For Reference

Not to be taken from this room

Digest of Education Statistics 2015
51st Edition

December 2016

Thomas D. Snyder
Cristobal de Brey
National Center for Education Statistics

Sally A. Dillow
American Institutes for Research

NCES 2016-014
U.S. DEPARTMENT OF EDUCATION

ISBN: 978-159888-957-4

U.S. Department of Education
John B. King, Jr.
Secretary

Institute of Education Sciences
Ruth Neild
Deputy Director for Policy and Research
Delegated Duties of the Director

National Center for Education Statistics
Peggy G. Carr
Acting Commissioner

The National Center for Education Statistics (NCES) is the primary federal entity for collecting, analyzing, and reporting data related to education in the United States and other nations. It fulfills a congressional mandate to collect, collate, analyze, and report full and complete statistics on the condition of education in the United States; conduct and publish reports and specialized analyses of the meaning and significance of such statistics; assist state and local education agencies in improving their statistical systems; and review and report on education activities in foreign countries.

NCES activities are designed to address high-priority education data needs; provide consistent, reliable, complete, and accurate indicators of education status and trends; and report timely, useful, and high-quality data to the U.S. Department of Education, the Congress, the states, other education policymakers, practitioners, data users, and the general public. Unless specifically noted, all information contained herein is in the public domain.

We strive to make our products available in a variety of formats and in language that is appropriate to a variety of audiences. You, as our customer, are the best judge of our success in communicating information effectively. If you have any comments or suggestions about this or any other NCES product or report, we would like to hear from you. Please direct your comments to

NCES, IES, U.S. Department of Education
Potomac Center Plaza (PCP)
550 12th Street SW
Washington, DC 20202

December 2016

The NCES Home Page address is http://nces.ed.gov.
The NCES Publications and Products address is http://nces.ed.gov/pubsearch.

This report was prepared for the National Center for Education Statistics under Contract No. ED-IES-12-D-0002 with American Institutes for Research. Mention of trade names, commercial products, or organizations does not imply endorsement by the U.S. Government.

Suggested Citation

Snyder, T.D., de Brey, C., and Dillow, S.A. (2016). *Digest of Education Statistics 2015* (NCES 2016-014). National Center for Education Statistics, Institute of Education Sciences, U.S. Department of Education. Washington, DC.

Content Contact

Thomas D. Snyder
(202) 245-7165
tom.snyder@ed.gov

FOREWORD

The 2015 edition of the *Digest of Education Statistics* is the 51st in a series of publications initiated in 1962. The *Digest* has been issued annually except for combined editions for the years 1977–78, 1983–84, and 1985–86. Its primary purpose is to provide a compilation of statistical information covering the broad field of American education from prekindergarten through graduate school. The *Digest* includes a selection of data from many sources, both government and private, and draws especially on the results of surveys and activities carried out by the National Center for Education Statistics (NCES). To qualify for inclusion in the *Digest*, material must be nationwide in scope and of current interest and value. The publication contains information on a variety of subjects in the field of education statistics, including the number of schools and colleges, teachers, enrollments, and graduates, in addition to data on educational attainment, finances, federal funds for education, libraries, and international comparisons. Supplemental information on population trends, attitudes on education, education characteristics of the labor force, government finances, and economic trends provides background for evaluating education data. Although the *Digest* contains important information on federal education funding, more detailed information on federal activities is available from federal education program offices.

The *Digest* contains seven chapters: All Levels of Education, Elementary and Secondary Education, Postsecondary Education, Federal Funds for Education and Related Activities, Outcomes of Education, International Comparisons of Education, and Libraries and Internet Use. Each chapter is divided into a number of topical subsections. Preceding the seven chapters is an Introduction that provides a brief overview of current trends in American education, which supplements the tabular materials in chapters 1 through 7. The *Digest* concludes with three appendixes. The first appendix, Guide to Sources, provides a brief synopsis of the surveys used to generate the *Digest* tables; the second, Definitions, is included to help readers understand terms used in the *Digest*; and the third, Index of Table Numbers, allows readers to quickly locate tables on specific topics.

In addition to providing updated versions of many statistics that have appeared in previous years, this edition incorporates new material on the following topics:

- Enrollment and percentage distribution of enrollment in public schools, by family poverty rate of 5- to 17-year-olds living in the school district, student race/ethnicity, region, and school locale (table 203.75)
- English language learner (ELL) students enrolled in public elementary and secondary schools, by grade and home language (table 204.27)
- Number and percentage distribution of public elementary and secondary school teachers who met licensing/certification requirements and of public school teachers who had less than 2 years of teaching experience, by state (table 209.25)
- Number and percentage of elementary and secondary school students retained in grade, by sex, race/ethnicity, and grade level (table 225.90)
- Percentage of public school students in grades 6 through 12 who had ever been suspended or expelled, by sex and race/ethnicity (table 233.20)
- Number and percentage of fall 2009 ninth-graders who were ever suspended or expelled through spring 2012, by when student was suspended or expelled and selected student characteristics (table 233.25)
- Number of students receiving selected disciplinary actions in public elementary and secondary schools, by type of disciplinary action, disability status, sex, and race/ethnicity (table 233.27)
- Percentage of students receiving selected disciplinary actions in public elementary and secondary schools, by type of disciplinary action, disability status, sex, and race/ethnicity (table 233.28)
- Number of discipline incidents resulting in removal of a student from a regular education program for at least an entire school day and rate of incidents per 100,000 students, by discipline reason and state (table 233.45)
- Percentage of public schools with a written plan for procedures to be performed in selected crises and percentage that have drilled students on the use of a plan, by selected school characteristics (table 233.65)
- Number of juvenile offenders in residential placement facilities, by selected juvenile and facility characteristics (table 233.90)
- Residential placement rate (number of juvenile offenders in residential facilities) per 100,000 juveniles, by sex and race/ethnicity (table 233.92)
- Percentage distribution of fall 2009 ninth-graders who had completed high school and selected measures of their high school achievement, by postsecondary enrollment status in fall 2013 and selected student characteristics (table 302.43)

- Number, percentage distribution, and median annual earnings of 25- to 34-year-olds with a bachelor's or higher degree, by sex, race/ethnicity, and selected employment and occupational characteristics (table 505.15)
- Average literacy and numeracy scale scores of 25- to 65-year-olds, by sex, age group, highest level of educational attainment, and country or other education system (table 604.10)
- Percentage distribution of 25- to 65-year-olds, by literacy proficiency level, numeracy proficiency level, selected levels of educational attainment, and country or other education system (table 604.20)

- Employment rates and mean monthly earnings of 25- to 65-year-olds, by literacy proficiency level, numeracy proficiency level, and country or other education system (table 604.30)

The *Digest* can be accessed from http://nces.ed.gov/programs/digest.

Thomas D. Snyder
Supervisor
Annual Reports and Information Staff

Contents

List of Figures

List of Text Tables

List of Reference Tables

Chapter 1. All Levels of Education

Summary of Enrollment, Teachers, and Schools

Summary of Finances

Chapter 2. Elementary and Secondary Education

Historical

Enrollment Status and Child Care Arrangements of Young Children

Enrollment in Public Schools

Teacher Attitudes and Teacher Mobility

Teacher Salaries

School Principals

School Staff

School Facilities

Computers and Technology

High School Completers and Dropouts

Science Achievement

Achievement in Other Subjects

Coursetaking, Grades, and Retention in Grade

Discipline, Safety and Security, and Juvenile Justice

Chapter 3. Postsecondary Education

Overview and Historical

Enrollment Rates

Total Fall Enrollment—General

Total Fall Enrollment—State-Level

First-Time Students and Admissions

Enrollment of Racial/Ethnic Groups

Large Institutions and Institutions Serving Specific Groups

Historically Black Colleges and Universities

Staff

Faculty and Instructional Staff

Faculty Salaries and Benefits

Institutions

Summary of Degrees Conferred

Degrees Conferred—State-Level

Certificates Below the Associate's Degree Level

Associate's Degrees

Financial Aid for Undergraduates

Financial Aid for Postbaccalaureate Students

Revenues

Expenditures

Chapter 4. Federal Funds for Education and Related Activities

On-Budget and Off-Budget Support

Federal Obligations for Research and Development

Chapter 5. Outcomes of Education

Labor Force Status by Educational Attainment

Occupation and Earnings by Educational Attainment

Employment of Students

Labor Force Status of Recent High School Completers and Dropouts

READER'S GUIDE

Data Sources

The data in this edition of the *Digest of Education Statistics* were obtained from many different sources—including students and teachers, state education agencies, local elementary and secondary schools, and colleges and universities—using surveys and compilations of administrative records. Users should be cautious when comparing data from different sources. Differences in aspects such as procedures, timing, question phrasing, and interviewer training can affect the comparability of results across data sources.

Most of the tables present data from surveys conducted by the National Center for Education Statistics (NCES) or conducted by other agencies and organizations with support from NCES. Some tables also include other data published by federal and state agencies, private research organizations, or professional organizations. Totals reported in the *Digest* are for the 50 states and the District of Columbia unless otherwise noted. Brief descriptions of the surveys and other data sources used in this volume can be found in Appendix A: Guide to Sources. For each NCES and non-NCES data source, the Guide to Sources also provides information on where to obtain further details about that source.

Data are obtained primarily from two types of surveys: universe surveys and sample surveys. In universe surveys, information is collected from every member of the population. For example, in a survey regarding certain expenditures of public elementary and secondary schools, data would be obtained from each school district in the United States. When data from an entire population are available, estimates of the total population or a subpopulation are made by simply summing the units in the population or subpopulation. As a result, there is no sampling error, and observed differences are reported as true.

Since a universe survey is often expensive and time consuming, many surveys collect data from a sample of the population of interest (sample survey). For example, the National Assessment of Educational Progress (NAEP) assesses a representative sample of students rather than the entire population of students. When a sample survey is used, statistical uncertainty is introduced, because the data come from only a portion of the entire population. This statistical uncertainty must be considered when reporting estimates and making comparisons. For information about how NCES accounts for statistical uncertainty when reporting sample survey results, see "Data Analysis and Interpretation," later in this Reader's Guide.

Common Measures and Indexes

Various types of statistics derived from universe and sample surveys are reported. Many tables report the size of a population or a subpopulation, and often the size of a subpopulation is expressed as a percentage of the total population.

In addition, the average (or *mean*) value of some characteristic of the population or subpopulation may be reported. The average is obtained by summing the values for all members of the population and dividing the sum by the size of the population. An example is the average annual salary of full-time instructional faculty at degree-granting postsecondary institutions. Another measure that is sometimes used is the *median*. The median is the midpoint value of a characteristic at or above which 50 percent of the population is estimated to fall, and at or below which 50 percent of the population is estimated to fall. An example is the median annual earnings of young adults who are full-time year-round workers. Some tables also present an *average per capita*, or per person, which represents an average computed for every person in a specified group or population. It is derived by dividing the total for an item (such as income or expenditures) by the number of persons in the specified population. An example is the per capita expenditure on education in each state.

Many tables report financial data in dollar amounts. Unless otherwise noted, all financial data are in *current dollars*, meaning not adjusted for changes in the purchasing power of the dollar over time due to inflation. For example, 1994–95 teacher salaries in current dollars are the amounts that the teachers earned in 1994–95, without any adjustments to account for inflation. *Constant dollar* adjustments attempt to remove the effects of price changes (inflation) from statistical series reported in dollars. For example, if teacher salaries over a 20-year period are adjusted to constant 2014–15 dollars, the salaries for all years are adjusted to the dollar values that presumably would exist if prices in each year were the same as in 2014–15, in other words, as if the dollar had constant purchasing power over the entire period. Any changes in the constant dollar amounts would reflect only changes in real values. Constant dollar amounts are computed using *price indexes*. Price indexes for inflation adjustments can be found in table 106.70. Each table that presents constant dollars includes a note indicating which index was used for the inflation adjustments; in most cases, the Consumer Price Index was used.

When presenting data for a time series, some tables include both *actual* and *projected* data. Actual data are data that have already been collected. Projected data can be used when data for a recent or future year are not yet available. Projections are estimates that are based on recent trends in relevant statistics and patterns associated with correlated variables. Unless otherwise noted, all data in this volume are actual.

Standard Errors

Using estimates calculated from data based on a sample of the population requires consideration of several factors before the estimates become meaningful. When using data from a sample, some margin of error will always be present in estimations of characteristics of the total population or subpopulation because the data are available from only a portion of the total population. Consequently, data from samples can provide only an approximation of the true or actual value. The margin of error of an estimate, or the range of potential true or actual values, depends on several factors such as the amount of variation in the responses, the size and representativeness of the sample, and the size of the subgroup for which the estimate is computed. The magnitude of this margin of error is measured by what statisticians call the "standard error" of an estimate.

When data from sample surveys are reported, the standard error is calculated for each estimate. In the tables, the standard error for each estimate generally appears in parentheses next to the estimate to which it applies. In order to caution the reader when interpreting findings, estimates from sample surveys are flagged with a "!" when the standard error is between 30 and 50 percent of the estimate, and suppressed with a "‡" when the standard error is 50 percent of the estimate or greater. The term "coefficient of variation (CV)" refers to the ratio of the standard error to the estimate; for example, if an estimate has a CV of 30 percent, this means that the standard error is equal to 30 percent of the value of the estimate.

Nonsampling Errors

In addition to standard errors, which apply only to sample surveys, all surveys are subject to nonsampling errors. Nonsampling errors may arise when individual respondents or interviewers interpret questions differently; when respondents must estimate values, or when coders, keyers, and other processors handle answers differently; when people who should be included in the universe are not; or when people fail to respond, either totally or partially. Total nonresponse means that people do not respond to the survey at all, while partial nonresponse (or item nonresponse) means that people fail to respond to specific survey items. To compensate for nonresponse, adjustments are often made. For universe surveys, an adjustment made for either type of nonresponse, total or partial, is often referred to as an imputation, which is often a substitution of the "average" questionnaire response for the nonresponse. For universe surveys, imputations are usually made separately within various groups of sample members that have similar survey characteristics. For sample surveys, total nonresponse is handled through nonresponse adjustments to the sample weights. For sample surveys, imputation for item nonresponse is usually made by substituting for a missing item the response to that item of a respondent having characteristics that are similar to those of the nonrespondent. For additional general information about imputations, see the *NCES Statistical Standards* (NCES 2014-097). Appendix A: Guide to Sources includes some information about specific surveys' response rates, nonresponse adjustments, and other efforts to reduce nonsampling error. Although the magnitude of nonsampling error is frequently unknown, idiosyncrasies that have been identified are noted in the appropriate tables.

Data Analysis and Interpretation

When estimates are from a sample, caution is warranted when drawing conclusions about one estimate in comparison to another, or about whether a time series of estimates is increasing, decreasing, or staying the same. Although one estimate may appear to be larger than another, a statistical test may find that the apparent difference between them is not reliably measurable due to the uncertainty around the estimates. In this case, the estimates will be described as having no measurable difference, meaning that the difference between them is not statistically significant.

Whether differences in means or percentages are statistically significant can be determined using the standard errors of the estimates. In reports produced by NCES, when differences are statistically significant, the probability that the difference occurred by chance is less than 5 percent, according to NCES standards.

Data presented in the text do not investigate more complex hypotheses, account for interrelationships among variables, or support causal inferences. We encourage readers who are interested in more complex questions and in-depth analysis to explore other NCES resources, including publications, online data tools, and public- and restricted-use datasets at http://nces.ed.gov.

In text that reports estimates based on samples, differences between estimates (including increases and decreases) are stated only when they are statistically significant. To determine whether differences reported are statistically significant, two-tailed *t* tests at the .05 level are typically used. The *t* test formula for determining statistical significance is adjusted when the samples being compared are dependent. The *t* test formula is not adjusted for multiple comparisons, with the exception of statistical tests conducted using the NAEP Data Explorer (http://nces.ed.gov/nationsreportcard/naepdata/). When the variables to be tested are postulated to form a trend, the relationship may be tested using linear regression, logistic regression, or ANOVA trend analysis instead of a series of *t* tests. These alternate methods of analysis test for specific relationships (e.g., linear, quadratic, or cubic) among variables. For more information on data analysis, please see the NCES Statistical Standards, Standard 5-1, available at http://nces.ed.gov/statprog/2012/pdf/Chapter5.pdf.

A number of considerations influence the ultimate selection of the data years to include in the tables and to feature in the text. To make analyses as timely as possible, the latest year of available data is shown. The choice of comparison years is often also based on the need to show the earliest available survey year, as in the case of NAEP and the international assessment surveys. The text typically compares the most current year's data with those from the initial year and then with those from a more recent year. In the case of surveys with long time frames, such as surveys measuring enrollment, changes over the course of a decade may be noted in the text. Where applicable, the text may also note years in which the data begin to diverge from previous trends. In figures and tables, intervening years are selected in increments in order to show the general trend.

Rounding and Other Considerations

All calculations are based on unrounded estimates. Therefore, the reader may find that a calculation, such as a difference or a percentage change, cited in the text or a figure may not be identical to the calculation obtained by using the rounded values shown in the accompanying tables. Although values reported in the tables are generally rounded to one decimal place (e.g., 76.5 percent), values reported in the text are generally rounded to whole numbers (with any value of 0.50 or above rounded to the next highest whole number). Due to rounding, cumulative percentages may sometimes equal 99 or 101 percent rather than 100 percent.

Race and Ethnicity

The Office of Management and Budget (OMB) is responsible for the standards that govern the categories used to collect and present federal data on race and ethnicity. The OMB revised the guidelines on racial/ethnic categories used by the federal government in October 1997, with a January 2003 deadline for implementation. The revised standards require a minimum of these five categories for data on race: American Indian or Alaska Native, Asian, Black or African American, Native Hawaiian or Other Pacific Islander, and White. The standards also require the collection of data on the ethnicity categories Hispanic or Latino and Not Hispanic or Latino. It is important to note that Hispanic origin is an ethnicity rather than a race, and therefore persons of Hispanic origin may be of any race. Origin can be viewed as the heritage, nationality group, lineage, or country of birth of the person or the person's parents or ancestors before their arrival in the United States. The race categories White, Black, Asian, Native Hawaiian or Other Pacific Islander, and American Indian or Alaska Native exclude persons of Hispanic origin unless otherwise noted.

For a description of each racial/ethnic category, please see the "Racial/ethnic group" entry in Appendix B: Definitions. Some of the category labels are shortened for more concise presentation in text, tables, and figures. American Indian or Alaska Native is denoted as American Indian/Alaska Native (except when separate estimates are available for American Indians alone or Alaska Natives alone); Black or African American is shortened to Black; and Hispanic or Latino is shortened to Hispanic. When discussed separately from Asian estimates, Native Hawaiian or Other Pacific Islander is shortened to Pacific Islander.

Many of the data sources used for this volume are federal surveys that collect data using the OMB standards for racial/ethnic classification described above; however, some sources have not fully adopted the standards, and some tables include historical data collected prior to the adoption of the OMB standards. Asians and Pacific Islanders are combined into a single category for years in which the data were not collected separately for the two groups. The combined category can sometimes mask significant differences between the two subgroups. For example, prior to 2011, NAEP collected data that did not allow for separate reporting of estimates for Asians and Pacific Islanders. The population counts presented in table 101.20, based on the U.S. Census Bureau's Current Population Reports, indicate that 96 percent of all Asian/Pacific Islander 5- to 17-year-olds were Asian in 2010. Thus, the combined category for Asians/Pacific Islanders is more representative of Asians than of Pacific Islanders.

Some surveys give respondents the option of selecting more than one race category, an "other" race category, or a "Two or more races" or "multiracial" category. Where possible, tables present data on the "Two or more races" category; however, in some cases this category may not be separately shown because the information was not collected or due to other data issues. Some tables include the "other" category. Any comparisons made between persons of one racial/ethnic group and persons of "all other racial/ethnic groups" include only the racial/ethnic groups shown in the reference table. In some surveys, respondents are not given the option to select more than one race category and also are not given an option such as "other" or "multiracial." In these surveys, respondents of Two or more races must select a single race category. Any comparisons between data from surveys that give the option to select more than one race and surveys that do not offer such an option should take into account the fact that there is a potential for bias if members of one racial group are more likely than members of the others to identify themselves as "Two or more races."[1] For postsecondary data, foreign students are counted separately and are therefore not included in any racial/ethnic category.

In addition to the major racial/ethnic categories, several tables include Hispanic ancestry subgroups (such as Mexican, Puerto Rican, Cuban, Dominican, Salvadoran, Other Central American, and South American) and Asian ancestry subgroups (such as Asian Indian, Chinese, Filipino, Japanese, Korean, and Vietnamese). In addition, selected tables include "Two or more races" subgroups (such as White and Black, White and Asian, and White and American Indian/Alaska Native).

---

[1] For discussion of such bias in responses to the 2000 Census, see Parker, J. et al. (2004). Bridging Between Two Standards for Collecting Information on Race and Ethnicity: An Application to Census 2000 and Vital Rates. *Public Health Reports, 119*(2): 192–205. Available at http://www.pubmed-central.nih.gov/articlerender.fcgi?artid=1497618.

Limitations of the Data

Due to large standard errors, some differences that seem substantial are not statistically significant and, therefore, are not cited in the text. This situation often applies to estimates involving American Indians/Alaska Natives and Pacific Islanders. The relatively small sizes of these populations pose many measurement difficulties when conducting statistical analysis. Even in larger surveys, the numbers of American Indians/Alaska Natives and Pacific Islanders included in a sample are often small. Researchers studying data on these two populations often face small sample sizes that increase the size of standard errors and reduce the reliability of results. Readers should keep these limitations in mind when comparing estimates presented in the tables.

As mentioned, caution should be exercised when comparing data from different sources. Differences in sampling, data collection procedures, coverage of target population, timing, phrasing of questions, scope of nonresponse, interviewer training, and data processing and coding mean that results from different sources may not be strictly comparable. For example, the racial/ethnic categories presented to a respondent, and the way in which the question is asked, can influence the response, especially for individuals who consider themselves of mixed race or ethnicity. In addition, data on American Indians/Alaska Natives are often subject to inaccuracies that can result from respondents self-identifying their race/ethnicity. Research on the collection of race/ethnicity data suggests that the categorization of American Indian and Alaska Native is the least stable self-identification (for example, the same individual may identify as American Indian when responding to one survey, but may not do so on a subsequent survey).[2]

---

[2] See U.S. Department of Labor, Bureau of Labor Statistics (1995). *A Test of Methods for Collecting Racial and Ethnic Information* (USDL 95-428). Washington DC: Author.

INTRODUCTION

The Introduction provides a brief overview of current trends in American education, highlighting key data that are presented in more detail later in this volume. Topics outlined include the participation of students, teachers, and faculty in U.S. educational institutions; the performance of U.S. elementary/secondary students overall and in comparison to students in other countries; the numbers of high school graduates and postsecondary degrees; and the amounts of expenditures on education at the elementary/secondary and postsecondary levels.

In fall 2015, about 75.8 million people were enrolled in American schools and colleges (table 105.10). About 4.6 million people were employed as elementary and secondary school teachers or as college faculty, in full-time equivalents (FTE). Other professional, administrative, and support staff at educational institutions totaled 5.3 million FTE employees. All data for 2015 in this Introduction are projected, except for data on educational attainment. Some data for other years are projected or estimated as noted. In discussions of historical trends, different time periods and specific years are cited, depending on the timing of important changes as well as the availability of relevant data.

Elementary/Secondary Education

Enrollment

A pattern of annual increases in total public elementary and secondary school enrollment began in 1985, but enrollment stabilized at 49.3 million between 2006 and 2008, before beginning to increase again (table 105.30). Overall, public school enrollment rose 28 percent, from 39.4 million to 50.3 million, between 1985 and 2015. Private school enrollment fluctuated during this period, with the fall 2015 enrollment of 5.3 million being 5 percent lower than the enrollment of 5.6 million in 1985. About 10 percent of elementary and secondary school students were enrolled in private schools in 2015, reflecting a decrease from 12 percent in 1985.

In public schools between 1985 and 2015, there was a 31 percent increase in elementary enrollment (prekindergarten through grade 8), compared with a 21 percent increase in secondary enrollment (grades 9 through 12) (table 105.30). Part of the higher growth in public elementary school enrollment resulted from the expansion of prekindergarten enrollment (table 203.10). Between fall 1985 and fall 2015, enrollment in prekindergarten increased 755 percent, while enrollment in other elementary grades (including kindergarten through grade 8 plus ungraded elementary programs) increased 26 percent. The number of children enrolled in prekindergarten increased from 0.2 million in 1985 to 1.3 million in 2015, and the number enrolled in other elementary grades increased from 26.9 million to 34.0 million. Public secondary school enrollment declined 8 percent from 1985 to 1990, but then increased 33 percent from 1990 to 2007; however, secondary school enrollment in 2015 was 1 percent lower than in 2007 (table 105.30). Between 1990 and 2015, the net increase in public secondary school enrollment was 32 percent, compared with an 18 percent increase in public elementary school enrollment. Over the most recent 10-year period (between 2005 and 2015), public school enrollment rose 2 percent. Elementary school enrollment increased 3 percent between 2005 and 2015, while secondary school enrollment was less than 1 percent higher in 2015 than in 2005.

Since the enrollment rates of 5- and 6-year-olds, 7- to 13-year-olds, and 14- to 17-year-olds changed by less than 3 percentage points from 1985 to 2014, increases in public elementary and secondary school enrollment primarily reflect increases in the number of children in the population in these age groups (tables 101.10 and 103.20). For example, the enrollment rate of 7- to 13-year-olds decreased from 99 to 98 percent between 1985 and 2014, but the number of 7- to 13-year-olds increased by 25 percent. Increases in both the enrollment rate of 3- and 4-year-old children (from 39 percent in 1985 to 54 percent in 2014) and the number of children in this age group (from 7.1 million to 8.0 million) also contributed to overall enrollment increases.

The National Center for Education Statistics (NCES) projects record levels of total public elementary and secondary school enrollment from 2015 (50.3 million) through at least 2025 (51.4 million) (table 105.30). The total public school enrollment projected for fall 2015 is a record-high number, and new records are expected every year through 2025, the last year for which NCES enrollment projections have been developed. Public elementary school enrollment (prekindergarten through grade 8) is projected to increase 2 percent between 2015 and 2025. Public secondary school enrollment (grades 9 through 12) is expected to increase 3 percent between 2015 and 2025. Overall, total public school enrollment is expected to increase 2 percent between 2015 and 2025.

Teachers

About 3.6 million full-time-equivalent (FTE) elementary and secondary school teachers were engaged in classroom instruction in fall 2015 (table 105.40). This number was less than 1 percent lower than in fall 2005. The 2015 number of FTE teachers includes 3.1 million public school teachers and 0.4 million private school teachers.

Public school enrollment was 2 percent higher in 2015 than in 2005, while the number of public school teachers was less than 1 percent lower (table 208.20). In fall 2015, the number of public school pupils per teacher was 16.1, which was higher than the ratio of 15.6 in 2005.

The average salary for public school teachers in 2014–15 was $57,379 in current dollars (i.e., dollars that are not adjusted for inflation) (table 211.50). In constant (i.e., inflation-adjusted) dollars, the average salary for teachers was 2 percent lower in 2014–15 than in 1990–91.

Student Performance

Most of the student performance data in the *Digest* are drawn from the National Assessment of Educational Progress (NAEP). The NAEP assessments have been conducted using three basic designs: the national main NAEP, state NAEP, and long-term trend NAEP. The national main NAEP and state NAEP provide current information about student performance in subjects including reading, mathematics, science, and writing, while long-term trend NAEP provides information on performance since the early 1970s in reading and mathematics only. Results from long-term trend NAEP are included in the discussion in chapter 2 of the *Digest*, while the information in this Introduction includes only selected results from the national main and state NAEP. Readers should keep in mind that comparisons of NAEP scores in the text (like all comparisons of estimates in the *Digest*) are based on statistical testing of unrounded values.

The main NAEP reports current information for the nation and specific geographic regions of the country. The assessment program includes students drawn from both public and private schools and reports results for student achievement at grades 4, 8, and 12. The main NAEP assessments follow the frameworks developed by the National Assessment Governing Board and use the latest advances in assessment methodology. The state NAEP is identical in content to the national main NAEP, but the state NAEP reports information only for public school students. Chapter 2 presents more information on the NAEP designs and methodology, and additional details appear in Appendix A: Guide to Sources.

Reading

The main NAEP reading assessment data are reported on a scale of 0 to 500. In 2015, the average reading score for 4th-grade students (223) was not measurably different from the 2013 score, but it was higher than the 1992 score (217) (table 221.10). At grade 4, the average 2015 reading scores for White (232), Black (206), Hispanic (208), and Asian/Pacific Islander students (239) were not measurably different from the corresponding scores in 2013, but their average scores were all higher than in 1992. For 8th-grade students, the average reading score in 2015 (265) was lower than in 2013 (268), but it was higher than in 1992 (260). At grade 8, average 2015 reading scores for White (274), Black (248), and Hispanic (253) students were lower than the scores in 2013 (276, 250, and 256, respectively), while the average 2015 reading score for Asian/Pacific Islander (280) students was not measurably different from the score in 2013. Consistent with the findings at grade 4, the average reading scores for White, Black, Hispanic, and Asian/Pacific Islander 8th-grade students were higher in 2015 than in 1992. For 12th-grade students, the average reading score in 2015 was not measurably different from that in 2013. At grade 12, the average 2015 reading scores for White (295), Hispanic (276), and Asian/Pacific Islander students (297) were not measurably different from the scores in 2013 and 1992. For Black students, the 2015 average score (266) was lower than the 1992 score (273) but was not measurably different from the 2013 score.

While there was no measurable change from 2013 to 2015 in the average reading score for 4th-grade public school students nationally, average scores were higher in 2015 than in 2013 in the District of Columbia and 12 states (table 221.40). Average 4th-grade scores were lower in 2015 than in 2013 in Maryland and Minnesota, while scores in all remaining states did not change measurably from 2013 to 2015. The average reading score for 8th-grade public school students was lower in 2015 than in 2013 nationally and in 8 states (table 221.60). However, 8th-grade students in West Virginia scored higher in 2015 than in 2013. In the remaining states and the District of Columbia, scores did not change measurably from 2013 to 2015.

Mathematics

The main NAEP mathematics assessment data for 4th- and 8th-graders are reported on a scale of 0 to 500 (table 222.10). The average 4th-grade mathematics score in 2015 (240) was lower than the score in 2013 (242), although it was higher than the score in 1990 (213). At grade 4, the average mathematics score in 2015 for White students (248) was lower than the score in 2013 (250), while the average scores in 2015 for Black (224), Hispanic (230), and Asian/Pacific Islander (257) students were not measurably different from the 2013 scores. However, the 4th-grade average scores for White, Black, Hispanic, and Asian/Pacific Islander students were all higher in 2015 than in 1990. The average 8th-grade mathematics score in 2015 (282) was lower than the score in 2013 (285), although it was higher than the score in 1990 (263). At grade 8, the average scores for White (292), Black (260), and Hispanic students (270) were lower in 2015 than in 2013 (294, 263, and 272, respectively). The 2015 average score for Asian/Pacific Islander students (306) was not measurably different from the score in 2013. However, the average scores for 8th-grade White, Black, Hispanic, and Asian/Pacific Islander students were all higher in 2015 than in 1990. Due to changes in the 12th-grade mathematics assessment framework, a new trend line started in 2005, with scores reported on a scale of 0 to 300. The average 12th-grade mathematics score in 2015 (152) was lower than the score in 2013 (153), but not measurably different from the score in 2005, the first year in which the revised assessment was administered.

The average mathematics score for 4th-grade public school students across the nation was lower in 2015 (240) than in 2013 (241) (table 222.50). Average 4th-grade mathematics scores for public school students were also lower in 2015 than in 2013 in 16 states. However, the mathematics average scores for 4th-grade students in Mississippi and the District of Columbia were higher in 2015 than in 2013. Scores were not measurably different in the other states during this period. The national public school average mathematics score for 8th-grade students was lower in 2015 (281) than in 2013 (284) (table 222.60). Similarly, 22 states had lower 8th-grade average scores in 2015 than in 2013, while scores for the remaining 28 states and the District of Columbia were not measurably different between 2013 and 2015. During this time, no state experienced a score increase at the 8th-grade level.

Science

NAEP has assessed the science abilities of students in grades 4, 8, and 12 in both public and private schools since 1996. As of 2009, however, NAEP science assessments are based on a new framework, so results from these assessments cannot be compared to results from earlier science assessments. The main NAEP science assessment data are reported on a scale of 0 to 300. The average 8th-grade science score increased from 150 in 2009 to 152 in 2011 (table 223.10). Average scores for both male and female students were higher in 2011 than in 2009. Male students scored 5 points higher on average than female students in 2011, which was not significantly different from the 4-point gap in 2009. Score gaps between White and Black students and between White and Hispanic students narrowed from 2009 to 2011. The 5-point gain from 2009 to 2011 for Hispanic students was larger than the 1-point gain for White students, narrowing the score gap from 30 points to 27 points. Black students scored 3 points higher in 2011 than in 2009. The 35-point score gap between White and Black students in 2011 was smaller than the 36-point gap in 2009. The average scores of Asian/Pacific Islander and American Indian/Alaska Native students were not significantly different in 2011 from their scores in 2009.

International Comparisons

The 2011 Trends in International Mathematics and Science Study (TIMSS) assessed students' mathematics and science performance at grade 4 in 45 countries and at grade 8 in 38 countries. In addition to countries, a number of subnational entities—including the public school systems in several U.S. states—also participated in TIMSS as separate education systems. Results for the participating states are included in the discussion in chapter 6 of the *Digest*, while this Introduction includes only results for the United States and other countries. TIMSS assessments are curriculum based and measure what students have actually learned against the subject matter that is expected to be taught in the participating countries by the end of grades 4 and 8. At both grades, TIMSS scores are reported on a scale of 0 to 1,000, with the scale average set at 500.

On the 2011 TIMSS, the average mathematics scores of U.S. 4th-graders (541) and 8th-graders (509) were higher than the scale average (tables 602.20 and 602.30). U.S. 4th-graders scored higher in mathematics, on average, than their counterparts in 37 countries and lower than those in 3 countries (table 602.20). Average mathematics scores in the other 4 countries were not measurably different from the U.S. average. At grade 8, the average U.S. mathematics score was higher than the average scores of students in 27 countries in 2011 and below the average scores of students in 4 countries (table 602.30). Average 8th-grade mathematics scores in the other 6 countries were not measurably different from the U.S. average. The average science scores of both U.S. 4th-graders (544) and U.S. 8th-graders (525) were higher than the TIMSS scale average of 500 in 2011. The average U.S. 4th-grade science score was higher than the average scores of students in 39 countries and lower than those of students in 5 countries. At grade 8, the average U.S. science score was higher than the average scores of students in 28 countries, lower than those in 6 countries, and not measurably different from those in the other 3 countries.

The Program for International Student Assessment (PISA), coordinated by the Organization for Economic Cooperation and Development (OECD), has measured the performance of 15-year-old students in reading, mathematics, and science literacy every 3 years since 2000. PISA assesses 15-year-old students' application of reading, mathematics, and science literacy to problems within a real-life context. In 2012, PISA assessed students in the 34 OECD countries as well as in a number of other education systems. Some subnational entities participated as separate education systems, including public school systems in the U.S. states of Connecticut, Florida, and Massachusetts. Results for the participating U.S. states are included in the discussion in chapter 6, while this Introduction includes only results for the United States in comparison with other OECD countries. PISA scores are reported on a scale of 0 to 1,000.

On the 2012 PISA assessment, U.S. 15-year-olds' average score in reading literacy was 498, which was not measurably different from the OECD average of 496 (table 602.50). The average reading literacy score in the United States was lower than the average score in 13 of the 33 other OECD countries, higher than the average score in 10 of the other OECD countries, and not measurably different from the average score in 10 of the OECD countries. In all countries, females outperformed males in reading (table 602.40). The U.S. gender gap in reading (31 points) was smaller than the OECD average gap (38 points) and smaller than the gaps in 14 of the OECD countries.

In mathematics literacy, U.S. 15-year-olds' average score of 481 on the 2012 PISA assessment was lower than the OECD average score of 494 (table 602.60). The average mathematics literacy score in the United States was lower than the average in 21 of the 33 other OECD countries, higher than the average in 5 OECD countries, and not measurably different from the average in 7 OECD countries. In 25 of the OECD countries, males outperformed females in mathematics literacy (table 602.40). In the United States, however, the average score of males (484) was not measurably different from that of females (479).

In science literacy, U.S. 15-year-olds' average score of 497 was not measurably different from the OECD average score of 501 (table 602.70). The average science literacy score in the United States was lower than the average in 15 OECD countries, higher than the average in 8 OECD countries, and not measurably different from the average in 10 OECD countries.

The Progress in International Reading Literacy Study (PIRLS) measures the reading knowledge and skills of 4th-graders over time. PIRLS scores are reported on a scale from 0 to 1,000, with the scale average set at 500. On the 2011 PIRLS, U.S. 4th-graders had an average reading literacy score of 556 (table 602.10). The U.S. average score in 2011 was 14 points higher than in 2001 and 16 points higher than in 2006. In all three assessment years, the U.S. average score was higher than the PIRLS scale average. In 2011, PIRLS assessed 4th-grade reading literacy in 40 countries. The average reading literacy score of 4th-graders in the United States was higher than the average score in 33 of the 39 other participating countries, lower than the average score in 3 countries, and not measurably different from the average in the remaining 3 countries.

High School Graduates and Dropouts

About 3,506,000 U.S. high school students were expected to graduate during the 2015–16 school year (table 219.10), including 3,192,000 public school graduates and 314,000 private school graduates. High school graduates include only recipients of diplomas, not recipients of equivalency credentials. The number of high school graduates projected for 2015–16 is higher than the prior record high in 2013–14, and exceeds the baby boom era's high point in 1975–76, when 3,142,000 students earned diplomas. In 2012–13, an estimated 81.9 percent of public high school students graduated on time—that is, received a diploma 4 years after beginning their freshman year.

The number of GED credentials issued by the states to GED test passers rose from 330,000 in 1977 to 487,000 in 2000 (table 219.60). A record number of 648,000 GED credentials were issued in 2001. In 2002, there were revisions to the GED test and to the data reporting procedures. In 2001, test takers were required to successfully complete all five components of the GED or else begin the five-part series again with the new test that was introduced in 2002. Prior to 2002, reporting was based on summary data from the states on the number of GED credentials issued. As of 2002, reporting has been based on individual GED candidate- and test-level records collected by the GED Testing Service.[1] Between 2003 and 2013, the number of persons passing the GED tests increased by 40 percent, from 387,000 to 541,000.

The percentage of dropouts among 16- to 24-year-olds (known as the status dropout rate) has decreased over the past two decades (table 219.70). The status dropout rate is the percentage of the civilian noninstitutionalized 16- to 24-year-old population who are not enrolled in school and who have not completed a high school program, regardless of when they left school. (People who left school but went on to receive a GED credential are not treated as dropouts in this measure.) Between 1990 and 2014, the status dropout rate declined from 12.1 percent to 6.5 percent (table 219.70). Although the status dropout rate declined for both Blacks and Hispanics during this period, their rates in 2014 (7.4 and 10.6 percent, respectively) remained higher than the rate for Whites (5.2 percent).

Postsecondary Education

College Enrollment

College enrollment was 20.2 million in fall 2014, reflecting a 4 percent decrease from the record enrollment in fall 2010 (table 105.30). College enrollment is expected to set new records from fall 2018 through fall 2025, the last year for which NCES enrollment projections have been developed. Between fall 2014 and fall 2025, enrollment is expected to increase by 15 percent. Despite decreases in the size of the traditional college-age population (18 to 24 years old) during the late 1980s and early 1990s, total enrollment increased during this period (tables 101.10 and 105.30). The traditional college-age population rose 7 percent between 2004 and 2014, and total college enrollment increased 17 percent during the same period. Between 2004 and 2014, the number of full-time students increased by 17 percent, compared with a 16 percent increase in part-time students (table 303.10). During the same time period, the number of males enrolled increased 19 percent, and the number of females enrolled increased 15 percent.

Faculty

In fall 2013, degree-granting institutions—defined as postsecondary institutions that grant an associate's or higher degree and are eligible for Title IV federal financial aid programs—employed 1.5 million faculty members, including 0.8 million full-time and 0.8 million part-time faculty (table 314.30). In addition, degree-granting institutions employed 0.4 million graduate assistants.

---

[1] Information on changes in GED test series and reporting is based on the 2003 edition of *Who Passed the GED Tests?*, by the GED Testing Service of the American Council on Education, as well as communication with staff of the GED Testing Service.

Postsecondary Degrees

During the 2015–16 academic year, postsecondary degrees conferred were projected to number 999,000 associate's degrees, 1,853,000 bachelor's degrees, 773,000 master's degrees, and 179,000 doctor's degrees (table 318.10). The doctor's degree total includes most degrees formerly classified as first-professional, such as M.D., D.D.S., and law degrees. Between 2003–04 and 2013–14 (the last year of actual data), the number of degrees conferred increased at all levels. The number of associate's degrees was 51 percent higher in 2013–14 than in 2003–04, the number of bachelor's degrees was 34 percent higher, the number of master's degrees was 34 percent higher, and the number of doctor's degrees was 41 percent higher.

Between 2003–04 and 2013–14, the number of bachelor's degrees awarded to males increased 35 percent, while the number of bachelor's degrees awarded to females increased 33 percent. Females earned 57 percent of all bachelor's degrees in 2013–14, the same percentage as in 2003–04. Between 2003–04 and 2013–14, the number of White students earning bachelor's degrees increased 19 percent, compared with larger increases of 46 percent for Black students, 114 percent for Hispanic students, and 43 percent for Asian/Pacific Islander students (table 322.20). The number of American Indian/Alaska Native students earning bachelor's degrees was 1 percent higher in 2013–14 than in 2003–04. In 2013–14, White students earned 68 percent of all bachelor's degrees awarded (vs. 76 percent in 2003–04), Black students earned 11 percent (vs. 10 percent in 2003–04), Hispanic students earned 11 percent (vs. 7 percent in 2003–04), and Asian/Pacific Islander students earned about 7 percent (increasing their share of the degrees from 6.8 percent in 2003–04 to 7.3 percent in 2013–14). American Indian/Alaska Native students earned less than 1 percent of the degrees in both years.

Undergraduate Prices

For the 2014–15 academic year, average annual prices for undergraduate tuition, fees, room, and board were estimated to be $16,188 at public institutions, $41,970 at private nonprofit institutions, and $23,372 at private for-profit institutions in current dollars (table 330.10). Between 2004–05 and 2014–15, prices for undergraduate tuition, fees, room, and board at public institutions rose 33 percent, and prices at private nonprofit institutions rose 26 percent, after adjustment for inflation. Prices for total tuition, fees, room, and board at private for-profit institutions decreased 18 percent between 2004–05 and 2014–15.

Educational Attainment

The U.S. Census Bureau collects annual statistics on the educational attainment of the population. Between 2005 and 2015, the percentage of the adult population 25 years of age and over who had completed high school rose from 85 percent to 88 percent, and the percentage of adults with a bachelor's degree increased from 28 percent to 33 percent (table 104.10). High school completers include those people who graduated from high school with a diploma, as well as those who completed high school through equivalency programs. The percentage of young adults (25- to 29-year-olds) who had completed high school increased from 86 percent in 2005 to 91 percent in 2015 (table 104.20). The percentage of young adults who had completed a bachelor's degree increased from 29 percent in 2005 to 36 percent in 2015. During this same period, the percentage of 25- to 29-year-olds who had completed a master's degree increased from 6 to 9 percent.

Adult Literacy and Numeracy Skills

The Program for the International Assessment of Adult Competencies (PIAAC) assesses the cognitive skills of adults in three areas—literacy, numeracy, and problem solving in technology-rich environments—that are seen as key to facilitating the social and economic participation of adults in advanced economies. The discussion below focuses on the areas of literacy and numeracy. PIAAC 2012 results are available for adults in 24 education systems, including 22 OECD education systems. The education systems that participated in the 2012 assessment were primarily countries, but also included three subnational education systems: Northern Ireland and England within the United Kingdom, and the Flemish community in Belgium. PIAAC literacy and numeracy scores are reported on a scale of 0 to 500.

In 2012, average scores on the PIAAC literacy scale for adults ages 25 to 65 ranged from 249 in Italy and 250 in Spain to 296 in Japan (table 604.10). U.S. 25- to 65-year-olds had an average PIAAC literacy score of 269, which was not measurably different from the OECD average score of 271. Across education systems, adults' average literacy scores generally increased with higher levels of educational attainment. In the United States, for example, 25- to 65-year-olds whose highest level of attainment was high school completion had an average literacy score of 259, compared with an average score of 302 for those who had a bachelor's or higher degree. The literacy score for U.S. high school completers in the 25- to 65-year-old age group was lower than the OECD average of 268 for high school completers in this age group, while the literacy score for U.S. 25- to 65-year-olds with a bachelor's or higher degree was not measurably different from the OECD average of 302 for those with a bachelor's or higher degree.

On the PIAAC numeracy scale, 2012 average scores for adults ages 25 to 65 ranged from 245 in Spain and 246 in Italy to 289 in Japan. U.S. 25- to 65-year-olds had an average PIAAC numeracy score of 254, which was lower than the OECD average score of 268. Across education systems, adults' average numeracy scores generally increased with higher levels of educational attainment. In the United States, for example, 25- to 65-year-olds whose highest level of attainment was high school completion had an average numeracy score of 241, compared with an average score of 293 for those who had a bachelor's or higher degree. The numeracy score for U.S. 25- to 65-year-olds who had completed only high school was lower than the OECD average of 265 for those with the same level of educational attainment. Likewise, the average numeracy score of U.S. 25- to 65-year-olds with a bachelor's or higher degree was lower than the OECD average of 303 for those with a bachelor's or higher degree.

Education Expenditures

Expenditures for public and private education, from pre-kindergarten through graduate school (excluding postsecondary schools not awarding associate's or higher degrees), were an estimated $1.2 trillion for 2014–15 (table 106.10). Expenditures of elementary and secondary schools totaled an estimated $696 billion, while those of degree-granting postsecondary institutions totaled an estimated $532 billion. Total expenditures for education were an estimated 7.1 percent of the gross domestic product in 2014–15. Education spending as a percentage of GDP increased from 7.1 in 2004–05 to 7.6 in 2009–10, but has declined since then.

CHAPTER 1
All Levels of Education

This chapter provides a broad overview of education in the United States. It brings together material from preprimary, elementary, secondary, and postsecondary education, as well as from the general population, to present a composite picture of the American educational system. Tables feature data on the total number of people enrolled in school, the number of teachers, the number of schools, and the total expenditures for education at all levels. This chapter also includes statistics on education-related topics such as educational attainment, family characteristics, and population. Economic indicators and price indexes have been added to facilitate analyses.

Many of the statistics in this chapter are derived from the statistical activities of the National Center for Education Statistics (NCES). In addition, substantial contributions have been drawn from the work of other groups, both governmental and nongovernmental, as shown in the source notes of the tables. Information on survey methodologies is contained in Appendix A: Guide to Sources and in the publications cited in the table source notes.

The U.S. System of Education

The U.S. system of education can be described as having three levels of formal education: elementary, secondary, and postsecondary (figure 1). Students may spend 1 to 3 years in preprimary programs (prekindergarten [PK] and kindergarten [K]), which may be offered either in separate schools or in elementary schools that also offer higher grades. (In *Digest of Education Statistics* tables, prekindergarten and kindergarten are generally defined as a part of elementary education.) Following kindergarten, students ordinarily spend from 6 to 8 years in elementary school. The elementary school program is followed by a 4- to 6-year program in secondary school. Students typically complete the entire program through grade 12 by age 18. Education at the elementary and secondary levels is provided in a range of institutional settings—including elementary schools (preprimary schools, middle schools, and schools offering broader ranges of elementary grades); secondary schools (junior high schools, high schools, and senior high schools); and combined elementary/secondary schools—that vary in structure from locality to locality.

High school graduates who decide to continue their education may enter a specialized career/technical institution, a 2-year community or junior college, or a 4-year college or university. A 2-year college typically offers the first 2 years of a standard 4-year college curriculum and a selection of terminal career and technical education programs. Academic courses completed at a 2-year college are usually transferable for credit at a 4-year college or university. A career/technical institution offers postsecondary technical training programs of varying lengths leading to a specific career.

An associate's degree requires at least 2 years of postsecondary coursework, and a bachelor's degree typically requires 4 years of postsecondary coursework. At least 1 year of coursework beyond the bachelor's is necessary for a master's degree, while a doctor's degree usually requires a minimum of 3 or 4 years beyond the bachelor's.

Professional schools differ widely in admission requirements and program length. Medical students, for example, generally complete a bachelor's program of premedical studies at a college or university before they can enter the 4-year program at a medical school. Law programs typically involve 3 years of coursework beyond the bachelor's degree level.

Enrollment

Total enrollment in public and private elementary and secondary schools (prekindergarten through grade 12) grew rapidly during the 1950s and 1960s, reaching a peak year in 1971 (table A, table 105.30, and figure 2). This enrollment rise reflected what is known as the "baby boom," a dramatic increase in births following World War II. Between 1971 and 1984, total elementary and secondary school enrollment decreased every year, reflecting the decline in the size of the school-age population over that period. After these years of decline, enrollment in elementary and secondary schools started increasing in fall 1985, began hitting new record levels in the mid-1990s, and continued to reach new record levels every year through 2006, after which enrollment declined slightly from its 2006 level. However, fall 2013 enrollment (55.4 million) was slightly higher than the fall 2006 record level of 55.3 million. A pattern of annual enrollment increases is projected to continue at least through fall 2025 (the last year for which NCES has projected school enrollment), when enrollment is expected to reach 56.5 million.

Table A. Total elementary and secondary school enrollment, by overall trends: Selected years, 1949–50 to fall 2025

Trend and year	Number of students (in millions)
"Baby boom" increases	
1949–50 school year	28.5
Fall 1959	40.9
Fall 1969	51.1
Fall 1971 (peak)..	51.3
13 years with annual declines	
Fall 1972 (first year of decline)...............................	50.7
Fall 1984 (final year of decline)...............................	44.9
Annual increases from 1985 to 2006	
Fall 1985	45.0
Fall 1996 (new record highs begin).........................	51.5
Fall 2006 (final year of record highs)	55.3
Slight declines or stable enrollment	
Fall 2007	55.2
Fall 2010	54.9
Fall 2012	55.1
Annual increases projected to start again	
Fall 2013	55.4
Fall 2014 (projected)..	55.5
Fall 2025 (projected)..	56.5

SOURCE: U.S. Department of Education, National Center for Education Statistics, *Biennial Survey of Education in the United States*, 1949–50; *Statistics of Public Elementary and Secondary School Systems*, 1959 through 1972; Common Core of Data (CCD), 1984 through 2013; Private School Universe Survey (PSS), 1997–98 through 2013–14; and National Elementary and Secondary Enrollment Projection Model, 1972 through 2025.

Between 1985 and 2014, the total public and private school enrollment rate for 5- and 6-year-olds decreased from 96 percent to 93 percent, while the enrollment rate for 7- to 13-year-olds decreased from 99 percent to 98 percent (table 103.20). The enrollment rate for 14- to 17-year-olds was 95 percent in 1985 and in 2014. Since these enrollment rates changed by 3 or fewer percentage points between 1985 and 2014, increases in public and private elementary and secondary school enrollment primarily reflect increases in the number of children in these age groups. Between 1985 and 2014, the number of 5- and 6-year-olds increased by 18 percent, the number of 7- to 13-year-olds increased by 25 percent, and the number of 14- to 17-year-olds increased by 12 percent (table 101.10). Increases in the enrollment rate of prekindergarten-age children (ages 3 and 4) from 39 percent in 1985 to 54 percent in 2014 (table 103.20) and in the number of 3- and 4-year-olds from 7.1 million to 8.0 million (table 101.10) also contributed to overall increases in prekindergarten through grade 12 enrollment.

Public school enrollment at the elementary level (prekindergarten through grade 8) rose from 29.9 million in fall 1990 to 34.2 million in fall 2003 (table 105.30). Elementary enrollment was less than 1 percent lower in fall 2004 than in fall 2003 and then generally increased to a projected total of 35.3 million for fall 2015. Public elementary enrollment is projected to increase 2 percent between 2015 and 2025. Public school enrollment at the secondary level (grades 9 through 12) rose from 11.3 million in 1990 to 15.1 million in 2007, but then declined 2 percent to 14.7 million in 2011. Public secondary enrollment is projected to increase 2 percent

between 2011 and 2015 and then show a further increase of 3 percent between 2015 and 2025. Total public elementary and secondary enrollment is projected to increase every year from 2015 to 2025.

The percentage of students in private elementary and secondary schools declined from 11.2 percent in fall 2003 to 9.7 percent in fall 2013 (table 105.30). In fall 2015, an estimated 5.3 million students were enrolled in private schools at the elementary and secondary levels.

Total enrollment in public and private degree-granting postsecondary institutions reached 14.5 million in fall 1992, but decreased every year through fall 1995 (table 105.30). Total enrollment increased 47 percent between 1995 and 2010 (to 21.0 million), but declined 4 percent between 2010 and 2014 (to 20.2 million). Total enrollment is expected to increase 15 percent between fall 2014 and fall 2025, reaching 23.3 million. The percentage of students who attended private institutions rose from 25 to 27 percent between 2004 and 2014. In fall 2014, about 5.6 million students attended private institutions, with about 4.0 million in nonprofit institutions and 1.6 million in for-profit institutions (table 303.10). Enrollment increases in degree-granting postsecondary institutions have been driven by increases in population, as well as by increases in enrollment rates for 20- to 24-year-olds. The percentage of 18- and 19-year-olds enrolled in degree-granting postsecondary institutions was 49 percent in 2014, which was not measurably different from the percentage in 2004. The number of 18- and 19-year-olds was 1 percent higher in 2014 than in 2004 (tables 101.10 and 103.20). The enrollment rate of 20- to 24-year-olds rose from 35 to 38 percent, and the number of 20- to 24-year-olds rose by 10 percent during the same period.

Educational Attainment

The percentages of adults 25 years old and over completing high school and higher education have been rising. Between 2005 and 2015, the percentage of the population 25 years old and over who had completed at least high school increased from 85 to 88 percent, and the percentage who had completed a bachelor's or higher degree increased from 28 to 33 percent (table 104.10 and figure 3). In 2015, about 9 percent of people 25 years old or over held a master's degree as their highest degree and 3 percent held a doctor's or first-professional degree (table 104.30).

Among young adults (25- to 29-year-olds), the percentage who had completed at least high school increased from 86 percent in 2005 to 91 percent in 2015 (table 104.20 and figure 4). The percentage of young adults who had completed a bachelor's or higher degree increased from 29 percent in 2005 to 36 percent in 2015. In 2015, about 7 percent of young adults held a master's degree as their highest degree and 2 percent held a doctor's or first-professional degree (table 104.30 and figure 5). Overall, the percentage of young adults who had a master's or higher degree rose from 6 percent in 2005 to 9 percent in 2015.

Between 2005 and 2015, changes occurred in the educational attainment of young adults (25- to 29-year-olds) by race/ethnicity. During this period, the percentages who had completed at least high school increased for Hispanic, White, and Black young adults, but there was no measurable change in the percentage for Asian young adults (96 percent in 2015) (table 104.20 and figure 6). The percentage of Hispanic young adults who had completed at least high school rose from 63 percent in 2005 to 77 percent in 2015, an increase of 14 percentage points. During the same period, the percentage of White young adults who had completed at least high school rose from 93 to 95 percent, an increase of 3 percentage points (based on unrounded data). Since the increase for White young adults was smaller than the increase for Hispanic young adults, the gap between the high school completion percentages for these two groups decreased from 30 percentage points in 2005 to 18 percentage points in 2015. Between 2005 and 2015, the percentage of Black young adults who had completed high school increased from 87 percent to 93 percent, and the gap between the White and Black high school completion percentages decreased from 6 to 3 percentage points. In 2015, the percentage of young adults who had completed at least high school was higher for Whites and Asians than for Blacks, Hispanics, and American Indians/Alaska Natives.

The percentage of bachelor's degree holders also varied among young adults of different racial/ethnic groups, with 66 percent of Asians in the 25- to 29-year-old age group holding a bachelor's or higher degree in 2015, compared with 43 percent of Whites, 21 percent of Blacks, 16 percent of Hispanics, 11 percent of Pacific Islanders, 15 percent of American Indians/Alaska Natives, and 30 percent of persons of Two or more races. Between 2005 and 2015, the percentages who had completed a bachelor's or higher degree increased for White, Black, and Hispanic young adults, but showed no measurable change for Asian young adults. During this 10-year period, the percentage of young adults who held a bachelor's or higher degree increased from 34 to 43

percent among Whites, from 18 to 21 percent among Blacks, and from 11 to 16 percent among Hispanics. With these increases for all three groups, the gap in bachelor's degree attainment percentages between Whites and Blacks increased by 5 percentage points between 2005 and 2015, and the gap between Whites and Hispanics increased by 3 percentage points.

Teachers and Faculty

A projected 3.6 million elementary and secondary school full-time-equivalent (FTE) teachers were engaged in classroom instruction in the fall of 2015 (table 105.40), which was not substantially different from the number in 2005. The number of FTE public school teachers in 2015 was 3.1 million, and the number of FTE private school teachers was 0.4 million. FTE faculty at degree-granting postsecondary institutions totaled a projected 1.0 million in 2015, including 0.7 million at public institutions and 0.4 million at private institutions (table 105.10).

Expenditures

Expenditures of educational institutions were an estimated $1.2 trillion for the 2014–15 school year (table 106.20 and figure 2). Elementary and secondary schools spent 57 percent of this total ($696 billion), and colleges and universities spent the remaining 43 percent ($532 billion). After adjustment for inflation, total expenditures of all educational institutions rose by an estimated 14 percent between 2004–05 and 2014–15. Inflation-adjusted expenditures of degree-granting postsecondary institutions rose by an estimated 29 percent. Expenditures of elementary and secondary schools were 4 percent higher in 2014–15 than in 2004–05. In 2014–15, expenditures of educational institutions were an estimated 7.1 percent of the gross domestic product (table 106.10).

Figure 1. The structure of education in the United States

NOTE: Figure is not intended to show relative number of institutions nor relative size of enrollment for the different levels of education. Figure reflects typical patterns of progression rather than all possible variations. Adult education programs, while not separately delineated above, may provide instruction at the adult basic, adult secondary, or postsecondary education levels.
SOURCE: U.S. Department of Education, National Center for Education Statistics, Annual Reports Program.

Figure 2. Enrollment, total expenditures in constant dollars, and expenditures as a percentage of the gross domestic product (GDP), by level of education: Selected years, 1965–66 through 2014–15

Fall enrollment, in millions

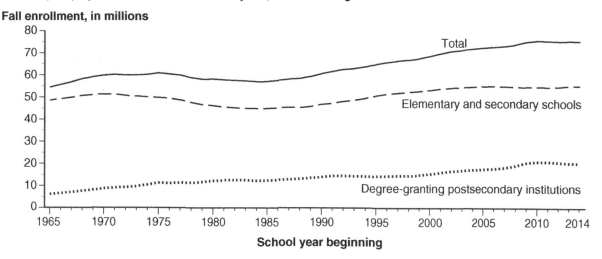

Total expenditures, in billions of constant 2014–15 dollars

Percent of GDP

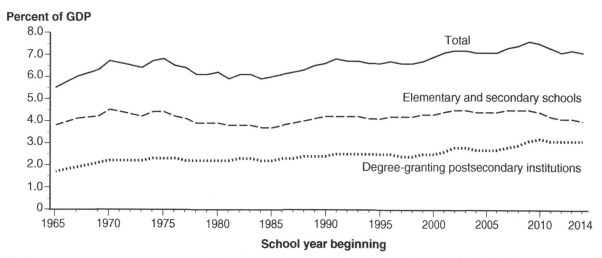

NOTE: Elementary and secondary enrollment data for school year 2014 (2014–15) are projected. Elementary and secondary expenditure data for school years 2013 and 2014 (2013–14 and 2014–15) are estimated. Postsecondary expenditure data for school year 2014 (2014–15) are estimated.

SOURCE: U.S. Department of Education, National Center for Education Statistics, *Statistics of State School Systems*, 1965–66 through 1969–70; *Statistics of Public Elementary and Secondary School Systems*, 1965 through 1980; *Revenues and Expenditures for Public Elementary and Secondary Education*, 1970–71 through 1986–87; Common Core of Data (CCD), "State Nonfiscal Survey of Public Elementary and Secondary Education," 1981–82 through 2013–14, and "National Public Education Financial Survey," 1987–88 through 2012–13; Private School Universe Survey (PSS), 1989–90 through 2013–14; National Elementary and Secondary Enrollment Projection Model, 1972 through 2025; Higher Education General Information Survey (HEGIS), "Fall Enrollment in Institutions of Higher Education" and "Financial Statistics of Institutions of Higher Education" surveys, 1965–66 through 1985–86; Integrated Postsecondary Education Data System (IPEDS), "Fall Enrollment Survey" (IPEDS-EF:86–99) and "Finance Survey" (IPEDS-F:FY87–99); and IPEDS Spring 2001 through Spring 2015, Fall Enrollment and Finance components. U.S. Department of Commerce, Bureau of Economic Analysis, National Income and Product Accounts Tables, retrieved January 29, 2016, from http://www.bea.gov/iTable/index_nipa.cfm.

Figure 3. Percentage of persons 25 years old and over, by highest level of educational attainment: Selected years, 1940 through 2015

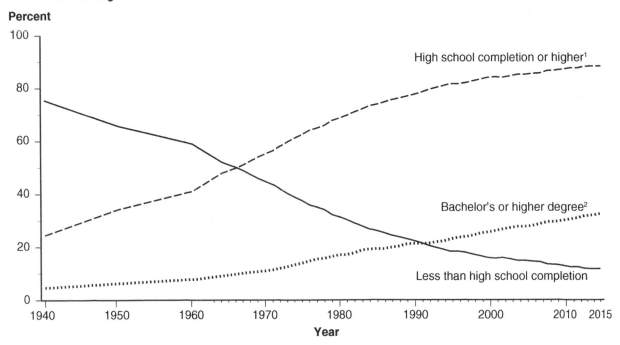

[1]Includes high school completion through equivalency programs, such as a GED program. For years prior to 1993, includes all persons with 4 or more years of high school.
[2]For years prior to 1993, includes all persons with 4 or more years of college.
SOURCE: U.S. Department of Commerce, Census Bureau, *U.S. Census of Population: 1960*, Vol. I, Part 1; J.K. Folger and C.B. Nam, *Education of the American Population* (1960 Census Monograph); Current Population Reports, Series P-20, various years; and Current Population Survey (CPS), Annual Social and Economic Supplement, 1961 through 2015.

Figure 4. Percentage of persons 25 through 29 years old, by highest level of educational attainment: Selected years, 1940 through 2015

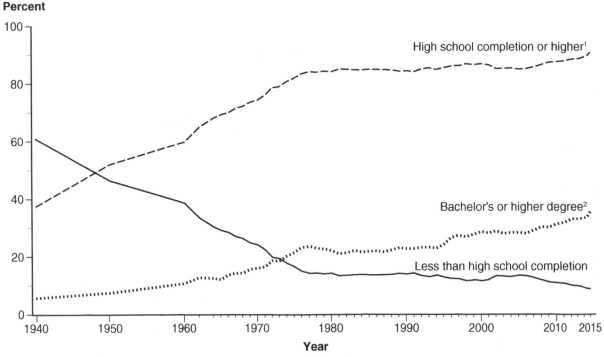

[1]Includes high school completion through equivalency programs, such as a GED program. For years prior to 1993, includes all persons with 4 or more years of high school.
[2]For years prior to 1993, includes all persons with 4 or more years of college.
SOURCE: U.S. Department of Commerce, Census Bureau, *U.S. Census of Population: 1960*, Vol. I, Part 1; J.K. Folger and C.B. Nam, *Education of the American Population* (1960 Census Monograph); Current Population Reports, Series P-20, various years; and Current Population Survey (CPS), Annual Social and Economic Supplement, 1961 through 2015.

Figure 5. Highest level of education attained by persons 25 through 29 years old: 2015

NOTE: High school completion includes equivalency programs, such as a GED program. Detail may not sum to totals because of rounding.
SOURCE: U.S. Department of Commerce, Census Bureau, Current Population Survey (CPS), Annual Social and Economic Supplement, 2015.

Figure 6. Percentage of persons 25 through 29 years old, by selected levels of educational attainment and race/ethnicity: 2005 and 2015

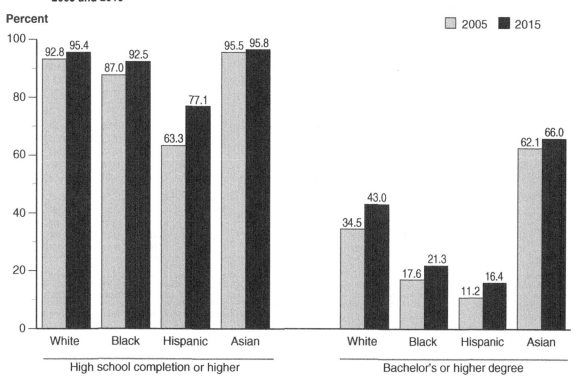

NOTE: High school completion includes equivalency programs, such as a GED program. Race categories exclude persons of Hispanic ethnicity.
SOURCE: U.S. Department of Commerce, Census Bureau, Current Population Survey (CPS), Annual Social and Economic Supplement, 2005 and 2015.

Table 101.10.   Estimates of resident population, by age group: 1970 through 2014

[In thousands]

Year	Total, all ages	Total, 3 to 34 years old	3 and 4 years old	5 and 6 years old	7 to 13 years old	14 to 17 years old	18 and 19 years old	20 and 21 years old	22 to 24 years old	25 to 29 years old	30 to 34 years old
1	2	3	4	5	6	7	8	9	10	11	12
1970	205,052	109,592	6,961	7,703	28,969	15,924	7,510	7,210	9,992	13,736	11,587
1971	207,661	111,202	6,805	7,344	28,892	16,328	7,715	7,350	10,809	14,041	11,917
1972	209,896	112,807	6,789	7,051	28,628	16,639	7,923	7,593	10,560	15,240	12,383
1973	211,909	114,426	6,938	6,888	28,158	16,867	8,114	7,796	10,725	15,786	13,153
1974	213,854	116,075	7,117	6,864	27,600	17,035	8,257	8,003	10,972	16,521	13,704
1975	215,973	117,435	6,912	7,013	26,905	17,128	8,478	8,196	11,331	17,280	14,191
1976	218,035	118,474	6,436	7,195	26,321	17,119	8,659	8,336	11,650	18,274	14,485
1977	220,239	119,261	6,190	6,978	25,877	17,045	8,675	8,550	11,949	18,277	15,721
1978	222,585	119,833	6,208	6,500	25,594	16,946	8,677	8,730	12,216	18,683	16,280
1979	225,055	120,544	6,252	6,256	25,175	16,611	8,751	8,754	12,542	19,178	17,025
1980	227,225	121,132	6,366	6,291	24,800	16,143	8,718	8,669	12,716	19,686	17,743
1981	229,466	121,999	6,535	6,315	24,396	15,609	8,582	8,759	12,903	20,169	18,731
1982	231,664	121,823	6,658	6,407	24,121	15,057	8,480	8,768	12,914	20,704	18,714
1983	233,792	122,302	6,877	6,572	23,709	14,740	8,290	8,652	12,981	21,414	19,067
1984	235,825	122,254	7,045	6,694	23,367	14,725	7,932	8,567	12,962	21,459	19,503
1985	237,924	122,512	7,134	6,916	22,976	14,888	7,637	8,370	12,895	21,671	20,025
1986	240,133	122,688	7,187	7,086	22,992	14,824	7,483	8,024	12,720	21,893	20,479
1987	242,289	122,672	7,132	7,178	23,325	14,502	7,502	7,742	12,450	21,857	20,984
1988	244,499	122,713	7,176	7,238	23,791	14,023	7,701	7,606	12,048	21,739	21,391
1989	246,819	122,655	7,315	7,184	24,228	13,536	7,898	7,651	11,607	21,560	21,676
1990	249,623	122,787	7,359	7,244	24,785	13,329	7,702	7,886	11,264	21,277	21,939
1991	252,981	123,210	7,444	7,393	25,216	13,491	7,208	8,029	11,205	20,923	22,301
1992	256,514	123,722	7,614	7,447	25,752	13,775	6,949	7,797	11,391	20,503	22,494
1993	259,919	124,371	7,887	7,549	26,212	14,096	6,985	7,333	11,657	20,069	22,584
1994	263,126	124,976	8,089	7,725	26,492	14,637	7,047	7,071	11,585	19,740	22,590
1995	266,278	125,478	8,107	8,000	26,825	15,013	7,182	7,103	11,197	19,680	22,372
1996	269,394	125,924	8,022	8,206	27,168	15,443	7,399	7,161	10,715	19,864	21,945
1997	272,647	126,422	7,915	8,232	27,683	15,769	7,569	7,309	10,601	19,899	21,446
1998	275,854	126,939	7,841	8,152	28,302	15,829	7,892	7,520	10,647	19,804	20,953
1999	279,040	127,446	7,772	8,041	28,763	16,007	8,094	7,683	10,908	19,575	20,603
2000	282,162	128,041	7,724	7,972	29,082	16,144	8,199	7,995	11,122	19,280	20,524
2001	284,969	128,467	7,630	7,883	29,210	16,280	8,235	8,290	11,467	18,819	20,652
2002	287,625	128,955	7,617	7,750	29,251	16,506	8,237	8,342	11,902	18,691	20,658
2003	290,108	129,346	7,678	7,661	29,153	16,694	8,325	8,324	12,267	18,772	20,472
2004	292,805	129,965	7,885	7,652	28,806	17,054	8,457	8,312	12,534	19,107	20,160
2005	295,517	130,280	7,973	7,721	28,527	17,358	8,482	8,392	12,568	19,535	19,724
2006	298,380	130,754	7,937	7,942	28,327	17,549	8,567	8,507	12,529	20,110	19,285
2007	301,231	131,417	8,002	8,040	28,256	17,597	8,730	8,500	12,578	20,543	19,171
2008	304,094	132,269	8,033	8,012	28,426	17,395	9,014	8,555	12,626	20,903	19,305
2009	306,772	133,202	8,059	8,088	28,569	17,232	9,146	8,691	12,693	21,078	19,645
2010[1]	309,347	134,105	8,189	8,138	28,730	17,066	9,062	8,956	12,748	21,145	20,070
2011[1]	311,722	134,930	8,225	8,163	28,756	16,873	8,923	9,197	12,975	21,292	20,528
2012[1]	314,112	135,555	8,096	8,230	28,778	16,723	8,791	9,184	13,422	21,402	20,928
2013[1]	316,498	136,165	7,986	8,267	28,817	16,659	8,686	9,041	13,807	21,604	21,298
2014	318,857	136,696	8,009	8,139	28,819	16,748	8,552	8,909	14,004	21,988	21,529

[1]Revised from previously published figures.
NOTE: Resident population includes civilian population and armed forces personnel residing within the United States; it excludes armed forces personnel residing overseas. Detail may not sum to totals because of rounding. Population estimates as of July 1 of the indicated reference year.

SOURCE: U.S. Department of Commerce, Census Bureau, Current Population Reports, Series P-25, Nos. 1000, 1022, 1045, 1057, 1059, 1092, and 1095; 2000 through 2009 Population Estimates, retrieved August 14, 2012, from http://www.census.gov/popest/data/national/asrh/2011/index.html; and 2010 through 2014 Population Estimates, retrieved September 15, 2015, from http://www.census.gov/popest/data/national/asrh/2014/index.html. (This table was prepared September 2015.)

Table 101.20. Estimates of resident population, by race/ethnicity and age group: Selected years, 1980 through 2014

Year and age group	Number (in thousands)								Percentage distribution							
	Total	White	Black	His-panic	Asian	Pacific Islander	American Indian/ Alaska Native	Two or more races	Total	White	Black	His-panic	Asian	Pacific Islander	American Indian/ Alaska Native	Two or more races
1	2	3	4	5	6	7	8	9	10	11	12	13	14	15	16	17
Total																
1980	227,225	181,140	26,215	14,869	3,665	(1)	1,336	—	100.0	79.7	11.5	6.5	1.6	(1)	0.6	—
1990	249,623	188,725	29,439	22,573	7,092	(1)	1,793	—	100.0	75.6	11.8	9.0	2.8	(1)	0.7	—
1995	266,278	194,389	32,500	28,158	9,188	(1)	2,044	—	100.0	73.0	12.2	10.6	3.5	(1)	0.8	—
2000[2]	282,162	195,702	34,406	35,662	10,469	370	2,102	3,452	100.0	69.4	12.2	12.6	3.7	0.1	0.7	1.2
2004[2]	292,805	196,462	35,798	41,501	12,220	421	2,169	4,234	100.0	67.1	12.2	14.2	4.2	0.1	0.7	1.4
2005[2]	295,517	196,621	36,147	43,024	12,658	434	2,186	4,447	100.0	66.5	12.2	14.6	4.3	0.1	0.7	1.5
2008[2]	304,094	197,184	37,291	47,794	13,956	475	2,237	5,158	100.0	64.8	12.3	15.7	4.6	0.2	0.7	1.7
2009[2]	306,772	197,275	37,657	49,327	14,361	488	2,252	5,411	100.0	64.3	12.3	16.1	4.7	0.2	0.7	1.8
2010[2]	309,347	197,387	38,013	50,756	14,774	500	2,269	5,648	100.0	63.8	12.3	16.4	4.8	0.2	0.7	1.8
2011[2]	311,722	197,498	38,394	51,951	15,250	510	2,289	5,830	100.0	63.4	12.3	16.7	4.9	0.2	0.7	1.9
2012[2]	314,112	197,668	38,778	53,086	15,737	521	2,310	6,013	100.0	62.9	12.3	16.9	5.0	0.2	0.7	1.9
2013[2]	316,498	197,777	39,156	54,237	16,264	534	2,330	6,200	100.0	62.5	12.4	17.1	5.1	0.2	0.7	2.0
2014[2]	318,857	197,871	39,528	55,388	16,787	546	2,350	6,388	100.0	62.1	12.4	17.4	5.3	0.2	0.7	2.0
Under 5 years old																
1980	16,451	11,904	2,413	1,677	319	(1)	137	—	100.0	72.4	14.7	10.2	1.9	(1)	0.8	—
1990	18,856	12,757	2,825	2,497	593	(1)	184	—	100.0	67.7	15.0	13.2	3.1	(1)	1.0	—
1995	19,627	12,415	3,050	3,245	734	(1)	182	—	100.0	63.3	15.5	16.5	3.7	(1)	0.9	—
2000[2]	19,178	11,253	2,753	3,748	686	30	171	538	100.0	58.7	14.4	19.5	3.6	0.2	0.9	2.8
2004[2]	19,786	10,940	2,714	4,439	810	34	170	678	100.0	55.3	13.7	22.4	4.1	0.2	0.9	3.4
2005[2]	19,917	10,847	2,706	4,607	839	35	171	712	100.0	54.5	13.6	23.1	4.2	0.2	0.9	3.6
2008[2]	20,271	10,557	2,753	5,032	885	38	176	831	100.0	52.1	13.6	24.8	4.4	0.2	0.9	4.1
2009[2]	20,245	10,395	2,776	5,101	890	39	176	868	100.0	51.3	13.7	25.2	4.4	0.2	0.9	4.3
2010[2]	20,190	10,276	2,780	5,127	892	39	176	899	100.0	50.9	13.8	25.4	4.4	0.2	0.9	4.5
2011[2]	20,126	10,160	2,777	5,159	901	39	174	916	100.0	50.5	13.8	25.6	4.5	0.2	0.9	4.5
2012[2]	19,980	10,036	2,756	5,138	914	39	171	925	100.0	50.2	13.8	25.7	4.6	0.2	0.9	4.6
2013[2]	19,868	9,931	2,739	5,120	935	40	169	933	100.0	50.0	13.8	25.8	4.7	0.2	0.9	4.7
2014[2]	19,877	9,896	2,737	5,131	961	40	168	944	100.0	49.8	13.8	25.8	4.8	0.2	0.8	4.7
5 to 17 years old																
1980	47,232	35,220	6,840	4,005	790	(1)	377	—	100.0	74.6	14.5	8.5	1.7	(1)	0.8	—
1990	45,359	—	—	—	—	—	—	—	—	—	—	—	—	—	—	—
1995	49,838	—	—	—	—	—	—	—	—	—	—	—	—	—	—	—
2000[2]	53,198	33,008	7,994	8,700	1,829	85	522	1,059	100.0	62.0	15.0	16.4	3.4	0.2	1.0	2.0
2004[2]	53,512	31,724	8,005	9,871	1,997	90	504	1,320	100.0	59.3	15.0	18.4	3.7	0.2	0.9	2.5
2005[2]	53,606	31,379	7,987	10,207	2,047	92	499	1,396	100.0	58.5	14.9	19.0	3.8	0.2	0.9	2.6
2008[2]	53,833	30,226	7,813	11,346	2,227	98	483	1,641	100.0	56.1	14.5	21.1	4.1	0.2	0.9	3.0
2009[2]	53,890	29,851	7,726	11,717	2,290	99	478	1,729	100.0	55.4	14.3	21.7	4.2	0.2	0.9	3.2
2010[2]	53,933	29,496	7,644	12,057	2,351	101	475	1,809	100.0	54.7	14.2	22.4	4.4	0.2	0.9	3.4
2011[2]	53,791	29,173	7,548	12,237	2,398	101	470	1,864	100.0	54.2	14.0	22.7	4.5	0.2	0.9	3.5
2012[2]	53,732	28,879	7,485	12,431	2,446	102	467	1,922	100.0	53.7	13.9	23.1	4.6	0.2	0.9	3.6
2013[2]	53,742	28,603	7,455	12,632	2,501	103	465	1,983	100.0	53.2	13.9	23.5	4.7	0.2	0.9	3.7
2014[2]	53,707	28,308	7,438	12,808	2,547	104	463	2,039	100.0	52.7	13.8	23.8	4.7	0.2	0.9	3.8
18 to 24 years old																
1980	30,103	23,278	3,872	2,284	468	(1)	201	—	100.0	77.3	12.9	7.6	1.6	(1)	0.7	—
1990	26,853	—	—	—	—	—	—	—	—	—	—	—	—	—	—	—
1995	25,482	—	—	—	—	—	—	—	—	—	—	—	—	—	—	—
2000[2]	27,315	16,913	3,780	4,786	1,158	50	239	389	100.0	61.9	13.8	17.5	4.2	0.2	0.9	1.4
2004[2]	29,302	17,765	4,072	5,313	1,328	57	261	506	100.0	60.6	13.9	18.1	4.5	0.2	0.9	1.7
2005[2]	29,442	17,741	4,092	5,406	1,351	57	263	531	100.0	60.3	13.9	18.4	4.6	0.2	0.9	1.8
2008[2]	30,194	17,712	4,283	5,813	1,445	62	266	613	100.0	58.7	14.2	19.3	4.8	0.2	0.9	2.0
2009[2]	30,530	17,705	4,363	6,006	1,481	64	266	645	100.0	58.0	14.3	19.7	4.9	0.2	0.9	2.1
2010[2]	30,767	17,618	4,436	6,183	1,520	66	266	678	100.0	57.3	14.4	20.1	4.9	0.2	0.9	2.2
2011[2]	31,094	17,615	4,564	6,304	1,558	66	272	716	100.0	56.6	14.7	20.3	5.0	0.2	0.9	2.3
2012[2]	31,397	17,611	4,664	6,428	1,596	66	276	756	100.0	56.1	14.9	20.5	5.1	0.2	0.9	2.4
2013[2]	31,534	17,525	4,705	6,541	1,627	65	277	794	100.0	55.6	14.9	20.7	5.2	0.2	0.9	2.5
2014[2]	31,464	17,340	4,671	6,639	1,645	65	276	829	100.0	55.1	14.8	21.1	5.2	0.2	0.9	2.6
25 years old and over																
1980	133,438	110,737	13,091	6,903	2,088	(1)	620	—	100.0	83.0	9.8	5.2	1.6	(1)	0.5	—
1990	158,555	125,653	16,322	11,447	4,190	(1)	944	—	100.0	79.2	10.3	7.2	2.6	(1)	0.6	—
1995	171,332	131,839	18,250	14,519	5,628	(1)	1,096	—	100.0	76.9	10.7	8.5	3.3	(1)	0.6	—
2000[2]	182,471	134,529	19,879	18,427	6,796	205	1,170	1,465	100.0	73.7	10.9	10.1	3.7	0.1	0.6	0.8
2004[2]	190,205	136,033	21,007	21,877	8,084	240	1,234	1,729	100.0	71.5	11.0	11.5	4.3	0.1	0.6	0.9
2005[2]	192,551	136,655	21,361	22,804	8,421	250	1,253	1,808	100.0	71.0	11.1	11.8	4.4	0.1	0.7	0.9
2008[2]	199,795	138,689	22,441	25,603	9,400	277	1,312	2,074	100.0	69.4	11.2	12.8	4.7	0.1	0.7	1.0
2009[2]	202,107	139,324	22,792	26,504	9,700	285	1,332	2,170	100.0	68.9	11.3	13.1	4.8	0.1	0.7	1.1
2010[2]	204,457	139,997	23,153	27,389	10,011	294	1,352	2,262	100.0	68.5	11.3	13.4	4.9	0.1	0.7	1.1
2011[2]	206,710	140,550	23,505	28,251	10,392	304	1,373	2,334	100.0	68.0	11.4	13.7	5.0	0.1	0.7	1.1
2012[2]	209,003	141,142	23,873	29,088	10,782	314	1,395	2,409	100.0	67.5	11.4	13.9	5.2	0.2	0.7	1.2
2013[2]	211,353	141,718	24,257	29,943	11,201	326	1,418	2,490	100.0	67.1	11.5	14.2	5.3	0.2	0.7	1.2
2014[2]	213,809	142,328	24,682	30,810	11,634	337	1,443	2,576	100.0	66.6	11.5	14.4	5.4	0.2	0.7	1.2

—Not available.
[1]Included under Asian.
[2]Data on persons of Two or more races were collected beginning in 2000. Direct comparability of the data (other than Hispanic) prior to 2000 with the data for 2000 and later years is limited by the extent to which people reporting more than one race in later years had been reported in specific race groups in earlier years.
NOTE: Resident population includes civilian population and armed forces personnel residing within the United States; it excludes armed forces personnel residing overseas. Race catego-ries exclude persons of Hispanic ethnicity. Detail may not sum to totals because of rounding. Some data have been revised from previously published figures. Population estimates as of July 1 of the indicated reference year.
SOURCE: U.S. Department of Commerce, Census Bureau, Current Population Reports, Series P-25, Nos. 1092 and 1095; 2000 through 2009 Population Estimates, retrieved August 14, 2012, from http://www.census.gov/popest/data/national/asrh/2011/index.html; and 2010 through 2014 Population Estimates, retrieved September 15, 2015, from http://www.census.gov/popest/data/national/asrh/2014/index.html. (This table was prepared September 2015.)

Table 101.30. Number, percentage, and percentage distribution of total resident population and population under 18 years old, by nativity, race/ethnicity, and selected racial/ethnic subgroups: 2004, 2009, and 2014

[Numbers in thousands. Standard errors appear in parentheses]

Year and race/ethnicity	Total, all ages						Under 18					
	Total number	U.S.-born[1] Number	U.S.-born[1] Percent	Foreign-born Number	Foreign-born Percent	Percentage distribution	Total number	U.S.-born[1] Number	U.S.-born[1] Percent	Foreign-born Number	Foreign-born Percent	Percentage distribution
1	2	3	4	5	6	7	8	9	10	11	12	13
2004												
Total	285,675 (328.7)	251,417 (227.7)	88.0 (0.08)	34,258 (227.7)	12.0 (0.08)	100.0 (†)	72,879 (305.5)	69,950 (301.4)	96.0 (0.10)	2,929 (70.6)	4.0 (0.10)	100.0 (†)
White	192,373 (327.3)	185,057 (334.8)	96.2 (0.06)	7,316 (110.7)	3.8 (0.06)	21.4 (0.29)	42,846 (250.3)	42,350 (249.1)	98.8 (0.09)	496 (29.2)	1.2 (0.09)	16.9 (0.91)
Black	34,132 (227.3)	31,659 (220.0)	92.8 (0.18)	2,473 (64.9)	7.2 (0.18)	7.2 (0.18)	10,646 (132.8)	10,436 (131.5)	98.0 (0.18)	210 (19.0)	2.0 (0.18)	7.2 (0.63)
Hispanic	40,451 (244.4)	24,609 (196.7)	60.8 (0.32)	15,842 (160.4)	39.2 (0.32)	46.2 (0.35)	13,891 (150.8)	12,320 (142.4)	88.7 (0.35)	1,571 (51.8)	11.3 (0.35)	53.6 (1.21)
Asian	11,937 (140.3)	3,827 (80.6)	32.1 (0.56)	8,110 (116.4)	67.9 (0.56)	23.7 (0.30)	2,716 (68.0)	2,124 (60.2)	78.2 (1.04)	592 (31.9)	21.8 (1.04)	20.2 (0.97)
Pacific Islander	362 (24.9)	286 (22.2)	79.0 (2.81)	76 (11.4)	21.0 (2.81)	0.2 ! (0.10)	101 (13.2)	93 (12.6)	91.7 (3.59)	8 ! (3.8)	8.3 ! (3.59)	‡ (†)
American Indian/Alaska Native	1,862 (56.4)	1,839 (56.1)	98.8 (0.43)	23 (6.3)	1.2 ! (0.43)	‡ (†)	545 (30.6)	544 (30.6)	99.7 (0.79)	‡ (†)	‡ (†)	‡ (†)
Some other race[2]	606 (32.2)	365 (25.0)	60.3 (2.61)	241 (20.3)	39.7 (2.61)	0.7 (0.10)	215 (19.2)	190 (18.1)	88.4 (2.87)	25 (6.5)	11.6 (2.87)	0.9 ! (0.34)
Two or more races	3,953 (81.9)	3,776 (80.0)	95.5 (0.43)	177 (17.4)	4.5 (0.43)	0.5 (0.10)	1,919 (57.3)	1,894 (56.9)	98.7 (0.42)	25 (6.5)	1.3 ! (0.42)	0.8 ! (0.34)
White and Black	975 (40.9)	955 (40.5)	98.0 (0.59)	19 (5.8)	2.0 (0.59)	‡ (†)	720 (35.1)	715 (35.0)	99.4 (0.68)	‡ (†)	‡ (†)	‡ (†)
White and Asian	809 (37.2)	742 (35.7)	91.8 (1.27)	66 (10.7)	8.2 (1.27)	‡ (†)	463 (28.2)	451 (27.8)	97.4 (0.96)	12 ! (4.5)	2.6 ! (0.96)	‡ (†)
White and American Indian/Alaska Native	1,202 (45.4)	1,197 (45.3)	99.6 (0.53)	† (12.2)	†	‡	336 (24.0)	335 (24.0)	100.0 (1.00)	‡ (†)	‡	‡ (†)
Other Two or more races	968 (40.7)	881 (38.9)	91.0 (1.20)	87 (12.2)	9.0 (1.20)	0.3 ! (0.10)	401 (26.2)	392 (26.0)	97.9 (0.95)	9 ! (3.8)	2.1 ! (0.95)	‡ (†)
2009												
Total	307,007 (9.9)	268,554 (89.9)	87.5 (0.03)	38,453 (84.3)	12.5 (0.03)	100.0 (†)	74,472 (23.1)	71,721 (33.0)	96.3 (0.03)	2,752 (23.7)	3.7 (0.03)	100.0 (†)
White	199,327 (19.1)	191,562 (51.8)	96.1 (0.02)	7,765 (45.7)	3.9 (0.02)	20.2 (0.10)	41,048 (8.6)	40,596 (13.1)	98.9 (0.03)	452 (10.8)	1.1 (0.03)	16.4 (0.35)
Black	37,178 (38.3)	34,297 (46.5)	92.3 (0.08)	2,881 (28.9)	7.7 (0.08)	7.5 (0.07)	10,219 (24.8)	9,984 (25.7)	97.7 (0.09)	236 (8.8)	2.3 (0.09)	8.6 (0.30)
Hispanic	48,348 (10.0)	30,279 (55.6)	62.6 (0.11)	18,069 (52.5)	37.4 (0.11)	47.0 (0.10)	16,694 (8.0)	15,312 (19.0)	91.7 (0.10)	1,382 (16.2)	8.3 (0.10)	50.2 (0.43)
Cuban	1,677 (19.1)	691 (14.1)	41.2 (0.62)	986 (13.9)	58.8 (0.62)	2.6 (0.04)	361 (8.6)	312 (8.4)	86.4 (0.78)	49 (2.9)	13.6 (0.78)	1.8 (0.11)
Dominican	1,360 (27.6)	580 (14.2)	42.6 (0.61)	780 (18.0)	57.4 (0.61)	2.0 (0.04)	414 (11.6)	354 (10.4)	85.6 (0.86)	60 (4.0)	14.4 (0.86)	2.2 (0.14)
Mexican	31,674 (59.1)	20,247 (45.1)	63.9 (0.14)	11,426 (57.1)	36.1 (0.14)	29.7 (0.13)	11,795 (29.3)	10,844 (31.8)	91.9 (0.13)	952 (15.1)	8.1 (0.13)	34.6 (0.43)
Puerto Rican	4,412 (36.1)	4,368 (36.3)	99.0 (0.09)	43 (3.9)	1.0 (0.09)	0.1 (0.01)	1,486 (14.6)	1,484 (14.6)	99.9 (0.03)	3 (0.9)	0.1 (0.03)	0.1 (0.02)
Spaniard	614 (13.8)	530 (13.2)	86.5 (0.67)	83 (4.3)	13.5 (0.67)	0.2 (0.01)	149 (6.4)	145 (6.3)	97.8 (0.61)	3 (0.9)	2.2 (0.61)	0.1 (0.03)
Central American[3]	4,140 (44.5)	1,460 (23.1)	35.3 (0.36)	2,680 (30.5)	64.7 (0.36)	7.0 (0.08)	1,195 (19.1)	1,028 (18.0)	86.0 (0.40)	167 (5.0)	14.0 (0.40)	6.1 (0.18)
Costa Rican	131 (6.1)	50 (3.3)	38.1 (1.85)	81 (4.6)	61.9 (1.85)	0.2 (0.01)	31 (2.5)	26 (2.4)	85.1 (2.63)	5 (0.8)	14.9 (2.63)	0.2 (0.03)
Guatemalan	1,077 (25.8)	340 (12.1)	31.5 (0.70)	738 (17.9)	68.5 (0.70)	1.9 (0.05)	324 (10.9)	259 (10.1)	80.0 (1.04)	65 (3.5)	20.0 (1.04)	2.3 (0.13)
Honduran	625 (15.7)	197 (7.2)	31.5 (0.75)	428 (11.2)	68.5 (0.75)	1.1 (0.03)	181 (7.0)	149 (6.4)	82.7 (1.28)	31 (2.5)	17.3 (1.28)	1.1 (0.09)
Nicaraguan	369 (13.9)	125 (5.9)	34.0 (1.09)	243 (10.3)	66.0 (1.09)	0.6 (0.03)	83 (4.3)	76 (4.2)	91.6 (1.49)	7 (1.3)	8.4 (1.49)	0.3 (0.05)
Panamanian	170 (7.5)	87 (4.7)	51.4 (1.75)	83 (4.8)	48.6 (1.75)	0.2 (0.01)	41 (3.4)	39 (3.4)	95.2 (1.69)	2 (0.6)	4.8 ! (1.69)	0.1 (0.03)
Salvadoran	1,736 (26.6)	647 (14.3)	37.3 (0.51)	1,089 (17.6)	62.7 (0.51)	2.8 (0.05)	528 (13.2)	470 (12.1)	89.1 (0.61)	57 (3.6)	10.9 (0.61)	2.1 (0.13)
South American	2,831 (36.4)	959 (17.8)	33.9 (0.43)	1,873 (26.2)	66.1 (0.43)	4.9 (0.07)	702 (13.6)	564 (13.4)	80.4 (0.73)	138 (5.0)	19.6 (0.73)	5.0 (0.18)
Chilean	123 (7.6)	48 (3.8)	39.3 (1.80)	75 (5.1)	60.7 (1.80)	0.2 (0.01)	31 (3.3)	25 (2.7)	81.4 (3.32)	6 (1.3)	18.6 (3.32)	0.2 (0.05)
Colombian	917 (19.5)	311 (9.3)	34.0 (0.63)	605 (13.4)	66.0 (0.63)	1.6 (0.04)	226 (7.9)	180 (6.8)	79.7 (1.02)	46 (2.7)	20.3 (1.02)	1.7 (0.10)
Ecuadorian	611 (16.3)	211 (7.7)	34.5 (0.87)	400 (11.9)	65.5 (0.87)	1.0 (0.03)	156 (6.2)	132 (5.9)	84.4 (1.58)	24 (2.6)	15.6 (1.58)	0.9 (0.09)
Peruvian	557 (16.4)	184 (8.4)	33.1 (1.00)	373 (11.6)	66.9 (1.00)	1.0 (0.03)	141 (7.3)	115 (7.0)	81.5 (1.68)	26 (2.4)	18.5 (1.68)	0.9 (0.09)
Venezuelan	198 (7.7)	60 (3.6)	30.3 (1.39)	138 (6.0)	69.7 (1.39)	0.4 (0.02)	49 (3.1)	34 (2.5)	69.0 (2.99)	15 (1.8)	31.0 (2.99)	0.5 (0.06)
Other South American	425 (10.6)	143 (5.9)	33.8 (1.10)	281 (8.4)	66.2 (1.10)	0.7 (0.02)	99 (4.6)	78 (4.1)	79.0 (1.91)	21 (2.1)	21.0 (1.91)	0.8 (0.08)
Other Hispanic	1,640 (23.7)	1,443 (20.9)	88.0 (0.42)	198 (7.9)	12.0 (0.42)	0.5 (0.02)	593 (12.7)	580 (12.7)	97.9 (0.23)	13 (1.4)	2.1 (0.23)	0.5 (0.05)
Asian	13,605 (20.9)	4,459 (22.1)	32.8 (0.15)	9,146 (24.8)	67.2 (0.15)	23.8 (0.06)	3,039 (12.6)	2,406 (14.6)	79.2 (0.33)	633 (10.1)	20.8 (0.33)	23.0 (0.34)
Chinese[4]	3,175 (25.7)	977 (11.7)	30.8 (0.31)	2,197 (21.6)	69.2 (0.31)	5.7 (0.06)	650 (9.0)	503 (8.0)	77.3 (0.78)	148 (5.7)	22.7 (0.78)	5.4 (0.20)
Filipino	2,425 (29.3)	788 (14.3)	32.5 (0.38)	1,636 (20.4)	67.5 (0.38)	4.3 (0.05)	454 (10.7)	359 (10.4)	79.1 (0.98)	95 (4.5)	20.9 (0.98)	3.4 (0.17)
Japanese	745 (14.7)	435 (9.4)	58.4 (0.79)	310 (9.3)	41.6 (0.79)	0.8 (0.02)	76 (4.5)	55 (3.4)	72.9 (2.22)	21 (2.3)	27.1 (2.22)	0.8 (0.08)
Korean	1,339 (17.4)	332 (8.8)	24.8 (0.52)	1,007 (13.7)	75.2 (0.52)	2.6 (0.04)	267 (7.7)	172 (6.2)	64.5 (1.41)	95 (4.7)	35.5 (1.41)	3.4 (0.17)
South Asian[5]	3,053 (31.5)	869 (14.4)	28.4 (0.33)	2,185 (23.2)	71.6 (0.33)	5.7 (0.06)	785 (11.3)	622 (10.6)	79.2 (0.65)	163 (5.5)	20.8 (0.65)	5.9 (0.19)
Asian Indian	2,591 (27.6)	730 (12.0)	28.2 (0.34)	1,861 (21.3)	71.8 (0.34)	4.8 (0.05)	645 (9.9)	516 (9.0)	79.9 (0.67)	130 (4.7)	20.1 (0.67)	4.7 (0.16)
Bangladeshi	93 (6.3)	26 (2.6)	28.3 (1.76)	67 (4.6)	71.7 (1.76)	0.2 (0.01)	31 (2.7)	23 (2.5)	73.8 (3.46)	8 (1.2)	26.2 (3.46)	0.3 (0.04)
Bhutanese	— (†)	— (†)	— (†)	— (†)	— (†)	— (†)	— (†)	— (†)	— (†)	— (†)	— (†)	— (†)
Nepalese	— (†)	— (†)	— (†)	— (†)	— (†)	— (†)	— (†)	— (†)	— (†)	— (†)	— (†)	— (†)
Pakistani	330 (13.4)	104 (5.8)	31.6 (1.11)	226 (9.6)	68.4 (1.11)	0.6 (0.02)	99 (4.9)	77 (4.3)	77.9 (1.99)	22 (2.2)	22.1 (1.99)	0.8 (0.08)

See notes at end of table.

Table 101.30. Number, percentage, and percentage distribution of total resident population and population under 18 years old, by nativity, race/ethnicity, and selected racial/ethnic subgroups: 2004, 2009, and 2014—Continued

[Numbers in thousands. Standard errors appear in parentheses]

Year and race/ethnicity	Total, all ages						Under 18					
	Total number	U.S.-born[1] Number	U.S.-born Percent	Foreign-born Number	Foreign-born Percent	Foreign-born Percentage distribution	Total number	U.S.-born[1] Number	U.S.-born Percent	Foreign-born Number	Foreign-born Percent	Foreign-born Percentage distribution
1	2	3	4	5	6	7	8	9	10	11	12	13
Southeast Asian	2,363 (29.9)	812 (14.1)	34.4 (0.36)	1,551 (20.4)	65.6 (0.36)	4.0 (0.05)	633 (13.2)	548 (11.5)	86.6 (0.59)	85 (4.3)	13.4 (0.59)	3.1 (0.16)
Burmese	— (†)	— (†)	— (†)	— (†)	— (†)	— (†)	— (†)	— (†)	— (†)	— (†)	— (†)	— (†)
Cambodian	229 (10.7)	94 (5.9)	40.9 (1.44)	135 (6.6)	59.1 (1.44)	0.4 (0.02)	62 (4.4)	56 (4.4)	90.3 (1.53)	6 (0.9)	9.7 (1.53)	0.2 (0.03)
Hmong	225 (8.4)	128 (6.0)	56.8 (1.37)	97 (4.4)	43.2 (1.37)	0.3 (0.01)	98 (5.0)	86 (4.9)	87.8 (2.17)	12 (2.2)	12.2 (2.17)	0.4 (0.08)
Laotian	200 (10.1)	80 (5.4)	40.1 (1.31)	120 (5.9)	59.9 (1.31)	0.3 (0.02)	50 (3.5)	48 (3.4)	96.1 (1.12)	‡ (†)	3.9 (1.12)	0.1 (0.02)
Thai	169 (6.9)	41 (3.1)	24.1 (1.35)	128 (5.3)	75.9 (1.35)	0.3 (0.01)	30 (2.8)	20 (2.2)	66.8 (3.80)	10 (1.5)	33.2 (3.80)	0.4 (0.05)
Vietnamese	1,469 (23.4)	450 (9.9)	30.6 (0.44)	1,019 (17.2)	69.4 (0.44)	2.7 (0.04)	380 (9.2)	327 (8.0)	86.0 (0.78)	53 (3.4)	14.0 (0.78)	1.9 (0.13)
Other Southeast Asian[6]	72 (5.5)	20 (2.1)	27.3 (2.00)	52 (4.2)	72.7 (2.00)	0.1 (0.01)	13 (2.0)	11 (1.8)	86.3 (4.80)	‡ (†)	13.7 ! (4.80)	0.1 ! (0.03)
Other Asian	505 (10.8)	247 (7.1)	48.8 (0.98)	259 (7.6)	51.2 (0.98)	0.7 (0.02)	174 (5.9)	147 (4.9)	84.3 (1.27)	27 (2.6)	15.7 (1.27)	1.0 (0.09)
Pacific Islander	417 (6.7)	328 (7.5)	78.6 (1.18)	89 (5.0)	21.4 (1.18)	0.2 (0.01)	106 (3.0)	99 (3.1)	93.1 (1.11)	7 (1.2)	6.9 (1.11)	0.3 (0.04)
American Indian/Alaska Native	1,969 (13.9)	1,944 (14.1)	98.7 (0.12)	25 (2.3)	1.3 (0.12)	0.1 (0.01)	541 (7.6)	538 (7.7)	99.5 (0.12)	‡ (†)	0.5 (0.12)	0.1 (0.02)
Some other race[2]	671 (17.3)	425 (12.1)	63.3 (1.10)	247 (10.5)	36.7 (1.10)	0.6 (0.03)	229 (8.1)	207 (7.9)	90.3 (0.94)	22 (2.2)	9.7 (0.94)	0.8 (0.08)
Two or more races	5,490 (45.0)	5,260 (43.6)	95.8 (0.11)	230 (6.5)	4.2 (0.11)	0.6 (0.02)	2,596 (24.0)	2,580 (24.0)	99.4 (0.05)	16 (1.4)	0.6 (0.05)	0.6 (0.05)
White and Black	1,530 (21.5)	1,498 (21.0)	97.9 (0.16)	32 (2.5)	2.1 (0.16)	0.1 (0.01)	1,036 (15.2)	1,034 (15.2)	99.8 (0.06)	‡ (†)	0.2 (0.06)	0.1 (0.02)
White and Asian	1,191 (15.4)	1,117 (14.6)	93.8 (0.29)	74 (3.7)	6.2 (0.29)	0.2 (0.01)	664 (9.8)	657 (9.6)	99.0 (0.14)	7 (0.9)	1.0 (0.14)	0.2 (0.03)
White and American Indian/Alaska Native	1,480 (13.8)	1,475 (13.7)	99.7 (0.05)	5 (0.7)	0.3 (0.05)	# (†)	398 (7.2)	398 (7.2)	100.0 (0.01)	‡ (†)	† (†)	† (†)
Other Two or more races	1,289 (17.5)	1,170 (16.8)	90.7 (0.35)	119 (4.7)	9.3 (0.35)	0.3 (0.01)	498 (9.3)	491 (9.2)	98.5 (0.18)	7 (0.9)	1.5 (0.18)	0.3 (0.03)
2014												
Total	318,857 (1.8)	276,621 (104.0)	86.8 (0.03)	42,236 (103.1)	13.2 (0.03)	100.0 (†)	73,492 (25.7)	70,987 (31.4)	96.6 (0.03)	2,505 (25.2)	3.4 (0.03)	100.0 (†)
White	197,441 (15.1)	189,786 (45.3)	96.1 (0.02)	7,655 (42.1)	3.9 (0.02)	18.1 (0.08)	38,057 (7.3)	37,685 (13.9)	99.0 (0.03)	373 (10.0)	1.0 (0.03)	14.9 (0.38)
Black	39,302 (42.8)	35,924 (45.3)	91.4 (0.07)	3,378 (28.0)	8.6 (0.07)	8.0 (0.06)	10,025 (25.9)	9,765 (26.3)	97.4 (0.08)	260 (8.5)	2.6 (0.08)	10.4 (0.32)
Hispanic	55,251 (9.7)	35,950 (67.3)	65.1 (0.12)	19,301 (65.5)	34.9 (0.12)	45.7 (0.10)	17,879 (8.4)	16,778 (20.7)	93.8 (0.11)	1,102 (19.1)	6.2 (0.11)	44.0 (0.57)
Cuban	2,046 (22.9)	879 (16.3)	42.9 (0.60)	1,167 (17.3)	57.1 (0.60)	2.8 (0.04)	414 (10.1)	358 (9.2)	86.4 (0.81)	56 (3.7)	13.6 (0.81)	2.2 (0.14)
Dominican	1,764 (28.7)	805 (16.8)	45.6 (0.55)	959 (17.8)	54.4 (0.55)	2.3 (0.04)	497 (12.9)	425 (11.0)	85.6 (0.86)	71 (5.0)	14.4 (0.86)	2.8 (0.20)
Mexican	35,371 (67.9)	23,742 (52.4)	67.1 (0.13)	11,630 (59.4)	32.9 (0.13)	27.5 (0.11)	12,344 (30.5)	11,706 (27.9)	94.8 (0.12)	638 (15.3)	5.2 (0.12)	25.5 (0.51)
Puerto Rican	5,320 (16.4)	5,237 (40.5)	98.4 (0.08)	83 (4.1)	1.6 (0.08)	0.2 (0.01)	1,687 (21.0)	1,683 (20.8)	99.8 (0.05)	4 (0.9)	0.2 (0.05)	0.2 (0.04)
Spaniard	754 (16.4)	643 (14.7)	85.4 (0.69)	110 (5.8)	14.6 (0.69)	0.3 (0.01)	200 (7.4)	191 (7.1)	95.5 (0.76)	9 (1.6)	4.5 (0.76)	0.4 (0.06)
Central American[3]	5,030 (52.6)	2,021 (25.9)	40.2 (0.30)	3,008 (34.9)	59.8 (0.30)	7.1 (0.08)	1,493 (22.0)	1,298 (21.3)	87.0 (0.44)	195 (6.7)	13.0 (0.44)	7.8 (0.25)
Costa Rican	141 (8.0)	67 (4.4)	47.6 (1.83)	74 (5.1)	52.4 (1.83)	0.2 (0.01)	34 (3.0)	32 (2.9)	93.5 (2.05)	‡ (†)	6.5 ! (2.05)	0.1 ! (0.03)
Guatemalan	1,325 (26.1)	490 (12.3)	37.0 (0.57)	834 (18.0)	63.0 (0.57)	2.0 (0.04)	406 (11.1)	341 (9.9)	84.0 (0.92)	65 (4.2)	16.0 (0.92)	2.6 (0.17)
Honduran	813 (24.2)	297 (11.1)	36.5 (0.80)	516 (16.5)	63.5 (0.80)	1.2 (0.04)	261 (11.4)	217 (9.6)	83.1 (1.31)	44 (4.2)	16.9 (1.31)	1.8 (0.16)
Nicaraguan	414 (14.7)	176 (7.8)	42.5 (0.96)	238 (8.9)	57.5 (0.96)	0.6 (0.02)	98 (5.5)	92 (5.3)	93.9 (1.07)	6 (1.1)	6.1 (1.07)	0.2 (0.04)
Panamanian	190 (8.0)	106 (5.6)	55.9 (1.64)	84 (4.6)	44.1 (1.64)	0.2 (0.01)	42 (3.3)	41 (3.3)	97.4 (1.18)	‡ (†)	2.6 ! (1.18)	# (†)
Salvadoran	2,100 (38.3)	860 (19.2)	41.0 (0.47)	1,240 (24.0)	59.0 (0.47)	2.9 (0.06)	638 (16.7)	564 (15.3)	88.3 (0.66)	74 (4.6)	11.7 (0.66)	3.0 (0.18)
South American	3,283 (37.6)	1,211 (17.5)	36.9 (0.36)	2,072 (27.2)	63.1 (0.36)	4.9 (0.06)	750 (13.8)	641 (12.4)	85.4 (0.63)	109 (5.3)	14.6 (0.63)	4.4 (0.21)
Chilean	149 (9.0)	65 (5.0)	43.3 (1.88)	84 (5.6)	56.7 (1.88)	0.2 (0.01)	33 (3.8)	29 (3.4)	87.5 (2.98)	4 (1.1)	12.5 (2.98)	0.2 (0.04)
Colombian	1,046 (21.2)	382 (9.7)	36.5 (0.69)	664 (14.7)	63.5 (0.69)	1.6 (0.04)	216 (8.0)	185 (7.2)	85.6 (1.07)	31 (2.6)	14.4 (1.07)	1.2 (0.10)
Ecuadorian	659 (23.8)	259 (12.0)	39.2 (0.92)	400 (14.7)	60.8 (0.92)	0.9 (0.03)	168 (9.3)	153 (9.2)	91.4 (1.06)	14 (1.7)	8.6 (1.06)	0.6 (0.07)
Peruvian	614 (17.4)	215 (8.9)	35.0 (1.00)	399 (12.5)	65.0 (1.00)	0.9 (0.03)	138 (6.5)	119 (6.0)	86.8 (1.31)	18 (2.0)	13.2 (1.31)	0.7 (0.08)
Venezuelan	303 (11.0)	94 (5.8)	31.2 (1.40)	208 (8.1)	68.8 (1.40)	0.5 (0.02)	74 (5.1)	53 (4.4)	72.3 (2.98)	20 (2.5)	27.7 (2.98)	0.8 (0.10)
Other South American	512 (13.5)	196 (7.5)	38.3 (1.01)	316 (9.5)	61.7 (1.01)	0.7 (0.02)	122 (6.0)	101 (5.6)	82.8 (1.69)	21 (2.2)	17.2 (1.69)	0.8 (0.09)
Other Hispanic	1,683 (28.4)	1,412 (24.8)	83.9 (0.48)	271 (9.5)	16.1 (0.48)	0.6 (0.02)	495 (14.1)	475 (13.8)	96.1 (0.48)	19 (2.4)	3.9 (0.48)	0.8 (0.10)
Asian	16,501 (27.9)	5,465 (24.1)	33.1 (0.13)	11,036 (27.1)	66.9 (0.13)	26.1 (0.07)	3,355 (15.7)	2,659 (15.0)	79.3 (0.31)	696 (11.5)	20.7 (0.31)	27.8 (0.39)
Chinese[7]	3,924 (33.0)	1,195 (15.1)	30.4 (0.30)	2,729 (26.0)	69.6 (0.30)	6.5 (0.06)	707 (10.8)	547 (9.9)	77.3 (0.62)	160 (4.8)	22.7 (0.62)	6.4 (0.19)
Filipino	2,696 (29.3)	896 (15.9)	33.2 (0.38)	1,800 (19.7)	66.8 (0.38)	4.3 (0.05)	451 (11.3)	354 (9.6)	78.5 (0.89)	97 (4.8)	21.5 (0.89)	3.9 (0.19)
Japanese	745 (11.6)	434 (9.2)	58.2 (0.84)	311 (7.9)	41.8 (0.84)	0.7 (0.02)	65 (3.7)	48 (3.4)	73.6 (2.59)	17 (1.8)	26.4 (2.59)	0.7 (0.07)
Korean	1,466 (21.7)	408 (10.4)	27.8 (0.54)	1,058 (16.8)	72.2 (0.54)	2.5 (0.04)	241 (7.0)	179 (6.2)	74.2 (1.40)	62 (3.8)	25.8 (1.40)	2.5 (0.15)

See notes at end of table.

Table 101.30. Number, percentage, and percentage distribution of total resident population and population under 18 years old, by nativity, race/ethnicity, and selected racial/ethnic subgroups: 2004, 2009, and 2014—Continued

[Numbers in thousands. Standard errors appear in parentheses]

Year and race/ethnicity	Total, all ages						Under 18					
	Total number	U.S.-born[1]		Foreign-born		Percentage distribution	Total number	U.S.-born[1]		Foreign-born		Percentage distribution
		Number	Percent	Number	Percent			Number	Percent	Number	Percent	
1	2	3	4	5	6	7	8	9	10	11	12	13
South Asian[5]	4,239 (43.4)	1,200 (17.1)	28.3 (0.29)	3,039 (33.7)	71.7 (0.29)	7.2 (0.08)	1,028 (13.7)	793 (12.5)	77.1 (0.68)	236 (7.8)	22.9 (0.68)	9.4 (0.29)
Asian Indian	3,437 (37.0)	989 (15.0)	28.8 (0.33)	2,448 (29.6)	71.2 (0.33)	5.8 (0.07)	816 (12.1)	644 (11.1)	78.9 (0.72)	172 (6.5)	21.1 (0.72)	6.9 (0.25)
Bangladeshi	157 (9.1)	39 (3.4)	25.0 (1.49)	118 (6.9)	75.0 (1.49)	0.3 (0.02)	44 (3.9)	31 (3.0)	70.0 (3.06)	13 (1.9)	30.0 (3.06)	0.5 (0.07)
Bhutanese	31 (5.6)	‡ (†)	8.7 (†)	28 (5.1)	91.3 (2.26)	0.1 (0.01)	8 (1.9)	‡ (†)	33.4 (8.82)	5 (1.5)	66.6 (8.82)	0.2 (0.06)
Nepalese	132 (8.4)	17 (1.9)	13.1 (1.26)	114 (7.6)	86.9 (1.26)	0.3 (0.02)	34 (2.8)	14 (1.7)	41.6 (3.77)	20 (2.1)	58.4 (3.77)	0.8 (0.08)
Pakistani	443 (13.4)	142 (6.2)	32.1 (1.03)	300 (10.3)	67.9 (1.03)	0.7 (0.02)	119 (5.4)	96 (4.8)	80.2 (1.78)	24 (2.4)	19.8 (1.78)	0.9 (0.09)
Southeast Asian	2,910 (34.8)	1,006 (14.8)	34.6 (0.34)	1,905 (25.5)	65.4 (0.34)	4.5 (0.06)	669 (12.4)	558 (10.8)	83.4 (0.64)	111 (4.9)	16.6 (0.64)	4.4 (0.19)
Burmese	142 (9.6)	18 (2.2)	12.7 (1.29)	124 (8.6)	87.3 (1.29)	0.3 (0.02)	45 (3.8)	17 (2.2)	37.2 (3.51)	28 (2.8)	62.8 (3.51)	1.1 (0.11)
Cambodian	267 (12.0)	110 (5.9)	41.1 (1.38)	157 (8.2)	58.9 (1.38)	0.4 (0.02)	60 (3.9)	57 (3.8)	94.0 (1.28)	4 (0.8)	6.0 (1.28)	0.1 (0.03)
Hmong	287 (11.6)	178 (8.0)	62.1 (1.55)	109 (6.6)	37.9 (1.55)	0.3 (0.02)	109 (6.4)	102 (6.2)	93.9 (1.73)	7 (1.9)	6.1 (1.73)	0.3 (0.08)
Laotian	221 (11.1)	88 (5.1)	39.8 (1.23)	133 (7.3)	60.2 (1.23)	0.3 (0.02)	50 (4.5)	46 (4.2)	91.6 (1.83)	4 (1.0)	8.4 (1.83)	0.2 (0.08)
Thai	189 (7.6)	43 (3.2)	23.0 (1.43)	145 (6.5)	77.0 (1.43)	0.3 (0.02)	27 (2.9)	15 (2.0)	57.9 (4.35)	11 (1.7)	42.1 (4.35)	0.4 (0.07)
Vietnamese	1,714 (24.7)	551 (10.8)	32.2 (0.44)	1,163 (18.6)	67.8 (0.44)	2.8 (0.04)	362 (9.0)	311 (8.4)	85.7 (0.79)	52 (3.0)	14.3 (0.79)	2.1 (0.12)
Other Southeast Asian[6]	91 (6.5)	17 (1.9)	19.0 (1.53)	74 (5.3)	81.0 (1.53)	0.2 (0.01)	16 (2.1)	11 (1.5)	67.7 (5.79)	5 (1.3)	32.3 (5.79)	0.2 (0.05)
Other Asian[4]	520 (12.6)	326 (8.7)	62.7 (0.94)	194 (7.3)	37.3 (0.94)	0.5 (0.02)	194 (7.6)	181 (7.2)	93.3 (0.78)	13 (1.6)	6.7 (0.78)	0.5 (0.06)
Pacific Islander	499 (7.7)	395 (8.3)	79.2 (1.18)	104 (6.2)	20.8 (1.18)	0.2 (0.01)	125 (4.3)	113 (3.6)	90.2 (1.28)	12 (1.8)	9.8 (1.28)	0.5 (0.07)
American Indian/ Alaska Native	2,085 (16.7)	2,061 (16.5)	98.9 (0.09)	24 (2.0)	1.1 (0.09)	0.1 (#)	563 (8.5)	561 (8.5)	99.6 (0.13)	‡ (†)	0.4 ! (0.13)	0.1 (0.03)
Some other race[2]	661 (16.8)	448 (12.0)	67.7 (1.03)	213 (9.5)	32.3 (1.03)	0.5 (0.02)	237 (7.9)	221 (7.4)	93.4 (0.83)	16 (2.1)	6.6 (0.83)	0.6 (0.08)
Two or more races	7,117 (51.3)	6,592 (48.9)	92.6 (0.19)	525 (13.9)	7.4 (0.19)	1.2 (0.03)	3,250 (28.4)	3,206 (26.8)	98.6 (0.13)	44 (4.4)	1.4 (0.13)	1.8 (0.18)
White and Black	2,151 (27.2)	2,109 (27.0)	98.0 (0.16)	43 (3.4)	2.0 (0.16)	0.1 (0.01)	1,375 (20.3)	1,372 (20.2)	99.8 (0.06)	3 (0.8)	0.2 (0.06)	0.1 (0.03)
White and Asian	1,768 (24.4)	1,528 (22.5)	86.4 (0.48)	240 (9.3)	13.6 (0.48)	0.6 (0.02)	888 (14.8)	858 (14.0)	96.7 (0.45)	29 (4.1)	3.3 (0.45)	1.2 (0.16)
White and American Indian/ Alaska Native	1,469 (16.5)	1,461 (16.7)	99.4 (0.11)	8 (1.7)	0.6 (0.11)	# (†)	377 (9.8)	376 (9.8)	99.9 (0.07)	‡ (†)	0.1 ! (0.07)	# (†)
Other Two or more races[3]	1,729 (22.9)	1,494 (22.1)	86.4 (0.50)	235 (9.0)	13.6 (0.50)	0.6 (0.02)	610 (11.6)	599 (11.6)	98.2 (0.22)	11 (1.4)	1.8 (0.22)	0.4 (0.06)

—Not available.
†Not applicable.
#Rounds to zero.
!Interpret data with caution. The coefficient of variation (CV) for this estimate is between 30 and 50 percent.
‡Reporting standards not met. Either there are too few cases for a reliable estimate or the coefficient of variation (CV) is 50 percent or greater.
[1]Includes those born in the 50 states, the District of Columbia, Puerto Rico, American Samoa, Guam, the U.S. Virgin Islands, and the Northern Marianas, as well as those born abroad to U.S.-citizen parents.
[2]Respondents who wrote in some other race that was not included as an option on the questionnaire.
[3]Includes other Central American subgroups not shown separately.

[4]Includes Taiwanese.
[5]In addition to the subgroups shown, also includes Sri Lankan.
[6]Consists of Indonesian and Malaysian.
NOTE: Resident population includes civilian population and armed forces personnel residing within the United States; it excludes armed forces personnel residing overseas. Data are from the American Community Survey and may differ from data shown in other tables obtained from the Current Population Survey. Race categories exclude persons of Hispanic ethnicity. Detail may not sum to totals because of rounding.
SOURCE: U.S. Department of Commerce, Census Bureau, American Community Survey (ACS), 2004, 2009, and 2014. (This table was prepared February 2016.)

Table 101.40. Estimated total and school-age resident populations, by state: Selected years, 1970 through 2014

[In thousands]

State	Total, all ages								5- to 17-year-olds							
	1970[1]	1980[1]	1990[1]	2000[2]	2010[2]	2012[2]	2013[2]	2014[2]	1970[1]	1980[1]	1990[1]	2000[2]	2010[2]	2012[2]	2013[2]	2014[2]
1	2	3	4	5	6	7	8	9	10	11	12	13	14	15	16	17
United States	203,302	226,546	248,765	282,162	309,347	314,112	316,498	318,857	52,540	47,407	45,178	53,198	53,933	53,732	53,742	53,707
Alabama	3,444	3,894	4,040	4,452	4,786	4,817	4,834	4,849	934	866	774	828	826	817	814	813
Alaska	303	402	550	628	714	731	737	737	88	92	117	143	134	133	133	132
Arizona	1,775	2,718	3,665	5,161	6,412	6,556	6,635	6,731	486	578	686	989	1,174	1,178	1,184	1,191
Arkansas........................	1,923	2,286	2,351	2,679	2,922	2,949	2,959	2,966	498	496	455	500	515	516	517	515
California	19,971	23,668	29,786	33,988	37,336	38,063	38,431	38,803	4,999	4,681	5,344	6,775	6,751	6,687	6,666	6,637
Colorado........................	2,210	2,890	3,294	4,327	5,049	5,192	5,272	5,356	589	592	607	808	883	896	904	911
Connecticut.....................	3,032	3,108	3,287	3,412	3,579	3,594	3,599	3,597	768	638	520	619	613	601	594	586
Delaware........................	548	594	666	786	900	917	925	936	148	125	114	143	150	149	147	148
District of Columbia	757	638	607	572	605	635	649	659	164	109	80	82	68	69	71	72
Florida............................	6,791	9,746	12,938	16,048	18,852	19,355	19,600	19,893	1,609	1,789	2,011	2,709	2,926	2,940	2,956	2,969
Georgia..........................	4,588	5,463	6,478	8,227	9,714	9,919	9,995	10,097	1,223	1,231	1,230	1,581	1,805	1,814	1,822	1,831
Hawaii...........................	770	965	1,108	1,214	1,364	1,393	1,409	1,420	204	198	196	217	216	216	217	217
Idaho.............................	713	944	1,007	1,299	1,571	1,596	1,613	1,634	200	213	228	272	308	311	314	317
Illinois............................	11,110	11,427	11,431	12,434	12,840	12,874	12,891	12,881	2,859	2,401	2,095	2,369	2,288	2,245	2,223	2,198
Indiana...........................	5,195	5,490	5,544	6,092	6,490	6,538	6,571	6,597	1,386	1,200	1,056	1,152	1,173	1,166	1,165	1,162
Iowa	2,825	2,914	2,777	2,929	3,050	3,076	3,092	3,107	743	604	525	544	526	527	529	531
Kansas...........................	2,249	2,364	2,478	2,694	2,859	2,886	2,896	2,904	573	468	472	525	522	524	523	522
Kentucky.........................	3,221	3,661	3,687	4,049	4,350	4,383	4,400	4,413	844	800	703	730	741	739	739	736
Louisiana........................	3,645	4,206	4,222	4,472	4,546	4,605	4,629	4,650	1,041	969	891	902	804	803	805	805
Maine.............................	994	1,125	1,228	1,277	1,327	1,329	1,329	1,330	260	243	223	231	204	199	197	194
Maryland.........................	3,924	4,217	4,781	5,311	5,788	5,892	5,939	5,976	1,038	895	803	1,004	987	980	979	981
Massachusetts.................	5,689	5,737	6,016	6,361	6,564	6,656	6,709	6,745	1,407	1,153	940	1,104	1,050	1,036	1,032	1,024
Michigan	8,882	9,262	9,295	9,952	9,876	9,885	9,898	9,910	2,450	2,067	1,754	1,924	1,740	1,692	1,673	1,653
Minnesota.......................	3,806	4,076	4,376	4,934	5,310	5,381	5,422	5,457	1,051	865	829	958	928	928	932	933
Mississippi	2,217	2,521	2,575	2,848	2,971	2,986	2,992	2,994	635	599	550	571	544	540	539	537
Missouri.........................	4,678	4,917	5,117	5,607	5,996	6,025	6,045	6,064	1,183	1,008	944	1,059	1,034	1,024	1,021	1,018
Montana..........................	694	787	799	904	991	1,005	1,015	1,024	197	167	163	175	161	161	163	164
Nebraska	1,485	1,570	1,578	1,714	1,830	1,855	1,869	1,882	389	324	309	333	328	332	334	336
Nevada	489	800	1,202	2,019	2,703	2,755	2,791	2,839	127	160	204	369	477	478	482	487
New Hampshire	738	921	1,109	1,240	1,317	1,321	1,323	1,327	189	196	194	235	216	209	206	203
New Jersey.....................	7,171	7,365	7,748	8,431	8,804	8,876	8,912	8,938	1,797	1,528	1,269	1,526	1,521	1,499	1,490	1,480
New Mexico	1,017	1,303	1,515	1,821	2,065	2,085	2,087	2,086	311	303	320	378	374	371	369	365
New York.........................	18,241	17,558	17,991	19,002	19,401	19,607	19,696	19,746	4,358	3,552	3,000	3,451	3,161	3,099	3,075	3,044
North Carolina	5,084	5,882	6,632	8,082	9,559	9,748	9,849	9,944	1,323	1,254	1,147	1,429	1,651	1,664	1,673	1,680
North Dakota	618	653	639	642	674	702	724	739	175	136	127	121	106	110	114	118
Ohio..............................	10,657	10,798	10,847	11,364	11,540	11,551	11,572	11,594	2,820	2,307	2,012	2,133	2,005	1,970	1,959	1,948
Oklahoma	2,559	3,025	3,146	3,454	3,759	3,817	3,853	3,878	640	622	609	656	667	675	683	687
Oregon...........................	2,092	2,633	2,842	3,430	3,837	3,899	3,928	3,970	534	525	521	624	628	627	627	629
Pennsylvania....................	11,801	11,864	11,883	12,284	12,711	12,770	12,781	12,787	2,925	2,376	1,996	2,192	2,057	2,019	2,002	1,986
Rhode Island	950	947	1,003	1,050	1,053	1,053	1,053	1,055	225	186	159	184	166	162	160	158
South Carolina..................	2,591	3,122	3,486	4,024	4,636	4,723	4,772	4,832	720	703	662	746	778	782	787	794
South Dakota...................	666	691	696	756	816	835	846	853	187	147	144	152	143	146	148	150
Tennessee	3,926	4,591	4,877	5,704	6,357	6,455	6,497	6,549	1,002	972	882	1,025	1,088	1,090	1,091	1,094
Texas	11,199	14,229	16,986	20,944	25,246	26,094	26,506	26,957	3,002	3,137	3,437	4,278	4,947	5,045	5,102	5,159
Utah	1,059	1,461	1,723	2,245	2,774	2,855	2,903	2,943	312	350	457	511	610	631	643	652
Vermont..........................	445	511	563	610	626	626	627	627	118	109	102	113	97	94	93	91
Virginia...........................	4,651	5,347	6,189	7,106	8,025	8,193	8,270	8,326	1,197	1,114	1,060	1,281	1,345	1,350	1,355	1,354
Washington......................	3,413	4,132	4,867	5,911	6,742	6,896	6,974	7,062	881	826	893	1,121	1,141	1,143	1,150	1,156
West Virginia....................	1,744	1,950	1,793	1,807	1,854	1,856	1,854	1,850	442	414	337	300	283	281	279	278
Wisconsin	4,418	4,706	4,892	5,374	5,689	5,725	5,743	5,758	1,203	1,011	927	1,027	979	968	964	959
Wyoming.........................	332	470	454	494	564	577	583	584	92	101	101	98	95	98	99	100

[1]As of April 1.
[2]Estimates as of July 1.
NOTE: Resident population includes civilian population and armed forces personnel residing within the United States and within each state; it excludes armed forces personnel residing overseas. Some data have been revised from previously published figures. Detail may not sum to totals because of rounding.

SOURCE: U.S. Department of Commerce, Census Bureau, Current Population Reports, Series P-25, No. 1095; CPH-L-74 (1990 data); 2000 through 2009 Population Estimates, retrieved August 17, 2012, from http://www.census.gov/popest/data/state/asrh/2011/index.html; and 2010 through 2014 Population Estimates, retrieved September 15, 2015, from http://factfinder.census.gov/faces/tableservices/jsf/pages/productview.xhtml?pid=PEP_2014_PEPANNRES&src=pt. (This table was prepared September 2015.)

Table 102.10. Number and percentage distribution of family households, by family structure and presence of own children under 18: Selected years, 1970 through 2015

[Standard errors appear in parentheses]

Number (in thousands)

Family structure and presence of own children	1970	1980	1990	2000	2010	2012	2013	2014	2015	Change, 2000 to 2010	Change, 2010 to 2015
1	2	3	4	5	6	7	8	9	10	11	12
All families	51,456 (257.3)	59,550 (271.4)	66,090 (307.8)	72,025 (311.6)	78,833 (241.0)	80,506 (242.4)	80,902 (242.8)	81,353 (311.8)	81,716 (267.6)	9.5 (0.58)	3.7 (0.46)
Married-couple families	44,728 (243.6)	49,112 (252.7)	52,317 (283.3)	55,311 (289.5)	58,410 (218.6)	58,949 (219.3)	59,204 (219.7)	59,629 (281.1)	60,010 (243.1)	5.6 (0.68)	2.7 (0.57)
Without own children under 18	19,196 (168.7)	24,151 (187.3)	27,780 (218.1)	30,062 (230.3)	33,835 (176.1)	35,245 (179.2)	35,333 (179.4)	35,697 (229.0)	35,970 (199.4)	12.6 (1.04)	6.3 (0.81)
With own children under 18	25,532 (192.0)	24,961 (190.1)	24,537 (206.4)	25,248 (214.1)	24,575 (153.1)	23,704 (150.6)	23,870 (151.1)	23,993 (191.9)	24,040 (167.3)	-2.7! (1.02)	-2.2! (0.91)
One own child under 18	8,163 (112.5)	9,671 (122.0)	9,583 (133.0)	9,402 (136.2)	9,567 (98.5)	9,215 (96.7)	9,157 (96.4)	9,298 (123.0)	9,163 (106.6)	‡	‡
Two own children under 18	8,045 (111.7)	9,488 (120.9)	9,784 (134.3)	10,274 (142.1)	9,658 (98.9)	9,442 (97.9)	9,597 (98.6)	9,536 (124.5)	9,662 (109.3)	-6.0 (1.62)	-4.2! (†)
Three or more own children under 18	9,325 (119.9)	5,802 (95.3)	5,170 (98.5)	5,572 (105.9)	5,351 (74.3)	5,047 (72.2)	5,117 (72.7)	5,099 (91.8)	5,215 (81.0)	‡	‡
Families with male householder, no spouse present	1,228 (44.2)	1,733 (52.5)	2,884 (73.9)	4,028 (90.4)	5,580 (75.8)	5,888 (77.8)	6,229 (80.0)	6,304 (101.8)	6,162 (87.9)	38.5 (3.63)	10.4 (2.18)
Without own children under 18	887 (37.6)	1,117 (42.2)	1,731 (57.4)	2,242 (67.7)	3,356 (59.0)	3,473 (60.0)	3,669 (61.7)	3,832 (79.8)	3,774 (69.1)	49.7 (5.23)	12.5 (2.86)
With own children under 18	341 (23.3)	616 (31.3)	1,153 (46.9)	1,786 (60.5)	2,224 (48.2)	2,415 (50.2)	2,560 (51.6)	2,472 (64.2)	2,388 (55.1)	24.5 (5.01)	7.4! (3.40)
One own child under 18	179 (16.9)	374 (24.4)	723 (37.2)	1,131 (48.2)	1,375 (37.9)	1,419 (38.5)	1,482 (39.4)	1,445 (49.2)	1,433 (42.8)	21.6 (6.17)	‡
Two own children under 18	87 (11.8)	165 (16.2)	307 (24.2)	483 (31.6)	576 (24.6)	704 (27.2)	766 (28.3)	731 (35.0)	653 (28.9)	19.3! (9.31)	‡
Three or more own children under 18	75 (10.9)	77 (11.1)	123 (15.3)	171 (18.8)	273 (16.9)	293 (17.5)	312 (18.1)	296 (22.3)	302 (19.7)	59.6! (20.15)	‡
Families with female householder, no spouse present	5,500 (92.8)	8,705 (116.0)	10,890 (141.4)	12,687 (156.9)	14,843 (121.4)	15,669 (124.5)	15,469 (123.8)	15,420 (156.6)	15,544 (137.0)	17.0 (1.73)	4.7 (1.26)
Without own children under 18	2,642 (64.7)	3,261 (71.8)	4,290 (89.9)	5,116 (101.6)	6,424 (81.2)	6,799 (83.5)	6,842 (83.7)	6,870 (106.2)	6,993 (93.5)	25.6 (2.96)	8.9 (2.00)
With own children under 18	2,858 (67.2)	5,445 (92.3)	6,599 (111.0)	7,571 (122.8)	8,419 (92.6)	8,869 (95.0)	8,627 (93.7)	8,550 (118.1)	8,551 (103.1)	11.2 (2.18)	‡
One own child under 18	1,008 (40.1)	2,398 (61.6)	3,225 (78.1)	3,777 (87.6)	4,207 (66.0)	4,399 (67.5)	4,144 (65.5)	4,167 (83.1)	4,192 (72.8)	11.4 (3.12)	‡
Two own children under 18	810 (35.9)	1,817 (53.7)	2,173 (64.2)	2,458 (70.9)	2,714 (53.2)	2,853 (54.5)	2,825 (54.2)	2,778 (68.0)	2,844 (60.1)	10.4! (3.85)	‡
Three or more own children under 18	1,040 (40.7)	1,230 (44.2)	1,202 (47.9)	1,336 (52.4)	1,499 (39.6)	1,618 (41.1)	1,658 (41.6)	1,605 (51.8)	1,515 (44.0)	12.2! (5.31)	‡

Percentage distribution of all families (Change columns: Change in percentage points)

Family structure and presence of own children	1970	1980	1990	2000	2010	2012	2013	2014	2015	Change, 2000 to 2010	Change, 2010 to 2015
All families	100.0 (†)	100.0 (†)	100.0 (†)	100.0 (†)	100.0 (†)	100.0 (†)	100.0 (†)	100.0 (†)	100.0 (†)	†	†
Married-couple families	86.9 (0.19)	82.5 (0.20)	79.2 (0.22)	76.8 (0.23)	74.1 (0.16)	73.2 (0.16)	73.2 (0.16)	73.3 (0.18)	73.4 (0.18)	-2.7 (0.28)	-0.7! (0.24)
Without own children under 18	37.3 (0.27)	40.6 (0.25)	42.0 (0.27)	41.7 (0.26)	42.9 (0.18)	43.8 (0.18)	43.7 (0.18)	43.9 (0.23)	44.0 (0.20)	1.2 (0.32)	1.1 (0.27)
With own children under 18	49.6 (0.28)	41.9 (0.26)	37.1 (0.26)	35.1 (0.26)	31.2 (0.17)	29.4 (0.16)	29.5 (0.16)	29.4 (0.21)	29.4 (0.18)	-3.9 (0.31)	-1.8 (0.25)
One own child under 18	15.9 (0.20)	16.2 (0.19)	14.5 (0.19)	13.1 (0.18)	12.1 (0.12)	11.4 (0.12)	11.3 (0.11)	11.4 (0.14)	11.2 (0.13)	-0.9 (0.22)	-0.9 (0.17)
Two own children under 18	15.6 (0.20)	15.9 (0.19)	14.8 (0.19)	14.3 (0.19)	12.3 (0.12)	11.7 (0.12)	11.9 (0.12)	11.7 (0.15)	11.8 (0.13)	-2.0 (0.22)	-0.4! (0.18)
Three or more own children under 18	18.1 (0.21)	9.7 (0.15)	7.8 (0.14)	7.7 (0.14)	6.8 (0.09)	6.3 (0.09)	6.3 (0.09)	6.3 (0.11)	6.4 (0.10)	-0.9 (0.17)	-0.4! (0.13)
Families with male householder, no spouse present	2.4 (0.09)	2.9 (0.09)	4.4 (0.11)	5.6 (0.12)	7.1 (0.09)	7.3 (0.09)	7.7 (0.10)	7.7 (0.12)	7.5 (0.10)	1.5 (0.15)	0.5! (0.14)
Without own children under 18	1.7 (0.07)	1.9 (0.07)	2.6 (0.09)	3.1 (0.09)	4.3 (0.07)	4.3 (0.07)	4.5 (0.08)	4.7 (0.10)	4.6 (0.08)	1.1 (0.12)	0.4! (0.11)
With own children under 18	0.7 (0.05)	1.0 (0.05)	1.7 (0.07)	2.5 (0.08)	2.8 (0.06)	3.0 (0.06)	3.2 (0.06)	3.0 (0.08)	2.9 (0.07)	0.3! (0.10)	‡
One own child under 18	0.3 (0.03)	0.6 (0.04)	1.1 (0.06)	1.6 (0.07)	1.7 (0.05)	1.8 (0.05)	1.8 (0.05)	1.8 (0.06)	1.8 (0.05)	0.2! (0.08)	‡
Two own children under 18	0.2 (0.02)	0.3 (0.03)	0.5 (0.04)	0.7 (0.04)	0.7 (0.03)	0.9 (0.03)	0.9 (0.03)	0.9 (0.04)	0.8 (0.04)	‡	‡
Three or more own children under 18	0.1 (0.02)	0.1 (0.02)	0.2 (0.02)	0.2 (0.03)	0.3 (0.02)	0.4 (0.02)	0.4 (0.02)	0.4 (0.03)	0.4 (0.02)	0.1! (0.03)	‡
Families with female householder, no spouse present	10.7 (0.17)	14.6 (0.18)	16.5 (0.20)	17.6 (0.20)	18.8 (0.14)	19.5 (0.14)	19.1 (0.14)	19.0 (0.18)	19.0 (0.16)	1.2 (0.25)	‡
Without own children under 18	5.1 (0.12)	5.5 (0.12)	6.5 (0.13)	7.1 (0.14)	8.1 (0.10)	8.4 (0.10)	8.5 (0.10)	8.4 (0.13)	8.6 (0.11)	1.0 (0.17)	0.4! (0.15)
With own children under 18	5.6 (0.13)	9.1 (0.15)	10.0 (0.16)	10.5 (0.16)	10.7 (0.11)	11.0 (0.11)	10.7 (0.11)	10.5 (0.14)	10.5 (0.12)	‡	‡
One own child under 18	2.0 (0.08)	4.0 (0.10)	4.9 (0.12)	5.2 (0.12)	5.3 (0.08)	5.5 (0.08)	5.1 (0.08)	5.1 (0.10)	5.1 (0.09)	‡	‡
Two own children under 18	1.6 (0.07)	3.1 (0.09)	3.3 (0.10)	3.4 (0.10)	3.4 (0.07)	3.5 (0.07)	3.5 (0.07)	3.4 (0.08)	3.5 (0.07)	‡	‡
Three or more own children under 18	2.0 (0.08)	2.1 (0.07)	1.8 (0.07)	1.9 (0.07)	1.9 (0.05)	2.0 (0.05)	2.0 (0.05)	2.0 (0.06)	1.9 (0.05)	‡	‡

†Not applicable.
!Interpret data with caution. The coefficient of variation (CV) for this estimate is between 30 and 50 percent.
‡Reporting standards not met. The coefficient of variation (CV) for this estimate is 50 percent or greater.
NOTE: A family household consists of two or more people who are related by birth, marriage, or adoption and are residing together. Own children are never-married sons and daughters, including stepchildren and adopted children, of the householder or married couple. Detail may not sum to totals because of rounding.

SOURCE: U.S. Department of Commerce, Census Bureau, Current Population Reports, Series P20, *Household and Family Characteristics*, 1994 and 1995; and Current Population Survey (CPS), Annual Social and Economic Supplement, *America's Families and Living Arrangements* (F table series), 2000 and 2010–2015, retrieved January 22, 2016, from http://www.census.gov/hhes/families/data/cps2015.html. (This table was prepared January 2016.)

Table 102.20. Number and percentage distribution of children under age 18 and under age 6, by living arrangements, race/ethnicity, and selected racial/ethnic subgroups: 2014

[Standard errors appear in parentheses]

Age and race/ethnicity	Number of children (in thousands)		Percentage distribution of children		Total		Married parents		Female parent, no spouse present		Male parent, no spouse present		All other children[2]	
1	2		3		4		5		6		7		8	
Under 18 years old														
Total	73,492	(25.7)	100.0	(†)	100.0	(†)	62.8	(0.12)	27.3	(0.10)	7.8	(0.06)	2.1	(0.03)
White	38,057	(7.3)	51.8	(0.02)	100.0	(†)	73.0	(0.18)	17.9	(0.14)	7.1	(0.08)	2.0	(0.04)
Black	10,025	(25.9)	13.6	(0.03)	100.0	(†)	32.5	(0.35)	57.0	(0.35)	8.0	(0.16)	2.5	(0.09)
Hispanic	17,879	(8.4)	24.3	(0.01)	100.0	(†)	56.1	(0.24)	32.3	(0.25)	9.7	(0.12)	1.9	(0.05)
Cuban	414	(10.1)	0.6	(0.01)	100.0	(†)	62.6	(1.29)	28.2	(1.41)	7.6	(0.71)	1.7	(0.34)
Dominican	497	(12.9)	0.7	(0.02)	100.0	(†)	40.6	(1.30)	48.1	(1.17)	9.7	(0.67)	1.7	(0.30)
Mexican	12,344	(30.5)	16.8	(0.04)	100.0	(†)	58.0	(0.27)	30.3	(0.28)	9.8	(0.14)	1.8	(0.06)
Puerto Rican	1,687	(21.0)	2.3	(0.03)	100.0	(†)	42.1	(0.73)	46.7	(0.75)	8.9	(0.45)	2.2	(0.18)
Spaniard	200	(7.4)	0.3	(0.01)	100.0	(†)	66.4	(2.24)	25.0	(2.22)	7.1	(0.81)	1.5	(0.30)
Central American[3]	1,493	(22.0)	2.0	(0.03)	100.0	(†)	53.5	(0.72)	32.6	(0.74)	11.5	(0.44)	2.4	(0.19)
Costa Rican	34	(3.0)	#	(†)	100.0	(†)	63.6	(5.24)	25.3	(4.31)	9.8 !	(3.10)	‡	(†)
Guatemalan	406	(11.1)	0.6	(0.02)	100.0	(†)	56.1	(1.56)	28.8	(1.48)	12.1	(0.96)	3.0	(0.41)
Honduran	261	(11.4)	0.4	(0.02)	100.0	(†)	45.9	(2.02)	40.7	(2.15)	10.1	(1.34)	3.3	(0.62)
Nicaraguan	98	(5.5)	0.1	(0.01)	100.0	(†)	52.5	(2.86)	37.9	(2.78)	8.7	(1.58)	0.9 !	(0.37)
Panamanian	42	(3.3)	0.1	(0.00)	100.0	(†)	58.8	(3.71)	34.0	(3.89)	6.8	(1.88)	‡	(†)
Salvadoran	638	(16.7)	0.9	(0.02)	100.0	(†)	54.1	(1.26)	31.1	(1.16)	12.7	(0.73)	2.1	(0.27)
South American	750	(13.8)	1.0	(0.02)	100.0	(†)	67.1	(0.84)	24.4	(0.86)	7.0	(0.53)	1.5	(0.23)
Chilean	33	(3.8)	#	(†)	100.0	(†)	76.8	(3.64)	17.3	(3.51)	5.3 !	(1.89)	‡	(†)
Colombian	216	(8.0)	0.3	(0.01)	100.0	(†)	67.1	(1.42)	24.9	(1.47)	6.6	(0.89)	1.4	(0.31)
Ecuadorian	168	(9.3)	0.2	(0.01)	100.0	(†)	60.1	(2.24)	27.4	(2.21)	9.4	(1.40)	3.1	(0.79)
Peruvian	138	(6.5)	0.2	(0.01)	100.0	(†)	65.7	(2.25)	24.7	(2.22)	8.2	(1.30)	1.4	(0.40)
Venezuelan	74	(5.1)	0.1	(0.01)	100.0	(†)	72.0	(2.98)	21.0	(2.81)	5.9 !	(2.15)	‡	(†)
Other South American	122	(6.0)	0.2	(0.01)	100.0	(†)	72.5	(1.99)	23.1	(1.91)	4.2	(0.84)	‡	(†)
Other Hispanic	495	(14.1)	0.7	(0.02)	100.0	(†)	55.9	(1.14)	32.1	(1.08)	9.6	(0.64)	2.4	(0.43)
Asian	3,355	(15.7)	4.6	(0.02)	100.0	(†)	82.3	(0.34)	11.7	(0.29)	4.6	(0.21)	1.4	(0.09)
Chinese[4]	707	(10.8)	1.0	(0.01)	100.0	(†)	82.4	(0.57)	11.6	(0.44)	4.1	(0.34)	1.9	(0.19)
Filipino	451	(11.3)	0.6	(0.02)	100.0	(†)	76.1	(0.99)	17.0	(0.92)	5.6	(0.55)	1.2	(0.19)
Japanese	65	(3.7)	0.1	(0.00)	100.0	(†)	85.1	(2.27)	11.1	(2.12)	2.3 !	(0.80)	1.5 !	(0.57)
Korean	241	(7.0)	0.3	(0.01)	100.0	(†)	86.6	(1.09)	7.8	(0.93)	3.9	(0.68)	1.7	(0.39)
South Asian[5]	1,028	(13.7)	1.4	(0.02)	100.0	(†)	92.4	(0.41)	5.1	(0.34)	2.0	(0.27)	0.6	(0.09)
Asian Indian	816	(12.1)	1.1	(0.02)	100.0	(†)	92.9	(0.41)	4.7	(0.35)	2.0	(0.29)	0.4	(0.08)
Bangladeshi	44	(3.9)	0.1	(0.01)	100.0	(†)	91.7	(2.59)	6.2 !	(2.50)	‡	(†)	1.2 !	(0.42)
Bhutanese	8	(1.9)	#	(†)	100.0	(†)	95.6	(2.80)	‡	(†)	‡	(†)	‡	(†)
Nepalese	34	(2.8)	#	(†)	100.0	(†)	83.4	(3.37)	6.9 !	(2.12)	5.6 !	(2.46)	4.1 !	(1.47)
Pakistani	119	(5.4)	0.2	(0.01)	100.0	(†)	91.4	(1.34)	6.8	(1.22)	1.4 !	(0.53)	‡	(†)
Southeast Asian	669	(12.4)	0.9	(0.02)	100.0	(†)	69.6	(0.91)	19.3	(0.76)	8.9	(0.64)	2.3	(0.27)
Burmese	45	(3.8)	0.1	(0.01)	100.0	(†)	84.9	(2.85)	8.4	(2.37)	4.9 !	(1.67)	‡	(†)
Cambodian	60	(3.9)	0.1	(0.01)	100.0	(†)	58.9	(3.12)	28.4	(3.27)	11.2	(2.08)	1.6 !	(0.65)
Hmong	109	(6.4)	0.1	(0.01)	100.0	(†)	55.5	(3.65)	25.5	(3.29)	16.6	(2.32)	2.5 !	(0.78)
Laotian	50	(4.5)	0.1	(0.01)	100.0	(†)	52.2	(4.27)	27.1	(4.26)	19.1	(3.53)	‡	(†)
Thai	27	(2.9)	#	(†)	100.0	(†)	76.6	(4.51)	12.6	(3.54)	5.6 !	(2.51)	5.2 !	(1.68)
Vietnamese	362	(9.0)	0.5	(0.01)	100.0	(†)	74.8	(1.36)	17.2	(0.94)	5.8	(0.68)	2.2	(0.37)
Other Southeast Asian[6]	16	(2.1)	#	(†)	100.0	(†)	86.4	(3.64)	8.5 !	(3.01)	‡	(†)	‡	(†)
Other Asian	194	(7.6)	0.3	(0.01)	100.0	(†)	81.1	(1.29)	13.4	(1.31)	4.4	(0.63)	1.1	(0.31)
Pacific Islander	125	(4.3)	0.2	(0.01)	100.0	(†)	64.7	(2.28)	24.8	(2.12)	8.0	(1.18)	2.5	(0.60)
American Indian/Alaska Native	563	(8.5)	0.8	(0.01)	100.0	(†)	43.0	(0.94)	38.8	(1.02)	14.0	(0.75)	4.3	(0.49)
Some other race[7]	237	(7.9)	0.3	(0.01)	100.0	(†)	62.4	(1.82)	27.3	(1.79)	8.1	(1.15)	2.3	(0.51)
Two or more races	3,250	(28.4)	4.4	(0.04)	100.0	(†)	56.2	(0.49)	34.0	(0.49)	7.5	(0.26)	2.3	(0.13)
White and Black	1,375	(20.3)	1.9	(0.03)	100.0	(†)	41.3	(0.85)	47.9	(0.87)	8.0	(0.45)	2.8	(0.20)
White and Asian	888	(14.8)	1.2	(0.02)	100.0	(†)	80.9	(0.72)	12.3	(0.58)	6.1	(0.38)	0.7	(0.13)
White and American Indian/ Alaska Native	377	(9.8)	0.5	(0.01)	100.0	(†)	56.3	(1.29)	30.4	(1.25)	10.5	(0.77)	2.9	(0.43)
Other Two or more races	610	(11.6)	0.8	(0.02)	100.0	(†)	53.7	(1.18)	36.3	(1.15)	6.9	(0.58)	3.1	(0.38)
Under 6 years old														
Total	23,704	(35.5)	100.0	(†)	100.0	(†)	62.3	(0.17)	27.7	(0.16)	8.3	(0.09)	1.7	(0.04)
White	11,844	(17.5)	50.0	(0.07)	100.0	(†)	74.6	(0.22)	16.8	(0.17)	7.0	(0.14)	1.6	(0.07)
Black	3,186	(18.3)	13.4	(0.07)	100.0	(†)	30.0	(0.48)	59.1	(0.45)	9.1	(0.26)	1.8	(0.10)
Hispanic	6,095	(19.1)	25.7	(0.06)	100.0	(†)	52.9	(0.36)	34.1	(0.36)	11.3	(0.20)	1.7	(0.09)
Cuban	139	(5.6)	0.6	(0.02)	100.0	(†)	60.5	(2.01)	27.7	(1.96)	10.3	(1.29)	1.6 !	(0.50)
Dominican	184	(6.0)	0.8	(0.03)	100.0	(†)	40.4	(2.03)	47.4	(1.90)	10.6	(1.25)	1.7	(0.44)
Mexican	4,179	(19.9)	17.6	(0.07)	100.0	(†)	54.3	(0.42)	32.9	(0.40)	11.3	(0.23)	1.6	(0.09)
Puerto Rican	581	(11.6)	2.5	(0.05)	100.0	(†)	40.8	(0.98)	46.5	(1.00)	10.9	(0.77)	1.9	(0.32)
Spaniard	62	(3.8)	0.3	(0.02)	100.0	(†)	69.2	(3.02)	23.7	(2.88)	6.6	(1.37)	‡	(†)
Central American[3]	544	(11.8)	2.3	(0.05)	100.0	(†)	48.7	(1.11)	33.5	(1.17)	15.0	(0.73)	2.7	(0.34)
Costa Rican	13	(1.7)	0.1	(0.01)	100.0	(†)	69.7	(6.53)	27.0	(6.57)	‡	(†)	‡	(†)
Guatemalan	149	(6.4)	0.6	(0.03)	100.0	(†)	50.4	(2.47)	31.1	(2.38)	15.4	(1.69)	3.1	(0.73)
Honduran	102	(5.9)	0.4	(0.03)	100.0	(†)	41.4	(2.40)	40.7	(2.71)	14.3	(2.17)	3.6	(0.87)
Nicaraguan	36	(2.9)	0.2	(0.01)	100.0	(†)	50.3	(4.51)	35.8	(4.02)	13.7	(3.05)	‡	(†)
Panamanian	13	(1.6)	0.1	(0.01)	100.0	(†)	65.5	(6.26)	27.1	(6.12)	7.4 !	(2.82)	‡	(†)
Salvadoran	227	(7.0)	1.0	(0.03)	100.0	(†)	48.6	(1.76)	32.1	(1.78)	16.5	(1.26)	2.8	(0.60)

See notes at end of table.

Table 102.20. Number and percentage distribution of children under age 18 and under age 6, by living arrangements, race/ethnicity, and selected racial/ethnic subgroups: 2014—Continued

[Standard errors appear in parentheses]

Age and race/ethnicity	Number of children (in thousands)		Percentage distribution of children		Percentage distribution of children, by living arrangements							
					Total		Children living with parent(s) or related to householder[1]						All other children[2]	
							Married parents		Female parent, no spouse present		Male parent, no spouse present			
1	2		3		4		5		6		7		8	
South American	251	(7.1)	1.1	(0.03)	100.0	(†)	67.4	(1.53)	23.4	(1.43)	7.8	(0.98)	1.4	(0.39)
Chilean	10	(1.6)	#	(†)	100.0	(†)	76.8	(5.51)	19.4	(5.48)	‡	(†)	‡	(†)
Colombian	71	(4.4)	0.3	(0.02)	100.0	(†)	67.5	(2.82)	24.6	(2.45)	7.0	(1.70)	‡	(†)
Ecuadorian	58	(4.6)	0.2	(0.02)	100.0	(†)	57.8	(3.36)	27.6	(3.27)	10.2	(2.11)	4.3 !	(1.58)
Peruvian	48	(3.1)	0.2	(0.01)	100.0	(†)	71.8	(3.40)	18.4	(2.69)	9.4	(2.28)	‡	(†)
Venezuelan	24	(2.8)	0.1	(0.01)	100.0	(†)	69.6	(5.70)	21.8	(4.55)	‡	(†)	‡	(†)
Other South American	40	(3.1)	0.2	(0.01)	100.0	(†)	71.9	(3.41)	22.9	(3.42)	4.7 !	(1.42)	‡	(†)
Other Hispanic	156	(6.7)	0.7	(0.03)	100.0	(†)	54.4	(1.86)	35.0	(2.03)	8.4	(0.95)	2.2	(0.54)
Asian	1,067	(9.4)	4.5	(0.04)	100.0	(†)	85.4	(0.47)	9.8	(0.42)	3.9	(0.27)	0.9	(0.13)
Chinese[4]	212	(5.6)	0.9	(0.02)	100.0	(†)	86.8	(1.07)	8.4	(0.89)	4.2	(0.68)	0.6 !	(0.19)
Filipino	116	(4.0)	0.5	(0.02)	100.0	(†)	76.0	(1.58)	17.0	(1.45)	5.8	(0.85)	1.2 !	(0.49)
Japanese	23	(2.2)	0.1	(0.01)	100.0	(†)	87.9	(3.38)	10.2 !	(3.33)	‡	(†)	‡	(†)
Korean	63	(3.2)	0.3	(0.01)	100.0	(†)	93.6	(1.21)	3.8	(0.92)	1.7 !	(0.77)	‡	(†)
South Asian[5]	392	(7.0)	1.7	(0.03)	100.0	(†)	94.8	(0.45)	3.6	(0.37)	1.4	(0.27)	0.2 !	(0.08)
Asian Indian	321	(6.6)	1.4	(0.03)	100.0	(†)	95.1	(0.49)	3.4	(0.43)	1.3	(0.31)	0.2 !	(0.09)
Bangladeshi	14	(1.9)	0.1	(0.01)	100.0	(†)	96.3	(1.75)	‡	(†)	‡	(†)	‡	(†)
Bhutanese	‡	(†)	#	(†)	100.0	(†)	‡	(†)	‡	(†)	‡	(†)	‡	(†)
Nepalese	13	(1.6)	0.1	(0.01)	100.0	(†)	90.6	(3.44)	‡	(†)	‡	(†)	‡	(†)
Pakistani	38	(2.8)	0.2	(0.01)	100.0	(†)	93.5	(2.15)	6.0 !	(2.05)	‡	(†)	‡	(†)
Southeast Asian	185	(5.8)	0.8	(0.02)	100.0	(†)	68.8	(1.48)	20.4	(1.52)	8.4	(1.07)	2.4	(0.56)
Burmese	21	(2.5)	0.1	(0.01)	100.0	(†)	88.6	(3.27)	5.2 !	(2.18)	‡	(†)	‡	(†)
Cambodian	17	(1.8)	0.1	(0.01)	100.0	(†)	63.2	(4.42)	21.4	(4.02)	12.8	(3.64)	‡	(†)
Hmong	39	(3.1)	0.2	(0.01)	100.0	(†)	49.6	(4.39)	31.1	(4.47)	17.4	(3.42)	‡	(†)
Laotian	11	(1.6)	#	(†)	100.0	(†)	47.2	(7.22)	41.7	(8.34)	11.1 !	(4.83)	‡	(†)
Thai	5	(1.0)	#	(†)	100.0	(†)	82.9	(6.07)	16.1 !	(6.32)	‡	(†)	‡	(†)
Vietnamese	87	(4.0)	0.4	(0.02)	100.0	(†)	74.0	(2.05)	17.5	(1.74)	5.3	(0.88)	3.2	(0.90)
Other Southeast Asian[6]	5	(1.0)	#	(†)	100.0	(†)	95.9	(3.01)	‡	(†)	‡	(†)	‡	(†)
Other Asian	75	(4.1)	0.3	(0.02)	100.0	(†)	80.7	(1.94)	14.2	(1.81)	4.4	(0.90)	0.7 !	(0.33)
Pacific Islander	36	(1.9)	0.2	(0.01)	100.0	(†)	62.2	(3.60)	25.0	(3.28)	9.2	(1.86)	3.7	(1.05)
American Indian/Alaska Native	178	(4.5)	0.8	(0.02)	100.0	(†)	38.4	(1.48)	42.8	(1.59)	14.9	(1.12)	3.9	(0.62)
Some other race[7]	92	(4.9)	0.4	(0.02)	100.0	(†)	64.5	(2.32)	24.5	(2.36)	9.4	(1.50)	1.6	(0.46)
Two or more races	1,205	(16.9)	5.1	(0.07)	100.0	(†)	56.3	(0.63)	33.8	(0.65)	7.9	(0.36)	2.0	(0.20)
White and Black	547	(11.1)	2.3	(0.05)	100.0	(†)	39.6	(1.10)	48.4	(1.13)	9.3	(0.71)	2.7	(0.31)
White and Asian	335	(7.3)	1.4	(0.03)	100.0	(†)	84.6	(0.88)	10.3	(0.83)	4.7	(0.52)	0.5 !	(0.16)
White and American Indian/ Alaska Native	114	(4.4)	0.5	(0.02)	100.0	(†)	55.8	(1.98)	29.8	(1.83)	12.2	(1.30)	2.1 !	(0.69)
Other Two or more races	208	(6.4)	0.9	(0.03)	100.0	(†)	54.7	(1.72)	35.4	(1.78)	7.3	(0.76)	2.5	(0.57)

†Not applicable.
#Rounds to zero.
!Interpret data with caution. The coefficient of variation (CV) for this estimate is between 30 and 50 percent.
‡Reporting standards not met. Either there are too few cases for a reliable estimate or the coefficient of variation (CV) is 50 percent or greater.
[1]Includes all children who live either with their parent(s) or with a householder to whom they are related by birth, marriage, or adoption (except a child who is the spouse of the householder). Children are classified by their parents' marital status or, if no parents are present in the household, by the marital status of the householder who is related to the children. Living arrangements with only a "female parent" or "male parent" are those in which the parent or the householder who is related to the child does not have a spouse living in the household. The householder is the person (or one of the people) who owns or rents (maintains) the housing unit.

[2]Includes foster children, children in unrelated subfamilies, children living in group quarters, and children who were reported as the householder or spouse of the householder.
[3]Includes other Central American subgroups not shown separately.
[4]Includes Taiwanese.
[5]In addition to the subgroups shown, also includes Sri Lankan.
[6]Consists of Indonesian and Malaysian.
[7]Respondents who wrote in some other race that was not included as an option on the questionnaire.
NOTE: Race categories exclude persons of Hispanic ethnicity. Detail may not sum to totals because of rounding.
SOURCE: U.S. Department of Commerce, Census Bureau, American Community Survey (ACS), 2014. (This table was prepared May 2016.)

Table 102.30.   Median household income, by state: Selected years, 1990 through 2014
[In constant 2014 dollars. Standard errors appear in parentheses]

State	1990[1]	2000[2]	2005		2009		2010		2011		2012		2013		2014	
1	2	3	4		5		6		7		8		9		10	
United States	$55,427	$59,687	$56,100	($80)	$55,500	($50)	$54,400	($40)	$53,200	($50)	$53,000	($30)	$53,100	($40)	$53,700	($60)
Alabama	43,516	48,517	44,700	(390)	44,700	(350)	44,000	(310)	43,600	(350)	42,900	(300)	43,600	(400)	42,800	(360)
Alaska	76,361	73,300	68,200	(1,330)	73,900	(1,560)	70,100	(1,380)	71,400	(1,250)	69,800	(1,190)	73,400	(1,170)	71,600	(1,080)
Arizona	50,787	57,646	53,700	(480)	53,800	(320)	50,800	(350)	49,200	(350)	49,300	(380)	49,300	(360)	50,100	(290)
Arkansas	38,997	45,741	42,500	(440)	41,800	(420)	41,600	(420)	40,800	(490)	41,400	(310)	41,200	(440)	41,300	(400)
California	66,016	67,503	65,100	(240)	65,100	(180)	62,700	(230)	60,300	(180)	60,100	(220)	61,200	(160)	61,900	(140)
Colorado	55,582	67,091	61,400	(410)	61,200	(470)	58,700	(480)	58,300	(390)	58,500	(370)	59,800	(500)	61,300	(300)
Connecticut	76,938	76,660	73,900	(600)	74,000	(670)	69,600	(720)	69,200	(550)	69,400	(540)	68,200	(650)	70,000	(500)
Delaware	64,313	67,344	63,700	(1,040)	62,800	(1,170)	60,700	(990)	61,900	(1,020)	60,200	(1,000)	58,800	(1,160)	59,700	(1,020)
District of Columbia	56,664	57,034	57,300	(1,430)	65,500	(1,150)	66,200	(1,020)	66,500	(1,540)	68,700	(1,280)	68,700	(2,090)	71,600	(1,210)
Florida	50,682	55,175	51,500	(200)	49,400	(190)	48,200	(210)	46,600	(260)	46,400	(220)	46,800	(190)	47,500	(200)
Georgia	53,518	60,311	55,300	(320)	52,500	(280)	50,400	(310)	48,400	(290)	48,700	(240)	48,600	(390)	49,300	(330)
Hawaii	71,605	70,811	70,500	(1,450)	70,800	(1,060)	68,500	(1,030)	65,100	(660)	68,300	(1,020)	69,100	(940)	70,000	(890)
Idaho	46,577	53,402	50,300	(620)	49,600	(640)	47,200	(660)	45,600	(840)	46,900	(580)	47,500	(570)	47,900	(780)
Illinois	59,476	66,220	61,000	(250)	59,600	(270)	57,500	(290)	56,100	(330)	56,900	(260)	57,100	(250)	57,400	(260)
Indiana	53,105	59,081	53,400	(370)	50,200	(310)	48,500	(300)	48,900	(290)	48,400	(260)	48,300	(320)	49,400	(300)
Iowa	48,369	56,099	52,900	(380)	53,000	(290)	52,100	(430)	52,000	(440)	52,500	(270)	53,100	(330)	53,700	(460)
Kansas	50,328	57,740	52,100	(540)	52,800	(450)	52,400	(570)	51,600	(480)	51,800	(330)	51,800	(380)	52,500	(430)
Kentucky	41,555	47,859	45,300	(350)	44,200	(360)	43,500	(330)	43,300	(300)	43,000	(260)	44,100	(400)	43,000	(420)
Louisiana	40,476	46,287	44,600	(420)	46,900	(420)	46,200	(470)	43,900	(340)	44,300	(430)	44,900	(540)	44,600	(450)
Maine	51,366	52,930	51,900	(710)	50,500	(630)	49,800	(630)	48,500	(510)	48,200	(560)	47,700	(490)	49,500	(680)
Maryland	72,632	75,143	74,700	(440)	76,500	(470)	74,800	(610)	73,700	(510)	73,300	(360)	73,700	(440)	74,000	(530)
Massachusetts	68,144	71,780	69,400	(510)	70,800	(460)	67,400	(270)	66,200	(580)	67,400	(400)	67,900	(440)	69,200	(580)
Michigan	57,204	63,487	55,900	(330)	50,000	(240)	49,300	(200)	48,400	(210)	48,300	(210)	49,100	(230)	48,800	(230)
Minnesota	57,000	66,960	63,100	(270)	61,400	(370)	60,200	(300)	60,000	(310)	60,700	(420)	61,700	(270)	61,500	(290)
Mississippi	37,133	44,530	40,000	(450)	40,500	(470)	40,000	(420)	38,900	(370)	38,200	(370)	38,600	(640)	39,700	(470)
Missouri	48,615	53,917	50,900	(270)	49,900	(350)	48,100	(330)	47,600	(340)	46,700	(260)	47,700	(260)	48,400	(340)
Montana	42,393	46,938	47,700	(710)	46,700	(720)	46,300	(750)	46,600	(690)	46,500	(680)	47,700	(700)	46,300	(740)
Nebraska	47,976	55,787	53,200	(560)	52,300	(540)	52,600	(600)	53,000	(440)	52,300	(360)	52,300	(300)	52,700	(420)
Nevada	57,188	63,364	59,600	(660)	58,900	(660)	55,400	(520)	51,500	(650)	51,300	(520)	52,100	(360)	51,500	(420)
New Hampshire	66,995	70,309	68,900	(740)	66,900	(930)	66,300	(760)	66,000	(910)	65,200	(960)	65,300	(830)	66,500	(270)
New Jersey	75,474	78,381	74,800	(390)	75,500	(440)	73,500	(500)	71,000	(460)	71,800	(450)	71,300	(340)	71,900	(270)
New Mexico	44,419	48,514	45,500	(550)	47,500	(690)	45,700	(480)	44,200	(510)	43,900	(570)	44,600	(590)	44,800	(520)
New York	60,791	61,676	60,000	(310)	60,400	(270)	58,800	(250)	58,200	(250)	58,200	(230)	58,300	(270)	58,900	(240)
North Carolina	49,140	55,693	49,400	(240)	48,200	(250)	47,100	(240)	46,200	(330)	46,600	(250)	46,700	(260)	46,600	(230)
North Dakota	42,807	49,184	49,800	(520)	52,800	(670)	52,900	(1,040)	54,400	(810)	55,300	(970)	56,700	(900)	59,000	(1,020)
Ohio	52,937	58,212	52,800	(250)	50,100	(230)	49,000	(190)	48,200	(200)	48,300	(180)	48,900	(250)	49,300	(220)
Oklahoma	43,479	47,472	45,000	(420)	46,000	(340)	45,700	(270)	45,500	(390)	45,700	(290)	46,400	(330)	47,500	(280)
Oregon	50,252	58,155	52,100	(430)	53,500	(420)	50,600	(360)	49,300	(460)	50,700	(510)	51,100	(330)	51,100	(300)
Pennsylvania	53,607	57,004	54,000	(290)	54,700	(190)	53,500	(290)	52,900	(190)	52,800	(170)	52,900	(160)	53,200	(260)
Rhode Island	59,345	59,824	62,400	(1,010)	59,800	(1,020)	56,800	(820)	56,500	(1,090)	56,300	(1,120)	56,800	(1,180)	54,900	(900)
South Carolina	48,419	52,706	47,700	(450)	46,900	(380)	45,600	(280)	44,600	(360)	44,400	(410)	44,900	(410)	45,200	(310)
South Dakota	41,498	50,147	48,900	(660)	49,700	(810)	49,900	(800)	50,900	(1,020)	49,900	(610)	49,700	(670)	51,000	(620)
Tennessee	45,747	51,680	47,200	(350)	46,100	(290)	45,000	(270)	43,900	(270)	44,100	(360)	45,000	(310)	44,400	(340)
Texas	49,821	56,750	51,100	(180)	53,300	(160)	52,800	(230)	52,000	(250)	52,300	(170)	52,600	(150)	53,000	(230)
Utah	54,346	64,992	58,100	(700)	60,900	(540)	59,500	(410)	58,800	(520)	58,800	(460)	60,700	(470)	60,900	(400)
Vermont	54,940	58,070	55,400	(880)	57,000	(640)	53,700	(980)	55,600	(910)	54,600	(790)	53,400	(960)	54,200	(1,050)
Virginia	61,461	66,344	65,800	(400)	65,500	(320)	65,900	(300)	65,200	(320)	63,700	(260)	63,700	(410)	64,900	(380)
Washington	57,505	65,063	59,800	(470)	62,400	(350)	60,400	(360)	59,800	(360)	59,400	(370)	59,400	(410)	61,400	(290)
West Virginia	38,348	42,208	40,600	(590)	41,300	(470)	41,500	(590)	40,500	(560)	41,400	(440)	41,900	(460)	41,100	(400)
Wisconsin	54,294	62,242	57,100	(290)	55,200	(270)	53,200	(330)	53,100	(270)	52,600	(200)	52,300	(230)	52,600	(260)
Wyoming	49,968	53,857	56,000	(1,120)	58,100	(1,260)	58,100	(1,250)	59,300	(1,210)	56,600	(930)	59,700	(1,110)	57,100	(1,210)

[1]Based on 1989 incomes collected in the 1990 census.
[2]Based on 1999 incomes collected in the 2000 census.
NOTE: Constant dollars adjusted by the Consumer Price Index research series using current methods (CPI-U-RS).
SOURCE: U.S. Department of Commerce, Census Bureau, 1990 Summary Tape File 3 (STF 3), "Median Household Income in 1989," retrieved May 12, 2005, from https://www.census.gov/hhes/ www/income/data/historical/state/state1.html; Decennial Census, 2000, *Summary Social, Economic, and Housing Characteristics*; Census 2000 Summary File 4 (SF 4), retrieved March 28, 2005, from https://www.census.gov/census2000/SF4.html; and American Community Survey (ACS), selected years, 2005 through 2014. (This table was prepared February 2016.)

Table 102.40. Poverty rates for all persons and poverty status of 5- to 17-year-olds, by region and state: Selected years, 1990 through 2014

[Standard errors appear in parentheses]

Region and state	Percent of persons in poverty					Poverty status of related children[1] 5 through 17 years old						
									2013[4]		2014[4]	
	1990[2]	2000[3]	2010[4]	2013[4]	2014[4]	1990,[2] percent in poverty	2000,[3] percent in poverty	2010,[4] percent in poverty	Number in poverty (in thousands)	Percent in poverty	Number in poverty (in thousands)	Percent in poverty
1	2	3	4	5	6	7	8	9	10	11	12	13
United States	13.1	12.4	14.9 (0.06)	15.4 (0.06)	15.1 (0.06)	17.0 (0.02)	15.4 (0.01)	19.7 (0.12)	10,892 (73.1)	20.7 (0.13)	10,681 (69.8)	20.3 (0.13)
Region												
Northeast	10.6	11.4	12.5 (0.09)	13.3 (0.11)	12.9 (0.11)	14.3 (0.54)	14.3 (0.39)	16.3 (0.24)	1,544 (20.9)	17.9 (0.24)	1,496 (21.2)	17.4 (0.24)
South	15.7	13.9	14.1 (0.10)	16.8 (0.08)	14.1 (0.11)	20.5 (0.90)	17.6 (0.64)	22.2 (0.20)	4,595 (39.3)	23.0 (0.19)	2,067 (28.5)	18.4 (0.25)
Midwest	12.0	10.2	16.5 (0.08)	14.4 (0.11)	16.5 (0.08)	14.9 (0.58)	12.0 (0.37)	18.4 (0.25)	2,112 (28.0)	18.7 (0.24)	4,583 (35.7)	22.8 (0.17)
West	12.6	13.0	15.0 (0.09)	15.7 (0.09)	15.3 (0.09)	16.2 (0.79)	16.2 (0.54)	19.4 (0.21)	2,641 (27.9)	20.8 (0.22)	2,536 (28.5)	20.0 (0.22)
Alabama	18.3	16.1	18.6 (0.39)	18.4 (0.31)	18.9 (0.39)	23.2 (0.16)	20.3 (0.11)	26.1 (0.90)	204 (6.5)	25.5 (0.79)	215 (6.6)	26.8 (0.80)
Alaska	9.0	9.4	10.6 (0.75)	8.7 (0.63)	12.0 (1.09)	9.6 (0.27)	10.3 (0.18)	11.2 (1.38)	14 (2.1)	10.5 (1.70)	20 (2.8)	15.3 (2.26)
Arizona	15.7	13.9	17.1 (0.35)	18.1 (0.31)	17.6 (0.30)	20.3 (0.15)	17.8 (0.11)	22.4 (0.77)	291 (8.1)	25.2 (0.69)	270 (8.1)	23.3 (0.68)
Arkansas	19.1	15.8	18.2 (0.41)	18.7 (0.44)	18.3 (0.43)	23.8 (0.20)	20.1 (0.13)	24.7 (1.00)	132 (5.3)	26.2 (1.03)	126 (5.7)	24.9 (1.13)
California	12.5	14.2	15.4 (0.13)	16.4 (0.12)	16.1 (0.15)	17.2 (0.06)	18.5 (0.04)	20.7 (0.30)	1,448 (19.1)	22.2 (0.29)	1,425 (21.3)	21.9 (0.32)
Colorado	11.7	9.3	12.8 (0.33)	12.6 (0.28)	11.9 (0.29)	13.7 (0.13)	10.0 (0.08)	14.9 (0.72)	141 (6.3)	15.9 (0.71)	136 (6.5)	15.1 (0.71)
Connecticut	6.8	7.9	9.6 (0.30)	10.2 (0.32)	9.9 (0.30)	9.8 (0.15)	9.6 (0.10)	11.2 (0.70)	76 (4.2)	13.1 (0.71)	74 (4.4)	12.8 (0.76)
Delaware	8.7	9.2	11.7 (0.73)	12.6 (0.75)	12.6 (0.72)	11.0 (0.27)	10.9 (0.22)	16.2 (1.55)	25 (2.7)	17.1 (1.89)	27 (2.9)	18.6 (1.97)
District of Columbia	16.9	20.2	18.3 (0.87)	18.3 (0.89)	15.9 (0.84)	24.1 (0.59)	30.4 (0.44)	30.2 (2.50)	21 (1.9)	30.7 (2.73)	20 (2.5)	28.1 (3.45)
Florida	12.7	12.5	16.2 (0.16)	16.6 (0.20)	16.2 (0.21)	17.5 (0.10)	16.6 (0.07)	21.7 (0.40)	662 (15.2)	23.0 (0.52)	655 (13.2)	22.5 (0.46)
Georgia	14.7	13.0	17.4 (0.27)	18.3 (0.26)	18.1 (0.26)	18.9 (0.14)	16.1 (0.09)	22.6 (0.48)	443 (11.7)	24.6 (0.65)	456 (10.9)	25.3 (0.59)
Hawaii	8.3	10.7	10.1 (0.50)	10.3 (0.51)	11.0 (0.60)	10.5 (0.25)	12.9 (0.18)	11.2 (1.28)	25 (2.9)	11.9 (1.38)	32 (3.3)	14.9 (1.56)
Idaho	13.3	11.8	15.0 (0.50)	15.5 (0.75)	14.6 (0.55)	14.4 (0.23)	12.6 (0.14)	15.0 (0.89)	61 (5.8)	19.7 (1.86)	54 (4.3)	17.1 (1.37)
Illinois	11.9	10.7	13.6 (0.19)	14.2 (0.21)	14.0 (0.23)	15.9 (0.08)	13.4 (0.05)	18.1 (0.41)	413 (11.7)	18.9 (0.53)	409 (11.8)	19.0 (0.54)
Indiana	10.7	9.5	14.9 (0.28)	15.3 (0.27)	14.9 (0.31)	12.8 (0.10)	10.6 (0.08)	20.0 (0.68)	221 (7.0)	19.6 (0.61)	226 (7.7)	20.1 (0.68)
Iowa	11.5	9.1	12.3 (0.41)	12.6 (0.41)	11.9 (0.46)	12.6 (0.14)	9.5 (0.09)	15.6 (0.95)	81 (5.5)	15.6 (1.07)	81 (5.9)	15.6 (1.15)
Kansas	11.5	9.9	12.7 (0.42)	13.2 (0.45)	13.2 (0.41)	12.8 (0.15)	10.4 (0.10)	15.7 (0.97)	84 (4.9)	16.7 (0.94)	84 (5.0)	16.4 (0.98)
Kentucky	19.0	15.8	18.1 (0.32)	17.8 (0.34)	18.0 (0.39)	23.2 (0.16)	19.4 (0.10)	23.3 (0.79)	165 (6.6)	22.8 (0.89)	169 (6.4)	23.4 (0.86)
Louisiana	23.6	19.6	17.9 (0.31)	19.1 (0.37)	19.0 (0.38)	30.4 (0.19)	25.3 (0.11)	24.2 (0.77)	207 (7.1)	26.2 (0.90)	200 (6.9)	25.3 (0.85)
Maine	10.8	10.9	13.3 (0.58)	13.0 (0.51)	14.2 (0.60)	12.3 (0.20)	12.0 (0.15)	17.0 (1.42)	29 (2.9)	15.5 (1.53)	33 (2.8)	17.2 (1.46)
Maryland	8.3	8.5	9.8 (0.25)	10.1 (0.23)	9.7 (0.25)	10.5 (0.12)	9.8 (0.09)	11.6 (0.50)	124 (6.6)	12.9 (0.67)	116 (5.8)	12.0 (0.60)
Massachusetts	8.9	9.3	11.0 (0.25)	11.5 (0.28)	11.2 (0.23)	12.2 (0.12)	11.4 (0.08)	12.6 (0.57)	150 (6.0)	14.9 (0.60)	141 (6.3)	14.0 (0.63)
Michigan	13.1	10.5	16.2 (0.24)	16.4 (0.23)	15.7 (0.23)	16.7 (0.09)	12.7 (0.05)	20.5 (0.58)	349 (8.9)	21.4 (0.53)	324 (8.4)	20.2 (0.53)
Minnesota	10.2	7.9	11.1 (0.32)	11.0 (0.32)	10.9 (0.31)	11.4 (0.10)	8.7 (0.06)	13.7 (0.81)	120 (7.2)	13.2 (0.79)	117 (6.6)	12.9 (0.71)
Mississippi	25.2	19.9	21.5 (0.51)	23.6 (0.49)	21.4 (0.47)	32.6 (0.21)	26.0 (0.13)	29.0 (1.03)	172 (5.7)	32.8 (1.08)	155 (6.4)	29.5 (1.19)
Missouri	13.3	11.7	15.1 (0.28)	15.8 (0.32)	14.9 (0.28)	16.2 (0.12)	14.4 (0.08)	18.1 (0.64)	214 (7.9)	21.5 (0.78)	187 (7.6)	18.9 (0.76)
Montana	16.1	14.6	14.1 (0.70)	16.9 (0.78)	15.7 (0.81)	18.4 (0.30)	17.1 (0.20)	17.8 (1.57)	34 (3.1)	21.6 (1.94)	29 (2.6)	18.1 (1.68)
Nebraska	11.1	9.7	12.7 (0.56)	12.6 (0.48)	12.3 (0.46)	12.0 (0.18)	11.1 (0.12)	16.4 (1.31)	45 (3.6)	13.7 (1.11)	52 (3.8)	15.7 (1.14)
Nevada	10.2	10.5	14.9 (0.49)	15.4 (0.51)	14.7 (0.45)	11.7 (0.26)	12.3 (0.16)	19.8 (1.08)	97 (5.9)	20.5 (1.22)	92 (5.5)	19.2 (1.15)
New Hampshire	6.4	6.5	8.0 (0.44)	8.5 (0.50)	9.1 (0.53)	6.4 (0.16)	6.7 (0.12)	8.1 (1.14)	18 (2.2)	9.3 (1.11)	25 (3.1)	12.6 (1.54)
New Jersey	7.6	8.5	10.0 (0.22)	11.1 (0.23)	10.9 (0.21)	10.8 (0.10)	10.5 (0.07)	12.9 (0.45)	217 (7.4)	14.8 (0.50)	223 (7.9)	15.3 (0.54)
New Mexico	20.6	18.4	19.9 (0.65)	22.8 (0.57)	20.9 (0.70)	26.3 (0.25)	23.6 (0.17)	28.2 (1.37)	115 (4.4)	31.6 (1.19)	98 (4.9)	27.7 (1.39)
New York	13.0	14.6	14.6 (0.19)	15.7 (0.16)	15.1 (0.18)	18.1 (0.09)	19.1 (0.06)	20.0 (0.39)	661 (11.5)	22.0 (0.38)	622 (12.7)	20.9 (0.42)
North Carolina	13.0	12.3	16.8 (0.24)	17.4 (0.23)	16.8 (0.25)	16.0 (0.11)	14.9 (0.07)	22.3 (0.55)	388 (10.0)	23.6 (0.61)	380 (10.9)	22.9 (0.65)
North Dakota	14.4	11.9	11.8 (0.77)	11.5 (0.71)	11.5 (0.92)	15.9 (0.30)	12.2 (0.17)	13.1 (1.76)	11 (1.9)	9.7 (1.70)	15 (2.4)	13.6 (2.16)
Ohio	12.5	10.6	15.4 (0.21)	15.1 (0.21)	15.4 (0.22)	16.2 (0.08)	12.9 (0.05)	21.0 (0.54)	388 (9.9)	20.4 (0.51)	399 (10.2)	21.0 (0.54)
Oklahoma	16.7	14.7	16.5 (0.39)	16.2 (0.32)	15.9 (0.37)	19.9 (0.16)	17.7 (0.11)	23.2 (1.04)	151 (5.4)	22.6 (0.80)	142 (5.7)	21.1 (0.85)
Oregon	12.4	11.6	15.6 (0.34)	16.2 (0.38)	15.8 (0.40)	13.4 (0.15)	12.8 (0.11)	19.5 (0.80)	116 (5.5)	19.0 (0.90)	108 (5.3)	17.7 (0.86)
Pennsylvania	11.1	11.0	12.8 (0.18)	13.3 (0.24)	13.1 (0.21)	14.5 (0.08)	13.6 (0.05)	17.3 (0.49)	349 (10.6)	17.9 (0.54)	339 (11.2)	17.6 (0.56)
Rhode Island	9.6	11.9	14.0 (0.59)	13.5 (0.60)	13.7 (0.66)	12.3 (0.30)	15.6 (0.25)	17.9 (1.57)	29 (2.4)	18.7 (1.52)	28 (2.6)	17.7 (1.69)
South Carolina	15.4	14.1	17.6 (0.33)	18.0 (0.36)	17.5 (0.37)	20.0 (0.19)	17.9 (0.12)	22.9 (0.86)	192 (6.3)	25.0 (0.81)	199 (7.3)	25.6 (0.93)
South Dakota	15.9	13.2	14.4 (0.89)	13.2 (0.73)	14.2 (0.61)	18.7 (0.33)	15.5 (0.21)	17.5 (2.26)	22 (2.6)	15.4 (1.76)	23 (2.1)	16.3 (1.45)
Tennessee	15.7	13.5	17.2 (0.30)	17.7 (0.28)	18.0 (0.33)	19.5 (0.13)	16.6 (0.10)	23.7 (0.76)	261 (6.0)	24.4 (0.56)	269 (8.2)	25.1 (0.74)
Texas	18.1	15.4	17.3 (0.16)	17.1 (0.17)	16.8 (0.16)	23.4 (0.09)	19.3 (0.06)	23.8 (0.32)	1,194 (19.0)	23.7 (0.38)	1,199 (18.5)	23.6 (0.37)
Utah	11.4	9.4	13.1 (0.46)	12.6 (0.41)	11.6 (0.39)	10.9 (0.16)	8.9 (0.09)	15.2 (0.91)	87 (5.8)	13.8 (0.91)	84 (5.1)	13.2 (0.79)
Vermont	9.9	9.4	11.4 (0.76)	12.4 (0.86)	9.7 (0.66)	10.7 (0.26)	9.9 (0.16)	12.4 (2.04)	14 (2.1)	14.8 (2.23)	12 (1.9)	13.2 (2.11)
Virginia	10.2	9.6	11.0 (0.18)	11.3 (0.22)	11.5 (0.26)	12.4 (0.12)	11.4 (0.08)	13.6 (0.46)	191 (6.9)	14.4 (0.52)	200 (8.1)	14.9 (0.60)
Washington	10.9	10.6	13.2 (0.27)	13.6 (0.30)	13.0 (0.24)	12.8 (0.10)	12.2 (0.09)	16.2 (0.59)	199 (8.0)	17.7 (0.72)	176 (5.8)	15.6 (0.51)
West Virginia	19.7	17.9	17.9 (0.54)	17.6 (0.53)	17.4 (0.49)	24.0 (0.23)	22.9 (0.17)	24.4 (1.50)	64 (3.9)	23.5 (1.43)	56 (3.5)	20.8 (1.32)
Wisconsin	10.7	8.7	12.7 (0.31)	13.3 (0.31)	12.6 (0.31)	13.3 (0.10)	10.0 (0.07)	17.0 (0.73)	163 (7.5)	17.3 (0.77)	152 (7.9)	16.3 (0.84)
Wyoming	11.9	11.4	10.4 (0.80)	10.3 (0.74)	11.7 (0.90)	12.6 (0.33)	12.5 (0.24)	11.7 (1.71)	11 (1.7)	11.0 (1.65)	12 (2.0)	12.9 (2.03)

[1]Related children in a family include all children in the household who are related to the householder by birth, marriage, or adoption (except a child who is the spouse of the householder). The householder is the person (or one of the people) who owns or rents (maintains) the housing unit.
[2]Based on 1989 incomes and family sizes collected in the 1990 census. May differ from Current Population Survey data that are shown in other tables.
[3]Based on 1999 incomes and family sizes collected in the 2000 census. May differ from Current Population Survey data that are shown in other tables.
[4]Based on income and family size data from the American Community Survey (ACS). May differ from Current Population Survey data that are shown in other tables. ACS respondents were interviewed throughout the given year and reported the income they received during the previous 12 months.

NOTE: For information about how the Census Bureau determines who is in poverty, see http://www.census.gov/hhes/www/poverty/about/overview/measure.html. Detail may not sum to totals because of rounding.
SOURCE: U.S. Department of Commerce, Census Bureau, 1990 Summary Tape File 3 (STF 3), "Median Household Income in 1989" and "Poverty Status in 1989 by Family Type and Age"; Decennial Census, 1990, Minority Economic Profiles, unpublished data; Decennial Census, 2000, Summary Social, Economic, and Housing Characteristics; Census 2000 Summary File 4 (SF 4), "Poverty Status in 1999 of Related Children Under 18 Years by Family Type and Age"; and American Community Survey (ACS), 2010, 2013, and 2014. (This table was prepared December 2015.)

Table 102.50.   Official and supplemental measures of poverty status for all persons, persons in families, and related children under age 18, by race/ethnicity: Selected years, 1960 through 2014

[Standard errors appear in parentheses]

Race/ethnicity, type of poverty measure, and year	All persons	Number below the poverty level (in thousands)					Percent below the poverty level					
		In all families			In families with female householder, no husband present		All persons	In all families			In families with female householder, no husband present	
		Total	Householder[1]	Related children under 18[2]	Total	Related children under 18[2]		Total	Householder[1]	Related children under 18[2]	Total	Related children under 18[2]
1	2	3	4	5	6	7	8	9	10	11	12	13
Total, official poverty measure[3]												
1960	39,851 (644.0)	34,925 (493.6)	8,243 (177.2)	17,288 (290.6)	7,247 (163.6)	4,095 (116.6)	22.2 (0.34)	20.7 (0.17)	18.1 (0.30)	26.5 (0.29)	48.9 (0.69)	68.4 (1.01)
1965	33,185 (595.4)	28,358 (419.2)	6,721 (156.2)	14,388 (255.6)	7,524 (167.4)	4,562 (124.1)	17.3 (0.30)	15.8 (0.14)	13.9 (0.26)	20.7 (0.26)	46.0 (0.66)	64.2 (0.96)
1970	25,420 (431.8)	20,330 (266.6)	5,260 (110.1)	10,235 (166.2)	7,503 (136.5)	4,689 (102.9)	12.6 (0.21)	10.9 (0.10)	10.1 (0.18)	14.9 (0.19)	38.1 (0.48)	53.0 (0.73)
1975	25,877 (435.2)	20,789 (271.0)	5,450 (112.4)	10,882 (173.0)	8,846 (151.3)	5,597 (114.2)	12.6 (0.20)	10.9 (0.10)	9.7 (0.17)	16.8 (0.20)	37.5 (0.43)	52.7 (0.67)
1980	29,272 (460.0)	22,601 (288.2)	6,217 (121.7)	11,114 (175.4)	10,120 (165.0)	5,866 (117.5)	13.0 (0.20)	11.5 (0.11)	10.3 (0.17)	17.9 (0.21)	36.7 (0.40)	50.8 (0.64)
1985	33,064 (513.3)	25,729 (336.0)	7,223 (141.0)	12,483 (200.4)	11,600 (190.8)	6,716 (134.8)	13.5 (0.21)	12.6 (0.11)	11.4 (0.18)	20.1 (0.23)	37.6 (0.40)	53.6 (0.65)
1990	33,585 (534.4)	25,232 (342.9)	7,098 (144.4)	12,715 (210.0)	12,578 (208.5)	7,363 (147.7)	13.8 (0.21)	12.0 (0.11)	10.7 (0.18)	19.9 (0.24)	37.2 (0.40)	53.4 (0.64)
1995	36,425 (553.5)	27,501 (366.1)	7,532 (149.8)	13,998 (224.2)	14,205 (228.5)	8,362 (159.9)	13.8 (0.21)	12.3 (0.10)	10.8 (0.18)	20.2 (0.23)	36.5 (0.37)	50.3 (0.58)
2000	31,581 (538.4)	22,347 (324.8)	6,400 (140.7)	11,005 (198.1)	10,926 (197.1)	6,300 (139.4)	11.3 (0.19)	9.6 (0.10)	8.7 (0.16)	15.6 (0.21)	28.5 (0.36)	40.1 (0.61)
2001	32,907 (548.1)	23,215 (334.2)	6,813 (146.2)	11,175 (200.1)	11,223 (200.6)	6,341 (140.0)	11.7 (0.20)	9.9 (0.10)	9.2 (0.17)	15.8 (0.21)	28.6 (0.36)	39.3 (0.60)
2002	34,570 (399.9)	24,534 (248.6)	7,229 (108.2)	11,646 (146.7)	11,657 (146.8)	6,564 (102.0)	12.1 (0.14)	10.4 (0.07)	9.6 (0.12)	16.3 (0.15)	28.8 (0.25)	39.6 (0.42)
2003	35,861 (407.8)	25,684 (257.4)	7,607 (111.6)	12,340 (152.5)	12,413 (153.1)	7,085 (106.9)	12.5 (0.14)	10.8 (0.07)	10.0 (0.12)	17.2 (0.16)	30.0 (0.25)	41.8 (0.42)
2004	37,040 (465.3)	26,544 (405.3)	7,835 (128.6)	12,473 (203.6)	12,832 (262.7)	7,152 (153.5)	12.7 (0.16)	11.0 (0.16)	10.2 (0.16)	17.3 (0.28)	30.5 (0.56)	41.9 (0.73)
2005	36,950 (466.0)	26,068 (410.7)	7,657 (124.4)	12,335 (215.9)	13,153 (303.2)	7,210 (178.4)	12.6 (0.16)	10.6 (0.15)	9.9 (0.15)	17.1 (0.30)	31.1 (0.62)	42.8 (0.86)
2006	36,460 (421.7)	25,915 (378.2)	7,668 (113.2)	12,299 (205.6)	13,199 (290.2)	7,341 (170.5)	12.3 (0.14)	10.8 (0.14)	9.8 (0.14)	16.9 (0.28)	30.7 (0.53)	42.1 (0.70)
2007	37,276 (511.9)	26,509 (441.4)	7,623 (136.3)	12,802 (241.1)	13,478 (317.4)	7,546 (193.5)	12.5 (0.17)	10.8 (0.17)	9.8 (0.17)	17.6 (0.33)	30.7 (0.61)	43.0 (0.87)
2008	39,829 (479.0)	28,564 (422.6)	8,147 (127.9)	13,507 (291.9)	13,812 (291.9)	7,587 (180.9)	13.2 (0.16)	11.3 (0.16)	10.3 (0.16)	18.5 (0.31)	31.4 (0.58)	43.5 (0.81)
2009	43,569 (487.0)	31,197 (439.7)	8,792 (131.1)	14,774 (233.1)	14,746 (307.2)	7,942 (178.2)	14.3 (0.16)	12.5 (0.16)	11.1 (0.16)	20.1 (0.32)	32.5 (0.61)	44.4 (0.80)
2010	46,180 (511.9)	33,007 (442.0)	9,221 (130.6)	15,730 (223.9)	15,895 (290.2)	8,648 (174.9)	15.1 (0.17)	13.2 (0.16)	11.7 (0.16)	21.5 (0.31)	34.2 (0.55)	46.9 (0.71)
2011	46,247 (462.7)	33,126 (442.9)	9,497 (132.7)	15,539 (229.0)	16,451 (326.0)	9,026 (196.8)	15.0 (0.15)	13.1 (0.16)	11.8 (0.16)	21.4 (0.32)	34.2 (0.59)	47.6 (0.80)
2012	46,496 (546.4)	33,198 (500.1)	9,520 (140.0)	15,435 (262.1)	15,957 (384.6)	8,664 (224.6)	15.0 (0.18)	13.1 (0.17)	11.8 (0.17)	21.3 (0.36)	33.9 (0.65)	47.2 (0.87)
2013	45,318 (616.6)	31,530 (513.4)	9,130 (150.1)	14,142 (270.2)	15,606 (375.3)	8,305 (217.6)	14.48 (0.20)	12.365 (0.21)	11.242 (0.18)	19.486 (0.37)	33.2 (0.71)	45.825 (0.89)
2014	46,657 (521.0)	32,615 (450.3)	9,467 (138.4)	14,987 (245.2)	15,905 (339.7)	8,491 (201.3)	14.8 (0.17)	12.7 (0.18)	11.6 (0.17)	20.7 (0.34)	33.1 (0.57)	46.5 (0.77)
Total, Supplemental Poverty Measure[4]												
2009	45,927 (529.5)	34,003 (482.6)	10,133 (139.0)	12,331 (233.6)	12,912 (323.0)	5,843 (168.8)	15.1 (0.17)	13.6 (0.20)	12.8 (0.17)	16.8 (0.32)	28.5 (0.65)	32.6 (0.82)
2010	48,631 (560.3)	35,603 (491.9)	10,535 (144.1)	12,951 (225.2)	14,133 (307.9)	6,507 (159.7)	15.9 (0.18)	14.2 (0.20)	13.4 (0.18)	17.7 (0.31)	30.4 (0.56)	35.3 (0.73)
2011	49,603 (384.1)	36,709 (506.3)	11,075 (152.7)	12,965 (220.0)	14,926 (302.0)	6,833 (164.2)	16.1 (0.18)	14.5 (0.20)	13.8 (0.18)	17.9 (0.30)	31.0 (0.57)	36.1 (0.77)
2012	49,690 (541.1)	36,709 (505.5)	11,118 (148.3)	12,945 (216.8)	14,105 (348.3)	6,477 (186.6)	16.0 (0.18)	14.5 (0.20)	13.7 (0.18)	17.8 (0.30)	30.0 (0.62)	35.3 (0.79)
2013	48,603 (629.7)	35,550 (549.9)	10,778 (155.0)	11,827 (233.1)	13,694 (378.8)	6,080 (188.6)	15.5 (0.20)	13.9 (0.22)	13.3 (0.19)	16.3 (0.32)	29.1 (0.73)	33.5 (0.88)
2014	48,253 (525.3)	35,217 (471.3)	10,787 (144.3)	11,907 (223.3)	13,784 (295.3)	6,075 (152.3)	15.3 (0.17)	13.7 (0.18)	13.2 (0.17)	16.4 (0.31)	28.7 (0.53)	33.2 (0.69)
White, official poverty measure[3]												
1970[5]	17,484 (363.3)	13,323 (198.0)	3,708 (90.0)	6,138 (120.7)	3,761 (90.7)	2,247 (68.2)	9.9 (0.20)	8.1 (0.09)	8.0 (0.17)	10.5 (0.17)	28.4 (0.54)	43.1 (0.94)
1975	17,770 (366.1)	13,799 (202.8)	3,838 (91.7)	6,748 (127.9)	4,577 (101.5)	2,813 (77.1)	9.7 (0.20)	8.3 (0.09)	7.7 (0.16)	12.5 (0.20)	29.4 (0.50)	44.2 (0.86)
1980[5]	19,699 (384.1)	14,587 (210.7)	4,195 (96.5)	6,817 (128.7)	4,940 (106.1)	2,813 (77.1)	10.2 (0.20)	8.6 (0.09)	8.0 (0.16)	13.4 (0.21)	28.0 (0.46)	41.6 (0.82)
1985[5]	22,860 (435.1)	17,125 (249.2)	4,983 (112.8)	7,838 (148.3)	5,990 (125.8)	3,372 (90.2)	11.4 (0.21)	9.9 (0.10)	9.1 (0.18)	15.6 (0.24)	29.8 (0.47)	45.2 (0.84)
1990	16,622 (388.2)	11,086 (191.7)	3,442 (94.4)	5,106 (148.4)	4,284 (106.9)	2,411 (75.5)	8.8 (0.20)	7.0 (0.10)	6.6 (0.16)	11.6 (0.23)	25.8 (0.50)	39.6 (0.94)
1995	16,267 (384.2)	10,599 (186.1)	3,384 (93.5)	4,745 (113.5)	4,183 (105.5)	2,299 (75.5)	8.5 (0.20)	6.6 (0.09)	6.4 (0.16)	10.6 (0.23)	22.8 (0.47)	33.5 (0.86)
2000	14,366 (375.9)	8,664 (169.7)	2,896 (89.0)	3,715 (102.4)	3,412 (097.6)	1,832 (69.4)	7.4 (0.19)	5.5 (0.09)	5.4 (0.15)	8.5 (0.21)	18.8 (0.45)	28.0 (0.87)
2001	15,271 (386.8)	9,122 (175.4)	3,051 (91.7)	3,887 (105.0)	3,661 (71.8)	1,953 (71.8)	7.8 (0.20)	5.7 (0.09)	5.7 (0.16)	8.9 (0.21)	19.9 (0.46)	29.0 (0.87)
2002	15,567 (278.6)	9,389 (127.5)	3,208 (67.3)	3,848 (74.5)	3,733 (73.2)	1,949 (51.2)	8.0 (0.14)	5.9 (0.07)	6.0 (0.11)	8.9 (0.15)	20.0 (0.33)	29.2 (0.62)
2003	15,902 (281.2)	9,658 (129.8)	3,270 (68.0)	3,957 (75.7)	3,959 (75.0)	2,033 (52.4)	8.2 (0.14)	6.1 (0.07)	6.1 (0.11)	9.3 (0.16)	21.1 (0.33)	30.7 (0.63)
2004	16,908 (303.0)	10,323 (254.5)	3,505 (92.4)	4,190 (120.4)	4,116 (84.1)	2,114 (84.1)	8.7 (0.16)	6.5 (0.16)	6.5 (0.17)	9.5 (0.28)	21.7 (0.70)	31.5 (1.02)
2005	16,227 (303.1)	9,604 (247.5)	3,285 (80.6)	3,973 (123.3)	4,278 (151.2)	2,158 (83.8)	8.3 (0.16)	6.0 (0.15)	6.1 (0.14)	9.5 (0.30)	22.6 (0.77)	33.1 (1.17)
2006	16,013 (280.1)	9,676 (239.5)	3,372 (79.5)	3,990 (123.5)	4,353 (151.2)	2,206 (85.3)	8.2 (0.14)	6.1 (0.14)	6.2 (0.14)	9.5 (0.30)	22.5 (0.66)	32.9 (1.00)
2007	16,032 (329.9)	9,553 (257.4)	3,184 (86.4)	3,996 (122.7)	4,099 (172.5)	2,101 (100.7)	8.2 (0.17)	6.0 (0.15)	5.9 (0.15)	9.7 (0.30)	21.4 (0.79)	32.4 (1.27)
2008	17,024 (313.4)	10,138 (255.5)	3,383 (83.7)	4,059 (130.7)	4,046 (154.6)	1,985 (88.5)	8.6 (0.16)	6.4 (0.15)	6.2 (0.15)	9.7 (0.32)	21.5 (0.73)	31.7 (1.17)
2009	18,530 (358.3)	11,211 (298.4)	3,797 (101.6)	4,518 (137.6)	4,532 (158.8)	2,144 (89.4)	9.4 (0.18)	7.1 (0.18)	7.0 (0.18)	11.2 (0.34)	23.8 (0.71)	33.5 (1.11)
2010	19,599 (342.7)	11,740 (281.8)	3,922 (96.1)	4,675 (134.0)	4,802 (165.2)	2,269 (83.1)	9.9 (0.17)	7.4 (0.17)	7.3 (0.17)	11.7 (0.33)	24.8 (0.78)	34.8 (1.03)
2011	19,171 (333.4)	11,562 (287.9)	3,955 (92.2)	4,554 (149.5)	4,746 (164.0)	2,321 (89.9)	9.8 (0.17)	7.4 (0.18)	7.3 (0.17)	11.9 (0.39)	23.8 (0.75)	35.5 (1.09)
2012	18,940 (361.6)	11,387 (298.3)	3,835 (93.5)	4,510 (150.1)	4,655 (164.0)	2,245 (91.8)	9.7 (0.19)	7.3 (0.20)	7.1 (0.18)	11.8 (0.37)	24.3 (0.75)	36.5 (1.17)
2013	18,796 (438.9)	10,710 (339.9)	3,717 (114.6)	3,833 (150.1)	4,325 (217.6)	2,001 (111.3)	9.6 (0.23)	6.9 (0.22)	6.9 (0.21)	10.1 (0.40)	22.9 (0.98)	33.6 (1.45)
2014	19,652 (318.3)	11,566 (267.8)	3,927 (92.6)	4,440 (128.4)	4,630 (160.0)	2,174 (94.1)	10.1 (0.16)	7.5 (0.18)	7.3 (0.17)	11.9 (0.34)	24.4 (0.75)	35.8 (1.18)

See notes at end of table.

Table 102.50. Official and supplemental measures of poverty status for all persons, persons in families, and related children under age 18, by race/ethnicity: Selected years, 1960 through 2014—Continued

[Standard errors appear in parentheses]

Race/ethnicity, type of poverty measure, and year	Number below the poverty level (in thousands)						Percent below the poverty level					
	In all families				In families with female householder, no husband present			In all families			In families with female householder, no husband present	
	All persons	Total	Householder[1]	Related children under 18[2]	Total	Related children under 18[2]	All persons	Total	Householder[1]	Related children under 18[2]	Total	Related children under 18[2]
1	2	3	4	5	6	7	8	9	10	11	12	13
White, Supplemental Poverty Measure												
2009	20,422 (351.3)	13,393 (299.8)	4,796 (104.0)	3,810 (122.2)	4,046 (164.4)	1,572 (77.5)	10.4 (0.18)	8.4 (0.19)	8.8 (0.19)	9.4 (0.30)	21.3 (0.76)	24.6 (1.05)
2010	21,746 (371.8)	13,972 (303.9)	4,917 (109.0)	3,894 (122.4)	4,242 (162.1)	1,660 (72.1)	11.0 (0.19)	8.9 (0.20)	9.1 (0.20)	9.8 (0.31)	21.9 (0.73)	25.5 (0.99)
2011	21,436 (344.0)	13,972 (305.6)	4,993 (105.1)	3,788 (122.9)	4,299 (156.4)	1,675 (75.3)	11.0 (0.18)	9.0 (0.19)	9.2 (0.19)	9.9 (0.32)	21.6 (0.66)	25.6 (0.96)
2012	20,923 (357.6)	13,561 (289.1)	4,870 (102.4)	3,582 (113.1)	3,972 (147.3)	1,510 (69.0)	10.7 (0.18)	8.7 (0.19)	9.0 (0.19)	9.4 (0.30)	20.7 (0.70)	24.6 (0.98)
2013	20,894 (396.1)	13,203 (336.1)	4,765 (116.7)	3,526 (128.2)	3,988 (201.2)	1,409 (83.9)	10.7 (0.20)	8.5 (0.22)	8.9 (0.21)	8.5 (0.34)	21.1 (0.95)	23.7 (1.26)
2014	20,837 (345.2)	13,278 (301.3)	4,717 (108.1)	3,513 (115.1)	3,980 (159.5)	1,478 (72.8)	10.7 (0.18)	8.6 (0.20)	8.8 (0.20)	9.4 (0.31)	20.9 (0.72)	24.3 (1.02)
Black, official poverty measure[3]												
1970[5]	7,548 (219.8)	6,683 (134.2)	1,481 (55.3)	3,922 (96.3)	3,656 (92.3)	2,383 (72.0)	33.5 (0.89)	32.2 (0.45)	29.5 (0.88)	41.5 (0.70)	58.7 (0.86)	67.7 (1.08)
1975[5]	7,545 (219.8)	6,533 (132.3)	1,513 (56.0)	3,884 (95.7)	4,168 (99.9)	2,724 (77.7)	31.3 (0.85)	30.1 (0.43)	27.1 (0.82)	41.4 (0.70)	54.3 (0.71)	66.0 (1.01)
1980[5]	8,579 (230.2)	7,190 (140.8)	1,826 (62.1)	3,906 (96.0)	4,984 (111.4)	2,944 (81.9)	32.5 (0.82)	31.1 (0.42)	28.9 (0.78)	42.1 (0.74)	53.4 (0.71)	64.8 (0.97)
1985[5]	8,926 (246.7)	7,504 (153.2)	1,983 (68.7)	4,057 (102.4)	5,342 (123.1)	3,181 (89.9)	31.3 (0.82)	30.5 (0.43)	28.7 (0.79)	43.1 (0.74)	53.2 (0.72)	66.9 (0.99)
1990	9,653 (262.0)	7,993 (165.4)	2,153 (74.4)	4,309 (111.5)	5,877 (135.3)	3,460 (97.8)	31.8 (0.83)	30.9 (0.43)	29.3 (0.80)	44.0 (0.75)	50.4 (0.70)	64.6 (0.98)
1995	9,562 (261.2)	7,924 (164.4)	2,063 (72.7)	4,481 (114.2)	6,391 (142.8)	3,848 (104.3)	29.0 (0.78)	28.2 (0.40)	26.2 (0.75)	41.1 (0.71)	48.1 (0.65)	61.3 (0.92)
2000	7,680 (249.9)	5,957 (134.8)	1,617 (63.9)	3,342 (115.6)	4,593 (115.6)	2,793 (104.2)	22.4 (0.73)	21.0 (0.38)	19.1 (0.67)	30.7 (0.69)	38.2 (0.69)	49.0 (1.03)
2001	7,752 (251.1)	6,076 (136.6)	1,744 (67.6)	3,248 (94.9)	4,490 (114.1)	2,610 (84.1)	22.4 (0.72)	21.1 (0.38)	20.4 (0.68)	29.7 (0.68)	37.0 (0.68)	46.1 (1.04)
2002	8,259 (183.3)	6,464 (101.0)	1,837 (49.6)	3,420 (69.7)	4,799 (84.6)	2,762 (61.9)	24.0 (0.53)	22.6 (0.28)	21.3 (0.49)	32.1 (0.50)	38.1 (0.48)	47.5 (0.73)
2003	8,463 (194.7)	6,609 (102.4)	1,921 (50.8)	3,599 (71.7)	4,947 (86.2)	2,927 (63.9)	24.3 (0.53)	23.0 (0.28)	22.3 (0.50)	33.5 (0.51)	38.8 (0.48)	49.7 (0.73)
2004	8,697 (207.2)	6,891 (192.5)	1,956 (58.6)	3,562 (107.3)	5,076 (171.6)	2,864 (102.9)	24.7 (0.59)	23.8 (0.66)	22.7 (0.65)	33.4 (0.99)	39.4 (1.06)	49.0 (1.34)
2005	8,850 (236.5)	6,917 (227.2)	1,922 (63.9)	3,615 (124.6)	5,127 (200.0)	2,859 (118.9)	24.9 (0.66)	23.8 (0.78)	22.0 (0.70)	34.2 (1.15)	39.3 (1.33)	50.2 (1.63)
2006	8,653 (196.5)	6,749 (184.3)	1,914 (56.2)	3,531 (107.1)	4,945 (162.5)	2,950 (103.1)	24.1 (0.55)	22.9 (0.63)	21.4 (0.62)	33.0 (0.99)	38.9 (1.20)	49.9 (1.30)
2007	8,821 (226.0)	6,966 (207.3)	1,941 (63.5)	3,646 (119.6)	5,181 (181.3)	2,950 (115.4)	24.3 (0.61)	24.3 (0.69)	21.7 (0.64)	34.1 (1.09)	39.3 (1.20)	49.9 (1.53)
2008	8,979 (225.6)	7,003 (221.1)	1,971 (70.4)	3,586 (124.7)	5,278 (198.0)	2,961 (119.8)	24.6 (0.62)	23.6 (0.74)	21.8 (0.72)	34.4 (1.17)	40.3 (1.22)	51.8 (1.50)
2009	9,419 (239.9)	7,223 (207.8)	2,036 (67.4)	3,682 (114.2)	5,179 (192.2)	2,853 (115.1)	25.5 (0.64)	24.2 (0.70)	22.5 (0.67)	35.3 (1.08)	39.6 (1.18)	50.8 (1.51)
2010	10,122 (240.9)	7,681 (217.0)	2,173 (69.1)	4,021 (119.7)	5,546 (171.4)	3,103 (106.3)	27.3 (0.64)	25.8 (0.74)	24.0 (0.69)	39.3 (1.17)	40.7 (1.15)	53.2 (1.51)
2011	10,108 (245.0)	7,665 (235.9)	2,175 (75.3)	3,872 (124.5)	5,540 (211.9)	3,053 (116.3)	27.3 (0.66)	25.9 (0.78)	23.8 (0.77)	38.0 (1.21)	41.9 (1.24)	54.2 (1.55)
2012	10,148 (245.0)	7,636 (245.4)	2,169 (78.0)	3,797 (132.4)	5,344 (211.9)	2,936 (123.5)	27.0 (0.66)	25.5 (0.80)	23.4 (0.78)	38.0 (1.30)	41.1 (1.28)	53.5 (1.61)
2013	10,264 (292.7)	7,761 (257.9)	2,116 (72.0)	3,863 (143.2)	5,439 (218.4)	2,972 (133.7)	27.2 (0.78)	25.8 (0.87)	22.7 (0.75)	38.9 (1.43)	42.5 (1.41)	54.6 (1.73)
2014	10,058 (209.7)	7,458 (196.9)	2,129 (65.8)	3,734 (119.5)	5,306 (179.8)	2,917 (112.2)	26.1 (0.55)	24.5 (0.65)	22.8 (0.61)	37.2 (1.15)	40.3 (1.15)	53.0 (1.48)
Black, Supplemental Poverty Measure												
2009	8,452 (214.3)	6,487 (191.4)	1,903 (55.9)	2,640 (96.4)	4,257 (168.4)	1,964 (89.4)	22.9 (0.58)	21.7 (0.64)	21.1 (0.56)	25.3 (0.94)	32.6 (1.07)	35.0 (1.35)
2010	9,327 (230.4)	7,080 (211.8)	2,081 (65.9)	2,936 (105.2)	4,739 (167.8)	2,218 (93.8)	25.1 (0.61)	23.8 (0.72)	23.0 (0.57)	28.7 (1.03)	34.8 (1.13)	38.0 (1.41)
2011	9,380 (242.4)	7,096 (227.8)	2,066 (69.8)	2,895 (114.6)	4,728 (185.2)	2,232 (102.1)	25.3 (0.65)	24.0 (0.76)	22.6 (0.71)	28.9 (1.13)	35.7 (1.16)	39.6 (1.54)
2012	9,623 (235.6)	7,348 (233.0)	2,213 (72.2)	2,877 (114.0)	4,633 (190.7)	2,147 (103.7)	25.6 (0.63)	24.6 (0.77)	23.8 (0.74)	28.8 (1.14)	35.6 (1.24)	39.1 (1.54)
2013	9,294 (275.9)	7,066 (252.1)	2,017 (67.3)	2,777 (121.2)	4,395 (200.6)	2,056 (111.1)	24.6 (0.74)	23.5 (0.85)	21.7 (0.74)	28.0 (1.22)	34.3 (1.39)	37.8 (1.80)
2014	8,904 (207.2)	6,664 (180.0)	1,979 (56.9)	2,621 (101.2)	4,232 (150.3)	1,964 (86.4)	23.1 (0.53)	21.9 (0.59)	21.2 (0.54)	26.1 (0.99)	32.1 (1.02)	35.7 (1.40)
Hispanic, official poverty measure[3]												
1975[5]	2,991 (176.8)	2,755 (90.2)	627 (41.3)	1,619 (67.7)	1,053 (54.0)	694 (43.5)	26.9 (1.41)	26.3 (0.70)	25.1 (1.09)	33.1 (1.09)	57.2 (1.88)	68.4 (2.37)
1980[5]	3,491 (189.8)	3,143 (97.0)	751 (45.3)	1,718 (69.8)	1,319 (60.7)	809 (47.1)	25.7 (1.26)	25.1 (0.63)	23.2 (1.06)	33.0 (1.06)	54.5 (1.65)	65.0 (2.20)
1985[5]	5,236 (202.8)	4,605 (107.7)	1,074 (48.7)	2,512 (76.6)	1,983 (67.4)	1,247 (52.7)	29.0 (1.01)	28.3 (0.51)	25.5 (0.98)	39.6 (0.89)	55.1 (1.21)	72.4 (1.57)
1990	6,006 (222.4)	5,091 (118.2)	1,244 (54.4)	2,750 (83.3)	2,115 (72.2)	1,314 (56.0)	28.1 (0.95)	26.9 (0.49)	25.0 (0.92)	37.7 (0.85)	53.0 (1.19)	68.4 (1.60)
1995	8,574 (256.1)	7,341 (147.4)	1,695 (64.1)	3,936 (101.9)	3,053 (88.3)	1,870 (67.6)	30.3 (0.85)	29.2 (0.43)	27.0 (0.84)	39.3 (0.73)	52.8 (0.99)	65.7 (1.34)
2000	7,747 (247.8)	6,430 (141.1)	1,540 (63.3)	3,342 (96.4)	2,444 (81.1)	1,407 (60.3)	21.5 (0.70)	20.3 (0.35)	19.2 (0.69)	27.6 (0.63)	37.8 (0.94)	49.8 (1.47)
2001	7,997 (251.7)	6,674 (144.4)	1,649 (65.6)	3,433 (97.9)	2,585 (83.6)	1,508 (62.6)	21.4 (0.68)	20.2 (0.34)	19.4 (0.67)	27.4 (0.62)	37.8 (0.92)	49.3 (1.41)
2002	8,555 (186.7)	7,184 (107.8)	1,792 (48.9)	3,653 (72.3)	2,554 (59.3)	1,501 (44.5)	21.8 (0.48)	20.8 (0.24)	19.7 (0.47)	28.2 (0.44)	36.4 (0.64)	47.9 (0.99)
2003	9,051 (192.6)	7,637 (111.9)	1,925 (50.8)	3,982 (76.0)	2,861 (63.1)	1,727 (48.0)	22.5 (0.48)	21.5 (0.24)	20.8 (0.47)	29.5 (0.44)	38.4 (0.63)	50.6 (0.95)
2004	9,122 (215.6)	7,705 (205.4)	1,953 (54.5)	3,985 (115.8)	3,072 (135.0)	1,840 (85.4)	21.9 (0.52)	21.1 (0.56)	20.5 (0.54)	28.6 (0.83)	39.3 (1.22)	51.9 (1.67)
2005	9,368 (202.4)	7,767 (192.2)	1,948 (51.0)	3,977 (113.4)	3,069 (120.9)	1,774 (103.4)	21.8 (0.47)	20.6 (0.51)	19.7 (0.48)	27.7 (0.78)	39.0 (1.41)	50.2 (1.59)
2006	9,243 (216.1)	7,650 (214.8)	1,922 (61.3)	3,959 (114.9)	3,189 (152.6)	1,848 (88.9)	20.6 (0.48)	19.5 (0.54)	18.9 (0.56)	26.6 (0.76)	36.9 (1.41)	47.2 (1.66)
2007	9,890 (244.8)	8,248 (229.3)	2,045 (60.4)	4,348 (134.9)	3,527 (158.7)	2,092 (98.1)	21.5 (0.53)	20.6 (0.58)	19.7 (0.56)	28.3 (0.87)	39.6 (1.32)	51.6 (1.59)
2008	10,987 (249.6)	9,303 (237.9)	2,239 (60.3)	4,888 (129.2)	3,751 (144.1)	2,218 (86.9)	23.2 (0.53)	22.3 (0.57)	21.3 (0.54)	30.3 (0.79)	40.5 (1.24)	51.9 (1.48)

See notes at end of table.

Table 102.50. Official and supplemental measures of poverty status for all persons, persons in families, and related children under age 18, by race/ethnicity: Selected years, 1960 through 2014—Continued

[Standard errors appear in parentheses]

Race/ethnicity, type of poverty measure, and year	Number below the poverty level (in thousands)						Percent below the poverty level					
	All persons	In all families			In families with female householder, no husband present		All persons	In all families			In families with female householder, no husband present	
		Total	Householder[1]	Related children under 18[2]	Total	Related children under 18[2]		Total	Householder[1]	Related children under 18[2]	Total	Related children under 18[2]
1	2	3	4	5	6	7	8	9	10	11	12	13
2009	12,350 (267.3)	10,345 (254.8)	2,369 (62.7)	5,419 (138.6)	4,176 (169.1)	2,437 (100.1)	25.3 (0.55)	24.2 (0.59)	22.7 (0.56)	32.5 (0.83)	40.6 (1.33)	52.2 (1.61)
2010	13,243 (254.4)	11,188 (242.8)	2,557 (64.4)	5,881 (139.4)	4,643 (167.5)	2,715 (107.1)	25.6 (0.51)	25.6 (0.55)	24.0 (0.54)	34.5 (0.81)	44.5 (1.24)	57.0 (1.49)
2011	13,244 (263.5)	11,143 (253.2)	2,651 (59.5)	5,820 (146.1)	4,996 (182.1)	2,955 (120.5)	25.3 (0.50)	24.3 (0.56)	22.9 (0.50)	33.7 (0.84)	44.0 (1.22)	56.8 (1.57)
2012	13,616 (278.2)	11,358 (276.3)	2,807 (71.8)	5,773 (145.5)	4,816 (187.7)	2,809 (114.9)	25.6 (0.52)	24.6 (0.59)	23.5 (0.54)	33.3 (0.84)	42.8 (1.19)	54.7 (1.49)
2013	12,744 (312.0)	10,536 (293.3)	2,613 (78.6)	5,273 (155.7)	4,860 (197.6)	2,763 (114.5)	23.3 (0.58)	22.3 (0.63)	21.6 (0.63)	30.0 (0.89)	41.6 (1.47)	52.3 (1.65)
2014	13,104 (269.8)	10,853 (246.1)	2,684 (60.6)	5,522 (136.1)	4,817 (191.3)	2,739 (113.3)	23.6 (0.47)	22.5 (0.52)	21.5 (0.46)	31.3 (0.76)	40.4 (1.26)	53.3 (1.49)
Hispanic, Supplemental Poverty Measure												
2009	13,329 (281.7)	11,239 (271.8)	2,674 (64.6)	4,879 (132.5)	3,842 (168.4)	1,953 (89.5)	27.3 (0.58)	26.3 (0.63)	25.7 (0.59)	29.3 (0.80)	37.4 (1.36)	41.9 (1.58)
2010	13,845 (279.4)	11,669 (262.5)	2,791 (63.3)	5,109 (136.5)	4,331 (160.6)	2,227 (94.3)	27.8 (0.56)	26.7 (0.59)	26.2 (0.53)	30.0 (0.80)	41.5 (1.19)	46.8 (1.51)
2011	14,571 (303.9)	12,397 (284.6)	3,081 (71.5)	5,210 (132.0)	4,907 (180.7)	2,473 (96.6)	27.9 (0.58)	27.1 (0.63)	26.6 (0.62)	30.2 (0.77)	43.2 (1.25)	47.5 (1.45)
2012	14,799 (273.5)	12,443 (264.0)	3,170 (69.8)	5,212 (127.6)	4,492 (172.7)	2,315 (99.3)	27.9 (0.52)	26.9 (0.56)	26.5 (0.52)	30.1 (0.74)	39.9 (1.16)	45.1 (1.49)
2013	14,062 (338.9)	11,883 (318.0)	3,032 (80.7)	4,747 (143.6)	4,371 (193.5)	2,175 (103.4)	26.0 (0.62)	25.1 (0.67)	25.0 (0.65)	27.0 (0.82)	37.4 (1.46)	41.2 (1.70)
2014	14,106 (269.5)	11,878 (258.3)	3,123 (65.7)	4,684 (130.6)	4,551 (177.6)	2,190 (92.8)	25.4 (0.49)	24.6 (0.53)	25.1 (0.51)	26.6 (0.73)	38.2 (1.20)	42.7 (1.41)
Asian, official poverty measure[3]												
1995[5]	1,379 (111.1)	1,087 (50.7)	258 (24.3)	520 (34.7)	253 (24.1)	139 (17.8)	14.6 (1.12)	12.9 (0.55)	12.3 (1.08)	18.5 (1.10)	28.7 (2.29)	41.8 (4.07)
2000[6]	1,210 (108.8)	863 (46.8)	227 (23.7)	390 (31.2)	272 (26.0)	151 (19.3)	9.8 (0.86)	8.0 (0.41)	7.8 (0.77)	12.3 (0.91)	22.8 (1.90)	37.0 (3.74)
2001[6]	1,242 (110.2)	854 (46.5)	225 (23.6)	344 (29.2)	190 (21.6)	99 (15.6)	10.1 (0.89)	8.1 (0.42)	7.7 (0.77)	11.4 (0.89)	14.7 (1.54)	26.3 (3.54)
2002	1,143 (75.4)	751 (31.0)	207 (16.1)	297 (19.3)	152 (13.8)	83 (13.8)	8.1 (0.65)	7.7 (0.30)	7.4 (0.55)	11.4 (0.69)	15.3 (1.28)	30.3 (3.09)
2003	1,372 (82.1)	992 (35.8)	305 (19.6)	313 (19.9)	226 (16.9)	107 (11.9)	9.7 (0.65)	9.7 (0.33)	10.0 (0.61)	11.7 (0.70)	22.6 (1.48)	35.5 (3.07)
2004	1,184 (76.3)	799 (70.5)	228 (21.4)	256 (32.4)	126 (23.6)	47 (11.9)	9.8 (0.64)	7.5 (0.67)	7.3 (0.69)	9.2 (1.16)	12.6 (2.20)	17.0 (4.09)
2005	1,391 (85.4)	960 (80.0)	286 (23.6)	309 (34.1)	182 (30.1)	65 (15.1)	11.2 (0.68)	8.9 (0.73)	9.0 (0.73)	11.1 (1.19)	17.9 (2.77)	26.2 (5.06)
2006	1,301 (95.4)	881 (86.5)	252 (24.1)	335 (42.0)	186 (34.5)	89 (20.7)	10.0 (0.73)	7.8 (0.76)	7.6 (0.72)	11.8 (1.45)	18.0 (2.99)	36.8 (6.58)
2007	1,329 (80.5)	916 (79.6)	255 (23.2)	340 (39.2)	205 (36.6)	95 (21.5)	10.2 (0.62)	8.1 (0.70)	7.8 (0.70)	11.8 (1.33)	16.8 (2.77)	32.2 (5.77)
2008	1,528 (89.1)	1,154 (88.6)	334 (24.8)	410 (41.7)	205 (34.2)	85 (18.7)	11.8 (0.68)	10.1 (0.76)	9.8 (0.71)	14.1 (1.41)	16.1 (2.38)	25.5 (4.53)
Asian, Supplemental Poverty Measure												
2009	1,684 (96.8)	1,201 (87.4)	327 (23.6)	434 (39.7)	227 (36.1)	88 (16.0)	12.3 (0.70)	10.0 (0.72)	9.3 (0.65)	13.7 (1.24)	17.4 (2.64)	25.8 (4.25)
2010	1,672 (95.0)	1,211 (90.2)	323 (23.4)	434 (42.0)	281 (45.4)	118 (19.6)	11.9 (0.68)	9.9 (0.74)	9.3 (0.66)	13.7 (1.31)	21.7 (3.09)	35.1 (4.61)
2011	1,871 (114.8)	1,317 (99.8)	385 (29.4)	422 (44.2)	295 (58.4)	124 (34.0)	12.2 (0.74)	9.8 (0.74)	9.6 (0.72)	12.7 (1.32)	20.6 (3.53)	34.4 (6.88)
2012	1,813 (113.6)	1,268 (109.7)	361 (29.4)	422 (46.4)	257 (45.0)	95 (18.9)	11.4 (0.70)	9.2 (0.78)	9.0 (0.69)	12.5 (1.37)	18.3 (2.81)	28.8 (5.46)
2013	1,733 (103.7)	1,134 (89.7)	374 (30.2)	346 (34.3)	227 (43.3)	89 (18.9)	10.4 (0.61)	7.8 (0.61)	8.7 (0.69)	9.9 (0.97)	14.2 (2.54)	24.2 (4.87)
2014	2,019 (121.2)	1,315 (103.3)	393 (31.3)	437 (42.6)	281 (41.5)	110 (19.2)	11.7 (0.69)	8.8 (0.68)	8.9 (0.68)	12.3 (1.20)	17.0 (2.32)	29.0 (4.18)

[1]Refers to the person who owns or rents (maintains) the housing unit.
[2]Refers to all children in the household who are related to the householder by birth, marriage, or adoption (except a child who is the spouse of the householder). For 1960 and 1965 only, the data exclude related children who have ever been married.
[3]The official poverty measure consists of a set of thresholds for families of different sizes and compositions that are compared to before-tax cash income to determine a family's poverty status. For more information about how the Census Bureau determines who is in poverty, see http://www.census.gov/hhes/www/poverty/about/overview/measure.html.
[4]For 2009 and later years, data based on the Supplemental Poverty Measure (SPM) are available. The SPM extends the information provided by the official poverty measure by adding to family income the value of benefits from many government programs designed to assist low-income families, subtracting taxes and necessary expenses such as child care costs (for working families) and medical expenses, and adjusting poverty thresholds for differences in housing costs. To match the population included in the current official poverty measure, SPM estimates presented in this table exclude unrelated children under age 15. For more information about the SPM, see http://www.census.gov/hhes/povmeas/methodology/supplemental/research/Short_ResearchSPM2011.pdf.

[5]Includes persons of Hispanic ethnicity, because data for the White, non-Hispanic and Black, non-Hispanic populations are not available for the indicated years.
[6]Includes Pacific Islanders as well as Asians.
NOTE: All data in this table are from the Current Population Survey (CPS); official poverty measure estimates may differ from those shown in other tables obtained from the Decennial Census and the American Community Survey (ACS). In all tables, poverty estimates are for the official measure unless otherwise noted. Supplemental Poverty Measure estimates can be generated only from the CPS, while estimates based on the official poverty measure can be generated from the CPS, Decennial Census, or ACS. Race categories exclude persons of Hispanic ethnicity except where otherwise noted. Some data have been revised from previously published figures.
SOURCE: U.S. Department of Commerce, Census Bureau, Current Population Reports, Series P-60, *Poverty in the United States*, selected years, 1960 through 2002; Current Population Survey (CPS), Annual Social and Economic Supplement, 1991 through 2015; and Supplemental Poverty Measure (SPM) Research Files, 2009 through 2014. (This table was prepared January 2016.)

Table 102.60. Number and percentage of children under age 18 living in poverty, by family structure, race/ethnicity, and selected racial/ethnic subgroups: 2009 and 2014

[Standard errors appear in parentheses]

Year and race/ethnicity	Number of related children[1] living in poverty (in thousands)		Percent of related children[1] living in poverty, by family structure					
			Total, all families		Married-couple household[2]		Mother-only household, no spouse present[2]	
1	2		3		4		5	
2009								
Total	14,299	(104.7)	19.6	(0.14)	9.6	(0.10)	42.2	(0.29)
White	4,674	(51.5)	11.6	(0.13)	6.0	(0.10)	33.1	(0.36)
Black	3,587	(37.7)	36.0	(0.34)	12.3	(0.38)	49.0	(0.46)
Hispanic	4,973	(41.2)	30.4	(0.25)	20.8	(0.28)	48.7	(0.47)
Cuban	56	(4.1)	15.7	(1.06)	8.4	(0.99)	32.7	(2.62)
Dominican	131	(7.0)	32.5	(1.47)	14.8	(1.80)	49.0	(1.90)
Mexican	3,729	(38.3)	32.3	(0.30)	23.8	(0.33)	50.1	(0.60)
Puerto Rican	466	(11.4)	32.1	(0.69)	11.2	(0.83)	51.5	(0.97)
Spaniard	20	(1.9)	13.4	(1.24)	5.5	(1.05)	31.6	(3.92)
Central American[3]	316	(11.4)	27.4	(0.81)	18.4	(0.93)	43.4	(1.56)
Costa Rican	4	(1.0)	12.4	(3.14)	‡	(†)	25.7 !	(8.23)
Guatemalan	98	(6.6)	31.6	(1.78)	25.4	(1.99)	48.0	(3.29)
Honduran	60	(4.1)	34.9	(2.08)	20.9	(2.66)	52.4	(4.17)
Nicaraguan	16	(2.4)	19.5	(2.81)	6.1 !	(2.04)	38.7	(4.83)
Panamanian	6	(1.4)	15.2	(3.38)	‡	(†)	33.4	(7.41)
Salvadoran	130	(8.2)	25.4	(1.34)	16.9	(1.34)	40.3	(2.63)
South American	109	(5.9)	15.7	(0.79)	9.0	(0.76)	32.9	(2.02)
Chilean	4	(1.0)	12.2	(2.95)	12.1 !	(3.73)	16.2 !	(7.43)
Colombian	30	(3.1)	13.7	(1.23)	7.9	(1.16)	31.0	(3.76)
Ecuadorian	32	(3.2)	20.9	(1.80)	14.2	(2.09)	33.2	(3.84)
Peruvian	21	(2.5)	15.0	(1.69)	7.6	(1.62)	30.4	(4.49)
Venezuelan	8	(1.5)	15.6	(2.89)	4.7 !	(1.65)	47.8	(7.16)
Other South American	14	(2.6)	14.4	(2.42)	7.2	(1.50)	37.2	(7.58)
Other Hispanic	146	(7.9)	25.0	(1.08)	12.5	(1.13)	47.5	(2.03)
Asian	351	(9.9)	11.7	(0.31)	8.9	(0.33)	28.2	(1.10)
Chinese[4]	69	(5.4)	10.8	(0.83)	8.3	(0.75)	25.9	(2.45)
Filipino	19	(2.3)	4.4	(0.48)	2.4	(0.36)	10.9	(1.83)
Japanese	5	(1.2)	6.1	(1.51)	3.3 !	(1.34)	35.0	(8.38)
Korean	31	(2.7)	11.9	(0.95)	9.8	(0.91)	28.0	(4.45)
South Asian[5]	53	(4.7)	7.8	(0.65)	6.5	(0.61)	34.1	(4.67)
Asian Indian	41	(4.0)	6.4	(0.59)	5.1	(0.54)	33.6	(4.83)
Bangladeshi	10	(1.8)	33.1	(4.35)	33.7	(5.01)	‡	(†)
Bhutanese	‡	(†)	‡	(†)	‡	(†)	‡	(†)
Nepalese	‡	(†)	‡	(†)	‡	(†)	‡	(†)
Pakistani	20	(2.7)	20.6	(2.47)	18.9	(2.54)	38.8 !	(12.92)
Southeast Asian	129	(6.8)	20.7	(0.92)	15.2	(1.03)	38.7	(2.29)
Burmese	‡	(‡)	‡	(†)	‡	(†)	‡	(†)
Cambodian	14	(2.7)	23.1	(3.77)	12.6	(3.63)	34.4	(7.07)
Hmong	35	(4.4)	35.7	(3.76)	29.7	(4.56)	44.9	(8.03)
Laotian	7	(1.7)	14.8	(3.40)	10.0 !	(4.24)	29.5	(6.23)
Thai	6	(1.4)	20.1	(4.41)	18.2	(4.97)	25.5 !	(10.67)
Vietnamese	66	(4.7)	17.6	(1.07)	12.7	(1.13)	41.3	(3.33)
Other Southeast Asian[6]	2 !	(0.7)	12.3 !	(4.67)	‡	(†)	‡	(†)
Other Asian	24	(2.6)	13.9	(1.36)	12.5	(1.50)	21.0	(3.69)
Pacific Islander	18	(2.5)	17.3	(2.39)	9.0	(2.16)	31.3	(4.37)
American Indian/Alaska Native[7]	172	(7.1)	33.0	(1.17)	13.1	(0.98)	52.7	(2.10)
American Indian	143	(6.7)	34.1	(1.36)	13.7	(1.23)	53.3	(2.51)
Alaska Native	6	(0.9)	24.0	(3.07)	13.5	(3.29)	43.1	(7.12)
Some other race[8]	38	(4.6)	16.9	(1.89)	8.3	(2.15)	35.4	(3.97)
Two or more races	487	(12.3)	19.3	(0.44)	6.9	(0.33)	39.2	(0.98)
2014								
Total	15,276	(98.6)	21.2	(0.13)	10.5	(0.11)	44.4	(0.27)
White	4,650	(45.7)	12.5	(0.12)	6.3	(0.09)	34.6	(0.39)
Black	3,725	(39.8)	38.1	(0.36)	14.9	(0.39)	51.6	(0.45)
Hispanic	5,559	(48.1)	31.7	(0.27)	21.3	(0.29)	50.2	(0.45)
Cuban	85	(5.2)	20.8	(1.10)	11.1	(0.90)	43.0	(2.69)
Dominican	166	(9.3)	34.0	(1.46)	20.8	(1.77)	46.4	(2.16)
Mexican	4,038	(45.5)	33.3	(0.34)	23.7	(0.34)	51.9	(0.61)
Puerto Rican	530	(13.4)	32.1	(0.70)	12.8	(0.73)	49.8	(1.10)
Spaniard	29	(3.5)	14.7	(1.57)	4.6	(1.03)	38.4	(4.19)
Central American[3]	475	(17.2)	32.6	(0.91)	23.4	(1.11)	49.6	(1.54)
Costa Rican	5	(1.3)	14.7	(3.46)	6.6 !	(2.52)	30.3	(9.07)
Guatemalan	156	(7.8)	39.6	(1.54)	32.1	(2.12)	54.4	(3.24)
Honduran	105	(7.6)	41.6	(1.81)	26.9	(2.72)	60.4	(2.78)
Nicaraguan	23	(3.0)	23.8	(2.95)	9.3	(2.42)	42.7	(5.48)
Panamanian	6	(1.3)	14.5	(2.78)	‡	(†)	33.1	(7.09)
Salvadoran	178	(10.9)	28.4	(1.33)	21.4	(1.84)	44.6	(2.02)
South American	126	(7.2)	17.0	(0.94)	10.0	(0.91)	36.2	(2.15)
Chilean	5	(1.0)	13.9	(2.84)	9.6 !	(2.94)	22.3 !	(7.75)
Colombian	34	(2.9)	16.0	(1.28)	8.7	(1.41)	36.7	(3.21)
Ecuadorian	40	(4.6)	24.8	(2.27)	13.9	(2.13)	46.7	(4.53)
Peruvian	16	(2.4)	11.9	(1.66)	6.9	(1.84)	26.0	(4.36)
Venezuelan	11	(2.2)	14.9	(2.85)	11.3	(2.61)	29.6	(7.73)
Other South American	20	(2.7)	16.1	(2.00)	10.1	(2.25)	36.5	(5.35)
Other Hispanic	111	(5.7)	23.0	(0.96)	12.7	(1.15)	42.8	(1.86)

Year and race/ethnicity	Father-only household, no spouse present[2]	
1	6	
2009		
Total	27.8	(0.35)
White	19.6	(0.41)
Black	40.1	(0.88)
Hispanic	33.3	(0.77)
Cuban	24.0	(5.21)
Dominican	39.8	(4.38)
Mexican	34.2	(1.00)
Puerto Rican	33.2	(2.41)
Spaniard	19.8	(4.71)
Central American[3]	31.5	(2.53)
Costa Rican	‡	(†)
Guatemalan	28.0	(4.70)
Honduran	54.4	(8.00)
Nicaraguan	34.4 !	(13.68)
Panamanian	‡	(†)
Salvadoran	29.2	(3.55)
South American	23.0	(3.43)
Chilean	‡	(†)
Colombian	17.1	(4.59)
Ecuadorian	33.5	(8.46)
Peruvian	22.1 !	(6.95)
Venezuelan	‡	(†)
Other South American	‡	(†)
Other Hispanic	31.4	(3.19)
Asian	23.4	(2.07)
Chinese[4]	22.7	(4.09)
Filipino	14.3 !	(4.58)
Japanese	‡	(†)
Korean	19.0	(5.11)
South Asian[5]	10.8 !	(5.33)
Asian Indian	11.8 !	(5.74)
Bangladeshi	‡	(†)
Bhutanese	‡	(†)
Nepalese	‡	(†)
Pakistani	‡	(†)
Southeast Asian	33.1	(4.41)
Burmese	‡	(†)
Cambodian	40.9	(12.24)
Hmong	61.9	(9.43)
Laotian	‡	(†)
Thai	‡	(†)
Vietnamese	21.5	(4.80)
Other Southeast Asian[6]	‡	(†)
Other Asian	22.8 !	(7.38)
Pacific Islander	33.0	(8.37)
American Indian/Alaska Native[7]	43.4	(2.56)
American Indian	44.5	(2.98)
Alaska Native	23.3 !	(9.42)
Some other race[8]	23.7	(4.24)
Two or more races	27.8	(1.65)
2014		
Total	28.2	(0.36)
White	21.0	(0.44)
Black	40.5	(0.90)
Hispanic	32.3	(0.75)
Cuban	20.2	(3.67)
Dominican	29.8	(3.62)
Mexican	34.2	(0.94)
Puerto Rican	34.2	(2.20)
Spaniard	26.7	(5.76)
Central American[3]	28.5	(2.30)
Costa Rican	‡	(†)
Guatemalan	39.7	(3.96)
Honduran	34.3	(5.87)
Nicaraguan	30.6	(9.15)
Panamanian	‡	(†)
Salvadoran	19.4	(2.67)
South American	18.5	(2.68)
Chilean	‡	(†)
Colombian	13.0 !	(4.05)
Ecuadorian	31.8	(5.76)
Peruvian	10.7 !	(4.60)
Venezuelan	‡	(†)
Other South American	‡	(†)
Other Hispanic	19.3	(2.99)

See notes at end of table.

Table 102.60. Number and percentage of children under age 18 living in poverty, by family structure, race/ethnicity, and selected racial/ethnic subgroups: 2009 and 2014—Continued

[Standard errors appear in parentheses]

Year and race/ethnicity	Number of related children[1] living in poverty (in thousands)		Percent of related children[1] living in poverty, by family structure							
			Total, all families		Married-couple household[2]		Mother-only household, no spouse present[2]		Father-only household, no spouse present[2]	
1	2		3		4		5		6	
Asian..................................	385	(9.6)	11.6	(0.28)	8.8	(0.28)	27.5	(1.50)	23.3	(1.91)
Chinese[4]................................	72	(4.4)	10.4	(0.64)	7.8	(0.62)	23.5	(2.31)	27.0	(4.84)
Filipino..................................	27	(3.0)	6.1	(0.65)	3.7	(0.59)	16.6	(2.61)	6.8	(1.87)
Japanese...............................	5	(1.3)	7.2	(1.87)	3.5 !	(1.22)	37.8	(10.14)	‡	(†)
Korean...................................	23	(2.5)	9.9	(1.05)	7.5	(1.01)	30.9	(4.72)	23.1 !	(9.16)
South Asian[5]...........................	98	(5.5)	9.5	(0.52)	8.6	(0.57)	21.4	(2.79)	24.6	(5.24)
Asian Indian......................	48	(4.3)	5.9	(0.51)	5.0	(0.52)	18.1	(2.86)	19.9	(5.18)
Bangladeshi......................	13	(1.8)	28.9	(3.40)	29.0	(3.70)	‡	(†)	‡	(†)
Bhutanese........................	4 !	(1.6)	51.8	(12.46)	51.4	(12.71)	‡	(†)	‡	(†)
Nepalese..........................	8	(1.4)	24.3	(3.82)	21.8	(3.92)	‡	(†)	‡	(†)
Pakistani..........................	25	(3.2)	21.1	(2.33)	20.1	(2.47)	24.6 !	(10.29)	‡	(†)
Southeast Asian......................	140	(6.9)	21.4	(0.88)	16.0	(0.85)	37.3	(2.81)	29.3	(4.11)
Burmese...........................	17	(2.2)	39.2	(4.14)	39.3	(4.74)	‡	(†)	‡	(†)
Cambodian........................	13	(2.1)	22.7	(2.97)	13.4	(3.32)	41.1	(6.76)	27.3 !	(9.13)
Hmong..............................	35	(4.2)	33.2	(3.32)	27.5	(3.97)	37.8	(7.27)	46.2	(9.76)
Laotian.............................	12	(2.1)	23.9	(3.54)	5.5 !	(2.10)	55.9	(7.33)	33.7 !	(11.05)
Thai..................................	6	(1.6)	24.1	(5.33)	17.7	(5.21)	57.0	(13.90)	‡	(†)
Vietnamese.......................	53	(3.7)	15.0	(0.95)	11.4	(1.14)	30.9	(2.96)	16.1	(3.88)
Other Southeast Asian[6].....	2 !	(1.0)	15.6 !	(5.44)	17.1 !	(5.93)	‡	(†)	‡	(†)
Other Asian............................	20	(2.7)	10.4	(1.24)	6.4	(0.97)	30.9	(5.46)	21.6 !	(6.78)
Pacific Islander........................	33	(3.4)	27.3	(2.33)	19.5	(2.66)	46.3	(4.88)	33.2	(8.18)
American Indian/Alaska Native[7]..........	188	(6.2)	34.9	(0.99)	19.4	(1.34)	50.2	(1.60)	42.1	(2.39)
American Indian....................	165	(5.4)	36.3	(1.01)	20.6	(1.51)	51.7	(1.58)	41.7	(2.60)
Alaska Native......................	9	(1.4)	28.5	(3.97)	19.1	(5.54)	38.8	(8.09)	33.3	(6.93)
Some other race[8]...................	52	(4.1)	22.6	(1.66)	11.9	(1.76)	44.9	(3.85)	31.0	(7.22)
Two or more races	683	(16.4)	21.5	(0.44)	8.7	(0.43)	42.5	(0.82)	25.2	(1.34)

†Not applicable.
!Interpret data with caution. The coefficient of variation (CV) for this estimate is between 30 and 50 percent.
‡Reporting standards not met. Either there are too few cases for a reliable estimate or the coefficient of variation (CV) is 50 percent or greater.
[1]Related children in a family include all children in the household who are related to the householder by birth, marriage, or adoption (except a child who is the spouse of the householder). The householder is the person (or one of the people) who owns or rents (maintains) the housing unit. This table includes only children related to the householder. It excludes unrelated children and householders who are themselves under the age of 18.
[2]To determine family structure, children are classified by their parents' marital status or, if no parents are present in the household, by the marital status of the householder who is related to the children. Mother-only households are those that have only a female householder, and father-only households are those that have only a male householder.
[3]Includes other Central American subgroups not shown separately.

[4]Includes Taiwanese.
[5]In addition to the subgroups shown, also includes Sri Lankan.
[6]Consists of Indonesian and Malaysian.
[7]Includes persons reporting American Indian alone, persons reporting Alaska Native alone, and persons from American Indian and/or Alaska Native tribes specified or not specified.
[8]Respondents who wrote in some other race that was not included as an option on the questionnaire.
NOTE: Data may differ from Current Population Survey data that are shown in other tables. American Community Survey respondents were interviewed throughout the given year and reported the income they received during the previous 12 months. For information about how the Census Bureau determines who is in poverty, see http://www.census.gov/hhes/www/poverty/about/overview/measure.html. Detail may not sum to totals because of rounding. Race categories exclude persons of Hispanic ethnicity.
SOURCE: U.S. Department of Commerce, Census Bureau, American Community Survey (ACS), 2009 and 2014. (This table was prepared December 2015.)

Table 103.10. Percentage of the population 3 to 34 years old enrolled in school, by sex, race/ethnicity, and age group: Selected years, 1980 through 2014

[Standard errors appear in parentheses]

Year and age group	Total				Male				Female			
	Total	White	Black	Hispanic	Total	White	Black	Hispanic	Total	White	Black	Hispanic
1	2	3	4	5	6	7	8	9	10	11	12	13
1980												
Total, 3 to 34 years old	49.7 (0.21)	48.8 (0.24)	54.0 (0.69)	49.8 (1.40)	50.9 (0.30)	50.0 (0.34)	56.2 (0.99)	49.9 (2.00)	48.5 (0.30)	47.7 (0.34)	52.1 (0.95)	49.8 (1.98)
3 and 4 years old	36.7 (0.95)	37.4 (1.12)	38.2 (2.85)	28.5 (5.13)	37.8 (1.34)	39.2 (1.59)	36.4 (3.98)	30.1 (7.03)	35.5 (1.35)	35.5 (1.59)	40.0 (4.08)	26.6 (7.48)
5 and 6 years old	95.7 (0.40)	95.9 (0.46)	95.5 (1.23)	94.5 (2.79)	95.0 (0.61)	95.4 (0.68)	94.1 (1.97)	94.0 (4.21)	96.4 (0.53)	96.5 (0.62)	97.0 (1.45)	94.9 (3.70)
7 to 9 years old	99.1 (0.15)	99.1 (0.18)	99.4 (0.36)	98.4 (1.19)	99.0 (0.22)	99.0 (0.26)	99.5 (0.46)	97.7 (2.05)	99.2 (0.20)	99.2 (0.24)	99.3 (0.55)	99.0 (1.29)
10 to 13 years old	99.4 (0.10)	99.4 (0.12)	99.4 (0.31)	99.7 (0.47)	99.4 (0.14)	99.6 (0.16)	99.4 (0.43)	98.9 (0.86)	99.3 (0.15)	99.7 (0.13)	99.3 (0.24)	99.9 (0.32)
14 and 15 years old	98.2 (0.22)	98.7 (0.22)	97.9 (0.73)	94.3 (2.46)	98.7 (0.27)	99.2 (0.30)	98.4 (0.89)	96.7 (2.74)	97.7 (0.36)	98.5 (0.34)	90.6 (0.79)	92.1 (3.91)
16 and 17 years old	89.0 (0.51)	89.2 (0.57)	90.7 (1.46)	81.8 (4.25)	89.1 (0.71)	89.4 (0.80)	90.7 (2.06)	81.5 (6.15)	88.8 (0.73)	89.0 (0.83)	90.5 (3.55)	82.2 (5.88)
18 and 19 years old	46.4 (0.80)	47.0 (0.91)	45.8 (2.58)	37.8 (5.16)	47.0 (1.15)	48.5 (1.30)	42.9 (3.76)	36.9 (7.12)	45.8 (1.12)	45.7 (1.27)	48.3 (3.02)	38.8 (7.47)
20 and 21 years old	31.0 (0.75)	33.0 (0.86)	23.3 (2.23)	19.5 (4.31)	32.6 (1.09)	34.8 (1.24)	22.8 (3.32)	21.4 (6.39)	29.5 (1.02)	31.3 (1.18)	23.7 (2.07)	17.6 (5.80) !
22 to 24 years old	16.3 (0.49)	16.8 (0.56)	13.6 (1.54)	11.7 (2.96)	17.8 (0.73)	18.7 (0.84)	13.4 (2.31)	10.7 (4.11)	14.9 (0.66)	15.0 (0.75)	13.7 (1.31)	12.6 (4.25) !
25 to 29 years old	9.3 (0.31)	9.4 (0.35)	8.8 (1.05)	6.9 (1.88)	9.8 (0.46)	9.8 (0.51)	9.8 (1.71)	6.8 (2.70)	8.8 (0.42)	9.1 (0.48)	7.5 (1.31)	6.9 (2.61) !
30 to 34 years old	6.4 (0.27)	6.4 (0.30)	6.9 (1.01)	5.1 (1.77) !	5.9 (0.38)	5.6 (0.40)	7.2 (1.56)	6.2 (2.72)	7.0 (0.39)	7.2 (0.45)	6.6 (1.33)	‡ (†)
1990												
Total, 3 to 34 years old	50.2 (0.23)	49.8 (0.27)	52.2 (0.71)	47.2 (1.06)	50.9 (0.32)	50.4 (0.38)	54.3 (1.02)	46.8 (1.48)	49.5 (0.32)	49.2 (0.38)	50.3 (0.99)	47.7 (1.52)
3 and 4 years old	44.4 (0.99)	47.2 (1.19)	41.8 (2.97)	30.7 (4.08)	43.9 (1.38)	47.9 (1.66)	38.1 (4.14)	28.0 (5.57)	44.9 (1.41)	46.6 (1.70)	45.5 (4.25)	33.6 (5.95)
5 and 6 years old	96.5 (0.37)	96.7 (0.43)	96.5 (1.05)	94.9 (1.96)	96.5 (0.51)	96.8 (0.59)	96.2 (1.53)	95.8 (2.48)	96.4 (0.53)	96.7 (0.62)	96.9 (1.43)	93.9 (3.05)
7 to 9 years old	99.7 (0.09)	99.7 (0.11)	99.8 (0.19)	99.5 (0.52)	99.7 (0.13)	99.7 (0.16)	99.9 (0.24)	99.0 (0.70)	99.6 (0.14)	99.7 (0.15)	99.8 (0.31)	99.4 (0.79)
10 to 13 years old	99.6 (0.09)	99.7 (0.10)	99.9 (0.15)	99.1 (0.64)	99.6 (0.13)	99.6 (0.14)	99.9 (0.19)	99.0 (0.93)	99.7 (0.12)	99.7 (0.13)	99.1 (0.24)	99.1 (0.87)
14 and 15 years old	99.0 (0.19)	99.0 (0.23)	99.4 (0.46)	99.0 (0.90)	99.1 (0.25)	99.2 (0.30)	99.7 (0.48)	99.1 (1.10)	99.4 (0.29)	98.9 (0.35)	99.1 (0.79)	98.8 (1.47)
16 and 17 years old	92.5 (0.52)	93.5 (0.58)	91.7 (1.59)	85.4 (3.22)	92.6 (0.72)	93.4 (0.82)	93.0 (2.09)	85.5 (4.39)	92.4 (0.74)	93.7 (0.81)	90.5 (2.41)	85.3 (4.73)
18 and 19 years old	57.2 (0.94)	59.1 (1.11)	55.0 (2.83)	44.0 (4.36)	58.2 (1.33)	59.7 (1.56)	60.4 (3.99)	40.7 (6.23)	56.3 (1.32)	58.5 (1.57)	49.8 (3.96)	47.2 (6.08)
20 and 21 years old	39.7 (0.92)	43.1 (1.10)	28.3 (2.56)	27.2 (3.82)	40.3 (1.32)	44.2 (1.59)	31.0 (3.81)	21.7 (4.94)	39.2 (1.28)	42.0 (1.53)	25.8 (3.45)	33.1 (5.79)
22 to 24 years old	21.0 (0.63)	21.9 (0.75)	19.7 (2.01)	9.9 (2.05)	22.3 (0.92)	23.7 (1.11)	19.3 (3.03)	11.2 (2.98)	19.9 (0.86)	20.3 (1.02)	20.0 (2.68)	8.4 (2.77) !
25 to 29 years old	9.7 (0.33)	10.4 (0.39)	6.1 (0.87)	6.3 (1.29)	9.2 (0.46)	10.0 (0.55)	4.7 (1.14)	4.6 (1.55) !	10.2 (0.47)	10.7 (0.56)	7.3 (1.27)	8.1 (2.05)
30 to 34 years old	5.8 (0.25)	6.2 (0.30)	4.5 (0.75)	3.6 (0.99)	4.8 (0.33)	5.0 (0.38)	2.3 (0.80)	4.0 (1.45) !	6.9 (0.38)	7.4 (0.46)	6.3 (1.19)	3.1 (1.32) !
1995												
Total, 3 to 34 years old	53.7 (0.21)	53.8 (0.25)	56.3 (0.58)	49.7 (0.65)	54.3 (0.30)	54.2 (0.36)	58.6 (0.83)	49.1 (0.90)	53.2 (0.30)	53.4 (0.36)	54.1 (0.81)	50.3 (0.93)
3 and 4 years old	48.7 (0.87)	52.2 (1.09)	47.8 (2.29)	36.9 (2.36)	49.4 (1.22)	51.1 (1.53)	52.4 (3.27)	40.8 (3.35)	48.1 (1.24)	53.5 (1.56)	43.4 (3.18)	32.7 (3.29)
5 and 6 years old	96.0 (0.34)	96.6 (0.39)	95.4 (0.97)	93.9 (1.23)	95.3 (0.52)	95.9 (0.60)	94.6 (1.48)	93.6 (1.75)	96.8 (0.53)	97.4 (0.49)	96.3 (1.24)	94.3 (1.72)
7 to 9 years old	98.7 (0.17)	98.9 (0.18)	97.7 (0.59)	98.5 (0.55)	98.9 (0.22)	99.0 (0.21)	98.1 (0.74)	98.8 (0.72)	98.5 (0.25)	98.9 (0.27)	97.2 (0.92)	98.2 (0.83)
10 to 13 years old	99.1 (0.12)	99.0 (0.15)	99.2 (0.30)	99.2 (0.36)	99.0 (0.17)	98.9 (0.30)	99.5 (0.34)	98.8 (0.59)	99.0 (0.18)	98.7 (0.22)	98.9 (0.50)	99.5 (0.39)
14 and 15 years old	98.8 (0.18)	98.8 (0.22)	99.0 (0.46)	98.8 (0.56)	99.0 (0.24)	98.8 (0.30)	98.8 (0.40)	98.4 (0.93)	98.6 (0.27)	98.8 (0.33)	98.3 (0.83)	99.4 (0.59)
16 and 17 years old	93.6 (0.42)	94.4 (0.47)	93.0 (1.16)	88.2 (1.83)	94.5 (0.55)	95.0 (0.63)	95.6 (1.30)	88.4 (2.59)	92.6 (0.64)	93.8 (0.72)	90.3 (1.94)	88.0 (2.58)
18 and 19 years old	59.4 (0.86)	61.8 (1.03)	57.5 (2.38)	46.1 (2.63)	59.5 (1.21)	61.9 (1.45)	59.2 (3.48)	47.4 (3.63)	59.2 (1.22)	61.8 (1.46)	56.1 (3.27)	44.8 (3.83)
20 and 21 years old	44.9 (0.90)	49.7 (1.10)	37.8 (2.47)	27.1 (2.37)	44.7 (1.29)	50.0 (1.57)	37.6 (3.67)	24.8 (3.30)	45.1 (1.25)	49.3 (1.54)	38.7 (3.35)	29.2 (3.40)
22 to 24 years old	23.2 (0.60)	24.4 (0.74)	20.0 (1.62)	15.6 (1.52)	22.8 (0.84)	24.1 (1.04)	20.6 (2.42)	14.8 (2.00)	23.6 (0.85)	24.8 (1.04)	19.5 (2.18)	16.6 (2.34)
25 to 29 years old	11.6 (0.34)	12.3 (0.42)	7.7 (0.95)	7.1 (0.88)	11.0 (0.48)	12.2 (0.59)	6.3 (1.16)	5.6 (1.10)	12.2 (0.49)	12.3 (0.59)	13.0 (1.41)	8.7 (1.38)
30 to 34 years old	5.9 (0.24)	5.7 (0.28)	7.7 (0.80)	4.7 (0.70)	5.4 (0.33)	5.0 (0.37)	6.9 (1.14)	4.5 (0.95)	6.5 (0.35)	6.3 (0.41)	8.3 (1.13)	4.9 (1.03)
2000												
Total, 3 to 34 years old	55.9 (0.22)	56.0 (0.27)	59.3 (0.59)	51.3 (0.63)	55.8 (0.31)	55.8 (0.38)	59.7 (0.85)	50.5 (0.88)	56.0 (0.31)	56.1 (0.38)	59.0 (0.83)	52.2 (0.89)
3 and 4 years old[1]	52.1 (0.93)	54.6 (1.19)	59.8 (2.50)	35.9 (2.36)	50.8 (1.30)	54.1 (1.66)	58.0 (3.53)	31.9 (3.23)	53.4 (1.32)	55.2 (1.70)	61.8 (3.55)	40.0 (3.43)
5 and 6 years old[1]	95.6 (0.38)	95.5 (0.49)	96.7 (0.89)	94.3 (1.13)	95.1 (0.56)	94.5 (0.76)	96.0 (1.38)	95.4 (1.41)	96.1 (0.51)	96.4 (0.63)	97.5 (1.12)	93.1 (1.79)
7 to 9 years old	98.1 (0.20)	98.4 (0.24)	97.5 (0.61)	97.5 (0.65)	98.0 (0.29)	98.1 (0.36)	98.2 (0.72)	96.6 (1.09)	98.3 (0.28)	98.6 (0.32)	96.7 (1.01)	96.4 (0.74)
10 to 13 years old	98.7 (0.17)	98.5 (0.19)	99.6 (0.42)	96.2 (0.99)	98.3 (0.23)	98.2 (0.30)	98.8 (0.52)	98.4 (0.65)	98.6 (0.24)	99.0 (0.25)	98.1 (0.66)	96.4 (1.01)
14 and 15 years old	98.7 (0.20)	98.9 (0.22)	99.6 (0.30)	96.2 (0.99)	98.7 (0.27)	98.8 (0.33)	99.6 (0.42)	96.9 (1.26)	98.6 (0.29)	99.0 (0.31)	99.6 (0.42)	95.4 (1.54)
16 and 17 years old	92.8 (0.45)	94.0 (0.50)	91.7 (1.32)	87.0 (1.77)	92.7 (0.63)	94.7 (0.66)	88.9 (2.09)	85.7 (2.60)	92.9 (0.64)	93.3 (0.76)	94.6 (1.54)	88.3 (2.40)
18 and 19 years old	61.2 (0.84)	63.9 (1.02)	57.2 (2.34)	49.5 (2.47)	58.3 (1.19)	61.2 (1.46)	51.5 (3.45)	48.0 (3.40)	64.2 (1.16)	66.7 (1.42)	62.2 (3.14)	51.1 (3.59)
20 and 21 years old	44.1 (0.88)	49.2 (1.10)	37.4 (2.38)	26.1 (2.22)	41.0 (1.23)	45.8 (1.54)	31.3 (3.42)	24.2 (3.02)	47.3 (1.26)	52.7 (1.58)	51.1 (3.59)	28.1 (3.26)
22 to 24 years old	24.6 (0.63)	24.9 (0.78)	24.0 (1.76)	18.2 (1.64)	23.9 (0.88)	25.0 (1.12)	22.0 (2.46)	15.2 (2.08)	25.3 (0.89)	24.8 (1.09)	25.8 (2.51)	21.6 (2.55)
25 to 29 years old	11.4 (0.37)	11.1 (0.45)	14.5 (1.18)	7.4 (0.88)	10.0 (0.50)	10.5 (0.62)	11.6 (1.63)	5.1 (1.06)	12.7 (0.53)	11.8 (0.65)	16.7 (1.66)	9.5 (1.38)
30 to 34 years old	6.7 (0.27)	6.1 (0.32)	9.9 (0.97)	5.6 (0.75)	5.6 (0.36)	4.7 (0.41)	8.5 (1.34)	5.7 (1.06)	7.7 (0.41)	7.4 (0.50)	11.2 (1.39)	5.5 (1.05)

See notes at end of table.

Table 103.10. Percentage of the population 3 to 34 years old enrolled in school, by sex, race/ethnicity, and age group: Selected years, 1980 through 2014—Continued

[Standard errors appear in parentheses]

Year and age group	Total				Male				Female			
	Total	White	Black	Hispanic	Total	White	Black	Hispanic	Total	White	Black	Hispanic
1	2	3	4	5	6	7	8	9	10	11	12	13
2005												
Total, 3 to 34 years old[1]	**56.5 (0.20)**	**57.6 (0.26)**	**58.5 (0.57)**	**50.9 (0.53)**	**55.8 (0.28)**	**57.1 (0.37)**	**58.8 (0.82)**	**48.4 (0.73)**	**57.2 (0.29)**	**58.0 (0.37)**	**58.1 (0.80)**	**53.7 (0.76)**
3 and 4 years old[1]	53.6 (0.86)	58.5 (1.14)	52.4 (2.39)	43.0 (2.07)	52.8 (1.21)	56.8 (1.61)	54.8 (3.42)	43.0 (2.91)	54.4 (1.23)	60.3 (1.63)	50.1 (3.32)	43.0 (2.96)
5 and 6 years old	95.4 (0.37)	95.9 (0.47)	95.9 (0.97)	93.8 (1.06)	94.8 (0.54)	95.4 (0.68)	94.8 (1.50)	92.4 (1.62)	96.1 (0.50)	96.3 (0.63)	97.1 (1.18)	95.3 (1.34)
7 to 9 years old	98.6 (0.17)	99.0 (0.19)	98.7 (0.45)	97.4 (0.58)	98.7 (0.27)	98.0 (0.27)	98.0 (0.81)	96.0 (1.00)	99.0 (0.20)	99.0 (0.27)	99.5 (0.41)	98.8 (0.57)
10 to 13 years old	98.6 (0.14)	98.6 (0.16)	98.5 (0.40)	97.9 (0.46)	98.4 (0.22)	99.1 (0.21)	97.6 (0.70)	97.2 (0.72)	98.9 (0.18)	98.8 (0.24)	99.0 (0.33)	98.6 (0.54)
14 and 15 years old	98.0 (0.22)	98.6 (0.24)	96.1 (0.83)	97.3 (0.70)	97.5 (0.34)	98.4 (0.35)	93.3 (1.52)	97.8 (0.90)	98.4 (0.28)	96.3 (0.33)	98.8 (0.66)	96.7 (1.09)
16 and 17 years old	95.1 (0.33)	96.1 (0.38)	93.6 (1.05)	92.6 (1.14)	95.1 (0.47)	95.9 (0.55)	93.6 (1.51)	92.5 (1.61)	95.1 (0.47)	96.3 (0.53)	93.6 (1.47)	92.6 (1.60)
18 and 19 years old	67.6 (0.79)	71.6 (0.95)	62.0 (2.30)	54.3 (2.33)	66.5 (1.11)	69.8 (1.35)	66.9 (3.20)	51.8 (3.22)	68.8 (1.12)	73.5 (1.34)	57.4 (3.27)	57.2 (3.37)
20 and 21 years old	48.7 (0.80)	54.4 (1.01)	37.9 (2.25)	30.0 (1.96)	45.3 (1.11)	50.5 (1.42)	35.5 (3.12)	25.2 (2.56)	52.3 (1.15)	58.5 (1.43)	40.4 (3.23)	35.3 (2.99)
22 to 24 years old	27.3 (0.59)	27.8 (0.76)	28.6 (1.75)	19.5 (1.41)	25.2 (0.83)	26.4 (1.07)	24.0 (2.45)	17.5 (1.85)	29.2 (0.85)	29.1 (1.09)	32.5 (2.45)	21.8 (2.17)
25 to 29 years old	11.9 (0.34)	12.5 (0.45)	11.9 (1.00)	7.8 (0.70)	9.6 (0.43)	10.2 (0.58)	9.1 (1.32)	5.6 (0.82)	14.2 (0.51)	14.7 (0.67)	14.2 (1.47)	10.4 (1.19)
30 to 34 years old	6.9 (0.27)	6.9 (0.34)	9.8 (0.94)	4.2 (0.54)	5.9 (0.35)	6.5 (0.47)	6.3 (1.15)	2.6 (0.58)	7.9 (0.40)	7.4 (0.50)	12.7 (1.42)	6.1 (0.94)
2010[2]												
Total, 3 to 34 years old[1]	**56.6 (0.17)**	**56.1 (0.25)**	**58.7 (0.58)**	**55.1 (0.35)**	**55.9 (0.23)**	**55.5 (0.29)**	**58.4 (0.78)**	**52.9 (0.45)**	**57.4 (0.26)**	**56.7 (0.36)**	**58.9 (0.77)**	**57.4 (0.49)**
3 and 4 years old[1]	53.2 (0.89)	56.1 (1.17)	57.2 (2.78)	44.2 (1.84)	53.0 (1.21)	55.9 (1.64)	57.0 (3.79)	43.3 (2.60)	53.4 (1.27)	56.3 (1.53)	57.4 (3.79)	45.0 (2.68)
5 and 6 years old	94.5 (0.46)	94.2 (0.66)	94.1 (1.12)	94.3 (0.96)	93.7 (0.69)	93.3 (1.04)	93.5 (1.94)	93.4 (1.31)	95.3 (0.54)	95.2 (0.77)	94.7 (1.38)	95.2 (1.20)
7 to 9 years old	97.7 (0.25)	97.4 (0.37)	96.9 (0.77)	98.5 (0.37)	97.6 (0.36)	97.1 (0.54)	97.3 (0.88)	98.1 (0.60)	98.0 (0.35)	97.7 (0.53)	96.5 (1.23)	98.9 (0.40)
10 to 13 years old	98.2 (0.21)	98.3 (0.26)	99.2 (0.41)	97.3 (0.54)	97.9 (0.30)	97.7 (0.42)	99.6 (0.37)	96.9 (0.77)	98.6 (0.26)	98.9 (0.24)	98.8 (0.74)	97.7 (0.61)
14 and 15 years old	98.1 (0.25)	98.0 (0.37)	95.7 (0.58)	97.9 (0.69)	98.0 (0.37)	98.0 (0.52)	98.4 (0.92)	97.5 (0.98)	98.3 (0.34)	98.1 (0.49)	99.3 (0.46)	98.3 (0.85)
16 and 17 years old	96.1 (0.33)	96.2 (0.47)	95.7 (0.82)	96.0 (0.83)	94.9 (0.51)	94.7 (0.74)	93.7 (1.41)	96.0 (1.17)	98.1 (0.38)	97.8 (0.47)	97.6 (0.95)	96.0 (1.10)
18 and 19 years old	69.2 (0.92)	71.0 (1.28)	62.9 (2.42)	66.2 (2.03)	66.9 (1.25)	67.8 (1.63)	62.3 (3.88)	64.9 (3.02)	71.5 (1.38)	74.3 (2.01)	63.4 (3.44)	67.6 (2.78)
20 and 21 years old	52.4 (1.08)	55.5 (1.28)	51.1 (2.93)	37.0 (2.34)	49.2 (1.31)	52.1 (1.76)	45.7 (4.18)	34.0 (3.08)	56.0 (1.47)	59.2 (1.78)	56.0 (3.84)	40.5 (3.36)
22 to 24 years old	28.9 (0.79)	29.1 (1.01)	29.8 (2.13)	23.8 (1.57)	27.0 (1.15)	27.8 (1.44)	29.5 (3.12)	18.6 (2.08)	30.8 (1.10)	30.4 (1.46)	30.0 (2.99)	29.2 (2.16)
25 to 29 years old	14.6 (0.47)	14.6 (0.64)	16.5 (1.34)	11.4 (0.90)	13.5 (0.65)	13.8 (0.84)	13.9 (2.06)	9.6 (1.21)	15.8 (0.66)	15.4 (0.88)	18.8 (1.97)	13.6 (1.44)
30 to 34 years old	8.3 (0.39)	8.5 (0.50)	11.0 (1.14)	5.7 (0.65)	6.7 (0.44)	7.2 (0.62)	6.6 (1.20)	4.9 (0.87)	9.9 (0.58)	9.8 (0.77)	14.8 (1.80)	6.6 (0.95)
2013[2]												
Total, 3 to 34 years old[1]	**55.8 (0.18)**	**54.7 (0.26)**	**57.8 (0.60)**	**55.5 (0.37)**	**55.2 (0.23)**	**54.1 (0.34)**	**57.3 (0.80)**	**54.0 (0.54)**	**56.4 (0.26)**	**55.4 (0.34)**	**58.3 (0.83)**	**57.0 (0.51)**
3 and 4 years old[1]	54.9 (1.00)	57.4 (1.50)	61.1 (2.54)	45.4 (2.14)	53.2 (1.46)	55.2 (2.09)	58.2 (4.15)	44.2 (2.78)	56.7 (1.48)	59.7 (1.92)	63.8 (4.13)	46.7 (3.18)
5 and 6 years old	93.8 (0.45)	93.6 (0.63)	94.7 (1.54)	93.9 (0.91)	93.8 (0.64)	93.7 (0.92)	95.2 (1.77)	93.6 (1.17)	93.7 (0.73)	93.5 (0.88)	94.1 (2.68)	94.1 (1.45)
7 to 9 years old	97.9 (0.26)	97.9 (0.34)	96.4 (1.03)	98.4 (0.34)	97.9 (0.34)	97.8 (0.42)	96.2 (1.55)	98.6 (0.43)	97.9 (0.37)	98.0 (0.51)	96.6 (1.35)	98.2 (0.61)
10 to 13 years old	98.2 (0.20)	98.5 (0.24)	97.6 (0.66)	98.3 (0.52)	98.1 (0.28)	98.4 (0.31)	97.6 (0.94)	97.7 (0.58)	98.2 (0.25)	98.5 (0.31)	97.6 (0.88)	97.7 (0.67)
14 and 15 years old	98.4 (0.27)	98.4 (0.38)	98.6 (0.58)	93.9 (0.56)	98.2 (0.40)	98.4 (0.50)	98.7 (0.91)	97.9 (0.90)	98.6 (0.32)	98.4 (0.47)	98.5 (0.81)	98.8 (0.60)
16 and 17 years old	93.7 (0.50)	93.6 (0.64)	92.7 (1.42)	93.9 (1.02)	93.3 (0.70)	92.8 (0.98)	93.7 (1.68)	93.5 (1.44)	94.1 (0.68)	94.5 (0.79)	91.7 (2.41)	94.3 (1.51)
18 and 19 years old	67.1 (0.97)	69.6 (1.23)	64.2 (2.92)	59.3 (1.98)	65.1 (1.31)	68.6 (1.49)	60.8 (4.26)	55.4 (2.99)	69.2 (1.40)	70.8 (1.72)	67.5 (3.92)	63.2 (2.96)
20 and 21 years old	52.8 (1.24)	55.2 (1.62)	48.7 (3.07)	43.9 (2.38)	48.5 (1.62)	51.0 (2.13)	43.5 (4.32)	38.0 (3.16)	57.3 (1.62)	59.6 (2.05)	53.5 (4.26)	50.6 (3.09)
22 to 24 years old	29.7 (0.81)	29.1 (1.02)	28.0 (2.18)	26.7 (1.66)	27.6 (1.14)	26.2 (1.42)	25.7 (3.27)	24.4 (2.18)	31.7 (1.01)	31.9 (1.31)	30.2 (3.01)	29.1 (2.39)
25 to 29 years old	13.3 (0.44)	12.9 (0.57)	17.1 (1.62)	10.4 (0.93)	12.2 (0.61)	11.4 (0.74)	13.2 (2.16)	10.8 (1.39)	14.4 (0.59)	14.3 (0.82)	11.8 (1.71)	10.0 (1.24)
30 to 34 years old	6.7 (0.32)	6.5 (0.37)	9.1 (1.12)	5.7 (0.61)	5.3 (0.37)	5.6 (0.46)	5.7 (1.37)	3.9 (0.75)	8.1 (0.53)	7.4 (0.60)		7.6 (0.97)
2014[2]												
Total, 3 to 34 years old[1]	**55.2 (0.21)**	**54.4 (0.27)**	**56.2 (0.54)**	**55.4 (0.40)**	**54.8 (0.28)**	**54.1 (0.38)**	**56.7 (0.71)**	**53.6 (0.54)**	**55.7 (0.28)**	**54.7 (0.35)**	**55.7 (0.81)**	**57.4 (0.55)**
3 and 4 years old[1]	54.5 (0.98)	57.6 (1.56)	59.2 (2.88)	45.5 (1.83)	53.5 (1.46)	56.5 (1.79)	60.0 (3.81)	43.1 (3.67)	55.5 (1.86)	58.8 (2.49)	58.4 (4.02)	47.8 (3.71)
5 and 6 years old	93.4 (0.53)	93.4 (0.67)	94.7 (1.38)	94.4 (0.88)	94.0 (0.74)	93.7 (0.82)	95.6 (1.69)	94.6 (1.47)	92.8 (0.76)	93.1 (1.01)	93.8 (1.95)	94.2 (1.27)
7 to 9 years old	97.7 (0.24)	97.3 (0.37)	98.9 (0.40)	98.2 (0.44)	98.9 (0.33)	96.9 (0.49)	99.0 (0.58)	97.8 (0.65)	97.9 (0.29)	97.7 (0.45)	98.6 (0.58)	98.6 (0.57)
10 to 13 years old	97.5 (0.26)	97.5 (0.34)	97.7 (0.72)	97.3 (0.53)	96.9 (0.35)	96.8 (0.49)	97.2 (0.97)	96.7 (0.77)	98.1 (0.30)	98.1 (0.38)	98.2 (0.89)	97.9 (0.67)
14 and 15 years old	97.8 (0.26)	97.8 (0.35)	99.4 (0.42)	97.1 (0.64)	97.5 (0.42)	97.1 (0.60)	98.8 (0.83)	97.8 (0.78)	98.2 (0.34)	98.5 (0.42)	100.0 (0.05)	96.4 (1.02)
16 and 17 years old	92.9 (0.51)	93.4 (0.62)	91.8 (1.44)	92.2 (1.24)	92.1 (0.74)	92.7 (0.88)	93.2 (1.85)	89.3 (1.90)	93.8 (0.68)	94.1 (0.84)	90.3 (2.42)	95.3 (1.52)
18 and 19 years old	68.4 (0.92)	69.3 (1.17)	65.3 (2.56)	64.7 (2.15)	64.9 (1.36)	66.0 (1.77)	59.3 (3.99)	61.6 (2.90)	72.1 (1.34)	72.9 (1.72)	71.1 (3.27)	67.8 (2.76)
20 and 21 years old	51.4 (1.24)	56.1 (1.63)	40.2 (2.97)	44.7 (2.70)	49.1 (1.72)	55.3 (2.35)	40.5 (4.77)	37.4 (3.73)	53.9 (1.67)	57.0 (2.16)	40.0 (3.67)	53.8 (3.73)
22 to 24 years old	29.6 (0.80)	29.9 (1.06)	24.8 (2.21)	24.0 (1.44)	28.1 (1.18)	28.3 (1.50)	23.9 (2.94)	21.5 (2.12)	31.0 (0.92)	31.4 (1.27)	25.8 (2.88)	26.3 (2.05)
25 to 29 years old	13.1 (0.44)	12.9 (0.55)	15.3 (1.33)	10.7 (0.95)	12.2 (0.61)	12.1 (0.77)	12.3 (1.91)	10.0 (1.37)	14.0 (0.60)	13.6 (0.77)	18.0 (1.91)	11.5 (1.26)
30 to 34 years old	6.4 (0.31)	6.3 (0.39)	8.6 (0.94)	5.3 (0.57)	5.3 (0.42)	5.8 (0.57)	6.8 (1.38)	3.2 (0.71)	7.4 (0.45)	6.9 (0.55)	10.1 (1.37)	7.6 (0.94)

†Not applicable.
!Interpret data with caution. The coefficient of variation (CV) for this estimate is between 30 and 50 percent.
‡Reporting standards not met. The coefficient of variation (CV) for this estimate is 50 percent or greater.
[1]Beginning in 1994, preprimary enrollment data were collected using new procedures. Data may not be comparable to figures for earlier years.
[2]Beginning in 2010, standard errors were computed using replicate weights, which produced more precise values than the generalized variance function methodology used in prior years.

NOTE: Includes enrollment in any type of graded public, parochial, or other private schools. Includes nursery schools, pre-schools, kindergartens, elementary schools, high schools, colleges, universities, and professional schools. Attendance may be on either a full-time or part-time basis and during the day or night. Total includes persons from other racial/ethnic groups not shown separately. Race categories exclude persons of Hispanic ethnicity.
SOURCE: U.S. Department of Commerce, Census Bureau, Current Population Survey (CPS), October, selected years, 1980 through 2014. (This table was prepared August 2015.)

Table 103.20. Percentage of the population 3 to 34 years old enrolled in school, by age group: Selected years, 1940 through 2014

[Standard errors appear in parentheses]

Year	Total, 3 to 34 years old	3 and 4 years old	5 and 6 years old	7 to 13 years old	14 to 17 years old			18 and 19 years old			20 to 24 years old			25 to 29 years old	30 to 34 years old
					Total	14 and 15	16 and 17	Total	In secondary education	In higher education	Total	20 and 21	22 to 24		
1	2	3	4	5	6	7	8	9	10	11	12	13	14	15	16
1940	— (†)	— (†)	— (†)	95.0 (—)	79.3 (—)	— (†)	— (†)	28.9 (†)	— (†)	— (†)	6.6 (†)	— (†)	— (†)	— (†)	— (†)
1945	— (†)	— (†)	— (†)	98.1 (—)	78.4 (—)	— (†)	— (†)	20.7 (†)	— (†)	— (†)	3.9 (†)	— (†)	— (†)	— (†)	— (†)
1947	— (†)	— (†)	73.8 (—)	98.5 (—)	79.3 (—)	91.6 (—)	67.6 (—)	24.3 (—)	— (†)	— (†)	10.2 (—)	— (†)	— (†)	3.0 (—)	1.0 (—)
1948	— (†)	— (†)	74.7 (—)	98.1 (—)	81.8 (—)	92.7 (—)	71.2 (—)	26.9 (—)	— (†)	— (†)	9.7 (—)	— (†)	— (†)	2.6 (—)	0.9 (—)
1949	— (†)	— (†)	76.2 (—)	98.6 (—)	81.6 (—)	93.5 (—)	69.5 (—)	25.3 (—)	— (†)	— (†)	9.2 (—)	— (†)	— (†)	3.8 (—)	1.1 (—)
1950	— (†)	— (†)	74.4 (—)	98.7 (—)	83.7 (—)	94.7 (—)	71.3 (—)	29.4 (—)	— (†)	— (†)	9.0 (—)	— (†)	— (†)	3.0 (—)	0.9 (—)
1951	— (†)	— (†)	73.6 (—)	99.1 (—)	85.2 (—)	94.8 (—)	75.1 (—)	26.2 (—)	— (†)	— (†)	8.6 (—)	— (†)	— (†)	2.5 (—)	0.7 (—)
1952	— (†)	— (†)	75.2 (—)	98.8 (—)	85.2 (—)	96.2 (—)	73.4 (—)	28.8 (—)	— (†)	— (†)	9.7 (—)	— (†)	— (†)	2.6 (—)	1.2 (—)
1953	— (†)	— (†)	78.6 (—)	99.4 (—)	85.9 (—)	96.5 (—)	74.7 (—)	31.2 (—)	— (†)	— (†)	11.1 (—)	— (†)	— (†)	2.9 (—)	1.7 (—)
1954	— (†)	— (†)	77.3 (—)	99.4 (—)	87.1 (—)	95.8 (—)	78.0 (—)	32.4 (—)	— (†)	— (†)	11.2 (—)	— (†)	— (†)	4.1 (—)	1.5 (—)
1955	— (†)	— (†)	78.1 (—)	99.2 (—)	86.9 (—)	95.9 (—)	77.4 (—)	31.5 (—)	— (†)	— (†)	11.1 (—)	— (†)	— (†)	4.2 (—)	1.6 (—)
1956	— (†)	— (†)	77.6 (—)	99.3 (—)	88.2 (—)	96.9 (—)	78.4 (—)	35.4 (—)	— (†)	— (†)	12.8 (—)	— (†)	— (†)	5.1 (—)	1.9 (—)
1957	— (†)	— (†)	78.6 (—)	99.5 (—)	89.5 (—)	97.1 (—)	80.5 (—)	34.9 (—)	— (†)	— (†)	14.0 (—)	— (†)	— (†)	5.5 (—)	1.8 (—)
1958	— (†)	— (†)	80.4 (—)	99.5 (—)	89.2 (—)	96.9 (—)	80.6 (—)	37.6 (—)	— (†)	— (†)	13.4 (—)	— (†)	— (†)	5.7 (—)	2.2 (—)
1959	— (†)	— (†)	80.0 (—)	99.4 (—)	90.2 (—)	97.5 (—)	82.9 (—)	36.8 (—)	— (†)	— (†)	12.7 (—)	18.8 (—)	8.6 (—)	5.1 (—)	2.2 (—)
1960	— (†)	— (†)	80.7 (—)	99.5 (—)	90.3 (—)	97.8 (—)	82.6 (—)	38.4 (—)	— (†)	— (†)	13.1 (—)	19.4 (—)	8.7 (—)	4.9 (—)	2.4 (—)
1961	— (†)	— (†)	81.7 (—)	99.3 (—)	91.4 (—)	97.6 (—)	83.6 (—)	38.0 (—)	— (†)	— (†)	13.7 (—)	21.5 (—)	8.4 (—)	4.4 (—)	2.0 (—)
1962	— (†)	— (†)	82.2 (—)	99.3 (—)	92.0 (—)	98.0 (—)	84.3 (—)	41.8 (—)	— (†)	— (†)	15.6 (—)	23.0 (—)	10.3 (—)	5.0 (—)	2.6 (—)
1963	— (†)	— (†)	82.7 (—)	99.3 (—)	92.9 (—)	98.4 (—)	87.1 (—)	40.9 (—)	10.9 (—)	29.8 (—)	17.3 (—)	25.0 (—)	11.4 (—)	4.9 (—)	2.5 (—)
1964	— (†)	9.5 (—)	83.3 (—)	99.0 (—)	93.1 (—)	98.6 (—)	87.7 (—)	41.6 (—)	11.0 (—)	30.6 (—)	16.8 (—)	26.3 (—)	9.9 (—)	5.2 (—)	2.6 (—)
1965	55.5 (—)	10.6 (—)	84.9 (—)	99.4 (—)	93.2 (—)	98.9 (—)	87.4 (—)	46.3 (—)	11.2 (—)	35.0 (—)	19.0 (—)	27.6 (—)	13.2 (—)	6.1 (—)	3.2 (—)
1966	56.1 (—)	12.5 (—)	85.8 (—)	99.3 (—)	93.7 (—)	98.6 (—)	88.5 (—)	47.2 (—)	10.8 (—)	36.3 (—)	19.9 (—)	29.9 (—)	13.2 (—)	6.5 (—)	2.7 (—)
1967	56.6 (—)	14.2 (—)	87.4 (—)	99.3 (—)	93.7 (—)	98.2 (—)	88.8 (—)	47.6 (—)	11.7 (—)	36.0 (—)	22.0 (—)	33.3 (—)	13.6 (—)	6.6 (—)	4.0 (—)
1968	56.7 (—)	15.7 (—)	87.6 (—)	99.1 (—)	94.2 (—)	98.0 (—)	90.2 (—)	50.4 (—)	12.4 (—)	38.0 (—)	21.4 (—)	31.2 (—)	13.8 (—)	7.0 (—)	3.9 (—)
1969	57.0 (—)	16.1 (—)	88.4 (—)	99.2 (—)	94.0 (—)	98.1 (—)	89.7 (—)	50.2 (—)	11.2 (—)	39.0 (—)	23.0 (—)	34.1 (—)	15.4 (—)	7.9 (—)	4.8 (—)
1970	56.4 (0.22)	20.5 (0.74)	89.5 (0.54)	99.2 (0.07)	94.1 (0.27)	98.1 (0.22)	90.0 (0.50)	47.7 (0.87)	10.5 (0.53)	37.3 (0.84)	21.5 (0.48)	31.9 (0.87)	14.9 (0.53)	7.5 (0.33)	4.2 (0.27)
1971	56.2 (0.22)	21.2 (0.76)	91.6 (0.50)	99.1 (0.08)	94.5 (0.26)	98.6 (0.19)	90.2 (0.49)	49.2 (0.85)	11.5 (0.54)	37.7 (0.83)	21.9 (0.47)	32.2 (0.85)	15.4 (0.52)	8.0 (0.33)	4.9 (0.29)
1972	54.9 (0.22)	24.4 (0.81)	91.9 (0.51)	99.2 (0.08)	93.3 (0.28)	97.6 (0.24)	88.9 (0.51)	46.3 (0.84)	10.4 (0.51)	35.9 (0.81)	21.6 (0.46)	31.4 (0.81)	14.8 (0.51)	8.6 (0.34)	4.6 (0.28)
1973	53.5 (0.22)	24.2 (0.80)	92.5 (0.50)	99.2 (0.08)	92.9 (0.29)	97.5 (0.25)	88.3 (0.52)	42.9 (0.82)	10.0 (0.50)	32.9 (0.78)	20.8 (0.44)	30.1 (0.79)	14.5 (0.50)	8.5 (0.33)	4.5 (0.27)
1974	53.6 (0.22)	28.8 (0.85)	94.2 (0.44)	99.3 (0.07)	92.9 (0.29)	97.9 (0.23)	87.9 (0.52)	43.1 (0.81)	9.9 (0.49)	33.2 (0.77)	21.4 (0.45)	30.2 (0.77)	15.1 (0.51)	9.6 (0.34)	5.7 (0.29)
1975	53.7 (0.22)	31.5 (0.89)	94.7 (0.42)	99.3 (0.08)	93.6 (0.27)	98.2 (0.21)	89.0 (0.50)	46.9 (0.81)	10.2 (0.49)	36.7 (0.78)	22.4 (0.45)	31.2 (0.77)	16.2 (0.52)	10.1 (0.34)	6.6 (0.31)
1976	53.1 (0.21)	31.3 (0.91)	95.5 (0.38)	99.2 (0.08)	93.7 (0.27)	98.2 (0.21)	89.1 (0.50)	46.2 (0.80)	10.2 (0.49)	36.0 (0.77)	23.3 (0.45)	32.0 (0.77)	17.1 (0.52)	10.0 (0.33)	6.0 (0.29)
1977	52.5 (0.21)	32.0 (0.94)	95.8 (0.38)	99.4 (0.07)	93.7 (0.28)	98.5 (0.20)	88.9 (0.50)	46.2 (0.80)	10.4 (0.49)	35.7 (0.77)	22.9 (0.44)	31.8 (0.76)	16.5 (0.51)	10.8 (0.34)	6.9 (0.30)
1978	51.2 (0.21)	34.2 (0.95)	95.3 (0.42)	99.1 (0.09)	93.7 (0.28)	98.4 (0.20)	89.1 (0.50)	45.4 (0.80)	9.8 (0.48)	35.6 (0.77)	21.8 (0.43)	29.5 (0.74)	16.3 (0.50)	9.4 (0.32)	6.4 (0.28)
1979	50.3 (0.21)	35.1 (0.95)	95.8 (0.40)	99.2 (0.08)	93.6 (0.28)	98.1 (0.22)	89.2 (0.50)	45.0 (0.80)	10.3 (0.49)	34.6 (0.76)	21.7 (0.43)	30.2 (0.74)	15.8 (0.49)	9.6 (0.32)	6.4 (0.28)
1980	49.7 (0.21)	36.7 (0.95)	95.7 (0.40)	99.3 (0.08)	93.4 (0.29)	98.2 (0.22)	89.0 (0.51)	46.4 (0.80)	10.5 (0.49)	35.9 (0.77)	22.3 (0.43)	31.0 (0.75)	16.3 (0.49)	9.3 (0.31)	6.4 (0.27)
1981	48.9 (0.21)	36.0 (0.93)	94.0 (0.46)	99.2 (0.08)	94.1 (0.28)	98.0 (0.24)	90.6 (0.47)	49.0 (0.81)	11.5 (0.51)	37.5 (0.78)	22.5 (0.42)	31.6 (0.74)	16.5 (0.48)	9.0 (0.30)	6.9 (0.27)
1982	48.6 (0.22)	36.4 (0.97)	95.0 (0.45)	99.2 (0.09)	94.4 (0.29)	98.5 (0.22)	90.6 (0.51)	47.8 (0.86)	11.3 (0.54)	36.5 (0.83)	23.5 (0.45)	34.0 (0.81)	16.8 (0.51)	9.6 (0.32)	6.3 (0.28)
1983	48.4 (0.22)	37.5 (0.96)	95.4 (0.43)	99.2 (0.09)	95.0 (0.28)	98.3 (0.23)	91.7 (0.50)	50.4 (0.87)	12.8 (0.58)	37.6 (0.84)	22.7 (0.45)	32.5 (0.80)	16.6 (0.51)	9.6 (0.32)	6.4 (0.28)
1984	47.9 (0.22)	36.3 (0.94)	94.5 (0.46)	99.2 (0.09)	94.7 (0.29)	97.8 (0.26)	91.5 (0.51)	50.1 (0.89)	11.5 (0.57)	38.6 (0.87)	23.7 (0.46)	33.9 (0.82)	17.3 (0.52)	9.1 (0.30)	6.3 (0.27)

See notes at end of table.

Table 103.20. Percentage of the population 3 to 34 years old enrolled in school, by age group: Selected years, 1940 through 2014—Continued

[Standard errors appear in parentheses]

Year	Total, 3 to 34 years old	3 and 4 years old	5 and 6 years old	7 to 13 years old	14 to 17 years old			18 and 19 years old			20 to 24 years old			25 to 29 years old	30 to 34 years old
					Total	14 and 15	16 and 17	Total	In secondary education	In higher education	Total	20 and 21	22 to 24		
1	2	3	4	5	6	7	8	9	10	11	12	13	14	15	16
1985	48.3 (0.22)	38.9 (0.95)	96.1 (0.38)	99.2 (0.09)	94.9 (0.28)	98.1 (0.24)	91.7 (0.50)	51.6 (0.91)	11.2 (0.57)	40.4 (0.89)	24.0 (0.47)	35.3 (0.84)	16.9 (0.52)	9.2 (0.31)	6.1 (0.26)
1986	48.2 (0.22)	38.9 (0.95)	95.3 (0.41)	99.2 (0.09)	94.9 (0.28)	97.6 (0.28)	92.3 (0.48)	54.6 (0.91)	13.1 (0.62)	41.5 (0.90)	23.6 (0.47)	33.0 (0.84)	17.9 (0.54)	8.8 (0.30)	6.0 (0.25)
1987	48.6 (0.22)	38.3 (0.95)	95.1 (0.42)	99.5 (0.07)	95.0 (0.28)	98.6 (0.22)	91.7 (0.49)	55.6 (0.90)	13.1 (0.61)	42.5 (0.90)	25.5 (0.49)	38.7 (0.89)	17.5 (0.54)	9.0 (0.30)	5.8 (0.25)
1988	48.7 (0.24)	38.2 (1.02)	96.0 (0.41)	99.7 (0.06)	95.1 (0.31)	98.9 (0.22)	91.6 (0.55)	55.6 (0.98)	13.9 (0.68)	41.8 (0.97)	26.1 (0.54)	39.1 (0.98)	18.2 (0.60)	8.3 (0.32)	5.9 (0.27)
1989	49.0 (0.23)	39.1 (0.97)	95.2 (0.43)	99.3 (0.08)	95.7 (0.28)	98.8 (0.21)	92.7 (0.50)	56.0 (0.92)	14.4 (0.65)	41.6 (0.91)	27.0 (0.53)	38.5 (0.94)	19.9 (0.60)	9.3 (0.32)	5.7 (0.25)
1990	50.2 (0.23)	44.4 (0.99)	96.5 (0.37)	99.6 (0.06)	95.8 (0.28)	99.0 (0.19)	92.5 (0.52)	57.2 (0.94)	14.5 (0.67)	42.7 (0.94)	28.6 (0.54)	39.7 (0.92)	21.0 (0.63)	9.7 (0.33)	5.8 (0.25)
1991	50.7 (0.23)	40.5 (0.96)	95.4 (0.41)	99.6 (0.06)	96.0 (0.27)	98.8 (0.22)	93.3 (0.49)	59.6 (0.96)	15.6 (0.71)	44.0 (0.97)	30.2 (0.55)	42.0 (0.92)	22.2 (0.64)	10.2 (0.34)	6.2 (0.26)
1992	51.4 (0.23)	39.7 (0.95)	95.5 (0.41)	99.4 (0.08)	96.7 (0.25)	99.1 (0.18)	94.1 (0.46)	61.4 (0.96)	17.1 (0.74)	44.3 (0.98)	31.6 (0.56)	44.0 (0.95)	23.7 (0.65)	9.8 (0.34)	6.1 (0.26)
1993	51.8 (0.23)	40.4 (0.93)	95.4 (0.41)	99.5 (0.07)	96.5 (0.25)	98.9 (0.20)	94.0 (0.46)	61.6 (0.95)	17.2 (0.74)	44.4 (0.97)	30.8 (0.56)	42.7 (0.97)	23.6 (0.65)	10.2 (0.35)	5.9 (0.25)
1994	53.3 (0.23)	47.3[1] (0.94)	96.7 (0.34)	99.4 (0.08)	96.6 (0.24)	98.8 (0.20)	94.4 (0.43)	60.2 (0.94)	16.2 (0.70)	43.9 (0.95)	32.0 (0.55)	44.9 (0.95)	24.0 (0.64)	10.8 (0.36)	6.7 (0.27)
1995	53.7 (0.21)	48.7[1] (0.87)	96.0 (0.34)	98.9 (0.09)	96.3 (0.23)	98.9 (0.18)	93.6 (0.42)	59.4 (0.86)	16.3 (0.64)	43.1 (0.86)	31.5 (0.52)	44.9 (0.90)	23.2 (0.60)	11.6 (0.34)	5.9 (0.24)
1996	54.1 (0.22)	48.3[1] (0.91)	94.0 (0.43)	97.7 (0.14)	95.4 (0.26)	98.0 (0.24)	92.8 (0.45)	61.5 (0.87)	16.7 (0.67)	44.9 (0.89)	32.5 (0.55)	44.4 (0.93)	24.8 (0.65)	11.9 (0.36)	6.1 (0.25)
1997	55.6 (0.22)	52.6[1] (0.92)	96.5 (0.33)	99.1 (0.09)	96.6 (0.22)	98.9 (0.18)	94.3 (0.40)	61.5 (0.86)	16.7 (0.66)	44.7 (0.88)	34.3 (0.55)	45.9 (0.91)	26.4 (0.66)	11.8 (0.36)	5.7 (0.25)
1998	55.8 (0.22)	52.1[1] (0.92)	95.6 (0.37)	98.9 (0.10)	96.1 (0.24)	98.4 (0.22)	93.9 (0.41)	62.2 (0.84)	15.7 (0.63)	46.4 (0.86)	33.0 (0.54)	44.8 (0.91)	24.9 (0.65)	11.9 (0.36)	6.6 (0.27)
1999	56.0 (0.22)	54.2[1] (0.93)	96.0 (0.36)	98.7 (0.10)	95.8 (0.24)	98.2 (0.23)	93.6 (0.42)	60.6 (0.84)	16.5 (0.64)	44.1 (0.85)	32.8 (0.54)	45.3 (0.90)	24.5 (0.64)	11.1 (0.36)	6.2 (0.27)
2000	55.9 (0.22)	52.1[1] (0.93)	95.6 (0.38)	98.2 (0.12)	95.7 (0.25)	98.7 (0.20)	92.8 (0.45)	61.2 (0.84)	16.5 (0.64)	44.7 (0.85)	32.5 (0.53)	44.1 (0.88)	24.6 (0.63)	11.4 (0.37)	6.7 (0.27)
2001	56.4 (0.20)	52.4[1] (0.88)	95.3 (0.37)	98.3 (0.11)	95.8 (0.23)	98.1 (0.22)	93.4 (0.40)	61.1 (0.79)	17.1 (0.61)	44.0 (0.80)	34.1 (0.50)	46.1 (0.82)	25.5 (0.61)	11.8 (0.36)	6.9 (0.26)
2002	56.2 (0.20)	56.3[1] (0.89)	95.5 (0.37)	98.3 (0.11)	96.4 (0.21)	98.4 (0.20)	94.3 (0.37)	63.3 (0.79)	18.0 (0.63)	45.3 (0.82)	34.4 (0.50)	47.8 (0.83)	25.6 (0.59)	12.1 (0.35)	6.6 (0.25)
2003	56.2 (0.20)	55.1[1] (0.85)	94.5 (0.40)	98.3 (0.11)	96.2 (0.21)	97.5 (0.25)	94.9 (0.34)	64.5 (0.80)	17.9 (0.64)	46.6 (0.84)	35.6 (0.50)	48.3 (0.83)	27.8 (0.59)	11.8 (0.34)	6.8 (0.26)
2004	56.2 (0.20)	54.0[1] (0.85)	95.4 (0.37)	98.4 (0.11)	96.5 (0.21)	98.5 (0.19)	94.5 (0.36)	64.4 (0.80)	16.6 (0.62)	47.8 (0.83)	35.2 (0.49)	48.9 (0.82)	26.3 (0.58)	13.0 (0.35)	6.6 (0.26)
2005	56.5 (0.20)	53.6[1] (0.86)	95.4 (0.37)	98.6 (0.10)	96.5 (0.20)	98.0 (0.22)	95.1 (0.33)	67.6 (0.79)	18.3 (0.65)	49.3 (0.84)	36.1 (0.49)	48.7 (0.80)	27.3 (0.59)	11.9 (0.34)	6.9 (0.27)
2006	56.0 (0.20)	55.7[1] (0.86)	94.6 (0.39)	98.3 (0.11)	96.4 (0.21)	98.3 (0.21)	94.6 (0.36)	65.5 (0.77)	19.3 (0.64)	46.2 (0.81)	35.0 (0.49)	47.5 (0.81)	26.7 (0.58)	11.7 (0.33)	7.2 (0.27)
2007	56.1 (0.20)	54.5[1] (0.86)	94.7 (0.39)	98.4 (0.11)	96.4 (0.21)	98.7 (0.18)	94.3 (0.36)	66.8 (0.75)	17.9 (0.61)	48.9 (0.80)	35.7 (0.49)	48.4 (0.81)	27.3 (0.59)	12.4 (0.33)	7.2 (0.27)
2008	56.2 (0.20)	52.8[1] (0.85)	93.8 (0.42)	98.7 (0.10)	96.8 (0.20)	98.6 (0.19)	95.2 (0.34)	66.0 (0.75)	17.4 (0.60)	48.6 (0.79)	36.9 (0.49)	50.1 (0.81)	28.2 (0.59)	13.2 (0.34)	7.3 (0.27)
2009	56.5 (0.20)	52.4[1] (0.85)	94.1 (0.40)	98.2 (0.12)	96.3 (0.22)	98.0 (0.23)	94.6 (0.36)	68.9 (0.73)	19.1 (0.62)	49.8 (0.79)	38.7 (0.50)	51.7 (0.81)	30.4 (0.60)	13.5 (0.34)	8.1 (0.28)
2010[2]	56.6 (0.17)	53.2[1] (0.89)	94.5 (0.46)	98.0 (0.16)	97.1 (0.21)	98.1 (0.25)	96.1 (0.33)	69.2 (0.92)	18.1 (0.71)	51.2 (1.05)	38.6 (0.71)	52.4 (1.08)	28.9 (0.79)	14.6 (0.47)	8.3 (0.39)
2011[2]	56.8 (0.19)	52.4[1] (0.90)	95.1 (0.43)	98.3 (0.14)	97.1 (0.22)	98.6 (0.21)	95.7 (0.38)	71.1 (0.95)	21.0 (0.78)	50.1 (1.08)	39.9 (0.68)	52.7 (1.05)	31.1 (0.82)	14.8 (0.44)	7.7 (0.32)
2012[2]	56.6 (0.22)	53.5[1] (1.11)	93.2 (0.49)	98.0 (0.17)	97.0 (0.28)	98.2 (0.31)	95.8 (0.40)	69.0 (0.98)	21.7 (0.77)	47.3 (0.96)	40.2 (0.72)	54.0 (1.04)	30.7 (0.84)	14.0 (0.48)	7.5 (0.33)
2013[2]	55.8 (0.18)	54.9[1] (1.00)	93.8 (0.45)	98.1 (0.16)	96.1 (0.28)	98.4 (0.27)	93.7 (0.50)	67.1 (0.97)	20.5 (0.80)	46.6 (1.00)	38.7 (0.76)	52.8 (1.24)	29.7 (0.81)	13.3 (0.44)	6.7 (0.32)
2014[2]	55.2 (0.21)	54.5[1] (0.98)	93.4 (0.53)	97.6 (0.19)	95.4 (0.29)	97.8 (0.26)	92.9 (0.51)	68.4 (0.92)	19.6 (0.79)	48.9 (1.09)	38.0 (0.76)	51.4 (1.24)	29.6 (0.80)	13.1 (0.44)	6.4 (0.31)

—Not available.
†Not applicable.
[1]Beginning in 1994, preprimary enrollment data were collected using new procedures. Data may not be comparable to figures for earlier years.
[2]Beginning in 2010, standard errors were computed using replicate weights, which produced more precise values than the generalized variance function methodology used in prior years.

NOTE: Data for 1940 are for April. Data for all other years are as of October. Includes enrollment in any type of graded public, parochial, or other private schools. Includes nursery schools, kindergartens, elementary schools, high schools, colleges, universities, and professional schools. Attendance may be on either a full-time or part-time basis and during the day or night. SOURCE: U.S. Department of Commerce, Census Bureau, *Historical Statistics of the United States, Colonial Times to 1970; Current Population Reports,* Series P-20, various years; CPS Historical Time Series Tables on School Enrollment, retrieved June 6, 2012, from http://www.census.gov/hhes/school/data/cps/historical/index.html; and Current Population Survey, October, 1970 through 2014. (This table was prepared August 2015.)

Table 104.10. Rates of high school completion and bachelor's degree attainment among persons age 25 and over, by race/ethnicity and sex: Selected years, 1910 through 2015

[Standard errors appear in parentheses]

Sex, high school or bachelor's degree attainment, and year	Total, percent of all persons age 25 and over		White[1]		Black[1]		Hispanic		Asian/Pacific Islander						American Indian/ Alaska Native		Two or more races	
									Total		Asian		Pacific Islander					
1	2		3		4		5		6		7		8		9		10	
Total																		
High school completion or higher[2]																		
1910[3]	13.5	(—)	—	(†)	—	(†)	—	(†)	—	(†)	—	(†)	—	(†)	—	(†)	—	(†)
1920[3]	16.4	(—)	—	(†)	—	(†)	—	(†)	—	(†)	—	(†)	—	(†)	—	(†)	—	(†)
1930[3]	19.1	(—)	—	(†)	—	(†)	—	(†)	—	(†)	—	(†)	—	(†)	—	(†)	—	(†)
1940	24.5	(—)	26.1	(—)	7.7	(—)	—	(†)	—	(†)	—	(†)	—	(†)	—	(†)	—	(†)
1950	34.3	(—)	36.4	(—)	13.7	(—)	—	(†)	—	(†)	—	(†)	—	(†)	—	(†)	—	(†)
1960	41.1	(—)	43.2	(—)	21.7	(—)	—	(†)	—	(†)	—	(†)	—	(†)	—	(†)	—	(†)
1970	55.2	(—)	57.4	(—)	36.1	(—)	—	(†)	—	(†)	—	(†)	—	(†)	—	(†)	—	(†)
1975	62.5	(—)	65.8	(—)	42.6	(—)	38.5	(—)	—	(†)	—	(†)	—	(†)	—	(†)	—	(†)
1980	68.6	(0.20)	71.9	(0.21)	51.4	(0.81)	44.5	(1.18)	—	(†)	—	(†)	—	(†)	—	(†)	—	(†)
1985	73.9	(0.18)	77.5	(0.19)	59.9	(0.74)	47.9	(0.99)	—	(†)	—	(†)	—	(†)	—	(†)	—	(†)
1986	74.7	(0.18)	78.2	(0.19)	62.5	(0.72)	48.5	(0.96)	—	(†)	—	(†)	—	(†)	—	(†)	—	(†)
1987	75.6	(0.17)	79.0	(0.18)	63.6	(0.71)	50.9	(0.94)	—	(†)	—	(†)	—	(†)	—	(†)	—	(†)
1988	76.2	(0.17)	79.8	(0.18)	63.5	(0.70)	51.0	(0.92)	—	(†)	—	(†)	—	(†)	—	(†)	—	(†)
1989	76.9	(0.17)	80.7	(0.18)	64.7	(0.69)	50.9	(0.89)	82.3	(1.17)	—	(†)	—	(†)	—	(†)	—	(†)
1990	77.6	(0.17)	81.4	(0.17)	66.2	(0.67)	50.8	(0.88)	84.2	(1.09)	—	(†)	—	(†)	—	(†)	—	(†)
1991	78.4	(0.16)	82.4	(0.17)	66.8	(0.66)	51.3	(0.86)	84.2	(1.05)	—	(†)	—	(†)	—	(†)	—	(†)
1992	79.4	(0.16)	83.4	(0.16)	67.7	(0.65)	52.6	(0.85)	83.7	(1.02)	—	(†)	—	(†)	—	(†)	—	(†)
1993	80.2	(0.16)	84.1	(0.16)	70.5	(0.63)	53.1	(0.83)	84.2	(1.00)	—	(†)	—	(†)	—	(†)	—	(†)
1994	80.9	(0.15)	84.9	(0.16)	73.0	(0.61)	53.3	(0.78)	84.8	(0.98)	—	(†)	—	(†)	—	(†)	—	(†)
1995	81.7	(0.15)	85.9	(0.16)	73.8	(0.61)	53.4	(0.78)	83.8	(1.06)	—	(†)	—	(†)	—	(†)	—	(†)
1996	81.7	(0.16)	86.0	(0.16)	74.6	(0.53)	53.1	(0.68)	83.5	(0.82)	—	(†)	—	(†)	—	(†)	—	(†)
1997	82.1	(0.14)	86.3	(0.15)	75.3	(0.52)	54.7	(0.54)	85.2	(0.75)	—	(†)	—	(†)	—	(†)	—	(†)
1998	82.8	(0.14)	87.1	(0.14)	76.4	(0.50)	55.5	(0.53)	84.9	(0.74)	—	(†)	—	(†)	—	(†)	—	(†)
1999	83.4	(0.14)	87.7	(0.14)	77.4	(0.49)	56.1	(0.52)	84.7	(0.73)	—	(†)	—	(†)	—	(†)	—	(†)
2000	84.1	(0.13)	88.4	(0.14)	78.9	(0.48)	57.0	(0.51)	85.7	(0.71)	—	(†)	—	(†)	—	(†)	—	(†)
2001	84.3	(0.13)	88.7	(0.13)	79.5	(0.47)	56.5	(0.50)	87.8	(0.60)	—	(†)	—	(†)	—	(†)	—	(†)
2002	84.1	(0.09)	88.7	(0.10)	79.2	(0.34)	57.0	(0.34)	87.7	(0.44)	—	(†)	—	(†)	—	(†)	—	(†)
2003	84.6	(0.09)	89.4	(0.09)	80.3	(0.33)	57.0	(0.33)	87.8	(0.43)	87.8	(0.44)	88.2	(1.87)	77.2	(1.64)	86.1	(0.97)
2004	85.2	(0.09)	90.0	(0.09)	81.1	(0.32)	58.4	(0.32)	86.9	(0.43)	86.9	(0.44)	88.5	(1.91)	77.8	(1.61)	87.2	(0.91)
2005	85.2	(0.14)	90.1	(0.16)	81.4	(0.44)	58.5	(0.53)	87.8	(0.62)	87.7	(0.62)	90.1	(2.69)	75.6	(2.02)	88.6	(0.83)
2006	85.5	(0.15)	90.5	(0.15)	81.2	(0.43)	59.3	(0.58)	87.5	(0.71)	87.5	(0.71)	85.7	(2.51)	78.5	(2.11)	88.1	(0.90)
2007	85.7	(0.15)	90.6	(0.15)	82.8	(0.39)	60.3	(0.56)	88.0	(0.79)	87.9	(0.81)	88.6	(2.30)	80.3	(2.27)	89.3	(0.87)
2008	86.6	(0.15)	91.5	(0.15)	83.3	(0.40)	62.3	(0.58)	89.0	(0.62)	88.8	(0.64)	94.4	(1.00)	78.4	(2.74)	89.5	(1.12)
2009	86.7	(0.15)	91.6	(0.15)	84.2	(0.44)	61.9	(0.56)	88.4	(0.61)	88.3	(0.63)	90.8	(1.76)	81.5	(1.83)	87.4	(0.96)
2010	87.1	(0.13)	92.1	(0.14)	84.6	(0.41)	62.9	(0.53)	89.1	(0.67)	89.1	(0.68)	90.2	(1.95)	80.8	(1.76)	88.9	(0.90)
2011	87.6	(0.13)	92.4	(0.14)	84.8	(0.41)	64.3	(0.54)	88.8	(0.55)	88.7	(0.57)	90.4	(1.61)	82.3	(1.77)	89.4	(1.00)
2012	87.6	(0.15)	92.5	(0.14)	85.7	(0.40)	65.0	(0.59)	89.2	(0.59)	89.0	(0.61)	91.6	(1.33)	81.8	(1.69)	91.0	(0.89)
2013	88.2	(0.14)	92.9	(0.13)	85.9	(0.42)	66.2	(0.52)	90.2	(0.51)	90.2	(0.53)	89.5	(1.72)	82.2	(1.68)	92.6	(0.75)
2014	88.3	(0.15)	93.1	(0.17)	86.7	(0.45)	66.5	(0.57)	89.5	(0.62)	89.5	(0.64)	88.8	(2.15)	81.0	(2.01)	93.3	(0.88)
2015	88.4	(0.12)	93.3	(0.13)	87.7	(0.37)	66.7	(0.48)	88.9	(0.49)	89.1	(0.51)	85.1	(2.04)	83.8	(1.64)	91.6	(0.87)
Bachelor's or higher degree[4]																		
1910[3]	2.7	(—)	—	(†)	—	(†)	—	(†)	—	(†)	—	(†)	—	(†)	—	(†)	—	(†)
1920[3]	3.3	(—)	—	(†)	—	(†)	—	(†)	—	(†)	—	(†)	—	(†)	—	(†)	—	(†)
1930[3]	3.9	(—)	—	(†)	—	(†)	—	(†)	—	(†)	—	(†)	—	(†)	—	(†)	—	(†)
1940	4.6	(—)	4.9	(—)	1.3	(—)	—	(†)	—	(†)	—	(†)	—	(†)	—	(†)	—	(†)
1950	6.2	(—)	6.6	(—)	2.2	(—)	—	(†)	—	(†)	—	(†)	—	(†)	—	(†)	—	(†)
1960	7.7	(—)	8.1	(—)	3.5	(—)	—	(†)	—	(†)	—	(†)	—	(†)	—	(†)	—	(†)
1970	11.0	(—)	11.6	(—)	6.1	(—)	—	(†)	—	(†)	—	(†)	—	(†)	—	(†)	—	(†)
1975	13.9	(—)	14.9	(—)	6.4	(—)	6.6	(—)	—	(†)	—	(†)	—	(†)	—	(†)	—	(†)
1980	17.0	(0.16)	18.4	(0.18)	7.9	(0.44)	7.6	(0.63)	—	(†)	—	(†)	—	(†)	—	(†)	—	(†)
1985	19.4	(0.16)	20.8	(0.19)	11.1	(0.47)	8.5	(0.55)	—	(†)	—	(†)	—	(†)	—	(†)	—	(†)
1986	19.4	(0.16)	20.9	(0.19)	10.9	(0.47)	8.4	(0.53)	—	(†)	—	(†)	—	(†)	—	(†)	—	(†)
1987	19.9	(0.16)	21.4	(0.19)	10.8	(0.46)	8.6	(0.53)	—	(†)	—	(†)	—	(†)	—	(†)	—	(†)
1988	20.3	(0.16)	21.8	(0.19)	11.2	(0.46)	10.0	(0.55)	—	(†)	—	(†)	—	(†)	—	(†)	—	(†)
1989	21.1	(0.16)	22.8	(0.19)	11.7	(0.46)	9.9	(0.53)	41.5	(1.51)	—	(†)	—	(†)	—	(†)	—	(†)
1990	21.3	(0.16)	23.1	(0.19)	11.3	(0.45)	9.2	(0.51)	41.7	(1.47)	—	(†)	—	(†)	—	(†)	—	(†)
1991	21.4	(0.16)	23.3	(0.19)	11.5	(0.45)	9.7	(0.51)	40.3	(1.42)	—	(†)	—	(†)	—	(†)	—	(†)
1992	21.4	(0.16)	23.2	(0.19)	11.9	(0.45)	9.3	(0.49)	39.3	(1.35)	—	(†)	—	(†)	—	(†)	—	(†)
1993	21.9	(0.16)	23.8	(0.19)	12.2	(0.45)	9.0	(0.48)	42.1	(1.35)	—	(†)	—	(†)	—	(†)	—	(†)
1994	22.2	(0.16)	24.3	(0.19)	12.9	(0.46)	9.1	(0.45)	41.3	(1.34)	—	(†)	—	(†)	—	(†)	—	(†)
1995	23.0	(0.16)	25.4	(0.19)	13.3	(0.47)	9.3	(0.45)	38.5	(1.40)	—	(†)	—	(†)	—	(†)	—	(†)
1996	23.6	(0.17)	25.9	(0.20)	13.8	(0.42)	9.3	(0.40)	42.3	(1.09)	—	(†)	—	(†)	—	(†)	—	(†)
1997	23.9	(0.16)	26.2	(0.19)	13.3	(0.41)	10.3	(0.33)	42.6	(1.04)	—	(†)	—	(†)	—	(†)	—	(†)
1998	24.4	(0.16)	26.6	(0.19)	14.8	(0.42)	11.0	(0.33)	42.3	(1.02)	—	(†)	—	(†)	—	(†)	—	(†)
1999	25.2	(0.16)	27.7	(0.19)	15.5	(0.43)	10.9	(0.33)	42.4	(1.01)	—	(†)	—	(†)	—	(†)	—	(†)
2000	25.6	(0.16)	28.1	(0.19)	16.6	(0.44)	10.6	(0.32)	44.4	(1.00)	—	(†)	—	(†)	—	(†)	—	(†)
2001	26.1	(0.16)	28.6	(0.19)	16.1	(0.43)	11.2	(0.32)	48.0	(0.92)	—	(†)	—	(†)	—	(†)	—	(†)
2002	26.7	(0.11)	29.4	(0.14)	17.2	(0.31)	11.1	(0.21)	47.7	(0.66)	—	(†)	—	(†)	—	(†)	—	(†)
2003	27.2	(0.11)	30.0	(0.14)	17.4	(0.31)	11.4	(0.21)	48.8	(0.65)	50.0	(0.67)	27.0	(2.56)	12.6	(1.30)	22.0	(1.17)
2004	27.7	(0.11)	30.6	(0.14)	17.7	(0.31)	12.1	(0.21)	48.9	(0.64)	49.7	(0.66)	32.4	(2.81)	14.3	(1.36)	21.8	(1.13)
2005	27.7	(0.23)	30.6	(0.29)	17.6	(0.45)	12.0	(0.31)	49.3	(0.91)	50.4	(0.93)	24.6	(3.67)	14.5	(1.51)	23.2	(1.19)

See notes at end of table.

Table 104.10. Rates of high school completion and bachelor's degree attainment among persons age 25 and over, by race/ethnicity and sex: Selected years, 1910 through 2015—Continued

[Standard errors appear in parentheses]

Sex, high school or bachelor's degree attainment, and year	Total, percent of all persons age 25 and over		White[1]		Black[1]		Hispanic		Asian/Pacific Islander						American Indian/ Alaska Native		Two or more races	
									Total		Asian		Pacific Islander					
1	2		3		4		5		6		7		8		9		10	
2006	28.0	(0.20)	31.0	(0.25)	18.6	(0.47)	12.4	(0.32)	49.1	(1.04)	50.0	(1.06)	26.9	(3.42)	12.9	(1.60)	23.1	(1.28)
2007	28.7	(0.21)	31.8	(0.27)	18.7	(0.51)	12.7	(0.31)	51.2	(1.02)	52.5	(1.03)	23.8	(3.30)	13.1	(1.24)	23.7	(1.30)
2008	29.4	(0.21)	32.6	(0.26)	19.7	(0.51)	13.3	(0.29)	51.9	(0.95)	52.9	(0.97)	28.4	(2.86)	14.9	(1.52)	24.4	(1.36)
2009	29.5	(0.21)	32.9	(0.26)	19.4	(0.45)	13.2	(0.34)	51.6	(0.91)	52.8	(0.95)	28.3	(2.68)	17.5	(2.08)	25.5	(1.34)
2010	29.9	(0.19)	33.2	(0.24)	20.0	(0.51)	13.9	(0.31)	51.6	(1.04)	52.8	(1.09)	25.6	(2.89)	16.0	(1.77)	25.3	(1.30)
2011	30.4	(0.19)	34.0	(0.24)	20.2	(0.50)	14.1	(0.34)	49.5	(0.92)	50.8	(0.96)	22.1	(2.73)	16.1	(1.73)	27.4	(1.27)
2012	30.9	(0.21)	34.5	(0.27)	21.4	(0.53)	14.5	(0.35)	50.7	(0.92)	51.9	(0.94)	24.5	(2.75)	16.7	(1.82)	27.1	(1.34)
2013	31.7	(0.21)	35.2	(0.26)	22.0	(0.49)	15.1	(0.34)	52.5	(0.92)	53.9	(0.93)	25.6	(2.66)	15.4	(1.72)	30.6	(1.35)
2014	32.0	(0.27)	35.6	(0.35)	22.8	(0.66)	15.2	(0.39)	51.3	(1.00)	52.7	(1.02)	22.3	(3.27)	13.8	(1.43)	31.2	(1.81)
2015	32.5	(0.22)	36.2	(0.28)	22.9	(0.52)	15.5	(0.31)	52.9	(0.84)	54.4	(0.87)	22.8	(2.39)	19.8	(1.32)	30.6	(1.52)
Males																		
High school completion or higher[2]																		
1940	22.7	(—)	24.2	(—)	6.9	(—)	—	(†)	—	(†)	—	(†)	—	(†)	—	(†)	—	(†)
1950	32.6	(—)	34.6	(—)	12.6	(—)	—	(†)	—	(†)	—	(†)	—	(†)	—	(†)	—	(†)
1960	39.5	(—)	41.6	(—)	20.0	(—)	—	(†)	—	(†)	—	(†)	—	(†)	—	(†)	—	(†)
1970	55.0	(—)	57.2	(—)	35.4	(—)	—	(†)	—	(†)	—	(†)	—	(†)	—	(†)	—	(†)
1980	69.2	(0.29)	72.4	(0.31)	51.2	(1.21)	44.9	(1.71)	—	(†)	—	(†)	—	(†)	—	(†)	—	(†)
1990	77.7	(0.24)	81.6	(0.25)	65.8	(1.01)	50.3	(1.25)	86.0	(1.49)	—	(†)	—	(†)	—	(†)	—	(†)
1995	81.7	(0.22)	86.0	(0.22)	73.5	(0.91)	52.9	(1.11)	85.8	(1.46)	—	(†)	—	(†)	—	(†)	—	(†)
1996	81.9	(0.23)	86.1	(0.23)	74.6	(0.80)	53.0	(0.97)	86.2	(1.10)	—	(†)	—	(†)	—	(†)	—	(†)
1997	82.0	(0.21)	86.3	(0.21)	73.8	(0.79)	54.9	(0.76)	87.5	(1.00)	—	(†)	—	(†)	—	(†)	—	(†)
1998	82.8	(0.20)	87.1	(0.21)	75.4	(0.77)	55.7	(0.74)	87.9	(0.98)	—	(†)	—	(†)	—	(†)	—	(†)
1999	83.4	(0.20)	87.7	(0.20)	77.2	(0.74)	56.0	(0.75)	86.9	(1.00)	—	(†)	—	(†)	—	(†)	—	(†)
2000	84.2	(0.19)	88.5	(0.20)	79.1	(0.72)	56.6	(0.73)	88.4	(0.94)	—	(†)	—	(†)	—	(†)	—	(†)
2001	84.4	(0.19)	88.6	(0.19)	80.6	(0.69)	55.6	(0.72)	90.6	(0.78)	—	(†)	—	(†)	—	(†)	—	(†)
2002	83.8	(0.14)	88.5	(0.14)	79.0	(0.51)	56.1	(0.48)	89.8	(0.58)	—	(†)	—	(†)	—	(†)	—	(†)
2003	84.1	(0.13)	89.0	(0.14)	79.9	(0.50)	56.3	(0.46)	89.8	(0.58)	89.8	(0.59)	89.8	(2.61)	76.5	(2.33)	87.2	(1.36)
2004	84.8	(0.13)	89.9	(0.13)	80.8	(0.49)	57.3	(0.45)	88.8	(0.59)	88.8	(0.60)	88.9	(2.65)	77.1	(2.31)	87.8	(1.29)
2005	84.9	(0.19)	89.9	(0.20)	81.4	(0.60)	57.9	(0.69)	90.4	(0.65)	90.5	(0.66)	88.5	(3.62)	75.6	(2.57)	89.0	(1.19)
2006	85.0	(0.20)	90.2	(0.21)	80.7	(0.63)	58.5	(0.77)	89.5	(0.84)	89.7	(0.86)	85.8	(3.10)	78.1	(2.77)	88.0	(1.36)
2007	85.0	(0.21)	90.2	(0.22)	82.5	(0.55)	58.2	(0.80)	90.0	(0.81)	90.1	(0.82)	88.1	(2.75)	78.3	(3.58)	89.4	(1.28)
2008	85.9	(0.19)	91.1	(0.20)	82.1	(0.61)	60.9	(0.72)	91.0	(0.66)	90.8	(0.69)	95.8	(1.40)	77.3	(3.37)	89.6	(1.21)
2009	86.2	(0.19)	91.4	(0.20)	84.2	(0.60)	60.6	(0.72)	90.8	(0.66)	90.7	(0.68)	92.1	(2.18)	80.0	(2.33)	87.3	(1.26)
2010	86.6	(0.17)	91.8	(0.19)	84.2	(0.57)	61.4	(0.68)	91.4	(0.78)	91.5	(0.79)	89.3	(2.84)	78.9	(2.46)	88.1	(1.36)
2011	87.1	(0.18)	92.0	(0.17)	84.2	(0.55)	63.6	(0.71)	90.6	(0.68)	90.6	(0.69)	91.5	(2.22)	80.6	(2.35)	88.1	(1.40)
2012	87.3	(0.19)	92.2	(0.18)	85.1	(0.56)	64.0	(0.73)	90.6	(0.68)	90.5	(0.70)	93.3	(1.84)	81.8	(2.39)	90.2	(1.45)
2013	87.6	(0.17)	92.7	(0.17)	84.9	(0.62)	64.6	(0.66)	91.6	(0.57)	91.7	(0.57)	89.3	(2.48)	81.0	(2.11)	93.3	(1.03)
2014	87.7	(0.19)	92.5	(0.22)	86.3	(0.58)	65.1	(0.74)	91.8	(0.70)	91.9	(0.72)	90.0	(2.68)	80.2	(2.30)	93.8	(1.08)
2015	88.0	(0.16)	93.0	(0.16)	87.2	(0.48)	65.5	(0.63)	90.9	(0.56)	91.3	(0.58)	84.9	(2.83)	81.9	(2.12)	92.5	(1.23)
Bachelor's or higher degree[4]																		
1940	5.5	(—)	5.9	(—)	1.4	(—)	—	(†)	—	(†)	—	(†)	—	(†)	—	(†)	—	(†)
1950	7.3	(—)	7.9	(—)	2.1	(—)	—	(†)	—	(†)	—	(†)	—	(†)	—	(†)	—	(†)
1960	9.7	(—)	10.3	(—)	3.5	(—)	—	(†)	—	(†)	—	(†)	—	(†)	—	(†)	—	(†)
1970	14.1	(—)	15.0	(—)	6.8	(—)	—	(†)	—	(†)	—	(†)	—	(†)	—	(†)	—	(†)
1980	20.9	(0.26)	22.7	(0.29)	7.7	(0.65)	9.2	(0.99)	—	(†)	—	(†)	—	(†)	—	(†)	—	(†)
1990	24.4	(0.25)	26.7	(0.28)	11.9	(0.69)	9.8	(0.74)	45.9	(2.14)	—	(†)	—	(†)	—	(†)	—	(†)
1995	26.0	(0.25)	28.9	(0.29)	13.7	(0.71)	10.1	(0.67)	42.3	(2.06)	—	(†)	—	(†)	—	(†)	—	(†)
1996	26.0	(0.26)	28.8	(0.30)	12.5	(0.61)	10.3	(0.59)	46.9	(1.59)	—	(†)	—	(†)	—	(†)	—	(†)
1997	26.2	(0.24)	29.0	(0.28)	12.5	(0.60)	10.6	(0.47)	48.0	(1.51)	—	(†)	—	(†)	—	(†)	—	(†)
1998	26.5	(0.24)	29.3	(0.28)	14.0	(0.62)	11.1	(0.47)	46.0	(1.50)	—	(†)	—	(†)	—	(†)	—	(†)
1999	27.5	(0.24)	30.6	(0.28)	14.3	(0.62)	10.7	(0.46)	46.3	(1.48)	—	(†)	—	(†)	—	(†)	—	(†)
2000	27.8	(0.24)	30.8	(0.28)	16.4	(0.65)	10.7	(0.45)	48.1	(1.47)	—	(†)	—	(†)	—	(†)	—	(†)
2001	28.0	(0.24)	30.9	(0.28)	15.9	(0.64)	11.1	(0.45)	52.9	(1.33)	—	(†)	—	(†)	—	(†)	—	(†)
2002	28.5	(0.17)	31.7	(0.20)	16.5	(0.47)	11.0	(0.30)	51.5	(0.96)	—	(†)	—	(†)	—	(†)	—	(†)
2003	28.9	(0.17)	32.3	(0.20)	16.8	(0.47)	11.2	(0.29)	52.8	(0.96)	54.2	(0.98)	25.7	(3.76)	13.1	(1.85)	21.9	(1.69)
2004	29.4	(0.17)	32.9	(0.20)	16.6	(0.46)	11.8	(0.30)	52.9	(0.93)	54.0	(0.95)	31.9	(3.94)	15.6	(1.99)	20.7	(1.60)
2005	28.9	(0.29)	32.4	(0.37)	16.0	(0.64)	11.8	(0.43)	53.0	(1.10)	54.3	(1.13)	25.1	(4.70)	17.0	(2.30)	23.1	(1.67)
2006	29.2	(0.24)	32.8	(0.31)	17.5	(0.63)	11.9	(0.40)	51.9	(1.33)	53.1	(1.35)	26.6	(4.67)	13.7	(2.07)	22.6	(1.75)
2007	29.5	(0.25)	33.2	(0.33)	18.1	(0.62)	11.8	(0.37)	54.2	(1.31)	55.8	(1.32)	19.2	(4.14)	12.7	(1.89)	21.5	(1.81)
2008	30.1	(0.25)	33.8	(0.33)	18.7	(0.67)	12.6	(0.39)	54.9	(1.24)	56.1	(1.24)	27.5	(3.64)	14.6	(2.15)	22.7	(1.62)
2009	30.1	(0.28)	33.9	(0.36)	17.9	(0.57)	12.5	(0.41)	54.8	(1.14)	56.5	(1.17)	23.0	(3.35)	16.1	(2.96)	24.4	(1.92)
2010	30.3	(0.23)	34.2	(0.30)	17.9	(0.59)	12.9	(0.37)	54.6	(1.26)	56.2	(1.30)	18.0	(3.74)	13.5	(2.61)	24.8	(1.86)
2011	30.8	(0.23)	35.0	(0.29)	18.4	(0.64)	13.1	(0.44)	52.4	(1.15)	54.0	(1.21)	19.1	(3.55)	14.1	(1.98)	25.7	(1.91)
2012	31.4	(0.27)	35.5	(0.33)	19.5	(0.62)	13.3	(0.45)	53.1	(1.26)	54.4	(1.29)	24.1	(3.34)	16.1	(2.27)	25.2	(1.85)
2013	32.0	(0.25)	36.0	(0.31)	20.2	(0.64)	13.9	(0.43)	55.1	(1.17)	56.9	(1.20)	23.1	(3.32)	14.0	(2.13)	29.0	(1.78)
2014	31.9	(0.32)	35.9	(0.41)	21.0	(0.88)	14.2	(0.51)	53.7	(1.33)	55.5	(1.34)	16.7	(3.42)	14.8	(2.46)	29.2	(2.56)
2015	32.3	(0.27)	36.3	(0.35)	21.1	(0.63)	14.3	(0.38)	55.6	(1.11)	57.3	(1.16)	24.4	(2.87)	18.1	(2.14)	27.2	(2.14)

See notes at end of table.

Table 104.10.   Rates of high school completion and bachelor's degree attainment among persons age 25 and over, by race/ethnicity and sex: Selected years, 1910 through 2015—Continued

[Standard errors appear in parentheses]

Sex, high school or bachelor's degree attainment, and year	Total, percent of all persons age 25 and over		White[1]		Black[1]		Hispanic		Asian/Pacific Islander Total		Asian		Pacific Islander		American Indian/ Alaska Native		Two or more races	
1	2		3		4		5		6		7		8		9		10	
Females																		
High school completion or higher[2]																		
1940	26.3	(—)	28.1	(—)	8.4	(—)	—	(†)	—	(†)	—	(†)	—	(†)	—	(†)	—	(†)
1950	36.0	(—)	38.2	(—)	14.7	(—)	—	(†)	—	(†)	—	(†)	—	(†)	—	(†)	—	(†)
1960	42.5	(—)	44.7	(—)	23.1	(—)	—	(†)	—	(†)	—	(†)	—	(†)	—	(†)	—	(†)
1970	55.4	(—)	57.7	(—)	36.6	(—)	—	(†)	—	(†)	—	(†)	—	(†)	—	(†)	—	(†)
1980	68.1	(0.28)	71.5	(0.30)	51.5	(1.08)	44.2	(1.63)	—	(†)	—	(†)	—	(†)	—	(†)	—	(†)
1990	77.5	(0.23)	81.3	(0.24)	66.5	(0.90)	51.3	(1.23)	82.5	(1.57)	—	(†)	—	(†)	—	(†)	—	(†)
1995	81.6	(0.21)	85.8	(0.22)	74.1	(0.81)	53.8	(1.09)	81.9	(1.54)	—	(†)	—	(†)	—	(†)	—	(†)
1996	81.6	(0.22)	85.9	(0.22)	74.6	(0.71)	53.3	(0.97)	81.0	(1.21)	—	(†)	—	(†)	—	(†)	—	(†)
1997	82.2	(0.20)	86.3	(0.20)	76.5	(0.68)	54.6	(0.76)	82.9	(1.11)	—	(†)	—	(†)	—	(†)	—	(†)
1998	82.9	(0.19)	87.1	(0.20)	77.1	(0.67)	55.3	(0.75)	82.3	(1.09)	—	(†)	—	(†)	—	(†)	—	(†)
1999	83.3	(0.19)	87.6	(0.19)	77.5	(0.66)	56.3	(0.73)	82.8	(1.06)	—	(†)	—	(†)	—	(†)	—	(†)
2000	84.0	(0.19)	88.4	(0.19)	78.7	(0.64)	57.5	(0.71)	83.4	(1.03)	—	(†)	—	(†)	—	(†)	—	(†)
2001	84.2	(0.18)	88.8	(0.19)	78.6	(0.64)	57.4	(0.70)	85.2	(0.91)	—	(†)	—	(†)	—	(†)	—	(†)
2002	84.4	(0.13)	88.9	(0.13)	79.4	(0.45)	57.9	(0.48)	85.7	(0.64)	—	(†)	—	(†)	—	(†)	—	(†)
2003	85.0	(0.13)	89.7	(0.13)	80.7	(0.44)	57.8	(0.46)	86.1	(0.62)	86.1	(0.64)	86.9	(2.63)	77.9	(2.30)	85.1	(1.38)
2004	85.4	(0.12)	90.1	(0.12)	81.2	(0.43)	59.5	(0.46)	85.3	(0.63)	85.1	(0.64)	88.1	(2.76)	78.6	(2.24)	86.5	(1.29)
2005	85.5	(0.15)	90.3	(0.18)	81.5	(0.53)	59.1	(0.63)	85.4	(0.76)	85.2	(0.78)	91.7	(2.46)	75.6	(2.29)	88.1	(1.12)
2006	85.9	(0.16)	90.8	(0.17)	81.5	(0.51)	60.1	(0.59)	85.6	(0.82)	85.6	(0.81)	85.7	(3.08)	78.9	(2.18)	88.2	(1.11)
2007	86.4	(0.15)	91.0	(0.16)	83.0	(0.49)	62.5	(0.56)	86.1	(0.93)	86.0	(0.97)	89.1	(2.40)	81.9	(1.91)	89.2	(1.22)
2008	87.2	(0.17)	91.8	(0.18)	84.2	(0.49)	63.7	(0.61)	87.2	(0.75)	87.0	(0.78)	93.0	(1.57)	79.2	(2.95)	89.5	(1.53)
2009	87.1	(0.16)	91.9	(0.17)	84.2	(0.48)	63.3	(0.59)	86.4	(0.73)	86.3	(0.75)	89.7	(2.33)	82.7	(1.96)	87.6	(1.16)
2010	87.6	(0.15)	92.3	(0.17)	85.0	(0.46)	64.4	(0.59)	87.2	(0.72)	87.1	(0.75)	90.9	(2.41)	82.5	(1.95)	89.7	(1.13)
2011	88.0	(0.15)	92.8	(0.16)	85.3	(0.50)	65.1	(0.57)	87.1	(0.64)	87.0	(0.66)	89.5	(2.25)	83.8	(2.00)	90.7	(1.22)
2012	88.0	(0.17)	92.7	(0.18)	86.1	(0.46)	66.0	(0.65)	87.9	(0.64)	87.8	(0.66)	90.1	(2.11)	81.8	(1.84)	91.6	(1.13)
2013	88.6	(0.16)	93.2	(0.16)	86.6	(0.46)	67.9	(0.55)	89.0	(0.61)	88.9	(0.63)	89.6	(2.01)	83.1	(2.16)	92.0	(0.95)
2014	88.9	(0.17)	93.7	(0.20)	87.0	(0.55)	67.9	(0.61)	87.4	(0.76)	87.4	(0.77)	87.8	(2.98)	81.6	(2.78)	92.8	(1.28)
2015	88.8	(0.14)	93.5	(0.15)	88.2	(0.43)	67.8	(0.53)	87.1	(0.60)	87.2	(0.62)	85.3	(2.46)	85.6	(2.10)	90.9	(1.14)
Bachelor's or higher degree[4]																		
1940	3.8	(—)	4.0	(—)	1.2	(—)	—	(†)	—	(†)	—	(†)	—	(†)	—	(†)	—	(†)
1950	5.2	(—)	5.4	(—)	2.4	(—)	—	(†)	—	(†)	—	(†)	—	(†)	—	(†)	—	(†)
1960	5.8	(—)	6.0	(—)	3.6	(—)	—	(†)	—	(†)	—	(†)	—	(†)	—	(†)	—	(†)
1970	8.2	(—)	8.6	(—)	5.6	(—)	—	(†)	—	(†)	—	(†)	—	(†)	—	(†)	—	(†)
1980	13.6	(0.20)	14.4	(0.23)	8.1	(0.59)	6.2	(0.79)	—	(†)	—	(†)	—	(†)	—	(†)	—	(†)
1990	18.4	(0.21)	19.8	(0.25)	10.8	(0.59)	8.7	(0.69)	37.8	(2.01)	—	(†)	—	(†)	—	(†)	—	(†)
1995	20.2	(0.22)	22.1	(0.26)	13.0	(0.62)	8.4	(0.61)	35.0	(1.90)	—	(†)	—	(†)	—	(†)	—	(†)
1996	21.4	(0.23)	23.2	(0.27)	14.8	(0.58)	8.3	(0.53)	38.0	(1.50)	—	(†)	—	(†)	—	(†)	—	(†)
1997	21.7	(0.21)	23.7	(0.25)	14.0	(0.56)	10.1	(0.46)	37.4	(1.43)	—	(†)	—	(†)	—	(†)	—	(†)
1998	22.4	(0.21)	24.1	(0.25)	15.4	(0.58)	10.9	(0.47)	38.9	(1.39)	—	(†)	—	(†)	—	(†)	—	(†)
1999	23.1	(0.22)	25.0	(0.26)	16.5	(0.59)	11.0	(0.46)	39.0	(1.37)	—	(†)	—	(†)	—	(†)	—	(†)
2000	23.6	(0.22)	25.5	(0.26)	16.8	(0.59)	10.6	(0.44)	41.0	(1.37)	—	(†)	—	(†)	—	(†)	—	(†)
2001	24.3	(0.22)	26.5	(0.26)	16.3	(0.58)	11.3	(0.45)	43.4	(1.26)	—	(†)	—	(†)	—	(†)	—	(†)
2002	25.1	(0.15)	27.3	(0.19)	17.7	(0.42)	11.2	(0.31)	44.2	(0.91)	—	(†)	—	(†)	—	(†)	—	(†)
2003	25.7	(0.15)	27.9	(0.19)	18.0	(0.43)	11.6	(0.30)	45.3	(0.89)	46.3	(0.92)	28.0	(3.50)	12.2	(1.81)	22.2	(1.61)
2004	26.1	(0.15)	28.4	(0.19)	18.5	(0.43)	12.3	(0.31)	45.2	(0.88)	45.7	(0.90)	32.9	(4.01)	13.1	(1.84)	22.7	(1.59)
2005	26.5	(0.23)	28.9	(0.30)	18.9	(0.51)	12.1	(0.42)	46.0	(1.08)	46.8	(1.10)	24.1	(4.08)	12.2	(2.00)	23.3	(1.43)
2006	26.9	(0.22)	29.3	(0.28)	19.5	(0.55)	12.9	(0.39)	46.6	(1.11)	47.3	(1.15)	27.2	(4.03)	12.3	(1.81)	23.6	(1.70)
2007	28.0	(0.23)	30.6	(0.29)	19.2	(0.59)	13.7	(0.44)	48.6	(1.07)	49.5	(1.10)	27.9	(4.16)	13.4	(1.53)	25.8	(1.58)
2008	28.8	(0.24)	31.5	(0.29)	20.5	(0.58)	14.1	(0.37)	49.3	(0.99)	50.1	(1.02)	29.3	(3.82)	15.1	(1.75)	26.1	(1.92)
2009	29.1	(0.21)	31.9	(0.26)	20.6	(0.56)	14.0	(0.41)	48.8	(0.98)	49.7	(1.02)	32.9	(3.74)	18.8	(1.91)	26.6	(1.67)
2010	29.6	(0.21)	32.4	(0.26)	21.6	(0.63)	14.9	(0.42)	49.1	(1.12)	49.9	(1.19)	32.2	(4.11)	18.2	(1.83)	25.7	(1.59)
2011	30.1	(0.22)	33.1	(0.28)	21.7	(0.60)	15.2	(0.43)	47.0	(1.04)	48.0	(1.07)	24.7	(3.52)	17.9	(2.17)	28.9	(1.70)
2012	30.6	(0.23)	33.5	(0.30)	22.9	(0.61)	15.8	(0.45)	48.6	(0.93)	49.7	(0.94)	24.9	(3.70)	17.2	(2.13)	28.8	(1.88)
2013	31.4	(0.24)	34.4	(0.31)	23.4	(0.61)	16.2	(0.42)	50.2	(0.94)	51.3	(0.96)	28.0	(3.44)	16.6	(2.05)	32.0	(1.89)
2014	32.0	(0.32)	35.3	(0.42)	24.2	(0.75)	16.1	(0.50)	49.3	(1.12)	50.4	(1.15)	27.1	(4.38)	13.1	(1.92)	33.1	(2.08)
2015	32.7	(0.25)	36.1	(0.32)	24.3	(0.60)	16.6	(0.42)	50.4	(0.82)	51.8	(0.85)	21.3	(3.13)	21.3	(1.71)	33.4	(1.96)

—Not available.

†Not applicable.

[1]Includes persons of Hispanic ethnicity for years prior to 1980.

[2]Data for years prior to 1993 are for persons with 4 or more years of high school. Data for later years are for high school completers—i.e., those persons who graduated from high school with a diploma as well as those who completed high school through equivalency programs, such as a GED program.

[3]Estimates based on Census Bureau reverse projection of 1940 census data on education by age.

[4]Data for years prior to 1993 are for persons with 4 or more years of college.

NOTE: Beginning in 2005, standard errors were computed using replicate weights, which produced more precise values than the generalized variance function methodology used in prior years. For 1960 and prior years, data were collected in April. For later years, data were collected in March. Race categories exclude persons of Hispanic ethnicity except where otherwise noted.
SOURCE: U.S. Department of Commerce, Census Bureau, *U.S. Census of Population: 1960*, Vol. I, Part 1; J.K. Folger and C.B. Nam, *Education of the American Population* (1960 Census Monograph); Current Population Reports, Series P-20, various years; and Current Population Survey (CPS), Annual Social and Economic Supplement, 1970 through 2015. (This table was prepared November 2015.)

Table 104.20. Percentage of persons 25 to 29 years old with selected levels of educational attainment, by race/ethnicity and sex: Selected years, 1920 through 2015

[Standard errors appear in parentheses]

Sex, selected level of educational attainment, and year	Total		White[1]		Black[1]		Hispanic		Asian/Pacific Islander Total		Asian		Pacific Islander		American Indian/ Alaska Native		Two or more races	
1	2		3		4		5		6		7		8		9		10	
Total																		
High school completion or higher[2]																		
1920[3]	—	(†)	22.0	(—)	6.3	(—)	—	(†)	—	(†)	—	(†)	—	(†)	—	(†)	—	(†)
1940	38.1	(—)	41.2	(—)	12.3	(—)	—	(†)	—	(†)	—	(†)	—	(†)	—	(†)	—	(†)
1950	52.8	(—)	56.3	(—)	23.6	(—)	—	(†)	—	(†)	—	(†)	—	(†)	—	(†)	—	(†)
1960	60.7	(—)	63.7	(—)	38.6	(—)	—	(†)	—	(†)	—	(†)	—	(†)	—	(†)	—	(†)
1970	75.4	(—)	77.8	(—)	58.4	(—)	—	(†)	—	(†)	—	(†)	—	(†)	—	(†)	—	(†)
1980	85.4	(0.40)	89.2	(0.40)	76.7	(1.64)	58.0	(2.59)	—	(†)	—	(†)	—	(†)	—	(†)	—	(†)
1990	85.7	(0.38)	90.1	(0.37)	81.7	(1.37)	58.2	(1.94)	91.5	(2.09)	—	(†)	—	(†)	—	(†)	—	(†)
1995	86.8	(0.39)	92.5	(0.36)	86.7	(1.23)	57.1	(1.80)	90.8	(2.26)	—	(†)	—	(†)	—	(†)	—	(†)
2000	88.1	(0.37)	94.0	(0.33)	86.8	(1.13)	62.8	(1.22)	93.7	(1.27)	—	(†)	—	(†)	—	(†)	—	(†)
2005	86.2	(0.42)	92.8	(0.39)	87.0	(1.03)	63.3	(1.32)	95.6	(0.88)	95.5	(0.92)	‡	(†)	80.2	(4.77)	91.4	(3.91)
2006	86.4	(0.36)	93.4	(0.35)	86.3	(1.09)	63.2	(1.17)	96.4	(0.88)	96.6	(0.86)	‡	(†)	79.8	(5.19)	89.3	(3.96)
2007	87.0	(0.36)	93.5	(0.33)	87.7	(1.16)	65.0	(1.06)	96.8	(0.91)	97.5	(0.73)	‡	(†)	84.5	(4.41)	90.5	(4.30)
2008	87.8	(0.36)	93.7	(0.38)	87.5	(1.29)	68.3	(1.16)	95.9	(0.86)	95.8	(0.91)	‡	(†)	86.7	(3.36)	94.2	(3.82)
2009	88.6	(0.36)	94.6	(0.33)	88.9	(0.98)	68.9	(1.16)	95.4	(0.91)	95.8	(0.95)	91.6	(3.46)	81.1	(4.26)	88.5	(3.61)
2010	88.8	(0.32)	94.5	(0.31)	89.6	(0.93)	69.4	(1.22)	93.7	(1.18)	94.0	(1.24)	89.7	(5.05)	89.9	(2.98)	88.5	(3.86)
2011	89.0	(0.34)	94.4	(0.34)	88.1	(0.98)	71.5	(1.12)	95.4	(0.87)	95.3	(0.91)	‡	(†)	84.9	(3.95)	90.7	(3.79)
2012	89.7	(0.38)	94.6	(0.37)	88.5	(0.96)	75.0	(1.16)	96.2	(0.73)	96.1	(0.77)	98.6	(0.83)	84.5	(3.94)	92.8	(2.22)
2013	89.9	(0.35)	94.1	(0.35)	90.3	(0.92)	75.8	(1.10)	95.4	(0.77)	95.4	(0.81)	95.5	(2.72)	84.7	(3.47)	97.4	(1.11)
2014	90.8	(0.39)	95.6	(0.41)	91.9	(0.93)	74.7	(1.31)	96.6	(0.76)	96.6	(0.79)	‡	(†)	83.9	(4.67)	96.0	(2.01)
2015	91.2	(0.31)	95.4	(0.32)	92.5	(0.78)	77.1	(1.02)	95.3	(0.92)	95.8	(0.87)	87.2	(6.60)	86.7	(2.65)	94.9	(1.54)
Bachelor's or higher degree[4]																		
1920[3]	—	(†)	4.5	(—)	1.2	(—)	—	(†)	—	(†)	—	(†)	—	(†)	—	(†)	—	(†)
1940	5.9	(—)	6.4	(—)	1.6	(—)	—	(†)	—	(†)	—	(†)	—	(†)	—	(†)	—	(†)
1950	7.7	(—)	8.2	(—)	2.8	(—)	—	(†)	—	(†)	—	(†)	—	(†)	—	(†)	—	(†)
1960	11.0	(—)	11.8	(—)	5.4	(—)	—	(†)	—	(†)	—	(†)	—	(†)	—	(†)	—	(†)
1970	16.4	(—)	17.3	(—)	10.0	(—)	—	(†)	—	(†)	—	(†)	—	(†)	—	(†)	—	(†)
1980	22.5	(0.47)	25.0	(0.55)	11.6	(1.24)	7.7	(1.39)	—	(†)	—	(†)	—	(†)	—	(†)	—	(†)
1990	23.2	(0.46)	26.4	(0.55)	13.4	(1.20)	8.1	(1.07)	43.0	(3.71)	—	(†)	—	(†)	—	(†)	—	(†)
1995	24.7	(0.49)	28.8	(0.62)	15.4	(1.31)	8.9	(1.04)	43.1	(3.87)	—	(†)	—	(†)	—	(†)	—	(†)
2000	29.1	(0.52)	34.0	(0.67)	17.8	(1.28)	9.7	(0.75)	54.3	(2.60)	—	(†)	—	(†)	—	(†)	—	(†)
2005	28.8	(0.55)	34.5	(0.78)	17.6	(1.21)	11.2	(0.81)	60.0	(2.20)	62.1	(2.25)	‡	(†)	16.4	(3.56)	28.0	(3.79)
2006	28.4	(0.52)	34.3	(0.78)	18.7	(1.33)	9.5	(0.66)	59.6	(2.39)	61.9	(2.44)	‡	(†)	9.5 !	(4.26)	23.3	(3.14)
2007	29.6	(0.54)	35.5	(0.75)	19.5	(1.21)	11.6	(0.61)	59.4	(2.24)	61.5	(2.26)	‡	(†)	6.4 !	(2.99)	26.3	(3.44)
2008	30.8	(0.51)	37.1	(0.70)	20.4	(1.35)	12.4	(0.69)	57.9	(2.26)	60.2	(2.32)	‡	(†)	14.3	(3.17)	26.6	(3.75)
2009	30.6	(0.57)	37.2	(0.85)	18.9	(1.36)	12.2	(0.80)	56.4	(2.25)	60.3	(2.28)	12.5 !	(4.44)	15.9	(3.73)	29.7	(3.84)
2010	31.7	(0.51)	38.6	(0.72)	19.4	(1.20)	13.5	(0.80)	52.5	(2.32)	55.8	(2.47)	10.0 !	(4.40)	18.6	(4.80)	29.8	(3.22)
2011	32.2	(0.62)	39.2	(0.88)	20.1	(1.25)	12.8	(0.73)	56.0	(2.50)	57.2	(2.52)	‡	(†)	17.3	(4.45)	32.4	(3.85)
2012	33.5	(0.58)	39.8	(0.78)	23.2	(1.38)	14.8	(0.90)	59.6	(2.17)	61.7	(2.24)	25.5	(6.12)	10.4	(2.87)	32.9	(3.72)
2013	33.6	(0.55)	40.4	(0.77)	20.5	(1.38)	15.7	(0.82)	58.0	(2.16)	60.1	(2.18)	24.7 !	(7.54)	16.6	(4.89)	29.6	(3.45)
2014	34.0	(0.75)	40.8	(1.05)	22.4	(1.82)	15.1	(0.97)	60.8	(2.44)	63.2	(2.50)	‡	(†)	5.6 !	(2.24)	32.4	(4.12)
2015	35.6	(0.55)	43.0	(0.83)	21.3	(1.33)	16.4	(0.78)	62.8	(2.25)	66.0	(2.27)	11.4 !	(4.64)	15.3	(3.21)	29.6	(3.62)
Master's or higher degree																		
1995	4.5	(0.24)	5.3	(0.31)	1.8	(0.48)	1.6	(0.46)	10.9	(1.85)	—	(†)	—	(†)	—	(†)	—	(†)
2000	5.4	(0.26)	5.8	(0.33)	3.7	(0.63)	2.1	(0.36)	15.5	(1.70)	—	(†)	‡	(†)	—	(†)	—	(†)
2005	6.3	(0.31)	7.5	(0.45)	2.6	(0.44)	2.1	(0.38)	16.9	(1.93)	17.5	(2.01)	‡	(†)	‡	(†)	7.0 !	(2.49)
2006	6.4	(0.29)	7.5	(0.42)	3.2	(0.58)	1.5	(0.25)	20.1	(2.00)	21.1	(2.10)	‡	(†)	‡	(†)	7.1	(1.83)
2007	6.3	(0.30)	7.6	(0.42)	3.5	(0.59)	1.5	(0.25)	17.5	(1.84)	18.5	(1.93)	‡	(†)	‡	(†)	6.2 !	(2.38)
2008	7.0	(0.28)	8.2	(0.40)	4.4	(0.64)	2.0	(0.28)	19.9	(1.84)	21.0	(1.96)	‡	(†)	‡	(†)	6.9 !	(2.57)
2009	7.4	(0.30)	8.9	(0.45)	4.2	(0.54)	1.9	(0.26)	21.1	(1.98)	22.9	(2.16)	‡	(†)	‡	(†)	6.5 !	(2.02)
2010	6.8	(0.26)	7.7	(0.38)	4.7	(0.60)	2.5	(0.37)	17.9	(1.87)	19.2	(1.99)	‡	(†)	‡	(†)	5.3 !	(1.63)
2011	6.9	(0.32)	8.1	(0.45)	4.0	(0.52)	2.7	(0.37)	16.7	(1.78)	17.5	(1.85)	‡	(†)	‡	(†)	6.1	(1.59)
2012	7.2	(0.35)	8.2	(0.51)	5.1	(0.66)	2.7	(0.36)	17.8	(1.85)	18.9	(1.92)	‡	(†)	2.6 !	(1.28)	4.1 !	(1.49)
2013	7.4	(0.31)	8.6	(0.50)	3.3	(0.50)	3.0	(0.37)	20.6	(1.73)	21.8	(1.79)	#	(†)	‡	(†)	4.8 !	(1.54)
2014	7.6	(0.41)	9.0	(0.58)	3.9	(0.77)	2.9	(0.43)	17.9	(1.84)	18.8	(1.92)	‡	(†)	#	(†)	7.1 !	(2.32)
2015	8.7	(0.33)	10.1	(0.51)	5.0	(0.60)	3.2	(0.41)	21.6	(1.85)	22.8	(1.97)	‡	(†)	‡	(†)	7.8	(1.79)
Males																		
High school completion or higher[2]																		
1980	85.4	(0.49)	89.1	(0.48)	74.7	(1.97)	57.0	(3.45)	—	(†)	—	(†)	—	(†)	—	(†)	—	(†)
1990	84.4	(0.56)	88.6	(0.57)	81.4	(2.03)	56.6	(2.69)	95.3	(1.78)	—	(†)	—	(†)	—	(†)	—	(†)
1995	86.3	(0.56)	92.0	(0.53)	88.4	(1.72)	55.7	(2.51)	90.5	(2.37)	—	(†)	—	(†)	—	(†)	—	(†)
2000	86.7	(0.55)	92.9	(0.51)	87.6	(1.67)	59.2	(1.76)	92.1	(1.83)	—	(†)	—	(†)	—	(†)	—	(†)
2005	85.0	(0.58)	91.8	(0.53)	86.6	(1.76)	63.2	(1.72)	96.8	(1.09)	96.7	(1.15)	‡	(†)	‡	(†)	89.1	(3.07)
2006	84.4	(0.54)	92.3	(0.52)	84.2	(2.02)	60.5	(1.64)	97.2	(1.01)	97.2	(1.06)	‡	(†)	‡	(†)	89.2	(3.81)
2007	84.9	(0.50)	92.7	(0.48)	87.4	(1.65)	60.5	(1.59)	95.9	(1.13)	96.3	(1.10)	‡	(†)	‡	(†)	92.9	(2.64)
2008	85.8	(0.54)	92.6	(0.58)	85.7	(1.99)	65.6	(1.55)	95.6	(1.23)	95.4	(1.31)	‡	(†)	‡	(†)	92.7	(2.68)
2009	87.5	(0.51)	94.4	(0.46)	88.8	(1.56)	66.2	(1.54)	96.4	(1.17)	96.2	(1.25)	‡	(†)	‡	(†)	92.0	(3.01)
2010	87.4	(0.44)	94.6	(0.42)	87.9	(1.52)	65.7	(1.52)	93.8	(1.83)	93.5	(1.95)	‡	(†)	93.2	(3.47)	87.9	(4.32)
2011	87.5	(0.49)	93.4	(0.48)	88.0	(1.43)	69.2	(1.62)	94.2	(1.30)	93.9	(1.36)	‡	(†)	84.5	(5.28)	86.2	(4.41)
2012	88.4	(0.51)	93.8	(0.50)	86.2	(1.58)	73.3	(1.57)	96.1	(1.04)	96.0	(1.09)	‡	(†)	‡	(†)	91.0	(3.58)
2013	88.3	(0.52)	93.3	(0.53)	87.8	(1.60)	73.1	(1.64)	94.4	(1.13)	94.3	(1.21)	‡	(†)	‡	(†)	96.8	(1.77)
2014	90.1	(0.53)	95.4	(0.60)	93.5	(1.18)	72.4	(1.76)	96.1	(1.10)	96.1	(1.14)	‡	(†)	‡	(†)	96.9	(2.02)
2015	90.5	(0.45)	95.1	(0.45)	91.8	(1.22)	75.7	(1.41)	95.9	(1.23)	97.1	(0.96)	75.8	(12.49)	83.2	(4.73)	98.0	(1.27)
Bachelor's or higher degree[4]																		
1980	24.0	(0.59)	26.8	(0.69)	10.5	(1.39)	8.4	(1.94)	—	(†)	—	(†)	—	(†)	—	(†)	—	(†)
1990	23.7	(0.65)	26.6	(0.79)	15.1	(1.87)	7.3	(1.41)	47.6	(4.19)	—	(†)	—	(†)	—	(†)	—	(†)
1995	24.5	(0.70)	28.4	(0.88)	17.4	(2.04)	7.8	(1.35)	42.0	(3.98)	—	(†)	—	(†)	—	(†)	—	(†)
2000	27.9	(0.73)	32.3	(0.93)	18.4	(1.96)	8.3	(0.98)	55.5	(3.37)	—	(†)	—	(†)	—	(†)	—	(†)
2005	25.5	(0.68)	30.7	(0.98)	14.2	(1.57)	10.2	(0.99)	58.5	(3.11)	61.0	(3.17)	‡	(†)	‡	(†)	24.5	(4.13)

See notes at end of table.

Table 104.20.   Percentage of persons 25 to 29 years old with selected levels of educational attainment, by race/ethnicity and sex: Selected years, 1920 through 2015—Continued

[Standard errors appear in parentheses]

Sex, selected level of educational attainment, and year	Total	White[1]	Black[1]	Hispanic	Asian/Pacific Islander Total	Asian/Pacific Islander Asian	Asian/Pacific Islander Pacific Islander	American Indian/ Alaska Native	Two or more races
1	2	3	4	5	6	7	8	9	10
2006	25.3 (0.67)	31.4 (0.98)	15.2 (1.66)	6.9 (0.70)	58.7 (3.46)	60.9 (3.52)	‡ (†)	‡ (†)	20.8 (4.65)
2007	26.3 (0.72)	31.9 (0.98)	18.9 (1.86)	8.6 (0.71)	58.5 (3.45)	60.4 (3.54)	‡ (†)	‡ (†)	23.3 (4.88)
2008	26.8 (0.64)	32.6 (0.89)	19.0 (1.94)	10.0 (0.86)	54.1 (3.41)	55.8 (3.53)	‡ (†)	‡ (†)	25.7 (4.45)
2009	26.6 (0.66)	32.6 (1.04)	14.8 (1.82)	11.0 (1.04)	55.2 (3.07)	59.2 (3.24)	‡ (†)	‡ (†)	24.6 (5.77)
2010	27.8 (0.68)	34.8 (0.96)	15.0 (1.72)	10.8 (1.06)	49.0 (3.12)	52.3 (3.31)	‡ (†)	18.9 ! (7.12)	24.9 (4.91)
2011	28.4 (0.82)	35.5 (1.16)	17.0 (1.83)	9.6 (0.90)	50.8 (3.42)	52.1 (3.55)	‡ (†)	15.4 ! (4.80)	34.1 (6.62)
2012	29.8 (0.82)	36.0 (1.06)	19.1 (1.74)	12.5 (1.20)	55.0 (3.15)	56.9 (3.16)	‡ (†)	‡ (†)	30.4 (5.44)
2013	30.2 (0.68)	37.1 (1.00)	17.4 (1.63)	13.1 (1.06)	53.0 (3.03)	55.1 (3.13)	‡ (†)	‡ (†)	29.3 (4.61)
2014	30.9 (0.93)	37.7 (1.36)	20.8 (2.40)	12.4 (1.22)	56.9 (3.55)	59.0 (3.59)	‡ (†)	‡ (†)	26.4 (6.13)
2015	32.4 (0.74)	39.5 (1.12)	17.6 (1.83)	14.5 (1.04)	60.9 (3.13)	63.8 (3.12)	‡ (†)	‡ (†)	26.7 (5.07)
Master's or higher degree									
1995	4.9 (0.35)	5.6 (0.45)	2.2 ! (0.80)	2.0 ! (0.70)	12.6 (2.68)	— (†)	— (†)	— (†)	— (†)
2000	4.7 (0.34)	4.9 (0.43)	2.1 ! (0.72)	1.5 (0.43)	17.2 (2.56)	— (†)	— (†)	— (†)	— (†)
2005	5.2 (0.38)	6.2 (0.55)	1.1 ! (0.43)	1.7 (0.46)	19.7 (3.13)	20.5 (3.30)	‡ (†)	‡ (†)	‡ (†)
2006	5.1 (0.37)	5.8 (0.51)	1.7 ! (0.52)	1.1 (0.32)	20.5 (2.68)	21.8 (2.83)	‡ (†)	‡ (†)	5.9 ! (2.66)
2007	5.0 (0.39)	5.7 (0.50)	3.3 (0.99)	0.6 ! (0.19)	18.4 (2.89)	19.3 (3.00)	‡ (†)	‡ (†)	9.8 ! (4.28)
2008	5.3 (0.34)	5.9 (0.49)	3.4 (0.90)	1.2 (0.32)	20.9 (2.94)	22.1 (3.07)	‡ (†)	‡ (†)	7.8 ! (2.85)
2009	6.1 (0.37)	7.4 (0.60)	3.2 (0.73)	1.2 (0.28)	20.4 (2.48)	22.0 (2.69)	‡ (†)	‡ (†)	5.0 ! (2.38)
2010	5.2 (0.32)	6.3 (0.50)	2.9 (0.69)	1.5 (0.39)	15.0 (2.19)	16.2 (2.36)	‡ (†)	‡ (†)	# (†)
2011	5.1 (0.38)	5.9 (0.49)	1.9 (0.54)	1.8 (0.41)	18.0 (2.58)	19.1 (2.71)	‡ (†)	‡ (†)	‡ (†)
2012	5.6 (0.42)	6.3 (0.59)	2.7 (0.72)	2.4 (0.50)	16.2 (2.46)	17.2 (2.60)	‡ (†)	‡ (†)	‡ (†)
2013	5.7 (0.38)	6.3 (0.53)	1.5 ! (0.56)	2.1 (0.43)	20.8 (2.49)	22.1 (2.60)	‡ (†)	‡ (†)	5.9 ! (2.47)
2014	5.9 (0.51)	7.0 (0.72)	2.6 ! (0.82)	2.2 (0.52)	15.9 (2.56)	16.6 (2.65)	‡ (†)	‡ (†)	‡ (†)
2015	7.0 (0.40)	8.2 (0.62)	2.5 (0.75)	2.3 (0.56)	21.1 (2.65)	22.4 (2.78)	‡ (†)	‡ (†)	5.6 ! (2.37)
Females									
High school completion or higher[2]									
1980	85.5 (0.48)	89.2 (0.48)	78.3 (1.71)	58.9 (3.38)	— (†)	— (†)	— (†)	— (†)	— (†)
1990	87.0 (0.51)	91.7 (0.49)	82.0 (1.85)	59.9 (2.79)	85.1 (2.82)	— (†)	— (†)	— (†)	— (†)
1995	87.4 (0.54)	93.0 (0.50)	85.3 (1.75)	58.7 (2.60)	91.2 (2.50)	— (†)	— (†)	— (†)	— (†)
2000	89.4 (0.49)	95.2 (0.43)	86.2 (1.53)	66.4 (1.69)	95.2 (1.39)	— (†)	— (†)	— (†)	— (†)
2005	87.4 (0.44)	93.8 (0.47)	87.3 (1.22)	63.4 (1.54)	94.6 (1.36)	94.4 (1.41)	‡ (†)	‡ (†)	94.2 (2.26)
2006	88.5 (0.44)	94.6 (0.41)	88.0 (1.14)	66.6 (1.41)	95.6 (1.44)	96.0 (1.31)	‡ (†)	90.2 (4.49)	89.4 (3.81)
2007	89.1 (0.45)	94.2 (0.44)	87.9 (1.46)	70.7 (1.30)	97.7 (1.05)	98.5 (0.68)	‡ (†)	84.2 (4.68)	87.9 (3.82)
2008	89.9 (0.39)	94.7 (0.44)	89.2 (1.43)	71.9 (1.34)	96.1 (1.12)	96.2 (1.18)	‡ (†)	83.4 (4.81)	95.9 (2.44)
2009	89.8 (0.41)	94.8 (0.44)	89.0 (1.12)	72.5 (1.34)	94.5 (1.20)	95.3 (1.18)	‡ (†)	86.8 (4.81)	84.8 (3.57)
2010	90.2 (0.39)	94.4 (0.42)	91.1 (0.96)	74.1 (1.53)	93.6 (1.25)	94.5 (1.27)	‡ (†)	86.8 (4.80)	89.1 (3.55)
2011	90.7 (0.36)	95.5 (0.42)	88.2 (1.24)	74.3 (1.26)	96.6 (0.89)	96.6 (0.92)	‡ (†)	85.3 (6.02)	94.0 (2.52)
2012	91.1 (0.44)	95.3 (0.46)	90.6 (1.11)	76.9 (1.39)	96.3 (0.98)	96.1 (1.04)	‡ (†)	85.8 (4.53)	94.7 (2.35)
2013	91.5 (0.38)	94.9 (0.43)	92.5 (0.95)	78.8 (1.17)	96.2 (0.96)	96.3 (1.01)	‡ (†)	82.0 (5.40)	98.2 (1.15)
2014	91.5 (0.50)	95.9 (0.54)	90.5 (1.62)	77.4 (1.56)	97.1 (0.96)	97.1 (0.99)	‡ (†)	84.1 (6.05)	95.2 (3.44)
2015	91.8 (0.39)	95.8 (0.41)	93.2 (0.90)	78.6 (1.34)	94.8 (1.18)	94.6 (1.25)	96.7 (1.86)	89.3 (3.52)	91.5 (2.99)
Bachelor's or higher degree[4]									
1980	21.0 (0.56)	23.2 (0.65)	12.4 (1.36)	6.9 (1.74)	— (†)	— (†)	— (†)	— (†)	— (†)
1990	22.8 (0.64)	26.2 (0.78)	11.9 (1.56)	9.1 (1.64)	37.4 (3.83)	— (†)	— (†)	— (†)	— (†)
1995	24.9 (0.70)	29.2 (0.89)	13.7 (1.70)	10.1 (1.59)	44.5 (4.38)	— (†)	— (†)	— (†)	— (†)
2000	30.1 (0.73)	35.8 (0.96)	17.4 (1.69)	11.0 (1.12)	53.1 (3.26)	— (†)	— (†)	— (†)	— (†)
2005	32.2 (0.75)	38.2 (1.00)	20.5 (1.68)	12.4 (1.07)	61.4 (3.06)	63.1 (3.11)	‡ (†)	‡ (†)	32.1 (5.70)
2006	31.6 (0.70)	37.2 (0.99)	21.7 (1.77)	12.8 (1.05)	60.4 (2.76)	62.8 (2.82)	‡ (†)	‡ (†)	25.7 (4.72)
2007	33.0 (0.72)	39.2 (1.03)	20.0 (1.38)	15.4 (1.10)	60.3 (2.83)	62.5 (2.88)	‡ (†)	‡ (†)	29.6 (5.17)
2008	34.9 (0.71)	41.7 (0.98)	21.6 (1.57)	15.5 (1.11)	61.6 (2.67)	64.4 (2.71)	‡ (†)	12.2 ! (3.69)	27.7 (5.57)
2009	34.8 (0.78)	42.0 (1.12)	22.6 (1.75)	13.8 (1.09)	57.6 (3.00)	61.3 (3.03)	‡ (†)	16.3 (4.42)	35.0 (5.07)
2010	35.7 (0.68)	42.4 (0.96)	23.3 (1.72)	16.8 (1.20)	55.8 (2.93)	58.9 (3.00)	‡ (†)	18.4 ! (6.68)	34.0 (4.96)
2011	36.1 (0.71)	43.0 (1.03)	22.9 (1.62)	16.8 (1.10)	61.0 (2.74)	62.0 (2.75)	‡ (†)	19.7 ! (6.64)	31.2 (4.36)
2012	37.2 (0.69)	43.6 (0.97)	26.7 (1.78)	17.4 (1.10)	64.0 (2.38)	66.2 (2.46)	‡ (†)	14.0 ! (4.55)	35.5 (5.50)
2013	37.0 (0.71)	43.8 (0.95)	23.2 (2.03)	18.6 (1.10)	62.4 (2.51)	64.3 (2.54)	‡ (†)	16.4 ! (6.57)	30.0 (5.26)
2014	37.2 (1.00)	43.9 (1.36)	23.8 (2.61)	18.3 (1.40)	64.3 (3.23)	66.9 (3.29)	‡ (†)	‡ (†)	38.4 (5.96)
2015	38.9 (0.74)	46.6 (1.06)	24.6 (1.72)	18.5 (1.21)	64.5 (2.74)	68.1 (2.73)	‡ (†)	21.8 (4.51)	32.9 (5.20)
Master's or higher degree									
1995	4.1 (0.32)	5.0 (0.42)	1.4 ! (0.59)	1.2 ! (0.58)	8.9 (2.50)	— (†)	— (†)	— (†)	— (†)
2000	6.2 (0.38)	6.7 (0.50)	4.9 (0.96)	2.7 (0.58)	13.9 (2.26)	— (†)	— (†)	— (†)	— (†)
2005	7.3 (0.44)	8.8 (0.64)	4.0 (0.70)	2.6 (0.51)	14.4 (2.08)	15.0 (2.15)	‡ (†)	‡ (†)	10.0 ! (4.26)
2006	7.8 (0.42)	9.2 (0.63)	4.5 (0.93)	2.0 (0.41)	19.7 (2.33)	20.4 (2.44)	‡ (†)	‡ (†)	8.3 ! (2.89)
2007	7.6 (0.43)	9.4 (0.63)	3.7 (0.66)	2.6 (0.53)	16.5 (2.39)	17.7 (2.54)	‡ (†)	‡ (†)	‡ (†)
2008	8.7 (0.44)	10.4 (0.64)	5.2 (0.87)	2.9 (0.46)	18.9 (2.30)	19.9 (2.44)	‡ (†)	‡ (†)	7.9 ! (2.84)
2009	8.8 (0.45)	10.4 (0.66)	5.1 (0.80)	2.7 (0.43)	21.7 (2.45)	23.7 (2.70)	‡ (†)	‡ (†)	10.0 ! (3.06)
2010	8.5 (0.39)	9.2 (0.56)	6.2 (0.94)	3.8 (0.56)	20.6 (2.60)	21.8 (2.75)	‡ (†)	‡ (†)	10.0 ! (3.06)
2011	8.8 (0.48)	10.4 (0.72)	5.8 (0.85)	3.8 (0.63)	15.4 (1.98)	15.9 (2.03)	‡ (†)	‡ (†)	9.9 (2.61)
2012	8.8 (0.45)	10.0 (0.67)	7.1 (1.00)	3.0 (0.45)	19.3 (2.23)	20.4 (2.31)	‡ (†)	‡ (†)	6.3 ! (2.49)
2013	9.2 (0.44)	10.8 (0.71)	4.8 (0.74)	4.0 (0.59)	20.4 (1.91)	21.6 (2.00)	‡ (†)	‡ (†)	3.3 ! (1.56)
2014	9.3 (0.56)	11.1 (0.84)	5.0 (1.17)	3.6 (0.63)	19.7 (2.33)	20.8 (2.47)	‡ (†)	# (†)	7.5 ! (3.00)
2015	10.4 (0.51)	12.0 (0.73)	7.2 (0.98)	4.1 (0.60)	22.0 (2.51)	23.2 (2.67)	‡ (†)	‡ (†)	10.2 ! (3.20)

—Not available.
†Not applicable.
#Rounds to zero.
!Interpret data with caution. The coefficient of variation (CV) for this estimate is between 30 and 50 percent.
‡Reporting standards not met. Either there are too few cases for a reliable estimate or the coefficient of variation (CV) is 50 percent or greater.
[1]Includes persons of Hispanic ethnicity for years prior to 1980.
[2]Data for years prior to 1993 are for persons with 4 or more years of high school. Data for later years are for high school completers—i.e., those persons who graduated from high school with a diploma as well as those who completed high school through equivalency programs, such as a GED program.

[3]Estimates based on Census Bureau reverse projection of 1940 census data on education by age.
[4]Data for years prior to 1993 are for persons with 4 or more years of college.
NOTE: Beginning in 2005, standard errors were computed using replicate weights, which produced more precise values than the generalized variance function methodology used in prior years. For 1960 and prior years, data were collected in April. For later years, data were collected in March. Race categories exclude persons of Hispanic ethnicity except where otherwise noted.
SOURCE: U.S. Department of Commerce, Census Bureau, U.S. Census of Population: 1960, Vol. I, Part 1; J.K. Folger and C.B. Nam, Education of the American Population (1960 Census Monograph); Current Population Reports, Series P-20, various years; and Current Population Survey (CPS), Annual Social and Economic Supplement, 1970 through 2015. (This table was prepared October 2015.)

Table 104.30. Number of persons age 18 and over, by highest level of educational attainment, sex, race/ethnicity, and age: 2015

[Numbers in thousands. Standard errors appear in parentheses]

Sex, race/ethnicity, and age	Total	Elementary school (kindergarten–8th grade)	High school — 1 to 3 years	High school — 4 years, no completion	High school — Completion[1]	Postsecondary — Some college, no degree	Postsecondary — Associate's degree	Postsecondary — Bachelor's degree	Postsecondary — Master's degree	Postsecondary — First-professional or doctor's degree
1	2	3	4	5	6	7	8	9	10	11
Total, 18 and over	**242,248** (96.9)	**10,353** (186.4)	**15,177** (209.1)	**4,130** (101.9)	**71,654** (411.7)	**46,212** (331.8)	**22,537** (242.5)	**46,515** (361.2)	**18,883** (225.6)	**6,988** (153.5)
18 and 19 years old	7,900 (82.2)	88 (14.2)	2,379 (61.6)	690 (34.6)	2,340 (68.3)	2,298 (65.1)	78 (13.7)	‡ (†)	‡ (†)	‡ (†)
20 to 24 years old	22,215 (21.7)	369 (33.8)	1,142 (56.8)	410 (33.5)	6,739 (113.8)	8,751 (137.2)	1,592 (69.2)	2,994 (103.0)	207 (23.5)	‡ (†)
25 years old and over	212,132 (45.8)	9,896 (179.2)	11,656 (185.2)	3,030 (82.3)	62,575 (382.7)	35,164 (285.3)	20,867 (213.8)	43,500 (327.7)	18,471 (223.8)	6,974 (153.9)
25 to 29 years old	21,867 (38.9)	496 (36.9)	1,048 (47.8)	384 (33.1)	5,690 (102.7)	4,259 (99.9)	2,197 (71.2)	5,889 (108.4)	1,492 (66.2)	412 (35.0)
30 to 34 years old	21,139 (35.6)	659 (36.1)	1,201 (51.0)	305 (24.3)	5,275 (96.8)	3,683 (86.2)	2,280 (63.4)	4,970 (94.9)	2,068 (75.6)	698 (48.5)
35 to 39 years old	19,916 (33.8)	923 (47.7)	1,134 (46.1)	270 (24.4)	5,134 (92.8)	3,228 (81.4)	2,049 (69.5)	4,457 (91.5)	2,002 (64.7)	719 (42.2)
40 to 49 years old	40,567 (41.6)	1,779 (63.2)	2,019 (68.2)	558 (34.2)	11,148 (148.0)	6,365 (110.9)	4,258 (84.4)	9,022 (136.2)	3,977 (105.2)	1,441 (58.6)
50 to 59 years old	43,652 (70.4)	1,818 (65.3)	2,249 (74.4)	631 (38.9)	13,581 (173.5)	7,113 (129.7)	4,724 (92.1)	8,542 (135.4)	3,624 (87.6)	1,369 (57.1)
60 to 64 years old	18,998 (113.0)	791 (40.2)	855 (48.6)	256 (26.4)	5,832 (123.3)	3,308 (87.7)	1,960 (70.3)	3,537 (89.8)	1,770 (68.8)	690 (41.1)
65 years old and over	45,994 (88.1)	3,431 (88.7)	3,150 (92.3)	626 (40.4)	15,915 (196.1)	7,207 (126.9)	3,398 (86.9)	7,082 (125.9)	3,539 (108.2)	1,645 (69.5)
Males, 18 and over	**117,051** (76.2)	**5,158** (118.1)	**7,580** (144.5)	**2,133** (72.6)	**36,008** (251.5)	**22,129** (208.1)	**9,718** (152.4)	**22,027** (222.7)	**8,221** (146.3)	**4,077** (106.8)
18 and 19 years old	3,962 (59.1)	46 (9.2)	1,246 (47.4)	381 (24.7)	1,228 (48.8)	1,019 (43.1)	‡ (†)	‡ (†)	‡ (†)	‡ (†)
20 to 24 years old	11,201 (21.1)	201 (24.2)	599 (39.6)	209 (21.3)	3,783 (79.4)	4,337 (92.9)	679 (42.9)	1,327 (67.2)	61 (11.7)	‡ (†)
25 years old and over	101,887 (44.2)	4,911 (113.9)	5,735 (129.4)	1,543 (61.6)	30,997 (234.9)	16,772 (177.0)	9,006 (139.4)	20,696 (203.7)	8,157 (145.2)	4,070 (107.3)
25 to 29 years old	10,984 (38.0)	269 (27.8)	550 (32.9)	223 (27.6)	3,286 (77.2)	2,122 (70.6)	980 (52.6)	2,783 (74.8)	599 (40.5)	172 (20.2)
30 to 34 years old	10,444 (35.3)	385 (25.8)	635 (37.4)	177 (18.4)	2,911 (64.5)	1,797 (62.4)	1,021 (44.8)	2,298 (59.3)	852 (47.2)	367 (30.3)
35 to 39 years old	9,830 (32.2)	500 (31.4)	641 (34.4)	146 (17.2)	2,799 (63.9)	1,597 (57.4)	903 (41.2)	2,071 (60.2)	839 (40.0)	334 (26.7)
40 to 49 years old	19,889 (40.1)	919 (45.7)	1,063 (48.7)	297 (26.1)	6,053 (108.3)	3,076 (73.0)	1,765 (56.7)	4,160 (84.3)	1,787 (68.8)	769 (40.0)
50 to 59 years old	21,174 (52.4)	914 (40.7)	1,237 (52.8)	336 (28.5)	6,884 (109.5)	3,323 (76.0)	2,039 (56.5)	4,000 (87.3)	1,604 (57.5)	836 (42.8)
60 to 64 years old	9,128 (105.2)	389 (25.7)	418 (31.1)	125 (16.9)	2,762 (80.9)	1,621 (62.1)	869 (44.4)	1,788 (60.9)	734 (43.3)	422 (33.4)
65 years old and over	20,439 (88.1)	1,535 (56.4)	1,191 (52.3)	240 (26.3)	6,301 (112.4)	3,236 (77.3)	1,428 (57.6)	3,596 (89.9)	1,742 (70.1)	1,170 (54.3)
Females, 18 and over	**125,197** (65.1)	**5,195** (101.4)	**7,597** (129.3)	**1,996** (62.4)	**35,646** (268.7)	**24,084** (230.8)	**12,819** (164.8)	**24,488** (238.3)	**10,462** (147.6)	**2,911** (83.1)
18 and 19 years old	3,938 (61.3)	‡ (†)	1,133 (45.4)	309 (23.9)	1,112 (44.8)	1,278 (46.7)	‡ (†)	‡ (†)	‡ (†)	‡ (†)
20 to 24 years old	11,014 (3.9)	168 (20.2)	543 (34.4)	200 (24.3)	2,956 (72.3)	4,414 (88.1)	913 (50.1)	1,668 (75.0)	146 (21.7)	‡ (†)
25 years old and over	110,245 (14.2)	4,985 (97.8)	5,921 (114.1)	1,487 (51.2)	31,578 (246.7)	18,391 (201.8)	11,861 (144.1)	22,804 (217.1)	10,314 (143.7)	2,903 (82.8)
25 to 29 years old	10,884 (36.2)	228 (21.9)	499 (34.7)	161 (18.7)	2,403 (65.8)	2,137 (60.5)	1,217 (44.1)	3,106 (73.5)	893 (50.1)	240 (24.3)
30 to 34 years old	10,695 (43.1)	273 (21.3)	566 (34.7)	128 (16.8)	2,364 (64.4)	1,886 (56.6)	1,260 (46.5)	2,672 (67.0)	1,216 (51.3)	330 (28.2)
35 to 39 years old	10,086 (7.6)	422 (27.9)	493 (28.4)	124 (15.4)	2,335 (62.0)	1,631 (51.0)	1,146 (46.9)	2,386 (58.5)	1,163 (47.2)	386 (27.0)
40 to 49 years old	20,678 (6.6)	860 (38.1)	956 (45.0)	261 (20.4)	5,095 (91.5)	3,289 (72.4)	2,493 (65.3)	4,862 (91.2)	2,190 (65.0)	672 (34.8)
50 to 59 years old	22,478 (45.3)	903 (43.1)	1,012 (43.6)	295 (24.1)	6,697 (117.2)	3,790 (93.2)	2,685 (70.2)	4,542 (91.3)	2,020 (67.6)	533 (36.8)
60 to 64 years old	9,870 (44.9)	402 (27.6)	437 (31.8)	131 (17.8)	3,070 (79.4)	1,687 (58.0)	1,091 (49.8)	1,750 (61.4)	1,035 (48.0)	267 (23.5)
65 years old and over	25,555 (0.6)	1,896 (55.9)	1,959 (67.5)	386 (29.3)	9,613 (129.3)	3,971 (99.9)	1,970 (65.5)	3,486 (89.4)	1,798 (68.2)	475 (32.9)
White, 18 and over	**157,151** (114.9)	**2,713** (107.6)	**7,273** (145.1)	**1,809** (72.8)	**46,241** (371.5)	**29,928** (284.8)	**15,957** (211.1)	**34,072** (306.4)	**13,904** (199.9)	**5,254** (137.3)
18 and 19 years old	4,293 (61.3)	‡ (†)	1,306 (46.1)	321 (25.5)	1,244 (49.3)	1,328 (52.5)	‡ (†)	‡ (†)	‡ (†)	‡ (†)
20 to 24 years old	12,219 (33.8)	143 (21.2)	409 (33.8)	126 (20.7)	3,471 (90.8)	4,857 (109.8)	955 (53.5)	2,129 (89.1)	124 (20.6)	‡ (†)
25 years old and over	140,638 (106.2)	2,536 (104.5)	5,558 (129.7)	1,362 (65.6)	41,526 (339.1)	23,743 (239.6)	14,964 (190.6)	31,927 (278.2)	13,776 (197.2)	5,247 (137.2)
25 to 29 years old	12,396 (36.2)	71 (13.0)	362 (32.2)	136 (18.9)	2,891 (78.5)	2,244 (74.5)	1,358 (58.3)	4,080 (92.0)	973 (55.5)	280 (29.6)
30 to 34 years old	12,185 (43.1)	107 (19.4)	421 (32.2)	109 (16.3)	2,682 (70.4)	2,100 (62.6)	1,530 (53.7)	3,351 (76.1)	1,401 (60.8)	484 (41.6)
35 to 39 years old	11,390 (41.2)	112 (16.7)	394 (28.6)	80 (12.1)	2,831 (77.6)	1,837 (62.8)	1,322 (65.8)	2,992 (52.7)	1,364 (88.3)	458 (34.1)
40 to 49 years old	24,868 (55.5)	255 (30.8)	748 (45.6)	204 (20.6)	6,614 (127.0)	4,060 (111.7)	2,860 (85.1)	6,362 (115.1)	2,766 (78.7)	997 (48.3)
50 to 59 years old	30,284 (52.0)	375 (31.0)	1,154 (59.5)	316 (21.0)	9,442 (152.7)	5,114 (89.0)	3,567 (61.9)	6,508 (117.5)	2,745 (64.7)	1,063 (50.3)
60 to 64 years old	13,788 (89.8)	184 (24.2)	402 (32.9)	136 (21.0)	4,201 (108.8)	2,518 (82.1)	1,543 (61.9)	2,744 (80.9)	1,486 (64.7)	574 (40.1)
65 years old and over	35,727 (91.2)	1,431 (65.7)	2,076 (73.3)	380 (35.2)	12,865 (180.6)	5,870 (118.4)	2,783 (84.6)	5,890 (121.8)	3,040 (103.3)	1,391 (63.4)
Black, 18 and over	**28,369** (81.3)	**703** (41.2)	**2,341** (73.9)	**712** (42.0)	**9,741** (146.4)	**6,490** (117.8)	**2,628** (79.2)	**3,742** (89.5)	**1,611** (65.0)	**401** (35.0)
18 and 19 years old	1,094 (35.6)	‡ (†)	379 (27.0)	106 (14.0)	328 (29.9)	252 (22.6)	‡ (†)	‡ (†)	‡ (†)	‡ (†)
20 to 24 years old	3,249 (23.7)	‡ (†)	205 (21.4)	93 (15.5)	1,153 (47.9)	1,346 (46.7)	187 (22.0)	238 (25.7)	‡ (†)	‡ (†)
25 years old and over	24,026 (64.2)	679 (40.8)	1,758 (64.4)	513 (36.6)	8,259 (130.4)	4,892 (99.6)	2,429 (75.4)	3,501 (85.6)	1,594 (64.2)	401 (35.0)
25 to 29 years old	2,858 (25.1)	‡ (†)	127 (16.1)	‡ (†)	997 (43.0)	760 (40.0)	280 (24.0)	466 (35.1)	119 (16.2)	‡ (†)
30 to 34 years old	2,585 (23.3)	‡ (†)	139 (18.5)	‡ (†)	876 (40.9)	597 (36.7)	290 (25.1)	434 (30.4)	172 (17.9)	‡ (†)
35 to 39 years old	2,482 (19.0)	62 (12.6)	121 (14.8)	95 (14.6)	765 (35.5)	550 (31.4)	291 (30.3)	446 (28.6)	209 (22.1)	‡ (†)
40 to 49 years old	4,937 (28.4)	109 (15.9)	261 (22.3)	128 (15.7)	1,698 (55.9)	971 (40.2)	527 (31.7)	777 (40.5)	422 (31.9)	124 (17.2)
50 to 59 years old	5,085 (54.5)	67 (10.4)	388 (22.8)	44 (8.1)	1,812 (53.1)	973 (39.7)	561 (31.7)	699 (35.5)	318 (27.8)	97 (13.4)
60 to 64 years old	2,066 (52.0)	‡ (†)	209 (21.3)	‡ (†)	710 (34.8)	401 (25.6)	193 (18.4)	271 (23.4)	132 (16.3)	‡ (†)
65 years old and over	4,013 (24.2)	374 (28.1)	513 (31.1)	101 (14.3)	1,400 (46.4)	641 (31.5)	286 (23.2)	407 (28.4)	221 (19.4)	69 (13.0)

See notes at end of table.

Table 104.30. Number of persons age 18 and over, by highest level of educational attainment, sex, race/ethnicity, and age: 2015—Continued

[Numbers in thousands. Standard errors appear in parentheses]

Sex, race/ethnicity, and age	Total	Elementary school (kindergarten–8th grade)	High school			Postsecondary education					
			1 to 3 years	4 years, no completion	Completion[1]	Some college, no degree	Associate's degree	Bachelor's degree	Master's degree	First-professional or doctor's degree
1	2	3	4	5	6	7	8	9	10	11
Hispanic, 18 and over	**37,509** (44.1)	**6,040** (133.4)	**4,546** (111.7)	**1,295** (58.6)	**11,529** (140.5)	**6,440** (113.9)	**2,565** (77.5)	**3,511** (85.2)	**1,099** (46.2)	**384** (27.6)
18 and 19 years old	1,771 (39.3)	‡ (†)	473 (25.9)	213 (20.2)	587 (32.5)	440 (23.3)	‡ (†)	‡ (†)	‡ (†)	‡ (†)
20 to 24 years old	4,717 (7.4)	198 (25.2)	466 (32.2)	155 (17.2)	1,685 (49.2)	1,603 (46.8)	322 (28.4)	270 (22.4)	‡ (†)	‡ (†)
25 years old and over	31,020 (13.0)	5,806 (124.9)	3,607 (95.9)	927 (49.3)	9,257 (121.3)	4,397 (99.5)	2,225 (65.5)	3,338 (80.9)	1,085 (46.4)	378 (27.8)
25 to 29 years old	4,487 (30.7)	366 (30.6)	496 (33.0)	166 (18.7)	1,399 (49.0)	907 (43.6)	416 (31.9)	595 (33.2)	120 (17.3)	‡ (†)
30 to 34 years old	4,307 (28.8)	518 (33.5)	563 (34.2)	140 (15.3)	1,366 (44.9)	697 (34.4)	307 (21.6)	513 (29.3)	154 (18.9)	50 (9.4)
35 to 39 years old	4,172 (30.6)	755 (40.4)	568 (36.8)	125 (15.5)	1,222 (40.3)	582 (35.2)	292 (23.5)	440 (28.8)	132 (14.7)	56 (9.9)
40 to 49 years old	7,246 (38.9)	1,361 (52.3)	880 (43.3)	217 (20.2)	2,125 (54.3)	936 (41.2)	535 (33.2)	814 (39.8)	292 (22.5)	87 (12.2)
50 to 59 years old	5,302 (46.8)	1,166 (51.8)	544 (30.2)	135 (15.6)	1,593 (54.0)	658 (34.7)	365 (26.2)	553 (29.0)	212 (21.2)	76 (11.6)
60 to 64 years old	1,870 (39.3)	437 (27.2)	178 (19.4)	59 (10.9)	576 (29.8)	225 (17.8)	127 (14.8)	184 (17.7)	56 (8.8)	‡ (†)
65 years old and over	3,636 (5.5)	1,204 (41.6)	378 (25.6)	85 (12.0)	976 (35.7)	392 (22.7)	183 (18.3)	239 (20.1)	120 (15.1)	60 (10.2)
Asian, 18 and over	**13,723** (106.4)	**754** (43.7)	**512** (33.4)	**208** (24.0)	**2,516** (84.4)	**1,974** (65.0)	**850** (40.3)	**4,247** (89.9)	**1,806** (67.9)	**857** (47.9)
18 and 19 years old	379 (21.2)	‡ (†)	77 (10.9)	‡ (†)	80 (10.9)	188 (16.0)	‡ (†)	‡ (†)	‡ (†)	‡ (†)
20 to 24 years old	1,268 (29.6)	‡ (†)	‡ (†)	‡ (†)	162 (20.2)	643 (33.9)	69 (13.0)	295 (26.2)	‡ (†)	‡ (†)
25 years old and over	12,077 (96.6)	740 (43.1)	418 (32.6)	159 (20.9)	2,274 (81.9)	1,143 (53.0)	776 (36.9)	3,952 (85.6)	1,760 (65.9)	855 (47.9)
25 to 29 years old	1,451 (30.9)	‡ (†)	‡ (†)	‡ (†)	202 (24.3)	147 (15.7)	83 (12.6)	627 (32.2)	256 (27.2)	75 (13.8)
30 to 34 years old	1,501 (34.9)	‡ (†)	‡ (†)	‡ (†)	189 (19.1)	165 (19.4)	96 (13.6)	543 (27.7)	306 (27.6)	135 (17.5)
35 to 39 years old	1,372 (39.0)	‡ (†)	‡ (†)	‡ (†)	181 (19.7)	124 (14.7)	99 (12.5)	484 (30.8)	260 (23.1)	164 (21.4)
40 to 49 years old	2,622 (51.0)	88 (13.6)	77 (13.8)	‡ (†)	478 (33.2)	181 (20.2)	210 (19.9)	899 (43.4)	448 (34.0)	214 (20.1)
50 to 59 years old	2,206 (53.8)	143 (18.3)	87 (14.6)	‡ (†)	473 (30.9)	235 (21.0)	136 (16.8)	666 (37.7)	301 (22.2)	120 (15.3)
60 to 64 years old	932 (36.5)	92 (14.6)	53 (11.1)	‡ (†)	239 (23.4)	99 (13.3)	65 (10.2)	262 (22.6)	72 (12.3)	43 (10.0)
65 years old and over	1,994 (37.8)	357 (31.3)	115 (16.8)	‡ (†)	511 (31.9)	191 (19.8)	86 (11.8)	470 (31.2)	117 (14.7)	105 (17.1)

†Not applicable.
‡Reporting standards not met. Either there are too few cases for a reliable estimate or the coefficient of variation (CV) is 50 percent or greater.
[1]Includes completion of high school through equivalency programs, such as a GED program.

NOTE: Total includes other racial/ethnic groups not shown separately. Race categories exclude persons of Hispanic ethnicity. Detail may not sum to totals because of rounding. Standard errors were computed using replicate weights.
SOURCE: U.S. Department of Commerce, Census Bureau, Current Population Survey (CPS), Annual Social and Economic Supplement, 2015. (This table was prepared November 2015.)

Table 104.40. Percentage of persons 18 to 24 years old and age 25 and over, by educational attainment, race/ethnicity, and selected racial/ethnic subgroups: 2009 and 2014

[Standard errors appear in parentheses]

Column groupings: Columns 2–8 = **18 to 24 years old**; Columns 9–14 = **Age 25 and over**. Within each age group, "High school completion[1] or higher" is broken into its components, and "At least some college" (18–24) is further broken out.

Year and race/ethnicity (1)	Less than high school completion (2)	Total, high school or higher (3)	High school only (4)	Total, at least some college (5)	Some college, no degree (6)	Associate's degree (7)	Bachelor's or higher degree (8)	Less than high school completion (9)	Total, high school or higher (10)	High school only (11)	Some college, no degree (12)	Associate's degree (13)	Bachelor's or higher degree (14)
2009													
Total[2]	16.4 (0.11)	83.6 (0.11)	30.2 (0.11)	53.4 (0.15)	39.7 (0.14)	4.7 (0.05)	9.0 (0.08)	14.7 (0.04)	85.3 (0.04)	28.5 (0.04)	21.4 (0.04)	7.5 (0.02)	27.9 (0.06)
White	11.7 (0.10)	88.3 (0.10)	29.2 (0.14)	59.1 (0.16)	42.6 (0.18)	5.4 (0.07)	11.2 (0.11)	9.6 (0.04)	90.4 (0.04)	29.3 (0.05)	22.0 (0.04)	8.0 (0.02)	31.1 (0.06)
Black	21.7 (0.27)	78.3 (0.27)	33.0 (0.36)	45.3 (0.39)	37.6 (0.36)	3.1 (0.12)	4.6 (0.12)	18.4 (0.11)	81.6 (0.11)	31.6 (0.14)	25.0 (0.12)	7.3 (0.06)	17.7 (0.12)
Hispanic	28.9 (0.32)	71.1 (0.32)	32.8 (0.25)	38.3 (0.32)	30.7 (0.29)	3.7 (0.10)	3.8 (0.11)	39.1 (0.16)	60.9 (0.16)	26.0 (0.11)	16.9 (0.10)	5.3 (0.06)	12.7 (0.11)
Cuban	13.4 (1.31)	86.6 (1.31)	31.4 (1.57)	55.2 (1.53)	37.0 (1.68)	3.8 (0.79)	14.4 (0.84)	24.4 (0.55)	75.6 (0.55)	27.4 (0.58)	15.8 (0.41)	8.6 (0.35)	23.8 (0.54)
Dominican	22.1 (1.55)	77.9 (1.55)	28.4 (1.52)	49.5 (1.65)	38.0 (1.58)	5.0 (0.72)	6.5 (0.83)	36.4 (0.74)	63.6 (0.74)	25.4 (0.73)	17.4 (0.55)	6.0 (0.35)	14.8 (0.67)
Mexican	30.8 (0.37)	69.2 (0.37)	34.6 (0.30)	35.0 (0.35)	28.9 (0.34)	3.2 (0.12)	2.9 (0.15)	44.8 (0.18)	55.2 (0.18)	25.8 (0.15)	15.9 (0.12)	4.4 (0.07)	9.0 (0.12)
Puerto Rican	14.6 (0.79)	85.4 (0.79)	26.7 (0.77)	58.7 (0.84)	46.4 (0.79)	4.2 (0.37)	8.1 (0.41)	27.2 (0.34)	72.8 (0.34)	28.9 (0.39)	25.7 (0.30)	8.1 (0.21)	15.6 (0.30)
Spaniard	24.6 (2.04)	75.4 (2.04)	26.5 (2.54)	48.9 (3.06)	36.3 (2.98)	3.4 (0.76)	9.2 (1.39)	11.7 (0.60)	88.3 (0.60)	22.8 (0.77)	20.8 (0.83)	4.0 (0.54)	31.7 (0.93)
Central American[3]	38.7 (0.88)	61.3 (0.88)	26.5 (0.86)	34.8 (0.92)	27.5 (0.84)	3.5 (0.31)	3.8 (0.35)	47.0 (0.49)	53.0 (0.49)	23.0 (0.40)	14.0 (0.32)	4.0 (0.16)	11.0 (0.28)
Costa Rican	21.2 (5.23)	78.8 (5.23)	24.5 (5.60)	54.4 (5.62)	23.3 (5.02)	8.4 (3.09)	22.7 (3.20)	17.9 (2.02)	82.1 (2.02)	23.9 (2.14)	23.0 (1.90)	7.0 (1.10)	25.0 (1.88)
Guatemalan	51.2 (1.59)	48.8 (1.59)	24.2 (1.48)	24.5 (1.54)	19.2 (1.38)	2.7 (0.52)	2.6 (0.58)	55.2 (1.01)	44.8 (1.01)	21.2 (0.87)	12.0 (0.55)	3.2 (0.30)	8.4 (0.50)
Honduran	44.3 (2.90)	55.7 (2.90)	26.0 (2.73)	29.7 (2.21)	23.1 (2.25)	2.6 (0.73)	4.1 (0.96)	49.3 (1.30)	50.7 (1.30)	24.1 (0.96)	12.4 (0.91)	4.3 (0.50)	9.9 (0.78)
Nicaraguan	17.5 (2.26)	82.5 (2.26)	29.1 (2.64)	53.4 (2.45)	39.6 (2.45)	7.2 (1.68)	6.6 (1.50)	24.5 (1.31)	75.5 (1.31)	29.8 (1.60)	18.0 (1.13)	7.3 (0.80)	20.4 (1.12)
Panamanian	10.5 (3.21)	89.5 (3.21)	28.4 (4.31)	61.1 (5.01)	47.2 (5.88)	6.2 (1.95)	7.8 (2.61)	9.5 (1.15)	90.5 (1.15)	25.5 (1.86)	25.9 (2.01)	7.7 (0.75)	31.4 (1.94)
Salvadoran	36.1 (1.36)	63.9 (1.36)	27.5 (1.00)	36.5 (1.16)	30.1 (1.31)	3.2 (0.51)	3.1 (0.44)	53.3 (0.67)	46.7 (0.67)	23.6 (0.47)	12.7 (0.47)	3.1 (0.22)	7.3 (0.34)
South American	14.3 (0.89)	85.7 (0.89)	28.3 (1.41)	57.5 (1.41)	42.7 (1.18)	6.5 (0.53)	8.2 (0.73)	17.4 (0.41)	82.6 (0.41)	26.3 (0.58)	19.8 (0.45)	7.5 (0.27)	29.0 (0.40)
Chilean	9.6 (2.74)	90.4 (2.74)	21.5 (4.23)	68.9 (5.05)	56.3 (5.07)	7.4 (3.49)	5.3 (2.11)	10.6 (1.26)	89.4 (1.26)	25.9 (1.92)	20.0 (1.93)	9.2 (1.11)	34.3 (2.14)
Colombian	13.8 (1.26)	86.2 (1.26)	29.7 (1.88)	56.6 (1.82)	41.0 (2.03)	7.6 (0.99)	7.9 (1.11)	15.7 (0.69)	84.3 (0.69)	27.0 (0.82)	20.3 (0.66)	7.7 (0.49)	29.3 (0.67)
Ecuadorian	21.4 (2.69)	78.6 (2.69)	26.0 (2.56)	52.6 (3.09)	39.4 (2.87)	7.2 (1.42)	6.1 (1.19)	31.2 (1.24)	68.8 (1.24)	26.7 (1.02)	18.4 (0.97)	6.1 (0.54)	17.6 (0.83)
Peruvian	9.7 (1.39)	90.3 (1.39)	27.8 (2.73)	62.5 (2.98)	50.2 (2.90)	3.9 (1.05)	8.3 (1.27)	12.0 (0.68)	88.0 (0.68)	30.4 (0.99)	20.7 (1.28)	7.5 (0.87)	29.4 (1.04)
Venezuelan	9.8 (2.53)	90.2 (2.53)	25.5 (4.53)	64.7 (4.93)	41.2 (4.56)	9.9 (2.90)	13.6 (3.42)	8.3 (1.12)	91.7 (1.12)	15.8 (1.18)	17.6 (1.01)	10.8 (0.58)	47.5 (1.91)
Other South American	13.9 (2.32)	86.1 (2.32)	33.2 (2.59)	52.9 (3.34)	37.5 (3.29)	4.6 (1.10)	11.2 (1.66)	15.0 (0.97)	85.0 (0.97)	24.7 (1.13)	19.7 (0.87)	7.0 (0.58)	33.6 (1.19)
Other Hispanic	23.4 (1.30)	76.6 (1.30)	30.6 (1.35)	46.0 (1.53)	38.0 (1.49)	4.0 (0.57)	4.1 (0.60)	23.5 (0.59)	76.5 (0.59)	29.0 (0.59)	24.4 (0.62)	6.8 (0.34)	16.4 (0.44)
Asian	8.8 (0.29)	91.2 (0.29)	20.7 (0.37)	70.5 (0.43)	46.6 (0.57)	5.0 (0.26)	19.0 (0.44)	14.6 (0.14)	85.4 (0.14)	16.0 (0.20)	13.0 (0.13)	6.6 (0.10)	49.9 (0.23)
Chinese[4]	6.5 (0.55)	93.5 (0.55)	18.2 (0.72)	75.3 (0.83)	49.2 (1.19)	2.9 (0.38)	23.2 (0.86)	18.7 (0.37)	81.3 (0.37)	14.7 (0.36)	8.8 (0.24)	5.9 (0.22)	51.9 (0.46)
Filipino	7.9 (0.70)	92.1 (0.70)	23.3 (1.14)	68.8 (1.27)	48.0 (1.48)	8.0 (0.67)	12.8 (0.90)	7.8 (0.22)	92.2 (0.22)	14.8 (0.32)	20.1 (0.32)	9.2 (0.29)	48.0 (0.48)
Japanese	7.1 (1.29)	92.9 (1.29)	22.2 (2.38)	70.8 (2.51)	46.0 (2.83)	8.3 (1.88)	16.4 (1.89)	5.6 (0.27)	94.4 (0.27)	20.9 (0.57)	16.3 (0.52)	9.6 (0.37)	47.5 (0.66)
Korean	8.7 (1.03)	91.3 (1.03)	18.4 (1.19)	72.8 (1.42)	53.4 (1.33)	3.7 (0.64)	15.8 (1.21)	9.3 (0.39)	90.7 (0.39)	19.6 (0.61)	13.8 (0.47)	5.9 (0.27)	52.3 (0.72)
South Asian[5]	7.8 (0.65)	92.2 (0.65)	16.1 (0.84)	76.2 (1.09)	41.3 (1.40)	4.7 (0.51)	30.1 (1.25)	8.4 (0.27)	91.6 (0.27)	10.8 (0.37)	7.4 (0.23)	4.1 (0.18)	68.4 (0.56)
Asian Indian	6.6 (0.62)	93.4 (0.62)	15.8 (0.92)	77.6 (1.09)	40.0 (1.40)	4.2 (0.54)	33.3 (1.40)	8.4 (0.30)	91.6 (0.30)	10.1 (0.37)	6.8 (0.26)	3.8 (0.18)	70.8 (0.56)
Bangladeshi	17.3 (6.46)	82.7 (6.46)	20.4 (4.11)	62.3 (6.84)	40.4 (6.65)	9.1 (2.78)	12.8 (4.66)	19.4 (2.21)	80.6 (2.21)	14.4 (1.69)	10.6 (2.27)	4.5 (0.86)	51.1 (2.76)
Bhutanese	— (†)	— (†)	— (†)	— (†)	— (†)	— (†)	— (†)	— (†)	— (†)	— (†)	— (†)	— (†)	— (†)
Nepalese	— (†)	— (†)	— (†)	— (†)	— (†)	— (†)	— (†)	— (†)	— (†)	— (†)	— (†)	— (†)	— (†)
Pakistani	12.1 (2.28)	87.9 (2.28)	18.5 (2.49)	69.4 (3.01)	45.9 (3.05)	7.1 (2.01)	16.4 (2.32)	14.2 (0.97)	85.8 (0.97)	15.8 (1.29)	11.2 (0.88)	5.7 (0.71)	53.0 (1.71)
Southeast Asian	13.1 (0.88)	86.9 (0.88)	28.1 (1.34)	58.8 (1.44)	43.6 (1.36)	4.9 (0.60)	10.2 (0.67)	30.3 (0.51)	69.7 (0.51)	21.8 (0.55)	16.0 (0.40)	7.5 (0.29)	24.5 (0.44)
Burmese	— (†)	— (†)	— (†)	— (†)	— (†)	— (†)	— (†)	— (†)	— (†)	— (†)	— (†)	— (†)	— (†)
Cambodian	19.9 (2.85)	80.1 (2.85)	39.0 (3.59)	41.0 (3.55)	32.2 (2.89)	4.5 (1.53)	4.4 (1.28)	39.0 (1.80)	61.0 (1.80)	24.8 (1.62)	16.9 (1.18)	6.3 (0.67)	13.0 (1.15)
Hmong	17.1 (2.54)	82.9 (2.54)	36.5 (3.15)	46.4 (3.28)	36.0 (2.89)	4.8 (1.17)	5.6 (1.64)	37.3 (2.30)	62.7 (2.30)	23.4 (1.94)	18.0 (1.54)	7.9 (1.17)	13.5 (1.80)
Laotian	16.3 (2.71)	83.7 (2.71)	35.0 (3.73)	48.7 (4.18)	37.8 (4.16)	6.0 (2.05)	4.9 (1.87)	30.0 (2.54)	70.0 (2.54)	27.5 (1.79)	16.5 (1.21)	6.2 (0.96)	11.4 (1.16)
Thai	7.8 (3.19)	92.2 (3.19)	19.9 (4.41)	72.3 (5.05)	49.7 (5.01)	5.8 (0.93)	16.6 (3.42)	18.7 (1.36)	81.3 (1.36)	16.8 (1.25)	12.9 (0.48)	6.6 (0.37)	44.9 (1.84)
Vietnamese	10.7 (1.16)	89.3 (1.16)	22.6 (1.59)	66.7 (1.93)	45.9 (2.02)	7.4 (1.42)	13.3 (1.01)	18.9 (0.59)	81.1 (0.59)	21.5 (0.66)	14.1 (0.73)	7.9 (0.37)	24.5 (0.52)
Other Southeast Asian[6]	0.9 (0.91)	99.1 (0.91)	19.0 (1.97)	80.2 (4.60)	59.6 (6.60)	4.2	16.3 (4.38)	8.8 (2.64)	91.2 (2.64)	15.2 (1.80)	14.3 (1.68)	8.0 (1.45)	53.8 (2.77)
Other Asian	12.9 (1.41)	87.1 (1.41)	19.4 (1.97)	67.7 (2.29)	45.9 (2.74)	8.4	13.4 (1.68)	18.5 (1.05)	81.5 (1.05)	16.4 (0.98)	16.1 (0.73)	6.5 (0.59)	44.4 (1.27)
Pacific Islander	17.9 (2.21)	82.1 (2.21)	39.8 (2.64)	42.4 (3.33)	34.3 (2.68)	3.1 (1.09)	4.9 (1.54)	19.6 (0.81)	80.4 (0.81)	37.4 (0.95)	26.1 (1.14)	7.7 (0.59)	14.4 (0.83)
American Indian/Alaska Native	27.0 (1.06)	73.0 (1.06)	36.6 (1.04)	36.4 (1.19)	29.4 (1.11)	3.6 (0.50)	3.4 (0.49)	19.6 (0.45)	80.4 (0.45)	31.7 (0.55)	28.1 (0.50)	7.8 (0.32)	13.7 (0.33)
Two or more races	15.1 (0.69)	84.9 (0.69)	32.0 (0.76)	52.9 (0.93)	41.0 (0.78)	4.5 (0.36)	7.5 (0.46)	14.4 (0.29)	85.6 (0.29)	25.1 (0.35)	27.8 (0.39)	9.1 (0.23)	26.1 (0.36)
White and Black	17.6 (1.30)	82.4 (1.30)	34.4 (1.67)	48.0 (1.71)	40.4 (1.79)	3.4 (0.60)	4.2 (0.68)	19.6 (0.87)	80.4 (0.87)	24.1 (1.09)	24.7 (0.97)	9.7 (0.64)	27.9 (1.14)
White and Asian	8.5 (0.85)	91.5 (0.85)	25.4 (1.44)	66.6 (1.53)	45.4 (1.64)	6.5 (0.97)	14.6 (1.14)	4.7 (0.40)	95.3 (0.40)	16.4 (0.75)	28.6 (0.81)	9.1 (0.55)	45.0 (0.88)
White and American Indian/Alaska Native	18.5 (1.28)	81.5 (1.28)	34.4 (1.53)	47.1 (1.87)	39.5 (1.70)	3.9 (0.58)	3.7 (0.69)	14.9 (0.48)	85.1 (0.48)	29.2 (0.57)	24.7 (0.55)	8.8 (0.37)	18.5 (0.47)
Other Two or more races	14.8 (1.25)	85.2 (1.25)	32.7 (1.59)	52.5 (1.66)	41.3 (1.45)	4.4 (0.76)	6.8 (0.99)	11.2 (0.47)	88.8 (0.47)	25.0 (0.59)	29.7 (0.74)	9.4 (0.37)	24.8 (0.64)

See notes at end of table.

Table 104.40. Percentage of persons 18 to 24 years old and age 25 and over, by educational attainment, race/ethnicity, and selected racial/ethnic subgroups: 2009 and 2014—Continued

[Standard errors appear in parentheses]

Year and race/ethnicity	18 to 24 years old							Age 25 and over					
	Less than high school completion	Total, high school or higher	High school only	Total, at least some college	Some college, no degree	Associate's degree	Bachelor's or higher degree	Less than high school completion	Total, high school or higher	High school only	Some college, no degree	Associate's degree	Bachelor's or higher degree
1	2	3	4	5	6	7	8	9	10	11	12	13	14
2014													
Total²	13.8 (0.08)	86.2 (0.08)	30.2 (0.11)	56.0 (0.11)	40.8 (0.14)	5.1 (0.06)	10.1 (0.08)	13.1 (0.04)	86.9 (0.04)	27.7 (0.05)	21.0 (0.04)	8.2 (0.03)	30.1 (0.06)
White	10.6 (0.09)	89.4 (0.09)	29.0 (0.14)	60.3 (0.16)	42.1 (0.20)	5.8 (0.07)	12.4 (0.11)	8.0 (0.03)	92.0 (0.03)	23.2 (0.15)	25.5 (0.05)	8.7 (0.03)	33.6 (0.06)
Black	17.6 (0.26)	82.4 (0.26)	33.3 (0.35)	49.1 (0.39)	40.0 (0.37)	3.6 (0.12)	5.5 (0.16)	15.5 (0.09)	84.5 (0.09)	31.7 (0.15)	25.0 (0.12)	8.1 (0.08)	19.8 (0.12)
Hispanic	20.8 (0.20)	79.2 (0.20)	33.1 (0.26)	46.1 (0.28)	36.8 (0.26)	4.4 (0.11)	4.9 (0.12)	34.6 (0.16)	65.4 (0.16)	27.1 (0.11)	17.9 (0.10)	6.0 (0.06)	14.4 (0.10)
Cuban	15.0 (1.19)	85.0 (1.19)	30.3 (1.61)	54.7 (1.46)	37.6 (1.41)	7.9 (0.85)	9.2 (0.85)	19.7 (0.45)	80.3 (0.45)	29.9 (0.62)	17.0 (0.41)	8.1 (0.31)	25.5 (0.53)
Dominican	18.8 (1.03)	81.2 (1.03)	28.7 (1.27)	52.5 (1.29)	36.9 (1.38)	6.4 (0.84)	9.2 (0.62)	30.5 (0.77)	69.5 (0.77)	26.0 (0.69)	18.0 (0.53)	7.5 (0.43)	18.1 (0.59)
Mexican	21.1 (0.24)	78.9 (0.24)	34.8 (0.30)	44.1 (0.33)	36.4 (0.31)	3.8 (0.10)	3.9 (0.14)	40.1 (0.21)	59.9 (0.21)	27.3 (0.17)	17.1 (0.12)	5.1 (0.08)	10.4 (0.11)
Puerto Rican	19.5 (0.78)	80.5 (0.78)	34.2 (0.88)	46.4 (0.90)	35.5 (0.78)	5.2 (0.44)	5.7 (0.38)	22.5 (0.43)	77.5 (0.43)	29.3 (0.42)	21.7 (0.33)	8.6 (0.23)	18.0 (0.36)
Spaniard	12.0 (1.69)	88.0 (1.69)	26.7 (2.20)	61.3 (2.91)	47.0 (3.00)	5.1 (0.88)	9.2 (1.53)	10.2 (0.56)	89.8 (0.56)	20.5 (0.80)	25.1 (0.89)	9.9 (0.61)	34.3 (0.91)
Central American³	29.6 (1.01)	70.4 (1.01)	30.1 (0.89)	40.2 (0.82)	31.8 (0.81)	3.9 (0.30)	4.5 (0.39)	44.1 (0.54)	55.9 (0.54)	28.4 (0.42)	14.7 (0.17)	4.8 (0.17)	11.8 (0.17)
Costa Rican	12.0 (4.00)	87.8 (4.00)	29.5 (5.43)	58.3 (6.07)	46.5 (5.71)	2.4 ! (0.47)	9.4 ! (3.07)	15.2 (1.77)	84.8 (1.77)	21.8 (2.14)	22.7 (1.67)	6.1 (0.97)	27.5 (2.08)
Guatemalan	40.2 (1.80)	59.8 (1.80)	27.9 (1.74)	31.9 (1.43)	25.1 (1.37)	2.6 (0.78)	4.2 (0.62)	53.6 (0.93)	46.4 (0.93)	26.5 (0.73)	12.2 (0.55)	4.1 (0.39)	8.3 (0.46)
Honduran	32.5 (2.41)	67.5 (2.41)	28.9 (2.19)	38.6 (2.46)	31.4 (2.40)	3.6 (0.88)	3.6 (0.88)	46.9 (1.08)	53.1 (1.08)	27.7 (1.09)	13.4 (0.68)	3.7 (0.36)	9.4 (0.68)
Nicaraguan	15.1 (1.99)	84.9 (1.99)	23.5 (2.75)	61.4 (3.12)	44.7 (3.11)	10.6 (2.25)	6.1 (1.16)	23.4 (1.39)	76.6 (1.39)	20.8 (1.19)	19.3 (1.06)	8.0 (0.66)	21.5 (1.16)
Panamanian	3.6 ! (1.18)	96.4 (1.18)	34.9 (3.88)	61.5 (3.92)	44.4 (4.30)	5.8 ! (1.82)	11.3 (2.73)	9.0 (1.03)	90.8 (1.03)	25.7 (1.87)	26.5 (1.68)	11.7 (1.29)	31.9 (1.73)
Salvadoran	28.2 (1.53)	71.8 (1.53)	32.1 (1.33)	39.5 (1.54)	31.6 (1.36)	3.9 (0.49)	4.0 (0.57)	48.1 (0.87)	51.9 (0.87)	24.8 (0.62)	12.9 (0.44)	4.0 (0.24)	9.2 (0.41)
South American	10.8 (0.79)	89.2 (0.79)	24.1 (0.85)	65.1 (1.06)	46.5 (1.11)	7.5 (0.65)	11.1 (0.84)	14.6 (0.36)	85.4 (0.36)	23.0 (0.47)	24.4 (0.35)	8.2 (0.22)	32.4 (0.45)
Chilean	6.4 ! (2.96)	93.6 (2.96)	28.9 (5.22)	67.9 (5.11)	43.7 (5.48)	8.6 ! (3.67)	15.6 (3.80)	9.9 (1.31)	90.1 (1.31)	25.6 (1.95)	18.8 (1.89)	7.1 (0.82)	35.6 (2.66)
Colombian	9.3 (1.28)	90.7 (1.28)	22.8 (1.64)	68.0 (3.20)	50.8 (1.93)	6.1 (1.23)	11.1 (1.17)	14.1 (0.57)	85.9 (0.57)	27.8 (1.07)	17.0 (0.70)	9.0 (0.40)	32.5 (0.67)
Ecuadorian	15.4 (1.68)	84.6 (1.68)	26.8 (2.24)	57.8 (3.20)	40.0 (2.69)	8.6 (1.38)	9.2 (1.46)	27.1 (1.35)	72.9 (1.35)	27.1 (1.07)	17.9 (0.92)	7.2 (0.65)	20.8 (0.79)
Peruvian	11.8 (1.97)	88.2 (1.97)	23.6 (2.41)	64.7 (2.99)	44.7 (3.14)	9.0 (1.70)	11.0 (1.84)	9.4 (0.64)	90.6 (0.64)	26.7 (0.91)	17.9 (1.19)	8.9 (0.66)	30.4 (0.96)
Venezuelan	7.6 (1.90)	92.4 (1.90)	24.2 (2.99)	68.3 (2.89)	50.1 (3.18)	3.6 (1.97)	14.6 (2.61)	5.4 (0.62)	94.6 (0.62)	14.4 (1.19)	20.7 (0.92)	9.0 (0.90)	53.2 (1.53)
Other South American	10.7 (1.90)	89.3 (1.90)	22.7 (2.54)	66.6 (2.83)	50.8 (2.47)	3.6 (1.02)	10.4 (1.75)	13.1 (0.89)	86.9 (0.89)	23.2 (1.15)	23.6 (0.96)	6.7 (0.56)	36.4 (1.27)
Other Hispanic	19.8 (1.15)	80.2 (1.15)	28.9 (1.42)	51.3 (1.62)	39.9 (1.81)	5.4 (0.63)	6.0 (0.73)	21.1 (0.61)	78.9 (0.61)	29.1 (0.66)	23.6 (0.62)	8.0 (0.33)	18.2 (0.57)
Asian	7.7 (0.27)	92.3 (0.27)	20.0 (0.39)	72.3 (0.44)	45.3 (0.49)	4.8 (0.17)	22.2 (0.43)	13.6 (0.12)	86.4 (0.12)	15.3 (0.15)	12.6 (0.14)	6.8 (0.09)	51.7 (0.22)
Chinese⁴	4.8 (0.36)	95.2 (0.36)	18.0 (0.63)	77.2 (0.60)	43.9 (1.12)	3.3 (0.37)	29.9 (1.01)	17.4 (0.31)	82.6 (0.31)	14.2 (0.30)	8.6 (0.23)	5.8 (0.15)	54.0 (0.42)
Filipino	7.8 (0.77)	92.2 (0.77)	22.6 (0.97)	69.6 (1.27)	46.9 (1.36)	8.0 (0.65)	14.7 (1.03)	4.5 (0.25)	95.5 (0.31)	14.8 (0.37)	20.0 (0.40)	9.9 (0.29)	48.2 (0.51)
Japanese	4.1 (1.16)	95.9 (1.16)	22.4 (2.82)	73.5 (2.88)	55.7 (2.84)	3.4 ! (1.09)	14.4 (1.96)	7.2 (0.32)	92.8 (0.32)	19.2 (0.65)	15.6 (0.53)	10.1 (0.48)	50.6 (0.69)
Korean	6.4 (0.76)	93.6 (0.76)	16.8 (1.19)	76.9 (1.31)	53.6 (1.74)	5.4 (0.65)	17.9 (1.39)	10.2 (0.29)	89.8 (0.26)	18.5 (0.31)	14.4 (0.48)	6.2 (0.27)	53.8 (0.66)
South Asian⁵	8.7 (0.70)	91.3 (0.70)	17.2 (0.78)	74.1 (0.93)	41.1 (1.00)	4.5 (0.42)	28.5 (1.13)	8.4 (0.25)	91.6 (0.29)	10.0 (0.31)	7.2 (0.22)	4.1 (0.16)	68.4 (0.41)
Asian Indian	6.2 (0.62)	93.8 (0.62)	15.3 (0.94)	78.5 (1.12)	40.9 (1.22)	4.1 (0.47)	33.4 (1.34)	15.8 (0.25)	84.2 (0.25)	8.9 (0.29)	6.6 (0.22)	3.5 (0.16)	72.6 (0.41)
Bangladeshi	11.3 (3.10)	88.7 (3.10)	17.1 (2.77)	71.6 (3.74)	48.8 (4.71)	8.2 ! (2.86)	14.6 (3.25)	15.8 (1.63)	84.2 (1.63)	17.7 (2.00)	11.2 (1.28)	8.6 (1.51)	46.8 (2.07)
Bhutanese	‡ (†)	† (†)	† (†)	† (†)	† (†)	† (†)	† (†)	59.0 (6.93)	41.0 (6.93)	22.1 (4.85)	9.7 ! (3.13)	5.1 ! (1.72)	4.1 ! (1.86)
Nepalese	40.2 (6.90)	59.8 (6.90)	17.9 (3.83)	41.9 (6.63)	27.5 (5.26)	4.2 ! (1.93)	10.2 (2.80)	14.3 (1.07)	85.7 (1.07)	14.3 (1.02)	7.6 (1.38)	6.8 (1.17)	39.7 (3.37)
Pakistani	8.9 (1.74)	91.1 (1.74)	24.4 (2.35)	66.7 (2.53)	44.5 (2.80)	6.0 (1.61)	16.2 (1.97)	26.6 (1.07)	73.4 (1.07)	22.2 (2.28)	10.9 (0.87)	7.1 (0.74)	53.4 (1.56)
Southeast Asian	12.1 (0.83)	87.9 (0.83)	24.8 (0.99)	63.1 (1.19)	45.6 (1.06)	4.4 (0.46)	13.1 (1.00)	26.6 (0.41)	73.4 (0.41)	14.8 (0.48)	16.2 (0.35)	7.9 (0.25)	27.3 (0.49)
Burmese	45.6 (6.19)	54.4 (6.19)	25.6 (5.53)	28.8 (5.20)	20.5 (4.96)	5.7 ! (1.32)	2.5 ! (1.00)	29.8 (3.09)	70.2 (3.09)	25.2 (2.05)	14.8 (1.57)	1.5 (0.92)	26.4 (2.31)
Cambodian	15.9 (6.19)	84.1 (6.19)	29.4 (3.74)	54.7 (3.60)	44.7 (3.62)	5.1 ! (1.31)	4.3 (1.18)	27.8 (1.45)	72.2 (1.45)	23.7 (2.14)	21.2 (1.32)	10.2 (1.06)	17.6 (1.20)
Hmong	13.1 (1.83)	86.9 (1.83)	34.4 (3.60)	52.5 (3.60)	40.9 (3.55)	‡ (†)	6.5 (1.74)	26.8 (1.72)	73.2 (1.72)	29.0 (1.88)	19.0 (1.40)	9.3 (1.17)	17.0 (1.34)
Laotian	19.8 (3.80)	80.2 (3.80)	30.5 (4.37)	49.7 (4.66)	41.0 (4.13)	‡ (†)	6.6 (2.01)	26.3 (1.13)	73.7 (1.13)	20.7 (1.63)	19.0 (1.16)	7.5 (1.04)	15.9 (1.87)
Thai	13.5 (3.29)	86.5 (3.29)	32.8 (4.75)	53.6 (5.62)	34.5 (5.62)	4.9 (0.67)	17.0 (4.36)	19.1 (0.56)	80.9 (0.56)	21.6 (1.63)	16.1 (0.43)	7.6 (0.33)	40.8 (0.62)
Vietnamese	7.8 (0.98)	92.2 (0.98)	20.8 (1.33)	71.4 (1.62)	51.3 (1.58)	3.1 ! (1.38)	16.4 (1.30)	26.3 (0.86)	73.7 (0.86)	16.0 (0.57)	16.1 (1.16)	7.6 (0.33)	28.3 (0.62)
Other Southeast Asian⁶	‡ (†)	98.0 (†)	19.7 (4.40)	78.3 (4.49)	47.6 (6.77)	‡ (†)	27.6 (5.81)	5.4 (1.30)	94.6 (1.30)	14.4 (1.90)	12.9 (1.86)	11.2 (1.72)	54.4 (2.68)
Other Asian	6.2 ! (1.20)	93.8 (1.20)	28.9 (1.99)	68.9 (2.23)	45.9 (2.72)	6.1 (1.41)	19.2 (1.96)	14.2 (0.86)	85.8 (0.86)	14.4 (0.86)	16.0 (0.81)	7.6 (0.62)	47.8 (1.27)
Pacific Islander	16.1 (1.72)	83.9 (1.72)	37.7 (2.66)	46.2 (3.20)	35.9 (3.09)	5.2 (1.30)	5.1 (1.18)	12.3 (0.82)	87.7 (0.82)	39.1 (1.26)	24.2 (0.97)	8.9 (0.55)	15.4 (0.84)
American Indian/Alaska Native	22.4 (1.06)	77.6 (1.06)	38.4 (1.28)	39.1 (1.50)	32.5 (1.42)	3.6 (0.54)	3.0 (0.50)	18.1 (0.39)	81.9 (0.39)	33.3 (0.46)	25.8 (0.48)	8.4 (0.27)	14.3 (0.38)
Two or more races	13.0 (0.47)	87.0 (0.47)	29.7 (0.63)	57.3 (0.73)	43.3 (0.72)	4.9 (0.32)	9.1 (0.44)	9.7 (0.24)	90.3 (0.24)	23.8 (0.32)	26.4 (0.32)	9.1 (0.23)	32.0 (0.35)
White and Black	15.3 (0.96)	84.7 (0.96)	32.6 (1.23)	52.1 (1.37)	42.0 (1.34)	3.6 (0.50)	6.4 (0.72)	9.2 (0.58)	90.8 (0.58)	23.8 (0.87)	30.4 (0.87)	8.6 (0.61)	28.0 (0.81)
White and Asian	9.1 (0.92)	90.9 (0.92)	24.7 (1.05)	66.2 (1.42)	44.5 (1.33)	5.6 (0.64)	16.1 (1.01)	6.2 (0.52)	93.8 (0.52)	15.7 (0.62)	21.6 (0.64)	8.1 (0.39)	48.4 (0.86)
White and American Indian/Alaska Native	16.8 (0.96)	83.2 (0.96)	32.0 (1.44)	51.2 (1.65)	40.5 (1.71)	4.3 (0.69)	6.3 (0.80)	11.9 (0.39)	88.1 (0.39)	27.2 (0.57)	28.2 (0.54)	9.7 (0.40)	23.0 (0.50)
Other Two or more races	10.8 (0.85)	89.2 (0.85)	28.9 (1.47)	60.2 (1.52)	45.9 (1.52)	6.4 (0.73)	7.9 (0.64)	10.2 (0.39)	89.8 (0.39)	23.1 (0.51)	26.2 (0.60)	9.3 (0.40)	31.2 (0.67)

—Not available.
†Not applicable.
‡Interpret data with caution. The coefficient of variation (CV) for this estimate is between 30 and 50 percent.
#Reporting standards not met. Either there were too few cases for a reliable estimate or the coefficient of variation (CV) is 50 percent or greater.
¹High school completers include diploma recipients and those completing high school through alternative credentials, such as a GED.
²Total includes other racial/ethnic groups not shown separately.
³Includes other Central American subgroups not shown separately.
⁴Includes Taiwanese.
⁵In addition to the subgroups shown, also includes Sri Lankan.
⁶Consists of Indonesian and Malaysian.
NOTE: Race categories exclude persons of Hispanic ethnicity. Detail may not sum to totals because of rounding.
SOURCE: U.S. Department of Commerce, Census Bureau, American Community Survey (ACS), 2009 and 2014. (This table was prepared January 2016.)

Table 104.50. Persons age 25 and over who hold a bachelor's or higher degree, by sex, race/ethnicity, age group, and field of bachelor's degree: 2014
[Standard errors appear in parentheses]

Field of bachelor's degree	Total	Sex		Race/ethnicity					Age		
		Males	Females	White	Black	Hispanic	Asian/Pacific Islander	American Indian/Alaska Native	25 to 29 years old	30 to 49 years old	50 years old and over
1	2	3	4	5	6	7	8	9	10	11	12
Total population, 25 and over (in thousands)	213,806 (50.0)	103,072 (31.3)	110,734 (31.9)	142,046 (14.8)	24,637 (23.9)	30,696 (21.0)	11,821 (21.2)	1,290 (12.0)	21,843 (23.1)	83,187 (30.3)	108,776 (37.8)
Percent of population with bachelor's degree	30.1 (0.01)	29.9 (0.06)	30.2 (0.07)	33.6 (0.06)	19.8 (0.12)	14.4 (0.10)	50.8 (0.22)	14.3 (0.38)	32.4 (0.15)	33.2 (0.09)	27.2 (0.05)
Bachelor's degree holders											
Total						Number (in thousands)					
Total	64,303 (137.5)	30,831 (71.4)	33,472 (81.9)	47,757 (92.0)	4,867 (30.8)	4,432 (33.3)	6,001 (28.6)	185 (5.4)	7,078 (33.6)	27,645 (78.4)	29,581 (63.2)
Agriculture/forestry	671 (9.6)	461 (7.0)	210 (5.7)	565 (8.2)	23 (1.8)	27 (2.1)	43 (2.8)	3 (0.6)	66 (3.5)	248 (6.5)	358 (5.5)
Art/architecture	3,058 (22.6)	1,328 (14.2)	1,729 (15.8)	2,368 (18.1)	145 (4.9)	228 (6.0)	247 (6.3)	7 (1.1)	465 (9.7)	1,362 (16.4)	1,231 (13.4)
Business/management	13,117 (40.1)	7,331 (30.2)	5,786 (23.7)	9,525 (32.6)	1,156 (15.0)	1,045 (13.4)	1,162 (11.6)	36 (2.4)	1,356 (16.4)	6,041 (30.2)	5,719 (24.5)
Communications	2,396 (18.8)	991 (12.2)	1,404 (14.6)	1,851 (14.8)	223 (7.4)	156 (4.9)	117 (4.3)	3 (0.7)	391 (8.1)	1,277 (13.9)	728 (10.0)
Computer and information sciences	1,902 (19.9)	1,366 (16.1)	536 (9.3)	1,103 (13.5)	176 (5.9)	125 (5.0)	451 (8.6)	5 (0.8)	245 (7.4)	1,149 (13.9)	508 (9.2)
Education	8,635 (39.5)	2,115 (17.9)	6,519 (34.0)	7,082 (32.2)	626 (9.7)	508 (10.0)	298 (6.8)	32 (1.8)	550 (7.9)	2,656 (22.0)	5,430 (27.8)
Engineering	5,016 (29.7)	4,293 (27.9)	723 (9.8)	3,327 (22.3)	207 (7.4)	381 (7.9)	1,010 (12.0)	9 (1.0)	499 (9.5)	2,123 (20.8)	2,393 (18.0)
English/literature	2,077 (17.3)	690 (9.4)	1,388 (14.2)	1,689 (15.4)	112 (4.7)	90 (3.6)	146 (4.8)	4 (0.7)	219 (5.6)	848 (11.9)	1,010 (10.3)
Foreign languages	692 (9.9)	196 (5.2)	496 (7.9)	512 (7.9)	24 (1.7)	69 (3.5)	71 (3.5)	‡ (†)	75 (3.1)	275 (6.3)	342 (6.5)
Health sciences	4,633 (28.3)	827 (11.4)	3,806 (24.0)	3,311 (22.9)	425 (8.6)	283 (7.3)	525 (8.3)	14 (1.4)	491 (8.5)	1,955 (19.6)	2,188 (17.2)
Liberal arts/humanities	942 (12.6)	377 (7.4)	566 (9.8)	694 (10.7)	72 (3.4)	78 (4.0)	76 (3.4)	3 (0.6)	79 (4.7)	410 (8.6)	453 (8.6)
Mathematics/statistics	972 (12.3)	576 (9.5)	396 (7.9)	738 (9.8)	52 (2.5)	40 (2.9)	126 (4.3)	‡ (†)	75 (3.3)	347 (7.6)	549 (8.5)
Natural sciences (biological and physical)	5,032 (27.0)	2,852 (19.6)	2,180 (16.3)	3,605 (21.3)	301 (6.9)	284 (8.3)	736 (10.9)	11 (1.3)	624 (9.5)	2,151 (18.9)	2,257 (15.8)
Philosophy/religion/theology	904 (11.8)	635 (10.0)	268 (6.9)	712 (10.3)	73 (3.3)	47 (3.0)	56 (2.9)	2 (0.5)	90 (4.0)	331 (7.4)	483 (8.7)
Pre-professional	1,081 (11.9)	651 (9.3)	430 (7.1)	727 (8.9)	169 (5.9)	129 (4.9)	28 (1.9)	7 (1.1)	171 (5.2)	610 (10.9)	301 (5.5)
Psychology	3,013 (20.1)	947 (11.4)	2,066 (18.9)	2,248 (15.5)	281 (6.6)	245 (6.9)	169 (4.8)	8 (1.1)	409 (7.9)	1,425 (15.2)	1,180 (11.9)
Social sciences/history	6,156 (33.1)	3,465 (24.0)	2,691 (18.1)	4,730 (27.6)	434 (8.8)	409 (8.3)	455 (7.1)	15 (1.4)	705 (12.2)	2,590 (19.4)	2,860 (20.6)
Other fields	4,008 (28.2)	1,730 (16.0)	2,278 (20.0)	2,972 (22.1)	370 (8.1)	287 (7.3)	286 (6.8)	21 (1.5)	568 (9.7)	1,848 (19.3)	1,591 (16.4)
						Percentage distribution, by field					
Total	100.0 (†)	100.0 (†)	100.0 (†)	100.0 (†)	100.0 (†)	100.0 (†)	100.0 (†)	100.0 (†)	100.0 (†)	100.0 (†)	100.0 (†)
Agriculture/forestry	1.0 (0.01)	1.5 (0.02)	0.6 (0.02)	1.2 (0.02)	0.5 (0.04)	0.6 (0.05)	0.7 (0.05)	1.8 (0.35)	0.9 (0.05)	0.9 (0.02)	1.2 (0.02)
Art/architecture	4.8 (0.03)	4.3 (0.04)	5.2 (0.04)	5.0 (0.04)	3.0 (0.10)	5.1 (0.12)	4.1 (0.10)	4.0 (0.59)	6.6 (0.14)	4.9 (0.06)	4.2 (0.04)
Business/management	20.4 (0.06)	23.8 (0.09)	17.3 (0.06)	19.9 (0.07)	23.8 (0.26)	23.6 (0.25)	19.4 (0.18)	19.3 (1.07)	19.2 (0.22)	21.9 (0.10)	19.3 (0.08)
Communications	3.7 (0.03)	3.2 (0.04)	4.2 (0.04)	3.9 (0.03)	4.6 (0.15)	3.5 (0.11)	1.9 (0.07)	1.9 (0.35)	5.5 (0.11)	4.6 (0.05)	2.5 (0.03)
Computer and information sciences	3.0 (0.03)	4.4 (0.05)	1.6 (0.03)	2.3 (0.03)	3.6 (0.12)	2.8 (0.12)	7.5 (0.14)	2.7 (0.43)	3.5 (0.10)	4.2 (0.05)	1.7 (0.03)
Education	13.4 (0.05)	6.9 (0.05)	19.5 (0.09)	14.8 (0.06)	12.9 (0.19)	11.5 (0.21)	5.0 (0.11)	17.6 (0.95)	7.8 (0.10)	9.6 (0.07)	18.4 (0.09)
Engineering	7.8 (0.04)	13.9 (0.08)	2.2 (0.03)	7.0 (0.04)	4.2 (0.16)	8.6 (0.17)	16.8 (0.16)	4.6 (0.51)	7.1 (0.13)	7.7 (0.07)	8.1 (0.06)
English/literature	3.2 (0.03)	2.2 (0.03)	4.1 (0.04)	3.5 (0.03)	2.3 (0.09)	2.0 (0.08)	2.4 (0.08)	2.1 (0.39)	3.1 (0.08)	3.1 (0.04)	3.4 (0.03)
Foreign languages	1.1 (0.01)	0.6 (0.02)	1.5 (0.02)	1.1 (0.02)	0.5 (0.03)	1.6 (0.08)	1.2 (0.06)	0.5 ! (0.20)	1.1 (0.04)	1.0 (0.02)	1.2 (0.02)
Health sciences	7.2 (0.04)	2.7 (0.04)	11.4 (0.07)	6.9 (0.05)	8.7 (0.17)	6.4 (0.16)	8.7 (0.14)	7.7 (0.73)	6.9 (0.12)	7.1 (0.07)	7.4 (0.06)
Liberal arts/humanities	1.5 (0.02)	1.2 (0.02)	1.7 (0.02)	1.5 (0.02)	1.5 (0.07)	1.8 (0.09)	1.3 (0.06)	1.6 (0.33)	1.1 (0.07)	1.5 (0.03)	1.5 (0.03)
Mathematics/statistics	1.5 (0.02)	1.9 (0.03)	1.2 (0.02)	1.5 (0.02)	1.1 (0.05)	0.9 (0.06)	2.1 (0.07)	0.9 (0.21)	1.1 (0.05)	1.3 (0.03)	1.9 (0.03)
Natural sciences (biological and physical)	7.8 (0.04)	9.2 (0.06)	6.5 (0.05)	7.5 (0.04)	6.2 (0.13)	6.4 (0.17)	12.3 (0.17)	6.1 (0.68)	8.8 (0.13)	7.8 (0.06)	7.6 (0.05)
Philosophy/religion/theology	1.4 (0.02)	2.1 (0.03)	0.8 (0.02)	1.5 (0.02)	1.5 (0.07)	1.1 (0.07)	0.9 (0.05)	1.3 (0.28)	1.3 (0.06)	1.2 (0.03)	1.6 (0.03)
Pre-professional	1.7 (0.02)	2.1 (0.03)	1.3 (0.02)	1.5 (0.02)	3.5 (0.12)	2.9 (0.11)	0.5 (0.03)	3.8 (0.58)	2.4 (0.07)	2.2 (0.04)	1.0 (0.02)
Psychology	4.7 (0.03)	3.1 (0.04)	6.2 (0.05)	4.7 (0.03)	5.8 (0.14)	5.5 (0.15)	2.8 (0.08)	4.4 (0.60)	5.8 (0.11)	5.2 (0.05)	4.0 (0.04)
Social sciences/history	9.6 (0.05)	11.2 (0.07)	8.0 (0.05)	9.9 (0.05)	8.9 (0.17)	9.2 (0.18)	7.6 (0.12)	8.4 (0.69)	10.0 (0.16)	9.4 (0.07)	9.7 (0.06)
Other fields	6.2 (0.04)	5.6 (0.05)	6.8 (0.06)	6.2 (0.05)	7.6 (0.15)	6.5 (0.16)	4.8 (0.11)	11.5 (0.78)	8.0 (0.13)	6.7 (0.07)	5.4 (0.06)

†Not applicable.
!Interpret data with caution. The coefficient of variation (CV) for this estimate is between 30 and 50 percent.
‡Reporting standards not met (too few cases for a reliable estimate).

NOTE: Totals include other racial/ethnic groups not separately shown. Race categories exclude persons of Hispanic ethnicity. Detail may not sum to totals because of rounding. SOURCE: U.S. Department of Commerce, Census Bureau, American Community Survey (ACS), 2014. (This table was prepared December 2015.)

Table 104.60. Number of persons 25 to 34 years old and percentage with a bachelor's or higher degree, by undergraduate field of study, sex, race/ethnicity, and U.S. nativity and citizenship status: 2014
[Standard errors appear in parentheses]

Sex, race/ethnicity, and U.S. nativity and citizenship status	Total population ages 25 to 34 (in thousands)	Percent of population with bachelor's or higher degree	Total, all fields	STEM total	Agriculture/natural resources	Architecture	Computer and information sciences	Engineering/engineering technologies	Biology/biomedical sciences	Mathematics/statistics	Physical/social sciences	Health studies	Non-STEM total	Business	Education	All other fields of study
1	2	3	4	5	6	7	8	9	10	11	12	13	14	15	16	17
Total	43,279 (33.9)	33.4 (0.12)	100.0 (†)	40.6 (0.16)	1.5 (0.05)	0.8 (0.03)	4.1 (0.08)	7.9 (0.10)	5.7 (0.07)	1.1 (0.03)	12.9 (0.12)	6.6 (0.08)	59.4 (0.16)	19.8 (0.13)	8.3 (0.09)	31.3 (0.17)
Sex																
Male	21,780 (23.5)	29.4 (0.13)	100.0	43.8 (0.28)	1.8 (0.07)	1.1 (0.05)	6.9 (0.15)	13.8 (0.18)	5.1 (0.10)	1.5 (0.06)	11.1 (0.18)	2.6 (0.07)	56.2 (0.28)	22.7 (0.20)	4.0 (0.10)	29.5 (0.23)
Female	21,500 (23.2)	37.5 (0.16)	100.0	38.0 (0.19)	1.3 (0.05)	0.6 (0.03)	1.8 (0.06)	3.2 (0.08)	6.2 (0.11)	0.8 (0.04)	14.3 (0.16)	9.9 (0.12)	62.0 (0.19)	17.6 (0.16)	11.6 (0.14)	32.8 (0.21)
Race/ethnicity																
White	24,638 (12.9)	39.7 (0.15)	100.0	37.6 (0.18)	1.9 (0.06)	0.8 (0.03)	3.0 (0.07)	6.4 (0.11)	5.4 (0.08)	1.1 (0.04)	12.5 (0.13)	6.5 (0.08)	62.4 (0.18)	19.4 (0.16)	9.8 (0.11)	33.2 (0.20)
Black	5,665 (20.1)	20.6 (0.24)	100.0	37.8 (0.62)	0.7 (0.10)	1.1 (0.07)	3.7 (0.25)	4.3 (0.31)	5.2 (0.23)	0.6 (0.09)	14.6 (0.45)	7.7 (0.37)	62.2 (0.62)	22.6 (0.58)	6.7 (0.30)	33.0 (0.60)
Hispanic	8,779 (19.8)	15.1 (0.19)	100.0	37.8 (0.58)	0.6 (0.10)	1.1 (0.10)	2.9 (0.21)	7.4 (0.33)	4.3 (0.23)	0.7 (0.10)	12.2 (0.37)	6.0 (0.28)	62.2 (0.58)	21.9 (0.50)	7.1 (0.30)	33.6 (0.60)
Asian	2,796 (16.5)	63.4 (0.40)	100.0	60.9 (0.51)	0.7 (0.07)	0.8 (0.09)	11.0 (0.32)	18.7 (0.41)	8.5 (0.21)	1.7 (0.12)	16.7 (0.42)	7.5 (0.24)	39.1 (0.51)	19.2 (0.38)	2.4 (0.16)	17.5 (0.38)
Pacific Islander	88 (3.5)	12.7	100.0	48.7 (5.44)	‡	(†)	4.3! (2.01)	9.1! (3.22)	10.2! (3.80)	‡	16.7! (4.28)	8.0! (3.29)	51.3 (5.44)	18.1 (5.16)	‡	30.7 (5.18)
American Indian/Alaska Native[1]	285 (6.1)	13.0 (0.77)	100.0	37.2 (3.33)	5.1! (1.55)	‡	2.8! (0.88)	6.6 (1.70)	4.8 (1.34)	‡	10.5 (1.77)	6.4 (1.79)	62.8 (3.33)	20.3 (2.65)	10.6 (1.72)	31.9 (3.06)
American Indian[1]	246 (5.5)	13.2 (0.85)	100.0	36.5 (3.51)	5.8 (1.72)	‡	1.9! (0.70)	6.5 (1.80)	4.4! (1.33)	‡	10.0 (1.86)	7.1 (2.07)	63.5 (3.51)	19.6 (2.89)	11.4 (1.87)	32.5 (3.42)
Alaska Native	14 (1.0)	6.0! (2.39)	100.0	‡	‡	‡	‡	‡	‡	‡	‡	‡	‡	‡	‡	‡
Some other race[2]	99 (5.4)	39.0 (2.01)	100.0	44.3 (4.19)	‡	‡	5.9! (2.21)	8.4 (2.14)	5.5! (1.44)	‡	11.6 (2.18)	6.9 (1.86)	55.7 (4.19)	22.5 (3.02)	3.9! (1.78)	29.3 (3.35)
Two or more races	928 (15.8)	35.5 (0.69)	100.0	43.9 (1.31)	1.5 (0.26)	0.9 (0.19)	3.7 (0.44)	8.6 (0.55)	8.1 (0.61)	1.2 (0.23)	14.5 (0.95)	5.4 (0.55)	56.1 (1.31)	17.1 (0.83)	4.4 (0.43)	34.6 (1.11)
Race/ethnicity by sex																
Male																
White	12,466 (9.0)	35.2 (0.17)	100.0	40.3 (0.30)	2.3 (0.09)	1.1 (0.06)	5.5 (0.13)	11.7 (0.21)	4.9 (0.11)	1.5 (0.07)	10.9 (0.19)	2.4 (0.08)	59.7 (0.30)	23.3 (0.25)	4.6 (0.12)	31.8 (0.27)
Black	2,706 (14.3)	16.5 (0.33)	100.0	36.5 (1.04)	1.0 (0.17)	0.6 (0.16)	6.5 (0.57)	8.2 (0.59)	4.8 (0.44)	0.8 (0.13)	11.5 (0.68)	3.1 (0.39)	63.5 (1.04)	24.1 (0.93)	4.9 (0.45)	34.4 (1.10)
Hispanic	4,590 (14.0)	12.4 (0.19)	100.0	40.6 (0.97)	0.7 (0.15)	1.5 (0.17)	5.6 (0.48)	13.3 (0.64)	4.1 (0.31)	1.0 (0.17)	11.9 (0.60)	2.5 (0.28)	59.4 (0.97)	24.0 (0.85)	4.1 (0.37)	31.3 (0.95)
Asian	1,326 (10.0)	61.8 (0.64)	100.0	68.4 (0.75)	0.7 (0.12)	0.7 (0.13)	15.2 (0.54)	28.0 (0.71)	6.8 (0.30)	2.1 (0.21)	11.4 (0.48)	3.5 (0.24)	31.6 (0.75)	18.0 (0.56)	0.7 (0.13)	12.9 (0.52)
Pacific Islander	43 (2.4)	10.7 (1.90)	100.0	48.5 (8.85)	‡	‡	9.5! (4.57)	11.3! (4.96)	‡	‡	11.6! (5.29)	‡	51.5 (8.85)	27.5! (8.51)	‡	23.1! (6.99)
American Indian/Alaska Native[1]	141 (4.2)	10.6 (1.12)	100.0	34.6 (5.20)	‡	‡	4.6! (1.82)	11.2! (3.43)	4.3! (1.45)	‡	8.9 (2.56)	‡	65.4 (5.20)	26.5 (5.32)	6.0! (2.19)	32.8 (5.32)
American Indian[1]	120 (4.0)	11.0 (1.20)	100.0	33.1 (5.41)	‡	‡	3.1! (1.42)	10.0! (3.47)	4.5! (1.54)	‡	9.3 (2.79)	‡	66.9 (5.41)	26.3 (5.73)	6.8! (2.48)	34.8 (5.88)
Alaska Native	7 (0.7)	‡	100.0	‡	‡	‡	‡	‡	‡	‡	‡	‡	‡	‡	‡	‡
Some other race[2]	52 (3.3)	33.3 (2.73)	100.0	49.7 (5.97)	‡	‡	11.5! (4.23)	16.0 (3.90)	4.1! (1.78)	‡	7.0! (2.14)	‡	50.3 (5.97)	20.0 (4.74)	‡	28.2 (4.63)
Two or more races	456 (11.2)	32.6 (0.89)	100.0	46.3 (1.88)	1.7 (0.44)	1.1 (0.30)	6.6 (0.89)	14.4 (1.11)	6.5 (0.87)	1.4 (0.40)	11.9 (1.11)	2.6 (0.53)	53.7 (1.88)	19.6 (1.29)	2.3 (0.63)	31.8 (1.51)
Female																
White	12,172 (7.0)	44.3 (0.20)	100.0	35.3 (0.23)	1.6 (0.07)	0.5 (0.04)	1.0 (0.06)	2.0 (0.08)	5.7 (0.12)	0.8 (0.05)	13.8 (0.18)	9.9 (0.14)	64.7 (0.23)	16.2 (0.20)	14.1 (0.19)	34.4 (0.27)
Black	2,960 (13.9)	24.4 (0.34)	100.0	37.6 (0.77)	0.5 (0.13)	0.2! (0.07)	1.9 (0.20)	1.9 (0.27)	5.4 (0.32)	0.6 (0.11)	16.6 (0.60)	10.5 (0.55)	62.4 (0.77)	21.6 (0.73)	7.8 (0.42)	33.0 (0.67)
Hispanic	4,189 (13.9)	18.1 (0.30)	100.0	35.6 (0.66)	0.6 (0.12)	0.9! (0.21)	1.0 (0.13)	3.0 (0.27)	4.4 (0.35)	0.5 (0.14)	12.8 (0.48)	8.6 (0.45)	64.4 (0.66)	20.3 (0.61)	9.4 (0.47)	34.7 (0.76)
Asian	1,470 (9.9)	64.9 (0.52)	100.0	54.5 (0.59)	0.7 (0.09)	0.8 (0.11)	7.4 (0.34)	10.7 (0.35)	9.9 (0.28)	1.3 (0.14)	20.4 (6.23)	10.9 (0.39)	45.5 (0.59)	20.2 (0.46)	3.8 (0.26)	21.5 (0.47)
Pacific Islander	45 (2.5)	14.6 (1.99)	100.0	44.8 (6.78)	‡	‡	‡	‡	‡	‡	‡	10.6! (4.72)	55.2 (6.78)	11.5! (4.52)	‡	36.1 (7.14)
American Indian/Alaska Native[1]	144 (3.6)	15.3 (1.12)	100.0	38.9 (4.22)	5.6! (2.16)	‡	‡	3.5! (1.46)	5.2! (2.05)	‡	11.6 (2.37)	10.1 (2.71)	61.1 (4.22)	16.1 (2.48)	13.7 (2.42)	31.3 (3.78)
American Indian[1]	126 (3.2)	15.3 (1.26)	100.0	38.9 (4.43)	6.5! (2.41)	‡	‡	4.0! (1.68)	4.4! (2.07)	‡	10.4 (2.48)	11.1 (3.21)	61.1 (4.43)	15.7 (2.62)	14.6 (2.55)	30.8 (4.12)
Alaska Native	7 (0.6)	8.7! (3.65)	100.0	‡	‡	‡	‡	‡	‡	‡	‡	‡	‡	‡	‡	‡
Some other race[2]	48 (3.1)	45.2 (2.79)	100.0	40.0 (4.88)	‡	‡	‡	‡	6.6! (2.13)	‡	15.3 (3.53)	8.7 (2.51)	60.0 (4.88)	24.5 (4.36)	5.3! (2.36)	30.2 (4.15)
Two or more races	473 (10.4)	38.3 (0.92)	100.0	42.0 (1.54)	1.3 (0.26)	0.8! (0.25)	1.4 (0.35)	3.9 (0.55)	9.4 (0.82)	1.0 (0.27)	16.6 (1.31)	7.6 (0.79)	58.0 (1.54)	15.1 (1.01)	6.0 (0.60)	36.9 (1.43)
Nativity																
Hispanic																
U.S.-born[3]	4,836 (28.5)	19.7 (0.27)	100.0	36.2 (0.61)	0.5 (0.09)	1.0 (0.12)	2.8 (0.21)	5.4 (0.32)	4.2 (0.27)	0.7 (0.11)	15.4 (0.51)	6.1 (0.34)	63.8 (0.61)	20.1 (0.56)	7.3 (0.32)	36.4 (0.61)
Foreign-born	3,943 (24.2)	9.5 (0.21)	100.0	41.8 (1.17)	1.0 (0.22)	1.5 (0.25)	3.3 (0.43)	12.5 (0.79)	4.4 (0.48)	0.7 (0.19)	12.7 (0.86)	5.8 (0.52)	58.2 (1.17)	26.5 (1.00)	6.6 (0.58)	25.1 (1.13)
Asian																
U.S.-born[3]	866 (11.7)	61.5 (0.68)	100.0	51.8 (0.83)	0.7 (0.14)	0.9 (0.18)	4.6 (0.35)	8.8 (0.49)	11.5 (0.51)	1.2 (0.21)	16.1 (0.72)	8.0 (0.53)	48.2 (0.83)	21.2 (0.77)	2.4 (0.29)	24.6 (0.81)
Foreign-born	1,930 (17.1)	64.3 (0.48)	100.0	64.9 (0.55)	0.6 (0.08)	0.8 (0.10)	13.7	22.9 (0.52)	7.2 (0.25)	1.9 (0.14)	10.5 (0.37)	7.3 (0.29)	35.1 (0.55)	18.3 (0.44)	2.4 (0.19)	14.5 (0.39)
Citizenship status																
U.S.-born citizen	35,600 (46.5)	33.8 (0.13)	100.0	37.4 (0.17)	1.7 (0.05)	0.8 (0.03)	2.9 (0.06)	5.9 (0.09)	5.5 (0.08)	1.0 (0.04)	13.1 (0.13)	6.6 (0.08)	62.6 (0.17)	19.6 (0.15)	9.2 (0.10)	33.8 (0.19)
Naturalized citizen	2,266 (22.1)	39.5 (0.43)	100.0	49.2 (0.76)	0.7 (0.10)	1.0 (0.16)	5.9 (0.34)	9.5 (0.46)	8.1 (0.30)	1.3 (0.15)	13.6 (0.47)	9.2 (0.49)	50.8 (0.76)	24.9 (0.62)	3.6 (0.36)	22.3 (0.57)
Noncitizen	5,413 (32.2)	28.2 (0.28)	100.0	60.4 (0.51)	0.9 (0.10)	1.0 (0.11)	11.9 (0.41)	22.2 (0.40)	6.1 (0.24)	1.9 (0.15)	10.9 (0.37)	5.5 (0.24)	39.6 (0.51)	18.4 (0.32)	3.6 (0.20)	17.6 (0.43)

†Not applicable.
!Interpret data with caution. The coefficient of variation (CV) for this estimate is between 30 and 50 percent.
‡Reporting standards not met. Either there are too few cases for a reliable estimate or the coefficient of variation (CV) is 50 percent or greater.
[1]Includes persons reporting American Indian alone, persons reporting Alaska Native alone, and persons from American Indian and/or Alaska Native tribes specified or not specified.
[2]Respondents who wrote in some other race that was not included as an option on the questionnaire.
[3]Includes those born in the 50 states, the District of Columbia, Puerto Rico, American Samoa, Guam, the U.S. Virgin Islands, and the Northern Marianas, as well as those born abroad to U.S.-citizen parents.

NOTE: Estimates are for the entire population in the indicated age range, including persons living in households and persons living in group quarters (such as college residence halls, residential treatment centers, military barracks, and correctional facilities). The first bachelor's degree major reported by respondents was used to classify their field of study, even though they were able to report a second bachelor's degree major and may possess advanced degrees in other fields. STEM fields, as defined here, consist of the fields specified in columns 6 through 13. Data were assembled based on major or field aggregations, except that management of STEM activities was counted as a STEM field instead of a business field. Detail may not sum to totals because of rounding. Race categories exclude persons of Hispanic ethnicity.
SOURCE: U.S. Department of Commerce, Census Bureau, American Community Survey (ACS), 2014. (This table was prepared December 2015.)

Table 104.70. Number and percentage distribution of 5- to 17-year-olds, by parent's highest level of educational attainment, household type, and child's race/ethnicity: 2009 and 2014

[Standard errors appear in parentheses]

Year, household type, and race/ethnicity	Total, all 5- to 17-year-olds — Number (in thousands)	Total, all 5- to 17-year-olds — Percentage distribution	Highest level of education attained by any parent residing with child[1] — Total, all levels	Less than high school completion	High school completion[2]	Some college, no degree	Associate's degree	Bachelor's or higher degree — Total	Bachelor's or higher degree — Bachelor's degree	Bachelor's or higher degree — Master's degree	Bachelor's or higher degree — Doctor's degree
	2	3	4	5	6	7	8	9	10	11	12
2009											
Total, both household types	50,507 (34.0)	100.0 (†)	100.0 (†)	11.2 (0.09)	20.3 (0.10)	23.3 (0.10)	10.0 (0.07)	35.2 (0.14)	20.5 (0.11)	9.9 (0.07)	4.8 (0.05)
White	28,882 (16.9)	57.2 (0.04)	100.0	3.8 (0.08)	17.6 (0.12)	22.8 (0.12)	11.3 (0.09)	44.5 (0.16)	25.6 (0.12)	12.8 (0.10)	6.1 (0.07)
Black	6,745 (22.9)	13.4 (0.04)	100.0	12.5 (0.24)	26.6 (0.23)	31.2 (0.32)	9.9 (0.18)	19.8 (0.26)	12.9 (0.20)	5.3 (0.16)	1.7 (0.09)
Hispanic	10,624 (15.0)	21.0 (0.02)	100.0	31.7 (0.27)	25.6 (0.23)	21.0 (0.22)	6.8 (0.14)	15.0 (0.19)	9.8 (0.16)	3.5 (0.08)	1.7 (0.06)
Asian	2,087 (11.6)	4.1 (0.02)	100.0	9.5 (0.32)	12.0 (0.34)	11.8 (0.38)	6.3 (0.24)	60.4 (0.58)	30.1 (0.49)	18.2 (0.42)	12.1 (0.33)
Pacific Islander	69 (3.0)	0.1 (0.01)	100.0	5.9 (1.29)	31.2 (3.05)	33.7 (3.56)	7.7 (1.31)	21.4 (2.37)	14.9 (2.12)	5.6 (1.48)	0.9 ! (0.28)
American Indian/Alaska Native	348 (6.7)	0.7 (0.01)	100.0	10.7 (0.81)	25.9 (1.06)	33.2 (1.16)	10.4 (0.83)	19.8 (1.09)	13.5 (0.96)	4.8 (0.53)	1.5 ! (0.31)
Some other race	155 (6.4)	0.3 (0.01)	100.0	13.4 (1.51)	17.7 (1.58)	17.8 (1.16)	8.9 (1.16)	42.1 (2.26)	20.8 (1.87)	12.8 (1.26)	8.6 (1.23)
Two or more races	1,597 (16.0)	3.2 (0.03)	100.0	5.2 (0.27)	17.8 (0.50)	28.2 (0.61)	11.6 (0.38)	37.2 (0.58)	20.8 (0.41)	10.5 (0.35)	5.9 (0.31)
Two-parent household	33,893 (61.5)	100.0 (†)	100.0	7.3 (0.07)	16.0 (0.12)	21.1 (0.12)	10.7 (0.09)	44.9 (0.13)	25.4 (0.12)	13.0 (0.09)	6.5 (0.06)
White	21,930 (40.9)	64.7 (0.09)	100.0	1.8 (0.06)	14.0 (0.12)	20.9 (0.13)	11.6 (0.11)	51.7 (0.15)	29.1 (0.13)	15.2 (0.12)	7.4 (0.08)
Black	2,315 (25.4)	6.8 (0.07)	100.0	3.3 (0.21)	17.3 (0.49)	29.6 (0.49)	12.8 (0.43)	37.0 (0.54)	22.7 (0.45)	10.4 (0.32)	3.9 (0.23)
Hispanic	6,619 (26.1)	19.5 (0.06)	100.0	27.9 (0.30)	24.1 (0.35)	21.0 (0.31)	7.7 (0.19)	19.3 (0.28)	12.4 (0.24)	4.6 (0.12)	2.4 (0.09)
Asian	1,753 (12.0)	5.2 (0.04)	100.0	7.6 (0.37)	10.5 (0.41)	10.6 (0.41)	6.3 (0.27)	65.0 (0.65)	31.4 (0.56)	20.1 (0.45)	13.5 (0.38)
Pacific Islander	45 (2.7)	0.1 (0.01)	100.0	2.4 ! (0.91)	29.0 (3.71)	32.0 (4.37)	13.4 (1.51)	23.2 (3.60)	16.2 (3.11)	5.6 (2.18)	1.4 ! (0.45)
American Indian/Alaska Native	173 (5.9)	0.5 (0.02)	100.0	4.1 (0.64)	20.5 (1.50)	32.9 (1.70)	8.5 (1.27)	29.0 (1.65)	18.5 (1.04)	8.5 (0.98)	2.0 (0.42)
Some other race	101 (5.1)	0.3 (0.01)	100.0	7.8 (1.87)	13.8 (1.60)	16.2 (1.76)	8.5 (1.44)	53.7 (2.79)	25.3 (2.23)	16.1 (1.80)	12.4 (1.75)
Two or more races	957 (12.4)	2.8 (0.04)	100.0	1.6 (0.17)	11.6 (0.51)	23.8 (0.63)	12.1 (0.48)	51.0 (0.84)	27.6 (0.64)	14.6 (0.51)	8.7 (0.45)
Single-parent household	16,614 (71.1)	100.0 (†)	100.0	19.1 (0.18)	29.2 (0.18)	27.8 (0.17)	8.6 (0.12)	15.4 (0.16)	10.6 (0.13)	3.5 (0.08)	1.3 (0.05)
White	6,952 (38.1)	41.8 (0.14)	100.0	10.2 (0.23)	29.0 (0.29)	28.8 (0.29)	10.4 (0.22)	21.6 (0.27)	14.7 (0.23)	4.9 (0.14)	2.0 (0.08)
Black	4,430 (29.5)	26.7 (0.14)	100.0	17.3 (0.33)	31.4 (0.42)	32.1 (0.43)	10.9 (0.25)	10.9 (0.25)	7.7 (0.19)	2.6 (0.14)	0.5 (0.05)
Hispanic	4,005 (28.2)	24.1 (0.13)	100.0	38.0 (0.41)	28.0 (0.38)	21.0 (0.35)	5.4 (0.21)	7.7 (0.22)	5.5 (0.19)	1.6 (0.09)	0.6 (0.06)
Asian	334 (8.6)	2.0 (0.05)	100.0	19.8 (1.05)	19.8 (1.23)	16.8 (1.20)	6.4 (0.57)	36.1 (1.30)	23.2 (1.09)	8.2 (0.69)	4.8 (0.55)
Pacific Islander	24 (2.4)	0.1 (0.01)	100.0	12.5 (3.25)	35.2 (4.63)	36.8 (5.27)	7.6 ! (2.42)	7.9 (2.31)	6.3 ! (2.31)	1.2 ! (0.34)	‡ (†)
American Indian/Alaska Native	175 (5.3)	1.1 (0.03)	100.0	17.2 (1.50)	31.2 (1.74)	33.5 (1.81)	7.4 (0.87)	10.6 (1.04)	8.6 (1.04)	1.2 (0.34)	0.9 ! (0.39)
Some other race	54 (3.9)	0.3 (0.02)	100.0	23.9 (3.26)	25.0 (3.34)	20.7 (2.90)	9.8 (2.16)	20.5 (2.95)	12.4 (2.54)	6.5 (2.54)	1.6 (†)
Two or more races	640 (10.5)	3.9 (0.06)	100.0	10.7 (0.59)	27.1 (0.85)	34.9 (0.98)	10.8 (0.63)	16.5 (0.60)	10.7 (0.46)	4.2 (0.38)	1.6 (0.23)
2014											
Total, both household types	50,852 (31.7)	100.0 (†)	100.0 (†)	10.8 (0.08)	19.0 (0.12)	21.6 (0.10)	10.4 (0.08)	38.1 (0.15)	21.2 (0.10)	11.8 (0.08)	5.2 (0.05)
White	26,906 (20.5)	52.9 (0.04)	100.0	3.6 (0.06)	15.3 (0.14)	20.4 (0.13)	11.9 (0.11)	48.8 (0.18)	26.8 (0.14)	15.3 (0.11)	6.8 (0.08)
Black	6,728 (22.5)	13.2 (0.04)	100.0	10.3 (0.25)	25.6 (0.21)	29.6 (0.37)	10.8 (0.23)	23.7 (0.31)	14.0 (0.25)	7.6 (0.20)	2.2 (0.10)
Hispanic	12,136 (17.0)	23.9 (0.03)	100.0	28.7 (0.26)	25.4 (0.19)	21.0 (0.19)	7.5 (0.15)	17.4 (0.17)	11.1 (0.14)	4.5 (0.11)	2.2 (0.07)
Asian	2,377 (14.4)	4.7 (0.03)	100.0	7.8 (0.28)	11.0 (0.36)	10.8 (0.33)	6.6 (0.24)	63.7 (0.48)	30.2 (0.48)	21.2 (0.42)	12.4 (0.31)
Pacific Islander	84 (3.2)	0.2 (0.01)	100.0	7.7 (1.62)	30.0 (2.47)	26.4 (2.40)	16.8 (2.23)	19.1 (2.14)	12.4 (1.87)	4.0 (1.08)	2.7 ! (0.91)
American Indian/Alaska Native	363 (7.2)	0.7 (0.01)	100.0	9.9 (0.73)	26.5 (0.98)	31.5 (1.07)	10.5 (0.71)	21.6 (0.98)	13.3 (0.91)	6.2 (0.53)	2.2 (0.34)
Some other race	152 (5.4)	0.3 (0.01)	100.0	13.7 (1.51)	18.0 (1.55)	18.9 (1.84)	6.4 (0.93)	43.0 (1.88)	23.1 (1.55)	13.1 (1.22)	6.8 (1.21)
Two or more races	2,107 (20.7)	4.1 (0.04)	100.0	5.4 (0.31)	15.7 (0.44)	25.7 (0.57)	11.9 (0.40)	41.3 (0.53)	21.9 (0.46)	12.5 (0.27)	6.9 (0.24)
Two-parent household	33,073 (60.6)	100.0 (†)	100.0	7.0 (0.09)	14.0 (0.12)	18.8 (0.12)	10.9 (0.10)	49.2 (0.17)	26.2 (0.14)	15.7 (0.11)	7.2 (0.07)
White	20,034 (54.6)	60.6 (0.13)	100.0	1.8 (0.06)	11.1 (0.13)	18.1 (0.16)	12.0 (0.13)	57.0 (0.20)	30.4 (0.18)	18.3 (0.14)	8.3 (0.10)
Black	2,340 (27.4)	7.1 (0.08)	100.0	2.6 (0.24)	15.1 (0.46)	25.9 (0.55)	13.0 (0.48)	43.5 (0.64)	23.5 (0.53)	15.1 (0.46)	4.8 (0.27)
Hispanic	7,185 (35.4)	21.7 (0.10)	100.0	24.5 (0.31)	23.8 (0.33)	20.5 (0.27)	8.1 (0.19)	23.1 (0.20)	14.2 (0.20)	6.2 (0.15)	2.6 (0.10)
Asian	1,974 (13.5)	6.0 (0.04)	100.0	6.1 (0.25)	9.2 (0.37)	9.9 (0.33)	6.1 (0.27)	68.7 (0.54)	31.2 (0.53)	23.5 (0.50)	14.0 (0.35)
Pacific Islander	55 (3.0)	0.2 (0.01)	100.0	3.7 ! (1.11)	27.1 (3.27)	28.7 (2.98)	14.6 (2.30)	26.0 (2.95)	17.3 (2.70)	4.7 (1.37)	4.0 ! (1.35)
American Indian/Alaska Native	172 (5.3)	0.5 (0.02)	100.0	2.6 (0.50)	20.9 (1.34)	31.5 (1.56)	17.0 (1.08)	28.0 (1.40)	13.3 (1.35)	10.2 (1.04)	4.5 (0.66)
Some other race	96 (5.2)	0.3 (0.02)	100.0	12.4 (1.79)	13.5 (1.67)	14.4 (1.79)	7.0 (1.27)	52.8 (2.46)	26.1 (1.94)	18.2 (1.74)	8.5 (1.42)
Two or more races	1,216 (16.7)	3.7 (0.05)	100.0	1.2 (0.25)	9.1 (0.49)	20.1 (0.60)	12.5 (0.53)	57.1 (0.72)	27.9 (0.64)	18.4 (0.45)	10.8 (0.40)
Single-parent household	17,779 (69.4)	100.0 (†)	100.0	17.8 (0.17)	28.2 (0.20)	26.8 (0.17)	9.6 (0.11)	17.6 (0.17)	11.8 (0.14)	4.4 (0.08)	1.4 (0.04)
White	6,872 (49.3)	38.7 (0.21)	100.0	8.9 (0.20)	27.5 (0.32)	28.0 (0.29)	11.6 (0.23)	25.0 (0.30)	16.5 (0.23)	6.3 (0.14)	2.3 (0.07)
Black	4,388 (31.2)	24.7 (0.15)	100.0	14.4 (0.32)	31.2 (0.44)	31.5 (0.44)	9.7 (0.27)	13.2 (0.28)	8.9 (0.19)	3.6 (0.11)	0.7 (0.05)
Hispanic	4,951 (35.6)	27.8 (0.18)	100.0	34.8 (0.43)	27.9 (0.34)	21.8 (0.31)	6.5 (0.21)	9.2 (0.23)	6.5 (0.19)	2.1 (0.11)	0.6 (0.05)
Asian	403 (9.7)	2.3 (0.05)	100.0	16.3 (0.97)	19.9 (1.07)	15.6 (0.97)	8.9 (0.70)	39.3 (1.05)	25.1 (1.19)	9.7 (0.75)	4.5 (0.46)
Pacific Islander	29 (2.7)	0.2 (0.02)	100.0	15.3 (3.77)	35.6 (4.80)	22.2 (2.98)	21.1 (5.19)	5.9 ! (1.22)	3.0 ! (1.38)	‡ (†)	‡ (†)
American Indian/Alaska Native	191 (5.4)	1.1 (0.03)	100.0	16.5 (1.28)	35.5 (1.40)	31.5 (1.52)	9.3 (0.89)	11.1 (1.11)	8.2 (1.11)	2.0 (0.66)	0.9 ! (0.40)
Some other race	56 (3.8)	0.3 (0.02)	100.0	16.1 (2.60)	25.7 (3.39)	26.7 (3.84)	5.3 (1.43)	26.1 (2.97)	18.0 (2.66)	4.3 (1.10)	3.8 ! (1.85)
Two or more races	890 (16.7)	5.0 (0.10)	100.0	11.0 (0.61)	24.8 (0.78)	33.3 (1.00)	11.1 (0.59)	19.8 (0.71)	13.6 (0.57)	4.5 (0.28)	1.6 (0.20)

†Not applicable.
!Interpret data with caution. The coefficient of variation (CV) for this estimate is between 30 and 50 percent.
‡Reporting standards not met. Either there are too few cases for a reliable estimate or the coefficient of variation (CV) is 50 percent or greater.
[1]Includes adoptive and stepparents, but excludes parents not residing in the same household as their children.
[2]Includes parents who completed high school through equivalency programs, such as a GED program.

NOTE: Table includes only 5- to 17-year-olds who resided with at least one of their parents (including an adoptive or stepparent). The 5- to 17-year-olds in single-parent households resided with only one parent, while those in two-parent households resided with two parents. Race categories exclude persons of Hispanic ethnicity. Detail may not sum to totals because of rounding.
SOURCE: U.S. Department of Commerce, Census Bureau, American Community Survey (ACS), 2009 and 2014. (This table was prepared January 2016.)

Table 104.80. Percentage of persons 18 to 24 years old and age 25 and over, by educational attainment and state: 2000 and 2014
[Standard errors appear in parentheses]

State	Percent of 18- to 24-year-olds who were high school completers[1]		Percent of population 25 years old and over, by educational attainment											
			2000					2014					
			Less than high school completion	High school completion[1] or higher	Bachelor's or higher degree			Less than high school completion	High school completion[1] or higher		Bachelor's or higher degree		
	2000	2014			Total	Bachelor's degree	Graduate degree		Total	High school only	Total	Bachelor's degree	Graduate degree
1	2	3	4	5	6	7	8	9	10	11	12	13	14
United States	74.7 (0.02)	86.2 (0.08)	19.6 (0.01)	80.4 (0.01)	24.4 (0.01)	15.5 (0.01)	8.9 (#)	13.1 (0.04)	86.9 (0.04)	27.7 (0.05)	30.1 (0.06)	18.6 (0.04)	11.4 (0.04)
Alabama	72.2 (0.15)	84.6 (0.74)	24.7 (0.06)	75.3 (0.06)	19.0 (0.05)	12.1 (0.04)	6.9 (0.03)	15.4 (0.29)	84.6 (0.29)	31.7 (0.38)	23.0 (0.30)	14.5 (0.25)	8.5 (0.20)
Alaska	76.9 (0.40)	86.6 (1.65)	11.7 (0.12)	88.3 (0.12)	24.7 (0.16)	16.1 (0.13)	8.6 (0.10)	8.1 (0.65)	91.9 (0.65)	25.8 (0.99)	29.1 (1.15)	18.7 (0.96)	10.4 (0.73)
Arizona	69.2 (0.19)	82.9 (0.61)	19.0 (0.06)	81.0 (0.06)	23.5 (0.07)	15.1 (0.06)	8.4 (0.04)	13.8 (0.22)	86.2 (0.22)	24.4 (0.29)	27.4 (0.24)	17.3 (0.23)	10.1 (0.17)
Arkansas	75.4 (0.19)	86.0 (0.83)	24.7 (0.07)	75.3 (0.07)	16.7 (0.06)	11.0 (0.05)	5.7 (0.04)	14.4 (0.34)	85.6 (0.34)	35.1 (0.46)	21.4 (0.47)	14.1 (0.35)	7.3 (0.27)
California	70.7 (0.07)	87.0 (0.20)	23.2 (0.03)	76.8 (0.03)	26.6 (0.03)	17.1 (0.02)	9.5 (0.02)	17.9 (0.09)	82.1 (0.09)	20.9 (0.10)	31.7 (0.13)	19.9 (0.10)	11.8 (0.08)
Colorado	75.1 (0.15)	86.7 (0.76)	13.1 (0.05)	86.9 (0.05)	32.7 (0.06)	21.6 (0.06)	11.1 (0.04)	9.5 (0.20)	90.5 (0.20)	21.9 (0.32)	38.0 (0.30)	24.1 (0.27)	13.9 (0.19)
Connecticut	78.2 (0.21)	88.9 (0.67)	16.0 (0.06)	84.0 (0.06)	31.4 (0.08)	18.1 (0.07)	13.3 (0.06)	9.9 (0.28)	90.1 (0.28)	27.5 (0.40)	37.9 (0.37)	21.3 (0.36)	16.7 (0.28)
Delaware	77.6 (0.41)	84.4 (1.47)	17.4 (0.14)	82.6 (0.14)	25.0 (0.16)	15.6 (0.14)	9.4 (0.11)	10.9 (0.56)	89.1 (0.56)	31.6 (0.76)	30.3 (0.69)	17.9 (0.56)	12.4 (0.57)
District of Columbia	79.4 (0.40)	88.8 (1.61)	22.2 (0.18)	77.8 (0.18)	39.1 (0.21)	18.1 (0.17)	21.0 (0.18)	9.9 (0.52)	90.1 (0.52)	17.8 (0.71)	54.8 (0.73)	24.5 (0.69)	30.2 (0.81)
Florida	71.7 (0.11)	83.5 (0.32)	20.1 (0.04)	79.9 (0.04)	22.3 (0.04)	14.2 (0.03)	8.1 (0.02)	12.8 (0.10)	87.2 (0.10)	29.5 (0.17)	27.4 (0.14)	17.5 (0.12)	9.9 (0.10)
Georgia	70.0 (0.15)	83.7 (0.55)	21.4 (0.05)	78.6 (0.05)	24.3 (0.05)	16.0 (0.05)	8.3 (0.04)	14.4 (0.17)	85.6 (0.17)	28.3 (0.25)	29.0 (0.22)	18.1 (0.19)	10.9 (0.15)
Hawaii	85.8 (0.25)	90.7 (1.15)	15.4 (0.10)	84.6 (0.10)	26.2 (0.12)	17.8 (0.10)	8.4 (0.08)	8.6 (0.36)	91.4 (0.36)	28.3 (0.63)	31.6 (0.70)	20.9 (0.63)	10.7 (0.37)
Idaho	77.3 (0.25)	86.4 (1.26)	15.3 (0.09)	84.7 (0.09)	21.7 (0.10)	14.9 (0.09)	6.8 (0.06)	9.9 (0.38)	90.1 (0.38)	28.3 (0.70)	25.2 (0.63)	17.1 (0.56)	8.2 (0.34)
Illinois	76.0 (0.09)	87.5 (0.36)	18.6 (0.03)	81.4 (0.03)	26.1 (0.03)	16.6 (0.03)	9.5 (0.02)	11.6 (0.13)	88.4 (0.13)	26.6 (0.23)	33.0 (0.19)	20.2 (0.18)	12.8 (0.15)
Indiana	76.5 (0.15)	83.2 (0.70)	17.9 (0.05)	82.1 (0.05)	19.4 (0.05)	12.2 (0.04)	7.2 (0.04)	11.3 (0.21)	88.7 (0.21)	34.4 (0.26)	24.8 (0.30)	15.8 (0.22)	9.0 (0.18)
Iowa	81.4 (0.16)	89.7 (0.86)	13.9 (0.06)	86.1 (0.06)	21.2 (0.07)	14.7 (0.06)	6.5 (0.04)	7.8 (0.26)	92.2 (0.26)	31.5 (0.44)	27.9 (0.41)	18.4 (0.35)	9.4 (0.29)
Kansas	78.3 (0.18)	86.5 (0.89)	14.0 (0.06)	86.0 (0.06)	25.8 (0.08)	17.1 (0.06)	8.7 (0.05)	9.8 (0.35)	90.2 (0.35)	26.7 (0.45)	31.5 (0.37)	20.1 (0.37)	11.5 (0.29)
Kentucky	74.9 (0.15)	86.3 (0.70)	25.9 (0.06)	74.1 (0.06)	17.1 (0.05)	10.2 (0.04)	6.9 (0.03)	15.5 (0.31)	84.5 (0.31)	33.3 (0.33)	22.7 (0.31)	13.3 (0.24)	9.4 (0.22)
Louisiana	72.3 (0.15)	80.3 (0.82)	25.2 (0.06)	74.8 (0.06)	18.7 (0.05)	12.2 (0.04)	6.5 (0.03)	16.4 (0.28)	83.6 (0.28)	33.9 (0.39)	22.9 (0.30)	15.0 (0.25)	7.8 (0.20)
Maine	78.9 (0.28)	88.4 (1.20)	14.6 (0.08)	85.4 (0.08)	22.9 (0.10)	15.0 (0.09)	7.9 (0.06)	7.8 (0.35)	92.2 (0.35)	32.1 (0.76)	29.7 (0.72)	19.5 (0.57)	10.2 (0.42)
Maryland	79.6 (0.16)	87.5 (0.59)	16.2 (0.05)	83.8 (0.05)	31.4 (0.07)	18.0 (0.06)	13.4 (0.05)	10.3 (0.23)	89.7 (0.23)	25.5 (0.26)	38.2 (0.31)	20.9 (0.25)	17.3 (0.25)
Massachusetts	82.2 (0.13)	89.9 (0.50)	15.2 (0.05)	84.8 (0.05)	33.2 (0.06)	19.5 (0.05)	13.7 (0.04)	10.4 (0.19)	89.6 (0.19)	24.6 (0.27)	41.4 (0.29)	23.3 (0.24)	18.0 (0.21)
Michigan	76.5 (0.10)	86.7 (0.41)	16.6 (0.03)	83.4 (0.03)	21.8 (0.04)	13.7 (0.03)	8.1 (0.02)	10.1 (0.18)	89.9 (0.18)	29.4 (0.22)	27.4 (0.21)	16.4 (0.17)	11.0 (0.14)
Minnesota	79.3 (0.13)	89.0 (0.67)	12.1 (0.04)	87.9 (0.04)	27.4 (0.06)	19.1 (0.05)	8.3 (0.03)	7.4 (0.19)	92.6 (0.19)	26.0 (0.33)	34.0 (0.36)	22.3 (0.31)	11.6 (0.26)
Mississippi	71.3 (0.18)	82.6 (0.88)	27.1 (0.08)	72.9 (0.08)	16.9 (0.06)	11.1 (0.05)	5.8 (0.04)	17.3 (0.37)	82.7 (0.37)	30.0 (0.44)	20.9 (0.44)	12.9 (0.35)	8.0 (0.28)
Missouri	76.5 (0.13)	86.9 (0.53)	18.7 (0.05)	81.3 (0.05)	21.6 (0.05)	14.0 (0.04)	7.6 (0.03)	11.2 (0.22)	88.8 (0.22)	31.2 (0.31)	27.5 (0.31)	17.1 (0.25)	10.5 (0.21)
Montana	78.6 (0.31)	87.2 (1.60)	12.8 (0.10)	87.2 (0.10)	24.4 (0.13)	17.2 (0.11)	7.2 (0.08)	7.8 (0.50)	92.2 (0.50)	30.8 (0.71)	28.1 (0.74)	18.5 (0.59)	9.6 (0.44)
Nebraska	80.0 (0.21)	88.7 (1.08)	13.4 (0.07)	86.6 (0.07)	23.7 (0.09)	16.4 (0.08)	7.3 (0.06)	9.5 (0.28)	90.5 (0.28)	27.9 (0.58)	30.2 (0.56)	20.8 (0.49)	9.5 (0.34)
Nevada	66.7 (0.32)	81.7 (1.00)	19.3 (0.10)	80.7 (0.10)	18.2 (0.10)	12.1 (0.08)	6.1 (0.06)	14.6 (0.34)	85.4 (0.34)	28.3 (0.47)	22.9 (0.36)	15.1 (0.31)	7.8 (0.21)
New Hampshire	77.8 (0.29)	89.4 (1.33)	12.6 (0.08)	87.4 (0.08)	28.7 (0.11)	18.7 (0.10)	10.0 (0.07)	7.4 (0.42)	92.6 (0.42)	28.7 (0.62)	35.3 (0.60)	22.0 (0.53)	13.2 (0.35)
New Jersey	76.3 (0.14)	87.5 (0.45)	17.9 (0.04)	82.1 (0.04)	29.8 (0.05)	18.8 (0.04)	11.0 (0.04)	11.0 (0.16)	89.0 (0.16)	28.5 (0.21)	37.2 (0.25)	23.0 (0.24)	14.2 (0.20)
New Mexico	70.5 (0.24)	81.9 (1.30)	21.1 (0.09)	78.9 (0.09)	23.5 (0.09)	13.7 (0.07)	9.8 (0.06)	15.5 (0.43)	84.5 (0.43)	26.2 (0.52)	26.6 (0.50)	15.4 (0.44)	11.2 (0.34)
New York	76.1 (0.09)	87.5 (0.32)	20.9 (0.03)	79.1 (0.03)	27.4 (0.04)	15.6 (0.03)	11.8 (0.03)	14.2 (0.13)	85.8 (0.13)	26.5 (0.17)	34.7 (0.16)	19.7 (0.16)	15.0 (0.14)
North Carolina	74.2 (0.11)	86.7 (0.46)	21.9 (0.04)	78.1 (0.04)	22.5 (0.04)	15.3 (0.04)	7.2 (0.03)	13.6 (0.19)	86.4 (0.19)	26.6 (0.20)	28.7 (0.23)	18.6 (0.18)	10.1 (0.13)
North Dakota	84.4 (0.24)	88.7 (1.52)	16.1 (0.10)	83.9 (0.10)	22.0 (0.12)	16.5 (0.10)	5.5 (0.06)	7.1 (0.44)	92.9 (0.44)	27.4 (0.95)	25.7 (0.96)	19.1 (0.87)	6.7 (0.50)
Ohio	76.8 (0.09)	86.1 (0.48)	17.0 (0.03)	83.0 (0.03)	21.1 (0.03)	13.7 (0.03)	7.4 (0.02)	10.7 (0.14)	89.3 (0.14)	34.0 (0.25)	26.5 (0.20)	16.6 (0.17)	9.9 (0.14)
Oklahoma	74.8 (0.16)	83.7 (0.77)	19.4 (0.06)	80.6 (0.06)	20.3 (0.06)	13.5 (0.05)	6.8 (0.04)	12.5 (0.23)	87.5 (0.23)	31.8 (0.44)	24.1 (0.42)	15.7 (0.35)	8.5 (0.21)
Oregon	74.2 (0.17)	86.8 (0.76)	14.9 (0.05)	85.1 (0.05)	25.1 (0.06)	16.4 (0.06)	8.7 (0.04)	10.3 (0.28)	89.7 (0.28)	24.0 (0.36)	30.6 (0.33)	19.0 (0.27)	11.5 (0.23)
Pennsylvania	79.8 (0.09)	87.8 (0.44)	18.1 (0.03)	81.9 (0.03)	22.4 (0.03)	14.0 (0.03)	8.4 (0.02)	10.5 (0.15)	89.5 (0.15)	36.3 (0.19)	28.8 (0.21)	17.5 (0.17)	11.3 (0.13)
Rhode Island	81.3 (0.32)	88.4 (1.10)	22.0 (0.13)	78.0 (0.13)	25.6 (0.14)	15.9 (0.12)	9.7 (0.10)	14.5 (0.55)	85.5 (0.55)	28.3 (0.67)	30.2 (0.73)	18.0 (0.54)	12.2 (0.49)
South Carolina	74.3 (0.18)	85.1 (0.59)	23.7 (0.07)	76.3 (0.07)	20.4 (0.07)	13.5 (0.06)	6.9 (0.04)	14.0 (0.29)	86.0 (0.29)	30.3 (0.31)	26.2 (0.30)	16.5 (0.23)	9.7 (0.20)
South Dakota	78.2 (0.33)	81.5 (2.15)	15.4 (0.12)	84.6 (0.12)	21.5 (0.13)	15.5 (0.12)	6.0 (0.08)	8.5 (0.45)	91.5 (0.45)	31.1 (0.84)	26.5 (0.86)	19.9 (0.87)	6.7 (0.42)
Tennessee	75.1 (0.16)	88.0 (0.45)	24.1 (0.06)	75.9 (0.06)	19.6 (0.06)	12.8 (0.05)	6.8 (0.03)	14.2 (0.21)	85.8 (0.21)	33.1 (0.27)	25.4 (0.28)	16.4 (0.23)	9.1 (0.15)
Texas	68.6 (0.08)	83.9 (0.29)	24.3 (0.03)	75.7 (0.03)	23.2 (0.03)	15.6 (0.03)	7.6 (0.02)	17.7 (0.12)	82.3 (0.12)	25.1 (0.16)	27.9 (0.14)	18.2 (0.13)	9.7 (0.08)
Utah	80.3 (0.16)	85.7 (0.87)	12.3 (0.07)	87.7 (0.07)	26.1 (0.09)	17.8 (0.08)	8.3 (0.06)	8.5 (0.32)	91.5 (0.32)	23.1 (0.48)	31.2 (0.44)	20.8 (0.35)	10.4 (0.27)
Vermont	83.0 (0.28)	92.1 (1.49)	13.6 (0.10)	86.4 (0.10)	29.4 (0.13)	18.3 (0.11)	11.1 (0.09)	8.0 (0.58)	92.0 (0.58)	29.9 (0.95)	36.2 (1.07)	21.9 (0.89)	14.2 (0.82)
Virginia	79.4 (0.13)	89.1 (0.53)	18.5 (0.05)	81.5 (0.05)	29.5 (0.06)	17.9 (0.05)	11.6 (0.04)	11.4 (0.19)	88.6 (0.19)	24.6 (0.23)	36.6 (0.26)	20.5 (0.20)	16.1 (0.20)
Washington	75.3 (0.16)	84.6 (0.61)	12.9 (0.05)	87.1 (0.05)	27.7 (0.06)	18.4 (0.05)	9.3 (0.04)	9.6 (0.19)	90.4 (0.19)	22.8 (0.22)	33.2 (0.29)	21.3 (0.23)	12.0 (0.18)
West Virginia	78.2 (0.22)	86.0 (1.07)	24.8 (0.09)	75.2 (0.09)	14.8 (0.07)	8.9 (0.06)	5.9 (0.05)	14.4 (0.42)	85.6 (0.42)	41.3 (0.48)	19.3 (0.41)	11.7 (0.36)	7.6 (0.27)
Wisconsin	78.9 (0.13)	89.1 (0.60)	14.9 (0.04)	85.1 (0.04)	22.4 (0.05)	15.2 (0.04)	7.2 (0.03)	8.5 (0.18)	91.5 (0.18)	32.1 (0.34)	28.5 (0.34)	18.8 (0.28)	9.7 (0.22)
Wyoming	79.0 (0.41)	88.1 (1.77)	12.1 (0.13)	87.9 (0.13)	21.9 (0.16)	14.9 (0.14)	7.0 (0.10)	7.8 (0.62)	92.2 (0.62)	27.5 (0.78)	25.9 (0.80)	16.9 (0.80)	9.0 (0.54)

#Rounds to zero.
[1]High school completers include those graduating from high school with a diploma as well as those completing high school through equivalency programs, such as a GED program.
NOTE: Detail may not sum to totals because of rounding.

SOURCE: U.S. Department of Commerce, Census Bureau, Census 2000 Summary File 3, retrieved October 11, 2006, from http://factfinder2.census.gov/faces/tableservices/jsf/pages/productview.xhtml?pid=DEC_00_SF3_QTP20&prodType=table; Census Briefs, *Educational Attainment: 2000*; and 2014 American Community Survey (ACS) 1-Year Public Use Microdata Sample (PUMS) data. (This table was prepared December 2015.)

Table 104.85. Rates of high school completion and bachelor's degree attainment among persons age 25 and over, by race/ethnicity and state: 2014

[Standard errors appear in parentheses]

State	Percent with high school completion[1] or higher						Percent with bachelor's degree or higher					
	Total[2]	White	Black	Hispanic	Asian	Two or more races	Total[2]	White	Black	Hispanic	Asian	Two or more races
1	2	3	4	5	6	7	8	9	10	11	12	13
United States	86.9 (0.16)	92.0 (0.24)	84.5 (0.12)	65.4 (0.16)	86.4 (0.12)	90.3 (0.24)	30.1 (0.16)	33.6 (0.16)	19.8 (0.12)	14.4 (0.10)	51.7 (0.22)	32.0 (0.35)
Alabama	84.6 (0.29)	87.4 (0.34)	79.8 (0.57)	59.4 (2.68)	86.5 (2.44)	89.2 (2.32)	23.0 (0.30)	25.6 (0.34)	15.1 (0.69)	17.4 (1.80)	52.1 (3.69)	24.5 (3.23)
Alaska	91.9 (0.65)	95.0 (0.65)	84.6 (7.68)	85.2 (4.46)	83.3 (4.17)	91.4 (3.54)	29.1 (1.15)	34.8 (1.47)	‡ (†)	23.1 (5.02)	37.8 (4.88)	15.4 (3.84)
Arizona	86.2 (0.22)	94.2 (0.16)	89.9 (0.94)	65.4 (0.62)	86.3 (1.27)	92.7 (1.30)	27.4 (0.24)	33.5 (0.32)	25.2 (1.39)	11.4 (0.41)	49.1 (1.64)	29.3 (2.16)
Arkansas	85.6 (0.34)	88.1 (0.33)	83.7 (0.91)	50.7 (2.53)	89.9 (2.56)	90.1 (2.41)	21.4 (0.47)	22.8 (0.55)	15.1 (0.87)	9.1 (1.03)	54.3 (4.22)	24.2 (3.61)
California	82.1 (0.09)	94.5 (0.09)	89.8 (0.32)	60.9 (0.24)	87.3 (0.20)	91.5 (0.54)	31.7 (0.13)	41.6 (0.20)	22.8 (0.47)	11.2 (0.15)	50.2 (0.36)	37.6 (0.84)
Colorado	90.5 (0.20)	95.6 (0.16)	89.9 (1.15)	69.7 (0.97)	83.5 (1.86)	93.1 (1.54)	38.0 (0.30)	43.9 (0.36)	24.1 (1.78)	13.9 (0.65)	51.6 (2.14)	36.0 (2.40)
Connecticut	90.1 (0.28)	93.5 (0.25)	86.8 (0.80)	72.3 (1.19)	91.1 (1.33)	88.2 (2.90)	37.9 (0.37)	41.7 (0.45)	22.9 (1.36)	17.8 (1.09)	66.3 (1.86)	33.2 (3.53)
Delaware	89.1 (0.56)	92.0 (0.62)	86.5 (1.41)	67.7 (3.70)	90.5 (3.09)	86.1 (5.59)	30.3 (0.69)	31.4 (0.82)	23.8 (1.60)	15.4 (2.50)	69.0 (4.37)	28.2 (9.40)
District of Columbia	90.1 (0.52)	98.9 (0.34)	86.9 (0.77)	67.2 (3.39)	91.7 (2.64)	98.9 (1.07)	54.8 (0.73)	89.6 (0.74)	24.7 (1.21)!	41.3 (3.42)	75.4 (3.71)	85.0 (4.62)
Florida	87.2 (0.10)	92.0 (0.11)	81.3 (0.39)	78.0 (0.35)	85.0 (0.76)	89.1 (1.07)	27.4 (0.14)	30.9 (0.20)	17.3 (0.35)	21.7 (0.32)	44.6 (1.09)	28.5 (1.67)
Georgia	85.6 (0.17)	89.5 (0.20)	84.1 (0.36)	58.9 (1.12)	85.9 (0.90)	90.3 (1.54)	29.0 (0.22)	33.3 (0.27)	20.7 (0.47)	15.2 (0.78)	51.5 (1.41)	36.5 (2.68)
Hawaii	91.4 (0.36)	96.7 (0.52)	97.9 (0.90)	91.4 (1.32)	87.3 (0.61)	94.1 (0.80)	31.6 (0.70)	45.8 (1.39)	28.4 (4.82)	20.7 (1.86)	31.2 (0.97)	25.5 (1.52)
Idaho	90.1 (0.38)	93.5 (0.34)	76.2 (10.48)	58.1 (2.45)	85.4 (6.54)	92.1 (2.01)	25.2 (0.63)	26.8 (0.70)	26.7 (9.49)!	8.1 (1.29)	45.7 (8.39)	22.0 (4.97)
Illinois	88.4 (0.13)	93.5 (0.12)	84.5 (0.47)	64.9 (0.64)	91.2 (0.60)	93.5 (0.95)	33.0 (0.19)	36.7 (0.25)	21.0 (0.53)	14.0 (0.51)	63.3 (1.03)	37.8 (2.50)
Indiana	88.7 (0.21)	90.3 (0.22)	86.3 (0.75)	65.1 (1.56)	87.5 (1.81)	88.8 (1.87)	24.8 (0.30)	25.5 (0.33)	16.5 (0.94)	13.6 (1.13)	58.3 (2.76)	26.2 (3.00)
Iowa	92.2 (0.26)	93.6 (0.29)	84.4 (2.30)	63.1 (2.49)	87.1 (2.20)	90.9 (3.23)	27.9 (0.41)	28.0 (0.46)	20.9 (3.13)	14.6 (1.72)	56.6 (4.49)	31.1 (6.12)
Kansas	90.2 (0.35)	93.6 (0.29)	85.9 (1.86)	60.2 (2.20)	86.2 (2.59)	92.3 (1.92)	31.5 (0.37)	33.9 (0.42)	17.7 (1.87)	12.4 (1.10)	53.0 (3.25)	28.0 (2.96)
Kentucky	84.5 (0.31)	84.9 (0.32)	86.3 (1.25)	64.5 (2.55)	83.5 (2.78)	85.2 (2.89)	22.7 (0.31)	23.1 (0.35)	15.2 (0.99)	17.1 (1.95)	54.4 (3.21)	23.9 (3.07)
Louisiana	83.6 (0.28)	87.3 (0.34)	78.0 (0.63)	73.2 (1.97)	75.5 (2.51)	81.6 (3.87)	22.9 (0.30)	26.8 (0.38)	14.0 (0.44)	19.9 (1.79)	40.7 (2.89)	20.4 (2.83)
Maine	92.2 (0.35)	92.4 (0.34)	76.8 (8.33)	95.9 (1.71)	84.4 (5.84)	88.9 (3.54)	29.7 (0.72)	29.7 (0.73)	20.3 (6.85)!	35.9 (6.94)	45.9 (8.79)	19.2 (4.60)
Maryland	89.7 (0.23)	93.0 (0.25)	89.8 (0.44)	63.6 (1.93)	91.1 (0.77)	91.1 (1.42)	38.2 (0.31)	43.2 (0.33)	27.8 (0.60)	21.4 (1.00)	61.7 (1.19)	40.3 (2.83)
Massachusetts	89.6 (0.19)	93.1 (0.16)	83.8 (0.88)	67.3 (1.20)	83.3 (0.98)	89.1 (1.87)	41.4 (0.29)	44.4 (0.36)	23.5 (1.08)	17.9 (0.85)	56.2 (1.48)	37.3 (2.66)
Michigan	89.9 (0.18)	91.8 (0.16)	84.0 (0.53)	72.2 (1.29)	87.5 (1.28)	87.1 (1.84)	27.4 (0.21)	28.4 (0.25)	17.1 (0.47)	16.7 (1.09)	63.8 (1.49)	26.0 (1.77)
Minnesota	92.6 (0.19)	95.0 (0.15)	83.0 (1.65)	68.3 (2.50)	78.8 (1.83)	91.1 (2.33)	34.0 (0.36)	35.4 (0.36)	19.0 (1.93)	19.7 (1.89)!	39.5 (2.41)	33.8 (3.57)
Mississippi	82.7 (0.37)	86.9 (0.37)	76.8 (0.64)	62.9 (3.25)	80.9 (3.77)	87.4 (4.34)	20.9 (0.44)	24.4 (0.50)	14.9 (0.72)	11.6 (1.80)	37.6 (4.40)	34.2 (6.62)
Missouri	88.8 (0.22)	89.9 (0.22)	85.3 (0.51)	70.4 (2.59)	87.5 (1.92)	82.6 (1.90)	27.5 (0.31)	28.5 (0.33)	17.2 (0.81)	20.6 (1.80)	61.3 (2.39)	25.1 (2.24)
Montana	92.2 (0.50)	93.0 (0.49)	‡ (†)	78.8 (0.94)	95.6 (2.73)	89.7 (4.02)	28.1 (0.74)	29.4 (0.78)	‡ (†)	19.1 (4.33)	34.5 (11.34)!	20.6 (5.80)
Nebraska	90.5 (0.28)	93.0 (0.23)	85.4 (2.29)	52.8 (2.68)	77.4 (4.28)	93.2 (2.38)	30.2 (0.56)	30.2 (0.65)	25.5 (3.28)	9.5 (1.47)	47.3 (5.51)	32.2 (6.49)
Nevada	85.4 (0.34)	92.7 (0.35)	85.8 (1.35)	63.6 (1.01)	90.3 (1.00)	94.3 (1.23)	22.9 (0.36)	27.6 (0.47)	13.6 (1.31)	9.0 (0.61)	37.6 (1.62)	28.0 (2.66)
New Hampshire	92.6 (0.42)	92.9 (0.43)	95.1 (2.69)	82.2 (3.83)	91.6 (2.81)	92.4 (3.19)	35.3 (0.60)	35.2 (0.64)	3 (5.89)	17.6 (3.09)	64.4 (4.78)	29.1 (4.97)
New Jersey	89.0 (0.16)	93.3 (0.15)	88.0 (0.51)	72.6 (0.71)	92.7 (0.43)	94.2 (1.17)	37.2 (0.25)	41.0 (0.33)	23.6 (0.60)	17.1 (0.48)	67.2 (0.91)	38.6 (2.72)
New Mexico	84.5 (0.43)	95.4 (0.29)	88.8 (2.25)	73.9 (0.94)	83.9 (4.19)	92.6 (2.46)	26.6 (0.50)	39.0 (0.81)	26.6 (4.01)	14.6 (0.62)	57.7 (4.18)	40.2 (6.35)
New York	85.8 (0.13)	92.5 (0.11)	83.4 (0.34)	67.6 (0.49)	78.5 (0.62)	86.5 (1.16)	34.7 (0.16)	40.7 (0.18)	23.4 (0.46)	17.7 (0.39)	44.8 (0.71)	36.1 (1.78)
North Carolina	86.4 (0.19)	90.3 (0.19)	84.0 (0.38)	55.2 (1.17)	85.6 (1.40)	88.8 (1.46)	28.7 (0.23)	32.4 (0.29)	19.3 (0.43)	11.9 (0.68)	53.6 (2.11)	32.9 (2.52)
North Dakota	92.9 (0.44)	94.0 (0.41)	‡ (†)	70.3 (9.12)	88.1 (6.94)	† (†)	25.7 (0.96)	26.6 (0.99)	‡ (†)	‡ (†)	59.1 (7.47)	‡ (†)
Ohio	89.3 (0.14)	90.5 (0.16)	83.8 (0.55)	73.8 (1.27)	88.8 (1.10)	87.1 (1.35)	26.5 (0.20)	27.4 (0.21)	16.2 (0.60)	19.7 (1.10)	63.0 (1.69)	22.4 (1.67)
Oklahoma	87.5 (0.23)	90.5 (0.23)	88.8 (0.88)	58.8 (1.76)	84.0 (2.75)	89.5 (1.02)	24.1 (0.42)	26.4 (0.50)	18.6 (1.40)	8.7 (0.62)	40.2 (3.69)	22.9 (1.55)
Oregon	89.7 (0.28)	92.9 (0.23)	87.5 (1.89)	62.0 (1.76)	88.2 (1.03)	88.2 (2.18)	30.6 (0.33)	32.3 (0.39)	24.2 (3.32)	12.0 (0.90)	47.9 (2.24)	25.6 (2.14)
Pennsylvania	89.5 (0.15)	91.7 (0.15)	85.3 (0.56)	67.7 (1.17)	81.2 (1.03)	89.2 (1.81)	28.8 (0.21)	30.3 (0.23)	16.5 (0.65)	13.6 (0.73)	54.3 (1.45)	31.7 (2.09)
Rhode Island	85.5 (0.55)	88.9 (0.53)	86.4 (2.63)	63.7 (2.30)	73.4 (4.65)	87.3 (3.78)	30.2 (0.73)	33.1 (0.84)	21.7 (2.89)	13.1 (1.76)	34.4 (4.96)	29.8 (5.95)
South Carolina	86.0 (0.29)	90.0 (0.29)	79.8 (0.55)	59.5 (2.17)	87.0 (1.95)	86.7 (2.48)	26.2 (0.30)	30.9 (0.38)	14.7 (0.51)	13.6 (1.29)	5 (3.50)	22.4 (3.61)
South Dakota	91.5 (0.45)	93.0 (0.45)	74.3 (16)	77.1 (5.50)	69.5 (8.01)	89.6 (3.67)	26.5 (0.86)	28.0 (0.93)	12.8 (6.30)	28.5 (7.94)	31.9 (9.92)!	20.4 (4.84)
Tennessee	85.8 (0.21)	87.2 (0.23)	85.2 (0.59)	58.6 (1.70)	84.5 (1.87)	82.6 (2.05)	25.4 (0.28)	26.9 (0.32)	18.5 (0.61)	13.4 (1.18)	50.2 (2.36)	22.9 (2.36)
Texas	82.3 (0.12)	93.4 (0.11)	88.2 (0.25)	62.7 (0.26)	86.9 (0.53)	91.8 (0.95)	27.9 (0.14)	36.4 (0.21)	13.0 (0.40)	13.0 (0.18)	58.1 (0.80)	34.9 (1.41)
Utah	91.5 (0.32)	95.5 (0.26)	89.1 (3.36)	65.5 (1.83)	87.3 (2.40)	91.8 (2.62)	31.2 (0.44)	34.0 (0.50)	27.8 (5.49)	12.2 (1.03)	39.8 (3.97)	38.0 (5.06)
Vermont	92.0 (0.58)	92.6 (0.53)	84.4 (0.45)!	96.3 (3.46)	60.4 (13.45)	97.6 (1.96)	36.2 (1.07)	36.2 (1.05)	‡ (†)	40.3 (9.32)	32.4 (9.77)!	28.4 (9.06)!
Virginia	88.6 (0.19)	91.7 (0.17)	87.9 (1.10)	69.3 (1.29)	89.1 (0.72)	92.9 (1.08)	36.6 (0.26)	40.1 (0.32)	22.5 (0.54)	22.5 (1.12)	59.9 (1.10)	44.3 (2.38)
Washington	90.4 (0.19)	94.2 (0.18)	87.9 (1.81)	63.1 (1.13)	86.9 (0.90)	93.0 (0.88)	33.2 (0.29)	34.8 (0.34)	14.5 (1.51)	14.5 (0.75)	47.8 (0.97)	33.0 (1.64)
West Virginia	85.6 (0.42)	85.5 (0.43)	84.1 (1.27)	85.2 (4.19)	82.0 (2.94)	89.0 (3.30)	19.3 (0.41)	19.1 (0.43)	15.3 (2.43)!	26.8 (7.30)	58.9 (5.45)	23.2 (4.39)
Wisconsin	91.5 (0.18)	93.6 (0.20)	† (†)	63.0 (1.64)	84.7 (1.80)	91.6 (2.25)	28.5 (0.34)	29.9 (0.38)	12.8 (1.21)!	14.6 (1.45)	44.5 (2.81)	30.6 (3.23)
Wyoming	92.2 (0.62)	94.6 (0.49)	‡ (†)	66.7 (4.14)	92.3 (3.32)	85.8 (6.51)	25.9 (0.80)	27.7 (0.83)	‡ (†)	9.3 (2.45)	50.8 (10.92)	22.4 (7.01)

†Not applicable.
!Interpret data with caution. The coefficient of variation (CV) for this estimate is between 30 and 50 percent.
‡Reporting standards not met. Either there are too few cases for a reliable estimate or the coefficient of variation (CV) is 50 percent or greater.
[1]Includes completion of high school through equivalency programs, such as a GED program.

[2]Total includes racial/ethnic groups not shown separately.
NOTE: Race categories exclude persons of Hispanic ethnicity.
SOURCE: U.S. Department of Commerce, Census Bureau, 2014 American Community Survey (ACS) 1-Year Public Use Microdata Sample (PUMS) data. (This table was prepared December 2015.)

Table 104.88. Rates of high school completion and bachelor's degree attainment among persons age 25 and over, by sex and state: 2014
[Standard errors appear in parentheses]

State	Number of persons age 25 and over (in thousands)						Percent with high school completion[1] or higher						Percent with bachelor's or higher degree					
	Total		Male		Female		Total		Male		Female		Total		Male		Female	
1	2		3		4		5		6		7		8		9		10	
United States	213,806	(50.5)	103,072	(31.5)	110,734	(32.0)	86.9	(0.04)	86.3	(0.05)	87.5	(0.05)	30.1	(0.06)	29.9	(0.06)	30.2	(0.07)
Alabama	3,259	(3.6)	1,536	(3.0)	1,723	(2.7)	84.6	(0.29)	83.7	(0.41)	85.5	(0.31)	23.0	(0.30)	22.7	(0.40)	23.3	(0.43)
Alaska	468	(2.5)	243	(2.3)	225	(2.2)	91.9	(0.65)	92.6	(0.69)	91.3	(1.05)	29.1	(1.15)	25.3	(1.30)	33.1	(1.56)
Arizona	4,438	(3.8)	2,167	(2.8)	2,271	(3.4)	86.2	(0.22)	85.6	(0.33)	86.7	(0.23)	27.4	(0.24)	27.8	(0.33)	27.0	(0.37)
Arkansas	1,970	(3.4)	946	(2.6)	1,024	(2.4)	85.6	(0.34)	85.0	(0.46)	86.1	(0.43)	21.4	(0.47)	20.7	(0.52)	22.0	(0.56)
California	25,656	(8.4)	12,515	(6.7)	13,141	(5.3)	82.1	(0.09)	81.8	(0.12)	82.3	(0.10)	31.7	(0.13)	32.0	(0.14)	31.4	(0.15)
Colorado	3,587	(3.3)	1,776	(3.2)	1,811	(2.9)	90.5	(0.20)	89.7	(0.29)	91.3	(0.24)	38.0	(0.30)	37.4	(0.43)	38.6	(0.38)
Connecticut	2,478	(2.8)	1,183	(2.7)	1,295	(2.1)	90.1	(0.28)	89.8	(0.38)	90.4	(0.31)	37.9	(0.37)	37.7	(0.47)	38.2	(0.50)
Delaware	639	(1.7)	302	(1.3)	337	(1.1)	89.1	(0.56)	88.0	(0.83)	90.1	(0.64)	30.3	(0.69)	29.3	(0.91)	31.2	(0.96)
District of Columbia	465	(1.0)	217	(0.9)	247	(0.7)	90.1	(0.52)	89.3	(0.76)	90.8	(0.60)	54.8	(0.73)	54.0	(1.03)	55.5	(0.88)
Florida	14,042	(6.4)	6,722	(5.8)	7,320	(4.4)	87.2	(0.10)	86.5	(0.18)	87.9	(0.12)	27.4	(0.14)	28.1	(0.23)	26.7	(0.18)
Georgia	6,576	(6.0)	3,114	(4.7)	3,462	(4.1)	85.6	(0.17)	84.2	(0.25)	86.9	(0.20)	29.0	(0.22)	28.8	(0.29)	29.3	(0.29)
Hawaii	974	(2.2)	481	(1.8)	493	(1.6)	91.4	(0.36)	92.4	(0.45)	90.4	(0.47)	31.6	(0.70)	30.5	(0.90)	32.6	(0.83)
Idaho	1,045	(2.1)	513	(2.2)	532	(1.9)	90.1	(0.38)	89.2	(0.55)	91.0	(0.40)	25.2	(0.63)	26.5	(0.80)	24.0	(0.84)
Illinois	8,640	(5.6)	4,153	(4.6)	4,487	(4.1)	88.4	(0.13)	87.9	(0.17)	88.8	(0.17)	33.0	(0.19)	32.7	(0.26)	33.3	(0.23)
Indiana	4,344	(4.2)	2,093	(3.2)	2,251	(3.3)	88.7	(0.21)	88.3	(0.29)	89.0	(0.23)	24.8	(0.30)	24.2	(0.33)	25.2	(0.38)
Iowa	2,063	(3.1)	1,007	(2.8)	1,056	(2.4)	92.2	(0.26)	91.0	(0.36)	93.2	(0.30)	27.9	(0.41)	26.8	(0.53)	28.8	(0.54)
Kansas	1,881	(4.0)	917	(3.2)	964	(2.8)	90.2	(0.35)	89.6	(0.42)	90.7	(0.40)	31.5	(0.37)	31.4	(0.52)	31.6	(0.44)
Kentucky	2,969	(4.1)	1,433	(3.0)	1,535	(2.6)	84.5	(0.31)	83.2	(0.34)	85.6	(0.36)	22.7	(0.31)	21.9	(0.39)	23.5	(0.40)
Louisiana	3,063	(4.3)	1,461	(3.4)	1,602	(2.8)	83.6	(0.28)	81.9	(0.37)	85.1	(0.36)	22.9	(0.30)	21.6	(0.33)	24.0	(0.40)
Maine	957	(1.6)	457	(1.7)	500	(1.6)	92.2	(0.35)	91.0	(0.51)	93.2	(0.47)	29.7	(0.72)	28.7	(0.94)	30.6	(0.77)
Maryland	4,066	(4.2)	1,924	(3.5)	2,142	(2.9)	89.7	(0.23)	88.8	(0.32)	90.5	(0.24)	38.2	(0.31)	38.2	(0.37)	38.3	(0.37)
Massachusetts	4,653	(3.3)	2,208	(3.3)	2,445	(2.4)	89.6	(0.19)	89.3	(0.27)	89.8	(0.24)	41.4	(0.29)	41.2	(0.36)	41.5	(0.38)
Michigan	6,689	(5.2)	3,219	(4.2)	3,471	(4.1)	89.9	(0.18)	89.1	(0.24)	90.7	(0.21)	27.4	(0.21)	27.1	(0.25)	27.7	(0.27)
Minnesota	3,683	(5.1)	1,807	(4.2)	1,876	(3.8)	92.6	(0.19)	92.6	(0.22)	92.6	(0.28)	34.0	(0.36)	32.9	(0.48)	35.0	(0.42)
Mississippi	1,948	(2.7)	920	(2.0)	1,029	(2.0)	82.7	(0.37)	81.0	(0.55)	84.3	(0.40)	20.9	(0.44)	18.9	(0.57)	22.7	(0.48)
Missouri	4,077	(4.6)	1,959	(3.5)	2,118	(3.2)	88.8	(0.22)	88.4	(0.29)	89.2	(0.27)	27.5	(0.31)	26.7	(0.37)	28.3	(0.42)
Montana	694	(2.0)	343	(1.5)	351	(1.7)	92.2	(0.50)	91.9	(0.71)	92.4	(0.58)	28.1	(0.74)	27.8	(0.92)	28.5	(1.00)
Nebraska	1,225	(2.7)	600	(2.4)	625	(2.2)	90.5	(0.28)	89.7	(0.46)	91.2	(0.36)	30.2	(0.56)	29.7	(0.71)	30.7	(0.69)
Nevada	1,919	(2.3)	953	(2.1)	967	(1.7)	85.4	(0.34)	85.2	(0.49)	85.6	(0.42)	22.9	(0.30)	23.3	(0.48)	22.6	(0.47)
New Hampshire	930	(1.5)	452	(1.4)	478	(1.3)	92.6	(0.42)	91.1	(0.68)	94.0	(0.43)	35.3	(0.60)	34.5	(0.76)	36.0	(0.81)
New Jersey	6,129	(3.5)	2,927	(3.1)	3,201	(3.1)	89.0	(0.16)	88.7	(0.23)	89.4	(0.21)	37.2	(0.25)	37.7	(0.33)	36.8	(0.31)
New Mexico	1,371	(3.3)	663	(2.8)	708	(2.2)	84.5	(0.43)	83.8	(0.50)	85.3	(0.56)	26.6	(0.50)	25.6	(0.62)	27.5	(0.62)
New York	13,546	(6.1)	6,423	(5.0)	7,123	(4.6)	85.8	(0.13)	85.7	(0.15)	85.9	(0.17)	34.7	(0.16)	34.2	(0.20)	35.1	(0.20)
North Carolina	6,666	(6.9)	3,155	(5.5)	3,511	(3.7)	86.4	(0.18)	84.7	(0.27)	87.9	(0.23)	28.7	(0.23)	27.8	(0.33)	29.4	(0.25)
North Dakota	477	(1.5)	239	(1.4)	238	(1.5)	92.9	(0.44)	92.4	(0.57)	93.3	(0.55)	25.7	(0.96)	23.3	(1.23)	28.2	(1.16)
Ohio	7,858	(4.9)	3,765	(4.4)	4,093	(3.5)	89.3	(0.14)	88.6	(0.20)	89.9	(0.20)	26.5	(0.20)	26.8	(0.26)	26.3	(0.24)
Oklahoma	2,536	(3.8)	1,230	(3.0)	1,306	(2.9)	87.5	(0.23)	86.8	(0.31)	88.1	(0.30)	24.1	(0.42)	23.3	(0.52)	25.0	(0.55)
Oregon	2,748	(3.7)	1,336	(3.0)	1,412	(2.7)	89.7	(0.28)	89.2	(0.36)	90.1	(0.35)	30.6	(0.33)	30.4	(0.37)	30.8	(0.48)
Pennsylvania	8,875	(6.1)	4,262	(5.3)	4,613	(4.4)	89.5	(0.15)	88.9	(0.20)	90.1	(0.19)	28.8	(0.21)	28.6	(0.30)	29.0	(0.24)
Rhode Island	726	(1.3)	344	(1.1)	382	(1.2)	85.5	(0.55)	84.3	(0.74)	86.5	(0.67)	30.2	(0.73)	31.1	(1.00)	29.3	(0.85)
South Carolina	3,261	(4.0)	1,546	(3.7)	1,715	(2.5)	86.0	(0.29)	84.5	(0.39)	87.4	(0.32)	26.2	(0.30)	26.0	(0.42)	26.4	(0.38)
South Dakota	556	(2.1)	276	(1.9)	280	(1.8)	91.5	(0.45)	90.1	(0.72)	92.8	(0.56)	26.5	(0.86)	24.3	(1.11)	28.7	(1.12)
Tennessee	4,422	(3.9)	2,105	(3.7)	2,317	(3.1)	85.8	(0.21)	84.8	(0.28)	86.7	(0.30)	25.4	(0.28)	25.4	(0.39)	25.5	(0.34)
Texas	17,099	(8.4)	8,325	(6.6)	8,774	(5.6)	82.3	(0.12)	81.6	(0.15)	82.8	(0.14)	27.9	(0.14)	27.8	(0.19)	28.0	(0.17)
Utah	1,708	(2.8)	849	(2.4)	860	(2.3)	91.5	(0.32)	91.1	(0.45)	91.8	(0.34)	31.2	(0.44)	34.1	(0.54)	28.3	(0.58)
Vermont	439	(1.2)	211	(1.0)	228	(1.1)	92.0	(0.58)	91.3	(0.77)	92.8	(0.74)	36.2	(1.07)	35.3	(1.50)	37.0	(1.18)
Virginia	5,622	(5.5)	2,707	(4.6)	2,915	(3.6)	88.6	(0.19)	87.6	(0.26)	89.5	(0.21)	36.6	(0.26)	36.8	(0.31)	36.5	(0.31)
Washington	4,787	(5.3)	2,357	(4.0)	2,431	(3.9)	90.4	(0.19)	90.2	(0.25)	90.7	(0.24)	33.2	(0.29)	34.0	(0.36)	32.5	(0.36)
West Virginia	1,296	(2.1)	630	(1.6)	666	(1.8)	85.6	(0.42)	85.1	(0.56)	86.0	(0.55)	19.3	(0.41)	18.2	(0.54)	20.4	(0.57)
Wisconsin	3,896	(4.6)	1,906	(4.0)	1,990	(3.3)	91.5	(0.18)	90.6	(0.29)	92.3	(0.24)	28.5	(0.34)	27.7	(0.43)	29.3	(0.46)
Wyoming	390	(1.9)	196	(1.5)	193	(1.3)	92.2	(0.62)	91.5	(0.84)	92.8	(0.80)	25.9	(0.80)	25.0	(1.20)	26.8	(1.03)

[1]Includes completion of high school through equivalency programs, such as a GED program.
NOTE: Detail may not sum to totals because of rounding.

SOURCE: U.S. Department of Commerce, Census Bureau, 2014 American Community Survey (ACS) 1-Year Public Use Microdata Sample (PUMS) data. (This table was prepared December 2015.)

Table 104.90. Percentage distribution of spring 2002 high school sophomores, by highest level of education completed through 2012 and selected student characteristics: 2012

[Standard errors appear in parentheses]

Selected student characteristic	Total		Less than high school completion		High school completion		Some post-secondary (no credential)		Postsecondary certificate		Associate's degree		Bachelor's degree		Master's or higher degree	
1	2		3		4		5		6		7		8		9	
Total, all students	100.0	(†)	3.1	(0.23)	12.6	(0.44)	32.3	(0.47)	10.1	(0.32)	8.7	(0.35)	26.6	(0.65)	6.7	(0.26)
Sex																
Male	100.0	(†)	3.7	(0.31)	16.0	(0.67)	33.9	(0.72)	8.4	(0.43)	8.0	(0.46)	25.1	(0.87)	4.9	(0.31)
Female	100.0	(†)	2.5	(0.26)	9.3	(0.51)	30.7	(0.68)	11.8	(0.46)	9.4	(0.50)	28.1	(0.80)	8.3	(0.42)
Race/ethnicity																
White	100.0	(†)	1.8	(0.22)	11.7	(0.51)	28.9	(0.60)	8.7	(0.40)	9.1	(0.47)	31.6	(0.80)	8.2	(0.36)
Black	100.0	(†)	4.7	(0.70)	13.2	(1.10)	40.2	(1.31)	14.6	(0.93)	7.5	(0.80)	16.1	(1.07)	3.7	(0.56)
Hispanic	100.0	(†)	6.6	(0.75)	14.6	(1.10)	38.7	(1.27)	12.3	(0.84)	9.1	(0.87)	15.8	(1.26)	2.8	(0.49)
Asian	100.0	(†)	1.6	(0.46)	5.9	(0.96)	27.6	(1.60)	8.5	(0.93)	5.6	(0.87)	39.8	(2.08)	11.1	(0.97)
Pacific Islander	100.0	(†)	#	(†)	22.7 !	(8.56)	35.0	(8.93)	‡	(†)	‡	(†)	29.5 !	(10.00)	‡	(†)
American Indian/Alaska Native	100.0	(†)	8.1 !	(3.31)	22.7	(5.00)	33.7	(4.82)	11.3 !	(3.57)	7.1 !	(2.59)	13.7 !	(4.28)	‡	(†)
Two or more races	100.0	(†)	3.4	(0.89)	18.5	(2.00)	32.6	(2.69)	9.0	(1.51)	8.6	(1.60)	22.2	(2.12)	5.7	(1.20)
Parents' educational attainment in 2002																
High school completion or less	100.0	(†)	6.4	(0.53)	21.1	(0.80)	33.5	(0.81)	12.5	(0.72)	9.3	(0.63)	14.7	(0.80)	2.5	(0.32)
Some college	100.0	(†)	2.2	(0.27)	13.4	(0.65)	36.8	(0.83)	12.1	(0.57)	9.5	(0.53)	21.7	(0.82)	4.3	(0.38)
Bachelor's degree	100.0	(†)	1.6	(0.30)	6.6	(0.58)	30.2	(1.13)	7.5	(0.58)	8.5	(0.74)	36.4	(1.21)	9.2	(0.76)
Master's or higher degree	100.0	(†)	1.3	(0.30)	4.4	(0.62)	23.5	(1.24)	5.5	(0.64)	6.1	(0.65)	44.0	(1.41)	15.1	(0.85)
Parents' socioeconomic status in 2012[1]																
Low quartile	100.0	(†)	7.0	(0.58)	21.3	(0.92)	36.2	(1.03)	12.8	(0.72)	8.2	(0.63)	12.3	(0.86)	2.2	(0.30)
Middle two quartiles	100.0	(†)	2.4	(0.26)	12.9	(0.54)	34.7	(0.68)	11.1	(0.48)	9.9	(0.52)	24.2	(0.78)	4.9	(0.32)
High quartile	100.0	(†)	0.5	(0.15)	3.1	(0.41)	23.6	(1.07)	5.4	(0.51)	6.7	(0.58)	45.9	(1.13)	14.7	(0.70)
Student's educational expectation in 10th grade																
High school completion or less	100.0	(†)	12.3	(1.44)	36.0	(1.88)	31.5	(1.94)	11.3	(1.38)	5.3	(0.92)	3.3	(0.70)	‡	(†)
Some college	100.0	(†)	5.7	(0.88)	22.8	(1.45)	37.5	(1.70)	14.5	(1.31)	10.7	(1.16)	7.9	(0.91)	1.0 !	(0.36)
Bachelor's degree	100.0	(†)	1.7	(0.27)	10.3	(0.66)	33.3	(0.88)	10.6	(0.57)	10.0	(0.64)	29.0	(0.92)	5.0	(0.37)
Master's or higher degree	100.0	(†)	1.0	(0.19)	4.1	(0.40)	29.3	(0.79)	8.0	(0.53)	7.7	(0.47)	37.9	(0.88)	12.1	(0.57)
Don't know	100.0	(†)	5.0	(0.88)	21.2	(1.58)	36.7	(1.92)	11.5	(1.06)	7.7	(0.98)	14.7	(1.38)	3.2	(0.66)
2002 high school type																
Public	100.0	(†)	3.3	(0.25)	13.4	(0.47)	33.0	(0.49)	10.4	(0.35)	8.8	(0.37)	25.0	(0.69)	6.1	(0.28)
Catholic	100.0	(†)	‡	(†)	1.6	(0.45)	23.7	(1.26)	6.4	(0.66)	6.2	(0.68)	47.3	(1.76)	14.6	(1.15)
Other private	100.0	(†)	‡	(†)	3.9	(0.98)	23.9	(2.00)	6.4	(1.01)	8.5	(1.26)	44.3	(2.44)	12.8	(1.38)
Cumulative high school grade point average																
0.00–1.99	100.0	(†)	11.3	(0.90)	25.7	(1.22)	41.8	(1.29)	12.5	(0.79)	5.4	(0.58)	3.1	(0.46)	‡	(†)
2.00–2.49	100.0	(†)	2.4	(0.47)	18.3	(1.00)	44.5	(1.11)	12.5	(0.77)	9.9	(0.79)	11.4	(0.83)	1.0	(0.24)
2.50–2.99	100.0	(†)	0.6	(0.17)	11.1	(0.91)	35.8	(1.21)	12.4	(0.86)	12.5	(0.90)	24.1	(1.13)	3.5	(0.50)
3.00–3.49	100.0	(†)	‡	(†)	5.0	(0.54)	25.9	(1.06)	9.0	(0.66)	9.8	(0.83)	41.9	(1.22)	8.2	(0.69)
3.50+	100.0	(†)	‡	(†)	1.6	(0.32)	13.1	(0.85)	2.9	(0.42)	5.7	(0.61)	55.0	(1.34)	21.7	(0.99)
Students with subsequent postsecondary enrollment																
Timing of first postsecondary enrollment																
Within 3 months of high school completion	100.0	(†)	†	(†)	†	(†)	28.8	(0.65)	8.5	(0.40)	10.2	(0.48)	41.9	(0.80)	10.7	(0.42)
Between 4 and 12 months of high school completion	100.0	(†)	†	(†)	†	(†)	45.2	(1.65)	17.8	(1.52)	10.7	(1.05)	21.2	(1.41)	5.1	(0.80)
13 or more months after high school completion	100.0	(†)	†	(†)	†	(†)	65.7	(1.27)	18.4	(1.05)	9.9	(0.85)	5.5	(0.74)	0.5 !	(0.17)
Type of postsecondary institution first attended																
Public	100.0	(†)	†	(†)	†	(†)	40.1	(0.67)	10.6	(0.43)	10.9	(0.50)	31.5	(0.75)	6.9	(0.33)
Private nonprofit	100.0	(†)	†	(†)	†	(†)	24.2	(1.31)	5.1	(0.65)	4.7	(0.65)	49.1	(1.42)	17.0	(0.98)
Private for-profit	100.0	(†)	†	(†)	†	(†)	46.8	(2.13)	30.4	(2.13)	15.5	(1.59)	6.6	(1.01)	0.7 !	(0.35)
Selectivity and level of postsecondary institution first attended																
Highly selective 4-year	100.0	(†)	†	(†)	†	(†)	14.8	(1.02)	2.5	(0.45)	1.7	(0.37)	60.7	(1.39)	20.3	(0.98)
Moderately selective 4-year	100.0	(†)	†	(†)	†	(†)	26.1	(1.17)	5.0	(0.51)	5.7	(0.62)	49.4	(1.19)	13.7	(0.91)
Inclusive 4-year	100.0	(†)	†	(†)	†	(†)	40.9	(2.01)	7.3	(1.04)	10.9	(1.51)	33.0	(2.06)	7.8	(1.08)
2-year	100.0	(†)	†	(†)	†	(†)	51.7	(0.92)	15.8	(0.71)	16.1	(0.79)	15.2	(0.78)	1.3	(0.20)
Less-than-2-year	100.0	(†)	†	(†)	†	(†)	41.8	(3.14)	51.9	(3.19)	4.9	(1.07)	1.3 !	(0.64)	‡	(†)

†Not applicable.
#Rounds to zero.
!Interpret data with caution. The coefficient of variation (CV) for this estimate is between 30 and 50 percent.
‡Reporting standards not met. Either there are too few cases for a reliable estimate or the coefficient of variation (CV) is 50 percent or greater.

[1]Socioeconomic status (SES) was measured by a composite score on parental education and occupations, and family income.
NOTE: Race categories exclude persons of Hispanic ethnicity. Detail may not sum to totals because of rounding.
SOURCE: U.S. Department of Education, National Center for Education Statistics, Education Longitudinal Study of 2002 (ELS:2002), Third Follow-up. (This table was prepared May 2014.)

Table 104.91. Number and percentage distribution of spring 2002 high school sophomores, by highest level of education completed, and socioeconomic status and selected student characteristics while in high school: 2013

[Standard errors appear in parentheses]

Socioeconomic status (SES) and selected student characteristic	Number (in thousands)		Percentage distribution		All levels		Less than high school completion		High school completion		Some post-secondary education (no credential)		Postsecondary certificate		Associate's degree		Bachelor's or higher degree	
1	2		3		4		5		6		7		8		9		10	
Total, all SES² groups	3,242	(49.0)	100.0	(†)	100.0	(†)	3.2	(0.23)	13.4	(0.47)	31.1	(0.53)	8.2	(0.31)	8.4	(0.31)	35.8	(0.79)
Low SES²	810	(24.4)	100.0	(†)	100.0	(†)	7.8	(0.61)	22.6	(0.92)	35.5	(1.07)	10.8	(0.68)	8.1	(0.59)	15.2	(0.90)
Sex																		
Male	370	(12.9)	45.7	(0.94)	100.0	(†)	10.4	(1.08)	27.7	(1.49)	34.8	(1.57)	7.4	(0.83)	7.3	(0.91)	12.4	(1.11)
Female	440	(15.8)	54.3	(0.94)	100.0	(†)	5.5	(0.64)	18.3	(1.11)	36.2	(1.45)	13.6	(0.95)	8.9	(0.77)	17.6	(1.21)
Race/ethnicity																		
White	311	(15.1)	38.4	(1.53)	100.0	(†)	5.5	(0.77)	27.4	(1.51)	31.4	(1.68)	11.0	(1.24)	9.1	(0.96)	15.7	(1.34)
Black	162	(10.6)	20.1	(1.26)	100.0	(†)	9.3	(1.54)	19.1	(2.07)	40.2	(2.66)	12.0	(1.62)	5.7	(1.08)	13.8	(1.75)
Hispanic	251	(16.9)	30.9	(1.71)	100.0	(†)	10.1	(1.20)	19.1	(2.04)	39.4	(2.21)	9.7	(1.12)	9.0	(1.34)	12.6	(1.64)
Asian	38	(3.5)	4.7	(0.45)	100.0	(†)	4.6	(1.32)	12.8	(2.71)	29.2	(3.08)	9.2	(1.76)	7.6	(1.76)	36.6	(3.39)
Pacific Islander	‡	(†)	0.2 !	(0.07)	100.0	(†)	‡	(†)	‡	(†)	‡	(†)	‡	(†)	‡	(†)	‡	(†)
American Indian/Alaska Native	11 !	(3.4)	1.4 !	(0.43)	100.0	(†)	‡	(†)	‡	(†)	36.7	(8.47)	‡	(†)	‡	(†)	‡	(†)
Two or more races	35	(3.8)	4.3	(0.45)	100.0	(†)	7.1 !	(2.69)	34.4	(5.23)	29.8	(5.46)	8.7 !	(3.22)	7.0 !	(3.10)	13.0	(3.66)
Reading achievement quartile³																		
First (lowest)	324	(14.0)	40.6	(1.16)	100.0	(†)	12.0	(1.17)	28.3	(1.62)	34.9	(1.69)	10.0	(1.08)	7.8	(0.85)	7.1	(1.04)
Second	246	(10.8)	30.8	(1.05)	100.0	(†)	6.4	(0.97)	21.6	(1.80)	37.6	(1.85)	13.8	(1.36)	6.9	(0.97)	13.7	(1.33)
Third	140	(8.6)	17.6	(0.89)	100.0	(†)	3.6	(0.95)	16.5	(1.84)	39.1	(2.51)	9.3	(1.54)	10.1	(1.64)	21.3	(2.24)
Fourth (highest)	88	(5.8)	11.0	(0.70)	100.0	(†)	‡	(†)	12.1	(2.27)	29.9	(3.23)	6.3	(1.63)	9.6	(2.12)	40.6	(3.27)
Math achievement quartile³																		
First (lowest)	320	(14.1)	40.2	(1.17)	100.0	(†)	11.9	(1.16)	29.4	(1.59)	35.3	(1.81)	11.6	(1.05)	6.3	(0.79)	5.5	(0.87)
Second	239	(12.0)	30.0	(1.09)	100.0	(†)	6.8	(1.00)	19.1	(1.51)	39.2	(2.19)	11.6	(1.33)	9.8	(1.19)	13.4	(1.35)
Third	160	(8.7)	20.1	(1.01)	100.0	(†)	3.6	(1.03)	17.7	(1.98)	37.5	(2.30)	8.3	(1.62)	8.1	(1.47)	24.8	(2.30)
Fourth (highest)	78	(5.4)	9.8	(0.68)	100.0	(†)	‡	(†)	12.8	(2.10)	25.0	(3.00)	8.5	(2.13)	10.7	(2.62)	42.0	(3.41)
Middle SES²	1,631	(31.5)	100.0	(†)	100.0	(†)	2.6	(0.28)	13.9	(0.58)	33.8	(0.72)	9.2	(0.44)	9.3	(0.47)	31.2	(0.85)
Sex																		
Male	810	(20.1)	49.6	(0.83)	100.0	(†)	2.7	(0.37)	18.5	(0.90)	36.8	(1.18)	7.9	(0.61)	7.9	(0.62)	26.2	(1.16)
Female	822	(21.3)	50.4	(0.83)	100.0	(†)	2.5	(0.40)	9.4	(0.70)	31.0	(0.89)	10.4	(0.61)	10.7	(0.72)	36.1	(1.08)
Race/ethnicity																		
White	1,027	(26.7)	62.9	(1.14)	100.0	(†)	1.8	(0.32)	13.7	(0.71)	31.2	(0.89)	8.3	(0.55)	9.4	(0.60)	35.6	(1.08)
Black	241	(14.2)	14.7	(0.82)	100.0	(†)	3.9	(0.82)	13.4	(1.51)	41.2	(1.99)	13.1	(1.42)	9.0	(1.07)	19.4	(1.61)
Hispanic	215	(12.3)	13.2	(0.70)	100.0	(†)	4.9	(1.01)	14.1	(1.47)	39.3	(1.92)	10.4	(1.33)	10.8	(1.52)	20.5	(1.79)
Asian	53	(4.2)	3.2	(0.26)	100.0	(†)	‡	(†)	6.1	(1.49)	27.7	(2.20)	6.0	(1.52)	6.5	(1.33)	53.0	(2.86)
Pacific Islander	‡	(†)	0.2	(0.06)	100.0	(†)	‡	(†)	‡	(†)	‡	(†)	‡	(†)	‡	(†)	‡	(†)
American Indian/Alaska Native	16	(3.3)	1.0	(0.20)	100.0	(†)	‡	(†)	32.6	(7.74)	29.0	(7.20)	‡	(†)	‡	(†)	15.5 !	(6.41)
Two or more races	77	(5.9)	4.7	(0.36)	100.0	(†)	2.7 !	(1.02)	18.5	(3.17)	36.4	(3.23)	7.9	(1.91)	8.2	(2.07)	26.3	(3.34)
Reading achievement quartile³																		
First (lowest)	358	(14.4)	22.0	(0.82)	100.0	(†)	6.2	(0.86)	23.5	(1.52)	39.7	(1.80)	12.6	(1.00)	8.7	(0.96)	9.3	(0.93)
Second	427	(15.5)	26.3	(0.72)	100.0	(†)	2.7	(0.56)	15.7	(1.05)	37.1	(1.48)	10.9	(1.01)	10.6	(0.92)	23.0	(1.28)
Third	462	(15.0)	28.4	(0.73)	100.0	(†)	1.1	(0.32)	10.7	(1.06)	32.3	(1.36)	8.8	(0.74)	10.1	(0.89)	37.1	(1.62)
Fourth (highest)	379	(13.5)	23.3	(0.76)	100.0	(†)	0.8 !	(0.29)	6.1	(0.67)	26.8	(1.45)	4.4	(0.71)	7.7	(0.90)	54.2	(1.72)
Math achievement quartile³																		
First (lowest)	353	(14.8)	21.7	(0.83)	100.0	(†)	6.6	(0.89)	24.1	(1.35)	39.1	(1.67)	13.1	(1.04)	8.8	(0.95)	8.4	(0.98)
Second	448	(15.5)	27.5	(0.71)	100.0	(†)	2.7	(0.55)	15.7	(1.11)	37.5	(1.35)	11.9	(0.93)	11.6	(0.95)	20.6	(1.22)
Third	443	(13.5)	27.2	(0.69)	100.0	(†)	1.1	(0.31)	10.6	(0.94)	32.5	(1.41)	7.9	(0.85)	9.6	(0.90)	38.3	(1.56)
Fourth (highest)	382	(13.9)	23.5	(0.76)	100.0	(†)	‡	(†)	5.6	(0.79)	26.6	(1.50)	3.9	(0.66)	7.0	(0.84)	56.6	(1.76)
High SES²	801	(27.1)	100.0	(†)	100.0	(†)	0.6	(0.17)	3.5	(0.43)	21.2	(1.11)	3.6	(0.43)	6.5	(0.54)	64.5	(1.19)
Sex																		
Male	411	(17.3)	51.3	(1.19)	100.0	(†)	0.8 !	(0.29)	4.7	(0.66)	25.8	(1.61)	2.8	(0.50)	6.8	(0.73)	59.1	(1.61)
Female	390	(15.7)	48.7	(1.19)	100.0	(†)	‡	(†)	2.3	(0.48)	16.3	(1.14)	4.6	(0.67)	6.2	(0.78)	70.3	(1.45)
Race/ethnicity																		
White	616	(23.3)	76.9	(1.08)	100.0	(†)	0.4 !	(0.16)	3.1	(0.43)	19.6	(1.12)	3.0	(0.47)	6.4	(0.63)	67.5	(1.26)
Black	61	(5.9)	7.7	(0.70)	100.0	(†)	‡	(†)	6.3 !	(2.19)	36.7	(4.72)	6.9	(2.04)	5.7 !	(1.88)	44.2	(4.45)
Hispanic	53	(5.3)	6.6	(0.63)	100.0	(†)	‡	(†)	6.5 !	(2.03)	28.5	(4.09)	6.8	(1.95)	7.1	(1.94)	48.8	(4.08)
Asian	39	(3.7)	4.9	(0.46)	100.0	(†)	‡	(†)	‡	(†)	12.6	(1.99)	3.3 !	(1.19)	4.1 !	(1.36)	78.2	(2.61)
Pacific Islander	‡	(†)	‡	(†)	100.0	(†)	‡	(†)	‡	(†)	‡	(†)	‡	(†)	‡	(†)	‡	(†)
American Indian/Alaska Native	‡	(†)	‡	(†)	100.0	(†)	‡	(†)	‡	(†)	‡	(†)	‡	(†)	‡	(†)	‡	(†)
Two or more races	27	(3.0)	3.4	(0.38)	100.0	(†)	‡	(†)	‡	(†)	19.8	(4.26)	5.4 !	(2.68)	11.4 !	(3.82)	58.6	(5.54)
Reading achievement quartile³																		
First (lowest)	70	(5.8)	8.7	(0.70)	100.0	(†)	5.3 !	(1.75)	15.4	(2.82)	34.5	(3.62)	14.9	(2.72)	7.0	(1.82)	22.8	(2.90)
Second	120	(7.9)	15.0	(0.86)	100.0	(†)	‡	(†)	4.7	(1.24)	30.2	(2.58)	6.5	(1.35)	9.6	(1.84)	49.0	(2.90)
Third	239	(11.9)	29.9	(0.99)	100.0	(†)	‡	(†)	3.0	(0.72)	22.6	(1.94)	2.6	(0.77)	7.4	(1.12)	64.3	(2.12)
Fourth (highest)	370	(15.3)	46.4	(1.18)	100.0	(†)	‡	(†)	1.1 !	(0.36)	14.9	(1.22)	1.3	(0.33)	4.8	(0.70)	77.9	(1.42)
Math achievement quartile³																		
First (lowest)	68	(6.6)	8.5	(0.79)	100.0	(†)	4.4 !	(1.67)	15.4	(3.14)	35.7	(3.82)	13.5	(2.49)	5.4	(1.27)	25.5	(3.38)
Second	125	(7.3)	15.6	(0.81)	100.0	(†)	‡	(†)	4.2	(1.21)	30.3	(2.81)	8.0	(1.44)	13.5	(1.95)	43.3	(2.82)
Third	222	(10.0)	27.9	(0.90)	100.0	(†)	‡	(†)	3.3	(0.81)	22.5	(1.59)	2.3	(0.66)	7.5	(1.10)	64.3	(1.85)
Fourth (highest)	383	(17.0)	48.0	(1.18)	100.0	(†)	‡	(†)	1.2	(0.35)	14.9	(1.27)	1.3	(0.33)	3.8	(0.61)	78.7	(1.46)

†Not applicable.
!Interpret data with caution. The coefficient of variation (CV) for this estimate is between 30 and 50 percent.
‡Reporting standards not met. Either there are too few cases for a reliable estimate or the coefficient of variation (CV) is 50 percent or greater.
[1]Postsecondary transcripts from 2013 were used to update self-reported attainment of highest degree for all respondents with complete transcripts as well as for respondents whose partial transcripts indicated higher attainment than was self-reported in 2012.
[2]Socioeconomic status (SES) was measured by a composite score on parental education and occupations, and family income in 2002. The "low" SES group is the lowest quartile; the "middle" SES group is the middle two quartiles; and the "high" SES group is the upper quartile.

[3]Reading and math achievement quartiles reflect students' scores on assessments conducted in 2002.
NOTE: Race categories exclude persons of Hispanic ethnicity. Detail may not sum to totals because of rounding and survey item nonresponse. Some data have been revised from previously published figures.
SOURCE: U.S. Department of Education, National Center for Education Statistics, Education Longitudinal Study of 2002 (ELS:2002), Base Year through Postsecondary Transcript Study. (This table was prepared June 2016.)

Table 104.92. Number and percentage distribution of spring 2002 high school sophomores, by highest level of education completed, socioeconomic status and educational expectations while in high school, and college enrollment status 2 years after high school: 2013

[Standard errors appear in parentheses]

Socioeconomic status (SES), educational expectations, and college enrollment status	Total				Highest level of education completed through 2013[1]									
	Number (in thousands)		Percentage distribution		All levels		Less than high school completion		High school completion		Some post-secondary education (no credential)		Postsecondary certificate		Associate's degree		Bachelor's or higher degree	
1	2		3		4		5		6		7		8		9		10	
Low SES[2]	810	(24.4)	100.0	(†)	100.0	(†)	7.8	(0.61)	22.6	(0.92)	35.5	(1.07)	10.8	(0.68)	8.1	(0.59)	15.2	(0.90)
Educational expectations in 2002																		
Don't know	94	(6.5)	12.6	(0.75)	100.0	(†)	8.9	(2.14)	29.1	(2.82)	35.5	(3.02)	9.7	(1.87)	6.4	(1.82)	10.4	(2.01)
Less than high school	13	(2.1)	1.7	(0.26)	100.0	(†)	21.3 !	(7.71)	42.0	(8.08)	34.6	(7.92)	‡	(†)	‡	(†)	‡	(†)
High school diploma or GED	92	(6.5)	12.4	(0.71)	100.0	(†)	16.2	(2.36)	43.4	(3.40)	26.1	(2.87)	8.6	(2.00)	4.4	(1.24)	1.3 !	(0.55)
Attend or complete 2-year college	66	(5.2)	8.8	(0.60)	100.0	(†)	9.7	(2.38)	28.8	(3.41)	33.9	(3.76)	15.2	(2.80)	6.6	(1.53)	5.8	(1.57)
Attend college, 4-year degree incomplete	43	(4.0)	5.7	(0.48)	100.0	(†)	11.3	(2.90)	26.1	(4.66)	35.8	(5.08)	8.2 !	(2.56)	10.5	(3.03)	8.2	(2.42)
Bachelor's degree	247	(10.9)	33.1	(0.94)	100.0	(†)	4.8	(0.98)	18.5	(1.59)	38.4	(1.88)	13.4	(1.33)	9.3	(1.05)	15.6	(1.51)
Advanced degree	191	(9.7)	25.6	(1.06)	100.0	(†)	3.9	(0.88)	10.4	(1.34)	38.3	(2.20)	8.3	(1.33)	9.9	(1.25)	29.2	(2.00)
Educational expectations in 2004																		
Don't know	114	(7.5)	14.3	(0.82)	100.0	(†)	14.3	(2.25)	34.6	(3.23)	33.1	(2.69)	9.6	(2.08)	5.4	(1.49)	3.1 !	(1.02)
Less than high school	‡	(†)	0.7	(0.21)	100.0	(†)	‡	(†)	‡	(†)	‡	(†)	‡	(†)	‡	(†)	‡	(†)
High school diploma or GED	88	(6.6)	11.0	(0.77)	100.0	(†)	17.1	(2.54)	47.2	(3.51)	22.2	(2.77)	7.3	(1.75)	4.2 !	(1.50)	2.0 !	(0.88)
Attend or complete 2-year college	176	(10.6)	22.0	(1.08)	100.0	(†)	6.3	(1.37)	26.7	(2.09)	40.1	(2.51)	15.7	(1.74)	8.5	(1.36)	2.8	(0.74)
Attend college, 4-year degree incomplete	40	(4.1)	5.0	(0.51)	100.0	(†)	‡	(†)	23.6	(4.56)	44.4	(4.99)	10.7 !	(3.39)	9.5 !	(3.33)	7.8 !	(2.97)
Bachelor's degree	202	(10.0)	25.2	(1.02)	100.0	(†)	2.8	(0.78)	9.8	(1.40)	39.9	(2.18)	9.7	(1.42)	12.2	(1.47)	25.6	(2.08)
Advanced degree	173	(8.8)	21.6	(0.93)	100.0	(†)	2.9 !	(1.02)	8.2	(1.25)	37.2	(2.82)	9.5	(1.74)	8.6	(1.29)	33.7	(2.50)
College enrollment status in 2006																		
Enrolled in a 4-year college	152	(7.7)	21.0	(1.00)	100.0	(†)	‡	(†)	‡	(†)	31.9	(2.39)	7.0	(1.24)	8.1	(1.60)	53.0	(2.62)
Enrolled in a 2-year college	207	(12.4)	28.6	(1.36)	100.0	(†)	‡	(†)	‡	(†)	50.6	(2.15)	16.2	(1.61)	16.9	(1.65)	15.9	(1.50)
Enrolled in a less-than-2-year college	25	(3.2)	3.5	(0.43)	100.0	(†)	‡	(†)	12.9 !	(4.56)	35.3	(7.00)	42.3	(6.72)	5.4 !	(2.28)	‡	(†)
Not enrolled	340	(14.3)	46.9	(1.39)	100.0	(†)	15.5	(1.31)	45.4	(1.60)	28.3	(1.51)	7.1	(0.93)	2.9	(0.54)	0.8 !	(0.26)
Middle SES[2]	1,631	(31.5)	100.0	(†)	100.0	(†)	2.6	(0.28)	13.9	(0.58)	33.8	(0.72)	9.2	(0.44)	9.3	(0.47)	31.2	(0.85)
Educational expectations in 2002																		
Don't know	149	(7.5)	9.8	(0.44)	100.0	(†)	5.3	(1.16)	21.7	(2.22)	36.7	(2.68)	11.8	(1.58)	6.3	(1.29)	18.2	(2.15)
Less than high school	14	(2.6)	0.9	(0.16)	100.0	(†)	20.9 !	(7.98)	34.2	(8.99)	31.4	(8.37)	‡	(†)	‡	(†)	‡	(†)
High school diploma or GED	105	(6.7)	6.9	(0.41)	100.0	(†)	9.7	(1.83)	34.5	(2.84)	34.6	(3.03)	11.7	(1.92)	5.5	(1.25)	4.1	(1.13)
Attend or complete 2-year college	110	(7.0)	7.2	(0.39)	100.0	(†)	3.2 !	(1.19)	24.8	(2.90)	38.0	(2.93)	13.0	(1.98)	12.9	(2.07)	8.0	(1.63)
Attend college, 4-year degree incomplete	59	(4.8)	3.9	(0.28)	100.0	(†)	‡	(†)	19.1	(3.05)	42.8	(4.20)	13.9	(2.59)	7.9	(2.11)	11.8	(2.37)
Bachelor's degree	562	(15.3)	36.9	(0.74)	100.0	(†)	1.2	(0.30)	11.5	(0.97)	34.1	(1.13)	8.4	(0.68)	11.4	(0.84)	33.5	(1.29)
Advanced degree	523	(15.8)	34.4	(0.74)	100.0	(†)	0.9 !	(0.27)	5.5	(0.66)	31.4	(1.40)	7.4	(0.72)	8.3	(0.71)	46.5	(1.33)
Educational expectations in 2004																		
Don't know	150	(8.8)	9.2	(0.50)	100.0	(†)	9.2	(1.55)	26.3	(2.33)	32.8	(2.48)	11.2	(1.82)	8.0	(1.51)	12.5	(1.98)
Less than high school	‡	(†)	‡	(†)	100.0	(†)	‡	(†)	‡	(†)	‡	(†)	‡	(†)	‡	(†)	‡	(†)
High school diploma or GED	97	(7.2)	5.9	(0.42)	100.0	(†)	7.9	(1.98)	46.9	(3.44)	27.3	(3.03)	8.1	(1.63)	4.6	(1.30)	5.2 !	(1.63)
Attend or complete 2-year college	281	(11.7)	17.2	(0.62)	100.0	(†)	3.1	(0.70)	23.9	(1.79)	39.2	(1.89)	17.2	(1.63)	11.6	(1.27)	4.9	(0.83)
Attend college, 4-year degree incomplete	68	(6.0)	4.2	(0.35)	100.0	(†)	‡	(†)	15.0	(2.87)	48.9	(3.85)	8.2	(2.32)	12.7	(2.93)	13.7	(2.91)
Bachelor's degree	547	(15.7)	33.5	(0.73)	100.0	(†)	0.8	(0.22)	7.1	(0.77)	34.7	(1.40)	6.7	(0.67)	11.2	(0.95)	39.5	(1.52)
Advanced degree	489	(14.8)	29.9	(0.78)	100.0	(†)	‡	(†)	3.6	(0.60)	28.8	(1.35)	5.9	(0.69)	7.5	(0.76)	53.7	(1.51)
College enrollment status in 2006																		
Enrolled in a 4-year college	574	(16.7)	39.4	(1.00)	100.0	(†)	‡	(†)	‡	(†)	24.4	(1.03)	3.9	(0.51)	7.3	(0.69)	64.3	(1.21)
Enrolled in a 2-year college	451	(16.7)	30.9	(0.94)	100.0	(†)	‡	(†)	‡	(†)	46.0	(1.52)	12.9	(1.01)	17.8	(1.11)	23.0	(1.23)
Enrolled in a less-than-2-year college	32	(3.8)	2.2	(0.26)	100.0	(†)	‡	(†)	14.6	(4.05)	31.5	(5.28)	39.6	(5.40)	7.7 !	(2.87)	‡	(†)
Not enrolled	402	(15.5)	27.5	(0.87)	100.0	(†)	8.6	(0.92)	43.6	(1.50)	31.4	(1.32)	9.7	(0.79)	4.4	(0.66)	2.3	(0.49)
High SES[2]	801	(27.1)	100.0	(†)	100.0	(†)	0.6	(0.17)	3.5	(0.43)	21.2	(1.11)	3.6	(0.43)	6.5	(0.54)	64.5	(1.19)
Educational expectations in 2002																		
Don't know	42	(4.0)	5.6	(0.48)	100.0	(†)	‡	(†)	6.3 !	(2.27)	34.3	(4.34)	4.2 !	(1.87)	9.2	(2.52)	45.6	(4.84)
Less than high school	‡	(†)	0.3 !	(0.10)	100.0	(†)	‡	(†)	‡	(†)	‡	(†)	‡	(†)	‡	(†)	‡	(†)
High school diploma or GED	14	(2.4)	1.9	(0.29)	100.0	(†)	‡	(†)	25.3	(7.29)	29.4	(8.30)	13.8 !	(6.19)	‡	(†)	16.3 !	(7.56)
Attend or complete 2-year college	19	(2.8)	2.5	(0.35)	100.0	(†)	‡	(†)	20.7 !	(7.21)	41.5	(7.90)	‡	(†)	20.6	(5.39)	12.0 !	(3.87)
Attend college, 4-year degree incomplete	13	(2.2)	1.7	(0.28)	100.0	(†)	‡	(†)	17.5 !	(7.75)	39.0	(8.02)	‡	(†)	‡	(†)	27.7	(7.47)
Bachelor's degree	262	(12.2)	35.0	(1.01)	100.0	(†)	‡	(†)	3.2	(0.64)	23.5	(1.70)	4.2	(0.75)	7.2	(0.97)	61.5	(2.02)
Advanced degree	396	(14.8)	52.9	(1.06)	100.0	(†)	‡	(†)	1.2 !	(0.37)	16.3	(1.21)	2.8	(0.53)	4.7	(0.58)	74.8	(1.42)
Educational expectations in 2004																		
Don't know	37	(4.2)	4.6	(0.51)	100.0	(†)	4.2 !	(1.98)	13.8	(3.78)	31.0	(4.77)	8.7	(2.58)	13.4	(3.94)	28.9	(4.40)
Less than high school	‡	(†)	‡	(†)	100.0	(†)	‡	(†)	‡	(†)	‡	(†)	‡	(†)	‡	(†)	‡	(†)
High school diploma or GED	13	(2.4)	1.7	(0.30)	100.0	(†)	‡	(†)	23.2 !	(9.42)	37.6	(11.14)	‡	(†)	‡	(†)	‡	(†)
Attend or complete 2-year college	43	(4.3)	5.3	(0.50)	100.0	(†)	‡	(†)	11.1 !	(3.57)	52.1	(5.15)	14.6	(3.61)	12.7	(3.31)	8.8	(2.25)
Attend college, 4-year degree incomplete	22	(3.3)	2.7	(0.40)	100.0	(†)	‡	(†)	18.3 !	(7.40)	37.1	(7.61)	‡	(†)	15.4 !	(5.72)	22.1	(6.52)
Bachelor's degree	268	(12.1)	33.2	(1.06)	100.0	(†)	‡	(†)	1.7	(0.39)	24.0	(1.71)	4.0	(0.80)	6.5	(0.90)	63.6	(1.87)
Advanced degree	423	(17.6)	52.4	(1.15)	100.0	(†)	‡	(†)	0.9 !	(0.30)	13.6	(1.15)	1.4	(0.34)	4.8	(0.67)	79.2	(1.32)
College enrollment status in 2006																		
Enrolled in a 4-year college	527	(21.4)	70.5	(1.27)	100.0	(†)	‡	(†)	‡	(†)	13.5	(1.00)	1.4	(0.32)	3.4	(0.46)	81.6	(1.05)
Enrolled in a 2-year college	150	(9.1)	20.1	(1.06)	100.0	(†)	‡	(†)	‡	(†)	38.0	(2.64)	7.9	(1.46)	16.6	(1.77)	37.4	(2.48)
Enrolled in a less-than-2-year college	6	(1.6)	0.8	(0.21)	100.0	(†)	‡	(†)	‡	(†)	36.6 !	(12.87)	30.3 !	(10.70)	‡	(†)	‡	(†)
Not enrolled	64	(5.4)	8.6	(0.70)	100.0	(†)	6.2 !	(1.98)	36.2	(4.18)	35.5	(4.21)	5.4	(1.55)	4.4 !	(1.77)	12.4	(2.42)

†Not applicable.
!Interpret data with caution. The coefficient of variation (CV) for this estimate is between 30 and 50 percent.
‡Reporting standards not met. Either there are too few cases for a reliable estimate or the coefficient of variation (CV) is 50 percent or greater.
[1]Postsecondary transcripts from 2013 were used to update self-reported attainment of highest degree for all respondents with complete transcripts as well as for respondents whose partial transcripts indicated higher attainment than was self-reported in 2012.

[2]Socioeconomic status (SES) was measured by a composite score on parental education and occupations, and family income in 2002. The "low" SES group is the lowest quartile; the "middle" SES group is the middle two quartiles; and the "high" SES group is the upper quartile.
NOTE: Detail may not sum to totals because of rounding and survey item nonresponse. Some data have been revised from previously published figures.
SOURCE: U.S. Department of Education, National Center for Education Statistics, Education Longitudinal Study of 2002 (ELS:2002), Base Year through Postsecondary Transcript Study. (This table was prepared June 2016.)

Table 104.93. Sources of college information for spring 2002 high school sophomores who expected to attend a postsecondary institution, by highest level of education completed and socioeconomic status while in high school: 2013

[Standard errors appear in parentheses]

Socioeconomic status (SES) and sources of college information	Percent of students obtaining college information from each source						
	All students who expected to attend a postsecondary institution	Highest level of education completed through 2013[1]					
		Less than high school completion	High school completion	Some postsecondary education (no credential)	Postsecondary certificate	Associate's degree	Bachelor's or higher degree
1	2	3	4	5	6	7	8
Low SES[2]							
Information sources as of 2002							
School counselor	40.8 (1.43)	25.9 (5.37)	35.5 (3.17)	40.5 (2.23)	39.4 (3.88)	41.9 (4.68)	50.8 (2.59)
Teacher	35.5 (1.29)	31.0 (5.50)	29.7 (2.65)	37.5 (2.18)	34.7 (3.96)	37.2 (4.50)	37.7 (3.10)
Coach	7.5 (0.68)	‡ (†)	6.4 (1.53)	10.4 (1.29)	3.1 ! (1.28)	6.4 ! (2.02)	6.5 (1.36)
Parent	42.0 (1.28)	29.8 (5.37)	36.9 (2.93)	42.7 (2.26)	41.7 (3.70)	48.8 (4.46)	45.6 (2.89)
Friend	39.5 (1.18)	30.0 (5.28)	35.9 (2.93)	40.8 (2.08)	41.3 (4.03)	31.2 (3.42)	46.0 (3.04)
Sibling	23.4 (1.13)	8.2 ! (2.86)	21.4 (2.70)	22.8 (1.91)	24.1 (3.81)	27.6 (3.86)	28.1 (2.64)
Other relative	27.2 (1.22)	26.3 (5.15)	21.9 (2.52)	29.2 (2.03)	29.2 (3.55)	28.8 (4.21)	26.6 (2.44)
College publication or website	29.9 (1.20)	12.8 ! (4.11)	21.8 (2.72)	30.3 (2.10)	22.0 (3.35)	36.4 (3.87)	43.1 (2.93)
College representative	15.2 (1.07)	‡ (†)	13.4 (1.83)	15.8 (1.71)	13.5 (2.86)	21.0 (3.88)	16.3 (2.55)
College search guide	28.7 (1.23)	18.8 (4.94)	21.6 (2.65)	28.6 (2.09)	21.5 (3.14)	26.3 (3.60)	43.9 (3.05)
Information sources as of 2004							
School counselor	77.7 (1.41)	‡ (†)	67.9 (3.96)	74.6 (2.44)	78.4 (3.54)	78.2 (4.23)	91.2 (1.81)
Teacher	46.1 (1.66)	‡ (†)	39.8 (3.79)	43.1 (2.65)	49.0 (4.52)	39.3 (5.45)	56.3 (3.59)
Coach	9.0 (0.89)	‡ (†)	‡ (†)	12.6 (1.68)	8.1 ! (3.43)	6.2 ! (2.36)	9.5 (1.76)
Parent	42.8 (1.41)	‡ (†)	36.7 (3.86)	41.7 (2.16)	47.7 (4.17)	40.2 (5.07)	47.4 (3.38)
Friend	25.9 (1.47)	‡ (†)	17.7 (2.72)	24.1 (2.18)	32.4 (4.40)	25.2 (4.69)	30.9 (2.89)
Sibling	32.6 (1.44)	‡ (†)	22.4 (3.42)	30.7 (2.01)	36.3 (4.05)	32.9 (4.91)	42.1 (3.10)
Other relative	53.1 (1.53)	‡ (†)	44.4 (4.32)	51.1 (2.56)	50.7 (4.21)	48.1 (5.39)	65.9 (3.06)
College publication or website	53.9 (1.50)	‡ (†)	36.8 (4.11)	52.9 (2.58)	56.1 (4.17)	53.5 (5.44)	67.8 (2.83)
College representative	50.7 (1.58)	‡ (†)	31.1 (3.78)	49.6 (2.43)	40.2 (4.36)	48.9 (5.31)	73.0 (3.10)
College search guide	43.0 (1.73)	‡ (†)	28.6 (3.51)	45.3 (2.59)	27.9 (4.02)	42.3 (4.65)	57.6 (3.03)
Middle SES[2]							
Information sources as of 2002							
School counselor	44.3 (1.06)	26.0 (6.59)	40.5 (2.83)	43.1 (1.41)	42.9 (2.72)	39.3 (2.77)	49.0 (1.64)
Teacher	31.6 (0.91)	41.4 (7.34)	32.0 (2.64)	32.0 (1.42)	31.0 (2.76)	24.1 (2.22)	32.9 (1.50)
Coach	9.3 (0.55)	‡ (†)	12.0 (1.86)	8.7 (0.81)	8.9 (1.66)	8.0 (1.56)	9.5 (0.96)
Parent	55.2 (0.90)	49.1 (8.17)	48.1 (2.89)	55.0 (1.39)	52.6 (3.23)	54.5 (2.60)	58.6 (1.51)
Friend	39.2 (0.86)	36.1 (9.25)	39.3 (2.89)	36.5 (1.50)	41.4 (2.81)	38.3 (2.71)	41.7 (1.40)
Sibling	23.6 (0.71)	20.8 ! (6.99)	17.4 (2.19)	20.7 (1.13)	24.0 (2.46)	23.9 (2.50)	28.3 (1.24)
Other relative	26.5 (0.84)	24.6 (6.88)	29.1 (2.46)	26.8 (1.47)	28.3 (2.72)	20.9 (2.11)	26.5 (1.34)
College publication or website	33.5 (0.86)	22.1 (5.71)	23.8 (2.58)	30.5 (1.32)	29.6 (2.81)	28.7 (2.62)	42.1 (1.44)
College representative	14.3 (0.67)	16.0 ! (6.32)	14.5 (1.87)	14.3 (1.05)	14.9 (1.94)	14.4 (2.24)	14.0 (1.04)
College search guide	31.0 (0.80)	30.5 (7.15)	20.8 (2.33)	28.4 (1.22)	28.8 (2.39)	28.3 (2.65)	37.8 (1.30)
Information sources as of 2004							
School counselor	79.6 (0.97)	‡ (†)	67.4 (3.23)	78.6 (1.44)	74.5 (3.09)	77.4 (2.86)	84.6 (1.23)
Teacher	43.6 (1.03)	‡ (†)	38.0 (3.39)	42.8 (1.97)	45.9 (3.48)	38.1 (3.05)	46.6 (1.71)
Coach	12.1 (0.77)	‡ (†)	8.2 (2.03)	11.8 (1.21)	6.9 (1.70)	11.5 (1.90)	14.2 (1.39)
Parent	58.5 (1.04)	‡ (†)	44.4 (3.47)	56.7 (1.89)	64.1 (3.33)	57.7 (2.98)	62.2 (1.48)
Friend	25.2 (0.81)	‡ (†)	22.9 (2.73)	20.9 (1.36)	21.9 (2.68)	23.7 (2.38)	30.1 (1.31)
Sibling	28.6 (1.00)	‡ (†)	28.3 (3.15)	27.8 (1.67)	34.6 (3.58)	26.2 (2.69)	28.8 (1.53)
Other relative	52.0 (0.97)	‡ (†)	45.8 (3.69)	49.7 (1.89)	50.6 (3.23)	47.8 (2.74)	56.7 (1.52)
College publication or website	59.3 (1.16)	‡ (†)	37.7 (3.47)	56.9 (2.01)	48.5 (3.49)	54.6 (2.91)	69.3 (1.72)
College representative	65.1 (1.01)	‡ (†)	38.6 (3.30)	58.4 (1.75)	49.6 (3.54)	64.9 (2.75)	79.6 (1.45)
College search guide	48.2 (1.11)	‡ (†)	31.8 (3.32)	41.1 (1.89)	42.7 (3.55)	45.7 (2.88)	59.3 (1.43)
High SES[2]							
Information sources as of 2002							
School counselor	46.3 (1.24)	‡ (†)	45.9 (7.73)	44.9 (2.32)	51.8 (6.69)	41.0 (5.26)	47.0 (1.41)
Teacher	30.7 (1.10)	‡ (†)	37.8 (8.19)	31.1 (2.36)	27.7 (6.30)	24.5 (3.78)	31.0 (1.32)
Coach	10.8 (0.70)	‡ (†)	14.9 ! (6.09)	10.2 (1.43)	12.5 ! (4.59)	5.4 ! (1.84)	11.2 (0.89)
Parent	68.4 (1.10)	‡ (†)	61.2 (8.52)	61.4 (2.54)	57.8 (6.34)	67.0 (4.61)	71.6 (1.22)
Friend	42.1 (1.09)	‡ (†)	45.4 (7.68)	37.4 (2.54)	36.8 (6.26)	43.5 (4.77)	43.5 (1.46)
Sibling	29.2 (0.94)	‡ (†)	23.7 (6.84)	26.1 (2.12)	20.5 (5.23)	29.8 (4.23)	30.7 (1.17)
Other relative	26.3 (0.97)	‡ (†)	37.1 (8.57)	26.8 (2.20)	23.2 (5.38)	23.6 (4.21)	26.0 (1.20)
College publication or website	44.4 (1.18)	‡ (†)	28.6 (7.35)	35.6 (2.52)	38.4 (6.87)	42.1 (4.83)	48.4 (1.49)
College representative	15.3 (0.78)	‡ (†)	10.9 ! (4.79)	17.9 (1.69)	23.7 (6.40)	14.2 (3.24)	14.4 (0.93)
College search guide	39.7 (1.13)	‡ (†)	21.1 ! (6.65)	34.2 (2.33)	29.4 (6.33)	33.5 (4.47)	43.3 (1.53)
Information sources as of 2004							
School counselor	80.9 (1.12)	‡ (†)	74.9 (8.21)	79.3 (2.48)	75.4 (6.62)	78.5 (4.24)	81.9 (1.23)
Teacher	42.7 (1.23)	‡ (†)	43.0 (8.66)	40.3 (2.97)	39.5 (7.32)	36.1 (5.21)	44.0 (1.45)
Coach	14.9 (0.88)	‡ (†)	‡ (†)	12.0 (1.82)	7.3 ! (3.50)	11.7 (3.23)	16.4 (1.13)
Parent	72.7 (1.29)	‡ (†)	69.5 (9.34)	65.9 (2.88)	61.4 (7.59)	67.0 (5.16)	75.5 (1.33)
Friend	30.0 (1.09)	‡ (†)	21.0 ! (7.21)	27.1 (2.34)	31.5 (6.84)	24.4 (4.56)	31.4 (1.20)
Sibling	28.0 (1.09)	‡ (†)	32.4 (8.55)	27.6 (2.89)	21.2 (5.48)	27.7 (4.46)	28.2 (1.35)
Other relative	53.2 (1.28)	‡ (†)	46.9 (8.79)	51.0 (2.78)	47.6 (7.90)	43.5 (4.84)	55.0 (1.48)
College publication or website	64.0 (1.23)	‡ (†)	40.2 (8.41)	55.5 (3.03)	49.4 (7.54)	44.7 (5.27)	69.0 (1.44)
College representative	79.5 (1.03)	‡ (†)	44.7 (9.51)	71.7 (2.75)	52.7 (8.05)	71.4 (4.38)	84.5 (1.10)
College search guide	59.6 (1.38)	‡ (†)	31.1 (8.61)	53.2 (3.12)	37.6 (7.23)	55.5 (4.71)	63.5 (1.52)

†Not applicable.
!Interpret data with caution. The coefficient of variation (CV) for this estimate is between 30 and 50 percent.
‡Reporting standards not met. Either there are too few cases for a reliable estimate or the coefficient of variation (CV) is 50 percent or greater.
[1]Postsecondary transcripts from 2013 were used to update self-reported attainment of highest degree for all respondents with complete transcripts as well as for respondents whose partial transcripts indicated higher attainment than was self-reported in 2012.

[2]Socioeconomic status (SES) was measured by a composite score on parental education and occupations, and family income in 2002. The "low" SES group is the lowest quartile; the "middle" SES group is the middle two quartiles; and the "high" SES group is the upper quartile.
NOTE: Students who reported that they planned to attend postsecondary education were asked, "Where have you gone for information about the entrance requirements of various colleges?" Because each student could indicate multiple sources, percentages do not sum to 100. Some data have been revised from previously published figures.
SOURCE: U.S. Department of Education, National Center for Education Statistics, Education Longitudinal Study of 2002 (ELS:2002), Base Year through Postsecondary Transcript Study. (This table was prepared June 2016.)

Table 104.95. Number of persons age 25 and over in metropolitan areas with populations greater than 1 million and rates of high school completion and bachelor's degree attainment among persons in this age group, by sex: 2014

[Standard errors appear in parentheses]

Metropolitan area	Number of persons 25 years old and over (in thousands)			Percent with high school completion or higher			Percent with bachelor's or higher degree		
	Total	Males	Females	Total	Male	Female	Total	Male	Female
1	2	3	4	5	6	7	8	9	10
Atlanta-Sandy Springs-Marietta, GA CBSA	3,591 (259.9)	1,719 (126.0)	1,873 (143.8)	90.9 (1.42)	88.9 (2.10)	92.8 (1.30)	38.7 (2.82)	39.9 (3.18)	37.6 (3.20)
Austin-Round Rock, TX CBSA	1,370 (133.2)	729 (76.4)	641 (65.8)	90.1 (2.68)	89.8 (3.21)	90.3 (2.50)	50.0 (4.08)	48.3 (5.10)	51.8 (4.06)
Birmingham-Hoover, AL CBSA	887 (93.5)	429 (52.4)	458 (46.0)	87.5 (2.32)	83.2 (4.42)	91.5 (2.49)	30.1 (4.53)	27.9 (5.18)	32.1 (5.16)
Boston-Worcester-Manchester, MA-NH-CT-ME CSA[1]	3,820 (132.2)	1,795 (77.1)	2,025 (69.7)	91.6 (1.32)	91.6 (1.74)	91.7 (1.31)	44.8 (2.31)	45.7 (2.54)	44.0 (2.67)
Buffalo-Niagara Falls, NY CBSA	759 (84.3)	354 (42.8)	405 (47.2)	92.3 (1.81)	89.1 (3.00)	95.0 (2.02)	24.4 (3.49)	23.9 (6.69)	24.9 (4.15)
Charlotte-Gastonia-Concord, NC-SC CBSA	1,291 (133.7)	602 (68.6)	689 (71.7)	82.5 (2.71)	81.7 (3.32)	83.2 (3.47)	30.9 (3.67)	32.3 (4.64)	29.6 (4.50)
Chicago-Naperville-Michigan City, IL-IN-WI CSA	6,218 (318.7)	2,993 (163.7)	3,224 (165.9)	89.0 (0.99)	87.7 (1.36)	90.3 (0.94)	38.2 (1.79)	37.2 (1.84)	39.1 (1.91)
Cincinnati-Middletown, OH-KY-IN CBSA[1]	1,344 (123.8)	668 (63.6)	676 (69.0)	89.0 (2.37)	87.0 (2.69)	92.0 (3.09)	29.3 (3.08)	31.8 (4.23)	26.9 (3.16)
Cleveland-Akron-Elyria, OH CSA	1,908 (145.4)	926 (81.0)	982 (77.2)	88.9 (1.63)	87.8 (2.43)	89.9 (1.60)	30.5 (3.09)	33.5 (3.98)	27.7 (2.91)
Columbus, OH CSA	1,174 (134.8)	565 (72.3)	608 (69.9)	90.9 (2.28)	90.9 (3.02)	90.9 (2.63)	32.3 (4.57)	34.3 (5.55)	30.5 (4.98)
Dallas-Fort Worth-Arlington, TX CBSA	4,565 (177.5)	2,248 (103.2)	2,317 (92.3)	85.6 (1.63)	84.2 (1.89)	86.9 (1.63)	33.7 (2.04)	35.4 (2.70)	32.1 (2.16)
Denver-Aurora-Boulder, CO CSA	2,086 (90.9)	1,042 (52.9)	1,044 (44.5)	93.1 (0.96)	92.7 (1.27)	93.6 (1.04)	48.7 (3.31)	47.2 (3.71)	50.2 (3.45)
Detroit-Warren-Flint, MI CSA	3,849 (249.4)	1,876 (132.9)	1,973 (123.8)	89.3 (1.35)	89.6 (1.65)	89.1 (1.56)	30.4 (2.06)	28.3 (2.63)	32.5 (2.38)
Fresno-Madera, CA CSA	688 (155.1)	345 (84.1)	342 (123.8)	84.5 (2.56)	84.5 (3.45)	83.0 (3.22)	18.4 (4.20)	17.0 (4.52)	19.8 (4.83)
Grand Rapids-Muskegon-Holland, MI CSA	895 (180.2)	418 (72.9)	477 (109.6)	96.7 (0.91)	96.7 (1.78)	96.7 (1.43)	33.2 (4.45)	30.3 (5.68)	35.7 (4.79)
Greensboro-Winston-Salem-High Point, NC CSA	1,040 (111.1)	488 (60.2)	551 (61.3)	86.8 (2.52)	86.8 (4.20)	88.7 (2.95)	21.4 (3.55)	22.3 (5.34)	20.7 (3.19)
Hartford-West Hartford, CT CBSA	789 (60.4)	384 (32.3)	406 (31.1)	89.7 (1.57)	87.7 (2.24)	91.6 (1.47)	38.5 (3.10)	37.3 (3.76)	39.7 (3.32)
Houston-Baytown-Sugarland, TX CBSA	4,044 (217.8)	1,944 (106.9)	2,100 (127.9)	83.0 (1.47)	81.1 (1.89)	84.8 (1.53)	31.8 (2.31)	30.5 (2.56)	32.9 (2.80)
Indianapolis-Anderson-Columbus, IN CSA	1,299 (108.4)	588 (54.0)	711 (61.4)	92.2 (2.00)	92.2 (2.69)	92.2 (1.81)	32.4 (4.20)	29.8 (5.06)	34.5 (4.22)
Jacksonville, FL CBSA	995 (99.7)	454 (49.3)	541 (55.4)	93.1 (1.87)	93.1 (1.89)	93.1 (2.19)	36.2 (4.26)	38.6 (5.45)	34.2 (4.69)
Kansas City, MO-KS CSRA	1,369 (92.3)	637 (49.1)	732 (49.7)	95.5 (0.96)	93.4 (1.44)	97.4 (0.92)	37.7 (3.03)	38.7 (3.92)	36.8 (3.39)
Las Vegas-Paradise, NV CBSA	1,259 (55.4)	630 (34.2)	630 (25.9)	89.9 (1.43)	90.6 (1.44)	89.1 (1.92)	23.4 (1.81)	22.5 (2.32)	24.4 (2.19)
Los Angeles-Long Beach-Riverside, CA CSA	11,824 (184.4)	5,696 (117.5)	6,128 (95.1)	80.7 (1.01)	80.7 (1.29)	80.6 (0.99)	32.4 (1.09)	33.0 (1.38)	31.8 (1.25)
Louisville, KY-IN CBSA	883 (112.4)	437 (74.5)	446 (44.4)	93.0 (1.37)	92.8 (2.01)	93.2 (2.21)	29.9 (2.87)	32.7 (5.19)	27.1 (4.31)
Memphis, TN-MS-AR CBSA[1]	896 (87.3)	396 (44.4)	500 (51.7)	84.8 (3.34)	88.7 (4.58)	82.6 (5.17)	31.6 (4.59)	26.8 (6.88)	35.4 (4.69)
Miami-Fort Lauderdale-Miami Beach, FL CBSA	3,893 (183.7)	1,822 (97.6)	2,071 (99.6)	88.9 (1.10)	89.7 (1.59)	89.7 (1.21)	31.7 (1.86)	32.7 (2.41)	30.8 (1.95)
Milwaukee-Racine-Waukesha, WI CSA	1,174 (243.7)	569 (119.6)	606 (126.4)	91.3 (1.68)	90.2 (2.54)	92.4 (1.44)	30.8 (3.49)	25.9 (4.42)	35.5 (3.41)
Minneapolis-St. Paul-St. Cloud, MN-WI CSA[1]	2,254 (97.4)	1,081 (54.3)	1,173 (50.9)	93.4 (0.90)	93.4 (1.10)	93.4 (1.07)	39.2 (1.97)	37.1 (2.17)	41.2 (2.34)
Nashville-Davidson-Murfreesboro, TN CBSA	1,159 (191.4)	552 (94.2)	607 (101.7)	87.5 (2.85)	89.6 (3.25)	85.6 (3.59)	37.2 (4.15)	39.5 (4.59)	35.1 (4.50)
New Orleans-Metairie-Kenner, LA CBSA	789 (88.1)	372 (46.0)	417 (47.9)	86.9 (2.95)	85.2 (4.23)	88.5 (3.02)	32.3 (4.08)	37.2 (5.40)	27.8 (5.40)
New York-Newark, NY-NJ-PA CSA	14,815 (254.8)	6,872 (160.0)	7,943 (128.1)	87.9 (0.72)	88.2 (0.92)	87.7 (0.74)	40.3 (1.12)	38.8 (1.44)	41.7 (1.19)
Oklahoma City, OK CBSA	937 (66.4)	412 (35.8)	524 (36.4)	89.5 (2.39)	88.0 (2.93)	90.7 (2.57)	29.4 (3.35)	32.1 (4.61)	27.4 (3.39)
Orlando, FL CBSA	1,496 (134.5)	750 (75.9)	746 (67.4)	92.7 (1.81)	91.0 (2.56)	94.5 (1.73)	29.4 (3.36)	28.4 (4.36)	30.4 (3.57)
Philadelphia-Camden-Vineland, PA-NJ-DE-MD CSA	4,274 (161.6)	2,029 (91.3)	2,244 (87.0)	93.1 (0.85)	92.6 (1.05)	93.6 (1.05)	36.6 (2.25)	37.4 (2.77)	35.9 (2.28)
Phoenix-Mesa-Scottsdale, AZ CBSA	2,805 ! (1,357.4)	1,425 ! (681.2)	1,380 ! (676.3)	85.0 (0.32)	83.1 (0.48)	86.9 (0.22)	31.3 (0.34)	33.3 (0.55)	29.2 (0.36)
Pittsburgh-New Castle, PA CBSA	1,742 (130.7)	818 (72.1)	923 (71.5)	93.2 (1.33)	96.0 (2.12)	96.0 (1.50)	37.7 (3.53)	37.6 (4.37)	37.7 (3.97)
Portland-Vancouver-Beaverton, OR-WA CBSA	1,552 (231.7)	773 (116.2)	779 (117.7)	92.7 (1.13)	95.4 (1.12)	90.1 (1.95)	36.2 (2.73)	34.6 (3.08)	37.7 (3.21)
Providence-Fall River-Warwick, RI-MA CBSA	876 (50.5)	419 (27.5)	457 (25.3)	84.8 (1.59)	86.0 (1.62)	83.8 (2.02)	35.8 (2.53)	38.5 (3.29)	33.4 (2.81)
Raleigh-Durham-Cary, NC CSA	1,382 (125.4)	648 (70.0)	734 (63.9)	86.3 (3.12)	83.6 (4.04)	88.7 (2.87)	44.7 (4.76)	45.6 (5.38)	44.0 (5.27)
Richmond, VA CBSA	976 (102.6)	466 (50.1)	510 (58.7)	90.4 (2.32)	89.3 (2.98)	91.4 (2.74)	34.5 (4.67)	30.4 (4.92)	38.3 (5.77)
Rochester, NY CBSA	806 (81.1)	398 (46.3)	408 (43.1)	93.6 (2.38)	92.3 (2.84)	94.9 (2.58)	34.7 (5.11)	34.1 (6.06)	35.2 (5.04)
Sacramento-Arden-Arcade-Roseville, CA CSA	1,462 (86.0)	704 (49.0)	758 (51.2)	88.1 (2.25)	88.1 (3.27)	88.1 (2.28)	30.9 (2.92)	35.0 (3.58)	27.1 (2.93)
Salt Lake City-Ogden-Clearfield, UT CSA	1,053 (64.3)	521 (37.5)	532 (32.0)	91.5 (1.75)	90.5 (2.38)	92.5 (1.65)	32.5 (3.11)	35.4 (4.20)	29.7 (2.84)
San Antonio, TX CBSA	1,433 (121.2)	748 (66.4)	685 (65.5)	78.9 (2.50)	75.5 (3.18)	82.5 (2.45)	24.1 (3.01)	24.5 (3.68)	23.7 (3.46)
San Diego-Carlsbad-San Marcos, CA CBSA	2,087 (111.4)	1,018 (60.0)	1,069 (61.6)	90.7 (1.59)	92.7 (1.83)	88.8 (1.93)	41.3 (2.82)	43.4 (3.69)	39.2 (3.14)
San Jose-San Francisco-Oakland, CA CSA	5,604 (233.3)	2,838 (124.4)	2,766 (123.1)	89.0 (1.09)	89.6 (1.33)	88.4 (1.10)	45.7 (1.99)	47.1 (2.19)	44.3 (2.34)
Seattle-Tacoma-Olympia, WA CSA	2,808 (128.6)	1,331 (68.7)	1,477 (67.8)	92.6 (1.19)	92.9 (1.42)	92.9 (1.29)	41.5 (2.46)	39.7 (2.85)	43.2 (2.70)
St. Louis, MO-IL CBSA	1,951 (124.6)	954 (69.0)	997 (65.3)	91.8 (1.57)	90.8 (1.68)	90.8 (1.95)	30.4 (2.63)	30.4 (3.12)	34.0 (3.03)
Tampa-St. Petersburg-Clearwater, FL CBSA	2,321 (220.5)	1,120 (114.2)	1,202 (114.4)	90.1 (1.47)	92.3 (1.88)	92.6 (1.99)	30.4 (3.15)	32.3 (3.61)	28.6 (3.69)
Virginia Beach-Norfolk-Newport News, VA-NC CBSA[1]	1,114 (85.2)	515 (42.1)	598 (50.6)	91.7 (1.82)	88.9 (2.79)	94.2 (1.55)	27.4 (3.15)	25.6 (3.96)	29.0 (3.40)
Washington-Baltimore-Northern Virginia, DC-MD-VA-WV CSA[1]	5,989 (143.3)	2,890 (78.8)	3,099 (81.6)	92.0 (0.82)	92.5 (0.99)	92.5 (0.96)	49.1 (1.42)	49.9 (1.53)	48.3 (1.75)

[1]Interpret data with caution. The coefficient of variation (CV) for this estimate is between 30 and 50 percent.

!Information on metropolitan status was suppressed for a small portion of sample observations. As a result, population estimates for these areas may be slightly underestimated.

NOTE: A Core Based Statistical Area (CBSA) consists of one or more counties associated with at least one population core of at least 10,000 people, plus adjacent counties having a high degree of social and economic integration with the core as measured through commuting ties. A Combined Statistical Area (CSA) consists of two or more adjacent CBSAs that have social and economic ties as measured by commuting, but at lower levels than are found within each component CBSA. Detail may not sum to totals because of rounding. Standard errors were computed using replicate weights.
SOURCE: U.S. Department of Commerce, Census Bureau, Current Population Survey (CPS), March 2014. (This table was prepared March 2015.)

Table 105.10.   Projected number of participants in educational institutions, by level and control of institution: Fall 2015

[In millions]

Participants	All levels (elementary, secondary, and degree-granting postsecondary)	Elementary and secondary schools			Degree-granting postsecondary institutions		
		Total	Public	Private	Total	Public	Private
1	2	3	4	5	6	7	8
Total...	**85.7**	**62.5**	**56.5**	**6.0**	**23.2**	**16.7**	**6.5**
Enrollment	75.8	55.5	50.3	5.3	20.3	14.8	5.5
Teachers and faculty.........................	4.6	3.6	3.1	0.4	1.0	0.7	0.4
Other professional, administrative, and support staff..	5.3	3.4	3.1	0.3	1.9	1.2	0.7

NOTE: Includes enrollments in local public school systems and in most private schools (religiously affiliated and nonsectarian). Excludes federal Bureau of Indian Education schools and Department of Defense schools. Excludes private preprimary enrollment in schools that do not offer kindergarten or above. Degree-granting institutions grant associate's or higher degrees and participate in Title IV federal financial aid programs. Data for teachers and other staff in public and private elementary and secondary schools and colleges and universities are reported in terms of full-time equivalents. Detail may not sum to totals because of rounding.

SOURCE: U.S. Department of Education, National Center for Education Statistics, National Elementary and Secondary Enrollment Projection Model, 1972 through 2025; Enrollment in Degree-Granting Institutions Projection Model, 1980 through 2025; Elementary and Secondary Teacher Projection Model, 1973 through 2025; and unpublished projections and estimates. (This table was prepared March 2016.)

Table 105.20. Enrollment in elementary, secondary, and degree-granting postsecondary institutions, by level and control of institution, enrollment level, and attendance status and sex of student: Selected years, fall 1990 through fall 2025

[In thousands]

Level and control of institution, enrollment level, and attendance status and sex of student	Actual				Projected											
	1990	2000	2010	2013	2014	2015	2016	2017	2018	2019	2020	2021	2022	2023	2024	2025
1	2	3	4	5	6	7	8	9	10	11	12	13	14	15	16	17
All levels...............	60,683	68,685	75,886	75,816	75,661	75,810	76,136	76,633	77,075	77,479	77,875	78,321	78,759	79,187	79,565	79,800
Elementary and secondary schools[1]............	**46,864**	**53,373**	**54,867**	**55,440**	**55,454**	**55,546**	**55,620**	**55,661**	**55,665**	**55,726**	**55,862**	**55,998**	**56,146**	**56,291**	**56,416**	**56,510**
Public..............................	41,217	47,204	49,484	50,045	50,132	50,268	50,385	50,477	50,528	50,618	50,774	50,928	51,084	51,225	51,338	51,420
Private	5,648[2]	6,169[2]	5,382[2]	5,396	5,322	5,278	5,235	5,183	5,136	5,108	5,088	5,070	5,062	5,065	5,078	5,090
Prekindergarten to grade 8....	34,388	38,592	38,708	39,335	39,255	39,265	39,339	39,350	39,365	39,410	39,430	39,418	39,443	39,616	39,802	39,995
Public[3]...........................	29,876	33,686	34,625	35,251	35,249	35,298	35,402	35,451	35,491	35,543	35,559	35,541	35,558	35,712	35,878	36,052
Private..............................	4,512[2]	4,906[2]	4,084[2]	4,084	4,006	3,968	3,938	3,899	3,873	3,867	3,871	3,877	3,885	3,904	3,923	3,943
Grades 9 to 12....................	12,476	14,781	16,159	16,106	16,199	16,281	16,281	16,311	16,300	16,316	16,432	16,580	16,703	16,675	16,614	16,515
Public[3]...........................	11,341	13,517	14,860	14,794	14,883	14,970	14,983	15,026	15,037	15,075	15,215	15,387	15,526	15,514	15,460	15,368
Private..............................	1,136[2]	1,264[2]	1,299[2]	1,312	1,316	1,311	1,298	1,284	1,263	1,242	1,217	1,194	1,177	1,161	1,155	1,147
Degree-granting postsecondary institutions..........	**13,819**	**15,312**	**21,019**	**20,376**	**20,207**[4]	**20,264**	**20,516**	**20,972**	**21,410**	**21,753**	**22,013**	**22,323**	**22,613**	**22,896**	**23,149**	**23,290**
Undergraduate...................	11,959	13,155	18,082	17,475	17,293[4]	17,298	17,490	17,853	18,214	18,496	18,704	18,954	19,187	19,417	19,631	19,756
Full-time	6,976	7,923	11,457	10,938	10,784[4]	10,801	10,930	11,164	11,386	11,551	11,670	11,814	11,950	12,098	12,229	12,285
Part-time	4,983	5,232	6,625	6,536	6,509[4]	6,497	6,561	6,689	6,828	6,944	7,034	7,140	7,236	7,318	7,403	7,471
Male	5,380	5,778	7,836	7,660	7,586[4]	7,499	7,528	7,634	7,774	7,889	7,970	8,074	8,176	8,274	8,367	8,433
Female	6,579	7,377	10,246	9,815	9,707[4]	9,799	9,962	10,219	10,440	10,607	10,734	10,880	11,011	11,143	11,264	11,323
2-year.............................	5,240	5,948	7,684	6,969	6,714[4]	7,114	7,194	7,346	7,500	7,622	7,706	7,810	7,912	8,007	8,096	8,157
4-year.............................	6,719	7,207	10,399	10,506	10,578[4]	10,184	10,296	10,507	10,714	10,874	10,998	11,144	11,275	11,410	11,535	11,599
Public.............................	9,710	10,539	13,703	13,347	13,245[4]	13,353	13,499	13,777	14,056	14,275	14,436	14,630	14,811	14,988	15,154	15,255
Private............................	2,250	2,616	4,379	4,128	4,048[4]	3,945	3,992	4,076	4,158	4,220	4,268	4,324	4,376	4,429	4,477	4,501
Postbaccalaureate..............	1,860	2,157	2,937	2,901	2,915[4]	2,966	3,025	3,119	3,196	3,257	3,308	3,369	3,427	3,479	3,517	3,534
Full-time	845	1,087	1,630	1,659	1,670[4]	1,684	1,721	1,778	1,821	1,852	1,879	1,912	1,944	1,973	1,991	1,994
Part-time	1,015	1,070	1,307	1,242	1,244[4]	1,282	1,304	1,341	1,375	1,405	1,429	1,457	1,483	1,506	1,526	1,541
Male	904	944	1,209	1,201	1,211[4]	1,261	1,279	1,311	1,344	1,371	1,394	1,422	1,449	1,473	1,492	1,504
Female	955	1,213	1,728	1,700	1,703[4]	1,704	1,746	1,809	1,852	1,886	1,914	1,947	1,978	2,006	2,026	2,030

[1]Includes enrollments in local public school systems and in most private schools (religiously affiliated and nonsectarian). Excludes homeschooled children who were not also enrolled in public and private schools. Private elementary enrollment includes preprimary students in schools offering kindergarten or higher grades.
[2]Estimated.
[3]Includes prorated proportion of students classified as ungraded.
[4]Data are actual.
NOTE: Postsecondary data for 1990 are for institutions of higher education, while later data are for degree-granting institutions. Degree-granting institutions grant associate's or higher degrees and participate in Title IV federal financial aid programs. The degree-granting classification is very similar to the earlier higher education classification, but it includes more 2-year

colleges and excludes a few higher education institutions that did not grant degrees. Detail may not sum to totals because of rounding. Some data have been revised from previously published figures.
SOURCE: U.S. Department of Education, National Center for Education Statistics, Common Core of Data (CCD), "State Nonfiscal Survey of Public Elementary and Secondary Education," 1990–91 through 2013–14; Private School Universe Survey (PSS), 1995–96 through 2013–14; National Elementary and Secondary Enrollment Projection Model, 1972 through 2025; Integrated Postsecondary Education Data System (IPEDS), "Fall Enrollment Survey" (IPEDS-EF:90–99); IPEDS Spring 2001 through Spring 2015, Fall Enrollment component; and Enrollment in Degree-Granting Institutions Projection Model, 1980 through 2025. (This table was prepared February 2016.)

Table 105.30. Enrollment in elementary, secondary, and degree-granting postsecondary institutions, by level and control of institution: Selected years, 1869–70 through fall 2025

[In thousands]

Year	Total enrollment, all levels	Elementary and secondary, total	Public elementary and secondary schools			Private elementary and secondary schools[1]			Degree-granting postsecondary institutions[2]		
			Total	Prekinder-garten through grade 8	Grades 9 through 12	Total	Prekinder-garten through grade 8	Grades 9 through 12	Total	Public	Private
1	2	3	4	5	6	7	8	9	10	11	12
1869–70	—	—	6,872	6,792	80	—	—	—	52	—	—
1879–80	—	—	9,868	9,757	110	—	—	—	116	—	—
1889–90	14,491	14,334	12,723	12,520	203	1,611	1,516	95	157	—	—
1899–1900	17,092	16,855	15,503	14,984	519	1,352	1,241	111	238	—	—
1909–10	19,728	19,372	17,814	16,899	915	1,558	1,441	117	355	—	—
1919–20	23,876	23,278	21,578	19,378	2,200	1,699	1,486	214	598	—	—
1929–30	29,430	28,329	25,678	21,279	4,399	2,651	2,310	341	1,101	—	—
1939–40	29,539	28,045	25,434	18,832	6,601	2,611	2,153	458	1,494	797	698
1949–50	31,151	28,492	25,111	19,387	5,725	3,380	2,708	672	2,659	1,355	1,304
Fall 1959	44,497	40,857	35,182	26,911	8,271	5,675	4,640	1,035	3,640	2,181	1,459
Fall 1969	59,055	51,050	45,550	32,513	13,037	5,500 [3]	4,200 [3]	1,300 [3]	8,005	5,897	2,108
Fall 1979	58,221	46,651	41,651	28,034	13,616	5,000 [3]	3,700 [3]	1,300 [3]	11,570	9,037	2,533
Fall 1985	57,226	44,979	39,422	27,034	12,388	5,557	4,195	1,362	12,247	9,479	2,768
Fall 1990	60,683	46,864	41,217	29,876	11,341	5,648 [3]	4,512 [3]	1,136 [3]	13,819	10,845	2,974
Fall 1991	62,087	47,728	42,047	30,503	11,544	5,681	4,550	1,131	14,359	11,310	3,049
Fall 1992	63,181	48,694	42,823	31,086	11,737	5,870 [3]	4,746 [3]	1,125 [3]	14,487	11,385	3,103
Fall 1993	63,837	49,532	43,465	31,502	11,963	6,067	4,950	1,118	14,305	11,189	3,116
Fall 1994	64,385	50,106	44,111	31,896	12,215	5,994 [3]	4,856 [3]	1,138 [3]	14,279	11,134	3,145
Fall 1995	65,020	50,759	44,840	32,338	12,502	5,918	4,756	1,163	14,262	11,092	3,169
Fall 1996	65,911	51,544	45,611	32,762	12,849	5,933 [3]	4,755 [3]	1,178 [3]	14,368	11,120	3,247
Fall 1997	66,574	52,071	46,127	33,071	13,056	5,944	4,759	1,185	14,502	11,196	3,306
Fall 1998	67,033	52,526	46,539	33,344	13,195	5,988 [3]	4,776 [3]	1,212 [3]	14,507	11,138	3,369
Fall 1999	67,725	52,875	46,857	33,486	13,371	6,018	4,789	1,229	14,850	11,376	3,474
Fall 2000	68,685	53,373	47,204	33,686	13,517	6,169 [3]	4,906 [3]	1,264 [3]	15,312	11,753	3,560
Fall 2001	69,920	53,992	47,672	33,936	13,736	6,320	5,023	1,296	15,928	12,233	3,695
Fall 2002	71,015	54,403	48,183	34,114	14,069	6,220 [3]	4,915 [3]	1,306 [3]	16,612	12,752	3,860
Fall 2003	71,551	54,639	48,540	34,201	14,339	6,099	4,788	1,311	16,911	12,859	4,053
Fall 2004	72,154	54,882	48,795	34,178	14,618	6,087 [3]	4,756 [3]	1,331 [3]	17,272	12,980	4,292
Fall 2005	72,674	55,187	49,113	34,204	14,909	6,073	4,724	1,349	17,487	13,022	4,466
Fall 2006	73,066	55,307	49,316	34,235	15,081	5,991 [3]	4,631 [3]	1,360 [3]	17,759	13,180	4,579
Fall 2007	73,449	55,201	49,291	34,204	15,086	5,910	4,546	1,364	18,248	13,491	4,757
Fall 2008	74,076	54,973	49,266	34,286	14,980	5,707 [3]	4,365 [3]	1,342 [3]	19,103	13,972	5,131
Fall 2009	75,163	54,849	49,361	34,409	14,952	5,488	4,179	1,309	20,314	14,811	5,503
Fall 2010	75,886	54,867	49,484	34,625	14,860	5,382 [3]	4,084 [3]	1,299 [3]	21,019	15,142	5,877
Fall 2011	75,800	54,790	49,522	34,773	14,749	5,268	3,977	1,291	21,011	15,116	5,894
Fall 2012	75,748	55,104	49,771	35,018	14,753	5,333 [3]	4,031 [3]	1,302 [3]	20,644	14,885	5,760
Fall 2013	75,816	55,440	50,045	35,251	14,794	5,396	4,084	1,312	20,376	14,746	5,630
Fall 2014[4]	75,661	55,454	50,132	35,249	14,883	5,322	4,006	1,316	20,207	14,655	5,552
Fall 2015[4]	75,810	55,546	50,268	35,298	14,970	5,278	3,968	1,311	20,264	14,789	5,475
Fall 2016[4]	76,136	55,620	50,385	35,402	14,983	5,235	3,938	1,298	20,516	14,964	5,552
Fall 2017[4]	76,633	55,661	50,477	35,451	15,026	5,183	3,899	1,284	20,972	15,287	5,686
Fall 2018[4]	77,075	55,665	50,528	35,491	15,037	5,136	3,873	1,263	21,410	15,604	5,807
Fall 2019[4]	77,479	55,726	50,618	35,543	15,075	5,108	3,867	1,242	21,753	15,852	5,900
Fall 2020[4]	77,875	55,862	50,774	35,559	15,215	5,088	3,871	1,217	22,013	16,038	5,975
Fall 2021[4]	78,321	55,998	50,928	35,541	15,387	5,070	3,877	1,194	22,323	16,261	6,062
Fall 2022[4]	78,759	56,146	51,084	35,558	15,526	5,062	3,885	1,177	22,613	16,471	6,143
Fall 2023[4]	79,187	56,291	51,225	35,712	15,514	5,065	3,904	1,161	22,896	16,673	6,223
Fall 2024[4]	79,565	56,416	51,338	35,878	15,460	5,078	3,923	1,155	23,149	16,858	6,291
Fall 2025[4]	79,800	56,510	51,420	36,052	15,368	5,090	3,943	1,147	23,290	16,967	6,323

—Not available.

[1]Beginning in fall 1985, data include estimates for an expanded universe of private schools. Therefore, direct comparisons with earlier years should be avoided.

[2]Data for 1869–70 through 1949–50 include resident degree-credit students enrolled at any time during the academic year. Beginning in 1959, data include all resident and extension students enrolled at the beginning of the fall term.

[3]Estimated.

[4]Projected data. Fall 2014 data for degree-granting institutions are actual.

NOTE: Data for 1869–70 through 1949–50 reflect enrollment for the entire school year. Elementary and secondary enrollment includes students in local public school systems and in most private schools (religiously affiliated and nonsectarian), but generally excludes homeschooled children and students in subcollegiate departments of colleges and in federal schools. Excludes preprimary pupils in private schools that do not offer kindergarten or above. Postsecondary data through 1995 are for institutions of higher education, while later data are for degree-granting institutions. Degree-granting institutions grant associate's or higher degrees and participate in Title IV federal financial aid programs. The degree-granting classification is very similar to the earlier higher education classification, but it includes more 2-year colleges and excludes a few higher education institutions that did not grant degrees. Some data have been revised from previously published figures. Detail may not sum to totals because of rounding.

SOURCE: U.S. Department of Education, National Center for Education Statistics, *Annual Report of the Commissioner of Education,* 1870 to 1910; *Biennial Survey of Education in the United States,* 1919–20 through 1949–50; *Statistics of Public Elementary and Secondary School Systems,* 1959 through 1979; Common Core of Data (CCD), "State Nonfiscal Survey of Public Elementary and Secondary Education," 1989–90 through 2013–14; Private School Universe Survey (PSS), 1991–92 through 2013–14; National Elementary and Secondary Enrollment Projection Model, 1972 through 2025; Opening (Fall) Enrollment in Higher Education, 1959; Higher Education General Information Survey (HEGIS), "Fall Enrollment in Institutions of Higher Education" surveys, 1969, 1979, and 1985; Integrated Postsecondary Education Data System (IPEDS), "Fall Enrollment Survey" (IPEDS-EF:90–99); IPEDS Spring 2001 through Spring 2015, Fall Enrollment component; and Enrollment in Degree-Granting Institutions Projection Model, 1980 through 2025. (This table was prepared February 2016.)

Table 105.40. Number of teachers in elementary and secondary schools, and faculty in degree-granting postsecondary institutions, by control of institution: Selected years, fall 1970 through fall 2025

[In thousands]

Year	All levels			Elementary and secondary teachers[1]			Degree-granting institutions instructional staff[2]		
	Total	Public	Private	Total	Public	Private	Total	Public	Private
1	2	3	4	5	6	7	8	9	10
1970	2,766	2,373	393	2,292	2,059	233	474	314	160
1975	3,081	2,641	440	2,453	2,198	255 [3]	628	443	185
1980	3,171	2,679	492	2,485	2,184	301	686 [3,4]	495 [3,4]	191 [3,4]
1981	3,145	2,636	509	2,440	2,127	313 [3]	705	509	196
1982	3,168	2,639	529	2,458	2,133	325 [3]	710 [3,4]	506 [3,4]	204 [3,4]
1983	3,200	2,651	549	2,476	2,139	337	724	512	212
1984	3,225	2,673	552	2,508	2,168	340 [3]	717 [3,4]	505 [3,4]	212 [3,4]
1985	3,264	2,709	555	2,549	2,206	343	715 [3,4]	503 [3,4]	212 [3,4]
1986	3,314	2,754	560	2,592	2,244	348 [3]	722 [3,4]	510 [3,4]	212 [3,4]
1987	3,424	2,832	592	2,631	2,279	352	793	553	240
1988	3,472	2,882	590	2,668	2,323	345	804 [3]	559 [3]	245 [3]
1989	3,537	2,934	603	2,713	2,357	356	824	577	247
1990	3,577	2,972	604	2,759	2,398	361 [3]	817 [3]	574 [3]	244 [3]
1991	3,623	3,013	610	2,797	2,432	365	826	581	245
1992	3,700	3,080	621	2,823	2,459	364 [3]	877 [3]	621 [3]	257 [3]
1993	3,784	3,154	629	2,868	2,504	364	915	650	265
1994	3,846	3,205	640	2,922	2,552	370 [3]	923 [3]	653 [3]	270 [3]
1995	3,906	3,255	651	2,974	2,598	376	932	657	275
1996	4,006	3,339	666	3,051	2,667	384 [3]	954 [3]	672 [3]	282 [3]
1997	4,127	3,441	687	3,138	2,746	391	990	695	295
1998	4,230	3,527	703	3,230	2,830	400 [3]	999 [3]	697 [3]	303 [3]
1999	4,347	3,624	723	3,319	2,911	408	1,028	713	315
2000	4,432	3,683	750	3,366	2,941	424 [3]	1,067 [3]	741 [3]	326 [3]
2001	4,554	3,771	783	3,440	3,000	441	1,113	771	342
2002	4,631	3,829	802	3,476	3,034	442 [3]	1,155 [3]	794 [3]	361 [3]
2003	4,663	3,840	823	3,490	3,049	441	1,174	792	382
2004	4,773	3,909	863	3,536	3,091	445 [3]	1,237 [3]	818 [3]	418 [3]
2005	4,883	3,984	899	3,593	3,143	450	1,290	841	449
2006	4,944	4,021	924	3,622	3,166	456 [3]	1,322 [3]	854 [3]	468 [3]
2007	5,028	4,077	951	3,656	3,200	456	1,371	877	494
2008	5,065	4,107	958	3,670	3,222	448 [3]	1,395 [3]	885 [3]	511 [3]
2009	5,086	4,123	963	3,647	3,210	437	1,439	914	525
2010	5,038	4,044	994	3,529	3,099	429 [3]	1,510 [3]	945 [3]	565 [3]
2011	5,049	4,057	991	3,524	3,103	421	1,524	954	570
2012	5,072	4,067	1,004	3,540	3,109	431 [3]	1,531 [3]	958 [3]	573 [3]
2013	5,101	4,082	1,018	3,555	3,114	441	1,545	969	577
2014[5]	—	—	—	3,555	3,119	435	—	—	—
2015[5]	—	—	—	3,560	3,128	432	—	—	—
2016[5]	—	—	—	3,563	3,135	428	—	—	—
2017[5]	—	—	—	3,565	3,141	424	—	—	—
2018[5]	—	—	—	3,592	3,168	424	—	—	—
2019[5]	—	—	—	3,615	3,192	424	—	—	—
2020[5]	—	—	—	3,636	3,213	423	—	—	—
2021[5]	—	—	—	3,661	3,237	424	—	—	—
2022[5]	—	—	—	3,686	3,261	425	—	—	—
2023[5]	—	—	—	3,712	3,285	427	—	—	—
2024[5]	—	—	—	3,739	3,309	430	—	—	—
2025[5]	—	—	—	3,761	3,327	433	—	—	—

—Not available.

[1]Includes teachers in local public school systems and in most private schools (religiously affiliated and nonsectarian). Teachers are reported in terms of full-time equivalents.

[2]Data through 1995 are for institutions of higher education, while later data are for degree-granting institutions. Degree-granting institutions grant associate's or higher degrees and participate in Title IV federal financial aid programs. The degree-granting classification is very similar to the earlier higher education classification, but it includes more 2-year colleges and excludes a few higher education institutions that did not grant degrees. Includes full-time and part-time faculty with the rank of instructor or above in colleges, universities, professional schools, and 2-year colleges. Excludes teaching assistants.

[3]Estimated.

[4]Inclusion of institutions is not consistent with surveys for 1987 and later years.

[5]Projected.

NOTE: Detail may not sum to totals because of rounding. Some data have been revised from previously published figures. Headcounts are used to report data for degree-granting institutions faculty.

SOURCE: U.S. Department of Education, National Center for Education Statistics, *Statistics of Public Elementary and Secondary Day Schools,* 1970 and 1975; Common Core of Data (CCD), "State Nonfiscal Survey of Public Elementary/Secondary Education," 1980 through 2013; Private School Universe Survey (PSS), 1989–90 through 2013–14; Elementary and Secondary Teacher Projection Model, 1973 through 2025; Higher Education General Information Survey (HEGIS), "Fall Staff" survey, 1970 and 1975; Integrated Postsecondary Education Data System (IPEDS), "Fall Staff Survey" (IPEDS-S:87–99); IPEDS Winter 2001–02 through Winter 2011–12, Human Resources component, Fall Staff section; IPEDS Spring 2014, Human Resources component, Fall Staff section; U.S. Equal Opportunity Commission, EEO-6, 1981 and 1983; and unpublished data. (This table was prepared March 2016.)

Table 105.50.　Number of educational institutions, by level and control of institution: Selected years, 1980–81 through 2013–14

Level and control of institution	1980–81	1990–91	1999–2000	2003–04	2004–05	2005–06	2006–07	2007–08	2008–09	2009–10	2010–11	2011–12	2012–13	2013–14
1	2	3	4	5	6	7	8	9	10	11	12	13	14	15
All institutions	—	—	131,414	136,819	—	138,899	—	139,207	—	138,925	—	136,423	—	139,126
Elementary and secondary schools	106,746	109,228	125,007	130,407	—	132,436	—	132,656	—	132,183	—	129,189	—	131,890
Elementary	72,659	74,716	86,433	89,252	—	88,896	—	88,982	—	88,565	—	86,386	—	89,543
Secondary	24,856	23,602	24,903	25,476	—	26,925	—	27,575	—	27,427	—	27,034	—	26,753
Combined	5,202	8,847	12,197	13,931	—	14,964	—	14,837	—	14,895	—	14,799	—	14,615
Other[1]	4,029	2,063	1,474	1,749	—	1,651	—	1,262	—	1,296	—	971	—	979
Public schools..................	85,982	84,538	92,012	95,726	96,513	97,382	98,793	98,916	98,706	98,817	98,817	98,328	98,454	98,271
Elementary....................	59,326	59,015	64,131	65,758	65,984	66,026	66,458	67,112	67,148	67,140	67,086	66,689	66,718	67,034
Secondary.....................	22,619	21,135	22,365	22,782	23,445	23,998	23,920	24,643	24,348	24,651	24,544	24,357	24,280	24,053
Combined	1,743	2,325	4,042	5,437	5,572	5,707	5,984	5,899	5,623	5,730	6,137	6,311	6,371	6,205
Other[1]	2,294	2,063	1,474	1,749	1,512	1,651	2,431	1,262	1,587	1,296	1,050	971	1,085	979
Private schools[2]...............	20,764	24,690	32,995	34,681	—	35,054	—	33,740	—	33,366	—	30,861	—	33,619
Elementary....................	13,333	15,701	22,302	23,494	—	22,870	—	21,870	—	21,425	—	19,697	—	22,509
Schools with highest grade of kindergarten.............	†	†	5,952	6,297	—	6,059	—	5,522	—	5,275	—	4,658	—	5,255
Secondary.....................	2,237	2,467	2,538	2,694	—	2,927	—	2,932	—	2,776	—	2,677	—	2,700
Combined	3,459	6,522	8,155	8,494	—	9,257	—	8,938	—	9,165	—	8,488	—	8,410
Other[1]	1,735	(3)	(3)	(3)	—	(3)	—	(3)	—	(3)	—	(3)	—	(3)
Postsecondary Title IV institutions.................	—	—	6,407	6,412	6,383	6,463	6,536	6,551	6,632	6,742	7,021	7,234	7,253	7,236
Public.....................................	—	—	2,078	2,047	2,027	2,013	2,009	2,004	1,997	1,989	2,015	2,011	1,981	1,980
Private	—	—	4,329	4,365	4,356	4,450	4,527	4,547	4,635	4,753	5,006	5,223	5,272	5,256
Nonprofit	—	—	1,936	1,913	1,875	1,866	1,848	1,815	1,809	1,809	1,812	1,830	1,820	1,834
For-profit	—	—	2,393	2,452	2,481	2,584	2,679	2,732	2,826	2,944	3,194	3,393	3,452	3,422
Title IV non-degree-granting institutions....................	—	—	2,323	2,176	2,167	2,187	2,222	2,199	2,223	2,247	2,422	2,528	2,527	2,512
Public..............................	—	—	396	327	327	320	321	319	321	317	359	362	358	355
Private.............................	—	—	1,927	1,849	1,840	1,867	1,901	1,880	1,902	1,930	2,063	2,166	2,169	2,157
Nonprofit......................	—	—	255	249	238	219	208	191	180	185	182	177	168	159
For-profit......................	—	—	1,672	1,600	1,602	1,648	1,693	1,689	1,722	1,745	1,881	1,989	2,001	1,998
Title IV degree-granting institutions........................	3,231	3,559	4,084	4,236	4,216	4,276	4,314	4,352	4,409	4,495	4,599	4,706	4,726	4,724
2-year colleges......................	1,274	1,418	1,721	1,706	1,683	1,694	1,685	1,677	1,690	1,721	1,729	1,738	1,700	1,685
Public	945	972	1,068	1,086	1,061	1,053	1,045	1,032	1,024	1,000	978	967	934	934
Private	329	446	653	620	622	641	640	645	666	721	751	771	766	751
Nonprofit......................	182	167	150	118	112	113	107	92	92	85	87	100	97	88
For-profit......................	147	279	503	502	510	528	533	553	574	636	664	671	669	663
4-year colleges......................	1,957	2,141	2,363	2,530	2,533	2,582	2,629	2,675	2,719	2,774	2,870	2,968	3,026	3,039
Public	552	595	614	634	639	640	643	653	652	672	678	682	689	691
Private	1,405	1,546	1,749	1,896	1,894	1,942	1,986	2,022	2,067	2,102	2,192	2,286	2,337	2,348
Nonprofit......................	1,387	1,482	1,531	1,546	1,525	1,534	1,533	1,532	1,537	1,539	1,543	1,553	1,555	1,587
For-profit......................	18	64	218	350	369	408	453	490	530	563	649	733	782	761

—Not available.
†Not applicable.
[1]Includes special education, alternative, and other schools not classified by grade span. Because of changes in survey definitions, figures for "other" schools are not comparable from year to year.
[2]Data for 1980–81 and 1990–91 include schools with first or higher grades. Data for later years include schools with kindergarten or higher grades.
[3]Included in the elementary, secondary, and combined categories.
NOTE: Postsecondary data for 1980–81 and 1990–91 are for institutions of higher education, while later data are for Title IV degree-granting and non-degree-granting institutions. Degree-granting institutions grant associate's or higher degrees and participate in Title IV federal financial aid programs. The degree-granting classification is very similar to the earlier higher education classification, but it includes more 2-year colleges and excludes a few higher education institutions that did not grant degrees.

SOURCE: U.S. Department of Education, National Center for Education Statistics, Common Core of Data (CCD), "Public Elementary/Secondary School Universe Survey," 1989–90 through 2013–14; Private Schools in American Education; Statistics of Public Elementary and Secondary Day Schools, 1980–81; Schools and Staffing Survey (SASS), "Private School Data File," 1990–91; Private School Universe Survey (PSS), 1995–96 through 2013–14; Higher Education General Information Survey (HEGIS), "Institutional Characteristics of Colleges and Universities" survey, 1980–81; Integrated Postsecondary Education Data System (IPEDS), "Institutional Characteristics Survey" (IPEDS-IC:90–99); and IPEDS Fall 2001 through Fall 2013, Institutional Characteristics component. (This table was prepared January 2016.)

Table 106.10.   Expenditures of educational institutions related to the gross domestic product, by level of institution: Selected years, 1929–30 through 2014–15

Year	Gross domestic product (GDP) (in billions of current dollars)	School year	Expenditures for education in current dollars					
			All educational institutions		All elementary and secondary schools		All degree-granting postsecondary institutions	
			Amount (in millions)	As a percent of GDP	Amount (in millions)	As a percent of GDP	Amount (in millions)	As a percent of GDP
1	2	3	4	5	6	7	8	9
1929	$104.6	1929–30	—	—	—	—	$632	0.6
1939	93.5	1939–40	—	—	—	—	758	0.8
1949	272.8	1949–50	$8,494	3.1	$6,249	2.3	2,246	0.8
1959	522.5	1959–60	22,314	4.3	16,713	3.2	5,601	1.1
1961	563.3	1961–62	26,828	4.8	19,673	3.5	7,155	1.3
1963	638.6	1963–64	32,003	5.0	22,825	3.6	9,178	1.4
1965	743.7	1965–66	40,558	5.5	28,048	3.8	12,509	1.7
1967	861.7	1967–68	51,558	6.0	35,077	4.1	16,481	1.9
1969	1,019.9	1969–70	64,227	6.3	43,183	4.2	21,043	2.1
1970	1,075.9	1970–71	71,575	6.7	48,200	4.5	23,375	2.2
1971	1,167.8	1971–72	76,510	6.6	50,950	4.4	25,560	2.2
1972	1,282.4	1972–73	82,908	6.5	54,952	4.3	27,956	2.2
1973	1,428.5	1973–74	91,084	6.4	60,370	4.2	30,714	2.2
1974	1,548.8	1974–75	103,903	6.7	68,846	4.4	35,058	2.3
1975	1,688.9	1975–76	114,004	6.8	75,101	4.4	38,903	2.3
1976	1,877.6	1976–77	121,793	6.5	79,194	4.2	42,600	2.3
1977	2,086.0	1977–78	132,515	6.4	86,544	4.1	45,971	2.2
1978	2,356.6	1978–79	143,733	6.1	93,012	3.9	50,721	2.2
1979	2,632.1	1979–80	160,075	6.1	103,162	3.9	56,914	2.2
1980	2,862.5	1980–81	176,378	6.2	112,325	3.9	64,053	2.2
1981	3,211.0	1981–82	190,825	5.9	120,486	3.8	70,339	2.2
1982	3,345.0	1982–83	204,661	6.1	128,725	3.8	75,936	2.3
1983	3,638.1	1983–84	220,993	6.1	139,000	3.8	81,993	2.3
1984	4,040.7	1984–85	239,351	5.9	149,400	3.7	89,951	2.2
1985	4,346.7	1985–86	259,336	6.0	161,800	3.7	97,536	2.2
1986	4,590.2	1986–87	280,964	6.1	175,200	3.8	105,764	2.3
1987	4,870.2	1987–88	301,786	6.2	187,999	3.9	113,787	2.3
1988	5,252.6	1988–89	333,245	6.3	209,377	4.0	123,867	2.4
1989	5,657.7	1989–90	365,825	6.5	231,170	4.1	134,656	2.4
1990	5,979.6	1990–91	395,318	6.6	249,230	4.2	146,088	2.4
1991	6,174.0	1991–92	417,944	6.8	261,755	4.2	156,189	2.5
1992	6,539.3	1992–93	439,676	6.7	274,435	4.2	165,241	2.5
1993	6,878.7	1993–94	460,756	6.7	287,407	4.2	173,351	2.5
1994	7,308.8	1994–95	485,169	6.6	302,200	4.1	182,969	2.5
1995	7,664.1	1995–96	508,523	6.6	318,046	4.1	190,476	2.5
1996	8,100.2	1996–97	538,854	6.7	338,951	4.2	199,903 [1]	2.5
1997	8,608.5	1997–98	570,471	6.6	361,615	4.2	208,856 [1]	2.4
1998	9,089.2	1998–99	603,847	6.6	384,638	4.2	219,209	2.4
1999	9,660.6	1999–2000	649,322	6.7	412,538	4.3	236,784	2.5
2000	10,284.8	2000–01	705,017	6.9	444,811	4.3	260,206	2.5
2001	10,621.8	2001–02	752,780	7.1	472,064	4.4	280,715	2.6
2002	10,977.5	2002–03	795,691	7.2	492,807	4.5	302,884	2.8
2003	11,510.7	2003–04	830,293	7.2	513,542	4.5	316,751	2.8
2004	12,274.9	2004–05	875,988	7.1	540,969	4.4	335,019	2.7
2005	13,093.7	2005–06	925,246	7.1	571,669	4.4	353,577	2.7
2006	13,855.9	2006–07	984,034	7.1	608,495	4.4	375,539	2.7
2007	14,477.6	2007–08	1,054,904	7.3	646,414	4.5	408,490	2.8
2008	14,718.6	2008–09	1,089,683	7.4	658,926	4.5	430,757	2.9
2009	14,418.7	2009–10	1,100,897	7.6	654,418	4.5	446,479	3.1
2010	14,964.4	2010–11	1,124,352	7.5	652,356	4.4	471,997	3.2
2011	15,517.9	2011–12	1,136,876	7.3	648,794	4.2	488,083	3.1
2012	16,155.3	2012–13	1,153,429	7.1	654,490	4.1	498,939	3.1
2013	16,663.2	2013–14 [2]	1,192,000	7.2	675,000	4.1	517,095	3.1
2014	17,348.1	2014–15 [3]	1,228,000	7.1	696,000	4.0	532,000	3.1

—Not available.

[1]Estimated by the National Center for Education Statistics based on enrollment data for the given year and actual expenditures for prior years.

[2]Data for elementary and secondary education are estimated; data for degree-granting institutions are actual.

[3]Estimated by the National Center for Education Statistics based on teacher and enrollment data, and actual expenditures for prior years.

NOTE: Total expenditures for public elementary and secondary schools include current expenditures, interest on school debt, and capital outlay. Data for private elementary and secondary schools are estimated. Expenditures for colleges and universities in 1929–30 and 1939–40 include current-fund expenditures and additions to plant value. Public and private degree-granting institutions data for 1949–50 through 1995–96 are for current-fund expenditures. Data for private degree-granting institutions for 1996–97 and later years are for total expenditures. Data for public degree-granting institutions for 1996–97 through 2000–01 are for current expenditures; data for later years are for total expenditures. Post-secondary data through 1995–96 are for institutions of higher education, while later data are for degree-granting institutions. Degree-granting institutions grant associate's or higher degrees and participate in Title IV federal financial aid programs. The degree-granting classification is very similar to the earlier higher education classification, but it includes more 2-year colleges and excludes a few higher education institutions that did not grant degrees. Some data have been revised from previously published figures. Detail may not sum to totals because of rounding.

SOURCE: U.S. Department of Education, National Center for Education Statistics, *Biennial Survey of Education in the United States*, 1929–30 through 1949–50; *Statistics of State School Systems*, 1959–60 through 1969–70; *Revenues and Expenditures for Public Elementary and Secondary Education*, 1970–71 through 1986–87; Common Core of Data (CCD), "National Public Education Financial Survey," 1987–88 through 2012–13; Higher Education General Information Survey (HEGIS), Financial Statistics of Institutions of Higher Education, 1965–66 through 1985–86; Integrated Postsecondary Education Data System (IPEDS), "Finance Survey" (IPEDS-F:FY87–99); and IPEDS Spring 2001 through Spring 2015, Finance component. U.S. Department of Commerce, Bureau of Economic Analysis, National Income and Product Accounts Tables, retrieved January 29, 2016, from http://www.bea.gov/iTable/index_nipa.cfm. (This table was prepared January 2016.)

Table 106.20. Expenditures of educational institutions, by level and control of institution: Selected years, 1899–1900 through 2014–15

[In millions]

School year	Current dollars							Constant 2014–15 dollars[1]			
	Total	Elementary and secondary schools			Degree-granting postsecondary institutions			Total	Elementary and secondary schools		Degree-granting post-secondary institutions
		Total	Public	Private[2]	Total	Public	Private		Total	Public	
1	2	3	4	5	6	7	8	9	10	11	12
1899–1900	—	—	$215	—	—	—	—	—	—	—	—
1909–10	—	—	426	—	—	—	—	—	—	—	—
1919–20	—	—	1,036	—	—	—	—	—	—	$12,868	—
1929–30	—	—	2,317	—	$632	$292	$341	—	—	32,034	$8,742
1939–40	—	—	2,344	—	758	392	367	—	—	39,698	12,845
1949–50	$8,494	$6,249	5,838	$411	2,246	1,154	1,092	$84,888	$62,446	58,339	22,442
1959–60	22,314	16,713	15,613	1,100	5,601	3,131	2,470	179,737	134,624	125,763	45,114
1969–70	64,227	43,183	40,683	2,500	21,043	13,250	7,794	402,408	270,563	254,900	131,844
1970–71	71,575	48,200	45,500	2,700	23,375	14,996	8,379	426,436	287,169	271,083	139,267
1971–72	76,510	50,950	48,050	2,900	25,560	16,484	9,075	440,052	293,044	276,364	147,008
1972–73	82,908	54,952	51,852	3,100	27,956	18,204	9,752	458,381	303,820	286,681	154,561
1973–74	91,084	60,370	56,970	3,400	30,714	20,336	10,377	462,359	306,451	289,192	155,908
1974–75	103,903	68,846	64,846	4,000	35,058	23,490	11,568	474,814	314,609	296,330	160,205
1975–76	114,004	75,101	70,601	4,500	38,903	26,184	12,719	486,532	320,505	301,301	166,026
1976–77	121,793	79,194	74,194	5,000	42,600	28,635	13,965	491,135	319,350	299,188	171,785
1977–78	132,515	86,544	80,844	5,700	45,971	30,725	15,246	500,747	327,033	305,494	173,714
1978–79	143,733	93,012	86,712	6,300	50,721	33,733	16,988	496,616	321,368	299,601	175,248
1979–80	160,075	103,162	95,962	7,200	56,914	37,768	19,146	488,015	314,505	292,555	173,510
1980–81	176,378	112,325	104,125	8,200	64,053	42,280	21,773	481,900	306,895	284,491	175,006
1981–82	190,825	120,486	111,186	9,300	70,339	46,219	24,120	479,917	303,016	279,627	176,900
1982–83	204,661	128,725	118,425	10,300	75,936	49,573	26,363	493,515	310,405	285,568	183,110
1983–84	220,993	139,000	127,500	11,500	81,993	53,087	28,907	513,878	323,218	296,477	190,660
1984–85	239,351	149,400	137,000	12,400	89,951	58,315	31,637	535,601	334,315	306,568	201,286
1985–86	259,336	161,800	148,600	13,200	97,536	63,194	34,342	564,055	351,915	323,205	212,140
1986–87	280,964	175,200	160,900	14,300	105,764	67,654	38,110	597,823	372,783	342,356	225,039
1987–88	301,786	187,999	172,699	15,300	113,787	72,641	41,145	616,580	384,101	352,841	232,479
1988–89	333,245	209,377	192,977	16,400	123,867	78,946	44,922	650,797	408,895	376,868	241,901
1989–90	365,825	231,170	212,770	18,400	134,656	85,771	48,885	681,885	430,892	396,595	250,993
1990–91	395,318	249,230	229,430	19,800	146,088	92,961	53,127	698,661	440,474	405,481	258,187
1991–92	417,944	261,755	241,055	20,700	156,189	98,847	57,342	715,716	448,247	412,799	267,469
1992–93	439,676	274,435	252,935	21,500	165,241	104,570	60,671	730,126	455,727	420,024	274,399
1993–94	460,757	287,407	265,307	22,100	173,351	109,310	64,041	745,814	465,216	429,444	280,597
1994–95	485,169	302,200	279,000	23,200	182,969	115,465	67,504	763,446	475,532	439,026	287,913
1995–96	508,523	318,046	293,646	24,400	190,476	119,525	70,952	779,001	487,212	449,834	291,789
1996–97	538,854	338,951	313,151	25,800	199,903 [2]	125,978	73,925 [2]	802,567	504,832	466,406	297,734 [2]
1997–98	570,471	361,615	334,315	27,300	208,856 [2]	132,846	76,010 [2]	834,770	529,151	489,203	305,619 [2]
1998–99	603,847	384,638	355,838	28,800	219,209	140,539	78,670	868,572	553,263	511,837	315,310
1999–2000	649,322	412,538	381,838	30,700	236,784	152,325	84,459	907,779	576,745	533,825	331,034
2000–01	705,017	444,811	410,811	34,000	260,206	170,345	89,861	952,992	601,264	555,306	351,728
2001–02	752,780	472,064	435,364	36,700	280,715	183,436	97,280	999,852	627,002	578,257	372,850
2002–03	795,691	492,807	454,907	37,900	302,884	197,026	105,858	1,034,122	640,477	591,221	393,644
2003–04	830,293	513,542	474,242	39,300	316,751	205,069	111,682	1,055,989	653,136	603,154	402,853
2004–05	875,988	540,969	499,569	41,400	335,019	215,794	119,225	1,081,559	667,920	616,804	413,639
2005–06	925,246	571,669	528,269	43,400	353,577	226,550	127,027	1,100,468	679,931	628,312	420,537
2006–07	984,034	608,495	562,195	46,300	375,539	238,829	136,710	1,140,886	705,487	651,807	435,399
2007–08	1,054,904	646,414	597,314	49,100	408,490	261,046	147,444	1,179,353	722,673	667,780	456,681
2008–09	1,089,683	658,926	610,326	48,600	430,757	273,019	157,739	1,201,460	726,517	672,931	474,943
2009–10	1,100,897	654,418	607,018	47,400	446,479	281,390	165,088	1,202,192	714,632	662,871	487,560
2010–11	1,124,352	652,356	604,356	48,000	471,997	296,863	175,134	1,203,636	698,357	646,972	505,279
2011–12	1,136,876	648,794	601,994	46,800	488,083	305,538	182,545	1,182,398	674,772	626,098	507,626
2012–13	1,153,429	654,490	606,490	48,000	498,939	311,425	187,514	1,179,977	669,555	620,450	510,423
2013–14[3]	1,192,000	675,000	625,000	51,000	517,095	323,888	193,207	1,201,000	680,000	630,000	521,000
2014–15[2]	1,228,000	696,000	646,000	50,000	532,000	335,000	197,000	1,228,000	696,000	646,000	532,000

—Not available.

[1]Constant dollars based on the Consumer Price Index, prepared by the Bureau of Labor Statistics, U.S. Department of Labor, adjusted to a school-year basis.

[2]Estimated by the National Center for Education Statistics based on enrollment data for the given year and actual expenditures for prior years.

[3]Data for elementary and secondary education are estimated; data for degree-granting institutions are actual.

NOTE: Total expenditures for public elementary and secondary schools include current expenditures, interest on school debt, and capital outlay. Expenditures for public and private colleges and universities in 1929–30 and 1939–40 include current-fund expenditures and additions to plant value. Public and private degree-granting institutions data for 1949–50 through 1995–96 are for current-fund expenditures. Data for private degree-granting institutions for 1996–97 and later years are for total expenditures. Data for public degree-granting institutions for 1996–97 through 2000–01 are for current expenditures; data for later years are for total expenditures. Postsecondary data through 1995–96 are for institutions of higher education, while later data are for degree-granting institutions. Degree-granting institutions grant associate's or higher degrees and participate in Title IV federal financial aid programs. The degree-granting classification is very similar to the earlier higher education classification, but it includes more 2-year colleges and excludes a few higher education institutions that did not grant degrees. Some data have been revised from previously published figures. Detail may not sum to totals because of rounding.

SOURCE: U.S. Department of Education, National Center for Education Statistics, *Annual Report of the Commissioner of Education,* 1899–1900 and 1909–10; *Biennial Survey of Education in the United States,* 1919–20 through 1949–50; *Statistics of State School Systems,* 1959–60 and 1969–70; *Revenues and Expenditures for Public Elementary and Secondary Education,* 1970–71 through 1986–87; Common Core of Data (CCD), "National Public Education Financial Survey," 1987–88 through 2012–13; Higher Education General Information Survey (HEGIS), Financial Statistics of Institutions of Higher Education, 1965–66 through 1985–86; Integrated Postsecondary Education Data System (IPEDS), "Finance Survey," (IPEDS-F:FY87–99); IPEDS Spring 2001 through Spring 2015, Finance component; and unpublished tabulations. (This table was prepared January 2016.)

Table 106.30. Amount and percentage distribution of direct general expenditures of state and local governments, by function: Selected years, 1970–71 through 2012–13

Function	1970–71	1980–81	1990–91	2000–01	2007–08	2008–09	2009–10	2010–11	2011–12	2012–13
1	2	3	4	5	6	7	8	9	10	11
Amount (in millions of current dollars)										
Total direct general expenditures	$150,674	$407,449	$908,109	$1,621,757	$2,401,417	$2,495,901	$2,537,892	$2,579,509	$2,589,022	$2,639,729
Education and public libraries	60,174	147,649	313,744	571,374	837,582	862,819	871,109	872,969	880,683	888,213
Education	59,413	145,784	309,302	563,572	826,061	851,689	860,118	862,271	869,223	876,566
Public libraries	761	1,865	4,442	7,802	11,521	11,130	10,991	10,699	11,460	11,647
Social services and income maintenance	30,376	92,555	214,919	396,086	619,237	661,411	689,435	729,846	732,358	770,101
Public welfare	18,226	54,121	130,402	257,350	404,198	432,428	456,200	490,645	485,513	516,389
Hospitals and health	11,205	36,101	81,110	134,010	209,904	223,180	227,285	233,018	240,891	247,786
Social insurance administration	945	2,276	3,250	4,359	4,055	4,570	5,157	5,256	5,116	4,901
Veterans' services	†	57	157	337	1,080	933	794	927	838	1,024
Transportation[1]	19,819	39,231	75,410	130,422	181,607	184,166	187,073	183,282	188,380	187,228
Public safety	9,416	31,233	79,932	146,544	216,471	225,735	224,346	225,202	225,631	232,176
Police and fire protection	7,531	21,283	46,568	84,554	128,768	135,904	137,106	138,147	139,375	144,707
Correction	1,885	7,393	27,356	52,370	72,753	75,096	73,100	73,243	72,688	73,324
Protective inspection and regulation	†	2,557	6,008	9,620	14,951	14,735	14,139	13,812	13,568	14,146
Environment and housing	11,832	35,223	76,167	124,203	191,828	196,750	198,223	200,491	196,184	196,353
Natural resources, parks, and recreation	5,191	13,239	28,505	50,082	70,380	71,714	68,680	67,053	66,424	66,695
Housing and community development	2,554	7,086	16,648	27,402	51,071	49,885	53,923	56,284	53,659	51,539
Sewerage and sanitation	4,087	14,898	31,014	46,718	70,378	75,152	75,620	77,154	76,101	78,118
Governmental administration	6,703	20,001	48,461	85,910	125,789	128,350	126,719	123,851	123,711	124,869
Financial administration	2,271	7,230	16,995	30,007	40,350	40,576	40,241	39,351	38,683	39,769
General control[2]	4,432	12,771	31,466	55,903	85,439	87,775	86,479	84,500	85,027	85,100
Interest on general debt	5,089	17,131	52,234	73,836	101,008	104,449	105,715	108,478	108,935	108,385
Other direct general expenditures	7,265	24,426	47,242	93,382	127,895	132,521	135,273	135,388	133,142	132,404
Amount (in millions of constant 2014–15 dollars)[3]										
Total direct general expenditures	$897,697	$1,113,231	$1,604,939	$2,192,177	$2,684,712	$2,751,922	$2,771,400	$2,761,397	$2,692,689	$2,700,479
Education and public libraries	358,509	403,406	554,493	772,343	936,391	951,324	951,258	934,525	915,946	908,654
Education	353,975	398,311	546,642	761,797	923,511	939,052	939,256	923,072	904,027	896,739
Public libraries	4,534	5,096	7,851	10,546	12,880	12,272	12,002	11,453	11,919	11,915
Social services and income maintenance	180,976	252,879	379,835	535,401	692,288	728,926	752,869	781,310	761,682	787,824
Public welfare	108,588	147,869	230,465	347,908	451,881	476,785	498,174	525,242	504,953	528,273
Hospitals and health	66,758	98,635	143,349	181,145	234,666	246,073	248,197	249,449	250,536	253,489
Social insurance administration	5,630	6,218	5,744	5,892	4,533	5,039	5,631	5,626	5,321	5,014
Veterans' services	†	156	277	455	1,208	1,029	867	992	872	1,048
Transportation[1]	118,079	107,187	133,275	176,296	203,032	203,057	204,285	196,206	195,923	191,537
Public safety	56,099	85,335	141,267	198,088	242,008	248,890	244,987	241,082	234,665	237,520
Police and fire protection	44,869	58,149	82,302	114,295	143,959	149,844	149,721	147,888	144,955	148,037
Correction	11,231	20,199	48,347	70,790	81,335	82,799	79,826	78,408	75,599	75,011
Protective inspection and regulation	†	6,986	10,618	13,004	16,715	16,247	15,440	14,786	14,111	14,472
Environment and housing	70,494	96,236	134,613	167,889	214,458	216,932	216,461	214,628	204,039	200,872
Natural resources, parks, and recreation	30,927	36,172	50,378	67,698	78,682	79,070	74,999	71,782	69,083	68,230
Housing and community development	15,216	19,360	29,423	37,040	57,096	55,002	58,885	60,252	55,808	52,725
Sewerage and sanitation	24,350	40,704	54,812	63,151	78,680	82,860	82,577	82,595	79,148	79,916
Governmental administration	39,936	54,647	85,647	116,127	140,628	141,516	138,379	132,584	128,664	127,742
Financial administration	13,530	19,754	30,036	40,561	45,110	44,738	43,943	42,126	40,232	40,684
General control[2]	26,405	34,893	55,611	75,565	95,518	96,778	94,436	90,458	88,432	87,058
Interest on general debt	30,320	46,805	92,315	99,806	112,923	115,163	115,442	116,128	113,297	110,879
Other direct general expenditures	43,284	66,737	83,493	126,227	142,982	146,115	147,719	144,935	138,473	135,451
Percentage distribution										
Total direct general expenditures	100.0	100.0	100.0	100.0	100.0	100.0	100.0	100.0	100.0	100.0
Education and public libraries	39.9	36.2	34.5	35.2	34.9	34.6	34.3	33.8	34.0	33.6
Education	39.4	35.8	34.1	34.8	34.4	34.1	33.9	33.4	33.6	33.2
Public libraries	0.5	0.5	0.5	0.5	0.5	0.4	0.4	0.4	0.4	0.4
Social services and income maintenance	20.2	22.7	23.7	24.4	25.8	26.5	27.2	28.3	28.3	29.2
Public welfare	12.1	13.3	14.4	15.9	16.8	17.3	18.0	19.0	18.8	19.6
Hospitals and health	7.4	8.9	8.9	8.3	8.7	8.9	9.0	9.0	9.3	9.4
Social insurance administration	0.6	0.6	0.4	0.3	0.2	0.2	0.2	0.2	0.2	0.2
Veterans' services	†	#	#	#	#	#	#	#	#	#
Transportation[1]	13.2	9.6	8.3	8.0	7.6	7.4	7.4	7.1	7.3	7.1
Public safety	6.2	7.7	8.8	9.0	9.0	9.0	8.8	8.7	8.7	8.8
Police and fire protection	5.0	5.2	5.1	5.2	5.4	5.4	5.4	5.4	5.4	5.5
Correction	1.3	1.8	3.0	3.2	3.0	3.0	2.9	2.8	2.8	2.8
Protective inspection and regulation	†	0.6	0.7	0.6	0.6	0.6	0.6	0.5	0.5	0.5
Environment and housing	7.9	8.6	8.4	7.7	8.0	7.9	7.8	7.8	7.6	7.4
Natural resources, parks, and recreation	3.4	3.2	3.1	3.1	2.9	2.9	2.7	2.6	2.6	2.5
Housing and community development	1.7	1.7	1.8	1.7	2.1	2.0	2.1	2.2	2.1	2.0
Sewerage and sanitation	2.7	3.7	3.4	2.9	2.9	3.0	3.0	3.0	2.9	3.0
Governmental administration	4.4	4.9	5.3	5.3	5.2	5.1	5.0	4.8	4.8	4.7
Financial administration	1.5	1.8	1.9	1.9	1.7	1.6	1.6	1.5	1.5	1.5
General control[2]	2.9	3.1	3.5	3.4	3.6	3.5	3.4	3.3	3.3	3.2
Interest on general debt	3.4	4.2	5.8	4.6	4.2	4.2	4.2	4.2	4.2	4.1
Other direct general expenditures	4.8	6.0	5.2	5.8	5.3	5.3	5.3	5.2	5.1	5.0

†Not applicable.
#Rounds to zero.
[1]Includes highways, air transportation (airports), parking facilities, and sea and inland port facilities. For 2000–01 and earlier years, also includes transit subsidies.
[2]Includes judicial and legal expenditures, expenditures on general public buildings, and other governmental administration expenditures.

[3]Constant dollars based on the Consumer Price Index, prepared by the Bureau of Labor Statistics, U.S. Department of Labor, adjusted to a school-year basis.
NOTE: Excludes monies paid by states to the federal government. Some data have been revised from previously published figures. Detail may not sum to totals because of rounding.
SOURCE: U.S. Department of Commerce, Census Bureau, Governmental Finances. Retrieved November 29, 2015, from http://www.census.gov/govs/local/. (This table was prepared December 2015.)

Table 106.40. Direct general expenditures of state and local governments for all functions and for education, by level of education and state: 2011–12 and 2012–13

[In millions of current dollars. Standard errors appear in parentheses]

State	Direct general expenditures, 2011–12 Total¹	Direct general expenditures, 2011–12 For education	Direct general expenditures, 2012–13 Total¹	Total for education	Elementary and secondary education Total for elementary and secondary	Elementary and secondary education Current expenditure	Elementary and secondary education Capital outlay	Colleges and universities Total for colleges and universities	Colleges and universities Current expenditure	Colleges and universities Capital outlay	Other education²
1	2	3	4	5	6	7	8	9	10	11	12
United States	$2,589,022	$869,223	$2,639,729 (2,375.8)	$876,566 (613.6)	$569,808 (569.8)	$521,988	$47,821	$261,153 (182.8)	$229,282	$31,872	$45,605
Alabama	34,788	12,614	36,239 (166.7)	13,373 (42.8)	7,543 (43.0)	6,899	644	4,977 (#)	4,038	940	853
Alaska	12,631	3,303	13,566 (77.3)	3,625 (13.4)	2,497 (13.2)	2,246	251	986 (#)	688	298	142
Arizona	41,517	13,520	41,310 (165.2)	13,456 (#)	7,464 (#)	6,905	559	5,075 (#)	4,285	790	916
Arkansas	21,354	8,275	21,427 (75.0)	8,168 (#)	4,910 (#)	4,376	534	2,607 (#)	2,274	333	651
California	349,223	107,599	361,925 (1,483.9)	106,084 (137.9)	66,340 (139.3)	60,190	6,150	34,610 (#)	31,106	3,504	5,134
Colorado	39,781	13,213	41,358 (384.6)	13,507 (1.4)	8,196 (0.8)	7,438	758	4,663 (#)	4,121	542	649
Connecticut	34,096	11,930	34,904 (209.4)	12,188 (142.6)	8,848 (142.5)	8,355	493	2,610 (#)	2,293	318	729
Delaware	9,043	3,339	9,406 (14.1)	3,479 (#)	1,847 (#)	1,690	158	1,252 (#)	1,070	182	379
District of Columbia	10,765	2,372	11,557 (#)	2,526 (#)	2,367 (#)	2,008	359	159 (#)	137	21	0
Florida	134,689	37,376	134,867 (674.3)	37,468 (#)	24,646 (#)	23,234	1,412	9,532 (#)	8,672	860	3,291
Georgia	64,424	25,277	65,267 (215.4)	25,184 (#)	17,045 (#)	15,412	1,633	6,298 (#)	5,505	793	1,841
Hawaii	12,359	3,503	12,309 (#)	3,404 (#)	1,886 (#)	1,704	182	1,411 (#)	1,103	308	107
Idaho	9,897	3,037	10,361 (65.3)	3,118 (0.3)	1,914 (0.2)	1,851	63	1,046 (#)	957	90	157
Illinois	102,734	35,372	107,509 (473.0)	35,944 (#)	25,012 (#)	23,070	1,943	9,254 (#)	8,497	757	1,678
Indiana	45,867	16,913	46,802 (107.6)	16,586 (#)	9,610 (#)	8,747	863	5,885 (#)	5,201	683	1,091
Iowa	27,930	9,803	27,945 (131.3)	9,965 (#)	5,961 (#)	5,178	784	3,555 (#)	3,112	443	449
Kansas	22,954	8,427	23,263 (174.5)	8,453 (#)	5,146 (#)	4,529	617	3,054 (#)	2,729	324	254
Kentucky	32,716	11,632	32,002 (89.6)	11,645 (#)	6,873 (#)	6,123	750	3,781 (#)	3,525	257	991
Louisiana	42,585	12,804	42,030 (163.9)	12,002 (#)	7,958 (#)	7,335	623	3,115 (#)	2,872	244	928
Maine	11,270	3,352	11,117 (56.7)	3,224 (29.7)	2,229 (29.6)	2,159	70	792 (#)	735	57	204
Maryland	53,834	18,606	52,691 (79.0)	18,446 (#)	12,108 (#)	11,152	956	5,632 (#)	4,990	642	706
Massachusetts	64,269	20,500	65,733 (387.8)	20,965 (195.0)	14,713 (194.2)	13,196	1,517	5,215 (#)	4,004	1,211	1,036
Michigan	73,890	28,695	74,702 (313.7)	27,993 (#)	16,473 (#)	15,511	963	10,483 (#)	9,152	1,331	1,037
Minnesota	48,500	15,438	49,238 (556.4)	16,013 (#)	10,346 (#)	9,330	1,017	4,648 (#)	4,144	504	1,018
Mississippi	24,137	7,445	23,963 (112.6)	7,319 (3.7)	4,311 (3.4)	4,025	286	2,573 (#)	2,329	243	436
Missouri	43,301	14,276	43,624 (279.2)	14,347 (#)	9,622 (#)	8,789	833	3,990 (#)	3,657	333	736
Montana	8,199	2,578	8,197 (22.1)	2,629 (#)	1,641 (#)	1,529	111	810 (#)	756	54	179
Nebraska	14,882	5,940	15,367 (107.6)	6,106 (#)	3,811 (#)	3,513	298	2,015 (#)	1,751	264	280
Nevada	18,644	5,406	18,127 (5.4)	5,441 (#)	3,844 (#)	3,622	222	1,231 (#)	1,171	59	366
New Hampshire	10,009	3,840	9,984 (25.0)	3,715 (#)	2,689 (#)	2,616	73	847 (#)	767	80	180
New Jersey	83,021	31,509	83,872 (251.6)	32,115 (48.2)	24,521 (49.0)	23,423	1,098	5,940 (#)	5,323	618	1,655
New Mexico	18,125	6,290	18,190 (54.6)	6,183 (#)	3,470 (#)	2,952	518	2,334 (#)	2,034	300	379
New York	237,767	71,490	244,724 (685.2)	71,144 (156.5)	55,769 (#)	51,794	3,975	13,642 (156.9)	11,096	2,546	1,733
North Carolina	71,047	23,692	73,098 (372.8)	24,871 (271.1)	14,178 (249.5)	13,458	721	9,436 (104.7)	8,476	960	1,257
North Dakota	7,200	2,353	7,458 (23.1)	2,522 (#)	1,441 (#)	1,216	225	981 (#)	874	107	101
Ohio	91,465	32,530	93,035 (502.4)	32,381 (13.0)	21,111 (12.7)	19,112	1,999	9,754 (#)	7,708	2,046	1,515
Oklahoma	26,600	9,446	27,301 (103.7)	9,595 (#)	5,714 (#)	5,156	558	3,348 (#)	3,045	303	533
Oregon	32,063	10,339	32,203 (132.0)	10,447 (#)	5,901 (#)	5,558	343	4,120 (#)	3,546	574	426
Pennsylvania	107,002	35,323	109,849 (527.3)	37,476 (#)	25,909 (#)	24,402	1,507	9,593 (#)	8,534	1,059	1,974
Rhode Island	9,301	3,142	9,431 (19.8)	3,201 (#)	2,271 (#)	2,214	56	660 (#)	629	31	270
South Carolina	34,340	12,134	35,050 (185.8)	12,606 (1.3)	7,666 (1.5)	6,839	827	3,697 (#)	3,315	382	1,244
South Dakota	6,101	2,001	6,216 (16.2)	2,058 (#)	1,292 (#)	1,113	179	652 (#)	572	80	113
Tennessee	42,941	13,783	42,733 (397.4)	13,746 (325.8)	9,041 (325.5)	8,521	520	3,670 (#)	3,323	346	1,035
Texas	183,263	70,407	187,243 (636.6)	71,861 (#)	45,040 (#)	39,568	5,472	24,649 (#)	22,209	2,440	2,172
Utah	21,256	8,207	21,257 (57.4)	8,468 (#)	4,466 (#)	3,768	698	3,620 (#)	3,281	339	382
Vermont	6,240	2,375	6,566 (20.4)	2,459 (#)	1,525 (#)	1,469	56	758 (#)	733	25	176
Virginia	63,095	23,519	65,558 (281.9)	24,529 (203.6)	15,901 (203.5)	14,414	1,487	7,715 (#)	6,426	1,288	913
Washington	58,371	19,284	59,513 (363.0)	19,713 (#)	11,677 (#)	10,234	1,443	6,221 (#)	5,317	905	1,815
West Virginia	14,564	5,507	14,685 (51.4)	5,482 (#)	3,167 (#)	2,882	285	1,684 (#)	1,435	249	631
Wisconsin	47,254	16,990	47,195 (226.5)	16,776 (3.4)	10,238 (3.1)	9,715	522	5,843 (#)	5,155	688	696
Wyoming	7,723	2,520	7,763 (31.1)	2,563 (#)	1,659 (#)	1,445	214	733 (#)	610	123	170

#Rounds to zero.
¹Includes state and local government expenditures for education services, social services and income maintenance, transportation, public safety, environment and housing, governmental administration, interest on general debt, and other general expenditures.
²Includes assistance and subsidies to individuals, private elementary and secondary schools, and private colleges and universities, as well as miscellaneous education expenditures. Does not include expenditures for public libraries.

NOTE: Current expenditure data in this table differ from figures appearing in other tables because of slightly varying definitions used in the Governmental Finances and Common Core of Data surveys. In 2011–12, a census of state and local governments was conducted; therefore, standard errors are not applicable. Detail may not sum to totals because of rounding. Some data have been revised from previously published figures.
SOURCE: U.S. Department of Commerce, Census Bureau, Governmental Finances. Retrieved January 15, 2016, from http://www.census.gov/govs/local/. (This table was prepared January 2016.)

Table 106.50.   Direct general expenditures of state and local governments per capita for all functions and for education, by level of education and state: 2011–12 and 2012–13

[Amounts in current dollars]

State	Direct general expenditures, 2011–12			Direct general expenditures, 2012–13									
		For education			For education								
					All education		Elementary and secondary education		Colleges and universities		Other education[2]		
	Total amount per capita[1]	Amount per capita	As a percent of all functions	Total amount per capita[1]	Amount per capita	As a percent of all functions	Amount per capita	As a percent of all functions	Amount per capita	As a percent of all functions	Amount per capita	As a percent of all functions	
1	2	3	4	5	6	7	8	9	10	11	12	13
United States	$8,242	$2,767	33.6	$8,340	$2,770	33.2	$1,800	21.6	$825	9.9	$144	1.7
Alabama	7,221	2,618	36.3	7,497	2,766	36.9	1,560	20.8	1,030	13.7	176	2.4
Alaska	17,277	4,518	26.1	18,401	4,917	26.7	3,387	18.4	1,337	7.3	193	1.1
Arizona	6,332	2,062	32.6	6,226	2,028	32.6	1,125	18.1	765	12.3	138	2.2
Arkansas	7,240	2,806	38.8	7,242	2,761	38.1	1,659	22.9	881	12.2	220	3.0
California	9,175	2,827	30.8	9,417	2,760	29.3	1,726	18.3	901	9.6	134	1.4
Colorado	7,662	2,545	33.2	7,845	2,562	32.7	1,555	19.8	884	11.3	123	1.6
Connecticut	9,486	3,319	35.0	9,697	3,386	34.9	2,458	25.4	725	7.5	203	2.1
Delaware	9,862	3,642	36.9	10,166	3,760	37.0	1,997	19.6	1,353	13.3	410	4.0
District of Columbia	16,952	3,735	22.0	17,804	3,891	21.9	3,647	20.5	244	1.4	0	0.0
Florida	6,959	1,931	27.8	6,881	1,912	27.8	1,257	18.3	486	7.1	168	2.4
Georgia	6,495	2,548	39.2	6,530	2,520	38.6	1,705	26.1	630	9.6	184	2.8
Hawaii	8,874	2,515	28.3	8,736	2,416	27.7	1,339	15.3	1,001	11.5	76	0.9
Idaho	6,202	1,903	30.7	6,424	1,933	30.1	1,187	18.5	649	10.1	98	1.5
Illinois	7,980	2,748	34.4	8,340	2,788	33.4	1,940	23.3	718	8.6	130	1.6
Indiana	7,016	2,587	36.9	7,123	2,524	35.4	1,463	20.5	896	12.6	166	2.3
Iowa	9,080	3,187	35.1	9,037	3,223	35.7	1,928	21.3	1,150	12.7	145	1.6
Kansas	7,954	2,920	36.7	8,033	2,919	36.3	1,777	22.1	1,055	13.1	88	1.1
Kentucky	7,463	2,654	35.6	7,274	2,647	36.4	1,562	21.5	859	11.8	225	3.1
Louisiana	9,248	2,781	30.1	9,079	2,593	28.6	1,719	18.9	673	7.4	200	2.2
Maine	8,483	2,523	29.7	8,367	2,427	29.0	1,677	20.0	596	7.1	153	1.8
Maryland	9,137	3,158	34.6	8,872	3,106	35.0	2,039	23.0	948	10.7	119	1.3
Massachusetts	9,656	3,080	31.9	9,798	3,125	31.9	2,193	22.4	777	7.9	154	1.6
Michigan	7,475	2,903	38.8	7,547	2,828	37.5	1,664	22.1	1,059	14.0	105	1.4
Minnesota	9,014	2,869	31.8	9,081	2,953	32.5	1,908	21.0	857	9.4	188	2.1
Mississippi	8,083	2,493	30.8	8,009	2,446	30.5	1,441	18.0	860	10.7	146	1.8
Missouri	7,186	2,369	33.0	7,217	2,373	32.9	1,592	22.1	660	9.1	122	1.7
Montana	8,157	2,565	31.4	8,077	2,591	32.1	1,617	20.0	798	9.9	176	2.2
Nebraska	8,021	3,201	39.9	8,222	3,267	39.7	2,039	24.8	1,078	13.1	150	1.8
Nevada	6,767	1,962	29.0	6,494	1,949	30.0	1,377	21.2	441	6.8	131	2.0
New Hampshire	7,575	2,906	38.4	7,549	2,809	37.2	2,033	26.9	640	8.5	136	1.8
New Jersey	9,353	3,550	38.0	9,412	3,604	38.3	2,752	29.2	667	7.1	186	2.0
New Mexico	8,695	3,017	34.7	8,716	2,963	34.0	1,663	19.1	1,118	12.8	182	2.1
New York	12,127	3,646	30.1	12,425	3,612	29.1	2,832	22.8	693	5.6	88	0.7
North Carolina	7,288	2,430	33.3	7,422	2,525	34.0	1,440	19.4	958	12.9	128	1.7
North Dakota	10,260	3,354	32.7	10,303	3,485	33.8	1,990	19.3	1,355	13.2	139	1.4
Ohio	7,918	2,816	35.6	8,040	2,798	34.8	1,824	22.7	843	10.5	131	1.6
Oklahoma	6,969	2,475	35.5	7,086	2,490	35.1	1,483	20.9	869	12.3	138	2.0
Oregon	8,224	2,652	32.2	8,198	2,659	32.4	1,502	18.3	1,049	12.8	108	1.3
Pennsylvania	8,379	2,766	33.0	8,595	2,932	34.1	2,027	23.6	751	8.7	154	1.8
Rhode Island	8,836	2,985	33.8	8,953	3,039	33.9	2,156	24.1	627	7.0	256	2.9
South Carolina	7,271	2,569	35.3	7,345	2,642	36.0	1,606	21.9	775	10.5	261	3.5
South Dakota	7,311	2,398	32.8	7,352	2,434	33.1	1,528	20.8	772	10.5	134	1.8
Tennessee	6,652	2,135	32.1	6,577	2,116	32.2	1,391	21.2	565	8.6	159	2.4
Texas	7,023	2,698	38.4	7,064	2,711	38.4	1,699	24.1	930	13.2	82	1.2
Utah	7,445	2,874	38.6	7,323	2,917	39.8	1,539	21.0	1,247	17.0	132	1.8
Vermont	9,965	3,794	38.1	10,475	3,923	37.5	2,432	23.2	1,209	11.5	282	2.7
Virginia	7,701	2,870	37.3	7,927	2,966	37.4	1,923	24.3	933	11.8	110	1.4
Washington	8,464	2,796	33.0	8,534	2,827	33.1	1,674	19.6	892	10.5	260	3.0
West Virginia	7,846	2,967	37.8	7,922	2,958	37.3	1,708	21.6	908	11.5	341	4.3
Wisconsin	8,254	2,968	36.0	8,218	2,921	35.5	1,783	21.7	1,017	12.4	121	1.5
Wyoming	13,387	4,367	32.6	13,310	4,394	33.0	2,845	21.4	1,257	9.4	292	2.2

[1]Includes state and local government expenditures for education services, social services and income maintenance, transportation, public safety, environment and housing, governmental administration, interest on general debt, and other general expenditures.
[2]Includes assistance and subsidies to individuals, private elementary and secondary schools, and private colleges and universities, as well as miscellaneous education expenditures. Does not include expenditures for public libraries.
NOTE: Per capita amounts for 2012–13 are based on population estimates for July 2013.

Per capita amounts for 2011–12 are based on the latest population estimates for July 2012 and have been revised from previously published figures. Detail may not sum to totals because of rounding.
SOURCE: U.S. Department of Commerce, Census Bureau, Governmental Finances, retrieved January 13, 2016, from http://www.census.gov/govs/local/; and GCT-T1 Population Estimates, retrieved January 13, 2016, from http://www.census.gov/popest/data/national/totals/2014/index.html. (This table was prepared January 2016).

Table 106.60. Gross domestic product, state and local expenditures, national income, personal income, disposable personal income, median family income, and population: Selected years, 1929 through 2015

Year	Gross domestic product (in billions)		State and local direct general expenditures (in millions)[1]		National income (in billions)	Personal income (in billions)	Disposable personal income (in billions of chained 2009 dollars)[2]	Disposable personal income per capita		Median family income		Population (in thousands)	
	Current dollars	Chained 2009 dollars[2]	All direct general expenditures	Education expenditures				Current dollars	Chained 2009 dollars[2]	Current dollars	Constant 2014 dollars[3]	Midyear data[4]	Resident as of July 1[5]
1	2	3	4	5	6	7	8	9	10	11	12	13	14
1929	$104.6	$1,056.6	—	—	$94.2	$85.3	$843.0	$685	$6,917	—	—	121,878	121,767
1939	93.5	1,163.6	—	—	82.5	73.6	923.2	551	7,046	—	—	131,028	130,880
1940	102.9	1,266.1	$9,229	$2,638	91.6	79.4	986.2	588	7,464	—	—	132,122	132,122
1950	300.2	2,184.0	22,787	7,177	267.0	233.9	1,521.9	1,417	10,033	$3,319	—	151,684	152,271
1960	543.3	3,108.7	51,876	18,719	479.9	422.5	2,146.9	2,083	11,877	5,620	$39,329	180,760	180,671
1970	1,075.9	4,722.0	131,332	52,718	940.1	864.6	3,413.2	3,713	16,643	9,867	53,705	205,089	205,052
1971	1,167.8	4,877.6	150,674	59,413	1,017.0	932.1	3,570.4	3,998	17,191	10,285	53,630	207,692	207,661
1972	1,282.4	5,134.3	168,550	65,814	1,123.0	1,023.6	3,741.2	4,287	17,821	11,116	56,276	209,924	209,896
1973	1,428.5	5,424.1	181,357	69,714	1,257.0	1,138.5	3,968.6	4,747	18,725	12,051	57,416	211,939	211,909
1974	1,548.8	5,396.0	198,959	75,833	1,350.8	1,249.3	3,923.6	5,135	18,343	12,902	55,882	213,898	213,854
1975	1,688.9	5,385.4	230,721	87,858	1,451.1	1,366.9	4,020.0	5,645	18,613	13,719	54,908	215,981	215,973
1976	1,877.6	5,675.4	256,731	97,216	1,614.8	1,498.5	4,144.0	6,079	19,002	14,958	56,609	218,086	218,035
1977	2,086.0	5,937.0	274,215	102,780	1,798.7	1,654.6	4,274.8	6,613	19,406	16,009	56,990	220,289	220,239
1978	2,356.6	6,267.2	296,984	110,758	2,029.9	1,859.7	4,470.5	7,322	20,080	17,640	58,766	222,629	222,585
1979	2,632.1	6,466.2	327,517	119,448	2,248.2	2,078.2	4,557.8	8,037	20,248	19,587	59,601	225,106	225,055
1980	2,862.5	6,450.4	369,086	133,211	2,426.8	2,317.5	4,590.5	8,861	20,158	21,023	57,528	227,726	227,225
1981	3,211.0	6,617.7	407,449	145,784	2,722.1	2,596.5	4,705.6	9,785	20,458	22,388	55,938	230,008	229,466
1982	3,345.0	6,491.3	436,733	154,282	2,840.4	2,779.5	4,803.3	10,442	20,685	23,433	55,217	232,218	231,664
1983	3,638.1	6,792.0	466,516	163,876	3,060.5	2,970.3	4,971.0	11,170	21,214	24,580	55,585	234,333	233,792
1984	4,040.7	7,285.0	505,008	176,108	3,444.0	3,281.8	5,314.0	12,284	22,480	26,433	57,387	236,394	235,825
1985	4,346.7	7,593.8	553,899	192,686	3,684.2	3,516.3	5,476.2	12,991	22,960	27,735	58,215	238,506	237,924
1986	4,590.2	7,860.5	605,623	210,819	3,848.2	3,725.7	5,687.8	13,661	23,632	29,458	60,732	240,683	240,133
1987	4,870.2	8,132.6	657,134	226,619	4,119.2	3,955.9	5,811.0	14,274	23,929	30,970	61,762	242,843	242,289
1988	5,252.6	8,474.5	704,921	242,683	4,493.4	4,276.3	6,083.9	15,386	24,826	32,191	61,925	245,061	244,499
1989	5,657.7	8,786.4	762,360	263,898	4,782.2	4,619.9	6,268.7	16,380	25,340	34,213	63,093	247,387	246,819
1990	5,979.6	8,955.0	834,818	288,148	5,036.1	4,906.4	6,393.5	17,235	25,555	35,353	62,131	250,181	249,623
1991	6,174.0	8,948.4	908,108	309,302	5,186.1	5,073.4	6,438.4	17,688	25,395	35,939	60,944	253,530	252,981
1992	6,539.3	9,266.6	981,253	324,652	5,499.7	5,413.0	6,714.2	18,684	26,133	36,573	60,485	256,922	256,514
1993	6,878.7	9,521.0	1,033,167	342,287	5,754.8	5,649.0	6,823.6	19,211	26,216	36,959	59,649	260,282	259,919
1994	7,308.8	9,905.4	1,077,665	353,287	6,140.2	5,937.3	7,010.7	19,906	26,611	38,782	61,311	263,455	263,126
1995	7,664.1	10,174.8	1,146,188	378,273	6,479.5	6,281.0	7,245.8	20,753	27,180	40,611	62,692	266,588	266,278
1996	8,100.2	10,561.0	1,189,356	398,859	6,899.4	6,667.0	7,476.1	21,615	27,719	42,300	63,578	269,714	269,394
1997	8,608.5	11,034.9	1,247,436	419,053	7,380.4	7,080.7	7,751.3	22,527	28,397	44,568	65,570	272,958	272,647
1998	9,089.2	11,525.9	1,314,496	450,365	7,857.3	7,593.7	8,208.1	23,759	29,723	46,737	67,843	276,154	275,854
1999	9,660.6	12,065.9	1,398,533	483,259	8,324.4	7,988.4	8,477.7	24,617	30,350	48,831	69,405	279,328	279,040
2000	10,284.8	12,559.7	1,502,768	521,612	8,907.0	8,637.1	8,902.2	26,206	31,524	50,732	69,741	282,398	282,162
2001	10,621.8	12,682.2	1,621,757	563,572	9,184.6	8,991.6	9,148.7	27,179	32,075	51,407	68,740	285,225	284,969
2002	10,977.5	12,908.8	1,732,478	594,694	9,436.8	9,153.9	9,431.6	28,127	32,754	51,680	68,007	287,955	287,625
2003	11,510.7	13,271.1	1,817,513	621,335	9,864.2	9,491.1	9,690.1	29,198	33,342	52,680	67,809	290,626	290,108
2004	12,274.9	13,773.5	1,903,915	655,182	10,540.9	10,052.9	10,035.7	30,697	34,221	54,061	67,756	293,262	292,805
2005	13,093.7	14,234.2	2,007,490	688,314	11,239.8	10,614.0	10,189.4	31,760	34,424	56,194	68,122	295,993	295,517
2006	13,855.9	14,613.8	2,117,161	728,917	12,004.8	11,393.9	10,595.4	33,589	35,458	58,407	68,582	298,818	298,380
2007	14,477.6	14,873.7	2,259,364	774,170	12,321.4	12,000.2	10,820.6	34,826	35,866	61,355	70,057	301,696	301,231
2008	14,718.6	14,830.4	2,401,417	826,061	12,427.8	12,502.2	10,987.3	36,101	36,078	61,521	67,648	304,543	304,094
2009	14,418.7	14,418.7	2,495,901	851,689	12,126.1	12,094.8	10,942.5	35,616	35,616	60,088	66,303	307,240	306,772
2010	14,964.4	14,783.8	2,537,892	860,118	12,739.5	12,477.1	11,055.1	36,274	35,684	60,236	65,408	309,807	309,347
2011	15,517.9	15,020.6	2,579,509	862,271	13,352.3	13,254.5	11,331.2	37,804	36,298	60,974	64,185	312,169	311,722
2012	16,155.3	15,354.6	2,589,022	869,223	14,061.9	13,915.1	11,688.3	39,441	37,166	62,241	64,179	314,490	314,112
2013	16,663.2	15,583.3	2,639,729	876,566	14,458.3	14,068.4	11,523.1	39,128	36,374	65,471	66,542	316,796	316,498
2014	17,348.1	15,961.7	—	—	15,076.5	14,694.2	11,836.3	40,453	37,077	66,632	66,632	319,233	318,857
2015	17,937.8	16,341.8	—	—	—	15,357.4	12,255.6	41,687	38,096	—	—	321,704	—

—Not available.

[1]Data for years prior to 1970 include expenditures for government fiscal years ending during that particular calendar year. Data for 1970 and later years are the aggregations of expenditures for government fiscal years that ended on June 30 of the stated year. General expenditures exclude expenditures of publicly owned utilities and liquor stores, and of insurance-trust activities. Intergovernmental payments between state and local governments are excluded. Payments to the federal government are included.

[2]Constant dollars based on a chain-price index, which uses the geometric mean of output weights of adjacent time periods compiled over a time series. Chain-price indexes reflect changes in prices, while implicit price deflators reflect both changes in prices and in the composition of output. More information is available at https://www.bea.gov/scb/account_articles/national/0597od/maintext.htm.

[3]Data adjusted by the CPU-RS, which is a price index of inflation that incorporates most of the improvements in methodology made to the current CPI-U since 1978 into a single, uniform series. See Census Bureau, *Money Income in the United States: 1999* (www.census.gov/prod/2000pubs/p60-209.pdf).

[4]Population of the United States including armed forces overseas. Includes Alaska and Hawaii beginning in 1960.

[5]Resident population of the United States. Includes Alaska and Hawaii beginning in 1958. Data for 1990 and later years include revisions based on the 2000 census. Excludes overseas armed forces personnel.

NOTE: Gross domestic product (GDP) data are adjusted by the GDP chained weight price deflator. Personal income data are adjusted by the personal consumption deflator. Some data have been revised from previously published figures.

SOURCE: Department of Commerce, Census Bureau, Current Population Survey, Income, retrieved February 1, 2016, from http://www.census.gov/hhes/www/income/data/historical/families/; Population Estimates, retrieved June 2, 2015, from http://www.census.gov/popest/data/historical/2010s/vintage_2013/national.html and September 15, 2015, from http://www.census.gov/popest/data/national/asrh/2014/index.html; and State and Local Government Finances, retrieved February 1, 2016, from http://www.census.gov/govs/local/. U.S. Department of Commerce, Bureau of Economic Analysis, National Income and Product Accounts Tables, retrieved February 1, 2016, from http://www.bea.gov/iTable/index_nipa.cfm. (This table was prepared February 2016.)

Table 106.70. Gross domestic product price index, Consumer Price Index, education price indexes, and federal budget composite deflator: Selected years, 1919 through 2015

Calendar year			School year					Federal fiscal year	
Year	Gross domestic product price index	Consumer Price Index[1]	Year	Consumer Price Index[2]	Higher Education Price Index[3]	Research and Development Index	Academic Library Operations Index	Year	Federal budget composite deflator
1	2	3	4	5	6	7	8	9	10
1919	—	17.3	1919–20	19.1	—	—	—	1919	—
1929	9.896	17.1	1929–30	17.1	—	—	—	1929	—
1939	8.033	13.9	1939–40	14.0	—	—	—	1939	—
1949	13.581	23.8	1949–50	23.7	—	—	—	1949	0.0958
1950	13.745	24.1	1950–51	25.1	—	—	—	1950	0.1005
1951	14.716	26.0	1951–52	26.3	—	—	—	1951	0.1009
1952	14.972	26.5	1952–53	26.7	—	—	—	1952	0.1006
1953	15.157	26.7	1953–54	26.9	—	—	—	1953	0.1080
1954	15.298	26.9	1954–55	26.8	—	—	—	1954	0.1113
1955	15.559	26.8	1955–56	26.9	—	—	—	1955	0.1151
1956	16.091	27.2	1956–57	27.7	—	—	—	1956	0.1202
1957	16.625	28.1	1957–58	28.6	—	—	—	1957	0.1261
1958	17.001	28.9	1958–59	29.0	—	—	—	1958	0.1336
1959	17.237	29.1	1959–60	29.4	—	—	—	1959	0.1391
1960	17.476	29.6	1960–61	29.8	25.6	26.7	—	1960	0.1411
1961	17.669	29.9	1961–62	30.1	26.5	27.5	—	1961	0.1443
1962	17.886	30.2	1962–63	30.4	27.6	28.5	—	1962	0.1446
1963	18.088	30.6	1963–64	30.8	28.6	29.5	—	1963	0.1507
1964	18.366	31.0	1964–65	31.2	29.8	30.7	—	1964	0.1531
1965	18.702	31.5	1965–66	31.9	31.3	32.0	—	1965	0.1553
1966	19.227	32.4	1966–67	32.9	32.9	33.8	—	1966	0.1596
1967	19.786	33.4	1967–68	34.0	34.9	35.7	—	1967	0.1632
1968	20.627	34.8	1968–69	35.7	37.1	38.0	—	1968	0.1692
1969	21.642	36.7	1969–70	37.8	39.5	40.3	—	1969	0.1798
1970	22.784	38.8	1970–71	39.7	42.1	42.7	—	1970	0.1899
1971	23.941	40.5	1971–72	41.2	44.3	45.0	—	1971	0.2031
1972	24.978	41.8	1972–73	42.8	46.7	47.1	—	1972	0.2166
1973	26.337	44.4	1973–74	46.6	49.9	50.1	—	1973	0.2267
1974	28.703	49.3	1974–75	51.8	54.3	54.8	—	1974	0.2455
1975	31.361	53.8	1975–76	55.5	57.8	59.0	57.3	1975	0.2696
1976	33.083	56.9	1976–77	58.7	61.5	62.7	61.6	1976	0.2890
1977	35.135	60.6	1977–78	62.6	65.7	66.8	65.8	1977	0.3099
1978	37.602	65.2	1978–79	68.5	70.5	71.7	71.4	1978	0.3294
1979	40.706	72.6	1979–80	77.6	77.5	78.3	78.5	1979	0.3578
1980	44.377	82.4	1980–81	86.6	85.8	86.6	86.1	1980	0.3953
1981	48.520	90.9	1981–82	94.1	93.9	94.0	94.0	1981	0.4393
1982	51.530	96.5	1982–83	98.2	100.0	100.0	100.0	1982	0.4722
1983	53.565	99.6	1983–84	101.8	104.8	104.3	105.1	1983	0.4958
1984	55.466	103.9	1984–85	105.8	110.8	109.8	111.2	1984	0.5185
1985	57.240	107.6	1985–86	108.8	116.3	115.2	117.6	1985	0.5373
1986	58.395	109.6	1986–87	111.2	120.9	120.0	124.2	1986	0.5487
1987	59.885	113.6	1987–88	115.8	126.2	126.8	130.0	1987	0.5644
1988	61.982	118.3	1988–89	121.2	132.8	132.1	138.6	1988	0.5835
1989	64.392	124.0	1989–90	127.0	140.8	139.0	147.4	1989	0.6059
1990	66.773	130.7	1990–91	133.9	148.2	145.8	155.7	1990	0.6238
1991	68.996	136.2	1991–92	138.2	153.5	150.6	163.3	1991	0.6527
1992	70.569	140.3	1992–93	142.5	157.9	155.2	169.8	1992	0.6772
1993	72.248	144.5	1993–94	146.2	163.3	160.1	176.7	1993	0.6973
1994	73.785	148.2	1994–95	150.4	168.1	165.4	183.9	1994	0.7100
1995	75.324	152.4	1995–96	154.5	173.0	170.8	192.6	1995	0.7307
1996	76.699	156.9	1996–97	158.9	178.4	—	—	1996	0.7460
1997	78.012	160.5	1997–98	161.7	184.7	—	—	1997	0.7612
1998	78.859	163.0	1998–99	164.5	189.1	—	—	1998	0.7681
1999	80.065	166.6	1999–2000	169.3	196.9	—	—	1999	0.7778
2000	81.887	172.2	2000–01	175.1	208.7	—	—	2000	0.7971
2001	83.754	177.1	2001–02	178.2	212.7	—	—	2001	0.8184
2002	85.039	179.9	2002–03	182.1	223.5	—	—	2002	0.8320
2003	86.735	184.0	2003–04	186.1	231.7	—	—	2003	0.8555
2004	89.120	188.9	2004–05	191.7	240.8	—	—	2004	0.8779
2005	91.988	195.3	2005–06	199.0	253.1	—	—	2005	0.9083
2006	94.814	201.6	2006–07	204.1	260.3	—	—	2006	0.9396
2007	97.337	207.3	2007–08	211.7	273.2	—	—	2007	0.9644
2008	99.246	215.3	2008–09	214.7	279.3	—	—	2008	0.9981
2009	100.000	214.5	2009–10	216.7	281.8	—	—	2009	1.0000
2010	101.221	218.1	2010–11	221.1	288.4	—	—	2010	1.0119
2011	103.311	224.9	2011–12	227.6	293.2	—	—	2011	1.0318
2012	105.214	229.6	2012–13	231.4	297.8	—	—	2012	1.0512
2013	106.929	233.0	2013–14	235.0	306.7	—	—	2013	1.0659
2014	108.686	236.7	2014–15	236.7	—	—	—	2014	1.0825
2015	109.767	237.0	2015–16	—	—	—	—	2015	1.0970

—Not available.
[1]Index for urban wage earners and clerical workers through 1977; 1978 and later figures are for all urban consumers.
[2]Consumer Price Index adjusted to a school-year basis (July through June).
[3]Beginning in 2001–02, components of index were weighted through a regression methodology.
NOTE: Some data have been revised from previously published figures.
SOURCE: U.S. Department of Commerce, Bureau of Economic Analysis, National Income and Product Accounts, retrieved February 1, 2016, from http://www.bea.gov/iTable/iTable.cfm?ReqID=

9&step=1#reqid=9&step=3&isuri=1&904=1929&903=13&906=a&905=2015&910=x&911=0. U.S. Department of Labor, Bureau of Labor Statistics, Consumer Price Index, retrieved July 29, 2015, from http://www.bls.gov/data/. Commonfund Institute, retrieved February 1, 2016, from https://www.commonfund.org/wp-content/uploads/2016/01/2014-Type-of-Institution-Summary.pdf. U.S. Office of Management and Budget, Composite Deflator, retrieved February 1, 2016, from http://www.whitehouse.gov/omb/budget/Historicals. (This table was prepared February 2016.)

CHAPTER 2
Elementary and Secondary Education

This chapter contains a variety of statistics on public and private elementary and secondary education. Data are presented for enrollments, teachers and other school staff, schools, dropouts, achievement, school violence, and revenues and expenditures. These data are derived from surveys, censuses, and administrative data collections conducted by the National Center for Education Statistics (NCES) and other public and private organizations. The information ranges from counts of students and schools to state graduation requirements.

Enrollments

Public elementary and secondary school enrollment rose from 49.3 million in 2008 to 50.0 million in 2013, an increase of 2 percent (table 203.10 and figure 7). Public elementary enrollment (prekindergarten through grade 8) increased 3 percent between 2008 and 2013 (from 34.3 million to 35.3 million), while public secondary enrollment (grades 9 through 12) decreased 1 percent (from 15.0 million to 14.8 million). Although public school enrollment increased overall between 2008 and 2013, there were increases in enrollment for some racial/ethnic groups and decreases for other groups (table 203.50). Between 2008 and 2013, the enrollment of Hispanic students increased 18 percent and the enrollment of Asian/Pacific Islander students increased 6 percent. In contrast, the enrollment of White students decreased 7 percent, the enrollment of Black students decreased 7 percent, and the enrollment of American Indian/Alaska Native students decreased 11 percent.

From 2008 to 2013, changes in public school enrollment varied from state to state. Thirty-six states and the District of Columbia had higher enrollment in 2013 than in 2008, while 14 states had lower enrollment in 2013 than in 2008 (table 203.20 and figure 8). The largest public school enrollment increases occurred in the District of Columbia (14 percent) and Utah (12 percent), and increases of more than 5 percent occurred in 8 other states (Colorado, Idaho, Kansas, Nebraska, North Dakota, Oklahoma, Texas, and Wyoming). The largest decrease in public school enrollment occurred in Michigan (a decrease of 7 percent), and decreases of at least 5 percent occurred in 3 other states (New Hampshire, Ohio, and Vermont).

Enrollment in private elementary and secondary schools in 2013 (5.4 million) was 5 percent lower than in 2008 (5.7 million) (table 208.20). In 2013, private school students made up 9.7 percent of all elementary and secondary school students.

In 2014, about 65 percent of 3- to 5-year-olds were enrolled in preprimary education (nursery school and kindergarten), not measurably different from the percentage enrolled in 2004 (table 202.10 and figure 9). However, the percentage of these children in full-day programs increased from 57 percent in 2004 to 62 percent in 2014.

A higher percentage of 4-year-old children (57 percent) were cared for primarily in center-based programs during the day in 2005–06 than had no regular nonparental care (20 percent) or were cared for primarily in home-based settings by relatives (13 percent) or by nonrelatives (8 percent) (table 202.50). There were differences in the average quality of care children received in these settings. A higher percentage of children in Head Start and other center-based programs (35 percent) received high-quality care than those in home-based relative and nonrelative care (9 percent), according to the ratings of trained observers (table 202.60).

The Individuals with Disabilities Education Act (IDEA), enacted in 1975, mandates that children and youth ages 3–21 with disabilities be provided a free and appropriate public school education. The percentage of total public school enrollment that represents children served by federally supported special education programs increased from 8.3 percent to 13.8 percent between 1976–77 and 2004–05 (table 204.30). Much of this overall increase can be attributed to a rise in the percentage of students identified as having specific learning disabilities from 1976–77 (1.8 percent) to 2004–05 (5.7 percent). The overall percentage of students being served in programs for those with disabilities decreased between 2004–05 (13.8 percent) and 2013–14 (12.9 percent). However, there were different patterns of change in the percentages served with some specific conditions between 2004–05 and 2013–14. The percentage of children identified as having other health impairments (limited strength, vitality, or alertness due to chronic or acute health problems such as a heart condition, tuberculosis, rheumatic fever, nephritis, asthma, sickle cell anemia, hemophilia, epilepsy, lead poisoning, leukemia, or diabetes) rose from 1.1 to 1.6 percent of total public school enrollment, the percentage with autism rose from 0.4 to 1.1 percent, and the percentage with developmental delay rose from 0.7 to 0.8 percent. The percentage of children with specific learning disabilities declined from 5.7 percent to 4.5 percent of total public school enrollment during this period. In fall 2013, some 95 percent of 6- to 21-year-old students with disabilities were served in regular schools; 3 percent were served in a separate school for students with disabilities; 1 percent were placed in regular private schools by their parents; and less than 1 percent each were served in one of the following environments: in a separate residential facility, homebound or in a hospital, or in a correctional facility (table 204.60).

Teachers and Other School Staff

During the 1970s and early 1980s, public school enrollment decreased, while the number of teachers generally increased. For public schools, the number of pupils per teacher—that is, the pupil/teacher ratio[1]—declined from 22.3 in 1970 to 17.9 in 1985 (table 208.20 and figure 7). After enrollment started increasing in 1985, the public school pupil/teacher ratio continued to decline, reaching 17.2 in 1989. After a period of relative stability from the late 1980s through the mid-1990s, the ratio declined from 17.3 in 1995 to 15.3 in 2008. After 2008, the public school pupil/teacher ratio increased, reaching 16.1 in 2013. By comparison, the pupil/teacher ratio for private schools was 12.2 in 2013. The average class size in 2011–12 was 21.2 pupils for public elementary schools and 26.8 pupils for public secondary schools (table 209.30).

In 2011–12, some 76 percent of public school teachers were female, 44 percent were under age 40, and 56 percent had a master's or higher degree (table 209.10). Compared with public school teachers, a lower percentage of private school teachers had a master's or higher degree (43 percent).

Public school principals tend to be older and have more advanced credentials than public school teachers. In 2011–12, some 20 percent of public school principals were under age 40, and 98 percent of public school principals had a master's or higher degree (table 212.10). Compared with public school principals, a lower percentage of private school principals had a master's or higher degree (69 percent). A lower percentage of principals than of teachers were female: About 52 percent of public school principals were female, compared with 76 percent of teachers. At private schools, 55 percent of principals were female in 2011–12, compared with 75 percent of teachers.

From 1969–70 to 1980, there was an 8 percent increase in the number of public school teachers, compared with a 48 percent increase in the number of all other public school staff[2] (table B and table 213.10). Consequently, the percentage of staff who were teachers declined from 60 percent in 1969–70

to 52 percent in 1980. From 1980 to 2013, the number of teachers and the number of all other staff grew at more similar rates (43 and 55 percent, respectively) than they did in the 1970s. As a result, the proportion of teachers among total staff was 2 percentage points lower in 2013 than in 1980, in contrast to the decrease of 8 percentage points during the 1970s. The numbers of staff in two categories increased more than 100 percent between 1980 and 2013: The number of instructional aides rose 127 percent, and the number of instruction coordinators rose 255 percent. Taken together, the percentage of staff with direct instructional responsibilities (teachers and instructional aides) increased from 60 to 62 percent between 1980 and 2013. In 2013, there were 8 pupils per staff member (total staff) at public schools, compared with 10 pupils per staff member in 1980 (table 213.10). At private schools in 2011–12, the number of pupils per staff member was 6 (table 205.60).

In more recent years, the numbers of some types of staff have increased while most others have decreased (table 213.10.). Overall, the number of public school staff decreased by 2 percent between fall 2008 and fall 2013. The number of officials and administrators rose 7 percent during this period. The number of principals and assistant principals was 5 percent higher in 2013 than in 2008, and the number of instructional aides was 1 percent higher. In contrast, the number of instruction coordinators was 1 percent lower in 2013 than in 2008, the number of support staff was 2 percent lower, and the number of teachers was 3 percent lower. The number of guidance counselors decreased by 5 percent, and the number of librarians decreased by 16 percent.

Table B. Number of public school staff, by selected categories: 1969–70, 1980, and 2013

[In thousands]

Selected staff category	1969–70	1980	2013
Total	3,361	4,168	6,188
Teachers	2,016	2,184	3,134
Instructional aides	57	326	738
Instruction coordinators	32	21	73

SOURCE: U.S. Department of Education, National Center for Education Statistics, *Statistics of State School Systems, 1969–70; Statistics of Public Elementary and Secondary Schools, 1980;* and Common Core of Data (CCD), "State Nonfiscal Survey of Public Elementary/Secondary Education," 2013–14.

Schools

During most of the last century, the trend of consolidating small schools brought declines in the total number of public schools in the United States. In 1929–30, there were approximately 248,000 public schools, compared with about 98,000 in 2013–14 (table 214.10). However, the number of public schools has increased in recent decades: Between 1988–89 and 2006–07, there was an increase of approximately 15,600 schools. Since 2006–07, the number of public schools has remained relatively stable, varying by about 500 schools or less from year to year.

---

[1] The pupil/teacher ratio is based on all teachers—including teachers for students with disabilities and other special teachers—and all students enrolled in the fall of the school year. Unlike the pupil/teacher ratio, the average class size excludes students and teachers in classes that are exclusively for special education students. Class size averages are based on surveys of teachers reporting on the counts of students in their classes.

[2] "All other public school staff" includes administrative staff, principals, librarians, guidance counselors, secretaries, custodial staff, food service workers, school bus drivers, and other professional and nonprofessional staff.

While the total number of public schools in the country has remained between 98,000 and 99,000 in recent years, new schools have opened and some schools have closed. In 2013–14, there were 1,737 school closures (table 216.95). The schools that closed had enrolled about 274,000 students in the prior school year (2012–13). Of the schools that closed, 1,179 were regular schools, 90 were special education schools, 20 were vocational schools, and 448 were alternative schools. The number of schools that closed in 2013–14 was higher than the number in 2000–01 (1,193); however, the number of annual school closures has fluctuated during this period, ranging from around 1,200 to 2,200. School closures do not necessarily reflect the number of school buildings that have been closed, since a school may share a building with another school, or one school may have multiple buildings.

Since the early 1970s, public school systems have been shifting away from junior high schools (schools consisting of either grades 7 and 8 or grades 7 to 9) and moving toward middle schools (a subset of elementary schools beginning with grade 4, 5, or 6 and ending with grade 6, 7, or 8) (table 216.10). Although the number of all elementary schools (schools beginning with grade 6 or below and having no grade higher than 8) was similar in 1970–71 and 2000–01 (64,000 and 64,600, respectively), the number of middle schools was 462 percent higher in 2000–01 than in 1970–71 (11,700 vs. 2,100). During the same period, the number of junior high schools declined by 57 percent (from 7,800 in 1970–71 to 3,300 in 2000–01). Between 2003–04 and 2013–14, the number of all elementary schools rose by 2 percent to 67,000, while the subset of middle schools rose by 8 percent to 13,300. During the same period, the number of junior high schools declined by 16 percent to 2,700.

The average number of students in public elementary schools in 2013–14 (483) was higher than in 2003–04 (476) (table 216.45). The average enrollment size of public secondary schools decreased from 722 students in 2003–04 to 694 students in 2013–14. The average size of regular public secondary schools—which exclude alternative, special education, and vocational education schools—decreased from 816 students in 2003–04 to 788 students in 2013–14.

School Choice

Over the past 2 decades, the range of options that parents have for the education of their children has expanded. Private schools have been a traditional alternative to public school education, but there are now more options for parents to choose public charter schools, and more parents are also homeschooling their children. Between fall 1999 and fall 2013, enrollment in private schools decreased from 6.0 million to 5.4 million, a decline of 0.6 million or 10 percent (table 105.30). During the same period, the percentage of elementary and secondary students who were enrolled in private schools declined from 11.4 percent to 9.7 percent. In contrast, enrollment in public charter schools increased between fall 1999 and fall 2013, rising from 0.3 million to 2.5 million, an increase of 2.2 million students (table 216.30). During this period, the percentage of public elementary and secondary school children who were in charter schools increased from 0.7 percent to 5.1 percent. In addition, there has been an increase in the number and percentage of 5- to 17-year-olds who are homeschooled (tables 206.10 and 206.20). About 1.8 million children were homeschooled in 2012, compared to 0.9 million in 1999.[3] Also, the percentage of 5- to 17-year-olds who were homeschooled in 2012 (3.4 percent) was higher than in 1999 (1.7 percent).

Charter schools are the typical form of choice available to parents within the public education sector; however, some opportunity for parental choice also can be found among traditional public schools. In 2012, the parents of 37 percent of all 1st- through 12th-grade students indicated that public school choice was available to them (table 206.40). Also in 2012, 13 percent of the students in traditional public schools were in a school chosen by their parents rather than an assigned school (table 206.30). There were differences in the characteristics of students attending their local assigned public schools in 2012 compared to those in public schools chosen by their parents. For example, White students made up a higher percentage of those in assigned schools (53 percent) than of those in chosen schools (40 percent). In contrast, Black students made up a higher percentage of those in chosen schools (22 percent) than of those in assigned schools (14 percent). Hispanic students also made up a higher percentage of those in chosen schools (27 percent) than of those in assigned schools (23 percent). Students in cities made up a higher percentage of those in chosen schools (46 percent) than of those in assigned schools (25 percent). In contrast, students in rural areas made up a higher percentage of those in assigned schools (26 percent) than of those in chosen schools (14 percent).

Compared with students in assigned public schools, a higher percentage of students in chosen public schools had parents who were very satisfied with some elements of their children's education in 2012 (table 206.50). Among students in grades 3 through 12, the percentage of students whose parents were very satisfied with their school was higher for students in chosen schools (56 percent) than for students in assigned schools (52 percent). Similarly, the percentage of students whose parents were very satisfied with their school's academic standards was higher for students in chosen schools (59 percent) than for students in assigned schools (53 percent). Also, higher percentages of students in chosen schools had parents who were very satisfied with school order and discipline (58 vs. 52 percent) as well as with staff interaction with parents (49 vs. 45 percent). However, there was no measurable difference between the percentages of students in chosen and assigned public schools whose parents were highly satisfied with the teachers in their school (52 percent each).

---

[3] The number of homeschooled children in 1999 is from *Homeschooling in the United States: 1999* (NCES 2001-033), available at http://nces.ed.gov/pubsearch/pubsinfo.asp?pubid=2001033. While National Household Education Surveys Program (NHES) administrations prior to 2012 were administered via telephone with an interviewer, NHES:2012 used self-administered paper-and-pencil questionnaires that were mailed to respondents. Measurable differences in estimates between 1999 and 2012 could reflect actual changes in the population, or the changes could be due to the mode change from telephone to mail.

High School Graduates and Dropouts

About 3,506,000 high school students are expected to graduate during the 2015–16 school year (table 219.10), including 3,192,000 public school graduates and 314,000 private school graduates. High school graduates include only recipients of diplomas, not recipients of equivalency credentials. The 2015–16 projection of high school graduates is higher than the prior record high of 3,480,000 graduates for 2013–14, and also exceeds the baby boom era's high point in 1975–76, when 3,142,000 students earned diplomas. In 2012–13, an estimated 81.9 percent of public high school students graduated on time—that is, received a diploma 4 years after beginning their freshman (9th-grade) year.

The number of GED credentials issued by the states to GED test passers rose from 330,000 in 1977 to 487,000 in 2000 (table 219.60). A record number of 648,000 GED credentials were issued in 2001. In 2002, there were revisions to the GED test and to the data reporting procedures. In 2001, test takers were required to successfully complete all five components of the GED or else begin the five-part series again with the new test that was introduced in 2002. Prior to 2002, reporting was based on summary data from the states on the number of GED credentials issued. As of 2002, reporting has been based on individual GED candidate- and test-level records collected by the GED Testing Service.[4] In 2013, some 541,000 people passed the GED tests, up from 387,000 in 2003.

The percentage of dropouts among 16- to 24-year-olds (known as the status dropout rate) has decreased over the past two decades (table 219.70). The status dropout rate is the percentage of the civilian noninstitutionalized 16- to 24-year-old population who are not enrolled in school and who have not completed a high school program, regardless of when they left school. (People who left school but went on to receive a GED credential are not treated as dropouts.) Between 1990 and 2014, the status dropout rate declined from 12.1 to 6.5 percent. Although the status dropout rate declined for both Blacks and Hispanics during this period, their rates in 2014 (7.4 and 10.6 percent, respectively) remained higher than the rate for Whites (5.2 percent).

Achievement

Most of the student performance data in the *Digest* are drawn from the National Assessment of Educational Progress (NAEP). The NAEP assessments have been conducted using three basic designs: the national main NAEP, state NAEP (which includes the Trial Urban District Assessment), and national long-term trend NAEP. The main NAEP reports current information for the nation and specific geographic regions of the country. The assessment program includes students drawn from both public and private schools and reports results for student achievement at grades 4, 8, and 12. The main

[4] Information on changes in GED test series and reporting is based on the 2003 edition of *Who Passed the GED Tests?*, by the GED Testing Service of the American Council on Education, as well as communication with staff of the GED Testing Service.

NAEP assessments follow the frameworks developed by the National Assessment Governing Board and use the latest advances in assessment methodology. Because the assessment items reflect curricula associated with specific grade levels, the main NAEP uses samples of students at those grade levels.

Since 1990, NAEP assessments have also been conducted at the state level. Each participating state receives assessment results that report on the performance of students in that state. In its content, the state assessment is identical to the assessment conducted nationally. From 1990 through 2001, the national sample was a subset of the combined sample of students assessed in each participating state along with an additional sample from the states that did not participate in the state assessment. For mathematics, reading, science, and writing assessments since 2002, a combined sample of public schools has been selected for 4th- and 8th-grade national NAEP and state NAEP (including the Trial Urban District Assessment).

NAEP long-term trend assessments are designed to give information on the changes in the basic achievement level of America's youth since the early 1970s. They are administered nationally and report student performance in reading and mathematics at ages 9, 13, and 17. Measuring long-term trends of student achievement requires the precise replication of past procedures. For example, students of specific ages are sampled in order to maintain consistency with the original sample design. Similarly, the long-term trend instrument does not evolve based on changes in curricula or in educational practices. The differences in procedures between the main NAEP and the long-term trend NAEP mean that their results cannot be compared directly.

The following paragraphs discuss results for the national main NAEP, state NAEP, and long-term trend NAEP. Readers should keep in mind that comparisons of NAEP scores in the text (like all comparisons of estimates in the *Digest*) are based on statistical testing of unrounded values.

Reading

The main NAEP reading assessment data are reported on a scale of 0 to 500. In 2015, the average reading score for 4th-grade students (223) was not measurably different from the 2013 score, but it was higher than the 1992 score (217) (table 221.10). At grade 4, the average 2015 reading scores for White (232), Black (206), Hispanic (208), and Asian/Pacific Islander students (239) were not measurably different from the corresponding scores in 2013, but their average scores were all higher than in 1992. For 8th-grade students, the average reading score in 2015 (265) was lower than in 2013 (268), but it was higher than in 1992 (260). At grade 8, average 2015 reading scores for White (274), Black (248), and Hispanic (253) students were lower than the scores in 2013 (276, 250, and 256, respectively), while the average 2015 reading score for Asian/Pacific Islander (280) students was not measurably different from the score in 2013. Consistent with the findings at grade 4, the average reading scores for White, Black, Hispanic, and Asian/Pacific Islander 8th-grade students were higher in 2015 than in 1992. For 12th grade students, the average reading score in 2015 was not measurably different from that in 2013. At grade 12, the average 2015 reading scores for White (295), Hispanic (276), and Asian/Pacific Islander students (297) were not measurably different from the scores in 2013 and 1992. For Black students, the 2015 average score (266) was lower than the 1992 score (273) but was not measurably different from the 2013 score.

From 1992 through 2015, the average reading scores for White 4th- and 8th-graders were higher than those of their Black and Hispanic peers (table 221.10). Although the White-Black and White-Hispanic achievement gaps did not change measurably from 2013 to 2015 at either grade 4 or 8, some of the racial/ethnic achievement gaps have narrowed since 1992. At grade 4, the White-Black gap narrowed from 32 points in 1992 to 26 points in 2015; at grade 8, the White-Hispanic gap narrowed from 26 points in 1992 to 21 points in 2015.

While there was no measurable change from 2013 to 2015 in the average reading score for 4th-grade public school students nationally, average scores were higher in 2015 than in 2013 in the District of Columbia and 12 states (table 221.40). Average 4th-grade scores were lower in 2015 than in 2013 in Maryland and Minnesota, while scores in all remaining states did not change measurably from 2013 to 2015. The average reading score for 8th-grade public school students was lower in 2015 than in 2013 nationally and in 8 states (table 221.60). However, 8th-grade students in West Virginia scored higher in 2015 than in 2013. In the remaining states and the District of Columbia, scores did not change measurably from 2013 to 2015.

Reported on a scale of 0 to 500, NAEP long-term trend results in reading are available for 13 assessment years going back to the first in 1971. The average reading score for 9-year-olds was higher in 2012 (221) than in assessment years prior to 2008, increasing 5 points since 2004 and 13 points in comparison to 1971 (table 221.85). The average score for 13-year-olds in 2012 (263) was higher than in all previous assessment years, except for 1992. The average reading score for 17-year-olds was higher in 2012 (287) than in 2004 (283), but was not significantly different from the score in 1971 (285).

White, Black, and Hispanic 9-, 13-, and 17-year-olds all had higher average reading scores in 2012 than they did in the first assessment year (which is 1975 for Hispanic students because separate data for Hispanics were not collected in 1971). Average reading scores were higher in 2012 than in 2004 for White, Black, and Hispanic students at all three ages (table 221.85). Reading results for 2012 continued to show gaps in scores between White and Black students (ranging from 23 to 26 points, depending on age) and between White and Hispanic students (about 21 points at all three ages). The White-Black and White-Hispanic reading gaps were smaller in 2012 than in the first assessment year at all three ages. For example, the White-Black reading gap for 17-year-olds was 53 points in 1971 compared with 26 points in 2012. Similarly the White-Hispanic reading gap for 17-year-olds narrowed from 41 points in 1975 to 21 points in 2012.

In 2012, female 9-, 13-, and 17-year-old students continued to have higher average reading scores than male students at all three ages (table 221.85). The gap between male and female 9-year-olds was 5 points in 2012; this was narrower than the gap in 1971 (13 points). The 8-point gender gap for 13-year-olds in 2012 was not significantly different from the gap in 1971. At age 17, the 8-point gap between males and females in 2012 was not significantly different from the gap in 1971.

Mathematics

The main NAEP mathematics assessment data for 4th- and 8th-graders are reported on a scale of 0 to 500 (table 222.10). The average 4th-grade mathematics score in 2015 (240) was lower than the score in 2013 (242), although it was higher than the score in 1990 (213). At grade 4, the average mathematics score in 2015 for White students (248) was lower than the score in 2013 (250), while the average scores in 2015 for Black (224), Hispanic (230), and Asian/Pacific Islander (257) students were not measurably different from the 2013 scores. However, the 4th-grade average scores for White, Black, Hispanic, and Asian/Pacific Islander students were all higher in 2015 than in 1990. The average 8th-grade mathematics score in 2015 (282) was lower than the score in 2013 (285), although it was higher than the score in 1990 (263). At grade 8, the average scores for White (292), Black (260), and Hispanic students (270) were lower in 2015 than in 2013 (294, 263, and 272, respectively). The 2015 average score for Asian/Pacific Islander students (306) was not measurably different from the score in 2013. However, the average scores for 8th-grade White, Black, Hispanic, and Asian/Pacific Islander students were all higher in 2015 than in 1990. Due to changes in the 12th-grade mathematics assessment framework, a new trend line started in 2005, with scores reported on a scale of 0 to 300. The average 12th-grade mathematics score in 2015 (152) was lower than the score in 2013 (153), but not measurably different from the score in 2005, the first year the revised assessment was administered.

From 1990 through 2015, the average mathematics scores for White students in grades 4 and 8 were higher than those of their Black and Hispanic peers. However, the White-Black achievement gap at grade 4 narrowed from 32 points in 1990 to 24 points in 2015. The gap of 24 points in 2015 also represented a decrease from the 4th-grade White-Black achievement gap in 2013 (26 points), which was due to a decrease in White 4th-graders' scores from 2013 to 2015. The 4th-grade White-Hispanic achievement gap in 2015 (18 points) was not measurably different from the gap in 2013. In 2015, the 8th-grade White-Black achievement gap (32 points) and White-Hispanic achievement gap (22 points) were not measurably different from the corresponding gaps in 2013.

The average mathematics score for 4th-grade public school students across the nation was lower in 2015 (240) than in 2013 (241) (table 222.50). Average 4th-grade mathematics scores for public school students were also lower in 2015 than in 2013 in 16 states. However, the average mathematics scores for 4th-grade students in Mississippi and the District of Columbia were higher in 2015 than in 2013. Scores were not measurably different in the other states during this period. The national public school average mathematics score for 8th-grade students was lower in 2015 (281) than in 2013 (284) (table 222.60). Similarly, 22 states had lower 8th-grade average scores in 2015 than in 2013, while scores for the remaining 28 states and the District of Columbia were not measurably different between 2013 and 2015. During this time, no state experienced a score increase at the 8th-grade level.

NAEP long-term trend mathematics results, reported on a scale of 0 to 500, are available for 12 assessment years, going back to the first in 1973. In 2012, the average mathematics score for 9-year-olds (244) was higher than in all previous assessment years prior to 2008 (table 222.85). The average score for 9-year-olds in 2012 was 5 points higher than in 2004 and 25 points higher than in 1973. The average mathematics score for 13-year-olds in 2012 (285) was higher than in all previous assessment years. For 13-year-olds, the average score in 2012 was 6 points higher than in 2004 and 19 points higher than in 1973. In contrast, the average score for 17-year-olds in 2012 (306) was not significantly different from the scores in 2004 and 1973.

White, Black, and Hispanic 9-, 13-, and 17-year-olds all had higher average mathematics scores in 2012 than in 1973 (table 222.85). In comparison to 2004, average mathematics scores were higher in 2012 for White 9-, 13-, and 17-year-olds, Hispanic 9- and 13-year-olds, and Black 13-year-olds. Mathematics results for 2012 continued to show score gaps between White and Hispanic students (ranging from 17 to 21 points [based on unrounded scores], depending on age) and between White and Black students (ranging from 25 to 28 points). Across all three age groups, both the White-Black and White-Hispanic gaps in mathematics scores were lower in 2012 than in 1973. For example, among 17-year-olds, the White-Black gap was 40 points in 1973 compared to 26 points in 2012, and the White-Hispanic gap was 33 points in 1973 compared to 19 points in 2012.

While there was no significant difference between the average mathematics scores of male and female 9- and 13-year-olds in 2012, male students did score higher than female students at age 17 (table 222.85). At both age 9 and age 13, the gap between males and females in 2012 was not significantly different from the gap in 1973. At age 17, the 4-point gender score gap in 2012 was smaller than the gap in 1973 (8 points).

Science

NAEP has assessed the science abilities of students in grades 4, 8, and 12 in both public and private schools since 1996. As of 2009, however, NAEP science assessments are based on a new framework, so results from these assess-ments cannot be compared to results from earlier science assessments. Scores are based on a scale ranging from 0 to 300. In 2009, White 4th-graders had a higher average science score (163) than did Black (127), Hispanic (131), Asian/Pacific Islander (160), and American Indian/Alaska Native (135) 4th-graders (table 223.10). The average science score was higher for male 4th-graders (151) than for female 4th-graders (149). In 2009, the pattern of differences in average science scores by students' race/ethnicity at grade 8 was similar to the pattern at grade 4. The average science score also was higher for male 8th-graders (152) than for female 8th-graders (148). At grade 12, average scores for White (159) and Asian/Pacific Islander (164) students were higher than the scores for Black (125), Hispanic (134), and American Indian/Alaska Native (144) students. The average science score in 2009 for male 12th-graders (153) was higher than the score for female 12th-graders (147). In 2011, a science assessment was conducted at grade 8 only. The average 8th-grade science score increased from 150 in 2009 to 152 in 2011. While there were no significant changes from 2009 to 2011 in the average scores for Asian/Pacific Islander or American Indian/Alaska Native 8th-graders, average scores increased 1 point for White 8th-graders, 3 points for Black 8th-graders, and 5 points for Hispanic 8th-graders. The average science score of White 8th-graders continued to be higher than the average scores of 8th-graders in all other racial/ethnic groups in 2011, but score gaps between White and Black 8th-graders and between White and Hispanic 8th-graders narrowed from 2009 to 2011. Average scores for both male and female 8th-graders were higher in 2011 than in 2009. In 2011, the average score was 5 points higher for male 8th-graders than for female 8th-graders, which was not significantly different from the 4-point gap in 2009.

Skills of Young Children

In addition to student performance data available through NAEP, the *Digest* presents data from other surveys to provide additional perspectives on student achievement. Differences among demographic groups in the acquisition of cognitive skills have been demonstrated at relatively early ages in the Early Childhood Longitudinal Survey's Birth Cohort (ECLS-B) study as well as its Kindergarten Class (ECLS-K) studies.

In 2003–04, about 64 percent of 2-year-olds demonstrated proficiency in expressive vocabulary, which measured toddlers' ability to communicate using gestures, words, and sentences (table 220.20). The percentage of 2-year-olds demonstrating expressive vocabulary was higher for females (69 percent) than for males (59 percent). Also, a higher percentage of White (71 percent) and Asian (62 percent) 2-year-olds demonstrated expressive vocabulary than of Black, Hispanic, or American Indian/Alaska Native 2-year-olds (56, 54, and 50 percent, respectively). The percentage of 2-year-olds from families with high socioeconomic status (SES) who demonstrated expressive vocabulary (75 percent) was higher than the percentage of children from low-SES families who did so (52 percent).

Patterns of differences were also observed by race/ethnicity and SES for children at about 4 years of age (48 to 57 months old). In 2005–06, average early reading scores were higher for White (27) and Asian (31) 48- to 57-month-old children than for Black (23), Hispanic (21), and American Indian/Alaska Native (20) children (table 220.30). Also, high-SES children (33) had higher average early reading scores than low-SES children (19) at this age. These same patterns were observed among 48- to 57-month-old children with respect to average mathematics scores. White (32) and Asian (35) 48- to 57-month-old children had higher mathematics scores than Black (27), Hispanic (26), and American Indian/Alaska Native children (23). High-SES 48- to 57-month-old children (36) had higher average mathematics scores than low-SES children (24).

Children who enrolled in kindergarten for the first time in 2010–11 showed similar patterns of score differences by race/ethnicity and SES. In fall 2010, average mathematics scores were higher for first-time kindergartners from high-SES families (37) than for those from low-SES families (24) (table 220.40). White (33) and Asian (36) first-time kindergartners had higher mathematics scores than their Black (27), Hispanic (26), and American Indian/Alaska Native (27) counterparts. Similarly, reading scores in fall 2010 were higher for White (39) and Asian (42) first-time kindergartners than for their Black (36), Hispanic (35), and American Indian/Alaska Native (34) counterparts. High-SES children (43) had higher average early reading scores than low-SES children (32). These same patterns were observed among these children during 1st grade in spring 2012. White (67) and Asian (68) 1st-graders had higher mathematics scores than their Black (57), Hispanic (58), and American Indian/Alaska Native (61) counterparts. Average mathematics scores were higher for 1st-graders from high-SES families (70) than for those from low-SES families (55). Average reading scores were also higher for White (72) and Asian (74) 1st-graders than for their Black (67), Hispanic (66), and American Indian/Alaska Native (67) counterparts; and 1st-graders from high-SES families (77) had higher average reading scores than those from low-SES families (62).

SAT Scores of College-Bound Seniors

The SAT (formerly known as the Scholastic Assessment Test and the Scholastic Aptitude Test) is not designed as an indicator of student achievement, but rather as an aid for predicting how well students will do in college. Possible scores on each section of the SAT range from 200 to 800. Between 1998–99 and 2004–05, the mathematics SAT average score increased by 9 points, but it decreased by 9 points between 2004–05 (520) and 2014–15 (511) (table 226.20). The critical reading average score decreased by 13 points between 2004–05 (508) and 2014–15 (495). Between 2005–06 (the year in which the SAT writing section was introduced) and 2014–15, the writing average score decreased by 13 points (from 497 to 484).

Coursetaking in High School

The average number of science and mathematics courses completed by public high school graduates increased between 1982 and 2009. The average number of mathematics courses (Carnegie units) completed in high school rose from 2.6 in 1982 to 3.9 in 2009, and the number of science courses rose from 2.2 to 3.5 (table 225.10). The average number of courses in career/technical areas completed by public high school graduates was lower in 2009 (2.5 units) than in 2000 (2.9 units). As a result of the increased academic course load, the percentage of public and private high school graduates completing the 1983 National Commission on Excellence recommendations (4 units of English, 3 units of social studies, 3 units of science, 3 units of mathematics, and 2 units of foreign language) rose from 10 percent in 1982 to 62 percent in 2009 (table 225.50).

School Violence

In 2013–14, some 65 percent of public schools reported one or more violent incidents, such as a serious violent incident, a physical attack, or a threat of a physical attack (table 229.10). This 2013–14 percentage was lower than the 71 percent of schools reporting violent incidents in 1999–2000. Serious violent victimization is a subcategory of violent victimization that includes the crimes of rape, sexual assault, robbery, and aggravated assault. The percentage of public schools reporting a serious violent crime in 2013–14 (13 percent) was lower than the percentage reporting a serious violent crime in 1999–2000 (20 percent). In addition, the percentage of public schools reporting an incident of a physical attack or a fight without a weapon in 2013–14 (58 percent) was lower than in 1999–2000 (64 percent). Also, the percentage of schools reporting an incident of a threat of a physical attack in 2013–14 (47 percent) was lower than in 1999–2000 (52 percent). Overall, public schools reported 15 violent incidents per 1,000 students in 2013–14, which was lower than the 31 violent incidents per 1,000 students reported in 1999–2000 (table 229.20).

On the National Crime Victimization Survey, students ages 12 to 18 reported a decrease in victimizations at school between 1992 and 2014 (table 228.20). The total victimization rates for students ages 12 to 18 declined 82 percent, from 181 victimizations per 1,000 students in 1992 to 33 victimizations per 1,000 students in 2014. This pattern of decline in total victimization rates between 1992 and 2014 also held for thefts, violent victimizations, and serious violent victimizations. Thefts at school declined from a rate of 114 per 1,000 students to 14 per 1,000. The rate of violent victimization at school declined overall from 68 victimizations per 1,000 students in 1992 to 19 per 1,000 in 2014. Serious violent victimizations at school declined from 8 per 1,000 students in 1992 to 4 per 1,000 in 2014.

Revenues and Expenditures

The state share of revenues for public elementary and secondary schools generally grew from the 1930s through the mid-1980s, while the local share declined during the same time period (table 235.10 and figure 10).[5] However, this pattern changed in the late 1980s, when the local share began to increase at the same time that the state share decreased. Between 1986–87 and 1993–94, the state share declined from 49.7 percent to 45.2 percent, while the local share rose from 43.9 percent to 47.8 percent. Between 1993–94 and 2000–01, the state share rose again to 49.7 percent, the highest share since 1986–87, but declined every school year thereafter until 2005–06, when the state share was 46.5 percent. In more recent years, the federal share in 2012–13 (9.3 percent) was lower than in 2009–10 (12.7 percent), but higher than in

2002–03 (8.5 percent). Between 2002–03 and 2012–13, the state share decreased from 48.7 to 45.2 percent. The local share in 2012–13 (45.5 percent) was higher than in 2002–03 (42.8 percent).

After adjustment for inflation, current expenditures per student in fall enrollment at public schools rose during the 1980s, but remained stable during the first part of the 1990s (table 236.55 and figure 11). There was an increase of 37 percent from 1980–81 to 1990–91, followed by minor fluctuations from 1990–91 to 1994–95. Current expenditures per student increased 34 percent from 1994–95 to 2008–09, but declined 5 percent from 2008–09 and 2012–13. In 2012–13, current expenditures per student in fall enrollment were $10,763 in unadjusted dollars. The expenditure for public school student transportation was $914 per student transported in 2012–13 (also in unadjusted dollars), and 55 percent of students were transported at public expense in 2007–08 (table 236.90).

---

[5] For data on individual years from 1980–81 through 1988–89, see *Digest of Education Statistics 2011* (NCES 2012-001), table 180.

Figure 7. Enrollment, number of teachers, pupil/teacher ratio, and expenditures in public elementary and secondary schools: 1960–61 through 2013–14

Fall enrollment, in millions

Teachers, in millions   Pupil/teacher ratio

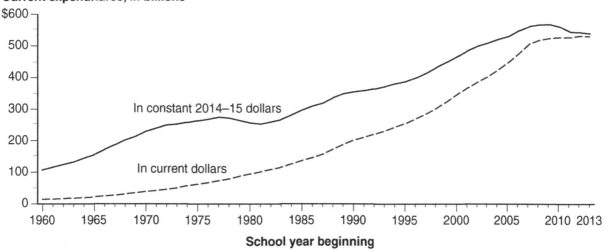

Current expenditures, in billions

NOTE: Expenditure data for school year 2013 (2013–14) are projected.
SOURCE: U.S. Department of Education, National Center for Education Statistics, *Statistics of State School Systems*, 1959–60 through 1969–70; *Statistics of Public Elementary and Secondary Day Schools*, 1959–60 through 1980–81; *Revenues and Expenditures for Public Elementary and Secondary Education*, 1970–71 through 1980–81; Common Core of Data (CCD), "State Nonfiscal Survey of Public Elementary/Secondary Education," 1981–82 through 2013–14, and "National Public Education Financial Survey," 1989–90 through 2012–13; and Public Elementary and Secondary Education Current Expenditure Projection Model, 1973–74 through 2025–26.

Figure 8. Percentage change in public elementary and secondary enrollment, by state: Fall 2008 to fall 2013

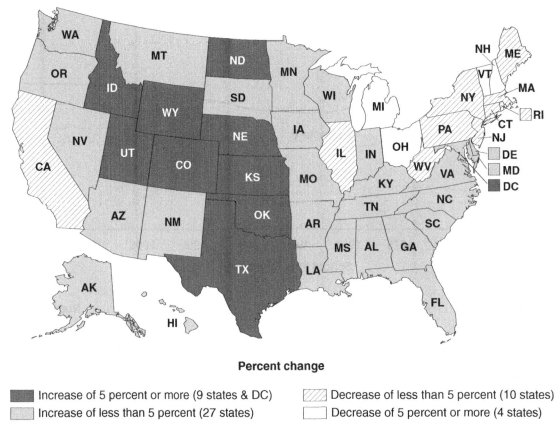

Percent change

▇ Increase of 5 percent or more (9 states & DC)	▨ Decrease of less than 5 percent (10 states)
░ Increase of less than 5 percent (27 states)	☐ Decrease of 5 percent or more (4 states)

SOURCE: U.S. Department of Education, National Center for Education Statistics, Common Core of Data (CCD), "State Nonfiscal Survey of Public Elementary/Secondary Education," 2008–09 and 2013–14.

Figure 9. Total and full-day preprimary enrollment of 3- to 5-year-olds: October 1970 through October 2014

Enrollment, in millions

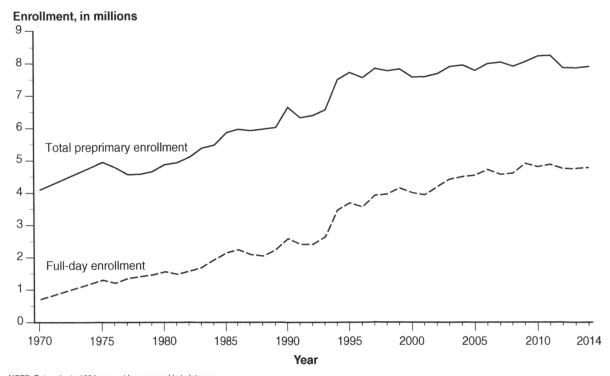

Year

NOTE: Data prior to 1994 may not be comparable to later years.
SOURCE: U.S. Department of Education, National Center for Education Statistics, *Preprimary Enrollment*, 1970 and 1975. U.S. Department of Commerce, Census Bureau, Current Population Survey (CPS), October 1976 through October 2014.

Figure 10. Percentage of revenue for public elementary and secondary schools, by source of funds: 1970–71 through 2012–13

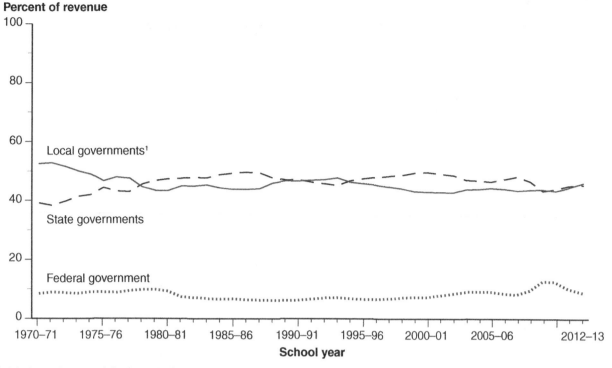

Percent of revenue

¹Includes intermediate sources below the state level.
SOURCE: U.S. Department of Education, National Center for Education Statistics, *Revenues and Expenditures for Public Elementary and Secondary Education,* 1970–71 through 1986–87; and Common Core of Data (CCD), "National Public Education Financial Survey," 1987–88 through 2012–13.

Figure 11. Current expenditure per pupil in fall enrollment in public elementary and secondary schools: 1970–71 through 2012–13

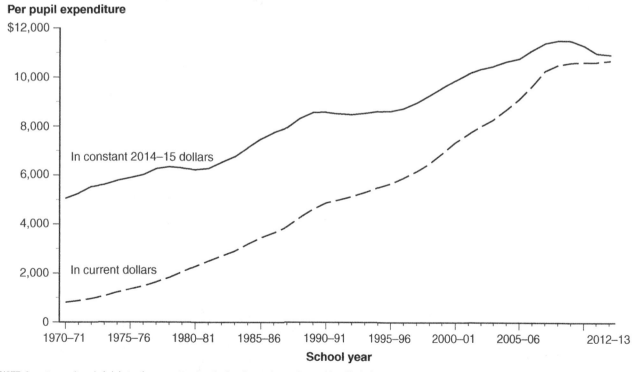

Per pupil expenditure

NOTE: Current expenditures include instruction, support services, food services, and enterprise operations. Beginning in 1988–89, extensive changes were made in the data collection procedures.
SOURCE: U.S. Department of Education, National Center for Education Statistics, *Revenues and Expenditures for Public Elementary and Secondary Education,* 1970–71 through 1986–87; and Common Core of Data (CCD), "National Public Education Financial Survey," 1987–88 through 2012–13.

Table 201.10.   Historical summary of public elementary and secondary school statistics: Selected years, 1869–70 through 2012–13

Selected characteristic	1869–70	1879–80	1889–90	1899–1900	1909–10	1919–20	1929–30	1939–40	1949–50	1959–60	1969–70	1979–80	1989–90	1999–2000	2008–09	2009–10	2010–11	2011–12	2012–13
1	2	3	4	5	6	7	8	9	10	11	12	13	14	15	16	17	18	19	20
Population, pupils, and instructional staff																			
Total population (in thousands)[1]	38,558	50,156	62,622	75,995	90,490	104,514	121,878	131,028	149,188	177,830	201,385	225,055	246,819	279,040	304,094	306,772	309,347	311,722	314,112
5- to 17-year-olds (in thousands)[1]	11,683	15,066	18,473	21,573	24,011	27,571	31,414	30,151	30,223	43,881	52,386	48,043	44,947	52,811	53,833	53,890	53,933	53,791	53,732
5- to 17-year-olds as a percent of total population	30.3	30.0	29.5	28.4	26.5	26.4	25.8	23.0	20.3	24.7	26.0	21.3	18.2	18.9	17.7	17.6	17.4	17.3	17.1
Total enrollment in elementary and secondary schools (in thousands)[2]	7,562[3]	9,867	12,723	15,503	17,814	21,578	25,678	25,434	25,112	36,087	45,550	41,651	40,543	46,857	49,266	49,361	49,484	49,522	49,771
Prekindergarten through grade 8 (in thousands)	7,481[3]	9,757	12,520	14,984	16,899	19,378	21,279	18,833	19,387	27,602	32,513	28,034	29,152	33,486	34,286	34,409	34,625	34,773	35,018
Grades 9–12 (in thousands)	80[3]	110	203	519	915	2,200	4,399	6,601	5,725	8,485	13,037	13,616	11,390	13,371	14,990	14,952	14,860	14,749	14,753
Enrollment as a percent of total population	19.6[3]	19.7	20.3	20.4	19.7	20.6	21.1	19.4	16.8	20.3	22.6	18.5	16.4	16.8	16.2	16.1	16.0	15.9	15.8
Enrollment as a percent of 5- to 17-year-olds	64.7[3]	65.5	68.9	71.9	74.2	78.3	81.7	84.4	83.1	82.2	87.0	86.7	90.2	88.7	91.5	91.6	91.8	92.1	92.6
Percent of total enrollment in grades 9–12	1.1[3]	1.1	1.6	3.3	5.1	10.2	17.1	26.0	22.8	23.5	28.6	32.7	28.1	28.5	30.4	30.3	30.0	29.8	29.6
High school graduates (in thousands)	—	—	22	62	111	231	592	1,143	1,063	1,627	2,589	2,748	2,320	2,554	3,039	3,128	3,144	3,149	3,169
Average daily attendance (in thousands)	4,077	6,144	8,154	10,633	12,827	16,150	21,265	22,042	22,284	32,477	41,934	38,289	37,799	43,807	46,173	45,919	46,119	43,400	46,568
Total number of days attended by pupils enrolled (in millions)	539	801	1,098	1,535	2,011	2,615	3,673	3,858	3,964	5,782	7,501	6,835[4]	—	7,858	8,264	8,199	8,235	3,298	8,357
Percent of enrolled pupils attending daily	59.3	62.3	64.1	66.6	72.1	74.8	82.8	86.7	88.7	90.0	90.4	90.1[4]	—	94.3	—	—	—	93.9	—
Average length of school term, in days	132.2	130.3	134.7	144.3	157.5	161.9	172.7	175.0	177.9	178.0	178.9	178.5[4]	—	179.4	179.0	178.6	178.6	178.8	179.5
Average number of days attended per pupil	78.4	81.1	86.3	99.0	113.0	121.2	143.0	151.7	157.9	160.2	161.7	160.8[4]	—	169.2	—	—	—	167.9	—
Total full-time-equivalent (FTE) instructional staff (in thousands)	—	—	—	—	—	678	880	912	963	1,457	2,286	2,406	2,986	3,819	4,278	4,279	4,151	4,134	4,158
Supervisors (in thousands)	—	—	—	—	—	7	7	5	—	—	—	—	—	—	—	—	—	—	—
Principals (in thousands)	—	—	—	—	—	14	31	32	43	64	91	106	126	137	160	168	165	166	169
Teachers, teacher aides, librarians, and guidance counselors (in thousands)[5]	201	287	364	423	523	657	843	875	920	1,393	2,195	2,300	2,860	3,682	4,118	4,111	3,986	3,967	3,989
Males (in thousands)	78	123	126	127	110	93	140	195	196	404[4]	711[4]	782[4]	—	—	—	—	—	—	—
Females (in thousands)	123	164	238	296	413	585	703	681	724	989[4]	1,484[4]	1,518[4]	—	—	—	—	—	—	—
Percent male	38.7	42.8	34.5	29.9	21.1	14.1	16.6	22.2	21.3	29.0[4]	32.4[4]	34.0[4]	—	—	—	—	—	—	—
Total revenues and expenditures											Amounts in current dollars								
Total revenue receipts (in millions)[6]	—	—	$143	$220	$433	$970	$2,089	$2,261	$5,437	$14,747	$40,267	$96,881	$208,548	$372,944	$592,422	$596,391	$604,229	$597,985	$603,687
Federal government	—	—	—	—	—	2	7	40	156	652	3,220	9,504	12,701	27,098	56,670	75,998	75,549	60,921	55,863
State governments	—	—	—	—	—	160	354	684	2,166	5,768	16,063	45,349	98,239	184,613	276,526	258,864	266,786	269,043	273,102
Local sources, including intermediate	—	—	—	—	—	808	1,728	1,536	3,116	8,327	20,985	42,029	97,608	161,233	259,226	261,529	261,893	267,921	274,723
Percentage distribution of revenue receipts																			
Federal government	—	—	—	—	—	0.3	0.4	1.8	2.9	4.4	8.0	9.8	6.1	7.3	9.6	12.7	12.5	10.2	9.3
State governments	—	—	—	—	—	16.5	16.9	30.3	39.8	39.1	39.9	46.8	47.1	49.5	46.7	43.4	44.2	45.0	45.2
Local sources, including intermediate	—	—	—	—	—	83.2	82.7	68.0	57.3	56.5	52.1	43.4	46.8	43.2	43.8	43.9	43.3	44.8	45.5
Total expenditures for public schools (in millions)[6]	$63	$78	$141	$215	$426	$1,036	$2,317	$2,344	$5,838	$15,613	$40,683	$95,962	$212,770	$381,838	$610,326	$607,018	$604,356	$607,994	$606,490
Current expenditures[6]	—	—	114	180	356	861	1,844	1,942	4,687	12,329[7]	34,218[7]	86,984[7]	188,229[7]	323,889[7]	518,923[7]	524,715[7]	527,291[7]	527,207[7]	535,665[7]
Capital outlay[8]	—	—	26	35	70	154	371	258	1,014	2,662	4,659	6,506	17,781	43,357	65,890	56,715	50,969	48,793	45,474
Interest on school debt	—	—	—	—	—	18	93	131	101	490	1,171	1,874	3,776	9,135	17,049	17,232	17,934	17,804	17,247
Other current expenditures[9]	—	—	—	—	—	3	10	13	36	133	636	598[10]	2,983	5,457	8,464	8,356	8,161	8,189	8,103
Percentage distribution of total expenditures																			
Current expenditures[6]	—	—	81.3	83.5	83.6	83.1	79.6	82.8	80.3	79.0[7]	84.1[7]	90.6[7]	88.5[7]	84.8[7]	85.0[7]	86.4[7]	87.2[7]	87.6[7]	88.3[7]
Capital outlay[8]	—	—	18.7	16.5	16.4	14.8	16.0	11.0	17.4	17.0	11.5	6.8	8.4	11.4	10.8	9.3	8.4	8.1	7.5
Interest on school debt	—	—	—	—	—	1.8	4.0	5.6	1.7	3.1	2.9	2.0	1.8	2.4	2.8	2.8	3.0	3.0	2.8
Other current expenditures[9]	—	—	—	—	—	0.3	0.4	0.6	0.6	0.8	1.6	0.6[10]	1.4	1.4	1.4	1.4	1.4	1.4	1.3

See notes at end of table.

Table 201.10. Historical summary of public elementary and secondary school statistics: Selected years, 1869–70 through 2012–13—Continued

Selected characteristic	1869–70	1879–80	1889–90	1899–1900	1909–10	1919–20	1929–30	1939–40	1949–50	1959–60	1969–70	1979–80	1989–90	1999–2000	2008–09	2009–10	2010–11	2011–12	2012–13
1	2	3	4	5	6	7	8	9	10	11	12	13	14	15	16	17	18	19	20
Teacher salaries; income and expenditures per pupil and per capita																			
Annual salary of classroom teachers[11]	$189	$195	$252	$325	$485	$971	$1,420	$1,441	$3,010	$4,995	$8,626	$15,970	$31,367	$41,807	$54,319	$55,202	$55,623	$55,418	$56,103
Personal income per member of labor force[1]	—	—	—	—	—	—	1,734	1,333	3,446	5,887	9,913	19,800	37,297	57,319	81,032	78,465	81,079	86,283	89,789
Total school expenditures per capita of total population[1]	2	2	2	3	5	10	19	18	39	88	202	426	862	1,368	2,007	1,979	1,954	1,931	1,931
National income per capita[1]	—	—	—	—	—	—	773	630	1,609	2,584	4,467	9,990	19,375	29,832	40,868	39,528	41,182	42,834	44,767
Current expenditure per pupil in ADA[6,12,13]	16	13	14	17	28	53	87	88	210	375	816	2,272	4,990	7,394	11,239	11,427	11,433	11,362	11,503
Total expenditure per pupil in ADA[13,14]	—	13	17	20	33	64	108	106	260	471	955	2,491	5,547	8,589	13,033	13,035	12,926	12,796	12,846
National income per pupil in ADA[13]	—	—	—	—	—	—	4,430	3,743	10,770	14,152	21,450	58,717	126,516	190,026	269,155	264,075	276,233	287,762	301,966
Current expenditure per day per pupil in ADA[6,13,15]	0.12	0.10	0.10	0.12	0.18	0.33	0.50	0.50	1.17	2.11	4.56	12.73	—	41.22	62.79	64.00	64.03	63.53	64.10
Total expenditure per day per pupil in ADA[13]	—	—	0.13	0.14	0.21	0.40	0.63	0.60	1.46	2.65	5.34	13.95	—	47.90	72.83	73.02	72.39	71.56	71.60
Amounts in constant 2014–15 dollars[16]																			
Annual salary of classroom teachers[11]	—	—	—	—	—	$10,817	$19,634	$24,404	$30,081	$40,234	$54,046	$48,687	$58,467	$58,448	$59,891	$60,281	$59,545	$57,637	$57,394
Personal income per member of labor force[1]	—	—	—	—	—	—	23,982	22,569	34,439	47,503	62,108	60,362	69,520	80,134	89,344	85,685	86,796	89,738	91,856
Total school expenditures per capita of total population[1]	—	—	—	—	—	123	263	303	391	707	1,266	1,300	1,607	1,913	2,213	2,161	2,091	2,009	1,975
National income per capita[1]	—	—	—	—	—	—	10,687	10,663	16,077	20,818	27,985	30,455	36,115	41,707	45,060	43,165	44,086	44,549	45,798
Current expenditure per pupil in ADA[6,12,13]	—	—	—	—	—	662	1,199	1,492	2,102	3,022	5,112	6,926	9,282	10,337	12,391	12,478	12,240	11,817	11,768
Total expenditure per pupil in ADA[13,14]	—	—	—	—	—	794	1,500	1,791	2,602	3,794	5,983	7,593	10,339	12,008	14,370	14,235	13,837	13,308	13,142
National income per pupil in ADA[13]	—	—	—	—	—	—	61,251	63,388	107,631	113,999	134,396	179,008	235,821	265,663	296,764	288,372	295,711	299,285	308,916
Current expenditure per day per pupil in ADA[6,13,15]	—	—	—	—	—	4.1	6.9	8.5	11.7	17.0	28.6	38.8	—	53.6	69.2	69.9	68.5	66.1	65.6
Total expenditure per day per pupil in ADA[13]	—	—	—	—	—	5.0	8.7	10.2	14.6	21.3	33.5	42.5	—	62.2	80.3	79.7	77.5	74.4	73.3

—Not available.

[1]Data on population and labor force are from the Census Bureau, and data on personal income and national income are from the Bureau of Economic Analysis, U.S. Department of Commerce. Population data through 1900 are based on total population from the decennial census. From 1909–10 to 1959–60, population data are total population, including armed forces overseas, as of July 1. Data for later years are for resident population that excludes armed forces overseas.
[2]Data for 1869–70 through 1959–60 are school year enrollment. Data for later years are fall enrollment. Total counts of ungraded students were prorated to prekindergarten through grade 8 and grades 9 through 12 based on prior reports.
[3]Data for 1870–71.
[4]Estimated by the National Center for Education Statistics.
[5]Prior to 1919–20, data are for the number of different persons employed rather than number of positions.
[6]Prior to 1919–20, includes interest on school debt.
[7]Because of the modification of the scope of "current expenditures for elementary and secondary schools," data for 1959–60 and later years are not entirely comparable with prior years.
[8]Beginning in 1969–70, includes capital outlay by state and local school building authorities.
[9]Includes summer schools, community colleges, and adult education. Beginning in 1959–60, also includes community services, formerly classified with "current expenditures for elementary and secondary schools."
[10]Excludes community colleges and adult education.
[11]Prior to 1959–60, average includes supervisors, principals, teachers, and other nonsupervisory instructional staff. Data for 1959–60 and later years are estimated by the National Education Association.

[12]Excludes current expenditures not allocable to pupil costs.
[13]"ADA" means average daily attendance in elementary and secondary schools.
[14]Expenditure figure is the sum of current expenditures allocable to pupil costs, capital outlay, and interest on school debt.
[15]Per-day rates derived by dividing annual rates by average length of term.
[16]Constant dollars based on the Consumer Price Index, prepared by the Bureau of Labor Statistics, U.S. Department of Labor, adjusted to a school-year basis.
NOTE: Some data have been revised from previously published figures. Beginning in 1959–60, data include Alaska and Hawaii. Detail may not sum to totals because of rounding.
SOURCE: U.S. Department of Education, National Center for Education Statistics, *Annual Report of the United States Commissioner of Education, 1869–70 through 1909–10; Biennial Survey of Education in the United States, 1919–20 through 1949–50; Statistics of State School Systems, 1959–60 and 1969–70; Statistics of Public Elementary and Secondary School Systems, 1979–80; Revenues and Expenditures for Public Elementary and Secondary Education, FY 1980;* Schools and Staffing Survey (SASS), "Public School Questionnaire," 1999–2000, 2007–08, and 2011–12; Common Core of Data (CCD), "State Nonfiscal Survey of Public Elementary/Secondary Education," 1989–90 through 2013–14, and "National Public Education Financial Survey," 1989–90 through 2012–13. U.S. Department of Commerce, Census Bureau, retrieved September 15, 2015, from http://www.census.gov/popest/data/national/asrh/2014/index.html. U.S. Department of Commerce, Bureau of Economic Analysis, retrieved January 29, 2016, from http://www.bea.gov/itable/. U.S. Department of Labor, Bureau of Labor Statistics, retrieved January 29, 2016, from http://stats.bls.gov/cpi/tables.htm#empstat. (This table was prepared January 2016.)

Table 201.20. Enrollment in grades 9 through 12 in public and private schools compared with population 14 to 17 years of age: Selected years, 1889–90 through fall 2015

[In thousands]

		Enrollment, grades 9 to 12[1]												Population 14 to 17 years of age[2]	Enrollment as a ratio of population 14 to 17 years of age[3]
		Public schools						Private schools							
Year	All schools	Total	9th grade	10th grade	11th grade	12th grade	Secondary ungraded	Total	9th grade	10th grade	11th grade	12th grade	Secondary ungraded		
1	2	3	4	5	6	7	8	9	10	11	12	13	14	15	16
1889–90............	298	203	—	—	—	—	—	95	—	—	—	—	—	5,355	5.6
1899–1900..........	630	519	—	—	—	—	—	111	—	—	—	—	—	6,152	10.2
1909–10.............	1,032	915	—	—	—	—	—	117	—	—	—	—	—	7,220	14.3
1919–20.............	2,414	2,200	917	576	396	312	0	214	—	—	—	—	—	7,736	31.2
1929–30.............	4,741	4,399	1,627	1,192	880	701	0	341 [4]	—	—	—	—	—	9,341	50.7
1939–40.............	7,059	6,601	2,011	1,767	1,486	1,282	55	458 [5]	—	—	—	—	—	9,720	72.6
1949–50.............	6,397	5,725	1,761	1,513	1,275	1,134	42	672	—	—	—	—	—	8,405	76.1
Fall 1959............	9,306	8,271	—	—	—	—	—	1,035	—	—	—	—	—	11,155	83.4
Fall 1963............	12,170	10,883	—	—	—	—	—	1,287	—	—	—	—	—	13,492	90.2
Fall 1965	13,002	11,602	3,215	2,993	2,741	2,477	176	1,400 [6]	—	—	—	—	—	14,146	91.9
Fall 1966	13,280	11,880	3,318	3,111	2,756	2,508	187	1,400 [6]	—	—	—	—	—	14,398	92.2
Fall 1967	13,647	12,247	3,395	3,221	2,879	2,525	226	1,400 [6]	—	—	—	—	—	14,727	92.7
Fall 1968	14,123	12,723	3,508	3,310	2,986	2,650	268	1,400 [6]	—	—	—	—	—	15,170	93.1
Fall 1969	14,337	13,037	3,568	3,405	3,047	2,732	285	1,300 [6]	—	—	—	—	—	15,549	92.2
Fall 1970	14,647	13,336	3,654	3,458	3,128	2,775	321	1,311	—	—	—	—	—	15,924	92.0
Fall 1971	15,053	13,753	3,781	3,571	3,200	2,864	337	1,300 [6]	—	—	—	—	—	16,328	92.2
Fall 1972	15,148	13,848	3,779	3,648	3,248	2,873	299	1,300 [6]	—	—	—	—	—	16,639	91.0
Fall 1973	15,344	14,044	3,801	3,650	3,323	2,918	352	1,300 [6]	—	—	—	—	—	16,867	91.0
Fall 1974	15,403	14,103	3,832	3,675	3,302	2,955	339	1,300 [6]	—	—	—	—	—	17,035	90.4
Fall 1975	15,604	14,304	3,879	3,723	3,354	2,986	362	1,300 [6]	—	—	—	—	—	17,128	91.1
Fall 1976	15,656	14,314	3,825	3,738	3,373	3,015	363	1,342	—	—	—	—	—	17,119	91.5
Fall 1977	15,546	14,203	3,779	3,686	3,388	3,026	324	1,343	—	—	—	—	—	17,045	91.2
Fall 1978	15,441	14,088	3,726	3,610	3,312	3,023	416	1,353	—	—	—	—	—	16,946	91.1
Fall 1979	14,916	13,616	3,526	3,532	3,241	2,969	348	1,300 [6]	—	—	—	—	—	16,611	89.8
Fall 1980	14,570	13,231	3,377	3,368	3,195	2,925	366	1,339	—	—	—	—	—	16,143	90.3
Fall 1981	14,164	12,764	3,286	3,218	3,039	2,907	314	1,400 [6]	—	—	—	—	—	15,609	90.7
Fall 1982	13,805	12,405	3,248	3,137	2,917	2,787	315	1,400 [6]	—	—	—	—	—	15,057	91.7
Fall 1983	13,671	12,271	3,330	3,103	2,861	2,678	299	1,400	—	—	—	—	—	14,740	92.7
Fall 1984	13,704	12,304	3,440	3,145	2,819	2,599	300	1,400 [6]	—	—	—	—	—	14,725	93.1
Fall 1985	13,750	12,388	3,439	3,230	2,866	2,550	303	1,362	—	—	—	—	—	14,888	92.4
Fall 1986	13,669	12,333	3,256	3,215	2,954	2,601	308	1,336 [6]	—	—	—	—	—	14,824	92.2
Fall 1987	13,323	12,076	3,143	3,020	2,936	2,681	296	1,247	—	—	—	—	—	14,502	91.9
Fall 1988	12,893	11,687	3,106	2,895	2,749	2,650	288	1,206 [6]	—	—	—	—	—	14,023	91.9
Fall 1989	12,524	11,393	3,141	2,868	2,629	2,473	281	1,131	303	284	267	273	5	13,536	92.5
Fall 1990	12,476	11,341	3,169	2,896	2,612	2,381	284	1,136 [6]	—	—	—	—	—	13,329	93.6
Fall 1991	12,675	11,544	3,313	2,915	2,645	2,392	278	1,131	309	286	272	260	4	13,491	94.0
Fall 1992	12,862	11,737	3,352	3,027	2,656	2,431	272	1,125 [6]	—	—	—	—	—	13,775	93.4
Fall 1993	13,081	11,963	3,487	3,050	2,751	2,424	250	1,118	312	286	266	249	5	14,096	92.8
Fall 1994	13,354	12,215	3,604	3,131	2,748	2,488	244	1,138 [6]	—	—	—	—	—	14,637	91.2
Fall 1995	13,665	12,502	3,704	3,237	2,826	2,487	247	1,163	325	304	276	255	2	15,013	91.0
Fall 1996	14,027	12,849	3,801	3,323	2,930	2,586	208	1,178 [6]	—	—	—	—	—	15,443	90.8
Fall 1997	14,241	13,056	3,819	3,376	2,972	2,673	216	1,185	326	306	283	266	4	15,769	90.3
Fall 1998	14,407	13,195	3,856	3,382	3,021	2,722	214	1,212 [6]	—	—	—	—	—	15,829	91.0
Fall 1999	14,600	13,371	3,935	3,415	3,034	2,782	205	1,229	336	313	295	280	5	16,007	91.2
Fall 2000	14,781	13,517	3,963	3,491	3,083	2,803	177	1,264 [6]	—	—	—	—	—	16,144	91.6
Fall 2001	15,032	13,736	4,012	3,528	3,174	2,863	159	1,296	350	333	316	293	3	16,280	92.3
Fall 2002	15,374	14,069	4,105	3,584	3,229	2,990	161	1,306 [6]	—	—	—	—	—	16,506	93.1
Fall 2003	15,651	14,339	4,190	3,675	3,277	3,046	150	1,311	351	334	317	304	5	16,694	93.8
Fall 2004	15,949	14,618	4,281	3,750	3,369	3,094	122	1,331 [6]	—	—	—	—	—	17,054	93.5
Fall 2005	16,258	14,909	4,287	3,866	3,454	3,180	121	1,349	356	348	326	315	3	17,358	93.7
Fall 2006	16,441	15,081	4,260	3,882	3,551	3,277	110	1,360 [6]	—	—	—	—	—	17,549	93.7
Fall 2007	16,451	15,086	4,200	3,863	3,557	3,375	92	1,364 [6]	357	347	334	324	2	17,597	93.5
Fall 2008	16,322	14,980	4,123	3,822	3,548	3,400	87	1,342 [6]	—	—	—	—	—	17,395	93.8
Fall 2009	16,261	14,952	4,080	3,809	3,541	3,432	90	1,309	333	330	324	319	3	17,232	94.4
Fall 2010	16,159	14,860	4,008	3,800	3,538	3,472	42	1,299 [6]	—	—	—	—	—	17,066	94.7
Fall 2011	16,040	14,749	3,957	3,751	3,546	3,452	43	1,291	330	325	318	315	4	16,873	95.1
Fall 2012	16,055	14,753	3,975	3,730	3,528	3,477	43	1,302 [6]	—	—	—	—	—	16,723	96.0
Fall 2013	16,106	14,794	3,980	3,761	3,526	3,476	52	1,312	334	331	325	320	3	16,659	96.7
Fall 2014[7]...........	16,199	14,883	4,038	3,765	3,555	3,474	52	1,316	—	—	—	—	—	16,748	96.7
Fall 2015[7]..........	16,281	14,970	4,038	3,820	3,558	3,502	52	1,311	—	—	—	—	—	—	—

—Not available.
[1]Includes a relatively small number of secondary ungraded students.
[2]Data for 1890 through 1950 are from the decennial censuses of population. Later data are Census Bureau estimates as of July 1 preceding the opening of the school year.
[3]Gross enrollment ratio based on school enrollment of all ages in grades 9 to 12 divided by the 14- to 17-year-old population. Differs from enrollment rates in other tables, which are based on the enrollment of persons in the given age group only.
[4]Data are for 1927–28.
[5]Data are for 1940–41.
[6]Estimated.
[7]Projected.
NOTE: Includes enrollment in public schools that are a part of state and local school systems and also in most private schools, both religiously affiliated and nonsectarian. The enrollment for ungraded public school students was estimated based on the secondary proportion of ungraded students in prior years. The enrollment of ungraded private school students was estimated based on the secondary proportion of ungraded students in individual high schools. Some data have been revised from previously published figures. Detail may not sum to totals because of rounding.
SOURCE: U.S. Department of Education, National Center for Education Statistics, *Annual Report of the Commissioner of Education,* 1890 through 1910; *Biennial Survey of Education in the United States,* 1919–20 through 1949–50; *Statistics of State School Systems,* 1951–52 through 1957–58; *Statistics of Public Elementary and Secondary School Systems,* 1959 through 1980; *Statistics of Nonpublic Elementary and Secondary Schools,* 1959 through 1980; Common Core of Data (CCD), "State Nonfiscal Survey of Public Elementary/Secondary Education," 1981–82 through 2013–14; Schools and Staffing Survey, Private School Data File, 1987–88; Private School Universe Survey (PSS), 1989–90 through 2013–14; National Elementary and Secondary Enrollment Projection Model, 1972 through 2025; and unpublished data. U.S. Department of Commerce, Census Bureau, Current Population Reports, Series P-25, Nos. 1000, 1022, 1045, 1057, 1059, 1092, and 1095; 2000 through 2009 Population Estimates, retrieved August 14, 2012, from http://www.census.gov/popest/data/national/asrh/2011/index.html; and 2010 through 2014 Population Estimates, retrieved September 15, 2015, from http://www.census.gov/popest/data/national/asrh/2014/index.html. (This table was prepared January 2016.)

Table 202.10. Enrollment of 3-, 4-, and 5-year-old children in preprimary programs, by age of child, level of program, control of program, and attendance status: Selected years, 1970 through 2014

[Standard errors appear in parentheses]

Age of child, level and control of program, and attendance status	1970	1980	1990	1995[1]	2000[1]	2003[1]	2005[1]	2010[1,2]	2012[1,2]	2013[1,2]	2014[1,2]
1	2	3	4	5	6	7	8	9	10	11	12
3 to 5 years old[3]											
Total population (in thousands)	10,949 (131.4)	9,284 (121.0)	11,207 (145.5)	12,518 (153.7)	11,858 (155.3)	12,204 (149.6)	12,134 (149.1)	12,949 (80.4)	12,259 (114.8)	12,166 (151.1)	12,191 (79.1)
Enrollment of 3- to 5-year-olds (in thousands)											
Total	4,104 (78.9)	4,878 (75.0)	6,659 (88.8)	7,739 (86.4)	7,592 (86.2)	7,921 (82.6)	7,801 (82.7)	8,246 (107.3)	7,883 (101.5)	7,878 (129.1)	7,890 (99.9)
Level and attendance status											
Preschool	1,094 (48.9)	1,981 (61.5)	3,379 (83.0)	4,331 (84.6)	4,326 (86.5)	4,859 (84.7)	4,529 (83.4)	4,797 (94.5)	4,602 (98.5)	4,625 (115.4)	4,658 (94.0)
Full-day	291 (26.2)	681 (39.1)	1,150 (54.9)	1,951 (64.5)	2,049 (67.9)	2,479 (69.6)	2,275 (67.3)	2,297 (81.4)	2,242 (78.3)	2,280 (76.8)	2,288 (76.9)
Part-day	803 (42.5)	1,301 (52.1)	2,229 (72.2)	2,381 (69.8)	2,277 (70.8)	2,380 (68.5)	2,255 (67.1)	2,500 (75.4)	2,359 (75.9)	2,345 (87.6)	2,370 (77.1)
Kindergarten	3,010 (72.8)	2,897 (69.6)	3,280 (82.3)	3,408 (79.2)	3,266 (80.3)	3,062 (75.0)	3,272 (76.6)	3,449 (75.9)	3,281 (74.9)	3,254 (72.0)	3,233 (75.0)
Full-day	407 (30.9)	870 (43.8)	1,428 (60.3)	1,738 (61.5)	1,959 (66.7)	1,950 (63.4)	2,274 (67.3)	2,516 (69.7)	2,517 (73.0)	2,473 (70.7)	2,576 (72.2)
Part-day	2,603 (69.4)	2,026 (62.0)	1,853 (67.2)	1,670 (60.5)	1,307 (56.3)	1,112 (49.8)	998 (47.4)	932 (53.4)	764 (43.8)	780 (47.0)	657 (42.9)
Control											
Public	2,830 (71.4)	3,066 (70.6)	3,971 (86.5)	4,750 (86.3)	4,847 (88.3)	5,051 (85.2)	5,213 (85.4)	5,829 (105.5)	5,638 (94.4)	5,448 (104.8)	5,543 (93.9)
Private	1,274 (52.3)	1,812 (59.5)	2,688 (77.2)	2,989 (75.8)	2,745 (75.8)	2,870 (73.4)	2,588 (70.7)	2,417 (77.1)	2,245 (78.9)	2,430 (84.9)	2,348 (76.5)
Attendance status											
Full-day	698 (39.8)	1,551 (56.0)	2,577 (76.1)	3,689 (81.1)	4,008 (85.0)	4,429 (83.2)	4,548 (83.5)	4,813 (98.5)	4,760 (97.2)	4,753 (100.4)	4,864 (100.4)
Part-day	3,406 (75.5)	3,327 (72.0)	4,082 (87.0)	4,051 (83.2)	3,584 (82.5)	3,492 (78.2)	3,253 (76.4)	3,432 (88.5)	3,123 (85.1)	3,125 (100.4)	3,027 (79.1)
Percent of 3- to 5-year-olds enrolled											
Total	37.5 (0.72)	52.5 (0.81)	59.4 (0.79)	61.8 (0.69)	64.0 (0.73)	64.9 (0.68)	64.3 (0.68)	63.7 (0.66)	64.3 (0.85)	64.8 (0.78)	64.7 (0.70)
Full-day as a percent of total enrollment	17.0 (0.91)	31.8 (1.04)	38.7 (1.02)	47.7 (0.90)	52.8 (0.95)	55.9 (0.87)	58.3 (0.87)	58.4 (0.92)	60.4 (0.95)	60.3 (0.99)	61.6 (0.93)
Full-day preschool as a percent of total preschool enrollment	26.6 (2.08)	34.3 (1.66)	34.0 (1.39)	45.0 (1.20)	47.4 (1.25)	51.0 (1.12)	50.2 (1.16)	47.9 (1.31)	48.7 (1.29)	49.3 (1.26)	49.1 (1.32)
Full-day kindergarten as a percent of total kindergarten enrollment	13.5 (0.97)	30.0 (1.33)	43.5 (1.48)	51.0 (1.36)	60.0 (1.41)	63.7 (1.36)	69.5 (1.26)	73.0 (1.38)	76.7 (1.26)	76.0 (1.35)	79.7 (1.24)
3 and 4 years old											
Total population (in thousands)	7,135 (106.1)	6,215 (99.0)	7,415 (118.3)	8,294 (125.1)	7,869 (126.5)	8,336 (123.6)	8,179 (122.4)	8,850 (63.8)	8,014 (124.2)	8,101 (126.7)	8,125 (92.2)
Age											
3 years old	3,516 (74.4)	3,143 (70.4)	3,692 (83.5)	4,148 (88.5)	3,929 (89.4)	4,260 (88.4)	4,151 (87.2)	4,492 (59.4)	3,983 (218.7)	4,000 (128.8)	4,043 (92.8)
4 years old	3,620 (75.5)	3,072 (69.6)	3,723 (83.8)	4,145 (88.5)	3,940 (89.5)	4,076 (86.4)	4,028 (85.9)	4,358 (57.7)	4,031 (124.6)	4,101 (67.1)	4,082 (57.5)
Enrollment of 3- and 4-year-olds (in thousands)											
Total	1,461 (53.1)	2,280 (59.2)	3,292 (73.1)	4,043 (72.4)	4,097 (73.1)	4,590 (71.1)	4,383 (70.6)	4,706 (84.1)	4,289 (89.1)	4,449 (104.4)	4,426 (98.1)
Age											
3 years old	454 (31.0)	857 (38.9)	1,205 (48.7)	1,489 (49.1)	1,541 (50.5)	1,806 (50.5)	1,715 (49.7)	1,718 (59.5)	1,614 (97.2)	1,674 (87.2)	1,721 (80.4)
4 years old	1,007 (42.0)	1,423 (43.1)	2,087 (51.7)	2,553 (49.8)	2,556 (49.4)	2,785 (46.5)	2,668 (47.0)	2,988 (67.2)	2,675 (87.8)	2,775 (69.5)	2,705 (60.2)
Level and attendance status											
Preschool	1,003 (45.8)	1,889 (56.5)	3,026 (72.3)	3,720 (72.0)	3,762 (73.1)	4,198 (71.5)	4,024 (70.8)	4,245 (85.3)	3,978 (89.1)	4,022 (106.3)	4,070 (90.1)
Full-day	263 (24.8)	649 (37.6)	1,028 (50.8)	1,715 (58.6)	1,763 (61.0)	2,135 (62.4)	1,986 (60.7)	2,018 (70.6)	1,951 (75.1)	2,003 (75.3)	2,026 (73.2)
Part-day	741 (40.1)	1,240 (49.1)	1,998 (65.3)	2,006 (62.0)	1,999 (63.7)	2,063 (61.7)	2,038 (61.3)	2,226 (73.0)	2,027 (67.3)	2,020 (79.6)	2,044 (70.7)
Kindergarten	458 (32.3)	391 (29.8)	266 (27.3)	322 (28.0)	335 (29.6)	392 (30.3)	359 (29.0)	462 (44.6)	312 (28.5)	427 (37.2)	356 (32.3)
Full-day	110 (16.2)	139 (18.2)	135 (19.7)	144 (18.9)	181 (21.9)	245 (24.1)	247 (24.2)	247 (31.4)	223 (22.4)	247 (28.6)	244 (27.6)
Part-day	348 (28.3)	252 (24.2)	131 (19.4)	178 (21.0)	154 (20.3)	147 (18.8)	112 (16.5)	214 (28.5)	89 (16.7)	179 (25.7)	112 (19.7)
Control											
Public	617 (37.0)	838 (42.0)	1,211 (54.4)	1,787 (59.5)	2,042 (64.2)	2,374 (64.5)	2,341 (64.0)	2,795 (82.2)	2,578 (75.9)	2,499 (80.2)	2,584 (81.1)
Private	844 (42.5)	1,441 (51.9)	2,081 (66.1)	2,256 (64.4)	2,055 (64.3)	2,216 (63.2)	2,042 (61.3)	1,911 (64.0)	1,711 (69.3)	1,950 (77.9)	1,842 (68.7)
Attendance status											
Full-day	373 (29.3)	788 (40.9)	1,163 (53.5)	1,858 (60.4)	1,944 (63.1)	2,380 (64.6)	2,233 (63.1)	2,265 (69.0)	2,174 (75.9)	2,250 (76.4)	2,269 (79.6)
Part-day	1,088 (47.3)	1,492 (52.5)	2,129 (66.6)	2,184 (63.8)	2,153 (65.3)	2,211 (63.1)	2,150 (62.4)	2,441 (76.5)	2,115 (68.7)	2,199 (83.1)	2,157 (71.7)
Percent of 3- and 4-year-olds enrolled											
Total	20.5 (1.65)	36.7 (1.57)	44.4 (1.48)	48.7 (1.25)	52.1 (1.29)	55.1 (1.15)	53.6 (1.18)	53.2 (0.89)	53.5 (1.11)	54.9 (1.00)	54.5 (0.98)
Age											
3 years old	12.9 (2.45)	27.3 (2.37)	32.6 (2.31)	35.9 (1.98)	39.2 (2.05)	42.4 (1.82)	41.3 (1.86)	38.2 (1.25)	40.5 (1.52)	41.8 (1.40)	42.6 (1.52)
4 years old	27.8 (2.20)	46.3 (2.06)	56.1 (1.86)	61.6 (1.53)	64.9 (1.56)	68.3 (1.38)	66.2 (1.43)	68.6 (1.25)	66.4 (1.31)	67.7 (1.37)	66.3 (1.28)
Full-day as a percent of total enrollment	25.5 (1.78)	34.5 (1.55)	35.3 (1.42)	46.0 (1.25)	47.4 (1.29)	51.8 (1.16)	50.9 (1.18)	48.1 (1.26)	50.7 (1.33)	50.6 (1.35)	51.3 (1.31)
Full-day preschool as a percent of total preschool enrollment	26.2 (2.16)	34.3 (1.70)	34.0 (1.47)	46.1 (1.30)	46.9 (1.34)	50.9 (1.21)	49.3 (1.23)	47.5 (1.36)	49.1 (1.40)	49.8 (1.39)	49.8 (1.39)
Full-day kindergarten as a percent of total kindergarten enrollment	24.0 (3.11)	35.6 (3.77)	50.8 (5.24)	44.6 (4.40)	54.0 (4.49)	62.4 (3.83)	68.8 (3.83)	53.6 (4.30)	71.6 (4.31)	58.0 (4.67)	68.4 (4.73)

See notes at end of table.

Table 202.10. Enrollment of 3-, 4-, and 5-year-old children in preprimary programs, by age of child, level of program, control of program, and attendance status: Selected years, 1970 through 2014—Continued

[Standard errors appear in parentheses]

Age of child, level and control of program, and attendance status	1970	1980	1990	1995[1]	2000[1]	2003[1]	2005[1]	2010[1,2]	2012[1,2]	2013[1,2]	2014[1,2]
1	2	3	4	5	6	7	8	9	10	11	12
5 years old[3]											
Total population (in thousands)	3,814 (77.5)	3,069 (69.6)	3,792 (84.6)	4,224 (89.3)	3,989 (90.1)	3,867 (84.2)	3,955 (85.1)	4,099 (57.9)	4,245 (77.0)	4,064 (69.1)	4,066 (80.9)
Enrollment of 5-year-olds (in thousands)											
Total	2,643 (44.4)	2,598 (31.1)	3,367 (33.2)	3,697 (34.1)	3,495 (34.3)	3,331 (33.7)	3,418 (33.7)	3,540 (56.2)	3,594 (71.1)	3,429 (72.1)	3,464 (70.0)
Level and attendance status											
Preschool	91 (14.7)	93 (14.8)	352 (30.5)	611 (36.3)	565 (36.3)	661 (36.7)	505 (32.9)	552 (35.8)	624 (45.1)	602 (42.0)	588 (44.4)
Full-day	28 (8.3)	32 (8.8)	122 (18.5)	236 (23.7)	286 (26.9)	344 (27.7)	289 (25.6)	279 (29.2)	291 (30.8)	277 (28.3)	262 (30.7)
Part-day	62 (12.2)	61 (12.0)	231 (25.2)	375 (29.4)	278 (26.6)	316 (26.7)	216 (22.4)	274 (26.9)	333 (33.3)	325 (30.2)	326 (31.0)
Kindergarten	2,552 (45.3)	2,505 (33.4)	3,015 (42.5)	3,086 (45.8)	2,931 (46.0)	2,670 (45.0)	2,913 (43.4)	2,987 (59.8)	2,970 (70.5)	2,827 (68.5)	2,877 (69.4)
Full-day	297 (25.8)	731 (36.8)	1,293 (49.9)	1,594 (50.1)	1,778 (51.8)	1,705 (48.4)	2,027 (49.2)	2,269 (60.2)	2,294 (69.3)	2,226 (68.2)	2,332 (69.8)
Part-day	2,255 (47.3)	1,774 (42.6)	1,722 (52.4)	1,492 (49.4)	1,152 (47.2)	965 (42.1)	886 (41.1)	718 (43.0)	675 (39.8)	601 (38.3)	545 (37.7)
Control											
Public	2,214 (47.5)	2,228 (38.5)	2,760 (46.8)	2,963 (47.3)	2,806 (47.6)	2,677 (45.0)	2,872 (43.9)	3,034 (57.8)	3,060 (70.8)	2,949 (68.2)	2,959 (69.7)
Private	429 (30.4)	370 (28.1)	607 (38.6)	733 (39.1)	690 (39.4)	654 (36.5)	546 (34.0)	506 (35.0)	534 (37.1)	480 (34.7)	505 (35.5)
Attendance status											
Full-day	326 (26.9)	763 (37.3)	1,414 (50.9)	1,830 (51.2)	2,065 (52.1)	2,050 (48.6)	2,316 (48.5)	2,548 (60.1)	2,585 (72.9)	2,503 (67.3)	2,594 (72.7)
Part-day	2,317 (47.0)	1,835 (42.3)	1,953 (52.6)	1,867 (51.3)	1,431 (50.0)	1,281 (45.8)	1,102 (44.2)	992 (44.6)	1,008 (50.4)	926 (46.2)	870 (43.8)
Percent of 5-year-olds enrolled											
Total	69.3 (1.16)	84.7 (1.01)	88.8 (0.88)	87.5 (0.81)	87.6 (0.86)	86.1 (0.87)	86.4 (0.85)	86.3 (0.92)	84.6 (0.94)	84.4 (1.04)	85.2 (1.04)
Full-day as a percent of total enrollment	12.3 (1.00)	29.4 (1.39)	42.0 (1.45)	49.5 (1.31)	59.1 (1.37)	61.5 (1.32)	67.7 (1.25)	72.0 (1.20)	71.9 (1.34)	73.0 (1.22)	74.9 (1.24)
Full-day preschool as a percent of total preschool enrollment	31.3 (7.58)	34.6 (7.70)	34.5 (4.33)	38.7 (3.13)	50.7 (3.47)	52.1 (3.04)	57.2 (3.45)	50.5 (3.90)	46.7 (3.67)	46.1 (3.33)	44.6 (3.62)
Full-day kindergarten as a percent of total kindergarten enrollment	11.6 (0.99)	29.2 (1.42)	42.9 (1.54)	51.7 (1.43)	60.7 (1.49)	63.9 (1.46)	69.6 (1.34)	76.0 (1.35)	77.3 (1.28)	78.7 (1.30)	81.1 (1.27)

[1]Beginning in 1994, preprimary enrollment data were collected using new procedures. Data may not be comparable to figures for earlier years.
[2]Beginning in 2010, standard errors were computed using replicate weights, which produced more precise values than the generalized variance function methodology used in prior years.
[3]Enrollment data for 5-year-olds include only those students in preprimary programs and do not include those enrolled in primary programs.

NOTE: Preprimary programs include kindergarten and preschool (or nursery school) programs. "Preschool," which was referred to as "nursery school" in previous versions of this table, is defined as a group or class that is organized to provide educational experiences for children during the year or years preceding kindergarten. Data are based on sample surveys of the civilian noninstitutionalized population. Detail may not sum to totals because of rounding.
SOURCE: U.S. Department of Commerce, Census Bureau, Current Population Survey (CPS), October, 1970 through 2014. (This table was prepared September 2015.)

Table 202.20. Percentage of 3-, 4-, and 5-year-old children enrolled in preprimary programs, by level of program, attendance status, and selected child and family characteristics: 2014

[Standard errors appear in parentheses]

Selected child or family characteristic	Total 3- to 5-year-old population (in thousands)	Total enrollment (in thousands)	Percent of 3- to 5-year-old population enrolled — Total	Preschool — Total	Preschool — Full-day	Preschool — Part-day	Kindergarten — Total	Kindergarten — Full-day	Kindergarten — Part-day	Percentage distribution of enrollment — Full-day	Percentage distribution of enrollment — Part-day
1	2	3	4	5	6	7	8	9	10	11	12
Total	12,191 (79.1)	7,890 (99.9)	64.7 (0.70)	38.2 (0.74)	18.8 (0.62)	19.4 (0.62)	26.5 (0.58)	21.1 (0.57)	5.4 (0.35)	61.6 (0.93)	38.4 (0.93)
Sex											
Male	6,189 (56.0)	3,981 (74.1)	64.3 (0.96)	37.5 (0.95)	19.0 (0.85)	18.5 (0.88)	26.8 (0.82)	21.4 (0.80)	5.4 (0.48)	62.9 (1.38)	37.1 (1.38)
Female	6,002 (62.8)	3,910 (84.0)	65.1 (1.13)	38.9 (1.31)	18.5 (0.96)	20.4 (1.03)	26.2 (0.84)	20.9 (0.77)	5.4 (0.48)	60.4 (1.39)	39.6 (1.39)
Age of child											
3 and 4 years old	8,125 (92.2)	4,426 (98.1)	54.5 (0.98)	50.1 (0.93)	24.9 (0.85)	25.2 (0.82)	4.4 (0.39)	3.0 (0.33)	1.4 (0.24)	51.3 (1.31)	48.7 (1.31)
3 years old	4,043 (92.8)	1,721 (80.4)	42.6 (1.52)	40.8 (1.51)	19.4 (1.13)	21.5 (1.20)	1.7 (0.35)	1.2 (0.31)	0.5! (0.19)	48.3 (2.15)	51.7 (2.15)
4 years old	4,082 (57.5)	2,705 (60.2)	66.3 (1.28)	59.3 (1.22)	30.4 (1.23)	28.8 (1.20)	7.0 (0.70)	4.8 (0.61)	2.2 (0.44)	53.2 (1.71)	46.8 (1.71)
5 years old	4,066 (80.9)	3,464 (70.0)	85.2 (1.04)	14.5 (1.02)	6.4 (0.73)	8.0 (0.73)	70.8 (1.43)	57.4 (1.51)	13.4 (0.92)	74.9 (1.24)	25.1 (1.24)
Race/ethnicity of child											
White	5,939 (43.4)	3,996 (67.6)	67.3 (1.04)	41.4 (1.23)	17.0 (0.92)	24.4 (0.96)	25.9 (0.88)	21.3 (0.84)	4.6 (0.42)	57.0 (1.25)	43.0 (1.25)
Black	1,758 (52.4)	1,185 (55.3)	67.4 (2.16)	39.2 (2.06)	27.2 (1.97)	12.0 (1.56)	28.2 (1.59)	23.4 (1.52)	4.7 (0.79)	75.1 (2.38)	24.9 (2.38)
Hispanic	3,154 (58.3)	1,853 (58.9)	58.7 (1.42)	32.0 (1.44)	17.8 (1.23)	14.2 (1.04)	26.7 (1.11)	20.3 (1.09)	6.4 (0.80)	64.9 (1.93)	35.1 (1.93)
Asian	639 (35.9)	408 (33.0)	63.9 (3.64)	40.1 (3.92)	19.7 (2.87)	20.4 (2.84)	23.8 (2.72)	15.8 (2.47)	8.1 (1.82)	55.5 (4.42)	44.5 (4.42)
Native Hawaiian/Pacific Islander	‡ (†)	‡ (†)	‡ (†)	‡ (†)	‡ (†)	‡ (†)	‡ (†)	‡ (†)	‡ (†)	‡ (†)	‡ (†)
American Indian/Alaska Native	134 (26.7)	73 (18.3)	54.7 (7.02)	31.2 (6.41)	17.3! (5.71)	13.9! (5.28)	23.5 (4.54)	12.2! (3.73)	11.3! (4.09)	53.8 (11.16)	46.2 (11.16)
Two or more races	538 (38.8)	354 (35.0)	65.7 (4.28)	35.2 (3.94)	15.5 (2.88)	19.7 (3.03)	30.6 (3.65)	24.8 (3.37)	5.8! (1.95)	61.3 (4.40)	38.7 (4.40)
Number of parents or guardians in household											
One parent or guardian	3,380 (96.4)	2,220 (77.7)	65.7 (1.41)	36.7 (1.60)	22.1 (1.39)	14.6 (1.18)	29.0 (1.33)	23.1 (1.25)	5.9 (0.69)	68.8 (1.88)	31.2 (1.88)
Two parents or guardians	8,811 (96.3)	5,671 (95.2)	64.4 (0.84)	38.8 (0.81)	17.5 (0.66)	21.3 (0.75)	25.6 (0.67)	20.4 (0.64)	5.2 (0.41)	58.8 (1.12)	41.2 (1.12)
Mother's current employment status[1]											
Employed	7,042 (112.1)	4,776 (97.0)	67.8 (0.88)	40.6 (0.92)	22.2 (0.92)	18.4 (0.79)	27.2 (0.83)	22.0 (0.79)	5.2 (0.41)	65.2 (1.16)	34.8 (1.16)
Unemployed	573 (53.4)	388 (38.7)	67.7 (3.79)	37.4 (3.78)	19.1 (3.25)	18.3 (2.90)	30.3 (3.67)	25.3 (3.26)	5.0! (1.64)	65.5 (4.15)	34.5 (4.15)
Not in the labor force	4,191 (104.6)	2,482 (90.1)	59.2 (1.39)	34.2 (1.44)	12.3 (0.93)	22.0 (1.36)	25.0 (1.04)	19.4 (0.92)	5.5 (0.58)	53.6 (1.93)	46.4 (1.93)
No mother in household	385 (33.5)	246 (26.3)	63.8 (3.81)	38.1 (4.60)	25.7 (3.87)	12.4 (3.16)	25.8 (3.82)	17.3 (3.34)	8.5! (2.84)	67.4 (5.27)	32.6 (5.27)
Father's current employment status[1]											
Employed	8,369 (100.5)	5,461 (94.7)	65.3 (0.84)	39.5 (0.84)	18.3 (0.71)	21.2 (0.75)	25.8 (0.69)	20.7 (0.67)	5.0 (0.41)	59.9 (1.12)	40.1 (1.12)
Unemployed	272 (32.4)	144 (21.7)	52.7 (4.91)	32.4 (4.67)	17.7 (3.60)	14.7 (3.82)	20.3 (4.30)	14.2 (3.59)	6.1! (2.33)	60.5 (6.52)	39.5 (6.52)
Not in the labor force	554 (49.1)	311 (32.9)	56.2 (3.60)	30.9 (3.19)	10.3 (2.01)	20.5 (3.01)	25.3 (2.70)	15.7 (2.34)	9.6 (2.19)	46.4 (5.00)	53.6 (5.00)
No father in household	2,996 (92.7)	1,974 (75.6)	65.9 (1.48)	36.5 (1.66)	21.6 (1.49)	14.9 (1.27)	29.4 (1.48)	23.9 (1.35)	5.5 (0.71)	69.0 (2.01)	31.0 (2.01)
Every parent or guardian employed[1]	6,936 (114.5)	4,740 (101.2)	68.3 (0.88)	40.9 (0.95)	22.9 (0.94)	18.0 (0.72)	27.4 (0.83)	22.3 (0.82)	5.1 (0.43)	66.1 (1.10)	33.9 (1.10)
No parent or guardian employed[1]	1,572 (80.0)	930 (63.8)	59.2 (2.48)	32.1 (2.18)	15.4 (1.78)	16.7 (1.82)	27.1 (1.76)	21.0 (1.55)	6.1 (0.92)	61.5 (2.93)	38.5 (2.93)
Highest educational attainment of parents or guardians[1]											
Less than high school	1,168 (59.5)	655 (43.6)	56.1 (2.48)	28.2 (2.57)	16.0 (1.90)	12.2 (1.80)	27.9 (2.16)	23.0 (2.20)	4.9 (1.04)	69.5 (3.07)	30.5 (3.07)
High school/GED	2,850 (98.0)	1,667 (75.2)	58.9 (1.64)	32.1 (1.65)	16.2 (1.39)	15.9 (1.29)	26.8 (1.39)	20.3 (1.16)	6.5 (0.81)	62.1 (2.08)	37.9 (2.08)
Some college, no degree	2,008 (88.5)	1,251 (63.3)	62.3 (1.72)	34.9 (1.88)	19.5 (1.64)	15.4 (1.38)	27.4 (1.78)	22.5 (1.68)	5.0 (0.84)	67.4 (2.41)	32.6 (2.41)
Associate's degree	1,304 (63.9)	846 (51.8)	64.9 (2.30)	38.1 (2.28)	16.3 (1.74)	21.8 (2.16)	26.8 (1.98)	22.1 (1.92)	4.6 (0.85)	59.3 (3.09)	40.7 (3.09)
Bachelor's degree	2,653 (86.3)	1,819 (65.5)	68.6 (1.42)	42.7 (1.55)	19.6 (1.25)	23.1 (1.28)	25.9 (1.42)	21.0 (1.35)	4.8 (0.67)	59.2 (1.89)	40.8 (1.89)
Graduate or professional degree	2,228 (87.8)	1,652 (75.3)	74.1 (1.72)	48.9 (1.83)	23.2 (1.67)	25.7 (1.60)	25.3 (1.39)	19.5 (1.29)	5.8 (0.76)	57.6 (2.05)	42.4 (2.05)

†Not applicable.
!Interpret data with caution. The coefficient of variation (CV) for this estimate is between 30 and 50 percent.
‡Reporting standards not met. Either there are too few cases for a reliable estimate or the coefficient of variation (CV) is 50 percent or greater.
[1]Data pertain only to parents or guardians who live in the household with the child.
NOTE: Preprimary programs include kindergarten and preschool (or nursery school) programs. "Preschool," which was referred to as "nursery school" in previous versions of this table, is defined as a group or class that is organized to provide educational experiences for children during the year or years preceding kindergarten. Enrollment data for 5-year-olds include only those students in preprimary programs and do not include those enrolled in primary programs. Race categories exclude persons of Hispanic ethnicity. Data are based on sample surveys of the civilian noninstitutionalized population. Detail may not sum to totals because of rounding.
SOURCE: U.S. Department of Commerce, Census Bureau, Current Population Survey (CPS), October, 2014. (This table was prepared September 2015.)

Table 202.30. Number of children under 6 years old and not yet enrolled in kindergarten, percentage in center-based programs, average weekly hours in nonparental care, and percentage in various types of primary care arrangements, by selected child and family characteristics: 2012

[Standard errors appear in parentheses]

Selected child or family characteristic	Number of children, ages 0 to 5 (in thousands)		Percent in center-based programs[2]		Average hours per week in nonparental care[3]		Percentage distribution, by type of primary care arrangement[1]										
							Parental care only		Nonparental care								
									Center-based care		Nonrelative home-based care						Relative		Multiple arrangements[4]	
											Total		In another home		In child's home					
1	2		3		4		5		6		7		8		9		10		11	
Total children	21,674	(1.0)	34.3	(0.66)	30.0	(0.37)	39.6	(0.78)	28.2	(0.62)	11.1	(0.49)	7.8	(0.43)	3.4	(0.27)	19.6	(0.62)	1.4	(0.15)
Age																				
Under 1 year	4,794	(130.9)	11.0	(1.11)	29.1	(0.98)	54.1	(1.92)	9.1	(0.90)	11.6	(1.11)	7.2	(0.80)	4.4	(0.72)	24.1	(1.48)	1.2 !	(0.38)
1 year old	4,468	(114.7)	17.9	(1.25)	31.0	(0.94)	49.3	(1.86)	15.4	(1.14)	13.3	(1.17)	10.0	(1.16)	3.3	(0.54)	21.0	(1.36)	1.0	(0.25)
2 years old	4,167	(133.9)	26.5	(1.43)	32.2	(0.88)	42.6	(1.57)	20.4	(1.30)	14.1	(1.13)	10.2	(1.12)	4.0	(0.61)	21.3	(1.38)	1.5	(0.39)
3 years old	3,674	(89.8)	48.8	(1.47)	29.7	(0.75)	30.5	(1.43)	40.0	(1.42)	9.4	(0.87)	6.3	(0.61)	3.1	(0.69)	18.5	(1.25)	1.6	(0.31)
4 years old	3,508	(90.4)	70.6	(1.57)	28.5	(0.65)	19.8	(1.68)	58.4	(1.50)	6.6	(0.65)	4.8	(0.57)	1.8	(0.37)	13.2	(1.15)	1.9	(0.36)
5 years old	1,062	(59.6)	68.3	(3.48)	29.7	(1.42)	18.5	(2.38)	58.4	(3.43)	9.0	(2.09)	6.7	(1.91)	2.3 !	(0.92)	12.1	(1.85)	2.0 !	(0.90)
Race/ethnicity of child and poverty status of household[5]																				
White	10,893	(99.5)	35.5	(0.90)	29.2	(0.38)	38.3	(0.95)	29.3	(0.84)	13.9	(0.78)	9.6	(0.72)	4.3	(0.33)	17.2	(0.73)	1.3	(0.20)
Poor	1,544	(63.3)	16.7	(1.72)	27.7	(1.65)	62.5	(2.84)	14.3	(1.52)	6.0	(1.36)	4.1 !	(1.24)	2.0 !	(0.73)	16.8	(1.78)	0.4 !	(0.15)
Near-poor	2,190	(82.6)	26.5	(1.83)	27.2	(1.20)	49.7	(2.35)	20.9	(1.72)	6.9	(0.91)	4.8	(0.73)	2.1	(0.57)	21.3	(1.79)	1.1 !	(0.37)
Nonpoor	7,159	(69.5)	42.4	(1.14)	29.9	(0.45)	29.5	(1.18)	35.2	(1.03)	17.7	(1.05)	12.3	(0.99)	5.4	(0.47)	16.1	(0.82)	1.5	(0.27)
Black	2,890	(#)	42.1	(2.28)	32.9	(1.21)	31.1	(2.46)	34.2	(2.39)	8.5	(1.66)	5.9	(1.29)	2.6 !	(1.07)	24.6	(1.94)	1.5 !	(0.50)
Poor	1,245	(34.2)	34.5	(3.33)	34.4	(1.68)	39.1	(3.99)	26.7	(3.16)	7.7 !	(2.62)	4.7 !	(2.22)	‡	(†)	25.2	(2.98)	1.3 !	(0.51)
Near-poor	729	(43.4)	44.0	(4.62)	33.4	(2.36)	29.2	(4.89)	36.3	(4.55)	8.2	(2.27)	7.2 !	(2.24)	‡	(†)	24.8	(3.93)	‡	(†)
Nonpoor	916	(24.9)	51.0	(3.92)	31.0	(2.34)	21.8	(3.32)	42.8	(4.39)	10.0 !	(3.45)	6.5 !	(2.29)	‡	(†)	23.5	(3.34)	‡	(†)
Hispanic	5,469	(1.0)	27.7	(1.15)	30.2	(0.80)	44.9	(1.62)	22.3	(1.13)	8.1	(0.97)	6.3	(0.71)	1.8	(0.54)	22.9	(1.58)	1.8	(0.44)
Poor	1,914	(42.0)	21.6	(1.81)	26.3	(1.54)	54.6	(2.57)	17.7	(1.78)	4.1	(0.80)	3.5	(0.75)	‡	(†)	21.0	(2.40)	2.5 !	(0.94)
Near-poor	1,575	(56.1)	24.3	(2.24)	31.5	(1.64)	47.1	(3.32)	20.0	(2.15)	7.7	(1.80)	6.1	(1.52)	‡	(†)	23.1	(2.47)	2.0 !	(0.68)
Nonpoor	1,980	(39.7)	36.3	(2.52)	32.0	(1.06)	33.8	(2.76)	28.4	(2.24)	12.3	(1.87)	9.2	(1.47)	3.1	(0.93)	24.6	(2.71)	0.9 !	(0.34)
Asian	1,030	(60.5)	37.3	(2.74)	28.8	(1.47)	44.9	(3.21)	32.9	(2.63)	5.2	(1.11)	3.1	(0.83)	2.1 !	(0.80)	15.7	(1.95)	1.3 !	(0.44)
Other[6]	1,393	(80.8)	31.5	(2.31)	29.1	(1.14)	42.9	(2.84)	26.9	(2.28)	11.1	(1.62)	6.5	(1.25)	4.7	(1.02)	18.1	(1.88)	1.0 !	(0.39)
Number of parents in the household[7]																				
Two parents	15,428	(139.0)	33.4	(0.73)	28.3	(0.36)	41.6	(0.87)	28.6	(0.68)	11.8	(0.61)	8.3	(0.55)	3.5	(0.27)	16.5	(0.68)	1.4	(0.18)
One parent	5,629	(131.2)	36.0	(1.36)	33.1	(0.79)	35.5	(1.55)	27.5	(1.31)	9.8	(1.00)	6.8	(0.84)	3.0	(0.62)	25.7	(1.36)	1.5	(0.31)
Mother in household																				
Yes	19,989	(91.0)	33.9	(0.70)	29.6	(0.37)	40.0	(0.84)	28.3	(0.62)	11.4	(0.51)	8.2	(0.47)	3.2	(0.24)	18.9	(0.63)	1.4	(0.16)
No	1,685	(91.0)	38.4	(2.65)	34.3	(1.68)	34.6	(2.74)	27.6	(2.38)	8.0	(1.93)	3.2 !	(1.00)	4.9 !	(1.68)	27.6	(2.85)	2.2 !	(0.69)
Mother's employment status[8]																				
Currently employed	10,801	(136.5)	43.1	(1.06)	32.2	(0.38)	17.9	(0.94)	34.9	(0.93)	18.1	(0.87)	13.7	(0.78)	4.4	(0.40)	26.9	(0.98)	2.2	(0.29)
35 or more hours per week	7,615	(148.0)	44.7	(1.25)	35.1	(0.44)	15.2	(1.13)	36.3	(1.13)	19.2	(0.99)	15.0	(0.93)	4.2	(0.46)	26.8	(1.14)	2.4	(0.38)
Less than 35 hours per week	3,186	(102.7)	39.4	(1.79)	24.6	(0.67)	24.5	(1.59)	31.4	(1.58)	15.3	(1.41)	10.5	(1.35)	4.8	(0.74)	27.0	(1.45)	1.7	(0.40)
Looking for work	1,478	(83.0)	26.8	(3.03)	29.4	(2.03)	55.1	(3.50)	22.2	(2.92)	3.8 !	(1.29)	2.4 !	(1.17)	1.4 !	(0.70)	18.5	(2.79)	‡	(†)
Not in labor force	7,710	(130.4)	22.3	(0.93)	20.1	(0.70)	68.1	(1.15)	20.2	(0.90)	3.5	(0.40)	1.5	(0.32)	1.9	(0.33)	7.9	(0.77)	0.3 !	(0.12)
Mother's highest education[8]																				
Less than high school	2,991	(71.5)	20.5	(1.83)	28.9	(1.69)	56.4	(2.74)	17.8	(1.75)	6.4	(1.40)	4.8	(1.27)	1.6 !	(0.59)	17.8	(2.06)	1.6 !	(0.65)
High school/GED	4,041	(96.1)	25.7	(1.75)	29.1	(1.11)	48.2	(2.24)	22.2	(1.68)	7.6	(1.32)	6.4	(1.26)	1.2 !	(0.39)	21.6	(1.68)	0.4 !	(0.16)
Vocational/technical or some college	4,084	(104.5)	31.4	(1.31)	28.6	(0.76)	42.7	(1.47)	26.0	(1.37)	9.2	(0.94)	7.4	(0.74)	1.8	(0.44)	20.4	(1.35)	1.7	(0.36)
Associate's degree	1,795	(80.2)	35.9	(2.30)	31.9	(1.14)	34.3	(2.49)	28.0	(2.04)	14.3	(1.96)	11.3	(1.85)	3.0	(0.77)	21.0	(2.04)	2.4 !	(0.77)
Bachelor's degree	5,056	(102.6)	43.4	(1.39)	29.4	(0.53)	31.3	(1.34)	36.1	(1.33)	14.3	(0.93)	9.9	(0.82)	4.4	(0.50)	17.3	(1.04)	1.1	(0.24)
Graduate/professional degree	2,022	(40.2)	49.7	(1.79)	31.0	(0.61)	21.2	(1.55)	41.2	(1.71)	21.1	(1.38)	11.2	(0.98)	9.8	(1.08)	14.7	(1.20)	1.8	(0.43)
Language spoken most at home by mother[8]																				
English	16,057	(127.9)	35.8	(0.83)	29.7	(0.35)	37.5	(0.91)	29.6	(0.75)	12.6	(0.63)	9.0	(0.57)	3.6	(0.26)	19.0	(0.67)	1.3	(0.15)
Non-English	3,932	(108.8)	26.1	(1.44)	28.9	(1.05)	50.3	(2.03)	22.7	(1.39)	6.6	(0.94)	4.9	(0.80)	1.7	(0.44)	18.7	(1.88)	1.7 !	(0.53)
Mother's age when first became parent[8]																				
Less than 18	1,628	(86.3)	28.9	(2.94)	31.3	(1.81)	48.3	(2.95)	23.3	(2.80)	5.5 !	(1.81)	4.9 !	(1.79)	‡	(†)	21.8	(2.36)	1.1 !	(0.44)
18 or 19	2,285	(110.7)	24.3	(2.03)	30.7	(1.49)	49.2	(2.78)	20.3	(1.92)	7.4	(1.64)	5.9	(1.25)	1.6 !	(0.59)	22.5	(2.18)	0.6 !	(0.26)
20 or older	15,935	(142.3)	35.7	(0.78)	29.3	(0.39)	37.9	(0.89)	29.8	(0.68)	12.6	(0.58)	8.9	(0.53)	3.8	(0.29)	18.1	(0.60)	1.5	(0.19)
Household income																				
$20,000 or less	3,955	(#)	24.6	(1.40)	29.7	(0.98)	52.0	(1.92)	19.3	(1.21)	6.7	(1.00)	4.5	(0.88)	2.2	(0.58)	20.6	(1.47)	1.4 !	(0.45)
$20,001 to $50,000	6,246	(1.0)	28.5	(1.20)	28.8	(0.80)	46.8	(1.46)	23.5	(1.18)	6.4	(0.62)	5.1	(0.54)	1.2	(0.28)	21.6	(1.18)	1.7	(0.29)
$50,001 to $75,000	3,881	(#)	34.3	(1.75)	29.4	(0.94)	38.7	(2.00)	28.9	(1.61)	10.4	(1.14)	8.6	(1.03)	1.8	(0.44)	20.9	(1.22)	1.0	(0.26)
$75,001 to $100,000	2,745	(#)	40.6	(1.86)	31.0	(0.98)	28.4	(1.89)	33.9	(1.73)	16.4	(1.66)	13.9	(1.64)	2.5	(0.63)	20.1	(1.73)	1.3 !	(0.46)
Over $100,000	4,847	(#)	45.9	(1.49)	31.2	(0.57)	27.3	(1.66)	37.8	(1.37)	18.5	(1.20)	9.8	(0.90)	8.8	(0.86)	14.9	(1.17)	1.5	(0.31)
Poverty status of household[5]																				
Poor	5,213	(75.9)	23.7	(1.31)	29.0	(0.86)	53.2	(1.73)	19.5	(1.24)	5.7	(0.76)	3.9	(0.69)	1.7	(0.45)	20.3	(1.21)	1.3	(0.37)
Near-poor	4,996	(96.6)	28.1	(1.41)	29.5	(0.92)	46.3	(1.66)	23.0	(1.29)	6.8	(0.80)	5.2	(0.68)	1.6	(0.35)	22.4	(1.26)	1.6	(0.31)
Nonpoor	11,464	(56.5)	41.7	(0.96)	30.5	(0.44)	30.5	(1.02)	34.5	(0.83)	15.5	(0.78)	10.6	(0.69)	4.9	(0.41)	18.1	(0.82)	1.4	(0.20)

See notes at end of table.

Table 202.30. Number of children under 6 years old and not yet enrolled in kindergarten, percentage in center-based programs, average weekly hours in nonparental care, and percentage in various types of primary care arrangements, by selected child and family characteristics: 2012—Continued

Selected child or family characteristic	Number of children, ages 0 to 5 (in thousands)	Percent in center-based programs[2]	Average hours per week in nonparental care[3]	Percentage distribution, by type of primary care arrangement[1]							
				Parental care only	Center-based care	Nonparental care					
						Nonrelative home-based care			Relative	Multiple arrangements[4]
						Total	In another home	In child's home		
1	2	3	4	5	6	7	8	9	10	11
Household size										
2 or 3 persons	5,427 (96.1)	37.4 (1.13)	32.5 (0.60)	33.2 (1.33)	30.2 (1.08)	13.1 (0.79)	9.4 (0.66)	3.7 (0.51)	21.7 (0.95)	1.8 (0.26)
4 persons	7,435 (96.1)	38.0 (1.21)	28.5 (0.55)	36.1 (1.18)	32.2 (1.12)	12.6 (0.94)	9.4 (0.85)	3.2 (0.43)	18.3 (0.93)	0.9 (0.18)
5 persons	4,243 (107.2)	34.0 (1.46)	28.8 (0.91)	43.5 (1.72)	27.7 (1.29)	9.6 (1.22)	6.4 (1.03)	3.2 (0.58)	17.8 (1.40)	1.4 (0.41)
6 or more persons	4,569 (107.1)	24.7 (1.48)	30.5 (1.13)	49.4 (2.00)	19.9 (1.44)	7.8 (0.95)	4.5 (0.70)	3.3 (0.70)	21.0 (1.54)	1.9 (0.49)
Locale										
City	7,165 (154.8)	34.3 (1.16)	30.4 (0.66)	38.3 (1.42)	28.3 (1.12)	11.3 (0.90)	7.1 (0.68)	4.3 (0.56)	20.5 (1.25)	1.5 (0.25)
Suburban	7,682 (173.4)	35.7 (1.18)	29.7 (0.56)	38.2 (1.23)	29.8 (1.12)	10.6 (0.68)	7.4 (0.61)	3.2 (0.38)	20.0 (0.95)	1.4 (0.29)
Town	2,208 (119.2)	29.4 (1.80)	29.5 (1.19)	45.1 (2.10)	23.4 (1.86)	10.0 (1.13)	7.1 (0.97)	2.9 (0.79)	19.6 (1.81)	2.0 ! (0.67)
Rural	4,619 (121.6)	34.0 (1.58)	30.1 (0.66)	41.4 (1.50)	27.7 (1.42)	12.2 (1.19)	9.8 (1.00)	2.5 (0.46)	17.6 (1.04)	1.1 (0.23)

†Not applicable.
#Rounds to zero.
!Interpret data with caution. The coefficient of variation (CV) for this estimate is between 30 and 50 percent.
‡Reporting standards not met. The coefficient of variation (CV) for this estimate is 50 percent or greater.
[1]A child's primary arrangement is the regular nonparental care arrangement or early childhood education program in which the child spent the most time per week.
[2]Center-based arrangements include day care centers, Head Start programs, preschools, prekindergartens, and other early childhood programs.
[3]Mean hours per week per child, among preschool children enrolled in any type of nonparental care arrangement. For children with more than one arrangement, the hours of each weekly arrangement were summed to calculate the total amount of time in child care per week.
[4]Children who spent an equal number of hours per week in multiple nonparental care arrangements.
[5]Poor children are those whose family incomes were below the Census Bureau's poverty threshold in the year prior to data collection; near-poor children are those whose family

incomes ranged from the poverty threshold to 199 percent of the poverty threshold; and non-poor children are those whose family incomes were at or above 200 percent of the poverty threshold. The poverty threshold is a dollar amount that varies depending on a family's size and composition and is updated annually to account for inflation. In 2011, for example, the poverty threshold for a family of four with two children was $22,811. Survey respondents are asked to select the range within which their income falls, rather than giving the exact amount of their income; therefore, the measure of poverty status is an approximation.
[6]Includes persons of all other races and Two or more races.
[7]Excludes children living apart from their parents.
[8]Excludes children living in households with no mother or female guardian present.
NOTE: Race categories exclude persons of Hispanic ethnicity. Detail may not sum to totals because of rounding.
SOURCE: U.S. Department of Education, National Center for Education Statistics, Early Childhood Program Participation Survey of the National Household Education Surveys Program (ECPP-NHES:2012). (This table was prepared April 2015.)

Table 202.35. Primary child care arrangements of 4- and 5-year-old children who are not yet enrolled in kindergarten, by race/ethnicity, poverty status, and mother's highest level of education: Selected years, 1995 through 2012

[Standard errors appear in parentheses]

Year and primary child care arrangement	Total	Race/ethnicity					Poverty status[1]			Mother's highest level of education[2]				
		White	Black	Hispanic	Asian/Pacific Islander	Other[3]	Poor	Near-poor	Nonpoor	Less than high school	High school/GED	Vocational/technical or some college	Associate's degree	Bachelor's or higher degree
1	2	3	4	5	6	7	8	9	10	11	12	13	14	15
1995														
Percent of all children	100.0 (†)	69.2 (1.09)	14.8 (0.79)	10.8 (0.53)	2.4 (0.36)	2.9 (0.46)	25.9 (1.11)	22.5 (1.11)	51.7 (1.28)	12.3 (0.97)	35.3 (1.31)	21.7 (1.10)	7.8 (0.68)	22.9 (0.95)
Percent in all types of care	100.0 (†)	100.0 (†)	100.0 (†)	100.0 (†)	100.0 (†)	100.0 (†)	100.0 (†)	100.0 (†)	100.0 (†)	100.0 (†)	100.0 (†)	100.0 (†)	100.0 (†)	100.0 (†)
Parental care only	21.7 (1.09)	20.9 (1.27)	15.8 (3.24)	33.7 (2.55)	15.5 ! (5.61)	30.0 (7.78)	28.4 (3.03)	32.1 (2.52)	13.8 (1.16)	40.2 (3.32)	26.2 (2.11)	18.9 (2.16)	17.4 (2.87)	9.0 (1.51)
Nonparental care	78.3 (1.09)	79.1 (1.27)	84.2 (3.24)	66.3 (2.55)	84.5 (5.61)	70.0 (7.78)	71.6 (3.03)	67.9 (2.52)	86.2 (1.16)	59.8 (3.32)	73.8 (2.11)	81.1 (2.16)	82.6 (2.87)	91.0 (1.51)
Primary arrangement[4]														
Center-based care[5]	55.1 (1.08)	55.0 (1.38)	59.7 (4.21)	44.3 (2.69)	73.7 (7.32)	58.3 (9.02)	51.4 (3.10)	45.4 (2.73)	61.0 (1.72)	41.2 (3.88)	50.0 (2.07)	57.5 (1.85)	57.7 (4.30)	67.4 (2.58)
Nonrelative care	11.0 (0.86)	12.7 (1.02)	7.8 (1.71)	6.6 (1.72)	7.1 ! (3.49)	‡	5.8 (1.18)	9.4 (1.27)	14.3 (1.25)	5.7 (1.69)	9.5 (1.15)	11.1 (1.64)	13.5 (3.15)	14.8 (1.94)
Relative care	10.8 (0.70)	10.0 (0.75)	14.2 (2.82)	14.7 (1.86)	‡	‡	11.8 (1.94)	12.3 (1.59)	9.7 (0.93)	11.6 (2.61)	12.1 (0.94)	12.1 (1.87)	10.6 (2.74)	7.1 (1.20)
Multiple arrangements[6]	1.4 ! (0.48)	1.4 ! (0.48)	‡	‡	‡	‡	‡	0.8 ! (0.38)	1.2 (0.33)	‡	2.2 ! (0.93)	‡	‡	1.7 ! (0.60)
2001														
Percent of all children	100.0 (†)	62.6 (0.89)	14.5 (0.82)	17.1 (0.73)	2.2 (0.41)	3.7 (0.47)	23.6 (1.26)	20.6 (1.15)	55.8 (1.21)	10.2 (0.67)	32.7 (1.44)	23.8 (1.23)	7.0 (0.66)	26.3 (1.20)
Percent in all types of care	100.0 (†)	100.0 (†)	100.0 (†)	100.0 (†)	100.0 (†)	100.0 (†)	100.0 (†)	100.0 (†)	100.0 (†)	100.0 (†)	100.0 (†)	100.0 (†)	100.0 (†)	100.0 (†)
Parental care only	20.5 (1.00)	20.3 (1.32)	10.6 (2.45)	31.6 (2.35)	22.6 ! (7.97)	10.7 ! (4.34)	25.1 (2.69)	30.0 (2.60)	15.1 (1.35)	35.0 (3.90)	25.0 (2.28)	17.3 (1.98)	14.0 (3.86)	13.3 (1.94)
Nonparental care	79.5 (1.00)	79.7 (1.32)	89.4 (2.45)	68.4 (2.35)	77.4 (7.97)	89.3 (4.34)	74.9 (2.69)	70.0 (2.60)	84.9 (1.35)	65.0 (3.90)	75.0 (2.28)	82.7 (1.98)	86.0 (3.86)	86.7 (1.94)
Primary arrangement[4]														
Center-based care[5]	56.2 (1.17)	57.3 (1.48)	63.4 (3.66)	44.1 (2.42)	59.6 (9.47)	62.4 (6.73)	47.4 (3.00)	50.8 (2.33)	61.9 (1.74)	42.6 (3.71)	49.5 (2.64)	59.3 (2.74)	68.0 (4.03)	66.0 (2.68)
Nonrelative care	9.6 (0.72)	11.5 (1.03)	4.3 ! (1.70)	8.4 (1.59)	12.6 ! (5.47)	8.5 ! (3.71)	5.2 (1.17)	8.3 (1.48)	12.0 (1.07)	7.0 (1.92)	8.6 (1.39)	8.3 (1.40)	9.7 ! (3.03)	13.1 (1.67)
Relative care	12.1 (0.95)	10.1 (0.99)	17.4 (3.64)	13.8 (1.98)	‡	17.0 ! (5.95)	19.5 (3.28)	8.7 (2.02)	10.2 (0.95)	12.5 (3.10)	15.5 (2.02)	12.5 (1.79)	7.8 (2.32)	6.7 (1.26)
Multiple arrangements[6]	1.6 (0.40)	0.7 ! (0.32)	‡	2.1 ! (0.76)	‡	‡	2.9 ! (1.31)	‡	0.8 ! (0.24)	‡	1.3 ! (0.61)	2.6 ! (1.27)	‡	0.9 ! (0.40)
2005														
Percent of all children	100.0 (†)	57.9 (1.14)	14.1 (1.02)	19.1 (0.94)	3.2 (0.58)	5.7 (0.65)	22.2 (1.15)	25.9 (1.48)	51.9 (1.42)	9.3 (0.89)	31.6 (1.61)	20.7 (1.44)	7.4 (0.68)	31.1 (1.25)
Percent in all types of care	100.0 (†)	100.0 (†)	100.0 (†)	100.0 (†)	100.0 (†)	100.0 (†)	100.0 (†)	100.0 (†)	100.0 (†)	100.0 (†)	100.0 (†)	100.0 (†)	100.0 (†)	100.0 (†)
Parental care only	21.1 (1.37)	19.3 (1.69)	13.8 (3.72)	32.6 (2.91)	14.7 ! (5.84)	21.2 (6.06)	25.8 (3.40)	29.7 (2.77)	14.7 (1.60)	36.2 (4.03)	27.4 (3.35)	22.5 (2.94)	14.7 (3.87)	11.2 (1.57)
Nonparental care	78.9 (1.37)	80.7 (1.69)	86.2 (3.72)	67.4 (2.91)	85.3 (5.84)	78.8 (6.06)	74.2 (3.40)	70.3 (2.77)	85.3 (1.60)	63.8 (4.03)	72.6 (3.35)	77.5 (2.94)	85.3 (3.87)	88.8 (1.57)
Primary arrangement[4]														
Center-based care[5]	59.2 (1.34)	60.2 (1.86)	66.1 (4.75)	49.7 (3.00)	70.2 (8.60)	57.5 (6.98)	51.8 (3.98)	48.4 (3.21)	67.7 (1.96)	50.6 (3.84)	48.4 (3.15)	57.1 (3.02)	65.7 (5.07)	72.4 (2.17)
Nonrelative care	5.5 (0.89)	7.3 (1.29)	2.6 ! (1.14)	3.2 (0.80)	3.6 ! (1.70)	2.8 ! (1.32)	4.7 ! (2.14)	3.0 (0.75)	7.1 (1.26)	‡	5.2 ! (1.64)	5.1 (1.48)	9.5 (2.63)	6.1 (1.52)
Relative care	12.0 (1.16)	10.7 (1.20)	15.7 ! (4.72)	13.6 (2.22)	‡	12.0 ! (4.59)	16.0 (3.18)	15.1 (2.98)	8.8 (1.12)	9.6 ! (3.27)	15.9 (2.42)	13.9 (2.62)	6.5 ! (2.68)	8.8 (1.52)
Multiple arrangements[6]	2.2 (0.44)	2.4 (0.51)	1.8 ! (0.86)	0.9 ! (0.40)	‡	‡	‡	3.8 (1.07)	1.7 (0.38)	‡	3.0 ! (0.94)	1.5 ! (0.66)	3.5 ! (1.73)	1.5 (0.44)
2012														
Percent of all children	100.0 (†)	50.6 (1.50)	14.6 (1.05)	23.9 (1.26)	5.2 (0.55)	5.7 (0.68)	22.9 (1.22)	23.6 (1.28)	53.5 (1.30)	16.9 (1.44)	21.3 (1.17)	21.8 (1.28)	8.1 (0.84)	31.9 (1.16)
Percent in all types of care	100.0 (†)	100.0 (†)	100.0 (†)	100.0 (†)	100.0 (†)	100.0 (†)	100.0 (†)	100.0 (†)	100.0 (†)	100.0 (†)	100.0 (†)	100.0 (†)	100.0 (†)	100.0 (†)
Parental care only	19.5 (1.43)	18.5 (1.83)	15.3 (3.50)	24.3 (3.38)	19.4 (5.00)	18.9 (5.51)	29.0 (2.87)	23.9 (2.66)	13.5 (1.96)	35.1 (5.53)	23.5 (3.23)	22.0 (2.23)	15.0 (3.11)	7.7 (1.12)
Nonparental care	80.5 (1.43)	81.5 (1.83)	84.7 (3.50)	75.7 (3.38)	80.6 (5.00)	81.1 (5.51)	71.0 (2.87)	76.1 (2.66)	86.5 (1.96)	64.9 (5.53)	76.5 (3.23)	78.0 (2.23)	85.0 (3.11)	92.3 (1.12)
Primary arrangement[4]														
Center-based care[5]	58.4 (1.32)	58.5 (1.82)	65.3 (4.10)	52.9 (3.60)	67.0 (5.41)	55.6 (6.52)	49.4 (3.05)	51.4 (3.04)	65.4 (1.88)	45.9 (5.65)	51.9 (3.68)	54.2 (2.93)	63.4 (4.02)	71.1 (1.88)
Nonrelative care	7.2 (0.72)	9.7 (1.19)	2.4 ! (0.93)	5.5 (1.47)	10.2 ! (3.64)	‡	5.2 (1.67)	5.9 (1.46)	8.6 (1.04)	‡	7.9 (1.98)	6.4 (1.33)	7.3 ! (2.24)	9.8 (1.36)
Relative care	13.0 (0.96)	11.3 (1.14)	16.3 (3.17)	14.4 (2.36)	‡	15.4 ! (4.69)	14.9 (2.19)	15.6 (2.78)	11.0 (1.37)	12.3 ! (3.01)	16.4 (2.63)	15.2 (2.26)	9.7 (2.45)	9.3 (1.35)
Multiple arrangements[6]	1.9 (0.33)	1.9 (0.44)	‡	2.9 ! (1.04)	‡	‡	1.5 ! (0.54)	3.2 ! (1.09)	1.5 (0.37)	‡	‡	2.2 (0.61)	4.6 ! (1.72)	2.2 (0.63)

†Not applicable.
!Interpret data with caution. The coefficient of variation (CV) for this estimate is between 30 and 50 percent.
‡Reporting standards not met. Either there are too few cases for a reliable estimate or the coefficient of variation (CV) is 50 percent or greater.
[1]Poor children are those whose family incomes were below the Census Bureau's poverty threshold in the year prior to data collection; near-poor children are those whose family incomes ranged from the poverty threshold to 199 percent of the poverty threshold; and nonpoor children are those whose family incomes were at or above 200 percent of the poverty threshold. The poverty threshold is a dollar amount that varies depending on a family's size and composition and is updated annually to account for inflation. In 2011, for example, the poverty threshold for a family of four with two children was $22,811. Survey respondents are asked to select the poverty status range within which their income falls, rather than giving the exact amount of their income; therefore, the measure of poverty status is an approximation.
[2]Excludes children living in households with no mother or female guardian present.
[3]Includes persons of all other races and Two or more races.

[4]A child's primary arrangement is the regular nonparental care arrangement or early childhood education program in which the child spent the most time per week.
[5]Center-based arrangements include day care centers, Head Start programs, preschools, prekindergartens, and other early childhood programs.
[6]Refers to children who spent an equal number of hours per week in multiple nonparental care arrangements
NOTE: While National Household Education Surveys Program (NHES) administrations prior to 2012 were administered via telephone with an interviewer, NHES:2012 used self-administered paper-and-pencil questionnaires that were mailed to respondents. Measurable differences in estimates between 2012 and prior years could reflect actual changes in the population, or the changes could be due to the mode change from telephone to mail. Race categories exclude persons of Hispanic ethnicity. Detail may not sum to totals because of rounding.
SOURCE: U.S. Department of Education, National Center for Education Statistics, Early Childhood Program Participation Survey of the National Household Education Surveys Program (ECPP-NHES:1995, 2001, 2005, and 2012). (This table was prepared November 2014.)

Table 202.40. Child care arrangements of 3- to 5-year-old children who are not yet in kindergarten, by age and race/ethnicity: Selected years, 1991 through 2012

[Standard errors appear in parentheses]

Year and child care arrangement	Total	Age			Race/ethnicity				
		3 years old	4 years old	5 years old	White	Black	Hispanic	Asian/Pacific Islander	Other[1]
1	2	3	4	5	6	7	8	9	10
1991									
All 3- to 5-year-olds									
In thousands	8,402 (40.9)	3,733 (7.1)	3,627 (14.6)	1,042 (38.6)	5,850 (59.9)	1,236 (41.0)	999 (31.3)	147 (19.0)	170 (29.9)
Percent	100.0 (†)	44.4 (0.21)	43.2 (0.24)	12.4 (0.40)	69.6 (0.67)	14.7 (0.47)	11.9 (0.37)	1.7 (0.23)	2.0 (0.35)
Percent in nonparental arrangements[2]	69.0 (0.80)	62.2 (1.19)	74.0 (1.05)	75.7 (2.10)	69.4 (0.87)	75.2 (2.02)	59.3 (2.35)	73.5 (4.94)	61.7 (6.08)
Relative care	16.9 (0.60)	16.2 (0.72)	18.0 (0.85)	15.6 (1.34)	14.8 (0.66)	24.1 (2.09)	19.6 (2.08)	22.5 (4.03)	16.6 ! (6.52)
Nonrelative care	14.8 (0.56)	14.8 (0.76)	14.7 (0.79)	14.9 (1.81)	17.3 (0.76)	7.9 (1.20)	9.4 (1.27)	11.2 (3.19)	12.9 (3.60)
Center-based programs[3]	52.8 (0.89)	42.3 (1.44)	60.4 (1.04)	63.9 (2.12)	54.0 (0.95)	58.3 (2.49)	38.8 (2.20)	56.4 (5.76)	49.9 (6.09)
Percent with parental care only	31.0 (0.80)	37.8 (1.19)	26.0 (1.05)	24.3 (2.10)	30.6 (0.87)	24.8 (2.02)	40.7 (2.35)	26.5 (4.94)	38.3 (6.08)
1995									
All 3- to 5-year-olds									
In thousands	9,222 (52.9)	4,123 (8.3)	4,061 (12.5)	1,038 (48.3)	6,334 (94.0)	1,389 (56.1)	1,042 (38.8)	208 (25.0)	249 (31.0)
Percent	100.0 (†)	44.7 (0.25)	44.0 (0.24)	11.3 (0.46)	68.7 (0.94)	15.1 (0.60)	11.3 (0.42)	2.3 (0.27)	2.7 (0.34)
Percent in nonparental arrangements[2]	74.1 (1.01)	68.0 (1.95)	77.9 (1.24)	83.8 (1.78)	74.8 (1.39)	80.1 (2.50)	61.6 (2.33)	80.1 (4.78)	72.2 (5.53)
Relative care	19.4 (0.64)	21.4 (1.23)	18.4 (0.95)	15.2 (2.14)	16.5 (0.84)	28.7 (2.78)	22.8 (2.01)	24.3 (5.61)	21.2 (4.73)
Nonrelative care	16.9 (0.84)	18.5 (1.35)	15.3 (1.03)	17.2 (2.19)	19.4 (1.04)	11.3 (1.65)	12.5 (1.64)	8.8 ! (3.96)	11.8 (3.40)
Center-based programs[3]	55.1 (0.97)	40.7 (1.55)	64.8 (1.45)	74.5 (2.35)	56.9 (1.44)	59.8 (3.19)	37.4 (2.15)	59.4 (6.51)	54.5 (6.96)
Percent with parental care only	25.9 (1.01)	32.0 (1.95)	22.1 (1.24)	16.2 (1.78)	25.2 (1.39)	19.9 (2.50)	38.4 (2.33)	19.9 (4.78)	27.8 (5.53)
1999									
All 3- to 5-year-olds									
In thousands	8,518 (139.7)	3,809 (79.1)	3,703 (79.9)	1,006 (54.2)	5,384 (77.4)	1,214 (59.2)	1,376 (52.3)	204 (25.5)	341 (33.5)
Percent	100.0 (†)	44.7 (0.93)	43.5 (0.93)	11.8 (0.64)	63.2 (0.91)	14.2 (0.69)	16.2 (0.61)	2.4 (0.30)	4.0 (0.39)
Percent in nonparental arrangements[2]	76.9 (0.72)	69.2 (1.42)	82.3 (0.99)	86.5 (1.78)	76.8 (0.91)	86.3 (1.97)	66.6 (2.04)	84.0 (5.25)	83.0 (4.28)
Relative care	22.8 (0.77)	24.3 (1.28)	22.0 (1.14)	20.2 (2.06)	18.7 (0.90)	33.4 (2.58)	26.5 (1.86)	22.5 ! (6.85)	34.4 (4.81)
Nonrelative care	16.1 (0.67)	16.3 (1.02)	15.9 (1.07)	16.1 (2.08)	19.4 (0.88)	7.4 (1.37)	12.7 (1.29)	9.1 ! (3.95)	11.2 (2.22)
Center-based programs[3]	59.7 (0.63)	45.7 (1.28)	69.6 (1.19)	76.5 (2.40)	60.0 (0.81)	73.2 (2.40)	44.2 (2.19)	61.1 (7.05)	68.9 (5.19)
Percent with parental care only	23.1 (0.72)	30.8 (1.42)	17.7 (0.99)	13.5 (1.78)	23.2 (0.91)	13.7 (1.97)	33.4 (2.04)	16.0 ! (5.25)	17.0 (4.28)
2001									
All 3- to 5-year-olds									
In thousands	8,551 (11.0)	3,795 (91.4)	3,861 (89.0)	896 (47.0)	5,313 (68.0)	1,251 (55.1)	1,506 (43.5)	202 (29.0)	280 (28.2)
Percent	100.0 (†)	44.4 (1.06)	45.1 (1.04)	10.5 (0.55)	62.1 (0.79)	14.6 (0.64)	17.6 (0.51)	2.4 (0.34)	3.3 (0.33)
Percent in nonparental arrangements[2]	73.9 (0.67)	66.2 (1.29)	79.6 (1.11)	82.0 (2.49)	74.7 (0.99)	84.9 (2.22)	61.0 (2.03)	69.9 (7.18)	80.9 (4.11)
Relative care	22.8 (0.89)	23.6 (1.39)	22.5 (1.33)	20.9 (2.66)	19.6 (1.01)	36.7 (3.42)	22.8 (1.89)	19.6 (4.68)	25.2 (5.16)
Nonrelative care	14.0 (0.65)	14.7 (1.17)	13.6 (0.95)	13.1 (2.13)	16.5 (0.98)	8.5 (1.65)	11.3 (1.43)	‡ (†)	14.0 (4.09)
Center-based programs[3]	56.4 (0.55)	42.8 (1.21)	65.9 (1.25)	73.0 (2.69)	59.1 (0.89)	63.1 (2.93)	39.9 (1.86)	63.4 (7.13)	60.6 (4.85)
Percent with parental care only	26.1 (0.67)	33.8 (1.29)	20.4 (1.11)	18.0 (2.49)	25.3 (0.99)	15.1 (2.22)	39.0 (2.03)	30.1 (7.18)	19.1 (4.11)
2005									
All 3- to 5-year-olds									
In thousands	9,066 (9.0)	4,070 (93.0)	3,873 (92.0)	1,123 (67.3)	5,177 (80.2)	1,233 (57.1)	1,822 (50.0)	282 (31.7)	552 (48.3)
Percent	100.0 (†)	44.9 (1.03)	42.7 (1.01)	12.4 (0.74)	57.1 (0.89)	13.6 (0.63)	20.1 (0.56)	3.1 (0.35)	6.1 (0.53)
Percent in nonparental arrangements[2]	73.7 (0.92)	66.6 (1.48)	79.4 (1.42)	79.6 (3.15)	75.9 (1.22)	80.5 (2.85)	62.0 (2.10)	79.8 (4.41)	72.9 (4.62)
Relative care	22.6 (1.02)	24.0 (1.44)	20.8 (1.56)	23.8 (3.17)	21.4 (1.34)	25.0 (3.42)	22.6 (1.79)	15.9 (4.68)	31.7 (4.49)
Nonrelative care	11.6 (0.73)	14.4 (1.12)	9.2 (1.03)	9.9 (2.00)	15.0 (1.13)	5.2 (1.31)	8.1 (1.36)	7.0 ! (3.34)	8.7 (2.41)
Center-based programs[3]	57.2 (0.83)	42.5 (1.67)	69.2 (1.36)	68.7 (3.51)	59.1 (1.32)	66.5 (3.41)	43.4 (2.10)	72.5 (4.99)	55.9 (4.89)
Percent with parental care only	26.3 (0.92)	33.4 (1.48)	20.6 (1.42)	20.4 (3.15)	24.1 (1.22)	19.5 (2.85)	38.0 (2.10)	20.2 (4.41)	27.1 (4.62)
2012									
All 3- to 5-year-olds									
In thousands	8,244 (85.1)	3,674 (89.8)	3,508 (90.4)	1,062 (59.6)	4,062 (97.4)	1,154 (63.4)	2,100 (76.1)	423 (32.7)	505 (44.4)
Percent	100.0 (†)	44.6 (0.97)	42.5 (1.01)	12.9 (0.72)	49.3 (1.12)	14.0 (0.75)	25.5 (0.84)	5.1 (0.38)	6.1 (0.55)
Percent in nonparental arrangements[2]	77.9 (1.02)	72.7 (1.32)	81.8 (1.62)	83.1 (2.32)	78.7 (1.41)	83.5 (2.97)	73.7 (2.24)	79.5 (3.76)	74.8 (4.21)
Relative care	26.2 (0.98)	27.9 (1.45)	25.1 (1.44)	24.6 (2.72)	24.0 (1.17)	30.2 (3.23)	29.3 (2.12)	21.7 (3.50)	26.6 (3.92)
Nonrelative care	13.3 (0.75)	15.4 (1.09)	11.0 (0.88)	13.9 (2.41)	16.1 (1.20)	11.4 (2.18)	10.8 (1.16)	5.9 (1.57)	12.1 (2.77)
Center-based programs[3]	60.6 (1.05)	48.8 (1.47)	70.6 (1.57)	68.3 (3.48)	63.0 (1.54)	68.0 (3.10)	51.5 (2.12)	67.8 (3.98)	55.5 (4.57)
Percent with parental care only	22.1 (1.02)	27.3 (1.32)	18.2 (1.62)	16.9 (2.32)	21.3 (1.41)	16.5 (2.97)	26.3 (2.24)	20.5 (3.76)	25.2 (4.21)

†Not applicable.
!Interpret data with caution. The coefficient of variation (CV) for this estimate is between 30 and 50 percent.
‡Reporting standards not met. The coefficient of variation (CV) for this estimate is 50 percent or greater.
[1]Includes persons of all other races and Two or more races.
[2]The total percentage of children who participated in nonparental arrangements. Counts each child only once, even if the child participated in more than one type of nonparental care.
[3]Center-based programs include day care centers, nursery schools, prekindergartens, preschools, and Head Start programs.
NOTE: While National Household Education Surveys Program (NHES) administrations prior to 2012 were administered via telephone with an interviewer, NHES:2012 used self-administered paper-and-pencil questionnaires that were mailed to respondents. Measurable differences in estimates between 2012 and prior years could reflect actual changes in the population, or the changes could be due to the mode change from telephone to mail. Race categories exclude persons of Hispanic ethnicity. Detail may not sum to totals because of rounding.
SOURCE: U.S. Department of Education, National Center for Education Statistics, Early Childhood Education Survey, Parent Survey, and Early Childhood Program Participation Survey of the National Household Education Surveys Program (ECE-NHES:1991; Parent-NHES:1999; ECPP-NHES:1995, 2001, 2005, and 2012). (This table was prepared September 2014.)

Table 202.50. Percentage distribution of children at about 2 and 4 years of age, by type of child care arrangement and selected child and family characteristics: 2003–04 and 2005–06

[Standard errors appear in parentheses]

Selected child and family characteristics	Children at about 2 years of age in 2003–04						Children at about 4 years of age in 2005–06							
	Percentage distribution of children[1]	No regular nonparental care	Home-based care		Center-based care[5]	Multiple arrangements[6]	Percentage distribution of children[7]	No regular nonparental care	Home-based care		Center-based care[5]			Multiple arrangements[6]
			Relative care[3]	Nonrelative care[4]					Relative care[3]	Nonrelative care[4]	Total	Head Start	Other than Head Start	
1	2	3	4	5	6	7	8	9	10	11	12	13	14	15
Total	100.0 (†)	50.5 (0.74)	18.5 (0.62)	14.6 (0.51)	15.8 (0.50)	0.5 (0.10)	100.0 (†)	20.0 (0.65)	13.1 (0.61)	7.6 (0.32)	57.4 (0.81)	12.6 (0.64)	44.8 (0.71)	1.9 (0.21)
Sex of child														
Male	51.2 (0.08)	50.0 (0.96)	19.1 (0.79)	14.3 (0.61)	16.3 (0.65)	0.3 (0.07)	51.2 (0.11)	19.3 (0.80)	13.1 (0.79)	7.5 (0.51)	58.0 (0.98)	12.9 (0.80)	45.1 (1.02)	2.1 (0.33)
Female	48.8 (0.08)	51.1 (1.01)	18.0 (0.78)	14.9 (0.71)	15.2 (0.63)	0.8 (0.19)	48.8 (0.11)	20.7 (0.90)	13.2 (0.86)	7.7 (0.52)	56.8 (1.02)	12.4 (0.74)	44.4 (0.92)	1.7 (0.20)
Race/ethnicity of child														
White	53.6 (0.54)	50.8 (1.08)	14.9 (0.88)	17.0 (0.74)	16.9 (0.74)	0.5 (0.13)	53.8 (0.59)	17.9 (0.98)	11.0 (0.74)	9.2 (0.49)	60.0 (1.04)	6.8 (0.61)	53.3 (1.00)	1.8 (0.28)
Black	13.7 (0.24)	37.3 (1.39)	25.8 (1.51)	12.0 (1.30)	24.2 (1.15)	0.8 ! (0.24)	13.8 (0.26)	16.3 (1.38)	13.9 (1.49)	4.4 (0.73)	62.1 (2.08)	25.1 (1.98)	37.0 (1.83)	3.3 (0.65)
Hispanic	25.3 (0.37)	57.5 (1.39)	21.4 (1.14)	11.5 (0.94)	9.2 (0.94)	‡ (†)	25.1 (0.42)	27.3 (1.36)	15.9 (1.14)	6.2 (0.78)	49.3 (1.57)	18.6 (1.23)	30.7 (1.64)	1.2 (0.29)
Asian	2.7 (0.09)	55.3 (2.17)	23.8 (1.44)	10.8 (1.05)	9.6 (1.39)	‡ (†)	2.6 (0.09)	17.1 (1.71)	16.1 (1.44)	3.6 (0.70)	60.9 (2.02)	5.5 (0.90)	55.3 (2.12)	2.3 ! (1.05)
Pacific Islander	0.2 (0.04)	73.2 (9.89)	23.8 ! (9.95)	‡ (†)	‡ (†)	‡ (†)	0.2 (0.05)	22.3 ! (6.82)	45.0 ! (14.27)	‡ (†)	19.9 ! (7.94)	‡ (†)	14.9 ! (6.47)	‡ (†)
American Indian/Alaska Native	0.5 (0.06)	57.3 (3.16)	17.4 (3.10)	11.6 ! (3.85)	13.8 (2.72)	‡ (†)	0.5 (0.05)	19.9 (2.40)	14.0 (2.60)	5.2 ! (1.45)	59.7 (3.57)	31.0 (4.71)	28.7 (5.61)	‡ (†)
Two or more races	4.0 (0.28)	46.3 (2.87)	20.0 (1.71)	13.2 (2.23)	19.3 (2.18)	‡ (†)	4.0 (0.28)	17.9 (2.14)	17.6 (2.43)	9.1 (2.16)	53.6 (3.47)	11.1 (2.35)	42.5 (3.22)	1.8 ! (0.86)
Age of child														
22 or fewer months	1.9 (0.29)	58.6 (4.73)	21.0 (4.62)	11.0 ! (3.41)	9.4 (2.77)	‡ (†)	‡	‡	‡	‡	‡	‡	‡	‡
23 months	38.3 (1.22)	54.1 (1.16)	17.0 (0.93)	13.6 (0.91)	14.5 (0.85)	0.7 (0.16)	‡	‡	‡	‡	‡	‡	‡	‡
24 months	38.0 (0.89)	49.1 (1.02)	18.5 (0.95)	15.6 (0.80)	16.6 (0.87)	0.2 ! (0.10)	‡	‡	‡	‡	‡	‡	‡	‡
25 months	12.4 (0.46)	44.9 (1.91)	23.1 (1.44)	14.7 (1.41)	16.8 (1.44)	‡ (†)	‡	‡	‡	‡	‡	‡	‡	‡
26 or more months	9.4 (0.60)	47.7 (2.37)	18.6 (1.82)	14.8 (1.39)	17.9 (1.60)	1.1 ! (0.54)	‡	‡	‡	‡	‡	‡	‡	‡
Less than 48 months	‡	‡	‡	‡	‡	‡	16.4 (0.57)	27.3 (1.63)	13.9 (1.48)	8.7 (0.95)	47.9 (1.77)	10.6 (1.25)	37.3 (1.91)	2.2 (0.55)
48 to 52 months	‡	‡	‡	‡	‡	‡	38.1 (0.55)	19.9 (1.01)	13.0 (0.87)	8.3 (0.60)	56.8 (1.29)	12.0 (0.79)	44.8 (1.31)	2.0 (0.37)
53 to 57 months	‡	‡	‡	‡	‡	‡	36.5 (0.57)	16.5 (0.93)	13.1 (0.83)	6.7 (0.52)	62.2 (1.33)	14.4 (1.01)	47.8 (1.23)	1.5 (0.25)
58 or more months	‡	‡	‡	‡	‡	‡	9.0 (0.41)	21.1 (1.98)	12.1 (1.66)	6.4 (1.09)	57.8 (2.80)	12.0 (1.70)	45.8 (2.50)	2.7 (0.75)
Mother's employment status[8]														
Employed full-time	34.7 (0.73)	15.7 (0.89)	30.4 (1.10)	26.0 (0.86)	27.1 (0.96)	0.8 (0.21)	34.7 (0.77)	11.3 (0.96)	16.2 (0.91)	12.1 (0.77)	58.7 (1.56)	11.5 (1.03)	47.2 (1.29)	1.7 (0.27)
Employed part-time	20.2 (0.62)	35.4 (1.53)	26.4 (1.53)	20.5 (1.37)	16.7 (1.23)	1.0 ! (0.34)	20.3 (0.63)	16.4 (1.33)	14.1 (1.20)	9.1 (0.86)	57.3 (1.70)	8.7 (1.00)	48.6 (1.65)	3.1 (0.57)
Looking for work	6.3 (0.35)	71.1 (2.30)	11.5 (1.58)	3.8 (0.95)	13.4 (2.02)	‡ (†)	6.3 (0.36)	22.3 (2.33)	18.5 (2.33)	5.4 (1.23)	52.4 (2.83)	25.9 (2.87)	26.5 (2.33)	1.4 ! (0.56)
Not in labor force	38.4 (0.78)	86.8 (0.75)	4.8 (0.48)	3.0 (0.35)	5.4 (0.46)	‡ (†)	38.3 (0.81)	29.4 (0.97)	8.6 (0.63)	3.3 (0.38)	57.1 (0.96)	13.7 (0.80)	43.5 (1.10)	1.6 (0.32)
No mother in household	0.4 (0.09)	21.2 ! (7.28)	33.5 (8.60)	19.5 ! (9.29)	25.9 ! (8.01)	‡ (†)	0.4 (0.10)	11.0 ! (6.13)	36.2 (9.59)	‡ (†)	52.5 (9.42)	21.0 ! (8.49)	31.5 (8.19)	‡ (†)
Parents' highest level of education														
Less than high school	12.8 (0.36)	67.6 (1.98)	17.5 (1.45)	6.8 (1.08)	7.7 (0.99)	‡ (†)	10.5 (0.36)	34.2 (2.10)	16.4 (1.77)	3.7 (1.04)	43.5 (2.59)	22.4 (2.13)	21.1 (2.06)	2.1 ! (0.80)
High school completion	25.7 (0.46)	50.1 (1.47)	23.1 (1.27)	12.3 (0.97)	14.1 (0.87)	0.4 ! (0.15)	23.1 (0.57)	22.0 (1.24)	17.0 (1.20)	6.9 (0.69)	52.1 (1.87)	21.6 (1.41)	30.6 (1.49)	1.9 (0.34)
Some college/vocational	29.7 (0.48)	46.9 (1.51)	21.6 (1.22)	15.1 (0.92)	15.7 (0.94)	0.7 ! (0.21)	33.4 (0.64)	21.0 (1.24)	15.2 (0.95)	7.1 (0.56)	54.9 (1.41)	13.3 (0.99)	41.6 (1.26)	1.8 (0.33)
Bachelor's degree	16.9 (0.46)	48.6 (1.14)	14.4 (1.18)	17.8 (1.18)	18.6 (1.14)	0.7 ! (0.23)	16.8 (0.45)	16.0 (1.57)	8.4 (1.02)	8.2 (0.93)	65.6 (1.88)	3.2 (0.75)	62.4 (2.00)	1.8 (0.48)
Any graduate education	14.9 (0.35)	46.0 (1.91)	10.5 (1.05)	20.7 (1.57)	22.4 (1.49)	0.4 ! (0.16)	16.2 (0.37)	9.7 (0.83)	6.2 (0.90)	11.3 (1.16)	70.8 (1.57)	2.0 (0.52)	68.8 (1.67)	2.0 (0.52)
Poverty status[9]														
Below poverty threshold	23.9 (0.75)	61.8 (1.40)	18.0 (1.15)	7.8 (0.79)	11.7 (0.92)	0.7 ! (0.24)	24.8 (0.64)	27.5 (1.27)	15.1 (1.19)	4.4 (0.54)	51.0 (1.61)	26.3 (1.45)	24.7 (1.20)	2.0 (0.40)
At or above poverty threshold	76.1 (0.75)	47.0 (0.90)	18.7 (0.68)	16.7 (0.62)	17.1 (0.60)	0.5 (0.11)	75.2 (0.64)	17.5 (0.71)	12.5 (0.64)	8.6 (0.39)	59.5 (0.86)	8.1 (0.57)	51.4 (0.65)	1.9 (0.22)
Socioeconomic status[10]														
Lowest 20 percent	20.0 (0.48)	66.7 (1.43)	17.2 (1.20)	6.8 (0.75)	8.9 (0.72)	0.4 ! (0.18)	20.0 (0.52)	30.5 (1.31)	14.9 (1.33)	5.0 (0.69)	47.2 (1.84)	24.9 (1.58)	22.4 (1.47)	2.3 (0.58)
Middle 60 percent	60.0 (0.67)	46.8 (0.98)	21.8 (0.78)	15.1 (0.63)	15.8 (0.58)	0.6 (0.15)	60.0 (0.67)	19.7 (0.86)	15.1 (0.82)	7.4 (0.49)	56.0 (1.09)	12.4 (0.80)	43.6 (0.90)	1.8 (0.23)
Highest 20 percent	20.0 (0.48)	45.9 (1.75)	10.2 (0.85)	20.8 (1.52)	22.6 (1.45)	0.5 ! (0.21)	20.0 (0.47)	10.4 (0.93)	5.4 (0.73)	10.7 (0.91)	71.6 (1.39)	1.0 (0.23)	70.5 (1.42)	1.9 (0.42)

†Not applicable.

!Interpret data with caution. The coefficient of variation (CV) for this estimate is between 30 and 50 percent.

‡Reporting standards not met. Either there are too few cases for a reliable estimate or the coefficient of variation (CV) is 50 percent or greater.

[1]Distribution of weighted Early Childhood Longitudinal Study, Birth Cohort survey population with data on primary care arrangements.

[2]Primary type of care arrangement is the type of nonparental care in which the child spent the most hours.

[3]Care provided in the child's home or in another home by a relative (excluding parents).

[4]Care provided in the child's home or in another private home by a person unrelated to the child.

[5]Care provided in places such as early learning centers, nursery schools, and preschools.

[6]Children who spent an equal amount of time in each of two or more arrangements.

[7]Distribution of weighted Early Childhood Longitudinal Study, Birth Cohort survey population between 44 and 65 months of age with data on primary care arrangements.

[8]Mothers who reported working at least 35 hours per week are defined as employed full time, while those who reported working less than 35 hours per week are defined as employed part time. Those neither employed nor looking for work are not in the labor force.

[9]Poverty status based on Census Bureau guidelines from 2002 (for 2-year-olds in 2003–04) and 2005 (for 4-year-olds in 2005–06), which identify a dollar amount determined to meet a household's needs, given its size and composition. In 2002, a family of four was considered to live below the poverty threshold if its income was less than or equal to $18,392 (in current dollars).

[10]Socioeconomic status (SES) was measured by a composite score on parental education and occupations, and family income.

NOTE: Data are based on a representative sample of children born in 2001. Estimates for children at about 2 years of age weighted by W1R0. Estimates for children at about 4 years of age weighted by W3R0. Race categories exclude persons of Hispanic ethnicity. Detail may not sum to totals because of rounding and suppression of cells that do not meet standards. Some data have been revised from previously published figures.

SOURCE: U.S. Department of Education, National Center for Education Statistics, Early Childhood Longitudinal Study, Birth Cohort, 9-month–Kindergarten Restricted-Use Data File and Electronic Codebook. (This table was prepared December 2010.)

Table 202.60. Percentage distribution of quality rating of child care arrangements of children at about 4 years of age, by type of arrangement and selected child and family characteristics: 2005–06

Selected child and family characteristics	Quality rating of primary type of child care arrangement[1]											
	Home-based relative and nonrelative care[2,3]			Head Start and other center-based programs[4]			All center-based programs					
							Head Start[4]			Center-based care other than Head Start[4,5]		
	Low	Medium	High	Low	Medium	High	Low	Medium	High	Low	Medium	High
1	2	3	4	5	6	7	8	9	10	11	12	13
Total	42.6 (4.01)	47.9 (4.22)	9.5 (2.37)	9.5 (1.40)	55.9 (2.44)	34.6 (2.58)	3.2 (0.78)	56.7 (3.27)	40.1 (3.34)	11.6 (1.74)	55.6 (3.05)	32.8 (3.10)
Sex of child												
Male	45.5 (5.48)	44.1 (5.58)	10.4 ! (3.88)	6.3 (1.47)	53.5 (3.35)	40.2 (3.29)	2.2 ! (0.97)	56.5 (3.94)	41.2 (3.95)	7.7 (1.82)	52.4 (4.07)	39.8 (4.08)
Female	39.3 (5.23)	52.2 (5.83)	8.5 (2.45)	12.7 (2.32)	58.2 (3.33)	29.1 (3.24)	4.3 (1.14)	56.8 (4.83)	38.9 (4.88)	15.2 (2.84)	58.7 (3.98)	26.2 (3.71)
Race/ethnicity of child												
White	29.9 (4.72)	55.3 (5.34)	14.9 (4.09)	9.3 (1.79)	54.7 (3.77)	36.0 (3.69)	4.0 ! (1.93)	47.5 (8.27)	48.5 (8.29)	10.2 (1.95)	55.8 (4.01)	34.0 (3.84)
Black	52.8 (8.64)	47.2 (8.64)	‡	14.8 ! (3.75)	59.9 (4.55)	25.3 (3.91)	6.9 (1.60)	67.0 (4.49)	26.1 (4.70)	20.8 (6.22)	54.6 (6.76)	24.6 (4.24)
Hispanic	62.5 (8.53)	33.4 (8.03)	‡	7.2 ! (2.79)	52.9 (4.25)	39.8 (4.77)	‡	56.2 (5.54)	43.4 (5.47)	11.7 ! (4.47)	50.8 (6.82)	37.6 (7.31)
Asian	‡	‡	‡	‡	61.7 (8.22)	32.8 (8.15)	‡	‡	‡	‡	64.8 (8.25)	29.3 (8.02)
Pacific Islander	‡	‡	‡	‡	‡	‡	‡	‡	‡	‡	‡	‡
American Indian/Alaska Native	‡	‡	‡	‡	73.5 (7.69)	23.5 (7.02)	‡	59.7 (10.79)	40.3 (10.79)	‡	68.4 (8.83)	19.7 ! (6.84)
Two or more races	‡	‡	‡	‡	66.0 (7.63)	25.5 (6.61)	‡	‡	‡	‡	‡	‡
Age of child												
Less than 48 months	31.8 (7.35)	64.3 (7.24)	‡	9.8 (2.35)	57.1 (5.33)	33.1 (5.51)	‡	62.3 (8.56)	35.3 (8.44)	12.5 (3.49)	55.2 (7.31)	32.3 (7.22)
48 to 52 months	40.3 (6.19)	47.2 (6.86)	12.5 ! (4.19)	12.3 (2.59)	54.9 (4.12)	32.8 (3.72)	‡	55.5 (6.29)	43.6 (6.31)	16.2 (3.23)	54.7 (5.00)	29.1 (4.37)
53 to 57 months	46.6 (6.49)	42.5 (6.69)	10.9 (3.14)	7.3 (1.67)	56.5 (3.22)	36.2 (3.36)	3.8 ! (1.34)	57.5 (4.02)	38.7 (4.06)	8.4 (2.08)	56.2 (4.22)	35.4 (4.29)
58 or more months	‡	‡	‡	‡	55.1 (4.81)	37.7 (4.57)	‡	46.7 (13.27)	38.4 (11.42)	‡	57.5 (5.77)	37.5 (5.88)
Mother's employment status[6]												
Full-time (35 hours or more)	36.6 (4.34)	56.6 (4.50)	6.9 ! (2.52)	14.9 (2.84)	55.5 (3.74)	29.6 (3.67)	4.9 (1.16)	47.7 (5.16)	47.4 (5.53)	17.6 (3.47)	57.6 (4.47)	24.8 (3.72)
Part-time (less than 35 hours)	48.9 (7.47)	35.1 (7.08)	16.0 (4.61)	5.7 ! (1.80)	60.9 (4.64)	33.4 (4.72)	‡	59.8 (8.26)	37.0 (7.97)	6.5 ! (2.17)	61.2 (6.14)	32.3 (5.97)
Looking for work	‡	‡	‡	14.0 ! (5.19)	53.4 (6.27)	32.5 (6.64)	‡	73.1 (8.42)	24.5 ! (8.27)	22.4 ! (8.52)	39.2 (8.58)	38.4 (9.45)
Not in labor force	‡	‡	‡	3.5 ! (1.31)	53.3 (4.81)	43.2 (4.98)	‡	59.0 (5.59)	39.2 (5.61)	4.2 ! (1.73)	51.2 (6.71)	44.7 (7.02)
No mother in household	‡	‡	‡	‡	‡	‡	‡	‡	‡	‡	‡	‡
Parents' highest level of education												
Less than high school	‡	‡	‡	12.6 ! (4.52)	59.6 (7.01)	27.8 (5.88)	‡	57.4 (7.36)	40.4 (7.28)	20.8 ! (7.99)	61.3 (10.74)	17.9 ! (7.65)
High school completion	62.0 (6.10)	32.8 (6.20)	‡	6.3 (1.81)	49.2 (3.34)	44.5 (4.07)	5.4 (1.47)	51.8 (6.12)	42.9 (6.28)	6.7 ! (2.48)	47.9 (4.55)	45.4 (5.62)
Some college/vocational	41.7 (6.68)	50.9 (6.75)	7.4 ! (3.39)	15.3 (2.78)	59.0 (2.92)	25.7 (2.68)	‡	62.0 (4.22)	35.3 (4.12)	21.5 (3.69)	57.5 (3.97)	21.0 (3.62)
Bachelor's degree	29.9 (8.51)	62.1 (8.63)	‡	6.7 ! (2.43)	59.8 (6.64)	33.4 (6.78)	‡	‡	‡	7.3 ! (2.64)	60.2 (7.18)	32.6 (7.32)
Any graduate education	‡	61.3 (8.63)	28.3 (7.99)	‡	53.6 (7.44)	41.4 (7.48)	‡	‡	‡	‡	54.5 (7.46)	40.2 (7.46)
Poverty status[7]												
Below poverty threshold	68.1 (6.76)	28.3 (6.86)	‡	9.0 (2.36)	59.2 (3.18)	31.8 (3.48)	2.6 ! (1.10)	57.8 (4.16)	39.7 (4.35)	15.0 (4.14)	60.6 (5.68)	24.4 (5.14)
At or above poverty threshold	35.8 (4.32)	53.2 (4.79)	11.1 (2.70)	9.7 (1.46)	54.8 (3.18)	35.6 (3.30)	3.8 ! (1.35)	55.6 (4.74)	40.5 (4.70)	10.8 (1.73)	54.6 (3.61)	34.6 (3.73)
Socioeconomic status[8]												
Lowest 20 percent	71.2 (7.12)	26.4 (7.02)	‡	6.7 (2.21)	58.6 (4.39)	34.7 (4.46)	3.5 ! (1.27)	53.0 (5.31)	43.6 (5.65)	9.8 ! (3.98)	63.9 (7.34)	26.4 (6.60)
Middle 60 percent	43.3 (5.26)	49.7 (5.50)	7.0 ! (2.57)	11.2 (1.83)	56.5 (2.69)	32.3 (2.68)	3.2 ! (1.22)	59.7 (4.07)	37.1 (4.05)	14.0 (2.28)	55.4 (3.37)	30.6 (3.37)
Highest 20 percent	‡	66.3 (7.41)	25.9 (6.85)	7.3 ! (2.54)	52.2 (6.27)	40.5 (6.19)	‡	‡	‡	7.5 ! (2.61)	52.7 (6.33)	39.8 (6.21)

†Not applicable.
!Interpret data with caution. The coefficient of variation (CV) for this estimate is between 30 and 50 percent.
‡Reporting standards not met. Either there are too few cases for a reliable estimate or the coefficient of variation (CV) is 50 percent or greater.
[1]Primary type of care arrangement is the type of nonparental care in which the child spent the most hours.
[2]Care provided in the child's home or in another private home by a relative (excluding parents) or by a person unrelated to the child.
[3]Quality rating based on the Family Day Care Rating Scale (FDCRS). Low quality = score of 1 but less than 3. Medium quality = score of 3 but less than 5. High quality = score of 5 to 7.
[4]Quality rating based on the Early Childhood Environment Rating Scale (ECERS). Low quality = score of 1 but less than 3. Medium quality = score of 3 but less than 5. High quality = score of 5 to 7.
[5]Care provided in places such as early learning centers, nursery schools, and preschools, not classified as Head Start.
[6]Mothers who reported working at least 35 hours per week are defined as employed full time, while those who reported working less than 35 hours per week are defined as employed part time. Those neither employed nor looking for work are not in the labor force.

[7]Poverty status based on Census Bureau guidelines from 2002, which identify a dollar amount determined to meet a household's needs, given its size and composition. In 2002, a family of four was considered to live below the poverty threshold if its income was less than or equal to $18,392 (in current dollars).
[8]Socioeconomic status (SES) was measured by a composite score based on parental education and occupations, and family income.
NOTE: Estimates weighted by W3SP0. Estimates pertain to children assessed between 44 months and 65 months of age. Rating is for child's primary type of care arrangement, which was the type of nonparental care in which the child spent the most hours. Children who were primarily cared for by parents or in multiple arrangements are not included in this table. Ratings of care arrangement quality using both the FDCRS and ECERS scales were based on interviewer observations of children's interactions with adults and peers, children's exposure to materials and activities, the extent to which and the manner in which routine care needs were met, and the furnishings and displays in the classroom. The FDCRS and ECERS metrics are designed to be equivalent. Race categories exclude persons of Hispanic ethnicity. Detail may not sum to totals because of rounding and suppression of cells that do not meet standards.
SOURCE: U.S. Department of Education, National Center for Education Statistics, Early Childhood Longitudinal Study, Birth Cohort, Longitudinal 9-month–Kindergarten Restricted-Use Data File. (This table was prepared January 2013.)

Table 202.65. Percentage distribution of first-time kindergartners, by primary type of child care arrangement during the year prior to kindergarten entry and selected child, family, and school characteristics: 2010–11

[Standard errors appear in parentheses]

Selected child, family, or school characteristic	Total, all children		Percent of first-time kindergartners during the year before starting kindergarten							
					Primary type of nonparental care arrangement[1]					
			No regular nonparental care	Total, any regular nonparental care	Home-based care				Center-based care	Multiple arrangements
					Relative care		Nonrelative care			
1	2		3	4	5		6		7	8
Total...................................	100.0	(†)	20.9 (0.82)	79.1 (0.82)	14.9 (0.46)		6.3 (0.36)		55.3 (0.97)	2.5 (0.18)
Sex of child										
Male..................................	100.0	(†)	21.0 (0.91)	79.0 (0.91)	14.3 (0.51)		6.6 (0.38)		55.6 (1.01)	2.6 (0.23)
Female..............................	100.0	(†)	20.8 (0.88)	79.2 (0.88)	15.6 (0.67)		6.0 (0.46)		55.1 (1.13)	2.4 (0.25)
Age of child at kindergarten entry, fall 2010										
Less than 5 years old................	100.0	(†)	19.5 (1.88)	80.5 (1.88)	14.4 (1.39)		4.3 (1.19)		59.3 (2.53)	2.5 (0.53)
5 years old to 5 1/2 years old............	100.0	(†)	21.5 (0.92)	78.5 (0.92)	15.8 (0.64)		5.9 (0.39)		54.5 (1.09)	2.3 (0.21)
More than 5 1/2 years old to 6 years old........	100.0	(†)	20.5 (0.89)	79.5 (0.89)	14.8 (0.62)		6.4 (0.45)		55.6 (1.05)	2.7 (0.26)
More than 6 years old................	100.0	(†)	21.1 (1.56)	78.9 (1.56)	11.8 (1.15)		8.6 (1.15)		55.8 (2.26)	2.6 (0.63)
Race/ethnicity of child										
White..................................	100.0	(†)	18.1 (0.86)	81.9 (0.86)	12.9 (0.57)		8.5 (0.65)		57.8 (1.15)	2.7 (0.25)
Black..................................	100.0	(†)	19.9 (1.93)	80.1 (1.93)	17.8 (1.29)		3.9 (0.59)		55.5 (2.06)	2.8 (0.47)
Hispanic..............................	100.0	(†)	28.3 (1.28)	71.7 (1.28)	18.1 (0.70)		4.0 (0.43)		47.8 (1.41)	1.8 (0.21)
Asian..................................	100.0	(†)	19.6 (2.37)	80.4 (2.37)	14.6 (1.43)		2.3 (0.57)		61.6 (3.25)	1.8 (0.52)
Pacific Islander......................	100.0	(†)	38.8 (6.02)	61.2 (6.02)	27.2 (7.27)		‡ (†)		27.6 (6.59)	‡ (†)
American Indian/Alaska Native......	100.0	(†)	23.5 (3.93)	76.5 (3.93)	13.2 ! (4.58)		‡ (†)		56.7 (2.41)	‡ (†)
Two or more races...................	100.0	(†)	17.2 (2.03)	82.8 (2.03)	13.8 (1.53)		5.2 (0.97)		60.9 (2.51)	2.9 ! (0.93)
Parents' employment status, fall 2010[2]										
Two parents										
Both employed full time................	100.0	(†)	8.4 (0.67)	91.6 (0.67)	17.6 (0.89)		12.9 (1.12)		57.1 (1.35)	4.0 (0.47)
One employed full time, one part time.......	100.0	(†)	16.5 (1.19)	83.5 (1.19)	14.7 (0.85)		7.1 (0.75)		58.8 (1.40)	2.8 (0.38)
One employed full time, one looking for work......	100.0	(†)	23.6 (2.19)	76.4 (2.19)	16.2 (1.87)		4.6 (0.86)		52.9 (2.82)	2.8 (0.80)
One employed full time, one not in labor force.....	100.0	(†)	33.7 (1.63)	66.3 (1.63)	4.7 (0.49)		1.6 (0.25)		58.9 (1.59)	1.0 (0.22)
Other combination......................	100.0	(†)	36.8 (1.48)	63.2 (1.48)	11.7 (1.29)		4.3 (0.90)		45.8 (1.92)	1.5 (0.43)
Single parent										
Employed full time....................	100.0	(†)	9.5 (0.97)	90.5 (0.97)	29.0 (1.23)		7.9 (0.95)		49.4 (1.39)	4.2 (0.41)
Employed part time....................	100.0	(†)	16.3 (1.75)	83.7 (1.75)	26.6 (1.99)		5.0 (1.14)		49.4 (2.56)	2.7 ! (0.97)
Looking for work......................	100.0	(†)	23.0 (2.23)	77.0 (2.23)	17.9 (2.32)		2.8 ! (1.19)		54.7 (2.38)	1.5 ! (0.72)
Not in labor force....................	100.0	(†)	35.2 (2.53)	64.8 (2.53)	14.2 (1.70)		‡ (†)		48.1 (2.69)	‡ (†)
No parent in household................	100.0	(†)	23.4 (2.65)	76.6 (2.65)	16.9 (3.28)		3.7 ! (1.29)		52.8 (4.15)	3.3 ! (1.45)
Parents' highest level of education[3]										
Less than high school................	100.0	(†)	37.7 (2.11)	62.3 (2.11)	15.8 (1.21)		3.1 (0.68)		42.5 (2.04)	0.9 ! (0.27)
High school completion................	100.0	(†)	28.3 (1.22)	71.7 (1.22)	19.1 (0.96)		5.1 (0.40)		45.5 (1.25)	1.9 (0.33)
Some college/vocational..............	100.0	(†)	20.2 (0.90)	79.8 (0.90)	18.1 (0.81)		7.0 (0.54)		51.6 (1.30)	3.0 (0.35)
Bachelor's degree....................	100.0	(†)	14.7 (0.96)	85.3 (0.96)	10.9 (0.69)		6.5 (0.71)		64.8 (1.23)	3.1 (0.31)
Any graduate education................	100.0	(†)	12.9 (1.14)	87.1 (1.14)	8.7 (0.70)		7.6 (0.67)		68.3 (1.38)	2.4 (0.33)
Household type, fall 2010										
Two-parent household................	100.0	(†)	21.5 (0.94)	78.5 (0.94)	12.4 (0.45)		6.9 (0.49)		56.7 (1.14)	2.5 (0.21)
Mother-only household................	100.0	(†)	17.5 (0.87)	82.5 (0.87)	23.9 (0.90)		5.2 (0.58)		50.4 (1.08)	3.1 (0.32)
Father-only household................	100.0	(†)	17.5 (2.96)	82.5 (2.96)	30.8 (3.51)		5.8 (1.69)		43.4 (3.66)	2.4 ! (1.16)
Other household type..................	100.0	(†)	23.4 (2.65)	76.6 (2.65)	16.9 (3.28)		3.7 ! (1.29)		52.8 (4.15)	3.3 ! (1.45)
Primary home language										
English................................	100.0	(†)	18.4 (0.72)	81.6 (0.72)	14.9 (0.56)		7.0 (0.41)		57.1 (0.98)	2.7 (0.21)
Non-English..........................	100.0	(†)	35.6 (2.10)	64.4 (2.10)	14.7 (0.95)		2.9 (0.48)		45.3 (1.84)	1.5 (0.25)
Primary language not identified........	100.0	(†)	22.1 (4.09)	77.9 (4.09)	18.2 (3.74)		‡ (†)		54.2 (4.62)	‡ (†)
Poverty status[4]										
Below poverty threshold..............	100.0	(†)	30.4 (1.46)	69.6 (1.46)	16.4 (0.90)		2.6 (0.36)		48.9 (1.46)	1.7 (0.30)
100 to 199 percent of poverty threshold......	100.0	(†)	24.9 (1.20)	75.1 (1.20)	16.5 (0.90)		5.0 (0.49)		51.8 (1.40)	1.7 (0.25)
200 percent or more of poverty threshold......	100.0	(†)	13.5 (0.69)	86.5 (0.69)	12.3 (0.64)		8.7 (0.58)		62.3 (1.12)	3.2 (0.29)
Socioeconomic status[5]										
Lowest 20 percent....................	100.0	(†)	35.2 (1.52)	64.8 (1.52)	15.6 (0.75)		3.4 (0.44)		44.3 (1.28)	1.6 (0.27)
Middle 60 percent....................	100.0	(†)	19.6 (0.71)	80.4 (0.71)	16.9 (0.54)		6.9 (0.45)		53.9 (1.09)	2.7 (0.23)
Highest 20 percent....................	100.0	(†)	12.3 (1.13)	87.7 (1.13)	8.7 (0.67)		7.1 (0.56)		69.1 (1.29)	2.7 (0.29)
School type										
Public................................	100.0	(†)	21.8 (0.80)	78.2 (0.80)	15.8 (0.51)		6.2 (0.35)		53.7 (0.98)	2.5 (0.20)
Private................................	100.0	(†)	14.5 (1.98)	85.5 (1.98)	8.3 (0.78)		7.0 (0.88)		67.9 (1.69)	2.3 (0.32)

†Not applicable.

!Interpret data with caution. The coefficient of variation (CV) for this estimate is between 30 and 50 percent.

‡Reporting standards not met. Either there are too few cases for a reliable estimate or the coefficient of variation (CV) is 50 percent or greater.

[1]The type of nonparental care in which the child spent the most hours. Multiple arrangements refers to children who spent an equal amount of time in each of two or more types of arrangements.

[2]Parents who reported working at least 35 hours per week are defined as employed full time, while those who reported working less than 35 hours per week are defined as employed part time. Those who neither employed nor looking for work are not in the labor force.

[3]Parents highest level of education is the highest level of education achieved by either of the parents or guardians in a two-parent household, by the only parent in a single-parent household, or by any guardian in a household with no parents.

[4]Poverty status is based on preliminary U.S. Census income thresholds for 2010, which identify incomes determined to meet household needs, given family size and composition.

For example, a family of three with one child was below the poverty threshold if its annual income was less than $17,552 in 2010.

[5]Socioeconomic status (SES) was measured by a composite score based on parental education and occupations and household income at the time of data collection.

NOTE: Estimates weighted by W1_2P0. Estimates pertain to a sample of children who were enrolled in kindergarten for the first time in the 2010–11 school year. Two parents may refer to two biological parents, two adoptive parents, or one biological/adoptive parent and one other parent/partner. Single parent refers to one biological or adoptive parent only. In households without parents, the guardian or guardians may be related or unrelated to the child. Race categories exclude persons of Hispanic ethnicity. Detail may not sum to totals because of rounding and survey item nonresponse. Some data have been revised from previously published figures.

SOURCE: U.S. Department of Education, National Center for Education Statistics, Early Childhood Longitudinal Study, Kindergarten Class of 2010–11 (ECLS-K:2011), Kindergarten–First Grade Restricted-Use Data File. (This table was prepared November 2014.)

Table 202.70. Number and percentage distribution of 3- to 5-year-olds not enrolled in school and all children enrolled in prekindergarten through second grade, by grade level and selected maternal and household characteristics: 2001, 2005, and 2012

[Standard errors appear in parentheses]

Selected maternal or household characteristic	3- to 5-year-olds, not enrolled in school			Enrolled in nursery school or prekindergarten			Enrolled in kindergarten			Enrolled in first grade			Enrolled in second grade		
	2001	2005	2012	2001	2005	2012	2001	2005	2012	2001	2005	2012	2001	2005	2012
1	2	3	4	5	6	7	8	9	10	11	12	13	14	15	16
Number of children (in thousands)	3,990 (3.2)	4,156 (5.0)	3,250 (90.6)	4,586 (#)	4,926 (#)	4,994 (103.8)	3,831 (#)	3,717 (#)	5,710 (115.2)	4,333 (#)	4,118 (#)	3,944 (136.3)	3,994 (#)	3,900 (#)	4,192 (151.8)
Percentage distribution															
Mother's highest level of education[1]	100.0 (†)	100.0 (†)	100.0 (†)	100.0 (†)	100.0 (†)	100.0 (†)	100.0 (†)	100.0 (†)	100.0 (†)	100.0 (†)	100.0 (†)	100.0 (†)	100.0 (†)	100.0 (†)	100.0 (†)
Less than high school	16.4 (1.26)	13.8 (1.24)	24.4 (1.60)	8.0 (0.76)	6.8 (0.76)	11.4 (1.06)	10.7 (1.31)	9.5 (1.16)	16.9 (1.83)	11.7 (1.28)	10.0 (1.20)	11.1 (1.56)	13.5 (1.26)	10.3 (1.21)	10.1 (1.93)
High school/GED	39.7 (1.59)	37.2 (2.17)	26.8 (1.61)	26.1 (1.34)	24.6 (1.34)	16.7 (1.04)	30.3 (1.86)	27.5 (1.92)	21.6 (1.92)	30.3 (2.17)	31.1 (2.13)	16.4 (1.45)	32.8 (2.11)	29.5 (1.77)	27.0 (2.94)
Vocational/technical or some college	19.1 (1.30)	21.2 (1.43)	24.1 (1.41)	24.6 (1.28)	19.2 (1.32)	19.5 (1.21)	23.5 (1.84)	20.7 (1.70)	21.3 (2.12)	24.3 (1.87)	19.9 (1.93)	25.4 (1.96)	22.5 (2.18)	19.8 (1.64)	20.0 (1.60)
Associate's degree	5.9 (0.67)	6.8 (0.82)	7.7 (0.82)	7.7 (0.71)	8.4 (0.71)	9.4 (0.86)	7.6 (1.18)	7.7 (0.96)	8.0 (1.06)	7.5 (1.01)	10.3 (1.22)	8.4 (0.81)	7.5 (0.92)	8.0 (0.98)	12.0 (1.50)
Bachelor's degree	13.0 (1.05)	14.9 (1.20)	13.9 (1.10)	20.4 (1.03)	25.5 (1.13)	30.6 (1.15)	18.8 (1.51)	21.3 (1.42)	23.4 (1.73)	18.5 (1.71)	18.0 (1.23)	28.1 (1.78)	14.9 (1.66)	18.7 (1.46)	20.7 (1.59)
Graduate/professional degree	6.0 (0.73)	6.1 (0.73)	3.1 (0.38)	13.2 (0.99)	15.5 (0.94)	12.4 (0.70)	9.1 (1.16)	13.4 (1.43)	8.7 (0.87)	7.7 (1.03)	10.6 (1.22)	10.6 (0.99)	8.8 (1.25)	13.6 (1.62)	10.1 (0.94)
Mother's employment status[1]	100.0 (†)	100.0 (†)	100.0 (†)	100.0 (†)	100.0 (†)	100.0 (†)	100.0 (†)	100.0 (†)	100.0 (†)	100.0 (†)	100.0 (†)	100.0 (†)	100.0 (†)	100.0 (†)	100.0 (†)
Working 35 hours/week or more	36.7 (1.55)	33.5 (1.92)	34.2 (2.03)	43.7 (1.18)	39.4 (1.42)	45.3 (1.23)	38.9 (1.99)	36.9 (2.25)	40.4 (2.32)	46.1 (2.33)	40.7 (2.35)	44.2 (1.98)	42.3 (2.30)	41.2 (2.19)	42.6 (2.26)
Working less than 35 hours/week	19.2 (1.30)	21.1 (1.50)	14.3 (1.34)	22.8 (1.00)	24.4 (1.36)	18.3 (0.94)	22.6 (1.57)	21.5 (1.62)	16.8 (1.63)	19.7 (1.59)	20.7 (1.42)	17.8 (1.68)	20.1 (1.60)	22.7 (1.72)	19.6 (1.65)
Looking for work	5.7 (0.75)	8.7 (1.37)	7.6 (1.01)	3.9 (0.55)	4.0 (0.59)	6.7 (0.90)	3.9 (0.87)	7.3 (1.06)	8.2 (1.59)	4.1 (0.89)	5.7 (1.07)	5.7 (1.01)	5.1 (1.09)	4.9 (0.82)	3.5 (0.58)
Not in labor force	38.4 (1.48)	36.8 (1.79)	43.9 (2.00)	29.6 (1.27)	32.2 (1.35)	29.7 (1.18)	34.7 (2.16)	34.3 (1.99)	34.6 (2.31)	30.1 (2.05)	32.8 (1.97)	32.3 (2.06)	32.5 (2.22)	31.2 (1.99)	34.4 (2.42)
Household income	100.0 (†)	100.0 (†)	100.0 (†)	100.0 (†)	100.0 (†)	100.0 (†)	100.0 (†)	100.0 (†)	100.0 (†)	100.0 (†)	100.0 (†)	100.0 (†)	100.0 (†)	100.0 (†)	100.0 (†)
$20,000 or less	28.6 (1.24)	22.2 (1.29)	24.0 (1.74)	21.2 (0.93)	17.3 (1.07)	14.0 (0.80)	22.6 (1.56)	19.3 (1.26)	20.8 (1.52)	23.1 (1.79)	18.2 (1.45)	12.6 (1.12)	21.8 (1.71)	20.1 (1.54)	14.8 (1.41)
$20,001 to $50,000	40.5 (1.50)	42.4 (1.65)	34.8 (1.92)	28.9 (1.20)	27.6 (1.39)	24.9 (1.07)	37.8 (1.95)	31.9 (1.76)	30.4 (1.86)	36.4 (2.18)	33.0 (1.95)	25.1 (1.52)	36.3 (2.11)	32.9 (2.10)	28.7 (1.90)
$50,001 to $75,000	18.8 (1.31)	19.9 (1.24)	17.4 (1.46)	21.2 (1.09)	20.8 (0.97)	18.9 (1.02)	20.9 (1.68)	18.4 (1.46)	13.9 (1.34)	18.3 (1.41)	20.4 (1.84)	19.5 (1.73)	19.6 (1.80)	20.3 (1.56)	18.5 (1.51)
$75,001 to $100,000	7.2 (0.76)	9.0 (1.08)	10.2 (1.08)	13.0 (0.92)	14.7 (0.93)	15.1 (0.88)	9.0 (1.04)	14.1 (1.29)	13.4 (1.02)	11.1 (1.41)	10.8 (1.22)	15.1 (1.26)	12.0 (1.33)	13.9 (1.41)	10.8 (1.08)
Over $100,000	4.9 (0.61)	6.4 (0.93)	13.7 (1.60)	15.7 (0.83)	19.7 (1.11)	27.1 (1.02)	9.6 (0.98)	16.3 (1.29)	21.5 (1.63)	11.0 (1.30)	17.6 (1.36)	27.8 (1.90)	10.3 (1.27)	12.8 (1.39)	27.3 (1.68)
Poverty status of household[2]	100.0 (†)	100.0 (†)	100.0 (†)	100.0 (†)	100.0 (†)	100.0 (†)	100.0 (†)	100.0 (†)	100.0 (†)	100.0 (†)	100.0 (†)	100.0 (†)	100.0 (†)	100.0 (†)	100.0 (†)
Poor	27.5 (1.24)	25.9 (1.53)	33.0 (1.79)	19.3 (0.94)	17.2 (1.10)	17.7 (1.00)	22.2 (1.67)	21.2 (1.53)	28.9 (2.16)	23.1 (2.00)	20.8 (1.47)	17.1 (1.46)	21.2 (1.70)	22.1 (1.50)	22.0 (1.76)
Near-poor	23.9 (1.27)	31.3 (1.73)	29.6 (1.78)	17.9 (0.99)	20.9 (1.24)	20.0 (1.18)	22.6 (1.86)	23.1 (2.05)	21.4 (1.84)	20.9 (1.93)	22.8 (1.35)	20.9 (1.39)	22.1 (1.92)	23.4 (1.66)	23.0 (1.81)
Nonpoor	48.6 (1.39)	42.8 (1.66)	37.5 (1.62)	62.8 (1.18)	61.9 (1.34)	62.3 (1.32)	55.2 (1.91)	55.7 (1.82)	49.7 (1.77)	56.0 (1.99)	56.4 (1.74)	62.1 (1.89)	56.7 (1.97)	54.5 (1.82)	55.0 (2.14)

†Not applicable.
#Rounds to zero.
[1]Excludes children living in households with no mother or female guardian present.
[2]Poor children are those whose family incomes were below the Census Bureau's poverty threshold in the year prior to data collection; near-poor children are those whose family incomes ranged from the poverty threshold to 199 percent of the poverty threshold; and nonpoor children are those whose family incomes were at or above 200 percent of the poverty threshold. The poverty threshold is a dollar amount that varies depending on a family's size and composition and is updated annually to account for inflation. In 2011, for example, the poverty threshold for a family of four with two children was $22,811. Survey respondents are asked to select the range within which their income falls, rather than giving the exact amount of their income; therefore, the measure of poverty status is an approximation.

NOTE: Enrollment data include homeschooled students and ungraded students if a grade equivalent was available. For 2001 and 2005, excludes students for whom no grade equivalent was available. For 2012, all students had a known grade level and were included. While National Household Education Surveys Program (NHES) administrations prior to 2012 were administered via telephone with an interviewer, NHES:2012 used self-administered paper-and-pencil questionnaires that were mailed to respondents. Measurable differences in estimates between 2012 and prior years could reflect actual changes in the population, or the changes could be due to the mode change from telephone to mail. Detail may not sum to totals because of rounding. SOURCE: U.S. Department of Education, National Center for Education Statistics, Early Childhood Program Participation Survey, Before- and After-School Programs and Activities Survey, and Parent and Family Involvement in Education Survey of the National Household Education Surveys Program (ECPP-NHES:2001, 2005, and 2012; ASPA-NHES:2001 and 2005; and PFI-NHES:2012). (This table was prepared October 2014.)

Table 203.10. Enrollment in public elementary and secondary schools, by level and grade: Selected years, fall 1980 through fall 2025

[In thousands]

Year	All grades	Elementary													Secondary					
		Total	Pre-kinder-garten	Kinder-garten	1st grade	2nd grade	3rd grade	4th grade	5th grade	6th grade	7th grade	8th grade	Un-graded	Total	9th grade	10th grade	11th grade	12th grade	Un-graded
1	2	3	4	5	6	7	8	9	10	11	12	13	14	15	16	17	18	19	20
1980	40,877	27,647	96	2,593	2,894	2,800	2,893	3,107	3,130	3,038	3,085	3,086	924	13,231	3,377	3,368	3,195	2,925	366
1985	39,422	27,034	151	3,041	3,239	2,941	2,895	2,771	2,776	2,789	2,938	2,982	511	12,388	3,439	3,230	2,866	2,550	303
1990	41,217	29,876	303	3,306	3,499	3,327	3,297	3,248	3,197	3,110	3,067	2,979	541	11,341	3,169	2,896	2,612	2,381	284
1991	42,047	30,503	375	3,311	3,556	3,360	3,334	3,315	3,268	3,239	3,181	3,020	542	11,544	3,313	2,915	2,645	2,392	278
1992	42,823	31,086	505	3,313	3,542	3,431	3,361	3,342	3,325	3,303	3,299	3,129	536	11,737	3,352	3,027	2,656	2,431	272
1993	43,465	31,502	545	3,377	3,529	3,429	3,437	3,361	3,350	3,356	3,355	3,249	513	11,963	3,487	3,050	2,751	2,424	250
1994	44,111	31,896	603	3,444	3,593	3,440	3,439	3,426	3,372	3,381	3,404	3,302	492	12,215	3,604	3,131	2,748	2,488	244
1995	44,840	32,338	637	3,536	3,671	3,507	3,445	3,431	3,438	3,395	3,422	3,356	500	12,502	3,704	3,237	2,826	2,487	247
1996	45,611	32,762	670	3,532	3,770	3,600	3,524	3,454	3,453	3,494	3,464	3,403	399	12,849	3,801	3,323	2,930	2,586	208
1997	46,127	33,071	695	3,503	3,755	3,689	3,597	3,507	3,458	3,492	3,520	3,415	440	13,056	3,819	3,376	2,972	2,673	216
1998	46,539	33,344	729	3,443	3,727	3,681	3,696	3,592	3,520	3,497	3,530	3,480	449	13,195	3,856	3,382	3,021	2,722	214
1999	46,857	33,486	751	3,397	3,684	3,656	3,691	3,686	3,604	3,564	3,541	3,497	415	13,371	3,935	3,415	3,034	2,782	205
2000	47,204	33,686	776	3,382	3,636	3,634	3,676	3,711	3,707	3,663	3,629	3,538	334	13,517	3,963	3,491	3,083	2,803	177
2001	47,672	33,936	865	3,379	3,614	3,593	3,653	3,695	3,727	3,769	3,720	3,616	304	13,736	4,012	3,528	3,174	2,863	159
2002	48,183	34,114	915	3,434	3,594	3,565	3,623	3,669	3,711	3,788	3,821	3,709	285	14,069	4,105	3,584	3,229	2,990	161
2003	48,540	34,201	950	3,503	3,613	3,544	3,611	3,619	3,685	3,772	3,841	3,809	255	14,339	4,190	3,675	3,277	3,046	150
2004	48,795	34,178	990	3,544	3,663	3,560	3,580	3,612	3,635	3,735	3,818	3,825	215	14,618	4,281	3,750	3,369	3,094	122
2005	49,113	34,204	1,036	3,619	3,691	3,606	3,586	3,578	3,633	3,670	3,777	3,802	205	14,909	4,287	3,866	3,454	3,180	121
2006	49,316	34,235	1,084	3,631	3,751	3,641	3,627	3,586	3,602	3,660	3,716	3,766	170	15,081	4,260	3,882	3,551	3,277	110
2007	49,291	34,204	1,081	3,609	3,750	3,704	3,659	3,624	3,600	3,628	3,700	3,709	139	15,086	4,200	3,863	3,557	3,375	92
2008	49,266	34,286	1,180	3,640	3,708	3,699	3,708	3,647	3,629	3,614	3,653	3,692	117	14,980	4,123	3,822	3,548	3,400	87
2009	49,361	34,409	1,223	3,678	3,729	3,665	3,707	3,701	3,652	3,644	3,641	3,651	119	14,952	4,080	3,809	3,541	3,432	90
2010	49,484	34,625	1,279	3,682	3,754	3,701	3,686	3,711	3,718	3,682	3,676	3,659	77	14,860	4,008	3,800	3,538	3,472	42
2011	49,522	34,773	1,291	3,746	3,773	3,713	3,703	3,672	3,699	3,724	3,696	3,679	77	14,749	3,957	3,751	3,546	3,452	43
2012	49,771	35,018	1,307	3,831	3,824	3,729	3,719	3,690	3,673	3,723	3,746	3,699	76	14,753	3,975	3,730	3,528	3,477	43
2013	50,045	35,251	1,328	3,834	3,885	3,791	3,738	3,708	3,697	3,684	3,748	3,753	85	14,794	3,980	3,761	3,526	3,476	52
Projected																			
2014	50,132	35,249	1,290	3,723	3,877	3,851	3,799	3,735	3,714	3,714	3,708	3,753	85	14,883	4,038	3,765	3,555	3,474	52
2015	50,268	35,298	1,294	3,733	3,765	3,843	3,859	3,796	3,741	3,731	3,737	3,713	85	14,970	4,038	3,820	3,558	3,502	52
2016	50,385	35,402	1,298	3,746	3,775	3,733	3,851	3,856	3,802	3,759	3,755	3,743	85	14,983	3,995	3,820	3,611	3,506	52
2017	50,477	35,451	1,293	3,730	3,788	3,742	3,740	3,848	3,862	3,820	3,782	3,761	85	15,026	4,027	3,779	3,611	3,557	52
2018	50,528	35,491	1,293	3,732	3,772	3,755	3,750	3,737	3,854	3,881	3,844	3,788	85	15,037	4,046	3,810	3,572	3,557	52
2019	50,618	35,543	1,303	3,761	3,774	3,739	3,763	3,747	3,744	3,872	3,905	3,850	85	15,075	4,075	3,827	3,601	3,519	52
2020	50,774	35,559	1,313	3,788	3,803	3,741	3,747	3,760	3,753	3,761	3,897	3,911	85	15,215	4,142	3,855	3,618	3,548	52
2021	50,928	35,541	1,322	3,816	3,831	3,770	3,749	3,744	3,766	3,771	3,785	3,903	85	15,387	4,208	3,918	3,644	3,564	52
2022	51,084	35,558	1,331	3,842	3,859	3,798	3,778	3,746	3,750	3,784	3,795	3,791	85	15,526	4,199	3,980	3,704	3,590	52
2023	51,225	35,712	1,340	3,867	3,886	3,825	3,806	3,775	3,752	3,768	3,807	3,800	85	15,514	4,078	3,972	3,762	3,649	52
2024	51,338	35,878	1,348	3,890	3,911	3,852	3,833	3,803	3,781	3,770	3,792	3,813	85	15,460	4,089	3,858	3,754	3,707	52
2025	51,420	36,052	1,355	3,911	3,934	3,877	3,860	3,830	3,809	3,799	3,794	3,798	86	15,368	4,103	3,868	3,647	3,699	52

NOTE: Due to changes in reporting and imputation practices, prekindergarten enrollment for years prior to 1992 represent an undercount compared to later years. The total ungraded counts of students were prorated to the elementary and secondary levels based on prior reports. Detail may not sum to totals because of rounding.

SOURCE: U.S. Department of Education, National Center for Education Statistics, *Statistics of Public Elementary and Secondary School Systems, 1980–81*; Common Core of Data (CCD), "State Nonfiscal Survey of Public Elementary/Secondary Education," 1985–86 through 2013–14; and National Elementary and Secondary Enrollment Projection Model, 1972 through 2025. (This table was prepared January 2016.)

Table 203.20. Enrollment in public elementary and secondary schools, by region, state, and jurisdiction: Selected years, fall 1990 through fall 2025

Columns 2–14 are "Actual total enrollment"; column 15 is "Percent change in total enrollment, 2008 to 2013"; columns 16–21 are "Projected total enrollment"; column 22 is "Percent change in total enrollment, 2013 to 2025".

Region, state, and jurisdiction	Fall 1990	Fall 2000	Fall 2003	Fall 2004	Fall 2005	Fall 2006	Fall 2007	Fall 2008	Fall 2009	Fall 2010	Fall 2011	Fall 2012	Fall 2013	% chg 2008→2013	Fall 2014	Fall 2015	Fall 2016	Fall 2017	Fall 2020	Fall 2025	% chg 2013→2025
1	2	3	4	5	6	7	8	9	10	11	12	13	14	15	16	17	18	19	20	21	22
United States	41,216,683	47,203,539	48,540,215	48,795,465	49,113,298	49,315,842	49,290,559	49,265,572	49,360,982	49,484,181	49,521,669	49,771,118	50,044,522	1.6	50,131,600	50,268,100	50,385,200	50,477,400	50,774,000	51,419,700	2.7
Region																					
Northeast	7,281,763	8,222,127	8,292,315	8,271,259	8,240,160	8,257,889	8,122,022	8,052,985	8,092,029	8,071,335	7,953,981	7,959,128	7,961,243	-1.1	7,918,000	7,888,600	7,866,000	7,841,700	7,761,000	7,578,400	-4.8
Midwest	9,943,761	10,729,987	10,608,977	10,775,409	10,818,815	10,819,248	10,770,210	10,742,973	10,672,171	10,609,604	10,573,792	10,559,230	10,572,920	-1.6	10,549,100	10,534,500	10,517,100	10,493,400	10,409,900	10,283,600	-2.7
South	14,807,016	17,007,261	17,672,745	17,891,987	18,103,166	18,293,633	18,422,773	18,490,770	18,651,889	18,805,000	18,955,932	19,128,376	19,298,714	4.4	19,432,000	19,576,400	19,699,500	19,804,500	20,134,800	20,810,400	7.8
West	9,184,143	11,244,164	11,766,178	11,856,810	11,951,157	11,945,072	11,975,554	11,978,844	11,944,893	11,998,242	12,037,964	12,124,384	12,211,645	1.9	12,232,500	12,268,600	12,302,700	12,337,800	12,468,300	12,747,200	4.4
State																					
Alabama	721,806	739,992	731,220	730,140	741,761	743,632	742,919	745,668	748,889	755,552	744,621	744,637	746,204	0.1	743,900	741,100	739,500	737,500	734,100	734,700	-1.5
Alaska	113,903	133,356	133,933	132,970	133,288	132,608	131,029	130,662	131,661	132,104	131,167	131,489	131,944	0.2	130,900	131,400	132,100	132,700	135,700	140,100	7.0
Arizona	639,853	877,696	1,012,068	1,043,298	1,094,454	1,068,249	1,087,447	1,087,817	1,077,831	1,071,751	1,090,319	1,089,384	1,102,445	1.3	1,108,100	1,116,000	1,123,900	1,134,900	1,174,100	1,250,700	13.4
Arkansas	436,286	449,989	454,523	463,115	474,206	476,409	479,016	478,965	480,559	482,114	483,114	486,157	489,979	2.3	490,500	490,800	491,300	491,700	493,600	500,400	2.1
California	4,950,474	6,140,814	6,413,867	6,441,557	6,437,202	6,406,750	6,343,471	6,322,528	6,263,438	6,289,578	6,287,834	6,299,451	6,312,623	-0.2	6,288,100	6,271,300	6,256,300	6,244,400	6,219,700	6,221,200	-1.4
Colorado	574,213	724,508	757,693	765,976	779,826	794,026	801,867	818,443	832,368	843,316	854,265	863,561	876,999	7.2	885,900	895,100	902,500	908,800	925,500	957,900	9.2
Connecticut	469,123	562,179	577,203	577,390	575,059	575,100	570,626	567,198	563,968	560,546	554,437	550,954	546,200	-3.7	538,200	531,700	525,100	518,000	498,500	468,600	-14.2
Delaware	99,658	114,676	117,668	119,091	120,937	122,254	122,574	125,430	126,801	129,403	128,946	129,026	132,040	5.0	132,400	133,300	134,500	135,500	138,100	139,900	6.2
District of Columbia	80,694	68,925	78,057	76,714	76,876	72,850	78,422	68,681	69,433	71,284	73,911	76,140	78,153	13.8	80,100	82,500	85,000	87,500	96,400	108,500	39.4
Florida	1,861,592	2,434,821	2,587,628	2,639,336	2,675,024	2,671,513	2,666,811	2,631,020	2,634,522	2,643,347	2,668,156	2,692,162	2,720,744	3.4	2,746,700	2,770,600	2,792,800	2,811,400	2,882,100	3,034,200	11.5
Georgia	1,151,687	1,444,937	1,522,611	1,553,437	1,598,461	1,629,157	1,649,589	1,655,792	1,667,685	1,677,067	1,685,016	1,703,332	1,723,909	4.1	1,737,800	1,750,500	1,760,400	1,768,500	1,797,200	1,873,600	8.7
Hawaii	171,708	184,360	183,609	183,185	182,818	180,728	179,897	179,478	180,196	179,601	182,706	184,760	186,825	4.1	187,700	188,900	190,400	191,800	194,900	195,800	4.8
Idaho	220,840	245,117	252,120	256,084	261,982	267,380	272,119	275,051	276,299	275,859	279,873	284,834	296,476	7.8	302,200	308,400	313,400	317,200	329,500	346,700	17.0
Illinois	1,821,407	2,048,792	2,100,961	2,097,503	2,111,706	2,118,276	2,112,805	2,119,707	2,104,175	2,091,654	2,083,097	2,072,880	2,066,990	-2.5	2,061,600	2,055,400	2,051,100	2,044,600	2,015,500	1,961,600	-5.1
Indiana	954,525	989,267	1,011,130	1,021,348	1,035,074	1,045,940	1,046,764	1,046,147	1,046,661	1,047,232	1,040,765	1,041,369	1,047,385	0.1	1,042,400	1,038,600	1,034,500	1,029,500	1,014,200	1,008,700	-3.7
Iowa	483,652	495,080	481,226	478,319	483,482	483,122	485,115	487,559	491,842	495,775	495,870	499,825	502,964	3.2	504,500	506,800	508,700	509,800	513,100	514,200	2.2
Kansas	437,034	470,610	470,490	469,136	467,525	469,506	468,295	471,060	474,489	483,701	486,108	489,043	496,440	5.4	498,600	502,100	504,800	507,300	512,800	517,600	4.3
Kentucky	636,401	665,850	663,369	663,886	679,878	683,152	666,225	670,030	680,089	673,128	681,987	685,167	677,389	1.1	673,300	671,000	669,200	667,600	663,300	661,800	-2.3
Louisiana	784,757	743,089	727,709	724,281	654,526	675,851	681,038	684,873	690,915	696,558	703,390	710,903	711,491	3.9	712,400	714,500	715,700	716,500	718,500	724,900	1.9
Maine	215,149	207,037	202,084	198,820	195,498	193,986	196,245	192,935	189,225	189,077	188,969	185,739	183,995	-4.6	182,000	180,100	178,000	176,100	170,800	161,900	-12.0
Maryland	715,176	852,920	869,113	865,561	860,020	851,640	845,700	843,861	848,412	852,211	854,086	859,638	866,169	2.6	871,800	879,200	886,800	894,400	912,200	922,200	6.5
Massachusetts	834,314	975,150	980,459	975,574	971,909	968,661	962,968	958,910	957,053	955,563	953,369	954,773	955,739	-0.3	951,500	947,900	943,700	939,700	927,900	910,700	-4.7
Michigan	1,584,431	1,720,626	1,757,604	1,751,290	1,742,282	1,722,656	1,692,739	1,659,921	1,649,082	1,587,067	1,573,537	1,555,370	1,548,841	-6.7	1,532,800	1,518,300	1,503,100	1,488,900	1,449,800	1,407,500	-9.1
Minnesota	756,374	854,340	842,854	838,503	839,243	840,565	837,578	836,048	837,053	838,037	839,738	845,404	850,973	1.8	858,900	864,900	871,700	877,300	890,100	893,200	5.0
Mississippi	502,417	497,871	493,540	493,360	494,954	495,026	494,122	492,590	492,481	490,526	490,619	493,596	492,586	0.1	490,900	489,900	488,400	486,200	479,800	471,200	-4.3
Missouri	816,558	912,744	905,941	905,449	917,705	920,353	917,188	917,871	917,982	918,710	916,584	917,900	918,288	#	916,200	915,300	913,800	912,500	911,000	911,100	-0.8
Montana	152,974	154,875	148,356	146,705	145,416	144,418	142,823	141,899	141,807	141,693	142,349	142,908	144,129	1.6	144,800	145,700	146,600	147,400	150,900	157,300	9.1
Nebraska	274,081	286,199	285,542	285,761	286,646	287,580	291,244	292,590	295,368	298,500	301,296	303,505	307,677	5.2	308,900	310,800	312,400	313,600	315,400	318,100	3.4
Nevada	201,316	340,706	385,401	400,083	412,395	424,766	429,362	433,371	428,947	437,149	439,634	445,707	451,831	4.3	455,700	461,500	466,800	471,700	487,500	516,200	14.2
New Hampshire	172,785	208,461	207,417	206,852	205,767	203,572	200,772	197,934	197,140	194,711	191,900	188,974	186,310	-5.9	183,300	180,500	177,700	175,200	168,200	159,100	-14.6
New Jersey	1,089,646	1,313,405	1,380,753	1,393,347	1,395,602	1,398,850	1,382,348	1,381,420	1,396,029	1,402,548	1,356,431	1,372,203	1,370,295	-0.8	1,365,700	1,362,000	1,358,700	1,355,200	1,341,400	1,309,600	-4.4
New Mexico	301,881	320,306	323,066	326,102	326,758	328,220	329,040	330,245	334,419	338,122	337,225	338,220	339,244	2.7	339,400	339,300	339,100	339,700	339,900	342,500	1.0
New York	2,598,337	2,882,188	2,864,775	2,836,337	2,815,581	2,809,649	2,765,435	2,740,592	2,766,052	2,734,955	2,704,718	2,710,703	2,732,770	-0.3	2,726,300	2,725,200	2,727,900	2,730,200	2,730,500	2,693,100	-1.5
North Carolina	1,086,871	1,293,638	1,360,209	1,385,754	1,416,436	1,444,481	1,489,492	1,488,645	1,483,397	1,490,605	1,507,864	1,518,465	1,530,857	2.8	1,536,900	1,544,000	1,553,300	1,553,700	1,566,500	1,610,100	5.2
North Dakota	117,825	109,201	102,233	100,513	98,283	96,670	95,059	94,728	95,073	96,323	97,646	101,111	103,947	9.7	106,900	110,000	112,900	115,900	125,000	135,000	29.9
Ohio	1,771,089	1,835,049	1,845,428	1,840,032	1,839,683	1,836,722	1,827,184	1,817,163	1,764,297	1,754,191	1,740,030	1,729,916	1,724,111	-5.1	1,714,400	1,707,600	1,698,700	1,689,500	1,660,900	1,621,000	-6.0
Oklahoma	579,087	623,110	626,160	629,476	634,739	639,391	642,065	645,108	654,802	659,911	666,120	673,483	681,848	5.7	686,400	693,100	700,800	703,500	717,200	736,300	8.0
Oregon	472,394	546,231	551,273	552,505	552,194	562,574	565,586	575,393	570,720	570,720	568,208	587,564	593,000	3.1	594,600	597,800	600,800	602,800	612,600	627,500	5.8
Pennsylvania	1,667,834	1,814,311	1,821,146	1,828,089	1,830,684	1,871,060	1,801,971	1,775,029	1,785,993	1,793,284	1,771,395	1,763,677	1,755,236	-1.1	1,742,300	1,734,200	1,729,200	1,722,700	1,703,400	1,662,000	-5.3
Rhode Island	138,813	157,347	159,375	156,498	153,422	151,612	147,629	145,342	145,118	143,793	142,854	142,481	142,008	-2.3	141,000	140,200	139,500	139,600	137,600	133,900	-5.7
South Carolina	622,112	677,411	699,198	699,736	701,544	708,021	712,317	718,113	723,143	725,838	727,186	735,998	745,657	3.8	754,600	763,200	769,900	775,100	791,200	815,900	9.4
South Dakota	129,164	128,603	125,537	122,798	122,012	121,158	121,606	126,128	123,713	126,128	128,016	130,471	130,890	3.5	131,600	132,900	134,100	135,800	139,800	142,600	9.0
Tennessee	824,595	909,161	936,682	941,091	953,928	978,368	964,259	971,950	972,549	987,422	999,693	993,496	993,556	2.2	995,800	999,100	1,002,700	1,005,300	1,018,600	1,051,300	5.8
Texas	3,382,887	4,059,619	4,331,751	4,405,215	4,525,394	4,599,509	4,674,832	4,752,148	4,850,210	4,935,715	5,000,470	5,077,659	5,153,702	8.4	5,221,000	5,291,000	5,348,300	5,399,800	5,545,700	5,825,000	13.0
Utah	446,652	481,485	495,981	503,607	508,430	523,386	576,244	559,778	571,586	585,552	598,832	613,279	625,461	11.7	635,600	646,100	655,300	663,200	688,800	739,300	18.2

See notes at end of table.

Table 203.20. Enrollment in public elementary and secondary schools, by region, state, and jurisdiction: Selected years, fall 1990 through fall 2025—Continued

Region, state, and jurisdiction	Actual total enrollment													Percent change in total enrollment, 2008 to 2013	Projected total enrollment						Percent change in total enrollment, 2013 to 2025
	Fall 1990	Fall 2000	Fall 2003	Fall 2004	Fall 2005	Fall 2006	Fall 2007	Fall 2008	Fall 2009	Fall 2010	Fall 2011	Fall 2012	Fall 2013		Fall 2014	Fall 2015	Fall 2016	Fall 2017	Fall 2020	Fall 2025	
1	2	3	4	5	6	7	8	9	10	11	12	13	14	15	16	17	18	19	20	21	22
Vermont	95,762	102,049	99,103	98,352	96,638	95,399	94,038	93,625	91,451	96,858	89,908	89,624	88,690	-5.3	87,800	86,900	86,100	85,100	83,100	79,600	-10.3
Virginia	998,601	1,144,915	1,192,092	1,204,739	1,213,616	1,220,440	1,230,857	1,235,795	1,245,340	1,251,440	1,257,883	1,265,419	1,273,825	3.1	1,279,200	1,286,000	1,292,000	1,297,000	1,310,700	1,331,100	4.5
Washington	839,709	1,004,770	1,021,349	1,020,005	1,031,985	1,026,774	1,030,247	1,037,018	1,035,347	1,043,788	1,045,453	1,051,694	1,058,936	2.1	1,065,400	1,072,200	1,079,200	1,086,200	1,109,600	1,149,300	8.5
West Virginia	322,389	286,367	281,215	280,129	280,866	281,939	282,535	282,662	282,729	282,879	282,870	283,044	280,958	-0.6	278,400	276,600	274,800	273,100	269,700	268,800	-4.3
Wisconsin	797,621	879,476	880,031	864,757	875,174	876,700	874,633	873,750	872,436	872,286	871,105	872,436	874,414	0.1	872,200	871,900	870,900	868,600	862,500	853,400	-2.4
Wyoming	98,226	89,940	87,462	84,733	84,409	85,193	86,422	87,161	88,155	89,009	90,099	91,533	92,732	6.4	93,900	95,000	96,000	96,900	99,800	102,700	10.8
Jurisdiction																					
Bureau of Indian Education	—	46,938	45,828	45,828	50,938	60,891	57,247	40,927	41,351	41,962	—	—	—	—	—	—	—	—	—	—	—
DoD, overseas	—	73,581	71,053	68,327	62,543	—	—	56,768	—	—	—	—	—	—	—	—	—	—	—	—	—
DoD, domestic	—	34,174	30,603	29,151	28,329	26,631	27,548	28,013	—	—	—	—	—	—	—	—	—	—	—	—	—
Other jurisdictions																					
American Samoa	12,463	15,702	15,893	16,126	16,438	16,400	—	—	—	—	—	—	—	—	—	—	—	—	—	—	—
Guam	26,391	32,473	31,572	30,605	30,986	—	—	—	—	31,618	31,243	31,186	33,414	—	—	—	—	—	—	—	—
Northern Marianas	6,449	10,004	11,244	11,601	11,718	11,695	11,299	10,913	10,961	11,105	11,011	10,646	10,638	-2.5	—	—	—	—	—	—	—
Puerto Rico	644,734	612,725	584,916	575,648	563,490	544,138	526,565	503,635	493,393	473,735	452,740	434,609	423,934	-15.8	—	—	—	—	—	—	—
U.S. Virgin Islands	21,750	19,459	17,716	16,429	16,750	16,284	15,903	15,768	15,493	15,495	15,711	15,192	14,953	-5.2	—	—	—	—	—	—	—

—Not available.
#Rounds to zero.
NOTE: DoD = Department of Defense. Detail may not sum to totals because of rounding. Some data have been revised from previously published figures.

SOURCE: U.S. Department of Education, National Center for Education Statistics, Common Core of Data (CCD), "State Nonfiscal Survey of Public Elementary/Secondary Education," 1990–91 through 2013–14; and State Public Elementary and Secondary Enrollment Projection Model, 1980 through 2025. (This table was prepared January 2016.)

Table 203.25. Public school enrollment in prekindergarten through grade 8, by region, state, and jurisdiction: Selected years, fall 1990 through fall 2025

Region, state, and jurisdiction	Fall 1990	Fall 2000	Fall 2003	Fall 2004	Fall 2005	Fall 2006	Fall 2007	Fall 2008	Fall 2009	Fall 2010	Fall 2011	Fall 2012	Fall 2013	Percent change in enrollment, 2008 to 2013	Fall 2014	Fall 2015	Fall 2016	Fall 2017	Fall 2020	Fall 2025	Percent change in enrollment, 2013 to 2025
	Actual enrollment														Projected enrollment						
1	2	3	4	5	6	7	8	9	10	11	12	13	14	15	16	17	18	19	20	21	22
United States	29,875,914	33,686,421	34,200,741	34,177,565	34,203,962	34,234,751	34,204,061	34,285,564	34,409,260	34,624,530	34,772,751	35,017,893	35,250,792	2.8	35,249,000	35,297,700	35,401,900	35,451,100	35,559,400	36,051,800	2.3
Region																					
Northeast	5,188,795	5,839,970	5,751,561	5,689,094	5,622,955	5,573,729	5,504,400	5,476,224	5,494,080	5,540,276	5,479,174	5,493,308	5,502,015	0.5	5,471,100	5,451,600	5,444,000	5,424,500	5,351,800	5,203,300	-5.4
Midwest	7,129,501	7,523,246	7,501,579	7,438,674	7,425,308	7,404,578	7,399,028	7,373,391	7,361,959	7,349,334	7,358,484	7,368,484	7,394,141	0.3	7,358,200	7,331,200	7,358,200	7,293,900	7,199,300	7,132,900	-3.5
South	10,858,800	12,314,176	12,675,179	12,760,160	12,881,836	12,989,696	13,085,045	13,166,590	13,300,643	13,434,553	13,578,211	13,711,284	13,830,129	5.0	13,883,100	13,953,300	14,047,100	14,129,500	14,378,800	14,808,200	7.1
West	6,698,818	8,009,029	8,272,422	8,289,637	8,273,863	8,266,748	8,255,608	8,268,969	8,252,578	8,300,367	8,356,574	8,444,817	8,524,507	3.1	8,536,600	8,561,600	8,592,100	8,603,200	8,629,500	8,907,400	4.5
State																					
Alabama	527,097	538,634	525,313	521,757	529,347	528,664	525,978	528,078	529,394	533,612	527,006	527,434	527,499	-0.1	524,300	522,800	523,200	523,800	525,300	522,800	-0.9
Alaska	85,297	94,442	93,695	91,981	91,225	90,167	88,980	89,263	90,824	91,990	92,057	93,069	92,714	3.9	93,000	93,600	94,600	95,700	97,700	100,000	7.9
Arizona	479,046	640,564	704,322	722,203	739,535	759,686	771,056	771,749	760,420	751,992	759,494	767,734	775,280	0.5	783,860	793,200	802,500	809,800	830,900	891,100	14.9
Arkansas	313,505	318,023	321,508	328,187	335,746	336,552	339,920	341,603	344,209	345,860	346,022	347,631	349,709	2.4	349,500	349,600	350,400	351,300	355,100	357,100	2.1
California	3,613,734	4,407,035	4,539,777	4,507,355	4,465,615	4,410,105	4,328,968	4,306,258	4,264,022	4,293,968	4,308,447	4,331,807	4,357,989	1.2	4,337,200	4,325,200	4,316,200	4,295,600	4,232,300	4,319,400	-0.9
Colorado	419,910	516,566	536,325	540,695	549,875	559,041	565,726	580,304	591,378	601,077	610,854	617,510	627,619	8.2	631,600	635,200	638,100	639,300	645,400	673,200	7.3
Connecticut	347,396	406,445	407,794	404,169	399,705	398,063	394,034	392,218	389,964	387,475	383,377	380,709	377,182	-3.8	371,400	366,100	361,700	355,900	341,300	323,100	-14.3
Delaware	72,606	80,801	82,898	83,599	84,639	84,996	85,019	86,811	87,710	90,279	90,624	91,004	93,204	7.4	93,700	94,500	95,200	96,500	95,800	97,600	4.7
District of Columbia	61,282	53,692	59,489	57,118	55,646	52,391	55,836	50,779	51,656	53,548	56,195	58,273	60,379	18.9	62,100	64,500	67,400	70,200	77,600	85,100	40.9
Florida	1,369,934	1,759,902	1,832,376	1,857,798	1,873,395	1,866,562	1,855,869	1,849,295	1,850,901	1,858,498	1,876,102	1,892,560	1,913,710	3.5	1,928,900	1,945,000	1,965,000	1,984,700	2,040,100	2,134,000	11.5
Georgia	849,082	1,059,983	1,103,181	1,118,379	1,145,446	1,166,508	1,178,577	1,185,684	1,194,751	1,202,479	1,211,250	1,222,289	1,233,877	4.1	1,237,600	1,241,600	1,248,100	1,255,300	1,278,900	1,336,500	8.3
Hawaii	122,840	132,293	130,054	128,788	127,472	126,008	125,556	125,910	127,477	127,525	131,005	133,590	135,925	8.0	136,700	138,100	139,100	139,700	140,700	139,900	2.9
Idaho	160,091	170,421	175,424	178,221	182,829	187,005	191,171	193,554	194,728	194,144	198,064	202,203	209,333	8.2	213,000	216,400	219,900	223,000	229,000	237,300	13.4
Illinois	1,309,516	1,473,933	1,492,725	1,483,644	1,480,320	1,477,679	1,472,909	1,479,195	1,463,713	1,454,793	1,453,156	1,448,201	1,445,459	-2.3	1,435,400	1,425,700	1,418,400	1,406,200	1,365,800	1,351,200	-6.5
Indiana	675,804	703,261	716,819	720,006	724,467	730,108	729,550	730,021	730,599	729,414	724,605	725,040	731,035	0.1	725,800	719,200	716,000	714,400	708,500	705,900	-3.4
Iowa	344,804	333,750	326,831	324,169	326,160	326,218	329,504	335,596	341,333	348,112	350,152	355,041	357,953	6.7	358,500	360,300	361,800	362,300	362,200	359,800	0.5
Kansas	319,648	323,157	322,491	321,176	320,513	326,201	326,771	331,079	332,997	342,927	347,129	349,695	355,929	7.5	356,600	358,000	360,000	361,000	362,800	364,400	2.4
Kentucky	459,020	471,429	478,254	481,174	484,639	487,165	469,373	472,204	480,334	480,334	488,456	491,310	485,001	2.7	481,600	478,500	478,300	476,700	474,700	476,400	-1.8
Louisiana	586,202	546,579	536,390	533,751	482,082	492,116	499,549	504,213	509,883	512,266	518,802	524,792	523,310	3.8	521,800	522,300	523,000	524,100	528,700	530,300	1.3
Maine	155,203	145,701	139,420	136,275	133,491	132,338	130,742	129,324	128,646	128,929	130,046	127,924	127,071	-1.7	125,600	124,300	123,300	122,000	117,500	111,500	-12.3
Maryland	526,744	609,043	605,682	597,417	598,571	579,065	576,479	576,473	581,785	588,156	594,216	602,802	612,580	6.3	618,700	626,400	631,900	635,900	642,200	638,200	4.2
Massachusetts	604,234	702,575	692,130	682,175	675,398	670,628	666,926	666,538	666,551	666,402	666,314	667,267	668,261	0.3	663,400	659,500	656,900	653,000	643,800	635,000	-5.0
Michigan	1,144,878	1,222,482	1,229,121	1,211,698	1,191,397	1,170,558	1,136,823	1,118,569	1,114,611	1,075,584	1,070,873	1,061,930	1,060,065	-5.2	1,044,900	1,032,700	1,024,400	1,015,200	990,100	970,900	-8.4
Minnesota	545,556	577,766	564,049	558,447	557,757	558,445	558,180	560,184	564,661	569,963	575,544	583,363	589,564	5.2	594,800	598,600	603,000	605,100	604,000	601,900	2.1
Mississippi	371,641	363,873	360,881	361,057	358,030	356,382	353,512	351,807	351,652	350,885	352,999	356,364	356,432	1.3	354,200	353,400	352,800	352,900	350,100	338,600	-5.0
Missouri	588,070	644,766	632,227	628,667	635,142	634,275	631,746	635,411	638,082	642,991	645,376	647,530	649,061	2.1	646,900	646,300	647,000	647,000	645,600	644,000	-0.8
Montana	111,169	105,226	100,160	98,673	97,770	97,021	96,354	96,869	97,868	98,491	99,725	100,819	101,991	5.3	103,000	103,800	104,600	105,300	107,300	111,900	9.7
Nebraska	198,080	195,496	195,417	194,816	195,055	195,769	200,095	202,912	206,860	210,292	213,504	215,432	219,122	8.0	218,600	219,200	219,900	218,600	216,600	222,100	1.4
Nevada	149,881	250,720	280,734	288,753	295,989	302,953	307,573	308,328	305,512	307,297	309,360	313,730	319,240	3.5	322,500	326,500	330,500	334,400	345,800	362,400	13.5
New Hampshire	126,301	147,121	142,031	140,241	138,584	136,188	134,359	132,995	132,768	131,576	129,632	128,169	126,933	-4.6	124,900	123,000	121,100	119,300	114,200	109,500	-13.8
New Jersey	783,422	967,533	978,440	975,856	970,592	963,418	954,418	956,785	968,332	981,265	947,576	956,070	956,379	#	951,900	949,100	947,600	944,100	930,400	903,800	-5.5
New Mexico	208,087	224,879	226,032	226,992	227,900	230,091	229,718	231,415	235,343	239,345	239,481	240,978	241,528	4.4	241,100	240,500	240,400	239,500	239,800	242,700	0.5
New York	1,827,418	2,028,906	1,978,181	1,942,575	1,909,028	1,887,284	1,856,315	1,843,080	1,847,003	1,869,150	1,857,574	1,868,561	1,884,845	2.3	1,879,000	1,880,500	1,886,900	1,888,400	1,884,200	1,838,400	-2.5
North Carolina	783,132	945,470	974,019	985,740	993,118	1,027,067	1,072,324	1,058,926	1,053,801	1,058,409	1,074,063	1,080,090	1,089,594	2.9	1,090,300	1,091,300	1,094,800	1,097,800	1,116,700	1,142,400	4.8
North Dakota	84,943	72,421	67,870	67,122	65,638	64,395	63,492	63,955	64,576	66,035	67,888	70,995	73,527	15.0	76,400	79,000	81,600	83,900	88,900	92,300	25.5
Ohio	1,257,580	1,293,646	1,278,202	1,267,088	1,261,331	1,253,193	1,241,322	1,239,494	1,225,346	1,222,808	1,217,299	1,211,299	1,208,500	-2.5	1,199,000	1,191,300	1,185,100	1,179,500	1,159,300	1,131,200	-6.4
Oklahoma	424,899	445,402	450,310	452,942	456,954	459,944	462,629	467,960	476,962	483,464	490,196	496,144	501,504	7.2	502,800	506,600	511,000	513,900	522,700	533,000	6.3
Oregon	340,243	379,264	378,052	376,933	379,680	380,576	383,598	395,421	404,451	392,601	391,310	409,325	414,405	4.8	416,100	418,900	422,100	424,600	431,200	437,700	5.6
Pennsylvania	1,172,164	1,257,824	1,235,624	1,234,828	1,227,625	1,220,074	1,205,361	1,194,327	1,200,046	1,209,786	1,204,232	1,204,732	1,201,169	0.6	1,195,500	1,190,800	1,189,500	1,185,700	1,168,400	1,134,600	-5.5
Rhode Island	101,797	113,545	111,209	107,040	103,870	101,996	99,159	97,983	98,184	97,734	97,659	97,809	98,738	0.8	98,500	97,800	97,200	96,500	94,500	92,100	-6.7
South Carolina	452,033	493,226	500,743	504,264	498,030	501,273	504,566	507,602	512,124	515,581	519,389	527,350	533,822	5.2	537,900	542,400	548,000	553,100	565,000	573,500	7.4
South Dakota	95,165	87,838	86,015	83,891	83,530	83,137	83,424	87,477	85,745	87,936	90,529	93,204	94,251	7.7	94,800	96,300	97,600	98,700	100,300	100,600	6.7
Tennessee	598,111	668,123	675,277	670,880	676,576	691,971	681,751	684,549	686,668	701,707	712,749	711,525	709,668	3.7	710,300	712,200	715,900	719,400	729,900	754,900	6.4
Texas	2,510,955	2,943,047	3,132,584	3,184,235	3,268,339	3,319,782	3,374,684	3,446,511	3,520,348	3,586,609	3,636,852	3,690,146	3,742,266	8.6	3,773,100	3,804,000	3,840,500	3,870,200	3,965,600	4,165,600	11.3
Utah	324,982	333,104	348,840	355,445	357,644	371,272	410,258	404,469	413,343	424,979	434,536	444,202	451,332	11.6	456,100	461,400	466,300	470,200	484,900	526,200	16.6

See notes at end of table.

Table 203.25. Public school enrollment in prekindergarten through grade 8, by region, state, and jurisdiction: Selected years, fall 1990 through fall 2025—Continued

Region, state, and jurisdiction	Actual enrollment													Percent change in enrollment, 2008 to 2013	Projected enrollment						Percent change in enrollment, 2013 to 2025
	Fall 1990	Fall 2000	Fall 2003	Fall 2004	Fall 2005	Fall 2006	Fall 2007	Fall 2008	Fall 2009	Fall 2010	Fall 2011	Fall 2012	Fall 2013		Fall 2014	Fall 2015	Fall 2016	Fall 2017	Fall 2020	Fall 2025	
1	2	3	4	5	6	7	8	9	10	11	12	13	14	15	16	17	18	19	20	21	22
Vermont	70,860	70,320	66,732	65,935	64,662	63,740	63,096	62,994	62,186	67,989	62,146	62,067	61,457	-2.4	60,900	60,400	59,900	59,400	57,600	55,200	-10.1
Virginia	728,280	815,748	837,258	839,687	841,299	841,685	850,444	855,008	864,020	871,446	881,225	889,444	896,573	4.9	897,900	900,700	905,000	908,900	915,800	927,300	3.4
Washington	612,597	694,367	699,248	695,405	699,482	694,858	697,407	704,794	705,387	714,172	718,184	724,560	730,868	3.7	735,200	740,700	748,700	755,600	774,200	793,600	8.6
West Virginia	224,097	201,201	198,836	197,555	197,189	197,573	198,545	199,477	200,313	201,472	202,065	202,371	201,001	0.8	198,500	197,300	196,500	195,900	194,800	195,100	-3.0
Wisconsin	565,457	594,740	589,812	577,950	583,998	584,600	585,212	589,528	593,436	598,479	602,810	606,754	609,675	3.4	606,100	604,700	604,000	601,900	595,200	588,500	-3.5
Wyoming	70,941	60,148	59,759	57,285	57,195	57,995	59,243	60,635	61,825	62,796	64,057	65,290	66,283	9.3	67,300	68,200	69,100	69,550	70,600	72,100	8.7
Jurisdiction																					
Bureau of Indian Education	—	35,746	33,671	33,671	36,133	—	—	30,612	31,381	31,985	—	—	—	—	—	—	—	—	—	—	—
DoD, overseas	—	59,299	56,226	53,720	48,691	47,589	44,418	43,931	—	—	—	—	—	—	—	—	—	—	—	—	—
DoD, domestic	—	30,697	27,500	26,195	25,558	24,052	24,807	25,255	—	—	—	—	—	—	—	—	—	—	—	—	—
Other jurisdictions																					
American Samoa	9,390	11,895	11,772	11,873	11,766	11,763	—	—	—	21,561	21,223	21,166	23,301	—	—	—	—	—	—	—	—
Guam	19,276	23,698	22,551	21,686	21,946	—	—	—	—	—	—	—	—	—	—	—	—	—	—	—	—
Northern Marianas	4,918	7,809	8,192	8,416	8,427	8,504	8,140	7,816	7,743	7,688	7,703	7,396	7,340	-6.1	—	—	—	—	—	—	—
Puerto Rico	480,356	445,524	418,649	408,671	399,447	382,647	372,514	355,115	347,638	334,613	318,924	305,048	294,976	-16.9	—	—	—	—	—	—	—
U.S. Virgin Islands	16,249	13,910	12,738	11,650	11,728	11,237	10,770	10,567	10,409	10,518	10,576	10,302	10,283	-2.7	—	—	—	—	—	—	—

—Not available.
#Rounds to zero.
NOTE: DoD = Department of Defense. Detail may not sum to totals because of rounding. Some data have been revised from previously published figures.

SOURCE: U.S. Department of Education, National Center for Education Statistics, Common Core of Data (CCD), "State Nonfiscal Survey of Public Elementary/Secondary Education," 1990–91 through 2013–14; and State Public Elementary and Secondary Enrollment Projection Model, 1980 through 2025. (This table was prepared January 2016.)

Table 203.30. Public school enrollment in grades 9 through 12, by region, state, and jurisdiction: Selected years, fall 1990 through fall 2025

Region, state, and jurisdiction	Fall 1990	Fall 2000	Fall 2003	Fall 2004	Fall 2005	Fall 2006	Fall 2007	Fall 2008	Fall 2009	Fall 2010	Fall 2011	Fall 2012	Fall 2013	Percent change in enrollment, 2008 to 2013	Fall 2014	Fall 2015	Fall 2016	Fall 2017	Fall 2020	Fall 2025	Percent change in enrollment, 2013 to 2025
1	2	3	4	5	6	7	8	9	10	11	12	13	14	15	16	17	18	19	20	21	22
United States	11,340,769	13,517,118	14,339,474	14,617,900	14,909,336	15,081,091	15,086,478	14,980,008	14,951,722	14,859,651	14,748,918	14,753,225	14,793,730	-1.2	14,882,600	14,970,400	14,983,400	15,026,300	15,214,600	15,367,900	3.9
Region																					
Northeast	2,092,968	2,382,157	2,540,754	2,582,165	2,617,205	2,684,160	2,617,622	2,576,761	2,597,949	2,531,059	2,474,807	2,465,820	2,459,228	-4.6	2,446,900	2,437,000	2,422,000	2,417,300	2,409,200	2,375,100	-3.4
Midwest	2,814,260	3,206,741	3,307,398	3,336,735	3,393,507	3,414,670	3,411,182	3,369,682	3,310,212	3,260,270	3,215,000	3,190,746	3,178,779	-5.7	3,190,900	3,203,300	3,198,200	3,199,500	3,210,600	3,150,700	-0.9
South	3,948,816	4,693,085	4,997,566	5,111,827	5,221,330	5,303,937	5,337,728	5,323,790	5,351,246	5,370,447	5,377,721	5,417,092	5,468,585	2.7	5,548,900	5,623,100	5,652,500	5,674,900	5,756,000	6,002,200	9.8
West	2,485,325	3,235,135	3,493,756	3,587,173	3,677,294	3,678,324	3,719,946	3,709,875	3,692,315	3,697,875	3,681,390	3,679,567	3,687,138	-0.6	3,695,900	3,707,000	3,710,600	3,734,600	3,638,800	3,839,800	4.1
State																					
Alabama	194,709	201,358	205,907	208,383	212,414	214,968	216,941	217,590	219,495	221,940	217,615	217,203	218,705	0.5	219,600	218,300	216,300	213,700	208,800	211,900	-3.1
Alaska	28,606	38,914	40,238	40,999	42,063	42,441	42,049	41,399	40,837	40,114	39,110	38,420	38,230	-7.7	37,900	37,800	37,500	37,000	38,000	40,100	4.8
Arizona	160,807	237,132	307,746	321,095	354,919	308,593	316,391	316,068	317,411	319,759	320,825	321,650	327,165	3.5	324,300	322,800	321,400	325,100	343,200	369,600	9.9
Arkansas	122,781	131,936	133,015	134,928	138,460	139,857	139,096	137,362	136,360	136,306	137,092	138,526	140,270	2.1	141,000	141,200	141,000	140,500	138,600	143,300	2.2
California	1,336,740	1,733,779	1,874,090	1,934,202	1,971,587	1,996,645	2,014,503	2,016,270	1,999,416	1,995,610	1,979,387	1,967,644	1,954,634	-3.1	1,951,000	1,946,100	1,940,100	1,948,800	1,987,500	1,901,800	-2.7
Colorado	154,303	207,942	221,368	225,281	229,951	234,985	236,141	238,139	240,990	242,239	243,411	246,051	249,380	4.7	254,400	259,900	264,400	269,500	280,100	284,700	14.1
Connecticut	121,727	155,734	169,409	173,221	175,354	177,037	176,592	174,980	174,004	173,071	171,060	170,245	169,038	-3.4	166,800	165,600	163,400	162,100	157,200	145,500	-13.9
Delaware	27,052	33,875	34,770	35,492	36,298	37,258	37,555	38,619	39,091	39,124	38,322	38,022	38,483	-0.4	38,600	38,900	39,300	40,000	42,300	42,300	10.0
District of Columbia	19,412	15,233	18,568	19,596	21,230	20,459	22,586	17,902	17,777	17,736	17,716	17,867	17,774	-0.7	18,000	18,000	17,800	17,700	18,800	23,900	34.2
Florida	491,658	674,919	755,252	781,538	801,629	804,951	810,952	781,725	783,621	784,849	792,054	799,602	807,034	3.2	817,800	825,600	827,800	826,700	842,000	900,300	11.6
Georgia	302,605	384,954	419,430	435,058	453,015	482,649	471,012	470,108	472,934	474,588	473,766	481,043	490,032	4.2	500,100	508,900	512,300	513,200	518,300	537,100	9.6
Hawaii	48,868	52,067	53,555	54,397	55,346	54,720	54,341	53,568	52,719	52,076	51,701	51,170	50,900	-5.0	51,100	50,700	51,200	52,100	54,200	55,900	9.8
Idaho	60,749	74,696	76,696	77,863	79,153	80,375	80,948	81,497	81,571	81,715	81,809	82,631	87,143	6.9	89,200	92,000	93,500	94,200	100,500	109,400	25.5
Illinois	511,891	574,859	608,236	613,859	631,386	640,597	639,896	640,512	640,462	636,861	629,941	624,679	621,531	-3.0	626,100	629,700	632,700	634,400	649,700	610,000	-1.9
Indiana	278,721	286,006	294,311	301,342	310,607	315,832	317,214	316,126	316,082	317,818	316,160	316,329	316,350	0.1	316,600	319,400	318,500	315,100	305,700	302,800	-4.3
Iowa	138,848	161,330	154,395	154,150	157,322	156,904	155,611	151,993	150,509	147,663	145,718	144,784	145,011	-4.6	146,000	146,500	146,900	147,600	150,900	154,400	6.5
Kansas	117,386	147,453	147,999	147,960	147,012	143,305	141,524	139,981	141,492	140,774	138,979	139,348	140,511	0.4	142,100	144,100	144,800	146,300	149,900	153,200	9.0
Kentucky	177,201	194,421	185,115	189,002	192,449	195,987	196,852	197,826	195,623	192,794	193,531	194,102	192,388	-2.7	191,900	192,300	190,800	190,900	188,600	185,300	-3.7
Louisiana	198,555	196,510	191,319	190,530	172,444	183,735	181,489	180,660	181,032	184,292	184,588	186,111	188,181	4.2	190,600	192,300	192,600	192,500	189,800	194,700	3.5
Maine	59,946	61,336	62,664	62,545	62,007	61,648	65,503	63,611	60,579	60,148	58,923	57,815	56,924	-10.5	56,400	55,700	54,700	54,000	53,300	50,400	-11.5
Maryland	188,432	243,877	263,251	268,144	271,449	272,575	269,221	267,388	266,627	264,055	259,870	256,836	253,589	-5.2	253,200	252,800	254,900	258,400	270,000	284,100	12.0
Massachusetts	230,080	272,575	288,329	293,399	296,511	298,033	296,032	292,372	290,502	289,161	287,055	287,506	287,478	-1.7	288,100	288,400	286,900	286,700	283,800	275,700	-4.1
Michigan	439,553	498,144	528,483	539,592	550,885	552,098	555,916	541,352	534,471	511,483	502,664	493,440	488,776	-9.7	487,800	485,600	478,800	473,700	459,700	436,600	-10.7
Minnesota	210,818	276,574	278,805	280,056	281,486	282,120	279,398	275,864	272,392	268,074	264,194	262,041	261,409	-5.2	264,100	266,300	268,700	272,100	286,000	291,200	11.4
Mississippi	130,776	133,998	132,659	134,319	136,924	138,644	140,610	140,155	140,829	139,641	137,620	137,286	136,154	-2.9	136,700	136,400	135,500	133,300	129,700	132,600	-2.6
Missouri	228,488	267,978	273,714	276,782	282,563	286,078	285,442	282,460	279,900	275,719	271,208	270,370	269,227	-4.7	269,400	269,000	266,800	265,400	265,300	267,200	-0.8
Montana	41,805	49,649	48,196	48,032	47,646	47,397	46,469	45,030	43,939	43,202	42,624	42,089	42,138	-6.4	41,900	41,900	42,000	42,100	43,600	45,400	7.7
Nebraska	76,001	90,713	90,125	90,945	91,591	91,811	91,149	89,678	88,508	88,208	87,792	88,073	88,555	-1.3	90,100	91,600	93,300	95,000	98,800	95,900	8.3
Nevada	51,435	89,986	104,667	111,330	116,406	121,813	121,789	125,043	123,435	129,852	130,274	131,971	132,591	6.0	133,100	135,100	136,400	137,400	141,800	153,800	16.0
New Hampshire	46,484	61,340	65,386	66,611	67,183	67,384	66,413	64,939	64,372	63,135	62,268	60,805	59,377	-8.6	58,500	57,500	56,600	55,900	54,000	49,600	-16.4
New Jersey	306,224	345,872	402,313	417,491	425,010	425,432	427,930	424,655	427,697	421,293	408,855	416,133	413,916	-2.5	413,700	412,900	411,100	411,100	410,900	405,800	-2.0
New Mexico	93,794	95,427	97,034	98,202	97,206	98,129	99,322	99,830	99,076	98,777	97,744	97,242	97,716	-1.1	98,300	98,800	99,500	99,300	100,000	99,800	2.1
New York	770,919	853,282	886,594	893,762	906,553	922,365	909,120	897,512	919,049	865,805	847,144	842,142	848,776	-5.5	847,300	844,600	841,000	841,700	846,200	854,700	0.8
North Carolina	303,739	348,168	386,190	400,014	413,318	417,414	417,168	429,719	429,596	432,196	433,801	438,375	441,263	2.7	446,600	452,000	454,400	455,800	449,900	467,600	6.0
North Dakota	32,882	36,780	34,363	33,391	32,645	32,275	31,567	30,773	30,497	30,288	29,758	30,116	30,420	-1.1	30,500	31,000	31,300	31,900	36,200	42,700	40.5
Ohio	513,509	541,403	567,226	572,944	578,352	583,529	585,882	577,669	538,951	531,383	522,804	518,617	518,611	-10.7	515,400	516,300	512,800	510,000	501,600	489,700	-5.0
Oklahoma	154,188	177,708	175,850	176,534	177,785	179,447	179,436	177,148	177,840	176,447	175,924	177,339	180,344	1.8	183,600	186,400	187,900	189,600	194,500	203,300	12.7
Oregon	132,151	166,967	173,221	175,572	172,514	181,998	181,988	179,972	178,388	178,119	176,898	178,239	178,595	-0.8	178,500	178,900	178,200	178,300	181,400	189,800	6.3
Pennsylvania	495,670	556,487	583,522	583,261	603,059	650,986	596,620	590,702	585,547	583,518	566,545	558,945	554,067	-4.6	546,800	543,400	539,700	536,900	535,100	527,300	-4.8
Rhode Island	37,016	43,802	48,166	49,458	49,552	49,616	48,470	47,369	46,059	46,050	45,195	44,672	43,270	-8.6	42,500	42,400	42,400	43,100	43,100	41,800	-3.5
South Carolina	170,079	184,185	198,455	199,472	203,514	206,748	207,751	210,511	211,019	210,257	207,797	208,648	211,835	0.6	216,700	220,800	222,000	222,000	226,200	242,300	14.4
South Dakota	33,999	40,765	39,522	38,907	38,482	38,021	38,182	38,952	37,968	38,192	37,487	37,267	36,639	-5.9	36,800	36,700	36,800	37,100	39,500	42,000	14.7
Tennessee	226,484	241,038	261,405	270,211	277,352	286,397	282,508	282,401	285,881	285,715	286,944	281,971	283,888	-1.2	285,500	286,900	286,800	285,800	288,700	296,400	4.4
Texas	871,032	1,116,572	1,199,167	1,220,980	1,257,055	1,279,727	1,300,148	1,305,637	1,329,862	1,349,106	1,363,618	1,387,513	1,411,436	8.1	1,447,900	1,487,000	1,507,800	1,529,600	1,580,100	1,659,500	17.6
Utah	121,670	148,381	147,141	148,162	150,786	152,114	165,986	155,309	158,243	160,573	164,296	169,077	174,129	12.1	179,600	184,600	189,000	193,100	203,900	213,200	22.4

See notes at end of table.

Table 203.30. Public school enrollment in grades 9 through 12, by region, state, and jurisdiction: Selected years, fall 1990 through fall 2025—Continued

Region, state, and jurisdiction	Fall 1990	Fall 2000	Fall 2003	Fall 2004	Fall 2005	Fall 2006	Fall 2007	Fall 2008	Fall 2009	Fall 2010	Fall 2011	Fall 2012	Fall 2013	Percent change in enrollment, 2008 to 2013	Fall 2014	Fall 2015	Fall 2016	Fall 2017	Fall 2020	Fall 2025	Percent change in enrollment, 2013 to 2025
1	2	3	4	5	6	7	8	9	10	11	12	13	14	15	16	17	18	19	20	21	22
Vermont	24,902	31,729	32,371	32,417	31,976	31,659	30,942	30,631	29,265	28,869	27,762	27,557	27,233	-11.1	26,900	26,500	26,200	25,700	25,600	24,400	-10.5
Virginia	270,321	329,167	354,834	365,052	372,317	378,755	380,413	380,787	381,320	379,994	376,658	375,975	377,282	-0.9	381,300	385,300	387,000	388,100	394,800	403,900	7.1
Washington	227,112	310,403	322,101	324,600	332,503	331,916	332,840	332,224	329,960	329,616	327,289	327,134	328,068	-1.3	330,200	331,500	330,500	330,600	335,400	355,700	8.4
West Virginia	98,292	85,166	82,379	82,574	83,677	84,366	83,990	83,252	82,349	81,407	80,805	80,673	79,957	-4.0	79,900	79,300	78,300	77,100	74,900	73,800	-7.7
Wisconsin	232,164	284,736	290,219	286,807	291,176	292,100	289,421	284,222	279,000	273,807	268,295	265,682	264,739	-6.9	266,000	267,200	266,800	266,600	267,300	285,000	0.1
Wyoming	27,285	29,792	27,703	27,448	27,214	27,198	27,179	26,526	26,330	26,223	26,042	26,243	26,449	-0.3	26,600	26,800	26,900	27,300	29,200	30,700	16.0
Jurisdiction																					
Bureau of Indian Education	—	11,192	12,157	12,157	14,805	13,302	12,829	10,315	9,970	9,977	—	—	—	—	—	—	—	—	—	—	—
DoD, overseas	—	14,282	14,827	14,607	13,852	—	—	12,837	—	—	—	—	—	—	—	—	—	—	—	—	—
DoD, domestic	—	3,477	3,103	2,956	2,771	2,579	2,741	2,758	—	—	—	—	—	—	—	—	—	—	—	—	—
Other jurisdictions																					
American Samoa	3,073	3,807	4,121	4,253	4,672	4,637	—	—	—	—	—	—	—	—	—	—	—	—	—	—	—
Guam	7,115	8,775	9,021	8,919	9,040	—	—	—	—	10,057	10,020	10,020	10,113	—	—	—	—	—	—	—	—
Northern Marianas	1,531	2,195	3,052	3,185	3,291	3,191	3,159	3,097	3,218	3,417	3,308	3,250	3,298	6.5	—	—	—	—	—	—	—
Puerto Rico	164,378	167,201	166,267	166,977	164,043	161,491	154,051	148,520	145,755	139,122	133,816	129,561	128,958	-13.2	—	—	—	—	—	—	—
U.S. Virgin Islands	5,501	5,549	4,978	4,779	5,022	5,047	5,133	5,201	5,084	4,977	5,135	4,890	4,670	-10.2	—	—	—	—	—	—	—

—Not available.
NOTE: DoD = Department of Defense. Detail may not sum to totals because of rounding. Some data have been revised from previously published figures.

SOURCE: U.S. Department of Education, National Center for Education Statistics, Common Core of Data (CCD), "State Nonfiscal Survey of Public Elementary/Secondary Education," 1990–91 through 2013–14; and State Public Elementary and Secondary Enrollment Projection Model, 1980 through 2025. (This table was prepared January 2016.)

Table 203.40. Enrollment in public elementary and secondary schools, by level, grade, and state or jurisdiction: Fall 2013

State or jurisdiction	Total, all grades	Elementary												Secondary					
		Total	Prekinder-garten	Kinder-garten	Grade 1	Grade 2	Grade 3	Grade 4	Grade 5	Grade 6	Grade 7	Grade 8	Elementary ungraded	Total	Grade 9	Grade 10	Grade 11	Grade 12	Secondary ungraded
1	2	3	4	5	6	7	8	9	10	11	12	13	14	15	16	17	18	19	20
United States	50,044,522	35,250,792	1,328,434	3,833,526	3,884,820	3,791,122	3,737,690	3,707,733	3,696,718	3,684,476	3,747,574	3,753,357	85,342	14,793,730	3,979,521	3,760,559	3,525,617	3,476,132	51,901
Alabama	746,204	527,499	9,415	59,757	60,315	56,909	56,003	55,719	55,699	56,428	58,455	58,799	0	218,705	62,069	56,144	51,527	48,965	0
Alaska	130,944	92,714	3,247	10,632	10,529	10,208	9,902	9,722	9,543	9,518	9,736	9,677	0	38,230	9,904	9,284	9,542	9,500	0
Arizona	1,102,445	775,280	8,791	86,258	88,553	85,814	85,149	84,282	84,535	83,495	84,315	83,849	239	327,165	83,995	81,410	77,448	84,291	21
Arkansas	489,979	349,709	14,984	39,900	39,720	36,244	36,090	36,321	36,146	36,564	36,876	36,660	204	140,270	37,934	36,447	34,158	31,646	85
California	6,312,623	4,357,989	75,951	506,831	470,812	485,674	474,323	470,515	469,645	462,125	465,592	472,381	4,140	1,954,634	491,493	484,993	477,425	498,403	2,320
Colorado	876,999	627,619	31,741	67,225	68,509	67,460	66,429	66,140	66,326	65,161	64,808	63,820	0	249,380	64,753	62,510	59,281	62,836	0
Connecticut	546,200	377,162	16,922	38,274	40,005	39,024	39,629	39,810	40,857	40,058	41,123	41,460	0	169,038	45,055	42,211	40,997	40,775	0
Delaware	131,687	93,204	1,413	10,488	10,370	10,487	10,220	10,069	10,209	9,965	9,990	9,993	0	38,483	11,418	9,718	8,811	8,536	0
District of Columbia	78,153	60,379	11,867	7,174	6,787	6,005	5,479	4,826	4,648	4,452	4,617	4,425	99	17,774	6,116	4,448	3,827	3,326	57
Florida	2,720,744	1,913,710	56,470	209,318	216,003	208,256	212,806	198,411	197,996	200,499	207,253	206,698	0	807,034	219,016	206,599	197,997	183,422	0
Georgia	1,723,909	1,233,877	45,427	136,658	137,101	133,003	131,114	129,329	128,527	129,456	131,967	131,295	0	490,032	148,721	128,105	110,112	103,094	0
Hawaii	186,825	135,925	1,577	17,561	16,271	15,419	15,269	14,810	14,631	13,952	13,090	13,228	117	50,900	14,595	13,132	12,154	10,925	94
Idaho	296,476	209,333	4,081	23,396	23,954	23,213	23,118	22,803	22,268	22,093	22,416	21,991	0	87,143	23,011	22,078	20,991	21,063	0
Illinois	2,066,990	1,445,459	80,953	145,117	152,879	149,990	151,750	152,779	151,364	152,129	153,920	154,578	0	621,531	165,333	159,174	152,458	144,566	0
Indiana	1,047,385	731,035	14,586	80,611	81,471	78,613	78,508	77,584	76,451	78,726	82,656	80,754	1,075	316,350	82,622	80,353	77,504	75,871	0
Iowa	502,964	357,953	28,075	41,240	37,397	36,717	36,026	35,617	35,606	35,371	35,666	36,238	0	145,011	36,944	36,349	35,460	36,258	0
Kansas	496,440	355,929	18,746	38,534	38,403	37,280	36,669	36,435	36,536	35,907	36,412	36,457	4,550	140,511	36,955	35,699	33,204	32,989	1,664
Kentucky	677,389	485,001	27,142	52,267	54,401	51,484	49,972	49,770	49,779	49,134	50,519	50,203	330	192,388	52,710	49,972	45,842	43,732	132
Louisiana	711,491	523,310	29,319	57,377	59,386	55,212	53,429	56,770	50,511	53,268	53,196	54,842	0	188,181	56,215	48,460	42,388	41,118	0
Maine	183,995	127,071	5,004	13,451	13,562	13,354	13,493	13,550	13,371	13,469	13,842	13,975	0	56,924	14,365	14,540	14,055	13,964	0
Maryland	866,169	612,580	29,811	67,548	68,373	66,320	64,855	64,629	63,817	63,243	61,662	62,322	0	253,589	69,952	64,688	59,835	59,114	0
Massachusetts	955,739	668,261	28,189	69,853	71,911	70,323	69,700	70,862	71,179	70,948	72,050	72,116	1,130	287,478	76,415	73,464	70,170	67,429	0
Michigan	1,548,841	1,060,065	40,660	106,166	113,323	111,911	110,437	113,400	112,175	113,458	117,440	118,440	2,645	488,776	126,842	127,799	116,270	116,607	1,258
Minnesota	850,973	589,564	14,556	65,618	65,960	64,575	63,654	63,979	62,900	61,871	63,552	62,899	0	261,409	64,424	63,815	64,080	69,090	0
Mississippi	492,586	356,432	4,329	41,948	42,925	39,096	37,301	36,959	36,118	37,018	37,516	37,896	5,326	136,154	37,991	34,605	30,560	29,412	3,586
Missouri	918,288	649,061	30,339	70,845	71,555	69,250	68,316	67,908	67,344	67,026	68,077	68,401	0	269,227	71,149	69,057	65,303	63,718	0
Montana	144,129	101,991	1,440	12,038	11,611	11,570	11,047	11,028	10,848	10,898	10,876	10,635	0	42,138	11,228	10,726	10,272	9,912	0
Nebraska	307,677	219,122	14,457	24,025	21,980	23,249	22,911	23,097	22,644	22,441	22,229	22,089	0	88,555	22,051	21,925	21,611	22,968	0
Nevada	451,831	319,240	4,707	35,073	37,162	35,414	34,491	33,827	33,863	34,478	34,886	34,541	798	132,591	34,497	33,935	32,682	31,450	27
New Hampshire	186,310	126,933	3,464	11,615	13,524	13,519	13,563	13,953	13,962	14,265	14,378	14,690	0	59,377	15,766	15,131	14,340	14,140	0
New Jersey	1,370,295	956,379	36,024	92,017	100,557	98,842	97,686	98,832	98,388	97,952	99,801	99,950	36,330	413,916	104,627	101,728	97,390	95,646	14,525
New Mexico	339,244	241,528	7,865	27,368	27,504	26,251	25,779	25,597	25,275	25,284	25,543	25,062	0	97,716	29,729	25,491	22,363	20,133	0
New York	2,732,770	1,884,845	48,968	201,930	209,128	203,908	198,174	196,988	198,824	197,036	199,676	203,267	26,946	847,925	223,440	213,861	192,944	190,081	27,599
North Carolina	1,530,857	1,089,594	30,978	122,209	123,140	119,088	115,962	108,034	116,515	116,654	119,049	117,965	0	441,263	126,737	114,718	103,355	96,453	0
North Dakota	103,947	73,527	2,054	8,822	8,608	8,405	7,857	7,824	7,536	7,471	7,598	7,352	0	30,420	7,813	7,749	7,469	7,389	0
Ohio	1,724,111	1,208,500	28,477	131,003	132,883	129,681	128,124	128,668	129,598	130,755	134,269	135,042	0	515,611	147,490	134,963	118,551	114,607	0
Oklahoma	681,848	501,504	42,770	54,923	56,067	51,556	49,975	49,603	49,276	48,587	48,751	48,583	1,413	180,344	50,284	47,179	42,850	39,498	533
Oregon	593,000	414,405	25,902	42,728	44,741	43,602	42,649	42,858	42,752	42,449	43,202	43,522	0	178,595	44,396	44,491	42,633	47,075	0
Pennsylvania	1,755,236	1,201,169	8,499	129,360	133,419	131,275	129,889	132,216	131,917	131,345	135,962	137,287	0	554,067	144,721	140,209	133,554	135,583	0
Rhode Island	142,008	98,738	2,242	10,490	10,823	10,697	10,676	11,037	10,751	10,865	10,864	10,293	0	43,270	10,912	11,304	10,651	10,403	0

See notes at end of table.

Table 203.40. Enrollment in public elementary and secondary schools, by level, grade, and state or jurisdiction: Fall 2013—Continued

State or jurisdiction	Total, all grades	Elementary												Secondary					
		Total	Prekindergarten	Kindergarten	Grade 1	Grade 2	Grade 3	Grade 4	Grade 5	Grade 6	Grade 7	Grade 8	Elementary ungraded	Total	Grade 9	Grade 10	Grade 11	Grade 12	Secondary ungraded
1	2	3	4	5	6	7	8	9	10	11	12	13	14	15	16	17	18	19	20
South Carolina	745,657	533,822	24,295	58,226	60,401	57,286	55,331	54,672	54,512	55,267	57,070	56,762	0	211,835	63,304	55,463	48,444	44,624	0
South Dakota	130,890	94,251	2,865	11,898	10,855	10,446	10,310	9,842	9,621	9,499	9,384	9,531	0	36,639	10,062	9,385	8,707	8,485	0
Tennessee	993,556	709,668	25,756	78,601	80,082	77,373	75,382	74,401	74,124	73,970	75,070	74,909	0	283,888	77,917	72,827	67,290	65,854	0
Texas	5,153,702	3,742,266	248,150	391,731	409,446	394,449	390,023	383,586	382,945	376,623	385,527	379,786	0	1,411,436	408,892	362,937	330,538	309,069	0
Utah	625,461	451,332	12,373	50,386	51,413	50,197	49,048	49,041	48,483	47,161	46,821	46,409	0	174,129	45,902	44,431	42,469	41,327	0
Vermont	88,690	61,457	5,667	6,215	6,246	6,017	6,254	6,159	6,108	6,163	6,296	6,332	0	27,233	7,137	6,828	6,723	6,545	0
Virginia	1,273,825	896,573	33,166	96,058	99,806	97,162	95,384	95,625	93,994	94,524	95,076	95,778	0	377,252	102,293	96,496	89,754	88,709	0
Washington	1,058,936	730,868	11,957	81,559	83,314	80,412	79,203	78,929	78,538	77,603	79,400	79,953	0	328,068	82,991	81,205	79,162	84,710	0
West Virginia	280,958	201,001	15,472	21,541	21,319	20,284	20,224	20,418	20,164	20,543	20,402	20,634	0	79,957	22,257	20,688	18,713	18,299	0
Wisconsin	874,414	609,675	56,777	61,522	62,479	60,999	60,697	61,393	60,768	60,505	61,814	62,721	0	264,739	67,985	64,958	65,450	66,346	0
Wyoming	92,732	66,283	514	8,141	7,837	7,609	7,410	7,086	7,131	6,804	6,884	6,867	0	26,449	7,093	6,877	6,303	6,176	0
Bureau of Indian Education	—	—	—	—	—	—	—	—	—	—	—	—	—	—	—	—	—	—	—
DoD, overseas	—	—	—	—	—	—	—	—	—	—	—	—	—	—	—	—	—	—	—
DoD, domestic	—	—	—	—	—	—	—	—	—	—	—	—	—	—	—	—	—	—	—
Other jurisdictions																			
American Samoa	—	—	—	—	—	—	—	—	—	—	—	—	—	—	—	—	—	—	—
Guam	33,414	23,301	828	3,113	2,818	2,788	2,243	2,337	2,244	2,251	2,315	2,364	0	10,113	3,284	3,063	2,000	1,766	0
Northern Marianas	10,638	7,340	462	544	770	730	720	750	773	782	926	814	69	3,298	1,084	862	696	656	0
Puerto Rico	423,934	294,976	1,410	27,752	32,864	30,684	31,193	31,076	30,264	31,073	34,510	34,365	9,785	128,958	33,525	32,990	29,971	27,374	5,098
U.S. Virgin Islands	14,953	10,283	—	1,167	1,112	1,141	1,117	1,150	1,137	1,175	1,213	1,071	0	4,670	1,573	1,093	992	1,012	0

—Not available.
NOTE: DoD = Department of Defense. The total ungraded counts of students were prorated to the elementary and secondary levels based on prior reports.

SOURCE: U.S. Department of Education, National Center for Education Statistics, Common Core of Data (CCD), "State Non-fiscal Survey of Public Elementary/Secondary Education," 2013–14. (This table was prepared August 2015.)

Table 203.45.　Enrollment in public elementary and secondary schools, by level, grade, and state or jurisdiction: Fall 2012

State or jurisdiction	Total, all grades	Elementary — Total	Prekindergarten	Kindergarten	Grade 1	Grade 2	Grade 3	Grade 4	Grade 5	Grade 6	Grade 7	Grade 8	Elementary ungraded	Secondary — Total	Grade 9	Grade 10	Grade 11	Grade 12	Secondary ungraded
1	2	3	4	5	6	7	8	9	10	11	12	13	14	15	16	17	18	19	20
United States	49,771,118	35,017,893	1,306,991	3,830,982	3,823,604	3,729,465	3,719,135	3,690,224	3,672,977	3,723,354	3,746,485	3,696,977	75,699	14,753,225	3,975,264	3,729,960	3,528,256	3,477,025	42,720
Alabama	744,637	527,434	9,032	59,428	58,287	56,361	55,868	55,859	56,523	58,240	59,685	58,151	0	217,203	61,642	56,229	50,387	48,945	0
Alaska	131,489	93,069	3,131	10,569	10,393	10,109	9,950	9,756	9,677	9,844	9,834	9,806	0	38,420	9,724	9,415	9,585	9,696	0
Arizona	1,089,384	767,734	9,304	86,265	86,474	84,763	83,883	83,892	83,093	83,540	83,568	82,769	183	321,650	82,291	80,074	77,518	81,751	16
Arkansas	486,157	347,631	14,290	40,463	37,093	36,450	36,362	36,140	36,569	36,727	36,693	36,607	237	138,526	37,978	36,343	33,373	30,734	98
California	6,299,451	4,331,807	74,360	489,274	489,420	474,656	470,243	468,007	462,439	463,024	470,054	465,967	4,363	1,967,644	497,945	487,566	482,903	496,754	2,476
Colorado	863,561	617,510	30,375	66,951	67,369	66,134	65,667	65,921	64,727	64,448	63,658	62,260	0	246,051	63,859	60,842	58,847	62,503	0
Connecticut	550,954	380,709	16,393	39,410	39,558	39,858	39,867	40,895	40,196	40,979	41,533	42,020	0	170,245	45,166	42,144	42,192	40,743	0
Delaware	129,026	91,004	1,291	10,128	10,393	10,123	9,963	10,089	9,619	9,699	9,983	9,716	0	38,022	11,056	9,670	8,931	8,365	0
District of Columbia	76,140	58,273	11,428	6,980	6,163	5,629	4,991	4,631	4,575	4,627	4,559	4,202	488	17,867	6,275	4,245	3,740	3,317	290
Florida	2,692,162	1,892,560	55,124	210,489	208,344	202,517	209,027	195,358	197,412	204,704	205,469	204,116	0	799,602	215,693	206,662	194,054	183,193	0
Georgia	1,703,332	1,222,289	45,252	136,837	133,482	130,176	129,257	128,538	129,054	130,803	130,458	128,432	0	481,043	146,953	124,928	108,084	101,078	0
Hawaii	184,760	133,590	1,509	17,497	15,555	15,264	14,810	14,572	14,383	13,315	13,772	12,791	122	51,170	14,786	13,307	12,255	10,721	101
Idaho	284,834	202,203	2,683	22,409	22,535	22,508	22,247	21,884	22,000	22,304	21,963	21,670	0	82,631	21,987	20,812	20,702	19,130	0
Illinois	2,072,880	1,448,201	81,475	147,315	150,312	150,336	154,232	151,409	151,508	154,031	155,078	152,505	0	624,679	165,536	160,924	151,946	146,273	0
Indiana	1,041,369	725,040	9,114	80,681	80,151	77,465	80,476	75,678	78,450	82,158	80,959	79,908	0	316,329	82,545	80,253	78,645	74,886	0
Iowa	499,825	355,041	27,729	41,381	36,730	35,891	35,455	35,492	35,142	35,469	36,058	35,694	0	144,784	36,752	36,240	35,538	36,254	0
Kansas	489,043	349,695	18,475	38,379	37,304	36,399	36,009	36,167	35,546	35,962	35,963	35,447	4,044	139,348	37,060	34,486	33,499	32,810	1,493
Kentucky	685,167	491,065	26,753	53,875	54,028	51,296	51,215	50,583	49,999	51,550	51,154	50,259	353	194,102	53,562	49,561	46,806	44,032	141
Louisiana	710,903	524,792	29,426	58,691	58,085	54,765	53,691	57,434	51,799	53,866	54,528	52,507	0	186,111	55,745	46,920	43,267	40,179	0
Maine	185,739	127,924	4,890	13,727	13,449	13,575	13,628	13,345	13,427	13,778	13,978	14,127	0	57,815	14,684	14,421	14,248	14,462	0
Maryland	859,638	602,802	29,671	66,896	66,274	64,595	64,272	63,703	63,204	61,120	62,159	60,908	0	256,836	71,360	64,841	60,657	59,978	0
Massachusetts	954,773	667,267	28,245	69,669	70,629	69,549	70,673	70,952	70,826	71,588	72,012	72,048	1,076	287,506	77,458	72,264	69,928	67,856	0
Michigan	1,555,370	1,061,930	36,769	107,986	113,035	110,939	113,332	112,952	112,720	116,465	118,538	117,640	2,438	493,440	128,111	128,144	117,453	118,564	1,168
Minnesota	845,404	583,363	14,695	65,745	64,520	63,357	63,659	62,523	61,355	62,547	62,627	62,335	0	262,041	63,743	64,278	63,510	70,510	0
Mississippi	493,650	356,364	4,026	43,208	40,851	38,001	37,735	36,663	37,336	37,646	39,034	36,745	5,119	137,286	37,825	34,874	31,434	29,676	3,477
Missouri	917,900	647,530	29,684	71,778	70,072	68,570	68,043	67,493	67,269	67,959	68,605	68,057	0	270,370	72,240	68,242	65,737	64,151	0
Montana	142,908	100,819	1,321	11,709	11,678	11,031	11,036	10,861	10,822	10,842	10,624	10,895	0	42,089	11,256	10,676	10,373	9,784	0
Nebraska	303,505	215,432	13,831	22,095	23,331	22,836	23,057	22,583	22,370	21,998	21,893	21,438	0	88,073	21,796	21,725	21,400	23,152	0
Nevada	445,707	313,730	4,599	35,008	35,429	34,266	33,557	33,462	33,787	34,364	34,373	34,192	693	131,977	34,025	33,462	32,527	31,939	24
New Hampshire	188,974	128,169	3,260	11,892	13,692	13,531	13,861	13,907	14,253	14,284	14,705	14,784	0	60,805	16,321	15,243	14,641	14,600	0
New Jersey	1,372,203	956,070	35,128	94,830	98,464	97,499	98,305	98,152	97,328	98,744	99,624	100,052	37,944	416,133	105,857	101,466	96,504	97,048	15,258
New Mexico	338,220	240,978	7,509	27,662	26,932	26,208	25,818	25,474	25,573	25,490	25,135	25,177	0	97,242	29,217	25,711	21,755	20,559	0
New York	2,710,703	1,868,561	48,712	202,670	205,963	199,600	199,088	198,361	196,709	198,595	202,583	200,642	15,638	842,142	225,291	215,312	193,257	192,112	16,170
North Carolina	1,518,465	1,080,090	30,329	121,389	120,038	116,691	107,832	116,264	116,351	118,514	117,535	115,147	0	438,375	126,694	113,605	103,428	94,648	0
North Dakota	101,111	70,995	1,848	8,578	8,367	7,710	7,725	7,380	7,292	7,339	7,256	7,500	0	30,116	7,801	7,536	7,432	7,347	0
Ohio	1,729,916	1,211,299	27,558	131,874	131,637	128,867	129,079	129,295	130,392	133,468	135,174	133,955	0	518,617	148,752	133,301	118,941	117,623	0
Oklahoma	673,483	496,144	42,154	55,115	54,039	50,660	49,840	49,274	48,675	48,486	48,640	47,856	1,405	177,339	49,577	45,628	42,200	39,407	527
Oregon	587,564	409,325	23,850	42,642	43,438	42,436	42,532	42,401	42,235	42,916	43,297	43,578	0	178,239	44,662	43,751	43,103	46,723	0
Pennsylvania	1,763,677	1,204,732	10,109	129,624	131,691	129,861	131,638	131,315	130,592	134,359	137,172	136,775	1,596	558,945	144,396	140,180	136,531	136,357	1,481
Rhode Island	142,481	97,809	2,068	10,786	10,429	10,737	10,968	10,831	10,820	10,900	10,299	9,971	0	44,672	12,014	11,330	10,819	10,509	0

See notes at end of table.

Table 203.45. Enrollment in public elementary and secondary schools, by level, grade, and state or jurisdiction: Fall 2012—Continued

State or jurisdiction	Total, all grades	Elementary													Secondary					
		Total	Prekinder-garten	Kinder-garten	Grade 1	Grade 2	Grade 3	Grade 4	Grade 5	Grade 6	Grade 7	Grade 8	Elementary ungraded	Total	Grade 9	Grade 10	Grade 11	Grade 12	Secondary ungraded
1	2	3	4	5	6	7	8	9	10	11	12	13	14	15	16	17	18	19	20
South Carolina	735,998	527,350	23,786	58,641	58,030	55,275	54,354	54,058	54,541	56,493	56,807	55,365	0	208,648	61,897	54,033	47,963	44,755	0
South Dakota	130,471	93,204	3,117	11,901	10,546	10,316	9,874	9,657	9,458	9,377	9,550	9,408	0	37,267	10,018	9,548	8,885	8,816	0
Tennessee	993,496	711,525	27,096	81,186	79,010	75,716	74,934	74,425	74,311	75,116	75,272	74,459	0	281,971	76,794	71,810	67,068	66,299	0
Texas	5,077,659	3,690,146	250,911	390,636	396,903	389,225	382,990	378,750	376,426	380,202	377,246	366,857	0	1,387,513	403,136	350,949	328,003	305,425	0
Utah	613,279	444,202	12,329	50,378	50,171	48,872	48,926	48,362	46,991	46,540	46,246	45,387	0	169,077	44,379	42,760	41,164	40,774	0
Vermont	89,624	62,067	5,705	6,273	6,096	6,269	6,196	6,133	6,190	6,291	6,373	6,541	0	27,557	7,004	6,980	6,817	6,756	0
Virginia	1,265,419	889,444	32,852	96,935	97,267	95,231	95,405	94,005	93,941	94,874	95,147	93,787	0	375,975	101,867	94,931	90,206	88,971	0
Washington	1,051,694	724,560	12,466	80,789	80,494	78,904	78,723	78,244	77,331	78,966	79,371	79,272	0	327,134	82,972	80,696	78,485	84,981	0
West Virginia	283,044	202,371	15,781	21,785	20,788	20,459	20,483	20,181	20,698	20,623	21,052	20,521	0	80,673	22,741	20,397	18,832	18,703	0
Wisconsin	872,436	606,754	55,008	62,422	61,037	60,585	61,243	60,670	60,253	61,369	62,310	61,857	0	265,682	67,699	64,507	66,346	67,130	0
Wyoming	91,533	65,290	540	8,131	7,628	7,394	7,116	7,127	6,790	6,811	6,879	6,874	0	26,243	7,122	6,738	6,337	6,046	0
Bureau of Indian Education	—	—	—	—	—	—	—	—	—	—	—	—	—	—	—	—	—	—	—
DoD, overseas	—	—	—	—	—	—	—	—	—	—	—	—	—	—	—	—	—	—	—
DoD, domestic	—	—	—	—	—	—	—	—	—	—	—	—	—	—	—	—	—	—	—
Other jurisdictions																			
American Samoa	31,186	21,166	13	2,207	2,329	2,317	2,408	2,325	2,348	2,364	2,383	2,472	0	10,020	3,101	3,269	2,089	1,561	0
Guam	10,646	7,396	462	582	745	686	740	776	799	825	934	792	55	3,250	1,078	794	748	630	0
Northern Marianas																			
Puerto Rico	434,609	305,048	1,050	27,887	33,453	32,372	31,647	31,345	32,116	33,811	36,096	35,547	9,724	129,561	34,414	32,839	30,216	27,169	4,923
U.S. Virgin Islands	15,192	10,302	—	1,052	1,146	1,118	1,108	1,144	1,243	1,129	1,278	1,084	0	4,890	1,651	1,193	1,051	995	0

—Not available.
NOTE: DoD = Department of Defense. The total ungraded counts of students were prorated to the elementary and secondary levels based on prior reports.

SOURCE: U.S. Department of Education, National Center for Education Statistics, Common Core of Data (CCD), "State Non-fiscal Survey of Public Elementary/Secondary Education," 2012–13. (This table was prepared October 2014.)

Table 203.50. Enrollment and percentage distribution of enrollment in public elementary and secondary schools, by race/ethnicity and region: Selected years, fall 1995 through fall 2025

Region and year	Enrollment (in thousands)							Percentage distribution						
	Total	White	Black	Hispanic	Asian/ Pacific Islander	American Indian/ Alaska Native	Two or more races	Total	White	Black	Hispanic	Asian/ Pacific Islander	American Indian/ Alaska Native	Two or more races
1	2	3	4	5	6	7	8	9	10	11	12	13	14	15
United States														
1995	44,840	29,044	7,551	6,072	1,668	505	—	100.0	64.8	16.8	13.5	3.7	1.1	†
2000	47,204	28,878	8,100	7,726	1,950	550	—	100.0	61.2	17.2	16.4	4.1	1.2	†
2001	47,672	28,735	8,177	8,169	2,028	564	—	100.0	60.3	17.2	17.1	4.3	1.2	†
2002	48,183	28,618	8,299	8,594	2,088	583	—	100.0	59.4	17.2	17.8	4.3	1.2	†
2003	48,540	28,442	8,349	9,011	2,145	593	—	100.0	58.6	17.2	18.6	4.4	1.2	†
2004	48,795	28,318	8,386	9,317	2,183	591	—	100.0	58.0	17.2	19.1	4.5	1.2	†
2005	49,113	28,005	8,445	9,787	2,279	598	—	100.0	57.0	17.2	19.9	4.6	1.2	†
2006	49,316	27,801	8,422	10,166	2,332	595	—	100.0	56.4	17.1	20.6	4.7	1.2	†
2007	49,291	27,454	8,392	10,454	2,396	594	—	100.0	55.7	17.0	21.2	4.9	1.2	†
2008	49,266	27,057	8,358	10,563	2,451	589	247 [1]	100.0	54.9	17.0	21.4	5.0	1.2	0.5 [1]
2009	49,361	26,702	8,245	10,991	2,484	601	338 [1]	100.0	54.1	16.7	22.3	5.0	1.2	0.7 [1]
2010	49,484	25,933	7,917	11,439	2,466	566	1,164	100.0	52.4	16.0	23.1	5.0	1.1	2.4
2011	49,522	25,602	7,827	11,759	2,513	547	1,272	100.0	51.7	15.8	23.7	5.1	1.1	2.6
2012	49,771	25,386	7,803	12,104	2,552	534	1,393	100.0	51.0	15.7	24.3	5.1	1.1	2.8
2013	50,045	25,160	7,805	12,452	2,593	523	1,511	100.0	50.3	15.6	24.9	5.2	1.0	3.0
2014 [2]	50,132	25,007	7,828	12,740	2,637	516	1,404	100.0	49.9	15.6	25.4	5.3	1.0	2.8
2015 [2]	50,268	24,789	7,817	13,030	2,678	508	1,445	100.0	49.3	15.6	25.9	5.3	1.0	2.9
2016 [2]	50,385	24,566	7,806	13,306	2,723	499	1,484	100.0	48.8	15.5	26.4	5.4	1.0	2.9
2017 [2]	50,477	24,340	7,796	13,563	2,769	490	1,519	100.0	48.2	15.4	26.9	5.5	1.0	3.0
2018 [2]	50,528	24,128	7,776	13,791	2,799	483	1,552	100.0	47.8	15.4	27.3	5.5	1.0	3.1
2019 [2]	50,618	23,993	7,754	13,964	2,846	472	1,590	100.0	47.4	15.3	27.6	5.6	0.9	3.1
2020 [2]	50,774	23,882	7,756	14,142	2,892	463	1,638	100.0	47.0	15.3	27.9	5.7	0.9	3.2
2021 [2]	50,928	23,777	7,774	14,300	2,934	457	1,685	100.0	46.7	15.3	28.1	5.8	0.9	3.3
2022 [2]	51,084	23,686	7,799	14,437	2,979	451	1,731	100.0	46.4	15.3	28.3	5.8	0.9	3.4
2023 [2]	51,225	23,614	7,819	14,541	3,029	447	1,777	100.0	46.1	15.3	28.4	5.9	0.9	3.5
2024 [2]	51,338	23,544	7,832	14,615	3,083	443	1,821	100.0	45.9	15.3	28.5	6.0	0.9	3.5
2025 [2]	51,420	23,465	7,836	14,677	3,139	439	1,863	100.0	45.6	15.2	28.5	6.1	0.9	3.6
Northeast														
1995	7,894	5,497	1,202	878	295	21	—	100.0	69.6	15.2	11.1	3.7	0.3	†
2000	8,222	5,545	1,270	1,023	361	24	—	100.0	67.4	15.4	12.4	4.4	0.3	†
2003	8,292	5,455	1,284	1,124	403	27	—	100.0	65.8	15.5	13.6	4.9	0.3	†
2005	8,240	5,317	1,282	1,189	425	27	—	100.0	64.5	15.6	14.4	5.2	0.3	†
2008	8,053	5,041	1,226	1,267	467	27	25 [1]	100.0	62.6	15.2	15.7	5.8	0.3	0.3 [1]
2009	8,092	5,010	1,230	1,308	487	27	30 [1]	100.0	61.9	15.2	16.2	6.0	0.3	0.4 [1]
2010	8,071	4,876	1,208	1,364	500	27	96	100.0	60.4	15.0	16.9	6.2	0.3	1.2
2011	7,954	4,745	1,166	1,394	510	27	113	100.0	59.7	14.7	17.5	6.4	0.3	1.4
2012	7,959	4,665	1,161	1,444	523	27	138	100.0	58.6	14.6	18.1	6.6	0.3	1.7
2013	7,961	4,593	1,158	1,492	533	28	158	100.0	57.7	14.5	18.7	6.7	0.3	2.0
Midwest														
1995	10,512	8,335	1,450	438	197	92	—	100.0	79.3	13.8	4.2	1.9	0.9	†
2000	10,730	8,208	1,581	610	239	92	—	100.0	76.5	14.7	5.7	2.2	0.9	†
2003	10,809	8,055	1,644	751	262	97	—	100.0	74.5	15.2	7.0	2.4	0.9	†
2005	10,819	7,950	1,654	836	283	96	—	100.0	73.5	15.3	7.7	2.6	0.9	†
2008	10,743	7,734	1,632	963	314	99	—	100.0	72.0	15.2	9.0	2.9	0.9	†
2009	10,672	7,622	1,606	1,000	318	98	29 [1]	100.0	71.4	15.0	9.4	3.0	0.9	0.3 [1]
2010	10,610	7,327	1,505	1,077	312	94	294	100.0	69.1	14.2	10.2	2.9	0.9	2.8
2011	10,574	7,240	1,485	1,127	321	90	311	100.0	68.5	14.0	10.7	3.0	0.9	2.9
2012	10,559	7,175	1,464	1,167	330	89	334	100.0	68.0	13.9	11.1	3.1	0.8	3.2
2013	10,573	7,111	1,464	1,212	341	87	358	100.0	67.3	13.8	11.5	3.2	0.8	3.4
South														
1995	16,118	9,565	4,236	1,890	280	148	—	100.0	59.3	26.3	11.7	1.7	0.9	†
2000	17,007	9,501	4,516	2,468	352	170	—	100.0	55.9	26.6	14.5	2.1	1.0	†
2003	17,673	9,437	4,656	2,980	410	189	—	100.0	53.4	26.3	16.9	2.3	1.1	†
2005	18,103	9,381	4,738	3,334	456	194	—	100.0	51.8	26.2	18.4	2.5	1.1	†
2008	18,491	9,190	4,771	3,790	537	203	—	100.0	49.7	25.8	20.5	2.9	1.1	†
2009	18,652	9,074	4,710	4,039	555	219	55 [1]	100.0	48.6	25.3	21.7	3.0	1.2	0.3 [1]
2010	18,805	8,869	4,545	4,206	555	207	424	100.0	47.2	24.2	22.4	3.0	1.1	2.3
2011	18,956	8,830	4,535	4,353	577	198	463	100.0	46.6	23.9	23.0	3.0	1.0	2.4
2012	19,128	8,780	4,545	4,513	595	191	504	100.0	45.9	23.8	23.6	3.1	1.0	2.6
2013	19,299	8,722	4,561	4,671	614	185	546	100.0	45.2	23.6	24.2	3.2	1.0	2.8
West														
1995	10,316	5,648	662	2,866	896	244	—	100.0	54.7	6.4	27.8	8.7	2.4	†
2000	11,244	5,624	733	3,625	998	264	—	100.0	50.0	6.5	32.2	8.9	2.4	†
2003	11,766	5,496	765	4,156	1,070	280	—	100.0	46.7	6.5	35.3	9.1	2.4	†
2005	11,951	5,356	771	4,428	1,115	281	—	100.0	44.8	6.5	37.1	9.3	2.4	†
2008	11,979	5,092	728	4,543	1,133	261	222 [1]	100.0	42.5	6.1	37.9	9.5	2.2	1.9 [1]
2009	11,945	4,997	699	4,645	1,124	256	223 [1]	100.0	41.8	5.9	38.9	9.4	2.1	1.9 [1]
2010	11,998	4,861	659	4,792	1,100	237	349	100.0	40.5	5.5	39.9	9.2	2.0	2.9
2011	12,038	4,787	642	4,886	1,105	233	385	100.0	39.8	5.3	40.6	9.2	1.9	3.2
2012	12,124	4,766	632	4,978	1,104	227	417	100.0	39.3	5.2	41.1	9.1	1.9	3.4
2013	12,212	4,733	623	5,077	1,105	224	449	100.0	38.8	5.1	41.6	9.1	1.8	3.7

—Not available.
†Not applicable.
[1] For this year, data on students of Two or more races were reported by only a small number of states. Therefore, the data are not comparable to figures for 2010 and later years.
[2] Projected.
NOTE: Race categories exclude persons of Hispanic ethnicity. Enrollment data for students not reported by race/ethnicity were prorated by state and grade to match state totals. Prior to 2008,

data on students of Two or more races were not collected. Some data have been revised from previously published figures. Detail may not sum to totals because of rounding.
SOURCE: U.S. Department of Education, National Center for Education Statistics, Common Core of Data (CCD), "State Nonfiscal Survey of Public Elementary and Secondary Education," 1995–96 through 2013–14; and National Elementary and Secondary Enrollment by Race/Ethnicity Projection Model, 1972 through 2025. (This table was prepared January 2016.)

Table 203.60. Enrollment and percentage distribution of enrollment in public elementary and secondary schools, by race/ethnicity and level of education: Fall 1999 through fall 2025

Level of education and year	Enrollment (in thousands)									Percentage distribution								
	Total	White	Black	His-panic	Asian/Pacific Islander			American Indian/Alaska Native	Two or more races	Total	White	Black	His-panic	Asian/Pacific Islander			American Indian/Alaska Native	Two or more races
					Total	Asian	Pacific Islander							Total	Asian	Pacific Islander		
1	2	3	4	5	6	7	8	9	10	11	12	13	14	15	16	17	18	19
Total																		
1999	46,857	29,035	8,066	7,327	1,887	—	—	542	—	100.0	62.0	17.2	15.6	4.0	†	†	1.2	†
2000	47,204	28,878	8,100	7,726	1,950	—	—	550	—	100.0	61.2	17.2	16.4	4.1	†	†	1.2	†
2001	47,672	28,735	8,177	8,169	2,028	—	—	564	—	100.0	60.3	17.2	17.1	4.3	†	†	1.2	†
2002	48,183	28,618	8,299	8,594	2,088	—	—	583	—	100.0	59.4	17.2	17.8	4.3	†	†	1.2	†
2003	48,540	28,442	8,349	9,011	2,145	—	—	593	—	100.0	58.6	17.2	18.6	4.4	†	†	1.2	†
2004	48,795	28,318	8,386	9,317	2,183	—	—	591	—	100.0	58.0	17.2	19.1	4.5	†	†	1.2	†
2005	49,113	28,005	8,445	9,787	2,279	—	—	598	—	100.0	57.0	17.2	19.9	4.6	†	†	1.2	†
2006	49,316	27,801	8,422	10,166	2,332	—	—	595	—	100.0	56.4	17.1	20.6	4.7	†	†	1.2	†
2007	49,291	27,454	8,392	10,454	2,396	—	—	594	—	100.0	55.7	17.0	21.2	4.9	†	†	1.2	†
2008	49,266	27,057	8,358	10,563	2,451	2,405	46	589	247[1]	100.0	54.9	17.0	21.4	5.0	4.9	0.1	1.2	0.5[1]
2009	49,361	26,702	8,245	10,991	2,484	2,435	49	601	338[1]	100.0	54.1	16.7	22.3	5.0	4.9	0.1	1.2	0.7[1]
2010	49,484	25,933	7,917	11,439	2,466	2,296	171	566	1,164	100.0	52.4	16.0	23.1	5.0	4.6	0.3	1.1	2.4
2011	49,522	25,602	7,827	11,759	2,513	2,334	179	547	1,272	100.0	51.7	15.8	23.7	5.1	4.7	0.4	1.1	2.6
2012	49,771	25,386	7,803	12,104	2,552	2,372	180	534	1,393	100.0	51.0	15.7	24.3	5.1	4.8	0.4	1.1	2.8
2013	50,045	25,160	7,805	12,452	2,593	2,417	176	523	1,511	100.0	50.3	15.6	24.9	5.2	4.8	0.4	1.0	3.0
2014[2]	50,132	25,007	7,828	12,740	2,637	2,463	174	516	1,404	100.0	49.9	15.6	25.4	5.3	4.9	0.3	1.0	2.8
2015[2]	50,268	24,789	7,817	13,030	2,678	2,506	172	508	1,445	100.0	49.3	15.6	25.9	5.3	5.0	0.3	1.0	2.9
2016[2]	50,385	24,566	7,806	13,306	2,723	2,553	170	499	1,484	100.0	48.8	15.5	26.4	5.4	5.1	0.3	1.0	2.9
2017[2]	50,477	24,340	7,796	13,563	2,769	2,600	168	490	1,519	100.0	48.2	15.4	26.9	5.5	5.2	0.3	1.0	3.0
2018[2]	50,528	24,128	7,776	13,791	2,799	2,633	167	483	1,552	100.0	47.8	15.4	27.3	5.5	5.2	0.3	1.0	3.1
2019[2]	50,618	23,993	7,754	13,964	2,846	2,682	164	472	1,590	100.0	47.4	15.3	27.6	5.6	5.3	0.3	0.9	3.1
2020[2]	50,774	23,882	7,756	14,142	2,892	2,730	162	463	1,638	100.0	47.0	15.3	27.9	5.7	5.4	0.3	0.9	3.2
2021[2]	50,928	23,777	7,774	14,300	2,934	2,775	160	457	1,685	100.0	46.7	15.3	28.1	5.8	5.4	0.3	0.9	3.3
2022[2]	51,084	23,686	7,799	14,437	2,979	2,821	158	451	1,731	100.0	46.4	15.3	28.3	5.8	5.5	0.3	0.9	3.4
2023[2]	51,225	23,614	7,819	14,541	3,029	2,872	157	447	1,777	100.0	46.1	15.3	28.4	5.9	5.6	0.3	0.9	3.5
2024[2]	51,338	23,544	7,832	14,615	3,083	2,926	157	443	1,821	100.0	45.9	15.3	28.5	6.0	5.7	0.3	0.9	3.5
2025[2]	51,420	23,465	7,836	14,677	3,139	2,981	158	439	1,863	100.0	45.6	15.2	28.5	6.1	5.8	0.3	0.9	3.6
Prekindergarten through grade 8																		
1999	33,486	20,327	5,952	5,512	1,303	—	—	391	—	100.0	60.7	17.8	16.5	3.9	†	†	1.2	†
2000	33,686	20,130	5,981	5,830	1,349	—	—	397	—	100.0	59.8	17.8	17.3	4.0	†	†	1.2	†
2001	33,936	19,960	6,004	6,159	1,409	—	—	405	—	100.0	58.8	17.7	18.1	4.2	†	†	1.2	†
2002	34,114	19,764	6,042	6,446	1,447	—	—	415	—	100.0	57.9	17.7	18.9	4.2	†	†	1.2	†
2003	34,201	19,558	6,015	6,729	1,483	—	—	415	—	100.0	57.2	17.6	19.7	4.3	†	†	1.2	†
2004	34,178	19,368	5,983	6,909	1,504	—	—	413	—	100.0	56.7	17.5	20.2	4.4	†	†	1.2	†
2005	34,204	19,051	5,954	7,216	1,569	—	—	412	—	100.0	55.7	17.4	21.1	4.6	†	†	1.2	†
2006	34,235	18,863	5,882	7,465	1,611	—	—	414	—	100.0	55.1	17.2	21.8	4.7	†	†	1.2	†
2007	34,204	18,679	5,821	7,632	1,660	—	—	412	—	100.0	54.6	17.0	22.3	4.9	†	†	1.2	†
2008	34,286	18,501	5,793	7,689	1,705	1,674	31	410	187[1]	100.0	54.0	16.9	22.4	5.0	4.9	0.1	1.2	0.5[1]
2009	34,409	18,316	5,713	7,977	1,730	1,697	33	419	254[1]	100.0	53.2	16.6	23.2	5.0	4.9	0.1	1.2	0.7[1]
2010	34,625	17,823	5,495	8,314	1,711	1,589	122	394	887	100.0	51.5	15.9	24.0	4.9	4.6	0.4	1.1	2.6
2011	34,773	17,654	5,470	8,558	1,744	1,616	128	384	963	100.0	50.8	15.7	24.6	5.0	4.6	0.4	1.1	2.8
2012	35,018	17,535	5,473	8,804	1,773	1,644	129	375	1,057	100.0	50.1	15.6	25.1	5.1	4.7	0.4	1.1	3.0
2013	35,251	17,390	5,483	9,054	1,809	1,683	126	367	1,148	100.0	49.3	15.6	25.7	5.1	4.8	0.4	1.0	3.3
2014[2]	35,249	17,258	5,486	9,246	1,834	1,710	124	361	1,064	100.0	49.0	15.6	26.2	5.2	4.9	0.4	1.0	3.0
2015[2]	35,298	17,079	5,473	9,438	1,860	1,737	122	355	1,093	100.0	48.4	15.5	26.7	5.3	4.9	0.3	1.0	3.1
2016[2]	35,402	16,940	5,480	9,623	1,886	1,765	121	349	1,123	100.0	47.9	15.5	27.2	5.3	5.0	0.3	1.0	3.2
2017[2]	35,451	16,791	5,495	9,764	1,905	1,786	120	344	1,152	100.0	47.4	15.5	27.5	5.4	5.0	0.3	1.0	3.2
2018[2]	35,491	16,662	5,510	9,881	1,920	1,802	118	341	1,177	100.0	46.9	15.5	27.8	5.4	5.1	0.3	1.0	3.3
2019[2]	35,543	16,618	5,507	9,930	1,952	1,836	116	333	1,204	100.0	46.8	15.5	27.9	5.5	5.2	0.3	0.9	3.4
2020[2]	35,559	16,560	5,500	9,948	1,985	1,871	115	327	1,238	100.0	46.6	15.5	28.0	5.6	5.3	0.3	0.9	3.5
2021[2]	35,541	16,496	5,482	9,949	2,021	1,907	114	323	1,271	100.0	46.4	15.4	28.0	5.7	5.4	0.3	0.9	3.6
2022[2]	35,558	16,449	5,468	9,966	2,054	1,940	114	319	1,301	100.0	46.3	15.4	28.0	5.8	5.5	0.3	0.9	3.7
2023[2]	35,712	16,456	5,480	10,029	2,099	1,985	114	316	1,331	100.0	46.1	15.3	28.1	5.9	5.6	0.3	0.9	3.7
2024[2]	35,878	16,469	5,501	10,087	2,142	2,027	114	314	1,365	100.0	45.9	15.3	28.1	6.0	5.6	0.3	0.9	3.8
2025[2]	36,052	16,483	5,523	10,150	2,184	2,070	115	313	1,399	100.0	45.7	15.3	28.2	6.1	5.7	0.3	0.9	3.9
Grades 9 through 12																		
1999	13,371	8,708	2,114	1,815	584	—	—	151	—	100.0	65.1	15.8	13.6	4.4	†	†	1.1	†
2000	13,517	8,747	2,119	1,896	601	—	—	153	—	100.0	64.7	15.7	14.0	4.4	†	†	1.1	†
2001	13,736	8,774	2,173	2,011	619	—	—	159	—	100.0	63.9	15.8	14.6	4.5	†	†	1.2	†
2002	14,069	8,854	2,257	2,148	642	—	—	168	—	100.0	62.9	16.0	15.3	4.6	†	†	1.2	†
2003	14,339	8,884	2,334	2,282	663	—	—	177	—	100.0	62.0	16.3	15.9	4.6	†	†	1.2	†
2004	14,618	8,950	2,403	2,408	679	—	—	178	—	100.0	61.2	16.4	16.5	4.6	†	†	1.2	†
2005	14,909	8,954	2,490	2,570	709	—	—	186	—	100.0	60.1	16.7	17.2	4.8	†	†	1.2	†
2006	15,081	8,938	2,540	2,701	720	—	—	181	—	100.0	59.3	16.8	17.9	4.8	†	†	1.2	†
2007	15,086	8,775	2,571	2,821	736	—	—	183	—	100.0	58.2	17.0	18.7	4.9	†	†	1.2	†
2008	14,980	8,556	2,565	2,874	746	731	15	179	59[1]	100.0	57.1	17.1	19.2	5.0	4.9	0.1	1.2	0.4[1]
2009	14,952	8,385	2,532	3,014	754	738	16	182	84[1]	100.0	56.1	16.9	20.2	5.0	4.9	0.1	1.2	0.6[1]
2010	14,860	8,109	2,422	3,125	755	707	49	171	277	100.0	54.6	16.3	21.0	5.1	4.8	0.3	1.2	1.9
2011	14,749	7,948	2,357	3,202	769	719	50	163	309	100.0	53.9	16.0	21.7	5.2	4.9	0.3	1.1	2.1
2012	14,753	7,851	2,330	3,300	779	727	51	158	335	100.0	53.2	15.8	22.4	5.3	4.9	0.3	1.1	2.3
2013	14,794	7,770	2,322	3,398	784	733	51	156	363	100.0	52.5	15.7	23.0	5.3	5.0	0.3	1.1	2.5

See notes at end of table.

Table 203.60. Enrollment and percentage distribution of enrollment in public elementary and secondary schools, by race/ethnicity and level of education: Fall 1999 through fall 2025—Continued

Level of education and year	Enrollment (in thousands)									Percentage distribution								
					Asian/Pacific Islander			American Indian/ Alaska Native	Two or more races					Asian/Pacific Islander			American Indian/ Alaska Native	Two or more races
	Total	White	Black	His-panic	Total	Asian	Pacific Islander			Total	White	Black	His-panic	Total	Asian	Pacific Islander		
1	2	3	4	5	6	7	8	9	10	11	12	13	14	15	16	17	18	19
2014[2]	14,883	7,749	2,342	3,494	804	753	50	155	340	100.0	52.1	15.7	23.5	5.4	5.1	0.3	1.0	2.3
2015[2]	14,970	7,710	2,345	3,592	819	769	50	153	352	100.0	51.5	15.7	24.0	5.5	5.1	0.3	1.0	2.3
2016[2]	14,983	7,626	2,326	3,683	837	788	49	150	361	100.0	50.9	15.5	24.6	5.6	5.3	0.3	1.0	2.4
2017[2]	15,026	7,550	2,300	3,800	863	815	48	146	367	100.0	50.2	15.3	25.3	5.7	5.4	0.3	1.0	2.4
2018[2]	15,037	7,466	2,266	3,909	879	831	48	142	375	100.0	49.6	15.1	26.0	5.8	5.5	0.3	0.9	2.5
2019[2]	15,075	7,375	2,247	4,034	894	846	48	139	386	100.0	48.9	14.9	26.8	5.9	5.6	0.3	0.9	2.6
2020[2]	15,215	7,322	2,256	4,194	907	860	47	136	400	100.0	48.1	14.8	27.6	6.0	5.7	0.3	0.9	2.6
2021[2]	15,387	7,281	2,292	4,351	913	868	46	134	415	100.0	47.3	14.9	28.3	5.9	5.6	0.3	0.9	2.7
2022[2]	15,526	7,237	2,331	4,470	924	880	44	133	430	100.0	46.6	15.0	28.8	6.0	5.7	0.3	0.9	2.8
2023[2]	15,514	7,158	2,339	4,512	929	886	43	131	445	100.0	46.1	15.1	29.1	6.0	5.7	0.3	0.8	2.9
2024[2]	15,460	7,075	2,331	4,528	942	899	43	129	455	100.0	45.8	15.1	29.3	6.1	5.8	0.3	0.8	2.9
2025[2]	15,368	6,982	2,313	4,527	955	912	43	127	464	100.0	45.4	15.1	29.5	6.2	5.9	0.3	0.8	3.0

—Not available.
†Not applicable.
[1]For this year, data on students of Two or more races were reported by only a small number of states. Therefore, the data are not comparable to figures for 2010 and later years.
[2]Projected.
NOTE: Race categories exclude persons of Hispanic ethnicity. Enrollment data for students not reported by race/ethnicity were prorated by state and grade to match state totals. Prior to 2008, data on students of Two or more races were not collected separately. Total counts

of ungraded students were prorated to prekindergarten through grade 8 and grades 9 through 12 based on prior reports. Some data have been revised from previously published figures. Detail may not sum to totals because of rounding.
SOURCE: U.S. Department of Education, National Center for Education Statistics, Common Core of Data (CCD), "State Nonfiscal Survey of Public Elementary and Secondary Education," 1998–99 through 2013–14; and National Elementary and Secondary Enrollment by Race/Ethnicity Projection Model, 1972 through 2025. (This table was prepared January 2016.)

Table 203.70. Percentage distribution of enrollment in public elementary and secondary schools, by race/ethnicity and state or jurisdiction: Fall 2003 and fall 2013

State or jurisdiction	Percentage distribution, fall 2003						Percentage distribution, fall 2013							
	Total	White	Black	Hispanic	Asian/ Pacific Islander	American Indian/ Alaska Native	Total	White	Black	Hispanic	Asian	Pacific Islander	American Indian/ Alaska Native	Two or more races
1	2	3	4	5	6	7	8	9	10	11	12	13	14	15
United States	100.0	58.7	17.2	18.5	4.4	1.2	100.0	50.3	15.6	24.8	4.8	0.4	1.0	3.0
Alabama	100.0	59.9	36.4	2.1	0.9	0.8	100.0	57.0	33.6	5.5	1.4	0.1	0.8	1.6
Alaska..............................	100.0	58.9	4.7	3.9	6.5	26.0	100.0	49.2	3.4	6.6	6.2	2.4	23.9	8.3
Arizona	100.0	49.2	4.8	37.2	2.2	6.6	100.0	40.7	5.2	44.1	2.8	0.3	4.8	2.2
Arkansas..........................	100.0	69.9	23.1	5.3	1.1	0.6	100.0	63.1	21.0	11.2	1.5	0.6	0.6	2.0
California	100.0	32.9	8.2	46.7	11.3	0.8	100.0	25.0	6.2	53.3	11.1	0.5	0.6	3.3
Colorado	100.0	64.5	5.8	25.3	3.1	1.2	100.0	55.0	4.7	32.8	3.1	0.2	0.7	3.5
Connecticut......................	100.0	68.3	13.6	14.6	3.2	0.3	100.0	58.5	12.9	21.2	4.7	0.1	0.3	2.4
Delaware	100.0	57.3	31.9	7.9	2.6	0.3	100.0	47.7	31.2	14.5	3.5	0.1	0.4	2.5
District of Columbia	100.0	4.3	84.7	9.5	1.5	0.1	100.0	8.8	73.6	14.4	1.4	0.1	0.1	1.6
Florida..............................	100.0	51.3	24.3	22.1	2.0	0.3	100.0	40.9	22.9	30.0	2.6	0.1	0.3	3.2
Georgia............................	100.0	52.1	38.3	6.9	2.5	0.2	100.0	42.7	37.0	13.3	3.5	0.1	0.2	3.1
Hawaii	100.0	20.2	2.4	4.5	72.4	0.5	100.0	13.6	2.1	10.0	32.0	32.0	0.4	9.9
Idaho................................	100.0	84.1	0.9	12.0	1.5	1.6	100.0	76.8	1.1	17.2	1.3	0.3	1.3	2.0
Illinois..............................	100.0	57.4	21.1	17.7	3.6	0.2	100.0	49.9	17.6	24.6	4.5	0.1	0.3	3.1
Indiana.............................	100.0	81.5	12.4	4.8	1.1	0.2	100.0	70.9	12.3	10.2	1.9	0.1	0.2	4.5
Iowa.................................	100.0	88.2	4.5	4.9	1.8	0.6	100.0	79.0	5.3	9.7	2.2	0.2	0.4	3.2
Kansas.............................	100.0	76.4	8.9	11.0	2.3	1.4	100.0	65.9	7.2	18.4	2.7	0.2	1.0	4.7
Kentucky	100.0	87.0	10.4	1.5	0.8	0.2	100.0	79.3	10.8	5.3	1.5	0.1	0.1	3.0
Louisiana	100.0	48.5	47.7	1.8	1.3	0.7	100.0	46.8	44.5	4.8	1.5	0.1	0.7	1.6
Maine...............................	100.0	95.8	1.7	0.8	1.2	0.5	100.0	90.9	3.2	1.8	1.5	0.1	0.8	1.6
Maryland...........................	100.0	50.4	37.9	6.4	4.9	0.4	100.0	40.9	34.9	13.6	6.1	0.1	0.3	4.1
Massachusetts.................	100.0	74.6	8.8	11.5	4.7	0.3	100.0	64.9	8.7	17.0	6.1	0.1	0.2	2.9
Michigan	100.0	72.7	20.1	4.1	2.2	1.0	100.0	68.3	18.3	6.8	2.9	0.1	0.7	2.8
Minnesota	100.0	80.2	7.8	4.6	5.4	2.1	100.0	70.7	9.7	8.2	6.4	0.1	1.7	3.3
Mississippi	100.0	47.3	50.7	1.1	0.7	0.2	100.0	45.4	49.3	2.9	1.0	#	0.2	1.1
Missouri	100.0	77.7	18.0	2.6	1.4	0.4	100.0	73.2	16.5	5.4	1.9	0.2	0.4	2.4
Montana...........................	100.0	85.1	0.7	2.1	1.0	11.0	100.0	80.0	0.9	4.1	0.8	0.2	11.3	2.6
Nebraska	100.0	79.5	7.1	10.1	1.7	1.6	100.0	68.9	6.7	17.3	2.3	0.1	1.4	3.3
Nevada	100.0	50.8	10.7	30.2	6.7	1.7	100.0	36.0	9.9	40.6	5.6	1.3	1.1	5.6
New Hampshire	100.0	94.2	1.4	2.4	1.7	0.3	100.0	88.0	1.9	4.4	3.0	0.1	0.3	2.3
New Jersey	100.0	57.9	17.7	17.2	7.0	0.2	100.0	48.9	16.1	24.2	9.3	0.2	0.1	1.2
New Mexico	100.0	32.8	2.4	52.5	1.2	11.2	100.0	24.6	1.9	60.7	1.2	0.1	10.1	1.4
New York	100.0	53.9	19.7	19.4	6.6	0.5	100.0	46.5	18.2	24.5	8.8	0.0	0.6	1.5
North Carolina	100.0	58.3	31.6	6.7	2.0	1.5	100.0	51.4	26.0	14.5	2.8	0.1	1.4	3.8
North Dakota	100.0	88.0	1.2	1.4	0.8	8.5	100.0	81.4	3.1	3.7	1.4	0.2	8.7	1.5
Ohio..................................	100.0	79.4	17.0	2.1	1.3	0.1	100.0	72.6	16.3	4.5	1.9	0.1	0.1	4.5
Oklahoma	100.0	61.5	10.9	7.6	1.5	18.5	100.0	51.7	9.2	15.0	1.8	0.3	15.0	7.1
Oregon	100.0	76.6	3.1	13.6	4.4	2.3	100.0	63.8	2.5	22.4	3.9	0.7	1.6	5.1
Pennsylvania....................	100.0	76.3	15.8	5.5	2.3	0.1	100.0	69.1	15.1	9.5	3.4	0.1	0.1	2.7
Rhode Island	100.0	71.2	8.5	16.4	3.2	0.6	100.0	61.5	8.1	23.4	2.9	0.2	0.7	3.2
South Carolina.................	100.0	54.2	41.3	3.2	1.1	0.3	100.0	52.5	35.1	7.5	1.4	0.1	0.3	3.1
South Dakota	100.0	84.9	1.5	1.8	1.0	10.7	100.0	76.9	2.7	4.5	1.7	0.1	11.5	2.6
Tennessee	100.0	70.7	25.0	2.8	1.3	0.2	100.0	65.6	22.9	7.8	1.8	0.1	0.2	1.6
Texas	100.0	38.7	14.3	43.8	2.9	0.3	100.0	29.5	12.7	51.8	3.7	0.1	0.4	1.9
Utah	100.0	83.4	1.1	11.0	2.9	1.5	100.0	76.3	1.3	16.0	1.7	1.5	1.1	2.0
Vermont	100.0	95.9	1.2	0.8	1.5	0.6	100.0	91.6	1.9	1.6	1.9	0.1	0.3	2.6
Virginia.............................	100.0	61.1	27.1	6.6	4.7	0.5	100.0	52.2	23.3	13.1	6.3	0.1	0.3	4.7
Washington......................	100.0	71.5	5.7	12.3	7.9	2.7	100.0	58.2	4.5	21.1	7.2	1.0	1.4	6.7
West Virginia....................	100.0	94.1	4.6	0.5	0.6	0.1	100.0	91.1	4.7	1.4	0.7	#	0.1	2.0
Wisconsin	100.0	78.8	10.5	5.8	3.4	1.4	100.0	72.4	9.7	10.5	3.6	0.1	1.2	2.4
Wyoming	100.0	86.0	1.4	8.2	1.0	3.5	100.0	79.4	1.2	13.1	0.9	0.1	3.4	1.9
Bureau of Indian Education.	100.0	0.0	0.0	0.0	0.0	100.0	—	—	—	—	—	—	—	—
DoD, overseas	100.0	55.2	20.0	13.5	10.5	0.9	—	—	—	—	—	—	—	—
DoD, domestic	100.0	48.6	23.6	22.7	4.2	1.0	—	—	—	—	—	—	—	—
Other jurisdictions American Samoa	100.0	0.0	0.0	0.0	100.0	0.0	100.0							
Guam	100.0	1.3	0.3	0.2	98.1	0.1	100.0	0.6	0.2	0.2	25.1	71.6	#	2.2
Northern Marianas.......	100.0	0.4	#	0.0	99.6	0.0	100.0	0.6	#	0.1	40.0	56.8	0.0	2.4
Puerto Rico..................	100.0	0.0	0.0	100.0	0.0	0.0	100.0	0.1	#	99.9	#	#	#	0.0
U.S. Virgin Islands........	100.0	0.8	84.3	14.5	0.2	0.2	100.0	1.5	78.5	18.6	0.5	0.1	0.1	0.7

—Not available.
#Rounds to zero.
NOTE: Percentage distribution based on students for whom race/ethnicity was reported, which may be less than the total number of students in the state. Race categories exclude persons of Hispanic ethnicity. DoD = Department of Defense. Detail may not sum to totals because of rounding.

SOURCE: U.S. Department of Education, National Center for Education Statistics, Common Core of Data (CCD), "State Nonfiscal Survey of Public Elementary/Secondary Education," 2003–04 and 2013–14. (This table was prepared August 2015.)

Table 203.75. Enrollment and percentage distribution of enrollment in public schools, by family poverty rate of 5- to 17-year-olds living in the school district, student race/ethnicity, region, and school locale: 2013–14

Student race/ethnicity, region, and school locale	Enrollment in public schools					Percentage distribution of enrollment				
	Total	Family poverty rate[1] of 5- to 17-year-olds[2] living in the school district				Total	Family poverty rate[1] of 5- to 17-year-olds[2] living in the school district			
		0 to 12.0 percent	12.1 to 20.0 percent	20.1 to 28.0 percent	More than 28.0 percent		0 to 12.0 percent	12.1 to 20.0 percent	20.1 to 28.0 percent	More than 28.0 percent
1	2	3	4	5	6	7	8	9	10	11
Total	49,481,720	12,301,079	12,922,300	12,094,711	12,163,630	100.0	24.9	26.1	24.4	24.6
White	24,845,481	8,692,937	7,476,122	5,691,098	2,985,324	100.0	35.0	30.1	22.9	12.0
Black	7,719,312	771,004	1,488,381	1,905,234	3,554,693	100.0	10.0	19.3	24.7	46.0
Hispanic	12,339,568	1,431,637	2,658,932	3,529,446	4,719,553	100.0	11.6	21.5	28.6	38.2
Asian	2,398,012	889,457	655,025	404,814	448,716	100.0	37.1	27.3	16.9	18.7
Pacific Islander	174,671	25,723	93,798	35,346	19,804	100.0	14.7	53.7	20.2	11.3
American Indian/Alaska Native	514,311	72,506	117,958	139,649	184,198	100.0	14.1	22.9	27.2	35.8
Two or more races	1,490,365	417,815	432,084	389,124	251,342	100.0	28.0	29.0	26.1	16.9
Region										
Northeast	7,868,890	3,384,038	1,474,912	756,386	2,253,554	100.0	43.0	18.7	9.6	28.6
White	4,530,450	2,644,675	1,025,428	435,433	424,914	100.0	58.4	22.6	9.6	9.4
Black	1,141,778	166,961	146,847	106,649	721,321	100.0	14.6	12.9	9.3	63.2
Hispanic	1,483,514	261,431	212,600	170,445	839,038	100.0	17.6	14.3	11.5	56.6
Asian	524,451	237,102	51,055	23,392	212,902	100.0	45.2	9.7	4.5	40.6
Pacific Islander	6,405	3,190	1,470	555	1,190	100.0	49.8	23.0	8.7	18.6
American Indian/Alaska Native .	26,723	6,379	4,654	2,860	12,830	100.0	23.9	17.4	10.7	48.0
Two or more races	155,569	64,300	32,858	17,052	41,359	100.0	41.3	21.1	11.0	26.6
Midwest	10,404,086	3,628,774	3,008,289	1,883,607	1,883,416	100.0	34.9	28.9	18.1	18.1
White	6,999,851	2,946,827	2,286,115	1,174,966	591,943	100.0	42.1	32.7	16.8	8.5
Black	1,433,910	166,580	209,790	272,151	785,389	100.0	11.6	14.6	19.0	54.8
Hispanic	1,197,286	232,755	304,204	282,979	377,348	100.0	19.4	25.4	23.6	31.5
Asian	326,685	156,921	78,301	53,191	38,272	100.0	48.0	24.0	16.3	11.7
Pacific Islander	10,657	3,324	3,147	2,684	1,502	100.0	31.2	29.5	25.2	14.1
American Indian/Alaska Native .	84,113	15,354	27,889	20,904	19,966	100.0	18.3	33.2	24.9	23.7
Two or more races	351,584	107,013	98,843	76,732	68,996	100.0	30.4	28.1	21.8	19.6
South	19,199,289	2,655,102	4,900,385	6,295,205	5,348,597	100.0	13.8	25.5	32.8	27.9
White	8,671,331	1,491,574	2,548,037	3,073,684	1,558,036	100.0	17.2	29.4	35.4	18.0
Black	4,531,913	370,816	974,166	1,324,676	1,862,255	100.0	8.2	21.5	29.2	41.1
Hispanic	4,657,701	443,158	1,004,917	1,520,883	1,688,743	100.0	9.5	21.6	32.7	36.3
Asian	586,656	208,822	174,145	127,583	76,106	100.0	35.6	29.7	21.7	13.0
Pacific Islander	25,989	3,897	6,479	8,281	7,332	100.0	15.0	24.9	31.9	28.2
American Indian/Alaska Native .	182,604	21,618	42,807	56,866	61,313	100.0	11.8	23.4	31.1	33.6
Two or more races	543,095	115,217	149,834	183,232	94,812	100.0	21.2	27.6	33.7	17.5
West	12,009,455	2,633,165	3,538,714	3,159,513	2,678,063	100.0	21.9	29.5	26.3	22.3
White	4,643,849	1,609,861	1,616,542	1,007,015	410,431	100.0	34.7	34.8	21.7	8.8
Black	611,711	66,647	157,578	201,758	185,728	100.0	10.9	25.8	33.0	30.4
Hispanic	5,001,067	494,293	1,137,211	1,555,139	1,814,424	100.0	9.9	22.7	31.1	36.3
Asian	960,220	286,612	351,524	200,648	121,436	100.0	29.8	36.6	20.9	12.6
Pacific Islander	131,620	15,312	82,702	23,826	9,780	100.0	11.6	62.8	18.1	7.4
American Indian/Alaska Native .	220,871	29,155	42,608	59,019	90,089	100.0	13.2	19.3	26.7	40.8
Two or more races	440,117	131,285	150,549	112,108	46,175	100.0	29.8	34.2	25.5	10.5
School locale										
City	15,033,168	1,534,603	2,801,732	3,828,456	6,868,377	100.0	10.2	18.6	25.5	45.7
White	4,469,681	832,736	1,259,612	1,333,178	1,044,155	100.0	18.6	28.2	29.8	23.4
Black	3,605,174	124,911	359,545	793,345	2,327,373	100.0	3.5	10.0	22.0	64.6
Hispanic	5,296,601	259,359	780,337	1,314,327	2,942,578	100.0	4.9	14.7	24.8	55.6
Asian	1,014,109	216,841	241,298	189,312	366,658	100.0	21.4	23.8	18.7	36.2
Pacific Islander	58,505	6,841	23,252	16,015	12,397	100.0	11.7	39.7	27.4	21.2
American Indian/Alaska Native .	108,738	14,031	21,442	35,715	37,550	100.0	12.9	19.7	32.8	34.5
Two or more races	480,360	79,884	116,246	146,564	137,666	100.0	16.6	24.2	30.5	28.7
Suburban	19,681,922	7,934,194	5,641,891	4,085,643	2,020,194	100.0	40.3	28.7	20.8	10.3
White	10,125,473	5,497,938	2,777,160	1,456,154	394,221	100.0	54.3	27.4	14.4	3.9
Black	2,688,333	553,707	892,296	738,779	503,551	100.0	20.6	33.2	27.5	18.7
Hispanic	4,889,909	962,617	1,354,169	1,561,821	1,011,302	100.0	19.7	27.7	31.9	20.7
Asian	1,183,661	605,471	349,149	172,738	56,303	100.0	51.2	29.5	14.6	4.8
Pacific Islander	73,890	15,103	41,847	13,326	3,614	100.0	20.4	56.6	18.0	4.9
American Indian/Alaska Native .	90,382	30,705	31,517	19,458	8,702	100.0	34.0	34.9	21.5	9.6
Two or more races	630,274	268,653	195,753	123,367	42,501	100.0	42.6	31.1	19.6	6.7
Town	5,656,097	757,138	1,660,327	1,699,017	1,539,615	100.0	13.4	29.4	30.0	27.2
White	3,659,321	634,632	1,239,716	1,143,382	641,591	100.0	17.3	33.9	31.2	17.5
Black	573,219	15,760	54,892	144,836	357,731	100.0	2.7	9.6	25.3	62.4
Hispanic	1,042,256	65,144	241,442	302,533	433,137	100.0	6.3	23.2	29.0	41.6
Asian	73,683	12,231	29,025	18,934	13,493	100.0	16.6	39.4	25.7	18.3
Pacific Islander	24,396	1,266	18,165	3,180	1,785	100.0	5.2	74.5	13.0	7.3
American Indian/Alaska Native .	124,190	10,245	27,541	31,038	55,366	100.0	8.2	22.2	25.0	44.6
Two or more races	159,032	17,860	49,546	55,114	36,512	100.0	11.2	31.2	34.7	23.0

See notes at end of table.

Table 203.75. Enrollment and percentage distribution of enrollment in public schools, by family poverty rate of 5- to 17-year-olds living in the school district, student race/ethnicity, region, and school locale: 2013–14—Continued

Student race/ethnicity, region, and school locale	Enrollment in public schools					Percentage distribution of enrollment				
		Family poverty rate[1] of 5- to 17-year-olds[2] living in the school district					Family poverty rate[1] of 5- to 17-year-olds[2] living in the school district			
	Total	0 to 12.0 percent	12.1 to 20.0 percent	20.1 to 28.0 percent	More than 28.0 percent	Total	0 to 12.0 percent	12.1 to 20.0 percent	20.1 to 28.0 percent	More than 28.0 percent
1	2	3	4	5	6	7	8	9	10	11
Rural	9,110,533	2,075,144	2,818,350	2,481,595	1,735,444	100.0	22.8	30.9	27.2	19.0
White	6,591,006	1,727,631	2,199,634	1,758,384	905,357	100.0	26.2	33.4	26.7	13.7
Black	852,586	76,626	181,648	228,274	366,038	100.0	9.0	21.3	26.8	42.9
Hispanic	1,110,802	144,517	282,984	350,765	332,536	100.0	13.0	25.5	31.6	29.9
Asian	126,559	54,914	35,553	23,830	12,262	100.0	43.4	28.1	18.8	9.7
Pacific Islander	17,880	2,513	10,534	2,825	2,008	100.0	14.1	58.9	15.8	11.2
American Indian/Alaska Native	191,001	17,525	37,458	53,438	82,580	100.0	9.2	19.6	28.0	43.2
Two or more races	220,699	51,418	70,539	64,079	34,663	100.0	23.3	32.0	29.0	15.7

[1]A family is in poverty if its income falls below the Census Bureau's poverty threshold, which is a dollar amount that varies depending on a family's size and composition and is updated annually to account for inflation. In 2013, for example, the poverty threshold for a family of four with two children was $23,624. The family poverty rate of 5- to 17-year-olds is the percentage of children in this age group whose families are in poverty. Includes only children classified as "related" and "relevant" (see footnote 2).

[2]Includes only those children who live in households and meet both of the following conditions: (1) The children are related to the householder by birth, marriage, or adoption (except a child who is the spouse of the householder). The householder is the person (or one of the people) who owns or rents (maintains) the housing unit. (2) The children are relevant to the school district. Children are relevant if they reside within the geographical boundaries of the district and are at a grade level served by the district, even if they do not attend a school in the district.

NOTE: School enrollment data were obtained from the Common Core of Data and poverty rate data were obtained from the Census Bureau. To create the school district categories, public school districts were ranked and divided into quarters based on the family poverty rate of their 5- to 17-year-old population; the cut points between the four quarters were chosen so that, at the national level, each quarter contains approximately the same number of students. For the approximately 3 percent of public school students who attended charter or other special districts, no data were available on their school district's family poverty rate. The rate for their district was imputed to be the same as the rate for the regular public school district within which their charter or other special district was geographically located. Race categories exclude persons of Hispanic ethnicity. Detail may not sum to totals because of rounding.

SOURCE: U.S. Department of Education, National Center for Education Statistics, Common Core of Data (CCD), "Public Elementary/Secondary School Universe Survey," 2013–14. U.S. Department of Commerce, Census Bureau, Small Area Income and Poverty Estimates (SAIPE) Program, 2013 Poverty Estimates for School Districts. (This table was prepared March 2016.)

Table 203.80. Average daily attendance (ADA) in public elementary and secondary schools, by state or jurisdiction: Selected years, 1969–70 through 2012–13

State or jurisdiction	1969–70	1979–80	1989–90	1999–2000	2004–05	2005–06	2006–07	2007–08	2008–09	2009–10	2010–11	2011–12	2012–13
1	2	3	4	5	6	7	8	9	10	11	12	13	14
United States	41,934,376	38,288,911	37,799,296	43,806,726	45,625,458	45,931,617	46,132,663	46,155,880	46,173,477	45,919,206	46,118,737	46,400,465	46,567,834
Alabama	777,123	711,432	683,833	725,212	706,588	714,197	714,302	731,161	712,179	698,208	709,225	715,402	688,614
Alaska	72,489	79,945	98,213	122,412	121,699	122,010	120,988	119,882	119,330	120,118	119,949	119,799	119,873
Arizona	391,526	481,905	557,252	782,851	911,640	933,663	972,404	973,689	999,386	968,764	964,683	969,825	973,369
Arkansas	414,158	423,610	403,025	422,958	430,290	435,278	436,804	439,347	439,432	435,676	443,118	443,125	470,644
California[1]	4,418,423	4,044,736	4,893,341	5,957,216	6,373,959	6,349,270	6,351,774	6,365,266	6,365,278	6,017,381 [2]	6,029,786 [2]	6,034,192 [2]	6,021,550 [2]
Colorado	500,388	513,475	519,419	656,700	700,485	712,476	722,168	735,549	747,845	762,190	763,147	779,747	784,242
Connecticut	618,881	507,362	439,524	533,779	559,478	558,423	555,428	553,445	549,776	548,787	537,104	534,846	534,350
Delaware	120,819	94,058	89,838	106,444	110,393	113,986	113,992	116,472	119,092	119,879	121,959	122,864	124,676
District of Columbia	138,600	91,576	71,468	65,371	70,817	59,137	61,799	61,636	68,447	68,217	69,575	71,910	76,486
Florida	1,312,693	1,464,461	1,646,583	2,175,453	2,463,323	2,494,778	2,527,431	2,494,397	2,468,060	2,493,694	2,541,022	2,575,910	2,600,989
Georgia	1,019,427	989,433	1,054,097	1,326,713	1,460,767	1,499,317	1,542,305	1,561,935	1,569,767	1,596,180	1,621,397	1,646,051	1,646,352
Hawaii	168,140	151,563	157,360	171,180	169,825	168,009	165,415	166,179	166,118	165,766	169,926	171,763	173,092
Idaho	170,920	189,199	203,987	230,828	241,590	247,009	251,278	255,523	258,712	262,238	263,001	263,377	264,786
Illinois	2,084,844	1,770,435	1,587,733	1,789,089	1,862,046	1,871,619	1,879,288	1,881,810	1,881,276	1,887,561	1,863,017	1,858,409	1,867,289
Indiana	1,111,043	983,444	884,568	929,281	944,944	966,967	976,373	969,976	973,342	976,503	976,225	976,337	977,509
Iowa	624,403	510,081	450,224	471,384	456,559	477,491	481,528	492,922	451,403	455,579	459,613	462,585	471,263
Kansas	470,296	382,019	388,986	426,853	411,455	407,812	422,142	418,751	418,495	435,745	443,131	454,740	453,778
Kentucky	647,970	619,868	569,795	565,693	574,380	580,937	583,102	585,775	585,556	587,102	593,323	594,440	618,774
Louisiana	776,555	727,601	727,125	701,957	670,238	648,243	625,916	631,163	637,764	643,374	654,093	664,640	673,721
Maine	225,146	211,400	195,089	194,554	184,374	180,223	178,870	175,161	173,357	168,213	165,067	166,483	164,339
Maryland	785,989	686,336	620,617	791,133	804,696	800,553	795,473	793,881	793,333	795,577	798,953	803,656	806,686
Massachusetts	1,056,207	935,960	763,231	913,502	930,338	930,151	933,697	917,181	913,976	912,792	910,568	906,736	907,954
Michigan	1,991,235	1,758,427	1,446,996	1,574,894	1,583,496	1,574,023	1,556,297	1,528,815	1,498,107	1,477,312	1,452,125	1,438,279	1,422,806
Minnesota	864,595	748,606	699,001	818,819	788,354	787,521	791,417	790,206	791,427	785,455	786,838	792,437	795,827
Mississippi	524,623	454,401	476,048	468,746	463,816	461,112	462,251	461,459	460,797	460,327	460,894	460,703	461,356
Missouri	906,132	777,269	729,693	836,105	851,114	859,441	858,821	852,106	853,580	852,460	839,997	840,917	843,762
Montana	162,664	144,608	135,406	142,313	130,998	129,948	128,872	132,104	131,982	130,704	130,949	133,266	132,579
Nebraska	314,516	270,524	254,754	261,767	260,725	262,805	263,800	264,810	266,536	269,590	271,468	285,837	288,023
Nevada	113,421	134,995	173,149	305,067	378,186	383,403	395,536	395,355	406,792	405,097	406,965	411,919	419,638
New Hampshire	140,203	154,187	154,915	200,283	201,242	199,952	198,004	195,383	192,890	191,969	188,913	185,947	183,571
New Jersey	1,322,124	1,140,111	997,561	1,222,438	1,341,156	1,358,562	1,348,279	1,340,220	1,342,419	1,343,405	1,339,012	1,340,367	1,336,336
New Mexico	259,997	253,453	290,245	323,963	322,046	323,964	327,244	326,034	327,562	331,152	334,272	335,165	335,773
New York	3,099,192	2,530,289	2,244,110	2,595,070	2,581,772	2,581,482	2,542,259	2,520,932	2,510,519	2,516,922	2,513,770	2,512,327	2,500,382
North Carolina	1,104,295	1,072,150	1,012,274	1,185,737	1,289,444	1,319,335	1,343,357	1,364,608	1,374,267	1,366,164	1,377,899	1,393,621	1,400,981
North Dakota	141,961	118,986	109,659	105,123	94,823	92,843	91,078	91,972	91,816	91,114	92,440	94,310	97,135
Ohio	2,246,282	1,849,283	1,584,735	1,659,903	1,719,566	1,730,080	1,691,206	1,660,981	1,628,515	1,609,008	1,601,188	1,605,571	1,587,878
Oklahoma	560,993	548,065	543,170	586,266	587,188	591,486	596,172	596,450	603,375	610,019	616,775	624,410	630,766
Oregon	436,736	418,593	419,771	479,321	506,638	513,650	516,258	515,834	518,119	515,644	517,373	518,896	520,326
Pennsylvania	2,169,225	1,808,630	1,524,839	1,684,913	1,698,795	1,702,566	1,701,044	1,693,569	1,680,772	1,661,990	1,668,916	1,659,616	1,649,205
Rhode Island	163,205	139,195	125,934	144,422	143,939	139,001	138,993	134,737	131,963	131,538	131,494	131,379	139,494
South Carolina	600,292	569,612	569,029	624,456	639,950	647,703	652,803	656,996	662,231	664,136	664,133	673,850	681,402
South Dakota	158,543	124,934	119,823	122,252	115,148	114,673	114,863	114,723	114,209	115,242	119,449	120,950	123,220
Tennessee	836,010	806,696	761,766	844,878	868,129	881,414	889,312	891,430	895,335	896,130	899,382	903,695	910,540
Texas	2,432,420	2,608,817	3,075,333	3,706,550	4,084,792	4,186,812	4,255,963	4,322,975	4,393,893	4,473,236	4,551,084	4,634,133	4,699,372
Utah	287,405	312,813	408,917	448,096	464,645	478,233	488,514	503,562	513,884	528,608	540,683	556,885	567,605
Vermont	97,772	95,045	87,832	98,894	93,608	92,508	91,437	89,880	87,931	86,378	85,501	85,184	84,326
Virginia	995,580	955,105	989,197	1,195,123	1,133,882	1,141,790	1,142,342	1,150,316	1,154,689	1,159,105	1,165,907	1,177,274	1,180,497
Washington	764,735	710,929	755,141	925,696	941,238	946,824	947,857	947,791	953,719	960,084	965,191	964,255	968,149
West Virginia	372,278	353,264	301,947	273,277	271,197	271,780	272,045	267,989	269,623	268,872	270,961	273,355	273,305
Wisconsin	880,609	770,554	711,466	825,699	831,809	834,177	835,072	823,754	823,595	817,284	825,622	825,949	829,261
Wyoming	81,293	89,471	91,277	86,092	77,878	77,757	79,090	79,788	81,006	80,717	81,654	83,131	83,983
Other jurisdictions													
American Samoa	—	—	11,448	15,102	15,302	15,237	14,606	14,646	14,646	14,403	15,451	15,541	13,355
Guam	20,315	—	23,883	—	—	29,617	29,515	28,358	28,521	28,075	28,765	28,735	29,591
Northern Marianas	—	—	6,809	8,712	10,301	10,871	10,277	9,927	9,815	9,900	9,965	9,731	9,564
Puerto Rico	—	656,709	597,436	540,676	540,365	522,655	531,273	494,880	477,918	466,483	411,164	429,799	422,560
U.S. Virgin Islands	—	—	18,924	18,676	15,841	15,241	14,927	15,903	15,768	15,493	15,747	15,711	15,192

—Not available.
[1]Data for California for 1989–90 and earlier years are not strictly comparable with those for other states because California's attendance figures included excused absences.
[2]Excludes average daily attendance for regional occupational programs and summer school programs that were reported in prior years.

NOTE: Some data have been revised from previously published figures.
SOURCE: U.S. Department of Education, National Center for Education Statistics, *Statistics of State School Systems, 1969–70; Revenues and Expenditures for Public Elementary and Secondary Education, 1979–80*; and Common Core of Data (CCD), "National Public Education Financial Survey," 1989–90 through 2012–13. (This table was prepared September 2015.)

Table 203.90. Average daily attendance (ADA) as a percentage of total enrollment, school day length, and school year length in public schools, by school level and state: 2007–08 and 2011–12

[Standard errors appear in parentheses]

State	2007–08 ADA as percent of enrollment	2007–08 Average hours in school day	2011–12 Total elementary, secondary, and combined elementary/secondary schools — ADA as percent of enrollment	Average hours in school day	Average days in school year	Average hours in school year	Elementary schools — ADA as percent of enrollment	Average hours in school day	Secondary schools — ADA as percent of enrollment	Average hours in school day
1	2	3	4	5	6	7	8	9	10	11
United States...............	93.1 (0.22)	6.6 (0.02)	93.9 (0.12)	6.7 (0.01)	179 (0.1)	1,203 (2.0)	94.9 (0.12)	6.7 (0.01)	91.7 (0.34)	6.7 (0.02)
Alabama	93.8 (1.24)	7.0 (0.07)	94.4 (0.94)	7.0 (0.04)	181 (0.8)	1,271 (8.5)	95.3 (0.92)	7.1 (0.04)	94.6 (0.65)	6.9 (0.13)
Alaska............................	89.9 (1.22)	6.5 (0.05)	91.4 (1.19)	6.7 (0.17)	177 (1.3)	1,183 (37.3)	‡ (†)	‡ (†)	‡ (†)	‡ (†)
Arizona	89.0 (2.95)	6.4 (0.09)	91.7 (0.99)	6.7 (0.08)	179 (1.3)	1,201 (12.5)	93.5 (0.53)	6.9 (0.06)	87.9 (2.40)	6.5 (0.26)
Arkansas........................	91.8 (1.35)	6.9 (0.06)	94.2 (0.58)	7.0 (0.07)	180 (0.5)	1,261 (14.1)	94.7 (0.36)	7.0 (0.08)	92.9 (1.93)	6.9 (0.14)
California	93.2 (0.71)	6.2 (0.07)	93.1 (0.46)	6.2 (0.05)	180 (0.3)	1,121 (9.0)	94.7 (0.51)	6.3 (0.06)	89.7 (1.08)	6.3 (0.08)
Colorado	93.9 (0.44)	7.0 (0.05)	93.1 (0.71)	7.1 (0.06)	172 (1.4)	1,215 (7.7)	94.6 (0.59)	7.0 (0.07)	88.0 (2.57)	7.1 (0.10)
Connecticut.....................	87.9 (2.98)	6.5 (0.09)	94.9 (0.47)	6.6 (0.04)	181 (0.1)	1,201 (7.5)	95.4 (0.61)	6.6 (0.05)	94.3 (0.53)	6.7 (0.09)
Delaware.........................	89.8 (1.75)	6.7 (0.09)	93.5 (0.50)	7.0 (0.10)	182 (1.2)	1,269 (23.7)	94.1 (0.50)	7.0 (0.12)	93.8 (0.71)	7.0 (0.09)
District of Columbia	91.2 (1.27)	6.9 (0.21)	‡ (†)	‡ (†)	‡ (†)	‡ (†)	‡ (†)	‡ (†)	‡ (†)	‡ (†)
Florida............................	92.7 (0.74)	6.4 (0.08)	93.2 (0.52)	6.6 (0.06)	181 (1.2)	1,193 (14.2)	94.3 (0.49)	6.6 (0.08)	90.7 (0.84)	6.7 (0.09)
Georgia	93.3 (1.28)	6.8 (0.06)	94.3 (0.53)	7.0 (0.04)	178 (0.4)	1,242 (8.5)	95.0 (0.59)	6.9 (0.05)	‡ (†)	‡ (†)
Hawaii............................	90.7 (4.58)	6.3 (0.10)	‡ (†)	‡ (†)	‡ (†)	‡ (†)	‡ (†)	‡ (†)	‡ (†)	‡ (†)
Idaho.............................	92.4 (2.27)	6.6 (0.09)	94.1 (1.01)	6.7 (0.13)	166 (5.1)	1,110 (21.7)	94.4 (0.75)	6.7 (0.08)	93.1 (0.83)	6.7 (0.20)
Illinois............................	94.0 (0.71)	6.5 (0.05)	94.1 (0.40)	6.5 (0.04)	176 (0.4)	1,151 (7.7)	95.1 (0.29)	6.5 (0.05)	92.4 (1.29)	6.8 (0.08)
Indiana...........................	95.7 (0.51)	6.8 (0.06)	95.9 (0.20)	6.8 (0.05)	180 (0.1)	1,226 (9.1)	96.1 (0.25)	6.7 (0.05)	95.5 (0.31)	7.0 (0.07)
Iowa..............................	94.8 (0.65)	6.9 (0.09)	95.7 (0.36)	6.7 (0.12)	180 (0.2)	1,213 (21.8)	96.4 (0.21)	6.9 (0.05)	93.6 (1.39)	6.3 (0.47)
Kansas...........................	95.4 (0.52)	7.0 (0.07)	94.9 (0.42)	7.0 (0.03)	177 (2.6)	1,245 (17.9)	95.5 (0.53)	7.0 (0.04)	94.0 (0.42)	7.1 (0.04)
Kentucky	93.1 (1.89)	6.7 (0.06)	93.2 (1.33)	6.8 (0.06)	179 (1.0)	1,211 (11.6)	95.9 (0.22)	6.8 (0.07)	87.0 (4.87)	6.8 (0.14)
Louisiana	90.3 (2.31)	7.1 (0.08)	92.8 (0.70)	7.2 (0.07)	178 (1.1)	1,283 (10.7)	93.0 (0.88)	7.3 (0.07)	93.5 (0.42)	7.1 (0.14)
Maine.............................	90.3 (2.41)	6.5 (0.06)	94.2 (0.73)	6.6 (0.06)	176 (0.2)	1,156 (10.7)	94.4 (1.00)	6.6 (0.07)	93.8 (0.45)	6.3 (0.08)
Maryland.........................	94.1 (0.44)	6.6 (0.07)	‡ (†)	‡ (†)	‡ (†)	‡ (†)	‡ (†)	‡ (†)	‡ (†)	‡ (†)
Massachusetts.................	94.6 (0.58)	6.5 (0.05)	93.5 (0.62)	6.4 (0.07)	180 (0.2)	1,157 (13.3)	94.4 (0.63)	6.4 (0.07)	90.3 (2.55)	6.6 (0.05)
Michigan.........................	93.0 (1.01)	6.6 (0.08)	91.6 (0.71)	6.8 (0.03)	177 (0.5)	1,196 (5.9)	92.3 (0.99)	6.8 (0.03)	89.4 (1.28)	6.7 (0.07)
Minnesota.......................	93.1 (0.91)	6.3 (0.12)	93.1 (0.49)	6.4 (0.08)	173 (1.3)	1,111 (14.0)	96.1 (0.16)	6.6 (0.07)	89.5 (1.21)	6.0 (0.20)
Mississippi	92.1 (2.00)	7.0 (0.12)	94.4 (0.47)	7.2 (0.09)	181 (0.4)	1,312 (16.4)	94.9 (0.57)	7.3 (0.06)	93.7 (0.86)	7.2 (0.24)
Missouri	94.8 (0.26)	6.7 (0.05)	95.1 (0.20)	6.9 (0.03)	175 (0.3)	1,197 (5.3)	95.6 (0.24)	6.9 (0.04)	94.3 (0.24)	6.8 (0.11)
Montana..........................	91.3 (1.39)	6.8 (0.05)	93.9 (0.81)	6.6 (0.06)	179 (0.4)	1,189 (11.2)	94.3 (0.79)	6.6 (0.09)	93.0 (0.48)	6.7 (0.08)
Nebraska........................	94.9 (1.21)	6.9 (0.08)	94.8 (0.60)	7.1 (0.05)	177 (1.0)	1,257 (9.6)	96.0 (0.53)	7.1 (0.04)	94.5 (0.66)	6.8 (0.19)
Nevada...........................	93.5 (1.27)	6.3 (0.06)	93.9 (0.39)	6.5 (0.07)	180 (1.1)	1,164 (10.9)	94.5 (0.30)	6.4 (0.10)	93.9 (0.70)	6.5 (0.07)
New Hampshire	92.2 (1.75)	6.5 (0.06)	91.1 (2.86)	6.6 (0.05)	180 (0.3)	1,181 (10.3)	95.9 (0.45)	6.5 (0.07)	75.1 (12.63)	6.7 (0.05)
New Jersey......................	94.6 (0.59)	6.4 (0.05)	93.5 (1.13)	6.6 (0.06)	181 (0.2)	1,201 (11.8)	93.7 (1.40)	6.6 (0.07)	92.6 (1.29)	6.7 (0.07)
New Mexico.....................	91.9 (1.76)	6.8 (0.08)	92.8 (0.80)	6.9 (0.09)	177 (0.6)	1,216 (15.7)	93.8 (0.80)	6.7 (0.08)	88.5 (2.41)	7.1 (0.14)
New York.........................	92.7 (1.30)	6.6 (0.09)	92.7 (0.94)	6.6 (0.06)	182 (0.2)	1,206 (10.6)	93.6 (1.28)	6.6 (0.07)	90.0 (1.32)	6.8 (0.07)
North Carolina	92.6 (1.73)	6.7 (0.06)	94.7 (0.37)	6.9 (0.04)	181 (0.2)	1,240 (7.4)	95.2 (0.23)	6.8 (0.04)	‡ (†)	‡ (†)
North Dakota	95.9 (0.59)	6.6 (0.04)	95.2 (0.46)	6.5 (0.06)	177 (0.3)	1,159 (10.0)	96.4 (0.35)	6.4 (0.08)	95.5 (0.45)	6.6 (0.14)
Ohio..............................	91.8 (2.01)	6.6 (0.10)	93.8 (0.48)	6.6 (0.03)	180 (0.5)	1,191 (6.2)	95.0 (0.30)	6.6 (0.04)	91.0 (1.45)	6.7 (0.07)
Oklahoma	92.1 (2.24)	6.6 (0.06)	94.4 (0.32)	6.7 (0.04)	174 (0.7)	1,176 (8.6)	94.9 (0.38)	6.7 (0.04)	93.3 (0.74)	6.8 (0.10)
Oregon...........................	94.4 (0.59)	6.6 (0.06)	94.2 (0.40)	6.6 (0.05)	170 (0.9)	1,118 (7.9)	95.1 (0.29)	6.5 (0.06)	91.1 (1.41)	6.7 (0.06)
Pennsylvania...................	94.9 (0.39)	6.4 (0.12)	94.4 (0.29)	6.7 (0.05)	181 (0.3)	1,212 (9.5)	94.9 (0.38)	6.7 (0.06)	92.9 (0.56)	6.9 (0.14)
Rhode Island	93.7 (1.27)	6.3 (0.03)	94.6 (0.36)	6.4 (0.05)	180 (0.1)	1,150 (8.2)	95.1 (0.38)	6.3 (0.05)	‡ (†)	‡ (†)
South Carolina.................	94.9 (0.71)	6.9 (0.07)	95.6 (0.26)	7.0 (0.04)	181 (0.4)	1,263 (7.3)	96.2 (0.27)	6.9 (0.05)	93.9 (0.84)	7.1 (0.05)
South Dakota	93.6 (2.53)	6.8 (0.08)	96.1 (0.24)	7.0 (0.07)	170 (1.1)	1,180 (6.7)	96.7 (0.30)	6.9 (0.08)	93.6 (0.53)	6.9 (0.17)
Tennessee	94.9 (0.23)	7.0 (0.05)	95.4 (0.30)	7.1 (0.03)	179 (0.4)	1,272 (7.8)	95.0 (0.28)	7.1 (0.04)	94.2 (0.54)	7.0 (0.02)
Texas	94.1 (1.34)	7.2 (0.11)	95.2 (0.43)	7.3 (0.04)	179 (0.7)	1,297 (8.8)	95.9 (0.41)	7.3 (0.03)	94.8 (0.29)	7.3 (0.06)
Utah..............................	91.4 (1.56)	6.3 (0.29)	93.3 (0.80)	6.5 (0.09)	179 (0.3)	1,165 (13.5)	94.4 (0.80)	6.5 (0.09)	93.6 (0.74)	6.6 (0.09)
Vermont..........................	92.7 (3.39)	6.7 (0.07)	94.0 (0.95)	6.7 (0.04)	178 (0.3)	1,183 (7.2)	93.7 (1.30)	6.8 (0.04)	94.7 (0.35)	6.2 (0.12)
Virginia...........................	94.7 (0.46)	6.6 (0.05)	95.0 (0.32)	6.6 (0.03)	185 (3.4)	1,222 (18.8)	95.8 (0.32)	6.7 (0.03)	93.3 (0.65)	6.6 (0.10)
Washington......................	82.9 (3.06)	6.2 (0.08)	92.2 (0.67)	6.3 (0.06)	179 (0.3)	1,129 (11.3)	94.3 (0.55)	6.4 (0.04)	88.0 (2.00)	6.1 (0.19)
West Virginia....................	94.0 (0.99)	6.9 (0.07)	94.9 (0.46)	7.0 (0.05)	181 (0.4)	1,272 (9.8)	96.2 (0.27)	7.0 (0.07)	89.8 (1.98)	7.3 (0.09)
Wisconsin	95.0 (0.57)	6.9 (0.04)	94.9 (0.31)	6.9 (0.11)	179 (0.2)	1,234 (19.2)	95.7 (0.21)	7.0 (0.03)	91.9 (1.08)	7.0 (0.12)
Wyoming.........................	92.4 (1.15)	6.9 (0.05)	93.6 (0.81)	7.0 (0.04)	174 (0.5)	1,209 (6.5)	94.8 (0.78)	6.9 (0.05)	89.9 (2.19)	7.0 (0.08)

†Not applicable.
‡Reporting standards not met. Either the response rate is under 50 percent or there are too few cases for a reliable estimate.
NOTE: Averages reflect data reported by schools rather than state requirements. School-reported length of day may exceed state requirements, and there is a range of statistical error in reported estimates.

SOURCE: U.S. Department of Education, National Center for Education Statistics, Schools and Staffing Survey (SASS), "Public School Data File," 2007–08 and 2011–12. (This table was prepared May 2013.)

Table 204.10. Number and percentage of public school students eligible for free or reduced-price lunch, by state: Selected years, 2000–01 through 2013–14

State	Number of students				Number of students eligible for free/reduced-price lunch				Percent of students eligible for free/reduced-price lunch			
	2000–01	2010–11	2012–13	2013–14	2000–01	2010–11	2012–13	2013–14	2000–01	2010–11	2012–13	2013–14
1	2	3	4	5	6	7	8	9	10	11	12	13
United States...............	46,579,068 [1]	48,941,267	49,084,316	49,235,065	17,839,867 [1]	23,544,479	25,188,294	25,596,274	38.3 [1]	48.1	51.3	52.0
Alabama......................	728,351	730,427	740,475	743,018	335,143	402,386	429,604	434,095	46.0	55.1	58.0	58.4
Alaska........................	105,333	132,104	131,483	130,386	32,468	50,701	53,082	56,053	30.8	38.4	40.4	43.0
Arizona.......................	877,696 [2]	1,067,210	990,378	1,018,883	274,277 [2]	482,044	514,193	543,811	31.2 [2]	45.2	51.9	53.4
Arkansas.....................	449,959	482,114	486,157	489,979	205,058	291,608	298,573	300,050	45.6	60.5	61.4	61.2
California.....................	6,050,753	6,169,427	6,178,788	6,210,899	2,820,611	3,335,885	3,478,407	3,610,385	46.6	54.1	56.3	58.1
Colorado.....................	724,349	842,864	863,121	875,866	195,148	336,426	358,876	367,665	26.9	39.9	41.6	42.0
Connecticut..................	562,179 [2]	552,919	549,295	546,020	143,030 [2]	190,554	201,085	202,514	25.4 [2]	34.5	36.6	37.1
Delaware.....................	114,676	128,342	127,791	130,849	37,766	61,564	66,413	51,939	32.9	48.0	52.0	39.7
District of Columbia	68,380	71,263	75,411	78,153	47,839	52,027	46,416	77,505	70.0	73.0	61.6	99.2
Florida........................	2,434,755	2,641,555	2,691,881	2,720,739	1,079,009	1,479,519	1,576,379	1,589,861	44.3	56.0	58.6	58.4
Georgia.......................	1,444,937	1,676,419	1,702,766	1,723,449	624,511	961,954	1,017,193	1,070,855	43.2	57.4	59.7	62.1
Hawaii........................	184,357	179,601	184,760	186,825	80,657	84,106	93,457	94,312	43.8	46.8	50.6	50.5
Idaho.........................	244,755	275,815	279,277	293,001	85,824	124,104	134,560	138,886	35.1	45.0	48.2	47.4
Illinois........................	2,048,792 [2]	1,973,401	2,031,835	2,030,536	759,973 [2]	921,471	1,027,336	1,044,588	37.1 [2]	46.7	50.6	51.4
Indiana.......................	977,219	1,038,817	1,039,797	1,045,996	285,267	485,728	509,604	514,937	29.2	46.8	49.0	49.2
Iowa..........................	492,021	484,856	490,630	493,505	131,553	188,486	200,417	201,703	26.7	38.9	40.8	40.9
Kansas.......................	462,594	479,953	470,283	491,553	154,693	228,852	233,322	246,033	33.4	47.7	49.6	50.1
Kentucky.....................	626,723	673,128	675,167	671,962	298,334	380,773	373,837	368,159	47.6	56.6	55.4	54.8
Louisiana	741,162	695,772	693,980	694,980	433,068	460,546	459,617	463,987	58.4	66.2	66.2	66.8
Maine.........................	198,532	183,477	179,323	176,881	60,162	78,915	80,636	80,952	30.3	43.0	45.0	45.8
Maryland.....................	852,911	852,202	856,775	866,169	255,872	341,557	366,695	382,440	30.0	40.1	42.8	44.2
Massachusetts..............	979,590	955,301	952,970	955,007	237,871	326,849	352,988	365,473	24.3	34.2	37.0	38.3
Michigan	1,703,260	1,551,861	1,511,030	1,505,679	504,044	719,800	724,340	726,974	29.6	46.4	47.9	48.3
Minnesota	854,154	837,930	845,291	850,232	218,867	306,136	323,459	326,864	25.6	36.5	38.3	38.4
Mississippi	497,421	489,462	491,220	492,586	319,670	345,734	352,084	355,484	64.3	70.6	71.7	72.2
Missouri......................	912,247	902,375	898,402	910,555	315,608	406,358	408,726	452,824	34.6	45.0	45.5	49.7
Montana......................	154,438	140,497	142,908	141,974	47,415	57,836	60,262	59,717	30.7	41.2	42.2	42.1
Nebraska	286,138	298,276	303,332	306,992	87,045	127,114	133,912	137,948	30.4	42.6	44.1	44.9
Nevada	282,621	436,840	443,158	449,895	92,978	219,904	228,660	238,936	32.9	50.3	51.6	53.1
New Hampshire	206,919	194,001	187,940	185,299	31,212	48,904	50,596	51,564	15.1	25.2	26.9	27.8
New Jersey	1,312,983	1,356,882	1,363,967	1,364,880	357,728	444,735	501,804	518,636	27.2	32.8	36.8	38.0
New Mexico	320,303	335,810	335,922	338,607	174,939	227,077	229,249	227,413	54.6	67.6	68.2	67.2
New York	2,859,927	2,722,761	2,708,341	2,571,749	1,236,945	1,315,564	1,297,148	1,292,077	43.3	48.3	47.9	50.2
North Carolina	1,194,371	1,487,699	1,506,080	1,484,672	470,316	747,978	809,732	801,350	39.4	50.3	53.8	54.0
North Dakota	109,201	94,273	98,993	101,656	31,840	29,929	30,330	30,676	29.2	31.7	30.6	30.2
Ohio..........................	1,745,237	1,747,851	1,656,390	1,712,279	494,829	745,121	674,438	763,448	28.4	42.6	40.7	44.6
Oklahoma....................	623,110	659,376	665,404	674,985	300,179	398,917	410,378	417,589	48.2	60.5	61.7	61.9
Oregon.......................	535,617	553,468	533,966	526,296	186,203	280,174	286,635	281,580	34.8	50.6	53.7	53.5
Pennsylvania................	1,798,977	1,742,608	1,716,262	1,728,190	510,121	686,641	712,584	753,224	28.4	39.4	41.5	43.6
Rhode Island	157,347	142,575	141,124	140,250	52,209	61,127	65,184	65,636	33.2	42.9	46.2	46.8
South Carolina................	677,411	722,203	735,998	742,324	320,254	395,033	427,396	426,387	47.3	54.7	58.1	57.4
South Dakota................	128,598	125,883	130,294	130,736	37,857	46,718	51,678	51,707	29.4	37.1	39.7	39.6
Tennessee...................	909,161 [2]	987,078	982,312	983,293	436,298 [2]	542,953	575,522	578,414	48.0 [2]	55.0	58.6	58.8
Texas	4,059,353	4,916,401	5,077,507	5,146,834	1,823,029	2,471,212	3,059,657	3,092,087	44.9	50.3	60.3	60.1
Utah..........................	470,265	585,552	600,146	625,093	135,428	223,943	362,933	231,165	28.8	38.2	60.5	37.0
Vermont......................	102,049	85,144	83,568	85,391	23,986	31,339	32,581	33,639	23.5	36.8	39.0	39.4
Virginia.......................	1,067,710	1,250,206	1,235,561	1,268,806	320,233	458,879	487,463	503,811	30.0	36.7	39.5	39.7
Washington..................	1,004,770 [2]	1,043,466	1,050,904	1,057,729	326,295 [2]	418,065	474,940	489,870	32.5 [2]	40.1	45.2	46.3
West Virginia................	286,285	282,879	283,044	168,180	143,446	145,605	148,493	80,479	50.1	51.5	52.5	47.9
Wisconsin....................	859,276	872,164	871,376	872,684	219,276	342,660	360,803	365,711	25.5	39.3	41.4	41.9
Wyoming.....................	89,895	88,779	91,533	92,563	43,483	32,968	34,617	34,861	48.4	37.1	37.8	37.7

[1]U.S. total includes imputation for nonreporting states.
[2]Imputation for survey nonresponse. State-level imputations for 2000–01 were based on the reported percentages for 2001–02 applied to the 2000–01 enrollments.
NOTE: Table reflects counts of students enrolled in all schools for which both enrollment data and free/reduced-price lunch eligibility data were reported.

SOURCE: U.S. Department of Education, National Center for Education Statistics, Common Core of Data (CCD), "Public Elementary/Secondary School Universe Survey," 2000–01, 2010–11, 2012–13, and 2013–14. (This table was prepared February 2016.)

Table 204.20. Number and percentage of public school students participating in programs for English language learners, by state: Selected years, 2003–04 through 2013–14

State	Number of public school students participating in programs for English language learners							Percent of students participating in programs for English language learners						
	2003–04	2008–09	2009–10	2010–11	2011–12	2012–13	2013–14	2003–04	2008–09	2009–10	2010–11	2011–12	2012–13	2013–14
1	2	3	4	5	6	7	8	9	10	11	12	13	14	15
United States...............	4,217,026 [1]	4,439,514 [1]	4,364,510 [1]	4,370,004 [1]	4,389,325	4,397,318 [1]	4,460,956 [1]	8.8 [1]	9.2 [1]	9.1 [1]	9.1 [1]	9.1	9.2 [1]	9.3 [1]
Alabama	10,825	19,523	19,497	17,559	17,895	17,837 [2]	17,457	1.5	2.6	2.6	2.4	2.4	2.4 [2]	2.3
Alaska	19,877	11,937	14,581	14,894	14,538	14,824	14,923	14.9	9.2	11.1	11.3	11.1	11.3	11.4
Arizona	152,447	118,868	78,793	70,716	70,527	58,512	63,242	16.5	12.1	8.2	7.5	7.5	6.2	6.7
Arkansas.....................	17,174	27,629	29,735	31,457	32,671	33,745	35,814	3.8	5.8	6.3	6.6	6.9	7.1	7.5
California	1,586,970	1,498,660	1,468,815 [3]	1,445,496 [2]	1,415,623	1,391,913	1,392,871	25.5	24.3	24.1 [3]	23.6 [2]	23.2	22.8	22.7
Colorado	97,024	88,254	94,391	98,809	101,262	101,913	105,856	12.8	10.9	11.4	11.8	12.0	12.0	12.2
Connecticut..................	24,892	28,886	29,266	29,671	29,318	30,077	30,261	4.5	5.4	5.4	5.6	5.6	5.8	5.9
Delaware.....................	3,947	7,111	7,615	6,766	6,972	7,280	7,927	3.5	6.1	6.5	5.6	5.9	6.1	6.6
District of Columbia	5,201	4,370	4,203	3,741	3,745	4,530	4,716	8.0	9.9	9.6	8.4	8.4	10.3	10.5
Florida........................	195,944	226,037	230,440	229,659	234,347	242,133	250,296	7.6	8.6	8.8	8.7	8.8	9.0	9.2
Georgia	65,876	82,000	86,668	80,965	83,400	87,104	90,481	4.3	5.0	5.2	4.9	5.0	5.2	5.3
Hawaii	12,850	18,564	18,097	19,092	24,750	16,474	15,949	7.0	10.3	10.0	10.6	13.5	8.9	8.5
Idaho..........................	19,649	17,657	15,931	15,361	15,143	16,615	13,147	7.8	6.6	6.0	5.8	5.7	6.1	4.7
Illinois........................	170,219 [2]	204,737	179,850	174,335	170,626	191,738	191,057	8.2 [2]	9.7	8.6	8.4	8.2	9.4	9.3
Indiana	42,563	45,527	48,364	48,574	50,082	50,750	54,364	4.2	4.4	4.7	4.7	5.0	5.0	5.4
Iowa...........................	15,238	20,334	20,867	21,733	22,503	21,839	23,137	3.2	4.2	4.2	4.4	4.5	4.4	4.6
Kansas........................	22,399	34,095	38,011	39,323	41,052	42,590	45,530	4.8	7.2	8.0	8.1	8.5	8.7	9.4
Kentucky	8,446	14,589	14,244	16,351	16,878	18,761	19,594	1.3	2.2	2.1	2.4	2.5	2.7	2.9
Louisiana	12,106	12,223	12,499	11,617	12,348	13,105	14,438	1.7	1.9	1.9	1.7	1.9	2.0	2.2
Maine.........................	2,796	4,128 [2]	4,467	4,792	5,104	4,980	5,194	1.4	2.2 [2]	2.4	2.5	2.7	2.7	2.8
Maryland......................	27,695	39,919 [2]	43,179	45,500	51,574	55,343	56,047	3.2	4.7 [2]	5.1	5.3	6.0	6.4	6.5
Massachusetts................	47,880	47,198	49,612	52,610	62,354	63,917	66,640	5.8	5.9	6.3	6.7	7.9	8.1	8.5
Michigan	57,374	55,593	53,565	50,773	52,811	56,865	63,322	3.5	3.6	3.5	3.5	3.7	4.1	4.6
Minnesota	51,257	55,738	54,349	40,778	54,034	50,837	55,875	6.2	7.0	6.8	5.1	6.8	6.3	6.9
Mississippi	2,916	6,543	6,061	5,617	6,175	8,485	6,574	0.6	1.3	1.2	1.1	1.3	1.7	1.3
Missouri	14,855	15,468	19,393	20,411	23,169	24,455	25,149	1.6	1.7	2.2	2.3	2.6	2.7	2.8
Montana......................	6,668	4,549	3,806	3,299	3,318	3,750	3,311	4.5	3.2	2.7	2.3	2.3	2.6	2.3
Nebraska.....................	15,586	18,388	19,323	20,062	17,532	16,895	15,416	5.5	6.3	6.6	6.7	5.8	5.6	5.0
Nevada	69,896	75,952	67,868	83,351	84,125	67,970	67,640	18.1	17.6	16.0	19.4	19.6	15.7	15.5
New Hampshire	2,755	3,496	3,821	3,965	3,892	3,709	3,506	1.3	1.8	1.9	2.0	2.0	2.0	1.9
New Jersey	58,349	53,960	55,450	52,580	53,543	57,838	60,655	4.1	4.0	4.1	3.8	4.0	4.3	4.5
New Mexico	54,528	55,978 [2]	51,257	52,029	53,071	51,554	49,917	16.9	17.0 [2]	15.5	15.7	16.1	15.8	15.3
New York......................	183,539 [2]	183,736	200,433	207,708	204,898	197,594	184,562 [4]	6.4 [2]	6.8	7.4	7.8	7.8	7.5	7.0 [4]
North Carolina	60,658	113,155	105,651	102,397	98,264	97,338	93,726	4.5	7.8	7.3	7.1	6.7	6.6	6.5
North Dakota	1,638	3,540	3,031	2,788	2,589	2,667	2,749	1.6	3.7	3.3	3.0	2.7	2.7	2.7
Ohio...........................	23,101	35,362	36,527	35,170	35,729	37,207	40,195	1.3	2.0	2.2	2.1	2.2	2.3	2.5
Oklahoma	40,041	38,314 [2]	39,259	41,431	44,593	46,155	46,736	6.4	5.9 [2]	6.0	6.3	6.7	6.9	7.0
Oregon........................	69,899	62,857	61,625	58,662	63,790	50,181	49,543	12.7	11.2	11.0	10.5	11.3	8.9	8.8
Pennsylvania.................	33,664 [2]	44,853	44,359	44,729	44,242	44,017	44,777	1.9 [2]	2.7	2.6	2.7	2.7	2.7	2.8
Rhode Island	9,558	6,466 [2]	6,340	7,161	7,724	7,856	8,562	6.1	4.9 [2]	4.9	5.5	6.1	6.2	6.8
South Carolina................	10,653	31,422	34,661	36,360	38,986	40,876	40,087	1.5	4.4	4.8	5.1	5.4	5.7	5.5
South Dakota	4,468	3,580	4,005	4,383	4,736	4,999	4,251	3.6	2.8	3.2	3.5	3.7	3.8	3.3
Tennessee	27,002 [2]	27,433	27,550	29,680	30,996	32,331	34,397	3.0 [2]	2.8	2.8	3.0	3.1	3.3	3.5
Texas	655,210	704,142	708,615	718,350	722,043	739,639	765,952	15.4	15.2	15.0	15.0	14.9	15.1	15.5
Utah...........................	49,436	43,957	46,591	41,805	32,423	31,810	32,775	10.1	8.3	8.5	7.7	5.9	5.7	5.7
Vermont	1,992	1,645 [2]	1,525	1,510	1,447	1,427	1,348 [5]	2.0	1.9 [2]	1.7	1.6	1.6	1.6	1.5 [5]
Virginia........................	60,101	86,745	86,475	87,752	91,431	92,937	93,995	5.1	7.1	7.0	7.1	7.4	7.4	7.5
Washington...................	58,523	82,711	65,101	90,282	82,070	93,940	99,650	5.7	8.0	6.3	8.7	7.9	8.9	9.4
West Virginia..................	1,477	1,617	1,605	1,786	1,914	2,084	1,878	0.5	0.6	0.6	0.6	0.7	0.7	0.7
Wisconsin	26,424	47,798	45,041	43,562	44,362	43,189	42,711	3.0	5.5	5.2	5.0	5.1	5.0	4.9
Wyoming......................	3,440	2,271	2,098	2,602	2,706	2,733	2,756	4.0	2.6	2.4	2.9	3.0	3.0	3.0

[1]U.S. total includes imputation for nonreporting states.
[2]Imputation for survey nonresponse. State-level imputations were based on the percentages reported by the state for other years applied to the enrollment for the given year.
[3]Based on data reported by the California Education Agency (http://www.cde.ca.gov/ds/sd/cb/cefelfacts.asp).
[4]For 2013–14, New York data on participation in programs for English language learners are from U.S. Department of Education, National Center for Education Statistics, EDFacts file 046, Data Group 123, extracted December 2, 2015, from the EDFacts Data Warehouse (internal U.S. Department of Education source).

[5]Includes students enrolled in all types of school districts.
NOTE: Includes students served in regular school districts, excluding regional education service agencies and supervisory union administrative centers, state-operated agencies, federally operated agencies, and other types of local education agencies, such as independent charter schools.
SOURCE: U.S. Department of Education, National Center for Education Statistics, Common Core of Data (CCD), "Local Education Agency Universe Survey," 2003–04 through 2013–14. (This table was prepared December 2015.)

Table 204.25. Public school students participating in programs for English language learners, by race/ethnicity: Fall 2009 through fall 2014

Year	Total	White	Black	Hispanic	Asian/Pacific Islander Total	Asian	Pacific Islander	American Indian/ Alaska Native[1]	Two or more races
1	2	3	4	5	6	7	8	9	10
Total enrollment in public schools									
2009	49,360,982	26,701,772	8,245,375	10,991,275	2,484,305	2,435,232	49,073	600,526	337,729
2010	49,484,181	25,932,691	7,917,019	11,438,797	2,466,199	2,295,692	170,507	565,629	1,163,846
2011	49,521,669	25,602,197	7,827,305	11,759,474	2,512,779	2,334,144	178,635	547,435	1,272,479
2012	49,771,118	25,385,841	7,803,273	12,103,504	2,552,088	2,371,747	180,341	533,583	1,392,829
2013	50,044,522	25,160,247	7,804,801	12,452,324	2,593,109	2,416,912	176,197	523,483	1,510,558
2014[2]	50,132,000	25,007,000	7,828,000	12,740,000	2,637,000	2,463,000	174,000	516,000	1,404,000
Number of students participating in English language learner (ELL) programs									
2009	4,437,388	218,285	142,626	3,406,735	509,540	—	—	38,148	(3)
2010	4,464,734	228,897	148,256	3,512,240	509,846	478,620	31,226	39,947	20,928
2011[4]	4,454,824	230,434	153,168	3,491,411	515,613	492,182	23,431	38,816	25,371
2012	4,505,849	242,341	155,625	3,534,292	511,310	486,946	24,364	36,820	25,461
2013	4,582,690	251,917	161,114	3,593,201	512,303	487,212	25,091	36,674	27,481
2014	4,668,515	270,854	163,588	3,648,211	521,975	496,359	25,616	35,442	28,445
Percentage distribution of ELL program participants									
2009	100.0	4.9	3.2	76.8	11.5	—	—	0.9	(3)
2010	100.0	5.1	3.3	78.7	11.4	10.7	0.7	0.9	0.5
2011[4]	100.0	5.2	3.4	78.4	11.6	11.0	0.5	0.9	0.6
2012	100.0	5.4	3.5	78.4	11.3	10.8	0.5	0.8	0.6
2013	100.0	5.5	3.5	78.4	11.2	10.6	0.5	0.8	0.6
2014	100.0	5.8	3.5	78.1	11.2	10.6	0.5	0.8	0.6
Number of ELL program participants as a percent of total enrollment									
2009	9.0	0.8	1.7	31.0	20.5	—	—	6.4	(3)
2010	9.0	0.9	1.9	30.7	20.7	20.8	18.3	7.1	1.8
2011[4]	9.0	0.9	2.0	29.7	20.5	21.1	13.1	7.1	2.0
2012	9.1	1.0	2.0	29.2	20.0	20.5	13.5	6.9	1.8
2013	9.2	1.0	2.1	28.9	19.8	20.2	14.2	7.0	1.8
2014[5]	9.3	1.1	2.1	28.6	19.8	20.2	14.7	6.9	2.0

—Not available.

[1]National totals do not include data for Bureau of Indian Education (BIE) schools. In fall 2014, there were 10,245 American Indian/Alaska Native ELL program participants in BIE schools.

[2]Projected.

[3]For 2009, data on students of Two or more races are included in the totals but are not shown separately. Only a small number of states reported these data, and they are not comparable to data for 2010 and later years.

[4]Includes imputations for missing data.

[5]Enrollment base for percentage of enrollment is projected.

NOTE: Race categories exclude persons of Hispanic ethnicity. Detail may not sum to totals because racial/ethnic categories were not reported for some students and because of rounding. SOURCE: U.S. Department of Education, National Center for Education Statistics, ED*Facts* file 046, Data Group 123, extracted April 24, 2016, from the ED*Facts* Data Warehouse (internal U.S. Department of Education source); Common Core of Data (CCD), "State Nonfiscal Survey of Public Elementary and Secondary Education," 2009–10 through 2013–14; and National Elementary and Secondary Enrollment Projection Model, 1972 through 2025. (This table was prepared April 2016.)

Table 204.27. English language learner (ELL) students enrolled in public elementary and secondary schools, by grade and home language: Selected years, 2008–09 through 2013–14

Grade and home language	Number of ELL students					Percentage distribution of ELL students					Number of ELL students as a percentage of total enrollment				
	2008–09[1]	2009–10[1]	2011–12[1]	2012–13	2013–14	2008–09[1]	2009–10[1]	2011–12[1]	2012–13	2013–14	2008–09[1]	2009–10[1]	2011–12[1]	2012–13	2013–14
1	2	3	4	5	6	7	8	9	10	11	12	13	14	15	16
Total	4,685,746	4,647,016	4,635,185	4,850,293	4,929,989	100.0	100.0	100.0	100.0	100.0	9.7	9.7	9.6	10.0	10.1
Grade															
Kindergarten	629,195	615,615	657,391	667,835	667,665	13.4	13.2	14.2	13.8	13.5	17.3	16.7	17.5	17.4	17.4
Grade 1	621,541	617,599	646,362	665,327	665,612	13.3	13.3	13.9	13.7	13.5	16.8	16.6	17.1	17.4	17.1
Grade 2	583,025	576,336	585,702	609,804	630,475	12.4	12.4	12.6	12.6	12.8	15.8	15.7	15.8	16.4	16.6
Grade 3	495,814	511,545	500,032	540,396	558,925	10.6	11.0	10.8	11.1	11.3	13.4	13.8	13.5	14.5	15.0
Grade 4	406,966	420,145	417,616	428,119	439,529	8.7	9.0	9.0	8.8	8.9	11.2	11.4	11.4	11.6	11.9
Grade 5	333,975	336,194	338,174	367,088	361,651	7.1	7.2	7.3	7.6	7.3	9.2	9.2	9.1	10.0	9.8
Grade 6	288,784	277,971	273,457	288,085	293,778	6.2	6.0	5.9	5.9	6.0	8.0	7.6	7.3	7.7	8.0
Grade 7	263,483	254,830	239,156	255,395	267,416	5.6	5.5	5.2	5.3	5.4	7.2	7.0	6.5	6.8	7.1
Grade 8	237,269	233,332	214,896	227,844	239,817	5.1	5.0	4.6	4.7	4.9	6.4	6.4	5.8	6.2	6.4
Grade 9	268,927	258,728	244,266	255,008	261,564	5.7	5.6	5.3	5.3	5.3	6.5	6.3	6.2	6.4	6.6
Grade 10	218,235	211,691	201,724	202,774	202,377	4.7	4.6	4.4	4.2	4.1	5.7	5.6	5.4	5.4	5.4
Grade 11	172,084	175,544	162,804	170,847	168,437	3.7	3.8	3.5	3.5	3.4	4.9	5.0	4.6	4.8	4.8
Grade 12	142,406	148,173	145,444	159,410	161,227	3.0	3.2	3.1	3.3	3.3	4.2	4.3	4.2	4.6	4.6
Ungraded	23,489	8,672	8,118	11,783	11,422	0.5	0.2	0.2	0.2	0.2	11.5	4.2	6.8	10.0	8.3
30 most commonly reported home languages of ELL students[2]															
Spanish, Castilian	3,617,597	3,577,649	3,562,860	3,718,047	3,770,816	77.2	77.0	76.9	76.7	76.5	7.5	7.4	7.4	7.7	7.7
Arabic	65,278	71,228	86,162	97,971	109,170	1.4	1.5	1.9	2.0	2.2	0.1	0.1	0.2	0.2	0.2
Chinese	77,240	80,124	96,509	104,799	107,825	1.6	1.7	2.1	2.2	2.2	0.2	0.2	0.2	0.2	0.2
English[3]	86,390	77,872	85,246	90,703	91,669	1.8	1.7	1.8	1.9	1.9	0.2	0.2	0.2	0.2	0.2
Vietnamese	91,607	93,204	89,536	92,560	89,705	2.0	2.0	1.9	1.9	1.8	0.2	0.2	0.2	0.2	0.2
Hmong	52,990	49,697	43,845	41,368	39,860	1.1	1.1	0.9	0.9	0.8	0.1	0.1	0.1	0.1	0.1
Haitian, Haitian Creole	37,074	39,736	39,883	38,768	37,371	0.8	0.9	0.9	0.8	0.8	0.1	0.1	0.1	0.1	0.1
Somali	26,264	27,771	27,861	30,959	34,472	0.6	0.6	0.6	0.6	0.7	0.1	0.1	0.1	0.1	0.1
Russian	34,085	33,349	32,225	33,678	33,821	0.7	0.7	0.7	0.7	0.7	0.1	0.1	0.1	0.1	0.1
Korean	43,169	39,739	33,704	34,874	32,445	0.9	0.9	0.7	0.7	0.7	0.1	0.1	0.1	0.1	0.1
Tagalog	38,849	37,038	32,766	35,395	32,141	0.8	0.8	0.7	0.7	0.7	0.1	0.1	0.1	0.1	0.1
Urdu	20,705	21,213	22,219	22,590	22,499	0.4	0.5	0.5	0.5	0.5	#	#	#	#	#
French	16,525	18,504	18,849	20,018	20,799	0.4	0.4	0.4	0.4	0.4	#	#	#	#	#
Portuguese	18,055	15,229	15,725	17,085	19,142	0.4	0.3	0.3	0.4	0.4	#	#	#	#	#
Japanese	16,212	14,582	15,011	16,727	16,591	0.3	0.3	0.3	0.3	0.3	#	#	#	#	#
Panjabi, Punjabi	14,262	14,331	14,055	15,622	15,842	0.3	0.3	0.3	0.3	0.3	#	#	#	#	#
Bengali	10,700	11,913	14,151	15,294	15,681	0.2	0.3	0.3	0.3	0.3	#	#	#	#	#
Nepali	3,205	6,283	12,200	14,254	15,331	0.1	0.1	0.3	0.3	0.3	#	#	#	#	#
Burmese	7,258	9,888	12,321	12,640	13,756	0.2	0.2	0.3	0.3	0.3	#	#	#	#	#
Hindi	11,112	11,176	11,625	13,042	13,667	0.2	0.2	0.3	0.3	0.3	#	#	#	#	#
Karen languages	3,021	4,478	9,576	11,370	12,607	0.1	0.1	0.2	0.2	0.3	#	#	#	#	#
Central Khmer	14,443	13,465	11,613	11,530	12,584	0.3	0.3	0.3	0.2	0.3	#	#	#	#	#
Gujarati	9,153	9,491	10,152	10,328	10,463	0.2	0.2	0.2	0.2	0.2	#	#	#	#	#
Persian	8,784	8,593	8,396	9,666	9,978	0.2	0.2	0.2	0.2	0.2	#	#	#	#	#
German	9,605	9,898	9,274	9,190	9,642	0.2	0.2	0.2	0.2	0.2	#	#	#	#	#
Amharic	5,838	6,950	7,902	9,147	9,400	0.1	0.1	0.2	0.2	0.2	#	#	#	#	#
Navajo, Navaho	11,333	10,813	9,684	9,614	9,205	0.2	0.2	0.2	0.2	0.2	#	#	#	#	#
Polish	11,126	9,061	8,981	9,001	9,203	0.2	0.2	0.2	0.2	0.2	#	#	#	#	#
Armenian	8,150	7,997	7,740	8,511	8,000	0.2	0.2	0.2	0.2	0.2	#	#	#	#	#
Ukrainian	8,941	8,736	7,577	7,786	7,756	0.2	0.2	0.2	0.2	0.2	#	#	#	#	#

#Rounds to zero.

[1]Includes data for California that reflect ELL students enrolled on a single date, rather than a cumulative count of all ELL students enrolled at any time during the school year.

[2]Ranking of the 30 most commonly reported home languages is based on 2013–14 data. In each year shown, home language data were unavailable for approximately 92,000–133,000 students identified as English language learners. Enrollments of children speaking less common languages are not separately listed.

[3]Examples of situations in which English might be reported as an English learner's home language include students who live in multilingual households and students adopted from other countries who speak English at home but also have been raised speaking another language.

NOTE: Includes all students identified as English language learners—both those participating in ELL programs and those not participating in ELL programs. Includes all ELLs enrolled at any time during the school year. Data exclude Puerto Rico and the Bureau of Indian Education. Detail may not sum to totals because grade levels were not reported for some students and because of rounding. 2010–11 not shown due to missing data.
SOURCE: U.S. Department of Education, National Center for Education Statistics, ED*Facts* file 141, Data Group 678, extracted May 13, 2016, from the ED*Facts* Data Warehouse (internal U.S. Department of Education source); Common Core of Data (CCD), "State Nonfiscal Survey of Public Elementary and Secondary Education," 2008–09 through 2013–14. (This table was prepared May 2016.)

Table 204.30. Children 3 to 21 years old served under Individuals with Disabilities Education Act (IDEA), Part B, by type of disability: Selected years, 1976–77 through 2013–14

Type of disability	1976–77	1980–81	1990–91	2000–01	2003–04	2004–05	2005–06	2006–07	2007–08[1]	2008–09[1]	2009–10	2010–11	2011–12	2012–13	2013–14
1	2	3	4	5	6	7	8	9	10	11	12	13	14	15	16
						Number served (in thousands)									
All disabilities	**3,694**	**4,144**	**4,710**	**6,296**	**6,634**	**6,720**	**6,718**	**6,687**	**6,597**	**6,483**	**6,481**	**6,436**	**6,401**	**6,429**	**6,464**
Autism	—	—	—	93	163	191	223	258	296	336	378	417	455	498	538
Deaf-blindness	—	3	1	1	2	2	2	2	2	2	2	2	2	1	1
Developmental delay	—	—	—	213	305	332	339	333	357	354	368	382	393	402	410
Emotional disturbance	283	347	389	480	489	489	477	464	442	420	407	390	373	362	354
Hearing impairment	88	79	58	77	79	79	79	80	79	78	79	78	78	77	77
Intellectual disability	961	830	534	624	593	578	556	534	500	478	463	448	435	430	425
Multiple disabilities	—	68	96	131	140	140	141	142	138	130	131	130	132	133	132
Orthopedic impairment	87	58	49	82	77	73	71	69	67	70	65	63	61	59	56
Other health impairment[2]	141	98	55	303	464	521	570	610	641	659	689	716	743	779	817
Preschool disabled[3]	†	†	390	†	†	†	†	†	†	†	†	†	†	†	†
Specific learning disability	796	1,462	2,129	2,860	2,831	2,798	2,740	2,665	2,569	2,476	2,431	2,361	2,303	2,277	2,264
Speech or language impairment	1,302	1,168	985	1,388	1,441	1,463	1,468	1,475	1,454	1,426	1,416	1,396	1,373	1,356	1,334
Traumatic brain injury	—	—	—	16	23	24	24	25	25	26	25	26	26	26	26
Visual impairment	38	31	23	29	28	29	29	29	29	29	29	28	28	28	28
					Percentage distribution of children served										
All disabilities	**100.0**	**100.0**	**100.0**	**100.0**	**100.0**	**100.0**	**100.0**	**100.0**	**100.0**	**100.0**	**100.0**	**100.0**	**100.0**	**100.0**	**100.0**
Autism	—	—	—	1.5	2.5	2.8	3.3	3.9	4.5	5.2	5.8	6.5	7.1	7.8	8.3
Deaf-blindness	—	0.1	#	#	#	#	#	#	#	#	#	#	#	#	#
Developmental delay	—	—	3.4	4.6	4.9	5.0	5.0	5.4	5.5	5.7	5.9	6.1	6.2	6.3	
Emotional disturbance	7.7	8.4	8.3	7.6	7.4	7.3	7.1	6.9	6.7	6.5	6.3	6.1	5.8	5.6	5.5
Hearing impairment	2.4	1.9	1.2	1.2	1.2	1.2	1.2	1.2	1.2	1.2	1.2	1.2	1.2	1.2	1.2
Intellectual disability	26.0	20.0	11.3	9.9	8.9	8.6	8.3	8.0	7.6	7.4	7.1	7.0	6.8	6.7	6.6
Multiple disabilities	—	1.6	2.0	2.1	2.1	2.1	2.1	2.1	2.1	2.0	2.0	2.0	2.1	2.1	2.0
Orthopedic impairment	2.4	1.4	1.0	1.3	1.2	1.1	1.1	1.0	1.0	1.1	1.0	1.0	1.0	0.9	0.9
Other health impairment[2]	3.8	2.4	1.2	4.8	7.0	7.7	8.5	9.1	9.7	10.2	10.6	11.1	11.6	12.1	12.6
Preschool disabled[3]	†	†	8.3	†	†	†	†	†	†	†	†	†	†	†	†
Specific learning disability	21.5	35.3	45.2	45.4	42.7	41.6	40.8	39.9	38.9	38.2	37.5	36.7	36.0	35.4	35.0
Speech or language impairment	35.2	28.2	20.9	22.0	21.7	21.8	21.8	22.1	22.0	22.0	21.8	21.7	21.4	21.1	20.6
Traumatic brain injury	—	—	—	0.2	0.4	0.4	0.4	0.4	0.4	0.4	0.4	0.4	0.4	0.4	0.4
Visual impairment	1.0	0.7	0.5	0.5	0.4	0.4	0.4	0.4	0.4	0.4	0.4	0.4	0.4	0.4	0.4
					Number served as a percent of total enrollment[4]										
All disabilities	**8.3**	**10.1**	**11.4**	**13.3**	**13.7**	**13.8**	**13.7**	**13.6**	**13.4**	**13.2**	**13.1**	**13.0**	**12.9**	**12.9**	**12.9**
Autism	—	—	—	0.2	0.3	0.4	0.5	0.5	0.6	0.7	0.8	0.8	0.9	1.0	1.1
Deaf-blindness	—	#	#	#	#	#	#	#	#	#	#	#	#	#	#
Developmental delay	—	—	—	0.5	0.6	0.7	0.7	0.7	0.7	0.7	0.7	0.8	0.8	0.8	0.8
Emotional disturbance	0.6	0.8	0.9	1.0	1.0	1.0	1.0	0.9	0.9	0.9	0.8	0.8	0.8	0.7	0.7
Hearing impairment	0.2	0.2	0.1	0.2	0.2	0.2	0.2	0.2	0.2	0.2	0.2	0.2	0.2	0.2	0.2
Intellectual disability	2.2	2.0	1.3	1.3	1.2	1.2	1.1	1.1	1.0	1.0	0.9	0.9	0.9	0.9	0.9
Multiple disabilities	—	0.2	0.2	0.3	0.3	0.3	0.3	0.3	0.3	0.3	0.3	0.3	0.3	0.3	0.3
Orthopedic impairment	0.2	0.1	0.1	0.2	0.2	0.2	0.1	0.1	0.1	0.1	0.1	0.1	0.1	0.1	0.1
Other health impairment[2]	0.3	0.2	0.1	0.6	1.0	1.1	1.2	1.2	1.3	1.3	1.4	1.4	1.5	1.6	1.6
Preschool disabled[3]	†	†	0.9	†	†	†	†	†	†	†	†	†	†	†	†
Specific learning disability	1.8	3.6	5.2	6.1	5.8	5.7	5.6	5.4	5.2	5.0	4.9	4.8	4.7	4.6	4.5
Speech or language impairment	2.9	2.9	2.4	2.9	3.0	3.0	3.0	3.0	2.9	2.9	2.9	2.8	2.8	2.7	2.7
Traumatic brain injury	—	—	—	#	#	#	#	0.1	0.1	0.1	0.1	0.1	0.1	0.1	0.1
Visual impairment	0.1	0.1	0.1	0.1	0.1	0.1	0.1	0.1	0.1	0.1	0.1	0.1	0.1	0.1	0.1

—Not available.
†Not applicable.
#Rounds to zero.
[1]Data do not include Vermont, for which 2007–08 and 2008–09 data were not available. In 2006–07, the total number of 3- to 21-year-olds served in Vermont was 14,010.
[2]Other health impairments include having limited strength, vitality, or alertness due to chronic or acute health problems such as a heart condition, tuberculosis, rheumatic fever, nephritis, asthma, sickle cell anemia, hemophilia, epilepsy, lead poisoning, leukemia, or diabetes.
[3]For 1990–91, preschool children are not included in the counts by disability condition but are separately reported. For other years, preschool children are included in the counts by disability condition.
[4]Based on the total enrollment in public schools, prekindergarten through 12th grade. For total enrollment in public schools, see table 203.20.
NOTE: Prior to October 1994, children and youth with disabilities were served under Chapter 1 of the Elementary and Secondary Education Act as well as under the Individuals with Disabilities

Education Act (IDEA), Part B. Data reported in this table for years prior to 1994–95 include children ages 0–21 served under Chapter 1. Data are for the 50 states and the District of Columbia only. Increases since 1987–88 are due in part to new legislation enacted in fall 1986, which added a mandate for public school special education services for 3- to 5-year-old children with disabilities. Detail may not sum to totals because of rounding.
SOURCE: U.S. Department of Education, Office of Special Education Programs, *Annual Report to Congress on the Implementation of the Individuals with Disabilities Education Act*, selected years, 1979 through 2006; and Individuals with Disabilities Education Act (IDEA) database, retrieved September 25, 2015, from http://www2.ed.gov/programs/osepidea/618-data/state-level-data-files/index.html#bcc. National Center for Education Statistics, *Statistics of Public Elementary and Secondary School Systems*, 1977–78 and 1980–81; and Common Core of Data (CCD), "State Nonfiscal Survey of Public Elementary/Secondary Education," 1990–91 through 2013–14. (This table was prepared October 2015.)

Table 204.40. Children 3 to 21 years old served under Individuals with Disabilities Education Act (IDEA), Part B, by race/ethnicity and age group: 2000–01 through 2013–14

Age group and year	Total	White	Black	Hispanic	Asian[1]	Pacific Islander	American Indian/ Alaska Native	Two or more races
1	2	3	4	5	6	7	8	9
				Number of children served				
3 to 21 years old								
2000–01	6,295,709	3,957,589	1,259,348	877,655	121,044	—	80,073	—
2001–02	6,407,417	3,989,528	1,281,803	928,776	123,434	—	83,876	—
2002–03	6,522,977	4,014,340	1,311,270	980,590	130,252	—	86,525	—
2003–04	6,633,902	4,035,880	1,334,666	1,035,463	137,544	—	90,349	—
2004–05	6,718,630	4,044,491	1,355,550	1,081,697	144,339	—	92,553	—
2005–06	6,712,614	4,003,865	1,346,177	1,119,140	149,954	—	93,478	—
2006–07	6,686,386	3,948,853	1,335,870	1,154,217	153,265	—	94,181	—
2007–08[2]	6,574,368	3,833,922	1,307,462	1,181,130	158,623	—	93,231	—
2008–09[2]	6,461,938	3,725,896	1,273,996	1,200,290	162,630	—	93,672	5,454 [3]
2009–10	6,461,226	3,659,194	1,262,799	1,252,493	167,144	—	92,646	26,950 [3]
2010–11	6,435,141	3,518,169	1,214,849	1,310,031	145,896	19,581	91,258	135,357
2011–12	6,401,238	3,436,105	1,196,679	1,352,435	147,697	19,203	88,665	160,458
2012–13[4]	6,429,331	3,396,135	1,189,148	1,406,540	150,913	20,343	86,884	180,268
2013–14[4]	6,464,096	3,356,261	1,191,817	1,469,282	155,668	19,606	86,307	185,274
3 to 5 years old								
2000–01	592,090	400,650	93,281	78,070	13,203	—	6,886	—
2005–06	698,608	453,531	102,310	112,883	20,791	—	9,093	—
2010–11	723,793	416,034	102,097	153,033	23,189	2,159	9,141	18,140
2011–12	730,558	408,973	103,051	158,507	23,023	2,146	8,729	26,133
2012–13[4]	735,890	399,019	102,677	163,997	23,101	2,087	8,291	36,774
2013–14[4]	729,703	394,227	103,829	170,939	24,497	1,972	8,338	25,917
6 to 21 years old								
2000–01	5,703,619	3,556,939	1,166,067	799,585	107,841	—	73,187	—
2005–06	6,014,006	3,550,334	1,243,867	1,006,257	129,163	—	84,385	—
2010–11	5,711,348	3,102,135	1,112,752	1,156,998	122,707	17,422	82,117	117,217
2011–12	5,670,680	3,027,132	1,093,628	1,193,928	124,674	17,057	79,936	134,325
2012–13[4]	5,693,441	2,997,116	1,086,471	1,242,543	127,812	18,256	78,593	143,494
2013–14[4]	5,734,393	2,962,034	1,087,988	1,298,343	131,171	17,634	77,969	159,357
				Percentage distribution of children served				
3 to 21 years old								
2000–01	100.0	62.9	20.0	13.9	1.9	†	1.3	†
2001–02	100.0	62.3	20.0	14.5	1.9	†	1.3	†
2002–03	100.0	61.5	20.1	15.0	2.0	†	1.3	†
2003–04	100.0	60.8	20.1	15.6	2.1	†	1.4	†
2004–05	100.0	60.2	20.2	16.1	2.1	†	1.4	†
2005–06	100.0	59.6	20.1	16.7	2.2	†	1.4	†
2006–07	100.0	59.1	20.0	17.3	2.3	†	1.4	†
2007–08[2]	100.0	58.3	19.9	18.0	2.4	†	1.4	†
2008–09[2]	100.0	57.7	19.7	18.6	2.5	†	1.4	0.1 [3]
2009–10	100.0	56.6	19.5	19.4	2.6	†	1.4	0.4 [3]
2010–11	100.0	54.7	18.9	20.4	2.3	0.3	1.4	2.1
2011–12	100.0	53.7	18.7	21.1	2.3	0.3	1.4	2.5
2012–13	100.0	52.8	18.5	21.9	2.3	0.3	1.4	2.8
2013–14	100.0	51.9	18.4	22.7	2.4	0.3	1.3	2.9
				Number served as a percent of total enrollment[5]				
3 to 21 years old								
2000–01	13.3	13.7	15.5	11.4	6.2	†	14.6	†
2001–02	13.4	13.9	15.7	11.4	6.1	†	14.9	†
2002–03	13.5	14.0	15.8	11.4	6.2	†	14.8	†
2003–04	13.7	14.2	16.0	11.5	6.4	†	15.2	†
2004–05	13.8	14.3	16.1	11.5	6.5	†	15.7	†
2005–06	13.7	14.3	15.9	11.4	6.6	†	15.6	†
2006–07	13.6	14.2	15.9	11.3	6.6	†	15.8	†
2007–08[2]	13.3	14.0	15.6	11.3	6.6	†	15.7	†
2008–09[2]	13.1	13.8	15.2	11.4	6.6	†	15.9	2.2 [3]
2009–10	13.1	13.7	15.2	11.5	6.7	†	15.6	8.0 [3]
2010–11	13.0	13.6	15.4	11.5	6.4	11.5	16.2	11.7
2011–12	12.9	13.4	15.3	11.5	6.4	10.8	16.2	12.6
2012–13	12.9	13.4	15.2	11.7	6.4	11.3	16.3	13.0
2013–14	12.9	13.4	15.3	11.8	6.5	11.2	16.5	12.3

—Not available.
†Not applicable.
[1]For years prior to 2010–11, Asian data include Pacific Islanders.
[2]Data do not include Vermont, for which 2007–08 and 2008–09 data were not available.
[3]For 2008–09 and 2009–10, data on children of Two or more races were reported by only a small number of states. Therefore, these data are not comparable to figures for later years.
[4]For 2012–13 and 2013–14, the total column shows the overall counts of children as reported by the 50 states and the District of Columbia rather than the sum of counts reported for individual racial/ethnic groups. (Due to data limitations, summing the data for the racial/ethnic groups can result in overcounts. For 2013–14, summing these data would result in a total overcount of 16 children in the 3- to 5-year-old age group and 103 children in the 6- to 21-year-old age group.)

[5]Based on the total enrollment in public schools, prekindergarten through 12th grade, by race/ethnicity. For total enrollment in public schools by race/ethnicity, see table 203.60.
NOTE: Data include only those children served for whom race/ethnicity was reported. Race categories exclude persons of Hispanic ethnicity. Detail may not sum to totals because of rounding.
SOURCE: U.S. Department of Education, Office of Special Education Programs, Individuals with Disabilities Education Act (IDEA) database, retrieved September 25, 2015, from http://www2.ed.gov/programs/osepidea/618-data/state-level-data-files/index.html#bcc; and National Center for Education Statistics, Common Core of Data (CCD), "State Nonfiscal Survey of Public Elementary and Secondary Education," 2000–01 through 2013–14. (This table was prepared October 2015.)

Table 204.50. Children 3 to 21 years old served under Individuals with Disabilities Education Act (IDEA), Part B, by age group and sex, race/ethnicity, and type of disability: 2013–14

Type of disability	Age group and sex[1]				Race/ethnicity						
	3 to 5 years old		6 to 21 years old		Total, 3 to 21 years old						
	Male	Female	Male	Female	White	Black	Hispanic	Asian	Pacific Islander	American Indian/ Alaska Native	Two or more races
1	2	3	4	5	6	7	8	9	10	11	12
	Number of children served										
All disabilities...................................	510,990	218,744	3,770,750	1,879,635	3,356,261	1,191,817	1,469,282	155,668	19,606	86,307	185,274
Autism...	—	—	399,598	73,681	307,112	74,464	103,919	29,564	1,351	4,011	17,594
Deaf-blindness....................................	—	—	680	582	832	166	345	59	10	22	34
Developmental delay	—	—	92,593	39,427	219,073	77,362	77,143	11,487	1,605	8,292	14,970
Emotional disturbance	—	—	256,362	86,710	186,308	92,141	53,121	3,208	931	4,851	13,299
Hearing impairment	—	—	35,822	31,093	36,443	10,876	21,895	4,218	424	820	1,956
Intellectual disability..........................	—	—	232,560	167,692	191,858	113,791	92,664	10,611	1,246	5,454	9,823
Multiple disabilities............................	—	—	76,672	47,079	74,546	24,468	23,787	4,031	509	1,967	3,133
Orthopedic impairment.......................	—	—	29,703	19,499	30,528	6,733	14,862	2,237	170	459	1,500
Other health impairment[2]..................	—	—	561,870	228,734	493,978	149,140	125,789	11,474	2,185	9,306	25,571
Specific learning disability	—	—	1,379,873	830,620	1,054,657	452,028	623,442	34,415	8,322	35,394	55,890
Speech or language impairment.........	—	—	675,197	334,488	729,813	182,318	321,543	42,525	2,662	15,029	39,949
Traumatic brain injury........................	—	—	15,974	9,063	15,937	4,032	4,554	667	84	339	783
Visual impairment	—	—	13,846	10,967	15,176	4,298	6,218	1,172	107	363	772
	Percentage distribution of children served										
All disabilities...................................	100.0	100.0	100.0	100.0	100.0	100.0	100.0	100.0	100.0	100.0	100.0
Autism...	—	—	10.6	3.9	9.2	6.2	7.1	19.0	6.9	4.6	9.5
Deaf-blindness....................................	—	—	#	#	#	#	#	#	0.1	#	#
Developmental delay	—	—	2.5	2.1	6.5	6.5	5.3	7.4	8.2	9.6	8.1
Emotional disturbance	—	—	6.8	4.6	5.6	7.7	3.6	2.1	4.7	5.6	7.2
Hearing impairment	—	—	0.9	1.7	1.1	0.9	1.5	2.7	2.2	1.0	1.1
Intellectual disability..........................	—	—	6.2	8.9	5.7	9.5	6.3	6.8	6.4	6.3	5.3
Multiple disabilities............................	—	—	2.0	2.5	2.2	2.1	1.6	2.6	2.6	2.3	1.7
Orthopedic impairment.......................	—	—	0.8	1.0	0.9	0.6	1.0	1.4	0.9	0.5	0.8
Other health impairment[2]..................	—	—	14.9	12.2	14.7	12.5	8.6	7.4	11.1	10.8	13.8
Specific learning disability	—	—	36.6	44.2	31.4	37.9	42.4	22.1	42.4	41.0	30.2
Speech or language impairment.........	—	—	17.9	17.8	21.7	15.3	21.9	27.3	13.6	17.4	21.6
Traumatic brain injury........................	—	—	0.4	0.5	0.5	0.3	0.3	0.4	0.4	0.4	0.4
Visual impairment	—	—	0.4	0.6	0.5	0.4	0.4	0.8	0.5	0.4	0.4
	Number served as a percent of total enrollment[3]										
All disabilities...................................	18.9	8.9	16.4	8.6	13.4	15.3	11.8	6.5	11.2	16.5	12.3
Autism...	—	—	1.7	0.3	1.2	1.0	0.8	1.2	0.8	0.8	1.2
Deaf-blindness....................................	—	—	#	#	#	#	#	#	#	#	#
Developmental delay	—	—	0.4	0.2	0.9	1.0	0.6	0.5	0.9	1.6	1.0
Emotional disturbance	—	—	1.1	0.4	0.7	1.2	0.4	0.1	0.5	0.9	0.9
Hearing impairment	—	—	0.2	0.1	0.1	0.1	0.2	0.2	0.2	0.2	0.1
Intellectual disability..........................	—	—	1.0	0.8	0.8	1.5	0.7	0.4	0.7	1.0	0.7
Multiple disabilities............................	—	—	0.3	0.2	0.3	0.3	0.2	0.2	0.3	0.4	0.2
Orthopedic impairment.......................	—	—	0.1	0.1	0.1	0.1	0.1	0.1	0.1	0.1	0.1
Other health impairment[2]..................	—	—	2.4	1.0	2.0	1.9	1.0	0.5	1.2	1.8	1.7
Specific learning disability	—	—	6.0	3.8	4.2	5.8	5.0	1.4	4.7	6.8	3.7
Speech or language impairment.........	—	—	2.9	1.5	2.9	2.3	2.6	1.8	1.5	2.9	2.7
Traumatic brain injury........................	—	—	0.1	#	0.1	0.1	#	#	#	0.1	0.1
Visual impairment	—	—	0.1	0.1	0.1	0.1	0.1	#	0.1	0.1	0.1

—Not available.
#Rounds to zero.
[1]For 3- to 5-year-olds, no data are available on type of disability by sex. For 6- to 21-year-olds, data include only those children served for whom both sex and type of disability were reported. About 1.5 percent of all 6- to 21-year-olds served are excluded from this table because of missing data.
[2]Other health impairments include having limited strength, vitality, or alertness due to chronic or acute health problems such as a heart condition, tuberculosis, rheumatic fever, nephritis, asthma, sickle cell anemia, hemophilia, epilepsy, lead poisoning, leukemia, or diabetes.
[3]Percentages for students 3 to 5 years old by sex are based on total public school enrollment in prekindergarten and kindergarten by sex. Percentages for students 6 to 21 years old by sex are based on total public school enrollment in grades 1 through 12 by sex. Percentages

for students of all ages (3 to 21 years old) by race/ethnicity are based on total enrollment in public schools, prekindergarten through grade 12, by race/ethnicity. For total enrollment in public schools by race/ethnicity, see table 203.50.
NOTE: Although data are for the 50 states and the District of Columbia, data limitations result in inclusion of a small (but unknown) number of students from other jurisdictions. Race categories exclude persons of Hispanic ethnicity. Detail may not sum to totals because of rounding.
SOURCE: U.S. Department of Education, Office of Special Education Programs, Individuals with Disabilities Education Act (IDEA) database, retrieved September 25, 2015, from http://www2.ed.gov/programs/osepidea/618-data/state-level-data-files/index.html#bcc; and National Center for Education Statistics, Common Core of Data (CCD), "State Nonfiscal Survey of Public Elementary/Secondary Education," 2013–14. (This table was prepared October 2015.)

Table 204.60. Percentage distribution of students 6 to 21 years old served under Individuals with Disabilities Education Act (IDEA), Part B, by educational environment and type of disability: Selected years, fall 1989 through fall 2013

Type of disability	All environments	Regular school, time inside general class			Separate school for students with disabilities	Separate residential facility	Parentally placed in regular private schools[1]	Homebound/hospital placement	Correctional facility
		Less than 40 percent	40–79 percent	80 percent or more					
1	2	3	4	5	6	7	8	9	10
All students with disabilities									
1989	100.0	24.9	37.5	31.7	4.5	1.0	—	0.6	—
1990	100.0	25.0	36.4	33.1	4.2	0.9	—	0.5	—
1994	100.0	22.4	28.5	44.8	3.0	0.7	—	0.6	—
1995	100.0	21.5	28.5	45.7	3.1	0.7	—	0.5	—
1996	100.0	21.4	28.3	46.1	3.0	0.7	—	0.5	—
1997	100.0	20.4	28.8	46.8	2.9	0.7	—	0.5	—
1998	100.0	20.0	29.9	46.0	2.9	0.7	—	0.5	—
1999	100.0	20.3	29.8	45.9	2.9	0.7	—	0.5	—
2000	100.0	19.5	29.8	46.5	3.0	0.7	—	0.5	—
2001	100.0	19.2	28.5	48.2	2.9	0.7	—	0.4	—
2002	100.0	19.0	28.7	48.2	2.9	0.7	—	0.5	—
2003	100.0	18.5	27.7	49.9	2.8	0.7	—	0.5	—
2004	100.0	17.9	26.5	51.5	3.0	0.6	—	0.4	—
2005	100.0	16.7	25.1	54.2	2.9	0.6	—	0.4	—
2006	100.0	16.4	23.8	54.8	2.9	0.4	1.0	0.4	0.4
2007	100.0	15.4	22.4	56.8	3.0	0.4	1.1	0.4	0.4
2008	100.0	14.9	21.4	58.5	2.9	0.4	1.1	0.4	0.4
2009	100.0	14.6	20.7	59.4	3.0	0.4	1.2	0.4	0.4
2010	100.0	14.2	20.0	60.5	3.0	0.4	1.2	0.4	0.3
2011									
All students with disabilities	100.0	14.0	19.8	61.1	3.0	0.3	1.1	0.4	0.3
Autism	100.0	33.7	18.2	39.0	7.7	0.5	0.6	0.3	#
Deaf-blindness	100.0	32.5	10.5	27.0	18.1	8.4	0.7	2.8	#
Developmental delay	100.0	16.3	19.6	62.5	0.8	0.1	0.6	0.2	#
Emotional disturbance	100.0	20.6	18.0	43.2	13.2	1.9	0.2	1.1	1.8
Hearing impairment	100.0	13.0	16.8	56.7	8.6	3.4	1.3	0.2	0.1
Intellectual disability	100.0	48.8	26.6	17.0	6.2	0.4	0.3	0.5	0.2
Multiple disabilities	100.0	46.2	16.4	13.0	19.2	1.7	0.3	3.0	0.1
Orthopedic impairment	100.0	22.2	16.3	54.0	4.7	0.2	0.8	1.7	0.1
Other health impairment[2]	100.0	10.0	22.7	63.5	1.6	0.2	1.0	0.9	0.3
Specific learning disability	100.0	6.8	25.1	66.2	0.5	0.1	0.8	0.1	0.3
Speech or language impairment	100.0	4.5	5.5	86.9	0.3	#	2.6	0.1	#
Traumatic brain injury	100.0	20.5	22.8	48.5	5.2	0.5	0.8	1.7	0.1
Visual impairment	100.0	11.3	13.1	64.3	5.9	3.8	1.1	0.6	#
2012									
All students with disabilities	100.0	13.9	19.7	61.2	3.0	0.3	1.2	0.4	0.3
Autism	100.0	33.3	18.1	39.5	7.7	0.5	0.7	0.3	#
Deaf-blindness	100.0	34.7	11.4	21.0	19.8	8.2	1.5	2.7	0.7
Developmental delay	100.0	16.6	19.5	62.3	0.8	0.1	0.6	0.2	#
Emotional disturbance	100.0	20.4	17.8	44.0	13.0	1.8	0.2	1.1	1.7
Hearing impairment	100.0	12.6	16.4	57.6	8.3	3.4	1.4	0.2	0.1
Intellectual disability	100.0	49.1	27.0	16.5	6.1	0.4	0.3	0.5	0.2
Multiple disabilities	100.0	46.4	16.3	12.9	19.1	1.7	0.4	3.1	0.1
Orthopedic impairment	100.0	21.8	16.2	54.6	4.5	0.2	0.9	1.7	0.1
Other health impairment[2]	100.0	9.8	22.4	63.7	1.7	0.2	1.1	0.8	0.3
Specific learning disability	100.0	6.4	25.0	66.7	0.5	0.1	0.9	0.1	0.3
Speech or language impairment	100.0	4.3	5.4	86.8	0.3	#	3.0	#	#
Traumatic brain injury	100.0	20.1	22.4	49.0	5.3	0.6	0.8	1.8	0.1
Visual impairment	100.0	11.3	13.3	64.0	6.0	3.6	1.2	0.6	0.1
2013									
All students with disabilities	100.0	13.8	19.4	61.8	2.9	0.3	1.1	0.4	0.3
Autism	100.0	33.3	18.2	39.7	7.4	0.4	0.7	0.3	#
Deaf-blindness	100.0	35.6	11.9	23.1	18.5	7.9	0.1	2.8	0.1
Developmental delay	100.0	16.1	19.4	63.0	0.8	#	0.5	0.2	#
Emotional disturbance	100.0	19.8	17.8	45.1	12.9	1.6	0.3	1.1	1.6
Hearing impairment	100.0	12.2	16.0	59.3	7.7	3.1	1.3	0.2	0.1
Intellectual disability	100.0	49.4	26.9	16.3	6.1	0.3	0.3	0.5	0.2
Multiple disabilities	100.0	46.4	16.4	13.3	18.7	1.6	0.3	3.2	0.1
Orthopedic impairment	100.0	21.5	16.1	55.1	4.4	0.1	0.8	1.9	0.1
Other health impairment[2]	100.0	9.6	21.9	64.5	1.7	0.2	1.0	0.8	0.3
Specific learning disability	100.0	6.1	24.4	67.8	0.5	0.1	0.8	0.1	0.3
Speech or language impairment	100.0	4.3	5.4	87.3	0.3	#	2.6	#	#
Traumatic brain injury	100.0	20.1	22.2	49.6	5.1	0.5	0.7	1.7	0.1
Visual impairment	100.0	10.8	13.0	64.8	6.1	3.5	1.2	0.6	#

—Not available.
#Rounds to zero.
[1]Students who are enrolled by their parents or guardians in regular private schools and have their basic education paid through private resources, but receive special education services at public expense. These students are not included under "Regular school, time inside general class" (columns 3 through 5).
[2]Other health impairments include having limited strength, vitality, or alertness due to chronic or acute health problems such as a heart condition, tuberculosis, rheumatic fever, nephritis, asthma, sickle cell anemia, hemophilia, epilepsy, lead poisoning, leukemia, or diabetes.

NOTE: Data are for the 50 United States, the District of Columbia, and the Bureau of Indian Education schools. Detail may not sum to totals because of rounding.
SOURCE: U.S. Department of Education, Office of Special Education Programs, Individuals with Disabilities Education Act (IDEA) database, retrieved October 29, 2015, from http://www2.ed.gov/programs/osepidea/618-data/state-level-data-files/index.html#bcc. (This table was prepared November 2015.)

Table 204.70. Number and percentage of children served under Individuals with Disabilities Education Act (IDEA), Part B, by age group and state or jurisdiction: Selected years, 1990–91 through 2013–14

State or jurisdiction	3- to 21-year-olds served						As a percent of public school enrollment, 2013–14[1]	Percent change in number served, 2000–01 to 2013–14	3- to 5-year-olds served					
	1990–91	2000–01	2010–11	2011–12	2012–13	2013–14			1990–91	2000–01	2010–11	2011–12	2012–13	2013–14
1	2	3	4	5	6	7	8	9	10	11	12	13	14	15
United States	4,710,089	6,295,816	6,434,916	6,401,238	6,429,331	6,464,096	12.9	2.7	389,751	592,087	723,738	730,558	735,890	729,703
Alabama	94,601	99,828	82,286	80,149	79,705	80,803	10.8	-19.1	7,154	7,554	7,492	7,355	7,344	7,238
Alaska	14,390	17,691	18,048	18,055	17,959	17,920	13.7	1.3	1,458	1,637	2,104	2,166	2,116	2,062
Arizona	56,629	96,442	125,816	127,198	128,281	129,801	11.8	34.6	4,330	9,144	14,756	15,235	15,386	15,278
Arkansas	47,187	62,222	64,881	64,790	64,698	65,166	13.3	4.7	4,626	9,376	13,034	13,275	12,789	12,529
California	468,420	645,287	672,174	679,269	688,346	698,947	11.1	8.3	39,627	57,651	72,404	73,720	75,285	76,345
Colorado	56,336	78,715	84,710	87,233	89,280	90,904	10.4	15.5	4,128	8,202	11,797	12,348	12,799	12,576
Connecticut	63,886	73,886	68,167	68,280	69,730	70,785	13.0	-4.2	5,466	7,172	7,933	7,956	8,025	8,034
Delaware	14,208	16,760	18,608	19,166	19,224	18,717	14.2	11.7	1,493	1,652	2,123	2,230	2,304	1,815
District of Columbia	6,290	10,559	11,947	12,536	12,585	11,774	15.1	11.5	411	374	957	1,431	1,550	1,441
Florida	234,509	367,335	368,808	358,922	354,352	356,488	13.1	-3.0	14,883	30,660	36,027	37,445	37,470	37,633
Georgia	101,762	171,292	177,544	179,423	185,037	190,587	11.1	11.3	7,098	16,560	15,911	16,539	17,395	17,528
Hawaii	12,705	23,951	19,716	19,605	19,696	19,221	10.3	-19.7	809	1,919	2,398	2,449	2,554	2,402
Idaho	21,703	29,174	27,388	26,864	27,086	27,592	9.3	-5.4	2,815	3,591	3,596	3,379	3,283	3,260
Illinois	236,060	297,316	302,830	292,956	292,430	294,227	14.2	-1.0	22,997	28,787	36,488	36,943	37,211	37,611
Indiana	112,949	156,320	166,073	164,147	168,815	169,830	16.2	8.6	7,243	15,101	18,725	18,172	18,476	18,014
Iowa	59,787	72,461	68,501	67,990	65,882	64,704	12.9	-10.7	5,421	5,580	7,378	7,467	7,109	6,534
Kansas	44,785	61,267	66,873	65,809	67,369	68,625	13.8	12.0	3,881	7,728	10,604	10,598	10,850	11,218
Kentucky	78,853	94,572	102,370	98,785	97,555	97,467	14.4	3.1	10,440	16,372	17,963	17,422	17,455	17,332
Louisiana	72,825	97,938	82,943	82,301	81,238	78,667	11.1	-19.7	6,703	9,957	10,427	11,206	11,209	9,784
Maine	27,987	35,633	32,261	32,078	32,194	32,219	17.5	-9.6	2,895	3,978	3,824	3,831	3,793	3,722
Maryland	88,017	112,077	103,490	103,563	103,429	103,788	12.0	-7.4	7,163	10,003	12,875	13,114	13,062	13,136
Massachusetts	149,743	162,216	167,526	166,236	166,437	166,859	17.5	2.9	12,141	14,328	16,662	16,491	16,583	16,759
Michigan	166,511	221,456	218,957	210,034	203,427	200,451	12.9	-9.5	14,547	19,937	23,183	21,086	20,831	20,511
Minnesota	79,013	109,880	122,850	123,353	123,785	124,507	14.6	13.3	8,646	11,522	15,076	15,361	15,289	15,175
Mississippi	60,872	62,281	64,038	64,334	64,860	65,687	13.3	5.5	5,642	6,944	10,191	10,498	10,244	10,070
Missouri	101,166	137,381	127,144	125,075	123,655	123,292	13.4	-10.3	4,100	11,307	15,891	15,984	16,040	16,047
Montana	16,955	19,313	16,761	16,032	16,450	16,473	11.4	-14.7	1,751	1,635	1,656	1,696	1,697	1,596
Nebraska	32,312	42,793	44,299	44,829	45,564	46,983	15.3	9.8	2,512	3,724	5,050	5,175	5,379	5,373
Nevada	18,099	38,160	48,148	49,117	50,332	52,052	11.5	36.4	1,401	3,676	6,947	7,598	8,047	8,241
New Hampshire	19,049	30,077	29,920	29,422	29,329	29,011	15.6	-3.5	1,468	2,387	3,135	3,158	3,227	3,173
New Jersey	178,870	221,715	232,002	223,935	232,317	228,844	16.7	3.2	14,741	16,361	17,073	16,925	17,954	17,821
New Mexico	36,000	52,256	46,628	46,555	46,498	47,283	13.9	-9.5	2,210	4,970	5,224	5,021	4,494	4,347
New York	307,366	441,333	454,542	452,319	450,794	454,971	16.6	3.1	26,266	51,665	64,923	64,082	65,031	65,705
North Carolina	122,942	173,067	185,107	187,767	190,098	193,092	12.6	11.6	10,516	17,361	18,433	18,787	18,665	18,801
North Dakota	12,294	13,652	13,170	13,093	13,234	13,366	12.9	-2.1	1,164	1,247	1,714	1,791	1,804	1,830
Ohio	205,440	237,643	259,454	259,064	255,953	254,541	14.8	7.1	12,487	18,664	22,454	23,904	23,401	22,933
Oklahoma	65,457	85,577	97,250	98,960	100,893	103,136	15.1	20.5	5,163	6,393	8,298	8,480	8,500	8,599
Oregon	54,422	75,204	81,050	81,718	82,183	82,717	13.9	10.0	2,854	6,926	9,392	9,913	10,052	10,122
Pennsylvania	214,254	242,655	295,080	294,963	295,502	296,249	16.9	22.1	17,982	21,477	31,072	32,722	33,041	32,464
Rhode Island	20,646	30,727	25,332	24,826	24,165	23,402	16.5	-23.8	1,682	2,614	2,945	2,984	2,910	2,906
South Carolina	77,367	105,922	100,289	99,624	99,530	98,930	13.3	-6.6	7,948	11,775	11,083	10,862	10,626	9,728
South Dakota	14,726	16,825	18,026	18,005	18,316	18,508	14.1	10.0	2,105	2,286	2,738	2,726	2,659	2,668
Tennessee	104,853	125,863	120,263	124,070	127,407	130,387	13.1	3.6	7,487	10,699	13,096	13,381	13,067	12,583
Texas	344,529	491,642	442,019	439,675	439,635	443,612	8.6	-9.8	24,848	36,442	41,494	40,756	43,981	42,868
Utah	46,606	53,921	70,278	71,233	78,270	75,428	12.1	39.9	3,424	5,785	8,990	8,856	9,890	9,516
Vermont	12,160	13,623	13,936	13,833	13,873	13,904	15.7	2.1	1,097	1,237	1,762	1,752	1,831	1,779
Virginia	112,072	162,212	162,338	161,198	161,498	161,160	12.7	-0.6	9,892	14,444	17,081	16,677	16,611	16,400
Washington	83,545	118,851	127,978	129,346	130,778	131,997	12.5	11.1	9,558	11,760	14,275	14,588	14,763	14,667
West Virginia	42,428	50,333	45,007	44,259	44,487	44,375	15.8	-11.8	2,923	5,445	5,607	5,488	5,483	5,363
Wisconsin	85,651	125,358	124,722	123,825	123,287	122,654	14.0	-2.2	10,934	14,383	16,079	16,106	16,325	16,166
Wyoming	10,852	13,154	15,348	15,419	11,883	11,993	12.9	-8.8	1,221	1,695	3,398	3,429	—	—
Bureau of Indian Education	6,997	8,448	6,801	—	6,504	—	—	—	1,092	338	396	—	305	—
Other jurisdictions	38,986	70,670	131,847	134,600	135,431	128,019	26.5	81.2	3,892	8,168	14,505	15,396	13,785	15,609
American Samoa	363	697	935	932	870	—	—	—	48	48	142	161	102	148
Guam	1,750	2,267	2,003	2,013	2,017	1,981	5.9	-12.6	198	205	165	179	161	166
Northern Marianas	411	569	944	931	895	906	8.5	59.2	211	53	104	104	86	87
Palau	—	131	—	—	119	104	—	-20.6	—	10	—	—	9	7
Puerto Rico	35,129	65,504	126,560	129,314	130,212	123,754	29.2	88.9	3,345	7,746	13,952	14,791	13,276	15,038
U.S. Virgin Islands	1,333	1,502	1,405	1,410	1,318	1,274	8.5	-15.2	90	106	142	161	151	163

—Not available.

[1]Based on the total enrollment in public schools, prekindergarten through 12th grade. For total enrollment in public schools, see table 203.40.

NOTE: Prior to October 1994, children and youth with disabilities were served under Chapter 1 of the Elementary and Secondary Education Act as well as under the Individuals with Disabilities Education Act (IDEA), Part B. Data reported in this table for 1990–91 include children ages 0–21 served under Chapter 1.

SOURCE: U.S. Department of Education, Office of Special Education Programs, *Annual Report to Congress on the Implementation of the Individuals with Disabilities Education Act*, selected years, 1992 through 2006, and Individuals with Disabilities Education Act (IDEA) database, retrieved October 29, 2015, from http://www2.ed.gov/programs/osepidea/618-data/state-level-data-files/index.html#bcc. National Center for Education Statistics, Common Core of Data (CCD), "State Nonfiscal Survey of Public Elementary/Secondary Education," 2013–14. (This table was prepared December 2015.)

Table 204.80. Number of public school students enrolled in gifted and talented programs, by sex, race/ethnicity, and state: 2004, 2006, and 2011–12

[Standard errors appear in parentheses]

| | | | | | 2011–12[1] | | | | | | | | |
| | | | | | | Sex | | Race/ethnicity | | | | | | |
State	2004, total		2006, total		Total	Male	Female	White	Black	Hispanic	Asian	Pacific Islander	American Indian/ Alaska Native	Two or more races
1	2		3		4	5	6	7	8	9	10	11	12	13
United States	3,202,760	(24,248)	3,236,990	(21,177)	3,189,757	1,570,453	1,619,304	1,939,266	281,135	538,529	301,633	11,053	30,103	88,038
Alabama	35,680	(798)	40,610	(361)	62,392	30,098	32,294	45,622	12,155	1,613	1,596	46	901	459
Alaska	5,390	(166)	5,620	(192)	6,320	3,041	3,279	4,182	133	403	584	74	270	674
Arizona	57,570	(1,275)	60,060	(711)	63,603	33,226	30,377	38,056	1,526	17,486	3,993	184	1,333	1,025
Arkansas	50,340	(3,219)	45,600	(1,870)	46,534	21,383	25,151	34,883	7,730	2,348	1,016	64	260	233
California	527,370	(10,256)	523,450	(13,209)	516,607	257,477	259,130	173,830	21,283	188,619	108,123	5,652	2,668	16,432
Colorado	50,350	(747)	54,000	(620)	55,743	29,048	26,695	40,561	1,126	9,193	2,625	93	272	1,873
Connecticut	15,980	(1,572)	20,170	(2,183)	13,153	6,179	6,974	9,196	1,117	1,379	1,168	4	32	257
Delaware	5,260 [1]	(†)	6,240 [1]	(†)	2,656	1,251	1,405	1,576	543	226	238	1–3	10	61
District of Columbia	—	(†)	—	(†)	62	27	35	0	60	0	1–3	0	0	0
Florida	114,400	(1,095)	132,440	(893)	145,079	72,777	72,302	79,722	13,486	38,513	8,204	108	426	4,620
Georgia	136,620	(3,954)	150,680	(5,291)	176,954	83,741	93,213	115,689	31,062	9,968	13,914	126	373	5,822
Hawaii	10,290	(993)	11,140 [1]	(†)	2,515	1,023	1,492	512	51	90	1,206	441	9	206
Idaho	9,920	(528)	10,650	(475)	8,494	4,365	4,129	7,498	38	517	224	22	46	149
Illinois	112,570	(4,554)	118,480	(5,016)	72,764	36,627	36,137	46,400	5,945	8,555	8,646	105	127	2,986
Indiana	74,780	(5,219)	82,830	(4,222)	131,797	63,729	68,068	108,500	7,355	6,542	4,496	68	272	4,564
Iowa	41,460	(1,657)	39,300	(1,030)	46,149	23,334	22,815	40,906	963	1,838	1,350	29	111	952
Kansas	15,150	(389)	14,430	(487)	14,015	7,644	6,371	11,380	355	777	849	9	105	540
Kentucky	85,660	(3,179)	96,600	(2,885)	87,214	41,311	45,903	79,288	3,525	1,394	1,709	75	68	1,155
Louisiana	28,020	(2,300)	22,010	(721)	20,802	9,530	11,272	12,830	5,627	771	1,111	19	120	324
Maine	5,640	(619)	6,030	(304)	8,160	4,010	4,150	7,702	109	81	184	8	30	46
Maryland	117,010 [1]	(†)	137,410 [1]	(†)	135,634	63,872	71,762	61,525	32,222	15,153	18,979	1,527	276	5,952
Massachusetts	7,440	(1,190)	6,130	(908)	6,242	3,005	3,237	4,183	533	625	711	4	17	169
Michigan	65,970	(6,408)	54,950	(4,750)	30,814	14,725	16,089	24,703	2,747	998	1,864	20	154	328
Minnesota	73,940	(2,585)	72,280	(2,154)	70,165	35,293	34,872	49,852	5,744	3,678	9,316	20	650	905
Mississippi	30,510	(837)	31,070	(1,015)	33,099	15,930	17,169	23,163	8,470	688	706	9	51	12
Missouri	34,470	(898)	33,070	(831)	37,175	18,780	18,395	30,109	3,280	1,110	1,951	36	125	564
Montana	8,760	(401)	7,490	(251)	5,900	3,120	2,780	5,255	35	102	102	10	320	76
Nebraska	32,160	(824)	32,650	(604)	35,469	17,673	17,796	28,850	1,381	2,713	1,187	34	252	1,052
Nevada	7,640	(23)	8,270 [1]	(†)	8,674	4,510	4,164	5,280	257	1,586	851	58	49	593
New Hampshire	4,450	(1,089)	4,700	(1,005)	2,579	1,222	1,357	2,423	10	20	106	1–3	4	14
New Jersey	88,960	(4,851)	97,260	(4,904)	88,990	41,222	47,768	55,282	7,927	9,288	15,509	218	92	674
New Mexico	36,410	(404)	12,950	(399)	14,891	7,853	7,038	7,027	233	5,957	512	10	894	258
New York	61,350	(5,223)	81,520	(3,741)	41,630	19,881	21,749	24,862	5,602	4,141	6,239	66	190	530
North Carolina	155,330	(10,613)	149,700	(4,678)	158,770	78,388	80,382	116,645	17,837	9,186	7,801	136	1,532	5,633
North Dakota	3,320	(305)	2,770	(162)	3,292	1,768	1,524	2,726	62	25	99	4	370	6
Ohio	133,690	(7,411)	127,610	(5,925)	65,821	33,263	32,558	55,946	3,403	1,021	3,296	19	55	2,081
Oklahoma	87,620	(2,447)	87,320	(2,151)	91,174	45,090	46,084	58,966	5,003	6,783	3,016	160	14,292	2,954
Oregon	39,440	(903)	38,570	(666)	37,767	20,072	17,695	28,241	498	3,019	3,498	120	301	2,090
Pennsylvania	85,070	(3,170)	75,930	(2,681)	66,867	34,353	32,514	54,609	4,170	1,797	5,274	59	67	891
Rhode Island	2,780	(531)	2,060	(300)	740	318	422	444	69	170	38	1–3	1–3	15
South Carolina	88,070	(6,564)	77,520	(3,781)	89,170	41,682	47,488	68,269	13,584	3,006	2,166	115	165	1,865
South Dakota	2,940	(241)	3,070	(175)	2,587	1,406	1,181	2,352	25	33	70	1–3	82	23
Tennessee	32,630	(1,451)	17,100	(904)	24,250	12,160	12,090	18,719	3,394	549	1,262	44	39	243
Texas	344,500	(3,483)	344,640	(2,413)	385,047	190,311	194,736	162,288	26,419	154,617	31,018	449	1,692	8,564
Utah	23,510	(1,218)	25,660	(170)	23,204	11,302	11,902	18,348	266	2,675	1,105	446	182	182
Vermont	740	(151)	730	(129)	268	124	144	252	4	4	6	0	0	1–3
Virginia	142,140	(3,772)	160,140	(3,319)	150,642	74,272	76,370	96,993	18,104	11,447	16,486	198	351	7,063
Washington	38,520	(843)	39,010	(1,289)	37,475	18,796	18,679	25,232	722	4,239	4,766	120	188	2,208
West Virginia	6,040	(493)	6,630	(559)	5,292	2,730	2,562	4,853	166	27	186	4	8	48
Wisconsin	62,000	(4,348)	56,450	(3,095)	52,058	25,957	26,101	40,742	4,767	3,410	2,231	29	241	638
Wyoming	2,910 !	(944)	2,030	(314)	3,061	1,555	1,506	2,794	12	151	44	4	29	27

—Not available.
†Not applicable.
!Interpret data with caution. The coefficient of variation (CV) for this estimate is between 30 and 50 percent.
[1]Data are based on universe counts of schools and school districts; therefore, these figures do not have standard errors.

NOTE: Race categories exclude persons of Hispanic ethnicity. Student counts between 1 and 3 are displayed as 1–3 to protect student privacy. Detail may not sum to totals because of rounding and because of privacy protection routines applied to universe data.
SOURCE: U.S. Department of Education, Office for Civil Rights, Civil Rights Data Collection: 2004, 2006, and 2011–12. (This table was prepared January 2016.)

Table 204.90. Percentage of public school students enrolled in gifted and talented programs, by sex, race/ethnicity, and state: 2004, 2006, and 2011–12
[Standard errors appear in parentheses]

State	2004, total		2006, total		2011–12[1]									
						Sex		Race/ethnicity						
					Total	Male	Female	White	Black	Hispanic	Asian	Pacific Islander	American Indian/ Alaska Native	Two or more races
1	2		3		4	5	6	7	8	9	10	11	12	13
United States	6.7	(0.05)	6.7	(0.04)	6.4	6.2	6.4	7.6	3.6	4.6	13.0	5.0	5.2	6.8
Alabama................	4.8	(0.11)	5.5	(0.06)	8.4	7.9	8.4	10.6	4.8	4.7	16.3	10.0	14.4	6.3
Alaska...................	4.1	(0.19)	4.1	(0.19)	4.7	4.4	4.7	6.2	2.7	4.7	6.8	2.5	0.9	6.4
Arizona.................	5.9	(0.17)	6.3	(0.11)	5.8	5.9	5.4	8.1	2.6	3.8	12.9	4.9	2.4	5.7
Arkansas..............	9.9	(0.65)	9.5	(0.43)	9.8	8.8	10.3	11.3	7.7	4.9	13.9	2.7	6.7	3.7
California..............	8.4	(0.18)	8.3	(0.21)	8.2	8.0	8.1	10.7	5.2	5.8	16.2	10.1	4.8	9.2
Colorado...............	6.7	(0.11)	6.8	(0.11)	6.5	6.6	6.0	8.4	2.7	3.4	9.7	5.0	3.6	7.1
Connecticut...........	3.0	(0.32)	3.8	(0.41)	2.3	2.1	2.4	2.7	1.6	1.3	4.7	0.8	1.4	2.2
Delaware...............	4.6 [1]	(†)	5.6 [1]	(†)	2.0	1.8	2.1	2.4	1.3	1.3	5.3	1.1-3.3	1.5	2.6
District of Columbia	—	(†)	—	(†)	0.1	0.1	0.1	0.0	0.1	0.0	0.1-0.3	0.0	0.0	0.0
Florida..................	4.5	(0.06)	4.7	(0.05)	5.4	5.3	5.3	7.1	2.2	5.1	12.1	3.6	4.3	5.8
Georgia................	8.9	(0.30)	9.3	(0.35)	10.4	9.6	10.7	15.5	4.9	4.9	24.3	6.8	9.6	11.4
Hawaii..................	5.7	(0.57)	6.2 [1]	(†)	1.4	1.1	1.6	2.0	1.2	0.7	1.9	0.7	0.9	1.4
Idaho...................	3.9	(0.23)	4.2	(0.20)	3.0	3.0	2.8	3.4	1.2	1.2	5.7	2.1	1.1	2.6
Illinois..................	5.4	(0.22)	5.8	(0.24)	3.5	3.4	3.4	4.4	1.6	1.7	9.8	5.0	2.0	5.0
Indiana.................	7.1	(0.49)	7.9	(0.40)	12.6	11.9	12.7	14.3	5.9	7.0	24.6	8.9	8.9	10.0
Iowa....................	8.5	(0.38)	8.2	(0.26)	9.3	9.1	8.9	10.2	3.7	4.3	12.6	3.7	4.6	7.8
Kansas.................	3.3	(0.11)	3.0	(0.12)	2.9	3.1	2.6	3.5	1.0	1.0	6.8	1.1	1.6	2.6
Kentucky...............	13.0	(0.54)	14.6	(0.50)	12.7	11.6	12.9	14.2	4.8	4.6	18.0	11.4	7.2	7.4
Louisiana..............	3.9	(0.32)	3.4	(0.13)	3.0	2.7	3.2	3.9	1.8	2.8	10.8	4.9	2.2	4.2
Maine...................	3.0	(0.36)	3.2	(0.19)	4.6	4.3	4.5	4.7	2.0	2.9	6.4	3.4	2.3	2.3
Maryland...............	13.8 [1]	(†)	16.1 [1]	(†)	15.8	14.5	16.3	19.6	9.6	14.4	37.7	7.5	9.4	19.0
Massachusetts........	0.8	(0.13)	0.7	(0.10)	0.7	0.6	0.7	0.7	0.7	0.4	1.3	0.4	0.7	0.6
Michigan	3.9	(0.37)	3.4	(0.29)	1.9	1.8	2.0	2.2	0.9	1.1	4.3	1.3	1.2	0.9
Minnesota	8.1	(0.37)	8.8	(0.28)	8.0	7.9	7.8	7.8	6.8	5.7	17.1	2.0	3.9	4.9
Mississippi	6.0	(0.19)	6.1	(0.20)	6.7	6.3	6.8	10.1	3.4	5.2	14.2	5.4	4.9	3.8
Missouri................	3.8	(0.12)	3.6	(0.11)	4.0	4.0	3.9	4.4	2.2	2.6	11.3	2.1	2.9	3.6
Montana	5.6	(0.28)	5.2	(0.20)	4.2	4.3	3.8	4.6	2.3	2.2	8.2	2.5	1.8	4.0
Nebraska	11.4	(0.31)	11.4	(0.24)	11.8	11.3	11.4	13.7	6.8	5.5	18.9	8.6	4.6	11.7
Nevada	1.9	(0.01)	1.9 [1]	(†)	2.0	2.0	1.8	3.2	0.6	0.9	3.4	1.0	1.0	2.6
New Hampshire	2.3	(0.55)	2.6	(0.54)	1.4	1.3	1.4	1.5	0.3	0.3	1.9	0.6-1.7	0.5	0.5
New Jersey	6.9	(0.38)	7.0	(0.35)	6.5	5.9	6.8	7.9	3.5	3.1	12.6	8.0	5.3	4.4
New Mexico	10.7	(0.26)	4.0	(0.14)	4.6	4.7	4.2	8.4	3.4	3.1	12.5	2.9	2.6	6.3
New York...............	2.2	(0.18)	2.9	(0.13)	1.5	1.4	1.5	1.9	1.1	0.7	2.7	1.3	1.2	2.0
North Carolina	10.9	(0.83)	10.8	(0.42)	10.6	10.2	10.5	14.9	4.5	4.6	20.0	7.5	6.6	10.6
North Dakota	3.1	(0.30)	2.8	(0.18)	3.3	3.4	2.9	3.3	2.1	0.9	7.9	1.7	3.8	1.3
Ohio....................	7.4	(0.40)	7.3	(0.33)	3.7	3.6	3.6	4.2	1.2	1.5	10.6	2.2	2.2	2.8
Oklahoma..............	14.0	(0.45)	13.7	(0.39)	13.9	13.4	13.7	16.9	7.8	7.8	24.4	9.1	13.2	9.1
Oregon.................	7.1	(0.20)	6.9	(0.16)	6.8	7.0	6.2	7.7	3.5	2.6	15.8	3.1	2.8	8.0
Pennsylvania..........	4.8	(0.19)	4.5	(0.17)	3.8	3.8	3.6	4.4	1.6	1.2	9.3	3.9	2.2	2.5
Rhode Island	1.8	(0.38)	1.4	(0.21)	0.5	0.4	0.6	0.5	0.6	0.6	1.0	0.5-1.6	0.1-0.3	0.3
South Carolina..............	12.7	(0.98)	11.0	(0.57)	12.0	10.9	12.4	17.3	5.1	6.2	21.2	11.7	7.0	9.7
South Dakota	2.2	(0.20)	2.7	(0.17)	2.0	2.1	1.8	2.3	0.7	0.7	3.5	0.8-2.5	0.6	0.9
Tennessee	3.3	(0.18)	1.7	(0.10)	2.5	2.4	2.4	2.8	1.5	1.1	7.4	3.8	1.9	2.6
Texas	8.0	(0.10)	7.6	(0.07)	7.7	7.4	7.6	10.7	4.1	6.1	17.5	6.7	6.9	9.6
Utah....................	4.6	(0.29)	5.0	(0.05)	3.9	3.7	3.9	4.0	3.2	2.9	10.2	4.9	2.4	2.0
Vermont	0.8	(0.17)	0.8	(0.15)	0.3	0.3	0.4	0.3	0.2	0.4	0.4	0.0	0.0	0.1-0.2
Virginia................	12.1	(0.38)	12.6	(0.32)	11.8	11.3	11.6	14.2	5.9	7.6	21.4	10.9	7.8	13.5
Washington............	3.8	(0.10)	3.9	(0.13)	3.5	3.4	3.4	4.0	1.4	2.0	6.3	1.3	1.2	3.5
West Virginia..........	2.2	(0.19)	2.2	(0.21)	1.9	1.8	1.7	1.9	1.1	0.8	9.3	3.6	2.4	1.3
Wisconsin	6.8	(0.47)	6.4	(0.35)	6.0	5.8	5.8	6.3	5.5	4.0	7.2	3.8	2.1	3.9
Wyoming...............	3.2 !	(1.04)	2.2	(0.35)	3.3	3.2	3.1	3.7	0.9	1.3	5.0	1.4	0.8	2.0

—Not available.
†Not applicable.
!Interpret data with caution. The coefficient of variation (CV) for this estimate is between 30 and 50 percent.
[1]Data are based on universe counts of schools and school districts; therefore, these figures do not have standard errors.

NOTE: Race categories exclude persons of Hispanic ethnicity. Percentages based on counts of between 1 and 3 gifted and talented students are displayed as ranges to protect student privacy.
SOURCE: U.S. Department of Education, Office for Civil Rights, Civil Rights Data Collection: 2004, 2006, and 2011–12. (This table was prepared January 2016.)

Table 205.10. Private elementary and secondary school enrollment and private enrollment as a percentage of total enrollment in public and private schools, by region and grade level: Selected years, fall 1995 through fall 2013

[Standard errors appear in parentheses]

Grade level and year	Total private enrollment		Private enrollment, by region							
			Northeast		Midwest		South		West	
	In thousands	Percent of total enrollment	In thousands	Percent of total enrollment in Northeast	In thousands	Percent of total enrollment in Midwest	In thousands	Percent of total enrollment in South	In thousands	Percent of total enrollment in West
1	2	3	4	5	6	7	8	9	10	11
Total, all grades										
1995	5,918 (31.8)	11.7 (0.06)	1,509 (18.8)	16.0 (0.20)	1,525 (14.2)	12.7 (0.12)	1,744 (12.8)	9.8 (0.07)	1,141 (11.5)	10.0 (0.10)
1997	5,944 (18.5)	11.4 (0.04)	1,496 (8.3)	15.6 (0.09)	1,528 (11.6)	12.5 (0.10)	1,804 (11.3)	9.8 (0.06)	1,116 (5.2)	9.4 (0.04)
1999	6,018 (30.2)	11.4 (0.06)	1,507 (7.9)	15.5 (0.08)	1,520 (10.3)	12.4 (0.09)	1,863 (26.7)	10.0 (0.14)	1,127 (5.4)	9.2 (0.04)
2001	6,320 (40.3)	11.7 (0.08)	1,581 (9.5)	16.1 (0.10)	1,556 (22.9)	12.6 (0.19)	1,975 (21.4)	10.3 (0.11)	1,208 (23.4)	9.6 (0.19)
2003	6,099 (41.2)	11.2 (0.08)	1,513 (25.8)	15.4 (0.27)	1,460 (15.1)	11.9 (0.12)	1,944 (21.0)	9.9 (0.11)	1,182 (19.1)	9.1 (0.15)
2005	6,073 (42.4)	11.0 (0.08)	1,430 (7.7)	14.8 (0.08)	1,434 (21.0)	11.7 (0.17)	1,976 (24.7)	9.8 (0.12)	1,234 (26.3)	9.4 (0.20)
2007	5,910 (28.4)	10.7 (0.05)	1,426 (11.0)	14.9 (0.12)	1,352 (8.3)	11.2 (0.07)	1,965 (21.5)	9.6 (0.11)	1,167 (12.3)	8.9 (0.09)
2009	5,488 (35.9)	10.0 (0.07)	1,310 (15.7)	14.0 (0.17)	1,296 (25.9)	10.8 (0.22)	1,842 (17.6)	9.1 (0.09)	1,041 (8.0)	8.0 (0.06)
2011	5,268 (24.9)	9.7 (0.04)	1,252 (18.0)	13.7 (0.17)	1,263 (17.1)	10.7 (0.13)	1,747 (2.6)	8.5 (0.01)	1,006 (0.4)	7.8 (#)
2013	5,396 (50.3)	9.8 (0.08)	1,201 (9.5)	13.2 (0.09)	1,326 (45.2)	11.2 (0.34)	1,840 (8.3)	8.7 (0.04)	1,028 (18.3)	7.9 (0.13)
Prekindergarten through grade 8										
1995	4,756 (28.4)	12.8 (0.08)	1,174 (16.8)	17.2 (0.25)	1,238 (13.5)	14.3 (0.16)	1,413 (11.9)	10.7 (0.09)	931 (9.2)	11.1 (0.11)
1997	4,759 (17.3)	12.6 (0.05)	1,165 (8.3)	16.8 (0.12)	1,235 (11.0)	14.1 (0.13)	1,449 (10.0)	10.8 (0.07)	909 (4.4)	10.5 (0.05)
1999	4,789 (23.1)	12.5 (0.06)	1,168 (7.5)	16.7 (0.11)	1,222 (8.4)	13.9 (0.10)	1,487 (19.6)	10.9 (0.14)	913 (4.4)	10.4 (0.05)
2001	5,023 (36.1)	12.9 (0.09)	1,216 (9.4)	17.3 (0.14)	1,253 (21.2)	14.3 (0.24)	1,584 (17.8)	11.3 (0.13)	969 (21.2)	10.6 (0.23)
2003	4,788 (30.3)	12.3 (0.08)	1,131 (7.8)	16.4 (0.11)	1,167 (13.6)	13.5 (0.16)	1,547 (18.6)	10.9 (0.13)	944 (18.1)	10.2 (0.20)
2005	4,724 (33.0)	12.1 (0.09)	1,063 (6.6)	15.9 (0.10)	1,142 (19.3)	13.3 (0.23)	1,551 (21.2)	10.7 (0.15)	969 (15.0)	10.5 (0.16)
2007	4,546 (21.9)	11.7 (0.06)	1,047 (6.3)	16.0 (0.10)	1,065 (7.7)	12.6 (0.09)	1,525 (17.7)	10.4 (0.12)	909 (8.1)	9.9 (0.09)
2009	4,179 (33.2)	10.8 (0.09)	938 (12.6)	14.6 (0.20)	1,016 (25.1)	12.1 (0.30)	1,424 (16.2)	9.8 (0.11)	802 (7.2)	8.8 (0.08)
2011	3,977 (18.2)	10.3 (0.04)	898 (12.8)	14.1 (0.17)	967 (12.8)	11.7 (0.14)	1,337 (1.8)	9.0 (0.01)	774 (0.3)	8.6 (#)
2013	4,084 (42.4)	10.5 (0.10)	859 (8.8)	13.5 (0.12)	1,036 (37.9)	12.4 (0.40)	1,403 (7.9)	9.2 (0.05)	786 (15.0)	8.6 (0.15)
Grades 9 through 12										
1995	1,163 (4.6)	8.5 (0.03)	335 (2.9)	13.0 (0.11)	287 (0.9)	8.6 (0.03)	331 (2.1)	7.1 (0.04)	209 (2.3)	6.8 (0.08)
1997	1,185 (2.4)	8.3 (0.02)	331 (0.5)	12.5 (0.02)	293 (0.7)	8.5 (0.02)	354 (1.7)	7.2 (0.03)	207 (1.2)	6.4 (0.04)
1999	1,229 (8.3)	8.4 (0.06)	340 (1.1)	12.6 (0.04)	299 (2.5)	8.6 (0.07)	376 (7.6)	7.5 (0.15)	215 (1.8)	6.3 (0.05)
2001	1,296 (6.7)	8.6 (0.04)	365 (0.8)	13.1 (0.03)	302 (2.0)	8.6 (0.06)	390 (4.4)	7.5 (0.08)	239 (4.5)	6.8 (0.13)
2003	1,311 (24.7)	8.4 (0.16)	382 (24.0)	13.1 (0.83)	294 (4.1)	8.2 (0.11)	397 (3.0)	7.4 (0.06)	238 (3.5)	6.4 (0.09)
2005	1,349 (18.1)	8.3 (0.11)	367 (1.7)	12.3 (0.06)	292 (5.0)	7.9 (0.14)	425 (7.2)	7.5 (0.13)	265 (15.7)	6.7 (0.40)
2007	1,364 (12.0)	8.3 (0.07)	379 (8.8)	12.7 (0.30)	287 (1.3)	7.8 (0.04)	440 (5.5)	7.6 (0.10)	257 (5.7)	6.5 (0.14)
2009	1,309 (6.5)	8.0 (0.04)	372 (5.7)	12.6 (0.20)	280 (2.2)	7.7 (0.06)	418 (1.7)	7.3 (0.03)	239 (1.1)	6.1 (0.03)
2011	1,291 (15.4)	8.1 (0.09)	353 (5.2)	12.6 (0.16)	295 (14.4)	8.4 (0.38)	411 (1.8)	7.1 (0.03)	232 (0.1)	5.9 (#)
2013	1,312 (14.9)	8.2 (0.09)	342 (0.8)	12.4 (0.03)	291 (13.1)	8.4 (0.35)	437 (1.3)	7.4 (0.02)	242 (7.0)	6.2 (0.17)

#Rounds to zero.
NOTE: Includes enrollment in prekindergarten through grade 12 in schools that offer kindergarten or higher grade. Ungraded students are prorated into prekindergarten through grade 8 and grades 9 through 12. Detail may not sum to totals because of rounding.

SOURCE: U.S. Department of Education, National Center for Education Statistics, Private School Universe Survey (PSS), 1995–96 through 2013–14; and Common Core of Data (CCD), "State Nonfiscal Survey of Public Elementary/Secondary Education," 1995–96 through 2013–14. (This table was prepared February 2016.)

Table 205.20. Enrollment and percentage distribution of students enrolled in private elementary and secondary schools, by school orientation and grade level: Selected years, fall 1995 through fall 2013

[Standard errors appear in parentheses]

Grade level and year	Total private enrollment	Catholic				Other religious				Nonsectarian
		Total	Parochial	Diocesan	Private	Total	Conservative Christian	Affiliated[1]	Unaffiliated[1]	
1	2	3	4	5	6	7	8	9	10	11

Enrollment

Total, all grades

Grade level and year	Total private enrollment	Total	Parochial	Diocesan	Private	Total	Conservative Christian	Affiliated[1]	Unaffiliated[1]	Nonsectarian
1995	5,918,040 (31,815)	2,660,450 (6,878)	1,458,990 (2,079)	850,560 (5,674)	350,900 (1,176)	2,094,690 (16,956)	786,660 (8,815)	697,280 (4,886)	610,750 (11,831)	1,162,900 (18,443)
1997	5,944,320 (18,543)	2,665,630 (5,472)	1,438,860 (5,331)	873,780 (761)	352,990 (1,405)	2,097,190 (13,733)	823,610 (7,342)	646,500 (3,104)	627,080 (11,133)	1,181,510 (12,013)
1999	6,018,280 (30,179)	2,660,600 (4,831)	1,397,570 (4,421)	880,650 (†)	382,190 (1,945)	2,193,370 (27,176)	871,060 (4,827)	646,280 (4,894)	676,030 (24,593)	1,164,500 (8,156)
2001	6,319,650 (40,272)	2,672,650 (12,460)	1,309,890 (5,626)	979,050 (6,976)	383,710 (3,152)	2,328,160 (17,281)	937,420 (6,070)	663,190 (8,636)	727,550 (13,303)	1,318,840 (27,300)
2003	6,099,220 (41,219)	2,520,120 (10,590)	1,183,250 (9,937)	963,140 (4,754)	373,740 (3,996)	2,228,230 (19,674)	889,710 (8,852)	650,530 (5,860)	688,000 (14,805)	1,350,870 (29,197)
2005	6,073,240 (42,446)	2,402,800 (9,293)	1,062,950 (6,355)	956,610 (6,325)	383,230 (3,996)	2,303,330 (22,368)	957,360 (9,561)	696,910 (6,677)	649,050 (14,200)	1,367,120 (27,558)
2007	5,910,210 (28,363)	2,308,150 (6,083)	945,860 (5,361)	969,940 (1,788)	392,340 (3,432)	2,283,210 (20,628)	883,180 (6,616)	527,040 (3,512)	872,990 (18,217)	1,318,850 (18,235)
2009	5,488,490 (35,857)	2,160,220 (3,494)	856,440 (3,088)	909,010 (4,393)	394,770 (1,087)	2,076,220 (32,751)	737,020 (1,891)	516,310 (4,366)	822,890 (31,180)	1,252,050 (8,849)
2011	5,268,090 (24,908)	2,087,870 (14,426)	804,410 (3,686)	899,810 (14,320)	383,650 (459)	1,991,950 (21,814)	730,570 (4,721)	565,340 (2,990)	696,040 (20,419)	1,188,270 (5,376)
2013	5,395,740 (50,342)	2,055,140 (37,142)	739,850 (18,829)	936,320 (32,000)	378,970 (980)	2,030,930 (30,090)	707,100 (7,544)	565,490 (5,884)	758,350 (28,152)	1,309,670 (14,800)

Prekindergarten through grade 8

Grade level and year	Total private enrollment	Total	Parochial	Diocesan	Private	Total	Conservative Christian	Affiliated[1]	Unaffiliated[1]	Nonsectarian
1995	4,755,540 (28,435)	2,041,990 (5,249)	1,368,340 (2,079)	575,190 (3,528)	98,460 (1,176)	1,752,510 (14,834)	651,050 (7,219)	574,820 (4,581)	526,630 (11,121)	961,040 (17,471)
1997	4,759,060 (17,323)	2,046,620 (5,469)	1,352,620 (5,331)	598,380 (761)	95,620 (1,393)	1,744,500 (12,194)	678,660 (5,957)	529,050 (2,504)	536,790 (10,120)	967,940 (11,050)
1999	4,788,990 (23,055)	2,033,900 (4,830)	1,317,300 (4,421)	607,860 (†)	108,740 (1,943)	1,818,260 (19,897)	713,020 (3,748)	529,280 (3,866)	575,970 (17,632)	936,820 (7,302)
2001	5,023,160 (36,096)	2,032,080 (10,751)	1,226,960 (4,494)	687,540 (6,976)	117,580 (2,978)	1,926,870 (15,459)	765,080 (5,110)	535,850 (7,370)	625,940 (12,240)	1,064,210 (24,703)
2003	4,788,070 (30,338)	1,886,530 (11,055)	1,108,320 (9,937)	670,910 (4,754)	107,300 (337)	1,835,930 (16,931)	722,460 (6,517)	519,310 (4,134)	594,160 (13,504)	1,065,620 (15,379)
2005	4,724,310 (33,034)	1,779,830 (9,318)	993,390 (6,355)	673,110 (6,286)	113,330 (2,896)	1,865,430 (19,380)	764,920 (8,028)	561,320 (5,730)	539,190 (12,633)	1,079,050 (15,497)
2007	4,545,910 (21,853)	1,685,220 (5,288)	878,830 (4,562)	688,260 (1,640)	118,130 (3,104)	1,833,540 (18,364)	698,930 (5,885)	417,610 (3,218)	717,000 (16,573)	1,027,150 (11,379)
2009	4,179,060 (33,168)	1,541,830 (3,250)	782,050 (3,085)	642,720 (846)	117,050 (578)	1,665,680 (30,216)	579,190 (1,685)	401,430 (3,952)	685,050 (28,928)	971,550 (8,113)
2011	3,976,960 (18,241)	1,481,620 (3,867)	737,090 (3,675)	630,970 (321)	113,560 (459)	1,583,610 (16,558)	568,150 (3,607)	443,780 (2,604)	571,690 (15,197)	911,730 (3,469)
2013	4,083,860 (42,441)	1,466,550 (27,646)	680,370 (18,826)	666,260 (20,228)	119,930 (843)	1,615,120 (29,311)	544,610 (5,638)	446,050 (5,316)	624,470 (27,948)	1,002,180 (11,849)

Grades 9 through 12

Grade level and year	Total private enrollment	Total	Parochial	Diocesan	Private	Total	Conservative Christian	Affiliated[1]	Unaffiliated[1]	Nonsectarian
1995	1,162,500 (4,625)	618,460 (2,786)	90,650 (†)	275,370 (2,786)	252,440 (†)	342,180 (3,174)	135,610 (2,338)	122,460 (645)	84,120 (1,720)	201,860 (1,495)
1997	1,185,260 (2,374)	619,010 (96)	86,240 (†)	275,400 (†)	257,370 (96)	352,690 (2,261)	144,950 (1,660)	117,450 (848)	90,290 (1,221)	213,560 (1,860)
1999	1,229,290 (8,260)	626,520 (70)	80,270 (†)	272,790 (†)	273,460 (70)	375,100 (7,920)	158,040 (1,640)	117,000 (1,237)	100,060 (7,461)	227,670 (2,208)
2001	1,296,480 (6,669)	640,570 (2,317)	82,930 (2,293)	291,520 (†)	266,130 (338)	401,290 (3,527)	172,340 (2,633)	127,340 (1,625)	101,600 (1,852)	254,620 (4,465)
2003	1,311,150 (24,733)	633,590 (3,888)	74,930 (†)	292,230 (†)	266,430 (3,888)	392,310 (4,195)	167,250 (3,144)	131,220 (1,924)	93,840 (2,031)	285,250 (23,952)
2005	1,348,930 (18,073)	622,970 (1,538)	69,560 (†)	283,510 (700)	269,900 (1,341)	437,900 (6,541)	192,440 (3,404)	135,590 (1,493)	109,860 (5,190)	288,070 (16,551)
2007	1,364,300 (11,958)	622,930 (1,377)	67,030 (1,201)	281,680 (566)	274,210 (364)	449,680 (3,796)	184,260 (1,768)	109,430 (374)	156,000 (3,052)	291,700 (11,156)
2009	1,309,430 (6,480)	618,390 (4,409)	74,380 (42)	266,290 (4,311)	277,720 (920)	410,540 (4,285)	157,830 (362)	114,880 (1,074)	137,840 (4,111)	280,500 (1,880)
2011	1,291,130 (15,396)	606,250 (14,313)	67,320 (10)	268,840 (14,313)	270,090 (†)	408,330 (5,747)	162,420 (1,349)	121,560 (513)	124,350 (5,792)	276,550 (3,485)
2013	1,311,880 (14,936)	588,580 (13,452)	59,480 (358)	270,060 (13,416)	259,040 (905)	415,810 (2,774)	162,490 (1,942)	119,440 (1,862)	133,880 (1,762)	307,490 (6,938)

Percentage distribution

Total, all grades

Grade level and year	Total private enrollment	Total	Parochial	Diocesan	Private	Total	Conservative Christian	Affiliated[1]	Unaffiliated[1]	Nonsectarian
1995	100.0	45.0 (0.19)	24.7 (0.13)	14.4 (0.08)	5.9 (0.03)	35.4 (0.19)	13.3 (0.12)	11.8 (0.08)	10.3 (0.18)	19.7 (0.23)
1997	100.0	44.8 (0.13)	24.2 (0.09)	14.7 (0.05)	5.9 (0.03)	35.3 (0.18)	13.9 (0.12)	10.9 (0.06)	10.5 (0.17)	19.9 (0.17)
1999	100.0	44.2 (0.24)	23.2 (0.14)	14.6 (0.07)	6.4 (0.04)	36.4 (0.28)	14.5 (0.09)	10.7 (0.08)	11.2 (0.36)	19.3 (0.11)
2001	100.0	42.3 (0.25)	20.7 (0.14)	15.5 (0.12)	6.1 (0.04)	36.8 (0.22)	14.8 (0.13)	10.5 (0.13)	11.5 (0.18)	20.9 (0.33)
2003	100.0	41.3 (0.27)	19.4 (0.17)	15.8 (0.14)	6.1 (0.07)	36.5 (0.25)	14.6 (0.13)	10.7 (0.10)	11.3 (0.22)	22.1 (0.36)
2005	100.0	39.6 (0.26)	17.5 (0.13)	15.8 (0.14)	6.3 (0.07)	37.9 (0.25)	15.8 (0.14)	11.5 (0.09)	10.7 (0.20)	22.5 (0.34)
2007	100.0	39.1 (0.20)	16.0 (0.11)	16.4 (0.09)	6.6 (0.06)	38.6 (0.25)	14.9 (0.12)	8.9 (0.06)	14.8 (0.26)	22.3 (0.25)
2009	100.0	39.4 (0.25)	15.6 (0.11)	16.6 (0.13)	7.2 (0.05)	37.8 (0.37)	13.4 (0.09)	9.4 (0.07)	15.0 (0.48)	22.8 (0.16)
2011	100.0	39.6 (0.25)	15.3 (0.09)	17.1 (0.25)	7.3 (0.04)	37.8 (0.28)	13.9 (0.09)	10.7 (0.08)	13.2 (0.34)	22.6 (0.15)
2013	100.0	38.1 (0.50)	13.7 (0.33)	17.4 (0.51)	7.0 (0.07)	37.6 (0.44)	13.1 (0.16)	10.5 (0.13)	14.1 (0.47)	24.3 (0.28)

See notes at end of table.

Table 205.20. Enrollment and percentage distribution of students enrolled in private elementary and secondary schools, by school orientation and grade level: Selected years, fall 1995 through fall 2013—Continued

[Standard errors appear in parentheses]

Grade level and year	Total private enrollment	Catholic				Other religious				Nonsectarian
		Total	Parochial	Diocesan	Private	Total	Conservative Christian	Affiliated[1]	Unaffiliated[1]	
1	2	3	4	5	6	7	8	9	10	11
Prekindergarten through grade 8										
1995	(†)	42.9 (0.20)	28.8 (0.17)	12.1 (0.06)	2.1 (0.02)	36.9 (0.22)	13.7 (0.13)	12.1 (0.09)	11.1 (0.21)	20.2 (0.28)
1997	(†)	43.0 (0.15)	28.4 (0.12)	12.6 (0.05)	2.0 (0.03)	36.7 (0.20)	14.3 (0.13)	11.1 (0.06)	11.3 (0.19)	20.3 (0.19)
1999	(†)	42.5 (0.23)	27.5 (0.16)	12.7 (0.06)	2.3 (0.04)	38.0 (0.26)	14.9 (0.09)	11.1 (0.07)	12.0 (0.32)	19.6 (0.12)
2001	(†)	40.5 (0.27)	24.4 (0.17)	13.7 (0.14)	2.3 (0.05)	38.4 (0.25)	15.2 (0.15)	10.7 (0.14)	12.5 (0.20)	21.2 (0.37)
2003	(†)	39.4 (0.25)	23.1 (0.18)	14.0 (0.13)	2.2 (0.01)	38.3 (0.23)	15.1 (0.12)	10.8 (0.09)	12.4 (0.24)	22.3 (0.22)
2005	(†)	37.7 (0.25)	21.0 (0.14)	14.2 (0.15)	2.4 (0.06)	39.5 (0.21)	16.2 (0.16)	11.9 (0.09)	11.4 (0.22)	22.8 (0.23)
2007	(†)	37.1 (0.20)	19.3 (0.13)	15.1 (0.09)	2.6 (0.07)	40.3 (0.27)	15.4 (0.14)	9.2 (0.07)	15.8 (0.30)	22.6 (0.21)
2009	(†)	36.9 (0.29)	18.7 (0.15)	15.4 (0.12)	2.8 (0.03)	39.9 (0.43)	13.9 (0.11)	9.6 (0.10)	16.4 (0.57)	23.2 (0.20)
2011	(†)	37.3 (0.18)	18.5 (0.11)	15.9 (0.08)	2.9 (0.02)	39.8 (0.24)	14.3 (0.08)	11.2 (0.08)	14.4 (0.32)	22.9 (0.11)
2013	(†)	35.9 (0.53)	16.7 (0.42)	16.3 (0.44)	2.9 (0.04)	39.5 (0.52)	13.3 (0.17)	10.9 (0.15)	15.3 (0.59)	24.5 (0.31)
Grades 9 through 12										
1995	(†)	53.2 (0.20)	7.8 (0.03)	23.7 (0.20)	21.7 (0.09)	29.4 (0.20)	11.7 (0.18)	10.5 (0.06)	7.2 (0.14)	17.4 (0.12)
1997	(†)	52.2 (0.10)	7.3 (0.01)	23.2 (0.05)	21.7 (0.04)	29.8 (0.16)	12.2 (0.13)	9.9 (0.08)	7.6 (0.10)	18.0 (0.14)
1999	(†)	51.0 (0.34)	6.5 (0.04)	22.2 (0.15)	22.2 (0.15)	30.5 (0.45)	12.9 (0.14)	9.5 (0.11)	8.1 (0.56)	18.5 (0.19)
2001	(†)	49.4 (0.26)	6.4 (0.17)	22.5 (0.12)	20.5 (0.10)	31.0 (0.19)	13.3 (0.17)	9.8 (0.12)	7.8 (0.13)	19.6 (0.28)
2003	(†)	48.3 (0.91)	5.7 (0.11)	22.3 (0.42)	20.3 (0.44)	29.9 (0.59)	12.8 (0.32)	10.0 (0.23)	7.2 (0.20)	21.8 (1.43)
2005	(†)	46.2 (0.60)	5.2 (0.07)	21.0 (0.28)	20.0 (0.27)	32.5 (0.52)	14.3 (0.28)	10.1 (0.16)	8.1 (0.37)	21.4 (0.97)
2007	(†)	45.7 (0.40)	4.9 (0.09)	20.6 (0.18)	20.1 (0.17)	33.0 (0.33)	13.5 (0.16)	8.0 (0.07)	11.4 (0.22)	21.4 (0.65)
2009	(†)	47.2 (0.25)	5.7 (0.03)	20.3 (0.27)	21.2 (0.12)	31.4 (0.25)	12.1 (0.06)	8.8 (0.08)	10.5 (0.28)	21.4 (0.15)
2011	(†)	47.0 (0.63)	5.2 (0.06)	20.8 (0.88)	20.9 (0.25)	31.6 (0.49)	12.6 (0.18)	9.4 (0.13)	9.6 (0.43)	21.4 (0.35)
2013	(†)	44.9 (0.64)	4.5 (0.06)	20.6 (0.83)	19.7 (0.24)	31.7 (0.42)	12.4 (0.19)	9.1 (0.17)	10.2 (0.19)	23.4 (0.47)

†Not applicable.
[1]Affiliated schools belong to associations of schools with a specific religious orientation other than Catholic or conservative Christian. Unaffiliated schools have a religious orientation or purpose but are not classified as Catholic, conservative Christian, or affiliated.

NOTE: Includes enrollment in prekindergarten through grade 12 in schools that offer kindergarten or higher grade. Ungraded students are prorated into prekindergarten through grade 8 and grades 9 through 12. Detail may not sum to totals because of rounding.
SOURCE: U.S. Department of Education, National Center for Education Statistics, Private School Universe Survey (PSS), 1995–96 through 2013–14. (This table was prepared December 2015.)

Table 205.30. Percentage distribution of students enrolled in private elementary and secondary schools, by school orientation and selected characteristics: Fall 2011 and fall 2013

[Standard errors appear in parentheses]

Selected characteristic	Total	Catholic				Other religious				Nonsectarian
		Total	Parochial	Diocesan	Private	Total	Conservative Christian	Affiliated[1]	Unaffiliated[1]	
1	2	3	4	5	6	7	8	9	10	11
Fall 2011										
Total	100.0 (†)	39.6 (0.25)	15.3 (0.09)	17.1 (0.25)	7.3 (0.04)	37.8 (0.26)	13.9 (0.09)	10.7 (0.08)	13.2 (0.34)	22.6 (0.15)
School level[2]										
Elementary	100.0 (†)	49.8 (0.16)	25.7 (0.12)	21.5 (0.07)	2.7 (0.02)	29.5 (0.19)	7.1 (0.05)	9.5 (0.05)	12.9 (0.23)	20.6 (0.12)
Secondary	100.0 (†)	74.0 (0.52)	8.1 (0.15)	34.3 (1.24)	31.6 (0.60)	14.1 (0.28)	2.6 (0.05)	5.9 (0.11)	5.7 (0.12)	11.9 (0.31)
Combined	100.0 (†)	8.3 (0.11)	1.7 (0.02)	2.6 (0.05)	4.1 (0.04)	61.4 (0.48)	29.6 (0.34)	14.8 (0.24)	17.1 (0.89)	30.3 (0.39)
Student race/ethnicity[3]										
White	100.0 (†)	41.9 (0.35)	15.9 (0.14)	18.3 (0.33)	7.7 (0.06)	39.5 (0.45)	14.3 (0.13)	11.5 (0.12)	13.7 (0.55)	18.7 (0.19)
Black	100.0 (†)	35.4 (0.15)	11.9 (0.05)	14.9 (0.08)	8.6 (0.03)	41.8 (0.18)	17.7 (0.08)	10.5 (0.10)	13.6 (0.06)	22.8 (0.30)
Hispanic	100.0 (†)	60.2 (0.22)	24.3 (0.12)	24.5 (0.32)	11.4 (0.05)	24.4 (0.19)	11.1 (0.19)	6.9 (0.04)	6.4 (0.06)	15.4 (0.10)
Asian	100.0 (†)	36.6 (0.10)	13.8 (0.02)	15.2 (0.11)	7.5 (0.01)	31.2 (0.05)	12.3 (0.04)	10.1 (0.01)	8.9 (0.01)	32.2 (0.07)
Pacific Islander	100.0 (†)	46.3 (0.33)	16.2 (0.08)	20.9 (0.36)	9.2 (0.04)	38.1 (0.28)	12.2 (0.18)	13.0 (0.06)	12.9 (0.06)	15.6 (0.30)
American Indian/Alaska Native	100.0 (†)	43.9 (0.18)	11.0 (0.05)	18.0 (0.08)	15.0 (0.06)	30.4 (0.29)	16.1 (0.35)	7.2 (0.03)	7.2 (0.06)	25.7 (0.11)
Two or more races	100.0 (†)	44.1 (0.14)	15.5 (0.04)	19.9 (0.14)	8.7 (0.06)	27.6 (0.10)	11.0 (0.04)	9.4 (0.02)	7.3 (0.09)	28.3 (0.12)
School enrollment										
Less than 50	100.0 (†)	2.9 (0.21)	0.8 (0.03)	0.8 (0.02)	1.4 (0.19)	54.4 (1.45)	14.5 (0.57)	8.2 (0.30)	31.7 (1.65)	42.7 (1.38)
50 to 149	100.0 (†)	15.4 (0.15)	6.7 (0.06)	6.5 (0.08)	2.2 (0.02)	46.9 (0.78)	16.1 (0.37)	11.1 (0.11)	19.7 (0.52)	37.7 (0.69)
150 to 299	100.0 (†)	44.0 (0.10)	21.2 (0.08)	19.5 (0.05)	3.3 (0.01)	37.3 (0.10)	14.4 (0.03)	10.8 (0.11)	12.2 (0.03)	18.7 (0.12)
300 to 499	100.0 (†)	51.2 (0.10)	23.1 (0.15)	21.6 (0.08)	6.5 (0.02)	31.9 (0.12)	12.9 (0.05)	9.6 (0.17)	9.4 (0.03)	16.8 (0.06)
500 to 749	100.0 (†)	55.6 (0.80)	18.6 (0.34)	24.9 (1.36)	12.2 (0.22)	29.7 (0.54)	12.5 (0.23)	9.5 (0.17)	7.7 (0.14)	14.7 (0.27)
750 or more	100.0 (†)	38.4 (0.80)	5.7 (0.12)	15.7 (0.33)	16.9 (0.35)	39.6 (1.25)	13.0 (0.27)	13.5 (0.28)	13.0 (1.80)	22.1 (0.46)
Region										
Northeast	100.0 (†)	43.3 (0.66)	17.0 (0.25)	16.5 (0.27)	9.8 (0.14)	30.9 (0.89)	4.7 (0.07)	11.9 (0.30)	14.2 (1.24)	25.8 (0.28)
Midwest	100.0 (†)	56.8 (0.79)	24.3 (0.38)	24.5 (0.94)	8.0 (0.13)	31.5 (0.90)	10.2 (0.32)	8.9 (0.18)	12.4 (0.66)	11.6 (0.43)
South	100.0 (†)	27.8 (0.04)	9.8 (0.01)	12.9 (0.02)	5.1 (0.01)	47.9 (0.07)	20.2 (0.06)	12.2 (0.02)	15.5 (0.02)	24.3 (0.09)
West	100.0 (†)	34.0 (0.01)	11.2 (0.01)	15.8 (0.01)	7.0 (0.00)	36.8 (0.02)	18.8 (0.01)	9.0 (0.01)	9.0 (0.02)	29.2 (0.01)
School locale										
City	100.0 (†)	44.2 (0.37)	15.4 (0.10)	19.3 (0.53)	9.5 (0.06)	33.9 (0.23)	10.4 (0.07)	11.1 (0.10)	12.4 (0.08)	21.9 (0.17)
Suburban	100.0 (†)	40.9 (0.14)	16.8 (0.15)	17.0 (0.06)	7.2 (0.02)	35.0 (0.08)	13.8 (0.05)	11.1 (0.10)	10.2 (0.04)	24.0 (0.15)
Town	100.0 (†)	49.4 (0.43)	23.9 (0.21)	23.4 (0.20)	2.1 (0.02)	39.3 (0.53)	16.8 (0.36)	8.6 (0.08)	14.0 (0.67)	11.3 (0.10)
Rural	100.0 (†)	16.7 (0.47)	6.3 (0.18)	7.2 (0.20)	3.2 (0.09)	57.2 (1.41)	23.4 (0.76)	9.7 (0.28)	24.1 (2.10)	26.2 (0.98)
Fall 2013										
Total	100.0 (†)	38.1 (0.50)	13.7 (0.33)	17.4 (0.51)	7.0 (0.07)	37.6 (0.44)	13.1 (0.16)	10.5 (0.13)	14.1 (0.47)	24.3 (0.28)
School level[2]										
Elementary	100.0 (†)	47.4 (0.64)	23.1 (0.57)	21.6 (0.37)	2.8 (0.04)	30.3 (0.73)	6.3 (0.08)	9.5 (0.20)	14.5 (0.85)	22.2 (0.38)
Secondary	100.0 (†)	71.4 (0.72)	6.9 (0.10)	34.1 (0.64)	30.3 (0.41)	15.3 (0.31)	2.5 (0.03)	6.5 (0.23)	6.3 (0.17)	13.3 (0.79)
Combined	100.0 (†)	9.8 (1.61)	1.7 (0.03)	3.9 (1.71)	4.2 (0.08)	58.3 (1.08)	28.2 (0.59)	13.6 (0.27)	16.6 (0.37)	31.9 (0.65)
Student race/ethnicity[3]										
White	100.0 (†)	40.2 (0.62)	14.0 (0.21)	18.9 (0.67)	7.3 (0.10)	39.7 (0.63)	13.5 (0.20)	11.6 (0.18)	14.6 (0.75)	20.1 (0.27)
Black	100.0 (†)	35.5 (1.81)	12.7 (2.34)	14.4 (0.45)	8.4 (0.26)	40.3 (1.27)	16.0 (0.50)	10.0 (0.40)	14.4 (0.55)	24.2 (1.35)
Hispanic	100.0 (†)	57.5 (0.50)	21.8 (0.25)	24.2 (0.39)	11.4 (0.10)	25.9 (0.49)	11.9 (0.41)	6.7 (0.06)	7.3 (0.16)	16.6 (0.17)
Asian	100.0 (†)	35.0 (0.48)	11.0 (0.14)	16.5 (0.56)	7.5 (0.07)	31.6 (0.33)	12.2 (0.18)	10.2 (0.17)	9.2 (0.09)	33.4 (0.31)
Pacific Islander	100.0 (†)	39.4 (0.43)	14.1 (0.19)	18.0 (0.53)	7.3 (0.08)	43.7 (0.33)	12.4 (0.14)	6.8 (0.05)	24.5 (0.25)	16.9 (0.20)
American Indian/Alaska Native	100.0 (†)	39.1 (0.37)	12.1 (0.11)	15.6 (0.28)	11.3 (0.10)	34.6 (0.49)	16.2 (0.14)	6.8 (0.65)	11.5 (0.11)	26.3 (0.36)
Two or more races	100.0 (†)	43.1 (0.43)	14.4 (0.30)	19.1 (0.32)	9.6 (0.08)	27.8 (0.41)	11.7 (0.25)	8.2 (0.22)	7.9 (0.12)	29.1 (0.34)
School enrollment										
Less than 50	100.0 (†)	2.9 (0.40)	0.8 (0.14)	0.9 (0.08)	1.2 (0.30)	58.4 (4.14)	10.5 (1.04)	6.4 (0.68)	41.6 (5.71)	38.7 (3.88)
50 to 149	100.0 (†)	14.8 (0.58)	6.0 (0.59)	6.8 (0.22)	2.0 (0.05)	46.9 (0.56)	14.5 (0.28)	10.9 (0.17)	21.6 (0.56)	38.3 (0.46)
150 to 299	100.0 (†)	42.9 (0.60)	20.3 (0.73)	18.9 (0.22)	3.7 (0.07)	36.5 (0.46)	13.2 (0.16)	10.5 (0.26)	12.8 (0.21)	20.6 (0.52)
300 to 499	100.0 (†)	50.7 (0.28)	21.0 (0.12)	23.0 (0.23)	6.6 (0.04)	32.3 (0.35)	14.1 (0.30)	9.6 (0.33)	8.6 (0.05)	17.0 (0.10)
500 to 749	100.0 (†)	51.8 (0.80)	16.4 (0.60)	23.6 (0.84)	11.8 (0.19)	30.7 (0.46)	12.2 (0.48)	9.9 (0.16)	8.6 (0.14)	17.5 (0.36)
750 or more	100.0 (†)	38.8 (2.22)	4.7 (0.17)	18.8 (2.92)	15.4 (0.57)	35.7 (1.31)	12.1 (0.45)	12.8 (0.47)	10.8 (0.40)	25.5 (1.10)

See notes at end of table.

Table 205.30. Percentage distribution of students enrolled in private elementary and secondary schools, by school orientation and selected characteristics: Fall 2011 and fall 2013—Continued

[Standard errors appear in parentheses]

Selected characteristic	Total	Catholic				Other religious					Nonsectarian
		Total	Parochial	Diocesan	Private	Total	Conservative Christian	Affiliated[1]	Unaffiliated[1]	
1	2	3	4	5	6	7	8	9	10	11
Region										
Northeast	100.0 (†)	42.0 (0.34)	15.1 (0.12)	16.5 (0.13)	10.3 (0.09)	29.9 (0.21)	4.8 (0.21)	11.4 (0.12)	13.7 (0.10)	28.1 (0.47)
Midwest	100.0 (†)	56.1 (1.68)	22.4 (1.27)	26.0 (1.90)	7.6 (0.27)	31.5 (1.69)	8.8 (1.69)	8.6 (0.36)	14.1 (1.83)	12.5 (0.47)
South	100.0 (†)	25.9 (0.29)	8.4 (0.28)	13.0 (0.06)	4.5 (0.04)	48.4 (0.30)	19.0 (0.30)	12.4 (0.18)	17.0 (0.32)	25.7 (0.21)
West	100.0 (†)	32.2 (0.60)	10.2 (0.18)	15.0 (0.36)	7.0 (0.12)	35.4 (0.52)	17.8 (0.52)	8.4 (0.26)	9.2 (0.17)	32.5 (0.65)
School locale										
City	100.0 (†)	42.1 (0.85)	13.9 (0.28)	19.3 (1.16)	8.9 (0.14)	33.6 (0.54)	10.0 (0.16)	11.5 (0.23)	12.2 (0.29)	24.2 (0.46)
Suburban	100.0 (†)	38.2 (0.38)	13.9 (0.12)	17.5 (0.34)	6.8 (0.07)	35.9 (0.37)	14.1 (0.27)	10.1 (0.19)	11.6 (0.14)	25.9 (0.30)
Town	100.0 (†)	48.2 (2.81)	25.2 (3.99)	20.9 (1.13)	2.1 (0.12)	38.6 (2.12)	15.6 (0.85)	8.2 (0.45)	14.8 (0.96)	13.2 (1.04)
Rural	100.0 (†)	14.4 (0.73)	4.8 (0.24)	6.3 (0.32)	3.3 (0.17)	61.1 (1.96)	20.4 (1.04)	9.1 (0.50)	31.5 (3.48)	24.5 (1.24)

†Not applicable.
[1]Affiliated schools belong to associations of schools with a specific religious orientation other than Catholic or conservative Christian. Unaffiliated schools have a religious orientation or purpose but are not classified as Catholic, conservative Christian, or affiliated.
[2]Elementary schools have grade 6 or lower and no grade higher than 8. Secondary schools have no grade lower than 7. Combined schools include those that have grades lower than 7 and higher than 8, as well as those that do not classify students by grade level.

[3]Race/ethnicity was not collected for prekindergarten students (773,240 out of 5,268,090 students in 2011 and 819,320 out of 5,395,740 students in 2013). Percentage distribution is based on the students for whom race/ethnicity was reported.
NOTE: Includes enrollment in prekindergarten through grade 12 in schools that offer kindergarten or higher grade. Race categories exclude persons of Hispanic ethnicity. Detail may not sum to totals because of rounding.
SOURCE: U.S. Department of Education, National Center for Education Statistics, Private School Universe Survey (PSS), 2011–12 and 2013–14. (This table was prepared December 2015.)

Table 205.40. Number and percentage distribution of private elementary and secondary students, teachers, and schools, by orientation of school and selected characteristics: Fall 1999, fall 2009, and fall 2013

[Standard errors appear in parentheses]

Selected characteristic	Fall 1999, total number	Fall 2009, total number	Fall 2013 Total — Number	Total — Percent	Catholic — Number	Catholic — Percent	Other religious — Number	Other religious — Percent	Nonsectarian — Number	Nonsectarian — Percent
1	2	3	4	5	6	7	8	9	10	11
Students[1]										
Total	6,018,280 (30,179)	5,488,490 (35,857)	5,395,740 (50,342)	100.0 (†)	2,055,140 (37,142)	100.0 (†)	2,030,930 (30,090)	100.0 (†)	1,309,670 (14,800)	100.0 (†)
School level[2]										
Elementary	3,595,020 (11,516)	2,937,090 (26,807)	2,848,140 (36,022)	52.8 (0.47)	1,351,380 (20,818)	65.8 (1.14)	863,250 (28,166)	42.5 (0.80)	633,510 (9,546)	48.4 (0.51)
Secondary	806,640 (2,395)	785,810 (4,810)	737,950 (9,211)	13.7 (0.19)	526,640 (6,315)	25.6 (0.51)	112,990 (2,036)	5.6 (0.13)	98,330 (6,627)	7.5 (0.46)
Combined	1,616,620 (23,949)	1,765,590 (15,909)	1,809,650 (34,220)	33.5 (0.48)	177,120 (32,247)	8.6 (1.45)	1,054,690 (7,776)	51.9 (0.72)	577,840 (7,819)	44.1 (0.54)
School enrollment										
Less than 50	238,980 (5,691)	296,000 (22,889)	292,310 (26,965)	5.4 (0.47)	8,360 (878)	0.4 (0.04)	170,830 (27,269)	8.4 (1.23)	113,130 (3,839)	8.6 (0.25)
50 to 149	939,110 (10,717)	950,050 (12,053)	925,150 (10,930)	17.1 (0.23)	136,820 (6,136)	6.7 (0.30)	434,100 (7,789)	21.4 (0.44)	354,230 (3,796)	27.0 (0.35)
150 to 299	1,615,970 (7,315)	1,423,220 (9,951)	1,378,460 (16,204)	25.5 (0.29)	591,210 (12,394)	28.8 (0.57)	502,810 (5,399)	24.8 (0.40)	284,430 (8,403)	21.7 (0.50)
300 to 499	1,419,360 (13,203)	1,154,950 (10,730)	1,102,200 (6,197)	20.4 (0.21)	558,370 (2,871)	27.2 (0.50)	356,170 (5,492)	17.5 (0.33)	187,660 (†)	14.3 (0.16)
500 to 749	917,670 (2,330)	768,540 (†)	782,570 (12,660)	14.5 (0.24)	405,250 (9,585)	19.7 (0.51)	240,020 (4,550)	11.8 (0.24)	137,300 (3,720)	10.5 (0.26)
750 or more	887,190 (18,232)	895,720 (6,538)	915,060 (33,650)	17.0 (0.54)	355,130 (32,844)	17.3 (1.35)	327,000 (†)	16.1 (0.24)	232,930 (7,318)	17.8 (0.49)
Student race/ethnicity[3]										
White	4,061,870 (24,242)	3,410,360 (31,067)	3,185,550 (38,542)	69.6 (0.31)	1,280,320 (25,768)	67.7 (0.51)	1,264,370 (28,385)	73.9 (0.45)	640,860 (6,026)	65.8 (0.47)
Black	494,530 (5,079)	430,970 (2,579)	424,480 (13,148)	9.3 (0.27)	150,840 (11,300)	8.0 (0.55)	170,950 (1,699)	10.0 (0.19)	102,690 (6,582)	10.5 (0.60)
Hispanic	435,890 (1,592)	443,290 (4,113)	468,790 (4,024)	10.2 (0.11)	269,520 (2,234)	14.2 (0.19)	121,310 (3,071)	7.1 (0.20)	77,960 (908)	8.0 (0.09)
Asian	239,510 (877)	239,320 (1,894)	268,690 (2,346)	5.9 (0.05)	94,100 (1,786)	5.0 (0.04)	84,790 (1,046)	5.0 (0.09)	89,790 (879)	9.2 (0.08)
Pacific Islander	[4] (†)	28,020 (884)	29,790 (221)	0.7 (0.01)	11,730 (200)	0.6 (0.01)	13,010 (80)	0.8 (0.01)	5,050 (57)	0.5 (0.01)
American Indian/ Alaska Native	22,690 (164)	21,080 (162)	22,030 (193)	0.5 (0.01)	8,610 (66)	0.5 (0.01)	7,620 (155)	0.4 (0.01)	5,800 (90)	0.6 (0.01)
Two or more races	— (†)	127,090 (781)	177,090 (1,538)	3.9 (0.03)	76,250 (837)	4.0 (0.04)	49,310 (953)	2.9 (0.06)	51,530 (763)	5.3 (0.05)
School locale										
City	— (†)	2,252,780 (12,708)	2,294,730 (35,960)	42.5 (0.50)	967,070 (33,365)	47.1 (1.01)	771,220 (5,625)	38.0 (0.59)	556,440 (9,732)	42.5 (0.47)
Suburban	— (†)	2,137,800 (20,891)	2,212,320 (18,866)	41.0 (0.44)	844,740 (8,428)	41.1 (0.85)	793,610 (12,105)	39.1 (0.66)	573,970 (8,821)	43.8 (0.52)
Town	— (†)	387,920 (9,565)	341,840 (18,483)	6.3 (0.33)	164,660 (18,120)	8.0 (0.82)	132,000 (2,105)	6.5 (0.14)	45,180 (2,976)	3.4 (0.21)
Rural	— (†)	709,990 (26,462)	546,850 (27,453)	10.1 (0.47)	78,660 (†)	3.8 (0.07)	334,100 (27,449)	16.5 (1.14)	134,090 (459)	10.2 (0.11)
Teachers[5]										
Total	408,400 (2,977)	437,410 (3,222)	441,500 (3,456)	100.0 (†)	138,990 (2,177)	100.0 (.00)	171,460 (2,192)	100.0 (†)	131,050 (1,516)	100.0 (†)
School level[2]										
Elementary	200,910 (735)	194,480 (1,878)	193,580 (2,206)	43.8 (0.40)	84,580 (1,000)	60.8 (1.08)	62,520 (1,957)	36.5 (0.73)	46,480 (394)	35.5 (0.43)
Secondary	62,740 (229)	67,530 (553)	64,770 (459)	14.7 (0.13)	39,460 (325)	28.4 (0.47)	12,030 (140)	7.0 (0.12)	13,280 (321)	10.1 (0.17)
Combined	144,750 (2,682)	175,410 (1,853)	183,150 (2,656)	41.5 (0.42)	14,960 (2,191)	10.8 (1.43)	96,910 (815)	56.5 (0.66)	71,280 (1,229)	54.4 (0.41)
School enrollment										
Less than 50	25,970 (488)	34,120 (1,642)	34,030 (1,966)	7.7 (0.41)	1,290 (192)	0.9 (0.14)	18,580 (1,933)	10.8 (1.01)	14,160 (420)	10.8 (0.25)
50 to 149	70,800 (963)	82,460 (1,102)	79,420 (703)	18.0 (0.21)	11,600 (283)	8.3 (0.31)	37,180 (606)	21.7 (0.39)	30,650 (282)	23.4 (0.31)
150 to 299	102,240 (486)	107,490 (1,873)	104,450 (883)	23.7 (0.23)	39,860 (708)	28.7 (0.54)	39,730 (439)	23.2 (0.33)	24,850 (244)	19.0 (0.26)
300 to 499	90,010 (1,316)	86,850 (751)	85,620 (395)	19.4 (0.17)	36,150 (164)	26.0 (0.42)	28,990 (360)	16.9 (0.27)	20,490 (†)	15.6 (0.18)
500 to 749	57,930 (79)	56,920 (†)	60,950 (711)	13.8 (0.17)	26,150 (499)	18.8 (0.41)	19,640 (444)	11.5 (0.25)	15,150 (†)	11.6 (0.14)
750 or more	61,440 (2,143)	69,570 (566)	77,030 (2,510)	17.4 (0.48)	23,950 (†)	17.2 (1.36)	27,340 (†)	15.9 (0.20)	25,740 (†)	19.6 (0.70)
School locale										
City	— (†)	176,740 (799)	187,910 (2,369)	42.6 (0.42)	64,630 (2,242)	46.5 (1.00)	66,360 (307)	38.7 (0.52)	56,920 (463)	43.4 (0.36)
Suburban	— (†)	166,170 (2,463)	175,370 (1,730)	39.7 (0.39)	56,380 (520)	40.6 (0.82)	64,900 (1,033)	37.8 (0.59)	54,090 (1,231)	41.3 (0.51)
Town	— (†)	30,390 (663)	26,640 (803)	6.0 (0.18)	11,600 (789)	8.3 (0.53)	10,940 (98)	6.4 (0.09)	4,100 (112)	3.1 (0.09)
Rural	— (†)	64,120 (1,960)	51,580 (1,942)	11.7 (0.40)	6,380 (†)	4.6 (0.07)	29,270 (1,939)	17.1 (0.94)	15,940 (105)	12.2 (0.15)
Schools										
Total	33,000 (301)	33,370 (834)	33,620 (1,665)	100.0 (†)	6,700 (93)	100.0 (.00)	16,390 (1,665)	100.0 (†)	10,540 (171)	100.0 (†)
School level[2]										
Elementary	22,300 (242)	21,420 (745)	22,510 (1,657)	67.0 (1.66)	5,290 (95)	79.0 (0.45)	10,240 (1,660)	62.5 (3.91)	6,980 (131)	66.3 (0.51)
Secondary	2,540 (62)	2,780 (39)	2,700 (59)	8.0 (0.43)	990 (11)	14.8 (0.25)	790 (39)	4.8 (0.56)	920 (41)	8.7 (0.31)
Combined	8,150 (160)	9,160 (153)	8,410 (142)	25.0 (1.28)	410 (21)	6.2 (0.32)	5,360 (130)	32.7 (3.42)	2,640 (59)	25.0 (0.56)
School enrollment										
Less than 50	9,160 (210)	11,070 (801)	11,990 (1,657)	35.7 (3.19)	250 (21)	3.8 (0.31)	7,620 (1,663)	46.5 (5.56)	4,130 (131)	39.2 (0.68)
50 to 149	10,260 (134)	10,470 (154)	10,120 (118)	30.1 (1.51)	1,300 (50)	19.5 (0.54)	4,730 (86)	28.9 (3.02)	4,090 (51)	38.8 (0.63)
150 to 299	7,440 (34)	6,690 (46)	6,480 (69)	19.3 (0.97)	2,680 (44)	40.1 (0.21)	2,400 (29)	14.7 (1.54)	1,390 (42)	13.2 (0.31)
300 to 499	3,730 (41)	3,010 (30)	2,880 (16)	8.6 (0.43)	1,450 (8)	21.6 (0.32)	940 (13)	5.7 (0.60)	490 (†)	4.7 (0.18)
500 to 749	1,530 (3)	1,280 (†)	1,300 (20)	3.9 (0.20)	680 (16)	10.1 (0.26)	400 (6)	2.4 (0.25)	230 (6)	2.1 (0.06)
750 or more	870 (20)	850 (7)	850 (22)	2.5 (0.14)	330 (†)	5.0 (0.32)	300 (†)	1.8 (0.19)	210 (8)	2.0 (0.08)
School locale										
City	— (†)	10,810 (171)	10,630 (138)	31.6 (1.60)	2,720 (26)	40.6 (0.66)	4,100 (75)	25.0 (2.63)	3,810 (84)	36.1 (0.60)
Suburban	— (†)	11,610 (176)	12,110 (141)	36.0 (1.82)	2,570 (33)	38.3 (0.65)	4,490 (66)	27.4 (2.87)	5,050 (87)	47.9 (0.76)
Town	— (†)	3,340 (154)	2,890 (136)	8.6 (0.59)	920 (89)	13.8 (1.14)	1,410 (51)	8.6 (0.93)	560 (90)	5.3 (0.79)
Rural	— (†)	7,610 (799)	7,990 (1,662)	23.8 (3.80)	490 (†)	7.2 (0.10)	6,390 (1,662)	39.0 (6.33)	1,120 (21)	10.6 (0.21)

—Not available.
†Not applicable.
[1]Includes students in prekindergarten through grade 12 in schools that offer kindergarten or higher grade.
[2]Elementary schools have grade 6 or lower and no grade higher than 8. Secondary schools have no grade lower than 7. Combined schools include those that have grades lower than 7 and higher than 8, as well as those that do not classify students by grade level.
[3]Race/ethnicity was not collected for prekindergarten students (819,320 in fall 2013). Percentage distribution is based on the students for whom race/ethnicity was reported.

[4]For 1999, Pacific Islander students are included under Asian. Prior to 2009, data were not collected on Pacific Islander students as a separate category.
[5]Reported in full-time equivalents (FTE). Excludes teachers who teach only prekindergarten students.
NOTE: Tabulation includes schools that offer kindergarten or higher grade. Detail may not sum to totals because of rounding.
SOURCE: U.S. Department of Education, National Center for Education Statistics, Private School Universe Survey (PSS), 1999–2000, 2009–10, and 2013–14. (This table was prepared December 2015.)

Table 205.50. Private elementary and secondary enrollment, number of schools, and average tuition, by school level, orientation, and tuition: Selected years, 1999–2000 through 2011–12
[Standard errors appear in parentheses]

School orientation and tuition	Kindergarten through 12th-grade enrollment[1]				Total schools	Average tuition charged[2] (in current dollars)				Average tuition charged[2] (in constant 2014–15 dollars), total
	Total	Elementary	Secondary	Combined		Total	Elementary	Secondary	Combined	
1	2	3	4	5	6	7	8	9	10	11
1999–2000										
Total..........	5,262,850 (131,001)	2,920,680 (55,057)	818,920 (34,102)	1,523,240 (88,816)	27,220 (239)	$4,980 (157)	$3,740 (249)	$6,080 (175)	$6,760 (261)	$5,960 (220)
Catholic..........	2,548,710 (23,352)	1,810,330 (18,134)	616,200 (25,935)	122,190 (15,613)	8,100 (24)	3,340 (57)	2,600 (47)	4,830 (92)	6,890 (690)	4,670 (80)
Other religious..........	1,871,850 (86,782)	831,060 (41,035)	115,010 (10,981)	925,780 (66,926)	13,270 (237)	4,440 (153)	4,070 (130)	6,400 (456)	4,520 (280)	6,210 (215)
Nonsectarian..........	842,290 (61,373)	279,290 (28,987)	87,720 (11,774)	475,270 (43,377)	5,850 (76)	11,120 (775)	10,130 (1,921)	14,450 (1,461)	11,090 (801)	15,550 (1,083)
2003–04										
Total..........	5,059,450 (104,287)	2,675,960 (55,714)	832,320 (54,051)	1,551,170 (82,059)	28,380 (262)	$6,600 (145)	$5,050 (120)	$8,410 (433)	$8,300 (290)	$8,390 (184)
Catholic..........	2,320,040 (49,156)	1,645,680 (41,231)	584,250 (32,236)	90,110 (14,746)	7,920 (35)	4,250 (96)	3,530 (106)	6,050 (131)	5,800 (883)	5,410 (122)
Other religious..........	1,746,460 (63,090)	714,860 (28,935)	107,980 ! (33,776)	923,630 (48,379)	13,660 (203)	5,840 (144)	5,400 (161)	9,540 (963)	5,750 (230)	7,430 (183)
Nonsectarian..........	992,940 (71,519)	315,430 (30,820)	140,080 (27,556)	537,440 (59,332)	6,810 (136)	13,420 (379)	12,170 (468)	17,410 (1,988)	13,110 (480)	17,070 (482)
2007–08										
Total..........	5,165,280 (104,435)	2,462,980 (58,830)	850,750 (38,553)	1,851,550 (91,348)	28,220 (328)	$8,550 (176)	$6,730 (181)	$10,550 (356)	$10,050 (372)	$9,560 (197)
Less than $3,500..........	1,122,300 (50,988)	750,020 (35,402)	143,510 (19,815)	342,100 (35,615)	10,030 (344)	2,710 (61)	2,900 (54)	5,080 (80)	2,350 (134)	3,030 (68)
$3,500 to $5,999..........	1,790,410 (77,850)	1,066,750 (45,444)	455,840 (33,376)	580,150 (53,528)	9,110 (341)	5,210 (42)	5,220 (49)	7,660 (105)	5,210 (89)	5,820 (46)
$6,000 to $9,999..........	1,155,290 (60,342)	366,470 (37,396)	‡	332,980 (36,574)	4,460 (232)	8,260 (101)	9,230 (287)	‡	8,030 (192)	9,230 (113)
$10,000 to $14,999..........	503,380 (45,776)	169,970 (26,731)	125,660 (15,623)	237,850 (37,089)	1,980 (154)	13,640 (319)	15,730 (696)	‡	12,910 (318)	15,250 (357)
$15,000 or more..........	593,900 (50,049)	109,770 (19,266)	‡	358,470 (43,060)	2,650 (187)	25,890 (768)	25,360 (1,940)	28,400 (1,327)	25,180 (1,061)	28,940 (858)
Catholic..........	2,224,470 (49,385)	1,457,960 (32,114)	620,840 (32,581)	145,680 (25,445)	7,400 (34)	6,020 (180)	4,940 (212)	7,830 (232)	9,070 (964)	6,730 (202)
Less than $3,500..........	619,410 (37,867)	571,560 (34,303)	‡	‡	2,810 (132)	2,980 (55)	3,010 (57)	‡	‡	3,330 (61)
$3,500 to $5,999..........	826,120 (37,974)	683,980 (32,576)	111,770 (16,043)	‡	3,040 (131)	4,900 (49)	4,860 (57)	5,150 (80)	‡	5,480 (55)
$6,000 to $9,999..........	607,980 (49,329)	165,120 (28,123)	395,900 (30,158)	‡	1,170 (102)	7,680 (116)	7,790 (240)	7,650 (117)	‡	8,590 (130)
$10,000 to $14,999..........	‡	‡	‡	‡	‡	‡	‡	‡	‡	‡
$15,000 or more..........	‡	‡	‡	‡	‡	‡	‡	‡	‡	‡
Other religious..........	1,975,980 (81,216)	709,730 (36,666)	128,550 (15,136)	1,137,700 (75,038)	13,950 (282)	7,120 (237)	6,580 (241)	10,490 (1,336)	7,070 (359)	7,960 (265)
Less than $3,500..........	430,010 (31,875)	172,660 (14,154)	‡	252,490 (29,920)	6,180 (291)	2,520 (106)	2,550 (167)	‡	2,510 (133)	2,820 (118)
$3,500 to $5,999..........	860,370 (59,588)	340,150 (27,800)	57,150 (10,809)	489,390 (49,116)	5,030 (257)	5,370 (75)	5,570 (111)	‡	5,270 (101)	6,000 (84)
$6,000 to $9,999..........	384,850 (39,687)	103,280 (15,561)	‡	224,420 (33,273)	1,640 (137)	8,050 (155)	8,810 (430)	7,680 (188)	5,790 (164)	9,000 (173)
$10,000 to $14,999..........	167,770 (25,960)	‡	‡	‡	620 (83)	13,230 (401)	‡	‡	‡	14,790 (448)
$15,000 or more..........	132,980 (24,657)	‡	‡	‡	480 (91)	22,880 (1,053)	‡	‡	‡	25,580 (1,178)
Nonsectarian..........	964,830 (55,074)	295,280 (25,191)	101,370 (12,739)	568,180 (48,321)	6,860 (119)	17,320 (555)	15,940 (702)	27,300 (1,506)	16,250 (795)	19,360 (621)
Less than $3,500..........	72,890 (10,998)	42,610 (7,809)	‡	59,910 (10,584)	1,030 (125)	1,610 (387)	‡	‡	1,640 (467)	1,800 (432)
$3,500 to $5,999..........	103,930 (18,494)	98,070 (16,434)	‡	‡	1,040 (143)	6,290 (352)	8,090 (687)	‡	‡	7,030 (394)
$6,000 to $9,999..........	162,450 (24,872)	77,450 (15,769)	‡	126,610 (25,784)	1,650 (168)	10,960 (530)	12,110 (792)	‡	13,230 (336)	12,250 (593)
$10,000 to $14,999..........	208,670 (29,194)	71,360 (14,776)	85,870 (13,205)	259,670 (38,826)	1,150 (124)	14,890 (567)	17,750 (1,501)	31,220 (1,647)	25,350 (1,334)	16,650 (634)
$15,000 or more..........	416,900 (39,779)	‡	‡	‡	2,000 (157)	26,500 (943)	25,010 (1,422)	‡	‡	29,630 (1,055)
2011–12										
Total..........	4,479,530 (105,651)	2,133,810 (59,964)	731,620 (53,646)	1,614,100 (98,602)	26,230 (541)	$10,740 (316)	$7,770 (211)	$13,030 (727)	$13,640 (753)	$11,170 (328)
Less than $3,500..........	618,710 (45,753)	404,700 (36,956)	42,580 ! (13,642)	171,430 (23,140)	7,950 (581)	2,190 (112)	2,410 (139)	1,370 (392)	1,870 (182)	2,280 (117)
$3,500 to $5,999..........	1,351,550 (64,739)	946,810 (56,403)	‡	364,520 (30,056)	7,800 (326)	5,300 (58)	5,350 (67)	5,250 (118)	5,250 (118)	5,510 (60)
$6,000 to $9,999..........	1,167,820 (80,517)	467,040 (41,842)	275,980 (29,528)	424,800 (62,852)	5,070 (279)	8,560 (124)	9,090 (230)	7,980 (172)	8,360 (251)	8,900 (129)
$10,000 to $14,999..........	534,560 (45,926)	143,500 (18,976)	208,750 (38,977)	182,310 (36,985)	1,840 (150)	13,400 (207)	15,050 (454)	11,960 (225)	13,750 (348)	13,940 (216)
$15,000 or more..........	806,880 (69,846)	171,760 (25,237)	164,090 (32,298)	471,040 (65,345)	3,570 (194)	27,820 (951)	24,020 (960)	28,000 (2,487)	29,140 (1,274)	28,930 (989)
Catholic..........	1,892,480 (59,899)	1,244,480 (36,762)	511,870 (43,761)	136,130 (19,283)	6,760 (39)	6,890 (185)	5,330 (128)	9,790 (405)	10,230 (1,230)	7,170 (192)
Less than $3,500..........	307,610 (35,036)	259,330 (33,704)	‡	‡	1,730 (170)	2,580 (123)	2,690 (122)	‡	‡	2,680 (128)
$3,500 to $5,999..........	781,420 (53,974)	716,630 (50,260)	‡	‡	3,070 (187)	5,110 (68)	5,120 (72)	‡	‡	5,310 (71)
$6,000 to $9,999..........	516,660 (48,765)	243,570 (35,924)	234,460 (29,418)	‡	1,320 (126)	7,850 (139)	7,820 (210)	7,970 (199)	‡	8,160 (144)
$10,000 to $14,999..........	221,150 (36,032)	‡	177,560 (34,919)	‡	440 (68)	12,290 (240)	‡	12,020 (252)	‡	12,780 (250)
$15,000 or more..........	‡	‡	‡	‡	‡	‡	‡	‡	‡	‡

See notes at end of table.

Table 205.50. Private elementary and secondary enrollment, number of schools, and average tuition, by school level, orientation, and tuition: Selected years, 1999–2000 through 2011–12—Continued
[Standard errors appear in parentheses]

School orientation and tuition	Kindergarten through 12th-grade enrollment[1]				Total schools	Average tuition charged[2] (in current dollars)				Average tuition charged[2] (in constant 2014–15 dollars), total
	Total	Elementary	Secondary	Combined		Total	Elementary	Secondary	Combined	
1	2	3	4	5	6	7	8	9	10	11
Other religious	1,604,900 (84,424)	609,930 (38,479)	116,660 (31,187)	878,320 (77,923)	13,040 (550)	8,690 (397)	7,960 (447)	16,520 (2,288)	8,160 (518)	9,040 (413)
Less than $3,500	243,840 (25,511)	136,240 (19,015)	† (†)	103,980 (13,231)	5,190 (518)	2,090 (156)	1,860 (245)	‡ (†)	2,440 (169)	2,170 (163)
$3,500 to $5,999	507,660 (38,017)	214,270 (23,446)	† (†)	286,370 (28,337)	4,280 (259)	5,540 (101)	5,980 (183)	‡ (†)	5,220 (123)	5,760 (105)
$6,000 to $9,999	532,720 (61,948)	144,110 (26,978)	40,740 (7,928)	347,870 (59,370)	2,220 (228)	8,460 (186)	9,010 (269)	8,030 (196)	8,280 (260)	8,800 (194)
$10,000 to $14,999	165,130 (32,486)	‡ (†)	‡ (†)	‡ (†)	630 (89)	13,490 (359)	‡ (†)	‡ (†)	‡ (†)	14,030 (373)
$15,000 or more	155,550 (33,317)	‡ (†)	‡ (†)	‡ (†)	720 (126)	25,000 (2,243)	‡ (†)	‡ (†)	‡ (†)	26,000 (2,333)
Nonsectarian	982,140 (67,032)	279,400 (21,508)	103,090 (19,049)	599,650 (61,512)	6,430 (68)	21,510 (1,018)	18,170 (906)	25,180 (2,907)	22,440 (1,503)	22,370 (1,059)
Less than $3,500	67,260 (15,092)	‡ (†)	‡ (†)	47,370 ! (14,470)	1,040 (140)	740 ! (285)	‡ (†)	‡ (†)	490 ! (244)	770 ! (297)
$3,500 to $5,999	‡ (†)	‡ (†)	‡ (†)	‡ (†)	‡ (†)	‡ (†)	‡ (†)	‡ (†)	‡ (†)	‡ (†)
$6,000 to $9,999	118,440 (21,597)	79,370 (7,976)	‡ (†)	‡ (†)	1,530 (119)	12,130 (628)	13,140 (683)	‡ (†)	‡ (†)	12,620 (653)
$10,000 to $14,999	148,280 (33,642)	59,130 (11,788)	‡ (†)	‡ (†)	770 (106)	14,950 (418)	15,960 (908)	‡ (†)	‡ (†)	15,550 (435)
$15,000 or more	585,680 (66,696)	115,850 (20,781)	74,630 (16,406)	395,200 (61,972)	2,640 (165)	29,160 (1,092)	25,490 (1,219)	32,120 (3,206)	29,670 (1,368)	30,330 (1,136)

†Not applicable.
!Interpret data with caution. The coefficient of variation (CV) for this estimate is between 30 and 50 percent.
‡Reporting standards not met. Either there are too few cases for a reliable estimate or the coefficient of variation (CV) is 50 percent or greater.
[1]Only includes kindergarten students who attend schools that offer first or higher grade.
[2]Each school reports the highest annual tuition charged for a full-time student; this amount does not take into account discounts that individual students may receive. This amount is weighted by the number of students enrolled in each school and averaged.

NOTE: Excludes schools not offering first or higher grade. Elementary schools have grade 6 or lower and no grade higher than 8. Secondary schools have no grade lower than 7. Combined schools include those that have grades lower than 7 and higher than 8, as well as those that do not classify students by grade level. Excludes prekindergarten students. Includes a small percentage of schools reporting tuition of 0; these private schools are often under contract to public school districts to provide special education services. Detail may not sum to totals because of rounding and cell suppression. Some data have been revised from previously published figures.
SOURCE: U.S. Department of Education, National Center for Education Statistics, Schools and Staffing Survey (SASS), "Private School Data File," 1999–2000, 2003–04, 2007–08, and 2011–12. (This table was prepared in December 2015.)

Table 205.60. Private elementary and secondary school full-time-equivalent (FTE) staff and student to FTE staff ratios, by orientation of school, school level, and type of staff: 2007–08 and 2011–12

[Standard errors appear in parentheses]

Type of staff	Total, 2007–08	2011–12 Total — Total	Elementary[1]	Secondary[2]	Combined[3]	Catholic — Total	Elementary[1]	Secondary[2]	Combined[3]
1	2	3	4	5	6	7	8	9	10
Number of FTE staff									
Number of schools	28,220 (328)	26,230 (541)	15,000 (434)	2,820 (153)	8,400 (220)	6,760 (39)	5,300 (24)	1,040 (37)	410 (26)
Enrollment (in thousands)	5,165 (104)	4,480 (106)	2,134 (60)	732 (54)	1,614 (99)	1,892 (60)	1,244 (37)	512 (44M)	136 (19)
Total FTE staff	**786,250 (16,261)**	**733,560 (17,373)**	**296,720 (8,627)**	**118,740 (8,321)**	**318,100 (17,125)**	**224,790 (7,201)**	**138,980 (3,830)**	**62,650 (5,069)**	**23,160 (2,739)**
Principals	30,550 (463)	26,290 (497)	12,670 (319)	3,040 (159)	10,580 (410)	7,070 (115)	5,240 (83)	1,250 (50)	580 (66)
Assistant principals	13,120 (487)	11,280 (418)	4,160 (274)	2,510 (253)	4,610 (326)	3,270 (208)	1,470 (147)	1,460 (138)	350 (68)
Other managers	26,110 (952)	25,950 (872)	9,710 (511)	5,160 (479)	11,070 (707)	6,690 (410)	3,010 (252)	2,710 (312)	970 (142)
Instruction coordinators	7,850 (538)	7,630 (733)	2,310 (296)	1,440 ! (443)	3,880 (572)	1,280 (176)	550 (124)	500 (107)	230 (54)
Teachers	436,910 (8,665)	413,140 (9,516)	174,930 (4,690)	64,390 (4,936)	173,810 (10,001)	130,210 (3,981)	82,300 (2,281)	36,000 (2,853)	11,900 (1,567)
Teacher aides	53,740 (2,591)	52,440 (3,563)	25,210 (1,664)	2,370 (384)	24,860 (2,940)	14,260 (1,102)	11,350 (720)	450 ! (136)	2,460 ! (763)
Other aides	11,350 (1,251)	11,060 (2,290)	3,480 (374)	1,250 ! (400)	6,330 ! (2,122)	2,040 (281)	1,800 (260)	70 ! (28)	‡ (†)
Guidance counselors	11,780 (506)	11,040 (501)	2,140 (188)	3,590 (288)	5,310 (390)	4,220 (259)	1,390 (146)	2,320 (209)	500 (86)
Librarians/media specialists	12,190 (351)	11,190 (393)	5,230 (228)	1,610 (134)	4,350 (319)	4,300 (164)	3,080 (147)	900 (78)	320 (51)
Library/media center aides	4,150 (261)	2,650 (443)	1,320 (246)	‡ (†)	900 (152)	1,210 (215)	910 (220)	200 (46)	100 ! (30)
Nurses	8,340 (399)	7,600 (372)	3,010 (203)	1,680 (246)	2,900 (279)	2,890 (180)	2,070 (158)	600 (122)	230 (51)
Student support staff[4]	24,920 (1,236)	23,010 (1,629)	5,510 (482)	4,190 (617)	13,300 (1,516)	4,420 (468)	2,210 (230)	1,350 (254)	860 ! (298)
Secretaries/clerical staff	50,360 (1,441)	42,730 (1,382)	15,420 (586)	8,210 (753)	19,090 (1,203)	13,460 (584)	7,080 (208)	5,160 (471)	1,220 (186)
Food service personnel	28,080 (1,019)	25,040 (1,196)	9,620 (549)	5,220 (583)	10,210 (998)	10,470 (625)	6,530 (435)	3,000 (383)	940 (142)
Custodial and maintenance	45,660 (1,469)	38,300 (1,482)	14,450 (614)	7,230 (527)	16,630 (1,369)	12,820 (576)	7,410 (325)	4,210 (393)	1,210 (185)
Other employees[5]	21,140 (2,717)	24,230 (3,023)	7,550 (1,820)	6,420 (1,602)	10,260 (1,975)	6,180 (1,381)	2,570 ! (921)	2,480 (735)	1,120 ! (508)
Students per FTE staff member									
Total FTE staff	**7 (0.1)**	**6 (0.1)**	**7 (0.1)**	**6 (0.3)**	**5 (0.2)**	**8 (0.1)**	**9 (0.1)**	**8 (0.2)**	**6 (0.6)**
Principals	169 (2.9)	170 (3.4)	168 (4.1)	241 (16.1)	153 (6.4)	268 (7.7)	237 (7.2)	409 (28.9)	235 (23.1)
Assistant principals	394 (12.3)	397 (14.5)	512 (30.9)	292 (20.2)	350 (23.5)	579 (28.4)	847 (77.4)	352 (19.1)	394 (69.0)
Other managers	198 (6.0)	173 (6.0)	220 (11.2)	142 (11.0)	146 (9.3)	283 (14.1)	413 (33.4)	189 (15.0)	140 (21.5)
Instruction coordinators	658 (43.1)	587 (54.5)	925 (125.5)	507 (128.0)	416 (64.9)	1,480 (198.3)	2,253 (653.7)	1,022 (226.7)	605 ! (223.6)
Teachers	12 (0.1)	11 (0.2)	12 (0.2)	11 (0.5)	9 (0.2)	15 (0.2)	15 (0.3)	14 (0.3)	11 (0.5)
Teacher aides	96 (4.8)	85 (5.9)	85 (5.0)	308 (57.9)	65 (8.9)	133 (10.6)	110 (6.3)	‡ (†)	‡ (†)
Other aides	455 (52.2)	405 (78.2)	614 (64.7)	‡ (†)	255 ! (80.4)	929 (144.9)	692 (107.9)	‡ (†)	‡ (†)
Guidance counselors	439 (16.1)	406 (15.0)	998 (84.7)	204 (9.3)	304 (16.0)	448 (21.0)	894 (96.6)	220 (7.9)	270 (34.6)
Librarians/media specialists	424 (9.5)	400 (13.0)	408 (15.7)	455 (35.2)	371 (20.6)	440 (17.9)	404 (22.0)	571 (30.4)	421 (46.3)
Library/media center aides	1,243 (75.1)	1,692 (229.0)	1,615 (281.5)	1,696 ! (636.7)	1,803 (329.9)	1,570 (259.6)	1,374 (328.5)	2,512 (665.0)	1,416 ! (510.9)
Nurses	619 (26.1)	590 (31.8)	709 (41.8)	434 (83.1)	556 (55.8)	654 (45.4)	602 (39.8)	860 ! (269.8)	594 (152.5)
Student support staff[4]	207 (9.9)	195 (14.1)	387 (32.3)	174 (26.7)	121 (12.7)	428 (49.0)	562 (61.8)	380 (98.6)	‡ (†)
Secretaries/clerical staff	103 (2.1)	105 (2.6)	138 (4.2)	89 (4.9)	85 (3.5)	141 (4.6)	176 (5.9)	99 (5.2)	112 (13.1)
Food service personnel	184 (6.2)	179 (7.8)	222 (12.1)	140 (15.9)	158 (13.9)	181 (9.1)	191 (12.0)	171 (17.8)	144 (26.5)
Custodial and maintenance	113 (2.8)	117 (3.8)	148 (5.0)	101 (5.4)	97 (6.2)	148 (4.5)	168 (5.8)	122 (6.2)	113 (15.5)
Other employees[5]	244 (29.0)	185 (24.0)	283 (62.5)	114 (32.0)	157 (37.1)	306 (71.6)	‡ (†)	206 ! (66.7)	‡ (†)

See notes at end of table.

Table 205.60. Private elementary and secondary school full-time-equivalent (FTE) staff and student to FTE staff ratios, by orientation of school, school level, and type of staff: 2007–08 and 2011–12—Continued

[Standard errors appear in parentheses]

Type of staff	2011–12							
	Other religious orientation				Nonsectarian			
	Total	Elementary[1]	Secondary[2]	Combined[3]	Total	Elementary[1]	Secondary[2]	Combined[3]
1	11	12	13	14	15	16	17	18
Number of schools	13,040 (550)	6,860 (433)	890 (146)	5,290 (226)	6,430 (68)	2,840 (48)	890 (19)	2,700 (65)
Enrollment (in thousands)	1,605 (84)	610 (38)	117 (31)	878 (78)	982 (67)	279 (22)	103 (19)	600 (62)
Number of FTE staff								
Total FTE staff	254,000 (11,431)	92,610 (6,078)	25,040 (6,246)	136,350 (10,252)	254,770 (14,961)	65,140 (3,983)	31,050 (4,110)	158,590 (13,610)
Principals	11,990 (419)	4,760 (291)	840 (141)	6,390 (350)	7,230 (249)	2,670 (106)	950 (63)	3,610 (215)
Assistant principals	4,000 (300)	1,320 (177)	540 (228)	2,140 (221)	4,020 (338)	1,380 (165)	510 (108)	2,130 (278)
Other managers	8,790 (592)	3,230 (280)	1,120 ! (377)	4,440 (375)	10,470 (734)	3,470 (322)	1,330 (238)	5,670 (620)
Instruction coordinators	2,790 (470)	790 (135)	‡ (†)	1,470 (236)	3,560 (529)	960 (200)	410 ! (125)	2,190 (487)
Teachers	154,650 (6,944)	56,490 (3,508)	13,990 (3,896)	84,170 (6,547)	128,280 (8,136)	36,140 (2,384)	14,400 (2,231)	77,740 (7,508)
Teacher aides	12,200 (1,070)	7,250 (987)	310 ! (132)	4,630 (522)	25,980 (3,077)	6,610 (809)	1,610 (354)	17,760 (2,705)
Other aides	2,990 (585)	780 (158)	320 ! (140)	1,900 (512)	6,020 ! (2,194)	900 (203)	870 ! (384)	4,260 ! (2,068)
Guidance counselors	3,080 (276)	370 (67)	600 ! (183)	2,120 (208)	3,740 (370)	380 (104)	670 (112)	2,690 (328)
Librarians/media specialists	3,630 (240)	1,290 (134)	390 (112)	1,960 (199)	3,260 (283)	870 (98)	320 (63)	2,070 (252)
Library/media center aides	730 ! (330)	240 (63)	‡ (†)	320 (88)	710 (146)	170 ! (60)	‡ (†)	470 (132)
Nurses	1,740 (182)	530 (71)	400 ! (121)	810 (115)	2,960 (310)	410 (74)	690 (190)	1,860 (258)
Student support staff[4]	4,050 (436)	1,550 (245)	810 ! (405)	1,680 (335)	14,540 (1,529)	1,750 (342)	2,030 (448)	10,760 (1,372)
Secretaries/clerical staff	16,000 (966)	5,510 (457)	1,610 ! (593)	8,890 (730)	13,270 (1,017)	2,830 (293)	1,450 (333)	8,980 (900)
Food service personnel	8,290 (813)	2,300 (238)	1,050 (264)	4,940 (718)	6,280 (886)	790 (155)	1,170 ! (392)	4,320 (756)
Custodial and maintenance	13,150 (904)	4,250 (358)	1,410 (323)	7,480 (804)	12,330 (1,101)	2,790 (347)	1,600 (348)	7,930 (998)
Other employees[5]	5,910 (1,690)	‡ (†)	970 ! (450)	2,990 (762)	12,130 (2,194)	3,020 (831)	2,970 ! (1,293)	6,150 (1,810)
Students per FTE staff member								
Total FTE staff	6 (0.2)	7 (0.2)	5 (0.5)	6 (0.2)	4 (0.2)	4 (0.2)	3 (0.4)	4 (0.2)
Principals	134 (5.5)	128 (6.4)	140 (26.9)	137 (8.9)	136 (7.6)	105 (7.9)	108 (21.6)	166 (13.0)
Assistant principals	402 (30.3)	464 (58.8)	217 (49.8)	410 (44.2)	245 (18.1)	203 (23.1)	202 (42.8)	282 (30.8)
Other managers	183 (11.8)	189 (16.7)	104 (17.1)	198 (16.3)	94 (6.1)	80 (5.5)	78 (16.8)	106 (11.1)
Instruction coordinators	575 (88.4)	769 (136.5)	‡ (†)	598 (107.7)	276 (40.2)	291 (64.2)	250 ! (116.8)	274 (66.3)
Teachers	10 (0.3)	11 (0.3)	8 (1.1)	10 (0.4)	8 (0.2)	8 (0.3)	7 (0.7)	8 (0.3)
Teacher aides	132 (12.6)	84 (9.7)	‡ (†)	190 (23.3)	38 (4.8)	42 (5.9)	64 (16.6)	34 (6.1)
Other aides	536 (110.3)	785 (171.8)	‡ (†)	462 ! (141.0)	163 ! (64.9)	310 (82.7)	‡ (†)	‡ (†)
Guidance counselors	520 (36.9)	1,653 (313.9)	195 (46.5)	415 (24.6)	263 (20.3)	743 (219.1)	154 (22.6)	223 (20.8)
Librarians/media specialists	442 (26.3)	475 (37.3)	301 ! (99.7)	448 (39.1)	301 (15.9)	322 (29.6)	319 (44.4)	290 (20.1)
Library/media center aides	2,196 (593.2)	2,512 (626.7)	‡ (†)	2,711 ! (866.0)	‡ (†)	‡ (†)	‡ (†)	1,262 (352.2)
Nurses	922 (107.2)	1,154 (131.9)	143 ! (65.7)	1,080 (160.3)	1,381 (257.5)	679 (160.0)	149 ! (54.5)	322 (46.9)
Student support staff[4]	396 (43.6)	394 (51.9)	‡ (†)	521 (105.2)	331 (34.0)	160 (33.7)	51 (14.7)	56 (7.4)
Secretaries/clerical staff	100 (4.6)	111 (6.7)	73 (11.9)	99 (6.0)	68 (7.4)	99 (7.3)	71 (11.0)	67 (4.6)
Food service personnel	194 (17.2)	265 (27.7)	‡ (†)	178 (21.3)	156 (19.4)	354 (82.1)	88 ! (32.9)	139 (24.1)
Custodial and maintenance	122 (6.7)	143 (10.7)	82 (16.4)	117 (9.1)	80 (4.6)	100 (9.0)	64 (11.3)	76 (6.7)
Other employees[5]	271 (64.9)	311 ! (131.9)	‡ (†)	294 ! (90.0)	81 (18.5)	93 ! (36.7)	‡ (†)	98 ! (45.5)

†Not applicable.
‡Reporting standards not met. The coefficient of variation (CV) for this estimate is 50 percent or greater.
!Interpret data with caution. The coefficient of variation (CV) for this estimate is between 30 and 50 percent.
[1]Includes schools beginning with grade 6 or below and with no grade higher than 8.
[2]Schools with no grade lower than 7.
[3]Schools with grades lower than 7 and higher than 8, as well as schools that do not classify students by grade level.
[4]Includes student support services professional staff, such as school psychologists, social workers, and speech therapists or pathologists.
[5]Includes other employees not identified by function.
NOTE: FTE staff consists of the total number of full-time staff, plus 48 percent of the part-time staff; this percentage was estimated based on the number of hours that part-time staff reported working. Data are based on a sample survey and may not be strictly comparable with data reported elsewhere. Excludes all prekindergarten students in calculations, but includes kindergarten students attending schools that offer first or higher grade. Includes only schools that offer first or higher grade. Detail may not sum to totals because of rounding. Some data have been revised from previously published figures.
SOURCE: U.S. Department of Education, National Center for Education Statistics, Schools and Staffing Survey (SASS), "Private School Data File," 2007–08 and 2011–12. (This table was prepared June 2013.)

Table 205.70. Enrollment and instructional staff in Catholic elementary and secondary schools, by level: Selected years, 1919–20 through 2014–15

School year	Number of schools			Enrollment[1]				Instructional staff[2]		
	Total	Elementary[3]	Secondary	Total	Pre-kindergarten	Elementary	Secondary	Total	Elementary[3]	Secondary
1	2	3	4	5	6	7	8	9	10	11
1919–20........................	8,103	6,551	1,552	1,925,521	([4])	1,795,673	129,848	49,516	41,592	7,924
1929–30........................	10,046	7,923	2,123	2,464,467	([4])	2,222,598	241,869	72,552	58,245	14,307
1939–40........................	10,049	7,944	2,105	2,396,305	([4])	2,035,182	361,123	81,057	60,081	20,976
1949–50........................	10,778	8,589	2,189	3,066,387	([4])	2,560,815	505,572	94,295	66,525	27,770
Fall 1960......................	12,893	10,501	2,392	5,253,791	([4])	4,373,422	880,369	151,902	108,169	43,733
1969–70........................	11,352	9,366	1,986	4,367,000	([4])	3,359,000	1,008,000	195,400 [5]	133,200 [5]	62,200 [5]
1970–71........................	11,350	9,370	1,980	4,363,566	([4])	3,355,478	1,008,088	166,208	112,750	53,458
1974–75........................	10,127	8,437	1,690	3,504,000	([4])	2,602,000	902,000	150,179	100,011	50,168
1975–76........................	9,993	8,340	1,653	3,415,000	([4])	2,525,000	890,000	149,276	99,319	49,957
1979–80........................	9,640	8,100	1,540	3,139,000	([4])	2,293,000	846,000	147,294	97,724	49,570
1980–81........................	9,559	8,043	1,516	3,106,000	([4])	2,269,000	837,000	145,777	96,739	49,038
1981–82........................	9,494	7,996	1,498	3,094,000	([4])	2,266,000	828,000	146,172	96,847	49,325
1982–83........................	9,432	7,950	1,482	3,007,189	([4])	2,211,412	795,777	146,460	97,337	49,123
1983–84........................	9,401	7,937	1,464	2,969,000	([4])	2,179,000	790,000	146,913	98,591	48,322
1984–85........................	9,325	7,876	1,449	2,903,000	([4])	2,119,000	784,000	149,888	99,820	50,068
1985–86........................	9,220	7,790	1,430	2,821,000	([4])	2,061,000	760,000	146,594	96,741	49,853
1986–87........................	9,102	7,693	1,409	2,726,000	([4])	1,998,000	728,000	141,930	93,554	48,376
1987–88........................	8,992	7,601	1,391	2,690,668	67,637	1,942,148	680,883	139,887	93,199	46,688
1988–89........................	8,867	7,505	1,362	2,627,745	76,626	1,911,911	639,208	137,700	93,154	44,546
1989–90........................	8,719	7,395	1,324	2,588,893	90,023	1,892,913	605,957	136,900	94,197	42,703
1990–91........................	8,587	7,291	1,296	2,575,815	100,376	1,883,906	591,533	131,198	91,039	40,159
1991–92........................	8,508	7,239	1,269	2,550,863	107,939	1,856,302	586,622	153,334	109,084	44,250
1992–93........................	8,423	7,174	1,249	2,567,630	122,788	1,860,937	583,905	154,816	109,825	44,991
1993–94........................	8,345	7,114	1,231	2,576,845	132,236	1,859,947	584,662	157,201	112,199	45,002
1994–95........................	8,293	7,055	1,238	2,618,567	143,360	1,877,782	597,425	164,219	117,620	46,599
1995–96........................	8,250	7,022	1,228	2,635,210	144,099	1,884,461	606,650	166,759	118,753	48,006
1996–97........................	8,231	7,005	1,226	2,645,462	148,264	1,885,037	612,161	153,276	107,548	45,728
1997–98........................	8,223	7,004	1,219	2,648,859	150,965	1,879,737	618,157	152,259	105,717	46,542
1998–99........................	8,217	6,990	1,227	2,648,844	152,356	1,876,211	620,277	153,081	105,943	47,138
1999–2000....................	8,144	6,923	1,221	2,653,038	152,622	1,877,236	623,180	157,134	109,404	47,730
2000–01........................	8,146	6,920	1,226	2,647,301	155,742	1,863,682	627,877	160,731	111,937	48,794
2001–02........................	8,114	6,886	1,228	2,616,330	159,869	1,827,319	629,142	155,658	108,485	47,173
2002–03........................	8,000	6,785	1,215	2,553,277	157,250	1,765,893	630,134	163,004	112,884	50,120
2003–04........................	7,955	6,727	1,228	2,484,252	150,422	1,708,501	625,329	162,337	112,303	50,034
2004–05........................	7,799	6,574	1,225	2,420,590	150,905	1,642,868	626,817	160,153	107,764	52,389
2005–06........................	7,589	6,386	1,203	2,325,220	146,327	1,568,687	610,206	152,502 [6]	103,481 [6]	49,021 [6]
2006–07........................	7,498	6,288	1,210	2,320,651	152,429	1,544,695	623,527	159,135	107,682	51,453
2007–08........................	7,378	6,165	1,213	2,270,913	152,980	1,494,979	622,954	160,075	107,217	52,858
2008–09........................	7,248	6,028	1,220	2,192,531	153,325	1,434,949	604,257	157,615	105,518	52,097
2009–10........................	7,094	5,889	1,205	2,119,341	150,262	1,375,982	593,097	154,316	103,460	50,856
2010–11........................	6,980	5,774	1,206	2,065,872	152,846	1,336,560	576,466	151,473	102,365	49,108
2011–12........................	6,841	5,636	1,205	2,031,455	154,282	1,303,028	574,145	151,395	100,365	51,030
2012–13........................	6,685	5,472	1,213	2,001,740	156,233	1,278,010	567,497	151,405	100,633	50,772
2013–14........................	6,594	5,399	1,195	1,974,578	158,537	1,252,397	563,644	151,351	100,244	51,107
2014–15........................	6,568	5,368	1,200	1,939,574	156,380	1,359,969	579,605	150,709	99,388	51,321

[1]Elementary enrollment is for kindergarten through grade 8, and secondary enrollment is for grades 9 through 12.
[2]From 1919–20 through fall 1960, includes part-time teachers. From 1969–70 through 1993–94, excludes part-time teachers. Beginning in 1994–95, reported in full-time equivalents (FTE). Prekindergarten teachers not counted separately but may be included with elementary teachers.
[3]Includes middle schools.
[4]Prekindergarten enrollment was not reported separately, but may be included in elementary enrollment.
[5]Includes estimates for the nonreporting schools.

[6]Excludes the Archdiocese of New Orleans.
NOTE: Data collected by the National Catholic Educational Association and data collected by the National Center for Education Statistics are not directly comparable because survey procedures and definitions differ.
SOURCE: National Catholic Educational Association, *A Statistical Report on Catholic Elementary and Secondary Schools for the Years 1967–68 to 1969–70; A Report on Catholic Schools,* 1970–71 through 1973–74; *A Statistical Report on U.S. Catholic Schools,* 1974–75 through 1980–81; and *United States Catholic Elementary and Secondary Schools,* 1981–82 through 2014–15, retrieved August 11, 2015, from http://www.ncea.org/data-information/catholic-school-data. (This table was prepared August 2015.)

Table 205.80. Private elementary and secondary schools, enrollment, teachers, and high school graduates, by state: Selected years, 2003 through 2013

[Standard errors appear in parentheses]

State	Schools, fall 2013		Enrollment in prekindergarten through grade 12												Teachers,[1] fall 2013		High school graduates, 2012–13	
			Fall 2003		Fall 2005		Fall 2007		Fall 2009		Fall 2011		Fall 2013					
1	2		3		4		5		6		7		8		9		10	
United States......	33,620	(1,665)	6,099,220	(41,219)	6,073,240	(42,446)	5,910,210	(28,363)	5,488,490	(35,857)	5,268,090	(24,908)	5,395,740	(50,342)	441,500	(3,456)	308,770	(3,801)
Alabama..............	400	(37)	99,580	(12,130)	92,280	(5,892)	83,840	(103)	95,570	(11,745)	81,070	(49)	76,400	(295)	6,180	(15)	4,770	(37)
Alaska.................	50	(†)	7,370	(424)	7,500	(1,028)	4,990	(†)	7,510 !	(2,740)	5,170	(†)	5,080	(†)	410	(†)	200	(†)
Arizona...............	340	(†)	75,360	(16,426)	66,840	(†)	64,910	(†)	55,390	(†)	53,120	(229)	55,070	(†)	4,060	(†)	3,010	(†)
Arkansas.............	190	(47)	31,300	(†)	35,390	(5,858)	40,120	(11,961)	28,900	(1,371)	29,930	(1,245)	30,340	(1,496)	2,530	(196)	1,600	(62)
California.............	3,390	(39)	740,460	(8,703)	737,490	(15,529)	703,810	(6,129)	623,150	(4,185)	608,070	(69)	596,160	(3,500)	45,710	(239)	32,700	(†)
Colorado	430	(33)	62,080	(476)	70,770	(1,160)	64,740	(†)	63,720	(3,486)	61,140	(148)	60,690	(4,498)	4,640	(137)	2,520	(50)
Connecticut.........	400	(34)	102,960	(25,024)	76,220	(1,619)	85,150	(9,241)	72,540	(464)	66,320	(142)	72,770	(8,293)	8,560	(1,410)	6,070	(17)
Delaware.............	120	(†)	33,020	(2,649)	29,830	(†)	32,520	(2,701)	26,640	(†)	25,090	(†)	23,640	(†)	2,070	(†)	1,790	(†)
District of Columbia......	90	(9)	23,510	(6,121)	19,880	(†)	19,640	(†)	17,810	(†)	16,950	(†)	19,790	(277)	2,460	(57)	1,820	(†)
Florida................	2,140	(41)	398,720	(14,590)	396,790	(7,429)	391,660	(6,123)	343,990	(1,023)	340,960	(230)	372,790	(2,812)	29,420	(104)	19,440	(73)
Georgia	740	(26)	144,850	(6,527)	152,600	(10,394)	157,430	(9,185)	150,300	(6,251)	138,080	(†)	150,360	(2,250)	13,760	(26)	9,370	(†)
Hawaii................	130	(3)	39,940	(†)	32,810	(†)	37,300	(290)	37,130	(†)	37,530	(†)	33,820	(32)	2,850	(9)	2,610	(†)
Idaho.................	200 !	(66)	12,570	(†)	15,320	(2,518)	24,700 !	(11,608)	18,680	(4,814)	13,670	(193)	18,580	(3,090)	1,360	(190)	670	(†)
Illinois...............	1,550	(8)	316,430	(1,698)	317,940	(4,263)	312,270	(6,638)	289,720	(9,237)	271,030	(1,289)	281,360	(6,026)	19,050	(323)	14,030	(†)
Indiana...............	870	(89)	124,500	(455)	139,370	(17,870)	119,910	(2,284)	120,770	(5,919)	129,120	(12,177)	121,230	(3,928)	8,390	(314)	5,100	(259)
Iowa...................	‡	(†)	53,850	(4,634)	60,960	(8,311)	47,820	(†)	45,160	(†)	63,840	(14,665)	56,150	(9,338)	4,580	(1,097)	2,400	(†)
Kansas...............	360 !	(160)	47,710	(2,151)	47,130	(1,654)	47,780	(2,414)	44,680	(1,668)	43,100	(1,640)	41,520	(3,286)	3,060	(240)	2,180	(†)
Kentucky	470	(83)	82,100	(1,525)	78,880	(1,228)	76,140	(2,074)	70,590	(2,132)	69,410	(12)	74,750	(4,226)	5,490	(166)	4,800	(783)
Louisiana............	420	(52)	155,780	(3,515)	138,270	(525)	137,460	(†)	147,040	(9,890)	125,720	(108)	129,720	(2,606)	9,230	(52)	7,900	(†)
Maine	190	(27)	24,740	(3,629)	20,680	(337)	21,260	(143)	18,310	(†)	18,350	(†)	18,380	(272)	2,040	(120)	2,630	(†)
Maryland.............	770	(36)	172,360	(†)	170,350	(4,201)	165,760	(1,160)	145,690	(160)	137,450	(564)	143,530	(2,030)	13,490	(208)	8,970	(†)
Massachusetts.....	800	(27)	164,390	(6,636)	157,770	(3,273)	151,640	(2,516)	137,110	(1,169)	130,940	(1,596)	134,560	(943)	15,050	(197)	11,020	(†)
Michigan.............	780	(6)	180,080	(†)	166,950	(407)	159,100	(2,047)	153,230	(5,828)	135,580	(544)	141,590	(6,240)	10,150	(296)	9,810	(1,735)
Minnesota...........	500	(†)	106,010	(3,011)	104,730	(3,467)	101,740	(3,903)	89,530	(†)	87,620	(†)	85,260	(†)	6,420	(†)	4,390	(†)
Mississippi..........	310 !	(97)	57,110	(2,981)	57,930	(4,104)	55,270	(†)	54,650	(2,458)	52,060	(†)	50,330	(3,333)	4,170	(386)	3,590	(193)
Missouri..............	‡	(†)	141,530	(9,966)	137,810	(10,580)	125,610	(3,685)	117,970	(2,065)	130,130	(8,715)	139,570	(25,980)	10,860	(1,695)	7,740	(326)
Montana..............	140	(21)	12,510	(2,091)	‡	(†)	15,030 !	(5,465)	10,390	(1,221)	10,550	(†)	10,560	(521)	880	(41)	390	(†)
Nebraska.............	220	(†)	41,650	(†)	42,420	(†)	40,320	(†)	39,040	(†)	40,750	(†)	42,300	(†)	3,000	(†)	2,380	(†)
Nevada...............	140	(†)	23,930	(†)	29,120	(†)	29,820	(2,009)	25,060	(†)	26,130	(†)	21,980	(†)	1,370	(†)	840	(†)
New Hampshire	280	(†)	33,780	(†)	33,220	(†)	30,920	(†)	26,470	(†)	27,350	(†)	26,700	(†)	2,690	(†)	2,460	(†)
New Jersey	1,270	(87)	269,530	(7,577)	256,160	(8,439)	253,250	(5,016)	232,020	(16,536)	210,220	(1,211)	211,150	(4,607)	17,440	(371)	13,100	(†)
New Mexico..........	170	(†)	29,310	(3,928)	25,030	(141)	27,290	(1,388)	23,730	(507)	22,680	(10)	21,750	(†)	2,020	(†)	1,060	(†)
New York.............	1,870	(25)	515,620	(4,071)	510,750	(3,596)	518,850	(7,196)	486,310	(5,211)	487,810	(19,574)	452,380	(901)	41,580	(415)	28,410	(†)
North Carolina......	690	(31)	126,230	(11,439)	117,280	(11,681)	121,660	(2,226)	110,740	(1,851)	119,070	(†)	118,090	(492)	11,050	(31)	7,120	(†)
North Dakota........	50	(†)	6,840	(†)	7,290	(†)	7,430	(†)	7,750	(†)	7,770	(†)	8,290	(†)	680	(†)	380	(†)
Ohio...................	1,160	(97)	270,660	(7,094)	254,530	(9,821)	239,520	(2,741)	246,250	(24,214)	213,990	(3,419)	238,620	(19,487)	16,890	(914)	12,750	(457)
Oklahoma............	170	(†)	34,300	(2,013)	35,350	(1,194)	40,320	(5,032)	34,000	(716)	35,750	(847)	32,740	(†)	2,950	(†)	1,990	(†)
Oregon...............	480	(42)	54,320	(†)	69,620	(14,139)	66,260	(5,188)	56,820	(3,502)	53,200	(†)	58,830	(3,109)	4,310	(213)	3,040	(313)
Pennsylvania........	2,320	(43)	357,580	(3,364)	332,740	(3,918)	324,020	(6,253)	301,640	(5,036)	276,300	(3,668)	253,800	(756)	20,510	(43)	14,760	(†)
Rhode Island........	130	(†)	31,960	(†)	30,600	(†)	28,260	(1,096)	24,940	(†)	25,420	(†)	22,180	(†)	1,970	(†)	1,750	(†)
South Carolina	430	(37)	73,800	(†)	70,240	(1,797)	71,430	(1,043)	62,320	(311)	60,890	(†)	65,350	(4,447)	5,310	(100)	3,010	(†)
South Dakota.......	70	(†)	11,980	(†)	12,700	(†)	12,280	(†)	11,470	(†)	12,490	(†)	9,950	(†)	780	(†)	260	(†)
Tennessee...........	560	(30)	93,390	(†)	105,240	(2,531)	117,540	(12,851)	98,310	(4,176)	92,430	(34)	93,990	(3,210)	8,720	(316)	5,510	(†)
Texas.................	1,740	(97)	271,380	(2,758)	304,170	(20,453)	296,540	(4,132)	313,360	(11,968)	285,320	(2,046)	312,640	(5,896)	26,600	(385)	14,060	(76)
Utah	160	(†)	19,990	(†)	21,220	(†)	20,860	(†)	21,990	(1,558)	18,660	(55)	23,310	(†)	1,720	(†)	1,600	(†)
Vermont..............	110	(†)	12,730	(†)	11,530	(†)	12,600	(232)	10,350	(†)	9,030	(†)	8,890	(†)	1,230	(†)	930	(†)
Virginia...............	910	(11)	131,160	(6,936)	155,220	(14,290)	143,140	(7,988)	128,140	(2,581)	123,780	(82)	131,330	(1,828)	12,080	(143)	6,530	(†)
Washington	800	(124)	101,130	(7,935)	119,640	(13,187)	104,070	(3,054)	94,340	(625)	93,630	(234)	119,730	(17,349)	8,720	(990)	5,960	(967)
West Virginia........	130	(†)	15,300	(†)	16,120	(†)	14,980	(†)	13,860	(†)	13,430	(1)	14,350	(†)	1,230	(†)	780	(†)
Wisconsin............	900	(44)	159,240	(11,743)	142,280	(137)	138,290	(1,597)	130,510	(†)	127,250	(†)	160,650	(32,980)	11,500	(2,244)	8,520 !	(3,248)
Wyoming.............	40	(†)	2,600	(†)	2,310	(†)	2,930	(†)	2,910	(†)	2,740	(†)	2,780	(†)	270	(†)	50	(†)

†Not applicable.
!Interpret data with caution. The coefficient of variation (CVV) for this estimate is between 30 and 50 percent.
‡Reporting standards not met. The coefficient of variation (CV) for this estimate is 50 percent or greater.
[1]Reported in full-time equivalents (FTE). Excludes teachers who teach only prekindergarten students.

NOTE: Includes special education, vocational/technical education, and alternative schools. Tabulation includes schools that offer kindergarten or higher grade. Includes enrollment of students in prekindergarten through grade 12 in schools that offer kindergarten or higher grade. Detail may not sum to totals because of rounding.
SOURCE: U.S. Department of Education, National Center for Education Statistics, Private School Universe Survey (PSS), 2003–04 through 2013–14. (This table was prepared December 2015.)

Table 206.10. Number and percentage of homeschooled students ages 5 through 17 with a grade equivalent of kindergarten through 12th grade, by selected child, parent, and household characteristics: 2003, 2007, and 2012

[Standard errors appear in parentheses]

Selected child, parent, or household characteristic	2003			2007			2012		
	Number of students[1] (in thousands)	Number homeschooled[2] (in thousands)	Percent homeschooled[2]	Number of students[1] (in thousands)	Number homeschooled[2] (in thousands)	Percent homeschooled[2]	Number of students[1] (in thousands)	Number homeschooled[2] (in thousands)	Percent homeschooled[2]
1	2	3	4	5	6	7	8	9	10
Total	50,707 (89.3)	1,096 (92.3)	2.2 (0.18)	51,135 (155.3)	1,520 (118.0)	3.0 (0.23)	51,657 (98.7)	1,773[3] (115.7)	3.4[3] (0.23)
Sex of child									
Male	25,819 (286.8)	569 (61.9)	2.2 (0.24)	26,286 (355.6)	639 (75.1)	2.4 (0.28)	26,620 (318.2)	499 (48.0)	1.9 (0.18)
Female	24,888 (277.7)	527 (58.2)	2.1 (0.23)	24,849 (386.9)	881 (97.4)	3.5 (0.39)	25,037 (314.0)	583 (63.4)	2.3 (0.25)
Race/ethnicity of child									
White	31,584 (187.2)	843 (77.5)	2.7 (0.25)	29,815 (197.9)	1,171 (102.2)	3.9 (0.34)	26,978 (161.7)	893 (81.2)	3.3 (0.30)
Black	7,985 (45.7)	‡ (†)	‡ (†)	7,523 (114.0)	‡ (†)	‡ (†)	7,191 (45.8)	‡ (†)	‡ (†)
Hispanic	8,075 (35.1)	‡ (†)	‡ (†)	9,589 (84.8)	147 (27.5)	1.5 (0.29)	11,514 (55.1)	72 (17.3)	0.6 (0.15)
Asian/Pacific Islander	1,432 (114.5)	‡ (†)	‡ (†)	1,580 (122.9)	‡ (†)	‡ (†)	2,849 (118.4)	‡ (†)	‡ (†)
Other	1,631 (127.7)	‡ (†)	‡ (†)	2,629 (141.0)	‡ (†)	‡ (†)	2,625 (120.0)	‡ (†)	‡ (†)
Grade equivalent[4]									
Kindergarten through grade 5	24,269 (24.7)	472 (55.3)	1.9 (0.23)	23,529 (68.1)	717 (83.8)	3.0 (0.36)	25,642 (141.1)	423 (61.1)	1.6 (0.24)
Kindergarten	3,643 (24.7)	‡ (#)	‡ (†)	3,669 (67.9)	‡ (†)	‡ (†)	5,295 (136.2)	‡ (†)	‡ (†)
Grades 1 through 3	12,098 (#)	214 (33.3)	1.8 (0.28)	11,965 (2.4)	406 (64.5)	3.4 (0.54)	12,101 (135.0)	203 (45.6)	1.7 (0.38)
Grades 4 through 5	8,528 (#)	160 (30.1)	1.9 (0.35)	7,895 (2.1)	197 (41.4)	2.5 (0.52)	8,446 (128.1)	142 (26.1)	1.7 (0.31)
Grades 6 through 8	12,472 (6.5)	302 (44.9)	2.4 (0.36)	12,435 (0.7)	371 (65.3)	3.0 (0.53)	12,006 (139.1)	317 (44.3)	2.6 (0.37)
Grades 9 through 12	13,958 (81.8)	315 (47.0)	2.3 (0.33)	15,161 (129.3)	422 (58.2)	2.8 (0.38)	13,808 (112.0)	341 (42.8)	2.5 (0.31)
Number of children in the household									
One child	8,033 (218.1)	110 (22.3)	1.4 (0.27)	8,463 (227.1)	197 (32.5)	2.3 (0.38)	10,899 (182.6)	179 (21.4)	1.6 (0.19)
Two children	20,530 (319.4)	306 (45.1)	1.5 (0.22)	20,694 (295.3)	414 (67.2)	2.0 (0.32)	20,337 (251.8)	314 (44.5)	1.5 (0.22)
Three or more children	22,144 (362.8)	679 (80.2)	3.1 (0.36)	21,979 (331.0)	909 (102.4)	4.1 (0.46)	20,421 (209.6)	589 (63.5)	2.9 (0.30)
Number of parents in the household									
Two parents	35,936 (315.1)	886 (82.7)	2.5 (0.23)	37,219 (300.7)	1,357 (111.5)	3.6 (0.30)	34,252 (254.7)	908 (79.2)	2.7 (0.23)
One parent	13,260 (319.2)	196 (42.6)	1.5 (0.32)	11,777 (296.8)	118 (28.4)	1.0 (0.24)	15,436 (250.8)	137 (34.5)	0.9 (0.22)
Nonparental guardians	1,511 (100.1)	‡ (†)	‡ (†)	2,139 (203.2)	‡ (†)	‡ (†)	1,968 (112.5)	‡ (†)	‡ (†)
Parent participation in the labor force									
Two parents—both in labor force	25,108 (373.1)	274 (44.1)	1.1 (0.18)	26,055 (318.3)	518 (76.2)	2.0 (0.29)	22,884 (293.3)	295 (41.3)	1.3 (0.18)
Two parents—one in labor force	10,545 (297.2)	594 (73.7)	5.6 (0.67)	10,754 (286.1)	808 (94.3)	7.5 (0.82)	11,581 (275.2)	618 (70.1)	5.3 (0.60)
One parent—in labor force	12,045 (267.9)	174 (39.8)	1.4 (0.33)	10,020 (277.1)	127 (29.5)	1.3 (0.30)	13,083 (238.6)	96 (19.2)	0.7 (0.15)
No parent participation in labor force	3,008 (171.4)	‡ (†)	‡ (†)	4,308 (228.9)	‡ (†)	‡ (†)	4,108 (187.3)	74 ! (26.9)	1.8 ! (0.65)
Highest education level of parents									
High school diploma or less	16,106 (272.3)	269 (51.6)	1.7 (0.32)	14,306 (292.9)	208 (35.5)	1.5 (0.24)	16,762 (83.8)	270 (53.3)	1.6 (0.32)
Vocational/technical or some college	16,068 (323.4)	338 (57.7)	2.1 (0.36)	14,581 (326.5)	559 (77.5)	3.8 (0.52)	15,621 (173.9)	344 (38.4)	2.2 (0.24)
Bachelor's degree/some graduate school	10,849 (275.0)	309 (48.5)	2.8 (0.45)	11,448 (276.5)	444 (64.7)	3.9 (0.57)	11,675 (168.4)	275 (41.9)	2.4 (0.36)
Graduate/professional degree	7,683 (239.5)	180 (41.6)	2.3 (0.55)	10,800 (236.0)	309 (50.0)	2.9 (0.46)	7,599 (34.1)	192 (26.5)	2.5 (0.35)
Household income									
$20,000 or less	9,079 (146.2)	164 (38.9)	1.8 (0.43)	8,488 (201.2)	186 (42.1)	2.2 (0.50)	7,593 (39.6)	59 (12.1)	0.8 (0.16)
$20,001 to $50,000	16,515 (336.1)	430 (60.3)	2.6 (0.36)	13,648 (306.1)	420 (59.8)	3.1 (0.42)	13,973 (84.7)	321 (44.2)	2.3 (0.32)
$50,001 to $75,000	10,961 (282.0)	264 (51.1)	2.4 (0.46)	10,289 (232.9)	414 (58.8)	4.0 (0.57)	9,406 (23.9)	278 (40.8)	3.0 (0.44)
$75,001 to $100,000	6,432 (238.0)	169 (42.9)	2.6 (0.66)	6,899 (210.8)	264 (57.2)	3.8 (0.83)	6,916 (29.5)	211 (42.4)	3.0 (0.61)
Over $100,000	7,718 (212.6)	‡ (†)	‡ (†)	11,891 (228.2)	236 (57.5)	2.0 (0.49)	13,769 (56.5)	214 (34.4)	1.6 (0.25)
Locale									
City	— (†)	—	—	15,998 (292.3)	327 (40.4)	2.0 (0.26)	15,191 (236.0)	226 (28.0)	1.5 (0.18)
Suburb	— (†)	—	—	18,988 (291.3)	503 (78.8)	2.6 (0.41)	19,356 (330.6)	303 (44.6)	1.6 (0.22)
Town	— (†)	—	—	5,574 (209.4)	168 (37.1)	3.0 (0.65)	4,839 (197.9)	112 (30.8)	2.3 (0.63)
Rural	— (†)	—	—	10,576 (110.9)	523 (75.9)	4.9 (0.71)	12,271 (249.1)	441 (65.0)	3.6 (0.52)

—Not available.
†Not applicable.
#Rounds to zero.
‡Reporting standards not met (too few cases for a reliable estimate).
[1]Refers to all students in public and private schools and homeschooled students.
[2]Numbers and percentages of homeschoolers exclude students who were enrolled in school for more than 25 hours a week or who were homeschooled only due to a temporary illness.
[3]The National Center for Education Statistics uses a statistical adjustment for estimates of total homeschoolers in 2012. For more information about this adjustment, please see *Homeschooling in the United States: 2012* (NCES 2015-019, forthcoming). All other estimates about homeschoolers do not use a statistical adjustment.
[4]Students whose grade equivalent was "ungraded" were excluded from the grade analysis. The percentage of students with an "ungraded" grade equivalent was 0.02 percent in 2003 and 2007. There were no students with an "ungraded" grade equivalent in 2012.

NOTE: While National Household Education Surveys Program (NHES) administrations prior to 2012 were administered via telephone with an interviewer, NHES:2012 used self-administered paper-and-pencil questionnaires that were mailed to respondents. Measurable differences in estimates between 2012 and prior years could reflect actual changes in the population, or the changes could be due to the mode change from telephone to mail. Race categories exclude persons of Hispanic ethnicity. Detail may not sum to totals because of rounding. Some data have been revised from previously published figures.
SOURCE: U.S. Department of Education, National Center for Education Statistics, Parent and Family Involvement in Education Survey of the National Household Education Surveys Program (PFI-NHES:2003, 2007, and 2012). (This table was prepared November 2014.)

Table 206.20. Percentage distribution of students ages 5 through 17 attending kindergarten through 12th grade, by school type or participation in homeschooling and selected child, parent, and household characteristics: 1999, 2003, and 2007

[Standard errors appear in parentheses]

Selected child, parent, or household characteristic	1999 Public school — Assigned	1999 Public school — Chosen	1999 Private school	1999 Homeschooled[1]	2003 Public school — Assigned	2003 Public school — Chosen	2003 Private school	2003 Homeschooled[1]	2007 Public school — Assigned	2007 Public school — Chosen	2007 Private school	2007 Homeschooled[1]
1	2	3	4	5	6	7	8	9	10	11	12	13
Total	74.1 (0.45)	14.3 (0.33)	10.0 (0.28)	1.7 (0.14)	72.1 (0.57)	15.0 (0.41)	10.8 (0.39)	2.2 (0.18)	70.6 (0.70)	15.0 (0.55)	11.4 (0.45)	2.9 (0.23)
Sex of child												
Male	74.8 (0.60)	13.9 (0.44)	9.7 (0.34)	1.6 (0.17)	72.1 (0.70)	15.0 (0.56)	10.7 (0.48)	2.2 (0.24)	70.7 (1.05)	15.3 (0.79)	11.5 (0.73)	2.4 (0.28)
Female	73.4 (0.61)	14.6 (0.45)	10.3 (0.41)	1.8 (0.19)	72.1 (0.78)	14.9 (0.54)	10.8 (0.51)	2.1 (0.23)	70.5 (0.88)	14.7 (0.64)	11.2 (0.54)	3.5 (0.39)
Race/ethnicity of child												
White	75.0 (0.54)	11.2 (0.35)	11.8 (0.39)	2.0 (0.19)	72.7 (0.67)	12.4 (0.47)	12.2 (0.48)	2.7 (0.25)	69.9 (0.80)	12.0 (0.46)	14.2 (0.61)	3.9 (0.34)
Black	70.2 (1.24)	22.6 (1.22)	6.2 (0.47)	1.0 (0.31)	66.6 (1.49)	23.4 (1.45)	8.6 (0.85)	1.3 ! (0.42)	68.4 (2.30)	23.0 (2.20)	7.8 (1.33)	0.8 ! (0.28)
Hispanic	76.0 (1.02)	17.6 (0.91)	5.2 (0.40)	1.1 (0.25)	77.2 (1.17)	15.0 (0.99)	7.1 (0.66)	0.7 ! (0.26)	74.6 (1.41)	17.5 (1.25)	6.3 (0.57)	1.5 (0.29)
Other	69.5 (2.20)	17.6 (1.99)	11.0 (1.35)	1.9 ! (0.65)	67.1 (2.59)	18.7 (1.94)	11.3 (1.61)	3.0 ! (1.02)	70.4 (2.23)	16.7 (1.79)	9.4 (1.12)	3.3 (0.86)
Disability status of child as reported by parent												
Has a disability	74.8 (0.93)	15.3 (0.78)	8.0 (0.49)	1.8 (0.27)	72.4 (1.12)	16.2 (0.75)	9.2 (0.70)	2.2 (0.35)	72.7 (1.35)	14.0 (0.91)	10.5 (0.96)	2.6 (0.48)
Does not have a disability	73.9 (0.51)	14.0 (0.36)	10.5 (0.34)	1.7 (0.16)	72.0 (0.67)	14.5 (0.51)	11.3 (0.44)	2.1 (0.21)	69.9 (0.76)	15.3 (0.63)	11.7 (0.48)	3.1 (0.28)
Grade equivalent[2]												
Kindergarten through 5th grade	71.5 (0.61)	15.1 (0.43)	11.6 (0.41)	1.8 (0.20)	70.1 (0.70)	16.2 (0.56)	11.8 (0.53)	1.9 (0.23)	68.5 (1.16)	16.2 (1.04)	12.2 (0.69)	3.0 (0.36)
Kindergarten	66.2 (1.67)	15.4 (1.13)	15.9 (1.29)	2.4 (0.52)	69.0 (1.50)	15.5 (1.18)	12.8 (1.21)	2.7 (0.64)	66.4 (2.20)	14.7 (1.60)	15.8 (1.61)	3.1 ! (0.96)
Grades 1 through 3	72.2 (0.87)	15.3 (0.67)	10.9 (0.53)	1.6 (0.29)	70.0 (1.18)	16.2 (0.96)	12.1 (0.73)	1.8 (0.28)	68.4 (1.68)	15.9 (1.63)	12.3 (0.93)	3.4 (0.54)
Grades 4 through 5	72.9 (1.17)	14.6 (0.79)	10.7 (0.77)	1.7 (0.28)	70.7 (1.12)	16.5 (0.96)	10.9 (0.76)	1.9 (0.35)	69.7 (1.44)	17.5 (1.34)	10.3 (1.08)	2.5 (0.52)
Grades 6 through 8	77.4 (0.79)	11.5 (0.65)	9.5 (0.47)	1.6 (0.24)	73.3 (1.03)	14.1 (0.81)	10.2 (0.59)	2.4 (0.36)	74.4 (1.44)	11.6 (0.81)	11.0 (1.14)	2.9 (0.52)
Grades 9 through 12	75.7 (0.75)	15.1 (0.60)	7.5 (0.44)	1.7 (0.24)	74.6 (0.97)	13.6 (0.76)	9.5 (0.63)	2.3 (0.33)	70.8 (1.07)	15.9 (0.84)	10.5 (0.75)	2.8 (0.38)
Number of parents in the household												
Two parents	74.5 (0.54)	12.0 (0.35)	11.5 (0.37)	2.1 (0.21)	71.8 (0.67)	13.6 (0.51)	12.1 (0.47)	2.5 (0.23)	69.5 (0.73)	13.8 (0.49)	12.9 (0.52)	3.6 (0.30)
One parent	73.5 (0.78)	18.2 (0.55)	7.3 (0.47)	0.9 (0.16)	72.9 (1.09)	18.0 (0.98)	7.6 (0.67)	1.5 (0.32)	73.6 (1.39)	17.2 (1.14)	8.1 (1.18)	1.0 (0.24)
Nonparental guardians	71.6 (2.70)	21.9 (2.72)	5.1 (0.84)	‡ (†)	73.2 (3.05)	20.1 (2.59)	5.8 (1.36)	‡ (†)	72.2 (5.91)	23.0 (6.19)	2.6 (0.74)	2.1 ! (0.81)
Highest education level of parents												
Less than a high school diploma	79.1 (1.38)	18.0 (1.46)	2.7 (0.51)	0.2 ! (0.10)	76.9 (2.06)	18.9 (1.76)	2.9 ! (1.18)	‡ (†)	83.3 (2.03)	12.7 (1.53)	3.5 ! (1.81)	0.5 ! (0.23)
High school diploma or GED	79.0 (0.84)	14.3 (0.72)	5.6 (0.44)	1.1 (0.19)	77.8 (1.01)	15.5 (0.89)	4.9 (0.45)	1.8 (0.34)	78.8 (1.90)	15.1 (1.84)	4.1 (0.63)	1.9 (0.36)
Vocational/technical or some college	74.7 (0.72)	14.7 (0.63)	7.7 (0.40)	1.9 (0.24)	74.0 (0.97)	15.5 (0.74)	8.3 (0.58)	2.1 (0.36)	72.0 (1.03)	15.3 (0.99)	8.8 (0.70)	3.8 (0.52)
Bachelor's degree/some graduate school	68.6 (1.06)	13.2 (0.75)	15.8 (0.75)	2.4 (0.37)	67.1 (1.00)	13.2 (0.84)	16.8 (0.90)	2.8 (0.45)	66.8 (1.24)	14.8 (1.02)	14.3 (0.87)	4.1 (0.57)
Graduate/professional degree	65.0 (1.14)	12.4 (0.77)	20.2 (0.91)	2.4 (0.54)	63.6 (1.50)	13.5 (1.14)	20.5 (1.28)	2.3 (0.55)	59.2 (1.37)	15.9 (1.01)	22.4 (1.22)	2.5 (0.41)
Poverty status of household												
Below poverty	74.8 (1.16)	19.2 (1.06)	4.3 (0.50)	1.7 (0.34)	76.3 (1.28)	17.7 (1.10)	3.7 (0.67)	2.3 (0.58)	76.6 (2.48)	17.8 (2.35)	3.7 (1.04)	1.8 (0.40)
Between poverty and 200 percent of poverty	76.8 (0.79)	15.3 (0.70)	5.9 (0.48)	2.0 (0.31)	75.1 (1.17)	16.0 (0.87)	5.9 (0.69)	3.1 (0.50)	74.4 (1.45)	16.2 (1.15)	5.2 (0.69)	4.1 (0.69)
At or above 200 percent of poverty	72.5 (0.57)	11.8 (0.34)	14.0 (0.47)	1.6 (0.18)	69.8 (0.70)	13.8 (0.54)	14.6 (0.54)	1.8 (0.21)	67.6 (0.75)	13.8 (0.48)	15.7 (0.54)	2.9 (0.30)
Urbanicity												
City	— (†)	— (†)	— (†)	— (†)	— (†)	— (†)	— (†)	— (†)	61.7 (1.46)	22.1 (1.38)	14.2 (0.97)	2.0 (0.26)
Suburb	— (†)	— (†)	— (†)	— (†)	— (†)	— (†)	— (†)	— (†)	72.7 (0.95)	11.8 (0.67)	12.8 (0.68)	2.6 (0.41)
Town	— (†)	— (†)	— (†)	— (†)	— (†)	— (†)	— (†)	— (†)	77.3 (1.77)	12.4 (1.43)	7.1 (0.75)	3.0 (0.66)
Rural	— (†)	— (†)	— (†)	— (†)	— (†)	— (†)	— (†)	— (†)	76.7 (1.36)	11.5 (1.03)	6.8 (1.09)	4.9 (0.71)
Region												
Northeast	72.8 (1.06)	13.4 (0.78)	12.6 (0.63)	1.1 (0.30)	71.6 (1.42)	11.9 (1.02)	14.6 (1.03)	1.8 ! (0.58)	72.5 (1.42)	11.8 (1.11)	13.6 (0.98)	2.1 (0.47)
South	75.4 (0.65)	13.2 (0.52)	9.3 (0.43)	2.0 (0.28)	74.2 (0.88)	14.9 (0.72)	8.3 (0.58)	2.6 (0.39)	71.9 (1.15)	13.6 (0.96)	10.8 (0.58)	3.7 (0.46)
Midwest	74.3 (0.80)	13.4 (0.72)	10.9 (0.61)	1.4 (0.24)	69.9 (1.27)	14.4 (0.92)	13.8 (1.04)	2.0 (0.37)	70.8 (1.54)	14.2 (1.06)	12.8 (1.14)	2.2 (0.53)
West	72.7 (0.95)	17.7 (0.73)	7.5 (0.49)	2.0 (0.34)	71.9 (1.07)	17.9 (0.97)	8.3 (0.59)	2.0 (0.34)	67.0 (1.40)	20.3 (1.17)	9.4 (0.75)	3.1 (0.42)

—Not available.
†Not applicable.
!Interpret data with caution. The coefficient of variation (CV) for this estimate is between 30 and 50 percent.
‡Reporting standards not met. The coefficient of variation (CV) for this estimate is 50 percent or greater.
[1]Excludes students who were enrolled in school for more than 25 hours a week; also excluded in 1999 and 2003 are students who were homeschooled only due to a temporary illness and, in 2007, students who were homeschooled primarily due to a temporary illness.
[2]Students whose grade equivalent was "ungraded" were excluded from the grade analysis. The percentage of students with an "ungraded" grade equivalent was 0.03 percent in 1999 and 0.02 percent in 2003 and 2007.
NOTE: Data are based on parent reports. Race categories exclude persons of Hispanic ethnicity. Detail may not sum to totals because of rounding. Some data have been revised from previously published figures.
SOURCE: U.S. Department of Education, National Center for Education Statistics, Parent Survey (Parent:1999) and Parent and Family Involvement in Education Survey (PFI:2003 and PFI:2007) of the National Household Education Surveys Program. (This table was prepared July 2010.)

Table 206.30. Percentage distribution of students enrolled in grades 1 through 12, by public school type and charter status, private school type, and selected child and household characteristics: 2012

[Standard errors appear in parentheses]

Selected child or household characteristic and public school type	Total		Public school										Private school					
			Total		Assigned or chosen type[1]				Traditional or charter status				Total		Religious		Nonsectarian	
					Assigned		Chosen		Traditional[2]		Charter							
1	2		3		4		5		6		7		8		9		10	
Total	100.0	(†)	100.0	(†)	100.0	(†)	100.0	(†)	100.0	(†)	100.0	(†)	100.0	(†)	100.0	(†)	100.0	(†)
Sex of child																		
Male	51.6	(0.60)	51.5	(0.63)	51.9	(0.68)	50.2	(1.48)	51.7	(0.63)	45.4	(3.46)	52.7	(1.89)	52.8	(2.24)	51.8	(3.71)
Female	48.4	(0.60)	48.5	(0.63)	48.1	(0.68)	49.8	(1.48)	48.3	(0.63)	54.6	(3.46)	47.3	(1.89)	47.2	(2.24)	48.2	(3.71)
Race/ethnicity of child																		
White	52.3	(0.39)	51.3	(0.43)	53.1	(0.49)	40.2	(1.36)	51.9	(0.43)	31.5	(2.85)	65.0	(1.77)	63.3	(1.94)	72.8	(3.35)
Black	14.4	(0.19)	14.7	(0.24)	13.5	(0.31)	21.6	(1.19)	14.3	(0.26)	29.9	(3.24)	10.2	(1.05)	11.0	(1.18)	6.6	(1.82)
Hispanic	22.7	(0.26)	23.3	(0.28)	22.7	(0.37)	27.4	(1.21)	23.1	(0.31)	30.8	(3.13)	15.2	(1.38)	16.8	(1.57)	7.6	(1.93)
Asian/Pacific Islander	5.2	(0.22)	5.2	(0.23)	5.1	(0.25)	5.5	(0.68)	5.2	(0.23)	5.4 !	(1.83)	5.2	(0.62)	5.1	(0.73)	6.0	(1.40)
Other	5.4	(0.26)	5.5	(0.27)	5.5	(0.30)	5.3	(0.55)	5.6	(0.28)	2.4 !	(0.84)	4.4	(0.70)	3.8	(0.79)	7.0	(1.95)
Disability status of child as reported by parent																		
Has a disability	17.3	(0.46)	17.7	(0.47)	17.7	(0.55)	17.7	(0.98)	17.8	(0.49)	15.5	(2.04)	12.2	(1.16)	11.1	(1.14)	17.7	(2.78)
Does not have a disability	82.7	(0.46)	82.3	(0.47)	82.3	(0.55)	82.3	(0.98)	82.2	(0.49)	84.5	(2.04)	87.8	(1.16)	88.9	(1.14)	82.3	(2.78)
Grade level																		
Grades 1 through 5	43.4	(0.26)	43.2	(0.32)	43.5	(0.40)	40.6	(1.19)	43.0	(0.33)	47.0	(3.65)	46.7	(1.73)	47.2	(1.84)	44.0	(3.84)
Grades 6 through 8	25.2	(0.33)	25.4	(0.34)	25.2	(0.42)	27.2	(1.05)	25.2	(0.36)	32.5	(3.12)	22.7	(1.42)	22.7	(1.60)	23.0	(3.26)
Grades 9 through 12	31.3	(0.23)	31.4	(0.30)	31.3	(0.34)	32.2	(1.13)	31.7	(0.30)	20.5	(2.41)	30.6	(1.74)	30.1	(1.84)	33.0	(3.77)
Number of parents in the household																		
Two parents	65.7	(0.50)	64.6	(0.54)	65.0	(0.62)	61.5	(1.29)	64.8	(0.55)	57.8	(3.61)	78.9	(1.18)	79.0	(1.33)	78.7	(2.54)
One parent	30.6	(0.49)	31.6	(0.53)	31.2	(0.63)	34.3	(1.37)	31.4	(0.55)	38.0	(3.61)	18.4	(1.19)	18.3	(1.35)	19.0	(2.40)
Nonparental guardians	3.8	(0.18)	3.8	(0.20)	3.8	(0.22)	4.2	(0.53)	3.8	(0.20)	4.2 !	(1.31)	2.7	(0.47)	2.8	(0.57)	2.3 !	(0.89)
Highest education level of parents																		
Less than a high school diploma	11.7	(0.21)	12.3	(0.23)	12.1	(0.28)	12.4	(1.06)	12.3	(0.24)	12.3	(3.08)	4.8	(1.09)	4.9	(1.11)	‡	(†)
High school diploma or GED	20.3	(0.22)	21.2	(0.26)	21.9	(0.33)	18.1	(1.26)	21.0	(0.27)	25.8	(3.53)	9.8	(1.30)	10.5	(1.44)	6.6 !	(2.24)
Vocational/technical or some college	30.4	(0.39)	31.3	(0.42)	31.6	(0.46)	30.4	(1.25)	31.4	(0.43)	26.4	(2.75)	20.0	(1.44)	20.7	(1.69)	16.8	(2.68)
Bachelor's degree/some graduate school	22.7	(0.34)	21.6	(0.35)	21.1	(0.41)	23.9	(1.27)	21.6	(0.36)	22.9	(2.72)	36.1	(1.68)	37.6	(1.92)	29.4	(3.97)
Graduate/professional degree	14.8	(0.13)	13.6	(0.17)	13.3	(0.21)	15.3	(0.65)	13.7	(0.18)	12.6	(1.82)	29.3	(1.38)	26.3	(1.48)	43.2	(3.30)
Poverty status of household[3]																		
Poor	18.6	(0.29)	19.5	(0.32)	19.6	(0.42)	19.3	(1.08)	19.4	(0.34)	25.2	(3.62)	7.1	(1.07)	6.9	(1.24)	8.1 !	(2.82)
Near-poor	22.1	(0.39)	23.0	(0.43)	23.1	(0.49)	22.9	(1.00)	22.9	(0.44)	27.7	(3.14)	10.7	(1.23)	11.2	(1.39)	8.0	(1.93)
Nonpoor	59.3	(0.30)	57.4	(0.37)	57.3	(0.42)	57.9	(1.21)	57.8	(0.39)	47.2	(3.19)	82.2	(1.54)	81.8	(1.71)	83.9	(3.18)
Locale																		
City	29.0	(0.49)	28.5	(0.48)	25.3	(0.49)	45.9	(1.41)	27.7	(0.46)	51.6	(3.10)	34.8	(1.81)	33.8	(2.03)	39.2	(3.41)
Suburban	38.0	(0.63)	37.7	(0.65)	38.5	(0.71)	33.8	(1.41)	37.9	(0.64)	30.8	(3.45)	41.6	(1.44)	42.8	(1.75)	35.7	(3.36)
Town	9.4	(0.34)	9.8	(0.36)	10.6	(0.43)	5.9	(0.82)	9.9	(0.37)	5.2 !	(2.08)	5.0	(0.65)	4.8	(0.72)	5.9	(1.63)
Rural	23.6	(0.49)	24.0	(0.50)	25.6	(0.57)	14.4	(1.03)	24.4	(0.50)	12.3	(2.18)	18.7	(1.50)	18.5	(1.68)	19.2	(2.99)
Region																		
Northeast	17.5	(0.39)	17.0	(0.39)	18.2	(0.44)	10.0	(0.79)	17.1	(0.41)	13.1	(2.05)	24.7	(1.53)	23.9	(1.88)	28.4	(4.04)
South	35.9	(0.57)	36.3	(0.60)	36.2	(0.69)	37.1	(1.36)	36.5	(0.61)	30.3	(3.20)	30.6	(1.52)	28.6	(1.69)	39.6	(3.32)
Midwest	22.2	(0.53)	22.1	(0.54)	22.4	(0.58)	20.0	(1.16)	22.0	(0.53)	23.8	(3.26)	23.2	(1.61)	26.6	(1.93)	7.2	(1.73)
West	24.4	(0.51)	24.7	(0.55)	23.2	(0.57)	33.0	(1.32)	24.4	(0.55)	32.8	(3.01)	21.5	(1.48)	20.8	(1.67)	24.8	(3.71)
Public school type[1]																		
Assigned	84.6 [4]	(0.46)	84.6	(0.46)	100.0	(†)	†	(†)	87.3	(0.40)	†	(†)	†	(†)	†	(†)	†	(†)
Chosen	15.4 [4]	(0.46)	15.4	(0.46)	†	(†)	100.0	(†)	12.7	(0.40)	100.0	(†)	†	(†)	†	(†)	†	(†)

†Not applicable.

!Interpret data with caution. The coefficient of variation (CV) for this estimate is between 30 and 50 percent.

‡Reporting standards not met. The coefficient of variation (CV) for this estimate is 50 percent or greater.

[1]In 160 cases, questions about whether the school was assigned were not asked because parents reported the school as a private school, and it was only later found to be a public school. These cases were excluded from the analysis of assigned versus chosen public schools, but were included in the charter school analysis as well as in the public school and overall totals.

[2]Includes all types of public noncharter schools.

[3]Poor children are those whose family incomes were below the Census Bureau's poverty threshold in the year prior to data collection; near-poor children are those whose family incomes ranged from the poverty threshold to 199 percent of the poverty threshold; and nonpoor children are those whose family incomes were at or above 200 percent of the poverty threshold. The poverty threshold is a dollar amount that varies depending on a family's size and composition and is updated annually to account for inflation. In 2011, for example, the poverty threshold for a family of four with two children was $22,811. Survey respondents are asked to select the range within which their income falls, rather than giving the exact amount of their income; therefore, the measure of poverty status is an approximation.

[4]Includes only students enrolled in public schools.

NOTE: Data exclude homeschooled children. Race categories exclude persons of Hispanic ethnicity. Detail may not sum to totals because of rounding.

SOURCE: U.S. Department of Education, National Center for Education Statistics, Parent and Family Involvement in Education Survey of the National Household Education Surveys Program (PFI-NHES:2012). (This table was prepared September 2014.)

Table 206.40. Percentage of students enrolled in grades 1 through 12 whose parents reported having public school choice, considered other schools, reported current school was their first choice, or moved to their current neighborhood for the public school, by school type and selected child and household characteristics: 2012

[Standard errors appear in parentheses]

School type and selected child or household characteristic	Public choice available		Considered other schools		School was parent's first choice		Moved to neighborhood for public school[1]	
1	2		3		4		5	
Total..	37.3	(0.54)	30.5	(0.51)	78.6	(0.43)	18.6	(0.54)
School type[2]								
Public, assigned...	27.8	(0.58)	24.2	(0.59)	77.5	(0.50)	20.3	(0.64)
Public, chosen[3]...	100.0	(†)	53.1	(1.49)	79.3	(1.05)	9.8	(0.97)
Private, religious..	20.7	(1.57)	46.5	(1.92)	87.2	(1.51)	†	(†)
Private, nonsectarian...	21.2	(3.58)	61.5	(3.63)	88.9	(2.37)	†	(†)
Sex of child								
Male...	36.3	(0.78)	29.9	(0.78)	79.0	(0.56)	17.6	(0.67)
Female...	38.5	(0.71)	31.2	(0.81)	78.1	(0.71)	19.7	(0.79)
Race/ethnicity of child								
White..	34.2	(0.64)	26.5	(0.67)	83.4	(0.60)	20.5	(0.60)
Black..	43.2	(1.56)	40.1	(1.56)	69.4	(1.69)	15.0	(1.70)
Hispanic...	38.9	(1.25)	31.5	(1.20)	74.3	(1.04)	16.5	(1.33)
Asian/Pacific Islander..	42.8	(2.51)	33.2	(2.50)	77.2	(2.12)	24.4	(1.75)
Other..	40.5	(2.33)	36.4	(2.55)	75.6	(1.99)	14.9	(1.55)
Disability status of child as reported by parent								
Has a disability..	37.8	(1.25)	32.5	(1.32)	75.4	(1.15)	18.3	(1.22)
Does not have a disability	37.2	(0.56)	30.1	(0.55)	79.2	(0.50)	18.7	(0.62)
Grade level								
Grades 1 through 5..	35.0	(0.87)	30.9	(0.94)	78.4	(0.81)	18.7	(0.86)
Grades 6 through 8..	39.0	(1.11)	30.3	(0.92)	78.1	(0.83)	19.4	(1.05)
Grades 9 through 12..	39.2	(0.86)	30.1	(0.80)	79.1	(0.73)	17.9	(1.06)
Number of parents in the household								
Two parents...	37.2	(0.62)	30.7	(0.61)	81.3	(0.45)	19.2	(0.57)
One parent...	37.4	(1.01)	30.4	(0.97)	73.1	(1.04)	18.5	(1.08)
Nonparental guardians	38.5	(2.63)	27.9	(2.67)	75.3	(2.87)	10.6	(1.74)
Highest education level of parents								
Less than a high school diploma	37.3	(1.71)	25.8	(1.63)	75.7	(1.65)	16.3	(1.89)
High school diploma or GED	34.7	(1.45)	23.9	(1.46)	77.9	(1.10)	13.5	(1.03)
Vocational/technical or some college......................	37.5	(0.90)	28.5	(0.74)	75.3	(0.87)	17.0	(0.85)
Bachelor's degree/some graduate school...............	38.4	(1.17)	35.1	(1.22)	81.9	(0.85)	21.6	(0.97)
Graduate/professional degree	39.0	(0.93)	40.2	(0.99)	83.3	(0.67)	27.8	(0.84)
Poverty status of household[4]								
Poor	37.7	(1.35)	26.8	(1.32)	72.5	(1.18)	14.8	(1.06)
Near-poor...	39.2	(1.14)	28.4	(1.13)	76.6	(1.01)	14.6	(0.92)
Nonpoor...	36.5	(0.67)	32.4	(0.75)	81.2	(0.56)	21.5	(0.69)
Locale								
City..	48.8	(1.07)	39.7	(1.05)	73.6	(0.77)	17.0	(0.80)
Suburban	32.0	(0.88)	30.0	(0.72)	78.1	(0.80)	22.5	(0.90)
Town..	33.1	(1.91)	19.6	(1.46)	82.2	(1.33)	14.0	(1.77)
Rural..	33.6	(1.15)	24.3	(1.02)	84.0	(0.88)	16.4	(0.96)
Region								
Northeast...	22.4	(1.01)	29.5	(1.08)	76.5	(1.13)	18.4	(1.10)
South...	34.2	(0.93)	28.9	(0.90)	78.3	(0.79)	18.3	(0.96)
Midwest..	41.8	(1.01)	28.5	(1.24)	80.1	(1.08)	21.1	(1.13)
West...	48.6	(1.21)	35.3	(0.98)	79.2	(0.80)	17.1	(0.89)

†Not applicable.

[1]This column shows percentages of public school students only. Private school students are excluded from the analysis.

[2]There were 160 cases excluded from the school type analysis because parents reported the school as a private school when it was later found to be a public school, and therefore questions about whether the school was assigned were not asked.

[3]Students who attended chosen public schools were automatically coded as yes for whether or not their district allowed public school choice.

[4]Poor children are those whose family incomes were below the Census Bureau's poverty threshold in the year prior to data collection; near-poor children are those whose family incomes ranged from the poverty threshold to 199 percent of the poverty threshold; and nonpoor children are those whose family incomes were at or above 200 per-

cent of the poverty threshold. The poverty threshold is a dollar amount that varies depending on a family's size and composition and is updated annually to account for inflation. In 2011, for example, the poverty threshold for a family of four with two children was $22,811. Survey respondents are asked to select the range within which their income falls, rather than giving the exact amount of their income; therefore, the measure of poverty status is an approximation.

NOTE: Data exclude homeschooled children. Race categories exclude persons of Hispanic ethnicity.

SOURCE: U.S. Department of Education, National Center for Education Statistics, Parent and Family Involvement in Education Survey of the National Household Education Surveys Program (PFI-NHES:2012). (This table was prepared September 2014.)

Table 206.50. Percentage of students enrolled in grades 3 through 12 whose parents were satisfied or dissatisfied with various aspects of their children's schools, by public and private school type: 2003, 2007, and 2012

[Standard errors appear in parentheses]

Parent satisfaction	2003 Public school Assigned	2003 Public school Chosen	2003 Private school Religious	2003 Private school Nonsectarian	2007 Public school Assigned	2007 Public school Chosen	2007 Private school Religious	2007 Private school Nonsectarian	2012 Public school Assigned	2012 Public school Chosen	2012 Private school Religious	2012 Private school Nonsectarian
1	2	3	4	5	6	7	8	9	10	11	12	13
Very satisfied												
School	53.7 (0.79)	64.2 (1.72)	77.0 (2.01)	71.7 (3.65)	52.1 (0.96)	62.1 (2.34)	78.7 (1.97)	78.6 (3.57)	52.5 (0.58)	56.2 (1.30)	80.0 (1.44)	77.8 (3.36)
Teachers	56.4 (0.74)	64.5 (1.62)	72.5 (1.88)	70.3 (3.68)	56.6 (0.88)	63.5 (2.32)	76.3 (1.96)	74.0 (3.67)	52.3 (0.65)	51.7 (1.48)	72.1 (1.80)	76.3 (3.23)
Academic standards	54.5 (0.78)	63.8 (1.75)	79.5 (1.77)	77.3 (3.32)	56.3 (0.84)	65.9 (2.09)	81.9 (1.70)	78.8 (3.81)	52.7 (0.58)	58.8 (1.48)	79.2 (1.76)	83.5 (2.89)
Order and discipline	55.9 (0.78)	64.8 (1.81)	81.2 (1.81)	80.5 (3.23)	55.0 (0.97)	60.9 (2.21)	82.7 (1.95)	80.5 (3.15)	52.4 (0.64)	57.9 (1.64)	82.2 (1.49)	79.8 (3.68)
Staff interaction with parents	— (†)	— (†)	— (†)	—	47.7 (1.00)	56.7 (2.24)	75.4 (1.85)	73.0 (4.03)	44.7 (0.72)	48.8 (1.67)	72.2 (1.66)	72.8 (3.53)
Somewhat satisfied												
School	35.3 (0.74)	27.6 (1.40)	18.7 (1.84)	22.6 (3.33)	34.9 (0.82)	30.5 (2.01)	18.4 (1.82)	17.8 (3.40)	37.6 (0.68)	34.0 (1.57)	16.4 (1.42)	19.4 (3.16)
Teachers	35.4 (0.71)	29.3 (1.57)	23.4 (1.69)	23.6 (3.25)	34.1 (0.84)	29.8 (1.87)	21.1 (1.90)	23.1 (3.78)	38.4 (0.64)	38.7 (1.47)	23.6 (1.70)	20.4 (3.16)
Academic standards	35.4 (0.79)	29.1 (1.59)	16.4 (1.52)	17.7 (2.97)	32.7 (0.84)	28.2 (1.99)	15.8 (1.58)	18.6 (3.67)	38.0 (0.67)	33.0 (1.49)	17.2 (1.56)	14.0 (2.70)
Order and discipline	30.5 (0.72)	26.0 (1.67)	14.7 (1.70)	15.6 (3.13)	30.1 (0.85)	27.6 (2.57)	14.6 (1.83)	16.8 (2.89)	35.3 (0.67)	30.8 (1.50)	15.2 (1.53)	16.9 (3.37)
Staff interaction with parents	— (†)	— (†)	— (†)	—	36.4 (0.92)	33.5 (2.03)	21.1 (1.83)	22.9 (3.92)	40.1 (0.79)	35.4 (1.69)	23.6 (1.54)	23.4 (3.40)
Somewhat dissatisfied												
School	7.4 (0.37)	5.6 (0.75)	3.2 (0.69)	4.5 ! (1.98)	8.4 (0.45)	5.5 (0.98)	2.6 (0.58)	3.3 ! (1.50)	7.4 (0.37)	7.6 (0.95)	2.9 (0.68)	‡ (†)
Teachers	6.2 (0.38)	4.1 (0.52)	3.4 (0.69)	3.8 ! (1.67)	6.6 (0.48)	5.6 (1.11)	1.7 (0.50)	2.9 ! (1.35)	7.2 (0.33)	7.7 (0.84)	4.0 (0.84)	2.0 ! (0.88)
Academic standards	6.6 (0.37)	4.3 (0.56)	3.3 (0.77)	4.5 ! (1.94)	6.8 (0.47)	4.9 (0.83)	2.0 ! (0.74)	‡ (†)	7.0 (0.40)	6.3 (0.77)	3.5 (0.92)	‡ (†)
Order and discipline	7.8 (0.42)	5.0 (0.69)	2.1 (0.52)	3.7 ! (1.45)	8.6 (0.50)	7.0 (1.00)	2.1 (0.52)	‡ (†)	8.6 (0.36)	7.3 (0.75)	1.8 (0.48)	‡ (†)
Staff interaction with parents	— (†)	— (†)	— (†)	—	10.7 (0.59)	6.7 (0.93)	2.3 (0.57)	‡ (†)	11.0 (0.41)	11.9 (1.03)	3.0 (0.58)	1.9 ! (0.77)
Very dissatisfied												
School	3.6 (0.26)	2.6 (0.54)	1.1 ! (0.50)	‡ (†)	4.6 (0.44)	1.8 (0.51)	0.4 ! (0.20)	‡ (†)	2.5 (0.21)	2.3 (0.39)	0.7 ! (0.33)	‡ (†)
Teachers	2.0 (0.16)	2.1 (0.45)	‡ (†)	‡ (†)	2.7 (0.39)	1.1 ! (0.34)	0.9 ! (0.32)	# (†)	2.0 (0.18)	2.0 (0.47)	‡ (†)	‡ (†)
Academic standards	3.4 (0.28)	2.7 (0.59)	‡ (†)	‡ (†)	4.3 (0.43)	1.0 ! (0.30)	‡ (†)	‡ (†)	2.3 (0.21)	1.8 (0.33)	‡ (†)	‡ (†)
Order and discipline	5.8 (0.38)	4.2 (0.72)	2.0 ! (0.80)	‡ (†)	8.6 (0.50)	4.5 (0.82)	‡ (†)	‡ (†)	3.6 (0.22)	4.1 (0.59)	0.7 ! (0.35)	‡ (†)
Staff interaction with parents	— (†)	— (†)	— (†)	—	5.3 (0.48)	3.2 (0.62)	1.2 ! (0.38)	‡ (†)	4.3 (0.28)	3.9 (0.55)	1.2 ! (0.42)	‡ (†)

—Not available.
†Not applicable.
#Rounds to zero.
!Interpret data with caution. The coefficient of variation (CV) for this estimate is between 30 and 50 percent.
‡Reporting standards not met. Either there are too few cases for a reliable estimate or the coefficient of variation (CV) is 50 percent or greater.
NOTE: Data exclude homeschooled children. While National Household Education Surveys Program (NHES) administrations prior to 2012 were administered via telephone with an interviewer. NHES:2012 used self-administered paper-and-pencil questionnaires that were mailed to respondents. Measurable differences in estimates between 2012 and prior years could reflect actual changes in the population, or the changes could be due to the mode change from telephone to mail. Detail may not sum to totals because of rounding.
SOURCE: U.S. Department of Education, National Center for Education Statistics, Parent and Family Involvement in Education Survey of the National Household Education Surveys Program (PFI-NHES:2003, 2007, and 2012). (This table was prepared September 2014.)

Table 207.10. Number of 3- to 5-year-olds not yet enrolled in kindergarten and percentage participating in home literacy activities with a family member, by type and frequency of activity and selected child and family characteristics: 2001, 2007, and 2012

[Standard errors appear in parentheses]

Selected child or family characteristic	Number of children (in thousands) 2001	2007	2012	Read by family member three or more times in past week 2001	2007	2012	Told a story by family member 2001	2007	2012	Taught letters, words, or numbers 2001	2007	2012	Did arts and crafts 2001	2007	2012	Visited a library at least once in past month 2001	2007	2012
1	2	3	4	5	6	7	8	9	10	11	12	13	14	15	16	17	18	19
Total	8,551 (11.0)	8,686 (18.1)	8,244 (85.1)	84 (0.8)	83 (1.1)	83 (0.8)	84 (0.8)	79 (1.1)	83 (0.9)	94 (0.6)	87 (1.1)	98 (0.3)	79 (0.9)	90 (1.1)	86 (0.8)	36 (1.1)	36 (1.2)	42 (1.2)
Age																		
3 years old	3,795 (91.4)	3,755 (108.1)	3,674 (89.8)	84 (1.1)	84 (1.5)	82 (1.3)	83 (1.2)	80 (2.0)	82 (1.4)	93 (1.0)	87 (1.4)	97 (0.5)	77 (1.3)	91 (1.3)	85 (1.1)	35 (1.9)	36 (2.0)	38 (1.6)
4 years old	3,861 (89.0)	3,738 (123.5)	3,508 (90.4)	85 (1.2)	83 (1.6)	84 (1.3)	84 (1.1)	76 (2.0)	84 (1.3)	95 (0.7)	86 (1.9)	98 (0.3)	82 (1.2)	89 (2.0)	87 (1.2)	37 (1.4)	35 (1.6)	43 (1.8)
5 years old	896 (47.0)	1,193 (78.0)	1,062 (59.6)	81 (2.7)	83 (3.0)	80 (2.7)	82 (2.4)	86 (2.6)	80 (2.7)	93 (1.8)	89 (2.2)	98 (0.7)	80 (2.4)	89 (2.7)	88 (1.9)	37 (3.4)	39 (3.4)	49 (3.8)
Sex																		
Male	4,292 (79.9)	4,364 (101.1)	4,251 (103.9)	82 (1.2)	81 (1.7)	82 (1.2)	82 (1.1)	77 (1.9)	82 (1.2)	94 (0.7)	86 (1.6)	97 (0.4)	76 (1.3)	87 (1.8)	84 (1.1)	35 (1.4)	34 (1.8)	41 (1.7)
Female	4,260 (79.6)	4,322 (100.8)	3,993 (104.2)	86 (1.0)	86 (1.2)	85 (1.4)	85 (1.0)	81 (1.6)	85 (1.0)	94 (0.8)	88 (1.5)	98 (0.4)	83 (1.3)	93 (1.1)	88 (1.1)	37 (1.6)	38 (1.8)	42 (1.4)
Race/ethnicity																		
White	5,313 (68.0)	4,664 (66.3)	4,062 (97.4)	89 (0.8)	91 (1.3)	90 (1.0)	86 (1.0)	85 (1.4)	90 (1.0)	95 (0.7)	88 (1.3)	98 (0.4)	85 (1.0)	92 (1.3)	90 (0.9)	39 (1.3)	41 (1.6)	44 (1.4)
Black	1,251 (55.1)	1,311 (6.0)	1,154 (63.4)	77 (2.6)	78 (4.0)	77 (3.3)	81 (2.1)	61 (5.0)	80 (2.3)	94 (1.8)	81 (5.2)	99 (0.6)	70 (3.1)	82 (5.1)	83 (2.8)	31 (2.6)	25 (3.6)	41 (3.8)
Hispanic	1,506 (43.5)	1,899 (13.6)	2,100 (76.1)	71 (1.9)	68 (2.4)	71 (2.0)	75 (2.2)	75 (2.2)	78 (2.2)	92 (1.1)	86 (1.6)	97 (0.7)	67 (2.2)	91 (1.4)	80 (1.9)	30 (2.0)	27 (2.2)	34 (2.2)
Asian/Pacific Islander	202 (29.0)	368 (44.3)	423 (32.7)	87 (4.1)	87 (3.7)	77 (3.0)	81 (5.8)	73 (7.2)	85 (2.7)	96 (2.2)	92 (2.7)	99 (1.1)	74 (6.9)	84 (5.8)	86 (2.6)	47 (7.5)	48 (7.2)	55 (4.4)
Other	280 (28.2)	444 (46.3)	505 (44.4)	87 (3.4)	86 (5.8)	87 (2.9)	92 (2.4)	95 (1.6)	84 (3.4)	94 (2.7)	90 (4.7)	99 (0.7)	85 (4.3)	90 (4.2)	88 (3.4)	31 (5.4)	43 (6.7)	46 (4.4)
Mother's highest level of education[2]																		
Less than high school	996 (54.5)	808 (71.6)	1,291 (71.9)	69 (2.8)	56 (5.1)	73 (3.1)	72 (2.7)	66 (4.5)	75 (3.5)	91 (2.0)	84 (3.3)	98 (0.8)	62 (3.0)	86 (4.4)	82 (2.6)	21 (2.4)	20 (3.7)	26 (3.1)
High school/GED	2,712 (89.0)	2,048 (108.7)	1,614 (64.0)	81 (1.6)	74 (2.8)	75 (2.5)	83 (1.3)	74 (3.2)	83 (1.8)	95 (0.9)	82 (3.3)	97 (0.9)	77 (1.8)	89 (2.3)	84 (1.8)	30 (1.9)	29 (2.9)	38 (2.8)
Vocational/technical or some college	1,833 (73.9)	1,838 (107.2)	1,663 (77.3)	85 (1.8)	84 (2.3)	85 (1.7)	85 (1.7)	75 (3.5)	83 (1.5)	94 (1.2)	85 (3.2)	97 (0.8)	81 (1.9)	87 (3.4)	86 (1.6)	38 (2.2)	28 (2.5)	40 (2.0)
Associate's degree	573 (40.9)	821 (59.4)	678 (50.0)	89 (2.5)	90 (2.1)	85 (2.3)	84 (2.7)	84 (2.8)	85 (2.3)	92 (2.3)	91 (2.1)	98 (0.7)	82 (3.2)	92 (2.2)	86 (2.3)	42 (4.3)	45 (4.5)	43 (3.9)
Bachelor's degree	1,553 (55.6)	1,990 (92.4)	1,870 (65.9)	93 (1.2)	95 (0.9)	92 (1.2)	88 (1.5)	86 (1.7)	92 (1.1)	95 (1.1)	90 (1.3)	99 (0.3)	89 (1.4)	92 (1.7)	92 (1.0)	46 (2.4)	43 (2.5)	49 (2.2)
Graduate/professional degree	685 (45.7)	1,053 (63.7)	680 (30.8)	96 (1.1)	95 (1.6)	95 (1.0)	89 (2.3)	90 (1.7)	89 (2.3)	94 (2.7)	93 (1.4)	97 (0.8)	86 (2.2)	92 (1.8)	91 (1.5)	55 (3.8)	54 (3.5)	64 (2.5)
Mother's employment status[2]																		
Employed	5,148 (84.2)	4,985 (130.1)	4,491 (88.6)	86 (1.0)	85 (1.2)	86 (0.9)	84 (1.0)	80 (1.4)	84 (1.2)	94 (0.7)	86 (1.5)	98 (0.3)	80 (1.2)	88 (1.5)	86 (0.9)	36 (1.2)	35 (1.7)	42 (1.5)
Unemployed	396 (36.9)	467 (61.5)	550 (52.0)	77 (5.0)	69 (7.5)	80 (4.4)	80 (4.7)	69 (7.9)	84 (3.5)	94 (3.3)	94 (2.0)	98 (1.1)	69 (5.5)	88 (7.1)	89 (4.0)	37 (4.8)	26 (5.8)	33 (4.2)
Not in labor force	2,809 (73.3)	3,105 (128.9)	2,756 (86.9)	83 (1.4)	83 (1.7)	84 (1.7)	82 (1.5)	79 (2.2)	84 (1.6)	94 (0.9)	87 (2.1)	97 (0.7)	80 (1.3)	89 (2.1)	87 (1.4)	38 (1.9)	38 (2.0)	43 (1.9)
Number of parents in the household																		
Two parents	6,416 (75.1)	6,826 (82.0)	5,702 (95.5)	87 (0.8)	85 (2.0)	86 (0.9)	84 (1.0)	82 (1.6)	86 (0.9)	94 (0.7)	88 (1.0)	98 (0.3)	81 (1.0)	90 (1.3)	88 (0.9)	38 (1.2)	37 (1.4)	42 (1.4)
None or one parent[3]	2,135 (75.1)	1,859 (83.9)	2,542 (86.2)	76 (2.0)	78 (3.2)	76 (2.0)	82 (1.6)	70 (3.6)	76 (2.0)	93 (1.2)	83 (3.7)	97 (0.6)	74 (2.3)	84 (3.5)	82 (1.7)	30 (2.1)	30 (3.1)	40 (2.3)
Poverty status[3]																		
Poor	2,008 (60.4)	1,934 (72.9)	1,958 (77.8)	74 (2.1)	71 (3.4)	74 (2.2)	81 (1.7)	69 (3.4)	74 (2.2)	92 (1.6)	86 (3.1)	96 (0.8)	73 (2.3)	85 (3.2)	83 (1.7)	27 (2.1)	28 (2.8)	39 (2.2)
Near-poor	1,782 (70.5)	1,939 (109.5)	1,960 (86.5)	81 (1.8)	81 (1.9)	81 (2.1)	82 (2.0)	76 (2.8)	81 (2.1)	95 (1.0)	81 (3.4)	98 (0.5)	76 (1.9)	89 (2.0)	82 (2.1)	33 (2.8)	34 (3.3)	38 (2.6)
Nonpoor	4,762 (71.9)	4,812 (83.0)	4,327 (87.6)	90 (0.9)	89 (1.3)	88 (1.0)	85 (1.0)	84 (1.2)	88 (1.0)	95 (0.6)	90 (0.9)	95 (0.4)	84 (1.0)	92 (1.1)	89 (1.0)	41 (1.4)	40 (1.7)	44 (1.5)

[1]The respondent was the parent most knowledgeable about the child's care and education. Responding parents reported on their own activities and the activities of their spouse/other adults in the household.
[2]Excludes children living in households with no mother or female guardian present.
[3]Poor children are those whose family incomes were below the Census Bureau's poverty threshold in the year prior to data collection; near-poor children are those whose family incomes ranged from the poverty threshold to 199 percent of the poverty threshold; and nonpoor children are those whose family incomes were at or above 200 percent of the poverty threshold. The poverty threshold is a dollar amount that varies depending on a family's size and composition and is updated annually to account for inflation. In 2011, for example, the poverty threshold for a family of four with two children was $22,811. Survey respondents are asked to select the range within which their income falls, rather than giving the exact amount of their income; therefore, the measure of poverty status is an approximation.

NOTE: While National Household Education Surveys Program (NHES) administrations prior to 2012 were administered via telephone with an interviewer, NHES:2012 used self-administered paper-and-pencil questionnaires that were mailed to respondents. Measurable differences in estimates between 2012 and prior years could reflect actual changes in the population, or the changes could be due to the mode change from telephone to mail. Totals include other racial/ethnic groups not separately shown. Race categories exclude persons of Hispanic ethnicity. Detail may not sum to totals because of rounding.
SOURCE: U.S. Department of Education, National Center for Education Statistics, Early Childhood Program Participation Survey (ECPP:2001 and 2012) and Parent and Family Involvement in Education Survey (PFI:2007) of the National Household Education Surveys Program. (This table was prepared October 2014.)

Table 207.20. Percentage of kindergartners through fifth-graders whose parents reported doing education-related activities with their children in the past month, by selected child, parent, and school characteristics: 2003, 2007, and 2012

[Standard errors appear in parentheses]

Selected child, parent, or school characteristic	Visited a library			Went to a play, concert, or other live show			Visited an art gallery, museum, or historical site			Visited a zoo or aquarium			Attended an event sponsored by a community, religious, or ethnic group[1]		
	2003	2007	2012	2003	2007	2012	2003	2007	2012	2003	2007	2012	2003	2007	2012
1	2	3	4	5	6	7	8	9	10	11	12	13	14	15	16
Total	50.2 (0.80)	48.8 (1.12)	46.5 (0.88)	35.5 (0.87)	31.4 (0.87)	32.0 (0.88)	22.2 (0.83)	26.3 (1.09)	25.9 (0.77)	16.5 (0.69)	19.0 (0.80)	24.6 (0.86)	62.0 (0.80)	58.9 (1.14)	57.3 (0.79)
Sex of child															
Male	47.3 (1.08)	46.8 (1.66)	44.8 (1.40)	33.6 (1.09)	28.7 (1.06)	30.0 (1.25)	23.1 (1.12)	27.1 (1.80)	25.6 (1.11)	16.3 (0.88)	18.5 (0.95)	24.1 (1.07)	61.0 (1.08)	57.3 (1.48)	57.2 (1.24)
Female	53.1 (1.11)	50.9 (1.52)	48.3 (1.37)	37.5 (1.09)	34.5 (1.57)	34.1 (1.16)	21.2 (1.07)	25.4 (1.30)	26.2 (1.09)	16.7 (0.87)	19.6 (1.41)	25.2 (1.18)	63.0 (1.09)	60.6 (1.49)	57.5 (1.15)
Race/ethnicity of child															
White	49.1 (1.03)	48.5 (1.22)	45.3 (1.14)	37.2 (1.26)	32.8 (1.13)	33.6 (1.10)	21.2 (1.09)	25.4 (1.18)	27.4 (1.00)	13.6 (0.85)	15.3 (0.85)	20.8 (0.99)	64.6 (1.12)	63.1 (1.19)	56.8 (1.13)
Black	52.3 (2.50)	56.1 (3.95)	50.2 (2.97)	36.7 (2.23)	34.5 (3.02)	35.9 (2.65)	24.4 (1.97)	32.7 (5.13)	25.1 (2.05)	18.9 (1.55)	24.2 (2.72)	27.5 (2.69)	66.3 (2.35)	61.7 (4.59)	68.7 (2.10)
Hispanic	48.2 (1.77)	44.6 (2.14)	43.5 (2.11)	28.0 (1.53)	25.1 (1.67)	26.8 (1.80)	20.8 (1.38)	23.5 (2.13)	23.3 (1.66)	23.7 (1.32)	25.4 (1.97)	29.3 (2.04)	49.3 (1.75)	44.9 (2.17)	53.5 (2.28)
Asian/Pacific Islander	70.9 (5.11)	58.8 (5.81)	58.6 (3.93)	36.0 (4.44)	34.8 (5.45)	36.9 (3.75)	34.3 (4.22)	30.8 (5.21)	24.5 (3.35)	22.3 (3.97)	22.2 (3.51)	32.8 (3.86)	65.4 (4.25)	56.7 (5.49)	51.2 (4.28)
Other	51.9 (4.57)	41.8 (5.09)	47.2 (3.48)	38.6 (4.28)	31.1 (4.18)	25.3 (2.76)	25.8 (3.65)	27.1 (4.05)	27.0 (3.19)	14.7 (3.13)	17.3 (3.02)	22.5 (3.13)	59.5 (5.41)	62.4 (4.60)	55.9 (3.54)
Grade of child															
Kindergarten and grade 1	48.7 (1.28)	48.0 (2.19)	46.0 (1.44)	34.2 (1.32)	29.8 (1.53)	31.9 (1.69)	21.1 (1.04)	25.7 (2.12)	28.5 (1.44)	18.2 (1.10)	21.5 (1.69)	28.7 (1.78)	59.3 (1.29)	55.9 (1.87)	55.9 (1.41)
Grades 2 and 3	50.5 (1.45)	46.9 (1.64)	48.6 (1.59)	33.2 (1.41)	31.5 (1.71)	32.8 (1.52)	22.2 (1.13)	25.3 (1.65)	27.1 (1.59)	17.5 (1.13)	16.7 (1.11)	26.1 (1.49)	61.5 (1.41)	60.5 (1.72)	59.0 (1.57)
Grades 4 and 5	51.2 (1.32)	51.4 (1.68)	45.0 (1.59)	38.9 (1.18)	33.0 (1.57)	31.3 (1.30)	23.1 (1.28)	27.8 (1.74)	21.8 (1.28)	14.0 (0.90)	18.8 (1.58)	18.5 (1.04)	65.0 (1.28)	60.2 (1.86)	57.3 (1.48)
Language spoken most at home by child[2]															
English	50.2 (0.86)	49.7 (1.23)	46.6 (1.00)	37.0 (0.93)	32.7 (0.93)	32.7 (0.91)	22.6 (0.90)	27.1 (1.20)	26.8 (0.76)	15.5 (0.71)	17.9 (0.80)	23.3 (0.87)	63.9 (0.85)	61.3 (1.20)	57.8 (0.78)
Spanish	41.8 (3.21)	37.5 (3.62)	33.8 (4.10)	16.4 (1.95)	16.7 (2.55)	20.0 (3.13)	14.9 (2.25)	16.2 (2.61)	12.8 (2.11)	26.0 (2.87)	27.0 (3.14)	30.4 (3.61)	34.7 (2.76)	33.4 (3.67)	54.9 (3.69)
English and Spanish equally	51.1 (4.40)	51.3 (5.65)	48.7 (4.14)	24.2 (3.77)	28.5 (5.18)	24.2 (3.38)	19.6 (3.35)	27.8 (5.45)	23.3 (4.60)	28.3 (4.06)	31.4 (5.49)	34.5 (4.78)	53.5 (4.92)	43.1 (5.88)	53.0 (5.31)
English and other language equally	‡ (†)	‡ (†)	61.5 (5.01)	‡ (†)	‡ (†)	42.8 (4.44)	‡ (†)	‡ (†)	31.2 (5.01)	‡ (†)	‡ (†)	38.7 (4.85)	‡ (†)	‡ (†)	64.2 (3.82)
Other language	69.8 (6.74)	41.4 (11.41)	47.0 (10.39)	30.5 (7.05)	28.8 (8.24)	32.0 (9.29)	26.3 (5.28)	22.5 ! (7.32)	17.6 ! (7.68)	27.8 (6.45)	14.5 ! (5.37)	21.9 ! (9.08)	55.8 (8.96)	66.0 (9.17)	42.5 (11.31)
Highest education level of parents/guardians in the household															
Less than high school	36.1 (3.39)	36.5 (4.20)	37.4 (3.31)	20.0 (3.10)	19.7 (3.46)	18.5 (2.69)	9.3 (1.75)	16.2 (2.82)	18.1 (3.19)	15.3 (2.05)	19.2 (3.08)	27.7 (3.58)	34.3 (3.06)	35.9 (4.70)	48.0 (2.88)
High school/GED	44.5 (1.64)	41.2 (3.13)	45.0 (2.43)	28.6 (1.83)	21.9 (2.08)	26.3 (2.17)	17.8 (1.73)	22.2 (3.16)	21.2 (2.12)	16.5 (1.18)	17.0 (2.00)	23.3 (1.90)	50.5 (1.81)	44.6 (2.88)	53.8 (2.41)
Vocational/technical or some college	44.3 (2.04)	43.5 (2.46)	41.0 (1.74)	32.8 (1.89)	29.6 (2.15)	30.7 (1.76)	19.1 (1.32)	18.6 (2.00)	23.7 (1.55)	15.2 (1.29)	16.4 (1.95)	23.8 (1.70)	62.1 (1.64)	58.2 (2.61)	54.0 (1.64)
Associate's degree	47.4 (3.04)	46.6 (2.74)	43.7 (3.08)	41.1 (3.24)	31.0 (2.46)	28.0 (2.74)	22.0 (2.40)	22.3 (2.72)	24.9 (2.39)	15.4 (2.09)	19.3 (2.56)	25.8 (2.72)	67.0 (2.85)	58.7 (2.84)	58.2 (2.38)
Bachelor's degree/some graduate school	57.7 (1.74)	51.9 (1.89)	51.2 (1.53)	40.1 (1.61)	37.1 (1.85)	38.3 (1.45)	27.6 (1.70)	32.1 (2.07)	30.2 (1.47)	16.0 (1.32)	21.1 (1.79)	24.3 (1.50)	71.3 (1.63)	66.7 (2.07)	61.5 (1.37)
Graduate/professional degree	65.2 (2.04)	62.2 (1.86)	57.8 (1.56)	47.2 (2.53)	40.0 (2.20)	45.0 (1.68)	31.7 (2.02)	34.7 (1.96)	35.6 (1.72)	20.7 (1.82)	20.3 (1.61)	24.7 (1.23)	75.6 (1.55)	72.3 (1.63)	67.0 (1.56)
Family income (in current dollars)															
$20,000 or less	44.2 (2.14)	42.5 (4.09)	43.6 (2.48)	29.0 (2.07)	20.4 (2.46)	22.1 (1.72)	19.4 (2.02)	20.6 (4.29)	19.4 (1.87)	20.1 (1.73)	16.8 (1.99)	25.7 (2.05)	51.3 (2.32)	44.4 (3.74)	51.5 (2.11)
$20,001 to $50,000	48.9 (1.45)	46.5 (2.05)	44.1 (2.11)	31.0 (1.51)	29.6 (1.75)	27.7 (1.58)	18.9 (1.25)	22.9 (2.06)	21.1 (1.47)	15.2 (1.01)	21.0 (2.19)	25.4 (1.84)	61.5 (1.65)	55.1 (2.06)	56.7 (2.01)
$50,001 to $75,000	50.0 (1.65)	49.2 (2.28)	47.1 (2.14)	39.0 (1.59)	31.9 (1.80)	33.7 (1.59)	23.1 (1.42)	23.9 (1.64)	29.7 (1.88)	14.9 (1.27)	15.8 (1.50)	27.4 (1.96)	64.5 (1.42)	61.2 (2.02)	56.3 (2.05)
$75,001 to $100,000	49.9 (2.36)	49.5 (2.44)	46.8 (2.16)	39.4 (2.27)	33.9 (2.03)	34.4 (2.01)	23.0 (2.22)	29.7 (2.25)	28.2 (2.07)	15.3 (1.52)	18.5 (2.17)	26.2 (2.03)	66.2 (2.25)	63.0 (2.18)	60.1 (2.18)
Over $100,000	60.9 (2.14)	56.0 (1.87)	50.1 (1.76)	45.3 (2.10)	40.7 (1.91)	40.0 (1.39)	30.9 (1.66)	35.2 (1.69)	31.2 (1.63)	18.3 (1.88)	21.4 (1.41)	20.5 (1.21)	69.4 (1.84)	70.5 (1.86)	60.7 (1.59)

See notes at end of table.

Table 207.20. Percentage of kindergartners through fifth-graders whose parents reported doing education-related activities with their children in the past month, by selected child, parent, and school characteristics: 2003, 2007, and 2012—Continued

[Standard errors appear in parentheses]

Selected child, parent, or school characteristic	Visited a library			Went to a play, concert, or other live show			Visited an art gallery, museum, or historical site			Visited a zoo or aquarium			Attended an event sponsored by a community, religious, or ethnic group[1]		
	2003	2007	2012	2003	2007	2012	2003	2007	2012	2003	2007	2012	2003	2007	2012
1	2	3	4	5	6	7	8	9	10	11	12	13	14	15	16
Poverty status[3]															
Poor	43.3 (2.30)	42.1 (3.38)	45.0 (2.53)	26.3 (1.98)	19.4 (2.18)	22.5 (1.63)	18.9 (1.97)	20.4 (3.83)	18.3 (1.55)	19.5 (1.67)	17.0 (2.04)	24.3 (2.09)	52.0 (2.14)	45.8 (3.76)	54.0 (2.18)
Near-poor	48.9 (1.63)	47.1 (2.40)	41.8 (1.86)	31.6 (2.10)	31.7 (2.15)	28.5 (2.10)	17.7 (1.50)	20.6 (1.96)	21.9 (1.77)	16.1 (1.28)	21.9 (2.17)	26.2 (1.99)	61.6 (2.24)	57.4 (2.28)	57.1 (2.10)
Nonpoor	52.8 (1.02)	51.7 (1.14)	48.8 (1.14)	39.8 (1.17)	35.7 (1.07)	36.9 (1.00)	24.9 (1.06)	30.2 (1.08)	30.4 (1.04)	15.8 (0.87)	18.8 (0.90)	24.1 (0.91)	65.2 (0.99)	64.0 (1.14)	58.7 (0.96)
Control of school															
Public	49.2 (0.87)	47.6 (1.22)	46.2 (0.94)	34.9 (0.88)	31.0 (0.93)	30.9 (0.96)	21.2 (0.92)	24.9 (1.12)	25.0 (0.82)	16.3 (0.71)	19.1 (0.88)	24.1 (0.94)	60.6 (0.85)	56.9 (1.25)	55.9 (0.87)
Private	57.0 (2.31)	57.0 (2.86)	49.0 (2.51)	40.0 (2.55)	34.3 (2.65)	41.8 (2.56)	29.0 (2.04)	35.6 (2.82)	34.4 (2.49)	17.9 (1.85)	18.5 (2.05)	28.8 (2.43)	72.2 (2.15)	71.8 (2.77)	70.0 (2.30)

†Not applicable.

!Interpret data with caution. The coefficient of variation (CV) for this estimate is between 30 and 50 percent.

‡Reporting standards not met (too few cases for a reliable estimate).

[1]In 2007 and 2012, a single item asked parents if they had attended an event sponsored by a community, ethnic, or religious group. In 2003, attendance at an event sponsored by a religious group was asked about separately from attendance at an event sponsored by a community or ethnic group.

[2]Excludes children who were not able to speak.

[3]Poor children are those whose family incomes were below the Census Bureau's poverty threshold in the year prior to data collection; near-poor children are those whose family incomes ranged from the poverty threshold to 199 percent of the poverty threshold; and nonpoor children are those whose family incomes were at or above 200 percent of the poverty threshold. The poverty threshold is a dollar amount that varies depending on a family's size and composition and is updated annually to account for inflation. In 2011, for example, the poverty threshold for a family of four with two children was $22,811. Survey respondents

are asked to select the range within which their income falls, rather than giving the exact amount of their income; therefore, the measure of poverty status is an approximation.

NOTE: While National Household Education Surveys Program (NHES) administrations prior to 2012 were administered via telephone with an interviewer, NHES:2012 used self-administered paper-and-pencil questionnaires that were mailed to respondents. Measurable differences in estimates between 2012 and prior years could reflect actual changes in the population, or the changes could be due to the mode change from telephone to mail. The respondent was the parent most knowledgeable about the child's education. Responding parents reported on their own activities and the activities of their spouse/other adults in the household. All information, including control of school, is based on parent reports. Excludes homeschooled children. Race categories exclude persons of Hispanic ethnicity. Some data have been revised from previously published figures.

SOURCE: U.S. Department of Education, National Center for Education Statistics, Parent and Family Involvement in Education Survey (PFI:2003, 2007, and 2012) of the National Household Education Surveys Program. (This table was prepared September 2014.)

Table 207.30. Percentage of kindergartners through fifth-graders whose parents reported doing education-related activities with their children in the past week, by selected child, parent, and school characteristics: 2003, 2007, and 2012

[Standard errors appear in parentheses]

Selected child, parent, or school characteristic	Told child a story			Did arts and crafts			Discussed family history/ethnic heritage			Played board games or did puzzles		
	2003	2007	2012	2003	2007	2012	2003	2007	2012	2003	2007	2012
	2	3	4	5	6	7	8	9	10	11	12	13
Total	74.9 (0.66)	70.3 (1.11)	68.8 (0.91)	74.9 (0.70)	75.7 (1.00)	67.0 (0.84)	53.1 (0.89)	53.5 (1.10)	49.4 (1.00)	72.9 (0.68)	69.0 (0.99)	64.0 (0.94)
Sex of child												
Male	73.3 (0.86)	68.7 (1.51)	68.2 (1.27)	69.7 (0.98)	70.3 (1.32)	60.7 (1.19)	51.1 (1.16)	52.9 (1.48)	47.6 (1.10)	71.8 (0.92)	69.0 (1.49)	63.0 (1.20)
Female	76.6 (0.96)	72.0 (1.47)	69.5 (1.22)	80.2 (1.01)	81.7 (1.33)	73.8 (1.25)	55.1 (1.28)	54.3 (1.45)	51.2 (1.47)	74.1 (1.05)	69.0 (1.43)	65.2 (1.14)
Race/ethnicity of child												
White	76.0 (0.96)	73.2 (1.20)	71.9 (0.98)	75.4 (0.89)	74.9 (1.23)	67.5 (1.08)	44.7 (1.13)	45.6 (1.28)	37.3 (1.21)	73.8 (0.87)	69.0 (1.19)	66.6 (1.03)
Black	69.6 (2.00)	61.6 (3.81)	64.3 (2.40)	68.1 (2.14)	73.0 (3.53)	64.0 (2.76)	66.6 (2.45)	66.9 (3.59)	67.4 (2.44)	72.9 (1.92)	72.8 (3.14)	60.1 (2.94)
Hispanic	74.2 (1.55)	67.6 (2.46)	65.4 (2.15)	79.6 (1.45)	81.2 (1.66)	67.7 (1.69)	64.5 (1.71)	61.1 (2.22)	58.1 (2.09)	68.5 (1.82)	67.5 (2.33)	62.2 (1.88)
Asian/Pacific Islander	75.8 (3.73)	71.4 (4.75)	70.9 (3.19)	70.4 (4.34)	70.4 (4.64)	65.0 (3.53)	68.2 (4.83)	74.6 (4.32)	69.3 (3.67)	67.0 (3.82)	63.7 (4.79)	61.1 (3.94)
Other	83.6 (4.37)	72.4 (4.43)	65.2 (3.20)	76.2 (3.58)	73.5 (4.00)	69.4 (2.66)	67.5 (5.02)	59.7 (4.90)	51.7 (3.72)	76.7 (3.81)	68.7 (4.34)	62.6 (3.64)
Grade of child												
Kindergarten through grade 1	84.5 (0.93)	74.1 (1.81)	78.0 (1.60)	89.1 (0.84)	89.3 (1.08)	81.2 (1.14)	47.7 (1.38)	45.7 (2.03)	44.4 (1.89)	77.5 (1.17)	73.5 (1.71)	69.3 (1.56)
Grades 2 through 3	74.5 (1.21)	70.7 (1.94)	66.9 (1.51)	74.0 (1.12)	75.4 (1.84)	66.7 (1.54)	54.7 (1.34)	55.7 (1.93)	52.1 (1.53)	72.7 (1.09)	68.9 (1.70)	65.5 (1.44)
Grades 4 through 5	66.4 (1.20)	66.1 (1.60)	60.2 (1.55)	62.2 (1.36)	62.6 (1.80)	51.2 (1.45)	56.5 (1.42)	59.3 (1.78)	52.3 (1.44)	68.9 (1.18)	64.6 (1.83)	56.6 (1.50)
Language spoken most at home by child[1]												
English	75.4 (0.73)	71.0 (1.22)	69.4 (1.00)	74.4 (0.72)	74.6 (1.04)	67.2 (0.81)	51.5 (0.93)	52.0 (1.10)	46.8 (1.13)	73.7 (0.73)	68.8 (1.06)	64.0 (1.06)
Spanish	65.6 (2.85)	60.7 (3.74)	56.4 (5.08)	81.7 (2.16)	84.5 (2.84)	70.7 (3.63)	60.2 (3.11)	62.2 (3.48)	64.7 (4.04)	58.1 (3.10)	69.2 (3.62)	60.2 (4.36)
English and Spanish equally	76.6 (3.83)	67.5 (4.69)	68.7 (4.01)	78.7 (3.88)	85.7 (3.23)	64.5 (4.01)	77.3 (4.18)	63.2 (3.98)	64.0 (3.84)	75.2 (3.73)	76.9 (4.06)	67.0 (3.51)
English and other language equally	‡ (†)	‡ (†)	74.6 (3.94)	‡ (†)	‡ (†)	66.9 (4.78)	‡ (†)	‡ (†)	72.2 (4.54)	‡ (†)	‡ (†)	68.2 (3.67)
Other language	81.7 (6.95)	80.3 (8.34)	66.1 (9.93)	76.7 (4.81)	84.4 (5.61)	55.2 (10.98)	75.1 (6.13)	74.8 (8.83)	63.1 (11.51)	74.8 (7.43)	66.3 (10.40)	65.5 (11.12)
Highest education level of parents/guardians in the household												
Less than high school	68.6 (2.73)	58.4 (3.93)	65.0 (3.19)	75.7 (2.63)	75.1 (3.55)	67.2 (3.32)	59.1 (3.11)	54.2 (3.05)	60.7 (3.45)	70.1 (2.69)	65.7 (3.57)	61.7 (3.09)
High school/GED	71.2 (1.56)	68.4 (2.75)	68.6 (1.87)	75.1 (1.41)	79.2 (2.57)	70.3 (2.50)	54.7 (2.01)	55.9 (3.56)	50.8 (2.04)	72.6 (1.39)	74.5 (2.61)	64.8 (2.32)
Vocational/technical or some college	75.9 (1.54)	70.0 (2.56)	69.1 (1.56)	76.2 (1.51)	76.4 (2.15)	64.4 (1.87)	50.8 (1.75)	53.1 (2.69)	47.0 (1.90)	71.6 (1.58)	69.0 (2.44)	63.9 (1.72)
Associate's degree	76.0 (2.00)	68.9 (2.58)	67.0 (3.80)	73.6 (2.47)	72.3 (3.13)	66.0 (2.45)	50.9 (2.16)	48.7 (3.17)	44.6 (3.22)	70.1 (2.50)	64.9 (2.77)	57.9 (3.69)
Bachelor's degree/some graduate school	77.3 (1.60)	70.6 (2.11)	71.3 (1.37)	74.0 (1.48)	74.2 (1.31)	66.8 (1.47)	47.3 (1.74)	51.8 (2.06)	45.6 (1.49)	75.8 (1.27)	69.4 (1.65)	65.1 (1.67)
Graduate/professional degree	78.6 (1.64)	77.9 (1.91)	72.7 (1.41)	73.9 (1.72)	74.1 (1.99)	67.3 (1.41)	60.1 (2.16)	55.9 (1.87)	51.9 (1.74)	74.9 (1.82)	66.8 (1.88)	67.8 (1.39)
Family income (in current dollars)												
$20,000 or less	73.9 (1.61)	64.9 (4.03)	68.7 (1.81)	76.0 (1.87)	79.8 (2.93)	71.4 (2.08)	61.6 (2.05)	57.8 (3.43)	54.3 (2.17)	73.3 (1.70)	73.9 (2.57)	61.7 (2.22)
$20,001 to $50,000	74.0 (1.31)	69.5 (2.19)	68.6 (1.87)	75.3 (1.05)	77.2 (1.86)	68.1 (1.86)	53.5 (1.59)	57.9 (2.05)	53.6 (2.07)	72.3 (1.45)	66.6 (2.01)	63.6 (1.80)
$50,001 to $75,000	74.9 (1.53)	69.1 (2.00)	68.5 (2.31)	75.3 (1.55)	75.5 (1.94)	67.5 (1.86)	49.6 (1.99)	44.4 (2.27)	47.7 (2.35)	72.1 (1.51)	66.6 (2.26)	63.3 (2.35)
$75,001 to $100,000	74.7 (2.02)	72.4 (2.29)	68.4 (2.03)	73.0 (1.98)	73.0 (2.03)	64.7 (2.13)	48.8 (2.28)	49.4 (2.77)	46.3 (2.46)	73.3 (2.30)	70.5 (2.41)	65.6 (2.29)
Over $100,000	78.6 (1.52)	75.3 (1.86)	69.4 (1.35)	75.1 (1.87)	73.9 (1.89)	64.1 (1.62)	50.1 (1.93)	55.4 (2.09)	44.5 (1.48)	74.7 (1.81)	69.1 (1.69)	65.5 (1.50)
Poverty status[2]												
Poor	73.2 (1.67)	65.5 (3.24)	68.6 (2.15)	76.9 (1.85)	77.7 (3.19)	72.0 (2.01)	60.9 (2.13)	59.8 (3.15)	57.6 (2.64)	72.4 (1.88)	72.5 (2.77)	61.7 (2.29)
Near-poor	74.3 (1.30)	68.5 (2.28)	68.3 (1.88)	76.7 (1.24)	81.3 (1.81)	67.5 (1.63)	53.3 (1.79)	56.0 (2.53)	49.8 (2.18)	73.6 (1.85)	68.7 (2.22)	63.3 (1.71)
Nonpoor	75.7 (0.85)	72.6 (1.07)	69.0 (1.07)	73.6 (0.92)	73.2 (1.13)	64.9 (0.98)	50.6 (1.11)	50.5 (1.26)	46.1 (1.09)	72.8 (0.87)	67.8 (1.05)	65.2 (1.16)
Control of school												
Public	75.0 (0.68)	69.6 (1.19)	68.2 (1.04)	75.9 (0.72)	76.9 (0.99)	67.0 (0.89)	52.4 (0.98)	54.0 (1.16)	49.6 (1.07)	73.4 (0.74)	68.9 (1.06)	63.7 (1.04)
Private	74.2 (2.09)	75.2 (2.51)	73.7 (2.08)	72.1 (1.94)	74.8 (2.76)	67.0 (2.45)	58.1 (2.17)	50.6 (2.72)	47.0 (2.75)	69.1 (1.99)	69.6 (2.40)	67.2 (2.25)

†Not applicable.
‡Reporting standards not met (too few cases for a reliable estimate).
[1]Excludes children who were not able to speak.
[2]Poor children are those whose family incomes were below the Census Bureau's poverty threshold in the year prior to data collection; near-poor children are those whose family incomes ranged from the poverty threshold to 199 percent of the poverty threshold; and nonpoor children are those whose family incomes were at or above 200 percent of the poverty threshold. The poverty threshold for a family with two children was $22,811. Survey respondents are asked to select the range within which their income falls, rather than giving the exact amount of their income; therefore, the measure of poverty status is an approximation.

NOTE: While National Household Education Surveys Program (NHES) administrations prior to 2012 were administered via telephone with an interviewer, NHES:2012 used self-administered paper-and-pencil questionnaires that were mailed to respondents. Measurable differences in estimates between 2012 and prior years could reflect actual changes in the population, or the changes could be due to the mode change from telephone to mail. The respondent was the parent most knowledgeable about the child's education. Responding parents reported on their own activities and the activities of their spouse/other adults in the household. All information, including control of school, is based on parent reports. Excludes homeschooled children. Race categories exclude persons of Hispanic ethnicity. Some data have been revised from previously published figures.
SOURCE: U.S. Department of Education, National Center for Education Statistics, Parent and Family Involvement in Education Survey (PFI:2003, 2007, and 2012) of the National Household Education Surveys Program. (This table was prepared October 2014.)

Table 207.40.   Percentage of elementary and secondary school children whose parents were involved in school activities, by selected child, parent, and school characteristics: 2003, 2007, and 2012

Percent of children whose parents report the following types of involvement in school activities

[Standard errors appear in parentheses]

Selected child, parent, or school characteristic	2003 Attended a general school meeting	2003 Attended parent-teacher conference	2003 Attended a class event	2003 Volunteered at school	2007 Attended a general school meeting	2007 Attended parent-teacher conference	2007 Attended a class event	2007 Volunteered at school	2012 Attended a general school meeting	2012 Attended parent-teacher conference	2012 Attended a class event	2012 Volunteered at school
1	2	3	4	5	6	7	8	9	10	11	12	13
Total	**87.7 (0.37)**	**77.1 (0.42)**	**69.9 (0.42)**	**41.8 (0.60)**	**89.4 (0.48)**	**78.1 (0.52)**	**74.5 (0.57)**	**46.4 (0.63)**	**87.4 (0.41)**	**75.8 (0.43)**	**74.4 (0.45)**	**41.7 (0.49)**
Sex of child												
Male	87.4 (0.49)	77.7 (0.63)	67.4 (0.75)	41.2 (0.87)	89.3 (0.70)	79.2 (0.65)	71.5 (0.90)	44.8 (0.95)	87.1 (0.66)	76.4 (0.61)	72.3 (0.65)	40.0 (0.71)
Female	87.9 (0.55)	76.5 (0.63)	72.6 (0.63)	42.4 (0.83)	89.6 (0.59)	76.8 (0.94)	77.7 (0.82)	48.1 (1.01)	87.7 (0.50)	75.1 (0.61)	76.7 (0.68)	43.5 (0.88)
Race/ethnicity of child												
White	88.7 (0.50)	76.4 (0.62)	74.1 (0.65)	48.3 (0.82)	90.9 (0.52)	77.8 (0.64)	80.1 (0.68)	54.2 (0.85)	89.1 (0.50)	77.2 (0.56)	81.5 (0.54)	49.6 (0.72)
Black	88.7 (0.85)	78.7 (1.35)	63.3 (1.54)	31.9 (1.64)	86.7 (1.77)	77.3 (1.98)	64.7 (2.31)	35.0 (1.89)	85.0 (1.35)	76.1 (1.35)	68.0 (1.66)	30.3 (1.33)
Hispanic	82.6 (1.05)	78.1 (1.10)	60.9 (1.36)	27.7 (1.23)	86.7 (1.14)	80.2 (1.05)	65.0 (1.46)	31.8 (1.34)	85.7 (1.08)	72.8 (1.08)	64.0 (1.34)	31.7 (1.14)
Asian/Pacific Islander	88.5 (2.14)	77.7 (3.03)	65.1 (3.65)	33.9 (2.69)	90.5 (1.98)	80.1 (2.80)	72.5 (2.86)	45.9 (3.78)	83.5 (1.73)	72.3 (1.91)	65.4 (2.56)	36.9 (2.30)
Asian	— (†)	— (†)	— (†)	— (†)	91.0 (2.06)	79.9 (2.87)	71.4 (2.89)	45.8 (3.78)	82.5 (1.80)	71.5 (2.03)	65.0 (2.30)	34.0 (2.33)
Pacific Islander	— (†)	— (†)	— (†)	— (†)	‡ (†)	‡ (†)	‡ (†)	‡ (†)	90.7 (3.96)	71.4 (8.97)	79.0 (6.32)	54.3 (11.37)
American Indian/Alaska Native[1]	— (†)	— (†)	— (†)	— (†)	94.2 (2.96)	79.7 (7.16)	80.8 (9.63)	58.4 (12.64)	85.1 (4.91)	79.9 (6.85)	75.6 (6.61)	42.3 (8.61)
Other	86.7 (2.22)	77.6 (3.17)	71.6 (2.95)	40.3 (3.86)	89.2 (1.76)	73.6 (3.48)	75.7 (2.83)	44.8 (3.13)	88.8 (1.30)	78.4 (2.31)	76.0 (2.52)	45.3 (2.57)
Highest education level of parents/guardians in the household												
Less than high school	73.5 (1.76)	70.2 (1.94)	47.0 (2.07)	17.5 (1.65)	77.1 (1.83)	72.0 (2.16)	49.8 (2.41)	20.2 (2.68)	77.0 (1.79)	63.3 (1.88)	48.0 (2.04)	18.3 (1.72)
High school/GED[3]	84.0 (0.93)	75.3 (1.03)	62.7 (1.30)	31.4 (1.25)	84.8 (1.28)	73.8 (1.25)	66.6 (1.63)	34.5 (1.71)	82.1 (1.42)	72.2 (1.23)	62.3 (1.45)	27.6 (1.38)
Vocational/technical or some college	88.5 (0.67)	78.0 (1.02)	69.1 (0.94)	38.8 (1.25)	87.5 (1.56)	75.7 (1.48)	69.3 (1.60)	40.3 (1.66)	87.5 (1.02)	75.4 (1.02)	76.1 (0.99)	39.0 (1.14)
Associate's degree	88.6 (1.27)	76.6 (1.68)	73.0 (1.76)	39.8 (1.67)	91.9 (1.18)	80.2 (1.75)	76.9 (2.14)	45.3 (2.32)	88.9 (0.91)	79.5 (1.13)	80.5 (1.37)	44.9 (1.77)
Bachelor's degree/some graduate school	92.0 (0.73)	79.8 (0.89)	80.1 (0.94)	53.9 (1.30)	93.6 (0.75)	81.4 (1.00)	83.2 (0.95)	57.1 (1.44)	92.1 (0.53)	79.9 (0.62)	85.0 (0.63)	55.0 (1.11)
Graduate/professional degree	94.6 (0.74)	79.5 (1.00)	80.8 (1.10)	61.7 (1.57)	95.6 (0.64)	82.3 (1.13)	87.3 (0.95)	64.1 (1.33)	95.1 (0.47)	83.0 (0.68)	90.1 (0.59)	61.8 (1.30)
Family income (in current dollars)												
$20,000 or less	79.8 (1.43)	74.6 (1.33)	56.6 (1.42)	26.1 (1.45)	78.9 (1.87)	75.1 (1.90)	54.8 (2.11)	24.8 (1.87)	79.9 (1.15)	69.4 (1.36)	57.2 (1.31)	24.1 (1.18)
$20,001 to $50,000	85.1 (0.67)	77.3 (0.85)	66.2 (0.94)	34.6 (1.14)	86.7 (1.02)	77.1 (1.21)	68.6 (1.15)	34.8 (1.10)	84.3 (0.73)	74.5 (1.04)	67.2 (1.28)	31.1 (1.22)
$50,001 to $75,000	89.9 (0.79)	76.9 (0.96)	74.5 (1.03)	46.0 (1.26)	92.0 (0.73)	78.6 (0.96)	79.0 (1.15)	51.7 (1.18)	88.7 (0.97)	77.3 (1.23)	77.3 (1.19)	43.7 (1.40)
$75,001 to $100,000	94.0 (0.80)	79.4 (1.28)	77.7 (1.34)	51.5 (1.71)	92.9 (0.85)	79.6 (1.47)	83.2 (1.20)	57.3 (1.90)	89.9 (0.88)	77.3 (1.15)	81.9 (1.13)	47.8 (1.24)
Over $100,000	93.9 (0.71)	77.9 (1.21)	80.7 (1.03)	61.1 (1.19)	96.1 (0.39)	80.1 (1.06)	86.7 (0.80)	64.7 (1.39)	92.5 (0.92)	79.0 (0.80)	85.5 (0.96)	57.6 (1.05)
Poverty status[2]												
Poor	79.4 (1.55)	74.5 (1.37)	56.7 (1.57)	26.8 (1.55)	80.9 (1.81)	76.8 (1.76)	55.8 (2.01)	26.5 (1.84)	82.5 (1.08)	71.3 (1.29)	60.0 (1.52)	26.8 (1.28)
Near-poor	85.1 (0.89)	77.9 (1.05)	64.8 (0.98)	32.5 (1.31)	86.2 (1.28)	76.8 (1.58)	68.1 (1.32)	35.2 (1.31)	83.7 (0.78)	75.2 (0.97)	66.5 (1.22)	31.2 (1.35)
Nonpoor	91.0 (0.46)	77.6 (0.58)	75.7 (0.51)	49.5 (0.76)	93.1 (0.34)	78.9 (0.58)	82.3 (0.57)	56.1 (0.77)	90.4 (0.51)	77.5 (0.55)	82.2 (0.61)	50.6 (0.71)
Control of school and enrollment level of child												
Public school	86.7 (0.40)	75.9 (0.45)	68.0 (0.47)	38.5 (0.64)	88.5 (0.53)	76.9 (0.59)	72.6 (0.66)	42.7 (0.69)	86.5 (0.45)	74.8 (0.45)	72.9 (0.50)	39.0 (0.52)
Elementary (kindergarten to grade 8)	90.9 (0.40)	85.1 (0.42)	71.7 (0.57)	42.8 (0.74)	91.7 (0.59)	85.1 (0.69)	76.1 (0.79)	48.5 (1.00)	90.0 (0.42)	82.4 (0.47)	76.0 (0.64)	44.1 (0.69)
Secondary (grades 9 to 12)	76.9 (1.06)	54.8 (1.02)	59.4 (1.06)	28.5 (0.98)	82.0 (1.12)	59.9 (1.14)	65.5 (1.20)	30.6 (1.05)	77.8 (0.92)	55.5 (1.04)	65.1 (0.90)	26.2 (0.71)
Private school	95.7 (0.61)	86.6 (1.03)	85.6 (1.23)	68.7 (1.57)	96.3 (1.08)	86.5 (1.84)	83.2 (1.27)	74.1 (1.75)	96.2 (0.58)	86.9 (1.13)	90.1 (1.18)	69.5 (1.63)
Elementary (kindergarten to grade 8)	96.6 (0.69)	91.6 (0.92)	88.4 (1.22)	73.4 (1.90)	96.8 (1.46)	92.5 (1.65)	89.2 (1.65)	80.3 (1.87)	97.4 (0.63)	91.8 (1.47)	91.8 (1.39)	74.4 (1.87)
Secondary (grades 9 to 12)	93.0 (1.56)	72.2 (2.54)	77.6 (2.93)	55.2 (2.78)	95.2 (1.11)	71.2 (4.05)	85.2 (2.21)	58.6 (3.50)	92.5 (1.20)	73.6 (2.19)	84.9 (2.08)	54.6 (2.44)

—Not available.
†Not applicable.
‡Reporting standards not met (too few cases for a reliable estimate).
[1]Included in "Other" in 2003 data.
[2]Poor children are those whose family incomes were below the Census Bureau's poverty threshold in the year prior to data collection; near-poor children are those whose family incomes ranged from the poverty threshold to 199 percent of the poverty threshold; and nonpoor children are those whose family incomes were at or above 200 percent of the poverty threshold. The poverty threshold is a dollar amount that varies depending on a family's size and composition and is updated annually to account for inflation. In 2011, for example, the poverty threshold for a family of four with two children was $22,811. Survey respondents are asked to select the range within which their income falls, rather than giving the exact amount of their income; therefore, the measure of poverty status is an approximation.
[3]High school diploma or equivalent, including a GED.

NOTE: While National Household Education Surveys Program (NHES) administrations prior to 2012 were administered via telephone with an interviewer, NHES:2012 used self-administered paper-and-pencil questionnaires that were mailed to respondents. Measurable differences in estimates between 2012 and prior years could reflect actual changes in the population, or the changes could be due to the mode change from telephone to mail. Includes children enrolled in kindergarten through grade 12 and ungraded students. Excludes homeschooled children. The respondent was the parent most knowledgeable about the child's education. Responding parents reported on their own activities and the activities of their spouse/other adults in the household. Race categories exclude persons of Hispanic ethnicity. Asian and Pacific Islander data were not collected separately prior to 2007. Some data have been revised from previously published figures.
SOURCE: U.S. Department of Education, National Center for Education Statistics, Parent and Family Involvement in Education: 2002–03 and Parent and Family Involvement in Education Survey (PFI:2003, 2007, and 2012) of the National Household Education Surveys Program. (This table was prepared October 2014.)

Table 208.10. Public elementary and secondary pupil/teacher ratios, by selected school characteristics: Selected years, fall 1990 through fall 2013

Selected school characteristic	1990	1994	1995	1996	1997	1998	1999	2000	2001	2002	2003	2004	2005	2006	2007	2008	2009	2010[1]	2011	2012	2013
1	2	3	4	5	6	7	8	9	10	11	12	13	14	15	16	17	18	19	20	21	22
All schools	**17.4**	**17.7**	**17.8**	**17.6**	**17.2**	**16.9**	**16.6**	**16.4**	**16.3**	**16.2**	**16.4**	**16.2**	**16.0**	**15.8**	**15.7**	**15.7**	**16.0**	**16.4**	**16.3**	**16.2**	**16.3**
Enrollment size of school																					
Under 300	14.0	14.1	14.1	14.0	13.7	13.6	13.3	13.1	12.9	12.8	13.0	12.8	12.7	12.7	12.7	12.5	12.6	12.9	12.8	12.7	12.7
300 to 499	17.0	17.2	17.1	16.9	16.5	16.2	15.8	15.5	15.4	15.3	15.5	15.2	15.0	14.9	15.0	14.8	15.2	15.4	15.4	15.3	15.4
500 to 999	18.0	18.1	18.2	17.9	17.5	17.1	16.8	16.7	16.5	16.5	16.6	16.4	16.2	15.9	15.9	15.9	16.3	16.7	16.7	16.6	16.7
1,000 to 1,499	17.9	18.6	18.7	18.5	18.1	17.7	17.6	17.4	17.4	17.4	17.6	17.3	16.9	16.7	16.5	16.5	16.8	17.3	17.1	17.0	17.1
1,500 or more	19.2	19.9	20.0	20.0	19.7	19.3	19.3	19.1	19.0	18.9	19.2	19.1	18.8	18.6	18.1	18.3	18.7	19.5	19.0	18.8	19.1
Type																					
Regular schools	17.6	17.8	17.9	17.7	17.3	17.0	16.7	16.5	16.4	16.3	16.5	16.3	16.1	15.9	15.8	15.8	16.1	16.5	16.4	16.4	16.5
Alternative	14.2	18.0	16.6	16.6	16.5	16.4	15.8	15.2	14.9	14.9	15.0	14.4	14.0	14.7	13.5	14.2	14.3	14.8	14.7	14.7	14.3
Special education	6.5	6.9	7.2	7.4	7.6	7.3	7.2	7.0	6.4	7.0	7.3	7.4	6.2	6.6	7.1	6.8	7.1	6.9	7.1	6.9	6.6
Vocational	13.0	12.9	12.7	12.9	12.9	13.1	13.0	12.7	12.7	9.9	10.3	11.5	12.0	13.3	11.3	10.7	10.2	11.7	11.8	11.6	11.7
Percent of students eligible for free or reduced-price lunch																					
25 percent or less	—	—	—	—	—	—	—	—	—	—	—	16.8	16.4	16.4	16.3	16.1	16.5	16.9	17.5	16.4	16.4
26 percent to 50 percent	—	—	—	—	—	—	—	—	—	—	—	16.2	16.1	15.8	15.7	15.7	16.1	16.5	16.2	16.3	16.3
51 percent to 75 percent	—	—	—	—	—	—	—	—	—	—	—	15.9	15.6	15.3	15.2	15.4	15.8	16.2	15.8	16.1	16.2
More than 75 percent	—	—	—	—	—	—	—	—	—	—	—	15.9	15.5	15.4	15.0	15.1	15.6	16.0	15.5	16.2	16.4
Level and size																					
Elementary schools	18.1	18.0	18.1	17.8	17.4	17.0	16.7	16.5	16.3	16.2	16.3	16.0	15.8	15.6	15.6	15.5	15.9	16.3	16.3	16.3	16.3
Regular	18.2	18.0	18.1	17.9	17.4	17.0	16.7	16.5	16.3	16.2	16.3	16.0	15.8	15.6	15.6	15.5	15.9	16.3	16.3	16.3	16.4
Under 300	16.0	15.7	15.7	15.6	15.3	15.1	14.6	14.4	14.1	13.9	14.0	13.7	13.6	13.5	13.7	13.5	13.7	14.0	14.0	13.9	14.0
300 to 499	17.6	17.5	17.5	17.2	16.8	16.4	16.1	15.8	15.6	15.5	15.6	15.3	15.2	15.1	15.2	15.0	15.4	15.6	15.7	15.6	15.6
500 to 999	18.8	18.5	18.6	18.3	17.8	17.4	17.1	16.9	16.8	16.7	16.8	16.5	16.3	16.0	16.0	16.0	16.5	16.9	16.9	16.9	17.0
1,000 to 1,499	19.5	19.6	19.7	19.4	18.8	18.4	18.3	18.1	18.0	18.0	18.1	17.7	17.2	17.0	16.7	16.8	17.2	17.8	17.7	17.7	17.7
1,500 or more	19.9	20.4	20.9	21.2	20.7	19.9	20.0	20.5	20.2	20.2	20.3	20.8	20.5	19.6	19.4	18.0	18.1	18.5	19.3	19.0	18.7	19.0
Secondary schools	16.6	17.5	17.6	17.5	17.3	17.0	16.8	16.6	16.6	16.6	16.7	16.9	16.8	16.6	16.3	16.2	16.4	16.8	16.5	16.5	16.6
Regular	16.7	17.6	17.7	17.6	17.4	17.1	16.9	16.7	16.7	16.8	17.0	16.9	16.8	16.6	16.4	16.3	16.6	16.9	16.7	16.6	16.7
Under 300	12.3	12.7	12.8	12.7	12.5	12.5	12.0	12.0	11.9	12.0	12.3	12.0	12.2	12.0	12.1	11.9	11.9	12.2	12.0	12.0	12.0
300 to 499	14.9	15.7	15.7	15.5	15.3	15.1	14.6	14.5	14.4	14.4	14.7	14.7	14.6	14.4	14.4	14.3	14.3	14.6	14.6	14.5	14.4
500 to 999	16.1	16.8	16.9	16.7	16.4	16.2	16.0	15.8	15.7	15.8	16.0	15.9	15.8	15.6	15.4	15.4	15.6	15.8	15.7	15.6	15.7
1,000 to 1,499	17.2	17.9	18.0	17.9	17.5	17.2	17.1	16.8	16.8	16.9	17.2	17.0	16.8	16.5	16.5	16.3	16.6	16.9	16.6	16.5	16.6
1,500 or more	19.3	19.9	20.0	20.0	19.7	19.3	19.2	18.9	18.8	18.8	19.0	19.0	18.8	18.5	18.2	18.2	18.6	19.3	18.8	18.7	18.9
Combined schools	14.5	15.1	15.0	14.7	14.4	13.4	13.4	13.7	13.4	13.5	13.8	13.9	14.1	14.7	13.4	13.9	14.0	15.4	14.4	14.3	14.6
Under 300	8.9	9.3	9.0	8.7	8.6	8.9	9.1	9.2	9.1	9.1	9.5	9.2	9.5	10.1	9.2	8.9	9.1	9.2	9.4	9.1	9.1
300 to 499	14.2	14.4	14.7	14.3	14.0	13.6	13.8	13.5	13.1	13.1	14.4	13.4	13.9	14.3	13.7	13.9	13.8	13.6	13.3	13.2	13.5
500 to 999	16.3	16.6	16.6	16.6	16.2	15.5	14.9	15.8	15.6	16.0	15.4	15.8	15.9	16.0	15.2	15.6	15.8	16.9	15.6	15.5	15.5
1,000 to 1,499	17.8	18.3	18.2	18.4	18.0	16.9	16.9	17.5	18.1	17.7	17.5	17.4	16.4	17.3	15.9	16.7	17.9	19.2	18.1	17.8	17.9
1,500 or more	17.7	19.5	19.6	19.3	19.3	18.7	19.2	18.6	18.9	19.1	19.2	18.7	20.0	20.3	18.0	21.7	21.7	25.7	23.4	23.0	24.6
Ungraded	6.4	6.7	6.9	5.9	6.2	5.9	5.3	7.0	6.3	6.8	9.6	8.0	7.7	7.2	7.3	5.5	8.5	5.3	6.0	5.6	2.9
Level, type, and percent of students eligible for free or reduced-price lunch																					
Elementary, regular																					
25 percent or less	—	—	—	—	—	—	—	—	—	—	—	16.6	16.4	16.2	16.2	16.0	16.4	16.8	17.4	16.4	16.4
26 to 50 percent	—	—	—	—	—	—	—	—	—	—	—	16.0	15.8	15.5	15.6	15.6	16.0	16.4	16.3	16.3	16.3
51 to 75 percent	—	—	—	—	—	—	—	—	—	—	—	15.7	15.5	15.1	15.2	15.2	15.7	16.0	15.9	16.1	16.1
More than 75 percent	—	—	—	—	—	—	—	—	—	—	—	16.0	15.6	15.4	15.1	15.2	15.8	16.1	15.7	16.4	16.6
Secondary, regular																					
25 percent or less	—	—	—	—	—	—	—	—	—	—	—	17.5	17.0	16.9	16.8	16.6	16.8	17.2	17.8	16.6	16.7
26 to 50 percent	—	—	—	—	—	—	—	—	—	—	—	16.9	16.8	16.4	16.4	16.2	16.5	16.8	16.4	16.6	16.5
51 to 75 percent	—	—	—	—	—	—	—	—	—	—	—	16.9	16.7	16.3	16.1	16.4	16.5	17.1	16.1	16.7	16.8
More than 75 percent	—	—	—	—	—	—	—	—	—	—	—	16.2	16.7	16.2	15.7	15.9	16.0	16.5	15.5	16.5	16.9

—Not available.
[1]Includes imputations for California and Wyoming.
NOTE: Pupil/teacher ratios are based on data reported by types of schools rather than by instructional programs within schools. Only includes schools that reported both enrollment and teacher data. Ratios are based on data reported by schools and may differ from data reported in other tables that reflect aggregate totals reported by states.

SOURCE: U.S. Department of Education, National Center for Education Statistics, Common Core of Data (CCD), "Public Elementary/Secondary School Universe Survey," 1990–91 through 2013–14. (This table was prepared October 2015.)

Table 208.20. Public and private elementary and secondary teachers, enrollment, pupil/teacher ratios, and new teacher hires: Selected years, fall 1955 through fall 2025

Year	Teachers (in thousands)			Enrollment (in thousands)			Pupil/teacher ratio			Number of new teacher hires (in thousands)[1]		
	Total	Public	Private	Total	Public	Private	Total	Public	Private	Total	Public	Private
1	2	3	4	5	6	7	8	9	10	11	12	13
1955	1,286	1,141	145 [2]	35,280	30,680	4,600 [2]	27.4	26.9	31.7 [2]	—	—	—
1960	1,600	1,408	192 [2]	42,181	36,281	5,900 [2]	26.4	25.8	30.7 [2]	—	—	—
1965	1,933	1,710	223	48,473	42,173	6,300	25.1	24.7	28.3	—	—	—
1970	2,292	2,059	233	51,257	45,894	5,363	22.4	22.3	23.0	—	—	—
1975	2,453	2,198	255 [2]	49,819	44,819	5,000 [2]	20.3	20.4	19.6 [2]	—	—	—
1976	2,457	2,189	268	49,478	44,311	5,167	20.1	20.2	19.3	—	—	—
1977	2,488	2,209	279	48,717	43,577	5,140	19.6	19.7	18.4	—	—	—
1978	2,479	2,207	272	47,637	42,551	5,086	19.2	19.3	18.7	—	—	—
1979	2,461	2,185	276 [2]	46,651	41,651	5,000 [2]	19.0	19.1	18.1 [2]	—	—	—
1980	2,485	2,184	301	46,208	40,877	5,331	18.6	18.7	17.7			
1981	2,440	2,127	313 [2]	45,544	40,044	5,500 [2]	18.7	18.8	17.6 [2]	—	—	—
1982	2,458	2,133	325 [2]	45,166	39,566	5,600 [2]	18.4	18.6	17.2 [2]	—	—	—
1983	2,476	2,139	337	44,967	39,252	5,715	18.2	18.4	17.0	—	—	—
1984	2,508	2,168	340 [2]	44,908	39,208	5,700 [2]	17.9	18.1	16.8 [2]	—	—	—
1985	2,549	2,206	343	44,979	39,422	5,557	17.6	17.9	16.2	—	—	—
1986	2,592	2,244	348 [2]	45,205	39,753	5,452 [2]	17.4	17.7	15.7 [2]	—	—	—
1987	2,631	2,279	352	45,488	40,008	5,479	17.3	17.6	15.6	—	—	—
1988	2,668	2,323	345 [2]	45,430	40,189	5,242 [2]	17.0	17.3	15.2 [2]	—	—	—
1989	2,713	2,357	356	46,141	40,543	5,599	17.0	17.2	15.7	—	—	—
1990	2,759	2,398	361 [2]	46,864	41,217	5,648 [2]	17.0	17.2	15.6 [2]	—	—	—
1991	2,797	2,432	365	47,728	42,047	5,681	17.1	17.3	15.6	—	—	—
1992	2,823	2,459	364 [2]	48,694	42,823	5,870 [2]	17.2	17.4	16.1 [2]	—	—	—
1993	2,868	2,504	364	49,532	43,465	6,067	17.3	17.4	16.7	—	—	—
1994	2,922	2,552	370 [2]	50,106	44,111	5,994 [2]	17.1	17.3	16.2 [2]	—	—	—
1995	2,974	2,598	376	50,759	44,840	5,918	17.1	17.3	15.7	—	—	—
1996	3,051	2,667	384 [2]	51,544	45,611	5,933 [2]	16.9	17.1	15.5 [2]	—	—	—
1997	3,138	2,746	391	52,071	46,127	5,944	16.6	16.8	15.2	—	—	—
1998	3,230	2,830	400 [2]	52,526	46,539	5,988 [2]	16.3	16.4	15.0 [2]	—	—	—
1999	3,319	2,911	408	52,875	46,857	6,018	15.9	16.1	14.7	305	222	83
2000	3,366	2,941	424 [2]	53,373	47,204	6,169 [2]	15.9	16.0	14.5 [2]	—	—	—
2001	3,440	3,000	441	53,992	47,672	6,320	15.7	15.9	14.3	—	—	—
2002	3,476	3,034	442 [2]	54,403	48,183	6,220 [2]	15.7	15.9	14.1 [2]	—	—	—
2003	3,490	3,049	441	54,639	48,540	6,099	15.7	15.9	13.8	311	236	74
2004	3,536	3,091	445 [2]	54,882	48,795	6,087 [2]	15.5	15.8	13.7 [2]	—	—	—
2005	3,593	3,143	450	55,187	49,113	6,073	15.4	15.6	13.5	—	—	—
2006	3,622	3,166	456 [2]	55,307	49,316	5,991 [2]	15.3	15.6	13.2 [2]	—	—	—
2007	3,656	3,200	456	55,201	49,291	5,910	15.1	15.4	13.0	241	173	68
2008	3,670	3,222	448 [2]	54,973	49,266	5,707 [2]	15.0	15.3	12.8 [2]	—	—	—
2009	3,647	3,210	437	54,849	49,361	5,488	15.0	15.4	12.5	—	—	—
2010	3,529	3,099	429 [2]	54,867	49,484	5,382 [2]	15.5	16.0	12.5 [2]	—	—	—
2011	3,524	3,103	421	54,790	49,522	5,268	15.5	16.0	12.5	241	173	68
2012	3,540	3,109	431 [2]	55,104	49,771	5,333 [2]	15.6	16.0	12.4 [2]	338	247	91
2013	3,555	3,114	441	55,440	50,045	5,396	15.6	16.1	12.2	334	244	90
2014[3]	3,555	3,119	435	55,454	50,132	5,322	15.6	16.1	12.2	322	246	76
2015[3]	3,560	3,128	432	55,546	50,268	5,278	15.6	16.1	12.2	328	251	77
2016[3]	3,563	3,135	428	55,620	50,385	5,235	15.6	16.1	12.2	325	249	76
2017[3]	3,565	3,141	424	55,661	50,477	5,183	15.6	16.1	12.2	322	247	76
2018[3]	3,592	3,168	424	55,665	50,528	5,136	15.5	15.9	12.1	347	268	78
2019[3]	3,615	3,192	424	55,726	50,618	5,108	15.4	15.9	12.1	343	265	79
2020[3]	3,636	3,213	423	55,862	50,774	5,088	15.4	15.8	12.0	342	263	79
2021[3]	3,661	3,237	424	55,998	50,928	5,070	15.3	15.7	12.0	346	267	79
2022[3]	3,686	3,261	425	56,146	51,084	5,062	15.2	15.7	11.9	348	268	80
2023[3]	3,712	3,285	427	56,291	51,225	5,065	15.2	15.6	11.9	350	269	82
2024[3]	3,739	3,309	430	56,416	51,338	5,078	15.1	15.5	11.8	353	270	83
2025[3]	3,761	3,327	433	56,510	51,420	5,090	15.0	15.5	11.8	350	267	83

—Not available.

[1]A teacher is considered to be a new hire for a public or private school if the teacher had not taught in that control of school in the previous year. A teacher who moves from a public to private or a private to public school is considered a new teacher hire, but a teacher who moves from one public school to another public school or one private school to another private school is not considered a new teacher hire.

[2]Estimated.

[3]Projected.

NOTE: Data for teachers are expressed in full-time equivalents (FTE). Counts of private school teachers and enrollment include prekindergarten through grade 12 in schools offering kindergarten or higher grades. Counts of public school teachers and enrollment include prekindergarten through grade 12. The pupil/teacher ratio includes teachers for students

with disabilities and other special teachers, while these teachers are generally excluded from class size calculations. Ratios for public schools reflect totals reported by states and differ from totals reported for schools or school districts. Some data have been revised from previously published figures. Detail may not sum to totals because of rounding.

SOURCE: U.S. Department of Education, National Center for Education Statistics, *Statistics of Public Elementary and Secondary Day Schools*, 1955–56 through 1980–81; Common Core of Data (CCD), "State Nonfiscal Survey of Public Elementary/Secondary Education," 1981–82 through 2013–14; Private School Universe Survey (PSS), 1989–90 through 2013–14; Schools and Staffing Survey (SASS), "Public School Teacher Data File" and "Private School Teacher Data File," 1999–2000 through 2011–12; Elementary and Secondary Teacher Projection Model, 1973 through 2025; and New Teacher Hires Projection Model, 1988 through 2025. (This table was prepared February 2016.)

Table 208.30. Public elementary and secondary teachers, by level and state or jurisdiction: Selected years, fall 2000 through fall 2013

State or jurisdiction	Fall 2000	Fall 2005	Fall 2009	Fall 2010	Fall 2011	Fall 2012				Fall 2013			
						Total	Elementary	Secondary	Ungraded	Total	Elementary	Secondary	Ungraded
1	2	3	4	5	6	7	8	9	10	11	12	13	14
United States	2,941,461 [1]	3,143,003 [1]	3,209,672 [1]	3,099,095 [1]	3,103,263 [1]	3,109,101 [1]	1,719,764 [1]	1,215,042 [1]	174,295	3,113,764 [1]	1,736,644 [1]	1,207,774 [1]	169,347
Alabama	48,194 [2]	57,757	47,492	49,363	47,723	51,877	30,428	21,450	0	47,162	33,029	14,133	0
Alaska.............................	7,880	7,912	8,083	8,171	8,088	7,682	4,191	3,491	0	7,898	4,255	3,643	0
Arizona...........................	44,438	51,376	51,947	50,031	50,800	48,866	34,248	14,619	0	48,359	33,890	14,468	0
Arkansas.........................	31,947	32,997	37,240	34,273	33,983	34,131	17,619	13,929	2,583	34,933	18,198	14,216	2,518
California.........................	298,021 [2]	309,222 [2]	316,299 [2]	260,806 [2]	268,689 [2]	266,255 [2]	172,533 [2]	87,675	6,048	259,506 [2]	175,937 [2]	80,911	2,657
Colorado.........................	41,983	45,841	49,060	48,543	48,078	48,922	28,033	20,889	0	50,157	28,807	21,350	0
Connecticut.....................	41,044	39,687	43,593	42,951	43,805	43,931	29,256	13,365	1,311	43,443	28,951	13,268	1,225
Delaware.........................	7,469	7,998	8,640	8,933	8,587	9,257	4,661	4,596	0	9,388	4,782	4,606	0
District of Columbia	4,949	5,481 [3]	5,854	5,925	6,278	5,925	2,975	2,295	655	5,991	3,068	1,726	1,198
Florida............................	132,030	158,962	183,827	175,609	175,006	176,537	76,564	66,930	33,043	177,853	77,076	66,896	33,881
Georgia...........................	91,043	108,535	115,918	112,460	111,133	109,365	50,808	42,795	15,763	109,441	50,826	42,831	15,785
Hawaii.............................	10,927	11,226	11,472	11,396	11,458	11,608	6,378	5,149	81	11,781	6,467	5,240	74
Idaho..............................	13,714	14,521	15,201	15,673	15,990	14,563	6,997	7,566	0	15,002	7,163	7,839	0
Illinois............................	127,620	133,857	138,483	132,983	131,777	135,701 [4]	92,561 [5]	42,044 [3]	1,095	136,355 [6]	91,826 [5]	43,459	1,070 [3]
Indiana............................	59,226	60,592	62,258	58,121 [2]	62,339	59,863	31,187	28,676	0	59,823	31,188	28,635	0
Iowa	34,636	35,181	35,842	34,642	34,658	35,080	24,443	10,637	0	35,397	24,719	10,677	0
Kansas............................	32,742	33,608	34,700	34,644	37,407	41,243	20,833	19,608	802	38,153	19,360	18,298	496
Kentucky.........................	39,589	42,413	41,981	42,042	41,860	42,769	21,874	10,120	10,776	41,820	24,751	9,959	7,110
Louisiana.........................	49,915	44,660	49,646	48,655	48,657	46,493	31,715	14,778	0	46,437	31,650	14,787	0
Maine..............................	16,559	16,684	16,331	15,384	14,888	15,222	10,561	4,661	0	15,452	10,699	4,744	9
Maryland..........................	52,433	56,685	58,463	58,428	57,589	57,718	34,453	23,266	0	58,611	35,332	23,279	0
Massachusetts.................	67,432	73,596	69,909	68,754	69,342	70,636	46,678	23,958	0	70,490	46,284	24,206	0
Michigan	97,031	98,069	92,691	88,615	86,997	86,154	35,430	33,967	16,757	85,786	35,535	33,666	16,585
Minnesota	53,457	51,107	52,839	52,672	52,832	53,585	28,561	23,413	1,611	54,413	29,197	23,650	1,565
Mississippi	31,006	31,433	33,103	32,255	32,007	32,613	15,401	13,187	4,026	32,292	15,291	13,068	3,934
Missouri	64,735	67,076	67,796	66,735	66,252	66,248	34,219	32,029	0	66,651	34,510	32,141	0
Montana	10,411	10,369	10,521	10,361	10,153	10,200	7,079	3,121	0	10,310	7,143	3,150	18
Nebraska	20,983	21,359	22,256	22,345	22,182	22,103	13,805	8,298	0	22,401	14,095	8,306	0
Nevada	18,293	21,744	22,104	21,839	21,132	20,695	10,088	7,683	2,924	21,921	10,760	8,071	3,090
New Hampshire	14,341	15,536	15,491	15,365	15,049	14,925	9,983	4,941	0	14,826	10,052	4,774	0
New Jersey......................	99,061	112,673	115,248	110,202	109,719	110,929	58,569	37,481	14,879	114,581	60,466	38,638	15,477
New Mexico	21,042	22,021	22,724	22,437	21,957	22,201	9,806	8,339	4,056	22,239	9,825	8,332	4,082
New York.........................	206,961	218,989	214,804	211,606	209,527	207,060	109,082	97,751	227	206,693	109,430	97,055	208
North Carolina	83,680	95,664	105,036 [7]	98,357	97,308	98,590	68,745	28,772	1,073	99,327	68,076	30,249	1,002
North Dakota	8,141	8,003	8,366	8,417	8,525	8,677	5,595	3,082	0	8,805	5,754	3,051	0
Ohio................................	118,361	117,982	111,378	109,282	107,972	106,000	50,217	47,953	7,830	106,010	49,680	47,207	9,123
Oklahoma	41,318	41,833	42,615	41,278	41,349	41,775	22,948	18,827	0	41,983	23,239	18,743	0
Oregon............................	28,094	28,346	28,768	28,109	26,791	26,410	18,541	7,869	0	26,733	18,776	7,957	0
Pennsylvania....................	116,963	122,397	130,984	129,911	124,646	123,147	58,769	54,682	9,696	121,330	58,121	53,270	9,938
Rhode Island	10,645	14,180 [2]	11,366	11,212	11,414	9,871	5,359	4,512	0	9,824	5,280	4,544	0
South Carolina.................	45,380	48,212	46,980	45,210	46,782	48,072	33,640	14,432	0	48,151	33,849	14,303	0
South Dakota	9,397	9,129	9,326	9,512	9,247	9,334	5,967	2,505	862	9,510	6,157	2,518	834
Tennessee	57,164	59,596	65,361	66,558	66,382	66,406	45,229	19,103	2,075	65,847	45,018	18,937	1,892
Texas	274,826	302,425	333,164	334,997	324,282	327,357	165,006	133,053	29,298	334,580	167,594	137,971	29,015
Utah................................	22,008	22,993	25,615	25,677	25,970	26,610	13,318	10,642	2,649	27,247	13,464	11,219	2,564
Vermont	8,414	8,851	8,734	8,382	8,364	8,403	3,377	3,186	1,840	8,375	3,369	3,152	1,854
Virginia............................	86,977 [2]	103,944	70,827	70,947	90,832	89,389	41,852	47,536	0	90,098	42,088	48,009	0
Washington......................	51,098	53,508	53,448	53,934	53,119	53,699	28,139	23,575	1,985	54,867	29,057	24,060	1,750
West Virginia....................	20,930	19,940	20,299	20,338	20,247	20,101	9,433	10,668	0	19,978	9,392	10,586	0
Wisconsin	60,165	60,127	58,426	57,625	56,245	57,551	28,658	28,543	350	57,980	29,092	28,496	392
Wyoming..........................	6,783	6,706	7,166	7,127	7,847	7,350	3,952	3,397	0	7,555	4,078	3,477	0
Bureau of Indian Education .	—	—	—	—	—	5,308	4,282	1,027	0	—	—	—	—
DoD, overseas	5,105	5,726	—	—	—	—	—	—	—	—	—	—	—
DoD, domestic	2,399	2,033	—	—	—	—	—	—	—	—	—	—	—
Other jurisdictions													
American Samoa	820	989	—	—	—	—	—	—	—	—	—	—	—
Guam...........................	1,975	1,804	—	1,843	2,291	2,291	925	991	375	2,291	925	991	375
Northern Marianas.........	526	614	552	607	496	409	249	156	4	417	243	170	4
Puerto Rico..................	37,620	42,036	39,102	36,506	33,079	30,986	14,293	11,765	4,928	33,412	15,209	12,642	5,560
U.S. Virgin Islands..........	1,511	1,434	1,425	1,457	1,217	1,129	489	351	289	1,082	470	276	336

—Not available.
[1]Includes imputed values for states.
[2]Includes imputations to correct for underreporting of prekindergarten teachers.
[3]Imputed.
[4]Includes imputations to correct for underreporting of prekindergarten, kindergarten, and secondary teachers.
[5]Includes imputations to correct for underreporting of prekindergarten and kindergarten teachers.
[6]Includes imputations to correct for underreporting of prekindergarten, kindergarten, and ungraded teachers.
[7]Includes imputations to correct for underreporting of kindergarten teachers.
NOTE: Distribution of elementary and secondary teachers determined by reporting units. DoD = Department of Defense.
SOURCE: U.S. Department of Education, National Center for Education Statistics, Common Core of Data (CCD), "State Nonfiscal Survey of Public Elementary/Secondary Education," 2000–01 through 2013–14. (This table was prepared August 2015.)

Table 208.40. Public elementary and secondary teachers, enrollment, and pupil/teacher ratios, by state or jurisdiction: Selected years, fall 2000 through fall 2013

State or jurisdiction	Pupil/teacher ratio				Fall 2011			Fall 2012			Fall 2013		
	Fall 2000	Fall 2008	Fall 2009	Fall 2010	Teachers	Enrollment	Pupil/ teacher ratio	Teachers	Enrollment	Pupil/ teacher ratio	Teachers	Enrollment	Pupil/ teacher ratio
1	2	3	4	5	6	7	8	9	10	11	12	13	14
United States	16.0 [1]	15.3 [1]	15.4 [1]	16.0 [1]	3,103,263 [1]	49,521,669	16.0 [1]	3,109,101 [1]	49,771,118	16.0 [1]	3,113,764 [1]	50,044,522	16.1 [1]
Alabama	15.4 [2]	15.6	15.8	15.3	47,723	744,621	15.6	51,877	744,637	14.4	47,162	746,204	15.8
Alaska	16.9	16.5	16.3	16.2	8,088	131,167	16.2	7,682	131,489	17.1	7,898	130,944	16.6
Arizona	19.8	19.9	20.7	21.4	50,800	1,080,319	21.3	48,866	1,089,384	22.3	48,359	1,102,445	22.8
Arkansas	14.1	12.9	12.9	14.1	33,983	483,114	14.2	34,131	486,157	14.2	34,933	489,979	14.0
California	20.6 [2]	20.8 [2]	19.8 [2]	24.1 [2]	268,689 [2]	6,287,834	23.4 [2]	266,255 [2]	6,299,451	23.7 [2]	259,506 [2]	6,312,623	24.3 [2]
Colorado	17.3	16.8	17.0	17.4	48,078	854,265	17.8	48,922	863,561	17.7	50,157	876,999	17.5
Connecticut	13.7	11.7	12.9	13.1	43,805	554,437	12.7	43,931	550,954	12.5	43,443	546,200	12.6
Delaware	15.4	15.1	14.7	14.5	8,587	128,946	15.0	9,257	129,026	13.9	9,388	131,687	14.0
District of Columbia	13.9	12.9	11.9	12.0	6,278	73,911	11.8	5,925	76,140	12.9	5,991	78,153	13.0
Florida	18.4	14.1	14.3	15.1	175,006	2,668,156	15.2	176,537	2,692,162	15.2	177,853	2,720,744	15.3
Georgia	15.9	13.9	14.4	14.9	111,133	1,685,016	15.2	109,365	1,703,332	15.6	109,441	1,723,909	15.8
Hawaii	16.9	15.9	15.7	15.8	11,458	182,706	15.9	11,608	184,760	15.9	11,781	186,825	15.9
Idaho	17.9	18.2	18.2	17.6	15,990	279,873	17.5	14,563	284,834	19.6	15,002	296,476	19.8
Illinois	16.1	15.6	15.2	15.7	131,777	2,083,097	15.8	135,701 [3]	2,072,880	15.3 [3]	136,355 [4]	2,066,990	15.2 [4]
Indiana	16.7	16.7	16.8	18.0 [2]	62,339	1,040,765	16.7 [2]	59,863	1,041,369	17.4	59,823	1,047,385	17.5
Iowa	14.3	13.6	13.7	14.3	34,658	495,870	14.3	35,080	499,825	14.2	35,397	502,964	14.2
Kansas	14.4	13.1	13.7	14.0	37,407	486,108	13.0	41,243	489,043	11.9	38,153	496,440	13.0
Kentucky	16.8	15.4	16.2	16.0	41,860	681,987	16.3	42,769	685,167	16.0	41,820	677,389	16.2
Louisiana	14.9	13.9	13.9	14.3	48,657	703,390	14.5	46,493	710,903	15.3	46,437	711,491	15.3
Maine	12.5	12.1	11.6	12.3	14,888	188,969	12.7	15,222	185,739	12.2	15,452	183,995	11.9
Maryland	16.3	14.3	14.5	14.6	57,589	854,086	14.8	57,718	859,638	14.9	58,611	866,169	14.8
Massachusetts	14.5	13.6	13.7	13.9	69,342	953,369	13.7	70,636	954,773	13.5	70,490	955,739	13.6
Michigan	17.7 [2]	17.5	17.8	17.9	86,997	1,573,537	18.1	86,154	1,555,370	18.1	85,786	1,548,841	18.1
Minnesota	16.0	15.7	15.8	15.9	52,832	839,738	15.9	53,585	845,404	15.8	54,413	850,973	15.6
Mississippi	16.1	14.7	14.9	15.2	32,007	490,619	15.3	32,613	493,650	15.1	32,292	492,586	15.3
Missouri	14.1	13.5	13.5	13.8	66,252	916,584	13.8	66,248	917,900	13.9	66,651	918,288	13.8
Montana	14.9	13.6	13.5	13.7	10,153	142,349	14.0	10,200	142,908	14.0	10,310	144,129	14.0
Nebraska	13.6	13.3	13.3	13.4	22,182	301,296	13.6	22,103	303,505	13.7	22,401	307,677	13.7
Nevada	18.6	19.7	19.4	20.0	21,132	439,634	20.8	20,695	445,707	21.5	21,921	451,831	20.6
New Hampshire	14.5	12.6	12.7	12.7	15,049	191,900	12.8	14,925	188,974	12.7	14,826	186,310	12.6
New Jersey	13.3	12.0	12.1	12.7	109,719	1,356,431	12.4	110,929	1,372,203	12.4	114,581	1,370,295	12.0
New Mexico	15.2	14.5	14.7	15.1	21,957	337,225	15.4	22,201	338,220	15.2	22,239	339,244	15.3
New York	13.9	12.6	12.9	12.9	209,527	2,704,718	12.9	207,060	2,710,703	13.1	206,693	2,732,770	13.2
North Carolina	15.5	13.6	14.1 [5]	15.2	97,308	1,507,864	15.5	98,590	1,518,465	15.4	99,327	1,530,857	15.4
North Dakota	13.4	11.6	11.4	11.4	8,525	97,646	11.5	8,677	101,111	11.7	8,805	103,947	11.8
Ohio	15.5	16.1	15.8	16.1	107,972	1,740,030	16.1	106,000	1,729,916	16.3	106,010	1,724,111	16.3
Oklahoma	15.1	13.9	15.4	16.0	41,349	666,120	16.1	41,775	673,483	16.1	41,983	681,848	16.2
Oregon	19.4	19.1	20.3	20.3	26,791	568,208	21.2	26,410	587,564	22.2	26,733	593,000	22.2
Pennsylvania	15.5	13.7	13.6	13.8	124,646	1,771,395	14.2	123,147	1,763,677	14.3	121,330	1,755,236	14.5
Rhode Island	14.8	12.8	12.8	12.8	11,414	142,854	12.5	9,871	142,481	14.4	9,824	142,008	14.5
South Carolina	14.9	14.4	15.4	16.1	46,782	727,186	15.5	48,072	735,998	15.3	48,151	745,657	15.5
South Dakota	13.7	13.7	13.3	13.3	9,247	128,016	13.8	9,334	130,471	14.0	9,510	130,890	13.8
Tennessee	15.9 [2]	15.0	14.9	14.8	66,382	999,693	15.1	66,406	993,496	15.0	65,847	993,556	15.1
Texas	14.8	14.5	14.6	14.7	324,282	5,000,470	15.4	327,357	5,077,659	15.5	334,580	5,153,702	15.4
Utah	21.9	23.7	22.3	22.8	25,970	598,832	23.1	26,610	613,279	23.0	27,247	625,461	23.0
Vermont	12.1	10.7	10.5	11.6	8,364	89,908	10.7	8,403	89,624	10.7	8,375	88,690	10.6
Virginia	13.2 [2]	17.3	17.6	17.6	90,832	1,257,883	13.8	89,389	1,265,419	14.2	90,098	1,273,825	14.1
Washington	19.7	19.1	19.4	19.4	53,119	1,045,453	19.7	53,699	1,051,694	19.6	54,867	1,058,936	19.3
West Virginia	13.7	14.0	13.9	13.9	20,247	282,870	14.0	20,101	283,044	14.1	19,978	280,958	14.1
Wisconsin	14.6	14.7	14.9	15.1	56,245	871,105	15.5	57,551	872,436	15.2	57,980	874,414	15.1
Wyoming	13.3	12.5	12.3	12.5	7,847	90,099	11.5	7,350	91,533	12.5	7,555	92,732	12.3
Bureau of Indian Education	—	—	—	—	—	—	—	5,308	—	—	—	—	—
DoD, overseas	14.4	12.5	—	—	—	—	—	—	—	—	—	—	—
DoD, domestic	14.2	13.1	—	—	—	—	—	—	—	—	—	—	—
Other jurisdictions American Samoa	19.1	—	—	—	—	—	—	—	—	—	—	—	—
Guam	16.4	—	—	17.2	2,291	31,243	13.6	2,291	31,186	13.6	2,291	33,414	14.6
Northern Marianas	19.0	21.2	19.9	18.3	496	11,011	22.2	409	10,646	26.0	417	10,638	25.5
Puerto Rico	16.3	12.8	12.6	13.0	33,079	452,740	13.7	30,986	434,609	14.0	33,412	423,934	12.7
U.S. Virgin Islands	12.9	11.8	10.9	10.6	1,217	15,711	12.9	1,129	15,192	13.5	1,082	14,953	13.8

—Not available.
[1]Includes imputed values for states.
[2]Includes imputations to correct for underreporting of prekindergarten teachers/enrollment.
[3]Includes imputations to correct for underreporting of prekindergarten, kindergarten, and secondary teachers.
[4]Includes imputations to correct for underreporting of prekindergarten, kindergarten, and unclassified teachers.
[5]Includes imputations to correct for underreporting of kindergarten teachers.

NOTE: Teachers reported in full-time equivalents (FTE). DoD = Department of Defense. The pupil/teacher ratio includes teachers for students with disabilities and other special teachers, while these teachers are generally excluded from class size calculations. Ratios reflect totals reported by states and differ from totals reported for schools or school districts.
SOURCE: U.S. Department of Education, National Center for Education Statistics, Common Core of Data (CCD), "State Nonfiscal Survey of Public Elementary/Secondary Education," 2000–01 through 2013–14. (This table was prepared August 2015.)

Table 209.10. Number and percentage distribution of teachers in public and private elementary and secondary schools, by selected teacher characteristics: Selected years, 1987–88 through 2011–12

[Standard errors appear in parentheses]

Selected teacher characteristic	Number of teachers (in thousands)							Percentage distribution of teachers						
	1987–88	1990–91	1993–94	1999–2000	2003–04	2007–08	2011–12	1987–88	1990–91	1993–94	1999–2000	2003–04	2007–08	2011–12
	2	3	4	5	6	7	8	9	10	11	12	13	14	15
Public schools														
Total	2,323 (13.2)	2,559 (20.7)	2,561 (20.8)	3,002 (19.4)	3,251 (29.2)	3,405 (44.0)	3,385 (41.4)	100.0 (†)	100.0 (†)	100.0 (†)	100.0 (†)	100.0 (†)	100.0 (†)	100.0 (†)
Sex														
Male	685 (6.8)	719 (11.2)	694 (11.8)	754 (10.7)	813 (13.3)	821 (20.4)	802 (22.2)	29.5 (0.22)	28.1 (0.31)	27.1 (0.36)	25.1 (0.30)	25.0 (0.32)	24.1 (0.47)	23.7 (0.49)
Female	1,638 (10.1)	1,840 (14.7)	1,867 (16.2)	2,248 (16.0)	2,438 (23.5)	2,584 (34.6)	2,584 (30.5)	70.5 (0.22)	71.9 (0.31)	72.9 (0.36)	74.9 (0.30)	75.0 (0.32)	75.9 (0.47)	76.3 (0.49)
Race/ethnicity														
White[1]	2,018 (12.6)	2,214 (20.0)	2,217 (19.5)	2,532 (17.2)	2,702 (30.1)	2,829 (38.7)	2,773 (30.5)	86.9 (0.24)	86.5 (0.29)	86.5 (0.33)	84.3 (0.30)	83.1 (0.53)	83.1 (0.53)	81.9 (0.53)
Black[1]	191 (4.6)	212 (6.4)	188 (5.4)	228 (6.0)	257 (11.0)	239 (15.8)	231 (12.1)	8.2 (0.19)	8.3 (0.25)	7.4 (0.21)	7.6 (0.19)	7.9 (0.34)	7.0 (0.45)	6.8 (0.31)
Hispanic[1]	69 (2.6)	87 (4.5)	109 (6.2)	169 (6.4)	202 (11.3)	240 (16.6)	264 (13.4)	3.0 (0.11)	3.4 (0.17)	4.2 (0.23)	5.6 (0.20)	6.2 (0.34)	7.1 (0.46)	7.8 (0.37)
Asian[1,2]	21 (1.1)	27 (1.7)	28 (1.2)	48 (2.7)	42 (2.5)	42 (7.2)	61 (7.3)	0.9 (0.05)	1.0 (0.06)	1.1 (0.05)	1.6 (0.09)	1.3 (0.08)	1.2 (0.21)	1.8 (0.21)
Pacific Islander	— (†)	— (†)	— (†)	— (†)	6 (0.8)	6 (1.3)	5 (1.4)	— (†)	— (†)	— (†)	— (†)	0.2 (0.03)	0.2 (0.04)	0.1 (0.04)
American Indian/Alaska Native[1]	24 (1.3)	20 (1.4)	20 (1.4)	26 (1.9)	17 (1.2)	17 (1.9)	17 (2.9)	1.0 (0.06)	0.8 (0.05)	0.8 (0.06)	0.9 (0.06)	0.5 (0.04)	0.5 (0.06)	0.5 (0.08)
Two or more races	— (†)	— (†)	— (†)	— (†)	24 (2.2)	31 (2.9)	35 (3.7)	— (†)	— (†)	— (†)	—	0.7 (0.07)	0.9 (0.09)	1.0 (0.11)
Age														
Under 30	313 (5.0)	257 (5.7)	280 (4.5)	509 (9.2)	540 (27.4)	612 (22.4)	518 (15.9)	13.5 (0.19)	10.0 (0.23)	10.9 (0.16)	17.0 (0.28)	16.6 (0.84)	18.0 (0.61)	15.3 (0.44)
30 to 39	823 (7.7)	684 (10.8)	573 (8.0)	661 (9.8)	798 (14.5)	898 (16.8)	979 (19.3)	35.4 (0.30)	26.7 (0.35)	22.4 (0.30)	22.0 (0.29)	24.5 (0.38)	26.4 (0.39)	28.9 (0.53)
40 to 49	762 (7.4)	1,034 (13.3)	1,070 (12.5)	953 (10.3)	840 (14.3)	808 (19.2)	849 (19.2)	32.8 (0.25)	40.4 (0.37)	41.8 (0.33)	31.8 (0.32)	25.9 (0.38)	23.7 (0.47)	25.1 (0.51)
50 to 59	357 (5.7)	477 (8.6)	540 (10.1)	786 (12.6)	942 (26.0)	879 (21.1)	783 (20.5)	15.4 (0.23)	18.7 (0.29)	21.1 (0.29)	26.2 (0.35)	29.0 (0.74)	25.8 (0.51)	23.1 (0.49)
60 and over	68 (2.5)	107 (4.1)	97 (3.5)	93 (4.0)	131 (4.8)	207 (10.3)	256 (13.2)	2.9 (0.11)	4.2 (0.16)	3.8 (0.14)	3.1 (0.13)	4.0 (0.14)	6.1 (0.29)	7.6 (0.34)
Highest degree earned														
Less than bachelor's	15 (1.0)	17 (1.2)	18 (1.4)	20 (1.3)	35 (2.5)	27 (2.1)	128 (8.6)	0.7 (0.04)	0.7 (0.05)	0.7 (0.06)	0.7 (0.04)	1.1 (0.08)	0.8 (0.06)	3.8 (0.24)
Bachelor's	1,214 (9.8)	1,327 (11.7)	1,331 (13.4)	1,560 (15.8)	1,651 (22.8)	1,612 (28.8)	1,350 (21.1)	52.3 (0.28)	51.9 (0.31)	52.0 (0.33)	52.0 (0.40)	50.8 (0.56)	47.4 (0.59)	39.9 (0.52)
Master's	932 (8.5)	1,077 (13.5)	1,075 (12.0)	1,257 (13.9)	1,331 (21.7)	1,517 (27.8)	1,614 (29.1)	40.1 (0.30)	42.1 (0.34)	42.0 (0.33)	41.9 (0.38)	40.9 (0.56)	44.5 (0.55)	47.7 (0.57)
Education specialist[3]	146 (3.4)	118 (5.3)	117 (3.8)	143 (5.2)	195 (6.8)	218 (8.6)	257 (9.7)	6.3 (0.14)	4.6 (0.20)	4.6 (0.14)	4.7 (0.17)	6.0 (0.19)	6.4 (0.25)	7.6 (0.27)
Doctor's	16 (1.2)	20 (1.7)	19 (1.7)	22 (1.8)	38 (3.5)	30 (2.7)	37 (4.0)	0.7 (0.05)	0.8 (0.07)	0.7 (0.07)	0.7 (0.06)	1.2 (0.11)	0.9 (0.08)	1.1 (0.11)
Years of full-time teaching experience														
Less than 3	188 (3.3)	223 (4.8)	249 (5.2)	387 (8.7)	396 (39.8)	457 (21.8)	305 (10.2)	8.1 (0.15)	8.7 (0.19)	9.7 (0.20)	12.9 (0.27)	12.2 (1.23)	13.4 (0.59)	9.0 (0.29)
3 to 9	605 (6.1)	634 (9.8)	653 (9.7)	865 (12.0)	1,070 (15.3)	1,143 (19.7)	1,128 (19.9)	26.0 (0.20)	24.8 (0.31)	25.5 (0.32)	28.8 (0.36)	32.9 (0.34)	33.6 (0.52)	33.3 (0.52)
10 to 20	1,034 (8.2)	1,025 (11.7)	898 (9.2)	854 (10.3)	924 (21.6)	997 (23.2)	1,232 (21.0)	44.5 (0.25)	40.0 (0.35)	35.0 (0.33)	28.5 (0.33)	28.4 (0.59)	29.3 (0.55)	36.4 (0.51)
Over 20	497 (5.8)	678 (10.4)	762 (12.4)	896 (12.8)	860 (26.6)	808 (22.9)	720 (23.7)	21.4 (0.21)	26.5 (0.30)	29.8 (0.32)	29.8 (0.34)	26.5 (0.77)	23.7 (0.60)	21.3 (0.54)
Level														
Elementary	1,292 (9.5)	1,442 (11.8)	1,331 (17.0)	1,602 (13.5)	1,716 (25.8)	1,725 (37.1)	1,726 (20.2)	55.6 (0.33)	56.3 (0.40)	52.0 (0.57)	53.3 (0.42)	52.8 (0.66)	50.7 (0.91)	51.0 (0.65)
General	788 (7.4)	887 (10.6)	881 (13.5)	1,042 (12.5)	1,130 (29.8)	1,100 (26.5)	1,078 (22.1)	33.9 (0.29)	34.6 (0.39)	34.4 (0.46)	34.7 (0.41)	34.8 (0.86)	32.3 (0.70)	31.8 (0.71)
Arts/music	116 (3.0)	110 (4.3)	83 (3.1)	99 (3.7)	101 (5.3)	103 (6.6)	82 (5.4)	5.0 (0.13)	4.3 (0.17)	3.2 (0.12)	3.3 (0.12)	3.1 (0.17)	3.0 (0.19)	2.4 (0.16)
English	60 (2.3)	72 (3.8)	49 (3.2)	66 (3.8)	70 (5.1)	104 (9.9)	92 (6.9)	2.6 (0.10)	2.8 (0.14)	1.9 (0.12)	2.2 (0.13)	2.2 (0.16)	3.0 (0.29)	2.7 (0.21)
ESL/bilingual	18 (1.1)	20 (1.3)	27 (2.2)	28 (1.8)	25 (3.6)	24 (3.3)	51 (6.8)	0.8 (0.05)	0.8 (0.05)	1.1 (0.09)	0.9 (0.06)	0.8 (0.11)	0.7 (0.10)	1.5 (0.20)
Health/physical ed.	56 (2.0)	66 (3.2)	58 (3.0)	57 (3.5)	73 (5.0)	63 (6.0)	79 (8.1)	2.4 (0.09)	2.6 (0.12)	2.3 (0.12)	1.9 (0.12)	2.2 (0.15)	1.8 (0.18)	2.3 (0.23)
Mathematics	31 (2.0)	30 (1.9)	24 (2.2)	23 (2.4)	19 (2.3)	28 (3.8)	32 (6.5)	1.3 (0.09)	1.2 (0.08)	0.9 (0.08)	0.8 (0.08)	0.6 (0.07)	0.8 (0.11)	0.9 (0.19)
Science	18 (1.5)	21 (1.9)	10 (1.2)	11 (1.3)	19 (3.0)	15 (3.4)	29 (3.3)	0.8 (0.06)	0.8 (0.07)	0.4 (0.05)	0.4 (0.04)	0.6 (0.09)	0.4 (0.10)	0.9 (0.10)
Special education	168 (3.9)	176 (5.9)	158 (4.2)	227 (5.6)	240 (20.6)	230 (13.0)	239 (10.3)	7.2 (0.16)	6.9 (0.23)	6.2 (0.16)	7.6 (0.18)	7.4 (0.63)	6.7 (0.37)	7.1 (0.31)
Other elementary	37 (2.4)	60 (3.2)	42 (2.9)	49 (3.5)	40 (3.5)	58 (3.5)	55 (5.2)	1.6 (0.10)	2.4 (0.12)	1.7 (0.11)	1.6 (0.12)	1.2 (0.11)	1.7 (0.12)	1.6 (0.15)
Secondary	1,031 (10.5)	1,118 (16.5)	1,230 (18.9)	1,401 (17.7)	1,534 (26.0)	1,680 (39.0)	1,659 (37.8)	44.4 (0.33)	43.7 (0.40)	48.0 (0.57)	46.7 (0.42)	47.2 (0.66)	49.3 (0.91)	49.0 (0.65)
Arts/music	73 (2.0)	74 (2.5)	92 (2.5)	110 (3.4)	112 (4.1)	121 (6.2)	121 (5.6)	3.1 (0.09)	2.9 (0.08)	3.6 (0.10)	3.7 (0.11)	3.4 (0.12)	3.6 (0.18)	3.6 (0.14)
English	171 (3.2)	195 (5.1)	209 (5.0)	245 (5.1)	269 (9.0)	306 (10.0)	289 (9.9)	7.4 (0.12)	7.6 (0.18)	8.2 (0.18)	8.2 (0.15)	8.3 (0.27)	9.0 (0.27)	8.5 (0.25)
ESL/bilingual	6 (0.5)	10 (0.7)	12 (1.3)	16 (1.2)	18 (2.5)	21 (2.5)	20 (2.4)	0.3 (0.05)	0.4 (0.03)	0.5 (0.05)	0.5 (0.04)	0.6 (0.08)	0.6 (0.07)	0.6 (0.07)
Foreign language	43 (1.2)	52 (2.4)	59 (2.0)	71 (2.4)	73 (3.3)	78 (5.0)	88 (4.5)	1.9 (0.05)	2.0 (0.09)	2.3 (0.07)	2.4 (0.08)	2.3 (0.10)	2.3 (0.14)	2.6 (0.12)
Health/physical ed.	76 (2.4)	76 (2.2)	88 (2.7)	99 (3.1)	102 (4.3)	119 (5.7)	101 (3.9)	3.3 (0.10)	3.0 (0.08)	3.4 (0.10)	3.3 (0.10)	3.1 (0.12)	3.5 (0.16)	3.0 (0.11)
Mathematics	139 (2.5)	155 (4.3)	174 (3.7)	207 (4.5)	213 (5.5)	252 (9.1)	250 (7.5)	6.0 (0.10)	6.0 (0.15)	6.8 (0.13)	6.9 (0.14)	6.5 (0.17)	7.4 (0.25)	7.4 (0.19)
Science	115 (2.9)	128 (4.0)	143 (3.4)	169 (4.0)	189 (6.8)	195 (8.3)	209 (6.1)	4.9 (0.11)	5.0 (0.15)	5.6 (0.11)	5.6 (0.12)	5.8 (0.24)	5.7 (0.24)	6.2 (0.16)
Social studies	118 (2.4)	124 (3.3)	138 (3.3)	163 (4.4)	178 (5.7)	209 (9.9)	197 (6.3)	5.1 (0.10)	4.8 (0.12)	5.4 (0.12)	5.4 (0.14)	5.5 (0.20)	6.1 (0.27)	5.8 (0.16)
Special education	100 (2.2)	113 (3.5)	126 (3.1)	113 (2.8)	174 (7.5)	165 (9.7)	191 (12.2)	4.3 (0.09)	4.4 (0.13)	4.9 (0.11)	3.8 (0.09)	5.4 (0.16)	4.9 (0.28)	5.7 (0.32)
Vocational/technical	166 (3.0)	160 (3.7)	153 (3.5)	161 (3.5)	169 (5.7)	164 (6.3)	147 (5.7)	7.1 (0.10)	6.3 (0.13)	6.0 (0.12)	5.4 (0.10)	5.2 (0.23)	4.8 (0.17)	4.3 (0.16)
Other secondary	25 (1.3)	30 (1.5)	36 (1.4)	47 (2.0)	36 (2.1)	47 (3.4)	46 (4.0)	1.1 (0.06)	1.2 (0.06)	1.4 (0.06)	1.6 (0.07)	1.1 (0.06)	1.4 (0.10)	1.4 (0.12)

See notes at end of table.

Table 209.10. Number and percentage distribution of teachers in public and private elementary and secondary schools, by selected teacher characteristics: Selected years, 1987–88 through 2011–12—Continued

[Standard errors appear in parentheses]

Selected teacher characteristic	Number of teachers (in thousands)							Percentage distribution of teachers						
	1987–88	1990–91	1993–94	1999–2000	2003–04	2007–08	2011–12	1987–88	1990–91	1993–94	1999–2000	2003–04	2007–08	2011–12
1	2	3	4	5	6	7	8	9	10	11	12	13	14	15
Private schools														
Total	307 (8.5)	356 (7.2)	378 (5.6)	449 (10.6)	467 (10.3)	490 (9.2)	465 (11.1)	100.0 (†)	100.0 (†)	100.0 (†)	100.0 (†)	100.0 (†)	100.0 (†)	100.0 (†)
Sex														
Male	67 (3.3)	82 (3.3)	93 (2.3)	107 (3.8)	110 (8.4)	127 (4.6)	117 (6.9)	21.8 (0.86)	22.9 (0.74)	24.6 (0.43)	23.9 (0.48)	23.6 (1.93)	26.0 (0.78)	25.2 (1.33)
Female	240 (7.2)	275 (5.8)	285 (4.2)	342 (7.7)	357 (14.3)	362 (7.7)	348 (10.1)	78.2 (0.86)	77.1 (0.74)	75.4 (0.43)	76.1 (0.48)	76.4 (1.93)	74.0 (0.78)	74.8 (1.33)
Race/ethnicity														
White[1]	285 (8.3)	329 (7.0)	348 (5.1)	402 (9.6)	411 (12.0)	423 (8.8)	411 (11.1)	92.8 (0.50)	92.2 (0.46)	91.9 (0.41)	89.5 (0.42)	88.0 (0.99)	86.4 (0.80)	88.3 (0.69)
Black[1]	7 (0.8)	9 (1.0)	12 (1.0)	17 (1.4)	19 (1.4)	20 (2.2)	17 (2.4)	2.3 (0.27)	2.7 (0.28)	3.1 (0.27)	3.7 (0.29)	4.0 (0.65)	4.0 (0.44)	3.6 (0.54)
Hispanic[1]	9 (1.1)	12 (1.0)	12 (1.0)	21 (1.5)	23 (3.1)	29 (2.1)	24 (2.4)	2.8 (0.36)	3.3 (0.26)	3.2 (0.26)	4.7 (0.30)	4.8 (0.71)	5.9 (0.38)	5.2 (0.51)
Asian[1,2]	4 (0.8)	5 (0.6)	5 (0.6)	7 (0.6)	9 (1.0)	11 (1.5)	9 (1.4)	1.2 (0.26)	1.5 (0.18)	1.4 (0.16)	1.6 (0.14)	1.8 (0.20)	2.2 (0.29)	1.8 (0.31)
Pacific Islander	—	—	—	—	‡	‡	‡	— (†)	— (†)	— (†)	—	0.2! (0.07)	0.3! (0.14)	‡ (†)
American Indian/Alaska Native[1]	3 (0.4)	1 (†)	2 (0.3)	2 (0.4)	‡ 3! (1.4)	‡ 4 (0.6)	‡ 4 (0.9)	0.9 (0.12)	0.4 (0.09)	0.4 (0.07)	0.6 (0.08)	0.6! (0.28)	0.7 (0.12)	0.8 (0.19)
Two or more races[2]	—	—	—	—	‡ 3! (1.4)	4	4	— (†)	— (†)	— (†)	—	‡	‡	‡
Age														
Under 30	67 (2.6)	60 (2.2)	65 (1.7)	87 (3.1)	88 (3.7)	80 (3.9)	78 (6.8)	21.8 (0.77)	16.7 (0.61)	17.2 (0.39)	19.3 (0.43)	18.9 (0.78)	16.3 (0.67)	16.7 (1.48)
30 to 39	106 (3.6)	100 (4.0)	94 (2.1)	101 (3.2)	103 (5.8)	109 (5.2)	112 (6.2)	34.5 (0.81)	28.1 (0.78)	24.8 (0.48)	22.4 (0.50)	22.0 (1.36)	22.3 (0.91)	24.0 (1.07)
40 to 49	84 (3.4)	121 (3.1)	131 (3.3)	131 (4.2)	119 (7.1)	116 (3.6)	110 (6.3)	27.4 (0.78)	33.9 (0.74)	34.8 (0.60)	29.2 (0.62)	25.4 (1.41)	23.8 (0.65)	23.8 (1.06)
50 to 59	34 (2.2)	53 (2.3)	66 (2.1)	106 (3.2)	121 (11.1)	128 (4.5)	99 (5.0)	11.1 (0.57)	14.8 (0.55)	17.4 (0.48)	23.5 (0.46)	25.8 (2.07)	26.2 (0.87)	21.3 (1.06)
60 and over	16 (1.7)	23 (1.6)	22 (1.1)	25 (1.2)	37 (4.7)	56 (3.1)	66 (5.0)	5.3 (0.49)	6.4 (0.41)	5.8 (0.27)	5.7 (0.24)	8.0 (0.99)	11.5 (0.62)	14.2 (1.05)
Highest degree earned														
Less than bachelor's	13 (1.4)	23 (1.6)	25 (1.8)	33 (2.3)	43! (21.5)	40 (2.9)	39 (5.2)	4.4 (0.42)	6.4 (0.45)	6.7 (0.46)	7.3 (0.46)	9.2! (4.41)	8.1 (0.58)	8.4 (1.07)
Bachelor's	189 (5.1)	221 (5.7)	223 (3.3)	258 (5.8)	259 (11.2)	264 (6.8)	225 (6.7)	61.4 (0.75)	61.9 (0.90)	59.0 (0.63)	57.5 (0.64)	55.5 (2.90)	53.9 (0.95)	48.5 (1.37)
Master's	92 (3.8)	96 (3.1)	113 (3.6)	136 (4.5)	138 (6.1)	161 (5.3)	166 (7.5)	29.8 (0.73)	27.0 (0.71)	29.8 (0.69)	30.3 (0.58)	29.5 (1.35)	32.8 (0.84)	35.8 (1.16)
Education specialist[3]	9 (0.9)	11 (0.9)	11 (0.7)	14 (1.0)	17 (2.4)	14 (1.3)	23 (2.3)	3.0 (0.30)	2.9 (0.24)	2.9 (0.19)	3.1 (0.19)	3.6 (0.54)	2.8 (0.25)	5.0 (0.48)
Doctor's	4 (0.7)	6 (0.8)	6 (0.6)	8 (0.8)	10 (1.2)	12 (1.9)	11 (2.0)	1.5 (0.23)	1.8 (0.22)	1.7 (0.15)	1.8 (0.16)	2.2 (0.26)	2.4 (0.38)	2.3 (0.41)
Years of full-time teaching experience														
Less than 3	59 (2.1)	73 (2.8)	79 (2.1)	108 (3.8)	116 (14.6)	116 (5.4)	91 (8.4)	19.0 (0.60)	20.4 (0.72)	20.9 (0.54)	23.9 (0.52)	24.8 (2.75)	23.6 (0.99)	19.5 (1.76)
3 to 9	115 (4.1)	123 (4.0)	128 (3.1)	139 (4.2)	154 (6.0)	152 (5.2)	145 (5.7)	37.6 (0.88)	34.6 (0.69)	33.9 (0.60)	31.0 (0.55)	33.0 (1.23)	31.0 (0.82)	31.3 (0.94)
10 to 20	92 (3.8)	107 (3.5)	112 (3.0)	122 (3.6)	112 (5.8)	120 (4.7)	129 (5.8)	29.8 (0.80)	30.0 (0.78)	29.6 (0.60)	27.2 (0.52)	23.9 (1.19)	24.6 (0.86)	27.7 (1.06)
Over 20	42 (2.4)	53 (2.5)	59 (2.1)	80 (2.6)	86 (8.0)	102 (4.0)	100 (7.2)	13.6 (0.62)	14.9 (0.67)	15.6 (0.51)	17.8 (0.45)	18.3 (1.87)	20.8 (0.75)	21.4 (1.47)
Level														
Elementary	179 (5.6)	225 (4.7)	221 (3.6)	261 (5.8)	263 (17.5)	258 (6.5)	245 (9.3)	58.3 (0.92)	63.2 (0.72)	58.4 (0.57)	58.1 (0.66)	56.4 (3.06)	52.8 (1.03)	52.8 (1.67)
Secondary	128 (4.7)	131 (4.0)	157 (3.4)	188 (6.2)	204 (13.4)	231 (7.1)	219 (9.9)	41.7 (0.92)	36.8 (0.72)	41.6 (0.57)	41.9 (0.66)	43.6 (3.06)	47.2 (1.03)	47.2 (1.67)

—Not available.
†Not applicable.
!Interpret data with caution. The coefficient of variation (CV) for this estimate is between 30 and 50 percent.
‡Reporting standards not met. Either there are too few cases for a reliable estimate or the coefficient of variation (CV) is 50 percent or greater.
[1]Data for years 1987–88 through 1999–2000 are only roughly comparable to data for later years, because the new category of Two or more races was introduced in 2003–04.
[2]Includes Pacific Islander for years 1987–88 through 1999–2000; and
[3]Education specialist degrees or certificates are generally awarded for 1 year's work beyond the master's level. Includes certificate of advanced graduate studies.
NOTE: Excludes prekindergarten teachers. Data are based on a head count of full-time and part-time teachers rather than on the number of full-time-equivalent teachers reported in other tables. Detail may not sum to totals because of rounding, missing data, and cell suppression. Race categories exclude persons of Hispanic ethnicity.
SOURCE: U.S. Department of Education, National Center for Education Statistics, Schools and Staffing Survey (SASS), "Public School Teacher Data File," 1987–88 through 2011–12; "Private School Teacher Data File," 1987–88 through 2011–12; and "Charter School Teacher Data File," 1999–2000. (This table was prepared July 2013.)

Table 209.20. Number, highest degree, and years of full-time teaching experience of teachers in public and private elementary and secondary schools, by selected teacher characteristics: 1999–2000 through 2011–12

[Standard error appears in parentheses]

Selected teacher characteristic	Number of teachers (in thousands)				Percent of teachers, by highest degree earned, 2011–12					Percent of teachers, by years of full-time teaching experience, 2011–12			
	1999–2000	2003–04	2007–08	2011–12	Less than bachelor's	Bachelor's	Master's	Education specialist[1]	Doctor's	Less than 3	3 to 9	10 to 20	Over 20
1	2	3	4	5	6	7	8	9	10	11	12	13	14
Public schools													
Total	3,002 (19.4)	3,251 (29.2)	3,405 (44.0)	3,385 (41.4)	3.8 (0.24)	39.9 (0.52)	47.7 (0.57)	7.6 (0.27)	1.1 (0.11)	9.0 (0.29)	33.3 (0.52)	36.4 (0.51)	21.3 (0.54)
Sex													
Males	754 (10.7)	813 (13.3)	821 (20.4)	802 (22.2)	5.7 (0.58)	39.7 (1.03)	46.3 (1.04)	6.6 (0.51)	1.7 (0.20)	9.7 (0.52)	32.3 (1.11)	38.3 (0.98)	19.7 (1.01)
Females	2,248 (16.0)	2,438 (23.5)	2,584 (34.6)	2,584 (30.5)	3.2 (0.22)	39.9 (0.59)	48.1 (0.64)	7.9 (0.33)	0.9 (0.13)	8.8 (0.34)	33.7 (0.59)	35.8 (0.61)	21.8 (0.61)
Race/ethnicity													
White	2,532 (17.2)[2]	2,702 (30.1)	2,829 (38.7)	2,773 (30.5)	3.7 (0.23)	39.3 (0.57)	48.7 (0.61)	7.4 (0.28)	0.9 (0.12)	8.7 (0.33)	32.5 (0.54)	36.5 (0.56)	22.3 (0.64)
Black	228 (6.0)[2]	257 (11.0)	239 (15.8)	231 (12.1)	4.2 (0.91)	39.6 (2.36)	45.0 (3.06)	8.7 (1.39)	2.5 (0.52)	9.5 (1.25)	32.4 (2.85)	34.7 (2.46)	23.4 (2.54)
Hispanic	169 (6.4)[2]	202 (11.3)	240 (16.6)	263 (13.4)	4.5 (1.16)	48.1 (2.31)	39.0 (2.18)	6.9 (0.98)	1.5 (0.41)	10.8 (2.05)	40.4 (2.44)	36.4 (2.54)	12.4 (1.63)
Asian	48 (2.7)[3]	42 (2.5)	42 (7.2)	61 (7.3)	1.8 ! (0.76)	27.9 (4.51)	53.4 (5.32)	15.8 ! (4.91)	1.1 ! (0.50)	10.1 (2.13)	45.0 (6.77)	33.7 (6.51)	11.2 (3.19)
Pacific Islander	— (†)	6 (0.8)	6 (1.3)	5 (1.4)	‡ (†)	39.2 ! (12.26)	39.2 ! (13.35)	‡ (†)	‡ (†)	‡ (†)	30.0 ! (13.01)	46.0 (12.75)	‡ (†)
American Indian/Alaska Native	26 (1.9)[2]	17 (1.2)	17 (1.9)	17 (2.9)	‡ (†)	48.0 (8.20)	30.7 (6.60)	7.6 ! (3.45)	‡ (†)	‡ (†)	24.3 (4.72)	49.5 (6.77)	18.0 ! (5.46)
Two or more races	— (†)	24 (2.2)	31 (2.9)	35 (3.8)	2.3 ! (0.84)	45.0 (5.56)	44.2 (5.15)	6.8 ! (2.58)	‡ (†)	17.6 (3.95)	37.6 (5.52)	35.0 (5.32)	9.8 (2.70)
Age													
Under 30	509 (9.2)	540 (27.4)	612 (22.4)	518 (15.9)	2.7 (0.36)	61.6 (1.27)	33.7 (1.27)	1.9 (0.33)	‡ (†)	35.9 (1.16)	64.1 (1.16)	‡ (†)	‡ (†)
30 to 39	661 (9.8)	798 (14.5)	898 (16.8)	979 (19.3)	3.3 (0.36)	37.0 (1.04)	51.1 (1.07)	7.8 (0.49)	0.9 (0.23)	6.3 (0.46)	51.5 (1.07)	42.2 (1.08)	‡ (†)
40 to 49	953 (10.3)	840 (14.3)	808 (19.2)	849 (19.2)	4.1 (0.42)	35.2 (1.15)	51.2 (1.17)	8.1 (0.64)	1.4 (0.23)	4.0 (0.41)	21.2 (0.88)	55.9 (1.08)	18.8 (0.98)
50 to 59	786 (12.6)	942 (26.0)	879 (21.1)	783 (20.5)	4.5 (0.52)	36.3 (1.18)	48.7 (1.06)	9.3 (0.56)	1.2 (0.19)	2.6 (0.31)	11.8 (0.74)	34.4 (1.31)	51.1 (1.25)
60 and over	93 (4.0)	131 (4.8)	207 (10.3)	256 (13.2)	4.8 (0.85)	33.6 (2.08)	48.1 (2.17)	11.3 (1.15)	2.2 (0.42)	1.4 (0.39)	7.3 (1.09)	28.8 (1.83)	62.5 (1.86)
Level of instruction[4]													
Elementary	1,602 (13.5)	1,716 (25.8)	1,725 (37.1)	1,726 (20.2)	3.2 (0.35)	41.3 (0.80)	47.1 (0.90)	7.9 (0.47)	0.4 (0.10)	8.3 (0.46)	33.6 (0.91)	36.1 (1.00)	22.0 (0.83)
General	1,019 (13.6)	1,130 (29.8)	1,100 (26.5)	1,078 (22.1)	3.3 (0.42)	43.5 (1.12)	46.0 (1.20)	6.8 (0.57)	0.3 ! (0.12)	8.0 (0.56)	33.8 (1.19)	36.9 (1.21)	21.3 (1.09)
Arts/music	‡ (†)	101 (5.3)	103 (6.6)	82 (5.4)	3.5 ! (1.24)	42.9 (3.71)	44.8 (3.76)	7.1 (2.12)	1.7 ! (0.75)	12.9 (2.56)	28.7 (3.00)	36.1 (3.60)	22.3 (3.98)
English	‡ (†)	70 (5.1)	104 (9.9)	92 (6.9)	‡ (†)	35.4 (3.93)	48.4 (3.71)	13.5 (2.88)	‡ (†)	7.5 (1.94)	20.7 (2.70)	41.2 (3.37)	30.6 (3.64)
ESL/bilingual	‡ (†)	25 (3.6)	24 (3.3)	51 (6.8)	‡ (†)	42.9 (5.52)	37.6 (6.42)	16.2 (4.09)	‡ (†)	‡ (†)	44.7 (6.79)	26.8 (5.75)	20.8 (5.95)
Health/physical ed.	‡ (†)	73 (5.0)	63 (6.0)	79 (8.1)	‡ (†)	48.4 (5.08)	42.7 (4.67)	4.3 ! (1.78)	‡ (†)	10.1 (2.24)	28.4 (4.53)	33.3 (4.84)	28.2 (4.70)
Mathematics	26 (2.5)	19 (2.3)	28 (3.8)	32 (6.5)	4.2 ! (2.04)	31.8 (5.90)	59.4 (6.33)	4.6 ! (1.79)	‡ (†)	5.9 ! (1.96)	29.9 (7.56)	41.0 (8.18)	23.1 (5.80)
Science	‡ (†)	19 (3.0)	15 (3.4)	18 (3.3)	‡ (†)	42.0 (6.99)	46.6 (7.72)	‡ (†)	‡ (†)	‡ (†)	42.6 (9.63)	38.5 (8.31)	12.6 ! (4.48)
Special education	210 (5.8)	240 (20.6)	230 (13.0)	239 (10.3)	2.7 ! (1.00)	33.6 (2.18)	53.0 (2.52)	10.6 (1.45)	‡ (†)	8.8 (1.39)	39.1 (2.38)	32.1 (2.16)	20.0 (1.72)
Other elementary	314 (8.4)	40 (3.5)	58 (4.2)	55 (5.2)	4.4 ! (2.11)	33.6 (4.12)	52.8 (4.77)	9.2 (2.31)	‡ (†)	7.1 (1.68)	30.6 (4.28)	39.4 (4.33)	22.9 (3.67)
Secondary	1,401 (17.7)	1,534 (26.0)	1,680 (39.0)	1,659 (37.8)	4.4 (0.26)	38.4 (0.60)	48.2 (0.61)	7.2 (0.32)	1.8 (0.20)	9.8 (0.31)	33.0 (0.59)	36.7 (0.53)	20.5 (0.61)
Arts/music	235 (5.0)	112 (4.1)	121 (6.2)	121 (5.6)	4.1 (0.59)	44.6 (2.01)	44.7 (1.87)	5.8 (1.23)	0.8 ! (0.29)	10.0 (1.01)	30.2 (1.79)	34.7 (1.94)	25.1 (1.64)
English	‡ (†)	269 (9.0)	306 (10.0)	289 (9.9)	3.4 (0.52)	36.6 (1.44)	49.0 (1.43)	9.1 (0.75)	1.9 (0.44)	9.6 (0.82)	33.3 (1.21)	38.3 (1.39)	18.7 (0.95)
ESL/bilingual	‡ (†)	18 (2.5)	21 (2.5)	20 (2.4)	8.0 ! (3.15)	27.6 (6.21)	51.4 (5.76)	11.1 (2.98)	1.6 ! (0.52)	6.9 ! (2.86)	41.4 (5.52)	35.7 (4.77)	16.1 (3.19)
Foreign language	‡ (†)	73 (3.3)	78 (5.0)	88 (4.5)	3.0 (0.76)	37.0 (2.42)	51.3 (2.48)	7.1 (1.08)	‡ (†)	11.6 (1.24)	31.7 (2.14)	37.5 (2.35)	19.2 (1.70)
Health/physical ed.	‡ (†)	102 (4.3)	119 (5.7)	101 (3.9)	4.9 (0.91)	44.6 (1.92)	44.9 (2.03)	4.9 (1.11)	0.6 ! (0.28)	9.2 (1.34)	25.6 (2.06)	37.7 (2.04)	27.5 (1.72)
Mathematics	191 (4.3)	213 (5.5)	252 (9.1)	250 (7.5)	2.7 (0.43)	41.4 (1.50)	48.9 (1.27)	5.6 (0.62)	1.4 ! (0.70)	12.0 (1.05)	33.9 (1.21)	35.0 (1.00)	19.1 (1.25)
Science	159 (3.7)	189 (6.8)	195 (8.3)	209 (6.1)	3.2 (0.51)	37.8 (1.57)	49.7 (1.51)	6.3 (0.73)	3.0 (0.54)	9.7 (0.95)	36.0 (1.75)	35.9 (1.34)	18.4 (1.40)
Social studies	147 (4.3)	174 (5.7)	209 (9.9)	197 (6.3)	3.2 (0.57)	39.2 (1.45)	49.1 (1.62)	5.8 (0.62)	2.8 (0.54)	8.8 (0.79)	34.4 (1.54)	38.5 (1.94)	18.3 (1.31)
Special education	99 (2.3)	169 (7.5)	165 (9.7)	191 (12.2)	3.1 ! (0.99)	31.3 (1.53)	52.7 (1.72)	11.8 (1.09)	1.1 ! (0.41)	8.1 (0.93)	35.5 (2.14)	35.3 (2.25)	21.1 (1.13)
Vocational/technical	125 (3.2)	125 (5.7)	164 (6.3)	147 (5.7)	12.8 (1.28)	38.7 (1.56)	41.2 (1.57)	5.7 (0.78)	1.6 ! (0.60)	9.8 ! (0.88)	30.2 (1.62)	35.8 (1.68)	24.2 (1.53)
Other secondary	443 (8.5)	36 (2.1)	47 (3.4)	46 (4.0)	9.8 (2.15)	37.9 (3.80)	42.2 (3.68)	8.2 (2.46)	1.8 ! (0.87)	8.6 ! (2.76)	28.4 (3.32)	40.5 (3.04)	22.6 (3.04)

See notes at end of table.

Table 209.20. Number, highest degree, and years of full-time teaching experience of teachers in public and private elementary and secondary schools, by selected teacher characteristics: 1999–2000 through 2011–12—Continued

[Standard error appears in parentheses]

Selected teacher characteristic	Number of teachers (in thousands)				Percent of teachers, by highest degree earned, 2011–12					Percent of teachers, by years of full-time teaching experience, 2011–12			
	1999–2000	2003–04	2007–08	2011–12	Less than bachelor's	Bachelor's	Master's	Education specialist[1]	Doctor's	Less than 3	3 to 9	10 to 20	Over 20
1	2	3	4	5	6	7	8	9	10	11	12	13	14
Private schools													
Total	449 (10.6)	467 (10.3)	490 (9.2)	465 (11.1)	8.4 (1.07)	48.5 (1.37)	35.8 (1.16)	5.0 (0.48)	2.3 (0.41)	19.5 (1.76)	31.3 (0.94)	27.7 (1.06)	21.4 (1.47)
Sex													
Males	107 (3.8)	110 (8.4)	127 (4.6)	117 (6.9)	10.0! (3.00)	40.0 (2.90)	40.1 (3.26)	5.4 (1.09)	4.6 (1.23)	18.3 (2.98)	31.2 (2.36)	25.4 (2.15)	25.0 (3.18)
Females	342 (7.7)	357 (14.3)	362 (7.7)	348 (10.1)	7.9 (0.97)	51.3 (1.53)	34.3 (1.21)	4.9 (0.56)	1.5 (0.41)	19.9 (1.67)	31.3 (1.28)	28.5 (1.29)	20.2 (1.28)
Race/ethnicity													
White	402 (9.6)[2]	411 (12.0)	423 (8.8)	411 (11.1)	8.0 (1.23)	48.1 (1.34)	36.7 (1.20)	5.0 (0.52)	2.2 (0.39)	18.5 (1.73)	30.7 (1.07)	27.9 (1.09)	22.9 (1.53)
Black	17 (1.4)[2]	19 (2.9)	20 (2.2)	17 (2.4)	10.5 (2.50)	53.4 (5.90)	29.1 (5.81)	4.8! (1.50)	‡ (†)	22.9 (6.38)	31.7 (5.60)	32.0 (5.94)	13.5 (3.97)
Hispanic	21 (1.5)[2]	23 (3.1)	29 (2.1)	24 (2.4)	13.3 (2.67)	47.0 (4.62)	29.5 (5.29)	6.0 (1.79)	‡ (†)	24.4 (3.44)	40.6 (4.88)	26.1 (5.05)	9.0! (3.01)
Asian	‡ (†)	‡ (†)	11 (1.5)	9 (1.4)	‡ (†)	55.5 (10.22)	27.3 (7.53)	‡ (†)	‡ (†)	42.4 (10.10)	26.6 (7.95)	24.8 (6.50)	‡ (†)
Pacific Islander[3]	— (†)	‡ (†)	‡ (†)	‡ (†)	‡ (†)	‡ (†)	‡ (†)	‡ (†)	‡ (†)	‡ (†)	‡ (†)	‡ (†)	‡ (†)
American Indian/Alaska Native	— (†)	‡ (†)	‡ (†)	‡ (†)	‡ (†)	‡ (†)	‡ (†)	‡ (†)	‡ (†)	‡ (†)	‡ (†)	‡ (†)	‡ (†)
Two or more races	—	‡ (†)	4 (0.6)	4 (0.9)	12.5! (5.87)	60.2 (11.13)	24.2! (10.48)	‡ (†)	‡ (†)	35.0! (11.38)	40.6! (12.49)	‡ (†)	‡ (†)
Age													
Under 30	87 (3.1)	88 (3.7)	80 (3.9)	78 (6.8)	10.4 (2.29)	63.0 (3.25)	24.7 (2.55)	1.7! (0.59)	‡ (†)	53.9 (4.80)	46.1 (4.80)	‡ (†)	‡ (†)
30 to 39	101 (3.2)	103 (5.8)	109 (5.2)	112 (6.2)	9.2 (2.51)	47.9 (2.57)	38.0 (2.56)	3.9 (0.80)	‡ (†)	18.0 (2.10)	55.0 (2.74)	27.0 (2.71)	‡ (†)
40 to 49	131 (4.2)	119 (7.1)	116 (3.6)	110 (6.3)	8.6 (1.57)	45.3 (2.66)	37.7 (2.47)	5.3 (1.26)	3.1! (0.99)	13.4 (1.63)	25.3 (2.34)	48.7 (2.38)	12.7 (1.87)
50 to 59	106 (3.2)	121 (11.1)	128 (4.5)	99 (5.0)	8.1 (1.16)	48.7 (2.50)	33.4 (2.47)	6.1 (1.07)	3.6! (0.82)	10.3 (1.51)	14.9 (1.47)	32.5 (2.08)	42.3 (2.31)
60 and over	25 (1.2)	37 (4.7)	56 (3.1)	66 (5.0)	5.0 (1.23)	37.2 (2.54)	45.5 (3.34)	9.0 (1.84)	3.4! (1.43)	5.7! (1.85)	8.2 (1.96)	19.5 (2.55)	66.6 (3.49)
Level of instruction[4]													
Elementary	261 (5.8)	263 (17.5)	258 (6.5)	245 (9.3)	11.1 (1.88)	53.0 (1.60)	29.3 (1.41)	5.7 (0.67)	0.9! (0.36)	20.0 (1.69)	31.5 (1.46)	28.3 (1.55)	20.2 (1.43)
General	168 (4.0)	174 (17.1)	163 (3.9)	151 (7.0)	12.5 (2.49)	55.4 (2.01)	26.1 (1.64)	5.3 (0.70)	‡ (†)	15.1 (1.68)	33.1 (1.99)	29.2 (1.81)	22.5 (1.77)
Arts/music	[5] (†)	21 (2.5)	20 (1.6)	20 (1.8)	10.7 (3.04)	59.9 (4.34)	18.6 (2.90)	10.0! (3.66)	‡ (†)	39.5 (5.51)	23.3 (4.04)	23.5 (6.09)	13.7 (3.17)
English	[5] (†)	8 (1.1)	13 (1.2)	16 (2.8)	‡ (†)	43.3 (9.17)	43.9 (8.21)	3.2! (1.57)	‡ (†)	17.6! (8.52)	25.9 (6.21)	31.1 (6.92)	25.5 (6.17)
Health/physical ed.	[5] (†)	14 (1.8)	14 (1.7)	11 (1.2)	8.7! (3.21)	57.1 (6.06)	30.1 (5.80)	‡ (†)	‡ (†)	29.3 (6.66)	31.3 (4.58)	24.7 (7.14)	14.7 (4.19)
Mathematics	[5] (†)	6 (0.7)	7 (1.0)	6 (1.1)	‡ (†)	51.2 (9.03)	38.8 (8.87)	‡ (†)	‡ (†)	24.6 (7.35)	35.3 (7.24)	29.0 (8.25)	11.1! (4.46)
Science	[5] (†)	5 (0.8)	6 (0.8)	5 (1.0)	‡ (†)	39.7 (9.14)	39.9 (10.37)	15.1! (6.05)	‡ (†)	17.0! (5.96)	25.7! (7.80)	35.6 (8.32)	21.6! (9.24)
Special education	16 (1.6)	12 (2.3)	9 (1.0)	10 (1.9)	‡ (†)	29.7 (6.55)	58.3 (7.50)	‡ (†)	‡ (†)	21.2 (6.23)	33.0 (8.47)	30.3 (7.24)	15.5! (5.20)
Other elementary	77 (2.2)	24 (3.5)	27 (2.3)	25 (2.8)	11.7 (3.14)	50.8 (4.16)	30.5 (3.48)	4.3! (1.98)	2.7! (1.22)	30.4 (4.23)	31.9 (5.04)	23.8 (3.64)	13.9 (3.01)
Secondary	188 (6.2)	204 (13.4)	231 (7.1)	219 (9.9)	5.4 (0.66)	43.3 (2.28)	43.1 (2.14)	4.4 (0.85)	3.8 (0.73)	19.0 (2.58)	31.0 (1.58)	27.1 (1.52)	22.9 (2.13)
Arts/music	[6] (†)	18 (1.9)	19 (1.8)	21 (2.2)	10.6! (4.00)	36.8 (5.86)	40.6 (7.37)	5.9! (2.68)	‡ (†)	24.7 (5.27)	27.1 (6.25)	33.8 (7.11)	14.3 (3.87)
English	33 (1.7)	38 (2.8)	39 (2.8)	39 (4.1)	3.1! (0.96)	46.0 (3.81)	41.6 (4.36)	7.5! (2.57)	1.8! (0.87)	12.8 (2.57)	35.7 (4.90)	29.7 (4.01)	21.9 (3.73)
Foreign language	[6] (†)	18 (2.1)	22 (2.6)	22 (3.5)	5.3! (2.42)	34.0 (6.40)	49.9 (5.92)	‡ (†)	‡ (†)	24.0 (5.59)	34.9 (7.22)	23.6 (7.03)	17.5 (3.50)
Health/physical ed.	[6] (†)	9 (1.0)	12 (1.8)	10 (1.8)	8.6! (3.75)	47.2 (10.06)	44.1 (9.51)	‡ (†)	‡ (†)	23.6! (9.69)	28.0! (9.59)	27.0! (8.24)	21.4! (9.03)
Mathematics	33 (1.6)	31 (3.2)	36 (2.6)	38 (5.1)	3.5! (1.09)	41.6 (4.57)	48.6 (5.38)	‡ (†)	4.8! (2.03)	16.9 (4.18)	27.8 (3.96)	27.5 (4.64)	27.8 (5.20)
Science	23 (1.3)	27 (1.8)	31 (1.9)	28 (2.7)	5.0! (2.23)	42.1 (5.15)	45.2 (4.66)	2.5! (1.22)	5.2! (1.97)	14.6 (3.18)	33.3 (5.88)	28.6 (5.57)	23.6 (5.05)
Social studies	19 (1.1)	27 (2.4)	31 (2.6)	28 (2.9)	‡ (†)	45.4 (5.22)	43.5 (5.25)	3.4! (1.25)	5.4! (2.50)	16.8 (4.16)	24.3 (3.63)	26.7 (5.51)	32.2 (5.76)
Special education	7 (1.0)	7 (1.5)	6 (1.0)	9 (1.5)	2.3! (1.12)	61.0 (6.98)	25.8 (5.34)	9.7! (3.69)	‡ (†)	18.9 (5.39)	50.9 (6.28)	19.8 (4.31)	10.3! (3.73)
Vocational/technical	4 (0.6)	5 (0.9)	5 (0.8)	5 (1.2)	‡ (†)	48.1 (11.53)	26.3! (9.50)	‡ (†)	‡ (†)	20.3! (9.08)	35.8! (11.28)	‡ (†)	37.8! (11.69)
Other secondary	69 (2.6)	24 (2.7)	29 (2.3)	20 (2.2)	10.8 (3.10)	45.6 (5.04)	38.7 (5.24)	‡ (†)	‡ (†)	29.9 (6.17)	25.4 (3.33)	24.8 (5.33)	19.9 (5.33)

—Not available.
†Not applicable.
!Interpret data with caution. The coefficient of variation (CV) for this estimate is between 30 and 50 percent.
‡Reporting standards not met. Either there are too few cases for a reliable estimate or the coefficient of variation (CV) is 50 percent or greater.
[1]Education specialist degrees or certificates are generally awarded for 1 year's work beyond the master's level. Includes certificate of advanced graduate studies.
[2]Data for 1999–2000 are only roughly comparable to data for later years, because the new category of Two or more races was introduced in 2003–04.
[3]Includes Pacific Islander.
[4]Teachers were classified as elementary or secondary on the basis of the grades they taught, rather than on the level of the school in which they taught. In general, elementary teachers include those teaching prekindergarten through grade 5 and those teaching multiple grades, with a preponderance of grades taught being kindergarten through grade 6. In general, secondary teachers include those teaching any of grades 7 through 12 and those teaching multiple grades, with a preponderance of grades taught being grades 7 through 12 and usually with no grade taught being lower than grade 5.
[5]Included under Other elementary.
[6]Included under Other secondary.
NOTE: Excludes prekindergarten teachers. Data are based on a head count of full-time and part-time teachers rather than on the number of full-time-equivalent teachers reported in other tables. Detail may not sum to totals because of rounding and cell suppression. Race categories exclude persons of Hispanic ethnicity.
SOURCE: U.S. Department of Education, National Center for Education Statistics, Schools and Staffing Survey (SASS), "Public School Teacher Data File," 1999–2000, 2003–04, 2007–08, and 2011–12; "Private School Teacher Data File," 1999–2000, 2003–04, 2007–08, and 2011–12; and "Charter School Teacher Data File," 1999–2000. (This table was prepared May 2013.)

Table 209.25. Number and percentage of public elementary and secondary school teachers who met licensing/certification requirements and of public school teachers who had less than 2 years of teaching experience, by state: 2011–12

State	Total number of public school teachers	Met all state licensing/ certification requirements[1]		Had less than 2 years of teaching experience[2]					
				Total		In first year of teaching		In second year of teaching	
		Number	Percent	Number	Percent	Number	Percent	Number	Percent
1	2	3	4	5	6	7	8	9	10
United States	3,129,363	3,046,577	97.4	310,298	9.9	172,611	5.5	137,686	4.4
Alabama	47,371	46,905	99.0	3,431	7.2	1,854	3.9	1,577	3.3
Alaska	7,800	7,764	99.5	1,114	14.3	655	8.4	458	5.9
Arizona	55,527	53,722	96.7	7,796	14.0	4,195	7.6	3,602	6.5
Arkansas	33,803	33,354	98.7	3,778	11.2	1,464	4.3	2,314	6.8
California	264,566	261,721	98.9	17,213	6.5	9,484	3.6	7,729	2.9
Colorado	48,479	47,399	97.8	5,262	10.9	2,738	5.6	2,524	5.2
Connecticut	43,467	42,851	98.6	3,677	8.5	2,034	4.7	1,643	3.8
Delaware	9,573	9,323	97.4	1,140	11.9	592	6.2	548	5.7
District of Columbia	5,745	5,165	89.9	1,449	25.2	842	14.7	607	10.6
Florida	179,972	153,680	85.4	42,145	23.4	34,944	19.4	7,201	4.0
Georgia	111,877	109,979	98.3	7,759	6.9	5,079	4.5	2,680	2.4
Hawaii	11,142	10,777	96.7	1,454	13.0	853	7.7	602	5.4
Idaho	14,589	14,463	99.1	1,389	9.5	738	5.1	651	4.5
Illinois	133,397	131,897	98.9	14,078	10.6	8,155	6.1	5,923	4.4
Indiana	61,053	60,688	99.4	7,561	12.4	2,941	4.8	4,620	7.6
Iowa	35,676	35,642	99.9	2,997	8.4	1,565	4.4	1,432	4.0
Kansas	34,039	33,654	98.9	3,119	9.2	1,693	5.0	1,425	4.2
Kentucky	42,747	42,645	99.8	4,875	11.4	2,444	5.7	2,431	5.7
Louisiana	46,810	45,581	97.4	3,996	8.5	2,191	4.7	1,805	3.9
Maine	14,567	14,326	98.3	1,030	7.1	561	3.9	469	3.2
Maryland	61,834	59,349	96.0	5,968	9.7	2,777	4.5	3,191	5.2
Massachusetts	71,204	68,828	96.7	7,491	10.5	3,982	5.6	3,509	4.9
Michigan	82,811	82,490	99.6	6,211	7.5	2,534	3.1	3,676	4.4
Minnesota	54,806	54,199	98.9	4,948	9.0	2,729	5.0	2,219	4.0
Mississippi	32,807	32,488	99.0	4,222	12.9	2,300	7.0	1,922	5.9
Missouri	65,759	63,733	96.9	7,018	10.7	3,976	6.0	3,042	4.6
Montana	10,831	10,781	99.5	1,284	11.9	489	4.5	795	7.3
Nebraska	23,154	23,077	99.7	2,357	10.2	1,139	4.9	1,217	5.3
Nevada	23,309	23,283	99.9	1,689	7.2	922	4.0	767	3.3
New Hampshire	14,823	14,674	99.0	1,302	8.8	523	3.5	778	5.3
New Jersey	118,746	118,099	99.5	10,831	9.1	6,041	5.1	4,790	4.0
New Mexico	21,576	21,501	99.7	2,107	9.8	1,138	5.3	969	4.5
New York	210,866	202,327	96.0	13,019	6.2	6,804	3.2	6,214	2.9
North Carolina	99,775	97,748	98.0	11,287	11.3	6,264	6.3	5,023	5.0
North Dakota	8,552	8,543	99.9	973	11.4	449	5.2	524	6.1
Ohio	108,717	107,757	99.1	6,916	6.4	3,428	3.2	3,489	3.2
Oklahoma	43,318	43,223	99.8	4,557	10.5	2,436	5.6	2,121	4.9
Oregon	25,902	25,789	99.6	1,495	5.8	731	2.8	764	2.9
Pennsylvania	123,514	116,752	94.5	8,888	7.2	2,958	2.4	5,930	4.8
Rhode Island	10,708	10,662	99.6	550	5.1	325	3.0	225	2.1
South Carolina	46,357	45,899	99.0	4,382	9.5	2,453	5.3	1,929	4.2
South Dakota	9,221	8,824	95.7	858	9.3	476	5.2	382	4.1
Tennessee	68,957	66,543	96.5	7,721	11.2	4,074	5.9	3,647	5.3
Texas	328,306	323,531	98.5	34,390	10.5	16,178	4.9	18,211	5.5
Utah	25,051	24,081	96.1	3,002	12.0	1,550	6.2	1,452	5.8
Vermont	7,237	7,122	98.4	563	7.8	303	4.2	259	3.6
Virginia	90,839	88,345	97.3	8,802	9.7	4,851	5.3	3,951	4.3
Washington	53,585	52,532	98.0	2,888	5.4	1,360	2.5	1,528	2.9
West Virginia	19,291	18,503	95.9	1,615	8.4	781	4.0	834	4.3
Wisconsin	58,136	57,200	98.4	6,969	12.0	3,204	5.5	3,766	6.5
Wyoming	7,173	7,160	99.8	737	10.3	417	5.8	319	4.4

[1]Requirements vary by state. Includes teachers who met all applicable state teacher certification requirements for a standard certificate (i.e., had a regular/standard certificate/license/endorsement issued by the state). Includes teachers who met the standard teacher education requirements, but had not completed a state-required probationary period. Excludes teachers with emergency, temporary, or provisional credentials.

[2]The number of years of teaching experience includes the current year and any prior years teaching in any school, subject, or grade. Does not include any student teaching or other similar preparation experiences.
NOTE: Teachers reported in full-time equivalents (FTE). Due to differing survey procedures, data in this table differ from data in tables based on other survey systems.
SOURCE: U.S. Department of Education, Office for Civil Rights, Civil Rights Data Collection, "2011–12 Classroom Teachers Estimations." (This table was prepared January 2016.)

Table 209.30. Highest degree earned, years of full-time teaching experience, and average class size for teachers in public elementary and secondary schools, by state: 2011–12

[Standard errors appear in parentheses]

State	Total number of teachers (in thousands)	Percent of teachers, by highest degree earned				Percent of teachers, by years of full-time teaching experience				Average class size, by level of instruction[1]	
		Less than bachelor's	Bachelor's	Master's	Education specialists[2] or doctor's	Less than 3	3 to 9	10 to 20	Over 20	Elementary	Secondary
1	2	3	4	5	6	7	8	9	10	11	12
United States	3,385.2 (41.42)	3.8 (0.24)	39.9 (0.52)	47.7 (0.57)	8.7 (0.28)	9.0 (0.29)	33.3 (0.52)	36.4 (0.51)	21.3 (0.54)	21.2 (0.18)	26.8 (0.22)
Alabama	45.0 (2.61)	3.8! (1.51)	34.5 (2.69)	52.8 (2.81)	8.9 (1.64)	8.0 (1.28)	30.9 (2.75)	39.2 (2.85)	21.9 (2.34)	19.2 (0.42)	27.4 (0.94)
Alaska	7.5 (0.70)	4.4! (1.78)	45.6 (4.44)	41.9 (4.01)	8.2 (2.37)	12.9 (3.30)	30.8 (4.15)	39.6 (4.16)	16.7 (3.76)	18.3 (1.35)	18.7 (1.22)
Arizona	61.7 (2.61)	4.6 (1.16)	44.4 (3.67)	44.1 (3.49)	6.9 (1.71)	16.4 (2.29)	38.0 (2.75)	28.5 (2.60)	17.2 (2.02)	24.1 (0.67)	27.7 (0.96)
Arkansas	37.7 (2.01)	3.7! (1.45)	54.7 (3.36)	35.0 (3.13)	6.6 (1.72)	11.5 (2.03)	28.9 (3.38)	32.3 (3.93)	27.3 (3.37)	20.4 (0.73)	25.4 (1.69)
California	285.5 (7.27)	4.8 (0.91)	43.4 (2.33)	39.2 (2.18)	12.7 (1.56)	9.4 (1.29)	29.1 (2.13)	42.3 (2.25)	19.1 (1.89)	25.0 (0.52)	32.0 (0.53)
Colorado	55.9 (3.14)	2.8! (1.00)	36.1 (3.51)	49.9 (4.26)	11.2 (2.79)	10.8 (2.25)	33.4 (3.50)	42.9 (3.96)	12.9 (2.51)	22.8 (1.29)	29.1 (1.25)
Connecticut	44.9 (2.51)	‡ (†)	15.3 (1.86)	64.4 (3.01)	17.7 (2.37)	10.0 (1.43)	29.1 (2.66)	37.1 (2.43)	23.8 (3.34)	19.6 (0.68)	22.0 (0.71)
Delaware	9.3 (0.70)	4.0! (1.50)	34.5 (4.36)	49.7 (4.55)	11.8 (2.85)	12.6 (3.31)	35.0 (3.59)	33.8 (4.04)	18.6 (2.75)	20.3 (0.82)	25.8 (2.09)
District of Columbia	‡ (†)	‡ (†)	‡ (†)	‡ (†)	‡ (†)	‡ (†)	‡ (†)	‡ (†)	‡ (†)	‡ (†)	‡ (†)
Florida	‡ (†)	‡ (†)	‡ (†)	‡ (†)	‡ (†)	‡ (†)	‡ (†)	‡ (†)	‡ (†)	‡ (†)	‡ (†)
Georgia	123.3 (3.97)	3.4 (1.15)	29.5 (3.48)	43.5 (3.79)	23.6 (3.00)	6.3 (1.70)	34.2 (3.42)	39.8 (3.34)	19.7 (2.58)	21.0 (0.91)	27.5 (1.42)
Hawaii	16.3 (1.83)	4.6 (1.37)	55.6 (3.30)	35.3 (3.18)	4.4 (1.20)	10.4 (1.93)	30.4 (3.18)	35.2 (3.02)	24.0 (2.89)	24.5 (0.63)	25.4 (2.13)
Idaho	‡ (†)	‡ (†)	‡ (†)	‡ (†)	‡ (†)	‡ (†)	‡ (†)	‡ (†)	‡ (†)	‡ (†)	‡ (†)
Illinois	140.9 (9.09)	2.7! (0.81)	32.6 (2.53)	57.8 (2.44)	7.0 (1.34)	9.3 (1.56)	36.4 (2.59)	34.4 (2.85)	20.0 (2.51)	22.9 (1.26)	27.7 (1.00)
Indiana	64.0 (2.98)	2.2 (0.52)	43.6 (3.04)	47.4 (3.29)	6.9 (1.45)	10.0 (1.92)	26.1 (2.42)	35.6 (3.01)	28.3 (3.02)	21.4 (0.45)	27.3 (1.07)
Iowa	36.1 (2.28)	3.5! (1.22)	52.8 (3.89)	39.7 (3.60)	4.1! (1.26)	8.8 (1.85)	29.0 (2.98)	32.7 (2.77)	29.5 (2.55)	20.3 (0.93)	27.4 (1.35)
Kansas	36.5 (2.27)	3.8 (0.83)	43.8 (3.52)	47.0 (3.66)	5.4 (1.38)	12.5 (2.98)	27.4 (3.00)	32.2 (3.15)	28.0 (2.83)	20.4 (0.86)	24.6 (1.21)
Kentucky	46.5 (2.51)	5.5 (1.22)	17.5 (2.24)	57.5 (2.58)	20.0 (2.11)	10.1 (1.83)	32.2 (2.82)	38.5 (2.81)	19.2 (2.02)	23.3 (1.92)	26.6 (1.09)
Louisiana	44.5 (2.39)	3.5! (1.72)	61.9 (3.12)	27.0 (2.68)	7.6 (1.55)	8.6 (1.51)	31.2 (3.13)	33.4 (3.31)	26.8 (3.10)	19.0 (0.80)	23.4 (0.78)
Maine	18.4 (0.90)	4.9! (1.60)	46.3 (3.41)	42.8 (3.30)	6.0 (1.36)	5.8 (1.47)	24.1 (2.57)	39.4 (3.32)	30.6 (2.81)	17.6 (0.64)	19.9 (1.76)
Maryland	‡ (†)	‡ (†)	‡ (†)	‡ (†)	‡ (†)	‡ (†)	‡ (†)	‡ (†)	‡ (†)	‡ (†)	‡ (†)
Massachusetts	79.2 (4.42)	3.9 (1.08)	21.8 (2.33)	67.5 (2.54)	6.8 (1.48)	12.4 (1.96)	33.4 (3.04)	36.8 (3.02)	17.4 (3.09)	19.9 (1.72)	24.5 (1.18)
Michigan	96.7 (3.73)	2.3 (0.55)	29.8 (2.50)	62.9 (2.52)	5.0 (1.40)	7.3 (1.00)	31.4 (2.68)	42.7 (2.44)	28.9 (2.12)	22.8 (0.93)	28.9 (0.81)
Minnesota	62.3 (2.99)	4.4 (0.77)	35.3 (2.06)	50.1 (1.87)	10.2 (1.40)	9.5 (1.20)	27.4 (2.05)	40.3 (2.14)	22.9 (2.00)	23.8 (0.70)	29.9 (0.86)
Mississippi	37.6 (2.11)	5.3 (1.45)	54.4 (3.87)	35.2 (3.57)	5.1 (1.51)	10.3 (1.97)	41.0 (3.45)	30.5 (3.35)	18.2 (3.18)	21.6 (1.01)	22.8 (1.15)
Missouri	68.7 (2.34)	4.4 (0.91)	33.3 (2.90)	57.5 (2.96)	4.8 (0.94)	10.4 (1.90)	35.3 (2.21)	35.0 (2.31)	19.6 (2.31)	20.2 (0.83)	26.8 (1.18)
Montana	12.4 (0.90)	6.4 (1.52)	55.2 (3.34)	34.6 (3.39)	3.7 (1.66)	9.6 (2.33)	31.3 (3.17)	30.4 (3.04)	28.6 (3.65)	18.9 (0.80)	21.7 (1.81)
Nebraska	23.9 (1.73)	5.5 (1.31)	44.9 (3.29)	45.9 (3.15)	3.7 (0.98)	10.6 (1.74)	27.2 (2.52)	34.6 (2.63)	27.6 (2.54)	17.9 (0.72)	23.5 (0.99)
Nevada	25.2 (2.63)	4.5! (1.85)	25.1 (3.92)	49.8 (4.26)	20.6 (3.23)	6.5! (2.17)	39.0 (4.02)	36.2 (4.29)	18.2 (2.02)	25.3 (1.41)	34.5 (1.54)
New Hampshire	15.7 (1.05)	3.0! (1.12)	40.2 (3.49)	48.7 (3.55)	8.1 (1.82)	8.1 (1.54)	32.8 (3.41)	31.5 (3.57)	27.5 (3.54)	20.4 (3.09)	21.7 (1.16)
New Jersey	125.2 (4.16)	3.0 (0.74)	48.5 (2.47)	40.8 (2.30)	7.6 (1.60)	7.3 (1.24)	35.4 (2.45)	37.4 (2.66)	20.0 (2.03)	18.5 (0.81)	23.9 (0.68)
New Mexico	21.7 (2.83)	4.3 (2.01)	43.3 (3.80)	42.1 (3.72)	10.3 (2.82)	8.0 (2.46)	30.9 (3.73)	40.3 (5.11)	20.8 (5.19)	19.8 (0.76)	23.7 (1.58)
New York	241.4 (14.58)	2.8! (1.00)	4.4 (1.09)	84.2 (1.56)	8.6 (1.32)	5.3 (1.38)	30.0 (2.81)	45.5 (2.35)	19.1 (2.41)	20.7 (1.36)	25.1 (1.25)
North Carolina	104.3 (5.71)	4.1! (1.57)	54.2 (3.16)	33.8 (2.80)	7.8 (1.84)	8.4 (1.52)	35.8 (3.13)	34.8 (3.05)	21.0 (2.74)	18.8 (0.65)	25.8 (1.25)
North Dakota	10.3 (0.74)	6.9 (1.63)	59.2 (3.08)	30.1 (2.60)	3.9 (1.13)	12.2 (2.09)	24.6 (3.06)	30.6 (3.28)	32.6 (3.45)	17.8 (0.60)	19.2 (1.41)
Ohio	122.1 (4.29)	5.3 (1.17)	24.0 (1.79)	64.5 (2.16)	6.2 (1.28)	7.1 (1.11)	28.8 (2.48)	40.8 (2.67)	23.3 (2.00)	21.3 (0.99)	26.7 (0.85)
Oklahoma	46.2 (2.49)	4.3 (1.04)	65.6 (2.66)	26.9 (2.56)	3.2! (1.12)	9.8 (1.84)	30.1 (2.58)	36.9 (2.93)	23.2 (2.27)	20.7 (0.56)	23.7 (0.88)
Oregon	31.0 (1.28)	4.2 (1.53)	26.3 (3.18)	59.8 (3.62)	9.7! (1.94)	7.2 (1.78)	37.0 (3.66)	34.1 (3.48)	20.2 (2.45)	26.4 (0.96)	30.0 (1.05)
Pennsylvania	148.8 (7.48)	4.5! (1.94)	32.9 (2.52)	53.9 (3.34)	‡ (†)	6.2 (2.43)	39.9 (4.49)	35.8 (4.52)	21.0 (2.30)	22.4 (0.99)	25.2 (0.96)
Rhode Island	10.3 (0.74)	‡ (†)	‡ (†)	‡ (†)	‡ (†)	‡ (†)	‡ (†)	‡ (†)	‡ (†)	‡ (†)	‡ (†)
South Carolina	51.8 (1.76)	3.0! (1.34)	28.8 (3.14)	57.9 (3.95)	10.3 (2.15)	8.4 (1.58)	30.5 (3.22)	32.3 (3.54)	28.9 (3.38)	19.1 (0.75)	26.0 (1.98)
South Dakota	10.8 (0.92)	2.3! (0.73)	68.8 (3.52)	26.6 (3.13)	2.3! (1.14)	8.8 (1.65)	24.6 (2.76)	32.9 (3.63)	33.7 (3.38)	20.4 (0.66)	22.3 (1.31)
Tennessee	76.5 (2.91)	4.4! (1.52)	35.1 (3.54)	46.3 (3.44)	14.2 (2.83)	10.6 (1.80)	34.0 (3.66)	34.1 (3.48)	21.3 (3.28)	17.7 (0.52)	26.9 (1.60)
Texas	350.8 (22.99)	3.3 (1.10)	66.4 (2.09)	25.8 (2.12)	4.6 (0.77)	8.9 (0.95)	40.4 (2.05)	31.1 (1.88)	19.7 (1.74)	18.2 (0.82)	26.9 (1.07)
Utah	27.9 (1.67)	4.2	56.8 (3.96)	27.3 (3.88)	11.7! (3.94)	15.0 (2.43)	39.9 (4.49)	25.6 (4.52)	19.5 (3.12)	27.4 (2.09)	31.5 (1.29)
Vermont	9.4 (0.34)	6.6 (1.46)	35.4 (2.78)	52.0 (2.87)	6.0 (1.59)	12.9 (1.60)	22.1 (2.38)	37.0 (2.56)	28.0 (2.73)	16.6 (0.40)	19.8 (1.25)
Virginia	88.5 (3.35)	3.3! (1.07)	47.5 (3.08)	41.6 (3.17)	7.6 (1.26)	9.1 (1.68)	31.5 (3.20)	34.2 (2.73)	25.2 (2.43)	20.4 (1.27)	23.8 (0.90)
Washington	55.5 (3.15)	2.9 (0.59)	23.1 (2.61)	62.9 (2.92)	11.1 (1.96)	6.2 (1.45)	32.2 (3.00)	34.8 (2.82)	26.8 (3.03)	23.7 (0.60)	29.7 (0.99)
West Virginia	24.2 (0.79)	3.1 (0.90)	46.6 (4.82)	43.2 (4.71)	7.1 (1.73)	11.1 (2.26)	31.2 (2.82)	30.5 (3.82)	26.3 (3.24)	18.7 (1.00)	24.0 (1.65)
Wisconsin	66.8 (3.42)	2.7 (0.79)	36.7 (2.96)	55.1 (2.98)	5.5 (1.41)	10.5 (1.67)	26.2 (4.12)	42.1 (3.24)	21.3 (2.73)	20.8 (0.55)	27.9 (0.95)
Wyoming	8.5 (0.57)	7.0! (3.08)	44.3 (4.47)	41.2 (4.18)	7.5! (2.74)	7.6! (2.62)	25.2 (4.09)	35.1 (3.73)	32.1 (4.30)	17.0 (1.05)	19.6 (1.22)

†Not applicable.

!Interpret data with caution. The coefficient of variation (CV) for this estimate is between 30 and 50 percent.

‡Reporting standards not met. Data may be suppressed because the response rate is under 50 percent, there are too few cases for a reliable estimate, or the coefficient of variation (CV) is 50 percent or greater.

[1] Elementary teachers are those who taught self-contained classes at the elementary level, and secondary teachers are those who taught departmentalized classes (e.g., science, art, social science, or other course subjects) at the secondary level. Teachers were classified as elementary or secondary on the basis of the grades they taught, rather than on the level of the school in which they taught. In general, elementary teachers include those teaching prekindergarten through grade 5 and those teaching multiple grades, with a preponderance of grades taught being kindergarten through grade 6. In general, secondary teachers include those teaching any of grades 7 through 12 and those teaching multiple grades, with a preponderance of grades taught being grades 7 through 12 and usually with no grade taught being lower than grade 5.

[2] Education specialist degrees or certificates are generally awarded for 1 year's work beyond the master's level. Includes certificate of advanced graduate studies.

NOTE: Data are based on a head count of all teachers rather than on the number of full-time-equivalent teachers appearing in other tables. Excludes prekindergarten teachers. Detail may not sum to totals because of rounding and cell suppression.

SOURCE: U.S. Department of Education, National Center for Education Statistics, Schools and Staffing Survey (SASS), "Public School Teacher Data File," 2011–12. (This table was prepared May 2013.)

Table 209.50. Percentage of public school teachers of grades 9 through 12, by field of main teaching assignment and selected demographic and educational characteristics: 2011–12

[Standard errors appear in parentheses]

Selected demographic or educational characteristic	Total		Field of main teaching assignment																		
			Arts and music		English or language arts		Foreign languages		Health and physical education		Mathematics		Natural sciences		Social sciences		Special education		Vocational/ technical		All other	
1	2		3		4		5		6		7		8		9		10		11		12	
Number of teachers (in thousands)	1,108.2	(32.76)	87.3	(4.85)	166.0	(7.03)	74.0	(4.18)	65.6	(3.47)	152.8	(6.67)	132.9	(5.35)	126.2	(5.35)	130.3	(10.33)	125.6	(5.49)	47.5	(3.92)
Total	100.0	(†)	100.0	(†)	100.0	(†)	100.0	(†)	100.0	(†)	100.0	(†)	100.0	(†)	100.0	(†)	100.0	(†)	100.0	(†)	100.0	(†)
Sex																						
Male	41.9	(0.66)	43.3	(2.45)	23.2	(1.73)	24.5	(2.38)	63.5	(2.62)	42.7	(1.88)	46.4	(2.16)	63.4	(1.79)	29.0	(2.10)	48.9	(1.99)	47.4	(3.75)
Female	58.1	(0.66)	56.7	(2.45)	76.8	(1.73)	75.5	(2.38)	36.5	(2.62)	57.3	(1.88)	53.6	(2.16)	36.6	(1.79)	71.0	(2.10)	51.1	(1.99)	52.6	(3.75)
Race/ethnicity																						
White	83.0	(0.75)	89.8	(2.53)	84.8	(1.55)	67.5	(2.43)	83.3	(2.44)	81.5	(1.90)	84.5	(1.50)	86.5	(1.30)	84.0	(1.83)	85.9	(1.81)	69.6	(3.48)
Black	6.2	(0.60)	4.4 !	(2.16)	6.1	(1.47)	2.1 !	(0.68)	9.2	(1.89)	6.4	(1.40)	5.4	(0.97)	4.4	(0.88)	8.4	(1.85)	6.2	(1.05)	11.2	(2.31)
Hispanic	6.8	(0.46)	3.5	(1.01)	6.3	(1.15)	25.5	(2.55)	4.5	(1.34)	6.2	(0.82)	5.1	(1.01)	5.9	(0.93)	4.4	(0.96)	4.0 !	(1.31)	12.6	(2.49)
Asian	2.0	(0.25)	0.8 !	(0.39)	0.9	(0.23)	3.1 !	(0.93)	‡	(†)	4.1	(1.01)	3.7	(0.93)	1.0 !	(0.38)	1.7 !	(0.52)	1.1 !	(0.41)	2.4 !	(0.97)
Pacific Islander	‡	(†)	‡	(†)	‡	(†)	‡	(†)	‡	(†)	‡	(†)	‡	(†)	‡	(†)	‡	(†)	‡	(†)	‡	(†)
American Indian/Alaska Native	0.6 !	(0.17)	‡	(†)	‡	(†)	‡	(†)	‡	(†)	0.6 !	(0.21)	0.4 !	(0.15)	‡	(†)	0.5 !	(0.20)	‡	(†)	‡	(†)
Two or more races	1.2	(0.15)	1.2 !	(0.38)	1.3	(0.27)	1.0 !	(0.46)	1.1	(0.32)	1.1	(0.31)	0.8	(0.23)	1.7 !	(0.51)	0.7 !	(0.23)	‡	(†)	1.9 !	(0.93)
Age																						
Under 30	15.4	(0.63)	17.2	(1.33)	17.4	(1.29)	15.3	(1.90)	13.0	(1.61)	20.9	(2.04)	16.0	(1.78)	16.5	(1.62)	12.2	(1.36)	10.5	(0.97)	8.0	(1.58)
30 to 39	28.1	(0.66)	27.2	(2.08)	29.4	(1.59)	28.8	(2.36)	29.6	(2.68)	28.1	(1.75)	29.6	(1.94)	33.8	(1.80)	27.0	(2.27)	21.3	(1.63)	22.8	(3.22)
40 to 49	25.0	(0.57)	21.1	(1.97)	24.6	(1.69)	25.8	(2.35)	29.1	(2.40)	24.7	(1.59)	25.7	(1.74)	25.4	(1.71)	23.1	(1.56)	26.6	(1.68)	25.1	(2.76)
50 to 59	22.8	(0.82)	26.2	(2.10)	20.1	(1.39)	20.9	(2.27)	22.2	(1.95)	18.1	(1.81)	21.5	(1.67)	16.7	(1.37)	28.3	(2.26)	30.3	(1.75)	30.8	(3.54)
60 and over	8.8	(0.43)	8.4	(1.43)	8.5	(0.87)	9.3	(1.39)	6.1	(1.33)	8.3	(1.31)	7.2	(1.39)	7.6	(0.98)	9.5	(1.12)	11.3	(1.00)	13.4	(2.31)
Age at which first began to teach full time or part time																						
25 or under	51.8	(0.66)	56.7	(2.46)	54.0	(1.75)	53.5	(2.42)	61.8	(2.57)	61.3	(1.79)	49.0	(1.86)	50.2	(1.89)	48.2	(2.54)	41.9	(1.78)	35.3	(3.21)
26 to 35	30.2	(0.55)	29.1	(2.50)	29.2	(1.48)	30.9	(2.26)	31.9	(2.54)	24.1	(1.49)	35.3	(1.73)	34.4	(1.84)	28.7	(1.84)	29.8	(1.81)	31.5	(3.82)
36 to 45	12.6	(0.51)	9.5	(1.40)	12.7	(1.19)	12.1	(1.68)	4.6	(1.03)	10.0	(1.05)	10.6	(1.20)	11.8	(1.28)	14.5	(1.86)	20.0	(1.62)	21.6	(3.23)
46 to 55	4.8	(0.32)	4.6 !	(1.42)	3.9	(0.79)	3.2 !	(0.98)	‡	(†)	4.2	(1.10)	4.5	(0.79)	3.0	(0.54)	8.2	(1.47)	6.6	(1.11)	9.4	(2.38)
56 or over	0.6	(0.12)	‡	(†)	‡	(†)	‡	(†)	‡	(†)	‡	(†)	‡	(†)	‡	(†)	0.4 !	(0.16)	1.7	(0.39)	2.2 !	(1.03)
Years of full-time teaching experience																						
Less than 3 years	9.9	(0.36)	10.8	(1.16)	9.7	(0.87)	11.2	(1.39)	10.1	(1.90)	11.6	(1.12)	10.0	(1.24)	8.8	(0.98)	7.9	(0.96)	10.4	(0.96)	7.4	(2.01)
3 to 9 years	32.7	(0.76)	30.7	(2.48)	34.3	(1.56)	31.1	(2.50)	23.9	(2.33)	33.8	(1.69)	33.5	(1.88)	34.7	(1.89)	34.8	(2.69)	30.9	(1.75)	34.0	(3.80)
10 to 20 years	36.7	(0.62)	34.4	(2.12)	37.1	(1.61)	37.2	(2.63)	38.4	(2.53)	34.5	(1.58)	35.8	(1.82)	40.2	(2.23)	37.3	(3.04)	35.2	(1.81)	38.6	(3.37)
Over 20 years	20.7	(0.68)	24.1	(1.82)	18.9	(1.42)	20.4	(2.04)	27.6	(2.37)	20.1	(1.49)	20.7	(1.77)	16.3	(1.31)	19.9	(1.53)	23.5	(1.74)	19.9	(2.97)
Highest degree earned																						
Less than bachelor's degree	4.9	(0.36)	4.2	(0.77)	3.4	(0.72)	3.3	(0.88)	5.4	(1.25)	2.6	(0.55)	2.9	(0.62)	3.1	(0.80)	3.3 !	(1.37)	14.2	(1.43)	11.4	(2.38)
Bachelor's degree	38.2	(0.73)	46.5	(2.67)	35.8	(1.99)	37.9	(2.64)	44.9	(2.41)	41.0	(2.03)	35.6	(1.86)	37.9	(1.70)	31.8	(1.97)	38.9	(1.76)	38.2	(3.72)
Master's degree	47.9	(0.74)	42.6	(2.41)	50.3	(2.26)	50.6	(2.77)	43.5	(2.31)	49.8	(1.74)	51.8	(1.96)	49.6	(1.79)	52.3	(2.08)	39.7	(1.82)	40.4	(3.48)
Education specialist[1]	6.8	(0.39)	5.8	(1.56)	8.6	(0.91)	6.8	(1.15)	5.3	(1.42)	4.8	(0.67)	5.6	(0.71)	5.9	(0.85)	11.2	(1.16)	5.6	(0.86)	8.1	(2.02)
Doctor's degree	2.1	(0.28)	0.9 !	(0.34)	1.9 !	(0.71)	1.4 !	(0.57)	0.8 !	(0.39)	‡	(†)	4.0	(0.85)	3.4	(0.78)	1.5 !	(0.58)	1.7 !	(0.64)	1.8 !	(0.88)
Major field of study in bachelor's or higher degree[2]																						
Arts and music	9.2	(0.42)	87.6	(1.37)	4.9	(0.84)	3.5	(0.78)	1.0 !	(0.51)	1.2	(0.34)	1.1 !	(0.36)	1.7 !	(0.52)	3.5	(0.79)	2.1 !	(0.93)	3.5 !	(1.49)
Education, elementary instruction	6.4	(0.32)	2.9	(0.77)	5.0	(0.63)	5.2 !	(1.62)	2.6	(0.65)	4.9	(0.68)	3.2	(0.66)	2.6	(0.52)	21.7	(1.81)	3.1	(0.56)	14.9	(2.17)
Education, secondary instruction	20.7	(0.64)	11.1	(1.83)	29.1	(1.68)	19.7	(1.91)	9.5	(1.38)	27.1	(1.36)	29.9	(1.76)	29.5	(2.00)	8.1 !	(2.96)	11.2	(1.06)	15.5	(2.80)
Education, special education	11.4	(0.58)	1.3	(0.36)	5.8	(0.81)	1.7 !	(0.68)	2.9 !	(1.19)	3.5 !	(1.20)	3.0 !	(0.98)	3.6	(0.65)	70.9	(1.84)	2.4 !	(0.89)	7.9	(1.75)
Education, other	17.7	(0.54)	12.8	(1.83)	17.4	(1.19)	17.3	(1.91)	20.5	(1.94)	18.2	(1.54)	17.8	(1.34)	21.5	(1.84)	17.0	(1.57)	17.2	(1.77)	16.3	(2.29)
English and language arts	17.1	(0.54)	6.7	(1.39)	77.9	(1.22)	15.0	(1.73)	2.3 !	(0.82)	3.8	(0.62)	1.6	(0.35)	6.4	(1.03)	11.5	(2.11)	2.4	(0.52)	15.4	(2.92)
Foreign languages	6.2	(0.32)	1.1 !	(0.50)	2.4	(0.47)	75.1	(2.32)	‡	(†)	1.2 !	(0.41)	‡	(†)	1.2 !	(0.43)	1.4	(0.38)	‡	(†)	3.9	(1.05)
Health and physical education	10.0	(0.43)	2.4 !	(0.80)	3.1	(0.61)	3.2 !	(1.20)	82.9	(2.11)	4.9	(0.83)	6.5	(0.96)	5.7	(0.96)	9.0	(1.38)	5.4	(0.99)	11.7	(2.79)
Mathematics	10.0	(0.31)	‡	(†)	‡	(†)	‡	(†)	‡	(†)	64.5	(2.00)	3.0	(0.58)	0.3 !	(0.09)	1.6 !	(0.52)	1.5	(0.40)	3.1 !	(1.03)
Natural sciences	12.0	(0.46)	0.5 !	(0.24)	0.7	(0.20)	0.9 !	(0.35)	3.2	(0.89)	8.4	(1.10)	78.3	(2.04)	1.1	(0.31)	2.4	(0.54)	4.1	(0.71)	4.8	(1.10)
Social sciences	18.6	(0.55)	4.0	(0.94)	10.6	(1.07)	15.9	(1.92)	6.8	(1.72)	9.2	(1.31)	7.3	(1.31)	78.6	(1.55)	21.5	(1.53)	6.4	(1.19)	20.1	(2.71)
Vocational/technical education	14.6	(0.51)	3.1	(0.85)	4.4	(0.78)	4.9	(1.15)	5.5	(1.26)	11.3	(1.55)	7.1	(1.18)	7.1	(1.10)	8.2	(1.07)	70.8	(1.81)	20.2	(3.24)
Other field	5.9	(0.31)	2.2	(0.49)	5.7	(0.88)	10.6	(1.80)	3.3	(0.85)	5.7	(0.65)	3.5	(0.65)	6.3	(0.93)	5.3	(1.15)	4.3	(0.66)	21.4	(2.77)
No degree	4.9	(0.36)	4.2	(0.77)	3.4	(0.72)	3.3	(0.88)	5.4	(1.25)	2.6	(0.55)	2.9	(0.62)	3.1	(0.80)	3.3 !	(1.37)	14.2	(1.43)	11.4	(2.38)

†Not applicable.
!Interpret data with caution. The coefficient of variation (CV) for this estimate is between 30 and 50 percent.
‡Reporting standards not met. Either there are too few cases for a reliable estimate or the coefficient of variation (CV) is 50 percent or greater.
[1]Education specialist degrees or certificates are generally awarded for 1 year's work beyond the master's level. Includes certificates of advanced graduate studies.

[2]Data may sum to more than 100 percent because (1) a teacher who reported more than one major is represented in more than one field of study and (2) a teacher with multiple degrees in different fields of study is represented in more than one field of study.
NOTE: Race categories exclude persons of Hispanic ethnicity. Detail may not sum to totals because of rounding.
SOURCE: U.S. Department of Education, National Center for Education Statistics, Schools and Staffing Survey (SASS), "Public School Teacher Data File," 2011–12. (This table was prepared May 2013.)

Table 210.10. Percentage of teachers indicating that certain issues are serious problems in their schools, by level and control of school: Selected years, 1987–88 through 2011–12

[Standard errors appear in parentheses]

Control of school and issue	1987–88 total	1993–94 total	1999–2000 total	2003–04 Total[1]	2003–04 Elementary schools	2003–04 Secondary schools	2007–08 Total	2007–08 Elementary schools	2007–08 Secondary schools	2007–08 Combined schools	2011–12 Total	2011–12 Elementary schools	2011–12 Secondary schools	2011–12 Combined schools
1	2	3	4	5	6	7	8	9	10	11	12	13	14	15
Public schools														
Student tardiness	10.5 (0.18)	10.5 (0.28)	10.2 (0.22)	13.8 (0.29)	9.8 (0.38)	23.1 (0.58)	9.8 (0.33)	5.8 (0.37)	17.9 (0.65)	9.0 (1.36)	11.9 (0.33)	8.5 (0.49)	17.6 (0.55)	16.4 (1.11)
Student absenteeism	16.4 (0.23)	14.4 (0.29)	13.9 (0.26)	13.1 (0.31)	8.3 (0.36)	23.7 (0.59)	11.7 (0.36)	6.5 (0.42)	21.4 (0.63)	14.2 (0.95)	13.9 (0.35)	8.6 (0.49)	22.6 (0.63)	21.9 (1.48)
Teacher absenteeism	2.3 (0.09)	1.5 (0.09)	2.2 (0.10)	1.1 (0.10)	0.9 (0.12)	1.7 (0.15)	1.5 (0.15)	1.2 (0.20)	2.0 (0.20)	2.3 (0.48)	1.6 (0.14)	1.3 (0.16)	1.8 (0.20)	3.3 (0.58)
Students cutting class	5.9 (0.16)	5.1 (0.12)	4.7 (0.12)	5.5 (0.23)	1.5 (0.17)	14.5 (0.59)	4.0 (0.20)	0.5 (0.12)	10.9 (0.52)	4.0 (0.64)	4.9 (0.22)	1.2 (0.16)	10.8 (0.47)	10.4 (1.05)
Physical conflicts among students	5.8 (0.18)	8.2 (0.25)	4.8 (0.19)	12.1 (0.29)	13.7 (0.43)	9.3 (0.38)	(†)	(†)	(†)	(†)	(†)	(†)	(†)	(†)
Robbery or theft	3.7 (0.12)	4.1 (0.17)	2.4 (0.11)	3.7 (0.17)	2.9 (0.23)	5.9 (0.24)	—	—	—	—	—	—	—	—
Vandalism of school property	6.1 (0.15)	6.7 (0.23)	3.4 (0.15)	3.7 (0.16)	2.5 (0.21)	6.3 (0.33)	—	—	—	—	—	—	—	—
Student pregnancy	6.9 (0.17)	7.3 (0.24)	3.7 (0.12)	2.4 (0.12)	‡	7.0 (0.34)	—	—	—	—	—	—	—	—
Student use of alcohol	11.4 (0.18)	9.3 (0.17)	7.4 (0.14)	3.0 (0.10)	0.3 (0.07)	9.0 (0.28)	—	—	—	—	—	—	—	—
Student drug abuse	8.0 (0.14)	5.7 (0.14)	6.0 (0.11)	4.5 (0.14)	0.5 (0.10)	13.0 (0.35)	—	—	—	—	—	—	—	—
Student possession of weapons	1.7 (0.06)	2.8 (0.12)	0.8 (0.06)	0.5 (0.05)	‡	1.2 (0.12)	(†)	(†)	(†)	(†)	(†)	(†)	(†)	(†)
Verbal abuse of teachers	8.1 (0.21)	11.1 (0.26)	—	11.8 (0.31)	9.3 (0.39)	17.1 (0.50)	(†)	(†)	(†)	(†)	(†)	(†)	(†)	(†)
Student disrespect for teachers	—	18.5 (0.35)	17.2 (0.34)	21.6 (0.45)	18.6 (0.62)	28.3 (0.58)	(†)	(†)	(†)	(†)	(†)	(†)	(†)	(†)
Students dropping out	—	5.8 (0.16)	4.6 (0.11)	3.3 (0.13)	0.4 (0.08)	9.6 (0.41)	3.5 (0.19)	0.8 (0.19)	8.7 (0.41)	5.3 (0.77)	3.1 (0.17)	0.9 (0.16)	6.3 (0.39)	7.7 (0.85)
Student apathy	—	23.6 (0.35)	20.6 (0.30)	16.6 (0.34)	9.9 (0.40)	30.4 (0.56)	16.5 (0.45)	10.0 (0.55)	28.5 (0.67)	21.4 (1.16)	20.0 (0.44)	13.4 (0.61)	31.4 (0.74)	27.3 (1.41)
Lack of parental involvement	—	27.6 (0.45)	23.7 (0.36)	21.6 (0.42)	19.3 (0.58)	26.3 (0.59)	19.5 (0.49)	16.8 (0.68)	24.0 (0.69)	23.5 (1.42)	24.6 (0.54)	22.1 (0.77)	28.3 (0.65)	29.4 (1.55)
Poverty	—	19.5 (0.52)	19.2 (0.43)	21.4 (0.46)	22.4 (0.64)	19.0 (0.57)	22.1 (0.59)	22.8 (0.83)	20.5 (0.68)	26.7 (1.36)	29.0 (0.59)	29.5 (0.86)	26.8 (0.79)	32.4 (2.00)
Students come unprepared to learn	—	28.8 (0.39)	29.5 (0.36)	26.8 (†)	23.7 (0.68)	33.5 (0.69)	24.2 (0.56)	20.7 (0.84)	30.5 (0.77)	28.5 (1.45)	30.2 (0.59)	27.1 (0.96)	35.4 (0.85)	34.9 (1.54)
Poor student health	—	—	—	(†)	—	—	3.3 (0.20)	3.4 (0.30)	2.8 (0.21)	4.2 (0.50)	5.0 (0.25)	5.1 (0.38)	4.4 (0.37)	6.3 (0.63)
Private schools														
Student tardiness	3.6 (0.38)	2.6 (0.23)	2.9 (0.21)	2.8 (0.40)	2.1 (0.45)	5.0 (0.83)	2.5 (0.28)	2.9 (0.37)	3.0 (0.83)	2.6 (0.47)	3.8 (0.59)	3.7 (0.61)	4.9 (1.11)	(†)
Student absenteeism	3.7 (0.39)	2.2 (0.19)	2.5 (0.21)	1.9 (0.23)	0.9 (0.17)	4.0 (0.75)	2.0 (0.23)	1.9 (0.23)	3.9 (0.99)	2.6 (0.40)	3.0 (0.34)	2.1 (0.44)	4.6 (0.99)	(†)
Teacher absenteeism	0.8 (0.13)	0.8 (0.10)	0.8 (0.11)	‡	‡	‡	0.5 (0.13)	0.3! (0.08)	‡	1.0! (0.32)	0.5 (0.12)	‡	0.7! (0.28)	(†)
Students cutting class	0.9 (0.16)	0.7 (0.11)	0.8 (0.12)	0.5 (0.11)	‡	‡	0.5! (0.18)	‡	1.1! (0.41)	‡	0.7 (0.20)	‡	‡	(†)
Physical conflicts among students	1.3 (0.19)	1.5 (0.15)	1.0 (0.18)	2.4 (0.31)	2.7 (0.55)	‡	(†)	(†)	(†)	(†)	(†)	(†)	(†)	(†)
Robbery or theft	1.3 (0.18)	0.8 (0.10)	0.9 (0.11)	0.4 (0.10)	0.4 (0.11)	1.3! (0.40)	—	—	—	—	—	—	—	—
Vandalism of school property	1.3 (0.19)	1.2 (0.11)	0.7 (0.11)	0.5 (0.11)	‡	‡	—	—	—	—	—	—	—	—
Student pregnancy	0.6 (0.12)	0.4 (0.06)	0.4 (0.09)	0.7! (0.17)	‡	3.3 (0.86)	—	—	—	—	—	—	—	—
Student use of alcohol	3.6 (0.30)	3.1 (0.19)	3.1 (0.16)	1.1 (0.25)	#	5.2 (1.31)	—	—	—	—	—	—	—	—
Student drug abuse	1.8 (0.24)	1.3 (0.15)	1.8 (0.14)	1.1 (0.25)	‡	6.6 (0.95)	—	—	—	—	—	—	—	—
Student possession of weapons	0.4 (0.11)	0.3 (0.06)	0.3 (0.06)	#	#	‡	(†)	(†)	(†)	(†)	(†)	(†)	(†)	(†)
Verbal abuse of teachers	2.0 (0.24)	2.3 (0.25)	—	2.4 (0.40)	1.1 (0.29)	4.0 (0.84)	(†)	(†)	(†)	(†)	(†)	(†)	(†)	(†)
Student disrespect for teachers	—	3.4 (0.27)	3.8 (0.31)	5.1 (0.37)	3.6 (0.54)	6.3 (1.05)	(†)	(†)	(†)	(†)	(†)	(†)	(†)	(†)
Students dropping out	—	0.6 (0.09)	0.5 (0.10)	0.3! (0.10)	‡	‡	0.4! (0.20)	‡	‡	‡	0.3! (0.13)	‡	7.1 (1.32)	(†)
Student apathy	—	4.5 (0.28)	4.3 (0.29)	3.0 (0.39)	1.4 (0.23)	6.6 (0.95)	3.9 (0.34)	1.7 (0.30)	6.9 (1.06)	5.1 (0.74)	3.6 (0.38)	1.7 (0.42)	7.1 (1.32)	(†)
Lack of parental involvement	—	4.0 (0.26)	3.4 (0.30)	2.5 (0.37)	1.6 (0.28)	3.6 (0.77)	2.5 (0.24)	1.9 (0.36)	2.8 (0.67)	3.0 (0.46)	2.7 (0.32)	1.8 (0.34)	3.2 (0.80)	(†)
Poverty	—	2.7 (0.23)	2.1 (0.21)	2.2 (0.26)	1.7 (0.31)	3.4 (0.78)	2.0 (0.21)	1.4 (0.28)	2.0 (0.56)	2.6 (0.44)	2.6 (0.33)	2.7 (0.52)	2.8 (0.79)	(†)
Students come unprepared to learn	—	4.1 (0.28)	4.9 (0.36)	3.5 (0.30)	2.1 (0.53)	6.8 (0.99)	3.6 (0.34)	1.9 (0.33)	6.2 (1.51)	4.4 (0.85)	3.9 (0.41)	2.0 (0.41)	6.7 (1.07)	(†)
Poor student health	—	—	—	—	—	—	0.7 (0.13)	0.3! (0.13)	‡	1.0 (0.25)	0.8 (0.21)	0.4! (0.17)	0.5! (0.25)	(†)

—Not available.
†Not applicable.
#Rounds to zero.
!Interpret data with caution. The coefficient of variation (CV) for this estimate is between 30 and 50 percent.
‡Reporting standards not met. Data may be suppressed because the response rate is under 50 percent, there are too few cases for a reliable estimate, or the coefficient of variation (CV) is 50 percent or greater.
[1]For 2003–04, combined schools are included in the total but not shown separately.

NOTE: Elementary schools are those with any of grades kindergarten through grade 6 and none of grades 7 through 12. Secondary schools have any of grades 7 through 12, and none of grades kindergarten through grade 6. Combined schools have both elementary and secondary grades, or have all students in ungraded classrooms.
SOURCE: U.S. Department of Education, National Center for Education Statistics, Schools and Staffing Survey (SASS), "Public School Teacher Data File," selected years, 1987–88 through 2011–12; "Private School Teacher Data File," selected years, 1987–88 through 2011–12; and "Charter School Teacher Data File," 1999–2000. (This table was prepared May 2013.)

Table 210.20. Percentage of teachers agreeing with statements about teaching and school conditions, by control and level of school: Selected years, 1993–94 through 2011–12

[Standard errors appear in parentheses]

Statement about conditions	Public school teachers								Private school teachers						
	1993–94 total	1999–2000 total	2003–04 total	2007–08 total	2011–12				1993–94 total	1999–2000 total	2003–04 total	2007–08 total	2011–12[1]		
					Total	Elementary schools	Secondary schools	Combined schools					Total	Elementary schools	Secondary schools
1	2	3	4	5	6	7	8	9	10	11	12	13	14	15	16
	Percent of teachers somewhat agreeing or strongly agreeing with statement														
The school administration's behavior toward the staff is supportive.	79.2 (0.36)	78.8 (0.38)	85.2 (0.33)	87.7 (0.39)	83.6 (0.44)	84.0 (0.67)	83.2 (0.57)	82.0 (1.18)	88.2 (0.42)	87.3 (0.45)	91.1 (0.78)	93.1 (0.43)	88.5 (0.90)	88.1 (1.20)	85.5 (2.41)
My principal enforces school rules for student conduct and backs me up when I need it.	80.8 (0.35)	82.2 (0.33)	87.2 (0.34)	88.0 (0.37)	83.7 (0.43)	84.5 (0.64)	82.2 (0.59)	83.1 (1.27)	88.4 (0.41)	88.3 (0.39)	92.2 (0.75)	92.2 (0.57)	89.4 (0.98)	90.1 (1.00)	87.0 (2.21)
In this school, staff members are recognized for a job well done.	67.9 (0.39)	68.3 (0.42)	75.5 (0.38)	76.7 (0.56)	74.3 (0.45)	75.6 (0.69)	72.5 (0.58)	71.0 (1.60)	81.1 (0.40)	78.9 (0.50)	83.8 (1.14)	84.0 (0.66)	80.6 (1.04)	80.7 (1.48)	79.9 (2.27)
Principal knows what kind of school he/she wants and has communicated it to the staff	80.5 (0.36)	83.2 (0.28)	87.3 (0.30)	88.4 (0.33)	84.7 (0.41)	85.8 (0.60)	83.1 (0.54)	82.7 (1.20)	88.6 (0.38)	88.4 (0.43)	91.9 (0.68)	91.7 (0.53)	87.6 (0.96)	88.2 (0.91)	85.7 (1.55)
Most of my colleagues share my beliefs and values about what the central mission of the school should be.	84.2 (0.22)	84.7 (0.26)	88.1 (0.26)	88.3 (0.35)	87.7 (0.38)	90.1 (0.52)	83.5 (0.49)	84.5 (1.47)	93.2 (0.37)	92.2 (0.31)	93.8 (0.49)	93.7 (0.44)	92.9 (0.66)	93.0 (0.82)	89.6 (1.75)
There is a great deal of cooperative effort among staff.	77.5 (0.31)	78.4 (0.32)	83.2 (0.36)	84.3 (0.33)	82.3 (0.41)	84.3 (0.61)	78.9 (0.53)	80.2 (1.11)	90.5 (0.29)	89.0 (0.42)	91.2 (0.77)	91.7 (0.63)	88.8 (0.83)	88.8 (1.05)	87.0 (1.45)
I receive a great deal of support from parents for the work I do.	52.5 (0.38)	57.9 (0.40)	61.1 (0.50)	64.3 (0.52)	58.6 (0.63)	61.9 (0.87)	52.8 (0.69)	55.1 (2.04)	84.6 (0.41)	84.0 (0.49)	86.1 (2.33)	87.7 (0.60)	85.0 (0.97)	85.8 (1.18)	80.2 (2.73)
I make a conscious effort to coordinate the content of my courses with that of other teachers.	85.0 (0.25)	84.1 (0.24)	86.3 (0.31)	— (†)	90.0 (0.32)	92.7 (0.39)	85.8 (0.48)	85.8 (1.25)	85.2 (0.44)	81.4 (0.55)	84.6 (0.90)	— (†)	87.3 (0.90)	89.9 (0.96)	83.4 (1.59)
Routine duties and paperwork interfere with my job of teaching.	70.8 (0.38)	71.1 (0.30)	70.8 (0.44)	69.0 (0.53)	69.2 (0.53)	70.5 (0.70)	67.3 (0.66)	65.9 (2.10)	40.1 (0.65)	44.5 (0.57)	40.7 (2.70)	42.7 (0.97)	41.1 (1.50)	43.9 (1.64)	46.2 (3.22)
Level of student misbehavior in this school interferes with my teaching.	44.1 (0.40)	40.8 (0.42)	37.2 (0.52)	36.0 (0.57)	40.7 (0.65)	40.1 (0.96)	41.9 (0.82)	41.3 (1.58)	22.4 (0.43)	24.1 (0.61)	20.7 (2.47)	20.6 (0.72)	22.0 (1.05)	23.7 (1.39)	20.4 (2.78)
Amount of student tardiness and class cutting in this school interferes with my teaching.	27.9 (0.32)	31.5 (0.35)	33.4 (0.45)	33.4 (0.64)	37.6 (0.51)	32.3 (0.76)	47.1 (0.69)	42.4 (1.56)	8.6 (0.42)	15.0 (0.43)	15.9 (1.11)	17.9 (0.72)	18.8 (1.06)	17.8 (1.05)	21.4 (2.45)
Rules for student behavior are consistently enforced by teachers in this school, even for students who are not in their classes.	61.8 (0.42)	62.6 (0.39)	71.1 (0.46)	70.6 (0.55)	67.6 (0.51)	75.2 (0.76)	53.4 (0.71)	62.0 (2.06)	77.6 (0.50)	75.9 (0.51)	81.0 (1.52)	80.1 (0.81)	77.4 (1.49)	80.2 (1.72)	68.3 (2.78)
I am satisfied with my teaching salary.	44.9 (0.45)	39.4 (0.36)	45.9 (0.46)	50.9 (0.64)	47.0 (0.50)	45.0 (0.71)	50.7 (0.70)	49.0 (1.67)	41.6 (0.59)	42.6 (0.73)	50.6 (1.76)	51.7 (0.86)	49.5 (1.44)	41.8 (1.84)	56.5 (2.28)
Necessary materials are available as needed by staff.	73.1 (0.42)	75.0 (0.32)	79.0 (0.42)	82.2 (0.55)	79.4 (0.45)	79.6 (0.68)	78.9 (0.59)	79.5 (1.42)	85.7 (0.44)	89.0 (0.38)	91.8 (0.74)	92.1 (0.54)	90.8 (0.68)	90.3 (0.84)	91.9 (1.25)
I worry about the security of my job because of the performance of my students on state or local tests.	— (†)	28.8 (0.37)	31.2 (0.43)	30.9 (0.58)	44.0 (0.54)	45.3 (0.78)	41.1 (0.60)	43.8 (2.05)	— (†)	6.7 (0.29)	7.8 (0.68)	7.6 (0.46)	9.8 (0.75)	11.0 (0.96)	9.8 (1.38)
State or district content standards have had a positive influence on my satisfaction with teaching.	— (†)	— (†)	— (†)	49.3 (0.62)	47.5 (0.52)	50.8 (0.74)	41.0 (0.63)	46.2 (1.86)	— (†)	— (†)	— (†)	41.1 (0.80)	38.9 (1.19)	46.9 (1.35)	33.8 (2.53)
I am given the support I need to teach students with special needs.	—	60.9 (0.33)	64.5 (0.47)	67.2 (0.57)	65.5 (0.51)	63.9 (0.73)	68.2 (0.61)	67.6 (1.74)	—	67.1 (0.58)	71.8 (2.00)	68.4 (0.84)	66.9 (1.22)	63.5 (1.71)	67.6 (2.70)
Stress and disappointments involved in teaching at this school aren't really worth it.	— (†)	— (†)	— (†)	18.9 (0.38)	22.0 (0.49)	21.9 (0.72)	21.4 (0.62)	25.5 (2.10)	— (†)	— (†)	— (†)	10.1 (0.52)	11.9 (0.82)	12.5 (1.12)	12.9 (1.93)
Teachers at this school like being here; I would describe us as a satisfied group.	— (†)	— (†)	— (†)	79.4 (0.47)	75.7 (0.53)	76.0 (0.75)	75.7 (0.71)	74.5 (1.66)	— (†)	— (†)	— (†)	89.0 (0.55)	87.5 (0.93)	85.2 (1.22)	87.7 (1.88)
I like the way things are run at this school.	— (†)	— (†)	— (†)	77.1 (0.55)	72.9 (0.51)	73.6 (0.73)	72.4 (0.62)	69.6 (2.22)	— (†)	— (†)	— (†)	84.5 (0.66)	79.6 (1.12)	78.6 (1.32)	79.0 (2.35)
If I could get a higher paying job I'd leave teaching as soon as possible.	— (†)	— (†)	— (†)	26.0 (0.45)	29.6 (0.59)	29.3 (0.83)	29.7 (0.61)	32.0 (1.52)	— (†)	— (†)	— (†)	18.3 (0.73)	21.6 (1.05)	23.6 (1.29)	19.1 (1.77)
I think about transferring to another school.	— (†)	— (†)	— (†)	28.5 (0.53)	29.1 (0.51)	29.0 (0.76)	28.2 (0.71)	33.6 (1.87)	— (†)	— (†)	— (†)	23.8 (0.92)	25.6 (1.31)	28.2 (1.58)	24.1 (2.27)
I am generally satisfied with being a teacher at this school.	— (†)	89.7 (0.24)	90.9 (0.29)	92.8 (0.31)	90.2 (0.33)	90.1 (0.48)	90.4 (0.42)	89.8 (1.39)	— (†)	93.3 (0.26)	95.2 (0.56)	95.7 (0.43)	94.2 (0.30)	94.1 (0.78)	93.0 (1.37)

—Not available.
†Not applicable.
[1]Data for combined private schools in 2011–12 are included in the total, but not shown separately due to low response rates (under 50 percent).

NOTE: Elementary schools are those with any of grades kindergarten through grade 6 and none of grades 9 through 12. Secondary schools have any of grades 7 through 12, and none of grades kindergarten through grade 6. Combined schools have both elementary and secondary grades, or have all students in ungraded classrooms.
SOURCE: U.S. Department of Education, National Center for Education Statistics, Schools and Staffing Survey (SASS), "Public School Teacher Data File," selected years 1993–94 through 2011–12; "Private School Teacher Data File," selected years 1993–94 through 2011–12; and "Charter School Teacher Data File," 1999–2000. (This table was prepared May 2013.)

Table 210.30. Mobility of public elementary and secondary teachers, by selected teacher and school characteristics: Selected years, 1987–88 through 2012–13

[Standard errors appear in parentheses]

Selected teacher or school characteristic	Left teaching 1987–88 to 1988–89	Left teaching 1993–94 to 1994–95	Left teaching 1999–2000 to 2000–01	Left teaching 2003–04 to 2004–05	Left teaching 2007–08 to 2008–09	2011–12 to 2012–13 Remained in same school	Moved to another school — Total moving to another school	Teachers who moved, by destination — Public school in same school district	Public school in different district	Private school	Left teaching
1	2	3	4	5	6	7	8	9	10	11	12
Total	5.6 (0.30)	6.6 (0.34)	7.4 (0.37)	8.4 (0.44)	8.0 (0.55)	84.3 (0.98)	8.1 (0.65)	58.8 (3.56)	38.2 (3.63)	2.9 (0.67)	7.7 (0.64)
Sex											
Male	5.1 (0.52)	5.2 (0.32)	7.4 (0.67)	7.7 (0.68)	7.9 (1.13)	85.7 (2.17)	7.9 (1.53)	46.4 (8.74)	51.2 (8.87)	2.3 ! (0.92)	6.4 (1.13)
Female	5.8 (0.39)	7.1 (0.44)	7.4 (0.45)	8.6 (0.50)	8.0 (0.65)	83.8 (1.03)	8.1 (0.70)	62.6 (3.80)	34.3 (3.85)	3.1 (0.86)	8.1 (0.70)
Race/ethnicity											
White	5.7 (0.32)	6.5 (0.36)	7.5 (0.45)	8.2 (0.50)	8.0 (0.67)	85.0 (0.86)	7.5 (0.63)	58.7 (3.94)	37.7 (3.93)	3.6 (0.90)	7.5 (0.56)
Black	5.1 ! (1.84)	6.6 (1.48)	7.4 (1.60)	11.0 (2.31)	9.0 (2.27)	78.2 (5.97)	11.7 ! (4.43)	64.2 (14.00)	35.2 ! (14.01)	‡ (†)	10.1 ! (3.47)
Hispanic	2.9 (0.84)	9.1 (2.14)	7.5 (1.67)	9.3 (1.89)	5.6 ! (1.81)	79.4 (5.00)	12.6 (3.13)	57.9 (10.56)	41.4 (10.56)	‡ (†)	8.0 ! (3.73)
Asian/Pacific Islander	‡ (†)	2.4 (0.71)	2.1 ! (0.87)	‡ (†)	8.0 ! (3.84)	95.5 (7.98)	‡ (†)	‡ (†)	‡ (†)	‡ (†)	‡ (†)
Asian	— (†)	— (†)	— (†)	‡ (†)	9.6 ! (4.38)	95.8 (7.75)	‡ (†)	‡ (†)	‡ (†)	‡ (†)	‡ (†)
Pacific Islander	— (†)	— (†)	— (†)	‡ (†)	‡ (†)	‡ (†)	‡ (†)	‡ (†)	‡ (†)	‡ (†)	‡ (†)
American Indian/Alaska Native	‡ (†)	3.5 ! (1.06)	7.6 ! (3.68)	1.9 ! (0.77)	‡ (†)	‡ (†)	‡ (†)	‡ (†)	‡ (†)	‡ (†)	‡ (†)
Two or more races	— (†)	— (†)	— (†)	‡ (†)	‡ (†)	88.8 (6.09)	‡ (†)	‡ (†)	‡ (†)	‡ (†)	‡ (†)
Age											
Less than 25	4.3 (0.91)	3.8 (1.05)	9.3 (2.20)	4.8 (1.24)	8.7 ! (3.11)	73.8 (6.02)	17.1 (3.97)	35.1 (9.35)	60.0 (8.85)	‡ (†)	‡ (†)
25 to 29	9.0 (1.18)	10.0 (1.25)	9.7 (1.39)	10.6 (1.98)	9.4 (2.09)	80.0 (2.93)	12.9 (2.59)	50.9 (9.17)	43.9 (9.14)	5.2 ! (1.88)	7.1 (1.26)
30 to 39	5.8 (0.59)	6.7 (0.94)	6.5 (0.88)	6.8 (0.87)	8.4 (1.46)	86.3 (1.50)	8.5 (0.98)	59.0 (6.36)	39.7 (6.42)	1.3 ! (0.78)	5.3 (1.10)
40 to 49	2.4 (0.32)	3.9 (0.54)	4.6 (0.62)	5.3 (0.73)	3.9 (0.91)	90.1 (1.46)	5.9 (1.00)	65.9 (6.57)	33.3 (6.52)	‡ (†)	4.0 (0.88)
50 to 59	5.7 (0.82)	6.3 (0.77)	8.1 (0.80)	9.8 (0.82)	8.4 (1.26)	83.0 (1.96)	6.6 (1.24)	67.5 (8.28)	29.0 (8.22)	‡ (†)	10.5 (1.44)
60 to 64	23.4 (4.90)	30.5 (4.78)	25.7 (5.44)	28.0 (4.35)	17.5 (5.10)	73.3 (6.04)	7.0 ! (2.77)	52.9 ! (20.56)	‡ (†)	‡ (†)	19.7 (4.44)
65 and over	‡ (†)	34.1 (7.79)	16.6 ! (5.44)	21.2 (5.95)	10.4 ! (4.84)	70.0 (14.55)	‡ (†)	‡ (†)	‡ (†)	‡ (†)	24.8 ! (11.73)
Full- and part-time teaching experience											
1 year or less	7.9 (0.96)	5.7 (0.82)	10.5 (1.93)	9.6 (1.66)	11.4 ! (3.94)	79.0 (6.34)	13.4 ! (4.63)	43.2 (8.33)	52.6 (7.94)	‡ (†)	7.6 ! (3.14)
2 years	7.3 (1.81)	9.1 (1.51)	8.5 (1.94)	6.4 (1.43)	8.8 ! (2.93)	78.0 (4.02)	14.5 (2.53)	26.0 (7.02)	68.1 (7.62)	5.9 ! (2.44)	7.5 ! (2.31)
3 years	9.3 (1.50)	9.8 (1.42)	7.5 (1.60)	7.7 (1.55)	9.0 ! (3.11)	84.0 (3.13)	9.8 (2.54)	46.1 (11.39)	48.0 (11.80)	‡ (†)	6.2 (1.56)
4 to 10 years	6.4 (0.89)	6.8 (0.94)	7.3 (0.72)	8.1 (0.98)	8.1 (1.27)	81.3 (1.95)	11.3 (1.33)	62.0 (6.39)	36.3 (6.42)	1.8 ! (0.72)	7.4 (1.48)
11 to 20 years	3.5 (0.42)	4.9 (0.64)	5.2 (0.74)	5.5 (0.70)	4.3 (0.89)	89.5 (1.51)	5.3 (1.04)	63.1 (6.55)	35.6 (6.48)	‡ (†)	5.2 (0.88)
21 to 25 years	3.5 (0.87)	4.0 (0.81)	4.2 (0.68)	6.6 (1.23)	5.8 ! (2.31)	87.5 (2.74)	6.6 ! (2.16)	63.1 (16.69)	35.1 ! (16.83)	‡ (†)	5.9 (1.33)
More than 25 years	11.3 (1.63)	12.0 (1.04)	11.4 (1.05)	14.3 (1.13)	12.6 (2.12)	79.4 (2.26)	4.5 (1.10)	73.5 (12.38)	‡ (†)	‡ (†)	16.1 (2.06)
Grade level taught											
Elementary (preK–grade 8)	5.5 (0.39)	6.4 (0.53)	6.8 (0.45)	8.4 (0.68)	7.9 (1.01)	84.1 (1.27)	8.9 (0.99)	66.5 (4.90)	30.5 (4.98)	3.0 ! (1.12)	7.1 (0.77)
Secondary (grades 9–12)	5.6 (0.42)	6.7 (0.53)	8.6 (0.71)	8.4 (0.59)	8.0 (0.75)	84.5 (1.37)	7.2 (0.82)	48.8 (5.19)	48.4 (5.16)	2.8 (0.74)	8.3 (0.94)
School size											
Less than 150	7.3 (1.36)	6.4 (1.15)	9.5 (2.29)	12.1 (2.92)	‡ (†)	85.4 (3.62)	7.6 ! (2.31)	36.5 (7.43)	59.0 (7.59)	‡ (†)	7.0 (1.97)
150 to 349	4.8 (0.45)	7.8 (1.03)	6.7 (0.99)	10.3 (1.58)	7.3 (1.26)	84.2 (2.66)	8.1 (1.83)	49.1 (8.80)	47.1 (8.52)	3.7 ! (1.64)	7.7 (1.60)
350 to 499	6.1 (0.98)	5.8 (0.73)	7.4 (0.85)	8.6 (1.16)	9.4 (2.28)	84.2 (1.93)	8.0 (1.17)	66.0 (5.53)	30.8 (5.13)	‡ (†)	7.8 (1.45)
500 to 749	5.6 (0.77)	7.6 (0.67)	7.1 (0.78)	7.0 (0.75)	5.3 (0.79)	82.9 (1.78)	9.2 (1.40)	68.6 (6.24)	28.2 (6.65)	‡ (†)	7.8 (1.24)
750 or more	5.0 (0.48)	5.7 (0.57)	7.7 (0.74)	8.2 (0.79)	8.9 (1.01)	85.1 (1.89)	7.3 (1.12)	51.9 (6.90)	45.9 (7.01)	2.2 ! (0.77)	7.5 (1.07)
Percent of students who are Black, Hispanic, Asian, Pacific Islander, American Indian/Alaska Native or Two or more races[1]											
Less than 5 percent	5.1 (0.56)	8.0 (0.93)	6.8 (0.96)	7.6 (1.13)	8.6 (1.97)	85.9 (3.16)	7.6 ! (2.83)	79.2 (11.49)	‡ (†)	2.6 ! (1.17)	6.5 (1.30)
5 to 19 percent	5.8 (0.74)	6.0 (0.71)	6.8 (0.65)	7.5 (0.75)	7.8 (1.75)	87.6 (1.37)	5.4 (0.86)	46.8 (6.94)	50.6 (7.02)	2.6 ! (1.17)	7.0 (1.04)
20 to 49 percent	5.2 (0.64)	6.2 (0.82)	9.4 (0.96)	6.5 (0.60)	8.1 (1.42)	86.4 (1.13)	7.3 (0.93)	62.0 (4.66)	34.2 (4.33)	3.8 ! (1.86)	6.3 (0.80)
50 percent or more	5.3 (0.66)	6.8 (0.72)	6.8 (0.62)	10.3 (0.84)	7.9 (0.82)	80.5 (1.88)	10.4 (1.26)	62.7 (4.94)	34.1 (5.04)	3.2 ! (1.00)	9.1 (1.23)
Percent of students approved for free or reduced-price lunch											
0 to 25.0 percent	— (†)	— (†)	— (†)	8.1 (0.69)	8.4 (1.06)	87.8 (1.79)	6.2 (1.30)	61.4 (7.11)	36.3 (6.82)	‡ (†)	6.0 (0.98)
25.1 to 50.0 percent	— (†)	— (†)	— (†)	7.3 (0.63)	9.8 (1.55)	85.8 (1.78)	6.2 (0.95)	58.4 (6.96)	39.1 (6.68)	‡ (†)	7.9 (1.36)
50.1 to 75.0 percent	— (†)	— (†)	— (†)	9.0 (1.21)	8.8 (1.77)	84.1 (1.75)	8.7 (1.23)	55.9 (7.11)	40.5 (7.05)	‡ (†)	7.1 (1.20)
More than 75.0 percent	— (†)	— (†)	— (†)	10.4 (1.49)	5.5 (0.90)	77.9 (2.88)	12.3 (1.79)	60.8 (6.16)	36.7 (6.16)	2.5 ! (1.14)	9.9 (1.85)
School did not respond or did not participate in program	— (†)	— (†)	— (†)	14.3 (2.44)	14.3 (1.73)	85.8 (4.95)	‡ (†)	40.0 ! (15.95)	36.7 ! (16.68)	‡ (†)	10.7 ! (3.67)
Locale											
City	— (†)	— (†)	— (†)	10.1 (1.05)	7.5 (1.01)	82.3 (2.35)	9.7 (1.54)	66.2 (6.58)	30.9 (6.59)	2.9 ! (1.20)	7.9 (1.44)
Suburban	— (†)	— (†)	— (†)	8.3 (0.83)	8.3 (1.08)	84.9 (1.43)	7.8 (1.12)	60.0 (6.03)	36.9 (6.33)	3.1 ! (1.52)	7.3 (0.90)
Town	— (†)	— (†)	— (†)	6.5 (0.76)	7.5 ! (2.51)	86.3 (2.15)	7.3 (1.56)	55.0 (9.53)	39.9 (8.77)	‡ (†)	6.4 (1.10)
Rural	— (†)	— (†)	— (†)	7.9 (0.99)	8.4 (1.44)	84.6 (1.69)	7.0 (1.08)	48.9 (7.30)	49.3 (7.18)	‡ (†)	8.4 (1.23)

—Not available.
†Not applicable.
!Interpret data with caution. The coefficient of variation (CV) for this estimate is between 30 and 50 percent.
‡Reporting standards not met. Either there are too few cases for a reliable estimate or the coefficient of variation (CV) is 50 percent or greater.
[1]Data were not available for approximately 4 percent of teachers for 2011–12 to 2012–13.
NOTE: Race categories exclude persons of Hispanic ethnicity. Detail may not sum to totals because of rounding.

SOURCE: U.S. Department of Education, National Center for Education Statistics, Schools and Staffing Survey (SASS), *Characteristics of Stayers, Movers, and Leavers: Results From the Teacher Follow-up Survey 1994–95; Teacher Attrition and Mobility: Results From the Teacher Follow-up Survey: 2000–01;* "Public School Teacher Data File" 2003–04, 2007–08, and 2011–12; and Teacher Follow-up Survey (TFS), "Current and Former Teacher Data Files," 1988–89, 2004–05, 2008–09, and 2012–13. (This table was prepared October 2014.)

Table 210.31. Mobility of private elementary and secondary teachers, by selected teacher and school characteristics: Selected years, 1987–88 through 2008–09

[Standard errors appear in parentheses]

Selected teacher or school characteristic	Percent of private school teachers											
	Left teaching								2007–08 to 2008–09					
	1987–88 to 1988–89		1993–94 to 1994–95		1999–2000 to 2000–01		2003–04 to 2004–05		Remained in same school		Changed schools		Left teaching	
1	2		3		4		5		6		7		8	
Total	**12.7**	**(0.85)**	**11.9**	**(0.70)**	**12.5**	**(0.69)**	**13.6**	**(2.18)**	**79.2**	**(1.72)**	**4.9**	**(0.60)**	**15.9**	**(1.53)**
Sex														
Male	10.2	(1.72)	13.1	(1.20)	11.7	(1.48)	14.2	(2.06)	80.0	(3.42)	5.7	(1.29)	14.3	(3.11)
Female	13.4	(0.92)	11.6	(0.78)	12.8	(0.76)	13.4	(2.88)	78.9	(1.84)	4.7	(0.68)	16.4	(1.63)
Race/ethnicity														
White	12.1	(0.90)	11.7	(0.69)	12.3	(0.73)	13.0	(2.33)	80.7	(1.82)	4.6	(0.59)	14.7	(1.59)
Black	34.7	(8.35)	12.6 !	(4.52)	14.8 !	(5.09)	‡	(†)	67.2	(10.90)	8.6 !	(3.78)	24.2 !	(10.11)
Hispanic	21.3 !	(6.46)	14.6	(4.31)	9.6	(2.85)	22.1	(5.72)	69.2	(8.37)	‡	(†)	23.7 !	(7.18)
Asian/Pacific Islander	‡	(†)	17.5 !	(8.67)	‡	(†)	7.6 !	(2.84)	‡	(†)	‡	(†)	‡	(†)
Asian	—	(†)	—	(†)	—	(†)	7.8 !	(3.01)	‡	(†)	‡	(†)	‡	(†)
Pacific Islander	—	(†)	—	(†)	—	(†)	‡	(†)	‡	(†)	‡	(†)	‡	(†)
American Indian/ Alaska Native	‡	(†)	‡	(†)	‡	(†)	‡	(†)	‡	(†)	‡	(†)	‡	(†)
Two or more races	—	(†)	—	(†)	—	(†)	‡	(†)	‡	(†)	‡	(†)	‡	(†)
Age														
Less than 25	19.0	(3.79)	20.0	(4.19)	29.9	(4.24)	18.0	(3.41)	67.0	(8.95)	6.5 !	(2.81)	26.5 !	(8.04)
25 to 29	17.6	(2.42)	13.1	(1.35)	18.6	(2.07)	21.2	(4.00)	69.7	(5.70)	11.6	(3.14)	18.7	(5.07)
30 to 39	12.4	(1.59)	14.9	(1.54)	13.7	(1.52)	14.2	(1.81)	76.9	(3.73)	4.9	(1.42)	18.2	(3.35)
40 to 49	10.5	(1.63)	8.7	(1.02)	8.5	(1.34)	10.7	(2.08)	83.7	(2.93)	5.4	(1.22)	10.9	(2.81)
50 to 59	11.3	(2.45)	8.2	(1.53)	5.9	(0.90)	‡	(†)	85.2	(2.11)	2.4	(0.63)	12.4	(2.06)
60 to 64	16.9 !	(5.93)	13.1	(2.74)	18.1	(3.72)	20.7	(5.27)	79.2	(6.44)	‡	(†)	17.6 !	(5.93)
65 and over	7.9 !	(3.16)	41.9	(8.67)	29.4	(7.60)	21.2 !	(7.31)	74.7	(9.34)	‡	(†)	23.3 !	(8.67)
Full- and part-time teaching experience														
1 year or less	15.9	(2.73)	18.2	(2.12)	28.9	(3.95)	20.2	(4.36)	66.1	(8.45)	‡	(†)	29.8	(7.86)
2 years	18.2	(3.32)	23.6	(2.72)	22.5	(3.24)	‡	(†)	72.8	(8.46)	6.5 !	(2.18)	20.7 !	(8.57)
3 years	15.4	(3.80)	12.8	(2.15)	17.8	(2.49)	15.3	(2.47)	73.9	(6.77)	9.6	(2.75)	16.5 !	(6.35)
4 to 10 years	14.0	(1.91)	13.1	(1.51)	12.6	(1.37)	16.0	(2.54)	76.9	(2.63)	6.9	(1.44)	16.3	(2.13)
11 to 20 years	11.5	(1.73)	7.1	(0.93)	6.9	(1.13)	8.2	(1.75)	83.4	(3.12)	3.1	(0.90)	13.5	(2.88)
21 to 25 years	5.2 !	(2.36)	6.0	(1.64)	5.5	(1.32)	8.9 !	(4.25)	88.7	(3.19)	2.7 !	(1.23)	8.6 !	(2.88)
More than 25 years	8.4	(2.03)	12.7	(2.53)	10.0	(1.40)	8.5	(1.77)	84.4	(3.25)	2.9 !	(1.01)	12.7	(2.95)
Level taught														
Elementary	12.5	(0.99)	11.5	(0.96)	13.4	(0.84)	14.4	(3.64)	79.8	(1.91)	5.9	(0.88)	14.3	(1.80)
Secondary	12.9	(2.38)	12.6	(1.51)	8.5	(0.90)	12.5	(1.35)	78.6	(2.64)	3.8	(0.93)	17.6	(2.44)
School size														
Less than 150	16.6	(1.72)	14.8	(1.43)	14.6	(1.45)	22.7	(6.32)	72.8	(3.77)	6.2	(1.43)	21.0	(3.32)
150 to 349	10.9	(1.62)	12.6	(1.21)	13.1	(1.24)	12.4	(1.40)	78.9	(2.92)	5.5	(1.35)	15.7	(2.38)
350 to 499	10.7	(2.63)	12.1	(1.95)	10.3	(1.26)	9.8	(1.40)	85.4	(2.87)	‡	(†)	11.5	(2.59)
500 to 749	9.6	(2.07)	7.1	(1.27)	11.1	(1.91)	9.8	(2.63)	86.7	(3.74)	3.8	(1.09)	9.6 !	(3.36)
750 or more	12.9	(3.14)	6.2	(1.18)	10.8	(1.64)	4.9	(0.90)	79.8	(5.61)	‡	(†)	16.6	(4.87)
Percent of students who are Black, Hispanic, Asian, Pacific Islander, American Indian/Alaska Native or Two or more races														
Less than 5 percent	13.2	(1.67)	11.0	(1.06)	12.3	(1.07)	‡	(†)	81.4	(3.29)	5.4	(1.40)	13.2	(2.87)
5 to 19 percent	10.3	(1.37)	11.1	(1.07)	11.4	(1.10)	12.5	(1.54)	78.9	(2.43)	5.0	(0.91)	16.1	(2.22)
20 to 49 percent	18.9	(4.18)	15.6	(2.28)	13.8	(1.82)	15.6	(2.00)	79.0	(3.19)	3.0	(0.84)	18.0	(2.97)
50 percent or more	13.6	(2.85)	13.2	(2.15)	14.7	(2.34)	18.5	(4.47)	77.0	(4.01)	7.3 !	(2.41)	15.6	(3.44)
Locale														
City	—	(†)	—	(†)	—	(†)	11.4	(1.42)	78.6	(2.81)	5.2	(0.96)	16.2	(2.55)
Suburban	—	(†)	—	(†)	—	(†)	12.4	(1.34)	79.1	(2.96)	4.8	(0.98)	16.2	(2.71)
Town	—	(†)	—	(†)	—	(†)	18.0	(3.63)	82.1	(4.47)	7.5 !	(2.43)	10.3	(3.08)
Rural	—	(†)	—	(†)	—	(†)	15.2	(3.30)	80.4	(4.50)	3.4 !	(1.59)	16.3	(3.86)

—Not available.
†Not applicable.
!Interpret data with caution. The coefficient of variation (CV) for this estimate is between 30 and 50 percent.
‡Reporting standards not met. Either there are too few cases for a reliable estimate or the coefficient of variation (CV) is 50 percent or greater.
NOTE: Race categories exclude persons of Hispanic ethnicity. Detail may not sum to totals because of rounding.

SOURCE: U.S. Department of Education, National Center for Education Statistics, Schools and Staffing Survey (SASS), *Characteristics of Stayers, Movers, and Leavers: Results From the Teacher Follow-up Survey 1994–95; Teacher Attrition and Mobility: Results From the Teacher Follow-up Survey: 2000–01;* "Private School Teacher Data File," 2003–04 and 2007–08; and Teacher Follow-up Survey (TFS), "Current and Former Teacher Data Files," 2004–05 and 2008–09. (This table was prepared October 2014.)

Table 211.10. Average salaries for full-time teachers in public and private elementary and secondary schools, by selected characteristics: 2011–12

[Amounts in current dollars. Standard errors appear in parentheses]

Selected characteristic	Number of full-time teachers (in thousands)	Total school-year and summer earned income from school and nonschool sources[1]	Base salary	School year supplemental contract[2]: Percent of teachers	School year supplemental contract[2]: Average supplement	Merit pay bonus: Percent of teachers	Merit pay bonus: Average amount	State supplements: Percent of teachers	State supplements: Average amount	Job outside the school system during the school year: Percent of teachers	Job outside the school system during the school year: Average income	Supplemental school system contract during summer[3]: Percent of teachers	Supplemental summer contract: Average supplement	Nonschool job during summer: Percent of teachers	Nonschool job during summer: Average income
(col) 1	2	3	4	5	6	7	8	9	10	11	12	13	14	15	16
Public schools															
Total	3,139.2 (38.34)	56,410 (251)	53,070 (213)	41.8 (0.53)	2,530 (74)	4.4 (0.23)	1,400 (85)	7.9 (0.31)	2,070 (96)	16.1 (0.39)	4,820 (172)	17.8 (0.41)	2,510 (69)	15.0 (0.41)	3,430 (112)
Sex															
Males	754.6 (20.70)	60,360 (464)	54,430 (385)	56.6 (0.92)	3,920 (134)	3.9 (0.35)	1,450 (101)	8.0 (0.54)	2,440 (189)	23.3 (0.76)	6,060 (309)	21.4 (0.90)	2,880 (86)	23.2 (0.75)	4,560 (201)
Females	2,384.6 (28.89)	55,160 (267)	52,640 (237)	37.1 (0.58)	1,860 (61)	4.6 (0.29)	1,390 (101)	7.9 (0.34)	1,950 (105)	13.9 (0.50)	4,150 (208)	16.6 (0.49)	2,360 (87)	12.4 (0.48)	2,770 (108)
Race/ethnicity															
White	2,556.2 (28.29)	56,400 (266)	53,020 (225)	42.8 (0.57)	2,560 (75)	4.1 (0.24)	1,390 (101)	7.9 (0.30)	2,130 (100)	17.0 (0.44)	4,740 (183)	16.7 (0.43)	2,410 (67)	16.1 (0.48)	3,310 (96)
Black	221.0 (10.15)	55,790 (985)	52,370 (901)	36.2 (2.58)	2,690 (371)	5.4 (1.28)	1,470 (263)	9.6 (1.52)	1,970 (339)	15.5 (2.23)	4,740 (775)	26.2 (2.58)	2,920 (274)	9.5 (1.40)	4,540 (727)
Hispanic	252.2 (12.62)	56,240 (891)	53,620 (872)	39.3 (2.29)	2,150 (219)	7.2 (1.29)	1,280 (202)	7.4 (1.23)	1,570 (367)	9.5 (1.13)	4,600 (456)	20.7 (1.85)	2,710 (233)	9.4 (1.19)	3,640 (509)
Asian	57.5 (7.30)	62,480 (2,702)	58,850 (2,253)	28.4 (5.19)	2,110 (477)	‡ (†)	2,320 ! (725)	‡ (†)	‡ (†)	7.9 (1.89)	7,000 (1,520)	19.7 (1.89)	3,080 (743)	7.0 (1.68)	5,400 ! (2,166)
Pacific Islander	4.4 (1.24)	57,280 (3,301)	52,920 (2,692)	‡ (†)	‡ (†)	‡ (†)	‡ (†)	‡ (†)	‡ (†)	‡ (†)	‡ (†)	‡ (†)	‡ (†)	‡ (†)	‡ (†)
American Indian/Alaska Native	15.4 (2.79)	53,000 (3,354)	46,630 (2,005)	43.9 (7.72)	2,360 (414)	‡ (†)	‡ (†)	‡ (†)	‡ (†)	22.4 (5.49)	‡ (†)	19.2 (3.74)	2,640 (639)	21.5 (6.15)	4,470 ! (1,464)
Two or more races	31.2 (3.64)	53,750 (1,306)	50,230 (1,195)	45.9 (6.50)	2,230 (293)	‡ (†)	‡ (†)	9.0 ! (3.13)	2,020 (537)	16.0 (3.39)	5,690 ! (1,977)	14.5 (2.76)	2,610 (268)	16.1 (3.24)	3,550 ! (1,848)
Age															
Less than 30	487.4 (15.04)	45,160 (393)	41,720 (405)	49.0 (1.53)	2,340 (86)	5.2 (0.61)	1,150 (134)	8.3 (0.76)	1,560 (143)	18.7 (1.05)	3,360 (239)	21.5 (1.10)	2,430 (150)	24.5 (1.16)	2,980 (181)
30 to 39	921.9 (19.46)	53,120 (392)	50,020 (350)	43.8 (0.96)	2,810 (182)	4.3 (0.41)	1,240 (113)	7.6 (0.63)	1,870 (148)	15.7 (0.73)	4,380 (340)	18.4 (0.90)	2,420 (83)	14.8 (0.86)	3,320 (218)
40 to 49	783.7 (18.62)	58,660 (394)	55,420 (368)	41.9 (1.12)	2,490 (81)	4.2 (0.45)	1,410 (135)	7.7 (0.58)	2,210 (183)	16.8 (0.79)	5,070 (339)	17.4 (0.77)	2,490 (108)	14.6 (0.70)	3,720 (199)
50 or more	946.2 (25.68)	63,550 (410)	59,940 (351)	36.1 (1.06)	2,370 (100)	4.2 (0.43)	1,710 (206)	8.3 (0.56)	2,390 (181)	14.6 (0.72)	6,000 (413)	15.6 (0.80)	2,680 (140)	10.6 (0.62)	3,800 (211)
Years of full-time teaching experience															
1 year or less	144.2 (7.55)	44,610 (519)	40,540 (512)	37.6 (2.48)	2,140 (137)	5.6 (1.29)	1,120 (271)	6.4 (1.10)	2,070 (420)	16.9 (1.67)	4,380 (668)	18.7 (2.01)	2,980 (390)	31.2 (1.90)	4,860 (524)
2 to 4 years	385.9 (12.54)	44,490 (305)	41,480 (244)	44.1 (1.42)	2,100 (85)	4.5 (0.59)	1,280 (127)	7.7 (0.70)	1,800 (179)	17.3 (1.02)	3,970 (275)	20.2 (0.86)	2,260 (116)	20.6 (0.89)	2,800 (181)
5 to 9 years	784.6 (18.32)	50,370 (360)	47,300 (312)	43.3 (1.10)	2,520 (96)	5.1 (0.59)	1,270 (129)	8.2 (0.68)	1,640 (137)	16.6 (0.97)	4,250 (321)	19.4 (0.97)	2,380 (113)	14.7 (1.00)	3,110 (239)
10 to 14 years	652.1 (16.57)	58,040 (412)	54,860 (369)	42.5 (1.28)	2,740 (178)	3.6 (0.38)	1,240 (135)	8.4 (0.69)	2,060 (166)	15.7 (0.81)	4,830 (318)	17.2 (0.83)	2,670 (152)	12.2 (0.76)	3,450 (213)
15 to 19 years	426.2 (14.56)	62,050 (623)	58,880 (596)	41.3 (1.51)	2,550 (179)	4.3 (0.85)	1,820 (332)	7.7 (0.94)	2,300 (239)	15.4 (1.13)	5,940 (861)	17.2 (1.34)	2,430 (124)	13.0 (0.84)	3,390 (277)
20 to 24 years	295.8 (10.26)	64,210 (602)	60,930 (593)	40.9 (1.51)	2,500 (146)	4.4 (0.85)	1,610 (365)	7.6 (0.94)	1,980 (230)	15.2 (1.07)	5,730 (612)	13.4 (1.09)	2,460 (158)	13.8 (1.29)	4,220 (498)
25 to 29 years	217.9 (11.00)	67,440 (1,044)	63,780 (838)	39.8 (2.37)	2,810 (278)	5.0 (0.90)	1,500 (274)	9.0 (1.30)	2,530 (304)	15.9 (1.49)	5,000 (781)	16.8 (1.62)	2,550 (214)	12.8 (1.42)	3,010 (316)
30 or more years	222.5 (11.58)	69,790 (763)	64,820 (646)	37.0 (1.98)	2,730 (186)	3.1 (0.58)	1,680 (270)	7.3 (1.14)	3,360 (558)	15.6 (1.35)	5,400 (433)	16.5 (1.57)	2,920 (376)	11.0 (1.12)	3,700 (401)
Highest degree earned															
Less than bachelor's degree	118.9 (8.32)	55,430 (960)	51,330 (794)	41.5 (2.79)	2,460 (199)	6.1 (1.29)	1,190 (363)	9.4 (2.00)	2,000 (420)	20.1 (1.76)	7,340 (1,356)	16.6 (2.16)	2,360 (200)	20.9 (2.38)	3,750 (468)
Bachelor's degree	1,278.2 (20.53)	49,410 (262)	46,340 (225)	42.4 (0.85)	2,370 (66)	5.2 (0.39)	1,350 (100)	8.6 (0.56)	1,790 (99)	14.5 (0.62)	4,600 (295)	16.8 (0.61)	2,360 (97)	16.2 (0.68)	3,400 (191)
Master's degree	1,479.3 (27.00)	61,230 (408)	57,830 (352)	41.5 (.71)	2,650 (125)	3.6 (0.26)	1,500 (148)	7.1 (0.38)	2,250 (178)	16.6 (0.61)	4,570 (160)	18.1 (0.67)	2,600 (104)	13.8 (0.58)	3,380 (145)
Education specialist[4]	228.7 (9.17)	63,420 (727)	59,680 (642)	39.4 (1.97)	2,640 (184)	3.6 (0.83)	1,450 (270)	9.0 (1.05)	2,480 (297)	17.7 (1.62)	5,330 (536)	20.4 (1.67)	2,650 (198)	12.2 (1.45)	3,620 (361)
Doctor's degree	34.2 (3.97)	66,140 (1,718)	60,230 (1,775)	49.2 (4.70)	3,110 (748)	‡ (†)	‡ (†)	‡ (†)	‡ (†)	30.8 (3.99)	6,610 (1,139)	26.9 (3.97)	2,810 (397)	18.8 (3.00)	3,940 (825)
Instructional level[5]															
Elementary	1,572.3 (22.63)	54,820 (349)	52,620 (303)	30.9 (0.87)	1,530 (104)	4.2 (0.37)	1,310 (157)	7.4 (0.41)	1,720 (127)	12.8 (0.62)	4,350 (313)	16.6 (0.68)	2,270 (113)	12.6 (0.67)	2,930 (178)
Secondary	1,566.9 (35.32)	58,000 (280)	53,520 (261)	52.8 (0.57)	3,110 (77)	4.6 (0.26)	1,480 (82)	8.5 (0.41)	2,370 (109)	19.5 (0.48)	5,130 (186)	19.0 (0.48)	2,720 (87)	17.4 (0.49)	3,790 (129)
School locale															
City	‡ (†)	‡ (†)	‡ (†)	‡ (†)	‡ (†)	‡ (†)	‡ (†)	‡ (†)	‡ (†)	‡ (†)	‡ (†)	‡ (†)	‡ (†)	‡ (†)	‡ (†)
Suburban	1,016.9 (30.46)	61,610 (476)	58,470 (427)	42.4 (1.09)	2,750 (136)	4.0 (0.43)	1,450 (140)	6.6 (0.53)	1,870 (148)	15.6 (0.65)	4,300 (188)	17.4 (0.75)	2,450 (94)	13.8 (0.63)	3,350 (161)
Town	382.9 (13.34)	51,060 (475)	47,780 (431)	43.6 (1.43)	2,580 (101)	3.0 (0.55)	1,110 (194)	7.4 (0.72)	1,940 (169)	16.3 (0.93)	4,910 (474)	15.6 (1.21)	2,030 (127)	16.0 (0.85)	3,520 (240)
Rural	853.0 (21.06)	50,670 (275)	47,130 (237)	44.3 (1.07)	2,520 (81)	3.7 (0.42)	1,390 (151)	10.0 (0.71)	2,070 (138)	16.3 (0.61)	5,340 (393)	15.1 (0.63)	2,290 (129)	16.9 (0.69)	3,600 (193)

See notes at end of table.

Table 211.10. Average salaries for full-time teachers in public and private elementary and secondary schools, by selected characteristics: 2011–12—Continued

[Amounts in current dollars. Standard errors appear in parentheses]

Selected characteristic	Number of full-time teachers (in thousands)	Total school-year and summer earned income from school and non-school sources[1]	Base salary	School year supplemental contract[2]		School year income from merit pay bonus		School year income from state supplements		Job outside the school system during the school year		Supplemental school system contract during summer[3]		Employed in a nonschool job during the summer	
				Percent of teachers	Average supplement	Percent of teachers	Average amount	Percent of teachers	Average amount	Percent of teachers	Average income	Percent of teachers	Average supplement	Percent of teachers	Average income
1	2	3	4	5	6	7	8	9	10	11	12	13	14	15	16
Private schools															
Total......	368.4 (10.95)	$44,130 (803)	$40,200 (732)	28.9 (1.30)	$2,730 (168)	‡	(†)	1.8 (0.48)	$1,960 ! (615)	19.6 (1.08)	$5,440 (373)	20.8 (1.15)	$3,370 (361)	17.1 (1.01)	$3,780 (484)
Sex															
Males......	92.9 (6.50)	51,150 (1,829)	44,470 (1,264)	42.7 (2.52)	3,850 (254)	‡	(†)	‡	(†)	26.9 (2.86)	6,550 (661)	29.3 (2.61)	3,600 (471)	23.3 (3.12)	4,650 (508)
Females......	275.5 (9.40)	41,760 (887)	38,760 (864)	24.3 (1.54)	2,070 (201)	‡	(†)	1.8 (0.52)	2,200 ! (806)	17.1 (1.14)	4,850 (431)	17.9 (1.27)	3,240 (483)	15.0 (1.03)	3,320 (665)
Race/ethnicity															
White......	326.0 (11.07)	44,390 (826)	40,450 (778)	29.1 (1.43)	2,750 (174)	‡	(†)	1.6 (0.47)	1,690 (252)	19.4 (1.21)	5,350 (373)	20.2 (1.25)	3,410 (408)	17.5 (1.06)	3,710 (519)
Black......	13.0 (1.83)	41,790 (2,813)	37,080 (2,201)	23.0 (5.65)	2,360 (414)	‡	(†)	‡	(†)	‡	‡	29.6 (4.67)	3,560 ! (1,145)	‡	‡
Hispanic......	19.8 (2.35)	42,550 (2,307)	39,530 (2,271)	27.2 (4.96)	2,180 (397)	‡	(†)	‡	(†)	15.3 (3.28)	6,090 (1,617)	18.0 (3.33)	2,590 (464)	‡	3,070 (765)
Asian......	6.3 (1.25)	40,170 (3,767)	36,720 (3,796)	‡	‡	‡	(†)	‡	(†)	‡	(†)	‡	‡	‡	‡
Pacific Islander......	‡	‡	‡	‡	‡	‡	(†)	‡	(†)	‡	(†)	‡	‡	‡	‡
American Indian/ Alaska Native......	‡ ! (0.86)	42,860 (7,642)	‡ (7,642)	‡	‡	‡	(†)	‡	(†)	‡	19,000	‡	‡	‡	‡
Two or more races......	2.8 ! (0.86)	46,660 (4,580)	39,640 (2,908)	‡	‡	‡	(†)	‡	(†)	‡	‡	‡	‡	‡	‡
Age															
Less than 30......	63.2 (5.13)	34,340 (710)	31,010 (680)	34.1 (2.76)	1,980 (298)	‡	(†)	‡	(†)	23.6 (2.55)	4,170 (575)	24.0 (2.23)	2,050 (141)	32.7 (2.70)	3,460 (454)
30 to 39......	94.3 (5.59)	42,110 (1,051)	38,420 (922)	34.6 (3.07)	3,080 (258)	‡	(†)	‡	(†)	19.4 (2.08)	4,950 (522)	23.9 (2.44)	4,270 (1,293)	15.4 (2.05)	3,590 (548)
40 to 49......	87.9 (5.74)	45,740 (1,316)	42,860 (1,282)	26.2 (2.96)	2,940 (486)	‡	(†)	‡	(†)	18.2 (2.19)	4,980 (965)	20.2 (2.75)	3,460 (451)	12.3 (1.91)	2,690 (403)
50 or more......	123.0 (6.67)	49,580 (1,439)	44,420 (1,203)	23.8 (1.87)	2,750 (263)	‡	(†)	‡	(†)	18.5 (2.14)	7,000 (712)	17.1 (1.56)	3,280 (644)	13.9 (1.88)	5,000 (1,398)
Years of full-time teaching experience															
1 year or less......	30.9 (4.65)	33,990 (1,396)	29,940 (1,139)	29.6 (5.24)	2,440 ! (768)	‡	(†)	‡	(†)	24.5 (4.12)	5,100 (1,103)	21.4 (5.20)	2,330 (511)	30.9 (4.68)	4,390 (1,170)
2 to 4 years......	61.5 (4.73)	36,760 (1,024)	33,540 (948)	31.6 (2.80)	2,760 (347)	‡	(†)	‡	(†)	22.0 (2.63)	4,250 (550)	23.9 (2.96)	2,540 (196)	23.5 (2.80)	2,820 (400)
5 to 9 years......	85.0 (4.67)	40,990 (1,036)	37,220 (995)	30.8 (2.80)	2,560 (299)	‡	(†)	‡	(†)	19.3 (2.34)	5,760 (734)	24.8 (3.29)	4,170 (1,277)	16.1 (1.92)	4,080 (637)
10 to 14 years......	58.6 (4.57)	43,570 (1,203)	40,440 (1,095)	27.4 (3.19)	3,050 (563)	‡	(†)	‡	(†)	19.3 (3.11)	5,310 (915)	18.6 (2.26)	3,740 (607)	14.2 (2.73)	3,340 (615)
15 to 19 years......	43.9 (3.38)	47,190 (2,185)	44,820 (2,386)	23.2 (4.67)	2,560 (478)	‡	(†)	‡	(†)	15.1 (3.05)	5,110 ! (2,128)	20.5 (3.62)	3,180 (768)	10.6 (2.01)	2,400 (528)
20 to 24 years......	27.7 (2.85)	52,380 (2,991)	48,170 (2,386)	30.8 (4.37)	1,900 (214)	‡	(†)	‡	(†)	20.3 (4.78)	6,230 (1,740)	16.0 (3.19)	1,790 (370)	15.4 (4.20)	3,860 ! (1,393)
25 to 29 years......	24.3 (2.53)	52,040 (2,524)	47,070 (2,091)	25.3 (4.04)	3,660 (999)	‡	(†)	‡	(†)	17.6 (4.16)	5,340 (1,069)	17.6 (4.29)	3,230 (628)	‡	‡
30 or more years......	36.5 (4.19)	57,950 (3,772)	50,390 (2,739)	29.4 (3.83)	3,200 (460)	‡	(†)	‡	(†)	18.4 (3.58)	7,420 (1,820)	15.1 (3.03)	4,700 (1,783)	14.8 (3.29)	2,410 (474)
Highest degree earned															
Less than bachelor's degree......	27.9 (4.18)	30,160 (1,733)	27,690 (1,749)	21.3 (5.09)	3,210 (653)	‡	(†)	‡	(†)	15.3 (4.03)	3,820 (1,216)	19.5 (3.96)	2,760 (363)	15.5 (4.10)	3,750 ! (1,158)
Bachelor's degree......	180.9 (5.98)	39,450 (887)	36,270 (830)	27.2 (1.73)	2,490 (251)	‡	(†)	‡ ! (0.36)	1,970 (540)	18.2 (1.32)	5,420 (549)	19.6 (1.36)	2,880 (333)	18.7 (1.16)	4,000 (840)
Master's degree......	134.3 (7.12)	50,670 (1,074)	46,400 (1,045)	32.9 (2.25)	2,850 (228)	‡	(†)	‡	(†)	20.7 (1.77)	5,070 (564)	21.8 (2.35)	4,160 (807)	16.3 (1.60)	3,470 (357)
Education specialist[4]......	17.7 (1.95)	55,230 (3,542)	47,450 (2,839)	22.5 (5.57)	3,230 ! (1,570)	‡	(†)	‡	(†)	25.2 (4.61)	7,280 (1,580)	24.6 (4.78)	2,820 (598)	‡	‡
Doctor's degree......	7.7 (1.84)	64,890 (11,118)	52,590 (6,259)	‡	‡	‡	(†)	‡	(†)	‡	‡	‡	‡	‡	‡
Instructional level[5]															
Elementary......	196.8 (8.15)	39,310 (794)	36,260 (632)	19.2 (1.39)	2,130 (251)	‡	(†)	‡	(†)	16.0 (1.21)	5,190 (720)	17.1 (1.23)	2,770 (349)	15.8 (1.37)	3,730 (853)
Secondary......	171.6 (8.24)	49,640 (1,319)	44,720 (1,174)	40.0 (2.23)	3,070 (224)	‡	(†)	2.6 ! (0.85)	1,600	23.7 (1.70)	5,640 (499)	25.0 (2.03)	3,840 (602)	18.7 (1.39)	3,820 (439)
School locale															
City......	157.9 (9.51)	48,980 (1,569)	44,770 (1,436)	29.3 (1.75)	30,100 (314)	‡	(†)	‡	(†)	19.2 (1.59)	59,700 (555)	21.1 (1.68)	39,400 (722)	16.3 (1.58)	3,750 (991)
Suburban......	‡	42,860 (7,642)	42,860 (7,642)	‡	‡	‡	(†)	‡	(†)	‡	19,000	‡	19,000	‡	‡
Town......	20.7 (2.54)	33,080 (1,479)	29,980 (1,134)	20.8 (3.66)	12,500 (257)	‡	(†)	‡	(†)	18.4 (3.49)	55,600 (1,536)	16.0 (2.82)	35,900 (1,418)	19.5 (3.41)	3,010 (670)
Rural......	‡	‡	‡	‡	‡	‡	(†)	‡	(†)	‡	‡	‡	‡	‡	‡

†Not applicable.

!Interpret data with caution. The coefficient of variation (CV) for this estimate is between 30 and 50 percent.

‡Reporting standards not met. Data may be suppressed because the response rate is under 50 percent, there are too few cases for a reliable estimate, or the coefficient of variation (CV) is 50 percent or greater.

[1]Includes retirement pension funds paid during the school year.

[2]Includes compensation for extracurricular or additional activities such as coaching, student activity sponsorship, or teaching evening classes.

[3]Includes teaching summer sessions and other non-teaching jobs at any school.

[4]Education specialist degrees or certificates are generally awarded for 1 year's work beyond the master's level. Includes certificates of advanced graduate studies.

[5]Teachers were classified as elementary or secondary on the basis of the grades they taught, rather than on the level of the school in which they taught. In general, elementary teachers include those teaching prekindergarten through grade 5 and those teaching multiple grades, with a preponderance of grades taught being kindergarten through grade 6. In general, secondary teachers include those teaching any of grades 7 through 12 and those teaching multiple grades, with a preponderance of grades taught being grades 7 through 12 and usually with no grade taught being lower than grade 5.

NOTE: This table includes regular full-time teachers only; it excludes other staff even when they have full-time teaching duties (regular part-time teachers, itinerant teachers, long-term substitutes, administrators, library media specialists, other professional staff, and support staff). Race categories exclude persons of Hispanic ethnicity. Detail may not sum to totals because of rounding and missing values in cells with too few cases to report.

SOURCE: U.S. Department of Education, National Center for Education Statistics, Schools and Staffing Survey (SASS), "Public School Teacher Data File" and "Private School Teacher Data File," 2011–12. (This table was prepared May 2013.)

Table 211.20. Average base salary for full-time teachers in public elementary and secondary schools, by highest degree earned and years of full-time teaching: Selected years, 1990–91 through 2011–12

[Standard errors appear in parentheses]

Years of full-time teaching experience	Number of full-time teachers	Salary (current dollars) Highest degree earned					Salary (constant 2014–15 dollars)[1] Highest degree earned				
		All teachers[2]	Bachelor's degree	Master's degree	Education specialist[3]	Doctor's degree	All teachers[2]	Bachelor's degree	Master's degree	Education specialist[3]	Doctor's degree
1	2	3	4	5	6	7	8	9	10	11	12
1990–91											
Total	2,336,750 (20,958)	$31,330 (97)	$27,740 (103)	$34,960 (125)	$34,960 (391)	$40,070 (817)	$55,370 (172)	$49,020 (182)	$61,780 (221)	$65,800 (690)	$70,810 (1,443)
1 year or less	94,000 (3,014)	22,210 (200)	21,510 (207)	26,440 (863)	26,630 (982)	‡ (†)	39,250 (354)	38,020 (366)	46,720 (1,526)	47,060 (1,736)	‡ (†)
2 years	86,900 (2,963)	22,120 (162)	21,650 (147)	25,060 (505)	‡ (†)	‡ (†)	39,090 (287)	38,260 (260)	44,300 (893)	‡ (†)	‡ (†)
3 years	80,340 (2,542)	23,010 (177)	22,440 (174)	25,960 (695)	‡ (†)	‡ (†)	40,670 (313)	39,670 (308)	45,880 (1,228)	‡ (†)	‡ (†)
4 years	79,610 (3,271)	23,960 (236)	23,150 (246)	26,340 (526)	29,160 (1,489)	‡ (†)	42,350 (418)	40,910 (434)	46,550 (930)	51,540 (2,632)	‡ (†)
5 years	83,540 (3,238)	25,080 (202)	24,070 (240)	27,220 (436)	29,870 (2,195)	‡ (†)	44,330 (356)	42,540 (425)	48,100 (771)	52,790 (3,879)	‡ (†)
6 to 9 years	316,210 (6,805)	26,500 (109)	25,010 (135)	28,800 (237)	30,210 (761)	‡ (†)	46,840 (192)	44,210 (239)	50,890 (420)	53,390 (1,345)	‡ (†)
10 to 14 years	408,300 (7,843)	29,620 (161)	27,320 (172)	31,760 (299)	33,640 (592)	37,900 (1,943)	52,350 (284)	48,280 (304)	56,130 (529)	59,450 (1,046)	66,990 (3,433)
15 to 19 years	444,930 (7,580)	33,590 (209)	30,820 (253)	35,240 (248)	37,800 (842)	40,340 (1,548)	59,360 (369)	54,470 (447)	62,290 (439)	66,800 (1,488)	71,290 (2,736)
20 to 24 years	392,330 (8,038)	36,960 (202)	34,050 (274)	38,460 (243)	39,520 (838)	43,740 (1,391)	65,310 (358)	60,180 (485)	67,960 (429)	69,850 (1,482)	77,300 (2,459)
25 to 29 years	219,140 (6,214)	38,100 (305)	34,770 (409)	39,830 (370)	42,460 (1,257)	43,110 (2,179)	67,340 (540)	61,460 (723)	70,390 (653)	75,040 (2,222)	76,190 (3,852)
30 to 34 years	100,460 (4,766)	38,530 (380)	35,040 (451)	40,660 (489)	40,900 (1,596)	‡ (†)	68,090 (671)	61,920 (797)	71,860 (865)	72,290 (2,821)	‡ (†)
35 years or more	30,980 (2,515)	39,150 (888)	34,120 (1,258)	41,730 (1,116)	‡ (†)	‡ (†)	69,200 (1,570)	60,290 (2,224)	73,760 (1,972)	‡ (†)	‡ (†)
1999–2000											
Total	2,742,210 (20,301)	$39,890 (118)	$35,310 (116)	$44,700 (174)	$47,990 (439)	$48,180 (1,418)	$55,770 (165)	$49,360 (162)	$62,500 (243)	$67,090 (614)	$67,350 (1,983)
1 year or less	172,710 (5,492)	29,280 (166)	28,110 (150)	34,010 (446)	33,360 (1,009)	‡ (†)	40,940 (232)	39,300 (209)	47,540 (624)	46,630 (1,411)	‡ (†)
2 years	161,220 (5,678)	29,670 (179)	28,800 (165)	33,030 (404)	‡ (†)	‡ (†)	41,480 (250)	40,260 (231)	46,170 (565)	‡ (†)	‡ (†)
3 years	145,290 (4,630)	30,690 (169)	29,650 (199)	34,360 (370)	34,540 (1,341)	‡ (†)	42,900 (237)	41,450 (278)	48,030 (517)	48,290 (1,874)	‡ (†)
4 years	133,840 (5,657)	32,380 (258)	30,810 (232)	35,870 (665)	37,130 (1,354)	‡ (†)	45,270 (361)	43,070 (325)	50,140 (930)	51,900 (1,894)	‡ (†)
5 years	120,490 (4,300)	32,440 (253)	31,040 (287)	34,880 (392)	35,800 (1,915)	‡ (†)	45,360 (354)	43,390 (401)	48,770 (548)	50,060 (2,678)	‡ (†)
6 to 9 years	385,840 (8,205)	34,960 (167)	32,630 (190)	37,800 (240)	40,170 (836)	41,260 (2,302)	48,880 (234)	45,620 (266)	52,840 (336)	56,160 (1,169)	57,680 (3,218)
10 to 14 years	382,730 (6,298)	39,340 (257)	36,160 (386)	42,070 (334)	44,840 (988)	36,500 (2,313)	54,990 (359)	50,550 (540)	58,810 (468)	62,680 (1,381)	51,030 (3,233)
15 to 19 years	321,740 (8,067)	43,400 (225)	40,280 (318)	45,930 (356)	47,270 (916)	34,890 (872)	60,670 (314)	56,310 (445)	64,210 (498)	66,080 (1,281)	48,780 (1,219)
20 to 24 years	351,730 (6,993)	45,650 (264)	41,260 (279)	48,480 (383)	49,000 (1,055)	33,430 (1,319)	63,820 (369)	57,680 (390)	67,780 (536)	68,500 (1,475)	46,730 (1,844)
25 to 29 years	329,170 (7,167)	48,540 (276)	44,750 (333)	50,170 (399)	54,230 (968)	38,150 (2,437)	67,860 (386)	62,570 (466)	70,130 (557)	75,820 (1,353)	53,340 (3,407)
30 to 34 years	185,470 (5,488)	52,150 (346)	47,270 (634)	54,240 (441)	55,990 (1,126)	‡ (†)	72,910 (484)	66,080 (886)	75,840 (616)	78,280 (1,574)	‡ (†)
35 years or more	51,990 (3,006)	50,620 (673)	46,690 (1,359)	52,270 (923)	56,200 (2,797)	‡ (†)	70,770 (941)	65,270 (1,900)	73,080 (1,291)	78,580 (3,911)	‡ (†)
2003–04											
Total	2,948,220 (28,203)	$44,360 (245)	$39,200 (300)	$49,440 (202)	$52,940 (458)	$53,750 (1,295)	$56,420 (311)	$49,850 (381)	$62,880 (257)	$67,330 (583)	$68,350 (1,646)
1 year or less	177,920 (17,391)	33,150 (381)	31,820 (342)	38,600 (732)	44,280 (5,030)	37,320 (1,690)	42,180 (485)	40,470 (435)	49,100 (931)	56,320 (6,397)	47,460 (2,150)
2 years	153,950 (17,695)	34,060 (284)	32,720 (334)	37,940 (646)	33,960 (1,299)	‡ (†)	43,310 (361)	41,620 (425)	48,260 (821)	43,190 (1,652)	‡ (†)
3 years	168,140 (9,009)	35,230 (349)	33,420 (282)	40,230 (683)	40,340 (3,173)	‡ (†)	44,810 (444)	42,500 (359)	51,160 (868)	51,310 (4,035)	‡ (†)
4 years	159,490 (6,723)	36,260 (265)	34,560 (279)	40,280 (530)	38,530 (1,799)	‡ (†)	46,120 (338)	43,950 (355)	51,230 (673)	49,000 (2,287)	‡ (†)
5 years	153,180 (6,194)	37,370 (403)	34,950 (324)	40,830 (763)	42,810 (1,957)	‡ (†)	47,530 (513)	44,450 (413)	51,940 (970)	54,450 (2,489)	‡ (†)
6 to 9 years	498,590 (13,859)	40,340 (201)	37,070 (209)	43,700 (300)	45,810 (1,308)	44,270 (2,321)	51,310 (255)	47,150 (266)	55,580 (381)	58,260 (1,664)	56,300 (2,951)
10 to 14 years	433,530 (14,595)	44,330 (257)	39,730 (267)	47,900 (393)	50,000 (956)	55,040 (3,584)	56,380 (327)	50,530 (340)	60,920 (500)	63,600 (1,216)	70,000 (4,559)
15 to 19 years	343,970 (9,606)	49,200 (356)	44,310 (482)	52,290 (469)	56,250 (1,349)	58,350 (3,443)	62,570 (453)	56,350 (613)	66,500 (597)	71,550 (1,716)	74,210 (4,378)
20 to 24 years	285,980 (8,434)	50,810 (362)	46,390 (374)	53,980 (583)	54,900 (999)	53,580 (3,531)	64,620 (461)	59,000 (476)	68,650 (741)	69,820 (1,270)	68,140 (4,491)
25 to 29 years	283,460 (11,809)	52,790 (281)	48,650 (488)	55,000 (411)	55,870 (975)	65,210 (3,524)	67,140 (357)	61,870 (620)	69,950 (523)	71,050 (1,240)	82,940 (4,482)
30 to 34 years	223,710 (11,435)	56,280 (428)	51,310 (606)	58,070 (566)	62,450 (1,389)	60,830 (2,664)	71,580 (544)	65,260 (771)	73,860 (720)	79,420 (1,767)	77,360 (3,388)
35 years or more	66,310 (3,427)	58,220 (755)	55,360 (1,296)	59,150 (978)	61,260 (2,224)	‡ (†)	74,050 (960)	70,410 (1,649)	75,230 (1,244)	77,910 (2,829)	‡ (†)

See notes at end of table.

Table 211.20. Average base salary for full-time teachers in public elementary and secondary schools, by highest degree earned and years of full-time teaching: Selected years, 1990–91 through 2011–12—Continued

[Standard errors appear in parentheses]

Years of full-time teaching experience	Number of full-time teachers	Salary (current dollars) — Highest degree earned					Salary (constant 2014–15 dollars)[1] — Highest degree earned				
		All teachers[2]	Bachelor's degree	Master's degree	Education specialist[3]	Doctor's degree	All teachers[2]	Bachelor's degree	Master's degree	Education specialist[3]	Doctor's degree
1	2	3	4	5	6	7	8	9	10	11	12
2007–08											
Total	3,114,690 (41,111)	$49,630 (203)	$43,650 (220)	$54,810 (281)	$58,420 (722)	$59,150 (1,620)	$55,480 (227)	$48,790 (246)	$61,280 (314)	$65,310 (807)	$66,130 (1,811)
1 year or less	211,500 (12,029)	38,210 (332)	36,670 (308)	42,840 (807)	47,410 (3,584)	†	42,710 (371)	41,000 (344)	47,900 (902)	53,010 (4,007)	†
2 years	185,130 (10,587)	38,640 (334)	36,900 (340)	42,640 (717)	47,420 (4,082)	†	43,200 (373)	41,260 (380)	47,670 (801)	53,010 (4,564)	†
3 years	177,230 (7,735)	40,070 (374)	37,740 (358)	44,430 (864)	52,230 (4,612)	†	44,800 (418)	42,190 (400)	49,680 (966)	58,400 (5,156)	†
4 years	174,350 (7,951)	41,180 (377)	38,550 (428)	45,490 (577)	47,590 (2,293)	†	46,040 (421)	43,100 (479)	50,860 (645)	53,210 (2,563)	†
5 years	148,540 (7,995)	42,830 (534)	39,690 (476)	46,470 (869)	46,670 (2,690)	†	47,890 (597)	44,380 (532)	51,950 (972)	52,180 (3,007)	†
6 to 9 years	557,050 (14,475)	46,330 (252)	41,800 (379)	50,190 (441)	51,740 (1,128)	52,850 (2,349)	51,800 (281)	46,730 (424)	56,110 (493)	57,840 (1,261)	59,090 (2,626)
10 to 14 years	508,300 (14,867)	50,470 (377)	45,380 (436)	53,430 (559)	56,550 (1,220)	60,400 (4,124)	56,420 (422)	50,740 (488)	59,730 (625)	63,220 (1,364)	67,520 (4,611)
15 to 19 years	350,690 (12,953)	55,000 (484)	48,500 (553)	59,180 (722)	59,620 (1,353)	63,280 (3,462)	61,490 (541)	54,230 (618)	66,160 (807)	66,650 (1,512)	70,740 (3,870)
20 to 24 years	288,110 (11,954)	57,830 (636)	52,760 (783)	60,640 (794)	65,300 (2,162)	67,960 (6,394)	64,650 (711)	58,990 (876)	67,790 (888)	73,010 (2,417)	75,980 (7,149)
25 to 29 years	221,950 (8,609)	60,260 (740)	54,420 (830)	63,280 (1,068)	66,830 (3,306)	†	67,370 (827)	60,840 (928)	70,750 (1,194)	74,710 (3,696)	†
30 to 34 years	197,490 (8,304)	61,120 (754)	54,860 (997)	64,280 (998)	63,820 (1,555)	†	68,330 (843)	61,340 (1,114)	71,870 (1,116)	71,350 (1,738)	†
35 years or more	94,340 (7,055)	61,920 (1,067)	55,350 (1,561)	64,400 (1,499)	68,780 (3,364)	†	69,220 (1,192)	61,880 (1,745)	71,990 (1,676)	76,890 (3,761)	†
2011–12											
Total	3,139,250 (38,342)	$53,070 (213)	$46,340 (225)	$57,830 (352)	$59,680 (642)	$60,230 (1,775)	$55,190 (222)	$48,200 (234)	$60,150 (366)	$62,070 (667)	$62,640 (1,846)
1 year or less	144,240 (7,545)	40,540 (512)	38,490 (578)	45,240 (1,122)	49,140 (3,732)	†	42,160 (532)	40,030 (601)	47,060 (1,167)	51,110 (3,882)	†
2 years	118,520 (5,799)	39,740 (356)	38,140 (381)	42,930 (725)	47,570 (4,451)	†	41,340 (370)	39,660 (397)	44,650 (755)	49,470 (4,629)	†
3 years	126,030 (7,109)	41,470 (450)	39,150 (478)	45,590 (800)	47,850 (2,277)	†	43,130 (468)	40,710 (497)	47,420 (832)	49,760 (2,368)	†
4 years	151,350 (8,219)	42,840 (422)	40,280 (461)	45,940 (637)	46,360 (2,122)	†	44,560 (438)	41,900 (479)	47,780 (663)	48,220 (2,207)	†
5 years	174,140 (8,549)	43,830 (789)	40,600 (422)	47,420 (1,610)	45,950 (2,262)	†	45,590 (820)	42,220 (439)	49,310 (1,674)	47,790 (2,352)	†
6 to 9 years	610,420 (16,507)	48,290 (327)	43,450 (419)	51,400 (457)	52,780 (1,237)	51,340 (2,507)	50,230 (340)	45,190 (435)	53,460 (475)	54,890 (1,287)	53,390 (2,608)
10 to 14 years	652,140 (16,569)	54,860 (369)	48,620 (537)	58,260 (541)	58,070 (1,044)	61,190 (2,548)	57,060 (384)	50,570 (558)	60,590 (563)	60,400 (1,086)	63,640 (2,650)
15 to 19 years	426,250 (14,564)	58,880 (596)	51,290 (749)	62,460 (775)	65,430 (1,673)	64,420 (3,910)	61,240 (620)	53,340 (779)	64,960 (806)	68,050 (1,740)	67,000 (4,066)
20 to 24 years	295,760 (10,256)	60,930 (593)	54,110 (849)	65,340 (871)	64,560 (1,665)	67,630 (4,095)	63,370 (617)	56,280 (883)	67,950 (906)	67,150 (1,732)	70,340 (4,259)
25 to 29 years	217,870 (11,000)	63,780 (838)	56,890 (1,046)	67,550 (1,253)	69,410 (2,890)	†	66,330 (872)	59,170 (1,088)	70,260 (1,303)	72,190 (3,006)	†
30 to 34 years	142,630 (9,117)	65,610 (791)	58,510 (1,069)	69,420 (1,083)	67,260 (2,406)	†	68,240 (822)	60,860 (1,112)	72,200 (1,126)	69,950 (2,502)	†
35 years or more	79,900 (5,008)	63,400 (947)	59,560 (1,548)	66,120 (1,133)	64,660 (2,385)	†	65,940 (985)	61,950 (1,610)	68,760 (1,178)	67,250 (2,480)	†

†Not applicable.
‡Reporting standards not met (too few cases for a reliable estimate).
[1]Constant dollars based on the Consumer Price Index, prepared by the Bureau of Labor Statistics, U.S. Department of Labor, adjusted to a school-year basis.
[2]Includes teachers with levels of education below the bachelor's degree (not shown separately).
[3]Education specialist degrees or certificates are generally awarded for 1 year's work beyond the master's level. Includes certificate of advanced graduate studies.

NOTE: This table includes regular full-time teachers only; it excludes other staff even when they have full-time teaching duties (regular part-time teachers, itinerant teachers, long-term substitutes, administrators, library media specialists, other professional staff, and support staff). Some data have been revised from previously published figures. Detail may not sum to totals because of rounding.
SOURCE: U.S. Department of Education, National Center for Education Statistics, Schools and Staffing Survey (SASS), "Public School Teacher Data File," 1990–91, 1999–2000, 2003–04, 2007–08, and 2011–12; and "Charter School Teacher Data File," 1999–2000. (This table was prepared October 2015.)

Table 211.30. Average base salary for full-time public elementary and secondary school teachers with a bachelor's degree as their highest degree, by years of full-time teaching experience and state: 1993–94 through 2011–12

[Amounts in current dollars. Standard errors appear in parentheses]

State	1993–94, total	1999–2000, total	2003–04, total	2007–08 Total	2007–08 2 or fewer years	2007–08 Over 20 years	2011–12 Total	2011–12 2 or fewer years	2011–12 3 to 5 years	2011–12 6 to 10 years	2011–12 11 to 20 years	2011–12 Over 20 years
1	2	3	4	5	6	7	8	9	10	11	12	13
United States	$30,150 (97)	$35,310 (116)	$39,200 (300)	$43,650 (220)	$36,780 (262)	$54,170 (463)	$46,340 (225)	$38,330 (341)	$40,030 (256)	$44,040 (456)	$50,440 (456)	$56,620 (604)
Alabama	24,450 (151)	31,300 (210)	32,750 (256)	39,210 (381)	34,810 (465)	44,220 (1,210)	41,010 (641)	35,030 (692)	39,070 (1,329)	40,150 (594)	43,490 (1,250)	46,810 (978)
Alaska	42,620 (308)	42,170 (269)	46,160 (720)	51,950 (747)	40,100 (746)	63,600 (1,932)	58,800 (2,016)	47,930 (1,664)	50,790 (2,385)	35,650 (†)	65,020 (2,320)	46,640 (3,131)
Arizona	28,050 (347)	36,960 (491)	33,370 (556)	36,880 (571)	33,640 (388)	45,670 (1,770)	36,960 (644)	32,850 (515)	35,170 (857)	35,540 (770)	41,010 (807)	46,640 (3,131)
Arkansas	24,970 (199)	29,810 (345)	32,710 (328)	40,220 (418)	33,090 (626)	44,610 (984)	41,830 (1,073)	37,390 (1,481)	36,200 (1,204)	39,540 (1,153)	43,390 (942)	48,000 (3,092)
California	37,330 (412)	41,930 (301)	51,210 (704)	56,950 (966)	44,770 (997)	72,680 (1,235)	62,010 (1,031)	47,310 (3,537)	48,930 (966)	58,570 (2,253)	66,030 (1,129)	73,980 (1,820)
Colorado	27,590 (391)	32,180 (428)	36,140 (699)	38,090 (884)	32,600 (621)	‡	40,770 (1,284)	33,270 (750)	35,140 (763)	40,420 (1,206)	49,250 (2,841)	‡
Connecticut	40,510 (645)	38,530 (883)	48,380 (997)	49,700 (1,286)	42,830 (1,348)	53,300 (†)	53,060 (1,578)	39,020 (1,497)	45,860 (1,365)	‡	‡	‡
Delaware	31,400 (375)	37,620 (893)	41,210 (991)	45,880 (960)	42,180 (†)	‡	47,000 (1,504)	‡	‡	‡	‡	‡
District of Columbia	37,690 (645)	40,980 (407)	48,350 (1,290)	54,970 (2,025)	42,180 (425)	‡	‡	‡	‡	‡	‡	‡
Florida	28,970 (229)	33,650 (407)	36,460 (624)	41,640 (554)	36,030 (473)	55,480 (1,182)	‡	‡	‡	‡	‡	‡
Georgia	25,650 (215)	33,610 (373)	37,160 (490)	41,640 (760)	34,580 (573)	54,330 (1,192)	42,490 (1,032)	38,060 (4,530)	37,820 (858)	40,760 (922)	46,140 (1,243)	‡
Hawaii	34,060 (460)	36,710 (533)	39,250 (887)	45,380 (922)	45,380 (1,496)	‡	38,680 (794)	32,230 (1,010)	33,770 (2,284)	32,270 (491)	43,270 (1,178)	47,650 (1,002)
Idaho	24,610 (252)	31,500 (208)	36,150 (627)	39,870 (609)	31,110 (619)	48,450 (1,122)	45,660 (1,156)	37,380 (1,287)	41,570 (1,299)	46,120 (1,710)	52,480 (2,868)	54,690 (2,716)
Illinois	29,480 (277)	35,250 (563)	38,730 (791)	42,740 (836)	36,030 (926)	52,950 (1,857)	42,900 (1,489)	34,240 (701)	37,420 (996)	39,960 (1,273)	47,630 (1,457)	‡
Indiana	25,400 (329)	30,760 (296)	34,600 (640)	38,670 (786)	32,850 (452)	‡	‡	‡	‡	‡	‡	‡
Iowa	24,950 (319)	28,910 (279)	33,600 (696)	35,240 (500)	28,580 (827)	40,400 (903)	41,040 (759)	33,900 (1,926)	36,410 (850)	39,280 (1,164)	45,250 (1,378)	45,100 (1,920)
Kansas	25,930 (135)	29,430 (264)	32,290 (326)	37,160 (476)	34,390 (523)	42,250 (880)	38,120 (438)	35,670 (955)	35,560 (445)	37,610 (872)	39,190 (659)	42,730 (1,282)
Kentucky	24,910 (457)	27,720 (358)	31,610 (468)	35,640 (608)	33,460 (1,011)	‡	38,840 (896)	36,060 (716)	36,670 (496)	‡	44,130 (980)	‡
Louisiana	22,520 (159)	28,020 (476)	32,590 (489)	39,880 (462)	36,300 (825)	44,800 (1,061)	43,040 (614)	39,120 (798)	39,560 (1,105)	42,510 (1,134)	45,230 (891)	47,540 (961)
Maine	22,550 (330)	34,690 (775)	36,650 (606)	38,770 (651)	31,260 (573)	46,260 (1,321)	43,710 (1,023)	‡	34,180 (1,538)	38,000 (1,033)	‡	52,570 (1,385)
Maryland	33,520 (476)	37,760 (683)	42,960 (1,313)	50,680 (1,213)	41,270 (492)	66,640 (1,644)	56,360 (2,123)	46,220 (3,395)	38,070 (839)	46,250 (1,873)	58,540 (2,167)	60,850 (2,504)
Massachusetts	34,340 (309)	40,410 (464)	43,930 (964)	50,880 (917)	37,720 (970)	58,510 (2,309)	47,260 (1,588)	36,620 (1,186)	39,570 (1,387)	41,950 (1,915)	48,040 (1,229)	56,320 (2,294)
Michigan	37,170 (670)	39,950 (838)	45,230 (682)	47,760 (1,612)	35,930 (664)	59,330 (1,506)	45,250 (1,184)	35,830 (2,261)	33,470 (490)	34,080 (658)	39,220 (802)	44,490 (1,504)
Minnesota	31,010 (419)	35,270 (685)	39,030 (566)	41,760 (593)	33,830 (574)	51,980 (924)	36,030 (520)	31,890 (761)	‡	‡	‡	‡
Mississippi	22,640 (106)	28,000 (186)	31,890 (425)	36,610 (344)	32,770 (434)	43,690 (850)	‡	‡	‡	‡	‡	‡
Missouri	23,510 (286)	28,020 (378)	31,340 (547)	34,730 (553)	31,200 (632)	39,320 (1,512)	36,640 (941)	36,210 (2,581)	34,100 (891)	35,460 (1,290)	38,370 (1,733)	52,550 (2,022)
Montana	24,070 (199)	27,920 (256)	31,870 (522)	35,880 (597)	27,090 (591)	44,080 (1,045)	38,470 (1,155)	28,560 (1,128)	31,410 (1,454)	34,980 (1,442)	41,240 (1,713)	48,570 (1,719)
Nebraska	22,580 (388)	26,090 (254)	30,300 (435)	34,190 (805)	29,400 (379)	36,690 (1,524)	33,970 (912)	33,970 (1,111)	34,240 (775)	39,260 (1,505)	41,330 (1,354)	44,090 (2,004)
Nevada	29,350 (285)	34,470 (434)	35,970 (700)	40,060 (619)	34,040 (462)	48,800 (2,143)	45,100 (1,913)	39,120 (†)	‡	44,300 (1,527)	51,190 (2,994)	‡
New Hampshire	31,280 (437)	34,210 (542)	38,800 (644)	43,910 (843)	33,810 (1,139)	52,430 (1,050)	48,320 (1,394)	‡	34,180 (†)	‡	51,260 (1,568)	56,980 (1,956)
New Jersey	41,330 (744)	46,720 (653)	49,780 (1,049)	54,580 (1,091)	45,370 (977)	72,840 (2,642)	61,120 (1,391)	50,880 (1,517)	49,590 (920)	54,610 (1,178)	66,830 (2,276)	78,660 (3,520)
New Mexico	25,260 (224)	29,290 (363)	29,360 (470)	39,830 (596)	32,520 (844)	48,430 (885)	41,460 (747)	34,900 (1,856)	36,750 (1,639)	42,620 (851)	42,480 (1,418)	46,950 (1,045)
New York	39,650 (1,152)	41,600 (1,094)	42,630 (1,074)	48,520 (2,004)	43,670 (1,652)	60,460 (2,704)	60,640 (2,704)	32,770 (895)	‡	‡	‡	‡
North Carolina	26,010 (220)	31,920 (331)	33,650 (479)	37,050 (489)	30,930 (499)	48,070 (843)	37,660 (545)	32,770 (895)	31,620 (913)	35,090 (613)	39,660 (832)	46,430 (1,154)
North Dakota	22,450 (193)	25,910 (279)	35,160 (490)	34,790 (695)	27,770 (579)	38,920 (1,069)	40,470 (1,666)	33,570 (722)	35,190 (720)	38,220 (1,096)	43,230 (1,248)	44,570 (2,866)
Ohio	30,370 (399)	35,120 (583)	41,600 (891)	41,670 (1,567)	35,350 (1,976)	54,890 (2,001)	46,070 (1,116)	34,980 (1,085)	36,990 (878)	43,670 (1,507)	51,930 (1,642)	59,950 (2,284)
Oklahoma	24,880 (108)	27,400 (224)	31,190 (211)	35,880 (226)	32,390 (458)	41,410 (477)	36,700 (371)	33,260 (868)	33,360 (469)	33,750 (416)	38,100 (409)	42,860 (1,104)
Oregon	32,580 (440)	42,620 (613)	40,040 (865)	46,930 (1,282)	32,050 (655)	52,750 (1,869)	51,260 (1,653)	‡	‡	‡	54,330 (2,170)	57,940 (1,849)
Pennsylvania	37,260 (523)	43,900 (357)	44,250 (963)	47,780 (1,162)	38,950 (780)	64,470 (1,680)	54,210 (1,485)	41,180 (1,073)	44,250 (1,367)	47,540 (1,414)	58,910 (2,455)	72,350 (2,919)
Rhode Island	38,000 (522)	43,900 (542)	49,360 (834)	56,680 (1,362)	‡	‡	48,320 (†)	‡	‡	‡	‡	‡
South Carolina	25,120 (280)	29,820 (300)	34,950 (483)	37,150 (606)	31,670 (625)	45,920 (1,013)	39,380 (1,077)	32,760 (668)	33,280 (601)	36,080 (1,103)	34,950 (900)	38,820 (1,345)
South Dakota	22,600 (186)	26,000 (230)	29,360 (301)	32,180 (445)	27,730 (422)	36,250 (784)	34,870 (601)	32,890 (2,513)	30,760 (639)	32,100 (490)	41,650 (832)	54,290 (1,561)
Tennessee	25,650 (291)	30,830 (378)	34,510 (432)	37,420 (553)	32,990 (481)	43,350 (1,430)	39,420 (877)	34,490 (2,730)	37,380 (1,322)	38,120 (1,301)	47,820 (639)	54,600 (1,206)
Texas	26,950 (295)	34,770 (386)	38,140 (278)	42,890 (480)	39,150 (706)	48,800 (753)	46,820 (440)	41,200 (935)	43,630 (571)	44,900 (590)	47,660 (1,248)	55,230 (1,500)
Utah	25,800 (195)	31,810 (375)	35,160 (525)	38,570 (863)	30,430 (745)	48,750 (1,469)	39,740 (1,087)	30,000 (1,831)	34,230 (411)	38,680 (1,059)	45,660 (1,248)	55,230 (1,500)
Vermont	29,750 (494)	33,470 (733)	39,040 (840)	43,430 (1,005)	37,170 (974)	52,160 (1,253)	48,240 (1,416)	38,080 (850)	38,200 (710)	41,220 (1,203)	50,670 (2,079)	55,660 (2,233)
Virginia	29,410 (378)	34,060 (424)	37,520 (583)	43,440 (569)	37,220 (2,053)	54,320 (1,391)	44,860 (999)	37,360 (2,125)	39,280 (1,702)	42,010 (878)	46,500 (2,085)	54,290 (1,561)
Washington	33,150 (490)	36,330 (359)	40,040 (916)	44,650 (905)	29,030 (491)	53,950 (1,445)	45,590 (1,439)	34,240 (1,737)	34,120 (595)	36,830 (775)	52,600 (2,364)	53,220 (4,347)
West Virginia	26,980 (183)	30,040 (246)	32,980 (344)	34,410 (475)	32,020 (651)	40,660 (581)	38,560 (646)	34,180 (637)	36,830 (775)	42,470 (1,338)	40,020 (1,158)	46,740 (1,211)
Wisconsin	31,490 (351)	35,470 (331)	37,150 (634)	41,390 (859)	32,020 (651)	49,630 (1,457)	42,790 (840)	34,180 (1,124)	38,830 (1,124)	42,910 (1,480)	46,880 (1,598)	54,890 (1,714)
Wyoming	27,310 (247)	29,470 (248)	34,080 (576)	45,750 (543)	38,230 (863)	51,210 (1,119)	50,610 (1,105)	43,440 (1,162)	47,530 (1,083)	42,910 (1,480)	52,180 (1,212)	55,710 (2,807)

†Not applicable.
‡Reporting standards not met. Data may be suppressed because the response rate is under 50 percent, there are too few cases for a reliable estimate, or the coefficient of variation (CV) is 50 percent or greater.
NOTE: This table includes regular full-time teachers only; it excludes other staff even when they have full-time teaching duties (regular part-time teachers, itinerant teachers, long-term substitutes, administrators, library media specialists, other professional staff, and support staff).

SOURCE: U.S. Department of Education, National Center for Education Statistics, Schools and Staffing Survey (SASS), "Public School Teacher Data File," 1993–94, 1999–2000, 2003–04, 2007–08, and 2011–12; and "Public Charter School Teacher Data File," 1999–2000. (This table was prepared June 2013.)

Table 211.40. Average base salary for full-time public elementary and secondary school teachers with a master's degree as their highest degree, by years of full-time teaching experience and state: 1993–94 through 2011–12

[Amounts in current dollars. Standard errors appear in parentheses]

State	1993–94, total	1999–2000, total	2003–04, total	2007–08 Total	2007–08 6 to 10 years	2007–08 11 to 20 years	2007–08 Over 20 years	2011–12 Total	2011–12 5 or fewer years	2011–12 6 to 10 years	2011–12 11 to 20 years	2011–12 Over 20 years
1	2	3	4	5	6	7	8	9	10	11	12	13
United States	$38,480 (154)	$44,700 (174)	$49,440 (202)	$54,810 (281)	$50,540 (380)	$56,770 (493)	$63,050 (576)	$57,830 (352)	$45,880 (550)	$52,260 (514)	$60,810 (504)	$67,150 (604)
Alabama	28,920 (156)	36,930 (145)	39,730 (383)	46,980 (436)	45,050 (828)	48,150 (480)	50,960 (1,102)	48,410 (367)	44,830 (666)	45,940 (757)	49,500 (483)	51,910 (557)
Alaska	50,900 (373)	51,170 (662)	53,720 (1,005)	58,640 (800)	54,480 (1,141)	61,530 (965)	65,260 (1,456)	64,240 (2,039)	53,330 (1,543)	‡	68,130 (3,724)	48,420 (1,191)
Arizona	35,280 (302)	38,150 (465)	41,310 (531)	43,910 (701)	39,600 (877)	44,910 (853)	52,300 (1,381)	42,560 (660)	36,780 (723)	39,270 (976)	45,220 (1,043)	‡
Arkansas	29,070 (322)	34,830 (483)	39,480 (639)	45,460 (678)	42,450 (1,355)	45,130 (1,150)	52,300 (971)	47,100 (921)	41,060 (337)	42,290 (1,199)	45,220 (1,574)	53,850 (1,869)
California	43,420 (636)	50,800 (537)	59,160 (761)	65,040 (982)	59,930 (1,076)	68,830 (1,477)	78,710 (1,186)	67,830 (981)	50,170 (1,334)	61,100 (1,091)	70,260 (1,776)	81,310 (1,116)
Colorado	36,580 (364)	41,200 (445)	47,960 (641)	50,140 (1,069)	46,050 (1,719)	54,760 (1,692)	60,770 (1,920)	52,760 (1,280)	42,580 (2,262)	45,800 (1,598)	54,990 (1,512)	67,830 (3,875)
Connecticut	49,310 (416)	50,620 (590)	57,340 (934)	62,480 (762)	57,870 (1,079)	68,270 (1,430)	72,230 (868)	67,040 (996)	52,510 (1,560)	59,060 (1,602)	72,890 (1,058)	77,630 (1,366)
Delaware	42,350 (535)	48,120 (910)	54,670 (913)	56,930 (1,117)	52,280 (1,679)	62,270 (2,243)	69,340 (1,947)	57,730 (1,420)	45,820 (1,361)	52,090 (1,343)	63,840 (1,647)	71,640 (1,769)
District of Columbia	45,360 (828)	51,040 (472)	55,450 (1,568)	66,250 (1,933)	41,600 (920)	70,100 (2,147)	81,410 (1,654)	‡	‡	‡	‡	‡
Florida	33,150 (487)	39,330 (476)	42,120 (784)	48,680 (985)	‡	45,760 (937)	61,650 (1,329)	‡	‡	‡	‡	‡
Georgia	31,890 (227)	41,950 (524)	47,540 (752)	51,600 (799)	48,020 (1,214)	53,320 (863)	57,920 (1,278)	50,700 (1,002)	43,240 (1,909)	46,510 (934)	53,010 (1,253)	60,350 (2,025)
Hawaii	36,430 (731)	39,280 (524)	42,910 (967)	49,380 (1,513)	41,150 (1,707)	51,410 (1,249)	53,120 (1,855)	45,920 (1,724)	‡	37,300 (1,627)	49,020 (2,067)	54,210 (2,258)
Idaho	31,590 (440)	42,380 (772)	44,140 (857)	47,020 (981)	41,930 (1,513)	51,410 (1,249)	53,120 (1,855)	‡	49,030 (2,082)	57,570 (1,787)	66,730 (2,353)	80,650 (2,944)
Illinois	42,400 (588)	47,770 (953)	54,110 (1,253)	61,330 (1,503)	53,930 (1,513)	62,610 (1,854)	74,860 (2,895)	64,670 (1,520)	49,030 (2,082)	57,570 (1,787)	66,730 (2,353)	80,650 (2,944)
Indiana	38,040 (292)	45,480 (413)	49,760 (670)	51,640 (686)	43,470 (1,128)	49,100 (883)	58,370 (655)	58,370 (735)	39,610 (943)	45,570 (1,258)	54,370 (908)	61,760 (753)
Iowa	32,220 (571)	38,010 (494)	41,880 (608)	44,770 (829)	39,040 (1,073)	43,130 (1,487)	50,980 (1,111)	49,630 (1,509)	39,350 (1,318)	42,010 (1,819)	51,650 (2,543)	53,420 (2,764)
Kansas	32,560 (314)	36,140 (428)	40,400 (755)	46,220 (955)	41,240 (1,390)	46,160 (1,036)	50,260 (1,519)	47,940 (1,090)	45,830 (1,882)	41,890 (638)	48,730 (1,461)	53,720 (1,554)
Kentucky	31,390 (396)	36,380 (310)	40,570 (457)	46,270 (578)	42,750 (762)	48,430 (1,162)	51,540 (866)	50,080 (751)	41,670 (1,457)	46,240 (922)	51,520 (975)	58,590 (1,585)
Louisiana	27,300 (262)	33,120 (806)	38,000 (558)	44,090 (854)	38,970 (871)	46,060 (1,135)	47,470 (974)	46,790 (986)	‡	45,420 (1,824)	48,690 (1,524)	50,220 (1,492)
Maine	33,060 (499)	38,770 (458)	42,460 (677)	44,820 (733)	44,820 (871)	45,960 (1,030)	51,680 (1,138)	48,890 (1,145)	41,670 (1,457)	42,190 (769)	48,160 (1,394)	57,530 (1,506)
Maryland	42,340 (406)	45,930 (1,055)	53,190 (1,307)	59,130 (1,422)	51,950 (1,240)	62,770 (2,878)	70,570 (1,880)	63,420 (†)	49,650 (1,399)	58,840 (1,673)	68,450 (1,821)	73,440 (1,603)
Massachusetts	39,710 (254)	47,630 (370)	53,500 (714)	58,680 (894)	57,660 (960)	62,000 (1,225)	68,590 (1,404)	64,130 (962)	54,060 (3,458)	55,250 (1,916)	67,590 (962)	70,610 (1,269)
Michigan	47,660 (488)	53,050 (651)	59,680 (906)	63,100 (1,116)	56,030 (1,790)	67,540 (1,494)	69,980 (1,434)	64,130 (700)	43,830 (1,531)	39,380 (640)	60,860 (847)	64,270 (1,098)
Minnesota	40,710 (552)	46,050 (674)	49,500 (731)	55,040 (730)	49,930 (1,041)	56,750 (900)	64,390 (1,203)	52,660 (700)	35,860 (749)	40,180 (1,742)	43,290 (841)	50,860 (1,612)
Mississippi	26,600 (200)	34,170 (326)	38,460 (479)	44,170 (617)	40,110 (537)	44,090 (798)	50,570 (804)	43,110 (767)	‡	‡	‡	‡
Missouri	33,180 (625)	37,400 (747)	40,880 (761)	45,830 (1,020)	41,260 (978)	46,150 (1,385)	54,300 (1,290)	47,480 (989)	39,240 (617)	43,430 (1,422)	47,790 (1,067)	58,230 (2,342)
Montana	32,270 (423)	35,960 (728)	39,980 (885)	45,970 (908)	39,360 (1,161)	45,700 (1,589)	51,300 (1,290)	49,060 (1,393)	42,210 (1,722)	42,210 (1,652)	47,620 (1,685)	60,160 (1,685)
Nebraska	30,290 (538)	33,540 (536)	39,980 (784)	40,410 (913)	37,490 (1,008)	38,420 (1,330)	43,880 (1,560)	47,260 (1,310)	39,320 (2,914)	44,930 (2,290)	48,880 (3,067)	50,660 (2,253)
Nevada	38,570 (353)	43,350 (429)	45,770 (1,083)	50,050 (906)	47,280 (840)	53,010 (757)	60,420 (1,134)	52,960 (1,713)	46,770 (891)	45,770 (1,824)	58,850 (1,524)	63,590 (1,751)
New Hampshire	36,970 (505)	41,310 (689)	45,140 (977)	51,320 (1,002)	46,650 (1,397)	55,020 (1,528)	59,610 (1,134)	54,350 (1,169)	36,970 (1,495)	48,480 (1,303)	48,160 (2,149)	63,000 (987)
New Jersey	50,950 (883)	57,410 (709)	60,200 (1,571)	62,580 (1,901)	54,270 (2,691)	66,070 (2,656)	81,170 (2,065)	68,910 (1,227)	56,040 (1,008)	59,390 (983)	72,360 (1,596)	85,460 (2,549)
New Mexico	28,400 (281)	35,570 (539)	40,100 (810)	47,200 (833)	44,420 (854)	48,890 (553)	53,050 (1,393)	47,360 (1,492)	37,280 (2,051)	44,620 (1,343)	50,160 (2,096)	53,570 (3,476)
New York	47,440 (840)	53,130 (923)	56,650 (746)	64,300 (1,698)	58,520 (2,054)	67,830 (2,458)	83,090 (3,081)	73,180 (1,462)	55,820 (2,523)	67,940 (1,897)	74,960 (1,693)	89,350 (2,861)
North Carolina	29,180 (306)	36,810 (542)	42,720 (641)	45,470 (1,321)	40,790 (1,636)	46,800 (1,948)	52,660 (2,098)	42,290 (1,149)	33,070 (985)	39,020 (2,025)	44,700 (912)	48,870 (2,335)
North Dakota	28,520 (730)	32,920 (559)	39,710 (789)	44,090 (885)	40,400 (1,690)	43,610 (1,629)	49,560 (1,644)	52,090 (1,471)	33,070 (1,130)	43,410 (1,130)	53,160 (2,149)	59,920 (1,552)
Ohio	37,960 (550)	43,420 (585)	50,000 (689)	55,680 (982)	49,420 (1,058)	58,470 (1,779)	63,100 (1,473)	57,430 (727)	42,660 (1,403)	49,940 (1,492)	61,280 (1,215)	65,380 (1,169)
Oklahoma	28,510 (186)	31,990 (261)	34,580 (319)	40,220 (486)	36,550 (718)	39,350 (769)	44,400 (592)	39,490 (936)	41,170 (640)	49,890 (1,301)	39,220 (639)	44,610 (1,204)
Oregon	36,930 (471)	42,180 (588)	45,850 (647)	48,170 (914)	46,830 (721)	53,310 (1,396)	57,740 (1,375)	51,520 (1,408)	45,940 (1,778)	54,790 (1,157)	57,300 (1,863)	61,040 (1,615)
Pennsylvania	44,830 (816)	50,790 (1,027)	54,800 (925)	62,340 (1,667)	52,120 (1,628)	64,360 (2,553)	74,360 (2,998)	62,650 (†)	‡	‡	67,650 (1,850)	75,380 (2,112)
Rhode Island	41,630 (303)	48,610 (204)	55,110 (909)	65,180 (1,137)	‡	67,950 (1,212)	69,950 (1,244)	‡	‡	‡	‡	‡
South Carolina	31,860 (208)	38,390 (528)	42,910 (625)	46,480 (529)	41,280 (1,209)	39,180 (812)	42,970 (892)	46,770 (966)	38,250 (1,216)	41,190 (1,777)	48,850 (851)	54,960 (1,263)
South Dakota	28,110 (449)	32,800 (443)	37,670 (801)	39,880 (764)	35,110 (1,125)	38,420 (1,199)	44,110 (1,224)	41,730 (910)	38,260 (947)	40,540 (949)	41,160 (1,285)	45,840 (1,731)
Tennessee	30,270 (350)	35,610 (414)	39,620 (543)	43,730 (694)	39,840 (999)	44,370 (1,197)	49,150 (964)	44,550 (984)	38,260 (989)	46,340 (854)	48,770 (2,096)	49,660 (1,879)
Texas	31,610 (355)	40,280 (453)	43,370 (723)	47,520 (1,129)	44,490 (2,023)	48,340 (1,242)	51,960 (2,138)	49,390 (593)	44,300 (1,495)	42,530 (1,558)	50,120 (1,102)	56,520 (1,316)
Utah	32,590 (277)	39,880 (586)	43,370 (636)	47,200 (1,092)	41,020 (748)	49,140 (866)	54,170 (1,687)	48,750 (1,772)	36,970 (1,495)	42,530 (1,724)	54,440 (1,724)	58,620 (1,332)
Vermont	36,770 (594)	37,260 (668)	44,740 (926)	51,320 (987)	44,780 (1,742)	51,310 (1,494)	58,040 (1,387)	56,190 (1,158)	44,410 (1,916)	50,380 (1,587)	56,450 (1,679)	64,460 (1,418)
Virginia	33,740 (579)	40,230 (668)	43,860 (948)	50,910 (1,572)	43,090 (1,865)	52,520 (2,135)	62,310 (2,889)	51,130 (1,408)	45,110 (2,671)	51,120 (1,317)	55,120 (1,603)	66,390 (3,502)
Washington	38,270 (398)	43,160 (364)	47,970 (500)	51,800 (649)	47,380 (1,210)	55,970 (831)	58,670 (882)	57,670 (1,077)	44,030 (1,130)	52,050 (3,153)	61,510 (1,406)	63,780 (785)
West Virginia	32,130 (195)	36,590 (226)	40,440 (716)	43,090 (477)	37,120 (580)	41,910 (762)	47,700 (513)	45,460 (805)	36,640 (1,543)	41,530 (1,333)	45,730 (1,133)	51,600 (1,012)
Wisconsin	40,920 (486)	46,420 (512)	47,750 (713)	52,210 (873)	46,650 (1,245)	53,120 (1,604)	58,010 (1,380)	55,430 (791)	‡	48,360 (1,235)	57,280 (924)	61,410 (1,797)
Wyoming	32,490 (371)	36,120 (497)	41,610 (1,014)	52,990 (932)	49,530 (1,444)	52,550 (1,243)	57,580 (1,495)	59,390 (817)	36,640 (†)	‡	59,700 (1,074)	63,230 (1,803)

†Not applicable.
‡Reporting standards not met. Data may be suppressed because the response rate is under 50 percent, there are too few cases for a reliable estimate, or the coefficient of variation (CV) is 50 percent or greater.
NOTE: This table includes regular full-time teachers only; it excludes other staff even when they have full-time teaching duties (regular part-time teachers, itinerant teachers, long-term substitutes, administrators, library media specialists, other professional staff, and support staff).

SOURCE: U.S. Department of Education, National Center for Education Statistics, Schools and Staffing Survey (SASS), "Public School Teacher Data File," 1993–94, 1999–2000, 2003–04, 2007–08, and 2011–12; and "Public Charter School Teacher Data File," 1999–2000. (This table was prepared June 2013.)

Table 211.50. Estimated average annual salary of teachers in public elementary and secondary schools: Selected years, 1959–60 through 2014–15

School year	Current dollars					Average public school teachers' salary in constant 2014–15 dollars[1]		
	Average public school teachers' salary			Wage and salary accruals per full-time-equivalent (FTE) employee[2]	Ratio of average teachers' salary to accruals per FTE employee			
	All teachers	Elementary teachers[3]	Secondary teachers[4]			All teachers	Elementary teachers[3]	Secondary teachers[4]
1	2	3	4	5	6	7	8	9
1959–60	$4,995	$4,815	$5,276	$4,749	1.05	$40,234	$38,784	$42,498
1961–62	5,515	5,340	5,775	5,063	1.09	43,425	42,047	45,472
1963–64	5,995	5,805	6,266	5,478	1.09	46,005	44,547	48,084
1965–66	6,485	6,279	6,761	5,934	1.09	48,102	46,574	50,150
1967–68	7,423	7,208	7,692	6,533	1.14	51,660	50,164	53,532
1969–70	8,626	8,412	8,891	7,486	1.15	54,046	52,705	55,706
1970–71	9,268	9,021	9,568	7,998	1.16	55,218	53,746	57,005
1971–72	9,705	9,424	10,031	8,521	1.14	55,819	54,203	57,694
1972–73	10,174	9,893	10,507	9,056	1.12	56,250	54,696	58,091
1973–74	10,770	10,507	11,077	9,667	1.11	54,670	53,335	56,229
1974–75	11,641	11,334	12,000	10,411	1.12	53,196	51,794	54,837
1975–76	12,600	12,280	12,937	11,194	1.13	53,773	52,407	55,211
1976–77	13,354	12,989	13,776	11,971	1.12	53,850	52,378	55,552
1977–78	14,198	13,845	14,602	12,811	1.11	53,651	52,317	55,178
1978–79	15,032	14,681	15,450	13,807	1.09	51,938	50,725	53,382
1979–80	15,970	15,569	16,459	15,050	1.06	48,687	47,465	50,178
1980–81	17,644	17,230	18,142	16,461	1.07	48,207	47,076	49,568
1981–82	19,274	18,853	19,805	17,795	1.08	48,473	47,414	49,809
1982–83	20,695	20,227	21,291	18,873	1.10	49,903	48,775	51,341
1983–84	21,935	21,487	22,554	19,781	1.11	51,006	49,964	52,445
1984–85	23,600	23,200	24,187	20,694	1.14	52,810	51,915	54,124
1985–86	25,199	24,718	25,846	21,685	1.16	54,808	53,762	56,215
1986–87	26,569	26,057	27,244	22,700	1.17	56,532	55,443	57,969
1987–88	28,034	27,519	28,798	23,777	1.18	57,276	56,224	58,837
1988–89	29,564	29,022	30,218	24,752	1.19	57,736	56,677	59,013
1989–90	31,367	30,832	32,049	25,762	1.22	58,467	57,470	59,738
1990–91	33,084	32,490	33,896	26,935	1.23	58,471	57,421	59,906
1991–92	34,063	33,479	34,827	28,169	1.21	58,332	57,332	59,640
1992–93	35,029	34,350	35,880	29,245	1.20	58,169	57,042	59,582
1993–94	35,737	35,233	36,566	30,030	1.19	57,846	57,030	59,188
1994–95	36,675	36,088	37,523	30,857	1.19	57,710	56,787	59,045
1995–96	37,642	37,138	38,397	31,822	1.18	57,663	56,891	58,820
1996–97	38,443	38,039	39,184	33,058	1.16	57,257	56,655	58,360
1997–98	39,350	39,002	39,944	34,635	1.14	57,581	57,072	58,450
1998–99	40,544	40,165	41,203	36,277	1.12	58,318	57,773	59,266
1999–2000	41,807	41,306	42,546	38,144	1.10	58,448	57,747	59,481
2000–01	43,378	42,910	44,053	39,727	1.09	58,635	58,003	59,548
2001–02	44,655	44,177	45,310	40,589	1.10	59,311	58,676	60,181
2002–03	45,686	45,408	46,106	41,629	1.10	59,376	59,014	59,922
2003–04	46,542	46,187	46,976	43,259	1.08	59,193	58,742	59,745
2004–05	47,516	47,122	47,688	44,908	1.06	58,667	58,180	58,879
2005–06	49,086	48,573	49,496	46,626	1.05	58,382	57,772	58,869
2006–07	51,052	50,740	51,529	48,713	1.05	59,189	58,828	59,743
2007–08	52,800	52,385	53,262	50,504	1.05	59,029	58,565	59,545
2008–09	54,319	53,998	54,552	51,409	1.06	59,891	59,537	60,148
2009–10	55,202	54,918	55,595	52,413	1.05	60,281	59,971	60,710
2010–11	55,623	55,217	56,225	53,975	1.03	59,545	59,110	60,190
2011–12	55,418	54,704	56,226	55,435	1.00	57,637	56,894	58,477
2012–13	56,103	55,344	57,077	56,361	1.00	57,394	56,618	58,391
2013–14	56,610	56,395	56,886	57,081	0.99	57,022	56,806	57,300
2014–15	57,379	57,225	57,609	—	—	57,379	57,225	57,609

—Not available.
[1]Constant dollars based on the Consumer Price Index, prepared by the Bureau of Labor Statistics, U.S. Department of Labor, adjusted to a school-year basis.
[2]The average monetary remuneration earned by FTE employees across all industries in a given year, including wages, salaries, commissions, tips, bonuses, voluntary employee contributions to certain deferred compensation plans, and receipts in kind that represent income. Calendar-year data from the U.S. Department of Commerce, Bureau of Economic Analysis, have been converted to a school-year basis by averaging the two appropriate calendar years in each case.
[3]Teachers at schools that are classified as elementary by state and local practice and composed of any span of grades not above grade 8. Preschool or kindergarten schools are included only if they are an integral part of an elementary school or a regularly established school system.

[4]Teachers at schools comprising any span of grades beginning with the next grade following an elementary or middle school (usually 7, 8, or 9) and ending with or below grade 12. Includes both junior high schools and senior high schools.
NOTE: Some data have been revised from previously published figures. Standard errors are not available for these estimates, which are based on state reports.
SOURCE: National Education Association, *Estimates of School Statistics*, 1959–60 through 2014–15; and unpublished tabulations. U.S. Department of Commerce, Bureau of Economic Analysis, National Income and Product Accounts, tables 6.6D, retrieved September 2, 2015, from http://www.bea.gov/iTable/iTable.cfm?ReqID=9&step=1#reqid=9&step=1&isuri=1. (This table was prepared September 2015.)

Table 211.60. Estimated average annual salary of teachers in public elementary and secondary schools, by state: Selected years, 1969–70 through 2014–15

State	Current dollars							Constant 2014–15 dollars[1]							Percent change, 1999–2000 to 2014–15
	1969–70	1979–80	1989–90	1999–2000	2009–10	2013–14	2014–15	1969–70	1979–80	1989–90	1999–2000	2009–10	2013–14	2014–15	
1	2	3	4	5	6	7	8	9	10	11	12	13	14	15	16
United States...	$8,626	$15,970	$31,367	$41,807	$55,202	$56,610	$57,379	$54,046	$48,687	$58,467	$58,448	$60,281	$57,022	$57,379	-1.8
Alabama	6,818	13,060	24,828	36,689	47,571	48,720	49,497	42,718	39,815	46,278	51,293	51,948	49,075	49,497	-3.5
Alaska	10,560	27,210	43,153	46,462	59,672	65,891	66,755	66,163	82,954	80,436	64,956	65,162	66,371	66,755	2.8
Arizona	8,711	15,054	29,402	36,902	46,952	45,335	45,406	54,578	45,894	54,804	51,590	51,272	45,665	45,406	-12.0
Arkansas	6,307	12,299	22,352	33,386	46,700	47,319	48,017	39,516	37,495	41,663	46,675	50,997	47,664	48,017	2.9
California	10,315	18,020	37,998	47,680	68,203	71,396	72,535	64,628	54,937	70,827	66,659	74,478	71,916	72,535	8.8
Colorado	7,761	16,205	30,758	38,163	49,202	49,615	49,828	48,626	49,403	57,332	53,353	53,729	49,976	49,828	-6.6
Connecticut	9,262	16,229	40,461	51,780	64,350	70,583	71,709	58,030	49,476	75,418	72,391	70,271	71,097	71,709	-0.9
Delaware	9,015	16,148	33,377	44,435	57,080	59,305	59,195	56,483	49,230	62,213	62,122	62,332	59,737	59,195	-4.7
District of Columbia..	10,285	22,190	38,402	47,076	64,548	73,162	75,490	64,440	67,649	71,580	65,814	70,487	73,695	75,490	14.7
Florida	8,412	14,149	28,803	36,722	46,708	47,780	48,992	52,705	43,135	53,688	51,339	51,006	48,128	48,992	-4.6
Georgia	7,276	13,853	28,006	41,023	53,112	52,924	53,382	45,587	42,233	52,202	57,352	57,999	53,309	53,382	-6.9
Hawaii	9,453	19,920	32,047	40,578	55,063	56,291	57,189	59,227	60,729	59,734	56,730	60,129	56,701	57,189	0.8
Idaho	6,890	13,611	23,861	35,547	46,283	44,465	45,218	43,169	41,495	44,476	49,696	50,541	44,789	45,218	-9.0
Illinois	9,569	17,601	32,794	46,486	62,077	60,124	61,083	59,954	53,659	61,127	64,989	67,789	60,562	61,083	-6.0
Indiana	8,833	15,599	30,902	41,850	49,986	50,289	50,502	55,343	47,556	57,600	58,508	54,585	50,655	50,502	-13.7
Iowa	8,355	15,203	26,747	35,678	49,626	52,032	52,862	52,348	46,349	49,855	49,879	54,192	52,411	52,862	6.0
Kansas	7,612	13,690	28,744	34,981	46,657	48,221	48,990	47,692	41,736	53,578	48,905	50,950	48,572	48,990	0.2
Kentucky	6,953	14,520	26,292	36,380	49,543	50,560	51,093	43,564	44,266	49,007	50,861	54,101	50,928	51,093	0.5
Louisiana	7,028	13,760	24,300	33,109	48,903	49,067	47,886	44,033	41,949	45,294	46,288	53,402	49,424	47,886	3.5
Maine	7,572	13,071	26,881	35,561	46,106	49,232	50,017	47,442	39,849	50,105	49,716	50,348	49,590	50,017	0.6
Maryland	9,383	17,558	36,319	44,048	63,971	64,546	64,845	58,789	53,528	67,697	61,581	69,857	65,016	64,845	5.3
Massachusetts	8,764	17,253	34,712	46,580	69,273	73,195	74,805	54,910	52,598	64,702	65,121	75,647	73,728	74,805	14.9
Michigan	9,826	19,663	37,072	49,044	57,958	62,166	62,778	61,564	59,946	69,101	68,565	63,291	62,619	62,778	-8.4
Minnesota	8,658	15,912	32,190	39,802	52,431	54,752	56,670	54,246	48,510	60,001	55,645	57,255	55,151	56,670	1.8
Mississippi	5,798	11,850	24,292	31,857	45,644	42,187	42,564	36,327	36,126	45,279	44,537	49,844	42,494	42,564	-4.4
Missouri	7,799	13,682	27,094	35,656	45,317	46,750	47,394	48,864	41,712	50,502	49,849	49,487	47,090	47,394	-4.9
Montana	7,606	14,537	25,081	32,121	45,759	49,893	50,999	47,655	44,318	46,750	44,906	49,969	50,256	50,999	13.6
Nebraska	7,375	13,516	25,522	33,237	46,227	49,539	50,318	46,208	41,206	47,572	46,467	50,480	49,900	50,318	8.3
Nevada	9,215	16,295	30,590	39,390	51,524	55,813	56,703	57,736	49,678	57,019	55,069	56,265	56,219	56,703	3.0
New Hampshire	7,771	13,017	28,986	37,734	51,443	57,057	58,554	48,689	39,684	54,029	52,754	56,176	57,472	58,554	11.0
New Jersey	9,130	17,161	35,676	52,015	65,130	68,238	69,038	57,203	52,318	66,499	72,719	71,123	68,735	69,038	-5.1
New Mexico	7,796	14,887	24,756	32,554	46,258	45,727	46,003	48,845	45,385	46,144	45,512	50,514	46,060	46,003	1.1
New York	10,336	19,812	38,925	51,020	71,633	76,409	77,628	64,759	60,400	72,555	71,328	78,224	76,965	77,628	8.8
North Carolina	7,494	14,117	27,883	39,404	46,850	44,990	47,783	46,953	43,038	51,973	55,088	51,161	45,318	47,783	-13.3
North Dakota	6,696	13,263	23,016	29,863	42,964	48,666	50,025	41,953	40,434	42,901	41,750	46,917	49,020	50,025	19.8
Ohio	8,300	15,269	31,218	41,436	55,958	55,913	56,172	52,003	46,550	58,189	57,929	61,107	56,320	56,172	-3.0
Oklahoma	6,882	13,107	23,070	31,298	47,691	44,549	44,628	43,119	39,959	43,002	43,756	52,079	44,873	44,628	2.0
Oregon	8,818	16,266	30,840	42,336	55,224	58,638	59,811	55,249	49,589	57,485	59,187	60,305	59,065	59,811	1.1
Pennsylvania	8,858	16,515	33,338	48,321	59,156	63,701	64,717	55,499	50,348	62,141	67,555	64,599	64,165	64,717	-4.2
Rhode Island	8,776	18,002	36,057	47,041	59,686	64,696	65,918	54,985	54,882	67,209	65,765	65,178	65,167	65,918	0.2
South Carolina	6,927	13,063	27,217	36,081	47,508	48,430	48,709	43,401	39,824	50,731	50,443	51,879	48,783	48,709	-3.4
South Dakota	6,403	12,348	21,300	29,071	38,837	40,023	40,661	40,118	37,645	39,702	40,642	42,410	40,314	40,661	#
Tennessee	7,050	13,972	27,052	36,328	46,290	47,742	48,503	44,171	42,596	50,424	50,788	50,549	48,090	48,503	-4.5
Texas	7,255	14,132	27,496	37,567	48,261	49,690	50,576	45,456	43,083	51,252	52,520	52,701	50,052	50,576	-3.7
Utah	7,644	14,909	23,686	34,946	45,885	45,695	45,848	47,893	45,452	44,150	48,856	50,107	46,028	45,848	-6.2
Vermont	7,968	12,484	29,012	37,758	49,084	55,958	57,642	49,923	38,059	54,077	52,787	53,600	56,365	57,642	9.2
Virginia	8,070	14,060	30,938	38,744	50,015	49,826	50,620	50,562	42,864	57,667	54,166	54,617	50,189	50,620	-6.5
Washington	9,225	18,820	30,457	41,043	53,003	52,969	53,714	57,799	57,376	56,771	57,380	57,880	53,355	53,714	-6.4
West Virginia	7,650	13,710	22,842	35,009	45,959	45,086	45,647	47,931	41,797	42,577	48,944	50,188	45,414	45,647	-6.7
Wisconsin	8,963	16,006	31,921	41,153	51,264	53,679	54,535	56,157	48,797	59,500	57,534	55,981	54,070	54,535	-5.2
Wyoming	8,232	16,012	28,141	34,127	55,861	56,583	57,715	51,577	48,815	52,454	47,711	61,001	56,995	57,715	21.0

#Rounds to zero.
[1]Constant dollars based on the Consumer Price Index (CPI), prepared by the Bureau of Labor Statistics, U.S. Department of Labor, adjusted to a school-year basis. The CPI does not account for differences in inflation rates from state to state.

NOTE: Some data have been revised from previously published figures. Standard errors are not available for these estimates, which are based on state reports.
SOURCE: National Education Association, *Estimates of School Statistics*, 1969–70 through 2014–15. (This table was prepared September 2015.)

Table 212.08. Number and percentage distribution of principals in public and private elementary and secondary schools, by selected characteristics: Selected years, 1993–94 through 2011–12

[Standard errors appear in parentheses]

Selected characteristic	Number of principals					Percentage distribution of principals				
	1993–94	1999–2000	2003–04	2007–08	2011–12	1993–94	1999–2000	2003–04	2007–08	2011–12
1	2	3	4	5	6	7	8	9	10	11
Public schools Total	79,620 (235)	83,790 (327)	87,620 (307)	90,470 (544)	89,810 (406)	100.0 (†)	100.0 (†)	100.0 (†)	100.0 (†)	100.0 (†)
Sex										
Male	52,110 (613)	47,130 (604)	45,930 (707)	44,950 (1,129)	43,450 (901)	65.5 (0.70)	56.2 (0.69)	52.4 (0.79)	49.7 (1.21)	48.4 (0.92)
Female	27,500 (542)	36,660 (598)	41,690 (708)	45,520 (1,129)	46,360 (801)	34.5 (0.70)	43.8 (0.69)	47.6 (0.79)	50.3 (1.21)	51.6 (0.92)
Race/ethnicity										
White[1]	67,080 (540)	68,930 (579)	72,200 (509)	73,160 (1,008)	72,070 (723)	84.3 (0.54)	82.3 (0.57)	82.4 (0.52)	80.9 (0.92)	80.3 (0.66)
Black[1]	8,020 (351)	9,240 (321)	9,250 (377)	9,620 (659)	9,110 (394)	10.1 (0.45)	11.0 (0.39)	10.6 (0.43)	10.6 (0.73)	10.1 (0.43)
Hispanic[1]	3,270 (258)	4,330 (300)	4,680 (355)	5,870 (540)	6,130 (404)	4.1 (0.33)	5.2 (0.36)	5.3 (0.40)	6.5 (0.60)	6.8 (0.46)
Asian[1,2]	620 (109)	630 (124)	460 (87)	570 (146)	820 (154)	0.8 (0.14)	0.8 (0.15)	0.5 (0.10)	0.6 (0.16)	0.9 (0.17)
Pacific Islander[2]	— (†)	— (†)	80 (18)	130 ! (52)	20 ! (9)	— (†)	— (†)	0.1 (0.02)	0.1 ! (0.06)	# (†)
American Indian/Alaska Native[1]	630 (67)	660 (60)	600 (80)	620 (179)	650 (123)	0.8 (0.08)	0.8 (0.07)	0.7 (0.09)	0.7 (0.20)	0.7 (0.14)
Two or more races[1]	— (†)	— (†)	350 (82)	490 ! (155)	1,010 (183)	— (†)	— (†)	0.4 (0.09)	0.5 ! (0.17)	1.1 (0.20)
Age										
Under 40	5,940 (273)	8,440 (302)	12,840 (477)	17,290 (785)	18,040 (523)	7.5 (0.34)	10.1 (0.35)	14.7 (0.55)	19.1 (0.84)	20.1 (0.58)
40 to 44	14,570 (496)	10,510 (317)	9,540 (449)	13,330 (706)	17,650 (565)	18.3 (0.61)	12.5 (0.37)	10.9 (0.51)	14.7 (0.78)	19.7 (0.62)
45 to 49	25,430 (429)	19,600 (535)	16,120 (526)	13,690 (767)	14,700 (541)	31.9 (0.55)	23.4 (0.63)	18.4 (0.59)	15.1 (0.86)	16.4 (0.60)
50 to 54	18,870 (539)	27,120 (606)	24,170 (669)	17,570 (746)	15,060 (668)	23.7 (0.68)	32.4 (0.71)	27.6 (0.75)	19.4 (0.82)	16.8 (0.73)
55 or over	14,820 (441)	18,130 (500)	24,960 (679)	28,590 (1,000)	24,350 (655)	18.6 (0.55)	21.6 (0.60)	28.5 (0.76)	31.6 (1.06)	27.1 (0.74)
School level										
Elementary	53,680[4] (294)	60,110 (253)	61,480 (361)	62,340 (584)	61,250 (443)	71.9 (0.21)	71.7 (0.21)	70.2 (0.32)	68.9 (0.54)	68.2 (0.38)
Secondary	18,260[4] (161)	20,450 (197)	19,700 (272)	21,550 (460)	20,470 (537)	24.4 (0.20)	24.4 (0.20)	22.5 (0.32)	23.8 (0.46)	22.8 (0.56)
Combined	2,750[4] (143)	3,230 (146)	6,450 (263)	6,580 (364)	8,090 (658)	3.7 (0.19)	3.9 (0.17)	7.4 (0.30)	7.3 (0.40)	9.0 (0.74)
Highest degree earned										
Bachelor's or less	1,150 (167)	1,540 (182)	1,650 (213)	1,320 (207)	1,960 (272)	1.4 (0.21)	1.8 (0.22)	1.9 (0.24)	1.5 (0.23)	2.2 (0.30)
Master's	50,470 (536)	45,440 (579)	51,840 (657)	55,250 (906)	55,420 (678)	63.4 (0.65)	54.2 (0.63)	59.2 (0.71)	61.1 (1.01)	61.7 (0.71)
Education specialist[3]	20,570 (459)	28,280 (493)	26,570 (619)	26,270 (930)	23,560 (492)	25.8 (0.57)	33.8 (0.60)	30.3 (0.69)	29.0 (0.97)	26.2 (0.54)
Doctor's or first professional	7,430 (263)	8,530 (386)	7,560 (376)	7,630 (512)	8,870 (442)	9.3 (0.33)	10.2 (0.46)	8.6 (0.43)	8.4 (0.57)	9.9 (0.49)
Number of years as a principal										
3 or fewer	24,450 (451)	25,080 (513)	30,400 (695)	31,500 (1,033)	29,520 (758)	30.7 (0.56)	29.9 (0.60)	34.7 (0.78)	34.8 (1.11)	32.9 (0.84)
4 to 9	26,600 (548)	25,900 (524)	29,160 (710)	32,140 (989)	35,500 (886)	33.4 (0.68)	30.9 (0.61)	33.3 (0.80)	35.5 (1.09)	39.5 (0.96)
10 to 19	19,730 (412)	23,230 (525)	21,330 (663)	20,470 (926)	19,870 (634)	24.8 (0.52)	27.7 (0.62)	24.3 (0.76)	22.6 (1.01)	22.1 (0.70)
20 or more	8,840 (377)	9,580 (331)	6,740 (314)	6,350 (414)	4,920 (273)	11.1 (0.47)	11.4 (0.39)	7.7 (0.35)	7.0 (0.46)	5.5 (0.31)
Years of full-time teaching experience prior to becoming a principal										
3 or fewer	5,690 (251)	3,210 (186)	4,820 (280)	4,150 (384)	4,040 (264)	7.1 (0.31)	3.8 (0.22)	5.5 (0.32)	4.6 (0.42)	4.5 (0.30)
4 to 9	29,500 (516)	22,510 (491)	26,260 (603)	30,260 (958)	34,240 (792)	37.1 (0.63)	26.9 (0.57)	30.0 (0.70)	33.4 (1.03)	38.1 (0.84)
10 to 19	36,680 (558)	38,110 (597)	39,790 (676)	40,200 (992)	39,160 (752)	46.1 (0.70)	45.5 (0.69)	45.4 (0.73)	44.4 (1.09)	43.6 (0.82)
20 or more	7,740 (275)	19,960 (485)	16,760 (552)	15,850 (781)	12,380 (519)	9.7 (0.34)	23.8 (0.57)	19.1 (0.62)	17.5 (0.86)	13.8 (0.58)
School locale										
City	— (†)	20,100 (328)	22,690 (425)	21,560 (731)	23,440 (274)	27.4 (0.34)	24.0 (0.40)	25.9 (0.49)	23.8 (0.81)	26.1 (0.28)
Suburban	— (†)	30,640 (440)	25,600 (506)	25,880 (921)	24,520 (356)	25.9 (0.45)	36.6 (0.53)	29.2 (0.56)	28.6 (1.01)	27.3 (0.36)
Town	— (†)	10,860 (228)	13,700 (424)	13,860 (669)	12,330 (341)	22.0 (0.43)	13.0 (0.26)	15.6 (0.48)	15.3 (0.74)	13.7 (0.40)
Rural	— (†)	22,200 (404)	25,640 (492)	29,170 (1,012)	29,520 (430)	24.7 (0.43)	26.5 (0.44)	29.3 (0.55)	32.2 (1.07)	32.9 (0.43)

See notes at end of table.

Table 212.08. Number and percentage distribution of principals in public and private elementary and secondary schools, by selected characteristics: Selected years, 1993–94 through 2011–12—Continued

[Standard errors appear in parentheses]

Selected characteristic	Number of principals					Percentage distribution of principals				
	1993–94	1999–2000	2003–04	2007–08	2011–12	1993–94	1999–2000	2003–04	2007–08	2011–12
1	2	3	4	5	6	7	8	9	10	11
Private schools										
Total	25,020 (198)	26,230 (259)	27,690 (677)	27,960 (328)	25,730 (605)	100.0 (†)	100.0 (†)	100.0 (†)	100.0 (†)	100.0 (†)
Sex										
Male	11,610 (301)	11,900 (308)	12,110 (552)	13,070 (457)	11,490 (501)	46.4 (1.10)	45.4 (1.06)	43.7 (1.43)	46.7 (1.38)	44.6 (1.48)
Female	13,410 (283)	14,330 (307)	15,580 (491)	14,890 (369)	14,240 (462)	53.6 (1.10)	54.6 (1.06)	56.3 (1.43)	53.3 (1.38)	55.4 (1.48)
Race/ethnicity										
White[1]	23,130 (270)	23,320 (309)	24,850 (715)	24,400 (409)	22,470 (628)	92.5 (0.70)	88.9 (0.76)	89.8 (0.88)	87.3 (0.91)	87.3 (1.08)
Black[1]	1,060 (124)	1,570 (164)	1,440 (155)	1,820 (184)	1,750 (193)	4.2 (0.50)	6.0 (0.62)	5.2 (0.57)	6.5 (0.67)	6.8 (0.75)
Hispanic[1]	520 (91)	830 (135)	820 (116)	1,110 (149)	860 (141)	2.1 (0.37)	3.2 (0.52)	3.0 (0.41)	4.0 (0.52)	3.3 (0.56)
Asian[1,2]	170 (43)	350 (64)	330 (82)	330 (77)	460 (101)	0.7 (0.17)	1.3 (0.25)	1.2 (0.29)	1.2 (0.28)	1.8 (0.38)
Pacific Islander	— (†)	— (†)	‡ (†)	‡ (†)	‡ (†)	† (†)	† (†)	† (†)	† (†)	‡ (†)
American Indian/Alaska Native[1]	130 (37)	150 ! (39)	160 ! (77)	‡ (†)	‡ (†)	0.5 (0.15)	0.6 (0.15)	0.6 ! (0.27)	‡ (†)	‡ (†)
Two or more races	— (†)	— (†)	60 ! (28)	200 ! (62)	90 ! (45)	— (†)	— (†)	0.2 ! (0.10)	0.7 ! (0.22)	0.4 ! (0.17)
Age										
Under 40	4,790 (302)	3,750 (223)	4,420 (267)	4,750 (318)	4,360 (392)	19.2 (1.21)	14.3 (0.80)	16.0 (0.94)	17.0 (1.09)	16.9 (1.44)
40 to 44	4,400 (217)	3,450 (212)	3,040 (250)	3,250 (277)	3,130 (300)	17.6 (0.83)	13.2 (0.83)	11.0 (0.85)	11.6 (1.00)	12.2 (1.05)
45 to 49	5,140 (216)	5,210 (261)	4,020 (250)	3,420 (246)	2,630 (281)	20.6 (0.87)	19.9 (0.96)	14.5 (0.82)	12.2 (0.86)	10.2 (1.00)
50 to 54	4,120 (228)	5,840 (291)	5,820 (337)	4,390 (263)	3,480 (247)	16.5 (0.90)	22.3 (1.11)	21.0 (1.00)	15.7 (0.94)	13.5 (0.93)
55 or over	6,550 (043)	7,980 (276)	10,390 (82)	12,150 (77)	12,120 (101)	26.2 (0.17)	30.4 (1.01)	37.5 (0.29)	43.5 (0.28)	47.1 (0.38)
School level										
Elementary	13,350[4] (244)	15,810 (245)	16,750 (327)	16,110 (297)	14,510 (505)	59.5 (0.74)	60.3 (0.85)	60.5 (1.07)	57.6 (0.81)	56.4 (0.90)
Secondary	2,300[4] (115)	2,630 (133)	2,510 (364)	2,930 (168)	2,660 (138)	10.3 (0.52)	10.0 (0.51)	9.1 (1.14)	10.5 (0.59)	10.3 (0.57)
Combined	6,770[4] (174)	7,800 (265)	8,430 (281)	8,920 (271)	8,570 (210)	30.2 (0.77)	29.7 (0.89)	30.4 (0.77)	31.9 (0.88)	33.3 (0.71)
Highest degree earned										
Bachelor's or less	8,590 (337)	8,050 (334)	9,170 (422)	9,120 (427)	7,990 (570)	34.3 (1.23)	30.7 (1.16)	33.1 (1.27)	32.6 (1.37)	31.0 (1.73)
Master's	12,900 (292)	13,370 (288)	13,720 (458)	14,030 (344)	12,800 (363)	51.6 (1.28)	51.0 (1.09)	49.5 (1.20)	50.2 (1.20)	49.7 (1.49)
Education specialist[3]	2,050 (103)	2,600 (159)	2,950 (183)	2,800 (203)	2,610 (200)	8.2 (0.41)	9.9 (0.60)	10.7 (0.61)	10.0 (0.75)	10.1 (0.80)
Doctor's or first professional	1,480 (138)	2,220 (167)	1,850 (190)	2,010 (177)	2,340 (224)	5.9 (0.54)	8.5 (0.64)	6.7 (0.63)	7.2 (0.63)	9.1 (0.87)
Number of years as a principal										
3 or fewer	8,270 (341)	7,540 (327)	8,990 (395)	9,190 (351)	7,100 (516)	33.1 (1.32)	28.7 (1.19)	32.5 (1.23)	32.9 (1.20)	27.6 (1.74)
4 to 9	7,080 (269)	6,990 (320)	6,830 (283)	7,230 (345)	6,750 (415)	28.3 (1.03)	26.6 (1.16)	24.6 (0.95)	25.9 (1.19)	26.2 (1.45)
10 to 19	6,950 (310)	7,340 (250)	7,260 (381)	6,430 (298)	6,910 (350)	27.8 (1.23)	28.0 (0.93)	26.2 (1.03)	23.0 (1.04)	26.8 (1.33)
20 or more	2,710 (189)	4,360 (230)	4,610 (275)	5,110 (260)	4,970 (318)	10.8 (0.77)	16.6 (0.90)	16.7 (0.88)	18.3 (0.91)	19.3 (1.27)
Years of full-time teaching experience prior to becoming a principal										
3 or fewer	6,290 (335)	3,610 (241)	7,350 (359)	7,850 (381)	6,820 (473)	25.2 (1.27)	13.8 (0.87)	26.6 (1.19)	28.1 (1.24)	26.5 (1.48)
4 to 9	6,940 (268)	5,560 (244)	6,690 (357)	7,030 (287)	6,810 (363)	27.8 (1.05)	21.2 (0.88)	24.2 (1.15)	25.1 (1.00)	26.5 (1.36)
10 to 19	9,240 (251)	9,070 (260)	9,110 (394)	8,510 (306)	7,790 (403)	36.9 (1.03)	34.6 (1.04)	32.9 (1.09)	30.4 (1.09)	30.3 (1.50)
20 or more	2,540 (136)	7,990 (265)	4,530 (275)	4,580 (247)	4,310 (249)	10.1 (0.54)	30.4 (0.98)	16.4 (0.83)	16.4 (0.89)	16.7 (0.99)
School locale										
City	— (†)	11,250 (226)	9,670 (374)	9,610 (268)	8,590 (267)	— (†)	42.9 (0.78)	34.9 (1.05)	34.4 (0.90)	33.4 (1.28)
Suburban	— (†)	9,190 (229)	11,690 (370)	9,510 (229)	8,110 (298)	— (†)	35.0 (0.80)	42.2 (1.14)	34.0 (0.83)	31.5 (1.27)
Town	— (†)	3,250 (190)	1,980 (179)	2,780 (205)	2,630 (323)	— (†)	12.4 (0.73)	7.2 (0.59)	10.0 (0.72)	10.2 (1.16)
Rural	— (†)	2,540 (211)	4,350 (293)	6,060 (296)	6,390 (510)	— (†)	9.7 (0.78)	15.7 (0.85)	21.7 (0.95)	24.8 (1.57)

—Not available.
†Not applicable.
#Rounds to zero.
!Interpret data with caution. The coefficient of variation (CV) for this estimate is between 30 and 50 percent.
‡Reporting standards not met. Either there are too few cases for a reliable estimate or the coefficient of variation (CV) is 50 percent or greater.
[1]Data for 1993–94 and 1999–2000 are only roughly comparable to data for later years, because the new category of Two or more races was introduced in 2003–04.
[2]Includes Pacific Islander for 1993–94 and 1999–2000.

[3]Education specialist degrees or certificates are generally awarded for 1 year's work beyond the master's level. Includes certificate of advanced graduate studies.
[4]Excludes data for 4,930 public and 2,690 private school principals whose school level could not be determined.
NOTE: Data are based on a head count of full-time and part-time principals rather than on the number of full-time-equivalent principals reported in other tables. Detail may not sum to totals because of rounding, missing data, and cell suppression. Race categories exclude persons of Hispanic ethnicity.
SOURCE: U.S. Department of Education, National Center for Education Statistics, Schools and Staffing Survey (SASS), "Public School Principal Data File" and "Private School Principal Data File," 1993–94, 1999–2000, 2003–04, 2007–08, and 2011–12; and "Charter School Principal Data File," 1999–2000. (This table was prepared November 2015.)

Table 212.10. Highest degree, average years of experience, and salaries of principals in public and private elementary and secondary schools, by selected characteristics: Selected years, 1993–94 through 2011–12

[Standard errors appear in parentheses]

Selected characteristic	Percentage distribution by highest degree earned, 2011–12 — Bachelor's or less	Master's	Education specialist[2]	Doctor's and first-professional	Average years of experience — As a principal, 1993–94	2003–04	2007–08	2011–12	Teaching experience, 2011–12	Average annual salary in constant 2014–15 dollars[1] — 1993–94	2003–04	2007–08	2011–12
1	2	3	4	5	6	7	8	9	10	11	12	13	14
Public schools Total	2.2 (0.30)	61.7 (0.71)	26.2 (0.54)	9.9 (0.49)	8.7 (0.10)	7.8 (0.10)	7.5 (0.14)	7.2 (0.09)	12.2 (0.12)	$88,800 (205)	$96,020 (236)	$95,860 (429)	$94,130 (258)
Sex													
Males	2.2 (0.37)	64.2 (0.95)	24.9 (0.77)	8.7 (0.57)	10.3 (0.16)	9.1 (0.16)	8.2 (0.20)	7.7 (0.12)	11.0 (0.17)	88,900 (259)	96,180 (369)	96,260 (743)	94,880 (454)
Females	2.1 (0.43)	59.4 (1.08)	27.5 (0.93)	11.0 (0.80)	5.6 (0.12)	6.3 (0.13)	6.8 (0.19)	6.6 (0.15)	13.3 (0.20)	88,600 (447)	95,850 (425)	95,470 (697)	93,430 (495)
Race/ethnicity													
White	1.8 (0.29)	62.0 (0.68)	26.9 (0.58)	9.3 (0.46)	9.0 (0.12)	8.0 (0.12)	7.8 (0.17)	7.3 (0.10)	12.4 (0.13)	88,160 (223)	95,490 (281)	94,840 (491)	93,540 (332)
Black	2.8 (0.74)	57.7 (2.67)	29.5 (2.17)	14.9 (1.89)	7.1 (0.21)	6.9 (0.33)	6.2 (0.38)	6.2 (0.30)	11.8 (0.39)	93,350 (736)	98,390 (846)	98,200 (1,449)	96,130 (1,188)
Hispanic	4.9! (1.70)	70.6 (3.73)	15.9 (2.69)	8.5 (2.18)	6.3 (0.37)	6.1 (0.43)	6.5 (0.62)	6.7 (0.42)	10.5 (0.45)	90,420 (1,292)	101,040 (1,741)	103,890 (2,967)	97,430 (1,469)
Asian	‡ (†)	62.8 (10.48)	‡ (†)	‡ (†)	6.0 ³ (0.60)	6.8 (1.17)	6.3 (0.97)	7.7 (1.13)	10.6 (1.16)	96,220 ³ (2,307)	105,110 (2,126)	115,650 (7,455)	106,650 (4,432)
Pacific Islander	‡	‡	‡	‡	†	—	—	—	—	—	—	—	—
American Indian/Alaska Native	‡	75.7 (7.38)	13.1!	10.9! (3.44)	12.6 (0.67)	6.9 (0.63)	6.4 (1.30)	9.2 (1.67)	13.7 (1.92)	82,740 (2,807)	78,860 (2,706)	111,440 (6,811)	83,760 (3,899)
Two or more races	‡	59.0 (8.49)	30.1	‡	†	5.6 (1.12)	5.8 (1.50)	7.8 (0.77)	11.3 (0.95)	—	96,410 (4,790)	91,310 (6,289)	95,330 (3,773)
Age													
Under 40	3.0 (0.63)	67.2 (1.67)	21.7 (1.26)	8.2 (0.99)	2.8 (0.12)	2.4 (0.10)	2.9 (0.14)	3.0 (0.10)	7.6 (0.11)	75,340 (766)	87,520 (692)	88,870 (1,012)	89,200 (727)
40 to 44	2.4 (0.60)	62.3 (1.69)	25.0 (1.48)	10.3 (1.30)	5.0 (0.12)	4.5 (0.18)	4.8 (0.22)	4.8 (0.13)	9.8 (0.16)	84,230 (624)	91,960 (842)	93,630 (1,249)	91,630 (675)
45 to 49	1.7 (0.52)	63.4 (2.01)	24.9 (1.54)	9.9 (1.11)	7.1 (0.13)	6.1 (0.16)	6.1 (0.26)	6.5 (0.18)	11.7 (0.23)	89,710 (422)	93,200 (670)	94,860 (1,074)	93,430 (891)
50 to 54	2.8! (0.93)	59.2 (2.13)	28.4 (1.70)	9.6 (1.39)	10.3 (0.18)	8.7 (0.19)	8.1 (0.28)	8.1 (0.24)	14.8 (0.24)	91,550 (590)	98,000 (556)	97,100 (1,031)	95,240 (927)
55 or over	1.3 (0.29)	57.7 (1.32)	30.0 (1.15)	11.0 (0.82)	15.1 (0.35)	11.9 (0.23)	11.8 (0.29)	11.8 (0.22)	16.0 (0.26)	93,600 (801)	101,860 (606)	100,850 (1,044)	99,340 (629)
School level													
Elementary	1.7 (0.30)	62.6 (0.93)	26.4 (0.72)	9.3 (0.68)	8.9 (0.14)	7.9 (0.13)	7.7 (0.17)	7.2 (0.13)	12.4 (0.16)	87,670 (273)	95,890 (286)	95,290 (547)	93,160 (315)
Secondary	2.2 (0.44)	59.6 (1.14)	26.2 (1.07)	12.0 (0.78)	8.0 (0.12)	7.5 (0.19)	7.1 (0.19)	7.1 (0.15)	11.5 (0.14)	91,620 (270)	100,940 (562)	100,910 (786)	100,170 (635)
Combined	5.5 (1.45)	60.3 (2.26)	25.4 (2.09)	8.9 (1.45)	7.5 (0.29)	7.4 (0.36)	7.1 (0.43)	7.1 (0.51)	12.2 (0.51)	85,510 (826)	82,230 (783)	84,700 (1,384)	86,250 (1,395)
School locale													
City	3.6 (0.76)	59.4 (1.76)	24.7 (1.42)	12.3 (1.15)	†	7.3 (0.17)	7.0 (0.25)	6.8 (0.21)	12.0 (0.24)	—	102,000 (479)	101,960 (831)	99,710 (588)
Suburban	1.2 (0.27)	59.0 (1.42)	26.9 (1.15)	12.9 (0.99)	†	7.9 (0.23)	7.7 (0.28)	7.3 (0.21)	11.6 (0.21)	—	108,590 (601)	108,360 (1,032)	105,670 (478)
Town	2.5! (0.79)	61.4 (1.94)	29.1 (1.74)	8.1 (0.81)	†	8.1 (0.28)	7.8 (0.34)	7.3 (0.24)	12.5 (0.30)	—	87,690 (640)	86,670 (795)	86,210 (576)
Rural	1.7 (0.33)	65.9 (0.99)	25.8 (0.91)	6.6 (0.66)	†	7.9 (0.22)	7.5 (0.27)	7.3 (0.15)	12.7 (0.20)	—	82,650 (447)	84,640 (734)	83,430 (373)
Private schools Total	31.0 (1.73)	49.7 (1.49)	10.1 (0.80)	9.1 (0.87)	8.8 (0.20)	10.0 (0.24)	10.0 (0.22)	10.8 (0.31)	13.9 (0.38)	$51,920 (588)	$63,820 (777)	$64,260 (896)	$67,900 (1,209)
Sex													
Males	32.7 (2.87)	45.9 (2.41)	8.8 (1.24)	12.6 (1.62)	9.0 (0.26)	11.0 (0.35)	10.6 (0.37)	11.4 (0.43)	12.7 (0.62)	57,620 (914)	70,450 (1,276)	70,390 (1,509)	76,870 (2,571)
Females	29.7 (1.93)	52.9 (1.84)	11.2 (1.10)	6.2 (0.81)	8.6 (0.27)	9.2 (0.28)	9.5 (0.26)	10.4 (0.41)	14.8 (0.43)	47,240 (984)	58,840 (1,072)	59,250 (1,076)	61,460 (1,309)
Race/ethnicity													
White	31.5 (1.81)	49.2 (1.61)	10.0 (0.79)	9.2 (0.94)	8.7 (0.22)	10.3 (0.24)	10.4 (0.25)	10.9 (0.31)	13.9 (0.42)	51,750 (648)	64,350 (767)	65,640 (981)	68,970 (1,390)
Black	24.0 (5.62)	50.5 (5.71)	12.4 (3.67)	13.0! (4.43)	8.3 (1.04)	7.1 (1.08)	7.1 (0.90)	11.3 (1.12)	14.9 (1.23)	55,660 (4,008)	56,360 (4,402)	55,220 (2,402)	60,700 (4,936)
Hispanic	41.1 (7.82)	43.1 (6.95)	10.7! (5.11)	‡	10.1 (1.43)	6.6 (1.29)	7.8 (0.87)	9.2 (0.93)	11.7 (1.34)	50,740 (3,169)	61,060 (5,010)	53,840 (3,684)	64,460 (6,240)
Age													
Under 40	53.4 (4.95)	36.4 (4.27)	4.8! (1.59)	5.1 (1.23)	3.5 (0.22)	2.9 (0.20)	3.0 (0.36)	3.3 (0.36)	6.4 (0.45)	42,580 (1,406)	52,050 (2,012)	52,170 (1,547)	50,970 (1,912)
40 to 44	35.4 (6.03)	47.0 (5.24)	10.6 (2.46)	‡	5.3 (0.24)	5.4 (0.38)	5.3 (0.35)	5.9 (0.56)	9.8 (0.82)	49,350 (1,502)	60,370 (2,187)	60,650 (2,991)	69,920 (7,372)
45 to 49	35.3 (5.89)	47.3 (4.78)	9.9 (2.36)	7.5! (2.32)	8.3 (0.27)	7.6 (0.38)	6.2 (0.38)	6.6 (0.50)	11.7 (1.08)	56,070 (1,191)	65,700 (1,865)	66,660 (2,303)	69,060 (3,904)
50 to 54	27.3 (3.71)	54.2 (3.78)	7.6 (1.88)	10.9 (3.33)	9.6 (0.34)	10.1 (0.35)	9.0 (0.43)	9.9 (0.59)	14.1 (0.75)	61,070 (1,616)	66,680 (1,994)	70,270 (2,044)	71,380 (3,797)
55 or over	21.9 (1.80)	54.5 (1.71)	12.7 (1.20)	10.9 (1.22)	14.8 (0.40)	15.2 (0.40)	15.4 (0.43)	16.1 (0.44)	18.0 (0.50)	51,440 (1,225)	68,680 (1,410)	68,680 (1,602)	71,300 (1,972)
School level													
Elementary	34.8 (2.23)	50.3 (1.92)	9.2 (1.06)	5.7 (0.80)	9.4 (0.27)	9.9 (0.30)	9.9 (0.38)	10.6 (0.39)	13.4 (0.47)	46,580 (719)	60,090 (856)	61,990 (1,084)	62,870 (1,207)
Secondary	9.1 (2.19)	57.1 (4.60)	15.4 (2.71)	18.9 (4.83)	7.8 (0.36)	9.3 (0.77)	9.3 (0.58)	11.0 (0.80)	15.4 (1.04)	70,710 (1,269)	82,680 (3,298)	83,960 (2,652)	88,270 (7,214)
Combined	31.5 (2.43)	46.6 (2.33)	10.0 (1.65)	11.9 (1.42)	8.0 (0.34)	10.3 (0.39)	10.2 (0.44)	11.2 (0.57)	14.2 (0.62)	54,440 (1,797)	66,600 (1,928)	65,640 (1,653)	69,590 (2,386)
School locale													
City	20.9 (2.16)	56.7 (2.60)	10.1 (1.39)	12.3 (2.05)	—	—	—	11.0 (0.53)	15.0 (0.58)	—	—	72,590 (1,448)	75,350 (2,176)
Suburban	26.3 (2.27)	52.4 (2.20)	11.1 (1.34)	10.2 (1.94)	—	—	—	11.8 (0.49)	14.8 (0.48)	—	—	68,850 (1,590)	70,770 (2,545)
Town	38.2 (5.31)	47.6 (5.43)	9.5! (3.17)	4.8! (2.19)	—	—	—	10.2 (1.00)	14.3 (1.01)	—	—	49,490 (2,404)	46,900 (2,384)
Rural	47.7 (3.97)	37.8 (3.29)	9.3 (1.77)	5.1 (1.18)	—	—	—	9.7 (0.76)	10.9 (0.93)	—	—	47,910 (1,835)	60,300 (2,821)

—Not available.
†Not applicable.
‡Reporting standards not met (too few cases for a reliable estimate).
!Interpret data with caution. The coefficient of variation (CV) for this estimate is between 30 and 50 percent.
[1]Constant dollars based on the Consumer Price Index, prepared by the Bureau of Labor Statistics, U.S. Department of Labor, adjusted to a school-year basis. Excludes principals reporting a salary of $0.
[2]Education specialist degrees or certificates are generally awarded for 1 year's work beyond the master's level. Includes certificate of advanced graduate studies.
[3]Data include Pacific Islanders.
NOTE: Race categories exclude persons of Hispanic ethnicity. Detail may not sum to totals because of rounding and survey item nonresponse.
SOURCE: U.S. Department of Education, National Center for Education Statistics, Schools and Staffing Survey (SASS), "Public School Principal Data File" and "Private School Principal Data File," 1993–94, 2003–04, 2007–08, and 2011–12. (This table was prepared December 2015.)

Table 212.20. Mobility of public elementary and secondary principals, by selected principal and school characteristics: 2007–08 to 2008–09 and 2011–12 to 2012–13

[Standard errors appear in parentheses]

Selected principal or school characteristic	Percent of public school principals											
	2007–08 to 2008–09						2011–12 to 2012–13					
	Remained in same school	Moved to another school[2]			Stopped working as a principal		Remained in same school	Moved to another school[2]			Stopped working as a principal	
		Total moving to another school[2]	Public school in same school district	Public school in different district	Working at a different type of job	Other[1]		Total moving to another school[2]	Public school in same school district	Public school in different district	Working at a different type of job	Other[1]
	2	3	4	5	6	7	8	9	10	11	12	13
Total	79.5 (1.85)	6.9 (1.25)	4.3 (0.99)	2.5! (0.77)	11.9 (1.35)	1.8! (0.64)	77.4 (1.23)	7.0 (0.92)	4.4 (0.79)	2.4 (0.47)	11.5 (1.00)	4.1 (0.72)
Sex												
Male	77.6 (2.57)	7.5 (1.69)	4.0! (1.38)	3.3! (1.00)	13.0 (2.10)	† (†)	77.1 (1.73)	7.0 (1.15)	3.8 (0.82)	3.1 (0.81)	11.6 (1.57)	4.3 (0.81)
Female	81.3 (2.55)	6.4 (1.71)	4.6! (1.39)	† (†)	10.8 (0.96)	† (†)	77.8 (2.01)	6.9 (1.33)	5.1 (1.33)	1.8! (0.55)	11.4 (1.48)	4.0 (1.08)
Race/ethnicity												
White	80.1 (2.14)	6.8 (1.37)	4.1 (0.98)	2.6! (0.87)	11.9 (1.60)	1.3! (0.55)	78.6 (1.15)	6.4 (0.92)	4.0 (0.76)	2.4 (0.50)	11.7 (1.05)	3.3 (0.68)
Black	77.4 (5.57)	† (†)	† (†)	† (†)	11.3! (4.32)	† (†)	73.2 (5.08)	9.7! (3.22)	6.6! (2.69)	† (†)	10.4! (3.30)	7.7! (3.10)
Hispanic	79.1 (8.27)	† (†)	† (†)	† (†)	† (†)	† (†)	73.6 (8.19)	† (†)	† (†)	† (†)	† (†)	‡ (†)
Age												
Under 40	81.6 (4.40)	9.5! (3.27)	5.2! (2.47)	† (†)	7.1 (2.78)	† (†)	81.1 (3.44)	7.5 (2.01)	3.7! (1.51)	3.8! (1.25)	7.9! (2.70)	3.5! (1.60)
40 to 44	83.7 (4.27)	7.5! (2.58)	4.6! (2.18)	2.9! (1.42)	6.9 (2.85)	† (†)	77.3 (3.75)	9.6 (2.60)	6.2! (2.21)	3.3! (1.41)	8.0 (2.29)	5.0! (2.28)
45 to 49	83.0 (4.64)	6.8! (3.23)	† (†)	† (†)	8.3! (3.43)	† (†)	82.8 (2.91)	7.4 (2.02)	5.2! (1.87)	2.0! (0.81)	6.9 (1.81)	† (†)
50 to 54	80.7 (3.38)	6.6 (2.49)	† (†)	† (†)	10.5 (2.82)	† (†)	80.4 (3.01)	6.8! (2.26)	5.0 (2.20)	† (†)	9.8 (2.06)	3.0! (1.33)
55 or over	73.7 (3.94)	5.3! (2.33)	3.1! (1.46)	† (†)	19.7 (3.35)	† (†)	69.7 (3.06)	4.5 (1.30)	2.9! (1.16)	1.4! (0.68)	20.5 (2.60)	5.4 (1.50)
Years of experience as a principal at any school												
Less than 3	81.3 (3.41)	8.5! (2.56)	5.4! (1.91)	3.0! (1.48)	8.0 (2.26)	† (†)	80.8 (2.30)	6.6 (1.34)	4.0! (1.29)	2.5 (0.70)	8.3 (1.68)	4.2! (1.43)
3 to 5	81.2 (5.55)	† (†)	† (†)	† (†)	9.8! (3.91)	† (†)	76.9 (3.88)	8.8! (2.65)	4.9! (1.99)	3.8! (1.78)	10.2 (2.39)	4.1! (1.79)
6 to 9	82.1 (3.88)	5.7! (1.89)	3.3! (1.50)	2.3! (1.07)	10.8 (3.01)	† (†)	77.1 (2.81)	7.5! (1.96)	5.2! (1.90)	2.2! (0.85)	11.4 (1.85)	4.0! (1.31)
10 or more	74.5 (3.68)	5.6! (1.94)	3.3! (1.59)	† (†)	18.2 (3.11)	† (†)	74.0 (2.67)	5.8 (1.62)	4.1 (1.47)	1.6! (0.62)	16.1 (2.44)	4.2! (1.44)
School level												
Elementary	80.4 (2.58)	7.0 (1.66)	4.5 (1.25)	2.4! (1.00)	11.0 (1.90)	1.5! (0.71)	77.9 (1.64)	7.1 (1.22)	5.0 (1.08)	2.0 (0.49)	10.9 (1.30)	4.1 (1.02)
Secondary	78.6 (2.62)	6.3! (1.98)	† (†)	2.7! (1.18)	13.1 (2.81)	† (†)	77.1 (2.32)	6.3 (1.34)	3.1 (1.04)	3.1 (0.92)	12.8 (1.77)	3.8 (1.04)
Combined	73.4 (5.74)	7.5! (3.13)	† (†)	† (†)	15.9! (5.15)	† (†)	74.7 (3.91)	7.2! (2.42)	3.4! (1.34)	† (0.80)	12.8 (2.73)	5.2! (1.87)
School size												
Less than 150	75.8 (6.40)	† (†)	† (†)	† (†)	12.6! (4.66)	† (†)	76.1 (4.43)	6.5 (1.91)	3.6! (1.60)	3.6! (1.60)	11.9! (3.56)	5.5! (2.32)
150 to 349	80.2 (4.27)	7.0! (2.60)	4.4! (1.99)	† (†)	11.0 (3.15)	† (†)	74.8 (3.31)	8.6 (2.20)	5.7 (2.10)	2.8! (0.93)	11.3 (2.45)	5.3! (1.98)
350 to 499	77.0 (4.78)	7.6! (3.22)	† (†)	† (†)	13.4 (3.59)	† (†)	78.0 (3.24)	6.6 (1.88)	4.4! (1.63)	2.1! (0.82)	11.4 (2.21)	4.1! (1.76)
500 to 749	82.2 (4.38)	5.8! (2.45)	3.4! (1.66)	† (†)	10.9 (3.22)	† (†)	78.1 (3.26)	7.4 (2.13)	4.8! (1.59)	2.1! (1.59)	10.7 (2.20)	3.8! (1.53)
750 or more	80.5 (3.27)	6.3! (2.10)	4.2! (1.89)	1.8! (0.84)	12.0 (2.53)	† (†)	79.6 (2.40)	5.3 (1.56)	3.5! (1.28)	1.6! (0.80)	12.4 (1.87)	2.6! (0.92)
Percent of students who are Black, Hispanic, Asian, Pacific Islander, American Indian/Alaska Native, or Two or more races												
Less than 5 percent	81.3 (4.15)	5.8! (2.79)	† (†)	† (†)	12.2 (3.20)	† (†)	80.0 (3.65)	4.4 (1.03)	† (†)	3.3 (0.92)	12.0 (2.94)	† (†)
5 to 19 percent	80.4 (4.44)	7.1! (3.41)	† (†)	† (†)	11.3 (2.59)	† (†)	79.5 (2.45)	5.9 (1.52)	3.6! (1.27)	2.2 (0.89)	11.7 (2.18)	2.8! (1.14)
20 to 49 percent	82.8 (3.41)	5.5! (1.80)	3.8! (1.53)	2.1 (0.98)	10.7 (2.77)	† (†)	79.4 (2.57)	6.9 (1.55)	4.5! (1.37)	2.2 (0.89)	10.8 (1.94)	2.9! (1.14)
50 percent or more	75.9 (3.13)	8.3 (2.20)	6.0! (1.97)	† (†)	12.9 (2.56)	3.0! (1.42)	74.3 (2.44)	8.3 (1.82)	5.8 (1.64)	2.4 (0.80)	11.6 (1.76)	5.8 (1.39)
Percent of students approved for free or reduced-price lunch												
0 to 25.0 percent	81.9 (3.34)	6.1! (2.03)	4.1! (1.64)	2.8! (1.34)	11.1 (2.83)	† (†)	79.2 (2.77)	6.4! (2.07)	4.4! (1.80)	1.7! (0.83)	11.4 (2.28)	† (†)
25.1 to 50.0 percent	81.8 (3.25)	6.8! (2.34)	4.1 (1.55)	† (†)	10.3 (2.14)	† (†)	79.8 (2.35)	5.4! (1.54)	3.2! (1.02)	2.1 (0.90)	11.7 (1.86)	3.1! (1.13)
50.1 to 75.0 percent	80.4 (3.92)	6.1! (1.93)	4.1 (1.55)	† (†)	12.2 (3.53)	† (†)	78.4 (2.80)	7.1 (1.62)	2.8 (0.98)	2.8 (0.98)	10.4 (2.02)	4.0! (1.53)
More than 75.0 percent	74.0 (4.56)	9.1! (3.29)	7.1 (3.11)	† (†)	13.4 (3.90)	† (†)	72.5 (2.89)	9.3 (2.29)	6.2! (2.06)	2.9! (0.94)	11.9 (2.52)	† (†)
Locale												
City	78.3 (4.25)	7.6! (2.71)	5.6! (2.41)	† (†)	11.4 (2.98)	† (†)	74.4 (3.35)	8.5 (2.50)	6.7! (2.28)	1.8! (0.75)	11.8 (2.72)	5.3 (1.51)
Suburban	82.0 (3.21)	5.5! (1.78)	3.7! (1.51)	† (†)	10.8 (2.61)	† (†)	78.3 (2.39)	7.0 (1.77)	4.5! (1.52)	2.3! (0.95)	10.9 (1.89)	3.8 (1.58)
Town	77.9 (4.88)	6.5! (2.70)	† (†)	† (†)	14.0! (4.59)	† (†)	79.5 (3.65)	6.3! (2.08)	4.1! (1.64)	2.3! (0.90)	10.3 (2.19)	3.8! (1.80)
Rural	78.8 (3.17)	7.9! (2.45)	4.0! (1.69)	3.9! (1.76)	12.3 (2.30)	† (†)	78.3 (1.77)	5.9 (1.11)	2.8 (0.73)	3.1 (0.78)	12.2 (1.46)	3.6! (1.18)

†Not applicable.
!Interpret data with caution. The coefficient of variation (CV) for this estimate is between 30 and 50 percent.
‡Reporting standards not met. Either there are too few cases for a reliable estimate or the coefficient of variation (CV) is 50 percent or greater.
[1]Includes retired, on leave (e.g., maternity/paternity or disability), deceased, and "other."
[2]Includes principals who moved from a public school to a private school, a category that is not shown separately.

NOTE: Race categories exclude persons of Hispanic ethnicity. Totals include other racial/ethnic groups not separately shown. Detail may not sum to totals because of rounding.
SOURCE: U.S. Department of Education, National Center for Education Statistics, Schools and Staffing Survey (SASS), "Public School Principal Data File," 2007–08 and 2011–12; and Principal Follow-up Survey (PFS), "Public School Principal Status Data File," 2008–09 and 2012–13. (This table was prepared January 2015.)

Table 212.30. Number and percentage distribution of public and private school principals who left the profession during the past year, by total years of experience as a principal and occupational status: 2012–13

[Standard errors appear in parentheses]

Occupational status	Total Number		Total Percent		Percentage distribution, by years of experience as a principal in any school Less than 3 years		3 to 5 years		6 to 9 years		10 or more years	
1	2		3		4		5		6		7	
All school principal leavers	13,160	(1,041)	100.0	(†)	18.3	(4.39)	22.2	(4.19)	20.3	(3.63)	39.2	(3.79)
Public school principal leavers	10,270	(875)	100.0	(†)	16.3	(4.23)	22.2	(4.36)	23.0	(4.30)	38.6	(4.54)
Private school principal leavers	2,880	(592)	100.0	(†)	25.3 !	(10.18)	22.3 !	(8.66)	‡	(†)	41.4	(10.35)
					Principals who left public schools							
All public school principal leavers	10,270	(875)	100.0	(†)	100.0	(†)	100.0	(†)	100.0	(†)	100.0	(†)
Retired, not working outside of home	3,860	(533)	37.6	(3.96)	15.5 !	(7.53)	22.1 !	(9.48)	35.3	(8.14)	57.1	(7.01)
Deceased	‡	(†)	‡	(†)	‡	(†)	‡	(†)	‡	(†)	‡	(†)
On leave (e.g., maternity/paternity or disability)	‡	(†)	‡	(†)	‡	(†)	‡	(†)	‡	(†)	‡	(†)
Working in a kindergarten through grade 12 school, but not as a principal	2,530	(440)	24.6	(3.89)	49.5	(11.42)	31.0 !	(9.72)	24.8 !	(9.95)	10.3 !	(3.99)
Working in current school, but not as a principal	890 !	(293)	8.6 !	(2.86)	21.7 !	(9.98)	‡	(†)	‡	(†)	‡	(†)
Working in a different public school, but not as a principal	1,440	(352)	14.0	(3.21)	‡	(†)	23.7 !	(9.08)	‡	(†)	5.9 !	(2.88)
Working in a private school, but not as a principal	‡	(†)	‡	(†)	‡	(†)	‡	(†)	‡	(†)	‡	(†)
Working in a different (not identified) school, but not as a principal	‡	(†)	‡	(†)	‡	(†)	‡	(†)	‡	(†)	‡	(†)
Working in kindergarten through grade 12 education, but not in a school	3,070	(538)	29.9	(4.44)	24.9 !	(9.97)	37.5 !	(11.37)	33.6	(8.28)	25.3	(7.06)
Working in a district or administrative office as a superintendent, assistant superintendent, or other higher level administrator	1,900	(424)	18.5	(3.95)	‡	(†)	20.3 !	(8.18)	24.9 !	(7.87)	16.2 !	(6.05)
Working in a district or administrative office, in a position other than that of a superintendent, assistant superintendent, or other higher level administrator	820 !	(315)	8.0 !	(2.87)	‡	(†)	‡	(†)	8.1 !	(3.84)	5.7 !	(2.45)
Working at a job associated with kindergarten through grade 12 education, but not directly associated with any schools or school systems	‡	(†)	‡	(†)	‡	(†)	‡	(†)	‡	(†)	‡	(†)
Position unknown	‡	(†)	‡	(†)	‡	(†)	‡	(†)	‡	(†)	‡	(†)
Working at a job outside of kindergarten through grade 12 education	710 !	(287)	6.9 !	(2.75)	‡	(†)	‡	(†)	‡	(†)	‡	(†)
Other	‡	(†)	‡	(†)	‡	(†)	‡	(†)	‡	(†)	‡	(†)
					Principals who left private schools							
All private school principal leavers	2,880	(592)	100.0	(†)	100.0	(†)	100.0	(†)	100.0	(†)	100.0	(†)
Retired, not working outside of home	860 !	(264)	29.9 !	(9.06)	‡	(†)	‡	(†)	‡	(†)	43.3 !	(15.36)
Deceased	‡	(†)	‡	(†)	‡	(†)	‡	(†)	‡	(†)	‡	(†)
On leave (e.g., maternity/paternity or disability)	‡	(†)	‡	(†)	‡	(†)	‡	(†)	‡	(†)	‡	(†)
Working in a kindergarten through grade 12 school, but not as a principal	1,100 !	(399)	38.2	(10.26)	60.3 !	(20.13)	‡	(†)	‡	(†)	30.0 !	(13.57)
Working in current school, but not as a principal	660 !	(281)	23.0 !	(7.77)	‡	(†)	‡	(†)	‡	(†)	‡	(†)
Working in a different public school, but not as a principal	‡	(†)	‡	(†)	‡	(†)	‡	(†)	‡	(†)	‡	(†)
Working in a private school, but not as a principal	‡	(†)	‡	(†)	‡	(†)	‡	(†)	‡	(†)	‡	(†)
Working in a different (not identified) school, but not as a principal	‡	(†)	‡	(†)	‡	(†)	‡	(†)	‡	(†)	‡	(†)
Working in kindergarten through grade 12 education, but not in a school	‡	(†)	‡	(†)	‡	(†)	‡	(†)	‡	(†)	‡	(†)
Working in a district or administrative office as a superintendent, assistant superintendent, or other higher level administrator	‡	(†)	‡	(†)	‡	(†)	‡	(†)	‡	(†)	‡	(†)
Working in a district or administrative office, in a position other than that of a superintendent, assistant superintendent, or other higher level administrator	‡	(†)	‡	(†)	‡	(†)	‡	(†)	‡	(†)	‡	(†)
Working at a job associated with kindergarten through grade 12 education, but not directly associated with any schools or school systems	‡	(†)	‡	(†)	‡	(†)	‡	(†)	‡	(†)	‡	(†)
Position unknown	‡	(†)	‡	(†)	‡	(†)	‡	(†)	‡	(†)	‡	(†)
Working at a job outside of kindergarten through grade 12 education	‡	(†)	20.3 !	(8.98)	‡	(†)	‡	(†)	‡	(†)	‡	(†)
Other	‡	(†)	‡	(†)	‡	(†)	‡	(†)	‡	(†)	‡	(†)

†Not applicable.
!Interpret data with caution. The coefficient of variation (CV) for this estimate is between 30 and 50 percent.
‡Reporting standards not met. Either there are too few cases for a reliable estimate or the coefficient of variation (CV) is 50 percent or greater.
NOTE: Detail may not sum to totals because of rounding.

SOURCE: U.S. Department of Education, National Center for Education Statistics, Schools and Staffing Survey (SASS), "Public School Principal Data File" and "Private School Principal Data File," 2011–12; and Principal Follow-up Survey (PFS), "Public School Principal Status Data File" and "Private School Principal Status Data File," 2012–13. (This table was prepared November 2014.)

Table 213.10. Staff employed in public elementary and secondary school systems, by type of assignment: Selected years, 1949–50 through fall 2013

[In full-time equivalents]

School year	Total	School district administrative staff			Instructional staff						Support staff[1]
		Total	Officials and administrators	Instruction coordinators	Total	Principals and assistant principals	Teachers	Instructional aides	Librarians	Guidance counselors	
1	2	3	4	5	6	7	8	9	10	11	12
					Number						
1949–50[2]	1,300,031	33,642	23,868	9,774	956,808	43,137	913,671	(3)	(3)	(3)	309,582
1959–60[2]	2,089,283	42,423	28,648	13,775	1,448,931	63,554	1,353,372	(3)	17,363	14,643	597,929
1969–70[2]	3,360,763	65,282	33,745	31,537	2,255,707	90,593	2,016,244	57,418	42,689	48,763	1,039,774
Fall 1980[2]	4,168,286	78,784	58,230	20,554	2,729,023	107,061	2,184,216	325,755	48,018	63,973	1,360,479
Fall 1990	4,494,076	75,868	—	—	3,051,404	127,417	2,398,169	395,959	49,909	79,950	1,366,804
Fall 1997	5,266,415	85,267	50,432	34,835	3,572,955	126,129	2,746,157	557,453	52,142	91,074	1,608,193
Fall 1998	5,419,181	88,939	52,975	35,964	3,693,630	129,317	2,830,286	588,108	52,805	93,114	1,636,612
Fall 1999	5,632,004	94,134	55,467	38,667	3,819,057	137,199	2,910,633	621,942	53,659	95,624	1,718,813
Fall 2000	5,709,753	97,270	57,837	39,433	3,876,628	141,792	2,941,461	641,392	54,246	97,737	1,735,855
Fall 2001	5,904,195	109,526	63,517	46,009	3,989,211	160,543	2,999,528	674,741	54,350	100,049	1,805,458
Fall 2002	5,954,661	110,777	62,781	47,996	4,016,963	164,171	3,034,123	663,552	54,205	100,912	1,826,921
Fall 2003	5,953,667	107,483	63,418	44,065	4,052,739	165,233	3,048,652	685,118	54,349	99,387	1,793,445
Fall 2004	6,058,174	111,832	64,101	47,731	4,120,063	165,657	3,090,925	707,514	54,145	101,822	1,826,279
Fall 2005	6,130,686	121,164	62,464	58,700	4,151,236	156,454	3,143,003	693,792	54,057	103,930	1,858,286
Fall 2006	6,153,735	118,707	53,722	64,985	4,186,968	153,673	3,166,391	709,715	54,444	102,745	1,848,060
Fall 2007	6,232,911	130,044	59,361	70,683	4,235,238	157,539	3,199,995	717,806	54,386	105,512	1,867,629
Fall 2008	6,326,702	135,706	62,153	73,553	4,277,674	159,897	3,222,154	734,010	53,805	107,808	1,913,322
Fall 2009	6,351,157	138,471	63,969	74,502	4,279,488	168,450	3,209,672	741,337	52,545	107,484	1,933,198
Fall 2010	6,195,207	133,833	64,597	69,236	4,151,225	165,047	3,099,095	731,705	50,300	105,079	1,910,150
Fall 2011	6,138,890	130,595	62,884	67,711	4,133,767	166,416	3,103,263	710,335	48,402	105,351	1,874,528
Fall 2012	6,181,238	136,387	65,420	70,967	4,158,000	169,240	3,109,101	729,756	46,685	103,218	1,886,851
Fall 2013	6,187,901	139,667	66,732	72,935	4,167,118	168,101	3,113,764	738,226	45,106	101,920	1,881,116
					Percentage distribution						
1949–50[2]	100.0	2.6	1.8	0.8	73.6	3.3	70.3	(3)	(3)	(3)	23.8
1959–60[2]	100.0	2.0	1.4	0.7	69.4	3.0	64.8	(3)	0.8	0.7	28.6
1969–70[2]	100.0	1.9	1.0	0.9	67.1	2.7	60.0	1.7	1.3	1.5	30.9
Fall 1980[2]	100.0	1.9	1.4	0.5	65.5	2.6	52.4	7.8	1.2	1.5	32.6
Fall 1990	100.0	1.7	—	—	67.9	2.8	53.4	8.8	1.1	1.8	30.4
Fall 1997	100.0	1.6	1.0	0.7	67.8	2.4	52.1	10.6	1.0	1.7	30.5
Fall 1998	100.0	1.6	1.0	0.7	68.2	2.4	52.2	10.9	1.0	1.7	30.2
Fall 1999	100.0	1.7	1.0	0.7	67.8	2.4	51.7	11.0	1.0	1.7	30.5
Fall 2000	100.0	1.7	1.0	0.7	67.9	2.5	51.5	11.2	1.0	1.7	30.4
Fall 2001	100.0	1.9	1.1	0.8	67.6	2.7	50.8	11.4	0.9	1.7	30.6
Fall 2002	100.0	1.9	1.1	0.8	67.5	2.8	51.0	11.1	0.9	1.7	30.7
Fall 2003	100.0	1.8	1.1	0.7	68.1	2.8	51.2	11.5	0.9	1.7	30.1
Fall 2004	100.0	1.8	1.1	0.8	68.0	2.7	51.0	11.7	0.9	1.7	30.1
Fall 2005	100.0	2.0	1.0	1.0	67.7	2.6	51.3	11.3	0.9	1.7	30.3
Fall 2006	100.0	1.9	0.9	1.1	68.0	2.5	51.5	11.5	0.9	1.7	30.0
Fall 2007	100.0	2.1	1.0	1.1	67.9	2.5	51.3	11.5	0.9	1.7	30.0
Fall 2008	100.0	2.1	1.0	1.2	67.6	2.5	50.9	11.6	0.9	1.7	30.2
Fall 2009	100.0	2.2	1.0	1.2	67.4	2.7	50.5	11.7	0.8	1.7	30.4
Fall 2010	100.0	2.2	1.0	1.1	67.0	2.7	50.0	11.8	0.8	1.7	30.8
Fall 2011	100.0	2.1	1.0	1.1	67.3	2.7	50.6	11.6	0.8	1.7	30.5
Fall 2012	100.0	2.2	1.1	1.1	67.3	2.7	50.3	11.8	0.8	1.7	30.5
Fall 2013	100.0	2.3	1.1	1.2	67.3	2.7	50.3	11.9	0.7	1.6	30.4
					Pupils per staff member						
1949–50[2]	19.3	746.4	1,052.1	2,569.2	26.2	582.1	27.5	(3)	(3)	(3)	81.1
1959–60[2]	16.8	829.3	1,228.1	2,554.1	24.3	553.6	26.0	(3)	2,026.3	2,402.7	58.8
1969–70[2]	13.6	697.7	1,349.8	1,444.3	20.2	502.8	22.6	793.3	1,067.0	934.1	43.8
Fall 1980[2]	9.8	518.9	702.0	1,988.8	15.0	381.8	18.7	125.5	851.3	639.0	30.0
Fall 1990	9.2	543.3	—	—	13.5	323.5	17.2	104.1	825.8	515.5	30.2
Fall 1997	8.8	541.0	914.6	1,324.2	12.9	365.7	16.8	82.7	884.6	506.5	28.7
Fall 1998	8.6	523.3	878.5	1,294.0	12.6	359.9	16.4	79.1	881.3	499.8	28.4
Fall 1999	8.3	497.8	844.8	1,211.8	12.3	341.5	16.1	75.3	873.2	490.0	27.3
Fall 2000	8.3	485.3	816.1	1,197.1	12.2	332.9	16.0	73.6	870.2	483.0	27.2
Fall 2001	8.1	435.3	750.5	1,036.1	12.0	296.9	15.9	70.7	877.1	476.5	26.4
Fall 2002	8.1	435.0	767.5	1,003.9	12.0	293.5	15.9	72.6	888.9	477.5	26.4
Fall 2003	8.2	451.6	765.4	1,101.6	12.0	293.8	15.9	70.8	893.1	488.4	27.1
Fall 2004	8.1	436.3	761.2	1,022.3	11.8	294.6	15.8	69.0	901.2	479.2	26.7
Fall 2005	8.0	405.3	786.3	836.7	11.8	313.9	15.6	70.8	908.5	472.6	26.4
Fall 2006	8.0	415.4	918.0	758.9	11.8	320.9	15.6	69.5	905.8	480.0	26.7
Fall 2007	7.9	379.0	830.4	697.3	11.6	312.9	15.4	68.7	906.3	467.2	26.4
Fall 2008	7.8	363.0	792.6	669.8	11.5	308.1	15.3	67.1	915.6	457.0	25.7
Fall 2009	7.8	356.5	771.6	662.5	11.5	293.0	15.4	66.6	939.4	459.2	25.5
Fall 2010	8.0	369.7	766.0	714.7	11.9	299.8	16.0	67.6	983.8	470.9	25.9
Fall 2011	8.1	379.2	787.5	731.4	12.0	297.6	16.0	69.7	1,023.1	470.1	26.4
Fall 2012	8.1	364.9	760.8	701.3	12.0	294.1	16.0	68.2	1,066.1	482.2	26.4
Fall 2013	8.1	358.3	749.9	686.2	12.0	297.7	16.1	67.8	1,109.5	491.0	26.6

—Not available.

[1]Includes school district administrative support staff, school and library support staff, student support staff, and other support services staff.
[2]Because of classification revisions, categories other than teachers, principals, librarians, and guidance counselors are only roughly comparable to figures for years after 1980.
[3]Data included in column 8.

NOTE: Data for 1949–50 through 1969–70 are cumulative for the entire school year, rather than counts as of the fall of the year. Detail may not sum to totals because of rounding.
SOURCE: U.S. Department of Education, National Center for Education Statistics, *Statistics of State School Systems*, various years; *Statistics of Public Elementary and Secondary Schools*, various years; and Common Core of Data (CCD), "State Nonfiscal Survey of Public Elementary/Secondary Education," 1986–87 through 2013–14. (This table was prepared August 2015.)

Table 213.20. Staff employed in public elementary and secondary school systems, by type of assignment and state or jurisdiction: Fall 2013
[In full-time equivalents]

State or jurisdiction	Total	School district staff			School staff						Student support staff	Other support services staff
		Officials and administrators	Administrative support staff	Instruction coordinators	Principals and assistant principals	School and library support staff	Teachers	Instructional aides	Guidance counselors	Librarians		
1	2	3	4	5	6	7	8	9	10	11	12	13
United States[1]	6,187,901	66,732	182,783	72,935	168,101	283,744	3,113,764	738,226	101,920	45,106	282,982	1,131,607
Alabama	91,753	605	880	882	4,170	2,976	47,162	6,243	1,789	1,356	2,966	22,724
Alaska[2]	17,127	613	780	198	635	1,142	7,898	2,422	301	137	623	2,378
Arizona	103,343	1,274	4,074	610	2,459	3,809	48,359	14,820	1,171	505	11,627	14,635
Arkansas	70,387	598	2,386	824	1,715	2,938	34,933	7,746	1,275	962	7,365	9,645
California[3,4]	541,762	2,949	19,261	16,808	16,509	34,673	259,506	64,664	7,676	780	17,328	101,609
Colorado	104,025	1,245	4,533	2,665	3,100	5,518	50,157	14,796	2,222	625	5,893	13,270
Connecticut	94,208	2,045	1,703	3,621	2,250	3,543	43,443	15,525	1,135	750	2,910	17,282
Delaware	18,253	420	453	273	469	376	9,388	1,876	302	126	1,176	3,394
District of Columbia	11,403	396	190	237	419	648	5,991	1,735	158	17	547	1,064
Florida	335,081	1,992	15,161	717	7,409	16,255	177,853	30,278	5,543	2,130	10,665	67,078
Georgia	218,097	2,420	2,465	2,492	6,095	9,989	109,441	23,604	3,521	2,116	7,804	48,150
Hawaii	22,438	231	677	637	602	1,000	11,781	2,478	625	185	1,720	2,501
Idaho[2]	23,803	125	135	234	640	1,084	15,002	2,758	447	54	760	2,566
Illinois[2,4,5,6,7,8,9]	266,645	3,189	4,801	508	7,714	16,803	136,355	34,573	2,947	1,434	9,883	48,437
Indiana	144,412	581	668	3,334	3,234	8,209	59,823	17,162	1,934	772	9,750	38,944
Iowa	71,551	1,220	1,957	490	1,777	2,747	35,397	11,529	1,190	458	4,373	10,414
Kansas	72,016	453	1,373	1,009	1,881	2,601	38,153	9,685	1,044	676	4,421	10,720
Kentucky	97,808	895	2,232	1,526	3,254	5,877	41,820	12,986	1,523	1,076	2,871	23,746
Louisiana	95,687	355	2,688	1,920	2,944	3,655	46,437	10,678	1,611	1,018	4,739	19,643
Maine	34,249	465	764	314	972	1,604	15,452	6,238	604	220	1,545	6,070
Maryland	115,066	3,536	2,173	1,634	3,544	6,385	58,611	11,064	2,335	1,164	4,889	19,731
Massachusetts	126,962	2,474	3,038	418	4,921	6,728	70,490	24,724	2,281	720	9,571	1,598
Michigan	184,175	4,063	1,139	1,283	6,608	11,383	85,786	20,758	2,116	531	13,141	37,367
Minnesota	112,735	2,249	2,278	2,208	2,234	4,577	54,413	17,769	1,145	633	12,520	12,709
Mississippi	68,252	974	2,057	662	2,004	2,538	32,292	8,171	1,119	832	3,160	14,442
Missouri	123,505	1,362	6,756	1,055	3,154	342	66,651	13,631	2,607	1,401	4,470	22,076
Montana[3]	20,885	440	673	171	509	853	10,310	2,547	450	367	764	3,801
Nebraska	45,907	594	1,097	808	975	1,981	22,401	6,604	783	535	1,473	8,657
Nevada[2,3,5,6,8]	34,003	191	965	1,421	1,072	1,628	21,921	4,199	890	340	73	1,304
New Hampshire	31,832	705	767	266	507	777	14,826	6,999	793	312	708	5,173
New Jersey[3]	231,012	1,438	5,520	3,799	4,997	10,885	114,581	36,198	3,766	1,514	13,091	35,223
New Mexico	46,380	860	120	642	1,321	3,921	22,239	6,066	758	237	3,385	6,830
New York	359,255	2,487	18,744	1,446	5,154	6,773	206,693	42,500	4,381	2,510	8,629	59,939
North Carolina	192,336	1,604	5,364	1,061	5,648	7,391	99,327	23,338	4,040	2,195	10,871	31,498
North Dakota	17,036	490	269	192	457	742	8,805	2,301	341	194	807	2,438
Ohio	248,469	2,449	13,662	1,552	5,360	12,620	106,010	19,389	3,733	921	23,013	59,760
Oklahoma	85,152	540	3,034	334	2,337	4,499	41,983	9,449	1,615	1,049	4,804	15,519
Oregon	59,768	426	2,592	379	1,539	4,526	26,733	9,184	982	129	2,486	10,791
Pennsylvania[2,9]	243,021	2,493	6,918	1,522	4,872	11,461	121,330	30,528	4,263	1,753	7,622	50,259
Rhode Island	17,312	75	507	177	493	752	9,824	2,281	351	191	531	2,130
South Carolina	72,401	771	1,809	1,875	2,707	1,354	48,151	9,098	1,955	1,072	3,280	329
South Dakota	19,205	693	369	160	425	602	9,510	2,554	333	108	917	3,535
Tennessee	125,506	171	819	747	3,533	5,427	65,847	15,808	2,913	1,912	1,344	26,986
Texas	658,340	6,279	22,711	3,548	22,826	27,043	334,580	62,300	11,079	4,605	24,741	138,629
Utah	54,945	780	1,045	1,909	1,403	2,733	27,247	8,545	915	243	1,184	8,942
Vermont	18,300	138	481	233	462	895	8,375	4,203	417	213	958	1,924
Virginia	178,202	1,719	4,383	1,728	3,864	8,461	90,098	19,096	3,344	1,593	4,559	39,357
Washington	105,365	2,446	1,920	318	2,973	5,069	54,867	10,582	2,110	1,066	3,390	20,624
West Virginia[3]	39,121	767	1,086	389	1,147	781	19,978	3,646	743	312	1,694	8,578
Wisconsin	102,476	1,063	2,829	1,353	2,425	4,170	57,980	10,498	1,905	946	5,257	14,049
Wyoming	16,931	384	475	350	385	1,000	7,555	2,410	440	112	682	3,139
Bureau of Indian Education	—	—	—	—	—	—	—	—	—	—	—	—
DoD, overseas	—	—	—	—	—	—	—	—	—	—	—	—
DoD, domestic	—	—	—	—	—	—	—	—	—	—	—	—
Other jurisdictions												
American Samoa	—	—	—	—	—	—	—	—	—	—	—	—
Guam	3,923	18	251	128	92	215	2,291	606	87	37	36	162
Northern Marianas	876	9	79	10	33	53	417	152	22	2	22	77
Puerto Rico	54,430	419	1,436	1,044	1,339	1,936	33,412	73	728	990	4,871	8,182
U.S. Virgin Islands	2,170	7	77	34	95	87	1,082	273	56	27	63	369

—Not available.
[1]Includes imputations to correct for undercounts in states as designated in footnotes 2 through 9.
[2]Includes imputations for instruction coordinators.
[3]Includes imputations for library support staff.
[4]Includes imputations for prekindergarten teachers.
[5]Includes imputations for administrative support staff.
[6]Includes imputations for school support staff.

[7]Includes imputations for kindergarten and ungraded teachers.
[8]Includes imputations for instructional aides.
[9]Includes imputations for student support staff.
NOTE: DoD = Department of Defense.
SOURCE: U.S. Department of Education, National Center for Education Statistics, Common Core of Data (CCD), "State Nonfiscal Survey of Public Elementary/Secondary Education," 2013–14. (This table was prepared August 2015.)

Table 213.30. Staff employed in public elementary and secondary school systems, by type of assignment and state or jurisdiction: Fall 2012

[In full-time equivalents]

State or jurisdiction	Total	School district staff			School staff						Student support staff	Other support services staff
		Officials and administrators	Administrative support staff	Instruction coordinators	Principals and assistant principals	School and library support staff	Teachers	Instructional aides	Guidance counselors	Librarians		
1	2	3	4	5	6	7	8	9	10	11	12	13
United States[1]	6,181,238	65,420	186,118	70,967	169,240	285,055	3,109,101	729,756	103,218	46,685	280,358	1,135,319
Alabama[2,3,4,5,6,7,8,9,10,11]	96,485	796	1,615	996	2,569	3,840	51,877	6,191	1,767	1,345	2,354	23,135
Alaska[4]	17,116	637	799	195	647	1,205	7,682	2,442	310	135	651	2,413
Arizona	103,228	1,230	4,161	592	2,497	3,903	48,866	14,804	1,238	595	11,527	13,813
Arkansas	71,279	612	2,410	969	1,651	4,005	34,131	7,519	1,264	964	8,194	9,559
California[6,12]	544,875	2,777	19,874	15,772	16,343	34,702	266,255	62,890	7,623	769	16,627	101,244
Colorado	102,480	1,158	4,417	2,579	2,940	5,540	48,922	15,137	2,198	630	5,696	13,264
Connecticut	91,264	1,919	2,860	3,618	2,462	2,088	43,931	13,703	1,111	742	2,678	16,151
Delaware	17,554	406	448	257	451	361	9,257	1,696	291	133	1,031	3,223
District of Columbia	12,480	260	1,147	304	595	584	5,925	1,494	258	82	1,020	811
Florida	335,100	1,925	14,670	695	8,237	16,504	176,537	29,900	5,517	2,266	10,572	68,276
Georgia	220,603	2,360	2,428	2,524	6,084	10,105	109,365	24,087	3,506	2,176	7,934	50,035
Hawaii	22,238	233	587	680	590	1,367	11,608	2,399	629	192	1,734	2,219
Idaho[3,4,10,11]	26,319	44	611	231	636	1,121	14,563	2,901	454	62	819	4,878
Illinois[2,4,5,9,10,12,13,14]	263,565	2,743	4,754	501	7,456	15,290	135,701	34,126	2,716	1,872	9,681	48,724
Indiana	147,936	1,267	727	3,200	3,147	8,278	59,863	16,648	1,925	781	13,115	38,985
Iowa	71,089	1,326	1,972	423	1,767	2,743	35,080	11,399	1,176	479	4,213	10,510
Kansas	73,020	508	1,349	1,103	1,969	2,602	41,243	9,327	1,123	742	2,474	10,579
Kentucky	99,176	892	2,243	1,049	3,290	5,962	42,769	13,630	1,511	1,087	2,848	23,893
Louisiana	95,585	340	2,614	2,003	2,874	3,622	46,493	10,658	1,708	1,066	4,718	19,486
Maine	32,859	446	732	315	913	1,550	15,222	5,906	580	219	1,395	5,581
Maryland	113,093	3,425	2,219	1,485	3,534	6,056	57,718	11,021	2,305	1,136	4,720	19,473
Massachusetts	125,347	2,605	3,006	404	4,621	6,465	70,636	24,255	2,231	752	8,888	1,483
Michigan	186,065	4,036	1,120	1,248	6,643	11,568	86,154	20,699	2,137	561	13,034	38,865
Minnesota	111,069	2,138	2,285	2,187	2,155	4,610	53,585	17,473	1,120	665	12,124	12,728
Mississippi	68,215	995	2,014	653	1,952	2,495	32,613	8,214	1,106	846	3,066	14,259
Missouri	126,937	1,354	7,847	1,110	3,113	372	66,248	13,445	2,569	1,394	4,368	25,116
Montana[3,6,7,11]	18,896	174	479	156	528	171	10,200	2,319	454	365	673	3,377
Nebraska	45,426	591	1,088	885	1,037	1,924	22,103	6,425	778	545	1,443	8,608
Nevada[3,4,6,7,8]	32,702	188	956	1,402	1,009	1,619	20,695	4,145	882	345	74	1,387
New Hampshire	31,734	721	716	223	554	793	14,925	6,853	805	312	704	5,131
New Jersey[6]	223,279	1,369	5,186	3,464	4,773	10,135	110,929	33,966	3,645	1,486	12,608	35,719
New Mexico	46,222	846	108	618	1,284	3,824	22,201	6,002	787	255	3,295	7,003
New York	370,214	2,485	19,266	1,666	9,144	9,536	207,060	42,866	6,443	2,610	10,025	59,114
North Carolina	191,732	1,607	5,216	1,026	5,368	7,290	98,590	24,474	3,988	2,198	10,495	31,479
North Dakota	16,713	475	261	197	450	733	8,677	2,174	321	195	804	2,425
Ohio	242,806	2,389	13,944	1,537	5,220	13,301	106,000	19,254	3,655	1,025	22,437	54,045
Oklahoma	84,380	544	2,975	318	2,286	4,405	41,775	9,006	1,619	1,054	4,724	15,676
Oregon	59,771	428	2,792	446	1,510	4,485	26,410	9,190	967	144	2,187	11,212
Pennsylvania	252,179	2,531	7,179	1,502	5,120	12,015	123,147	32,168	4,480	1,842	7,467	54,729
Rhode Island	16,934	177	491	102	477	700	9,871	2,211	353	193	489	1,868
South Carolina	72,511	765	1,720	1,879	2,689	1,451	48,072	9,263	1,930	1,110	3,332	301
South Dakota	19,146	757	380	177	417	595	9,334	2,511	327	126	1,001	3,520
Tennessee	127,643	172	977	844	3,494	5,183	66,406	16,090	2,912	1,911	1,387	28,266
Texas	644,442	6,042	21,598	3,300	22,027	26,422	327,357	60,362	10,828	4,644	23,950	137,911
Utah	53,730	397	730	1,958	1,366	2,732	26,610	8,396	887	259	1,322	9,074
Vermont	18,422	140	492	230	482	883	8,403	4,197	417	213	924	2,042
Virginia	177,357	1,751	4,470	1,675	4,058	8,891	89,389	19,477	3,306	1,727	4,713	37,901
Washington	102,540	2,326	1,869	290	2,852	4,982	53,699	10,139	2,035	1,056	3,282	20,011
West Virginia[6]	39,267	757	1,104	369	1,145	773	20,101	3,699	736	324	1,672	8,588
Wisconsin	101,644	984	2,730	1,261	2,439	4,283	57,551	10,229	1,880	935	5,207	14,144
Wyoming	16,573	373	481	346	373	996	7,350	2,377	409	122	661	3,085
Bureau of Indian Education	12,373 [15]	—	—	244	558	1,128	5,308	1,654	317	182	1,014	1,968
DoD, overseas	—	—	—	—	—	—	—	—	—	—	—	—
DoD, domestic	—	—	—	—	—	—	—	—	—	—	—	—
Other jurisdictions												
American Samoa	—	—	—	—	—	—	—	—	—	—	—	—
Guam	3,923	18	251	128	92	215	2,291	606	87	37	36	162
Northern Marianas	891	9	76	8	34	64	409	164	23	1	24	79
Puerto Rico	54,381	400	1,710	1,883	1,401	2,159	30,986	81	728	1,004	4,865	9,164
U.S. Virgin Islands	2,208	7	76	30	97	87	1,129	280	60	29	68	345

—Not available.
[1]Includes imputations to correct for undercounts in states as designated in footnotes 2 through 14.
[2]Includes imputations for officials and administrators.
[3]Includes imputations for administrative support staff.
[4]Includes imputations for instruction coordinators.
[5]Includes imputations for principals and assistant principals.
[6]Includes imputations for library support staff.
[7]Includes imputations for school support staff.
[8]Includes imputations for instructional aides.
[9]Includes imputations for librarians.
[10]Includes imputations for student support staff.
[11]Includes imputations for other support services staff.
[12]Includes imputations for prekindergarten teachers.
[13]Includes imputations for kindergarten teachers.
[14]Includes imputations for secondary teachers.
[15]Excludes counts for officials and administrators and for administrative support staff, which were not reported.
NOTE: DoD = Department of Defense.
SOURCE: U.S. Department of Education, National Center for Education Statistics, Common Core of Data (CCD), "State Nonfiscal Survey of Public Elementary/Secondary Education," 2012–13. (This table was prepared October 2014.)

Table 213.40. Staff, teachers, and teachers as a percentage of staff in public elementary and secondary school systems, by state or jurisdiction: Selected years, fall 2000 through fall 2013

[In full-time equivalents]

State or jurisdiction	Teachers as a percent of staff						Fall 2011			Fall 2012			Fall 2013		
	Fall 2000	Fall 2005	Fall 2007	Fall 2008	Fall 2009	Fall 2010	All staff	Teachers	Teachers as a percent of staff	All staff	Teachers	Teachers as a percent of staff	All staff	Teachers	Teachers as a percent of staff
1	2	3	4	5	6	7	8	9	10	11	12	13	14	15	16
United States[1]	51.5	51.3	51.3	50.9	50.5	50.0	6,138,890	3,103,263	50.6	6,181,238	3,109,101	50.3	6,187,901	3,113,764	50.3
Alabama	53.7 [2]	55.7	45.2 [2]	50.1	50.5	51.9	92,289	47,723	51.7	96,485 [2]	51,877	53.8 [2]	91,753	47,162	51.4
Alaska	49.3 [2]	44.1 [2]	45.9 [2]	46.2 [2]	45.6 [2]	45.1 [2]	17,747 [2]	8,088	45.6 [2]	17,116 [2]	7,682	44.9 [2]	17,127 [2]	7,898	46.1 [2]
Arizona	49.3	51.3	51.6	51.8	51.8	51.8	98,712	50,800	51.5	103,228	48,866	47.3	103,343	48,359	46.8
Arkansas	50.6	46.7	48.2	52.1	50.1	47.5	72,650	33,983	46.8	71,279	34,131	47.9	70,387 [2]	34,933	49.6
California	54.1 [2]	53.4 [2]	52.3 [2]	51.5 [2]	51.9 [2]	49.2 [2]	547,188 [2]	268,689 [2]	49.1 [2]	544,875 [2]	266,255 [2]	48.9 [2]	541,762 [2]	259,506 [2]	47.9 [2]
Colorado	50.7	49.2	48.1	47.5	47.5	47.9	100,349	48,078	47.9	102,480	48,922	47.7	104,025	50,157	48.2
Connecticut	50.0	46.9	45.3	52.4	46.9	46.1	92,955	43,805	47.1	91,264	43,931	48.1	94,208	43,443	46.1
Delaware	59.2	51.7	52.8	56.2	50.9	54.2	15,449	8,587	55.6	17,554	9,257	52.7	18,253	9,388	51.4
District of Columbia	46.2	44.3 [2]	50.6	43.9	50.1	52.1	11,541	6,278	54.4	12,480	5,925	47.5	11,403	5,991	52.5
Florida	47.8	50.6	54.9	54.7	54.8	52.7	328,709	175,006	53.2	335,100	176,537	52.7	335,081	177,853	53.1
Georgia	49.2	49.6	49.7	49.7	49.4	49.5	224,207	111,133	49.6	220,603	109,365	49.6	218,097	109,441	50.2
Hawaii	59.5	53.3	52.6	52.3	52.9	52.5	22,065	11,458	51.9	22,238	11,608	52.2	22,438	11,781	52.5
Idaho	56.2	55.8	55.3	55.6	54.9	56.4	28,065	15,990	57.0	26,319 [2]	14,563	55.3 [2]	23,803 [2]	15,002	63.0 [2]
Illinois	51.1 [2]	53.2 [2]	63.7 [2]	61.4 [2]	62.4 [2]	61.6 [2]	213,578 [2]	131,777	61.7 [2]	263,565 [2]	135,701 [2]	51.5 [2]	266,645 [2]	136,355 [2]	51.1 [2]
Indiana	46.7	45.5	44.7	44.1	43.6	41.9 [2]	150,191	62,339	41.5	147,936	59,863	40.5	144,412	59,823	41.4
Iowa	51.1	50.9	50.3	49.7	49.4	49.8	69,901	34,658	49.6	71,089	35,080	49.3	71,551	35,397	49.5
Kansas	50.9	51.3	65.2	64.8	51.4	51.1	70,631	37,407	53.0	73,020	41,243	56.5	72,016	38,153	53.0
Kentucky	44.1	43.3	43.4	43.4	42.3	42.4	92,287	41,860	45.4	99,176	42,769	43.1	97,808	41,820	42.8
Louisiana	49.3	48.2	48.8	48.9	48.3	48.2	100,880	48,657	48.2	95,585	46,493	48.6	95,687	46,437	48.5
Maine	49.7	47.3	41.5	43.6	43.8	47.3	39,946 [2]	14,888	37.3 [2]	32,859	15,222	46.3	34,249	15,452	45.1
Maryland	54.3	51.0	50.8	50.4	50.7	50.6	113,351	57,589	50.8	113,093	57,718	51.0	115,066	58,611	50.9
Massachusetts	55.1	53.0 [2]	57.4	56.9	56.8	56.3	122,880	69,342	56.4	125,347	70,636	56.4	126,962	70,490	55.5
Michigan	46.1	47.9 [2]	46.0	45.5	45.3	45.8	188,428	86,997	46.2	186,065	86,154	46.3	184,175	85,786	46.6
Minnesota	51.6 [2]	48.9	48.9	48.6	48.4	48.3	109,119	52,832	48.4	111,069	53,585	48.2	112,735	54,413	48.3
Mississippi	47.9	46.5	47.2	46.3	46.8	47.5	67,850	32,007	47.2	68,215	32,613	47.8	68,252	32,292	47.3
Missouri	53.2	52.1	51.2	51.3	51.3	52.0	132,167	66,252	50.1	126,937	66,248	52.2	123,505	66,651	54.0
Montana	53.5 [2]	52.9 [2]	54.8 [2]	54.5 [2]	54.1 [2]	53.8 [2]	18,790 [2]	10,153	54.0 [2]	18,896 [2]	10,200	54.0 [2]	20,885 [2]	10,310	49.4 [2]
Nebraska	52.6	51.9	50.2	48.8	48.6	49.1	45,290	22,182	49.0	45,426	22,103	48.7	45,907	22,401	48.8
Nevada	58.6	67.2 [2]	65.8 [2]	65.6 [2]	65.5 [2]	65.4 [2]	32,533 [2]	21,132	65.0 [2]	32,702 [2]	20,695	63.3 [2]	34,003 [2]	21,921	64.5 [2]
New Hampshire	51.1	48.5	47.5	47.7	47.1	46.6	31,971	15,049	47.1	31,734	14,925	47.0	31,832	14,826	46.6
New Jersey	53.4	53.2 [2]	55.3	55.8 [2]	53.9 [2]	54.4 [2]	202,928 [2]	109,719	54.1 [2]	223,279 [2]	110,929	49.7 [2]	231,012 [2]	114,581	49.6 [2]
New Mexico	46.8	45.9	47.8	47.7	47.8	48.2	45,907	21,957	47.8	46,222	22,201	48.0	46,380	22,239	47.9
New York	49.7	58.6	56.6	50.9	50.9	51.1	406,625	209,527	51.5	370,214	207,060	55.9	359,255	206,693	57.5
North Carolina	51.5	52.5	52.4	52.7	52.4 [2]	51.0	188,553	97,308	51.6	191,732	98,590	51.4	192,336	99,327	51.6
North Dakota	53.9	52.9	52.4	52.3	52.3	51.8	16,401	8,525	52.0	16,713	8,677	51.9	17,036	8,805	51.7
Ohio	53.1	49.4	45.1	46.1	45.6	45.3	243,586	107,972	44.3	242,806	106,000	43.7	248,469	106,010	42.7
Oklahoma	55.0	51.1	53.9	53.2	50.3	50.2	82,719	41,349	50.0	84,380	41,775	49.5	85,152	41,983	49.3
Oregon	50.0	47.0	46.4	46.3	45.7	44.2	60,715	26,791	44.1	59,771	26,410	44.2	59,768	26,733	44.7
Pennsylvania	52.2	50.9	53.1	51.5	51.6	48.7	254,297	124,646	49.0	252,179	123,147	48.8	243,021 [2]	121,330	49.9 [2]
Rhode Island	60.0	58.4 [2]	64.2	60.8	60.4	60.2	18,743	11,414	60.9	16,934	9,871	58.3	17,312	9,824	56.7
South Carolina	65.7 [2]	70.9 [2]	71.7	71.6	69.7	69.0	69,272	46,782	67.5	72,511	48,072	66.3	72,401	48,151	66.5
South Dakota	52.0	48.0	55.3	50.3	50.1	48.7	19,059	9,247	48.5	19,146	9,334	48.8	19,205	9,510	49.5
Tennessee	52.1	52.2	51.1	51.2	51.2	51.9	127,781	66,382	51.9	127,643	66,406	52.0	125,506	65,847	52.5
Texas	50.6	50.5	50.6	50.5	50.3	50.3	640,166	324,282	50.7	644,442	327,357	50.8	658,340	334,580	50.8
Utah	54.1	50.2	50.2	48.2	49.4	49.1	51,994	25,970	49.9	53,730	26,610	49.5	54,945	27,247	49.6
Vermont	47.3	46.5	45.6	45.3	45.2	45.3	18,385	8,364	45.5	18,422	8,403	45.6	18,300	8,375	45.8
Virginia	54.1 [2]	44.4	35.2	35.1	34.8	35.3	180,086	90,832	50.4	177,357	89,389	50.4	178,202	90,098	50.6
Washington	52.3	47.0	52.0	52.0	51.4	52.0	101,914	53,119	52.1	102,540	53,699	52.4	105,365	54,867	52.1
West Virginia	54.3	52.3	53.0 [2]	52.4	51.8 [2]	51.8 [2]	39,380 [2]	20,247	51.4 [2]	39,267 [2]	20,101	51.2 [2]	39,121 [2]	19,978	51.1 [2]
Wisconsin	56.3	57.0	56.1	55.7	55.5	55.5	101,533	56,245	55.4	101,644	57,551	56.6	102,476	57,980	56.6
Wyoming	48.6	46.2	44.7	44.2	43.5	43.4	17,128	7,847	45.8	16,573	7,350	44.3	16,931	7,555	44.6
Bureau of Indian Education	—	—	—	—	—	—	—	—	—	12,373	5,308	42.9 [3]	—	—	—
DoD, overseas	66.0	62.9	66.2	60.5	—	—	—	—	—	—	—	—	—	—	—
DoD, domestic	59.2	55.4	56.2	55.8	—	—	—	—	—	—	—	—	—	—	—
Other jurisdictions															
American Samoa	50.0	68.4	—	—	—	—	—	—	—	—	—	—	—	—	—
Guam	51.5	52.2	—	—	—	54.5	3,923	2,291	58.4	3,923	2,291	58.4	3,923	2,291	58.4
Northern Marianas	50.2	49.8	49.5	49.3	47.8	50.0	1,042	496	47.6	891	409	45.9	876	417	47.6
Puerto Rico	54.4	56.0	56.8	56.2	61.9	61.6	55,797	33,079	59.3	54,381	30,986	57.0	54,430	33,412	61.4
U.S. Virgin Islands	52.1	53.8	48.4	53.8	49.9	49.9	2,391	1,217	50.9	2,208	1,129	51.1	2,170	1,082	49.9

—Not available.
[1]U.S. totals include imputations for underreporting and nonreporting states.
[2]Includes imputations to correct for underreporting.
[3]Total staff count excludes officials and administrators and administrative support staff, so computed percentage of teachers may be overstated.

NOTE: DoD = Department of Defense.
SOURCE: U.S. Department of Education, National Center for Education Statistics, Common Core of Data (CCD), "State Nonfiscal Survey of Public Elementary/Secondary Education," 2000–01 through 2013–14. (This table was prepared August 2015.)

Table 213.50. Staff, enrollment, and pupil/staff ratios in public elementary and secondary school systems, by state or jurisdiction: Selected years, fall 2000 through fall 2013

State or jurisdiction	Pupil/staff ratio						Fall 2011			Fall 2012			Fall 2013		
	Fall 2000	Fall 2005	Fall 2007	Fall 2008	Fall 2009	Fall 2010	Staff	Enrollment	Pupil/ staff ratio	Staff	Enrollment	Pupil/ staff ratio	Staff	Enrollment	Pupil/ staff ratio
1	2	3	4	5	6	7	8	9	10	11	12	13	14	15	16
United States[1]....	8.3	8.0	7.9	7.8	7.8	8.0	6,138,890	49,521,669	8.1	6,181,238	49,771,118	8.1	6,187,901	50,044,522	8.1
Alabama	8.2 [2]	7.1	6.7 [2]	7.8	8.0	7.9	92,289	744,621	8.1	96,485 [2]	744,637	7.7 [2]	91,753	746,204	8.1
Alaska....................	8.3 [2]	7.4 [2]	7.9 [2]	7.6 [2]	7.4 [2]	7.3 [2]	17,747 [2]	131,167	7.4 [2]	17,116 [2]	131,489	7.7 [2]	17,127 [2]	130,944	7.6 [2]
Arizona..................	9.7	10.9	10.4	10.3	10.7	11.1	98,712	1,080,319	10.9	103,228	1,089,384	10.6	103,343	1,102,445	10.7
Arkansas.................	7.1	6.7	6.8	6.7	6.5	6.7	72,650	483,114	6.6	71,279	486,157	6.8	70,387	489,979	7.0
California	11.1 [2]	11.1 [2]	10.9 [2]	10.7 [2]	10.3 [2]	11.9 [2]	547,188 [2]	6,287,834	11.5 [2]	544,875 [2]	6,299,451	11.6 [2]	541,762 [2]	6,312,623	11.7 [2]
Colorado	8.7	8.4	8.1	8.0	8.1	8.3	100,349	854,265	8.5	102,480	863,561	8.4	104,025	876,999	8.4
Connecticut..............	6.8	6.8	6.6	6.1	6.1	6.0	92,955	554,437	6.0	91,264	550,954	6.0	94,208	546,200	5.8
Delaware.................	9.1	7.8	7.9	8.5	7.5	7.9	15,449	128,946	8.3	17,554	129,026	7.4	18,253	131,687	7.2
District of Columbia	6.4	6.2 [2]	6.3	5.7	5.9	6.3	11,541	73,911	6.4	12,480	76,140	6.1	11,403	78,153	6.9
Florida....................	8.8	8.5	7.7	7.7	7.9	7.9	328,709	2,668,156	8.1	335,100	2,692,162	8.0	335,081	2,720,744	8.1
Georgia...................	7.8	7.3	7.0	6.9	7.1	7.4	224,207	1,685,016	7.5	220,603	1,703,332	7.7	218,097	1,723,909	7.9
Hawaii....................	10.0	8.7	8.3	8.3	8.3	8.3	22,065	182,706	8.3	22,238	184,760	8.3	22,438	186,825	8.3
Idaho.....................	10.1	10.1	10.0	10.1	10.0	9.9	28,065	279,873	10.0	26,319 [2]	284,834	10.8 [2]	23,803 [2]	296,476	12.5 [2]
Illinois...................	8.2 [2]	8.4 [2]	9.9 [2]	9.6 [2]	9.5 [2]	9.7 [2]	213,578 [2]	2,083,097	9.8 [2]	263,565 [2]	2,072,880	7.9 [2]	266,645 [2]	2,066,990	7.8 [2]
Indiana...................	7.8	7.8	7.5	7.4	7.3	7.5 [2]	150,191	1,040,765	6.9	147,936	1,041,369	7.0	144,412	1,047,385	7.3
Iowa	7.3	7.0	6.8	6.7	6.8	7.1	69,901	495,870	7.1	71,089	499,825	7.0	71,551	502,964	7.0
Kansas...................	7.3	7.1	8.6	8.5	7.0	7.1	70,631	486,108	6.9	73,020	489,043	6.7	72,016	496,440	6.9
Kentucky.................	7.4	6.9	6.6 [2]	6.7	6.9	6.8	92,287	681,987	7.4	99,176	685,167	6.9	97,808	677,389	6.9
Louisiana................	7.3	7.1	6.8	6.8	6.7	6.9	100,880	703,390	7.0	95,585	710,903	7.4	95,687	711,491	7.4
Maine....................	6.2	5.5	4.9	5.3	5.1	5.8	39,946 [2]	188,969	4.7 [2]	32,859	185,739	5.7	34,249	183,995	5.4
Maryland.................	8.8	7.7	7.2	7.2	7.4	7.4	113,351	854,086	7.5	113,093	859,638	7.6	115,066	866,169	7.5
Massachusetts...........	8.0	7.0 [2]	7.8	7.8	7.8	7.8	122,880	953,369	7.8	125,347	954,773	7.6	126,962	955,739	7.5
Michigan.................	8.2 [2]	8.5 [2]	8.1	8.0	8.1	8.2	188,428	1,573,537	8.4	186,065	1,555,370	8.4	184,175	1,548,841	8.4
Minnesota	8.2 [2]	8.0	7.7	7.7	7.7	7.7	109,119	839,738	7.7	111,069	845,404	7.6	112,735	850,973	7.5
Mississippi	7.7	7.3	6.9	6.8	7.0	7.2	67,850	490,619	7.2	68,215	493,650	7.2	68,252	492,586	7.2
Missouri	7.5	7.1	6.9	6.9	7.0	7.2	132,167	916,584	6.9	126,937	917,900	7.2	123,505	918,288	7.4
Montana	8.0 [2]	7.4 [2]	7.4 [2]	7.4 [2]	7.3 [2]	7.4 [2]	18,790 [2]	142,349	7.6 [2]	18,896 [2]	142,908	7.6 [2]	20,885 [2]	144,129	6.9 [2]
Nebraska	7.2	7.0	6.7	6.5	6.4	6.6	45,290	301,296	6.7	45,426	303,505	6.7	45,907	307,677	6.7
Nevada	10.9	12.7 [2]	12.1 [2]	12.9 [2]	12.7 [2]	13.1 [2]	32,533 [2]	439,634	13.5 [2]	32,702 [2]	445,707	13.6 [2]	34,003 [2]	451,831	13.3 [2]
New Hampshire	7.4	6.4	6.2	6.0	6.0	5.9	31,971	191,900	6.0	31,734	188,974	6.0	31,832	186,310	5.9
New Jersey	7.1	6.6 [2]	6.9 [2]	6.7 [2]	6.5 [2]	6.9 [2]	202,928 [2]	1,356,431	6.7 [2]	223,279 [2]	1,372,203	6.1 [2]	231,012 [2]	1,370,295	5.9 [2]
New Mexico	7.1	6.8	7.0	6.9	7.0	7.3	45,907	337,225	7.3	46,222	338,220	7.3	46,380	339,244	7.3
New York.................	6.9	7.5	7.4	6.4	6.6	6.6	406,625	2,704,718	6.7	370,214	2,710,703	7.3	359,255	2,732,770	7.6
North Carolina	8.0	7.8	7.3	7.2	7.4 [2]	7.7	188,553	1,507,864	8.0	191,732	1,518,465	7.9	192,336	1,530,857	8.0
North Dakota	7.2	6.5	6.2	6.1	5.9	5.9	16,401	97,646	6.0	16,713	101,111	6.0	17,036	103,947	6.1
Ohio	8.2	7.7	7.5	7.4	7.2	7.3	243,586	1,740,030	7.1	242,806	1,729,916	7.1	248,469	1,724,111	6.9
Oklahoma	8.3	7.8	7.4	7.4	7.7	8.0	82,719	666,120	8.1	84,380	673,483	8.0	85,152	681,848	8.0
Oregon...................	9.7	9.2	8.8	8.8	9.3	9.0	60,715	568,208	9.4	59,771	587,564	9.8	59,768	593,000	9.9
Pennsylvania.............	8.1	7.6	7.1	7.0	7.0	6.7	254,297	1,771,395	7.0	252,179	1,763,677	7.0	243,021 [2]	1,755,236	7.2 [2]
Rhode Island	8.9	6.3 [2]	8.4	7.8	7.7	7.7	18,743	142,854	7.6	16,934	142,481	8.4	17,312	142,008	8.2
South Carolina	9.8 [2]	10.3 [2]	10.8	10.3	10.7	11.1	69,272	727,186	10.5	72,511	735,998	10.2	72,401	745,657	10.3
South Dakota	7.1	6.4	7.1	6.9	6.6	6.5	19,059	128,016	6.7	19,146	130,471	6.8	19,205	130,890	6.8
Tennessee	8.3 [2]	8.4	7.6	7.7	7.6	7.7	127,781	999,693	7.8	127,643	993,496	7.8	125,506	993,556	7.9
Texas	7.5	7.6	7.4	7.3	7.3	7.4	640,166	5,000,470	7.8	644,442	5,077,659	7.9	658,340	5,153,702	7.8
Utah	11.8	11.1	11.9	11.4	11.0	11.2	51,994	598,832	11.5	53,730	613,279	11.4	54,945	625,461	11.4
Vermont	5.7	5.1	4.9	4.8	4.7	5.2	18,385	89,908	4.9	18,422	89,624	4.9	18,300	88,690	4.8
Virginia..................	7.1 [2]	5.2	6.0	6.1	6.1	6.2	180,086	1,257,883	7.0	177,357	1,265,419	7.1	178,202	1,273,825	7.1
Washington	10.3	9.1	9.9	9.9	10.0	10.1	101,914	1,045,453	10.3	102,540	1,051,694	10.3	105,365	1,058,936	10.1
West Virginia.............	7.4	7.4	7.4 [2]	7.3	7.2 [2]	7.2 [2]	39,380 [2]	282,870	7.2 [2]	39,267 [2]	283,044	7.2 [2]	39,121 [2]	280,958	7.2 [2]
Wisconsin	8.2	8.3	8.3	8.2	8.3	8.4	101,533	871,105	8.6	101,644	872,436	8.6	102,476	874,414	8.5
Wyoming.................	6.4	5.8	5.6	5.5	5.4	5.4	17,128	90,099	5.3	16,573	91,533	5.5	16,931	92,732	5.5
Bureau of Indian Education..............	—	—	—	—	—	—	—	—	—	12,373 [3]	—	—	—	—	—
DoD, overseas	9.5	6.9	9.1	7.5	—	—	—	—	—	—	—	—	—	—	—
DoD, domestic	8.4	7.7	6.9	7.3	—	—	—	—	—	—	—	—	—	—	—
Other jurisdictions															
American Samoa	9.6	11.4	—	—	—	—	—	—	—	—	—	—	—	—	—
Guam	8.5	9.0	—	—	—	9.3	3,923	31,243	8.0	3,923	31,186	7.9	3,923	33,414	8.5
Northern Marianas..	9.6	9.5	10.2	10.5	9.5	9.1	1,042	11,011	10.6	891	10,646	11.9	876	10,638	12.1
Puerto Rico............	8.9	7.5	7.3	7.2	7.8	8.0	55,797	452,740	8.1	54,381	434,609	8.0	54,430	423,934	7.8
U.S. Virgin Islands...	6.7	6.3	5.1	6.4	5.4	5.3	2,391	15,711	6.6	2,208	15,192	6.9	2,170	14,953	6.9

—Not available.
[1]U.S. totals include imputations for underreporting and nonreporting states.
[2]Includes imputations to correct for underreporting.
[3]Excludes counts for officials and administrators and for administrative support staff, which were not reported.

NOTE: Staff reported in full-time equivalents. DoD = Department of Defense.
SOURCE: U.S. Department of Education, National Center for Education Statistics, Common Core of Data (CCD), "State Nonfiscal Survey of Public Elementary/Secondary Education," 2000–01 through 2013–14. (This table was prepared August 2015.)

Table 214.10. Number of public school districts and public and private elementary and secondary schools: Selected years, 1869–70 through 2013–14

School year	Regular public school districts[1]	Total, all public and private schools	Total, all public schools[4]	Total, schools with reported grade spans[5]	Schools with elementary grades — Total	Schools with elementary grades — One-teacher	Schools with secondary grades	Total, all private schools	Schools with elementary grades	Schools with secondary grades
1	2	3	4	5	6	7	8	9	10	11
1869–70	—	—	116,312	—	—	—	—	—	—	—
1879–80	—	—	178,122	—	—	—	—	—	—	—
1889–90	—	—	224,526	—	—	—	—	—	—	—
1899–1900	—	—	248,279	—	—	—	—	—	—	—
1909–10	—	—	265,474	—	—	212,448	—	—	—	—
1919–20	—	—	271,319	—	—	187,948	—	—	—	—
1929–30	—	—	248,117	—	238,306	148,712	23,930	—	9,275 [6]	3,258 [6]
1939–40	117,108 [7]	—	226,762	—	—	113,600	—	—	11,306 [6]	3,568 [6]
1949–50	83,718 [7]	—	—	—	128,225	59,652	24,542	—	10,375 [6]	3,331 [6]
1951–52	71,094 [7]	—	—	—	123,763	50,742	23,746	—	10,666 [6]	3,322 [6]
1959–60	40,520 [7]	—	—	—	91,853	20,213	25,784	—	13,574 [6]	4,061 [6]
1961–62	35,676 [7]	125,634	107,260	—	81,910	13,333	25,350	18,374	14,762 [6]	4,129 [6]
1963–64	31,705 [7]	—	104,015	—	77,584	9,895	26,431	—	—	4,451 [6]
1965–66	26,983 [7]	117,662	99,813	—	73,216	6,491	26,597	17,849 [6]	15,340 [6]	4,606 [6]
1967–68	22,010 [7]	—	—	94,197	70,879	4,146	27,011	—	—	—
1970–71	17,995 [7]	—	—	89,372	65,800	1,815	25,352	—	14,372 [6]	3,770 [6]
1973–74	16,730 [7]	—	—	88,655	65,070	1,365	25,906	—	—	—
1975–76	16,376 [7]	—	88,597	87,034	63,242	1,166	25,330	—	—	—
1976–77	16,271 [7]	—	—	86,501	62,644	1,111	25,378	19,910 [6]	16,385 [6]	5,904 [6]
1978–79	16,014 [7]	—	—	84,816	61,982	1,056	24,504	19,489 [6]	16,097 [6]	5,766 [6]
1979–80	15,944 [7]	—	87,004	—	—	—	—	—	—	—
1980–81	15,912 [7]	106,746	85,982	83,688	61,069	921	24,362	20,764 [6]	16,792 [6]	5,678 [6]
1982–83	15,824 [7]	—	84,740	82,039	59,656	798	23,988	—	—	—
1983–84	15,747 [7]	111,872	84,178	81,418	59,082	838	23,947	27,694	20,872	7,862
1984–85	—	—	84,007	81,147	58,827	825	23,916	—	—	—
1985–86	—	—	—	—	—	—	—	25,616	20,252	7,387
1986–87	15,713	—	83,421	82,316	60,811	763	23,481	—	—	—
1987–88	15,577	110,055	83,248	81,416	59,754	729	23,841	26,807	22,959	8,418
1988–89	15,376	—	83,165	81,579	60,176	583	23,638	—	—	—
1989–90	15,367	110,137	83,425	81,880	60,699	630	23,461	26,712	24,221	10,197
1990–91	15,358	109,228	84,538	82,475	61,340	617	23,460	24,690	22,223	8,989
1991–92	15,173	110,576	84,578	82,506	61,739	569	23,248	25,998	23,523	9,282
1992–93	15,025	—	84,497	82,896	62,225	430	23,220	—	—	—
1993–94	14,881	111,486	85,393	83,431	62,726	442	23,379	26,093	23,543	10,555
1994–95	14,772	—	86,221	84,476	63,572	458	23,668	—	—	—
1995–96	14,766	121,519	87,125	84,958	63,961	474	23,793	34,394	32,401	10,942
1996–97	14,841	—	88,223	86,092	64,785	487	24,287	—	—	—
1997–98	14,805	123,403	89,508	87,541	65,859	476	24,802	33,895	31,408	10,779
1998–99	14,891	—	90,874	89,259	67,183	463	25,797	—	—	—
1999–2000	14,928	125,007	92,012	90,538	68,173	423	26,407	32,995	30,457	10,693
2000–01	14,859	—	93,273	91,691	69,697	411	27,090	—	—	—
2001–02	14,559	130,007	94,112	92,696	70,516	408	27,468	35,895	33,191	11,846
2002–03	14,465	—	95,615	93,869	71,270	366	28,151	—	—	—
2003–04	14,383	130,407	95,726	93,977	71,195	376	28,219	34,681	31,988	11,188
2004–05	14,205	—	96,513	95,001	71,556	338	29,017	—	—	—
2005–06	14,166	132,436	97,382	95,731	71,733	326	29,705	35,054	32,127	12,184
2006–07	13,856	—	98,793	96,362	72,442	313	29,904	—	—	—
2007–08	13,838	132,656	98,916	97,654	73,011	288	30,542	33,740	30,808	11,870
2008–09	13,809	—	98,706	97,119	72,771	237	29,971	—	—	—
2009–10	13,625	132,183	98,817	97,521	72,870	217	30,381	33,366	30,590	11,491
2010–11	13,588	—	98,817	97,767	73,323	224	30,681	—	—	—
2011–12	13,567	129,189	98,328	97,357	73,000	205	30,668	30,861	28,184	11,165
2012–13	13,515	—	98,454	97,369	73,089	196	30,651	—	—	—
2013–14	13,491	131,890	98,271	97,292	73,239	193	30,258	33,619	30,919	11,110

—Not available.

[1]Regular districts exclude regional education service agencies and supervisory union administrative centers, state-operated agencies, federally operated agencies, and other types of local education agencies, such as independent charter schools.
[2]Schools with both elementary and secondary grades are included under elementary schools and also under secondary schools.
[3]Data for most years prior to 1976–77 are partly estimated. Prior to 1995–96, excludes schools with highest grade of kindergarten.
[4]Includes schools not classified by grade span, which are not shown separately.
[5]Includes elementary, secondary, and combined elementary/secondary schools.
[6]These data cannot be compared directly with the data for years after 1980–81.
[7]Because of expanded survey coverage, data are not directly comparable with figures after 1983–84.

SOURCE: U.S. Department of Education, National Center for Education Statistics, *Annual Report of the Commissioner of Education*, 1870 through 1910; *Biennial Survey of Education in the United States*, 1919–20 through 1949–50; *Statistics of State School Systems*, 1951–52 through 1967–68; *Statistics of Public Elementary and Secondary School Systems*, 1970–71 through 1980–81; *Statistics of Public and Nonpublic Elementary and Secondary Day Schools, 1968–69*; *Statistics of Nonpublic Elementary and Secondary Schools*, 1970–71; *Private Schools in American Education*; Schools and Staffing Survey (SASS), "Private School Questionnaire," 1987–88 and 1990–91; Private School Universe Survey (PSS), 1989–90 through 2013–14; and Common Core of Data (CCD), "Local Education Agency Universe Survey" and "Public Elementary/Secondary School Universe Survey," 1982–83 through 2013–14. (This table was prepared January 2016.)

Table 214.20. Number and percentage distribution of regular public school districts and students, by enrollment size of district: Selected years, 1979–80 through 2013–14

Year	Total	25,000 or more	10,000 to 24,999	5,000 to 9,999	2,500 to 4,999	1,000 to 2,499	600 to 999	300 to 599	1 to 299	Size not reported
1	2	3	4	5	6	7	8	9	10	11
Number of districts										
1979–80	15,944	181	478	1,106	2,039	3,475	1,841	2,298	4,223	303
1989–90	15,367	179	479	913	1,937	3,547	1,801	2,283	3,910	318
1999–2000	14,928	238	579	1,036	2,068	3,457	1,814	2,081	3,298	357
2001–02	14,559	243	573	1,067	2,031	3,429	1,744	2,015	3,127	330
2002–03	14,465	248	587	1,062	2,033	3,411	1,745	1,987	3,117	275
2003–04	14,383	256	594	1,058	2,031	3,421	1,728	1,981	2,994	320
2004–05	14,205	264	589	1,056	2,018	3,391	1,739	1,931	2,881	336
2005–06	14,166	269	594	1,066	2,015	3,335	1,768	1,895	2,857	367
2006–07	13,856	275	598	1,066	2,006	3,334	1,730	1,898	2,685	264
2007–08	13,838	281	589	1,062	2,006	3,292	1,753	1,890	2,692	273
2008–09	13,809	280	594	1,049	1,995	3,272	1,766	1,886	2,721	246
2009–10	13,625	284	598	1,044	1,985	3,242	1,750	1,891	2,707	124
2010–11	13,588	282	600	1,052	1,975	3,224	1,738	1,887	2,687	143
2011–12	13,567	286	592	1,044	1,952	3,222	1,755	1,911	2,676	129
2012–13	13,515	290	588	1,048	1,924	3,227	1,751	1,908	2,678	101
2013–14	13,491	286	596	1,046	1,920	3,186	1,791	1,894	2,668	104
Percentage distribution of districts										
1979–80	100.0	1.1	3.0	6.9	12.8	21.8	11.5	14.4	26.5	1.9
1989–90	100.0	1.2	3.1	5.9	12.6	23.1	11.7	14.9	25.4	2.1
1999–2000	100.0	1.6	3.9	6.9	13.9	23.2	12.2	13.9	22.1	2.4
2001–02	100.0	1.7	3.9	7.3	14.0	23.6	12.0	13.8	21.5	2.3
2002–03	100.0	1.7	4.1	7.3	14.1	23.6	12.1	13.7	21.5	1.9
2003–04	100.0	1.8	4.1	7.4	14.1	23.8	12.0	13.8	20.8	2.2
2004–05	100.0	1.9	4.1	7.4	14.2	23.9	12.2	13.6	20.3	2.4
2005–06	100.0	1.9	4.2	7.5	14.2	23.5	12.5	13.4	20.2	2.6
2006–07	100.0	2.0	4.3	7.7	14.5	24.1	12.5	13.7	19.4	1.9
2007–08	100.0	2.0	4.3	7.7	14.5	23.8	12.7	13.7	19.5	2.0
2008–09	100.0	2.0	4.3	7.6	14.4	23.7	12.8	13.7	19.7	1.8
2009–10	100.0	2.1	4.4	7.7	14.6	23.8	12.8	13.9	19.9	0.9
2010–11	100.0	2.1	4.4	7.7	14.5	23.7	12.8	13.9	19.8	1.1
2011–12	100.0	2.1	4.4	7.7	14.4	23.7	12.9	14.1	19.7	1.0
2012–13	100.0	2.1	4.4	7.8	14.2	23.9	13.0	14.1	19.8	0.7
2013–14	100.0	2.1	4.4	7.8	14.2	23.6	13.3	14.0	19.8	0.8
Number of students										
1979–80	41,882,000	11,415,000	7,004,000	7,713,000	7,076,000	5,698,000	1,450,000	1,005,000	521,000	†
1989–90	40,069,756	11,209,889	7,107,362	6,347,103	6,731,334	5,763,282	1,402,623	997,434	510,729	†
1999–2000	46,318,635	14,886,636	8,656,672	7,120,704	7,244,407	5,620,962	1,426,280	911,127	451,847	†
2001–02	46,906,607	15,356,867	8,756,777	7,393,237	7,129,358	5,576,508	1,375,571	885,061	433,228	†
2002–03	47,379,395	15,690,805	8,957,891	7,348,643	7,150,205	5,547,189	1,375,070	874,163	435,429	†
2003–04	47,685,982	15,939,776	9,039,697	7,342,745	7,160,367	5,558,125	1,355,563	867,599	422,110	†
2004–05	47,800,967	16,182,672	8,980,096	7,346,960	7,134,861	5,533,156	1,368,546	851,455	403,221	†
2005–06	48,013,931	16,376,213	9,055,547	7,394,010	7,114,942	5,442,588	1,391,314	835,430	403,887	†
2006–07	48,105,666	16,496,573	9,083,944	7,395,889	7,092,532	5,433,770	1,363,287	840,032	399,639	†
2007–08	48,096,140	16,669,611	8,946,432	7,408,553	7,103,274	5,358,492	1,381,342	834,295	394,141	†
2008–09	48,033,126	16,634,807	9,043,665	7,324,565	7,079,061	5,329,406	1,392,110	832,262	397,250	†
2009–10	48,021,335	16,788,789	9,053,144	7,265,111	7,034,640	5,266,945	1,381,415	835,035	396,256	†
2010–11	48,059,830	16,803,247	9,150,912	7,318,413	6,973,720	5,215,389	1,372,759	833,764	391,626	†
2011–12	47,973,834	16,934,369	9,031,528	7,266,770	6,907,658	5,218,533	1,381,289	842,134	391,553	†
2012–13	48,033,002	17,101,040	8,967,874	7,300,285	6,817,724	5,232,487	1,377,490	841,150	394,952	†
2013–14	48,124,386	17,125,416	9,128,194	7,270,070	6,792,172	5,169,748	1,412,987	832,091	393,708	†
Percentage distribution of students										
1979–80	100.0	27.3	16.7	18.4	16.9	13.6	3.5	2.4	1.2	†
1989–90	100.0	28.0	17.7	15.8	16.8	14.4	3.5	2.5	1.3	†
1999–2000	100.0	32.1	18.7	15.4	15.6	12.1	3.1	2.0	1.0	†
2001–02	100.0	32.7	18.7	15.8	15.2	11.9	2.9	1.9	0.9	†
2002–03	100.0	33.1	18.9	15.5	15.1	11.7	2.9	1.8	0.9	†
2003–04	100.0	33.4	19.0	15.4	15.0	11.7	2.8	1.8	0.9	†
2004–05	100.0	33.9	18.8	15.4	14.9	11.6	2.9	1.8	0.8	†
2005–06	100.0	34.1	18.9	15.4	14.8	11.3	2.9	1.7	0.8	†
2006–07	100.0	34.3	18.9	15.4	14.7	11.3	2.8	1.7	0.8	†
2007–08	100.0	34.7	18.6	15.4	14.8	11.1	2.9	1.7	0.8	†
2008–09	100.0	34.6	18.8	15.2	14.7	11.1	2.9	1.7	0.8	†
2009–10	100.0	35.0	18.9	15.1	14.6	11.0	2.9	1.7	0.8	†
2010–11	100.0	35.0	19.0	15.2	14.5	10.9	2.9	1.7	0.8	†
2011–12	100.0	35.3	18.8	15.1	14.4	10.9	2.9	1.8	0.8	†
2012–13	100.0	35.6	18.7	15.2	14.2	10.9	2.9	1.8	0.8	†
2013–14	100.0	35.6	19.0	15.1	14.1	10.7	2.9	1.7	0.8	†

†Not applicable.
NOTE: Size not reported (column 11) includes school districts reporting enrollment of zero and school districts whose enrollment counts were suppressed because they failed data quality edits. Regular districts exclude regional education service agencies and supervisory union administrative centers, state-operated agencies, federally operated agencies, and other types of local education agencies, such as independent charter schools. Enrollment totals differ from other tables because this table represents data reported by regular school districts rather than states or schools. Detail may not sum to totals because of rounding.
SOURCE: U.S. Department of Education, National Center for Education Statistics, Common Core of Data (CCD), "Local Education Agency Universe Survey," 1979–80 through 2013–14. (This table was prepared September 2015.)

Table 214.30. Number of public elementary and secondary education agencies, by type of agency and state or jurisdiction: 2012–13 and 2013–14

State or jurisdiction	Total agencies		Regular school districts[1]		Regional education service agencies and supervisory union administrative centers		State-operated agencies		Federally operated agencies		Independent charter schools and other agencies	
	2012–13	2013–14	2012–13	2013–14	2012–13	2013–14	2012–13	2013–14	2012–13	2013–14	2012–13	2013–14
1	2	3	4	5	6	7	8	9	10	11	12	13
United States	18,087	18,194	13,515	13,491	1,540	1,522	265	255	3	3	2,764	2,923
Alabama	173	177	135	137	0	0	38	40	0	0	0	0
Alaska...............................	54	54	53	53	0	0	1	1	0	0	0	0
Arizona	665	684	223	223	19	19	10	10	0	0	413	432
Arkansas...........................	288	288	238	237	15	15	5	5	0	0	30	31
California	1,181	1,172	948	944	198	197	4	4	0	0	31	27
Colorado	259	261	178	178	79	81	1	1	0	0	1	1
Connecticut.......................	200	201	169	169	6	6	7	7	0	0	18	19
Delaware...........................	44	43	19	19	1	1	2	2	0	0	22	21
District of Columbia	60	62	1	1	0	0	2	1	0	0	57	60
Florida...............................	76	76	67	67	0	0	3	3	0	0	6	6
Georgia.............................	218	218	180	180	16	16	7	7	0	0	15	15
Hawaii	1	1	1	1	0	0	0	0	0	0	0	0
Idaho.................................	149	152	116	115	0	2	3	3	0	0	30	32
Illinois...............................	1,070	1,068	863	861	197	195	5	5	0	0	5	7
Indiana..............................	407	408	297	295	32	31	4	4	0	0	74	78
Iowa..................................	357	355	348	346	9	9	0	0	0	0	0	0
Kansas..............................	321	321	309	309	0	0	12	12	0	0	0	0
Kentucky	194	194	174	174	18	18	2	2	0	0	0	0
Louisiana	131	133	70	70	0	0	6	6	0	0	55	57
Maine................................	255	254	231	237	18	8	4	4	0	0	2	5
Maryland............................	25	25	24	24	0	0	1	1	0	0	0	0
Massachusetts...................	404	409	237	238	89	89	1	1	0	0	77	81
Michigan	890	907	550	548	56	56	6	6	0	0	278	297
Minnesota	553	548	336	332	66	63	3	3	0	0	148	150
Mississippi	162	162	151	151	0	0	11	11	0	0	0	0
Missouri	567	568	521	521	0	0	5	5	0	0	41	42
Montana............................	496	493	410	407	77	77	4	4	0	0	5	5
Nebraska...........................	286	287	249	249	32	33	5	5	0	0	0	0
Nevada	18	19	17	18	0	0	0	0	0	0	1	1
New Hampshire	288	292	178	179	93	95	0	0	0	0	17	18
New Jersey	691	680	601	590	1	0	3	3	0	0	86	87
New Mexico	146	150	89	89	0	0	6	6	0	0	51	55
New York[2]	950	970	696	694	37	37	6	6	0	0	211	233
North Carolina	244	265	115	115	0	0	4	4	2	2	123	144
North Dakota	223	222	177	176	43	43	3	3	0	0	0	0
Ohio..................................	1,093	1,116	616	618	105	104	4	4	0	0	368	390
Oklahoma	584	598	521	517	0	0	3	3	0	0	60	78
Oregon..............................	220	220	180	180	19	19	4	4	0	0	17	17
Pennsylvania.....................	799	789	500	500	103	99	19	8	0	0	177	182
Rhode Island	54	61	32	35	4	4	5	6	0	0	13	16
South Carolina..................	103	102	84	84	12	11	4	4	0	0	3	3
South Dakota.....................	170	170	151	151	15	15	4	4	0	0	0	0
Tennessee	141	140	141	140	0	0	0	0	0	0	0	0
Texas	1,254	1,252	1,029	1,027	20	20	3	3	0	0	202	202
Utah..................................	132	138	41	41	4	4	3	3	0	0	84	90
Vermont	361	360	294	294	60	59	2	2	0	0	5	5
Virginia..............................	227	227	134	134	71	71	21	21	1	1	0	0
Washington........................	322	318	295	298	9	9	2	0	0	0	16	11
West Virginia......................	57	57	55	55	0	0	2	2	0	0	0	0
Wisconsin..........................	464	466	423	422	16	16	3	3	0	0	22	25
Wyoming............................	60	61	48	48	0	0	12	13	0	0	0	0
Bureau of Indian Education .	196	196	174	174	22	22	0	0	0	0	0	0
DoD, domestic and overseas	16	16	0	0	0	0	0	0	16	16	0	0
Other jurisdictions												
American Samoa	1	1	1	1	0	0	0	0	0	0	0	0
Guam............................	1	1	1	1	0	0	0	0	0	0	0	0
Northern Marianas........	1	1	1	1	0	0	0	0	0	0	0	0
Puerto Rico...................	1	1	1	1	0	0	0	0	0	0	0	0
U.S. Virgin Islands..........	2	2	2	2	0	0	0	0	0	0	0	0

[1]Regular school districts include both independent districts and those that are a dependent segment of a local government. Also includes components of supervisory unions that operate schools, but share superintendent services with other districts.
[2]New York City counted as one school district.

NOTE: DoD = Department of Defense.
SOURCE: U.S. Department of Education, National Center for Education Statistics, Common Core of Data (CCD), "Local Education Agency Universe Survey," 2012–13 and 2013–14. (This table was prepared September 2015.)

Table 214.40. Public elementary and secondary school enrollment, number of schools, and other selected characteristics, by locale: 2010–11 through 2013–14

Enrollment, number of schools, and other characteristics	Total	City				Suburban				Town				Rural				Locale unknown[12]
		Total	Large[1]	Midsize[2]	Small[3]	Total	Large[4]	Midsize[5]	Small[6]	Total	Fringe[7]	Distant[8]	Remote[9]	Total	Fringe[10]	Distant[11]	Remote[12]	
1	2	3	4	5	6	7	8	9	10	11	12	13	14	15	16	17	18	19
Fall 2010																		
Enrollment (in thousands)	49,178	14,425	7,545	3,186	3,694	16,872	14,290	1,580	1,001	5,841	939	3,066	1,835	12,032	7,418	3,460	1,154	8
Percentage distribution of enrollment, by race/ethnicity	100.0	100.0	100.0	100.0	100.0	100.0	100.0	100.0	100.0	100.0	100.0	100.0	100.0	100.0	100.0	100.0	100.0	100.0
White	52.5	30.3	20.4	34.1	47.0	53.5	51.7	62.8	64.7	66.3	70.0	67.6	62.5	70.8	65.7	80.3	75.3	62.1
Black	16.0	25.2	28.4	25.7	18.3	14.3	15.0	10.2	10.0	10.5	6.2	11.6	10.9	10.0	11.6	7.8	6.8	16.4
Hispanic	23.1	34.3	40.5	30.3	25.1	22.9	23.6	19.4	18.5	17.1	18.8	15.8	18.4	12.8	15.9	7.6	8.4	12.9
Asian	4.6	6.6	7.5	5.8	5.6	5.8	6.2	3.3	3.5	1.5	1.5	1.2	1.9	2.2	3.2	0.6	0.5	4.2
Pacific Islander	0.3	0.3	0.4	0.4	0.3	0.4	0.4	0.6	0.2	0.5	0.1	0.2	1.1	0.2	0.2	0.1	0.2	0.1
American Indian/Alaska Native	1.1	0.8	0.8	0.7	0.9	0.5	0.5	0.7	0.8	2.0	1.0	1.5	3.3	2.0	1.1	2.0	7.4	0.9
Two or more races	2.4	2.5	2.0	3.1	2.8	2.6	2.5	3.1	2.3	2.2	2.4	2.2	2.1	2.0	2.3	1.6	1.4	3.4
Schools	98,817	25,879	13,279	5,737	6,863	27,108	22,425	2,805	1,878	13,838	1,906	7,004	4,928	31,952	13,348	11,593	7,011	40
Average school size[13]	517	579	584	583	568	640	655	579	555	447	511	462	400	391	583	307	170	481
Pupil/teacher ratio[14]	16.4	16.9	17.1	17.0	16.6	16.8	16.8	16.8	17.1	15.8	16.8	15.8	15.4	15.5	16.6	14.6	12.7	16.2
Enrollment (percentage distribution)	100.0	29.3	15.3	6.5	7.5	34.3	29.1	3.2	2.0	11.9	1.9	6.2	3.7	24.5	15.1	7.0	2.3	#
Schools (percentage distribution)	100.0	26.2	13.4	5.8	6.9	27.4	22.7	2.8	1.9	14.0	1.9	7.1	5.0	32.3	13.5	11.7	7.1	#
Fall 2011																		
Enrollment (in thousands)	49,256	14,457	7,559	3,180	3,718	16,709	14,193	1,549	967	5,671	907	2,953	1,812	12,418	7,859	3,416	1,143	†
Percentage distribution of enrollment, by race/ethnicity	100.0	100.0	100.0	100.0	100.0	100.0	100.0	100.0	100.0	100.0	100.0	100.0	100.0	100.0	100.0	100.0	100.0	†
White	51.7	29.7	20.2	33.3	46.1	52.5	50.7	61.9	63.9	65.5	69.1	66.8	61.6	70.0	65.0	79.9	75.0	†
Black	15.8	24.8	27.9	25.4	18.2	14.2	14.9	9.9	9.7	10.4	6.1	11.5	10.8	10.0	11.5	7.5	6.8	†
Hispanic	23.7	34.9	41.0	31.0	25.8	23.8	24.4	20.3	19.3	17.7	19.8	16.4	19.0	13.4	16.4	8.1	8.7	†
Asian	4.7	6.7	7.5	5.9	5.6	5.9	6.4	3.4	3.5	1.5	1.6	1.2	1.9	2.2	3.2	0.6	0.5	†
Pacific Islander	0.4	0.4	0.4	0.4	0.3	0.4	0.4	0.6	0.2	0.5	0.1	0.2	1.1	0.2	0.3	0.2	0.2	†
American Indian/Alaska Native	1.1	0.8	0.8	0.6	0.9	0.5	0.4	0.6	0.8	2.0	1.0	1.5	3.4	1.9	1.1	2.0	7.3	†
Two or more races	2.6	2.7	2.2	3.3	3.1	2.8	2.7	3.3	2.7	2.4	2.3	2.5	2.3	2.2	2.5	1.8	1.6	†
English language learners (in thousands)[15]	4,389	2,035	1,211	430	394	1,604	1,439	97	68	336	63	159	114	414	294	77	42	†
English language learners as a percent of enrollment[15]	9.1	14.2	16.7	12.6	10.9	9.0	9.4	6.4	7.6	6.2	8.4	5.7	6.1	3.9	4.7	2.5	3.9	†
Schools	98,328	25,800	13,266	5,666	6,868	26,840	22,263	2,760	1,817	13,387	1,844	6,720	4,823	32,301	13,904	11,445	6,952	†
Average school size[13]	520	581	585	588	568	641	656	577	552	448	509	463	402	399	592	307	170	†
Pupil/teacher ratio[14]	16.3	16.9	17.1	17.0	16.4	16.6	16.5	16.6	17.0	15.9	16.9	15.9	15.4	15.5	16.5	14.6	12.5	†
Enrollment (percentage distribution)	100.0	29.4	15.3	6.5	7.5	33.9	28.8	3.1	2.0	11.5	1.8	6.0	3.7	25.2	16.0	6.9	2.3	†
Schools (percentage distribution)	100.0	26.2	13.5	5.8	7.0	27.3	22.6	2.8	1.8	13.6	1.9	6.8	4.9	32.9	14.1	11.6	7.1	†
Fall 2012																		
Enrollment (in thousands)	49,474	15,018	7,976	3,368	3,674	19,641	16,851	1,807	983	5,672	1,435	2,499	1,738	9,143	5,189	2,918	1,036	†
Percentage distribution of enrollment, by race/ethnicity	100.0	100.0	100.0	100.0	100.0	100.0	100.0	100.0	100.0	100.0	100.0	100.0	100.0	100.0	100.0	100.0	100.0	†
White	51.0	30.4	20.9	33.6	48.1	52.4	50.6	62.4	65.7	65.4	69.2	66.4	60.9	73.1	68.7	80.5	73.9	†
Black	15.7	24.2	26.8	24.8	17.9	13.6	14.3	10.3	8.4	10.3	7.2	11.8	10.6	9.4	10.8	7.6	7.1	†
Hispanic	24.3	34.6	41.0	31.8	23.3	24.2	25.0	19.6	19.0	17.8	17.8	16.4	19.9	11.6	14.5	7.4	9.0	†
Asian	4.8	6.7	7.5	5.4	5.9	5.9	6.4	3.0	3.2	1.3	1.5	1.1	1.5	1.4	2.1	0.5	0.5	†
Pacific Islander	0.4	0.4	0.4	0.4	0.4	0.4	0.4	0.5	0.2	0.4	0.5	0.1	0.9	0.2	0.2	0.1	0.3	†
American Indian/Alaska Native	1.1	0.7	0.8	0.6	0.8	0.5	0.4	0.7	0.7	2.2	1.2	1.7	3.7	2.2	1.1	2.1	7.5	†
Two or more races	2.8	3.0	2.5	3.5	3.5	3.0	2.9	3.6	2.8	2.6	2.7	2.6	2.5	2.2	2.5	1.9	1.8	†

See notes at end of table.

Table 214.40. Public elementary and secondary school enrollment, number of schools, and other selected characteristics, by locale: 2010–11 through 2013–14—Continued

Enrollment, number of schools, and other characteristics	Total	City				Suburban				Town				Rural				Locale unknown
		Total	Large[1]	Midsize[2]	Small[3]	Total	Large[4]	Midsize[5]	Small[6]	Total	Fringe[7]	Distant[8]	Remote[9]	Total	Fringe[10]	Distant[11]	Remote[12]	
1	2	3	4	5	6	7	8	9	10	11	12	13	14	15	16	17	18	19
English language learners (in thousands)[15]	4,397	2,063	1,293	430	340	1,753	1,581	108	64	334	75	147	112	248	153	59	36	†
English language learners as a percent of enrollment[15]	9.2	14.0	16.7	12.6	9.4	8.5	8.9	5.9	7.0	6.0	6.0	5.9	6.2	3.5	4.4	2.2	3.6	†
Schools..........	98,454	26,545	13,873	5,916	6,756	30,922	25,780	3,226	1,916	13,530	2,973	5,916	4,641	27,457	10,368	10,545	6,544	†
Average school size[13]	522	588	590	601	571	655	674	578	534	444	500	447	404	345	522	285	164	†
Pupil/teacher ratio[14]	16.2	16.8	17.1	16.9	16.2	16.6	16.6	16.5	16.7	15.8	16.5	15.7	15.4	14.9	15.8	14.2	12.6	†
Enrollment (percentage distribution)...	100.0	30.4	16.1	6.8	7.4	39.7	34.1	3.7	2.0	11.5	2.9	5.1	3.5	18.5	10.5	5.9	2.1	†
Schools (percentage distribution)...	100.0	27.0	14.1	6.0	6.9	31.4	26.2	3.3	1.9	13.7	3.0	6.0	4.7	27.9	10.5	10.7	6.6	†
Fall 2013																		
Enrollment (in thousands)...	49,710	15,118	8,027	3,394	3,696	19,777	16,972	1,821	984	5,683	1,436	2,506	1,741	9,133	5,216	2,887	1,029	†
Percentage distribution of enrollment, by race/ethnicity...	100.0	100.0	100.0	100.0	100.0	100.0	100.0	100.0	100.0	100.0	100.0	100.0	100.0	100.0	100.0	100.0	100.0	†
White.....................	50.3	30.0	20.7	33.1	47.2	51.5	49.7	61.4	65.1	64.8	68.7	65.6	60.3	72.4	67.9	80.1	73.6	†
Black.....................	15.6	23.9	26.5	24.6	17.8	13.7	14.3	10.3	8.3	10.1	7.0	11.6	10.5	9.3	10.9	7.5	6.9	†
Hispanic.................	24.9	35.1	41.4	32.3	23.9	24.8	25.6	20.3	19.5	18.4	18.3	17.0	20.4	12.2	15.2	7.7	9.3	†
Asian....................	4.8	6.7	7.6	5.4	6.0	6.0	6.5	3.0	3.2	1.3	1.5	1.0	1.5	1.4	2.1	0.5	0.5	†
Pacific Islander.........	0.4	0.4	0.4	0.4	0.4	0.4	0.4	0.5	0.2	0.4	0.4	0.1	0.9	0.2	0.2	0.1	0.3	†
American Indian/Alaska Native......	1.0	0.7	0.7	0.6	0.8	0.5	0.4	0.7	0.7	2.2	1.2	1.7	3.7	2.1	1.1	2.0	7.4	†
Two or more races.....	3.0	3.2	2.7	3.7	3.8	3.2	3.1	3.9	3.1	2.8	2.9	2.8	2.7	2.4	2.7	2.1	2.0	†
English language learners (in thousands)[15]	4,461	2,076	1,301	439	336	1,796	1,620	112	64	338	75	151	112	251	153	59	39	†
English language learners as a percent of enrollment[15]	9.3	14.1	16.6	12.8	9.6	8.7	9.0	6.0	6.9	6.1	6.0	6.0	6.2	3.5	4.5	2.2	3.9	†
Schools..........	98,271	26,581	13,910	5,916	6,755	30,941	25,795	3,224	1,922	13,485	2,962	5,893	4,630	27,264	10,333	10,442	6,489	†
Average school size[13]	525	590	592	605	574	657	675	582	536	446	500	450	404	347	526	285	164	†
Pupil/teacher ratio[14]	16.3	17.0	17.3	17.1	16.3	16.7	16.7	16.4	17.0	15.8	16.5	15.7	15.4	14.9	15.9	14.2	12.5	†
Enrollment (percentage distribution)...	100.0	30.4	16.1	6.8	7.4	39.8	34.1	3.7	2.0	11.4	2.9	5.0	3.5	18.4	10.5	5.8	2.1	†
Schools (percentage distribution)...	100.0	27.0	14.2	6.0	6.9	31.5	26.2	3.3	2.0	13.7	3.0	6.0	4.7	27.7	10.5	10.6	6.6	†

†Not applicable.
#Rounds to zero.
[1]Located inside an urbanized area and inside a principal city with a population of at least 250,000 or more.
[2]Located inside an urbanized area and inside a principal city with a population of at least 100,000, but less than 250,000.
[3]Located inside an urbanized area and inside a principal city with a population less than 100,000.
[4]Located inside an urbanized area and outside a principal city with a population of 250,000 or more.
[5]Located inside an urbanized area and outside a principal city with a population of at least 100,000, but less than 250,000.
[6]Located inside an urbanized area and outside a principal city with a population less than 100,000.
[7]Located inside an urban cluster that is 10 miles or less from an urbanized area.
[8]Located inside an urban cluster that is more than 10 but less than or equal to 35 miles from an urbanized area.
[9]Located inside an urban cluster that is more than 35 miles from an urbanized area.
[10]Located outside any urbanized area or urban cluster, but 5 miles or less from an urbanized area or 2.5 miles or less from an urban cluster.
[11]Located outside any urbanized area or urban cluster and more than 5 miles but less than or equal to 25 miles from an urbanized area, or more than 2.5 miles but less than or equal to 10 miles from an urban cluster.

[12]Located outside any urbanized area or urban cluster, more than 25 miles from an urbanized area, and more than 10 miles from an urban cluster.
[13]Average for schools reporting enrollment. Enrollment data were available for 95,111 out of 98,817 schools in 2010–11, 94,743 out of 98,328 schools in 2011–12, 94,771 out of 98,454 schools in 2012–13, and 94,758 out of 98,271 schools in 2013–14.
[14]Ratio for schools reporting both full-time-equivalent teachers and fall enrollment data.
[15]Data are based on locales of school districts rather than locales of schools as in the rest of the table. Includes imputed data for Alabama in 2012 and New York in 2013. Includes only students served in regular school districts—excluding other types of districts, such as regional education service agencies and charter schools—with the exception of Vermont data in 2013, which are for students served in all types of districts.
NOTE: Detail may not sum to totals because of rounding. Race categories exclude persons of Hispanic ethnicity. Enrollment and ratios are based on data reported by schools and may differ from data reported in other tables that reflect aggregate totals reported by states.
SOURCE: U.S. Department of Education, National Center for Education Statistics, Common Core of Data (CCD), "Public Elementary/Secondary School Universe Survey," 2010–11, 2011–12, 2012–13, and 2013–14; and "Local Education Agency Universe Survey," 2011–12, 2012–13, and 2013–14. (This table was prepared October 2015.)

Table 215.10. Selected statistics on enrollment, teachers, dropouts, and graduates in public school districts enrolling more than 15,000 students: Selected years, 1990 through 2013

Name of district	State	Enrollment, fall 1990	Enrollment, fall 2000	Enrollment, fall 2010	Enrollment, fall 2013	Number of English language learners, 2013	Percent eligible for free or reduced-price lunch, 2013[1]	White	Black	Hispanic	Asian	Pacific Islander	American Indian/Alaska Native	Two or more races	Number of classroom teachers	Pupil/teacher ratio	Total number of staff	Student/staff ratio	Teachers as a percentage of total staff	ACGR 2010–11[2]	ACGR 2011–12[2]	ACGR 2012–13[2]	ACGR 2013–14[2]	Number of schools, fall 2013
1	2	3	4	5	6	7	8	9	10	11	12	13	14	15	16	17	18	19	20	21	22	23	24	25
Districts with more than 15,000 students[3]	†	**16,924,003**	**20,347,275**	**21,888,865**	**22,152,435**	**2,772,771**	**57.4**	**34.7**	**20.7**	**33.8**	**6.5**	**0.6**	**0.6**	**3.2**	**1,295,029**	**17.1**	**2,506,749**	**8.8**	**51.7**	**—**	**—**	**—**	**—**	**32,906**
Baldwin County	AL	17,479	22,656	28,199	30,281	644	48.4	77.5	13.3	5.6	0.9	0.1	0.6	2.0	1,746	17.3	3,439	8.8	50.8	74	74	80	84	47
Birmingham City	AL	41,710	37,843	25,914	24,858	609	85.4	1.1	94.4	3.8	0.2	#	0.1	0.5	1,398	17.8	2,296	10.8	60.9	55	56	65	79	83
Huntsville City	AL	24,024	22,832	23,364	23,656	926	51.7	44.8	41.2	7.6	2.1	0.3	0.5	3.5	1,399	16.9	2,509	9.4	55.7	66	77	82	87	50
Jefferson County	AL	40,752	40,726	35,860	36,203	1,068	56.7	46.3	45.2	6.4	0.5	0.1	0.1	1.3	2,210	16.4	3,046	11.9	72.5	81	81	83	88	62
Madison County	AL	13,861	15,675	19,897	19,741	127	38.7	68.2	19.0	3.0	1.6	0.1	6.0	2.1	1,168	16.9	2,338	8.4	50.0	76	76	86	89	29
Mobile County	AL	67,286	64,976	62,016	58,808	839	71.2	42.7	50.6	2.3	2.3	0.1	1.1	1.0	3,412	17.2	6,755	8.7	50.5	64	68	76	82	111
Montgomery County	AL	35,973	33,267	31,464	31,802	1,110	75.6	12.7	77.5	5.1	3.1	0.1	0.1	1.4	1,768	18.0	2,583	12.3	68.4	66	64	64	76	66
Shelby County	AL	16,096	20,129	28,063	22,809	899	30.7	72.3	14.5	8.7	2.3	#	0.2	1.8	1,426	16.0	3,031	7.5	47.0	86	89	91	95	35
Tuscaloosa County	AL	14,514	15,666	17,785	17,860	394	53.6	64.6	28.5	4.6	0.8	0.1	0.2	1.2	1,007	17.7	1,378	13.0	73.1	68	74	77	83	35
Anchorage	AK	41,992	49,526	49,206	48,159	5,804	47.4	44.2	6.1	11.3	10.7	5.0	8.6	14.1	2,902	16.6	5,775	8.3	50.3	72	73	76	74	97
Mazanuska-Susitna Borough	AK	9,810	13,008	17,079	17,784	456	33.4	72.2	2.2	3.4	2.9	1.2	18.0	#	894	19.9	1,836	9.7	48.7	70	72	74	75	45
Cartwright Elementary	AZ	14,368	17,746	17,672	19,119	4,053	99.7	4.0	4.1	89.4	0.4	0.1	1.2	0.7	925	20.7	1,915	10.0	48.3	†	†	†	†	20
Chandler Unified	AZ	11,041	21,703	38,876	41,257	1,516	29.3	56.0	5.8	26.4	8.3	0.1	1.6	1.7	2,116	19.5	3,947	10.8	53.6	92	93	92	91	42
Deer Valley Unified	AZ	15,889	27,158	35,190	33,395	729	29.0	71.3	2.9	18.0	3.4	0.4	1.0	2.9	1,732	19.3	3,572	9.4	48.5	91	91	91	92	38
Dysart Unified	AZ	3,804	5,459	24,175	26,121	901	51.1	49.5	7.5	36.0	2.3	0.3	0.9	3.5	1,310	19.9	2,338	11.2	56.0	88	84	81	85	24
Gilbert Unified	AZ	10,862	29,188	38,086	37,852	455	0.7	69.0	3.7	19.7	4.3	0.3	0.9	2.1	2,055	18.4	4,169	9.3	49.3	88	87	85	89	42
Glendale Union High	AZ	12,189	13,453	14,839	15,235	320	64.1	31.3	7.8	53.4	3.8	0.1	2.6	1.0	713	21.4	1,485	10.3	48.0	89	88	86	88	10
Kyrene Elementary	AZ	10,483	19,446	17,815	17,401	391	28.8	51.5	9.4	24.0	6.6	0.3	3.5	4.7	963	18.1	1,746	10.0	55.2	†	†	†	†	26
Mesa Unified	AZ	62,748	73,587	65,123	64,161	4,243	57.3	47.5	4.1	40.6	2.1	0.2	4.3	1.3	3,305	19.4	7,532	8.5	43.9	76	75	74	76	79
Paradise Valley Unified	AZ	26,695	34,882	33,017	32,464	1,834	11.4	60.3	3.0	28.4	3.4	0.2	1.1	3.7	1,745	18.6	3,289	9.9	53.1	88	88	85	88	47
Peoria Unified	AZ	20,850	32,608	36,873	36,706	1,004	40.6	58.0	4.6	30.0	2.6	0.3	1.0	3.5	1,854	19.8	3,477	10.6	53.3	94	93	93	93	41
Phoenix Union High	AZ	18,297	22,192	24,949	26,582	965	79.9	5.3	9.1	80.0	2.0	0.2	2.5	1.0	1,308	20.3	2,573	10.3	50.9	79	75	74	76	15
Scottsdale Unified	AZ	19,752	26,958	26,235	24,866	681	25.9	67.5	3.8	20.0	4.8	0.3	2.3	1.3	1,292	19.2	2,735	9.1	47.2	91	90	88	87	32
Sunnyside Unified	AZ	13,067	14,518	17,323	17,697	2,460	77.0	4.5	2.6	88.2	0.4	0.2	3.8	0.4	869	20.4	2,053	8.6	42.3	72	73	70	70	23
Tucson Unified	AZ	56,174	61,869	53,275	49,308	3,170	67.4	22.7	5.3	62.7	1.6	0.4	3.7	3.5	2,594	19.0	5,263	9.4	49.3	82	80	80	80	87
Washington Elementary	AZ	22,446	24,723	22,349	23,343	3,308	81.1	30.7	7.4	52.2	2.6	0.3	4.2	2.6	1,228	19.0	2,879	8.1	42.6	†	†	†	†	32
Bentonville	AR	4,164	6,906	13,530	15,081	839	27.2	75.6	2.9	10.7	5.8	0.3	1.3	3.4	1,031	14.6	1,929	7.8	53.5	87	85	86	88	18
Little Rock	AR	25,813	25,502	25,685	25,110	2,391	60.7	18.5	66.0	11.7	2.5	#	0.3	1.0	1,757	14.3	3,905	6.4	45.0	66	82	75	78	48
Pulaski County Special	AR	21,495	18,735	17,501	17,750	531	56.5	44.3	43.3	6.7	2.0	0.1	0.5	3.1	1,244	14.3	2,719	6.5	45.7	61	66	73	73	36
Rogers	AR	6,790	10,976	14,340	15,094	4,916	61.9	49.7	1.6	43.3	2.0	0.8	0.9	1.6	913	16.5	1,962	7.7	46.6	85	83	88	93	22
Springdale	AR	7,877	11,422	19,411	21,369	9,199	68.2	38.4	2.3	45.5	1.7	10.0	0.5	1.6	1,346	15.9	2,554	8.4	52.7	80	82	81	84	28
ABC Unified	CA	20,972	22,303	20,682	20,846	4,609	49.9	6.9	9.0	44.3	35.9	0.8	0.3	2.8	818	25.5	1,647	12.7	49.7	91	92	93	94	30
Alhambra Unified	CA	20,313	19,776	18,413	17,826	4,986	64.2	1.9	0.7	42.8	51.7	0.1	0.2	2.6	655	27.2	1,345	13.3	48.7	91	92	91	94	18
Alvord Unified	CA	14,853	17,664	19,803	19,480	8,048	77.8	11.0	3.8	78.4	4.9	0.1	0.2	1.3	751	25.9	1,430	13.6	52.5	77	79	80	84	23
Anaheim City	CA	14,972	22,275	19,095	19,308	11,254	85.2	4.6	1.4	86.6	6.0	0.5	0.1	0.8	677	28.5	1,318	14.6	51.4	†	†	†	†	25
Anaheim Union High	CA	23,086	29,363	33,156	31,889	6,866	69.0	13.2	2.8	63.5	15.8	0.6	0.5	3.5	—	—	—	—	—	83	82	84	85	21
Antelope Valley Union High	CA	10,937	19,056	26,084	24,468	2,696	60.6	19.6	18.6	54.7	3.1	0.9	0.9	2.8	1,031	23.7	2,141	11.4	48.2	76	78	78	80	15
Antioch Unified	CA	13,045	20,018	19,081	18,523	3,247	61.5	18.7	25.3	40.1	8.9	0.9	0.7	5.4	722	23.7	1,498	12.4	48.2	74	74	78	77	28
Bakersfield City	CA	24,911	27,674	27,590	29,684	9,136	85.2	10.1	8.4	78.2	1.3	0.1	0.6	1.3	1,308	22.7	2,661	11.2	49.2	†	†	†	†	42
Baldwin Park Unified	CA	15,878	17,473	19,923	18,767	4,535	86.1	2.9	3.4	86.9	5.6	0.2	0.3	0.6	965	19.4	1,697	11.1	56.9	89	88	93	92	22
Burbank Unified	CA	12,057	16,170	16,630	16,207	1,723	39.9	44.7	2.6	38.9	9.4	0.2	0.2	4.1	695	23.3	1,271	12.7	54.7	91	93	92	94	22
Cajon Valley Union	CA	17,328	16,065	16,065	16,420	5,148	64.2	46.7	7.1	36.3	2.8	0.4	0.4	6.2	685	24.0	1,366	12.0	50.1	†	†	†	†	30
Capistrano Unified	CA	26,852	45,074	53,192	53,833	5,403	21.6	59.1	1.3	25.6	7.1	0.3	0.4	6.5	1,871	28.8	3,532	15.2	53.0	97	97	97	97	63
Central Unified	CA	5,070	10,290	14,817	15,490	1,989	68.5	18.0	10.0	55.7	13.8	0.5	0.6	1.7	589	26.3	1,297	11.9	45.5	72	77	80	81	21
Chaffey Joint Union High	CA	13,505	19,851	25,427	24,747	2,502	53.9	18.4	8.4	63.4	6.7	0.5	0.3	2.3	946	26.2	1,763	14.0	53.7	84	85	86	86	11
Chino Valley Unified	CA	23,257	31,763	31,608	30,206	4,082	43.4	20.3	3.4	57.1	6.7	0.2	0.1	2.4	1,127	26.8	2,176	13.9	51.8	85	87	89	89	35
Chula Vista Elementary	CA	17,604	23,132	27,723	29,472	10,603	49.3	11.8	3.6	69.2	11.7	0.2	0.2	3.0	1,248	23.6	2,179	13.5	57.3	†	†	†	†	47
Clovis Unified	CA	23,224	32,717	38,495	40,783	2,536	41.9	44.4	3.2	33.6	14.6	0.3	0.7	3.3	1,547	26.4	3,541	11.5	43.7	93	93	92	92	47

See notes at end of table.

Table 215.10. Selected statistics on enrollment, teachers, dropouts, and graduates in public school districts enrolling more than 15,000 students: Selected years, 1990 through 2013—Continued

Name of district	State	Enrollment, fall 1990	Enrollment, fall 2000	Enrollment, fall 2010	Enrollment, fall 2013	Number of English language learners, 2013	Percent eligible for free or reduced-price lunch, 2013[1]	Percentage distribution of enrollment, by race/ethnicity, fall 2013							Teachers and staff, fall 2013					Public high school 4-year adjusted cohort graduation rate (ACGR)[2]				Number of schools, fall 2013
								White	Black	Hispanic	Asian	Pacific Islander	American Indian/Alaska Native	Two or more races	Number of classroom teachers	Pupil/teacher ratio	Total number of staff	Student/staff ratio	Teachers as a percentage of total staff	2010–11	2011–12	2012–13	2013–14	
1	2	3	4	5	6	7	8	9	10	11	12	13	14	15	16	17	18	19	20	21	22	23	24	25
Coachella Valley Unified	CA	9,091	12,636	18,464	18,850	9,908	79.3	1.1	0.2	97.0	0.2	#	0.5	1.2	834	22.6	1,669	11.3	50.0	74	78	79	78	23
Colton Joint Unified	CA	16,415	22,118	23,382	23,362	6,181	80.6	7.9	5.7	82.1	2.9	0.3	0.3	0.8	996	23.5	1,987	11.8	50.1	74	78	78	85	27
Compton Unified	CA	27,585	31,037	24,224	22,452	8,428	92.9	0.3	19.4	79.0	0.1	0.7	0.2	0.3	995	22.6	2,092	10.7	47.6	58	57	65	60	38
Conejo Valley Unified	CA	17,209	20,999	21,091	20,142	2,202	22.5	60.1	1.5	23.9	10.5	0.3	0.4	3.4	835	24.1	1,497	13.5	55.8	95	96	96	97	27
Corona-Norco Unified	CA	23,036	37,487	53,149	53,782	7,019	40.8	29.0	6.1	51.7	10.9	0.3	0.3	1.6	2,016	26.7	3,568	15.1	56.5	87	91	92	92	52
Cupertino Union	CA	12,227	15,670	18,370	19,194	2,298	5.2	17.4	0.7	5.3	73.9	0.1	0.2	2.3	785	24.4	1,430	13.4	54.9	†	†	†	†	25
Desert Sands Unified	CA	16,058	23,500	29,123	29,156	7,081	59.5	21.8	1.9	71.5	2.6	0.1	0.3	1.8	1,087	26.8	2,064	14.1	52.7	83	86	86	88	34
Downey Unified	CA	15,418	21,474	22,844	22,878	3,862	72.2	5.8	3.0	87.5	2.8	0.2	0.3	0.4	881	26.0	1,661	13.8	53.0	92	91	93	94	20
East Side Union High	CA	21,973	24,282	25,676	26,489	5,258	51.2	6.7	2.9	51.6	36.0	0.5	0.3	1.9	1,093	24.2	1,851	14.3	59.0	77	80	80	83	23
Elk Grove Unified	CA	27,246	47,736	62,455	62,499	10,479	49.3	22.6	14.6	26.0	27.0	1.7	0.6	7.5	3,012	20.8	4,981	12.5	60.5	82	86	88	90	66
Escondido Union	CA	14,663	19,312	19,242	19,446	8,335	65.7	20.4	2.1	69.5	4.3	0.2	0.3	3.1	799	24.3	1,709	11.4	46.8	†	†	†	†	26
Fairfield-Suisun Unified	CA	20,227	22,263	21,534	21,574	3,268	58.4	19.7	17.2	38.7	13.6	1.1	0.8	8.8	855	25.2	1,604	13.4	53.3	83	88	90	91	29
Folsom-Cordova Unified	CA	12,656	16,277	18,893	19,356	2,271	35.8	56.0	6.9	17.9	14.1	0.8	0.7	3.6	740	26.1	1,415	13.7	52.3	90	91	93	92	34
Fontana Unified	CA	27,043	37,244	40,841	39,982	14,197	83.0	4.7	6.1	85.9	2.1	0.3	0.1	0.7	1,613	24.8	3,375	11.8	47.8	81	82	86	87	43
Fremont Unified	CA	27,172	31,078	32,607	33,887	6,703	16.5	15.1	3.2	15.9	61.3	0.6	0.1	3.5	1,330	25.5	2,305	14.7	57.7	89	90	82	93	43
Fresno Unified	CA	71,500	79,007	74,833	73,353	17,589	82.8	11.5	8.9	65.6	11.8	0.3	0.6	1.2	3,036	24.2	6,524	11.2	46.5	73	75	76	79	108
Garden Grove Unified	CA	37,969	48,742	48,659	46,936	19,220	76.7	9.6	0.7	53.9	34.3	0.7	0.1	0.7	1,706	27.5	3,496	13.4	48.8	86	88	89	90	67
Glendale Unified	CA	25,459	30,329	26,371	26,070	6,381	47.1	54.7	1.3	23.1	18.7	0.1	0.2	1.9	995	26.2	1,981	13.2	50.2	88	92	92	90	34
Grossmont Union High	CA	18,647	23,639	24,224	22,555	2,463	50.0	46.1	7.2	34.8	3.2	0.6	0.6	7.4	863	26.1	1,922	11.7	44.9	77	78	78	75	18
Hacienda La Puente Unified	CA	23,267	24,646	20,942	20,032	4,121	75.6	3.8	1.0	80.6	13.4	0.3	0.2	0.8	846	23.7	1,854	10.8	45.6	46	90	88	90	36
Hayward Unified	CA	19,122	24,205	21,744	22,272	6,886	68.7	5.6	11.8	61.3	14.5	3.4	0.4	2.9	895	24.9	1,935	10.5	46.3	69	71	79	80	36
Hemet Unified	CA	12,811	17,451	22,294	21,507	2,915	79.7	32.0	7.9	52.6	2.1	0.7	1.0	4.0	842	25.5	2,045	10.5	41.2	81	80	79	81	27
Hesperia Unified	CA	13,113	15,360	23,137	23,528	4,159	65.6	26.3	7.6	60.3	1.6	0.3	0.5	3.4	910	25.9	1,966	12.0	46.3	79	83	83	87	30
Huntington Beach Union High	CA	14,039	14,359	16,320	16,431	1,311	29.6	39.4	1.1	25.7	24.2	0.7	0.2	3.6	613	26.8	1,223	13.4	50.1	91	94	93	94	9
Irvine Unified	CA	20,735	23,961	27,262	30,123	4,744	13.1	33.0	2.2	10.6	46.8	0.3	0.3	6.8	1,008	29.9	2,226	13.5	45.3	97	96	95	96	36
Jurupa Unified	CA	15,419	19,839	20,088	19,471	7,308	74.6	11.0	2.1	84.3	1.4	0.3	0.4	0.8	752	25.9	1,523	12.8	49.4	80	82	82	82	27
Kern Union High	CA	20,183	29,333	37,452	37,100	3,324	59.7	24.8	6.3	62.8	3.8	0.2	0.7	1.5	1,406	26.4	3,132	11.8	44.9	82	81	80	84	25
Lake Elsinore Unified	CA	11,000	17,178	22,065	22,316	3,287	60.4	33.0	4.6	55.3	2.7	0.4	0.5	3.3	884	25.3	1,928	11.6	45.8	89	90	83	89	31
Lodi Unified	CA	23,954	27,339	30,528	30,256	7,698	66.2	24.5	7.3	42.8	21.0	0.7	0.5	3.2	1,256	24.1	2,363	12.8	53.2	77	83	83	81	54
Long Beach Unified	CA	71,342	93,694	84,812	81,155	19,277	67.2	14.3	14.7	55.0	10.7	1.7	0.2	3.4	2,967	27.4	6,975	11.6	42.5	78	80	81	81	86
Los Angeles Unified	CA	625,073	721,346	667,273	653,826	179,322	75.5	9.3	9.2	73.8	6.1	0.4	0.4	0.9	27,748	23.6	62,858	10.4	44.1	61	67	68	70	983
Madera Unified	CA	13,728	15,957	19,576	20,200	6,961	85.9	7.8	2.1	87.5	1.4	0.1	0.5	0.5	776	26.0	1,396	14.5	55.6	82	86	83	87	27
Manteca Unified	CA	13,356	19,746	23,406	23,079	5,031	63.4	22.8	8.1	52.1	13.2	0.9	0.7	2.3	870	26.5	1,554	14.9	56.0	88	89	92	93	30
Modesto City Elementary	CA	17,405	18,740	15,088	15,385	6,104	83.9	18.3	3.0	67.0	4.1	0.6	0.5	6.5	634	24.3	1,378	11.2	46.0	†	†	†	†	26
Montebello Unified	CA	32,938	34,794	32,046	29,951	9,313	85.6	1.4	0.3	95.5	2.2	0.1	0.2	0.3	1,112	26.9	2,433	12.3	45.7	81	80	82	83	30
Moreno Valley Unified	CA	29,064	32,730	36,901	34,468	8,265	81.3	9.1	16.5	67.7	3.6	0.7	0.3	2.2	1,350	25.5	2,607	13.2	51.8	69	75	82	83	40
Mount Diablo Unified	CA	32,840	36,648	34,116	31,955	7,385	45.6	37.0	4.4	40.2	11.9	0.9	0.4	5.2	1,324	24.1	2,353	13.6	56.3	82	81	83	85	52
Murrieta Valley Unified	CA	3,990	12,065	22,318	23,023	1,060	33.1	46.3	5.5	33.9	7.7	0.6	0.4	5.5	817	28.2	1,854	12.4	44.1	89	92	88	94	20
Napa Valley Unified	CA	13,705	16,392	18,003	18,497	4,017	44.5	31.0	2.6	52.4	8.5	0.4	0.4	4.7	756	24.5	1,481	12.5	51.1	85	88	88	87	32
Newport-Mesa Unified	CA	16,434	21,658	21,811	22,018	5,443	44.1	46.9	1.1	44.0	5.1	0.4	0.6	2.1	859	25.6	1,962	11.2	43.8	93	94	93	93	31
Norwalk-La Mirada Unified	CA	19,179	23,610	20,421	19,370	3,347	74.7	9.8	2.4	79.1	6.3	0.5	0.2	1.8	764	25.4	1,524	12.7	50.1	90	92	94	93	28
Oakland Unified	CA	52,095	54,863	46,586	47,194	14,483	74.7	9.8	27.9	42.8	14.1	1.1	0.3	4.1	2,105	22.4	4,306	11.0	48.9	59	59	63	60	123
Oceanside Unified	CA	17,034	22,354	21,082	21,244	3,448	62.2	28.9	6.0	54.0	6.3	2.2	0.4	3.3	839	25.3	1,842	11.5	45.6	81	84	87	89	25
Ontario-Montclair Elementary	CA	21,033	26,407	22,591	22,767	10,564	85.8	4.0	2.6	88.7	1.9	0.1	0.5	1.6	989	23.0	1,903	12.0	52.0	†	†	†	†	32
Orange Unified	CA	25,224	31,097	30,373	29,750	7,204	45.5	31.0	1.4	52.9	11.5	0.4	0.3	2.5	1,118	26.6	2,361	12.6	47.4	90	92	94	93	41
Oxnard	CA	12,212	16,249	15,870	16,803	8,972	86.7	3.5	1.4	91.5	2.6	0.2	0.1	0.6	658	25.5	1,306	12.9	50.4	†	†	†	†	21
Oxnard Union High	CA	11,512	14,552	16,676	16,876	3,102	59.2	15.5	2.0	74.1	6.3	0.4	0.2	1.5	654	25.8	1,173	14.4	55.7	79	82	78	80	10
Pajaro Valley Unified	CA	16,355	19,864	19,542	20,362	9,464	76.2	16.2	0.5	81.1	1.9	0.1	0.2	0.1	821	24.8	1,909	10.7	43.0	81	86	89	90	33
Palm Springs Unified	CA	14,427	20,847	23,626	23,360	7,541	79.3	14.1	5.3	75.1	3.4	0.6	0.6	1.3	899	26.0	1,763	13.2	51.0	80	84	87	87	28
Palmdale Elementary	CA	13,199	20,853	21,049	21,623	6,077	82.8	7.5	16.1	71.4	1.8	0.7	0.3	2.3	825	26.2	1,442	15.0	57.2	†	†	†	†	28
Panama-Buena Vista Union	CA	10,066	12,843	16,562	17,484	2,739	62.0	25.1	10.2	53.6	8.9	0.4	0.4	1.3	679	25.8	1,560	11.2	43.5	†	†	†	†	23
Paramount Unified	CA	12,855	16,862	15,792	15,911	5,765	87.5	1.1	8.6	87.4	1.4	0.7	0.1	0.7	506	31.5	1,125	14.1	45.0	74	78	81	86	19
Pasadena Unified	CA	21,802	23,559	19,803	19,102	3,824	68.0	16.8	14.7	58.7	5.8	0.2	0.3	3.5	817	23.4	1,839	10.4	44.4	76	79	83	81	34

See notes at end of table.

Table 215.10. Selected statistics on enrollment, teachers, dropouts, and graduates in public school districts enrolling more than 15,000 students: Selected years, 1990 through 2013—Continued

Name of district	State	Enrollment, fall 1990	Enrollment, fall 2000	Enrollment, fall 2010	Enrollment, fall 2013	Number of English language learners, 2013	Percent eligible for free or reduced-price lunch, 2013[1]	Percentage distribution of enrollment, by race/ethnicity, fall 2013							Number of classroom teachers	Pupil/teacher ratio	Total number of staff	Student/staff ratio	Teachers as a percentage of total staff	Public high school 4-year adjusted cohort graduation rate (ACGR)[2]				Number of schools, fall 2013
								White	Black	Hispanic	Asian	Pacific Islander	American Indian/Alaska Native	Two or more races						2010–11	2011–12	2012–13	2013–14	
1	2	3	4	5	6	7	8	9	10	11	12	13	14	15	16	17	18	19	20	21	22	23	24	25
Placentia-Yorba Linda Unified	CA	21,438	26,046	25,821	25,843	3,596	34.5	40.8	1.6	40.2	14.5	0.2	0.2	2.5	937	27.6	1,863	13.9	50.3	92	92	93	94	34
Pomona Unified	CA	26,918	34,479	28,298	26,264	9,641	79.0	3.6	5.2	84.6	5.0	0.1	0.2	1.2	1,029	25.5	2,090	12.6	49.3	77	78	79	83	43
Poway Unified	CA	24,662	32,532	34,135	35,498	4,279	15.8	50.9	2.5	14.1	25.7	0.4	0.2	6.2	1,299	27.3	2,782	12.8	46.7	94	96	95	96	37
Redlands Unified	CA	16,002	19,411	21,398	21,233	1,966	54.8	31.5	6.5	45.8	10.9	0.5	0.4	4.4	841	25.2	1,491	14.2	56.4	86	90	91	91	26
Rialto Unified	CA	19,794	28,060	27,026	26,468	6,788	80.1	4.1	11.5	81.2	1.5	0.5	0.4	0.9	1,014	26.1	2,095	12.6	48.4	78	78	80	81	30
Riverside Unified	CA	31,326	38,124	42,532	42,587	7,370	63.8	24.5	7.1	60.0	4.5	0.3	0.4	2.9	1,621	26.3	3,152	13.5	51.4	80	82	85	87	50
Rowland Unified	CA	19,143	18,972	15,711	15,209	4,168	68.2	4.2	2.4	63.1	27.9	0.3	0.3	1.9	660	23.0	1,405	10.8	47.0	84	84	84	88	24
Sacramento City Unified	CA	49,557	52,794	47,897	47,031	10,222	71.8	18.5	17.3	37.8	18.5	1.7	0.7	5.4	1,870	25.1	3,558	13.2	52.6	74	80	85	85	80
Saddleback Valley Unified	CA	25,130	35,199	31,724	29,731	4,576	27.9	50.2	1.5	31.9	10.1	0.2	0.3	5.8	1,052	28.2	1,963	15.1	53.6	94	95	95	85	35
San Bernardino City Unified	CA	40,589	52,031	54,518	53,785	14,867	91.1	7.4	13.7	73.6	2.0	0.4	0.5	2.3	2,292	23.5	4,735	11.4	48.4	68	74	76	80	86
San Diego Unified	CA	121,107	141,804	131,785	130,303	33,877	59.0	23.1	9.7	46.8	13.6	0.6	0.3	6.1	5,461	23.9	11,803	11.0	46.3	85	87	88	90	225
San Francisco Unified	CA	61,688	59,979	55,571	57,620	16,136	60.5	12.9	9.7	27.2	40.9	1.6	0.5	7.2	2,787	20.7	5,059	11.4	55.1	82	82	82	84	127
San Jose Unified	CA	29,630	33,015	33,018	33,152	8,166	44.2	29.2	2.9	53.1	14.3	0.4	0.4	3.7	1,414	23.4	2,738	12.1	51.7	84	84	81	86	53
San Juan Unified	CA	47,600	50,266	47,116	49,035	5,229	49.6	59.6	7.9	21.1	6.1	0.9	1.1	3.4	1,923	25.5	4,237	11.6	45.4	80	81	81	82	77
San Marcos Unified	CA	9,108	12,804	18,642	20,107	4,123	44.3	41.5	2.4	45.8	7.5	0.6	0.4	1.9	750	26.8	1,629	12.3	46.1	94	97	94	98	19
San Ramon Valley Unified	CA	16,119	20,742	28,987	31,398	1,690	4.2	48.5	1.8	8.5	33.3	0.2	0.1	7.5	1,262	24.9	2,266	13.9	55.7	97	97	86	87	36
Santa Ana Unified	CA	45,964	60,643	57,319	57,499	27,458	88.0	2.7	0.3	92.5	2.8	0.1	0.2	1.3	2,145	26.8	4,069	14.2	52.8	83	85	86	87	60
Santa Barbara Unified	CA	13,370	16,957	16,003	15,518	4,808	46.9	32.7	1.0	59.5	3.2	0.1	0.4	3.0	653	23.8	1,352	11.5	48.3	—	90	90	87	26
Santa Clara Unified	CA	14,043	14,107	15,383	15,434	4,379	45.1	32.7	3.6	36.7	31.7	0.1	0.4	4.5	636	24.3	1,183	13.1	53.8	81	83	81	82	25
Santa Maria-Bonita	CA	8,904	11,312	14,182	15,544	10,162	74.1	3.6	0.7	93.1	2.0	0.1	0.6	0.3	605	25.7	1,140	13.6	53.1	—	—	—	—	19
Simi Valley Unified	CA	18,262	21,181	19,933	18,353	1,668	30.6	54.0	1.1	32.2	9.2	0.1	0.4	3.1	735	25.0	1,485	12.4	49.5	82	86	85	84	29
Stockton Unified	CA	32,687	37,573	38,252	39,486	11,223	82.9	7.1	11.0	62.7	14.0	0.4	2.7	1.9	1,434	27.5	3,488	11.3	41.1	67	71	83	76	62
Sweetwater Union High	CA	27,894	35,330	41,426	40,901	8,339	57.7	6.4	2.8	75.9	9.7	0.4	0.3	4.6	1,575	26.0	3,451	11.9	45.6	80	83	83	82	31
Temecula Valley Unified	CA	7,596	18,980	30,272	30,065	1,547	19.8	46.4	3.8	31.4	8.9	0.3	1.1	8.0	1,160	25.9	2,342	12.8	49.5	92	93	94	94	30
Torrance Unified	CA	19,645	24,118	24,370	24,213	3,678	27.3	25.5	4.3	27.4	34.2	0.6	0.4	7.7	864	28.0	1,832	13.2	47.2	93	95	96	95	32
Tracy Joint Unified	CA	7,626	13,816	17,530	17,442	4,291	43.7	24.1	6.9	48.2	15.5	0.9	0.4	3.9	725	24.1	1,355	12.9	53.5	83	87	87	90	24
Tustin Unified	CA	10,831	16,963	23,093	23,949	5,209	40.6	29.2	2.1	46.6	18.7	0.4	0.2	2.7	827	28.9	1,715	14.0	48.3	96	95	97	97	29
Twin Rivers Unified	CA	—	—	31,632	31,122	8,693	86.9	29.4	14.7	39.4	9.1	1.5	0.9	5.0	1,367	22.8	2,662	11.7	51.3	68	72	75	78	53
Val Verde Unified	CA	19,049	11,242	19,687	19,796	4,642	79.0	5.9	14.7	73.0	3.2	0.2	0.2	2.6	761	26.0	1,464	13.5	52.0	82	90	91	91	22
Vallejo City Unified	CA	15,383	20,270	15,604	15,080	2,808	70.0	9.0	30.4	35.8	19.2	2.0	0.4	3.3	602	25.1	1,298	11.6	46.4	54	59	65	72	26
Ventura Unified	CA	21,309	17,527	17,509	17,430	2,800	46.0	41.9	1.4	49.1	3.2	0.2	0.5	3.7	666	26.2	1,490	11.7	44.7	90	86	90	92	29
Visalia Unified	CA	21,309	23,989	27,118	27,835	4,451	63.7	24.2	2.0	64.7	5.1	0.9	1.2	2.6	1,046	26.6	2,226	12.5	47.0	84	87	88	83	40
Vista Unified	CA	18,489	27,651	25,843	25,670	6,231	63.8	26.1	3.3	61.6	3.6	0.8	0.4	4.1	1,043	24.6	2,156	11.9	48.4	81	83	81	83	34
West Contra Costa Unified	CA	31,292	34,499	29,842	30,720	10,672	70.3	10.6	19.4	52.4	15.7	0.2	0.2	1.0	1,304	23.6	2,625	11.7	49.7	74	76	80	78	58
William S. Hart Union High	CA	10,278	17,001	26,161	25,640	2,320	23.9	45.6	4.5	34.8	10.7	0.2	0.3	4.0	1,072	23.9	1,991	12.9	53.8	94	93	93	95	21
Academy, No. 20	CO	10,986	17,628	23,119	24,481	396	13.2	74.5	2.9	12.5	3.8	0.4	0.4	5.5	1,463	16.7	2,962	8.3	49.4	89	89	91	90	32
Adams 12 Five Star Schools	CO	20,838	30,079	41,957	42,230	5,858	37.9	54.4	2.2	35.3	5.2	0.1	0.8	1.9	2,093	20.2	4,315	9.8	48.5	65	70	74	74	55
Aurora, Joint District No. 28	CO	25,897	30,453	38,605	40,877	14,456	67.7	18.0	17.9	54.1	4.5	0.5	0.8	4.2	2,083	19.6	4,607	8.9	45.2	48	48	53	56	58
Boulder Valley, No. RE2	CO	21,502	27,508	29,526	30,546	2,546	18.6	70.1	0.9	17.8	5.8	0.1	0.4	5.0	1,689	18.1	3,602	8.5	46.9	88	90	91	92	57
Brighton, No. 27J	CO	3,953	5,796	15,089	16,717	1,974	37.2	48.4	1.7	44.0	2.5	0.1	0.5	2.8	803	20.8	1,560	10.7	51.5	73	71	79	80	26
Cherry Creek, No. 5	CO	29,210	42,320	52,232	54,228	4,169	26.0	55.4	11.6	18.6	8.2	0.3	0.5	5.4	2,983	18.2	6,355	8.5	46.9	84	87	87	87	60
Colorado Springs, No. 11	CO	30,009	32,699	29,498	28,448	2,057	56.6	52.7	7.2	29.7	1.9	0.3	0.9	7.2	1,686	16.9	3,688	7.7	45.7	64	67	66	68	58
Denver	CO	59,013	70,847	78,339	86,046	27,084	72.0	21.2	13.8	57.7	3.3	0.3	0.7	3.0	5,356	16.1	10,271	8.4	52.2	56	59	61	63	184
Douglas County, No. RE1	CO	13,125	34,918	61,465	66,230	2,984	12.1	75.7	1.7	13.9	4.0	0.1	0.4	4.1	3,271	20.2	6,872	9.6	47.6	84	87	89	89	85
Falcon, No. 49	CO	2,488	6,026	14,708	18,880	885	30.0	60.8	6.2	23.2	2.5	0.4	0.6	6.4	914	20.7	1,831	10.3	49.9	87	90	90	64	22
Greeley, No. 6	CO	11,657	15,998	19,623	20,461	4,149	64.7	35.6	1.8	58.9	1.8	0.1	0.3	1.4	1,142	17.9	2,260	9.1	50.5	72	79	80	78	32
Jefferson County, No. R1	CO	76,275	87,703	85,979	86,011	5,643	32.8	67.4	1.1	24.2	3.1	0.2	0.6	3.3	4,780	18.0	10,446	8.2	45.8	79	81	81	83	164
Littleton, No. 6	CO	15,524	16,516	15,733	15,830	637	20.9	74.8	1.3	16.9	3.1	0.1	0.3	3.3	843	18.8	1,821	8.7	46.3	89	90	92	91	23
Mesa County Valley, No. 51	CO	17,024	19,688	22,109	21,906	805	42.3	71.5	0.6	22.7	0.7	0.1	0.7	3.7	1,263	17.3	2,661	8.2	47.4	76	78	78	77	46
Poudre, No. R1	CO	18,589	24,052	26,923	28,439	1,595	29.0	73.8	1.2	17.8	3.2	0.1	0.5	3.4	1,626	17.5	3,425	8.3	47.5	84	86	87	82	52
Pueblo, No. 60	CO	18,364	17,636	18,443	18,012	976	68.8	26.2	2.0	69.4	0.6	0.1	0.6	1.1	1,048	17.2	2,023	8.9	51.8	63	64	70	72	34
Saint Vrain Valley, No. RE1J	CO	15,070	19,620	27,379	30,195	3,885	36.5	64.9	0.9	28.7	3.2	0.2	0.5	1.5	1,616	18.7	3,193	9.5	50.6	79	82	83	83	51
Thompson, No. R2J	CO	12,019	14,766	15,310	16,210	462	37.0	75.3	0.9	19.6	1.2	0.2	0.6	2.2	868	18.7	2,026	8.0	42.8	81	77	78	75	35

See notes at end of table.

Table 215.10. Selected statistics on enrollment, teachers, dropouts, and graduates in public school districts enrolling more than 15,000 students: Selected years, 1990 through 2013—Continued

Name of district	State	Enrollment, fall 1990	Enrollment, fall 2000	Enrollment, fall 2010	Enrollment, fall 2013	Number of English language learners, 2013	Percent eligible for free or reduced-price lunch, 2013[1]	Percentage distribution of enrollment, by race/ethnicity, fall 2013							Teachers and staff, fall 2013					Public high school 4-year adjusted cohort graduation rate (ACGR)[2]				Number of schools, fall 2013
								White	Black	Hispanic	Asian	Pacific Islander	American Indian/Alaska Native	Two or more races	Number of classroom teachers	Pupil/teacher ratio	Total number of staff	Student/staff ratio	Teachers as a percentage of total staff	2010-11	2011-12	2012-13	2013-14	
1	2	3	4	5	6	7	8	9	10	11	12	13	14	15	16	17	18	19	20	21	22	23	24	25
Bridgeport	CT	19,687	22,432	20,205	20,753	2,690	99.4	10.1	37.5	48.7	2.8	0.1	0.4	0.4	1,348	15.4	2,896	7.2	46.6	60	66	67	72	39
Hartford	CT	25,418	22,543	21,021	21,286	3,551	84.6	12.4	31.1	49.6	3.2	0.2	0.3	3.2	1,601	13.3	3,111	6.8	51.5	63	65	71	72	49
New Haven	CT	17,881	19,549	20,003	21,298	2,725	65.9	15.1	42.8	39.3	2.1	#	0.2	0.4	1,646	12.9	4,211	5.1	39.1	64	71	71	75	47
Stamford	CT	11,574	14,791	15,309	15,860	1,895	46.2	33.7	19.2	37.3	8.5	#	0.1	1.1	1,242	12.8	2,090	7.6	59.4	85	85	89	89	21
Waterbury	CT	13,323	16,282	18,152	18,614	2,119	82.4	21.3	23.9	49.5	1.5	0.1	0.4	3.3	1,415	13.2	2,946	6.3	48.0	66	63	66	68	32
Christina	DE	17,872	19,882	17,190	16,326	1,480	43.4	33.0	40.1	19.1	4.4	0.1	0.3	3.0	1,256	13.0	3,074	5.3	40.9	63	68	67	75	30
Red Clay Consolidated	DE	14,551	15,827	15,954	16,538	1,986	44.3	44.0	23.0	25.9	5.3	#	0.2	1.6	1,144	14.5	2,194	7.5	52.2	82	84	80	87	27
District of Columbia	DC	80,694	68,925	44,199	44,942	4,716	99.3	12.1	67.6	16.3	2.0	0.2	0.1	1.9	3,374	13.3	5,983	7.5	56.4	53	54	56	58	115
Alachua	FL	26,387	29,712	27,513	28,157	529	52.8	45.5	35.6	8.4	4.5	0.1	0.2	5.7	1,804	15.6	4,253	6.6	42.4	63	69	73	72	69
Bay	FL	21,875	25,755	25,935	27,053	484	58.0	71.3	15.1	5.9	2.1	0.1	0.4	5.0	1,794	15.1	3,577	7.6	50.2	68	74	73	71	51
Brevard	FL	56,639	70,597	71,866	71,232	2,186	44.7	63.0	14.6	13.1	2.1	0.1	0.2	6.9	4,723	15.1	9,013	7.9	52.4	81	85	87	86	123
Broward	FL	161,100	251,129	256,472	262,666	26,323	59.9	24.1	39.7	29.7	3.5	0.1	0.3	2.6	15,214	17.3	27,777	9.5	54.8	72	76	75	74	349
Charlotte	FL	13,030	17,170	16,640	16,264	286	61.0	71.5	9.1	13.0	1.4	0.1	0.3	4.5	1,345	12.1	2,690	6.0	50.0	73	79	76	76	24
Citrus	FL	11,697	15,199	15,675	15,070	135	63.3	81.6	4.8	7.5	1.8	0.1	0.4	3.8	1,077	14.0	2,230	6.8	48.3	75	78	80	77	24
Clay	FL	21,933	28,115	35,812	35,523	576	41.0	68.7	13.6	10.3	2.6	0.3	0.2	4.4	2,414	14.7	4,605	7.7	52.4	74	74	78	80	46
Collier	FL	20,878	34,233	42,919	44,418	5,913	61.9	37.0	12.2	46.8	1.1	0.1	0.8	2.0	2,941	15.1	5,413	8.2	54.3	73	78	81	82	71
Dade	FL	292,000	368,625	347,366	356,233	72,437	74.1	7.7	23.1	67.4	1.1	#	0.1	0.5	20,527	17.4	34,218	10.4	60.0	71	76	77	77	534
Duval	FL	111,100	125,846	123,997	127,653	4,416	50.2	37.8	44.3	9.1	4.3	0.2	0.2	4.1	7,751	16.5	12,405	6.5	62.5	63	68	64	74	205
Escambia	FL	43,091	45,012	40,753	40,753	444	63.4	49.6	35.1	5.2	2.5	0.2	0.8	6.5	2,802	14.5	5,154	7.9	54.4	58	62	64	66	73
Hernando	FL	12,861	17,215	22,684	22,069	585	63.7	70.5	7.3	16.1	1.6	0.1	0.3	4.0	1,508	14.6	2,889	7.6	52.2	71	74	74	77	37
Hillsborough	FL	123,900	164,311	194,525	203,439	24,054	60.0	36.8	21.4	33.9	3.4	0.2	0.3	4.0	14,266	14.3	26,640	7.6	53.6	69	73	80	73	310
Indian River	FL	11,838	14,979	17,740	18,060	1,028	57.0	57.2	16.5	21.3	1.4	0.1	0.3	3.3	1,074	16.8	1,956	9.2	54.9	72	81	78	79	37
Lake	FL	21,065	29,293	41,110	41,794	1,915	57.9	56.1	15.0	21.9	2.7	#	0.5	3.7	2,862	14.6	5,837	7.2	49.0	75	78	74	77	61
Lee	FL	43,240	58,401	81,967	87,425	6,064	65.3	45.2	15.0	35.4	1.6	0.1	0.3	2.4	5,517	15.8	11,072	7.9	49.8	74	72	74	80	120
Leon	FL	27,241	32,050	33,326	33,747	617	39.9	44.9	43.0	4.7	3.6	0.1	0.3	3.4	2,192	15.4	4,536	7.4	48.3	74	81	80	84	60
Manatee	FL	26,326	36,569	44,249	46,705	4,628	58.3	49.9	14.1	30.9	1.8	0.1	0.2	3.1	3,011	15.5	6,028	7.7	50.0	73	71	78	76	81
Marion	FL	29,577	38,562	41,955	42,107	2,091	54.7	53.5	19.8	19.6	1.4	0.1	0.6	4.9	2,599	16.2	5,889	7.2	44.5	71	77	74	78	67
Martin	FL	11,808	16,308	18,170	18,792	2,272	43.5	62.0	7.6	26.0	1.6	0.1	0.3	2.5	1,193	15.8	2,514	7.5	47.4	76	77	77	89	38
Okaloosa	FL	26,140	30,344	28,695	30,223	767	41.7	68.5	12.6	8.6	2.2	0.2	0.4	7.5	1,808	16.7	3,392	8.9	53.3	82	85	88	83	52
Orange	FL	103,000	150,681	176,008	187,092	24,771	61.0	29.7	27.3	35.6	4.5	0.2	0.3	2.3	11,760	15.9	22,944	8.2	51.3	85	83	83	83	249
Osceola	FL	19,570	34,566	53,357	58,204	9,962	65.4	26.3	11.4	56.9	2.4	0.1	0.4	2.6	3,517	16.5	7,093	8.2	49.6	71	74	76	75	69
Palm Beach	FL	106,000	153,871	174,663	182,895	20,527	59.6	34.1	28.9	30.6	2.9	0.1	0.7	2.7	12,694	14.4	22,615	8.1	56.1	76	78	76	78	269
Pasco	FL	33,891	49,704	66,994	68,109	2,697	52.7	65.9	6.4	20.4	2.5	0.1	0.4	4.2	5,392	12.6	10,481	6.5	51.4	74	77	76	79	110
Pinellas	FL	94,364	113,027	104,001	103,411	5,592	42.6	58.1	18.8	14.5	4.6	0.1	0.3	3.9	6,913	15.0	13,787	7.5	50.1	65	72	72	76	170
Polk	FL	65,218	79,477	95,178	97,953	10,516	59.7	44.3	21.1	29.4	1.6	0.1	0.5	3.0	6,489	15.1	13,061	7.5	49.7	66	68	69	69	162
Saint Johns	FL	22,224	20,090	30,710	33,583	218	22.8	79.5	7.4	7.3	3.3	0.1	0.2	2.2	2,420	13.9	4,454	7.5	54.3	86	86	87	88	48
Saint Lucie	FL	12,080	29,540	39,259	39,477	2,828	66.8	37.7	29.8	26.8	1.7	0.1	0.3	3.5	2,280	17.3	4,621	8.5	49.3	65	71	68	83	49
Santa Rosa	FL	15,741	22,633	25,533	25,893	157	41.8	80.1	5.1	5.7	1.5	0.2	0.5	6.9	1,660	15.6	2,599	10.0	63.9	78	78	79	83	39
Sarasota	FL	27,888	35,533	40,899	41,395	2,439	44.8	65.1	9.0	18.6	2.3	0.1	0.3	4.4	2,958	14.0	5,661	7.3	52.3	71	80	79	81	59
Seminole	FL	49,027	60,869	64,229	64,851	2,486	45.6	54.5	14.5	22.9	4.3	0.3	0.2	3.3	5,044	12.9	8,373	7.7	60.2	79	76	84	85	76
Volusia	FL	48,403	61,517	61,559	61,238	3,363	61.7	60.4	15.5	18.0	1.8	0.1	0.3	3.8	4,019	15.2	7,387	8.3	54.4	62	67	68	71	90
Atlanta	GA	60,795	58,230	49,796	50,131	1,508	76.9	14.3	76.1	6.7	1.0	0.1	0.1	1.6	3,659	13.7	6,574	7.6	55.7	52	51	59	59	103
Bibb County	GA	24,413	24,739	24,961	24,180	383	81.9	18.7	73.6	3.9	1.6	0.1	0.1	2.0	1,529	15.8	3,370	7.2	45.4	51	52	61	59	45
Chatham County	GA	34,100	35,344	35,246	37,445	798	65.4	30.0	57.2	4.8	2.0	0.1	0.3	5.6	2,579	14.5	4,703	8.0	54.8	54	63	70	69	58
Cherokee County	GA	16,006	26,043	38,760	39,760	1,880	32.4	72.7	7.1	15.3	1.7	0.1	0.2	3.0	2,316	17.2	4,207	8.0	55.1	75	73	78	82	40
Clayton County	GA	34,754	46,930	50,366	52,296	4,064	99.7	3.1	70.4	19.3	4.3	0.1	0.1	2.6	3,098	16.9	6,374	9.5	48.6	51	54	56	60	63
Cobb County	GA	69,441	95,781	107,315	110,001	8,344	45.3	41.2	31.7	18.5	5.0	0.1	0.2	3.3	6,975	15.8	13,094	8.4	53.3	73	76	77	78	114
Columbia County	GA	14,096	18,756	23,722	24,907	356	33.6	63.1	19.1	8.3	4.0	0.1	0.3	5.1	1,408	17.7	2,915	8.5	48.3	76	74	80	85	30
Coweta County	GA	10,430	16,766	22,490	22,526	487	44.5	64.3	21.7	7.8	1.9	#	0.4	3.9	1,419	15.9	2,955	7.6	48.0	75	80	79	82	29
DeKalb County	GA	74,404	95,958	98,115	99,388	11,364	72.8	10.9	66.6	14.6	6.0	0.1	0.2	1.5	6,316	15.7	12,395	8.0	51.0	59	57	59	62	135
Dougherty County	GA	18,877	16,799	15,906	15,663	203	99.6	8.0	88.4	1.0	0.5	0.2	0.9	1.0	1,018	15.4	2,282	6.9	44.6	54	57	60	59	24

See notes at end of table.

Table 215.10. Selected statistics on enrollment, teachers, dropouts, and graduates in public school districts enrolling more than 15,000 students: Selected years, 1990 through 2013—Continued

Name of district	State	Enrollment, fall 1990	Enrollment, fall 2000	Enrollment, fall 2010	Enrollment, fall 2013	Number of English language learners, 2013	Percent eligible for free or reduced-price lunch, 2013[1]	Percentage distribution of enrollment, by race/ethnicity, fall 2013							Teachers and staff, fall 2013					Public high school 4-year adjusted cohort graduation rate (ACGR)[2]				Number of schools, fall 2013
								White	Black	Hispanic	Asian	Pacific Islander	American Indian/Alaska Native	Two or more races	Number of classroom teachers	Pupil/teacher ratio	Total number of staff	Student/staff ratio	Teachers as a percentage of total staff	2010-11	2011-12	2012-13	2013-14	
1	2	3	4	5	6	7	8	9	10	11	12	13	14	15	16	17	18	19	20	21	22	23	24	25
Douglas County	GA	14,002	17,489	24,601	25,577	1,333	62.2	30.8	50.6	12.8	1.3	0.2	0.1	4.1	1,593	16.1	3,275	7.8	48.6	71	72	71	76	36
Fayette County	GA	13,105	19,590	21,274	20,159	587	26.1	53.4	25.5	9.9	5.4	0.1	0.4	5.2	1,293	15.6	2,469	8.2	52.4	78	86	87	90	24
Forsyth County	GA	7,742	17,131	35,920	40,691	1,814	18.7	71.4	2.9	12.5	10.1	0.1	0.4	2.6	2,375	17.1	4,296	9.5	55.3	86	88	90	90	36
Fulton County	GA	41,935	68,583	91,864	95,232	5,311	45.8	31.0	42.5	13.9	9.7	0.1	0.1	2.8	6,330	15.0	11,896	8.0	53.2	70	71	76	79	104
Gwinnett County	GA	64,980	110,075	160,744	169,150	18,957	55.5	28.2	30.9	26.9	10.1	0.1	0.3	3.6	10,357	16.3	19,687	8.6	52.6	68	71	73	75	132
Hall County	GA	13,833	20,330	25,946	26,919	4,174	60.4	52.7	4.7	38.9	1.4	0.1	0.1	2.1	1,683	16.0	3,132	8.6	53.7	73	74	75	78	33
Henry County	GA	10,929	23,601	40,909	40,720	641	52.0	36.6	48.2	8.1	2.8	0.1	0.1	4.0	2,539	16.0	4,586	8.9	55.4	72	76	79	75	50
Houston County	GA	16,249	21,529	27,061	27,948	790	58.4	48.1	36.4	8.1	2.6	0.1	0.2	4.5	1,838	15.2	3,849	7.3	47.7	73	76	79	77	39
Muscogee County	GA	30,125	32,916	32,288	32,128	582	71.9	28.0	57.9	7.0	2.2	0.1	0.2	4.5	2,142	15.0	4,720	6.8	45.4	68	68	73	77	58
Newton County	GA	8,054	11,734	19,478	19,522	527	68.5	36.3	52.4	6.5	0.8	0.2	0.1	3.8	1,265	15.4	2,523	7.7	50.1	64	76	73	77	24
Paulding County	GA	7,604	16,587	28,407	28,434	410	43.2	66.5	20.4	7.8	0.9	0.1	0.3	3.9	1,666	17.1	3,227	8.8	51.6	76	75	78	78	33
Richmond County	GA	33,660	35,424	32,322	31,997	275	96.8	19.0	72.8	3.8	0.8	1.0	0.1	2.5	2,006	15.9	4,144	7.7	48.4	55	59	58	62	61
Rockdale County	GA	10,942	13,519	15,864	16,047	576	68.8	18.6	62.9	13.0	1.8	0.2	0.2	3.3	1,040	15.4	2,048	7.8	50.8	66	72	78	76	18
Hawaii Department of Education	HI	159,285	184,360	179,601	186,825	15,949	50.5	13.6	2.1	10.0	32.0	32.0	0.4	9.9	11,781	15.9	22,438	8.3	52.5	80	81	82	82	288
Boise Independent	ID	23,394	26,598	25,039	27,275	1,794	41.2	77.0	3.5	11.9	4.1	0.6	0.6	2.3	1,468	18.6	2,355	11.6	62.3	—	—	—	81	49
Meridian Joint	ID	14,802	23,854	35,537	38,006	985	28.9	83.7	1.3	8.7	2.2	0.4	0.5	3.1	1,775	21.4	2,673	14.2	66.4	—	—	—	81	55
Nampa	ID	7,878	11,403	15,181	16,241	988	62.3	62.8	1.1	33.4	0.9	0.8	0.9	0.1	714	22.8	901	18.0	79.2	—	—	—	77	26
Carpentersville (CUSD 300)	IL	11,196	16,711	20,678	20,884	2,291	46.2	51.3	5.1	34.4	5.9	0.1	0.2	3.0	1,249	16.7	1,509	13.8	82.7	89	88	89	90	27
City of Chicago (SD 299)	IL	408,830	435,261	405,644	396,641	65,489	85.6	9.3	39.4	45.8	3.5	0.1	0.3	1.5	23,320	17.0	45,545	8.7	51.2	74	69	70	81	595
Elgin (SDU-46)	IL	27,726	36,767	40,551	40,551	9,585	59.5	31.3	6.7	49.6	8.5	0.1	1.2	2.6	2,170	18.7	3,109	13.0	69.8	88	80	80	86	57
Indian Prairie (CUSD 204)	IL	7,670	23,173	29,522	28,711	1,678	17.9	52.8	9.1	10.6	23.0	#	0.2	4.3	1,758	16.3	1,864	15.4	94.3	98	97	—	98	33
Naperville (CUSD 203)	IL	16,212	18,762	17,834	17,276	794	13.3	66.5	5.0	9.3	15.5	#	0.1	3.5	1,080	16.0	1,573	11.0	68.6	98	97	95	98	22
Oswego (CUSD 308)	IL	4,108	6,846	16,729	17,644	761	26.3	61.3	7.6	18.9	6.6	#	0.2	5.4	985	17.9	1,554	11.4	63.4	95	94	96	96	23
Plainfield (SD 202)	IL	3,324	11,986	28,921	28,559	1,638	21.1	58.7	9.1	22.8	5.5	0.1	0.2	3.4	1,580	18.1	2,002	14.3	78.9	91	93	93	91	30
Rockford (SD 205)	IL	27,255	27,399	28,961	29,046	3,335	78.6	32.9	29.8	26.4	4.0	#	0.2	6.6	1,876	15.5	2,458	11.8	76.3	72	62	64	68	51
Springfield (SD 186)	IL	15,813	15,387	15,176	15,249	112	66.6	47.1	38.5	2.6	2.0	0.1	0.2	9.5	1,049	14.5	1,460	10.4	71.9	76	68	67	70	34
Valley View (CUSD 365U)	IL	11,781	13,558	17,874	17,710	2,224	63.7	27.4	20.1	41.3	6.8	0.3	0.3	3.9	1,181	15.0	1,914	9.3	61.7	83	86	84	85	20
Waukegan (CUSD 60)	IL	12,116	15,510	16,462	16,876	4,783	69.2	3.8	15.1	77.3	1.3	0.2	0.4	1.8	948	17.8	1,192	14.2	79.5	68	71	75	76	24
Carmel Clay	IN	8,449	12,073	15,550	15,912	546	10.2	76.4	3.5	2.5	11.7	0.3	0.2	5.4	829	19.2	1,906	8.3	43.5	94	96	97	97	15
Evansville Vanderburgh	IN	22,918	22,875	23,440	22,688	485	59.4	71.0	14.0	3.7	1.3	0.3	0.2	9.5	1,700	13.3	3,534	6.4	48.1	81	82	81	81	37
Fort Wayne	IN	31,611	31,843	31,401	30,783	2,809	70.6	46.8	24.2	15.2	4.7	0.1	0.4	8.5	1,644	18.7	3,499	8.8	47.0	88	84	89	87	50
Hamilton Southeastern	IN	3,113	8,777	18,687	20,524	553	13.7	77.1	6.9	5.5	5.5	0.1	0.1	4.6	1,036	19.8	2,328	8.8	44.5	94	93	94	94	21
Indianapolis	IN	48,140	41,008	33,079	30,813	4,492	82.0	20.4	52.2	21.9	0.6	0.1	0.2	4.7	2,498	12.3	5,276	5.8	47.3	65	60	63	61	68
MSD Wayne Township	IN	12,229	13,263	16,002	15,874	2,484	78.2	39.3	30.5	23.0	0.8	#	0.2	6.2	1,051	15.1	2,457	6.5	42.8	86	73	76	78	18
South Bend	IN	21,425	21,536	19,998	19,680	2,259	73.0	36.2	34.6	18.6	1.3	0.1	0.3	9.0	1,032	19.1	2,738	7.2	37.7	77	76	72	76	38
Vigo County	IN	16,982	16,545	15,881	15,573	217	55.7	82.7	5.3	3.1	1.7	#	0.3	7.1	864	18.0	1,632	9.5	53.0	88	91	91	93	28
Cedar Rapids	IA	17,003	17,780	17,272	17,372	480	49.2	71.0	14.5	5.9	2.0	0.3	0.3	6.0	1,131	15.4	2,452	7.1	46.1	82	83	81	85	31
Davenport	IA	17,846	16,874	17,096	16,836	496	62.7	57.3	18.7	13.6	1.9	0.3	0.3	8.1	1,110	15.2	2,140	7.9	51.8	77	79	79	83	33
Des Moines Independent	IA	30,888	32,435	33,091	34,230	5,711	69.8	44.4	17.6	23.9	7.0	0.2	0.4	6.5	2,402	14.3	4,682	7.3	51.3	76	79	79	82	61
Blue Valley	KS	9,433	17,111	21,641	22,400	414	8.4	77.4	3.2	4.9	10.3	0.1	0.3	3.8	1,456	15.4	2,811	8.0	51.8	96	97	95	97	34
Kansas City	KS	22,118	21,173	20,229	21,677	7,132	90.7	12.6	34.0	45.4	5.5	0.2	0.3	2.0	1,540	14.1	3,113	7.0	49.4	63	67	65	64	43
Olathe	KS	14,870	20,703	27,882	29,080	1,760	28.5	70.6	7.0	13.7	4.7	0.1	0.4	3.5	2,101	13.8	3,919	7.4	53.6	92	91	90	92	47
Shawnee Mission	KS	30,619	30,765	27,822	27,404	2,518	37.8	65.5	8.8	17.2	3.0	0.2	0.3	5.1	1,745	15.7	3,137	8.7	55.6	91	91	91	91	43
Wichita	KS	47,222	48,228	49,329	50,629	8,555	77.9	34.5	18.1	33.0	4.6	0.2	1.3	8.4	3,250	15.6	6,169	8.2	52.7	66	74	77	75	89
Boone County	KY	9,911	13,445	19,306	20,046	914	33.4	84.4	3.6	6.3	2.2	0.2	0.1	3.1	1,216	16.5	2,708	7.4	44.9	—	—	92	93	24
Fayette County	KY	32,083	33,130	37,819	40,079	3,636	48.0	55.1	22.8	13.6	4.1	0.1	0.2	4.2	2,799	14.3	5,793	6.9	48.3	—	—	83	85	80
Jefferson County	KY	91,450	96,860	97,331	100,529	6,216	59.1	48.3	36.8	8.2	3.3	0.2	0.1	3.2	5,853	17.2	14,271	7.0	41.0	—	—	77	79	174
Ascension Parish	LA	13,001	15,038	19,953	21,367	406	48.3	60.6	30.5	6.0	1.0	0.1	0.3	1.5	1,388	15.4	2,736	7.8	50.7	80	87	87	87	27
Bossier Parish	LA	17,804	18,797	20,656	21,844	554	46.3	59.5	27.8	6.8	1.6	0.2	0.4	3.7	1,346	16.2	2,786	7.8	48.3	77	74	79	80	33

See notes at end of table.

Table 215.10. Selected statistics on enrollment, teachers, dropouts, and graduates in public school districts enrolling more than 15,000 students: Selected years, 1990 through 2013—Continued

Name of district	State	Enrollment, fall 1990	Enrollment, fall 2000	Enrollment, fall 2010	Enrollment, fall 2013	Number of English language learners, 2013	Percent eligible for free or reduced-price lunch, 2013[1]	Percentage distribution of enrollment, by race/ethnicity, fall 2013							Teachers and staff, fall 2013					Public high school 4-year adjusted cohort graduation rate (ACGR)[2]				Number of schools, fall 2013
								White	Black	Hispanic	Asian	Pacific Islander	American Indian/ Alaska Native	Two or more races	Number of classroom teachers	Pupil/ teacher ratio	Total number of staff	Student/ staff ratio	Teachers as a percentage of total staff	2010–11	2011–12	2012–13	2013–14	
1	2	3	4	5	6	7	8	9	10	11	12	13	14	15	16	17	18	19	20	21	22	23	24	25
Caddo Parish	LA	51,375	45,119	41,894	40,913	432	66.3	31.4	63.3	2.6	1.1	0.1	0.1	1.3	2,536	16.1	5,657	7.2	44.8	61	63	64	68	66
Calcasieu Parish	LA	32,917	32,261	33,063	32,481	308	59.1	60.5	33.2	2.9	1.2	0.1	0.2	1.8	2,353	13.8	4,720	6.9	49.8	78	78	78	78	58
East Baton Rouge Parish	LA	61,669	54,246	42,723	41,937	1,773	81.5	10.9	79.6	5.3	3.2	0.2	0.1	0.7	2,786	15.1	5,597	7.5	49.8	63	66	69	66	85
Jefferson Parish	LA	58,177	50,891	45,230	46,312	4,416	77.0	28.0	43.7	20.4	4.7	0.3	0.6	2.3	2,945	15.7	6,017	7.7	48.9	67	70	69	72	82
Lafayette Parish	LA	29,403	28,931	30,218	30,961	971	61.4	48.5	43.0	5.0	2.2	#	0.3	1.0	1,979	15.6	4,121	7.5	48.0	73	70	72	69	42
Livingston Parish	LA	16,310	19,723	24,468	25,603	236	50.0	87.5	7.3	3.8	0.7	0.1	0.2	0.5	1,520	16.8	3,127	8.2	48.6	78	76	80	80	44
Ouachita Parish	LA	17,667	17,479	19,680	19,923	152	59.4	62.0	34.5	2.0	0.9	#	0.1	0.6	1,249	15.9	2,859	7.0	43.7	73	73	79	81	36
Rapides Parish	LA	24,765	23,467	23,989	24,099	426	70.0	51.6	43.1	2.9	0.9	#	0.6	0.4	1,631	14.8	3,224	7.5	50.6	67	70	67	73	50
Saint Tammany Parish	LA	27,522	32,392	36,651	37,684	621	47.9	73.2	18.7	4.7	1.4	#	0.3	1.6	2,511	15.0	5,143	7.3	48.8	79	79	67	80	55
Tangipahoa Parish	LA	16,724	18,197	19,400	19,962	274	77.5	46.3	47.3	4.0	0.7	#	0.1	1.6	1,202	16.6	2,567	7.8	46.8	71	71	69	72	33
Terrebonne Parish	LA	21,116	19,774	18,722	18,522	353	68.1	53.7	27.8	5.6	1.1	#	8.9	2.9	1,054	17.6	2,107	8.8	50.0	70	77	81	76	38
Anne Arundel County	MD	65,011	74,491	75,481	78,489	3,559	31.9	59.1	20.3	10.8	3.6	0.3	0.3	5.6	5,337	14.7	9,778	8.0	54.6	84	85	86	88	121
Baltimore City	MD	108,663	99,859	83,800	84,730	3,005	84.9	8.0	83.8	6.2	1.0	0.3	0.3	0.4	5,272	16.1	9,905	8.6	53.2	66	66	69	70	189
Baltimore County	MD	96,737	106,898	104,160	108,191	4,031	47.5	43.2	38.7	7.2	6.4	0.1	0.4	4.0	7,306	14.8	14,264	7.6	51.2	82	84	86	88	173
Calvert County	MD	10,398	16,170	16,795	16,221	125	24.2	73.6	13.9	4.6	1.5	0.1	0.2	6.1	1,040	15.6	2,128	7.6	48.9	91	92	92	94	26
Carroll County	MD	21,835	27,528	27,334	26,331	201	18.9	87.1	3.6	4.4	2.2	0.1	0.2	2.3	1,865	14.1	3,354	7.9	55.6	93	95	94	96	47
Cecil County	MD	12,868	15,905	15,937	15,824	145	43.1	79.5	8.4	5.7	0.8	0.1	0.3	5.2	1,147	13.8	2,083	7.6	55.1	83	84	87	89	29
Charles County	MD	18,708	23,468	26,850	26,455	272	33.7	31.6	52.5	6.0	3.1	0.1	0.5	6.1	1,702	15.5	3,237	8.2	52.6	88	90	90	91	37
Frederick County	MD	26,848	36,885	40,188	40,648	1,727	26.2	65.5	11.2	12.6	5.0	0.1	0.4	5.2	2,647	15.4	5,487	7.4	48.2	92	93	93	93	67
Harford County	MD	31,500	39,520	38,394	37,842	357	30.5	66.7	18.1	6.0	3.1	0.2	0.3	5.5	2,811	13.5	5,461	6.9	51.5	87	88	90	90	54
Howard County	MD	29,949	44,946	50,994	52,806	2,096	19.2	44.4	21.5	9.1	18.4	0.1	0.2	6.3	3,832	13.8	7,701	6.9	49.8	91	90	93	93	75
Montgomery County	MD	103,757	134,180	144,023	151,295	20,465	34.2	32.0	21.4	27.4	14.4	0.2	0.2	4.6	10,112	15.0	20,595	7.3	49.1	87	87	88	90	207
Prince George's County	MD	108,868	133,723	126,671	125,136	17,768	61.5	4.5	64.6	25.8	2.8	0.2	0.4	1.7	8,326	15.0	16,997	7.4	49.0	75	73	74	77	209
Saint Mary's County	MD	12,549	15,151	17,271	17,841	189	32.1	67.2	18.5	5.9	2.7	#	0.4	5.2	1,067	16.7	2,059	8.7	51.8	84	88	92	93	27
Washington County	MD	17,778	19,782	22,206	22,495	377	48.8	72.2	12.5	6.4	1.8	#	0.3	6.8	1,519	14.8	2,936	7.7	51.7	90	90	91	91	46
Boston	MA	60,543	63,024	56,037	54,300	15,022	77.6	13.6	34.5	40.4	8.6	0.2	0.3	2.4	4,001	13.6	7,128	7.6	56.1	64	66	66	67	118
Brockton	MA	14,529	16,791	15,828	17,011	3,291	80.7	23.5	54.9	14.4	2.4	0.2	0.4	4.1	1,113	15.3	2,104	8.1	52.9	69	75	74	73	24
Springfield	MA	24,194	26,526	25,213	25,826	4,084	87.3	12.4	20.2	62.2	2.6	#	0.1	2.5	2,106	12.3	3,844	6.7	54.8	52	57	55	62	54
Worcester	MA	21,066	25,828	24,192	24,562	6,271	73.0	35.8	14.5	38.0	7.7	#	0.2	3.8	1,413	17.4	2,798	8.8	50.5	72	72	73	79	45
Ann Arbor	MI	14,190	16,539	16,764	16,454	856	23.5	55.3	14.1	6.6	14.9	#	0.4	8.7	927	17.8	2,736	6.0	33.9	84	87	87	89	32
Chippewa Valley	MI	9,340	12,329	16,088	16,477	1,134	25.7	80.9	9.0	3.4	3.0	#	0.2	3.4	818	20.1	1,543	10.7	53.0	85	87	88	89	20
Dearborn City	MI	13,380	17,129	18,653	19,190	8,693	68.9	92.5	4.2	2.1	0.9	#	0.2	0.1	1,157	16.6	2,123	9.0	54.5	76	86	86	87	36
Detroit City	MI	168,956	162,194	77,757	49,043	5,540	81.6	2.4	83.8	12.1	1.3	#	0.5	6.3	3,084	15.9	6,957	7.0	44.3	60	65	65	71	92
Grand Rapids	MI	26,871	25,625	18,125	16,452	3,846	82.2	20.3	34.3	37.4	1.1	0.1	0.5	6.3	1,159	14.2	2,663	6.2	43.5	48	45	47	50	49
Plymouth-Canton	MI	14,955	16,518	18,905	17,646	716	16.8	72.2	9.5	3.4	10.6	0.1	0.3	3.8	913	19.3	1,811	9.7	50.4	86	86	88	89	24
Rochester Community	MI	11,350	13,862	14,890	15,051	681	13.8	76.3	4.9	4.0	11.4	0.1	0.2	3.1	839	17.9	1,778	8.5	47.2	93	94	94	95	22
Utica	MI	23,960	27,786	28,985	28,316	1,993	29.9	88.2	4.8	2.4	3.1	0.1	0.2	1.2	1,408	20.1	2,561	11.1	55.0	90	90	91	91	38
Warren Consolidated	MI	14,336	14,602	15,820	15,116	2,836	58.6	73.6	12.2	1.6	9.7	0.3	0.3	2.5	777	19.5	1,463	10.3	53.1	80	78	78	80	27
Anoka-Hennepin	MN	34,524	41,314	39,158	38,250	2,152	32.9	76.1	9.4	4.5	6.2	0.1	0.9	2.7	2,198	17.4	4,557	8.4	48.2	77	76	81	82	50
Minneapolis	MN	41,050	48,834	34,934	36,817	8,316	64.9	32.7	36.3	18.6	6.9	0.1	4.1	1.3	2,457	15.0	5,707	6.5	43.1	47	50	54	59	91
Osseo Public	MN	19,579	22,017	21,053	20,913	1,986	40.8	47.7	22.4	7.9	16.0	#	0.4	5.6	1,222	17.1	2,671	7.8	45.8	81	81	84	86	34
Rochester	MN	14,045	15,929	16,353	16,761	1,920	36.9	64.3	12.0	8.8	10.4	#	0.3	4.2	1,006	16.7	2,103	8.0	47.8	79	81	83	84	38
Rosemount-Apple Valley-Eagan	MN	20,547	28,330	27,590	27,289	1,489	25.5	69.5	10.1	7.6	8.1	0.1	0.4	4.3	1,583	17.2	3,197	8.5	49.5	86	89	92	92	36
Saint Paul	MN	35,932	45,115	38,316	38,228	12,491	73.1	22.8	27.6	13.9	30.5	0.1	1.3	3.9	2,628	14.5	5,730	6.7	45.9	64	66	73	76	98
South Washington County	MN	11,417	14,953	17,456	18,137	241	19.0	71.3	7.2	7.0	9.6	0.1	0.3	4.6	1,124	16.1	2,150	8.4	52.3	91	91	90	93	27
DeSoto County	MS	13,470	19,812	31,916	33,054	1,151	52.8	58.4	33.0	6.3	1.6	0.1	0.2	0.4	1,926	17.2	3,974	8.3	48.5	86	85	90	90	41
Jackson	MS	33,546	31,351	30,366	29,488	224	92.1	1.4	96.9	1.2	0.1	0.0	#	0.4	1,720	17.1	4,195	7.0	41.0	63	64	64	67	63
Rankin County	MS	12,824	15,013	18,937	19,382	282	42.3	73.2	22.0	2.1	1.4	#	0.1	1.1	1,354	14.3	2,446	7.9	55.3	84	84	86	84	27
Columbia, 93	MO	12,786	16,178	17,550	17,872	920	42.0	61.7	20.3	6.1	5.5	0.0	0.4	5.9	1,300	13.7	2,610	6.8	49.8	83	85	86	90	32
Fort Zumwalt, R-III	MO	10,110	16,521	18,951	18,654	400	24.7	83.5	5.6	3.9	3.2	0.2	0.2	3.4	1,142	16.3	1,492	12.5	76.6	83	90	89	91	24

See notes at end of table.

Table 215.10. Selected statistics on enrollment, teachers, dropouts, and graduates in public school districts enrolling more than 15,000 students: Selected years, 1990 through 2013—Continued

Name of district	State	Enrollment, fall 1990	Enrollment, fall 2000	Enrollment, fall 2010	Enrollment, fall 2013	Number of English language learners, 2013	Percent eligible for free or reduced-price lunch, 2013[1]	White	Black	Hispanic	Asian	Pacific Islander	American Indian/Alaska Native	Two or more races	Number of classroom teachers	Pupil/teacher ratio	Total number of staff	Student/staff ratio	Teachers as a percentage of total staff	2010–11	2011–12	2012–13	2013–14	Number of schools, fall 2013
1	2	3	4	5	6	7	8	9	10	11	12	13	14	15	16	17	18	19	20	21	22	23	24	25
Francis Howell, R-III	MO	13,391	19,497	19,981	19,975	228	18.7	82.4	8.6	3.0	3.6	0.2	0.1	2.0	1,185	16.9	1,616	12.4	73.3	88	89	92	94	23
Hazelwood	MO	16,985	18,855	18,655	18,402	422	63.1	22.9	72.7	2.1	1.1	0.1	0.1	1.0	1,112	16.6	1,199	15.4	92.7	75	83	86	85	33
Kansas City, 33	MO	34,486	37,298	17,326	15,230	3,426	76.0	8.6	58.4	27.9	3.7	0.1	0.3	0.9	1,137	13.4	2,367	6.4	48.0	50	63	67	63	34
Lee's Summit, R-VII	MO	7,132	14,340	17,803	17,844	224	19.4	76.2	14.4	5.6	2.9	0.3	0.5	0.0	1,146	15.6	2,412	7.4	47.5	86	91	94	94	27
North Kansas City, 74	MO	15,732	17,258	18,764	19,726	1,294	44.3	63.5	12.3	12.8	3.5	0.7	0.6	6.6	1,222	16.1	2,681	7.4	45.6	85	88	91	93	32
Parkway, C-2	MO	21,542	20,433	17,458	17,955	614	19.9	64.2	15.4	4.9	11.0	0.1	0.1	4.3	1,181	15.2	2,472	7.3	47.8	92	93	93	92	28
Rockwood, R-VI	MO	15,608	21,203	22,823	21,883	329	15.9	79.4	9.3	2.9	6.4	0.1	0.2	1.7	1,449	15.1	3,529	6.2	41.1	91	95	94	96	31
Saint Louis City	MO	43,284	44,412	25,084	27,017	1,687	87.8	11.5	82.6	3.1	2.6	0.0	0.2	0.0	2,006	13.5	2,890	9.3	69.4	54	62	68	71	78
Springfield, R-XII	MO	23,631	24,630	24,730	25,609	788	56.6	80.7	7.9	4.9	2.6	0.4	0.5	3.0	1,662	15.4	2,412	10.6	68.9	79	85	87	89	55
Lincoln	NE	27,986	31,354	35,896	37,879	2,158	44.4	68.3	6.3	12.7	4.6	0.1	0.7	7.3	2,747	13.8	5,332	7.1	51.5	80	83	84	84	71
Millard	NE	16,784	19,160	22,783	23,549	288	18.7	81.3	3.0	7.1	5.1	0.2	0.3	3.0	1,499	15.7	2,748	8.6	54.5	93	93	94	95	37
Omaha	NE	41,699	45,197	49,405	51,069	6,988	73.4	31.4	25.7	32.3	4.0	0.1	1.1	5.5	3,147	16.2	6,390	8.0	49.3	73	76	78	81	105
Clark County	NV	121,994	231,655	314,059	320,532	52,744	56.9	28.5	12.8	44.2	6.5	1.5	0.5	6.1	15,321	20.9	18,244	17.6	84.0	59	62	72	71	363
Washoe County	NV	38,466	56,268	64,380	65,550	10,348	47.1	46.4	2.4	38.7	4.5	1.0	1.6	5.4	3,198	20.5	3,640	18.0	87.9	70	70	73	73	106
Elizabeth	NJ	15,266	19,674	24,258	24,875	3,390	85.0	8.1	20.9	69.0	1.7	0.2	#	0.1	2,084	11.9	2,512	9.9	83.0	67	66	71	73	34
Jersey City	NJ	28,585	31,347	34,505	27,571	3,331	70.8	11.4	32.1	38.2	16.9	0.6	0.4	0.4	2,400	11.5	3,528	7.8	68.0	70	67	67	67	38
Newark	NJ	48,433	42,150	41,235	34,976	3,108	84.3	7.9	50.9	40.1	0.8	0.1	0.2	#	3,057	11.4	6,057	5.8	50.5	61	69	68	69	72
Paterson	NJ	22,109	24,629	31,350	34,598	4,613	90.2	5.9	26.7	63.0	4.0	0.1	0.2	#	2,182	11.3	4,331	5.7	50.4	64	66	72	75	48
Toms River Regional	NJ	16,002	17,621	17,285	16,324	119	28.5	77.2	4.8	12.0	3.9	0.1	0.1	1.9	1,179	13.8	2,163	7.5	54.5	90	91	90	91	18
Albuquerque	NM	88,295	85,276	95,415	93,202	15,556	65.0	21.3	2.2	66.9	2.1	0.1	4.5	3.0	6,185	15.1	12,339	7.6	50.1	63	65	69	62	162
Las Cruces	NM	19,216	22,185	25,488	25,130	3,127	63.3	19.9	2.5	75.2	0.9	0.4	0.9	0.4	1,628	15.4	3,337	7.5	48.8	71	71	67	68	41
Rio Rancho	NM	—	10,219	16,751	17,202	578	42.2	37.7	2.8	50.9	1.6	0.2	3.6	3.2	1,052	16.4	2,100	8.2	50.1	73	79	84	84	19
Brentwood Union Free	NY	11,749	15,565	16,833	17,963	5,789	57.6	5.6	12.3	79.3	2.2	0.0	0.3	0.3	1,045	17.2	2,181	8.2	47.9	76	72	74	74	17
Buffalo City	NY	47,224	45,721	33,543	34,854	4,220	43.3	21.4	50.1	17.4	7.3	0.0	1.1	2.8	2,859	12.2	4,296	8.1	66.5	50	56	49	56	56
New York City	NY	943,969	1,066,516	995,336	989,012	139,740	77.5	15.2	26.2	40.7	16.4	0.0	0.7	0.7	66,153	15.0	—	—	—	66	66	65	66	1,634
Rochester City	NY	32,730	36,294	32,223	30,295	2,971	68.6	10.3	60.3	25.5	3.7	0.0	0.2	0.1	2,543	11.9	5,100	5.9	49.9	51	50	48	49	53
Syracuse City	NY	22,561	23,015	21,247	21,212	2,608	66.0	24.3	49.6	13.2	7.4	0.0	1.3	4.2	1,568	13.5	3,100	6.8	50.6	51	53	51	52	30
Yonkers City	NY	18,621	26,237	25,568	26,516	3,133	69.2	17.8	20.2	55.1	5.4	0.1	0.3	1.2	1,534	17.3	3,264	8.1	47.0	69	72	84	84	39
Alamance-Burlington	NC	10,322	20,729	22,811	22,615	2,146	57.6	50.1	21.0	23.2	1.3	0.1	0.4	3.8	1,503	15.0	2,777	8.1	54.1	76	75	78	79	36
Buncombe County	NC	22,026	24,708	25,572	25,495	1,641	55.5	73.5	6.5	13.6	1.5	0.2	0.3	4.4	1,647	15.5	3,470	7.3	47.5	78	80	80	83	42
Cabarrus County	NC	12,853	19,115	28,980	30,088	1,713	42.2	59.7	19.1	14.1	2.9	0.1	0.4	3.8	1,905	15.8	3,715	8.1	51.3	84	86	87	88	38
Catawba County	NC	12,770	16,250	17,370	16,876	1,156	51.9	70.0	5.3	13.4	6.7	0.1	0.5	4.4	1,054	16.0	2,003	8.4	52.6	86	89	91	91	28
Charlotte-Mecklenburg	NC	77,069	103,336	135,954	142,991	13,740	54.7	30.8	41.2	19.5	5.5	0.1	0.5	2.4	8,662	16.5	17,310	8.3	50.0	74	76	81	85	160
Cleveland County	NC	8,131	9,663	16,417	15,118	267	64.9	63.7	25.9	4.9	0.8	#	0.1	4.5	1,120	13.5	2,166	7.0	51.7	73	78	83	85	29
Cumberland County	NC	44,612	50,850	53,307	51,471	912	60.1	32.3	45.1	11.4	1.8	0.4	1.9	7.2	3,580	14.4	6,923	7.4	51.7	78	81	82	85	87
Davidson County	NC	16,426	19,136	20,648	19,887	400	45.8	86.1	3.2	6.9	1.2	0.1	0.4	2.2	1,199	16.6	2,306	8.6	52.0	81	83	85	85	35
Durham	NC	18,517	29,728	32,479	33,349	4,619	64.2	18.8	49.6	25.3	2.5	0.1	0.5	3.2	2,291	14.6	4,563	7.3	50.2	74	77	80	82	56
Gaston County	NC	29,631	30,603	32,326	31,256	1,441	60.8	63.8	20.5	10.0	1.5	0.1	0.2	4.0	1,911	16.4	3,605	8.7	53.0	75	78	81	84	56
Guilford County	NC	24,575	63,417	73,205	72,081	5,638	59.8	36.1	41.1	12.6	5.7	0.1	0.5	3.8	4,976	14.5	9,978	7.2	49.9	83	85	86	89	125
Harnett County	NC	11,890	16,338	19,704	20,243	1,254	58.5	49.8	24.5	18.1	0.6	1.1	1.1	5.7	1,362	14.9	2,465	8.2	55.3	73	75	77	79	27
Iredell-Statesville	NC	10,610	17,235	21,393	20,858	1,007	43.3	68.9	14.0	11.4	2.8	0.2	0.4	2.6	1,291	16.2	2,501	8.3	51.6	85	87	88	89	36
Johnston County	NC	14,647	21,334	32,454	33,852	2,797	45.7	59.2	15.9	20.4	0.6	#	0.4	3.4	2,259	15.0	3,970	8.5	56.9	79	82	83	85	44
Nash-Rocky Mount	NC	11,653	18,342	17,448	16,007	742	68.9	34.2	50.0	10.3	0.8	0.1	0.5	4.1	939	17.0	1,954	8.2	48.1	75	77	79	77	29
New Hanover County	NC	19,090	21,605	24,806	25,398	861	47.6	61.7	22.0	10.3	1.7	0.1	0.4	3.8	1,717	14.8	3,472	7.3	49.4	74	80	82	81	41
Onslow County	NC	18,605	20,984	23,890	25,161	324	44.1	59.7	19.2	11.7	1.4	0.1	0.6	7.2	1,616	15.6	3,204	7.9	50.4	82	87	87	83	35
Pitt County	NC	17,693	20,040	23,630	23,622	924	59.9	37.5	47.5	10.0	1.4	#	0.2	3.4	1,619	14.6	3,038	7.8	53.3	70	73	78	78	36
Randolph County	NC	13,572	17,271	18,935	18,098	1,050	55.9	76.5	3.7	15.1	1.3	#	0.6	2.8	1,183	15.3	2,287	7.9	51.7	83	84	89	87	31
Robeson County	NC	23,251	23,911	23,933	23,557	1,508	84.2	14.8	25.7	13.3	0.8	0.1	41.9	3.4	1,531	15.4	3,061	7.7	50.0	79	83	85	85	42
Rowan-Salisbury	NC	16,403	20,472	20,460	19,831	1,293	61.9	62.8	18.7	13.7	1.1	#	0.3	3.2	1,309	15.1	2,569	7.7	51.0	77	81	83	81	35
Union County	NC	12,864	22,862	40,153	41,074	2,163	34.3	67.1	12.8	15.0	2.2	#	0.3	2.5	2,561	16.0	4,914	8.4	52.1	89	90	91	93	52

See notes at end of table.

Table 215.10. Selected statistics on enrollment, teachers, dropouts, and graduates in public school districts enrolling more than 15,000 students: Selected years, 1990 through 2013—Continued

Name of district	State	Enrollment, fall 1990	Enrollment, fall 2000	Enrollment, fall 2010	Enrollment, fall 2013	Number of English language learners, 2013	Percent eligible for free or reduced-price lunch, 2013[1]	Percentage distribution of enrollment, by race/ethnicity, fall 2013							Number of classroom teachers	Pupil/teacher ratio	Total number of staff	Student/staff ratio	Teachers as a percentage of total staff	Public high school 4-year adjusted cohort graduation rate (ACGR)[2]				Number of schools, fall 2013
								White	Black	Hispanic	Asian	Pacific Islander	American Indian/ Alaska Native	Two or more races						2010–11	2011–12	2012–13	2013–14	
1	2	3	4	5	6	7	8	9	10	11	12	13	14	15	16	17	18	19	20	21	22	23	24	25
Wake County	NC	64,266	98,950	144,173	153,534	11,351	33.5	48.6	24.4	15.7	6.8	0.1	0.3	4.1	9,869	15.6	17,435	8.8	56.6	81	81	81	83	170
Wayne County	NC	13,653	19,279	19,471	19,197	1,592	64.1	40.1	35.0	18.5	1.4	0.1	0.2	4.8	1,233	15.6	2,456	7.8	50.2	75	80	80	83	31
Winston-Salem/Forsyth County	NC	37,625	44,769	53,367	53,413	5,973	55.9	42.4	28.6	22.2	2.3	0.1	0.3	4.1	3,714	14.4	6,905	7.7	53.8	79	81	82	84	81
Akron City	OH	33,213	31,464	23,113	21,708	1,171	77.5	38.2	45.5	3.4	5.3	0.1	0.1	7.4	1,380	15.7	2,767	7.8	49.9	75	76	78	74	49
Cincinnati City	OH	51,148	46,562	33,783	31,801	1,507	64.4	25.6	63.4	3.7	1.2	0.1	0.1	5.9	1,947	16.3	4,597	6.9	42.4	64	66	74	70	56
Cleveland Municipal	OH	70,019	75,684	44,974	38,562	2,764	87.7	14.7	66.5	14.8	1.0	0.1	0.2	2.8	2,469	15.6	6,775	5.7	36.4	56	59	64	64	98
Columbus City	OH	64,280	64,511	51,134	50,478	6,419	70.5	26.2	56.4	8.8	2.9	#	0.2	5.4	3,074	16.4	6,904	7.3	44.5	76	79	77	74	115
Hilliard City	OH	6,533	12,423	15,455	15,566	1,074	23.8	76.4	6.0	6.2	6.8	0.1	0.2	4.3	842	18.5	1,868	8.3	45.1	93	94	94	93	23
Lakota Local	OH	9,356	14,659	18,135	16,223	855	21.4	73.3	10.2	5.6	6.1	0.1	0.1	4.5	724	22.4	1,628	10.0	44.5	92	94	95	94	20
Olentangy Local	OH	2,140	5,417	15,815	17,988	298	6.9	81.0	3.8	2.6	8.8	#	0.1	3.7	922	19.5	1,994	9.0	46.2	98	98	98	98	23
South-Western City	OH	16,605	19,216	20,725	21,107	2,579	54.0	67.5	11.6	13.8	2.4	#	0.1	4.5	1,121	18.8	2,483	8.5	45.1	83	85	86	85	33
Toledo City	OH	40,452	37,738	24,283	21,669	331	69.5	39.1	40.9	11.2	0.5	#	0.1	8.2	1,410	15.4	3,074	7.0	45.9	62	65	65	65	52
Broken Arrow, 48J	OK	13,872	14,990	16,732	17,947	725	41.8	65.7	4.6	10.5	2.9	0.2	7.6	8.5	1,017	17.7	2,220	8.1	45.8	—	—	88	87	25
Edmond	OK	13,041	17,084	21,344	23,020	848	26.6	65.5	10.3	9.1	5.1	0.3	2.2	7.7	1,285	17.9	2,427	9.5	53.0	—	—	96	92	24
Lawton	OK	17,727	17,338	16,199	15,463	602	64.2	40.8	27.1	16.2	1.9	0.7	6.1	7.2	972	15.9	2,239	6.9	43.4	—	—	86	80	32
Moore	OK	16,630	18,101	22,226	23,019	530	43.5	52.6	6.4	13.6	5.0	0.1	6.1	16.1	1,284	17.9	2,547	9.0	50.4	—	—	83	83	31
Norman	OK	11,572	12,596	14,644	15,601	840	47.6	62.5	5.8	11.7	3.1	0.1	5.4	11.4	931	16.8	1,757	8.9	53.0	—	—	81	73	25
Oklahoma City	OK	36,066	39,750	42,989	40,913	13,427	87.2	16.8	24.9	49.6	2.1	0.1	3.7	2.8	2,415	16.9	3,526	11.6	68.5	—	—	79	73	80
Putnam City	OK	18,071	19,506	19,068	19,378	2,348	76.2	36.1	25.2	23.9	4.2	0.2	3.1	7.3	1,216	15.9	2,200	8.8	55.3	—	—	80	79	27
Tulsa	OK	40,732	42,812	41,501	40,152	7,150	85.0	27.8	26.7	29.1	1.3	0.2	6.4	8.4	2,377	16.9	5,635	7.1	42.2	—	—	65	63	79
Union	OK	9,563	13,054	14,931	15,526	2,783	66.1	38.4	14.4	27.8	6.9	0.1	5.2	7.1	828	18.7	1,865	8.3	44.4	—	—	89	90	17
Beaverton, 48J	OR	24,874	33,600	38,902	39,625	5,077	36.7	50.8	2.7	24.1	14.0	0.8	0.5	7.2	1,803	22.0	3,622	10.9	49.8	77	77	77	80	53
Bend-Lapine, SD1	OR	9,481	13,128	16,173	16,834	594	42.5	84.3	0.8	10.9	1.2	0.3	0.9	1.6	744	22.6	1,554	10.8	47.9	68	72	79	77	28
Eugene, SD4J	OR	17,904	18,432	17,379	16,886	384	42.7	69.8	1.8	13.5	3.7	0.8	1.4	9.5	737	22.9	1,676	10.1	44.0	71	66	64	72	36
Hillsboro, SD1J	OR	10,396	18,315	20,923	21,118	2,745	51.4	50.2	2.1	34.9	6.4	0.8	0.8	4.8	860	24.6	2,016	10.5	42.6	78	75	80	81	35
North Clackamas, SD12	OR	12,403	14,876	17,420	17,053	1,918	46.4	67.1	1.9	16.8	7.1	0.6	0.8	5.7	699	24.4	1,608	10.6	43.4	66	72	74	78	31
Portland, SD1J	OR	53,042	53,141	45,818	47,323	3,224	43.3	56.7	10.4	15.7	7.9	0.9	0.9	7.4	2,480	19.1	4,897	9.7	50.6	62	63	67	70	86
Salem-Keizer, SD24J	OR	27,756	35,108	40,403	40,565	6,411	61.3	50.2	1.0	39.2	2.1	2.0	1.0	4.7	1,754	23.1	3,658	11.1	48.0	70	69	72	72	65
Allentown City	PA	13,519	16,424	17,637	17,006	1,804	85.4	13.0	15.7	66.0	1.4	0.1	0.1	3.6	976	17.4	1,921	8.9	50.8	66	62	68	68	21
Central Bucks	PA	10,286	17,305	20,432	19,621	119	9.4	87.5	1.5	3.1	5.7	#	0.1	2.0	1,170	16.8	2,148	9.1	54.5	98	97	—	98	23
Philadelphia City	PA	190,979	201,190	166,233	137,674	11,885	85.8	14.3	53.0	18.9	8.1	#	0.2	5.4	7,646	18.0	14,909	9.2	51.3	55	62	64	68	214
Pittsburgh	PA	39,896	38,560	27,982	26,041	721	76.4	33.4	53.7	2.2	3.6	0.1	0.2	6.8	1,864	14.0	3,788	6.9	49.2	68	73	77	74	58
Reading	PA	11,965	15,487	18,194	17,487	3,153	93.6	6.8	9.2	81.0	0.5	0.0	0.2	2.5	999	17.5	1,645	10.6	60.7	61	61	67	72	19
Providence	RI	20,908	26,937	23,573	23,827	4,947	81.3	8.5	17.5	64.9	5.0	0.1	0.9	3.1	1,394	17.1	2,879	8.3	48.4	66	65	71	71	39
Aiken, 01	SC	23,970	25,147	24,632	24,716	1,332	58.9	54.6	33.4	7.8	0.8	0.1	0.3	3.0	1,493	16.6	2,340	10.6	63.8	74	76	80	83	40
Beaufort 01	SC	12,518	16,721	19,648	20,725	3,291	55.0	43.1	29.9	22.2	1.0	0.1	0.3	3.3	1,427	14.5	2,089	9.9	68.3	70	75	75	78	30
Berkeley 01	SC	27,384	26,635	29,400	31,766	1,866	58.8	53.3	31.0	8.3	1.8	0.2	0.3	5.1	1,895	16.8	2,864	11.1	66.2	75	74	77	80	40
Charleston, 01	SC	43,637	44,767	43,654	45,650	2,566	51.7	46.1	42.4	7.5	1.4	0.1	0.1	2.3	3,265	14.0	4,818	9.5	67.8	73	75	77	80	80
Dorchester, 02	SC	13,735	16,678	22,762	24,334	721	43.7	56.7	29.9	6.0	1.7	0.3	0.4	4.9	1,442	16.9	2,026	12.0	71.2	75	77	81	85	21
Florence, 01	SC	14,731	13,930	15,919	16,280	394	62.6	41.3	51.9	2.6	1.9	0.1	0.2	2.0	1,073	15.2	1,808	9.0	59.3	79	80	80	80	26
Greenville, 01	SC	51,434	59,875	71,930	74,475	7,608	48.2	57.5	23.2	13.1	2.2	0.3	0.2	3.6	4,462	16.7	7,067	10.5	63.1	74	77	82	82	96
Horry, 01	SC	24,080	29,894	38,534	40,943	2,787	60.0	64.3	20.3	9.2	1.1	0.2	0.3	4.5	2,636	15.5	4,143	9.9	63.6	75	78	79	79	53
Lexington, 01	SC	11,202	17,285	22,694	24,210	911	38.2	76.7	10.6	7.0	1.7	0.3	0.3	3.6	1,598	15.2	2,400	10.1	66.6	84	84	88	88	29
Lexington, 05	SC	11,883	15,064	16,999	16,644	398	33.5	62.0	27.9	3.3	2.7	0.3	0.3	3.5	1,232	13.5	1,591	10.5	77.5	87	87	87	87	21
Pickens, 01	SC	14,289	15,938	16,319	16,716	541	47.7	82.1	6.8	5.5	1.2	#	0.1	4.2	1,023	16.3	1,486	11.3	68.9	72	75	75	80	26
Richland, 01	SC	27,051	27,061	24,220	24,372	728	68.0	18.2	73.1	4.0	1.2	0.1	0.1	3.4	1,842	13.2	2,493	9.8	73.9	69	68	72	74	49
Richland, 02	SC	12,788	17,409	25,667	26,780	1,272	47.7	27.3	59.1	7.1	2.9	0.1	0.2	3.2	1,783	15.0	2,319	11.5	76.9	76	80	81	83	31
Sumter, 01	SC	18,531	19,063	17,060	16,794	275	69.6	31.6	61.4	3.5	0.9	0.3	0.2	2.3	994	16.9	1,550	10.8	64.1	—	82	80	79	27
York, 03	SC	12,685	14,925	17,343	17,617	803	55.1	49.6	37.3	7.2	1.6	0.1	1.6	2.6	1,059	16.6	1,387	12.7	76.4	74	77	79	81	28

See notes at end of table.

Table 215.10. Selected statistics on enrollment, teachers, dropouts, and graduates in public school districts enrolling more than 15,000 students: Selected years, 1990 through 2013—Continued

Name of district	State	Enrollment, fall 1990	Enrollment, fall 2000	Enrollment, fall 2010	Enrollment, fall 2013	Number of English language learners, 2013	Percent eligible for free or reduced-price lunch, 2013[1]	White	Black	Hispanic	Asian	Pacific Islander	American Indian/Alaska Native	Two or more races	Number of classroom teachers	Pupil/teacher ratio	Total number of staff	Student/staff ratio	Teachers as a percentage of total staff	2010–11	2011–12	2012–13	2013–14	Number of schools, fall 2013
1	2	3	4	5	6	7	8	9	10	11	12	13	14	15	16	17	18	19	20	21	22	23	24	25
Sioux Falls	SD	16,092	19,097	21,390	23,384	2,083	44.3	68.4	10.3	8.8	3.8	0.1	5.1	3.5	1,472	15.9	2,783	8.4	52.9	79	79	81	82	48
Davidson County	TN	68,452	67,669	78,782	82,806	10,186	72.7	31.2	44.1	19.6	3.9	0.1	0.1	1.0	5,497	15.1	10,503	7.9	52.3	76	78	77	79	158
Hamilton County	TN	22,785	39,915	42,589	43,540	1,736	58.7	57.7	30.6	8.4	2.2	0.1	0.2	0.7	3,046	14.3	5,174	8.4	58.9	82	81	85	83	78
Knox County	TN	50,750	51,944	57,977	59,236	1,810	49.5	74.4	14.1	6.4	2.0	0.1	0.2	2.8	3,936	15.0	7,452	7.9	52.8	87	90	88	89	89
Montgomery County	TN	16,591	23,339	29,780	31,271	572	47.5	56.5	23.6	10.9	1.4	0.5	0.4	6.7	2,064	15.1	4,047	7.7	51.0	94	95	94	93	38
Rutherford County	TN	17,996	25,356	38,846	41,495	1,672	42.2	66.6	16.4	10.8	4.1	0.1	0.2	1.9	2,750	15.1	4,435	9.4	62.0	91	91	92	92	47
Shelby County	TN	144,778	160,702	159,540	149,832	7,699	68.9	20.2	66.9	9.1	2.5	0.1	0.1	1.1	9,282	16.1	14,167	10.6	65.5	—	—	—	75	290
Sumner County	TN	19,630	22,347	27,907	28,715	415	40.6	81.4	9.8	5.9	1.6	0.1	0.2	1.0	1,927	14.9	3,720	7.7	51.8	89	91	89	90	46
Williamson County	TN	11,472	19,545	31,616	34,350	421	11.9	83.1	3.8	5.1	4.1	#	#	3.7	2,170	15.8	4,043	8.5	53.7	92	92	94	94	41
Wilson County	TN	10,175	11,430	15,705	16,753	233	30.3	85.3	7.3	4.0	1.9	0.2	0.2	1.0	1,009	16.6	1,983	8.4	50.9	90	96	95	96	21
Abilene ISD	TX	18,217	18,118	17,161	17,329	561	65.3	40.0	11.8	42.1	1.9	0.1	0.4	3.8	1,121	15.5	2,258	7.7	49.6	90	92	91	90	37
Aldine ISD	TX	41,372	52,520	63,154	67,381	17,768	85.3	2.0	25.1	70.8	1.3	0.1	0.1	0.7	4,036	16.7	8,432	8.0	47.9	78	79	78	79	76
Alief ISD	TX	29,774	42,151	45,768	46,258	15,147	80.9	3.6	30.5	51.8	12.5	0.2	0.8	0.6	3,135	14.8	6,073	7.6	51.6	91	93	93	93	46
Allen ISD	TX	5,240	10,604	18,888	20,381	1,107	15.8	56.0	10.7	12.7	15.3	0.3	0.6	4.3	1,277	16.0	2,262	9.0	56.4	98	98	—	97	24
Alvin ISD	TX	9,323	11,324	17,367	19,809	2,997	50.4	30.5	14.7	43.9	8.6	0.3	0.4	1.8	1,209	16.4	2,445	8.1	49.4	84	89	90	92	23
Amarillo ISD	TX	27,374	28,908	32,682	33,456	4,293	66.8	36.1	9.9	45.4	5.1	0.1	0.5	2.9	2,271	14.7	4,130	8.1	55.0	85	84	85	84	54
Arlington ISD	TX	44,958	58,866	64,484	64,688	12,147	68.4	23.0	24.2	43.8	6.3	0.2	0.5	2.0	4,113	15.7	8,055	8.0	51.1	81	83	84	83	77
Austin ISD	TX	65,885	77,816	85,697	85,372	21,321	61.1	25.5	8.2	59.9	3.5	0.1	0.2	2.6	5,899	14.5	11,539	7.4	51.1	80	83	84	86	128
Beaumont ISD	TX	20,627	20,696	19,883	19,875	1,177	73.6	12.9	60.6	21.1	2.9	0.1	0.2	2.2	1,358	14.6	2,496	8.0	54.4	87	90	90	84	30
Birdville ISD	TX	18,477	21,246	23,545	24,326	3,253	56.4	45.0	7.9	38.7	4.9	0.3	0.7	2.5	1,569	15.5	2,929	8.3	53.6	86	87	88	87	32
Brownsville ISD	TX	37,489	40,898	49,879	49,370	14,576	96.0	1.0	0.1	98.7	0.2	#	0.2	#	3,157	15.6	7,183	6.9	44.0	88	87	88	90	60
Bryan ISD	TX	11,413	13,501	15,751	15,741	3,092	73.4	25.2	19.6	53.4	0.4	0.1	0.2	1.2	1,028	15.3	2,192	7.2	46.9	81	83	77	76	27
Carrollton-Farmers Branch ISD	TX	17,561	24,134	26,159	26,347	6,046	62.2	16.1	16.5	54.9	10.6	0.1	0.3	1.6	1,639	16.1	3,033	8.7	54.0	87	91	93	94	40
Clear Creek ISD	TX	22,372	29,875	38,406	39,998	2,896	27.4	50.1	8.2	28.0	9.8	0.2	0.2	3.5	2,504	16.0	4,850	8.2	51.6	96	95	96	95	45
Comal ISD	TX	5,883	10,695	17,239	19,500	812	30.7	56.3	2.2	37.2	1.2	0.2	0.3	2.6	1,180	16.5	2,369	8.2	49.8	93	93	93	94	29
Conroe ISD	TX	23,288	34,928	51,170	55,009	5,430	36.1	52.7	6.3	34.2	3.4	0.2	0.5	2.7	3,311	16.6	6,403	8.6	51.7	93	93	92	92	55
Corpus Christi ISD	TX	41,881	39,138	38,409	39,414	1,757	66.2	13.8	4.0	79.3	1.7	0.1	0.2	0.8	2,275	17.3	4,858	8.1	46.8	81	85	84	82	60
Crowley ISD	TX	5,832	9,137	15,240	15,080	1,374	62.5	21.9	41.1	29.4	4.1	0.7	0.7	2.6	941	16.0	1,581	9.5	59.5	86	90	90	86	23
Cypress-Fairbanks ISD	TX	41,196	63,497	106,097	111,440	14,100	49.3	28.3	16.5	43.6	8.6	0.1	0.2	2.3	6,675	16.7	13,313	8.4	50.1	90	90	91	91	84
Dallas ISD	TX	135,000	161,548	157,162	159,713	59,070	89.1	4.7	23.4	69.7	1.2	0.1	0.4	0.5	9,830	16.2	16,778	9.5	58.6	77	81	85	86	234
Denton ISD	TX	10,690	13,645	23,994	26,312	3,567	42.6	51.4	12.1	31.0	2.8	0.1	0.4	1.8	1,898	13.9	3,227	8.2	58.8	95	93	94	94	37
Donna ISD	TX	7,906	10,332	15,028	15,376	7,292	97.1	0.2	0.1	99.6	#	0.0	#	#	1,023	15.0	2,481	6.2	41.2	75	76	79	84	24
Eagle Mt-Saginaw ISD	TX	4,691	6,567	16,709	18,197	1,144	40.3	47.1	9.5	35.5	3.7	0.3	0.6	3.2	1,071	17.0	2,042	8.9	52.5	91	93	94	91	26
Eagle Pass ISD	TX	10,584	12,515	14,850	15,117	4,977	77.2	0.7	0.1	97.4	0.2	#	0.4	0.1	908	16.6	2,071	7.3	43.8	81	85	85	81	24
Ector County ISD	TX	26,993	26,831	28,126	30,857	4,305	50.7	21.5	4.0	72.1	0.9	0.2	0.2	1.0	1,762	17.5	3,367	9.2	52.3	75	77	80	81	39
Edinburg CISD	TX	15,645	22,005	33,223	34,104	10,089	85.1	1.0	0.2	98.1	0.6	#	0.1	0.1	2,229	15.3	4,584	7.4	48.6	86	88	88	88	45
El Paso ISD	TX	64,092	62,325	64,330	61,620	12,692	69.5	10.4	3.9	82.9	1.1	0.2	0.4	1.3	4,121	15.0	8,172	7.5	50.4	81	82	80	80	95
Fort Bend ISD	TX	36,296	53,999	68,948	70,931	9,341	35.8	18.5	29.3	26.4	22.8	0.1	0.4	2.4	4,129	17.2	8,109	8.7	50.9	91	91	92	92	73
Fort Worth ISD	TX	69,163	79,661	81,651	84,588	24,593	77.1	11.1	22.7	62.8	2.0	0.1	0.2	1.3	5,217	16.2	9,775	8.7	53.4	80	80	79	81	144
Frisco ISD	TX	1,419	7,234	37,279	46,053	1,654	11.3	55.3	10.6	14.8	15.4	0.6	0.2	3.2	3,052	15.1	5,410	8.5	56.4	97	98	98	98	55
Galena Park ISD	TX	15,593	18,885	21,680	22,572	6,641	80.5	5.3	16.6	76.1	0.8	0.1	0.4	0.7	1,473	15.3	2,958	7.6	49.8	87	88	88	89	23
Garland ISD	TX	37,978	50,312	57,833	57,616	11,536	60.8	21.3	17.2	50.8	8.2	0.1	0.5	2.0	3,647	15.8	7,308	7.9	49.9	88	90	89	91	72
Goose Creek CISD	TX	17,654	18,003	21,283	22,320	2,635	64.5	22.9	15.7	58.1	1.4	0.1	0.3	1.6	1,457	15.3	2,938	7.6	49.6	86	91	92	90	27
Grand Prairie ISD	TX	16,482	20,257	26,541	27,740	6,723	71.6	11.9	17.5	65.3	3.3	0.3	0.3	1.7	1,756	15.8	2,968	9.3	59.2	84	89	89	89	40
Harlandale ISD	TX	15,089	14,468	14,895	15,324	2,417	88.1	2.0	0.4	97.3	0.1	0.0	0.1	0.1	989	15.5	2,108	7.3	46.9	81	88	87	85	30
Harlingen CISD	TX	14,863	15,857	18,422	18,568	2,535	78.5	7.2	0.5	91.4	0.6	#	0.2	0.1	1,214	15.3	2,704	6.9	44.9	86	84	86	85	32
Hays CISD	TX	4,166	7,402	15,325	17,255	2,558	50.6	31.3	3.1	62.7	0.8	0.2	0.2	1.9	1,070	16.1	2,230	7.7	48.0	86	89	90	89	23
Houston ISD	TX	194,000	208,462	204,245	211,552	55,717	80.4	8.2	25.2	61.9	3.5	0.1	0.2	0.9	11,336	18.7	23,114	9.2	49.0	79	79	79	89	283
Humble ISD	TX	19,560	24,684	35,913	38,235	2,895	34.3	43.5	18.6	32.0	2.9	0.1	0.4	2.1	2,450	15.6	4,716	8.1	51.9	93	94	94	93	43
Hurst-Euless-Bedford ISD	TX	18,740	19,203	21,046	22,180	1,814	53.1	41.6	17.1	29.0	6.6	0.4	0.5	2.8	1,307	17.0	2,440	9.1	53.6	96	96	95	86	40
Irving ISD	TX	23,509	29,097	34,243	35,328	12,488	80.5	9.6	12.8	71.7	3.3	2.3	1.3	1.2	2,351	15.0	4,081	8.7	57.6	84	86	87	86	40
Judson ISD	TX	13,145	16,603	22,040	22,972	1,639	70.4	16.4	23.2	54.8	1.8	0.3	0.3	3.2	1,335	17.2	2,903	7.9	46.0	81	82	83	85	30

See notes at end of table.

Table 215.10. Selected statistics on enrollment, teachers, dropouts, and graduates in public school districts enrolling more than 15,000 students: Selected years, 1990 through 2013—Continued

Name of district	State	Enrollment, fall 1990	Enrollment, fall 2000	Enrollment, fall 2010	Enrollment, fall 2013	Number of English language learners, 2013	Percent eligible for free or reduced-price lunch, 2013[1]	Percentage distribution of enrollment, by race/ethnicity, fall 2013[1]							Number of classroom teachers	Pupil/teacher ratio	Total number of staff	Student/staff ratio	Teachers as a percentage of total staff	Public high school 4-year adjusted cohort graduation rate (ACGR)[2]				Number of schools, fall 2013
								White	Black	Hispanic	Asian	Pacific Islander	American Indian/ Alaska Native	Two or more races						2010–11	2011–12	2012–13	2013–14	
1	2	3	4	5	6	7	8	9	10	11	12	13	14	15	16	17	18	19	20	21	22	23	24	25
Katy ISD	TX	19,507	34,503	60,803	67,213	7,819	29.0	41.1	9.5	34.0	12.2	0.1	0.5	2.6	4,303	15.6	8,163	8.2	52.7	92	93	93	92	61
Keller ISD	TX	8,212	17,083	32,746	33,763	1,682	23.5	58.7	8.0	21.2	7.6	0.2	0.6	3.7	2,033	16.6	3,622	9.3	56.1	94	94	94	94	40
Killeen ISD	TX	22,131	29,687	40,231	41,402	2,776	57.3	26.5	33.6	28.1	2.6	1.6	0.7	6.9	2,754	15.0	5,813	7.1	47.4	87	86	86	89	56
Klein ISD	TX	26,220	32,376	45,310	48,253	5,315	41.2	36.3	14.0	38.0	8.4	0.1	0.4	2.8	3,127	15.4	6,097	7.9	51.3	87	88	89	91	49
La Joya ISD	TX	9,844	17,641	28,846	29,711	13,712	94.8	0.2	#	99.6	#	0.0	0.1	#	1,953	15.2	4,132	7.2	47.3	78	83	89	83	38
Lamar CISD	TX	12,335	15,159	24,637	27,079	2,853	47.5	28.4	18.6	45.4	5.9	0.1	0.3	1.5	1,543	17.5	3,013	9.0	51.2	90	91	94	94	37
Laredo ISD	TX	23,304	22,547	24,706	24,995	14,532	97.6	0.4	0.1	99.5	0.1	#	#	0.0	1,455	17.2	3,547	7.0	41.0	82	85	81	81	30
Leander ISD	TX	5,419	14,499	32,152	35,450	1,493	18.9	62.6	3.9	23.9	5.5	0.2	0.3	3.7	2,301	15.4	4,243	8.4	54.2	91	94	95	95	40
Lewisville ISD	TX	20,776	39,096	51,484	52,801	6,922	30.8	47.9	9.4	27.5	11.7	0.1	0.4	3.0	3,705	14.3	6,248	8.5	59.3	93	94	95	94	68
Lubbock ISD	TX	30,991	29,026	28,905	29,287	898	66.6	25.3	13.5	57.3	1.7	0.1	0.4	1.9	1,961	14.9	3,382	8.7	58.0	80	83	83	85	51
Mansfield ISD	TX	7,570	14,888	32,251	32,779	3,094	38.1	37.4	26.5	24.7	6.4	0.1	0.4	4.5	2,105	15.6	4,129	7.9	51.0	90	91	91	93	42
McAllen ISD	TX	21,120	21,747	25,622	25,217	7,052	67.2	4.5	0.4	93.2	1.4	#	0.1	0.3	1,633	15.4	3,417	7.4	47.8	80	85	86	86	34
McKinney ISD	TX	5,052	12,000	24,422	24,565	2,193	30.3	52.8	12.8	27.3	3.4	0.3	0.6	2.8	1,649	14.9	2,589	9.5	63.7	95	95	96	95	32
Mesquite ISD	TX	25,920	32,334	37,747	39,909	6,862	70.5	18.1	24.5	53.0	1.8	0.1	0.6	1.9	2,529	15.8	4,965	8.0	50.9	89	89	91	90	47
Midland ISD	TX	21,082	20,522	21,746	23,560	2,239	46.3	28.6	8.2	60.0	1.7	0.1	0.3	1.3	1,505	15.7	2,777	8.5	54.2	82	83	80	81	35
Mission CISD	TX	11,032	12,464	15,841	15,372	4,453	83.9	0.9	0.1	98.8	0.1	0.0	#	#	1,009	15.2	2,140	7.2	47.1	81	85	82	82	24
North East ISD	TX	39,909	50,875	66,604	68,205	5,480	46.4	29.2	7.1	56.8	3.6	0.0	0.3	2.9	4,258	16.0	8,448	8.1	50.4	88	89	89	89	74
Northside ISD	TX	50,229	63,739	95,581	102,129	6,479	52.1	18.9	6.1	68.8	3.0	0.2	0.1	2.8	6,462	15.8	12,835	8.0	50.3	92	92	92	93	113
Northwest ISD	TX	3,197	5,556	15,370	18,950	532	19.0	67.4	6.3	20.1	2.9	0.3	0.6	2.5	1,184	16.0	1,877	10.1	63.1	90	93	93	93	26
Pasadena ISD	TX	37,643	42,577	52,218	54,535	13,601	78.6	7.1	7.0	82.2	2.9	#	0.2	0.6	3,540	15.4	7,404	7.4	47.8	83	85	86	85	68
Pearland ISD	TX	6,739	10,618	18,769	20,034	1,249	27.7	41.1	16.1	29.7	9.8	0.1	0.5	2.8	1,208	16.6	2,397	8.4	50.4	93	96	95	97	24
Pflugerville ISD	TX	6,482	14,545	22,763	23,543	3,809	53.7	24.4	18.1	45.9	7.4	0.2	0.4	3.6	1,618	14.5	2,834	8.3	57.1	90	93	93	94	28
Pharr-San Juan-Alamo ISD	TX	18,773	22,537	31,508	31,997	12,915	89.1	0.8	0.1	98.9	0.2	0.0	#	#	2,048	15.6	4,234	7.6	48.4	88	90	90	90	46
Plano ISD	TX	30,585	47,161	55,568	54,822	5,472	27.5	40.3	11.4	23.0	21.5	0.1	0.3	3.4	3,825	14.3	6,526	8.4	58.6	93	95	94	94	80
Richardson ISD	TX	32,555	35,138	36,070	38,283	6,948	57.5	27.9	22.2	40.0	6.9	0.1	0.4	2.5	2,497	15.3	4,806	8.0	51.9	91	89	91	88	58
Round Rock ISD	TX	19,636	31,536	44,776	46,666	3,467	29.1	43.4	8.9	30.3	12.6	0.2	0.4	4.1	3,120	15.0	5,798	8.0	53.8	90	95	95	96	54
San Angelo ISD	TX	16,497	16,092	14,696	15,009	696	58.6	33.8	4.4	59.1	1.0	0.1	0.1	1.4	931	16.1	1,896	7.9	49.1	82	88	88	88	27
San Antonio ISD	TX	60,161	57,273	55,116	53,857	8,575	93.3	1.8	6.3	91.2	0.6	0.2	0.1	0.4	3,329	16.2	7,424	7.3	44.8	75	79	81	81	99
Socorro ISD	TX	14,350	26,711	42,569	44,517	7,966	72.1	5.0	2.2	91.1	0.6	0.2	0.3	0.5	2,383	18.7	4,684	9.5	50.9	86	90	90	88	46
Spring Branch ISD	TX	26,495	31,669	32,948	35,312	10,471	58.2	27.8	5.0	58.5	6.2	0.1	0.9	1.5	2,122	16.6	4,119	8.6	51.5	90	83	88	88	49
Spring ISD	TX	18,537	23,034	36,323	36,484	6,240	73.4	11.6	38.7	43.3	3.8	0.1	0.9	1.3	2,360	15.5	4,728	7.7	49.9	82	82	86	93	41
Tyler ISD	TX	16,182	16,626	18,549	18,029	3,344	71.7	22.1	30.3	44.3	1.3	#	0.3	1.7	1,273	14.2	2,533	7.1	50.2	85	89	89	93	27
United ISD	TX	12,553	27,556	41,876	43,575	16,753	73.3	1.0	0.1	98.5	0.3	#	#	0.1	2,523	17.3	6,104	7.1	41.3	94	94	94	93	41
Weslaco ISD	TX	11,903	13,407	17,839	17,731	4,669	85.6	1.3	0.1	98.3	0.3	#	0.2	0.0	1,091	16.2	2,292	7.7	47.6	82	83	83	81	22
Ysleta ISD	TX	49,974	46,394	44,746	43,063	9,459	80.9	4.5	1.7	92.9	0.3	0.1	0.2	0.4	2,933	14.7	6,046	7.1	48.5	85	86	86	86	62
Alpine	UT	38,854	47,117	67,076	73,975	2,086	27.4	84.8	0.7	9.6	0.9	1.2	0.5	2.4	3,078	24.0	5,741	12.9	53.6	76	79	88	91	81
Cache	UT	12,280	13,026	15,648	16,279	517	32.3	88.2	0.6	8.5	0.6	0.4	0.3	1.4	641	25.4	1,561	10.4	41.1	89	90	92	93	27
Canyons	UT			33,714	34,394	1,387	30.0	76.5	1.1	14.2	2.3	1.1	0.6	4.3	1,504	22.9	2,756	12.5	54.6	83	83	83	84	49
Davis	UT	54,558	59,578	67,452	70,411	1,802	22.9	84.9	1.3	8.9	1.4	1.1	0.5	1.8	2,853	24.7	5,954	11.8	47.9	82	83	90	89	89
Granite	UT	78,554	71,328	70,083	70,407	10,491	45.5	55.0	3.2	31.8	4.3	3.6	1.5	0.6	2,983	23.6	6,057	11.6	49.3	65	73	74	72	92
Jordan	UT	64,991	73,158	50,048	53,355	1,455	28.8	79.1	1.0	13.0	1.7	1.6	0.5	3.1	2,236	23.9	4,114	13.0	54.4	77	83	84	85	55
Nebo	UT	16,393	21,094	29,848	31,905	816	37.8	86.5	0.6	10.0	0.5	0.8	0.4	1.2	1,281	24.9	2,709	11.8	47.3	86	84	91	91	43
Provo	UT	13,625	13,302	13,753	15,181	1,428	45.9	65.5	0.9	26.1	2.3	2.7	0.9	1.6	646	23.5	1,457	10.4	44.3	70	78	69	73	24
Salt Lake	UT	24,766	25,367	24,647	24,597	4,135	61.2	40.8	4.0	42.0	4.3	4.2	1.1	3.5	1,139	21.6	2,595	9.5	43.9	62	65	70	71	42
Washington	UT	13,264	18,374	26,091	28,085	1,465	45.5	81.1	0.9	12.8	0.7	1.8	1.8	1.0	1,255	22.4	2,514	11.2	43.9	75	81	86	82	47
Weber	UT	25,661	27,783	30,431	31,281	848	36.2	82.2	0.8	12.2	1.1	0.5	0.5	2.6	1,356	23.1	2,858	10.9	47.4	77	79	84	82	48
Arlington County	VA	14,825	18,870	21,485	23,499	5,233	31.4	45.7	10.8	28.7	9.3	0.1	0.5	4.9	1,925	12.2	3,849	6.1	50.0	81	84	84	87	37
Chesapeake City	VA	29,533	37,645	39,748	39,737	709	32.7	50.1	33.4	7.2	2.7	0.2	0.3	6.3	2,634	15.1	5,462	7.3	48.2	85	88	88	88	47
Chesterfield County	VA	44,480	51,212	59,243	59,186	3,012	22.8	54.3	26.3	11.5	3.5	0.1	0.3	4.0	3,840	15.4	6,996	8.5	54.9	83	88	88	89	62
Fairfax County	VA	128,840	156,412	174,479	183,417	35,696	27.4	41.7	10.3	23.3	19.5	0.2	0.2	4.9	14,344	12.8	30,029	6.1	47.8	86	80	87	87	218
Hampton City	VA	21,383	23,290	21,568	21,157	339	55.6	26.3	59.6	5.9	2.2	0.1	0.3	5.5	1,649	12.8	3,229	6.6	51.1	80	80	86	81	31
Hanover County	VA	11,328	16,611	18,628	18,264	156	14.0	82.0	9.5	3.5	1.7	0.1	0.4	2.8	1,340	13.6	2,617	7.0	51.2	91	92	92	93	26

See notes at end of table.

Table 215.10. Selected statistics on enrollment, teachers, dropouts, and graduates in public school districts enrolling more than 15,000 students: Selected years, 1990 through 2013—Continued

Name of district	State	Enrollment, fall 1990	Enrollment, fall 2000	Enrollment, fall 2010	Enrollment, fall 2013	Number of English language learners, 2013	Percent eligible for free or reduced-price lunch, 2013[1]	White	Black	Hispanic	Asian	Pacific Islander	American Indian/ Alaska Native	Two or more races	Number of classroom teachers	Pupil/ teacher ratio	Total number of staff	Student/ staff ratio	Teachers as a percentage of total staff	2010–11	2011–12	2012–13	2013–14	Number of schools, fall 2013
1	2	3	4	5	6	7	8	9	10	11	12	13	14	15	16	17	18	19	20	21	22	23	24	25
Henrico County	VA	32,638	41,655	49,405	50,569	2,681	39.8	42.9	36.5	7.7	8.8	0.1	0.3	3.7	2,769	18.3	3,877	13.0	71.4	80	83	85	85	81
Loudoun County	VA	14,485	31,804	63,142	70,759	5,825	17.5	54.8	6.7	15.6	17.2	0.1	0.6	5.0	5,026	14.1	10,784	6.6	46.6	92	92	93	91	85
Newport News City	VA	28,925	33,008	30,488	29,777	1,015	58.2	26.8	53.7	11.7	2.7	0.2	0.4	4.5	2,108	14.1	4,354	6.8	48.4	76	78	82	84	44
Norfolk City	VA	36,541	37,349	33,787	32,597	639	64.7	22.7	61.3	6.6	2.3	0.3	0.5	6.3	1,992	16.4	3,849	8.5	51.7	68	71	73	75	52
Prince William County	VA	41,888	54,646	79,358	85,451	13,658	38.3	34.2	20.6	30.4	7.8	0.2	0.3	6.5	5,308	16.1	9,814	8.7	54.1	84	84	84	86	89
Richmond City	VA	27,021	27,237	23,454	23,775	1,173	73.0	9.6	78.3	10.0	0.7	0.1	0.1	1.2	2,058	11.6	3,704	6.4	55.6	59	61	65	71	51
Spotsylvania County	VA	12,227	18,876	23,585	23,838	885	36.7	61.3	18.2	12.3	2.7	0.1	0.3	5.1	1,465	16.3	2,635	9.0	55.6	82	83	85	87	34
Stafford County	VA	12,555	21,124	27,257	27,462	1,121	25.8	55.9	18.3	15.2	2.7	0.3	0.4	7.2	1,670	16.4	3,388	8.1	49.3	89	89	89	88	30
Virginia Beach City	VA	70,266	76,596	71,185	70,556	871	35.5	51.0	24.1	10.3	5.7	0.5	0.3	8.2	4,028	17.5	8,382	8.4	48.1	82	83	84	85	86
Auburn	WA	10,295	13,135	14,697	15,027	2,027	56.0	48.1	6.8	24.5	7.6	3.0	1.5	8.6	779	19.3	1,465	10.3	53.2	74	81	75	78	23
Bellevue	WA	14,971	15,431	18,330	19,153	1,796	14.9	44.4	2.7	11.6	32.5	0.2	0.2	8.5	982	19.5	1,935	9.9	50.7	90	92	89	92	31
Bethel	WA	11,319	16,029	17,779	18,234	270	48.6	59.0	8.8	14.6	5.3	2.9	1.7	7.7	877	20.8	1,739	10.5	50.4	71	70	71	77	38
Edmonds	WA	18,452	22,067	20,757	20,817	2,237	41.6	52.4	6.1	17.6	13.1	0.6	0.6	9.6	1,012	20.6	1,981	10.5	51.1	76	74	76	83	40
Everett	WA	14,846	18,683	18,992	19,217	1,996	41.1	59.3	4.0	16.4	12.4	1.3	0.6	5.9	902	21.3	1,693	11.4	53.3	82	85	80	89	32
Evergreen (Clark)	WA	14,242	21,650	25,750	26,382	2,754	57.4	63.2	3.2	17.2	6.8	1.7	0.8	7.4	1,445	18.3	2,462	10.7	58.7	82	85	73	80	38
Federal Way	WA	17,263	22,623	22,258	22,499	3,217	57.4	33.9	11.3	25.6	12.1	4.4	0.8	12.1	1,194	18.8	2,170	10.4	55.1	72	70	73	76	47
Highline	WA	15,900	18,024	17,992	18,686	4,254	70.9	24.2	11.5	36.9	14.4	4.3	1.1	7.6	1,015	18.4	2,039	9.2	49.8	62	66	62	63	42
Issaquah	WA	8,533	14,259	17,358	18,806	838	10.4	61.3	1.9	7.5	23.2	0.3	0.3	5.5	900	20.9	1,663	11.3	54.1	90	92	93	92	27
Kennewick	WA	11,147	13,629	16,467	16,968	2,327	53.4	64.9	2.5	27.4	2.2	0.3	0.6	2.2	834	20.3	1,551	10.9	53.8	73	72	75	77	28
Kent	WA	20,212	26,535	27,079	27,681	4,817	53.8	37.8	12.2	20.9	17.3	2.4	0.6	8.9	1,395	19.8	2,621	10.6	53.2	69	80	79	79	43
Lake Washington	WA	22,431	23,662	24,677	26,283	1,728	13.8	61.6	1.6	10.0	20.1	0.2	0.3	6.2	1,360	19.3	2,355	11.2	57.7	94	92	89	90	53
Mukilteo	WA	8,519	13,544	14,723	15,121	2,650	50.3	42.7	5.4	12.5	15.3	1.1	0.5	8.0	759	19.9	1,390	10.9	54.6	82	83	82	74	21
Northshore	WA	17,213	20,255	19,750	20,647	1,196	17.7	63.7	1.8	12.5	13.8	0.4	0.1	7.4	1,016	20.3	1,854	11.1	54.8	91	91	90	90	35
Pasco	WA	6,677	8,850	15,164	16,712	5,846	74.0	25.6	2.1	68.8	1.1	0.2	0.1	2.1	872	19.2	1,616	10.3	54.0	64	71	70	74	19
Puyallup	WA	14,325	19,757	20,986	21,097	777	35.3	64.2	3.7	14.4	4.6	1.2	0.8	10.9	1,037	20.4	1,934	10.9	53.6	84	80	84	85	39
Renton	WA	11,857	12,729	14,535	15,206	2,454	53.2	28.5	17.8	21.2	24.9	0.5	0.6	6.1	790	19.3	1,584	9.6	49.8	77	78	74	77	29
Seattle	WA	40,917	47,575	47,735	50,509	4,600	40.5	45.1	16.7	12.5	16.8	1.5	0.8	7.5	2,868	17.6	5,301	9.5	54.1	76	75	73	76	103
Spokane	WA	27,965	31,725	29,446	29,446	1,276	59.2	70.1	2.6	9.5	2.4	2.3	1.7	12.1	1,677	17.6	3,172	9.3	52.9	75	77	81	83	62
Tacoma	WA	29,465	34,093	27,407	29,168	2,628	63.0	44.9	20.1	17.2	10.2	3.4	1.3	4.0	1,569	18.6	3,068	9.5	51.1	60	74	70	78	66
Vancouver	WA	15,943	21,892	22,669	23,077	2,515	51.2	62.6	3.1	22.0	3.4	1.9	0.7	6.3	1,156	20.0	2,299	10.0	50.3	71	73	73	74	41
Yakima	WA	12,076	13,985	14,927	15,697	4,908	84.7	19.1	1.0	75.9	0.4	0.1	0.9	2.6	818	19.2	1,545	10.2	53.0	66	56	57	63	28
Berkeley County	WV	10,415	13,076	17,720	18,221	376	45.3	78.5	9.1	6.1	0.8	0.1	0.2	5.2	1,328	13.7	2,644	6.9	50.2	81	79	84	86	31
Kanawha County	WV	34,284	29,250	28,458	28,378	192	42.6	83.3	11.9	0.8	1.4	#	#	2.4	1,926	14.7	3,784	7.5	50.9	71	72	71	76	69
Appleton Area	WI	12,876	14,793	15,194	16,224	1,117	37.3	74.8	4.9	8.4	11.2	0.0	0.8	0.0	990	16.4	1,644	9.9	60.2	89	87	88	86	39
Green Bay Area	WI	18,048	20,104	20,376	21,006	3,477	60.7	52.4	7.7	25.0	6.7	0.1	4.1	4.1	1,476	14.2	2,453	8.6	60.2	78	80	81	78	41
Kenosha	WI	16,219	20,099	22,996	22,602	1,911	52.3	53.3	15.4	25.6	1.5	0.1	0.3	3.9	1,352	16.7	2,332	9.7	58.0	79	80	85	85	42
Madison Metropolitan	WI	23,214	25,087	24,806	27,185	4,879	48.3	44.2	18.4	19.3	9.2	0.1	0.4	8.4	2,156	12.6	4,027	6.8	53.5	74	75	77	79	54
Milwaukee	WI	92,789	97,985	80,934	78,516	7,418	82.7	13.7	55.3	24.1	5.7	#	0.7	0.5	4,082	19.2	8,729	9.0	46.8	63	62	61	61	165
Racine Unified	WI	22,159	21,102	21,100	20,301	2,433	65.2	43.6	26.5	25.3	1.3	#	0.3	3.0	1,418	14.3	2,507	8.1	56.6	68	70	72	78	34

—Not available.
†Not applicable.
#Rounds to zero.
[1] Percentages are for those schools that reported on free and reduced-price lunch eligibility.
[2] The ACGR is the percentage of public high school freshmen who graduate with a regular diploma within 4 years of starting 9th grade. Students who are entering 9th grade for the first time form a cohort for the graduating class. This cohort is "adjusted" by adding any students who subsequently transfer into the cohort and subtracting any students who subsequently transfer out, emigrate to another country, or die.

[3] Total for districts reporting data. Includes imputations for total staff in New York City.
NOTE: Total enrollment, staff, and teacher data in this table reflect totals reported by school districts and may differ from data derived from summing school-level data to school district aggregates. ISD = independent school district. CISD = consolidated independent school district. Race categories exclude persons of Hispanic ethnicity. Detail may not sum to totals because of rounding.
SOURCE: U.S. Department of Education, National Center for Education Statistics, Common Core of Data (CCD), "Public Elementary/Secondary School Universe Survey," 2013–14; "Local Education Agency Universe Survey," 1990–91, 2000–01, 2010–11, and 2013–14; and Regulatory Adjusted Cohort Graduation Rates (ACGR), 2010–11 through 2013–14, retrieved February 3, 2016, from http://www2.ed.gov/about/inits/ed/edfacts/data-files/index.html. (This table was prepared February 2016.)

Table 215.20. Revenues, expenditures, poverty rate, and Title I allocations of public school districts enrolling more than 15,000 students: 2012–13 and fiscal year 2015

Name of district	State	Revenues by source of funds, 2012–13 (in thousands of current dollars)				Percentage distribution of revenues, 2012–13				Expenditures, 2012–13 (in thousands of current dollars)					Poverty rate of 5- to 17-year-olds, 2014[1]	Current expenditure per pupil[2] 2012–13 (in current dollars)	Title I allocations, federal fiscal year 2015	
		Total	Federal	State	Local	Total	Federal	State	Local	Total[3]	Current expenditures						Total[4] (in thousands of current dollars)	Per poverty child[6] (in current dollars)
											Total	Instruction	Capital outlay	Interest on school debt				
1	2	3	4	5	6	7	8	9	10	11	12	13	14	15	16	17	18	19
Districts with more than 15,000 students......	†	$254,517,606	$25,607,430	$114,929,078	$113,981,098	100.0	10.1	45.2	44.8	$259,052,643	$219,577,466	$135,939,498	$21,763,084	$8,370,034	22.3	$9,982	$7,391,161	$1,326
Baldwin County...........	AL	294,249	22,266	122,616	149,367	100.0	7.6	41.7	50.8	264,079	238,294	139,776	11,220	9,007	18.9	8,100	6,367	1,032
Birmingham City..........	AL	260,624	43,386	121,766	95,472	100.0	16.6	46.7	36.6	297,451	246,435	136,788	40,005	3,254	41.5	9,817	14,994	1,177
Huntsville City............	AL	257,889	25,093	111,925	120,871	100.0	9.7	43.4	46.9	274,014	235,133	133,368	27,401	8,652	23.5	10,033	6,433	1,029
Jefferson County.........	AL	332,957	36,354	186,535	110,068	100.0	10.9	56.0	33.1	335,896	312,745	179,942	13,451	4,200	18.2	8,671	7,388	1,039
Madison County..........	AL	175,756	12,982	103,776	58,998	100.0	7.4	59.0	33.6	190,287	159,843	94,079	19,580	6,545	13.5	8,088	2,660	850
Mobile County............	AL	552,138	78,340	299,116	174,682	100.0	14.2	54.2	31.6	589,569	523,345	273,846	47,397	13,952	28.4	8,927	23,185	1,199
Montgomery County.....	AL	283,295	42,257	159,134	81,904	100.0	14.9	56.2	28.9	294,254	260,762	147,137	25,419	2,276	29.9	8,315	13,190	1,127
Shelby County............	AL	273,821	16,296	141,875	115,650	100.0	6.0	51.8	42.2	296,889	237,231	139,977	44,163	9,647	11.3	8,279	2,639	866
Tuscaloosa County......	AL	170,388	14,101	93,275	63,012	100.0	8.3	54.7	37.0	185,132	140,462	79,399	39,791	1,832	18.0	7,908	3,329	970
Anchorage..................	AK	770,180	76,535	487,629	206,016	100.0	9.9	63.3	26.7	786,647	750,908	439,272	32,205	23	9.4	15,391	12,763	2,556
Matanuska-Susitna Borough..	AK	270,675	19,653	198,826	52,196	100.0	7.3	73.5	19.3	303,290	266,648	153,678	36,606	8	10.0	15,251	3,918	2,020
Cartwright Elementary..	AZ	132,673	28,081	72,921	31,671	100.0	21.2	55.0	23.9	141,586	129,442	78,872	10,476	858	45.3	6,839	11,300	1,167
Chandler Unified.........	AZ	293,685	21,357	122,139	150,189	100.0	7.3	41.6	51.1	283,066	252,177	150,725	16,370	9,362	12.1	6,279	4,897	889
Deer Valley Unified......	AZ	273,562	21,491	95,241	156,830	100.0	7.9	34.8	57.3	237,770	213,054	124,923	21,743	752	12.1	6,261	5,286	906
Dysart Unified............	AZ	205,806	17,996	85,903	101,907	100.0	8.7	41.7	49.5	177,671	167,385	95,644	539	9,160	17.4	6,445	5,801	998
Gilbert Unified............	AZ	290,154	18,312	126,188	145,654	100.0	6.3	43.5	50.2	261,526	242,651	148,149	7,491	8,173	9.6	6,384	3,566	861
Glendale Union High.....	AZ	135,491	15,207	51,319	68,965	100.0	11.2	37.9	50.9	136,729	119,888	65,841	10,270	3,562	29.9	7,981	5,922	999
Kyrene Elementary.......	AZ	157,073	9,920	51,128	96,025	100.0	6.3	32.6	61.1	127,604	112,983	67,524	6,878	7,497	9.2	6,352	1,333	771
Mesa Unified..............	AZ	549,773	74,829	220,609	254,335	100.0	13.6	40.1	46.3	480,253	456,178	270,896	13,679	8,846	25.4	7,110	24,242	1,166
Paradise Valley Unified..	AZ	292,910	27,732	69,622	195,556	100.0	9.5	23.8	66.8	297,031	222,997	128,715	58,661	12,716	17.2	6,774	7,104	1,021
Peoria Unified............	AZ	269,518	26,646	126,320	116,552	100.0	9.9	46.9	43.2	255,388	229,000	129,341	16,799	7,984	15.1	6,234	5,997	1,006
Phoenix Union High......	AZ	289,169	38,453	53,399	197,317	100.0	13.3	18.5	68.2	378,903	333,258	191,123	29,290	11,297	37.1	12,890	18,014	1,139
Scottsdale Unified.......	AZ	241,406	15,796	30,048	195,562	100.0	6.5	12.4	81.0	258,518	200,849	120,209	40,360	15,822	11.8	7,956	3,255	866
Sunnyside Unified.......	AZ	132,626	23,160	63,105	46,361	100.0	17.5	47.6	35.0	115,228	104,449	54,182	9,207	1,223	36.5	5,979	9,809	1,359
Tucson Unified...........	AZ	470,812	58,134	141,581	271,097	100.0	12.3	30.1	57.6	587,894	505,283	251,236	48,124	14,294	26.4	9,952	23,894	1,237
Washington Elementary..	AZ	201,343	33,578	81,465	86,300	100.0	16.7	40.5	42.9	188,507	165,457	94,913	19,406	480	34.1	7,227	10,460	1,079
Bentonville................	AR	149,395	7,031	64,339	78,025	100.0	4.7	43.1	52.2	173,615	134,123	81,550	28,204	8,216	10.2	9,014	1,507	907
Little Rock.................	AR	358,324	41,383	157,391	159,550	100.0	11.5	43.9	44.5	369,570	315,766	172,194	19,681	6,955	26.9	12,582	9,534	1,170
Pulaski County Special..	AR	208,222	18,817	86,468	102,937	100.0	9.0	41.5	49.4	204,250	178,714	96,254	12,647	5,812	17.1	9,963	5,140	1,122
Rogers.....................	AR	151,947	14,538	64,885	72,524	100.0	9.6	42.7	47.7	153,013	130,505	79,976	15,462	5,574	17.9	8,822	3,252	1,054
Springdale................	AR	205,492	19,365	121,151	64,976	100.0	9.4	59.0	31.6	210,982	180,694	108,260	23,379	6,633	28.1	8,712	6,360	1,082
ABC Unified...............	CA	195,535	20,919	132,337	42,279	100.0	10.7	67.7	21.6	194,243	176,213	107,978	4,198	978	18.6	8,458	3,446	1,004
Alhambra Unified.........	CA	245,162	33,635	146,436	65,091	100.0	13.7	59.7	26.6	244,718	162,802	92,416	19,758	5,378	26.5	9,007	4,924	1,036
Alvord Unified............	CA	182,562	18,518	122,640	41,404	100.0	10.1	67.2	22.7	159,776	151,335	96,210	3,300	5,037	23.5	7,708	5,644	1,053
Anaheim City.............	CA	181,226	17,404	89,211	74,611	100.0	9.6	49.2	41.2	204,960	150,491	93,679	36,349	5,327	30.4	7,868	6,711	1,046
Anaheim Union High.....	CA	319,952	33,647	201,703	84,602	100.0	10.5	63.0	26.4	320,630	296,654	185,195	5,838	5,105	22.6	9,246	8,810	1,070
Antelope Valley Union High..	CA	236,039	24,475	161,592	49,972	100.0	10.4	68.5	21.2	235,064	224,391	139,711	4,043	3,944	23.9	9,042	7,260	1,062
Antioch Unified...........	CA	148,051	15,059	94,533	38,459	100.0	10.2	63.9	26.0	164,202	152,095	97,356	8,383	2,729	17.2	8,068	3,997	1,024
Bakersfield City..........	CA	279,489	43,081	207,006	29,402	100.0	15.4	74.1	10.5	305,809	261,067	159,596	41,093	2,213	41.0	9,006	14,531	1,207
Baldwin Park Unified....	CA	171,823	18,353	110,298	43,172	100.0	10.7	64.2	25.1	178,658	143,566	85,882	13,470	3,826	28.7	7,618	4,691	1,032
Burbank Unified..........	CA	140,392	8,657	59,977	71,758	100.0	6.2	42.7	51.1	130,136	123,289	77,850	1,936	2,277	14.5	7,481	1,974	923
Cajon Valley Union......	CA	153,027	16,368	81,227	55,432	100.0	10.7	53.1	36.2	171,432	140,036	90,021	26,007	5,137	28.3	8,628	5,562	1,038
Capistrano Unified.......	CA	413,762	22,301	113,402	278,059	100.0	5.4	27.4	67.2	384,371	366,335	241,189	4,299	1,314	9.1	6,811	5,296	921
Central Unified............	CA	129,761	13,522	86,579	29,660	100.0	10.4	66.7	22.9	134,592	116,990	63,467	8,554	6,751	29.6	7,665	4,925	1,032
Chaffey Joint Union High..	CA	265,315	16,346	133,884	115,085	100.0	6.2	50.5	43.4	224,768	202,555	128,464	8,975	4,004	16.5	8,096	4,682	1,043

See notes at end of table.

Table 215.20. Revenues, expenditures, poverty rate, and Title I allocations of public school districts enrolling more than 15,000 students: 2012–13 and fiscal year 2015—Continued

Name of district	State	Revenues by source of funds, 2012–13 (in thousands of current dollars)				Percentage distribution of revenues, 2012–13				Expenditures, 2012–13 (in thousands of current dollars)					Poverty rate of 5- to 17-year-olds, 2014[1]	Current expenditure per pupil,[2] 2012–13 (in current dollars)	Title I allocations, federal fiscal year 2015	
		Total	Federal	State	Local	Total	Federal	State	Local	Total[3]	Current expenditures						Total[4] (in thousands of current dollars)	Per poverty child[5] (in current dollars)
											Total	Instruction	Capital outlay	Interest on school debt				
1	2	3	4	5	6	7	8	9	10	11	12	13	14	15	16	17	18	19
Chino Valley Unified	CA	275,472	20,872	166,751	87,849	100.0	7.6	60.5	31.9	246,073	217,956	139,358	15,737	6,021	13.2	7,098	4,106	921
Chula Vista Elementary	CA	269,881	23,066	119,627	127,188	100.0	8.5	44.3	47.1	276,982	235,624	146,366	28,597	10,046	18.6	8,261	5,585	1,038
Clovis Unified	CA	391,532	25,848	244,982	120,702	100.0	6.6	62.6	30.8	394,485	330,832	200,026	49,365	8,587	17.4	8,293	7,055	1,060
Coachella Valley Unified	CA	191,419	30,224	116,269	44,926	100.0	15.8	60.7	23.5	209,834	189,224	112,499	11,515	7,253	40.2	10,108	10,049	1,165
Colton Joint Unified	CA	209,669	23,429	138,859	47,381	100.0	11.2	66.2	22.6	233,578	193,842	118,515	30,794	6,773	23.6	8,365	6,308	1,081
Compton Unified	CA	252,171	39,137	179,055	33,979	100.0	15.5	71.0	13.5	252,965	236,687	136,871	2,848	5,018	33.7	9,579	13,472	1,151
Conejo Valley Unified	CA	196,101	8,442	58,630	129,029	100.0	4.3	29.9	65.8	182,868	167,097	110,545	2,780	2,970	8.2	8,113	1,640	816
Corona-Norco Unified	CA	457,599	31,925	272,309	153,355	100.0	7.0	59.5	33.5	460,326	405,675	260,136	39,010	13,726	13.5	7,592	8,129	1,078
Cupertino Union	CA	174,703	4,350	38,122	132,231	100.0	2.5	21.8	75.7	169,617	151,171	103,000	13,823	4,480	4.4	7,942	463	499
Desert Sands Unified	CA	307,510	24,877	118,113	164,520	100.0	8.1	38.4	53.5	326,952	245,265	148,388	58,580	22,992	22.7	8,411	7,234	1,069
Downey Unified	CA	224,663	21,319	148,191	55,153	100.0	9.5	66.0	24.5	209,780	188,814	125,289	12,520	3,331	20.0	8,264	4,719	1,033
East Side Union High	CA	284,154	16,149	117,929	150,076	100.0	5.7	41.5	52.8	328,782	206,062	127,649	83,068	31,469	15.8	7,836	5,018	1,033
Elk Grove Unified	CA	549,526	54,840	389,954	104,732	100.0	10.0	71.0	19.1	555,236	523,096	341,025	13,416	11,487	19.5	8,418	15,708	1,172
Escondido Union	CA	169,424	21,648	83,129	64,647	100.0	12.8	49.1	38.2	156,923	151,456	93,594	1,735	3,611	22.1	7,821	4,677	1,025
Fairfield-Suisun Unified	CA	180,466	14,991	97,964	67,511	100.0	8.3	54.3	37.4	177,383	158,254	93,196	4,557	9,649	17.5	7,395	4,379	1,031
Folsom-Cordova Unified	CA	172,884	10,909	95,477	66,498	100.0	6.3	55.2	38.5	162,418	148,860	91,652	5,052	7,400	14.5	7,787	3,183	981
Fontana Unified	CA	377,129	44,671	276,714	55,744	100.0	11.8	73.4	14.8	376,709	349,036	210,071	3,005	23,356	25.5	8,645	12,308	1,148
Fremont Unified	CA	303,718	18,573	158,398	126,747	100.0	6.1	52.2	41.7	315,635	266,717	181,712	8,279	18,786	8.6	8,008	2,869	871
Fresno Unified	CA	775,739	128,551	542,650	104,538	100.0	16.6	70.0	13.5	793,385	676,659	396,631	91,537	14,567	50.1	9,183	50,504	1,271
Garden Grove Unified	CA	506,887	52,738	325,496	128,653	100.0	10.4	64.2	25.4	475,386	417,209	267,920	46,001	7,402	26.4	8,765	15,348	1,152
Glendale Unified	CA	254,231	30,456	137,147	86,628	100.0	12.0	53.9	34.1	276,976	235,723	158,864	25,722	5,906	20.2	9,004	6,282	1,053
Grossmont Union High	CA	256,080	19,813	94,180	142,087	100.0	7.7	36.8	55.5	275,573	187,772	106,536	58,661	15,152	16.7	8,176	4,601	1,034
Hacienda La Puente Unified	CA	222,851	23,020	157,478	42,353	100.0	10.3	70.7	19.0	216,043	189,426	109,491	1,454	4,181	22.6	9,305	5,080	1,039
Hayward Unified	CA	219,596	30,388	113,378	75,830	100.0	13.8	51.6	34.5	233,854	199,624	127,838	16,761	11,197	19.0	9,100	5,578	1,036
Hemet Unified	CA	225,359	24,473	128,509	72,377	100.0	10.9	57.0	32.1	235,075	211,464	130,719	12,819	10,477	26.0	9,750	7,057	1,067
Hesperia Unified	CA	168,724	19,198	126,995	22,531	100.0	11.4	75.3	13.4	168,378	163,268	96,576	2,347	1,200	26.7	6,963	6,544	1,065
Huntington Beach Union High	CA	195,733	16,836	60,585	118,312	100.0	8.6	31.0	60.4	190,414	145,718	85,913	2,188	11,016	15.0	8,885	2,438	952
Irvine Unified	CA	265,639	11,824	55,281	198,534	100.0	4.5	20.8	74.7	270,363	231,348	144,363	19,212	14,276	9.7	7,958	2,395	849
Jurupa Unified	CA	170,688	18,944	115,467	36,277	100.0	11.1	67.6	21.3	171,397	164,647	104,161	3,654	2,674	25.2	8,410	5,758	1,054
Kern Union High	CA	419,552	34,236	241,170	144,146	100.0	8.2	57.5	34.4	422,711	368,306	203,745	33,279	9,360	25.0	9,935	12,255	1,135
Lake Elsinore Unified	CA	189,239	18,740	116,408	54,091	100.0	9.9	61.5	28.6	191,999	181,616	113,025	5,329	2,020	18.1	8,204	4,865	1,055
Lodi Unified	CA	263,918	31,232	176,439	56,247	100.0	11.8	66.9	21.3	266,241	243,468	151,914	12,351	8,699	22.0	8,056	8,042	1,072
Long Beach Unified	CA	810,505	116,859	487,891	205,755	100.0	14.4	60.2	25.4	856,996	710,575	456,397	89,396	24,682	25.9	8,639	27,575	1,222
Los Angeles Unified	CA	8,318,105	1,091,741	4,858,628	2,367,736	100.0	13.1	58.4	28.5	8,366,970	6,985,426	4,162,680	687,399	587,475	31.4	10,657	344,219	1,478
Madera Unified	CA	182,879	21,435	117,068	44,376	100.0	11.7	64.0	24.3	164,484	155,978	92,786	3,996	2,768	32.0	7,805	7,695	1,143
Manteca Unified	CA	197,534	17,508	122,382	57,644	100.0	8.9	62.0	29.2	202,059	166,508	103,922	26,529	4,775	18.1	7,252	4,874	1,040
Modesto City[6]	CA	271,507	33,942	169,301	68,264	100.0	12.5	62.4	25.1	271,445	245,835	143,204	12,591	1,400	41.9	8,201	7,760	1,169
Montebello Unified	CA	309,750	39,194	192,125	78,431	100.0	12.7	62.0	25.3	311,484	280,600	164,030	8,706	6,903	29.0	9,181	10,476	1,111
Moreno Valley Unified	CA	307,165	33,743	226,634	46,788	100.0	11.0	73.8	15.2	288,721	277,237	173,840	2,206	8,405	26.7	7,939	12,036	1,140
Mount Diablo Unified	CA	336,040	35,675	147,903	152,462	100.0	10.6	44.0	45.4	378,438	289,819	180,831	64,237	20,492	13.3	9,057	5,621	1,019
Murrieta Valley Unified	CA	197,065	10,800	107,211	79,054	100.0	5.5	54.4	40.1	183,899	167,903	107,157	6,675	7,741	10.4	7,323	2,122	849
Napa Valley Unified	CA	178,078	15,285	52,184	110,609	100.0	8.6	29.3	62.1	168,598	144,334	90,881	7,631	13,221	12.5	7,876	2,157	850
Newport-Mesa Unified	CA	283,523	19,127	40,426	223,970	100.0	6.7	14.3	79.0	276,491	238,531	141,601	29,666	4,498	17.0	10,841	4,788	1,023
Norwalk-La Mirada Unified	CA	208,016	24,443	138,342	45,231	100.0	11.8	66.5	21.7	213,708	183,616	112,407	6,459	2,571	18.7	9,288	4,408	1,027
Oakland Unified	CA	604,008	74,530	325,280	204,198	100.0	12.3	53.9	33.8	595,132	438,090	243,203	96,401	41,385	25.9	9,429	17,582	1,173
Oceanside Unified	CA	207,443	28,871	103,978	74,594	100.0	13.9	50.1	36.0	211,799	174,936	104,957	28,615	5,908	21.2	8,246	4,866	1,028
Ontario-Montclair Elementary	CA	212,682	28,246	145,746	38,690	100.0	13.3	68.5	18.2	214,634	202,269	131,465	9,346	2,612	29.2	8,897	7,694	1,089
Orange Unified	CA	256,209	20,956	73,397	161,856	100.0	8.2	28.6	63.2	250,552	233,625	147,979	12,013	2,036	15.3	7,826	5,894	1,037
Oxnard	CA	150,842	17,290	91,163	42,389	100.0	11.5	60.4	28.1	175,936	136,596	88,236	31,361	5,135	27.5	8,262	4,895	1,034

See notes at end of table.

Table 215.20. Revenues, expenditures, poverty rate, and Title I allocations of public school districts enrolling more than 15,000 students: 2012–13 and fiscal year 2015—Continued

Name of district	State	Revenues by source of funds, 2012–13 (in thousands of current dollars)				Percentage distribution of revenues, 2012–13				Expenditures, 2012–13 (in thousands of current dollars)					Poverty rate of 5- to 17-year-olds, 2014[1]	Current expenditure per pupil[2] 2012–13 (in current dollars)	Title I allocations, federal fiscal year 2015	
		Total	Federal	State	Local	Total	Federal	State	Local	Total[3]	Current expenditures		Capital outlay	Interest on school debt			Total[4] (in thousands of current dollars)	Per poverty child[5] (in current dollars)
											Total	Instruction						
1	2	3	4	5	6	7	8	9	10	11	12	13	14	15	16	17	18	19
Oxnard Union High	CA	159,993	19,135	72,463	68,395	100.0	12.0	45.3	42.7	166,194	136,494	83,860	20,835	5,035	17.9	8,134	3,483	1,003
Pajaro Valley Unified	CA	212,141	39,434	111,390	61,317	100.0	18.6	52.5	28.9	210,798	205,001	119,371	1,282	2,073	23.7	10,250	5,515	1,043
Palm Springs Unified	CA	303,245	25,767	182,438	95,040	100.0	8.5	60.2	31.3	268,468	202,903	121,915	51,050	14,410	29.5	8,605	8,864	1,139
Palmdale Elementary	CA	262,078	56,465	169,991	35,622	100.0	21.5	64.9	13.6	265,070	187,397	109,264	11,643	3,290	32.8	8,813	7,197	1,061
Panama-Buena Vista Union	CA	143,374	11,676	109,840	21,858	100.0	8.1	76.6	15.2	145,265	131,790	80,677	4,629	120	19.9	7,607	3,567	1,006
Paramount Unified	CA	144,285	19,048	94,754	30,483	100.0	13.2	65.7	21.1	154,372	135,931	80,683	10,460	3,534	28.7	8,578	5,138	1,039
Pasadena Unified	CA	244,049	30,229	89,941	123,879	100.0	12.4	36.9	50.8	230,036	187,821	108,626	22,498	19,263	20.1	9,612	5,762	1,048
Placentia-Yorba Linda Unified	CA	242,202	18,460	98,652	125,090	100.0	7.6	40.7	51.6	249,575	209,333	131,991	19,061	15,029	12.3	8,170	3,124	878
Pomona Unified	CA	319,430	62,570	197,896	58,964	100.0	19.6	62.0	18.5	348,202	270,382	154,872	45,635	10,544	28.4	9,946	10,364	1,110
Poway Unified	CA	358,425	11,977	119,223	227,225	100.0	3.3	33.3	63.4	359,432	298,055	179,651	37,644	22,000	6.5	8,468	1,942	825
Redlands Unified	CA	194,159	15,806	121,279	57,074	100.0	8.1	62.5	29.4	181,243	168,744	104,809	3,323	4,838	16.1	7,893	3,584	1,022
Rialto Unified	CA	243,738	26,769	175,006	41,963	100.0	11.0	71.8	17.2	248,353	227,662	126,896	16,722	2,550	26.4	8,560	7,995	1,077
Riverside Unified	CA	382,543	42,841	237,972	101,730	100.0	11.2	62.2	26.6	405,139	359,163	227,667	34,200	7,474	20.9	8,439	10,817	1,124
Rowland Unified	CA	176,601	22,385	118,926	35,290	100.0	12.7	67.3	20.0	196,098	134,825	82,329	34,727	7,403	23.9	8,698	4,483	1,029
Sacramento City Unified	CA	488,458	82,038	301,350	105,070	100.0	16.8	61.7	21.5	473,966	442,326	272,619	8,250	16,853	31.5	9,289	19,817	1,200
Saddleback Valley Unified	CA	276,369	14,966	93,522	167,881	100.0	5.4	33.8	60.7	260,479	228,470	158,682	7,379	6,288	9.3	7,527	2,873	870
San Bernardino City Unified	CA	558,440	90,300	413,021	55,119	100.0	16.2	74.0	9.9	646,287	492,707	274,992	130,235	9,016	37.8	9,107	26,908	1,269
San Diego Unified	CA	1,427,717	164,044	431,908	831,765	100.0	11.5	30.3	58.3	1,438,489	1,221,364	727,756	161,155	53,267	22.9	9,376	39,812	1,245
San Francisco Unified	CA	752,645	80,673	198,811	473,161	100.0	10.7	26.4	62.9	737,509	566,150	282,971	70,261	31,691	14.2	9,938	12,017	1,142
San Jose Unified	CA	356,595	24,459	102,127	230,009	100.0	6.9	28.6	64.5	336,127	302,227	177,359	11,660	21,115	13.6	9,108	5,637	1,007
San Juan Unified	CA	436,242	45,645	267,790	122,807	100.0	10.5	61.4	28.2	442,274	403,213	241,465	19,155	15,127	21.5	8,444	12,326	1,152
San Marcos Unified	CA	180,399	13,120	74,867	92,412	100.0	7.3	41.5	51.2	253,632	149,978	96,054	84,301	13,311	14.4	7,645	2,899	970
San Ramon Valley Unified	CA	293,880	6,700	96,999	190,181	100.0	2.3	33.0	64.7	302,282	253,777	163,868	25,588	21,170	4.1	8,251	647	504
Santa Ana Unified	CA	554,940	85,915	315,946	153,079	100.0	15.5	56.9	27.6	618,649	522,139	314,982	80,017	13,334	31.4	9,095	20,195	1,182
Santa Barbara Unified	CA	155,423	12,452	26,897	116,074	100.0	8.0	17.3	74.7	162,980	127,381	73,402	23,090	7,210	14.7	8,224	2,307	938
Santa Clara Unified	CA	192,735	11,140	23,502	158,093	100.0	5.8	12.2	82.0	236,790	143,224	87,947	69,101	20,243	9.3	9,453	1,477	810
Santa Maria-Bonita	CA	123,584	19,173	84,195	20,216	100.0	15.5	68.1	16.4	124,582	122,465	75,939	1,800	276	29.1	8,137	4,352	1,022
Simi Valley Unified	CA	175,717	9,306	87,156	79,255	100.0	5.3	49.6	45.1	178,340	156,032	98,770	10,432	5,878	9.2	8,274	1,759	819
Stockton Unified	CA	390,195	64,398	260,338	65,459	100.0	16.5	66.7	16.8	409,731	348,466	212,275	44,401	13,900	38.5	9,066	19,250	1,195
Sweetwater Union High	CA	421,164	29,948	240,683	150,533	100.0	7.1	57.1	35.7	425,442	349,127	204,095	39,816	23,319	20.8	8,533	10,293	1,109
Temecula Valley Unified	CA	239,603	12,164	131,284	96,155	100.0	5.1	54.8	40.1	225,044	212,987	144,829	8,524	1,402	8.6	7,021	2,507	880
Torrance Unified	CA	227,972	14,625	127,354	85,993	100.0	6.4	55.9	37.7	240,735	181,336	122,039	35,342	10,770	10.1	7,455	1,964	833
Tracy Joint Unified	CA	139,696	10,223	90,427	39,046	100.0	7.3	64.7	28.0	155,183	132,174	81,586	17,700	3,288	15.5	7,594	2,884	988
Tustin Unified	CA	202,767	15,745	74,921	112,101	100.0	7.8	36.9	55.3	228,991	173,760	109,883	43,419	7,568	14.3	7,310	3,129	878
Twin Rivers Unified	CA	337,321	48,073	221,686	67,562	100.0	14.3	65.7	20.0	321,786	293,377	169,307	10,524	12,208	34.3	9,337	13,315	1,147
Val Verde Unified	CA	367,095	69,239	244,114	53,742	100.0	18.9	66.5	14.6	382,283	170,477	102,192	5,718	4,356	24.5	8,596	5,298	1,049
Vallejo City Unified	CA	141,715	16,223	89,038	36,454	100.0	11.4	62.8	25.7	137,196	123,745	71,378	4,090	6,768	21.0	8,164	4,182	1,027
Ventura Unified	CA	158,708	13,979	71,348	73,381	100.0	8.8	45.0	46.2	158,229	144,812	82,306	4,101	2,897	12.9	8,322	2,080	843
Visalia Unified	CA	235,501	25,205	151,556	58,740	100.0	10.7	64.4	24.9	228,040	206,344	129,023	16,298	908	27.6	7,472	9,481	1,108
Vista Unified	CA	221,233	21,810	108,243	91,180	100.0	9.9	48.9	41.2	214,019	191,933	121,691	11,946	5,534	20.0	7,485	5,439	1,038
West Contra Costa Unified	CA	364,176	42,801	180,179	141,196	100.0	11.8	49.5	38.8	400,603	285,015	158,214	78,622	33,845	17.8	9,376	7,655	1,071
William S. Hart Union High	CA	236,962	9,217	151,072	76,673	100.0	3.9	63.8	32.4	228,144	195,568	111,384	20,844	9,971	9.2	7,415	1,955	832
Academy, No. 20	CO	226,291	13,704	107,152	105,435	100.0	6.1	47.4	46.6	211,209	190,505	115,283	7,848	11,296	4.8	7,947	555	521
Adams 12 Five Star Schools	CO	405,051	22,447	221,472	161,132	100.0	5.5	54.7	39.8	386,054	343,032	217,724	16,597	23,527	11.0	7,928	4,656	963
Aurora, Joint District No. 28	CO	395,801	41,210	215,642	138,949	100.0	10.4	54.5	35.1	395,175	337,229	192,926	34,453	18,402	26.7	8,466	12,559	1,149
Boulder Valley, No. RE2	CO	338,885	14,665	70,977	253,243	100.0	4.3	20.9	74.7	333,238	289,673	179,250	18,787	16,918	8.5	9,643	2,242	844
Brighton, No. 27J	CO	138,629	9,423	78,092	51,114	100.0	6.8	56.3	36.9	130,472	116,903	65,281	4,600	7,663	8.9	7,223	1,332	860
Cherry Creek, No. 5	CO	548,930	26,039	220,886	302,005	100.0	4.7	40.2	55.0	532,278	479,737	325,699	28,331	21,911	9.9	8,980	5,152	933
Colorado Springs, No. 11	CO	297,913	28,671	125,107	144,135	100.0	9.6	42.0	48.4	281,236	258,207	144,869	8,267	10,855	15.7	8,894	7,513	1,348

See notes at end of table.

Table 215.20. Revenues, expenditures, poverty rate, and Title I allocations of public school districts enrolling more than 15,000 students: 2012–13 and fiscal year 2015—Continued

Name of district	State	Revenues by source of funds, 2012–13 (in thousands of current dollars)				Percentage distribution of revenues, 2012–13				Expenditures, 2012–13 (in thousands of current dollars)					Poverty rate of 5- to 17-year-olds, 2014[1]	Current expenditure per pupil,[2] 2012–13 (in current dollars)	Title I allocations, federal fiscal year 2015	
		Total	Federal	State	Local	Total	Federal	State	Local	Total[3]	Current expenditures						Total[4] (in thousands of current dollars)	Per poverty child[5] (in current dollars)
											Total	Instruction	Capital outlay	Interest on school debt				
1	2	3	4	5	6	7	8	9	10	11	12	13	14	15	16	17	18	19
Denver	CO	1,057,142	125,850	293,572	637,720	100.0	11.9	27.8	60.3	1,087,297	835,041	455,882	108,152	99,192	28.7	10,015	32,896	1,258
Douglas County, No. RE1	CO	603,241	18,184	271,165	313,892	100.0	3.0	45.0	52.0	598,873	504,280	293,176	57,072	35,076	3.4	7,799	1,115	476
Falcon, No. 49	CO	125,042	6,245	75,957	42,840	100.0	5.0	60.7	34.3	117,399	102,249	56,858	7,088	7,081	6.9	6,606	1,083	927
Greeley, No. 6	CO	173,783	20,430	100,951	52,402	100.0	11.8	58.1	30.2	184,111	160,371	93,592	15,000	5,804	21.2	8,091	4,950	1,041
Jefferson County, No. R1	CO	842,074	53,795	339,822	448,457	100.0	6.4	40.4	53.2	834,668	723,169	410,007	65,306	40,560	11.9	8,454	12,297	1,175
Littleton, No. 6	CO	161,849	7,340	62,221	92,288	100.0	4.5	38.4	57.0	158,899	142,733	85,304	11,849	3,620	9.5	9,060	1,198	798
Mesa County Valley, No. 51	CO	186,246	16,419	89,928	79,899	100.0	8.8	48.3	42.9	177,978	165,796	102,615	4,948	4,477	18.7	7,624	4,647	1,057
Poudre, No. R1	CO	274,346	17,895	101,316	155,135	100.0	6.5	36.9	56.5	281,016	243,253	144,538	23,203	13,021	12.5	8,716	3,075	884
Pueblo, No. 60	CO	152,635	23,705	86,623	42,307	100.0	15.5	56.8	27.7	146,045	138,968	79,011	1,708	3,697	30.0	7,846	5,933	1,079
Saint Vrain Valley, No. RE1J	CO	295,768	16,919	118,006	160,843	100.0	5.7	39.9	54.4	292,516	221,698	128,499	42,983	24,080	12.9	7,545	3,582	902
Thompson, No. R2J	CO	141,777	9,791	65,563	66,423	100.0	6.9	46.2	46.9	137,534	122,964	71,070	3,058	9,254	11.6	7,665	1,761	815
Bridgeport	CT	387,186	37,029	289,487	60,670	100.0	9.6	74.8	15.7	396,769	306,925	194,311	62,974	5,653	28.3	15,228	12,057	1,688
Hartford	CT	518,922	42,586	382,587	93,749	100.0	8.2	73.7	18.1	518,678	396,359	225,511	66,559	5,086	40.4	18,397	16,705	1,885
New Haven	CT	441,149	41,786	269,943	129,420	100.0	9.5	61.2	29.3	417,635	361,335	230,103	21,588	13,538	31.4	17,084	11,983	1,949
Stamford	CT	316,199	11,242	56,201	248,756	100.0	3.6	17.8	78.7	309,320	286,613	171,549	4,658	5,244	13.8	18,188	3,283	1,314
Waterbury	CT	359,556	31,574	230,689	97,293	100.0	8.8	64.2	27.1	364,773	291,663	165,320	62,024	1,524	29.4	15,859	10,418	1,821
Christina	DE	287,938	24,845	129,583	133,510	100.0	8.6	45.0	46.4	300,047	273,022	153,106	4,201	2,376	17.6	16,664	8,753	1,880
Red Clay Consolidated	DE	243,303	23,868	122,529	96,906	100.0	9.8	50.4	39.8	244,721	226,324	149,023	2,936	2,394	16.8	14,008	6,760	1,825
District of Columbia	DC	1,300,036	129,874	0	1,170,162	100.0	10.0	0.0	90.0	1,258,826	793,155	475,854	375,676		29.1	17,953	42,820	2,084
Alachua	FL	251,276	34,759	101,873	114,644	100.0	13.8	40.5	45.6	256,779	239,276	132,067	10,427	3,041	24.2	8,599	7,712	1,012
Bay	FL	238,607	25,419	81,255	131,933	100.0	10.7	34.1	55.3	227,920	204,350	131,504	13,403	4,744	24.4	7,673	6,669	1,019
Brevard	FL	599,412	62,930	290,283	246,199	100.0	10.5	48.4	41.1	603,010	565,138	347,535	11,332	23,519	19.7	7,934	16,940	1,097
Broward	FL	2,302,764	263,763	897,604	1,141,397	100.0	11.5	39.0	49.6	2,370,326	2,112,288	1,314,953	94,625	92,341	17.7	8,117	62,226	1,199
Charlotte	FL	157,273	21,361	31,710	104,202	100.0	13.6	20.2	66.3	167,557	143,710	79,129	3,471	3,650	21.5	8,787	3,471	962
Citrus	FL	137,642	15,381	47,929	74,332	100.0	11.2	34.8	54.0	149,680	132,339	75,997	12,543	980	26.2	8,646	4,062	978
Clay	FL	289,722	24,410	172,498	92,814	100.0	8.4	59.5	32.0	292,110	277,934	180,068	10,837	2,846	12.9	7,886	4,233	876
Collier	FL	491,985	55,854	77,715	358,416	100.0	11.4	15.8	72.9	491,934	438,396	261,008	23,849	22,244	22.4	10,012	10,933	1,053
Dade	FL	3,266,516	488,124	1,071,630	1,706,762	100.0	14.9	32.8	52.3	3,405,385	3,090,883	1,985,933	118,735	103,279	26.1	8,725	126,439	1,242
Duval	FL	1,106,654	152,989	494,665	459,000	100.0	13.8	44.7	41.5	1,142,394	1,054,683	631,959	67,941	16,933	22.1	8,391	36,213	1,139
Escambia	FL	361,945	52,498	161,612	147,835	100.0	14.5	44.7	40.8	360,162	334,485	192,949	19,115	2,106	27.1	8,224	13,356	1,077
Hernando	FL	192,138	22,346	91,239	78,553	100.0	11.6	47.5	40.9	188,684	176,171	102,620	4,508	7,550	23.4	7,929	5,898	996
Hillsborough	FL	1,845,716	279,601	897,747	668,368	100.0	15.1	48.6	36.2	1,894,010	1,650,271	1,004,006	88,592	48,033	22.4	8,232	58,474	1,192
Indian River	FL	172,699	16,900	36,394	119,405	100.0	9.8	21.1	69.1	170,280	144,004	86,849	18,377	6,977	22.1	7,995	4,110	969
Lake	FL	340,131	38,288	160,908	140,935	100.0	11.3	47.3	41.4	360,281	320,522	191,135	25,299	14,343	21.9	7,724	10,580	1,048
Lee	FL	795,969	92,386	241,823	461,760	100.0	11.6	30.4	58.0	852,352	740,301	447,962	76,780	19,168	26.0	8,632	27,011	1,125
Leon	FL	317,045	38,266	128,960	149,819	100.0	12.1	40.7	47.3	340,846	277,744	157,253	43,928	6,827	21.3	8,308	8,585	1,032
Manatee	FL	415,726	48,375	145,953	221,398	100.0	11.6	35.1	53.3	432,826	380,762	232,191	22,903	13,674	26.0	8,248	14,098	1,079
Marion	FL	361,558	51,208	168,448	141,902	100.0	14.2	46.6	39.2	382,138	340,069	195,793	25,810	5,977	27.6	8,099	13,932	1,076
Martin	FL	184,778	17,019	33,043	134,716	100.0	9.2	17.9	72.9	192,376	158,783	90,323	26,045	2,095	18.1	8,497	3,519	991
Okaloosa	FL	259,417	25,507	105,743	128,167	100.0	9.8	40.8	49.4	260,639	244,014	160,505	7,920	2,863	21.1	8,192	6,402	1,008
Orange	FL	1,879,014	206,990	662,965	1,009,059	100.0	11.0	35.3	53.7	1,775,937	1,495,127	895,431	183,960	65,625	24.5	8,167	58,949	1,181
Osceola	FL	492,781	61,964	252,942	177,875	100.0	12.6	51.3	36.1	494,352	446,888	271,227	23,569	15,354	31.8	7,922	19,815	1,104
Palm Beach	FL	1,778,291	178,941	419,188	1,180,162	100.0	10.1	23.6	66.4	1,867,496	1,647,841	1,040,314	89,218	85,588	21.2	9,179	49,530	1,170
Pasco	FL	596,027	62,571	312,533	220,923	100.0	10.5	52.4	37.1	584,858	532,403	313,351	32,328	16,771	17.7	7,928	14,168	1,087
Pinellas	FL	921,475	106,001	298,106	517,368	100.0	11.5	32.4	56.1	960,314	888,018	548,111	50,049	2,180	22.0	8,572	29,490	1,132
Polk	FL	913,627	110,493	458,721	344,413	100.0	12.1	50.2	37.7	940,629	878,547	586,356	33,181	19,011	27.5	9,063	33,100	1,137
Saint Johns	FL	266,793	17,829	94,740	174,224	100.0	6.2	33.0	60.7	285,975	255,926	151,411	19,850	7,120	10.5	7,888	3,260	856

See notes at end of table.

Table 215.20. Revenues, expenditures, poverty rate, and Title I allocations of public school districts enrolling more than 15,000 students: 2012–13 and fiscal year 2015—Continued

Name of district	State	Revenues by source of funds, 2012–13 (in thousands of current dollars)				Percentage distribution of revenues, 2012–13				Expenditures, 2012–13 (in thousands of current dollars)					Poverty rate of 5- to 17-year-olds, 2014[1]	Current expenditure per pupil,[2] 2012–13 (in current dollars)	Title I allocations, federal fiscal year 2015	
										Total[3]	Current expenditures						Total[4] (in thousands of current dollars)	Per poverty child[5] (in current dollars)
		Total	Federal	State	Local	Total	Federal	State	Local		Total	Instruction	Capital outlay	Interest on school debt				
1	2	3	4	5	6	7	8	9	10	11	12	13	14	15	16	17	18	19
Saint Lucie	FL	361,338	42,321	157,248	161,769	100.0	11.7	43.5	44.8	362,954	329,859	191,051	17,195	14,990	25.7	8,321	12,576	1,069
Santa Rosa	FL	212,658	23,007	107,163	82,488	100.0	10.8	50.4	38.8	219,646	197,192	114,100	12,906	2,231	16.1	7,620	4,361	985
Sarasota	FL	470,782	38,325	70,987	361,470	100.0	8.1	15.1	76.8	526,125	415,985	268,707	92,596	9,837	17.3	10,122	7,884	1,022
Seminole	FL	522,697	50,596	249,252	222,849	100.0	9.7	47.7	42.6	515,802	489,059	310,504	13,675	9,721	15.8	7,587	12,131	1,067
Volusia	FL	548,917	61,284	225,372	262,261	100.0	11.2	41.1	47.8	522,991	480,215	282,220	18,204	20,219	23.7	7,864	19,165	1,199
Atlanta	GA	771,985	84,743	146,818	540,424	100.0	11.0	19.0	70.0	805,195	629,983	332,621	123,408	6,683	36.4	12,712	31,528	1,503
Bibb County	GA	279,356	49,926	105,234	124,196	100.0	17.9	37.7	44.5	264,692	239,351	137,679	23,807	1,143	39.1	9,766	12,315	1,133
Chatham County	GA	409,049	49,177	128,288	231,584	100.0	12.0	31.4	56.6	400,683	343,717	221,997	53,517	3,027	28.6	9,389	13,517	1,108
Cherokee County	GA	403,642	20,988	191,873	190,781	100.0	5.2	47.5	47.3	387,661	321,292	213,187	50,212	14,271	12.0	8,182	5,003	925
Clayton County	GA	471,535	59,213	234,529	177,793	100.0	12.6	49.7	37.7	498,137	409,994	252,111	87,638	0	34.1	7,922	23,200	1,265
Cobb County	GA	1,091,899	86,718	420,998	584,183	100.0	7.9	38.6	53.5	1,099,583	955,945	628,099	126,487	0	16.2	8,814	22,795	1,162
Columbia County	GA	214,116	11,579	99,911	102,626	100.0	5.4	46.7	47.9	226,802	193,681	123,763	31,292	1,623	9.8	7,928	2,214	834
Coweta County	GA	205,105	15,539	91,608	97,958	100.0	7.6	44.7	47.8	203,200	188,397	119,846	12,501	826	17.4	8,303	4,633	1,008
DeKalb County	GA	1,120,290	120,025	445,743	554,522	100.0	10.7	39.8	49.5	939,285	864,053	520,727	69,592	5,574	28.6	8,736	38,216	1,215
Dougherty County	GA	163,875	21,978	80,028	61,869	100.0	13.4	48.8	37.8	154,014	148,726	86,960	4,761	0	42.4	9,404	7,886	1,133
Douglas County	GA	250,075	27,396	120,316	102,363	100.0	11.0	48.1	40.9	263,598	224,372	139,332	23,790	9,002	23.0	8,912	6,739	1,052
Fayette County	GA	209,144	8,756	84,530	115,858	100.0	4.2	40.4	55.4	197,923	180,618	119,486	10,707	4,219	8.5	8,897	1,491	803
Forsyth County	GA	361,212	14,905	142,535	203,772	100.0	4.1	39.5	56.4	327,321	305,161	208,550	4,014	16,487	7.9	7,855	3,074	878
Fulton County	GA	1,090,818	74,519	314,734	701,565	100.0	6.8	28.9	64.3	1,022,219	908,134	562,089	78,239	9,259	17.3	9,671	22,025	1,143
Gwinnett County	GA	1,582,099	132,604	718,476	731,019	100.0	8.4	45.4	46.2	1,615,198	1,458,088	889,987	98,691	54,482	18.3	8,838	38,079	1,169
Hall County	GA	246,287	26,443	114,483	105,361	100.0	10.7	46.5	42.8	248,321	226,455	145,455	20,202	1,108	24.1	8,489	7,564	1,043
Henry County	GA	386,427	27,607	192,293	166,527	100.0	7.1	49.8	43.1	399,677	344,376	225,453	41,572	11,481	14.8	8,571	7,536	1,123
Houston County	GA	277,017	24,370	141,003	111,644	100.0	8.8	50.9	40.3	288,715	257,285	166,471	28,566	2,022	19.7	9,319	5,933	1,088
Muscogee County	GA	356,170	46,047	158,733	151,390	100.0	12.9	44.6	42.5	354,583	320,672	190,585	30,216	1,661	32.6	9,967	11,953	1,101
Newton County	GA	186,519	19,437	106,071	61,011	100.0	10.4	56.9	32.7	194,839	165,985	106,964	22,608	3,708	20.9	8,654	4,467	1,011
Paulding County	GA	244,208	17,467	150,234	76,507	100.0	7.2	61.5	31.3	240,201	221,750	143,726	12,383	5,707	13.5	7,806	4,174	972
Richmond County	GA	324,269	52,449	143,428	128,382	100.0	16.2	44.2	39.6	322,042	296,135	176,960	19,223	6,055	43.2	9,239	16,453	1,136
Rockdale County	GA	162,263	17,354	69,624	75,285	100.0	10.7	42.9	46.4	162,456	152,741	88,727	9,715	0	21.5	9,624	3,671	997
Hawaii Department of Education	HI	2,331,770	310,778	1,962,923	58,069	100.0	13.3	84.2	2.5	2,345,917	2,184,393	1,283,872	146,656	0	13.6	11,823	47,116	1,604
Boise Independent	ID	228,405	20,348	118,732	89,325	100.0	8.9	52.0	39.1	224,533	213,511	131,813	5,166	3,959	17.0	8,292	5,665	1,110
Meridian Joint	ID	239,693	16,709	164,316	58,668	100.0	7.0	68.6	24.5	227,334	209,487	127,765	8,614	9,042	10.4	5,687	4,490	983
Nampa	ID	99,323	13,374	72,861	13,088	100.0	13.5	73.4	13.2	93,951	87,772	56,056	470	5,709	24.9	5,461	5,444	1,107
Carpentersville (CUSD 300)	IL	248,565	14,443	55,779	178,343	100.0	5.8	22.4	71.7	244,509	224,234	118,418	5,870	14,076	11.7	9,734	3,083	1,182
City of Chicago (SD 299)	IL	5,388,477	806,318	1,911,744	2,670,415	100.0	15.0	35.5	49.6	5,744,617	4,863,728	3,113,082	510,450	304,787	32.8	12,284	279,268	2,023
Elgin (SDU-46)	IL	503,502	35,700	161,534	306,268	100.0	7.1	32.1	60.8	476,427	423,749	244,087	27,580	12,851	16.4	10,504	10,775	1,496
Indian Prairie (CUSD 204)	IL	369,899	10,212	86,061	273,626	100.0	2.8	23.3	74.0	344,180	320,104	216,469	8,262	14,885	5.1	11,040	1,669	1,116
Naperville (CUSD 203)	IL	286,438	7,410	58,574	220,454	100.0	2.6	20.4	77.0	276,290	253,732	151,944	12,506	1,765	4.9	14,463	648	699
Oswego (CUSD 308)	IL	206,628	4,255	67,624	134,749	100.0	2.1	32.7	65.2	223,636	154,153	91,191	39,289	14,038	7.2	8,761	1,447	1,116
Plainfield (SD 202)	IL	298,877	10,864	108,312	179,701	100.0	3.6	36.2	60.1	283,645	254,618	167,406	7,394	15,131	6.5	8,864	2,252	1,152
Rockford (SD 205)	IL	406,540	44,912	168,360	193,268	100.0	11.0	41.4	47.5	378,780	338,438	191,094	16,538	1,789	28.7	11,761	15,170	1,607
Springfield (SD 186)	IL	211,542	24,527	77,576	109,439	100.0	11.6	36.7	51.7	230,648	196,101	107,047	22,026	4,081	25.9	13,035	6,924	1,491
Valley View (CUSD 365U)	IL	249,337	14,403	69,432	165,502	100.0	5.8	27.8	66.4	241,293	223,720	135,065	11,986	5,465	15.1	12,555	3,982	1,391
Waukegan (CUSD 60)	IL	239,314	18,249	140,549	80,516	100.0	7.6	58.7	33.6	231,401	197,968	108,292	29,338	2,689	26.2	11,775	6,431	1,441
Carmel Clay	IN	185,425	8,004	101,053	76,368	100.0	4.3	54.5	41.2	168,281	141,932	85,818	19,068	6,866	3.6	9,026	366	502
Evansville Vanderburgh	IN	269,977	34,480	174,981	60,516	100.0	12.8	64.8	22.4	258,020	231,669	129,255	14,106	8,915	24.6	10,064	8,314	1,193
Fort Wayne	IN	351,290	40,298	239,384	71,608	100.0	11.5	68.1	20.4	333,397	299,858	182,686	26,580	3,727	28.5	9,861	14,268	1,285
Hamilton Southeastern	IN	205,244	5,130	124,367	75,747	100.0	2.5	60.6	36.9	177,100	163,022	97,673	12,822	16	4.5	8,067	503	502

See notes at end of table.

Table 215.20. Revenues, expenditures, poverty rate, and Title I allocations of public school districts enrolling more than 15,000 students: 2012–13 and fiscal year 2015—Continued

Name of district	State	Revenues by source of funds, 2012–13 (in thousands of current dollars)				Percentage distribution of revenues, 2012–13				Expenditures, 2012–13 (in thousands of current dollars)					Poverty rate of 5- to 17-year-olds, 2014[1]	Current expenditure per pupil[2] 2012–13 (in current dollars)	Title I allocations, federal fiscal year 2015	
		Total	Federal	State	Local	Total	Federal	State	Local	Total[3]	Current expenditures						Total[4] (in thousands of current dollars)	Per poverty child[5] (in current dollars)
											Total	Instruction	Capital outlay	Interest on school debt				
1	2	3	4	5	6	7	8	9	10	11	12	13	14	15	16	17	18	19
Indianapolis	IN	474,483	73,642	289,792	111,049	100.0	15.5	61.1	23.4	510,759	405,831	207,660	65,554	26,502	42.5	13,616	30,813	1,470
MSD Wayne Township	IN	221,013	25,187	135,688	60,138	100.0	11.4	61.4	27.2	200,503	181,040	109,893	5,988	1,060	27.8	11,500	4,691	1,140
South Bend	IN	295,328	34,483	162,258	98,587	100.0	11.7	54.9	33.4	235,894	215,025	126,658	8,523	8,583	32.7	11,041	10,552	1,214
Vigo County	IN	166,672	13,938	117,864	34,870	100.0	8.4	70.7	20.9	157,577	139,700	88,877	12,130	3,000	27.2	9,069	5,065	1,145
Cedar Rapids	IA	225,856	15,836	109,936	100,084	100.0	7.0	48.7	44.3	236,498	185,337	119,744	30,155	9,186	14.6	10,826	3,815	1,312
Davenport	IA	201,115	18,815	106,747	75,553	100.0	9.4	53.1	37.6	181,203	164,570	109,324	12,944	0	24.0	9,816	5,712	1,308
Des Moines Independent	IA	428,673	50,406	242,003	136,264	100.0	11.8	56.5	31.8	435,547	351,188	228,161	60,941	6,348	23.4	10,301	12,008	1,426
Blue Valley	KS	300,505	6,491	98,512	195,502	100.0	2.2	32.8	65.1	260,227	212,137	129,547	32,355	14,628	2.6	9,572	469	666
Kansas City	KS	257,008	33,958	169,103	53,947	100.0	13.2	65.8	21.0	248,816	213,585	128,849	32,854	2,377	40.3	10,213	14,013	1,492
Olathe	KS	317,752	15,787	172,625	129,340	100.0	5.0	54.3	40.7	316,642	271,494	182,572	31,497	13,648	6.5	9,445	2,016	1,000
Shawnee Mission	KS	309,790	18,302	115,143	176,345	100.0	5.9	37.2	56.9	300,666	260,326	170,295	31,799	8,528	8.8	9,489	3,259	1,068
Wichita	KS	597,576	73,149	361,455	162,972	100.0	12.2	60.5	27.3	617,744	533,752	295,703	61,675	22,085	25.3	10,603	21,881	1,514
Boone County	KY	196,244	12,401	85,101	98,742	100.0	6.3	43.4	50.3	185,153	166,783	97,170	9,769	7,875	10.5	8,412	2,373	940
Fayette County	KY	455,348	38,917	170,997	245,434	100.0	8.5	37.6	53.9	514,755	427,850	258,107	70,348	13,957	20.4	10,901	11,183	1,196
Jefferson County	KY	1,241,582	162,705	485,779	593,098	100.0	13.1	39.1	47.8	1,243,108	1,135,349	587,451	80,162	18,326	20.3	11,318	37,683	1,505
Ascension Parish	LA	246,802	21,690	102,553	122,559	100.0	8.8	41.6	49.7	282,506	213,390	126,358	34,143	4,594	14.4	10,160	3,767	1,113
Bossier Parish	LA	218,012	19,889	103,184	94,939	100.0	9.1	47.3	43.5	215,107	204,706	117,900	7,572	2,149	18.9	9,539	5,049	1,206
Caddo Parish	LA	472,055	60,771	206,001	205,283	100.0	12.9	43.6	43.5	473,950	440,140	252,386	28,544	4,365	30.5	10,651	18,263	1,361
Calcasieu Parish	LA	355,955	46,047	153,778	156,130	100.0	12.9	43.2	43.9	343,154	324,243	190,134	11,573	6,953	21.5	10,049	9,494	1,251
East Baton Rouge Parish	LA	565,614	71,584	177,987	316,043	100.0	12.7	31.5	55.9	529,770	491,612	264,478	36,763	262	28.3	11,438	24,139	1,401
Jefferson Parish	LA	557,140	85,506	195,745	275,889	100.0	15.3	35.1	49.5	586,409	526,369	281,515	50,666	5,650	27.7	11,418	26,469	1,402
Lafayette Parish	LA	340,201	40,600	121,040	178,561	100.0	11.9	35.6	52.5	320,232	306,405	179,978	10,420	2,521	20.0	9,973	9,954	1,254
Livingston Parish	LA	232,722	20,571	152,000	60,151	100.0	8.8	65.3	25.8	228,105	213,806	129,699	11,035	2,925	16.8	8,453	5,349	1,207
Ouachita Parish	LA	214,185	21,103	122,436	70,646	100.0	9.9	57.2	33.0	202,960	187,190	100,649	10,026	5,569	24.7	9,339	5,865	1,207
Rapides Parish	LA	236,950	28,961	130,896	77,093	100.0	12.2	55.2	32.5	232,649	220,329	134,210	8,474	3,665	27.3	9,156	8,526	1,263
Saint Tammany Parish	LA	458,389	41,724	210,754	205,911	100.0	9.1	46.0	44.9	436,904	413,030	240,304	13,606	9,022	13.8	11,010	8,114	1,276
Tangipahoa Parish	LA	188,153	35,419	106,105	46,629	100.0	18.8	56.4	24.8	185,756	176,300	100,605	8,991	343	31.1	8,889	8,579	1,237
Terrebonne Parish	LA	180,823	28,308	88,526	63,989	100.0	15.7	49.0	35.4	174,353	162,965	97,042	10,670	142	21.7	8,742	5,439	1,204
Anne Arundel County	MD	1,125,008	60,765	398,054	666,189	100.0	5.4	35.4	59.2	1,159,942	1,009,442	639,364	108,212	20,516	8.2	12,980	11,731	1,564
Baltimore City	MD	1,432,281	178,834	980,398	273,049	100.0	12.5	68.5	19.1	1,426,977	1,275,425	760,541	81,626	6,236	29.8	15,050	49,459	1,852
Baltimore County	MD	1,579,381	96,279	691,632	791,470	100.0	6.1	43.8	50.1	1,562,450	1,412,140	860,662	101,770	11,597	11.5	13,207	25,860	1,753
Calvert County	MD	241,560	9,319	101,743	130,498	100.0	3.9	42.1	54.0	234,896	216,164	136,733	13,110	1,948	7.6	13,243	1,586	1,210
Carroll County	MD	377,348	14,909	166,739	195,700	100.0	4.0	44.2	51.9	368,080	350,098	218,259	12,712	4,852	6.5	13,119	2,358	1,210
Cecil County	MD	211,038	13,731	113,497	83,810	100.0	6.5	53.8	39.7	208,357	194,803	121,622	7,185	2,595	12.6	12,460	2,928	1,281
Charles County	MD	411,753	19,056	195,298	197,399	100.0	4.6	47.4	47.9	393,920	346,256	199,043	39,163	2,861	9.5	12,996	3,567	1,279
Frederick County	MD	619,784	21,894	276,534	321,356	100.0	3.5	44.6	51.8	562,025	507,450	321,129	35,319	9,997	7.5	12,543	4,294	1,313
Harford County	MD	563,734	28,177	252,026	283,531	100.0	5.0	44.7	50.3	550,318	483,969	291,309	38,990	12,849	8.4	12,780	4,990	1,355
Howard County	MD	934,547	23,580	307,545	603,422	100.0	2.5	32.9	64.6	902,049	774,761	517,199	97,914	15,985	5.7	14,884	4,247	1,300
Montgomery County	MD	2,764,729	105,027	799,882	1,859,820	100.0	3.8	28.9	67.3	2,499,433	2,243,603	1,434,428	171,346	45,078	8.8	15,080	25,876	1,702
Prince George's County	MD	2,138,117	141,722	1,064,292	932,103	100.0	6.6	49.8	43.6	2,006,738	1,744,765	1,003,338	189,343	18,262	12.9	14,101	31,665	1,723
Saint Mary's County	MD	225,194	16,419	109,577	99,198	100.0	7.3	48.7	44.1	225,122	217,128	128,337	4,238	1,655	10.3	12,441	2,540	1,228
Washington County	MD	306,909	21,095	182,837	102,977	100.0	6.9	59.6	33.6	304,119	281,730	169,994	18,191	1,496	14.6	12,576	5,765	1,602
Boston	MA	1,262,641	98,227	263,349	901,065	100.0	7.8	20.9	71.4	1,264,531	1,050,818	583,048	71,757	12,938	28.4	19,066	39,078	1,910
Brockton	MA	225,240	15,332	155,115	54,793	100.0	6.8	68.9	24.3	223,302	202,627	124,244	1,817	1,184	23.2	12,210	6,090	1,564
Springfield	MA	502,525	60,874	363,929	77,722	100.0	12.1	72.4	15.5	483,537	364,871	202,435	58,661	8,756	40.8	14,431	21,908	1,865
Worcester	MA	390,515	37,548	239,590	113,377	100.0	9.6	61.4	29.0	383,203	322,578	212,823	381	9,070	30.1	13,039	14,099	1,739

See notes at end of table.

Table 215.20. Revenues, expenditures, poverty rate, and Title I allocations of public school districts enrolling more than 15,000 students: 2012–13 and fiscal year 2015—Continued

Name of district	State	Revenues by source of funds, 2012–13 (in thousands of current dollars)				Percentage distribution of revenues, 2012–13				Expenditures, 2012–13 (in thousands of current dollars)					Poverty rate of 5- to 17-year-olds, 2014[1]	Current expenditure per pupil,[2] 2012–13 (in current dollars)	Title I allocations, federal fiscal year 2015	
										Total[3]	Current expenditures						Total[4] (in thousands of current dollars)	Per poverty child[5] (in current dollars)
		Total	Federal	State	Local	Total	Federal	State	Local		Total	Instruction	Capital outlay	Interest on school debt				
1	2	3	4	5	6	7	8	9	10	11	12	13	14	15	16	17	18	19
Ann Arbor	MI	224,288	6,015	93,098	125,175	100.0	2.7	41.5	55.8	234,898	196,819	119,549	18,198	8,519	11.2	11,818	2,185	971
Chippewa Valley	MI	167,606	4,974	113,261	49,371	100.0	3.0	67.6	29.5	177,548	140,660	92,263	14,798	20,301	9.9	8,565	1,671	951
Dearborn City	MI	223,516	18,273	134,267	70,976	100.0	8.2	60.1	31.8	215,787	204,128	122,816	2,548	6,175	41.5	10,792	13,089	1,485
Detroit City	MI	851,989	228,390	389,089	234,510	100.0	26.8	45.7	27.5	882,693	702,097	359,121	59,253	112,938	51.3	14,259	139,667	2,118
Grand Rapids	MI	260,571	42,609	121,032	96,930	100.0	16.4	46.4	37.2	263,934	228,059	126,726	4,813	5,577	27.1	13,385	13,249	1,614
Plymouth-Canton	MI	184,213	3,659	118,522	62,032	100.0	2.0	64.3	33.7	175,073	159,630	100,175	2,067	8,027	6.7	8,870	1,401	947
Rochester Community	MI	183,124	2,330	117,064	63,730	100.0	1.3	63.9	34.8	171,429	157,510	98,664	3,031	6,572	5.3	10,496	863	946
Utica	MI	280,831	8,131	202,454	70,246	100.0	2.9	72.1	25.0	284,367	258,682	181,070	12,335	8,055	12.1	9,104	4,030	1,053
Warren Consolidated	MI	183,396	13,063	108,448	61,885	100.0	7.1	59.1	33.7	199,557	175,914	106,281	14,895	7,350	21.6	11,579	4,376	1,185
Anoka-Hennepin	MN	469,899	21,171	315,512	133,216	100.0	4.5	67.1	28.3	444,904	395,682	264,981	23,495	3,468	8.7	10,286	4,767	1,245
Minneapolis	MN	634,167	68,315	370,952	194,900	100.0	10.8	58.5	30.7	653,743	529,081	352,860	74,704	16,871	26.7	14,761	21,918	1,582
Osseo Public	MN	283,489	14,167	173,712	95,610	100.0	5.0	61.3	33.7	282,009	239,148	165,252	15,276	5,921	12.7	11,474	3,971	1,178
Rochester	MN	195,048	10,971	133,395	50,682	100.0	5.6	68.4	26.0	212,745	162,707	106,380	26,205	13,622	10.2	9,890	2,319	1,076
Rosemount-Apple Valley-Eagan	MN	339,661	11,573	224,716	103,372	100.0	3.4	66.2	30.4	322,623	290,336	205,383	16,809	3,660	7.7	10,657	2,382	1,067
Saint Paul	MN	631,296	70,292	408,337	152,667	100.0	11.1	64.7	24.2	635,813	548,835	372,869	35,490	18,109	27.5	14,286	22,109	1,583
South Washington County	MN	217,646	7,453	138,316	71,877	100.0	3.4	63.6	33.0	217,920	171,474	113,529	16,937	12,730	4.9	9,501	996	1,014
DeSoto County	MS	252,277	22,607	139,487	90,183	100.0	9.0	55.3	35.7	230,690	211,949	122,280	11,384	6,766	15.1	6,470	5,178	989
Jackson	MS	281,273	57,444	128,322	95,507	100.0	20.4	45.6	34.0	269,324	253,146	137,488	9,528	5,906	46.5	8,513	17,570	1,180
Rankin County	MS	166,239	14,675	80,600	70,964	100.0	8.8	48.5	42.7	159,521	149,364	88,212	6,268	3,167	14.0	7,680	2,832	934
Columbia, 93	MO	214,547	15,724	55,896	142,927	100.0	7.3	26.1	66.6	224,407	171,821	95,381	38,801	7,952	15.8	9,697	3,620	1,163
Fort Zumwalt, R-II	MO	207,675	8,879	62,694	136,102	100.0	4.3	30.2	65.5	200,396	180,305	112,669	5,504	11,639	6.6	9,555	1,381	912
Francis Howell, R-III	MO	203,782	7,826	47,575	148,381	100.0	3.8	23.3	72.8	203,066	175,406	109,457	10,785	9,272	6.2	8,843	1,216	897
Hazelwood	MO	209,171	15,820	61,192	132,159	100.0	7.6	29.3	63.2	257,660	183,679	105,646	59,003	11,521	19.3	10,023	4,940	1,222
Kansas City, 33	MO	226,124	38,765	16,158	171,201	100.0	17.1	7.1	75.7	232,608	192,337	86,518	25,744	3,561	36.3	11,427	14,091	1,323
Lee's Summit, R-VII	MO	207,908	6,593	63,800	137,515	100.0	3.2	30.7	66.1	187,348	186,244	105,482	6,077	9,455	9.2	9,348	1,657	934
North Kansas City, 74	MO	219,304	13,878	57,299	148,127	100.0	6.3	26.1	67.5	218,226	191,184	111,184	10,990	9,641	13.8	9,831	3,215	1,081
Parkway, C-2	MO	229,879	5,163	10,691	214,025	100.0	2.2	4.7	93.1	231,800	208,075	117,368	12,441	6,658	6.0	12,850	1,198	896
Rockwood, R-VI	MO	256,100	6,127	37,293	212,680	100.0	2.4	14.6	83.0	237,994	208,651	125,103	9,252	9,542	4.2	10,203	557	534
Saint Louis City	MO	388,521	68,192	68,498	251,831	100.0	17.6	17.6	64.8	427,624	344,831	186,450	59,472	11,202	41.8	10,655	28,825	1,588
Springfield, R-XII	MO	255,945	27,916	63,874	164,155	100.0	10.9	25.0	64.1	248,475	213,512	128,987	20,833	11,814	24.4	8,358	8,674	1,249
Lincoln	NE	408,746	41,230	128,818	238,698	100.0	10.1	31.5	58.4	422,577	376,457	256,959	30,356	15,731	15.4	10,190	9,915	1,493
Millard	NE	227,638	6,927	93,125	127,586	100.0	3.0	40.9	56.0	241,020	218,701	138,664	7,340	13,410	5.6	9,348	1,924	1,372
Omaha	NE	613,144	97,243	212,407	303,494	100.0	15.9	34.6	49.5	612,960	577,088	383,773	25,090	9,520	21.8	11,414	23,901	1,733
Clark County	NV	2,964,019	281,548	971,614	1,710,857	100.0	9.5	32.8	57.7	2,837,439	2,541,464	1,465,591	109,604	171,404	21.7	8,023	93,091	1,203
Washoe County	NV	594,199	60,924	215,740	317,535	100.0	10.3	36.3	53.4	629,197	543,663	303,291	56,686	25,190	17.2	8,365	14,801	1,193
Elizabeth	NJ	530,269	32,269	445,808	52,192	100.0	6.1	84.1	9.8	540,149	503,385	285,909	3,555	0	26.5	20,985	9,419	1,604
Jersey City	NJ	698,809	46,470	535,040	117,299	100.0	6.6	76.6	16.8	697,120	589,727	371,250	8,715	3,500	32.9	21,819	20,432	1,782
Newark	NJ	1,143,555	78,227	881,877	183,451	100.0	6.8	77.1	16.0	1,164,481	877,966	455,112	17,349	5,000	35.9	24,670	33,609	1,907
Paterson	NJ	589,486	44,940	486,631	57,915	100.0	7.6	82.6	9.8	576,670	460,467	264,607	12,306	550	36.6	18,740	18,240	1,744
Toms River Regional	NJ	245,087	9,162	81,815	154,110	100.0	3.7	33.4	62.9	234,393	226,126	134,029	1,202	3,018	9.8	13,492	2,320	1,290
Albuquerque	NM	964,205	106,368	682,462	175,375	100.0	11.0	70.8	18.2	952,320	797,281	480,829	133,258	20,728	25.2	8,474	35,282	1,224
Las Cruces	NM	252,821	31,950	182,840	38,031	100.0	12.6	72.3	15.0	259,773	214,507	128,367	39,872	4,007	30.9	8,450	6,190	1,039
Rio Rancho	NM	151,491	7,531	111,678	32,282	100.0	5.0	73.7	21.3	154,106	130,084	79,067	18,433	4,473	14.1	7,705	2,157	814
Brentwood Union Free	NY	339,200	21,468	220,207	97,525	100.0	6.3	64.9	28.8	349,096	321,401	221,887	18,304	4,139	17.7	18,374	3,768	1,348
Buffalo City	NY	910,087	104,880	677,857	127,350	100.0	11.5	74.5	14.0	919,509	615,048	370,306	105,116	60,613	46.1	18,773	32,278	1,672

See notes at end of table.

Table 215.20. Revenues, expenditures, poverty rate, and Title I allocations of public school districts enrolling more than 15,000 students: 2012–13 and fiscal year 2015—Continued

Name of district	State	Revenues by source of funds, 2012–13 (in thousands of current dollars)				Percentage distribution of revenues, 2012–13				Expenditures, 2012–13 (in thousands of current dollars)						Poverty rate of 5- to 17-year-olds, 2014[1]	Current expenditure per pupil,[2] 2012–13 (in current dollars)	Title I allocations, federal fiscal year 2015	
		Total	Federal	State	Local	Total	Federal	State	Local	Total[3]	Current expenditures			Capital outlay	Interest on school debt			Total[4] (in thousands of current dollars)	Per poverty child[5] (in current dollars)
											Total	Instruction							
1	2	3	4	5	6	7	8	9	10	11	12	13	14	15	16	17	18	19
New York City	NY	23,438,719	1,780,098	8,635,858	13,022,763	100.0	7.6	36.8	55.6	24,974,898	20,115,726	15,276,343	2,187,904	478,921	30.2	20,331	701,094	1,886
Rochester City	NY	714,523	92,927	497,666	123,930	100.0	13.0	69.7	17.3	790,024	612,929	346,327	106,021	13,919	47.7	20,333	27,871	1,681
Syracuse City	NY	441,343	64,410	310,039	66,894	100.0	14.6	70.2	15.2	453,002	364,783	244,959	54,655	9,374	42.2	17,689	15,003	1,605
Yonkers City	NY	506,211	37,159	274,949	194,103	100.0	7.3	54.3	38.3	532,892	483,374	317,737	17,208	6,556	23.0	18,934	10,501	1,471
Alamance-Burlington	NC	181,704	25,341	116,943	39,420	100.0	13.9	64.4	21.7	184,233	180,117	118,217	2,396	0	24.8	7,875	6,760	1,034
Buncombe County	NC	233,483	32,268	134,707	66,508	100.0	13.8	57.7	28.5	229,775	219,847	134,345	8,885	0	19.7	8,513	6,632	1,078
Cabarrus County	NC	233,235	24,255	147,080	61,900	100.0	10.4	63.1	26.5	235,544	225,727	141,663	6,819	0	13.0	7,421	4,343	1,006
Catawba County	NC	139,779	15,568	89,923	34,288	100.0	11.1	64.3	24.5	141,629	136,555	86,753	4,282	0	20.7	7,913	4,039	1,035
Charlotte-Mecklenburg	NC	1,235,570	129,228	711,653	394,689	100.0	10.5	57.6	31.9	1,278,989	1,174,943	732,859	86,125	0	19.6	8,132	40,660	1,185
Cleveland County	NC	150,740	22,365	92,433	35,942	100.0	14.8	61.3	23.8	154,309	142,119	91,498	11,330	0	27.5	8,910	5,019	1,126
Cumberland County	NC	425,630	65,617	262,137	97,876	100.0	15.4	61.6	23.0	451,760	428,538	271,578	16,646	0	25.5	8,097	15,900	1,147
Davidson County	NC	154,278	16,364	103,975	33,939	100.0	10.6	67.4	22.0	155,392	145,629	92,906	9,078	0	21.0	7,188	4,824	1,023
Durham County	NC	345,454	41,363	173,729	130,362	100.0	12.0	50.3	37.7	370,307	339,620	206,394	24,837	0	22.2	10,267	10,568	1,109
Gaston County	NC	246,053	33,477	161,113	51,463	100.0	13.6	65.5	20.9	266,174	239,600	148,163	25,296	0	26.7	7,534	10,349	1,082
Guilford County	NC	686,284	99,692	381,631	204,961	100.0	14.5	55.6	29.9	729,482	670,054	409,228	55,855	0	27.2	9,035	26,822	1,164
Harnett County	NC	156,105	15,832	114,121	26,152	100.0	10.1	73.1	16.8	157,589	149,833	95,316	7,047	0	21.5	7,284	5,481	1,024
Iredell-Statesville	NC	171,788	20,072	109,184	42,532	100.0	11.7	63.6	24.8	175,394	164,602	100,318	8,268	0	15.7	7,692	4,020	1,025
Johnston County	NC	268,472	28,877	178,728	60,867	100.0	10.8	66.6	22.7	278,019	272,847	176,312	4,095	0	19.2	8,094	7,560	1,101
Nash-Rocky Mount	NC	154,202	21,207	98,419	34,576	100.0	13.8	63.8	22.4	159,811	156,165	101,284	2,978	0	26.3	9,312	4,942	1,030
New Hanover County	NC	230,735	24,740	134,708	71,287	100.0	10.7	58.4	30.9	228,862	221,902	132,991	6,293	0	23.2	8,589	7,391	1,048
Onslow County	NC	207,407	33,986	122,943	50,478	100.0	16.4	59.3	24.3	204,158	197,711	123,526	4,899	0	24.1	7,743	6,505	1,039
Pitt County	NC	200,999	29,868	128,398	42,733	100.0	14.9	63.9	21.3	201,568	195,876	130,361	3,626	0	29.3	8,233	8,488	1,053
Randolph County	NC	149,565	18,460	103,585	27,520	100.0	12.3	69.3	18.4	150,114	144,483	90,257	4,841	0	23.6	7,756	4,981	1,021
Robeson County	NC	211,881	39,118	146,951	25,812	100.0	18.5	69.4	12.2	217,180	204,431	125,979	11,179	0	40.8	8,293	12,419	1,200
Rowan-Salisbury	NC	175,107	23,726	108,098	43,283	100.0	13.5	61.7	24.7	177,347	171,515	106,550	4,831	0	25.9	8,506	6,014	1,036
Union County	NC	325,803	26,222	199,367	100,214	100.0	8.0	61.2	30.8	334,742	315,508	197,757	13,435	0	13.2	7,760	5,866	921
Wake County	NC	1,216,116	97,321	759,712	359,083	100.0	8.0	62.5	29.5	1,276,435	1,166,957	760,854	97,061	0	13.2	7,730	28,156	1,173
Wayne County	NC	165,298	29,077	109,488	26,733	100.0	17.6	66.2	16.2	167,977	153,415	104,064	13,810	0	30.7	7,764	6,858	1,034
Winston-Salem/Forsyth County	NC	477,178	55,778	287,162	134,238	100.0	11.7	60.2	28.1	488,367	456,737	298,920	28,720	0	26.1	8,477	19,010	1,163
Akron City	OH	351,045	26,952	197,837	126,256	100.0	7.7	56.4	36.0	376,088	290,769	162,355	45,507	0	35.3	12,984	15,690	1,506
Cincinnati City	OH	579,274	45,183	205,158	328,933	100.0	7.8	35.4	56.8	622,452	390,801	184,263	98,270	34,273	35.9	12,361	32,109	1,861
Cleveland Municipal	OH	809,193	52,963	507,441	248,789	100.0	6.5	62.7	30.7	795,528	556,584	312,410	62,218	6,964	45.8	13,980	51,960	1,729
Columbus City	OH	855,757	63,211	320,043	472,503	100.0	7.4	37.4	55.2	928,345	694,998	355,318	73,074	22,139	39.2	13,794	46,439	1,674
Hilliard City	OH	194,710	5,963	56,497	132,250	100.0	3.1	29.0	67.9	183,151	169,492	106,139	4,296	4,494	9.6	10,981	1,757	1,044
Lakota Local	OH	160,891	5,939	55,904	99,048	100.0	3.7	34.7	61.6	159,254	145,685	79,513	3,757	6,313	7.4	8,816	1,632	1,050
Olentangy Local	OH	215,530	3,095	26,124	186,311	100.0	1.4	12.1	86.4	191,630	165,908	103,953	6,440	17,535	3.7	9,544	430	607
South-Western City	OH	266,499	14,136	122,107	130,256	100.0	5.3	45.8	48.9	243,715	204,842	119,312	14,435	6,782	23.2	9,798	8,245	1,413
Toledo City	OH	358,884	26,422	221,425	111,037	100.0	7.4	61.7	30.9	383,453	264,484	135,054	25,824	6,388	37.8	11,964	23,182	1,609
Broken Arrow	OK	140,501	9,839	65,894	64,768	100.0	7.0	46.9	46.1	136,240	117,815	60,721	15,340	2,064	10.7	6,847	1,756	836
Edmond	OK	189,586	9,539	61,287	118,760	100.0	5.0	32.3	62.6	190,536	153,385	84,726	33,494	2,056	8.9	6,820	1,980	867
Lawton	OK	137,043	23,267	79,227	34,549	100.0	17.0	57.8	25.2	126,329	119,478	62,699	5,483	435	28.4	7,618	4,699	1,058
Moore	OK	201,784	13,203	89,154	99,427	100.0	6.5	44.2	49.3	177,403	161,037	92,437	14,284	1,439	11.8	6,949	2,636	912
Norman	OK	129,304	10,320	55,269	63,715	100.0	8.0	42.7	49.3	141,081	112,186	64,529	27,014	1,306	15.8	7,415	2,609	1,046
Oklahoma City	OK	466,293	74,665	200,088	191,540	100.0	16.0	42.9	41.1	403,192	375,948	196,180	21,847	3,575	34.1	8,407	22,463	1,265
Putnam City	OK	167,277	18,904	77,934	70,439	100.0	11.3	46.6	42.1	161,197	141,606	80,063	17,625	1,638	23.3	7,353	5,073	1,059
Tulsa	OK	401,508	63,430	161,472	176,606	100.0	15.8	40.2	44.0	399,220	345,549	172,142	45,332	3,589	29.8	8,412	17,757	1,232
Union	OK	139,092	13,303	59,477	66,312	100.0	9.6	42.8	47.7	133,296	110,829	55,251	16,295	1,337	17.0	7,245	2,705	992

See notes at end of table.

Table 215.20. Revenues, expenditures, poverty rate, and Title I allocations of public school districts enrolling more than 15,000 students: 2012–13 and fiscal year 2015—Continued

Name of district	State	Revenues by source of funds, 2012–13 (in thousands of current dollars)				Percentage distribution of revenues, 2012–13				Expenditures, 2012–13 (in thousands of current dollars)					Poverty rate of 5- to 17-year-olds, 2014[1]	Current expenditure per pupil,[2] 2012–13 (in current dollars)	Title I allocations, federal fiscal year 2015	
		Total	Federal	State	Local	Total	Federal	State	Local	Total[3]	Current expenditures						Total[4] (in thousands of current dollars)	Per poverty child[5] (in current dollars)
											Total	Instruction	Capital outlay	Interest on school debt				
1	2	3	4	5	6	7	8	9	10	11	12	13	14	15	16	17	18	19
Beaverton, 48J	OR	383,894	24,901	177,953	181,040	100.0	6.5	46.4	47.2	381,249	328,027	205,023	8,034	42,926	10.8	8,265	5,469	1,091
Bend-Lapine, SD1	OR	161,616	13,003	60,668	87,945	100.0	8.0	37.5	54.4	170,227	139,049	81,985	4,611	24,360	14.5	8,384	2,947	1,131
Eugene, SD4J	OR	176,885	14,164	67,061	95,660	100.0	8.0	37.9	54.1	193,806	163,063	93,245	13,689	12,478	16.4	9,576	3,876	1,249
Hillsboro, SD1J	OR	208,199	16,736	98,163	93,300	100.0	8.0	47.1	44.8	205,472	184,196	106,093	4,517	14,774	13.1	8,706	3,707	1,161
North Clackamas, SD12	OR	173,130	10,499	84,204	78,427	100.0	6.1	48.6	45.3	174,075	139,748	74,027	4,747	20,003	9.7	8,197	2,196	1,182
Portland, SD1J	OR	534,955	55,347	170,112	309,496	100.0	10.3	31.8	57.9	574,339	490,236	283,949	36,465	26,319	16.8	10,487	12,056	1,294
Salem-Keizer, SD24J	OR	410,239	40,043	246,214	123,982	100.0	9.8	60.0	30.2	421,994	369,907	224,888	29,013	18,080	25.3	9,165	15,256	1,329
Allentown City	PA	242,082	32,490	127,829	81,743	100.0	13.4	52.8	33.8	272,977	216,406	150,472	10,504	8,337	38.6	12,755	13,371	1,638
Central Bucks	PA	295,554	3,337	48,162	244,055	100.0	1.1	16.3	82.6	259,413	222,987	144,867	12,970	10,970	4.4	11,254	698	722
Philadelphia City	PA	2,743,433	429,562	1,333,752	980,119	100.0	15.7	48.6	35.7	3,627,516	2,357,138	1,666,917	80,438	101,169	33.5	16,381	170,023	2,146
Pittsburgh	PA	609,890	78,929	245,315	285,646	100.0	12.9	40.2	46.8	626,633	440,866	263,004	21,249	20,982	29.8	16,768	17,420	1,719
Reading	PA	219,528	25,200	153,856	40,472	100.0	11.5	70.1	18.4	224,745	172,926	109,566	10,445	14,290	43.1	9,797	15,544	1,969
Providence	RI	445,603	63,549	250,870	131,184	100.0	14.3	56.3	29.4	426,225	371,695	199,242	5,786	14,539	39.8	15,570	20,271	1,799
Aiken, 01	SC	233,133	23,676	125,964	83,493	100.0	10.2	54.0	35.8	236,682	205,611	121,176	26,585	1,421	26.3	8,329	8,131	1,131
Beaufort, 01	SC	288,092	24,963	80,086	183,043	100.0	8.7	27.8	63.5	255,223	223,923	126,556	10,164	15,880	21.4	10,954	5,787	1,109
Berkeley, 01	SC	318,591	34,763	161,136	122,692	100.0	10.9	50.6	38.5	318,984	265,897	146,050	27,340	22,108	23.1	8,593	8,997	1,147
Charleston, 01	SC	707,221	72,128	211,939	423,154	100.0	10.2	30.0	59.8	686,455	471,105	259,583	145,299	30,127	25.1	10,563	16,571	1,257
Dorchester, 02	SC	223,012	15,759	126,697	80,556	100.0	7.1	56.8	36.1	213,011	192,647	116,036	8,457	9,142	16.8	8,115	4,804	1,124
Florence, 01	SC	173,450	15,861	88,409	69,180	100.0	9.1	51.0	39.9	181,432	148,091	85,227	29,801	1,121	23.5	9,172	4,288	1,093
Greenville, 01	SC	739,657	63,797	370,991	304,869	100.0	8.6	50.2	41.2	737,151	600,432	336,094	67,152	49,038	22.7	8,153	25,126	1,319
Horry, 01	SC	489,684	39,692	172,812	277,180	100.0	8.1	35.3	56.6	474,241	407,157	240,567	43,514	16,373	29.0	10,179	14,829	1,238
Lexington, 01	SC	278,165	11,663	147,260	119,242	100.0	4.2	52.9	42.9	321,566	233,972	128,698	65,561	21,890	12.3	9,933	3,294	1,096
Lexington, 05	SC	215,884	12,297	111,392	92,195	100.0	5.7	51.6	42.7	288,741	180,436	103,249	98,640	8,344	11.7	10,979	1,803	868
Pickens, 01	SC	163,227	14,742	83,569	64,916	100.0	9.0	51.2	39.8	184,710	130,670	77,295	36,982	15,921	19.1	7,808	3,650	1,082
Richland, 01	SC	373,491	36,433	120,146	216,912	100.0	9.8	32.2	58.1	358,960	313,682	173,804	18,750	21,937	29.4	12,995	9,633	1,175
Richland, 02	SC	328,139	23,575	160,310	144,254	100.0	7.2	48.9	44.0	340,505	278,280	156,105	33,520	25,745	15.4	10,476	4,484	1,090
Sumter, 01	SC	161,572	21,122	89,237	51,213	100.0	13.1	55.2	31.7	153,461	141,866	75,383	3,551	5,691	31.8	8,446	6,756	1,121
York, 03	SC	188,076	13,760	97,568	76,748	100.0	7.3	51.9	40.8	176,818	159,645	93,803	9,174	6,939	17.5	9,110	3,939	1,121
Sioux Falls	SD	207,079	21,026	68,945	117,108	100.0	10.2	33.3	56.6	217,436	177,691	111,997	32,380	4,494	13.2	7,650	5,310	1,591
Davidson County	TN	904,316	113,884	256,788	533,644	100.0	12.6	28.4	59.0	860,543	785,830	433,433	49,603	23,987	28.4	9,686	32,165	1,176
Hamilton County	TN	398,221	50,421	135,667	212,133	100.0	12.7	34.1	53.3	386,423	372,439	227,846	5,316	5,800	22.7	8,521	13,776	1,132
Knox County	TN	524,707	60,904	177,135	286,668	100.0	11.6	33.8	54.6	510,347	461,784	272,921	44,723	3,175	19.0	7,836	15,139	1,142
Montgomery County	TN	248,887	32,697	128,857	87,333	100.0	13.1	51.8	35.1	283,340	242,410	141,701	30,093	10,311	19.4	7,916	7,612	1,203
Rutherford County	TN	321,222	25,493	166,009	129,720	100.0	7.9	51.7	40.4	315,247	298,948	190,604	11,670	4,061	12.5	7,400	4,442	912
Shelby County	TN	1,179,930	253,751	449,576	476,603	100.0	21.5	38.1	40.4	1,163,418	1,071,609	622,370	55,990	0	31.7	9,960	69,472	1,266
Sumner County	TN	224,212	19,543	120,405	84,264	100.0	8.7	53.7	37.6	219,838	209,420	131,384	1,739	6,732	13.9	7,362	4,205	976
Williamson County	TN	277,733	11,067	108,008	158,658	100.0	4.0	38.9	57.1	296,877	260,787	166,911	18,095	15,397	4.8	7,829	895	466
Wilson County	TN	127,433	9,202	62,116	56,115	100.0	7.2	48.7	44.0	196,846	114,570	72,027	73,162	5,522	11.3	7,024	1,713	818
Abilene ISD	TX	150,649	24,643	75,534	50,472	100.0	16.4	50.1	33.5	149,076	137,869	82,084	6,820	2,407	25.5	8,038	4,326	998
Aldine ISD	TX	626,345	86,783	346,842	192,720	100.0	13.9	55.4	30.8	568,695	521,809	320,862	26,085	18,812	37.3	7,944	27,624	1,166
Alief ISD	TX	452,367	63,375	239,316	149,676	100.0	14.0	52.9	33.1	419,159	394,984	251,800	13,611	6,664	35.8	8,627	21,504	1,146
Allen ISD	TX	199,156	5,044	49,365	144,747	100.0	2.5	24.8	72.7	215,889	150,894	94,236	42,612	21,717	6.0	7,585	952	750
Alvin ISD	TX	165,042	13,492	91,938	59,612	100.0	8.2	55.7	36.1	173,006	144,961	87,522	10,952	16,105	17.0	7,676	2,866	950
Amarillo ISD	TX	285,353	37,635	148,650	99,068	100.0	13.2	52.1	34.7	288,750	267,247	169,060	15,129	3,803	25.1	8,019	8,516	1,037
Arlington ISD	TX	574,291	66,478	241,953	265,860	100.0	11.6	42.1	46.3	551,537	480,081	310,571	46,656	20,349	22.7	7,386	17,542	1,125
Austin ISD	TX	1,054,072	146,954	109,965	797,153	100.0	13.9	10.4	75.6	1,048,370	820,532	477,700	57,151	34,710	24.8	9,484	29,892	1,227

See notes at end of table.

Table 215.20. Revenues, expenditures, poverty rate, and Title I allocations of public school districts enrolling more than 15,000 students: 2012–13 and fiscal year 2015—Continued

Name of district	State	Revenues by source of funds, 2012–13 (in thousands of current dollars)				Percentage distribution of revenues, 2012–13				Expenditures, 2012–13 (in thousands of current dollars)					Poverty rate of 5- to 17-year-olds, 2014[1]	Current expenditure per pupil,[2] 2012–13 (in current dollars)	Title I allocations, federal fiscal year 2015	
		Total	Federal	State	Local	Total	Federal	State	Local	Total[3]	Current expenditures		Capital outlay	Interest on school debt			Total[4] (in thousands of current dollars)	Per poverty child[5] (in current dollars)
											Total	Instruction						
1	2	3	4	5	6	7	8	9	10	11	12	13	14	15	16	17	18	19
Beaumont ISD	TX	183,145	25,326	45,168	112,651	100.0	13.8	24.7	61.5	204,640	188,454	106,528	13,830	52	32.4	9,494	6,876	1,008
Birdville ISD	TX	233,328	26,826	97,094	109,408	100.0	11.5	41.6	46.9	218,780	192,467	122,882	4,172	17,289	17.7	7,956	4,297	972
Brownsville ISD	TX	501,016	110,950	327,277	62,789	100.0	22.1	65.3	12.5	484,309	453,666	264,424	11,693	10,235	43.4	9,223	24,905	1,214
Bryan ISD	TX	152,085	23,196	55,952	72,937	100.0	15.3	36.8	48.0	137,978	129,952	77,372	4,075	3,455	32.6	8,317	5,640	1,003
Carrollton-Farmers Branch ISD	TX	268,039	20,564	56,188	191,287	100.0	7.7	21.0	71.4	232,499	211,512	124,637	6,876	13,361	19.2	8,016	5,430	992
Clear Creek ISD	TX	355,832	19,461	110,331	226,040	100.0	5.5	31.0	63.5	328,568	287,233	183,743	12,868	27,228	10.7	7,247	3,899	865
Comal ISD	TX	186,100	9,924	25,986	150,190	100.0	5.3	14.0	80.7	189,016	139,926	82,020	22,949	23,272	11.5	7,485	1,903	842
Conroe ISD	TX	460,425	27,482	134,933	298,010	100.0	6.0	29.3	64.7	515,730	369,961	234,097	100,642	44,188	13.1	6,860	7,570	1,014
Corpus Christi ISD	TX	357,620	53,311	155,024	149,285	100.0	14.9	43.3	41.7	384,199	310,795	178,541	52,143	15,823	24.8	7,926	11,859	1,079
Crowley ISD	TX	144,392	12,416	49,872	82,104	100.0	8.6	34.5	56.9	137,672	118,125	73,616	1,674	17,297	16.5	7,844	2,994	938
Cypress-Fairbanks ISD	TX	982,181	77,092	387,467	517,622	100.0	7.8	39.4	52.7	944,151	747,861	486,448	83,553	106,117	15.0	6,798	19,358	1,136
Dallas ISD	TX	1,632,183	255,315	398,911	977,957	100.0	15.6	24.4	59.9	1,764,754	1,324,736	767,652	293,336	131,349	37.3	8,335	92,559	1,306
Denton ISD	TX	267,198	17,419	84,751	165,028	100.0	6.5	31.7	61.8	282,698	211,583	134,506	45,132	24,507	13.8	8,209	3,365	863
Donna ISD	TX	165,313	30,089	120,683	14,541	100.0	18.2	73.0	8.8	177,608	139,852	83,755	31,778	4,144	50.5	9,155	9,829	1,202
Eagle Mt.-Saginaw ISD	TX	171,684	10,105	63,126	98,453	100.0	5.9	36.8	57.3	171,304	140,011	84,811	6,473	24,665	11.6	7,898	1,628	773
Eagle Pass ISD	TX	137,208	20,419	93,503	23,286	100.0	14.9	68.1	17.0	130,839	124,058	73,779	1,575	3,002	34.5	8,219	6,954	1,522
Ector County ISD	TX	250,077	25,117	85,994	138,966	100.0	10.0	34.4	55.6	238,559	219,101	130,774	9,232	8,188	19.4	7,390	5,968	997
Edinburg CISD	TX	326,432	53,020	203,757	69,655	100.0	16.2	62.4	21.3	309,323	287,433	180,771	9,503	9,420	38.1	8,536	14,660	1,107
El Paso ISD	TX	590,906	94,183	295,803	200,920	100.0	15.9	50.1	34.0	572,954	523,138	314,717	22,230	24,242	31.8	8,276	26,610	1,317
Fort Bend ISD	TX	613,872	39,064	222,109	352,699	100.0	6.4	36.2	57.5	580,513	510,223	319,380	22,214	40,676	12.1	7,332	10,903	1,090
Fort Worth ISD	TX	841,701	129,752	340,167	371,782	100.0	15.4	40.4	44.2	793,501	696,683	404,054	51,857	32,580	31.8	7,674	34,506	1,187
Frisco ISD	TX	431,286	9,830	132,028	289,428	100.0	2.3	30.6	67.1	477,670	327,730	206,205	83,240	62,655	5.4	8,343	5,338	777
Galena Park ISD	TX	237,513	24,445	112,164	100,904	100.0	10.3	47.2	42.5	205,700	185,242	106,827	6,945	11,049	26.6	8,377	14,623	989
Garland ISD	TX	516,152	49,404	285,512	181,236	100.0	9.6	55.3	35.1	517,465	438,237	267,588	60,311	16,054	21.6	7,548	5,094	1,106
Goose Creek CISD	TX	223,217	22,982	67,973	132,262	100.0	10.3	30.5	59.3	207,504	186,852	109,166	7,672	10,751	23.9	8,563	7,031	986
Grand Prairie ISD	TX	264,758	31,473	154,925	78,360	100.0	11.9	58.5	29.6	276,493	215,369	127,742	35,173	23,074	24.1	8,000	5,276	1,005
Harlandale ISD	TX	154,600	24,763	109,181	20,656	100.0	16.0	70.6	13.4	147,543	132,354	77,114	5,565	8,553	34.5	8,722	6,214	1,171
Harlingen CISD	TX	178,811	28,920	106,237	43,654	100.0	16.2	59.4	24.4	215,278	157,216	93,652	48,318	6,116	37.8	8,494	8,032	1,176
Hays CISD	TX	157,594	11,375	82,826	63,393	100.0	7.2	52.6	40.2	147,033	146,964	74,705	4,708	12,942	12.8	7,784	1,729	789
Houston ISD	TX	1,987,654	301,816	346,401	1,339,437	100.0	15.2	17.4	67.4	2,096,600	1,686,869	970,020	263,921	130,453	33.6	8,295	105,461	1,320
Humble ISD	TX	356,363	17,815	157,601	180,947	100.0	5.0	44.2	50.8	344,814	278,542	171,625	32,523	32,664	11.2	7,509	3,566	857
Hurst-Euless-Bedford ISD	TX	205,524	17,404	60,721	127,399	100.0	8.5	29.5	62.0	252,648	162,845	103,709	70,448	19,061	17.2	7,465	3,844	962
Irving ISD	TX	347,296	41,544	168,888	136,864	100.0	12.0	48.6	39.4	358,938	282,022	174,971	44,298	28,839	29.5	8,051	10,751	1,064
Judson ISD	TX	209,304	21,464	94,578	93,262	100.0	10.3	45.2	44.6	192,825	169,778	105,076	3,640	17,961	18.9	7,510	4,815	1,003
Katy ISD	TX	630,967	39,276	229,009	362,682	100.0	6.2	36.3	57.5	650,992	494,152	315,325	100,120	55,662	9.8	7,654	6,214	988
Keller ISD	TX	310,422	11,964	95,224	203,234	100.0	3.9	30.7	65.5	292,457	234,396	151,581	14,094	42,949	6.6	7,025	2,020	805
Killeen ISD	TX	372,750	87,277	205,686	79,787	100.0	23.4	55.2	21.4	359,161	327,448	206,758	25,464	4,126	21.9	7,842	9,597	1,061
Klein ISD	TX	432,348	31,330	196,262	204,756	100.0	7.2	45.4	47.4	466,601	357,301	221,335	75,551	34,139	14.5	7,595	7,186	1,007
Le Joya ISD	TX	315,983	60,994	222,410	32,579	100.0	19.3	70.4	10.3	302,091	271,759	157,956	14,856	12,717	50.3	9,296	16,614	1,229
Lamar CISD	TX	242,071	17,701	73,651	150,719	100.0	7.3	30.4	62.3	258,185	194,033	124,980	37,858	25,207	14.5	7,424	4,006	992
Laredo ISD	TX	258,339	55,466	169,850	33,023	100.0	21.5	65.7	12.8	258,886	205,817	122,419	38,545	10,662	54.2	8,291	15,362	1,300
Leander ISD	TX	336,952	13,465	100,526	222,961	100.0	4.0	29.8	66.2	311,570	257,646	160,881	10,110	39,965	6.2	7,494	1,785	787
Lewisville ISD	TX	525,467	34,064	121,900	369,503	100.0	6.5	23.2	70.3	612,012	423,017	272,622	138,979	45,275	8.7	8,053	4,659	883
Lubbock ISD	TX	278,223	43,426	109,312	125,485	100.0	15.6	39.3	45.1	319,139	239,654	146,255	66,913	6,612	27.2	8,202	8,943	1,062
Mansfield ISD	TX	303,918	17,323	128,006	158,509	100.0	5.7	42.1	52.2	325,940	252,141	153,407	43,791	29,542	10.9	7,669	3,259	848
McAllen ISD	TX	233,061	38,690	119,096	75,275	100.0	16.6	51.1	32.3	242,219	205,587	125,587	27,323	6,049	34.7	8,246	9,845	1,058
McKinney ISD	TX	240,250	11,270	72,637	156,343	100.0	4.7	30.2	65.1	277,635	192,524	122,781	61,072	21,052	10.2	7,876	2,301	814
Mesquite ISD	TX	370,468	33,184	241,932	95,352	100.0	9.0	65.3	25.7	353,926	294,397	186,609	41,531	16,427	24.2	7,524	9,949	1,052
Midland ISD	TX	222,591	22,483	28,207	171,901	100.0	10.1	12.7	77.2	204,158	180,888	110,133	16,198	4,843	15.4	7,757	4,129	983

See notes at end of table.

Table 215.20. Revenues, expenditures, poverty rate, and Title I allocations of public school districts enrolling more than 15,000 students: 2012–13 and fiscal year 2015—Continued

Name of district	State	Revenues by source of funds, 2012–13 (in thousands of current dollars)				Percentage distribution of revenues, 2012–13				Expenditures, 2012–13 (in thousands of current dollars)					Poverty rate of 5- to 17-year-olds, 2014[1]	Current expenditure per pupil[2] 2012–13 (in current dollars)	Title I allocations, federal fiscal year 2015	
		Total	Federal	State	Local	Total	Federal	State	Local	Total[3]	Current expenditures						Total[4] (in thousands of current dollars)	Per poverty child[5] (in current dollars)
											Total	Instruction	Capital outlay	Interest on school debt				
1	2	3	4	5	6	7	8	9	10	11	12	13	14	15	16	17	18	19
Mission CISD	TX	167,891	29,241	114,896	23,754	100.0	17.4	68.4	14.1	166,840	140,911	83,849	16,438	7,121	44.1	9,071	8,044	1,203
North East ISD	TX	650,475	55,278	180,772	414,425	100.0	8.5	27.8	63.7	712,129	539,309	332,088	110,729	60,958	16.1	7,943	13,641	1,111
Northside ISD	TX	917,293	85,183	333,335	498,775	100.0	9.3	36.3	54.4	999,831	752,092	474,310	167,219	69,997	16.1	7,509	19,503	1,165
Northwest ISD	TX	202,187	8,607	36,574	157,006	100.0	4.3	18.1	77.7	246,042	149,468	87,375	50,451	34,900	6.5	8,392	862	745
Pasadena ISD	TX	523,346	74,357	300,502	148,487	100.0	14.2	57.4	28.4	563,113	451,878	272,630	81,245	26,938	28.5	8,420	17,950	1,129
Pearland ISD	TX	183,001	7,992	88,315	86,694	100.0	4.4	48.3	47.4	161,952	145,578	86,184	8,402	7,127	7.8	7,409	1,256	769
Pflugerville ISD	TX	224,952	18,102	85,964	120,886	100.0	8.0	38.2	53.7	218,075	180,136	111,567	21,757	14,181	15.8	7,716	4,065	996
Pharr-San Juan-Alamo ISD	TX	344,376	62,574	225,645	56,157	100.0	18.2	65.5	16.3	371,120	275,970	161,257	72,177	18,094	42.2	8,611	14,329	1,106
Plano ISD	TX	588,710	31,117	57,279	500,314	100.0	5.3	9.7	85.0	605,486	453,889	294,290	78,415	45,878	9.5	8,225	5,579	896
Richardson ISD	TX	356,407	37,196	94,633	224,578	100.0	10.4	26.6	63.0	365,702	287,522	185,778	57,218	18,405	25.5	7,558	10,456	1,060
Round Rock ISD	TX	442,949	29,811	104,707	308,431	100.0	6.7	23.6	69.6	450,456	361,349	221,137	49,804	35,348	8.0	7,899	3,568	871
San Angelo ISD	TX	129,027	17,860	60,434	50,733	100.0	13.8	46.8	39.3	145,940	111,959	68,108	26,923	6,174	22.6	7,586	3,507	974
San Antonio ISD	TX	582,725	135,767	277,726	169,232	100.0	23.3	47.7	29.0	602,204	494,724	285,667	67,255	31,640	37.5	9,116	27,710	1,254
Socorro ISD	TX	383,072	40,997	235,682	106,393	100.0	10.7	61.5	27.8	465,118	323,413	194,579	117,388	21,121	24.5	7,307	11,520	1,068
Spring Branch ISD	TX	353,951	40,687	41,736	271,528	100.0	11.5	11.8	76.7	395,015	288,832	171,049	63,606	38,060	26.9	8,286	10,066	1,054
Spring ISD	TX	353,249	37,142	194,374	121,733	100.0	10.5	55.0	34.5	322,315	277,763	169,580	10,936	31,732	25.8	7,695	10,294	1,058
Tyler ISD	TX	183,238	26,464	51,670	105,104	100.0	14.4	28.2	57.4	177,529	153,709	92,590	14,087	8,492	25.0	8,416	5,441	1,021
United ISD	TX	395,105	50,435	194,718	149,952	100.0	12.8	49.3	38.0	372,563	341,989	198,721	19,276	9,475	31.4	7,973	14,583	1,103
Weslaco ISD	TX	171,598	31,153	116,592	23,853	100.0	18.2	67.9	13.9	163,385	154,931	89,614	2,650	3,373	46.0	8,638	9,467	1,225
Ysleta ISD	TX	423,790	61,548	272,495	89,747	100.0	14.5	64.3	21.2	425,904	387,945	237,199	13,772	19,060	35.9	8,882	15,793	1,143
Alpine	UT	473,461	40,700	282,417	150,344	100.0	8.6	59.6	31.8	505,173	401,347	271,853	80,626	16,216	9.6	5,539	8,734	1,104
Cache	UT	113,090	9,870	71,303	31,917	100.0	8.7	63.0	28.2	105,524	96,498	63,304	4,264	3,228	10.2	5,988	1,522	820
Canyons	UT	284,990	18,359	126,447	140,184	100.0	6.4	44.4	49.2	389,257	230,917	139,456	141,263	9,455	10.3	6,801	4,058	914
Davis	UT	502,664	38,175	281,320	183,169	100.0	7.6	56.0	36.4	511,456	430,243	277,639	51,151	18,862	8.6	6,130	7,232	1,068
Granite	UT	491,011	62,052	262,433	166,526	100.0	12.6	53.4	33.9	634,151	479,232	316,092	146,615	8,304	19.0	6,914	8,594	1,207
Jordan	UT	362,061	23,316	206,102	132,643	100.0	6.4	56.9	36.6	356,555	299,547	189,458	46,971	3,556	8.2	5,708	4,641	941
Nebo	UT	220,589	14,955	140,764	64,870	100.0	6.8	63.8	29.4	214,564	183,428	107,243	17,459	8,564	9.1	5,871	3,004	909
Provo	UT	113,146	16,804	58,287	38,055	100.0	14.9	51.5	33.6	108,296	97,608	66,291	5,864	1,678	19.5	6,707	3,352	1,005
Salt Lake	UT	237,507	38,049	77,584	121,874	100.0	16.0	32.7	51.3	246,900	204,312	137,187	18,249	4,175	21.8	8,278	6,634	1,055
Washington	UT	214,876	21,048	98,571	95,257	100.0	9.8	45.9	44.3	225,706	179,535	115,019	34,581	8,792	20.0	6,583	6,592	1,053
Weber	UT	213,347	16,073	132,717	64,557	100.0	7.5	62.2	30.3	231,900	198,716	136,007	29,081	4,103	10.4	6,432	3,193	899
Arlington County	VA	532,105	13,595	55,378	463,132	100.0	2.6	10.4	87.0	534,718	416,231	254,706	81,834	13,134	11.1	18,464	2,892	1,083
Chesapeake City	VA	461,273	35,274	204,414	221,585	100.0	7.6	44.3	48.0	458,987	413,697	259,624	23,512	10,911	11.2	10,439	5,581	1,173
Chesterfield County	VA	581,811	32,908	280,338	268,565	100.0	5.7	48.2	46.2	589,981	532,015	330,448	40,798	14,704	9.4	9,039	6,917	1,191
Fairfax County	VA	2,543,509	110,231	562,643	1,870,635	100.0	4.3	22.1	73.5	2,746,699	2,469,067	1,526,811	186,926	75,401	7.0	13,670	20,550	1,506
Hampton City	VA	222,079	22,144	123,082	76,853	100.0	10.0	55.4	34.6	223,826	210,881	122,226	4,637	6,203	20.5	9,878	5,761	1,314
Hanover County	VA	188,054	8,020	80,866	99,168	100.0	4.3	43.0	52.7	176,334	166,917	112,882	3,416	4,992	5.8	9,086	1,080	985
Henrico County	VA	545,496	34,931	232,125	278,440	100.0	6.4	42.6	51.0	512,207	448,002	272,307	15,439	14,107	12.2	8,945	9,049	1,351
Loudoun County	VA	1,027,126	21,204	255,954	749,968	100.0	2.1	24.9	73.0	1,077,291	853,718	555,570	186,319	36,435	3.6	12,517	1,687	607
Newport News City	VA	340,542	46,217	165,356	128,969	100.0	13.6	48.6	37.9	335,157	306,665	176,525	18,082	0	26.1	10,296	10,464	1,359
Norfolk City	VA	373,720	58,976	184,660	130,084	100.0	15.8	49.4	34.8	376,833	345,789	211,987	20,157	24	32.2	10,522	15,699	1,474
Prince William County	VA	1,004,075	47,983	428,753	527,339	100.0	4.8	42.7	52.5	1,015,911	857,627	489,191	93,217	27,975	8.6	10,226	10,311	1,356
Richmond City	VA	318,967	58,528	122,057	138,382	100.0	18.3	38.3	43.4	324,956	302,922	175,688	8,597	6,035	35.6	12,809	16,030	1,739
Spotsylvania County	VA	264,118	17,073	121,460	125,585	100.0	6.5	46.0	47.5	250,213	233,745	139,363	6,385	8,410	8.9	9,834	2,377	1,056
Stafford County	VA	274,079	16,427	132,913	124,739	100.0	6.0	48.5	45.5	290,213	266,885	166,292	22,537	72	7.0	9,718	2,045	1,031
Virginia Beach City	VA	765,695	70,068	319,412	376,215	100.0	9.2	41.7	49.1	829,642	744,310	437,281	46,830	17,648	11.2	10,594	11,525	1,394
Auburn	WA	166,612	12,848	91,794	61,970	100.0	7.7	55.1	37.2	173,430	140,578	83,746	26,965	4,372	22.8	9,515	4,406	1,186
Bellevue	WA	264,930	11,034	110,761	143,135	100.0	4.2	41.8	54.0	269,868	186,002	112,397	60,692	14,540	9.7	9,785	1,887	954

See notes at end of table.

Table 215.20. Revenues, expenditures, poverty rate, and Title I allocations of public school districts enrolling more than 15,000 students: 2012–13 and fiscal year 2015—Continued

Name of district	State	Revenues by source of funds, 2012–13 (in thousands of current dollars)				Percentage distribution of revenues, 2012–13				Expenditures, 2012–13 (in thousands of current dollars)					Poverty rate of 5- to 17-year-olds, 2014[1]	Current expenditure per pupil,[2] 2012–13 (in current dollars)	Title I allocations, federal fiscal year 2015	
											Current expenditures						Total[4] (in thousands of current dollars)	Per poverty child[5] (in current dollars)
		Total	Federal	State	Local	Total	Federal	State	Local	Total[3]	Total	Instruction	Capital outlay	Interest on school debt				
1	2	3	4	5	6	7	8	9	10	11	12	13	14	15	16	17	18	19
Bethel	WA	207,368	12,719	138,782	55,867	100.0	6.1	66.9	26.9	193,522	162,501	89,268	20,408	9,128	14.6	9,012	3,432	1,177
Edmonds	WA	231,681	12,072	125,203	94,406	100.0	5.2	54.0	40.7	210,522	187,819	111,714	11,151	9,706	13.6	9,055	3,411	1,041
Everett	WA	227,700	14,816	125,482	87,402	100.0	6.5	55.1	38.4	236,499	189,307	113,519	36,138	10,221	13.7	10,011	3,323	1,116
Evergreen (Clark)	WA	280,848	18,506	187,388	74,954	100.0	6.6	66.7	26.7	264,870	239,531	144,382	16,719	7,545	17.2	9,041	5,951	1,216
Federal Way	WA	236,406	18,826	139,743	77,837	100.0	8.0	59.1	32.9	228,516	207,017	121,501	11,284	9,444	20.3	9,312	6,207	1,215
Highline	WA	222,471	20,539	119,808	82,124	100.0	9.2	53.9	36.9	231,019	189,402	107,915	27,250	13,324	27.4	10,309	6,989	1,228
Issaquah	WA	217,815	5,894	102,496	109,425	100.0	2.7	47.1	50.2	237,418	158,514	99,418	59,843	13,826	4.7	8,589	530	539
Kennewick	WA	171,664	13,040	122,270	36,354	100.0	7.6	71.2	21.2	174,519	147,725	88,775	23,176	3,368	19.5	8,910	4,175	1,211
Kent	WA	292,358	21,957	166,560	103,841	100.0	7.5	57.0	35.5	273,699	250,146	148,140	14,566	8,199	19.8	9,090	7,537	1,228
Lake Washington	WA	316,900	13,093	156,980	146,827	100.0	4.1	49.5	46.3	384,891	234,073	142,801	135,857	22,916	6.2	9,171	1,816	965
Mukilteo	WA	164,654	10,497	95,079	59,078	100.0	6.4	57.7	35.9	155,287	146,632	93,577	6,268	2,261	17.2	9,837	3,139	1,138
Northshore	WA	244,924	9,813	126,785	108,326	100.0	4.0	51.8	44.2	231,838	189,111	116,558	25,197	16,536	7.4	9,303	1,598	960
Pasco	WA	163,359	15,132	113,219	35,008	100.0	9.3	69.3	21.4	160,826	144,555	84,083	10,611	5,468	23.2	8,997	4,952	1,193
Puyallup	WA	222,923	10,346	135,075	77,502	100.0	4.6	60.6	34.8	209,468	193,080	109,859	6,344	9,216	11.0	9,361	2,601	1,025
Renton	WA	186,476	12,881	91,884	81,711	100.0	6.9	49.3	43.8	196,944	143,334	86,899	37,734	14,250	19.7	9,568	4,285	1,185
Seattle	WA	703,137	52,494	317,728	332,915	100.0	7.5	45.2	47.3	629,926	572,138	340,037	49,139	6,353	15.2	11,295	12,740	1,305
Spokane	WA	358,154	35,647	213,169	109,338	100.0	10.0	59.5	30.5	380,902	299,151	171,766	59,169	14,831	23.6	10,304	10,226	1,283
Tacoma	WA	370,091	38,536	187,595	143,960	100.0	10.4	50.7	38.9	356,429	324,583	175,976	20,153	11,295	25.3	10,740	10,740	1,275
Vancouver	WA	238,510	19,783	145,192	73,535	100.0	8.3	60.9	30.8	217,130	210,866	117,229	934	4,103	21.7	9,198	6,539	1,221
Yakima	WA	229,539	26,236	178,253	25,050	100.0	11.4	77.7	10.9	266,419	159,738	92,706	101,632	4,861	31.8	10,381	6,182	1,243
Berkeley County	WV	211,979	18,725	124,603	68,651	100.0	8.8	58.8	32.4	216,467	190,181	111,445	22,695	1,909	16.2	10,466	4,256	1,343
Kanawha County	WV	330,105	39,428	181,883	108,794	100.0	11.9	55.1	33.0	342,004	300,806	184,099	31,495	0	20.4	10,537	8,569	1,473
Appleton Area	WI	171,846	12,348	83,454	76,044	100.0	7.2	48.6	44.3	172,370	162,540	101,096	3,844	1,391	11.4	10,672	2,018	1,098
Green Bay Area	WI	259,648	23,828	148,538	87,282	100.0	9.2	57.2	33.6	243,278	218,646	128,752	11,136	1,037	20.0	10,570	6,428	1,385
Kenosha	WI	284,266	20,795	161,706	101,765	100.0	7.3	56.9	35.8	259,266	247,194	156,092	2,972	5,780	20.2	10,952	6,616	1,383
Madison Metropolitan	WI	388,792	31,475	92,654	264,663	100.0	8.1	23.8	68.1	391,118	346,794	206,185	17,140	1,888	19.4	12,791	7,278	1,394
Milwaukee	WI	1,184,781	204,823	631,627	348,331	100.0	17.3	53.3	29.4	1,186,315	1,012,830	570,346	25,801	10,952	40.2	12,925	74,998	1,676
Racine Unified	WI	259,373	26,609	142,431	90,333	100.0	10.3	54.9	34.8	259,493	227,994	137,183	20,785	1,296	20.4	11,080	6,904	1,404

†Not applicable.
[1]Poverty is defined based on the number of persons and related children in the family and their income. For information on poverty thresholds, see http://www.census.gov/hhes/www/poverty/data/threshld.
[2]Current expenditure per pupil based on fall enrollment collected through the "Local Education Agency (School District) Finance Survey (F33)."
[3]Includes other expenditures not shown separately.
[4]Fiscal year 2015 Department of Education funds available for spending by school districts beginning with the 2015–16 school year.

[5]Fiscal year 2015 Department of Education funds available for spending by school districts beginning with the 2015–16 school year divided by number of poverty children in 2014.
[6]Includes data for both Modesto City Elementary and Modesto City High.
NOTE: Detail may not sum to totals because of rounding. ISD = independent school district. CISD = consolidated independent school district.
SOURCE: U.S. Department of Education, National Center for Education Statistics, Common Core of Data (CCD), "Local Education Agency Universe Survey," 2013–14; "Local Education Agency (School District) Finance Survey (F33)," 2012–13; and unpublished Department of Education budget data. (This table was prepared February 2016.)

Table 215.30. Enrollment, poverty, and federal funds for the 120 largest school districts, by enrollment size in 2013: Selected years, 2012–13 through 2015

Name of district	State	Rank order	Enrollment, fall 2013	5- to 17-year-old population, 2014	5- to 17-year-olds in poverty, 2014[1]	Poverty rate of 5- to 17-year-olds, 2014[1]	Revenues by source of funds, 2012–13: Total (in thousands)	Federal (in thousands)	Federal as a percent of total	Federal revenue per student[3]	Revenue from selected federal programs (in thousands), 2012–13: Title I basic and concentration grants	School lunch	Individuals with Disabilities Education Act (IDEA)	Eisenhower math and science	Vocational education	Drug-free schools	Federal Title I allocations (in thousands), federal fiscal year 2015[2]: Total	Basic grants	Concentration grants	Targeted grants	Education finance incentive grants
1	2	3	4	5	6	7	8	9	10	11	12	13	14	15	16	17	18	19	20	21	22
New York City	NY	1	989,012	1,229,623	371,720	30.2	$23,438,719	$1,780,098	7.6	$1,799	$661,541	$401,378	$282,453	$52,933	$11,907	$117	$701,094	$262,524	$63,969	$197,973	$176,629
Los Angeles Unified	CA	2	653,826	740,867	232,853	31.4	8,318,105	1,091,741	13.1	1,666	362,695	299,444	128,108	33,204	8,893	617	344,219	119,183	28,242	95,019	101,776
City of Chicago (SD 299)	IL	3	396,641	420,432	138,024	32.8	5,388,477	806,318	15.0	2,036	304,801	190,093	106,902	—	8,268	—	279,268	96,913	22,964	75,399	83,992
Dade	FL	4	356,233	390,870	101,841	26.1	3,266,516	488,124	14.9	1,378	163,180	122,149	80,223	9,017	4,935	—	126,439	47,391	11,230	36,089	31,730
Clark County	NV	5	320,532	356,617	77,378	21.7	2,964,019	281,548	9.5	889	99,076	86,172	50,043	—	3,720	—	93,091	36,308	8,604	26,964	21,215
Broward	FL	6	262,666	293,180	51,909	17.7	2,302,764	263,763	11.5	1,014	69,820	72,166	55,480	10,563	2,813	84	62,226	24,328	5,765	17,100	15,034
Houston ISD	TX	7	211,552	237,925	79,916	33.6	1,987,654	301,816	15.2	1,484	110,863	98,315	36,563	12,776	2,452	—	105,461	37,265	8,919	27,752	31,526
Hillsborough	FL	8	203,439	219,108	49,055	22.4	1,845,716	279,601	15.1	1,395	62,793	68,507	41,644	10,700	3,316	—	58,474	22,980	5,445	15,990	14,058
Orange	FL	9	187,092	203,372	49,895	24.5	1,879,014	206,990	11.0	1,131	56,709	64,616	42,287	5,245	2,162	—	58,949	23,151	5,486	16,131	14,182
Hawaii Department of Education	HI	10	186,825	216,496	29,375	13.6	2,331,770	310,778	13.3	1,682	46,636	43,837	38,832	962	2,225	—	47,116	19,490	4,588	11,414	11,684
Fairfax County	VA	11	183,417	195,333	13,643	7.0	2,543,509	110,231	4.3	610	19,176	31,405	33,797	4,251	1,663	—	20,550	8,205	1,944	4,746	5,655
Palm Beach	FL	12	182,895	199,881	42,336	21.2	1,778,291	178,941	10.1	997	54,120	52,677	39,119	—	1,669	—	49,530	19,768	4,684	13,345	11,733
Gwinnett County	GA	13	169,150	178,365	32,573	18.3	1,582,099	132,604	8.4	804	32,880	59,527	26,917	3,007	1,136	200	38,079	15,319	3,630	9,818	9,312
Dallas ISD	TX	14	159,713	190,136	70,878	37.3	1,632,183	255,315	15.6	1,606	85,861	79,876	30,211	9,194	2,655	—	92,559	33,055	7,833	24,285	27,386
Wake County	NC	15	153,534	181,251	24,013	13.2	1,216,116	97,321	8.0	645	24,655	27,656	30,521	2,710	—	—	28,156	11,216	2,658	7,012	7,271
Montgomery County	MD	16	151,295	173,396	15,202	8.8	2,764,729	105,027	3.8	706	20,951	29,211	30,081	3,929	1,230	—	25,876	10,672	2,529	6,297	6,379
Shelby County	TN	17	149,832	172,997	54,891	31.7	1,179,930	253,751	21.5	2,358	92,876	53,789	26,564	—	3,200	793	69,472	25,911	6,140	18,403	19,019
Charlotte-Mecklenburg	NC	18	142,991	174,930	34,323	19.6	1,235,570	229,228	10.5	894	37,718	44,442	26,927	3,387	—	—	40,660	15,962	3,782	10,269	10,647
Philadelphia City	PA	19	137,674	236,225	79,210	33.5	2,743,433	429,562	15.7	2,985	222,083	71,108	—	29,863	5,798	—	170,023	58,117	13,761	43,633	54,512
San Diego Unified	CA	20	130,303	139,328	31,967	22.9	1,427,717	164,044	11.5	1,259	46,889	48,420	26,953	9,128	995	267	39,812	16,032	3,799	10,274	9,707
Duval	FL	21	127,653	143,628	31,807	22.1	1,106,654	152,989	13.8	1,217	48,470	38,221	33,981	5,686	1,265	1	36,213	14,843	3,517	9,501	8,353
Prince George's County	MD	22	125,136	142,561	18,373	12.9	2,138,117	141,722	6.6	1,145	34,793	42,789	25,907	4,208	1,129	—	31,665	12,883	3,053	7,814	7,915
Cypress-Fairbanks ISD	TX	23	111,440	113,304	17,037	15.0	982,181	77,092	7.8	701	14,588	31,397	13,911	1,173	977	—	19,358	7,944	1,882	4,767	4,764
Cobb County	GA	24	110,001	121,444	19,620	16.2	1,091,899	86,718	7.9	800	20,382	27,476	20,398	2,517	790	1,830	22,795	9,311	2,206	5,696	5,582
Baltimore County	MD	25	108,191	128,226	14,754	11.5	1,579,381	96,279	6.1	900	22,849	25,954	24,085	3,778	960	174	25,860	10,666	2,527	6,293	6,374
Pinellas	FL	26	103,411	118,224	26,051	22.0	921,475	106,001	11.5	1,023	28,112	28,698	30,506	3,841	1,859	—	29,490	12,182	2,887	7,675	6,747
Northside ISD	TX	27	102,129	103,742	16,738	16.1	917,293	85,183	9.3	850	17,647	29,838	14,519	2,140	970	—	19,503	7,965	1,886	4,848	4,803
Jefferson County	KY	28	100,529	123,168	25,043	20.3	1,241,582	162,705	13.1	1,622	46,151	38,217	26,897	8,151	1,166	—	37,683	14,048	3,323	8,903	11,408
DeKalb County	GA	29	99,388	109,957	31,444	28.6	1,120,290	120,025	10.7	1,213	45,081	39,054	14,942	3,156	1,692	518	38,216	14,995	3,551	9,643	10,027
Polk	FL	30	97,953	105,795	29,108	27.5	913,627	110,493	12.1	1,140	28,396	32,206	21,066	3,219	1,268	—	33,100	13,610	3,225	8,655	7,609
Fulton County	GA	31	95,232	111,576	19,273	17.3	1,090,818	74,519	6.8	794	24,424	22,916	17,889	2,353	578	—	22,025	9,081	2,152	5,539	5,253
Albuquerque	NM	32	93,202	114,253	28,822	25.2	964,205	106,368	11.0	1,131	35,713	11	25,909	4,658	1,089	—	35,282	13,737	3,255	8,742	9,549
Lee	FL	33	87,425	92,340	24,017	26.0	795,969	92,386	11.6	1,077	19,261	29,041	21,314	—	983	—	27,011	11,200	2,654	7,001	6,155
Denver	CO	34	86,046	91,237	26,159	28.7	1,057,142	125,850	11.9	1,509	40,506	31,377	16,663	4,637	1,299	—	32,896	12,527	2,968	7,901	9,500
Jefferson County, No. R1	CO	35	86,011	88,260	10,463	11.9	842,074	53,795	6.4	629	11,596	13,195	14,082	1,083	432	—	12,297	5,132	1,216	2,826	3,123
Prince William County	VA	36	85,451	88,432	7,606	8.6	1,004,075	47,983	4.8	572	6,299	16,309	14,273	1,166	730	—	10,311	4,559	1,080	2,261	2,410
Austin ISD	TX	37	85,372	98,159	24,367	24.8	1,054,072	146,954	13.9	1,699	39,323	28,258	17,354	3,165	1,166	—	29,892	11,899	2,817	7,536	7,639
Baltimore City	MD	38	84,730	89,707	26,703	29.8	1,432,281	178,834	12.5	2,110	62,103	37,902	26,897	8,151	1,692	—	49,459	19,660	4,655	12,500	12,644
Fort Worth ISD	TX	39	84,588	91,520	29,068	31.8	841,701	129,752	15.4	1,554	46,882	34,116	14,942	3,156	1,128	—	34,506	13,611	3,320	8,674	8,901
Davidson County	TN	40	82,806	96,427	27,359	28.4	904,316	113,884	12.6	1,404	28,917	32,509	18,155	—	3,016	—	32,165	12,748	3,021	8,063	8,333
Long Beach Unified	CA	41	81,155	87,044	22,571	25.9	810,505	116,859	14.4	1,421	33,912	27,744	15,651	4,672	736	—	27,575	11,316	2,681	7,038	6,540
Milwaukee	WI	42	78,516	111,407	44,749	40.2	1,184,781	204,823	17.3	2,614	100,835	35,590	21,129	—	1,886	—	74,998	26,825	6,356	18,337	23,480
Anne Arundel County	MD	43	78,489	91,526	7,502	8.2	1,125,008	60,765	5.4	781	10,642	12,350	17,500	2,116	580	—	11,731	5,250	1,244	2,602	2,635
Greenville, 01	SC	44	74,475	84,024	19,048	22.7	739,657	63,797	8.6	866	21,428	20,145	14,975	1,983	1,116	—	25,126	9,735	2,307	5,937	7,148
Alpine	UT	45	73,975	82,407	7,913	9.6	473,461	40,700	8.6	562	4,374	10,668	12,232	1,157	633	—	8,734	3,775	895	1,906	2,158

See notes at end of table.

Table 215.30. Enrollment, poverty, and federal funds for the 120 largest school districts, by enrollment size in 2013: Selected years, 2012–13 through 2015—Continued

Column groups: Columns 8–11 = "Revenues by source of funds, 2012–13"; Columns 12–17 = "Revenue from selected federal programs (in thousands), 2012–13"; Columns 18–22 = "Federal Title I allocations (in thousands), federal fiscal year 2015[2]".

Name of district	State	Rank order	Enrollment, fall 2013	5- to 17-year-old population, 2014	5- to 17-year-olds in poverty, 2014[1]	Poverty rate of 5- to 17-year-olds, 2014[1]	Total (in thousands)	Federal (in thousands)	Federal as a percent of total	Federal revenue per student[3]	Title I basic and concentration grants	School lunch	Individuals with Disabilities Education Act (IDEA)	Eisenhower math and science	Vocational education	Drug-free schools	Total	Basic grants	Concentration grants	Targeted grants	Education finance incentive grants
1	2	3	4	5	6	7	8	9	10	11	12	13	14	15	16	17	18	19	20	21	22
Fresno Unified	CA	46	73,353	79,385	39,743	50.1	775,739	128,551	16.6	1,745	55,287	35,393	15,624	6,701	1,144	—	50,504	19,796	4,691	13,245	12,772
Guilford County	NC	47	72,081	84,854	23,052	27.2	686,284	99,692	14.5	1,344	25,763	25,671	18,110	1,896	—	—	26,822	10,709	2,538	6,664	6,910
Brevard	FL	48	71,232	78,341	15,442	19.7	599,412	62,930	10.5	884	14,626	17,346	15,685	2,618	619	—	16,940	7,214	1,709	4,266	3,751
Fort Bend ISD	TX	49	70,931	82,427	10,001	12.1	613,872	39,064	6.4	561	7,876	11,646	10,015	896	598	—	10,903	4,767	1,129	2,587	2,420
Loudoun County	VA	50	70,759	76,328	2,780	3.6	1,027,126	21,204	2.1	311	1,183	6,127	9,774	579	241	—	1,687	1,687	—	—	—
Virginia Beach City	VA	51	70,556	73,625	8,265	11.2	765,695	70,068	9.2	997	12,139	12,735	18,683	2,499	837	—	11,525	5,008	1,187	2,552	2,778
Davis	UT	52	70,411	78,643	6,769	8.6	502,664	38,175	7.6	544	2,702	11,420	10,685	1,376	553	—	7,232	3,182	754	1,560	1,737
Granite	UT	53	70,407	81,256	15,402	19.0	491,011	62,052	12.6	895	15,923	19,048	14,446	2,700	932	—	18,594	7,216	1,710	4,267	5,402
North East ISD	TX	54	68,205	76,118	12,276	16.1	650,475	55,278	8.5	814	11,850	16,783	12,847	1,478	688	—	13,641	5,796	1,373	3,293	3,179
Pasco	FL	55	68,109	73,537	13,030	17.7	596,027	62,571	10.5	932	15,284	20,731	12,233	1,864	593	81	14,168	6,117	1,449	3,513	3,089
Aldine	TX	56	67,381	63,532	23,699	37.3	626,345	86,783	13.9	1,321	19,622	37,024	11,253	2,454	944	—	27,624	11,051	2,619	6,899	7,055
Katy ISD	TX	57	67,213	63,833	6,287	9.8	630,967	39,276	6.2	608	4,694	10,345	7,029	736	456	—	6,214	2,939	610	1,426	1,239
Douglas County No. RE1	CO	58	66,230	69,001	2,343	3.4	603,241	18,184	3.0	281	1,065	3,599	10,681	458	182	—	1,115	1,115	—	—	—
Washoe County	NV	59	65,550	72,033	12,408	17.2	594,199	60,924	10.3	937	14,019	14,445	10,200	1,811	786	96	14,801	6,591	1,561	3,907	2,742
Seminole	FL	60	64,851	71,952	11,369	15.8	522,697	50,596	9.7	785	10,290	15,911	15,317	1,960	444	—	12,131	5,310	1,258	2,960	2,602
Arlington ISD	TX	61	64,688	68,697	15,593	22.7	574,291	66,478	11.6	1,023	14,107	23,234	12,012	1,727	766	—	17,542	7,262	1,721	4,299	4,260
Mesa Unified	AZ	62	64,161	81,861	20,782	25.4	549,773	74,829	13.6	1,166	24,497	22,105	12,299	3,293	1,354	510	24,242	10,057	2,383	6,217	5,586
Elk Grove Unified	CA	63	62,499	68,820	13,407	19.5	549,526	54,840	10.0	883	12,988	17,783	9,552	3,249	524	—	15,708	6,742	1,598	3,900	3,468
El Paso ISD	TX	64	61,620	63,519	20,205	31.8	590,906	94,183	15.9	1,490	30,492	23,110	11,408	4,201	988	—	26,610	10,475	2,670	6,966	6,498
Volusia	FL	65	61,238	67,567	15,988	23.7	548,917	61,284	11.2	1,004	18,064	17,811	14,535	—	659	—	19,165	8,056	1,908	4,910	4,291
Knox County	TN	66	59,236	69,627	13,253	19.0	524,707	60,904	11.6	1,034	12,471	16,909	12,690	—	1,041	364	15,139	6,280	1,488	3,625	3,746
Chesterfield County	VA	67	59,186	61,727	5,808	9.4	581,811	32,908	5.7	559	6,832	7,773	12,144	1,490	583	—	6,917	3,483	610	1,670	1,765
Mobile County	AL	68	58,808	67,973	19,338	28.4	552,138	78,340	14.2	1,336	29,650	24,557	18,069	3,111	907	461	23,185	9,036	2,141	5,516	6,492
Osceola	FL	69	58,204	56,477	17,946	31.8	492,781	61,964	12.6	1,098	18,559	21,804	9,222	—	585	2	19,815	8,352	1,979	5,047	4,437
San Francisco Unified	CA	70	57,620	73,913	10,527	14.2	752,645	80,673	10.7	1,416	31,718	14,168	—	3,514	347	211	12,017	5,255	1,245	2,924	2,592
Garland ISD	TX	71	57,616	61,166	13,227	21.6	516,152	49,404	9.6	851	12,180	17,632	10,671	1,110	706	—	14,623	6,165	1,461	3,546	3,451
Santa Ana Unified	CA	72	57,499	54,420	17,084	31.4	554,940	85,915	15.5	1,497	29,500	26,037	11,810	3,728	443	—	20,195	8,472	2,007	5,086	4,630
Conroe ISD	TX	73	55,009	56,948	7,463	13.1	460,425	27,482	6.0	510	6,765	8,719	6,998	1,135	408	—	7,570	3,496	828	1,732	1,513
Plano ISD	TX	74	54,822	65,316	6,230	9.5	588,710	31,117	5.3	564	5,360	8,003	8,713	1,172	381	—	5,579	2,926	—	1,419	1,233
Pasadena ISD	TX	75	54,535	55,870	15,902	28.5	523,346	74,357	14.2	1,386	20,564	24,955	10,758	1,638	729	—	17,950	7,415	1,757	4,404	4,374
Boston	MA	76	54,300	72,057	20,458	28.4	1,262,641	98,227	7.8	1,782	24,779	17,134	20,657	—	1,452	—	39,078	14,511	3,438	8,931	12,198
Cherry Creek No. 5	CO	77	54,228	55,930	5,520	9.9	548,930	26,039	4.7	487	4,820	7,565	9,503	804	220	—	5,152	2,631	—	1,254	1,268
San Antonio ISD	TX	78	53,857	58,889	22,093	37.5	582,725	135,767	23.3	2,502	36,312	35,652	13,475	4,311	832	—	27,710	11,187	2,786	7,012	6,725
Capistrano Unified	CA	79	53,833	63,230	5,751	9.1	413,762	22,301	5.4	415	3,916	4,672	10,194	783	240	—	5,296	2,852	—	1,367	1,078
San Bernardino City Unified	CA	80	53,785	56,077	21,197	37.8	558,440	90,300	16.2	1,669	43,826	23,733	10,908	4,283	557	—	26,908	11,009	2,607	6,855	6,438
Corona-Norco Unified	CA	81	53,782	55,882	7,540	13.5	457,589	31,925	7.0	597	5,969	10,648	9,259	1,446	259	—	8,129	3,805	902	1,890	1,532
Winston-Salem/Forsyth County	NC	82	53,413	62,708	16,346	26.1	477,178	55,778	11.7	1,035	17,434	16,466	9,217	1,596	—	—	19,010	7,675	1,817	4,649	4,868
Jordan	UT	83	53,355	60,105	4,934	8.2	362,061	23,316	6.4	444	3,057	7,787	7,585	579	426	—	4,641	2,338	—	1,096	1,206
Howard County	MD	84	52,806	57,534	3,268	5.7	934,547	23,580	2.5	453	2,885	4,842	9,900	1,346	322	—	4,247	2,286	—	974	987
Lewisville ISD	TX	85	52,801	60,889	5,274	8.7	525,467	34,064	6.5	648	3,538	9,251	8,750	611	384	—	4,659	2,475	—	1,172	1,011
Clayton County	GA	86	52,296	53,836	18,335	34.1	471,535	59,213	12.6	1,144	14,319	26,058	8,788	895	488	—	23,200	9,378	2,221	5,760	5,842
Cumberland County	NC	87	51,471	54,436	13,857	25.5	425,630	65,617	15.4	1,240	17,728	17,926	11,953	2,792	—	—	15,900	6,564	1,555	3,820	3,961
Omaha	NE	88	51,069	63,358	13,793	21.8	613,144	97,243	15.9	1,923	35,653	20,674	11,354	2,932	503	202	23,901	9,054	2,145	5,306	7,395
Wichita	KS	89	50,629	57,069	14,452	25.3	597,576	73,149	12.2	1,453	28,987	18,597	—	—	—	—	21,881	8,295	1,966	4,891	6,729
Henrico County	VA	90	50,629	54,985	6,700	12.2	545,496	34,931	6.4	697	4,370	10,460	9,548	1,813	1,234	—	9,049	4,030	955	1,971	2,093

See notes at end of table.

Table 215.30. Enrollment, poverty, and federal funds for the 120 largest school districts, by enrollment size in 2013: Selected years, 2012–13 through 2015—Continued

Name of district	State	Rank order	Enrollment, fall 2013	5- to 17-year-old population, 2014	5- to 17-year-olds in poverty, 2014[1]	Poverty rate of 5- to 17-year-olds, 2014[1]	Total (in thousands)	Federal (in thousands)	Federal as a percent of total	Federal revenue per student[3]	Title I basic and concentration grants	School lunch	Individuals with Disabilities Education Act (IDEA)	Eisenhower math and science	Vocational education	Drug-free schools	Total	Basic grants	Concentration grants	Targeted grants	Education finance incentive grants
							Revenues by source of funds, 2012–13				Revenue from selected federal programs (in thousands), 2012–13						Federal Title I allocations (in thousands), federal fiscal year 2015[2]				
1	2	3	4	5	6	7	8	9	10	11	12	13	14	15	16	17	18	19	20	21	22
Seattle	WA	91	50,509	64,156	9,766	15.2	703,137	52,494	7.5	1,036	11,899	9,626	11,831	153	376	—	12,740	5,254	1,245	2,825	3,415
Columbus City	OH	92	50,478	70,736	27,741	39.2	855,757	63,211	7.4	1,255	0	24,785	11,983	—	2,054	—	46,439	17,424	4,129	11,061	13,826
Atlanta	GA	93	50,131	57,606	20,970	36.4	771,985	84,743	11.0	1,710	30,480	21,009	10,400	4,783	499	1,270	31,528	12,228	2,983	7,662	8,655
Brownsville ISD	TX	94	49,370	47,291	20,521	43.4	501,016	110,950	22.1	2,256	37,154	33,573	10,941	3,198	968		24,905	9,835	2,402	6,358	6,310
Tucson Unified	AZ	95	49,308	73,274	19,315	26.4	470,812	58,134	12.3	1,145	22,803	17,108	13	3,907	1,416	813	23,894	9,559	2,263	5,939	6,133
Detroit City	MI	96	49,043	128,676	65,949	51.3	851,989	228,390	26.8	4,638	126,653	37,999	14,987	—	2,197	—	139,667	45,887	11,696	36,374	45,710
San Juan Unified	CA	97	49,035	49,829	10,698	21.5	436,242	45,645	10.5	956	13,324	9,876	9,380	1,800	339	406	12,326	5,439	1,289	3,006	2,593
Klein ISD	TX	98	48,253	49,135	7,135	14.5	432,348	31,330	7.2	666	6,088	10,024	8,092	556	215	—	7,186	3,328	789	1,640	1,431
Anchorage	AK	99	48,159	53,216	4,994	9.4	770,180	76,535	9.9	1,569	13,938	15,529	12,306	3,206	967	—	12,763	5,118	651	3,464	3,529
Portland, SD1J	OR	100	47,323	55,527	9,319	16.8	534,955	55,347	10.3	1,184	15,777	10,498	13,107	2,697	435	—	12,056	4,936	1,170	2,622	3,329
Oakland Unified	CA	101	47,194	57,818	14,988	25.9	604,008	74,530	12.3	1,604	26,581	15,427	11,515	3,098	489	323	17,582	7,464	1,769	4,395	3,953
Sacramento City Unified	CA	102	47,031	52,506	16,515	31.5	488,458	82,038	16.8	1,723	22,342	19,862	10,365	3,863	544	535	19,817	8,297	1,966	4,974	4,580
Garden Grove Unified	CA	103	46,936	50,483	13,318	26.4	506,887	52,738	10.4	1,108	14,586	19,494	9,126	1,561	357	—	15,348	6,604	1,565	3,805	3,375
Manatee	FL	104	46,705	50,242	13,063	26.0	415,726	48,375	11.6	1,048	11,210	15,279	9,750	1,486	660	—	14,098	6,089	1,443	3,494	3,072
Round Rock ISD	TX	105	46,666	51,345	4,095	8.0	442,949	29,811	6.7	652	3,043	7,504	6,489	466	318	—	3,568	1,941	—	878	749
Jefferson Parish	LA	106	46,312	68,154	18,877	27.7	557,140	85,506	15.3	1,855	29,878	17,183	9,675	2,343	721	—	26,469	10,548	2,499	6,414	7,008
Alief ISD	TX	107	46,258	52,409	18,767	35.8	452,367	63,375	14.0	1,384	16,130	20,850	8,830	1,085	673	—	21,504	8,751	2,074	5,321	5,359
Frisco ISD	TX	108	46,053	40,585	2,184	5.4	431,286	9,830	2.3	230	1,013	2,845	4,820	117	219	—	1,696	1,020	376	376	300
Charleston, 01	SC	109	45,650	52,565	13,179	25.1	707,221	72,128	10.2	1,617	27,445	16,264	10,421	2,448	646	—	16,571	6,683	1,584	3,843	4,461
District of Columbia	DC	110	44,942	70,507	20,544	29.1	1,300,036	129,874	10.0	2,940	32,760	22,088	13,622	7,795	2,527	320	42,820	17,744	3,994	10,557	10,525
Socorro ISD	TX	111	44,517	44,018	10,791	24.5	383,072	40,997	10.7	926	9,285	17,728	6,670	999	578	—	11,520	4,999	1,184	2,746	2,591
Collier	FL	112	44,418	46,316	10,384	22.4	491,985	55,854	11.4	1,276	17,776	16,115	8,987	1,309	515	—	10,933	4,836	1,146	2,635	2,316
United ISD	TX	113	43,575	42,174	13,223	31.4	395,105	50,435	12.8	1,176	14,065	19,433	7,413	1,050	409	—	14,583	6,150	1,457	3,536	3,440
Hamilton County	TN	114	43,540	53,541	12,166	22.7	398,221	50,421	12.7	1,154	16,521	14,689	9,826		729	529	13,776	5,762	1,365	3,270	3,379
Ysleta ISD	TX	115	43,063	38,453	13,819	35.9	423,790	61,548	14.5	1,409	19,099	19,418	8,184	2,571	674	—	15,793	6,416	1,635	4,006	3,736
Riverside Unified	CA	116	42,587	46,032	9,624	20.9	382,543	42,841	11.2	1,007	10,804	15,392	8,189	2,835	347	—	10,817	4,857	1,151	2,606	2,202
Adams 12 Five Star Schools	CO	117	42,230	44,089	4,834	11.0	405,051	22,447	5.5	519	4,651	6,112	6,995	1,162	199	—	4,656	2,337		1,122	1,197
Marion	FL	118	42,107	46,865	12,945	27.6	361,558	51,208	14.2	1,220	13,801	17,540	9,932	1,642	585	—	13,932	6,023	1,427	3,449	3,033
East Baton Rouge Parish	LA	119	41,937	60,888	17,228	28.3	565,614	71,584	12.7	1,665	24,044	20,549	8,668	4,879	679	25	24,139	9,650	2,287	5,798	6,404
Lake	FL	120	41,794	46,136	10,094	21.9	340,131	38,288	11.3	923	10,350	13,244	9,025	1,385	483	—	10,580	4,697	1,113	2,539	2,232

—Not available.
[1] Poverty is defined based on the number of persons and related children in the family and their income. For information on poverty thresholds, see http://www.census.gov/hhes/www/poverty/data/threshld/.
[2] Fiscal year 2015 Department of Education funds available for spending by school districts in the 2015–16 school year.
[3] Federal revenue per student is based on fall enrollment collected through the "Local Education Agency (School District) Finance Survey (F33)."

NOTE: Detail may not sum to totals because of rounding. ISD = independent school district.
SOURCE: U.S. Department of Education, National Center for Education Statistics, Common Core of Data (CCD), "Local Education Agency Universe Survey," 2013–14; "Local Education Agency (School District) Finance Survey (F33)," 2012–13; and unpublished Department of Education budget data. U.S. Department of Commerce, Census Bureau, Small Area Income and Poverty Estimates (SAIPE) Program, 2014 Poverty Estimates for School Districts. (This table was prepared January 2016.)

Table 216.10. Public elementary and secondary schools, by level of school: Selected years, 1967–68 through 2013–14

| | | Schools with reported grade spans | | | | | | | | | | | |
| | | | Elementary schools | | | | Secondary schools | | | | | Combined elementary/ secondary schools[2] | Other schools[1] |
Year	Total, all public schools	Total	Total[3]	Middle schools[4]	One-teacher schools	Other elementary schools	Total[5]	Junior high[6]	3-year or 4-year high schools	5-year or 6-year high schools	Other secondary schools		
1	2	3	4	5	6	7	8	9	10	11	12	13	14
1967–68	—	94,197	67,186	—	4,146	63,040	23,318	7,437	10,751	4,650	480	3,693	—
1970–71	—	89,372	64,020	2,080	1,815	60,125	23,572	7,750	11,265	3,887	670	1,780	—
1972–73	—	88,864	62,942	2,308	1,475	59,159	23,919	7,878	11,550	3,962	529	2,003	—
1974–75	—	87,456	61,759	3,224	1,247	57,288	23,837	7,690	11,480	4,122	545	1,860	—
1975–76	88,597	87,034	61,704	3,916	1,166	56,622	23,792	7,521	11,572	4,113	586	1,538	1,563
1976–77	—	86,501	61,123	4,180	1,111	55,832	23,857	7,434	11,658	4,130	635	1,521	—
1978–79	—	84,816	60,312	5,879	1,056	53,377	22,834	6,282	11,410	4,429	713	1,670	—
1980–81	85,982	83,688	59,326	6,003	921	52,402	22,619	5,890	10,758	4,193	1,778	1,743	2,294
1982–83	84,740	82,039	58,051	6,875	798	50,378	22,383	5,948	11,678	4,067	690	1,605	2,701
1983–84	84,178	81,418	57,471	6,885	838	49,748	22,336	5,936	11,670	4,046	684	1,611	2,760
1984–85	84,007	81,147	57,231	6,893	825	49,513	22,320	5,916	11,671	4,021	712	1,596	2,860
1986–87	83,421	82,316	58,835	7,483	763	50,589	21,505	5,109	11,430	4,196	770	1,976	1,105 [7]
1987–88	83,248	81,416	57,575	7,641	729	49,205	21,662	4,900	11,279	4,048	1,435	2,179	1,832 [7]
1988–89	83,165	81,579	57,941	7,957	583	49,401	21,403	4,687	11,350	3,994	1,372	2,235	1,586 [7]
1989–90	83,425	81,880	58,419	8,272	630	49,517	21,181	4,512	11,492	3,812	1,365	2,280	1,545 [7]
1990–91	84,538	82,475	59,015	8,545	617	49,853	21,135	4,561	11,537	3,723	1,314	2,325	2,063
1991–92	84,578	82,506	59,258	8,829	569	49,860	20,767	4,298	11,528	3,699	1,242	2,481	2,072
1992–93	84,497	82,896	59,676	9,152	430	50,094	20,671	4,115	11,661	3,613	1,292	2,549	1,601
1993–94	85,393	83,431	60,052	9,573	442	50,037	20,705	3,970	11,858	3,595	1,282	2,674	1,962
1994–95	86,221	84,476	60,808	9,954	458	50,396	20,904	3,859	12,058	3,628	1,359	2,764	1,745
1995–96	87,125	84,958	61,165	10,205	474	50,486	20,997	3,743	12,168	3,621	1,465	2,796	2,167
1996–97	88,223	86,092	61,805	10,499	487	50,819	21,307	3,707	12,424	3,614	1,562	2,980	2,131
1997–98	89,508	87,541	62,739	10,944	476	51,319	21,682	3,599	12,734	3,611	1,738	3,120	1,967
1998–99	90,874	89,259	63,462	11,202	463	51,797	22,076	3,607	13,457	3,707	1,305	3,721	1,615
1999–2000	92,012	90,538	64,131	11,521	423	52,187	22,365	3,566	13,914	3,686	1,199	4,042	1,474
2000–01	93,273	91,691	64,601	11,696	411	52,494	21,994	3,318	13,793	3,974	909	5,096	1,582
2001–02	94,112	92,696	65,228	11,983	408	52,837	22,180	3,285	14,070	3,917	908	5,288	1,416
2002–03	95,615	93,869	65,718	12,174	366	53,178	22,599	3,263	14,330	4,017	989	5,552	1,746
2003–04	95,726	93,977	65,758	12,341	376	53,041	22,782	3,251	14,595	3,840	1,096	5,437	1,749
2004–05	96,513	95,001	65,984	12,530	338	53,116	23,445	3,250	14,854	3,945	1,396	5,572	1,512
2005–06	97,382	95,731	66,026	12,545	326	53,155	23,998	3,249	15,103	3,910	1,736	5,707	1,651
2006–07	98,793	96,362	66,458	12,773	313	53,372	23,920	3,112	15,043	4,048	1,717	5,984	2,431
2007–08	98,916	97,654	67,112	13,014	288	53,810	24,643	3,117	16,146	3,981	1,399	5,899	1,262
2008–09	98,706	97,119	67,148	13,060	237	53,851	24,348	3,037	16,246	3,761	1,304	5,623	1,587
2009–10	98,817	97,521	67,140	13,163	217	53,760	24,651	2,953	16,706	3,778	1,214	5,730	1,296
2010–11	98,817	97,767	67,086	13,045	224	53,817	24,544	2,855	16,321	4,047	1,321	6,137	1,050
2011–12	98,328	97,357	66,689	12,963	205	53,521	24,357	2,865	16,586	3,899	1,007	6,311	971
2012–13	98,454	97,369	66,718	13,061	196	53,461	24,280	2,810	16,657	3,871	942	6,371	1,085
2013–14	98,271	97,292	67,034	13,322	193	53,519	24,053	2,719	16,937	3,498	899	6,205	979

—Not available.
[1]Includes special education, alternative, and other schools not reported by grade span.
[2]Includes schools beginning with grade 6 or below and ending with grade 9 or above.
[3]Includes schools beginning with grade 6 or below and with no grade higher than 8.
[4]Includes schools with grade spans beginning with 4, 5, or 6 and ending with 6, 7, or 8.
[5]Includes schools with no grade below 7, and at least one higher grade.
[6]Includes schools with grades 7 and 8 or grades 7 through 9.

[7]Because of revision in data collection procedures, figures not comparable to data for other years.
SOURCE: U.S. Department of Education, National Center for Education Statistics, *Statistics of State School Systems*, 1967–68 and 1975–76; *Statistics of Public Elementary and Secondary Day Schools*, 1970–71, 1972–73, 1974–75, and 1976–77 through 1980–81; and Common Core of Data (CCD), "Public Elementary/Secondary School Universe Survey," 1982–83 through 2013–14. (This table was prepared September 2015.)

Table 216.20. Number and enrollment of public elementary and secondary schools, by school level, type, and charter and magnet status: Selected years, 1990–91 through 2013–14

School level, type, and charter and magnet status	Number of schools										Enrollment									
	1990–91	2000–01	2003–04	2007–08	2008–09	2009–10	2010–11	2011–12	2012–13	2013–14	1990–91	2000–01	2003–04	2007–08	2008–09	2009–10	2010–11	2011–12	2012–13	2013–14
1	2	3	4	5	6	7	8	9	10	11	12	13	14	15	16	17	18	19	20	21
Total, all schools	84,538	93,273	95,726	98,916	98,706	98,817	98,817	98,328	98,454	98,271	41,141,366	47,060,714	48,353,523	48,910,025	49,053,786	49,081,519	49,177,617	49,256,120	49,474,030	49,709,977
School type																				
Regular	80,395	85,422	86,340	88,274	88,801	89,018	88,929	88,663	89,031	89,183	40,599,943	46,194,730	47,415,655	47,962,492	48,168,727	48,186,142	48,259,245	48,273,539	48,539,891	48,800,105
Special education	1,932	2,008	2,328	2,267	2,289	2,089	2,206	2,087	2,034	2,010	209,145	174,577	211,623	207,030	164,874	192,999	190,910	195,161	198,417	213,077
Vocational	1,060	1,025	1,100	1,409	1,409	1,417	1,485	1,434	1,403	1,380	198,117	199,669	182,343	163,003	156,390	129,840	164,013	159,905	159,917	148,451
Alternative[1]	1,151	4,818	5,958	6,966	6,207	6,293	6,197	6,144	5,986	5,698	134,161	491,738	543,902	577,500	563,795	572,548	563,449	627,515	575,805	548,344
School level and type																				
Elementary[2]	59,015	64,601	65,758	67,112	67,148	67,140	67,086	66,689	66,718	67,034	26,503,677	30,673,453	31,204,774	31,225,474	31,446,040	31,547,988	31,581,751	31,724,573	31,893,347	32,183,080
Regular	58,440	63,674	64,721	65,721	65,999	65,947	65,874	65,461	65,581	65,948	26,400,740	30,582,610	31,098,893	31,093,502	31,325,566	31,413,221	31,441,027	31,545,896	31,747,440	32,040,651
Special education	419	496	487	563	538	520	587	544	540	543	58,204	63,371	44,908	56,999	49,661	56,999	56,967	58,844	59,537	62,580
Vocational	31	8	5	7	1	24	16	17	15	7	17,686	2,409	1,917	1,634	16	1,892	3,495	4,558	3,734	1,791
Alternative[1]	125	423	545	801	610	649	609	667	582	536	27,047	46,307	69,056	66,967	70,797	75,916	78,242	115,285	82,636	78,058
Secondary[3]	21,135	21,994	22,782	24,643	24,348	24,651	24,544	24,357	24,280	24,053	13,569,787	15,038,171	15,751,624	16,184,724	16,055,123	15,830,401	15,692,610	15,708,815	15,644,214	15,618,300
Regular	19,459	18,456	18,810	19,371	19,349	19,604	19,449	19,441	19,470	19,409	13,313,097	14,567,969	15,279,073	15,680,507	15,568,281	15,454,043	15,197,786	15,194,153	15,137,814	15,148,323
Special education	165	219	274	375	325	354	359	339	330	329	11,913	12,607	17,743	30,680	24,266	30,443	27,990	27,905	27,731	28,014
Vocational	1,010	997	1,069	1,356	1,326	1,343	1,387	1,349	1,324	1,311	174,105	193,981	176,022	159,270	154,522	126,827	154,088	154,187	154,275	144,070
Alternative[1]	501	2,322	2,629	3,541	3,348	3,350	3,349	3,228	3,156	3,004	70,672	263,614	278,786	314,267	308,054	319,088	312,746	332,570	324,394	297,893
Combined elementary/secondary[4]	2,325	5,096	5,437	5,899	5,623	5,730	6,137	6,311	6,371	6,205	925,887	1,266,778	1,310,435	1,472,248	1,520,246	1,542,734	1,897,712	1,818,020	1,934,697	1,896,908
Regular	1,784	2,780	2,657	2,786	2,793	3,028	3,363	3,435	3,572	3,448	855,814	1,007,368	1,030,665	1,187,281	1,253,785	1,288,109	1,620,031	1,533,002	1,654,256	1,610,750
Special education	376	715	801	904	938	847	964	970	960	951	43,992	86,253	99,668	88,000	80,245	76,691	99,120	104,344	109,992	111,175
Vocational	19	20	26	46	82	50	82	68	64	62	6,326	3,279	4,404	2,099	1,852	1,121	6,430	1,160	1,908	2,590
Alternative[1]	146	1,581	1,953	2,163	1,810	1,805	1,728	1,838	1,775	1,744	19,755	169,878	176,698	194,868	184,364	176,813	172,131	179,514	168,541	172,393
Other (not classified by grade span)	2,063	1,582	1,749	1,262	1,587	1,296	1,050	971	1,085	979	142,015	82,312	86,690	27,579	32,377	60,396	5,544	4,712	1,772	11,689
Regular	712	512	152	396	660	439	243	326	408	378	30,292	36,783	17,024	1,202	21,095	30,769	401	498	381	381
Special education	972	578	766	405	488	368	296	234	204	187	95,036	33,590	50,304	24,979	10,702	28,896	4,813	4,068	1,157	11,308
Vocational[1]	0	0	0	0	0	0	0	0	0	0	0	0	0	0	0	0	0	0	0	0
Alternative[1]	379	492	831	461	439	489	511	411	473	414	16,687	11,939	19,362	1,398	580	731	330	146	234	0
Charter status and level																				
All charter schools[5]	—	1,993	2,977	4,388	4,694	4,952	5,274	5,696	6,079	6,465	—	448,343	789,479	1,276,731	1,433,116	1,610,285	1,787,091	2,057,599	2,267,814	2,519,065
Elementary[2]	—	1,011	1,549	2,340	2,513	2,679	2,866	3,127	3,391	3,636	—	249,101	414,225	674,990	746,950	824,297	905,575	1,045,492	1,156,384	1,297,378
Secondary[3]	—	467	779	1,218	1,255	1,329	1,368	1,418	1,463	1,521	—	79,588	158,999	264,402	291,016	327,289	341,534	386,482	398,430	441,762
Combined elementary/secondary[4]	—	448	626	803	865	929	1,027	1,112	1,204	1,269	—	117,377	215,462	337,195	395,122	458,075	539,653	625,429	712,634	789,777
Other (not classified by grade span)	—	67	23	27	61	15	13	39	21	39	—	2,277	793	144	28	624	329	196	366	148
Magnet status and level																				
All magnet schools[5]	—	1,469	2,108	2,793	3,021	2,213	2,722	2,949	3,151	3,254	—	1,213,976	1,619,779	2,132,395	2,307,712	1,515,562	2,055,133	2,248,177	2,479,188	2,554,828
Elementary[2]	—	1,111	1,566	2,015	2,193	1,530	1,849	2,012	2,150	2,164	—	704,763	946,815	1,157,470	1,267,944	799,546	1,035,298	1,158,405	1,287,509	1,298,904
Secondary[3]	—	328	478	688	728	582	746	802	862	939	—	484,684	633,080	926,314	976,483	668,832	944,434	1,015,267	1,119,369	1,177,869
Combined elementary/secondary[4]	—	29	59	83	92	79	103	116	121	133	—	24,529	39,011	48,593	63,285	46,467	75,411	74,505	72,192	78,055
Other (not classified by grade span)	—	1	5	7	8	22	24	19	18	18	—	—	873	18	580	717	0	0	98	0

—Not available.

[1]Includes schools that provide nontraditional education, address needs of students that typically cannot be met in regular schools, serve as adjuncts to regular schools, or fall outside the categories of regular, special education, or vocational education.

[2]Includes schools beginning with grade 6 or below and with no grade higher than 8.

[3]Includes schools with no grade lower than 7.

[4]Includes schools beginning with grade 6 or below and ending with grade 9 or above.

[5]Magnet and charter schools are also included under regular, special education, vocational, or alternative schools as appropriate.

SOURCE: U.S. Department of Education, National Center for Education Statistics, Common Core of Data (CCD), "Public Elementary/Secondary School Universe Survey," 1990–91 through 2013–14. (This table was prepared September 2015.)

Table 216.30. Number and percentage distribution of public elementary and secondary students and schools, by traditional or charter school status and selected characteristics: Selected years, 1999–2000 through 2013–14

Selected characteristic	1999–2000 Total, all public schools	1999–2000 Traditional (noncharter) schools	1999–2000 Charter schools	2003–04 Total, all public schools	2003–04 Traditional (noncharter) schools	2003–04 Charter schools	Charter schools 2007–08	Charter schools 2009–10	Charter schools 2011–12	Charter schools 2012–13	2013–14 Total, all public schools	2013–14 Traditional (noncharter) schools	2013–14 Charter schools
1	2	3	4	5	6	7	8	9	10	11	12	13	14
Enrollment (in thousands)	46,689	46,350	340	48,354	47,564	789	1,277	1,610	2,058	2,268	49,710	47,191	2,519
Percentage distribution of students													
Sex	100.0	100.0	100.0	100.0	100.0	100.0	100.0	100.0	100.0	100.0	100.0	100.0	100.0
Male	51.4	51.4	51.0	51.4	51.5	50.3	49.5	49.5	49.6	49.6	51.4	51.4	49.6
Female	48.6	48.6	49.0	48.6	48.5	49.7	50.5	50.5	50.4	50.4	48.6	48.6	50.4
Race/ethnicity	100.0	100.0	100.0	100.0	100.0	100.0	100.0	100.0	100.0	100.0	100.0	100.0	100.0
White	61.8	61.9	42.5	58.4	58.7	41.8	38.8	37.3	35.6	35.4	50.3	51.1	34.9
Black	17.1	16.9	33.5	17.1	16.9	31.9	31.8	30.3	28.7	27.6	15.6	15.0	27.1
Hispanic	15.9	15.9	19.6	18.8	18.7	21.5	24.5	26.0	28.0	29.1	24.9	24.6	30.0
Asian/Pacific Islander	4.1	4.1	2.8	4.5	4.5	3.2	3.8	3.9	4.0	4.2	5.2	5.2	4.1
American Indian/Alaska Native	1.2	1.2	1.5	1.2	1.2	1.5	1.2	1.0	0.9	0.8	1.0	1.1	0.8
Two or more races	—	—	—	—	—	—	—	1.4	2.8	2.9	3.0	3.0	3.0
Percent of students eligible for free or reduced-price lunch program[1]	100.0	100.0	100.0	100.0	100.0	100.0	100.0	100.0	100.0	100.0	100.0	100.0	100.0
0 to 25.0	44.9	45.0	36.9	31.7	31.6	33.2	19.8	20.6	21.9	19.5	20.2	20.2	19.7
25.1 to 50.0	25.4	25.5	12.7	26.0	26.1	17.1	16.5	18.8	18.4	19.8	27.1	27.6	18.9
50.1 to 75.0	16.0	16.1	13.0	18.1	18.2	16.1	18.9	20.2	21.0	22.0	26.9	27.1	21.8
More than 75.0	12.2	12.2	14.3	13.4	13.3	18.4	21.2	30.7	30.8	35.5	24.8	24.2	36.7
Missing/school does not participate	1.4	1.2	23.2	10.8	10.7	15.2	23.6	9.7	7.9	3.1	1.0	0.8	3.0
Number of teachers[2]	2,636,277	2,622,678	13,599	2,714,733	2,678,327	36,406	69,725	84,983	107,929	117,037	2,973,522	2,844,844	128,678
Pupil/teacher ratio[2]	16.6	16.6	18.8	16.4	16.4	17.6	15.9	17.3	17.6	17.7	16.3	16.2	17.9
Total number of schools	92,012	90,488	1,524	95,726	92,749	2,977	4,388	4,952	5,696	6,079	98,271	91,806	6,465
Percentage distribution of schools													
School level	100.0	100.0	100.0	100.0	100.0	100.0	100.0	100.0	100.0	100.0	100.0	100.0	100.0
Elementary[3]	69.7	70.0	54.6	68.7	69.2	52.0	53.3	54.1	54.9	55.8	68.2	69.1	56.2
Secondary[4]	24.3	24.3	25.9	23.8	23.7	26.2	27.8	26.8	24.9	24.1	24.5	24.5	23.5
Combined[5]	4.4	4.2	18.6	5.7	5.2	21.0	18.3	18.8	19.5	19.8	6.3	5.4	19.6
Other	1.6	1.6	0.9	1.8	1.9	0.8	0.6	0.3	0.7	0.3	1.0	1.0	0.6
Size of enrollment	100.0	100.0	100.0	100.0	100.0	100.0	100.0	100.0	100.0	100.0	100.0	100.0	100.0
Less than 300	31.4	30.7	77.1	32.4	31.2	71.1	65.6	61.5	55.8	54.1	30.2	28.6	51.7
300 to 499	26.4	26.7	12.0	26.6	27.0	15.6	19.3	20.8	23.1	23.5	27.3	27.5	24.3
500 to 999	32.6	33.0	8.6	31.0	31.7	10.1	12.0	14.0	17.0	18.0	33.4	34.4	19.0
1,000 or more	9.5	9.7	2.4	9.9	10.2	3.2	3.1	3.7	4.2	4.4	9.1	9.4	4.9
Racial/ethnic concentration													
More than 50 percent White	70.9	71.2	51.1	67.2	67.8	48.7	43.2	40.3	37.5	36.6	58.2	59.8	35.8
More than 50 percent Black	11.1	10.8	26.5	11.4	10.9	24.5	26.5	25.8	25.3	24.9	10.1	9.1	24.4
More than 50 percent Hispanic	8.8	8.7	11.4	10.8	10.7	13.6	17.8	19.8	21.8	22.6	15.8	15.3	23.4
Percent of students eligible for free or reduced-price lunch program[1]	100.0	100.0	100.0	100.0	100.0	100.0	100.0	100.0	100.0	100.0	100.0	100.0	100.0
0 to 25.0	42.3	42.3	44.5	26.9	26.8	28.7	20.2	19.3	18.7	18.3	17.5	17.5	17.7
25.1 to 50.0	25.6	25.9	11.1	25.8	26.1	16.0	15.5	17.2	17.9	18.7	25.6	26.1	18.0
50.1 to 75.0	16.8	16.9	10.2	18.9	19.0	16.0	18.8	20.9	19.9	20.9	27.0	27.4	20.6
More than 75.0	11.9	11.9	12.4	14.1	13.9	19.9	22.4	32.8	33.8	36.9	25.0	24.1	38.9
Missing/school does not participate	3.3	3.0	21.9	14.3	14.1	19.5	23.0	9.8	9.7	5.2	4.9	4.9	4.8
Locale	—	—	—	100.0	100.0	100.0	100.0	100.0	100.0	100.0	100.0	100.0	100.0
City	—	—	—	25.7	24.8	52.7	54.3	54.8	55.4	56.7	27.0	25.0	56.5
Suburban	—	—	—	27.8	28.0	22.0	22.0	21.1	21.2	25.5	31.5	31.9	26.1
Town	—	—	—	15.2	15.4	9.6	8.5	8.0	7.4	7.0	13.7	14.2	7.0
Rural	—	—	—	31.3	31.8	15.8	15.2	16.1	16.0	10.8	27.7	29.0	10.4
Region	100.0	100.0	100.0	100.0	100.0	100.0	100.0	100.0	100.0	100.0	100.0	100.0	100.0
Northeast	16.1	16.3	7.2	16.0	16.2	9.2	8.6	9.1	9.7	10.0	15.4	15.8	10.1
Midwest	28.9	29.0	24.9	28.1	28.3	23.7	26.5	24.0	22.3	21.9	25.9	26.2	21.7
South	33.1	33.2	28.9	33.6	33.8	26.7	28.2	29.5	30.8	30.7	35.1	35.4	31.2
West	21.8	21.6	38.9	22.3	21.8	40.3	36.6	37.4	37.2	37.3	23.6	22.7	37.0

—Not available.

[1]The National School Lunch Program is a federally assisted meal program. To be eligible for free lunch under the program, a student must be from a household with an income at or below 130 percent of the poverty threshold; to be eligible for reduced-price lunch, a student must be from a household with an income between 130 percent and 185 percent of the poverty threshold.
[2]Pupil/teacher ratio based on schools that reported both enrollment and teacher data.
[3]Includes schools beginning with grade 6 or below and with no grade higher than 8.

[4]Includes schools with no grade lower than 7.
[5]Includes schools beginning with grade 6 or below and ending with grade 9 or above.
NOTE: Detail may not sum to totals because of rounding. Race categories exclude persons of Hispanic ethnicity.
SOURCE: U.S. Department of Education, National Center for Education Statistics, Common Core of Data (CCD), "Public Elementary/Secondary School Universe Survey," 1999–2000 through 2013–14. (This table was prepared September 2015.)

Table 216.40. Number and percentage distribution of public elementary and secondary schools and enrollment, by level, type, and enrollment size of school: 2011–12, 2012–13, and 2013–14

| | Number and percentage distribution of schools, by level and type | | | | | | Enrollment totals and percentage distribution, by level and type of school[1] | | | | | |
| | | | Secondary[4] | | Combined elementary/secondary[5] | Other[6] | | | Secondary[4] | | Combined elementary/secondary[5] | Other[6] |
Enrollment size of school	Total[2]	Elementary[3]	All schools	Regular schools[7]			Total[2]	Elementary[3]	All schools	Regular schools[7]		
1	2	3	4	5	6	7	8	9	10	11	12	13
2011–12												
Total	98,328	66,689	24,357	19,441	6,311	971	49,256,120	31,724,573	15,708,815	15,194,153	1,818,020	4,712
Percent[8]	100.00	100.00	100.00	100.00	100.00	100.00	100.00	100.00	100.00	100.00	100.00	100.00
Under 100	10.32	5.46	17.47	9.31	37.92	67.86	0.89	0.57	1.08	0.65	4.80	35.93
100 to 199	9.09	7.65	11.57	10.59	15.72	28.57	2.62	2.43	2.47	2.00	7.05	49.79
200 to 299	10.96	11.68	9.12	9.36	10.02	1.79	5.31	6.18	3.29	2.96	7.68	4.69
300 to 399	13.79	16.20	8.12	8.88	8.45	0.00	9.29	11.88	4.10	3.93	9.10	0.00
400 to 499	13.92	17.08	6.56	7.40	6.55	1.79	12.00	16.00	4.26	4.21	9.16	9.59
500 to 599	11.65	14.14	5.87	6.68	5.90	0.00	12.27	16.17	4.66	4.64	10.01	0.00
600 to 699	8.58	10.23	4.92	5.56	4.04	0.00	10.67	13.82	4.61	4.56	8.12	0.00
700 to 799	6.13	6.98	4.48	5.12	2.96	0.00	8.80	10.88	4.85	4.85	6.80	0.00
800 to 999	6.56	6.77	6.79	7.87	3.13	0.00	11.17	12.49	8.80	8.94	8.65	0.00
1,000 to 1,499	5.40	3.48	11.51	13.30	3.28	0.00	12.42	8.42	20.53	20.76	12.20	0.00
1,500 to 1,999	2.02	0.29	7.26	8.53	1.24	0.00	6.71	1.02	18.24	18.77	6.49	0.00
2,000 to 2,999	1.33	0.03	5.36	6.29	0.44	0.00	6.03	0.13	18.26	18.78	3.27	0.00
3,000 or more	0.25	#	0.97	1.13	0.35	0.00	1.80	0.01	4.85	4.93	6.67	0.00
Average enrollment[8]	520	479	690	788	322	84	520	479	690	788	322	84
2012–13												
Total	98,454	66,718	24,280	19,470	6,371	1,085	49,474,030	31,893,347	15,644,214	15,137,814	1,934,697	1,772
Percent[8]	100.00	100.00	100.00	100.00	100.00	100.00	100.00	100.00	100.00	100.00	100.00	100.00
Under 100	10.14	5.34	17.35	9.30	36.73	86.21	0.88	0.56	1.08	0.65	4.42	57.73
100 to 199	9.20	7.74	11.66	10.60	16.30	6.90	2.63	2.44	2.48	1.99	6.94	12.64
200 to 299	10.90	11.50	9.30	9.66	10.23	6.90	5.28	6.08	3.36	3.07	7.52	29.63
300 to 399	13.62	16.05	7.95	8.65	8.11	0.00	9.15	11.71	4.02	3.84	8.37	0.00
400 to 499	13.86	16.93	6.87	7.72	6.07	0.00	11.91	15.80	4.46	4.40	8.06	0.00
500 to 599	11.72	14.24	5.85	6.63	5.93	0.00	12.28	16.19	4.64	4.62	9.63	0.00
600 to 699	8.64	10.35	4.91	5.54	3.71	0.00	10.70	13.90	4.62	4.57	7.13	0.00
700 to 799	6.14	7.06	4.23	4.87	3.21	0.00	8.78	10.94	4.59	4.64	7.10	0.00
800 to 999	6.70	6.94	6.70	7.76	3.87	0.00	11.36	12.74	8.69	8.84	10.13	0.00
1,000 to 1,499	5.47	3.52	11.60	13.37	3.68	0.00	12.53	8.47	20.74	20.97	13.08	0.00
1,500 to 1,999	2.04	0.29	7.38	8.64	1.17	0.00	6.77	1.00	18.63	19.13	5.88	0.00
2,000 to 2,999	1.30	0.03	5.23	6.12	0.49	0.00	5.86	0.14	17.85	18.34	3.29	0.00
3,000 or more	0.27	#	0.97	1.14	0.51	0.00	1.87	0.02	4.84	4.95	8.44	0.00
Average enrollment[8]	522	481	689	785	337	61	522	481	689	785	337	61
2013–14												
Total	98,271	67,034	24,053	19,409	6,205	979	49,709,977	32,183,080	15,618,300	15,148,323	1,896,908	11,689
Percent[8]	100.00	100.00	100.00	100.00	100.00	100.00	100.00	100.00	100.00	100.00	100.00	100.00
Under 100	10.12	5.35	17.33	9.46	37.63	45.45	0.88	0.56	1.10	0.67	4.49	6.07
100 to 199	9.04	7.68	11.29	10.28	16.23	11.36	2.58	2.41	2.39	1.93	6.86	5.40
200 to 299	10.91	11.49	9.35	9.61	10.28	18.18	5.25	6.04	3.34	3.03	7.44	16.39
300 to 399	13.40	15.70	8.00	8.76	7.83	9.09	8.96	11.41	4.03	3.88	8.06	11.94
400 to 499	13.90	16.95	6.88	7.72	5.88	2.27	11.89	15.75	4.45	4.40	7.77	4.12
500 to 599	11.81	14.41	5.80	6.52	5.06	4.55	12.32	16.33	4.57	4.52	8.13	8.74
600 to 699	8.71	10.35	4.98	5.61	4.32	2.27	10.74	13.85	4.64	4.61	8.24	5.62
700 to 799	6.13	7.07	4.10	4.71	3.20	0.00	8.72	10.91	4.42	4.48	7.03	0.00
800 to 999	6.85	7.13	6.89	7.95	3.41	2.27	11.57	13.04	8.86	9.01	9.01	7.98
1,000 to 1,499	5.49	3.57	11.58	13.33	3.84	2.27	12.52	8.56	20.54	20.83	13.66	10.77
1,500 to 1,999	2.04	0.29	7.44	8.64	1.25	0.00	6.73	0.99	18.61	19.03	6.35	0.00
2,000 to 2,999	1.33	0.03	5.37	6.27	0.55	2.27	5.95	0.13	18.19	18.70	3.92	22.96
3,000 or more	0.27	#	0.98	1.13	0.52	0.00	1.88	0.02	4.86	4.91	9.05	0.00
Average enrollment[8]	525	483	694	788	339	266	525	483	694	788	339	266

#Rounds to zero.
[1]Totals differ from those reported in other tables because this table represents data reported by schools rather than by states or school districts. Percentage distribution and average enrollment calculations exclude data for schools not reporting enrollment.
[2]Includes elementary, secondary, combined elementary/secondary, and other schools.
[3]Includes schools beginning with grade 6 or below and with no grade higher than 8.
[4]Includes schools with no grade lower than 7.
[5]Includes schools beginning with grade 6 or below and ending with grade 9 or above.
[6]Includes special education, alternative, and other schools not reported by grade span.

[7]Excludes special education schools, vocational schools, and alternative schools.
[8]Data are for schools reporting enrollments greater than zero. Enrollments greater than zero were reported for 94,743 out of 98,328 schools in 2011–12, 94,771 out of 98,454 in 2012–13, and 94,758 out of 98,271 in 2013–14.
NOTE: Detail may not sum to totals because of rounding.
SOURCE: U.S. Department of Education, National Center for Education Statistics, Common Core of Data (CCD), "Public Elementary/Secondary School Universe Survey," 2011–12, 2012–13, 2013–14. (This table was prepared September 2015.)

Table 216.45. Average enrollment and percentage distribution of public elementary and secondary schools, by level, type, and enrollment size: Selected years, 1982–83 through 2013–14

Year	Average enrollment in schools, by level and type						Percentage distribution of schools, by enrollment size							
	Total[1]	Elementary[2]	Secondary[3]		Combined elementary/ secondary[4]	Other[5]	Under 200	200 to 299	300 to 399	400 to 499	500 to 599	600 to 699	700 to 999	1,000 or more
			All schools	Regular schools[6]										
1	2	3	4	5	6	7	8	9	10	11	12	13	14	15
1982–83...............	478	399	719	—	478	142	21.9	13.8	15.5	13.1	10.2	7.1	10.2	8.3
1983–84...............	480	401	720	—	475	145	21.7	13.7	15.5	13.2	10.2	7.1	10.3	8.3
1984–85...............	482	403	721	—	476	146	21.5	13.6	15.5	13.2	10.3	7.1	10.4	8.4
1986–87...............	489	416	707	714	426	118	21.1	13.1	15.0	13.5	10.8	7.5	10.7	8.1
1987–88...............	490	424	695	711	420	122	20.3	12.9	14.9	13.8	11.1	7.8	11.2	8.0
1988–89...............	494	433	689	697	412	142	20.0	12.5	14.7	13.8	11.4	8.0	11.6	8.0
1989–90...............	493	441	669	689	402	142	19.8	12.2	14.5	13.7	11.5	8.3	12.0	7.9
1990–91...............	497	449	663	684	398	150	19.7	11.9	14.2	13.6	11.7	8.5	12.3	8.1
1991–92...............	507	458	677	717	407	152	19.1	11.7	14.1	13.5	11.8	8.6	12.8	8.5
1992–93...............	513	464	688	733	423	135	18.6	11.6	13.9	13.5	11.9	8.7	13.1	8.7
1993–94...............	518	468	693	748	418	136	18.6	11.5	13.6	13.5	11.7	8.8	13.3	9.0
1994–95...............	520	471	696	759	412	131	18.6	11.4	13.6	13.4	11.8	8.7	13.3	9.2
1995–96...............	525	476	703	771	401	136	18.5	11.2	13.5	13.4	11.8	8.8	13.4	9.4
1996–97...............	527	478	703	777	387	135	18.7	11.3	13.2	13.2	11.8	8.8	13.6	9.5
1997–98...............	525	478	699	779	374	121	19.3	11.2	13.1	13.3	11.6	8.6	13.4	9.6
1998–99...............	524	478	707	786	290	135	19.6	11.2	13.1	13.2	11.5	8.5	13.3	9.6
1999–2000...............	521	477	706	785	282	123	20.0	11.3	13.3	13.2	11.2	8.4	13.1	9.5
2000–01...............	519	477	714	795	274	136	20.4	11.4	13.2	13.3	11.0	8.2	12.9	9.6
2001–02...............	520	477	718	807	270	138	20.5	11.5	13.3	13.1	10.9	8.1	12.7	9.7
2002–03...............	519	476	720	813	265	136	20.7	11.6	13.4	13.0	10.9	8.1	12.4	9.8
2003–04...............	521	476	722	816	269	142	20.7	11.6	13.5	13.2	10.8	8.0	12.3	9.9
2004–05...............	521	474	713	815	298	143	20.7	11.6	13.5	13.2	10.8	8.1	12.2	9.9
2005–06...............	521	473	709	819	318	128	20.7	11.5	13.6	13.2	11.0	8.1	12.2	9.8
2006–07...............	521	473	711	818	325	138	20.3	11.5	13.8	13.4	11.0	8.2	12.2	9.6
2007–08...............	516	469	704	816	292	136	20.4	11.5	13.9	13.6	11.1	8.1	12.0	9.3
2008–09...............	517	470	704	807	308	177	20.0	11.4	13.8	13.9	11.3	8.3	12.2	9.1
2009–10...............	516	473	692	796	300	191	20.0	11.3	13.7	13.9	11.4	8.5	12.3	9.0
2010–11...............	517	475	684	790	343	57	19.8	11.0	13.9	13.9	11.5	8.5	12.5	9.0
2011–12...............	520	479	690	788	322	84	19.4	11.0	13.8	13.9	11.7	8.6	12.7	9.0
2012–13...............	522	481	689	785	337	61	19.3	10.9	13.6	13.9	11.7	8.6	12.8	9.1
2013–14...............	525	483	694	788	339	266	19.2	10.9	13.4	13.9	11.8	8.7	13.0	9.1

—Not available.
[1]Includes elementary, secondary, combined elementary/secondary, and other schools.
[2]Includes schools beginning with grade 6 or below and with no grade higher than 8.
[3]Includes schools with no grade lower than 7.
[4]Includes schools beginning with grade 6 or below and ending with grade 9 or above.
[5]Includes special education, alternative, and other schools not reported by grade span.
[6]Excludes special education schools, vocational schools, and alternative schools.

NOTE: Data reflect reports by schools rather than by states or school districts. Percentage distribution and average enrollment calculations include data only for schools reporting enrollments greater than zero. Enrollments greater than zero were reported for 94,758 out of 98,271 schools in 2013–14. Detail may not sum to totals because of rounding.
SOURCE: U.S. Department of Education, National Center for Education Statistics, Common Core of Data (CCD), "Public Elementary/Secondary School Universe Survey," 1982–83 through 2013–14. (This table was prepared September 2015.)

Table 216.50. Number and percentage distribution of public elementary and secondary school students, by percentage of minority enrollment in the school and student's racial/ethnic group: Selected years, fall 1995 through fall 2013

Year and racial/ethnic group	Number of students in racial/ethnic group, by percent minority enrollment in the school							Percentage distribution of students in racial/ethnic group, by percent minority enrollment in the school						
	Total	Less than 10 percent	10 to 24 percent	25 to 49 percent	50 to 74 percent	75 to 89 percent	90 percent or more	Total	Less than 10 percent	10 to 24 percent	25 to 49 percent	50 to 74 percent	75 to 89 percent	90 percent or more
1	2	3	4	5	6	7	8	9	10	11	12	13	14	15
Total, 1995	44,424,467	14,508,573	8,182,484	8,261,110	5,467,784	2,876,302	5,128,214	100.0	32.7	18.4	18.6	12.3	6.5	11.5
White	28,736,961	13,939,633	6,812,196	5,246,785	2,094,440	499,884	144,023	100.0	48.5	23.7	18.3	7.3	1.7	0.5
Minority	15,687,506	568,940	1,370,288	3,014,325	3,373,344	2,376,418	4,984,191	100.0	3.6	8.7	19.2	21.5	15.1	31.8
Black	7,510,678	198,386	598,716	1,588,850	1,622,448	941,335	2,560,943	100.0	2.6	8.0	21.2	21.6	12.5	34.1
Hispanic	6,016,293	174,140	415,761	932,949	1,289,184	1,099,109	2,105,150	100.0	2.9	6.9	15.5	21.4	18.3	35.0
Asian/Pacific Islander	1,656,787	142,886	259,335	367,888	379,110	297,680	209,888	100.0	8.6	15.7	22.2	22.9	18.0	12.7
American Indian/Alaska Native	503,748	53,528	96,476	124,638	82,602	38,294	108,210	100.0	10.6	19.2	24.7	16.4	7.6	21.5
Total, 2000	46,120,425	12,761,478	8,736,252	8,760,300	6,013,131	3,472,083	6,377,181	100.0	27.7	18.9	19.0	13.0	7.5	13.8
White	28,146,613	12,218,862	7,271,285	5,566,681	2,303,106	596,478	190,201	100.0	43.4	25.8	19.8	8.2	2.1	0.7
Minority	17,973,812	542,616	1,464,967	3,193,619	3,710,025	2,875,605	6,186,980	100.0	3.0	8.2	17.8	20.6	16.0	34.4
Black	7,854,032	178,185	561,488	1,485,130	1,652,393	1,043,907	2,932,929	100.0	2.3	7.1	18.9	21.0	13.3	37.3
Hispanic	7,649,728	181,685	505,612	1,121,809	1,542,982	1,432,639	2,865,001	100.0	2.4	6.6	14.7	20.2	18.7	37.5
Asian/Pacific Islander	1,924,875	132,813	295,437	441,769	423,175	353,395	278,286	100.0	6.9	15.3	23.0	22.0	18.4	14.5
American Indian/Alaska Native	545,177	49,933	102,430	144,911	91,475	45,664	110,764	100.0	9.2	18.8	26.6	16.8	8.4	20.3
Total, 2005	48,584,980	10,711,307	9,283,783	9,865,121	6,839,850	4,149,802	7,735,117	100.0	22.0	19.1	20.3	14.1	8.5	15.9
White	27,742,612	10,208,608	7,720,632	6,259,485	2,604,846	707,603	241,438	100.0	36.8	27.8	22.6	9.4	2.6	0.9
Minority	20,842,368	502,699	1,563,151	3,605,636	4,235,004	3,442,199	7,493,679	100.0	2.4	7.5	17.3	20.3	16.5	36.0
Black	8,366,722	162,455	560,928	1,513,020	1,752,207	1,176,649	3,201,463	100.0	1.9	6.7	18.1	20.9	14.1	38.3
Hispanic	9,638,712	182,039	581,533	1,388,496	1,873,877	1,803,567	3,809,200	100.0	1.9	6.0	14.4	19.4	18.7	39.5
Asian/Pacific Islander	2,242,628	115,084	319,524	543,952	496,515	406,788	360,765	100.0	5.1	14.2	24.3	22.1	18.1	16.1
American Indian/Alaska Native	594,306	43,121	101,166	160,168	112,405	55,195	122,251	100.0	7.3	17.0	27.0	18.9	9.3	20.6
Total, 2010	49,212,031	7,395,549	9,177,649	11,236,328	7,904,340	4,718,126	8,780,039	100.0	15.0	18.6	22.8	16.1	9.6	17.8
White	25,801,021	6,987,898	7,614,557	7,097,284	3,003,599	808,637	289,046	100.0	27.1	29.5	27.5	11.6	3.1	1.1
Minority	23,411,010	407,651	1,563,092	4,139,044	4,900,741	3,909,489	8,490,993	100.0	1.7	6.7	17.7	20.9	16.7	36.3
Black	7,873,809	95,108	415,807	1,335,674	1,697,727	1,236,333	3,093,160	100.0	1.2	5.3	17.0	21.6	15.7	39.3
Hispanic	11,367,157	142,927	583,019	1,654,084	2,238,071	2,063,492	4,685,564	100.0	1.3	5.1	14.6	19.7	18.2	41.2
Asian	2,281,908	63,974	259,910	585,447	552,633	390,731	429,213	100.0	2.8	11.4	25.7	24.2	17.1	18.8
Pacific Islander	169,678	4,958	13,772	27,478	32,241	41,652	49,577	100.0	2.9	8.1	16.2	19.0	24.5	29.2
American Indian/Alaska Native	561,126	26,066	77,990	157,300	116,787	58,476	124,507	100.0	4.6	13.9	28.0	20.8	10.4	22.2
Two or more races	1,157,332	74,618	212,594	379,061	263,282	118,805	108,972	100.0	6.4	18.4	32.8	22.7	10.3	9.4
Total, 2011	49,246,537	6,943,209	9,090,845	11,325,084	8,087,862	4,909,344	8,890,193	100.0	14.1	18.5	23.0	16.4	10.0	18.1
White	25,464,162	6,549,257	7,535,852	7,154,879	3,086,247	842,317	295,610	100.0	25.7	29.6	28.1	12.1	3.3	1.2
Minority	23,782,375	393,952	1,554,993	4,170,205	5,001,615	4,067,027	8,594,583	100.0	1.7	6.5	17.5	21.0	17.1	36.1
Black	7,782,146	85,682	393,118	1,302,027	1,686,653	1,255,240	3,059,426	100.0	1.1	5.1	16.7	21.7	16.1	39.3
Hispanic	11,693,788	141,593	594,874	1,678,320	2,302,100	2,161,819	4,815,082	100.0	1.2	5.1	14.4	19.7	18.5	41.2
Asian	2,321,362	58,414	249,943	587,291	570,921	415,832	438,961	100.0	2.5	10.8	25.3	24.6	17.9	18.9
Pacific Islander	177,871	5,170	13,635	27,828	34,546	42,851	53,841	100.0	2.9	7.7	15.6	19.4	24.1	30.3
American Indian/Alaska Native	541,986	23,215	69,953	152,088	112,568	58,106	126,056	100.0	4.3	12.9	28.1	20.8	10.7	23.3
Two or more races	1,265,222	79,878	233,470	422,651	294,827	133,179	101,217	100.0	6.3	18.5	33.4	23.3	10.5	8.0
Total, 2012	49,460,399	6,512,145	9,106,399	11,465,619	8,280,130	4,994,550	9,101,556	100.0	13.2	18.4	23.2	16.7	10.1	18.4
White	25,238,825	6,136,381	7,549,183	7,233,482	3,153,892	859,415	306,472	100.0	24.3	29.9	28.7	12.5	3.4	1.2
Minority	24,221,574	375,764	1,557,216	4,232,137	5,126,238	4,135,135	8,795,084	100.0	1.6	6.4	17.5	21.2	17.1	36.3
Black	7,745,244	76,614	377,613	1,275,975	1,690,994	1,260,621	3,063,427	100.0	1.0	4.9	16.5	21.8	16.3	39.6
Hispanic	12,028,116	137,254	601,847	1,721,620	2,374,944	2,210,057	4,982,394	100.0	1.1	5.0	14.3	19.7	18.4	41.4
Asian	2,358,015	52,671	244,691	595,541	589,235	417,742	458,135	100.0	2.2	10.4	25.3	25.0	17.7	19.4
Pacific Islander	179,353	4,899	13,819	28,583	34,480	40,876	56,696	100.0	2.7	7.7	15.9	19.2	22.8	31.6
American Indian/Alaska Native	528,024	20,847	65,566	147,080	110,908	59,210	124,413	100.0	3.9	12.4	27.9	21.0	11.2	23.6
Two or more races	1,382,822	83,479	253,680	463,338	325,677	146,629	110,019	100.0	6.0	18.3	33.5	23.6	10.6	8.0
Total, 2013	49,700,391	6,121,290	9,029,047	11,604,239	8,505,389	5,179,379	9,261,047	100.0	12.3	18.2	23.3	17.1	10.4	18.6
White	25,002,213	5,761,258	7,482,233	7,319,117	3,241,142	886,628	311,835	100.0	23.0	29.9	29.3	13.0	3.5	1.2
Minority	24,698,178	360,032	1,546,814	4,285,122	5,264,247	4,292,751	8,949,212	100.0	1.5	6.3	17.3	21.3	17.4	36.2
Black	7,743,485	69,458	360,023	1,251,977	1,696,184	1,298,309	3,067,534	100.0	0.9	4.6	16.2	21.9	16.8	39.6
Hispanic	12,363,677	132,910	603,028	1,755,809	2,448,589	2,304,721	5,118,620	100.0	1.1	4.9	14.2	19.8	18.6	41.4
Asian	2,401,305	48,171	238,017	603,725	613,063	430,727	467,602	100.0	2.0	9.9	25.1	25.5	17.9	19.5
Pacific Islander	175,236	4,200	13,249	28,616	35,507	39,899	53,765	100.0	2.4	7.6	16.3	20.3	22.8	30.7
American Indian/Alaska Native	516,705	18,685	61,576	142,536	110,727	59,304	123,877	100.0	3.6	11.9	27.6	21.4	11.5	24.0
Two or more races	1,497,770	86,608	270,921	502,459	360,177	159,791	117,814	100.0	5.8	18.1	33.5	24.0	10.7	7.9

NOTE: Data reflect racial/ethnic data reported by schools. Because some schools do not report complete racial/ethnic data, totals may differ from figures in other tables. Excludes 1995 data for Idaho and 2000 data for Tennessee because racial/ethnic data were not reported. Race categories exclude persons of Hispanic ethnicity. Detail may not sum to totals because of rounding.

SOURCE: U.S. Department of Education, National Center for Education Statistics, Common Core of Data (CCD), "Public Elementary/Secondary School Universe Survey," 1995–96 through 2013–14. (This table was prepared January 2016.)

Table 216.55. Number and percentage distribution of public elementary and secondary school students, by percentage of student's racial/ethnic group enrolled in the school and student's racial/ethnic group: Selected years, fall 1995 through fall 2013

Year and racial/ ethnic group	Total	Less than 10 percent of group	10 to 24 percent of group	25 to 49 percent of group	50 to 74 percent of group	75 to 89 percent of group	90 percent or more of group	Total	Less than 10 percent of group	10 to 24 percent of group	25 to 49 percent of group	50 to 74 percent of group	75 to 89 percent of group	90 percent or more of group
1	2	3	4	5	6	7	8	9	10	11	12	13	14	15
1995														
White	28,736,961	143,787	498,649	2,084,689	5,244,015	6,813,804	13,952,017	100.0	0.5	1.7	7.3	18.2	23.7	48.6
Black	7,510,678	657,403	1,119,556	1,873,303	1,386,802	811,898	1,661,716	100.0	8.8	14.9	24.9	18.5	10.8	22.1
Hispanic	6,016,293	646,364	847,792	1,359,649	1,360,020	874,878	927,590	100.0	10.7	14.1	22.6	22.6	14.5	15.4
Asian/Pacific Islander	1,656,787	703,101	435,495	301,984	135,001	67,558	13,648	100.0	42.4	26.3	18.2	8.1	4.1	0.8
American Indian/ Alaska Native	503,748	223,244	75,019	63,070	39,200	15,084	88,131	100.0	44.3	14.9	12.5	7.8	3.0	17.5
2000														
White	28,146,613	189,779	595,137	2,294,232	5,556,108	7,279,301	12,232,056	100.0	0.7	2.1	8.2	19.7	25.9	43.5
Black	7,854,032	735,459	1,199,865	1,899,982	1,366,363	871,399	1,780,964	100.0	9.4	15.3	24.2	17.4	11.1	22.7
Hispanic	7,649,728	738,509	1,054,396	1,696,944	1,739,038	1,134,466	1,286,375	100.0	9.7	13.8	22.2	22.7	14.8	16.8
Asian/Pacific Islander	1,924,875	799,220	524,279	331,576	171,739	81,461	16,600	100.0	41.5	27.2	17.2	8.9	4.2	0.9
American Indian/ Alaska Native	545,177	251,983	81,119	75,831	39,944	15,363	80,937	100.0	46.2	14.9	13.9	7.3	2.8	14.8
2005														
White	27,742,612	240,614	705,300	2,596,310	6,256,109	7,718,175	10,226,104	100.0	0.9	2.5	9.4	22.6	27.8	36.9
Black	8,366,722	849,399	1,396,670	2,004,856	1,453,759	884,663	1,777,375	100.0	10.2	16.7	24.0	17.4	10.6	21.2
Hispanic	9,638,712	848,160	1,316,558	2,071,303	2,218,616	1,545,322	1,638,753	100.0	8.8	13.7	21.5	23.0	16.0	17.0
Asian/Pacific Islander	2,242,628	925,411	616,762	363,562	214,304	100,845	21,744	100.0	41.3	27.5	16.2	9.6	4.5	1.0
American Indian/ Alaska Native	594,306	276,846	86,978	84,665	43,272	21,275	81,270	100.0	46.6	14.6	14.2	7.3	3.6	13.7
2010														
White	25,801,021	288,136	807,107	2,991,928	7,090,581	7,620,071	7,003,198	100.0	1.1	3.1	11.6	27.5	29.5	27.1
Black	7,873,809	904,777	1,453,068	1,907,158	1,328,164	859,843	1,420,799	100.0	11.5	18.5	24.2	16.9	10.9	18.0
Hispanic	11,367,157	896,796	1,603,546	2,473,080	2,657,108	1,791,161	1,945,466	100.0	7.9	14.1	21.8	23.4	15.8	17.1
Asian	2,281,908	944,657	633,149	431,446	219,381	43,509	9,766	100.0	41.4	27.7	18.9	9.6	1.9	0.4
Pacific Islander	169,678	104,646	15,170	27,558	14,860	5,146	2,298	100.0	61.7	8.9	16.2	8.8	3.0	1.4
American Indian/ Alaska Native	561,126	276,859	76,874	78,978	38,349	21,156	68,910	100.0	49.3	13.7	14.1	6.8	3.8	12.3
Two or more races	1,157,332	996,181	128,813	15,347	6,709	3,286	6,996	100.0	86.1	11.1	1.3	0.6	0.3	0.6
2011														
White	25,464,162	294,998	840,764	3,072,182	7,153,778	7,543,427	6,559,013	100.0	1.2	3.3	12.1	28.1	29.6	25.8
Black	7,782,146	909,399	1,448,983	1,912,335	1,301,165	864,856	1,345,408	100.0	11.7	18.6	24.6	16.7	11.1	17.3
Hispanic	11,693,788	909,247	1,658,024	2,543,266	2,720,777	1,877,108	1,985,366	100.0	7.8	14.2	21.7	23.3	16.1	17.0
Asian	2,321,362	946,520	644,479	441,656	232,408	43,530	12,769	100.0	40.8	27.8	19.0	10.0	1.9	0.6
Pacific Islander	177,871	112,805	14,759	28,211	15,688	4,471	1,937	100.0	63.4	8.3	15.9	8.8	2.5	1.1
American Indian/ Alaska Native	541,986	267,993	72,148	77,142	36,010	22,095	66,598	100.0	49.4	13.3	14.2	6.6	4.1	12.3
Two or more races	1,265,222	1,107,727	139,250	8,444	3,484	5,324	993	100.0	87.6	11.0	0.7	0.3	0.4	0.1
2012														
White	25,238,825	306,146	857,049	3,139,878	7,229,221	7,552,960	6,153,571	100.0	1.2	3.4	12.4	28.6	29.9	24.4
Black	7,745,244	912,607	1,458,854	1,902,995	1,326,005	854,903	1,289,880	100.0	11.8	18.8	24.6	17.1	11.0	16.7
Hispanic	12,028,116	918,483	1,709,042	2,610,291	2,818,279	1,916,973	2,055,048	100.0	7.6	14.2	21.7	23.4	15.9	17.1
Asian	2,358,015	954,868	649,405	460,219	235,915	44,832	12,776	100.0	40.5	27.5	19.5	10.0	1.9	0.5
Pacific Islander	179,353	115,282	14,614	28,687	14,860	4,542	1,368	100.0	64.3	8.1	16.0	8.3	2.5	0.8
American Indian/ Alaska Native	528,024	260,268	70,477	77,044	33,558	20,767	65,910	100.0	49.3	13.3	14.6	6.4	3.9	12.5
Two or more races	1,382,822	1,205,382	164,423	7,702	1,229	3,114	972	100.0	87.2	11.9	0.6	0.1	0.2	0.1
2013														
White	25,002,213	311,182	883,277	3,231,085	7,315,466	7,487,804	5,773,399	100.0	1.2	3.5	12.9	29.3	29.9	23.1
Black	7,743,485	911,504	1,477,015	1,921,631	1,336,048	860,336	1,236,951	100.0	11.8	19.1	24.8	17.3	11.1	16.0
Hispanic	12,363,677	919,255	1,750,152	2,690,698	2,918,707	1,969,011	2,115,854	100.0	7.4	14.2	21.8	23.6	15.9	17.1
Asian	2,401,305	956,000	661,825	479,668	243,021	48,169	12,622	100.0	39.8	27.6	20.0	10.1	2.0	0.5
Pacific Islander	175,236	112,227	14,772	30,051	12,430	5,136	620	100.0	64.0	8.4	17.1	7.1	2.9	0.4
American Indian/ Alaska Native	516,705	254,656	69,669	74,838	33,702	18,951	64,889	100.0	49.3	13.5	14.5	6.5	3.7	12.6
Two or more races	1,497,770	1,290,200	195,092	8,046	2,822	1,397	213	100.0	86.1	13.0	0.5	0.2	0.1	#

#Rounds to zero.
NOTE: Data reflect racial/ethnic data reported by schools. Because some schools do not report complete racial/ethnic data, totals may differ from figures in other tables. Excludes 1995 data for Idaho and 2000 data for Tennessee because racial/ethnic data were not reported. Race categories exclude persons of Hispanic ethnicity. Detail may not sum to totals because of rounding.
SOURCE: U.S. Department of Education, National Center for Education Statistics, Common Core of Data (CCD), "Public Elementary/Secondary School Universe Survey," 1995–96 through 2013–14. (This table was prepared January 2016.)

Table 216.60. Number and percentage distribution of public school students, by percentage of students in school who are eligible for free or reduced-price lunch, school level, locale, and student race/ethnicity: 2013–14

School level, locale, and student race/ethnicity	Number of students, by percent of students in school eligible for free or reduced-price lunch						Percentage distribution of students, by percent of students in school eligible for free or reduced-price lunch					
	Total[1]	0 to 25.0 percent	25.1 to 50.0 percent	50.1 to 75.0 percent	More than 75.0 percent	Missing/ school does not participate	Total[1]	0 to 25.0 percent	25.1 to 50.0 percent	50.1 to 75.0 percent	More than 75.0 percent	Missing/ school does not participate
1	2	3	4	5	6	7	8	9	10	11	12	13
Total[2]	49,700,391	10,034,137	13,490,958	13,356,867	12,343,741	474,688	100.0	20.2	27.1	26.9	24.8	1.0
White	25,002,213	7,301,646	8,960,889	6,541,027	1,885,498	313,153	100.0	29.2	35.8	26.2	7.5	1.3
Black	7,743,485	512,623	1,259,165	2,261,276	3,652,903	57,518	100.0	6.6	16.3	29.2	47.2	0.7
Hispanic	12,363,677	942,396	2,053,535	3,386,043	5,913,177	68,526	100.0	7.6	16.6	27.4	47.8	0.6
Asian	2,401,305	880,078	598,242	499,840	408,341	14,804	100.0	36.6	24.9	20.8	17.0	0.6
Pacific Islander	175,236	20,511	47,529	63,727	42,877	592	100.0	11.7	27.1	36.4	24.5	0.3
American Indian/ Alaska Native	516,705	42,312	112,860	171,850	182,777	6,906	100.0	8.2	21.8	33.3	35.4	1.3
Two or more races	1,497,770	334,571	458,738	433,104	258,168	13,189	100.0	22.3	30.6	28.9	17.2	0.9
School level[3]												
Elementary[4]	32,175,213	6,018,352	7,704,642	8,635,843	9,508,930	307,446	100.0	18.7	23.9	26.8	29.6	1.0
White	15,751,282	4,346,966	5,151,807	4,511,613	1,533,505	207,391	100.0	27.6	32.7	28.6	9.7	1.3
Black	5,043,598	273,226	675,159	1,304,427	2,753,907	36,879	100.0	5.4	13.4	25.9	54.6	0.7
Hispanic	8,344,356	564,016	1,151,154	2,056,521	4,530,456	42,209	100.0	6.8	13.8	24.6	54.3	0.5
Asian	1,542,059	578,232	350,545	302,863	302,864	7,555	100.0	37.5	22.7	19.6	19.6	0.5
Pacific Islander	110,748	11,644	24,699	40,143	33,945	317	100.0	10.5	22.3	36.2	30.7	0.3
American Indian/ Alaska Native	322,836	20,935	58,245	105,048	134,925	3,683	100.0	6.5	18.0	32.5	41.8	1.1
Two or more races	1,060,334	223,333	293,033	315,228	219,328	9,412	100.0	21.1	27.6	29.7	20.7	0.9
Secondary[5]	15,617,444	3,659,280	5,332,383	4,163,053	2,352,910	109,818	100.0	23.4	34.1	26.7	15.1	0.7
White	8,269,298	2,695,839	3,499,775	1,730,805	274,026	68,853	100.0	32.6	42.3	20.9	3.3	0.8
Black	2,341,741	211,470	544,303	853,299	718,123	14,546	100.0	9.0	23.2	36.4	30.7	0.6
Hispanic	3,604,199	343,316	832,614	1,212,456	1,196,949	18,864	100.0	9.5	23.1	33.6	33.2	0.5
Asian	797,676	284,628	232,735	183,865	92,575	3,873	100.0	35.7	29.2	23.1	11.6	0.5
Pacific Islander	56,269	7,656	21,128	20,677	6,657	151	100.0	13.6	37.5	36.7	11.8	0.3
American Indian/ Alaska Native	161,158	18,197	50,293	56,978	33,990	1,700	100.0	11.3	31.2	35.4	21.1	1.1
Two or more races	387,103	98,174	151,535	104,973	30,590	1,831	100.0	25.4	39.1	27.1	7.9	0.5
School locale												
City	15,114,922	1,791,693	2,913,971	3,785,675	6,504,136	119,447	100.0	11.9	19.3	25.0	43.0	0.8
White	4,527,499	1,071,551	1,534,934	1,214,590	654,696	51,728	100.0	23.7	33.9	26.8	14.5	1.1
Black	3,615,068	123,521	395,180	889,890	2,176,775	29,702	100.0	3.4	10.9	24.6	60.2	0.8
Hispanic	5,305,056	240,032	605,356	1,238,056	3,195,421	26,191	100.0	4.5	11.4	23.3	60.2	0.5
Asian	1,015,350	256,116	217,399	253,019	283,364	5,452	100.0	25.2	21.4	24.9	27.9	0.5
Pacific Islander	58,778	5,432	12,953	20,425	19,690	278	100.0	9.2	22.0	34.7	33.5	0.5
American Indian/ Alaska Native	109,831	10,176	24,126	30,327	43,628	1,574	100.0	9.3	22.0	27.6	39.7	1.4
Two or more races	483,340	84,865	124,023	139,368	130,562	4,522	100.0	17.6	25.7	28.8	27.0	0.9
Suburban	19,773,710	6,348,192	5,559,004	4,193,326	3,516,067	157,121	100.0	32.1	28.1	21.2	17.8	0.8
White	10,187,181	4,643,800	3,354,988	1,626,949	459,771	101,673	100.0	45.6	32.9	16.0	4.5	1.0
Black	2,699,895	322,694	628,336	851,530	879,443	17,892	100.0	12.0	23.3	31.5	32.6	0.7
Hispanic	4,902,880	579,961	999,072	1,330,180	1,969,636	24,031	100.0	11.8	20.4	27.1	40.2	0.5
Asian	1,185,234	565,708	313,550	191,845	106,161	7,970	100.0	47.7	26.5	16.2	9.0	0.7
Pacific Islander	74,107	12,703	24,457	22,824	13,990	133	100.0	17.1	33.0	30.8	18.9	0.2
American Indian/ Alaska Native	91,282	19,167	30,600	25,322	15,413	780	100.0	21.0	33.5	27.7	16.9	0.9
Two or more races	633,131	204,159	208,001	144,676	71,653	4,642	100.0	32.2	32.9	22.9	11.3	0.7
Town	5,680,267	421,943	1,829,156	2,276,395	1,071,025	81,748	100.0	7.4	32.2	40.1	18.9	1.4
White	3,679,384	357,329	1,477,785	1,472,132	310,858	61,280	100.0	9.7	40.2	40.0	8.4	1.7
Black	574,829	12,060	63,536	218,362	276,423	4,448	100.0	2.1	11.1	38.0	48.1	0.8
Hispanic	1,043,352	28,783	179,093	422,734	401,853	10,889	100.0	2.8	17.2	40.5	38.5	1.0
Asian	73,932	7,992	26,247	28,864	10,215	614	100.0	10.8	35.5	39.0	13.8	0.8
Pacific Islander	24,429	608	5,558	13,628	4,549	86	100.0	2.5	22.8	55.8	18.6	0.4
American Indian/ Alaska Native	124,378	5,073	27,656	49,931	39,308	2,410	100.0	4.1	22.2	40.1	31.6	1.9
Two or more races	159,963	10,098	49,281	70,744	27,819	2,021	100.0	6.3	30.8	44.2	17.4	1.3
Rural	9,131,492	1,472,309	3,188,827	3,101,471	1,252,513	116,372	100.0	16.1	34.9	34.0	13.7	1.3
White	6,608,149	1,228,966	2,593,182	2,227,356	460,173	98,472	100.0	18.6	39.2	33.7	7.0	1.5
Black	853,693	54,348	172,113	301,494	320,262	5,476	100.0	6.4	20.2	35.3	37.5	0.6
Hispanic	1,112,389	93,620	270,014	395,073	346,267	7,415	100.0	8.4	24.3	35.5	31.1	0.7
Asian	126,789	50,262	41,046	26,112	8,601	768	100.0	39.6	32.4	20.6	6.8	0.6
Pacific Islander	17,922	1,768	4,561	6,850	4,648	95	100.0	9.9	25.4	38.2	25.9	0.5
American Indian/ Alaska Native	191,214	7,896	30,478	66,270	84,428	2,142	100.0	4.1	15.9	34.7	44.2	1.1
Two or more races	221,336	35,449	77,433	78,316	28,134	2,004	100.0	16.0	35.0	35.4	12.7	0.9

[1]Includes students enrolled in schools that did not report free or reduced-price lunch eligibility.
[2]Excludes 9,586 students whose race/ethnicity was not available. Includes students who attended combined elementary/secondary schools and schools not reported by grade span, which are not shown separately.
[3]Combined elementary/secondary schools and schools not reported by grade span are not shown separately.
[4]Includes schools beginning with grade 6 or below and with no grade higher than 8.
[5]Includes schools with no grade lower than 7.
NOTE: Students with household incomes under 185 percent of the poverty threshold are eligible for free or reduced price lunch under the National School Lunch Program (NSLP). In addition, some groups of children—such as foster children, children participating in the Head Start and Migrant Education programs, and children receiving services under the Runaway and Homeless Youth Act—are assumed to be categorically eligible to participate in the NSLP. Also, under the Community Eligibility option, some nonpoor children who attend school in a low-income area may participate if the district decides that it would be more efficient to provide free lunch to all children in the school. For more information, see http://www.fns.usda.gov/nslp/national-school-lunch-program-nslp. Race categories exclude persons of Hispanic ethnicity. Detail may not sum to totals because of rounding.
SOURCE: U.S. Department of Education, National Center for Education Statistics, Common Core of Data (CCD), "Public Elementary/Secondary School Universe Survey," 2013–14. (This table was prepared September 2015.)

Table 216.70. Public elementary and secondary schools, by level, type, and state or jurisdiction: 1990–91, 2000–01, 2010–11, and 2013–14

State or jurisdiction	Total, all schools, 1990–91	Total, all schools, 2000–01	Total, all schools, 2010–11	Total, all schools	Elementary[1]	Secondary[2]	Combined elementary/secondary[3] Total	Prekindergarten, kindergarten, or 1st grade to grade 12	Other schools ending with grade 12	Other combined schools	Other[4]	Alternative[5]	Special education[5]	One-teacher schools[5]
1	2	3	4	5	6	7	8	9	10	11	12	13	14	15
United States	84,538	93,273	98,817	98,271	67,034	24,053	6,205	3,123	2,484	598	979	5,698	2,010	193
Alabama	1,297	1,517	1,600	1,637	990	434	182	118	60	4	31	119	44	1
Alaska	498	515	509	507	199	83	225	210	12	3	0	61	3	7
Arizona	1,049	1,724	2,265	2,252	1,335	734	157	83	50	24	26	61	21	3
Arkansas	1,098	1,138	1,110	1,112	718	368	24	6	11	7	2	9	4	0
California	7,913	8,773	10,124	10,276	6,954	2,606	601	452	135	14	115	1,238	151	36
Colorado	1,344	1,632	1,796	1,832	1,300	389	143	61	67	15	0	92	6	2
Connecticut	985	1,248	1,157	1,152	815	286	41	9	19	13	10	50	44	0
Delaware	173	191	214	219	159	36	19	11	6	2	5	7	19	0
District of Columbia	181	198	228	225	166	39	11	4	4	3	9	11	5	0
Florida	2,516	3,316	4,131	4,295	2,829	695	631	245	367	19	140	398	186	1
Georgia	1,734	1,946	2,449	2,379	1,776	457	61	16	29	16	85	72	60	1
Hawaii	235	261	289	288	208	52	28	24	3	1	0	1	1	1
Idaho	582	673	748	706	449	197	57	38	15	4	3	51	13	8
Illinois	4,239	4,342	4,361	4,204	3,107	937	159	46	100	13	1	144	137	0
Indiana	1,915	1,976	1,936	1,928	1,370	460	98	56	32	10	0	9	27	0
Iowa	1,588	1,534	1,436	1,382	969	371	42	6	36	0	0	26	7	3
Kansas	1,477	1,430	1,378	1,346	943	352	49	13	35	1	2	2	10	0
Kentucky	1,400	1,526	1,554	1,565	983	422	142	40	98	4	18	152	5	0
Louisiana	1,533	1,530	1,471	1,412	930	281	117	67	39	11	84	97	30	0
Maine	747	714	631	619	453	149	13	10	2	1	4	0	3	3
Maryland	1,220	1,383	1,449	1,442	1,130	246	51	20	24	7	15	54	38	1
Massachusetts	1,842	1,905	1,829	1,865	1,430	382	47	12	30	5	6	22	22	1
Michigan	3,313	3,998	3,877	3,538	2,213	939	378	203	157	18	8	310	183	4
Minnesota	1,590	2,362	2,392	2,414	1,280	836	297	144	140	13	1	479	279	0
Mississippi	972	1,030	1,083	1,066	626	325	106	65	40	1	9	62	4	0
Missouri	2,199	2,368	2,410	2,410	1,591	642	157	73	82	2	20	104	63	0
Montana	900	879	827	824	485	339	0	0	0	0	0	4	2	62
Nebraska	1,506	1,326	1,096	1,102	730	307	13	11	1	1	52	52	26	4
Nevada	354	511	645	653	480	132	41	13	28	0	0	35	13	12
New Hampshire	439	526	480	482	376	106	0	0	0	0	0	0	0	0
New Jersey	2,272	2,410	2,607	2,508	1,956	494	56	34	18	4	2	23	58	0
New Mexico	681	765	862	880	611	238	30	9	18	3	1	40	8	0
New York	4,010	4,336	4,757	4,801	3,307	1,130	330	128	140	62	34	30	128	0
North Carolina	1,955	2,207	2,567	2,588	1,899	536	146	60	69	17	7	82	26	0
North Dakota	663	579	516	512	297	183	0	0	0	0	32	0	33	5
Ohio	3,731	3,916	3,758	3,656	2,488	1,013	150	49	63	38	5	4	50	1
Oklahoma	1,880	1,821	1,785	1,789	1,222	561	6	2	4	0	0	4	4	0
Oregon	1,199	1,273	1,296	1,246	882	277	87	57	29	1	0	39	1	9
Pennsylvania	3,260	3,252	3,233	3,068	2,165	805	96	47	43	6	2	10	5	0
Rhode Island	309	328	317	304	224	73	6	3	2	1	1	5	1	0
South Carolina	1,097	1,127	1,214	1,243	914	288	34	11	17	6	7	20	9	0
South Dakota	802	769	710	699	437	239	23	9	13	1	0	31	9	12
Tennessee	1,543	1,624	1,784	1,855	1,387	384	82	37	42	3	2	23	16	0
Texas	5,991	7,519	8,732	8,748	5,983	2,097	663	294	215	154	5	977	21	0
Utah	714	793	1,016	1,006	649	261	96	43	8	45	0	26	69	6
Vermont	397	393	320	316	232	68	16	11	5	0	0	1	0	1
Virginia	1,811	1,969	2,175	2,166	1,495	406	34	24	9	1	231	187	53	0
Washington	1,936	2,305	2,338	2,381	1,504	617	260	158	72	30	0	325	96	0
West Virginia	1,015	840	757	758	568	124	66	43	18	5	0	30	3	0
Wisconsin	2,018	2,182	2,238	2,249	1,576	560	109	36	71	2	4	95	11	3
Wyoming	415	393	360	366	244	97	25	12	6	7	0	24	3	6
Bureau of Indian Education	—	189	173	174	110	19	45	39	3	3	0	0	0	—
DoD, domestic and overseas	—	227	191	191	141	35	14	10	4	0	1	0	0	—
Other jurisdictions														
American Samoa	30	31	28	28	22	6	0	0	0	0	0	0	0	—
Guam	35	38	40	38	32	4	2	1	0	1	0	0	0	0
Northern Marianas	26	29	30	29	22	6	0	0	0	0	1	0	0	0
Puerto Rico	1,619	1,543	1,473	1,452	852	398	171	4	1	166	31	10	23	0
U.S. Virgin Islands	33	36	32	31	22	9	0	0	0	0	0	0	0	0

—Not available.
[1]Includes schools beginning with grade 6 or below and with no grade higher than 8.
[2]Includes schools with no grade lower than 7.
[3]Includes schools beginning with grade 6 or below and ending with grade 9 or above.
[4]Includes schools not reported by grade span.
[5]Schools are also included under elementary, secondary, combined, or other as appropriate.
NOTE: DoD = Department of Defense.
SOURCE: U.S. Department of Education, National Center for Education Statistics, Common Core of Data (CCD), "Public Elementary/Secondary School Universe Survey," 1990–91, 2000–01, 2010–11, and 2013–14. (This table was prepared September 2015.)

Table 216.75. Public elementary schools, by grade span, average school enrollment, and state or jurisdiction: 2013–14

State or jurisdiction	Total, all elementary schools	Total, all regular elementary schools[1]	Schools, by grade span						Average school enrollment[2]	
			Prekindergarten, kindergarten, or 1st grade to grades 3 or 4	Prekindergarten, kindergarten, or 1st grade to grade 5	Prekindergarten, kindergarten, or 1st grade to grade 6	Prekindergarten, kindergarten, or 1st grade to grade 8	Grade 4, 5, or 6 to grade 6, 7, or 8	Other grade spans	All elementary schools	Regular elementary schools[1]
1	2	3	4	5	6	7	8	9	10	11
United States	67,034	65,948	5,090	25,309	10,213	6,553	13,322	6,547	483	488
Alabama	990	977	91	331	141	74	229	124	496	499
Alaska	199	190	2	45	89	26	25	12	333	329
Arizona	1,335	1,316	44	243	355	453	167	73	516	518
Arkansas	718	715	116	164	156	9	161	112	431	432
California	6,954	6,765	134	2,443	2,124	1,006	1,045	202	559	569
Colorado	1,300	1,295	28	617	212	121	248	74	441	441
Connecticut	815	805	93	251	72	99	153	147	428	432
Delaware	159	154	15	78	6	9	37	14	560	570
District of Columbia	166	164	11	68	6	32	26	23	347	345
Florida	2,829	2,765	33	1,675	138	255	593	135	656	668
Georgia	1,776	1,774	38	1,057	30	36	463	152	676	677
Hawaii	208	208	0	84	86	9	28	1	573	573
Idaho	449	439	35	152	129	26	76	31	410	415
Illinois	3,107	3,067	288	782	312	664	583	478	437	441
Indiana	1,370	1,369	174	467	310	42	264	113	476	476
Iowa	969	966	125	334	136	12	234	128	338	338
Kansas	943	939	89	354	175	65	197	63	340	342
Kentucky	983	971	26	488	104	82	202	81	477	482
Louisiana	930	890	68	321	119	104	193	125	488	487
Maine	453	453	61	98	51	87	85	71	264	264
Maryland	1,130	1,113	13	667	82	92	221	55	532	538
Massachusetts	1,430	1,418	193	482	115	98	297	245	437	438
Michigan	2,213	2,166	243	782	201	237	473	277	419	422
Minnesota	1,280	1,127	108	376	285	75	245	191	431	471
Mississippi	626	623	71	134	96	37	160	128	511	511
Missouri	1,591	1,580	149	502	295	115	319	211	381	382
Montana	485	482	19	59	206	111	60	30	189	190
Nebraska	730	723	57	171	273	26	105	98	277	278
Nevada	480	470	9	263	81	23	89	15	627	638
New Hampshire	376	376	54	115	36	54	81	36	329	329
New Jersey	1,956	1,940	271	566	141	293	371	314	463	466
New Mexico	611	600	19	256	115	33	129	59	369	373
New York	3,307	3,273	300	1,260	351	268	724	404	518	519
North Carolina	1,899	1,886	79	1,088	66	120	461	85	537	539
North Dakota	297	296	14	72	111	61	29	10	227	228
Ohio	2,488	2,467	372	619	346	262	545	344	431	433
Oklahoma	1,222	1,218	84	297	166	283	237	155	385	385
Oregon	882	876	30	410	120	118	177	27	410	410
Pennsylvania	2,165	2,165	301	660	389	188	421	206	488	488
Rhode Island	224	223	32	83	37	3	41	28	411	412
South Carolina	914	911	40	459	53	39	224	99	559	561
South Dakota	437	433	17	134	68	91	101	26	209	210
Tennessee	1,387	1,376	168	548	54	177	326	114	508	511
Texas	5,983	5,841	610	2,763	463	140	1,356	651	571	581
Utah	649	612	13	114	399	33	42	48	552	575
Vermont	232	232	13	25	103	62	18	11	235	235
Virginia	1,495	1,495	47	839	150	12	312	135	575	575
Washington	1,504	1,428	42	579	414	88	257	124	440	456
West Virginia	568	568	73	265	35	39	115	41	350	350
Wisconsin	1,576	1,566	155	606	134	150	333	198	365	367
Wyoming	244	242	23	63	77	14	44	23	231	232
Bureau of Indian Education	110	110	6	5	25	68	4	2	—	—
DoD, domestic and overseas	141	141	20	43	26	9	28	15	—	—
Other jurisdictions										
American Samoa	22	22	0	0	0	22	0	0	—	—
Guam	32	32	0	4	20	0	7	1	615	615
Northern Marianas	22	22	0	1	11	0	1	9	266	266
Puerto Rico	852	852	38	4	782	2	18	8	226	226
U.S. Virgin Islands	22	22	1	1	17	2	1	0	390	390

—Not available.
[1]Excludes special education and alternative schools.
[2]Average for schools reporting enrollment data. Enrollment data were available for 66,605 out of 67,034 public elementary schools in 2013–14.

NOTE: Includes schools beginning with grade 6 or below and with no grade higher than 8. Excludes schools not reported by grade level, such as some special education schools for the disabled. DoD = Department of Defense.
SOURCE: U.S. Department of Education, National Center for Education Statistics, Common Core of Data (CCD), "Public Elementary/Secondary School Universe Survey," 2013–14. (This table was prepared September 2015.)

Table 216.80. Public secondary schools, by grade span, average school enrollment, and state or jurisdiction: 2013–14

State or jurisdiction	Total, all secondary schools	Total, all regular secondary schools[1]	Schools, by grade span							Vocational schools[2]	Average school enrollment[3]	
			Grades 7 to 8 and 7 to 9	Grades 7 to 12	Grades 8 to 12	Grades 9 to 12	Grades 10 to 12	Other spans ending with grade 12	Other grade spans		All secondary schools	Regular secondary schools[1]
1	2	3	4	5	6	7	8	9	10	11	12	13
United States.............	24,053	19,409	2,719	3,002	496	16,361	576	321	578	1,380	694	788
Alabama........................	434	326	40	78	8	262	32	3	11	72	706	721
Alaska...........................	83	60	12	21	1	47	1	1	0	3	436	549
Arizona.........................	734	491	70	43	7	584	12	5	13	227	617	713
Arkansas......................	368	335	47	119	12	136	35	0	19	26	499	507
California......................	2,606	1,642	372	300	10	1,819	63	27	15	76	860	1,234
Colorado.......................	389	330	39	43	2	292	5	1	7	6	642	722
Connecticut...................	286	207	30	13	7	195	10	21	10	16	638	815
Delaware......................	36	28	1	1	12	22	0	0	0	6	1,033	1,067
District of Columbia.......	39	31	1	1	0	31	0	0	6	2	405	460
Florida..........................	695	513	16	44	39	571	6	15	4	51	1,210	1,489
Georgia.........................	457	424	17	5	7	391	4	1	32	1	1,074	1,147
Hawaii...........................	52	51	12	7	0	33	0	0	0	0	1,134	1,155
Idaho............................	197	141	33	39	2	119	3	1	0	9	501	622
Illinois..........................	937	819	138	72	15	675	9	13	15	0	716	802
Indiana..........................	460	439	73	95	4	272	3	5	8	27	813	820
Iowa.............................	371	346	37	73	0	243	10	2	6	0	430	456
Kansas..........................	352	346	38	88	4	218	1	2	1	1	443	449
Kentucky.......................	422	245	25	35	7	350	2	1	2	122	676	819
Louisiana......................	281	243	28	42	53	135	4	12	7	8	707	776
Maine............................	149	120	10	11	4	121	1	0	2	27	461	463
Maryland.......................	246	190	5	3	2	221	3	6	6	26	1,077	1,244
Massachusetts..............	382	327	34	36	15	288	1	5	3	39	799	819
Michigan.......................	939	695	73	96	34	681	32	15	8	6	542	680
Minnesota.....................	836	448	46	276	26	394	48	42	4	11	393	606
Mississippi...................	325	227	24	58	2	212	23	2	4	90	645	645
Missouri........................	642	560	59	184	1	362	15	9	12	64	536	540
Montana........................	339	336	168	0	0	171	0	0	0	0	155	156
Nebraska......................	307	301	29	160	1	112	1	4	0	0	364	364
Nevada.........................	132	117	21	7	2	96	2	4	0	1	1,023	1,129
New Hampshire.............	106	106	14	0	0	88	2	0	2	0	585	585
New Jersey....................	494	410	50	37	4	390	2	3	8	57	918	1,032
New Mexico...................	238	207	35	35	1	153	8	0	6	1	478	519
New York.......................	1,130	1,057	70	133	21	825	20	2	59	25	736	749
North Carolina...............	536	509	25	7	5	480	2	6	11	7	826	858
North Dakota.................	183	171	7	93	0	78	1	1	3	12	202	202
Ohio..............................	1,013	934	136	142	37	655	17	11	15	69	593	603
Oklahoma......................	561	557	91	1	0	429	29	1	10	0	364	366
Oregon..........................	277	255	27	49	3	195	1	2	0	0	654	693
Pennsylvania.................	805	711	112	143	12	511	17	3	7	85	805	816
Rhode Island.................	73	59	10	0	1	59	1	0	2	12	704	737
South Carolina..............	288	234	20	9	1	237	10	4	7	42	880	922
South Dakota................	239	222	61	2	0	173	1	2	0	3	167	173
Tennessee....................	384	361	14	18	1	328	11	3	9	19	813	834
Texas...........................	2,097	1,535	283	166	50	1,322	40	44	192	0	751	986
Utah.............................	261	234	84	45	8	67	42	1	14	4	856	922
Vermont........................	68	52	7	19	0	27	0	0	15	15	493	502
Virginia.........................	406	343	33	4	28	337	2	0	2	58	1,160	1,176
Washington...................	617	432	71	55	38	398	26	18	11	20	633	833
West Virginia.................	124	105	2	18	4	92	2	0	6	30	634	727
Wisconsin.....................	560	497	51	63	4	401	14	23	4	4	497	541
Wyoming.......................	97	80	18	13	1	63	2	0	0	0	332	383
Bureau of Indian Education..	19	19	1	5	0	13	0	0	0	0	—	—
DoD, domestic and overseas.	35	35	3	11	0	21	0	0	0	0	—	—
Other jurisdictions												
American Samoa.............	6	5	0	0	0	6	0	0	0	1	—	—
Guam............................	4	4	0	0	0	4	0	0	0	0	1,853	1,853
Northern Marianas...........	6	6	1	2	0	3	0	0	0	0	787	787
Puerto Rico	398	367	196	26	1	5	159	0	11	30	431	416
U.S. Virgin Islands...........	9	8	4	0	0	5	0	0	0	1	798	798

—Not available.
[1]Excludes vocational, special education, and alternative schools.
[2]Vocational schools are also included under appropriate grade span. Includes vocational schools not classified as secondary schools.
[3]Average for schools reporting enrollment data. Enrollment data were available for 22,513 out of 24,053 public secondary schools in 2013–14.

NOTE: Includes schools with no grade lower than 7. Excludes schools not reported by grade level, such as some special education schools for the disabled. DoD = Department of Defense.
SOURCE: U.S. Department of Education, National Center for Education Statistics, Common Core of Data (CCD), "Public Elementary/Secondary School Universe Survey," 2013–14. (This table was prepared September 2015.)

Table 216.90. Public elementary and secondary charter schools and enrollment, by state: Selected years, 1999–2000 through 2013–14

State	Number of charter schools					Charter school enrollment					Charter schools as a percent of total public schools				Charter school enrollment as a percent of total public school enrollment			
	1999–2000	2003–04	2009–10	2012–13	2013–14	1999–2000	2003–04	2009–10	2012–13	2013–14	1999–2000	2003–04	2009–10	2013–14	1999–2000	2003–04	2009–10	2013–14
1	2	3	4	5	6	7	8	9	10	11	12	13	14	15	16	17	18	19
United States	1,524	2,977	4,952	6,079	6,465	339,678	789,479	1,610,285	2,267,814	2,519,065	1.7	3.1	5.0	6.6	0.7	1.6	3.3	5.1
Alabama	0	0	0	0	0	0	0	0	0	0	0.0	0.0	0.0	0.0	0.0	0.0	0.0	0.0
Alaska	18	19	25	27	27	2,300	3,476	5,196	5,869	6,118	3.6	3.7	4.9	5.3	1.7	2.6	3.9	4.7
Arizona	245	505	504	542	600	31,176	81,725	113,974	151,086	195,027	14.9	25.0	22.4	26.6	3.7	8.1	10.6	17.8
Arkansas	0	13	38	45	52	0	2,719	8,662	13,261	17,176	0.0	1.1	3.4	4.7	0.0	0.6	1.8	3.5
California	238	444	813	1,085	1,125	104,730	166,208	316,658	470,880	513,350	2.8	4.8	8.1	10.9	1.8	2.6	5.1	8.3
Colorado	69	96	158	187	200	17,822	31,529	66,826	89,451	95,860	4.3	5.7	8.8	10.9	2.5	4.2	8.0	10.9
Connecticut	16	12	18	17	18	2,148	2,222	5,215	6,518	7,094	1.5	1.0	1.5	1.6	0.4	0.4	0.9	1.3
Delaware	1	13	18	22	21	115	6,241	9,173	9,942	11,064	0.5	6.4	8.3	9.6	0.1	5.3	7.3	8.4
District of Columbia	27	37	99	102	109	6,432	12,958	25,813	31,580	33,158	14.3	18.0	42.5	48.4	8.3	16.6	37.3	42.4
Florida	113	257	412	581	623	17,251	67,472	137,887	204,132	230,173	3.5	7.5	10.2	14.5	0.7	2.6	5.2	8.5
Georgia	18	51	63	93	94	11,005	26,756	37,545	64,233	70,544	1.0	2.1	2.6	4.0	0.8	1.8	2.3	4.1
Hawaii	2	26	31	32	33	790	4,502	7,869	9,635	9,816	0.8	9.2	10.7	11.5	0.4	2.5	4.4	5.3
Idaho	8	17	36	47	49	915	4,811	14,529	18,188	19,375	1.2	2.5	4.9	6.9	0.3	1.9	5.3	6.6
Illinois	17	28	39	58	65	6,152	11,750	35,836	53,829	59,817	0.4	0.6	0.9	1.5	0.3	0.6	1.7	2.9
Indiana	0	17	53	72	76	0	2,908	18,488	33,297	35,676	0.0	0.9	2.7	3.9	0.0	0.3	1.8	3.4
Iowa	0	0	9	3	3	0	0	593	352	315	0.0	0.0	0.6	0.2	0.0	0.0	0.1	0.1
Kansas	0	17	35	16	11	0	1,395	4,684	2,888	2,518	0.0	1.2	2.5	0.8	0.0	0.3	1.0	0.5
Kentucky	0	0	0	0	0	0	0	0	0	0	0.0	0.0	0.0	0.0	0.0	0.0	0.0	0.0
Louisiana	16	16	77	104	118	2,449	4,585	31,467	45,293	50,049	1.0	1.0	5.2	8.4	0.3	0.6	4.6	7.2
Maine	0	0	0	2	5	0	0	0	106	384	0.0	0.0	0.0	0.8	0.0	0.0	0.0	0.2
Maryland	0	1	42	52	53	0	196	11,995	18,943	20,269	0.0	0.1	2.9	3.7	0.0	0.0	1.4	2.3
Massachusetts	40	51	62	77	81	12,518	17,971	27,393	31,830	34,631	2.1	2.7	3.4	4.3	1.3	1.8	2.9	3.6
Michigan	193	212	294	346	370	46,078	72,096	110,504	126,602	139,110	4.9	5.3	7.6	10.5	2.8	4.1	6.8	9.2
Minnesota	62	105	181	176	186	7,794	14,256	35,375	41,615	43,937	2.6	4.1	7.4	7.7	0.9	1.7	4.2	5.2
Mississippi	1	1	1	0	0	347	338	375	—	—	0.1	0.1	0.0	0.0	0.1	0.1	0.1	0.0
Missouri	15	26	48	57	59	4,303	10,304	18,415	17,925	19,462	0.6	1.1	2.0	2.4	0.5	1.1	2.0	2.1
Montana	0	0	0	0	0	0	0	0	0	0	0.0	0.0	0.0	0.0	0.0	0.0	0.0	0.0
Nebraska	0	0	0	0	0	0	0	0	0	0	0.0	0.0	0.0	0.0	0.0	0.0	0.0	0.0
Nevada	5	15	35	40	41	898	3,917	11,613	22,199	24,621	1.0	2.7	5.5	6.3	0.3	1.0	2.7	5.4
New Hampshire	0	0	15	22	23	0	0	816	1,739	2,097	0.0	0.0	3.1	4.8	0.0	0.0	0.4	1.1
New Jersey	0	51	70	86	87	0	12,806	22,981	29,540	33,430	0.0	2.1	2.7	3.5	0.0	0.9	1.7	2.4
New Mexico	1	34	72	94	95	22	6,225	13,090	19,916	21,485	0.1	4.2	8.4	10.8	0.0	1.9	3.9	6.3
New York	5	50	140	211	233	—	14,572	43,963	78,139	92,143	0.1	1.1	3.0	4.9	—	0.5	1.6	3.4
North Carolina	82	93	96	108	128	12,691	21,955	38,973	50,060	58,307	3.8	4.1	3.8	4.9	1.0	1.6	2.6	3.9
North Dakota	0	0	0	0	0	0	0	0	0	0	0.0	0.0	0.0	0.0	0.0	0.0	0.0	0.0
Ohio	48	165	323	368	390	9,809	46,130	90,989	114,459	120,224	1.2	4.2	8.5	10.7	0.5	2.5	5.2	7.0
Oklahoma	0	12	18	23	25	0	3,491	6,315	12,037	13,473	0.0	0.7	1.0	1.4	0.0	0.6	1.0	2.0
Oregon	1	24	102	123	124	109	2,487	18,334	27,077	28,241	0.1	1.9	7.8	10.0	0.0	0.5	3.3	5.1
Pennsylvania	47	102	134	175	181	11,413	41,114	79,167	118,430	128,261	1.5	3.1	4.1	5.9	0.6	2.3	4.5	7.4
Rhode Island	2	8	12	18	23	446	1,024	3,233	5,131	5,950	0.6	2.3	3.7	7.6	0.3	0.7	2.3	4.2
South Carolina	7	18	39	55	60	327	3,155	13,035	20,067	23,432	0.6	1.6	3.2	4.8	#	0.5	1.8	3.2
South Dakota	0	0	0	0	0	0	0	0	0	0	0.0	0.0	0.0	0.0	0.0	0.0	0.0	0.0
Tennessee	0	4	20	51	72	0	324	4,343	11,698	15,690	0.0	0.2	1.1	3.9	0.0	#	0.4	1.6
Texas	176	274	536	628	658	25,687	60,833	148,392	215,082	235,634	2.4	3.4	6.2	7.5	0.6	1.4	3.1	4.6
Utah	6	19	72	88	95	390	3,253	33,968	50,694	54,795	0.8	2.1	6.9	9.4	0.1	0.7	5.8	8.8
Vermont	0	0	0	0	0	0	0	0	0	0	0.0	0.0	0.0	0.0	0.0	0.0	0.0	0.0
Virginia	0	6	3	4	6	0	478	179	399	603	0.0	0.3	0.1	0.3	0.0	#	#	#
Washington	0	0	0	0	0	0	0	0	0	0	0.0	0.0	0.0	0.0	0.0	0.0	#	0.0
West Virginia	0	0	0	0	0	0	0	0	0	0	0.0	0.0	0.0	0.0	0.0	0.0	0.0	0.0
Wisconsin	45	137	206	238	242	3,561	21,165	36,153	43,323	44,853	2.1	6.2	9.2	10.8	0.4	2.4	4.1	5.1
Wyoming	0	1	3	4	4	0	132	269	369	463	0.0	0.3	0.8	1.1	0.0	0.2	0.3	0.5

—Not available.
#Rounds to zero.
NOTE: Some data have been revised from previously published figures.

SOURCE: U.S. Department of Education, National Center for Education Statistics, Common Core of Data (CCD), "Public Elementary/Secondary School Universe Survey," 1999–2000 through 2013–14. (This table was prepared September 2015.)

Table 216.95. Number and enrollment of public elementary and secondary schools that have closed, by school level, type, and charter status: Selected years, 1995–96 through 2013–14

School level, type, and charter status	1995–96	2000–01	2001–02	2002–03	2003–04	2004–05	2005–06	2006–07	2007–08	2008–09	2009–10	2010–11	2011–12	2012–13	2013–14
1	2	3	4	5	6	7	8	9	10	11	12	13	14	15	16
							Number of schools that closed								
Total, all schools	954	1,193	1,412	1,368	2,168	1,913	1,553	1,877	2,120	1,515	1,822	1,929	1,840	1,493	1,737
School type															
Regular	686	908	1,018	985	1,248	1,190	1,171	1,348	1,450	1,059	1,321	1,486	1,340	1,075	1,179
Special education	110	84	118	91	114	271	88	160	195	99	235	72	87	83	90
Vocational	17	17	90	27	33	18	28	14	30	15	11	7	11	66	20
Alternative[1]	141	184	186	265	773	434	266	355	445	342	255	364	402	269	448
School level and type															
Elementary[2]	497	601	697	721	947	901	770	846	844	769	936	1,073	1,020	776	864
Regular	449	563	648	660	870	847	725	771	804	713	893	1,010	959	726	778
Special education	28	20	21	26	23	25	13	53	20	22	13	18	18	18	33
Vocational	0	2	0	0	0	0	1	1	0	1	0	0	0	0	1
Alternative[1]	20	16	28	35	54	29	31	21	20	33	30	45	43	32	52
Secondary[3]	199	302	313	245	347	302	342	308	394	368	346	436	451	421	502
Regular	114	173	141	127	144	177	192	171	233	186	212	237	238	204	231
Special education	12	19	12	9	10	4	11	24	19	21	12	15	15	24	15
Vocational	17	14	89	27	33	18	27	13	29	13	11	7	10	64	19
Alternative[1]	56	96	71	82	160	103	112	100	113	148	111	177	188	129	237
Combined elementary/secondary[4]	42	146	168	124	158	321	184	193	172	164	91	157	207	170	183
Regular	10	83	76	57	54	68	82	65	65	50	42	74	82	64	67
Special education	13	22	29	22	30	28	38	45	48	34	16	24	34	34	33
Vocational	0	1	1	0	0	0	0	0	1	1	0	0	1	2	0
Alternative[1]	19	40	62	45	74	225	64	83	58	79	33	59	90	70	83
Other (not classified by grade span)	216	144	234	278	716	389	257	530	710	214	449	263	162	126	188
Regular	113	89	153	141	180	98	172	341	348	110	174	165	61	81	103
Special education	57	23	56	34	51	214	26	38	108	22	194	15	20	7	9
Vocational	0	0	0	0	0	0	0	0	0	0	0	0	0	0	0
Alternative[1]	46	32	25	103	485	77	59	151	254	82	81	83	81	38	76
All charter schools[5]	—	72	111	85	74	171	206	267	133	161	189	216	202	183	284
							Prior year enrollment of schools that have closed								
Total, enrollment	173,766	209,228	171,669	195,033	262,183	297,487	229,259	242,388	268,212	243,166	306,806	321,246	300,764	240,704	274,397
School type															
Regular	151,574	198,699	161,663	185,536	242,383	282,432	216,360	227,260	253,409	227,714	292,915	304,001	281,961	227,444	252,172
Special education	4,475	1,665	2,840	1,789	4,144	2,799	3,068	4,745	4,060	1,916	2,173	1,709	3,765	1,168	4,331
Vocational	1,613	632	75	223	719	2,975	73	429	183	1,665	767	22	26	289	1,578
Alternative[1]	16,104	8,232	7,091	7,485	14,937	9,281	9,758	9,954	10,560	11,871	10,951	15,514	15,012	11,803	16,316
School level and type															
Elementary[2]	112,328	134,934	125,753	146,709	194,752	213,607	161,649	172,403	179,554	171,722	221,681	242,193	225,205	174,885	195,776
Regular	108,440	134,060	124,170	144,013	192,117	211,822	158,744	169,895	176,862	169,815	219,469	239,913	222,186	173,272	190,138
Special education	2,991	338	591	1,020	1,040	1,153	1,158	1,892	2,131	651	727	404	1,539	272	2,042
Vocational	0	2	0	0	0	0	0	9	0	569	0	0	0	0	308
Alternative[1]	897	534	992	1,676	1,595	632	1,747	607	561	687	1,485	1,876	1,480	1,341	3,288
Secondary[3]	48,074	47,950	30,817	33,243	52,437	60,029	54,489	55,834	66,163	55,261	68,548	56,935	54,558	51,820	59,920
Regular	39,307	42,666	27,752	30,271	42,750	51,547	49,335	48,797	60,085	45,800	60,734	48,430	46,345	43,775	49,374
Special education	398	121	175	357	172	108	83	1,126	440	501	508	520	404	500	633
Vocational	1,613	592	72	223	719	2,975	73	420	183	1,096	767	22	19	202	1,270
Alternative[1]	6,756	4,571	2,818	2,392	8,796	5,399	4,998	5,491	5,455	7,864	6,539	7,963	7,790	7,343	8,643
Combined elementary/secondary[4]	12,418	25,031	12,622	12,957	13,150	22,022	12,993	12,157	19,349	16,093	12,151	21,360	20,931	13,963	18,614
Regular	3,743	21,973	8,999	9,451	7,484	18,415	8,281	7,682	16,295	12,081	8,342	14,941	13,430	10,361	12,660
Special education	326	701	410	365	1,328	840	1,791	1,293	1,008	692	882	744	1,752	396	1,569
Vocational	0	38	3	0	0	0	0	0	0	0	0	0	7	87	0
Alternative[1]	8,349	2,319	3,210	3,141	4,338	2,767	2,921	3,182	2,046	3,320	2,927	5,675	5,742	3,119	4,385
Other (not classified by grade span)	946	1,313	2,477	2,124	1,844	1,829	128	1,994	3,146	90	4,426	758	70	36	87
Regular	84	0	742	1,801	32	648	0	886	167	18	4,370	717	0	36	0
Special education	760	505	1,664	47	1,604	698	36	434	481	72	56	41	70	0	87
Vocational	0	0	0	0	0	0	0	0	0	0	0	0	0	0	0
Alternative[1]	102	808	71	276	208	483	92	674	2,498	0	0	0	0	0	0
All charter schools[5]	—	5,925	11,134	11,894	6,797	21,505	14,118	15,340	12,226	20,537	17,954	24,165	29,095	24,437	38,327

—Not available.

[1]Includes schools that provide nontraditional education, address needs of students that typically cannot be met in regular schools, serve as adjuncts to regular schools, or fall outside the categories of regular, special education, or vocational education.
[2]Includes schools beginning with grade 6 or below and with no grade higher than 8.
[3]Includes schools with no grade lower than 7.
[4]Includes schools beginning with grade 6 or below and ending with grade 9 or above.
[5]Charter schools are also included under the school level and type categories, as appropriate.

NOTE: This table indicates the school year by which the school no longer operated (generally it closed between that school year and the prior school year). The closure of a school does not necessarily mean that a building is no longer used for educational purposes. A single school may share a building with another school, or one school may be housed in several buildings. SOURCE: U.S. Department of Education, National Center for Education Statistics, Common Core of Data (CCD), "Public Elementary/Secondary School Universe Survey," 1995–96 through 2013–14. (This table was prepared February 2016.)

Table 217.10. Functional age of public schools' main instructional buildings and percentage of schools with permanent and portable (temporary) buildings, by selected school characteristics and condition of permanent and portable buildings: 2012

[Standard errors appear in parentheses]

Functional age of main instructional building; presence and condition of permanent and portable buildings	All public schools[1]	Instructional level			Community type				Percent of students eligible for free or reduced-price lunch			
		Elementary	Secondary	Combined	City	Suburban	Town	Rural	Less than 35 percent	35 to 49 percent	50 to 74 percent	75 percent or more
1	2	3	4	5	6	7	8	9	10	11	12	13
Estimated number of schools	84,000 (†)	62,600 (†)	18,900 (†)	2,400 (†)	21,200 (†)	23,500 (†)	10,900 (†)	28,400 (†)	31 (†)	18 (†)	27 (†)	23 (†)
Main instructional building												
Percent of schools, by functional age[2]												
Less than 5 years old	21 (1.1)	19 (1.2)	25 (2.2)	27 (6.8)	24 (2.6)	23 (2.2)	19 (2.9)	17 (1.9)	20 (2.1)	23 (2.9)	18 (2.0)	24 (2.5)
5 to 14 years old	38 (1.2)	37 (1.4)	39 (2.3)	34 (7.2)	33 (2.5)	39 (2.7)	37 (4.1)	40 (2.3)	40 (2.2)	34 (3.3)	39 (2.6)	35 (3.0)
15 to 34 years old	23 (1.2)	25 (1.6)	17 (1.8)	28 (7.5)	20 (2.3)	20 (1.8)	27 (3.6)	28 (2.3)	25 (2.1)	22 (2.9)	25 (2.3)	20 (2.7)
35 or more years old	18 (1.2)	19 (1.4)	18 (1.7)	11 ! (4.3)	22 (2.4)	19 (2.2)	17 (3.0)	15 (1.9)	15 (2.0)	21 (2.9)	17 (2.1)	21 (2.8)
Average years												
Since construction	44 (0.7)	45 (0.9)	43 (1.2)	50 (4.2)	50 (1.7)	43 (1.2)	48 (1.8)	40 (1.2)	42 (1.3)	46 (1.8)	43 (1.4)	48 (1.9)
Since major renovation[3]	12 (0.4)	12 (0.5)	11 (0.7)	12 (2.0)	11 (0.7)	11 (0.7)	14 (1.2)	12 (0.8)	11 (0.6)	12 (1.1)	12 (0.8)	11 (0.8)
Permanent buildings *(percent of schools)*												
School has permanent buildings[4]	99 (0.2)	99 (0.3)	100 (0.3)	100 (#)	99 (0.7)	100 (0.4)	99 (0.6)	100 (0.3)	100 (0.4)	99 (0.6)	100 (#)	98 (0.8)
Overall condition of buildings[4]												
Excellent	20 (1.1)	20 (1.4)	20 (1.5)	15 ! (5.5)	17 (2.0)	23 (2.2)	18 (3.3)	20 (1.8)	24 (2.0)	18 (2.3)	20 (2.1)	16 (2.0)
Good	56 (1.4)	57 (1.7)	57 (2.2)	44 (7.0)	55 (2.6)	56 (2.6)	57 (3.8)	57 (2.5)	56 (2.3)	63 (3.5)	56 (2.7)	52 (3.2)
Fair	21 (1.0)	21 (1.3)	20 (2.0)	38 (7.4)	23 (2.3)	20 (2.1)	23 (3.2)	20 (2.0)	18 (1.9)	17 (2.5)	22 (2.0)	28 (2.7)
Poor	3 (0.5)	3 (0.6)	2 ! (0.7)	‡ (†)	5 (1.3)	‡ (†)	‡ (†)	2 ! (0.8)	2 ! (0.8)	2 ! (0.9)	2 ! (1.0)	4 (1.3)
Environmental factors are unsatisfactory[5]												
Lighting, artificial	8 (0.9)	8 (1.1)	7 (1.4)	‡ (†)	9 (1.6)	7 (1.4)	8 (2.1)	9 (1.4)	6 (1.4)	7 (1.8)	8 (1.8)	11 (1.9)
Lighting, natural	16 (1.1)	17 (1.4)	16 (1.7)	15 ! (5.3)	16 (2.2)	15 (2.0)	20 (3.2)	16 (1.9)	14 (1.7)	17 (2.7)	17 (2.0)	19 (2.6)
Heating	14 (0.9)	13 (1.2)	16 (2.1)	20 ! (6.2)	16 (2.1)	10 (1.6)	14 (2.4)	14 (1.7)	12 (1.6)	14 (2.4)	14 (2.2)	15 (2.3)
Air conditioning	17 (1.1)	16 (1.4)	20 (2.3)	21 ! (6.7)	21 (2.5)	13 (1.9)	18 (3.2)	17 (2.0)	17 (1.9)	16 (2.7)	15 (2.5)	19 (2.7)
Ventilation	17 (1.2)	16 (1.4)	16 (1.8)	28 (7.3)	18 (2.0)	12 (1.9)	16 (3.2)	20 (2.1)	15 (1.9)	16 (2.6)	16 (2.0)	20 (2.7)
Indoor air quality	9 (0.8)	9 (1.0)	9 (1.4)	13 ! (5.0)	11 (1.8)	4 (1.0)	7 (2.2)	12 (1.7)	7 (1.2)	9 (2.1)	11 (1.8)	10 (1.9)
Water quality	5 (0.6)	5 (0.8)	6 (1.1)	16 ! (6.4)	6 (1.5)	3 (0.9)	5 (1.6)	7 (1.3)	4 (1.0)	5 (1.5)	6 (1.4)	7 (1.4)
Acoustics or noise control	14 (1.0)	14 (1.3)	12 (1.5)	25 (6.2)	14 (2.1)	10 (1.5)	15 (3.0)	16 (2.0)	12 (1.7)	13 (2.4)	13 (1.8)	17 (2.3)
Portable (temporary) buildings *(percent of schools)*												
School has portable buildings[6]	31 (1.4)	33 (1.8)	24 (2.0)	29 (6.8)	40 (2.8)	32 (2.2)	27 (3.6)	25 (2.1)	25 (2.0)	30 (2.9)	31 (2.2)	39 (3.4)
Overall condition of buildings[6]												
Excellent	6 (1.1)	6 (1.4)	5 ! (1.5)	‡ (†)	4 ! (1.8)	5 ! (1.8)	10 ! (4.7)	7 ! (2.3)	8 ! (2.7)	7 ! (3.0)	4 ! (1.9)	5 ! (2.0)
Good	49 (2.8)	49 (3.2)	46 (4.4)	56 (14.2)	53 (4.2)	51 (4.9)	43 (7.7)	44 (5.0)	51 (4.8)	53 (6.1)	45 (4.4)	48 (5.0)
Fair	36 (2.4)	36 (2.9)	43 (4.8)	‡ (†)	34 (4.1)	38 (4.8)	38 (7.5)	36 (4.8)	29 (4.1)	36 (5.9)	41 (4.2)	38 (4.6)
Poor	9 (1.4)	9 (1.7)	7 ! (2.3)	‡ (†)	8 ! (2.6)	6 ! (2.0)	9 ! (4.1)	13 (3.5)	12 (3.2)	‡ (†)	10 ! (3.2)	8 ! (3.0)
Environmental factors are unsatisfactory[7]												
Lighting, artificial	11 (1.8)	11 (2.1)	12 (3.3)	# (†)	10 (2.9)	6 ! (2.6)	14 ! (5.7)	15 (4.0)	10 ! (3.0)	8 ! (3.5)	12 (3.3)	12 (3.3)
Lighting, natural	28 (2.5)	29 (3.0)	28 (4.3)	‡ (†)	26 (4.2)	26 (4.4)	41 (8.0)	28 (4.4)	26 (4.1)	28 (4.9)	29 (4.8)	30 (4.5)
Heating	12 (1.8)	11 (2.0)	16 (3.3)	# (†)	11 (2.9)	7 ! (2.4)	17 ! (5.7)	16 (4.0)	13 (3.5)	8 ! (3.5)	15 (3.5)	10 (3.1)
Air conditioning	15 (2.2)	16 (2.6)	14 (3.3)	‡ (†)	15 (3.6)	12 (3.1)	14 ! (5.3)	18 (4.3)	17 (3.9)	13 ! (4.1)	16 (3.9)	14 (3.7)
Ventilation	19 (2.2)	19 (2.6)	22 (3.9)	‡ (†)	18 (3.7)	14 (3.1)	26 (6.7)	24 (4.4)	18 (3.9)	18 ! (5.7)	23 (4.6)	18 (4.0)
Indoor air quality	16 (2.0)	17 (2.3)	14 (3.1)	# (†)	17 (3.6)	11 (2.8)	18 ! (5.5)	19 (4.2)	14 (3.4)	15 ! (4.4)	19 ! (4.1)	16 (3.6)
Water quality	10 (1.7)	10 (2.0)	8 ! (3.1)	‡ (†)	7 ! (2.7)	7 ! (2.8)	16 ! (6.7)	14 ! (4.6)	9 ! (3.8)	‡ (†)	11 ! (3.8)	14 (3.8)
Acoustics or noise control	21 (2.5)	21 (2.9)	21 (4.1)	‡ (†)	19 (3.6)	17 (3.9)	24 (7.1)	26 (4.6)	19 (4.2)	11 ! (4.2)	26 (4.6)	23 (4.7)

†Not applicable.
#Rounds to zero.
!Interpret data with caution. The coefficient of variation (CV) for this estimate is between 30 and 50 percent.
‡Reporting standards not met. Either there are too few cases for a reliable estimate or the coefficient of variation (CV) for this estimate is 50 percent or greater.
[1]Excludes special education, vocational, and alternative schools; schools without enrollment data; and schools offering only preprimary education.
[2]The functional age of the main instructional building is the number of years since its most recent major renovation or since its construction if no major renovation has ever occurred.
[3]Based on schools whose main instructional building has undergone a major renovation.

[4]Based on the 99 percent of public schools with permanent buildings.
[5]Based on schools with the specified environmental factor in their permanent buildings. Includes ratings of "unsatisfactory" and "very unsatisfactory."
[6]Based on the 31 percent of public schools with portable (temporary) buildings.
[7]Based on schools with the specified environmental factor in their portable (temporary) buildings. Includes ratings of "unsatisfactory" and "very unsatisfactory."
NOTE: Detail may not sum to totals because of rounding.
SOURCE: U.S. Department of Education, National Center for Education Statistics, Fast Response Survey System (FRSS), "Condition of Public School Facilities: 2012–13," FRSS 105, 2013. (This table was prepared June 2014.)

Table 217.15. Percentage of public schools with plans for major repair, renovation, or replacement of building systems or features in the next 2 years and percentage distribution of schools with such plans, by selected school characteristics, type of system or feature, and main reason for the plans: 2012–13

[Standard errors appear in parentheses]

Type of system or feature and main reason for major repair, renovation, or replacement plans	All public schools	Instructional level			Community type				Percent of students eligible for free or reduced-priced lunch			
		Elementary	Secondary	Combined	City	Suburban	Town	Rural	Less than 35 percent	35 to 49 percent	50 to 74 percent	75 percent or more
1	2	3	4	5	6	7	8	9	10	11	12	13
Roofs—percent of schools with plans	**19** (1.1)	**17** (1.3)	**25** (1.8)	**25** (6.8)	**19** (2.1)	**19** (2.0)	**20** (3.0)	**19** (1.9)	**22** (1.8)	**18** (2.4)	**17** (2.0)	**18** (2.3)
Percentage distribution by main reason for the plans	100 (†)	100 (†)	100 (†)	100 (†)	100 (†)	100 (†)	100 (†)	100 (†)	100 (†)	100 (†)	100 (†)	100 (†)
Functional problem in existing system or feature	39 (3.1)	38 (3.9)	41 (4.4)	31 ! (14.2)	35 (6.0)	40 (5.6)	50 (10.0)	35 (5.3)	33 (4.5)	45 (7.5)	40 (5.8)	42 (7.1)
Improve operational or energy efficiency	9 (1.7)	8 (2.1)	9 (2.6)	30 ! (15.1)	6 ! (2.9)	8 ! (3.0)	‡ (†)	13 ! (4.1)	6 ! (2.2)	‡ (†)	8 ! (3.2)	17 ! (5.4)
Replacement cycle	46 (3.1)	47 (4.2)	45 (4.7)	38 ! (12.3)	50 (5.9)	46 (5.3)	36 (9.0)	49 (5.8)	55 (5.0)	46 (7.6)	49 (5.4)	30 (6.5)
Other reason	6 (1.5)	7 ! (2.2)	5 ! (1.7)	# (†)	8 ! (3.7)	‡ (†)	‡ (†)	‡ (†)	7 ! (2.9)	‡ (†)	‡ (†)	11 ! (4.9)
Framing, floors, foundations—percent of schools with plans	**7** (0.7)	**5** (0.9)	**8** (1.4)	**22** ! (6.8)	**7** (1.2)	**7** (1.3)	**7** (2.0)	**5** (1.1)	**6** (1.1)	**5** (1.3)	**6** (1.4)	**8** (1.6)
Percentage distribution by main reason for the plans	100 (†)	100 (†)	100 (†)	100 (†)	100 (†)	100 (†)	100 (†)	100 (†)	100 (†)	100 (†)	100 (†)	100 (†)
Functional problem in existing system or feature	41 (4.9)	40 (6.2)	42 (7.1)	48 ! (19.9)	37 (9.4)	38 (9.9)	53 (15.6)	41 (11.6)	27 ! (8.1)	58 (12.6)	37 ! (11.3)	51 (9.8)
Improve operational or energy efficiency	16 (3.8)	12 ! (4.7)	17 ! (6.6)	43 ! (18.9)	19 ! (8.9)	14 ! (6.8)	20 ! (9.6)	‡ (†)	15 ! (6.7)	‡ (†)	21 ! (9.0)	‡ (†)
Replacement cycle	27 (4.5)	30 (6.0)	26 (6.9)	‡ (†)	27 (7.5)	23 ! (9.4)	‡ (†)	32 ! (10.6)	38 (9.7)	‡ (†)	33 ! (11.0)	17 ! (7.5)
Other reason	16 (3.9)	19 ! (5.7)	15 ! (7.1)	# (†)	16 ! (7.4)	24 ! (9.1)	‡ (†)	‡ (†)	20 ! (8.9)	‡ (†)	‡ (†)	16 ! (7.5)
Exterior walls, finishes—percent of schools with plans	**9** (0.7)	**8** (0.9)	**10** (1.3)	**17** ! (6.0)	**9** (1.5)	**8** (1.3)	**9** (1.9)	**8** (1.3)	**9** (1.3)	**9** (1.7)	**8** (1.3)	**10** (1.8)
Percentage distribution by main reason for the plans	100 (†)	100 (†)	100 (†)	100 (†)	100 (†)	100 (†)	100 (†)	100 (†)	100 (†)	100 (†)	100 (†)	100 (†)
Functional problem in existing system or feature	38 (4.5)	36 (5.6)	46 (7.5)	‡ (†)	33 (7.1)	39 (9.5)	53 (11.8)	35 (8.9)	38 (8.1)	37 ! (11.4)	46 (10.5)	31 (8.8)
Improve operational or energy efficiency	21 (3.6)	19 (4.5)	23 ! (7.1)	‡ (†)	20 ! (7.0)	17 ! (6.6)	18 ! (7.3)	26 ! (8.5)	14 ! (5.4)	20 ! (7.7)	23 ! (9.3)	29 ! (8.8)
Replacement cycle	23 (3.7)	26 (5.1)	18 (4.9)	‡ (†)	31 (7.7)	25 ! (7.7)	‡ (†)	23 ! (8.1)	32 (8.1)	18 ! (8.8)	21 ! (7.6)	19 ! (8.0)
Other reason	18 (3.9)	20 (5.2)	14 ! (5.9)	# (†)	16 ! (7.3)	19 ! (8.1)	24 ! (11.5)	15 ! (6.6)	16 ! (7.4)	25 ! (10.5)	‡ (†)	20 ! (8.3)
Windows, doors—percent of schools with plans	**15** (0.9)	**13** (1.1)	**21** (2.1)	**21** ! (6.7)	**15** (2.1)	**14** (1.8)	**18** (2.7)	**16** (1.8)	**15** (1.8)	**15** (2.2)	**15** (1.9)	**16** (2.2)
Percentage distribution by main reason for the plans	100 (†)	100 (†)	100 (†)	100 (†)	100 (†)	100 (†)	100 (†)	100 (†)	100 (†)	100 (†)	100 (†)	100 (†)
Functional problem in existing system or feature	30 (3.4)	29 (4.5)	31 (4.8)	40 ! (16.8)	24 (5.4)	30 (7.0)	40 (9.6)	31 (6.3)	28 (6.2)	27 (7.7)	37 (7.5)	30 (6.4)
Improve operational or energy efficiency	43 (3.9)	41 (4.7)	45 (6.1)	60 (16.8)	34 (6.7)	36 (7.2)	43 (9.8)	54 (7.1)	39 (6.9)	52 (9.2)	46 (7.3)	36 (8.0)
Replacement cycle	17 (2.6)	19 (3.4)	14 (3.8)	# (†)	31 (6.7)	21 (5.8)	‡ (†)	10 ! (3.9)	20 (4.9)	12 ! (5.5)	13 ! (4.4)	22 ! (6.6)
Other reason	10 (2.3)	11 (2.9)	10 ! (3.3)	# (†)	11 (5.1)	13 ! (4.8)	14 ! (6.3)	‡ (†)	13 ! (4.8)	‡ (†)	‡ (†)	12 ! (4.9)
Interior finishes, trim—percent of schools with plans	**12** (0.8)	**11** (1.0)	**13** (1.5)	**25** (6.8)	**13** (1.7)	**13** (1.6)	**12** (2.3)	**11** (1.3)	**14** (1.6)	**9** (1.7)	**11** (1.7)	**12** (1.9)
Percentage distribution by main reason for the plans	100 (†)	100 (†)	100 (†)	100 (†)	100 (†)	100 (†)	100 (†)	100 (†)	100 (†)	100 (†)	100 (†)	100 (†)
Functional problem in existing system or feature	19 (3.1)	17 (3.7)	27 (5.3)	‡ (†)	19 (5.5)	20 ! (6.1)	32 ! (11.5)	13 ! (5.7)	17 ! (5.4)	16 ! (6.2)	27 (7.0)	16 ! (5.8)
Improve operational or energy efficiency	20 (3.2)	17 (3.7)	24 (6.2)	33 ! (16.4)	18 (5.4)	17 ! (5.2)	33 ! (10.9)	19 ! (6.2)	14 ! (4.8)	‡ (†)	20 (5.7)	31 (8.0)
Replacement cycle	44 (3.9)	48 (5.1)	31 (5.1)	49 ! (15.3)	45 (7.6)	46 (6.9)	30 ! (10.8)	47 (7.7)	50 (6.9)	44 (9.0)	39 (7.8)	39 (9.0)
Other reason	17 (3.0)	18 (4.0)	19 ! (5.7)	# (†)	18 ! (6.5)	18 ! (5.7)	‡ (†)	22 (6.2)	19 ! (5.9)	26 ! (8.4)	13 ! (5.8)	14 ! (5.7)

See notes at end of table.

Table 217.15. Percentage of public schools with plans for major repair, renovation, or replacement of building systems or features in the next 2 years and percentage distribution of schools with such plans, by selected school characteristics, type of system or feature, and main reason for the plans: 2012–13—Continued

[Standard errors appear in parentheses]

Type of system or feature and main reason for major repair, renovation, or replacement plans	All public schools	Instructional level			Community type				Percent of students eligible for free or reduced-priced lunch			
		Elementary	Secondary	Combined	City	Suburban	Town	Rural	Less than 35 percent	35 to 49 percent	50 to 74 percent	75 percent or more
1	2	3	4	5	6	7	8	9	10	11	12	13
Plumbing/lavatories—percent of schools with plans	13 (1.0)	12 (1.2)	17 (1.8)	28 (7.2)	15 (2.0)	13 (1.9)	16 (2.4)	11 (1.5)	13 (1.8)	13 (2.0)	13 (1.7)	13 (2.2)
Percentage distribution by main reason for the plans	100 (†)	100 (†)	100 (†)	100 (†)	100 (†)	100 (†)	100 (†)	100 (†)	100 (†)	100 (†)	100 (†)	100 (†)
Functional problem in existing system or feature	25 (3.7)	25 (4.6)	21 (3.8)	46 ! (16.6)	29 (7.0)	22 (6.1)	26 ! (7.9)	24 (7.2)	26 (7.4)	29 (8.6)	27 (6.1)	20 ! (6.5)
Improve operational or energy efficiency	35 (3.8)	32 (4.7)	41 (5.9)	44 ! (15.0)	27 (6.4)	33 (6.9)	49 (9.6)	39 (7.7)	24 (5.7)	29 (8.0)	47 (7.6)	42 (7.6)
Replacement cycle	26 (3.1)	28 (4.4)	25 (5.0)	‡ (†)	34 (6.7)	22 (4.8)	19 ! (7.7)	27 (6.5)	29 (5.8)	25 ! (7.6)	23 (6.3)	28 (7.3)
Other reason	13 (2.5)	14 (3.5)	13 ! (4.1)	# (†)	10 ! (4.5)	24 (5.6)	‡ (†)	10 ! (4.8)	22 (5.5)	16 ! (6.6)	‡ (†)	10 ! (4.9)
Heating system—percent of schools with plans	16 (1.1)	14 (1.2)	21 (2.1)	29 (6.8)	15 (2.0)	17 (1.9)	15 (2.5)	16 (1.8)	18 (1.7)	15 (2.0)	16 (1.9)	15 (2.2)
Percentage distribution by main reason for the plans	100 (†)	100 (†)	100 (†)	100 (†)	100 (†)	100 (†)	100 (†)	100 (†)	100 (†)	100 (†)	100 (†)	100 (†)
Functional problem in existing system or feature	26 (2.9)	23 (3.7)	31 (4.7)	33 ! (14.0)	24 (6.1)	24 (6.0)	32 (8.8)	27 (6.0)	23 (5.3)	31 (8.1)	23 (5.3)	30 (7.6)
Improve operational or energy efficiency	41 (3.1)	34 (3.7)	54 (5.4)	54 ! (14.1)	34 (6.8)	37 (5.4)	38 (9.6)	51 (6.8)	31 (5.0)	38 (8.1)	53 (6.8)	45 (7.6)
Replacement cycle	27 (2.9)	35 (4.0)	13 ! (4.4)	‡ (†)	35 (6.5)	31 (6.0)	23 ! (8.4)	20 (5.1)	38 (5.4)	30 (7.9)	20 (5.5)	17 ! (6.4)
Other reason	6 (1.7)	8 ! (2.7)	‡ (†)	# (†)	‡ (†)	8 ! (3.5)	‡ (†)	‡ (†)	8 ! (3.8)	‡ (†)	‡ (†)	‡ (†)
Air conditioning system—percent of schools with plans	16 (1.1)	14 (1.3)	22 (2.2)	17 ! (5.2)	18 (2.4)	16 (2.0)	14 (2.7)	16 (1.9)	14 (1.7)	18 (2.6)	17 (2.3)	16 (2.5)
Percentage distribution by main reason for the plans	100 (†)	100 (†)	100 (†)	100 (†)	100 (†)	100 (†)	100 (†)	100 (†)	100 (†)	100 (†)	100 (†)	100 (†)
Functional problem in existing system or feature	28 (3.5)	26 (4.4)	34 (4.9)	‡ (†)	25 (6.2)	29 (6.7)	31 ! (10.4)	30 (6.4)	28 (6.0)	31 (7.9)	22 (6.2)	34 (7.7)
Improve operational or energy efficiency	44 (3.5)	39 (4.6)	52 (5.0)	57 ! (19.0)	44 (7.4)	43 (5.7)	39 ! (11.1)	46 (7.1)	36 (5.9)	44 (8.0)	54 (6.4)	40 (7.5)
Replacement cycle	23 (2.8)	29 (3.9)	11 ! (3.6)	‡ (†)	26 (6.0)	21 (5.6)	27 ! (9.6)	20 (5.9)	31 (6.0)	19 ! (6.4)	23 (5.9)	16 ! (5.9)
Other reason	5 (1.5)	6 ! (2.2)	4 ! (1.8)	# (†)	‡ (†)	8 ! (3.4)	‡ (†)	‡ (†)	‡ (†)	‡ (†)	‡ (†)	‡ (†)
Ventilation/filtration system—percent of schools with plans	11 (0.8)	10 (0.9)	15 (1.7)	13 ! (4.3)	11 (1.6)	11 (1.6)	11 (2.6)	11 (1.5)	13 (1.4)	11 (1.9)	11 (1.5)	9 (1.7)
Percentage distribution by main reason for the plans	100 (†)	100 (†)	100 (†)	100 (†)	100 (†)	100 (†)	100 (†)	100 (†)	100 (†)	100 (†)	100 (†)	100 (†)
Functional problem in existing system or feature	31 (4.3)	30 (5.6)	32 (5.6)	‡ (†)	30 (7.4)	26 (7.5)	37 (13.5)	33 (7.3)	27 (6.5)	37 (10.8)	26 (7.4)	38 (10.7)
Improve operational or energy efficiency	38 (4.3)	39 (5.3)	55 (6.1)	41 ! (19.2)	39 (8.4)	39 (7.2)	28 ! (10.5)	41 (7.8)	33 (6.1)	36 (10.0)	49 (8.3)	35 (10.1)
Replacement cycle	23 (3.4)	29 (5.0)	8 ! (3.0)	‡ (†)	19 ! (5.7)	24 (7.0)	32 ! (11.6)	22 (6.4)	30 (6.7)	25 ! (8.8)	22 ! (6.8)	‡ (†)
Other reason	8 (2.4)	10 ! (3.5)	5 ! (2.4)	# (†)	‡ (†)	11 ! (4.9)	‡ (†)	‡ (†)	‡ (†)	‡ (†)	‡ (†)	18 ! (7.3)
Electrical system—percent of schools with plans	9 (0.8)	9 (0.9)	10 (1.4)	17 ! (6.1)	11 (1.5)	10 (1.6)	9 (2.1)	8 (1.4)	11 (1.5)	8 (1.6)	8 (1.3)	10 (1.7)
Percentage distribution by main reason for the plans	100 (†)	100 (†)	100 (†)	100 (†)	100 (†)	100 (†)	100 (†)	100 (†)	100 (†)	100 (†)	100 (†)	100 (†)
Functional problem in existing system or feature	28 (4.0)	28 (5.0)	27 (5.8)	‡ (†)	31 (8.2)	32 (7.6)	25 ! (12.3)	21 ! (8.4)	23 (6.2)	46 (12.9)	24 ! (8.2)	28 ! (8.3)
Improve operational or energy efficiency	37 (4.5)	31 (6.0)	51 (7.7)	52 ! (19.2)	29 (7.1)	35 (8.5)	42 ! (13.5)	45 (9.7)	37 (7.4)	29 ! (11.1)	42 (9.6)	38 (9.4)
Replacement cycle	22 (3.5)	26 (4.9)	11 ! (4.5)	‡ (†)	33 (8.3)	16 ! (5.7)	19 ! (9.2)	18 ! (7.5)	32 (7.0)	‡ (†)	23 ! (7.5)	15 ! (7.5)
Other reason	13 (3.2)	15 (4.2)	11 ! (5.4)	# (†)	‡ (†)	17 ! (6.2)	‡ (†)	15 ! (7.0)	‡ (†)	‡ (†)	‡ (†)	19 ! (7.7)

See notes at end of table.

Table 217.15. Percentage of public schools with plans for major repair, renovation, or replacement of building systems or features in the next 2 years and percentage distribution of schools with such plans, by selected school characteristics, type of system or feature, and main reason for the plans: 2012–13—Continued

[Standard errors appear in parentheses]

Type of system or feature and main reason for major repair, renovation, or replacement plans	All public schools	Instructional level			Community type				Percent of students eligible for free or reduced-priced lunch			
		Elementary	Secondary	Combined	City	Suburban	Town	Rural	Less than 35 percent	35 to 49 percent	50 to 74 percent	75 percent or more
1	2	3	4	5	6	7	8	9	10	11	12	13
Interior lighting—percent of schools with plans	13 (0.9)	13 (1.1)	13 (1.4)	18 ! (6.5)	14 (1.9)	14 (1.7)	10 (2.3)	12 (1.6)	15 (1.6)	10 (1.9)	13 (1.7)	12 (2.1)
Percentage distribution by main reason for the plans	100 (†)	100 (†)	100 (†)	100 (†)	100 (†)	100 (†)	100 (†)	100 (†)	100 (†)	100 (†)	100 (†)	100 (†)
Functional problem in existing system or feature	12 (2.6)	13 (3.4)	11 ! (3.8)	‡ (†)	12 ! (4.5)	12 ! (5.3)	22 ! (9.5)	‡ (†)	11 ! (4.4)	‡ (†)	13 ! (5.4)	19 ! (6.5)
Improve operational or energy efficiency	70 (3.9)	68 (4.9)	74 (5.6)	73 (17.7)	66 (7.2)	67 (7.4)	62 (11.2)	78 (6.1)	65 (7.1)	78 (8.6)	78 (5.9)	60 (8.4)
Replacement cycle	9 (2.0)	10 (2.6)	6 ! (2.8)	‡ (†)	13 ! (5.5)	8 ! (3.4)	‡ (†)	8 ! (3.5)	13 ! (4.3)	‡ (†)	7 ! (3.2)	‡ (†)
Other reason	9 (2.3)	10 ! (2.9)	‡ (†)	‡ (†)	‡ (†)	13 ! (4.9)	‡ (†)	‡ (†)	10 ! (4.6)	‡ (†)	‡ (†)	11 ! (5.4)
Exterior lighting—percent of schools with plans	10 (0.8)	9 (1.0)	10 (1.3)	18 ! (6.0)	9 (1.5)	10 (1.5)	9 (2.1)	10 (1.6)	12 (1.6)	8 (1.7)	7 (1.2)	10 (1.8)
Percentage distribution by main reason for the plans	100 (†)	100 (†)	100 (†)	100 (†)	100 (†)	100 (†)	100 (†)	100 (†)	100 (†)	100 (†)	100 (†)	100 (†)
Functional problem in existing system or feature	19 (3.5)	20 (4.6)	19 ! (5.8)	‡ (†)	12 ! (5.2)	14 ! (6.3)	39 ! (14.2)	22 ! (7.2)	13 ! (5.5)	‡ (†)	29 ! (9.9)	21 ! (8.1)
Improve operational or energy efficiency	56 (4.7)	53 (5.9)	62 (6.9)	73 (17.2)	50 (9.2)	67 (8.8)	47 (13.9)	56 (8.5)	57 (7.8)	66 (10.9)	48 (10.2)	56 (10.2)
Replacement cycle	14 (3.0)	15 (3.9)	10 ! (3.9)	‡ (†)	27 ! (8.6)	‡ (†)	‡ (†)	15 ! (6.2)	17 ! (5.1)	‡ (†)	17 ! (7.5)	‡ (†)
Other reason	11 (3.2)	12 ! (3.8)	‡ (†)	# (†)	‡ (†)	14 ! (6.1)	‡ (†)	‡ (†)	13 ! (5.7)	‡ (†)	‡ (†)	‡ (†)
Energy management system—percent of schools with plans	14 (0.9)	13 (1.2)	16 (1.9)	34 (7.9)	13 (2.0)	14 (1.9)	17 (2.9)	15 (1.9)	17 (1.9)	12 (2.0)	14 (1.9)	14 (2.0)
Percentage distribution by main reason for the plans	100 (†)	100 (†)	100 (†)	100 (†)	100 (†)	100 (†)	100 (†)	100 (†)	100 (†)	100 (†)	100 (†)	100 (†)
Functional problem in existing system or feature	14 (2.4)	13 (3.2)	15 (4.1)	‡ (†)	19 ! (5.9)	‡ (†)	21 ! (7.9)	11 ! (4.2)	16 (4.4)	‡ (†)	16 ! (5.7)	11 ! (5.2)
Improve operational or energy efficiency	65 (3.6)	64 (4.5)	66 (6.0)	68 (14.8)	59 (8.7)	63 (7.3)	64 (10.3)	71 (5.6)	58 (6.8)	68 (8.4)	72 (6.3)	67 (8.4)
Replacement cycle	14 (2.7)	16 (3.5)	9 ! (4.3)	‡ (†)	13 ! (5.6)	16 ! (6.2)	13 ! (5.1)	14 ! (5.0)	20 (5.8)	15 ! (6.7)	8 ! (3.4)	‡ (†)
Other reason	7 (2.0)	7 ! (2.6)	9 ! (4.1)	# (†)	‡ (†)	12 ! (4.8)	‡ (†)	‡ (†)	‡ (†)	‡ (†)	‡ (†)	11 ! (5.3)
Life safety features[1]—percent of schools with plans	12 (0.8)	11 (1.0)	12 (1.5)	16 ! (5.8)	11 (1.6)	13 (1.8)	16 (2.7)	10 (1.5)	13 (1.8)	12 (2.0)	11 (1.8)	9 (1.7)
Percentage distribution by main reason for the plans	100 (†)	100 (†)	100 (†)	100 (†)	100 (†)	100 (†)	100 (†)	100 (†)	100 (†)	100 (†)	100 (†)	100 (†)
Functional problem in existing system or feature	24 (3.7)	23 (4.4)	23 (5.8)	‡ (†)	22 ! (7.5)	30 (7.8)	21 ! (7.7)	21 ! (6.6)	26 (6.2)	36 (9.4)	20 ! (6.3)	12 ! (4.7)
Improve operational or energy efficiency	37 (4.2)	34 (4.9)	41 (6.9)	60 ! (22.4)	42 (8.3)	33 (7.6)	40 (8.5)	35 (8.1)	31 (6.9)	29 (7.9)	41 (8.2)	51 (9.6)
Replacement cycle	21 (3.0)	22 (4.0)	19 (4.9)	‡ (†)	24 ! (7.5)	19 ! (6.6)	24 ! (8.7)	18 ! (6.0)	23 (6.0)	17 ! (6.2)	20 ! (6.2)	20 ! (8.6)
Other reason	19 (3.5)	21 (4.2)	16 ! (5.5)	# (†)	‡ (†)	19 ! (5.8)	16 ! (6.7)	26 ! (8.2)	19 ! (6.0)	19 ! (8.1)	19 ! (6.7)	17 ! (7.2)
Security systems—percent of schools with plans	21 (1.2)	20 (1.5)	20 (1.9)	32 (7.4)	16 (2.1)	19 (2.0)	24 (3.1)	24 (2.2)	23 (2.2)	19 (2.7)	21 (2.2)	17 (2.3)
Percentage distribution by main reason for the plans	100 (†)	100 (†)	100 (†)	100 (†)	100 (†)	100 (†)	100 (†)	100 (†)	100 (†)	100 (†)	100 (†)	100 (†)
Functional problem in existing system or feature	22 (2.8)	22 (3.5)	25 (4.4)	‡ (†)	19 ! (5.7)	16 (4.7)	33 (7.5)	24 (4.6)	17 (3.8)	33 (7.7)	22 (4.9)	21 (6.1)
Improve operational or energy efficiency	46 (3.0)	44 (3.7)	50 (5.5)	67 (12.3)	43 (7.2)	53 (6.2)	51 (7.6)	41 (5.3)	48 (5.2)	36 (7.2)	48 (5.7)	48 (8.0)
Replacement cycle	9 (1.8)	10 (2.3)	10 ! (3.1)	# (†)	14 ! (5.1)	8 ! (2.5)	‡ (†)	9 ! (3.1)	13 (3.6)	‡ (†)	7 ! (3.0)	‡ (†)
Other reason	22 (3.0)	25 (3.9)	15 (4.3)	‡ (†)	24 (6.9)	22 (5.5)	9 ! (4.2)	26 (4.8)	21 (4.7)	25	22 (4.8)	22 (6.6)

See notes at end of table.

Table 217.15. Percentage of public schools with plans for major repair, renovation, or replacement of building systems or features in the next 2 years and percentage distribution of schools with such plans, by selected school characteristics, type of system or feature, and main reason for the plans: 2012–13—Continued

[Standard errors appear in parentheses]

Type of system or feature and main reason for major repair, renovation, or replacement plans	All public schools	Instructional level			Community type				Percent of students eligible for free or reduced-priced lunch			
		Elementary	Secondary	Combined	City	Suburban	Town	Rural	Less than 35 percent	35 to 49 percent	50 to 74 percent	75 percent or more
1	2	3	4	5	6	7	8	9	10	11	12	13
Internal communication systems— percent of schools with plans	**14** (1.0)	**13** (1.2)	**16** (2.1)	**23** ! (7.0)	**13** (2.0)	**13** (1.7)	**16** (2.6)	**14** (1.7)	**15** (1.8)	**12** (2.1)	**14** (1.8)	**14** (2.5)
Percentage distribution by main reason for the plans	100 (†)	100 (†)	100 (†)	100 (†)	100 (†)	100 (†)	100 (†)	100 (†)	100 (†)	100 (†)	100 (†)	100 (†)
Functional problem in existing system or feature	24 (3.3)	21 (4.2)	28 (5.5)	37 ! (18.4)	24 (6.4)	19 ! (5.9)	17 ! (6.7)	30 (6.2)	21 (5.2)	31 (8.0)	23 (6.3)	24 (7.0)
Improve operational or energy efficiency	43 (3.5)	39 (4.7)	49 (6.9)	63 (18.4)	41 (7.3)	50 (8.1)	42 (9.1)	39 ! (7.0)	43 (6.3)	47 (9.5)	39 (7.5)	44 (7.1)
Replacement cycle	21 (3.1)	25 (4.2)	12 ! (3.8)	‡ (†)	21 (6.4)	15 ! (5.2)	34 (9.3)	19 ! (5.7)	25 (6.2)	‡ (†)	22 (6.5)	19 ! (6.3)
Other reason	13 (2.7)	15 (3.5)	11 ! (4.6)	# (†)	14 ! (6.2)	16 ! (5.7)	‡ (†)	12 ! (4.8)	12 ! (4.8)	‡ (†)	16 ! (5.3)	13 ! (5.5)
Technology infrastructure—percent of schools with plans	**20** (1.0)	**19** (1.2)	**23** (2.2)	**33** (7.4)	**17** (2.1)	**20** (2.1)	**23** (2.8)	**21** (2.0)	**23** (2.0)	**20** (2.6)	**18** (2.1)	**19** (2.6)
Percentage distribution by main reason for the plans	100 (†)	100 (†)	100 (†)	100 (†)	100 (†)	100 (†)	100 (†)	100 (†)	100 (†)	100 (†)	100 (†)	100 (†)
Functional problem in existing system or feature	17 (2.4)	16 (3.0)	19 (4.1)	‡ (†)	16 ! (5.0)	11 ! (4.1)	16 ! (5.6)	22 (4.7)	14 (3.8)	17 ! (5.9)	16 (4.6)	23 (5.3)
Improve operational or energy efficiency	51 (3.3)	46 (4.2)	59 (5.0)	71 (14.0)	53 (6.5)	51 (6.5)	65 (7.3)	44 (5.3)	44 (4.9)	53 (7.3)	59 (6.6)	51 (6.5)
Replacement cycle	21 (2.6)	25 (3.4)	14 (3.4)	‡ (†)	21 (5.5)	21 (4.5)	10 ! (4.6)	26 (5.1)	28 (5.1)	19 ! (6.0)	19 (5.4)	15 ! (4.8)
Other reason	11 (2.0)	13 (2.7)	8 ! (2.9)	# (†)	9 ! (4.3)	17 (4.5)	‡ (†)	8 ! (3.6)	13 (3.7)	11 ! (4.5)	6 ! (2.9)	12 ! (4.8)

†Not applicable.
#Rounds to zero.
!Interpret data with caution. The coefficient of variation (CV) for this estimate is between 30 and 50 percent.
‡Reporting standards not met. Either there are too few cases for a reliable estimate or the coefficient of variation (CV) for this estimate is 50 percent or greater.

[1]Life safety features include sprinklers, fire alarms, and smoke detectors.
NOTE: Percentage of schools with major repair, renovation, or replacement plans is based on schools having the specified building system or feature. Detail may not sum to totals because of rounding.
SOURCE: U.S. Department of Education, National Center for Education Statistics, Fast Response Survey System (FRSS), "Condition of Public School Facilities: 2012–13," FRSS 105, 2013. (This table was prepared April 2014.)

Table 217.20. Percentage of public schools with enrollment under, at, or over capacity, by selected school characteristics: 1999 and 2005

[Standard errors appear in parentheses]

School enrollment versus design capacity	All public schools[1]		Instructional level				Size of school enrollment						Percent of students eligible for free or reduced-price lunch							
			Elementary		Secondary/ combined		Less than 350		350 to 699		700 or more		Less than 35 percent		35 to 49 percent		50 to 74 percent		75 percent or more	
1	2		3		4		5		6		7		8		9		10		11	
1999, total	100	(†)	100	(†)	100	(†)	100	(†)	100	(†)	100	(†)	100	(†)	100	(†)	100	(†)	100	(†)
Underenrolled by more than 25 percent	19	(1.5)	17	(1.7)	22	(2.5)	39	(4.0)	11	(2.0)	8	(1.7)	16	(2.0)	18	(3.1)	17	(4.1)	27	(4.4)
Underenrolled by 6 to 25 percent	33	(1.7)	31	(2.1)	39	(2.9)	32	(3.8)	36	(2.4)	31	(2.8)	38	(2.6)	32	(4.6)	29	(4.6)	25	(4.5)
Enrollment within 5 percent of capacity	26	(1.5)	28	(2.0)	20	(2.2)	16	(2.9)	34	(2.6)	25	(2.0)	25	(2.2)	26	(4.4)	32	(4.5)	23	(4.1)
Overenrolled by 6 to 25 percent	14	(1.2)	15	(1.5)	11	(1.8)	10	(2.4)	14	(2.0)	20	(1.8)	14	(2.1)	18	(3.6)	14	(3.3)	11	(3.0)
Overenrolled by more than 25 percent	8	(0.9)	8	(1.1)	8	(1.6)	3 !	(1.3)	6	(1.3)	16	(2.4)	6	(1.2)	6	(1.8)	7 !	(2.4)	14	(3.4)
2005, total	100	(†)	100	(†)	100	(†)	100	(†)	100	(†)	100	(†)	100	(†)	100	(†)	100	(†)	100	(†)
Underenrolled by more than 25 percent	21	(1.4)	20	(1.7)	24	(2.6)	41	(3.3)	14	(1.7)	6	(1.4)	19	(2.6)	25	(4.6)	24	(2.7)	19	(3.0)
Underenrolled by 6 to 25 percent	38	(1.8)	39	(2.1)	36	(2.6)	39	(3.4)	44	(2.9)	29	(2.4)	38	(2.7)	43	(4.0)	37	(2.8)	36	(4.1)
Enrollment within 5 percent of capacity	22	(1.5)	23	(1.9)	21	(1.9)	14	(2.3)	27	(2.5)	26	(2.4)	27	(2.5)	19	(3.3)	18	(3.1)	22	(2.9)
Overenrolled by 6 to 25 percent	10	(1.0)	10	(1.4)	11	(1.2)	4	(1.1)	9	(1.9)	20	(2.1)	11	(1.8)	6 !	(2.0)	12	(2.6)	9	(1.6)
Overenrolled by more than 25 percent	8	(1.0)	8	(1.3)	8	(1.0)	2 !	(0.9)	6	(1.4)	19	(2.5)	5	(1.0)	7 !	(2.3)	8	(2.2)	14	(2.9)

†Not applicable.
!Interpret data with caution. The coefficient of variation (CV) for this estimate is between 30 and 50 percent.
[1]Excludes special education, vocational, and alternative schools; schools without enrollment data; and schools offering only preprimary education.

NOTE: Detail may not sum to totals because of rounding.
SOURCE: U.S. Department of Education, National Center for Education Statistics, Fast Response Survey System (FRSS), "Condition of America's Public School Facilities, 1999," FRSS 73, 1999, and "Public School Principals' Perceptions of Their School Facilities: Fall 2005," FRSS 88, 2005. (This table was prepared July 2007.)

CHAPTER 2: Elementary and Secondary Education 231
Computers and Technology

Table 218.10. Number and internet access of instructional computers and rooms in public schools, by selected school characteristics: Selected years, 1995 through 2008
[Standard errors appear in parentheses]

Instructional computers and rooms, and access	All public schools	Instructional level[1]		Size of school enrollment			Community type[2]				Percent of students eligible for free or reduced-price lunch[3]			
		Elementary	Secondary	Less than 300	300 to 999	1,000 or more	City	Suburban	Town	Rural	Less than 35 percent	35 to 49 percent	50 to 74 percent	75 percent or more
1	2	3	4	5	6	7	8	9	10	11	12	13	14	15
Computers for instructional purposes														
Number (in thousands)														
1995[4]	5,621 (—)	3,453 (—)	2,021 (—)	850 (—)	3,600 (—)	1,171 (—)	1,497 (—)	1,526 (—)	1,404 (—)	1,195 (—)	2,905 (—)	806 (—)	950 (—)	882 (—)
2000	8,776 (174)	5,296 (149)	3,271 (113)	1,135 (73)	5,524 (121)	2,117 (103)	2,537 (179)	3,396 (213)	1,155 (132)	1,689 (131)	4,394 (147)	1,373 (93)	1,606 (112)	1,384 (107)
2005	12,672 (281)	7,701 (251)	4,783 (148)	1,566 (98)	7,966 (243)	3,139 (163)	3,132 (177)	4,058 (242)	1,819 (193)	3,663 (255)	5,352 (261)	2,193 (185)	2,687 (244)	2,440 (152)
2008	15,434 (193)	9,711 (159)	5,415 (125)	1,746 (68)	9,486 (144)	4,202 (130)	3,611 (155)	5,787 (255)	2,062 (159)	3,974 (180)	6,195 (174)	2,364 (155)	3,805 (190)	3,070 (175)
Average number per school														
1995[4]	72 (—)	60 (—)	112 (—)	41 (—)	72 (—)	164 (—)	84 (—)	83 (—)	72 (—)	54 (—)	78 (—)	59 (—)	74 (—)	67 (—)
2000	110 (2.0)	89 (2.4)	178 (5.3)	57 (3.1)	106 (2.3)	259 (9.0)	120 (4.9)	128 (4.3)	97 (5.6)	82 (3.6)	120 (3.4)	111 (5.9)	94 (5.7)	99 (5.5)
2005	154 (3.4)	124 (3.8)	253 (6.8)	75 (4.2)	149 (4.2)	388 (13.5)	165 (7.2)	170 (6.3)	154 (13.4)	132 (5.9)	166 (5.5)	153 (9.3)	147 (6.9)	139 (7.4)
2008	189 (2.9)	157 (2.8)	301 (6.5)	87 (3.4)	179 (2.9)	486 (10.4)	205 (7.5)	221 (6.1)	189 (8.0)	147 (4.2)	209 (5.6)	182 (7.7)	181 (6.8)	170 (8.2)
Number with internet access (in thousands)														
1995[4]	447 (—)	232 (—)	187 (—)	59 (—)	315 (—)	73 (—)	96 (—)	131 (—)	126 (—)	94 (—)	286 (—)	46 (—)	57 (—)	36 (—)
2000	6,759 (174)	3,813 (136)	2,779 (113)	882 (69)	4,191 (114)	1,686 (97)	1,782 (148)	2,688 (178)	955 (111)	1,335 (91)	3,608 (139)	1,064 (80)	1,215 (93)	858 (87)
2005	12,245 (274)	7,361 (246)	4,706 (151)	1,515 (98)	7,642 (239)	3,089 (162)	3,009 (173)	3,912 (238)	1,784 (193)	3,541 (239)	5,239 (259)	2,090 (176)	2,583 (228)	2,332 (146)
2008	15,162 (204)	9,508 (169)	5,356 (128)	1,710 (69)	9,308 (153)	4,144 (130)	3,517 (154)	5,716 (253)	2,028 (154)	3,901 (178)	6,131 (174)	2,321 (153)	3,739 (188)	2,971 (175)
Percent with internet access														
1995[4]	8 (—)	7 (—)	9 (—)	7 (—)	9 (—)	6 (—)	6 (—)	9 (—)	9 (—)	8 (—)	10 (—)	6 (—)	6 (—)	4 (—)
2000	77 (1.1)	72 (1.5)	85 (1.2)	78 (2.6)	76 (1.3)	80 (1.8)	70 (2.1)	79 (1.7)	83 (2.5)	79 (2.1)	82 (1.2)	77 (2.9)	76 (2.6)	62 (3.1)
2005	97 (0.4)	96 (0.5)	98 (0.4)	97 (0.7)	96 (0.5)	98 (0.5)	96 (0.7)	96 (1.1)	96 (1.1)	97 (0.7)	98 (0.6)	95 (1.0)	96 (1.0)	96 (0.8)
2008	98 (0.2)	98 (0.3)	99 (0.2)	98 (0.7)	98 (0.3)	99 (0.4)	97 (0.5)	99 (0.3)	98 (0.7)	98 (0.4)	99 (0.3)	98 (0.5)	98 (0.4)	97 (0.7)
Ratio of students to instructional computers with internet access														
2000	6.6 (0.10)	7.8 (0.20)	5.2 (0.20)	3.9 (0.30)	7.0 (0.20)	7.2 (0.30)	8.2 (0.40)	6.6 (0.20)	6.2 (0.30)	5.0 (0.30)	6.0 (0.20)	6.3 (0.40)	7.2 (0.40)	9.1 (0.70)
2005	3.8 (0.10)	4.1 (0.10)	3.3 (0.10)	2.4 (0.10)	3.9 (0.10)	4.0 (0.10)	4.2 (0.20)	4.1 (0.10)	3.4 (0.20)	3.0 (0.10)	3.8 (0.10)	3.4 (0.20)	3.6 (0.20)	4.0 (0.20)
2008	3.1 (0.04)	3.2 (0.05)	2.9 (0.05)	2.2 (0.07)	3.2 (0.05)	3.2 (0.06)	3.4 (0.12)	3.2 (0.08)	2.7 (0.09)	2.9 (0.07)	3.1 (0.06)	3.2 (0.08)	2.9 (0.08)	3.2 (0.14)
Instructional rooms[5]														
Number (in thousands)														
2000	2,905 (35)	1,864 (28)	972 (24)	377 (22)	1,871 (23)	657 (23)	866 (56)	1,086 (61)	413 (47)	541 (39)	1,380 (46)	465 (28)	570 (36)	482 (29)
2005	3,283 (71)	2,152 (70)	1,078 (27)	426 (23)	2,152 (70)	705 (30)	849 (62)	1,050 (61)	439 (41)	945 (67)	1,339 (50)	593 (51)	695 (56)	655 (39)
2008[6]	2,663 (21)	1,723 (20)	887 (15)	282 (9)	1,692 (20)	689 (18)	639 (26)	1,003 (35)	338 (24)	683 (28)	1,053 (27)	425 (26)	653 (27)	532 (22)
Percent with internet access[6]														
1995	8 (0.7)	8 (1.0)	8 (1.0)	9 (1.6)	8 (1.0)	4 (1.0)	6 (1.3)	8 (1.4)	8 (2.0)	8 (1.5)	10 (1.2)	6 (1.4)	6 ! (1.9)	3 ! (1.0)
2000	77 (1.1)	76 (1.5)	79 (1.6)	83 (2.8)	78 (1.5)	70 (2.2)	66 (2.2)	78 (2.0)	87 (2.6)	85 (1.7)	82 (1.5)	81 (2.9)	77 (2.8)	60 (3.3)
2005	94 (1.3)	93 (1.9)	95 (0.9)	92 (1.9)	94 (1.9)	94 (1.5)	88 (3.7)	96 (0.8)	98 (0.7)	95 (1.8)	96 (0.8)	88 (4.3)	96 (0.8)	91 (2.5)
2008	— (†)	— (†)	— (†)	— (†)	— (†)	— (†)	— (—)	— (†)	— (†)	— (†)	— (†)	— (†)	— (†)	— (†)

—Not available.
†Not applicable.
!Interpret data with caution. The coefficient of variation (CV) for this estimate is between 30 and 50 percent.
[1]Data for combined schools are included in the totals and in analyses by other school characteristics, but are not shown separately.
[2]Due to definitional changes for community type, estimates for years prior to 2005 may not be directly comparable with estimates for later years.
[3]Free or reduced-price lunch information was obtained on the questionnaire and supplemented, if necessary, with data from the Common Core of Data (CCD).
[4]Includes computers used for instructional or administrative purposes.

[5]In 2008, instructional rooms included classrooms only and excluded computer labs and library/media centers. Prior to 2008, instructional rooms included classrooms, computer labs and other labs, library/media centers, and other rooms used for instructional purposes.
[6]Some data differ slightly (e.g., by 1 percent) from previously published figures.
NOTE: Detail may not sum to totals because of rounding.
SOURCE: U.S. Department of Education, National Center for Education Statistics, Fast Response Survey System (FRSS), *Internet Access in U.S. Public Schools and Classrooms: 1994–2005* and *Educational Technology in U.S. Public Schools: Fall 2008*; and unpublished tabulations. (This table was prepared August 2010.)

Table 218.20. Percentage of public school districts with students enrolled in technology-based distance education courses and number of enrollments in such courses, by instructional level and district characteristics: 2002–03, 2004–05, and 2009–10

[Standard errors appear in parentheses]

District characteristic	Percent of districts enrolling distance education students		Number of enrollments in technology-based distance education courses,[1] by instructional level									
			All instructional levels		Elementary schools		Middle or junior high schools		High schools		Combined or ungraded schools[2]	
1	2		3		4		5		6		7	
2002–03												
Total	36	(1.2)	317,070	(27,437)	2,780 !	(977)	6,390	(1,067)	214,140	(16,549)	93,760	(22,593)
District enrollment size												
Less than 2,500	37	(1.5)	116,300	(21,698)	‡	(†)	1,250 !	(450)	72,730	(6,924)	42,240 !	(20,502)
2,500 to 9,999	32	(1.8)	82,370	(6,384)	230 !	(109)	1,870 !	(642)	44,170	(5,832)	36,110	(1,210)
10,000 or more	50	(2.1)	118,390	(15,703)	2,480 !	(968)	3,270	(723)	97,240	(13,853)	‡	(†)
Region												
Northeast	21	(2.2)	41,950 !	(20,821)	100 !	(49)	‡	(†)	17,300	(3,656)	‡	(†)
Southeast	45	(2.6)	59,240	(6,251)	‡	(†)	2,530	(632)	50,640	(5,698)	4,680	(1,254)
Central	46	(2.3)	106,690	(7,726)	940 !	(441)	1,050 !	(412)	59,110	(6,455)	45,590	(2,529)
West	32	(2.2)	109,190	(16,010)	350 !	(165)	2,620	(782)	87,090	(14,825)	19,130 !	(8,619)
Poverty concentration												
Less than 10 percent	33	(2.1)	75,740	(11,177)	‡	(†)	2,020	(564)	55,670	(7,556)	17,470 !	(8,591)
10 to 19 percent	42	(2.1)	95,510	(7,962)	‡	(†)	1,830	(392)	78,680	(7,050)	13,560	(2,446)
20 percent or more	42	(2.5)	86,110	(13,518)	760 !	(249)	2,540 !	(837)	75,930	(13,532)	6,880	(1,557)
2004–05												
Total	37	(1.2)	506,950	(56,959)	12,540 !	(6,107)	15,150	(3,367)	309,630	(24,350)	169,630 !	(51,753)
District enrollment size												
Less than 2,500	37	(1.6)	210,200	(54,063)	610 !	(275)	‡	(†)	103,190	(17,659)	‡	(†)
2,500 to 9,999	35	(1.6)	102,730	(13,404)	‡	(†)	2,570	(731)	48,420	(5,136)	45,080	(9,429)
10,000 or more	50	(2.5)	193,440	(16,415)	5,280 !	(2,202)	6,520	(1,101)	157,440	(16,044)	24,210	(5,298)
Region												
Northeast	22	(2.0)	108,300 !	(49,777)	570 !	(206)	‡	(†)	16,860	(2,621)	‡	(†)
Southeast	46	(3.2)	112,830	(6,341)	‡	(†)	5,030	(732)	89,800	(5,276)	16,090	(1,913)
Central	45	(2.4)	128,650	(22,055)	‡	(†)	2,130 !	(953)	70,450	(13,024)	46,190 !	(15,067)
West	35	(2.1)	157,180	(22,608)	200 !	(161)	4,110 !	(1,732)	132,520	(21,287)	20,350 !	(7,587)
Poverty concentration												
Less than 10 percent	35	(1.9)	112,320	(16,778)	‡	(†)	4,070	(1,123)	80,150	(10,651)	‡	(†)
10 to 19 percent	42	(2.2)	151,050	(12,379)	‡	(†)	4,800	(602)	124,540	(10,283)	19,700	(5,835)
20 percent or more	43	(2.7)	106,610	(14,709)	‡	(†)	6,280 !	(3,111)	78,590	(13,367)	21,340	(2,905)
2009–10												
Total	55	(1.4)	1,816,390	(251,054)	78,040 !	(25,180)	154,970	(30,828)	1,348,920	(135,979)	‡	(†)
District enrollment size												
Less than 2,500	51	(1.8)	509,030 !	(167,570)	‡	(†)	‡	(†)	408,030 !	(123,883)	6,570 !	2,753
2,500 to 9,999	66	(1.5)	579,250 !	(185,243)	‡	(†)	23,960 !	(9,196)	312,130	(50,963)	‡	(†)
10,000 or more	74	(0.8)	728,110	(27,105)	11,540	(1,862)	77,750	(4,730)	628,760	(23,545)	10,060	2,756
Metropolitan status												
City	37	(4.0)	653,660 !	(201,665)	‡	(†)	40,400 !	(15,671)	405,740	(79,507)	‡	(†)
Suburban	47	(2.6)	527,250	(34,188)	22,900 !	(11,293)	62,210	(4,106)	434,260	(30,904)	7,880	2,347
Town	67	(2.7)	306,840 !	(145,000)	‡	(†)	‡	(†)	246,850 !	(107,079)	9,310 !	3,908
Rural	59	(2.5)	328,640	(36,233)	‡	(†)	15,360	(2,420)	262,070	(27,077)	‡	(†)
Region												
Northeast	39	(3.3)	77,670	(7,358)	‡	(†)	4,970	(989)	71,330	(6,651)	‡	(†)
Southeast	78	(3.7)	518,770	(63,187)	12,070 !	(4,154)	57,500	(9,828)	443,770	(50,079)	5,440 !	1,678
Central	62	(2.2)	697,140 !	(235,103)	37,920 !	(18,915)	‡	(†)	416,550	(122,633)	‡	(†)
West	51	(2.4)	522,810	(42,673)	‡	(†)	41,620	(3,384)	417,270	(33,400)	36,510 !	14,278
Poverty concentration												
Less than 10 percent	54	(2.5)	287,680	(34,577)	‡	(†)	12,620	(2,997)	231,890	(27,672)	‡	(†)
10 to 19 percent	56	(2.1)	1,009,290	(193,646)	23,540 !	(11,116)	97,220	(16,126)	682,380	(78,795)	‡	(†)
20 percent or more	56	(2.4)	519,420	(146,507)	‡	(†)	‡	(†)	434,640	(108,046)	5,750 !	2,484

†Not applicable.
!Interpret data with caution. The coefficient of variation (CV) for this estimate is between 30 and 50 percent.
‡Reporting standards not met. Either there are too few cases for a reliable estimate or the coefficient of variation (CV) is 50 percent or greater.
[1]Based on students regularly enrolled in the districts. Enrollments may include duplicated counts of students, since districts were instructed to count a student enrolled in multiple courses for each course in which he or she was enrolled.
[2]Combined or ungraded schools are those in which the grades offered in the school span both elementary and secondary grades or that are not divided into grade levels.

NOTE: Percentages are based on unrounded numbers. For the 2002–03 FRSS study sample, there were 3 cases for which district enrollment size was missing and 112 cases for which poverty concentration was missing. For the 2004–05 FRSS study sample, there were 7 cases for which district enrollment size was missing and 103 cases for which poverty concentration was missing. Detail may not sum to totals because of rounding or missing data.
SOURCE: U.S. Department of Education, National Center for Education Statistics, Fast Response Survey System (FRSS), *Technology-Based Distance Education Courses for Public Elementary and Secondary Schools: 2002–03 and 2004–05* and "Distance Education Courses for Public Elementary and Secondary School Students: 2009–10," FRSS 98. (This table was prepared November 2011.)

Table 219.10. High school graduates, by sex and control of school: Selected years, 1869–70 through 2025–26

School year	High school graduates							Averaged freshman graduation rate for public schools[3]	Population 17 years old[4]	Graduates as a ratio of 17-year-old population
	Total[1]	Sex		Control						
		Males	Females	Public[2]			Private, total			
				Total	Males	Females				
1	2	3	4	5	6	7	8	9	10	11
1869–70	16,000	7,064	8,936	—	—	—	—	—	815,000	2.0
1879–80	23,634	10,605	13,029	—	—	—	—	—	946,026	2.5
1889–90	43,731	18,549	25,182	21,882	—	—	21,849 [5]	—	1,259,177	3.5
1899–1900	94,883	38,075	56,808	61,737	—	—	33,146 [5]	—	1,489,146	6.4
1909–10	156,429	63,676	92,753	111,363	—	—	45,066 [5]	—	1,786,240	8.8
1919–20	311,266	123,684	187,582	230,902	—	—	80,364 [5]	—	1,855,173	16.8
1929–30	666,904	300,376	366,528	591,719	—	—	75,185 [5]	—	2,295,822	29.0
1939–40	1,221,475	578,718	642,757	1,143,246	538,273	604,973	78,229 [5]	—	2,403,074	50.8
1949–50	1,199,700	570,700	629,000	1,063,444	505,394	558,050	136,256 [5]	—	2,034,450	59.0
1959–60	1,858,023	895,000	963,000	1,627,050	791,426	835,624	230,973	—	2,672,000	69.5
1969–70	2,888,639	1,430,000	1,459,000	2,588,639	1,285,895	1,302,744	300,000 [5]	78.7	3,757,000	76.9
1975–76	3,142,120	1,552,000	1,590,000	2,837,129	1,401,064	1,436,065	304,991	74.9	4,272,000	73.6
1979–80	3,042,214	1,503,000	1,539,000	2,747,678	—	—	294,536	71.5	4,262,000	71.4
1980–81	3,020,285	1,492,000	1,528,000	2,725,285	—	—	295,000 [5]	72.2	4,212,000	71.7
1981–82	2,994,758	1,479,000	1,515,000	2,704,758	—	—	290,000 [5]	72.9	4,134,000	72.4
1982–83	2,887,604	1,426,000	1,461,000	2,597,604	—	—	290,000 [5]	73.8	3,962,000	72.9
1983–84	2,766,797	—	—	2,494,797	—	—	272,000 [5]	74.5	3,784,000	73.1
1984–85	2,676,917	—	—	2,413,917	—	—	263,000 [5]	74.2	3,699,000	72.4
1985–86	2,642,616	—	—	2,382,616	—	—	260,000 [5]	74.3	3,670,000	72.0
1986–87	2,693,803	—	—	2,428,803	—	—	265,000 [5]	74.3	3,754,000	71.8
1987–88	2,773,020	—	—	2,500,020	—	—	273,000 [5]	74.2	3,849,000	72.0
1988–89	2,743,743	—	—	2,458,800	—	—	284,943	73.4	3,842,000	71.4
1989–90[6]	2,574,162	—	—	2,320,337	—	—	253,825 [7]	73.6	3,505,000	73.4
1990–91	2,492,988	—	—	2,234,893	—	—	258,095	73.7	3,417,913	72.9
1991–92	2,480,399	—	—	2,226,016	—	—	254,383 [7]	74.2	3,398,884	73.0
1992–93	2,480,519	—	—	2,233,241	—	—	247,278	73.8	3,449,143	71.9
1993–94	2,463,849	—	—	2,220,849	—	—	243,000 [5]	73.1	3,442,521	71.6
1994–95	2,519,084	—	—	2,273,541	—	—	245,543	71.8	3,635,803	69.3
1995–96	2,518,109	—	—	2,273,109	—	—	245,000 [5]	71.0	3,640,132	69.2
1996–97	2,611,988	—	—	2,358,403	—	—	253,585	71.3	3,792,207	68.9
1997–98	2,704,050	—	—	2,439,050	1,187,647	1,251,403	265,000 [5]	71.3	4,008,416	67.5
1998–99	2,758,655	—	—	2,485,630	1,212,924	1,272,706	273,025	71.1	3,917,885	70.4
1999–2000	2,832,844	—	—	2,553,844	1,241,631	1,312,213	279,000 [5]	71.7	4,056,639	69.8
2000–01	2,847,973	—	—	2,569,200	1,251,931	1,317,269	278,773	71.7	4,023,686	70.8
2001–02	2,906,534	—	—	2,621,534	1,275,813	1,345,721	285,000 [5]	72.6	4,023,968	72.2
2002–03	3,015,735	—	—	2,719,947	1,330,973	1,388,974	295,788	73.9	4,125,087	73.1
2003–04[6,8]	3,054,438	—	—	2,753,438	1,347,800	1,405,638	301,000 [5]	74.3	4,113,074	74.3
2004–05	3,106,499	—	—	2,799,250	1,369,749	1,429,501	307,249	74.7	4,120,073	75.4
2005–06[6]	3,122,544	—	—	2,815,544	1,376,458	1,439,086	307,000 [5]	73.4	4,200,554	74.3
2006–07	3,199,650	—	—	2,893,045	1,414,069	1,478,976	306,605	73.9	4,297,239	74.5
2007–08	3,312,337	—	—	3,001,337	1,467,180	1,534,157	311,000 [5]	74.7	4,436,955	74.7
2008–09[6]	3,347,828	—	—	3,039,015	1,490,317	1,548,698	308,813	75.5	4,336,950	77.2
2009–10	3,439,102	—	—	3,128,022	1,542,684 [9]	1,585,338 [9]	311,080	78.2	4,311,831	79.8
2010–11	3,449,940	—	—	3,144,100	1,552,981	1,591,113	305,840 [5]	79.6	4,368,154	79.0
2011–12	3,455,405	—	—	3,149,185	1,558,489	1,590,694	306,220	80.8	4,294,956	80.5
2012–13	3,478,027	—	—	3,169,257	1,569,675	1,599,579	308,770 [5]	81.9	4,257,599	81.7
2013–14[10]	3,480,130	—	—	3,168,650	—	—	311,480	—	4,187,691	83.1
2014–15[10]	3,477,620	—	—	3,166,260	—	—	311,360	—	4,172,212	83.4
2015–16[10]	3,505,920	—	—	3,192,220	—	—	313,700	—	—	—
2016–17[10]	3,510,330	—	—	3,195,630	—	—	314,700	—	—	—
2017–18[10]	3,558,100	—	—	3,242,620	—	—	315,480	—	—	—
2018–19[10]	3,549,010	—	—	3,242,630	—	—	306,380	—	—	—
2019–20[10]	3,509,360	—	—	3,208,110	—	—	301,250	—	—	—
2020–21[10]	3,535,980	—	—	3,233,840	—	—	302,140	—	—	—
2021–22[10]	3,543,910	—	—	3,248,980	—	—	294,930	—	—	—
2022–23[10]	3,558,600	—	—	3,272,620	—	—	285,980	—	—	—
2023–24[10]	3,604,410	—	—	3,326,230	—	—	278,180	—	—	—
2024–25[10]	3,658,340	—	—	3,378,810	—	—	279,530	—	—	—
2025–26[10]	3,650,620	—	—	3,371,680	—	—	278,940	—	—	—

—Not available.
[1]Includes graduates of public and private schools.
[2]Data for 1929–30 and preceding years are from *Statistics of Public High Schools* and exclude graduates from high schools that failed to report to the Office of Education. Includes estimates for jurisdictions not reporting counts of graduates by sex.
[3]The averaged freshman graduation rate provides an estimate of the percentage of students who receive a regular diploma within 4 years of entering ninth grade. The rate uses aggregate student enrollment data to estimate the size of an incoming freshman class and aggregate counts of the number of diplomas awarded 4 years later. Averaged freshman graduation rates in this table are based on reported totals of enrollment by grade and high school graduates, rather than on details reported by race/ethnicity.
[4]Derived from Current Population Reports, Series P-25. For years 1869–70 through 1989–90, 17-year-old population is an estimate of the October 17-year-old population based on July data. Data for 1990–91 and later years are October resident population estimates prepared by the Census Bureau.
[5]Estimated.
[6]Includes imputations for nonreporting states.
[7]Projected by private schools responding to the Private School Universe Survey.
[8]Includes estimates for public schools in New York and Wisconsin. Without estimates for these two states, the averaged freshman graduation rate for the remaining 48 states and the District of Columbia is 75.0 percent.

[9]Includes estimate for Connecticut, which did not report graduates by sex.
[10]Projected by NCES.
NOTE: Includes graduates of regular day school programs. Excludes graduates of other programs, when separately reported, and recipients of high school equivalency certificates. Some data have been revised from previously published figures. Detail may not sum to totals because of rounding and adjustments to protect student privacy.
SOURCE: U.S. Department of Education, National Center for Education Statistics, *Annual Report of the Commissioner of Education*, 1870 through 1910; *Biennial Survey of Education in the United States*, 1919–20 through 1949–50; *Statistics of State School Systems*, 1951–52 through 1957–58; *Statistics of Public Elementary and Secondary School Systems*, 1958–59 through 1980–81; *Statistics of Nonpublic Elementary and Secondary Schools*, 1959 through 1980; Common Core of Data (CCD), "State Nonfiscal Survey of Public Elementary/Secondary Education," 1981–82 through 2009–10; "State Dropout and Completion Data File," 2005–06 through 2012–13; *Public School Graduates and Dropouts From the Common Core of Data*, 2007–08 and 2008–09; Private School Universe Survey (PSS), 1989 through 2013; and National High School Graduates Projection Model, 1972–73 through 2025–26. U.S. Department of Commerce, Census Bureau, Population Estimates, retrieved August 11, 2011, from http://www.census.gov/popest/data/national/asrh/2009/2009-nat-res.html and Population Estimates, retrieved December 18, 2015, from http://www.census.gov/popest/data/national/asrh/2014/2014-nat-res.html. (This table was prepared January 2016.)

Table 219.20. Public high school graduates, by region, state, and jurisdiction: Selected years, 1980–81 through 2025–26

Region, state, and jurisdiction	Actual data										Projected data													Percent change 2012–13 to 2025–26
	1980–81	1989–90	1999–2000	2006–07	2007–08	2008–09	2009–10	2010–11	2011–12	2012–13	2013–14	2014–15	2015–16	2016–17	2017–18	2018–19	2019–20	2020–21	2021–22	2022–23	2023–24	2024–25	2025–26	
1	2	3	4	5	6	7	8	9	10	11	12	13	14	15	16	17	18	19	20	21	22	23	24	25
United States	**2,725,285**	**2,320,337**[1]	**2,553,844**	**2,893,045**	**3,001,337**	**3,039,015**[1]	**3,128,022**	**3,144,100**	**3,149,185**	**3,169,257**	**3,168,650**	**3,166,260**	**3,192,220**	**3,195,630**	**3,242,620**	**3,242,630**	**3,208,110**	**3,233,840**	**3,248,980**	**3,272,620**	**3,326,230**	**3,378,810**	**3,371,680**	**6.4**
Region																								
Northeast	593,727	446,045	453,814	536,697	552,289	562,973	556,400	556,611	554,705	555,202	546,940	541,890	539,000	534,910	536,910	532,910	525,990	530,150	529,890	526,380	532,000	541,880	535,840	-3.5
Midwest	784,071	616,700	648,020	702,987	721,220	717,536	726,844	718,779	716,072	713,662	705,590	702,490	704,950	703,690	715,240	713,800	701,690	705,420	714,230	709,600	717,090	724,370	718,480	0.7
South	868,068	796,385	861,498	986,801	1,031,773	1,068,270	1,104,770	1,119,414	1,121,400	1,138,965	1,145,650	1,154,890	1,176,960	1,188,240	1,213,240	1,220,330	1,206,310	1,210,460	1,213,120	1,234,320	1,257,450	1,289,490	1,303,110	14.4
West	479,419	461,207	590,512	666,560	696,055	700,236	740,008	749,296	757,008	761,428	770,470	766,990	771,310	768,800	777,230	775,590	774,120	787,810	791,740	802,310	819,690	813,070	814,240	6.9
State																								
Alabama	44,894	40,485	37,819	38,912	41,346	42,082	43,166	46,035	45,394	44,233	44,540	45,210	44,450	44,660	45,200	44,250	43,020	42,590	42,440	42,620	43,000	44,510	44,140	-0.2
Alaska	5,343	5,396	6,615	7,666	7,855	8,008	8,245	8,064	7,999	7,860	7,720	7,450	7,360	7,520	7,430	7,370	7,130	7,130	7,350	7,540	7,810	8,000	7,980	1.6
Arizona	28,416	32,103	38,304	55,954	61,667	62,374	61,145	64,472	63,208	62,208	66,710	65,520	65,740	63,730	64,390	64,220	64,670	66,470	67,500	69,390	70,890	72,970	72,970	17.3
Arkansas	29,577	26,475	27,336	27,166	28,725	28,057	28,276	28,205	28,419	28,928	29,610	30,360	30,520	30,330	30,330	30,480	30,320	29,910	30,040	29,850	29,690	31,820	31,490	8.8
California	242,172	236,291	309,866	356,641	374,561	372,310[2]	404,987	410,467	418,664	422,125	424,110	420,920	420,140	415,710	420,520	416,700	414,980	422,540	422,530	427,010	436,140	417,570	417,430	-1.1
Colorado	35,897	32,957	39,924	45,628	46,082	47,459	49,321	50,122	50,087	50,968	51,310	51,890	53,470	54,340	55,580	56,580	57,260	58,550	58,600	59,360	60,440	61,580	61,550	20.8
Connecticut	38,369	27,878	31,562	37,541	38,419	34,968	34,495	38,854	38,681	38,722	37,860	36,660	36,650	36,520	35,910	35,580	34,750	35,330	34,360	34,200	33,490	33,910	33,130	-14.4
Delaware	7,349	5,550	6,108	7,205	7,398	7,889	8,133	8,043	8,247	8,070	8,480	8,150	8,099	8,330	8,350	8,350	8,480	8,860	8,800	8,800	9,290	9,190	9,160	13.5
District of Columbia	4,848	3,686	2,695	2,944	3,352	3,517	3,602	3,477	3,860	3,961	3,890	3,920	3,910	3,830	3,920	3,940	3,750	3,750	3,830	4,160	4,300	4,710	4,880	23.1
Florida	88,755	88,934	106,708	142,284	149,046	153,461	156,130	155,493	151,964	158,029	158,450	162,200	162,630	165,540	167,270	168,390	164,800	164,770	166,990	170,250	174,690	181,370	183,470	16.1
Georgia	62,963	56,605	62,563	77,829	83,505	88,003	91,561	92,338	90,582	92,416	94,390	96,530	99,150	100,540	102,560	103,750	102,380	102,700	102,220	103,710	105,840	108,930	109,110	18.1
Hawaii	11,472	10,325	10,437	11,063	11,613	11,508	10,998	10,716	11,360	10,790	11,050	10,900	10,760	10,660	11,080	10,640	11,140	10,700	11,400	11,670	11,640	12,170	12,100	12.1
Idaho	12,679	11,971	16,170	16,242	16,567	16,807	17,793	17,525	17,568	17,198	19,120	18,800	19,820	20,790	20,930	21,340	21,160	22,430	22,250	23,110	23,770	25,190	25,150	46.2
Illinois	136,795	108,119	111,835	130,220	135,143	131,670	139,035	134,956	139,575	139,228	137,650	139,000	136,900	137,350	141,510	141,890	139,730	142,530	145,760	143,530	143,900	143,390	139,980	0.5
Indiana	73,381	60,012	57,012	59,887	61,901	63,663	64,551	66,133	65,667	66,595	67,560	66,840	66,690	67,120	67,700	69,160	66,250	64,380	65,710	64,220	65,020	66,210	65,920	-1.0
Iowa	42,635	31,796	33,926	34,127	34,573	33,926	34,462	33,863	33,230	32,548	32,600	32,640	32,820	33,000	33,490	33,120	33,180	33,550	33,630	34,210	34,960	35,660	35,730	9.8
Kansas	29,397	35,357	29,102	30,139	30,737	30,368	31,642	31,370	31,898	31,922	32,150	31,750	32,750	32,650	33,530	33,630	33,430	34,080	34,120	34,600	35,210	36,250	36,040	12.9
Kentucky	41,714	38,015	36,830	39,099	39,339	41,851	42,664	43,031	42,642	42,888	42,400	41,640	41,900	41,440	41,980	41,990	40,710	41,480	41,450	40,530	40,640	41,370	41,110	-4.2
Louisiana	46,199	36,053	38,400	34,274	34,401	35,622	36,573	35,844	36,675	37,508	38,190	37,240	38,440	38,170	39,780	38,900	38,840	38,250	37,840	38,260	38,880	40,300	40,090	6.9
Maine	15,554	13,839	12,211	13,151	14,350[4]	14,093[4]	14,069	13,653	13,473	13,170	12,730	12,650	12,730	12,410	12,240	12,110	11,830	11,780	11,930	11,890	11,720	11,820	11,630	-11.7
Maryland	54,050	41,566	47,849	57,564	59,171	58,304	59,078	58,745	58,811	58,896	58,130	57,350	57,290	56,300	57,550	57,020	58,930	59,420	60,260	61,010	62,600	64,900	65,310	10.9
Massachusetts	74,831	55,941[5]	52,950	63,903	65,197	65,258	64,462	64,724	65,157	66,360	65,200	65,570	66,560	65,730	65,850	65,830	65,210	65,450	65,100	64,300	64,880	66,130	64,750	-2.4
Michigan	124,372	93,807	97,679	111,838	115,183	112,742	110,682	106,017	105,446	104,210	102,520	101,310	101,840	100,160	101,570	99,430	96,400	96,040	96,650	94,000	94,610	94,670	93,490	-10.3
Minnesota	64,166	49,087	57,372	59,497	60,409	59,729	59,667	59,357	57,501	58,255	56,380	57,150	56,590	57,300	58,200	59,130	58,620	60,270	61,880	62,390	63,860	65,150	64,690	11.0
Mississippi	28,083	25,182	24,232	24,186	24,735	24,505	25,478	27,321	26,158	26,502	26,650	25,910	25,890	26,070	26,830	25,820	25,370	24,480	24,730	24,620	25,370	26,770	26,230	-1.0
Missouri	60,359	48,967	52,848	60,275	61,717	62,969	63,994	62,994	61,313	61,407	60,900	60,780	61,640	60,860	61,060	60,530	58,930	59,420	59,880	60,290	60,820	62,060	62,050	1.0
Montana	11,634	9,370	10,903	10,122	10,396	10,077	10,075	9,732	9,750	9,369	9,470	9,420	9,480	9,480	9,250	9,480	9,530	9,580	9,690	9,720	10,190	10,160	10,330	10.2
Nebraska	21,411	17,664	20,149	19,873	20,035	19,501	19,370	20,331	20,464	20,442	20,580	20,860	21,120	21,420	22,000	22,350	22,760	22,970	23,490	23,420	23,790	22,450	23,190	13.4
Nevada	9,069	9,477	14,551	17,149	18,815	19,904[2]	20,956	21,182	21,891	23,038	22,720	22,100	22,490	22,860	23,040	23,420	23,390	23,520	23,640	24,270	24,940	26,210	26,520	15.1
New Hampshire	11,552	10,766	11,829	14,452	14,982	14,757	15,034	14,495	14,426	14,262	13,790	13,560	13,510	13,050	12,970	12,690	12,660	12,400	12,410	12,130	12,080	11,960	11,740	-17.7
New Jersey	93,168	69,824	74,420	93,013	94,994	95,085	96,225	95,186	93,819	96,490	95,230	95,640	95,400	94,520	94,950	94,780	93,810	93,810	94,980	93,870	94,710	96,890	95,970	-0.5
New Mexico	17,915	14,884	18,031	16,131	18,264	17,931	18,585	19,352	20,315	19,232	18,850	19,180	18,690	19,010	19,000	19,440	19,290	19,020	19,290	19,550	19,810	20,100	19,860	3.2
New York	198,465	143,318	141,731	168,333	176,310	180,917	183,826	182,759	180,806	180,351	178,820	179,220	178,550	177,440	179,510	176,920	175,600	177,800	176,670	177,240	181,430	185,130	183,720	1.9
North Carolina	69,395	64,782	62,140	76,031	83,307	66,712	88,704	89,882	93,977	94,339	96,220	96,520	98,260	98,540	100,790	101,870	100,130	100,090	99,300	100,230	103,100	105,800	105,360	11.7
North Dakota	9,924	7,660	8,606	7,159	6,999	7,232	7,155	7,156	6,942	6,900	6,960	7,020	7,200	7,250	7,080	7,420	7,540	7,810	8,230	8,460	9,230	9,540	9,940	44.0
Ohio	143,503	114,513	111,668	117,658	120,758	122,203	123,437	124,229	123,135	122,491	119,520	116,970	118,530	117,520	119,010	117,970	115,700	115,150	114,750	114,380	115,230	116,470	115,580	-5.6
Oklahoma	38,875	36,606	37,646	37,100	37,630	37,219	38,503	37,744	37,305	37,033	37,260	37,640	38,930	39,530	40,160	40,160	40,210	40,910	41,150	41,350	42,140	43,800	43,870	18.5
Oregon	28,729	25,473	30,151	33,446	34,949	35,138	34,671	34,723	34,261	33,899	34,450	34,010	34,020	34,400	34,410	34,300	34,050	34,440	34,650	34,800	35,730	36,880	37,070	9.4
Pennsylvania	144,645	110,527	113,959	128,603	130,298	130,658	131,182	130,284	131,733	129,777	127,210	122,630	119,790	120,200	120,440	119,470	116,730	117,680	118,720	117,430	118,670	120,470	119,630	-7.8
Rhode Island	10,719	7,825	8,477	10,384	10,347	10,028	9,908	9,724	9,751	9,579	9,730	9,630	9,630	8,750	9,020	9,530	9,500	9,420	9,610	9,280	9,240	9,600	9,420	-1.6

See notes at end of table.

Table 219.20. Public high school graduates, by region, state, and jurisdiction: Selected years, 1980–81 through 2025–26—Continued

Region, state, and jurisdiction	Actual data										Projected data													Percent change, 2012–13 to 2025–26
	1980–81	1989–90	1999–2000	2006–07	2007–08	2008–09	2009–10	2010–11	2011–12	2012–13	2013–14	2014–15	2015–16	2016–17	2017–18	2018–19	2019–20	2020–21	2021–22	2022–23	2023–24	2024–25	2025–26	
1	2	3	4	5	6	7	8	9	10	11	12	13	14	15	16	17	18	19	20	21	22	23	24	25
South Carolina	39,347	32,483	31,617	35,108	35,303	39,114	40,438	40,708	41,442	42,246	41,720	42,300	43,500	44,600	45,630	45,830	44,800	44,760	45,220	46,000	47,810	49,850	50,160	18.7
South Dakota	10,385	7,650	9,278	8,346	8,582	8,123	8,162	8,248	8,196	8,239	7,960	7,910	7,800	7,880	8,040	7,830	7,970	8,100	8,280	8,750	8,820	9,120	9,180	11.4
Tennessee	50,648	46,034	41,568	54,502	57,486	60,368	62,408	61,862	62,454	61,323	60,980	60,770	61,180	62,040	62,310	62,080	61,210	61,220	61,460	62,400	63,910	64,850	64,930	5.9
Texas	171,665	172,480	212,925	241,193	252,121	264,275	280,894	290,470	292,531	301,390	304,390	308,820	320,520	325,890	336,640	344,000	340,310	345,840	349,080	355,970	360,340	372,450	375,720	24.7
Utah	19,886	21,196	32,501	28,276	28,167	30,463	31,481	30,888	31,157	33,186	33,400	34,260	35,550	36,970	37,770	38,360	39,050	40,210	40,750	41,040	42,180	43,400	43,420	30.8
Vermont	6,424	6,127	6,675	7,317	7,392	7,209	7,199	6,932	6,889	6,491	6,360	6,330	6,170	6,300	6,020	5,990	5,900	5,850	5,910	6,040	5,810	5,970	5,850	-9.8
Virginia	67,126	60,605	65,596	73,997	77,369	79,651	81,511	82,895	83,336	83,279	83,100	82,900	84,560	85,030	86,650	86,570	86,180	86,010	87,720	87,890	89,570	92,150	91,550	9.9
Washington	50,046	45,941	57,597	62,801	61,625	62,764	66,046	66,453	65,205	66,066	66,240	66,990	67,500	67,540	68,000	67,980	66,700	67,550	68,060	68,670	69,930	72,530	73,190	10.8
West Virginia	23,580	21,854	19,437	17,407	17,489	17,690	17,661	17,311	17,603	17,924	17,520	17,420	17,740	17,400	17,470	16,940	16,730	16,420	16,590	16,410	16,270	16,720	16,540	-7.7
Wisconsin	67,743	52,038	58,545	63,968	65,183	65,410	64,687	64,135	62,705	61,425	60,820	60,240	60,850	61,180	62,020	61,350	60,470	60,950	61,610	61,240	61,630	63,200	62,710	2.1
Wyoming	6,161	5,823	6,462	5,441	5,494	5,493	5,695	5,600	5,553	5,489	5,590	5,560	5,700	5,700	5,730	5,750	5,750	6,070	6,030	6,300	6,480	6,670	6,680	21.9
Jurisdiction																								
Bureau of Indian Education	—	—	—	—	—	—	—	—	—	—	—	—	—	—	—	—	—	—	—	—	—	—	—	—
DoD, overseas	—	—	2,642	—	—	—	—	—	—	—	—	—	—	—	—	—	—	—	—	—	—	—	—	—
DoD, domestic	—	—	560	—	—	—	—	—	—	—	—	—	—	—	—	—	—	—	—	—	—	—	—	—
Other jurisdictions																								
American Samoa	—	703	698	954	—	—	—	—	—	—	—	—	—	—	—	—	—	—	—	—	—	—	—	—
Guam	—	1,033	1,406	—	—	—	—	—	—	—	—	—	—	—	—	—	—	—	—	—	—	—	—	—
Northern Marianas	—	227	360	643	—	—	—	—	—	—	—	—	—	—	—	—	—	—	—	—	—	—	—	—
Puerto Rico	—	29,049	30,856	31,718	30,016	29,286	25,514	26,231	25,720	—	—	—	—	—	—	—	—	—	—	—	—	—	—	—
U.S. Virgin Islands	—	1,260	1,060	820	820	940	958	1,014	1,046	897	—	—	—	—	—	—	—	—	—	—	—	—	—	—

—Not available.
[1]U.S. total includes estimates for nonreporting states.
[2]Estimated high school graduates from NCES 2011-312, *Public School Graduates and Dropouts from the Common Core of Data: School Year 2008–09.*
[3]Beginning in 1989–90, graduates from adult programs are excluded.
[4]Includes 1,161 graduates in 2007–08 and 1,169 graduates in 2008–09 from private high schools that received a majority of their funding from public sources.
[5]Projected data from NCES 91-490, *Projections of Education Statistics to 2002.*

NOTE: Data include regular diploma recipients, but exclude students receiving a certificate of attendance and persons receiving high school equivalency certificates. DoD = Department of Defense. Some data have been revised from previously published figures. Detail may not sum to totals because of rounding.
SOURCE: U.S. Department of Education, National Center for Education Statistics, Common Core of Data (CCD), "State Nonfiscal Survey of Public Elementary/Secondary Education," 1981–82 through 2005–06; "State Dropout and Completion Data File," 2005–06 through 2012–13; *Public School Graduates and Dropouts From the Common Core of Data,* 2007–08 and 2008–09; and State High School Graduates Projection Model, 1980–81 through 2025–26. (This table was prepared January 2016.)

Table 219.30. Public high school graduates, by race/ethnicity: 1998–99 through 2025–26

Year	Number of high school graduates							Percentage distribution of graduates						
	Total	White	Black	Hispanic	Asian/ Pacific Islander	American Indian/ Alaska Native	Two or more races	Total	White	Black	Hispanic	Asian/ Pacific Islander	American Indian/ Alaska Native	Two or more races
1	2	3	4	5	6	7	8	9	10	11	12	13	14	15
1998–99	2,485,630	1,749,561	325,708	270,836	115,216	24,309	—	100.0	70.4	13.1	10.9	4.6	1.0	†
1999–2000	2,553,844	1,778,370	338,116	289,139	122,344	25,875	—	100.0	69.6	13.2	11.3	4.8	1.0	†
2000–01	2,569,200	1,775,036	339,578	301,740	126,465	26,381	—	100.0	69.1	13.2	11.7	4.9	1.0	†
2001–02	2,621,534	1,796,110	348,969	317,197	132,182	27,076	—	100.0	68.5	13.3	12.1	5.0	1.0	†
2002–03	2,719,947	1,856,454	359,920	340,182	135,588	27,803	—	100.0	68.3	13.2	12.5	5.0	1.0	†
2003–04	2,753,438	1,829,177	383,443	374,492	137,496	28,830	—	100.0	66.4	13.9	13.6	5.0	1.0	†
2004–05	2,799,250	1,855,198	385,987	383,714	143,729	30,622	—	100.0	66.3	13.8	13.7	5.1	1.1	†
2005–06	2,815,544	1,838,765	399,406	396,820	150,925	29,628	—	100.0	65.3	14.2	14.1	5.4	1.1	†
2006–07	2,893,045	1,868,056	418,113	421,036	154,837	31,003	—	100.0	64.6	14.5	14.6	5.4	1.1	†
2007–08	3,001,337	1,898,367	429,840	448,887	159,410	32,036	32,797 [1]	100.0	63.3	14.3	15.0	5.3	1.1	1.1 [1]
2008–09	3,039,015	1,883,382	451,384	481,698	163,575	32,213	26,763 [1]	100.0	62.0	14.9	15.9	5.4	1.1	0.9 [1]
2009–10	3,128,022	1,871,980	472,261	545,518	167,840	34,131	36,292 [1]	100.0	59.8	15.1	17.4	5.4	1.1	1.2 [1]
2010–11	3,144,100	1,835,332	471,461	583,907	168,875	32,768	51,748	100.0	58.4	15.0	18.6	5.4	1.0	1.6
2011–12	3,149,185	1,807,528	467,932	608,726	173,835	32,450	58,703	100.0	57.4	14.9	19.3	5.5	1.0	1.9
2012–13	3,169,257	1,791,147	461,919	640,413	179,101	31,100	65,569	100.0	56.5	14.6	20.2	5.7	1.0	2.1
2013–14[2]	3,168,650	1,771,690	453,800	657,520	183,210	30,230	72,190	100.0	55.9	14.3	20.8	5.8	1.0	2.3
2014–15[2]	3,166,260	1,754,090	457,250	673,030	186,540	29,800	65,560	100.0	55.4	14.4	21.3	5.9	0.9	2.1
2015–16[2]	3,192,220	1,754,840	462,620	690,090	186,490	30,370	67,810	100.0	55.0	14.5	21.6	5.8	1.0	2.1
2016–17[2]	3,195,630	1,749,280	461,500	696,570	188,240	30,040	70,000	100.0	54.7	14.4	21.8	5.9	0.9	2.2
2017–18[2]	3,242,620	1,743,650	467,080	729,510	201,350	29,370	71,650	100.0	53.8	14.4	22.5	6.2	0.9	2.2
2018–19[2]	3,242,630	1,724,920	461,930	752,130	201,860	28,560	73,230	100.0	53.2	14.2	23.2	6.2	0.9	2.3
2019–20[2]	3,208,110	1,684,190	450,920	765,430	204,560	27,810	75,200	100.0	52.5	14.1	23.9	6.4	0.9	2.3
2020–21[2]	3,233,840	1,681,980	443,170	791,050	213,430	26,900	77,310	100.0	52.0	13.7	24.5	6.6	0.8	2.4
2021–22[2]	3,248,980	1,668,640	440,250	817,460	217,020	26,410	79,190	100.0	51.4	13.6	25.2	6.7	0.8	2.4
2022–23[2]	3,272,620	1,648,490	446,110	853,780	216,980	25,980	81,290	100.0	50.4	13.6	26.1	6.6	0.8	2.5
2023–24[2]	3,326,230	1,645,150	457,510	896,570	217,630	25,860	83,510	100.0	49.5	13.8	27.0	6.5	0.8	2.5
2024–25[2]	3,378,810	1,651,690	471,750	922,660	221,420	25,500	85,790	100.0	48.9	14.0	27.3	6.6	0.8	2.5
2025–26[2]	3,371,680	1,635,040	473,570	920,630	228,750	25,420	88,260	100.0	48.5	14.0	27.3	6.8	0.8	2.6

—Not available.
†Not applicable.
[1]Data on students of Two or more races were not reported by all states; therefore, the data are not comparable to figures for 2010–11 and later years.
[2]Projected.
NOTE: Race categories exclude persons of Hispanic ethnicity. Prior to 2007–08, data on students of Two or more races were not collected separately. Some data have been revised from previously published figures. Detail may not sum to totals because of rounding and statistical methods used to prevent the identification of individual students.
SOURCE: U.S. Department of Education, National Center for Education Statistics, Common Core of Data (CCD), "State Nonfiscal Survey of Public Elementary/Secondary Education," 1999–2000 through 2005–06; "State Dropout and Completion Data File," 2005–06 through 2012–13; and National Public High School Graduates by Race/Ethnicity Projection Model, 1995–96 through 2025–26. (This table was prepared January 2016.)

Table 219.32. Public high school graduates, by sex, race/ethnicity, and state or jurisdiction: 2012–13

State or jurisdiction	Total, male and female				Asian/Pacific Islander			American Indian/Alaska Native	Two or more races	Male				Asian/Pacific Islander	American Indian/Alaska Native	Two or more races	Female				Asian/Pacific Islander	American Indian/Alaska Native	Two or more races
	Total	White	Black	Hispanic	Total	Asian	Pacific Islander			Total	White	Black	Hispanic				Total	White	Black	Hispanic			
1	2	3	4	5	6	7	8	9	10	11	12	13	14	15	16	17	18	19	20	21	22	23	24
United States	3,169,257	1,791,147	461,919	640,413	179,101	168,782	10,319	31,100	65,569	1,569,675	899,883	219,989	312,878	90,150	15,407	31,370	1,599,579	891,264	241,930	327,535	88,959	15,692	34,200
Alabama	44,233	26,963	14,709	1,338	595	574	21	486	142	21,701	13,618	6,815	675	284	246	63	22,532	13,345	7,894	663	311	240	79
Alaska	7,860	4,428	271	482	725	567	158	1,495	459	3,945	2,224	133	238	379	738	233	3,915	2,204	138	244	346	757	226
Arizona	62,206	29,357	3,332	23,542	2,313	2,166	147	2,837	827	30,337	14,505	1,635	11,281	1,185	1,348	383	31,871	14,852	1,697	12,261	1,128	1,489	444
Arkansas	28,928	19,426	6,007	2,413	513	428	85	180	389	14,369	9,787	2,815	1,235	262	90	180	14,559	9,639	3,192	1,178	251	90	209
California	422,125	125,492	27,069	198,993	57,667	55,083	2,584	2,998	9,906	208,126	62,954	13,102	96,324	29,437	1,441	4,868	213,999	62,538	13,967	102,669	29,230	1,557	5,038
Colorado	50,968	31,552	2,441	13,219	1,916	1,797	119	432	1,408	25,170	15,703	1,234	6,434	911	213	675	25,798	15,849	1,207	6,785	1,005	219	733
Connecticut	38,722	25,828	4,758	5,838	1,707	1,642	65	142	449	19,435	13,084	2,368	2,859	831	75	218	19,287	12,744	2,390	2,979	876	67	231
Delaware	8,070	4,334	2,561	805	295	292	≤3	26	46	3,948	2,144	1,229	381	159	13	22	4,122	2,190	1,332	424	139	13	24
District of Columbia	3,961	142	3,028	422	59	54	≤3	7	303	1,732	64	1,285	192	26	≤3	164	2,228	78	1,743	230	34	4	139
Florida	158,029	73,953	32,454	42,010	4,804	4,652	152	629	4,179	77,301	36,500	15,484	20,638	2,372	326	1,981	80,728	37,453	16,970	21,372	2,432	303	2,198
Georgia	92,416	44,875	32,811	8,275	3,776	3,699	77	207	2,472	44,872	22,315	15,271	4,062	1,954	101	1,169	47,544	22,560	17,540	4,213	1,822	106	1,303
Hawaii	10,790	1,379	224	504	8,017	4,753	3,264	42	624	5,350	659	103	240	3,997	21	330	5,440	720	121	264	4,020	21	294
Idaho	17,198	13,883	199	2,375	329	258	71	198	214	8,524	6,914	102	1,137	168	99	104	8,674	6,969	97	1,238	161	99	110
Illinois	139,228	80,496	22,016	26,687	6,390	6,278	112	363	3,276	68,855	40,673	10,235	12,992	3,199	201	1,555	70,373	39,823	11,781	13,695	3,191	162	1,721
Indiana	66,595	51,519	6,877	4,643	1,209	1,176	33	223	2,124	32,674	25,530	3,150	2,263	593	106	1,032	33,921	25,989	3,727	2,380	616	117	1,082
Iowa	32,548	27,495	1,314	2,228	724	687	37	154	633	16,388	13,871	674	1,095	358	76	314	16,160	13,624	640	1,133	366	78	319
Kansas	31,922	22,933	2,235	4,352	901	756	45	369	1,232	16,057	11,654	1,125	2,131	396	196	555	15,865	11,279	1,110	2,221	405	173	677
Kentucky	42,888	35,865	4,581	1,236	577	550	27	119	510	21,653	18,215	2,237	609	297	56	239	21,235	17,650	2,344	627	280	63	271
Louisiana	37,508	19,635	15,307	1,259	747	722	25	272	288	17,728	9,529	6,974	600	379	130	116	19,780	10,106	8,333	659	368	142	172
Maine	13,170	12,175	319	191	294	284	10	92	99	6,660	6,162	157	104	145	47	45	6,510	6,013	162	87	149	45	54
Maryland	58,896	27,409	20,361	5,463	3,752	3,700	52	246	1,665	29,049	13,791	9,715	2,756	1,863	133	791	29,847	13,618	10,646	2,707	1,889	113	874
Massachusetts	66,360	47,254	5,870	7,941	3,874	3,800	74	153	1,268	33,048	23,642	2,859	3,937	1,934	82	594	33,312	23,612	3,011	4,004	1,940	71	674
Michigan	104,210	77,503	16,949	3,324	3,087	2,973	114	833	2,514	51,453	38,637	7,974	1,658	1,582	418	1,184	52,757	38,866	8,975	1,666	1,505	415	1,330
Minnesota	58,255	46,012	4,231	2,827	3,670	3,644	26	664	851	29,164	23,177	2,113	1,398	1,773	322	381	29,091	22,885	2,118	1,429	1,897	342	470
Mississippi	26,502	12,883	12,740	448	304	297	7	44	83	12,382	6,256	5,687	230	154	21	34	14,120	6,627	7,053	218	150	23	49
Missouri	61,407	47,112	9,671	2,317	1,273	1,202	71	283	751	31,258	24,158	4,764	1,172	666	142	356	30,149	22,954	4,907	1,145	607	141	395
Montana	9,369	8,041	65	281	128	109	19	738	116	4,794	4,122	34	154	60	366	58	4,575	3,919	31	127	68	372	58
Nebraska	20,442	15,329	1,264	2,666	413	393	20	230	540	10,340	7,815	615	1,318	207	124	261	10,102	7,514	649	1,348	206	106	279
Nevada	23,038	10,028	1,873	7,548	2,064	1,735	329	230	1,295	10,953	4,820	904	3,480	1,030	111	608	12,085	5,208	969	4,068	1,034	119	687
New Hampshire	14,282	13,022	261	457	353	344	9	37	132	7,176	6,569	143	214	175	15	83	7,086	6,453	118	243	178	22	72
New Jersey	96,490	54,591	14,930	17,711	8,788	8,555	233	111	359	48,698	27,864	7,409	8,736	4,453	48	188	47,792	26,727	7,521	8,975	4,335	63	171
New Mexico	19,232	5,509	426	10,628	303	288	15	2,146	220	9,390	2,745	218	5,114	155	1,054	104	9,842	2,764	208	5,514	148	1,092	116
New York[1]	180,351	98,641	30,059	33,532	16,496	16,295	201	785	838	88,740	49,507	14,149	16,174	8,169	376	365	91,611	49,134	15,910	17,358	8,327	409	473
North Carolina	94,339	52,914	25,497	9,078	2,568	2,482	86	1,301	2,981	46,526	26,687	12,125	4,412	1,239	660	1,403	47,813	26,227	13,372	4,666	1,329	641	1,578
North Dakota	6,900	6,051	164	134	103	92	11	417	31	3,486	3,073	81	70	56	194	12	3,414	2,978	83	64	47	223	19
Ohio	122,491	96,889	16,229	3,286	2,100	2,054	46	154	3,833	61,315	48,901	7,768	1,659	1,030	86	1,871	61,176	47,988	8,461	1,627	1,070	68	1,962
Oklahoma	37,033	21,386	3,434	3,601	928	857	71	6,441	1,243	18,444	10,761	1,670	1,756	450	3,205	602	18,589	10,625	1,764	1,845	478	3,236	641
Oregon	33,899	23,534	848	5,807	1,723	1,535	188	514	1,473	16,610	11,688	379	2,737	846	292	728	17,289	11,846	469	3,070	877	282	745
Pennsylvania	129,777	97,199	17,765	8,706	4,429	4,344	85	163	1,515	65,092	49,267	8,544	4,285	2,207	78	711	64,685	47,932	9,221	4,421	2,222	85	804
Rhode Island	9,579	6,592	770	1,740	298	282	16	36	153	4,749	3,305	371	842	141	19	71	4,830	3,277	399	898	157	17	82
South Carolina	42,246	23,802	14,769	2,070	707	647	60	123	775	20,566	11,845	6,945	1,022	351	65	338	21,680	11,957	7,824	1,048	356	58	437
South Dakota	8,239	7,025	209	229	149	144	5	543	83	4,147	3,553	104	101	75	274	40	4,092	3,472	105	128	75	269	43
Tennessee	61,323	42,682	14,509	2,800	1,185	1,113	72	147	—	30,378	21,452	6,836	1,408	601	82	—	30,943	21,230	7,673	1,392	584	65	—
Texas	301,390	104,466	38,772	139,783	12,044	11,650	394	1,311	5,014	151,002	53,036	19,177	69,495	6,174	701	2,419	150,388	51,430	19,595	70,288	5,870	610	2,595
Utah	33,186	26,757	402	4,100	1,135	669	466	373	419	16,436	13,259	212	1,994	613	165	193	16,750	13,498	190	2,106	522	208	226
Vermont	6,491	5,949	135	83	152	143	9	12	160	3,317	3,051	57	43	71	4	91	3,174	2,898	78	40	81	8	69
Virginia	83,279	47,825	18,565	8,055	5,293	5,183	110	265	3,276	41,383	24,168	8,820	4,000	2,710	265	1,555	41,896	23,657	9,745	4,055	2,583	135	1,721
Washington	66,066	43,132	2,905	10,092	5,826	5,380	446	740	3,371	32,968	21,235	1,416	4,860	2,865	381	1,611	33,698	21,897	1,489	5,232	2,961	359	1,760
West Virginia	17,924	16,572	917	174	134	131	≤3	19	105	9,033	8,344	475	84	69	13	48	8,891	8,228	442	90	68	6	57
Wisconsin	61,425	48,675	4,754	4,155	2,297	2,268	29	682	862	30,832	24,717	2,263	2,024	1,070	341	417	30,593	23,958	2,491	2,131	1,227	341	445
Wyoming	5,489	4,643	62	565	67	55	12	88	64	2,721	2,333	34	255	29	40	30	2,768	2,310	28	310	38	48	34

See notes at end of table.

Table 219.32. Public high school graduates, by sex, race/ethnicity, and state or jurisdiction: 2012–13—Continued

State or jurisdiction	Total, male and female									Male							Female						
	Total	White	Black	Hispanic	Asian/Pacific Islander Total	Asian	Pacific Islander	American Indian/Alaska Native	Two or more races	Total	White	Black	Hispanic	Asian/Pacific Islander	American Indian/Alaska Native	Two or more races	Total	White	Black	Hispanic	Asian/Pacific Islander	American Indian/Alaska Native	Two or more races
1	2	3	4	5	6	7	8	9	10	11	12	13	14	15	16	17	18	19	20	21	22	23	24
Bureau of Indian Education	—	—	—	—	—	—	—	—	—	—	—	—	—	—	—	—	—	—	—	—	—	—	—
DoD, overseas	—	—	—	—	—	—	—	—	—	—	—	—	—	—	—	—	—	—	—	—	—	—	—
DoD, domestic	—	—	—	—	—	—	—	—	—	—	—	—	—	—	—	—	—	—	—	—	—	—	—
Other jurisdictions																							
American Samoa	—	—	—	—	—	—	—	—	—	—	—	—	—	—	—	—	—	—	—	—	—	—	—
Guam	—	—	—	—	—	—	—	—	—	—	—	—	—	—	—	—	—	—	—	—	—	—	—
Northern Marianas	—	—	—	—	—	—	—	—	—	—	—	—	—	—	—	—	—	—	—	—	—	—	—
Puerto Rico	897	7	727	139	≤3	≤3	≤3	≤3	20	383	≤3	321	55	≤3	≤3	≤3	514	4	406	84	≤3	≤3	≤3
U.S. Virgin Islands																17						≤3	17

—Not available.
[1]Distribution of Asian and Pacific Islander students is estimated by the National Center for Education Statistics.
NOTE: Race categories exclude persons of Hispanic ethnicity. DoD = Department of Defense. To protect the confidentiality of individual students, small cell sizes have been bottom coded to less than or equal to three. Detail may not sum to totals because of statistical methods used to prevent the identification of individual students.
SOURCE: U.S. Department of Education, National Center for Education Statistics, Common Core of Data (CCD), State Dropout and Completion Data File, 2012–13. (This table was prepared January 2016.)

Table 219.35. Public high school averaged freshman graduation rate (AFGR), by state or jurisdiction: Selected years, 1990–91 through 2012–13

State or jurisdiction	1990–91	1995–96	1999–2000	2000–01	2002–03	2003–04	2004–05	2005–06	2006–07	2007–08	2008–09	2009–10	2010–11	2011–12	2012–13
1	2	3	4	5	6	7	8	9	10	11	12	13	14	15	16
United States	73.7	71.0	71.7	71.7	73.9	74.3 [1]	74.7	73.4 [2]	73.9	74.7	75.5 [2]	78.2	79.6	80.8	81.9
Alabama	69.8	62.7	64.1	63.7	64.7	65.0	65.9	66.2	67.1	69.0	69.9	71.8	76.1	75.1	74.2
Alaska	74.6	68.3	66.7	68.0	68.0	67.2	64.1	66.5	69.0	69.1	72.6	75.5	77.9	78.6	79.9
Arizona	76.7	60.8	63.6	74.2	75.9	66.8	84.7	70.5	69.6	70.7	72.5	74.7	78.9	77.3	76.5
Arkansas	76.6	74.2	74.6	73.9	76.6	76.8	75.7	80.4	74.4	76.4	74.0	75.0	77.0	78.1	80.1
California	69.6	67.6	71.7	71.6	74.1	73.9	74.6	69.2	70.7	71.2	71.0 [3]	78.2	79.7	81.7	83.6
Colorado	76.3	74.8	74.1	73.2	76.4	78.7	76.7	75.5	76.6	75.4	77.6	79.8	82.0	82.3	83.3
Connecticut	80.2	76.1	81.9	77.5	80.9	80.7	80.9	80.9	81.8	82.2	75.4	75.1	84.7	86.1	87.4
Delaware	72.5	70.4	66.8	71.0	73.0	72.9	73.0	76.3	71.9	72.1	73.7	75.5	76.1	77.1	77.0
District of Columbia	54.5	49.7	54.5	60.2	59.6	68.2	66.3	65.4 [4]	54.8	56.0	62.4	59.9	64.9	70.8	77.7
Florida	65.6	62.3	61.0	61.2	66.7	66.4	64.6	63.6	65.0	66.9	68.9	70.8	72.0	74.7	75.8
Georgia	70.3	61.9	59.7	58.7	60.8	61.2	61.7	62.4	64.1	65.4	67.8	69.9	69.6	69.6	70.5
Hawaii	75.9	74.5	70.9	68.3	71.3	72.6	75.1	75.5	75.4	76.0	75.3	75.4	73.7	77.9	78.0
Idaho	79.6	80.5	79.4	79.6	81.4	81.5	81.0	80.5	80.4	80.1	80.6	84.0	83.2	83.9	82.1
Illinois	76.6	75.2	76.3	75.6	75.9	80.3	79.4	79.7	79.5	80.4	77.7	81.9	80.0	82.1	82.7
Indiana	76.9	73.6	71.8	72.1	75.5	73.5	73.2	73.3	73.9	74.1	75.2	77.2	79.9	80.0	81.0
Iowa	84.4	84.3	83.1	82.8	85.3	85.8	86.6	86.9	86.5	86.4	85.7	87.9	89.0	89.3	89.4
Kansas	80.8	77.1	77.1	76.5	76.9	77.9	79.2	77.5	78.8	79.0	80.2	84.5	86.5	88.3	88.4
Kentucky	72.9	71.3	69.7	69.8	71.7	73.0	75.9	77.2	76.4	74.4	77.6	79.9	80.9	81.9	83.1
Louisiana	57.5	61.7	62.2	63.7	64.1	69.4	63.9	59.5	61.3	63.5	67.3	68.8	71.2	71.9	72.7
Maine	80.7	73.7	75.9	76.4	76.3	77.6	78.6	76.3	78.5	79.1 [5]	79.9 [5]	82.8 [6]	85.7	86.7	87.5
Maryland	77.5	78.3	77.6	78.7	79.2	79.5	79.3	79.9	80.0	80.4	80.1	82.2	83.8	84.5	85.6
Massachusetts	79.1	78.0	78.0	78.9	75.7	79.3	78.7	79.5	80.8	81.5	83.3	82.6	85.4	86.5	88.4
Michigan	72.1	71.4	75.3	75.4	74.0	72.5	73.0	72.2	77.0	76.3	75.3	75.9	74.7	77.5	78.3
Minnesota	90.8	86.1	84.9	83.6	84.8	84.7	85.9	86.2	86.5	86.4	87.4	88.2	89.2	88.4	91.0
Mississippi	63.3	59.7	59.4	59.7	62.7	62.7	63.3	63.5	63.5	63.9	62.0	63.8	68.5	67.3	68.4
Missouri	76.0	75.0	76.3	75.5	78.3	80.4	80.6	81.0	81.9	82.4	83.1	83.7	84.7	85.9	86.6
Montana	84.4	83.9	80.8	80.0	81.0	80.4	81.5	81.9	81.5	82.0	82.0	81.9	83.7	85.7	84.7
Nebraska	86.7	85.6	85.7	83.8	85.2	87.6	87.8	87.0	86.3	83.8	82.9	83.8	89.8	92.7	93.3
Nevada	77.0	65.8	69.7	70.0	72.3	57.4	55.8	55.8	54.2	56.3	56.3 [3]	57.8	58.7	59.5	67.5
New Hampshire	78.6	77.5	76.1	77.8	78.2	78.7	80.1	81.1	81.7	83.3	84.3	86.3	86.6	87.0	87.3
New Jersey	81.4	82.8	83.6	85.4	87.0	86.3	85.1	84.8	84.4	84.6	85.3	87.2	86.6	86.4	89.1
New Mexico	70.1	63.7	64.7	65.9	63.1	67.0	65.4	67.3	59.1	66.8	64.8	67.3	70.7	74.3	71.6
New York	66.1	63.6	61.8	61.5	60.9	60.9 [7]	65.3	67.4	68.9	70.9	73.5	76.0	77.6	77.1	78.5
North Carolina	71.3	66.5	65.8	66.5	70.1	71.4	72.6	71.8	68.6	72.8	75.1	76.9	76.8	78.7	80.5
North Dakota	87.6	89.5	86.0	85.4	86.4	86.1	86.3	82.2	83.1	83.8	87.4	88.4	90.2	91.1	91.4
Ohio	77.5	74.5	75.2	76.5	79.0	81.3	80.2	79.2	78.7	79.0	79.6	81.4	82.3	83.9	84.9
Oklahoma	76.5	75.6	75.8	75.8	76.0	77.0	76.9	77.8	77.8	78.0	77.3	78.5	79.9	79.3	79.4
Oregon	72.7	68.3	69.6	68.3	73.7	74.2	74.2	73.0	73.8	76.7	76.5	76.3	78.1	78.0	76.8
Pennsylvania	79.7	80.0	78.7	79.0	81.7	82.2	82.5	83.5 [4]	83.0	82.7	80.5	84.1	85.8	88.3	88.4
Rhode Island	75.0	72.7	72.8	73.5	77.7	75.9	78.4	77.8	78.4	76.4	75.3	76.4	76.6	77.1	79.0
South Carolina	66.6	60.9	58.6	56.5	59.7	60.6	60.1	61.0 [4]	58.9	62.2	66.0	68.2	69.0	71.6	74.2
South Dakota	83.8	84.5	77.6	77.4	83.0	83.7	82.3	84.5	82.5	84.4	81.7	81.8	81.6	83.1	83.8
Tennessee	69.8	66.6	59.5	59.0	63.4	66.1	68.5	70.7	72.6	74.9	77.4	80.4	81.1	83.6	82.4
Texas	72.2	66.1	71.0	70.8	75.5	76.7	74.0	72.5	71.9	73.1	75.4	78.9	81.4	83.0	83.6
Utah	77.5	76.9	82.5	81.6	80.2	83.0	84.4	78.6	76.6	74.3	79.4	78.6	78.5	77.6	81.6
Vermont	79.5	85.3	81.0	80.2	83.6	85.4	86.5	82.3	88.5	89.3	89.6	91.4	92.7	91.9	89.3
Virginia	76.2	76.2	76.9	77.5	80.6	79.3	79.6	74.5	75.5	77.0	78.4	81.2	82.7	83.9	84.8
Washington	75.7	75.5	73.7	69.2	74.2	74.6	75.0	72.9	74.8	71.9	73.7	77.2	79.0	79.2	80.4
West Virginia	76.6	77.0	76.7	75.9	75.7	76.9	77.3	76.9	78.2	77.3	77.0	78.3	78.1	80.3	81.5
Wisconsin	85.2	83.6	82.7	83.3	85.8	85.8 [7]	86.7	87.5	88.5	89.6	90.7	91.1	92.2	92.2	93.0
Wyoming	81.1	77.7	76.3	73.4	73.9	76.0	76.7	76.1	75.8	76.0	75.2	80.3	80.4	80.2	82.5
Other jurisdictions															
American Samoa	85.3	79.7	71.9	77.0	81.0	80.2	81.1	81.0	84.6	—	—	—	—	—	—
Guam	48.2	44.6	52.9	51.7	56.3	48.4	—	—	—	—	—	—	—	—	—
Northern Marianas	—	63.3	61.1	62.7	65.2	75.3	75.4	80.3	73.6	—	—	—	—	—	—
Puerto Rico	60.9	60.8	64.7	65.7	67.8	64.8	61.7	68.6	66.7	64.5	67.2	60.2	61.6	61.7	—
U.S. Virgin Islands	53.2	54.2	53.8	57.3	53.5	—	—	—	57.8	58.3	63.1	65.5	96.8	72.5	67.8

—Not available.
[1]Includes estimates for New York and Wisconsin. Without estimates for these two states, the averaged freshman graduation rate for the remaining 48 states and the District of Columbia is 75.0 percent.
[2]U.S. total includes estimates for nonreporting states.
[3]Estimated high school graduates from NCES 2011-312, *Public School Graduates and Dropouts From the Common Core of Data: School Year 2008–09.*
[4]Projected high school graduates from NCES 2009-062, *Projections of Education Statistics to 2018.*
[5]Includes 1,161 graduates in 2007–08 and 1,169 graduates in 2008–09 from private high schools that received a majority of their funding from public sources.
[6]Includes 1,419 fall 2006 9th-graders who attended publicly funded private schools that were not reported in the 2006–07 Common Core of Data, but were reported in data for later years.
[7]Estimated high school graduates from NCES 2006-606rev, *The Averaged Freshman Graduation Rate for Public High Schools From the Common Core of Data: School Years 2002–03 and 2003–04.*

NOTE: The averaged freshman graduation rate provides an estimate of the percentage of students who receive a regular diploma within 4 years of entering ninth grade. The rate uses aggregate student enrollment data to estimate the size of an incoming freshman class and aggregate counts of the number of diplomas awarded 4 years later. Averaged freshman graduation rates in this table are based on reported totals of enrollment by grade and high school graduates, rather than on details reported by race/ethnicity.
SOURCE: U.S. Department of Education, National Center for Education Statistics, Common Core of Data (CCD), "State Nonfiscal Survey of Public Elementary/Secondary Education," 1986–87 through 2010–11; "State Dropout and Completion Data File," 2005–06 through 2012–13; *The Averaged Freshman Graduation Rate for Public High Schools From the Common Core of Data: School Years 2002–03 and 2003–04; Public School Graduates and Dropouts From the Common Core of Data,* 2007–08 and 2008–09; and *Projections of Education Statistics to 2018.* (This table was prepared January 2016.)

Table 219.40. Public high school averaged freshman graduation rate (AFGR), by sex, race/ethnicity, and state or jurisdiction: 2012–13

State or jurisdiction	Total, male and female						Male						Female					
	Total[1]	White	Black	Hispanic	Asian/ Pacific Islander	American Indian/ Alaska Native	Total[1]	White	Black	Hispanic	Asian/ Pacific Islander	American Indian/ Alaska Native	Total[1]	White	Black	Hispanic	Asian/ Pacific Islander	American Indian/ Alaska Native
1	2	3	4	5	6	7	8	9	10	11	12	13	14	15	16	17	18	19
United States	81.9	85.6	69.4	78.2	94.6	67.7	78.8	83.5	64.3	74.1	92.6	65.3	85.2	87.8	74.8	82.6	96.7	70.2
Alabama	74.2	78.1	67.6	67.5	87.2	84.7	70.5	75.8	61.3	64.9	86.7	83.4	78.2	80.6	74.3	70.5	87.8	86.0
Alaska	79.9	82.3	74.7	87.6	94.1	68.6	77.7	80.7	67.3	87.7	92.1	64.7	82.2	83.9	83.6	87.6	96.5	72.8
Arizona	76.5	80.1	70.0	72.1	90.1	64.2	72.7	77.1	67.3	66.9	89.0	61.3	80.6	83.1	72.8	77.6	91.4	67.0
Arkansas	80.1	81.0	74.5	81.1	87.8	67.0	77.1	78.8	69.0	78.5	86.7	65.5	83.3	83.5	80.2	83.9	89.0	68.5
California	83.6	88.7	72.7	79.7	97.3	73.5	80.1	86.3	68.9	75.2	95.5	68.9	87.3	91.3	76.8	84.4	99.2	78.4
Colorado	83.3	84.5	68.7	77.7	90.4	62.7	79.8	81.7	66.5	73.0	87.2	60.3	87.0	87.6	71.1	82.7	93.5	65.2
Connecticut	87.4	90.4	76.6	77.7	100.0	79.5	84.9	89.1	72.0	73.0	99.6	80.1 [2]	90.0	91.7	81.8	82.8	100.0	78.8 [2]
Delaware	77.0	79.8	70.6	75.8	94.2	83.0 [2]	72.7	76.1	65.2	71.8	92.8	‡	81.6	83.8	76.5	79.7	98.1	‡
District of Columbia	77.7	94.8	69.8	80.7	87.1 [2]	‡	68.9	84.6 [2]	59.8	76.8	82.9 [2]	‡	86.2	100.0 [2]	79.7	84.3	93.5 [2]	‡
Florida	75.8	77.8	67.2	79.1	93.3	85.2	72.1	74.4	62.3	75.7	91.7	82.3	79.7	81.4	72.5	82.6	95.0	88.7
Georgia	70.5	76.5	63.7	64.4	90.8	66.9	66.5	73.3	58.0	60.9	89.3	63.3	74.9	79.8	69.6	68.1	92.5	70.8
Hawaii	78.0	57.5	70.6	84.8	79.8	57.0 [2]	74.8	53.9	60.2	76.2	77.0	49.1 [2]	81.4	61.3	82.8	94.4	82.9	67.7 [2]
Idaho	82.1	82.4	77.3	78.7	88.8	55.2	79.8	80.0	84.5	75.1	87.8	55.1	84.5	84.8	71.0	82.2	89.8	55.2
Illinois	82.7	90.6	63.6	78.3	97.8	78.5	80.7	90.5	58.1	75.1	96.7	81.8	84.7	90.7	69.4	81.6	98.9	74.7
Indiana	81.0	83.1	66.4	85.7	99.2	92.7	77.0	79.8	59.3	80.2	96.8	89.6	85.2	86.6	73.9	91.6	100.0	95.6
Iowa	89.4	90.2	69.0	85.5	98.0	67.2	87.3	88.3	65.9	82.1	96.1	69.1	91.6	92.2	72.6	89.0	100.0	65.5
Kansas	88.4	89.6	75.5	85.9	95.9	68.8	86.3	88.6	73.6	79.8	94.2	68.1	90.6	90.6	77.5	92.7	97.5	69.6
Kentucky	83.1	83.4	79.5	86.8	99.7	100.0 [2]	81.7	81.6	75.0	79.8	100.0	100.0 [2]	86.6	85.4	84.4	94.9	99.0	100.0 [2]
Louisiana	72.7	78.0	64.3	94.4	97.1	69.5	67.3	73.7	57.7	87.4	94.5	64.6	78.4	82.6	71.1	100.0	99.9	74.7
Maine	87.5	86.5	92.7	92.9	100.0	76.9	86.0	85.0	95.7	87.6	100.0	79.2 [2]	89.1	88.2	90.0	100.0 [2]	100.0	74.6 [2]
Maryland	85.6	88.6	76.2	84.5	99.3	85.0	81.8	86.5	70.7	79.8	97.8	83.6	89.7	90.9	82.1	89.9	100.0	86.7
Massachusetts	88.4	90.9	87.0	72.7	100.0	67.6	86.1	89.3	81.2	69.6	100.0	71.5	90.8	92.6	93.4	76.0	100.0	63.6
Michigan	78.3	83.4	60.6	52.6	95.3	68.2	74.5	80.3	54.8	49.8	93.3	66.6	82.3	86.7	67.0	55.7	97.5	69.8
Minnesota	91.0	93.2	74.2	77.1	97.8	50.7	88.5	91.3	70.4	73.1	94.3	48.5	93.6	95.3	78.4	81.6	100.0	53.0
Mississippi	68.4	74.2	63.1	64.7	88.7	60.8 [2]	63.1	70.5	56.4	62.5	85.1	52.6 [2]	73.7	78.1	69.8	67.1	92.7	71.1 [2]
Missouri	86.6	88.2	73.6	91.2	95.7	86.8	84.8	87.0	69.9	89.9	96.6	84.2	88.4	89.6	77.6	92.6	94.7	89.6
Montana	84.7	86.9	66.6 [2]	94.6	92.3	60.1	83.7	85.8	66.7 [2]	94.1	90.9 [2]	59.1	85.8	88.0	66.4 [2]	95.3	93.6 [2]	61.2
Nebraska	93.3	94.6	71.3	90.7	93.4	65.5	91.3	93.4	67.4	85.7	90.5	66.0	95.5	95.9	75.5	96.1	96.6	64.9
Nevada	67.5	69.5	48.6	62.0	73.4	45.1	63.2	65.6	45.6	56.9	70.9	42.0	71.9	73.7	51.7	67.2	76.1	48.5
New Hampshire	87.3	86.7	85.9	87.0	97.3	68.5 [2]	84.9	84.5	85.3	77.6	99.6	‡	89.8	89.1	86.8	97.3	95.2	71.0 [2]
New Jersey	89.1	92.7	79.4	83.3	98.6	70.3	86.9	91.3	75.7	79.9	98.5	60.5 [2]	91.4	94.3	83.4	86.8	98.8	80.2 [2]
New Mexico	71.6	76.9	64.9	68.3	94.8	71.8	67.6	73.7	58.4	63.9	92.6	67.8	76.0	80.2	73.6	73.0	97.2	76.2
New York	78.5	87.1	65.2	66.4	90.9	71.9	76.1	87.1	60.5	62.1	86.1	65.2	81.0	87.1	70.1	70.9	96.1	79.4
North Carolina	80.5	83.4	69.7	79.9	91.9	76.3	76.6	80.8	64.3	74.7	89.5	72.5	84.7	86.2	75.4	85.7	94.3	80.6
North Dakota	91.4	93.8	100.0	85.4	100.0 [2]	59.1	89.1	91.8	100.0 [2]	89.7 [2]	100.0 [2]	54.5	93.8	95.8	100.0 [2]	81.0 [2]	100.0 [2]	63.7
Ohio	84.9	89.4	65.2	85.7	98.8	73.9	82.7	87.7	60.5	84.0	96.5	81.6	87.3	91.1	70.3	87.6	100.0	66.0
Oklahoma	79.4	81.0	66.2	76.6	92.8	71.5	76.9	78.7	63.1	73.0	92.4	70.0	82.0	83.5	69.5	80.3	93.2	73.1
Oregon	76.8	76.7	66.4	76.0	87.3	56.5	73.2	73.7	59.9	70.3	86.2	49.2	80.6	80.0	72.7	82.0	88.4	64.3
Pennsylvania	88.4	92.0	76.4	77.4	100.0	68.4	86.0	89.2	71.7	73.2	100.0	63.0	91.0	92.6	81.2	81.9	100.0	74.3
Rhode Island	79.0	80.5	69.7	74.6	81.1	46.2 [2]	75.3	77.2	64.0	70.4	77.8	53.3 [2]	83.0	84.1	76.0	79.1	84.3	40.2 [2]
South Carolina	74.2	78.2	66.3	74.7	86.3	57.4	69.4	74.4	60.0	70.7	85.6	56.2	79.5	82.3	73.1	79.0	87.0	58.8 [2]
South Dakota	83.8	87.9	76.7	80.5	100.0	47.7	81.3	85.3	72.6	71.0	100.0 [2]	47.9	86.3	90.7	81.4	90.1	100.0 [2]	47.6
Tennessee	82.4	83.8	77.6	82.7	100.0	96.1	79.2	81.6	71.6	78.4	100.0	100.0 [2]	85.8	86.2	83.8	87.5	100.0	85.2 [2]
Texas	83.6	85.8	77.0	82.1	97.4	71.5	80.9	84.3	73.1	78.6	96.9	71.5	86.6	87.4	81.2	85.7	98.0	71.4
Utah	81.6	83.2	67.4	71.4	82.5	62.5	78.9	80.9	66.3	67.2	85.2	55.3	84.4	85.7	68.7	75.9	79.6	69.6
Vermont	89.3	89.2	88.0	97.3 [2]	100.0	‡	88.9	88.9	79.2 [2]	100.0 [2]	100.0 [2]	‡	89.7	89.6	95.9 [2]	83.9 [2]	100.0 [2]	‡
Virginia	84.8	86.4	72.7	89.7	98.5	76.2	81.5	84.2	67.2	84.5	97.1	74.4	88.4	88.7	78.6	95.5	100.0	78.0
Washington	80.4	80.1	62.7	80.7	84.5	40.3	76.8	76.8	58.5	74.8	82.1	40.5	84.6	83.7	67.2	86.9	87.0	40.1
West Virginia	81.5	81.5	73.5	83.4	93.7	‡	79.7	79.7	73.5	80.0	92.8 [2]	‡	83.3	83.5	73.5	86.8	99.0 [2]	‡
Wisconsin	93.0	96.3	68.1	83.7	97.7	72.9	90.7	95.1	61.5	78.5	93.5	68.6	95.5	97.5	75.5	89.3	100.0	77.9
Wyoming	82.5	84.0	75.3 [2]	77.9	100.0 [2]	42.6	80.0	82.1	73.9 [2]	69.4	‡	41.0 [2]	85.0	85.9	77.1 [2]	86.8	100.0 [2]	44.2
Bureau of Indian Education	—	—	—	—	—	—	—	—	—	—	—	—	—	—	—	—	—	—
DoD, overseas	—	—	—	—	—	—	—	—	—	—	—	—	—	—	—	—	—	—
DoD, domestic	—	—	—	—	—	—	—	—	—	—	—	—	—	—	—	—	—	—
Other jurisdictions																		
American Samoa	—	—	—	—	—	—	—	—	—	—	—	—	—	—	—	—	—	—
Guam	—	—	—	—	—	—	—	—	—	—	—	—	—	—	—	—	—	—
Northern Marianas	—	—	—	—	—	—	—	—	—	—	—	—	—	—	—	—	—	—
Puerto Rico	—	—	—	—	—	—	—	—	—	—	—	—	—	—	—	—	—	—
U.S. Virgin Islands	67.8	‡	67.2	63.8	‡	‡	59.1	‡	59.6	54.5	‡	‡	76.1	‡	74.7	71.8	‡	‡

—Not available.

‡Reporting standards not met (too few cases).

[1] Total averaged freshman graduation rate (AFGR) is based on reported totals of enrollment by grade and high school graduates, rather than on details reported by race/ethnicity.

[2] AFGR is based on an estimate of 30 to 99 students entering ninth grade and may show large variation from year to year.

NOTE: The AFGR provides an estimate of the percentage of students who receive a regular diploma within 4 years of entering ninth grade. The rate uses aggregate student enrollment data to estimate the size of an incoming freshman class and aggregate counts of the number of diplomas awarded 4 years later. The enrollment data used in computing the AFGR for race/ethnicity categories include only students for whom race/ethnicity was reported. Race categories exclude persons of Hispanic ethnicity. DoD = Department of Defense.

SOURCE: U.S. Department of Education, National Center for Education Statistics, Common Core of Data (CCD), "State Dropout and Completion Data File," 2012–13. (This table was prepared January 2016.)

Table 219.50. Number and percentage of 9th- to 12th-graders who dropped out of public schools (event dropout rate), by race/ethnicity, grade, and state or jurisdiction: 2009–10

State or jurisdiction	Percent of 9th- to 12th-graders who dropped out (event dropout rate), by race/ethnicity							Number and percent of 9th- to 12th-graders who dropped out (event dropout rate), by grade							
								Grade 9		Grade 10		Grade 11		Grade 12	
	Total	White	Black	Hispanic	Asian/ Pacific Islander	American Indian/ Alaska Native	Two or more races	Number of dropouts	Event dropout rate	Number of dropouts	Event dropout rate	Number of dropouts	Event dropout rate	Number of dropouts	Event dropout rate
1	2	3	4	5	6	7	8	9	10	11	12	13	14	15	16
United States	3.4	2.3	5.5	5.0	1.9	6.7	‡	104,756	2.6	113,370	3.0	117,536	3.3	175,806	5.1
Alabama	1.8	1.6	2.0	0.9	1.4	1.3	—	864	1.4	1,128	2.0	1,048	2.1	862	1.8
Alaska	6.9	5.1	6.4	6.1	4.8	11.6	9.6	404	4.0	551	5.5	1,014	9.3	851	8.7
Arizona	7.8	6.8	8.8	8.1	4.9	14.6	—	4,207	5.1	4,594	5.7	5,269	7.0	10,795	13.6
Arkansas	3.6	3.1	5.0	4.1	2.0	4.9	3.1	720	1.9	1,130	3.2	1,427	4.4	1,613	5.3
California	4.6	2.8	8.4	5.8	2.0	6.5	5.0	13,849	2.6	15,518	3.1	20,625	4.2	42,587	8.9
Colorado	5.3	3.2	8.6	9.9	2.4	10.1	—	1,957	3.1	2,216	3.7	3,045	5.3	5,673	9.7
Connecticut	3.0	1.4	6.8	6.9	1.1	3.0	—	1,316	2.8	1,127	2.6	1,452	3.4	1,299	3.2
Delaware	3.9	3.1	4.9	4.7	3.2	10.3	—	546	4.7	386	3.7	299	3.4	288	3.5
District of Columbia[1]	7.0	4.9	6.9	8.3	5.4	#	—	501	8.1	262	5.9	153	4.2	133	4.0
Florida	2.3	1.6	3.5	2.8	0.8	2.7	—	4,189	1.9	4,348	2.2	4,678	2.4	4,816	2.8
Georgia	3.8	3.1	4.6	4.3	1.5	4.2	3.4	5,800	4.0	5,095	4.2	4,074	3.8	2,800	2.9
Hawaii	5.2	6.4	7.9	5.9	4.7	9.0	—	562	3.7	816	5.7	726	5.8	632	6.0
Idaho	1.4	1.2	1.9	2.2	1.2	2.5	—	211	1.0	235	1.1	301	1.5	386	2.0
Illinois	2.9	1.8	5.7	3.8	0.9	3.0	—	3,482	2.0	5,287	3.1	3,970	2.7	5,801	4.0
Indiana	1.6	1.3	3.1	2.4	1.1	2.2	—	373	0.4	945	1.2	1,349	1.7	2,346	3.2
Iowa	3.4	2.8	9.1	6.9	2.1	8.9	4.9	363	1.0	713	1.9	1,276	3.5	2,747	7.1
Kansas	2.1	1.8	3.7	2.9	0.7	4.1	2.0	442	1.2	661	1.9	765	2.3	1,105	3.3
Kentucky	3.2	2.9	5.5	5.6	2.0	1.9	—	1,076	2.0	1,769	3.5	1,762	3.8	1,615	3.7
Louisiana	4.8	3.2	6.8	3.9	2.0	4.8	—	3,229	5.7	1,920	4.2	1,663	4.1	1,892	4.9
Maine	4.2	4.2	4.9	5.0	3.8	8.6	—	252	1.7	349	2.3	703	4.8	1,260	8.3
Maryland	2.7	2.0	3.4	4.2	0.9	3.2	—	1,998	2.7	2,029	3.0	1,686	2.7	1,369	2.2
Massachusetts	2.8	1.7	5.0	7.3	1.7	3.3	3.1	2,356	3.0	2,045	2.8	1,837	2.6	1,847	2.7
Michigan	4.3	2.7	9.2	6.2	3.1	5.4	—	4,305	3.1	6,661	4.9	5,318	4.2	6,699	5.3
Minnesota	1.6	1.0	3.9	4.2	1.6	5.7	—	337	0.5	453	0.7	796	1.2	2,752	3.7
Mississippi	7.4	5.6	9.3	5.9	2.8	4.6	#	2,399	6.0	2,651	7.3	2,339	7.3	2,023	7.0
Missouri	3.5	2.4	8.4	4.1	1.5	3.0	—	2,139	2.9	2,009	2.9	2,449	3.6	3,245	4.8
Montana	4.3	3.5	7.0	6.2	2.0	10.3	—	340	2.9	435	3.9	527	4.9	599	5.7
Nebraska	2.2	1.6	4.1	4.0	1.8	7.0	—	186	0.8	372	1.7	538	2.5	825	3.7
Nevada	4.5	3.4	6.5	5.4	3.1	4.7	—	790	2.3	1,389	4.0	1,294	4.4	2,071	8.0
New Hampshire	1.2	1.1	1.6	2.9	1.1	1.5	1.0	3	#	6	#	90	0.6	667	4.3
New Jersey	1.6	0.9	3.5	2.8	0.4	1.5	3.4	1,696	1.6	1,667	1.6	1,522	1.5	1,594	1.6
New Mexico	6.9	5.3	9.0	7.2	4.6	8.8	4.7	2,229	7.5	2,075	7.8	1,484	6.6	1,021	5.1
New York	3.6	1.7	6.5	5.9	2.4	5.6	—	7,354	3.1	8,222	3.5	6,674	3.4	8,931	4.7
North Carolina	4.7	4.0	5.4	6.1	2.0	6.1	—	6,553	5.1	5,535	4.9	4,769	4.8	3,338	3.8
North Dakota	2.2	1.7	2.6	3.5	0.9	7.5	—	40	0.5	174	2.3	207	2.7	259	3.4
Ohio	4.2	2.8	9.4	7.4	1.4	7.8	—	6,968	4.4	3,853	2.8	4,574	3.7	7,011	5.9
Oklahoma	2.4	2.1	3.3	3.5	1.1	2.5	—	949	1.9	1,062	2.3	1,188	2.8	1,086	2.7
Oregon	3.4	2.9	6.2	4.7	1.4	6.7	—	465	1.0	771	1.7	1,451	3.3	3,299	7.2
Pennsylvania	2.1	1.5	3.7	5.1	1.3	2.2	—	1,643	1.1	3,029	2.0	3,268	2.3	4,302	3.1
Rhode Island	4.6	3.8	6.6	6.8	4.5	8.5	—	573	4.4	613	5.0	509	4.7	471	4.4
South Carolina	3.0	2.7	3.3	3.6	1.3	5.6	—	1,691	2.7	1,811	3.3	1,547	3.2	1,220	2.7
South Dakota	2.6	1.6	3.4	5.2	2.7	10.5	—	184	1.8	267	2.7	258	2.8	291	3.3
Tennessee	2.7	1.8	4.9	3.3	1.2	2.7	—	1,370	1.8	1,579	2.1	1,790	2.6	2,843	4.3
Texas	2.7	1.2	4.2	3.6	0.5	3.6	—	6,945	1.8	8,253	2.5	6,824	2.2	14,048	4.8
Utah	2.6	2.1	3.8	5.5	2.8	5.7	—	207	0.5	555	1.4	927	2.3	2,444	6.1
Vermont	2.4	2.4	1.5	2.6	2.0	#	4.1	76	1.0	180	2.4	215	3.0	250	3.4
Virginia	2.1	1.4	3.0	4.6	1.2	1.6	—	1,741	1.7	1,857	1.9	1,934	2.1	2,467	2.8
Washington	4.2	3.6	6.1	5.8	3.0	8.2	—	2,881	3.4	2,792	3.4	3,472	4.4	4,815	5.8
West Virginia	4.0	4.0	4.6	4.6	0.5	3.6	1.9	809	3.4	848	4.1	839	4.4	798	4.3
Wisconsin	2.2	1.2	7.5	4.7	1.6	5.2	—	971	1.4	611	0.9	1,222	1.7	3,260	4.6
Wyoming	6.0	5.0	13.1	#	1.7	20.8	94.9	215	3.2	516	7.3	389	6.1	460	7.5
Bureau of Indian Education .	—	—	—	—	—	—	—	—	—	—	—	—	—	—	—
DoD, overseas	—	—	—	—	—	—	—	—	—	—	—	—	—	—	—
DoD, domestic	—	—	—	—	—	—	—	—	—	—	—	—	—	—	—
Other jurisdictions															
American Samoa	—	—	—	—	—	—	—	—	—	—	—	—	—	—	—
Guam	—	—	—	—	—	—	—	—	—	—	—	—	—	—	—
Northern Marianas	—	—	—	—	—	—	—	—	—	—	—	—	—	—	—
Puerto Rico	—	—	—	—	—	—	—	—	—	—	—	—	—	—	—
U.S. Virgin Islands	5.5	#	5.3	7.4	#	#	—	122	7.2	68	5.5	53	4.7	38	3.7

—Not available.
#Rounds to zero.
‡Reporting standards not met (too few cases for a reliable estimate).
[1]Data were imputed based on prior year rates.
NOTE: Race categories exclude persons of Hispanic ethnicity. Event dropout rates measure the percentage of public school students in grades 9 through 12 who dropped out of school between one October and the next. Enrollment and dropout data for ungraded students were prorated into grades 9 through 12 based on the counts for graded students. DoD stands for Department of Defense.
SOURCE: U.S. Department of Education, National Center for Education Statistics, Common Core of Data (CCD), "State Dropout and Completion Data File," 2009–10. (This table was prepared November 2012.)

Table 219.55. Among 15- to 24-year-olds enrolled in grades 10 through 12, percentage who dropped out (event dropout rate), by sex and race/ethnicity: 1972 through 2014

[Standard errors appear in parentheses]

Year	Total[2]		Sex				Race/ethnicity					
			Male		Female		White		Black		Hispanic	
1	2		3		4		5		6		7	
1972	6.1	(0.34)	5.9	(0.47)	6.3	(0.49)	5.3	(0.35)	9.6	(1.36)	11.2 !	(3.70)
1973	6.3	(0.34)	6.8	(0.50)	5.7	(0.46)	5.5	(0.35)	10.0	(1.39)	10.0 !	(3.50)
1974	6.7	(0.35)	7.4	(0.52)	6.0	(0.47)	5.8	(0.36)	11.6	(1.44)	9.9 !	(3.34)
1975	5.8	(0.32)	5.4	(0.45)	6.1	(0.47)	5.1	(0.34)	8.7	(1.28)	10.9 !	(3.30)
1976	5.9	(0.33)	6.6	(0.49)	5.2	(0.44)	5.6	(0.36)	7.4	(1.18)	7.3 !	(2.71)
1977	6.5	(0.34)	6.9	(0.49)	6.1	(0.47)	6.1	(0.37)	8.6	(1.21)	7.8 !	(2.79)
1978	6.7	(0.35)	7.5	(0.52)	5.9	(0.46)	5.8	(0.36)	10.2	(1.32)	12.3	(3.60)
1979	6.7	(0.35)	6.8	(0.50)	6.7	(0.49)	6.1	(0.37)	10.0	(1.34)	9.8 !	(3.20)
1980	6.1	(0.33)	6.7	(0.49)	5.5	(0.45)	5.3	(0.35)	8.3	(1.22)	11.7	(3.36)
1981	5.9	(0.33)	6.0	(0.47)	5.8	(0.46)	4.9	(0.34)	9.7	(1.30)	10.7	(3.00)
1982	5.5	(0.34)	5.8	(0.50)	5.2	(0.47)	4.8	(0.37)	7.8	(1.23)	9.2 !	(3.04)
1983	5.2	(0.34)	5.8	(0.50)	4.7	(0.46)	4.4	(0.36)	7.0	(1.20)	10.1 !	(3.18)
1984	5.1	(0.34)	5.5	(0.50)	4.8	(0.47)	4.5	(0.37)	5.8	(1.08)	11.1	(3.28)
1985	5.3	(0.35)	5.4	(0.51)	5.1	(0.49)	4.4	(0.37)	7.8	(1.29)	9.8	(2.58)
1986	4.7	(0.33)	4.7	(0.46)	4.7	(0.46)	3.8	(0.34)	5.5	(1.08)	11.9	(2.70)
1987	4.1	(0.31)	4.4	(0.45)	3.8	(0.42)	3.6	(0.33)	6.4	(1.16)	5.6 !	(1.94)
1988	4.8	(0.37)	5.4	(0.55)	4.6	(0.53)	4.4	(0.42)	6.3	(1.28)	11.0	(3.08)
1989	4.5	(0.35)	4.6	(0.50)	4.6	(0.50)	3.6	(0.37)	8.2	(1.40)	8.1	(2.43)
1990	4.0	(0.33)	4.2	(0.49)	4.1	(0.49)	3.5	(0.37)	5.2	(1.17)	8.4	(2.41)
1991	4.0	(0.33)	3.9	(0.47)	4.4	(0.51)	3.3	(0.37)	6.4	(1.27)	7.8	(2.33)
1992	4.4	(0.35)	3.9	(0.46)	4.9	(0.53)	3.7	(0.38)	5.0	(1.09)	8.2	(2.23)
1993	4.5	(0.36)	4.6	(0.51)	4.3	(0.50)	3.9	(0.40)	5.8	(1.20)	6.7 !	(2.02)
1994	5.3	(0.37)	5.2	(0.51)	5.4	(0.53)	4.2	(0.40)	6.6	(1.21)	10.0	(2.18)
1995	5.7	(0.35)	6.2	(0.51)	5.3	(0.48)	4.5	(0.38)	6.4	(1.01)	12.4	(1.62)
1996	5.0	(0.34)	5.0	(0.48)	5.1	(0.49)	4.1	(0.38)	6.7	(1.05)	9.0	(1.49)
1997	4.6	(0.32)	5.0	(0.47)	4.1	(0.43)	3.6	(0.35)	5.0	(0.91)	9.5	(1.45)
1998	4.8	(0.33)	4.6	(0.45)	4.9	(0.47)	3.9	(0.36)	5.2	(0.91)	9.4	(1.46)
1999	5.0	(0.33)	4.6	(0.44)	5.4	(0.49)	4.0	(0.36)	6.5	(0.99)	7.8	(1.27)
2000	4.8	(0.33)	5.5	(0.49)	4.1	(0.43)	4.1	(0.37)	6.1	(1.00)	7.4	(1.24)
2001	5.0	(0.32)	5.6	(0.46)	4.3	(0.42)	4.1	(0.35)	6.3	(0.96)	8.8	(1.31)
2002	3.5	(0.27)	3.7	(0.39)	3.4	(0.37)	2.6	(0.28)	4.9	(0.87)	5.8	(1.01)
2003	4.0	(0.28)	4.2	(0.40)	3.8	(0.38)	3.2	(0.31)	4.8	(0.85)	7.1	(1.06)
2004	4.7	(0.30)	5.1	(0.44)	4.3	(0.41)	3.7	(0.34)	5.7	(0.94)	8.9	(1.20)
2005	3.8	(0.27)	4.2	(0.40)	3.4	(0.36)	2.8	(0.29)	7.3	(1.03)	5.0	(0.87)
2006	3.8	(0.27)	4.1	(0.39)	3.4	(0.36)	2.9	(0.30)	3.8	(0.77)	7.0	(1.01)
2007	3.5	(0.26)	3.7	(0.37)	3.3	(0.35)	2.2	(0.26)	4.5	(0.80)	6.0	(0.98)
2008	3.5	(0.26)	3.1	(0.34)	4.0	(0.39)	2.3	(0.27)	6.4	(0.94)	5.3	(0.85)
2009	3.4	(0.25)	3.5	(0.36)	3.4	(0.35)	2.4	(0.28)	4.8	(0.83)	5.8	(0.87)
2010	3.0	(0.24)	3.0	(0.33)	2.9	(0.34)	2.3	(0.27)	3.6	(0.70)	4.1	(0.75)
2011	3.4	(0.25)	3.6	(0.36)	3.1	(0.35)	2.7	(0.30)	4.4	(0.77)	4.6	(0.75)
2012	3.4	(0.32)	3.6	(0.48)	3.3	(0.49)	1.6	(0.24)	6.8	(1.35)	5.4	(0.93)
2013	4.7	(0.40)	4.8	(0.53)	4.5	(0.55)	4.3	(0.51)	5.8	(1.17)	5.7	(0.95)
2014	5.2	(0.38)	5.4	(0.58)	5.0	(0.53)	4.7	(0.43)	5.7	(1.21)	7.9	(1.05)

!Interpret data with caution. The coefficient of variation (CV) for this estimate is between 30 and 50 percent.
[1]The event dropout rate is the percentage of 15- to 24-year-olds in grades 10 through 12 who dropped out between one October and the next (e.g., the 2014 data refer to 10th-through 12th-graders who were enrolled in October 2013 but had dropped out by October 2014). Dropping out is defined as leaving school without a high school diploma or alternative credential such as a GED certificate.
[2]Includes other racial/ethnic groups not separately shown.

NOTE: Data are based on sample surveys of the civilian noninstitutionalized population, which excludes persons in prisons, persons in the military, and other persons not living in households. Because of changes in data collection procedures, data for 1992 and later years may not be comparable with figures for prior years. Beginning in 2010, standard errors were computed using replicate weights, which produced more precise values than the generalized variance function methodology used in prior years. Race categories exclude persons of Hispanic ethnicity. Detail may not sum to totals because of rounding.
SOURCE: U.S. Department of Commerce, Census Bureau, Current Population Survey (CPS), October, 1972 through 2014. (This table was prepared March 2016.)

Table 219.57. Population of 15- to 24-year-olds enrolled in grades 10 through 12, number who dropped out (event dropouts), percentage who dropped out (event dropout rate), and percentage distribution, by selected characteristics: 2014

[Standard errors appear in parentheses]

Selected characteristic	15- to 24-year-olds enrolled in grades 10 through 12									
	Number (in thousands)						Percentage distribution			
	Total population[1]		Event dropouts[2]		Event dropout rate (percent)[3]		Total population[1]		Event dropouts[2]	
1	2		3		4		5		6	
Total..............................	10,889	(138.4)	567	(42.4)	5.2	(0.38)	100.0	(†)	100.0	(†)
Sex										
Male..........................	5,558	(88.5)	300	(32.7)	5.4	(0.58)	51.0	(0.54)	53.0	(3.99)
Female.......................	5,330	(92.9)	267	(29.3)	5.0	(0.53)	49.0	(0.54)	47.0	(3.99)
Race/ethnicity										
White.........................	6,104	(94.2)	285	(27.4)	4.7	(0.43)	56.1	(0.64)	50.2	(3.90)
Black.........................	1,463	(46.3)	83	(17.9)	5.7	(1.21)	13.4	(0.38)	14.6	(2.84)
Hispanic.....................	2,274	(67.4)	179	(25.6)	7.9	(1.05)	20.9	(0.52)	31.5	(3.52)
Asian.........................	507	(34.5)	‡	(†)	‡	(†)	4.7	(0.30)	‡	(†)
Pacific Islander...........	‡	(†)	‡	(†)	‡	(†)	‡	(†)	‡	(†)
American Indian/Alaska Native..............	118	(21.0)	12 !	(4.9)	10.1 !	(3.91)	1.1	(0.19)	2.1 !	(0.86)
Two or more races	378	(32.5)	‡	(†)	‡	(†)	3.5	(0.30)	‡	(†)
Family income[4]										
Low income.................	1,603	(76.5)	150	(23.9)	9.4	(1.41)	14.7	(0.65)	26.5	(3.43)
Middle income.............	6,273	(123.3)	339	(30.6)	5.4	(0.48)	57.6	(0.90)	59.8	(3.76)
High income................	3,012	(90.8)	78	(15.8)	2.6	(0.50)	27.7	(0.77)	13.7	(2.55)
Age[5]										
15–16.........................	3,058	(84.0)	190	(25.8)	6.2	(0.82)	28.1	(0.62)	33.5	(3.85)
17.............................	3,684	(56.1)	120	(22.3)	3.3	(0.60)	33.8	(0.49)	21.2	(3.51)
18.............................	2,871	(63.2)	121	(21.4)	4.2	(0.73)	26.4	(0.54)	21.3	(3.39)
19.............................	930	(56.1)	68	(14.1)	7.4	(1.38)	8.5	(0.48)	12.1	(2.35)
20–24.........................	346	(39.8)	68	(16.1)	19.5	(4.25)	3.2	(0.35)	11.9	(2.73)
Recency of immigration[6]										
Born outside the United States										
Hispanic..................	387	(35.5)	72	(16.8)	18.7	(3.82)	3.6	(0.32)	12.8	(2.74)
Non-Hispanic	480	(42.5)	24 !	(10.5)	4.9 !	(2.11)	4.4	(0.38)	4.2 !	(1.75)
First generation										
Hispanic..................	1,183	(60.6)	63	(15.7)	5.3	(1.29)	10.9	(0.54)	11.0	(2.65)
Non-Hispanic	952	(60.8)	27 !	(9.3)	2.8 !	(0.96)	8.7	(0.56)	4.7 !	(1.58)
Second or later generation										
Hispanic..................	703	(47.6)	44 !	(14.6)	6.2 !	(1.95)	6.5	(0.41)	7.7 !	(2.43)
Non-Hispanic	7,183	(117.9)	338	(27.8)	4.7	(0.37)	66.0	(0.72)	59.6	(3.66)
Disability status[7]										
With a disability...........	450	(40.8)	18 !	(6.2)	4.0 !	(1.39)	4.1	(0.37)	3.2 !	(1.10)
Without a disability........	10,439	(136.3)	549	(42.3)	5.3	(0.39)	95.9	(0.37)	96.8	(1.10)
Region										
Northeast....................	1,983	(80.2)	96	(20.3)	4.8	(0.98)	18.2	(0.69)	16.9	(3.29)
Midwest......................	2,533	(75.8)	118	(17.2)	4.6	(0.68)	23.3	(0.65)	20.7	(2.90)
South	3,715	(100.2)	190	(25.9)	5.1	(0.67)	34.1	(0.82)	33.5	(3.93)
West	2,659	(84.5)	164	(26.0)	6.2	(0.93)	24.4	(0.69)	28.9	(3.80)

†Not applicable.

!Interpret data with caution. The coefficient of variation (CV) for this estimate is between 30 and 50 percent.

‡Reporting standards not met. Either there are too few cases for a reliable estimate or the coefficient of variation (CV) is 50 percent or greater.

[1]Includes all 15- to 24-year-olds who were enrolled in grades 10 through 12 in October 2013.

[2]Includes only those 15- to 24-year-olds who dropped out of grades 10 through 12 between October 2013 and October 2014. Dropping out is defined as leaving school without a high school diploma or alternative credential such as a GED certificate.

[3]Among 15- to 24-year-olds who were enrolled in grades 10 through 12 in October 2013, the percentage who had dropped out by October 2014.

[4]Low income refers to the bottom 20 percent of all family incomes; high income refers to the top 20 percent of all family incomes; and middle income refers to the 60 percent in between. In 2014, low income was defined as $19,716 or less, and high income was defined as $95,433 or more.

[5]Age at the time of data collection. A person's age at the time of dropping out may be 1 year younger, because the dropout event could occur at any time over the previous 12-month period.

[6]The United States includes the 50 states and the District of Columbia. Individuals defined as "first generation" were born in the United States, but one or both of their parents were born outside the United States. Individuals defined as "second or later generation" were born in the United States, as were both of their parents.

[7]Individuals identified as having a disability reported difficulty with at least one of the following: hearing, seeing even when wearing glasses, walking or climbing stairs, dressing or bathing, doing errands alone, concentrating, remembering, or making decisions.

NOTE: Data are based on sample surveys of the civilian noninstitutionalized population, which excludes persons in prisons, persons in the military, and other persons not living in households. Race categories exclude persons of Hispanic ethnicity. Detail may not sum to totals because of rounding. Standard errors were computed using replicate weights.

SOURCE: U.S. Department of Commerce, Census Bureau, Current Population Survey (CPS), October 2014. (This table was prepared March 2016.)

Table 219.60. Number of people taking the GED test and percentage distribution of those who passed, by age group: 1971 through 2013

Year	Number of test takers (in thousands)			Percentage distribution of test passers, by age group[1]				
	Total[2]	Completing test battery[3]	Passing tests[4]	16 to 18 years old	19 to 24 years old	25 to 29 years old	30 to 34 years old	35 years old or over
1	2	3	4	5	6	7	8	9
1971[5]	377	—	227	—	—	—	—	—
1972[5]	419	—	245	—	—	—	—	—
1973[5]	423	—	249	—	—	—	—	—
1974	—	—	294	35 [6]	27 [6]	13	9	17
1975	—	—	340	33 [6]	26 [6]	14	9	18
1976	—	—	333	31 [6]	28 [6]	14	10	17
1977	—	—	330	40 [6]	24 [6]	13	8	14
1978	—	—	381	31 [6]	27 [6]	13	10	18
1979	—	—	426	37 [6]	28 [6]	12	13	11
1980	—	—	479	37 [6]	27 [6]	13	8	15
1981	—	—	489	37 [6]	27 [6]	13	8	14
1982	—	—	486	37 [6]	28 [6]	13	8	15
1983	—	—	465	34 [6]	29 [6]	14	8	15
1984	—	—	427	32 [6]	28 [6]	15	9	16
1985	—	—	413	32 [6]	26 [6]	15	10	16
1986	—	—	428	32 [6]	26 [6]	15	10	17
1987	—	—	444	33 [6]	24 [6]	15	10	18
1988	—	—	410	35 [6]	22 [6]	14	10	18
1989	632	541	357	22	37	13	—	—
1990	714	615	410	22	39	13	10	15
1991	755	657	462	20	40	13	10	16
1992	739	639	457	22	39	13	9	17
1993	746	651	469	22	38	13	10	16
1994	774	668	491	25	37	13	10	15
1995	787	682	504	27	36	13	9	15
1996	824	716	488	27	37	13	9	14
1997	785	681	460	31	36	12	8	13
1998	776	673	481	32	36	11	7	13
1999	808	702	498	32	37	11	7	13
2000	811	699	487	33	37	11	7	13
2001[7]	1,016	928	648	29	38	11	8	14
2002[7]	557	467	330	38	36	10	6	11
2003	657	552	387	35	37	10	7	11
2004	666	570	406	35	38	11	6	10
2005	681	588	424	34	37	12	7	11
2006	676	580	398	35	36	12	6	11
2007	692	600	429	35	35	12	7	11
2008	737	642	469	34	35	13	7	11
2009	748	645	448	31	36	13	8	12
2010	720	623	452	27	37	14	9	14
2011	691	602	434	27	37	13	9	14
2012	674	581	401	26	37	14	9	13
2013	816	714	541	22	35	15	11	17

—Not available.

[1]Age data for 1988 and prior years are for all test takers and may not be comparable to data for later years. For 1989 and later years, age data are only for test passers. The less than 1 percent of people who failed to report their date of birth—2,948 of the 540,535 test passers in 2013—were excluded from the calculation.
[2]All people taking the GED tests (one or more subtests).
[3]People completing the entire GED battery of five tests.
[4]Data for 2002 and later years are for people passing the GED tests (i.e., earning both a passing total score on the test battery and a passing score on each individual test). Data for 2001 and prior years are for high school equivalency credentials issued by the states to GED test passers. In order to receive high school equivalency credentials in some states, GED test passers must meet additional state requirements (e.g., complete an approved course in civics or government).

[5]Includes other jurisdictions, such as Puerto Rico, Guam, and American Samoa.
[6]For 1988 and prior years, 19-year-olds are included with the 16- to 18-year-olds instead of the 19- to 24-year-olds.
[7]A revised GED test was introduced in 2002. In 2001, test takers were required to successfully complete all five components of the GED or else begin the five-part series again with the new test that was introduced in 2002.
NOTE: Data are for the United States only and exclude other jurisdictions, except where noted. Detail may not sum to totals because of rounding.
SOURCE: American Council on Education, General Educational Development Testing Service, the GED annual *Statistical Report*, 1971 through 1992; *Who Took the GED?* 1993 through 2001; *Who Passed the GED Tests?* 2002 through 2005; and *GED Testing Program Statistical Report*, 2006 through 2013, retrieved November 5, 2014, from http://www.gedtesting service.com/educators/historical-testing-data. (This table was prepared November 2014.)

Table 219.67. High school completion rate of 18- to 24-year-olds not enrolled in high school (status completion rate) and number and percentage distribution of 18- to 24-year-olds not enrolled in high school, by selected characteristics: Selected years, 2004 through 2014

[Standard errors appear in parentheses]

Selected characteristic	Status completion rate[1]				2014				
					Number of 18- to 24-year-olds not enrolled in high school (in thousands)		Percentage distribution of 18- to 24-year-olds not enrolled in high school		
	2004	2009	2013	2014	Total population[2]	Status completers only[3]	Total population[2]	Status completers only[3]	
1	2	3	4	5	6	7	8	9	
Total	86.9 (0.30)	89.8 (0.27)	92.0 (0.35)	92.4 (0.32)	28,402 (99.9)	26,255 (137.6)	100.0 (†)	100.0 (†)	
Sex									
Male	84.9 (0.46)	88.3 (0.40)	91.4 (0.47)	91.8 (0.46)	14,151 (70.1)	12,986 (94.1)	49.8 (0.20)	49.5 (0.26)	
Female	88.8 (0.40)	91.2 (0.35)	92.6 (0.45)	93.1 (0.38)	14,251 (81.9)	13,269 (99.3)	50.2 (0.20)	50.5 (0.26)	
Race/ethnicity									
White	91.7 (0.31)	93.8 (0.27)	94.3 (0.38)	94.2 (0.40)	15,767 (123.5)	14,847 (136.0)	55.5 (0.40)	56.6 (0.45)	
Black	83.5 (0.98)	87.1 (0.84)	91.5 (1.13)	91.7 (0.91)	4,092 (102.0)	3,750 (102.8)	14.4 (0.35)	14.3 (0.38)	
Hispanic	69.9 (1.12)	76.8 (1.00)	85.0 (0.98)	87.1 (0.88)	6,101 (76.5)	5,313 (88.9)	21.5 (0.26)	20.2 (0.32)	
Asian	95.2 (1.00)	97.6 (0.72)	96.3 (1.27)	98.8 (0.47)	1,467 (44.6)	1,450 (45.5)	5.2 (0.16)	5.5 (0.17)	
Pacific Islander	94.7 (4.07)	77.2 (6.63)	99.3 (0.79)	94.3 (5.59)	97 (22.4)	91 (21.7)	0.3 (0.08)	0.3 (0.08)	
American Indian/Alaska Native	76.7 (4.70)	82.4 (4.47)	91.7 (2.97)	78.7 (4.18)	244 (25.2)	192 (24.0)	0.9 (0.09)	0.7 (0.09)	
Two or more races	93.1 (1.86)	89.2 (2.18)	93.6 (1.83)	96.6 (1.16)	633 (42.5)	612 (41.9)	2.2 (0.15)	2.3 (0.16)	
Race/ethnicity by sex									
Male									
White	91.2 (0.46)	92.4 (0.42)	93.8 (0.48)	93.7 (0.53)	7,911 (75.4)	7,411 (85.6)	55.9 (0.43)	57.1 (0.50)	
Black	79.9 (1.56)	85.0 (1.31)	90.3 (1.41)	91.2 (1.30)	1,944 (39.4)	1,773 (46.3)	13.7 (0.27)	13.7 (0.34)	
Hispanic	64.2 (1.59)	74.9 (1.43)	83.8 (1.35)	86.0 (1.22)	3,095 (51.4)	2,663 (53.4)	21.9 (0.37)	20.5 (0.40)	
Asian	96.7 (1.18)	98.7 (0.74)	97.6 (1.17)	98.0 (0.86)	755 (32.7)	739 (33.3)	5.3 (0.23)	5.7 (0.25)	
Pacific Islander	‡ (†)	‡ (†)	‡ (†)	‡ (†)	41 ! (12.3)	36 ! (11.1)	0.3 ! (0.09)	0.3 ! (0.09)	
American Indian/Alaska Native	81.0 (6.37)	85.0 (6.06)	90.5 (6.44)	78.0 (5.79)	115 (16.2)	89 (14.3)	0.8 (0.11)	0.7 (0.11)	
Two or more races	92.1 (2.79)	90.0 (3.00)	94.7 (2.65)	94.7 (2.14)	290 (26.2)	275 (25.6)	2.1 (0.18)	2.1 (0.20)	
Female									
White	92.2 (0.43)	95.1 (0.34)	94.7 (0.45)	94.7 (0.52)	7,856 (75.2)	7,436 (83.7)	55.1 (0.55)	56.0 (0.61)	
Black	86.5 (1.22)	88.9 (1.09)	92.6 (1.39)	92.0 (1.16)	2,148 (84.5)	1,977 (81.9)	15.1 (0.55)	14.9 (0.57)	
Hispanic	76.5 (1.52)	78.8 (1.40)	86.2 (1.30)	88.1 (1.16)	3,006 (47.6)	2,649 (61.2)	21.1 (0.31)	20.0 (0.42)	
Asian	93.6 (1.62)	96.5 (1.23)	94.9 (1.94)	99.6 (0.31)	713 (27.1)	710 (26.9)	5.0 (0.19)	5.4 (0.20)	
Pacific Islander	‡ (†)	‡ (†)	‡ (†)	100.0 (#)	56 (16.4)	56 (16.4)	0.4 (0.11)	0.4 (0.12)	
American Indian/Alaska Native	73.0 (6.79)	80.1 (6.50)	92.5 (4.02)	79.4 (4.56)	129 (17.5)	103 (16.5)	0.9 (0.12)	0.8 (0.12)	
Two or more races	94.2 (2.45)	88.5 (3.16)	92.5 (2.88)	98.2 (1.05)	343 (29.4)	337 (29.3)	2.4 (0.21)	2.5 (0.22)	
Age									
18–19	85.9 (0.63)	89.0 (0.55)	91.4 (0.69)	90.7 (0.70)	6,643 (71.6)	6,028 (81.5)	23.4 (0.20)	23.0 (0.25)	
20–21	87.2 (0.55)	89.8 (0.50)	92.4 (0.63)	92.8 (0.53)	8,369 (171.4)	7,765 (166.7)	29.5 (0.60)	29.6 (0.61)	
22–24	87.1 (0.44)	90.2 (0.39)	92.1 (0.51)	93.1 (0.44)	13,389 (167.8)	12,463 (162.9)	47.1 (0.59)	47.5 (0.61)	
Recency of immigration[4]									
Born outside the United States									
Hispanic	54.7 (1.84)	63.0 (1.88)	73.0 (2.36)	74.7 (2.29)	1,462 (76.0)	1,093 (63.3)	5.1 (0.27)	4.2 (0.24)	
Non-Hispanic	91.0 (1.06)	92.5 (0.99)	93.3 (1.34)	95.7 (1.08)	1,669 (91.1)	1,597 (88.4)	5.9 (0.32)	6.1 (0.34)	
First generation									
Hispanic	81.0 (1.70)	83.7 (1.49)	89.1 (1.36)	91.3 (1.05)	2,718 (97.9)	2,481 (90.1)	9.6 (0.34)	9.4 (0.34)	
Non-Hispanic	95.9 (0.77)	95.2 (0.74)	95.3 (1.22)	97.9 (0.69)	1,883 (82.1)	1,843 (82.0)	6.6 (0.29)	7.0 (0.31)	
Second generation or higher									
Hispanic	82.0 (1.86)	86.7 (1.53)	89.8 (1.46)	90.5 (1.46)	1,921 (91.0)	1,739 (92.0)	6.8 (0.32)	6.6 (0.35)	
Non-Hispanic	90.0 (0.32)	92.3 (0.28)	93.8 (0.38)	93.4 (0.36)	18,748 (137.9)	17,502 (149.0)	66.0 (0.42)	66.7 (0.47)	
Disability[5]									
With a disability	— (†)	80.0 (1.90)	81.3 (2.27)	83.7 (2.10)	1,050 (64.1)	878 (57.3)	3.7 (0.23)	3.3 (0.22)	
Without a disability	— (†)	90.1 (0.27)	92.4 (0.33)	92.8 (0.31)	27,352 (115.1)	25,377 (144.9)	96.3 (0.23)	96.7 (0.22)	
Region									
Northeast	88.7 (0.62)	90.9 (0.62)	93.4 (0.79)	94.3 (0.71)	5,017 (125.5)	4,731 (120.4)	17.7 (0.43)	18.0 (0.45)	
Midwest	89.7 (0.55)	90.3 (0.58)	93.2 (0.71)	93.6 (0.70)	5,897 (145.8)	5,520 (146.8)	20.8 (0.50)	21.0 (0.54)	
South	85.5 (0.57)	89.3 (0.47)	91.2 (0.60)	91.2 (0.62)	10,459 (166.6)	9,538 (174.3)	36.8 (0.58)	36.3 (0.63)	
West	84.5 (0.73)	89.1 (0.56)	91.2 (0.70)	92.0 (0.68)	7,029 (135.9)	6,466 (139.7)	24.7 (0.48)	24.6 (0.53)	

—Not available.
†Not applicable.
#Rounds to zero.
!Interpret data with caution. The coefficient of variation for this estimate is between 30 and 50 percent.
‡Reporting standards not met (too few cases for a reliable estimate).
[1]The status completion rate is the number of 18- to 24-year-olds who are high school completers as a percentage of the total number of 18- to 24-year-olds who are not enrolled in high school or a lower level of education. High school completers include those with a high school diploma, as well as those with an alternative credential, such as a GED.
[2]Includes all 18- to 24-year-olds who are not enrolled in high school or a lower level of education.
[3]Status completers are 18- to 24-year-olds who are not enrolled in high school or a lower level of education and who also are high school completers—that is, have either a high school diploma or an alternative credential, such as a GED.

[4]The United States includes the 50 states and the District of Columbia. Individuals defined as "first generation" were born in the United States, but one or both of their parents were born outside the United States. Individuals defined as "second generation or higher" were born in the United States, as were both of their parents.
[5]Individuals identified as having a disability reported difficulty in at least one of the following: hearing, seeing even when wearing glasses, walking or climbing stairs, dressing or bathing, doing errands alone, concentrating, remembering, or making decisions.
NOTE: Data are based on sample surveys of the civilian noninstitutionalized population, which excludes persons in prisons, persons in the military, and other persons not living in households. Race categories exclude persons of Hispanic ethnicity. Detail may not sum to totals because of rounding.
SOURCE: U.S. Department of Commerce, Census Bureau, Current Population Survey (CPS), October, 2004 through 2014. (This table was prepared March 2016.)

Table 219.70. Percentage of high school dropouts among persons 16 to 24 years old (status dropout rate), by sex and race/ethnicity: Selected years, 1960 through 2014

[Standard errors appear in parentheses]

Year	Total status dropout rate				Male status dropout rate				Female status dropout rate			
	All races[1]	White	Black	Hispanic	All races[1]	White	Black	Hispanic	All races[1]	White	Black	Hispanic
1	2	3	4	5	6	7	8	9	10	11	12	13
1960[2]	27.2 (—)	— (†)	— (†)	— (†)	27.8 (—)	— (†)	— (†)	— (†)	26.7 (—)	— (†)	— (†)	— (†)
1967[3]	17.0 (—)	15.4 (—)	28.6 (—)	— (†)	16.5 (—)	14.7 (—)	30.6 (—)	— (†)	17.3 (—)	16.1 (—)	26.9 (—)	— (†)
1968[3]	16.2 (—)	14.7 (—)	27.4 (—)	— (†)	15.8 (—)	14.4 (—)	27.1 (—)	— (†)	16.5 (—)	15.0 (—)	27.6 (—)	— (†)
1969[3]	15.2 (—)	13.6 (—)	26.7 (—)	— (†)	14.3 (—)	12.6 (—)	26.9 (—)	— (†)	16.0 (—)	14.6 (—)	26.7 (—)	— (†)
1970[3]	15.0 (0.29)	13.2 (0.30)	27.9 (1.22)	— (†)	14.2 (0.42)	12.2 (0.42)	29.4 (1.82)	— (†)	15.7 (0.41)	14.1 (0.42)	26.6 (1.65)	— (†)
1971[3]	14.7 (0.28)	13.4 (0.29)	24.0 (1.14)	— (†)	14.2 (0.41)	12.6 (0.41)	25.5 (1.70)	— (†)	15.2 (0.40)	14.2 (0.42)	22.6 (1.54)	— (†)
1972	14.6 (0.28)	12.3 (0.29)	21.3 (1.07)	34.3 (2.22)	14.1 (0.40)	11.6 (0.40)	22.3 (1.59)	33.7 (3.23)	15.1 (0.39)	12.8 (0.41)	20.5 (1.44)	34.8 (3.05)
1973	14.1 (0.27)	11.6 (0.28)	22.2 (1.06)	33.5 (2.24)	13.7 (0.38)	11.5 (0.39)	21.5 (1.53)	30.4 (3.16)	14.5 (0.38)	11.8 (0.39)	22.8 (1.47)	36.4 (3.16)
1974	14.3 (0.27)	11.9 (0.28)	21.2 (1.05)	33.0 (2.08)	14.2 (0.39)	12.0 (0.40)	20.1 (1.51)	33.8 (2.99)	14.3 (0.38)	11.8 (0.39)	22.1 (1.45)	32.2 (2.90)
1975	13.9 (0.27)	11.4 (0.27)	22.9 (1.06)	29.2 (2.02)	13.3 (0.37)	11.0 (0.38)	23.0 (1.56)	26.7 (2.84)	14.5 (0.38)	11.8 (0.39)	22.9 (1.44)	31.6 (2.86)
1976	14.1 (0.27)	12.0 (0.28)	20.5 (1.00)	31.4 (2.01)	14.1 (0.38)	12.1 (0.39)	21.2 (1.49)	30.3 (2.94)	14.2 (0.37)	11.8 (0.39)	19.9 (1.35)	32.3 (2.76)
1977	14.1 (0.27)	11.9 (0.28)	19.8 (0.99)	33.0 (2.02)	14.5 (0.38)	12.6 (0.40)	19.5 (1.45)	31.6 (2.89)	13.8 (0.37)	11.2 (0.38)	20.0 (1.36)	34.3 (2.83)
1978	14.2 (0.27)	11.9 (0.28)	20.2 (1.00)	33.3 (2.00)	14.6 (0.38)	12.2 (0.40)	22.5 (1.52)	33.6 (2.88)	13.9 (0.37)	11.6 (0.39)	18.3 (1.31)	33.1 (2.78)
1979	14.6 (0.27)	12.0 (0.28)	21.1 (1.01)	33.8 (1.98)	15.0 (0.39)	12.6 (0.40)	22.4 (1.52)	33.0 (2.83)	14.2 (0.37)	11.5 (0.38)	20.0 (1.35)	34.5 (2.77)
1980	14.1 (0.26)	11.4 (0.27)	19.1 (0.97)	35.2 (1.89)	15.1 (0.39)	12.3 (0.40)	20.8 (1.47)	37.2 (2.72)	13.1 (0.36)	10.5 (0.37)	17.7 (1.28)	33.2 (2.61)
1981	13.9 (0.26)	11.3 (0.27)	18.4 (0.93)	33.2 (1.80)	15.1 (0.38)	12.5 (0.40)	19.9 (1.40)	36.0 (2.61)	12.8 (0.35)	10.2 (0.36)	17.1 (1.24)	30.4 (2.48)
1982	13.9 (0.27)	11.4 (0.29)	18.4 (0.97)	31.7 (1.93)	14.5 (0.40)	12.0 (0.42)	21.2 (1.50)	30.5 (2.73)	13.3 (0.38)	10.8 (0.40)	15.9 (1.26)	32.8 (2.71)
1983	13.7 (0.27)	11.1 (0.29)	18.0 (0.97)	31.6 (1.93)	14.9 (0.41)	12.2 (0.43)	19.9 (1.46)	34.3 (2.84)	12.5 (0.37)	10.1 (0.39)	16.2 (1.28)	29.1 (2.61)
1984	13.1 (0.27)	11.0 (0.29)	15.5 (0.91)	29.8 (1.91)	14.0 (0.40)	11.9 (0.43)	16.8 (1.37)	30.6 (2.78)	12.3 (0.37)	10.1 (0.39)	14.3 (1.22)	29.0 (2.63)
1985	12.6 (0.27)	10.4 (0.29)	15.2 (0.92)	27.6 (1.93)	13.4 (0.40)	11.1 (0.42)	16.1 (1.37)	29.9 (2.76)	11.8 (0.37)	9.8 (0.39)	14.3 (1.23)	25.2 (2.68)
1986	12.2 (0.27)	9.7 (0.28)	14.2 (0.90)	30.1 (1.88)	13.1 (0.40)	10.3 (0.42)	15.0 (1.33)	32.8 (2.66)	11.4 (0.37)	9.1 (0.39)	13.5 (1.21)	27.2 (2.63)
1987	12.6 (0.28)	10.4 (0.30)	14.1 (0.90)	28.6 (1.84)	13.2 (0.40)	10.8 (0.43)	15.0 (1.35)	29.1 (2.57)	12.1 (0.38)	10.0 (0.41)	13.3 (1.21)	28.1 (2.64)
1988	12.9 (0.30)	9.6 (0.31)	14.5 (1.00)	35.8 (2.30)	13.5 (0.44)	10.3 (0.46)	15.0 (1.48)	36.0 (3.19)	12.2 (0.42)	8.9 (0.43)	14.0 (1.36)	35.4 (3.31)
1989	12.6 (0.31)	9.4 (0.32)	13.9 (0.98)	33.0 (2.19)	13.6 (0.45)	10.3 (0.47)	14.9 (1.46)	34.4 (3.08)	11.7 (0.42)	8.5 (0.43)	13.0 (1.32)	31.6 (3.11)
1990	12.1 (0.29)	9.0 (0.30)	13.2 (0.94)	32.4 (1.91)	12.3 (0.42)	9.3 (0.44)	11.9 (1.30)	34.3 (2.71)	11.8 (0.41)	8.7 (0.42)	14.4 (1.34)	30.3 (2.70)
1991	12.5 (0.30)	8.9 (0.31)	13.6 (0.95)	35.3 (1.93)	13.0 (0.43)	8.9 (0.44)	13.5 (1.37)	39.2 (2.74)	11.9 (0.41)	8.9 (0.43)	13.7 (1.31)	31.1 (2.70)
1992[4]	11.0 (0.28)	7.7 (0.29)	13.7 (0.95)	29.4 (1.86)	11.3 (0.41)	8.0 (0.42)	12.5 (1.32)	32.1 (2.67)	10.7 (0.39)	7.4 (0.40)	14.8 (1.36)	26.6 (2.56)
1993[4]	11.0 (0.28)	7.9 (0.29)	13.6 (0.94)	27.5 (1.79)	11.2 (0.40)	8.2 (0.42)	12.6 (1.32)	28.1 (2.54)	10.9 (0.40)	7.6 (0.41)	14.4 (1.34)	26.9 (2.52)
1994[4]	11.4 (0.26)	7.7 (0.27)	12.6 (0.75)	30.0 (1.16)	12.3 (0.38)	8.0 (0.38)	14.1 (1.14)	31.6 (1.60)	10.6 (0.36)	7.5 (0.37)	11.3 (0.99)	28.1 (1.66)
1995[4]	12.0 (0.27)	8.6 (0.28)	12.1 (0.74)	30.0 (1.15)	12.2 (0.38)	9.0 (0.40)	11.1 (1.05)	30.0 (1.59)	11.7 (0.37)	8.2 (0.39)	12.9 (1.05)	30.0 (1.66)
1996[4]	11.1 (0.27)	7.3 (0.27)	13.0 (0.80)	29.4 (1.19)	11.4 (0.38)	7.3 (0.38)	13.5 (1.18)	30.3 (1.67)	10.9 (0.38)	7.3 (0.39)	12.5 (1.08)	28.3 (1.69)
1997[4]	11.0 (0.27)	7.6 (0.28)	13.4 (0.80)	25.3 (1.11)	11.9 (0.39)	8.5 (0.41)	13.3 (1.16)	27.0 (1.55)	10.1 (0.36)	6.7 (0.37)	13.5 (1.11)	23.4 (1.59)
1998[4]	11.8 (0.27)	7.7 (0.28)	13.8 (0.81)	29.5 (1.12)	13.3 (0.40)	8.6 (0.41)	15.5 (1.24)	33.5 (1.59)	10.3 (0.36)	6.9 (0.37)	12.2 (1.05)	25.0 (1.56)
1999[4]	11.2 (0.26)	7.3 (0.27)	12.6 (0.77)	28.6 (1.11)	11.9 (0.38)	7.7 (0.39)	12.1 (1.10)	31.0 (1.58)	10.5 (0.36)	6.9 (0.37)	13.0 (1.08)	26.0 (1.54)
2000[4]	10.9 (0.26)	6.9 (0.26)	13.1 (0.78)	27.8 (1.08)	12.0 (0.38)	7.0 (0.37)	15.3 (1.20)	31.8 (1.56)	9.9 (0.35)	6.9 (0.37)	11.1 (1.00)	23.5 (1.48)
2001[4]	10.7 (0.25)	7.3 (0.26)	10.9 (0.71)	27.0 (1.06)	12.2 (0.38)	7.9 (0.39)	13.0 (1.12)	31.6 (1.55)	9.3 (0.34)	6.7 (0.36)	9.0 (0.90)	22.1 (1.42)
2002[4]	10.5 (0.24)	6.5 (0.24)	11.3 (0.70)	25.7 (0.93)	11.8 (0.35)	6.7 (0.35)	12.8 (1.07)	29.6 (1.32)	9.2 (0.32)	6.3 (0.34)	9.9 (0.91)	21.2 (1.27)
2003[4,5]	9.9 (0.23)	6.3 (0.24)	10.9 (0.69)	23.5 (0.90)	11.3 (0.34)	7.1 (0.35)	12.5 (1.05)	26.7 (1.29)	8.4 (0.30)	5.6 (0.32)	9.5 (0.89)	20.1 (1.23)
2004[4,5]	10.3 (0.23)	6.8 (0.24)	11.8 (0.70)	23.8 (0.89)	11.6 (0.34)	7.1 (0.35)	13.5 (1.08)	28.5 (1.30)	9.0 (0.31)	6.4 (0.34)	10.2 (0.92)	18.5 (1.18)
2005[4,5]	9.4 (0.22)	6.0 (0.23)	10.4 (0.66)	22.4 (0.87)	10.8 (0.33)	6.6 (0.34)	12.0 (1.02)	26.4 (1.26)	8.0 (0.29)	5.3 (0.31)	9.0 (0.86)	18.1 (1.16)
2006[4,5]	9.3 (0.22)	5.8 (0.23)	10.7 (0.66)	22.1 (0.86)	10.3 (0.33)	6.4 (0.33)	9.7 (0.91)	25.7 (1.25)	8.3 (0.30)	5.3 (0.31)	11.7 (0.96)	18.1 (1.15)
2007[4,5]	8.7 (0.21)	5.3 (0.22)	8.4 (0.59)	21.4 (0.83)	9.8 (0.32)	6.0 (0.32)	8.0 (0.82)	24.7 (1.22)	7.7 (0.29)	4.5 (0.28)	8.8 (0.84)	18.0 (1.13)
2008[4,5]	8.0 (0.20)	4.8 (0.21)	9.9 (0.63)	18.3 (0.78)	8.5 (0.30)	5.4 (0.30)	8.7 (0.85)	19.9 (1.12)	7.5 (0.28)	4.2 (0.28)	11.1 (0.93)	16.7 (1.08)
2009[4,5]	8.1 (0.20)	5.2 (0.21)	9.3 (0.61)	17.6 (0.76)	9.1 (0.31)	6.3 (0.33)	10.6 (0.93)	19.0 (1.10)	7.0 (0.27)	4.1 (0.27)	8.1 (0.80)	16.1 (1.06)
2010[4,5,6]	7.4 (0.27)	5.1 (0.30)	8.0 (0.76)	15.1 (0.87)	8.5 (0.40)	5.9 (0.42)	9.5 (1.11)	17.3 (1.24)	6.3 (0.28)	4.2 (0.35)	6.7 (0.85)	12.8 (0.97)
2011[4,5,6]	7.1 (0.26)	5.0 (0.31)	7.3 (0.67)	13.6 (0.78)	7.7 (0.36)	5.4 (0.41)	8.3 (0.98)	14.6 (1.09)	6.5 (0.34)	4.6 (0.38)	6.4 (0.94)	12.4 (0.97)
2012[4,5,6]	6.6 (0.25)	4.3 (0.31)	7.5 (0.76)	12.7 (0.72)	7.3 (0.36)	4.8 (0.40)	8.1 (1.15)	13.9 (1.04)	5.9 (0.33)	3.8 (0.37)	7.0 (1.01)	11.3 (1.00)
2013[4,5,6]	6.8 (0.28)	5.1 (0.31)	7.3 (0.87)	11.7 (0.74)	7.2 (0.37)	5.5 (0.39)	8.2 (1.11)	12.6 (1.01)	6.3 (0.34)	4.7 (0.36)	6.6 (1.07)	10.8 (0.98)
2014[4,5,6]	6.5 (0.25)	5.2 (0.32)	7.4 (0.74)	10.6 (0.68)	7.1 (0.37)	5.7 (0.42)	7.1 (1.02)	11.8 (1.04)	5.9 (0.29)	4.8 (0.41)	7.7 (1.02)	9.3 (0.84)

—Not available.
†Not applicable.
[1]Includes other racial/ethnic categories not separately shown.
[2]Based on the April 1960 decennial census.
[3]For 1967 through 1971, White and Black include persons of Hispanic ethnicity.
[4]Because of changes in data collection procedures, data may not be comparable with figures for years prior to 1992.
[5]White and Black exclude persons identifying themselves as Two or more races.
[6]Beginning in 2010, standard errors were computed using replicate weights, which produced more precise values than the generalized variance function methodology used in prior years.

NOTE: "Status" dropouts are 16- to 24-year-olds who are not enrolled in school and who have not completed a high school program, regardless of when they left school. People who have received GED credentials are counted as high school completers. All data except for 1960 are based on October counts. Data are based on sample surveys of the civilian noninstitutionalized population, which excludes persons in prisons, persons in the military, and other persons not living in households. Race categories exclude persons of Hispanic ethnicity except where otherwise noted.
SOURCE: U.S. Department of Commerce, Census Bureau, Current Population Survey (CPS), October, 1967 through 2014. (This table was prepared August 2015.)

Table 219.71. Population 16 to 24 years old and number of 16- to 24-year-old high school dropouts (status dropouts), by sex and race/ethnicity: 1970 through 2014

[Standard errors appear in parentheses]

Year	Total — All races[1]	Total — White	Total — Black	Total — Hispanic	Males — All races[1]	Males — White	Males — Black	Males — Hispanic	Females — All races[1]	Females — White	Females — Black	Females — Hispanic
	2	3	4	5	6	7	8	9	10	11	12	13
					Population 16 to 24 years old (in thousands)							
1970[2]	30,251 (260.7)	26,241 (245.8)	3,669 (93.6)	— (†)	14,260 (175.6)	12,403 (165.7)	1,703 (62.5)	— (†)	15,991 (177.3)	13,838 (167.3)	1,966 (63.7)	— (†)
1971[2]	31,538 (265.1)	27,299 (249.8)	3,871 (95.5)	— (†)	15,060 (179.5)	13,076 (169.4)	1,809 (64.0)	— (†)	16,478 (179.4)	14,223 (169.2)	2,062 (64.8)	— (†)
1972	32,643 (268.8)	26,502 (246.8)	4,024 (96.9)	1,774 (81.5)	15,787 (183.0)	12,913 (168.5)	1,878 (64.8)	830 (55.2)	16,856 (181.0)	13,589 (166.1)	2,145 (65.7)	944 (55.3)
1973	33,430 (271.4)	27,100 (249.1)	4,190 (98.3)	1,718 (80.4)	16,248 (185.1)	13,259 (170.4)	1,976 (66.0)	821 (54.9)	17,182 (182.3)	13,841 (167.4)	2,214 (66.4)	896 (54.1)
1974	33,968 (273.1)	27,301 (249.9)	4,153 (98.0)	1,981 (85.6)	16,508 (186.2)	13,361 (171.0)	1,921 (65.3)	972 (59.2)	17,460 (183.4)	13,941 (167.8)	2,232 (66.6)	1,009 (57.0)
1975	34,700 (275.4)	27,867 (252.0)	4,310 (99.3)	1,962 (85.3)	16,925 (188.0)	13,711 (172.8)	1,992 (66.2)	940 (58.3)	17,775 (184.7)	14,157 (168.9)	2,319 (67.4)	1,022 (57.3)
1976	35,222 (277.0)	28,146 (253.1)	4,429 (100.2)	2,060 (87.1)	17,210 (189.3)	13,925 (173.9)	2,054 (66.9)	944 (58.4)	18,012 (185.6)	14,221 (169.2)	2,375 (67.9)	1,115 (59.4)
1977	35,658 (278.3)	28,393 (254.0)	4,516 (100.9)	2,123 (88.3)	17,431 (190.2)	14,027 (174.4)	2,086 (67.2)	1,018 (60.4)	18,227 (186.4)	14,366 (169.9)	2,430 (68.4)	1,106 (59.2)
1978	35,931 (279.1)	28,490 (254.3)	4,584 (101.4)	2,183 (89.3)	17,582 (190.8)	14,084 (174.7)	2,113 (67.5)	1,059 (61.5)	18,349 (186.9)	14,406 (170.1)	2,471 (68.8)	1,123 (59.6)
1979	36,131 (279.7)	28,602 (254.8)	4,618 (101.7)	2,242 (90.4)	17,708 (191.4)	14,172 (175.2)	2,128 (67.7)	1,085 (62.1)	18,423 (187.2)	14,430 (170.2)	2,490 (69.0)	1,157 (60.3)
1980	36,143 (279.7)	28,253 (253.5)	4,651 (101.9)	2,518 (95.0)	17,715 (191.4)	13,979 (174.2)	2,148 (67.9)	1,240 (65.8)	18,428 (187.2)	14,274 (169.5)	2,503 (69.1)	1,277 (62.8)
1981	36,945 (282.1)	28,483 (254.3)	4,895 (103.7)	2,684 (97.5)	18,167 (193.2)	14,111 (174.4)	2,286 (69.2)	1,333 (67.8)	18,778 (188.5)	14,372 (169.9)	2,608 (69.9)	1,352 (64.3)
1982	36,452 (296.5)	27,979 (266.7)	4,912 (109.6)	2,598 (103.0)	17,938 (203.2)	13,841 (183.3)	2,303 (73.3)	1,263 (70.9)	18,514 (198.1)	14,139 (178.4)	2,609 (73.9)	1,335 (64.0)
1983	35,884 (294.7)	27,385 (264.3)	4,907 (109.6)	2,587 (101.7)	17,712 (202.2)	13,616 (182.0)	2,329 (73.6)	1,242 (69.8)	18,172 (196.7)	13,769 (176.4)	2,578 (73.6)	1,345 (68.1)
1984	35,204 (292.6)	26,758 (261.8)	4,890 (109.5)	2,558 (101.4)	17,387 (200.8)	13,325 (180.4)	2,329 (73.6)	1,226 (69.4)	17,817 (195.3)	13,433 (174.7)	2,561 (73.5)	1,332 (67.8)
1985	34,382 (289.9)	25,772 (257.7)	4,749 (108.4)	2,887 (86.4)	16,892 (198.5)	12,715 (176.9)	2,239 (72.7)	1,472 (60.7)	17,490 (193.0)	13,057 (172.6)	2,510 (73.0)	1,415 (69.4)
1986	33,945 (288.4)	24,959 (254.2)	4,698 (108.0)	3,206 (93.7)	16,709 (197.7)	12,276 (174.3)	2,222 (72.5)	1,667 (66.4)	17,236 (192.9)	12,684 (170.5)	2,476 (72.7)	1,538 (60.5)
1987	33,452 (286.8)	24,479 (252.1)	4,631 (107.5)	3,234 (94.1)	16,458 (196.5)	12,058 (173.0)	2,176 (72.0)	1,680 (66.6)	16,994 (191.8)	12,420 (169.1)	2,455 (72.5)	1,554 (60.7)
1988	32,893 (310.4)	23,908 (272.0)	4,584 (116.5)	3,267 (107.8)	16,134 (212.5)	11,725 (186.3)	2,156 (78.2)	1,696 (76.3)	16,759 (207.9)	12,184 (182.7)	2,429 (78.7)	1,571 (61.0)
1989	32,007 (291.9)	22,947 (254.0)	4,593 (111.1)	3,459 (98.1)	15,783 (200.2)	11,314 (174.4)	2,193 (74.8)	1,783 (69.1)	16,224 (195.2)	11,634 (170.3)	2,399 (74.6)	1,676 (69.8)
1990	31,443 (289.8)	22,360 (251.1)	4,487 (110.2)	3,443 (99.8)	15,502 (198.8)	11,059 (172.7)	2,117 (73.9)	1,773 (70.4)	15,941 (193.8)	11,302 (168.2)	2,370 (74.3)	1,669 (64.6)
1991	31,171 (288.8)	21,883 (248.8)	4,475 (110.1)	3,519 (100.1)	15,408 (198.3)	10,819 (171.1)	2,126 (74.0)	1,829 (71.2)	15,763 (193.0)	11,064 (166.7)	2,350 (74.1)	1,690 (64.9)
1992[3]	30,944 (287.9)	21,697 (247.9)	4,527 (110.6)	3,476 (100.2)	15,375 (198.1)	10,826 (171.0)	2,169 (74.5)	1,760 (70.2)	15,569 (192.0)	10,871 (165.5)	2,358 (74.2)	1,716 (65.3)
1993[3]	30,845 (287.5)	21,499 (246.9)	4,536 (110.7)	3,595 (101.5)	15,355 (198.0)	10,742 (170.5)	2,179 (74.6)	1,802 (70.8)	15,490 (191.6)	10,757 (164.7)	2,357 (74.2)	1,793 (66.3)
1994[3]	32,560 (293.9)	22,080 (248.9)	4,805 (112.8)	4,411 (109.3)	16,304 (202.8)	11,016 (172.4)	2,298 (75.9)	2,355 (77.9)	16,257 (195.3)	11,064 (166.7)	2,507 (75.7)	2,056 (69.5)
1995[3]	32,379 (293.2)	21,991 (249.3)	4,732 (112.2)	4,485 (109.9)	16,208 (202.3)	11,062 (172.7)	2,236 (75.3)	2,338 (77.7)	16,170 (194.9)	10,929 (165.8)	2,496 (75.6)	2,147 (70.5)
1996[3]	32,452 (304.7)	21,527 (256.4)	4,745 (116.6)	4,481 (115.4)	16,296 (210.5)	10,836 (177.7)	2,251 (78.2)	2,313 (81.4)	16,156 (202.3)	10,690 (170.5)	2,494 (78.4)	2,168 (70.7)
1997[3]	32,960 (306.6)	21,800 (257.8)	4,847 (117.4)	4,660 (115.6)	16,619 (212.1)	11,001 (178.8)	2,308 (78.9)	2,487 (82.3)	16,341 (203.2)	10,799 (171.3)	2,540 (78.8)	2,173 (73.4)
1998[3]	33,445 (308.5)	21,920 (258.4)	4,893 (117.7)	5,034 (118.5)	16,854 (213.3)	11,067 (179.3)	2,305 (78.8)	2,683 (84.2)	16,592 (204.4)	10,854 (171.6)	2,588 (79.3)	2,351 (73.4)
1999[3]	34,169 (310.9)	22,408 (260.9)	4,939 (118.1)	5,060 (118.7)	17,106 (214.5)	11,325 (181.1)	2,336 (79.2)	2,603 (83.5)	17,063 (206.6)	11,084 (173.2)	2,603 (79.4)	2,457 (76.2)
2000[3]	34,568 (312.4)	22,574 (261.8)	5,058 (119.0)	5,237 (120.0)	17,402 (215.9)	11,390 (181.5)	2,417 (80.0)	2,725 (84.6)	17,166 (207.0)	11,184 (173.9)	2,641 (79.7)	2,513 (76.7)
2001[3]	35,167 (298.5)	22,874 (249.9)	5,119 (113.3)	5,344 (112.0)	17,663 (206.1)	11,598 (173.6)	2,418 (75.9)	2,744 (78.6)	17,504 (198.0)	11,276 (165.6)	2,701 (76.2)	2,601 (77.4)
2002[3]	35,495 (299.6)	22,358 (247.4)	4,991 (112.4)	6,120 (118.8)	17,893 (207.2)	11,183 (170.9)	2,375 (75.5)	3,281 (84.3)	17,602 (198.4)	11,175 (165.0)	2,617 (75.5)	2,838 (77.5)
2003[3,4]	36,017 (301.3)	22,565 (248.4)	4,973 (115.6)	6,103 (118.8)	18,099 (208.1)	11,329 (171.9)	2,385 (78.1)	3,214 (83.9)	17,918 (199.7)	11,236 (165.4)	2,588 (77.7)	2,888 (75.3)
2004[3,4]	36,504 (302.8)	22,654 (248.8)	5,048 (116.3)	6,301 (119.8)	18,406 (209.4)	11,395 (172.3)	2,425 (78.5)	3,326 (84.6)	18,097 (200.5)	11,259 (165.5)	2,623 (78.0)	2,975 (75.8)
2005[3,4]	36,761 (303.6)	22,806 (249.6)	5,111 (116.8)	6,364 (120.1)	18,547 (210.7)	11,492 (173.0)	2,457 (78.9)	3,341 (84.7)	18,214 (201.0)	11,314 (165.9)	2,654 (78.4)	3,023 (76.0)
2006[3,4]	37,047 (304.5)	22,863 (249.8)	5,260 (118.0)	6,439 (120.4)	18,707 (210.7)	11,537 (173.3)	2,573 (80.1)	3,357 (84.7)	18,340 (201.5)	11,327 (165.9)	2,688 (78.7)	3,083 (76.3)
2007[3,4]	37,480 (305.9)	22,962 (250.3)	5,363 (118.7)	6,632 (121.2)	18,940 (211.6)	11,641 (173.9)	2,639 (80.7)	3,447 (85.2)	18,541 (202.3)	11,320 (165.9)	2,724 (79.1)	3,186 (76.8)
2008[3,4]	37,569 (306.2)	22,956 (250.6)	5,387 (118.8)	6,721 (121.5)	18,948 (211.7)	11,628 (173.9)	2,616 (80.5)	3,472 (85.4)	18,621 (202.6)	11,328 (165.9)	2,771 (79.5)	3,249 (77.1)
2009[3,4]	37,616 (306.3)	22,809 (249.6)	5,445 (119.4)	6,809 (121.9)	18,949 (211.7)	11,542 (173.8)	2,633 (80.7)	3,497 (85.4)	18,667 (202.8)	11,267 (165.9)	2,812 (79.9)	3,313 (77.3)
2010[3,4,5]	37,949 (#)	22,607 (38.0)	5,450 (33.5)	7,193 (10.0)	19,126 (#)	11,437 (27.6)	2,609 (24.1)	3,714 (5.8)	18,823 (#)	11,170 (24.6)	2,841 (20.2)	3,479 (8.6)
2011[3,4,5]	38,205 (133.8)	22,359 (138.0)	5,444 (86.7)	7,656 (59.0)	19,430 (40.3)	11,290 (36.9)	2,627 (58.2)	4,123 (41.9)	18,775 (135.4)	11,068 (133.6)	2,817 (36.2)	3,533 (23.1)
2012[3,4,5]	38,800 (306.3)	21,708 (137.5)	5,540 (64.1)	8,201 (73.5)	19,557 (266.3)	10,963 (120.5)	2,699 (47.9)	4,241 (85.8)	19,243 (54.1)	10,745 (44.8)	2,841 (35.0)	3,959 (22.9)
2013[3,4,5]	38,804 (210.7)	21,542 (196.8)	5,570 (48.4)	8,263 (43.2)	19,561 (150.8)	10,911 (119.0)	2,708 (40.5)	4,248 (30.3)	19,243 (71.7)	10,631 (89.5)	2,863 (33.1)	4,015 (22.0)
2014[3,4,5]	38,650 (67.1)	21,290 (111.6)	5,590 (99.2)	8,345 (61.6)	19,484 (46.7)	10,775 (67.6)	2,739 (31.6)	4,278 (41.7)	19,166 (57.8)	10,515 (57.9)	2,851 (81.4)	4,066 (26.8)

See notes at end of table.

Table 219.71. Population 16 to 24 years old and number of 16- to 24-year-old high school dropouts (status dropouts), by sex and race/ethnicity: 1970 through 2014—Continued

[Standard errors appear in parentheses]

Year	Total				Number of 16- to 24-year-old (status) dropouts (in thousands)							
	All races[1]	White	Black	Hispanic	All races[1]	Males White	Males Black	Males Hispanic	Females All races[1]	Females White	Females Black	Females Hispanic
1	2	3	4	5	6	7	8	9	10	11	12	13
1970[2]	4,525 (108.5)	3,459 (95.1)	1,022 (53.6)	— (†)	2,022 (71.1)	1,508 (61.6)	500 (36.8)	— (†)	2,503 (76.3)	1,951 (67.6)	522 (36.0)	— (†)
1971[1,2]	4,641 (109.8)	3,663 (97.8)	919 (50.9)	— (†)	2,137 (73.0)	1,649 (64.3)	462 (35.5)	— (†)	2,504 (76.3)	2,013 (68.6)	456 (33.8)	— (†)
1972	4,770 (111.3)	3,250 (92.2)	858 (49.3)	609 (49.4)	2,226 (74.5)	1,504 (61.5)	419 (33.9)	280 (33.1)	2,545 (76.9)	1,745 (64.0)	439 (33.2)	329 (34.0)
1973	4,716 (110.7)	3,150 (90.8)	930 (51.2)	576 (48.1)	2,220 (74.4)	1,519 (61.8)	425 (34.1)	250 (31.3)	2,496 (76.2)	1,631 (61.9)	504 (35.4)	326 (33.9)
1974	4,849 (112.2)	3,240 (92.1)	878 (49.9)	653 (51.1)	2,343 (76.4)	1,601 (63.4)	386 (32.6)	328 (35.7)	2,505 (76.2)	1,638 (62.0)	493 (35.0)	325 (33.9)
1975	4,824 (111.9)	3,185 (91.3)	987 (52.7)	573 (48.0)	2,248 (74.9)	1,509 (61.6)	457 (35.3)	251 (31.3)	2,577 (77.4)	1,676 (62.8)	530 (36.3)	323 (33.7)
1976	4,981 (113.7)	3,366 (93.8)	908 (50.7)	646 (50.8)	2,432 (77.8)	1,688 (65.1)	435 (34.5)	286 (33.4)	2,549 (77.0)	1,678 (62.8)	473 (34.4)	360 (35.5)
1977	5,031 (114.2)	3,374 (94.0)	893 (50.3)	701 (52.9)	2,519 (79.1)	1,767 (66.5)	407 (33.4)	322 (35.4)	2,512 (76.4)	1,607 (61.5)	487 (34.8)	379 (36.4)
1978	5,114 (115.1)	3,384 (94.1)	928 (51.2)	728 (53.8)	2,572 (79.9)	1,715 (65.6)	475 (36.0)	356 (37.1)	2,541 (76.9)	1,670 (62.6)	453 (33.7)	371 (36.1)
1979	5,265 (116.8)	3,433 (94.8)	975 (52.4)	758 (54.9)	2,650 (81.1)	1,779 (66.8)	477 (36.0)	358 (37.2)	2,614 (77.9)	1,653 (62.3)	499 (35.2)	400 (37.4)
1980	5,085 (114.8)	3,211 (91.7)	889 (50.2)	885 (59.1)	2,672 (81.4)	1,715 (65.6)	446 (34.9)	462 (42.0)	2,413 (75.0)	1,496 (59.3)	444 (33.3)	424 (38.4)
1981	5,143 (115.4)	3,232 (92.0)	901 (50.5)	891 (59.3)	2,746 (82.5)	1,762 (66.5)	454 (35.2)	480 (42.8)	2,397 (74.7)	1,470 (58.8)	447 (33.4)	411 (37.9)
1982	5,055 (121.0)	3,202 (96.7)	902 (53.4)	823 (60.7)	2,601 (84.9)	1,668 (68.3)	488 (38.5)	386 (41.0)	2,454 (79.6)	1,534 (63.5)	414 (34.1)	437 (39.0)
1983	4,905 (119.2)	3,053 (94.5)	882 (52.8)	816 (60.3)	2,631 (85.4)	1,661 (68.2)	463 (37.6)	426 (42.9)	2,274 (76.9)	1,392 (60.5)	418 (34.2)	391 (39.2)
1984	4,626 (115.8)	2,952 (92.9)	758 (49.1)	762 (58.4)	2,438 (82.3)	1,592 (66.8)	391 (34.7)	375 (40.4)	2,188 (75.5)	1,360 (59.8)	367 (32.2)	387 (39.0)
1985	4,324 (112.1)	2,688 (88.8)	719 (47.9)	797 (49.8)	2,264 (79.4)	1,406 (62.8)	360 (33.3)	440 (36.4)	2,060 (73.3)	1,282 (58.1)	360 (31.9)	357 (37.6)
1986	4,142 (109.8)	2,418 (84.2)	667 (46.2)	966 (55.1)	2,183 (78.0)	1,260 (59.5)	333 (32.1)	547 (40.7)	1,959 (71.5)	1,158 (55.2)	334 (30.7)	419 (34.2)
1987	4,230 (110.9)	2,538 (86.3)	653 (45.7)	926 (54.0)	2,169 (77.7)	1,299 (60.4)	326 (31.8)	490 (38.7)	2,061 (73.3)	1,239 (57.1)	327 (30.4)	437 (34.8)
1988	4,232 (120.9)	2,301 (89.6)	664 (50.2)	1,168 (53.8)	2,184 (85.0)	1,214 (63.7)	323 (34.5)	611 (48.3)	2,049 (79.7)	1,087 (58.4)	341 (33.9)	557 (39.0)
1989	4,038 (112.3)	2,152 (82.4)	639 (46.9)	1,142 (61.4)	2,145 (80.1)	1,160 (59.2)	327 (32.9)	613 (44.2)	1,893 (72.9)	991 (53.0)	312 (30.8)	529 (42.6)
1990	3,797 (108.9)	2,007 (79.6)	594 (45.2)	1,114 (61.0)	1,909 (75.6)	1,027 (55.8)	252 (29.1)	608 (44.3)	1,887 (72.8)	980 (52.7)	342 (32.2)	506 (38.7)
1991	3,881 (110.1)	1,953 (78.5)	609 (45.8)	1,241 (64.2)	2,001 (77.4)	967 (54.1)	288 (31.0)	717 (47.8)	1,880 (72.6)	985 (52.8)	321 (31.3)	525 (39.3)
1992	3,410 (103.1)	1,676 (72.8)	621 (46.2)	1,022 (58.6)	1,742 (72.3)	866 (51.3)	271 (30.1)	565 (42.8)	1,668 (68.5)	810 (48.0)	350 (32.6)	457 (36.9)
1993	3,396 (103.1)	1,707 (73.4)	615 (46.0)	989 (57.7)	1,715 (71.8)	884 (51.8)	275 (30.3)	507 (40.7)	1,681 (68.7)	823 (48.3)	340 (32.1)	483 (37.8)
1994	3,727 (108.0)	1,709 (73.5)	607 (45.7)	1,322 (66.1)	2,000 (77.4)	880 (51.6)	324 (32.8)	744 (48.6)	1,727 (69.7)	829 (48.5)	284 (29.4)	578 (41.1)
1995[3]	3,876 (110.1)	1,887 (77.2)	571 (44.4)	1,345 (66.6)	1,978 (77.0)	996 (54.9)	249 (28.9)	701 (47.3)	1,898 (73.0)	891 (50.3)	322 (31.3)	644 (43.2)
1996[3]	3,611 (110.3)	1,569 (73.1)	615 (47.8)	1,315 (68.6)	1,854 (77.4)	792 (50.9)	304 (33.0)	701 (49.3)	1,757 (72.9)	777 (48.8)	312 (32.0)	614 (42.3)
1997[3]	3,624 (110.6)	1,656 (75.1)	649 (49.0)	1,180 (65.1)	1,970 (79.7)	934 (55.2)	306 (33.2)	671 (48.2)	1,654 (70.8)	722 (47.0)	343 (33.5)	509 (40.3)
1998[3]	3,942 (115.2)	1,697 (76.0)	675 (50.0)	1,487 (72.4)	2,241 (84.9)	950 (55.7)	358 (35.7)	899 (55.0)	1,701 (71.8)	747 (47.8)	317 (32.2)	587 (43.0)
1999[3]	3,829 (113.6)	1,636 (74.7)	621 (48.0)	1,445 (71.5)	2,032 (81.0)	873 (53.4)	282 (31.9)	807 (52.4)	1,797 (73.7)	763 (48.3)	338 (33.3)	638 (44.7)
2000	3,776 (112.8)	1,564 (73.0)	663 (49.5)	1,456 (71.7)	2,082 (81.9)	795 (51.0)	369 (36.3)	866 (54.1)	1,694 (71.6)	769 (48.5)	294 (31.1)	590 (43.1)
2001[3]	3,766 (106.9)	1,668 (71.6)	557 (43.2)	1,442 (67.5)	2,151 (79.0)	916 (51.9)	314 (31.8)	865 (51.0)	1,615 (66.4)	752 (45.6)	243 (26.9)	577 (42.7)
2002	3,721 (106.3)	1,457 (66.9)	564 (43.5)	1,572 (70.5)	2,108 (78.2)	752 (47.1)	305 (31.4)	971 (54.0)	1,612 (66.4)	705 (44.1)	259 (27.7)	601 (41.3)
2003[3,4]	3,552 (103.9)	1,431 (66.3)	544 (42.8)	1,437 (67.7)	2,045 (77.1)	802 (48.6)	298 (31.2)	858 (51.1)	1,506 (64.2)	630 (41.7)	246 (27.1)	579 (40.6)
2004[3,4]	3,766 (106.9)	1,530 (68.5)	594 (44.7)	1,499 (69.0)	2,140 (78.8)	808 (48.8)	326 (32.6)	949 (53.5)	1,626 (66.6)	722 (44.6)	268 (28.3)	549 (39.6)
2005[4]	3,458 (102.5)	1,358 (64.6)	534 (42.4)	1,429 (67.5)	2,009 (76.4)	760 (47.3)	295 (31.0)	883 (51.8)	1,449 (63.0)	599 (40.7)	239 (26.7)	546 (39.5)
2006[4]	3,462 (102.6)	1,337 (64.1)	565 (43.6)	1,421 (67.3)	1,935 (75.0)	739 (46.7)	250 (28.6)	864 (51.3)	1,527 (64.6)	598 (40.7)	315 (30.6)	557 (39.8)
2007[4]	3,278 (99.9)	1,210 (61.0)	451 (39.1)	1,422 (67.3)	1,859 (73.6)	704 (45.6)	212 (26.4)	850 (50.9)	1,419 (62.3)	507 (37.4)	239 (26.8)	572 (40.3)
2008[4]	3,010 (95.8)	1,103 (58.3)	535 (42.5)	1,232 (63.0)	1,606 (68.5)	623 (42.9)	227 (27.3)	690 (46.3)	1,403 (62.0)	480 (36.5)	308 (30.3)	541 (39.3)
2009[4]	3,030 (96.1)	1,188 (60.5)	508 (41.4)	1,199 (62.2)	1,731 (71.0)	725 (46.2)	280 (30.2)	665 (45.5)	1,299 (59.7)	464 (35.8)	228 (26.2)	534 (39.1)
2010[3,4,5]	2,816 (100.8)	1,147 (67.9)	437 (41.5)	1,090 (62.3)	1,625 (77.3)	675 (48.4)	247 (29.2)	644 (46.2)	1,192 (53.0)	472 (38.7)	190 (24.1)	446 (33.9)
2011[3,4,5]	2,714 (99.1)	1,118 (68.1)	400 (37.5)	1,040 (60.1)	1,501 (69.9)	614 (46.0)	218 (26.4)	602 (44.9)	1,213 (64.6)	505 (42.9)	182 (27.2)	439 (34.0)
2012[3,4,5]	2,562 (101.1)	930 (67.7)	418 (42.3)	1,040 (59.0)	1,427 (74.2)	526 (43.8)	219 (31.2)	591 (46.1)	1,135 (63.8)	404 (39.4)	199 (28.9)	449 (39.6)
2013[3,4,5]	2,622 (109.3)	1,100 (66.7)	409 (48.4)	969 (61.2)	1,406 (73.6)	596 (42.8)	221 (29.9)	536 (43.1)	1,216 (66.0)	504 (38.5)	188 (31.1)	432 (39.5)
2014[3,4,5]	2,527 (94.9)	1,114 (68.1)	415 (42.8)	882 (57.4)	1,389 (71.1)	612 (44.6)	195 (27.9)	506 (45.4)	1,138 (55.7)	502 (43.2)	219 (30.5)	377 (33.9)

—Not available.
†Not applicable.
#Rounds to zero.
[1]Includes other racial/ethnic categories not separately shown.
[2]For 1970 and 1971, White and Black include persons of Hispanic ethnicity.
[3]Because of changes in data collection procedures, data may not be comparable with figures for years prior to 1992.
[4]White and Black exclude persons of two or more races.
[5]Beginning in 2010, standard errors were computed using replicate weights, which produced more precise values than the generalized variance function methodology used in prior years.

NOTE: "Status" dropouts are 16- to 24-year-olds who are not enrolled in school and who have not completed a high school program, regardless of when they left school. People who have received GED credentials are counted as high school completers. All data are based on October counts. Data are based on sample surveys of the civilian noninstitutionalized population, which excludes persons in prisons, persons in the military, and other persons not living in households. Race categories exclude persons of Hispanic ethnicity except where otherwise noted. Detail may not sum to totals because of rounding.
SOURCE: U.S. Department of Commerce, Census Bureau, Current Population Survey (CPS), October, 1970 through 2014. (This table was prepared August 2015.)

Table 219.73. Percentage of high school dropouts among persons 16 to 24 years old (status dropout rate) and number and percentage distribution of 16- to 24-year-olds, by selected characteristics: Selected years, 2004 to 2014

Selected characteristic	Status dropout rate[1] 2004		2009		2013		2014		2014 Number of 16- to 24-year-olds (in thousands) Total population[2]		Status dropouts only[3]		2014 Percentage distribution of 16- to 24-year-olds Total population[2]		Status dropouts only[3]	
1	2		3		4		5		6		7		8		9	
Total	10.3	(0.23)	8.1	(0.20)	6.8	(0.28)	6.5	(0.25)	38,650	(67.1)	2,527	(94.9)	100.0	(†)	100.0	(†)
Sex																
Male	11.6	(0.34)	9.1	(0.31)	7.2	(0.37)	7.1	(0.37)	19,484	(46.7)	1,389	(71.1)	50.4	(0.10)	55.0	(1.66)
Female	9.0	(0.31)	7.0	(0.27)	6.3	(0.34)	5.9	(0.29)	19,166	(57.8)	1,138	(55.7)	49.6	(0.10)	45.0	(1.66)
Race/ethnicity																
White	6.8	(0.24)	5.2	(0.21)	5.1	(0.31)	5.2	(0.32)	21,290	(111.6)	1,114	(68.1)	55.1	(0.28)	44.1	(2.03)
Black	11.8	(0.70)	9.3	(0.61)	7.3	(0.87)	7.4	(0.74)	5,590	(99.2)	415	(42.8)	14.5	(0.26)	16.4	(1.60)
Hispanic	23.8	(0.89)	17.6	(0.76)	11.7	(0.74)	10.6	(0.68)	8,345	(61.6)	882	(57.4)	21.6	(0.16)	34.9	(1.85)
Asian	3.5	(0.74)	2.1	(0.58)	3.2	(0.95)	1.0 !	(0.35)	1,966	(43.1)	21 !	(6.8)	5.1	(0.11)	0.8 !	(0.27)
Pacific Islander	‡	(†)	18.4	(5.42)	‡	(†)	12.1 !	(6.05)	125	(26.3)	‡	(†)	0.3	(0.07)	‡	(†)
American Indian/Alaska Native	17.0	(3.46)	13.2	(3.28)	7.0 !	(2.27)	15.7	(3.02)	339	(32.9)	53	(10.6)	0.9	(0.08)	2.1	(0.42)
Two or more races	6.1	(1.47)	6.5	(1.41)	5.7	(1.37)	2.7	(0.80)	996	(51.7)	27	(7.8)	2.6	(0.13)	1.1	(0.30)
Race/ethnicity by sex																
Male																
White	7.1	(0.35)	6.3	(0.33)	5.5	(0.39)	5.7	(0.42)	10,775	(67.6)	612	(44.6)	55.3	(0.28)	44.1	(2.48)
Black	13.5	(1.08)	10.6	(0.93)	8.2	(1.11)	7.1	(1.02)	2,739	(31.6)	195	(27.9)	14.1	(0.17)	14.1	(1.89)
Hispanic	28.5	(1.30)	19.0	(1.10)	12.6	(1.01)	11.8	(1.04)	4,278	(41.7)	506	(45.4)	22.0	(0.24)	36.4	(2.41)
Asian	2.1 !	(0.82)	‡	(†)	2.3 !	(0.96)	1.9 !	(0.66)	978	(29.8)	18 !	(6.4)	5.0	(0.15)	1.3 !	(0.47)
Pacific Islander	‡	(†)	26.9 !	(8.45)	‡	(†)	‡	(†)	58	(13.6)	‡	(†)	0.3	(0.07)	‡	(†)
American Indian/Alaska Native	12.6 !	(4.26)	12.3 !	(4.59)	‡	(†)	13.7	(3.48)	186	(24.3)	25	(7.3)	1.0	(0.12)	1.8	(0.53)
Two or more races	6.3 !	(2.09)	5.5 !	(1.86)	4.2 !	(2.01)	4.1 !	(1.45)	469	(29.5)	19 !	(6.7)	2.4	(0.15)	1.4 !	(0.47)
Female																
White	6.4	(0.34)	4.1	(0.27)	4.7	(0.36)	4.8	(0.41)	10,515	(57.9)	502	(43.2)	54.9	(0.34)	44.1	(2.98)
Black	10.2	(0.92)	8.1	(0.80)	6.6	(1.07)	7.7	(1.02)	2,851	(81.4)	219	(30.5)	14.9	(0.40)	19.3	(2.48)
Hispanic	18.5	(1.18)	16.1	(1.06)	10.8	(0.98)	9.3	(0.84)	4,066	(26.8)	377	(33.9)	21.2	(0.12)	33.1	(2.62)
Asian	4.9	(1.24)	3.0 !	(0.99)	4.1 !	(1.35)	‡	(†)	988	(22.2)	‡	(†)	5.2	(0.11)	‡	(†)
Pacific Islander	‡	(†)	‡	(†)	‡	(†)	‡	(†)	67	(18.6)	‡	(†)	0.3	(0.10)	‡	(†)
American Indian/Alaska Native	21.7	(5.44)	14.1 !	(4.69)	8.0 !	(3.56)	18.1	(4.01)	153	(19.3)	28	(6.2)	0.8	(0.10)	2.4	(0.56)
Two or more races	5.8 !	(2.06)	7.5	(2.10)	7.2	(2.07)	1.5 !	(0.72)	527	(32.3)	8 !	(3.8)	2.8	(0.17)	0.7 !	(0.33)
Age																
16	3.8	(0.42)	2.7	(0.37)	5.2	(0.64)	5.2	(0.62)	4,101	(50.9)	213	(25.1)	10.6	(0.13)	8.4	(0.96)
17	5.2	(0.51)	4.4	(0.46)	4.7	(0.62)	5.2	(0.67)	4,245	(50.0)	223	(28.6)	11.0	(0.13)	8.8	(1.10)
18	10.6	(0.73)	7.8	(0.59)	5.4	(0.64)	7.0	(0.72)	4,145	(45.9)	291	(30.4)	10.7	(0.12)	11.5	(1.15)
19	11.2	(0.74)	9.3	(0.65)	7.1	(0.78)	7.2	(0.76)	4,116	(46.5)	297	(31.5)	10.7	(0.13)	11.7	(1.12)
20 to 24	12.6	(0.34)	9.7	(0.30)	7.6	(0.38)	6.8	(0.33)	22,043	(65.5)	1,503	(72.9)	57.0	(0.08)	59.5	(1.72)
Recency of immigration[4]																
Born outside the United States																
Hispanic	38.4	(1.61)	31.3	(1.64)	22.8	(1.97)	21.0	(1.84)	1,889	(88.1)	397	(41.3)	4.9	(0.23)	15.7	(1.51)
Non-Hispanic	6.5	(0.81)	6.2	(0.81)	5.5	(1.06)	3.9	(0.91)	2,134	(102.5)	84	(20.2)	5.5	(0.27)	3.3	(0.79)
First generation																
Hispanic	14.7	(1.27)	11.8	(1.04)	8.2	(0.98)	7.1	(0.82)	3,808	(112.6)	270	(33.3)	9.9	(0.29)	10.7	(1.25)
Non-Hispanic	2.6	(0.51)	3.9	(0.57)	3.9	(0.90)	2.2	(0.59)	2,689	(106.8)	60	(15.8)	7.0	(0.27)	2.4	(0.61)
Second generation or higher																
Hispanic	13.7	(1.39)	10.2	(1.13)	8.3	(1.10)	8.1	(1.17)	2,648	(109.4)	215	(31.7)	6.9	(0.28)	8.5	(1.22)
Non-Hispanic	8.0	(0.24)	6.1	(0.21)	5.6	(0.31)	5.9	(0.29)	25,483	(135.2)	1,500	(74.1)	65.9	(0.34)	59.4	(1.94)
Disability[5]																
With a disability	—	(†)	15.5	(1.44)	14.9	(1.87)	13.9	(1.59)	1,530	(75.0)	212	(26.4)	4.0	(0.19)	8.4	(0.98)
Without a disability	—	(†)	7.8	(0.21)	6.4	(0.27)	6.2	(0.24)	37,121	(103.8)	2,314	(89.0)	96.0	(0.19)	91.6	(0.98)
Region																
Northeast	8.8	(0.47)	7.1	(0.47)	5.5	(0.61)	5.3	(0.54)	6,750	(134.1)	359	(37.4)	17.5	(0.34)	14.2	(1.42)
Midwest	8.0	(0.42)	7.6	(0.44)	6.0	(0.60)	5.4	(0.52)	8,186	(149.1)	443	(43.4)	21.2	(0.38)	17.5	(1.62)
South	11.4	(0.44)	8.4	(0.36)	7.6	(0.48)	7.6	(0.49)	14,294	(171.5)	1,083	(70.8)	37.0	(0.45)	42.9	(2.05)
West	12.2	(0.56)	8.6	(0.44)	7.1	(0.53)	6.8	(0.55)	9,420	(153.4)	642	(52.5)	24.4	(0.39)	25.4	(1.92)

—Not available.
†Not applicable.
!Interpret data with caution. The coefficient of variation (CV) for this estimate is 30 percent or greater.
‡Reporting standards not met. Either there are too few cases for a reliable estimate or the coefficient of variation (CV) is 50 percent or greater.
[1]The status dropout rate is the percentage of 16- to 24-year-olds who are not enrolled in high school and who lack a high school credential. High school credentials include high school diplomas and alternative credentials, such as a GED certificate.
[2]Includes all 16- to 24-year-olds.
[3]Status dropouts are 16- to 24-year-olds who are not enrolled in high school and who lack a high school credential. High school credentials include high school diplomas and alternative credentials, such as a GED certificate.

[4]The United States includes the 50 states and the District of Columbia. Individuals defined as "first generation" were born in the United States, but one or both of their parents were born outside the United States. Individuals defined as "second generation or higher" were born in the United States, as were both of their parents.
[5]Individuals identified as having a disability reported difficulty in at least one of the following: hearing, seeing even when wearing glasses, walking or climbing stairs, dressing or bathing, doing errands alone, concentrating, remembering, or making decisions.
NOTE: Data are based on sample surveys of the civilian noninstitutionalized population, which excludes persons in prisons, persons in the military, and other persons not living in households. Race categories exclude persons of Hispanic ethnicity. Detail may not sum to totals because of rounding.
SOURCE: U.S. Department of Commerce, Census Bureau, Current Population Survey (CPS), October, 2004 through 2014. (This table was prepared March 2016.)

Table 219.75. Percentage of high school dropouts among persons 16 to 24 years old (status dropout rate), by income level, and percentage distribution of status dropouts, by labor force status and years of school completed: 1970 through 2014

[Standard errors appear in parentheses]

Year	Status dropout rate	Status dropout rate, by family income quartile — Lowest quartile	Middle low quartile	Middle high quartile	Highest quartile	Percentage distribution of status dropouts, by labor force status — Total	Employed[1]	Unemployed	Not in labor force	Percentage distribution of status dropouts, by years of school completed — Total	Less than 9 years	9 years	10 years	11 or 12 years
1	2	3	4	5	6	7	8	9	10	11	12	13	14	15
1970	15.0 (0.29)	28.0 (0.92)	21.2 (0.65)	11.7 (0.50)	5.2 (0.34)	100.0 (†)	49.8 (1.06)	10.3 (0.65)	39.9 (1.04)	100.0 (†)	28.5 (0.96)	20.6 (0.86)	26.8 (0.94)	24.0 (0.91)
1971	14.7 (0.28)	28.8 (0.90)	20.7 (0.63)	10.9 (0.49)	5.1 (0.32)	100.0 (†)	49.5 (1.05)	10.9 (0.65)	39.6 (1.02)	100.0 (†)	27.9 (0.94)	21.7 (0.86)	27.8 (0.94)	22.7 (0.88)
1972	14.6 (0.28)	27.6 (0.85)	20.8 (0.62)	10.2 (0.46)	5.4 (0.33)	100.0 (†)	51.2 (1.03)	10.2 (0.63)	38.6 (1.01)	100.0 (†)	27.5 (0.92)	21.7 (0.84)	29.0 (0.94)	22.7 (0.87)
1973	14.1 (0.27)	28.0 (0.80)	19.6 (0.60)	9.9 (0.45)	4.9 (0.31)	100.0 (†)	53.2 (1.04)	9.2 (0.60)	37.5 (1.01)	100.0 (†)	26.5 (0.92)	20.9 (0.84)	27.4 (0.93)	25.3 (0.90)
1974	14.3 (0.27)	— (†)	— (†)	— (†)	— (†)	100.0 (†)	51.8 (1.02)	12.3 (0.67)	35.9 (0.98)	100.0 (†)	25.4 (0.89)	20.1 (0.82)	28.7 (0.93)	25.8 (0.90)
1975	13.9 (0.27)	28.8 (0.82)	18.0 (0.58)	10.2 (0.45)	5.0 (0.30)	100.0 (†)	46.0 (1.02)	15.6 (0.74)	38.4 (1.00)	100.0 (†)	23.5 (0.87)	21.1 (0.84)	27.5 (0.92)	27.9 (0.92)
1976	14.1 (0.27)	28.1 (0.79)	19.2 (0.60)	10.1 (0.45)	4.9 (0.29)	100.0 (†)	48.8 (1.01)	16.0 (0.74)	35.2 (0.97)	100.0 (†)	24.3 (0.87)	21.7 (0.81)	27.3 (0.91)	27.8 (0.91)
1977	14.1 (0.27)	28.5 (0.80)	19.0 (0.60)	10.4 (0.46)	4.5 (0.29)	100.0 (†)	52.9 (1.02)	13.6 (0.70)	33.5 (0.96)	100.0 (†)	24.3 (0.87)	21.7 (0.84)	27.3 (0.91)	26.6 (0.90)
1978	14.2 (0.27)	28.2 (0.80)	18.9 (0.60)	10.5 (0.46)	5.5 (0.31)	100.0 (†)	54.3 (1.01)	12.4 (0.67)	33.3 (0.95)	100.0 (†)	22.9 (0.85)	20.2 (0.81)	28.2 (0.91)	28.8 (0.91)
1979	14.6 (0.27)	28.1 (0.79)	18.5 (0.60)	11.5 (0.47)	5.6 (0.32)	100.0 (†)	54.0 (0.99)	12.7 (0.66)	33.3 (0.94)	100.0 (†)	22.5 (0.83)	21.0 (0.81)	28.6 (0.90)	27.8 (0.89)
1980	14.1 (0.26)	27.0 (0.77)	18.1 (0.57)	10.7 (0.46)	5.7 (0.32)	100.0 (†)	50.4 (1.01)	17.0 (0.76)	32.6 (0.95)	100.0 (†)	23.6 (0.86)	19.7 (0.80)	29.8 (0.93)	27.0 (0.90)
1981	13.9 (0.26)	26.4 (0.75)	17.8 (0.57)	11.1 (0.47)	5.2 (0.30)	100.0 (†)	49.8 (1.01)	18.3 (0.78)	31.9 (0.94)	100.0 (†)	24.3 (0.86)	18.6 (0.78)	30.2 (0.92)	26.9 (0.89)
1982	13.9 (0.27)	27.2 (0.78)	18.3 (0.63)	10.2 (0.48)	4.4 (0.29)	100.0 (†)	45.2 (1.06)	21.1 (0.87)	33.7 (1.01)	100.0 (†)	22.9 (0.90)	20.8 (0.87)	28.8 (0.96)	27.6 (0.95)
1983	13.7 (0.27)	26.5 (0.77)	17.8 (0.62)	10.5 (0.50)	4.1 (0.29)	100.0 (†)	48.4 (1.08)	18.2 (0.83)	33.4 (1.02)	100.0 (†)	23.0 (0.91)	19.3 (0.85)	28.8 (0.98)	28.8 (0.98)
1984	13.1 (0.27)	25.9 (0.76)	16.5 (0.61)	9.9 (0.48)	3.8 (0.29)	100.0 (†)	49.7 (1.11)	17.3 (0.84)	32.9 (1.05)	100.0 (†)	22.5 (0.95)	21.4 (0.91)	27.5 (1.00)	27.5 (0.99)
1985	12.6 (0.27)	27.1 (0.78)	14.7 (0.60)	8.3 (0.46)	4.0 (0.29)	100.0 (†)	50.1 (1.15)	17.5 (0.88)	32.4 (1.08)	100.0 (†)	23.9 (0.98)	21.0 (0.94)	27.9 (1.03)	27.2 (1.03)
1986	12.2 (0.27)	25.4 (0.75)	14.8 (0.60)	8.0 (0.45)	3.4 (0.28)	100.0 (†)	51.1 (1.18)	16.4 (0.87)	32.5 (1.10)	100.0 (†)	25.4 (1.03)	21.5 (0.97)	25.7 (1.03)	27.4 (1.05)
1987	12.6 (0.28)	25.5 (0.76)	16.6 (0.63)	8.0 (0.46)	3.6 (0.28)	100.0 (†)	52.4 (1.16)	13.6 (0.80)	34.0 (1.10)	100.0 (†)	25.9 (1.02)	20.7 (0.94)	25.1 (1.02)	27.5 (1.04)
1988	12.9 (0.30)	27.2 (0.85)	15.4 (0.68)	8.2 (0.51)	3.4 (0.30)	100.0 (†)	52.9 (1.27)	— (†)	— (†)	100.0 (†)	28.9 (1.15)	19.3 (1.00)	25.1 (1.10)	26.8 (1.12)
1989	12.6 (0.31)	25.0 (0.84)	16.2 (0.71)	8.7 (0.52)	3.3 (0.31)	100.0 (†)	53.2 (1.30)	13.8 (0.90)	33.0 (1.22)	100.0 (†)	29.4 (1.18)	20.8 (1.05)	24.9 (1.12)	25.0 (1.13)
1990	12.1 (0.29)	24.3 (0.82)	15.1 (0.65)	8.7 (0.51)	2.9 (0.28)	100.0 (†)	52.5 (1.29)	13.3 (0.88)	34.2 (1.23)	100.0 (†)	28.6 (1.17)	20.9 (1.05)	24.4 (1.11)	26.1 (1.14)
1991	12.5 (0.30)	25.9 (0.83)	15.5 (0.66)	7.7 (0.49)	3.0 (0.29)	100.0 (†)	47.5 (1.28)	15.8 (0.93)	36.7 (1.23)	100.0 (†)	28.6 (1.15)	20.5 (1.03)	26.1 (1.12)	24.9 (1.10)
1992	11.0 (0.28)	23.4 (0.79)	12.9 (0.62)	7.3 (0.48)	2.4 (0.26)	100.0 (†)	47.6 (1.36)	15.0 (0.97)	37.4 (1.32)	100.0 (†)	21.6 (1.12)	17.5 (1.04)	24.4 (1.17)	36.5 (1.31)
1993	11.0 (0.28)	22.9 (0.77)	12.7 (0.62)	6.6 (0.46)	2.9 (0.29)	100.0 (†)	48.7 (1.37)	12.8 (0.91)	38.5 (1.33)	100.0 (†)	20.5 (1.10)	16.6 (1.02)	24.1 (1.17)	38.8 (1.33)
1994	11.4 (0.26)	20.7 (0.71)	13.7 (0.58)	8.7 (0.45)	4.9 (0.33)	100.0 (†)	49.5 (1.21)	13.0 (0.81)	37.5 (1.17)	100.0 (†)	23.9 (1.03)	16.2 (0.89)	20.3 (0.97)	39.6 (1.18)
1995[2]	12.0 (0.27)	23.2 (0.69)	13.8 (0.59)	8.3 (0.46)	3.6 (0.29)	100.0 (†)	48.9 (1.19)	14.2 (0.83)	37.0 (1.14)	100.0 (†)	22.2 (0.99)	17.0 (0.89)	22.5 (0.99)	38.3 (1.15)
1996[2]	11.1 (0.27)	22.0 (0.72)	13.6 (0.60)	7.0 (0.45)	3.2 (0.28)	100.0 (†)	47.3 (1.28)	15.0 (0.91)	37.7 (1.24)	100.0 (†)	20.3 (1.03)	17.7 (0.98)	22.6 (1.07)	39.4 (1.25)
1997[2]	11.0 (0.27)	21.8 (0.71)	13.5 (0.59)	6.2 (0.42)	3.4 (0.29)	100.0 (†)	53.3 (1.28)	13.2 (0.86)	33.5 (1.21)	100.0 (†)	19.9 (1.02)	15.7 (0.93)	22.3 (1.06)	42.1 (1.26)
1998[2]	11.8 (0.27)	22.3 (0.71)	14.9 (0.62)	7.7 (0.45)	3.5 (0.29)	100.0 (†)	55.1 (1.22)	10.3 (0.74)	34.6 (1.17)	100.0 (†)	21.0 (1.02)	14.9 (0.87)	21.4 (1.01)	42.6 (1.21)
1999[2]	11.2 (0.26)	21.0 (0.70)	14.3 (0.60)	7.4 (0.44)	3.9 (0.30)	100.0 (†)	55.6 (1.24)	10.0 (0.75)	34.4 (1.18)	100.0 (†)	22.2 (1.03)	16.3 (0.92)	22.5 (1.04)	39.0 (1.21)
2000	10.9 (0.26)	20.7 (0.70)	12.8 (0.56)	8.3 (0.46)	3.5 (0.29)	100.0 (†)	56.9 (1.24)	12.3 (0.82)	30.8 (1.16)	100.0 (†)	21.5 (1.03)	15.3 (0.90)	23.1 (1.06)	40.0 (1.23)
2001	10.7 (0.25)	19.3 (0.68)	13.4 (0.57)	9.0 (0.47)	3.8 (0.27)	100.0 (†)	58.3 (1.24)	14.8 (0.89)	26.9 (1.11)	100.0 (†)	18.4 (0.97)	16.8 (0.94)	23.8 (1.07)	40.9 (1.23)
2002	10.5 (0.24)	18.8 (0.62)	12.3 (0.53)	8.4 (0.43)	3.8 (0.28)	100.0 (†)	57.4 (1.18)	13.3 (0.81)	29.2 (1.09)	100.0 (†)	22.8 (1.00)	17.1 (0.90)	21.3 (0.98)	38.9 (1.17)
2003	9.9 (0.23)	19.5 (0.64)	10.8 (0.49)	7.3 (0.40)	3.4 (0.26)	100.0 (†)	53.5 (1.22)	13.7 (0.84)	36.9 (1.15)	100.0 (†)	21.2 (1.00)	18.2 (0.94)	20.7 (0.99)	40.0 (1.20)
2004	10.3 (0.23)	18.0 (0.60)	12.7 (0.52)	8.2 (0.42)	3.7 (0.27)	100.0 (†)	53.0 (1.19)	14.3 (0.83)	32.7 (1.12)	100.0 (†)	21.4 (0.97)	15.9 (0.87)	22.5 (0.99)	40.3 (1.17)
2005	9.4 (0.22)	17.9 (0.60)	11.5 (0.51)	7.1 (0.39)	2.7 (0.23)	100.0 (†)	56.9 (1.23)	11.9 (0.80)	31.2 (1.15)	100.0 (†)	18.9 (0.97)	16.8 (0.93)	21.4 (1.02)	42.9 (1.23)
2006	9.3 (0.22)	16.5 (0.58)	12.1 (0.51)	6.3 (0.37)	3.8 (0.27)	100.0 (†)	56.4 (1.23)	11.7 (0.80)	32.0 (1.16)	100.0 (†)	22.1 (1.03)	13.4 (0.85)	20.7 (1.01)	43.9 (1.23)
2007	8.7 (0.21)	16.7 (0.59)	10.5 (0.48)	6.4 (0.36)	3.2 (0.25)	100.0 (†)	55.5 (1.27)	11.2 (0.80)	33.3 (1.20)	100.0 (†)	21.2 (1.04)	16.9 (0.96)	22.9 (1.07)	39.0 (1.24)
2008	8.0 (0.20)	16.4 (0.58)	9.4 (0.45)	5.4 (0.34)	2.2 (0.21)	100.0 (†)	46.8 (1.33)	16.3 (1.06)	36.9 (1.28)	100.0 (†)	18.4 (1.08)	15.2 (0.96)	23.8 (1.13)	42.6 (1.32)
2009	8.1 (0.20)	15.8 (0.57)	9.7 (0.45)	5.4 (0.34)	2.5 (0.22)	100.0 (†)	43.2 (1.31)	19.9 (1.06)	36.9 (1.28)	100.0 (†)	17.7 (1.01)	13.6 (0.91)	24.4 (1.14)	44.3 (1.32)
2010[2,3]	7.4 (0.27)	13.8 (0.83)	8.9 (0.54)	5.1 (0.48)	2.5 (0.31)	100.0 (†)	45.8 (1.64)	18.7 (1.38)	35.5 (1.70)	100.0 (†)	19.2 (1.48)	13.1 (1.07)	22.5 (1.59)	45.2 (1.89)
2011[2,3]	7.1 (0.26)	13.0 (0.73)	9.0 (0.53)	4.8 (0.45)	2.3 (0.32)	100.0 (†)	49.8 (1.77)	16.0 (1.33)	34.1 (1.69)	100.0 (†)	18.1 (1.72)	12.9 (1.15)	21.2 (1.39)	47.7 (1.87)
2012[2,3]	6.6 (0.25)	11.8 (0.70)	8.2 (0.65)	4.1 (0.44)	1.9 (0.31)	100.0 (†)	44.8 (2.07)	18.1 (1.49)	37.1 (1.83)	100.0 (†)	18.3 (1.76)	10.2 (1.21)	21.9 (1.57)	49.6 (2.20)
2013[2,3]	6.8 (0.28)	10.7 (0.73)	8.8 (0.67)	5.0 (0.44)	3.2 (0.36)	100.0 (†)	41.1 (2.01)	16.8 (1.58)	42.1 (1.84)	100.0 (†)	18.3 (1.70)	13.3 (1.34)	21.1 (1.63)	47.4 (2.31)
2014[2,3]	6.5 (0.25)	11.6 (0.68)	7.6 (0.57)	4.7 (0.43)	2.8 (0.31)	100.0 (†)	44.7 (1.84)	17.0 (1.41)	38.3 (1.61)	100.0 (†)	15.0 (1.58)	13.7 (1.28)	21.3 (1.56)	50.0 (1.94)

—Not available.
†Not applicable.
[1]Includes persons who were employed but not at work during the survey week.
[2]Because of changes in data collection procedures, data may not be comparable with figures for years prior to 1992.
[3]Beginning in 2010, standard errors were computed using replicate weights, which produced more precise values than the generalized variance function methodology used in prior years.

NOTE: "Status" dropouts are 16- to 24-year-olds who are not enrolled in school and who have not completed a high school program, regardless of when they left school. People who have received GED credentials are counted as high school completers. Data are based on sample surveys of the civilian noninstitutional population, which excludes persons in prisons, persons in the military, and other persons not living in households. Detail may not sum to totals because of rounding.
SOURCE: U.S. Department of Commerce, Census Bureau, Current Population Survey (CPS), October, 1970 through 2014. (This table was prepared August 2015.)

Table 219.80. Percentage of high school dropouts among persons 16 to 24 years old (status dropout rate) and number of status dropouts, by noninstitutionalized or institutionalized status, birth in or outside of the United States, and selected characteristics: Selected years, 2006 through 2014

[Standard errors appear in parentheses]

Selected characteristic	Total status dropout rate — 2006	2009	2013	2014	2014 Noninst. — Number of status dropouts (in thousands)	Percentage distribution of status dropouts	Status dropout rate — Total for noninst. population	For those born in the United States	For those born outside of the United States	Institutionalized population — Number of status dropouts (in thousands)	Status dropout rate
	2	3	4	5	6	7	8	9	10	11	12
Total	9.7 (0.07)	8.6 (0.08)	6.8 (0.06)	6.3 (0.05)	2,346 (21.5)	100.0 (†)	6.0 (0.05)	5.3 (0.05)	12.4 (0.27)	151 (3.4)	33.1 (0.64)
Sex											
Male	11.3 (0.11)	10.1 (0.10)	8.0 (0.08)	7.2 (0.09)	1,343 (17.2)	57.2 (0.46)	6.7 (0.09)	5.9 (0.08)	14.2 (0.35)	138 (3.6)	34.1 (0.72)
Female	7.9 (0.08)	7.1 (0.09)	5.6 (0.08)	5.2 (0.07)	1,003 (13.3)	42.8 (0.46)	5.2 (0.07)	4.7 (0.07)	10.4 (0.33)	13 (1.1)	24.7 (1.76)
Race/ethnicity											
White	6.4 (0.07)	5.6 (0.07)	4.7 (0.06)	4.4 (0.06)	936 (12.5)	39.9 (0.41)	4.3 (0.06)	4.3 (0.06)	4.0 (0.36)	33 (1.7)	23.9 (1.18)
Black	11.5 (0.21)	10.7 (0.18)	9.0 (0.19)	7.9 (0.17)	385 (9.5)	16.4 (0.38)	6.8 (0.17)	6.9 (0.17)	5.7 (0.59)	74 (2.6)	39.2 (1.12)
Hispanic	21.0 (0.26)	17.9 (0.22)	11.8 (0.20)	10.7 (0.15)	872 (12.5)	37.2 (0.39)	10.4 (0.15)	7.6 (0.15)	20.8 (0.47)	38 (1.6)	37.2 (1.30)
Cuban	7.2 (0.83)	7.0 (0.87)	6.2 (0.63)	6.3 (0.85)	14 (2.0)	0.6 (0.08)	6.1 (0.85)	4.3 (0.68)	10.4 (1.89)	† (†)	† (†)
Dominican	10.0 (0.92)	10.8 (0.94)	8.3 (0.70)	8.0 (0.67)	22 (2.2)	1.0 (0.09)	7.7 (0.70)	6.2 (0.78)	10.7 (1.35)	† (†)	30.8 (8.29)
Mexican	23.6 (0.31)	19.3 (0.26)	12.8 (0.26)	11.0 (0.16)	592 (9.2)	25.2 (0.34)	10.6 (0.16)	7.8 (0.17)	22.0 (0.61)	26 (1.5)	39.2 (1.55)
Puerto Rican	15.2 (0.64)	14.1 (0.58)	9.5 (0.49)	9.6 (0.51)	76 (3.9)	3.2 (0.16)	9.4 (0.51)	9.3 (0.51)	13.3 ! (5.35)	3 (0.7)	25.9 (3.82)
Spaniard	6.9 (1.50)	7.4 (1.46)	4.9 (1.04)	4.5 (0.90)	4 (0.9)	0.2 (0.04)	4.1 (0.86)	4.0 (0.88)	‡ (‡)	† (†)	† (†)
Central American[4]	29.8 (0.93)	27.0 (0.83)	17.1 (0.69)	17.8 (0.73)	123 (5.6)	5.2 (0.23)	17.4 (0.75)	6.5 (0.51)	32.7 (1.53)	4 (0.7)	46.0 (5.36)
Costa Rican	13.6 (3.84)	12.5 (3.59)	4.7 ! (2.06)	6.1 ! (2.38)	‡ (†)	# (0.16)	6.1 (2.56)	5.6 ! (1.21)	† (†)	† (†)	† (†)
Guatemalan	43.4 (2.17)	41.0 (1.57)	27.0 (1.75)	28.7 (1.66)	52 (3.8)	2.2 (0.16)	28.4 (1.68)	7.8 (1.21)	46.3 (2.51)	† (†)	50.5 (9.24)
Honduran	34.2 (2.75)	32.0 (2.45)	19.9 (1.66)	19.5 (1.76)	20 (2.2)	0.9 (0.09)	18.7 (1.78)	6.3 (1.55)	28.7 (3.07)	† (†)	67.4 (9.27)
Nicaraguan	13.6 (2.41)	7.5 (1.51)	7.6 (1.55)	7.3 (1.24)	4 (0.7)	0.2 (0.03)	7.4 (1.25)	6.4 (1.34)	11.3 ! (3.99)	† (†)	† (†)
Panamanian	7.4 ! (2.95)	5.6 ! (2.07)	3.0 ! (1.13)	1.8 ! (0.81)	‡ (†)	# (†)	1.8 ! (0.82)	‡ (†)	‡ (†)	† (†)	41.9 (9.74)
Salvadoran	23.9 (1.46)	23.1 (1.36)	13.4 (0.95)	14.9 (0.92)	45 (3.1)	1.9 (0.13)	14.6 (0.93)	6.8 (0.80)	27.8 (1.94)	† (†)	38.3 ! (11.97)
South American	8.1 (0.71)	6.8 (0.63)	4.3 ! (0.43)	4.1 (0.45)	17 (1.9)	0.7 (0.08)	3.9 (0.43)	2.7 (0.40)	5.4 (0.79)	† (†)	† (†)
Chilean	4.9 ! (2.19)	‡ (†)	4.3 ! (1.81)	‡ (†)	‡ (†)	# (†)	‡ (†)	‡ (†)	‡ (†)	† (†)	† (†)
Colombian	5.6 (0.89)	6.1 (0.80)	3.4 (0.56)	3.4 (0.79)	5 (1.1)	0.2 (0.05)	3.1 (0.73)	2.2 (0.53)	4.3 ! (1.37)	† (†)	† (†)
Ecuadorian	14.1 (2.31)	13.8 (2.08)	10.8 (1.67)	7.3 (1.38)	6 (1.2)	0.3 (0.05)	7.1 (1.37)	3.3 ! (1.07)	12.8 (2.76)	† (†)	† (†)
Peruvian	6.2 ! (1.88)	3.5 (0.96)	1.7 (0.42)	3.1 (0.88)	‡ (†)	0.1 (0.03)	3.0 (0.87)	‡ (†)	4.4 (1.28)	† (†)	† (†)
Venezuelan	5.1 ! (1.69)	2.6 ! (1.00)	4.1 ! (1.26)	4.1 (1.26)	‡ (†)	0.1 ! (0.02)	4.1 (1.26)	3.8 ! (1.85)	4.3 ! (1.66)	† (†)	† (†)
Other South American	9.5 (2.38)	6.5 (1.50)	1.5 (0.41)	2.7 (0.79)	‡ (†)	0.1 (0.02)	2.5 ! (0.75)	2.7 (1.05)	2.3 ! (1.03)	† (†)	† (†)
Other Hispanic	13.4 (0.70)	11.9 (0.87)	9.0 (0.75)	10.0 (0.77)	24 (2.2)	1.0 (0.09)	9.6 (0.80)	9.0 (0.86)	15.1 (3.14)	† (†)	27.8 (6.34)
Asian	3.1 (0.20)	3.3 (0.17)	2.5 (0.16)	2.5 (0.14)	51 (2.9)	2.2 (0.12)	2.5 (0.14)	1.8 (0.14)	3.4 (0.28)	† (†)	21.5 ! (10.04)
Chinese[5]	3.1 (0.45)	2.1 (0.34)	1.2 (0.25)	1.2 (0.18)	6 (1.0)	0.3 (0.04)	1.2 (0.18)	1.0 (0.23)	1.3 (0.25)	† (†)	† (†)
Filipino	2.6 (0.37)	3.2 (0.43)	1.9 (0.35)	1.9 (0.35)	6 (1.1)	0.2 (0.05)	1.9 (0.35)	1.4 (0.37)	2.5 (0.62)	† (†)	† (†)
Japanese	1.0 ! (0.39)	2.5 ! (0.82)	1.6 ! (0.60)	1.3 ! (0.51)	‡ (†)	# (†)	1.3 ! (0.51)	1.5 ! (0.72)	‡ (†)	† (†)	† (†)
Korean	0.9 (0.21)	2.4 (0.56)	1.0 ! (0.36)	0.9 ! (0.28)	‡ (†)	0.1 ! (0.02)	0.9 ! (0.28)	1.3 ! (0.47)	0.6 ! (0.65)	† (†)	† (†)
South Asian[6]	2.7 (0.41)	2.4 (0.35)	2.8 (0.40)	3.2 (0.38)	14 (1.8)	0.6 (0.08)	3.1 (0.39)	1.4 (0.34)	4.6 (0.65)	† (†)	† (†)
Asian Indian	2.6 (0.47)	2.1 (0.34)	1.8 (0.31)	2.0 (0.31)	7 (1.1)	0.3 (0.05)	1.9 (0.31)	1.3 (0.38)	2.6 (0.51)	† (†)	† (†)
Bangladeshi	‡ (†)	‡ (†)	‡ (†)	6.1 ! (2.34)	‡ (†)	# (†)	5.2 ! (2.35)	‡ (†)	8.0 ! (3.45)	† (†)	† (†)
Bhutanese	— (†)	— (†)	36.8 (8.18)	19.6 (5.67)	‡ (†)	0.2 ! (0.06)	19.9 (5.80)	‡ (†)	21.6 (6.24)	† (†)	† (†)
Nepalese	3.5 ! (1.22)	4.1 (1.18)	11.1 ! (3.36)	2.6 (0.76)	‡ (†)	0.1 (0.02)	2.6 (0.76)	2.4 ! (1.14)	2.8 ! (1.01)	† (†)	† (†)
Pakistani	5.7 (0.55)	6.0 (0.55)	4.7 (0.48)	5.3 (0.50)	21 (2.1)	0.9 (0.09)	5.2 (0.50)	3.4 (0.45)	8.5 (1.24)	† (†)	† (†)
Southeast Asian	6.5 (1.59)	9.7 (0.83)	8.4 (1.49)	8.3 (1.71)	‡ (†)	0.2 (0.06)	8.3 (1.71)	3.4 (1.14)	28.4 (5.91)	† (†)	† (†)
Burmese	— (†)	— (†)	8.4 (4.13)	27.5 (5.70)	‡ (†)	0.2 (0.09)	27.5 (5.70)	8.2 (2.00)	28.9 (5.91)	† (†)	† (†)
Cambodian	6.7 (1.56)	9.7 (2.10)	6.2 (1.49)	8.4 (1.71)	‡ (†)	0.1 (0.03)	8.3 (1.71)	3.3 (0.91)	8.9 ! (4.45)	† (†)	† (†)
Hmong	8.0 (1.93)	7.3 (1.33)	4.3 (1.12)	8.9 (1.20)	‡ (†)	0.1 (0.03)	8.8 (1.20)	8.9 (2.80)	17.6 ! (5.64)	† (†)	† (†)
Laotian	2.5 ! (1.24)	9.7 (2.15)	5.7 ! (1.91)	6.3 ! (2.51)	‡ (†)	0.1 (0.03)	5.5 ! (2.53)	8.9 ! (2.80)	‡ (‡)	† (†)	† (†)
Thai	‡ (†)	‡ (†)	‡ (†)	2.4 (2.02)	‡ (†)	# (†)	1.98	1.6 (0.37)	4.41	† (†)	† (†)
Vietnamese	5.4 (0.76)	4.6 (0.74)	3.5 (0.55)	2.4 (0.45)	6 (1.0)	0.2 (0.04)	2.5 (0.45)	1.6 (0.37)	4.0 (1.08)	† (†)	† (†)
Other Southeast Asian[7]	‡ (†)	‡ (†)	‡ (†)	‡ (†)	‡ (†)	# (†)	‡ (†)	‡ (†)	‡ (†)	† (†)	† (†)
Other Asian	3.0 (0.69)	6.0 (1.01)	1.7 (0.49)	2.2 (0.64)	‡ (†)	0.1 (0.02)	2.2 (0.64)	1.0 ! (0.51)	6.3 ! (2.41)	† (†)	† (†)
Pacific Islander	7.4 (1.13)	9.5 (1.45)	5.0 (1.03)	10.6 (1.66)	8 (1.4)	0.3 (0.06)	10.2 (1.67)	7.1 (1.37)	23.4 (5.65)	‡ (†)	‡ (†)
American Indian/Alaska Native[8]	15.1 (0.63)	15.9 (0.83)	12.8 (0.76)	11.5 (0.77)	32 (2.3)	1.4 (0.09)	11.3 (0.77)	11.1 (0.77)	21.8 ! (7.44)	2 (0.5)	22.2 (5.70)
American Indian	15.0 (0.79)	16.3 (0.95)	13.2 (0.83)	11.5 (0.83)	27 (2.0)	1.2 (0.08)	11.2 (0.82)	11.0 (0.84)	‡ (‡)	‡ (†)	23.8 ! (7.36)
Alaska Native	17.2 (3.93)	19.5 (3.42)	9.1 (1.73)	10.6 (1.73)	2 (0.3)	0.1 (0.01)	10.7 (1.78)	10.7 (1.78)	‡ (‡)	‡ (†)	‡ (†)

See notes at end of table.

Table 219.80. Percentage of high school dropouts among persons 16 to 24 years old (status dropout rate) and number of status dropouts, by noninstitutionalized or institutionalized status, birth in or outside of the United States, and selected characteristics: Selected years, 2006 through 2014—Continued

[Standard errors appear in parentheses]

Selected characteristic	Total status dropout rate 2006	2009	2013	2014	2014 Noninstitutionalized population[1] — Number of status dropouts (in thousands)	Percentage distribution of status dropouts	Status dropout rate — Total for noninstitutionalized population	For those born in the United States[3]	For those born outside of the United States[3]	2014 Institutionalized population[2] — Number of status dropouts (in thousands)	Status dropout rate
1	2	3	4	5	6	7	8	9	10	11	12
Some other race[9]	10.2 (1.23)	9.1 (1.48)	5.1 (1.13)	5.6 (1.03)	5 (1.0)	0.2 (0.04)	5.4 (1.03)	3.8 (1.05)	10.9 (2.94)	‡ (†)	‡ (†)
Two or more races	7.8 (0.39)	6.5 (0.36)	5.2 (0.28)	5.0 (0.26)	56 (3.2)	2.4 (0.14)	4.8 (0.26)	4.7 (0.27)	5.4 (1.04)	3 (0.4)	20.8 (2.67)
Race/ethnicity by sex											
Male											
White	7.2 (0.10)	6.3 (0.10)	5.4 (0.08)	5.0 (0.08)	528 (9.2)	39.3 (0.52)	4.8 (0.08)	4.8 (0.09)	4.6 (0.59)	29 (1.6)	25.3 (1.38)
Black	14.0 (0.31)	13.1 (0.27)	10.9 (0.27)	9.5 (0.22)	211 (6.7)	15.7 (0.42)	7.6 (0.23)	7.7 (0.23)	5.6 (0.84)	69 (2.6)	39.5 (1.22)
Hispanic	24.8 (0.36)	21.2 (0.31)	13.9 (0.26)	12.7 (0.23)	526 (9.9)	39.1 (0.56)	12.2 (0.23)	8.8 (0.23)	23.6 (0.60)	35 (1.6)	37.6 (1.41)
Asian	3.5 (0.28)	3.7 (0.26)	2.8 (0.19)	2.5 (0.19)	25 (2.0)	1.9 (0.14)	2.5 (0.19)	2.0 (0.20)	3.1 (0.36)	‡ (†)	21.5! (10.04)
Pacific Islander	7.7 (1.54)	9.4 (2.06)	4.2 (1.00)	12.6 (2.45)	‡ (1.5)	0.4 (0.08)	11.9 (2.48)	7.8 (1.82)	24.9! (8.06)	‡ (†)	‡ (†)
American Indian/Alaska Native	17.3 (1.08)	17.6 (1.20)	14.3 (1.11)	13.1 (1.13)	18 (1.5)	1.3 (0.11)	12.6 (1.08)	12.5 (1.12)	10.3! (3.79)	‡ (†)	24.4 (6.33)
Some other race[9]	11.4 (1.78)	12.0 (2.43)	6.2 (1.75)	5.5 (1.36)	‡ (†)	0.2 (0.05)	5.3 (1.37)	3.6! (1.25)	4.5! (1.48)	‡ (†)	‡ (†)
Two or more races	8.8 (0.59)	7.4 (0.56)	5.5 (0.43)	5.0 (0.34)	27 (2.1)	2.0 (0.16)	4.7 (0.35)	4.7 (0.37)	‡ (†)	3 (0.4)	19.6 (2.97)
Female											
White	5.5 (0.08)	4.9 (0.08)	4.0 (0.08)	3.9 (0.09)	408 (9.3)	40.7 (0.68)	3.8 (0.09)	3.9 (0.09)	3.3 (0.41)	5 (0.7)	17.5 (2.49)
Black	9.0 (0.23)	8.2 (0.21)	7.1 (0.23)	6.3 (0.21)	174 (5.8)	17.3 (0.60)	6.1 (0.21)	6.1 (0.22)	5.9 (0.82)	5 (0.7)	35.0 (4.13)
Hispanic	16.7 (0.29)	14.3 (0.26)	9.6 (0.23)	8.5 (0.20)	347 (7.9)	34.5 (0.60)	8.5 (0.20)	6.3 (0.19)	17.3 (0.59)	3 (0.5)	31.9 (4.88)
Asian	2.7 (0.22)	2.1 (0.22)	2.1 (0.22)	2.6 (0.21)	26 (2.1)	2.6 (0.20)	2.6 (0.21)	1.5 (0.21)	3.8 (0.39)	‡ (†)	‡ (†)
Pacific Islander	7.2 (1.49)	9.7 (2.00)	5.8! (1.76)	8.3 (1.64)	3 (0.6)	0.3 (0.06)	8.4 (1.63)	6.4 (1.73)	20.6 (6.14)	‡ (†)	‡ (†)
American Indian/Alaska Native	12.9 (0.98)	14.2 (1.18)	11.3 (0.96)	9.9 (0.93)	15 (1.4)	1.4 (0.14)	9.9 (0.93)	9.7 (0.92)	‡ (†)	‡ (†)	‡ (†)
Some other race[9]	8.9 (1.72)	6.4 (1.60)	3.9 (1.16)	5.6 (1.48)	‡ (†)	0.3 (0.07)	5.6 (1.48)	4.1! (1.70)	11.8! (4.54)	‡ (†)	‡ (†)
Two or more races	6.8 (0.51)	5.6 (0.43)	4.8 (0.36)	5.0 (0.39)	29 (2.4)	2.8 (0.24)	4.9 (0.39)	4.8 (0.39)	6.5 (1.62)	‡ (†)	27.8 (7.47)
Age											
16	3.3 (0.10)	2.8 (0.10)	2.2 (0.08)	2.2 (0.10)	88 (4.2)	3.8 (0.17)	2.1 (0.10)	2.0 (0.10)	4.3 (0.58)	3 (0.5)	7.2 (1.32)
17	5.5 (0.14)	4.4 (0.12)	3.1 (0.09)	3.0 (0.12)	121 (4.8)	5.2 (0.20)	2.9 (0.12)	2.8 (0.12)	4.6 (0.57)	5 (0.8)	14.0 (1.88)
18	8.0 (0.18)	7.5 (0.17)	5.0 (0.17)	4.8 (0.15)	207 (6.4)	8.8 (0.24)	4.6 (0.14)	4.3 (0.14)	7.6 (0.63)	11 (1.1)	35.7 (3.00)
19	10.0 (0.18)	9.1 (0.20)	6.4 (0.16)	6.0 (0.18)	237 (7.6)	10.1 (0.30)	5.6 (0.18)	5.3 (0.19)	9.7 (0.72)	16 (1.1)	41.3 (2.35)
20–24	12.2 (0.11)	10.8 (0.11)	8.7 (0.09)	7.9 (0.07)	1,693 (15.6)	72.2 (0.42)	7.5 (0.07)	6.6 (0.07)	15.4 (0.34)	117 (3.2)	37.0 (0.87)
English speaking ability											
Spoke English at home or spoke English very well	7.9 (0.06)	7.2 (0.07)	6.0 (0.06)	5.5 (0.05)	1,946 (20.4)	82.9 (0.39)	5.2 (0.05)	5.2 (0.05)	5.5 (0.18)	140 (3.3)	32.2 (0.64)
Spoke a language other than English at home and spoke English less than very well	34.7 (0.47)	32.8 (0.42)	23.5 (0.53)	21.8 (0.47)	400 (9.8)	17.1 (0.39)	21.5 (0.47)	12.7 (0.53)	25.8 (0.65)	11 (1.0)	49.4 (3.17)
Region											
Northeast	7.4 (0.14)	6.8 (0.12)	5.4 (0.12)	5.2 (0.11)	337 (7.4)	14.4 (0.30)	4.9 (0.11)	4.3 (0.11)	10.7 (0.50)	22 (1.4)	30.3 (1.65)
Midwest	8.1 (0.13)	7.4 (0.13)	5.9 (0.12)	5.7 (0.10)	454 (8.5)	19.4 (0.29)	5.4 (0.10)	5.1 (0.09)	10.7 (0.76)	26 (1.5)	30.0 (1.44)
South	11.0 (0.13)	9.7 (0.13)	7.8 (0.11)	6.9 (0.10)	956 (14.5)	40.8 (0.45)	6.5 (0.10)	5.8 (0.09)	13.7 (0.46)	74 (2.7)	36.8 (1.02)
West	10.7 (0.13)	9.5 (0.14)	7.1 (0.10)	6.6 (0.10)	599 (9.4)	25.5 (0.37)	6.3 (0.10)	5.4 (0.10)	13.2 (0.43)	29 (1.7)	30.0 (1.61)

—Not available.
†Not applicable.
#Rounds to zero.
!Interpret data with caution. The coefficient of variation (CV) for this estimate is between 30 and 50 percent.
‡Reporting standards not met. Either there are too few cases for a reliable estimate or the coefficient of variation (CV) is 50 percent or greater.
[1] Persons living in households as well as persons living in noninstitutional group quarters. Noninstitutionalized group quarters include college and university housing, military quarters, facilities for workers and religious groups, and temporary shelters for the homeless.
[2] Persons living in institutionalized group quarters, including adult and juvenile correctional facilities, nursing facilities, and other health care facilities.
[3] United States refers to the 50 states and the District of Columbia, Puerto Rico, American Samoa, Guam, the U.S. Virgin Islands, and the Northern Marianas.
[4] Includes other Central American subgroups not shown separately.
[5] Includes Taiwanese.
[6] In addition to the subgroups shown, also includes Sri Lankan.
[7] Consists of Indonesian and Malaysian.
[8] Includes persons reporting American Indian alone, persons reporting Alaska Native alone, and persons from American Indian and/or Alaska Native tribes specified or not specified.
[9] Respondents who wrote in some other race that was not included as an option on the questionnaire.
NOTE: "Status" dropouts are 16- to 24-year-olds who are not enrolled in school and who have not completed a high school program, regardless of when they left school and whether they ever attended school in the United States. People who have received GED credentials are counted as high school completers. Detail may not sum to totals because of rounding. Race categories exclude persons of Hispanic ethnicity. Status dropout rates in this table may differ from those in tables based on the Current Population Survey (CPS) because of differences in survey design and target populations.
SOURCE: U.S. Department of Commerce, Census Bureau, American Community Survey (ACS), 2006, 2009, 2013, and 2014. (This table was prepared November 2015.)

Table 219.90. Number and percentage distribution of 14- through 21-year-old students served under Individuals with Disabilities Education Act (IDEA), Part B, who exited school, by exit reason, sex, race/ethnicity, age, and type of disability: 2011–12 and 2012–13

Year, sex, race/ethnicity, age, and type of disability	Total	Exited school Graduated with regular diploma	Received alternative certificate[1]	Reached maximum age[2]	Dropped out[3]	Died	Transferred to regular education[4]	Moved, known to be continuing[5]
1	2	3	4	5	6	7	8	9
2011–12								
Total number	392,200	250,672	53,914	5,567	80,469	1,578	64,709	175,719
Percentage distribution of total	100.0	63.9	13.7	1.4	20.5	0.4	†	†
Number by sex								
Male	256,276	161,429	34,184	3,709	55,866	1,088	43,014	118,347
Female	135,924	89,243	19,730	1,858	24,603	490	21,695	57,372
Number by race/ethnicity								
White	207,262	147,512	22,073	2,945	33,945	787	36,934	85,875
Black	87,018	46,782	15,744	1,281	22,839	372	11,060	46,587
Hispanic	77,201	42,954	13,578	989	19,351	329	12,714	32,690
Asian	6,131	4,297	1,002	213	591	28	1,388	1,701
Pacific Islander	1,542	1,026	180	32	297	7	404	452
American Indian/Alaska Native	6,105	3,634	536	46	1,863	26	895	3,723
Two or more races	6,941	4,467	801	61	1,583	29	1,314	4,691
Number by type of disability								
Autism	16,732	10,806	3,791	847	1,224	64	1,815	4,958
Deaf-blindness	83	39	15	12	12	5	6	28
Emotional disturbance	40,966	21,190	3,671	362	15,589	154	6,072	32,505
Hearing impairment	4,704	3,452	696	60	482	14	726	1,505
Intellectual disability	38,622	15,546	13,388	2,197	7,243	248	2,210	14,196
Multiple disabilities	8,712	4,235	2,121	717	1,375	264	338	3,048
Orthopedic impairment	3,737	2,308	731	183	425	90	505	1,183
Other health impairment[6]	54,515	38,080	5,439	270	10,443	283	9,712	25,030
Specific learning disability	209,813	144,445	22,520	768	41,667	413	34,197	87,482
Speech or language impairment	9,997	7,462	910	51	1,563	11	8,736	4,651
Traumatic brain injury	2,583	1,771	412	60	319	21	204	671
Visual impairment	1,735	1,337	220	40	127	11	188	460
2012–13								
Total number	396,292	258,028	56,404	5,846	74,575	1,439	57,677	162,901
Percentage distribution of total	100.0	65.1	14.2	1.5	18.8	0.4	†	†
Number by sex								
Male	258,321	166,023	35,705	3,786	51,810	997	38,328	109,036
Female	137,971	92,005	20,699	2,060	22,765	442	19,349	53,865
Number by race/ethnicity								
White	208,030	149,809	22,314	3,035	32,105	767	33,817	79,442
Black	84,905	46,520	16,360	1,296	20,391	338	9,795	42,779
Hispanic	82,015	47,671	15,032	1,062	18,007	243	10,548	30,722
Asian	6,450	4,547	1,054	264	555	30	1,263	1,638
Pacific Islander	1,617	1,061	159	50	338	9	300	474
American Indian/Alaska Native	5,645	3,559	518	51	1,498	19	754	3,092
Two or more races	7,630	4,861	967	88	1,681	33	1,200	4,754
Number by age[7]								
14	2,687	13	21	†	2,461	192	15,210	33,807
15	5,280	46	32	†	4,974	228	13,229	34,883
16	15,964	3,537	560	†	11,574	293	12,766	35,506
17	147,525	111,224	15,493	5	20,525	278	10,158	31,521
18	149,844	107,060	22,095	1	20,467	221	4,464	18,570
19	43,275	25,284	8,319	73	9,483	116	1,126	5,915
20	18,536	7,624	5,512	1,588	3,741	71	506	1,981
21	13,181	3,240	4,372	4,179	1,350	40	218	718
Number by type of disability								
Autism	19,429	12,467	4,506	1,027	1,375	54	1,802	5,276
Deaf-blindness	82	46	13	9	12	2	2	18
Emotional disturbance	39,493	21,249	3,787	344	13,984	129	5,557	29,392
Hearing impairment	4,623	3,335	768	70	441	9	637	1,470
Intellectual disability	40,690	17,384	13,438	2,315	7,302	251	1,781	15,880
Multiple disabilities	9,205	4,184	2,602	718	1,397	304	320	2,901
Orthopedic impairment	3,586	2,268	708	165	382	63	414	1,093
Other health impairment[6]	58,413	41,526	5,814	267	10,550	256	9,245	24,801
Specific learning disability	206,054	144,530	23,260	754	37,191	319	28,869	76,001
Speech or language impairment	10,488	7,990	907	45	1,525	21	8,622	4,845
Traumatic brain injury	2,525	1,741	405	81	280	18	219	758
Visual impairment	1,704	1,308	196	51	136	13	209	466

†Not applicable.

[1]Received a certificate of completion, modified diploma, or some similar document, but did not meet the same standards for graduation as those for students without disabilities.

[2]Students may exit special education services due to maximum age beginning at age 18, depending on state law or practice or order of any court.

[3]"Dropped out" is defined as the total who were enrolled at some point in the reporting year, were not enrolled at the end of the reporting year, and did not exit for any of the other reasons described. Includes students previously categorized as "moved, not known to continue."

[4]"Transferred to regular education" was previously labeled "no longer receives special education."

[5]"Moved, known to be continuing" is the total number of students who moved out of the administrative area or transferred to another district and are known to be continuing in an educational program.

[6]Other health impairments include having limited strength, vitality, or alertness due to chronic or acute health problems such as a heart condition, tuberculosis, rheumatic fever, nephritis, asthma, sickle cell anemia, hemophilia, epilepsy, lead poisoning, leukemia, or diabetes.

[7]Age data are as of fall of the school year, so some students may have been 1 year older at the time they exited school.

NOTE: Data are for the 50 states, the District of Columbia, the Bureau of Indian Education, American Samoa, the Federated States of Micronesia, Guam, the Northern Marianas, Puerto Rico, the Republic of Palau, the Republic of the Marshall Islands, and the U.S. Virgin Islands. Data on number by age are not available for 2011–12, so these rows have been omitted. Detail may not sum to totals because of rounding.

SOURCE: U.S. Department of Education, Office of Special Education Programs, Individuals with Disabilities Education Act (IDEA) Section 618 Data Products: State Level Data Files. Retrieved November 30, 2015, from http://www2.ed.gov/programs/osepidea/618-data/state-level-data-files/index.html. (This table was prepared December 2015.)

Table 220.10. Percentage of children demonstrating specific cognitive and motor skills at about 9 months of age, by child's age and selected characteristics: 2001–02

[Standard errors appear in parentheses]

Age and selected characteristic	Number of children (in thousands)		Percentage distribution of children		Percent of children who demonstrate skills[1]																		
					Specific cognitive skills										Specific motor skills								
					Explores objects[2]		Explores purposefully[3]		Jabbers expressively[4]		Early problem solving[5]		Names objects[6]		Eye-hand coordination[7]		Sitting[8]		Prewalking[9]		Stands alone[10]		Skillful walking[11]		Balance[12]	
1	2		3		4		5		6		7		8		9		10		11		12		13		14	
8 through 10 months																										
Total	**2,882**	**(39.1)**	**100.0**	**(†)**	**98.6**	**(0.06)**	**83.2**	**(0.54)**	**29.6**	**(0.57)**	**3.7**	**(0.13)**	**0.6**	**(0.03)**	**89.1**	**(0.26)**	**86.8**	**(0.24)**	**64.7**	**(0.60)**	**18.6**	**(0.50)**	**8.4**	**(0.21)**	**1.7**	**(0.09)**
Sex of child																										
Male	1,460	(23.0)	50.7	(0.38)	98.6	(0.06)	82.7	(0.51)	28.8	(0.56)	3.5	(0.14)	0.6	(0.03)	89.3	(0.30)	87.0	(0.27)	65.1	(0.69)	18.5	(0.55)	8.3	(0.23)	1.7	(0.10)
Female	1,422	(22.0)	49.3	(0.38)	98.7	(0.09)	83.8	(0.68)	30.4	(0.71)	3.9	(0.18)	0.7	(0.05)	88.9	(0.36)	86.6	(0.33)	64.4	(0.78)	18.7	(0.67)	8.4	(0.29)	1.8	(0.14)
Race/ethnicity of child																										
White	1,569	(29.2)	54.5	(0.63)	98.8	(0.07)	84.0	(0.69)	30.4	(0.72)	3.9	(0.17)	0.7	(0.04)	88.8	(0.37)	86.5	(0.33)	63.8	(0.81)	18.0	(0.66)	8.1	(0.27)	1.6	(0.10)
Black	381	(11.1)	13.3	(0.38)	98.1	(0.16)	80.8	(0.92)	27.8	(0.99)	3.3	(0.25)	0.6	(0.07)	91.0	(0.33)	88.6	(0.32)	69.7	(0.94)	22.8	(1.15)	10.4	(0.58)	2.6	(0.35)
Hispanic	717	(18.5)	24.9	(0.54)	98.5	(0.13)	82.9	(0.82)	29.0	(0.84)	3.4	(0.21)	0.6	(0.05)	88.4	(0.47)	86.1	(0.43)	63.4	(1.00)	17.0	(0.77)	7.8	(0.32)	1.6	(0.15)
Asian	79	(3.1)	2.7	(0.10)	98.8	(0.13)	83.3	(0.96)	28.2	(0.92)	3.1	(0.20)	0.5	(0.04)	89.5	(0.53)	87.1	(0.49)	65.2	(1.21)	18.2	(1.00)	8.2	(0.39)	1.6	(0.14)
Pacific Islander	6	(1.5)	0.2	(0.05)	98.9	(0.23)	81.8	(3.58)	23.8	(3.22)	2.0	(0.47)	0.3	(0.07)	95.4	(0.97)	93.0	(1.13)	79.9	(3.81)	34.8	(8.69)	15.1	(3.90)	3.9 !	(1.67)
American Indian/Alaska Native	10	(1.1)	0.4	(0.04)	98.4	(0.30)	80.3	(2.72)	27.2	(2.49)	3.4	(0.70)	0.6	(0.18)	90.2	(0.99)	87.8	(0.91)	66.8	(2.15)	19.6	(2.08)	8.4	(0.80)	1.5	(0.29)
Two or more races	115	(9.8)	4.0	(0.33)	98.6	(0.14)	83.0	(1.24)	29.8	(1.51)	3.9	(0.55)	0.8	(0.21)	90.0	(0.94)	87.8	(0.87)	67.7	(2.20)	22.1	(2.03)	9.6	(0.79)	2.0	(0.30)
Months of age																										
8 months	642	(32.8)	29.5	(0.90)	97.5	(0.14)	67.9	(1.04)	15.7	(0.53)	1.1	(0.09)	0.1	(0.02)	84.0	(0.52)	82.0	(0.46)	52.7	(1.08)	8.8	(0.63)	4.5	(0.22)	0.5	(0.05)
9 months	1,389	(28.2)	22.3	(0.99)	98.7	(0.06)	84.5	(0.60)	27.5	(0.44)	2.7	(0.09)	0.4	(0.02)	89.1	(0.32)	86.7	(0.30)	64.2	(0.74)	16.1	(0.55)	7.2	(0.21)	1.2	(0.07)
10 months	851	(24.2)	48.2	(0.76)	99.3	(0.07)	92.7	(0.33)	43.5	(0.74)	7.1	(0.27)	1.4	(0.08)	92.8	(0.26)	90.5	(0.25)	74.6	(0.63)	30.1	(0.85)	13.3	(0.42)	3.6	(0.25)
Primary type of nonparental care arrangement[13]																										
No regular nonparental arrangement	1,459	(28.0)	50.7	(0.90)	98.5	(0.09)	82.4	(0.59)	28.7	(0.55)	3.4	(0.14)	0.6	(0.04)	88.2	(0.34)	86.0	(0.30)	63.1	(0.70)	17.7	(0.52)	8.0	(0.22)	1.6	(0.10)
Home-based care																										
Relative care[14]	759	(27.1)	26.4	(0.81)	98.8	(0.08)	84.3	(0.67)	30.6	(0.79)	3.9	(0.22)	0.7	(0.06)	90.3	(0.35)	87.9	(0.33)	67.3	(0.84)	20.4	(0.81)	9.2	(0.38)	2.0	(0.19)
Nonrelative care[15]	430	(17.1)	14.9	(0.53)	98.8	(0.08)	84.7	(0.80)	31.3	(1.00)	4.3	(0.29)	0.8	(0.08)	90.0	(0.45)	87.6	(0.45)	66.1	(1.14)	19.3	(1.35)	8.7	(0.58)	1.8	(0.23)
Center-based care[16]	211	(13.9)	7.3	(0.48)	98.6	(0.19)	82.8	(1.43)	29.3	(1.54)	3.5	(0.39)	0.6	(0.09)	89.0	(0.77)	86.7	(0.71)	64.0	(1.72)	18.0	(1.51)	8.3	(0.66)	1.9	(0.32)
Multiple arrangements[17]	19	(4.0)	0.7	(0.14)	98.1	(0.36)	77.5	(3.54)	24.8	(3.12)	2.8	(0.65)	0.4	(0.12)	86.8	(2.89)	84.6	(2.55)	61.8	(5.09)	14.4	(2.71)	6.4	(0.94)	0.9	(0.19)
Parents' highest level of education																										
Less than high school	388	(12.4)	13.5	(0.42)	98.4	(0.11)	80.0	(0.87)	25.9	(0.79)	2.8	(0.20)	0.5	(0.06)	88.9	(0.62)	86.5	(0.58)	54.4	(1.20)	17.3	(0.96)	8.0	(0.42)	1.7	(0.20)
High school completion	702	(19.8)	24.4	(0.60)	98.4	(0.13)	82.6	(0.89)	29.2	(0.81)	3.6	(0.21)	0.7	(0.06)	89.6	(0.45)	87.3	(0.42)	56.8	(0.91)	20.6	(0.84)	9.1	(0.36)	1.9	(0.17)
Some college/vocational	847	(24.8)	29.4	(0.68)	98.7	(0.08)	84.4	(0.60)	30.8	(0.69)	3.9	(0.20)	0.7	(0.05)	90.0	(0.35)	87.7	(0.33)	56.7	(0.84)	20.8	(0.82)	9.3	(0.35)	2.0	(0.16)
Bachelor's degree	497	(16.2)	17.3	(0.54)	98.8	(0.07)	83.9	(0.60)	30.2	(0.71)	3.8	(0.20)	0.7	(0.05)	88.4	(0.46)	86.1	(0.41)	52.5	(1.05)	16.3	(0.85)	7.4	(0.34)	1.4	(0.12)
Any graduate education	446	(15.7)	15.5	(0.52)	98.8	(0.11)	84.0	(0.94)	30.4	(0.88)	3.8	(0.22)	0.7	(0.06)	87.5	(0.58)	85.4	(0.52)	50.5	(1.23)	15.2	(0.91)	7.0	(0.40)	1.4	(0.18)
Poverty status[18]																										
Below poverty threshold	682	(23.0)	23.7	(0.74)	98.3	(0.14)	80.9	(0.75)	27.1	(0.79)	3.1	(0.21)	0.5	(0.05)	89.1	(0.47)	86.8	(0.43)	55.5	(0.98)	19.2	(0.86)	8.7	(0.42)	1.9	(0.24)
At or above poverty threshold	2,200	(37.2)	76.3	(0.74)	98.7	(0.07)	84.0	(0.58)	30.4	(0.63)	3.8	(0.15)	0.7	(0.04)	89.1	(0.27)	86.8	(0.25)	54.5	(0.66)	18.4	(0.56)	8.3	(0.23)	1.7	(0.10)
Socioeconomic status[19]																										
Lowest 20 percent	557	(16.8)	19.3	(0.58)	98.3	(0.13)	80.7	(0.72)	26.8	(0.69)	3.0	(0.17)	0.5	(0.04)	89.1	(0.46)	86.7	(0.43)	55.4	(0.90)	18.8	(0.83)	8.5	(0.35)	1.8	(0.18)
Middle 60 percent	1,719	(38.2)	59.7	(0.83)	98.6	(0.08)	83.5	(0.63)	30.2	(0.67)	3.8	(0.18)	0.7	(0.05)	89.5	(0.30)	87.2	(0.28)	55.6	(0.73)	19.6	(0.67)	8.8	(0.28)	1.9	(0.11)
Highest 20 percent	606	(18.4)	21.0	(0.63)	98.8	(0.09)	84.8	(0.73)	30.5	(0.79)	3.8	(0.18)	0.6	(0.04)	88.0	(0.45)	85.8	(0.40)	51.5	(0.96)	15.6	(0.66)	7.1	(0.28)	1.3	(0.13)

See notes at end of table.

Table 220.10. Percentage of children demonstrating specific cognitive and motor skills at about 9 months of age, by child's age and selected characteristics: 2001–02—Continued

[Standard errors appear in parentheses]

Age and selected characteristic	Number of children (in thousands)	Percentage distribution of children	Percent of children who demonstrate skills[1]										
			Specific cognitive skills						Specific motor skills				
			Explores objects[2]	Explores purposefully[3]	Jabbers expressively[4]	Early problem solving[5]	Names objects[6]	Eye-hand coordination[7]	Sitting[8]	Prewalking[9]	Stands alone[10]	Skillful walking[11]	Balance[12]
1	2	3	4	5	6	7	8	9	10	11	12	13	14
11 through 13 months													
Total..........	839 (32.2)	100.0 (†)	99.7 (0.05)	97.3 (0.15)	67.9 (0.54)	22.5 (0.55)	8.2 (0.37)	97.1 (0.17)	95.6 (0.19)	89.0 (0.54)	62.5 (1.29)	34.9 (0.95)	19.1 (0.84)
Months of age													
11 months..........	425 (19.6)	50.6 (1.54)	99.5 (0.10)	95.8 (0.28)	57.6 (0.77)	14.2 (0.59)	4.0 (0.33)	95.8 (0.28)	93.9 (0.29)	84.4 (0.86)	49.0 (1.74)	24.3 (1.05)	10.5 (0.77)
12 months..........	251 (14.8)	30.0 (1.29)	99.8 (0.03)	98.4 (0.13)	74.3 (0.83)	26.9 (0.94)	10.2 (0.65)	98.1 (0.21)	96.8 (0.26)	92.6 (0.71)	70.9 (2.09)	40.2 (1.65)	22.9 (1.50)
13 months..........	163 (12.1)	19.4 (1.16)	100.0 (†)	99.5 (0.08)	85.0 (0.62)	37.7 (1.04)	16.0 (0.87)	99.0 (0.27)	98.2 (0.30)	95.8 (0.85)	84.8 (2.24)	54.4 (1.81)	36.0 (1.83)
14 through 22 months..........	260 (19.7)	100.0 (†)	100.0 (†)	99.5 (0.14)	90.0 (0.60)	58.4 (1.44)	40.8 (1.71)	99.5 (0.12)	99.1 (0.13)	98.3 (0.28)	94.1 (0.91)	74.0 (1.35)	61.7 (1.82)

†Not applicable.

!Interpret data with caution. The coefficient of variation (CV) for this estimate is between 30 and 50 percent.

[1]Based on assessments collected using the Bayley Short Form Research Edition (BSF-R), a shortened field method of administering the Bayley Scales of Infant Development-II (BSID-II) (Bayley 1993). The scores are fully equated with the BSID-II; for more information, see NCES's *Early Childhood Longitudinal Study, Birth Cohort (ECLS-B) Psychometric Report for the 2-year Data Collection.* The proficiency probabilities indicate mastery of a specific skill or ability within cognitive or physical domains.

[2]Ability to explore objects, for example, reaching for and holding objects. The child may have no specific purpose except to play or discover.

[3]Ability to explore objects with a purpose, such as to explore a bell to understand the source of the sound.

[4]Measures proficiency in communication through diverse nonverbal sounds and gestures, such as vowel and vowel-consonant sounds.

[5]Measures proficiency in engaging in early problem solving, such as using a tool to reach an out-of-reach toy or locating a hidden toy.

[6]Measures proficiency in early communication skills, such as saying simple words like "mama" and "dada."

[7]Measures proficiency in being able to use visual tracking to guide hand movements to pick up a small object.

[8]Measures proficiency in ability to maintain control of the muscles used in sitting with and without support.

[9]Measures proficiency in ability to engage in various prewalking types of mobility, with and without support, such as shifting weight from one foot to the other.

[10]Measures proficiency in ability to walk with help and to stand independently.

[11]Measures proficiency in being able to walk independently.

[12]Measures proficiency in ability to maintain balance while changing position.

[13]The type of nonparental care in which the child spent the most hours.

[14]Care provided in the child's home or in another private home by a relative (excluding parents).

[15]Care provided in the child's home or in another private home by a person unrelated to the child.

[16]Care provided in places such as early learning centers, nursery schools, and preschools.

[17]Children who spent an equal amount of time in each of two or more types of arrangements.

[18]Poverty status based on Census Bureau guidelines from 2002, which identify a dollar amount determined to meet a household's needs, given its size and composition. In 2002, a family of four was considered to live below the poverty threshold if its income was less than or equal to $18,392.

[19]Socioeconomic status (SES) was measured by a composite score based on parental education and occupations, and family income.

NOTE: Estimates weighted by W1C0. This table is based on a survey that sampled children born in 2001 and was designed to collect information about them for the first time when the children were about 9 months of age (i.e., 8 to 10 months). As shown in the table, some children were older than this at the time data were collected, although only 6.5 percent were over 13 months of age. Race categories exclude persons of Hispanic ethnicity. Detail may not sum to totals because of rounding and survey item nonresponse. Some data have been revised from previously published figures.

SOURCE: U.S. Department of Education, National Center for Education Statistics, Early Childhood Longitudinal Study, Birth Cohort 9-month–Kindergarten 2007 Restricted-Use Data File and Electronic Codebook. (This table was prepared December 2010.)

Table 220.20. Percentage of children demonstrating specific cognitive skills, motor skills, and secure emotional attachment to parents at about 2 years of age, by selected characteristics: 2003–04

[Standard errors appear in parentheses]

Selected characteristic	Percentage distribution of children[1]	Specific cognitive skills[2]					Specific motor skills[2]						Secure emotional attachment to parent[3]
		Receptive vocabulary[4]	Expressive vocabulary[5]	Listening comprehension[6]	Matching/discrimination[7]	Early counting[8]	Skillful walking[9]	Balance[10]	Fine motor control[11]	Uses stairs[12]	Alternating balance[13]	Motor planning[14]	
1	2	3	4	5	6	7	8	9	10	11	12	13	14
Total	100.0 (†)	84.5 (0.38)	63.9 (0.53)	36.6 (0.42)	31.9 (0.39)	3.9 (0.14)	92.6 (0.20)	89.4 (0.33)	55.5 (0.48)	48.1 (0.41)	30.0 (0.47)	10.2 (0.21)	61.6 (1.12)
Sex of child													
Male	51.1 (0.21)	81.4 (0.56)	59.3 (0.75)	32.9 (0.58)	28.4 (0.53)	3.0 (0.16)	92.0 (0.26)	88.4 (0.43)	54.2 (0.53)	46.9 (0.44)	28.7 (0.48)	9.6 (0.20)	55.0 (1.23)
Female	48.9 (0.21)	87.7 (0.38)	68.9 (0.59)	40.6 (0.50)	35.6 (0.48)	4.8 (0.20)	93.2 (0.20)	90.5 (0.32)	56.8 (0.53)	49.3 (0.47)	31.3 (0.55)	10.9 (0.26)	68.4 (1.27)
Race/ethnicity of child													
White	54.6 (0.61)	88.7 (0.40)	70.7 (0.63)	42.2 (0.52)	37.1 (0.49)	5.2 (0.21)	92.8 (0.23)	89.9 (0.38)	55.8 (0.58)	48.4 (0.50)	30.2 (0.58)	10.4 (0.26)	65.7 (1.41)
Black	13.4 (0.29)	79.4 (0.93)	55.7 (1.18)	29.9 (0.86)	25.5 (0.75)	2.2 (0.21)	93.3 (0.40)	90.6 (0.66)	58.0 (0.94)	50.2 (0.79)	32.5 (0.87)	11.2 (0.37)	53.3 (2.13)
Hispanic	24.5 (0.45)	78.3 (0.99)	53.7 (1.19)	28.2 (0.83)	24.1 (0.73)	1.9 (0.16)	91.6 (0.42)	87.9 (0.69)	53.5 (0.76)	46.3 (0.65)	28.2 (0.66)	9.4 (0.27)	57.3 (1.84)
Asian	2.7 (0.10)	82.5 (1.23)	61.8 (1.40)	35.2 (0.93)	30.5 (0.82)	3.6 (0.27)	92.4 (0.39)	89.2 (0.65)	54.7 (0.91)	47.4 (0.72)	29.2 (0.76)	9.9 (0.29)	61.1 (2.29)
Pacific Islander	0.2 (0.05)	78.8 (4.16)	54.1 (5.83)	27.8 (4.30)	23.2 (3.61)	1.1 ! (0.36)	92.8 (1.34)	90.0 (2.29)	54.0 (4.00)	46.5 (2.99)	27.4 (3.24)	8.9 (1.22)	61.9 (12.63)
American Indian/Alaska Native	0.5 (0.06)	75.3 (3.99)	50.5 (4.17)	25.9 (2.69)	22.0 (2.23)	1.5 (0.27)	92.4 (0.70)	89.1 (1.28)	55.1 (1.14)	47.9 (0.90)	29.8 (1.05)	10.1 (0.45)	46.3 (5.14)
Two or more races	4.1 (0.31)	85.1 (0.91)	64.7 (1.47)	37.2 (1.26)	32.3 (1.26)	3.7 (0.55)	92.4 (0.54)	89.1 (0.93)	54.4 (1.35)	47.2 (1.11)	28.9 (1.22)	9.7 (0.53)	61.4 (3.03)
Age of child													
22 months	2.0 (0.30)	78.1 (2.15)	53.1 (2.77)	28.4 (2.34)	24.5 (2.31)	2.9 ! (1.01)	90.9 (1.68)	86.5 (2.78)	53.4 (3.05)	46.5 (2.70)	29.2 (2.77)	10.6 (1.58)	65.1 (5.06)
23 months	42.3 (1.22)	81.9 (0.54)	60.1 (0.66)	33.4 (0.47)	28.8 (0.41)	2.9 (0.13)	92.2 (0.27)	88.7 (0.45)	54.3 (0.59)	47.0 (0.49)	28.8 (0.53)	9.7 (0.22)	62.7 (1.40)
24 months	42.0 (1.02)	86.5 (0.42)	66.9 (0.65)	39.1 (0.56)	34.3 (0.54)	4.6 (0.23)	92.9 (0.22)	90.0 (0.37)	56.1 (0.57)	43.6 (0.48)	30.4 (0.57)	10.4 (0.25)	60.8 (1.65)
25 months	13.7 (0.54)	87.4 (0.58)	68.3 (0.91)	40.3 (0.78)	35.4 (0.77)	5.0 (0.35)	93.0 (0.35)	90.2 (0.56)	57.5 (0.79)	50.0 (0.68)	32.4 (0.81)	11.4 (0.40)	59.8 (1.90)
Primary type of nonparental care arrangement[15]													
No regular nonparental arrangement	50.8 (0.75)	83.4 (0.50)	62.0 (0.70)	34.8 (0.56)	30.2 (0.52)	3.3 (0.17)	92.2 (0.26)	88.8 (0.43)	54.5 (0.55)	47.2 (0.47)	29.0 (0.52)	9.7 (0.22)	62.1 (1.35)
Home-based care													
Relative care[16]	18.6 (0.63)	83.2 (0.70)	61.6 (1.04)	34.7 (0.84)	30.1 (0.84)	3.6 (0.29)	92.7 (0.30)	89.7 (0.49)	55.8 (0.79)	43.3 (0.67)	30.1 (0.77)	10.3 (0.35)	57.5 (1.94)
Nonrelative care[17]	14.5 (0.57)	86.7 (0.72)	67.8 (1.00)	39.8 (0.81)	34.8 (0.76)	4.4 (0.29)	93.3 (0.27)	90.6 (0.46)	57.1 (0.73)	49.5 (0.63)	31.5 (0.74)	10.8 (0.35)	61.1 (2.23)
Center-based care[18]	15.6 (0.51)	87.5 (0.69)	69.4 (0.99)	41.6 (0.84)	36.8 (0.82)	5.5 (0.47)	93.0 (0.31)	90.2 (0.50)	56.9 (0.70)	49.5 (0.61)	31.8 (0.74)	11.2 (0.37)	64.6 (1.87)
Multiple arrangements[19]	0.5 (0.09)	81.7 (5.66)	63.1 (7.07)	38.0 (5.92)	33.8 (5.68)	6.2 ! (2.87)	91.3 (1.70)	87.1 (2.97)	52.4 (3.41)	45.8 (2.92)	27.9 (3.29)	9.8 (1.62)	72.2 (8.48)
Mother's employment status													
Full-time (35 hours or more)	34.3 (0.76)	85.6 (0.56)	65.8 (0.83)	38.2 (0.66)	33.4 (0.62)	4.2 (0.24)	93.0 (0.25)	90.1 (0.43)	56.6 (0.65)	49.1 (0.57)	31.2 (0.66)	10.8 (0.31)	59.8 (1.58)
Part-time (less than 35 hours)	20.3 (0.69)	86.6 (0.64)	67.6 (0.98)	39.7 (0.84)	34.8 (0.80)	4.7 (0.37)	92.8 (0.28)	89.8 (0.47)	55.5 (0.70)	48.1 (0.58)	29.8 (0.66)	10.1 (0.30)	65.2 (1.53)
Looking for work	6.3 (0.33)	80.1 (1.28)	56.6 (1.77)	30.2 (1.33)	25.8 (1.20)	1.9 (0.24)	92.0 (0.48)	88.4 (0.81)	53.8 (1.04)	46.7 (0.85)	28.5 (0.91)	9.6 (0.37)	58.8 (3.07)
Not in labor force	38.8 (0.82)	83.1 (0.56)	61.6 (0.77)	34.7 (0.63)	30.1 (0.60)	3.4 (0.21)	92.2 (0.26)	88.8 (0.43)	54.6 (0.56)	47.3 (0.49)	29.2 (0.54)	9.9 (0.24)	61.4 (1.41)
No mother in household	0.4 (0.09)	82.1 (4.44)	58.8 (6.94)	33.5 (6.05)	29.3 (5.73)	‡ (†)	94.4 (1.25)	92.4 (2.19)	59.7 (3.58)	51.6 (2.90)	33.5 (3.30)	11.3 (1.37)	62.1 (9.92)
Parents' highest level of education													
Less than high school	12.2 (0.37)	76.6 (1.00)	50.5 (1.32)	25.4 (0.95)	21.6 (0.81)	1.3 (0.14)	91.2 (0.43)	87.3 (0.70)	52.7 (0.84)	45.6 (0.69)	27.4 (0.71)	9.0 (0.28)	51.8 (2.90)
High school completion	25.2 (0.52)	81.9 (0.61)	58.7 (0.88)	31.8 (0.68)	27.2 (0.62)	2.3 (0.18)	92.4 (0.29)	89.3 (0.47)	55.2 (0.66)	47.8 (0.56)	29.7 (0.63)	10.0 (0.27)	54.3 (1.78)
Some college/vocational	29.7 (0.53)	84.4 (0.62)	64.0 (0.85)	36.6 (0.68)	31.8 (0.65)	3.7 (0.21)	92.5 (0.31)	89.4 (0.51)	55.6 (0.70)	48.2 (0.60)	30.2 (0.67)	10.4 (0.30)	62.6 (1.77)
Bachelor's degree	17.5 (0.46)	88.6 (0.66)	71.1 (1.11)	42.6 (0.99)	37.4 (0.98)	5.3 (0.47)	93.2 (0.30)	90.5 (0.52)	56.7 (0.79)	49.1 (0.67)	31.0 (0.78)	10.7 (0.37)	67.2 (2.09)
Any graduate education	15.4 (0.39)	90.4 (0.60)	74.8 (0.93)	46.5 (0.79)	41.4 (0.78)	7.1 (0.37)	93.0 (0.36)	90.2 (0.61)	56.5 (0.80)	48.9 (0.68)	30.9 (0.77)	10.6 (0.35)	72.8 (1.90)
Poverty status[20]													
Below poverty threshold	23.0 (0.80)	78.7 (0.85)	54.6 (1.11)	29.0 (0.81)	24.8 (0.72)	2.1 (0.18)	91.8 (0.32)	88.1 (0.53)	54.1 (0.70)	46.8 (0.60)	28.8 (0.67)	9.6 (0.28)	52.7 (1.73)
At or above poverty threshold	77.0 (0.80)	86.2 (0.37)	66.7 (0.53)	38.9 (0.44)	34.0 (0.42)	4.4 (0.18)	92.8 (0.21)	89.8 (0.35)	55.9 (0.53)	48.4 (0.45)	30.3 (0.51)	10.4 (0.23)	64.2 (1.22)

See notes at end of table.

Table 220.20. Percentage of children demonstrating specific cognitive skills, motor skills, and secure emotional attachment to parents at about 2 years of age, by selected characteristics: 2003–04—Continued

[Standard errors appear in parentheses]

Selected characteristic	Percentage distribution of children[1]	Percent of children who demonstrate skills or secure emotional attachment											Secure emotional attachment to parent[3]
		Specific cognitive skills[2]					Specific motor skills[2]						
		Receptive vocabulary[4]	Expressive vocabulary[5]	Listening comprehension[6]	Matching/ discrimination[7]	Early counting[8]	Skillful walking[9]	Balance[10]	Fine motor control[11]	Uses stairs[12]	Alternating balance[13]	Motor planning[14]	
1	2	3	4	5	6	7	8	9	10	11	12	13	14
Socioeconomic status[21]													
Lowest 20 percent............	19.1 (0.53)	77.3 (0.89)	51.7 (1.12)	26.5 (0.78)	22.5 (0.67)	1.5 (0.12)	91.7 (0.37)	88.1 (0.60)	53.7 (0.75)	46.5 (0.63)	28.3 (0.66)	9.4 (0.26)	51.5 (1.90)
Middle 60 percent............	60.3 (0.73)	84.5 (0.47)	63.8 (0.69)	36.3 (0.56)	31.5 (0.53)	3.5 (0.17)	92.5 (0.24)	89.4 (0.41)	55.4 (0.60)	48.0 (0.52)	30.0 (0.60)	10.2 (0.27)	61.3 (1.49)
Highest 20 percent............	20.6 (0.56)	91.1 (0.43)	75.4 (0.80)	46.7 (0.70)	41.5 (0.70)	7.0 (0.38)	93.4 (0.24)	90.9 (0.40)	57.2 (0.64)	49.5 (0.54)	31.5 (0.63)	10.9 (0.29)	71.7 (1.86)

†Not applicable.
!Interpret data with caution. The coefficient of variation (CV) for this estimate is between 30 and 50 percent.
‡Reporting standards not met. The coefficient of variation (CV) for this estimate is 50 percent or greater.
[1]Weighted distribution of Early Childhood Longitudinal Study, Birth Cohort survey population between 22 and 25 months of age.
[2]Based on assessments collected using the Bayley Short Form Research Edition (BSF-R), a shortened field method of administering the Bayley Scales of Infant Development-II (BSID-II) (Bayley 1993). The scores are fully equated with the BSID-II; for more information, see NCES's *Early Childhood Longitudinal Study, Birth Cohort (ECLS-B) Psychometric Report for the 2-year Data Collection.* The proficiency probabilities indicate mastery of a specific skill or ability within cognitive or physical domains.
[3]Attachment was measured by trained observers using the Toddler Attachment Sort-45 Item (TAS-45) assessment. The formation of secure attachments in early childhood is an indicator that the child is able to use the parent as a secure base from which to explore novel stimuli in the environment freely and acquire a sense of self-confidence and adaptability to new and challenging situations. Other possible attachment classifications were avoidant, ambivalent, and disorganized/disoriented.
[4]Ability to recognize and understand spoken words or to indicate a named object by pointing.
[5]Verbal expressiveness using gestures, words, and sentences.
[6]Ability to understand actions depicted by a story, in pictures, or by verbal instructions.
[7]Ability to match objects by their properties (e.g., color) or differentiate one object from another.
[8]Knowledge of counting words, knowledge of ordinality, and understanding of simple quantities.
[9]Ability to walk independently.
[10]Ability to maintain balance when changing position.
[11]Ability to use fine motor control with hands, such as grasping a pencil or holding a piece of paper while scribbling.

[12]Ability to walk up and down stairs, with or without *alternating feet.*
[13]Ability to maintain balance when changing position or when in motion, such as jumping.
[14]Ability to anticipate, regulate, and execute motor movements, such as being able to replicate the motions of others.
[15]The type of nonparental care in which the child spent the most hours.
[16]Care provided in the child's home or in another private home by a relative (excluding parents).
[17]Care provided in the child's home or in another private home by a person unrelated to the child.
[18]Care provided in places such as early learning centers, nursery schools, and preschools.
[19]Children who spent an equal amount of time in each of two or more types of arrangements.
[20]Poverty status based on Census Bureau guidelines from 2002, which identify a dollar amount determined to meet a household's needs, given its size and composition. In 2002, a family of four was considered to live below the poverty threshold if its income was less than or equal to $18,392.
[21]Socioeconomic status (SES) was measured by a composite score based on parental education and occupations, and family income.
NOTE: Estimates weighted by W2R0. Estimates pertain to sample of children born in 2001 and assessed between 22 months and 25 months of age. Children younger than 22 months (less than 1 percent of the survey population) and children older than 25 months (approximately 9 percent of the survey population) are excluded from this table. Race categories exclude persons of Hispanic ethnicity. Detail may not sum to totals because of rounding and survey item nonresponse. Some data have been revised from previously published figures.
SOURCE: U.S. Department of Education, National Center for Education Statistics, Early Childhood Longitudinal Study, Birth Cohort 9-month-Kindergarten 2007 Restricted-Use Data File and Electronic Codebook. (This table was prepared December 2010.)

Table 220.30. Children's reading, language, mathematics, color knowledge, and fine motor skills at about 4 years of age, by child's age and selected characteristics: 2005–06

[Standard errors appear in parentheses]

Age and selected characteristic	Number of children (in thousands)		Percentage distribution of children		Average early reading scale score[1]		Expressive vocabulary (telling stories) score[2]		Average mathematics scale score[3]		Color knowledge— percent scoring 10 out of 10[4]		Fine motor score[5]	
1	2		3		4		5		6		7		8	
Less than 48 months														
Total	645	(22.3)	100.0	(†)	21.5	(0.32)	2.1	(0.04)	24.5	(0.31)	49.0	(1.89)	2.5	(0.05)
Sex of child														
Male	324	(15.8)	50.3	(1.79)	20.7	(0.48)	1.9	(0.05)	23.5	(0.44)	41.8	(3.03)	2.3	(0.07)
Female	321	(16.3)	49.7	(1.79)	22.4	(0.43)	2.2	(0.06)	25.5	(0.45)	56.1	(2.40)	2.8	(0.06)
Socioeconomic status[6]														
Lowest 20 percent	121	(11.3)	18.7	(1.50)	16.7	(0.35)	1.8	(0.09)	19.1	(0.52)	16.2	(3.65)	2.0	(0.10)
Middle 60 percent	380	(16.7)	58.9	(1.67)	21.0	(0.39)	2.1	(0.04)	24.2	(0.39)	50.9	(2.57)	2.6	(0.06)
Highest 20 percent	144	(10.7)	22.4	(1.59)	26.3	(0.67)	2.2	(0.07)	29.2	(0.64)	67.8	(2.97)	2.9	(0.09)
48 through 57 months														
Total	2,939	(23.2)	100.0	(†)	25.5	(0.22)	2.4	(0.02)	29.7	(0.20)	63.6	(0.84)	3.4	(0.02)
Sex of child														
Male	1,516	(18.2)	51.6	(0.48)	24.6	(0.26)	2.3	(0.03)	29.2	(0.25)	61.2	(1.12)	3.1	(0.04)
Female	1,423	(18.4)	48.4	(0.48)	26.4	(0.29)	2.6	(0.02)	30.3	(0.24)	66.1	(1.29)	3.7	(0.04)
Race/ethnicity of child														
White	1,604	(22.9)	54.7	(0.69)	27.4	(0.30)	2.6	(0.03)	31.6	(0.28)	71.0	(1.11)	3.5	(0.03)
Black	391	(11.5)	13.3	(0.37)	22.9	(0.46)	2.4	(0.04)	26.9	(0.44)	55.3	(2.44)	3.2	(0.06)
Hispanic	729	(18.1)	24.9	(0.56)	21.2	(0.36)	2.1	(0.04)	26.2	(0.34)	50.2	(1.79)	3.3	(0.06)
Asian	74	(3.6)	2.5	(0.12)	30.5	(0.56)	2.1	(0.05)	34.7	(0.42)	70.7	(2.37)	4.5	(0.09)
Pacific Islander	4	(0.7)	0.1	(0.03)	22.2	(2.24)	2.1	(0.18)	26.3	(3.41)	39.0	(9.21)	3.0	(0.34)
American Indian/Alaska Native	15	(1.5)	0.5	(0.05)	20.1	(0.89)	2.1	(0.09)	23.2	(0.98)	44.1	(3.83)	3.0	(0.18)
Two or more races	115	(9.0)	3.9	(0.31)	27.3	(0.89)	2.5	(0.06)	30.2	(0.82)	62.7	(3.04)	3.5	(0.12)
Primary type of nonparental care arrangement[7]														
No regular nonparental arrangement	535	(20.8)	18.2	(0.69)	22.9	(0.41)	2.3	(0.04)	26.9	(0.41)	51.6	(2.04)	3.1	(0.05)
Home-based care														
Relative care[8]	384	(18.8)	13.1	(0.65)	23.0	(0.44)	2.3	(0.05)	27.3	(0.42)	53.4	(2.58)	3.2	(0.07)
Nonrelative care[9]	220	(11.8)	7.5	(0.40)	25.1	(0.51)	2.5	(0.07)	30.2	(0.58)	63.8	(2.72)	3.3	(0.09)
Head Start	386	(22.3)	13.2	(0.73)	22.2	(0.35)	2.3	(0.05)	26.8	(0.40)	52.8	(2.55)	3.2	(0.07)
Other center-based care[10]	1,358	(26.2)	46.3	(0.83)	28.0	(0.32)	2.6	(0.03)	32.2	(0.27)	73.5	(1.19)	3.6	(0.04)
Multiple arrangements[11]	52	(6.8)	1.8	(0.23)	24.6	(0.93)	2.5	(0.10)	29.3	(0.92)	67.1	(5.44)	3.2	(0.23)
Mother's employment status														
Full-time (35 hours or more)	1,149	(26.5)	39.4	(0.85)	25.6	(0.30)	2.5	(0.03)	30.3	(0.24)	67.5	(1.09)	3.5	(0.05)
Part-time (less than 35 hours)	573	(17.7)	19.6	(0.60)	26.3	(0.35)	2.5	(0.04)	30.6	(0.35)	63.5	(2.06)	3.5	(0.05)
Looking for work	163	(9.9)	5.6	(0.34)	21.7	(0.57)	2.2	(0.07)	25.8	(0.74)	47.1	(3.83)	3.0	(0.11)
Not in labor force	1,010	(27.1)	34.6	(0.88)	25.5	(0.39)	2.4	(0.03)	29.3	(0.35)	62.1	(1.42)	3.3	(0.04)
No mother in household	22	(4.0)	0.8	(0.14)	21.6	(1.35)	2.3	(0.24)	26.3	(1.25)	57.3	(8.79)	3.0	(0.21)
Parents' highest level of education														
Less than high school	292	(11.9)	9.9	(0.41)	18.7	(0.41)	1.9	(0.06)	23.6	(0.47)	37.3	(2.74)	3.1	(0.09)
High school completion	672	(24.1)	22.9	(0.79)	21.6	(0.28)	2.3	(0.03)	25.9	(0.30)	52.0	(1.64)	3.1	(0.04)
Some college/vocational	998	(23.5)	34.0	(0.76)	24.3	(0.30)	2.5	(0.03)	28.9	(0.28)	63.4	(1.29)	3.4	(0.04)
Bachelor's degree	498	(17.6)	17.0	(0.57)	28.8	(0.40)	2.7	(0.04)	33.2	(0.28)	75.6	(1.69)	3.7	(0.08)
Any graduate education	475	(14.6)	16.2	(0.49)	33.0	(0.43)	2.7	(0.04)	36.2	(0.33)	81.0	(1.48)	3.9	(0.05)
Poverty status[12]														
Below poverty threshold	732	(21.0)	24.9	(0.71)	20.5	(0.26)	2.1	(0.03)	24.6	(0.28)	46.9	(1.76)	3.1	(0.05)
At or above poverty threshold	2,207	(28.4)	75.1	(0.71)	27.0	(0.24)	2.5	(0.02)	31.3	(0.21)	68.8	(0.91)	3.5	(0.03)
Socioeconomic status[6]														
Lowest 20 percent	576	(17.2)	19.6	(0.57)	19.3	(0.31)	2.0	(0.04)	23.6	(0.35)	43.1	(2.15)	3.0	(0.06)
Middle 60 percent	1,768	(27.3)	60.2	(0.77)	24.7	(0.22)	2.5	(0.03)	29.3	(0.23)	63.5	(1.07)	3.4	(0.03)
Highest 20 percent	594	(20.4)	20.2	(0.68)	32.7	(0.43)	2.8	(0.03)	36.2	(0.33)	81.6	(1.51)	3.9	(0.05)
58 months or more														
Total	356	(16.4)	100.0	(†)	29.7	(0.58)	2.6	(0.04)	34.5	(0.44)	71.1	(2.09)	4.1	(0.07)
Sex of child														
Male	179	(12.1)	50.3	(2.21)	29.0	(0.77)	2.6	(0.06)	34.2	(0.64)	66.5	(3.05)	3.7	(0.10)
Female	177	(10.5)	49.7	(2.21)	30.4	(0.76)	2.7	(0.06)	34.8	(0.51)	75.9	(2.49)	4.4	(0.10)
Socioeconomic status[6]														
Lowest 20 percent	91	(8.0)	25.5	(2.26)	22.3	(0.91)	2.1	(0.11)	28.4	(0.97)	47.4	(5.25)	3.6	(0.14)
Middle 60 percent	215	(14.7)	60.5	(2.47)	30.0	(0.75)	2.7	(0.05)	34.9	(0.54)	76.0	(2.63)	4.1	(0.10)
Highest 20 percent	50	(6.9)	14.0	(1.84)	40.3	(2.31)	2.9	(0.10)	42.8	(1.15)	88.5	(2.89)	4.7	(0.18)

†Not applicable.
[1]Reflects performance on language and literacy items (e.g., conventions of print, letter recognition, understanding of letter-sound relationships, phonological awareness, sight word recognition, and understanding words in the context of simple sentences). Potential score ranges from 0 to 85.
[2]Verbal expressiveness using gestures, words, and sentences. Potential score ranges from 0 to 5.
[3]Includes number sense, geometry, counting, operations, and patterns. Potential score ranges from 0 to 71.
[4]Percentage of children who scored 10 on a test with a potential score range of 0 to 10. These children were able to name the colors of five pictured objects (2 points per correct answer).
[5]Measures the ability to use fine motor skills in drawing basic forms and shapes. Potential score ranges from 0 to 7.
[6]Socioeconomic status (SES) was measured by a composite score based on parental education and occupations, and family income.
[7]The type of nonparental care in which the child spent the most hours.
[8]Care provided in the child's home or in another private home by a relative (excluding parents).
[9]Care provided in the child's home or in another private home by a person unrelated to the child.

[10]Care provided in places such as early learning centers, nursery schools, and preschools, excluding Head Start.
[11]Children who spent an equal amount of time in each of two or more types of arrangements.
[12]Poverty status based on Census Bureau guidelines from 2005, which identify a dollar amount determined to meet a household's needs, given its size and composition. In 2005, a family of four was considered to live below the poverty threshold if its income was less than or equal to $19,971.
NOTE: Estimates weighted by W3R0. Estimates pertain to a sample of children who were born in 2001. This table was designed to present data collected when the children were about 4 years of age (i.e., 48 to 57 months old). As shown in the table, some children were younger or older than this at the time data were collected, although 75 percent were within the target age range. Race categories exclude persons of Hispanic ethnicity. Detail may not sum to totals because of rounding and survey item nonresponse. Some data have been revised from previously published figures.
SOURCE: U.S. Department of Education, National Center for Education Statistics, Early Childhood Longitudinal Study, Birth Cohort (ECLS-B), Longitudinal 9-Month–Kindergarten 2007 Restricted-Use Data File. (This table was prepared December 2010.)

Table 220.40. Fall 2010 first-time kindergartners' reading, mathematics, and science scale scores, by selected child, family, and school characteristics: Fall 2010, spring 2011, spring 2012, and spring 2013

[Standard errors appear in parentheses]

Selected child, family, or school characteristic	Number of children (in thousands)	Percentage distribution of children	Mean reading score[1] — Kindergarten Fall 2010	Mean reading score[1] — Kindergarten Spring 2011	Mean reading score[1] — First grade, spring 2012	Mean reading score[1] — Second grade, spring 2013	Mean mathematics score[2] — Kindergarten Fall 2010	Mean mathematics score[2] — Kindergarten Spring 2011	Mean mathematics score[2] — First grade, spring 2012	Mean mathematics score[2] — Second grade, spring 2013	Mean science score[3] — Kindergarten, spring 2011	Mean science score[3] — First grade, spring 2012	Mean science score[3] — Second grade, spring 2013
1	2	3	4	5	6	7	8	9	10	11	12	13	14
Total	3,770 (26.0)	100.0 (†)	47.4 (0.29)	62.0 (0.37)	85.2 (0.39)	97.1 (0.27)	32.3 (0.29)	45.8 (0.33)	67.7 (0.37)	81.7 (0.32)	28.6 (0.21)	36.8 (0.27)	43.8 (0.24)
Sex of child													
Male	1,920 (20.5)	50.9 (0.46)	47.0 (0.32)	61.3 (0.43)	84.0 (0.46)	96.0 (0.32)	32.7 (0.33)	46.0 (0.40)	68.6 (0.47)	82.8 (0.37)	28.8 (0.20)	37.2 (0.26)	44.2 (0.25)
Female	1,850 (22.7)	49.1 (0.46)	47.8 (0.34)	62.8 (0.40)	86.5 (0.42)	98.2 (0.29)	31.8 (0.34)	45.6 (0.36)	66.8 (0.39)	80.7 (0.39)	28.5 (0.25)	36.4 (0.32)	43.4 (0.27)
Age of child at kindergarten entry, fall 2010													
Less than 5 years old	137 (19.9)	3.6 (0.53)	44.4 (0.95)	57.5 (1.20)	80.7 (1.35)	93.8 (0.99)	27.4 (0.88)	40.3 (1.07)	61.3 (1.11)	78.1 (1.07)	25.8 (0.55)	33.7 (0.79)	41.1 (0.70)
5 years old to 5 1/2 years old	1,620 (32.1)	43.0 (0.72)	45.9 (0.35)	60.2 (0.43)	83.6 (0.46)	96.0 (0.30)	29.8 (0.34)	43.5 (0.36)	65.3 (0.43)	80.2 (0.43)	27.4 (0.25)	35.2 (0.31)	42.7 (0.29)
More than 5 1/2 years old to 6 years old	1,663 (24.6)	44.1 (0.64)	48.4 (0.33)	63.4 (0.39)	86.5 (0.47)	97.9 (0.37)	34.0 (0.35)	47.5 (0.39)	69.5 (0.35)	83.0 (0.35)	29.6 (0.22)	37.9 (0.30)	44.7 (0.25)
More than 6 years old	350 (17.6)	9.3 (0.46)	50.7 (0.59)	65.4 (0.72)	88.7 (0.68)	99.3 (0.55)	37.3 (0.67)	50.7 (0.70)	72.8 (0.68)	84.6 (0.63)	30.9 (0.42)	39.9 (0.46)	45.7 (0.45)
Race/ethnicity of child													
White	1,973 (65.8)	52.3 (1.69)	49.2 (0.39)	64.2 (0.44)	88.2 (0.47)	99.4 (0.29)	35.0 (0.36)	48.7 (0.42)	71.9 (0.41)	85.2 (0.32)	31.6 (0.18)	40.1 (0.21)	46.4 (0.16)
Black	494 (45.3)	13.1 (1.20)	45.7 (0.50)	59.3 (0.69)	81.8 (0.90)	93.7 (0.68)	28.3 (0.46)	40.3 (0.51)	60.1 (0.85)	73.3 (0.93)	24.9 (0.52)	32.1 (0.71)	39.4 (0.70)
Hispanic	919 (46.0)	24.4 (1.23)	43.3 (0.38)	57.9 (0.42)	79.7 (0.63)	93.2 (0.54)	27.5 (0.36)	41.7 (0.46)	61.9 (0.61)	77.4 (0.57)	24.2 (0.30)	31.8 (0.45)	39.9 (0.44)
Asian	168 (25.5)	4.4 (0.68)	52.1 (0.95)	65.8 (1.06)	89.1 (1.11)	100.0 (0.59)	36.3 (0.80)	48.9 (0.60)	71.7 (0.74)	87.5 (0.55)	26.5 (0.44)	36.1 (0.63)	45.1 (0.53)
Pacific Islander	17 (4.8)	0.4 (0.13)	42.2 (2.40)	56.7 (2.79)	82.7 (3.76)	96.4 (2.92)	30.8 (3.62)	44.9 (4.10)	66.1 (4.25)	82.2 (3.90)	25.1 (1.61)	33.3 (1.64)	40.7 (2.68)
American Indian/Alaska Native	43 ! (20.0)	1.1 ! (0.53)	44.1 (0.83)	56.9 (1.31)	81.8 (1.56)	93.0 (1.57)	29.1 (0.99)	44.4 (1.02)	65.3 (1.36)	79.8 (1.33)	29.5 (0.83)	38.1 (1.09)	43.6 (0.69)
Two or more races	156 (8.0)	4.1 (0.21)	50.4 (0.84)	65.2 (0.92)	88.3 (0.90)	99.3 (0.66)	35.0 (0.68)	48.5 (0.87)	70.6 (0.98)	84.3 (0.91)	31.1 (0.41)	40.4 (0.45)	46.2 (0.41)
How often child exhibited positive learning behaviors, fall 2010[4]													
Never	51 (6.0)	1.4 (0.16)	36.8 (0.80)	46.9 (1.23)	63.2 (1.39)	80.1 (1.37)	19.5 (0.68)	30.0 (0.99)	47.7 (1.38)	62.0 (2.00)	22.5 (0.92)	27.6 (0.95)	34.0 (1.24)
Sometimes	886 (24.0)	24.1 (0.62)	42.3 (0.39)	55.8 (0.44)	77.2 (0.59)	91.2 (0.44)	26.5 (0.35)	39.6 (0.42)	60.4 (0.51)	75.7 (0.51)	25.9 (0.29)	33.2 (0.37)	40.6 (0.39)
Often	1,784 (32.0)	48.5 (0.84)	47.6 (0.28)	62.6 (0.39)	86.5 (0.41)	98.2 (0.27)	32.7 (0.35)	46.7 (0.40)	68.9 (0.41)	82.9 (0.37)	29.0 (0.24)	37.4 (0.28)	44.3 (0.25)
Very often	954 (33.4)	26.0 (0.85)	52.5 (0.48)	67.9 (0.57)	92.0 (0.47)	101.8 (0.37)	37.4 (0.38)	51.1 (0.40)	73.9 (0.45)	86.6 (0.35)	30.9 (0.23)	39.8 (0.35)	46.5 (0.25)
Primary type of nonparental care arrangement prior to kindergarten entry[5]													
No regular nonparental arrangement	746 (33.6)	20.4 (0.89)	44.8 (0.46)	59.3 (0.55)	82.2 (0.61)	94.8 (0.45)	29.4 (0.42)	43.4 (0.42)	64.4 (0.54)	79.6 (0.47)	26.9 (0.31)	35.0 (0.38)	42.1 (0.36)
Home-based care													
Relative care	550 (21.6)	15.1 (0.57)	45.0 (0.45)	60.4 (0.46)	83.2 (0.65)	95.9 (0.51)	30.2 (0.47)	43.9 (0.44)	65.8 (0.58)	79.8 (0.58)	27.9 (0.31)	36.0 (0.39)	42.9 (0.39)
Nonrelative care	239 (16.7)	6.5 (0.46)	48.3 (0.62)	63.7 (0.79)	88.3 (0.67)	99.0 (0.46)	34.7 (0.67)	48.3 (0.82)	71.2 (0.77)	84.4 (0.65)	30.7 (0.41)	38.6 (0.47)	45.4 (0.33)
Center-based care	2,030 (39.3)	55.5 (1.05)	49.0 (0.30)	63.3 (0.39)	86.6 (0.45)	98.0 (0.30)	33.7 (0.32)	47.0 (0.39)	69.1 (0.42)	82.7 (0.39)	29.2 (0.23)	37.4 (0.29)	44.4 (0.26)
Multiple arrangements	89 (7.6)	2.4 (0.21)	48.4 (0.63)	63.6 (0.80)	86.8 (1.09)	98.5 (0.77)	33.0 (0.58)	46.7 (0.80)	70.1 (0.94)	83.4 (0.90)	30.7 (0.53)	39.6 (0.65)	46.0 (0.63)
Parents' employment status, fall 2010[6]													
Two parents													
Both employed full time	907 (25.7)	26.5 (0.73)	50.1 (0.33)	65.2 (0.42)	88.9 (0.42)	99.7 (0.34)	35.1 (0.36)	48.9 (0.43)	71.8 (0.46)	84.8 (0.41)	30.4 (0.25)	39.0 (0.29)	45.6 (0.24)
One employed full time, one part time	570 (21.4)	16.6 (0.57)	49.6 (0.54)	64.5 (0.61)	88.8 (0.63)	100.3 (0.38)	35.2 (0.52)	48.9 (0.49)	71.8 (0.55)	85.5 (0.45)	30.8 (0.28)	39.5 (0.34)	46.0 (0.31)
One employed full time, one looking for work	152 (10.4)	4.4 (0.30)	46.0 (0.84)	61.4 (1.00)	82.9 (1.07)	96.8 (0.82)	30.8 (0.70)	44.5 (0.82)	66.6 (0.81)	81.1 (0.93)	27.4 (0.60)	35.6 (0.71)	42.7 (0.71)
One employed full time, one not in labor force	823 (31.0)	24.0 (0.89)	43.4 (0.51)	62.2 (0.55)	85.6 (0.67)	97.4 (0.53)	32.7 (0.74)	46.3 (0.53)	68.5 (0.59)	82.8 (0.53)	29.0 (0.25)	37.1 (0.33)	44.3 (0.29)
Other combination	210 (13.9)	6.1 (0.39)	45.2 (0.68)	59.5 (0.86)	81.2 (0.98)	93.8 (0.81)	29.0 (0.57)	43.2 (0.68)	63.8 (0.91)	78.2 (0.81)	26.8 (0.47)	34.4 (0.63)	41.5 (0.55)
Single parent													
Employed full time	342 (17.4)	10.0 (0.49)	45.2 (0.50)	59.3 (0.64)	81.9 (0.74)	93.8 (0.58)	29.4 (0.50)	42.2 (0.58)	63.4 (0.72)	76.9 (0.88)	26.5 (0.46)	34.1 (0.55)	41.3 (0.51)
Employed part time	133 (10.1)	3.9 (0.29)	44.0 (0.54)	58.6 (0.77)	82.7 (0.89)	94.8 (0.70)	29.0 (0.67)	42.0 (0.70)	63.7 (1.04)	77.6 (0.73)	27.0 (0.54)	35.0 (0.55)	41.7 (0.66)
Looking for work	104 (10.1)	3.0 (0.29)	42.3 (0.87)	56.2 (1.06)	77.8 (1.86)	92.4 (1.16)	26.8 (0.74)	39.6 (0.93)	59.8 (1.37)	74.2 (1.30)	25.7 (0.70)	33.1 (0.87)	40.8 (0.85)
Not in labor force	116 (9.5)	3.4 (0.28)	43.4 (0.78)	56.4 (1.06)	78.0 (1.45)	91.2 (1.27)	27.1 (0.74)	40.6 (1.10)	60.2 (1.59)	74.9 (1.78)	25.9 (0.71)	33.2 (0.89)	39.5 (0.86)
No parent in household	68 (6.5)	2.0 (0.19)	42.4 (0.82)	56.8 (0.85)	79.2 (1.32)	93.0 (1.01)	26.5 (0.86)	39.6 (0.88)	59.1 (1.38)	74.0 (1.51)	26.3 (0.76)	33.2 (0.89)	40.6 (0.81)
Parents' highest level of education[7]													
Less than high school	296 (18.3)	7.9 (0.48)	40.0 (0.61)	53.7 (0.55)	74.5 (0.66)	88.5 (0.71)	23.9 (0.58)	38.0 (0.70)	57.5 (0.76)	72.9 (0.83)	21.7 (0.33)	28.6 (0.42)	36.9 (0.54)
High school completion	767 (32.6)	20.4 (0.58)	43.1 (0.40)	57.4 (0.39)	79.5 (0.52)	92.4 (0.41)	27.7 (0.40)	40.9 (0.35)	62.0 (0.44)	76.9 (0.43)	25.3 (0.31)	32.9 (0.35)	40.4 (0.34)
Some college/vocational	1,267 (33.2)	33.7 (0.84)	46.2 (0.29)	60.9 (0.49)	83.7 (0.45)	96.6 (0.33)	31.2 (0.31)	44.7 (0.40)	66.5 (0.48)	80.8 (0.41)	28.4 (0.23)	36.5 (0.30)	43.6 (0.25)
Bachelor's degree	783 (27.7)	20.8 (0.73)	50.7 (0.38)	65.8 (0.43)	89.7 (0.49)	100.8 (0.24)	35.9 (0.32)	49.8 (0.35)	72.5 (0.41)	85.8 (0.34)	31.2 (0.22)	39.8 (0.28)	46.8 (0.21)
Any graduate education	650 (27.3)	17.3 (0.72)	54.2 (0.49)	69.0 (0.51)	93.1 (0.43)	103.0 (0.27)	39.2 (0.40)	52.6 (0.43)	75.8 (0.43)	88.5 (0.35)	32.8 (0.22)	42.0 (0.30)	48.1 (0.20)
Household type, fall 2010													
Two-parent household	2,725 (42.6)	77.7 (0.90)	48.5 (0.32)	63.3 (0.38)	86.8 (0.42)	98.4 (0.28)	33.5 (0.33)	47.3 (0.37)	69.6 (0.36)	83.5 (0.32)	29.5 (0.20)	37.9 (0.25)	44.8 (0.21)
Mother-only household	670 (29.2)	19.1 (0.82)	44.3 (0.40)	58.2 (0.55)	80.9 (0.63)	93.3 (0.44)	28.6 (0.43)	41.5 (0.42)	62.4 (0.65)	76.2 (0.63)	26.3 (0.43)	33.9 (0.47)	40.9 (0.49)
Father-only household	45 (5.3)	1.3 (0.15)	43.9 (0.85)	57.1 (1.11)	80.2 (1.57)	93.1 (1.14)	29.0 (0.93)	42.0 (1.06)	63.4 (1.37)	76.9 (1.30)	28.3 (0.61)	34.5 (1.02)	42.1 (1.05)
Other household type	68 (6.5)	1.9 (0.19)	42.4 (0.82)	56.8 (0.85)	79.2 (1.32)	93.0 (1.01)	26.5 (0.86)	39.6 (0.88)	59.1 (1.38)	74.0 (1.51)	26.3 (0.76)	33.2 (0.89)	40.6 (0.81)

See notes at end of table.

Table 220.40. Fall 2010 first-time kindergartners' reading, mathematics, and science scale scores, by selected child, family, and school characteristics: Fall 2010, spring 2011, spring 2012, and spring 2013—Continued

[Standard errors appear in parentheses]

Selected child, family, or school characteristic	Number of children (in thousands)	Percentage distribution of children	Mean reading score[1]				Mean mathematics score[2]				Mean science score[3]		
			Kindergarten		First grade, spring 2012	Second grade, spring 2013	Kindergarten		First grade, spring 2012	Second grade, spring 2013	Kindergarten, spring 2011	First grade, spring 2012	Second grade, spring 2013
			Fall 2010	Spring 2011			Fall 2010	Spring 2011					
1	2	3	4	5	6	7	8	9	10	11	12	13	14
Primary home language													
English	3,138 (39.4)	83.4 (0.80)	48.4 (0.29)	63.1 (0.40)	86.5 (0.40)	98.0 (0.27)	33.3 (0.29)	46.8 (0.34)	69.0 (0.38)	82.6 (0.34)	29.9 (0.21)	38.2 (0.26)	44.8 (0.24)
Non-English	581 (29.0)	15.4 (0.77)	42.5 (0.53)	56.5 (0.62)	78.6 (0.82)	92.1 (0.61)	26.6 (0.55)	40.9 (0.63)	61.3 (0.70)	77.4 (0.71)	21.8 (0.29)	29.6 (0.48)	38.8 (0.56)
Primary language not identified	44 (7.1)	1.2 (0.19)	45.5 (1.51)	61.2 (1.81)	82.0 (2.39)	95.1 (2.09)	29.1 (1.44)	41.8 (1.46)	62.9 (1.92)	80.2 (1.88)	24.5 (0.90)	32.4 (1.12)	40.4 (1.46)
Poverty status, spring 2011[8]													
Below poverty threshold	810 (34.8)	23.7 (0.99)	42.4 (0.40)	56.3 (0.44)	77.7 (0.58)	90.9 (0.50)	26.7 (0.43)	40.4 (0.48)	60.2 (0.59)	75.2 (0.66)	24.3 (0.31)	31.6 (0.45)	39.4 (0.46)
100 to 199 percent of poverty threshold	809 (24.3)	23.7 (0.68)	45.8 (0.32)	60.6 (0.56)	84.1 (0.62)	96.2 (0.42)	30.6 (0.40)	44.0 (0.48)	66.2 (0.58)	80.7 (0.48)	27.7 (0.31)	35.8 (0.38)	43.2 (0.33)
200 percent or more of poverty threshold	1,798 (43.4)	52.6 (1.13)	50.8 (0.31)	65.5 (0.38)	89.6 (0.38)	100.6 (0.25)	36.0 (0.29)	49.5 (0.34)	72.4 (0.32)	85.7 (0.30)	31.3 (0.18)	40.0 (0.21)	46.4 (0.18)
Socioeconomic status[9]													
Lowest 20 percent	741 (31.1)	19.7 (0.83)	41.3 (0.45)	55.2 (0.41)	76.3 (0.54)	89.9 (0.48)	25.4 (0.44)	38.9 (0.50)	58.9 (0.58)	74.2 (0.61)	23.5 (0.34)	30.7 (0.40)	38.5 (0.42)
Middle 60 percent	2,249 (35.8)	59.8 (0.77)	47.0 (0.25)	61.8 (0.40)	85.4 (0.40)	97.4 (0.27)	32.1 (0.27)	45.7 (0.35)	67.8 (0.39)	81.9 (0.33)	28.8 (0.20)	37.0 (0.26)	44.0 (0.23)
Highest 20 percent	773 (31.6)	20.5 (0.84)	54.3 (0.47)	69.1 (0.47)	93.2 (0.44)	103.1 (0.27)	39.2 (0.34)	52.8 (0.38)	75.8 (0.37)	88.5 (0.29)	32.8 (0.20)	42.1 (0.29)	48.2 (0.19)
School type, fall 2010													
Public	3,369 (19.1)	89.4 (0.27)	47.0 (0.32)	61.7 (0.40)	84.8 (0.43)	96.7 (0.30)	31.8 (0.32)	45.3 (0.36)	67.3 (0.40)	81.4 (0.34)	28.3 (0.23)	36.5 (0.29)	43.5 (0.26)
Private	401 (12.0)	10.6 (0.27)	50.7 (0.73)	65.0 (0.90)	88.8 (0.95)	100.7 (0.55)	36.2 (0.59)	50.1 (0.85)	71.4 (0.96)	84.8 (0.70)	31.1 (0.37)	39.3 (0.50)	45.9 (0.41)

†Not applicable.
!Interpret data with caution. The coefficient of variation (CV) for this estimate is between 30 and 50 percent.

[1]Reflects performance on questions measuring basic skills (print familiarity, letter recognition, beginning and ending sounds, rhyming words, and word recognition); vocabulary knowledge; and reading comprehension, including identifying information specifically stated in text (e.g., definitions, facts, and supporting details), making complex inferences from texts, and considering the text objectively and judging its appropriateness and quality. Possible scores for the reading assessment range from 0 to 120.

[2]Reflects performance on questions on number sense, properties, and operations; measurement; geometry and spatial sense; data analysis, statistics, and probability (measured with a set of simple questions assessing children's ability to read a graph); and prealgebra skills such as identification of patterns. Possible scores for the mathematics assessment range from 0 to 113.

[3]Science was not assessed in the fall of kindergarten. Reflects performance on questions on physical sciences, life sciences, environmental sciences, and scientific inquiry. Possible scores for the science assessment range from 0 to 64.

[4]Derived from child's approaches to learning scale score in fall of the kindergarten year. This score is based on teachers' reports on how often students exhibit positive learning behaviors in seven areas: attentiveness, task persistence, eagerness to learn, learning independence, ability to adapt easily to changes in routine, organization, and ability to follow classroom rules. Possible scores range from 1 to 4, with higher scores indicating that a child exhibits positive learning behaviors more often. Fall 2010 scores were categorized into the four anchor points on the original scale—1 (never), 2 (sometimes), 3 (often), and 4 (very often)—by rounding the mean score to the nearest whole number.

[5]The type of nonparental care in which the child spent the most hours. "Multiple arrangements" refers to children who spent an equal amount of time in each of two or more arrangements.

[6]Parents who reported working at least 35 hours per week are defined as employed full time, while those who reported working less than 35 hours per week are defined as employed part time. Those neither employed nor looking for work are not in the labor force.

[7]Parents' highest level of education is the highest level of education achieved by either of the parents or guardians in a two-parent household, by the only parent in a single-parent household, or by any guardian in a household with no parents. These data were collected during the child's kindergarten year.

[8]Poverty status is based on preliminary U.S. Census income thresholds for 2010, which identify incomes determined to meet household needs, given family size and composition. For example, a family of three with one child was below the poverty threshold if its income was less than $17,552 in 2010.

[9]Socioeconomic status (SES) was measured by a composite score based on parental education and occupations and household income during the child's kindergarten year.

NOTE: Estimates weighted by W6C6P_6T0. Estimates pertain to a sample of children who were enrolled in kindergarten for the first time in the 2010–11 school year. Most of the children were in second grade in 2012–13, but 6 percent were in first grade or other grades (e.g., third grade, ungraded classrooms). Two parents may refer to two biological parents, two adoptive parents, or one biological/adoptive parent and one other parent/partner. Single parent refers to one biological or adoptive parent only. In households without parents, the guardian or guardians may be related or unrelated to the child. Estimates differ from previously published figures because scale scores were recalculated to represent the kindergarten through second-grade assessment item pools and weights were adjusted to account for survey nonresponse at each data collection wave. Race categories exclude persons of Hispanic ethnicity. Detail may not sum to totals because of rounding and survey item nonresponse.

SOURCE: U.S. Department of Education, National Center for Education Statistics, Early Childhood Longitudinal Study, Kindergarten Class of 2010–11 (ECLS-K:2011), Kindergarten–Second Grade Restricted-Use Data File. (This table was prepared August 2015.)

Table 220.45. Fall 2010 first-time kindergartners' approaches to learning, interpersonal skills, and self-control scale scores, by selected child, family, and school characteristics: Fall 2010, spring 2011, spring 2012, and spring 2013

[Standard errors appear in parentheses]

Selected child, family, or school characteristic	Mean approaches to learning score[1] — Kindergarten Fall 2010	Kindergarten Spring 2011	First grade, spring 2012	Second grade, spring 2013	Mean interpersonal skills score[2] — Kindergarten Fall 2010	Kindergarten Spring 2011	First grade, spring 2012	Second grade, spring 2013	Mean self-control score[3] — Kindergarten Fall 2010	Kindergarten Spring 2011	First grade, spring 2012	Second grade, spring 2013
	2	3	4	5	6	7	8	9	10	11	12	13
Total	3.0 (0.01)	3.1 (0.01)	3.1 (0.01)	3.1 (0.01)	3.0 (0.01)	3.2 (0.01)	3.2 (0.01)	3.1 (0.01)	3.1 (0.01)	3.2 (0.01)	3.2 (0.01)	3.2 (0.01)
Sex of child												
Male	2.8 (0.01)	3.0 (0.01)	2.9 (0.01)	2.9 (0.02)	2.9 (0.01)	3.0 (0.02)	3.0 (0.01)	3.0 (0.02)	3.0 (0.01)	3.1 (0.01)	3.1 (0.01)	3.1 (0.01)
Female	3.1 (0.02)	3.3 (0.02)	3.3 (0.02)	3.3 (0.01)	3.1 (0.02)	3.3 (0.02)	3.3 (0.02)	3.3 (0.02)	3.2 (0.01)	3.3 (0.01)	3.3 (0.01)	3.3 (0.02)
Age of child at kindergarten entry, fall 2010												
Less than 5 years old	2.8 (0.06)	3.0 (0.06)	3.1 (0.07)	3.0 (0.06)	3.0 (0.05)	3.2 (0.05)	3.2 (0.07)	3.1 (0.07)	3.1 (0.05)	3.2 (0.04)	3.3 (0.05)	3.2 (0.06)
5 years old to 5 1/2 years old	2.9 (0.02)	3.1 (0.02)	3.0 (0.01)	3.0 (0.02)	3.0 (0.02)	3.1 (0.02)	3.1 (0.01)	3.1 (0.01)	3.1 (0.02)	3.2 (0.02)	3.2 (0.01)	3.2 (0.01)
More than 5 1/2 years old to 6 years old	3.0 (0.02)	3.1 (0.02)	3.1 (0.02)	3.1 (0.02)	3.0 (0.01)	3.2 (0.01)	3.2 (0.02)	3.1 (0.02)	3.1 (0.01)	3.2 (0.03)	3.2 (0.02)	3.3 (0.02)
More than 6 years old	3.1 (0.03)	3.3 (0.03)	3.2 (0.03)	3.2 (0.03)	3.1 (0.03)	3.2 (0.03)	3.2 (0.03)	3.2 (0.03)	3.2 (0.03)	3.3 (0.03)	3.3 (0.03)	3.3 (0.03)
Race/ethnicity of child												
White	3.0 (0.02)	3.2 (0.02)	3.2 (0.01)	3.1 (0.01)	3.1 (0.02)	3.2 (0.02)	3.2 (0.01)	3.2 (0.01)	3.1 (0.02)	3.3 (0.02)	3.3 (0.01)	3.3 (0.01)
Black	2.8 (0.02)	3.0 (0.02)	2.9 (0.03)	2.9 (0.03)	3.0 (0.02)	3.0 (0.04)	3.0 (0.02)	3.0 (0.03)	3.0 (0.03)	3.0 (0.02)	3.0 (0.03)	3.0 (0.03)
Hispanic	2.9 (0.02)	3.1 (0.02)	3.1 (0.02)	3.1 (0.02)	3.0 (0.02)	3.1 (0.02)	3.1 (0.02)	3.1 (0.02)	3.1 (0.02)	3.2 (0.02)	3.3 (0.02)	3.4 (0.04)
Asian	3.0 (0.05)	3.2 (0.05)	3.3 (0.05)	3.3 (0.05)	3.0 (0.06)	3.1 (0.05)	3.2 (0.05)	3.2 (0.06)	3.1 (0.06)	3.2 (0.06)	3.3 (0.04)	3.3 (0.04)
Pacific Islander	‡ (†)	3.2 (0.14)	3.0 (0.16)	3.1 (0.11)	‡ (†)	3.3 (0.17)	3.3 (0.14)	3.2 (0.16)	‡ (†)	3.3 (0.13)	‡ (†)	3.3 (0.11)
American Indian/Alaska Native	3.0 (0.08)	3.1 (0.08)	3.1 (0.05)	3.2 (0.07)	3.2 (0.04)	3.3 (0.08)	3.3 (0.08)	3.1 (0.12)	3.1 (0.05)	3.3 (0.09)	3.2 (0.06)	3.2 (0.06)
Two or more races	3.0 (0.04)	3.2 (0.04)	3.1 (0.04)	3.2 (0.04)	3.1 (0.04)	3.2 (0.04)	3.2 (0.04)	3.2 (0.03)	3.1 (0.03)	3.2 (0.04)	3.3 (0.03)	3.2 (0.04)
How often child exhibited positive learning behaviors, fall 2010[4]												
Never	† (†)	1.8 (0.06)	2.3 (0.09)	2.2 (0.10)	1.9 (0.07)	2.2 (0.06)	2.6 (0.06)	2.6 (0.09)	2.1 (0.06)	2.4 (0.07)	2.8 (0.06)	2.7 (0.07)
Sometimes	† (†)	2.5 (0.02)	2.6 (0.02)	2.6 (0.02)	2.5 (0.01)	2.7 (0.02)	2.8 (0.02)	2.8 (0.02)	2.5 (0.02)	2.8 (0.02)	2.9 (0.02)	2.9 (0.02)
Often	† (†)	3.2 (0.01)	3.1 (0.01)	3.1 (0.02)	3.0 (0.01)	3.1 (0.02)	3.2 (0.01)	3.2 (0.01)	3.1 (0.01)	3.3 (0.01)	3.2 (0.01)	3.3 (0.01)
Very often	† (†)	3.7 (0.01)	3.5 (0.02)	3.5 (0.01)	3.6 (0.01)	3.6 (0.01)	3.4 (0.02)	3.4 (0.01)	3.6 (0.01)	3.6 (0.01)	3.5 (0.01)	3.5 (0.01)
Primary type of nonparental care arrangement prior to kindergarten entry[5]												
No regular nonparental arrangement	2.9 (0.02)	3.2 (0.02)	3.1 (0.02)	3.1 (0.02)	3.0 (0.02)	3.2 (0.02)	3.2 (0.02)	3.1 (0.02)	3.1 (0.02)	3.2 (0.02)	3.2 (0.02)	3.3 (0.02)
Home-based care												
Relative care	2.9 (0.03)	3.1 (0.03)	3.1 (0.03)	3.1 (0.03)	3.0 (0.03)	3.1 (0.03)	3.2 (0.02)	3.1 (0.02)	3.1 (0.02)	3.2 (0.02)	3.2 (0.02)	3.2 (0.02)
Nonrelative care	3.0 (0.03)	3.2 (0.08)	3.1 (0.02)	3.1 (0.03)	3.1 (0.03)	3.2 (0.03)	3.2 (0.03)	3.1 (0.03)	3.1 (0.03)	3.2 (0.05)	3.2 (0.03)	3.2 (0.04)
Center-based care	3.0 (0.01)	3.1 (0.02)	3.2 (0.02)	3.1 (0.01)	3.0 (0.01)	3.2 (0.01)	3.2 (0.01)	3.1 (0.01)	3.1 (0.01)	3.1 (0.02)	3.2 (0.01)	3.2 (0.01)
Multiple arrangements	3.0 (0.05)	3.1 (0.05)	3.1 (0.05)	3.0 (0.05)	3.0 (0.06)	3.2 (0.05)	3.2 (0.05)	3.1 (0.05)	3.1 (0.05)	3.2 (0.05)	3.2 (0.05)	3.2 (0.04)
Parents' employment status, fall 2010[6]												
Two parents												
Both employed full time	3.1 (0.02)	3.2 (0.02)	3.2 (0.02)	3.2 (0.01)	3.1 (0.02)	3.2 (0.02)	3.2 (0.01)	3.2 (0.02)	3.2 (0.02)	3.3 (0.02)	3.3 (0.01)	3.3 (0.01)
One employed full time, one part time	3.1 (0.02)	3.2 (0.02)	3.1 (0.03)	3.2 (0.02)	3.1 (0.02)	3.2 (0.02)	3.3 (0.02)	3.2 (0.02)	3.3 (0.02)	3.3 (0.05)	3.3 (0.02)	3.2 (0.02)
One employed full time, one looking for work	2.9 (0.06)	3.1 (0.05)	2.9 (0.05)	3.0 (0.05)	3.0 (0.04)	3.1 (0.05)	3.1 (0.04)	3.1 (0.05)	3.1 (0.05)	3.1 (0.05)	3.3 (0.05)	3.2 (0.05)
One employed full time, one not in labor force	3.0 (0.02)	3.2 (0.02)	3.2 (0.02)	3.2 (0.02)	3.1 (0.02)	3.2 (0.02)	3.2 (0.02)	3.1 (0.02)	3.2 (0.02)	3.3 (0.02)	3.3 (0.02)	3.3 (0.03)
Other combination	2.9 (0.03)	3.1 (0.03)	3.0 (0.03)	3.0 (0.04)	3.0 (0.03)	3.2 (0.04)	3.1 (0.04)	3.1 (0.04)	3.1 (0.03)	3.2 (0.04)	3.1 (0.04)	3.2 (0.03)
Single parent												
Employed full time	2.8 (0.03)	3.0 (0.03)	2.9 (0.03)	2.9 (0.03)	2.9 (0.03)	3.0 (0.04)	3.0 (0.03)	3.0 (0.04)	3.0 (0.03)	3.0 (0.04)	3.0 (0.04)	3.0 (0.03)
Employed part time	2.7 (0.08)	3.0 (0.08)	3.0 (0.06)	2.8 (0.07)	2.8 (0.06)	2.9 (0.07)	3.0 (0.05)	2.8 (0.06)	2.9 (0.08)	3.0 (0.07)	3.1 (0.07)	3.0 (0.05)
Looking for work	2.8 (0.05)	2.9 (0.08)	2.8 (0.08)	2.9 (0.07)	2.9 (0.05)	2.9 (0.06)	2.9 (0.07)	2.9 (0.06)	2.9 (0.04)	3.1 (0.06)	3.1 (0.04)	3.0 (0.06)
Not in labor force	2.8 (0.05)	2.9 (0.05)	2.7 (0.08)	2.7 (0.07)	2.8 (0.05)	2.9 (0.06)	2.9 (0.08)	2.9 (0.06)	2.8 (0.06)	2.9 (0.06)	3.1 (0.06)	2.9 (0.06)
No parent in household	2.7 (0.05)	2.9 (0.05)	2.7 (0.08)	2.7 (0.07)	2.8 (0.05)	2.9 (0.06)	2.9 (0.08)	2.8 (0.06)	2.8 (0.06)	2.9 (0.06)	3.1 (0.04)	2.8 (0.06)
Parents' highest level of education[7]												
Less than high school	2.8 (0.04)	3.0 (0.03)	3.0 (0.03)	2.9 (0.03)	2.9 (0.04)	3.0 (0.04)	3.0 (0.02)	3.0 (0.03)	3.0 (0.04)	3.1 (0.03)	3.1 (0.02)	3.0 (0.03)
High school completion	2.9 (0.02)	3.1 (0.02)	3.0 (0.03)	3.0 (0.02)	3.0 (0.02)	3.0 (0.02)	3.1 (0.02)	3.1 (0.02)	3.0 (0.02)	3.1 (0.03)	3.2 (0.02)	3.1 (0.02)
Some college/vocational	2.9 (0.02)	3.1 (0.02)	3.0 (0.02)	3.0 (0.02)	3.0 (0.02)	3.1 (0.02)	3.1 (0.02)	3.1 (0.02)	3.1 (0.02)	3.2 (0.02)	3.2 (0.02)	3.2 (0.02)
Bachelor's degree	3.1 (0.02)	3.3 (0.02)	3.2 (0.02)	3.2 (0.02)	3.1 (0.02)	3.3 (0.02)	3.3 (0.02)	3.3 (0.02)	3.2 (0.02)	3.3 (0.02)	3.3 (0.02)	3.3 (0.02)
Any graduate education	3.1 (0.02)	3.3 (0.03)	3.3 (0.02)	3.3 (0.02)	3.1 (0.01)	3.3 (0.02)	3.3 (0.02)	3.3 (0.02)	3.2 (0.02)	3.3 (0.02)	3.4 (0.02)	3.4 (0.02)
Household type, fall 2010												
Two-parent household	3.0 (0.01)	3.2 (0.02)	3.2 (0.01)	3.2 (0.01)	3.1 (0.01)	3.2 (0.01)	3.1 (0.01)	3.2 (0.01)	3.2 (0.01)	3.3 (0.01)	3.3 (0.01)	3.3 (0.01)
Mother-only household	2.8 (0.02)	3.0 (0.02)	2.9 (0.03)	2.9 (0.02)	2.9 (0.02)	3.0 (0.03)	3.0 (0.02)	3.0 (0.02)	3.0 (0.02)	3.0 (0.02)	3.1 (0.02)	3.1 (0.02)
Father-only household	2.8 (0.06)	2.9 (0.06)	2.8 (0.07)	2.8 (0.09)	2.9 (0.08)	3.0 (0.08)	2.9 (0.08)	2.9 (0.09)	3.0 (0.09)	3.1 (0.06)	3.0 (0.08)	3.0 (0.08)
Other household type	2.7 (0.05)	2.9 (0.05)	2.7 (0.08)	2.7 (0.07)	2.8 (0.05)	2.9 (0.06)	2.9 (0.08)	2.8 (0.06)	2.8 (0.06)	2.9 (0.06)	2.9 (0.06)	2.8 (0.06)

See notes at end of table.

Table 220.45. Fall 2010 first-time kindergartners' approaches to learning, interpersonal skills, and self-control scale scores, by selected child, family, and school characteristics: Fall 2010, spring 2011, spring 2012, and spring 2013—Continued

[Standard errors appear in parentheses]

Selected child, family, or school characteristic	Mean approaches to learning score[1]				Mean interpersonal skills score[2]				Mean self-control score[3]			
	Kindergarten		First grade, spring 2012	Second grade, spring 2013	Kindergarten		First grade, spring 2012	Second grade, spring 2013	Kindergarten		First grade, spring 2012	Second grade, spring 2013
	Fall 2010	Spring 2011			Fall 2010	Spring 2011			Fall 2010	Spring 2011		
1	2	3	4	5	6	7	8	9	10	11	12	13
Primary home language												
English	3.0 (0.01)	3.2 (0.02)	3.1 (0.01)	3.1 (0.01)	3.0 (0.01)	3.2 (0.02)	3.2 (0.01)	3.1 (0.01)	3.1 (0.01)	3.2 (0.01)	3.2 (0.01)	3.2 (0.01)
Non-English	3.0 (0.03)	3.1 (0.02)	3.1 (0.02)	3.1 (0.02)	2.9 (0.03)	3.1 (0.03)	3.1 (0.02)	3.1 (0.02)	3.1 (0.03)	3.2 (0.02)	3.2 (0.02)	3.3 (0.02)
Primary language not identified	2.8 (0.08)	3.0 (0.10)	3.1 (0.10)	3.1 (0.10)	2.9 (0.07)	3.1 (0.08)	3.2 (0.10)	3.2 (0.09)	3.0 (0.08)	3.2 (0.10)	3.2 (0.11)	3.4 (0.07)
Poverty status, spring 2011[8]												
Below poverty threshold	2.8 (0.02)	3.0 (0.02)	2.9 (0.02)	2.9 (0.02)	2.9 (0.02)	3.1 (0.03)	3.0 (0.02)	3.0 (0.02)	3.0 (0.02)	3.1 (0.02)	3.1 (0.02)	3.1 (0.02)
100 to 199 percent of poverty threshold	3.0 (0.02)	3.2 (0.02)	3.1 (0.03)	3.1 (0.02)	3.0 (0.02)	3.2 (0.02)	3.1 (0.02)	3.1 (0.02)	3.1 (0.02)	3.2 (0.02)	3.2 (0.02)	3.2 (0.02)
200 percent or more of poverty threshold	3.1 (0.02)	3.2 (0.02)	3.2 (0.01)	3.2 (0.01)	3.1 (0.02)	3.2 (0.02)	3.3 (0.01)	3.2 (0.01)	3.2 (0.01)	3.3 (0.01)	3.3 (0.01)	3.3 (0.01)
Socioeconomic status[9]												
Lowest 20 percent	2.8 (0.02)	3.0 (0.02)	2.9 (0.02)	2.9 (0.02)	2.9 (0.02)	3.1 (0.02)	3.0 (0.02)	3.0 (0.02)	3.0 (0.02)	3.1 (0.02)	3.1 (0.02)	3.1 (0.02)
Middle 60 percent	3.0 (0.02)	3.1 (0.02)	3.1 (0.01)	3.1 (0.01)	3.0 (0.01)	3.2 (0.02)	3.2 (0.01)	3.1 (0.01)	3.1 (0.01)	3.2 (0.02)	3.2 (0.01)	3.2 (0.01)
Highest 20 percent	3.1 (0.02)	3.3 (0.01)	3.3 (0.01)	3.3 (0.01)	3.1 (0.02)	3.3 (0.01)	3.3 (0.01)	3.3 (0.02)	3.2 (0.02)	3.3 (0.01)	3.4 (0.01)	3.4 (0.02)
School type, fall 2010												
Public	3.0 (0.01)	3.1 (0.02)	3.1 (0.01)	3.1 (0.01)	3.0 (0.01)	3.2 (0.02)	3.2 (0.01)	3.1 (0.01)	3.1 (0.01)	3.2 (0.01)	3.2 (0.01)	3.2 (0.01)
Private	3.1 (0.03)	3.2 (0.03)	3.2 (0.03)	3.1 (0.04)	3.2 (0.03)	3.2 (0.03)	3.2 (0.03)	3.2 (0.03)	3.2 (0.04)	3.2 (0.03)	3.2 (0.03)	3.2 (0.03)

†Not applicable.

‡Reporting standards not met (too few cases for a reliable estimate).

[1]The approaches to learning scale is based on teachers' reports on how students rate in seven areas: attentiveness, task persistence, eagerness to learn, learning independence, ability to adapt easily to changes in routine, organization, and ability to follow classroom rules. Possible scores on the scale range from 1 to 4, with higher scores indicating that a child exhibits positive learning behaviors more often.

[2]The interpersonal skills scale is based on teachers' reports on the student's skill in forming and maintaining friendships; getting along with people who are different; comforting or helping other children; expressing feelings, ideas, and opinions in positive ways; and showing sensitivity to the feelings of others. Possible scores on the scale range from 1 to 4, with higher scores indicating that a child interacted with others in a positive way more often.

[3]The self-control scale is based on teachers' reports on the student's ability to control behavior by respecting the property rights of others, controlling temper, accepting peer ideas for group activities, and responding appropriately to pressure from peers. Possible scores on the scale range from 1 to 4, with higher scores indicating that a child exhibited behaviors indicative of self-control more often.

[4]Derived from child's approaches to learning scale score in fall of the kindergarten year. This score is based on teachers' reports on how often students exhibit positive learning behaviors in seven areas: attentiveness, task persistence, eagerness to learn, learning independence, ability to adapt easily to changes in routine, organization, and ability to follow classroom rules. Possible scores range from 1 to 4. Fall 2010 scores were categorized into the four anchor points on the original scale—1 (never), 2 (sometimes), 3 (often), and 4 (very often)—by rounding the mean score to the nearest whole number.

[5]The type of nonparental care in which the child spent the most hours. Multiple arrangements refers to children who spent an equal amount of time in each of two or more arrangements.

[6]Parents who reported working at least 35 hours per week are defined as employed full time, while those who reported working less than 35 hours per week are defined as employed part time. Those neither employed nor looking for work are not in the labor force.

[7]Parents' highest level of education is the highest level of education achieved by either of the parents or guardians in a two-parent household, by the only parent in a single-parent household, or by any guardian in a household with no parents. These data were collected during the child's kindergarten year.

[8]Poverty status is based on preliminary U.S. Census income thresholds for 2010, which identify incomes determined to meet household needs, given family size and composition. For example, a family of three with one child was below the poverty threshold if its income was less than $17,552 in 2010.

[9]Socioeconomic status (SES) was measured by a composite score based on parental education and occupations and household income during the child's kindergarten year.

NOTE: Estimates weighted by W6C6P_6T0. Estimates pertain to a sample of children who were enrolled in kindergarten for the first time in the 2010–11 school year. Most of the children were in second grade in 2012–13, but 6 percent were in first grade or other grades (e.g., third grade, ungraded classrooms). Two parents may refer to two biological parents, two adoptive parents, or one biological/adoptive parent and one other parent/partner. Single parent refers to one biological or adoptive parent only. In households without parents, the guardian or guardians may be related or unrelated to the child. Estimates differ from previously published figures because weights were adjusted to account for survey nonresponse at each data collection wave. Race categories exclude persons of Hispanic ethnicity. Detail may not sum to totals because of rounding and survey item nonresponse.

SOURCE: U.S. Department of Education, National Center for Education Statistics, Early Childhood Longitudinal Study, Kindergarten Class of 2010–11 (ECLS-K:2011), Kindergarten–Second Grade Restricted-Use Data File. (This table was prepared August 2015.)

Table 220.50. Number and percentage distribution of kindergartners, by fall 2010 kindergarten entry status and selected child, family, and school characteristics: 2010–11

[Standard errors appear in parentheses]

Selected child, family, or school characteristic	All kindergartners[1]		Percentage distribution of kindergartners, by entry status[2]					
	Number (in thousands)	Percentage distribution, by selected characteristics	Total[1]		Early kindergarten entrants	On-time kindergarten entrants	Delayed kindergarten entrants	Kindergarten repeaters
1	2	3	4		5	6	7	8
Total..........	4,054 (5.7)	100.0 (†)	100.0 (†)		1.5 (0.17)	86.6 (0.91)	5.9 (0.41)	6.0 (0.87)
Sex of child								
Male..........	2,097 (18.9)	51.7 (0.47)	100.0 (†)		1.1 (0.16)	85.0 (1.03)	6.8 (0.63)	7.1 (0.90)
Female..........	1,957 (19.7)	48.3 (0.47)	100.0 (†)		1.9 (0.24)	88.3 (0.96)	4.9 (0.35)	4.9 (0.90)
Age of child at first kindergarten entry[3]								
Less than 5 years old..........	234 (33.2)	6.4 (0.90)	100.0 (†)		12.3 (2.57)	47.2 (7.36)	1.2 (0.32)	39.3 (8.87)
5 years old to 5 1/2 years old..........	1,557 (31.0)	42.3 (0.62)	100.0 (†)		1.0 (0.18)	92.3 (0.56)	1.3 (0.18)	5.4 (0.42)
More than 5 1/2 years old to 6 years old..........	1,572 (31.6)	42.7 (0.68)	100.0 (†)		0.5 (0.11)	92.3 (0.49)	4.7 (0.48)	2.5 (0.29)
More than 6 years old..........	315 (15.7)	8.6 (0.41)	100.0 (†)		‡ (†)	60.4 (3.20)	38.3 (3.14)	1.1 ! (0.47)
Race/ethnicity of child								
White..........	2,080 (70.5)	51.3 (1.75)	100.0 (†)		1.0 (0.17)	86.5 (0.75)	7.4 (0.64)	5.1 (0.59)
Black..........	547 (52.2)	13.5 (1.29)	100.0 (†)		1.8 ! (0.64)	85.4 (3.29)	3.1 (0.40)	9.7 ! (3.26)
Hispanic..........	1,004 (54.0)	24.8 (1.33)	100.0 (†)		1.7 (0.32)	88.3 (0.93)	3.7 (0.40)	6.3 (0.84)
Asian..........	186 (28.4)	4.6 (0.70)	100.0 (†)		5.1 ! (1.55)	84.0 (2.27)	6.1 (1.15)	4.8 ! (1.70)
Pacific Islander..........	17 (3.0)	0.4 (0.07)	100.0 (†)		‡ (†)	90.3 (4.38)	‡ (†)	‡ (†)
American Indian/Alaska Native..........	49 ! (21.4)	1.2 ! (0.53)	100.0 (†)		‡ (†)	81.3 (2.01)	8.0 (1.87)	8.2 (2.37)
Two or more races..........	169 (9.2)	4.2 (0.23)	100.0 (†)		1.5 ! (0.49)	86.4 (1.85)	6.6 (1.28)	5.5 (1.19)
Primary type of nonparental care arrangement prior to kindergarten entry[4]								
No regular nonparental arrangement..........	815 (29.3)	21.5 (0.75)	100.0 (†)		1.3 (0.25)	85.1 (1.21)	5.6 (0.55)	8.1 (1.12)
Home-based care								
Relative care..........	560 (17.3)	14.8 (0.44)	100.0 (†)		1.6 (0.31)	87.3 (1.06)	4.7 (0.51)	6.5 (0.85)
Nonrelative care..........	225 (12.7)	5.9 (0.33)	100.0 (†)		0.9 ! (0.35)	87.9 (1.46)	7.4 (1.26)	3.8 (0.74)
Center-based care..........	2,103 (33.3)	55.4 (0.90)	100.0 (†)		1.7 (0.25)	87.0 (1.02)	6.2 (0.53)	5.1 (0.96)
Multiple arrangements..........	90 (6.5)	2.4 (0.17)	100.0 (†)		0.7 ! (0.34)	86.6 (1.87)	5.9 (1.51)	6.7 (1.87)
Parents' employment status, fall 2010[5]								
Two parents								
Both employed full time..........	824 (24.5)	25.0 (0.68)	100.0 (†)		1.8 (0.25)	87.3 (0.97)	6.4 (0.75)	4.5 (0.59)
One employed full time, one part time..........	524 (20.1)	15.9 (0.51)	100.0 (†)		1.5 (0.35)	88.1 (0.77)	6.8 (0.59)	3.5 (0.65)
One employed full time, one looking for work..........	141 (8.0)	4.3 (0.23)	100.0 (†)		2.4 ! (0.87)	86.8 (2.08)	3.5 ! (1.31)	7.3 (1.51)
One employed full time, one not in labor force..........	779 (28.2)	23.6 (0.81)	100.0 (†)		1.1 (0.22)	86.8 (1.11)	6.7 (0.64)	5.4 (0.90)
Other combination..........	220 (12.5)	6.7 (0.35)	100.0 (†)		1.7 (0.46)	84.8 (1.56)	5.8 (1.05)	7.7 (1.41)
Single parent								
Employed full time..........	348 (17.0)	10.5 (0.47)	100.0 (†)		1.6 (0.41)	88.4 (1.49)	4.1 (0.53)	5.9 (1.46)
Employed part time..........	135 (8.3)	4.1 (0.24)	100.0 (†)		1.0 ! (0.45)	87.6 (2.03)	5.5 (1.16)	5.8 (1.51)
Looking for work..........	116 (8.9)	3.5 (0.26)	100.0 (†)		‡ (†)	84.3 (2.53)	6.1 (1.48)	8.8 (2.31)
Not in labor force..........	137 (10.1)	4.1 (0.30)	100.0 (†)		‡ (†)	83.0 (2.42)	5.7 (1.14)	9.9 (2.02)
No parent in household..........	79 (5.6)	2.4 (0.17)	100.0 (†)		‡ (†)	82.2 (2.26)	3.8 ! (1.52)	12.1 (2.28)
Parents' highest level of education[6]								
Less than high school..........	388 (18.6)	9.6 (0.46)	100.0 (†)		2.0 (0.50)	82.7 (1.48)	4.7 (0.85)	10.7 (1.58)
High school completion..........	852 (23.0)	21.1 (0.56)	100.0 (†)		1.1 (0.26)	86.3 (1.20)	4.4 (0.53)	8.1 (1.15)
Some college/vocational..........	1,292 (27.3)	32.0 (0.67)	100.0 (†)		1.0 (0.18)	88.4 (1.23)	4.8 (0.55)	5.9 (1.09)
Bachelor's degree..........	792 (24.6)	19.6 (0.60)	100.0 (†)		1.8 (0.34)	85.3 (0.98)	8.4 (0.67)	4.5 (0.79)
Any graduate education..........	711 (29.2)	17.6 (0.73)	100.0 (†)		2.2 (0.44)	87.0 (0.75)	7.4 (0.64)	3.4 (0.60)
Household type, fall 2010								
Two-parent household..........	2,563 (50.1)	75.1 (0.92)	100.0 (†)		1.5 (0.19)	87.1 (0.75)	6.3 (0.50)	5.1 (0.65)
Mother-only household..........	719 (31.1)	21.1 (0.84)	100.0 (†)		1.2 (0.27)	86.8 (1.59)	4.6 (0.48)	7.3 (1.57)
Father-only household..........	51 (3.5)	1.5 (0.10)	100.0 (†)		‡ (†)	83.5 (2.75)	9.7 ! (2.96)	4.6 ! (2.04)
Other household type..........	79 (5.6)	2.3 (0.17)	100.0 (†)		‡ (†)	82.2 (2.26)	3.8 ! (1.52)	12.1 (2.28)
Primary home language								
English..........	3,338 (36.8)	82.6 (0.89)	100.0 (†)		1.3 (0.17)	86.8 (0.90)	6.3 (0.45)	5.7 (0.84)
Non-English..........	663 (33.7)	16.4 (0.84)	100.0 (†)		2.6 (0.67)	85.1 (1.64)	4.0 (0.53)	8.3 (1.56)
Primary language not identified..........	42 (4.9)	1.0 (0.12)	100.0 (†)		1.9 ! (0.89)	90.6 (2.55)	‡ (†)	5.6 ! (2.18)
Poverty status[7]								
Below poverty threshold..........	893 (35.8)	26.3 (1.03)	100.0 (†)		1.2 (0.30)	84.5 (1.64)	4.4 (0.53)	9.9 (1.63)
100 to 199 percent of poverty threshold..........	762 (18.1)	22.5 (0.51)	100.0 (†)		0.9 (0.20)	87.1 (1.31)	5.7 (0.64)	6.3 (1.07)
200 percent or more of poverty threshold..........	1,736 (44.5)	51.2 (1.25)	100.0 (†)		1.8 (0.26)	87.2 (0.64)	7.3 (0.57)	3.8 (0.52)
Socioeconomic status[8]								
Lowest 20 percent..........	799 (29.9)	19.8 (0.75)	100.0 (†)		1.5 (0.33)	84.1 (1.46)	4.3 (0.51)	10.1 (1.55)
Middle 60 percent..........	2,429 (30.6)	60.2 (0.73)	100.0 (†)		1.2 (0.16)	87.1 (1.01)	5.9 (0.52)	5.7 (0.88)
Highest 20 percent..........	808 (33.5)	20.0 (0.83)	100.0 (†)		2.4 (0.47)	87.2 (0.70)	7.2 (0.61)	3.2 (0.59)
School type								
Public..........	3,329 (48.4)	88.5 (0.18)	100.0 (†)		0.8 (0.11)	87.8 (0.86)	5.6 (0.42)	5.8 (0.77)
Private..........	432 (5.1)	11.5 (0.18)	100.0 (†)		6.8 (1.12)	78.0 (1.87)	7.8 (0.90)	7.5 (2.18)

†Not applicable.

!Interpret data with caution. The coefficient of variation (CV) for this estimate is between 30 and 50 percent.

‡Reporting standards not met. Either there are too few cases for a reliable estimate or the coefficient of variation (CV) is 50 percent or greater.

[1]Includes students with missing kindergarten entry status information.

[2]A child who enrolled in kindergarten for the first time in 2010–11 is classified as an early, on-time, or delayed kindergarten entrant depending on whether the parent reported enrolling the child early, enrolling the child when he or she was old enough, or waiting until the child was older relative to school guidelines about when children can start school based on their birth date. A child is classified as a kindergarten repeater if the parent reported that 2010–11 was the child's second (or third or more) year of kindergarten.

[3]Most of the children first entered kindergarten in 2010–11, but the children who were repeating kindergarten in 2010–11—that is, the "Kindergarten repeaters" shown in column 8—had first entered kindergarten in an earlier school year.

[4]The type of nonparental care in which the child spent the most hours. "Multiple arrangements" refers to children who spent an equal amount of time in each of two or more arrangements.

[5]Parents who reported working at least 35 hours per week are defined as employed full time, while those who reported working less than 35 hours per week are defined as employed part time. Those neither employed nor looking for work are not in the labor force.

[6]Parents' highest level of education is the highest level of education achieved by either of the parents or guardians in a two-parent household, by the only parent in a single-parent household, or by any guardian in a household with no parents.

[7]Poverty status is based on preliminary U.S. Census income thresholds for 2010, which identify incomes determined to meet household needs, given family size and composition. For example, a family of three with one child was below the poverty threshold if its income was less than $17,552 in 2010.

[8]Socioeconomic status (SES) was measured by a composite score based on parental education and occupations and household income at the time of data collection.

NOTE: Estimates weighted by W1_2P0. Estimates pertain to a sample of children who were enrolled in kindergarten in the 2010–11 school year. Two parents may refer to two biological parents, two adoptive parents, or one biological/adoptive parent and one other parent/partner. Single parent refers to one biological or adoptive parent only. In households without parents, the guardian or guardians may be related or unrelated to the child. Race categories exclude persons of Hispanic ethnicity. Detail may not sum to totals because of rounding and survey item nonresponse. Some data have been revised from previously published figures.

SOURCE: U.S. Department of Education, National Center for Education Statistics, Early Childhood Longitudinal Study, Kindergarten Class of 2010–11 (ECLS-K:2011), Kindergarten-First Grade Restricted-Use Data File. (This table was prepared February 2015.)

Table 220.60. Fall 2010 kindergartners' reading, mathematics, science, and approaches to learning scale scores, by kindergarten entry status and time of assessment: Fall 2010, spring 2011, spring 2012, and spring 2013

[Standard errors appear in parentheses]

Type and time of assessment	Overall mean score[1]		Mean score by fall 2010 kindergarten entry status[2]							
			Early kindergarten entrants		On-time kindergarten entrants		Delayed kindergarten entrants		Kindergarten repeaters	
1	2		3		4		5		6	
Reading scale score[3]										
Kindergarten										
Fall 2010........................	47.2	(0.26)	45.9	(1.39)	47.2	(0.28)	48.8	(0.67)	49.1	(0.79)
Spring 2011........................	61.6	(0.34)	58.5	(2.21)	61.9	(0.35)	63.1	(0.74)	60.4	(0.81)
First grade, spring 2012........................	84.3	(0.34)	80.9	(2.29)	84.9	(0.38)	86.2	(0.72)	79.2	(1.10)
Second grade, spring 2013........................	96.3	(0.24)	94.3	(1.48)	96.8	(0.27)	97.7	(0.60)	91.2	(1.13)
Mathematics scale score[4]										
Kindergarten										
Fall 2010........................	32.0	(0.28)	28.6	(1.32)	31.9	(0.30)	35.7	(0.76)	32.4	(0.70)
Spring 2011........................	45.4	(0.33)	42.0	(1.93)	45.6	(0.35)	48.6	(0.84)	44.6	(0.76)
First grade, spring 2012........................	67.1	(0.35)	62.3	(2.21)	67.4	(0.38)	71.2	(0.95)	63.5	(0.92)
Second grade, spring 2013........................	81.1	(0.29)	77.3	(2.18)	81.5	(0.31)	83.4	(0.67)	76.8	(1.12)
Science scale score[5]										
Kindergarten, spring 2011........................	28.3	(0.20)	25.4	(0.98)	28.6	(0.20)	30.7	(0.42)	27.4	(0.53)
First grade, spring 2012........................	36.4	(0.25)	33.5	(1.25)	36.7	(0.26)	38.9	(0.43)	34.6	(0.70)
Second grade, spring 2013........................	43.4	(0.22)	41.7	(1.26)	43.7	(0.23)	45.0	(0.42)	41.3	(0.67)
Approaches to learning score[6]										
Kindergarten										
Fall 2010........................	3.0	(0.01)	3.0	(0.07)	3.0	(0.01)	3.0	(0.03)	2.9	(0.05)
Spring 2011........................	3.1	(0.01)	3.0	(0.08)	3.1	(0.01)	3.1	(0.03)	3.0	(0.05)
First grade, spring 2012........................	3.1	(0.01)	3.1	(0.12)	3.1	(0.01)	3.1	(0.04)	2.8	(0.05)
Second grade, spring 2013........................	3.1	(0.01)	3.1	(0.09)	3.1	(0.01)	3.1	(0.04)	2.8	(0.06)

[1]Includes students with missing kindergarten entry status information.
[2]A child who enrolled in kindergarten for the first time in 2010–11 is classified as an early, on-time, or delayed kindergarten entrant depending on whether the parent reported enrolling the child early, enrolling the child when he or she was old enough, or waiting until the child was older relative to school guidelines about when children can start school based on their birth date. A child is classified as a kindergarten repeater if the parent reported that 2010–11 was the child's second (or more) year of kindergarten.
[3]Reflects performance on questions measuring basic skills (print familiarity, letter recognition, beginning and ending sounds, rhyming words, and word recognition); vocabulary knowledge; and reading comprehension, including identifying information specifically stated in text (e.g., definitions, facts, and supporting details), making complex inferences from texts, and considering the text objectively and judging its appropriateness and quality. Possible scores for the reading assessment range from 0 to 120.
[4]Reflects performance on questions on number sense, properties, and operations; measurement; geometry and spatial sense; data analysis, statistics, and probability (measured with a set of simple questions assessing children's ability to read a graph); and prealgebra skills such as identification of patterns. Possible scores for the mathematics assessment range from 0 to 113.

[5]Science was not assessed in the fall of kindergarten. Reflects performance on questions on physical sciences, life sciences, environmental sciences, and scientific inquiry. Possible scores for the science assessment range from 0 to 64.
[6]The approaches to learning scale is based on teachers' reports on how students rate in seven areas: attentiveness, task persistence, eagerness to learn, learning independence, ability to adapt easily to changes in routine, organization, and ability to follow classroom rules. Possible scores on the scale range from 1 to 4, with higher scores indicating that a child exhibits positive learning behaviors more often.
NOTE: Estimates weighted by W6C6P_20. Estimates pertain to a sample of children who were enrolled in kindergarten in the 2010–11 school year. The same children were assessed in spring 2012 (when the majority were in first grade) and in spring 2013 (when the majority were in second grade). Estimates differ from previously published figures because reading, mathematics, and science scale scores were recalculated to represent the kindergarten through second-grade assessment item pools and because weights were adjusted to account for survey nonresponse at each data collection wave, including the latest round of data collection (spring 2013).
SOURCE: U.S. Department of Education, National Center for Education Statistics, Early Childhood Longitudinal Study, Kindergarten Class of 2010–11 (ECLS-K:2011), Kindergarten-Second Grade Restricted-Use Data File. (This table was prepared October 2015.)

Table 220.70. Mean reading scale scores and specific reading skills of fall 1998 first-time kindergartners, by time of assessment and selected characteristics: Selected years, fall 1998 through spring 2007

[Standard errors appear in parentheses]

Selected characteristic	Mean reading scale score						Percentage of children with specific reading skills, eighth grade, spring 2007			
	Kindergarten		First grade, spring 2000	Third grade, spring 2002	Fifth grade, spring 2004	Eighth grade, spring 2007	Deriving meaning from text	Interpreting beyond text	Evaluating nonfiction	Evaluating complex syntax
	Fall 1998	Spring 1999								
1	2	3	4	5	6	7	8	9	10	11
Total......	36 (0.2)	47 (0.3)	79 (0.6)	128 (0.8)	151 (0.7)	169 (0.8)	83 (0.8)	66 (0.8)	29 (0.9)	6 (0.3)
Sex										
Male......	35 (0.3)	46 (0.4)	77 (0.9)	126 (1.0)	149 (1.0)	166 (1.2)	80 (1.1)	63 (1.2)	26 (1.3)	5 (0.4)
Female......	36 (0.3)	48 (0.5)	81 (0.8)	131 (1.0)	153 (0.9)	172 (0.9)	85 (0.8)	69 (1.0)	31 (1.2)	7 (0.4)
Race/ethnicity										
White......	37 (0.3)	48 (0.4)	83 (0.8)	135 (0.9)	158 (0.8)	176 (0.8)	89 (0.7)	74 (0.8)	36 (1.1)	8 (0.4)
Black......	32 (0.5)	42 (0.8)	70 (1.3)	114 (2.0)	135 (1.9)	149 (2.4)	66 (2.6)	45 (2.4)	10 (1.6)	2 (0.3)
Hispanic......	33 (0.5)	44 (0.8)	72 (1.1)	118 (1.3)	142 (1.1)	160 (1.3)	76 (1.3)	57 (1.4)	18 (1.4)	3 (0.3)
Asian......	41 (1.3)	53 (1.7)	90 (2.0)	135 (2.3)	157 (1.8)	178 (2.0)	89 (1.6)	75 (2.2)	41 (3.3)	10 (1.2)
Other[1]......	34 (1.4)	46 (1.7)	76 (2.4)	125 (3.9)	150 (4.3)	167 (3.8)	82 (3.3)	64 (4.1)	25 (3.6)	5 (0.8)
Parents' highest level of education[2]										
Less than high school......	30 (0.5)	39 (0.7)	64 (1.5)	103 (1.7)	128 (1.8)	141 (2.2)	58 (2.5)	37 (2.1)	5 (0.7)	1 (0.1)
High school......	32 (0.3)	42 (0.5)	71 (1.0)	118 (1.2)	140 (1.2)	159 (1.3)	75 (1.3)	55 (1.4)	16 (1.3)	3 (0.3)
Some college......	35 (0.4)	46 (0.4)	78 (0.8)	128 (1.1)	151 (1.0)	169 (1.1)	84 (1.1)	66 (1.2)	25 (1.1)	4 (0.3)
Bachelor's or higher degree......	40 (0.5)	52 (0.7)	89 (1.1)	143 (0.8)	165 (0.8)	183 (0.8)	93 (0.6)	81 (0.8)	49 (1.3)	12 (0.6)
Primary home language[2]										
English......	36 (0.2)	47 (0.3)	80 (0.7)	130 (0.8)	152 (0.7)	170 (0.9)	84 (0.8)	67 (0.9)	30 (0.9)	6 (0.3)
Non-English......	33 (0.6)	44 (0.8)	70 (1.1)	113 (1.3)	138 (1.4)	157 (1.6)	73 (1.6)	54 (1.4)	17 (1.4)	4 (0.5)
Socioeconomic status[2]										
Lowest 20 percent......	30 (0.3)	39 (0.5)	64 (1.1)	105 (1.3)	129 (1.3)	145 (1.5)	62 (1.7)	41 (1.5)	8 (0.9)	1 (0.2)
Middle 60 percent......	35 (0.3)	46 (0.3)	78 (0.7)	128 (0.8)	151 (0.7)	169 (0.8)	84 (0.8)	66 (0.9)	26 (0.9)	5 (0.3)
Highest 20 percent......	41 (0.6)	54 (0.8)	92 (1.4)	145 (0.9)	167 (0.9)	186 (0.8)	95 (0.6)	84 (0.9)	52 (1.5)	14 (0.8)
Grade level in spring 2007										
Eighth grade or above......	36 (0.2)	48 (0.4)	82 (0.6)	133 (0.7)	155 (0.7)	173 (0.9)	86 (0.8)	70 (0.9)	32 (1.0)	7 (0.3)
Below eighth grade......	30 (0.5)	37 (0.6)	57 (1.4)	100 (1.9)	126 (2.2)	143 (2.5)	58 (2.7)	39 (2.5)	9 (2.0)	2 ! (0.7)
School type across all waves of the study										
Public school all years......	35 (0.3)	46 (0.4)	77 (0.6)	126 (0.9)	149 (0.8)	166 (0.9)	80 (0.9)	63 (1.0)	25 (1.0)	5 (0.2)
Private school all years......	39 (0.6)	52 (0.9)	88 (1.5)	140 (1.4)	163 (1.0)	184 (1.2)	94 (0.7)	81 (1.4)	47 (2.5)	10 (0.8)
Change in school type during study......	38 (0.8)	51 (1.1)	84 (1.9)	134 (1.8)	158 (1.4)	177 (1.8)	89 (1.4)	74 (1.9)	38 (2.7)	9 (1.1)

! Interpret data with caution. The coefficient of variation (CV) for this estimate is between 30 and 50 percent.
[1] Includes persons of all other races and Two or more races.
[2] Status during kindergarten year.
NOTE: Reading scale ranges from 0 to 209. Estimates for each assessment round include all children assessed in English in that round, even if they were not assessed in English in a previous round. In fall 1998, 8 percent of the kindergarten sample was not administered the English battery because of nonpassing scores on the OLDS (Oral Language Development Scale) English proficiency assessment. By spring of first grade, this percentage had decreased to 2 percent. In the third grade and subsequent years, the OLDS was not administered and all children were assessed in English. Most of the children were in first grade in 1999–2000, but 5 percent were in kindergarten or other grades (e.g., second grade, ungraded classrooms); most were in third

grade in 2001–02, but 11 percent were in second grade or other grades (e.g., fourth grade, ungraded classrooms); most were in fifth grade in 2003–04, but 14 percent were in fourth grade or other grades (e.g., sixth grade, ungraded classrooms); most were in eighth grade in 2006–07, but 14 percent were in seventh grade or other grades (e.g., ninth grade or ungraded classrooms). Data were calculated using C1_7FC0 weight. Estimates differ from previously published figures because the data were recalibrated to represent the kindergarten through eighth-grade reading assessment item pool. Race categories exclude persons of Hispanic ethnicity.
SOURCE: U.S. Department of Education, National Center for Education Statistics, Early Childhood Longitudinal Study, Kindergarten Class of 1998–99 (ECLS-K), Longitudinal Kindergarten–Eighth Grade Full Sample Public-Use Data File, fall 1998, spring 1999, spring 2000, spring 2002, spring 2004, and spring 2007. (This table was prepared September 2009.)

Table 220.80. Mean mathematics and science scale scores and specific mathematics skills of fall 1998 first-time kindergartners, by time of assessment and selected characteristics: Selected years, fall 1998 through spring 2007

[Standard errors appear in parentheses]

Selected characteristic	Mathematics — Mean scale score						Percentage of children with specific skills, eighth grade, spring 2007			Science — Mean scale score		
	Kindergarten Fall 1998	Kindergarten Spring 1999	First grade, spring 2000	Third grade, spring 2002	Fifth grade, spring 2004	Eighth grade, spring 2007	Rate and measurement	Fractions	Area and volume	Third grade, spring 2002	Fifth grade, spring 2004	Eighth grade, spring 2007
1	2	3	4	5	6	7	8	9	10	11	12	13
Total	26 (0.2)	37 (0.3)	62 (0.4)	100 (0.7)	124 (0.7)	140 (0.6)	68 (0.9)	38 (1.0)	16 (0.8)	51 (0.4)	65 (0.4)	84 (0.5)
Sex												
Male	26 (0.3)	37 (0.4)	63 (0.6)	103 (0.8)	126 (0.9)	141 (0.8)	70 (1.3)	40 (1.3)	18 (1.0)	53 (0.6)	67 (0.6)	85 (0.5)
Female	26 (0.3)	37 (0.4)	61 (0.5)	97 (0.9)	121 (1.0)	139 (0.8)	65 (1.3)	35 (1.4)	14 (1.0)	49 (0.6)	63 (0.6)	82 (0.6)
Race/ethnicity												
White	29 (0.3)	40 (0.4)	67 (0.6)	106 (0.8)	130 (0.8)	146 (0.6)	77 (1.0)	46 (1.3)	21 (1.1)	56 (0.5)	70 (0.4)	89 (0.5)
Black	22 (0.4)	31 (0.6)	52 (0.8)	84 (1.8)	105 (1.8)	123 (1.6)	40 (2.3)	13 (1.8)	4 (1.2)	40 (1.1)	52 (1.1)	69 (1.3)
Hispanic	22 (0.4)	32 (0.5)	57 (0.9)	93 (1.1)	119 (1.1)	136 (1.0)	62 (1.7)	29 (2.1)	10 (1.1)	44 (0.7)	60 (0.7)	78 (0.8)
Asian	30 (1.0)	40 (1.2)	65 (1.7)	107 (2.7)	135 (2.4)	150 (2.3)	81 (3.1)	59 (3.8)	38 (3.7)	53 (1.5)	67 (1.6)	89 (1.1)
Other[1]	25 (1.0)	36 (1.3)	60 (2.1)	97 (3.3)	122 (3.6)	138 (3.2)	65 (5.2)	34 (4.7)	15 (3.2)	49 (2.0)	63 (2.2)	82 (2.6)
Parents' highest level of education[2]												
Less than high school	20 (0.4)	28 (0.6)	49 (1.1)	81 (1.4)	105 (1.9)	122 (2.1)	41 (2.9)	14 (1.9)	3 (0.8)	37 (0.9)	50 (1.0)	68 (1.2)
High school	23 (0.3)	33 (0.5)	56 (0.7)	91 (1.0)	114 (1.0)	131 (0.8)	53 (1.4)	21 (1.2)	7 (0.7)	45 (0.6)	59 (0.7)	77 (0.7)
Some college	26 (0.3)	37 (0.4)	62 (0.6)	100 (1.0)	124 (0.9)	141 (0.8)	70 (1.3)	35 (1.5)	13 (1.0)	51 (0.6)	65 (0.6)	84 (0.6)
Bachelor's or higher degree	31 (0.3)	42 (0.4)	70 (0.6)	111 (0.9)	136 (0.8)	152 (0.7)	85 (1.2)	59 (1.5)	30 (1.4)	59 (0.6)	73 (0.5)	92 (0.4)
Primary home language[2]												
English	27 (0.2)	38 (0.3)	63 (0.4)	101 (0.7)	125 (0.8)	141 (0.6)	69 (0.9)	38 (1.0)	16 (0.8)	52 (0.4)	66 (0.5)	84 (0.5)
Non-English	21 (0.4)	30 (0.6)	55 (0.8)	91 (1.1)	117 (1.2)	135 (1.1)	58 (1.7)	30 (1.9)	13 (1.2)	41 (0.8)	57 (0.8)	77 (0.9)
Socioeconomic status[2]												
Lowest 20 percent	20 (0.3)	28 (0.4)	50 (0.8)	83 (1.1)	105 (1.3)	123 (1.2)	42 (1.8)	14 (1.1)	4 (0.5)	38 (0.8)	51 (0.9)	70 (0.9)
Middle 60 percent	26 (0.2)	37 (0.3)	62 (0.4)	99 (0.7)	123 (0.7)	140 (0.6)	67 (0.9)	35 (1.0)	13 (0.8)	51 (0.4)	65 (0.4)	84 (0.5)
Highest 20 percent	32 (0.4)	43 (0.5)	72 (0.7)	115 (0.9)	139 (0.9)	154 (0.7)	88 (1.0)	63 (1.8)	33 (1.8)	60 (0.6)	75 (0.6)	94 (0.5)
Grade level in spring 2007												
Eighth-grade or above	27 (0.2)	38 (0.3)	65 (0.4)	103 (0.7)	127 (0.8)	143 (0.6)	73 (1.0)	41 (1.1)	18 (0.8)	53 (0.4)	67 (0.4)	86 (0.5)
Below eighth grade	20 (0.4)	27 (0.6)	47 (1.2)	79 (1.6)	103 (1.9)	121 (1.8)	37 (2.5)	14 (2.5)	5 (1.5)	40 (1.1)	53 (1.3)	69 (1.4)
School type across all waves of the study												
Public school all years	26 (0.2)	36 (0.4)	61 (0.5)	99 (0.9)	122 (0.9)	139 (0.7)	66 (1.1)	35 (1.2)	15 (0.8)	50 (0.5)	64 (0.5)	82 (0.6)
Private school all years	31 (0.6)	43 (0.8)	69 (1.0)	107 (1.7)	133 (1.5)	149 (1.3)	82 (2.4)	50 (3.0)	22 (1.9)	56 (1.0)	71 (0.9)	90 (0.8)
Change in school type during study	28 (0.7)	39 (0.8)	66 (1.1)	103 (1.5)	128 (1.6)	144 (1.3)	73 (2.0)	44 (2.6)	20 (2.1)	55 (1.0)	69 (1.0)	88 (0.9)

[1]Includes persons of all other races and Two or more races.
[2]Status during kindergarten year.
NOTE: Mathematics scale ranges from 0 to 172, and science scale ranges from 0 to 108. Estimates for each assessment round include all children assessed in that round, including children assessed in Spanish. In kindergarten and first grade, the mathematics assessment was administered in Spanish for Spanish-speaking children who did not pass the English OLDS (Oral Language Development Scale). All assessments were administered in English in third grade through eighth grade. Most of the children were in first grade in 1999–2000, but 5 percent were in kindergarten or other grades (e.g., second grade, ungraded classrooms); most were in third grade in 2001–02, but 11 percent were in second grade or other grades (e.g., fourth grade, ungraded classrooms); most were in fifth grade in 2003–04, but 14 percent were in fourth grade or other grades (e.g., sixth grade, ungraded classrooms); most were in eighth grade in 2006–07, but 14 percent were in seventh grade or other grades (e.g., ninth grade or ungraded classrooms). Data were calculated using C1_7FC0 weight. Estimates differ from previously published figures because the data were recalibrated to represent the kindergarten through eighth-grade mathematics assessment item pool and the third-grade through eighth-grade science assessment item pool. Race categories exclude persons of Hispanic ethnicity.
SOURCE: U.S. Department of Education, National Center for Education Statistics, Early Childhood Longitudinal Study, Kindergarten Class of 1998–99 (ECLS-K), Longitudinal Kindergarten–Eighth Grade Full Sample Public-Use Data File, fall 1998, spring 1999, spring 2000, spring 2002, spring 2004, and spring 2007. (This table was prepared September 2009.)

Table 221.10. Average National Assessment of Educational Progress (NAEP) reading scale score, by sex, race/ethnicity, and grade: Selected years, 1992 through 2015

[Standard errors appear in parentheses]

Grade and year	All students	Sex — Average reading scale score — Male	Female	Gap between female and male score	Race/ethnicity — Average reading scale score — White	Black	Hispanic	Asian/Pacific Islander — Total	Asian[1]	Pacific Islander[1]	American Indian/ Alaska Native	Two or more races[1]	Gap between White and Black score	Gap between White and Hispanic score
1	2	3	4	5	6	7	8	9	10	11	12	13	14	15
Grade 4														
1992[2]	217 (0.9)	213 (1.2)	221 (1.0)	8 (1.6)	224 (1.2)	192 (1.7)	197 (2.6)	216 (2.9)	— (†)	— (†)	‡ (†)	— (†)	32 (2.1)	27 (2.9)
1994[2]	214 (1.0)	209 (1.3)	220 (1.1)	10 (1.7)	224 (1.3)	185 (1.8)	188 (3.4)	220 (3.8)	— (†)	— (†)	211 (6.6)	— (†)	38 (2.2)	35 (3.6)
1998	215 (1.1)	212 (1.3)	217 (1.3)	5 (1.8)	225 (1.0)	193 (1.9)	193 (3.2)	215 (5.6)	— (†)	— (†)	‡ (†)	— (†)	32 (2.2)	32 (3.3)
2000	213 (1.3)	208 (1.3)	219 (1.4)	11 (1.9)	224 (1.1)	190 (1.8)	190 (2.9)	225 (5.2)	— (†)	— (†)	214 (6.0)	— (†)	34 (2.1)	35 (3.1)
2002	219 (0.4)	215 (0.4)	222 (0.5)	6 (0.7)	229 (0.3)	199 (0.5)	201 (1.3)	224 (1.6)	— (†)	— (†)	207 (2.0)	— (†)	30 (0.6)	28 (1.4)
2003	218 (0.3)	215 (0.3)	222 (0.3)	7 (0.5)	229 (0.3)	198 (0.4)	200 (0.6)	226 (1.2)	— (†)	— (†)	202 (1.4)	— (†)	31 (0.5)	28 (0.6)
2005	219 (0.2)	216 (0.2)	222 (0.3)	6 (0.4)	229 (0.2)	200 (0.3)	203 (0.5)	229 (0.7)	— (†)	— (†)	204 (1.3)	— (†)	29 (0.4)	26 (0.5)
2007	221 (0.3)	218 (0.3)	224 (0.3)	7 (0.4)	231 (0.2)	203 (0.4)	205 (0.5)	232 (1.0)	— (†)	— (†)	203 (1.2)	— (†)	27 (0.5)	26 (0.6)
2009	221 (0.3)	218 (0.3)	224 (0.3)	7 (0.4)	230 (0.3)	205 (0.5)	205 (0.5)	235 (1.0)	— (†)	— (†)	204 (1.3)	— (†)	26 (0.6)	25 (0.6)
2011	221 (0.3)	218 (0.3)	225 (0.3)	7 (0.5)	231 (0.2)	205 (0.5)	206 (0.5)	235 (1.2)	236 (1.3)	216 (1.9)	202 (1.3)	227 (1.2)	25 (0.5)	24 (0.6)
2013	222 (0.3)	219 (0.3)	225 (0.3)	7 (0.5)	232 (0.3)	206 (0.5)	207 (0.5)	235 (1.1)	237 (1.1)	212 (2.5)	205 (1.3)	227 (1.0)	26 (0.6)	25 (0.6)
2015	223 (0.4)	219 (0.4)	226 (0.4)	7 (0.6)	232 (0.3)	206 (0.5)	208 (0.8)	239 (1.4)	241 (1.6)	215 (2.9)	205 (1.5)	227 (1.2)	26 (0.6)	24 (0.9)
Grade 8														
1992[2]	260 (0.9)	254 (1.1)	267 (1.0)	13 (1.5)	267 (1.1)	237 (1.7)	241 (1.6)	268 (3.9)	— (†)	— (†)	‡ (†)	— (†)	30 (2.0)	26 (2.0)
1994[2]	260 (0.8)	252 (1.0)	267 (1.0)	15 (1.4)	267 (1.0)	236 (1.8)	243 (1.2)	265 (3.0)	— (†)	— (†)	248 (4.7)	— (†)	30 (2.1)	24 (1.5)
1998	263 (0.8)	256 (1.0)	270 (0.8)	14 (1.3)	270 (0.9)	244 (1.2)	243 (1.7)	264 (7.1)	— (†)	— (†)	‡ (†)	— (†)	26 (1.5)	27 (1.9)
2000	— (†)	— (†)	— (†)	— (†)	— (†)	— (†)	— (†)	— (†)	— (†)	— (†)	— (†)	— (†)	— (†)	— (†)
2002	264 (0.4)	260 (0.5)	269 (0.5)	9 (0.7)	272 (0.4)	245 (0.7)	247 (0.8)	267 (1.7)	— (†)	— (†)	250 (3.5)	— (†)	27 (0.9)	26 (0.9)
2003	263 (0.3)	258 (0.3)	269 (0.3)	11 (0.4)	272 (0.4)	244 (0.5)	245 (0.7)	270 (1.1)	— (†)	— (†)	246 (3.0)	— (†)	28 (0.5)	27 (0.7)
2005	262 (0.2)	257 (0.2)	267 (0.2)	10 (0.3)	271 (0.2)	243 (0.4)	246 (0.4)	271 (0.8)	— (†)	— (†)	249 (1.4)	— (†)	28 (0.5)	25 (0.5)
2007	263 (0.2)	258 (0.3)	268 (0.3)	10 (0.4)	272 (0.2)	245 (0.4)	247 (0.4)	271 (1.1)	— (†)	— (†)	247 (1.2)	— (†)	27 (0.4)	25 (0.5)
2009	264 (0.3)	259 (0.3)	269 (0.3)	9 (0.5)	273 (0.2)	246 (0.4)	249 (0.6)	274 (1.1)	— (†)	— (†)	251 (1.2)	— (†)	26 (0.5)	24 (0.7)
2011	265 (0.2)	261 (0.3)	270 (0.2)	9 (0.4)	274 (0.2)	249 (0.5)	252 (0.5)	275 (1.0)	277 (1.0)	254 (2.2)	252 (1.2)	269 (1.2)	25 (0.5)	22 (0.5)
2013	268 (0.3)	263 (0.3)	273 (0.3)	10 (0.4)	276 (0.3)	250 (0.4)	256 (0.5)	280 (0.9)	282 (0.9)	259 (2.6)	251 (1.0)	271 (0.9)	26 (0.5)	21 (0.5)
2015	265 (0.2)	261 (0.2)	270 (0.3)	10 (0.4)	274 (0.2)	248 (0.5)	253 (0.4)	280 (1.3)	281 (1.3)	255 (2.4)	251 (1.7)	269 (1.1)	26 (0.5)	21 (0.5)
Grade 12														
1992[2]	292 (0.6)	287 (0.7)	297 (0.7)	10 (1.0)	297 (0.6)	273 (1.4)	279 (2.7)	290 (3.2)	— (†)	— (†)	‡ (†)	— (†)	24 (1.5)	19 (2.7)
1994[2]	287 (0.7)	280 (0.8)	294 (0.8)	14 (1.2)	293 (0.7)	265 (1.6)	270 (1.7)	278 (2.4)	— (†)	— (†)	274 (5.8)	— (†)	29 (1.8)	23 (1.9)
1998	290 (0.6)	282 (0.8)	298 (0.8)	16 (1.1)	297 (0.7)	269 (1.4)	275 (1.5)	287 (2.7)	— (†)	— (†)	‡ (†)	— (†)	27 (1.6)	22 (1.6)
2000	— (†)	— (†)	— (†)	— (†)	— (†)	— (†)	— (†)	— (†)	— (†)	— (†)	— (†)	— (†)	— (†)	— (†)
2002	287 (0.7)	279 (0.9)	295 (0.7)	16 (1.1)	292 (0.7)	267 (1.3)	273 (1.5)	286 (2.0)	— (†)	— (†)	‡ (†)	— (†)	25 (1.5)	20 (1.6)
2003	— (†)	— (†)	— (†)	— (†)	— (†)	— (†)	— (†)	— (†)	— (†)	— (†)	— (†)	— (†)	— (†)	— (†)
2005	286 (0.6)	279 (0.8)	292 (0.7)	13 (1.1)	293 (0.7)	267 (1.2)	272 (1.2)	287 (1.9)	— (†)	— (†)	279 (6.3)	— (†)	26 (1.4)	21 (1.4)
2007	— (†)	— (†)	— (†)	— (†)	— (†)	— (†)	— (†)	— (†)	— (†)	— (†)	— (†)	— (†)	— (†)	— (†)
2009	288 (0.7)	282 (0.7)	294 (0.8)	12 (1.1)	296 (0.6)	269 (1.1)	274 (1.0)	298 (2.4)	— (†)	— (†)	283 (3.7)	— (†)	27 (1.3)	22 (1.2)
2011	— (†)	— (†)	— (†)	— (†)	— (†)	— (†)	— (†)	— (†)	— (†)	— (†)	— (†)	— (†)	— (†)	— (†)
2013	288 (0.6)	284 (0.6)	293 (0.7)	10 (0.9)	297 (0.6)	268 (0.9)	276 (0.9)	296 (1.9)	296 (2.0)	289 (6.0)	277 (3.5)	291 (2.5)	30 (1.0)	22 (1.0)
2015	287 (0.5)	282 (0.6)	292 (0.7)	10 (1.0)	295 (0.7)	266 (1.1)	276 (0.9)	297 (2.1)	297 (2.1)	‡ (†)	279 (6.2)	295 (2.9)	30 (1.3)	20 (1.1)

—Not available.
†Not applicable.
‡Reporting standards not met (too few cases for a reliable estimate).
[1]Prior to 2011, separate data for Asian students, Pacific Islander students, and students of Two or more races were not collected.
[2]Accommodations were not permitted for this assessment.
NOTE: Scale ranges from 0 to 500. Includes public and private schools. For 1998 and later years, includes students tested with accommodations (1 to 13 percent of all students, depending on grade level and year); excludes only those students with disabilities and Eng-lish language learners who were unable to be tested even with accommodations (2 to 6 percent of all students). Data on race/ethnicity are based on school reports. Race categories exclude persons of Hispanic ethnicity.
SOURCE: U.S. Department of Education, National Center for Education Statistics, National Assessment of Educational Progress (NAEP), 1992, 1994, 1998, 2000, 2002, 2003, 2005, 2007, 2009, 2011, 2013, and 2015 Reading Assessments, retrieved June 10, 2016, from the Main NAEP Data Explorer (http://nces.ed.gov/nationsreportcard/naepdata/). (This table was prepared June 2016.)

Table 221.12. Average National Assessment of Educational Progress (NAEP) reading scale score and percentage of students attaining selected NAEP reading achievement levels, by selected school and student characteristics and grade: Selected years, 1992 through 2015

[Standard errors appear in parentheses]

Grade and year	Percent of students in school eligible for free or reduced-price lunch					English language learner (ELL) status			Disability status[1]			Percent of all students attaining reading achievement levels		
	Average reading scale score[2]				Gap between low-poverty and high-poverty score	Average reading scale score[2]		Gap between non-ELL and ELL score	Average reading scale score[2]		Gap between non-SD and SD score	Below Basic[3]	At or above Basic[3]	At or above Proficient[4]
	0–25 percent eligible (low poverty)	26–50 percent eligible	51–75 percent eligible	76–100 percent eligible (high poverty)		ELL	Non-ELL		Identified as student with disability (SD)	Not identified as SD				
1	2	3	4	5	6	7	8	9	10	11	12	13	14	15
Grade 4														
1992[5]	— (†)	— (†)	— (†)	— (†)	— (†)	‡ (†)	‡ (†)	‡ (†)	‡ (†)	‡ (†)	‡ (†)	38 (1.1)	62 (1.1)	29 (1.2)
1994[5]	— (†)	— (†)	— (†)	— (†)	— (†)	‡ (†)	‡ (†)	‡ (†)	‡ (†)	‡ (†)	‡ (†)	40 (1.0)	60 (1.0)	30 (1.1)
1998	231 (1.4)	218 (1.6)	205 (1.8)	187 (3.1)	44 (3.4)	174 (5.2)	217 (1.0)	43 (5.3)	176 (4.6)	217 (1.1)	41 (4.7)	40 (1.2)	60 (1.2)	29 (0.9)
2000	231 (1.5)	218 (1.3)	205 (2.1)	184 (2.8)	48 (3.2)	167 (5.2)	216 (1.1)	49 (5.3)	167 (4.8)	217 (1.2)	50 (4.9)	41 (1.4)	59 (1.4)	29 (1.1)
2002	233 (0.4)	221 (0.5)	210 (0.7)	196 (0.7)	37 (0.9)	183 (2.1)	221 (0.3)	38 (2.1)	187 (0.8)	221 (0.5)	34 (0.9)	36 (0.5)	64 (0.5)	31 (0.4)
2003	233 (0.4)	221 (0.5)	211 (0.5)	194 (0.5)	39 (0.7)	186 (0.8)	221 (0.3)	35 (0.8)	185 (0.6)	221 (0.3)	36 (0.6)	37 (0.3)	63 (0.3)	31 (0.3)
2005	234 (0.3)	221 (0.3)	211 (0.4)	197 (0.4)	37 (0.5)	187 (0.5)	222 (0.2)	35 (0.6)	190 (0.5)	222 (0.2)	32 (0.6)	36 (0.3)	64 (0.3)	31 (0.2)
2007	235 (0.4)	223 (0.4)	212 (0.4)	200 (0.5)	35 (0.7)	188 (0.6)	224 (0.3)	36 (0.6)	191 (0.6)	224 (0.3)	33 (0.7)	33 (0.3)	67 (0.3)	33 (0.3)
2009	237 (0.4)	223 (0.5)	215 (0.5)	202 (0.5)	35 (0.6)	188 (0.8)	224 (0.3)	36 (0.8)	190 (0.7)	224 (0.3)	35 (0.7)	33 (0.3)	67 (0.3)	33 (0.4)
2011	238 (0.5)	226 (0.5)	217 (0.4)	203 (0.5)	35 (0.7)	188 (0.7)	225 (0.3)	36 (0.9)	186 (0.5)	225 (0.3)	39 (0.6)	33 (0.3)	67 (0.3)	34 (0.4)
2013	240 (0.4)	227 (0.5)	218 (0.6)	203 (0.4)	37 (0.6)	187 (0.7)	226 (0.3)	38 (0.7)	184 (0.6)	227 (0.3)	42 (0.7)	32 (0.3)	68 (0.3)	35 (0.3)
2015	241 (0.5)	228 (0.5)	219 (0.6)	205 (0.6)	36 (0.8)	189 (1.1)	226 (0.3)	37 (1.1)	187 (0.7)	228 (0.3)	41 (0.8)	31 (0.4)	69 (0.4)	36 (0.4)
Grade 8														
1992[5]	— (†)	— (†)	— (†)	— (†)	— (†)	‡ (†)	‡ (†)	‡ (†)	‡ (†)	‡ (†)	‡ (†)	31 (1.0)	69 (1.0)	29 (1.1)
1994[5]	— (†)	— (†)	— (†)	— (†)	— (†)	‡ (†)	‡ (†)	‡ (†)	‡ (†)	‡ (†)	‡ (†)	30 (0.9)	70 (0.9)	30 (0.9)
1998	273 (1.1)	262 (1.3)	252 (2.1)	240 (1.8)	33 (2.1)	218 (2.5)	264 (0.7)	46 (2.6)	224 (3.7)	266 (0.7)	42 (3.7)	27 (0.8)	73 (0.8)	32 (1.1)
2000	— (†)	— (†)	— (†)	— (†)	— (†)	— (†)	— (†)	— (†)	— (†)	— (†)	— (†)	— (†)	— (†)	— (†)
2002	276 (0.6)	264 (0.6)	254 (0.8)	240 (1.1)	36 (1.3)	224 (1.4)	266 (0.4)	42 (1.4)	228 (1.0)	268 (0.4)	39 (1.0)	25 (0.5)	75 (0.5)	33 (0.5)
2003	275 (0.4)	263 (0.4)	253 (0.6)	239 (1.0)	36 (1.1)	222 (1.5)	265 (0.3)	43 (1.5)	225 (0.6)	267 (0.3)	42 (0.6)	26 (0.3)	74 (0.3)	32 (0.3)
2005	274 (0.3)	262 (0.3)	252 (0.4)	240 (0.6)	34 (0.7)	224 (0.9)	264 (0.2)	40 (0.9)	227 (0.5)	266 (0.2)	39 (0.5)	27 (0.2)	73 (0.2)	31 (0.2)
2007	275 (0.4)	263 (0.4)	253 (0.5)	241 (0.7)	34 (0.8)	223 (1.1)	265 (0.2)	42 (1.1)	227 (0.6)	266 (0.2)	39 (0.6)	26 (0.2)	74 (0.2)	31 (0.2)
2009	277 (0.4)	265 (0.4)	256 (0.6)	243 (0.7)	34 (0.8)	219 (1.0)	266 (0.2)	47 (1.0)	230 (0.6)	267 (0.3)	37 (0.7)	25 (0.3)	75 (0.3)	32 (0.4)
2011	279 (0.4)	268 (0.4)	258 (0.5)	247 (0.5)	32 (0.7)	224 (1.0)	267 (0.2)	44 (1.0)	231 (0.5)	269 (0.2)	38 (0.6)	24 (0.3)	76 (0.3)	34 (0.3)
2013	282 (0.5)	270 (0.5)	261 (0.4)	249 (0.5)	33 (0.7)	225 (0.9)	270 (0.2)	45 (1.0)	232 (0.6)	272 (0.2)	39 (0.7)	22 (0.3)	78 (0.3)	36 (0.3)
2015	281 (0.5)	269 (0.5)	261 (0.6)	248 (0.6)	33 (0.8)	223 (0.9)	268 (0.2)	45 (0.9)	230 (0.6)	270 (0.2)	40 (0.6)	24 (0.3)	76 (0.3)	34 (0.3)
Grade 12														
1992[5]	— (†)	— (†)	— (†)	— (†)	— (†)	‡ (†)	‡ (†)	‡ (†)	‡ (†)	‡ (†)	‡ (†)	20 (0.6)	80 (0.6)	40 (0.8)
1994[5]	— (†)	— (†)	— (†)	— (†)	— (†)	‡ (†)	‡ (†)	‡ (†)	‡ (†)	‡ (†)	‡ (†)	25 (0.7)	75 (0.7)	36 (1.0)
1998	296 (0.9)	284 (1.7)	275 (2.0)	272 (3.3)	23 (3.4)	244 (2.6)	291 (0.6)	46 (2.7)	244 (3.2)	292 (0.6)	48 (3.2)	24 (0.7)	76 (0.7)	40 (0.7)
2000	— (†)	— (†)	— (†)	— (†)	— (†)	— (†)	— (†)	— (†)	— (†)	— (†)	— (†)	— (†)	— (†)	— (†)
2002	293 (0.9)	282 (1.6)	275 (2.6)	268 (2.4)	25 (2.6)	245 (2.4)	288 (0.7)	43 (2.5)	247 (2.0)	289 (0.7)	42 (2.1)	26 (0.8)	74 (0.8)	36 (0.8)
2003	— (†)	— (†)	— (†)	— (†)	— (†)	— (†)	— (†)	— (†)	— (†)	— (†)	— (†)	— (†)	— (†)	— (†)
2005	292 (1.1)	282 (1.1)	273 (1.8)	266 (2.0)	26 (2.3)	247 (2.4)	288 (0.6)	40 (2.4)	244 (1.8)	289 (0.6)	45 (1.9)	27 (0.8)	73 (0.8)	35 (0.7)
2007	— (†)	— (†)	— (†)	— (†)	— (†)	— (†)	— (†)	— (†)	— (†)	— (†)	— (†)	— (†)	— (†)	— (†)
2009	299 (1.1)	286 (0.8)	276 (1.1)	266 (1.0)	33 (1.5)	240 (2.1)	290 (0.7)	50 (2.2)	253 (1.4)	291 (0.7)	38 (1.6)	26 (0.6)	74 (0.6)	38 (0.8)
2011	— (†)	— (†)	— (†)	— (†)	— (†)	— (†)	— (†)	— (†)	— (†)	— (†)	— (†)	— (†)	— (†)	— (†)
2013	302 (1.1)	289 (0.9)	280 (0.9)	268 (1.5)	35 (1.9)	237 (1.9)	290 (0.5)	53 (2.0)	252 (1.4)	292 (0.6)	40 (1.5)	25 (0.6)	75 (0.6)	38 (0.7)
2015	— (†)	— (†)	— (†)	— (†)	— (†)	— (†)	— (†)	— (†)	— (†)	— (†)	— (†)	— (†)	— (†)	— (†)

—Not available.
†Not applicable.
‡Reporting standards not met (too few cases for a reliable estimate).
[1]The student with disability (SD) variable used in this table includes students who have a 504 plan, even if they do not have an Individualized Education Plan (IEP).
[2]Scale ranges from 0 to 500.
[3]*Basic* denotes partial mastery of the knowledge and skills that are fundamental for proficient work at a given grade.
[4]*Proficient* represents solid academic performance. Students reaching this level have demonstrated competency over challenging subject matter.

[5]Accommodations were not permitted for this assessment.
NOTE: Includes public and private schools. For 1998 and later years, includes students tested with accommodations (1 to 13 percent of all students, depending on grade level and year); excludes only those students with disabilities and English language learners who were unable to be tested even with accommodations (2 to 6 percent of all students).
SOURCE: U.S. Department of Education, National Center for Education Statistics, National Assessment of Educational Progress (NAEP), 1992, 1994, 1998, 2000, 2002, 2003, 2005, 2007, 2009, 2011, 2013, and 2015 Reading Assessments, retrieved October 28, 2015, from the Main NAEP Data Explorer (http://nces.ed.gov/nationsreportcard/naepdata/). (This table was prepared October 2015.)

Table 221.20. Percentage of students at or above selected National Assessment of Educational Progress (NAEP) reading achievement levels, by grade and selected student characteristics: Selected years, 1998 through 2015

[Standard errors appear in parentheses]

Grade and selected student characteristic	1998 Basic[1]	1998 Prof.[2]	2003 Basic[1]	2003 Prof.[2]	2005 Basic[1]	2005 Prof.[2]	2007 Basic[1]	2007 Prof.[2]	2009 Basic[1]	2009 Prof.[2]	2011 Basic[1]	2011 Prof.[2]	2013 Basic[1]	2013 Prof.[2]	2015 Basic[1]	2015 Prof.[2]
1	2	3	4	5	6	7	8	9	10	11	12	13	14	15	16	17
4th grade, all students	60 (1.2)	29 (0.9)	63 (0.3)	31 (0.3)	64 (0.3)	31 (0.2)	67 (0.3)	33 (0.3)	67 (0.3)	33 (0.4)	67 (0.3)	34 (0.4)	68 (0.3)	35 (0.3)	69 (0.4)	36 (0.4)
Sex																
Male	57 (1.3)	27 (1.1)	60 (0.4)	28 (0.3)	61 (0.4)	29 (0.3)	64 (0.3)	30 (0.3)	64 (0.3)	30 (0.4)	64 (0.4)	31 (0.4)	65 (0.3)	32 (0.4)	66 (0.5)	33 (0.5)
Female	62 (1.5)	32 (1.2)	67 (0.4)	35 (0.4)	67 (0.3)	34 (0.3)	70 (0.3)	36 (0.4)	70 (0.4)	36 (0.4)	71 (0.4)	37 (0.5)	72 (0.4)	38 (0.4)	72 (0.4)	39 (0.5)
Race/ethnicity																
White	70 (1.3)	37 (1.2)	75 (0.3)	41 (0.4)	76 (0.3)	41 (0.3)	78 (0.3)	43 (0.4)	78 (0.3)	42 (0.3)	78 (0.3)	44 (0.3)	79 (0.3)	46 (0.4)	79 (0.3)	46 (0.5)
Black	36 (1.8)	10 (1.1)	40 (0.5)	13 (0.4)	42 (0.5)	13 (0.3)	46 (0.6)	14 (0.4)	48 (0.7)	16 (0.5)	49 (0.6)	17 (0.5)	50 (0.6)	18 (0.5)	52 (0.6)	18 (0.5)
Hispanic	37 (3.2)	13 (1.7)	44 (0.7)	15 (0.5)	46 (0.7)	16 (0.5)	50 (0.6)	17 (0.4)	49 (0.7)	17 (0.5)	51 (0.8)	19 (0.6)	53 (0.6)	20 (0.6)	55 (1.3)	21 (0.7)
Asian/Pacific Islander	58 (6.1)	30 (4.5)	70 (1.5)	38 (1.4)	73 (0.9)	42 (0.9)	77 (1.0)	46 (1.4)	80 (1.0)	49 (1.3)	80 (1.2)	49 (1.7)	80 (1.0)	51 (1.2)	82 (1.3)	55 (1.8)
Asian	—	—	—	—	—	—	—	—	—	—	81 (1.2)	50 (1.5)	82 (1.0)	53 (1.3)	84 (1.4)	57 (2.0)
Pacific Islander	—	—	—	—	—	—	—	—	—	—	61 (2.4)	28 (3.2)	57 (3.2)	27 (3.0)	60 (3.7)	28 (3.7)
American Indian/Alaska Native	‡	‡	47 (2.0)	16 (1.5)	48 (1.5)	18 (1.0)	49 (1.4)	18 (1.1)	50 (1.7)	20 (1.4)	47 (1.7)	18 (1.4)	51 (1.6)	21 (1.4)	52 (2.1)	21 (1.9)
Two or more races	—	—	—	—	—	—	—	—	—	—	—	—	73 (1.2)	40 (1.4)	73 (1.4)	40 (1.6)
Eligibility for free or reduced-price lunch																
Eligible	39 (1.8)	13 (1.0)	45 (0.4)	15 (0.5)	46 (0.4)	16 (0.3)	50 (0.4)	17 (0.3)	51 (0.4)	17 (0.3)	52 (0.4)	18 (0.3)	53 (0.4)	20 (0.3)	56 (0.5)	21 (0.6)
Not eligible	73 (1.0)	40 (1.2)	76 (0.3)	42 (0.5)	77 (0.2)	42 (0.2)	79 (0.3)	44 (0.3)	80 (0.3)	45 (0.4)	82 (0.3)	45 (0.4)	83 (0.4)	51 (0.5)	83 (0.3)	52 (0.6)
Unknown	69 (3.0)	37 (3.8)	76 (0.9)	43 (1.1)	77 (1.1)	45 (1.1)	80 (1.3)	46 (1.8)	81 (1.9)	50 (1.9)	82 (1.0)	48 (1.3)	83 (1.6)	51 (2.1)	81 (1.3)	52 (1.8)
8th grade, all students	73 (0.8)	32 (1.1)	74 (0.3)	32 (0.3)	73 (0.2)	31 (0.2)	74 (0.2)	31 (0.2)	75 (0.3)	32 (0.4)	76 (0.3)	34 (0.3)	78 (0.3)	36 (0.3)	76 (0.3)	34 (0.3)
Sex																
Male	67 (1.2)	26 (1.2)	69 (0.3)	27 (0.3)	68 (0.3)	26 (0.3)	69 (0.4)	26 (0.3)	71 (0.4)	28 (0.4)	72 (0.4)	29 (0.4)	74 (0.4)	31 (0.4)	72 (0.3)	29 (0.4)
Female	80 (0.9)	39 (1.3)	79 (0.3)	38 (0.3)	78 (0.2)	36 (0.2)	79 (0.3)	36 (0.3)	79 (0.4)	37 (0.5)	80 (0.3)	38 (0.4)	82 (0.3)	42 (0.4)	80 (0.3)	39 (0.5)
Race/ethnicity																
White	81 (0.9)	39 (1.3)	83 (0.3)	41 (0.4)	82 (0.2)	39 (0.4)	84 (0.3)	40 (0.3)	84 (0.2)	41 (0.3)	85 (0.2)	43 (0.4)	86 (0.2)	46 (0.4)	85 (0.2)	44 (0.4)
Black	53 (1.8)	13 (1.5)	54 (0.6)	13 (0.4)	52 (0.6)	12 (0.4)	55 (0.6)	12 (0.4)	57 (0.6)	14 (0.6)	59 (0.7)	15 (0.5)	61 (0.6)	17 (0.5)	58 (0.7)	16 (0.5)
Hispanic	53 (2.4)	14 (1.0)	56 (0.9)	15 (0.6)	56 (0.6)	15 (0.4)	58 (0.5)	15 (0.4)	58 (0.8)	17 (0.6)	64 (0.8)	19 (0.5)	68 (0.7)	22 (0.6)	66 (0.6)	21 (0.5)
Asian/Pacific Islander	75 (8.8)	33 (5.6)	79 (1.2)	40 (1.6)	80 (0.8)	40 (1.2)	80 (1.1)	41 (1.2)	83 (1.1)	45 (1.7)	83 (1.0)	47 (1.4)	86 (0.7)	52 (1.3)	86 (1.0)	52 (1.8)
Asian	—	—	—	—	—	—	—	—	—	—	84 (1.0)	49 (1.5)	87 (0.7)	54 (1.3)	87 (0.7)	54 (1.9)
Pacific Islander	—	—	—	—	—	—	—	—	—	—	63 (2.7)	24 (3.0)	70 (3.5)	27 (3.7)	66 (3.3)	24 (3.0)
American Indian/Alaska Native	‡	‡	57 (3.3)	17 (1.7)	59 (2.1)	17	56 (1.9)	18	62 (2.0)	21 (1.2)	63 (1.4)	24 (1.7)	62 (1.8)	19 (1.6)	63 (2.2)	22 (1.8)
Two or more races	—	—	—	—	—	—	—	—	—	—	79 (1.7)	39 (1.5)	81 (1.1)	40 (1.4)	79 (1.2)	38 (1.6)
Eligibility for free or reduced-price lunch																
Eligible	56 (1.3)	14 (1.0)	57 (0.5)	16 (0.3)	57 (0.4)	15 (0.3)	58 (0.4)	15	60 (0.5)	16 (0.3)	63 (0.5)	18 (0.3)	66 (0.3)	20 (0.2)	64 (0.3)	20 (0.3)
Not eligible	80 (1.0)	38 (1.5)	82 (0.3)	40 (0.4)	81 (0.3)	39 (0.2)	83 (0.3)	40 (0.3)	85 (0.3)	42 (0.4)	86 (0.3)	45 (0.4)	87 (0.3)	48 (0.4)	87 (0.3)	47 (0.4)
Unknown	80 (1.9)	43 (2.5)	81 (0.9)	42 (1.2)	84 (1.0)	45 (1.3)	86 (1.0)	48 (1.6)	89 (1.3)	51 (1.8)	90 (0.8)	54 (1.4)	92 (0.9)	59 (2.4)	89 (0.9)	53 (1.5)
12th grade, all students	76 (0.7)	40 (0.7)	—	—	73 (0.8)	35 (0.7)	—	—	74 (0.6)	38 (0.8)	—	—	75 (0.6)	38 (0.7)	—	(†)
Sex																
Male	70 (0.9)	32 (0.9)	—	—	67 (0.9)	29 (0.9)	—	—	69 (0.8)	32 (0.8)	—	—	70 (0.7)	33 (0.7)	—	—
Female	83 (0.8)	48 (1.1)	—	—	78 (0.9)	41 (0.9)	—	—	80 (0.6)	43 (1.0)	—	—	79 (0.7)	42 (0.9)	—	—
Race/ethnicity																
White	82 (0.7)	47 (0.9)	—	—	79 (0.8)	43 (0.9)	—	—	81 (0.5)	46 (0.8)	—	—	83 (0.6)	47 (0.8)	—	—
Black	57 (1.9)	17 (1.4)	—	—	54 (1.5)	16 (1.2)	—	—	57 (1.3)	17 (1.2)	—	—	56 (1.2)	16 (0.9)	—	—
Hispanic	62 (2.5)	24 (1.5)	—	—	60 (1.9)	20 (1.3)	—	—	61 (1.5)	22 (1.3)	—	—	64 (1.8)	23 (1.0)	—	—
Asian/Pacific Islander	74 (3.1)	38 (2.9)	—	—	74 (2.3)	36 (2.3)	—	—	81 (1.5)	49 (2.9)	—	—	80 (1.8)	48 (2.5)	—	—
Asian	—	—	—	—	—	—	—	—	—	—	—	—	80 (1.9)	48 (2.6)	—	—
Pacific Islander	—	—	—	—	—	—	—	—	—	—	—	—	75 (8.0)	39 (8.4)	—	—
American Indian/Alaska Native	‡	‡	—	—	67 (10.1)	26 (8.6)	—	—	70 (6.4)	29 (5.5)	—	—	65 (5.0)	26 (4.8)	—	—
Two or more races	—	—	—	—	—	—	—	—	—	—	—	—	77 (2.9)	38 (3.4)	—	—

—Not available.
†Not applicable.
‡Reporting standards not met (too few cases for a reliable estimate).
[1]Basic denotes partial mastery of the knowledge and skills that are fundamental for proficient work at a given grade.
[2]Proficient represents solid academic performance. Students reaching this level have demonstrated competency over challenging subject matter.

NOTE: Includes public and private schools. Includes students tested with accommodations (1 to 12 percent of all students, depending on grade level and year); excludes only those students with disabilities and English language learners who were unable to be tested even with accommodations (2 to 6 percent of all students). Race categories exclude persons of Hispanic ethnicity. Prior to 2011, separate data for Asian students, Pacific Islander students, and students of Two or more races were not collected.
SOURCE: U.S. Department of Education, National Center for Education Statistics, National Assessment of Educational Progress (NAEP), 1998, 2003, 2005, 2007, 2009, 2011, 2013, and 2015 Reading Assessments, retrieved November 3, 2015, from the Main NAEP Data Explorer (http://nces.ed.gov/nationsreportcard/naepdata/). (This table was prepared November 2015.)

Table 221.30. Average National Assessment of Educational Progress (NAEP) reading scale score and percentage distribution of students, by age, amount of reading for school and for fun, and time spent on homework and watching TV/video: Selected years, 1984 through 2012

[Standard errors appear in parentheses]

Amount of reading for school and for fun, time spent on homework and watching TV/video	9-year-olds 1984	1994	1999	2008	2012	13-year-olds 1984	1994	1999	2008	2012	17-year-olds 1984	1994	1999	2008	2012
1	2	3	4	5	6	7	8	9	10	11	12	13	14	15	16
Average scale score[1]															
Pages read daily in school and for homework															
5 or fewer	208 (0.9)	203 (2.3)	202 (1.8)	210 (1.1)	207 (1.1)	250 (0.8)	249 (1.7)	249 (2.0)	250 (1.2)	251 (1.8)	273 (0.8)	271 (1.9)	273 (2.7)	271 (1.3)	274 (1.1)
6–10	215 (1.0)	214 (1.7)	212 (1.7)	219 (1.3)	219 (1.5)	261 (0.6)	261 (1.4)	262 (1.7)	258 (1.2)	261 (1.5)	287 (0.9)	284 (2.1)	285 (1.7)	284 (1.4)	283 (1.2)
11–15	220 (1.4)	217 (2.3)	221 (2.4)	224 (1.4)	225 (1.3)	264 (1.1)	266 (1.8)	263 (2.1)	263 (1.6)	266 (1.8)	294 (0.9)	288 (1.9)	292 (2.1)	290 (1.6)	289 (1.5)
16–20	215 (1.4)	209 (2.9)	214 (2.9)	225 (1.4)	226 (1.2)	263 (1.1)	263 (2.3)	264 (2.6)	267 (1.6)	268 (1.8)	296 (1.1)	298 (2.2)	292 (2.9)	296 (1.5)	297 (1.5)
More than 20	215 (1.6)	217 (2.4)	217 (2.1)	226 (1.2)	227 (1.0)	261 (1.5)	261 (2.0)	265 (2.0)	267 (1.4)	271 (1.3)	300 (1.2)	304 (2.2)	302 (1.9)	303 (1.3)	301 (1.5)
Frequency of reading for fun															
Almost every day	214 (1.1)	215 (2.3)	215 (2.4)	225 (1.2)	226 (0.9)	264 (1.4)	272 (3.2)	272 (3.2)	274 (1.4)	276 (1.4)	297 (1.5)	302 (4.2)	301 (4.9)	302 (1.3)	302 (1.3)
Once or twice a week	212 (1.7)	214 (3.1)	215 (2.6)	225 (1.3)	226 (0.9)	255 (1.4)	255 (3.1)	263 (3.2)	264 (1.1)	267 (1.4)	290 (1.7)	286 (4.1)	289 (2.9)	291 (1.7)	294 (1.4)
Once or twice a month	204 (3.3)	213 (5.8)	211 (4.2)	217 (1.7)	219 (2.0)	255 (1.4)	255 (5.7)	260 (3.7)	261 (1.3)	264 (1.7)	290 (1.8)	286 (8.2)	286 (4.8)	288 (1.5)	288 (1.5)
A few times a year	197 (4.2)	197 (†)	‡ (†)	212 (2.0)	211 (1.9)	252 (3.6)	252 (5.4)	253 (4.4)	254 (1.6)	258 (1.6)	279 (2.7)	281 (5.2)	283 (4.4)	287 (1.5)	288 (1.3)
Never or hardly ever	198 (2.7)	193 (3.9)	195 (3.3)	211 (1.2)	208 (1.9)	239 (2.5)	237 (5.1)	242 (5.3)	247 (0.9)	249 (1.3)	269 (2.4)	258 (5.1)	262 (5.0)	269 (1.1)	272 (1.4)
TV/video watched on school day															
1 hour or less	212 (3.4)	212 (4.8)	221 (4.6)	223 (3.0)	222 (3.1)	264 (2.7)	264 (5.1)	265 (6.0)	267 (3.0)	276 (3.5)	300 (1.6)	308 (3.4)	300 (2.8)	292 (2.4)	292 (2.5)
2 hours	217 (1.5)	216 (1.8)	218 (2.1)	225 (1.2)	229 (1.2)	269 (1.1)	269 (1.5)	270 (1.6)	266 (1.1)	269 (1.2)	300 (1.2)	299 (1.8)	298 (2.0)	293 (1.2)	290 (1.3)
3 hours	222 (1.1)	219 (2.1)	221 (1.7)	227 (1.3)	227 (1.1)	268 (0.8)	268 (1.4)	268 (1.6)	262 (1.3)	266 (1.5)	295 (0.9)	292 (2.0)	292 (2.1)	290 (1.1)	290 (1.2)
4 hours	220 (1.2)	218 (2.2)	218 (2.3)	223 (1.4)	224 (1.4)	264 (0.7)	264 (2.2)	263 (1.5)	262 (1.5)	261 (1.5)	288 (1.0)	276 (4.0)	282 (2.3)	284 (1.3)	284 (1.2)
5 hours	219 (1.0)	212 (1.8)	214 (2.4)	219 (2.2)	213 (2.1)	257 (0.9)	257 (3.0)	254 (2.4)	255 (2.6)	259 (1.5)	277 (1.5)	269 (2.7)	273 (3.8)	276 (2.3)	275 (3.9)
6 hours or more	199 (0.8)	192 (2.7)	191 (1.7)	205 (1.2)	205 (1.2)	245 (1.0)	245 (3.1)	238 (1.8)	238 (1.4)	241 (1.4)	269 (1.5)	256 (3.7)	256 (5.2)	256 (2.3)	261 (2.6)
Percentage distribution															
Pages read daily in school and for homework															
5 or fewer	36 (0.8)	28 (1.4)	28 (1.4)	25 (0.9)	22 (0.7)	27 (0.7)	26 (0.9)	23 (1.0)	26 (0.8)	23 (0.8)	21 (0.8)	21 (1.2)	23 (1.4)	30 (0.9)	29 (0.7)
6–10	25 (0.4)	26 (0.6)	24 (0.9)	20 (0.5)	17 (0.6)	34 (0.5)	31 (0.9)	31 (1.1)	24 (0.6)	22 (0.8)	26 (0.6)	25 (0.9)	24 (0.8)	23 (0.5)	22 (0.6)
11–15	14 (0.4)	14 (0.5)	15 (0.7)	14 (0.5)	12 (0.4)	18 (0.2)	17 (0.6)	18 (0.8)	17 (0.5)	17 (0.5)	18 (0.3)	18 (0.6)	17 (0.6)	16 (0.5)	15 (0.4)
16–20	14 (0.4)	14 (0.9)	14 (0.9)	14 (0.5)	15 (0.6)	11 (0.4)	11 (0.5)	13 (0.7)	13 (0.4)	13 (0.5)	14 (0.5)	13 (0.6)	14 (0.8)	12 (0.4)	12 (0.5)
More than 20	13 (0.5)	17 (1.0)	19 (1.0)	28 (0.8)	34 (1.1)	11 (0.5)	14 (0.8)	16 (1.0)	22 (0.9)	24 (1.1)	21 (0.9)	23 (1.5)	22 (1.2)	19 (0.7)	22 (0.7)
Frequency of reading for fun															
Almost every day	53 (1.0)	58 (1.6)	54 (1.7)	48 (0.7)	53 (0.8)	35 (1.0)	32 (1.8)	28 (1.7)	26 (0.6)	27 (0.7)	31 (0.8)	30 (2.6)	25 (1.7)	20 (0.6)	19 (0.6)
Once or twice a week	28 (0.8)	25 (1.5)	25 (1.5)	23 (0.6)	23 (0.6)	35 (1.2)	32 (2.1)	36 (1.6)	25 (0.6)	26 (0.6)	33 (1.1)	31 (1.9)	28 (2.7)	22 (0.5)	21 (0.6)
Once or twice a month	7 (0.6)	5 (0.6)	6 (0.6)	8 (0.4)	7 (0.4)	14 (0.8)	14 (1.7)	17 (1.6)	13 (0.4)	14 (0.4)	17 (0.5)	15 (1.5)	19 (1.7)	17 (0.5)	16 (0.4)
A few times a year	3 (0.3)	3 (0.6)	4 (0.7)	8 (0.4)	7 (0.3)	7 (0.5)	7 (1.2)	10 (1.1)	12 (0.3)	11 (0.4)	10 (0.5)	12 (1.5)	12 (1.4)	16 (0.5)	18 (0.6)
Never or hardly ever	9 (0.5)	9 (0.8)	10 (0.8)	14 (0.6)	11 (0.4)	8 (0.6)	12 (1.7)	9 (1.4)	24 (0.7)	22 (0.7)	9 (0.6)	12 (1.4)	16 (2.4)	24 (0.6)	27 (0.6)
Time spent on homework yesterday															
No homework assigned	35 (1.3)	32 (2.1)	26 (1.6)	18 (1.3)	22 (1.6)	22 (0.7)	23 (1.4)	24 (1.2)	23 (1.2)	21 (1.2)	22 (0.9)	23 (1.4)	26 (1.0)	28 (0.8)	27 (0.9)
Didn't do assignment	4 (0.3)	4 (0.4)	4 (0.3)	5 (0.3)	4 (0.4)	4 (0.2)	6 (0.6)	5 (0.4)	7 (0.3)	5 (0.3)	11 (0.3)	11 (0.6)	13 (0.7)	12 (0.4)	11 (0.4)
Less than 1 hour	41 (1.0)	48 (1.7)	53 (1.4)	60 (1.2)	57 (1.3)	36 (0.5)	34 (1.0)	37 (1.4)	43 (1.2)	44 (0.8)	26 (0.4)	27 (1.2)	23 (1.0)	27 (0.5)	26 (0.6)
1 to 2 hours	13 (0.4)	11 (0.7)	12 (0.6)	12 (0.5)	12 (0.6)	29 (0.6)	28 (1.0)	26 (1.0)	21 (0.7)	23 (0.9)	27 (0.5)	26 (0.9)	23 (0.8)	22 (0.5)	23 (0.6)
More than 2 hours	6 (0.2)	4 (0.4)	5 (0.5)	5 (0.3)	5 (0.3)	9 (0.3)	9 (0.7)	8 (0.8)	6 (0.4)	7 (0.5)	13 (0.5)	13 (0.9)	12 (0.9)	10 (0.5)	13 (0.7)
TV/video watched on school day															
None	3 (0.2)	2 (0.2)	4 (0.8)	4 (0.3)	6 (0.3)	2 (0.2)	3 (0.3)	4 (0.6)	5 (0.3)	6 (0.3)	5 (0.3)	6 (0.8)	6 (0.3)	6 (0.3)	10 (0.3)
1 hour or less	14 (0.3)	23 (1.0)	24 (0.9)	24 (0.6)	27 (0.7)	12 (0.4)	20 (1.0)	22 (0.8)	25 (0.7)	29 (0.6)	25 (0.5)	31 (0.9)	34 (0.9)	33 (0.6)	34 (0.6)
2 hours	16 (0.4)	23 (0.7)	21 (0.9)	18 (0.5)	18 (0.5)	23 (0.4)	22 (0.8)	29 (0.9)	26 (0.5)	27 (0.7)	26 (0.3)	26 (0.8)	26 (0.9)	27 (0.5)	25 (0.5)
3 hours	15 (0.2)	16 (0.5)	14 (0.6)	12 (0.4)	12 (0.4)	23 (0.4)	23 (0.8)	20 (0.9)	18 (0.5)	15 (0.5)	20 (0.3)	18 (0.8)	17 (0.7)	16 (0.5)	16 (0.5)
4 hours	12 (0.2)	11 (0.5)	9 (0.4)	9 (0.3)	8 (0.3)	17 (0.3)	17 (0.7)	11 (0.6)	10 (0.4)	10 (0.3)	12 (0.2)	9 (0.6)	8 (0.5)	8 (0.4)	8 (0.4)
5 hours or more	30 (0.7)	20 (0.8)	22 (1.2)	26 (0.8)	23 (0.8)	13 (0.4)	13 (0.9)	9 (0.6)	13 (0.4)	10 (0.5)	6 (0.2)	5 (0.4)	5 (0.6)	4 (0.2)	3 (0.2)

†Not applicable.
‡Reporting standards not met (too few cases for a reliable estimate).
[1]Scale ranges from 0 to 500. Students scoring 150 (or higher) are able to follow brief written directions and carry out simple, discrete reading tasks. Students scoring 200 are able to understand, combine ideas, and make inferences based on short uncomplicated passages about specific or sequentially related information. Students scoring 250 are able to search for specific information, interrelate ideas, and make generalizations about literature, science, and social studies materials. Students scoring 300 are able to find, understand, summarize, and explain relatively complicated literary and informational material. For 1984, 1994, and 1999, accommodations were not permitted. For 2008 and later years, includes students tested with accommodations; excludes only those students with disabilities and English language learners who were unable to be tested even with accommodations (2 to 4 percent of all students, depending on age and assessment year). Detail may not sum to totals because of rounding.

SOURCE: U.S. Department of Education, National Center for Education Statistics, National Assessment of Educational Progress (NAEP), NAEP Trends in Academic Progress, 1996 and 1999; and 2008 and 2012 NAEP Long-Term Trend Reading Assessments, retrieved June 24, 2009, and July 02, 2013, from the Long-Term Trend NAEP Data Explorer (http://nces.ed.gov/nationsreportcard/naepdata/). (This table was prepared July 2013.)

NOTE: Includes public and private schools. For 1984, 1994, and 1999, accommodations were not permitted. For 2008 and later

Table 221.40. Average National Assessment of Educational Progress (NAEP) reading scale score of 4th-grade public school students and percentage attaining reading achievement levels, by state: Selected years, 1992 through 2015

[Standard errors appear in parentheses]

State	Average scale score[1] 1992[2]	1994[2]	1998	2002	2003	2005	2007	2009	2011	2013	2015	Percent attaining reading achievement levels, 2015 At or above Basic[3]	At or above Proficient[4]	At Advanced[5]
1	2	3	4	5	6	7	8	9	10	11	12	13	14	15
United States	215 (1.0)	212 (1.1)	213 (1.2)	217 (0.5)	216 (0.3)	217 (0.2)	220 (0.3)	220 (0.3)	220 (0.3)	221 (0.3)	221 (0.4)	68 (0.4)	35 (0.4)	8 (0.2)
Alabama	207 (1.7)	208 (1.5)	211 (1.9)	207 (1.4)	207 (1.7)	208 (1.2)	216 (1.3)	216 (1.2)	220 (1.3)	219 (1.2)	217 (1.4)	65 (1.8)	29 (1.7)	5 (0.7)
Alaska	— (†)	— (†)	— (†)	— (†)	212 (1.6)	211 (1.4)	214 (1.0)	211 (1.2)	208 (1.1)	209 (1.0)	213 (1.3)	61 (1.4)	30 (1.4)	6 (0.8)
Arizona	209 (1.2)	206 (1.9)	206 (1.4)	205 (1.5)	209 (1.2)	207 (1.6)	210 (1.6)	210 (1.2)	212 (1.2)	213 (1.4)	215 (1.3)	62 (1.6)	30 (1.5)	7 (0.8)
Arkansas	211 (1.2)	209 (1.7)	209 (1.6)	213 (1.4)	214 (1.4)	217 (1.1)	217 (1.2)	216 (1.1)	217 (1.0)	219 (0.9)	218 (1.1)	65 (1.3)	32 (1.5)	6 (0.8)
California[6,7]	202 (2.0)	197 (1.8)	202 (2.5)	206 (2.5)	206 (1.2)	207 (0.7)	209 (1.0)	210 (1.5)	211 (1.8)	213 (1.2)	213 (1.7)	59 (2.1)	28 (1.7)	6 (0.9)
Colorado	217 (1.1)	213 (1.3)	220 (1.4)	— (†)	224 (1.2)	224 (1.1)	224 (1.1)	226 (1.2)	223 (1.3)	227 (1.0)	224 (1.6)	71 (1.7)	39 (1.8)	10 (1.0)
Connecticut	222 (1.3)	222 (1.6)	230 (1.6)	229 (1.1)	228 (1.1)	226 (1.0)	227 (1.3)	229 (1.1)	227 (1.3)	230 (0.9)	229 (1.1)	74 (1.2)	43 (1.5)	13 (1.0)
Delaware[8]	213 (0.6)	206 (1.1)	207 (1.7)	224 (0.6)	224 (0.7)	226 (0.8)	225 (0.7)	226 (0.5)	225 (0.7)	226 (0.8)	224 (0.8)	70 (1.2)	37 (1.2)	9 (0.7)
District of Columbia	188 (0.8)	179 (0.9)	179 (1.2)	191 (0.9)	188 (0.9)	191 (1.0)	197 (0.9)	202 (1.0)	201 (0.8)	206 (0.9)	212 (0.9)	56 (1.2)	27 (0.9)	8 (0.7)
Florida	208 (1.2)	205 (1.7)	206 (1.4)	214 (1.4)	218 (1.1)	219 (0.9)	224 (0.8)	226 (1.0)	225 (1.1)	227 (1.1)	227 (1.0)	75 (1.2)	39 (1.5)	8 (0.9)
Georgia	212 (1.5)	207 (2.4)	209 (1.4)	215 (1.0)	214 (1.3)	214 (1.2)	219 (0.9)	218 (1.1)	221 (1.1)	222 (1.1)	222 (1.2)	68 (1.5)	34 (1.6)	7 (1.0)
Hawaii	203 (1.7)	201 (1.7)	200 (1.5)	208 (0.9)	208 (1.4)	210 (1.0)	213 (1.1)	211 (1.0)	214 (1.0)	215 (1.0)	215 (1.0)	61 (1.2)	29 (1.2)	6 (0.6)
Idaho	219 (0.9)	‡ (†)	— (†)	220 (1.1)	218 (1.0)	222 (0.9)	223 (0.8)	221 (0.9)	221 (0.8)	219 (0.9)	222 (1.0)	69 (1.3)	36 (1.4)	8 (0.7)
Illinois	— (†)	— (†)	‡ (†)	‡ (†)	216 (1.6)	216 (1.2)	219 (1.2)	219 (1.4)	219 (1.1)	219 (1.4)	222 (1.2)	68 (1.3)	35 (1.5)	9 (0.9)
Indiana	221 (1.3)	220 (1.3)	— (†)	222 (1.4)	220 (1.0)	218 (1.1)	222 (0.9)	223 (1.1)	221 (0.9)	225 (1.0)	227 (1.1)	75 (1.3)	40 (1.6)	9 (0.8)
Iowa[6,7]	225 (1.1)	223 (1.3)	220 (1.6)	223 (1.1)	223 (1.1)	221 (0.9)	225 (1.1)	221 (1.2)	224 (0.8)	224 (1.1)	224 (1.1)	71 (1.4)	38 (1.6)	9 (0.8)
Kansas[6,7]	— (†)	— (†)	221 (1.4)	222 (1.4)	220 (1.2)	220 (1.3)	225 (1.1)	224 (1.3)	224 (1.0)	223 (1.3)	221 (1.5)	68 (1.6)	35 (1.8)	9 (1.0)
Kentucky	213 (1.3)	212 (1.6)	218 (1.5)	219 (1.1)	219 (1.3)	220 (1.1)	222 (1.1)	226 (1.1)	225 (1.0)	224 (1.2)	228 (1.2)	75 (1.3)	40 (1.6)	10 (1.1)
Louisiana	204 (1.2)	197 (1.3)	200 (1.6)	207 (1.7)	205 (1.4)	209 (1.3)	207 (1.6)	207 (1.1)	210 (1.4)	210 (1.3)	216 (1.5)	63 (1.9)	29 (1.6)	6 (1.0)
Maine[8]	227 (1.1)	228 (1.3)	225 (1.4)	225 (1.4)	224 (0.9)	225 (0.9)	226 (0.9)	224 (0.9)	222 (0.7)	225 (1.0)	224 (0.9)	71 (1.2)	36 (1.3)	8 (0.7)
Maryland	211 (1.6)	210 (1.5)	212 (1.6)	217 (1.5)	219 (1.4)	220 (1.3)	225 (1.1)	226 (1.4)	231 (0.9)	232 (1.3)	223 (1.3)	68 (1.5)	37 (1.7)	10 (0.9)
Massachusetts[6]	226 (0.9)	223 (1.3)	223 (1.4)	234 (1.1)	228 (1.2)	231 (0.9)	236 (1.1)	234 (1.1)	237 (1.0)	232 (1.1)	235 (1.0)	82 (1.2)	50 (1.5)	14 (1.0)
Michigan	216 (1.5)	‡ (†)	216 (1.5)	219 (1.1)	219 (1.2)	218 (1.5)	220 (1.4)	218 (1.0)	219 (1.2)	217 (1.4)	216 (1.3)	63 (1.8)	29 (1.6)	5 (0.8)
Minnesota[6,7]	221 (1.2)	218 (1.4)	219 (1.7)	225 (1.4)	223 (1.2)	225 (1.3)	225 (1.1)	223 (1.3)	222 (1.2)	227 (1.2)	223 (1.3)	71 (1.4)	39 (1.5)	9 (1.0)
Mississippi	199 (1.3)	202 (1.6)	203 (1.3)	203 (1.3)	205 (1.3)	204 (1.3)	208 (1.0)	211 (1.1)	209 (1.2)	209 (0.9)	214 (1.0)	60 (1.4)	26 (1.3)	5 (0.6)
Missouri	220 (1.2)	217 (1.5)	216 (1.3)	220 (1.3)	222 (1.2)	221 (0.9)	221 (1.1)	224 (1.1)	220 (0.9)	222 (1.0)	223 (1.1)	70 (1.2)	36 (1.5)	9 (0.8)
Montana[6,7,9]	— (†)	222 (1.4)	225 (1.5)	224 (1.8)	223 (1.2)	225 (1.1)	227 (1.0)	225 (0.8)	225 (0.6)	223 (0.8)	225 (0.8)	72 (1.2)	37 (1.2)	8 (0.6)
Nebraska[8,9]	221 (1.1)	220 (1.5)	— (†)	222 (1.5)	221 (1.0)	221 (1.2)	223 (1.3)	223 (1.0)	223 (1.0)	223 (1.0)	227 (1.1)	74 (1.3)	40 (1.5)	9 (1.0)
Nevada	— (†)	— (†)	206 (1.8)	209 (1.2)	207 (1.2)	207 (1.2)	211 (1.2)	211 (1.1)	213 (1.0)	214 (1.1)	214 (1.2)	61 (1.4)	29 (1.3)	6 (0.7)
New Hampshire[6,8,9]	228 (1.2)	223 (1.5)	226 (1.7)	— (†)	228 (1.0)	227 (0.9)	229 (0.9)	229 (1.0)	230 (0.8)	232 (0.9)	232 (1.0)	79 (1.2)	46 (1.5)	12 (0.8)
New Jersey[8]	223 (1.4)	219 (1.2)	— (†)	— (†)	225 (1.2)	223 (1.3)	231 (1.2)	229 (0.9)	231 (1.2)	229 (1.3)	229 (1.1)	75 (1.5)	43 (1.8)	12 (1.2)
New Mexico	211 (1.5)	205 (1.7)	205 (1.4)	208 (1.6)	203 (1.5)	207 (1.3)	212 (1.3)	208 (1.4)	208 (1.0)	206 (1.1)	207 (1.0)	54 (1.4)	23 (1.2)	4 (0.5)
New York[6,7,8]	215 (1.4)	212 (1.4)	215 (1.6)	222 (1.5)	222 (1.1)	223 (1.0)	224 (1.0)	224 (1.0)	222 (1.1)	224 (1.2)	223 (1.1)	68 (1.2)	36 (1.5)	9 (0.9)
North Carolina	212 (1.1)	214 (1.5)	213 (1.6)	222 (1.0)	221 (1.0)	217 (1.0)	218 (0.9)	219 (1.1)	221 (1.2)	222 (1.1)	226 (1.1)	73 (1.4)	38 (1.5)	9 (1.0)
North Dakota[7]	226 (1.1)	225 (1.2)	— (†)	224 (1.0)	222 (0.9)	225 (0.7)	226 (0.9)	226 (0.8)	226 (0.5)	224 (0.5)	225 (0.7)	73 (1.0)	37 (0.9)	7 (0.7)
Ohio	217 (1.3)	— (†)	— (†)	222 (1.3)	222 (1.2)	223 (1.4)	226 (1.1)	225 (1.1)	224 (1.0)	224 (1.0)	225 (1.2)	72 (1.3)	38 (1.7)	8 (1.0)
Oklahoma	220 (0.9)	— (†)	219 (1.2)	213 (1.2)	214 (1.2)	214 (1.1)	217 (1.1)	217 (1.1)	215 (1.1)	217 (1.1)	222 (1.1)	71 (1.4)	33 (1.5)	6 (0.7)
Oregon	— (†)	— (†)	212 (1.8)	220 (1.4)	218 (1.3)	217 (1.4)	215 (1.4)	218 (1.2)	216 (1.1)	219 (1.3)	220 (1.4)	67 (1.6)	34 (1.6)	8 (0.9)
Pennsylvania[9]	221 (1.3)	215 (1.6)	— (†)	221 (1.2)	219 (1.3)	223 (1.3)	226 (1.0)	224 (1.4)	227 (1.2)	226 (1.3)	227 (1.0)	74 (1.9)	41 (2.0)	11 (1.0)
Rhode Island[9]	217 (1.8)	220 (1.3)	218 (1.4)	220 (1.2)	216 (1.3)	216 (1.2)	219 (1.0)	223 (1.1)	222 (0.8)	223 (0.9)	225 (0.9)	72 (1.1)	40 (1.3)	10 (0.8)
South Carolina	210 (1.3)	203 (1.4)	209 (1.4)	214 (1.3)	215 (1.3)	213 (1.3)	214 (1.2)	216 (1.1)	215 (1.2)	214 (1.2)	218 (1.4)	65 (1.4)	33 (1.6)	8 (0.9)
South Dakota	— (†)	— (†)	— (†)	— (†)	222 (1.2)	222 (0.5)	223 (1.0)	222 (0.6)	220 (0.9)	218 (1.0)	220 (0.9)	68 (1.2)	35 (1.1)	8 (0.7)
Tennessee[7,9]	212 (1.4)	213 (1.7)	212 (1.4)	214 (1.2)	212 (1.6)	214 (1.4)	216 (1.2)	217 (1.2)	215 (1.1)	220 (1.4)	219 (1.4)	66 (1.7)	33 (1.7)	8 (1.0)
Texas	213 (1.6)	212 (1.9)	214 (1.9)	217 (1.7)	215 (1.0)	219 (0.8)	220 (0.9)	219 (1.2)	218 (1.5)	217 (1.7)	218 (1.7)	64 (1.9)	31 (1.9)	7 (0.9)
Utah	220 (1.1)	217 (1.3)	216 (1.2)	222 (1.0)	219 (1.0)	221 (1.0)	221 (1.2)	219 (1.0)	220 (1.0)	223 (1.1)	226 (1.1)	74 (1.1)	40 (1.5)	10 (1.1)
Vermont	— (†)	— (†)	— (†)	227 (1.1)	226 (0.9)	227 (0.9)	228 (0.8)	229 (0.8)	227 (0.6)	228 (0.6)	230 (0.8)	76 (1.0)	45 (1.4)	12 (0.9)
Virginia	221 (1.4)	213 (1.5)	217 (1.2)	225 (1.3)	223 (1.5)	226 (0.8)	227 (1.1)	227 (1.2)	226 (1.1)	229 (1.3)	229 (1.7)	74 (1.8)	43 (2.1)	14 (1.4)
Washington[7]	— (†)	213 (1.5)	218 (1.4)	224 (1.2)	221 (1.1)	223 (1.1)	224 (1.4)	221 (1.2)	221 (1.1)	225 (1.4)	226 (1.5)	71 (1.5)	40 (1.8)	12 (1.2)
West Virginia	216 (1.3)	213 (1.1)	216 (1.7)	219 (1.2)	219 (1.0)	215 (0.8)	215 (1.1)	215 (1.0)	214 (0.8)	215 (0.8)	216 (1.2)	64 (1.3)	30 (1.5)	6 (0.7)
Wisconsin[6,9]	224 (1.0)	224 (1.1)	222 (1.1)	‡ (†)	221 (0.8)	221 (1.0)	223 (1.2)	220 (1.1)	221 (0.8)	221 (1.6)	223 (1.1)	71 (1.4)	37 (1.5)	8 (0.7)
Wyoming	223 (1.1)	221 (1.2)	218 (1.5)	221 (1.0)	222 (0.8)	223 (0.7)	225 (0.5)	223 (0.7)	224 (0.8)	226 (0.6)	228 (0.7)	75 (1.0)	41 (1.2)	10 (0.7)
Department of Defense dependents schools[10]	— (†)	— (†)	220 (0.7)	224 (0.4)	224 (0.5)	226 (0.6)	229 (0.5)	228 (0.5)	229 (0.5)	232 (0.6)	234 (0.7)	83 (1.1)	47 (1.3)	9 (0.9)

—Not available.

†Not applicable.

‡Reporting standards not met. Participation rates fell below the required standards for reporting.

[1]Scale ranges from 0 to 500.

[2]Accommodations were not permitted for this assessment.

[3]Basic denotes partial mastery of the knowledge and skills that are fundamental for proficient work at the 4th-grade level.

[4]Proficient represents solid academic performance for 4th-graders. Students reaching this level have demonstrated competency over challenging subject matter.

[5]Advanced signifies superior performance.

[6]Did not meet one or more of the guidelines for school participation in 1998. Data are subject to appreciable nonresponse bias.

[7]Did not meet one or more of the guidelines for school participation in 2002. Data are subject to appreciable nonresponse bias.

[8]Did not meet one or more of the guidelines for school participation in 1992. Data are subject to appreciable nonresponse bias.

[9]Did not meet one or more of the guidelines for school participation in 1994. Data are subject to appreciable nonresponse bias.

[10]Prior to 2005, NAEP divided the Department of Defense (DoD) schools into two jurisdictions, domestic and overseas. In 2005, NAEP began combining the DoD domestic and overseas schools into a single jurisdiction. Data shown in this table for years prior to 2005 were recalculated for comparability.

NOTE: For 1998 and later years, includes public school students who were tested with accommodations; excludes only those students with disabilities (SD) and English language learners (ELL) who were unable to be tested even with accommodations. SD and ELL populations, accommodation rates, and exclusion rates vary from state to state. Some data have been revised from previously published estimates.

SOURCE: U.S. Department of Education, National Center for Education Statistics, National Assessment of Educational Progress (NAEP), 1992, 1994, 1998, 2002, 2003, 2005, 2007, 2009, 2011, 2013, and 2015 Reading Assessments, retrieved November 11, 2015, from the Main NAEP Data Explorer (http://nces.ed.gov/nationsreportcard/naepdata/). (This table was prepared November 2015.)

Table 221.50. Average National Assessment of Educational Progress (NAEP) reading scale score of 4th-grade public school students, by race/ethnicity, school's level of free or reduced-price lunch eligibility, and state: 2015

[Standard errors appear in parentheses]

State	Race/ethnicity							Percent of students in school eligible for free or reduced-price lunch			
	White	Black	Hispanic	Asian	Pacific Islander	American Indian/Alaska Native	Two or more races	0–25 percent eligible (low poverty)	26–50 percent eligible	51–75 percent eligible	76–100 percent eligible (high poverty)
1	2	3	4	5	6	7	8	9	10	11	12
United States	232 (0.3)	206 (0.5)	208 (0.8)	240 (1.7)	212 (2.2)	206 (1.5)	226 (1.0)	241 (0.5)	228 (0.5)	219 (0.7)	205 (0.7)
Alabama	226 (1.6)	204 (2.0)	199 (3.1)	‡ (†)	‡ (†)	‡ (†)	‡ (†)	232 (3.5)	226 (3.0)	218 (2.0)	205 (2.2)
Alaska	228 (1.6)	209 (5.4)	215 (3.0)	210 (3.8)	211 (5.0)	184 (3.4)	217 (3.1)	232 (2.4)	219 (2.0)	213 (3.3)	190 (4.7)
Arizona	229 (1.7)	217 (3.7)	204 (1.7)	‡ (†)	‡ (†)	191 (4.1)	‡ (†)	241 (3.2)	232 (2.7)	212 (3.0)	200 (1.7)
Arkansas	224 (1.2)	202 (2.2)	210 (2.9)	‡ (†)	‡ (†)	‡ (†)	‡ (†)	‡ (†)	227 (2.7)	219 (1.3)	209 (2.0)
California	231 (1.8)	198 (4.0)	201 (2.1)	237 (4.3)	‡ (†)	‡ (†)	228 (7.5)	243 (2.6)	220 (2.5)	212 (2.9)	197 (2.5)
Colorado	236 (1.4)	214 (5.0)	206 (1.9)	‡ (†)	‡ (†)	‡ (†)	232 (4.7)	243 (2.1)	225 (2.5)	222 (3.3)	201 (2.5)
Connecticut............	240 (1.5)	205 (2.3)	210 (1.8)	235 (3.5)	‡ (†)	‡ (†)	‡ (†)	241 (1.8)	225 (2.2)	216 (2.9)	204 (2.5)
Delaware................	236 (1.1)	210 (1.7)	210 (2.2)	240 (4.4)	‡ (†)	‡ (†)	229 (5.1)	246 (2.1)	229 (1.7)	223 (1.6)	210 (1.6)
District of Columbia	260 (2.3)	204 (1.0)	207 (2.8)	‡ (†)	‡ (†)	‡ (†)	‡ (†)	243 (2.1)	235 (4.0)	211 (3.6)	201 (1.2)
Florida..................	235 (1.5)	213 (1.9)	224 (1.4)	250 (3.2)	‡ (†)	‡ (†)	226 (3.1)	243 (2.0)	234 (1.5)	232 (1.5)	216 (1.7)
Georgia..................	232 (1.4)	212 (1.8)	211 (2.3)	241 (4.5)	‡ (†)	‡ (†)	222 (4.5)	243 (5.2)	232 (1.8)	224 (1.6)	211 (1.9)
Hawaii...................	233 (2.2)	‡ (†)	212 (4.2)	220 (1.4)	201 (1.5)	‡ (†)	225 (2.9)	241 (2.5)	221 (2.0)	211 (1.8)	195 (2.6)
Idaho....................	227 (1.0)	‡ (†)	200 (2.4)	‡ (†)	‡ (†)	‡ (†)	‡ (†)	232 (3.2)	230 (1.4)	218 (1.6)	207 (3.2)
Illinois................	233 (1.5)	202 (2.2)	211 (1.5)	248 (4.5)	‡ (†)	‡ (†)	224 (4.4)	240 (3.2)	229 (2.5)	222 (2.4)	204 (2.4)
Indiana..................	231 (1.1)	212 (2.3)	216 (3.0)	‡ (†)	‡ (†)	‡ (†)	228 (4.3)	241 (1.8)	229 (1.5)	227 (1.6)	214 (2.8)
Iowa.....................	228 (1.2)	195 (3.8)	209 (2.3)	233 (5.7)	‡ (†)	‡ (†)	227 (4.5)	239 (1.8)	226 (1.5)	216 (1.4)	205 (4.5)
Kansas...................	227 (1.4)	198 (5.4)	208 (1.9)	237 (5.4)	‡ (†)	‡ (†)	218 (4.3)	245 (2.9)	228 (1.9)	219 (1.6)	200 (2.3)
Kentucky.................	231 (1.3)	212 (2.4)	216 (2.8)	‡ (†)	‡ (†)	‡ (†)	225 (4.7)	‡ (†)	238 (2.0)	226 (1.4)	218 (1.3)
Louisiana...............	226 (1.6)	204 (1.8)	217 (4.3)	‡ (†)	‡ (†)	‡ (†)	‡ (†)	‡ (†)	229 (3.0)	223 (1.8)	210 (2.1)
Maine....................	225 (0.9)	196 (8.4)	‡ (†)	‡ (†)	‡ (†)	‡ (†)	‡ (†)	238 (2.1)	227 (1.4)	219 (1.5)	207 (4.8)
Maryland.................	235 (1.7)	208 (1.4)	210 (3.2)	238 (3.9)	‡ (†)	‡ (†)	236 (4.0)	242 (2.5)	228 (2.9)	213 (2.5)	202 (1.9)
Massachusetts............	242 (1.1)	217 (2.9)	215 (1.8)	249 (3.9)	‡ (†)	‡ (†)	233 (4.3)	248 (1.6)	236 (2.0)	221 (5.2)	212 (2.5)
Michigan.................	221 (1.5)	192 (2.3)	206 (3.3)	236 (4.2)	‡ (†)	‡ (†)	223 (5.2)	233 (2.1)	222 (2.3)	212 (1.8)	198 (2.6)
Minnesota................	232 (1.2)	195 (4.0)	199 (4.5)	222 (6.0)	‡ (†)	198 (6.8)	218 (4.0)	237 (2.3)	225 (1.8)	221 (2.5)	197 (4.8)
Mississippi..............	227 (1.2)	202 (1.4)	210 (3.9)	‡ (†)	‡ (†)	‡ (†)	‡ (†)	‡ (†)	230 (2.3)	218 (1.6)	206 (1.7)
Missouri.................	229 (1.1)	202 (3.0)	209 (4.6)	‡ (†)	‡ (†)	‡ (†)	215 (5.8)	239 (1.9)	228 (1.9)	221 (2.0)	207 (2.3)
Montana..................	229 (0.8)	‡ (†)	219 (3.9)	‡ (†)	‡ (†)	199 (3.1)	222 (3.3)	235 (1.7)	229 (1.3)	224 (1.9)	204 (2.5)
Nebraska.................	234 (1.0)	208 (3.1)	208 (2.1)	‡ (†)	‡ (†)	‡ (†)	219 (4.7)	240 (1.8)	228 (1.6)	226 (1.9)	210 (2.5)
Nevada...................	228 (1.9)	200 (2.9)	204 (1.5)	234 (3.6)	‡ (†)	‡ (†)	223 (3.6)	236 (2.7)	222 (2.2)	215 (3.0)	201 (2.2)
New Hampshire............	233 (1.0)	‡ (†)	217 (3.1)	241 (3.5)	‡ (†)	‡ (†)	‡ (†)	238 (1.1)	229 (1.7)	218 (3.1)	‡ (†)
New Jersey...............	239 (1.7)	213 (2.3)	216 (2.7)	250 (3.7)	‡ (†)	‡ (†)	‡ (†)	243 (2.6)	229 (1.9)	218 (2.9)	210 (4.1)
New Mexico...............	225 (1.6)	‡ (†)	202 (1.2)	‡ (†)	‡ (†)	184 (4.9)	‡ (†)	‡ (†)	216 (2.7)	213 (1.9)	196 (2.1)
New York.................	234 (1.4)	208 (2.5)	209 (1.5)	236 (3.6)	‡ (†)	‡ (†)	‡ (†)	238 (2.6)	229 (2.9)	222 (2.7)	208 (2.4)
North Carolina..........	236 (1.3)	214 (1.6)	212 (2.0)	242 (5.2)	‡ (†)	198 (7.4)	228 (4.6)	245 (2.0)	233 (2.4)	221 (2.0)	213 (1.6)
North Dakota.............	229 (0.7)	208 (3.8)	205 (4.0)	‡ (†)	‡ (†)	204 (2.9)	‡ (†)	230 (1.1)	225 (1.1)	221 (2.5)	202 (3.9)
Ohio.....................	230 (1.3)	205 (1.8)	210 (4.5)	‡ (†)	‡ (†)	‡ (†)	221 (3.8)	241 (2.3)	228 (1.4)	221 (2.0)	209 (2.8)
Oklahoma.................	226 (1.3)	205 (3.1)	213 (2.3)	‡ (†)	‡ (†)	223 (2.1)	225 (2.9)	242 (4.5)	227 (1.6)	223 (2.2)	212 (1.8)
Oregon...................	227 (1.4)	‡ (†)	202 (2.4)	232 (4.2)	‡ (†)	192 (7.5)	223 (3.4)	239 (2.4)	232 (3.0)	217 (2.1)	208 (2.2)
Pennsylvania.............	234 (1.4)	205 (2.8)	201 (2.9)	233 (5.9)	‡ (†)	‡ (†)	222 (4.7)	244 (1.8)	229 (1.7)	222 (2.4)	197 (3.0)
Rhode Island	234 (1.0)	215 (2.9)	207 (1.7)	223 (4.1)	‡ (†)	‡ (†)	221 (3.8)	240 (1.1)	231 (1.5)	224 (2.4)	205 (2.2)
South Carolina..........	230 (1.6)	200 (1.8)	203 (4.6)	‡ (†)	‡ (†)	‡ (†)	219 (4.9)	241 (3.3)	230 (2.9)	218 (2.0)	204 (2.0)
South Dakota.............	227 (1.0)	202 (5.4)	202 (4.0)	‡ (†)	‡ (†)	192 (3.2)	220 (3.8)	233 (1.5)	225 (1.3)	213 (2.7)	194 (2.9)
Tennessee................	225 (1.6)	199 (2.2)	214 (3.5)	‡ (†)	‡ (†)	‡ (†)	225 (5.2)	236 (6.1)	235 (3.2)	216 (2.4)	204 (2.1)
Texas....................	235 (2.3)	205 (2.9)	210 (1.8)	248 (6.1)	‡ (†)	‡ (†)	225 (5.5)	241 (2.7)	229 (2.1)	218 (2.8)	206 (1.6)
Utah.....................	231 (1.2)	‡ (†)	204 (2.3)	‡ (†)	‡ (†)	‡ (†)	‡ (†)	234 (1.5)	226 (2.5)	219 (3.0)	203 (3.5)
Vermont..................	231 (0.8)	‡ (†)	‡ (†)	‡ (†)	‡ (†)	‡ (†)	‡ (†)	239 (1.9)	233 (1.3)	225 (1.5)	211 (4.0)
Virginia.................	238 (1.5)	208 (2.6)	217 (3.1)	248 (3.8)	‡ (†)	‡ (†)	237 (3.7)	246 (2.3)	230 (3.0)	219 (2.0)	205 (3.6)
Washington...............	234 (1.6)	215 (4.2)	203 (2.0)	248 (3.7)	‡ (†)	198 (8.9)	225 (3.5)	243 (2.7)	231 (2.8)	217 (2.1)	207 (3.5)
West Virginia............	217 (1.3)	210 (4.6)	‡ (†)	‡ (†)	‡ (†)	‡ (†)	211 (4.4)	‡ (†)	227 (2.1)	215 (1.8)	208 (2.1)
Wisconsin................	231 (1.0)	193 (3.0)	209 (2.7)	222 (5.0)	‡ (†)	207 (7.1)	‡ (†)	238 (2.0)	228 (2.0)	214 (2.5)	198 (2.3)
Wyoming..................	232 (0.8)	‡ (†)	216 (1.9)	‡ (†)	‡ (†)	204 (4.5)	‡ (†)	233 (1.7)	231 (0.9)	221 (1.7)	214 (4.1)
Department of Defense dependents schools.....	237 (1.1)	228 (2.1)	228 (1.6)	236 (2.9)	‡ (†)	‡ (†)	237 (2.0)	237 (1.4)	234 (1.2)	228 (2.3)	‡ (†)

†Not applicable.
‡Reporting standards not met (too few cases for a reliable estimate).
NOTE: Scale ranges from 0 to 500. Includes public school students who were tested with accommodations; excludes only those students with disabilities (SD) and English language learners (ELL) who were unable to be tested even with accommodations. SD and ELL popula-tions, accommodation rates, and exclusion rates vary from state to state. Race/ethnicity based on school records. Race categories exclude persons of Hispanic ethnicity.
SOURCE: U.S. Department of Education, National Center for Education Statistics, National Assessment of Educational Progress (NAEP), 2015 Reading Assessment, retrieved November 4, 2015, from the Main NAEP Data Explorer (http://nces.ed.gov/nationsreportcard/naepdata/). (This table was prepared November 2015.)

Table 221.60. Average National Assessment of Educational Progress (NAEP) reading scale score of 8th-grade public school students and percentage attaining reading achievement levels, by state: Selected years, 1998 through 2015

[Standard errors appear in parentheses]

State	Average scale score[1]									Percent attaining reading achievement levels, 2015		
	1998	2002	2003	2005	2007	2009	2011	2013	2015	At or above Basic[2]	At or above Proficient[3]	At Advanced[4]
1	2	3	4	5	6	7	8	9	10	11	12	13
United States	261 (0.8)	263 (0.5)	261 (0.2)	260 (0.2)	261 (0.2)	262 (0.3)	264 (0.2)	266 (0.2)	264 (0.2)	75 (0.3)	33 (0.3)	3 (0.1)
Alabama..........................	255 (1.4)	253 (1.3)	253 (1.5)	252 (1.4)	252 (1.0)	255 (1.1)	258 (1.5)	257 (1.2)	259 (1.1)	71 (1.6)	26 (1.4)	2 (0.4)
Alaska............................	— (†)	— (†)	256 (1.1)	259 (0.9)	259 (1.0)	259 (0.9)	261 (0.9)	261 (0.8)	260 (1.1)	71 (1.4)	31 (1.5)	3 (0.4)
Arizona...........................	260 (1.1)	257 (1.3)	255 (1.4)	255 (1.0)	255 (1.2)	258 (1.2)	260 (1.2)	260 (1.1)	263 (1.2)	74 (1.3)	31 (1.7)	2 (0.5)
Arkansas........................	256 (1.3)	260 (1.1)	258 (1.3)	258 (1.1)	258 (1.0)	258 (1.2)	259 (0.9)	262 (1.1)	259 (1.2)	70 (1.5)	27 (1.6)	2 (0.5)
California[5,6]....................	252 (1.6)	250 (1.8)	251 (1.3)	250 (0.6)	251 (0.8)	253 (1.2)	255 (1.0)	262 (1.2)	259 (1.2)	70 (1.4)	28 (1.5)	3 (0.4)
Colorado.........................	264 (1.0)	— (†)	268 (1.2)	265 (1.1)	266 (1.0)	266 (0.8)	271 (1.4)	271 (1.1)	268 (1.4)	78 (1.3)	38 (2.0)	3 (0.6)
Connecticut.....................	270 (1.0)	267 (1.2)	267 (1.1)	264 (1.3)	267 (1.6)	272 (0.9)	275 (0.9)	274 (1.0)	273 (1.1)	82 (1.0)	43 (1.7)	6 (0.9)
Delaware........................	254 (1.3)	267 (0.5)	265 (0.7)	266 (0.6)	265 (0.7)	265 (0.7)	266 (0.6)	266 (0.7)	263 (0.8)	73 (1.1)	31 (1.0)	3 (0.5)
District of Columbia	236 (2.1)	240 (2.0)	239 (0.8)	238 (0.9)	241 (0.7)	242 (0.9)	242 (0.9)	248 (0.9)	248 (1.0)	56 (1.4)	19 (1.0)	3 (0.4)
Florida............................	255 (1.4)	261 (1.6)	257 (1.3)	256 (1.2)	260 (1.2)	264 (1.2)	262 (1.0)	266 (1.1)	263 (1.0)	75 (1.1)	30 (1.4)	2 (0.4)
Georgia...........................	257 (1.4)	258 (1.0)	258 (1.1)	257 (1.3)	259 (1.0)	260 (1.0)	262 (1.1)	265 (1.2)	262 (1.3)	73 (1.5)	30 (1.8)	3 (0.7)
Hawaii............................	249 (1.0)	252 (0.9)	251 (0.9)	249 (0.9)	251 (0.8)	255 (0.6)	257 (0.7)	260 (0.8)	257 (0.9)	68 (1.2)	26 (1.1)	2 (0.4)
Idaho..............................	— (†)	266 (1.1)	264 (0.9)	264 (1.1)	265 (0.9)	265 (0.9)	268 (0.7)	270 (0.8)	269 (0.9)	81 (1.0)	37 (1.4)	3 (0.5)
Illinois............................	‡ (†)	‡ (†)	266 (1.0)	264 (1.0)	263 (1.0)	265 (1.2)	266 (0.8)	267 (1.0)	267 (1.0)	77 (1.1)	35 (1.5)	4 (0.7)
Indiana...........................	— (†)	265 (1.3)	265 (1.0)	261 (1.1)	264 (1.1)	266 (1.0)	265 (1.0)	267 (1.2)	268 (1.1)	80 (1.1)	37 (1.6)	4 (0.6)
Iowa...............................	— (†)	— (†)	268 (1.0)	267 (0.9)	267 (0.9)	265 (0.9)	265 (1.0)	269 (0.8)	268 (1.0)	81 (1.2)	36 (1.6)	3 (0.6)
Kansas[5,6]......................	268 (1.4)	269 (1.3)	266 (1.5)	267 (1.0)	267 (0.8)	267 (0.8)	267 (1.0)	267 (1.0)	267 (1.2)	79 (1.3)	35 (1.8)	3 (0.5)
Kentucky.........................	262 (1.4)	265 (1.3)	266 (1.3)	264 (1.1)	262 (1.0)	267 (0.9)	269 (0.8)	270 (0.8)	268 (1.0)	78 (1.2)	36 (1.5)	4 (0.6)
Louisiana........................	252 (1.4)	256 (1.5)	253 (1.6)	253 (1.6)	253 (1.1)	253 (1.6)	255 (1.5)	257 (1.0)	255 (1.2)	66 (1.8)	23 (1.4)	2 (0.3)
Maine.............................	271 (1.2)	270 (0.9)	268 (1.0)	270 (1.0)	270 (0.8)	268 (0.7)	270 (0.8)	269 (0.8)	268 (0.9)	81 (1.0)	36 (1.5)	2 (0.5)
Maryland[5]......................	261 (1.8)	263 (1.7)	262 (1.4)	261 (1.2)	265 (1.2)	267 (1.1)	271 (1.2)	274 (1.1)	268 (1.1)	76 (1.1)	37 (1.6)	5 (0.6)
Massachusetts.................	269 (1.4)	271 (1.3)	273 (1.3)	274 (1.0)	273 (1.0)	274 (1.2)	275 (1.0)	277 (1.0)	274 (1.1)	83 (1.2)	46 (1.5)	6 (0.8)
Michigan.........................	— (†)	265 (1.6)	264 (1.8)	261 (1.2)	260 (1.2)	262 (1.4)	265 (0.9)	266 (1.0)	264 (1.2)	76 (1.3)	32 (1.6)	3 (0.5)
Minnesota[5]....................	265 (1.4)	‡ (†)	268 (1.1)	268 (0.9)	268 (0.9)	270 (1.0)	270 (1.0)	271 (1.0)	270 (1.1)	81 (1.1)	40 (1.5)	4 (0.8)
Mississippi......................	251 (1.2)	255 (0.9)	255 (1.4)	251 (1.3)	250 (1.1)	251 (1.0)	254 (1.2)	253 (1.0)	252 (1.0)	63 (1.5)	20 (1.1)	1 (0.3)
Missouri..........................	262 (1.3)	268 (1.0)	267 (1.0)	265 (1.0)	263 (1.0)	267 (1.0)	267 (1.1)	267 (1.1)	267 (1.1)	77 (1.3)	36 (1.5)	3 (0.5)
Montana[5,6]....................	271 (1.3)	270 (1.0)	270 (1.0)	269 (0.7)	271 (0.8)	270 (0.6)	273 (0.6)	272 (0.8)	270 (0.8)	82 (1.0)	37 (1.4)	3 (0.5)
Nebraska........................	— (†)	270 (0.9)	266 (0.9)	267 (0.9)	267 (0.9)	267 (0.9)	268 (0.7)	269 (0.8)	269 (0.9)	81 (1.1)	38 (1.5)	3 (0.5)
Nevada...........................	258 (1.0)	251 (0.8)	252 (0.8)	253 (0.9)	252 (0.8)	254 (0.9)	258 (0.9)	262 (0.7)	259 (0.9)	71 (1.2)	27 (1.4)	2 (0.4)
New Hampshire.................	— (†)	— (†)	271 (0.9)	270 (1.2)	270 (0.9)	271 (1.0)	272 (0.7)	274 (0.8)	275 (0.9)	85 (0.9)	45 (1.3)	5 (0.7)
New Jersey......................	— (†)	— (†)	268 (1.2)	269 (1.2)	270 (1.1)	273 (1.3)	275 (1.2)	276 (1.1)	271 (1.0)	80 (1.3)	41 (1.4)	6 (0.8)
New Mexico.....................	258 (1.2)	254 (1.0)	252 (0.9)	251 (1.0)	251 (0.8)	254 (1.2)	256 (0.9)	256 (0.8)	253 (0.9)	65 (1.3)	20 (1.3)	1 (0.3)
New York[5,6]...................	265 (1.5)	264 (1.5)	265 (1.3)	265 (1.0)	264 (1.1)	264 (1.2)	266 (1.1)	266 (1.1)	263 (1.4)	73 (1.4)	33 (1.7)	4 (0.7)
North Carolina..................	262 (1.1)	265 (1.1)	262 (1.0)	258 (0.9)	259 (1.1)	260 (1.2)	263 (0.9)	265 (1.1)	261 (1.3)	72 (1.4)	30 (1.6)	3 (0.6)
North Dakota[6].................	— (†)	268 (0.8)	270 (0.8)	270 (0.6)	268 (0.7)	269 (0.6)	269 (0.7)	268 (0.6)	267 (0.6)	80 (0.9)	34 (1.1)	2 (0.4)
Ohio...............................	— (†)	268 (1.6)	267 (1.3)	267 (1.3)	268 (1.2)	269 (1.3)	268 (1.1)	269 (1.0)	266 (1.5)	76 (1.7)	36 (1.7)	4 (0.5)
Oklahoma.......................	265 (1.2)	262 (0.8)	262 (0.9)	260 (1.4)	260 (0.8)	259 (0.9)	260 (1.1)	262 (0.9)	263 (1.3)	76 (1.5)	29 (1.6)	2 (0.4)
Oregon[6]........................	266 (1.5)	268 (1.3)	264 (1.2)	263 (1.1)	266 (0.9)	265 (1.0)	264 (0.9)	268 (0.9)	268 (1.3)	79 (1.2)	36 (1.8)	4 (0.7)
Pennsylvania...................	— (†)	265 (1.0)	264 (1.2)	267 (1.3)	268 (1.2)	271 (0.8)	268 (1.3)	272 (1.0)	269 (1.5)	78 (1.6)	39 (2.0)	5 (0.7)
Rhode Island	264 (0.9)	262 (0.8)	261 (0.7)	261 (0.7)	258 (0.9)	260 (0.6)	265 (0.7)	267 (0.6)	265 (0.7)	76 (0.9)	35 (1.2)	4 (0.6)
South Carolina..................	255 (1.1)	258 (1.1)	258 (1.3)	257 (1.1)	257 (0.9)	257 (1.2)	260 (0.9)	261 (1.0)	260 (1.2)	71 (1.5)	28 (1.5)	2 (0.4)
South Dakota....................	— (†)	— (†)	270 (0.8)	269 (0.6)	270 (0.7)	270 (0.5)	269 (0.8)	268 (0.8)	267 (1.0)	80 (1.4)	34 (1.3)	2 (0.4)
Tennessee[6]....................	258 (1.2)	260 (1.4)	258 (1.2)	259 (0.9)	259 (1.0)	261 (1.1)	259 (1.0)	265 (1.1)	265 (1.4)	76 (1.5)	33 (1.8)	3 (0.7)
Texas.............................	261 (1.4)	262 (1.4)	259 (1.1)	258 (1.0)	261 (0.9)	260 (1.1)	261 (1.0)	264 (1.1)	261 (1.0)	72 (1.1)	28 (1.6)	2 (0.4)
Utah...............................	263 (1.0)	263 (1.1)	264 (0.8)	262 (0.8)	262 (1.0)	266 (0.8)	267 (0.8)	270 (0.9)	269 (1.0)	81 (1.2)	38 (1.4)	4 (0.6)
Vermont..........................	— (†)	272 (0.9)	271 (0.8)	269 (0.7)	273 (0.8)	272 (0.6)	274 (0.9)	274 (0.7)	274 (0.8)	83 (1.0)	44 (1.4)	6 (0.7)
Virginia...........................	266 (1.1)	269 (1.0)	268 (1.1)	268 (1.0)	267 (1.1)	266 (1.1)	267 (1.2)	268 (1.3)	267 (1.2)	77 (1.2)	36 (1.8)	3 (0.6)
Washington[6]...................	264 (1.2)	268 (1.2)	264 (0.9)	265 (1.3)	265 (0.9)	267 (1.1)	268 (1.0)	272 (1.0)	267 (1.2)	77 (1.2)	37 (1.6)	4 (0.6)
West Virginia....................	262 (1.0)	264 (1.0)	260 (1.0)	255 (1.2)	255 (1.0)	255 (0.9)	256 (0.9)	257 (0.9)	260 (0.9)	72 (1.3)	27 (1.3)	2 (0.5)
Wisconsin[5].....................	265 (1.8)	‡ (†)	266 (1.3)	266 (1.1)	264 (1.0)	266 (1.0)	267 (0.9)	268 (0.9)	270 (1.1)	79 (1.1)	39 (1.7)	4 (0.7)
Wyoming.........................	263 (1.3)	265 (0.7)	267 (0.5)	268 (0.7)	266 (0.7)	268 (1.0)	270 (1.0)	271 (0.6)	269 (0.7)	81 (1.0)	36 (1.2)	3 (0.5)
Department of Defense dependents schools[7]	269 (1.3)	273 (0.5)	272 (0.6)	271 (0.7)	273 (1.0)	272 (0.7)	272 (0.7)	277 (0.7)	277 (0.7)	90 (0.9)	47 (1.6)	3 (0.7)

—Not available.
†Not applicable.
‡Reporting standards not met. Either there are too few cases for a reliable estimate or item response rates fell below the required standards for reporting.
[1]Scale ranges from 0 to 500.
[2]*Basic* denotes partial mastery of the knowledge and skills that are fundamental for proficient work at the 8th-grade level.
[3]*Proficient* represents solid academic performance for 8th-graders. Students reaching this level have demonstrated competency over challenging subject matter.
[4]*Advanced* signifies superior performance.
[5]Did not meet one or more of the guidelines for school participation in 1998. Data are subject to appreciable nonresponse bias.
[6]Did not meet one or more of the guidelines for school participation in 2002. Data are subject to appreciable nonresponse bias.

[7]Prior to 2005, NAEP divided the Department of Defense (DoD) schools into two jurisdictions, domestic and overseas. In 2005, NAEP began combining the DoD domestic and overseas schools into a single jurisdiction. Data shown in this table for years prior to 2005 were recalculated for comparability.
NOTE: Includes public school students who were tested with accommodations; excludes only those students with disabilities (SD) and English language learners (ELL) who were unable to be tested even with accommodations. SD and ELL populations, accommodation rates, and exclusion rates vary from state to state. Some data have been revised from previously published figures.
SOURCE: U.S. Department of Education, National Center for Education Statistics, National Assessment of Educational Progress (NAEP), 1998, 2002, 2003, 2005, 2007, 2009, 2011, 2013, and 2015 Reading Assessments, retrieved November 11, 2015, from the Main NAEP Data Explorer (http://nces.ed.gov/nationsreportcard/naepdata/). (This table was prepared November 2015.)

Table 221.65. Average National Assessment of Educational Progress (NAEP) reading scale score of 8th-grade public school students, by race/ethnicity, parent's highest level of education, and state: 2015

[Standard errors appear in parentheses]

State	Race/ethnicity														Highest level of education attained by either parent[1]							
	White		Black		Hispanic		Asian		Pacific Islander		American Indian/ Alaska Native		Two or more races		Did not finish high school		Graduated high school		Some education after high school		Graduated college	
1	2		3		4		5		6		7		8		9		10		11		12	
United States	273	(0.2)	247	(0.5)	253	(0.4)	280	(1.4)	254	(2.4)	253	(1.7)	267	(1.0)	249	(0.6)	253	(0.4)	267	(0.5)	274	(0.3)
Alabama	267	(1.0)	243	(2.0)	252	(3.9)	‡	(†)	‡	(†)	‡	(†)	‡	(†)	250	(2.9)	246	(2.0)	265	(2.2)	268	(1.4)
Alaska	276	(1.3)	248	(4.1)	263	(3.0)	260	(3.0)	242	(4.0)	231	(2.3)	270	(3.1)	‡	(†)	‡	(†)	‡	(†)	‡	(†)
Arizona	276	(1.4)	249	(4.0)	254	(1.3)	‡	(†)	‡	(†)	244	(4.4)	‡	(†)	254	(2.4)	254	(1.9)	267	(1.8)	274	(1.5)
Arkansas	266	(1.6)	238	(1.9)	255	(2.7)	‡	(†)	‡	(†)	‡	(†)	‡	(†)	252	(2.4)	249	(2.0)	262	(2.0)	268	(1.9)
California	274	(1.6)	248	(2.6)	249	(1.2)	279	(3.5)	‡	(†)	‡	(†)	263	(6.4)	246	(2.3)	249	(1.8)	266	(2.4)	273	(1.5)
Colorado	277	(1.7)	255	(3.8)	253	(1.7)	290	(4.0)	‡	(†)	‡	(†)	272	(5.1)	244	(2.7)	254	(2.4)	269	(2.4)	280	(1.5)
Connecticut	282	(1.3)	251	(2.5)	256	(2.6)	282	(3.9)	‡	(†)	‡	(†)	‡	(†)	249	(4.1)	260	(2.4)	271	(2.5)	282	(1.1)
Delaware	273	(1.1)	249	(1.4)	253	(2.3)	284	(5.3)	‡	(†)	‡	(†)	‡	(†)	249	(2.6)	248	(2.2)	272	(2.0)	271	(1.3)
District of Columbia	299	(3.2)	242	(1.1)	249	(2.9)	‡	(†)	‡	(†)	‡	(†)	‡	(†)	238	(3.4)	236	(1.9)	253	(2.6)	259	(1.6)
Florida	272	(1.1)	251	(1.8)	260	(1.3)	283	(4.9)	‡	(†)	‡	(†)	261	(5.3)	255	(2.4)	257	(1.7)	265	(1.5)	271	(1.2)
Georgia	273	(1.7)	248	(1.7)	257	(2.1)	281	(5.4)	‡	(†)	‡	(†)	279	(6.0)	249	(3.0)	255	(1.6)	269	(2.0)	269	(2.0)
Hawaii	270	(2.3)	258	(4.2)	258	(3.1)	263	(1.2)	245	(1.3)	‡	(†)	264	(3.1)	249	(4.8)	244	(1.6)	260	(1.6)	266	(1.3)
Idaho	273	(1.0)	‡	(†)	253	(2.3)	‡	(†)	‡	(†)	‡	(†)	‡	(†)	253	(3.3)	254	(1.9)	274	(2.0)	277	(1.1)
Illinois	276	(1.3)	247	(1.5)	257	(1.8)	290	(3.4)	‡	(†)	‡	(†)	‡	(†)	253	(3.2)	256	(1.8)	269	(1.8)	276	(1.3)
Indiana	272	(1.3)	252	(2.5)	257	(3.0)	‡	(†)	‡	(†)	‡	(†)	260	(4.7)	255	(3.1)	258	(1.9)	272	(1.9)	277	(1.5)
Iowa	271	(1.1)	245	(3.1)	256	(2.7)	‡	(†)	‡	(†)	‡	(†)	‡	(†)	250	(3.6)	254	(1.8)	270	(2.4)	275	(1.3)
Kansas	272	(1.2)	246	(3.8)	254	(2.6)	‡	(†)	‡	(†)	‡	(†)	258	(4.0)	255	(3.1)	255	(2.9)	267	(1.9)	276	(1.2)
Kentucky	271	(1.2)	247	(2.0)	266	(3.0)	275	(7.7)	‡	(†)	‡	(†)	261	(5.6)	251	(2.4)	260	(1.7)	270	(1.8)	277	(1.4)
Louisiana	266	(1.5)	243	(1.6)	258	(3.6)	‡	(†)	‡	(†)	‡	(†)	‡	(†)	245	(3.0)	248	(2.1)	263	(1.8)	261	(1.4)
Maine	269	(0.9)	246	(4.7)	‡	(†)	‡	(†)	‡	(†)	‡	(†)	‡	(†)	‡	(†)	257	(2.0)	271	(1.8)	275	(0.9)
Maryland	279	(1.4)	251	(1.5)	258	(2.3)	292	(4.3)	‡	(†)	‡	(†)	275	(4.2)	251	(3.6)	255	(2.1)	264	(2.0)	277	(1.3)
Massachusetts	281	(0.9)	252	(2.6)	249	(2.3)	290	(3.3)	‡	(†)	‡	(†)	279	(5.0)	248	(2.9)	260	(2.4)	272	(1.9)	284	(1.2)
Michigan	270	(1.1)	243	(1.8)	263	(3.7)	282	(3.6)	‡	(†)	‡	(†)	‡	(†)	249	(4.5)	252	(1.7)	263	(1.7)	272	(1.3)
Minnesota	276	(1.2)	247	(3.0)	260	(3.3)	264	(3.8)	‡	(†)	250	(5.9)	260	(5.1)	242	(4.2)	253	(2.7)	271	(2.0)	279	(1.2)
Mississippi	266	(1.0)	240	(1.4)	‡	(†)	‡	(†)	‡	(†)	‡	(†)	‡	(†)	243	(3.1)	244	(1.8)	258	(2.0)	258	(1.6)
Missouri	271	(1.1)	246	(2.0)	258	(4.8)	‡	(†)	‡	(†)	‡	(†)	‡	(†)	254	(3.5)	258	(2.1)	272	(2.2)	274	(1.3)
Montana	273	(0.9)	‡	(†)	257	(3.9)	‡	(†)	‡	(†)	249	(2.2)	‡	(†)	256	(3.1)	260	(1.7)	269	(1.9)	278	(1.0)
Nebraska	275	(1.0)	245	(3.5)	257	(1.9)	‡	(†)	‡	(†)	‡	(†)	‡	(†)	257	(2.9)	253	(2.5)	269	(2.4)	278	(1.2)
Nevada	270	(1.6)	249	(2.4)	250	(1.1)	276	(3.1)	‡	(†)	‡	(†)	265	(4.0)	247	(2.2)	254	(1.9)	269	(1.9)	270	(1.4)
New Hampshire	275	(0.8)	‡	(†)	262	(4.6)	290	(6.5)	‡	(†)	‡	(†)	‡	(†)	252	(4.2)	264	(2.3)	276	(2.1)	281	(1.1)
New Jersey	278	(1.3)	253	(2.3)	254	(2.0)	294	(2.5)	‡	(†)	‡	(†)	‡	(†)	253	(4.7)	256	(2.3)	272	(2.1)	279	(1.3)
New Mexico	268	(1.5)	‡	(†)	249	(1.0)	‡	(†)	‡	(†)	243	(3.1)	‡	(†)	241	(2.4)	245	(1.8)	259	(1.9)	263	(1.3)
New York	273	(1.6)	248	(2.1)	254	(2.0)	272	(3.0)	‡	(†)	‡	(†)	‡	(†)	247	(3.2)	251	(2.1)	264	(2.2)	274	(1.6)
North Carolina	271	(1.6)	243	(2.0)	252	(1.9)	279	(4.8)	‡	(†)	250	(6.4)	269	(4.5)	245	(2.6)	249	(2.1)	263	(2.4)	272	(1.6)
North Dakota	270	(0.6)	255	(2.9)	261	(3.4)	‡	(†)	‡	(†)	245	(3.0)	‡	(†)	249	(3.8)	257	(1.9)	266	(2.2)	273	(0.8)
Ohio	271	(1.2)	245	(3.2)	255	(6.0)	272	(19.6)	‡	(†)	‡	(†)	‡	(†)	260	(4.9)	253	(2.0)	265	(2.1)	277	(1.4)
Oklahoma	268	(1.3)	244	(3.2)	257	(1.9)	‡	(†)	‡	(†)	261	(2.4)	263	(4.0)	248	(3.3)	255	(1.9)	268	(1.6)	270	(1.5)
Oregon	274	(1.4)	‡	(†)	252	(1.9)	274	(4.8)	‡	(†)	‡	(†)	272	(3.7)	252	(2.5)	259	(2.5)	272	(2.2)	278	(1.5)
Pennsylvania	276	(1.3)	245	(2.7)	250	(4.2)	291	(5.3)	‡	(†)	‡	(†)	260	(4.5)	250	(3.8)	257	(1.9)	267	(2.4)	279	(1.5)
Rhode Island	275	(1.0)	248	(3.0)	245	(1.5)	279	(5.9)	‡	(†)	‡	(†)	266	(4.8)	247	(3.0)	253	(2.0)	268	(1.9)	277	(1.0)
South Carolina	271	(1.6)	244	(1.6)	249	(3.6)	‡	(†)	‡	(†)	‡	(†)	267	(4.8)	248	(3.0)	252	(2.0)	263	(2.1)	268	(1.5)
South Dakota	271	(0.9)	259	(3.7)	260	(3.1)	‡	(†)	‡	(†)	247	(2.2)	‡	(†)	254	(3.2)	257	(2.2)	269	(2.4)	273	(1.1)
Tennessee	270	(1.5)	247	(2.3)	257	(3.2)	‡	(†)	‡	(†)	‡	(†)	‡	(†)	247	(2.9)	254	(1.7)	267	(1.6)	275	(1.7)
Texas	274	(1.7)	251	(2.2)	252	(1.2)	284	(3.9)	‡	(†)	‡	(†)	274	(5.2)	251	(2.0)	252	(1.9)	265	(1.7)	271	(1.3)
Utah	274	(1.1)	‡	(†)	252	(2.4)	‡	(†)	‡	(†)	247	(7.1)	270	(4.9)	‡	(†)	‡	(†)	‡	(†)	‡	(†)
Vermont	275	(0.8)	‡	(†)	‡	(†)	‡	(†)	‡	(†)	‡	(†)	‡	(†)	‡	(†)	255	(2.3)	277	(2.2)	284	(1.0)
Virginia	274	(1.6)	249	(2.1)	257	(2.7)	287	(3.1)	‡	(†)	‡	(†)	267	(3.1)	249	(3.0)	252	(1.9)	265	(2.2)	278	(1.5)
Washington	275	(1.2)	250	(4.6)	250	(2.1)	282	(2.8)	‡	(†)	251	(4.5)	262	(3.2)	252	(2.6)	257	(2.5)	271	(1.7)	279	(1.4)
West Virginia	261	(1.0)	250	(3.1)	‡	(†)	‡	(†)	‡	(†)	‡	(†)	‡	(†)	248	(3.4)	248	(1.6)	264	(1.9)	269	(1.2)
Wisconsin	275	(1.2)	241	(2.6)	255	(2.4)	271	(6.0)	‡	(†)	253	(6.8)	‡	(†)	243	(4.4)	253	(2.2)	269	(2.1)	278	(1.4)
Wyoming	272	(0.7)	‡	(†)	258	(2.2)	‡	(†)	‡	(†)	‡	(†)	‡	(†)	252	(2.6)	257	(1.9)	269	(1.9)	278	(1.1)
Department of Defense dependents schools	281	(1.4)	273	(1.9)	273	(1.8)	274	(3.7)	‡	(†)	‡	(†)	279	(2.6)	‡	(†)	268	(2.4)	279	(2.1)	281	(1.0)

†Not applicable.

‡Reporting standards not met. Either there are too few cases for a reliable estimate or item response rates fell below the required standards for reporting.

[1]Excludes students who responded "I don't know" to the question about educational level of parents.

NOTE: Scale ranges from 0 to 500. Includes public school students who were tested with accommodations; excludes only those students with disabilities (SD) and English language learners (ELL) who were unable to be tested even with accommodations. SD and ELL populations, accommodation rates, and exclusion rates vary from state to state. Race/ethnicity based on school records. Race categories exclude persons of Hispanic ethnicity.

SOURCE: U.S. Department of Education, National Center for Education Statistics, National Assessment of Educational Progress (NAEP), 2015 Reading Assessment, retrieved November 13, 2015, from the Main NAEP Data Explorer (http://nces.ed.gov/nationsreportcard/naepdata/). (This table was prepared November 2015.)

Table 221.70. Average National Assessment of Educational Progress (NAEP) reading scale scores of 4th- and 8th-graders in public schools and percentage scoring at or above selected reading achievement levels, by English language learner (ELL) status and state: 2015

[Standard errors appear in parentheses]

| | 4th-graders | | | | | | | 8th-graders | | | | | | |
| | English language learners | | | | Not English language learners | | | English language learners | | | | Not English language learners | | |
State	Percent of all students assessed	Average scale score[1]	At or above Basic[2]	At or above Proficient[3]	Average scale score[1]	At or above Basic[2]	At or above Proficient[3]	Percent of all students assessed	Average scale score[1]	At or above Basic[2]	At or above Proficient[3]	Average scale score[1]	At or above Basic[2]	At or above Proficient[3]
1	2	3	4	5	6	7	8	9	10	11	12	13	14	15
United States	11 (0.3)	189 (1.1)	32 (1.2)	8 (0.6)	225 (0.3)	72 (0.3)	38 (0.4)	6 (0.2)	223 (0.9)	28 (1.2)	3 (0.4)	267 (0.2)	78 (0.3)	35 (0.4)
Alabama	2 (0.3)	‡ (†)	‡ (†)	‡ (†)	218 (1.3)	65 (1.8)	29 (1.7)	1 (0.2)	‡ (†)	‡ (†)	‡ (†)	259 (1.1)	72 (1.6)	26 (1.4)
Alaska	15 (1.0)	165 (4.3)	19 (2.9)	4 (1.2)	221 (1.1)	69 (1.4)	34 (1.6)	11 (1.0)	211 (2.8)	18 (3.7)	1 (0.6)	266 (1.2)	77 (1.4)	35 (1.8)
Arizona	10 (0.8)	165 (3.8)	12 (2.7)	1 (#)	221 (1.3)	67 (1.6)	33 (1.6)	4 (0.6)	206 (4.1)	8 (3.1)	# (†)	265 (1.2)	76 (1.4)	32 (1.8)
Arkansas	8 (1.1)	204 (3.1)	50 (4.3)	16 (3.4)	219 (1.1)	66 (1.8)	33 (1.5)	7 (0.7)	245 (2.6)	56 (4.6)	11 (2.8)	260 (1.3)	71 (1.4)	28 (1.7)
California	28 (1.7)	183 (2.7)	27 (2.9)	6 (1.1)	224 (1.4)	71 (1.7)	36 (2.0)	14 (0.9)	215 (2.4)	21 (2.7)	2 (0.9)	266 (1.2)	78 (1.4)	33 (1.7)
Colorado	14 (1.2)	185 (2.3)	29 (3.1)	5 (1.5)	230 (1.4)	77 (1.5)	44 (1.9)	11 (0.8)	229 (2.7)	33 (4.1)	3 (1.4)	273 (1.4)	84 (1.3)	43 (2.1)
Connecticut	7 (0.6)	190 (3.2)	33 (4.8)	7 (2.4)	232 (1.1)	77 (1.2)	46 (1.6)	3 (0.4)	217 (6.1)	24 (6.6)	2 (#)	275 (1.0)	84 (1.0)	45 (1.7)
Delaware	5 (0.4)	177 (4.1)	23 (5.1)	4 (2.2)	226 (0.8)	72 (1.2)	39 (1.3)	2 (0.2)	‡ (†)	‡ (†)	‡ (†)	263 (0.8)	74 (1.2)	32 (1.0)
District of Columbia	6 (0.3)	177 (4.5)	20 (4.7)	3 (#)	214 (0.9)	58 (1.2)	29 (1.0)	5 (0.4)	218 (4.1)	26 (6.3)	3 (#)	249 (1.0)	57 (1.4)	19 (1.0)
Florida	9 (0.7)	201 (1.8)	41 (3.5)	9 (1.6)	230 (1.1)	78 (1.3)	42 (1.6)	5 (0.4)	226 (2.9)	30 (4.9)	2 (1.1)	265 (0.9)	77 (1.1)	32 (1.4)
Georgia	5 (1.0)	188 (4.2)	23 (6.6)	5 (#)	224 (1.2)	70 (1.5)	35 (1.6)	3 (0.4)	233 (4.8)	42 (6.5)	6 (3.9)	263 (1.3)	74 (1.5)	31 (1.8)
Hawaii	7 (0.5)	164 (4.3)	12 (4.1)	2 (1.1)	219 (1.0)	65 (1.2)	31 (1.2)	6 (0.4)	214 (3.0)	17 (4.0)	1 (#)	260 (0.9)	71 (1.2)	27 (1.2)
Idaho	4 (0.4)	160 (4.8)	8 (3.9)	# (†)	225 (1.0)	72 (1.4)	38 (1.4)	2 (0.3)	‡ (†)	‡ (†)	‡ (†)	270 (0.9)	83 (0.9)	38 (1.4)
Illinois	10 (1.1)	184 (2.7)	25 (3.1)	4 (1.7)	226 (1.3)	73 (1.5)	39 (1.6)	5 (0.5)	219 (3.1)	26 (5.5)	3 (#)	269 (1.1)	80 (1.2)	37 (1.5)
Indiana	7 (1.0)	199 (3.6)	42 (4.4)	14 (4.2)	230 (1.1)	77 (1.4)	42 (1.7)	5 (0.6)	249 (3.8)	61 (7.2)	13 (4.1)	269 (1.1)	80 (1.0)	38 (1.7)
Iowa	7 (1.0)	197 (3.0)	42 (4.1)	11 (3.0)	226 (1.2)	74 (1.5)	40 (1.7)	4 (0.5)	235 (3.6)	44 (6.1)	6 (2.4)	270 (1.1)	82 (1.3)	37 (1.6)
Kansas	13 (1.2)	201 (3.0)	45 (4.2)	15 (2.8)	224 (1.5)	71 (1.6)	38 (1.9)	11 (0.8)	250 (4.1)	61 (4.9)	18 (4.7)	269 (1.1)	81 (1.1)	37 (1.8)
Kentucky	3 (0.3)	201 (5.4)	40 (8.1)	13 (6.1)	229 (1.3)	75 (1.3)	41 (1.6)	1 (0.2)	236 (6.2)	42 (8.9)	5 (3.3)	268 (1.0)	78 (1.1)	37 (1.5)
Louisiana	2 (0.4)	‡ (†)	‡ (†)	‡ (†)	217 (1.5)	64 (1.8)	29 (1.6)	1 (0.2)	‡ (†)	‡ (†)	‡ (†)	256 (1.2)	66 (1.8)	23 (1.4)
Maine	3 (0.3)	186 (8.3)	33 (7.9)	6 (3.7)	225 (0.9)	72 (1.2)	37 (1.3)	3 (0.3)	239 (5.1)	45 (7.1)	11 (5.0)	269 (0.9)	82 (1.0)	36 (1.5)
Maryland	8 (1.4)	193 (4.1)	35 (5.5)	7 (2.2)	225 (1.3)	70 (1.5)	39 (1.8)	2 (0.3)	232 (4.8)	36 (9.0)	7 (4.3)	269 (1.1)	77 (1.1)	38 (1.6)
Massachusetts	9 (0.8)	200 (2.7)	44 (3.8)	12 (2.5)	239 (1.0)	85 (1.1)	53 (1.5)	5 (0.6)	225 (3.8)	35 (5.5)	6 (2.8)	277 (1.0)	86 (1.1)	48 (1.5)
Michigan	4 (0.8)	202 (4.9)	48 (6.5)	16 (4.8)	217 (1.4)	64 (1.8)	29 (1.6)	3 (0.6)	237 (4.0)	43 (7.1)	6 (4.4)	265 (1.2)	77 (1.4)	33 (1.6)
Minnesota	10 (0.9)	179 (4.8)	28 (4.5)	6 (2.3)	228 (1.1)	75 (1.3)	42 (1.5)	6 (0.7)	234 (3.5)	43 (5.2)	6 (2.6)	273 (1.0)	84 (1.1)	42 (1.5)
Mississippi	2 (0.4)	‡ (†)	‡ (†)	‡ (†)	214 (1.0)	61 (1.4)	26 (1.3)	1 (0.2)	‡ (†)	‡ (†)	‡ (†)	253 (1.0)	63 (1.5)	20 (1.1)
Missouri	3 (0.4)	203 (4.4)	50 (7.7)	14 (5.6)	223 (1.2)	70 (1.3)	37 (1.5)	2 (0.4)	‡ (†)	‡ (†)	‡ (†)	268 (1.1)	78 (1.3)	37 (1.5)
Montana	3 (0.3)	175 (5.8)	17 (6.1)	1 (#)	226 (0.8)	74 (1.2)	38 (1.2)	2 (0.2)	‡ (†)	‡ (†)	‡ (†)	271 (0.8)	83 (1.0)	37 (1.4)
Nebraska	7 (0.7)	193 (3.1)	32 (4.6)	7 (2.6)	229 (1.0)	77 (1.3)	42 (1.5)	2 (0.3)	‡ (†)	‡ (†)	‡ (†)	270 (0.9)	83 (1.1)	39 (1.5)
Nevada	24 (1.1)	190 (1.8)	33 (2.1)	8 (1.5)	222 (1.2)	70 (1.5)	36 (1.5)	15 (0.6)	226 (1.8)	30 (2.7)	3 (1.2)	265 (1.1)	78 (1.3)	32 (1.6)
New Hampshire	3 (0.3)	206 (4.4)	51 (6.2)	19 (6.4)	233 (0.9)	80 (1.1)	47 (1.5)	1 (0.2)	‡ (†)	‡ (†)	‡ (†)	275 (0.9)	85 (1.0)	45 (1.3)
New Jersey	3 (0.6)	‡ (†)	‡ (†)	‡ (†)	231 (1.5)	77 (1.5)	44 (1.8)	2 (0.3)	‡ (†)	‡ (†)	‡ (†)	272 (1.0)	81 (1.2)	41 (1.4)
New Mexico	16 (0.7)	171 (2.9)	18 (2.3)	4 (1.2)	214 (0.9)	61 (1.4)	27 (1.3)	13 (0.7)	219 (1.9)	22 (3.1)	2 (1.0)	258 (0.9)	72 (1.4)	23 (1.4)
New York	7 (0.8)	184 (3.1)	26 (3.5)	5 (2.0)	226 (1.0)	72 (1.3)	38 (1.5)	6 (0.6)	215 (3.2)	22 (4.3)	3 (1.4)	266 (1.3)	76 (1.3)	35 (1.7)
North Carolina	6 (0.5)	187 (3.0)	29 (4.7)	5 (2.1)	229 (1.1)	76 (1.4)	41 (1.6)	4 (0.5)	217 (4.0)	25 (5.0)	1 (#)	263 (1.3)	74 (1.4)	32 (1.7)
North Dakota	2 (0.2)	‡ (†)	‡ (†)	‡ (†)	226 (0.7)	74 (1.0)	37 (1.0)	2 (0.2)	‡ (†)	‡ (†)	‡ (†)	268 (0.6)	81 (1.0)	34 (1.1)
Ohio	4 (0.7)	202 (4.8)	49 (7.0)	12 (5.2)	226 (1.2)	73 (1.3)	39 (1.7)	3 (1.5)	227 (11.8)	31 (14.2)	7 (#)	267 (1.3)	77 (1.6)	36 (1.6)
Oklahoma	6 (0.5)	197 (4.4)	42 (7.0)	9 (3.4)	224 (1.1)	73 (1.3)	34 (1.5)	5 (0.7)	239 (3.3)	47 (5.6)	7 (3.5)	264 (1.3)	77 (1.6)	31 (1.8)
Oregon	13 (1.0)	180 (3.1)	26 (3.5)	3 (1.2)	226 (1.2)	74 (1.4)	39 (1.6)	3 (0.3)	207 (5.6)	11 (5.2)	1 (#)	269 (1.2)	81 (1.2)	37 (1.9)
Pennsylvania	3 (0.5)	170 (5.5)	16 (4.4)	3 (#)	229 (1.6)	76 (1.8)	43 (1.9)	2 (0.4)	218 (6.7)	20 (7.2)	6 (3.5)	270 (1.4)	79 (1.5)	40 (2.0)
Rhode Island	7 (0.5)	182 (3.3)	25 (3.6)	5 (2.1)	229 (0.9)	76 (1.1)	43 (1.4)	5 (0.3)	209 (3.8)	17 (5.1)	1 (#)	268 (0.7)	78 (0.9)	36 (1.3)
South Carolina	8 (1.0)	201 (4.7)	47 (5.1)	21 (3.9)	219 (1.3)	66 (1.4)	35 (1.6)	4 (0.5)	242 (4.3)	48 (7.6)	11 (3.8)	261 (1.2)	72 (1.4)	29 (1.6)
South Dakota	3 (0.2)	170 (7.5)	20 (6.0)	5 (2.8)	222 (0.9)	69 (1.2)	35 (1.2)	2 (0.3)	‡ (†)	‡ (†)	‡ (†)	268 (1.0)	81 (1.3)	35 (1.3)
Tennessee	4 (0.6)	200 (5.1)	47 (7.1)	16 (5.2)	219 (1.4)	66 (1.8)	34 (1.7)	2 (0.4)	‡ (†)	‡ (†)	‡ (†)	266 (1.3)	77 (1.4)	33 (1.8)
Texas	22 (1.9)	198 (2.1)	41 (3.3)	12 (2.2)	224 (1.8)	70 (1.9)	36 (2.2)	11 (0.6)	224 (2.2)	29 (3.3)	2 (1.2)	265 (1.2)	78 (1.3)	31 (1.8)
Utah	4 (0.5)	174 (6.3)	19 (5.5)	8 (3.5)	228 (1.0)	77 (1.0)	41 (1.5)	3 (0.4)	213 (4.6)	16 (6.1)	1 (#)	271 (0.9)	83 (1.1)	39 (1.4)
Vermont	3 (0.3)	‡ (†)	‡ (†)	‡ (†)	231 (0.8)	76 (1.0)	45 (1.4)	1 (0.2)	‡ (†)	‡ (†)	‡ (†)	275 (0.8)	84 (1.0)	44 (1.4)
Virginia	6 (0.9)	189 (3.0)	30 (4.0)	7 (2.5)	232 (1.8)	77 (1.8)	45 (2.2)	5 (0.6)	231 (2.7)	31 (5.8)	3 (1.8)	269 (1.3)	80 (1.3)	38 (1.9)
Washington	13 (1.2)	189 (2.1)	28 (2.8)	5 (1.6)	231 (1.5)	77 (1.5)	46 (2.0)	6 (0.7)	223 (3.5)	26 (4.9)	3 (1.6)	270 (1.1)	80 (1.1)	40 (1.6)
West Virginia	1 (0.2)	‡ (†)	‡ (†)	‡ (†)	216 (1.2)	64 (1.3)	30 (1.5)	1 (0.2)	‡ (†)	‡ (†)	‡ (†)	260 (0.9)	72 (1.3)	27 (1.3)
Wisconsin	7 (0.8)	198 (2.9)	40 (4.5)	9 (2.1)	225 (1.1)	73 (1.4)	39 (1.5)	4 (0.5)	234 (3.2)	38 (5.4)	6 (3.0)	271 (1.2)	81 (1.2)	40 (1.7)
Wyoming	3 (0.2)	‡ (†)	‡ (†)	‡ (†)	229 (0.7)	77 (1.0)	42 (1.3)	2 (0.2)	‡ (†)	‡ (†)	‡ (†)	270 (0.8)	82 (1.0)	37 (1.2)
Department of Defense dependents schools	8 (0.4)	213 (2.5)	62 (4.2)	18 (3.5)	236 (0.7)	85 (1.1)	50 (1.4)	5 (0.5)	249 (4.1)	61 (7.5)	12 (5.5)	279 (0.8)	92 (0.9)	49 (1.8)

†Not applicable.
#Rounds to zero.
‡Reporting standards not met (too few cases for a reliable estimate).
[1]Scale ranges from 0 to 500.
[2]Basic denotes partial mastery of the knowledge and skills that are fundamental for proficient work at a given grade.
[3]Proficient represents solid academic performance. Students reaching this level have demonstrated competency over challenging subject matter.

NOTE: The results for English language learners are based on students who were assessed and cannot be generalized to the total population of such students. Although testing accommodations were permitted, some English language learners did not have a sufficient level of English proficiency to participate in the 2015 Reading Assessment.
SOURCE: U.S. Department of Education, National Center for Education Statistics, National Assessment of Educational Progress (NAEP), 2015 Reading Assessment, retrieved November 9, 2015, from the Main NAEP Data Explorer (http://nces.ed.gov/nationsreport card/naepdata/). (This table was prepared November 2015.)

Table 221.75. Average National Assessment of Educational Progress (NAEP) reading scale score and standard deviation, by selected student characteristics, percentile, and grade: Selected years, 1992 through 2015

[Standard errors appear in parentheses]

Selected student characteristic, percentile, and grade	1992[1]	1994[1]	1998	2000	2002	2003	2005	2007	2009	2011	2013	2015 Total	2015 Male	2015 Female
1	2	3	4	5	6	7	8	9	10	11	12	13	14	15
Average reading scale score[2]														
All students														
4th grade	217 (0.9)	214 (1.0)	215 (1.1)	213 (1.3)	219 (0.4)	218 (0.3)	219 (0.2)	221 (0.3)	221 (0.3)	221 (0.3)	222 (0.3)	223 (0.4)	219 (0.4)	226 (0.4)
8th grade	260 (0.9)	260 (0.8)	263 (0.8)	— (†)	264 (0.4)	263 (0.3)	262 (0.2)	263 (0.2)	264 (0.3)	265 (0.2)	268 (0.3)	265 (0.2)	261 (0.2)	270 (0.3)
12th grade	292 (0.6)	287 (0.7)	290 (0.6)	— (†)	287 (0.7)	— (†)	286 (0.6)	— (†)	288 (0.7)	— (†)	288 (0.6)	— (†)	— (†)	— (†)
Eligibility for free or reduced-price lunch														
4th grade														
Eligible	— (†)	— (†)	196 (1.7)	193 (1.7)	203 (0.7)	201 (0.3)	203 (0.3)	205 (0.3)	206 (0.3)	207 (0.3)	207 (0.3)	209 (0.4)	206 (0.5)	213 (0.4)
Not eligible	— (†)	— (†)	227 (0.9)	226 (1.2)	230 (0.4)	229 (0.3)	230 (0.2)	232 (0.3)	232 (0.3)	235 (0.3)	236 (0.3)	237 (0.3)	234 (0.4)	240 (0.4)
Unknown	— (†)	— (†)	223 (2.7)	225 (2.3)	226 (1.6)	230 (0.9)	232 (0.9)	233 (1.3)	236 (1.3)	235 (0.8)	237 (1.4)	236 (1.3)	234 (1.9)	239 (1.6)
8th grade														
Eligible	— (†)	— (†)	245 (1.0)	— (†)	249 (0.5)	247 (0.4)	247 (0.3)	247 (0.3)	249 (0.3)	252 (0.3)	254 (0.2)	253 (0.3)	248 (0.4)	258 (0.3)
Not eligible	— (†)	— (†)	269 (1.1)	— (†)	272 (0.4)	271 (0.3)	270 (0.2)	271 (0.3)	273 (0.3)	275 (0.3)	278 (0.3)	277 (0.3)	272 (0.4)	282 (0.4)
Unknown	— (†)	— (†)	272 (2.0)	— (†)	271 (1.4)	272 (1.0)	275 (1.1)	277 (1.3)	280 (1.3)	283 (0.9)	286 (1.8)	282 (0.9)	278 (1.3)	285 (1.1)
12th grade														
Eligible	— (†)	— (†)	270 (1.1)	— (†)	273 (1.4)	— (†)	271 (1.0)	— (†)	273 (0.7)	— (†)	274 (0.7)	— (†)	— (†)	— (†)
Not eligible	— (†)	— (†)	293 (0.6)	— (†)	289 (0.9)	— (†)	290 (0.7)	— (†)	294 (0.8)	— (†)	296 (0.6)	— (†)	— (†)	— (†)
Unknown	— (†)	— (†)	295 (1.6)	— (†)	294 (1.5)	— (†)	295 (1.9)	— (†)	296 (2.4)	— (†)	302 (2.6)	— (†)	— (†)	— (†)
Read for fun on own time														
4th grade														
Almost every day	223 (1.2)	223 (1.2)	219 (1.5)	218 (1.7)	225 (0.5)	225 (0.3)	225 (0.3)	227 (0.3)	228 (0.4)	228 (0.4)	229 (0.4)	229 (0.5)	227 (0.6)	232 (0.5)
1–2 times a week	218 (1.2)	213 (1.1)	217 (1.2)	216 (1.2)	220 (0.5)	219 (0.3)	220 (0.3)	223 (0.3)	221 (0.4)	221 (0.4)	223 (0.4)	224 (0.5)	222 (0.6)	226 (0.6)
1–2 times a month	210 (1.6)	208 (2.1)	211 (1.9)	212 (1.6)	210 (0.8)	211 (0.5)	213 (0.4)	216 (0.4)	214 (0.4)	214 (0.4)	216 (0.4)	219 (0.5)	217 (0.7)	221 (0.6)
Never or hardly ever	199 (1.8)	197 (1.9)	202 (1.9)	201 (1.8)	208 (0.5)	207 (0.4)	208 (0.3)	211 (0.4)	210 (0.3)	210 (0.5)	211 (0.4)	212 (0.5)	210 (0.5)	214 (0.7)
8th grade														
Almost every day	277 (1.1)	277 (1.4)	277 (1.0)	— (†)	279 (0.6)	279 (0.4)	279 (0.3)	281 (0.4)	282 (0.4)	284 (0.4)	286 (0.4)	284 (0.4)	278 (0.7)	286 (0.5)
1–2 times a week	263 (1.1)	264 (1.1)	267 (1.1)	— (†)	266 (0.5)	265 (0.4)	265 (0.3)	265 (0.3)	267 (0.4)	268 (0.3)	271 (0.4)	269 (0.4)	266 (0.6)	272 (0.5)
1–2 times a month	258 (1.2)	257 (0.8)	263 (0.9)	— (†)	264 (0.6)	262 (0.3)	261 (0.3)	261 (0.3)	261 (0.4)	263 (0.3)	266 (0.3)	263 (0.4)	260 (0.4)	266 (0.6)
Never or hardly ever	246 (1.4)	246 (1.1)	251 (1.1)	— (†)	255 (0.4)	253 (0.3)	252 (0.3)	253 (0.3)	253 (0.4)	255 (0.3)	257 (0.3)	255 (0.3)	253 (0.4)	258 (0.6)
12th grade														
Almost every day	304 (0.9)	302 (1.1)	304 (1.0)	— (†)	304 (1.1)	— (†)	302 (1.2)	— (†)	305 (0.9)	— (†)	306 (0.8)	— (†)	— (†)	— (†)
1–2 times a week	296 (0.7)	294 (1.0)	298 (0.9)	— (†)	292 (1.1)	— (†)	292 (1.0)	— (†)	295 (1.0)	— (†)	297 (0.8)	— (†)	— (†)	— (†)
1–2 times a month	290 (0.9)	285 (1.0)	289 (0.7)	— (†)	288 (0.9)	— (†)	285 (0.8)	— (†)	288 (0.8)	— (†)	289 (0.6)	— (†)	— (†)	— (†)
Never or hardly ever	279 (1.0)	273 (1.1)	275 (1.0)	— (†)	275 (1.0)	— (†)	274 (0.8)	— (†)	275 (0.6)	— (†)	276 (0.7)	— (†)	— (†)	— (†)
Percentile[3]														
4th grade														
10th	170 (1.9)	159 (1.5)	163 (2.1)	159 (2.3)	170 (0.9)	169 (0.5)	171 (0.4)	174 (0.4)	175 (0.5)	174 (0.4)	174 (0.6)	174 (0.7)	169 (1.0)	179 (0.6)
25th	194 (1.1)	189 (1.1)	191 (1.7)	189 (1.4)	196 (0.5)	195 (0.4)	196 (0.3)	199 (0.3)	199 (0.4)	200 (0.4)	200 (0.3)	201 (0.5)	197 (0.6)	205 (0.5)
50th	219 (1.3)	219 (1.3)	217 (1.3)	218 (1.7)	221 (0.5)	221 (0.3)	221 (0.2)	224 (0.3)	223 (0.3)	224 (0.3)	225 (0.3)	226 (0.4)	223 (0.5)	229 (0.4)
75th	242 (1.1)	243 (1.3)	242 (0.9)	243 (0.8)	244 (0.5)	244 (0.3)	244 (0.3)	246 (0.3)	245 (0.3)	246 (0.3)	247 (0.3)	248 (0.4)	246 (0.5)	250 (0.4)
90th	261 (1.4)	263 (1.7)	262 (0.9)	262 (1.4)	263 (0.4)	264 (0.3)	263 (0.3)	264 (0.4)	264 (0.3)	264 (0.4)	265 (0.4)	266 (0.4)	264 (0.4)	268 (0.6)
8th grade														
10th	213 (1.2)	211 (1.9)	216 (1.7)	— (†)	220 (0.5)	217 (0.6)	216 (0.3)	217 (0.4)	219 (0.5)	221 (0.3)	223 (0.4)	220 (0.5)	214 (0.6)	226 (0.5)
25th	237 (1.1)	236 (1.1)	241 (0.7)	— (†)	244 (0.5)	242 (0.3)	240 (0.2)	242 (0.3)	243 (0.4)	244 (0.3)	246 (0.2)	244 (0.3)	239 (0.5)	249 (0.3)
50th	262 (1.1)	262 (0.7)	266 (0.7)	— (†)	267 (0.5)	266 (0.3)	265 (0.2)	265 (0.2)	267 (0.3)	267 (0.2)	269 (0.3)	268 (0.2)	263 (0.3)	272 (0.4)
75th	285 (0.8)	286 (1.1)	288 (1.0)	— (†)	288 (0.4)	288 (0.3)	286 (0.2)	287 (0.2)	288 (0.4)	289 (0.3)	291 (0.3)	290 (0.3)	285 (0.4)	294 (0.4)
90th	305 (1.3)	305 (1.2)	306 (0.8)	— (†)	305 (0.5)	306 (0.2)	305 (0.2)	305 (0.2)	305 (0.4)	305 (0.2)	307 (0.2)	310 (0.4)	308 (0.3)	303 (0.4)	312 (0.4)
12th grade														
10th	249 (0.8)	239 (0.9)	240 (0.6)	— (†)	237 (1.5)	— (†)	235 (1.1)	— (†)	238 (0.8)	— (†)	239 (1.0)	— (†)	— (†)	— (†)
25th	271 (0.8)	264 (0.9)	267 (0.8)	— (†)	263 (1.3)	— (†)	262 (0.8)	— (†)	264 (0.8)	— (†)	264 (0.8)	— (†)	— (†)	— (†)
50th	294 (0.8)	290 (0.6)	293 (0.6)	— (†)	289 (0.7)	— (†)	288 (0.8)	— (†)	291 (0.7)	— (†)	290 (0.7)	— (†)	— (†)	— (†)
75th	315 (0.5)	313 (0.8)	317 (0.7)	— (†)	312 (0.6)	— (†)	313 (1.1)	— (†)	315 (0.9)	— (†)	315 (0.7)	— (†)	— (†)	— (†)
90th	333 (0.7)	332 (1.2)	336 (0.8)	— (†)	332 (0.9)	— (†)	333 (1.1)	— (†)	335 (0.9)	— (†)	335 (0.6)	— (†)	— (†)	— (†)
Standard deviation of the reading scale score[4]														
All students														
4th grade	36 (0.6)	41 (0.6)	39 (0.7)	42 (0.9)	36 (0.3)	37 (0.2)	36 (0.1)	36 (0.2)	35 (0.2)	36 (0.1)	37 (0.2)	37 (0.3)	38 (0.3)	36 (0.3)
8th grade	36 (0.3)	37 (0.4)	35 (0.5)	— (†)	34 (0.3)	35 (0.2)	35 (0.1)	35 (0.2)	34 (0.2)	34 (0.1)	34 (0.1)	35 (0.2)	35 (0.2)	34 (0.2)
12th grade	33 (0.4)	37 (0.5)	38 (0.4)	— (†)	37 (0.4)	— (†)	38 (0.4)	— (†)	38 (0.3)	— (†)	38 (0.3)	— (†)	— (†)	— (†)

—Not available.
†Not applicable.
[1]Accommodations were not permitted for this assessment.
[2]Scale ranges from 0 to 500.
[3]The percentile represents a specific point on the percentage distribution of all students ranked by their reading score from low to high. For example, 10 percent of students scored at or below the 10th percentile score, while 90 percent of students scored above it.
[4]The standard deviation provides an indication of how much the test scores varied. The lower the standard deviation, the closer the scores were clustered around the average score. About two-thirds of the student scores can be expected to fall within the range of one standard deviation above and one standard deviation below the average score. For example, the average score for all 4th-graders in 2015 was 223, and the standard deviation was 37. This means that we would expect about two-thirds of the students to have scores between 260 (one standard deviation above the average) and 186 (one standard deviation below). Standard errors also must be taken into account when making comparisons of these ranges.

NOTE: Includes public and private schools. For 1998 and later years, includes students tested with accommodations (1 to 13 percent of all students, depending on grade level and year); excludes only those students with disabilities and English language learners who were unable to be tested even with accommodations (2 to 6 percent of all students). On the student questionnaire, the format of the question about reading for fun on your own time changed slightly beginning with the 2002 assessment year. In 1992 through 2000, reading for fun was one of several activities included in the same question ("How often do you do each of the following?"), and the response options were listed in order from most frequent to least frequent (that is, "Almost every day" was listed first, and "Never or hardly ever" was listed last); starting in 2002, reading for fun was the only activity in the question, and the order of the response options was reversed.
SOURCE: U.S. Department of Education, National Center for Education Statistics, National Assessment of Educational Progress (NAEP), 1992, 1994, 1998, 2000, 2002, 2003, 2005, 2007, 2009, 2011, 2013, and 2015 Reading Assessments, retrieved November 10, 2015, from the Main NAEP Data Explorer (http://nces.ed.gov/nationsreportcard/naepdata/). (This table was prepared November 2015.)

Table 221.80. Average National Assessment of Educational Progress (NAEP) reading scale scores of 4th- and 8th-grade public school students and percentage attaining selected reading achievement levels, by race/ethnicity and jurisdiction or specific urban district: 2009, 2011, 2013, and 2015

[Standard errors appear in parentheses]

Grade level and jurisdiction or specific urban district	2009 All students	2011 All students	2013 All students	2013 White	2013 Black	2013 Hispanic	2013 Asian	2015 All students	2015 White	2015 Black	2015 Hispanic	2015 Asian	Percent of students 2015 At or above Basic[2]	Percent of students 2015 At or above Proficient[3]
1	2	3	4	5	6	7	8	9	10	11	12	13	14	15
4th grade														
United States..................	220 (0.3)	220 (0.3)	221 (0.3)	231 (0.3)	205 (0.5)	207 (0.5)	237 (1.1)	221 (0.4)	232 (0.3)	206 (0.5)	208 (0.8)	240 (1.7)	68 (0.4)	35 (0.4)
All large cities[4].................	210 (0.7)	211 (0.7)	212 (0.7)	235 (1.0)	202 (0.8)	204 (0.8)	229 (2.5)	214 (0.8)	235 (1.2)	204 (0.9)	206 (0.8)	233 (4.1)	59 (0.9)	27 (1.0)
Selected urban districts														
Albuquerque (NM)..........	— (†)	209 (1.6)	207 (1.5)	232 (2.4)	‡ (†)	199 (1.7)	‡ (†)	207 (1.6)	227 (2.6)	‡ (†)	202 (1.8)	‡ (†)	54 (1.9)	24 (1.7)
Atlanta (GA).................	209 (1.5)	212 (1.4)	214 (1.3)	252 (1.9)	204 (1.4)	208 (3.5)	‡ (†)	212 (1.6)	251 (2.2)	202 (1.9)	205 (4.7)	‡ (†)	54 (2.0)	26 (1.6)
Austin (TX).................	220 (1.8)	224 (2.3)	221 (1.6)	250 (2.2)	206 (5.4)	208 (2.1)	‡ (†)	220 (1.8)	248 (2.3)	‡ (†)	207 (2.2)	‡ (†)	65 (2.1)	35 (2.1)
Baltimore City (MD)	202 (1.7)	200 (1.7)	204 (1.6)	233 (5.2)	201 (1.7)	‡ (†)	‡ (†)	199 (1.7)	217 (3.8)	196 (1.9)	200 (4.4)	‡ (†)	40 (2.1)	11 (1.3)
Boston (MA)..................	215 (1.2)	217 (0.8)	214 (1.1)	237 (2.2)	205 (1.9)	210 (1.7)	234 (3.3)	219 (1.4)	241 (2.5)	214 (2.1)	214 (1.8)	230 (3.7)	65 (1.8)	29 (2.0)
Charlotte (NC)...............	225 (1.6)	224 (1.2)	226 (1.6)	245 (1.8)	215 (2.0)	212 (2.9)	238 (4.9)	226 (1.6)	245 (2.1)	216 (2.3)	212 (2.6)	246 (5.4)	72 (1.9)	39 (1.8)
Chicago (IL).................	202 (1.5)	203 (1.3)	206 (1.6)	239 (4.1)	198 (2.5)	203 (1.6)	235 (4.7)	213 (1.4)	250 (2.3)	205 (2.4)	205 (1.6)	248 (5.0)	58 (1.6)	27 (1.5)
Cleveland (OH)	194 (2.0)	193 (0.9)	190 (1.9)	206 (3.7)	185 (2.2)	191 (4.1)	‡ (†)	197 (2.0)	210 (3.1)	193 (2.7)	199 (4.3)	‡ (†)	39 (2.3)	11 (1.3)
Dallas (TX).................	— (†)	204 (1.6)	205 (1.4)	231 (4.9)	201 (2.1)	204 (1.8)	‡ (†)	204 (1.9)	240 (4.6)	202 (3.4)	200 (2.1)	‡ (†)	47 (2.4)	17 (1.8)
Detroit (MI).................	187 (1.9)	191 (2.0)	190 (2.2)	‡ (†)	188 (2.6)	199 (3.4)	‡ (†)	186 (2.0)	‡ (†)	184 (2.2)	195 (4.0)	‡ (†)	27 (2.5)	6 (1.2)
District of Columbia (DC) .	203 (1.2)	201 (1.0)	206 (1.2)	260 (2.6)	192 (1.4)	211 (2.6)	‡ (†)	214 (1.0)	262 (2.5)	202 (1.3)	206 (3.2)	‡ (†)	56 (1.4)	30 (1.3)
Duval County (FL).........	— (†)	— (†)	— (†)	— (†)	— (†)	— (†)	— (†)	225 (1.5)	236 (2.0)	212 (2.1)	225 (2.7)	‡ (†)	73 (1.9)	35 (2.4)
Fresno (CA).................	197 (1.7)	194 (2.4)	196 (1.7)	218 (2.9)	187 (3.0)	192 (1.9)	199 (3.0)	199 (1.6)	220 (4.7)	186 (3.8)	196 (2.0)	207 (3.8)	42 (2.1)	13 (1.6)
Hillsborough County (FL).	— (†)	231 (1.7)	228 (1.3)	237 (1.8)	214 (3.1)	223 (1.6)	247 (4.0)	230 (1.9)	242 (2.0)	216 (3.2)	221 (2.0)	‡ (†)	76 (2.4)	41 (2.7)
Houston (TX)	211 (1.7)	213 (1.6)	208 (1.3)	238 (3.3)	202 (2.7)	204 (1.3)	245 (4.7)	210 (1.9)	246 (4.3)	207 (3.3)	204 (1.9)	‡ (†)	54 (2.1)	23 (2.1)
Jefferson County (KY)....	219 (1.8)	223 (1.3)	221 (1.2)	233 (1.7)	203 (1.9)	221 (3.5)	‡ (†)	222 (2.0)	232 (2.4)	208 (2.3)	217 (3.6)	‡ (†)	67 (2.2)	36 (2.6)
Los Angeles (CA)..........	197 (1.1)	201 (1.2)	205 (1.6)	237 (3.4)	204 (2.9)	199 (1.3)	222 (4.3)	204 (1.8)	233 (4.2)	202 (4.9)	197 (1.7)	237 (5.0)	50 (1.8)	21 (1.6)
Miami-Dade (FL)............	221 (1.2)	221 (1.5)	223 (1.5)	239 (2.8)	209 (2.2)	225 (1.7)	‡ (†)	226 (1.3)	239 (4.5)	210 (3.3)	229 (1.6)	‡ (†)	74 (1.6)	39 (2.0)
Milwaukee (WI)	196 (2.0)	195 (1.7)	199 (1.9)	223 (3.8)	190 (2.3)	200 (2.6)	201 (8.2)	— (†)	— (†)	— (†)	— (†)	— (†)	— (†)	— (†)
New York City (NY)	217 (1.4)	216 (1.2)	216 (1.4)	231 (3.1)	210 (1.8)	208 (1.6)	233 (3.2)	214 (1.5)	233 (4.7)	206 (1.7)	205 (2.0)	236 (2.6)	59 (1.8)	26 (1.7)
Philadelphia (PA)...........	195 (1.8)	199 (1.8)	200 (1.7)	214 (3.2)	196 (2.0)	193 (3.0)	215 (4.9)	201 (2.2)	216 (4.3)	198 (1.8)	188 (4.4)	221 (4.6)	44 (2.7)	14 (1.8)
San Diego (CA).............	213 (2.1)	215 (1.7)	218 (1.6)	240 (2.2)	205 (4.0)	204 (2.4)	229 (3.9)	216 (2.0)	240 (3.1)	201 (6.2)	204 (2.7)	223 (4.5)	61 (2.3)	30 (2.0)
8th grade														
United States..................	262 (0.3)	264 (0.2)	266 (0.2)	275 (0.2)	250 (0.4)	255 (0.4)	280 (1.0)	264 (0.2)	273 (0.2)	247 (0.5)	253 (0.4)	280 (1.4)	75 (0.3)	33 (0.3)
All large cities[4].................	252 (0.5)	255 (0.5)	258 (0.8)	276 (1.0)	246 (0.9)	253 (0.7)	273 (2.8)	257 (0.9)	277 (1.3)	246 (0.8)	251 (1.0)	272 (2.4)	67 (0.9)	25 (1.0)
Selected urban districts														
Albuquerque (NM)..........	— (†)	254 (1.2)	256 (1.0)	275 (2.6)	‡ (†)	250 (1.1)	‡ (†)	251 (1.2)	267 (2.2)	‡ (†)	246 (1.3)	‡ (†)	62 (1.6)	19 (1.6)
Atlanta (GA).................	250 (1.5)	253 (1.0)	255 (1.0)	294 (2.8)	249 (1.2)	254 (4.5)	‡ (†)	252 (1.4)	290 (2.9)	246 (1.5)	258 (3.7)	‡ (†)	61 (2.0)	20 (1.6)
Austin (TX).................	261 (2.0)	261 (1.5)	261 (1.4)	286 (2.9)	245 (3.5)	251 (1.6)	‡ (†)	261 (1.5)	290 (3.1)	241 (5.0)	249 (1.6)	‡ (†)	70 (1.6)	33 (2.3)
Baltimore City (MD)	245 (1.7)	246 (1.6)	252 (1.5)	275 (5.6)	249 (1.5)	‡ (†)	‡ (†)	243 (1.7)	268 (5.9)	240 (2.0)	246 (5.1)	‡ (†)	51 (2.7)	13 (1.7)
Boston (MA)..................	257 (1.5)	255 (1.2)	257 (1.0)	281 (2.8)	247 (1.8)	250 (1.5)	278 (3.5)	258 (1.2)	282 (3.1)	250 (2.1)	249 (2.3)	281 (3.9)	67 (1.7)	28 (1.4)
Charlotte (NC)...............	259 (1.0)	265 (0.9)	266 (1.2)	286 (2.0)	253 (1.8)	259 (3.1)	‡ (†)	263 (1.6)	284 (2.1)	251 (2.4)	254 (3.7)	‡ (†)	73 (1.8)	33 (2.0)
Chicago (IL).................	249 (1.6)	253 (1.1)	253 (1.0)	279 (2.6)	244 (1.6)	255 (1.6)	278 (4.3)	257 (1.8)	289 (5.0)	247 (1.6)	257 (1.6)	‡ (†)	67 (1.6)	24 (2.2)
Cleveland (OH)	242 (1.6)	240 (1.7)	239 (1.6)	250 (3.2)	235 (1.8)	241 (3.6)	‡ (†)	240 (1.6)	251 (3.4)	238 (2.1)	238 (3.3)	‡ (†)	48 (2.5)	11 (1.4)
Dallas (TX).................	— (†)	248 (1.0)	251 (1.3)	‡ (†)	244 (2.4)	253 (1.6)	‡ (†)	250 (1.3)	‡ (†)	241 (2.5)	251 (1.5)	‡ (†)	60 (2.2)	17 (1.7)
Detroit (MI).................	232 (2.4)	237 (1.0)	239 (1.6)	‡ (†)	239 (1.6)	242 (4.7)	‡ (†)	237 (1.2)	‡ (†)	235 (1.5)	245 (3.1)	‡ (†)	44 (2.4)	7 (1.2)
District of Columbia (DC) .	240 (1.5)	237 (1.2)	245 (1.3)	301 (4.0)	237 (1.4)	247 (3.6)	‡ (†)	245 (1.4)	299 (3.8)	236 (1.8)	244 (3.7)	‡ (†)	52 (1.9)	19 (1.4)
Duval County (FL).........	— (†)	— (†)	— (†)	— (†)	— (†)	— (†)	— (†)	264 (1.4)	272 (2.2)	254 (1.5)	262 (3.6)	‡ (†)	75 (2.0)	31 (2.0)
Fresno (CA).................	240 (2.4)	238 (1.8)	245 (1.4)	265 (3.4)	236 (3.3)	241 (1.6)	247 (3.1)	242 (1.9)	256 (4.5)	238 (3.9)	238 (2.2)	249 (3.9)	51 (2.5)	13 (1.7)
Hillsborough County (FL).	— (†)	264 (1.5)	267 (1.2)	277 (1.6)	252 (2.3)	263 (1.8)	‡ (†)	261 (1.7)	274 (2.1)	246 (3.4)	254 (2.3)	‡ (†)	71 (2.5)	29 (2.3)
Houston (TX)	252 (1.2)	252 (0.9)	252 (1.2)	284 (3.2)	245 (2.2)	250 (1.4)	284 (5.6)	252 (1.8)	280 (4.1)	246 (2.6)	247 (1.5)	‡ (†)	61 (1.6)	20 (2.2)
Jefferson County (KY)....	259 (1.0)	260 (1.1)	261 (1.0)	271 (1.6)	243 (1.4)	258 (4.5)	‡ (†)	261 (1.8)	271 (2.7)	247 (1.9)	260 (4.6)	‡ (†)	70 (2.2)	31 (2.2)
Los Angeles (CA)..........	244 (1.1)	246 (1.1)	250 (1.4)	276 (3.2)	240 (3.8)	245 (1.1)	272 (3.1)	251 (1.4)	273 (3.2)	248 (5.3)	246 (1.3)	274 (4.8)	62 (2.0)	20 (1.6)
Miami-Dade (FL)............	261 (1.4)	260 (1.4)	259 (1.0)	278 (2.8)	245 (2.0)	261 (1.1)	‡ (†)	265 (1.8)	279 (4.5)	254 (3.1)	266 (1.9)	‡ (†)	77 (2.0)	32 (2.4)
Milwaukee (WI)	241 (2.0)	238 (1.6)	242 (1.4)	262 (3.3)	232 (1.7)	253 (2.5)	‡ (†)	— (†)	— (†)	— (†)	— (†)	— (†)	— (†)	— (†)
New York City (NY)	252 (1.4)	254 (1.8)	256 (1.2)	274 (4.0)	253 (2.0)	249 (2.0)	271 (3.1)	258 (1.7)	276 (3.7)	247 (2.0)	254 (2.2)	270 (3.5)	67 (1.8)	27 (2.2)
Philadelphia (PA)...........	247 (2.5)	247 (1.5)	249 (1.8)	261 (3.1)	244 (2.4)	243 (3.3)	265 (5.4)	248 (2.0)	263 (4.8)	240 (2.2)	244 (3.6)	276 (5.3)	58 (2.1)	16 (2.4)
San Diego (CA).............	254 (2.8)	256 (2.1)	260 (1.5)	281 (2.4)	244 (3.7)	247 (2.1)	266 (3.6)	262 (2.0)	283 (2.9)	252 (4.4)	248 (2.9)	266 (4.1)	73 (2.3)	32 (2.2)

—Not available.
†Not applicable.
‡Reporting standards not met (too few cases for a reliable estimate).
[1]Scale ranges from 0 to 500.
[2]Basic denotes partial mastery of prerequisite knowledge and skills that are fundamental for proficient work at a given grade.
[3]Proficient represents solid academic performance. Students reaching this level have demonstrated competency over challenging subject matter.

[4]Includes public school students from all cities in the nation with populations of 250,000 or more, including the participating districts.
NOTE: Race categories exclude persons of Hispanic ethnicity. Totals include racial/ethnic groups not shown separately.
SOURCE: U.S. Department of Education, National Center for Education Statistics, National Assessment of Educational Progress (NAEP), 2009, 2011, 2013, and 2015 Reading Assessments, retrieved November 3, 2015, from the Main NAEP Data Explorer (http://nces.ed.gov/nationsreportcard/naepdata/). (This table was prepared November 2015.)

Table 221.85. Average National Assessment of Educational Progress (NAEP) reading scale score, by age and selected student characteristics: Selected years, 1971 through 2012

[Standard errors appear in parentheses]

Selected student characteristic	1971	1975	1980	1984	1988	1990	1992	1994	1996	1999	2004[1] Previous format	2004[1] Revised format	2008	2012
1	2	3	4	5	6	7	8	9	10	11	12	13	14	15
9-year-olds														
All students	208 (1.0)	210 (0.7)	215 (1.0)	211 (0.8)	212 (1.1)	209 (1.2)	211 (0.9)	211 (1.2)	212 (1.0)	212 (1.3)	219 (1.1)	216 (1.0)	220 (0.9)	221 (0.8)
Sex														
Male	201 (1.1)	204 (0.8)	210 (1.1)	207 (1.0)	207 (1.4)	204 (1.7)	206 (1.3)	207 (1.3)	207 (1.4)	209 (1.6)	216 (1.4)	212 (1.1)	216 (1.1)	218 (0.9)
Female	214 (1.0)	216 (0.8)	220 (1.1)	214 (0.9)	216 (1.3)	215 (1.2)	215 (0.9)	215 (1.4)	218 (1.1)	215 (1.5)	221 (1.0)	219 (1.1)	224 (0.9)	223 (0.9)
Gap between female and male score	13 (1.5)	12 (1.1)	10 (1.6)	7 (1.3)	9 (1.9)	11 (2.0)	10 (1.6)	7 (1.9)	11 (1.8)	6 (2.2)	5 (1.8)	8 (1.5)	7 (1.4)	5 (1.3)
Race/ethnicity														
White	214 [2] (0.9)	217 (0.7)	221 (0.8)	218 (0.9)	218 (1.4)	217 (1.3)	218 (1.0)	218 (1.3)	220 (1.2)	221 (1.6)	226 (1.1)	224 (0.9)	228 (1.0)	229 (0.8)
Black	170 [2] (1.7)	181 (1.2)	189 (1.8)	186 (1.3)	189 (2.4)	182 (2.9)	185 (2.2)	185 (2.3)	191 (2.6)	186 (2.3)	200 (2.2)	197 (1.8)	204 (1.7)	206 (1.9)
Hispanic	[3] (†)	183 (2.2)	190 (2.3)	187 (3.0)	194 (3.5)	189 (2.3)	192 (3.1)	186 (3.9)	195 (3.4)	193 (2.7)	205 (1.7)	199 (1.5)	207 (1.5)	208 (1.5)
Gap between White and Black score	44 (1.9)	35 (1.4)	32 (1.9)	32 (1.6)	29 (2.8)	35 (3.2)	33 (2.4)	33 (2.6)	29 (2.8)	35 (2.8)	26 (2.5)	27 (2.1)	24 (2.0)	23 (2.1)
Gap between White and Hispanic score	† (†)	34 (2.4)	31 (2.4)	31 (3.1)	24 (3.8)	28 (2.6)	26 (3.2)	32 (4.1)	25 (3.6)	28 (3.2)	21 (2.1)	25 (1.8)	21 (1.8)	21 (1.7)
13-year-olds														
All students	255 (0.9)	256 (0.8)	258 (0.9)	257 (0.6)	257 (1.0)	257 (0.8)	260 (1.2)	258 (0.9)	258 (1.0)	259 (1.0)	259 (1.0)	257 (1.0)	260 (0.8)	263 (1.0)
Sex														
Male	250 (1.0)	250 (0.8)	254 (1.1)	253 (0.7)	252 (1.3)	251 (1.1)	254 (1.7)	251 (1.2)	251 (1.2)	254 (1.3)	254 (1.2)	252 (1.1)	256 (1.0)	259 (1.3)
Female	261 (0.9)	262 (0.9)	263 (0.9)	262 (0.7)	263 (1.0)	263 (1.1)	265 (1.2)	266 (1.2)	264 (1.2)	265 (1.2)	264 (1.3)	262 (1.2)	264 (0.9)	267 (0.9)
Gap between female and male score	11 (1.3)	13 (1.2)	8 (1.4)	9 (1.0)	11 (1.7)	13 (1.6)	11 (2.1)	15 (1.7)	13 (1.7)	12 (1.8)	10 (1.8)	10 (1.6)	8 (1.3)	8 (1.6)
Race/ethnicity														
White	261 [2] (0.7)	262 (0.7)	264 (0.7)	263 (0.6)	261 (1.1)	262 (0.9)	266 (1.2)	265 (1.1)	266 (1.0)	267 (1.2)	266 (1.0)	265 (1.0)	268 (1.0)	270 (1.3)
Black	222 [2] (1.2)	226 (1.2)	233 (1.5)	236 (1.2)	243 (2.4)	241 (2.2)	238 (2.3)	234 (2.4)	234 (2.6)	238 (2.4)	244 (2.0)	239 (1.9)	247 (1.6)	247 (1.6)
Hispanic	[3] (†)	232 (3.0)	237 (2.0)	240 (2.0)	240 (3.5)	238 (2.3)	239 (3.5)	235 (1.9)	238 (2.9)	244 (2.9)	242 (1.6)	241 (2.1)	242 (1.5)	249 (1.3)
Gap between White and Black score	39 (1.4)	36 (1.4)	32 (1.6)	26 (1.3)	18 (2.6)	21 (2.4)	29 (2.7)	31 (2.7)	32 (2.8)	29 (2.7)	22 (2.3)	25 (2.1)	21 (1.9)	23 (2.1)
Gap between White and Hispanic score	† (†)	30 (3.1)	27 (2.1)	23 (2.1)	21 (3.6)	24 (2.5)	27 (3.7)	30 (2.2)	28 (3.1)	23 (3.1)	24 (1.9)	24 (2.4)	26 (1.8)	21 (1.8)
Parents' highest level of education														
Did not finish high school	— (†)	— (†)	239 (1.1)	240 (1.2)	246 (2.1)	241 (1.8)	239 (2.6)	237 (2.4)	239 (2.8)	238 (3.4)	240 (2.7)	238 (2.3)	239 (1.9)	248 (2.0)
Graduated high school	— (†)	— (†)	253 (0.9)	253 (0.8)	253 (1.2)	251 (0.9)	252 (1.7)	251 (1.4)	251 (1.5)	251 (1.8)	251 (1.6)	249 (1.1)	251 (1.1)	248 (1.7)
Some education after high school	— (†)	— (†)	268 (1.0)	266 (1.1)	265 (1.7)	267 (1.7)	265 (2.7)	266 (1.9)	268 (2.3)	269 (2.4)	264 (2.0)	261 (1.4)	265 (1.1)	264 (1.5)
Graduated college	— (†)	— (†)	273 (0.9)	268 (0.9)	265 (1.6)	267 (1.1)	271 (1.5)	269 (1.2)	269 (1.4)	270 (1.2)	270 (1.0)	266 (1.2)	270 (1.2)	273 (1.3)
17-year-olds														
All students	285 (1.2)	286 (0.8)	285 (1.2)	289 (0.8)	290 (1.0)	290 (1.1)	290 (1.1)	288 (1.3)	288 (1.1)	288 (1.3)	285 (1.2)	283 (1.1)	286 (0.9)	287 (0.9)
Sex														
Male	279 (1.2)	280 (1.0)	282 (1.3)	284 (0.8)	286 (1.5)	284 (1.6)	284 (1.6)	282 (2.2)	281 (1.3)	281 (1.6)	278 (1.5)	276 (1.4)	280 (1.1)	283 (1.1)
Female	291 (1.3)	291 (1.0)	289 (1.2)	294 (0.9)	294 (1.5)	296 (1.2)	296 (1.1)	295 (1.5)	295 (1.2)	295 (1.4)	292 (1.3)	289 (1.2)	291 (1.0)	291 (1.0)
Gap between female and male score	12 (1.8)	12 (1.4)	7 (1.8)	10 (1.2)	8 (2.1)	12 (2.0)	11 (1.9)	13 (2.7)	15 (1.8)	13 (2.1)	14 (2.0)	14 (1.8)	11 (1.5)	8 (1.5)
Race/ethnicity														
White	291 [2] (1.0)	293 (0.6)	293 (0.9)	295 (0.9)	295 (1.2)	297 (1.2)	297 (1.4)	296 (1.5)	295 (1.2)	295 (1.4)	293 (1.1)	289 (1.2)	295 (1.0)	295 (1.0)
Black	239 [2] (1.7)	241 (2.0)	243 (1.8)	264 (1.2)	274 (2.4)	267 (2.3)	261 (2.1)	266 (3.9)	266 (2.7)	264 (1.7)	264 (2.7)	262 (1.9)	266 (2.4)	269 (1.6)
Hispanic	[3] (†)	252 (3.6)	261 (2.7)	268 (2.9)	271 (4.3)	275 (3.6)	271 (3.7)	263 (4.9)	265 (4.1)	271 (3.9)	264 (2.9)	267 (2.5)	269 (1.3)	274 (1.5)
Gap between White and Black score	53 (2.0)	52 (2.1)	50 (2.0)	32 (1.5)	20 (2.7)	29 (2.6)	37 (2.5)	30 (4.2)	29 (3.0)	31 (2.3)	29 (2.9)	27 (2.3)	29 (2.6)	26 (1.9)
Gap between White and Hispanic score	† (†)	41 (3.6)	31 (2.9)	27 (3.0)	24 (4.4)	22 (3.8)	26 (3.9)	33 (5.2)	30 (4.2)	24 (4.2)	29 (3.1)	22 (2.8)	26 (1.6)	21 (1.9)
Parents' highest level of education														
Did not finish high school	— (†)	— (†)	262 (1.5)	269 (1.4)	267 (2.0)	270 (2.8)	271 (3.9)	268 (2.7)	267 (3.2)	265 (3.6)	259 (3.4)	259 (2.7)	266 (2.1)	266 (2.1)
Graduated high school	— (†)	— (†)	277 (1.0)	281 (0.8)	282 (1.3)	283 (1.4)	280 (1.6)	276 (1.9)	273 (1.7)	274 (2.1)	274 (1.6)	271 (1.4)	274 (1.4)	270 (1.6)
Some education after high school	— (†)	— (†)	295 (1.2)	298 (0.9)	299 (2.2)	295 (1.9)	293 (1.9)	294 (1.6)	295 (2.2)	295 (1.8)	286 (1.9)	285 (1.5)	288 (1.1)	287 (1.1)
Graduated college	— (†)	— (†)	301 (1.0)	302 (0.9)	300 (1.4)	302 (1.5)	301 (1.7)	300 (1.7)	299 (1.5)	298 (1.3)	298 (1.3)	295 (1.4)	298 (1.1)	300 (1.0)

—Not available.
†Not applicable.
[1]In 2004, two assessments were conducted—one using the same format that was used in previous assessments, and one using a revised assessment format that provides accommodations for students with disabilities and for English language learners. The 2004 data in column 12 are for the format that was used in previous assessment years, while the 2004 data in column 13 are for the revised format. In subsequent years, only the revised format was used.
[2]Data for 1971 include persons of Hispanic ethnicity.
[3]Test scores of Hispanics were not tabulated separately.
NOTE: Scale ranges from 0 to 500. Students scoring 150 (or higher) are able to follow brief written directions and carry out simple, discrete reading tasks. Students scoring 200 are able to understand, combine ideas, and make inferences based on short uncomplicated passages about specific or sequentially related information. Students scoring 250 are able to search for specific information, interrelate ideas, and make generalizations about literature, science, and social studies materials. Students scoring 300 are able to find, understand, summarize, and explain relatively complicated literary and informational material. Includes public and private schools. For assessment years prior to 2004, accommodations were not permitted. For 2004 (revised format) and later years, includes students tested with accommodations; excludes only those students with disabilities and English language learners who were unable to be tested even with accommodations (2 to 5 percent of all students, depending on age and assessment year). Race categories exclude persons of Hispanic ethnicity, except where noted. Totals include other racial/ethnic groups not shown separately.
SOURCE: U.S. Department of Education, National Center for Education Statistics, National Assessment of Educational Progress (NAEP), *NAEP 2012 Trends in Academic Progress*; and 2012 NAEP Long-Term Trend Reading Assessment, retrieved June 27, 2013, from Long-Term Trend NAEP Data Explorer (http://nces.ed.gov/nationsreportcard/naepdata/). (This table was prepared June 2013.)

Table 221.90. Percentage of students at or above selected National Assessment of Educational Progress (NAEP) reading score levels, by age, sex, and race/ethnicity: Selected years, 1971 through 2012

[Standard errors appear in parentheses]

Age, sex, race/ethnicity, and score level	1971	1975	1980	1984	1988	1990	1992	1994	1996	1999	2004	2008	2012
1	2	3	4	5	6	7	8	9	10	11	12	13	14
9-year-olds													
Total													
Level 150[1]	91 (0.5)	93 (0.4)	95 (0.4)	92 (0.4)	93 (0.7)	90 (0.9)	92 (0.4)	92 (0.7)	93 (0.6)	93 (0.7)	94 (0.5)	96 (0.4)	96 (0.4)
Level 200[2]	59 (1.0)	62 (0.8)	68 (1.0)	62 (0.8)	63 (1.3)	59 (1.3)	62 (1.1)	63 (1.4)	64 (1.3)	64 (1.4)	69 (1.0)	73 (0.9)	74 (0.9)
Level 250[3]	16 (0.6)	15 (0.6)	18 (0.8)	17 (0.7)	17 (1.1)	18 (1.0)	16 (0.8)	17 (1.2)	17 (0.8)	16 (1.0)	19 (0.7)	21 (0.8)	22 (0.7)
Male													
Level 150[1]	88 (0.7)	91 (0.5)	93 (0.5)	90 (0.5)	90 (0.9)	88 (1.4)	90 (0.8)	90 (1.0)	92 (0.8)	91 (1.1)	92 (0.6)	94 (0.6)	94 (0.6)
Level 200[2]	53 (1.2)	56 (1.0)	63 (1.1)	58 (1.0)	58 (1.8)	54 (1.9)	57 (1.6)	59 (1.5)	58 (2.0)	61 (1.8)	64 (1.3)	70 (1.2)	71 (1.0)
Level 250[3]	12 (0.6)	12 (0.6)	15 (0.9)	16 (0.8)	16 (1.4)	16 (1.2)	14 (1.0)	15 (1.2)	14 (1.3)	15 (1.3)	17 (0.8)	19 (1.0)	21 (0.8)
Female													
Level 150[1]	93 (0.5)	95 (0.3)	96 (0.4)	94 (0.5)	95 (1.0)	92 (1.1)	94 (0.6)	94 (0.8)	95 (0.6)	95 (0.8)	96 (0.5)	97 (0.4)	97 (0.4)
Level 200[2]	65 (1.1)	68 (0.8)	73 (1.0)	65 (1.0)	67 (1.4)	64 (1.2)	67 (1.2)	67 (1.9)	70 (1.6)	67 (1.6)	73 (1.2)	77 (1.1)	77 (1.1)
Level 250[3]	19 (0.8)	18 (0.8)	21 (1.0)	18 (0.8)	19 (1.2)	21 (1.2)	18 (1.1)	18 (1.5)	19 (1.3)	17 (1.3)	20 (1.0)	22 (1.0)	23 (0.9)
White													
Level 150[1]	94 [5] (0.4)	96 (0.3)	97 (0.2)	95 (0.3)	95 (0.7)	94 (0.9)	96 (0.5)	96 (0.5)	96 (0.6)	97 (0.4)	97 (0.4)	98 (0.4)	98 (0.4)
Level 200[2]	65 [5] (1.0)	69 (0.8)	74 (0.7)	69 (0.9)	68 (1.6)	66 (1.4)	69 (1.2)	70 (1.5)	71 (1.5)	73 (1.6)	77 (1.0)	81 (1.0)	82 (0.8)
Level 250[3]	18 [5] (0.7)	17 (0.7)	21 (0.9)	21 (0.8)	20 (1.5)	23 (1.2)	20 (1.0)	20 (1.5)	20 (1.1)	20 (1.4)	24 (0.8)	27 (1.1)	28 (0.8)
Black													
Level 150[1]	70 [5] (1.7)	81 (1.1)	85 (1.4)	81 (1.2)	83 (2.4)	77 (2.7)	80 (2.2)	79 (2.4)	84 (1.9)	82 (2.5)	88 (1.7)	91 (1.1)	94 (1.0)
Level 200[2]	22 [5] (1.5)	32 (1.5)	41 (1.9)	37 (1.5)	39 (2.9)	34 (3.4)	37 (2.2)	38 (2.8)	42 (3.2)	36 (3.0)	50 (2.3)	58 (2.3)	61 (2.1)
Level 250[3]	2 [5] (0.5)	2 (0.3)	4 (0.6)	5 (0.6)	6 (1.2)	5 (1.5)	5 (0.8)	4 (1.5)	6 (1.1)	4 (1.1)	7 (0.8)	9 (0.9)	10 (1.1)
Hispanic													
Level 150[1]	[6] (†)	81 (2.5)	84 (1.8)	82 (3.0)	86 (3.5)	84 (1.8)	83 (2.6)	80 (4.6)	86 (2.4)	87 (3.3)	89 (1.3)	93 (0.8)	92 (1.1)
Level 200[2]	[6] (†)	35 (3.0)	42 (2.6)	40 (2.7)	46 (3.3)	41 (2.7)	43 (3.5)	37 (4.6)	48 (3.8)	44 (3.4)	53 (1.7)	62 (1.7)	63 (1.8)
Level 250[3]	[6] (†)	3 (0.5)	5 (1.4)	4 (0.7)	9 (2.3)	6 (2.0)	7 (2.3)	6 (1.6)	7 (3.2)	6 (1.7)	7 (0.8)	10 (1.2)	11 (1.0)
13-year-olds													
Total													
Level 200[2]	93 (0.5)	93 (0.4)	95 (0.4)	94 (0.3)	95 (0.6)	94 (0.6)	93 (0.7)	92 (0.6)	92 (0.7)	93 (0.7)	92 (0.6)	94 (0.4)	94 (0.4)
Level 250[3]	58 (1.1)	59 (1.0)	61 (1.1)	59 (0.8)	59 (1.3)	59 (1.0)	62 (1.4)	60 (1.2)	60 (1.3)	61 (1.5)	59 (1.1)	63 (0.8)	66 (1.3)
Level 300[4]	10 (0.5)	10 (0.5)	11 (0.5)	11 (0.4)	11 (0.8)	11 (0.6)	15 (0.9)	14 (0.8)	14 (1.0)	15 (1.1)	12 (0.8)	13 (0.5)	15 (1.0)
Male													
Level 200[2]	91 (0.7)	91 (0.5)	93 (0.6)	92 (0.4)	93 (1.0)	91 (0.9)	90 (1.1)	89 (1.1)	91 (0.9)	89 (0.8)	92 (0.6)	93 (0.7)
Level 250[3]	52 (1.2)	52 (1.1)	56 (1.2)	54 (0.9)	52 (1.9)	52 (1.5)	55 (2.0)	53 (1.9)	53 (1.6)	55 (1.9)	55 (1.3)	59 (1.2)	62 (1.6)
Level 300[4]	7 (0.5)	7 (0.4)	9 (0.7)	9 (0.5)	9 (0.9)	8 (0.8)	13 (1.1)	10 (0.7)	10 (1.0)	11 (1.1)	11 (0.9)	11 (0.7)	13 (1.1)
Female													
Level 200[2]	95 (0.4)	95 (0.4)	96 (0.4)	96 (0.3)	97 (0.6)	96 (0.6)	95 (0.7)	95 (0.6)	95 (0.6)	96 (0.7)	95 (0.6)	96 (0.5)	96 (0.4)
Level 250[3]	64 (1.1)	65 (1.2)	65 (1.1)	64 (0.8)	65 (1.4)	65 (1.5)	68 (1.4)	68 (1.7)	66 (1.6)	66 (1.9)	65 (1.3)	66 (1.0)	69 (1.4)
Level 300[4]	12 (0.6)	13 (0.7)	13 (0.6)	13 (0.6)	13 (0.9)	13 (0.9)	14 (0.9)	18 (1.1)	18 (1.1)	17 (1.3)	18 (1.7)	14 (1.0)	16 (0.9)	17 (1.1)
White													
Level 200[2]	96 [5] (0.3)	96 (0.2)	97 (0.2)	96 (0.2)	96 (0.6)	96 (0.6)	96 (0.6)	95 (0.7)	95 (0.5)	96 (0.6)	95 (0.5)	96 (0.4)	96 (0.6)
Level 250[3]	64 [5] (0.9)	65 (0.9)	68 (0.8)	65 (0.8)	64 (1.5)	65 (1.2)	68 (1.4)	68 (1.3)	69 (1.4)	69 (1.7)	68 (1.1)	72 (1.2)	74 (1.8)
Level 300[4]	11 [5] (0.5)	12 (0.5)	14 (0.6)	13 (0.6)	12 (0.9)	13 (0.9)	18 (1.1)	17 (1.0)	17 (1.3)	18 (1.4)	16 (0.9)	18 (0.8)	19 (1.0)
Black													
Level 200[2]	74 [5] (1.7)	77 (1.3)	84 (1.7)	85 (1.2)	91 (2.2)	88 (2.3)	82 (2.7)	81 (2.3)	82 (3.2)	85 (2.3)	86 (1.5)	91 (1.1)	90 (1.3)
Level 250[3]	21 [5] (1.6)	25 (1.6)	30 (2.0)	35 (1.3)	40 (2.3)	42 (3.5)	38 (2.7)	36 (3.5)	34 (3.9)	38 (2.7)	40 (2.3)	48 (2.3)	48 (2.5)
Level 300[4]	1 [5] (0.2)	2 (0.3)	2 (0.5)	3 (0.6)	5 (1.2)	5 (0.8)	6 (1.4)	4 (1.2)	3 (0.9)	5 (1.4)	4 (0.7)	6 (0.8)	6 (0.9)
Hispanic													
Level 200[2]	[6] (†)	81 (2.3)	87 (2.4)	86 (1.7)	87 (2.6)	86 (2.4)	83 (3.5)	82 (2.7)	85 (3.2)	89 (2.8)	85 (1.9)	87 (1.3)	91 (1.2)
Level 250[3]	[6] (†)	32 (3.6)	35 (2.6)	39 (2.3)	38 (4.4)	37 (2.9)	41 (5.1)	34 (3.9)	38 (3.7)	43 (3.8)	44 (2.3)	44 (1.8)	51 (1.7)
Level 300[4]	[6] (†)	2 (1.0)	2 (0.6)	4 (1.0)	4 (1.9)	4 (1.2)	6 (1.8)	4 (1.8)	5 (1.7)	6 (1.8)	5 (1.2)	5 (0.6)	6 (0.5)
17-year-olds													
Total													
Level 250[3]	79 (0.9)	80 (0.7)	81 (0.9)	83 (0.6)	86 (0.8)	84 (1.0)	83 (0.8)	81 (1.0)	82 (0.8)	82 (1.0)	79 (0.9)	80 (0.6)	82 (0.6)
Level 300[4]	39 (1.0)	39 (0.8)	38 (1.1)	40 (1.0)	41 (1.5)	41 (1.0)	43 (1.1)	41 (1.2)	39 (1.4)	40 (1.4)	36 (1.2)	39 (0.8)	39 (0.9)
Male													
Level 250[3]	74 (1.0)	76 (0.8)	78 (1.0)	80 (0.7)	83 (1.4)	80 (1.4)	78 (1.2)	76 (1.5)	77 (1.2)	77 (1.5)	73 (1.2)	76 (0.8)	79 (0.8)
Level 300[4]	34 (1.1)	34 (1.0)	35 (1.3)	36 (1.0)	37 (2.3)	36 (1.5)	38 (1.6)	36 (1.9)	34 (1.9)	34 (1.7)	32 (1.2)	35 (0.9)	36 (1.2)
Female													
Level 250[3]	83 (1.0)	84 (0.9)	84 (1.0)	87 (0.6)	88 (1.1)	89 (1.0)	87 (1.1)	86 (1.2)	87 (1.0)	87 (1.0)	84 (0.9)	84 (0.8)	85 (0.7)
Level 300[4]	44 (1.2)	44 (0.9)	41 (1.2)	45 (1.1)	44 (2.0)	47 (1.3)	48 (1.5)	46 (1.5)	45 (1.7)	45 (1.8)	41 (1.6)	43 (1.0)	42 (1.1)
White													
Level 250[3]	84 [5] (0.7)	86 (0.6)	87 (0.6)	88 (0.5)	89 (0.9)	88 (1.1)	88 (0.9)	86 (1.1)	87 (0.8)	87 (1.3)	83 (0.9)	87 (0.6)	87 (0.6)
Level 300[4]	43 [5] (0.9)	44 (0.8)	43 (1.1)	47 (1.1)	45 (1.6)	48 (1.2)	50 (1.4)	48 (1.4)	46 (1.5)	46 (1.5)	42 (1.3)	47 (1.0)	47 (1.3)
Black													
Level 250[3]	40 [5] (1.6)	43 (1.6)	44 (2.0)	65 (1.5)	76 (2.4)	69 (2.8)	61 (2.3)	66 (4.1)	68 (4.0)	66 (2.5)	64 (2.2)	67 (2.4)	70 (1.4)
Level 300[4]	8 [5] (0.9)	8 (0.7)	7 (0.8)	16 (1.0)	25 (3.1)	20 (1.8)	17 (2.5)	22 (3.7)	18 (2.2)	17 (1.7)	16 (1.8)	21 (1.5)	22 (1.5)
Hispanic													
Level 250[3]	[6] (†)	53 (4.1)	62 (3.1)	68 (2.4)	71 (4.8)	75 (4.7)	69 (4.0)	63 (4.4)	65 (4.2)	68 (4.3)	67 (2.4)	70 (1.5)	74 (1.3)
Level 300[4]	[6] (†)	13 (2.7)	17 (2.1)	21 (3.0)	23 (3.7)	27 (3.3)	27 (3.2)	20 (3.0)	20 (4.8)	24 (3.8)	23 (2.1)	22 (1.0)	26 (1.3)

†Not applicable.

[1]Students scoring 150 (or higher) are able to follow brief written directions and carry out simple, discrete reading tasks.

[2]Students scoring 200 (or higher) are able to understand, combine ideas, and make inferences based on short uncomplicated passages about specific or sequentially related information.

[3]Students scoring 250 (or higher) are able to search for specific information, interrelate ideas, and make generalizations about literature, science, and social studies materials.

[4]Students scoring 300 (or higher) are able to find, understand, summarize, and explain relatively complicated literary and informational material.

[5]Data for 1971 include persons of Hispanic ethnicity.

[6]Test scores of Hispanics were not tabulated separately.

NOTE: The NAEP reading scores have been evaluated at certain performance levels, as outlined in footnotes 1 through 4. Scale ranges from 0 to 500. Includes public and private schools. For assessment years prior to 2004, accommodations were not permitted. For 2004 and later years, includes students tested with accommodations; excludes only those students with disabilities and English language learners who were unable to be tested even with accommodations (2 to 5 percent of all students, depending on age and assessment year). Race categories exclude persons of Hispanic ethnicity, except where noted. Totals include other racial/ethnic groups not shown separately.

SOURCE: U.S. Department of Education, National Center for Education Statistics, National Assessment of Educational Progress (NAEP), *NAEP 1999 Trends in Academic Progress*; and 2004, 2008, and 2012 Long-Term Trend Reading Assessments, retrieved May 12, 2009, and July 15, 2013, from the Long-Term Trend NAEP Data Explorer (http://nces.ed.gov/nationsreportcard/naepdata/). (This table was prepared July 2013.)

Table 222.10. Average National Assessment of Educational Progress (NAEP) mathematics scale score, by sex, race/ethnicity, and grade: Selected years, 1990 through 2015

[Standard errors appear in parentheses]

Grade and year	All students	Sex			Race/ethnicity								Gap between White and Black score	Gap between White and Hispanic score
		Average mathematics scale score		Gap between female and male score	Average mathematics scale score									
		Male	Female		White	Black	Hispanic	Asian/Pacific Islander Total	Asian[1]	Pacific Islander[1]	American Indian/ Alaska Native	Two or more races[1]		
1	2	3	4	5	6	7	8	9	10	11	12	13	14	15
Grade 4														
1990[2]	213 (0.9)	214 (1.2)	213 (1.1)	-1 (1.7)	220 (1.0)	188 (1.8)	200 (2.2)	225 (4.1)	— (†)	— (†)	‡ (†)	— (†)	32 (2.0)	20 (2.4)
1992[2]	220 (0.7)	221 (0.8)	219 (1.0)	-2 (1.2)	227 (0.8)	193 (1.4)	202 (1.5)	231 (2.1)	— (†)	— (†)	‡ (†)	— (†)	35 (1.6)	25 (1.7)
1996	224 (1.0)	224 (1.0)	223 (1.1)	# (†)	232 (1.0)	198 (1.6)	207 (1.9)	229 (4.2)	— (†)	— (†)	217 (5.6)	— (†)	34 (1.8)	25 (2.1)
2000	226 (0.9)	227 (1.0)	224 (0.9)	-3 (1.4)	234 (0.8)	203 (1.2)	208 (1.5)	‡ (†)	— (†)	— (†)	208 (3.5)	— (†)	31 (1.5)	27 (1.7)
2003	235 (0.2)	236 (0.3)	233 (0.2)	-3 (0.3)	243 (0.2)	216 (0.4)	222 (0.4)	246 (1.1)	— (†)	— (†)	223 (1.0)	— (†)	27 (0.4)	22 (0.5)
2005	238 (0.1)	239 (0.2)	237 (0.2)	-3 (0.2)	246 (0.1)	220 (0.3)	226 (0.3)	251 (0.7)	— (†)	— (†)	226 (0.9)	— (†)	26 (0.3)	20 (0.3)
2007	240 (0.2)	241 (0.2)	239 (0.2)	-2 (0.2)	248 (0.2)	222 (0.3)	227 (0.3)	253 (0.8)	— (†)	— (†)	228 (0.7)	— (†)	26 (0.4)	21 (0.4)
2009	240 (0.2)	241 (0.3)	239 (0.3)	-2 (0.4)	248 (0.2)	222 (0.3)	227 (0.4)	255 (1.0)	— (†)	— (†)	225 (0.9)	— (†)	26 (0.4)	21 (0.5)
2011	241 (0.2)	241 (0.2)	240 (0.2)	-1 (0.3)	249 (0.2)	224 (0.4)	229 (0.3)	256 (1.0)	257 (1.0)	236 (2.1)	225 (0.9)	245 (0.6)	25 (0.4)	20 (0.4)
2013	242 (0.2)	242 (0.3)	241 (0.2)	-1 (0.4)	250 (0.2)	224 (0.3)	231 (0.4)	258 (0.8)	259 (0.8)	236 (2.0)	227 (1.1)	245 (0.7)	26 (0.4)	19 (0.5)
2015	240 (0.3)	241 (0.3)	239 (0.3)	-2 (0.4)	248 (0.3)	224 (0.4)	230 (0.5)	257 (1.2)	259 (1.2)	231 (2.3)	227 (1.0)	245 (0.8)	24 (0.5)	18 (0.5)
Grade 8														
1990[2]	263 (1.3)	263 (1.6)	262 (1.3)	-1 (2.1)	270 (1.3)	237 (2.7)	246 (4.3)	275 (5.0)	— (†)	— (†)	‡ (†)	— (†)	33 (3.0)	24 (4.5)
1992[2]	268 (0.9)	268 (1.1)	269 (1.0)	1 (1.5)	277 (1.0)	237 (1.3)	249 (1.2)	290 (5.9)	— (†)	— (†)	‡ (†)	— (†)	40 (1.7)	28 (1.5)
1996	270 (0.9)	271 (1.1)	269 (1.1)	-2 (1.5)	281 (1.1)	240 (1.9)	251 (1.7)	‡ (†)	— (†)	— (†)	‡ (†)	— (†)	41 (2.2)	30 (2.0)
2000	273 (0.8)	274 (0.9)	272 (0.9)	-2 (1.3)	284 (0.8)	244 (1.2)	253 (1.3)	288 (3.5)	— (†)	— (†)	259 (7.5)	— (†)	40 (1.5)	31 (1.6)
2003	278 (0.3)	278 (0.3)	277 (0.3)	-2 (0.4)	288 (0.3)	252 (0.5)	259 (0.6)	291 (1.3)	— (†)	— (†)	263 (1.8)	— (†)	35 (0.6)	29 (0.7)
2005	279 (0.2)	280 (0.2)	278 (0.3)	-2 (0.3)	289 (0.2)	255 (0.4)	262 (0.4)	295 (0.9)	— (†)	— (†)	264 (0.9)	— (†)	34 (0.4)	27 (0.5)
2007	281 (0.3)	282 (0.3)	280 (0.3)	-2 (0.4)	291 (0.3)	260 (0.4)	265 (0.4)	297 (0.9)	— (†)	— (†)	264 (1.2)	— (†)	32 (0.5)	26 (0.5)
2009	283 (0.3)	284 (0.3)	282 (0.4)	-2 (0.5)	293 (0.3)	261 (0.5)	266 (0.6)	301 (1.2)	— (†)	— (†)	266 (1.1)	— (†)	32 (0.5)	26 (0.6)
2011	284 (0.2)	284 (0.3)	283 (0.2)	-1 (0.4)	293 (0.2)	262 (0.5)	270 (0.5)	303 (1.0)	305 (1.1)	269 (2.4)	265 (0.9)	288 (1.3)	31 (0.5)	23 (0.5)
2013	285 (0.3)	285 (0.3)	284 (0.3)	-1 (0.4)	294 (0.3)	263 (0.4)	272 (0.5)	306 (1.1)	309 (1.1)	275 (2.3)	269 (1.2)	288 (1.2)	31 (0.5)	22 (0.5)
2015	282 (0.3)	282 (0.3)	282 (0.4)	# (†)	292 (0.3)	260 (0.5)	270 (0.5)	306 (1.5)	307 (1.5)	276 (2.9)	267 (1.3)	285 (1.1)	32 (0.6)	22 (0.6)
Grade 12														
1990[2]	[3] (†)	[3] (†)	[3] (†)	[3] (†)	[3] (†)	[3] (†)	[3] (†)	[3] (†)	[3] (†)	[3] (†)	[3] (†)	[3] (†)	[3] (†)	[3] (†)
1992[2]	[3] (†)	[3] (†)	[3] (†)	[3] (†)	[3] (†)	[3] (†)	[3] (†)	[3] (†)	[3] (†)	[3] (†)	[3] (†)	[3] (†)	[3] (†)	[3] (†)
1996	[3] (†)	[3] (†)	[3] (†)	[3] (†)	[3] (†)	[3] (†)	[3] (†)	[3] (†)	[3] (†)	[3] (†)	[3] (†)	[3] (†)	[3] (†)	[3] (†)
2000	[3] (†)	[3] (†)	[3] (†)	[3] (†)	[3] (†)	[3] (†)	[3] (†)	[3] (†)	[3] (†)	[3] (†)	[3] (†)	[3] (†)	[3] (†)	[3] (†)
2003	— (†)	— (†)	— (†)	— (†)	— (†)	— (†)	— (†)	— (†)	— (†)	— (†)	— (†)	— (†)	— (†)	— (†)
2005	150 (0.6)	151 (0.7)	149 (0.7)	-3 (1.0)	157 (0.6)	127 (1.1)	133 (1.3)	163 (2.0)	— (†)	— (†)	134 (4.1)	— (†)	31 (1.2)	24 (1.4)
2007	— (†)	— (†)	— (†)	— (†)	— (†)	— (†)	— (†)	— (†)	— (†)	— (†)	— (†)	— (†)	— (†)	— (†)
2009	153 (0.7)	155 (0.9)	152 (0.7)	-3 (1.1)	161 (0.6)	131 (0.8)	138 (0.8)	175 (2.7)	— (†)	— (†)	144 (2.8)	— (†)	30 (1.0)	23 (1.0)
2011	— (†)	— (†)	— (†)	— (†)	— (†)	— (†)	— (†)	— (†)	— (†)	— (†)	— (†)	— (†)	— (†)	— (†)
2013	153 (0.5)	155 (0.6)	152 (0.6)	-3 (0.9)	162 (0.6)	132 (0.8)	141 (0.8)	172 (1.3)	174 (1.3)	151 (2.8)	142 (3.2)	155 (1.7)	30 (1.0)	21 (1.0)
2015	152 (0.5)	153 (0.7)	150 (0.6)	-3 (0.9)	160 (0.6)	130 (1.0)	139 (0.8)	170 (2.0)	171 (1.9)	‡ (†)	138 (2.8)	157 (2.2)	30 (1.2)	22 (1.0)

—Not available.
†Not applicable.
#Rounds to zero.
‡Reporting standards not met (too few cases for a reliable estimate).
[1]Prior to 2011, separate data for Asian students, Pacific Islander students, and students of Two or more races were not collected.
[2]Accommodations were not permitted for this assessment.
[3]Because of major changes to the framework and content of the grade 12 assessment, scores from 2005 and later assessment years cannot be compared with scores from earlier assessment years. Therefore, this table does not include scores from the earlier grade 12 assessment years (1990, 1992, 1996, and 2000). For data pertaining to scale score comparisons between earlier years, see the *Digest of Education Statistics 2009*, table 138 (http://nces.ed.gov/programs/digest/d09/tables/dt09_138.asp).

NOTE: For the grade 4 and grade 8 assessments, the scale ranges from 0 to 500. For the grade 12 assessment, the scale ranges from 0 to 300. Includes public and private schools. For 1996 and later years, includes students tested with accommodations (1 to 14 percent of all students, depending on grade level and year); excludes only those students with disabilities and English language learners who were unable to be tested even with accommodations (1 to 4 percent of all students). Race categories exclude persons of Hispanic ethnicity. SOURCE: U.S. Department of Education, National Center for Education Statistics, National Assessment of Educational Progress (NAEP), 1990, 1992, 1996, 2000, 2003, 2005, 2007, 2009, 2011, 2013, and 2015 Mathematics Assessments, retrieved June 10, 2016, from the Main NAEP Data Explorer (http://nces.ed.gov/nationsreportcard/naepdata/). (This table was prepared June 2016.)

Table 222.12. Average National Assessment of Educational Progress (NAEP) mathematics scale score and percentage of students attaining selected NAEP mathematics achievement levels, by selected school and student characteristics and grade: Selected years, 1990 through 2015

[Standard errors appear in parentheses]

Grade and year	Percent of students in school eligible for free or reduced-price lunch					English language learner (ELL) status			Disability status[1]			Percent of all students attaining mathematics achievement levels		
	Average mathematics scale score[2]				Gap between low-poverty and high-poverty score	Average mathematics scale score[2]		Gap between non-ELL and ELL score	Average mathematics scale score[2]		Gap between non-SD and SD score			
	0–25 percent eligible (low poverty)	26–50 percent eligible	51–75 percent eligible	76–100 percent eligible (high poverty)		ELL	Non-ELL		Identified as student with disability (SD)	Not identified as SD		Below Basic[3]	At or above Basic[3]	At or above Proficient[4]
1	2	3	4	5	6	7	8	9	10	11	12	13	14	15
Grade 4														
1990[5]	— (†)	— (†)	— (†)	— (†)	— (†)	‡ (†)	‡ (†)	‡ (†)	‡ (†)	‡ (†)	‡ (†)	50 (1.4)	50 (1.4)	13 (1.2)
1992[5]	— (†)	— (†)	— (†)	— (†)	— (†)	‡ (†)	‡ (†)	‡ (†)	‡ (†)	‡ (†)	‡ (†)	41 (1.0)	59 (1.0)	18 (1.0)
1996	— (†)	— (†)	— (†)	— (†)	— (†)	201 (3.6)	225 (0.9)	24 (3.7)	204 (2.9)	225 (1.1)	22 (3.1)	37 (1.3)	63 (1.3)	21 (1.1)
2000	239 (1.2)	227 (1.2)	216 (1.5)	205 (1.2)	34 (1.7)	199 (2.0)	227 (0.8)	28 (2.1)	198 (2.2)	228 (0.9)	30 (2.4)	35 (1.3)	65 (1.3)	24 (1.0)
2003	247 (0.3)	237 (0.3)	229 (0.4)	216 (0.5)	31 (0.6)	214 (0.6)	237 (0.2)	23 (0.6)	214 (0.4)	237 (0.2)	23 (0.4)	23 (0.3)	77 (0.3)	32 (0.3)
2005	250 (0.3)	240 (0.3)	232 (0.3)	220 (0.3)	30 (0.4)	216 (0.5)	240 (0.1)	24 (0.5)	219 (0.4)	240 (0.2)	22 (0.4)	20 (0.2)	80 (0.2)	36 (0.2)
2007	252 (0.3)	242 (0.3)	234 (0.3)	222 (0.4)	30 (0.5)	217 (0.5)	242 (0.2)	25 (0.5)	220 (0.4)	242 (0.2)	22 (0.4)	18 (0.2)	82 (0.2)	39 (0.3)
2009	254 (0.4)	242 (0.4)	234 (0.4)	223 (0.4)	31 (0.6)	218 (0.6)	242 (0.2)	24 (0.7)	221 (0.5)	242 (0.2)	21 (0.5)	18 (0.3)	82 (0.3)	39 (0.3)
2011	255 (0.4)	245 (0.4)	237 (0.3)	226 (0.3)	29 (0.6)	219 (0.5)	243 (0.2)	24 (0.5)	218 (0.4)	244 (0.2)	26 (0.5)	18 (0.2)	82 (0.2)	40 (0.3)
2013	257 (0.4)	246 (0.4)	238 (0.5)	226 (0.5)	31 (0.6)	219 (0.6)	244 (0.2)	25 (0.6)	218 (0.5)	245 (0.2)	26 (0.5)	17 (0.2)	83 (0.2)	42 (0.3)
2015	257 (0.7)	245 (0.5)	237 (0.5)	226 (0.5)	30 (0.8)	218 (0.7)	243 (0.3)	25 (0.7)	218 (0.5)	244 (0.3)	26 (0.5)	18 (0.3)	82 (0.3)	40 (0.4)
Grade 8														
1990[5]	— (†)	— (†)	— (†)	— (†)	— (†)	‡ (†)	‡ (†)	‡ (†)	‡ (†)	‡ (†)	‡ (†)	48 (1.4)	52 (1.4)	15 (1.1)
1992[5]	— (†)	— (†)	— (†)	— (†)	— (†)	‡ (†)	‡ (†)	‡ (†)	‡ (†)	‡ (†)	‡ (†)	42 (1.1)	58 (1.1)	21 (1.0)
1996	— (†)	— (†)	— (†)	— (†)	— (†)	226 (3.2)	272 (1.0)	46 (3.4)	231 (2.7)	273 (0.9)	42 (2.9)	39 (1.0)	61 (1.0)	23 (1.0)
2000	287 (1.1)	270 (1.4)	260 (1.8)	246 (2.2)	41 (2.4)	234 (2.7)	274 (0.8)	40 (2.8)	230 (2.1)	276 (0.8)	47 (2.3)	37 (0.9)	63 (0.9)	26 (0.8)
2003	291 (0.4)	278 (0.4)	266 (0.7)	251 (0.7)	40 (0.8)	242 (1.0)	279 (0.3)	38 (1.0)	242 (0.6)	282 (0.3)	39 (0.6)	32 (0.3)	68 (0.3)	29 (0.3)
2005	293 (0.4)	280 (0.3)	268 (0.4)	254 (0.6)	38 (0.7)	244 (0.8)	281 (0.2)	37 (0.8)	245 (0.5)	283 (0.2)	38 (0.5)	31 (0.2)	69 (0.2)	30 (0.2)
2007	296 (0.4)	282 (0.4)	271 (0.6)	259 (0.7)	37 (0.8)	246 (0.8)	283 (0.3)	38 (0.8)	246 (0.6)	285 (0.3)	38 (0.7)	29 (0.3)	71 (0.3)	32 (0.3)
2009	298 (0.5)	284 (0.5)	274 (0.7)	260 (0.7)	38 (0.8)	243 (0.9)	285 (0.3)	42 (0.9)	249 (0.5)	287 (0.3)	38 (0.6)	27 (0.3)	73 (0.3)	34 (0.3)
2011	300 (0.5)	287 (0.5)	276 (0.7)	264 (0.5)	36 (0.9)	244 (1.0)	286 (0.2)	42 (1.0)	250 (0.6)	288 (0.2)	38 (0.7)	27 (0.2)	73 (0.2)	35 (0.2)
2013	301 (0.5)	289 (0.5)	277 (0.4)	265 (0.6)	36 (0.8)	246 (0.8)	287 (0.3)	41 (0.8)	249 (0.5)	289 (0.3)	40 (0.6)	26 (0.3)	74 (0.3)	35 (0.3)
2015	301 (0.6)	287 (0.5)	276 (0.7)	264 (0.7)	38 (1.0)	246 (0.8)	284 (0.3)	38 (0.8)	247 (0.5)	287 (0.3)	40 (0.6)	29 (0.3)	71 (0.3)	33 (0.3)
Grade 12														
1990[5]	[6] (†)	[6] (†)	[6] (†)	[6] (†)	[6] (†)	[6] (†)	[6] (†)	[6] (†)	[6] (†)	[6] (†)	[6] (†)	[6] (†)	[6] (†)	[6] (†)
1992[5]	[6] (†)	[6] (†)	[6] (†)	[6] (†)	[6] (†)	[6] (†)	[6] (†)	[6] (†)	[6] (†)	[6] (†)	[6] (†)	[6] (†)	[6] (†)	[6] (†)
1996	[6] (†)	[6] (†)	[6] (†)	[6] (†)	[6] (†)	[6] (†)	[6] (†)	[6] (†)	[6] (†)	[6] (†)	[6] (†)	[6] (†)	[6] (†)	[6] (†)
2000	[6] (†)	[6] (†)	[6] (†)	[6] (†)	[6] (†)	[6] (†)	[6] (†)	[6] (†)	[6] (†)	[6] (†)	[6] (†)	[6] (†)	[6] (†)	[6] (†)
2003	— (†)	— (†)	— (†)	— (†)	— (†)	— (†)	— (†)	— (†)	— (†)	— (†)	— (†)	— (†)	— (†)	— (†)
2005	158 (1.0)	147 (1.0)	136 (1.3)	122 (2.7)	36 (2.8)	120 (2.5)	151 (0.6)	31 (2.5)	114 (1.8)	153 (0.6)	39 (1.9)	39 (0.8)	61 (0.8)	23 (0.7)
2007	— (†)	— (†)	— (†)	— (†)	— (†)	— (†)	— (†)	— (†)	— (†)	— (†)	— (†)	— (†)	— (†)	— (†)
2009	166 (1.3)	150 (0.7)	140 (1.2)	130 (1.7)	36 (2.1)	117 (1.7)	154 (0.7)	38 (1.9)	120 (1.2)	156 (0.7)	36 (1.4)	36 (0.8)	64 (0.8)	26 (0.8)
2011	— (†)	— (†)	— (†)	— (†)	— (†)	— (†)	— (†)	— (†)	— (†)	— (†)	— (†)	— (†)	— (†)	— (†)
2013	169 (1.0)	155 (0.6)	143 (1.0)	134 (1.2)	35 (1.6)	109 (1.7)	155 (0.5)	46 (1.8)	119 (1.0)	157 (0.5)	38 (1.2)	35 (0.7)	65 (0.7)	26 (0.6)
2015	— (†)	— (†)	— (†)	— (†)	— (†)	— (†)	— (†)	— (†)	— (†)	— (†)	— (†)	— (†)	— (†)	— (†)

—Not available.
†Not applicable.
‡Reporting standards not met (too few cases for a reliable estimate).
[1]The student with disability (SD) variable used in this table includes students who have a 504 plan, even if they do not have an Individualized Education Plan (IEP).
[2]For the grade 4 and grade 8 assessments, the scale ranges from 0 to 500. For the grade 12 assessment, the scale ranges from 0 to 300.
[3]*Basic* denotes partial mastery of the knowledge and skills that are fundamental for proficient work at a given grade.
[4]*Proficient* represents solid academic performance. Students reaching this level have demonstrated competency over challenging subject matter.
[5]Accommodations were not permitted for this assessment.
[6]Because of major changes to the framework and content of the grade 12 assessment, results from 2005 and later assessment years cannot be compared with results from earlier assessment years. Therefore, this table does not include results from the earlier grade 12 assessment years (1990, 1992, 1996, and 2000). For data pertaining to comparisons between earlier years, see the *Digest of Education Statistics 2009*, table 138 (http://nces.ed.gov/programs/digest/d09/tables/dt09_138.asp).
NOTE: Includes public and private schools. For 1996 and later years, includes students tested with accommodations (1 to 14 percent of all students, depending on grade level and year); excludes only those students with disabilities and English language learners who were unable to be tested even with accommodations (1 to 4 percent of all students).
SOURCE: U.S. Department of Education, National Center for Education Statistics, National Assessment of Educational Progress (NAEP), 1990, 1992, 1996, 2000, 2003, 2005, 2007, 2009, 2011, 2013, and 2015 Mathematics Assessments, retrieved October 29, 2015, from the Main NAEP Data Explorer (http://nces.ed.gov/nationsreportcard/naepdata/). (This table was prepared October 2015.)

Table 222.20. Percentage of students at or above selected National Assessment of Educational Progress (NAEP) mathematics achievement levels, by grade and selected student characteristics: Selected years, 1996 through 2015

[Standard errors appear in parentheses]

Grade and selected student characteristic	1996 At or above Basic[1]	1996 At or above Proficient[2]	2003 At or above Basic[1]	2003 At or above Proficient[2]	2005 At or above Basic[1]	2005 At or above Proficient[2]	2007 At or above Basic[1]	2007 At or above Proficient[2]	2009 At or above Basic[1]	2009 At or above Proficient[2]	2011 At or above Basic[1]	2011 At or above Proficient[2]	2013 At or above Basic[1]	2013 At or above Proficient[2]	2015 At or above Basic[1]	2015 At or above Proficient[2]
1	2	3	4	5	6	7	8	9	10	11	12	13	14	15	16	17
4th grade, all students	63 (1.3)	21 (1.1)	77 (0.3)	32 (0.3)	80 (0.2)	36 (0.2)	82 (0.2)	39 (0.3)	82 (0.3)	39 (0.3)	82 (0.2)	40 (0.3)	83 (0.2)	42 (0.3)	82 (0.3)	40 (0.4)
Sex																
Male	63 (1.5)	22 (1.2)	78 (0.4)	35 (0.4)	81 (0.2)	38 (0.2)	82 (0.2)	41 (0.3)	82 (0.3)	41 (0.3)	83 (0.3)	42 (0.3)	82 (0.3)	43 (0.4)	82 (0.3)	42 (0.5)
Female	63 (1.4)	20 (1.4)	76 (0.3)	30 (0.3)	80 (0.2)	34 (0.3)	82 (0.2)	37 (0.4)	82 (0.3)	37 (0.3)	82 (0.3)	39 (0.3)	83 (0.2)	41 (0.4)	82 (0.3)	38 (0.5)
Race/ethnicity																
White	76 (1.2)	27 (1.3)	87 (0.2)	43 (0.3)	90 (0.2)	47 (0.2)	91 (0.2)	51 (0.4)	91 (0.3)	51 (0.5)	91 (0.6)	52 (0.6)	91 (0.6)	54 (0.4)	90 (0.3)	51 (0.5)
Black	27 (2.0)	3 (0.6)	54 (0.6)	10 (0.6)	60 (0.5)	13 (0.5)	64 (0.6)	15 (0.4)	64 (0.6)	16 (0.6)	66 (0.6)	17 (0.5)	66 (0.6)	18 (0.5)	65 (0.7)	19 (0.6)
Hispanic	40 (2.7)	7 (1.4)	62 (0.7)	16 (0.7)	68 (0.5)	19 (0.3)	70 (0.5)	22 (0.4)	71 (0.7)	22 (0.7)	72 (0.6)	24 (0.6)	73 (0.7)	26 (0.6)	73 (0.6)	26 (0.7)
Asian/Pacific Islander	67 (5.7)	27 (5.0)	87 (0.8)	48 (1.9)	90 (0.5)	55 (1.1)	91 (0.7)	58 (1.3)	92 (0.6)	60 (1.5)	—	—	—	—	—	—
Asian	—	—	—	—	—	—	—	—	—	—	93 (0.5)	64 (1.6)	92 (0.6)	66 (1.6)	93 (0.7)	65 (1.7)
Pacific Islander	—	—	—	—	—	—	—	—	—	—	77 (2.7)	34 (3.2)	77 (3.1)	33 (3.2)	68 (4.0)	30 (2.8)
American Indian/Alaska Native	57 (7.5)	‡ (†)	64 (1.7)	17 (1.7)	68 (1.5)	21 (1.2)	70 (1.2)	25 (1.1)	66 (1.6)	21 (1.2)	66 (2.7)	22 (1.7)	68 (1.8)	23 (1.7)	69 (1.8)	23 (1.7)
Two or more races	—	—	—	—	—	—	—	—	—	—	87 (1.7)	45 (1.7)	85 (1.0)	46 (1.4)	86 (0.9)	45 (1.3)
Eligibility for free or reduced-price lunch																
Eligible	40 (1.8)	8 (0.9)	62 (0.5)	15 (0.3)	67 (0.3)	19 (0.2)	70 (0.4)	22 (0.3)	70 (0.4)	22 (0.3)	72 (0.3)	24 (0.3)	73 (0.4)	25 (0.4)	72 (0.4)	24 (0.4)
Not eligible	76 (1.2)	27 (1.2)	88 (0.3)	45 (0.3)	90 (0.2)	49 (0.2)	91 (0.2)	53 (0.4)	91 (0.3)	54 (0.3)	92 (0.2)	57 (0.4)	93 (0.2)	59 (0.4)	92 (0.3)	58 (0.6)
Unknown	72 (3.0)	28 (4.1)	84 (0.9)	41 (1.2)	87 (0.7)	45 (1.2)	90 (0.9)	48 (1.5)	88 (1.3)	47 (1.7)	90 (0.8)	52 (1.7)	90 (1.0)	52 (2.2)	89 (1.2)	50 (1.7)
8th grade, all students	61 (1.0)	23 (1.0)	68 (0.3)	29 (0.3)	69 (0.2)	30 (0.2)	71 (0.3)	32 (0.3)	73 (0.3)	34 (0.3)	73 (0.2)	35 (0.2)	74 (0.3)	35 (0.3)	71 (0.3)	33 (0.3)
Sex																
Male	62 (1.2)	25 (1.2)	69 (0.4)	30 (0.4)	70 (0.3)	31 (0.3)	72 (0.3)	34 (0.3)	73 (0.3)	36 (0.3)	73 (0.4)	35 (0.4)	74 (0.3)	36 (0.3)	71 (0.4)	34 (0.4)
Female	60 (1.2)	22 (1.2)	67 (0.4)	27 (0.4)	69 (0.3)	28 (0.3)	71 (0.3)	30 (0.3)	72 (0.4)	32 (0.4)	73 (0.2)	34 (0.3)	74 (0.4)	35 (0.4)	72 (0.4)	33 (0.4)
Race/ethnicity																
White	73 (1.3)	30 (1.3)	80 (0.3)	37 (0.4)	80 (0.2)	39 (0.3)	82 (0.3)	42 (0.3)	83 (0.3)	44 (0.3)	84 (0.3)	44 (0.3)	84 (0.2)	45 (0.5)	82 (0.3)	43 (0.4)
Black	25 (1.8)	4 (0.8)	39 (0.8)	7 (0.5)	42 (0.5)	9 (0.4)	47 (0.7)	11 (0.4)	50 (0.6)	12 (0.6)	51 (0.7)	13 (0.6)	52 (0.6)	14 (0.5)	48 (0.9)	13 (0.5)
Hispanic	39 (2.0)	8 (1.1)	48 (0.8)	12 (0.7)	52 (0.6)	13 (0.4)	55 (0.7)	15 (0.4)	57 (0.7)	17 (0.6)	61 (0.7)	20 (0.6)	62 (0.7)	21 (0.5)	60 (0.7)	19 (0.6)
Asian/Pacific Islander	‡ (†)	‡ (†)	78 (1.1)	43 (1.3)	81 (0.8)	47 (1.2)	83 (0.8)	50 (1.1)	85 (1.0)	54 (1.1)	—	—	—	—	—	—
Asian	—	—	—	—	—	—	—	—	—	—	88 (1.0)	58 (1.3)	89 (0.8)	63 (1.3)	87 (0.9)	61 (1.7)
Pacific Islander	—	—	—	—	—	—	—	—	—	—	67 (4.7)	24 (2.9)	67 (3.5)	24 (2.9)	63 (4.2)	29 (3.9)
American Indian/Alaska Native	‡ (†)	‡ (†)	52 (2.7)	15 (1.7)	53 (1.3)	14 (1.2)	53 (1.8)	16 (1.2)	56 (1.5)	18 (1.3)	55 (1.5)	17 (1.5)	59 (1.5)	21 (1.5)	57 (1.8)	20 (1.7)
Two or more races	—	—	—	—	—	—	—	—	—	—	78 (1.1)	39 (1.1)	76 (1.2)	38 (1.4)	74 (1.3)	36 (1.3)
Eligibility for free or reduced-price lunch																
Eligible	38 (2.1)	8 (1.3)	48 (0.5)	12 (0.4)	51 (0.4)	13 (0.2)	55 (0.5)	15 (0.3)	57 (0.5)	17 (0.3)	59 (0.4)	19 (0.4)	60 (0.3)	20 (0.3)	58 (0.4)	18 (0.4)
Not eligible	69 (1.5)	28 (1.3)	79 (0.3)	37 (0.3)	79 (0.2)	39 (0.3)	81 (0.3)	42 (0.4)	83 (0.3)	45 (0.3)	84 (0.2)	47 (0.4)	86 (0.3)	49 (0.4)	84 (0.5)	48 (0.5)
Unknown	70 (2.6)	30 (2.6)	75 (1.1)	36 (1.1)	79 (1.1)	40 (1.4)	81 (1.7)	43 (1.7)	83 (1.3)	48 (1.7)	85 (0.9)	48 (0.9)	84 (1.3)	50 (2.6)	81 (1.5)	46 (1.9)
12th grade, all students	[3]	[3]	†	†	61 (0.8)	23 (0.7)	†	†	64 (0.8)	26 (0.8)	†	†	65 (0.7)	26 (0.6)	†	†
Sex																
Male	[3]	[3]	†	†	62 (0.9)	25 (1.0)	†	†	65 (0.9)	28 (1.0)	†	†	66 (0.8)	28 (0.8)	†	†
Female	[3]	[3]	†	†	60 (1.0)	21 (0.8)	†	†	63 (0.8)	24 (0.8)	†	†	64 (0.9)	24 (0.7)	†	†
Race/ethnicity																
White	[3]	[3]	†	†	70 (0.8)	29 (0.8)	†	†	75 (0.7)	33 (0.7)	†	†	75 (0.8)	33 (0.8)	†	†
Black	[3]	[3]	†	†	30 (1.7)	6 (0.8)	†	†	37 (1.1)	6 (0.6)	†	†	38 (1.5)	7 (0.6)	†	†
Hispanic	[3]	[3]	†	†	40 (2.1)	8 (1.0)	†	†	45 (1.1)	11 (0.8)	†	†	50 (1.4)	12 (0.7)	†	†
Asian/Pacific Islander	[3]	[3]	†	†	73 (2.6)	36 (3.0)	†	†	84 (1.9)	52 (3.4)	†	†	—	—	†	†
Asian	[3]	[3]	†	†	—	—	†	†	—	—	†	†	83 (1.5)	49 (2.0)	†	†
Pacific Islander	[3]	[3]	†	†	—	—	†	†	—	—	†	†	65 (7.3)	16 (6.0)	†	†
American Indian/Alaska Native	[3]	[3]	†	†	42 (8.6)	6 (2.9)	†	†	56 (5.4)	12 (3.3)	†	†	54 (5.8)	12 (4.0)	†	†
Two or more races	[3]	[3]	†	†	—	—	†	†	—	—	†	†	67 (3.0)	26 (2.7)	†	†

—Not available.
†Not applicable.
‡Reporting standards not met (too few cases for a reliable estimate).
[1] Basic denotes partial mastery of the knowledge and skills that are fundamental for proficient work.
[2] Proficient represents solid academic performance. Students reaching this level have demonstrated competency over challenging subject matter.
[3] Because of major changes to the framework and content of the grade 12 assessment, results from 2005 and later assessment years cannot be compared with results from earlier assessment years. Therefore, this table excludes grade 12 results from 1996.

NOTE: Includes public and private schools. Includes students tested with accommodations (1 to 14 percent of all students, depending on grade level and year); excludes only those students with disabilities and English language learners who were unable to be tested even with accommodations (1 to 4 percent of all students). Race categories exclude persons of Hispanic ethnicity. Prior to 2011, separate data for Asian students, Pacific Islander students, and students of Two or more races were not collected.
SOURCE: U.S. Department of Education, National Center for Education Statistics, National Assessment of Educational Progress (NAEP), 1996, 2003, 2005, 2007, 2009, 2011, 2013, and 2015 Mathematics Assessments, retrieved October 29, 2015, from the Main NAEP Data Explorer (http://nces.ed.gov/nationsreportcard/naepdata/). (This table was prepared October 2015.)

Table 222.30. Average National Assessment of Educational Progress (NAEP) mathematics scale score of 8th-graders with various attitudes toward mathematics and percentage reporting these attitudes, by selected student characteristics: 2015

[Standard errors appear in parentheses]

Average scale score[1]

Student characteristic	Math work is engaging and interesting — Never or hardly ever	Sometimes	Often	Always/ almost always	Math work is challenging — Never or hardly ever	Sometimes	Often	Always/ almost always	Math work is too easy — Never or hardly ever	Sometimes	Often	Always/ almost always
1	2	3	4	5	6	7	8	9	10	11	12	13
All students	276 (0.4)	282 (0.4)	288 (0.4)	286 (0.6)	295 (0.6)	284 (0.4)	281 (0.4)	272 (0.6)	282 (0.5)	281 (0.3)	286 (0.5)	289 (0.8)
Sex												
Male	277 (0.5)	282 (0.5)	287 (0.5)	285 (0.7)	297 (0.9)	284 (0.4)	281 (0.5)	270 (0.8)	281 (0.6)	281 (0.4)	286 (0.6)	291 (0.9)
Female	275 (0.5)	282 (0.4)	288 (0.6)	286 (0.8)	293 (0.8)	284 (0.5)	281 (0.6)	273 (0.7)	283 (0.7)	281 (0.4)	285 (0.6)	287 (1.1)
Race/ethnicity												
White	282 (0.5)	292 (0.4)	298 (0.4)	298 (0.6)	301 (0.6)	293 (0.4)	291 (0.5)	281 (0.7)	289 (0.6)	291 (0.3)	296 (0.5)	298 (0.9)
Black	258 (1.0)	260 (0.8)	264 (0.7)	263 (0.9)	272 (1.6)	263 (0.6)	260 (0.8)	252 (1.2)	261 (1.1)	260 (0.6)	265 (0.8)	265 (1.5)
Hispanic	264 (1.0)	269 (0.7)	274 (0.8)	273 (1.0)	281 (1.6)	272 (0.7)	269 (0.8)	264 (1.3)	271 (1.0)	269 (0.5)	273 (0.9)	277 (1.9)
Asian	300 (2.0)	306 (2.0)	312 (2.2)	310 (2.8)	325 (2.7)	308 (1.3)	305 (1.7)	293 (3.3)	305 (2.9)	305 (2.0)	311 (1.8)	318 (2.9)
Pacific Islander	271 (5.3)	273 (5.1)	291 (4.2)	266 (6.2)	296 (6.1)	277 (3.9)	277 (6.3)	260 (4.2)	286 (7.7)	275 (4.7)	274 (5.9)	287 (7.4)
American Indian/ Alaska Native	262 (3.0)	269 (2.2)	272 (2.3)	270 (3.9)	284 (6.1)	272 (1.9)	265 (2.2)	259 (2.9)	268 (2.8)	266 (1.7)	273 (3.3)	279 (5.9)
Two or more races	274 (1.8)	287 (1.8)	289 (2.0)	291 (2.5)	294 (2.9)	285 (1.4)	286 (2.2)	275 (2.9)	283 (2.3)	286 (1.5)	284 (2.1)	292 (3.7)
Eligibility for free or reduced-price lunch												
Eligible	264 (0.5)	267 (0.5)	273 (0.5)	271 (0.6)	280 (0.8)	271 (0.4)	267 (0.5)	258 (0.6)	266 (0.5)	267 (0.4)	272 (0.5)	275 (1.2)
Not eligible	286 (0.5)	295 (0.4)	302 (0.6)	303 (0.8)	306 (0.7)	297 (0.4)	295 (0.5)	287 (0.8)	294 (0.6)	295 (0.4)	299 (0.6)	304 (1.0)
Unknown	282 (2.4)	298 (1.7)	298 (1.7)	299 (2.6)	308 (3.9)	294 (1.6)	294 (1.8)	283 (2.7)	292 (2.3)	294 (1.7)	300 (2.6)	303 (3.3)
Highest education level of either parent[2]												
Did not finish high school	260 (1.2)	265 (0.9)	269 (1.3)	268 (1.7)	275 (2.2)	269 (1.0)	263 (1.1)	256 (1.6)	261 (1.4)	264 (0.8)	270 (1.3)	276 (2.2)
Graduated high school	265 (0.8)	267 (0.8)	272 (0.7)	269 (1.2)	279 (1.5)	270 (0.6)	267 (0.7)	257 (1.1)	267 (1.1)	267 (0.6)	271 (0.9)	270 (1.6)
Some education after high school	278 (0.9)	282 (0.7)	285 (0.8)	286 (1.1)	293 (1.3)	284 (0.6)	281 (0.7)	272 (1.1)	278 (0.9)	282 (0.6)	287 (0.9)	292 (1.7)
Graduated college	285 (0.5)	294 (0.5)	299 (0.6)	298 (0.7)	305 (0.8)	295 (0.5)	293 (0.5)	285 (0.7)	293 (0.6)	293 (0.4)	296 (0.6)	300 (0.8)

Percent of students

Student characteristic	Math work is engaging and interesting — Never or hardly ever	Sometimes	Often	Always/ almost always	Math work is challenging — Never or hardly ever	Sometimes	Often	Always/ almost always	Math work is too easy — Never or hardly ever	Sometimes	Often	Always/ almost always
All students	20 (0.2)	35 (0.3)	29 (0.3)	15 (0.2)	11 (0.2)	44 (0.3)	34 (0.3)	12 (0.1)	18 (0.2)	55 (0.2)	20 (0.2)	7 (0.1)
Sex												
Male	20 (0.3)	33 (0.3)	30 (0.3)	16 (0.2)	11 (0.2)	43 (0.3)	35 (0.3)	11 (0.2)	16 (0.2)	55 (0.3)	22 (0.3)	7 (0.2)
Female	20 (0.3)	37 (0.3)	29 (0.3)	15 (0.2)	11 (0.3)	44 (0.4)	33 (0.4)	12 (0.2)	20 (0.4)	55 (0.3)	19 (0.3)	6 (0.2)
Race/ethnicity												
White	23 (0.3)	35 (0.4)	28 (0.3)	14 (0.3)	12 (0.3)	43 (0.4)	34 (0.4)	11 (0.2)	21 (0.3)	54 (0.3)	18 (0.2)	6 (0.2)
Black	18 (0.5)	34 (0.6)	28 (0.5)	20 (0.5)	9 (0.3)	43 (0.6)	33 (0.6)	15 (0.3)	16 (0.4)	55 (0.6)	22 (0.5)	7 (0.3)
Hispanic	17 (0.4)	36 (0.5)	31 (0.6)	16 (0.5)	9 (0.4)	44 (0.6)	35 (0.6)	11 (0.3)	13 (0.4)	58 (0.6)	22 (0.5)	7 (0.3)
Asian	14 (1.0)	33 (1.4)	34 (0.9)	19 (1.3)	14 (0.4)	48 (1.3)	29 (1.1)	9 (0.7)	10 (0.9)	54 (1.2)	27 (1.2)	10 (0.7)
Pacific Islander	17 (4.1)	29 (3.4)	36 (4.1)	18 (2.6)	11 (2.6)	43 (3.7)	35 (2.9)	11 (1.8)	13 (2.5)	56 (3.7)	21 (3.2)	10 (2.6)
American Indian/Alaska Native	19 (1.5)	35 (1.9)	32 (2.1)	14 (1.0)	9 (1.3)	41 (2.2)	38 (2.3)	12 (1.0)	18 (1.4)	55 (2.1)	20 (1.8)	7 (1.0)
Two or more races	22 (1.0)	34 (1.3)	30 (1.3)	14 (0.9)	12 (0.8)	42 (1.6)	36 (1.8)	11 (0.7)	19 (1.1)	55 (1.3)	20 (1.1)	6 (0.6)
Eligibility for free or reduced-price lunch												
Eligible	19 (0.3)	35 (0.3)	30 (0.3)	17 (0.3)	10 (0.2)	44 (0.4)	34 (0.4)	12 (0.2)	15 (0.3)	56 (0.3)	22 (0.3)	7 (0.2)
Not eligible	22 (0.3)	35 (0.4)	29 (0.3)	14 (0.3)	12 (0.2)	43 (0.4)	34 (0.4)	11 (0.2)	20 (0.3)	55 (0.4)	19 (0.3)	6 (0.2)
Unknown	21 (1.2)	34 (1.1)	29 (1.3)	17 (0.9)	11 (0.9)	41 (1.1)	37 (1.2)	11 (0.7)	23 (1.3)	55 (1.2)	16 (1.0)	5 (0.5)
Highest education level of either parent[2]												
Did not finish high school	20 (0.6)	36 (0.7)	29 (0.7)	15 (0.7)	9 (0.5)	43 (1.0)	35 (1.0)	13 (0.6)	15 (0.6)	56 (0.9)	22 (0.9)	7 (0.5)
Graduated high school	21 (0.5)	36 (0.6)	28 (0.5)	15 (0.4)	9 (0.3)	44 (0.5)	35 (0.6)	12 (0.3)	16 (0.4)	58 (0.6)	20 (0.5)	6 (0.3)
Some education after high school	21 (0.4)	36 (0.5)	29 (0.5)	14 (0.4)	11 (0.5)	45 (0.7)	33 (0.7)	11 (0.4)	19 (0.4)	55 (0.5)	20 (0.5)	6 (0.3)
Graduated college	20 (0.3)	34 (0.4)	30 (0.3)	16 (0.3)	12 (0.2)	43 (0.3)	34 (0.3)	11 (0.2)	19 (0.3)	54 (0.3)	20 (0.3)	7 (0.2)

[1]Scale ranges from 0 to 500.
[2]Based on student reports. The category of students whose parents have an unknown level of education is not shown, although data for these students is included in table totals.
NOTE: Includes public and private schools. Includes students tested with accommodations (12 percent of all 8th-grade students); excludes only those students with disabilities and English language learners who were unable to be tested even with accommodations (2 percent of all 8th-grade students). Race categories exclude persons of Hispanic ethnicity. Detail may not sum to totals because of rounding.
SOURCE: U.S. Department of Education, National Center for Education Statistics, National Assessment of Educational Progress (NAEP), 2015 Mathematics Assessment, retrieved October 29, 2015, from the Main NAEP Data Explorer (http://nces.ed.gov/nationsreportcard/naepdata/). (This table was prepared October 2015.)

Table 222.35. Average National Assessment of Educational Progress (NAEP) mathematics scale score of 12th-graders with various attitudes toward mathematics and percentage reporting these attitudes, by selected student characteristics: 2013

[Standard errors appear in parentheses]

Student characteristic	Math work is engaging and interesting				Math work is challenging				Math work is too easy			
	Never or hardly ever	Sometimes	Often	Always/ almost always	Never or hardly ever	Sometimes	Often	Always/ almost always	Never or hardly ever	Sometimes	Often	Always/ almost always
1	2	3	4	5	6	7	8	9	10	11	12	13
	Average scale score[1]											
All students	145 (0.6)	155 (0.6)	165 (0.8)	166 (1.0)	158 (1.4)	157 (0.7)	158 (0.6)	154 (1.0)	156 (0.7)	156 (0.6)	158 (1.0)	162 (1.1)
Sex												
Male	146 (0.9)	158 (0.8)	167 (1.1)	169 (1.3)	161 (1.8)	160 (0.9)	158 (0.8)	155 (1.2)	157 (1.1)	157 (0.8)	163 (1.2)	165 (1.5)
Female	145 (0.8)	153 (0.8)	163 (1.0)	164 (1.4)	154 (1.8)	153 (0.9)	157 (0.9)	154 (1.3)	156 (0.8)	154 (0.8)	152 (1.2)	157 (1.8)
Race/ethnicity												
White	152 (0.8)	164 (0.7)	175 (1.1)	179 (1.4)	165 (1.5)	165 (0.8)	166 (0.8)	163 (1.2)	163 (0.9)	165 (0.8)	168 (1.1)	169 (1.4)
Black	127 (1.3)	133 (1.3)	139 (1.4)	135 (2.4)	136 (2.4)	134 (1.3)	134 (1.3)	129 (1.6)	133 (1.7)	132 (1.1)	134 (1.9)	136 (2.6)
Hispanic	135 (1.3)	142 (1.0)	147 (1.3)	154 (1.7)	141 (3.5)	144 (0.9)	144 (1.1)	141 (1.5)	144 (1.4)	142 (0.9)	144 (1.6)	150 (2.7)
Asian	167 (2.9)	173 (2.3)	182 (2.3)	187 (3.1)	188 (4.0)	179 (2.0)	174 (2.2)	176 (3.3)	181 (2.2)	174 (2.3)	176 (2.7)	185 (3.6)
Pacific Islander	‡	‡	‡	‡	‡	‡	‡	‡	‡	‡	‡	‡
American Indian/Alaska Native	137 (7.7)	149 (4.3)	140 (5.8)	‡	‡	140 (7.3)	145 (5.2)	‡	145 (3.8)	141 (4.8)	‡	‡
Two or more races	145 (3.9)	156 (2.4)	168 (5.3)	‡	‡	159 (3.8)	158 (3.3)	153 (3.7)	158 (3.7)	153 (3.1)	160 (6.2)	‡
Eligibility for free or reduced-price lunch												
Eligible	133 (0.9)	139 (0.8)	146 (1.2)	148 (1.9)	143 (1.8)	142 (0.9)	141 (1.0)	137 (1.3)	139 (1.2)	139 (1.0)	143 (1.4)	149 (1.8)
Not eligible	151 (0.8)	164 (0.7)	175 (0.9)	177 (1.2)	166 (1.6)	165 (0.7)	166 (0.7)	163 (1.2)	163 (0.8)	165 (0.7)	167 (1.1)	169 (1.5)
Unknown	155 (2.8)	165 (2.3)	175 (3.6)	183 (3.9)	174 (4.8)	169 (3.1)	166 (2.8)	165 (2.9)	166 (2.6)	167 (2.9)	169 (4.3)	‡
Highest education level of either parent[2]												
Did not finish high school	131 (2.0)	136 (1.4)	144 (1.8)	148 (3.2)	137 (4.3)	139 (1.6)	140 (1.7)	136 (1.5)	136 (1.6)	138 (1.5)	141 (2.0)	148 (3.9)
Graduated high school	134 (1.2)	141 (1.1)	147 (1.4)	152 (2.4)	147 (2.9)	142 (1.1)	142 (1.2)	137 (1.8)	140 (1.5)	141 (0.9)	142 (2.1)	150 (2.9)
Some education after high school	141 (1.1)	153 (1.0)	161 (1.4)	162 (1.9)	156 (2.5)	152 (1.2)	153 (1.2)	152 (1.3)	151 (1.0)	152 (0.9)	155 (1.5)	159 (2.0)
Graduated college	155 (0.9)	167 (0.8)	177 (1.0)	178 (1.4)	169 (1.7)	168 (0.8)	169 (0.8)	166 (1.2)	167 (0.9)	167 (0.8)	171 (1.2)	171 (1.5)
	Percent of students											
All students	26 (0.5)	36 (0.5)	27 (0.5)	11 (0.4)	7 (0.2)	35 (0.5)	37 (0.5)	21 (0.4)	32 (0.5)	47 (0.5)	15 (0.3)	6 (0.3)
Sex												
Male	25 (0.6)	35 (0.6)	28 (0.7)	12 (0.5)	8 (0.4)	36 (0.7)	37 (0.7)	18 (0.5)	27 (0.6)	48 (0.7)	18 (0.4)	7 (0.4)
Female	27 (0.7)	37 (0.7)	25 (0.5)	11 (0.4)	6 (0.3)	34 (0.7)	36 (0.6)	23 (0.6)	36 (0.8)	47 (0.7)	13 (0.4)	4 (0.3)
Race/ethnicity												
White	28 (0.6)	35 (0.6)	27 (0.6)	10 (0.4)	8 (0.4)	35 (0.6)	37 (0.7)	21 (0.5)	34 (0.7)	45 (0.7)	14 (0.4)	6 (0.3)
Black	27 (1.0)	37 (1.0)	24 (1.0)	13 (0.9)	8 (0.5)	37 (1.3)	34 (1.0)	22 (1.2)	32 (1.0)	48 (1.2)	14 (0.8)	6 (0.5)
Hispanic	24 (0.9)	35 (1.0)	28 (0.8)	13 (0.7)	6 (0.3)	35 (1.0)	35 (1.0)	20 (0.8)	25 (0.8)	52 (1.0)	18 (0.8)	6 (0.5)
Asian	13 (1.1)	37 (1.5)	32 (1.6)	17 (1.4)	6 (1.1)	36 (1.8)	36 (1.7)	21 (1.6)	24 (1.7)	49 (2.1)	20 (1.7)	8 (1.1)
Pacific Islander	20 (5.5)	42 (7.2)	18 (4.6)	20 (6.7)	7 (3.9)	32 (7.0)	31 (7.1)	31 (5.8)	36 (7.7)	41 (6.5)	19 (6.1)	10 (4.5)
American Indian/Alaska Native	27 (4.9)	40 (5.1)	22 (4.8)	11 (3.0)	10 (3.1)	30 (6.9)	38 (5.8)	22 (4.0)	30 (6.0)	50 (6.0)	11 (4.2)	4 (3.6)
Two or more races	28 (2.6)	40 (3.3)	22 (2.7)	10 (1.7)	6 (1.3)	36 (3.3)	37 (3.2)	21 (2.7)	35 (3.3)	46 (3.0)	13 (2.2)	6 (1.6)
Eligibility for free or reduced-price lunch												
Eligible	25 (0.6)	35 (0.7)	27 (0.7)	12 (0.6)	7 (0.4)	36 (0.8)	35 (0.8)	21 (0.6)	27 (0.6)	50 (0.9)	17 (0.5)	6 (0.5)
Not eligible	27 (0.7)	36 (0.6)	26 (0.6)	11 (0.4)	7 (0.3)	35 (0.7)	37 (0.6)	21 (0.6)	34 (0.7)	46 (0.6)	15 (0.4)	6 (0.3)
Unknown	25 (2.0)	37 (1.5)	28 (1.8)	10 (1.3)	6 (0.9)	33 (1.9)	40 (1.6)	21 (1.6)	38 (2.1)	44 (1.9)	14 (1.6)	4 (0.8)
Highest education level of either parent[2]												
Did not finish high school	25 (1.3)	35 (1.0)	26 (1.1)	14 (1.1)	7 (0.7)	38 (1.5)	35 (1.4)	20 (1.2)	24 (1.3)	49 (1.4)	20 (1.0)	7 (0.8)
Graduated high school	29 (1.1)	36 (1.0)	26 (0.9)	10 (0.6)	8 (0.5)	36 (1.1)	37 (1.1)	19 (0.7)	29 (1.0)	49 (1.1)	15 (0.8)	6 (0.5)
Some education after high school	27 (0.9)	38 (1.0)	25 (0.9)	9 (0.6)	8 (0.5)	35 (0.9)	36 (0.9)	21 (0.8)	32 (0.8)	47 (0.8)	15 (0.6)	5 (0.4)
Graduated college	25 (0.7)	35 (0.6)	28 (0.6)	12 (0.5)	7 (0.3)	35 (0.7)	37 (0.8)	21 (0.6)	34 (0.7)	46 (0.7)	14 (0.4)	6 (0.3)

† Not applicable.

‡ Reporting standards not met (too few cases for a reliable estimate).

[1] Scale ranges from 0 to 300.

[2] Based on student reports. The category of students whose parents have an unknown level of education is not shown, although data for these students is included in table totals.

NOTE: Includes public and private schools. Includes students tested with accommodations (9 percent of all 12th-grade students); excludes only those students with disabilities and English language learners who were unable to be tested even with accommodations (2 percent of all 12th-grade students). Race categories exclude persons of Hispanic ethnicity. Detail may not sum to totals because of rounding.

SOURCE: U.S. Department of Education, National Center for Education Statistics, National Assessment of Educational Progress (NAEP), 2013 Mathematics Assessment, retrieved October 20, 2014, from the Main NAEP Data Explorer (http://nces.ed.gov/nationsreportcard/naepdata/). (This table was prepared October 2014.)

Table 222.40. Average National Assessment of Educational Progress (NAEP) mathematics scale score of high school graduates at grade 12, by highest mathematics course taken in high school and selected student and school characteristics: 2009

[Standard errors appear in parentheses]

Selected student or school characteristic	Algebra I or below[1]		Geometry		Algebra II/ trigonometry		Analysis/ precalculus		Statistics/ probability		Advanced mathematics, other[2]		Calculus	
1		2		3		4		5		6		7		8
Total[3]	114	(1.1)	127	(1.0)	143	(0.6)	166	(0.9)	164	(1.8)	154	(1.3)	193	(1.2)
Sex														
Male	117	(1.7)	128	(1.2)	145	(0.8)	169	(1.0)	165	(2.2)	156	(1.5)	197	(1.4)
Female	111	(1.6)	126	(1.1)	142	(0.8)	163	(1.0)	162	(2.0)	153	(1.4)	190	(1.2)
Race/ethnicity														
White	117	(1.6)	133	(1.3)	150	(0.8)	172	(0.9)	169	(1.5)	160	(1.3)	194	(1.1)
Black	104	(2.8)	114	(1.8)	129	(0.9)	147	(1.6)	139	(4.0)	138	(2.1)	170	(2.7)
Hispanic	109	(2.2)	122	(1.0)	136	(0.8)	155	(1.6)	154	(3.2)	142	(2.3)	179	(2.5)
Asian/Pacific Islander	‡	(†)	129	(3.9)	149	(4.1)	170	(2.3)	176	(4.1)	164	(2.9)	203	(1.8)
American Indian/Alaska Native	‡	(†)	‡	(†)	143	(3.8)	‡	(†)	‡	(†)	‡	(†)	‡	(†)
Student with disabilities (SD) status														
SD[4]	103	(1.7)	114	(2.5)	126	(2.1)	166	(5.0)	136	(6.3)	134	(3.5)	197	(3.7)
Non-SD	122	(1.2)	129	(0.9)	144	(0.6)	166	(0.9)	164	(1.7)	156	(1.3)	193	(1.2)
English language learner (ELL) status														
ELL	104	(4.5)	113	(2.8)	121	(2.1)	144	(6.1)	‡	(†)	129	(4.8)	‡	(†)
Non-ELL	114	(1.2)	128	(1.0)	144	(0.6)	166	(0.9)	164	(1.8)	155	(1.3)	193	(1.2)
School type														
Traditional public	114	(1.2)	127	(1.0)	143	(0.7)	166	(0.9)	164	(1.8)	155	(1.4)	193	(1.3)
Public charter	‡	(†)	‡	(†)	137	(10.3)	141	(6.8)	132	(1.6)	‡	(†)	‡	(†)
Private	‡	(†)	123	(3.3)	146	(3.3)	169	(2.7)	168	(3.9)	146	(4.0)	193	(3.3)
Percentage of students eligible for free or reduced-price lunch														
0–25 percent	116	(3.0)	134	(2.0)	151	(1.3)	173	(1.5)	173	(1.5)	162	(1.9)	199	(1.6)
26–50 percent	115	(1.5)	127	(1.4)	144	(1.0)	165	(1.1)	162	(2.9)	154	(1.7)	189	(1.0)
51–75 percent	111	(3.0)	123	(1.8)	136	(1.1)	156	(1.3)	149	(3.6)	146	(3.7)	179	(2.8)
76–100 percent	107	(5.4)	115	(3.1)	126	(2.0)	144	(3.7)	137	(4.1)	131	(2.6)	163	(3.9)
School locale														
City	110	(2.6)	125	(1.7)	140	(1.8)	163	(2.1)	163	(3.3)	151	(3.0)	195	(2.3)
Suburban	112	(2.3)	127	(1.9)	144	(1.0)	169	(1.4)	167	(2.4)	157	(2.0)	195	(2.0)
Town	114	(2.5)	129	(1.9)	144	(1.6)	166	(1.6)	164	(3.1)	152	(3.8)	191	(2.1)
Rural	117	(2.0)	129	(1.4)	145	(1.3)	165	(1.9)	157	(4.9)	155	(2.1)	187	(2.0)

†Not applicable.

‡Reporting standards not met (too few cases for a reliable estimate).

[1]Includes basic math, general math, applied math, prealgebra, and algebra I.

[2]Includes courses such as actuarial sciences, pure mathematics, discrete math, and advanced functions and modeling.

[3]Includes other racial/ethnic groups not shown separately, as well as students for whom information on race/ethnicity or sex was missing.

[4]SD estimates include both students with an Individualized Education Plan (IEP) and students with a plan under Section 504 of the Rehabilitation Act (a "504 plan"). IEPs are only for students who require specialized instruction, whereas 504 plans apply to students who require accommodations but may not require specialized instruction.

NOTE: Scale ranges from 0 to 300. Includes students tested with accommodations (6 percent of all 12th-graders); excludes only those students with disabilities and English language learners who were unable to be tested even with accommodations (3 percent of all 12th-graders). For a transcript to be included in the analyses, it had to meet three requirements: (1) the graduate received either a standard or honors diploma, (2) the graduate's transcript contained 16 or more Carnegie credits, and (3) the graduate's transcript contained more than 0 Carnegie credits in English courses. Race categories exclude persons of Hispanic ethnicity.

SOURCE: U.S. Department of Education, National Center for Education Statistics, National Assessment of Educational Progress (NAEP), 2009 Mathematics Assessment; and 2009 High School Transcript Study (HSTS). (This table was prepared September 2012.)

Table 222.50. Average National Assessment of Educational Progress (NAEP) mathematics scale score of 4th-grade public school students and percentage attaining mathematics achievement levels, by state: Selected years, 1992 through 2015

[Standard errors appear in parentheses]

State	Average scale score[1]										Percent attaining mathematics achievement levels, 2015		
	1992[2]	1996[3]	2000	2003	2005	2007	2009	2011	2013	2015	At or above Basic[4]	At or above Proficient[5]	At Advanced[6]
1	2	3	4	5	6	7	8	9	10	11	12	13	14
United States	219 (0.8)	222 (1.0)	224 (1.0)	234 (0.2)	237 (0.2)	239 (0.2)	239 (0.2)	240 (0.2)	241 (0.2)	240 (0.3)	81 (0.3)	39 (0.4)	7 (0.2)
Alabama	208 (1.6)	212 (1.2)	217 (1.2)	223 (1.2)	225 (0.9)	229 (1.3)	228 (1.1)	231 (1.0)	233 (1.0)	231 (0.9)	75 (1.4)	26 (1.5)	2 (0.5)
Alaska[7].....................	— (†)	224 (1.3)	— (†)	233 (0.8)	236 (1.0)	237 (1.0)	237 (0.9)	236 (0.9)	236 (0.8)	236 (1.1)	78 (1.3)	35 (1.5)	6 (0.8)
Arizona	215 (1.1)	218 (1.7)	219 (1.3)	229 (1.1)	230 (1.1)	232 (1.0)	230 (1.1)	235 (1.1)	240 (1.2)	238 (1.0)	79 (1.2)	38 (1.5)	6 (0.9)
Arkansas[7]	210 (0.9)	216 (1.5)	216 (1.1)	229 (0.9)	236 (0.9)	238 (1.1)	238 (0.9)	238 (0.8)	240 (0.9)	235 (0.8)	79 (1.2)	32 (1.5)	3 (0.5)
California[8]	208 (1.6)	209 (1.8)	213 (1.6)	227 (0.9)	230 (0.6)	230 (0.7)	232 (1.2)	234 (1.4)	234 (1.2)	232 (1.4)	72 (1.5)	29 (2.1)	5 (1.0)
Colorado	221 (1.0)	226 (1.0)	— (†)	235 (1.0)	239 (1.1)	240 (1.0)	243 (1.0)	244 (0.9)	247 (0.8)	242 (1.0)	82 (1.1)	43 (1.5)	8 (0.8)
Connecticut.................	227 (1.1)	232 (1.1)	234 (1.1)	241 (0.8)	242 (0.8)	243 (1.1)	245 (1.0)	242 (1.3)	243 (0.9)	240 (0.9)	81 (1.2)	41 (1.4)	7 (0.7)
Delaware....................	218 (0.8)	215 (0.6)	— (†)	236 (0.5)	240 (0.5)	242 (0.4)	239 (0.5)	240 (0.6)	243 (0.7)	239 (0.6)	82 (0.9)	37 (1.1)	5 (0.5)
District of Columbia	193 (0.5)	187 (1.1)	192 (1.1)	205 (0.7)	211 (0.8)	214 (0.8)	219 (0.7)	222 (0.7)	229 (0.7)	231 (0.6)	69 (1.1)	31 (1.0)	7 (0.6)
Florida........................	214 (1.5)	216 (1.2)	— (†)	234 (1.1)	239 (1.0)	242 (0.8)	242 (1.0)	240 (0.8)	242 (0.8)	243 (1.0)	85 (1.0)	42 (1.8)	7 (0.7)
Georgia......................	216 (1.2)	215 (1.5)	219 (1.1)	230 (1.0)	234 (1.0)	235 (1.0)	236 (0.9)	238 (0.7)	240 (1.0)	236 (1.2)	78 (1.4)	35 (1.8)	5 (0.8)
Hawaii	214 (1.3)	215 (1.5)	216 (1.0)	227 (1.0)	230 (0.8)	234 (0.8)	236 (1.1)	239 (0.7)	243 (0.8)	238 (0.9)	79 (1.1)	38 (1.3)	7 (0.8)
Idaho[8]......................	222 (1.0)	— (†)	224 (1.4)	235 (0.7)	242 (0.7)	241 (0.7)	241 (0.8)	241 (0.8)	240 (0.6)	241 (0.9)	80 (1.1)	38 (1.5)	6 (0.7)
Illinois[8].....................	— (†)	— (†)	223 (1.9)	233 (1.1)	233 (1.0)	237 (1.1)	238 (1.0)	239 (1.1)	239 (1.2)	237 (1.2)	77 (1.4)	37 (1.5)	8 (0.9)
Indiana[8]....................	221 (1.0)	229 (1.0)	233 (1.1)	238 (1.0)	240 (0.8)	245 (0.8)	243 (0.9)	244 (1.0)	249 (0.9)	248 (1.1)	89 (1.1)	50 (1.8)	9 (1.2)
Iowa[7,8].....................	230 (1.0)	229 (1.1)	231 (1.2)	238 (0.7)	240 (0.7)	243 (0.8)	243 (0.8)	243 (0.8)	246 (0.9)	243 (0.9)	84 (1.0)	44 (1.5)	9 (0.9)
Kansas[8]....................	— (†)	— (†)	232 (1.6)	242 (1.0)	246 (1.0)	248 (0.9)	245 (1.0)	246 (0.9)	246 (0.8)	241 (1.0)	83 (1.1)	41 (1.7)	7 (0.8)
Kentucky	215 (1.0)	220 (1.1)	219 (1.4)	229 (1.1)	231 (0.9)	235 (0.9)	239 (1.1)	241 (0.8)	241 (0.9)	242 (1.1)	84 (1.2)	40 (1.8)	7 (1.1)
Louisiana	204 (1.5)	209 (1.1)	218 (1.4)	226 (1.0)	230 (0.9)	230 (1.0)	229 (1.0)	231 (1.0)	231 (1.2)	234 (1.1)	78 (1.3)	30 (1.9)	4 (0.6)
Maine[8]......................	232 (1.0)	232 (1.0)	230 (1.0)	238 (0.7)	241 (0.8)	242 (0.8)	244 (1.0)	244 (0.7)	244 (0.7)	242 (0.8)	85 (1.0)	41 (1.4)	7 (0.8)
Maryland....................	217 (1.3)	221 (1.6)	222 (1.2)	233 (1.3)	238 (1.0)	240 (0.9)	244 (0.9)	247 (0.9)	245 (1.3)	239 (1.0)	79 (1.2)	40 (1.5)	8 (0.9)
Massachusetts...............	227 (1.2)	229 (1.3)	233 (1.2)	242 (0.8)	247 (0.8)	252 (0.8)	252 (0.9)	253 (0.8)	253 (1.0)	251 (1.2)	90 (1.1)	54 (1.9)	13 (1.2)
Michigan[7,8]................	220 (1.7)	226 (1.3)	229 (1.6)	236 (0.9)	238 (1.2)	238 (1.3)	236 (1.0)	236 (1.1)	237 (1.1)	236 (1.2)	77 (1.5)	34 (1.6)	5 (0.9)
Minnesota[8]................	228 (0.9)	232 (1.1)	234 (1.3)	242 (0.9)	246 (1.0)	247 (1.0)	249 (1.1)	249 (0.9)	253 (1.1)	250 (1.2)	87 (1.1)	53 (1.8)	14 (1.2)
Mississippi	202 (1.1)	208 (1.2)	211 (1.1)	223 (1.0)	227 (0.9)	228 (1.0)	227 (1.0)	230 (0.9)	231 (0.7)	234 (0.9)	78 (1.3)	30 (1.5)	3 (0.5)
Missouri	222 (1.2)	225 (1.1)	228 (1.2)	235 (0.9)	235 (0.9)	239 (0.9)	241 (1.2)	240 (0.9)	240 (0.8)	239 (0.9)	82 (1.1)	38 (1.5)	5 (0.7)
Montana[7,8]................	— (†)	228 (1.2)	228 (1.7)	236 (0.8)	241 (0.8)	244 (0.8)	244 (0.8)	244 (0.6)	244 (0.6)	241 (0.7)	84 (0.9)	41 (1.4)	6 (0.6)
Nebraska....................	225 (1.2)	228 (1.2)	225 (1.8)	236 (0.8)	238 (0.9)	238 (1.1)	239 (1.0)	240 (1.0)	243 (1.0)	244 (0.9)	86 (1.0)	46 (1.5)	7 (0.8)
Nevada[7]....................	— (†)	218 (1.3)	220 (1.0)	228 (0.8)	230 (0.8)	232 (0.9)	235 (0.9)	237 (0.8)	236 (0.8)	234 (1.1)	76 (1.5)	32 (1.7)	4 (0.6)
New Hampshire	230 (1.2)	— (†)	— (†)	243 (0.9)	246 (0.8)	249 (0.8)	251 (0.8)	252 (0.6)	253 (0.8)	249 (0.8)	91 (0.7)	51 (1.5)	10 (0.7)
New Jersey[7]................	227 (1.5)	227 (1.5)	— (†)	239 (1.1)	244 (1.1)	249 (1.1)	247 (1.0)	248 (0.9)	247 (1.1)	245 (1.2)	86 (1.3)	47 (2.0)	9 (1.2)
New Mexico	213 (1.4)	214 (1.8)	213 (1.3)	223 (1.1)	224 (0.8)	228 (0.9)	230 (1.0)	233 (0.8)	233 (0.7)	231 (0.8)	73 (1.3)	27 (1.2)	3 (0.4)
New York[7,8]...............	218 (1.2)	223 (1.2)	225 (1.4)	236 (0.9)	238 (0.9)	243 (0.8)	241 (0.7)	238 (0.8)	240 (1.0)	237 (0.9)	79 (1.2)	35 (1.4)	5 (0.7)
North Carolina	213 (1.1)	224 (1.2)	230 (1.1)	242 (0.8)	241 (0.9)	242 (0.8)	244 (0.8)	245 (0.7)	245 (0.9)	244 (1.0)	85 (1.0)	44 (1.5)	8 (1.0)
North Dakota	229 (0.8)	231 (1.2)	231 (1.2)	238 (0.7)	243 (0.5)	245 (0.5)	245 (0.6)	245 (0.4)	246 (0.5)	245 (0.5)	88 (0.7)	45 (1.1)	8 (0.6)
Ohio[8].......................	219 (1.2)	— (†)	230 (1.5)	238 (1.0)	242 (1.0)	245 (1.0)	244 (1.1)	244 (0.8)	246 (1.1)	244 (1.2)	85 (1.2)	45 (1.9)	8 (0.9)
Oklahoma	220 (1.0)	— (†)	224 (1.0)	229 (1.0)	234 (1.0)	237 (0.8)	237 (0.9)	237 (0.8)	239 (0.7)	240 (1.0)	84 (1.2)	37 (1.8)	5 (0.8)
Oregon[8]....................	— (†)	223 (1.4)	224 (1.8)	236 (0.9)	238 (0.8)	236 (1.0)	238 (0.9)	237 (0.9)	240 (1.3)	238 (1.1)	79 (1.2)	37 (1.7)	6 (0.8)
Pennsylvania[7].............	224 (1.3)	226 (1.2)	— (†)	236 (1.1)	241 (1.2)	244 (0.8)	244 (1.1)	246 (1.1)	244 (1.0)	243 (1.4)	83 (1.4)	45 (2.0)	10 (1.1)
Rhode Island	215 (1.5)	220 (1.4)	224 (1.1)	230 (1.0)	233 (0.9)	236 (0.9)	239 (0.8)	242 (0.7)	241 (0.8)	238 (0.7)	80 (1.0)	37 (1.2)	6 (0.6)
South Carolina[7].............	212 (1.1)	213 (1.3)	220 (1.4)	236 (0.9)	238 (0.9)	237 (0.8)	236 (0.9)	237 (1.0)	237 (1.0)	237 (1.1)	79 (1.2)	36 (1.9)	6 (0.8)
South Dakota	— (†)	— (†)	— (†)	237 (0.7)	242 (0.5)	241 (0.7)	242 (0.5)	241 (0.6)	241 (0.5)	240 (0.7)	83 (1.0)	40 (1.4)	4 (0.6)
Tennessee	211 (1.4)	219 (1.4)	220 (1.4)	228 (1.0)	232 (1.2)	233 (0.9)	232 (1.1)	233 (0.9)	240 (0.9)	241 (1.1)	82 (1.2)	40 (1.9)	7 (0.9)
Texas........................	218 (1.2)	229 (1.4)	231 (1.1)	237 (0.9)	242 (0.6)	242 (0.7)	240 (0.7)	241 (1.1)	242 (0.9)	244 (1.3)	86 (1.2)	44 (2.1)	8 (1.1)
Utah.........................	224 (1.0)	227 (1.2)	227 (1.3)	235 (0.8)	239 (0.8)	239 (0.9)	240 (1.0)	243 (0.8)	243 (0.9)	243 (1.0)	84 (1.1)	44 (1.6)	7 (0.8)
Vermont[7,8].................	— (†)	225 (1.2)	232 (1.6)	242 (0.8)	244 (0.5)	246 (0.5)	248 (0.4)	247 (0.5)	248 (0.6)	243 (0.7)	85 (1.0)	43 (1.3)	9 (0.8)
Virginia......................	221 (1.3)	223 (1.4)	230 (1.0)	239 (1.1)	240 (0.9)	244 (0.9)	243 (1.0)	245 (0.8)	246 (1.1)	247 (1.3)	87 (1.2)	47 (1.9)	10 (1.2)
Washington	— (†)	225 (1.2)	— (†)	238 (1.0)	242 (0.9)	243 (1.0)	242 (0.8)	243 (0.9)	246 (1.1)	245 (1.3)	83 (1.2)	47 (1.7)	12 (1.3)
West Virginia................	215 (1.1)	223 (1.0)	223 (1.3)	231 (0.8)	231 (0.7)	236 (0.9)	233 (0.8)	235 (0.7)	237 (0.8)	235 (0.8)	78 (1.3)	33 (1.4)	5 (0.6)
Wisconsin	229 (1.1)	231 (1.0)	‡ (†)	237 (0.9)	241 (0.9)	244 (0.9)	244 (0.9)	245 (0.8)	245 (1.0)	243 (1.1)	83 (1.1)	45 (1.8)	9 (1.0)
Wyoming.....................	225 (0.9)	223 (1.4)	229 (1.1)	241 (0.6)	243 (0.6)	244 (0.5)	242 (0.6)	244 (0.4)	247 (0.4)	247 (0.6)	88 (0.8)	48 (1.2)	9 (0.7)
Department of Defense dependents schools[9] .	— (†)	224 (0.6)	227 (0.6)	237 (0.4)	239 (0.5)	240 (0.4)	240 (0.5)	241 (0.4)	245 (0.4)	248 (0.5)	90 (0.8)	49 (1.1)	8 (0.8)

—Not available.
†Not applicable.
‡Reporting standards not met. Participation rates fell below the required standards for reporting.
[1]Scale ranges from 0 to 500.
[2]Accommodations were not permitted for this assessment.
[3]The 1996 data in this table do not include students who were tested with accommodations. Data for students tested with accommodations are not available at the state level for 1996.
[4]*Basic* denotes partial mastery of the knowledge and skills that are fundamental for proficient work at the 4th-grade level.
[5]*Proficient* represents solid academic performance for 4th-graders. Students reaching this level have demonstrated competency over challenging subject matter.
[6]*Advanced* signifies superior performance.
[7]Did not meet one or more of the guidelines for school participation in 1996. Data are subject to appreciable nonresponse bias.

[8]Did not meet one or more of the guidelines for school participation in 2000. Data are subject to appreciable nonresponse bias.
[9]Prior to 2005, NAEP divided the Department of Defense (DoD) schools into two jurisdictions, domestic and overseas. In 2005, NAEP began combining the DoD domestic and overseas schools into a single jurisdiction. Data shown in this table for years prior to 2005 were recalculated for comparability.
NOTE: For 2000 and later years, includes public school students who were tested with accommodations; excludes only those students with disabilities (SD) and English language learners (ELL) who were unable to be tested even with accommodations. SD and ELL populations, accommodation rates, and exclusion rates vary from state to state. Some data have been revised from previously published figures.
SOURCE: U.S. Department of Education, National Center for Education Statistics, National Assessment of Educational Progress (NAEP), 1992, 1996, 2000, 2003, 2005, 2007, 2009, 2011, 2013, and 2015 Mathematics Assessments, retrieved November 4, 2015, from the Main NAEP Data Explorer (http://nces.ed.gov/nationsreportcard/naepdata/). (This table was prepared November 2015.)

Table 222.55. Average National Assessment of Educational Progress (NAEP) mathematics scale score of 4th-grade public school students, by race/ethnicity, school's level of free or reduced-price lunch eligibility, and state: 2015

[Standard errors appear in parentheses]

State	White		Black		Hispanic		Asian		Pacific Islander		American Indian/ Alaska Native		Two or more races		0–25 percent eligible (low poverty)		26–50 percent eligible		51–75 percent eligible		76–100 percent eligible (high poverty)	
1	2		3		4		5		6		7		8		9		10		11		12	
United States	248	(0.3)	224	(0.4)	230	(0.5)	259	(1.2)	226	(2.2)	228	(1.1)	244	(0.8)	257	(0.7)	245	(0.5)	237	(0.5)	226	(0.5)
Alabama	239	(1.3)	217	(1.4)	221	(2.3)	‡	(†)	‡	(†)	‡	(†)	‡	(†)	250	(3.1)	238	(2.5)	232	(1.7)	219	(1.5)
Alaska	246	(1.3)	221	(2.9)	235	(2.8)	239	(3.0)	216	(4.2)	219	(2.2)	243	(2.2)	254	(2.4)	240	(1.5)	232	(2.0)	219	(2.5)
Arizona	251	(1.6)	231	(3.1)	229	(1.1)	‡	(†)	‡	(†)	220	(3.1)	‡	(†)	257	(3.3)	248	(2.7)	233	(2.1)	227	(1.4)
Arkansas	240	(0.9)	221	(1.6)	231	(2.2)	‡	(†)	‡	(†)	‡	(†)	‡	(†)	‡	(†)	243	(2.1)	236	(1.1)	228	(1.7)
California	246	(1.9)	222	(2.5)	222	(1.2)	254	(3.2)	‡	(†)	‡	(†)	257	(7.0)	260	(3.0)	237	(2.5)	230	(2.3)	219	(1.7)
Colorado	253	(1.0)	221	(4.3)	227	(1.2)	‡	(†)	‡	(†)	‡	(†)	252	(3.1)	258	(1.4)	244	(2.1)	235	(2.3)	224	(2.0)
Connecticut	249	(1.0)	218	(2.0)	224	(1.5)	259	(2.8)	‡	(†)	‡	(†)	‡	(†)	251	(1.5)	240	(1.9)	229	(2.0)	218	(2.4)
Delaware	247	(0.8)	227	(0.9)	232	(1.4)	258	(2.7)	‡	(†)	‡	(†)	241	(2.8)	255	(1.6)	243	(1.2)	237	(1.4)	230	(1.1)
District of Columbia	274	(1.7)	223	(0.8)	231	(1.8)	‡	(†)	‡	(†)	‡	(†)	‡	(†)	257	(1.7)	244	(3.1)	232	(2.5)	222	(0.9)
Florida	251	(1.3)	228	(1.8)	240	(1.1)	262	(3.5)	‡	(†)	‡	(†)	244	(3.7)	259	(1.8)	251	(2.2)	245	(1.2)	232	(1.4)
Georgia	245	(1.5)	224	(1.6)	234	(1.8)	262	(5.5)	‡	(†)	‡	(†)	238	(3.4)	257	(5.3)	246	(2.2)	241	(1.4)	226	(1.8)
Hawaii	248	(1.8)	‡	(†)	236	(2.4)	244	(1.4)	226	(1.5)	‡	(†)	241	(3.1)	257	(1.6)	244	(1.7)	234	(1.5)	220	(2.9)
Idaho	243	(1.0)	‡	(†)	221	(1.5)	‡	(†)	‡	(†)	‡	(†)	‡	(†)	254	(2.0)	243	(1.6)	236	(1.3)	224	(2.0)
Illinois	248	(1.4)	215	(1.9)	228	(1.7)	262	(3.7)	‡	(†)	‡	(†)	244	(4.0)	253	(4.2)	243	(2.5)	236	(2.3)	221	(1.8)
Indiana	252	(1.0)	229	(1.9)	240	(2.2)	‡	(†)	‡	(†)	‡	(†)	244	(3.3)	260	(2.5)	252	(1.7)	246	(1.6)	236	(3.5)
Iowa	248	(0.9)	222	(3.1)	226	(2.2)	251	(5.1)	‡	(†)	‡	(†)	235	(3.5)	255	(1.7)	247	(1.3)	237	(1.9)	226	(3.4)
Kansas	247	(1.0)	218	(2.3)	228	(1.7)	255	(3.8)	‡	(†)	‡	(†)	240	(2.8)	258	(2.0)	243	(1.6)	241	(1.3)	225	(2.1)
Kentucky	244	(1.2)	226	(1.3)	234	(2.4)	258	(9.3)	‡	(†)	‡	(†)	243	(3.1)	‡	(†)	251	(2.6)	241	(1.6)	233	(1.4)
Louisiana	242	(1.2)	224	(1.3)	238	(2.4)	‡	(†)	‡	(†)	‡	(†)	‡	(†)	‡	(†)	244	(2.6)	238	(1.8)	230	(1.6)
Maine	243	(0.8)	223	(4.1)	‡	(†)	‡	(†)	‡	(†)	‡	(†)	‡	(†)	258	(2.7)	243	(1.1)	239	(1.3)	229	(3.4)
Maryland	252	(1.4)	224	(1.1)	229	(1.5)	262	(3.1)	‡	(†)	‡	(†)	245	(3.2)	255	(2.0)	245	(1.7)	231	(1.6)	221	(1.8)
Massachusetts	256	(1.3)	230	(2.2)	232	(1.9)	273	(3.5)	‡	(†)	‡	(†)	253	(4.3)	263	(2.1)	249	(1.6)	237	(3.9)	231	(2.3)
Michigan	241	(1.0)	212	(2.6)	223	(3.7)	254	(7.4)	‡	(†)	‡	(†)	‡	(†)	252	(2.4)	240	(1.7)	232	(1.3)	216	(2.8)
Minnesota	257	(1.1)	227	(3.1)	232	(3.1)	244	(6.1)	‡	(†)	223	(3.8)	248	(3.2)	263	(2.6)	251	(1.5)	245	(2.4)	226	(3.0)
Mississippi	245	(1.1)	224	(1.1)	229	(3.6)	‡	(†)	‡	(†)	‡	(†)	‡	(†)	‡	(†)	247	(2.4)	238	(1.3)	226	(1.4)
Missouri	244	(0.9)	220	(2.4)	233	(3.5)	‡	(†)	‡	(†)	‡	(†)	243	(4.7)	253	(3.0)	246	(1.6)	236	(1.7)	226	(1.6)
Montana	245	(0.8)	‡	(†)	231	(2.9)	‡	(†)	‡	(†)	216	(2.1)	239	(3.1)	249	(1.9)	245	(1.0)	240	(1.5)	224	(2.0)
Nebraska	251	(1.0)	217	(1.8)	230	(1.4)	‡	(†)	‡	(†)	‡	(†)	234	(3.0)	257	(1.6)	247	(1.3)	240	(1.8)	227	(1.6)
Nevada	246	(1.3)	218	(2.5)	227	(1.1)	251	(3.5)	‡	(†)	‡	(†)	237	(2.7)	253	(2.1)	242	(2.6)	231	(2.2)	223	(1.7)
New Hampshire	250	(0.8)	‡	(†)	237	(3.5)	262	(3.3)	‡	(†)	‡	(†)	‡	(†)	255	(0.9)	246	(1.2)	237	(2.7)	‡	(†)
New Jersey	254	(1.4)	228	(1.9)	232	(1.4)	270	(2.7)	‡	(†)	‡	(†)	‡	(†)	258	(2.5)	244	(1.8)	236	(2.7)	228	(2.3)
New Mexico	241	(1.5)	‡	(†)	229	(1.0)	‡	(†)	‡	(†)	218	(3.2)	‡	(†)	‡	(†)	236	(2.3)	236	(1.6)	224	(1.3)
New York	245	(1.1)	221	(1.8)	228	(1.2)	253	(3.6)	‡	(†)	‡	(†)	‡	(†)	248	(3.3)	244	(2.6)	234	(1.8)	226	(2.3)
North Carolina	253	(1.3)	229	(1.5)	235	(1.4)	260	(5.9)	‡	(†)	229	(4.4)	249	(3.8)	258	(2.3)	251	(2.2)	242	(1.4)	229	(1.5)
North Dakota	249	(0.6)	231	(3.2)	224	(3.4)	‡	(†)	‡	(†)	225	(1.9)	‡	(†)	251	(0.9)	243	(0.7)	238	(1.7)	228	(2.5)
Ohio	249	(1.2)	220	(1.6)	236	(2.5)	‡	(†)	‡	(†)	‡	(†)	237	(2.8)	258	(1.8)	248	(1.5)	240	(2.8)	227	(2.9)
Oklahoma	245	(1.2)	223	(2.9)	232	(1.4)	‡	(†)	‡	(†)	235	(1.7)	242	(2.5)	262	(4.4)	244	(2.3)	243	(1.8)	230	(1.4)
Oregon	243	(1.1)	217	(4.6)	224	(1.5)	253	(4.4)	‡	(†)	‡	(†)	240	(2.8)	256	(2.2)	246	(1.7)	233	(1.4)	229	(1.5)
Pennsylvania	250	(1.3)	219	(2.1)	226	(2.8)	260	(3.1)	‡	(†)	‡	(†)	243	(4.4)	258	(3.1)	246	(1.9)	239	(3.3)	216	(2.5)
Rhode Island	246	(0.9)	222	(2.7)	223	(1.2)	239	(4.7)	‡	(†)	‡	(†)	231	(3.5)	253	(1.3)	241	(1.7)	234	(2.0)	223	(1.5)
South Carolina	247	(1.2)	221	(1.1)	233	(3.9)	‡	(†)	‡	(†)	‡	(†)	240	(3.7)	254	(2.8)	249	(2.1)	238	(1.8)	225	(1.5)
South Dakota	246	(0.8)	218	(4.2)	227	(2.6)	‡	(†)	‡	(†)	216	(1.7)	236	(2.8)	251	(1.4)	242	(1.0)	236	(1.9)	219	(2.0)
Tennessee	246	(1.3)	226	(2.0)	235	(2.5)	‡	(†)	‡	(†)	‡	(†)	‡	(†)	258	(5.0)	247	(2.6)	240	(1.5)	231	(1.7)
Texas	255	(1.9)	233	(2.1)	239	(1.4)	271	(3.8)	‡	(†)	‡	(†)	252	(5.3)	272	(3.2)	248	(2.3)	242	(1.8)	234	(1.5)
Utah	247	(0.9)	‡	(†)	226	(2.4)	‡	(†)	‡	(†)	‡	(†)	‡	(†)	249	(1.5)	243	(1.9)	238	(1.7)	221	(3.2)
Vermont	244	(0.7)	‡	(†)	‡	(†)	‡	(†)	‡	(†)	‡	(†)	‡	(†)	255	(1.7)	244	(1.1)	236	(1.3)	233	(2.7)
Virginia	253	(1.2)	231	(1.9)	235	(1.9)	270	(2.3)	‡	(†)	‡	(†)	249	(3.3)	258	(2.1)	251	(2.4)	240	(1.6)	230	(3.2)
Washington	251	(1.2)	229	(4.4)	228	(2.1)	268	(3.8)	‡	(†)	216	(4.2)	244	(3.3)	263	(2.8)	250	(2.2)	236	(2.1)	230	(3.1)
West Virginia	236	(0.8)	218	(3.0)	‡	(†)	‡	(†)	‡	(†)	‡	(†)	228	(5.2)	‡	(†)	244	(2.4)	233	(1.3)	228	(1.5)
Wisconsin	250	(1.1)	212	(2.9)	229	(2.8)	251	(4.6)	‡	(†)	231	(4.5)	246	(4.0)	259	(1.9)	247	(1.4)	235	(2.2)	218	(2.7)
Wyoming	250	(0.6)	‡	(†)	234	(1.6)	‡	(†)	‡	(†)	220	(4.0)	‡	(†)	252	(1.3)	249	(0.7)	241	(1.4)	244	(2.9)
Department of Defense dependents schools	251	(0.8)	236	(1.5)	244	(1.3)	257	(2.6)	‡	(†)	‡	(†)	249	(1.8)	250	(1.2)	246	(1.0)	241	(2.2)	‡	(†)

†Not applicable.
‡Reporting standards not met (too few cases for a reliable estimate).
NOTE: Scale ranges from 0 to 500. Includes public school students who were tested with accommodations; excludes only those students with disabilities (SD) and English language learners (ELL) who were unable to be tested even with accommodations. SD and ELL populations, accommodation rates, and exclusion rates vary from state to state. Race/ethnicity based on school records. Race categories exclude persons of Hispanic ethnicity.
SOURCE: U.S. Department of Education, National Center for Education Statistics, National Assessment of Educational Progress (NAEP), 2015 Mathematics Assessment, retrieved November 16, 2015, from the Main NAEP Data Explorer (http://nces.ed.gov/nationsreportcard/naepdata/). (This table was prepared November 2015.)

Table 222.60. Average National Assessment of Educational Progress (NAEP) mathematics scale score of 8th-grade public school students and percentage attaining mathematics achievement levels, by state: Selected years, 1990 through 2015

[Standard errors appear in parentheses]

State	Average scale score[1]											Percent attaining mathematics achievement levels, 2015		
	1990[2]	1992[2]	1996[3]	2000	2003	2005	2007	2009	2011	2013	2015	At or above Basic[4]	At or above Proficient[5]	At Advanced[6]
1	2	3	4	5	6	7	8	9	10	11	12	13	14	15
United States	262 (1.4)	267 (1.0)	271 (1.2)	272 (0.9)	276 (0.3)	278 (0.2)	280 (0.3)	282 (0.3)	283 (0.2)	284 (0.2)	281 (0.3)	70 (0.3)	32 (0.3)	8 (0.2)
Alabama	253 (1.1)	252 (1.7)	257 (2.1)	264 (1.8)	262 (1.5)	262 (1.5)	266 (1.5)	269 (1.2)	269 (1.4)	269 (1.3)	267 (1.2)	56 (1.6)	17 (1.2)	3 (0.4)
Alaska[7]	— (†)	— (†)	278 (1.8)	— (†)	279 (0.9)	279 (0.8)	283 (1.1)	283 (1.0)	283 (0.8)	282 (0.9)	280 (1.0)	71 (1.2)	32 (1.2)	7 (0.7)
Arizona[8]	260 (1.3)	265 (1.3)	268 (1.6)	269 (1.8)	271 (1.2)	274 (1.1)	276 (1.2)	277 (1.4)	279 (1.2)	280 (1.2)	283 (1.4)	72 (1.4)	35 (1.8)	8 (1.0)
Arkansas[7]	256 (0.9)	256 (1.2)	262 (1.5)	257 (1.5)	266 (1.2)	272 (1.2)	274 (1.1)	276 (1.1)	279 (1.0)	278 (1.1)	275 (1.4)	66 (2.0)	25 (1.5)	4 (0.7)
California[8]	256 (1.3)	261 (1.7)	263 (1.9)	260 (2.1)	267 (1.2)	269 (0.6)	270 (0.8)	270 (1.3)	273 (1.2)	276 (1.2)	275 (1.3)	64 (1.5)	27 (1.3)	6 (1.0)
Colorado	267 (0.9)	272 (1.0)	276 (1.1)	— (†)	283 (1.1)	281 (1.2)	286 (0.9)	287 (1.4)	292 (1.1)	290 (1.2)	286 (1.5)	73 (1.6)	37 (1.7)	10 (1.0)
Connecticut	270 (1.0)	274 (1.1)	280 (1.1)	281 (1.3)	284 (1.2)	281 (1.4)	282 (1.5)	289 (1.0)	287 (1.1)	285 (1.1)	284 (1.2)	72 (1.4)	36 (1.4)	10 (0.8)
Delaware	261 (0.9)	263 (1.0)	267 (0.9)	— (†)	277 (0.7)	281 (0.6)	283 (0.6)	284 (0.5)	283 (0.7)	282 (0.7)	280 (0.7)	69 (1.4)	30 (0.9)	7 (0.6)
District of Columbia	231 (0.9)	235 (0.9)	233 (1.3)	235 (1.1)	243 (0.8)	245 (0.9)	248 (0.9)	254 (0.9)	260 (0.7)	265 (0.9)	263 (0.9)	51 (1.3)	19 (0.9)	4 (0.5)
Florida	255 (1.2)	260 (1.5)	264 (1.8)	— (†)	271 (1.5)	274 (1.1)	277 (1.3)	279 (1.1)	278 (0.8)	281 (0.8)	275 (1.4)	64 (1.7)	26 (1.2)	5 (0.5)
Georgia	259 (1.3)	259 (1.2)	262 (1.6)	265 (1.2)	270 (1.2)	272 (1.1)	275 (1.0)	278 (0.9)	278 (1.0)	279 (1.2)	279 (1.2)	67 (1.4)	28 (1.4)	7 (0.8)
Hawaii	251 (0.8)	257 (0.9)	262 (1.0)	262 (1.4)	266 (0.8)	266 (0.7)	269 (0.8)	274 (0.7)	278 (0.7)	281 (0.8)	279 (0.8)	70 (1.2)	30 (1.1)	6 (0.7)
Idaho[8]	271 (0.8)	275 (0.7)	— (†)	277 (1.0)	280 (0.9)	281 (0.9)	284 (0.9)	287 (0.8)	287 (0.8)	286 (0.7)	284 (0.9)	75 (1.1)	34 (1.4)	6 (0.6)
Illinois[8]	261 (1.7)	— (†)	— (†)	275 (1.7)	277 (1.2)	278 (1.1)	280 (1.1)	282 (1.2)	283 (1.1)	285 (1.0)	282 (1.3)	72 (1.4)	32 (1.6)	7 (1.0)
Indiana[8]	267 (1.2)	270 (1.1)	276 (1.4)	281 (1.4)	281 (1.1)	282 (1.0)	285 (1.1)	287 (0.9)	285 (1.0)	288 (1.1)	287 (1.2)	77 (1.3)	39 (1.5)	9 (0.9)
Iowa[7]	278 (1.1)	283 (1.0)	284 (1.3)	— (†)	284 (0.8)	284 (0.9)	285 (0.9)	284 (1.0)	285 (0.9)	285 (0.9)	286 (1.2)	76 (1.2)	37 (1.6)	9 (0.8)
Kansas[8]	— (†)	— (†)	— (†)	283 (1.7)	284 (1.3)	284 (1.0)	290 (1.1)	289 (1.0)	290 (0.9)	290 (1.0)	284 (1.3)	76 (1.5)	33 (1.6)	6 (0.7)
Kentucky	257 (1.2)	262 (1.1)	267 (1.1)	270 (1.3)	274 (1.2)	274 (1.2)	279 (1.1)	279 (1.1)	282 (0.9)	281 (0.9)	278 (0.9)	68 (1.3)	28 (1.3)	5 (0.6)
Louisiana	246 (1.2)	250 (1.7)	252 (1.6)	259 (1.5)	266 (1.5)	268 (1.4)	272 (1.1)	272 (1.6)	273 (1.2)	273 (0.9)	268 (1.4)	57 (1.8)	18 (1.5)	3 (0.5)
Maine[8]	— (†)	279 (1.0)	284 (1.3)	281 (1.1)	282 (0.9)	281 (0.8)	286 (0.8)	286 (0.7)	289 (0.8)	289 (0.7)	285 (0.7)	76 (0.8)	35 (1.1)	8 (0.7)
Maryland[7]	261 (1.4)	265 (1.3)	270 (2.1)	272 (1.7)	278 (1.0)	278 (1.1)	286 (1.2)	288 (1.1)	288 (1.2)	287 (1.1)	283 (1.2)	71 (1.5)	35 (1.7)	10 (0.8)
Massachusetts	— (†)	273 (1.0)	278 (1.7)	279 (1.5)	287 (0.9)	292 (0.9)	298 (1.3)	299 (1.3)	299 (0.8)	301 (0.9)	297 (1.4)	81 (1.5)	51 (1.6)	18 (1.1)
Michigan[7,8]	264 (1.4)	267 (1.4)	277 (1.8)	277 (1.9)	276 (2.0)	277 (1.5)	277 (1.4)	278 (1.6)	280 (1.4)	280 (1.3)	278 (1.3)	68 (1.6)	29 (1.5)	7 (0.7)
Minnesota[8]	275 (0.9)	282 (1.0)	284 (1.3)	287 (1.4)	291 (1.1)	290 (1.2)	292 (1.0)	294 (1.0)	295 (1.0)	295 (1.0)	294 (1.0)	82 (1.0)	48 (1.4)	13 (1.0)
Mississippi	— (†)	246 (1.2)	250 (1.2)	254 (1.1)	261 (1.1)	262 (1.2)	265 (0.8)	265 (1.2)	269 (1.4)	271 (0.9)	271 (1.1)	60 (1.5)	22 (1.1)	3 (0.4)
Missouri	— (†)	271 (1.2)	273 (1.4)	271 (1.5)	279 (1.1)	276 (1.3)	281 (1.0)	286 (1.0)	282 (1.1)	283 (1.0)	281 (1.2)	71 (1.6)	31 (1.5)	7 (0.8)
Montana[7,8]	280 (0.9)	— (†)	283 (1.3)	285 (1.4)	286 (0.8)	286 (0.7)	287 (0.7)	292 (0.9)	293 (0.6)	289 (0.9)	287 (0.8)	79 (1.0)	39 (1.1)	8 (0.8)
Nebraska	276 (1.0)	278 (1.1)	283 (1.0)	280 (1.2)	282 (0.9)	284 (1.0)	284 (1.0)	284 (1.1)	283 (0.8)	285 (0.9)	286 (0.8)	77 (1.0)	38 (1.2)	8 (0.8)
Nevada	— (†)	— (†)	‡ (†)	265 (0.8)	268 (0.8)	270 (0.8)	271 (0.8)	274 (0.7)	278 (0.8)	278 (0.7)	275 (0.7)	65 (1.1)	26 (0.9)	5 (0.5)
New Hampshire	273 (0.9)	278 (1.0)	‡ (†)	— (†)	286 (0.8)	285 (0.8)	288 (0.7)	292 (0.9)	292 (0.7)	296 (0.8)	294 (0.9)	84 (0.9)	46 (1.3)	12 (1.0)
New Jersey	270 (1.1)	272 (1.6)	‡ (†)	— (†)	281 (1.1)	284 (1.4)	289 (1.2)	293 (1.4)	294 (1.2)	296 (1.1)	293 (1.2)	79 (1.1)	46 (1.4)	16 (1.5)
New Mexico	256 (0.7)	260 (0.9)	262 (1.2)	259 (1.3)	263 (1.0)	263 (0.9)	268 (0.9)	270 (1.1)	274 (0.8)	273 (0.7)	271 (1.0)	61 (1.3)	21 (1.2)	3 (0.4)
New York[7,8]	261 (1.4)	266 (2.1)	270 (1.7)	271 (2.2)	280 (1.1)	280 (0.9)	280 (1.2)	283 (1.2)	280 (0.9)	282 (0.9)	281 (1.4)	69 (1.4)	31 (1.7)	7 (0.8)
North Carolina	250 (1.1)	258 (1.4)	268 (1.4)	276 (1.3)	281 (1.0)	282 (0.9)	284 (1.1)	284 (1.3)	286 (1.0)	286 (1.1)	281 (1.6)	69 (1.5)	33 (1.8)	9 (1.1)
North Dakota	281 (1.2)	283 (1.1)	284 (0.9)	282 (1.1)	287 (0.8)	287 (0.6)	292 (0.7)	293 (0.7)	292 (0.6)	291 (0.5)	288 (0.7)	80 (1.0)	39 (1.0)	7 (0.6)
Ohio	264 (1.0)	268 (1.5)	— (†)	281 (1.6)	282 (1.3)	283 (1.1)	285 (1.2)	286 (1.0)	289 (1.0)	290 (1.1)	285 (1.6)	75 (1.6)	35 (1.6)	9 (0.8)
Oklahoma	263 (1.3)	268 (1.1)	— (†)	270 (1.3)	272 (1.1)	271 (1.0)	275 (0.9)	276 (1.0)	279 (1.0)	276 (1.0)	275 (1.3)	67 (1.8)	23 (1.6)	3 (0.4)
Oregon[8]	271 (1.0)	— (†)	276 (1.5)	280 (1.5)	281 (1.3)	282 (1.0)	284 (1.1)	285 (1.0)	283 (1.0)	284 (1.1)	283 (1.2)	73 (1.2)	34 (1.5)	7 (0.8)
Pennsylvania	266 (1.6)	271 (1.5)	— (†)	— (†)	279 (1.1)	281 (1.5)	286 (1.1)	288 (1.3)	286 (1.2)	290 (1.0)	284 (1.5)	72 (1.7)	36 (1.7)	10 (1.0)
Rhode Island	260 (0.6)	266 (0.7)	269 (0.9)	269 (1.3)	272 (0.7)	272 (0.8)	275 (0.7)	278 (0.8)	283 (0.5)	284 (0.6)	281 (0.7)	72 (0.8)	32 (1.2)	6 (0.6)
South Carolina[7]	— (†)	261 (1.0)	261 (1.5)	265 (1.5)	277 (1.3)	281 (0.9)	282 (1.0)	280 (1.3)	281 (1.1)	280 (1.1)	276 (1.3)	65 (1.5)	26 (1.5)	5 (0.6)
South Dakota	— (†)	— (†)	— (†)	— (†)	285 (0.8)	287 (0.6)	288 (0.8)	291 (0.5)	291 (0.5)	287 (0.7)	285 (0.9)	77 (1.2)	34 (1.2)	6 (0.6)
Tennessee	— (†)	259 (1.4)	263 (1.4)	262 (1.5)	268 (1.8)	271 (1.1)	274 (1.1)	275 (1.4)	274 (1.2)	278 (1.3)	278 (1.8)	68 (1.8)	29 (2.0)	6 (1.0)
Texas	258 (1.4)	265 (1.3)	270 (1.4)	273 (1.6)	277 (1.1)	281 (0.6)	286 (1.0)	287 (1.3)	290 (0.9)	288 (1.0)	284 (1.2)	75 (1.4)	32 (1.6)	7 (0.7)
Utah	— (†)	274 (0.7)	277 (1.0)	274 (1.2)	281 (1.0)	279 (0.7)	281 (0.9)	284 (0.9)	283 (0.8)	284 (0.9)	286 (1.1)	76 (1.3)	38 (1.4)	8 (0.8)
Vermont[7,8]	— (†)	— (†)	279 (1.0)	281 (1.5)	286 (0.8)	287 (0.7)	291 (0.7)	293 (0.6)	294 (0.7)	295 (0.7)	290 (0.7)	79 (0.9)	42 (1.2)	11 (0.9)
Virginia	264 (1.5)	268 (1.2)	270 (1.6)	275 (1.3)	282 (1.3)	284 (1.1)	288 (1.1)	286 (1.1)	289 (1.1)	288 (1.2)	288 (1.2)	76 (1.2)	38 (1.6)	10 (1.1)
Washington	— (†)	— (†)	276 (1.3)	— (†)	281 (0.9)	285 (1.0)	285 (1.0)	289 (1.0)	288 (1.0)	290 (1.0)	287 (1.3)	74 (1.2)	39 (1.5)	11 (0.9)
West Virginia	256 (1.0)	259 (1.0)	265 (1.0)	266 (1.2)	271 (1.2)	269 (1.0)	270 (1.0)	270 (1.0)	273 (0.7)	274 (0.9)	271 (0.9)	62 (1.5)	21 (1.1)	3 (0.5)
Wisconsin[7]	274 (1.3)	278 (1.5)	283 (1.5)	‡ (†)	284 (1.3)	285 (1.1)	286 (1.1)	288 (0.9)	289 (1.0)	289 (0.9)	289 (1.3)	78 (1.5)	41 (1.5)	11 (1.0)
Wyoming	272 (0.7)	275 (0.9)	275 (0.9)	276 (1.0)	284 (0.7)	282 (0.7)	287 (0.7)	286 (0.6)	288 (0.6)	288 (0.5)	287 (0.7)	78 (0.9)	35 (1.2)	7 (0.7)
Department of Defense dependents schools[9]	— (†)	— (†)	274 (0.9)	277 (1.1)	285 (0.7)	284 (0.7)	285 (0.8)	287 (0.9)	288 (0.8)	290 (0.8)	291 (0.7)	83 (1.2)	40 (1.1)	9 (1.0)

—Not available.
†Not applicable.
‡Reporting standards not met. Participation rates fell below the required standards for reporting.
[1]Scale ranges from 0 to 500.
[2]Accommodations were not permitted for this assessment.
[3]The 1996 data in this table do not include students who were tested with accommodations. Data for students tested with accommodations are not available at the state level for 1996.
[4]*Basic* denotes partial mastery of the knowledge and skills that are fundamental for proficient work at the 8th-grade level.
[5]*Proficient* represents solid academic performance for 8th-graders. Students reaching this level have demonstrated competency over challenging subject matter.
[6]*Advanced* signifies superior performance.
[7]Did not meet one or more of the guidelines for school participation in 1996. Data are subject to appreciable nonresponse bias.

[8]Did not meet one or more of the guidelines for school participation in 2000. Data are subject to appreciable nonresponse bias.
[9]Prior to 2005, NAEP divided the Department of Defense (DoD) schools into two jurisdictions, domestic and overseas. In 2005, NAEP began combining the DoD domestic and overseas schools into a single jurisdiction. Data shown in this table for years prior to 2005 were recalculated for comparability.
NOTE: For 2000 and later years, includes public school students who were tested with accommodations; excludes only those students with disabilities (SD) and English language learners (ELL) who were unable to be tested even with accommodations. SD and ELL populations, accommodation rates, and exclusion rates vary from state to state. Some data have been revised from previously published figures.
SOURCE: U.S. Department of Education, National Center for Education Statistics, National Assessment of Educational Progress (NAEP), 1990, 1992, 1996, 2000, 2003, 2005, 2007, 2009, 2011, 2013, and 2015 Mathematics Assessments, retrieved October 29, 2015, from the Main NAEP Data Explorer (http://nces.ed.gov/nationsreportcard/naepdata/). (This table was prepared November 2015.)

Table 222.70. Average National Assessment of Educational Progress (NAEP) mathematics scale score of 8th-grade public school students, by race/ethnicity, parents' highest level of education, and state: 2015

[Standard errors appear in parentheses]

State	Race/ethnicity														Highest level of education attained by either parent[1]							
	White		Black		Hispanic		Asian		Pacific Islander		American Indian/Alaska Native		Two or more races		Did not finish high school		Graduated high school		Some education after high school		Graduated college	
1	2		3		4		5		6		7		8		9		10		11		12	
United States	291	(0.3)	260	(0.5)	269	(0.6)	307	(1.5)	277	(2.5)	267	(1.3)	283	(1.1)	265	(0.6)	268	(0.5)	282	(0.4)	293	(0.4)
Alabama	276	(1.4)	248	(1.8)	260	(3.2)	‡	(†)	‡	(†)	‡	(†)	‡	(†)	254	(2.5)	252	(2.3)	271	(1.9)	276	(1.4)
Alaska	295	(1.2)	269	(4.5)	279	(2.9)	282	(2.5)	‡	(†)	257	(2.6)	285	(2.6)	‡	(†)	‡	(†)	‡	(†)	‡	(†)
Arizona	297	(1.9)	269	(4.1)	273	(1.2)	‡	(†)	‡	(†)	260	(4.4)	‡	(†)	269	(2.3)	271	(2.7)	285	(1.9)	297	(2.0)
Arkansas	283	(1.5)	255	(2.2)	269	(2.8)	‡	(†)	‡	(†)	‡	(†)	‡	(†)	266	(2.4)	262	(2.4)	280	(1.9)	283	(1.6)
California	291	(1.8)	260	(3.3)	263	(1.5)	304	(3.6)	‡	(†)	‡	(†)	289	(9.7)	261	(2.0)	263	(2.3)	278	(2.2)	293	(1.7)
Colorado	297	(1.7)	260	(4.9)	269	(1.6)	308	(5.3)	‡	(†)	‡	(†)	290	(4.8)	266	(2.6)	270	(2.3)	284	(2.3)	299	(1.6)
Connecticut	295	(1.2)	256	(2.9)	261	(2.3)	310	(5.6)	‡	(†)	‡	(†)	‡	(†)	254	(4.2)	265	(2.1)	275	(2.4)	297	(1.4)
Delaware	291	(1.1)	263	(1.3)	270	(2.2)	317	(4.0)	‡	(†)	‡	(†)	‡	(†)	264	(2.8)	267	(2.0)	280	(1.8)	290	(1.1)
District of Columbia	316	(2.7)	257	(1.0)	265	(2.6)	‡	(†)	‡	(†)	‡	(†)	‡	(†)	258	(3.6)	250	(2.0)	269	(2.3)	276	(1.6)
Florida	285	(1.6)	258	(2.2)	272	(1.4)	297	(3.6)	‡	(†)	‡	(†)	282	(3.5)	264	(2.5)	266	(2.1)	280	(2.0)	285	(1.6)
Georgia	291	(1.7)	264	(1.5)	270	(2.1)	317	(6.2)	‡	(†)	‡	(†)	277	(5.3)	269	(2.4)	264	(1.9)	281	(2.0)	289	(1.5)
Hawaii	286	(2.2)	‡	(†)	271	(2.9)	289	(1.4)	268	(1.4)	‡	(†)	285	(2.6)	270	(4.4)	264	(1.7)	284	(1.6)	289	(1.2)
Idaho	288	(0.9)	‡	(†)	264	(2.2)	‡	(†)	‡	(†)	‡	(†)	‡	(†)	262	(2.6)	267	(2.5)	286	(1.9)	294	(1.2)
Illinois	290	(1.5)	261	(2.4)	273	(1.4)	309	(4.6)	‡	(†)	‡	(†)	‡	(†)	270	(3.1)	268	(2.0)	282	(1.7)	293	(1.8)
Indiana	294	(1.2)	257	(3.2)	271	(3.1)	‡	(†)	‡	(†)	‡	(†)	281	(4.6)	268	(3.1)	274	(1.7)	288	(2.0)	297	(1.4)
Iowa	291	(1.2)	254	(3.0)	269	(3.1)	292	(5.1)	‡	(†)	‡	(†)	283	(5.6)	261	(3.5)	272	(2.4)	283	(2.0)	296	(1.3)
Kansas	289	(1.2)	263	(3.8)	274	(2.8)	302	(5.5)	‡	(†)	‡	(†)	278	(3.1)	268	(4.1)	272	(2.4)	282	(1.8)	293	(1.3)
Kentucky	281	(1.0)	257	(2.3)	274	(2.9)	‡	(†)	‡	(†)	‡	(†)	266	(5.9)	260	(2.6)	268	(1.6)	281	(1.6)	288	(1.1)
Louisiana	280	(1.7)	255	(1.4)	271	(3.7)	‡	(†)	‡	(†)	‡	(†)	‡	(†)	258	(2.5)	259	(2.2)	270	(1.9)	277	(1.6)
Maine	286	(0.7)	‡	(†)	‡	(†)	‡	(†)	‡	(†)	‡	(†)	‡	(†)	267	(4.4)	272	(1.9)	283	(1.8)	295	(1.0)
Maryland	297	(1.5)	263	(1.3)	273	(2.4)	314	(3.6)	‡	(†)	‡	(†)	290	(3.9)	265	(3.4)	263	(1.9)	282	(2.0)	295	(1.6)
Massachusetts	304	(1.3)	268	(3.6)	271	(3.1)	324	(4.3)	‡	(†)	‡	†	‡	(†)	267	(4.6)	277	(2.7)	293	(2.2)	308	(1.4)
Michigan	285	(1.3)	251	(2.2)	269	(4.0)	313	(4.7)	‡	(†)	‡	†	‡	(†)	261	(3.7)	263	(2.1)	275	(2.2)	288	(1.5)
Minnesota	302	(1.2)	262	(2.7)	272	(3.2)	293	(4.1)	‡	(†)	261	(5.8)	284	(5.0)	275	(3.3)	278	(2.9)	290	(1.8)	304	(1.2)
Mississippi	284	(1.2)	257	(1.7)	269	(4.9)	‡	(†)	‡	(†)	‡	(†)	‡	(†)	258	(3.0)	259	(2.0)	279	(2.5)	277	(1.5)
Missouri	285	(1.3)	258	(2.7)	270	(3.5)	‡	(†)	‡	(†)	‡	(†)	‡	(†)	257	(2.9)	268	(2.0)	285	(2.0)	291	(1.4)
Montana	292	(0.8)	‡	(†)	275	(4.9)	‡	(†)	‡	(†)	256	(2.9)	287	(4.1)	272	(3.7)	270	(2.3)	286	(1.8)	296	(1.0)
Nebraska	295	(0.9)	254	(3.6)	266	(2.1)	‡	(†)	‡	(†)	‡	(†)	285	(5.3)	262	(2.7)	267	(2.1)	288	(2.3)	298	(1.0)
Nevada	288	(1.3)	256	(2.6)	266	(1.1)	300	(3.8)	‡	(†)	‡	(†)	281	(3.3)	263	(2.0)	266	(1.5)	283	(1.7)	288	(1.3)
New Hampshire	295	(0.9)	‡	(†)	270	(4.3)	313	(6.9)	‡	(†)	‡	(†)	‡	(†)	269	(4.4)	278	(1.9)	290	(1.7)	304	(1.0)
New Jersey	301	(1.3)	269	(3.0)	272	(2.0)	332	(3.6)	‡	(†)	‡	(†)	‡	(†)	267	(4.5)	273	(2.4)	291	(2.1)	303	(1.6)
New Mexico	285	(2.1)	‡	(†)	266	(1.1)	‡	(†)	‡	(†)	259	(2.8)	‡	(†)	261	(2.2)	260	(1.6)	277	(1.9)	283	(1.4)
New York	290	(1.5)	264	(2.9)	268	(1.7)	298	(3.7)	‡	(†)	‡	(†)	‡	(†)	267	(3.0)	269	(2.5)	283	(1.9)	290	(1.6)
North Carolina	292	(1.7)	263	(2.0)	273	(2.5)	311	(6.3)	‡	(†)	261	(4.7)	274	(4.4)	264	(2.4)	267	(2.1)	281	(1.8)	294	(2.0)
North Dakota	293	(0.7)	263	(4.7)	276	(3.3)	‡	(†)	‡	(†)	260	(3.1)	‡	(†)	266	(3.4)	274	(2.3)	286	(1.6)	296	(0.9)
Ohio	291	(1.3)	259	(3.1)	266	(8.8)	304	(25.4)	‡	(†)	‡	(†)	280	(3.6)	259	(4.6)	272	(2.1)	284	(2.0)	296	(1.4)
Oklahoma	281	(1.4)	260	(2.7)	266	(2.9)	‡	(†)	‡	(†)	269	(1.8)	273	(3.8)	263	(3.0)	265	(1.8)	277	(2.1)	284	(1.7)
Oregon	289	(1.4)	‡	(†)	266	(1.7)	308	(5.9)	‡	(†)	‡	(†)	281	(4.2)	268	(2.4)	271	(1.9)	283	(2.1)	295	(1.6)
Pennsylvania	292	(1.3)	253	(2.3)	261	(3.7)	317	(6.1)	‡	(†)	‡	(†)	274	(4.9)	261	(3.4)	265	(3.3)	284	(2.3)	297	(1.6)
Rhode Island	290	(0.8)	258	(3.1)	265	(1.1)	300	(4.0)	‡	(†)	‡	(†)	274	(4.3)	268	(2.5)	269	(1.8)	285	(2.0)	293	(1.0)
South Carolina	288	(1.3)	256	(1.9)	272	(4.3)	‡	(†)	‡	(†)	‡	(†)	‡	(†)	271	(3.6)	263	(2.3)	278	(2.2)	284	(1.3)
South Dakota	290	(0.7)	‡	(†)	272	(4.5)	‡	(†)	‡	(†)	260	(2.9)	‡	(†)	265	(4.1)	269	(1.9)	287	(1.9)	292	(1.1)
Tennessee	285	(1.7)	253	(3.0)	273	(4.0)	‡	(†)	‡	(†)	‡	(†)	‡	(†)	265	(3.1)	266	(2.0)	281	(2.0)	291	(2.2)
Texas	298	(1.5)	267	(2.9)	277	(1.4)	312	(3.2)	‡	(†)	‡	(†)	293	(6.1)	272	(1.9)	275	(1.8)	284	(2.0)	296	(1.6)
Utah	292	(1.0)	‡	(†)	262	(2.6)	‡	(†)	‡	(†)	240	(9.0)	‡	(†)	‡	(†)	‡	(†)	‡	(†)	‡	(†)
Vermont	291	(0.8)	‡	(†)	‡	(†)	‡	(†)	‡	(†)	‡	(†)	‡	(†)	266	(3.6)	277	(2.0)	288	(2.5)	301	(1.1)
Virginia	295	(1.4)	265	(1.8)	279	(2.4)	317	(4.1)	‡	(†)	‡	(†)	293	(3.3)	268	(3.2)	272	(2.0)	281	(1.9)	298	(1.6)
Washington	294	(1.4)	257	(3.4)	269	(2.5)	312	(3.7)	‡	(†)	264	(7.0)	285	(3.7)	266	(3.0)	272	(2.6)	288	(1.8)	300	(1.4)
West Virginia	272	(0.9)	256	(3.1)	‡	(†)	‡	(†)	‡	(†)	‡	(†)	‡	(†)	255	(2.9)	261	(1.6)	275	(1.8)	280	(1.4)
Wisconsin	296	(1.1)	249	(4.2)	271	(2.6)	296	(4.8)	‡	(†)	274	(7.0)	‡	(†)	263	(3.8)	271	(2.4)	289	(2.1)	299	(1.2)
Wyoming	290	(0.8)	‡	(†)	273	(1.9)	‡	(†)	‡	(†)	251	(4.0)	‡	(†)	272	(2.8)	272	(1.7)	285	(1.8)	297	(1.0)
Department of Defense dependents schools.....	298	(1.2)	271	(2.1)	287	(2.1)	298	(3.3)	‡	(†)	‡	(†)	290	(2.6)	‡	(†)	276	(2.5)	291	(1.9)	295	(1.0)

†Not applicable.
‡Reporting standards not met. Either there are too few cases for a reliable estimate or item response rates fell below the required standards for reporting.
[1]Excludes students who responded "I don't know" to the question about educational level of parents.
NOTE: Scale ranges from 0 to 500. Includes public school students who were tested with accommodations; excludes only those students with disabilities (SD) and English language learners (ELL) who were unable to be tested even with accommodations. SD and ELL populations, accommodation rates, and exclusion rates vary from state to state. Race/ethnicity based on school records. Race categories exclude persons of Hispanic ethnicity.
SOURCE: U.S. Department of Education, National Center for Education Statistics, National Assessment of Educational Progress (NAEP), 2015 Mathematics Assessment, retrieved October 29, 2015, from the Main NAEP Data Explorer (http://nces.ed.gov/nationsreportcard/naepdata/). (This table was prepared October 2015.)

Table 222.80. Average National Assessment of Educational Progress (NAEP) mathematics scale scores of 4th- and 8th-grade public school students and percentage attaining selected mathematics achievement levels, by race/ethnicity and jurisdiction or specific urban district: 2009, 2011, 2013, and 2015

[Standard errors appear in parentheses]

Grade level and jurisdiction or specific urban district	2009 All students	2011 All students	2013 All students	2013 White	2013 Black	2013 Hispanic	2013 Asian	2015 All students	2015 White	2015 Black	2015 Hispanic	2015 Asian	2015 At or above Basic[2]	2015 At or above Proficient[3]
1	2	3	4	5	6	7	8	9	10	11	12	13	14	15
4th grade														
United States	239 (0.2)	240 (0.2)	241 (0.2)	250 (0.2)	224 (0.3)	230 (0.4)	260 (0.8)	240 (0.3)	248 (0.3)	224 (0.4)	230 (0.5)	259 (1.2)	81 (0.3)	39 (0.4)
All large cities[4]	231 (0.5)	233 (0.6)	235 (0.7)	254 (0.9)	223 (0.6)	229 (0.8)	258 (2.1)	234 (0.6)	251 (1.0)	222 (0.6)	230 (0.7)	253 (2.0)	75 (0.6)	32 (0.9)
Selected urban districts														
Albuquerque (NM)	— (†)	235 (1.3)	235 (1.0)	253 (2.0)	‡ (†)	229 (1.2)	‡ (†)	231 (1.1)	249 (2.2)	‡ (†)	226 (1.3)	‡ (†)	72 (1.7)	28 (1.6)
Atlanta (GA)	225 (0.8)	228 (0.7)	233 (0.7)	269 (1.4)	222 (0.9)	233 (2.7)	‡ (†)	228 (1.2)	267 (1.9)	218 (1.4)	225 (3.6)	‡ (†)	65 (2.1)	26 (1.4)
Austin (TX)	240 (1.0)	245 (1.1)	245 (0.9)	264 (1.7)	228 (3.4)	237 (1.2)	‡ (†)	246 (1.4)	268 (2.0)	226 (3.1)	237 (1.6)	‡ (†)	85 (1.5)	47 (1.9)
Baltimore City (MD)	222 (1.0)	226 (1.1)	223 (1.2)	250 (4.0)	220 (1.2)	227 (3.9)	‡ (†)	215 (1.5)	232 (3.6)	212 (1.6)	223 (3.3)	‡ (†)	51 (2.2)	12 (1.6)
Boston (MA)	236 (0.7)	237 (0.6)	237 (0.8)	255 (1.6)	228 (1.4)	233 (1.1)	259 (2.2)	236 (1.3)	253 (2.5)	228 (1.8)	230 (2.0)	259 (3.3)	78 (1.9)	33 (1.8)
Charlotte (NC)	245 (1.3)	247 (1.1)	247 (1.6)	264 (2.0)	235 (2.2)	242 (2.0)	255 (4.1)	248 (1.3)	264 (2.0)	236 (1.7)	243 (2.2)	268 (4.2)	87 (1.2)	51 (2.3)
Chicago (IL)	222 (1.2)	224 (0.9)	231 (1.3)	261 (2.8)	221 (2.1)	230 (1.2)	256 (5.8)	232 (1.2)	262 (2.7)	221 (1.8)	230 (1.6)	265 (4.3)	71 (1.5)	30 (1.7)
Cleveland (OH)	213 (1.0)	216 (0.7)	216 (0.9)	233 (2.2)	210 (1.1)	221 (2.6)	‡ (†)	219 (1.3)	233 (2.4)	215 (1.6)	221 (3.4)	‡ (†)	58 (2.1)	13 (1.5)
Dallas (TX)	— (†)	233 (1.3)	234 (1.0)	‡ (†)	226 (1.7)	235 (1.1)	‡ (†)	238 (1.3)	259 (7.8)	228 (2.8)	238 (1.2)	‡ (†)	82 (1.9)	34 (1.9)
Detroit (MI)	200 (1.7)	203 (1.4)	204 (1.6)	‡ (†)	201 (1.6)	214 (2.9)	‡ (†)	205 (1.6)	‡ (†)	202 (1.8)	215 (3.1)	‡ (†)	36 (2.9)	5 (1.1)
District of Columbia (DC)	220 (0.8)	222 (1.0)	229 (0.8)	277 (2.2)	218 (1.0)	226 (2.3)	‡ (†)	232 (0.9)	275 (1.9)	220 (1.1)	233 (2.3)	‡ (†)	68 (1.5)	33 (1.2)
Duval County (FL)	— (†)	— (†)	— (†)	— (†)	— (†)	— (†)	— (†)	243 (1.3)	254 (1.8)	230 (1.7)	240 (2.4)	‡ (†)	86 (1.5)	41 (2.3)
Fresno (CA)	219 (1.4)	218 (0.9)	220 (1.2)	241 (2.2)	211 (2.5)	217 (1.5)	221 (2.7)	218 (1.3)	235 (3.6)	213 (3.8)	214 (1.5)	226 (3.1)	55 (2.2)	14 (1.5)
Hillsborough County (FL)	— (†)	243 (1.1)	243 (0.9)	254 (1.4)	227 (1.9)	238 (1.3)	263 (3.2)	244 (1.4)	253 (1.9)	230 (1.6)	237 (1.9)	‡ (†)	86 (1.5)	43 (2.7)
Houston (TX)	236 (1.2)	237 (0.8)	236 (1.1)	261 (1.9)	227 (2.3)	235 (1.0)	‡ (†)	239 (1.4)	266 (2.8)	231 (2.4)	235 (1.1)	‡ (†)	80 (1.5)	36 (2.4)
Jefferson County (KY)	233 (1.6)	235 (0.9)	234 (1.0)	245 (1.2)	220 (1.4)	224 (3.0)	‡ (†)	236 (1.5)	245 (1.7)	225 (1.6)	226 (3.1)	‡ (†)	77 (1.8)	34 (2.3)
Los Angeles (CA)	222 (1.2)	223 (0.8)	228 (1.3)	254 (3.4)	223 (2.3)	224 (0.9)	252 (2.4)	224 (1.4)	247 (2.6)	216 (3.6)	218 (1.1)	255 (3.2)	64 (1.8)	22 (1.8)
Miami-Dade (FL)	236 (1.3)	236 (1.0)	237 (1.1)	251 (2.2)	227 (1.9)	238 (1.2)	‡ (†)	242 (1.1)	257 (2.6)	230 (2.2)	243 (1.1)	‡ (†)	86 (1.3)	41 (2.0)
Milwaukee (WI)	220 (1.5)	220 (1.0)	221 (1.6)	246 (2.8)	209 (1.8)	227 (2.2)	234 (7.5)	— (†)	— (†)	— (†)	— (†)	— (†)	— (†)	— (†)
New York City (NY)	237 (1.0)	234 (1.2)	236 (1.1)	251 (2.7)	225 (1.5)	228 (1.5)	257 (2.6)	231 (1.0)	242 (2.5)	220 (1.5)	226 (1.4)	254 (1.9)	73 (1.2)	26 (1.4)
Philadelphia (PA)	222 (1.4)	225 (1.2)	223 (1.5)	237 (3.3)	218 (1.3)	217 (2.2)	246 (3.9)	217 (1.9)	235 (4.1)	211 (1.7)	211 (2.3)	246 (4.0)	54 (2.5)	15 (2.0)
San Diego (CA)	236 (1.6)	239 (1.3)	241 (1.2)	260 (1.9)	228 (3.1)	228 (1.6)	253 (2.8)	233 (1.5)	254 (2.5)	217 (3.6)	222 (2.0)	243 (3.3)	73 (2.0)	31 (2.0)
8th grade														
United States	282 (0.3)	283 (0.2)	284 (0.2)	293 (0.3)	263 (0.4)	271 (0.4)	308 (1.1)	281 (0.3)	291 (0.3)	260 (0.5)	269 (0.6)	307 (1.5)	70 (0.3)	32 (0.3)
All large cities[4]	271 (0.7)	274 (0.7)	276 (0.8)	295 (1.2)	261 (0.8)	269 (0.8)	301 (2.2)	274 (1.0)	296 (1.4)	258 (0.9)	268 (1.2)	301 (2.0)	62 (1.1)	26 (0.9)
Selected urban districts														
Albuquerque (NM)	— (†)	275 (1.0)	274 (1.2)	295 (2.6)	‡ (†)	267 (1.5)	‡ (†)	271 (1.4)	289 (2.9)	‡ (†)	264 (1.5)	‡ (†)	61 (1.7)	21 (1.4)
Atlanta (GA)	259 (1.6)	266 (1.3)	267 (1.2)	311 (3.0)	261 (1.3)	262 (3.7)	‡ (†)	266 (1.2)	318 (2.4)	258 (1.2)	271 (4.4)	‡ (†)	51 (1.7)	20 (1.0)
Austin (TX)	287 (0.9)	287 (1.2)	285 (1.0)	312 (1.9)	267 (2.5)	273 (1.3)	‡ (†)	284 (1.3)	313 (2.4)	260 (3.4)	271 (1.4)	‡ (†)	70 (1.5)	35 (1.7)
Baltimore City (MD)	257 (1.9)	261 (1.3)	260 (2.0)	286 (6.0)	257 (2.0)	‡ (†)	‡ (†)	255 (1.8)	281 (6.4)	251 (1.9)	261 (5.2)	‡ (†)	41 (2.5)	12 (1.6)
Boston (MA)	279 (1.3)	282 (0.9)	283 (1.2)	309 (2.4)	271 (1.8)	275 (1.8)	318 (3.7)	281 (1.2)	311 (3.3)	269 (2.1)	271 (2.1)	318 (5.0)	67 (1.6)	34 (1.4)
Charlotte (NC)	283 (0.9)	285 (0.8)	289 (1.2)	313 (1.9)	271 (1.8)	279 (3.4)	314 (6.1)	286 (1.5)	312 (2.1)	268 (1.9)	275 (3.8)	314 (5.1)	71 (1.7)	39 (2.0)
Chicago (IL)	264 (1.4)	270 (1.0)	269 (1.0)	294 (2.4)	259 (1.5)	270 (1.4)	306 (5.4)	275 (2.4)	317 (5.6)	262 (1.5)	275 (1.8)	‡ (†)	62 (2.1)	25 (2.4)
Cleveland (OH)	256 (1.0)	256 (2.1)	253 (1.3)	265 (2.9)	249 (1.5)	252 (3.4)	‡ (†)	254 (1.5)	273 (3.1)	249 (2.1)	257 (3.5)	‡ (†)	40 (1.9)	9 (1.0)
Dallas (TX)	— (†)	274 (0.9)	275 (1.0)	304 (4.7)	263 (2.0)	277 (1.1)	‡ (†)	271 (1.3)	‡ (†)	261 (2.1)	272 (1.5)	‡ (†)	60 (1.9)	20 (1.5)
Detroit (MI)	238 (2.7)	246 (1.2)	240 (1.7)	‡ (†)	239 (1.7)	243 (4.0)	‡ (†)	244 (1.7)	‡ (†)	242 (1.9)	253 (3.3)	‡ (†)	27 (1.8)	4 (0.7)
District of Columbia (DC)	251 (1.3)	255 (0.9)	260 (1.3)	315 (4.1)	253 (1.4)	262 (3.6)	‡ (†)	258 (1.3)	314 (3.3)	248 (1.5)	263 (3.3)	‡ (†)	46 (1.8)	17 (1.3)
Duval County (FL)	— (†)	— (†)	— (†)	— (†)	— (†)	— (†)	— (†)	275 (1.0)	285 (1.6)	264 (1.4)	266 (3.3)	298 (4.9)	64 (1.7)	22 (1.3)
Fresno (CA)	258 (1.2)	256 (0.9)	260 (1.4)	279 (3.0)	247 (4.0)	256 (1.6)	270 (2.8)	257 (1.5)	281 (3.7)	242 (5.0)	252 (1.9)	270 (3.8)	44 (1.8)	12 (1.1)
Hillsborough County (FL)	— (†)	282 (1.5)	284 (1.1)	296 (1.8)	264 (2.5)	278 (1.9)	‡ (†)	276 (1.7)	290 (2.1)	260 (2.6)	266 (2.2)	‡ (†)	64 (2.3)	27 (1.6)
Houston (TX)	277 (1.2)	279 (1.0)	280 (1.1)	312 (3.3)	271 (1.7)	279 (1.2)	314 (7.2)	276 (1.4)	313 (3.7)	265 (2.6)	273 (1.2)	319 (6.6)	65 (1.7)	27 (1.5)
Jefferson County (KY)	271 (0.9)	274 (1.0)	273 (1.0)	285 (1.5)	257 (1.7)	265 (3.7)	‡ (†)	272 (1.7)	285 (2.2)	252 (2.2)	266 (4.5)	‡ (†)	58 (1.8)	26 (1.8)
Los Angeles (CA)	258 (1.0)	261 (1.3)	264 (1.5)	293 (3.2)	256 (3.4)	258 (1.3)	298 (3.3)	263 (1.6)	285 (4.4)	255 (4.1)	259 (1.4)	296 (5.9)	52 (2.0)	15 (1.4)
Miami-Dade (FL)	273 (1.1)	272 (1.1)	274 (1.5)	295 (3.4)	259 (2.9)	275 (1.3)	‡ (†)	274 (1.8)	299 (2.8)	255 (3.3)	277 (2.0)	‡ (†)	64 (2.1)	26 (1.7)
Milwaukee (WI)	251 (1.5)	254 (1.7)	257 (1.4)	282 (3.5)	247 (1.8)	266 (2.2)	‡ (†)	— (†)	— (†)	— (†)	— (†)	— (†)	— (†)	— (†)
New York City (NY)	273 (1.5)	272 (1.6)	274 (1.1)	301 (3.8)	263 (1.9)	263 (1.7)	304 (3.1)	275 (2.1)	294 (4.6)	261 (3.2)	267 (1.8)	303 (3.1)	62 (2.1)	27 (2.3)
Philadelphia (PA)	265 (2.0)	265 (2.0)	266 (1.7)	287 (2.8)	258 (2.2)	261 (4.1)	297 (4.9)	267 (1.9)	282 (4.0)	257 (2.1)	259 (3.2)	303 (6.0)	53 (2.3)	20 (1.9)
San Diego (CA)	280 (2.0)	278 (1.7)	277 (1.4)	300 (2.3)	260 (4.5)	260 (2.2)	294 (2.9)	280 (1.6)	302 (2.3)	261 (4.0)	266 (2.2)	293 (3.3)	70 (1.9)	32 (1.8)

—Not available.
†Not applicable.
‡Reporting standards not met (too few cases for a reliable estimate).
[1]Scale ranges from 0 to 500.
[2]Basic denotes partial mastery of the knowledge and skills that are fundamental for proficient work at a given grade.
[3]Proficient represents solid academic performance. Students reaching this level have demonstrated competency over challenging subject matter.

[4]Includes public school students from all cities in the nation with populations of 250,000 or more, including the participating districts.
NOTE: Race categories exclude persons of Hispanic ethnicity. Totals include racial/ethnic groups not shown separately.
SOURCE: U.S. Department of Education, National Center for Education Statistics, National Assessment of Educational Progress (NAEP), 2009, 2011, 2013, and 2015 Mathematics Assessments, retrieved October 29, 2015, from the Main NAEP Data Explorer (http://nces.ed.gov/nationsreportcard/naepdata/). (This table was prepared October 2015.)

Table 222.85. Average National Assessment of Educational Progress (NAEP) mathematics scale score, by age and selected student characteristics: Selected years, 1973 through 2012

[Standard errors appear in parentheses]

Selected student characteristic	1973	1978	1982	1986	1990	1992	1994	1996	1999	2004[1] Previous format	2004[1] Revised format	2008	2012
1	2	3	4	5	6	7	8	9	10	11	12	13	14
9-year-olds													
All students	219 (0.8)	219 (0.8)	219 (1.1)	222 (1.0)	230 (0.8)	230 (0.8)	231 (0.8)	231 (0.8)	232 (0.8)	241 (0.9)	239 (0.9)	243 (0.8)	244 (1.0)
Sex													
Male	218 (0.7)	217 (0.7)	217 (1.2)	222 (1.1)	229 (0.9)	231 (1.0)	232 (1.0)	233 (1.2)	233 (1.0)	243 (1.1)	239 (1.0)	242 (0.9)	244 (1.2)
Female	220 (1.1)	220 (1.0)	221 (1.2)	222 (1.2)	230 (1.1)	228 (1.0)	230 (0.9)	229 (0.7)	231 (0.9)	240 (1.1)	240 (1.0)	243 (1.0)	244 (1.0)
Gap between female and male score	2 (1.3)	3 (1.3)	4 (1.7)	# (†)	1 (1.4)	-2 (1.4)	-2 (1.4)	-4 (1.4)	-2 (1.3)	-3 (1.5)	1 (1.4)	1 (1.3)	# (†)
Race/ethnicity													
White	225 (1.0)	224 (0.9)	224 (1.1)	227 (1.1)	235 (0.8)	235 (0.8)	237 (1.0)	237 (1.0)	239 (0.9)	247 (0.9)	245 (0.8)	250 (0.8)	252 (1.1)
Black	190 (1.8)	192 (1.1)	195 (1.6)	202 (1.6)	208 (2.2)	208 (2.0)	212 (1.6)	212 (1.4)	211 (1.6)	224 (2.1)	221 (2.1)	224 (1.9)	226 (1.8)
Hispanic	202 (2.4)	203 (2.2)	204 (1.3)	205 (2.1)	214 (2.1)	212 (2.3)	210 (2.3)	215 (1.7)	213 (1.9)	230 (2.0)	229 (2.0)	234 (1.2)	234 (0.9)
Gap between White and Black score	35 (2.1)	32 (1.5)	29 (2.0)	25 (2.0)	27 (2.4)	27 (2.2)	25 (1.8)	25 (1.8)	28 (1.8)	23 (2.2)	24 (2.2)	26 (2.1)	25 (2.1)
Gap between White and Hispanic score	23 (2.6)	21 (2.4)	20 (1.7)	21 (2.3)	21 (2.3)	23 (2.5)	27 (2.5)	22 (2.0)	26 (2.1)	18 (2.2)	16 (2.1)	16 (1.4)	17 (1.5)
13-year-olds													
All students	266 (1.1)	264 (1.1)	269 (1.1)	269 (1.2)	270 (0.9)	273 (0.9)	274 (1.0)	274 (0.8)	276 (0.8)	281 (1.0)	279 (1.0)	281 (0.9)	285 (1.1)
Sex													
Male	265 (1.3)	264 (1.3)	269 (1.4)	270 (1.1)	271 (1.2)	274 (1.1)	276 (1.3)	276 (0.9)	277 (0.9)	283 (1.2)	279 (1.0)	284 (1.0)	286 (1.3)
Female	267 (1.1)	265 (1.1)	268 (1.1)	268 (1.5)	270 (0.9)	272 (1.0)	273 (1.0)	272 (1.0)	274 (1.1)	279 (1.0)	278 (1.2)	279 (1.0)	284 (1.1)
Gap between female and male score	2 (1.7)	1 (1.7)	-1 (1.7)	-2 (1.9)	-2 (1.5)	-2 (1.5)	-3 (1.6)	-4 (1.4)	-3 (1.4)	-3 (1.6)	-1 (1.6)	-4 (1.4)	-2 (1.7)
Race/ethnicity													
White	274 (0.9)	272 (0.8)	274 (1.0)	274 (1.3)	276 (1.1)	279 (0.9)	281 (0.9)	281 (0.9)	283 (0.8)	288 (0.9)	287 (0.9)	290 (1.2)	293 (1.1)
Black	228 (1.9)	230 (1.9)	240 (1.6)	249 (2.3)	249 (2.3)	250 (1.9)	252 (3.5)	252 (1.3)	251 (2.6)	262 (1.6)	257 (1.8)	262 (1.2)	264 (1.9)
Hispanic	239 (2.2)	238 (2.0)	252 (1.7)	254 (2.9)	255 (1.8)	259 (1.8)	256 (1.9)	256 (1.6)	259 (1.7)	265 (2.0)	264 (1.5)	268 (1.2)	271 (1.4)
Gap between White and Black score	46 (2.1)	42 (2.1)	34 (1.9)	24 (2.6)	27 (2.6)	29 (2.1)	29 (3.7)	29 (1.6)	32 (2.7)	27 (1.8)	30 (2.1)	28 (1.7)	28 (2.2)
Gap between White and Hispanic score	35 (2.4)	34 (2.1)	22 (1.9)	19 (3.2)	22 (2.1)	20 (2.0)	25 (2.1)	25 (1.9)	24 (1.9)	23 (2.2)	23 (1.8)	23 (1.7)	21 (1.8)
Parents' highest level of education													
Did not finish high school	— (†)	245 (1.2)	251 (1.4)	252 (2.3)	253 (1.8)	256 (1.0)	255 (2.1)	254 (2.4)	256 (2.8)	262 (2.2)	263 (1.9)	268 (1.3)	266 (2.5)
Graduated high school	— (†)	263 (1.0)	263 (0.8)	263 (1.2)	263 (1.2)	263 (1.2)	266 (1.1)	267 (1.1)	264 (1.1)	271 (1.7)	270 (1.3)	272 (1.1)	270 (1.1)
Some education after high school	— (†)	273 (1.2)	275 (0.9)	274 (0.8)	277 (1.0)	278 (1.0)	277 (1.6)	277 (1.4)	279 (0.9)	283 (1.0)	282 (1.4)	285 (1.1)	286 (1.4)
Graduated college	— (†)	284 (1.2)	282 (1.5)	280 (1.4)	280 (1.0)	283 (1.0)	285 (1.2)	283 (1.2)	286 (1.0)	292 (0.9)	289 (1.1)	291 (1.0)	296 (1.3)
17-year-olds													
All students	304 (1.1)	300 (1.0)	298 (0.9)	302 (0.9)	305 (0.9)	307 (0.9)	306 (1.0)	307 (1.2)	308 (1.0)	307 (0.8)	305 (0.7)	306 (0.6)	306 (0.8)
Sex													
Male	309 (1.2)	304 (1.0)	301 (1.0)	305 (1.2)	306 (1.1)	309 (1.1)	309 (1.4)	310 (1.3)	310 (1.4)	308 (1.0)	307 (0.9)	309 (0.7)	308 (1.0)
Female	301 (1.1)	297 (1.0)	296 (1.0)	299 (1.0)	303 (1.1)	305 (1.1)	304 (1.1)	305 (1.4)	307 (1.0)	305 (0.9)	304 (0.8)	303 (0.8)	304 (0.8)
Gap between female and male score	-8 (1.6)	-7 (1.4)	-6 (1.4)	-5 (1.5)	-3 (1.5)	-4 (1.5)	-4 (1.8)	-5 (1.9)	-3 (1.7)	-3 (1.4)	-3 (1.2)	-5 (1.1)	-4 (1.3)
Race/ethnicity													
White	310 (1.1)	306 (0.9)	304 (0.9)	308 (1.0)	309 (1.0)	312 (0.8)	312 (1.1)	313 (1.4)	315 (1.1)	313 (0.7)	311 (0.7)	314 (0.7)	314 (1.0)
Black	270 (1.3)	268 (1.3)	272 (1.2)	279 (2.1)	289 (2.8)	286 (2.2)	286 (1.8)	286 (1.7)	283 (1.5)	285 (1.6)	284 (1.4)	287 (1.2)	288 (1.3)
Hispanic	277 (2.2)	276 (2.3)	277 (1.8)	283 (2.9)	284 (2.9)	292 (2.6)	291 (3.7)	292 (2.1)	293 (2.5)	289 (1.8)	292 (1.2)	293 (1.1)	294 (1.1)
Gap between White and Black score	40 (1.7)	38 (1.6)	32 (1.5)	29 (2.3)	21 (3.0)	26 (2.4)	27 (2.1)	27 (2.2)	31 (1.9)	28 (1.8)	27 (1.6)	26 (1.4)	26 (1.6)
Gap between White and Hispanic score	33 (2.5)	30 (2.4)	27 (2.0)	24 (3.0)	26 (3.1)	20 (2.8)	22 (3.9)	21 (2.5)	22 (2.7)	24 (1.9)	19 (1.4)	21 (1.3)	19 (1.5)
Parents' highest level of education													
Did not finish high school	— (†)	280 (1.2)	279 (1.0)	279 (2.3)	285 (2.2)	285 (2.3)	284 (2.4)	281 (2.4)	289 (1.8)	287 (2.4)	287 (1.2)	292 (1.3)	290 (1.4)
Graduated high school	— (†)	294 (0.8)	293 (0.8)	293 (1.0)	294 (0.9)	298 (1.7)	295 (1.1)	297 (2.4)	299 (1.6)	295 (1.1)	294 (0.9)	296 (1.2)	291 (1.1)
Some education after high school	— (†)	305 (0.9)	304 (0.9)	305 (1.2)	308 (1.0)	308 (1.1)	305 (1.3)	307 (1.5)	308 (1.6)	306 (1.1)	305 (0.9)	306 (0.8)	306 (0.9)
Graduated college	— (†)	317 (1.0)	312 (1.0)	314 (1.4)	316 (1.3)	316 (1.0)	318 (1.4)	317 (1.3)	317 (1.2)	317 (0.9)	315 (0.9)	316 (0.7)	317 (0.8)

—Not available.
†Not applicable.
#Rounds to zero.
[1]In 2004, two assessments were conducted—one using the same format that was used in previous assessments, and one using a revised assessment format that provides accommodations for students with disabilities and for English language learners. The 2004 data in column 11 are for the format that was used in previous assessment years, while the 2004 data in column 12 are for the revised format. In subsequent years, only the revised format was used.
NOTE: Scale ranges from 0 to 500. Students scoring 150 (or higher) know some basic addition and subtraction facts. Students scoring 200 have a considerable understanding of two-digit numbers and know some basic multiplication and division facts. Students scoring 250 have an initial understanding of the four basic operations and are developing an ability to analyze simple logical relations. Students scoring 300 can perform reasoning and problem solving involving fractions, decimals, percents, elementary geometry, and simple algebra. Students scoring 350 can perform reasoning and problem solving involving geometry, algebra, and beginning statistics and probability. Includes public and private schools. For assessment years prior to 2004, accommodations were not permitted. For 2004 (revised format) and later years, includes students tested with accommodations; excludes only those students with disabilities and English language learners who were unable to be tested even with accommodations (1 to 4 percent of all students, depending on age and assessment year). Race categories exclude persons of Hispanic ethnicity. Totals include other racial/ethnic groups not shown separately.
SOURCE: U.S. Department of Education, National Center for Education Statistics, National Assessment of Educational Progress (NAEP), *NAEP 2012 Trends in Academic Progress*; and 2012 NAEP Long-Term Trend Mathematics Assessment, retrieved August 29, 2013, from Long-Term Trend NAEP Data Explorer (http://nces.ed.gov/nationsreportcard/naepdata/). (This table was prepared August 2013.)

Table 222.90. Percentage of students at or above selected National Assessment of Educational Progress (NAEP) mathematics score levels, by age, sex, and race/ethnicity: Selected years, 1978 through 2012

[Standard errors appear in parentheses]

Sex, race/ ethnicity, and year	9-year-olds						13-year-olds						17-year-olds					
	Level 150[1]		Level 200[2]		Level 250[3]		Level 200[2]		Level 250[3]		Level 300[4]		Level 250[3]		Level 300[4]		Level 350[5]	
1	2		3		4		5		6		7		8		9		10	
Total																		
1978	96.7	(0.25)	70.4	(0.92)	19.6	(0.73)	94.6	(0.46)	64.9	(1.18)	18.0	(0.73)	92.0	(0.50)	51.5	(1.14)	7.3	(0.44)
1982	97.1	(0.35)	71.4	(1.18)	18.8	(0.96)	97.7	(0.37)	71.4	(1.18)	17.4	(0.95)	93.0	(0.50)	48.5	(1.28)	5.5	(0.43)
1986	97.9	(0.29)	74.1	(1.24)	20.7	(0.88)	98.6	(0.25)	73.3	(1.59)	15.8	(1.01)	95.6	(0.48)	51.7	(1.43)	6.5	(0.52)
1990	99.1	(0.21)	81.5	(0.96)	27.7	(0.86)	98.5	(0.21)	74.7	(1.03)	17.3	(0.99)	96.0	(0.52)	56.1	(1.43)	7.2	(0.63)
1996	99.1	(0.18)	81.5	(0.76)	29.7	(1.02)	98.8	(0.20)	78.6	(0.87)	20.6	(1.24)	96.8	(0.42)	60.1	(1.72)	7.4	(0.77)
1999	98.9	(0.17)	82.5	(0.84)	30.9	(1.07)	98.7	(0.25)	78.8	(1.02)	23.2	(0.95)	96.8	(0.45)	60.7	(1.63)	8.4	(0.83)
2004	98.7	(0.19)	87.0	(0.77)	40.9	(0.89)	98.1	(0.19)	81.1	(0.98)	27.8	(1.09)	95.8	(0.40)	58.3	(1.12)	6.1	(0.47)
2008	99.0	(0.18)	89.1	(0.69)	44.5	(1.01)	98.2	(0.19)	83.4	(0.63)	30.0	(1.08)	96.0	(0.37)	59.4	(0.87)	6.2	(0.40)
2012	98.7	(0.21)	88.7	(0.69)	46.7	(1.28)	98.5	(0.21)	84.7	(0.71)	34.0	(1.38)	95.7	(0.31)	59.7	(1.22)	7.0	(0.51)
Male																		
1978	96.2	(0.48)	68.9	(0.98)	19.2	(0.64)	93.9	(0.49)	63.9	(1.32)	18.4	(0.85)	93.0	(0.52)	55.1	(1.21)	9.5	(0.57)
1982	96.5	(0.55)	68.8	(1.29)	18.1	(1.06)	97.5	(0.55)	71.3	(1.44)	18.9	(1.18)	93.9	(0.58)	51.9	(1.51)	6.9	(0.70)
1986	98.0	(0.51)	74.0	(1.45)	20.9	(1.10)	98.5	(0.32)	73.8	(1.76)	17.6	(1.12)	96.1	(0.63)	54.6	(1.78)	8.4	(0.91)
1990	99.0	(0.26)	80.6	(1.05)	27.5	(0.96)	98.2	(0.34)	75.1	(1.75)	19.0	(1.24)	95.8	(0.77)	57.6	(1.42)	8.8	(0.76)
1996	99.1	(0.20)	82.5	(1.10)	32.7	(1.74)	98.7	(0.25)	79.8	(1.43)	23.0	(1.64)	97.0	(0.66)	62.7	(1.77)	9.5	(1.32)
1999	98.8	(0.28)	82.6	(0.92)	32.4	(1.25)	98.5	(0.27)	79.3	(1.12)	25.4	(1.19)	96.5	(0.81)	63.1	(2.12)	9.8	(1.09)
2004	98.3	(0.27)	86.1	(0.89)	40.7	(1.03)	97.7	(0.29)	80.5	(1.08)	29.9	(1.27)	95.6	(0.45)	60.8	(1.31)	7.3	(0.68)
2008	99.0	(0.27)	88.4	(0.87)	44.4	(1.18)	98.2	(0.28)	84.3	(0.75)	33.4	(1.29)	96.2	(0.47)	62.9	(0.96)	7.6	(0.61)
2012	98.6	(0.24)	88.0	(0.79)	47.0	(1.47)	98.2	(0.27)	84.7	(0.84)	35.7	(1.55)	95.5	(0.43)	61.5	(1.33)	9.0	(0.75)
Female																		
1978	97.2	(0.27)	72.0	(1.05)	19.9	(1.00)	95.2	(0.49)	65.9	(1.17)	17.5	(0.75)	91.0	(0.57)	48.2	(1.29)	5.2	(0.66)
1982	97.6	(0.33)	74.0	(1.30)	19.6	(1.11)	98.0	(0.27)	71.4	(1.29)	15.9	(1.00)	92.1	(0.56)	45.3	(1.37)	4.1	(0.42)
1986	97.8	(0.38)	74.3	(1.32)	20.6	(1.28)	98.6	(0.31)	72.7	(1.95)	14.1	(1.31)	95.1	(0.65)	48.9	(1.73)	4.7	(0.59)
1990	99.1	(0.26)	82.3	(1.26)	27.9	(1.31)	98.9	(0.18)	74.4	(1.32)	15.7	(1.00)	96.2	(0.84)	54.7	(1.84)	5.6	(0.79)
1996	99.1	(0.36)	80.7	(0.93)	26.7	(1.07)	98.8	(0.27)	77.4	(1.09)	18.4	(1.48)	96.7	(0.57)	57.6	(2.21)	5.3	(0.80)
1999	99.0	(0.19)	82.5	(1.15)	29.4	(1.36)	99.0	(0.40)	78.4	(1.22)	21.0	(1.38)	97.2	(0.40)	58.5	(1.89)	7.1	(1.06)
2004	99.0	(0.22)	87.8	(0.96)	41.1	(1.13)	98.4	(0.25)	81.7	(1.10)	25.7	(1.24)	95.9	(0.58)	55.9	(1.18)	4.9	(0.48)
2008	99.0	(0.21)	89.9	(0.78)	44.6	(1.18)	98.2	(0.25)	82.5	(0.86)	26.7	(1.13)	95.7	(0.43)	55.8	(1.25)	4.6	(0.34)
2012	98.8	(0.29)	89.4	(0.80)	46.5	(1.34)	98.8	(0.23)	84.7	(0.91)	32.2	(1.42)	96.0	(0.37)	57.9	(1.45)	5.1	(0.60)
White																		
1978	98.3	(0.19)	76.3	(1.00)	22.9	(0.87)	97.6	(0.27)	72.9	(0.85)	21.4	(0.73)	95.6	(0.30)	57.6	(1.14)	8.5	(0.48)
1982	98.5	(0.25)	76.8	(1.22)	21.8	(1.13)	99.1	(0.14)	78.3	(0.94)	20.5	(1.00)	96.2	(0.33)	54.7	(1.41)	6.4	(0.54)
1986	98.8	(0.24)	79.6	(1.33)	24.6	(1.03)	99.3	(0.27)	78.9	(1.69)	18.6	(1.17)	98.0	(0.36)	59.1	(1.69)	7.9	(0.68)
1990	99.6	(0.16)	86.9	(0.86)	32.7	(1.04)	99.4	(0.14)	82.0	(1.01)	21.0	(1.23)	97.6	(0.28)	63.2	(1.59)	8.3	(0.73)
1996	99.6	(0.15)	86.6	(0.80)	35.7	(1.38)	99.6	(0.16)	86.4	(1.02)	25.4	(1.50)	98.7	(0.37)	68.7	(2.18)	9.2	(1.02)
1999	99.6	(0.12)	88.6	(0.78)	37.1	(1.35)	99.4	(0.29)	86.7	(0.92)	29.0	(1.26)	98.7	(0.40)	69.9	(1.96)	10.4	(1.07)
2004	99.2	(0.18)	91.9	(0.61)	47.2	(0.97)	99.1	(0.16)	89.3	(0.82)	35.1	(1.21)	97.5	(0.28)	66.8	(1.08)	7.6	(0.63)
2008	99.6	(0.12)	94.0	(0.52)	52.9	(1.29)	98.9	(0.17)	90.4	(0.83)	39.2	(1.60)	98.2	(0.26)	70.5	(1.09)	8.1	(0.55)
2012	99.4	(0.18)	93.2	(0.58)	55.9	(1.54)	99.2	(0.15)	91.6	(0.57)	41.4	(1.65)	97.9	(0.33)	70.3	(1.56)	9.1	(0.71)
Black																		
1978	88.4	(1.01)	42.0	(1.44)	4.1	(0.64)	79.7	(1.48)	28.7	(2.06)	2.3	(0.48)	70.7	(1.73)	16.8	(1.57)	0.5	(—)
1982	90.2	(0.97)	46.1	(2.35)	4.4	(0.81)	90.2	(1.60)	37.9	(2.51)	2.9	(0.96)	76.4	(1.47)	17.1	(1.51)	0.5	(—)
1986	93.9	(1.37)	53.4	(2.47)	5.6	(0.92)	95.4	(0.95)	49.0	(3.70)	4.0	(1.42)	85.6	(2.53)	20.8	(2.83)	0.2	(—)
1990	96.9	(0.88)	60.0	(2.76)	9.4	(1.72)	95.4	(1.10)	48.7	(3.56)	3.9	(1.61)	92.4	(2.20)	32.8	(4.49)	2.0	(1.04)
1996	97.3	(0.84)	65.3	(2.38)	10.0	(1.24)	96.2	(1.27)	53.7	(2.56)	4.8	(1.08)	90.6	(1.33)	31.2	(2.51)	0.9	(—)
1999	96.4	(0.64)	63.3	(2.11)	12.3	(1.48)	96.5	(1.06)	50.8	(4.01)	4.4	(1.37)	88.6	(1.95)	26.6	(2.70)	1.0	(—)
2004	97.1	(0.65)	74.3	(2.61)	22.0	(1.72)	95.3	(0.78)	61.5	(2.47)	9.7	(1.35)	89.1	(1.63)	29.4	(2.07)	0.4	(—)
2008	96.9	(0.86)	75.6	(2.31)	24.6	(1.67)	96.6	(0.68)	67.6	(1.69)	10.2	(1.17)	90.6	(1.42)	31.8	(1.60)	0.8	(0.23)
2012	97.5	(0.66)	77.2	(1.56)	26.3	(2.01)	96.7	(0.66)	67.3	(2.10)	14.2	(1.61)	89.8	(1.03)	33.8	(2.04)	1.1	(0.32)
Hispanic																		
1978	93.0	(1.20)	54.2	(2.80)	9.2	(2.49)	86.4	(0.94)	36.0	(2.92)	4.0	(0.95)	78.3	(2.29)	23.4	(2.67)	1.4	(0.58)
1982	94.3	(1.19)	55.7	(2.26)	7.8	(1.74)	95.9	(0.95)	52.2	(2.48)	6.3	(0.97)	81.4	(1.86)	21.6	(2.16)	0.7	(0.36)
1986	96.4	(1.29)	57.6	(2.95)	7.3	(2.81)	96.9	(1.43)	56.0	(5.01)	5.5	(1.15)	89.3	(2.52)	26.5	(4.48)	1.1	(—)
1990	98.0	(0.76)	68.4	(3.03)	11.3	(3.49)	96.8	(1.06)	56.7	(3.32)	6.4	(1.70)	85.8	(4.18)	30.1	(3.09)	1.9	(0.78)
1996	98.1	(0.73)	67.1	(2.14)	13.8	(2.26)	96.2	(0.78)	58.3	(2.28)	6.7	(1.17)	92.2	(2.24)	40.1	(3.47)	1.8	(—)
1999	98.1	(0.71)	67.5	(2.47)	10.5	(1.63)	97.2	(0.60)	62.9	(2.50)	8.2	(1.37)	93.6	(2.21)	37.7	(4.15)	3.1	(1.12)
2004	98.0	(0.46)	80.5	(2.03)	30.2	(2.17)	96.4	(0.66)	68.5	(1.86)	13.7	(1.44)	92.3	(1.05)	38.1	(2.12)	1.9	(0.60)
2008	98.9	(0.28)	85.1	(1.25)	33.5	(1.46)	97.0	(0.44)	73.3	(1.71)	14.4	(1.09)	92.2	(1.10)	41.1	(1.69)	1.5	(0.41)
2012	98.3	(0.40)	84.7	(1.00)	34.6	(1.22)	97.3	(0.54)	76.4	(1.94)	18.5	(1.45)	92.9	(0.59)	43.3	(1.91)	2.4	(0.44)

—Not available.
[1]Students scoring 150 (or higher) know some basic addition and subtraction facts.
[2]Students scoring 200 (or higher) have a considerable understanding of two-digit numbers and know some basic multiplication and division facts.
[3]Students scoring 250 (or higher) have an initial understanding of the four basic operations and are developing an ability to analyze simple logical relations.
[4]Students scoring 300 (or higher) can perform reasoning and problem solving involving fractions, decimals, percents, elementary geometry, and simple algebra.
[5]Students scoring 350 (or above) can perform reasoning and problem solving involving geometry, algebra, and beginning statistics and probability.
NOTE: The NAEP mathematics scores have been evaluated at certain performance levels, as outlined in footnotes 1 through 5. Scale ranges from 0 to 500. Includes public and pri-

vate schools. For assessment years prior to 2004, accommodations were not permitted. For 2004 and later years, includes students tested with accommodations; excludes only those students with disabilities and English language learners who were unable to be tested even with accommodations (1 to 4 percent of all students, depending on age and assessment year). Race categories exclude persons of Hispanic ethnicity. Totals include other racial/ethnic groups not shown separately.
SOURCE: U.S. Department of Education, National Center for Education Statistics, National Assessment of Educational Progress (NAEP), *NAEP Trends in Academic Progress*, 1996 and 1999; and 2004, 2008, and 2012 Long-Term Trend Mathematics Assessments, retrieved May 4, 2009, and July 20, 2013, from the Long-Term Trend NAEP Data Explorer (http://nces.ed.gov/nationsreportcard/naepdata/). (This table was prepared July 2013.)

Table 222.95. National Assessment of Educational Progress (NAEP) mathematics performance of 17-year-olds, by highest mathematics course taken, sex, and race/ethnicity: Selected years, 1978 through 2012

[Standard errors appear in parentheses]

Year, sex, and race/ethnicity	Percent of students	Average scale score by highest mathematics course taken						Percent of students at or above score levels			
		All students	Prealgebra or general mathematics	Algebra I	Geometry	Algebra II	Precalculus or calculus	200	250	300	350
1	2	3	4	5	6	7	8	9	10	11	12
1978											
All students	100 (†)	300 (1.0)	267 (0.8)	286 (0.7)	307 (0.7)	321 (0.7)	334 (1.4)	100 (†)	92 (0.5)	52 (1.1)	7 (0.4)
Sex											
Male	49 (0.5)	304 (1.0)	269 (1.0)	289 (0.9)	310 (1.0)	325 (0.8)	337 (2.0)	100 (†)	93 (0.5)	55 (1.2)	10 (0.6)
Female	51 (0.5)	297 (1.0)	264 (0.9)	284 (1.0)	304 (0.8)	318 (0.9)	329 (1.8)	100 (†)	91 (0.6)	48 (1.3)	5 (0.7)
Race/ethnicity											
White	83 (1.3)	306 (0.9)	272 (0.6)	291 (0.6)	310 (0.6)	325 (0.6)	338 (1.1)	100 (†)	96 (0.3)	58 (1.1)	8 (0.5)
Black	12 (1.1)	268 (1.3)	247 (1.6)	264 (1.5)	281 (1.9)	292 (1.4)	297 (6.5)	99 (0.3)	71 (1.7)	17 (1.6)	# (†)
Hispanic	4 (0.5)	276 (2.3)	256 (2.3)	273 (2.8)	294 (4.4)	303 (2.9)	‡ (†)	99 (0.4)	78 (2.3)	23 (2.7)	1 (0.6)
Other[1]	1 (0.1)	313 (3.3)	‡ (†)	‡ (†)	‡ (†)	323 (2.9)	‡ (†)	100 (†)	94 (2.6)	65 (4.9)	15 (3.2)
1990											
All students	100 (†)	305 (0.9)	273 (1.1)	288 (1.2)	299 (1.5)	319 (1.0)	344 (2.7)	100 (†)	96 (0.5)	56 (1.4)	7 (0.6)
Sex											
Male	49 (0.9)	306 (1.1)	274 (1.7)	291 (1.6)	302 (1.6)	323 (1.2)	347 (2.4)	100 (†)	96 (0.8)	58 (1.4)	9 (0.8)
Female	51 (0.9)	303 (1.1)	271 (1.8)	285 (1.8)	296 (1.8)	316 (1.1)	340 (4.0)	100 (†)	96 (0.8)	55 (1.8)	6 (0.8)
Race/ethnicity											
White	73 (0.5)	309 (1.0)	277 (1.1)	292 (1.6)	304 (1.3)	323 (0.9)	347 (2.8)	100 (†)	98 (0.3)	63 (1.6)	8 (0.7)
Black	16 (0.3)	289 (2.8)	264 (2.2)	278 (4.0)	285 (3.5)	302 (3.2)	‡ (†)	100 (†)	92 (2.2)	33 (4.5)	2 (1.0)
Hispanic	7 (0.4)	284 (2.9)	‡ (†)	‡ (†)	‡ (†)	306 (3.3)	‡ (†)	100 (†)	86 (4.2)	30 (3.1)	2 (0.8)
Other[1]	4 (0.5)	312 (5.2)	‡ (†)	‡ (†)	‡ (†)	321 (3.8)	‡ (†)	100 (†)	98 (‡)	62 (7.0)	16 (4.3)
1996											
All students	100 (†)	307 (1.2)	269 (1.9)	283 (1.3)	298 (1.3)	316 (1.3)	339 (1.7)	100 (†)	97 (0.4)	60 (1.7)	7 (0.8)
Sex											
Male	50 (1.2)	310 (1.3)	272 (2.5)	286 (1.5)	302 (1.7)	320 (1.7)	342 (2.3)	100 (†)	97 (0.7)	63 (1.8)	9 (1.3)
Female	50 (1.2)	305 (1.4)	265 (2.2)	278 (2.2)	294 (1.5)	313 (1.4)	335 (2.2)	100 (†)	97 (0.6)	58 (2.2)	5 (0.8)
Race/ethnicity											
White	71 (0.6)	313 (1.4)	273 (2.3)	287 (2.0)	304 (1.6)	320 (1.4)	342 (1.9)	100 (†)	99 (0.4)	69 (2.2)	9 (1.0)
Black	15 (0.3)	286 (1.7)	‡ (†)	272 (2.4)	280 (3.0)	299 (2.2)	‡ (†)	100 (†)	91 (1.3)	31 (2.5)	1 (—)
Hispanic	9 (0.7)	292 (2.1)	‡ (†)	‡ (†)	‡ (†)	306 (2.8)	‡ (†)	100 (†)	92 (2.2)	40 (3.5)	2 (—)
Other[1]	4 (0.7)	312 (5.7)	‡ (†)	‡ (†)	‡ (†)	‡ (†)	‡ (†)	100 (†)	97 (1.2)	64 (7.2)	14 (5.0)
1999											
All students	100 (†)	308 (1.0)	278 (2.8)	285 (1.7)	298 (1.2)	315 (0.8)	341 (1.4)	100 (†)	97 (0.5)	61 (1.6)	8 (0.8)
Sex											
Male	48 (1.0)	310 (1.4)	281 (3.2)	288 (2.6)	301 (1.8)	317 (1.3)	343 (1.9)	100 (†)	96 (0.8)	63 (2.1)	10 (1.1)
Female	52 (1.0)	307 (1.0)	274 (3.2)	282 (2.5)	295 (1.3)	314 (1.1)	340 (2.0)	100 (†)	97 (0.4)	58 (1.9)	7 (1.1)
Race/ethnicity											
White	72 (0.5)	315 (1.1)	282 (3.4)	290 (2.2)	303 (1.5)	320 (0.9)	343 (1.5)	100 (†)	99 (0.4)	70 (2.0)	10 (1.1)
Black	15 (0.4)	283 (1.5)	‡ (†)	267 (2.9)	281 (2.5)	293 (1.4)	‡ (†)	100 (†)	89 (2.0)	27 (2.7)	1 (—)
Hispanic	10 (0.5)	293 (2.5)	‡ (†)	‡ (†)	‡ (†)	308 (3.0)	‡ (†)	100 (†)	94 (2.2)	38 (4.1)	3 (1.1)
Other[1]	4 (0.2)	320 (4.0)	‡ (†)	‡ (†)	‡ (†)	320 (4.4)	‡ (†)	100 (†)	100 (†)	76 (6.3)	14 (4.1)
2008											
All students	100 (†)	306 (0.6)	270 (1.9)	280 (1.1)	295 (0.8)	307 (0.7)	333 (0.8)	— (†)	96 (0.4)	59 (0.9)	6 (0.4)
Sex								— (†)			
Male	50 (0.5)	309 (0.7)	273 (2.9)	283 (1.5)	300 (0.8)	310 (0.8)	336 (1.1)	— (†)	96 (0.5)	63 (1.0)	8 (0.6)
Female	50 (0.5)	303 (0.8)	267 (2.8)	276 (1.6)	289 (1.0)	303 (0.8)	331 (0.9)	— (†)	96 (0.4)	56 (1.3)	5 (0.3)
Race/ethnicity								— (†)			
White	59 (1.5)	314 (0.7)	275 (2.3)	287 (1.3)	301 (0.9)	314 (0.8)	337 (0.8)	— (†)	98 (0.3)	71 (1.1)	8 (0.5)
Black	14 (1.4)	287 (1.2)	‡ (†)	266 (2.6)	282 (1.6)	291 (1.5)	312 (2.6)	— (†)	91 (1.4)	32 (1.6)	1 (0.2)
Hispanic	19 (1.2)	293 (1.1)	261 (3.2)	274 (2.3)	289 (1.3)	296 (1.2)	320 (1.9)	— (†)	92 (1.1)	41 (1.7)	1 (0.4)
Other[1]	7 (0.5)	316 (1.8)	‡ (†)	‡ (†)	297 (2.8)	311 (1.9)	340 (2.2)	— (†)	98 (0.7)	71 (2.2)	13 (1.8)
2012											
All students	100 (†)	306 (0.8)	263 (3.6)	272 (1.5)	290 (1.3)	305 (1.0)	334 (0.8)	— (†)	96 (0.3)	60 (1.2)	7 (0.5)
Sex											
Male	49 (0.5)	308 (1.0)	266 (4.4)	276 (1.7)	293 (1.6)	308 (1.1)	337 (1.2)	— (†)	95 (0.4)	62 (1.3)	9 (0.8)
Female	51 (0.5)	304 (0.8)	‡ (†)	267 (2.0)	287 (1.3)	302 (1.1)	331 (1.0)	— (†)	96 (0.4)	58 (1.4)	5 (0.6)
Race/ethnicity											
White	56 (1.6)	314 (1.0)	268 (5.2)	278 (2.1)	298 (1.8)	311 (1.2)	337 (0.8)	— (†)	98 (0.3)	70 (1.6)	9 (0.7)
Black	13 (1.3)	288 (1.3)	‡ (†)	260 (2.7)	280 (1.6)	290 (1.0)	317 (2.5)	— (†)	90 (1.0)	34 (2.0)	1 (0.3)
Hispanic	22 (1.5)	294 (1.1)	‡ (†)	269 (2.5)	284 (1.4)	296 (1.0)	324 (2.0)	— (†)	93 (0.6)	43 (1.9)	2 (0.4)
Other[1]	8 (0.8)	318 (2.4)	‡ (†)	‡ (†)	293 (3.7)	308 (2.4)	338 (2.1)	— (†)	98 (0.8)	73 (3.0)	14 (2.3)

—Not available.
†Not applicable.
#Rounds to zero.
‡Reporting standards not met (too few cases for a reliable estimate).
[1]Includes Asians/Pacific Islanders and American Indians/Alaska Natives.
NOTE: Scale ranges from 0 to 500. Students scoring 200 (or higher) have a considerable understanding of two-digit numbers and know some basic multiplication and division facts. Students scoring 250 have an initial understanding of the four basic operations and are developing an ability to analyze simple logical relations. Students scoring 300 can perform reasoning and problem solving involving fractions, decimals, percents, elementary geometry, and simple algebra. Students scoring 350 can perform reasoning and problem solving involving geometry, alge-

bra, and beginning statistics and probability. Includes public and private schools. For assessment years prior to 2004, accommodations were not permitted. For 2004 and later years, includes students tested with accommodations; excludes only those students with disabilities and English language learners who were unable to be tested even with accommodations (1 to 4 percent of all students, depending on age and assessment year). Race categories exclude persons of Hispanic ethnicity. Detail may not sum to totals because of rounding.
SOURCE: U.S. Department of Education, National Center for Education Statistics, National Assessment of Educational Progress (NAEP), NAEP Trends in Academic Progress, 1996 and 1999; and 2004, 2008, and 2012 Long-Term Trend Mathematics Assessments, retrieved June 4, 2009, and August 12, 2013, from the Long-Term Trend NAEP Data Explorer (http://nces.ed.gov/nationsreportcard/naepdata/). (This table was prepared August 2013.)

Table 223.10. Average National Assessment of Educational Progress (NAEP) science scale score, standard deviation, and percentage of students attaining science achievement levels, by grade level, selected student and school characteristics, and percentile: 2009 and 2011

[Standard errors appear in parentheses]

Selected characteristic, percentile, and achievement level	Grade 4 — 2009			Grade 8 — 2009			Grade 8 — 2011			Grade 12 — 2009		
	Total, all students	Male	Female	Total, all students	Male	Female	Total, all students	Male	Female	Total, all students	Male	Female
	2	3	4	5	6	7	8	9	10	11	12	13
	(0.3)	(0.3)	(0.3)	(0.3)	(0.4)	(0.3)	(0.3)	(0.3)	(0.3)	(0.8)	(0.9)	(0.9)
Average science scale score[1]												
All students	150 (0.3)	151 (0.3)	149 (0.3)	150 (0.3)	152 (0.4)	148 (0.3)	152 (0.3)	154 (0.3)	149 (0.3)	150 (0.8)	153 (0.9)	147 (0.9)
Race/ethnicity												
White	163 (0.2)	164 (0.3)	162 (0.3)	162 (0.2)	164 (0.3)	160 (0.3)	163 (0.2)	166 (0.7)	161 (0.3)	159 (0.7)	162 (0.9)	156 (0.8)
Black	127 (0.4)	126 (0.6)	128 (0.5)	126 (0.4)	125 (0.6)	126 (0.5)	129 (0.5)	130 (0.7)	128 (0.6)	125 (1.2)	127 (1.6)	123 (1.5)
Hispanic	131 (0.5)	132 (0.7)	130 (0.6)	132 (0.6)	134 (0.8)	130 (0.7)	137 (0.5)	140 (0.8)	134 (0.8)	134 (1.3)	138 (2.3)	130 (1.5)
Asian/Pacific Islander	160 (1.2)	159 (1.4)	160 (1.4)	160 (1.0)	162 (1.3)	158 (1.3)	159 (1.3)	161 (1.6)	157 (1.7)	164 (3.0)	161 (2.9)	166 (3.8)
American Indian/Alaska Native	135 (1.3)	135 (1.5)	135 (1.8)	141 (1.4)	141 (1.8)	133 (2.0)	141 (1.4)	143 (2.1)	139 (1.5)	144 (3.7)	‡ (†)	‡ (†)
Highest education level of either parent												
Did not finish high school	—	—	—	131 (0.6)	135 (1.0)	128 (0.7)	132 (0.7)	136 (1.2)	130 (1.0)	131 (1.4)	136 (1.9)	128 (1.8)
Graduated high school	—	—	—	139 (0.4)	141 (0.5)	137 (0.5)	138 (0.4)	143 (0.7)	138 (0.6)	138 (1.2)	140 (1.5)	136 (1.4)
Some education after high school	—	—	—	152 (0.4)	154 (0.5)	150 (0.4)	147 (0.3)	156 (0.4)	151 (0.6)	147 (0.9)	150 (1.3)	144 (1.1)
Graduated college	—	—	—	161 (0.4)	162 (0.5)	159 (0.3)	162 (0.3)	164 (0.4)	160 (0.4)	161 (0.7)	163 (0.9)	159 (1.0)
Eligibility for free or reduced-price lunch												
Eligible	134 (0.3)	134 (0.4)	133 (0.3)	135 (0.4)	135 (0.5)	131 (0.4)	137 (0.3)	139 (0.4)	135 (0.4)	132 (1.0)	135 (1.1)	130 (1.1)
Not eligible	163 (0.3)	164 (0.3)	163 (0.3)	163 (0.3)	163 (0.4)	159 (0.4)	164 (0.3)	166 (0.4)	161 (0.4)	157 (0.9)	159 (1.1)	154 (1.0)
Unknown	162 (1.3)	163 (1.7)	161 (1.3)	167 (1.2)	167 (1.4)	161 (1.2)	164 (1.6)	168 (2.2)	159 (2.2)	156 (2.7)	156 (3.6)	156 (3.0)
School type												
Public	149 (0.3)	149 (0.3)	148 (0.3)	151 (0.3)	151 (0.4)	147 (0.3)	151 (0.2)	153 (0.3)	148 (0.3)	—	—	—
Private	163 (0.9)	165 (1.2)	162 (1.0)	167 (0.9)	167 (1.2)	161 (1.0)	163 (1.4)	168 (1.9)	158 (1.9)	—	—	—
School locale												
City	142 (0.6)	142 (0.6)	142 (0.7)	144 (0.6)	144 (0.7)	141 (0.7)	144 (0.6)	146 (0.8)	142 (0.7)	146 (1.8)	148 (1.6)	144 (2.2)
Suburban	154 (0.4)	154 (0.6)	153 (0.4)	155 (0.5)	155 (0.6)	152 (0.5)	158 (0.5)	158 (0.5)	153 (0.6)	154 (1.4)	157 (1.8)	150 (1.5)
Town	150 (0.6)	151 (0.8)	149 (0.6)	152 (1.0)	152 (1.1)	147 (0.9)	153 (0.7)	155 (0.9)	150 (0.8)	150 (1.2)	153 (1.5)	146 (1.6)
Rural	155 (0.5)	156 (0.7)	154 (0.5)	156 (0.4)	156 (0.5)	152 (0.5)	156 (0.5)	159 (0.6)	153 (0.6)	150 (1.2)	153 (1.5)	146 (1.4)
Percentile[2]												
10th	103 (0.6)	103 (0.6)	104 (0.5)	103 (0.6)	103 (0.7)	103 (0.6)	106 (0.5)	107 (0.9)	105 (0.7)	104 (1.2)	106 (1.8)	103 (1.1)
25th	128 (0.4)	128 (0.5)	128 (0.4)	130 (0.4)	130 (0.5)	127 (0.5)	131 (0.4)	133 (0.5)	129 (0.6)	126 (0.8)	128 (1.0)	125 (1.1)
50th	153 (0.3)	154 (0.4)	152 (0.4)	156 (0.3)	156 (0.4)	151 (0.3)	155 (0.3)	158 (0.5)	152 (0.3)	151 (1.1)	154 (1.4)	148 (1.1)
75th	175 (0.3)	176 (0.4)	174 (0.4)	178 (0.2)	178 (0.4)	172 (0.2)	176 (0.4)	179 (0.4)	173 (0.4)	174 (1.1)	178 (1.2)	171 (1.1)
90th	192 (0.3)	194 (0.4)	191 (0.5)	195 (0.3)	195 (0.2)	188 (0.4)	193 (0.4)	196 (0.4)	189 (0.5)	194 (1.0)	198 (0.9)	190 (1.4)
Standard deviation of the science scale score[3]												
All students	35 (0.2)	36 (0.2)	34 (0.2)	36 (0.2)	36 (0.2)	34 (0.2)	34 (0.2)	35 (0.2)	33 (0.3)	35 (0.4)	36 (0.5)	34 (0.5)
Percent of students attaining science achievement levels												
Below Basic[4]	28 (0.3)	27 (0.4)	28 (0.3)	37 (0.4)	35 (0.5)	38 (0.4)	35 (0.3)	32 (0.4)	37 (0.5)	40 (1.0)	37 (1.1)	42 (1.3)
At or above Basic	72 (0.3)	73 (0.4)	72 (0.3)	63 (0.4)	65 (0.5)	62 (0.4)	65 (0.3)	68 (0.4)	63 (0.5)	60 (1.0)	63 (1.1)	58 (1.3)
At or above Proficient[5]	34 (0.3)	35 (0.3)	32 (0.3)	30 (0.3)	34 (0.4)	27 (0.3)	32 (0.4)	35 (0.5)	28 (0.5)	21 (0.8)	24 (1.0)	18 (0.8)
At Advanced[6]	1 (0.1)	1 (0.1)	1 (0.1)	2 (0.1)	2 (0.1)	1 (0.1)	2 (0.1)	2 (0.1)	1 (0.1)	1 (0.2)	2 (0.3)	0 (0.2)

—Not available.
†Not applicable.
‡Reporting standards not met (too few cases for a reliable estimate).
[1]Scale ranges from 0 to 300 for all three grades, but scores cannot be compared across grades. For example, the average score of 163 for White 4th-graders does not denote higher performance than the score of 159 for White 12th-graders.
[2]The percentile represents a specific point on the percentage distribution of all students ranked by their science score from low to high. For example, 10 percent of students scored at or below the 10th percentile score, while 90 percent of students scored above it.
[3]The standard deviation provides an indication of how much the test scores varied. The lower the standard deviation, the closer the scores were clustered around the average score. About two-thirds of the student scores can be expected to fall within the range of one standard deviation above and one standard deviation below the average score. For example, the average score for all 4th-graders was 150, and the standard deviation was 35. This means that we would expect about two-thirds of the students to have scores between 185 (one standard deviation above the average) and 115 (one standard deviation below). Standard errors also must be taken into account when making comparisons of these ranges. For a discussion of standard errors, see Appendix A: Guide to Sources.
[4]Basic denotes partial mastery of the knowledge and skills that are fundamental for proficient work.
[5]Proficient represents solid academic performance. Students reaching this level have demonstrated competency over challenging subject matter.
[6]Advanced signifies superior performance.
NOTE: In 2011, only 8th-grade students were assessed in science. Includes students tested with accommodations (7 to 11 percent of all students, depending on grade level and year); excludes only those students with disabilities and English language learners who were unable to be tested even with accommodations (2 to 3 percent of all students). Race categories exclude persons of Hispanic ethnicity.
SOURCE: U.S. Department of Education, National Center for Education Statistics, National Assessment of Educational Progress (NAEP), 2011 Science Assessment, retrieved August 1, 2012, from the Main NAEP Data Explorer (http://nces.ed.gov/nationsreportcard/naepdata/). (This table was prepared August 2012.)

Table 223.20. Average National Assessment of Educational Progress (NAEP) science scale scores of 8th-grade public school students, by race/ethnicity and state: 2009 and 2011

[Standard errors appear in parentheses]

State	2009 Total, all students	2009 White	2009 Black	2009 Hispanic	2009 Asian/Pacific Islander	2011 Total, all students	2011 White	2011 Black	2011 Hispanic	2011 Asian/Pacific Islander
1	2	3	4	5	6	7	8	9	10	11
United States	149 (0.3)	161 (0.2)	125 (0.4)	131 (0.6)	159 (1.0)	151 (0.2)	163 (0.2)	128 (0.5)	136 (0.5)	159 (1.2)
Alabama	139 (1.1)	152 (1.1)	115 (1.8)	129 (3.5)	‡ (†)	140 (1.4)	152 (1.3)	118 (1.4)	136 (3.6)	‡ (†)
Alaska	— (†)	— (†)	— (†)	— (†)	— (†)	153 (0.7)	166 (0.9)	133 (3.2)	147 (2.7)	145 (2.2)
Arizona	141 (1.3)	157 (1.3)	126 (3.2)	127 (1.5)	159 (5.5)	144 (1.3)	158 (1.3)	128 (2.9)	132 (1.6)	‡ (†)
Arkansas	144 (1.3)	154 (0.9)	111 (2.1)	134 (3.0)	‡ (†)	148 (1.1)	158 (1.0)	119 (2.1)	138 (2.1)	‡ (†)
California	137 (1.4)	157 (2.0)	122 (2.8)	122 (1.3)	154 (2.2)	140 (1.3)	159 (1.6)	124 (3.4)	128 (1.4)	157 (2.8)
Colorado	156 (1.0)	166 (1.0)	135 (3.7)	137 (1.6)	161 (3.7)	161 (1.3)	171 (1.4)	149 (3.7)	141 (1.8)	162 (4.5)
Connecticut	155 (0.9)	164 (0.8)	126 (2.3)	128 (1.8)	169 (3.5)	155 (1.1)	165 (1.0)	128 (2.3)	129 (2.5)	170 (4.2)
Delaware	148 (0.6)	159 (0.9)	133 (1.0)	141 (2.2)	160 (4.3)	150 (0.6)	161 (0.8)	134 (1.3)	139 (2.0)	168 (3.3)
District of Columbia	— (†)	— (†)	— (†)	— (†)	— (†)	112 (1.0)	174 (3.3)	107 (1.1)	116 (2.6)	‡ (†)
Florida	146 (1.0)	158 (1.4)	126 (1.4)	139 (1.2)	163 (4.1)	148 (1.1)	161 (1.1)	127 (2.0)	144 (1.5)	161 (4.5)
Georgia	147 (1.0)	161 (1.2)	129 (1.3)	137 (2.2)	172 (2.7)	151 (1.4)	166 (1.6)	133 (1.8)	143 (3.1)	168 (3.9)
Hawaii	139 (0.7)	153 (1.5)	133 (5.0)	148 (4.3)	136 (1.0)	142 (0.7)	157 (1.8)	‡ (†)	144 (3.3)	139 (0.9)
Idaho	158 (0.9)	162 (0.9)	‡ (†)	137 (1.4)	‡ (†)	159 (0.7)	163 (0.7)	‡ (†)	139 (1.8)	‡ (†)
Illinois	148 (1.4)	162 (1.2)	118 (1.5)	131 (1.5)	167 (3.2)	147 (1.0)	161 (1.1)	120 (1.9)	135 (1.2)	163 (4.4)
Indiana	152 (1.2)	159 (1.0)	126 (3.9)	135 (3.5)	‡ (†)	153 (0.9)	160 (1.0)	125 (2.7)	136 (3.7)	‡ (†)
Iowa	156 (0.9)	160 (0.8)	127 (3.5)	133 (3.2)	‡ (†)	157 (0.8)	161 (0.8)	128 (3.7)	143 (3.1)	‡ (†)
Kansas	— (†)	— (†)	— (†)	— (†)	— (†)	156 (0.8)	163 (0.8)	129 (3.2)	134 (2.1)	156 (5.2)
Kentucky	156 (0.8)	159 (0.9)	137 (1.8)	145 (3.5)	‡ (†)	157 (0.8)	160 (0.9)	135 (1.7)	149 (3.0)	‡ (†)
Louisiana	139 (1.7)	155 (1.5)	120 (1.9)	‡ (†)	‡ (†)	143 (1.7)	156 (1.6)	125 (2.1)	142 (5.2)	‡ (†)
Maine	158 (0.8)	159 (0.8)	126 (4.5)	‡ (†)	‡ (†)	160 (0.5)	160 (0.6)	‡ (†)	‡ (†)	‡ (†)
Maryland	148 (1.1)	164 (1.2)	127 (1.5)	136 (2.8)	169 (2.5)	152 (1.2)	167 (1.2)	131 (1.8)	142 (2.2)	164 (4.3)
Massachusetts	160 (1.1)	167 (1.1)	132 (2.6)	131 (2.7)	168 (4.1)	161 (1.1)	169 (1.1)	133 (4.3)	130 (2.6)	170 (4.1)
Michigan	153 (1.4)	162 (1.0)	121 (2.1)	139 (3.4)	‡ (†)	157 (1.0)	165 (0.8)	124 (2.8)	146 (3.3)	166 (6.9)
Minnesota	159 (1.0)	166 (0.9)	128 (2.8)	132 (3.7)	141 (3.0)	161 (1.0)	168 (1.0)	129 (2.5)	137 (4.0)	149 (3.9)
Mississippi	132 (1.2)	150 (1.2)	114 (1.1)	‡ (†)	‡ (†)	137 (1.3)	156 (1.1)	119 (1.4)	‡ (†)	‡ (†)
Missouri	156 (1.1)	161 (0.9)	129 (2.5)	150 (3.8)	167 (4.7)	156 (1.1)	162 (0.8)	130 (3.5)	‡ (†)	‡ (†)
Montana	162 (0.7)	166 (0.7)	‡ (†)	155 (3.3)	‡ (†)	163 (0.7)	167 (0.7)	‡ (†)	‡ (†)	‡ (†)
Nebraska	— (†)	— (†)	— (†)	— (†)	— (†)	157 (0.7)	164 (0.7)	126 (3.5)	135 (1.9)	‡ (†)
Nevada	141 (0.7)	153 (0.9)	127 (2.4)	129 (1.0)	148 (2.4)	144 (0.8)	157 (1.3)	123 (3.3)	133 (1.1)	154 (2.6)
New Hampshire	160 (0.8)	161 (0.8)	‡ (†)	131 (4.2)	‡ (†)	162 (0.7)	164 (0.6)	‡ (†)	137 (4.3)	‡ (†)
New Jersey	155 (1.5)	165 (1.0)	127 (3.3)	138 (2.7)	174 (2.6)	155 (1.2)	166 (1.2)	131 (2.5)	134 (1.9)	173 (2.8)
New Mexico	143 (1.4)	163 (1.4)	‡ (†)	135 (1.4)	‡ (†)	145 (0.8)	161 (1.4)	‡ (†)	139 (0.8)	‡ (†)
New York	149 (1.2)	164 (1.0)	123 (1.8)	125 (1.7)	161 (2.3)	149 (1.0)	163 (1.3)	130 (2.2)	129 (1.7)	154 (2.6)
North Carolina	144 (1.3)	158 (1.3)	121 (1.6)	132 (2.3)	165 (7.1)	148 (1.1)	160 (1.1)	125 (1.8)	138 (2.4)	160 (6.5)
North Dakota	162 (0.5)	166 (0.6)	‡ (†)	‡ (†)	‡ (†)	164 (0.7)	168 (0.8)	‡ (†)	‡ (†)	‡ (†)
Ohio	158 (1.0)	164 (0.9)	126 (2.1)	140 (4.6)	‡ (†)	158 (1.0)	165 (1.0)	132 (2.6)	151 (5.3)	‡ (†)
Oklahoma	146 (0.9)	155 (1.0)	124 (2.6)	127 (2.6)	‡ (†)	148 (1.1)	156 (1.0)	126 (3.6)	135 (2.8)	‡ (†)
Oregon	154 (1.0)	160 (1.1)	135 (4.1)	130 (1.8)	160 (3.5)	155 (0.9)	162 (1.0)	‡ (†)	135 (1.4)	159 (4.3)
Pennsylvania	154 (1.1)	162 (0.9)	123 (2.0)	121 (4.4)	159 (4.1)	151 (1.3)	163 (0.9)	120 (2.3)	118 (4.8)	163 (4.9)
Rhode Island	146 (0.6)	155 (0.8)	125 (2.6)	119 (1.9)	146 (5.3)	149 (0.7)	161 (0.7)	122 (3.4)	120 (1.9)	151 (4.6)
South Carolina	143 (1.6)	158 (1.1)	124 (1.7)	129 (4.2)	‡ (†)	149 (1.0)	163 (1.0)	128 (1.6)	139 (3.0)	‡ (†)
South Dakota	161 (0.6)	165 (0.6)	141 (5.5)	135 (4.1)	‡ (†)	162 (0.5)	166 (0.6)	‡ (†)	151 (4.1)	‡ (†)
Tennessee	148 (1.2)	157 (0.9)	122 (2.0)	139 (3.8)	‡ (†)	150 (1.0)	160 (0.9)	121 (1.6)	137 (3.1)	‡ (†)
Texas	150 (1.2)	167 (1.4)	133 (2.5)	141 (1.5)	170 (3.6)	153 (1.0)	167 (1.2)	137 (2.3)	146 (1.3)	172 (4.3)
Utah	158 (1.0)	164 (1.1)	‡ (†)	129 (1.7)	147 (3.9)	161 (0.8)	167 (0.8)	‡ (†)	137 (2.0)	153 (4.7)
Vermont	— (†)	— (†)	— (†)	— (†)	— (†)	163 (0.8)	164 (0.9)	‡ (†)	‡ (†)	‡ (†)
Virginia	156 (1.1)	166 (1.1)	135 (2.0)	144 (2.2)	168 (3.1)	160 (1.0)	169 (1.3)	138 (1.7)	145 (2.8)	172 (2.4)
Washington	155 (1.0)	161 (1.1)	135 (3.7)	132 (2.3)	157 (3.0)	156 (0.9)	163 (1.0)	133 (3.1)	141 (2.5)	156 (2.8)
West Virginia	145 (0.8)	146 (0.8)	127 (2.8)	‡ (†)	‡ (†)	149 (1.0)	150 (1.0)	136 (2.7)	‡ (†)	‡ (†)
Wisconsin	157 (0.9)	165 (0.8)	120 (1.5)	134 (3.9)	152 (3.5)	159 (1.0)	166 (0.9)	121 (3.1)	140 (4.8)	149 (4.7)
Wyoming	158 (0.7)	162 (0.7)	‡ (†)	137 (1.8)	‡ (†)	160 (0.5)	164 (0.6)	‡ (†)	143 (2.0)	‡ (†)
Department of Defense dependents schools	162 (0.7)	170 (1.0)	144 (1.4)	155 (2.0)	160 (2.3)	161 (0.8)	169 (1.1)	143 (2.2)	158 (2.5)	155 (3.2)

—Not available.
†Not applicable.
‡Reporting standards not met (too few cases for a reliable estimate).
NOTE: Scale ranges from 0 to 300. Includes students tested with accommodations (10 percent of all students in 2009 and 9 percent of all students in 2011); excludes only those students with disabilities and English language learners who were unable to be tested even with accommodations (2 percent of all students in both years). Race categories exclude persons of Hispanic ethnicity. Totals include other racial/ethnic groups not shown separately.
SOURCE: U.S. Department of Education, National Center for Education Statistics, National Assessment of Educational Progress (NAEP), 2009 and 2011 Science Assessment, retrieved August 12, 2012, from the Main NAEP Data Explorer (http://nces.ed.gov/nationsreportcard/naepdata/). (This table was prepared August 2012.)

Table 223.25. Average National Assessment of Educational Progress (NAEP) science scale scores of 8th-graders with various attitudes toward science and percentage reporting these attitudes, by selected student characteristics: 2011

[Standard errors appear in parentheses]

Student characteristic	Take science only because it will help in future				Like science				Take science only because required			
	Strongly disagree	Disagree	Agree	Strongly agree	Strongly disagree	Disagree	Agree	Strongly agree	Strongly disagree	Disagree	Agree	Strongly agree
1	2	3	4	5	6	7	8	9	10	11	12	13
Average scale score[1]												
All students	154 (0.5)	161 (0.4)	150 (0.3)	143 (0.5)	136 (0.6)	144 (0.5)	155 (0.3)	166 (0.5)	164 (0.5)	160 (0.4)	146 (0.3)	138 (0.5)
Sex												
Male	156 (0.7)	163 (0.4)	153 (0.4)	145 (0.7)	136 (0.9)	146 (0.7)	157 (0.4)	168 (0.7)	166 (0.6)	162 (0.5)	148 (0.5)	140 (0.7)
Female	152 (0.9)	158 (0.5)	148 (0.5)	141 (0.6)	136 (0.8)	144 (0.6)	153 (0.5)	162 (0.7)	161 (0.7)	158 (0.6)	144 (0.5)	137 (0.6)
Race/ethnicity												
White	164 (0.6)	169 (0.4)	161 (0.3)	158 (0.6)	148 (0.6)	156 (0.5)	165 (0.3)	175 (0.5)	174 (0.5)	170 (0.4)	157 (0.4)	150 (0.6)
Black	132 (1.3)	137 (1.3)	130 (0.8)	123 (0.9)	120 (1.1)	124 (0.8)	131 (0.6)	141 (1.2)	139 (1.6)	137 (0.7)	126 (0.7)	121 (0.8)
Hispanic	140 (1.6)	145 (1.0)	135 (0.7)	132 (1.0)	124 (1.3)	129 (1.1)	140 (0.6)	151 (1.3)	149 (1.1)	144 (0.9)	132 (0.9)	129 (0.9)
Asian	165 (2.8)	170 (1.9)	159 (2.1)	156 (2.0)	140 (3.3)	151 (2.2)	162 (1.7)	177 (2.1)	176 (2.4)	167 (3.4)	155 (2.0)	144 (2.3)
Pacific Islander	143 (6.5)	146 (3.9)	139 (2.2)	137 (5.1)	117 (5.3)	130 (3.4)	147 (3.1)	153 (3.6)	150 (4.8)	150 (3.4)	134 (3.8)	126 (3.4)
American Indian/Alaska Native	140 (4.4)	151 (2.2)	141 (1.9)	134 (2.2)	126 (3.2)	138 (2.3)	146 (2.2)	150 (3.1)	149 (2.0)	150 (2.0)	140 (2.7)	132 (3.2)
Two or more races	158 (5.0)	161 (1.8)	153 (1.6)	155 (4.2)	139 (4.6)	147 (2.3)	159 (1.2)	170 (3.6)	167 (3.9)	163 (1.7)	152 (2.2)	139 (2.6)
Eligibility for free or reduced-price lunch												
Eligible	140 (0.7)	146 (0.5)	136 (0.4)	130 (0.6)	125 (0.7)	131 (0.7)	140 (0.4)	149 (0.6)	147 (0.5)	145 (0.5)	133 (0.5)	128 (0.6)
Not eligible	165 (0.7)	170 (0.4)	162 (0.4)	158 (0.6)	147 (0.6)	156 (0.6)	166 (0.4)	176 (0.5)	175 (0.6)	170 (0.5)	158 (0.5)	150 (0.5)
Unknown	168 (3.9)	170 (2.3)	161 (2.4)	154 (3.7)	147 (5.4)	156 (2.6)	166 (1.9)	177 (3.4)	174 (3.1)	157 (2.5)	157 (2.4)	147 (5.1)
Parents' highest level of education												
Did not finish high school	134 (1.9)	142 (1.3)	130 (1.4)	128 (1.5)	125 (1.8)	126 (1.6)	136 (0.9)	144 (1.8)	140 (1.6)	140 (1.3)	128 (1.2)	129 (1.5)
Graduated high school	143 (1.4)	148 (0.9)	139 (0.6)	132 (1.1)	129 (1.0)	135 (0.8)	143 (0.6)	153 (1.0)	151 (1.2)	148 (0.7)	136 (0.7)	132 (0.7)
Some education after high school	156 (1.3)	160 (0.8)	152 (0.6)	145 (0.9)	140 (1.3)	146 (0.9)	156 (0.5)	165 (1.0)	164 (0.9)	160 (0.8)	149 (0.7)	141 (0.9)
Graduated college	165 (0.8)	170 (0.4)	161 (0.4)	153 (0.7)	145 (0.9)	155 (0.6)	164 (0.4)	174 (0.5)	173 (0.6)	169 (0.4)	156 (0.5)	146 (0.8)
Percent of students												
All students	12 (0.2)	32 (0.3)	39 (0.2)	18 (0.2)	12 (0.2)	19 (0.3)	50 (0.3)	19 (0.3)	18 (0.2)	34 (0.3)	30 (0.2)	17 (0.2)
Sex												
Male	14 (0.3)	33 (0.4)	36 (0.4)	16 (0.3)	11 (0.2)	16 (0.3)	51 (0.4)	22 (0.4)	21 (0.3)	35 (0.4)	27 (0.3)	17 (0.2)
Female	10 (0.2)	30 (0.4)	41 (0.4)	19 (0.3)	12 (0.3)	23 (0.4)	49 (0.4)	16 (0.3)	15 (0.2)	34 (0.4)	33 (0.4)	18 (0.3)
Race/ethnicity												
White	13 (0.2)	36 (0.4)	37 (0.4)	13 (0.2)	10 (0.2)	19 (0.3)	50 (0.4)	20 (0.3)	20 (0.2)	37 (0.4)	28 (0.3)	16 (0.2)
Black	12 (0.5)	22 (0.7)	37 (0.7)	29 (0.6)	16 (0.5)	20 (0.6)	46 (0.6)	19 (0.6)	17 (0.7)	28 (0.6)	30 (0.7)	25 (0.5)
Hispanic	11 (0.4)	27 (0.6)	42 (0.6)	20 (0.6)	13 (0.5)	21 (0.7)	50 (0.6)	16 (0.5)	15 (0.5)	33 (0.6)	35 (0.6)	18 (0.5)
Asian	9 (0.8)	26 (1.4)	42 (1.7)	22 (1.1)	8 (0.8)	16 (0.8)	57 (1.4)	19 (1.1)	19 (0.9)	37 (1.4)	30 (1.4)	14 (0.8)
Pacific Islander	11 (2.5)	26 (3.3)	39 (3.7)	23 (3.3)	15 (2.9)	21 (3.1)	50 (4.3)	15 (2.6)	14 (2.9)	37 (3.9)	30 (2.8)	18 (2.9)
American Indian/Alaska Native	10 (1.2)	27 (1.8)	44 (2.0)	18 (1.1)	14 (1.3)	19 (1.2)	52 (1.6)	15 (1.3)	14 (1.3)	29 (1.5)	37 (1.7)	19 (1.5)
Two or more races	13 (1.4)	33 (2.0)	36 (1.9)	18 (1.7)	14 (1.8)	18 (1.0)	47 (2.0)	21 (1.8)	20 (2.4)	34 (1.9)	28 (1.7)	19 (1.5)
Eligibility for free or reduced-price lunch												
Eligible	12 (0.2)	27 (0.3)	40 (0.3)	21 (0.3)	14 (0.3)	20 (0.3)	49 (0.3)	17 (0.3)	16 (0.3)	31 (0.4)	32 (0.3)	21 (0.3)
Not eligible	12 (0.2)	35 (0.3)	38 (0.3)	15 (0.3)	10 (0.2)	18 (0.3)	51 (0.4)	20 (0.3)	20 (0.3)	37 (0.4)	28 (0.3)	15 (0.2)
Unknown	12 (1.9)	38 (2.9)	35 (2.7)	15 (1.6)	10 (1.2)	20 (2.1)	48 (2.5)	22 (2.1)	22 (2.1)	36 (2.5)	30 (2.4)	12 (1.4)
Parents' highest level of education												
Did not finish high school	12 (0.6)	27 (1.1)	40 (1.0)	20 (0.9)	16 (0.7)	23 (0.9)	45 (1.1)	15 (0.7)	14 (0.6)	29 (0.9)	34 (1.0)	23 (0.9)
Graduated high school	12 (0.4)	31 (0.6)	39 (0.6)	18 (0.5)	13 (0.4)	21 (0.5)	50 (0.6)	16 (0.6)	15 (0.5)	32 (0.6)	32 (0.6)	20 (0.4)
Some education after high school	12 (0.3)	31 (0.5)	39 (0.5)	17 (0.4)	12 (0.4)	20 (0.5)	50 (0.6)	18 (0.5)	18 (0.4)	35 (0.6)	29 (0.5)	18 (0.5)
Graduated college	12 (0.3)	33 (0.4)	38 (0.4)	17 (0.3)	10 (0.3)	18 (0.4)	51 (0.5)	22 (0.3)	21 (0.3)	37 (0.5)	28 (0.4)	15 (0.3)

[1]Scale ranges from 0 to 300.

NOTE: Includes public and private schools. Includes students tested with accommodations (11 percent of all 8th-graders); excludes only those students with disabilities and English language learners who were unable to be tested even with accommodations (2 percent of all 8th-graders). Detail may not sum to totals because of rounding. Race categories exclude persons of Hispanic ethnicity.

SOURCE: U.S. Department of Education, National Center for Education Statistics, National Assessment of Educational Progress (NAEP), 2011 Science Assessment, retrieved November 22, 2013, from the Main NAEP Data Explorer (http://nces.ed.gov/nationsreportcard/naepdata/). (This table was prepared November 2013.)

Table 223.30. Average National Assessment of Educational Progress (NAEP) science scale scores of 12th-graders with various educational goals and attitudes toward science, and percentage reporting these goals and attitudes, by selected student characteristics: 2009

[Standard errors appear in parentheses]

Student characteristic	Educational goals[1]				Like science				Take science only because required			
	Graduate high school	Some education after high school	Graduate college	Go to graduate school	Strongly disagree	Disagree	Agree	Strongly agree	Strongly disagree	Disagree	Agree	Strongly agree
1	2	3	4	5	6	7	8	9	10	11	12	13
Average scale score[2]												
All students	114 (1.9)	131 (1.3)	148 (0.6)	171 (1.0)	132 (1.3)	141 (0.9)	153 (0.9)	172 (1.1)	169 (1.1)	159 (0.9)	142 (0.9)	134 (1.0)
Sex												
Male	121 (2.6)	134 (1.8)	152 (0.8)	177 (1.3)	130 (1.7)	141 (1.4)	155 (1.2)	175 (1.3)	172 (1.4)	162 (1.2)	143 (1.2)	134 (1.3)
Female	103 (2.6)	127 (1.9)	143 (0.8)	166 (1.2)	133 (1.8)	141 (1.1)	150 (0.9)	169 (1.8)	165 (1.8)	156 (0.9)	140 (1.2)	134 (1.4)
Race/ethnicity												
White	127 (2.1)	140 (1.6)	156 (0.7)	178 (1.0)	140 (1.6)	150 (1.1)	161 (0.9)	180 (1.0)	176 (1.1)	167 (0.8)	151 (1.0)	143 (1.4)
Black	89 (3.6)	107 (3.2)	124 (1.1)	144 (1.8)	113 (2.0)	120 (2.0)	128 (1.5)	142 (2.4)	140 (2.6)	135 (2.3)	121 (1.6)	115 (1.7)
Hispanic	106 (3.7)	122 (2.7)	136 (1.2)	154 (2.3)	123 (2.6)	127 (1.5)	135 (1.8)	157 (2.4)	152 (2.9)	143 (1.7)	128 (1.6)	125 (2.3)
Asian/Pacific Islander	‡ (†)	‡ (†)	154 (2.9)	181 (3.4)	141 (5.2)	149 (3.8)	166 (2.9)	188 (4.5)	181 (4.2)	171 (3.3)	154 (3.2)	141 (4.5)
American Indian/Alaska Native	‡ (†)	‡ (†)	‡ (†)	‡ (†)	‡ (†)	‡ (†)	‡ (†)	‡ (†)	‡ (†)	‡ (†)	‡ (†)	‡ (†)
Eligibility for free or reduced-price lunch												
Eligible	105 (2.9)	120 (2.0)	134 (0.8)	151 (2.0)	120 (1.8)	125 (1.4)	135 (1.1)	152 (2.0)	147 (2.7)	142 (1.4)	127 (1.1)	121 (1.6)
Not eligible	122 (2.0)	138 (1.8)	153 (0.8)	176 (1.0)	137 (1.5)	148 (1.1)	159 (1.1)	179 (1.3)	175 (1.2)	165 (1.0)	148 (1.1)	140 (1.4)
Unknown	‡ (†)	‡ (†)	151 (2.4)	169 (3.5)	139 (3.1)	146 (3.6)	158 (2.9)	177 (3.8)	175 (3.6)	164 (3.3)	149 (2.6)	138 (3.3)
Parents' highest level of education												
Did not finish high school	112 (3.7)	124 (2.8)	134 (1.5)	145 (3.1)	119 (2.7)	125 (2.5)	134 (2.0)	153 (3.5)	147 (3.1)	138 (2.5)	127 (2.3)	121 (2.2)
Graduated high school	109 (2.8)	129 (2.7)	141 (1.3)	158 (2.1)	124 (2.2)	132 (1.5)	141 (1.3)	158 (2.7)	149 (2.7)	149 (1.6)	133 (1.8)	126 (1.9)
Some education after high school	126 (4.0)	135 (2.2)	146 (0.9)	162 (2.1)	133 (1.5)	138 (1.2)	149 (1.2)	168 (1.7)	164 (2.3)	156 (1.3)	140 (1.1)	133 (1.7)
Graduated college	120 (3.9)	140 (2.4)	155 (0.8)	177 (0.9)	141 (1.7)	151 (1.3)	163 (1.0)	181 (1.3)	180 (1.3)	168 (1.0)	152 (1.0)	143 (1.2)
Percent of students												
All students	5 (0.3)	7 (0.3)	59 (0.7)	26 (0.8)	14 (0.4)	21 (0.4)	48 (0.5)	16 (0.3)	15 (0.4)	34 (0.5)	31 (0.4)	19 (0.4)
Sex												
Male	6 (0.4)	9 (0.4)	59 (0.8)	22 (0.8)	12 (0.5)	18 (0.5)	52 (0.7)	18 (0.5)	17 (0.5)	37 (0.6)	29 (0.7)	17 (0.5)
Female	4 (0.3)	6 (0.4)	58 (0.9)	31 (1.0)	16 (0.5)	25 (0.6)	45 (0.7)	14 (0.5)	14 (0.6)	31 (0.7)	33 (0.6)	21 (0.6)
Race/ethnicity												
White	4 (0.3)	7 (0.3)	60 (0.7)	26 (0.8)	13 (0.5)	21 (0.5)	49 (0.7)	17 (0.5)	17 (0.5)	36 (0.6)	29 (0.6)	18 (0.5)
Black	6 (0.8)	6 (0.6)	60 (1.3)	25 (1.4)	20 (1.0)	23 (0.9)	43 (1.3)	14 (0.9)	11 (0.8)	28 (1.2)	33 (1.0)	28 (1.1)
Hispanic	7 (0.7)	12 (0.8)	59 (1.4)	18 (1.1)	13 (0.7)	24 (0.9)	49 (1.1)	14 (0.9)	12 (0.8)	31 (1.1)	38 (1.0)	19 (1.0)
Asian/Pacific Islander	3 (0.8)	2 (0.5)	42 (2.6)	50 (2.8)	9 (1.0)	18 (1.7)	55 (1.5)	18 (1.5)	19 (1.6)	40 (1.3)	28 (1.9)	13 (1.1)
American Indian/Alaska Native	‡ (†)	‡ (†)	‡ (†)	‡ (†)	‡ (†)	‡ (†)	‡ (†)	‡ (†)	‡ (†)	‡ (†)	‡ (†)	‡ (†)
Eligibility for free or reduced-price lunch												
Eligible	8 (0.5)	10 (0.6)	60 (1.2)	18 (1.1)	16 (0.7)	23 (0.9)	47 (1.0)	14 (0.6)	13 (0.7)	30 (0.8)	34 (0.7)	22 (0.8)
Not eligible	4 (0.3)	7 (0.4)	59 (0.8)	29 (0.9)	13 (0.4)	21 (0.5)	49 (0.6)	17 (0.4)	16 (0.5)	35 (0.6)	30 (0.6)	18 (0.5)
Unknown	2 (0.7)	4 (1.0)	56 (2.4)	35 (2.7)	13 (1.2)	21 (1.3)	48 (1.9)	18 (1.6)	16 (1.6)	36 (2.3)	29 (1.8)	19 (1.6)
Parents' highest level of education												
Did not finish high school	11 (1.1)	13 (1.0)	53 (2.2)	16 (1.8)	19 (1.4)	22 (1.4)	47 (1.7)	13 (1.2)	13 (1.2)	30 (1.6)	35 (1.7)	23 (1.3)
Graduated high school	10 (0.6)	12 (0.8)	62 (1.4)	13 (1.0)	16 (0.8)	25 (1.0)	46 (1.2)	12 (0.7)	12 (0.7)	31 (1.3)	35 (1.1)	22 (1.1)
Some education after high school	4 (0.4)	9 (0.5)	65 (1.0)	20 (1.1)	15 (0.8)	22 (1.0)	48 (1.2)	15 (0.8)	14 (0.9)	33 (1.0)	32 (0.9)	21 (0.8)
Graduated college	2 (0.2)	4 (0.3)	56 (0.8)	37 (0.9)	12 (0.6)	19 (0.6)	50 (0.7)	19 (0.5)	18 (0.4)	37 (0.7)	28 (0.6)	17 (0.6)

†Not applicable.
‡Reporting standards not met (too few cases for a reliable estimate).
[1]The educational goals columns exclude the 1 percent of students who reported that they would not finish high school and the 2 percent who reported that they did not know how much education they would complete.
[2]Scale ranges from 0 to 300.

NOTE: Includes students tested with accommodations (7 percent of all 12th-graders); excludes only those students with disabilities and English language learners who were unable to be tested even with accommodations (3 percent of all 12th-graders). Race categories exclude persons of Hispanic ethnicity.
SOURCE: U.S. Department of Education, National Center for Education Statistics, National Assessment of Educational Progress (NAEP), 2009 Science Assessment, retrieved May 26, 2011, from the Main NAEP Data Explorer (http://nces.ed.gov/nationsreportcard/naepdata/). (This table was prepared May 2011.)

Table 224.10. Average National Assessment of Educational Progress (NAEP) arts scale score of 8th-graders, percentage distribution by frequency of instruction, and percentage participating in selected activities, by subject and selected characteristics: 2008

[Standard errors appear in parentheses]

Selected characteristic	Average score			Percentage distribution of students by school-reported frequency of instruction								Percent of students reporting participation in musical activities in school		
	Music,[1] responding scale score (0 to 300)	Visual arts[2]		Music				Visual arts				Play in band	Play in orchestra	Sing in chorus or choir
		Responding scale score (0 to 300)	Creating task score (0 to 100)	Subject not offered	Less than once a week	Once or twice a week	At least 3 or 4 times a week	Subject not offered	Less than once a week	Once or twice a week	At least 3 or 4 times a week			
1	2	3	4	5	6	7	8	9	10	11	12	13	14	15
All students	150 (1.2)	150 (1.2)	52 (0.6)	8 (2.0)	8 (2.0)	27 (3.1)	57 (3.2)	14 (2.4)	10 (2.5)	30 (3.5)	47 (3.9)	16 (0.9)	5 (0.5)	17 (1.2)
Sex														
Male	145 (1.3)	145 (1.4)	49 (0.7)	9 (2.1)	8 (2.1)	27 (3.1)	56 (3.2)	14 (2.6)	10 (2.5)	30 (3.6)	46 (4.1)	18 (1.0)	3 (0.5)	9 (1.2)
Female	155 (1.4)	155 (1.2)	54 (0.7)	8 (2.0)	7 (1.9)	28 (3.2)	57 (3.2)	13 (2.3)	10 (2.5)	29 (3.3)	48 (3.8)	14 (1.0)	6 (0.6)	26 (1.8)
Race/ethnicity														
White	161 (1.3)	160 (1.2)	55 (0.5)	6 (2.5)	8 (2.5)	29 (4.0)	57 (3.6)	11 (2.6)	11 (3.4)	34 (4.4)	44 (4.6)	19 (1.2)	5 (0.6)	19 (1.6)
Black	130 (2.0)	129 (2.4)	43 (1.5)	10 (2.9)	8 (4.5)	26 (5.5)	56 (7.0)	18 (4.9)	10 (4.9)	24 (4.5)	49 (5.7)	13 (1.2)	4 (1.0)	21 (1.9)
Hispanic	129 (1.9)	134 (1.9)	46 (1.1)	14 (4.3)	6 (2.3)	21 (4.1)	59 (4.5)	17 (4.5)	5 (2.0)	23 (4.7)	56 (6.0)	8 (1.2)	3 (0.6)	10 (1.6)
Asian/Pacific Islander	159 (4.7)	156 (4.2)	54 (2.0)	7 (4.1)	8 (3.4)	25 (6.6)	60 (8.7)	5 (2.5)	11 (4.6)	29 (6.0)	54 (8.4)	21 (3.5)	6 (2.1)	16 (2.9)
Free or reduced-price lunch eligibility														
Eligible	132 (1.3)	132 (1.4)	46 (1.0)	10 (2.1)	6 (2.1)	26 (3.4)	58 (3.9)	18 (3.4)	9 (3.2)	26 (3.7)	47 (4.7)	12 (1.2)	3 (0.6)	15 (1.4)
Not eligible	161 (1.4)	161 (1.2)	55 (0.6)	8 (2.6)	8 (2.6)	26 (4.0)	59 (4.0)	10 (2.4)	10 (3.2)	30 (4.1)	50 (4.6)	19 (1.0)	5 (0.6)	19 (1.6)
Unknown	156 (5.6)	156 (5.9)	57 (2.6)	4 (†)	19 (8.7)	54 (11.5)	23 (10.5)	16 (10.3)	13 (8.4)	47 (13.6)	24 (10.6)	14 (6.3)	5 (2.3)	13 (2.0)
Control of school														
Public	149 (1.3)	149 (1.2)	51 (0.7)	8 (2.1)	7 (2.1)	24 (3.2)	61 (3.5)	13 (2.4)	10 (2.7)	26 (3.5)	51 (4.2)	17 (0.9)	5 (0.5)	18 (1.3)
Private	163 (2.8)	159 (5.2)	60 (1.3)	10 (6.0)	15 (6.9)	71 (8.8)	3 (†)	17 (8.2)	10 (6.1)	70 (10.2)	3 (0.9)	9 (1.9)	1 (0.4)	13 (2.1)
School location														
City	142 (2.0)	144 (2.1)	49 (1.2)	13 (4.0)	10 (3.8)	24 (5.7)	52 (5.6)	12 (2.6)	9 (3.5)	24 (4.9)	55 (5.4)	14 (1.0)	4 (0.6)	13 (1.3)
Suburban	155 (1.9)	155 (1.8)	54 (0.7)	3 (2.2)	7 (3.5)	32 (5.6)	57 (6.3)	10 (3.1)	9 (4.6)	33 (6.4)	46 (6.1)	14 (1.5)	6 (1.0)	16 (1.6)
Town	156 (3.5)	149 (2.8)	50 (1.5)	4 (1.0)	# (†)	18 (9.0)	78 (9.0)	16 (8.4)	# (†)	23 (9.2)	60 (10.5)	23 (3.0)	4 (1.3)	23 (3.4)
Rural	150 (2.6)	151 (3.0)	52 (1.5)	13 (5.0)	8 (4.8)	29 (5.7)	50 (7.7)	20 (7.3)	17 (6.8)	35 (7.8)	28 (6.7)	18 (2.5)	3 (1.0)	21 (3.4)
Region														
Northeast	154 (3.1)	160 (2.3)	52 (0.9)	10 (5.3)	13 (5.8)	40 (9.0)	37 (8.6)	5 (3.3)	5 (†)	50 (6.2)	39 (9.3)	16 (2.7)	6 (0.9)	17 (2.6)
Midwest	158 (2.9)	155 (2.3)	53 (1.3)	12 (6.6)	# (†)	25 (7.2)	63 (5.8)	9 (2.0)	15 (7.7)	26 (6.7)	50 (7.3)	22 (2.1)	6 (1.3)	24 (3.1)
South	147 (1.9)	147 (2.2)	51 (1.0)	6 (1.8)	10 (4.0)	25 (3.9)	59 (5.7)	19 (5.3)	9 (3.8)	26 (5.0)	46 (6.4)	16 (1.2)	4 (0.6)	16 (2.0)
West	144 (2.0)	143 (2.1)	51 (1.1)	8 (3.7)	8 (3.5)	24 (6.9)	60 (5.4)	15 (4.9)	9 (4.0)	25 (9.0)	51 (8.2)	9 (1.2)	3 (0.6)	12 (1.7)
Frequency of instruction														
Subject not offered	139 (6.3)	138 (4.2)	— (†)	(†)	(†)	(†)	(†)	(†)	(†)	(†)	(†)	17 (4.0)	4 (1.5)	11 (2.1)
Less than once a week	149 (6.4)	154 (5.3)	— (†)	(†)	(†)	(†)	(†)	(†)	(†)	(†)	(†)	11 (2.4)	4 (1.5)	10 (2.0)
Once or twice a week	152 (2.8)	154 (2.6)	— (†)	(†)	(†)	(†)	(†)	(†)	(†)	(†)	(†)	12 (1.7)	3 (0.8)	17 (2.2)
At least 3 or 4 times a week	149 (1.8)	149 (1.8)	— (†)	(†)	(†)	(†)	(†)	(†)	(†)	(†)	(†)	17 (1.4)	5 (0.7)	20 (1.6)

—Not available.
†Not applicable.
#Rounds to zero.
[1]Students were asked to analyze and describe aspects of music they heard, critique instrumental and vocal performances, and demonstrate their knowledge of standard musical notation and music's role in society.
[2]The visual arts assessment measured students' ability to respond to and create visual arts. Responding questions asked students to analyze and describe works of art and design, while creating questions required students to create works of art and design of their own.

NOTE: Excludes students unable to be tested due to limited proficiency in English or due to a disability (if the accommodations provided were not sufficient to enable the test to properly reflect the students' music or visual arts proficiency). Detail may not sum to totals because of rounding. Race categories exclude persons of Hispanic ethnicity. Totals include other racial/ethnic groups not shown separately.
SOURCE: U.S. Department of Education, National Center for Education Statistics, National Assessment of Educational Progress (NAEP), 2008 Arts Assessment, retrieved June 30, 2009, from the Main NAEP Data Explorer (http://nces.ed.gov/nationsreportcard/naepdata/). (This table was prepared June 2009.)

Table 224.20. Average National Assessment of Educational Progress (NAEP) civics scale score and percentage of students attaining civics achievement levels, by grade level, selected student characteristics, and percentile: 1998, 2006, 2010, and 2014

[Standard errors appear in parentheses]

Selected student characteristic	4th-graders 1998		2006		2010		8th-graders 1998		2006		2010		2014		12th-graders 1998		2006		2010	
1	2		3		4		5		6		7		8		9		10		11	
Average civics scale score[1]
All students	150	(0.7)	154	(1.0)	157	(0.8)	150	(0.7)	150	(0.8)	151	(0.8)	154	(1.1)	150	(0.8)	151	(0.9)	148	(0.8)
Sex
Male	149	(1.0)	153	(1.1)	153	(1.0)	148	(0.9)	149	(1.0)	150	(0.9)	154	(1.2)	148	(1.1)	150	(1.1)	148	(0.9)
Female	151	(0.9)	155	(1.1)	160	(0.8)	152	(0.8)	151	(0.8)	152	(0.8)	154	(1.1)	152	(0.8)	152	(1.0)	148	(0.9)
Race/ethnicity
White	158	(0.9)	164	(0.9)	167	(0.8)	158	(0.9)	161	(0.8)	160	(0.8)	164	(1.0)	157	(1.0)	158	(1.0)	156	(0.9)
Black	130	(1.1)	140	(1.5)	143	(1.2)	131	(1.2)	133	(1.5)	135	(1.6)	137	(2.1)	130	(1.6)	131	(1.4)	127	(1.6)
Hispanic	123	(2.2)	138	(1.3)	140	(1.6)	127	(1.3)	131	(1.1)	137	(1.1)	141	(1.4)	132	(1.1)	134	(1.1)	137	(1.4)
Asian/Pacific Islander	147	(4.0)	154	(3.8)	164	(2.0)	151	(8.9)	154	(3.2)	158	(2.5)	165	(3.1)	149	(5.2)	155	(3.1)	153	(2.6)
Asian[2]	—	(†)	—	(†)	—	(†)	—	(†)	—	(†)	—	(†)	166	(3.1)	—	(†)	—	(†)	—	(†)
Pacific Islander[2]	—	(†)	—	(†)	—	(†)	—	(†)	—	(†)	—	(†)	‡	(†)	—	(†)	—	(†)	—	(†)
American Indian/Alaska Native	‡	(†)	124	(7.6)	143	(7.0)	‡	(†)	127	(7.3)	136	(12.6)	‡	(†)	‡	(†)	131	(3.5)	134	(14.6)
Two or more races[2]	—	(†)	—	(†)	—	(†)	—	(†)	—	(†)	—	(†)	160	(2.8)	—	(†)	—	(†)	—	(†)
Parents' highest level of education[3]
Did not finish high school	—	(†)	—	(†)	—	(†)	123	(3.2)	129	(1.6)	134	(1.3)	134	(1.5)	124	(2.1)	126	(1.8)	128	(1.4)
Graduated high school	—	(†)	—	(†)	—	(†)	144	(1.2)	140	(1.3)	139	(1.1)	140	(1.7)	140	(1.2)	138	(1.0)	137	(1.2)
Some education after high school	—	(†)	—	(†)	—	(†)	143	(1.0)	153	(1.0)	155	(1.1)	155	(1.1)	145	(1.1)	150	(0.9)	147	(1.1)
Graduated college	—	(†)	—	(†)	—	(†)	160	(0.8)	162	(0.9)	162	(0.8)	164	(1.0)	160	(0.9)	162	(1.1)	158	(0.9)
Eligibility for free or reduced-price lunch
Eligible	132	(0.9)	139	(1.1)	143	(0.9)	131	(1.1)	132	(1.0)	136	(0.9)	139	(1.2)	130	(1.4)	133	(1.0)	132	(1.0)
Not eligible	160	(1.1)	166	(0.8)	169	(0.8)	157	(1.0)	160	(0.8)	163	(0.7)	166	(1.1)	153	(1.0)	156	(1.0)	155	(0.9)
Unknown	154	(2.2)	167	(2.1)	171	(2.7)	156	(2.2)	171	(2.4)	166	(2.3)	166	(2.1)	153	(1.3)	160	(2.4)	159	(3.3)
Percentile[4]
10th	102	(1.6)	111	(1.9)	115	(1.6)	103	(1.6)	102	(1.6)	106	(1.9)	110	(1.8)	103	(1.2)	104	(1.2)	101	(1.8)
25th	128	(0.9)	134	(1.2)	138	(1.0)	128	(1.1)	128	(1.5)	131	(1.1)	133	(1.7)	128	(1.4)	128	(1.2)	126	(1.4)
50th	153	(1.3)	156	(1.1)	159	(1.2)	153	(0.7)	154	(1.1)	155	(0.9)	157	(1.2)	153	(0.8)	154	(1.1)	152	(1.0)
75th	175	(0.8)	176	(0.9)	179	(1.2)	175	(1.0)	175	(1.0)	175	(0.8)	177	(1.4)	175	(0.8)	176	(1.0)	173	(0.8)
90th	192	(0.7)	192	(1.1)	194	(1.0)	192	(0.7)	191	(0.6)	191	(0.5)	193	(1.0)	192	(0.7)	194	(0.9)	190	(1.3)
Standard deviation of the civics scale score[5]
All students	35	(0.5)	31	(0.5)	31	(0.5)	35	(0.4)	35	(0.5)	34	(0.4)	33	(0.5)	35	(0.4)	35	(0.4)	35	(0.4)
Percent of students achieving civics achievement levels
Achievement level
Below *Basic*	31	(1.0)	27	(1.2)	23	(1.0)	30	(0.9)	30	(1.1)	28	(1.0)	26	(1.3)	35	(0.9)	34	(1.1)	36	(1.0)
At or above *Basic*[6]	69	(1.0)	73	(1.2)	77	(1.0)	70	(0.9)	70	(1.1)	72	(1.0)	74	(1.3)	65	(0.9)	66	(1.1)	64	(1.0)
At or above *Basic* by sex
Male	68	(1.2)	72	(1.3)	73	(1.3)	67	(1.1)	68	(1.3)	70	(1.1)	74	(1.4)	62	(1.2)	64	(1.5)	63	(1.0)
Female	70	(1.0)	75	(1.4)	81	(1.0)	73	(1.2)	72	(1.2)	74	(1.1)	75	(1.4)	68	(1.2)	67	(1.2)	64	(1.3)
At or above *Basic* by sex by race/ethnicity
White	78	(1.3)	85	(1.0)	87	(0.9)	78	(1.1)	82	(0.9)	82	(1.0)	86	(1.0)	73	(1.1)	74	(1.1)	73	(1.0)
Black	45	(1.7)	57	(2.3)	62	(2.2)	49	(1.7)	50	(2.0)	53	(2.3)	55	(3.4)	41	(2.0)	42	(1.9)	38	(1.9)
Hispanic	40	(2.8)	55	(2.0)	58	(2.3)	44	(2.3)	50	(2.2)	56	(1.4)	61	(1.7)	45	(1.9)	46	(1.7)	50	(1.8)
Asian/Pacific Islander	66	(5.5)	75	(4.5)	82	(2.3)	69	(9.5)	73	(4.0)	78	(2.5)	83	(2.8)	63	(4.8)	68	(3.7)	70	(3.1)
Asian[2]	—	(†)	—	(†)	—	(†)	—	(†)	—	(†)	—	(†)	84	(2.8)	—	(†)	—	(†)	—	(†)
Pacific Islander[2]	—	(†)	—	(†)	—	(†)	—	(†)	—	(†)	—	(†)	‡	(†)	—	(†)	—	(†)	—	(†)
American Indian/Alaska Native	‡	(†)	38	(11.3)	63	(10.9)	‡	(†)	46	(9.5)	56	(18.0)	‡	(†)	‡	(†)	42	(8.0)	47	(17.3)
Two or more races[2]	—	(†)	—	(†)	—	(†)	—	(†)	—	(†)	—	(†)	80	(3.4)	—	(†)	—	(†)	—	(†)
At or above *Proficient*[7]	23	(0.9)	24	(1.0)	27	(0.9)	22	(0.8)	22	(0.8)	22	(0.8)	23	(1.1)	26	(0.9)	27	(1.0)	24	(0.9)
At *Advanced*[8]	2	(0.3)	1	(0.2)	2	(0.2)	2	(0.2)	2	(0.2)	1	(0.1)	2	(0.3)	4	(0.4)	5	(0.4)	4	(0.3)

—Not available.
†Not applicable.
‡Reporting standards not met (too few cases for a reliable estimate).
[1]Scale ranges from 0 to 300 for all three grades, but scores cannot be compared across grades. For example, the average score of 167 for White 4th-graders in 2010 does not denote higher performance than the score of 160 for White 8th-graders in 2010.
[2]In civics assessments prior to 2014, separate data for Asians, Pacific Islanders, and students of Two or more races were not collected.
[3]These data are based on students' responses to questions about their parents' education level. Because the wording of the questions was different in 1998 than in the later assessment years, data from 1998 are not directly comparable to data from 2006, 2010, and 2014. For all assessment years, data for students whose parents have an unknown level of education are included in table totals, but not shown separately.
[4]The percentile represents a specific point on the percentage distribution of all students ranked by their civics score from low to high. For example, 10 percent of students scored at or below the 10th percentile score, while 90 percent of students scored above it.
[5]The standard deviation provides an indication of how much the test scores varied. The lower the standard deviation, the closer the scores were clustered around the average score. About two-thirds of the student scores can be expected to fall within the range of one standard deviation above and one standard deviation below the average score. For exam-

ple, the average score for all 8th-graders in 2014 was 154, and the standard deviation was 33. This means that about two-thirds of the students would be expected to have scores between 187 (one standard deviation above the average) and 121 (one standard deviation below). Standard errors also must be taken into account when making comparisons of these ranges.
[6]*Basic* denotes partial mastery of the knowledge and skills that are fundamental for proficient work.
[7]*Proficient* represents solid academic performance. Students reaching this level have demonstrated competency over challenging subject matter.
[8]*Advanced* signifies superior performance.
NOTE: In 2014, only 8th-grade students were assessed in civics. Includes public and private schools. Includes students tested with accommodations (1 to 13 percent of all students, depending on grade level and year); excludes only those students with disabilities and English language learners who were unable to be tested even with accommodations (1 to 5 percent of all students). Race categories exclude persons of Hispanic ethnicity. Detail may not sum to totals because of rounding.
SOURCE: U.S. Department of Education, National Center for Education Statistics, National Assessment of Educational Progress (NAEP), 1998, 2006, 2010, and 2014 Civics Assessments, retrieved April 30, 2015, from the Main NAEP Data Explorer (http://nces.ed.gov/nationsreportcard/naepdata/). (This table was prepared April 2015.)

Table 224.30. Average National Assessment of Educational Progress (NAEP) economics scale score of 12th-graders, percentage attaining economics achievement levels, and percentage with different levels of economics coursework, by selected characteristics: 2006 and 2012

[Standard errors appear in parentheses]

Selected characteristic	Average scale score[1]		Percent of students attaining achievement levels						Percentage distribution of students by highest level of economics coursework taken								
			At or above Basic[2]		At or above Proficient[3]		At Advanced[4]		No economics courses		Combined course		Consumer economics/ business		General economics		Advanced economics[5]
1	2		3		4		5		6		7		8		9		10
2006																	
All students	150	(0.9)	79	(0.8)	42	(1.1)	3	(0.3)	13	(0.9)	12	(0.7)	11	(0.7)	49	(1.4)	16	(0.7)
Sex																	
Male	152	(1.0)	79	(0.8)	45	(1.3)	4	(0.5)	13	(1.0)	10	(0.6)	10	(0.7)	50	(1.4)	16	(0.8)
Female	148	(0.9)	79	(0.9)	38	(1.3)	2	(0.3)	12	(0.9)	13	(0.9)	11	(0.8)	48	(1.6)	15	(0.8)
Race/ethnicity																	
White	158	(0.8)	87	(0.7)	51	(1.2)	4	(0.4)	15	(1.1)	12	(0.8)	11	(0.8)	49	(1.6)	13	(0.9)
Black	127	(1.2)	57	(1.9)	16	(1.3)	#	(†)	8	(0.8)	11	(0.9)	11	(1.2)	49	(1.7)	21	(1.1)
Hispanic	133	(1.2)	64	(1.6)	21	(1.2)	#	(†)	8	(1.7)	13	(1.1)	7	(0.9)	55	(2.6)	18	(1.2)
Asian/Pacific Islander	153	(3.5)	80	(4.0)	44	(4.5)	4	(1.4)	13	(1.8)	10	(1.8)	10	(1.4)	45	(4.1)	22	(1.9)
American Indian/Alaska Native	137	(4.1)	72	(5.6)	26	(4.8)	2	(†)	11	(3.9)	18	(2.7)	17	(3.2)	41	(4.9)	13	(3.1)
Parents' highest level of education																	
Not high school graduate	129	(1.4)	59	(2.1)	17	(1.7)	#	(†)	10	(1.7)	13	(1.4)	10	(1.4)	53	(3.2)	14	(1.3)
Graduated high school	138	(1.2)	69	(1.5)	27	(1.4)	1	(0.3)	11	(1.2)	12	(1.0)	12	(1.0)	52	(1.7)	13	(0.9)
Some college	150	(0.8)	82	(1.1)	39	(1.4)	1	(0.4)	11	(1.0)	13	(0.9)	12	(1.0)	51	(1.9)	14	(1.0)
Graduated college	160	(0.9)	87	(0.8)	54	(1.3)	5	(0.6)	14	(1.0)	11	(0.8)	10	(0.7)	47	(1.5)	17	(1.0)
Free or reduced-price lunch eligibility																	
Eligible	132	(0.9)	62	(1.1)	20	(1.1)	1	(0.2)	9	(0.7)	13	(1.1)	10	(0.9)	50	(1.6)	18	(0.8)
Not eligible	155	(0.9)	84	(0.8)	48	(1.2)	4	(0.4)	13	(1.1)	12	(0.8)	12	(0.9)	48	(1.6)	16	(0.9)
Unknown	157	(1.9)	86	(1.7)	50	(2.8)	4	(1.1)	16	(3.0)	12	(1.6)	7	(1.1)	54	(3.1)	11	(1.4)
Region																	
Northeast	153	(2.0)	81	(1.7)	46	(2.6)	4	(0.9)	26	(2.6)	7	(1.1)	11	(1.3)	43	(3.2)	13	(1.4)
Midwest	153	(1.5)	83	(1.4)	45	(2.0)	3	(0.6)	12	(2.2)	12	(1.6)	15	(1.5)	51	(2.6)	10	(1.0)
South	147	(1.4)	77	(1.4)	37	(1.7)	2	(0.5)	6	(1.1)	14	(1.2)	9	(1.3)	49	(2.0)	22	(1.5)
West	‡	(†)	‡	(†)	‡	(†)	‡	(†)	‡	(†)	‡	(†)	‡	(†)	‡	(†)	‡	(†)
2012																	
All students	152	(0.8)	82	(0.8)	42	(1.1)	3	(0.3)	9	(1.0)	9	(0.8)	10	(1.2)	54	(2.0)	18	(0.9)
Sex																	
Male	155	(0.9)	83	(1.0)	47	(1.3)	4	(0.4)	8	(0.9)	9	(0.8)	10	(1.2)	54	(2.0)	18	(1.0)
Female	149	(0.9)	80	(1.0)	37	(1.3)	2	(0.2)	10	(1.2)	9	(0.9)	10	(1.3)	53	(2.2)	18	(1.1)
Race/ethnicity																	
White	160	(1.0)	89	(0.9)	53	(1.6)	4	(0.4)	10	(1.4)	9	(1.0)	11	(1.6)	54	(2.4)	15	(1.1)
Black	131	(1.4)	61	(2.1)	16	(1.3)	1	(0.2)	6	(1.2)	8	(1.1)	9	(1.2)	54	(2.9)	23	(1.4)
Hispanic	138	(1.4)	71	(2.0)	25	(1.4)	1	(0.3)	5	(1.1)	9	(1.0)	7	(1.2)	57	(2.9)	21	(2.0)
Asian	160	(1.9)	86	(1.9)	53	(2.4)	6	(1.3)	10	(1.5)	9	(1.2)	7	(1.2)	45	(2.7)	29	(2.6)
Pacific Islander	‡	(†)	‡	(†)	‡	(†)	‡	(†)	‡	(†)	‡	(†)	‡	(†)	‡	(†)	‡	(†)
American Indian/Alaska Native	136	(4.7)	72	(7.8)	20	(5.6)	2	(†)	4	(2.7)	7	(2.9)	19	(9.9)	54	(8.0)	16	(4.6)
Two or more races	154	(3.4)	87	(3.0)	42	(5.2)	3	(1.8)	10	(2.9)	6	(1.4)	7	(1.8)	57	(4.5)	20	(2.8)
Parents' highest level of education																	
Not high school graduate	134	(1.5)	66	(2.1)	21	(1.9)	#	(†)	4	(0.7)	10	(1.3)	10	(1.4)	59	(2.4)	17	(1.5)
Graduated high school	139	(1.1)	71	(1.7)	27	(1.6)	1	(0.2)	7	(1.2)	9	(1.1)	11	(1.2)	56	(2.3)	16	(1.0)
Some college	150	(0.8)	84	(1.0)	38	(1.2)	1	(0.3)	8	(1.2)	9	(0.9)	10	(1.5)	56	(2.3)	16	(1.6)
Graduated college	161	(0.9)	89	(1.0)	55	(1.4)	5	(0.5)	10	(1.4)	9	(1.0)	10	(1.3)	51	(2.3)	20	(1.2)
Free or reduced-price lunch eligibility																	
Eligible	138	(0.9)	70	(1.3)	25	(1.1)	#	(†)	7	(0.9)	9	(0.7)	10	(1.2)	57	(2.1)	18	(1.3)
Not eligible	159	(0.9)	88	(0.8)	52	(1.4)	4	(0.4)	10	(1.3)	9	(1.1)	11	(1.4)	51	(2.3)	19	(1.1)
Unknown	164	(3.3)	90	(2.3)	59	(4.2)	5	(1.4)	13	(4.7)	8	(1.8)	6	(1.6)	58	(5.0)	15	(1.9)
School location																	
City	147	(1.8)	77	(1.9)	37	(2.3)	3	(0.5)	8	(1.5)	9	(1.3)	8	(1.4)	54	(3.3)	22	(1.8)
Suburb	156	(0.9)	85	(1.0)	48	(1.1)	4	(0.4)	12	(1.8)	10	(1.1)	11	(1.6)	50	(2.1)	17	(1.5)
Town	149	(2.7)	81	(2.4)	39	(3.8)	2	(0.6)	9	(2.8)	8	(1.2)	10	(2.4)	57	(3.5)	16	(3.8)
Rural	152	(1.5)	83	(1.5)	42	(2.5)	2	(0.6)	5	(1.2)	9	(1.4)	12	(2.8)	57	(4.0)	17	(2.1)
Region																	
Northeast	154	(1.7)	84	(1.8)	46	(2.0)	3	(0.7)	27	(4.0)	9	(1.9)	11	(1.4)	39	(5.5)	14	(2.2)
Midwest	157	(1.6)	86	(1.1)	50	(2.2)	4	(0.7)	5	(1.2)	9	(2.3)	18	(3.4)	57	(4.3)	11	(1.0)
South	149	(1.8)	79	(1.7)	38	(2.7)	2	(0.5)	3	(1.5)	8	(1.2)	5	(0.9)	55	(3.6)	29	(2.0)
West	148	(1.1)	79	(1.4)	40	(1.5)	2	(0.3)	7	(1.2)	11	(1.1)	9	(3.1)	60	(3.0)	13	(1.0)

†Not applicable.
#Rounds to zero.
‡Reporting standards not met. Either there are too few cases for a reliable estimate or item response rates fell below the required standards for reporting.
[1]Scale ranges from 0 to 300.
[2]Basic denotes partial mastery of the knowledge and skills that are fundamental for proficient work at a given grade.
[3]Proficient represents solid academic performance. Students reaching this level have demonstrated competency over challenging subject matter.
[4]Advanced signifies superior performance for a given grade.

[5]Advanced economics includes Advanced Placement, International Baccalaureate, and honors courses.
NOTE: Includes public and private schools. Includes students tested with accommodations; excludes only those students with disabilities and English language learners who were unable to be tested even with accommodations (3 percent of all students in both assessment years). Detail may not sum to totals because of rounding. Race categories exclude persons of Hispanic ethnicity. Totals include other racial/ethnic groups not shown separately.
SOURCE: U.S. Department of Education, National Center for Education Statistics, National Assessment of Educational Progress (NAEP), 2006 and 2012 Economics Assessment, retrieved May 08, 2013, from the NAEP Data Explorer (http://nces.ed.gov/nationsreportcard/naepdata/). (This table was prepared May 2013.)

Table 224.40. Average National Assessment of Educational Progress (NAEP) geography scale score, standard deviation, and percentage of students attaining geography achievement levels, by grade level, selected student characteristics, and percentile: Selected years, 1994 through 2014

[Standard errors appear in parentheses]

Selected student characteristic	4th-graders						8th-graders								12th-graders					
	1994[1]		2001		2010		1994[1]		2001		2010		2014		1994[1]		2001		2010	
1	2		3		4		5		6		7		8		9		10		11	
	Average geography scale score[2]																			
All students	206	(1.2)	208	(0.9)	213	(0.8)	260	(0.7)	260	(1.0)	261	(0.7)	261	(1.0)	285	(0.7)	284	(0.8)	282	(0.6)
Sex																				
Male	208	(1.4)	210	(1.0)	215	(0.9)	262	(0.9)	262	(1.2)	263	(0.8)	263	(1.1)	288	(0.8)	287	(1.0)	285	(0.6)
Female	203	(1.4)	206	(1.3)	211	(0.9)	258	(0.8)	258	(1.0)	259	(0.8)	260	(1.0)	281	(0.9)	281	(0.8)	280	(0.8)
Race/ethnicity																				
White	218	(1.5)	219	(1.1)	224	(0.9)	269	(0.8)	269	(1.4)	272	(0.6)	273	(1.0)	290	(0.8)	291	(0.8)	290	(0.5)
Black	166	(2.4)	180	(1.8)	192	(1.3)	229	(1.7)	233	(1.6)	241	(1.1)	240	(1.1)	258	(1.4)	258	(1.5)	261	(1.2)
Hispanic	177	(3.3)	185	(2.5)	197	(1.2)	238	(2.0)	237	(2.0)	244	(1.0)	248	(1.1)	269	(1.7)	268	(1.6)	270	(1.2)
Asian/Pacific Islander	211	(4.0)	214	(3.5)	224	(3.3)	262	(5.3)	264	(2.7)	268	(2.7)	275	(2.5)	283	(3.1)	284	(5.0)	285	(1.7)
Asian[3]	—	(†)	—	(†)	—	(†)	—	(†)	—	(†)	—	(†)	275	(2.6)	—	(†)	—	(†)	—	(†)
Pacific Islander[3]	—	(†)	—	(†)	—	(†)	—	(†)	—	(†)	—	(†)	‡	(†)	—	(†)	—	(†)	—	(†)
American Indian/Alaska Native	‡	(†)	‡	(†)	201	(3.5)	251	(5.5)	261	(5.3)	250	(3.9)	‡	(†)	‡	(†)	‡	(†)	277	(2.5)
Two or more races[3]	—	(†)	—	(†)	—	(†)	—	(†)	—	(†)	—	(†)	264	(2.5)	—	(†)	—	(†)	—	(†)
Parents' highest level of education[4]																				
Did not finish high school	—	(†)	—	(†)	—	(†)	238	(1.7)	236	(1.8)	243	(1.3)	243	(1.2)	263	(1.2)	266	(1.7)	263	(1.2)
Graduated high school	—	(†)	—	(†)	—	(†)	250	(1.2)	251	(1.2)	251	(1.1)	250	(1.0)	274	(1.1)	275	(0.9)	274	(0.8)
Some education after high school	—	(†)	—	(†)	—	(†)	265	(1.0)	264	(1.1)	262	(1.0)	261	(0.9)	286	(1.0)	284	(0.9)	280	(0.7)
Graduated college	—	(†)	—	(†)	—	(†)	272	(1.0)	273	(1.0)	272	(1.0)	272	(1.2)	294	(0.9)	293	(1.0)	291	(0.7)
Eligibility for free or reduced-price lunch																				
Eligible	—	(†)	185	(1.4)	197	(0.7)	—	(†)	239	(1.3)	246	(0.9)	248	(1.0)	—	(†)	268	(1.7)	269	(0.8)
Not eligible	—	(†)	221	(1.1)	227	(0.8)	—	(†)	269	(1.2)	272	(0.7)	274	(1.2)	—	(†)	287	(1.0)	288	(0.5)
Unknown	—	(†)	219	(2.8)	227	(3.7)	—	(†)	265	(2.3)	276	(2.6)	277	(3.0)	—	(†)	288	(1.6)	289	(2.2)
Percentile[5]																				
10th	146	(1.9)	159	(2.6)	169	(1.8)	213	(1.3)	213	(1.2)	220	(1.2)	220	(1.2)	244	(0.9)	246	(1.1)	247	(0.8)
25th	179	(1.5)	184	(1.4)	192	(1.2)	237	(1.0)	238	(1.3)	241	(0.7)	242	(1.3)	265	(1.1)	266	(1.2)	265	(0.8)
50th	211	(1.1)	211	(1.0)	216	(1.1)	263	(1.1)	264	(1.2)	263	(0.9)	263	(1.0)	287	(0.9)	286	(0.9)	284	(0.7)
75th	237	(1.3)	235	(1.4)	236	(0.7)	285	(0.9)	285	(1.1)	284	(0.9)	283	(0.9)	306	(1.0)	304	(0.9)	301	(0.7)
90th	257	(2.0)	254	(1.3)	253	(0.9)	302	(1.9)	302	(1.1)	300	(0.7)	300	(1.3)	321	(1.0)	319	(1.3)	315	(0.7)
	Standard deviation of the geography scale score[6]																			
All students	44	(0.8)	37	(0.8)	33	(0.4)	35	(0.4)	35	(0.5)	31	(0.3)	31	(0.5)	30	(0.4)	28	(0.4)	26	(0.3)
	Percent of students achieving geography achievement levels																			
Achievement level																				
Below *Basic*[7]	30	(1.1)	27	(1.0)	21	(0.9)	29	(1.0)	28	(1.2)	26	(0.9)	25	(1.1)	30	(0.9)	29	(1.0)	30	(0.9)
At or above *Basic*[7]	70	(1.1)	73	(1.0)	79	(0.9)	71	(1.0)	72	(1.2)	74	(0.9)	75	(1.1)	70	(0.9)	71	(1.0)	70	(0.9)
At or above *Basic* by sex																				
Male	71	(1.3)	74	(0.9)	80	(1.0)	72	(1.3)	73	(1.5)	75	(1.0)	76	(1.1)	73	(1.1)	74	(1.3)	73	(1.0)
Female	68	(1.4)	71	(1.5)	78	(1.1)	69	(1.1)	71	(1.1)	73	(1.1)	74	(1.2)	67	(1.2)	68	(1.2)	66	(1.2)
At or above *Basic* by race/ethnicity																				
White	81	(1.3)	84	(1.1)	89	(1.0)	81	(0.9)	82	(1.5)	86	(0.7)	88	(0.9)	78	(0.9)	81	(0.9)	81	(0.8)
Black	33	(2.4)	43	(2.5)	57	(2.1)	34	(3.0)	39	(2.4)	49	(1.7)	48	(2.1)	33	(2.3)	33	(2.0)	36	(1.8)
Hispanic	44	(3.1)	50	(3.1)	64	(1.7)	49	(3.8)	45	(2.5)	55	(1.5)	61	(1.7)	48	(3.0)	48	(2.9)	52	(2.0)
Asian/Pacific Islander	72	(4.4)	77	(4.2)	87	(3.2)	72	(6.7)	77	(3.6)	80	(3.3)	87	(2.0)	67	(3.8)	70	(6.2)	73	(2.7)
Asian[3]	—	(†)	—	(†)	—	(†)	—	(†)	—	(†)	—	(†)	87	(2.0)	—	(†)	—	(†)	—	(†)
Pacific Islander[3]	—	(†)	—	(†)	—	(†)	—	(†)	—	(†)	—	(†)	‡	(†)	—	(†)	—	(†)	—	(†)
American Indian/Alaska Native	‡	(†)	‡	(†)	68	(6.4)	62	(7.7)	74	(4.8)	62	(7.2)	‡	(†)	‡	(†)	‡	(†)	62	(5.1)
Two or more races[3]	—	(†)	—	(†)	—	(†)	—	(†)	—	(†)	—	(†)	79	(3.5)	—	(†)	—	(†)	—	(†)
At or above *Proficient*[8]	22	(1.2)	20	(0.9)	21	(0.8)	28	(1.0)	29	(1.3)	27	(0.8)	27	(1.2)	27	(1.2)	24	(1.2)	20	(0.8)
At *Advanced*[9]	3	(0.4)	2	(0.3)	2	(0.2)	4	(0.4)	4	(0.5)	3	(0.2)	3	(0.4)	2	(0.5)	1	(0.3)	1	(0.1)

—Not available.
†Not applicable.
‡Reporting standards not met (too few cases for a reliable estimate).
[1]Accommodations were not permitted for this assessment.
[2]Scale ranges from 0 to 500.
[3]In geography assessments prior to 2014, separate data for Asians, Pacific Islanders, and students of Two or more races were not collected.
[4]Based on student reports. Data for students whose parents have an unknown level of education are included in table totals, but not shown separately.
[5]The percentile represents a specific point on the percentage distribution of all students ranked by their geography score from low to high. For example, 10 percent of students scored at or below the 10th percentile score, while 90 percent of students scored above it.
[6]The standard deviation provides an indication of how much the test scores varied. The lower the standard deviation, the closer the scores were clustered around the average score. About two-thirds of the student scores can be expected to fall within the range of one standard deviation above and one standard deviation below the average score. For example, the average score for all 8th-graders in 2014 was 261, and the standard deviation was 31. This means that about two-thirds of the students would be expected to have scores between 292 (one

standard deviation above the average) and 230 (one standard deviation below). Standard errors also must be taken into account when making comparisons of these ranges.
[7]*Basic* denotes partial mastery of the knowledge and skills that are fundamental for proficient work.
[8]*Proficient* represents solid academic performance. Students reaching this level have demonstrated competency over challenging subject matter.
[9]*Advanced* signifies superior performance.
NOTE: In 2014, only 8th-grade students were assessed in geography. Includes public and private schools. For 2001 and later years, includes students tested with accommodations (3 to 13 percent of all students, depending on grade level and year); excludes only those students with disabilities and English language learners who were unable to be tested even with accommodations (1 to 4 percent of all students). Race categories exclude persons of Hispanic ethnicity. Detail may not sum to totals because of rounding.
SOURCE: U.S. Department of Education, National Center for Education Statistics, National Assessment of Educational Progress (NAEP), 1994, 2001, 2010, and 2014 Geography Assessments, retrieved April 30, 2015, from the Main NAEP Data Explorer (http://nces.ed.gov/nationsreportcard/naepdata/). (This table was prepared April 2015.)

Table 224.50. Average National Assessment of Educational Progress (NAEP) U.S. history scale score, standard deviation, and percentage of students attaining achievement levels, by grade level, selected student characteristics, and percentile: Selected years, 1994 through 2014

[Standard errors appear in parentheses]

Selected student characteristic	4th-graders				8th-graders					12th-graders			
	1994[1]	2001	2006	2010	1994[1]	2001	2006	2010	2014	1994[1]	2001	2006	2010
1	2	3	4	5	6	7	8	9	10	11	12	13	14
Average U.S. history scale score[2]													
All students	205 (1.0)	208 (0.9)	211 (1.1)	214 (0.8)	259 (0.6)	260 (0.8)	263 (0.8)	266 (0.8)	267 (1.0)	286 (0.8)	287 (0.9)	290 (0.7)	288 (0.8)
Sex													
Male	203 (1.5)	207 (1.1)	211 (1.2)	215 (1.0)	259 (0.8)	261 (0.9)	264 (0.9)	268 (0.8)	270 (1.1)	288 (0.8)	288 (1.1)	292 (0.9)	290 (0.8)
Female	206 (1.1)	209 (1.2)	211 (1.1)	213 (0.9)	259 (0.7)	260 (0.9)	261 (0.8)	263 (0.8)	265 (0.9)	285 (0.9)	286 (0.9)	288 (0.8)	286 (1.0)
Race/ethnicity													
White	214 (1.3)	217 (1.3)	223 (1.1)	224 (1.1)	266 (0.8)	268 (0.9)	273 (0.6)	274 (0.7)	277 (0.9)	292 (0.8)	292 (1.0)	297 (0.8)	296 (0.7)
Black	176 (1.6)	186 (2.0)	191 (1.9)	198 (1.9)	238 (1.6)	240 (1.9)	244 (1.2)	250 (1.1)	251 (1.3)	265 (1.5)	267 (1.4)	270 (1.3)	268 (1.5)
Hispanic	175 (2.6)	184 (2.6)	194 (1.9)	198 (1.2)	243 (1.4)	240 (2.0)	248 (1.2)	252 (1.0)	257 (0.9)	267 (1.7)	271 (1.9)	275 (1.0)	275 (1.3)
Asian/Pacific Islander	204 (3.6)	216 (3.7)	214 (5.1)	221 (2.4)	261 (5.0)	264 (2.8)	270 (3.0)	275 (1.8)	279 (2.5)	283 (3.5)	294 (6.0)	296 (2.6)	293 (2.5)
Asian[3]	— (†)	— (†)	— (†)	— (†)	— (†)	— (†)	— (†)	— (†)	280 (2.5)	— (†)	— (†)	— (†)	— (†)
Pacific Islander[3]	— (†)	— (†)	— (†)	— (†)	— (†)	— (†)	— (†)	— (†)	— (†)	— (†)	— (†)	— (†)	— (†)
American Indian/Alaska Native	‡ (†)	‡ (†)	190 (5.9)	193 (6.2)	245 (3.4)	255 (4.4)	244 (6.3)	259 (5.0)	‡ (†)	272 (3.0)	283 (4.2)	278 (4.1)	278 (4.2)
Two or more races[3]	— (†)	— (†)	— (†)	— (†)	— (†)	— (†)	— (†)	— (†)	276 (1.9)	— (†)	— (†)	— (†)	— (†)
Parents' highest level of education[4]													
Did not finish high school	— (†)	— (†)	— (†)	— (†)	241 (1.3)	241 (2.8)	244 (1.2)	249 (0.9)	250 (1.3)	263 (1.4)	266 (1.6)	268 (1.3)	268 (1.7)
Graduated high school	— (†)	— (†)	— (†)	— (†)	251 (0.8)	251 (1.0)	252 (1.3)	255 (0.9)	255 (1.1)	276 (1.1)	274 (1.1)	278 (1.0)	277 (1.0)
Some education after high school	— (†)	— (†)	— (†)	— (†)	264 (0.8)	264 (1.0)	265 (0.9)	267 (0.9)	269 (0.8)	287 (1.2)	286 (0.8)	290 (0.8)	286 (0.8)
Graduated college	— (†)	— (†)	— (†)	— (†)	270 (0.8)	273 (0.9)	274 (0.8)	276 (0.8)	277 (1.1)	296 (0.9)	298 (1.2)	300 (0.8)	298 (0.8)
Eligibility for free or reduced-price lunch													
Eligible	— (†)	188 (1.4)	195 (1.1)	199 (0.9)	— (†)	242 (1.3)	247 (1.1)	253 (0.7)	254 (0.9)	— (†)	269 (1.4)	273 (1.0)	273 (1.0)
Not eligible	— (†)	219 (1.4)	224 (1.0)	227 (0.8)	— (†)	267 (1.1)	273 (0.7)	275 (0.8)	279 (1.0)	— (†)	289 (1.2)	295 (0.8)	294 (0.7)
Unknown	— (†)	217 (2.8)	227 (3.9)	225 (6.1)	— (†)	266 (2.0)	281 (2.7)	278 (2.0)	281 (2.5)	— (†)	294 (2.1)	300 (2.4)	300 (2.5)
Percentile[5]													
10th	147 (2.1)	157 (1.4)	165 (2.3)	169 (1.4)	217 (1.1)	216 (1.3)	221 (1.4)	227 (1.2)	229 (1.1)	243 (1.2)	244 (1.2)	249 (1.3)	246 (1.3)
25th	180 (1.5)	184 (1.4)	189 (1.3)	192 (1.6)	239 (0.9)	239 (0.9)	243 (0.9)	246 (0.9)	248 (1.0)	265 (1.2)	266 (1.1)	270 (1.0)	267 (1.3)
50th	210 (0.9)	211 (1.1)	213 (1.0)	216 (0.6)	261 (1.1)	262 (1.1)	265 (0.7)	267 (0.9)	269 (1.0)	288 (0.8)	288 (1.1)	291 (0.9)	290 (0.7)
75th	234 (1.2)	234 (1.0)	235 (1.1)	238 (0.9)	282 (0.7)	284 (1.0)	285 (0.7)	286 (0.7)	288 (1.0)	309 (0.9)	309 (1.0)	312 (0.7)	311 (0.6)
90th	253 (1.4)	254 (1.4)	254 (1.0)	256 (1.4)	299 (0.6)	302 (0.7)	302 (1.0)	302 (1.1)	303 (1.0)	326 (1.0)	326 (1.5)	329 (0.9)	328 (1.0)
Standard deviation of the U.S. history scale score[6]													
All students	41 (0.7)	38 (0.7)	34 (0.5)	34 (0.7)	32 (0.3)	33 (0.4)	32 (0.4)	29 (0.3)	29 (0.4)	32 (0.4)	32 (0.6)	31 (0.3)	32 (0.4)
Percent of students achieving U.S. history achievement levels													
Achievement level													
Below *Basic*[7]	36 (1.1)	34 (1.2)	30 (1.3)	27 (0.8)	39 (0.9)	38 (1.0)	35 (1.0)	31 (1.0)	29 (1.3)	57 (1.1)	57 (1.2)	53 (1.1)	55 (1.0)
At or above *Basic*[7]	64 (1.1)	66 (1.2)	70 (1.3)	73 (0.8)	61 (0.9)	62 (1.0)	65 (1.0)	69 (1.0)	71 (1.3)	43 (1.1)	43 (1.2)	47 (1.1)	45 (1.0)
At or above *Basic* by sex													
Male	62 (1.6)	65 (1.3)	69 (1.5)	73 (1.0)	61 (1.0)	62 (1.1)	67 (1.3)	71 (1.1)	74 (1.5)	45 (1.2)	45 (1.6)	50 (1.2)	49 (1.1)
Female	65 (1.4)	67 (1.4)	70 (1.2)	73 (1.0)	61 (1.3)	61 (1.2)	64 (1.0)	67 (1.2)	69 (1.4)	40 (1.4)	40 (1.2)	44 (1.2)	41 (1.4)
At or above *Basic* by race/ethnicity													
White	73 (1.3)	76 (1.5)	84 (1.2)	83 (1.0)	70 (1.1)	71 (1.1)	79 (0.8)	80 (0.9)	84 (1.2)	50 (1.2)	49 (1.3)	56 (1.3)	55 (1.2)
Black	35 (1.5)	41 (2.3)	46 (2.5)	54 (2.6)	32 (2.4)	35 (2.1)	40 (1.7)	48 (2.1)	47 (2.5)	17 (1.5)	19 (1.5)	20 (1.6)	20 (1.2)
Hispanic	36 (3.2)	40 (2.8)	49 (2.7)	56 (1.6)	41 (2.2)	36 (2.6)	46 (2.2)	52 (1.7)	59 (1.5)	22 (2.4)	24 (2.3)	27 (1.4)	28 (1.4)
Asian/Pacific Islander	62 (4.3)	74 (4.5)	71 (4.8)	82 (3.1)	60 (6.9)	65 (3.0)	75 (4.4)	78 (2.1)	82 (2.6)	40 (4.7)	51 (6.7)	54 (3.5)	50 (3.2)
Asian[3]	— (†)	— (†)	— (†)	— (†)	— (†)	— (†)	— (†)	— (†)	84 (2.6)	— (†)	— (†)	— (†)	— (†)
Pacific Islander[3]	— (†)	— (†)	— (†)	— (†)	— (†)	— (†)	— (†)	— (†)	— (†)	— (†)	— (†)	— (†)	— (†)
American Indian/Alaska Native	‡ (†)	‡ (†)	41 (7.7)	49 (5.4)	42 (6.2)	57 (6.5)	43 (6.1)	61 (6.3)	‡ (†)	21 (6.3)	37 (7.8)	32 (7.3)	29 (5.9)
Two or more races[3]	— (†)	— (†)	— (†)	— (†)	— (†)	— (†)	— (†)	— (†)	81 (2.5)	— (†)	— (†)	— (†)	— (†)
At or above *Proficient*[8]	17 (1.0)	18 (0.9)	18 (1.0)	20 (0.7)	14 (0.6)	16 (0.7)	17 (0.8)	17 (0.8)	18 (0.9)	11 (0.7)	11 (0.9)	13 (0.7)	12 (0.5)
At *Advanced*[9]	2 (0.3)	2 (0.3)	2 (0.3)	2 (0.3)	1 (0.1)	1 (0.2)	1 (0.1)	1 (0.1)	1 (0.1)	1 (0.2)	1 (0.3)	1 (0.2)	1 (0.1)

—Not available.
†Not applicable.
‡Reporting standards not met (too few cases for a reliable estimate).
[1]Accommodations were not permitted for this assessment.
[2]Scale ranges from 0 to 500.
[3]In U.S. history assessments prior to 2014, separate data for Asians, Pacific Islanders, and students of Two or more races were not collected.
[4]Based on student reports. Data for students whose parents have an unknown level of education are included in table totals, but not shown separately.
[5]The percentile represents a specific point on the percentage distribution of all students ranked by their U.S. history score from low to high. For example, 10 percent of students scored at or below the 10th percentile score, while 90 percent of students scored above it.
[6]The standard deviation provides an indication of how much the test scores varied. The lower the standard deviation, the closer the scores were clustered around the average score. About two-thirds of the student scores can be expected to fall within the range of one standard deviation above and one standard deviation below the average score. For example, the average score for all 8th-graders in 2014 was 267, and the standard deviation was 29. This means that about two-thirds of the students would be expected to have scores between 296 (one

standard deviation above the average) and 238 (one standard deviation below). Standard errors also must be taken into account when making comparisons of these ranges.
[7]*Basic* denotes partial mastery of the knowledge and skills that are fundamental for proficient work.
[8]*Proficient* represents solid academic performance. Students reaching this level have demonstrated competency over challenging subject matter.
[9]*Advanced* signifies superior performance.
NOTE: In 2014, only 8th-grade students were assessed in U.S. history. Includes public and private schools. For 2001 and later years, includes students tested with accommodations (3 to 13 percent of all students, depending on grade level and year); excludes only those students with disabilities and English language learners who were unable to be tested even with accommodations (1 to 3 percent of all students). Race categories exclude persons of Hispanic ethnicity. Detail may not sum to totals because of rounding.
SOURCE: U.S. Department of Education, National Center for Education Statistics, National Assessment of Educational Progress (NAEP), 1994, 2001, 2006, 2010, and 2014 U.S. History Assessments, retrieved April 30, 2015, from the Main NAEP Data Explorer (http://nces.ed.gov/nationsreportcard/naepdata/). (This table was prepared April 2015.)

Table 224.60. Average National Assessment of Educational Progress (NAEP) writing scale score of 8th- and 12th-graders, standard deviation, and percentage of students attaining writing achievement levels, by selected student and school characteristics and percentile: 2011

[Standard errors appear in parentheses]

Selected student or school characteristic	8th-graders Total, all students		8th-graders Eligibility for free or reduced-price lunch — Eligible		Not eligible		Unknown		12th-graders Total, all students		12th-graders Eligibility for free or reduced-price lunch — Eligible		Not eligible		Unknown	
1	2		3		4		5		6		7		8		9	
Average writing scale score[1]																
All students	**150**	**(0.7)**	**134**	**(0.6)**	**161**	**(0.8)**	**163**	**(2.2)**	**150**	**(0.5)**	**133**	**(0.7)**	**157**	**(0.6)**	**167**	**(1.7)**
Sex																
Male	140	(0.7)	125	(0.7)	151	(0.9)	154	(2.6)	143	(0.6)	126	(0.8)	150	(0.6)	162	(1.9)
Female	160	(0.7)	144	(0.6)	171	(0.8)	171	(2.5)	157	(0.6)	140	(0.7)	165	(0.6)	173	(1.9)
Race/ethnicity																
White	158	(0.8)	142	(0.8)	163	(0.9)	166	(2.3)	159	(0.7)	144	(1.0)	161	(0.7)	172	(1.6)
Black	132	(1.1)	127	(1.1)	145	(1.4)	140	(4.6)	130	(1.0)	124	(1.1)	140	(1.2)	148	(3.6)
Hispanic	136	(0.7)	130	(0.8)	150	(1.0)	150	(5.4)	134	(0.7)	128	(0.8)	142	(1.0)	149	(3.6)
Asian/Pacific Islander	163	(2.4)	146	(2.8)	171	(2.4)	175	(4.0)	158	(1.6)	146	(2.3)	163	(2.0)	162	(4.9)
Asian	165	(2.0)	148	(2.7)	172	(2.2)	175	(4.0)	158	(1.5)	146	(2.5)	164	(1.7)	162	(5.0)
Native Hawaiian/Pacific Islander	141	(6.3)	‡	(†)	‡	(†)	‡	(†)	144	(6.0)	‡	(†)	‡	(†)	‡	(†)
American Indian/Alaska Native	145	(4.0)	139	(4.3)	‡	(†)	‡	(†)	145	(3.5)	135	(4.4)	153	(4.4)	‡	(†)
Two or more races	155	(1.9)	141	(2.3)	165	(2.5)	‡	(†)	158	(2.3)	137	(4.2)	163	(2.8)	‡	(†)
Parents' highest level of education																
Did not finish high school	133	(1.0)	131	(1.0)	142	(2.0)	‡	(†)	129	(0.9)	127	(1.0)	135	(1.6)	‡	(†)
Graduated high school	138	(0.8)	131	(0.8)	149	(1.3)	146	(4.4)	138	(0.7)	131	(1.0)	145	(0.9)	153	(3.5)
Some education after high school	150	(0.9)	143	(0.9)	158	(1.2)	155	(3.8)	149	(0.5)	140	(0.9)	155	(0.6)	158	(2.2)
Graduated college	160	(0.8)	141	(0.8)	166	(0.9)	167	(2.3)	160	(0.7)	139	(1.1)	164	(0.7)	173	(1.5)
Student's attitude and experience																
Agreed or strongly agreed that "Writing is one of my favorite activities"	157	(0.8)	141	(0.8)	170	(0.9)	172	(2.5)	157	(0.6)	139	(0.8)	165	(0.6)	175	(2.0)
Uses a computer for writing school assignments once or twice a week	157	(0.9)	140	(0.7)	168	(1.2)	169	(2.9)	154	(0.6)	136	(0.8)	161	(0.7)	167	(1.4)
School locale																
City	144	(1.2)	130	(1.0)	160	(1.4)	164	(4.3)	146	(1.0)	131	(0.8)	156	(1.2)	168	(2.5)
Suburban	155	(1.3)	137	(1.0)	165	(1.3)	164	(4.4)	154	(0.9)	135	(1.1)	160	(0.9)	167	(2.1)
Town	148	(1.1)	137	(1.3)	156	(1.3)	157	(3.8)	149	(2.0)	134	(3.1)	156	(1.8)	‡	(†)
Rural	150	(1.4)	137	(1.5)	158	(1.3)	158	(5.3)	149	(1.1)	135	(1.5)	154	(1.0)	164	(5.4)
Percentile[2]																
10th	104	(1.0)	92	(1.1)	119	(1.1)	121	(3.8)	104	(0.9)	90	(0.9)	114	(1.1)	126	(4.6)
25th	127	(0.8)	113	(0.6)	140	(1.0)	142	(2.6)	127	(0.8)	111	(0.9)	136	(0.8)	149	(2.3)
50th	151	(0.8)	135	(0.6)	163	(0.9)	163	(2.6)	152	(0.7)	135	(1.1)	159	(0.8)	170	(2.2)
75th	175	(0.7)	157	(0.8)	184	(1.1)	185	(2.6)	175	(0.6)	156	(0.6)	180	(0.5)	189	(1.7)
90th	194	(0.9)	176	(0.9)	201	(1.4)	203	(3.5)	194	(0.7)	176	(0.8)	198	(0.8)	205	(3.2)
Standard deviation of the writing scale score[3]																
All students	35	(0.3)	33	(0.3)	32	(0.3)	32	(1.1)	35	(0.3)	33	(0.3)	33	(0.3)	31	(0.9)
Percent of students attaining writing achievement levels																
Achievement level																
Below *Basic*[4]	20	(0.6)	32	(0.8)	10	(0.6)	10	(1.6)	21	(0.6)	36	(0.9)	14	(0.5)	9	(1.3)
At or above *Basic*	80	(0.6)	68	(0.8)	90	(0.6)	90	(1.6)	79	(0.6)	64	(0.9)	86	(0.5)	91	(1.3)
At or above *Basic* by race/ethnicity																
White	87	(0.6)	76	(1.1)	91	(0.6)	94	(1.6)	87	(0.6)	76	(1.2)	88	(0.6)	95	(1.1)
Black	65	(1.7)	59	(1.7)	79	(2.1)	74	(6.4)	61	(1.5)	54	(1.7)	71	(1.9)	82	(3.9)
Hispanic	69	(0.9)	63	(1.1)	82	(1.2)	80	(5.4)	65	(0.9)	59	(1.1)	74	(1.4)	79	(4.7)
Asian/Pacific Islander	88	(2.3)	76	(3.4)	93	(1.8)	96	(2.1)	85	(1.4)	78	(2.7)	89	(1.4)	83	(4.4)
Asian	89	(1.9)	79	(3.0)	94	(1.7)	95	(2.2)	85	(1.4)	78	(2.9)	89	(1.3)	83	(4.4)
Native Hawaiian/Pacific Islander	70	(7.3)	‡	(†)	‡	(†)	‡	(†)	78	(5.0)	‡	(†)	‡	(†)	‡	(†)
American Indian/Alaska Native	78	(4.7)	74	(6.6)	‡	(†)	‡	(†)	76	(4.3)	66	(7.2)	84	(5.0)	‡	(†)
Two or more races	87	(1.7)	79	(3.9)	92	(1.9)	‡	(†)	86	(2.7)	70	(7.1)	90	(3.1)	‡	(†)
At or above *Proficient*[5]	27	(0.7)	12	(0.4)	37	(1.0)	39	(2.9)	27	(0.6)	12	(0.5)	33	(0.7)	46	(2.3)
At *Advanced*[6]	3	(0.2)	1	(0.1)	5	(0.4)	5	(1.2)	3	(0.2)	1	(0.1)	4	(0.3)	7	(1.2)

†Not applicable.

‡Reporting standards not met (too few cases for a reliable estimate).

[1]Scale ranges from 0 to 300.

[2]The percentile represents a specific point on the percentage distribution of all students ranked by their writing score from low to high. For example, 10 percent of students scored at or below the 10th percentile score, while 90 percent of students scored above it.

[3]The standard deviation provides an indication of how much the test scores varied. The lower the standard deviation, the closer the scores were clustered around the average score. About two-thirds of the student scores can be expected to fall within the range of one standard deviation above and one standard deviation below the average score. For example, the average score for all 12th-graders was 150 and the standard deviation was 35. This means that we would expect about two-thirds of the students to have scores between 185 (one standard deviation above the average) and 115 (one standard deviation below). Standard errors also must be taken into account when making comparisons of these ranges.

[4]*Basic* denotes partial mastery of the knowledge and skills that are fundamental for proficient work.

[5]*Proficient* represents solid academic performance. Students reaching this level have demonstrated competency over challenging subject matter.

[6]*Advanced* signifies superior performance.

NOTE: Writing scores from 2011 cannot be compared with writing scores from earlier assessment years. The 2011 writing assessment was developed under a new framework and is NAEP's first computer-based writing assessment. Includes public and private schools. Includes students tested with accommodations (8 percent of all 8th-graders and 7 percent of all 12th-graders); excludes only those students with disabilities and English language learners who were unable to be tested even with accommodations (2 percent of all students at both grades). Race categories exclude persons of Hispanic ethnicity. Detail may not sum to totals because of rounding.

SOURCE: U.S. Department of Education, National Center for Education Statistics, National Assessment of Educational Progress (NAEP), 2011 Writing Assessment, retrieved October 1, 2012, from the Main NAEP Data Explorer (http://nces.ed.gov/nationsreportcard/naepdata/). (This table was prepared October 2012.)

Table 225.10. Average number of Carnegie units earned by public high school graduates in various subject fields, by sex and race/ethnicity: Selected years, 1982 through 2009

[Standard errors appear in parentheses]

Graduation year, sex, and race/ethnicity	Total	English	History/ social studies	Mathematics	Science					Foreign languages	Arts	Career/ technical (occupational) education[1]	Labor market, family, and consumer education[2]	Personal use[3]
					Total	Biology	Chemistry	Physics	Other science[4]					
1	2	3	4	5	6	7	8	9	10	11	12	13	14	15
1982 graduates	**21.58 (0.090)**	**3.93 (0.022)**	**3.16 (0.028)**	**2.63 (0.022)**	**2.20 (0.025)**	**0.94 (0.014)**	**0.34 (0.010)**	**0.17 (0.008)**	**0.73 (0.016)**	**0.99 (0.029)**	**1.47 (0.035)**	**(†)**	**(†)**	**2.58 (0.048)**
Sex														
Male	21.40 (0.108)	3.88 (0.026)	3.16 (0.034)	2.71 (0.030)	2.27 (0.031)	0.91 (0.016)	0.36 (0.014)	0.23 (0.012)	0.76 (0.018)	0.80 (0.030)	1.29 (0.044)	‡	—	2.69 (0.056)
Female	21.75 (0.101)	3.98 (0.026)	3.15 (0.029)	2.57 (0.024)	2.13 (0.029)	0.97 (0.017)	0.33 (0.013)	0.12 (0.008)	0.71 (0.017)	1.17 (0.036)	1.63 (0.044)	‡	—	2.48 (0.049)
Race/ethnicity														
White	21.69 (0.107)	3.90 (0.025)	3.19 (0.032)	2.68 (0.026)	2.27 (0.029)	0.97 (0.015)	0.38 (0.013)	0.20 (0.010)	0.73 (0.017)	1.06 (0.033)	1.53 (0.042)	‡	—	2.52 (0.052)
Black	21.15 (0.169)	4.08 (0.050)	3.08 (0.054)	2.61 (0.043)	2.06 (0.049)	0.90 (0.033)	0.26 (0.023)	0.09 (0.011)	0.81 (0.033)	0.72 (0.067)	1.26 (0.063)	‡	—	2.60 (0.094)
Hispanic	21.23 (0.122)	3.94 (0.037)	3.00 (0.037)	2.33 (0.040)	1.80 (0.038)	0.81 (0.025)	0.16 (0.012)	0.07 (0.007)	0.75 (0.026)	0.77 (0.042)	1.29 (0.054)	‡	—	2.87 (0.081)
Asian/Pacific Islander	22.46 (0.216)	4.01 (0.091)	3.16 (0.094)	3.15 (0.095)	2.64 (0.125)	1.11 (0.048)	0.61 (0.046)	0.42 (0.048)	0.51 (0.061)	1.79 (0.105)	1.31 (0.124)	‡	—	3.05 (0.146)
American Indian/ Alaska Native	21.45 (0.330)	3.98 (0.114)	3.25 (0.207)	2.35 (0.129)	2.04 (0.090)	0.84 (0.124)	0.42 (0.087)	0.12 ! (0.039)	0.67 (0.087)	0.48 (0.117)	1.72 (0.338)	‡	—	2.84 (0.128)
1987 graduates	**23.00 (0.157)**	**4.12 (0.022)**	**3.32 (0.037)**	**3.01 (0.029)**	**2.55 (0.046)**	**1.10 (0.020)**	**0.47 (0.015)**	**0.21 (0.011)**	**0.76 (0.033)**	**1.35 (0.049)**	**1.44 (0.044)**	**(†)**	**(†)**	**2.67 (0.073)**
Sex														
Male	22.88 (0.162)	4.08 (0.021)	3.29 (0.037)	3.05 (0.029)	2.59 (0.049)	1.05 (0.021)	0.47 (0.016)	0.26 (0.013)	0.79 (0.032)	1.16 (0.051)	1.24 (0.046)	‡	—	2.83 (0.081)
Female	23.12 (0.156)	4.15 (0.026)	3.35 (0.041)	2.96 (0.030)	2.52 (0.048)	1.14 (0.022)	0.47 (0.017)	0.17 (0.012)	0.74 (0.035)	1.53 (0.051)	1.63 (0.050)	‡	—	2.51 (0.069)
Race/ethnicity														
White	23.11 (0.189)	4.08 (0.028)	3.29 (0.045)	3.01 (0.034)	2.61 (0.058)	1.12 (0.025)	0.50 (0.020)	0.23 (0.012)	0.75 (0.040)	1.38 (0.055)	1.50 (0.055)	‡	—	2.60 (0.082)
Black	22.40 (0.251)	4.22 (0.038)	3.34 (0.073)	2.99 (0.060)	2.33 (0.060)	1.01 (0.036)	0.31 (0.021)	0.10 (0.020)	0.90 (0.051)	1.08 (0.094)	1.20 (0.064)	‡	—	2.73 (0.120)
Hispanic	22.84 (0.162)	4.30 (0.055)	3.22 (0.071)	2.81 (0.056)	2.24 (0.045)	1.07 (0.028)	0.29 (0.015)	0.13 (0.013)	0.78 (0.028)	1.25 (0.071)	1.34 (0.056)	‡	—	3.19 (0.096)
Asian/Pacific Islander	24.47 (0.332)	4.37 (0.076)	3.65 (0.163)	3.71 (0.094)	3.14 (0.116)	1.17 (0.027)	0.87 (0.069)	0.50 (0.045)	0.59 (0.048)	2.07 (0.105)	1.18 (0.077)	‡	—	3.23 (0.185)
American Indian/ Alaska Native	23.23 (0.153)	4.22 (0.033)	3.18 (0.044)	2.98 (0.113)	2.44 (0.104)	1.22 (0.073)	0.32 (0.035)	0.09 ! (0.027)	0.81 (0.041)	0.75 (0.138)	1.68 (0.112)	‡	—	3.06 (0.050)
1990 graduates	**23.53 (0.127)**	**4.19 (0.034)**	**3.47 (0.040)**	**3.15 (0.028)**	**2.75 (0.028)**	**1.14 (0.019)**	**0.53 (0.014)**	**0.23 (0.010)**	**0.85 (0.026)**	**1.54 (0.041)**	**1.55 (0.045)**	**(†)**	**(†)**	**2.68 (0.073)**
Sex														
Male	23.35 (0.130)	4.13 (0.035)	3.45 (0.041)	3.16 (0.028)	2.78 (0.033)	1.11 (0.021)	0.52 (0.017)	0.28 (0.012)	0.88 (0.027)	1.33 (0.040)	1.31 (0.047)	‡	—	2.87 (0.077)
Female	23.69 (0.132)	4.25 (0.036)	3.50 (0.041)	3.14 (0.033)	2.73 (0.027)	1.17 (0.019)	0.53 (0.014)	0.19 (0.010)	0.83 (0.027)	1.72 (0.045)	1.76 (0.050)	‡	—	2.51 (0.072)
Race/ethnicity														
White	23.54 (0.133)	4.12 (0.036)	3.46 (0.045)	3.13 (0.032)	2.80 (0.033)	1.15 (0.020)	0.55 (0.016)	0.25 (0.011)	0.84 (0.022)	1.58 (0.049)	1.61 (0.056)	‡	—	2.61 (0.076)
Black	23.40 (0.255)	4.34 (0.044)	3.49 (0.058)	3.20 (0.064)	2.68 (0.061)	1.11 (0.042)	0.42 (0.024)	0.16 (0.020)	0.98 (0.068)	1.20 (0.075)	1.34 (0.052)	‡	—	2.74 (0.124)
Hispanic	23.83 (0.210)	4.51 (0.139)	3.42 (0.071)	3.13 (0.058)	2.50 (0.046)	1.10 (0.034)	0.42 (0.034)	0.14 (0.016)	0.83 (0.041)	1.57 (0.060)	1.48 (0.072)	‡	—	3.10 (0.103)
Asian/Pacific Islander	24.07 (0.236)	4.50 (0.117)	3.70 (0.126)	3.52 (0.060)	2.97 (0.114)	1.12 (0.085)	0.74 (0.057)	0.42 (0.047)	0.68 (0.080)	2.06 (0.150)	1.29 (0.084)	‡	—	2.96 (0.221)
American Indian/ Alaska Native	22.64 (0.267)	4.08 (0.092)	3.34 (0.083)	3.04 (0.152)	2.48 (0.175)	1.09 (0.090)	0.42 (0.072)	0.15 (0.039)	0.83 (0.090)	1.15 (0.188)	1.11 (0.126)	‡	—	2.81 (0.148)
1994 graduates	**24.17 (0.144)**	**4.29 (0.028)**	**3.55 (0.041)**	**3.33 (0.021)**	**3.04 (0.028)**	**1.26 (0.018)**	**0.62 (0.013)**	**0.28 (0.011)**	**0.88 (0.024)**	**1.71 (0.033)**	**1.66 (0.041)**	**(†)**	**(†)**	**2.63 (0.077)**
Sex														
Male	23.79 (0.146)	4.26 (0.028)	3.51 (0.041)	3.32 (0.022)	3.03 (0.030)	1.20 (0.020)	0.59 (0.015)	0.32 (0.014)	0.91 (0.026)	1.49 (0.034)	1.43 (0.038)	‡	—	2.83 (0.081)
Female	24.11 (0.147)	4.32 (0.030)	3.59 (0.041)	3.34 (0.023)	3.06 (0.028)	1.31 (0.018)	0.64 (0.014)	0.24 (0.010)	0.86 (0.024)	1.93 (0.034)	1.87 (0.051)	‡	—	2.44 (0.078)
Race/ethnicity														
White	24.08 (0.183)	4.23 (0.035)	3.56 (0.049)	3.36 (0.023)	3.13 (0.032)	1.29 (0.022)	0.65 (0.014)	0.30 (0.014)	0.89 (0.030)	1.76 (0.039)	1.74 (0.049)	‡	—	2.61 (0.096)
Black	23.28 (0.132)	4.36 (0.044)	3.51 (0.050)	3.23 (0.030)	2.80 (0.042)	1.21 (0.036)	0.49 (0.028)	0.17 (0.013)	0.92 (0.051)	1.35 (0.052)	1.36 (0.066)	‡	—	2.69 (0.101)
Hispanic	23.71 (0.131)	4.51 (0.075)	3.45 (0.046)	3.28 (0.041)	2.69 (0.046)	1.19 (0.027)	0.49 (0.047)	0.17 (0.021)	0.83 (0.058)	1.73 (0.062)	1.51 (0.046)	‡	—	2.93 (0.086)
Asian/Pacific Islander	23.84 (0.256)	4.60 (0.091)	3.66 (0.097)	3.66 (0.082)	3.35 (0.131)	1.22 (0.042)	0.81 (0.062)	0.48 (0.058)	0.80 (0.034)	2.09 (0.085)	1.32 (0.121)	‡	—	2.78 (0.123)
American Indian/ Alaska Native	23.40 (0.541)	4.27 (0.113)	3.57 (0.201)	3.11 (0.038)	2.82 (0.073)	1.28 (0.069)	0.50 (0.065)	0.13 (0.039)	0.91 (0.057)	1.30 (0.150)	2.01 (0.351)	‡	—	3.12 (0.355)
1998 graduates	**25.14 (0.162)**	**4.25 (0.037)**	**3.74 (0.038)**	**3.40 (0.024)**	**3.12 (0.026)**	**1.26 (0.021)**	**0.66 (0.015)**	**0.31 (0.015)**	**0.89 (0.024)**	**1.85 (0.039)**	**1.90 (0.079)**	**(†)**	**(†)**	**2.89 (0.076)**
Sex														
Male	24.64 (0.162)	4.19 (0.038)	3.68 (0.040)	3.37 (0.024)	3.09 (0.028)	1.20 (0.021)	0.62 (0.014)	0.33 (0.018)	0.93 (0.026)	1.62 (0.040)	1.61 (0.072)	‡	—	3.12 (0.079)
Female	25.04 (0.166)	4.31 (0.039)	3.80 (0.036)	3.42 (0.025)	3.17 (0.029)	1.32 (0.023)	0.70 (0.018)	0.28 (0.015)	0.87 (0.023)	2.06 (0.041)	2.15 (0.094)	‡	—	2.67 (0.080)
Race/ethnicity														
White	24.87 (0.178)	4.19 (0.049)	3.77 (0.046)	3.40 (0.028)	3.18 (0.028)	1.28 (0.025)	0.69 (0.017)	0.33 (0.019)	0.87 (0.027)	1.90 (0.049)	1.74 (0.078)	‡	—	2.80 (0.088)
Black	24.37 (0.250)	4.28 (0.045)	3.69 (0.050)	3.42 (0.042)	3.03 (0.064)	1.24 (0.038)	0.58 (0.025)	0.22 (0.022)	0.97 (0.045)	1.58 (0.062)	1.57 (0.152)	‡	—	2.94 (0.080)
Hispanic	24.69 (0.218)	4.51 (0.055)	3.60 (0.051)	3.28 (0.041)	2.81 (0.054)	1.13 (0.026)	0.50 (0.036)	0.20 (0.020)	0.97 (0.042)	1.78 (0.055)	1.78 (0.113)	‡	—	3.36 (0.121)
Asian/Pacific Islander	24.67 (0.195)	4.37 (0.068)	3.92 (0.086)	3.62 (0.029)	3.43 (0.079)	1.26 (0.027)	0.83 (0.037)	0.51 (0.036)	0.81 (0.041)	2.29 (0.129)	1.52 (0.056)	‡	—	2.95 (0.208)
American Indian/ Alaska Native	23.81 (0.350)	4.18 (0.082)	3.67 (0.093)	3.10 (0.081)	2.68 (0.081)	1.07 (0.056)	0.49 (0.038)	0.15 (0.024)	0.98 (0.070)	1.45 (0.132)	1.94 (0.146)	‡	—	3.40 (0.212)

See notes at end of table.

Table 225.10. Average number of Carnegie units earned by public high school graduates in various subject fields, by sex and race/ethnicity: Selected years, 1982 through 2009—Continued

[Standard errors appear in parentheses]

Graduation year, sex, and race/ethnicity	Total	English	History/ social studies	Mathematics	Science					Foreign languages	Arts	Career/ technical (occupational) education[1]	Labor market, family, and consumer education[2]	Personal use[3]
					Total	Biology	Chemistry	Physics	Other science[4]					
1	2	3	4	5	6	7	8	9	10	11	12	13	14	15
2000 graduates	26.15 (0.204)	4.26 (0.037)	3.89 (0.036)	3.62 (0.029)	3.20 (0.038)	1.28 (0.028)	0.71 (0.020)	0.37 (0.018)	0.84 (0.030)	2.01 (0.045)	2.03 (0.054)	2.86 (0.105)	1.35 (0.044)	3.49 (0.071)
Sex														
Male	26.01 (0.210)	4.18 (0.036)	3.83 (0.036)	3.60 (0.032)	3.15 (0.039)	1.20 (0.030)	0.67 (0.020)	0.42 (0.020)	0.87 (0.029)	1.77 (0.045)	1.75 (0.051)	3.24 (0.133)	1.35 (0.049)	3.76 (0.079)
Female	26.26 (0.204)	4.34 (0.040)	3.95 (0.038)	3.64 (0.028)	3.24 (0.041)	1.36 (0.030)	0.74 (0.022)	0.33 (0.018)	0.81 (0.031)	2.25 (0.050)	2.29 (0.065)	2.48 (0.086)	1.34 (0.047)	3.22 (0.068)
Race/ethnicity														
White	26.31 (0.256)	4.26 (0.037)	3.93 (0.042)	3.63 (0.032)	3.24 (0.038)	1.30 (0.034)	0.72 (0.024)	0.39 (0.021)	0.83 (0.033)	1.98 (0.054)	2.11 (0.068)	2.97 (0.136)	1.37 (0.055)	3.37 (0.080)
Black	25.85 (0.233)	4.36 (0.078)	3.81 (0.068)	3.57 (0.046)	3.12 (0.059)	1.25 (0.041)	0.66 (0.030)	0.30 (0.027)	0.91 (0.043)	1.71 (0.070)	1.94 (0.134)	2.74 (0.143)	1.54 (0.075)	3.60 (0.134)
Hispanic	25.59 (0.358)	4.29 (0.125)	3.84 (0.076)	3.48 (0.069)	2.86 (0.112)	1.18 (0.068)	0.58 (0.055)	0.25 (0.026)	0.84 (0.044)	2.22 (0.063)	1.76 (0.062)	2.64 (0.152)	1.20 (0.082)	3.95 (0.173)
Asian/Pacific Islander	26.23 (0.332)	4.12 (0.060)	3.80 (0.055)	4.01 (0.108)	3.70 (0.162)	1.35 (0.066)	0.97 (0.050)	0.67 (0.042)	0.71 (0.086)	2.90 (0.089)	1.78 (0.085)	1.99 (0.149)	0.81 (0.050)	3.52 (0.221)
American Indian/ Alaska Native	25.24 (0.342)	4.08 (0.069)	3.82 (0.102)	3.35 (0.117)	2.88 (0.086)	1.25 (0.080)	0.45 (0.045)	0.19 (0.042)	0.98 (0.038)	1.41 (0.105)	1.99 (0.220)	3.23 (0.380)	1.60 (0.151)	3.60 (0.365)
2005 graduates	26.88 (0.102)	4.33 (0.022)	4.08 (0.027)	3.80 (0.018)	3.35 (0.019)	1.28 (0.016)	0.75 (0.011)	0.37 (0.012)	0.95 (0.019)	2.07 (0.022)	2.06 (0.035)	2.64 (0.045)	1.38 (0.030)	3.83 (0.047)
Sex														
Male	26.70 (0.107)	4.26 (0.024)	4.01 (0.030)	3.78 (0.021)	3.29 (0.023)	1.19 (0.016)	0.71 (0.012)	0.41 (0.014)	0.98 (0.019)	1.87 (0.025)	1.71 (0.035)	3.01 (0.050)	1.36 (0.032)	4.17 (0.055)
Female	27.05 (0.104)	4.39 (0.022)	4.16 (0.028)	3.83 (0.018)	3.41 (0.019)	1.37 (0.017)	0.79 (0.012)	0.33 (0.012)	0.92 (0.020)	2.25 (0.023)	2.38 (0.045)	2.29 (0.049)	1.41 (0.033)	3.52 (0.050)
Race/ethnicity														
White	27.06 (0.127)	4.30 (0.030)	4.12 (0.030)	3.80 (0.022)	3.44 (0.021)	1.31 (0.018)	0.77 (0.014)	0.39 (0.012)	0.96 (0.021)	2.03 (0.025)	2.17 (0.043)	2.75 (0.059)	1.39 (0.036)	3.64 (0.059)
Black	26.76 (0.151)	4.50 (0.039)	4.10 (0.054)	3.86 (0.036)	3.22 (0.035)	1.27 (0.025)	0.69 (0.017)	0.28 (0.025)	0.99 (0.037)	1.77 (0.041)	1.77 (0.056)	2.58 (0.074)	1.56 (0.065)	4.32 (0.096)
Hispanic	26.18 (0.147)	4.33 (0.026)	3.88 (0.052)	3.64 (0.034)	2.93 (0.036)	1.11 (0.021)	0.64 (0.022)	0.25 (0.017)	0.94 (0.031)	2.39 (0.047)	1.78 (0.055)	2.41 (0.086)	1.30 (0.046)	4.44 (0.100)
Asian/Pacific Islander	26.58 (0.183)	4.28 (0.043)	4.02 (0.048)	4.08 (0.051)	3.65 (0.057)	1.31 (0.035)	0.98 (0.028)	0.59 (0.036)	0.77 (0.061)	2.70 (0.066)	1.80 (0.076)	1.94 (0.116)	0.98 (0.052)	3.53 (0.122)
American Indian/ Alaska Native	26.66 (0.454)	4.42 (0.136)	4.15 (0.151)	3.60 (0.175)	3.00 (0.075)	1.27 (0.061)	0.52 (0.053)	0.17 (0.036)	1.04 (0.063)	1.55 (0.125)	2.45 (0.179)	2.45 (0.208)	1.70 (0.184)	4.24 (0.294)
2009 graduates	27.15 (0.100)	4.37 (0.013)	4.19 (0.027)	3.91 (0.017)	3.47 (0.022)	1.35 (0.014)	0.78 (0.011)	0.42 (0.013)	0.92 (0.017)	2.21 (0.027)	2.12 (0.036)	2.47 (0.059)	1.11 (0.030)	3.86 (0.059)
Sex														
Male	26.98 (0.111)	4.30 (0.015)	4.13 (0.028)	3.88 (0.018)	3.46 (0.027)	1.27 (0.014)	0.74 (0.012)	0.48 (0.017)	0.96 (0.017)	2.01 (0.028)	1.76 (0.034)	2.77 (0.068)	1.13 (0.036)	4.18 (0.070)
Female	27.31 (0.095)	4.42 (0.014)	4.25 (0.027)	3.93 (0.018)	3.49 (0.020)	1.43 (0.015)	0.82 (0.011)	0.37 (0.012)	0.88 (0.019)	2.40 (0.028)	2.46 (0.046)	2.19 (0.055)	1.10 (0.028)	3.57 (0.060)
Race/ethnicity														
White	27.30 (0.151)	4.32 (0.016)	4.23 (0.037)	3.91 (0.021)	3.55 (0.026)	1.37 (0.015)	0.80 (0.013)	0.44 (0.016)	0.94 (0.022)	2.19 (0.032)	2.26 (0.042)	2.55 (0.071)	1.16 (0.040)	3.70 (0.075)
Black	27.42 (0.141)	4.56 (0.039)	4.26 (0.036)	4.02 (0.035)	3.31 (0.027)	1.33 (0.025)	0.68 (0.022)	0.30 (0.019)	1.00 (0.028)	1.87 (0.044)	1.87 (0.067)	2.72 (0.127)	1.21 (0.052)	4.29 (0.102)
Hispanic	26.47 (0.194)	4.43 (0.024)	4.04 (0.040)	3.70 (0.029)	3.13 (0.028)	1.24 (0.019)	0.70 (0.015)	0.32 (0.015)	0.87 (0.024)	2.34 (0.034)	1.85 (0.046)	2.31 (0.101)	1.04 (0.040)	4.26 (0.095)
Asian/Pacific Islander	26.94 (0.190)	4.19 (0.039)	4.13 (0.083)	4.16 (0.052)	4.06 (0.091)	1.56 (0.077)	1.08 (0.035)	0.75 (0.033)	0.68 (0.063)	2.98 (0.090)	1.99 (0.065)	1.63 (0.074)	0.62 (0.054)	3.47 (0.100)
American Indian/ Alaska Native	26.17 (0.409)	4.39 (0.085)	4.11 (0.083)	3.76 (0.125)	3.20 (0.070)	1.38 (0.062)	0.50 (0.051)	0.24 (0.046)	1.09 (0.066)	1.56 (0.097)	2.19 (0.157)	2.35 (0.188)	1.20 (0.117)	4.54 (0.370)

—Not available.
†Not applicable.
‡Interpret data with caution. The coefficient of variation (CV) for this estimate is between 30 and 50 percent.
[1]Includes occupational education in agriculture; business and marketing; communications and design; computer and information sciences; construction and architecture; engineering technologies; health sciences; manufacturing; repair and transportation; and personal, public, and legal services. Does not include general labor market preparation courses and family and consumer sciences education courses.
[2]Includes general labor market preparation courses and family and consumer sciences education courses.
[3]Includes general skills, personal health and physical education, religion, military sciences, special education, and other courses not included in other academic subject fields. Some personal-use courses are also included in the Career/technical (occupational) education column and the Labor market, family, and consumer education column.
[4]Includes all science credits earned outside of biology, chemistry, and physics.
NOTE: The Carnegie unit is a standard of measurement that represents one credit for the completion of a 1-year course. Data differ slightly from figures appearing in other NCES reports because of differences in taxonomies and case exclusion criteria. Race categories exclude persons of Hispanic ethnicity. Totals include other racial/ethnic groups not separately shown. Detail may not sum to totals because of rounding.
SOURCE: U.S. Department of Education, National Center for Education Statistics, High School and Beyond Longitudinal Study of 1980 Sophomores (HS&B-So:80/82), "High School Transcript Study"; and 1987, 1990, 1994, 1998, 2000, 2005, and 2009 High School Transcript Study (HSTS). (This table was prepared September 2011.)

Table 225.20. Average number of Carnegie units earned by public high school graduates in career/technical education courses in various occupational fields, by sex and race/ethnicity, and percentage distribution of students, by units earned: Selected years, 2000 through 2009

[Standard errors appear in parentheses]

Graduation year, sex, and race/ethnicity	Total, all occupational education courses[1]	Agriculture	Business and marketing	Communications and design	Computer and information sciences	Construction and architecture	Engineering technologies	Health sciences	Manufacturing	Repair and transportation	Personal, public, and legal services
1	2	3	4	5	6	7	8	9	10	11	12
2000 graduates											
Average units earned, all students[2]	2.86 (0.105)	0.25 (0.029)	0.82 (0.041)	0.30 (0.016)	0.27 (0.021)	0.14 (0.018)	0.20 (0.020)	0.15 (0.019)	0.24 (0.021)	0.18 (0.015)	0.32 (0.018)
Units earned, by sex											
Male	3.24 (0.133)	0.34 (0.041)	0.71 (0.043)	0.28 (0.018)	0.33 (0.026)	0.25 (0.035)	0.34 (0.034)	0.07 (0.013)	0.40 (0.035)	0.33 (0.028)	0.18 (0.015)
Female	2.48 (0.086)	0.16 (0.022)	0.91 (0.042)	0.32 (0.017)	0.21 (0.020)	0.02 (0.003)	0.06 (0.008)	0.22 (0.026)	0.10 (0.011)	0.03 (0.004)	0.46 (0.027)
Units earned, by race/ethnicity											
White	2.97 (0.136)	0.31 (0.038)	0.79 (0.049)	0.31 (0.019)	0.26 (0.023)	0.16 (0.027)	0.22 (0.025)	0.13 (0.019)	0.27 (0.027)	0.20 (0.021)	0.31 (0.020)
Black	2.74 (0.143)	0.11 (0.027)	0.98 (0.068)	0.29 (0.026)	0.24 (0.024)	0.08 (0.017)	0.15 (0.029)	0.17 (0.022)	0.17 (0.023)	0.11 (0.016)	0.44 (0.050)
Hispanic	2.64 (0.152)	0.13 (0.020)	0.86 (0.083)	0.29 (0.024)	0.26 (0.021)	0.09 (0.018)	0.14 (0.019)	0.24 ! (0.100)	0.17 (0.027)	0.15 (0.017)	0.31 (0.029)
Asian/Pacific Islander	1.99 (0.149)	0.06 (0.014)	0.54 (0.065)	0.25 (0.035)	0.45 (0.098)	0.02 ! (0.007)	0.17 (0.033)	0.15 (0.037)	0.12 (0.030)	0.07 (0.018)	0.16 (0.022)
American Indian/Alaska Native	3.23 (0.380)	0.37 ! (0.131)	0.80 (0.088)	0.24 (0.050)	0.32 (0.072)	0.08 ! (0.029)	0.20 ! (0.067)	0.11 (0.030)	0.49 ! (0.160)	‡ (†)	0.41 (0.121)
Percentage distribution of students, by units earned											
0 units	11.1 (0.79)	88.3 (0.86)	49.0 (1.83)	74.5 (1.29)	75.7 (1.61)	93.1 (0.51)	85.8 (1.10)	89.4 (1.23)	83.6 (0.98)	90.7 (0.61)	74.5 (1.34)
More than 0, but less than 1	7.9 (0.57)	2.3 (0.37)	12.1 (1.18)	8.9 (0.72)	8.7 (1.22)	1.8 (0.26)	3.4 (0.44)	5.6 (1.22)	5.4 (0.53)	2.7 (0.43)	11.8 (1.01)
At least 1, but less than 2	22.1 (0.77)	4.5 (0.37)	22.7 (0.91)	12.1 (0.72)	11.9 (0.94)	3.0 (0.33)	7.5 (0.67)	2.3 (0.32)	7.0 (0.61)	3.5 (0.38)	8.6 (0.64)
At least 2, but less than 3	17.0 (0.56)	1.7 (0.18)	8.1 (0.50)	3.0 (0.25)	2.5 (0.39)	0.7 (0.11)	2.1 (0.23)	0.8 (0.13)	2.1 (0.27)	0.9 (0.11)	2.5 (0.29)
3 or more units	41.8 (1.53)	3.3 (0.44)	8.1 (0.63)	1.6 (0.20)	1.1 (0.20)	1.4 (0.21)	1.3 (0.18)	1.9 (0.39)	1.9 (0.27)	2.1 (0.21)	2.6 (0.22)
4 or more units	28.9 (1.48)	2.1 (0.37)	4.0 (0.47)	0.8 (0.13)	0.6 (0.15)	1.0 (0.20)	0.6 (0.13)	1.1 ! (0.37)	1.2 (0.20)	1.4 (0.18)	1.5 (0.19)
2005 graduates											
Average units earned, all students[2]	2.64 (0.045)	0.23 (0.013)	0.64 (0.020)	0.36 (0.012)	0.24 (0.011)	0.12 (0.007)	0.15 (0.008)	0.16 (0.010)	0.21 (0.011)	0.18 (0.011)	0.35 (0.013)
Units earned, by sex											
Male	3.01 (0.050)	0.32 (0.020)	0.62 (0.022)	0.34 (0.014)	0.33 (0.015)	0.21 (0.014)	0.26 (0.014)	0.07 (0.007)	0.33 (0.019)	0.33 (0.019)	0.20 (0.011)
Female	2.29 (0.049)	0.15 (0.011)	0.66 (0.023)	0.38 (0.014)	0.15 (0.010)	0.03 (0.003)	0.05 (0.005)	0.25 (0.016)	0.10 (0.008)	0.03 (0.005)	0.49 (0.018)
Units earned, by race/ethnicity											
White	2.75 (0.059)	0.28 (0.017)	0.63 (0.024)	0.39 (0.015)	0.24 (0.013)	0.13 (0.010)	0.17 (0.010)	0.15 (0.012)	0.25 (0.015)	0.19 (0.014)	0.33 (0.015)
Black	2.58 (0.074)	0.10 (0.018)	0.80 (0.041)	0.28 (0.019)	0.23 (0.021)	0.11 (0.012)	0.11 (0.015)	0.25 (0.023)	0.11 (0.013)	0.13 (0.023)	0.45 (0.030)
Hispanic	2.41 (0.086)	0.14 (0.019)	0.63 (0.033)	0.30 (0.016)	0.21 (0.015)	0.10 (0.014)	0.12 (0.019)	0.16 (0.019)	0.17 (0.022)	0.19 (0.020)	0.39 (0.030)
Asian/Pacific Islander	1.94 (0.116)	0.06 ! (0.022)	0.49 (0.045)	0.32 (0.040)	0.36 (0.032)	0.04 (0.010)	0.13 (0.021)	0.10 (0.022)	0.13 (0.024)	0.09 (0.018)	0.21 (0.020)
American Indian/Alaska Native	2.45 (0.208)	0.46 (0.127)	0.46 (0.080)	0.33 (0.056)	0.24 ! (0.076)	0.09 ! (0.038)	0.02 ! (0.009)	0.10 (0.029)	0.24 (0.055)	0.21 ! (0.069)	0.31 (0.057)
Percentage distribution of students, by units earned											
0 units	13.0 (0.45)	88.4 (0.54)	55.8 (1.05)	69.8 (0.79)	80.5 (0.91)	93.3 (0.33)	88.2 (0.53)	90.4 (0.67)	83.6 (0.82)	91.2 (0.38)	74.9 (0.85)
More than 0, but less than 1	8.2 (0.35)	2.0 (0.20)	11.5 (0.62)	10.6 (0.50)	6.3 (0.36)	1.6 (0.17)	3.7 (0.34)	3.3 (0.52)	6.2 (0.48)	2.6 (0.26)	9.7 (0.61)
At least 1, but less than 2	22.0 (0.41)	4.8 (0.28)	20.7 (0.65)	14.2 (0.59)	9.5 (0.62)	2.9 (0.20)	5.7 (0.28)	2.9 (0.21)	6.4 (0.35)	2.8 (0.17)	9.6 (0.47)
At least 2, but less than 3	17.3 (0.34)	1.8 (0.12)	6.5 (0.29)	3.4 (0.16)	2.3 (0.19)	0.9 (0.11)	1.4 (0.12)	1.1 (0.11)	2.0 (0.18)	1.1 (0.12)	2.7 (0.20)
3 or more units	39.5 (0.76)	3.0 (0.21)	5.4 (0.32)	2.1 (0.17)	1.4 (0.12)	1.2 (0.12)	1.0 (0.13)	2.2 (0.19)	1.8 (0.16)	2.3 (0.20)	3.0 (0.20)
4 or more units	26.5 (0.67)	1.9 (0.16)	2.7 (0.20)	0.9 (0.09)	0.6 (0.09)	0.8 (0.09)	0.5 (0.08)	1.1 (0.13)	0.8 (0.11)	1.5 (0.16)	1.7 (0.15)
2009 graduates											
Average units earned, all students[2]	2.47 (0.059)	0.20 (0.013)	0.51 (0.017)	0.36 (0.011)	0.23 (0.010)	0.11 (0.009)	0.14 (0.008)	0.20 (0.015)	0.17 (0.010)	0.17 (0.015)	0.37 (0.020)
Units earned, by sex											
Male	2.77 (0.068)	0.27 (0.020)	0.52 (0.020)	0.35 (0.012)	0.31 (0.013)	0.20 (0.015)	0.24 (0.013)	0.09 (0.010)	0.26 (0.017)	0.32 (0.027)	0.22 (0.013)
Female	2.19 (0.055)	0.14 (0.009)	0.50 (0.018)	0.38 (0.013)	0.16 (0.009)	0.03 (0.004)	0.05 (0.005)	0.31 (0.021)	0.09 (0.007)	0.03 (0.005)	0.51 (0.028)
Units earned, by race/ethnicity											
White	2.55 (0.071)	0.27 (0.020)	0.50 (0.022)	0.38 (0.013)	0.22 (0.011)	0.13 (0.011)	0.16 (0.010)	0.16 (0.013)	0.20 (0.014)	0.17 (0.012)	0.35 (0.020)
Black	2.72 (0.127)	0.09 (0.010)	0.69 (0.035)	0.34 (0.026)	0.26 (0.026)	0.10 (0.021)	0.10 (0.015)	0.31 (0.044)	0.12 (0.015)	0.19 ! (0.056)	0.52 (0.037)
Hispanic	2.31 (0.101)	0.14 (0.018)	0.43 (0.027)	0.34 (0.015)	0.23 (0.025)	0.08 (0.011)	0.10 (0.009)	0.24 (0.031)	0.13 (0.012)	0.20 (0.026)	0.43 (0.044)
Asian/Pacific Islander	1.63 (0.074)	0.03 (0.009)	0.42 (0.054)	0.26 (0.026)	0.27 (0.024)	0.04 (0.009)	0.13 (0.034)	0.20 (0.048)	0.08 (0.012)	0.07 (0.015)	0.14 (0.020)
American Indian/Alaska Native	2.35 (0.188)	0.17 ! (0.069)	0.43 (0.065)	0.44 (0.065)	0.24 ! (0.079)	‡ (†)	0.07 ! (0.028)	0.12 ! (0.050)	0.30 (0.071)	0.19 ! (0.068)	0.26 (0.057)

See notes at end of table.

Table 225.20. Average number of Carnegie units earned by public high school graduates in career/technical education courses in various occupational fields, by sex and race/ethnicity, and percentage distribution of students, by units earned: Selected years, 2000 through 2009—Continued

[Standard errors appear in parentheses]

Graduation year, sex, and race/ethnicity	Total, all occupational education courses[1]	Agriculture	Business and marketing	Communications and design	Computer and information sciences	Construction and architecture	Engineering technologies	Health sciences	Manufacturing	Repair and transportation	Personal, public, and legal services
1	2	3	4	5	6	7	8	9	10	11	12
Percentage distribution of students, by units earned											
0 units	15.0 (0.61)	89.3 (0.58)	63.4 (1.04)	70.2 (0.91)	78.5 (0.89)	93.3 (0.43)	88.8 (0.62)	89.6 (0.64)	87.1 (0.52)	92.0 (0.43)	74.6 (0.73)
More than 0, but less than 1	8.7 (0.33)	2.1 (0.26)	10.1 (0.51)	10.2 (0.55)	8.3 (0.64)	1.7 (0.18)	2.8 (0.24)	2.3 (0.28)	4.5 (0.30)	2.0 (0.21)	9.2 (0.40)
At least 1, but less than 2	23.0 (0.59)	4.3 (0.32)	17.0 (0.60)	13.8 (0.53)	10.1 (0.50)	2.9 (0.23)	6.1 (0.51)	4.1 (0.44)	5.6 (0.31)	2.8 (0.20)	10.2 (0.45)
At least 2, but less than 3	17.0 (0.33)	1.7 (0.15)	5.4 (0.35)	3.6 (0.20)	2.1 (0.16)	1.0 (0.17)	1.3 (0.12)	1.4 (0.13)	1.6 (0.12)	1.1 (0.10)	2.9 (0.22)
3 or more units	36.2 (1.02)	2.7 (0.24)	4.1 (0.23)	2.2 (0.13)	1.1 (0.14)	1.1 (0.11)	0.9 (0.09)	2.6 (0.25)	1.3 (0.15)	2.1 (0.24)	3.2 (0.24)
4 or more units	23.8 (0.89)	1.6 (0.15)	1.8 (0.16)	1.0 (0.07)	0.4 (0.07)	0.7 (0.08)	0.4 (0.05)	1.7 (0.19)	0.6 (0.09)	1.5 (0.21)	1.9 (0.19)

†Not applicable.
!Interpret data with caution. The coefficient of variation (CV) for this estimate is between 30 and 50 percent.
‡Reporting standards not met. The coefficient of variation (CV) for this estimate is 50 percent or greater.
[1]Includes Carnegie units earned in all occupational education courses. This table does not include general labor market preparation courses and family and consumer sciences education courses.
[2]Total includes other racial/ethnic groups not separately shown.

NOTE: The Carnegie unit is a standard of measurement that represents one credit for the completion of a 1-year course. Data may differ from figures appearing in other NCES reports because of differences in course taxonomies and/or inclusion criteria. The analysis was restricted to graduates who attained either a standard or honors diploma and whose transcripts reflected a total of 16 or more Carnegie credits, with credits in English making up some part of the total. Race categories exclude persons of Hispanic ethnicity. Totals include other racial/ethnic groups not separately shown. Detail may not sum to totals because of rounding.
SOURCE: U.S. Department of Education, National Center for Education Statistics, 2000, 2005, and 2009 High School Transcript Study (HSTS). (This table was prepared September 2011.)

Table 225.30. Percentage of public and private high school graduates taking selected mathematics and science courses in high school, by sex and race/ethnicity: Selected years, 1982 through 2009

[Standard errors appear in parentheses]

Course (Carnegie units)	1982	1990	1994	1998	2000	2005	2009 Total	2009 Sex Male	2009 Sex Female	2009 Race/ethnicity White	2009 Race/ethnicity Black	2009 Race/ethnicity Hispanic	2009 Race/ethnicity Asian/Pacific Islander	2009 Race/ethnicity American Indian/ Alaska Native
1	2	3	4	5	6	7	8	9	10	11	12	13	14	15
Mathematics[1]														
Any mathematics (≥1.0)	98.5 (0.21)	99.6 (0.07)	99.5 (0.07)	99.9 (0.05)	99.8 (0.05)	99.9 (0.02)	100.0 (†)	100.0 (†)	100.0 (†)	100.0 (†)	100.0 (†)	100.0 (†)	100.0 (†)	100.0 (†)
Algebra I (≥1.0)[2]	55.2 (1.01)	64.5 (1.55)	66.9 (1.33)	63.4 (1.44)	66.5 (1.75)	68.4 (0.99)	68.9 (0.94)	68.5 (0.98)	69.3 (1.01)	67.0 (1.09)	77.2 (1.26)	75.4 (1.60)	53.3 (3.52)	74.8 (5.85)
Geometry (≥1.0)	47.1 (0.99)	64.1 (1.33)	70.6 (1.25)	75.3 (1.06)	78.3 (1.08)	83.8 (0.63)	88.3 (0.53)	86.6 (0.75)	89.9 (0.54)	88.8 (0.73)	88.4 (1.07)	87.0 (0.96)	86.1 (1.47)	81.6 (4.09)
Algebra II (≥0.5)[3]	39.9 (0.93)	48.8 (1.39)	61.5 (1.38)	61.7 (1.77)	67.6 (1.43)	70.3 (1.01)	75.5 (0.92)	73.5 (1.09)	77.6 (0.91)	77.1 (1.09)	70.5 (1.68)	71.1 (1.83)	82.8 (2.57)	66.3 (4.12)
Trigonometry (≥0.5)	8.1 (0.54)	18.2 (1.28)	11.8 (1.16)	8.9 (1.06)	7.9 (1.33)	8.4 (0.88)	6.1 (0.77)	5.8 (0.78)	6.4 (0.81)	7.1 (1.01)	3.2 (0.55)	3.6 (0.69)	8.5 (1.96)	6.5 (1.84)
Analysis/precalculus (≥0.5)	6.2 (0.46)	13.4 (0.95)	17.4 (0.87)	23.2 (1.44)	26.6 (1.40)	29.4 (0.98)	35.3 (0.84)	33.8 (1.02)	36.6 (0.89)	37.9 (0.98)	22.7 (1.29)	26.5 (1.36)	60.5 (2.88)	18.5 (2.98)
Statistics/probability (≥0.5)	1.0 (0.16)	1.0 (0.21)	2.0 (0.33)	3.7 (0.54)	5.7 (0.85)	7.7 (0.53)	10.8 (0.49)	10.7 (0.51)	10.9 (0.58)	11.6 (0.64)	7.9 (1.04)	7.5 (0.77)	17.6 (1.69)	5.9 ! (2.07)
Calculus (≥1.0)	5.0 (0.43)	6.5 (0.46)	9.4 (0.56)	11.0 (0.85)	11.6 (0.72)	13.6 (0.53)	15.9 (0.66)	16.1 (0.75)	15.7 (0.69)	17.5 (0.69)	6.1 (0.59)	8.6 (0.64)	42.2 (5.11)	6.3 (1.60)
AP/honors calculus (≥1.0)[4]	1.6 (0.26)	4.2 (0.44)	7.0 (0.54)	6.8 (0.49)	7.8 (0.58)	9.2 (0.44)	11.0 (0.55)	11.3 (0.65)	10.7 (0.54)	11.5 (0.52)	4.0 (0.37)	6.3 (0.46)	34.8 (2.77)	4.9 (1.44)
Science[1]														
Any science (≥1.0)	96.4 (0.39)	99.4 (0.13)	99.5 (0.09)	99.5 (0.10)	99.4 (0.12)	99.7 (0.05)	99.9 (0.02)	99.8 (0.04)	99.9 (0.02)	99.9 (0.03)	99.9 (0.04)	99.8 (0.06)	100.0 (†)	100.0 (†)
Biology (≥1.0)	77.4 (0.87)	91.3 (0.98)	93.7 (0.98)	92.9 (0.68)	91.1 (1.01)	92.5 (0.60)	95.6 (0.40)	94.9 (0.45)	96.2 (0.43)	95.6 (0.51)	96.3 (0.56)	94.8 (0.67)	95.8 (0.95)	94.5 (1.64)
AP/honors biology (≥1.0)[4]	10.0 (0.64)	5.0 (0.76)	12.0 (0.93)	16.3 (1.32)	16.3 (1.45)	16.0 (0.83)	22.4 (0.78)	19.7 (0.76)	25.0 (0.89)	24.2 (0.88)	14.1 (0.80)	16.1 (0.88)	39.7 (3.58)	15.4 (3.38)
Chemistry (≥1.0)	32.1 (0.84)	49.2 (1.22)	56.1 (1.01)	60.5 (1.29)	61.8 (1.48)	66.4 (0.94)	70.4 (0.75)	67.4 (0.95)	73.4 (0.76)	71.5 (0.87)	55.3 (1.80)	65.7 (1.41)	84.8 (1.72)	44.5 (4.78)
AP/honors chemistry (≥1.0)[4]	3.0 (0.33)	3.5 (0.47)	3.9 (0.53)	4.8 (0.50)	5.7 (0.84)	7.6 (0.53)	5.9 (0.43)	6.1 (0.52)	5.8 (0.39)	6.5 (0.47)	2.5 (0.46)	2.6 (0.35)	17.0 (2.36)	3.4 ! (1.39)
Physics (≥1.0)	15.0 (0.62)	21.3 (0.84)	24.8 (0.86)	28.8 (1.49)	31.3 (1.16)	32.9 (0.91)	36.1 (1.01)	39.2 (1.29)	33.0 (0.92)	37.6 (1.24)	26.9 (1.72)	28.6 (1.33)	61.1 (2.35)	19.8 (3.89)
AP/honors physics (≥1.0)[4]	1.2 (0.17)	2.0 (0.38)	2.7 (0.34)	3.0 (0.37)	3.9 (0.60)	5.3 (0.33)	5.7 (0.46)	7.7 (0.63)	3.7 (0.38)	6.1 (0.54)	2.5 (0.39)	3.4 (0.39)	15.1 (2.51)	† (†)
Engineering (≥1.0)	1.2 (0.21)	0.1 (0.04)	4.5 (0.80)	6.7 (1.76)	4.1 (0.98)	4.8 (0.56)	8.2 (0.93)	9.0 (1.02)	7.4 (0.93)	8.2 (1.18)	10.1 (1.75)	7.1 (1.06)	6.4 (.17)	9.0 ! (3.15)
Astronomy (≥0.5)	1.2 (0.24)	1.2 (0.31)	1.7 (0.50)	1.9 (0.46)	2.8 (0.59)	2.8 (0.37)	3.3 (0.40)	3.9 (0.51)	2.7 (0.33)	4.0 (0.57)	1.8 (0.38)	2.0 (0.36)	1.9 (0.43)	5.3 ! (2.51)
Geology/earth science (≥0.5)	13.6 (1.04)	25.3 (2.47)	23.1 (2.44)	20.9 (2.35)	18.5 (1.92)	24.7 (1.43)	27.7 (1.70)	28.9 (1.88)	26.5 (1.66)	28.2 (2.04)	30.1 (2.57)	27.1 (2.15)	19.1 (2.38)	26.0 (5.25)
Biology and chemistry (≥2.0)[5]	29.3 (0.83)	47.8 (1.23)	53.8 (1.18)	59.1 (1.22)	59.2 (1.50)	64.3 (0.97)	68.3 (0.77)	65.0 (0.91)	71.4 (0.84)	68.9 (0.93)	54.3 (1.74)	64.2 (1.45)	82.7 (1.93)	43.9 (4.77)
Biology, chemistry, and physics (≥3.0)[5]	11.2 (0.51)	18.7 (0.71)	21.4 (0.83)	25.6 (1.34)	25.0 (1.10)	27.4 (0.89)	30.1 (0.87)	31.9 (1.08)	28.3 (0.85)	31.4 (1.04)	21.9 (1.48)	22.7 (1.19)	54.4 (2.77)	13.6 (2.87)

†Not applicable.
!Interpret data with caution. The coefficient of variation (CV) for this estimate is between 30 and 50 percent.
‡Reporting standards not met. The coefficient of variation (CV) for this estimate is 50 percent or greater.
[1]For each course category, percentages include only students who earned at least the number of credits shown in parentheses.
[2]Excludes prealgebra.
[3]Includes courses where trigonometry or geometry has been combined with algebra II.
[4]For 2000 and later years, includes International Baccalaureate (IB) courses in addition to Advanced Placement (AP) and honors courses.
[5]Percentages include only students who earned at least one credit in each of the indicated courses.

NOTE: For a transcript to be included in the analyses, it had to meet three requirements: (1) the student graduated with either a standard or honors diploma, (2) the student's transcript contained 16 or more Carnegie units, and (3) the student's transcript contained more than 0 Carnegie units in English courses. The Carnegie unit is a standard of measurement that represents one credit for the completion of a 1-year course (0.5 = one semester; 1.0 = one academic year). Data differ slightly from figures appearing in other National Center for Education Statistics reports because of differences in taxonomies and case exclusion criteria. Race categories exclude persons of Hispanic ethnicity. Totals include other racial/ethnic groups not separately shown. Some data have been revised from previously published figures.
SOURCE: U.S. Department of Education, National Center for Education Statistics, High School and Beyond Longitudinal Study of 1980 Sophomores (HS&B-So:80/82), "High School Transcript Study", and 1990, 1994, 1998, 2000, 2005, and 2009 High School Transcript Study (HSTS). (This table was prepared October 2012.)

Table 225.40. Percentage of public and private high school graduates taking selected mathematics and science courses in high school, by selected student and school characteristics: Selected years, 1990 through 2009

[Standard errors appear in parentheses]

Year and student or school characteristic	Mathematics						Science				
	Algebra I[1,2]	Geometry[1]	Algebra II/ trigonometry[3]	Analysis/ precalculus[3]	Statistics/ probability[3]	Calculus[1]	Biology[1]	Chemistry[1]	Physics[1]	Biology and chemistry[4]	Biology, chemistry, and physics[5]
1	2	3	4	5	6	7	8	9	10	11	12
1990											
Total[6]	**64.5** (1.55)	**64.1** (1.33)	**53.6** (1.32)	**13.4** (0.95)	**1.0** (0.21)	**6.5** (0.46)	**91.3** (0.98)	**49.2** (1.22)	**21.3** (0.84)	**47.8** (1.23)	**18.7** (0.71)
Sex											
Male	62.0 (1.57)	63.0 (1.57)	51.8 (1.44)	14.1 (1.14)	1.2 (0.27)	7.6 (0.64)	90.0 (1.09)	48.1 (1.40)	25.1 (0.95)	46.6 (1.40)	21.8 (0.82)
Female	66.7 (1.69)	65.0 (1.31)	55.2 (1.45)	12.8 (0.94)	0.8 (0.20)	5.6 (0.37)	92.5 (0.94)	50.2 (1.29)	17.7 (0.87)	48.9 (1.30)	16.0 (0.76)
Race/ethnicity											
White	64.6 (1.83)	66.4 (1.43)	56.9 (1.53)	14.9 (1.04)	1.0 (0.22)	6.9 (0.53)	91.5 (1.06)	51.8 (1.33)	22.8 (0.91)	50.5 (1.35)	20.5 (0.82)
Black	65.1 (2.42)	56.3 (2.58)	43.9 (2.77)	6.2 (0.96)	1.1 ! (0.44)	2.8 (0.55)	91.3 (2.19)	40.3 (2.19)	14.5 (1.85)	39.5 (2.24)	12.0 (1.23)
Hispanic	64.8 (2.75)	54.1 (2.89)	39.9 (2.80)	7.1 (0.82)	‡ (†)	3.8 (0.67)	90.2 (1.40)	38.3 (2.90)	12.7 (1.33)	36.4 (2.70)	10.0 (1.21)
Asian/Pacific Islander	63.5 (3.01)	71.5 (2.90)	69.3 (5.51)	25.2 (6.54)	‡ (†)	18.4 (3.23)	90.2 (2.73)	63.5 (4.01)	38.0 (3.36)	60.0 (3.45)	33.4 (2.56)
American Indian/Alaska Native	61.7 (8.40)	55.7 (2.85)	53.9 (4.80)	‡ (†)	‡ (†)	‡ (†)	90.5 (4.37)	35.5 (4.50)	‡ (†)	34.2 (4.46)	‡ (†)
Student with disabilities (SD) status											
SD[7]	20.6 (3.09)	11.8 (2.42)	8.3 (2.04)	‡ (†)	‡ (†)	‡ (†)	65.0 (4.73)	7.7 (1.53)	‡ (†)	‡ (†)	‡ (†)
Non-SD	65.4 (1.59)	65.1 (1.32)	54.5 (1.35)	13.6 (0.97)	1.0 (0.21)	6.7 (0.47)	91.8 (0.92)	50.0 (1.24)	21.6 (0.84)	48.6 (1.23)	19.1 (0.71)
English language learner (ELL) status											
ELL	57.7 (5.79)	42.2 (6.30)	37.1 (6.64)	‡ (†)	‡ (†)	‡ (†)	70.5 (4.66)	‡ (†)	‡ (†)	‡ (†)	‡ (†)
Non-ELL	64.5 (1.56)	64.2 (1.34)	53.7 (1.34)	13.4 (0.95)	1.0 (0.21)	6.6 (0.47)	91.4 (0.98)	49.3 (1.23)	21.3 (0.84)	48.0 (1.23)	18.8 (0.71)
School type											
Traditional public	62.9 (1.66)	61.9 (1.41)	51.4 (1.32)	12.2 (1.11)	0.8 (0.20)	6.2 (0.48)	90.7 (1.08)	47.4 (1.32)	20.2 (0.86)	46.0 (1.33)	17.8 (0.71)
Public charter	— (†)	— (†)	— (†)	— (†)	— (†)	— (†)	— (†)	— (†)	— (†)	— (†)	— (†)
Private	79.9 (2.22)	85.5 (1.98)	75.5 (3.55)	25.3 (3.44)	2.6 ! (1.03)	9.7 (1.33)	97.2 (0.55)	66.7 (2.71)	31.4 (2.30)	65.2 (2.67)	28.2 (2.07)
Percentage of students eligible for free or reduced-price lunch											
0–25 percent	64.9 (2.16)	67.4 (1.67)	57.8 (2.05)	15.3 (1.38)	1.1 (0.31)	7.5 (0.70)	92.4 (1.09)	54.0 (1.60)	22.8 (1.27)	52.8 (1.59)	21.0 (1.12)
26–50 percent	60.6 (3.97)	45.4 (2.90)	44.6 (2.74)	5.5 (1.43)	‡ (†)	3.8 (0.89)	88.8 (4.60)	36.5 (3.08)	15.3 (2.08)	35.5 (3.33)	12.8 (1.71)
51–75 percent	74.2 (7.31)	56.0 (14.72)	40.1 (5.12)	5.6 (1.54)	# (†)	‡ (†)	93.6 (2.87)	33.5 (4.28)	12.7 (3.12)	33.0 (4.42)	11.7 (2.83)
76–100 percent	96.0 (4.01)	89.4 (0.92)	78.7 (2.96)	‡ (†)	# (†)	# (†)	99.0 (0.99)	‡ (†)	‡ (†)	‡ (†)	‡ (†)
2000											
Total[6]	**66.5** (1.75)	**78.3** (1.08)	**68.3** (1.45)	**26.6** (1.40)	**5.7** (0.85)	**11.6** (0.72)	**91.1** (1.01)	**61.8** (1.48)	**31.3** (1.16)	**59.2** (1.50)	**25.0** (1.10)
Sex											
Male	65.0 (1.72)	74.8 (1.31)	65.2 (1.46)	25.3 (1.39)	5.8 (0.97)	12.1 (0.79)	88.9 (1.32)	57.7 (1.42)	34.1 (1.29)	54.3 (1.49)	26.3 (1.23)
Female	68.0 (1.87)	81.4 (1.01)	71.1 (1.69)	27.8 (1.61)	5.6 (0.85)	11.1 (0.77)	93.2 (0.82)	65.5 (1.75)	28.9 (1.22)	63.6 (1.76)	23.9 (1.14)
Race/ethnicity											
White	65.1 (2.08)	79.2 (1.21)	69.6 (1.57)	28.1 (1.74)	6.1 (1.00)	12.5 (0.77)	91.7 (1.15)	62.9 (1.66)	32.3 (1.34)	60.1 (1.72)	25.6 (1.20)
Black	70.1 (3.20)	77.8 (1.93)	64.7 (2.32)	16.1 (1.52)	3.7 ! (1.24)	4.6 (0.55)	92.4 (1.09)	59.5 (2.38)	25.1 (1.97)	57.8 (2.31)	20.0 (1.76)
Hispanic	73.2 (2.43)	72.6 (3.30)	60.0 (5.06)	19.3 (2.95)	2.3 (0.52)	5.6 (0.86)	87.8 (2.69)	52.0 (4.13)	23.1 (2.32)	50.3 (4.30)	17.7 (2.19)
Asian/Pacific Islander	58.1 (3.28)	81.3 (2.03)	81.3 (2.00)	48.7 (2.79)	11.4 (2.44)	30.4 (5.02)	87.8 (3.20)	75.1 (2.89)	53.8 (2.80)	70.6 (3.03)	47.0 (2.70)
American Indian/Alaska Native	68.7 (5.80)	65.0 (6.18)	60.3 (5.51)	‡ (†)	‡ (†)	‡ (†)	88.4 (2.88)	43.6 (4.03)	‡ (†)	39.4 (3.81)	‡ (†)
Student with disabilities (SD) status											
SD[7]	45.2 (2.96)	36.1 (2.90)	22.9 (2.88)	6.7 ! (2.23)	‡ (†)	‡ (†)	72.0 (2.71)	21.2 (2.88)	13.6 (2.63)	19.9 (2.84)	7.9 ! (2.45)
Non-SD	67.3 (1.77)	79.9 (1.08)	70.1 (1.46)	27.4 (1.43)	5.9 (0.87)	11.9 (0.74)	91.9 (1.02)	63.4 (1.47)	32.0 (1.18)	60.7 (1.51)	25.7 (1.11)
English language learner (ELL) status											
ELL	62.3 (5.71)	57.8 (4.11)	45.8 (4.82)	15.0 (2.20)	‡ (†)	‡ (†)	73.4 (7.02)	34.9 (4.50)	20.8 (4.16)	31.3 (4.97)	11.2 (2.53)
Non-ELL	66.5 (1.75)	78.5 (1.07)	68.6 (1.44)	26.7 (1.41)	5.7 (0.86)	11.6 (0.73)	91.3 (0.98)	62.1 (1.47)	31.4 (1.18)	59.5 (1.50)	25.2 (1.11)
School type											
Traditional public	65.3 (1.76)	77.0 (1.20)	67.1 (1.57)	24.1 (1.43)	5.5 (0.85)	10.9 (0.71)	90.5 (1.11)	59.5 (1.42)	30.0 (1.22)	56.8 (1.44)	23.5 (1.10)
Public charter	— (†)	— (†)	— (†)	— (†)	— (†)	— (†)	— (†)	— (†)	— (†)	— (†)	— (†)
Private	79.1 (3.29)	92.3 (2.52)	81.9 (6.49)	53.8 (5.88)	7.8 ! (3.33)	18.2 (3.99)	98.2 (0.53)	86.6 (3.88)	45.1 (7.62)	85.4 (3.87)	41.5 (7.38)
Percentage of students eligible for free or reduced-price lunch											
0–25 percent	66.8 (2.64)	80.3 (1.47)	68.1 (2.36)	29.6 (2.41)	6.5 (1.53)	13.4 (1.32)	91.4 (1.53)	65.2 (2.51)	34.5 (2.05)	61.9 (2.59)	28.6 (1.83)
26–50 percent	64.8 (3.65)	72.5 (2.90)	67.2 (1.86)	19.1 (2.12)	3.5 (1.00)	8.8 (1.09)	93.4 (1.49)	56.0 (2.10)	26.3 (2.50)	55.0 (2.15)	19.1 (1.19)
51–75 percent	72.7 (3.97)	77.5 (3.48)	66.7 (5.53)	18.0 (2.97)	3.4 ! (1.62)	4.8 (1.11)	90.8 (3.02)	58.9 (3.11)	22.5 (1.75)	57.4 (3.47)	17.5 (1.85)
76–100 percent	81.7 (3.87)	83.1 (5.61)	68.1 (9.69)	23.9 (4.40)	‡ (†)	5.4 (1.05)	91.4 (5.08)	60.8 (9.48)	35.0 (6.03)	59.5 (9.38)	26.1 (5.80)

See notes at end of table.

Table 225.40. Percentage of public and private high school graduates taking selected mathematics and science courses in high school, by selected student and school characteristics: Selected years, 1990 through 2009—Continued

[Standard errors appear in parentheses]

Year and student or school characteristic	Mathematics						Science				
	Algebra I [1,2]	Geometry [1]	Algebra II/ trigonometry [3]	Analysis/ precalculus [3]	Statistics/ probability [3]	Calculus [1]	Biology [1]	Chemistry [1]	Physics [1]	Biology and chemistry [4]	Biology, chemistry, and physics [5]
1	2	3	4	5	6	7	8	9	10	11	12
2005											
Total[6]	68.4 (0.99)	83.8 (0.63)	71.3 (0.97)	29.4 (0.98)	7.7 (0.53)	13.6 (0.53)	92.5 (0.60)	66.4 (0.94)	32.9 (0.91)	64.3 (0.97)	27.4 (0.89)
Sex											
Male	66.8 (1.04)	81.9 (0.70)	68.0 (1.09)	28.0 (1.02)	7.7 (0.57)	14.0 (0.62)	91.0 (0.68)	62.7 (1.08)	34.9 (0.90)	60.3 (1.08)	28.2 (0.86)
Female	69.8 (1.06)	85.6 (0.66)	74.4 (0.98)	30.8 (1.05)	7.8 (0.55)	13.2 (0.58)	93.9 (0.58)	70.0 (0.99)	31.0 (1.09)	68.0 (1.03)	26.5 (1.10)
Race/ethnicity											
White	66.8 (1.17)	83.9 (0.79)	72.4 (1.17)	32.0 (1.18)	8.5 (0.65)	15.3 (0.61)	92.8 (0.67)	67.4 (1.06)	34.8 (0.87)	65.3 (1.10)	29.0 (0.85)
Black	75.4 (1.60)	85.0 (1.04)	69.3 (1.63)	17.9 (1.61)	5.8 (0.83)	5.5 (0.53)	93.7 (0.60)	63.6 (1.61)	25.8 (2.31)	62.0 (1.60)	21.3 (2.25)
Hispanic	70.2 (1.79)	81.0 (1.16)	63.1 (1.55)	20.4 (1.42)	3.4 (0.48)	6.4 (0.63)	89.2 (1.22)	59.3 (2.09)	23.4 (1.66)	57.2 (2.28)	18.8 (1.63)
Asian/Pacific Islander	65.4 (2.71)	87.1 (1.29)	79.5 (2.94)	48.8 (2.84)	12.9 (1.21)	30.0 (1.63)	92.4 (1.83)	79.7 (1.60)	50.3 (2.35)	75.5 (2.16)	42.9 (2.49)
American Indian/Alaska Native	70.1 (4.82)	73.8 (3.36)	67.2 (3.54)	15.8 (3.07)	‡ (†)	‡ (†)	91.5 (1.92)	48.9 (4.70)	18.1 (3.82)	47.6 (4.69)	‡ (†)
Student with disabilities (SD) status											
SD[7]	49.5 (2.05)	47.8 (1.83)	27.9 (1.67)	6.0 (0.71)	2.2 (0.46)	2.0 (0.54)	71.6 (1.58)	26.6 (1.88)	13.2 (1.27)	24.8 (1.75)	6.6 (0.74)
Non-SD	69.9 (1.04)	87.0 (0.68)	75.2 (0.98)	31.6 (1.07)	8.3 (0.56)	14.7 (0.56)	94.4 (0.57)	69.9 (0.92)	34.5 (0.94)	67.8 (0.96)	29.0 (0.93)
English language learner (ELL) status											
ELL	63.7 (2.75)	70.1 (2.10)	48.0 (2.97)	13.8 (1.85)	3.9 (0.88)	6.1 (1.79)	81.4 (1.96)	46.1 (2.61)	20.2 (2.40)	43.0 (2.85)	13.8 (2.02)
Non-ELL	68.4 (1.00)	84.3 (0.67)	72.0 (1.00)	30.0 (1.02)	7.9 (0.54)	13.8 (0.54)	92.9 (0.62)	67.0 (0.97)	33.2 (0.93)	64.9 (1.01)	27.6 (0.91)
School type											
Traditional public	67.6 (1.09)	83.0 (0.71)	69.3 (1.07)	27.6 (0.92)	7.7 (0.55)	12.5 (0.53)	92.1 (0.59)	64.2 (0.87)	30.6 (0.94)	62.0 (0.85)	24.8 (0.86)
Public charter	84.5 (5.72)	78.1 (7.06)	69.3 (11.47)	‡ (†)	‡ (†)	‡ (†)	91.6 (2.47)	72.2 (11.52)	36.7 ! (13.63)	67.0 (10.91)	33.9 ! (13.67)
Private	74.4 (3.27)	91.2 (1.41)	89.6 (1.88)	45.3 (3.93)	8.3 (1.84)	23.9 (2.45)	96.1 (2.31)	86.8 (2.79)	53.8 (2.46)	85.1 (3.10)	49.9 (2.72)
Percentage of students eligible for free or reduced-price lunch											
0–25 percent	65.4 (1.85)	82.2 (1.41)	70.9 (1.73)	34.0 (1.64)	10.2 (0.97)	15.7 (0.92)	92.8 (1.01)	68.4 (1.34)	35.3 (1.40)	65.9 (1.39)	28.7 (1.32)
26–50 percent	69.5 (1.93)	84.2 (1.04)	69.8 (1.37)	23.4 (1.30)	6.7 (0.93)	10.8 (0.58)	93.0 (0.97)	61.0 (1.60)	26.9 (1.44)	59.1 (1.72)	21.8 (1.42)
51–75 percent	74.3 (2.78)	82.2 (1.99)	68.3 (2.80)	19.2 (2.26)	3.3 (0.91)	6.9 (0.86)	86.7 (2.05)	57.0 (2.80)	20.9 (2.38)	54.1 (2.90)	16.1 (2.06)
76–100 percent	75.1 (3.73)	88.2 (1.61)	69.4 (3.05)	18.2 (2.90)	2.8 ! (0.87)	4.9 (0.90)	90.2 (3.04)	67.6 (3.04)	21.2 (3.16)	64.1 (3.60)	17.8 (2.80)
2009											
Total[6]	68.9 (0.94)	88.3 (0.53)	75.8 (0.92)	35.3 (0.84)	10.8 (0.49)	15.9 (0.66)	95.6 (0.40)	70.4 (0.75)	36.1 (1.01)	68.3 (0.77)	30.1 (0.87)
Sex											
Male	68.5 (0.98)	86.6 (0.75)	73.8 (1.09)	33.8 (1.02)	10.7 (0.51)	16.1 (0.75)	94.9 (0.45)	67.4 (0.95)	39.2 (1.29)	65.0 (0.91)	31.9 (1.08)
Female	69.3 (1.01)	89.9 (0.54)	77.8 (0.91)	36.6 (0.89)	10.9 (0.58)	15.7 (0.69)	96.2 (0.43)	73.4 (0.76)	33.0 (0.92)	71.4 (0.84)	28.3 (0.85)
Race/ethnicity											
White	67.0 (1.09)	88.8 (0.73)	77.4 (1.08)	37.9 (0.98)	11.6 (0.64)	17.5 (0.69)	95.6 (0.51)	71.5 (0.87)	37.6 (1.24)	68.9 (0.93)	31.4 (1.04)
Black	77.2 (1.26)	88.4 (1.07)	70.6 (1.69)	22.7 (1.29)	7.9 (1.04)	6.1 (0.59)	96.3 (0.56)	65.3 (1.80)	26.9 (1.72)	64.3 (1.74)	21.9 (1.48)
Hispanic	75.4 (1.60)	87.0 (0.96)	71.4 (1.81)	26.5 (1.36)	7.5 (0.77)	8.6 (0.64)	94.8 (0.67)	65.7 (1.41)	28.6 (1.33)	64.2 (1.45)	22.7 (1.19)
Asian/Pacific Islander	53.3 (3.52)	86.1 (1.47)	83.0 (2.59)	60.5 (2.88)	17.6 (1.69)	42.2 (3.11)	95.8 (0.95)	84.8 (1.72)	61.1 (2.35)	82.7 (1.93)	54.4 (2.77)
American Indian/Alaska Native	74.8 (5.85)	81.6 (4.09)	66.6 (4.12)	18.5 (2.98)	‡ (†)	‡ (†)	94.5 (1.64)	44.5 (4.78)	19.8 (3.89)	43.9 (4.77)	13.6 (2.87)
Student with disabilities (SD) status											
SD[7]	56.0 (1.63)	61.1 (1.82)	39.5 (1.67)	9.7 (1.26)	3.9 (0.57)	3.0 (0.55)	82.4 (1.30)	35.4 (1.69)	19.3 (1.67)	33.8 (1.67)	12.0 (1.51)
Non-SD	70.1 (0.97)	90.7 (0.53)	79.1 (0.93)	37.6 (0.90)	11.4 (0.53)	17.1 (0.71)	96.8 (0.41)	73.6 (0.75)	37.6 (1.06)	71.4 (0.79)	31.7 (0.94)
English language learner (ELL) status											
ELL	73.3 (2.33)	76.2 (1.99)	58.1 (2.54)	19.4 (2.36)	4.4 (1.03)	4.7 (0.87)	86.9 (2.12)	47.4 (2.99)	23.2 (2.41)	43.8 (3.03)	15.4 (2.02)
Non-ELL	68.8 (0.95)	88.5 (0.54)	76.2 (0.93)	35.6 (0.86)	10.9 (0.50)	16.2 (0.67)	95.7 (0.41)	70.9 (0.77)	36.3 (1.02)	68.7 (0.79)	30.3 (0.89)
School type											
Traditional public	68.2 (0.99)	88.1 (0.53)	74.9 (0.96)	34.0 (0.97)	10.7 (0.51)	15.4 (0.73)	95.3 (0.44)	68.9 (0.75)	34.6 (1.03)	66.9 (0.78)	28.8 (0.83)
Public charter	79.0 (4.21)	86.9 (3.57)	77.8 (6.64)	34.1 (9.95)	‡ (†)	‡ (†)	94.0 (1.92)	56.8 (11.13)	40.0 (7.36)	55.7 (10.77)	23.2 ! (7.52)
Private	74.7 (2.95)	90.0 (3.98)	84.6 (4.01)	47.5 (3.76)	12.5 (1.86)	23.3 (2.05)	98.6 (0.28)	87.4 (1.87)	49.5 (3.73)	83.3 (2.67)	43.9 (3.77)
Percentage of students eligible for free or reduced-price lunch											
0–25 percent	61.3 (1.72)	89.7 (0.82)	80.1 (1.75)	43.1 (1.88)	14.8 (1.03)	22.6 (1.37)	96.4 (1.03)	76.3 (1.58)	46.5 (2.02)	74.9 (1.70)	40.4 (2.07)
26–50 percent	70.9 (1.82)	88.4 (0.87)	74.7 (1.38)	29.7 (1.44)	8.6 (0.80)	11.8 (0.76)	94.5 (0.98)	64.0 (1.52)	27.6 (1.79)	61.6 (1.59)	22.2 (1.54)
51–75 percent	75.8 (1.85)	87.4 (1.45)	69.3 (3.35)	25.4 (1.52)	7.5 (1.14)	9.8 (1.05)	95.6 (0.72)	65.6 (2.03)	29.4 (2.56)	64.2 (1.97)	22.7 (2.12)
76–100 percent	80.1 (3.75)	88.8 (2.26)	70.7 (4.02)	25.5 (2.80)	5.1 (1.08)	7.5 (1.34)	95.6 (1.42)	69.4 (3.68)	26.6 (3.07)	68.2 (3.69)	22.8 (2.97)

See notes at end of table.

Table 225.40. Percentage of public and private high school graduates taking selected mathematics and science courses in high school, by selected student and school characteristics: Selected years, 1990 through 2009—Continued

[Standard errors appear in parentheses]

Year and student or school characteristic	Mathematics						Science				
	Algebra II[1][2]	Geometry[1]	Algebra II/ trigonometry[3]	Analysis/ precalculus[3]	Statistics/ probability[3]	Calculus[1]	Biology[1]	Chemistry[1]	Physics[1]	Biology and chemistry[4]	Biology, chemistry, and physics[5]
1	2	3	4	5	6	7	8	9	10	11	12
School locale											
City	72.5 (1.85)	89.1 (0.91)	74.9 (2.06)	36.7 (1.98)	10.6 (0.91)	15.5 (1.42)	96.4 (0.53)	74.0 (1.59)	38.8 (1.99)	70.8 (1.97)	31.6 (1.97)
Suburban	62.8 (1.62)	89.4 (1.27)	78.7 (1.79)	39.0 (1.71)	13.1 (0.97)	19.5 (1.12)	97.1 (0.30)	76.7 (1.14)	43.8 (1.42)	75.4 (1.04)	38.6 (1.21)
Town	76.9 (2.25)	86.4 (1.08)	71.4 (3.00)	30.1 (2.40)	8.4 (1.25)	10.7 (1.02)	92.2 (2.23)	62.3 (1.84)	24.0 (2.45)	60.4 (1.87)	18.9 (1.94)
Rural	70.2 (2.19)	86.3 (0.95)	74.5 (1.38)	30.0 (1.35)	8.6 (1.12)	13.5 (0.87)	93.7 (1.66)	59.6 (1.82)	26.0 (1.95)	57.2 (1.77)	19.7 (1.41)

—Not available.
†Not applicable.
#Rounds to zero.
!Interpret data with caution. The coefficient of variation (CV) for this estimate is between 30 and 50 percent.
‡Reporting standards not met (too few cases for a reliable estimate)
[1]Percentages are for students who earned at least one Carnegie credit.
[2]Excludes prealgebra.
[3]Percentages are for students who earned at least one-half of a Carnegie credit in a course that includes a focus on at least one of the listed content areas.
[4]Percentages are for students who earned at least one Carnegie credit each in biology and chemistry.
[5]Percentages are for students who earned at least one Carnegie credit each in biology, chemistry, and physics.

[6]Includes other racial/ethnic groups not shown separately, as well as students for whom information on race/ethnicity or sex was missing.
[7]SD data include both students with an Individualized Education Plan (IEP) and students with a plan under Section 504 of the Rehabilitation Act (a "504 plan"). IEPs are only for students who require specialized instruction, whereas 504 plans apply to students who require accommodations but may not require specialized instruction.
NOTE: For a transcript to be included in the analyses, it had to meet three requirements: (1) the graduate received either a standard or honors diploma, (2) the graduate's transcript contained 16 or more Carnegie credits, and (3) the graduate's transcript contained more than 0 Carnegie credits in English courses. Race categories exclude persons of Hispanic ethnicity.
SOURCE: U.S. Department of Education, National Center for Education Statistics, 1990, 2000, 2005, and 2009 High School Transcript Study (HSTS). (This table was prepared September 2012.)

Table 225.50. Percentage of public and private high school graduates earning minimum credits in selected combinations of academic courses, by sex and race/ethnicity: Selected years, 1982 through 2009

[Standard errors appear in parentheses]

Year of graduation and course combination taken[1]	All students[2]		Sex				Race/ethnicity								
			Male		Female		White		Black		Hispanic		Asian/Pacific Islander		American Indian/ Alaska Native	
1	2		3		4		5		6		7		8		9	
1982 graduates																
4 Eng, 3 SS, 3 Sci, 3 Math, and 2 FL[3]..	9.5	(0.57)	9.1	(0.70)	9.9	(0.71)	10.9	(0.69)	5.2	(1.02)	3.9	(0.57)	17.0	(2.49)	‡	(†)
4 Eng, 3 SS, 3 Sci, 3 Math....................	14.3	(0.66)	15.2	(0.86)	13.4	(0.79)	15.9	(0.79)	11.0	(1.39)	6.7	(0.79)	21.1	(2.65)	8.1 !	(3.02)
4 Eng, 3 SS, 2 Sci, 2 Math....................	31.5	(1.07)	31.7	(1.26)	31.3	(1.22)	32.4	(1.21)	30.8	(2.32)	25.6	(1.76)	32.0	(3.40)	23.6	(5.39)
1987 graduates																
4 Eng, 3 SS, 3 Sci, 3 Math, and 2 FL[3]..	18.1	(0.91)	18.0	(1.13)	18.3	(1.01)	19.0	(1.10)	12.7	(1.15)	10.8	(1.70)	35.7	(4.49)	4.9	(1.40)
4 Eng, 3 SS, 3 Sci, 3 Math....................	24.8	(1.03)	25.9	(1.27)	23.7	(1.07)	26.1	(1.21)	19.6	(1.99)	14.5	(1.69)	39.8	(4.51)	24.3	(3.69)
4 Eng, 3 SS, 2 Sci, 2 Math....................	48.1	(1.74)	48.0	(2.22)	48.4	(1.56)	48.1	(2.15)	48.3	(2.63)	43.9	(1.92)	57.9	(4.82)	61.8	(5.56)
1990 graduates																
4 Eng, 3 SS, 3 Sci, 3 Math, and 2 FL[3]..	29.9	(1.26)	28.8	(1.38)	31.0	(1.36)	31.7	(1.46)	22.9	(2.27)	25.4	(2.41)	42.6	(2.95)	9.9 !	(3.70)
4 Eng, 3 SS, 3 Sci, 3 Math....................	38.2	(1.50)	38.5	(1.69)	37.9	(1.54)	39.2	(1.63)	39.0	(3.57)	29.8	(2.51)	47.4	(3.04)	19.2	(4.70)
4 Eng, 3 SS, 2 Sci, 2 Math....................	65.5	(1.96)	64.3	(2.09)	66.4	(1.98)	64.9	(2.28)	71.3	(3.00)	63.7	(3.01)	69.1	(3.90)	46.3	(6.39)
1994 graduates																
4 Eng, 3 SS, 3 Sci, 3 Math, and 2 FL[3]..	39.0	(1.12)	35.0	(1.11)	42.7	(1.33)	41.6	(1.32)	29.6	(1.52)	35.6	(2.94)	50.1	(2.39)	22.5	(4.31)
4 Eng, 3 SS, 3 Sci, 3 Math....................	49.3	(1.45)	47.0	(1.45)	51.5	(1.58)	52.4	(1.67)	43.7	(2.39)	40.3	(3.25)	54.9	(2.46)	46.0	(3.30)
4 Eng, 3 SS, 2 Sci, 2 Math....................	73.9	(1.50)	71.2	(1.63)	76.4	(1.46)	75.1	(1.69)	74.5	(2.32)	74.7	(2.61)	72.3	(3.62)	76.3	(3.60)
1998 graduates																
4 Eng, 3 SS, 3 Sci, 3 Math, and 2 FL[3]..	44.2	(1.92)	40.5	(2.19)	48.2	(2.05)	46.2	(2.16)	40.0	(3.41)	32.0	(2.94)	57.8	(4.51)	28.3	(4.53)
4 Eng, 3 SS, 3 Sci, 3 Math....................	55.0	(2.44)	52.9	(2.64)	57.8	(2.48)	56.8	(2.69)	55.6	(4.39)	40.0	(3.28)	66.1	(5.69)	40.0	(4.73)
4 Eng, 3 SS, 2 Sci, 2 Math....................	74.5	(2.18)	72.8	(2.34)	77.0	(2.14)	74.7	(2.64)	76.0	(3.21)	70.1	(2.57)	79.5	(4.76)	76.4	(5.21)
2000 graduates																
4 Eng, 3 SS, 3 Sci, 3 Math, and 2 FL[3]..	47.8	(1.53)	41.5	(1.68)	53.4	(1.65)	48.9	(1.60)	45.6	(2.27)	40.3	(5.47)	58.2	(3.48)	26.8	(3.63)
4 Eng, 3 SS, 3 Sci, 3 Math....................	58.6	(1.64)	54.4	(1.70)	62.3	(1.75)	59.2	(1.74)	64.1	(2.51)	48.3	(5.74)	62.7	(3.44)	42.5	(5.84)
4 Eng, 3 SS, 2 Sci, 2 Math....................	78.2	(1.60)	74.9	(1.88)	81.2	(1.43)	78.3	(1.85)	82.5	(2.26)	75.4	(3.16)	75.0	(3.27)	72.6	(4.48)
2005 graduates																
4 Eng, 3 SS, 3 Sci, 3 Math, and 2 FL[3]..	54.7	(0.96)	49.0	(1.14)	60.1	(0.94)	55.5	(1.19)	54.3	(1.87)	46.3	(2.08)	66.7	(2.10)	38.1	(3.37)
4 Eng, 3 SS, 3 Sci, 3 Math....................	67.4	(1.02)	63.5	(1.22)	71.0	(0.94)	68.5	(1.29)	72.3	(1.76)	53.5	(2.20)	72.2	(2.05)	60.9	(3.40)
4 Eng, 3 SS, 2 Sci, 2 Math....................	83.0	(1.02)	80.3	(1.19)	85.4	(0.94)	82.1	(1.34)	89.7	(0.91)	79.6	(1.38)	85.0	(1.68)	81.0	(3.10)
2009 graduates																
4 Eng, 3 SS, 3 Sci, 3 Math, and 2 FL[3]..	61.8	(0.84)	57.4	(1.06)	66.0	(0.82)	62.4	(0.94)	58.4	(1.71)	58.4	(1.65)	73.1	(2.28)	43.0	(3.44)
4 Eng, 3 SS, 3 Sci, 3 Math....................	74.3	(0.81)	72.1	(0.96)	76.4	(0.77)	75.0	(1.04)	78.1	(1.20)	67.2	(1.49)	76.9	(2.08)	64.7	(4.23)
4 Eng, 3 SS, 2 Sci, 2 Math....................	87.7	(0.74)	86.2	(0.82)	89.1	(0.73)	86.8	(0.97)	92.0	(0.63)	88.0	(0.87)	86.1	(1.52)	86.6	(2.99)

†Not applicable.
!Interpret data with caution. The coefficient of variation (CV) for this estimate is between 30 and 50 percent.
‡Reporting standards not met. The coefficient of variation (CV) for this estimate is 50 percent or greater.
[1]Eng = English; SS = social studies; Sci = science; and FL = foreign language.
[2]Totals include other racial/ethnic groups not separately shown.
[3]In 1983, the National Commission on Excellence in Education recommended that all college-bound high school students take these courses plus 0.5 credits of computer science as a minimum.

NOTE: Data differ slightly from figures appearing in other NCES reports because of differences in taxonomies and case exclusion criteria. Race categories exclude persons of Hispanic ethnicity.
SOURCE: U.S. Department of Education, National Center for Education Statistics, High School and Beyond Longitudinal Study of 1980 Sophomores (HS&B-So:80/82), "High School Transcript Study"; and 1987, 1990, 1994, 1998, 2000, 2005, and 2009 High School Transcript Study (HSTS). (This table was prepared October 2011.)

Table 225.60. Number and percentage of public high school graduates taking dual credit, Advanced Placement (AP), and International Baccalaureate (IB) courses in high school and average credits earned, by selected student and school characteristics: 2000, 2005, and 2009

[Standard errors appear in parentheses]

Year and student or school characteristic	Number of graduates who earned credits in dual credit, AP, or IB courses				Percentage of graduates who earned credits in dual credit, AP, or IB courses				Average total credits[2] in dual credit, AP, and IB courses per graduate taking such courses
	Total	Dual credit courses[1]	AP courses	IB courses	Total	Dual credit courses[1]	AP courses	IB courses	
1	2	3	4	5	6	7	8	9	10
2000, all public high school graduates	747,000 (42,700)	—	728,000 (39,200)	35,000 ! (15,100)	27.6 (1.59)	— (†)	26.9 (1.48)	1.3 ! (0.56)	0.60 (0.048)
Sex									
Male	325,000 (20,800)	—	317,000 (19,700)	16,000 ! (7,200)	24.7 (1.60)	— (†)	24.1 (1.51)	1.2 ! (0.55)	0.55 (0.049)
Female	422,000 (23,700)	—	410,000 (21,300)	19,000 ! (8,100)	30.4 (1.70)	— (†)	29.5 (1.55)	1.4 ! (0.58)	0.66 (0.050)
Race/ethnicity									
White	513,000 (31,200)	—	499,000 (27,000)	‡ (†)	27.7 (1.70)	— (†)	26.9 (1.50)	1.4 ! (0.69)	0.61 (0.050)
Black	69,000 (7,300)	—	68,000 (7,400)	2,000 ! (1,000)	19.0 (2.08)	— (†)	18.7 (2.09)	0.5 ! (0.26)	0.36 (0.048)
Hispanic	96,000 (13,500)	—	96,000 (13,500)	1,000 ! (600)	28.9 (3.89)	— (†)	28.7 (3.89)	0.4 ! (0.17)	0.51 (0.074)
Asian/Pacific Islander	62,000 (6,700)	—	60,000 (6,400)	‡ (†)	50.6 (3.32)	— (†)	48.6 (3.29)	4.6 ! (2.28)	1.61 (0.216)
American Indian/Alaska Native	4,000 (1,000)	—	4,000 (1,000)	‡ (†)	17.4 (3.02)	— (†)	17.4 (3.02)	‡ (†)	0.21 (0.036)
School enrollment size									
Less than 500	47,000 (11,100)	—	47,000 (11,100)	‡ (†)	13.2 (3.35)	— (†)	13.1 (3.35)	‡ (†)	0.19 ! (0.060)
500 to 1,499	313,000 (36,100)	—	308,000 (35,700)	‡ (†)	26.5 (2.17)	— (†)	26.1 (2.15)	‡ (†)	0.53 (0.062)
1,500 or more	386,000 (44,500)	—	373,000 (43,200)	‡ (†)	33.0 (2.22)	— (†)	31.8 (2.24)	2.3 ! (1.16)	0.80 (0.081)
Region									
Northeast	102,000 (12,900)	—	102,000 (12,700)	‡ (†)	23.6 (3.43)	— (†)	23.5 (3.39)	‡ (†)	0.42 (0.070)
Midwest	164,000 (24,200)	—	152,000 (18,000)	‡ (†)	23.8 (3.55)	— (†)	22.0 (2.73)	‡ (†)	0.49 (0.107)
South	296,000 (34,400)	—	294,000 (34,300)	‡ (†)	29.8 (2.60)	— (†)	29.6 (2.60)	‡ (†)	0.73 (0.085)
West	184,000 (15,700)	—	180,000 (15,400)	‡ (†)	31.2 (2.33)	— (†)	30.5 (2.28)	‡ (†)	0.65 (0.055)
Percent of students eligible for free or reduced-price lunch									
0 to 25 percent	386,000 (36,700)	—	374,000 (36,100)	‡ (†)	28.4 (1.89)	— (†)	27.6 (1.84)	‡ (†)	0.65 (0.066)
26 to 50 percent	140,000 (23,500)	—	139,000 (23,300)	‡ (†)	24.5 (2.88)	— (†)	24.2 (2.88)	‡ (†)	0.49 (0.065)
More than 50 percent	93,000 (21,700)	—	93,000 (21,700)	‡ (†)	26.5 (4.51)	— (†)	26.4 (4.51)	‡ (†)	0.50 (0.086)
School did not participate or data missing	128,000 (23,700)	—	122,000 (22,400)	‡ (†)	29.7 (4.41)	— (†)	28.4 (4.20)	‡ (†)	0.70 (0.154)
2005, all public high school graduates	842,000 (23,800)	216,000 (14,900)	695,000 (20,700)	44,000 (12,600)	34.9 (0.79)	8.9 (0.60)	28.8 (0.68)	1.8 (0.53)	1.04 (0.043)
Sex									
Male	367,000 (12,100)	98,000 (7,600)	294,000 (10,200)	21,000 ! (6,400)	31.2 (0.83)	8.4 (0.63)	25.0 (0.70)	1.8 ! (0.55)	0.94 (0.046)
Female	475,000 (14,100)	117,000 (8,000)	401,000 (12,500)	22,000 (6,500)	38.3 (0.89)	9.5 (0.64)	32.3 (0.78)	1.8 (0.53)	1.13 (0.045)
Race/ethnicity									
White	603,000 (20,900)	165,000 (12,500)	490,000 (18,700)	30,000 ! (9,900)	36.7 (0.95)	10.0 (0.73)	29.8 (0.86)	1.8 ! (0.60)	1.08 (0.047)
Black	72,000 (4,700)	16,000 (2,600)	60,000 (4,300)	5,000 (1,100)	21.8 (1.09)	4.7 (0.80)	18.3 (0.97)	1.4 (0.34)	0.55 (0.044)
Hispanic	100,000 (6,400)	23,000 (3,300)	84,000 (5,800)	4,000 (1,300)	33.8 (1.43)	7.7 (1.10)	28.5 (1.29)	1.3 ! (0.45)	0.93 (0.073)
Asian/Pacific Islander	56,000 (5,100)	10,000 (1,400)	51,000 (4,800)	4,000 ! (2,000)	52.0 (2.37)	9.2 (1.25)	47.2 (2.25)	3.9 ! (1.79)	2.12 (0.174)
American Indian/Alaska Native	5,000 (900)	1,000 ! (400)	4,000 (800)	‡ (†)	22.3 (3.83)	5.6 ! (2.00)	17.4 (3.45)	‡ (†)	0.51 (0.131)
Combined Black and Hispanic enrollment in school									
Less than 5 percent	231,000 (19,200)	60,000 (9,500)	189,000 (17,100)	‡ (†)	31.4 (1.62)	8.2 (1.20)	25.7 (1.49)	‡ (†)	0.77 (0.061)
5 to 50 percent	452,000 (23,400)	126,000 (12,400)	363,000 (18,800)	31,000 ! (11,100)	38.1 (1.29)	10.6 (1.04)	30.6 (0.91)	2.6 ! (0.94)	1.22 (0.075)
More than 50 percent	152,000 (11,400)	24,000 (4,800)	138,000 (10,600)	10,000 ! (3,200)	31.8 (1.30)	5.1 (0.94)	28.9 (1.23)	2.1 ! (0.68)	0.96 (0.069)
School enrollment size									
Less than 500	65,000 (8,900)	36,000 (7,300)	41,000 (6,200)	‡ (†)	25.6 (2.73)	14.1 (2.66)	16.2 (1.89)	‡ (†)	0.83 (0.230)
500 to 1,499	309,000 (21,200)	78,000 (9,200)	252,000 (17,500)	19,000 ! (8,000)	33.6 (1.30)	8.5 (0.93)	27.4 (1.13)	2.1 ! (0.83)	1.00 (0.077)
1,500 or more	384,000 (25,200)	81,000 (12,100)	331,000 (21,600)	21,000 ! (9,400)	38.7 (1.38)	8.2 (1.14)	33.4 (1.14)	2.1 ! (0.95)	1.16 (0.061)
Region									
Northeast	128,000 (9,600)	13,000 ! (4,900)	119,000 (8,300)	‡ (†)	26.6 (1.70)	2.7 ! (1.01)	24.6 (1.43)	‡ (†)	0.80 (0.079)
Midwest	196,000 (10,500)	53,000 (7,100)	158,000 (10,700)	‡ (†)	34.7 (1.62)	9.4 (1.32)	27.9 (1.59)	‡ (†)	0.87 (0.062)
South	300,000 (15,500)	92,000 (12,200)	241,000 (10,300)	24,000 ! (8,300)	36.7 (1.42)	11.3 (1.38)	29.5 (0.94)	2.9 ! (1.01)	1.20 (0.100)
West	218,000 (15,100)	57,000 (10,300)	178,000 (10,500)	17,000 ! (8,000)	39.8 (1.98)	10.4 (1.72)	32.4 (1.43)	3.1 ! (1.45)	1.17 (0.089)

See notes at end of table.

Table 225.60. Number and percentage of public high school graduates taking dual credit, Advanced Placement (AP), and International Baccalaureate (IB) courses in high school and average credits earned, by selected student and school characteristics: 2000, 2005, and 2009—Continued

[Standard errors appear in parentheses]

Year and student or school characteristic	Number of graduates who earned credits in dual credit, AP, or IB courses				Percentage of graduates who earned credits in dual credit, AP, or IB courses				Average total credits[2] in dual credit, AP, and IB courses per graduate taking such courses
	Total	Dual credit courses[1]	AP courses	IB courses	Total	Dual credit courses[1]	AP courses	IB courses	
1	2	3	4	5	6	7	8	9	10
Percent of students eligible for free or reduced-price lunch									
0 to 25 percent	410,000 (26,700)	102,000 (14,800)	344,000 (23,200)	22,000! (10,500)	39.3 (1.36)	9.8 (1.32)	32.9 (1.27)	2.1! (1.00)	1.24 (0.083)
26 to 50 percent	223,000 (19,400)	67,000 (10,700)	174,000 (13,900)	13,000 (4,300)	32.0 (1.55)	9.6 (1.31)	24.9 (1.16)	1.9! (0.62)	0.91 (0.058)
More than 50 percent	103,000 (10,100)	22,000 (4,900)	89,000 (8,700)	6,000! (2,500)	28.3 (1.83)	5.9 (1.32)	24.5 (1.46)	1.6! (0.69)	0.77 (0.066)
School did not participate or data missing	105,000 (13,900)	25,000 (5,500)	88,000 (12,300)	‡ (†)	34.4 (2.39)	8.2 (1.72)	28.8 (2.04)	‡ (†)	0.94 (0.092)
2009, all public high school graduates	**1,104,000 (36,400)**	**249,000 (20,700)**	**968,000 (33,900)**	**50,000 (10,500)**	**41.4 (1.00)**	**9.3 (0.76)**	**36.3 (0.94)**	**1.9 (0.40)**	**1.39 (0.051)**
Sex									
Male	477,000 (17,900)	110,000 (10,800)	413,000 (16,200)	21,000 (4,900)	36.8 (1.05)	8.5 (0.80)	31.9 (0.98)	1.7 (0.38)	1.24 (0.057)
Female	628,000 (20,100)	139,000 (10,700)	554,000 (19,100)	29,000 (5,800)	45.8 (1.07)	10.1 (0.78)	40.4 (1.01)	2.1 (0.43)	1.53 (0.049)
Race/ethnicity									
White	702,000 (25,700)	160,000 (16,300)	617,000 (23,700)	29,000 (7,100)	42.5 (1.04)	9.7 (1.00)	37.3 (0.95)	1.8 (0.43)	1.41 (0.049)
Black	106,000 (6,600)	25,000 (3,700)	86,000 (5,100)	7,000 (1,700)	27.3 (1.50)	6.4 (0.99)	22.2 (1.00)	1.7 (0.44)	0.75 (0.054)
Hispanic	170,000 (9,300)	46,000 (5,900)	144,000 (7,800)	7,000 (2,000)	39.8 (1.45)	10.8 (1.18)	33.8 (1.30)	1.6 (0.47)	1.17 (0.059)
Asian/Pacific Islander	115,000 (14,800)	15,000 (2,300)	111,000 (14,800)	7,000 (1,900)	69.1 (2.36)	9.2 (1.46)	66.3 (2.56)	4.1! (1.23)	3.25 (0.263)
American Indian/Alaska Native	4,000 (900)	1,000! (400)	3,000 (900)	‡ (†)	25.0 (3.97)	7.0! (2.20)	20.3 (3.74)	‡ (†)	0.79 (0.187)
Combined Black and Hispanic enrollment in school									
Less than 5 percent	239,000 (28,100)	45,000 (13,300)	209,000 (25,500)	‡ (†)	35.9 (2.27)	6.8 (1.92)	31.5 (2.13)	‡ (†)	1.01 (0.102)
5 to 50 percent	601,000 (38,100)	132,000 (15,000)	533,000 (35,200)	32,000 (8,400)	45.4 (1.36)	10.0 (0.96)	40.3 (1.34)	2.5 (0.62)	1.64 (0.092)
More than 50 percent	265,000 (17,900)	72,000 (10,800)	225,000 (15,900)	13,000 (3,600)	39.0 (1.55)	10.6 (1.47)	33.1 (1.34)	1.9 (0.52)	1.26 (0.063)
School enrollment size									
Less than 500	93,000 (12,500)	46,000 (9,400)	61,000 (9,000)	‡ (†)	28.2 (3.13)	13.9 (2.77)	18.3 (2.19)	‡ (†)	0.90 (0.199)
500 to 1,499	355,000 (28,300)	71,000 (11,500)	314,000 (27,900)	6,000! (2,100)	36.8 (1.50)	7.4 (1.11)	32.5 (1.73)	0.7! (0.21)	1.13! (0.100)
1,500 or more	551,000 (32,800)	111,000 (16,200)	500,000 (30,600)	35,000 (8,600)	47.6 (1.24)	9.6 (1.40)	43.1 (1.14)	3.0 (0.70)	1.71 (0.066)
School locale									
City	354,000 (27,500)	81,000 (10,200)	311,000 (24,300)	28,000 (8,100)	48.1 (2.03)	11.0 (1.26)	42.3 (1.78)	3.8 (1.05)	1.72 (0.105)
Suburb	434,000 (26,300)	81,000 (14,800)	396,000 (25,300)	13,000 (3,200)	44.4 (1.52)	8.3 (1.51)	40.5 (1.51)	1.4 (0.33)	1.60 (0.102)
Town	120,000 (14,800)	31,000 (6,900)	101,000 (13,700)	‡ (†)	35.8 (2.05)	9.4 (1.88)	30.3 (2.06)	‡ (†)	0.99 (0.073)
Rural	197,000 (17,100)	56,000 (8,000)	159,000 (16,700)	‡ (†)	31.7 (2.02)	9.0 (1.47)	25.7 (1.77)	‡ (†)	0.89 (0.064)
Region									
Northeast	220,000 (17,600)	46,000 (13,500)	198,000 (15,900)	5,000! (1,800)	40.9 (2.54)	8.5 (2.52)	37.0 (2.20)	0.9! (0.34)	1.28! (0.120)
Midwest	224,000 (13,500)	40,000 (8,000)	194,000 (12,500)	‡ (†)	35.4 (2.00)	6.4 (1.30)	30.6 (1.86)	‡ (†)	0.98 (0.078)
South	385,000 (17,100)	128,000 (12,400)	320,000 (16,800)	16,000 (4,500)	43.8 (1.24)	14.5 (1.37)	36.4 (1.30)	1.9 (0.53)	1.64 (0.084)
West	275,000 (25,800)	35,000 (7,200)	255,000 (25,200)	17,000! (5,800)	44.7 (2.34)	5.7 (1.14)	41.4 (2.41)	2.8! (0.92)	1.54! (0.165)
Percent of students eligible for free or reduced-price lunch									
0 to 25 percent	481,000 (39,800)	91,000 (16,000)	442,000 (37,100)	14,000! (6,400)	48.8 (1.83)	9.3 (1.56)	44.9 (1.72)	1.5! (0.63)	1.75! (0.108)
26 to 50 percent	311,000 (24,700)	77,000 (11,900)	261,000 (21,600)	18,000 (5,700)	37.1 (1.41)	9.2 (1.25)	31.3 (1.40)	2.1! (0.69)	1.17! (0.058)
More than 50 percent	193,000 (16,100)	51,000 (8,400)	160,000 (12,900)	16,000! (5,900)	34.4 (1.92)	9.1 (1.33)	28.6 (1.64)	2.8! (1.02)	1.05! (0.083)
School did not participate or data missing	120,000 (17,500)	30,000 (7,600)	104,000 (16,000)	‡ (†)	42.1 (2.84)	10.4 (2.50)	36.5 (2.42)	‡ (†)	1.44 (0.214)

—Not available.
†Not applicable.
!Interpret data with caution. The coefficient of variation (CV) for this estimate is between 30 and 50 percent.
‡Reporting standards not met. Either there are too few cases for a reliable estimate or the coefficient of variation (CV) is 50 percent or greater.
[1]Dual credit courses are those in which high school students can earn both high school and postsecondary credits for the same course. For 2009, includes some courses for which college credits were conditional upon the student meeting additional requirements. For example, one school offered a consumer economics course for which the student earned college credits only if the student later attended that college and took an advanced consumer economics course there. If the student did not attend that college and take the advanced course, then no college credits would be earned for the course (only high school credits would be earned). In 2009, such conditional college credit courses made up an unweighted 15 percent of the dual credit courses in the sample.

[2]Credits are shown in Carnegie units. The Carnegie unit is a standard unit of measurement that represents one credit for the completion of a 1-year course.
NOTE: For a transcript to be included in the analyses, it had to meet three requirements: (1) the graduate graduated with either a standard or honors diploma, (2) the graduate's transcript contained 16 or more Carnegie credits, and (3) the graduate's transcript contained more than 0 Carnegie credits in English courses. Race categories exclude persons of Hispanic ethnicity. Totals include other racial/ethnic groups not separately shown. Percentages are based on unrounded numbers. Each student is counted only once in each column, regardless of the number of courses taken. Students are counted only once in the total columns even if they earned credits in more than one category—e.g., a student may take both AP courses and dual credit courses, or a single course may fall into both the AP and the dual credit categories. Detail may not sum to totals because of rounding.
SOURCE: U.S. Department of Education, National Center for Education Statistics, 2000, 2005, and 2009 High School Transcript Study (HSTS). (This table was prepared November 2012.)

Table 225.70. Number and percentage of high school graduates who took foreign language courses in high school and average number of credits earned, by language and number of credits: 2000, 2005, and 2009

[Standard errors appear in parentheses]

Language and number of credits	2000 Number of graduates (in thousands)	2000 Percent of graduates	2000 Average credits[1]	2005 Number of graduates (in thousands)	2005 Percent of graduates	2005 Average credits[1]	2009 Number of graduates (in thousands)	2009 Percent of graduates	2009 Average credits[1]
1	2	3	4	5	6	7	8	9	10
All foreign languages Any credit	2,487 (33.8)	84.0 (0.92)	2.5 (0.03)	2,295 (51.1)	85.7 (0.49)	2.5 (0.02)	2,599 (52.7)	88.5 (0.45)	2.6 (0.02)
Spanish									
Any credit	1,780 (31.9)	60.1 (0.90)	2.2 (0.03)	1,705 (42.2)	63.7 (0.66)	2.2 (0.02)	2,032 (45.0)	69.2 (0.70)	2.3 (0.02)
2 or more credits	1,369 (32.2)	46.2 (1.04)	2.6 (0.03)	1,344 (35.9)	50.2 (0.67)	2.6 (0.01)	1,638 (39.2)	55.8 (0.73)	2.6 (0.02)
3 or more credits	554 (26.3)	18.7 (0.90)	3.4 (0.03)	531 (20.1)	19.8 (0.57)	3.4 (0.01)	721 (30.2)	24.5 (0.78)	3.4 (0.02)
French									
Any credit	528 (21.5)	17.8 (0.73)	2.3 (0.05)	414 (14.1)	15.5 (0.49)	2.3 (0.03)	411 (16.1)	14.0 (0.47)	2.4 (0.04)
2 or more credits	398 (17.8)	13.4 (0.61)	2.7 (0.04)	309 (11.1)	11.5 (0.38)	2.7 (0.03)	314 (14.1)	10.7 (0.42)	2.8 (0.03)
3 or more credits	190 (12.1)	6.4 (0.42)	3.5 (0.04)	143 (7.2)	5.4 (0.25)	3.5 (0.03)	167 (10.6)	5.7 (0.32)	3.5 (0.03)
German									
Any credit	142 (17.2)	4.8 (0.57)	2.3 (0.08)	139 (10.0)	5.2 (0.36)	2.3 (0.04)	122 (8.6)	4.2 (0.29)	2.3 (0.06)
2 or more credits	104 (14.6)	3.5 (0.49)	2.8 (0.07)	102 (8.2)	3.8 (0.29)	2.8 (0.04)	91 (7.8)	3.1 (0.27)	2.8 (0.05)
3 or more credits	55 (8.6)	1.8 (0.29)	3.5 (0.06)	53 (4.7)	2.0 (0.17)	3.5 (0.04)	46 (5.3)	1.6 (0.18)	3.5 (0.03)
Latin									
Any credit	120 (15.3)	4.0 (0.52)	2.1 (0.08)	106 (10.4)	4.0 (0.36)	2.1 (0.05)	108 (10.6)	3.7 (0.35)	2.2 (0.07)
Italian									
Any credit	29 (5.5)	1.0 (0.19)	2.2 (0.20)	29 (5.3)	1.1 (0.20)	2.4 (0.16)	36 (7.0)	1.2 (0.23)	2.3 (0.18)
Japanese									
Any credit	36 (7.3)	1.2 (0.25)	2.3 (0.15)	30 (4.4)	1.1 (0.16)	2.1 (0.12)	28 (4.3)	1.0 (0.15)	2.5 (0.12)
Chinese									
Any credit	12 (3.1)	0.4 (0.10)	2.4 (0.20)	8 (2.1)	0.3 (0.08)	2.1 (0.23)	20 (4.1)	0.7 (0.14)	1.9 (0.13)
Arabic									
Any credit	‡ (†)	‡ (†)	‡ (†)	‡ (†)	‡ (†)	‡ (†)	‡ (†)	‡ (†)	2.8 (0.36)
Russian									
Any credit	10 (2.7)	0.3 (0.09)	1.9 (0.24)	5 (1.3)	0.2 (0.05)	1.5 (0.17)	3 ! (1.3)	0.1 ! (0.04)	2.4 (0.14)
Other foreign languages									
Any credit	106 (12.0)	3.6 (0.40)	2.5 (0.17)	89 (5.9)	3.3 (0.23)	2.8 (0.10)	105 (10.6)	3.6 (0.37)	2.5 (0.18)
AP/IB/honors foreign languages									
Any credit	183 (23.9)	6.2 (0.81)	1.2 (0.04)	157 (10.3)	5.9 (0.38)	1.2 (0.02)	233 (15.9)	7.9 (0.52)	1.2 (0.02)

†Not applicable.

!Interpret data with caution. The coefficient of variation (CV) for this estimate is between 30 and 50 percent.

‡Reporting standards not met. Either there are too few cases for a reliable estimate or the coefficient of variation (CV) is 50 percent or greater.

[1]Average credits earned are shown only for those graduates who earned any credit in the specified language while in high school. For these students, however, credits earned include both courses taken in high school and courses taken prior to entering high school. Credits are shown in Carnegie units. The Carnegie unit is a standard unit of measurement that represents one credit for the completion of a 1-year course.

NOTE: For a transcript to be included in the analyses, it had to meet three requirements: (1) the graduate received either a standard or honors diploma, (2) the graduate's transcript contained 16 or more Carnegie credits, and (3) the graduate's transcript contained more than 0 Carnegie credits in English courses.

SOURCE: U.S. Department of Education, National Center for Education Statistics, 2000, 2005, and 2009 High School Transcript Study (HSTS). (This table was prepared April 2014.)

Table 225.80. Percentage distribution of elementary and secondary school children, by average grades and selected child and school characteristics: 2003, 2007, and 2012
[Standard errors appear in parentheses]

Selected child or school characteristic	2003				2007				2012			
	Mostly A's	Mostly B's	Mostly C's	Mostly D's or F's	Mostly A's	Mostly B's	Mostly C's	Mostly D's or F's	Mostly A's	Mostly B's	Mostly C's	Mostly D's or F's
1	2	3	4	5	6	7	8	9	10	11	12	13
All students	43.6 (0.62)	37.0 (0.58)	15.9 (0.52)	3.6 (0.24)	47.2 (0.75)	35.0 (0.80)	14.1 (0.72)	3.8 (0.36)	49.2 (0.53)	35.6 (0.57)	12.8 (0.37)	2.5 (0.21)
Sex of child												
Male	36.4 (0.72)	38.6 (0.86)	19.8 (0.74)	5.2 (0.40)	40.3 (1.01)	37.1 (1.17)	17.0 (1.25)	5.7 (0.64)	42.9 (0.74)	37.7 (0.78)	16.1 (0.58)	3.3 (0.34)
Female	51.0 (0.84)	35.3 (0.76)	11.9 (0.61)	1.9 (0.24)	54.7 (0.99)	32.7 (0.97)	11.0 (0.62)	1.7 (0.24)	55.9 (0.82)	33.3 (0.80)	9.3 (0.51)	1.5 (0.22)
Race/ethnicity of child												
White	47.8 (0.86)	35.2 (0.75)	14.0 (0.63)	3.1 (0.25)	53.9 (0.97)	32.2 (0.91)	11.7 (0.68)	2.1 (0.27)	53.6 (0.74)	33.5 (0.77)	10.8 (0.48)	2.1 (0.22)
Black	34.5 (1.75)	39.5 (1.65)	20.9 (1.33)	5.0 (0.82)	28.3 (2.04)	40.5 (2.75)	24.9 (2.89)	6.3 (1.41)	37.0 (1.88)	39.7 (1.97)	19.9 (1.19)	3.4 (0.75)
Hispanic	34.9 (1.14)	42.3 (1.24)	18.6 (1.03)	4.2 (0.48)	40.8 (1.68)	39.2 (1.66)	14.1 (1.24)	6.0 (1.15)	43.2 (1.09)	39.9 (1.05)	14.3 (0.83)	2.6 (0.41)
Asian/Pacific Islander	62.0 (3.47)	25.5 (2.76)	11.3 (3.06)	‡	68.7 (4.52)	25.7 (4.29)	3.5 (1.03)	‡	60.6 (2.70)	32.9 (2.79)	5.8 (0.97)	0.7! (0.27)
Asian	—	—	—	—	74.5 (3.67)	20.7 (3.60)	3.2! (1.10)	‡	63.2 (2.82)	31.8 (2.86)	4.6 (0.98)	0.4! (0.20)
Pacific Islander	† (†)	† (†)	† (†)	—	‡	29.2 (8.22)	19.9! (6.67)	‡	23.7! (7.70)	43.4 (10.65)	27.5! (8.38)	‡ (†)
American Indian/Alaska Native	29.5 (6.53)	53.3 (6.42)	12.1! (4.90)	5.1! (2.54)	39.7 (9.13)	29.2 (8.22)	‡	‡	54.6 (8.07)	28.2 (6.56)	16.3! (5.26)	‡ (†)
Other	41.4 (4.34)	36.2 (3.91)	18.8 (2.81)	3.5! (1.38)	43.4 (3.98)	39.0 (4.33)	11.3 (2.39)	6.4 (1.73)	56.0 (2.82)	27.6 (2.61)	11.3 (1.71)	5.1! (2.33)
Highest education level of parents												
Less than high school	27.8 (2.17)	41.6 (2.05)	22.7 (2.27)	7.8 (1.46)	26.8 (3.18)	41.9 (4.27)	22.0 (2.55)	9.3 (2.02)	39.5 (2.25)	39.7 (2.02)	16.8 (1.73)	4.0 (0.93)
High school/GED	32.1 (1.20)	41.4 (1.23)	21.7 (1.12)	4.8 (0.57)	32.9 (1.70)	39.8 (1.64)	21.9 (2.02)	5.4 (0.82)	37.7 (1.51)	40.8 (1.62)	17.6 (1.31)	4.0 (0.71)
Vocational/technical or some college	39.8 (1.34)	38.3 (1.36)	17.2 (0.95)	4.7 (0.58)	40.7 (1.65)	38.6 (2.03)	16.6 (1.43)	4.0 (0.78)	43.5 (1.07)	38.1 (1.05)	15.6 (0.87)	2.8 (0.32)
Associate's degree	46.7 (2.13)	34.5 (1.94)	16.4 (1.51)	2.4 (0.57)	40.3 (2.27)	38.4 (2.00)	15.7 (1.76)	5.5! (2.10)	47.0 (1.82)	34.9 (1.78)	15.4 (1.29)	2.7 (0.52)
Bachelor's degree/some graduate school	53.0 (1.26)	34.2 (1.29)	11.1 (0.85)	1.7 (0.28)	58.9 (1.62)	32.2 (1.52)	7.3 (0.85)	1.6 (0.38)	60.1 (1.05)	31.4 (1.02)	7.5 (0.53)	1.0 (0.19)
Graduate/professional degree	61.9 (1.71)	30.5 (1.75)	6.7 (0.67)	0.9 (0.24)	68.2 (1.59)	24.1 (1.37)	6.6 (1.33)	1.2! (0.38)	68.1 (1.04)	27.3 (1.04)	4.2 (0.36)	0.5 (0.10)
Family income (in current dollars)												
$20,000 or less	33.1 (1.53)	38.9 (1.56)	22.0 (1.30)	6.0 (0.85)	29.0 (2.20)	39.4 (2.61)	24.7 (2.83)	6.8 (1.14)	37.2 (1.35)	40.2 (1.19)	18.3 (1.04)	4.4 (0.59)
$20,001 to $50,000	37.8 (1.20)	40.0 (1.19)	17.7 (0.85)	4.5 (0.42)	37.6 (1.47)	37.9 (1.65)	18.0 (1.39)	6.4 (0.91)	41.3 (1.22)	38.9 (1.19)	16.7 (0.90)	3.1 (0.44)
$50,001 to $75,000	48.0 (1.29)	35.0 (1.22)	14.0 (0.81)	3.0 (0.45)	53.0 (1.50)	33.8 (1.42)	11.0 (0.97)	2.2 (0.42)	49.3 (1.45)	35.8 (1.37)	12.9 (1.07)	1.9 (0.32)
$75,001 to $100,000	51.8 (1.66)	33.7 (1.45)	13.3 (1.23)	1.3 (0.32)	55.7 (1.74)	33.3 (1.84)	9.7 (1.00)	1.4 (0.33)	53.7 (1.64)	33.5 (1.42)	10.6 (1.03)	2.3 (0.50)
Over $100,000	55.8 (1.74)	33.9 (1.72)	9.1 (1.09)	1.2 (0.24)	61.6 (1.44)	30.2 (1.31)	7.0 (0.88)	1.2 (0.36)	61.8 (1.15)	30.4 (1.19)	6.6 (0.61)	1.1! (0.41)
Poverty status[1]												
Poor	33.1 (1.61)	39.4 (1.65)	21.9 (1.39)	5.6 (0.91)	30.4 (2.07)	39.0 (2.52)	23.3 (2.38)	7.2 (1.09)	39.1 (1.39)	38.9 (1.33)	17.8 (1.06)	4.2 (0.54)
Near-poor	34.8 (1.39)	42.0 (1.26)	18.2 (1.08)	5.0 (0.59)	38.4 (1.85)	36.5 (1.85)	18.6 (1.84)	6.5 (1.18)	40.1 (1.19)	40.3 (1.07)	17.0 (0.93)	2.7 (0.45)
Nonpoor	49.9 (0.83)	34.5 (0.76)	13.2 (0.54)	2.4 (0.23)	55.1 (0.89)	33.2 (0.91)	9.8 (0.56)	1.8 (0.21)	56.0 (0.75)	32.7 (0.75)	9.5 (0.45)	1.8 (0.25)
Control of school and enrollment level of child												
Public school	41.8 (0.64)	37.5 (0.62)	16.8 (0.57)	3.8 (0.26)	45.5 (0.80)	35.5 (0.84)	14.9 (0.77)	4.1 (0.39)	47.9 (0.55)	36.0 (0.60)	13.5 (0.39)	2.6 (0.23)
Elementary (kindergarten to grade 8)	46.1 (0.80)	35.9 (0.84)	14.6 (0.74)	3.4 (0.32)	50.0 (0.99)	33.1 (1.00)	13.4 (1.12)	3.5 (0.43)	52.9 (0.69)	34.2 (0.73)	11.0 (0.49)	1.8 (0.22)
Secondary (grades 9 to 12)	34.6 (0.96)	40.2 (0.97)	20.6 (0.94)	4.6 (0.46)	38.6 (1.36)	39.1 (1.27)	17.2 (1.08)	5.2 (0.71)	37.5 (0.83)	39.7 (1.03)	18.4 (0.84)	4.4 (0.54)
Private school	57.6 (1.72)	33.0 (1.68)	8.1 (0.91)	1.3! (0.45)	60.6 (2.79)	30.8 (2.85)	7.8 (1.73)	0.9! (0.35)	63.4 (1.63)	30.8 (1.51)	5.4 (0.68)	0.4! (0.20)
Elementary (kindergarten to grade 8)	61.6 (2.39)	30.3 (2.28)	7.3 (1.03)	0.8! (0.28)	66.1 (3.73)	26.6 (4.05)	6.6 (1.66)	‡	67.3 (1.95)	28.2 (1.91)	3.5 (0.61)	‡
Secondary (grades 9 to 12)	48.8 (3.22)	38.9 (2.94)	10.0 (1.77)	‡ (†)	51.2 (3.91)	37.8 (3.43)	9.8! (3.87)	‡	52.8 (2.70)	37.2 (2.58)	9.9 (1.60)	‡ (†)

—Not available.
†Not applicable.
!Interpret data with caution. The coefficient of variation (CV) for this estimate is between 30 and 50 percent.
‡Reporting standards not met. Either there are too few cases for a reliable estimate or the coefficient of variation (CV) is 50 percent or greater.
[1]Poor children are those whose family incomes were below the Census Bureau's poverty threshold in the year prior to data collection; near-poor children are those whose family incomes ranged from the poverty threshold to 199 percent of the poverty threshold; and nonpoor children are those whose family incomes were at or above 200 percent of the poverty threshold. The poverty threshold is a dollar amount that varies depending on a family's size and composition and is updated annually to account for inflation. In 2011, for example, the poverty threshold for a family of four with two children was $22,811. Survey respondents are asked to select the range within which their income falls, rather than giving the exact amount of their income; therefore, the measure of poverty status is an approximation.

NOTE: While National Household Education Surveys Program (NHES) administrations prior to 2012 were administered via telephone with an interviewer, NHES:2012 used self-administered paper-and-pencil questionnaires that were mailed to respondents. Measurable differences in estimates between 2012 and prior years could reflect actual changes in the population, or the changes could be due to the mode change from telephone to mail. Includes children enrolled in kindergarten through grade 12. Excludes children whose programs have no classes with lettered grades. Race categories exclude persons of Hispanic ethnicity. Detail may not sum to totals because of rounding. Some data have been revised from previously published figures.
SOURCE: U.S. Department of Education, National Center for Education Statistics, Parent and Family Involvement in Education Survey of the National Household Education Surveys Program (PFI-NHES:2003, 2007, and 2012). (This table was prepared September 2014.)

Table 225.90. Number and percentage of elementary and secondary school students retained in grade, by sex, race/ethnicity, and grade level: 1994 through 2014

[Standard errors appear in parentheses]

| | Number of students retained (in thousands) | | | | | | Percent of students retained — Students retained in grade (in same grade as in previous year) | | | | | |
| | | Sex | | Race/ethnicity | | | | Sex | | Race/ethnicity | | |
Grade level and year	Total	Male	Female	White	Black	Hispanic	Total	Male	Female	White	Black	Hispanic
1	2	3	4	5	6	7	8	9	10	11	12	13
Total, all grades												
1994	1,368 (58.6)	747 (43.4)	621 (39.5)	772 (43.9)	333 (31.0)	222 (26.9)	2.9 (0.12)	3.1 (0.18)	2.7 (0.17)	2.5 (0.14)	4.5 (0.40)	3.7 (0.43)
1995	1,479 (61.0)	803 (45.0)	676 (41.2)	893 (47.3)	336 (31.1)	208 (26.0)	3.1 (0.12)	3.3 (0.18)	2.9 (0.17)	2.8 (0.14)	4.4 (0.39)	3.3 (0.40)
1996	1,223 (57.4)	717 (44.0)	506 (36.8)	629 (41.1)	312 (31.0)	233 (28.5)	2.4 (0.11)	2.7 (0.16)	2.1 (0.15)	1.9 (0.12)	3.9 (0.37)	3.3 (0.39)
1997	1,253 (58.1)	715 (44.0)	538 (38.0)	674 (42.6)	310 (30.9)	222 (27.8)	2.6 (0.12)	2.9 (0.17)	2.3 (0.16)	2.1 (0.13)	3.9 (0.38)	3.3 (0.40)
1998	1,335 (60.1)	734 (44.6)	601 (40.3)	713 (43.8)	345 (32.7)	213 (27.2)	2.7 (0.12)	2.9 (0.17)	2.5 (0.16)	2.3 (0.14)	4.3 (0.39)	3.1 (0.38)
1999	1,524 (64.3)	916 (50.0)	608 (40.5)	835 (47.5)	316 (31.3)	318 (33.5)	3.1 (0.13)	3.6 (0.19)	2.5 (0.16)	2.6 (0.15)	4.0 (0.38)	4.4 (0.44)
2000	1,521 (64.2)	946 (50.8)	575 (39.4)	737 (44.5)	391 (35.0)	306 (32.8)	3.1 (0.13)	3.7 (0.19)	2.4 (0.16)	2.3 (0.14)	5.0 (0.42)	4.1 (0.42)
2001	1,569 (61.9)	880 (46.4)	689 (41.0)	745 (42.5)	397 (33.5)	354 (33.6)	3.1 (0.12)	3.4 (0.17)	2.8 (0.16)	2.4 (0.13)	5.1 (0.41)	4.5 (0.41)
2002	1,475 (56.9)	803 (42.0)	672 (38.4)	744 (40.3)	311 (27.9)	348 (31.5)	2.9 (0.11)	3.1 (0.16)	2.7 (0.16)	2.4 (0.13)	4.0 (0.34)	4.0 (0.35)
2003	1,568 (58.7)	856 (43.4)	711 (39.5)	773 (41.1)	376 (30.8)	323 (30.3)	3.1 (0.11)	3.3 (0.16)	2.9 (0.16)	2.5 (0.13)	4.8 (0.38)	3.7 (0.34)
2004	1,515 (57.7)	858 (43.5)	657 (37.9)	717 (39.6)	368 (30.5)	316 (30.0)	3.0 (0.11)	3.3 (0.16)	2.7 (0.15)	2.4 (0.13)	4.9 (0.38)	3.5 (0.32)
2005	1,544 (58.2)	825 (42.6)	719 (39.7)	756 (40.6)	369 (30.6)	319 (30.1)	3.0 (0.11)	3.2 (0.16)	2.9 (0.16)	2.5 (0.13)	4.9 (0.38)	3.4 (0.31)
2006	1,418 (55.8)	756 (40.7)	663 (38.1)	689 (38.8)	295 (27.2)	321 (30.2)	2.8 (0.11)	2.9 (0.15)	2.7 (0.15)	2.3 (0.13)	4.0 (0.35)	3.4 (0.31)
2007	1,164 (50.4)	615 (36.6)	548 (34.6)	595 (36.0)	213 (23.0)	296 (28.9)	2.3 (0.10)	2.4 (0.14)	2.2 (0.14)	2.0 (0.12)	2.8 (0.30)	3.0 (0.28)
2008	999 (46.6)	543 (34.4)	456 (31.4)	506 (33.1)	231 (23.9)	225 (25.1)	2.0 (0.09)	2.1 (0.13)	1.8 (0.12)	1.7 (0.11)	3.1 (0.31)	2.2 (0.24)
2009	1,018 (47.1)	556 (34.8)	462 (31.7)	491 (32.6)	206 (22.6)	232 (25.5)	2.0 (0.09)	2.2 (0.13)	1.9 (0.13)	1.7 (0.11)	2.8 (0.30)	2.2 (0.24)
2010[1]	1,061 (47.6)	557 (34.0)	504 (36.4)	506 (41.9)	191 (24.0)	305 (31.0)	2.1 (0.09)	2.2 (0.13)	2.0 (0.15)	1.8 (0.15)	2.6 (0.30)	2.8 (0.28)
2011[1]	945 (60.5)	490 (41.9)	455 (37.7)	454 (41.7)	181 (24.9)	245 (29.7)	1.8 (0.12)	1.9 (0.16)	1.8 (0.15)	1.6 (0.15)	2.5 (0.34)	2.1 (0.26)
2012[1]	1,106 (66.7)	603 (48.6)	503 (42.7)	437 (40.4)	210 (30.2)	363 (38.2)	2.2 (0.13)	2.3 (0.18)	2.0 (0.17)	1.6 (0.15)	2.9 (0.42)	3.1 (0.32)
2013[1]	1,124 (71.1)	661 (50.5)	463 (40.4)	458 (49.0)	259 (31.6)	334 (35.3)	2.2 (0.14)	2.5 (0.19)	1.9 (0.16)	1.7 (0.18)	3.6 (0.44)	2.8 (0.29)
2014[1]	1,313 (72.1)	723 (49.1)	590 (45.6)	523 (42.3)	218 (30.3)	430 (41.3)	2.6 (0.14)	2.8 (0.19)	2.4 (0.18)	2.0 (0.16)	3.0 (0.42)	3.6 (0.34)
Kindergarten through grade 8												
1994	1,006 (51.2)	552 (38.0)	454 (34.3)	583 (38.9)	250 (27.4)	141 (21.8)	3.1 (0.15)	3.3 (0.22)	2.9 (0.21)	2.7 (0.17)	4.8 (0.50)	3.3 (0.50)
1995	1,089 (53.3)	570 (38.6)	519 (36.8)	677 (42.0)	259 (27.9)	122 (20.2)	3.3 (0.16)	3.4 (0.22)	3.2 (0.22)	3.1 (0.18)	4.9 (0.50)	2.7 (0.44)
1996	831 (48.1)	482 (36.7)	350 (31.2)	430 (34.5)	215 (26.2)	155 (23.6)	2.3 (0.13)	2.6 (0.20)	2.0 (0.18)	1.9 (0.15)	3.8 (0.45)	3.1 (0.46)
1997	863 (49.1)	508 (37.7)	356 (31.5)	464 (35.9)	227 (27.0)	143 (22.7)	2.6 (0.14)	2.9 (0.21)	2.2 (0.19)	2.1 (0.16)	4.2 (0.48)	3.0 (0.46)
1998	965 (52.0)	536 (38.8)	429 (34.6)	542 (38.9)	225 (26.8)	143 (22.7)	2.8 (0.15)	3.1 (0.21)	2.6 (0.20)	2.5 (0.17)	4.1 (0.47)	2.9 (0.44)
1999	994 (52.8)	600 (41.1)	393 (33.1)	533 (38.6)	217 (26.4)	213 (27.9)	2.9 (0.15)	3.4 (0.23)	2.4 (0.19)	2.5 (0.17)	4.0 (0.46)	4.1 (0.51)
2000	1,121 (56.1)	701 (44.6)	420 (34.2)	545 (39.0)	298 (31.1)	214 (27.9)	3.3 (0.16)	4.0 (0.24)	2.5 (0.20)	2.5 (0.18)	5.3 (0.53)	4.0 (0.50)
2001	1,047 (51.4)	588 (38.6)	459 (34.0)	524 (36.3)	266 (27.8)	233 (27.7)	3.0 (0.14)	3.3 (0.21)	2.7 (0.20)	2.4 (0.16)	4.9 (0.49)	4.1 (0.47)
2002	1,009 (50.5)	563 (37.8)	445 (33.5)	529 (36.5)	213 (24.8)	225 (27.1)	2.9 (0.14)	3.2 (0.21)	2.7 (0.19)	2.5 (0.17)	3.9 (0.43)	3.6 (0.42)
2003	1,110 (53.0)	596 (38.9)	514 (36.1)	550 (37.2)	259 (27.4)	229 (27.4)	3.3 (0.15)	3.4 (0.21)	3.2 (0.21)	2.7 (0.18)	4.9 (0.50)	3.8 (0.43)
2004	1,121 (53.3)	618 (39.6)	504 (35.7)	548 (37.1)	276 (28.4)	218 (26.7)	3.3 (0.15)	3.5 (0.22)	3.1 (0.21)	2.7 (0.18)	5.4 (0.52)	3.4 (0.40)
2005	1,129 (53.5)	594 (38.8)	535 (36.8)	567 (37.8)	256 (27.3)	235 (27.7)	3.3 (0.15)	3.4 (0.21)	3.2 (0.21)	2.8 (0.18)	5.0 (0.51)	3.6 (0.40)
2006	955 (49.1)	521 (36.3)	434 (33.0)	469 (34.3)	207 (24.5)	206 (25.9)	2.8 (0.14)	3.0 (0.21)	2.6 (0.20)	2.4 (0.17)	4.2 (0.48)	3.1 (0.38)
2007	749 (43.3)	394 (31.4)	355 (29.8)	392 (31.3)	131 (19.3)	193 (25.0)	2.2 (0.12)	2.2 (0.18)	2.2 (0.18)	2.0 (0.16)	2.7 (0.38)	2.7 (0.34)
2008	660 (40.6)	374 (30.6)	287 (26.8)	343 (29.3)	154 (21.0)	132 (20.6)	1.9 (0.12)	2.1 (0.17)	1.7 (0.16)	1.8 (0.15)	3.0 (0.40)	1.9 (0.28)
2009	619 (39.3)	316 (28.1)	302 (27.5)	324 (28.4)	109 (17.6)	128 (20.3)	1.8 (0.11)	1.8 (0.16)	1.8 (0.16)	1.7 (0.14)	2.3 (0.36)	1.7 (0.27)
2010[1]	621 (37.9)	333 (28.2)	288 (27.9)	296 (33.1)	122 (17.2)	155 (23.0)	1.8 (0.11)	1.9 (0.16)	1.7 (0.17)	1.6 (0.17)	2.5 (0.36)	2.0 (0.29)
2011[1]	631 (49.7)	342 (35.1)	289 (30.0)	318 (32.2)	94 (17.5)	183 (28.2)	1.8 (0.14)	1.8 (0.19)	1.7 (0.18)	1.7 (0.17)	1.9 (0.36)	2.2 (0.34)
2012[1]	698 (52.9)	404 (39.3)	293 (29.8)	280 (33.3)	127 (23.6)	226 (30.6)	2.0 (0.15)	2.3 (0.22)	1.7 (0.18)	1.5 (0.18)	2.7 (0.49)	2.7 (0.37)
2013[1]	668 (58.6)	377 (42.5)	292 (31.9)	268 (41.0)	153 (24.2)	215 (29.0)	1.9 (0.17)	2.1 (0.24)	1.7 (0.19)	1.5 (0.22)	3.2 (0.50)	2.5 (0.34)
2014[1]	896 (58.4)	482 (39.2)	414 (37.8)	331 (32.6)	159 (24.3)	300 (31.5)	2.6 (0.17)	2.7 (0.22)	2.4 (0.22)	1.8 (0.18)	3.3 (0.49)	3.5 (0.37)

See notes at end of table.

Table 225.90. Number and percentage of elementary and secondary school students retained in grade, by sex, race/ethnicity, and grade level: 1994 through 2014—Continued

[Standard errors appear in parentheses]

Grade level and year	Number of students retained (in thousands)						Students retained in grade (in same grade as in previous year) Percent of students retained					
	Total	Sex		Race/ethnicity			Total	Sex		Race/ethnicity		
		Male	Female	White	Black	Hispanic		Male	Female	White	Black	Hispanic
1	2	3	4	5	6	7	8	9	10	11	12	13
Grades 9 through 12												
1994	363 (30.1)	196 (22.1)	167 (20.4)	189 (21.7)	83 (15.4)	81 (16.3)	2.6 (0.21)	2.7 (0.30)	2.4 (0.29)	2.0 (0.22)	3.6 (0.65)	4.6 (0.88)
1995	390 (31.3)	232 (24.2)	157 (19.8)	216 (23.2)	76 (14.8)	87 (16.9)	2.7 (0.21)	3.2 (0.32)	2.2 (0.28)	2.2 (0.23)	3.3 (0.62)	5.0 (0.93)
1996	392 (32.5)	236 (25.3)	156 (20.5)	200 (23.1)	97 (17.3)	78 (16.6)	2.6 (0.21)	3.0 (0.31)	2.1 (0.27)	2.0 (0.23)	4.1 (0.70)	3.9 (0.79)
1997	389 (32.4)	207 (23.6)	182 (22.1)	211 (23.8)	82 (15.9)	78 (16.6)	2.6 (0.21)	2.7 (0.30)	2.5 (0.29)	2.1 (0.23)	3.3 (0.62)	4.0 (0.81)
1998	370 (31.6)	198 (23.1)	172 (21.5)	171 (21.4)	120 (19.4)	70 (15.6)	2.5 (0.21)	2.6 (0.29)	2.3 (0.29)	1.7 (0.21)	4.9 (0.76)	3.6 (0.77)
1999	530 (38.0)	316 (29.4)	215 (24.1)	302 (28.6)	98 (17.5)	106 (19.4)	3.5 (0.24)	4.0 (0.36)	2.9 (0.32)	3.0 (0.28)	4.2 (0.71)	5.0 (0.88)
2000	400 (32.9)	245 (25.8)	155 (20.4)	192 (22.7)	94 (17.1)	91 (18.0)	2.6 (0.21)	3.1 (0.32)	2.1 (0.27)	1.9 (0.22)	4.1 (0.72)	4.3 (0.81)
2001	521 (35.7)	291 (26.8)	230 (23.7)	221 (23.1)	131 (19.3)	121 (19.8)	3.4 (0.22)	3.7 (0.32)	3.1 (0.31)	2.2 (0.22)	5.5 (0.76)	5.7 (0.88)
2002	466 (32.0)	240 (22.9)	227 (22.3)	216 (21.7)	98 (15.7)	123 (18.8)	3.0 (0.20)	3.0 (0.28)	3.0 (0.28)	2.1 (0.21)	4.2 (0.64)	5.0 (0.73)
2003	458 (31.7)	260 (23.9)	197 (20.7)	223 (22.1)	117 (17.2)	95 (16.4)	2.8 (0.19)	3.1 (0.28)	2.4 (0.25)	2.2 (0.21)	4.6 (0.65)	3.7 (0.61)
2004	393 (29.3)	240 (22.9)	153 (18.2)	170 (19.2)	92 (15.2)	98 (16.7)	2.4 (0.18)	3.0 (0.27)	1.9 (0.22)	1.7 (0.19)	3.8 (0.60)	3.7 (0.61)
2005	415 (30.1)	231 (22.5)	184 (20.0)	188 (20.2)	113 (16.9)	84 (15.4)	2.5 (0.18)	2.7 (0.25)	2.3 (0.24)	1.8 (0.19)	4.6 (0.66)	3.0 (0.53)
2006	463 (31.9)	234 (22.7)	229 (22.4)	221 (21.9)	‡ (†)	115 (18.1)	2.8 (0.19)	2.8 (0.26)	2.9 (0.27)	2.2 (0.22)	3.5 (0.56)	4.0 (0.61)
2007	415 (30.1)	221 (22.0)	194 (20.6)	203 (21.0)	82 (14.2)	103 (17.1)	2.5 (0.18)	2.6 (0.25)	2.4 (0.25)	2.1 (0.21)	3.2 (0.54)	3.6 (0.57)
2008	338 (27.1)	169 (19.2)	169 (19.2)	163 (18.8)	‡ (†)	92 (16.2)	2.1 (0.16)	2.1 (0.23)	2.1 (0.24)	1.7 (0.19)	3.2 (0.55)	3.1 (0.52)
2009	400 (29.6)	240 (23.0)	160 (18.6)	167 (19.0)	97 (15.6)	104 (17.2)	2.5 (0.18)	2.9 (0.27)	2.1 (0.23)	1.8 (0.20)	3.9 (0.60)	3.5 (0.55)
2010[1]	440 (31.8)	224 (24.3)	216 (22.9)	210 (23.1)	69 (14.3)	150 (19.8)	2.7 (0.20)	2.7 (0.30)	2.8 (0.29)	2.3 (0.25)	2.9 (0.59)	4.8 (0.62)
2011[1]	314 (32.8)	148 (23.6)	166 (23.1)	137 (20.4)	‡ (†)	‡ (†)	1.9 (0.20)	1.8 (0.28)	2.1 (0.29)	1.5 (0.22)	3.6 (0.74)	1.9 (0.38)
2012[1]	408 (38.9)	198 (27.5)	210 (28.6)	157 (22.7)	‡ (†)	137 (20.9)	2.5 (0.23)	2.4 (0.33)	2.6 (0.34)	1.8 (0.25)	3.4 (0.77)	3.8 (0.56)
2013[1]	456 (39.3)	284 (31.0)	172 (22.6)	190 (25.1)	107 (19.6)	119 (20.1)	2.8 (0.24)	3.5 (0.37)	2.2 (0.28)	2.2 (0.29)	4.5 (0.82)	3.3 (0.56)
2014[1]	417 (37.8)	241 (27.3)	176 (23.6)	192 (24.5)	‡ (†)	129 (23.9)	2.6 (0.23)	3.0 (0.33)	2.2 (0.30)	2.2 (0.28)	2.5 (0.64)	3.7 (0.67)

†Not applicable.
‡Reporting standards not met (too few cases for a reliable estimate).
[1]Beginning in 2010, standard errors were computed using replicate weights, which produced more precise values than the generalized variance function methodology used in prior years.

NOTE: Data are as of October of each year. Excludes students who were reported as being in a higher grade the previous year than the given year. Race categories exclude persons of Hispanic ethnicity. Totals include other racial/ethnic categories not separately shown. Detail may not sum to totals because of rounding.
SOURCE: U.S. Department of Commerce, Census Bureau, Current Population Survey, October, 1994 through 2014. (This table was prepared July 2015.)

Table 226.10. SAT mean scores of college-bound seniors, by race/ethnicity: Selected years, 1986–87 through 2014–15

Race/ethnicity	1986–87	1990–91	1996–97	2000–01	2003–04	2004–05	2005–06	2006–07	2007–08	2008–09	2009–10	2010–11	2011–12	2012–13	2013–14	2014–15	Score change 1990–91 to 2004–05	2004–05 to 2014–15	2009–10 to 2014–15	2013–14 to 2014–15
1	2	3	4	5	6	7	8	9	10	11	12	13	14	15	16	17	18	19	20	21
SAT—Critical reading																				
All students	507	499	505	506	508	508	503	502	502	501	501	497	496	496	497	495	9	-13	-6	-2
White	524	518	526	529	528	532	527	527	528	528	528	528	527	527	529	529	14	-3	1	0
Black	428	427	434	433	430	433	434	433	430	429	428	428	428	431	431	431	6	-2	2	0
Mexican American	457	454	451	451	451	453	454	455	454	453	454	451	448	449	450	448	-1	-5	-6	-2
Puerto Rican	436	436	454	457	457	460	459	459	456	452	454	452	452	456	456	456	24	-4	2	0
Other Hispanic	464	458	466	460	461	463	458	459	455	455	454	452	447	450	451	449	5	-14	-5	-2
Asian/Pacific Islander	479	485	496	501	507	511	510	514	513	516	519	517	518	521	523	525	26	14	6	2
American Indian/Alaska Native	471	470	475	481	483	489	487	487	485	486	485	484	482	480	483	481	19	-8	-4	-2
Other	480	486	512	503	494	495	494	497	496	494	494	493	491	492	493	490	9	-5	-4	-3
SAT—Mathematics																				
All students	501	500	511	514	518	520	518	515	515	515	516	514	514	514	513	511	20	-9	-5	-2
White	514	513	526	531	531	536	536	534	537	536	536	535	536	534	534	534	23	-2	-2	0
Black	411	419	423	426	427	431	429	429	426	426	428	427	428	429	429	428	12	-3	0	-1
Mexican American	455	459	458	458	458	463	465	466	463	463	467	466	465	464	461	457	4	-6	-10	-4
Puerto Rican	432	439	447	451	452	457	456	454	453	450	452	452	452	453	450	449	18	-8	-3	-1
Other Hispanic	462	462	468	465	465	469	463	463	461	461	462	462	461	461	459	457	7	-12	-5	-2
Asian/Pacific Islander	541	548	560	566	577	580	578	578	581	587	591	595	595	597	598	598	32	18	7	0
American Indian/Alaska Native	463	468	475	479	488	493	494	494	491	493	492	488	489	486	484	482	25	-11	-10	-2
Other	482	492	514	512	508	513	513	512	512	514	514	517	516	519	520	519	21	6	5	-1
SAT—Writing																				
All students	†	†	†	†	†	†	497	494	494	493	492	489	488	488	487	484	†	†	-8	-3
White	†	†	†	†	†	†	519	518	518	517	516	516	515	515	513	513	†	†	-3	0
Black	†	†	†	†	†	†	428	425	424	421	420	417	417	418	418	418	†	†	-2	0
Mexican American	†	†	†	†	†	†	452	450	447	446	448	445	443	442	443	438	†	†	-10	-5
Puerto Rican	†	†	†	†	†	†	448	447	445	443	443	442	442	445	443	442	†	†	-1	-1
Other Hispanic	†	†	†	†	†	†	450	450	448	448	447	444	442	443	443	439	†	†	-8	-4
Asian/Pacific Islander	†	†	†	†	†	†	512	513	516	520	526	528	528	527	530	531	†	†	5	1
American Indian/Alaska Native	†	†	†	†	†	†	474	473	470	469	467	465	462	461	461	460	†	†	-7	-1
Other	†	†	†	†	†	†	493	493	494	493	492	492	491	490	491	487	†	†	-5	-4

†Not applicable.
NOTE: Data for 2009–10 and earlier years are for seniors who took the SAT any time during their high school years through March of their senior year. Data for 2010–11 onwards are for seniors who took the SAT any time during their high school years through June of their senior year. If a student took the SAT more than once, the most recent score on each section was used. Possible scores on each section of the SAT range from 200 to 800. Prior to 2006, the critical reading section was known as the verbal section. The writing section was introduced in March 2005. The SAT was formerly known as the Scholastic Assessment Test and the Scholastic Aptitude Test.
SOURCE: College Entrance Examination Board, *College-Bound Seniors: Total Group Profile [National] Report,* selected years, 1986–87 through 2014–15, retrieved September 10, 2015, from https://secure-media.collegeboard.org/digitalServices/pdf/sat/total-group-2015.pdf. (This table was prepared September 2015.)

Table 226.20. SAT mean scores of college-bound seniors, by sex: 1966–67 through 2014–15

| | SAT[1] | | | | | | | | | Scholastic Aptitude Test (old scale) | | | | | |
| | Critical reading score | | | Mathematics score | | | Writing score[2] | | | Verbal score | | | Mathematics score | | |
School year	Total	Male	Female	Total	Male	Female	Total	Male	Female	Total	Male	Female	Total	Male	Female
1	2	3	4	5	6	7	8	9	10	11	12	13	14	15	16
1966–67	543	540	545	516	535	495	†	†	†	466	463	468	492	514	467
1967–68	543	541	543	516	533	497	†	†	†	466	464	466	492	512	470
1968–69	540	536	543	517	534	498	†	†	†	463	459	466	493	513	470
1969–70	537	536	538	512	531	493	†	†	†	460	459	461	488	509	465
1970–71	532	531	534	513	529	494	†	†	†	455	454	457	488	507	466
1971–72	530	531	529	509	527	489	†	†	†	453	454	452	484	505	461
1972–73	523	523	521	506	525	489	†	†	†	445	446	443	481	502	460
1973–74	521	524	520	505	524	488	†	†	†	444	447	442	480	501	459
1974–75	512	515	509	498	518	479	†	†	†	434	437	431	472	495	449
1975–76	509	511	508	497	520	475	†	†	†	431	433	430	472	497	446
1976–77	507	509	505	496	520	474	†	†	†	429	431	427	470	497	445
1977–78	507	511	503	494	517	474	†	†	†	429	433	425	468	494	444
1978–79	505	509	501	493	516	473	†	†	†	427	431	423	467	493	443
1979–80	502	506	498	492	515	473	†	†	†	424	428	420	466	491	443
1980–81	502	508	496	492	516	473	†	†	†	424	430	418	466	492	443
1981–82	504	509	499	493	516	473	†	†	†	426	431	421	467	493	443
1982–83	503	508	498	494	516	474	†	†	†	425	430	420	468	493	445
1983–84	504	511	498	497	518	478	†	†	†	426	433	420	471	495	449
1984–85	509	514	503	500	522	480	†	†	†	431	437	425	475	499	452
1985–86	509	515	504	500	523	479	†	†	†	431	437	426	475	501	451
1986–87	507	512	502	501	523	481	†	†	†	430	435	425	476	500	453
1987–88	505	512	499	501	521	483	†	†	†	428	435	422	476	498	455
1988–89	504	510	498	502	523	482	†	†	†	427	434	421	476	500	454
1989–90	500	505	496	501	521	483	†	†	†	424	429	419	476	499	455
1990–91	499	503	495	500	520	482	†	†	†	422	426	418	474	497	453
1991–92	500	504	496	501	521	484	†	†	†	423	428	419	476	499	456
1992–93	500	504	497	503	524	484	†	†	†	424	428	420	478	502	457
1993–94	499	501	497	504	523	487	†	†	†	423	425	421	479	501	460
1994–95	504	505	502	506	525	490	†	†	†	428	429	426	482	503	463
1995–96	505	507	503	508	527	492	†	†	†	—	—	—	—	—	—
1996–97	505	507	503	511	530	494	†	†	†	—	—	—	—	—	—
1997–98	505	509	502	512	531	496	†	†	†	—	—	—	—	—	—
1998–99	505	509	502	511	531	495	†	†	†	—	—	—	—	—	—
1999–2000	505	507	504	514	533	498	†	†	†	†	†	†	†	†	†
2000–01	506	509	502	514	533	498	†	†	†	†	†	†	†	†	†
2001–02	504	507	502	516	534	500	†	†	†	†	†	†	†	†	†
2002–03	507	512	503	519	537	503	†	†	†	†	†	†	†	†	†
2003–04	508	512	504	518	537	501	†	†	†	†	†	†	†	†	†
2004–05	508	513	505	520	538	504	†	†	†	†	†	†	†	†	†
2005–06	503	505	502	518	536	502	497	491	502	†	†	†	†	†	†
2006–07	502	504	502	515	533	499	494	489	500	†	†	†	†	†	†
2007–08	502	504	500	515	533	500	494	488	501	†	†	†	†	†	†
2008–09	501	503	498	515	534	499	493	486	499	†	†	†	†	†	†
2009–10	501	503	498	516	534	500	492	486	498	†	†	†	†	†	†
2010–11	497	500	495	514	531	500	489	482	496	†	†	†	†	†	†
2011–12	496	498	493	514	532	499	488	481	494	†	†	†	†	†	†
2012–13	496	499	494	514	531	499	488	482	493	†	†	†	†	†	†
2013–14	497	499	495	513	530	499	487	481	492	†	†	†	†	†	†
2014–15	495	497	493	511	527	496	484	478	490	†	†	†	†	†	†

—Not available.
†Not applicable.
[1]Data for 1966–67 to 1985–86 were converted to the recentered scale by using a formula applied to the original mean and standard deviation. For 1986–87 to 1994–95, individual student scores were converted to the recentered scale and then the mean was recomputed. For 1995–96 to 1998–99, nearly all students received scores on the recentered scale; any score on the original scale was converted to the recentered scale prior to recomputing the mean. From 1999–2000 on, all scores have been reported on the recentered scale.
[2]The SAT writing section was introduced in March 2005.
NOTE: Data for 1966–67 through 1970–71 are estimates derived from the test scores of all participants. Data for 1971–72 through 2009–10 are for seniors who took the SAT any time during their high school years through March of their senior year. Data for 2010–11 onwards are for seniors who took the SAT any time during their high school years through June of their senior year. If a student took the SAT more than once, the most recent score on each section was used. Possible scores on each section of the SAT range from 200 to 800. Prior to 2006, the critical reading section was known as the verbal section. The SAT was formerly known as the Scholastic Assessment Test and the Scholastic Aptitude Test.
SOURCE: College Entrance Examination Board, College-Bound Seniors: Total Group Profile [National] Report, 1966–67 through 2014–15, retrieved September 10, 2015, from https://secure-media.collegeboard.org/digitalServices/pdf/sat/total-group-2015.pdf. (This table was prepared September 2015.)

Table 226.30. SAT mean scores and percentage distribution of college-bound seniors, by selected student characteristics: Selected years, 1995–96 through 2014–15

	1995–96			2000–01			2005–06				2010–11				2014–15			
Selected student characteristic	Critical reading score	Mathematics score	Percentage distribution	Critical reading score	Mathematics score	Percentage distribution	Critical reading score	Mathematics score	Writing score	Percentage distribution	Critical reading score	Mathematics score	Writing score	Percentage distribution	Critical reading score	Mathematics score	Writing score	Percentage distribution
1	2	3	4	5	6	7	8	9	10	11	12	13	14	15	16	17	18	19
All students	**505**	**508**	**100**	**506**	**514**	**100**	**503**	**518**	**497**	**100**	**497**	**514**	**489**	**100**	**495**	**511**	**484**	**100**
High school rank																		
Top decile	591	606	22	588	607	24	580	604	577	31	575	606	572	35	574	605	568	35
Second decile	530	539	22	526	540	23	516	537	511	25	510	535	503	27	511	532	499	26
Second quintile	494	496	28	490	497	26	484	498	476	20	482	498	470	18	482	494	467	18
Bottom three quintiles[1]	—	—	—	—	—	—	443	449	435	23	438	448	426	20	438	443	423	21
Third quintile	455	448	24	454	452	22	—	—	—	—	—	—	—	—	—	—	—	—
Fourth quintile	429	418	4	423	417	4	—	—	—	—	—	—	—	—	—	—	—	—
Fifth quintile	411	401	1	407	401	1	—	—	—	—	—	—	—	—	—	—	—	—
High school grade point average																		
A+ (97–100)	617	632	6	609	626	7	602	621	599	7	596	620	595	7	592	617	587	7
A (93–96)	573	583	14	566	581	17	563	582	559	18	560	583	556	18	558	578	551	21
A- (90–92)	545	554	15	540	552	17	534	552	529	18	528	548	521	19	523	540	513	20
B (80–89)	486	485	49	482	486	47	479	489	471	46	469	480	458	45	463	472	450	43
C (70–79)	432	426	15	428	425	12	426	428	414	11	416	421	401	10	407	412	393	9
D, E, or F (below 70)	414	408	#	403	404	#	406	413	389	#	409	425	398	#	386	404	372	#
High school type																		
Public	502	506	83	502	510	83	500	514	492	83	494	506	483	84	489	498	475	84
Private, religiously affiliated	525	510	12	530	523	12	531	529	528	11	531	533	528	10	533	536	527	9
Private, independent	547	556	5	549	567	5	544	573	550	5	541	579	550	6	532	579	538	7
Intended college major[2]																		
Agriculture, agriculture operations, and related sciences	491	484	2	487	484	1	481	485	469	1	475	484	461	1	470	474	455	1
Architecture and related services	492	519	3	493	521	2	488	528	485	3	490	534	485	2	482	522	474	1
Area, ethnic, cultural and gender studies	†	†	†	†	†	†	†	†	†	†	545	513	531	#	537	505	521	#
Arts: visual/performing	520	497	6	518	501	8	516	502	507	8	508	497	499	8	503	490	490	7
Biological and biomedical sciences	546	545	6	545	549	9	540	554	532	6	540	557	533	6	537	549	527	7
Business and management, marketing, and related support services	483	500	13	489	511	14	486	511	481	15	488	522	484	15	494	520	486	12
Communication, journalism, and related programs	527	497	4	527	506	4	522	504	520	4	519	502	516	4	516	496	509	3
Computer and information sciences and support services	497	522	3	501	533	7	503	534	482	4	511	539	485	4	530	559	505	3
Construction trades	†	†	†	†	†	†	†	†	†	†	422	451	399	#	429	450	403	#
Education	487	477	8	483	481	9	480	484	478	8	480	487	476	8	481	480	473	4
Engineering	525	569	8	523	572	9	519	577	506	8	528	584	513	8	526	575	509	11
Engineering technologies/technicians	†	†	†	†	†	†	†	†	†	†	464	511	447	2	475	523	458	1
English language and literature/letters	605	545	1	606	549	1	597	541	584	2	584	529	570	1	573	519	557	1
Family and consumer sciences/human sciences[3]	458	452	#	459	458	#	462	466	461	1	456	461	452	1	450	451	445	#
Foreign languages, literatures, and linguistics	556	534	1	557	540	1	572	549	563	1	567	542	557	#	555	530	540	1
General/interdisciplinary	576	553	#	554	539	#	542	532	532	#	†	†	†	†	†	†	†	†
Health professions and related clinical services	500	505	19	494	502	15	485	498	483	18	487	502	484	19	484	492	477	19
History	†	†	†	†	†	†	†	†	†	†	542	510	511	1	539	504	507	1
Legal professions and studies	†	†	†	†	†	†	†	†	†	†	512	507	500	3	520	509	505	2
Liberal arts and sciences, general studies, and humanities	†	†	†	†	†	†	†	†	†	†	552	532	541	1	549	530	538	1
Library science and administration	554	512	#	574	504	#	579	509	542	#	564	505	516	#	550	502	511	#
Mathematics and statistics	552	628	#	549	625	1	539	624	537	1	518	603	519	1	541	616	538	1
Mechanic and repair technologies/technician	†	†	†	†	†	†	†	†	†	†	421	451	400	#	416	441	396	#
Military technologies and applied sciences	503	505	#	507	511	#	510	521	487	1	467	471	433	#	483	490	455	1
Multi/interdisciplinary studies	†	†	†	†	†	†	†	†	†	†	582	580	570	#	579	585	567	1

See notes at end of table.

Table 226.30. SAT mean scores and percentage distribution of college-bound seniors, by selected student characteristics: Selected years, 1995–96 through 2014–15—Continued

Selected student characteristic	1995–96			2000–01			2005–06				2010–11				2014–15			
	Critical reading score	Mathematics score	Percentage distribution	Critical reading score	Mathematics score	Percentage distribution	Critical reading score	Mathematics score	Writing score	Percentage distribution	Critical reading score	Mathematics score	Writing score	Percentage distribution	Critical reading score	Mathematics score	Writing score	Percentage distribution
1	2	3	4	5	6	7	8	9	10	11	12	13	14	15	16	17	18	19
Natural resources and conservation	†	†	†	†	†	†	†	†	†	†	525	524	506	1	523	519	502	#
Parks, recreation, leisure, and fitness studies	†	†	†	†	†	†	†	†	†	†	444	468	435	1	436	455	427	1
Personal and culinary services	†	†	†	†	†	†	†	†	†	†	457	456	440	#	444	440	426	#
Philosophy and religious studies	560	536	#	561	539	1	557	537	535	1	557	535	530	#	542	523	518	#
Physical sciences	575	595	1	568	588	1	557	589	542	2	553	582	537	1	559	584	539	1
Precision production	†	†	†	†	†	†	†	†	†	†	436	468	422	#	461	467	419	#
Psychology	458	448	3	461	455	2	462	461	454	3	505	494	497	5	500	484	489	5
Public administration and social services	532	509	11	531	512	10	539	519	525	9	467	459	462	#	466	455	458	#
Security and protective services	†	†	†	†	†	†	†	†	†	†	445	454	432	2	445	448	432	3
Social sciences and history	435	441	1	444	451	1	437	454	421	1	†	†	†	†	†	†	†	†
Social sciences	†	†	†	†	†	†	†	†	†	†	573	558	559	2	560	545	544	2
Technical and vocational	†	†	†	†	†	†	†	†	†	†	†	†	†	†	†	†	†	†
Theology and religious vocations	†	†	†	†	†	†	†	†	†	†	539	522	513	#	533	515	509	#
Transportation and materials moving	†	†	†	†	†	†	†	†	†	†	465	496	446	2	463	481	441	2
Other	†	†	†	†	†	†	†	†	†	†	453	462	443	#	450	456	439	#
Undecided	500	507	7	515	524	7	512	530	502	3	530	545	522	8	532	543	520	7
Degree-level goal																		
Certificate program	434	439	1	443	455	1	443	462	435	1	445	464	434	1	435	454	424	1
Associate's degree	422	415	2	419	416	2	416	420	409	2	412	416	400	1	408	409	395	1
Bachelor's degree	476	476	23	478	483	25	477	487	469	25	478	490	467	30	482	490	468	31
Master's degree	514	518	29	516	526	31	512	525	505	31	506	524	499	29	510	525	499	31
Doctor's or related degree	548	552	24	547	554	21	539	553	532	21	534	550	527	21	535	547	525	21
Other	430	438	1	438	449	1	439	456	436	1	425	451	423	1	408	437	405	1
Undecided	502	503	20	511	517	19	515	528	508	19	509	522	499	16	504	517	492	14
Family income																		
Less than $20,000	—	—	—	—	—	—	—	—	—	—	434	460	429	13	433	454	426	14
$20,000, but less than $40,000	—	—	—	—	—	—	—	—	—	—	464	480	454	16	466	479	454	16
$40,000, but less than $60,000	—	—	—	—	—	—	—	—	—	—	487	499	475	15	488	497	473	14
$60,000, but less than $80,000	—	—	—	—	—	—	—	—	—	—	502	512	489	14	503	510	487	12
$80,000, but less than $100,000	—	—	—	—	—	—	—	—	—	—	515	527	503	12	517	526	501	11
$100,000, but less than $120,000	—	—	—	—	—	—	—	—	—	—	526	539	515	10	528	539	514	10
$120,000, but less than $140,000	—	—	—	—	—	—	—	—	—	—	530	544	520	5	531	542	518	5
$140,000, but less than $160,000	—	—	—	—	—	—	—	—	—	—	538	552	529	4	539	551	526	4
$160,000, but less than $200,000	—	—	—	—	—	—	—	—	—	—	543	557	536	5	545	557	534	5
More than $200,000	—	—	—	—	—	—	—	—	—	—	568	586	567	7	570	587	563	8
Highest level of parental education																		
No high school diploma	414	439	4	411	438	4	418	445	418	4	421	449	418	6	420	443	415	7
High school diploma	475	474	35	472	476	32	467	478	460	31	463	476	452	31	461	471	448	29
Associate's degree	489	487	8	489	491	9	484	493	474	8	480	489	466	8	479	483	462	8
Bachelor's degree	525	529	28	525	533	29	522	536	514	30	522	538	514	31	521	537	509	31
Graduate degree	556	558	25	559	567	26	558	571	552	27	559	574	554	25	560	575	550	25

—Not available.
†Not applicable.
#Rounds to zero.
[1]Beginning in 2005–06, the College Board has reported third, fourth, and fifth quintiles as the bottom three quintiles instead of reporting them separately as in previous years.
[2]Data may not be comparable over time because of additions to the list of majors and changes in subspecialties within majors.
[3]Prior to 2006–07, family and consumer sciences/human sciences was called home economics.
NOTE: Prior to 2010–11, data are for seniors who took the SAT any time during their high school years through March of their senior year. Data for 2010–11 onwards are for seniors who took the SAT any time during their high school years through June of their senior year. If a student took the SAT more than once, the most recent score on each section was used. Possible scores on each section of the SAT range from 200 to 800. Prior to 2006, the critical reading section was known as the verbal section. The writing section was introduced in March 2005. The SAT was formerly known as the Scholastic Assessment Test and the Scholastic Aptitude Test. Detail may not sum to totals because of rounding.

SOURCE: College Entrance Examination Board, College-Bound Seniors: Total Group Profile [National] Report, selected years, 1995–96 through 2014–15, retrieved September 11, 2015, from https://secure-media.collegeboard.org/digitalServices/pdf/sat/total-group-2015.pdf. (This table was prepared September 2015.)

Table 226.40. Mean SAT scores of college-bound seniors and percentage of graduates taking SAT, by state: Selected years, 1995–96 through 2014–15

State	1995–96		2000–01		2005–06			2010–11			2013–14			2014–15			Percent taking SAT[1]	
	Critical reading score	Mathe-matics score	Critical reading score	Mathe-matics score	Critical reading score	Mathe-matics score	Writing score	Critical reading score	Mathe-matics score	Writing score	Critical reading score	Mathe-matics score	Writing score	Critical reading score	Mathe-matics score	Writing score	2013–14	2014–15
1	2	3	4	5	6	7	8	9	10	11	12	13	14	15	16	17	18	19
United States	505	508	506	514	503	518	497	497	514	489	497	513	487	495	511	484	48	49
Alabama	565	558	559	554	565	561	565	546	541	536	547	538	532	545	538	533	7	6
Alaska	521	513	514	510	517	517	493	515	511	487	507	503	475	509	503	482	54	52
Arizona	525	521	523	525	521	528	507	517	523	499	522	525	500	523	527	502	36	34
Arkansas	566	550	562	550	574	568	567	568	570	554	573	571	554	568	569	551	4	4
California	495	511	498	517	501	518	501	499	515	499	498	510	496	495	506	491	60	60
Colorado	536	538	539	542	558	564	548	570	573	556	582	586	567	582	587	567	14	12
Connecticut	507	504	509	510	512	516	511	509	513	513	507	510	508	504	506	504	88	89
Delaware[2]	508	495	501	499	495	500	484	489	490	476	456	459	444	462	461	445	100	100
District of Columbia[2] ..	489	473	482	474	487	472	482	469	457	459	440	438	431	441	440	432	100	100
Florida	498	496	498	499	496	497	480	487	489	471	491	485	472	486	480	468	72	74
Georgia	484	477	491	489	494	496	487	485	487	473	488	485	472	490	485	475	77	77
Hawaii	485	510	486	515	482	509	472	479	500	469	484	504	472	487	508	477	63	61
Idaho[2]	543	536	543	542	543	545	525	542	539	517	458	456	450	467	463	442	100	100
Illinois	564	575	576	589	591	609	586	599	617	591	599	616	587	599	616	587	5	4
Indiana	494	494	499	501	498	509	486	493	501	475	497	500	477	496	499	478	71	71
Iowa	590	600	593	603	602	613	591	596	606	575	605	611	578	589	600	566	3	3
Kansas	579	571	577	580	582	590	566	580	591	563	591	596	566	588	592	568	5	5
Kentucky	549	544	550	550	562	562	555	576	572	563	589	585	572	588	587	574	5	4
Louisiana	559	550	564	562	570	571	571	555	550	546	561	556	550	563	559	553	5	5
Maine[3]	504	498	506	500	501	501	491	469	469	453	467	471	449	468	473	451	96	96
Maryland	507	504	508	510	503	509	499	499	502	491	492	495	481	491	493	478	79	79
Massachusetts	507	504	511	515	513	524	510	513	527	509	516	531	509	516	529	507	84	86
Michigan	557	565	561	572	568	583	555	583	604	573	593	610	581	594	609	585	4	4
Minnesota	582	593	580	589	591	600	574	593	608	577	598	610	578	595	607	576	6	5
Mississippi	569	557	566	551	556	541	562	564	543	553	583	566	565	580	563	570	3	3
Missouri	570	569	577	577	587	591	582	592	593	579	595	597	579	596	599	582	4	4
Montana	546	547	539	539	538	545	524	539	537	516	555	552	530	561	556	538	18	15
Nebraska	567	568	562	568	576	583	566	585	591	569	589	587	569	589	590	576	4	4
Nevada	508	507	509	515	498	508	481	494	496	470	495	494	469	494	494	470	54	50
New Hampshire	520	514	520	516	520	524	509	523	525	511	524	530	512	525	530	511	70	70
New Jersey	498	505	499	513	496	515	496	495	516	497	501	523	502	500	521	499	79	81
New Mexico	554	548	551	542	557	549	543	548	541	529	548	543	526	551	544	528	12	12
New York	497	499	495	505	493	510	483	485	499	476	488	502	478	489	502	478	76	75
North Carolina	490	486	493	499	495	513	485	493	508	474	499	507	477	498	504	476	64	63
North Dakota	596	599	592	599	610	617	588	586	612	561	612	620	584	597	608	586	2	2
Ohio	536	535	534	539	535	544	521	539	545	522	555	562	535	557	563	537	15	14
Oklahoma	566	557	567	561	576	574	563	571	565	547	576	571	550	576	569	548	5	4
Oregon	523	521	526	526	523	529	503	520	521	499	523	522	499	523	521	502	48	47
Pennsylvania	498	492	500	499	493	500	483	493	501	479	497	504	480	499	504	482	71	71
Rhode Island	501	491	501	499	495	502	490	495	493	489	497	496	487	494	494	484	73	77
South Carolina	480	474	486	488	487	498	480	482	490	464	488	490	465	488	487	467	65	65
South Dakota	574	566	577	582	590	604	578	584	591	562	604	609	579	592	597	564	3	3
Tennessee	563	552	562	553	573	569	572	575	568	567	578	570	566	581	574	568	8	7
Texas	495	500	493	499	491	506	487	479	502	465	476	495	461	470	486	454	62	64
Utah	583	575	575	570	560	557	550	563	559	545	571	568	551	579	575	554	5	5
Vermont	506	500	511	506	513	519	502	515	518	505	522	525	507	523	524	507	63	61
Virginia	507	496	510	501	512	513	500	512	509	495	518	515	497	518	516	499	73	72
Washington	519	519	527	527	527	532	511	523	529	508	510	518	491	502	510	484	63	66
West Virginia	526	506	527	512	519	510	515	514	501	497	517	505	500	509	497	495	15	15
Wisconsin	577	586	584	596	588	600	577	590	602	575	596	608	578	591	605	575	4	4
Wyoming	544	544	547	545	548	555	537	572	569	551	590	599	573	589	586	562	3	3

[1]Members of the graduating class who had taken the SAT as a percentage of the total number of high school graduates. State percentages were calculated by the College Entrance Examination Board based on the number of high school graduates in each state as projected by the Western Interstate Commission for Higher Education (WICHE). The total percentage for the United States was calculated by the National Center for Education Statistics (NCES) based on NCES projections of the total number of U.S. high school graduates.
[2]The SAT is administered to all public high school juniors in Delaware (as of spring 2011), the District of Columbia (as of spring 2013), and Idaho (as of spring 2012).
[3]Beginning with the spring SAT administration in 2006, all Maine high school juniors, including all students in their third year of high school, are required to take the SAT.
NOTE: Data for 2005–06 and earlier years are for seniors who took the SAT any time during their high school years through March of their senior year. Data for 2010–11 onwards are for seniors who took the SAT any time during their high school years through June of their senior year. If a student took the SAT more than once, the most recent score on each section was used. Possible scores on each section of the SAT range from 200 to 800. Prior to 2006, the critical reading section was known as the verbal section. The writing section was introduced in March 2005. The SAT was formerly known as the Scholastic Assessment Test or the Scholastic Aptitude Test.
SOURCE: College Entrance Examination Board, College-Bound Seniors Tables and Related Items, selected years, 1995–96 through 2014–15, retrieved September 11, 2015, from http://research.collegeboard.org/programs/sat/data/cb-seniors-2015 and https://www.collegeboard.org/release/2015-program-results. (This table was prepared September 2015.)

Table 226.50. Number and percentage of graduates taking the ACT test; average scores and standard deviations, by sex and race/ethnicity; and percentage of test takers with selected composite scores and planned fields of postsecondary study: Selected years, 1995 through 2015

Score type and test-taker characteristic	1995	2000	2005	2006	2007	2008	2009	2010	2011	2012	2013	2014	2015
1	2	3	4	5	6	7	8	9	10	11	12	13	14
Total test takers													
Number (in thousands)	945	1,065	1,186	1,206	1,301	1,422	1,480	1,569	1,623	1,666	1,799	1,846	1,924
Percent of all graduates[1]	37.5	37.6	38.2	38.6	40.6	42.9	44.2	45.6	47.0	48.2	51.7	53.0	55.3
						Average test score[2]							
Composite score, total	20.8	21.0	20.9	21.1	21.2	21.1	21.1	21.0	21.1	21.1	20.9	21.0	21.0
Sex													
Male	21.0	21.2	21.1	21.2	21.2	21.2	21.3	21.2	21.2	21.2	20.9	21.1	21.1
Female	20.7	20.9	20.9	21.0	21.0	21.0	20.9	20.9	21.0	21.0	20.9	20.9	21.0
Race/ethnicity													
White	—	21.8	21.9	22.0	22.1	22.1	22.2	22.3	22.4	22.4	22.2	22.3	22.4
Black	—	17.0	17.0	17.1	17.0	16.9	16.9	16.9	17.0	17.0	16.9	17.0	17.1
Hispanic	—	—	18.6	18.6	18.7	18.7	18.7	18.6	18.7	18.9	18.8	18.8	18.9
Asian/Pacific Islander	—	21.7	22.1	22.3	22.6	22.9	23.2	23.4	—	—	—	—	—
Asian	—	—	—	—	—	—	—	—	23.6	23.6	23.5	23.5	23.9
Pacific Islander	—	—	—	—	—	—	—	—	19.5	19.8	19.5	18.6	18.8
American Indian/Alaska	—	19.0	18.7	18.8	18.9	19.0	18.9	19.0	18.6	18.4	18.0	18.0	17.9
Two or more races	—	—	—	—	—	—	—	—	21.1	21.4	21.1	21.2	21.2
Subject-area scores													
English	20.2	20.5	20.4	20.6	20.7	20.6	20.6	20.5	20.6	20.5	20.2	20.3	20.4
Male	19.8	20.0	20.0	20.1	20.2	20.1	20.2	20.1	20.2	20.2	19.8	20.0	20.0
Female	20.6	20.9	20.8	21.0	21.0	21.0	20.9	20.8	20.9	20.9	20.6	20.7	20.8
Mathematics	20.2	20.7	20.7	20.8	21.0	21.0	21.0	21.0	21.1	21.1	20.9	20.9	20.8
Male	20.9	21.4	21.3	21.5	21.6	21.6	21.6	21.6	21.6	21.7	21.4	21.4	21.3
Female	19.7	20.2	20.2	20.3	20.4	20.4	20.4	20.5	20.6	20.6	20.5	20.5	20.4
Reading	21.3	21.4	21.3	21.4	21.5	21.4	21.4	21.3	21.3	21.3	21.1	21.3	21.4
Male	21.1	21.2	21.0	21.1	21.2	21.2	21.3	21.1	21.1	21.2	20.9	21.1	21.2
Female	21.4	21.5	21.5	21.6	21.6	21.5	21.4	21.4	21.4	21.4	21.4	21.5	21.6
Science reasoning	21.0	21.0	20.9	20.9	21.0	20.8	20.9	20.9	20.9	20.9	20.7	20.8	20.9
Male	21.6	21.6	21.4	21.4	21.4	21.3	21.4	21.4	21.4	21.4	21.2	21.2	21.3
Female	20.5	20.6	20.5	20.5	20.5	20.4	20.4	20.5	20.5	20.5	20.4	20.5	20.6
						Standard deviation[3]							
Composite score, total	—	4.7	—	4.8	5.0	5.0	5.1	5.2	5.2	5.3	5.4	5.4	5.5
Sex													
Male	—	4.9	5.0	—	—	—	—	—	—	—	—	—	—
Female	—	4.6	4.7	—	—	—	—	—	—	—	—	—	—
Subject-area scores													
English	—	5.5	—	5.9	6.0	6.1	6.3	6.4	6.5	6.5	6.5	6.6	6.7
Male	—	5.6	6.0	—	—	—	—	—	—	—	—	—	—
Female	—	5.5	5.9	—	—	—	—	—	—	—	—	—	—
Mathematics	—	5.0	—	5.0	5.1	5.2	5.3	5.3	5.3	5.3	5.3	5.3	5.4
Male	—	5.2	5.3	—	—	—	—	—	—	—	—	—	—
Female	—	4.8	4.8	—	—	—	—	—	—	—	—	—	—
Reading	—	6.1	—	6.0	6.1	6.1	6.2	6.2	6.2	6.2	6.3	6.3	6.4
Male	—	6.1	6.1	—	—	—	—	—	—	—	—	—	—
Female	—	6.0	6.0	—	—	—	—	—	—	—	—	—	—
Science reasoning	—	4.5	—	4.6	4.9	4.9	5.0	5.1	5.1	5.2	5.3	5.5	5.5
Male	—	4.8	4.9	—	—	—	—	—	—	—	—	—	—
Female	—	4.3	4.3	—	—	—	—	—	—	—	—	—	—
						Percent of ACT test takers							
Composite score													
28 or above	—	10	10	11	11	12	12	12	13	13	13	13	14
17 or below	—	25	26	25	25	26	27	28	28	28	30	30	30
Planned major field of study													
Business[4]	13	11	9	9	8	11	12	11	10	9	9	9	9
Education[5]	8	9	6	6	5	6	7	7	6	6	5	5	5
Engineering[6]	8	8	6	6	5	7	8	8	8	8	9	9	10
Health sciences and technologies	—	17	16	15	14	17	19	20	19	19	19	19	18
Social sciences[7]	9	9	7	6	5	6	7	7	8	9	8	8	8

—Not available.

[1]Those members of the graduating class who had taken the ACT test as a percentage of all students who graduated in that school year. For example, the 2015 column shows test-taking members of the class of 2015 as a percentage of all 2014–15 high school graduates.

[2]Minimum score is 1 and maximum score is 36.

[3]Standard deviations not available for racial/ethnic groups.

[4]For years prior to 2011, includes business and management, business and office, and marketing and distribution.

[5]For years prior to 2011, includes education and teacher education.

[6]Includes engineering as well as engineering technology and drafting.

[7]Includes social sciences and philosophy, religion, and theology. For 2011 and later years, also includes law.

NOTE: Data are for high school graduates who took the ACT test during their sophomore, junior, or senior year. If a student took the ACT test more than once, the composite and subject-area scores from the most recent test were used. Race categories exclude persons of Hispanic ethnicity. Some data have been revised from previously published figures.
SOURCE: ACT, High School Profile Report, selected years, 1995 through 2015. U.S. Department of Education, National Center for Education Statistics, Common Core of Data (CCD), "State Nonfiscal Survey of Public Elementary/Secondary Education," 1995–96 through 2009–10; "State Dropout and Completion Data File," 2005–06 through 2012–13; Public School Graduates and Dropouts from the Common Core of Data, 2007–08 and 2008–09; Private School Universe Survey (PSS), 1995 through 2013; and National High School Graduates Projection Model, 1972–73 through 2025–26. (This table was prepared January 2016.)

Table 227.10. Percentage of 9th-grade students participating in various school-sponsored and non-school-sponsored activities, by sex and race/ethnicity: 2009

[Standard errors appear in parentheses]

Sex and race/ethnicity	School-sponsored activities			Non-school-sponsored activities							
	Math-related[1]	Science-related[1]	At least one of the math- or science-related activities	Music, dance, art, or theater	Organized sports	Religious youth group or instruction	Scouting or other group or club activity	Academic instruction[2]	Math or science camp	Another camp	At least one of the non-school-sponsored activities
1	2	3	4	5	6	7	8	9	10	11	12
Total	9.8 (0.39)	6.4 (0.36)	13.4 (0.50)	34.6 (0.91)	54.9 (0.81)	51.4 (0.93)	22.8 (0.64)	17.7 (0.62)	4.1 (0.31)	23.8 (0.76)	85.7 (0.60)
Sex											
Male	8.9 (0.44)	6.3 (0.59)	12.6 (0.69)	27.9 (0.93)	59.8 (0.93)	49.5 (1.10)	21.6 (0.87)	17.5 (0.80)	4.1 (0.51)	23.2 (0.92)	86.1 (0.79)
Female	10.7 (0.55)	6.5 (0.45)	14.2 (0.67)	41.3 (1.20)	50.0 (1.10)	53.4 (1.12)	24.1 (0.88)	17.9 (0.80)	4.0 (0.40)	24.4 (0.91)	85.4 (0.75)
Race/ethnicity											
White	8.3 (0.35)	6.4 (0.43)	12.2 (0.46)	36.8 (0.78)	60.5 (0.87)	56.7 (1.04)	24.0 (0.83)	13.2 (0.65)	2.7 (0.26)	30.6 (0.92)	89.7 (0.47)
Black	12.5 (1.54)	5.4 (0.77)	15.3 (1.71)	33.8 (2.90)	49.1 (2.39)	52.3 (2.31)	26.3 (2.02)	32.8 (2.55)	7.4 (1.24)	14.8 (1.79)	84.9 (1.72)
Hispanic	10.5 (0.92)	5.5 (0.72)	13.4 (1.07)	27.5 (1.47)	46.9 (2.46)	39.1 (2.36)	16.6 (1.27)	18.6 (1.20)	3.6 (0.77)	14.5 (1.66)	76.9 (2.28)
Asian	17.3 (2.25)	13.0 (1.93)	22.3 (2.48)	44.4 (3.43)	38.5 (2.87)	38.8 (3.31)	25.8 (2.28)	31.1 (3.49)	15.0 (2.06)	16.2 (2.14)	82.1 (2.76)
Native Hawaiian/Pacific Islander	‡ (†)	‡ (†)	‡ (†)	‡ (†)	‡ (†)	‡ (†)	‡ (†)	‡ (†)	‡ (†)	‡ (†)	‡ (†)
American Indian/Alaska Native	9.1! (2.95)	‡ (†)	12.8! (3.87)	20.0! (6.56)	48.8 (6.60)	42.3 (6.00)	31.6 (6.00)	16.8 (4.36)	‡ (†)	19.1! (8.31)	78.9 (5.22)
Two or more races	10.5 (1.19)	7.6 (1.02)	14.2 (1.41)	36.4 (2.49)	55.8 (2.46)	53.6 (2.47)	24.9 (2.13)	15.4 (1.57)	3.4 (0.81)	21.2 (1.60)	86.8 (1.53)
Race/ethnicity by sex											
Male											
White	7.6 (0.45)	6.1 (0.61)	11.5 (0.73)	29.1 (0.95)	63.3 (1.06)	54.5 (1.19)	23.2 (1.12)	14.2 (0.93)	2.8 (0.36)	29.6 (1.22)	89.0 (0.61)
Black	12.2 (1.74)	5.8 (1.10)	15.4 (1.92)	27.4 (2.88)	58.2 (3.15)	49.0 (3.03)	21.0 (2.85)	31.1 (3.11)	7.5 (2.01)	14.6 (2.46)	87.3 (1.95)
Hispanic	9.2 (1.22)	5.5 (1.15)	12.1 (1.50)	22.4 (2.04)	54.4 (2.86)	37.1 (2.92)	15.3 (1.69)	16.9 (1.83)	2.9! (0.88)	13.1 (2.11)	78.4 (2.70)
Asian	18.4 (2.96)	11.5 (2.38)	22.8 (3.23)	36.9 (4.02)	42.9 (3.89)	32.8 (5.50)	26.1 (3.78)	31.0 (4.54)	18.4 (3.34)	20.3 (3.47)	78.9 (3.87)
Native Hawaiian/Pacific Islander	‡ (†)	‡ (†)	‡ (†)	‡ (†)	‡ (†)	‡ (†)	‡ (†)	‡ (†)	‡ (†)	‡ (†)	‡ (†)
American Indian/Alaska Native	10.9! (4.96)	‡ (†)	‡ (†)	18.8! (9.40)	49.9 (9.31)	38.2 (9.74)	31.3 (8.35)	‡ (†)	‡ (†)	‡ (†)	78.4 (6.67)
Two or more races	8.3 (1.37)	9.0 (1.85)	13.4 (2.04)	29.9 (2.96)	59.2 (3.78)	56.9 (3.48)	26.2 (2.99)	16.0 (2.30)	3.4! (1.22)	20.4 (2.28)	88.6 (1.82)
Female											
White	9.0 (0.56)	6.7 (0.61)	13.0 (0.71)	44.9 (1.16)	57.5 (1.13)	59.0 (1.17)	24.8 (1.04)	12.1 (0.76)	2.7 (0.34)	31.7 (1.08)	90.4 (0.62)
Black	12.8 (2.14)	5.0 (1.09)	15.2 (2.38)	39.0 (4.64)	41.8 (3.87)	55.0 (3.33)	30.5 (2.59)	34.2 (3.75)	7.3 (1.53)	14.9 (2.58)	83.0 (2.66)
Hispanic	11.9 (1.16)	5.5 (0.76)	14.6 (1.28)	32.9 (2.06)	39.0 (3.27)	41.1 (2.95)	17.9 (1.83)	20.3 (1.85)	4.4 (1.12)	16.0 (2.15)	75.4 (2.71)
Asian	16.1 (2.49)	14.6 (2.92)	21.8 (3.16)	51.8 (4.88)	34.2 (3.19)	44.8 (3.24)	25.6 (3.53)	31.2 (3.72)	11.7 (3.07)	12.2 (2.55)	85.3 (3.16)
Native Hawaiian/Pacific Islander	‡ (†)	‡ (†)	‡ (†)	‡ (†)	‡ (†)	‡ (†)	‡ (†)	‡ (†)	‡ (†)	‡ (†)	‡ (†)
American Indian/Alaska Native	‡ (†)	‡ (†)	‡ (†)	21.4! (8.36)	47.4 (9.63)	47.0 (11.74)	32.0 (8.98)	‡ (†)	‡ (†)	‡ (†)	79.5 (8.44)
Two or more races	12.7 (1.71)	6.3 (1.00)	15.0 (1.73)	42.4 (3.39)	52.5 (4.18)	50.4 (3.62)	23.7 (2.95)	14.8 (2.05)	3.4! (1.19)	22.0 (2.24)	85.1 (2.47)

†Not applicable.

!Interpret data with caution. The coefficient of variation (CV) for this estimate is between 30 and 50 percent.

‡Reporting standards not met. Either there are too few cases for a reliable estimate or the coefficient of variation (CV) is 50 percent or greater.

[1]Students could indicate that they participated in clubs, competitions, camps, study groups, or tutoring programs.

[2]Academic instruction outside of school such as from a Saturday academy, learning center, personal tutor, or summer school program.

NOTE: Data on school-sponsored activities are based on student responses and are weighted by W1STUDENT. Student reports about school-sponsored activities refer to the period "since the beginning of the last school year," which for most of these students was 8th grade, or the fall of 2008. Data on non-school-sponsored activities are based on parent responses and are weighted by W1PARENT. Parent reports about non-school-sponsored activities refer to the last 12 months. Race categories exclude persons of Hispanic ethnicity.
SOURCE: U.S. Department of Education, National Center for Education Statistics, High School Longitudinal Study of 2009, Base-Year Public-Use Data File. (This table was prepared September 2012.)

Table 227.20. Percentage of high school seniors who say they engage in various activities, by selected student and school characteristics: 1992 and 2004

[Standard errors appear in parentheses]

Activity	Total	Sex		Race/ethnicity					Socioeconomic status[1]			Control of school attended		
		Male	Female	White	Black	Hispanic	Asian/Pacific Islander	American Indian/Alaska Native	Low	Middle	High	Public	Catholic	Other private
1	2	3	4	5	6	7	8	9	10	11	12	13	14	15
1992														
At least once a week														
Use personal computer[2]	23.6 (0.52)	28.1 (0.76)	19.3 (0.64)	23.9 (0.58)	23.3 (1.71)	20.7 (1.49)	26.6 (1.90)	22.0 (3.88)	18.7 (1.10)	23.4 (0.73)	27.6 (0.91)	23.3 (0.50)	26.0 (2.58)	29.0 (3.04)
Work on hobbies	40.9 (0.62)	44.4 (0.85)	37.6 (0.86)	42.2 (0.71)	34.5 (1.99)	39.7 (1.71)	37.7 (2.16)	51.8 (4.20)	36.3 (1.29)	41.1 (0.84)	43.6 (1.14)	40.6 (0.59)	42.4 (2.69)	41.1 (2.60)
Perform community service	11.3 (0.48)	10.7 (0.80)	11.9 (0.52)	11.1 (0.60)	12.1 (1.26)	11.1 (1.03)	13.8 (1.58)	8.0 ! (2.56)	7.6 (0.61)	9.6 (0.46)	16.9 (1.22)	9.6 (0.37)	23.6 (2.50)	22.9 (2.63)
Driving or riding around	73.2 (0.59)	74.4 (0.84)	72.1 (0.75)	75.7 (0.64)	67.8 (2.15)	66.0 (1.82)	66.5 (2.05)	67.6 (4.40)	69.6 (1.26)	75.3 (0.75)	72.4 (1.13)	74.0 (0.55)	76.1 (2.41)	68.7 (2.91)
Visiting with friends at a local hangout	88.0 (0.45)	88.2 (0.62)	87.9 (0.62)	90.6 (0.41)	79.8 (2.02)	82.1 (1.27)	85.7 (1.46)	73.0 (4.89)	80.6 (1.05)	88.0 (0.66)	83.7 (0.57)	88.2 (0.39)	93.3 (1.23)	95.1 (0.78)
Talk on phone with friends	80.5 (0.56)	72.6 (0.88)	88.3 (0.64)	81.7 (0.62)	81.3 (2.01)	71.8 (1.60)	77.2 (1.82)	73.7 (6.12)	72.8 (1.13)	81.6 (0.71)	83.7 (1.10)	80.4 (0.54)	86.8 (1.84)	77.9 (2.77)
Take music, art, or dance class	10.2 (0.35)	7.9 (0.44)	12.4 (0.52)	10.0 (0.40)	9.6 (1.11)	9.9 (1.27)	14.1 (1.21)	10.7 ! (3.40)	7.2 (0.67)	8.9 (0.43)	14.2 (0.75)	9.7 (0.35)	12.4 (1.55)	14.9 (1.49)
Take sports lessons	7.3 (0.38)	9.7 (0.62)	5.0 (0.45)	7.0 (0.46)	7.5 (0.80)	8.0 (1.14)	9.3 (1.06)	10.0 ! (4.07)	5.5 (0.61)	6.6 (0.40)	9.5 (0.96)	6.5 (0.29)	9.2 (1.60)	7.3 (1.13)
Play nonschool sports	26.2 (0.62)	38.7 (0.91)	14.0 (0.70)	27.1 (0.73)	28.6 (1.79)	23.4 (1.55)	28.1 (2.13)	27.3 (4.25)	20.4 (1.01)	24.5 (0.73)	32.9 (1.29)	25.6 (0.56)	35.1 (2.71)	28.0 (3.00)
Reading 3 or more hours per week (not for school)	33.7 (0.56)	30.9 (0.78)	36.4 (0.78)	34.5 (0.64)	28.6 (1.81)	32.8 (1.75)	35.3 (2.03)	34.4 (3.90)	29.7 (1.10)	33.4 (0.77)	36.7 (1.01)	33.2 (0.59)	32.4 (2.35)	38.8 (2.51)
Plays video/computer games 3 or more hours per day on weekdays	2.0 (0.16)	3.2 (0.29)	0.8 (0.12)	1.8 (0.18)	3.3 (0.64)	2.1 (0.43)	2.7 ! (0.88)	2.5 ! (1.19)	3.4 (0.40)	2.1 (0.23)	1.1 (0.19)	2.1 (0.18)	1.6 ! (0.50)	0.6 ! (0.26)
Watches television 3 or more hours per day on weekdays	27.0 (0.62)	27.7 (0.88)	26.4 (0.77)	23.6 (0.67)	49.2 (2.29)	26.6 (1.54)	25.0 (2.20)	36.4 (4.85)	34.1 (1.24)	29.3 (0.89)	18.1 (1.03)	26.4 (0.56)	26.1 (2.29)	15.5 (2.34)
2004														
At least once a week														
Use personal computer at home	79.3 (0.52)	79.6 (0.65)	79.0 (0.69)	84.7 (0.54)	62.8 (1.34)	71.4 (1.32)	89.5 (1.06)	68.8 (2.31)	61.9 (1.07)	79.8 (0.63)	92.3 (0.53)	78.2 (0.56)	93.2 (0.69)	89.6 (1.90)
Work on hobbies	46.5 (0.56)	49.6 (0.80)	43.3 (0.71)	46.8 (0.68)	44.3 (1.46)	44.8 (1.39)	49.3 (1.75)	58.4 (1.90)	42.2 (1.07)	46.6 (0.76)	49.6 (0.93)	46.3 (0.60)	47.2 (1.41)	48.6 (1.90)
Perform community service	18.7 (0.45)	15.1 (0.54)	22.3 (0.63)	17.9 (0.52)	21.1 (1.22)	17.5 (1.11)	27.4 (1.36)	11.6 (2.05)	15.7 (0.74)	17.4 (0.64)	23.5 (0.81)	18.3 (0.48)	23.8 (1.29)	22.1 (1.81)
Driving or riding around	65.7 (0.61)	67.5 (0.78)	64.0 (0.79)	70.0 (0.40)	63.9 (1.28)	54.0 (1.28)	58.3 (1.93)	77.0 (3.70)	59.0 (1.17)	67.2 (0.82)	68.4 (0.93)	65.7 (0.66)	68.8 (1.36)	62.8 (2.24)
Visiting with friends at a local hangout	86.1 (0.41)	88.4 (0.46)	83.9 (0.63)	90.7 (0.40)	79.0 (1.03)	77.7 (1.16)	82.6 (1.37)	82.6 (2.52)	76.6 (0.94)	87.7 (0.51)	90.9 (0.56)	85.7 (0.44)	89.2 (0.65)	89.2 (1.05)
Talk on phone with friends	72.1 (0.48)	65.2 (0.71)	78.9 (0.58)	71.6 (0.61)	80.5 (0.98)	66.6 (1.24)	64.7 (1.75)	73.1 (2.68)	66.0 (0.95)	73.5 (0.66)	74.2 (0.82)	71.8 (0.52)	77.5 (1.30)	72.7 (1.53)
Take music, art, or language class	17.7 (0.46)	13.8 (0.52)	21.7 (0.66)	17.5 (0.61)	18.7 (0.96)	15.2 (1.02)	21.2 (1.42)	17.8 (1.30)	13.6 (0.78)	17.0 (0.61)	22.4 (0.71)	17.4 (0.49)	19.6 (1.22)	22.6 (1.75)
Take sports lessons	13.2 (0.41)	15.8 (0.61)	10.7 (0.48)	12.5 (0.47)	15.7 (1.09)	12.9 (1.07)	12.1 (1.31)	12.1 (0.43)	10.8 (0.70)	12.6 (0.57)	16.4 (0.71)	12.9 (0.44)	18.8 (0.92)	14.4 (1.07)
Play nonschool sports	27.4 (0.53)	39.2 (0.77)	15.7 (0.62)	26.8 (0.70)	28.3 (1.14)	27.5 (1.27)	30.7 (1.57)	38.7 (1.61)	24.3 (0.91)	27.3 (0.73)	30.0 (1.06)	27.3 (0.57)	31.2 (1.47)	24.8 (1.74)
Reading 3 or more hours per week (not for school)	32.0 (0.51)	29.5 (0.70)	34.5 (0.71)	31.5 (0.66)	32.7 (1.24)	32.8 (1.28)	30.5 (1.43)	34.4 (3.73)	30.3 (0.99)	30.8 (0.72)	35.6 (0.89)	32.0 (0.55)	29.6 (1.47)	34.9 (1.74)
Pays video/computer games 3 or more hours per day on weekdays	5.9 (0.27)	10.4 (0.48)	1.5 (0.18)	5.1 (0.31)	7.8 (0.78)	6.6 (0.66)	6.1 (0.81)	8.9 (1.17)	7.2 (0.54)	6.3 (0.40)	4.2 (0.35)	6.1 (0.29)	3.8 (0.50)	3.5 (0.59)
Watches television/DVDs 3 or more hours per day on weekdays	28.1 (0.54)	29.3 (0.76)	26.9 (0.69)	21.9 (0.61)	51.7 (1.37)	33.0 (1.06)	24.6 (1.72)	29.9 (3.81)	35.6 (1.00)	29.3 (0.76)	20.0 (0.75)	28.8 (0.58)	24.3 (1.60)	15.8 (1.43)
Hours of homework per week														
Less than 1 hour	13.3 (0.44)	17.3 (0.67)	9.4 (0.48)	14.0 (0.56)	15.1 (0.93)	10.7 (0.83)	6.5 (1.09)	14.9 (1.38)	15.6 (0.78)	14.8 (0.62)	8.7 (0.55)	14.0 (0.47)	5.5 (0.70)	5.4 (1.19)
1 to 3 hours	28.7 (0.52)	30.2 (0.72)	27.3 (0.75)	27.3 (0.64)	32.6 (1.18)	33.9 (1.27)	16.6 (1.52)	29.6 (2.75)	32.7 (0.97)	30.3 (0.71)	22.8 (0.89)	29.7 (0.56)	19.5 (1.32)	16.9 (1.57)
4 to 6 hours	25.0 (0.49)	24.5 (0.68)	25.5 (0.66)	25.8 (0.64)	24.7 (1.18)	23.0 (1.20)	26.7 (1.59)	21.4 (2.19)	25.1 (0.94)	25.1 (0.67)	25.6 (0.89)	25.0 (0.53)	27.3 (1.23)	24.0 (1.48)
7 to 12 hours	21.7 (0.51)	19.8 (0.68)	23.6 (0.68)	22.4 (0.65)	18.0 (0.98)	21.7 (1.26)	27.3 (1.46)	26.9 (3.86)	18.2 (0.81)	20.5 (0.66)	26.8 (0.90)	20.9 (0.55)	29.1 (1.13)	32.2 (1.87)
More than 12 hours	11.2 (0.39)	8.2 (0.43)	14.2 (0.61)	10.5 (0.47)	9.6 (0.85)	10.7 (0.99)	22.8 (1.66)	7.2 ! (2.20)	9.2 (0.76)	9.4 (0.46)	16.1 (0.73)	10.4 (0.40)	18.6 (1.52)	21.5 (2.83)

!Interpret data with caution. The coefficient of variation (CV) for this estimate is between 30 and 50 percent.

[1]Socioeconomic status (SES) was measured by a composite score on parental education and occupations, and family income. The "low" SES group is the lowest quartile; the "middle" SES group is the middle two quartiles; and the "high" SES group is the upper quartile.

[2]Question does not specify where computer is used.

NOTE: Race categories exclude persons of Hispanic ethnicity. Total includes other racial/ethnic groups not separately shown.
SOURCE: U.S. Department of Education, National Center for Education Statistics, National Education Longitudinal Study of 1988 (NELS:88/92), "Second Follow-up Student Survey, 1992"; and Education Longitudinal Study of 2002 (ELS:2002/04), "First Follow-up, 2004." (This table was prepared December 2009.)

Table 227.30. Percentage of high school seniors who participate in various school-sponsored extracurricular activities, by selected student characteristics: 1992 and 2004

[Standard errors appear in parentheses]

Selected student characteristic	Academic clubs		Sports				Cheerleading and drill team[2]	Hobby clubs (photography, chess, etc.)		Music (band, orchestra, chorus, or choir)		Vocational clubs (Future Farmers of America, Skills USA, etc.)	
			Any sport		Interscholastic[1]	Intramural[1]							
	1992	2004	1992	2004	2004	2004	1992	1992	2004	1992	2004	1992	2004
1	2	3	4	5	6	7	8	9	10	11	12	13	14
All seniors	25.0 (0.58)	21.3 (0.49)	42.7 (0.67)	44.4 (0.56)	38.8 (0.56)	19.2 (0.47)	7.6 (0.34)	7.7 (0.32)	11.7 (0.38)	19.8 (0.51)	21.0 (0.55)	17.6 (0.58)	15.6 (0.55)
Sex													
Male	22.7 (0.80)	17.8 (0.58)	55.5 (0.92)	50.6 (0.80)	44.5 (0.79)	24.2 (0.71)	2.0 (0.24)	8.1 (0.44)	11.9 (0.51)	15.1 (0.62)	16.3 (0.66)	14.7 (0.68)	14.8 (0.68)
Female	27.1 (0.76)	24.7 (0.73)	30.1 (0.80)	38.2 (0.76)	33.2 (0.74)	14.3 (0.57)	13.0 (0.60)	7.4 (0.44)	11.6 (0.48)	24.3 (0.75)	25.5 (0.73)	20.4 (0.75)	16.3 (0.69)
Race/ethnicity													
White	24.3 (4.66)	22.6 (0.62)	41.4 (5.81)	46.9 (0.70)	42.1 (0.69)	18.8 (0.58)	13.3 ! (4.87)	10.1 ! (5.01)	11.4 (0.51)	15.4 (3.65)	22.0 (0.68)	12.2 (2.98)	16.8 (0.74)
Black	21.2 (1.64)	16.5 (0.90)	41.6 (2.29)	45.4 (1.21)	37.5 (1.05)	24.4 (1.05)	10.0 (1.73)	6.9 (0.94)	9.1 (0.75)	24.6 (1.57)	24.0 (1.21)	23.1 (1.82)	17.5 (1.17)
Hispanic	26.1 (0.72)	18.3 (1.15)	44.0 (0.79)	35.3 (1.25)	29.5 (1.25)	16.9 (1.02)	7.6 (0.35)	7.4 (0.37)	11.8 (0.87)	20.0 (0.62)	14.3 (0.97)	17.8 (0.71)	11.8 (1.04)
Asian/Pacific Islander	22.0 (1.55)	34.7 (1.90)	36.2 (1.84)	40.6 (1.81)	33.4 (1.71)	18.0 (1.48)	7.6 (1.16)	8.1 (1.05)	20.3 (1.50)	19.1 (1.68)	19.0 (1.57)	17.6 (1.59)	9.2 (0.78)
American Indian/Alaska Native	31.9 (2.31)	19.7 (2.88)	43.9 (2.25)	45.8 (1.42)	40.8 (2.29)	20.7 (0.34)	5.3 (0.97)	11.2 (1.51)	6.3 (0.37)	18.6 (2.01)	15.9 (2.10)	10.4 (1.53)	22.6 (2.23)
Test performance quartile[3]													
Lowest test quartile	17.0 (1.40)	13.4 (0.74)	40.5 (1.46)	34.5 (1.09)	28.0 (1.02)	20.4 (1.00)	7.6 (0.70)	7.9 (0.64)	8.4 (0.63)	18.7 (1.06)	17.7 (0.90)	25.0 (1.38)	17.8 (0.94)
Second test quartile	20.6 (1.10)	16.1 (0.86)	37.5 (1.22)	42.4 (1.06)	36.1 (1.04)	21.3 (0.85)	7.0 (0.86)	7.0 (0.66)	9.7 (0.63)	17.2 (0.88)	17.7 (0.86)	23.2 (1.19)	17.9 (0.92)
Third test quartile	24.1 (1.02)	20.9 (0.86)	44.0 (1.14)	46.5 (1.05)	41.3 (1.04)	19.2 (0.76)	8.3 (0.62)	7.1 (0.58)	11.2 (0.65)	19.7 (0.94)	20.6 (0.90)	16.6 (0.81)	15.5 (0.82)
Highest test quartile	36.1 (1.10)	31.8 (0.91)	48.3 (1.17)	52.7 (0.98)	48.0 (0.96)	17.1 (0.82)	7.8 (0.54)	8.7 (0.59)	16.7 (0.78)	24.1 (0.94)	26.3 (0.92)	11.9 (0.78)	12.5 (0.75)
Socioeconomic status[4]													
Low	18.3 (0.94)	16.4 (0.89)	32.3 (1.23)	33.1 (1.05)	26.4 (1.01)	16.5 (0.79)	6.7 (0.96)	6.6 (0.62)	8.0 (0.61)	17.6 (0.96)	16.6 (0.75)	24.4 (1.25)	17.3 (0.94)
Middle	24.1 (0.78)	19.6 (0.65)	41.3 (0.84)	43.7 (0.77)	38.5 (0.75)	19.6 (0.62)	8.0 (0.43)	7.0 (0.41)	11.2 (0.48)	19.6 (0.71)	20.7 (0.68)	19.6 (0.79)	16.8 (0.71)
High	30.9 (1.12)	28.3 (0.89)	52.2 (1.21)	54.6 (0.95)	49.3 (0.99)	20.7 (0.86)	7.8 (0.53)	9.3 (0.59)	15.7 (0.77)	22.0 (0.96)	24.9 (0.98)	9.9 (0.59)	12.1 (0.70)
Region													
Northeast	23.3 (1.06)	21.1 (0.93)	48.0 (1.41)	47.6 (1.27)	41.8 (1.19)	21.7 (1.19)	6.9 (0.67)	9.2 (0.79)	14.0 (0.99)	20.8 (1.07)	20.4 (1.19)	8.4 (0.91)	9.9 (1.03)
Midwest	25.2 (1.17)	20.1 (1.00)	45.6 (1.29)	48.3 (1.13)	41.9 (1.02)	20.9 (1.02)	8.3 (0.61)	6.5 (0.54)	9.8 (0.78)	23.8 (1.07)	25.6 (1.22)	18.0 (1.30)	16.3 (1.40)
South	28.4 (1.14)	23.5 (0.83)	38.6 (1.17)	42.1 (0.93)	36.7 (0.90)	17.6 (0.74)	8.4 (0.70)	6.8 (0.60)	10.5 (0.55)	17.8 (0.82)	20.1 (0.86)	27.4 (1.14)	21.4 (0.94)
West	21.3 (1.08)	19.5 (1.17)	40.7 (1.41)	40.9 (1.22)	36.2 (1.19)	17.7 (0.97)	6.3 (0.62)	9.4 (0.72)	13.9 (0.92)	17.6 (1.12)	17.6 (1.19)	10.2 (0.84)	10.8 (0.94)
Senior's school sector													
Public	24.9 (0.61)	20.5 (0.52)	41.4 (0.69)	42.9 (0.60)	37.5 (0.59)	18.5 (0.49)	7.7 (0.36)	7.4 (0.33)	11.1 (0.41)	19.8 (0.53)	20.6 (0.58)	19.0 (0.62)	16.6 (0.60)
Catholic	27.7 (2.50)	29.5 (1.61)	54.5 (2.98)	60.8 (1.64)	53.1 (1.46)	28.1 (1.96)	7.8 (1.39)	10.4 (1.60)	18.8 (1.22)	14.2 (1.96)	19.2 (1.53)	2.7 (0.61)	4.2 (0.66)
Other private	21.6 (2.80)	29.3 (2.40)	58.3 (3.06)	60.5 (2.72)	51.7 (2.98)	25.8 (2.82)	5.7 (1.49)	11.4 (2.32)	18.1 (1.76)	29.9 (2.67)	31.6 (3.51)	2.2 ! (0.76)	4.0 (0.81)

!Interpret data with caution. The coefficient of variation (CV) for this estimate is between 30 and 50 percent.
[1]Interscholastic refers to competition between teams from different schools. Intramural refers to competition between teams or students within the same school. Data on these categories are available only for 2004.
[2]These data were not collected in 2004.
[3]Composite test performance quartile on mathematics, reading, science, and social studies in 1990 (for 1992 seniors) and composite test performance quartile on mathematics, reading, and science in 2002 (for 2004 seniors).
[4]Socioeconomic status (SES) was measured by a composite score on parental education and occupations, and family income.
NOTE: Race categories exclude persons of Hispanic ethnicity.
SOURCE: U.S. Department of Education, National Center for Education Statistics, National Education Longitudinal Study of 1988 (NELS:88/92), "Second Follow-up, 1992"; and Education Longitudinal Study of 2002 (ELS:2002/04), "First Follow-up, 2004." (This table was prepared December 2009.)

Table 227.40. Percentage of elementary and secondary school students who do homework, average time spent, percentage whose parents check that homework is done, and percentage whose parents help with homework, by frequency and selected characteristics: 2007 and 2012

[Standard errors appear in parentheses]

Year and selected characteristic	Percent of students who do homework outside of school	Average hours spent per week doing homework	Students who do homework outside of school				Percent whose parents¹ check that homework is done[2]	Percentage distribution by how frequently their parents¹ help with homework				
			Percentage distribution by how frequently they do homework					No help given	Less than once per week	1 to 2 days per week	3 to 4 days per week	5 or more days per week
			Less than once per week	1 to 2 days per week	3 to 4 days per week	5 or more days per week						
1	2	3	4	5	6	7	8	9	10	11	12	13
2007												
All students	**94.4** (0.30)	**5.4** (0.06)	**3.1** (0.34)	**13.1** (0.47)	**43.6** (0.62)	**40.2** (0.60)	**85.4** (0.46)	**10.2** (0.41)	**20.3** (0.51)	**31.7** (0.64)	**25.3** (0.59)	**12.4** (0.41)
All elementary school students (kindergarten through grade 8)	**95.0** (0.37)	**4.7** (0.07)	**2.1** (0.23)	**12.3** (0.56)	**46.2** (0.73)	**39.4** (0.68)	**95.0** (0.34)	**4.3** (0.34)	**13.1** (0.52)	**32.6** (0.77)	**32.9** (0.76)	**17.0** (0.56)
Sex												
Male	94.6 (0.51)	4.6 (0.09)	2.1 (0.31)	12.4 (0.71)	47.9 (1.19)	37.6 (1.09)	95.3 (0.47)	4.3 (0.39)	12.9 (0.63)	32.3 (1.02)	32.7 (1.28)	17.8 (0.85)
Female	95.4 (0.53)	4.9 (0.10)	2.1 (0.31)	12.2 (0.96)	44.4 (1.13)	41.3 (1.08)	94.6 (0.48)	4.3 (0.56)	13.4 (0.76)	32.9 (1.17)	33.2 (1.17)	16.1 (0.79)
Race/ethnicity												
White	94.7 (0.48)	4.4 (0.07)	2.7 (0.36)	13.7 (0.74)	48.3 (1.05)	35.3 (0.99)	94.0 (0.42)	3.8 (0.37)	15.7 (0.74)	34.9 (0.94)	31.3 (0.92)	14.3 (0.63)
Black	95.5 (1.07)	5.6 (0.27)	1.3! (0.53)	7.0 (1.19)	44.4 (3.40)	47.2 (3.11)	98.1 (0.63)	3.5 (1.03)	7.4 (1.14)	25.2 (2.22)	38.3 (3.36)	25.5 (2.38)
Hispanic	94.8 (0.85)	4.7 (0.11)	1.3 (0.33)	13.5 (1.39)	40.7 (1.94)	44.4 (1.74)	96.1 (0.70)	7.1 (0.95)	10.3 (0.91)	30.1 (1.79)	34.0 (1.78)	18.6 (1.52)
Asian/Pacific Islander	95.9 (2.14)	5.7 (0.36)	‡ (†)	4.7 (1.35)	40.1 (4.35)	54.3 (4.73)	89.4 (3.22)	3.7! (1.35)	15.4 (4.07)	34.7 (4.39)	29.3 (4.03)	17.0 (2.54)
Asian	97.7 (0.97)	5.7 (0.39)	‡ (†)	5.1! (1.53)	39.1 (4.31)	54.8 (4.48)	88.5 (3.44)	3.1! (1.36)	12.8 (2.84)	37.5 (4.52)	30.7 (4.22)	15.9 (2.56)
Pacific Islander	‡ (†)	‡ (†)	‡ (†)	‡ (†)	‡ (†)	‡ (†)	‡ (†)	‡ (†)	‡ (†)	‡ (†)	‡ (†)	‡ (†)
American Indian/Alaska Native	‡ (†)	‡ (†)	‡ (†)	‡ (†)	‡ (†)	‡ (†)	‡ (†)	‡ (†)	‡ (†)	‡ (†)	‡ (†)	‡ (†)
Other	96.7 (1.24)	4.8 (0.25)	1.2! (0.56)	8.5 (1.73)	57.1 (3.81)	33.1 (3.69)	95.1 (1.81)	‡ (†)	12.3 (2.30)	35.5 (3.99)	33.8 (3.81)	16.1 (2.71)
School control												
Public	95.1 (0.38)	4.7 (0.08)	2.0 (0.25)	12.4 (0.62)	46.1 (0.76)	39.4 (0.73)	95.4 (0.36)	4.4 (0.38)	13.1 (0.55)	32.4 (0.86)	32.9 (0.81)	17.2 (0.64)
Private	94.0 (1.01)	4.8 (0.19)	2.7 (0.63)	11.4 (1.96)	46.7 (2.64)	39.2 (2.46)	91.5 (1.19)	3.6 (0.85)	13.6 (1.48)	34.3 (2.10)	33.5 (2.36)	15.2 (1.68)
Poverty status[3]												
Poor	94.2 (0.99)	4.7 (0.20)	2.9 (0.72)	16.3 (2.18)	39.0 (2.53)	41.7 (2.21)	97.9 (0.55)	6.1 (1.01)	8.8 (1.29)	28.5 (2.44)	35.2 (2.41)	21.3 (1.90)
Near-poor	93.1 (1.03)	4.7 (0.16)	2.2 (0.49)	13.4 (1.37)	47.0 (1.89)	37.5 (1.91)	95.8 (1.05)	5.2 (0.92)	11.5 (1.13)	31.8 (1.79)	33.3 (1.63)	18.2 (1.60)
Nonpoor	95.9 (0.38)	4.8 (0.08)	1.8 (0.24)	10.7 (0.59)	48.3 (0.94)	39.2 (0.89)	93.7 (0.48)	3.5 (0.32)	15.1 (0.68)	34.2 (0.85)	32.1 (0.79)	15.2 (0.59)
Locale												
City	95.2 (0.65)	5.1 (0.13)	1.5 (0.31)	9.1 (0.91)	43.4 (1.58)	46.0 (1.43)	95.4 (0.54)	4.8 (0.67)	11.3 (1.02)	29.1 (1.39)	36.0 (1.41)	18.7 (1.15)
Suburb	95.4 (0.51)	4.9 (0.11)	1.9 (0.37)	9.3 (0.71)	46.1 (1.24)	42.7 (1.19)	93.5 (0.67)	4.4 (0.55)	14.5 (0.85)	33.1 (1.05)	30.8 (1.14)	17.1 (0.91)
Town	93.0 (1.50)	4.1 (0.14)	2.7 (0.79)	18.8 (1.98)	46.4 (2.29)	32.2 (2.08)	96.0 (1.04)	3.2 (0.80)	14.2 (1.62)	35.7 (2.68)	31.1 (2.31)	15.7 (1.62)
Rural	95.0 (0.85)	4.2 (0.15)	3.2 (0.69)	19.5 (1.79)	50.6 (1.90)	26.8 (1.63)	96.3 (0.72)	4.1 (0.94)	13.1 (1.30)	35.5 (2.29)	32.8 (2.23)	14.6 (1.37)
All secondary school students (grades 9 through 12)	**93.0** (0.55)	**6.8** (0.11)	**5.4** (0.85)	**14.8** (0.96)	**38.0** (1.15)	**41.9** (1.18)	**64.6** (1.21)	**23.1** (1.08)	**35.9** (1.26)	**29.7** (1.19)	**8.8** (0.81)	**2.5** (0.34)
Sex												
Male	91.2 (0.80)	6.0 (0.19)	7.4 (1.53)	18.3 (1.59)	38.2 (1.78)	36.0 (1.64)	67.8 (1.88)	24.1 (1.56)	36.9 (1.97)	29.1 (1.84)	8.2 (1.11)	1.8 (0.41)
Female	94.9 (0.79)	7.5 (0.16)	3.3 (0.72)	11.2 (1.10)	37.7 (1.79)	47.9 (1.85)	61.4 (1.78)	22.0 (1.32)	35.0 (1.44)	30.4 (1.35)	9.3 (1.11)	3.3 (0.60)
Race/ethnicity												
White	94.5 (0.52)	6.8 (0.13)	4.2 (0.58)	12.9 (0.91)	38.6 (1.51)	44.3 (1.42)	57.2 (1.54)	22.5 (1.28)	41.1 (1.36)	27.7 (1.43)	6.3 (0.66)	2.3 (0.42)
Black	91.8 (1.98)	6.3 (0.38)	‡ (†)	20.1 (3.86)	41.0 (4.72)	29.7 (3.43)	83.1 (2.84)	19.5 (2.97)	26.5 (4.77)	34.4 (4.03)	16.7 (4.45)	2.9! (1.13)
Hispanic	90.7 (2.11)	6.4 (0.34)	5.9 (1.29)	17.7 (3.55)	36.6 (2.93)	39.9 (3.03)	75.6 (2.71)	26.2 (2.94)	25.8 (2.38)	33.8 (3.49)	11.0 (1.76)	3.3! (1.00)
Asian/Pacific Islander	94.2 (4.66)	10.9 (1.22)	# (†)	12.2! (4.84)	22.3 (6.26)	63.6 (7.16)	65.0 (7.41)	27.1 (7.15)	34.0 (6.73)	27.0 (6.87)	9.2! (3.24)	‡ (†)
Asian	93.6 (5.45)	10.3 (1.37)	‡ (†)	13.8! (5.51)	18.5! (6.12)	67.7 (7.18)	59.0 (7.69)	26.4 (7.58)	36.1 (7.55)	26.8 (7.61)	7.6! (3.11)	‡ (†)
Pacific Islander	‡ (†)	‡ (†)	‡ (†)	‡ (†)	‡ (†)	‡ (†)	‡ (†)	‡ (†)	‡ (†)	‡ (†)	‡ (†)	‡ (†)
American Indian/Alaska Native	‡ (†)	‡ (†)	‡ (†)	‡ (†)	‡ (†)	‡ (†)	‡ (†)	‡ (†)	‡ (†)	‡ (†)	‡ (†)	‡ (†)
Other	86.7 (4.90)	7.2 (0.72)	‡ (†)	9.9 (2.55)	34.1 (4.90)	50.2 (5.29)	64.4 (6.36)	27.2 (6.80)	35.6 (5.57)	27.8 (5.30)	7.9! (2.41)	‡ (†)
School control												
Public	92.3 (0.60)	6.5 (0.11)	5.9 (0.96)	15.9 (1.06)	39.7 (1.26)	38.5 (1.17)	66.1 (1.24)	22.8 (1.16)	35.4 (1.29)	30.0 (1.26)	9.1 (0.87)	2.7 (0.37)
Private	98.5 (0.54)	9.3 (0.39)	0.8! (0.35)	5.9 (1.34)	24.0 (2.72)	69.4 (2.89)	53.1 (3.98)	25.0 (2.64)	40.1 (3.68)	27.5 (4.07)	6.1 (1.36)	1.4! (0.61)
Poverty status[3]												
Poor	89.5 (2.21)	5.5 (0.32)	‡ (†)	19.2 (3.62)	38.7 (4.32)	33.7 (3.69)	81.0 (3.03)	24.2 (3.80)	24.0 (4.21)	36.1 (3.76)	14.0 (3.21)	1.7! (0.63)
Near-poor	89.5 (1.86)	6.4 (0.35)	6.6 (1.58)	20.5 (3.32)	44.2 (3.43)	28.7 (3.10)	70.8 (3.38)	22.9 (2.90)	32.4 (2.97)	28.7 (3.42)	13.0 (2.22)	3.0! (1.02)
Nonpoor	94.9 (0.57)	7.2 (0.13)	4.3 (0.54)	12.1 (0.74)	36.1 (1.41)	47.5 (1.34)	58.9 (1.28)	22.8 (1.11)	39.9 (1.29)	28.4 (1.17)	6.3 (0.68)	2.6 (0.45)

See notes at end of table.

Table 227.40. Percentage of elementary and secondary school students who do homework, average time spent, percentage whose parents check that homework is done, and percentage whose parents help with homework, by frequency and selected characteristics: 2007 and 2012—Continued

[Standard errors appear in parentheses]

Year and selected characteristic	Percent of students who do homework outside of school	Average hours spent per week doing homework	Less than once per week	1 to 2 days per week	3 to 4 days per week	5 or more days per week	Percent whose parents' check that homework is done[2]	No help given	Less than once per week	1 to 2 days per week	3 to 4 days per week	5 or more days per week
1	2	3	4	5	6	7	8	9	10	11	12	13
Coursework												
Enrolled in AP classes	96.9 (0.59)	8.5 (0.22)	2.4 (0.70)	7.5 (0.93)	31.9 (1.81)	58.2 (1.97)	56.3 (2.06)	27.4 (1.90)	36.3 (1.69)	28.3 (1.74)	6.0 (0.99)	1.9 (0.43)
Not enrolled in AP classes	90.6 (0.81)	5.7 (0.13)	7.3 (1.31)	19.5 (1.40)	41.9 (1.56)	31.2 (1.42)	70.1 (1.46)	20.2 (1.14)	35.7 (1.70)	30.7 (1.59)	10.5 (1.23)	2.9 (0.51)
Locale												
City	92.8 (1.01)	6.8 (0.22)	6.3 ! (2.46)	14.1 (1.90)	35.9 (2.32)	43.7 (2.53)	71.5 (1.89)	22.6 (1.88)	33.4 (2.64)	29.3 (2.00)	12.0 (1.80)	2.7 (0.55)
Suburb	93.6 (0.95)	7.5 (0.17)	4.8 (0.86)	11.4 (1.27)	36.5 (1.71)	47.4 (2.07)	58.9 (2.00)	23.6 (1.74)	39.1 (1.79)	27.8 (1.68)	7.5 (1.01)	2.0 (0.47)
Town	89.7 (2.16)	6.4 (0.27)	5.4 (1.48)	13.2 (1.74)	45.9 (3.46)	35.5 (3.17)	64.8 (3.12)	24.3 (2.81)	34.4 (2.96)	27.9 (3.41)	9.3 (1.80)	4.2 ! (1.54)
Rural	93.9 (1.23)	5.6 (0.29)	5.1 (1.20)	22.7 (2.76)	39.6 (3.04)	32.6 (2.79)	65.5 (2.94)	22.1 (2.69)	34.4 (2.71)	34.8 (3.43)	6.2 (1.53)	2.5 ! (0.88)
2012												
All students	96.0 (0.27)	5.2 (0.05)	5.3 (0.22)	15.3 (0.46)	43.5 (0.58)	35.9 (0.59)	96.6 (0.18)	8.5 (0.24)	22.0 (0.43)	26.5 (0.43)	26.5 (0.52)	16.6 (0.41)
All elementary school students (kindergarten through grade 8)	96.3 (0.29)	4.7 (0.06)	4.1 (0.27)	12.8 (0.50)	46.7 (0.74)	36.3 (0.68)	99.0 (0.12)	3.0 (0.24)	14.5 (0.40)	27.0 (0.54)	33.7 (0.64)	21.9 (0.57)
Sex												
Male	96.2 (0.37)	4.5 (0.09)	4.7 (0.41)	13.5 (0.64)	46.7 (0.91)	35.1 (0.90)	99.1 (0.18)	3.3 (0.35)	14.7 (0.60)	26.0 (0.73)	34.5 (0.88)	21.5 (0.83)
Female	96.5 (0.46)	4.8 (0.09)	3.4 (0.37)	12.1 (0.69)	46.8 (1.21)	37.7 (1.04)	98.9 (0.15)	2.7 (0.31)	14.3 (0.59)	28.0 (0.90)	32.7 (1.03)	22.3 (0.88)
Race/ethnicity												
White	95.4 (0.54)	4.4 (0.07)	5.3 (0.40)	14.3 (0.69)	47.4 (0.95)	33.0 (0.91)	98.8 (0.16)	2.5 (0.27)	17.7 (0.61)	27.5 (0.68)	33.4 (0.92)	18.9 (0.82)
Black	96.2 (0.83)	5.5 (0.19)	3.5 (0.86)	14.0 (1.63)	47.9 (2.16)	34.7 (1.75)	99.1 (0.37)	3.7 (0.92)	9.8 (1.62)	24.3 (1.80)	37.0 (2.40)	25.1 (1.80)
Hispanic	98.1 (0.40)	4.7 (0.12)	3.0 (0.57)	10.0 (0.82)	44.7 (1.65)	42.3 (1.53)	99.6 (0.13)	3.8 (0.46)	11.0 (0.96)	28.1 (1.25)	32.7 (1.58)	24.4 (1.34)
Asian	97.3 (0.85)	5.6 (0.27)	1.0 ! (0.39)	11.1 (2.03)	39.1 (3.03)	48.7 (3.11)	98.4 (0.64)	4.1 (0.91)	14.0 (1.64)	25.7 (2.60)	26.9 (2.49)	29.3 (3.15)
Pacific Islander	97.0 (0.93)	5.7 (0.29)	1.1 ! (0.42)	11.6 (1.98)	37.2 (2.71)	50.1 (2.96)	98.2 (0.70)	3.9 (0.99)	14.9 (1.73)	27.4 (2.55)	26.5 (2.54)	27.3 (3.10)
American Indian/Alaska Native	97.9 ! (2.15)	4.5 (0.41)	‡ (†)	8.1 ! (3.18)	71.2 (7.78)	14.5 ! (4.82)	100.0 (†)	‡ (†)	9.3 ! (3.95)	18.8 ! (6.52)	48.0 (11.41)	23.2 ! (10.28)
Other	96.9 (0.79)	4.6 (0.25)	2.3 ! (0.73)	11.2 (1.97)	51.7 (2.94)	34.7 (2.48)	99.1 (0.42)	1.8 ! (0.58)	14.3 (2.12)	26.8 (2.95)	35.9 (2.76)	21.2 (2.40)
School control												
Public	96.7 (0.30)	4.7 (0.06)	4.1 (0.26)	13.3 (0.54)	47.0 (0.78)	35.7 (0.72)	99.1 (0.12)	3.0 (0.25)	14.5 (0.45)	27.4 (0.57)	33.5 (0.69)	21.6 (0.60)
Private	92.5 (1.23)	4.8 (0.15)	4.0 (1.15)	8.5 (1.19)	43.9 (1.77)	43.5 (1.95)	98.7 (0.49)	3.0 (0.78)	14.2 (1.41)	23.0 (1.83)	35.5 (1.88)	24.3 (1.70)
Poverty status[3]												
Poor	94.9 (1.00)	4.7 (0.16)	4.2 (0.64)	13.7 (1.15)	42.2 (1.87)	39.9 (1.68)	99.2 (0.33)	4.7 (0.74)	10.0 (0.87)	24.9 (1.50)	31.9 (1.83)	28.5 (1.49)
Near-poor	95.4 (0.71)	4.6 (0.14)	4.4 (0.56)	14.6 (1.10)	46.9 (1.51)	34.1 (1.44)	99.1 (0.26)	3.6 (0.57)	12.5 (1.12)	27.2 (1.58)	35.3 (1.61)	21.4 (1.38)
Nonpoor	97.2 (0.30)	4.7 (0.07)	3.9 (0.36)	11.9 (0.60)	48.3 (1.00)	35.9 (0.88)	99.0 (0.14)	2.2 (0.25)	16.8 (0.56)	27.7 (0.68)	33.7 (0.79)	19.7 (0.72)
Locale												
City	96.0 (0.49)	5.0 (0.12)	3.3 (0.51)	11.4 (0.90)	43.7 (1.47)	41.5 (1.39)	98.9 (0.21)	4.0 (0.60)	12.3 (0.77)	26.8 (1.21)	32.0 (1.17)	24.9 (1.21)
Suburb	96.8 (0.64)	4.8 (0.08)	2.9 (0.34)	11.0 (0.84)	46.2 (1.25)	39.9 (1.19)	99.1 (0.18)	2.7 (0.26)	15.6 (0.84)	27.2 (0.93)	32.6 (1.22)	21.9 (0.92)
Town	97.1 (0.65)	4.2 (0.21)	6.2 (1.25)	15.5 (1.52)	28.3 (2.66)	49.9 (2.44)	99.2 (0.36)	2.0 (0.53)	13.7 (1.95)	25.4 (2.12)	35.8 (2.64)	23.1 (2.25)
Rural	95.6 (0.62)	4.3 (0.14)	6.1 (0.73)	16.5 (1.15)	50.2 (1.31)	27.2 (1.35)	99.0 (0.22)	2.7 (0.48)	15.9 (1.03)	27.5 (1.34)	36.6 (1.35)	17.2 (1.08)
All secondary school students (grades 9 through 12)	95.1 (0.58)	6.6 (0.10)	8.4 (0.48)	21.8 (0.92)	35.0 (0.91)	34.9 (0.97)	90.4 (0.55)	22.7 (0.70)	41.5 (1.00)	25.3 (0.84)	7.8 (0.63)	2.8 (0.28)
Sex												
Male	93.4 (1.02)	5.7 (0.15)	10.8 (0.73)	24.7 (1.28)	35.2 (1.24)	29.3 (1.19)	92.5 (0.59)	22.4 (0.92)	41.7 (1.25)	23.9 (1.01)	8.7 (1.07)	3.3 (0.41)
Female	97.0 (0.42)	7.5 (0.15)	5.8 (0.64)	18.7 (1.15)	34.7 (1.19)	40.7 (1.42)	88.2 (0.92)	23.0 (1.13)	41.3 (1.59)	26.6 (1.43)	6.8 (0.62)	3.2 (0.42)
Race/ethnicity												
White	94.9 (1.01)	6.5 (0.10)	8.6 (0.59)	21.2 (0.88)	34.6 (1.04)	35.6 (1.22)	89.0 (0.85)	20.1 (0.85)	48.1 (1.21)	24.2 (1.07)	5.8 (0.49)	1.8 (0.32)
Black	94.5 (0.94)	6.3 (0.24)	7.7 (1.28)	27.2 (2.52)	34.4 (2.51)	30.7 (2.31)	95.2 (0.93)	20.5 (2.12)	32.0 (3.05)	28.7 (2.51)	12.1 (2.23)	6.7 (1.23)
Hispanic	95.3 (0.86)	6.1 (0.22)	8.9 (1.32)	22.3 (2.29)	36.4 (2.72)	32.4 (2.10)	91.7 (1.27)	27.9 (2.10)	33.7 (1.80)	27.6 (1.80)	7.6 (1.54)	3.2 (0.59)
Asian/Pacific Islander	98.4 (0.59)	10.5 (0.76)	5.5 ! (1.78)	10.0 ! (3.24)	53.9 (3.66)	30.6 (3.64)	87.3 (3.15)	38.4 (3.90)	33.4 (3.72)	14.8 (2.49)	11.5 (2.25)	‡ (†)
Asian	98.6 (0.61)	10.9 (0.82)	5.0 ! (1.85)	10.4 ! (3.58)	53.7 (3.96)	31.0 (3.64)	87.0 (3.44)	40.8 (4.08)	34.7 (3.97)	14.4 (2.52)	9.2 (1.78)	‡ (†)
Pacific Islander	‡ (†)	‡ (†)	‡ (†)	‡ (†)	‡ (†)	‡ (†)	‡ (†)	‡ (†)	‡ (†)	‡ (†)	‡ (†)	‡ (†)
American Indian/Alaska Native	99.7 (0.33)	‡ (†)	‡ (†)	‡ (†)	‡ (†)	‡ (†)	‡ (†)	‡ (†)	‡ (†)	‡ (†)	‡ (†)	‡ (†)
Other	93.9 (2.11)	6.6 (0.63)	6.8 (1.84)	24.6 (6.65)	37.7 (5.27)	31.0 (4.48)	90.2 (3.09)	17.5 (3.71)	38.7 (4.64)	27.0 (4.28)	15.9 ! (6.95)	‡ (†)

See notes at end of table.

Table 227.40. Percentage of elementary and secondary school students who do homework, average time spent, percentage whose parents check that homework is done, and percentage whose parents help with homework, by frequency and selected characteristics: 2007 and 2012—Continued

[Standard errors appear in parentheses]

Year and selected characteristic	Percent of students who do homework outside of school	Average hours spent per week doing homework	Students who do homework outside of school									
			Percentage distribution by how frequently they do homework				Percent whose parents[1] check that homework is done[2]	Percentage distribution by how frequently their parents[1] help with homework				
			Less than once per week	1 to 2 days per week	3 to 4 days per week	5 or more days per week		No help given	Less than once per week	1 to 2 days per week	3 to 4 days per week	5 or more days per week
1	2	3	4	5	6	7	8	9	10	11	12	13
School control												
Public	94.9 (0.63)	6.3 (0.11)	8.9 (0.52)	22.9 (1.00)	35.8 (0.95)	32.4 (1.04)	90.8 (0.56)	22.7 (0.77)	41.0 (1.07)	25.6 (0.91)	7.9 (0.67)	2.8 (0.31)
Private	97.5 (0.88)	9.4 (0.28)	1.9 ! (0.69)	8.7 (1.32)	25.4 (2.07)	64.0 (2.52)	85.8 (1.87)	22.4 (2.41)	47.4 (2.70)	21.5 (1.94)	6.5 (1.37)	2.2 ! (0.76)
Poverty status[3]												
Poor	90.8 (1.20)	5.5 (0.26)	14.3 (1.36)	24.1 (2.02)	33.8 (1.96)	27.8 (2.37)	90.1 (1.87)	28.2 (2.12)	28.8 (2.12)	27.7 (2.18)	11.3 (1.36)	4.1 (0.91)
Near-poor	94.9 (0.73)	5.8 (0.23)	9.6 (1.05)	26.9 (2.04)	36.6 (2.14)	26.8 (1.58)	90.7 (1.32)	25.8 (2.19)	35.4 (2.36)	27.5 (2.24)	7.1 (1.33)	4.2 (0.84)
Nonpoor	96.3 (0.83)	7.1 (0.12)	6.4 (0.55)	19.2 (0.88)	34.6 (1.12)	39.8 (1.15)	90.4 (0.56)	20.1 (0.82)	47.1 (1.27)	23.8 (0.97)	7.1 (0.86)	1.9 (0.26)
Coursework												
Enrolled in AP classes	98.7 (0.32)	8.3 (0.16)	4.6 (0.50)	13.6 (0.93)	34.3 (1.35)	47.5 (1.30)	88.1 (0.81)	26.5 (1.23)	45.2 (1.44)	21.6 (1.08)	4.6 (0.60)	2.2 (0.39)
Not enrolled in AP classes	92.9 (0.95)	5.4 (0.14)	11.0 (0.79)	27.6 (1.27)	35.5 (1.12)	25.9 (1.18)	92.2 (0.73)	19.9 (1.05)	39.0 (1.34)	28.0 (1.21)	9.9 (0.98)	3.2 (0.39)
Locale												
City	95.1 (0.66)	7.1 (0.21)	7.3 (0.78)	20.0 (1.54)	33.7 (1.85)	39.0 (1.61)	92.8 (0.78)	24.4 (1.49)	37.8 (1.96)	25.4 (1.51)	9.1 (1.23)	3.2 (0.57)
Suburb	96.4 (0.43)	7.0 (0.16)	5.8 (0.66)	19.9 (1.62)	34.9 (1.31)	39.4 (1.42)	89.7 (1.05)	23.4 (1.25)	41.4 (1.48)	24.0 (1.33)	8.1 (1.24)	3.0 (0.51)
Town	94.9 (1.13)	5.1 (0.21)	14.1 (2.02)	26.9 (2.75)	36.5 (2.99)	22.5 (2.89)	89.0 (2.16)	19.7 (2.21)	41.3 (3.45)	28.8 (2.72)	7.3 (1.56)	2.9 ! (0.98)
Rural	93.1 (2.06)	5.8 (0.20)	11.7 (1.13)	25.1 (1.89)	35.9 (1.92)	27.3 (1.55)	89.3 (1.09)	20.5 (1.41)	46.2 (2.07)	25.9 (1.77)	5.7 (0.70)	1.8 (0.49)

†Not applicable.

#Rounds to zero.

!Interpret data with caution. The coefficient of variation (CV) for this estimate is between 30 and 50 percent.

‡Reporting standards not met. Either there are too few cases for a reliable estimate or the coefficient of variation (CV) is 50 percent or greater.

[1]Refers to one or more parent or other household adult.

[2]The wording of the questionnaire item changed from 2007 to 2012. In 2007, parents responded "yes" or "no" to an item asking whether they check that homework is done. In 2012, parents responded to a multiple-choice question asking how often they check that homework is done, and the 2012 estimates include all parents who "rarely," "sometimes," or "always" check. Therefore, the 2007 and 2012 estimates are not comparable.

[3]Poor children are those whose family incomes were below the Census Bureau's poverty threshold in the year prior to data collection; near-poor children are those whose family incomes ranged from the poverty threshold to 199 percent of the poverty threshold; and nonpoor children are those whose family incomes were at or above 200 percent of the poverty threshold. The poverty threshold is a dollar amount that varies depending on a family's size and composition and is updated annually to account for inflation. In 2011, for example, the poverty threshold for a family of four with two children was $22,811. Survey respondents are asked to select the range within which their income falls, rather than giving the exact amount of their income; therefore, the measure of poverty status is an approximation.

NOTE: While National Household Education Surveys Program (NHES) administrations prior to 2012 were administered via telephone with an interviewer, NHES:2012 used self-administered paper-and-pencil questionnaires that were mailed to respondents. Measurable differences in estimates between 2012 and prior years could reflect actual changes in the population, or the changes could be due to the mode change from telephone to mail. Includes children enrolled in kindergarten through grade 12 and ungraded students. Excludes homeschooled students. Data based on responses of the parent most knowledgeable about the student's education. Race categories exclude persons of Hispanic ethnicity. Detail may not sum to totals because of rounding.

SOURCE: U.S. Department of Education, National Center for Education Statistics, Parent and Family Involvement in Education Survey of the National Household Education Surveys Program (PFI-NHES:2007 and 2012). (This table was prepared May 2015.)

Table 227.50. Average National Assessment of Educational Progress (NAEP) reading and mathematics scale scores of 4th-, 8th-, and 12th-graders and percentage absent from school, by selected characteristics and number of days absent in the last month: 2013 and 2015

[Standard errors appear in parentheses]

Grade level and days absent from school in the last month	All students	Sex		Race/ethnicity							Eligibility for free or reduced-price lunch (public schools only)			Control of school		
		Male	Female	White	Black	Hispanic	Asian	Pacific Islander	American Indian/ Alaska Native	Two or more races	Eligible	Not eligible	Unknown	Public	Catholic	Other private
1	2	3	4	5	6	7	8	9	10	11	12	13	14	15	16	17
Average mathematics scale score[1]																
4th-graders (2015)																
0 days	245 (0.3)	246 (0.4)	244 (0.3)	252 (0.3)	229 (0.6)	235 (0.5)	264 (1.2)	240 (3.1)	232 (1.5)	249 (1.1)	233 (0.3)	257 (0.4)	250 (3.0)	245 (0.3)	250 (1.3)	‡ (†)
1–2 days	240 (0.4)	240 (0.5)	239 (0.6)	248 (0.4)	223 (0.7)	230 (0.7)	255 (1.4)	231 (3.5)	228 (1.7)	244 (1.3)	230 (0.4)	252 (0.4)	245 (2.6)	239 (0.4)	246 (1.6)	‡ (†)
3–4 days	233 (0.4)	234 (0.6)	232 (0.6)	241 (0.6)	220 (0.8)	225 (1.0)	250 (2.8)	223 (4.3)	226 (1.9)	240 (2.0)	225 (0.5)	247 (0.7)	238 (2.7)	233 (0.5)	240 (2.6)	‡ (†)
5–10 days	231 (0.6)	231 (0.8)	231 (0.8)	242 (0.7)	215 (1.1)	221 (1.6)	240 (5.4)	218 (†)	220 (4.6)	232 (4.6)	220 (0.9)	247 (1.1)	239 (4.4)	230 (0.6)	‡ (†)	‡ (†)
More than 10 days	216 (1.0)	215 (1.5)	216 (1.1)	227 (1.3)	204 (1.7)	208 (2.0)	232 (4.8)	‡ (†)	203 (4.1)	219 (3.4)	209 (1.0)	231 (1.8)	‡ (†)	215 (1.0)	‡ (†)	‡ (†)
8th-graders (2015)																
0 days	288 (0.4)	288 (0.4)	288 (0.5)	297 (0.4)	266 (0.7)	275 (0.7)	311 (1.8)	282 (4.7)	272 (2.4)	292 (1.4)	274 (0.5)	300 (0.5)	299 (3.4)	288 (0.4)	296 (2.1)	‡ (†)
1–2 days	283 (0.4)	282 (0.5)	283 (0.5)	292 (0.4)	261 (0.8)	271 (0.8)	306 (1.9)	278 (6.0)	270 (2.8)	282 (1.6)	268 (0.4)	296 (0.4)	297 (3.5)	282 (0.4)	295 (1.9)	‡ (†)
3–4 days	272 (0.5)	271 (0.7)	272 (0.6)	282 (0.6)	252 (1.1)	261 (0.8)	295 (3.8)	270 (8.2)	262 (2.6)	281 (2.4)	260 (0.6)	287 (0.7)	281 (4.6)	271 (0.4)	281 (3.2)	‡ (†)
5–10 days	266 (0.8)	266 (1.0)	265 (1.1)	277 (1.0)	249 (1.5)	255 (1.7)	281 (5.9)	270 (7.4)	264 (5.6)	269 (6.0)	256 (0.9)	282 (1.1)	273 (6.0)	265 (0.8)	‡ (†)	‡ (†)
More than 10 days	251 (1.5)	250 (2.2)	252 (2.2)	264 (2.0)	235 (2.6)	240 (2.4)	‡ (†)	‡ (†)	236 (7.0)	261 (8.4)	241 (1.5)	269 (2.5)	‡ (†)	250 (1.5)	‡ (†)	‡ (†)
12th-graders (2013)																
0 days	157 (0.6)	159 (0.7)	156 (0.8)	165 (0.7)	135 (1.2)	146 (0.9)	176 (1.8)	‡ (†)	156 (5.5)	159 (3.3)	143 (0.9)	165 (0.7)	142 (6.1)	—	—	—
1–2 days	155 (0.7)	157 (0.8)	154 (0.8)	163 (0.7)	134 (1.3)	141 (1.1)	174 (2.0)	‡ (†)	146 (6.6)	157 (2.5)	140 (0.9)	163 (0.7)	140 (6.2)	—	—	—
3–4 days	147 (0.9)	149 (1.1)	146 (1.1)	157 (1.0)	126 (1.5)	133 (1.3)	167 (3.3)	‡ (†)	131 (6.7)	150 (4.1)	134 (1.1)	156 (1.1)	‡ (†)	—	—	—
5–10 days	144 (1.4)	145 (2.0)	143 (2.0)	150 (1.7)	125 (2.4)	133 (2.5)	172 (6.3)	‡ (†)	‡ (†)	‡ (†)	131 (1.8)	152 (1.9)	‡ (†)	—	—	—
More than 10 days	135 (2.2)	133 (2.9)	137 (2.9)	139 (3.2)	113 (3.5)	126 (3.8)	‡ (†)	‡ (†)	‡ (†)	‡ (†)	124 (3.3)	142 (2.5)	‡ (†)	—	—	—
Average reading scale score[2]																
4th-graders (2015)																
0 days	227 (0.4)	224 (0.5)	231 (0.4)	236 (0.4)	212 (0.5)	213 (0.8)	244 (1.5)	216 (4.1)	212 (2.1)	233 (1.6)	213 (0.4)	240 (0.4)	232 (3.3)	226 (0.4)	240 (1.3)	‡ (†)
1–2 days	222 (0.5)	219 (0.7)	225 (0.6)	232 (0.5)	206 (0.8)	208 (1.1)	238 (2.7)	217 (8.5)	209 (2.7)	225 (2.0)	210 (0.6)	236 (0.6)	228 (4.3)	221 (0.5)	237 (1.8)	‡ (†)
3–4 days	215 (0.6)	211 (0.8)	219 (0.9)	226 (0.7)	200 (1.2)	202 (1.5)	230 (3.7)	218 (5.6)	200 (2.7)	222 (1.9)	204 (0.8)	232 (0.8)	225 (5.0)	214 (0.6)	232 (3.0)	‡ (†)
5–10 days	214 (0.7)	209 (1.4)	218 (1.0)	225 (0.9)	195 (2.1)	203 (1.8)	237 (4.4)	203 (6.2)	200 (5.5)	221 (3.8)	202 (1.1)	231 (1.2)	‡ (†)	213 (0.8)	‡ (†)	‡ (†)
More than 10 days	192 (1.4)	189 (2.2)	197 (1.7)	206 (1.6)	184 (2.7)	181 (2.6)	204 (7.7)	‡ (†)	182 (6.0)	199 (4.3)	186 (1.4)	208 (2.1)	‡ (†)	192 (1.3)	‡ (†)	‡ (†)
8th-graders (2015)																
0 days	270 (0.3)	266 (0.4)	275 (0.4)	278 (0.4)	253 (0.6)	258 (0.6)	284 (1.4)	265 (3.1)	260 (2.2)	273 (1.4)	257 (0.5)	279 (0.4)	277 (3.0)	269 (0.3)	287 (1.2)	‡ (†)
1–2 days	266 (0.3)	261 (0.4)	271 (0.4)	275 (0.3)	248 (1.0)	254 (0.6)	280 (1.8)	249 (4.7)	256 (2.5)	271 (1.7)	254 (0.4)	277 (0.4)	276 (3.3)	265 (0.3)	283 (1.7)	‡ (†)
3–4 days	257 (0.5)	252 (0.8)	262 (0.7)	267 (0.6)	241 (1.0)	247 (1.1)	269 (3.0)	251 (4.6)	249 (2.8)	261 (3.1)	247 (0.6)	269 (0.6)	268 (4.6)	256 (0.5)	275 (3.1)	‡ (†)
5–10 days	251 (1.0)	244 (1.2)	257 (1.3)	262 (1.1)	236 (1.8)	240 (1.8)	271 (5.8)	236 (7.3)	239 (8.0)	257 (4.1)	241 (1.1)	266 (1.6)	250 (8.3)	250 (1.0)	‡ (†)	‡ (†)
More than 10 days	236 (1.5)	232 (2.0)	240 (2.1)	246 (2.2)	224 (2.7)	227 (2.6)	256 (7.8)	‡ (†)	223 (10.6)	‡ (†)	229 (1.7)	248 (2.7)	‡ (†)	235 (1.5)	‡ (†)	‡ (†)
12th-graders (2013)																
0 days	292 (0.7)	287 (0.8)	297 (0.8)	301 (0.8)	271 (1.4)	280 (1.1)	298 (2.4)	‡ (†)	266 (6.5)	300 (4.8)	276 (1.1)	299 (0.8)	281 (3.1)	—	—	—
1–2 days	290 (0.6)	286 (0.8)	295 (0.7)	299 (0.8)	269 (1.2)	276 (1.1)	300 (2.3)	‡ (†)	288 (4.4)	289 (4.4)	275 (0.7)	298 (0.7)	284 (6.0)	—	—	—
3–4 days	286 (0.8)	281 (1.1)	290 (1.1)	295 (1.0)	264 (1.6)	273 (1.7)	291 (4.8)	‡ (†)	270 (9.3)	285 (4.3)	272 (1.2)	294 (1.0)	‡ (†)	—	—	—
5–10 days	278 (1.4)	271 (1.6)	283 (2.1)	285 (1.8)	265 (4.2)	266 (2.7)	‡ (†)	‡ (†)	‡ (†)	‡ (†)	270 (2.3)	283 (1.9)	‡ (†)	—	—	—
More than 10 days	259 (3.0)	251 (3.6)	269 (3.9)	266 (4.6)	239 (4.4)	247 (4.3)	‡ (†)	‡ (†)	‡ (†)	‡ (†)	252 (3.3)	260 (4.0)	‡ (†)	—	—	—

See notes at end of table.

Table 227.50. Average National Assessment of Educational Progress (NAEP) reading and mathematics scale scores of 4th-, 8th-, and 12th-graders and percentage absent from school, by selected characteristics and number of days absent in the last month: 2013 and 2015—Continued

[Standard errors appear in parentheses]

Grade level and days absent from school in the last month	All students	Sex		Race/ethnicity							Eligibility for free or reduced-price lunch (public schools only)			Control of school		
		Male	Female	White	Black	Hispanic	Asian	Pacific Islander	American Indian/ Alaska Native	Two or more races	Eligible	Not eligible	Unknown	Public	Catholic	Other private
1	2	3	4	5	6	7	8	9	10	11	12	13	14	15	16	17
							Percent of students absent[3]									
4th-graders (2015)																
0 days............	52 (0.2)	54 (0.3)	50 (0.4)	52 (0.3)	49 (0.6)	51 (0.6)	67 (1.3)	45 (4.4)	44 (1.9)	49 (1.4)	48 (0.3)	56 (0.4)	59 (3.2)	52 (0.3)	55 (1.6)	‡ (†)
1–2 days........	29 (0.2)	28 (0.2)	31 (0.3)	30 (0.3)	28 (0.5)	29 (0.5)	22 (1.0)	28 (3.0)	31 (1.8)	31 (1.4)	30 (0.3)	29 (0.3)	24 (2.2)	29 (0.2)	28 (1.3)	‡ (†)
3–4 days........	11 (0.1)	11 (0.2)	12 (0.2)	11 (0.2)	13 (0.3)	12 (0.3)	7 (0.5)	17 (3.0)	15 (0.9)	12 (0.9)	13 (0.2)	9 (0.2)	12 (1.5)	11 (0.1)	11 (0.9)	‡ (†)
5–10 days......	5 (0.1)	5 (0.1)	5 (0.2)	5 (0.1)	6 (0.3)	5 (0.2)	3 (0.3)	6 (1.8)	7 (0.8)	5 (0.5)	5 (0.1)	4 (0.2)	4 (1.1)	5 (0.1)	4 (0.6)	‡ (†)
More than 10 days......	3 (0.1)	3 (0.1)	2 (0.1)	2 (0.1)	4 (0.3)	3 (0.2)	2 (0.2)	3 (0.7)	4 (0.6)	3 (0.4)	4 (0.1)	2 (0.1)	1 (0.4)	3 (0.1)	1 (0.4)	‡ (†)
8th-graders (2015)																
0 days............	45 (0.3)	47 (0.4)	43 (0.4)	44 (0.3)	45 (0.6)	44 (0.7)	65 (1.3)	47 (4.0)	32 (1.7)	45 (1.5)	41 (0.4)	49 (0.4)	45 (1.5)	45 (0.3)	51 (1.6)	‡ (†)
1–2 days........	36 (0.2)	35 (0.3)	38 (0.3)	38 (0.3)	33 (0.4)	37 (0.5)	26 (1.1)	28 (2.7)	40 (1.7)	35 (1.2)	36 (0.3)	37 (0.3)	35 (1.4)	36 (0.2)	36 (1.4)	‡ (†)
3–4 days........	12 (0.2)	12 (0.2)	13 (0.3)	12 (0.2)	14 (0.4)	13 (0.4)	6 (0.6)	14 (2.4)	20 (1.2)	14 (0.9)	15 (0.2)	10 (0.2)	14 (1.1)	13 (0.1)	10 (0.9)	‡ (†)
5–10 days......	4 (0.1)	4 (0.1)	5 (0.1)	4 (0.1)	6 (0.3)	5 (0.2)	2 (0.3)	7 (1.5)	6 (0.9)	5 (0.5)	6 (0.1)	3 (0.1)	5 (0.9)	5 (0.1)	2 (0.5)	‡ (†)
More than 10 days......	1 (0.1)	2 (0.1)	1 (0.1)	1 (0.1)	2 (0.2)	2 (0.1)	1 (0.1)	5 (1.8)	3 (0.6)	1 (0.3)	2 (0.1)	1 (0.1)	1 (0.3)	2 (0.1)	1 (0.2)	‡ (†)
12th-graders (2013)																
0 days............	36 (0.4)	40 (0.6)	32 (0.6)	35 (0.6)	41 (1.1)	35 (0.8)	50 (1.7)	44 (6.8)	24 (4.5)	34 (3.3)	34 (0.7)	37 (0.6)	41 (4.3)	— (†)	— (†)	—
1–2 days........	40 (0.4)	38 (0.6)	42 (0.5)	42 (0.5)	36 (0.9)	40 (0.7)	34 (1.5)	36 (6.7)	42 (4.2)	40 (3.0)	39 (0.6)	40 (0.5)	31 (4.1)	— (†)	— (†)	—
3–4 days........	16 (0.3)	14 (0.3)	17 (0.4)	16 (0.4)	16 (0.7)	16 (0.6)	11 (1.3)	15 (4.8)	21 (4.0)	17 (2.6)	17 (0.4)	16 (0.4)	20 (3.5)	— (†)	— (†)	—
5–10 days......	6 (0.2)	5 (0.2)	6 (0.3)	6 (0.2)	6 (0.6)	6 (0.5)	4 (0.7)	5 (2.8)	11 (3.5)	6 (1.4)	7 (0.4)	5 (0.3)	6 (2.3)	— (†)	— (†)	—
More than 10 days......	2 (0.1)	2 (0.2)	2 (0.2)	2 (0.2)	2 (0.2)	2 (0.3)	1 (0.3)	# (†)	2 (0.9)	3 (1.6)	2 (0.2)	2 (0.1)	1 (0.4)	— (†)	— (†)	—

—Not available.
†Not applicable.
#Rounds to zero.
‡Reporting standards not met (too few cases for a reliable estimate).
[1]For grades 4 and 8, mathematics scale ranges from 0 to 500. For grade 12, mathematics scale ranges from 0 to 300.
[2]Reading scale ranges from 0 to 500.
[3]Absenteeism percentages based on the 2015 Reading Assessment for 4th- and 8th-graders and the 2013 Reading Assessment for 12th-graders, who were not assessed in 2015.

NOTE: Includes public and private schools except where otherwise noted. Includes students tested with accommodations (9 to 13 percent of all students, depending on assessment, grade level, and year); excludes only those students with disabilities and English language learners who were unable to be tested even with accommodations (2 percent of all students). Race categories exclude persons of Hispanic ethnicity. Some data have been revised from previously published figures. Detail may not sum to totals because of rounding.
SOURCE: U.S. Department of Education, National Center for Education Statistics, National Assessment of Educational Progress (NAEP), 2013 and 2015 Mathematics and Reading Assessments, retrieved November 4, 2015, from the Main NAEP Data Explorer (http://nces.ed.gov/nationsreportcard/naepdata/). (This table was prepared November 2015.)

Table 228.10. School-associated violent deaths of all persons, homicides and suicides of youth ages 5–18 at school, and total homicides and suicides of youth ages 5–18, by type of violent death: 1992–93 to 2012–13

Year	School-associated violent deaths[1] of all persons (includes students, staff, and other nonstudents)					Homicides of youth ages 5–18		Suicides of youth ages 5–18	
	Total	Homicides	Suicides	Legal interventions	Unintentional firearm-related deaths	Homicides at school[2]	Total homicides	Suicides at school[2]	Total suicides[3]
1	2	3	4	5	6	7	8	9	10
1992–93	57	47	10	0	0	34	2,721	6	1,680
1993–94	48	38	10	0	0	29	2,932	7	1,723
1994–95	48	39	8	0	1	28	2,696	7	1,767
1995–96	53	46	6	1	0	32	2,545	6	1,725
1996–97	48	45	2	1	0	28	2,221	1	1,633
1997–98	57	47	9	1	0	34	2,100	6	1,626
1998–99	47	38	6	2	1	33	1,777	4	1,597
1999–2000	37[4]	26[4]	11[4]	0[4]	0[4]	14[4]	1,567	8[4]	1,415
2000–01	34[4]	26[4]	7[4]	1[4]	0[4]	14[4]	1,509	6[4]	1,493
2001–02	36[4]	27[4]	8[4]	1[4]	0[4]	16[4]	1,498	5[4]	1,400
2002–03	36[4]	25[4]	11[4]	0[4]	0[4]	18[4]	1,553	10[4]	1,331
2003–04	45[4]	37[4]	7[4]	1[4]	0[4]	23[4]	1,474	5[4]	1,285
2004–05	52[4]	40[4]	10[4]	2[4]	0[4]	22[4]	1,554	8[4]	1,471
2005–06	44[4]	37[4]	6[4]	1[4]	0[4]	21[4]	1,697	3[4]	1,408
2006–07	63[4]	48[4]	13[4]	2[4]	0[4]	32[4]	1,801	9[4]	1,296
2007–08	48[4]	39[4]	7[4]	2[4]	0[4]	21[4]	1,744	5[4]	1,231
2008–09	44[4]	29[4]	15[4]	0[4]	0[4]	18[4]	1,605	7[4]	1,344
2009–10	35[4]	27[4]	5[4]	3[4]	0[4]	19[4]	1,410	2[4]	1,467
2010–11	32[4]	26[4]	6[4]	0[4]	0[4]	11[4]	1,339	3[4]	1,456
2011–12	45[4]	26[4]	14[4]	5[4]	0[4]	15[4]	1,201	5[4]	1,568
2012–13	53[4]	41[4]	11[4]	1[4]	0[4]	31[4]	1,186	6[4]	1,590

[1]A school-associated violent death is defined as "a homicide, suicide, or legal intervention (involving a law enforcement officer), in which the fatal injury occurred on the campus of a functioning elementary or secondary school in the United States," while the victim was on the way to or from regular sessions at school, or while the victim was attending or traveling to or from an official school-sponsored event.

[2]"At school" includes on school property, on the way to or from regular sessions at school, and while attending or traveling to or from a school-sponsored event.

[3]Total youth suicides are reported for calendar years 1992 through 2012 (instead of school years 1992–93 through 2012–13).

[4]Data from 1999–2000 onward are subject to change until interviews with school and law enforcement officials have been completed. The details learned during the interviews can occasionally change the classification of a case.

NOTE: Unless otherwise noted, data are reported for the school year, defined as July 1 through June 30. Some data have been revised from previously published figures.
SOURCE: Centers for Disease Control and Prevention (CDC), 1992–2013 School-Associated Violent Deaths Surveillance Study (SAVD) (partially funded by the U.S. Department of Education, Office of Safe and Healthy Students), previously unpublished tabulation (September 2015); CDC, National Center for Injury Prevention and Control, Web-based Injury Statistics Query and Reporting System Fatal (WISQARS™ Fatal), 1999–2012, retrieved September 2015 from http://www.cdc.gov/injury/wisqars/index.html; and Federal Bureau of Investigation and Bureau of Justice Statistics, Supplementary Homicide Reports (SHR), preliminary data (November 2015). (This table was prepared December 2015.)

Table 228.20. Number of nonfatal victimizations against students ages 12–18 and rate of victimization, by type of victimization, location, and year: 1992 through 2014

[Standard errors appear in parentheses]

Location and year	Number of nonfatal victimizations		Violent		Rate of victimization per 1,000 students		Violent	
	Total	Theft	All violent	Serious violent[1]	Total	Theft	All violent	Serious violent[1]
1	2	3	4	5	6	7	8	9
At school[2]								
1992	4,281,200 (225,600)	2,679,400 (147,660)	1,601,800 (121,630)	197,600 (35,430)	181.5 (7.99)	113.6 (5.64)	67.9 (4.77)	8.4 (1.48)
1993	4,692,800 (321,220)	2,477,100 (121,200)	2,215,700 (194,520)	535,500 (76,050)	193.5 (11.02)	102.1 (4.61)	91.4 (7.23)	22.1 (3.02)
1994	4,721,000 (271,730)	2,474,100 (121,260)	2,246,900 (165,530)	459,100 (58,110)	187.7 (9.04)	98.4 (4.46)	89.3 (5.95)	18.3 (2.24)
1995	4,400,700 (267,610)	2,468,400 (120,690)	1,932,200 (152,670)	294,500 (42,890)	172.2 (8.82)	96.6 (4.37)	75.6 (5.44)	11.5 (1.64)
1996	4,130,400 (281,640)	2,205,200 (107,650)	1,925,300 (166,690)	371,900 (54,150)	158.4 (9.17)	84.5 (3.88)	73.8 (5.81)	14.3 (2.01)
1997	3,610,900 (282,430)	1,975,000 (111,830)	1,635,900 (164,530)	376,200 (60,990)	136.6 (9.25)	74.7 (3.95)	61.9 (5.74)	14.2 (2.24)
1998	3,247,300 (254,250)	1,635,100 (104,210)	1,612,200 (155,840)	314,500 (49,770)	121.3 (8.27)	61.1 (3.69)	60.2 (5.34)	11.7 (1.80)
1999	3,152,400 (258,560)	1,752,200 (104,970)	1,400,200 (148,230)	281,100 (50,060)	117.0 (8.43)	65.1 (3.69)	52.0 (5.11)	10.4 (1.81)
2000	2,301,000 (211,140)	1,331,500 (95,940)	969,500 (115,680)	214,200 (40,980)	84.9 (7.00)	49.1 (3.34)	35.8 (4.02)	7.9 (1.48)
2001	2,521,300 (202,890)	1,348,500 (93,240)	1,172,700 (120,560)	259,400 (44,110)	92.3 (6.67)	49.4 (3.23)	42.9 (4.14)	9.5 (1.58)
2002	2,082,600 (212,520)	1,088,800 (77,110)	993,800 (126,210)	173,500 (37,300)	75.4 (6.96)	39.4 (2.69)	36.0 (4.29)	6.3 (1.32)
2003	2,308,800 (210,930)	1,270,500 (88,550)	1,038,300 (121,490)	188,400 (38,240)	87.4 (7.16)	48.1 (3.18)	39.3 (4.32)	7.1 (1.42)
2004	1,762,200 (154,390)	1,065,400 (75,160)	696,800 (83,100)	107,300 (25,110)	67.2 (5.40)	40.6 (2.76)	26.6 (3.03)	4.1 (0.95)
2005	1,678,600 (169,040)	875,900 (70,140)	802,600 (102,360)	140,300 (32,400)	63.2 (5.85)	33.0 (2.56)	30.2 (3.66)	5.3 (1.20)
2006[3]	1,799,900 (170,490)	859,000 (68,730)	940,900 (109,880)	249,900 (45,670)	67.5 (5.86)	32.2 (2.52)	35.3 (3.90)	9.4 (1.68)
2007	1,801,200 (188,450)	896,700 (66,230)	904,400 (114,320)	116,100 (25,430)	67.8 (6.40)	33.7 (2.41)	34.0 (4.02)	4.4 (0.94)
2008	1,435,500 (161,330)	648,000 (61,170)	787,500 (108,480)	128,700 (34,370)	54.3 (5.67)	24.5 (2.26)	29.8 (3.91)	4.9 (1.28)
2009	1,322,800 (168,370)	594,500 (54,480)	728,300 (111,550)	233,700 (51,610)	51.0 (6.00)	22.9 (2.05)	28.1 (4.08)	9.0 (1.94)
2010	892,000 (124,260)	469,800 (45,300)	422,300 (73,310)	155,000 (36,500)	34.9 (4.55)	18.4 (1.75)	16.5 (2.75)	6.1 (1.40)
2011	1,246,200 (139,940)	647,700 (61,500)	598,600 (84,090)	89,500 (23,360)	49.3 (5.11)	25.6 (2.36)	23.7 (3.16)	3.5 (0.91)
2012	1,364,900 (133,810)	615,600 (51,440)	749,200 (90,250)	89,000 (23,850)	52.4 (4.78)	23.6 (1.93)	28.8 (3.31)	3.4 (0.91)
2013	1,420,900 (176,390)	454,900 (43,390)	966,000 (134,140)	125,500 (32,110)	55.0 (6.24)	17.6 (1.65)	37.4 (4.84)	4.9 (1.22)
2014	850,100 (109,100)	363,700 (39,120)	486,400 (74,790)	93,800 (25,550)	33.0 (4.00)	14.1 (1.50)	18.9 (2.79)	3.6 (0.98)
Away from school								
1992	4,084,100 (218,910)	1,857,600 (118,610)	2,226,500 (149,210)	1,025,100 (92,600)	173.1 (7.81)	78.7 (4.66)	94.4 (5.70)	43.5 (3.72)
1993	3,835,900 (280,790)	1,731,100 (96,700)	2,104,800 (187,960)	1,004,300 (114,870)	158.2 (9.90)	71.4 (3.75)	86.8 (7.01)	41.4 (4.47)
1994	4,147,100 (234,640)	1,713,900 (96,250)	2,433,200 (174,580)	1,074,900 (101,370)	164.9 (8.44)	68.1 (3.61)	96.7 (6.24)	42.7 (3.80)
1995	3,626,600 (234,640)	1,604,800 (92,000)	2,021,800 (157,470)	829,700 (85,830)	141.9 (7.91)	62.8 (3.41)	79.1 (5.59)	32.5 (3.19)
1996	3,483,200 (250,620)	1,572,700 (87,830)	1,910,600 (165,810)	870,000 (96,510)	133.5 (8.32)	60.3 (3.22)	73.3 (5.79)	33.4 (3.50)
1997	3,717,600 (288,080)	1,710,700 (101,810)	2,006,900 (189,180)	853,300 (105,660)	140.7 (9.41)	64.7 (3.62)	75.9 (6.51)	32.3 (3.79)
1998	3,047,800 (243,270)	1,408,000 (94,900)	1,639,800 (157,700)	684,900 (85,520)	113.8 (7.96)	52.6 (3.38)	61.3 (5.40)	25.6 (3.04)
1999	2,713,600 (233,350)	1,129,200 (79,770)	1,584,500 (161,350)	675,400 (90,150)	100.8 (7.71)	41.9 (2.85)	58.8 (5.53)	25.1 (3.20)
2000	2,303,600 (211,310)	1,228,900 (90,770)	1,074,800 (124,280)	402,100 (62,950)	85.0 (7.01)	45.3 (3.17)	39.6 (4.30)	14.8 (2.24)
2001	1,780,300 (160,090)	961,400 (74,230)	819,000 (94,590)	314,800 (50,070)	65.2 (5.39)	35.2 (2.60)	30.0 (3.30)	11.5 (1.79)
2002	1,619,500 (178,050)	820,100 (64,530)	799,400 (108,260)	341,200 (59,590)	58.6 (5.92)	29.7 (2.27)	28.9 (3.71)	12.4 (2.09)
2003	1,824,100 (179,240)	780,900 (64,210)	1,043,200 (121,880)	412,800 (64,660)	69.1 (6.19)	29.6 (2.34)	39.5 (4.33)	15.6 (2.37)
2004	1,371,800 (130,480)	718,000 (59,070)	653,700 (79,660)	272,500 (45,080)	52.3 (4.63)	27.4 (2.19)	24.9 (2.91)	10.4 (1.68)
2005	1,429,000 (151,460)	637,700 (57,740)	791,300 (101,180)	257,100 (47,950)	53.8 (5.29)	24.0 (2.12)	29.8 (3.63)	9.7 (1.77)
2006[3]	1,413,100 (144,660)	714,200 (61,900)	698,900 (89,980)	263,600 (47,280)	53.0 (5.04)	26.8 (2.27)	26.2 (3.22)	9.9 (1.73)
2007	1,371,700 (154,740)	614,300 (52,740)	757,400 (100,440)	337,700 (55,630)	51.6 (5.34)	23.1 (1.94)	28.5 (3.55)	12.7 (2.01)
2008	1,132,600 (137,840)	498,500 (52,350)	634,100 (94,160)	258,600 (52,980)	42.8 (4.90)	18.9 (1.94)	24.0 (3.42)	9.8 (1.96)
2009	857,200 (124,770)	484,200 (48,320)	372,900 (70,660)	176,800 (42,890)	33.1 (4.54)	18.7 (1.83)	14.4 (2.63)	6.8 (1.62)
2010	689,900 (103,620)	378,800 (40,200)	311,200 (59,190)	167,300 (38,460)	27.0 (3.83)	14.8 (1.55)	12.2 (2.24)	6.5 (1.47)
2011	966,100 (117,200)	541,900 (55,160)	424,300 (66,350)	137,600 (31,000)	38.2 (4.33)	21.4 (2.13)	16.8 (2.52)	5.4 (1.20)
2012	991,200 (108,370)	470,800 (44,070)	520,400 (71,280)	169,900 (35,260)	38.0 (3.93)	18.1 (1.66)	20.0 (2.64)	6.5 (1.33)
2013	778,500 (115,110)	403,000 (40,470)	375,500 (68,800)	151,200 (36,490)	30.1 (4.19)	15.6 (1.54)	14.5 (2.56)	5.8 (1.38)
2014	621,300 (88,190)	288,900 (34,370)	332,400 (58,000)	165,000 (36,650)	24.1 (3.27)	11.2 (1.32)	12.9 (2.18)	6.4 (1.40)

[1] Serious violent victimization is also included in all violent victimization.
[2] "At school" includes inside the school building, on school property, and on the way to and from school.
[3] Due to methodological differences, use caution when comparing 2006 estimates to other years.
NOTE: "Serious violent victimization" includes the crimes of rape, sexual assault, robbery, and aggravated assault. "All violent victimization" includes serious violent crimes as well as simple assault. "Theft" includes attempted and completed purse-snatching, completed pickpocketing, and all attempted and completed thefts, with the exception of motor vehicle thefts. Theft does not include robbery, which involves the threat or use of force or use of force and s classified as a violent crime. "Total victimization" includes theft and violent crimes. Data in this table are from the National Crime Victimization Survey (NCVS); due to differences in time coverage and administration between the NCVS and the School Crime Supplement (SCS) to the NCVS, data in this table cannot be compared with data in tables that are based on the SCS. Detail may not sum to totals because of rounding.

SOURCE: U.S. Department of Justice, Bureau of Justice Statistics, National Crime Victimization Survey (NCVS), 1992 through 2014. (This table was prepared August 2015).

Table 228.25. Number of nonfatal victimizations against students ages 12–18 and rate of victimization, by type of victimization, location, and selected student characteristics: 2014

[Standard errors appear in parentheses]

Location and student characteristic	Number of nonfatal victimizations				Rate of victimization per 1,000 students				
	Total	Theft	Violent		Total	Theft	Violent		
			All violent	Serious violent[1]			All violent	Serious violent[1]	
1	2	3	4	5	6	7	8	9	
At school[2]									
Total	850,100 (109,100)	363,700 (39,120)	486,400 (74,790)	93,800 (25,550)	33.0 (4.00)	14.1 (1.50)	18.9 (2.79)	3.6 (0.98)	
Sex									
Male	461,800 (72,230)	202,000 (28,180)	259,900 (49,290)	69,500 ! (21,170)	34.8 (5.12)	15.2 (2.09)	19.6 (3.57)	5.2 ! (1.57)	
Female	388,300 (64,320)	161,800 (24,940)	226,600 (45,040)	24,300 ! (11,190)	31.0 (4.85)	12.9 (1.97)	18.1 (3.46)	1.9 ! (0.89)	
Age									
12–14	421,200 (67,910)	182,600 (26,650)	238,700 (46,610)	18,700 ! (9,580)	33.9 (5.13)	14.7 (2.11)	19.2 (3.60)	1.5 ! (0.77)	
15–18	428,900 (68,740)	181,200 (26,540)	247,700 (47,770)	75,100 (22,220)	32.2 (4.86)	13.6 (1.96)	18.6 (3.44)	5.6 (1.64)	
Race/ethnicity[3]									
White	473,400 (73,440)	211,500 (28,900)	262,000 (49,550)	59,800 ! (19,280)	34.6 (5.04)	15.4 (2.08)	19.1 (3.47)	4.4 ! (1.39)	
Black	111,300 (28,460)	51,600 (13,470)	59,700 (19,260)	10,800 ! (6,980)	27.6 (6.73)	12.8 (3.31)	14.8 (4.64)	2.7 ! (1.72)	
Hispanic	102,600 (27,040)	48,200 (12,980)	54,500 (18,200)	13,700 ! (7,990)	17.3 (4.40)	8.1 (2.17)	9.2 (3.00)	2.3 ! (1.34)	
Other	162,800 (36,330)	52,500 (13,600)	110,300 ! (28,300)	9,600 ! (6,520)	76.5 (15.41)	24.7 (6.27)	51.8 ! (12.34)	4.5 ! (3.03)	
Urbanicity[4]									
Urban	245,800 (47,520)	121,100 (21,290)	124,800 (30,620)	31,300 ! (12,990)	32.5 (5.91)	16.0 (2.77)	16.5 (3.90)	4.1 ! (1.69)	
Suburban	391,100 (64,630)	189,700 (27,220)	201,500 (41,720)	16,900 ! (9,050)	27.6 (4.33)	13.4 (1.90)	14.2 (2.85)	1.2 ! (0.64)	
Rural	213,200 (43,290)	53,000 (13,660)	160,200 (35,950)	45,600 ! (16,330)	52.8 (9.88)	13.1 (3.34)	39.7 (8.34)	11.3 ! (3.95)	
Household income									
Less than $15,000	125,800 (30,770)	41,400 (11,980)	84,400 ! (23,890)	8,400 ! (6,070)	66.9 (14.94)	22.0 (6.26)	44.9 ! (11.89)	4.5 ! (3.20)	
$15,000–29,999	75,900 (22,360)	44,200 (12,410)	31,700 (13,100)	14,100 ! (8,120)	26.1 (7.36)	15.2 (4.22)	10.9 (4.41)	4.8 ! (2.77)	
$30,000–49,999	156,500 (35,420)	61,200 (14,750)	95,300 (25,810)	10,700 ! (6,960)	35.6 (7.58)	13.9 (3.31)	21.7 (5.63)	2.4 ! (1.57)	
$50,000–74,999	119,200 (29,740)	35,600 (11,070)	83,600 (23,760)	6,000 ! (5,020)	36.1 (8.48)	10.8 (3.32)	25.3 (6.88)	1.8 ! (1.51)	
$75,000 or more	202,300 (41,880)	128,400 (21,990)	73,800 (21,980)	9,700 ! (6,570)	27.1 (5.33)	17.2 (2.90)	9.9 (2.88)	1.3 ! (0.88)	
Not reported	170,500 (37,430)	52,900 (13,650)	117,600 (29,480)	44,800 ! (16,160)	29.2 (6.08)	9.1 (2.32)	20.1 (4.85)	7.7 ! (2.71)	
Away from school									
Total	621,300 (88,190)	288,900 (34,370)	332,400 (58,000)	165,000 (36,650)	24.1 (3.27)	11.2 (1.32)	12.9 (2.18)	6.4 (1.40)	
Sex									
Male	332,100 (57,970)	150,100 (23,930)	182,000 (39,060)	107,100 (27,780)	25.0 (4.16)	11.3 (1.78)	13.7 (2.85)	8.1 (2.05)	
Female	289,200 (52,890)	138,800 (22,940)	150,300 (34,510)	57,900 (18,900)	23.1 (4.03)	11.1 (1.81)	12.0 (2.68)	4.6 (1.49)	
Age									
12–14	269,400 (50,470)	116,800 (20,880)	152,600 (34,840)	69,600 (21,180)	21.7 (3.88)	9.4 (1.66)	12.3 (2.72)	5.6 (1.67)	
15–18	351,900 (60,240)	172,100 (25,800)	179,800 (38,740)	95,400 (25,820)	26.4 (4.29)	12.9 (1.91)	13.5 (2.81)	7.2 (1.90)	
Race/ethnicity[3]									
White	373,200 (62,640)	191,900 (27,400)	181,300 (38,950)	79,300 (22,990)	27.2 (4.34)	14.0 (1.97)	13.2 (2.76)	5.8 (1.65)	
Black	103,300 (27,140)	36,600 (11,240)	66,600 (20,620)	32,500 (13,310)	25.7 (6.43)	9.1 (2.77)	16.6 (4.95)	8.1 ! (3.24)	
Hispanic	100,600 (26,700)	37,000 (11,300)	63,600 (20,030)	42,900 (15,730)	17.0 (4.35)	6.2 (1.89)	10.7 (3.30)	7.2 (2.61)	
Other	44,200 (16,020)	23,300 (8,870)	20,900 ! (10,230)	10,200 ! (6,780)	20.8 (7.26)	11.0 (4.13)	9.8 ! (4.71)	4.8 ! (3.15)	
Urbanicity[4]									
Urban	193,300 (40,610)	95,400 (18,710)	97,900 (26,240)	37,600 ! (14,530)	25.5 (5.10)	12.6 (2.44)	12.9 (3.36)	5.0 (1.89)	
Suburban	308,400 (55,180)	139,400 (22,990)	169,000 (37,210)	100,900 (26,750)	21.8 (3.73)	9.8 (1.61)	11.9 (2.55)	7.1 (1.85)	
Rural	119,600 (29,810)	54,100 (13,810)	65,500 (20,410)	26,400 (11,760)	29.6 (7.00)	13.4 (3.38)	16.2 (4.89)	6.5 ! (2.87)	
Household income									
Less than $15,000	85,800 ! (24,140)	20,800 ! (8,360)	64,900 (20,290)	22,900 (10,810)	45.6 (12.00)	11.1 ! (4.41)	34.5 (10.23)	12.2 (5.62)	
$15,000–29,999	105,600 (27,520)	49,500 (13,180)	56,000 (18,520)	34,000 (13,670)	36.4 (8.94)	17.1 (4.48)	19.3 (6.15)	11.7 (4.60)	
$30,000–49,999	93,000 (25,400)	40,200 (11,800)	52,800 (17,850)	23,400 (10,920)	21.1 (5.54)	9.1 (2.66)	12.0 (3.95)	5.3 (2.45)	
$50,000–74,999	103,600 (27,200)	51,000 (13,390)	52,600 (17,810)	19,100 (9,720)	31.4 (7.81)	15.5 (4.00)	15.9 (5.23)	5.8 ! (2.90)	
$75,000 or more	109,700 (28,210)	57,300 (14,240)	52,400 (17,770)	35,500 ! (14,020)	14.7 (3.66)	7.7 (1.90)	7.0 (2.34)	4.8 (1.86)	
Not reported	123,700 (30,450)	70,000 (15,840)	53,700 (18,050)	30,100 (12,690)	21.2 (5.00)	12.0 (2.68)	9.2 (3.02)	5.1 (2.14)	

! Interpret data with caution. Estimate based on 10 or fewer sample cases, or the coefficient of variation is greater than 50 percent.
[1] Serious violent victimization is also included in all violent victimization.
[2] "At school" includes inside the school building, on school property, and on the way to and from school.
[3] Race categories exclude persons of Hispanic ethnicity. "Other" includes Asians, Pacific Islanders, American Indians/Alaska Natives, and persons of Two or more races.
[4] Refers to the Standard Metropolitan Statistical Area (MSA) status of the respondent's household as defined in 2000 by the U.S. Census Bureau. Categories include "central city of an MSA (Urban)," "in MSA but not in central city (Suburban)," and "not MSA (Rural)."
NOTE: "Serious violent victimization" includes the crimes of rape, sexual assault, robbery, and aggravated assault. "All violent victimization" includes serious violent crimes as well as simple assault. "Theft" includes attempted and completed purse-snatching, completed pickpocketing, and all attempted and completed thefts, with the exception of motor vehicle thefts. Theft does not include robbery, which involves the threat or use of force and is classified as a violent crime. "Total victimization" includes theft and violent crimes. Data in this table are from the National Crime Victimization Survey (NCVS) and are reported in accordance with Bureau of Justice Statistics standards. Detail may not sum to totals because of rounding and missing data on student characteristics. The population size for students ages 12–18 was 25,773,800 in 2014.
SOURCE: U.S. Department of Justice, Bureau of Justice Statistics, National Crime Victimization Survey (NCVS), 2014. (This table was prepared August 2015.)

Table 228.30. Percentage of students ages 12–18 who reported criminal victimization at school during the previous 6 months, by type of victimization and selected student and school characteristics: Selected years, 1995 through 2013

[Standard errors appear in parentheses]

Type of victimization and student or school characteristic	1995		1999		2001		2003		2005		2007		2009		2011		2013	
1	2		3		4		5		6		7		8		9		10	
Total	**9.5**	**(0.35)**	**7.6**	**(0.35)**	**5.5**	**(0.31)**	**5.1**	**(0.24)**	**4.3**	**(0.31)**	**4.3**	**(0.30)**	**3.9**	**(0.28)**	**3.5**	**(0.28)**	**3.0**	**(0.25)**
Sex																		
Male	10.0	(0.46)	7.8	(0.46)	6.1	(0.41)	5.4	(0.33)	4.6	(0.42)	4.5	(0.43)	4.6	(0.40)	3.7	(0.35)	3.2	(0.40)
Female	9.0	(0.47)	7.3	(0.46)	4.9	(0.39)	4.8	(0.36)	3.9	(0.38)	4.0	(0.39)	3.2	(0.35)	3.4	(0.38)	2.8	(0.34)
Race/ethnicity[1]																		
White	9.8	(0.37)	7.5	(0.44)	5.8	(0.39)	5.4	(0.31)	4.7	(0.35)	4.3	(0.38)	3.9	(0.37)	3.6	(0.35)	3.0	(0.32)
Black	10.2	(1.04)	9.9	(0.85)	6.1	(0.78)	5.3	(0.80)	3.8	(0.80)	4.3	(0.83)	4.4	(0.74)	4.6	(0.89)	3.2	(0.71)
Hispanic	7.6	(0.90)	5.7	(0.77)	4.6	(0.64)	3.9	(0.50)	3.9	(0.70)	3.6	(0.54)	3.9	(0.75)	2.9	(0.47)	3.2	(0.46)
Asian	—	(†)	—	(†)	—	(†)	—	(†)	1.5 !	(0.68)	3.6 !	(1.38)	‡	(†)	2.5 !	(1.23)	2.6 !	(1.08)
Other	8.8	(1.54)	6.4	(1.28)	3.1	(0.91)	5.0	(1.08)	4.3 !	(2.00)	8.1	(2.01)	‡	(†)	3.7 !	(1.37)	2.2 !	(1.08)
Grade																		
6th	9.6	(0.97)	8.0	(1.24)	5.9	(0.90)	3.8	(0.77)	4.6	(0.83)	4.1	(0.87)	3.7	(0.91)	3.8	(0.85)	4.1	(0.92)
7th	11.2	(0.81)	8.2	(0.81)	5.8	(0.66)	6.3	(0.74)	5.4	(0.71)	4.7	(0.69)	3.4	(0.70)	3.1	(0.61)	2.5	(0.51)
8th	10.5	(0.78)	7.6	(0.84)	4.3	(0.61)	5.2	(0.65)	3.6	(0.63)	4.4	(0.63)	3.8	(0.78)	3.8	(0.67)	2.3	(0.52)
9th	11.9	(0.88)	8.9	(0.79)	7.9	(0.81)	6.3	(0.70)	4.7	(0.69)	5.3	(0.75)	5.3	(0.85)	5.1	(0.83)	4.1	(0.76)
10th	9.1	(0.76)	8.0	(0.82)	6.5	(0.77)	4.8	(0.63)	4.3	(0.71)	4.4	(0.67)	4.2	(0.79)	3.0	(0.58)	3.3	(0.57)
11th	7.3	(0.74)	7.2	(0.88)	4.8	(0.62)	5.1	(0.68)	3.6	(0.51)	4.0	(0.75)	4.7	(0.88)	3.1	(0.65)	3.3	(0.65)
12th	6.1	(0.74)	4.8	(0.81)	2.9	(0.52)	3.6	(0.71)	3.8	(0.85)	2.7	(0.70)	2.0	(0.52)	2.9	(0.68)	2.0 !	(0.67)
Urbanicity[2]																		
Urban	9.3	(0.64)	8.4	(0.69)	5.9	(0.58)	6.1	(0.58)	5.3	(0.65)	4.5	(0.58)	4.2	(0.56)	4.3	(0.56)	3.3	(0.47)
Suburban	10.3	(0.49)	7.6	(0.43)	5.7	(0.40)	4.8	(0.33)	4.2	(0.34)	4.1	(0.38)	4.0	(0.36)	3.3	(0.34)	3.2	(0.35)
Rural	8.3	(0.79)	6.4	(0.96)	4.7	(0.93)	4.7	(0.75)	2.8	(0.69)	4.4	(0.55)	3.1	(0.66)	2.8	(0.57)	2.0	(0.58)
Sector																		
Public	9.8	(0.38)	7.9	(0.37)	5.7	(0.34)	5.2	(0.26)	4.4	(0.32)	4.6	(0.32)	4.1	(0.30)	3.7	(0.29)	3.1	(0.27)
Private	6.6	(0.90)	4.5	(0.80)	3.4	(0.72)	4.9	(0.79)	2.7	(0.77)	1.1 !	(0.50)	1.8 !	(0.76)	1.9 !	(0.68)	2.8 !	(0.89)
Theft	**7.1**	**(0.29)**	**5.7**	**(0.32)**	**4.2**	**(0.24)**	**4.0**	**(0.21)**	**3.1**	**(0.27)**	**3.0**	**(0.23)**	**2.8**	**(0.23)**	**2.6**	**(0.23)**	**1.9**	**(0.20)**
Sex																		
Male	7.1	(0.38)	5.7	(0.41)	4.5	(0.34)	4.0	(0.27)	3.1	(0.34)	3.0	(0.34)	3.4	(0.36)	2.6	(0.29)	2.0	(0.30)
Female	7.1	(0.41)	5.7	(0.43)	3.8	(0.33)	4.1	(0.32)	3.2	(0.36)	3.0	(0.33)	2.1	(0.28)	2.6	(0.33)	1.8	(0.28)
Race/ethnicity[1]																		
White	7.4	(0.32)	5.8	(0.43)	4.2	(0.30)	4.3	(0.28)	3.4	(0.32)	3.1	(0.29)	2.9	(0.31)	2.5	(0.28)	1.6	(0.22)
Black	7.1	(0.85)	7.4	(0.77)	5.0	(0.68)	4.0	(0.66)	2.7	(0.65)	3.0	(0.70)	2.5	(0.61)	3.7	(0.78)	2.7	(0.67)
Hispanic	5.8	(0.78)	3.9	(0.61)	3.7	(0.69)	3.0	(0.41)	3.1	(0.64)	2.2	(0.47)	3.0	(0.63)	2.0	(0.41)	1.8	(0.39)
Asian	—	(†)	—	(†)	—	(†)	—	(†)	‡	(†)	3.2 !	(1.32)	‡	(†)	2.5 !	(1.23)	2.6 !	(1.08)
Other	6.5	(1.40)	4.4	(0.98)	2.9	(0.87)	4.4	(1.04)	‡	(†)	4.5 !	(1.57)	‡	(†)	2.8 !	(1.21)	‡	(†)
Grade																		
6th	5.4	(0.66)	5.2	(0.97)	4.0	(0.70)	2.2	(0.63)	2.8	(0.75)	2.7	(0.77)	1.3 !	(0.52)	2.7	(0.70)	1.4 !	(0.57)
7th	8.1	(0.71)	6.0	(0.73)	3.4	(0.51)	4.8	(0.67)	2.9	(0.50)	2.7	(0.54)	2.1	(0.57)	1.9	(0.44)	1.4	(0.38)
8th	7.9	(0.72)	5.9	(0.81)	3.3	(0.50)	4.1	(0.56)	2.4	(0.53)	2.5	(0.54)	2.0	(0.55)	2.0	(0.48)	1.0 !	(0.33)
9th	9.1	(0.77)	6.5	(0.71)	6.2	(0.76)	5.3	(0.62)	3.7	(0.61)	4.6	(0.70)	4.9	(0.80)	4.4	(0.78)	2.7	(0.58)
10th	7.7	(0.72)	6.5	(0.73)	5.7	(0.72)	3.7	(0.59)	3.8	(0.66)	3.6	(0.63)	3.5	(0.72)	2.1	(0.50)	2.6	(0.48)
11th	5.5	(0.66)	5.5	(0.67)	3.8	(0.57)	4.1	(0.64)	2.8	(0.45)	2.6	(0.61)	3.3	(0.74)	2.7	(0.58)	2.3	(0.50)
12th	4.6	(0.67)	4.0	(0.71)	2.3	(0.45)	3.1	(0.68)	3.5	(0.85)	1.9	(0.55)	1.5	(0.44)	2.4	(0.62)	1.6 !	(0.62)
Urbanicity[2]																		
Urban	6.6	(0.51)	6.9	(0.59)	4.5	(0.52)	4.5	(0.47)	3.6	(0.51)	2.8	(0.48)	2.9	(0.45)	3.0	(0.45)	2.4	(0.44)
Suburban	7.6	(0.40)	5.4	(0.36)	4.3	(0.32)	3.8	(0.27)	3.2	(0.31)	3.0	(0.31)	2.8	(0.32)	2.5	(0.30)	1.9	(0.27)
Rural	6.8	(0.66)	5.0	(0.95)	3.4	(0.65)	3.9	(0.66)	2.2 !	(0.68)	3.2	(0.46)	2.3	(0.59)	2.0	(0.47)	0.8	(0.24)
Sector																		
Public	7.3	(0.32)	5.9	(0.34)	4.4	(0.26)	4.0	(0.22)	3.3	(0.28)	3.2	(0.25)	2.9	(0.25)	2.7	(0.24)	1.9	(0.21)
Private	5.2	(0.74)	4.3	(0.78)	2.5	(0.67)	4.0	(0.77)	1.3 !	(0.48)	1.1 !	(0.50)	‡	(†)	1.2 !	(0.52)	2.0 !	(0.76)
Violent	**3.0**	**(0.21)**	**2.3**	**(0.18)**	**1.8**	**(0.19)**	**1.3**	**(0.15)**	**1.2**	**(0.15)**	**1.6**	**(0.18)**	**1.4**	**(0.17)**	**1.1**	**(0.15)**	**1.2**	**(0.15)**
Sex																		
Male	3.5	(0.27)	2.5	(0.26)	2.1	(0.26)	1.8	(0.24)	1.6	(0.25)	1.7	(0.26)	1.6	(0.25)	1.2	(0.21)	1.3	(0.23)
Female	2.4	(0.25)	2.0	(0.22)	1.5	(0.24)	0.9	(0.16)	0.8	(0.15)	1.4	(0.23)	1.1	(0.21)	0.9	(0.17)	1.1	(0.23)
Race/ethnicity[1]																		
White	3.0	(0.23)	2.1	(0.22)	2.0	(0.24)	1.4	(0.18)	1.3	(0.20)	1.5	(0.22)	1.2	(0.21)	1.2	(0.17)	1.5	(0.24)
Black	3.4	(0.61)	3.5	(0.55)	1.3 !	(0.40)	1.6	(0.41)	1.3 !	(0.46)	1.6 !	(0.50)	2.3	(0.62)	1.1 !	(0.42)	‡	(†)
Hispanic	2.7	(0.43)	1.9	(0.38)	1.5	(0.41)	1.1	(0.28)	0.9	(0.24)	1.4	(0.42)	1.3 !	(0.40)	1.0	(0.28)	1.5	(0.26)
Asian	—	(†)	—	(†)	—	(†)	—	(†)	‡	(†)	‡	(†)	#	(†)	#	(†)	‡	(†)
Other	2.5 !	(0.87)	2.2 !	(0.81)	‡	(†)	‡	(†)	‡	(†)	4.5 !	(1.50)	‡	(†)	‡	(†)	‡	(†)
Grade																		
6th	5.1	(0.73)	3.8	(0.76)	2.6	(0.66)	1.9	(0.53)	1.9	(0.55)	1.5 !	(0.54)	2.6 !	(0.83)	1.3 !	(0.49)	2.7	(0.73)
7th	3.8	(0.54)	2.6	(0.43)	2.6	(0.47)	1.7	(0.43)	2.6	(0.53)	2.4	(0.50)	1.2 !	(0.42)	1.2 !	(0.41)	1.2 !	(0.38)
8th	3.1	(0.44)	2.4	(0.44)	1.3 !	(0.34)	1.5	(0.35)	1.4	(0.39)	2.1	(0.47)	2.0	(0.60)	2.1	(0.50)	1.4	(0.42)
9th	3.4	(0.50)	3.2	(0.47)	2.4	(0.46)	1.5	(0.31)	1.0	(0.29)	1.2 !	(0.37)	0.9 !	(0.37)	1.1 !	(0.35)	1.4 !	(0.44)
10th	2.1	(0.36)	1.7	(0.39)	1.2	(0.31)	1.4	(0.36)	0.5 !	(0.24)	1.2 !	(0.39)	1.0 !	(0.37)	0.9 !	(0.34)	1.0 !	(0.35)
11th	1.9	(0.40)	1.8 !	(0.58)	1.6	(0.39)	1.0 !	(0.33)	0.7 !	(0.31)	1.5 !	(0.46)	1.5 !	(0.51)	‡	(†)	1.0 !	(0.43)
12th	1.9	(0.41)	0.8 !	(0.31)	0.9 !	(0.31)	0.5 !	(0.26)	‡	(†)	0.8 !	(0.35)	‡	(†)	‡	(†)	‡	(†)
Urbanicity[2]																		
Urban	3.3	(0.40)	2.3	(0.38)	1.7	(0.29)	1.8	(0.32)	1.8	(0.34)	2.0	(0.35)	1.8	(0.41)	1.4	(0.31)	0.9	(0.21)
Suburban	3.5	(0.30)	2.4	(0.26)	1.7	(0.20)	1.2	(0.19)	1.1	(0.18)	1.3	(0.23)	1.3	(0.23)	0.9	(0.16)	1.4	(0.21)
Rural	1.8	(0.31)	1.9	(0.50)	2.0 !	(0.64)	0.9 !	(0.31)	0.6 !	(0.26)	1.7	(0.36)	0.8 !	(0.32)	1.0 !	(0.31)	1.1 !	(0.46)
Sector																		
Public	3.1	(0.22)	2.5	(0.20)	1.9	(0.20)	1.4	(0.15)	1.2	(0.15)	1.7	(0.20)	1.4	(0.19)	1.1	(0.15)	1.2	(0.16)
Private	1.7	(0.45)	‡	(†)	1.0 !	(0.32)	0.9 !	(0.39)	1.4 !	(0.60)	‡	(†)	‡	(†)	‡	(†)	‡	(†)

See notes at end of table.

Table 228.30. Percentage of students ages 12–18 who reported criminal victimization at school during the previous 6 months, by type of victimization and selected student and school characteristics: Selected years, 1995 through 2013—Continued

[Standard errors appear in parentheses]

Type of victimization and student or school characteristic	1995		1999		2001		2003		2005		2007		2009		2011		2013	
1	2		3		4		5		6		7		8		9		10	
Serious violent[3]	**0.7**	**(0.09)**	**0.5**	**(0.09)**	**0.4**	**(0.08)**	**0.2**	**(0.06)**	**0.3**	**(0.07)**	**0.4**	**(0.08)**	**0.3**	**(0.09)**	**0.1 !**	**(0.05)**	**0.2 !**	**(0.07)**
Sex																		
Male	0.9	(0.14)	0.6	(0.12)	0.5	(0.11)	0.3 !	(0.10)	0.3 !	(0.10)	0.5 !	(0.14)	0.6	(0.16)	0.2 !	(0.08)	0.2 !	(0.10)
Female	0.4	(0.10)	0.5	(0.12)	0.4 !	(0.12)	‡	(†)	0.3	(0.07)	0.2 !	(0.08)	‡	(†)	‡	(†)	0.2 !	(0.10)
Race/ethnicity[1]																		
White	0.6	(0.09)	0.4	(0.09)	0.4	(0.08)	0.2 !	(0.06)	0.3 !	(0.09)	0.2 !	(0.08)	0.3 !	(0.10)	0.2 !	(0.07)	0.2 !	(0.09)
Black	1.0 !	(0.31)	1.2	(0.33)	0.5 !	(0.25)	‡	(†)	‡	(†)	‡	(†)	‡	(†)	‡	(†)	‡	(†)
Hispanic	0.9 !	(0.30)	0.6 !	(0.22)	0.8 !	(0.33)	0.4 !	(0.18)	0.4 !	(0.16)	0.8 !	(0.32)	‡	(†)	‡	(†)	0.4 !	(0.17)
Asian	—	(†)	—	(†)	—	(†)	—	(†)	‡	(†)	‡	(†)	#	(†)	#	(†)	‡	(†)
Other	‡	(†)	#	(†)	#	(†)	‡	(†)	‡	(†)	‡	(†)	#	(†)	#	(†)	‡	(†)
Grade																		
6th	1.5	(0.42)	1.3 !	(0.40)	‡	(†)	#	(†)	‡	(†)	‡	(†)	‡	(†)	‡	(†)	0.8 !	(0.42)
7th	0.9	(0.24)	0.9 !	(0.27)	0.6 !	(0.24)	‡	(†)	‡	(†)	0.4 !	(0.20)	‡	(†)	0.5 !	(0.23)	‡	(†)
8th	0.8 !	(0.23)	0.5 !	(0.22)	0.3 !	(0.14)	0.3 !	(0.15)	‡	(†)	‡	(†)	‡	(†)	#	(†)	‡	(†)
9th	0.7	(0.21)	0.6 !	(0.18)	0.8 !	(0.31)	0.6 !	(0.21)	‡	(†)	‡	(†)	‡	(†)	‡	(†)	‡	(†)
10th	0.4 !	(0.17)	‡	(†)	0.4 !	(0.18)	#	(†)	‡	(†)	‡	(†)	‡	(†)	#	(†)	‡	(†)
11th	0.4 !	(0.16)	‡	(†)	‡	(†)	‡	(†)	‡	(†)	0.6 !	(0.27)	‡	(†)	#	(†)	‡	(†)
12th	‡	(†)	‡	(†)	‡	(†)	#	(†)	‡	(†)	‡	(†)	‡	(†)	#	(†)	‡	(†)
Urbanicity[2]																		
Urban	1.3	(0.24)	0.7	(0.19)	0.5	(0.15)	0.4 !	(0.14)	0.4 !	(0.17)	0.7 !	(0.23)	0.6 !	(0.22)	‡	(†)	0.3 !	(0.16)
Suburban	0.6	(0.12)	0.5	(0.11)	0.4	(0.09)	0.1 !	(0.05)	0.3 !	(0.08)	0.2 !	(0.09)	0.3 !	(0.11)	‡	(†)	0.2 !	(0.08)
Rural	0.3 !	(0.10)	0.4 !	(0.18)	0.5 !	(0.24)	‡	(†)	‡	(†)	‡	(†)	‡	(†)	‡	(†)	‡	(†)
Sector																		
Public	0.7	(0.10)	0.6	(0.10)	0.5	(0.09)	0.2	(0.06)	0.3	(0.06)	0.4	(0.09)	0.4	(0.10)	0.1 !	(0.06)	0.2 !	(0.08)
Private	‡	(†)	#	(†)	#	(†)	#	(†)	‡	(†)	‡	(†)	‡	(†)	#	(†)	‡	(†)

—Not available.
†Not applicable.
#Rounds to zero.
!Interpret data with caution. The coefficient of variation (CV) for this estimate is between 30 and 50 percent.
‡Reporting standards not met. Either there are too few cases for a reliable estimate or the coefficient of variation (CV) is 50 percent or greater.
[1]Race categories exclude persons of Hispanic ethnicity. "Other" includes American Indians/Alaska Natives, Asians (prior to 2005), Pacific Islanders, and, from 2003 onward, persons of Two or more races. Due to changes in racial/ethnic categories, comparisons of race/ethnicity across years should be made with caution.
[2]Refers to the Standard Metropolitan Statistical Area (MSA) status of the respondent's household as defined in 2000 by the U.S. Census Bureau. Categories include "central city of an MSA (Urban)," "in MSA but not in central city (Suburban)," and "not MSA (Rural)."

[3]Serious violent victimization is also included in violent victimization.
NOTE: "Total victimization" includes theft and violent victimization. A single student could report more than one type of victimization. In the total victimization section, students who reported both theft and violent victimization are counted only once. "Theft" includes attempted and completed purse-snatching, completed pickpocketing, and all attempted and completed thefts, with the exception of motor vehicle thefts. Theft does not include robbery, which involves the threat or use of force and is classified as a violent crime. "Serious violent victimization" includes the crimes of rape, sexual assault, robbery, and aggravated assault. "Violent victimization" includes the serious violent crimes as well as simple assault. "At school" includes the school building, on school property, on a school bus, and, from 2001 onward, going to and from school.
SOURCE: U.S. Department of Justice, Bureau of Justice Statistics, School Crime Supplement (SCS) to the National Crime Victimization Survey, selected years, 1995 through 2013. (This table was prepared August 2014.)

Table 228.40. Percentage of students in grades 9–12 who reported being threatened or injured with a weapon on school property during the previous 12 months, by selected student characteristics and number of times threatened or injured: Selected years, 1993 through 2013

[Standard errors appear in parentheses]

Number of times and year	Total	Sex		Race/ethnicity[1]							Grade			
		Male	Female	White	Black	Hispanic	Asian[2]	Pacific Islander[2]	American Indian/ Alaska Native[2]	Two or more races[2]	9th grade	10th grade	11th grade	12th grade
1	2	3	4	5	6	7	8	9	10	11	12	13	14	15
At least once														
1993	7.3 (0.44)	9.2 (0.64)	5.4 (0.40)	6.3 (0.58)	11.2 (0.95)	8.6 (0.83)	(†)	(†)	11.7 (2.50)	—	9.4 (0.92)	7.3 (0.59)	7.3 (0.64)	5.5 (0.62)
1995	8.4 (0.52)	10.9 (0.57)	5.8 (0.68)	7.0 (0.53)	11.0 (1.61)	12.4 (1.44)	(†)	(†)	11.4 ! (4.22)	—	9.6 (0.96)	9.6 (1.03)	7.7 (0.64)	6.7 (0.57)
1997	7.4 (0.45)	10.2 (0.71)	4.0 (0.32)	6.2 (0.56)	9.9 (0.91)	9.0 (0.63)	(†)	(†)	12.5 ! (5.15)	—	10.1 (1.02)	7.9 (1.14)	5.9 (0.70)	5.8 (0.80)
1999	7.7 (0.42)	9.5 (0.80)	5.8 (0.64)	6.6 (0.35)	7.6 (0.85)	9.8 (1.09)	7.7 (1.05)	15.6 (4.46)	13.2 ! (5.45)	9.3 (1.22)	10.5 (0.95)	8.2 (0.92)	6.1 (0.46)	5.1 (0.79)
2001	8.9 (0.55)	11.5 (0.66)	6.5 (0.52)	8.5 (0.66)	9.3 (0.71)	8.9 (1.05)	11.3 (2.73)	24.8 (7.16)	15.2 ! (4.57)	10.3 (2.33)	12.7 (0.89)	9.1 (0.75)	6.9 (0.65)	5.3 (0.52)
2003	9.2 (0.75)	11.6 (0.96)	6.5 (0.61)	7.8 (0.77)	10.9 (0.80)	9.4 (1.23)	11.5 (2.66)	16.3 (4.31)	22.1 (4.79)	18.7 (3.11)	12.1 (1.25)	9.2 (1.02)	7.3 (0.69)	6.3 (0.92)
2005	7.9 (0.35)	9.7 (0.42)	6.1 (0.41)	7.2 (0.46)	8.1 (0.69)	9.8 (0.86)	4.6 (1.10)	14.5 ! (4.93)	9.8 (2.67)	10.7 (2.33)	10.5 (0.63)	8.8 (0.72)	5.5 (0.43)	5.8 (0.52)
2007	7.8 (0.44)	10.2 (0.59)	5.4 (0.41)	6.9 (0.52)	9.7 (0.86)	8.7 (0.60)	7.6 ! (2.29)	8.1 ! (2.45)	5.9 (1.24)	13.3 (2.25)	9.2 (0.69)	8.4 (0.51)	6.8 (0.57)	6.3 (0.64)
2009	7.7 (0.37)	9.6 (0.59)	5.5 (0.37)	6.4 (0.43)	9.4 (0.80)	9.1 (0.61)	5.5 (0.91)	12.5 (3.11)	16.5 (2.68)	9.2 (1.50)	8.7 (0.53)	8.4 (0.72)	7.9 (0.60)	5.2 (0.53)
2011	7.4 (0.31)	9.5 (0.39)	5.2 (0.37)	6.1 (0.35)	8.9 (0.64)	9.2 (0.81)	7.0 (0.99)	11.3 (3.23)	8.2 (1.52)	9.9 (1.35)	8.3 (0.63)	7.7 (0.58)	7.3 (0.61)	5.9 (0.45)
2013	6.9 (0.38)	7.7 (0.54)	6.1 (0.40)	5.8 (0.32)	8.4 (0.82)	8.5 (0.73)	5.3 (1.41)	8.7 ! (2.71)	18.5 (5.24)	7.7 (2.11)	8.5 (0.75)	7.0 (0.67)	6.8 (0.60)	4.9 (0.61)
Number of times, 2013														
0 times	93.1 (0.38)	92.3 (0.54)	93.9 (0.40)	94.2 (0.32)	91.6 (0.82)	91.5 (0.73)	94.7 (1.41)	91.3 (2.71)	81.5 (5.24)	92.3 (2.11)	91.5 (0.75)	93.0 (0.67)	93.2 (0.60)	95.1 (0.61)
1 time	3.0 (0.22)	3.0 (0.25)	3.0 (0.33)	2.7 (0.27)	3.8 (0.51)	3.3 (0.51)	1.7 ! (0.51)	2.0 (0.59)	9.6 ! (3.14)	3.1 ! (0.96)	3.5 (0.50)	3.0 (0.52)	3.4 (0.39)	2.0 (0.27)
2 or 3 times	1.7 (0.14)	1.7 (0.21)	1.6 (0.20)	1.6 (0.17)	1.8 (0.35)	1.6 (0.29)	‡	‡	(†)	2.2 ! (0.67)	2.5 (0.37)	1.7 (0.26)	1.3 (0.24)	1.1 (0.21)
4 to 11 times	1.3 (0.14)	1.7 (0.21)	0.9 (0.18)	0.8 (0.12)	1.7 (0.36)	2.3 (0.34)	‡	‡	4.9 ! (2.34)	1.5 ! (0.63)	1.5 (0.22)	1.4 (0.30)	1.3 (0.28)	1.0 (0.21)
12 or more times	0.9 (0.11)	1.3 (0.19)	0.6 (0.08)	0.7 (0.17)	1.2 (0.23)	1.2 (0.25)	‡	‡	(†)	‡	1.0 (0.20)	0.9 (0.20)	0.9 (0.22)	0.9 (0.25)

—Not available.
†Not applicable.
!Interpret data with caution. The coefficient of variation (CV) for this estimate is between 30 and 50 percent.
‡Reporting standards not met. Either there are too few cases for a reliable estimate or the coefficient of variation (CV) is 50 percent or greater.
[1]Race categories exclude persons of Hispanic ethnicity.

[2]Before 1999, Asian students and Pacific Islander students were not categorized separately, and students could not be classified as Two or more races. Because the response categories changed in 1999, caution should be used in comparing data on race from 1993, 1995, and 1997 with data from later years.
NOTE: Survey respondents were asked about being threatened or injured "with a weapon such as a gun, knife, or club on school property." "On school property" was not defined for respondents. Detail may not sum to totals because of rounding.
SOURCE: Centers for Disease Control and Prevention, Division of Adolescent and School Health, Youth Risk Behavior Surveillance System (YRBSS), 1993 through 2013. (This table was prepared June 2014.)

Table 228.50. Percentage of public school students in grades 9–12 who reported being threatened or injured with a weapon on school property at least one time during the previous 12 months, by state: Selected years, 2003 through 2013

[Standard errors appear in parentheses]

State	2003		2005		2007		2009		2011		2013	
1	2		3		4		5		6		7	
United States[1]	9.2	(0.75)	7.9	(0.35)	7.8	(0.44)	7.7	(0.37)	7.4	(0.31)	6.9	(0.38)
Alabama	7.2	(0.91)	10.6	(0.86)	—	(†)	10.4	(1.56)	7.6	(1.20)	9.9	(1.17)
Alaska	8.1	(1.01)	—	(†)	7.7	(0.88)	7.3	(0.90)	5.6	(0.70)	—	(†)
Arizona	9.7	(1.10)	10.7	(0.55)	11.2	(0.79)	9.3	(0.92)	10.4	(0.74)	9.1	(1.32)
Arkansas	—	(†)	9.6	(1.06)	9.1	(1.03)	11.9	(1.38)	6.3	(0.85)	10.9	(1.14)
California	—	(†)	—	(†)	—	(†)	—	(†)	—	(†)	—	(†)
Colorado	—	(†)	7.6	(0.75)	—	(†)	8.0	(0.74)	6.7	(0.80)	—	(†)
Connecticut	—	(†)	9.1	(0.91)	7.7	(0.59)	7.0	(0.62)	6.8	(0.71)	7.1	(0.74)
Delaware	7.7	(0.60)	6.2	(0.63)	5.6	(0.50)	7.8	(0.63)	6.4	(0.62)	5.6	(0.46)
District of Columbia	12.7	(1.42)	12.1	(0.78)	11.3	(0.98)	—	(†)	8.7	(0.92)	—	(†)
Florida	8.4	(0.44)	7.9	(0.45)	8.6	(0.57)	8.2	(0.39)	7.2	(0.31)	7.1	(0.37)
Georgia	8.2	(0.75)	8.3	(2.08)	8.1	(0.81)	8.2	(0.83)	11.7	(2.08)	7.2	(0.81)
Hawaii	—	(†)	6.8	(0.87)	6.4	(1.10)	7.7	(1.03)	6.3	(0.62)	—	(†)
Idaho	9.4	(0.82)	8.3	(0.59)	10.2	(1.07)	7.9	(0.62)	7.3	(0.99)	5.8	(0.59)
Illinois	—	(†)	—	(†)	7.8	(0.69)	8.8	(0.86)	7.6	(0.48)	8.5	(0.82)
Indiana	6.7	(0.91)	8.8	(0.96)	9.6	(0.68)	6.5	(0.66)	6.8	(1.14)	—	(†)
Iowa	—	(†)	7.8	(1.02)	7.1	(0.86)	—	(†)	6.3	(0.85)	—	(†)
Kansas	—	(†)	7.4	(0.82)	8.6	(1.12)	6.2	(0.62)	5.6	(0.68)	5.3	(0.65)
Kentucky	5.2	(0.72)	8.0	(0.75)	8.3	(0.53)	7.9	(1.00)	7.4	(0.98)	5.4	(0.57)
Louisiana	—	(†)	—	(†)	—	(†)	9.5	(1.29)	8.7	(1.18)	10.5	(0.99)
Maine	8.5	(0.78)	7.1	(0.68)	6.8	(0.84)	7.7	(0.32)	6.8	(0.26)	5.3	(0.29)
Maryland	—	(†)	11.7	(1.30)	9.6	(0.86)	9.1	(0.75)	8.4	(0.67)	9.4	(0.22)
Massachusetts	6.3	(0.54)	5.4	(0.44)	5.3	(0.47)	7.0	(0.58)	6.8	(0.67)	4.4	(0.38)
Michigan	9.7	(0.57)	8.6	(0.81)	8.1	(0.77)	9.4	(0.63)	6.8	(0.50)	6.7	(0.52)
Minnesota	—	(†)	—	(†)	—	(†)	—	(†)	—	(†)	—	(†)
Mississippi	6.6	(0.82)	—	(†)	8.3	(0.59)	8.0	(0.69)	7.5	(0.63)	8.8	(0.78)
Missouri	7.5	(0.93)	9.1	(1.19)	9.3	(1.03)	7.8	(0.76)	—	(†)	—	(†)
Montana	7.1	(0.46)	8.0	(0.64)	7.0	(0.51)	7.4	(0.99)	7.5	(0.53)	6.3	(0.40)
Nebraska	8.8	(0.80)	9.7	(0.68)	—	(†)	—	(†)	6.4	(0.54)	6.4	(0.57)
Nevada	6.0	(0.65)	8.1	(0.96)	7.8	(0.70)	10.7	(0.84)	—	(†)	6.4	(0.80)
New Hampshire	7.5	(0.98)	8.6	(0.91)	7.3	(0.69)	—	(†)	—	(†)	—	(†)
New Jersey	—	(†)	8.0	(1.07)	—	(†)	6.6	(0.75)	5.7	(0.51)	6.2	(0.81)
New Mexico	—	(†)	10.4	(0.96)	10.1	(0.68)	—	(†)	—	(†)	—	(†)
New York	7.2	(0.44)	7.2	(0.47)	7.3	(0.57)	7.5	(0.55)	7.3	(0.60)	7.3	(0.61)
North Carolina	7.2	(0.74)	7.9	(0.92)	6.6	(0.62)	6.8	(0.61)	9.1	(0.95)	6.9	(0.45)
North Dakota	5.9	(0.89)	6.6	(0.58)	5.2	(0.59)	—	(†)	—	(†)	—	(†)
Ohio[2]	7.7	(1.30)	8.2	(0.67)	8.3	(0.77)	—	(†)	—	(†)	—	(†)
Oklahoma	7.4	(1.10)	6.0	(0.65)	7.0	(0.72)	5.8	(0.66)	5.7	(0.88)	4.6	(0.53)
Oregon	—	(†)	—	(†)	—	(†)	—	(†)	—	(†)	—	(†)
Pennsylvania	—	(†)	—	(†)	—	(†)	5.6	(0.73)	—	(†)	—	(†)
Rhode Island	8.2	(0.84)	8.7	(0.87)	8.3	(0.42)	6.5	(0.65)	—	(†)	6.4	(0.51)
South Carolina	—	(†)	10.1	(0.93)	9.8	(0.85)	8.8	(1.48)	9.2	(0.92)	6.5	(0.83)
South Dakota[2]	6.5	(0.71)	8.1	(1.04)	5.9	(0.87)	6.8	(0.87)	6.1	(0.77)	5.0	(0.69)
Tennessee	8.4	(1.17)	7.4	(0.79)	7.3	(0.76)	7.0	(0.71)	5.8	(0.52)	9.3	(0.73)
Texas	—	(†)	9.3	(0.84)	8.7	(0.52)	7.2	(0.52)	6.8	(0.40)	7.1	(0.62)
Utah	7.3	(1.44)	9.8	(1.32)	11.4	(1.92)	7.7	(0.88)	7.0	(0.98)	5.5	(0.59)
Vermont	7.3	(0.20)	6.3	(0.46)	6.2	(0.56)	6.0	(0.30)	5.5	(0.37)	6.4	(0.43)
Virginia	—	(†)	—	(†)	—	(†)	—	(†)	7.0	(0.86)	6.1	(0.43)
Washington	—	(†)	—	(†)	—	(†)	—	(†)	—	(†)	—	(†)
West Virginia	8.5	(1.26)	8.0	(0.78)	9.7	(0.77)	9.2	(0.77)	6.6	(0.93)	5.6	(0.51)
Wisconsin	5.5	(0.70)	7.6	(0.73)	5.6	(0.66)	6.7	(0.75)	5.1	(0.48)	4.3	(0.64)
Wyoming	9.7	(1.00)	7.8	(0.67)	8.3	(0.67)	9.4	(0.58)	7.3	(0.58)	6.8	(0.47)

—Not available.
†Not applicable.
[1]Data for the U.S. total include both public and private schools and were collected through a national survey representing the entire country.
[2]Data include both public and private schools.
NOTE: Survey respondents were asked about being threatened or injured "with a weapon such as a gun, knife, or club on school property." "On school property" was not defined for respondents. State-level data include public schools only, with the exception of data for Ohio and South Dakota. Data for the U.S. total, Ohio, and South Dakota include both public and private schools. For specific states, a given year's data may be unavailable (1) because the state did not participate in the survey that year; (2) because the state omitted this particular survey item from the state-level questionnaire; or (3) because the state had an overall response rate of less than 60 percent (the overall response rate is the school response rate multiplied by the student response rate).
SOURCE: Centers for Disease Control and Prevention, Division of Adolescent and School Health, Youth Risk Behavior Surveillance System (YRBSS), 2003 through 2013. (This table was prepared June 2014.)

Table 228.70. Number and percentage of public and private school teachers who reported that they were threatened with injury or physically attacked by a student from school during the previous 12 months, by selected teacher and school characteristics: Selected years, 1993–94 through 2011–12

[Standard errors appear in parentheses]

Year	Sex			Race/ethnicity				Instructional level[1]		Control of school	
	Total	Male	Female	White	Black	Hispanic	Other[2]	Elementary	Secondary	Public[3]	Private
1	2	3	4	5	6	7	8	9	10	11	12
Threatened with injury							Number of teachers				
1993–94	342,700 (7,140)	115,900 (3,870)	226,800 (5,570)	295,700 (6,320)	23,900 (1,380)	15,900 (1,850)	7,300 (680)	135,200 (4,520)	207,500 (5,380)	326,800 (7,040)	15,900 (1,130)
1999–2000	304,900 (7,090)	95,100 (3,610)	209,800 (5,490)	252,500 (5,670)	28,300 (2,150)	17,200 (1,980)	7,000 (850)	148,100 (5,560)	156,900 (4,360)	287,400 (7,060)	17,500 (1,700)
2003–04	252,800 (8,750)	78,400 (3,930)	174,400 (7,260)	198,900 (6,980)	32,500 (3,050)	12,400 (1,810)	9,000 (1,250)	113,600 (7,240)	139,200 (5,280)	242,100 (7,840)	10,700 (1,780)
2007–08	289,900 (10,660)	88,300 (5,970)	201,600 (8,140)	234,700 (8,850)	28,700 (3,080)	17,900 (3,230)	8,600 (1,630)	130,000 (7,720)	160,000 (7,220)	276,600 (10,570)	13,300 (1,460)
2011–12	352,900 (17,080)	84,500 (5,220)	268,400 (15,450)	279,900 (13,300)	34,200 (4,380)	27,100 (4,660)	11,800 (2,200)	189,800 (13,430)	163,200 (7,520)	338,400 (17,290)	14,500 (1,450)
Physically attacked											
1993–94	121,100 (3,950)	30,800 (1,770)	90,300 (3,900)	104,300 (4,020)	7,700 (860)	6,200 (1,290)	2,800 (450)	77,300 (3,240)	43,800 (1,980)	112,400 (3,730)	8,700 (860)
1999–2000	134,800 (4,820)	30,600 (1,990)	104,200 (4,390)	111,700 (3,810)	11,600 (1,540)	8,800 (1,660)	2,600 (460)	102,200 (4,360)	32,600 (2,270)	125,000 (4,630)	9,800 (1,070)
2003–04	129,200 (7,810)	23,600 (2,610)	105,700 (6,460)	102,200 (5,920)	15,100 (2,300)	7,000 (1,860)	5,000 (1,110)	89,800 (6,680)	39,400 (3,410)	121,400 (7,180)	7,800 (1,450)
2007–08	156,000 (8,090)	34,900 (4,760)	121,100 (6,120)	132,300 (6,860)	12,300 (2,350)	8,200 (2,040)	3,200 ! (1,250)	114,700 (7,220)	41,300 (3,220)	146,400 (8,200)	9,600 (1,170)
2011–12	209,800 (11,880)	32,500 (3,330)	177,300 (11,310)	171,300 (10,950)	18,800 (3,580)	11,800 (2,890)	7,900 (1,990)	160,700 (10,210)	49,100 (4,310)	197,400 (11,730)	12,400 (1,490)
Threatened with injury							Percent of teachers				
1993–94	11.7 (0.23)	14.7 (0.40)	10.5 (0.25)	11.5 (0.24)	11.9 (0.61)	13.1 (1.32)	13.4 (1.08)	8.7 (0.30)	15.0 (0.28)	12.8 (0.26)	4.2 (0.29)
1999–2000	8.8 (0.20)	11.0 (0.38)	8.1 (0.20)	8.6 (0.19)	11.6 (0.84)	9.1 (1.01)	8.3 (0.98)	8.0 (0.29)	9.9 (0.26)	9.6 (0.22)	3.9 (0.35)
2003–04	6.8 (0.24)	8.5 (0.39)	6.2 (0.27)	6.4 (0.24)	11.8 (0.96)	5.5 (0.82)	8.7 (1.25)	5.7 (0.37)	8.0 (0.27)	7.4 (0.24)	2.3 (0.40)
2007–08	7.4 (0.26)	9.3 (0.59)	6.8 (0.27)	7.2 (0.26)	11.1 (0.93)	6.7 (1.19)	7.6 (1.36)	6.6 (0.38)	8.4 (0.36)	8.1 (0.30)	2.7 (0.30)
2011–12	9.2 (0.42)	9.2 (0.49)	9.2 (0.50)	8.8 (0.40)	13.8 (1.72)	9.4 (1.54)	9.1 (1.54)	9.6 (0.67)	8.7 (0.34)	10.0 (0.48)	3.1 (0.32)
Physically attacked											
1993–94	4.1 (0.13)	3.9 (0.21)	4.2 (0.18)	4.1 (0.16)	3.9 (0.40)	5.2 (0.99)	5.2 (0.76)	5.0 (0.20)	3.2 (0.14)	4.4 (0.14)	2.3 (0.23)
1999–2000	3.9 (0.14)	3.5 (0.22)	4.0 (0.17)	3.8 (0.13)	4.8 (0.59)	4.6 (0.83)	3.1 (0.54)	5.5 (0.23)	2.1 (0.14)	4.2 (0.15)	2.2 (0.22)
2003–04	3.5 (0.21)	2.6 (0.27)	3.8 (0.24)	3.3 (0.20)	5.5 (0.78)	3.1 (0.85)	4.8 (1.10)	4.5 (0.35)	2.3 (0.19)	3.7 (0.22)	1.7 (0.32)
2007–08	4.0 (0.21)	3.7 (0.49)	4.1 (0.21)	4.1 (0.22)	4.7 (0.89)	3.1 (0.73)	2.8 ! (0.97)	5.8 (0.38)	2.2 (0.16)	4.3 (0.24)	2.0 (0.24)
2011–12	5.4 (0.30)	3.5 (0.35)	6.0 (0.37)	5.4 (0.33)	7.6 (1.41)	4.1 (0.96)	6.1 (1.43)	8.2 (0.50)	2.6 (0.21)	5.8 (0.33)	2.7 (0.33)

! Interpret data with caution. The coefficient of variation (CV) for this estimate is between 30 and 50 percent.

[1]Teachers were classified as elementary or secondary on the basis of the grades they taught, rather than on the level of the school in which they taught. In general, elementary teachers include those teaching prekindergarten through grade 5 and those teaching multiple grades, with a preponderance of grades taught being kindergarten through grade 6. In general, secondary teachers include those teaching any of grades 7 through 12 and those teaching multiple grades, with a preponderance of grades taught being grades 7 through 12 and usually with no grade taught being lower than grade 5.

[2]Includes American Indians/Alaska Natives, Asians, and Pacific Islanders; for 2003–04 and later years, also includes persons of Two or more races.

[3]Includes traditional public and public charter schools.

NOTE: Teachers who taught only prekindergarten students are excluded. Instructional level divides teachers into elementary or secondary based on a combination of the grades taught, main teaching assignment, and the structure of the teachers' class(es). Race categories exclude persons of Hispanic ethnicity. Detail may not sum to totals because of rounding. Some data have been revised from previously published figures.

SOURCE: U.S. Department of Education, National Center for Education Statistics, Schools and Staffing Survey (SASS), "Public School Teacher Data File" and "Private School Teacher Data File," 1993–94, 1999–2000, 2003–04, 2007–08, and 2011–12; and "Charter School Teacher Data File," 1999–2000. (This table was prepared October 2013.)

Table 228.80. Percentage of public school teachers who reported that they were threatened with injury or physically attacked by a student from school during the previous 12 months, by state: Selected years, 1993–94 through 2011–12

[Standard errors appear in parentheses]

State	Threatened with injury										Physically attacked										
	1993–94		1999–2000		2003–04		2007–08		2011–12		1993–94		1999–2000		2003–04		2007–08		2011–12	
1	2		3		4		5		6		7		8		9		10		11	
United States	12.8	(0.26)	9.6	(0.22)	7.4	(0.24)	8.1	(0.30)	10.0	(0.48)	4.4	(0.14)	4.2	(0.15)	3.7	(0.22)	4.3	(0.24)	5.8	(0.33)
Alabama	13.3	(1.29)	8.8	(0.99)	6.1	(0.88)	6.8	(1.41)	7.6	(1.92)	3.2	(0.84)	3.8	(0.57)	2.7	(0.75)	3.2 !	(1.12)	3.1 !	(0.94)
Alaska	13.7	(0.92)	10.9	(0.80)	8.9	(1.25)	7.8	(1.24)	12.3	(2.82)	6.5	(0.48)	5.2	(0.51)	6.0	(0.94)	6.7	(1.50)	5.1 !	(1.78)
Arizona	13.0	(1.07)	9.5	(1.16)	6.8	(0.98)	6.4	(1.04)	9.1	(2.08)	3.6	(0.67)	4.5	(0.95)	2.6	(0.58)	4.9	(1.29)	4.7 !	(1.43)
Arkansas	13.8	(1.38)	10.1	(1.18)	4.8	(0.81)	5.9	(1.18)	7.8	(1.48)	3.0	(0.67)	2.5	(0.59)	2.7	(0.72)	4.1	(1.07)	5.2 !	(1.80)
California	7.4	(0.91)	5.8	(0.70)	6.0	(1.00)	8.5	(1.31)	7.7	(1.17)	2.9	(0.61)	2.5	(0.46)	2.0	(0.53)	3.6	(0.78)	4.4	(0.95)
Colorado	13.1	(1.29)	6.6	(0.97)	3.8	(0.82)	6.8	(1.64)	7.3	(1.69)	4.9	(0.82)	3.1	(0.60)	1.5 !	(0.45)	4.7	(1.33)	3.6 !	(1.26)
Connecticut	11.8	(0.86)	9.1	(0.88)	6.9	(1.28)	7.2	(1.39)	7.5 !	(3.03)	3.5	(0.46)	4.1	(0.55)	2.8	(0.70)	3.3 !	(1.04)	6.2 !	(2.91)
Delaware	18.7	(1.56)	11.4	(1.37)	7.7	(1.35)	11.7	(1.93)	15.8	(3.49)	7.2	(1.10)	5.3	(0.92)	3.2 !	(1.00)	5.4	(1.46)	9.8	(2.80)
District of Columbia	24.0	(1.80)	22.3	(1.30)	17.3	(2.63)	16.9	(3.06)	‡	(†)	8.3	(1.34)	9.1	(0.83)	5.2	(1.24)	7.3	(2.00)	‡	(†)
Florida	20.1	(1.65)	12.2	(1.07)	11.2	(1.26)	11.4	(2.11)	‡	(†)	4.9	(0.78)	6.7	(0.91)	6.5	(1.58)	4.0	(1.04)	‡	(†)
Georgia	14.0	(1.29)	9.5	(1.42)	6.4	(1.21)	5.8	(1.18)	9.5 !	(2.98)	3.4	(0.66)	3.6	(0.84)	4.6	(1.30)	4.0	(1.04)	6.3 !	(2.60)
Hawaii	9.9	(1.48)	9.4	(0.99)	9.0	(1.33)	8.0	(1.84)	‡	(†)	2.9	(0.57)	3.2	(0.57)	5.7	(1.18)	4.5	(1.30)	‡	(†)
Idaho	9.7	(1.02)	7.8	(0.44)	5.4	(0.98)	5.9	(1.24)	6.7	(1.42)	4.2	(0.76)	4.3	(0.39)	2.5 !	(0.75)	2.9 !	(0.87)	3.6 !	(1.34)
Illinois	10.9	(0.76)	8.2	(0.89)	7.9	(1.60)	8.1	(1.42)	7.3	(1.41)	4.5	(0.50)	2.7	(0.39)	2.3 !	(0.77)	3.9	(0.90)	4.1	(1.11)
Indiana	13.8	(1.28)	7.6	(1.12)	7.2	(1.18)	10.2	(1.78)	11.2	(2.87)	3.0	(0.66)	3.0	(0.75)	4.1 !	(1.28)	4.7	(0.93)	6.4	(1.88)
Iowa	9.4	(1.19)	10.7	(0.93)	4.9	(1.13)	7.2	(1.32)	11.7	(2.43)	4.3	(0.88)	3.9	(0.73)	2.4	(0.64)	3.4	(0.93)	7.6	(2.11)
Kansas	10.9	(0.91)	6.0	(0.78)	3.9	(0.81)	5.7	(1.07)	7.2	(1.66)	3.8	(0.61)	2.9	(0.55)	3.3	(0.79)	5.0	(1.36)	5.5 !	(1.77)
Kentucky	14.0	(1.33)	12.6	(1.22)	7.8	(1.46)	9.8	(1.86)	10.6	(1.48)	3.8	(0.72)	4.5	(0.62)	2.7	(0.79)	5.8	(1.60)	7.0	(1.25)
Louisiana	17.0	(1.17)	13.4	(2.31)	9.8	(1.42)	10.3	(2.35)	18.3	(2.95)	6.6	(0.82)	5.0	(1.31)	2.7	(0.69)	4.0 !	(1.40)	7.2 !	(2.27)
Maine	9.0	(1.11)	11.7	(1.13)	5.2	(1.09)	9.5	(1.49)	9.1	(1.98)	2.4	(0.62)	6.3	(0.96)	3.3 !	(1.00)	5.2	(1.37)	5.2	(1.55)
Maryland	19.8	(2.15)	10.7	(1.31)	13.5	(2.24)	12.6	(2.47)	‡	(†)	8.6	(1.34)	4.6	(0.93)	6.5	(1.40)	8.4	(1.57)	‡	(†)
Massachusetts	10.8	(0.83)	11.3	(1.48)	6.4	(1.23)	9.7	(1.98)	6.2	(1.69)	4.7	(0.64)	4.3	(0.67)	3.8	(0.75)	4.1	(0.93)	5.3	(1.51)
Michigan	10.7	(1.54)	8.0	(0.93)	9.2	(1.55)	6.0	(1.15)	11.8	(1.62)	6.4	(1.13)	3.8	(0.91)	5.4	(1.04)	3.5 !	(1.32)	9.0	(2.00)
Minnesota	9.6	(1.13)	9.5	(1.11)	8.1	(1.17)	7.3	(1.16)	11.4	(1.49)	4.5	(0.85)	4.4	(1.04)	3.6	(0.68)	6.5	(1.38)	6.5	(1.27)
Mississippi	13.4	(1.48)	11.1	(0.99)	5.5	(0.92)	10.7	(1.59)	7.7	(1.42)	4.1	(0.78)	3.7	(0.58)	0.9 !	(0.34)	2.9	(0.83)	3.1 !	(1.14)
Missouri	12.6	(1.11)	11.3	(1.73)	8.3	(1.27)	8.7	(1.17)	12.3	(2.25)	3.2	(0.73)	5.6	(1.41)	5.5	(1.43)	5.3	(1.15)	7.5	(1.73)
Montana	7.7	(0.58)	8.3	(0.97)	6.0	(0.78)	6.3	(1.25)	7.6	(2.24)	2.7	(0.48)	2.7	(0.38)	1.9	(0.47)	4.0	(0.81)	4.2 !	(1.37)
Nebraska	10.4	(0.61)	9.9	(0.70)	7.5	(1.12)	7.2	(1.27)	8.0	(1.46)	3.6	(0.64)	3.8	(0.57)	4.1	(0.89)	4.2	(1.11)	5.8	(1.36)
Nevada	13.2	(1.22)	11.6	(1.34)	7.3	(1.89)	9.2	(2.21)	9.1	(2.65)	4.5	(0.86)	8.1	(1.07)	4.1 !	(1.28)	3.7 !	(1.41)	4.7 !	(2.25)
New Hampshire	11.1	(1.30)	8.8	(1.43)	5.8	(1.37)	6.5	(1.47)	5.6 !	(2.11)	3.0	(0.70)	4.2	(1.09)	2.8 !	(0.91)	2.2 !	(0.91)	‡	(†)
New Jersey	7.9	(0.87)	7.5	(0.80)	4.3	(1.20)	4.6	(1.26)	6.9	(1.08)	2.4	(0.45)	3.4	(0.78)	2.0 !	(0.67)	2.2 !	(0.82)	3.6	(0.97)
New Mexico	12.8	(1.27)	10.2	(1.75)	7.8	(1.25)	12.8	(1.85)	10.0	(2.76)	4.4	(0.72)	6.8	(1.77)	5.9	(0.97)	4.5	(1.33)	9.9 !	(3.17)
New York	16.2	(1.32)	11.5	(1.06)	10.4	(1.62)	10.5	(1.85)	11.9	(1.86)	6.7	(0.97)	5.2	(0.79)	6.5	(1.12)	6.4	(1.56)	7.0	(1.48)
North Carolina	17.1	(1.32)	12.8	(1.63)	8.7	(1.44)	9.6	(1.71)	13.4	(2.79)	6.0	(0.95)	5.5	(1.23)	4.4	(0.95)	5.9 !	(1.84)	6.3	(1.58)
North Dakota	5.5	(0.62)	5.7	(0.57)	5.0	(0.95)	2.5	(0.70)	6.1	(1.48)	2.9	(0.66)	2.1	(0.37)	2.1	(0.49)	1.6 !	(0.50)	3.3 !	(1.06)
Ohio	15.2	(1.48)	9.6	(1.35)	6.2	(1.14)	8.7	(1.59)	9.9	(1.20)	3.6	(0.69)	2.9	(0.83)	2.5 !	(0.83)	2.2 !	(0.70)	3.9	(0.88)
Oklahoma	11.0	(1.21)	8.5	(1.17)	6.0	(0.79)	7.4	(0.87)	9.6	(2.12)	4.1	(0.81)	4.5	(1.12)	3.0	(0.53)	3.2	(0.63)	6.2	(1.66)
Oregon	11.5	(1.00)	6.9	(1.33)	5.5	(1.11)	6.3	(1.30)	5.3	(1.56)	3.4	(0.64)	3.0	(0.60)	1.4 !	(0.55)	3.9 !	(1.18)	3.4 !	(1.27)
Pennsylvania	11.0	(1.75)	9.5	(1.28)	9.5	(1.29)	4.6	(1.04)	10.1	(1.54)	3.6	(1.02)	4.5	(0.97)	5.0	(0.82)	3.8	(0.90)	4.4	(0.99)
Rhode Island	13.4	(1.78)	10.2	(0.64)	4.6 !	(1.39)	8.6	(2.13)	‡	(†)	4.2	(0.91)	4.8	(0.59)	2.4 !	(0.92)	‡	(†)	‡	(†)
South Carolina	15.2	(1.62)	11.5	(1.10)	8.5	(1.30)	8.5	(1.46)	13.1	(2.70)	3.8	(0.92)	5.3	(0.94)	3.1	(0.82)	2.9 !	(1.18)	‡	(†)
South Dakota	6.5	(0.83)	7.7	(0.91)	4.7	(1.23)	6.9	(1.88)	10.0	(2.28)	2.6	(0.46)	3.9	(0.50)	2.9	(0.79)	4.3	(0.88)	5.2 !	(1.66)
Tennessee	12.4	(1.45)	13.3	(1.65)	6.5	(1.24)	7.7	(1.26)	9.4	(2.11)	3.5	(0.91)	2.6	(0.67)	3.7	(1.02)	4.1	(1.11)	3.2 !	(1.04)
Texas	12.6	(1.15)	8.9	(0.89)	7.6	(1.13)	7.6	(1.31)	10.0	(1.81)	4.2	(0.65)	4.8	(0.75)	3.9	(0.92)	4.2	(1.18)	5.7	(1.30)
Utah	11.1	(0.87)	8.0	(1.15)	5.2	(0.82)	5.7	(1.18)	7.2	(1.96)	7.2	(0.72)	2.6	(0.58)	4.1	(0.90)	3.8 !	(1.26)	5.4	(1.53)
Vermont	12.4	(1.28)	9.9	(1.46)	4.9	(1.18)	7.6	(1.82)	8.7	(1.86)	8.6	(1.38)	5.3	(0.94)	1.8 !	(0.90)	4.2	(1.22)	5.3	(1.29)
Virginia	14.9	(1.37)	12.1	(1.19)	6.5	(1.11)	8.1	(1.38)	9.9	(1.58)	6.9	(1.23)	4.9	(0.76)	2.9 !	(0.88)	6.0	(1.32)	6.5	(1.68)
Washington	13.0	(1.33)	10.0	(0.98)	6.7	(1.29)	7.0	(1.34)	7.4	(1.36)	4.9	(0.74)	5.0	(0.61)	4.1	(0.85)	4.4	(1.28)	6.8	(1.80)
West Virginia	11.7	(0.86)	10.0	(1.19)	7.4	(1.13)	8.1	(1.67)	9.4	(2.08)	3.4	(0.67)	3.4	(0.67)	3.4	(0.82)	4.0	(1.07)	4.3 !	(1.72)
Wisconsin	13.7	(1.82)	10.1	(0.99)	4.7	(0.99)	8.8	(1.51)	13.7	(2.37)	3.9	(0.77)	4.4	(0.79)	2.5	(0.71)	6.5	(1.29)	11.3	(2.56)
Wyoming	9.0	(0.79)	6.7	(0.96)	3.8 !	(1.31)	5.1	(1.00)	10.9	(3.10)	2.7	(0.49)	2.6	(0.47)	2.5 !	(1.04)	3.0	(0.86)	‡	(†)

†Not applicable.

!Interpret data with caution. The coefficient of variation (CV) for this estimate is between 30 and 50 percent.

‡Reporting standards not met. Data may be suppressed because the response rate is under 50 percent, there are too few cases for a reliable estimate, or the coefficient of variation (CV) is 50 percent or greater.

NOTE: Teachers who taught only prekindergarten students are excluded. Includes traditional public and public charter schools. Detail may not sum to totals because of rounding. Some data have been revised from previously published figures.
SOURCE: U.S. Department of Education, National Center for Education Statistics, Schools and Staffing Survey (SASS), "Public School Teacher Data File," 1993–94, 1999–2000, 2003–04, 2007–08, and 2011–12; and "Charter School Teacher Data File," 1999–2000. (This table was prepared October 2013.)

Table 229.10. Percentage of public schools recording incidents of crime at school and reporting incidents to police, number of incidents, and rate per 1,000 students, by type of crime: Selected years, 1999–2000 through 2013–14

[Standard errors appear in parentheses]

Type of crime recorded or reported to police	Percent of schools					2013–14[1]		
	1999–2000	2003–04	2005–06	2007–08	2009–10	Percent of schools	Number of incidents	Rate per 1,000 students[2]
1	2	3	4	5	6	7	8	9
Recorded incidents								
Total[3]	86.4 (1.23)	88.5 (0.85)	85.7 (1.07)	85.5 (0.87)	85.0 (0.87)	— (†)	— (†)	— (†)
Violent incidents	71.4 (1.37)	81.4 (1.05)	77.7 (1.11)	75.5 (1.09)	73.8 (1.09)	65.0 (1.46)	757,000 (48,540)	15.4 (1.04)
Serious violent incidents	19.7 (0.98)	18.3 (0.99)	17.1 (0.91)	17.2 (1.06)	16.4 (1.06)	13.1 (1.00)	25,700 (2,730)	0.5 (0.06)
Rape or attempted rape	0.7 (0.10)	0.8 (0.17)	0.3 (0.07)	0.8 (0.17)	0.5 (0.10)	0.2! (0.10)	‡ (†)	# (†)
Sexual battery other than rape	2.5 (0.33)	3.0 (0.32)	2.8 (0.24)	2.5 (0.33)	2.3 (0.17)	1.8 (0.37)	1,800 (480)	# (0.01)
Physical attack or fight with a weapon	5.2 (0.60)	4.0 (0.46)	3.8 (0.38)	3.0 (0.33)	3.9 (0.33)	1.8 (0.34)	2,900 (700)	0.1 (0.01)
Threat of physical attack with a weapon	11.1 (0.70)	8.6 (0.71)	8.8 (0.66)	9.3 (0.77)	7.7 (0.77)	8.7 (0.78)	15,100 (1,820)	0.3 (0.04)
Robbery with a weapon	0.5! (0.15)	0.6 (0.15)	0.4 (0.12)	0.4! (0.14)	0.2 (0.14)	‡ (†)	‡ (†)	‡ (†)
Robbery without a weapon	5.3! (0.56)	6.3 (0.60)	6.4 (0.59)	5.2 (0.56)	4.4 (0.56)	2.5 (0.42)	5,200 (920)	0.1 (0.02)
Physical attack or fight without a weapon	63.7 (1.52)	76.7 (1.21)	74.3 (1.20)	72.7 (1.07)	70.5 (1.07)	57.5 (1.43)	453,100 (41,330)	9.1 (0.87)
Threat of physical attack without a weapon	52.2 (1.47)	53.0 (1.34)	52.2 (1.27)	47.8 (1.19)	46.4 (1.19)	47.1 (1.50)	278,100 (13,820)	5.7 (0.30)
Theft[4]	45.6 (1.37)	46.0 (1.29)	46.0 (1.07)	47.3 (1.29)	44.1 (1.29)	— (†)	— (†)	— (†)
Other incidents[5]	72.7 (1.30)	64.0 (1.27)	68.2 (1.07)	67.4 (1.13)	68.1 (1.13)	— (†)	— (†)	— (†)
Possession of a firearm/explosive device	5.5 (0.44)	6.1 (0.49)	7.2 (0.60)	4.7 (0.38)	4.7 (0.38)	— (†)	— (†)	— (†)
Possession of a knife or sharp object	42.6 (1.28)	—	42.8 (1.23)	40.6 (1.10)	39.7 (1.10)	— (†)	— (†)	— (†)
Distribution of illegal drugs[6]	12.3 (0.50)	12.9 (0.55)	— (†)	— (†)	— (†)	— (†)	— (†)	— (†)
Possession or use of alcohol or illegal drugs[7]	26.6 (0.72)	29.3 (0.87)	25.9 (0.68)	23.2 (0.68)	24.6 (0.68)	— (†)	— (†)	— (†)
Distribution, possession, or use of illegal drugs[6]	— (†)	—	16.2 (0.68)	14.9 (0.57)	12.1	— (†)	— (†)	— (†)
Inappropriate distribution, possession, or use of prescription drugs[8]	—	—	—	—	14.1 (0.57)	— (†)	— (†)	— (†)
Distribution, possession, or use of alcohol	36.3 (1.26)	—	—	—	—	— (†)	— (†)	— (†)
Sexual harassment	—	—	—	—	—	— (†)	— (†)	— (†)
Vandalism	51.4 (1.61)	51.4 (1.17)	50.5 (1.17)	49.3 (1.16)	45.8 (1.16)	— (†)	— (†)	— (†)
Reported incidents to police								
Total	62.5 (1.37)	65.2 (1.35)	60.9 (1.15)	62.0 (1.24)	60.0 (1.24)	— (†)	— (†)	— (†)
Violent incidents	36.0 (1.26)	43.6 (1.15)	37.7 (1.09)	37.8 (1.16)	39.9 (1.16)	— (†)	— (†)	— (†)
Serious violent incidents	14.8 (0.82)	13.3 (0.88)	12.6 (0.70)	12.6 (0.86)	10.4 (0.86)	— (†)	— (†)	— (†)
Rape or attempted rape	0.6 (0.10)	0.6 (0.17)	0.7 (0.07)	0.8 (0.17)	0.5 (0.17)	— (†)	— (†)	— (†)
Sexual battery other than rape	2.3 (0.34)	2.6 (0.28)	2.2 (0.26)	2.1 (0.29)	1.4 (0.29)	— (†)	— (†)	— (†)
Physical attack or fight with a weapon	3.9 (0.50)	2.8 (0.38)	2.2 (0.27)	2.1 (0.27)	2.2 (0.27)	— (†)	— (†)	— (†)
Threat of physical attack with a weapon	8.5 (0.59)	6.0 (0.55)	5.9 (0.49)	5.7 (0.59)	4.5 (0.59)	— (†)	— (†)	— (†)
Robbery with a weapon	0.3! (0.09)	0.6 (0.15)	0.4 (0.12)	0.4! (0.14)	0.2 (0.14)	— (†)	— (†)	— (†)
Robbery without a weapon	3.4 (0.41)	4.2 (0.51)	4.9 (0.48)	4.1 (0.42)	3.5 (0.42)	— (†)	— (†)	— (†)
Physical attack or fight without a weapon	25.8 (0.91)	35.6 (0.98)	29.2 (1.00)	28.2 (0.90)	34.3 (0.90)	— (†)	— (†)	— (†)
Threat of physical attack without a weapon	18.9 (0.94)	21.0 (0.82)	19.7 (0.69)	19.5 (0.76)	15.2 (0.76)	— (†)	— (†)	— (†)
Theft[4]	28.5 (1.04)	30.5 (1.17)	27.9 (0.97)	31.0 (1.12)	25.4 (1.12)	— (†)	— (†)	— (†)
Other incidents[5]	52.0 (1.14)	50.0 (1.18)	50.6 (1.00)	48.7 (1.17)	46.3 (1.17)	— (†)	— (†)	— (†)
Possession of a firearm/explosive device	4.5 (0.41)	4.9 (0.44)	5.5 (0.51)	3.6 (0.32)	3.1 (0.32)	— (†)	— (†)	— (†)
Possession of a knife or sharp object	23.0 (0.84)	—	25.0 (1.00)	23.3 (0.69)	20.0 (0.69)	— (†)	— (†)	— (†)
Distribution of illegal drugs[6]	11.4 (0.48)	12.4 (0.57)	— (†)	— (†)	— (†)	— (†)	— (†)	— (†)
Possession or use of alcohol or illegal drugs[7]	22.2 (0.67)	26.0 (0.76)	22.8 (0.62)	20.7 (0.60)	21.4 (0.60)	— (†)	— (†)	— (†)
Distribution, possession, or use of illegal drugs[6]	—	—	11.6 (0.61)	10.6 (0.55)	9.6	— (†)	— (†)	— (†)
Inappropriate distribution, possession, or use of prescription drugs[8]	—	—	—	—	10.0 (0.55)	— (†)	— (†)	— (†)
Distribution, possession, or use of alcohol	14.7 (0.78)	—	—	—	—	— (†)	— (†)	— (†)
Sexual harassment	—	—	—	—	—	— (†)	— (†)	— (†)
Vandalism	32.7 (1.10)	34.3 (1.06)	31.9 (1.02)	30.8 (1.18)	26.8 (1.18)	— (†)	— (†)	— (†)

—Not available.
†Not applicable.
#Rounds to zero.
!Interpret data with caution. The coefficient of variation (CV) for this estimate is between 30 and 50 percent.
‡Reporting standards not met. Either there are too few cases for a reliable estimate or the coefficient of variation (CV) for this estimate is 50 percent or greater.
[1]Data for 2013–14 were collected using the Fast Response Survey System, while data for earlier years were collected using the School Survey on Crime and Safety (SSOCS). The 2013–14 survey was designed to allow comparisons with SSOCS data. However, respondents to SSOCS did not have the option of completing the survey online. The 2013–14 survey also relied on a smaller sample. The smaller sample size and change in survey administration may have impacted 2013–14 results.
[2]Because the 2013–14 survey did not collect school enrollment counts, the rate per 1,000 students was calculated by dividing the number of incidents by the total number of students obtained from the Common Core of Data.
[3]Total not presented for 2013–14 because the survey did not collect information regarding theft and other incidents. Therefore, the total incident rate is not comparable with earlier years.
[4]Theft/larceny (taking things worth over $10 without personal confrontation) was defined for respondents as "the unlawful taking of another person's property without personal confrontation, threat, violence, or bodily harm." This includes pocket picking, stealing a purse or backpack (if left unattended or no force was used to take it from owner), theft from a building, theft from a motor vehicle or motor vehicle parts or accessories, theft of a bicycle, theft from a vending machine, and all other types of thefts.
[5]Caution should be used when making direct comparisons of "Other incidents" between years because the survey questions about alcohol and drugs changed, as outlined in footnotes 6, 7, and 8.
[6]The survey items "Distribution of illegal drugs" and "Possession or use of alcohol or illegal drugs" appear only on the 1999–2000 and 2003–04 questionnaires. Different alcohol- and drug-related survey items were used on the questionnaires for later years.
[7]The survey items "Distribution, possession, or use of illegal drugs" and "Distribution, possession, or use of alcohol" appear only on the questionnaires for 2005–06 and later years.
[8]The 2009–10 questionnaire was the first to include the survey item "Inappropriate distribution, possession, or use of prescription drugs."
NOTE: Responses were provided by the principal or the person most knowledgeable about crime and safety issues at the school. "At school" was defined to include activities that happen in school buildings, on school grounds, on school buses, and at places that hold school-sponsored events or activities. Respondents were instructed to include incidents that occurred before, during, and after normal school hours or when school activities or events were in session. Detail may not sum to totals because of rounding and because schools that recorded or reported more than one type of crime incident were counted only once in the total percentage of schools recording or reporting incidents.
SOURCE: U.S. Department of Education, National Center for Education Statistics, 1999–2000, 2003–04, 2005–06, 2007–08, and 2009–10 School Survey on Crime and Safety (SSOCS), 2000, 2004, 2006, 2008, and 2010; Fast Response Survey System (FRSS), "School Safety and Discipline: 2013–14," FRSS 106, 2014; and Common Core of Data (CCD), "Public Elementary/Secondary School Universe Survey," 2013–14. (This table was prepared September 2015.)

Table 229.20. Number and percentage of public schools recording at least one crime incident that occurred at school, and number and rate of incidents, by school characteristics and type of incident: 1999–2000 and 2009–10

[Standard errors appear in parentheses]

Type of incident	All public schools, 1999–2000	2009–10 All public schools	Instruction level of school — Primary	Middle	High	Locale — City	Suburban	Town	Rural	Percent of students eligible for free or reduced-price lunch — 0 to 20	21 to 50	51 or more
	2	3	4	5	6	7	8	9	10	11	12	13
Number of public schools (in thousands)												
All schools	82 (#)	83 (0.5)	49 (0.3)	15 (0.1)	12 (0.1)	22 (0.2)	24 (0.2)	12 (0.1)	25 (0.3)	14 (0.7)	26 (1.2)	43 (1.1)
Schools with incident	71 (1.0)	70 (1.0)	38 (0.9)	15 (0.1)	12 (0.1)	19 (0.4)	20 (0.6)	11 (0.3)	21 (0.5)	10 (0.7)	23 (1.1)	38 (1.2)
Percent of schools with incident	86.4 (1.23)	85.0 (1.07)	77.9 (1.69)	96.2 (0.66)	98.3 (0.49)	86.9 (1.71)	84.3 (2.07)	89.4 (2.63)	82.1 (2.04)	73.0 (3.28)	85.8 (1.78)	88.4 (1.30)
Violent incidents	71.4 (1.37)	73.8 (1.07)	64.4 (1.63)	90.5 (1.10)	90.9 (1.21)	74.9 (2.12)	73.5 (2.21)	80.3 (3.14)	70.2 (1.91)	61.7 (3.40)	74.6 (2.04)	77.2 (1.66)
Serious violent incidents	19.7 (0.98)	16.4 (0.94)	13.0 (1.42)	18.9 (1.46)	27.6 (1.35)	21.7 (2.12)	15.5 (1.80)	15.6 (2.33)	13.2 (1.51)	10.5 (1.41)	15.4 (1.65)	18.9 (1.50)
Rape or attempted rape	0.7 (0.10)	0.5 (0.10)	— (†)	1.3! (0.42)	2.0 (0.41)	0.7! (0.26)	0.6! (0.25)	0.6! (0.28)	0.3! (0.13)	0.4! (0.20)	0.6 (0.17)	0.5 (0.15)
Sexual battery other than rape	2.5 (0.33)	2.3 (0.34)	1.0! (0.38)	3.2 (0.56)	5.1 (0.73)	3.2 (0.76)	1.6 (0.32)	2.7 (0.82)	1.9! (0.68)	1.4 (0.33)	2.7 (0.72)	2.3 (0.44)
Physical attack or fight with weapon	5.2 (0.60)	3.9 (0.48)	3.0 (0.68)	3.9 (0.75)	7.1 (1.02)	5.5 (1.18)	4.6 (1.00)	4.1! (1.28)	1.8 (0.48)	2.3! (0.77)	3.6 (0.69)	4.6 (0.73)
Threat of attack with weapon	11.1 (0.70)	7.7 (0.72)	6.8 (1.11)	10.3 (1.04)	10.0 (0.99)	10.2 (1.69)	7.7 (1.15)	6.3 (1.57)	6.2 (1.13)	4.7 (1.06)	5.9 (0.72)	9.7 (1.32)
Robbery with weapon	0.5! (0.15)	0.2 (0.05)	— (†)	0.5! (0.20)	1.0 (0.30)	0.6! (0.19)	0.2! (0.10)	‡ (†)	— (†)	‡ (†)	0.2! (0.09)	0.3! (0.09)
Robbery without weapon	5.3 (0.56)	4.4 (0.49)	2.7 (0.66)	5.5 (0.74)	10.6 (0.87)	6.5 (0.84)	3.4 (0.55)	3.0 (1.05)	4.3 (0.97)	3.4 (0.74)	4.5 (0.86)	4.7 (0.74)
Physical attack or fight without weapon	63.7 (1.52)	70.5 (1.11)	60.3 (1.65)	88.8 (1.13)	88.4 (1.36)	71.7 (2.02)	69.9 (2.11)	76.8 (2.93)	67.2 (2.26)	57.9 (3.19)	70.4 (2.30)	74.6 (1.63)
Threat of attack without weapon	52.2 (1.47)	46.4 (1.33)	38.0 (1.94)	61.5 (1.73)	61.9 (1.58)	48.6 (2.43)	46.3 (2.44)	56.2 (3.86)	40.0 (2.15)	34.7 (2.84)	47.7 (2.21)	49.4 (1.97)
Theft/larceny[1]	45.6 (1.37)	44.1 (1.31)	25.7 (1.82)	65.2 (1.48)	82.6 (1.35)	47.6 (2.70)	43.1 (1.97)	46.2 (3.22)	41.1 (2.51)	38.0 (2.26)	48.8 (2.50)	43.1 (1.98)
Other incidents[2]	— (†)	68.1 (1.12)	57.3 (1.72)	81.9 (1.25)	92.2 (1.10)	73.5 (2.39)	66.1 (2.23)	74.1 (2.97)	62.6 (2.62)	54.8 (3.31)	67.3 (2.10)	72.9 (1.79)
Possession of firearm/explosive device	5.5 (0.44)	4.7 (0.52)	3.5 (0.81)	5.8 (0.79)	9.4 (1.20)	6.0 (0.99)	4.9 (0.89)	3.8! (1.37)	3.1 (1.01)	3.1 (0.64)	3.3 (0.58)	6.0 (0.93)
Possession of knife or sharp object	42.6 (1.28)	39.7 (1.06)	33.5 (1.51)	51.5 (1.94)	55.2 (1.51)	41.1 (2.36)	38.7 (1.75)	49.8 (3.16)	34.7 (2.13)	26.7 (2.20)	38.0 (1.96)	44.8 (1.72)
Distribution, possession, or use of illegal drugs	— (†)	24.6 (0.57)	3.5 (0.69)	44.7 (1.17)	77.2 (1.51)	27.8 (1.22)	22.4 (0.83)	25.5 (1.42)	23.4 (1.17)	20.3 (1.39)	27.9 (1.67)	23.8 (0.96)
Inappropriate distribution, possession, or use of prescription drugs	— (†)	12.1 (0.47)	1.5! (0.48)	18.8 (1.13)	43.0 (1.64)	10.3 (0.92)	12.1 (0.79)	12.3 (1.12)	13.5 (1.18)	13.1 (1.20)	15.2 (0.98)	9.8 (0.76)
Distribution, possession, or use of alcohol	— (†)	14.1 (0.50)	2.1 (0.52)	19.7 (1.31)	51.6 (1.60)	14.9 (1.14)	15.5 (0.92)	12.8 (1.17)	12.7 (1.03)	14.7 (1.01)	16.5 (1.21)	12.5 (0.76)
Vandalism	51.4 (1.61)	45.8 (1.12)	37.9 (1.69)	55.5 (1.38)	62.5 (1.86)	56.9 (2.11)	47.2 (2.44)	44.7 (3.54)	35.7 (2.25)	38.5 (2.96)	47.0 (2.27)	47.5 (1.92)
Number of incidents (in thousands)	2,259 (117.0)	1,877 (50.9)	626 (39.6)	548 (23.6)	590 (18.2)	642 (32.5)	585 (37.5)	255 (23.1)	395 (19.5)	211 (15.1)	560 (25.6)	1,106 (51.1)
Violent incidents	1,466 (103.7)	1,184 (44.4)	482 (37.3)	375 (19.3)	264 (12.9)	396 (27.4)	371 (33.0)	166 (21.2)	250 (15.9)	110 (10.6)	322 (20.5)	752 (43.2)
Serious violent incidents	61 (7.0)	52 (5.5)	22 (3.8)	14 (2.4)	14 (1.7)	17 (2.8)	16 (3.1)	6 (1.4)	13 (2.9)	6 (1.4)	13 (2.0)	33 (5.4)
Rape or attempted rape	1 (0.1)	1 (0.1)	— (†)	# (†)	# (†)	# (†)	# (†)	# (†)	# (†)	# (†)	# (†)	2 (0.4)
Sexual battery other than rape	4 (1.1)	4 (0.6)	1! (0.4)	1 (0.2)	1 (0.2)	1 (0.4)	1 (0.2)	# (†)	# (†)	# (†)	1! (0.5)	3 (0.6)
Physical attack or fight with weapon	12 (2.5)	14 (3.6)	8! (2.9)	3 (0.7)	3 (0.7)	3! (1.0)	5! (2.1)	3! (1.0)	1 (0.4)	1! (0.3)	3 (0.9)	10! (3.6)
Threat of attack with weapon	21 (1.9)	19 (2.9)	8 (1.9)	8 (1.9)	3 (0.6)	7 (1.8)	7 (1.5)	2! (1.1)	3 (0.9)	2! (0.7)	5 (1.3)	12 (2.7)
Robbery with weapon	‡ (†)	# (†)	# (†)	# (†)	# (†)	# (†)	# (†)	# (†)	# (†)	# (†)	# (†)	# (†)
Robbery without weapon	20 (3.2)	14 (1.9)	6! (1.9)	3 (0.6)	6 (0.8)	6 (0.9)	3 (0.7)	1! (0.3)	5! (1.6)	3! (0.9)	4 (1.2)	8 (1.4)
Physical attack or fight without weapon	807 (59.6)	725 (27.8)	295 (24.0)	239 (12.7)	157 (10.6)	249 (19.7)	232 (17.9)	93 (15.1)	152 (10.7)	68 (5.9)	194 (14.3)	464 (27.5)
Threat of attack without weapon	599 (52.7)	406 (23.0)	165 (21.6)	123 (8.8)	94 (5.4)	130 (10.7)	123 (17.0)	67 (9.4)	86 (7.1)	36 (4.6)	115 (11.7)	255 (20.8)
Theft/larceny[1]	218 (9.2)	259 (8.6)	42 (5.7)	69 (4.8)	125 (5.1)	85 (7.0)	81 (4.0)	33 (3.3)	59 (4.6)	41 (3.3)	96 (5.7)	121 (8.4)
Other incidents[2]	— (†)	435 (11.1)	102 (6.4)	104 (4.4)	200 (7.7)	160 (9.2)	133 (6.4)	55 (4.0)	86 (4.5)	60 (4.1)	142 (7.2)	233 (11.7)
Possession of firearm/explosive device	9 (2.2)	5 (0.6)	2 (0.4)	2 (0.3)	2 (0.2)	2 (0.3)	2 (0.3)	1 (0.2)	1 (0.3)	1 (0.1)	1 (0.2)	3 (0.5)
Possession of knife or sharp object	86 (4.0)	72 (2.6)	29 (1.7)	18 (0.9)	22 (1.5)	21 (1.3)	22 (1.9)	12 (0.9)	17 (1.3)	7 (0.6)	22 (1.3)	44 (0.0)
Distribution, possession, or use of illegal drugs	— (†)	116 (4.7)	3 (0.8)	25 (1.6)	79 (3.6)	44 (4.0)	36 (2.0)	15 (1.5)	20 (1.5)	17 (1.4)	42 (2.6)	56 (4.4)
Inappropriate distribution, possession, or use of prescription drugs	— (†)	29 (1.9)	1! (0.3)	6 (0.6)	19 (1.5)	7 (0.9)	10 (1.2)	5 (0.9)	8 (0.9)	5 (0.6)	13 (1.5)	11 (1.1)
Distribution, possession, or use of alcohol	— (†)	41 (1.8)	1! (0.3)	7 (0.6)	29 (1.5)	14 (1.3)	14 (1.1)	5 (0.8)	8 (0.9)	9 (0.9)	16 (1.3)	15 (1.3)
Vandalism	211 (13.6)	172 (7.3)	66 (5.8)	46 (3.1)	49 (4.5)	72 (5.7)	49 (3.6)	18 (1.8)	32 (3.5)	21 (2.6)	47 (3.4)	103 (6.9)

See notes at end of table.

Table 229.20. Number and percentage of public schools recording at least one crime incident that occurred at school, and number and rate of incidents, by school characteristics and type of incident: 1999–2000 and 2009–10—Continued

[Standard errors appear in parentheses]

Type of incident	All public schools, 1999–2000	All public schools 2009–10	Instruction level of school			Locale				Percent of students eligible for free or reduced-price lunch		
			Primary	Middle	High	City	Suburban	Town	Rural	0 to 20	21 to 50	51 or more
1	2	3	4	5	6	7	8	9	10	11	12	13
Number of incidents per 100,000 students	4,849 (252.4)	3,965 (103.7)	2,766 (172.3)	5,840 (249.6)	4,773 (149.9)	4,672 (250.7)	3,527 (210.5)	4,320 (350.6)	3,554 (184.8)	2,220 (131.3)	3,613 (149.4)	4,950 (200.9)
Violent incidents	3,147 (223.8)	2,500 (90.9)	2,131 (163.6)	3,997 (203.9)	2,141 (105.3)	2,885 (210.8)	2,236 (192.4)	2,820 (335.6)	2,250 (149.0)	1,153 (93.1)	2,081 (127.4)	3,364 (177.9)
Serious violent incidents	130 (15.2)	111 (11.5)	97 (16.8)	145 (25.2)	110 (13.7)	126 (21.3)	98 (18.4)	107 (23.2)	113 (26.4)	62 (14.3)	86 (13.2)	149 (24.4)
Rape or attempted rape	1 (0.2)	1 (0.3)	— (†)	3! (1.0)	3 (0.6)	1 (0.5)	1! (0.5)	2! (0.9)	1! (0.3)	1! (0.4)	1! (0.3)	2 (0.5)
Sexual battery other than rape	9 (2.4)	8 (1.3)	4! (2.0)	10 (2.4)	11 (1.8)	11 (2.7)	4 (1.2)	8 (2.5)	8! (3.5)	3 (0.8)	8 (2.9)	9 (1.8)
Physical attack or fight with weapon	26 (5.4)	30 (7.5)	34! (13.0)	19! (7.4)	23 (5.5)	22! (7.5)	32! (12.7)	43! (16.7)	‡ (†)	9! (3.1)	21 (6.1)	46! (16.0)
Threat of attack with weapon	45 (4.1)	41 (6.1)	34 (8.4)	81 (20.4)	26 (4.8)	49 (13.2)	40 (9.2)	38! (17.9)	31 (7.6)	22! (7.7)	30 (8.3)	56 (12.3)
Robbery with weapon	‡ (†)	1! (0.3)	— (†)	‡ (†)	‡ (†)	2! (1.2)	# (†)	# (†)	— (†)	# (†)	# (†)	2! (0.7)
Robbery without weapon	43 (6.8)	30 (4.1)	25! (8.2)	31 (6.2)	45 (6.5)	40 (6.6)	19 (4.3)	15! (4.6)	45! (14.3)	28! (9.6)	25 (7.6)	35 (6.3)
Physical attack or fight without weapon	1,732 (128.8)	1,532 (57.9)	1,305 (106.9)	2,545 (132.7)	1,271 (85.0)	1,814 (148.1)	1,398 (104.3)	1,571 (242.2)	1,364 (100.3)	713 (49.9)	1,251 (89.8)	2,076 (117.2)
Threat of attack without weapon	1,285 (113.2)	857 (47.4)	730 (94.0)	1,307 (94.3)	760 (45.4)	945 (81.4)	741 (100.8)	1,142 (154.3)	775 (64.6)	378 (44.0)	744 (73.4)	1,139 (86.5)
Theft/larceny[1]	468 (20.2)	546 (18.5)	185 (24.8)	736 (50.7)	1,012 (43.5)	622 (53.0)	488 (21.6)	565 (52.2)	526 (40.7)	436 (34.0)	619 (37.3)	542 (36.2)
Other incidents[2]	— (†)	918 (23.2)	450 (27.9)	1,108 (47.1)	1,620 (60.8)	1,166 (62.6)	803 (32.2)	935 (65.7)	776 (42.2)	631 (41.1)	914 (37.1)	1,044 (46.9)
Possession of firearm/explosive device	18 (4.8)	11 (1.2)	8! (1.9)	15 (2.8)	13 (1.9)	13 (2.2)	10! (1.8)	10! (3.5)	9 (2.4)	6 (1.1)	7 (1.2)	15 (2.3)
Possession of knife or sharp object	184 (8.7)	153 (5.2)	126 (7.3)	193 (9.8)	175 (12.5)	156 (9.7)	131 (10.9)	208 (15.1)	151 (10.1)	72 (5.4)	140 (6.6)	196 (11.2)
Distribution, possession, or use of illegal drugs	— (†)	245 (9.8)	14 (3.4)	262 (17.4)	637 (28.9)	321 (27.1)	220 (10.4)	250 (25.6)	184 (13.5)	183 (13.8)	273 (15.8)	251 (18.4)
Inappropriate distribution, possession, or use of prescription drugs	— (†)	62 (4.0)	4! (1.3)	68 (6.5)	157 (12.4)	48 (6.4)	60 (7.2)	84 (15.3)	70 (8.3)	55 (6.2)	83 (9.3)	50 (4.8)
Distribution, possession, or use of alcohol	— (†)	86 (3.9)	5 (1.3)	77 (6.9)	238 (13.7)	100 (9.9)	85 (6.2)	82 (14.2)	72 (8.0)	95 (10.6)	105 (8.6)	69 (5.7)
Vandalism	453 (28.6)	362 (15.3)	293 (25.6)	492 (32.4)	400 (35.4)	527 (40.4)	297 (20.5)	301 (30.3)	289 (32.3)	221 (27.0)	305 (18.2)	462 (29.6)

—Not available.
†Not applicable.
#Rounds to zero.
!Interpret data with caution. The coefficient of variation (CV) for this estimate is 30 percent or greater.
‡Reporting standards not met. The coefficient of variation (CV) for this estimate is 50 percent or greater.
[1]Theft/larceny (taking things worth over $10 without personal confrontation) includes pocket picking, stealing a purse or back-pack (if left unattended or if no force was used to take it from owner), theft from a building, theft from a motor vehicle or of motor vehicle parts or accessories, theft of bicycles, theft from vending machines, and all other types of thefts.
[2]This table shows only the "Other incidents" that were included on the 2009–10 questionnaire. In 1999–2000, most of the "Other incidents" differed from those shown in this table.

NOTE: "At school" was defined to include activities that happen in school buildings, on school grounds, on school buses, and at places holding school-sponsored events or activities. Includes incidents that occurred before, during, or after normal school hours or when school activities or events were in session. Primary schools are defined as schools in which the lowest grade is not higher than grade 3 and the highest grade is not higher than grade 8. Middle schools are defined as schools in which the lowest grade is not lower than grade 4 and the highest grade is not higher than grade 9. High schools are defined as schools in which the lowest grade is not lower than grade 9 and the highest grade is not higher than grade 12. All public schools also includes schools with other combinations of grades (including K–12 schools), which are not shown separately. Detail may not sum to totals because of rounding.
SOURCE: U.S. Department of Education, National Center for Education Statistics, 1999–2000 and 2009–10 School Survey on Crime and Safety (SSOCS), 2000 and 2010. (This table was prepared August 2011.)

Table 229.30. Percentage of public schools recording violent incidents of crime at school, number of incidents, and rate per 1,000 students, by category of violent incident and selected school characteristics: 2009–10 and 2013–14

[Standard errors appear in parentheses]

School characteristic	2009–10 Total number of public schools	2009–10 All violent incidents[2] — Percent of schools recording	Number of incidents	Rate per 1,000 students	2009–10 Serious violent incidents[3] — Percent of schools recording	Number of incidents	Rate per 1,000 students	2013–14[1] Total number of public schools	2013–14 All violent incidents[2] — Percent of schools recording	Number of incidents	Rate per 1,000 students	2013–14 Serious violent incidents[3] — Percent of schools recording	Number of incidents	Rate per 1,000 students[4]
1	2	3	4	5	6	7	8	9	10	11	12	13	14	15
Total	82,800 (460)	73.8 (1.07)	1,183,700 (44,390)	25.0 (0.91)	16.4 (0.94)	52,500 (5,510)	1.1 (0.12)	84,100 (840)	65.0 (1.46)	757,000 (48,540)	15.4 (1.04)	13.1 (1.00)	25,700 (2,730)	0.5 (0.06)
School level[5]														
Primary	48,900 (340)	64.4 (1.63)	482,100 (37,320)	21.3 (1.64)	13.0 (1.42)	21,900 (3,780)	1.0 (0.17)	49,700 (800)	52.8 (2.18)	318,300 (43,530)	13.0 (1.85)	9.2 (1.25)	7,700 (1,250)	0.3 (0.05)
Middle	15,300 (100)	90.5 (1.10)	375,200 (19,310)	40.0 (2.04)	18.9 (1.46)	13,600 (2,360)	1.5 (0.25)	16,100 (250)	87.6 (1.93)	228,700 (15,050)	23.3 (1.59)	18.3 (1.92)	7,600 (1,150)	0.8 (0.12)
High school/combined	— (†)	— (†)	— (†)	— (†)	— (†)	— (†)	— (†)	18,400 (330)	78.0 (2.53)	209,900 (15,680)	13.9 (0.98)	19.3 (1.85)	10,400 (1,960)	0.7 (0.13)
High school	12,200 (70)	90.9 (1.21)	264,400 (12,910)	21.4 (1.05)	27.6 (1.35)	13,500 (1,690)	1.1 (0.14)	— (†)	— (†)	— (†)	— (†)	— (†)	— (†)	— (†)
Combined	6,400 (200)	73.7 (5.33)	62,000 (7,570)	20.8 (2.21)	15.5 (3.72)	‡ (†)	‡ (†)	— (†)	— (†)	— (†)	— (†)	— (†)	— (†)	— (†)
Enrollment size														
Less than 300	18,900 (400)	62.8 (3.25)	111,300 (17,230)	27.2 (4.08)	10.4 (2.11)	6,100! (2,100)	1.5! (0.51)	19,500 (1,540)	54.6 (4.18)	72,200 (15,010)	16.0 (2.74)	11.3 (2.58)	‡ (†)	0.8 (0.19)
300–499	25,200 (180)	71.3 (2.34)	274,400 (25,110)	26.5 (2.44)	15.7 (2.14)	14,200 (3,560)	1.4 (0.35)	25,400 (1,250)	60.7 (2.80)	202,700 (38,450)	19.5 (3.80)	10.7 (1.77)	5,000 (1,090)	0.5 (0.10)
500–999	29,800 (100)	76.4 (1.75)	487,900 (35,630)	25.0 (1.78)	15.9 (1.42)	16,400 (2,420)	0.8 (0.12)	30,700 (950)	69.1 (1.98)	316,200 (24,810)	14.9 (1.14)	12.9 (1.57)	11,500 (2,290)	0.8 (0.11)
1,000 or more	8,900 (60)	95.4 (1.22)	310,100 (16,110)	23.2 (1.19)	32.8 (1.61)	15,700 (2,080)	1.2 (0.15)	8,500 (300)	86.4 (2.18)	165,900 (12,860)	12.7 (0.92)	25.3 (2.57)	6,300 (900)	0.5 (0.07)
Locale														
City	21,500 (190)	74.9 (2.12)	396,300 (27,430)	28.8 (2.11)	21.7 (2.12)	17,400 (2,830)	1.3 (0.21)	21,100 (570)	68.0 (2.96)	300,200 (39,830)	20.7 (2.87)	17.5 (2.30)	10,100 (2,010)	0.7 (0.15)
Suburban	23,800 (240)	73.5 (2.21)	371,000 (33,010)	22.4 (1.92)	15.5 (1.80)	16,200 (3,070)	1.0 (0.18)	23,500 (630)	60.4 (3.13)	202,140 (20,140)	11.9 (1.23)	11.2 (1.62)	6,000 (1,010)	0.4 (0.06)
Town	12,100 (110)	80.3 (3.14)	166,300 (11,190)	28.2 (3.36)	15.6 (2.33)	6,300 (1,390)	1.1 (0.23)	10,800 (750)	76.4 (3.51)	103,100 (12,540)	18.3 (2.01)	17.4 (3.46)	4,400 (1,040)	0.8 (0.18)
Rural	25,300 (300)	70.2 (1.91)	250,100 (15,910)	22.5 (1.49)	13.2 (1.51)	12,600 (2,920)	1.1 (0.26)	28,600 (1,030)	62.2 (3.21)	161,700 (16,780)	12.4 (1.23)	9.9 (1.51)	5,200 (840)	0.4 (0.07)
Percent combined enrollment of Black, Hispanic, Asian/Pacific Islander, and American Indian/Alaska Native students														
Less than 5 percent	11,700 (980)	69.6 (3.33)	108,500 (20,340)	23.3 (3.62)	12.6 (2.52)	5,400! (2,090)	1.2! (0.44)	7,300 (920)	59.7 (5.75)	30,500 (4,910)	11.6 (1.37)	5.7! (2.37)	‡ (†)	0.2! (0.09)
5 percent to less than 20 percent	20,900 (1,080)	67.9 (2.82)	192,800 (15,450)	17.2 (1.19)	9.9 (1.29)	6,500 (1,490)	0.6 (0.13)	22,800 (1,130)	62.1 (3.55)	111,600 (10,320)	10.3 (0.93)	10.2 (1.80)	5,400 (1,090)	0.5 (0.10)
20 percent to less than 50 percent	20,000 (650)	75.9 (2.14)	293,600 (20,960)	23.1 (1.76)	18.6 (1.58)	15,100 (3,000)	1.2 (0.23)	22,700 (1,290)	62.1 (2.81)	173,500 (15,540)	11.9 (1.01)	14.9 (2.06)	6,800 (1,020)	0.5 (0.07)
50 percent or more	30,100 (1,270)	78.2 (1.75)	588,800 (43,670)	31.4 (1.96)	21.1 (1.82)	25,400 (4,360)	1.4 (0.23)	31,300 (1,120)	70.4 (2.29)	441,400 (44,490)	20.9 (2.13)	15.7 (1.62)	13,000 (2,170)	0.6 (0.11)
Percent of students eligible for free or reduced-price lunch[4]														
0–25	17,100 (690)	62.6 (3.07)	141,700 (11,440)	11.9 (0.82)	10.5 (1.22)	6,700 (1,400)	0.6 (0.11)	15,100 (1,090)	50.8 (3.79)	62,400 (9,970)	6.1 (0.93)	10.3 (2.01)	3,200 (680)	0.3 (0.06)
26–50	22,700 (1,050)	76.0 (2.13)	290,500 (20,440)	22.1 (1.48)	16.2 (1.89)	12,500 (1,970)	1.0 (0.16)	22,900 (1,290)	66.9 (2.82)	141,200 (12,280)	10.7 (0.89)	10.9 (1.69)	4,600 (770)	0.4 (0.06)
51–75	23,800 (1,020)	73.8 (2.49)	334,400 (24,050)	27.3 (1.82)	15.8 (1.67)	13,100 (2,840)	1.1 (0.24)	23,200 (1,200)	67.4 (3.00)	219,300 (19,270)	17.2 (1.29)	14.6 (1.88)	8,500 (1,460)	0.7 (0.11)
76–100	19,100 (940)	81.4 (2.49)	417,200 (42,360)	41.3 (3.73)	22.9 (2.60)	20,100 (4,550)	2.0 (0.45)	19,800 (1,100)	71.2 (2.91)	301,800 (43,350)	27.6 (3.94)	16.2 (2.16)	8,700 (1,920)	0.8 (0.18)

—Not available.
†Not applicable.
!Interpret data with caution. The coefficient of variation (CV) for this estimate is between 30 and 50 percent.
‡Reporting standards not met. Either there are too few cases for a reliable estimate or the coefficient of variation (CV) is 50 percent or greater.
[1]Data for 2013–14 were collected using the Fast Response Survey System, while data for 2009–10 were collected using the School Survey on Crime and Safety (SSOCS). The 2013–14 survey was designed to allow comparisons with SSOCS data. However, respondents to the 2013–14 survey could choose either to complete the survey on paper (and mail it back) or to complete the survey online, whereas respondents to SSOCS did not have the option of completing the survey online. The 2013–14 survey also relied on a smaller sample. The smaller sample size and change in survey administration may have impacted 2013–14 results.
[2]All violent incidents include serious violent incidents (see footnote 3) as well as physical attack or fight without a weapon and threat of physical attack without a weapon.
[3]Serious violent incidents include rape, sexual battery other than rape, physical attack or fight with a weapon, threat of physical attack with a weapon, and robbery with or without a weapon.
[4]The 2013–14 survey collected neither school enrollment counts nor data on the percentage of students eligible for free or reduced-price lunch. For 2013–14, the rate per 1,000 students was calculated by dividing the number of incidents by the total number of stu-

dents obtained from the Common Core of Data (CCD). For 2013–14, the classification of schools by the percentage of students eligible for free or reduced-price lunch was also computed from CCD data.
[5]Primary schools are defined as schools in which the lowest grade is not higher than grade 3 and the highest grade is not higher than grade 8. Middle schools are defined as schools in which the lowest grade is not lower than grade 4 and the highest grade is not higher than grade 9. High schools are defined as schools in which the lowest grade is not lower than grade 9 and the highest grade is not higher than grade 12. Combined schools include all other combinations of grades, including K–12 schools. Separate data on high schools and combined schools are not available for 2013–14.
NOTE: Responses were provided by the principal or the person most knowledgeable about crime and safety issues at the school. "At school" was defined to include activities that happen in school buildings, on school grounds, on school buses, and at places that hold school-sponsored events or activities. Respondents were instructed to include incidents that occurred before, during, or after normal school hours or when school activities or events were in session. Detail may not sum to totals because of rounding.
SOURCE: U.S. Department of Education, National Center for Education Statistics, 2009–10 School Survey on Crime and Safety (SSOCS), 2010; Fast Response Survey System (FRSS), "School Safety and Discipline: 2013–14," FRSS 106, 2014; and Common Core of Data (CCD), "Public Elementary/Secondary School Universe Survey," 2013–14. (This table was prepared September 2015.)

Table 229.40. Percentage of public schools reporting incidents of crime at school to the police, number of incidents, and rate per 1,000 students, by type of crime and selected school characteristics: 2009–10

[Standard errors appear in parentheses]

School characteristic	Total number of schools	Violent incidents — All violent[1] — Percent of schools	All violent — Number of incidents	All violent — Rate per 1,000 students	Serious violent[2] — Percent of schools	Serious violent — Number of incidents	Serious violent — Rate per 1,000 students	Theft[3] — Percent of schools	Theft — Number of incidents	Theft — Rate per 1,000 students	Other incidents[4] — Percent of schools	Other incidents — Number of incidents	Other incidents — Rate per 1,000 students
1	2	3	4	5	6	7	8	9	10	11	12	13	14
Total	82,800 (460)	39.9 (1.13)	303,900 (13,310)	6.4 (0.28)	10.4 (0.62)	23,500 (2,320)	0.5 (0.05)	25.4 (1.01)	122,800 (4,180)	2.6 (0.09)	46.3 (1.23)	262,400 (8,260)	5.5 (0.17)
School level[5]													
Primary	48,900 (340)	21.1 (1.60)	35,300 (5,400)	1.6 (0.23)	5.5 (0.84)	6,100 (1,450)	0.3 (0.06)	9.3 (1.18)	9,500 (1,950)	0.4 (0.09)	30.3 (1.78)	40,100 (3,810)	1.8 (0.17)
Middle	15,300 (100)	65.9 (1.53)	100,100 (6,140)	10.7 (0.64)	15.5 (1.25)	6,300 (850)	0.7 (0.09)	41.1 (1.81)	27,100 (2,110)	2.9 (0.23)	65.4 (1.32)	60,300 (2,600)	6.4 (0.29)
High school	12,200 (70)	76.6 (1.61)	146,200 (10,520)	11.8 (0.84)	24.9 (1.16)	10,200 (1,120)	0.8 (0.09)	64.1 (1.59)	73,800 (3,370)	6.0 (0.31)	83.6 (1.32)	146,200 (5,850)	11.8 (0.50)
Combined	6,400 (200)	51.0 (5.72)	22,300 (3,820)	7.5 (1.20)	8.4 (2.41)	1,000 ! (400)	0.3 ! (0.13)	36.9 (5.41)	12,500 (2,420)	4.2 (0.84)	52.0 (4.86)	15,900 (2,350)	5.3 (0.82)
Enrollment size													
Less than 300	18,900 (400)	22.6 (2.54)	14,800 (2,740)	3.6 (0.67)	4.7 ! (1.44)	1,400 (380)	0.3 (0.09)	14.6 (2.73)	7,800 (2,210)	1.9 (0.53)	30.1 (2.59)	16,000 (2,590)	3.9 (0.66)
300–499	25,200 (180)	31.4 (2.29)	36,800 (4,240)	3.6 (0.42)	7.1 (1.32)	3,700 (860)	0.4 (0.08)	17.1 (1.91)	12,800 (1,780)	1.2 (0.17)	40.2 (2.58)	33,100 (2,720)	3.2 (0.27)
500–999	29,800 (100)	45.6 (1.79)	93,400 (6,070)	4.8 (0.31)	10.6 (1.04)	7,900 (1,440)	0.4 (0.07)	26.4 (1.40)	31,000 (2,410)	1.6 (0.12)	48.9 (2.08)	74,300 (4,010)	3.8 (0.20)
1,000 or more	8,900 (60)	81.1 (1.67)	159,000 (12,100)	11.9 (0.90)	31.1 (1.67)	10,600 (1,100)	0.8 (0.08)	68.4 (1.70)	71,200 (3,640)	5.3 (0.29)	89.0 (1.72)	139,000 (5,870)	10.4 (0.46)
Locale													
City	21,500 (190)	42.5 (2.01)	94,100 (4,900)	6.8 (0.35)	14.0 (1.45)	9,200 (1,460)	0.7 (0.11)	23.7 (1.65)	37,000 (3,420)	2.7 (0.24)	50.6 (1.85)	91,000 (4,370)	6.6 (0.31)
Suburban	23,800 (240)	39.9 (1.80)	107,600 (12,150)	6.5 (0.72)	10.0 (1.11)	7,300 (1,280)	0.4 (0.08)	26.3 (1.46)	39,900 (2,430)	2.4 (0.14)	47.5 (2.11)	85,700 (5,410)	5.2 (0.28)
Town	12,100 (110)	43.1 (3.06)	39,100 (3,510)	6.6 (0.56)	9.9 (1.91)	2,100 (350)	0.4 (0.06)	26.9 (2.33)	16,400 (1,720)	2.8 (0.27)	48.1 (3.27)	35,900 (3,090)	6.1 (0.52)
Rural	25,300 (300)	36.0 (1.93)	63,200 (5,590)	5.7 (0.52)	8.1 (1.22)	4,900 (1,110)	0.4 (0.10)	25.3 (2.00)	29,500 (2,930)	2.7 (0.27)	40.8 (1.89)	49,800 (2,620)	4.5 (0.26)
Percent combined enrollment of Black, Hispanic, Asian/Pacific Islander, and American Indian/Alaska Native students													
Less than 5 percent	11,700 (980)	36.5 (3.00)	20,000 (2,360)	4.3 (0.42)	7.1 (1.64)	1,400 (400)	0.3 (0.09)	23.5 (2.54)	10,200 (1,490)	2.2 (0.32)	38.5 (3.20)	20,200 (2,820)	4.3 (0.49)
5 percent to less than 20 percent	20,900 (1,080)	35.8 (1.72)	48,800 (3,620)	4.4 (0.32)	6.5 (0.80)	3,200 (450)	0.3 (0.04)	24.8 (1.66)	30,100 (2,970)	2.7 (0.26)	40.1 (2.31)	53,200 (3,810)	4.7 (0.32)
20 percent to less than 50 percent	20,000 (650)	41.7 (2.20)	75,000 (6,600)	5.9 (0.50)	10.3 (1.01)	5,000 (710)	0.4 (0.06)	26.8 (1.71)	34,900 (2,900)	2.7 (0.23)	46.3 (2.29)	65,500 (4,240)	5.1 (0.33)
50 percent or more	30,100 (1,270)	42.8 (2.36)	160,200 (13,150)	8.5 (0.67)	14.5 (1.27)	14,100 (2,310)	0.7 (0.12)	25.7 (1.78)	47,500 (3,470)	2.5 (0.19)	53.7 (2.25)	123,500 (6,250)	6.6 (0.34)
Percent of students eligible for free or reduced-price lunch													
0–25	17,100 (690)	33.8 (1.98)	42,200 (3,270)	3.6 (0.25)	7.4 (0.76)	3,600 (560)	0.3 (0.04)	26.8 (1.72)	30,500 (2,420)	2.6 (0.20)	40.6 (2.55)	54,200 (3,980)	4.6 (0.31)
26–50	22,700 (1,050)	42.7 (1.92)	76,100 (4,170)	5.8 (0.33)	10.7 (1.31)	5,000 (670)	0.4 (0.05)	31.2 (1.83)	43,300 (3,740)	3.3 (0.29)	48.0 (2.92)	76,900 (5,010)	5.9 (0.36)
51–75	23,800 (1,020)	40.3 (2.50)	87,200 (6,600)	7.1 (0.51)	8.8 (1.01)	5,400 (1,160)	0.4 (0.09)	22.9 (1.95)	31,200 (3,220)	2.6 (0.25)	47.5 (2.55)	72,300 (5,400)	5.9 (0.40)
76–100	19,100 (940)	41.4 (2.91)	98,400 (13,140)	9.8 (1.28)	14.7 (1.92)	9,500 (2,230)	0.9 (0.22)	20.3 (1.88)	17,800 (2,030)	1.8 (0.19)	48.0 (2.76)	59,000 (4,970)	5.8 (0.49)
Student/teacher ratio[6]													
Less than 12	12,300 (960)	36.8 (3.46)	29,000 (3,330)	6.9 (0.74)	8.7 (1.85)	2,200 (450)	0.5 (0.11)	24.8 (3.36)	11,400 (1,470)	2.7 (0.38)	46.4 (3.51)	22,100 (2,730)	5.3 (0.65)
12–16	32,600 (960)	41.5 (1.96)	128,500 (13,490)	7.4 (0.75)	10.0 (1.10)	7,900 (900)	0.5 (0.05)	25.8 (1.43)	42,100 (3,230)	2.4 (0.18)	45.6 (1.77)	88,900 (6,080)	5.1 (0.33)
More than 16	37,900 (1,000)	39.4 (1.76)	146,400 (8,760)	5.7 (0.33)	11.3 (0.83)	13,400 (2,210)	0.5 (0.08)	25.3 (1.55)	69,300 (3,600)	2.7 (0.15)	46.9 (1.67)	151,500 (6,510)	5.9 (0.26)

! Interpret data with caution. The coefficient of variation (CV) for this estimate is between 30 and 50 percent.

[1] All violent incidents include serious violent incidents (see footnote 2) as well as physical attack or fight without a weapon and threat of physical attack without a weapon.

[2] Serious violent incidents include rape, sexual battery other than rape, physical attack or fight with a weapon, threat of physical attack with a weapon, and robbery with or without a weapon.

[3] Theft/larceny (taking things worth over $10 without personal confrontation) was defined for respondents as "the unlawful taking of another person's property without personal confrontation, threat, violence, or bodily harm." This includes pocket picking, stealing a purse or backpack (if left unattended or no force was used to take it from owner), theft from a building, theft from a motor vehicle or motor vehicle parts or accessories, theft of a bicycle, theft from a vending machine, and all other types of thefts.

[4] "Other incidents" include possession of a firearm or explosive device; possession of a knife or sharp object; distribution, possession, or use of illegal drugs or alcohol; inappropriate distribution, possession, or use of prescription drugs; and vandalism.

[5] Primary schools are defined as schools in which the lowest grade is not higher than grade 3 and the highest grade is not higher than grade 8. Middle schools are defined as schools in which the lowest grade is not lower than grade 4 and the highest grade is not higher than grade 9. High schools are defined as schools in which the lowest grade is not lower than grade 9 and the highest grade is not higher than grade 12. Combined schools include all other combinations of grades, including K-12 schools.

[6] Student/teacher ratio was calculated by dividing the total number of students enrolled in the school by the total number of full-time-equivalent (FTE) teachers. Information regarding the total number of FTE teachers was obtained from the Common Core of Data (CCD), the sampling frame for SSOCS.

NOTE: Responses were provided by the principal or the person most knowledgeable about crime and safety issues at the school. "At school" was defined to include activities that happen in school buildings, on school grounds, on school buses, and at places that hold school-sponsored events or activities. Respondents were instructed to include incidents that occurred before, during, or after normal school hours or when school activities or events were in session. Detail may not sum to totals because of rounding.

SOURCE: U.S. Department of Education, National Center for Education Statistics, 2009–10 School Survey on Crime and Safety (SSOCS), 2010. (This table was prepared September 2013.)

Table 229.50. Percentage distribution of public schools, by number of violent incidents of crime at school recorded and reported to the police and selected school characteristics: 2009–10

[Standard errors appear in parentheses]

School characteristic	Number of violent incidents recorded							Number of violent incidents reported to the police						
	None	1–2 incidents	3–5 incidents	6–9 incidents	10–14 incidents	15–19 incidents	20 or more incidents	None	1–2 incidents	3–5 incidents	6–9 incidents	10–14 incidents	15–19 incidents	20 or more incidents
1	2	3	4	5	6	7	8	9	10	11	12	13	14	15
Total	26.2 (1.07)	7.6 (0.64)	14.5 (0.82)	14.5 (0.94)	11.1 (0.67)	6.6 (0.54)	19.4 (0.79)	60.1 (1.13)	17.9 (1.08)	7.8 (0.54)	4.3 (0.39)	3.1 (0.26)	1.7 (0.23)	5.0 (0.27)
School level[1]														
Primary	35.6 (1.63)	7.6 (1.09)	15.6 (1.40)	15.9 (1.46)	9.0 (1.03)	4.7 (0.75)	11.4 (1.11)	78.9 (1.60)	16.9 (1.63)	1.9! (0.58)	1.3 (0.38)	‡ (†)	‡ (†)	0.7! (0.25)
Middle	9.5 (1.10)	6.0 (0.86)	12.2 (1.18)	13.7 (1.09)	15.6 (1.03)	8.8 (0.96)	34.3 (1.36)	34.1 (1.53)	22.1 (1.44)	17.1 (1.20)	8.8 (1.09)	5.9 (0.59)	3.1 (0.58)	9.0 (0.70)
High school	9.1 (1.21)	8.4 (1.01)	12.1 (1.30)	10.6 (1.07)	14.0 (1.26)	11.0 (1.17)	34.8 (1.47)	23.4 (1.61)	17.8 (1.39)	15.6 (1.14)	9.4 (1.04)	9.8 (0.81)	5.7 (0.83)	18.3 (1.05)
Combined	26.3 (5.33)	10.3! (3.69)	15.4 (3.74)	13.6 (3.50)	11.0! (3.51)	7.6! (3.19)	15.8 (3.49)	49.0 (5.72)	16.2 (4.12)	16.6 (3.20)	7.2! (2.68)	6.9! (2.75)	‡ (†)	2.5! (1.22)
Enrollment size														
Less than 300	37.2 (3.25)	12.7 (2.05)	19.9 (2.84)	12.4 (2.17)	7.7 (1.72)	2.9! (1.00)	7.3 (1.72)	77.4 (2.54)	13.7 (2.18)	4.8 (1.06)	1.8! (0.72)	2.0! (0.94)	‡ (†)	‡ (†)
300–499	28.7 (2.34)	8.2 (1.55)	13.2 (1.83)	15.9 (2.03)	11.5 (1.35)	6.4 (1.11)	16.0 (1.80)	68.6 (2.29)	18.2 (2.09)	7.2 (1.09)	2.7 (0.63)	1.2! (0.41)	0.9! (0.36)	1.2! (0.38)
500–999	23.6 (1.75)	5.2 (1.01)	15.1 (1.52)	15.6 (1.39)	12.7 (1.16)	8.1 (0.88)	19.8 (1.21)	54.4 (1.79)	22.8 (1.47)	9.4 (0.79)	5.3 (0.73)	2.8 (0.34)	1.4 (0.37)	3.8 (0.44)
1,000 or more	4.6 (1.22)	3.6 (0.91)	4.2 (0.81)	11.3 (1.76)	12.3 (1.34)	10.3 (1.07)	53.7 (2.49)	18.9 (1.67)	9.7 (1.05)	10.7 (1.12)	11.2 (1.36)	12.1 (1.28)	8.1 (1.15)	29.5 (1.92)
Locale														
City	25.1 (2.12)	4.5 (1.11)	13.4 (2.08)	14.4 (1.65)	10.5 (1.39)	7.2 (1.27)	25.0 (1.84)	57.5 (2.01)	19.3 (1.65)	6.2 (0.81)	4.5 (0.74)	3.4 (0.54)	2.1 (0.54)	7.1 (0.61)
Suburban	26.5 (2.21)	6.3 (1.10)	15.5 (1.61)	14.1 (1.60)	11.8 (1.42)	6.5 (1.00)	19.3 (1.43)	60.1 (1.80)	17.1 (1.63)	8.7 (1.14)	4.0 (0.56)	2.7 (0.37)	1.3 (0.23)	6.1 (0.61)
Town	19.7 (3.14)	8.1 (1.92)	14.8 (2.51)	16.5 (2.87)	12.2 (1.77)	8.0 (1.68)	20.8 (2.50)	56.9 (3.06)	17.9 (2.47)	10.4 (1.48)	4.7 (1.03)	3.9 (0.64)	2.4! (0.76)	4.0 (0.70)
Rural	29.8 (1.91)	11.4 (1.58)	14.2 (1.55)	14.1 (1.38)	10.5 (1.57)	5.8 (1.07)	14.2 (1.47)	64.0 (1.93)	17.6 (1.93)	7.2 (0.87)	4.3 (0.83)	2.9 (0.74)	1.4 (0.39)	2.6 (0.42)
Percent combined enrollment of Black, Hispanic, Asian/Pacific Islander, and American Indian/Alaska Native students														
Less than 5 percent	30.4 (3.33)	15.1 (2.68)	12.1 (2.01)	13.8 (2.08)	11.7 (2.26)	4.5! (1.53)	12.4 (2.47)	63.5 (3.00)	18.8 (2.45)	10.5 (1.68)	3.2! (1.08)	1.7! (0.52)	0.9! (0.42)	1.5 (0.35)
5 percent to less than 20 percent	32.1 (2.82)	7.0 (1.44)	16.5 (1.91)	14.3 (1.81)	9.3 (1.20)	7.3 (1.28)	13.5 (1.38)	64.2 (1.72)	16.3 (1.42)	8.2 (1.09)	4.5 (0.79)	2.8 (0.36)	1.4 (0.42)	2.5 (0.34)
20 percent to less than 50 percent	24.1 (2.14)	8.4 (1.33)	14.7 (2.07)	15.1 (1.87)	9.5 (1.26)	6.6 (1.06)	21.6 (1.83)	58.3 (2.20)	19.8 (1.98)	7.2 (1.48)	3.8 (0.72)	3.8 (0.62)	1.9 (0.34)	5.3 (0.57)
50 percent or more	21.8 (1.75)	4.7 (1.04)	13.8 (1.59)	14.6 (1.55)	13.2 (1.31)	7.0 (1.05)	24.9 (1.65)	57.2 (2.36)	17.4 (1.99)	6.9 (0.87)	5.0 (0.59)	3.5 (0.64)	2.0 (0.46)	7.9 (0.70)
Percent of students eligible for free or reduced-price lunch														
0–25	37.4 (3.07)	7.4 (1.32)	14.9 (2.01)	13.1 (1.64)	10.0 (1.43)	5.1 (0.96)	12.1 (1.38)	66.2 (1.98)	14.4 (1.52)	7.9 (0.93)	3.4 (0.53)	3.8 (0.54)	1.4 (0.32)	3.0 (0.36)
26–50	24.0 (2.13)	9.0 (1.60)	16.2 (1.99)	14.3 (1.88)	10.9 (1.37)	6.7 (1.06)	18.9 (1.39)	57.3 (1.92)	19.6 (1.88)	9.7 (1.18)	4.0 (0.55)	2.9 (0.41)	1.8 (0.32)	4.7 (0.46)
51–75	26.2 (2.49)	7.9 (1.40)	13.2 (1.58)	14.2 (1.87)	10.0 (1.20)	7.5 (1.17)	21.0 (1.69)	59.7 (2.50)	18.0 (2.04)	7.1 (0.97)	4.9 (0.81)	3.3 (0.70)	2.1 (0.51)	5.1 (0.60)
76–100	18.6 (2.49)	5.9 (1.50)	13.5 (2.18)	16.5 (2.21)	13.8 (2.01)	6.9 (1.28)	24.7 (2.30)	58.6 (2.91)	19.0 (3.03)	6.5 (1.12)	4.9 (0.82)	2.7 (0.52)	1.4! (0.51)	6.9 (0.91)
Student/teacher ratio[2]														
Less than 12	30.3 (3.05)	11.1 (2.42)	15.7 (2.01)	16.7 (2.54)	8.1 (2.03)	5.9 (1.64)	12.3 (2.14)	63.2 (3.46)	19.4 (2.97)	6.5 (1.13)	3.9! (1.25)	2.4! (0.96)	1.7! (0.61)	2.8 (0.54)
12–16	24.7 (1.89)	7.9 (1.14)	15.2 (1.49)	14.0 (1.31)	12.0 (1.13)	6.1 (0.79)	20.0 (1.33)	58.5 (1.96)	18.2 (1.33)	9.2 (0.92)	4.6 (0.63)	3.2 (0.37)	1.9 (0.44)	4.4 (0.43)
More than 16	26.1 (1.35)	6.3 (0.96)	13.4 (1.28)	14.3 (1.44)	11.3 (1.10)	7.3 (0.81)	21.3 (1.29)	60.6 (1.76)	17.2 (1.56)	7.1 (0.79)	4.2 (0.54)	3.4 (0.47)	1.5 (0.22)	6.1 (0.52)

†Not applicable.

!Interpret data with caution. The coefficient of variation (CV) for this estimate is between 30 and 50 percent.

‡Reporting standards not met. Either there are too few cases for a reliable estimate or the coefficient of variation (CV) is 50 percent or greater.

[1]Primary schools are defined as schools in which the lowest grade is not higher than grade 3 and the highest grade is not higher than grade 8. Middle schools are defined as schools in which the lowest grade is not lower than grade 4 and the highest grade is not higher than grade 9. High schools are defined as schools in which the lowest grade is not lower than grade 9 and the highest grade is not higher than grade 12. Combined schools include all other combinations of grades, including K–12 schools.

[2]Student/teacher ratio was calculated by dividing the total number of students enrolled in the school by the total number of full-time-equivalent (FTE) teachers. Information regarding the total number of FTE teachers was obtained from the Common Core of Data (CCD), the sampling frame for SSOCS.

NOTE: Violent incidents include rape, sexual battery other than rape, physical attack or fight with or without a weapon, threat of physical attack with or without a weapon, and robbery with or without a weapon. Responses were provided by the principal or the person most knowledgeable about crime and safety issues at the school. "At school" was defined to include activities that happen in school buildings, on school grounds, on school buses, and at places that hold school-sponsored events or activities. Respondents were instructed to include incidents that occurred before, during, or after normal school hours or when school activities or events were in session. Detail may not sum to totals because of rounding.

SOURCE: U.S. Department of Education, National Center for Education Statistics, 2009–10 School Survey on Crime and Safety (SSOCS), 2010. (This table was prepared September 2013.)

Table 229.60. Percentage distribution of public schools, by number of serious violent incidents of crime at school recorded and reported to the police and selected school characteristics: 2009–10

[Standard errors appear in parentheses]

School characteristic	Number of serious violent incidents recorded						Number of serious violent incidents reported to the police					
	None	1 incident	2 incidents	3–5 incidents	6–9 incidents	10 or more incidents	None	1 incident	2 incidents	3–5 incidents	6–9 incidents	10 or more incidents
1	2	3	4	5	6	7	8	9	10	11	12	13
Total [1]	**83.6** (0.94)	**7.9** (0.70)	**3.0** (0.38)	**2.8** (0.40)	**1.2** (0.27)	**1.5** (0.31)	**89.6** (0.62)	**5.9** (0.57)	**1.9** (0.26)	**1.6** (0.23)	**0.5** (0.07)	**0.6** (0.16)
School level [1]												
Primary	87.0 (1.42)	6.8 (1.06)	1.8! (0.55)	2.2 (0.62)	1.3! (0.44)	0.9! (0.30)	94.5 (0.84)	3.8 (0.75)	0.7! (0.29)	0.6! (0.25)	# (†)	‡ (†)
Middle	81.1 (1.46)	8.6 (0.97)	4.5 (0.89)	2.9 (0.65)	1.0! (0.29)	1.9 (0.41)	84.5 (1.25)	8.3 (0.94)	4.0 (0.62)	1.7 (0.48)	0.8! (0.27)	0.6! (0.22)
High school	72.4 (1.35)	11.2 (1.01)	5.2 (0.66)	6.4 (0.83)	2.0 (0.43)	2.9 (0.56)	75.1 (1.16)	10.8 (1.04)	4.5 (0.72)	5.9 (0.83)	2.1 (0.42)	1.6 (0.43)
Combined	84.5 (3.72)	8.6! (2.89)	3.9! (1.85)	‡ (†)	# (†)	‡ (†)	91.6 (2.41)	6.3! (2.27)	‡ (†)	‡ (†)	# (†)	‡ (†)
Enrollment size												
Less than 300	89.6 (2.11)	5.7 (1.60)	‡ (†)	1.8! (0.90)	‡ (†)	‡ (†)	95.3 (1.44)	3.9! (1.45)	‡ (†)	0.6! (0.28)	‡ (†)	‡ (†)
300–499	84.3 (2.14)	8.4 (1.69)	3.2 (0.96)	1.9! (0.73)	1.4! (0.60)	‡ (†)	92.9 (1.32)	4.7 (1.14)	1.4! (0.55)	0.7! (0.35)	‡ (†)	‡ (†)
500–999	84.1 (1.42)	7.8 (1.13)	2.9 (0.58)	2.8 (0.57)	1.1! (0.39)	1.4! (0.43)	89.4 (1.04)	6.3 (0.93)	2.1 (0.40)	1.3 (0.38)	0.3! (0.11)	0.6! (0.30)
1,000 or more	67.2 (1.61)	11.7 (1.02)	6.3 (0.70)	7.5 (1.05)	2.2 (0.49)	5.2 (1.01)	68.9 (1.67)	11.9 (1.11)	6.2 (0.83)	7.3 (1.02)	2.4 (0.41)	3.2 (0.87)
Locale												
City	78.3 (2.12)	10.4 (1.43)	4.0 (0.80)	4.5 (0.93)	1.1! (0.41)	1.7 (0.45)	86.0 (1.45)	7.5 (1.11)	2.7 (0.59)	2.2 (0.41)	0.6 (0.14)	0.9! (0.30)
Suburban	84.5 (1.80)	6.5 (0.92)	3.4 (0.96)	2.7 (0.73)	1.0! (0.43)	2.0! (0.76)	90.0 (1.11)	4.7 (0.63)	2.3 (0.57)	1.5 (0.38)	0.7 (0.16)	0.8! (0.34)
Town	84.4 (2.33)	9.3 (2.05)	1.3 (0.39)	1.1 (0.33)	3.0! (1.20)	0.9! (0.36)	90.1 (1.91)	7.0 (1.85)	1.4! (0.41)	1.0! (0.31)	‡ (†)	0.8! (0.31)
Rural	86.8 (1.51)	6.4 (1.30)	2.5 (0.57)	2.3! (0.69)	‡ (†)	1.3! (0.48)	91.9 (1.22)	5.0 (1.19)	1.1 (0.28)	1.5 (0.44)	‡ (†)	‡ (†)
Percent combined enrollment of Black, Hispanic, Asian/Pacific Islander, and American Indian/Alaska Native students												
Less than 5 percent	87.4 (2.52)	6.7 (1.64)	1.0! (0.47)	2.9! (1.33)	# (†)	‡ (†)	92.9 (1.64)	5.5 (1.45)	‡ (†)	‡ (†)	‡ (†)	# (†)
5 percent to less than 20 percent	90.1 (1.29)	5.0 (0.84)	2.3 (0.59)	1.0! (0.31)	‡ (†)	0.4! (0.14)	93.5 (0.80)	3.6 (0.66)	1.6! (0.49)	0.7 (0.21)	0.3! (0.13)	0.2! (0.11)
20 percent to less than 50 percent	81.4 (1.58)	9.5 (1.48)	2.3 (0.43)	3.5 (0.99)	1.1! (0.49)	2.2 (0.64)	89.7 (1.16)	6.3 (1.12)	2.0 (0.45)	1.2 (0.32)	0.3! (0.12)	0.5! (0.26)
50 percent or more	78.9 (1.82)	9.3 (1.35)	4.6 (0.82)	3.6 (0.55)	1.9 (0.53)	1.6 (0.48)	85.5 (1.27)	7.3 (0.93)	2.6 (0.54)	2.7 (0.48)	0.8 (0.20)	1.1! (0.40)
Percent of students eligible for free or reduced-price lunch												
0–25	89.5 (1.22)	5.2 (0.93)	2.0 (0.47)	1.3 (0.39)	0.4! (0.16)	1.5! (0.47)	92.6 (0.76)	4.1 (0.55)	1.2 (0.30)	1.3 (0.36)	0.5! (0.20)	0.4! (0.14)
26–50	83.8 (1.89)	8.1 (1.43)	3.2 (0.69)	2.6! (0.82)	‡ (†)	1.0 (0.24)	89.3 (1.31)	6.5 (1.28)	2.5 (0.50)	1.1 (0.25)	0.5 (0.14)	‡ (†)
51–75	84.2 (1.67)	7.7 (1.24)	2.7 (0.78)	3.2 (0.67)	1.2! (0.51)	1.0! (0.44)	91.2 (1.01)	4.8 (0.90)	1.7 (0.45)	1.6 (0.41)	0.2! (0.09)	0.5! (0.30)
76–100	77.1 (2.60)	10.3 (1.90)	3.9 (0.89)	3.9 (0.97)	2.1! (0.74)	2.7! (1.13)	85.3 (1.92)	7.9 (1.55)	2.1 (0.58)	2.7 (0.67)	0.7! (0.26)	1.4! (0.57)
Student/teacher ratio [2]												
Less than 12	86.8 (2.24)	7.8 (1.94)	1.4! (0.55)	1.7! (0.65)	‡ (†)	1.5! (0.56)	91.3 (1.85)	5.5 (1.61)	1.7! (0.72)	0.8! (0.32)	‡ (†)	‡ (†)
12–16	84.0 (1.44)	8.0 (1.13)	2.7 (0.56)	2.6 (0.54)	1.2! (0.50)	1.5! (0.56)	90.0 (1.10)	6.0 (1.04)	1.5 (0.25)	1.8 (0.38)	0.3! (0.12)	0.5! (0.16)
More than 16	82.1 (1.35)	7.8 (0.89)	3.8 (0.72)	3.4 (0.62)	1.1! (0.39)	1.8 (0.45)	88.7 (0.83)	5.9 (0.64)	2.3 (0.50)	1.8 (0.37)	0.6 (0.11)	0.8! (0.32)

†Not applicable.
#Rounds to zero.
!Interpret data with caution. The coefficient of variation (CV) for this estimate is between 30 and 50 percent.
‡Reporting standards not met. Either there are too few cases for a reliable estimate or the coefficient of variation (CV) is 50 percent or greater.
[1]Primary schools are defined as schools in which the lowest grade is not higher than grade 3 and the highest grade is not higher than grade 8. Middle schools are defined as schools in which the lowest grade is not lower than grade 4 and the highest grade is not higher than grade 9. High schools are defined as schools in which the lowest grade is not lower than grade 9 and the highest grade is not higher than grade 12. Combined schools include all other combinations of grades, including K–12 schools.
[2]Student/teacher ratio was calculated by dividing the total number of students enrolled in the school by the total number of full-

time-equivalent (FTE) teachers. Information regarding the total number of FTE teachers was obtained from the Common Core of Data (CCD), the sampling frame for SSOCS.
NOTE: Serious violent incidents include rape, sexual battery other than rape, physical attack or fight with a weapon, threat of physical attack with a weapon, and robbery with or without a weapon. Responses were provided by the principal or the person most knowledgeable about crime and safety issues at the school. "At school" was defined to include activities that happen in school buildings, on school grounds, on school buses, and at places that hold school-sponsored events or activities. Respondents were instructed to include incidents that occurred before, during, or after normal school hours or when school activities or events were in session. Detail may not sum to totals because of rounding.
SOURCE: U.S. Department of Education, National Center for Education Statistics, 2009–10 School Survey on Crime and Safety (SSOCS), 2010. (This table prepared September 2013.)

Table 230.10. Percentage of public schools reporting selected discipline problems that occurred at school, by frequency and selected school characteristics: Selected years, 1999–2000 through 2013–14

[Standard errors appear in parentheses]

Year and school characteristic	Happens at least once a week[1]							Happens at all[2]	
	Student racial/ ethnic tensions[3]	Student bullying	Student sexual harassment of other students	Student harassment of other students based on sexual orientation or gender identity	Student verbal abuse of teachers	Widespread disorder in classrooms	Student acts of disrespect for teachers other than verbal abuse	Gang activities	Cult or extremist group activities
1	2	3	4	5	6	7	8	9	10
All schools									
1999–2000	3.4 (0.41)	29.3 (1.21)	— (†)	— (†)	12.5 (0.69)	3.1 (0.44)	— (†)	18.7 (0.85)	6.7 (0.46)
2003–04	2.1 (0.28)	26.8 (1.09)	4.0 (0.40)	— (†)	10.7 (0.80)	2.8 (0.39)	— (†)	16.7 (0.78)	3.4 (0.35)
2005–06	2.8 (0.31)	24.5 (1.14)	3.5 (0.40)	— (†)	9.5 (0.61)	2.3 (0.24)	— (†)	16.9 (0.76)	3.7 (0.41)
2007–08	3.7 (0.49)	25.3 (1.11)	3.0 (0.39)	— (†)	6.0 (0.48)	4.0 (0.45)	10.5 (0.71)	19.8 (0.88)	2.6 (0.36)
2009–10									
All schools	2.8 (0.39)	23.1 (1.12)	3.2 (0.55)	2.5 (0.41)	4.8 (0.49)	2.5 (0.37)	8.6 (0.67)	16.4 (0.84)	1.7 (0.31)
School level[4]									
Primary	2.1 (0.62)	19.6 (1.75)	1.8! (0.70)	0.8! (0.35)	3.4 (0.67)	1.9! (0.60)	6.1 (0.92)	7.5 (1.11)	1.4! (0.48)
Middle	5.4 (0.81)	38.6 (1.60)	6.1 (0.89)	6.2 (0.92)	6.8 (0.83)	4.1 (0.67)	13.7 (1.15)	29.2 (1.48)	1.4 (0.36)
High school	3.3 (0.56)	19.8 (1.41)	3.2 (0.58)	3.1 (0.55)	8.6 (1.00)	4.4 (0.80)	14.3 (1.27)	38.4 (1.50)	3.9 (0.48)
Combined	‡ (†)	18.6 (4.38)	7.5! (2.92)	6.0! (2.74)	‡ (†)	# (†)	4.4! (2.05)	11.1 (2.89)	‡ (†)
Enrollment size									
Less than 300	‡ (†)	16.5 (2.48)	4.5! (1.38)	4.3! (1.33)	‡ (†)	‡ (†)	3.3! (1.09)	6.5 (1.34)	‡ (†)
300–499	2.5 (0.72)	24.0 (2.19)	2.4! (0.75)	1.0 (0.28)	5.2 (1.03)	2.4 (0.70)	9.5 (1.57)	11.9 (1.49)	‡ (†)
500–999	3.0 (0.54)	25.3 (1.55)	2.6 (0.55)	2.4 (0.48)	4.3 (0.64)	2.6 (0.60)	8.3 (1.00)	16.4 (1.24)	1.3! (0.44)
1,000 or more	5.5 (1.10)	27.0 (2.12)	4.7 (1.01)	3.8 (0.82)	11.2 (1.37)	4.3 (0.96)	18.2 (1.64)	49.8 (1.72)	5.6 (0.95)
Locale									
City	5.3 (1.14)	27.0 (2.08)	3.6! (1.16)	2.9! (1.06)	9.1 (1.38)	4.5 (0.85)	11.7 (1.46)	28.3 (2.10)	2.5 (0.72)
Suburban	2.7 (0.61)	19.9 (1.96)	2.6 (0.69)	2.0 (0.42)	4.7 (0.92)	3.0 (0.77)	8.1 (1.10)	14.6 (1.16)	2.1 (0.41)
Town	1.0! (0.36)	26.2 (2.71)	2.9! (0.99)	2.0 (0.56)	3.3! (1.24)	0.6! (0.26)	11.6 (2.16)	13.9 (1.56)	1.7! (0.75)
Rural	1.6! (0.63)	21.2 (2.11)	3.6 (1.01)	2.9 (0.69)	1.9! (0.58)	1.3! (0.62)	5.0 (0.93)	9.1 (1.13)	1.6! (0.70)
Percent combined enrollment of Black, Hispanic, Asian/Pacific Islander, and American Indian/Alaska Native students									
Less than 5 percent	‡ (†)	22.0 (3.36)	4.5! (1.91)	2.7! (1.19)	‡ (†)	‡ (†)	3.6! (1.18)	1.5 (0.39)	0.4! (0.19)
5 percent to less than 20 percent	1.5 (0.33)	21.3 (1.66)	1.8! (0.58)	1.9 (0.46)	1.8! (0.48)	0.5! (0.16)	6.1 (1.22)	5.8 (0.80)	1.8! (0.75)
20 percent to less than 50 percent	3.2 (0.96)	22.3 (1.70)	2.6 (0.45)	2.6 (0.47)	4.5 (1.08)	1.1! (0.48)	9.6 (1.12)	16.9 (1.40)	1.4 (0.23)
50 percent or more	4.3 (0.95)	25.2 (2.35)	4.1! (1.25)	2.9! (0.87)	8.5 (1.17)	5.7 (0.94)	11.7 (1.22)	29.1 (1.88)	2.4 (0.64)
Percent of students eligible for free or reduced-price lunch									
0–25	1.9 (0.40)	19.7 (1.99)	2.6 (0.74)	2.1 (0.55)	1.5 (0.28)	0.7! (0.21)	3.6 (0.60)	7.9 (0.91)	1.4 (0.39)
26–50	2.6! (0.85)	21.9 (1.58)	3.2 (0.80)	3.0 (0.67)	2.3 (0.52)	1.3! (0.43)	6.9 (0.91)	13.2 (1.33)	1.9! (0.68)
51–75	2.4! (0.83)	24.1 (2.24)	3.2 (0.98)	2.7 (0.86)	5.6 (0.95)	1.0! (0.37)	10.7 (1.42)	17.4 (1.46)	1.3! (0.57)
76–100	4.3 (1.16)	26.1 (3.07)	3.9! (1.47)	2.1! (0.87)	9.6 (1.64)	7.5 (1.38)	12.5 (1.49)	26.5 (2.19)	2.3! (0.87)
2013–14[5]									
All schools	1.4 (0.31)	15.7 (1.12)	1.4 (0.26)	0.8 (0.19)	5.1 (0.54)	2.3 (0.45)	8.6 (0.74)	— (†)	— (†)
School level[4]									
Primary	1.2! (0.47)	12.2 (1.64)	‡ (†)	‡ (†)	4.4 (0.83)	2.1! (0.64)	6.2 (1.11)	— (†)	— (†)
Middle	2.5! (0.84)	24.5 (2.11)	3.4 (0.84)	2.4! (0.81)	6.1 (1.08)	2.5! (0.87)	11.1 (1.58)	— (†)	— (†)
High school/combined	1.1! (0.37)	17.2 (1.84)	1.8! (0.54)	1.4! (0.54)	6.2 (1.10)	2.8 (0.76)	12.8 (1.68)	— (†)	— (†)
Enrollment size									
Less than 300	‡ (†)	13.5 (2.93)	‡ (†)	‡ (†)	‡ (†)	‡ (†)	5.1! (1.72)	— (†)	— (†)
300–499	‡ (†)	14.6 (2.10)	1.8! (0.69)	0.7! (0.34)	6.1 (1.41)	3.7! (1.20)	7.8 (1.53)	— (†)	— (†)
500–999	2.1! (0.73)	16.1 (1.54)	1.3 (0.36)	0.4! (0.22)	5.4 (0.94)	2.4 (0.71)	9.5 (1.23)	— (†)	— (†)
1,000 or more	3.7 (1.01)	22.1 (2.40)	3.8! (1.19)	2.0! (0.74)	8.4 (1.47)	2.6! (0.85)	15.6 (2.53)	— (†)	— (†)
Locale									
City	3.1! (1.08)	14.8 (2.11)	2.5! (0.84)	‡ (†)	8.1 (1.52)	4.9 (1.38)	12.5 (1.72)	— (†)	— (†)
Suburban	2.0! (0.59)	12.9 (1.66)	1.5! (0.47)	1.0! (0.35)	6.2 (1.35)	2.4! (0.99)	9.0 (1.81)	— (†)	— (†)
Town	‡ (†)	24.0 (3.39)	‡ (†)	‡ (†)	3.9! (1.67)	‡ (†)	8.6 (2.08)	— (†)	— (†)
Rural	‡ (†)	15.4 (2.35)	‡ (†)	‡ (†)	2.5 (0.70)	1.2! (0.52)	5.4 (1.15)	— (†)	— (†)

See notes at end of table.

Table 230.10. Percentage of public schools reporting selected discipline problems that occurred at school, by frequency and selected school characteristics: Selected years, 1999–2000 through 2013–14—Continued

[Standard errors appear in parentheses]

Year and school characteristic	Happens at least once a week[1]							Happens at all[2]	
	Student racial/ethnic tensions[3]	Student bullying	Student sexual harassment of other students	Student harassment of other students based on sexual orientation or gender identity	Student verbal abuse of teachers	Widespread disorder in classrooms	Student acts of disrespect for teachers other than verbal abuse	Gang activities	Cult or extremist group activities
1	2	3	4	5	6	7	8	9	10
Percent combined enrollment of Black, Hispanic, Asian/Pacific Islander, and American Indian/Alaska Native students									
Less than 5 percent	‡	14.6 ! (4.52)	‡	‡	‡	‡	‡	—	†
5 percent to less than 20 percent	‡	11.9 (2.03)	‡	‡	1.6 ! (0.71)	‡	4.1 (1.00)	—	†
20 percent to less than 50 percent	1.5 ! (0.57)	18.1 (2.52)	2.2 ! (0.79)	‡	6.0 (1.36)	3.6 ! (1.13)	10.1 (1.72)	—	†
50 percent or more	2.5 (0.72)	16.8 (1.67)	1.5 (0.38)	1.1 ! (0.39)	7.8 (1.15)	3.4 (0.86)	11.6 (1.51)	—	†
Percent of students eligible for free or reduced-price lunch[6]									
0–25	‡	8.2 (2.15)	‡	1.0 ! (0.45)	‡	‡	2.0 (0.59)	—	†
26–50	1.4 ! (0.56)	14.2 (2.02)	1.2 ! (0.42)	‡	3.0 ! (0.94)	1.6 ! (0.76)	5.7 (1.28)	—	†
51–75	‡	18.3 (2.26)	2.2 ! (0.69)	‡	6.2 (1.19)	1.9 ! (0.70)	11.1 (1.75)	—	†
76–100	3.4 ! (1.18)	20.2 (2.36)	1.4 ! (0.67)	‡	8.2 (1.80)	5.1 (1.39)	12.4 (1.72)	—	†

—Not available.
†Not applicable.
#Rounds to zero.
!Interpret data with caution. The coefficient of variation (CV) for this estimate is between 30 and 50 percent.
‡Reporting standards not met. Either there are too few cases for a reliable estimate or the coefficient of variation (CV) is 50 percent or greater.
[1]Includes schools that reported the activity happens either at least once a week or daily.
[2]Includes schools that reported the activity happens at all at their school during the school year. In the 1999–2000 survey administration, the questionnaire specified "undesirable" gang activities and "undesirable" cult or extremist group activities.
[3]Prior to the 2007–08 survey administration, the questionnaire wording was "student racial tensions."
[4]Primary schools are defined as schools in which the lowest grade is not higher than grade 3 and the highest grade is not higher than grade 8. Middle schools are defined as schools in which the lowest grade is not lower than grade 4 and the highest grade is not higher than grade 9. High schools are defined as schools in which the lowest grade is not lower than grade 9 and the highest grade is not higher than grade 12. Combined schools include all other combinations of grades, including K–12 schools. Separate data on high schools and combined schools are not available for 2013–14.
[5]Data for 2013–14 were collected using the Fast Response Survey System, while data for earlier years were collected using the School Survey on Crime and Safety (SSOCS). The 2013–14 survey was designed to allow comparisons with SSOCS

data. However, respondents to the 2013–14 survey could choose either to complete the survey on paper (and mail it back) or to complete the survey online, whereas respondents to SSOCS did not have the option of completing the survey online. The 2013–14 survey also relied on a smaller sample. The smaller sample size and change in survey administration may have impacted 2013–14 results.
[6]Because the 2013–14 survey did not collect data on the percentage of students eligible for free or reduced-price lunch, the classification of schools by the percentage of students eligible for free or reduced-price lunch was computed based on data obtained from the Common Core of Data.
NOTE: Responses were provided by the principal or the person most knowledgeable about crime and safety issues at the school. "At school" was defined to include activities that happen in school buildings, on school grounds, on school buses, and at places that hold school-sponsored events or activities. Respondents were instructed to respond only for those times that were during normal school hours or when school activities or events were in session, unless the survey specified otherwise.
SOURCE: U.S. Department of Education, National Center for Education Statistics, 1999–2000, 2003–04, 2005–06, 2007–08, and 2009–10 School Survey on Crime and Safety (SSOCS), 2000, 2004, 2006, 2008, and 2010; Fast Response Survey System (FRSS), "School Safety and Discipline: 2013–14," FRSS 106, 2014; and Common Core of Data (CCD), "Public Elementary/Secondary School Universe Survey," 2013–14. (This table was prepared September 2015.)

Table 230.20. Percentage of students ages 12–18 who reported that gangs were present at school during the school year, by selected student and school characteristics and urbanity: Selected years, 2001 through 2013

Year and urbanity	Total	Sex		Race/ethnicity[1]					Grade							Control of school	
		Male	Female	White	Black	Hispanic	Asian	Other	6th grade	7th grade	8th grade	9th grade	10th grade	11th grade	12th grade	Public	Private
1	2	3	4	5	6	7	8	9	10	11	12	13	14	15	16	17	18
2001 Total	20.1 (0.71)	21.4 (0.86)	18.8 (0.90)	15.5 (0.72)	28.6 (1.90)	32.0 (1.82)	—	21.4 (2.18)	11.2 (1.28)	15.7 (1.09)	17.3 (1.22)	24.3 (1.27)	23.6 (1.48)	24.2 (1.56)	21.1 (1.54)	21.6 (0.77)	4.9 (1.05)
Urban	28.9 (1.23)	31.9 (1.62)	25.9 (1.52)	20.5 (1.28)	32.4 (2.79)	40.3 (2.45)	—	27.0 (4.41)	14.9 (2.45)	23.7 (2.54)	24.0 (2.66)	35.3 (2.77)	33.1 (3.08)	34.2 (3.18)	34.1 (3.21)	31.9 (1.35)	5.0 (1.38)
Suburban	18.3 (0.72)	18.9 (0.92)	17.5 (1.08)	15.4 (0.75)	25.4 (2.79)	27.1 (2.25)	—	20.0 (2.95)	9.0 (1.52)	13.7 (1.16)	16.6 (1.50)	20.8 (1.48)	22.3 (1.58)	22.7 (1.71)	18.6 (1.81)	19.5 (0.60)	4.3 ! (1.45)
Rural	13.3 (1.71)	14.0 (2.08)	12.5 (1.84)	12.1 (1.70)	22.5 (5.78)	16.8 ! (7.49)	—	‡ (†)	11.0 (2.78)	8.9 (1.87)	10.1 (2.24)	18.9 (3.03)	14.4 (3.05)	15.8 (3.65)	11.5 ! (4.51)	13.7 (1.90)	‡ (†)
2003 Total	20.9 (0.70)	22.3 (0.95)	19.5 (0.79)	14.2 (0.59)	29.5 (2.14)	37.2 (1.76)	—	22.0 (2.54)	10.9 (1.28)	16.3 (1.14)	17.9 (1.29)	26.1 (1.44)	26.3 (1.37)	23.4 (1.64)	22.2 (1.50)	22.5 (0.78)	3.9 (0.82)
Urban	30.9 (1.33)	32.1 (1.71)	29.7 (1.84)	19.8 (1.71)	32.8 (2.43)	42.6 (2.17)	—	30.6 (4.09)	21.6 (3.42)	25.5 (2.32)	25.2 (2.63)	38.2 (3.25)	35.3 (2.82)	34.6 (2.81)	34.8 (2.75)	33.7 (1.50)	6.0 (1.62)
Suburban	18.4 (0.84)	20.5 (1.07)	16.3 (0.92)	13.8 (0.67)	28.3 (3.93)	34.6 (2.14)	—	18.2 (2.96)	7.5 (1.25)	13.2 (1.28)	16.2 (1.65)	24.3 (1.58)	24.1 (1.72)	20.4 (2.34)	19.3 (1.91)	19.9 (0.91)	2.4 ! (0.78)
Rural	12.3 (1.81)	12.2 (2.00)	12.4 (2.34)	10.7 (1.42)	21.8 ! (7.17)	12.7 ! (4.11)	—	‡ (†)	‡ (†)	9.4 (2.56)	10.9 ! (3.26)	13.8 (3.00)	18.0 (3.50)	15.0 (3.30)	13.3 (3.60)	12.8 (2.02)	‡ (†)
2005 Total	24.2 (0.93)	25.3 (1.07)	22.9 (1.09)	16.8 (0.83)	37.6 (2.41)	38.9 (2.69)	20.2 (2.59)	27.7 (4.62)	12.1 (1.41)	17.3 (1.21)	19.1 (1.79)	28.3 (1.59)	32.6 (1.89)	28.0 (1.99)	27.9 (2.16)	25.8 (1.01)	4.2 (0.94)
Urban	36.2 (2.00)	37.4 (2.31)	35.0 (2.42)	23.7 (1.87)	41.8 (2.93)	48.9 (4.44)	25.0 (5.16)	33.9 (8.68)	19.9 (3.11)	24.2 (2.64)	30.5 (3.81)	40.3 (3.70)	50.6 (3.79)	44.3 (3.89)	39.5 (3.73)	39.1 (2.12)	7.7 (2.26)
Suburban	20.8 (0.93)	22.4 (1.14)	19.1 (1.15)	16.0 (0.87)	36.2 (4.41)	32.1 (2.52)	18.1 (2.87)	29.0 (6.12)	8.9 (1.52)	14.9 (1.46)	14.6 (2.01)	24.8 (1.92)	27.9 (2.37)	25.5 (2.21)	25.1 (2.60)	22.3 (1.01)	3.0 ! (1.02)
Rural	16.4 (2.53)	16.1 (3.20)	16.7 (2.79)	14.1 (2.46)	24.4 (6.75)	26.2 (6.51)	19.0 ! (9.22)	‡ (†)	8.3 (3.29)	15.2 (3.46)	14.7 (4.22)	21.0 (4.00)	22.0 (3.61)	13.3 ! (4.36)	15.8 ! (5.82)	17.2 (2.67)	‡ (†)
2007[2] Total	23.2 (0.80)	25.1 (1.07)	21.3 (0.87)	16.0 (0.70)	37.6 (2.26)	36.1 (2.04)	17.4 (2.72)	26.4 (3.63)	15.3 (1.99)	17.4 (1.28)	20.6 (1.68)	28.0 (1.51)	28.1 (1.73)	25.9 (1.61)	24.4 (1.69)	24.9 (0.87)	5.2 (1.14)
Urban	32.3 (1.49)	35.3 (2.01)	29.2 (1.62)	23.4 (1.98)	39.7 (3.07)	40.4 (2.90)	18.4 (4.30)	31.9 (6.10)	17.8 (3.45)	24.1 (2.96)	25.9 (2.90)	41.1 (3.40)	38.6 (3.36)	34.7 (3.05)	38.4 (4.01)	35.6 (1.61)	7.3 (2.07)
Suburban	21.0 (0.97)	23.1 (1.36)	18.9 (1.19)	15.9 (0.92)	35.5 (3.16)	33.3 (2.66)	16.3 (3.63)	29.0 (5.14)	14.0 (2.40)	15.4 (1.67)	19.6 (2.23)	23.1 (1.78)	26.6 (2.01)	23.6 (2.22)	22.4 (2.26)	22.7 (1.05)	2.8 ! (1.09)
Rural	15.5 (2.78)	14.9 (2.69)	16.1 (3.18)	10.9 (1.59)	36.8 (10.42)	27.5 ! (10.34)	‡ (†)	14.3 ! (6.01)	15.6 ! (6.21)	13.1 (2.79)	14.7 (4.26)	21.7 (4.43)	15.2 (3.39)	18.7 (3.98)	7.6 ! (2.90)	15.6 (2.91)	11.8 (5.84)
2009[2] Total	20.4 (0.85)	20.9 (1.12)	19.9 (1.03)	14.1 (0.79)	31.4 (2.62)	33.0 (2.20)	17.2 (3.21)	15.3 (4.07)	11.0 (1.76)	14.8 (1.70)	15.9 (1.60)	24.9 (2.01)	27.7 (1.75)	22.6 (1.53)	21.9 (2.02)	22.0 (0.89)	2.3 ! (0.82)
Urban	30.7 (1.86)	32.8 (2.35)	28.6 (2.29)	19.4 (1.99)	40.0 (3.76)	38.9 (3.31)	18.9 (4.63)	23.2 ! (9.05)	14.5 (4.13)	21.0 (3.37)	24.4 (3.24)	34.2 (4.01)	44.8 (3.41)	34.9 (4.08)	36.0 (4.32)	33.7 (1.94)	4.1 ! (1.83)
Suburban	16.6 (0.80)	17.2 (1.10)	16.0 (1.17)	13.5 (0.91)	20.2 (2.75)	28.3 (2.64)	14.5 (3.95)	14.8 ! (6.41)	9.7 (1.90)	11.2 (1.89)	11.8 (1.73)	22.4 (2.10)	21.0 (2.07)	19.4 (1.88)	17.6 (2.29)	18.1 (0.85)	‡ (†)
Rural	16.0 (3.08)	13.7 (3.37)	18.1 (3.18)	11.8 (2.09)	35.4 (9.77)	27.3 ! (10.84)	‡ (†)	‡ (†)	8.3 ! (3.11)	16.5 (4.19)	14.2 ! (4.41)	18.8 (5.04)	19.6 (5.02)	13.4 (3.50)	17.3 ! (5.37)	16.2 (3.18)	‡ (†)
2011[2] Total	17.5 (0.71)	17.5 (0.95)	17.5 (0.88)	11.1 (0.67)	32.7 (2.23)	26.4 (1.55)	9.9 (2.24)	9.9 (2.12)	8.2 (1.20)	10.2 (1.08)	11.3 (1.02)	21.7 (1.47)	23.0 (1.63)	23.2 (1.74)	21.3 (1.82)	18.9 (0.77)	1.9 ! (0.69)
Urban	22.8 (1.34)	23.0 (1.90)	22.6 (1.53)	13.9 (1.60)	31.6 (2.75)	31.0 (2.34)	7.6 ! (2.29)	12.3 (3.41)	5.4 ! (1.98)	11.7 (2.02)	16.2 (2.29)	27.5 (3.12)	31.1 (3.13)	28.1 (3.17)	32.9 (3.88)	25.7 (1.47)	‡ (†)
Suburban	16.1 (0.97)	16.5 (1.24)	15.6 (1.18)	11.3 (0.89)	33.5 (4.08)	23.2 (1.95)	12.0 ! (3.69)	10.4 ! (3.54)	8.6 (1.79)	9.3 (1.37)	9.0 (1.22)	18.9 (1.79)	21.5 (2.10)	23.7 (2.46)	18.5 (2.27)	17.1 (1.01)	2.9 ! (1.20)
Rural	12.1 (2.42)	10.2 (2.23)	14.1 (3.18)	7.7 (1.31)	34.5 (6.62)	22.1 ! (10.47)	‡ (†)	‡ (†)	11.1 (2.97)	10.1 (2.64)	9.6 ! (2.89)	19.3 (4.99)	13.9 (4.02)	10.6 (3.69)	9.2 ! (3.04)	12.5 (2.49)	‡ (†)
2013[2] Total	12.4 (0.62)	12.9 (0.85)	12.0 (0.73)	7.5 (0.63)	18.6 (1.72)	20.1 (1.34)	9.4 (1.85)	14.3 (2.68)	5.0 (1.15)	7.7 (0.96)	7.8 (0.96)	13.9 (1.43)	17.7 (1.46)	17.1 (1.65)	14.6 (1.58)	13.3 (0.67)	2.3 ! (0.94)
Urban	18.3 (1.23)	18.6 (1.61)	18.0 (1.38)	14.3 (1.73)	20.6 (2.36)	22.6 (2.15)	10.4 (2.61)	17.9 ! (5.59)	9.6 (2.75)	12.0 (2.44)	13.2 (2.30)	19.6 (2.53)	24.8 (2.86)	26.7 (3.21)	18.2 (3.07)	19.9 (1.36)	4.6 ! (2.08)
Suburban	10.8 (0.76)	11.7 (1.09)	9.8 (0.92)	6.5 (0.76)	17.3 (3.02)	19.3 (1.69)	8.2 ! (2.59)	13.0 (3.29)	3.0 ! (1.25)	6.6 (1.14)	6.3 (1.19)	12.2 (1.95)	15.4 (1.91)	15.1 (2.00)	14.1 (2.06)	11.7 (0.82)	‡ (†)
Rural	6.8 (1.44)	5.7 (1.38)	7.9 (1.92)	4.1 (1.20)	16.1 (4.49)	9.4 ! (4.52)	‡ (†)	11.9 ! (5.43)	‡ (†)	4.2 ! (1.88)	‡ (†)	8.0 ! (3.19)	11.3 (3.37)	8.1 ! (3.32)	9.0 (3.56)	6.8 (1.47)	‡ (†)

—Not available.
†Not applicable.
!Interpret data with caution. The coefficient of variation (CV) for this estimate is between 30 and 50 percent.
‡Reporting standards not met. Either there are too few cases for a reliable estimate or the coefficient of variation (CV) is 50 percent or greater.
[1]Race categories exclude persons of Hispanic ethnicity. "Other" includes American Indians/Alaska Natives, Asians (prior to 2005), Pacific Islanders, and, from 2003 onward, persons of Two or more races. Due to changes in racial/ethnic categories, comparisons of race/ethnicity across years should be made with caution.

[2]Starting in 2007, the reference period was the school year, whereas in prior survey years the reference period was the previous 6 months. Cognitive testing showed that estimates from 2007 onward are comparable to previous years.
NOTE: Urbanicity refers to the Standard Metropolitan Statistical Area (MSA) status of the respondents household as defined in 2000 by the U.S. Census Bureau. Categories include "central city of an MSA (Urban)," "in MSA but not in central city (Suburban)," and "not MSA (Rural)." All gangs, whether or not they are involved in violent or illegal activity, are included. "At school" includes in the school building, on school property, on a school bus, and going to and from school.
SOURCE: U.S. Department of Justice, Bureau of Justice Statistics, School Crime Supplement (SCS) to the National Crime Victimization Survey, selected years, 2001 through 2013. (This table was prepared August 2014.)

Table 230.30. Percentage of students ages 12–18 who reported being the target of hate-related words and seeing hate-related graffiti at school during the school year, by selected student and school characteristics: Selected years, 1999 through 2013

[Standard errors appear in parentheses]

Student or school characteristic	1999	2001	2003	2005	2007[1]	2009[1]	2011[1]	2013[3]
1	2	3	4	5	6	7	8	9
Hate-related words								
Total............	— (†)	12.3 (0.46)	11.7 (0.47)	11.2 (0.50)	9.7 (0.43)	8.7 (0.52)	9.1 (0.48)	6.6 (0.40)
Sex								
Male............	— (†)	12.8 (0.65)	12.0 (0.61)	11.7 (0.68)	9.9 (0.61)	8.5 (0.62)	9.0 (0.60)	6.6 (0.51)
Female........	— (†)	11.7 (0.52)	11.3 (0.64)	10.7 (0.64)	9.6 (0.57)	8.9 (0.72)	9.1 (0.68)	6.7 (0.53)
Race/ethnicity[2]								
White..........	— (†)	12.1 (0.58)	10.9 (0.56)	10.3 (0.60)	8.9 (0.50)	7.2 (0.59)	8.3 (0.59)	5.3 (0.43)
Black..........	— (†)	13.9 (1.08)	14.2 (1.35)	15.1 (1.48)	11.4 (1.35)	11.1 (1.35)	10.7 (1.30)	7.8 (1.20)
Hispanic......	— (†)	11.0 (1.15)	11.4 (0.96)	10.5 (1.15)	10.6 (1.18)	11.2 (1.13)	9.8 (0.98)	7.4 (0.84)
Asian..........	— (†)	— (†)	— (†)	10.9 (2.56)	11.1 (1.97)	10.7 (2.81)	9.0 (2.00)	10.3 (2.19)
Other..........	— (†)	13.6 (2.05)	14.1 (2.03)	14.2 (3.27)	10.6 (2.71)	10.0 (2.37)	10.4 (2.61)	11.2 (2.47)
Grade								
6th.............	— (†)	12.1 (1.26)	11.9 (1.31)	11.1 (1.58)	12.1 (1.54)	8.3 (1.39)	9.0 (1.43)	6.7 (1.33)
7th.............	— (†)	14.1 (1.13)	12.5 (1.04)	13.1 (1.16)	10.7 (1.02)	9.6 (1.22)	9.9 (1.02)	7.5 (0.89)
8th.............	— (†)	13.0 (1.07)	12.8 (0.92)	11.2 (1.04)	11.0 (1.19)	10.9 (1.22)	8.4 (0.94)	7.4 (1.01)
9th.............	— (†)	12.1 (1.00)	13.5 (1.23)	12.8 (1.12)	10.9 (1.08)	8.0 (1.18)	10.2 (1.10)	6.6 (0.94)
10th...........	— (†)	13.1 (0.95)	11.6 (1.12)	10.9 (1.04)	9.0 (0.99)	9.7 (1.18)	9.6 (1.14)	6.4 (0.97)
11th...........	— (†)	12.7 (1.13)	8.3 (0.97)	9.0 (1.17)	8.6 (1.01)	8.4 (1.14)	8.7 (1.01)	7.5 (1.01)
12th...........	— (†)	7.9 (0.87)	10.8 (1.25)	9.7 (1.35)	6.0 (0.98)	5.8 (0.96)	7.5 (1.01)	4.1 (0.78)
Urbanicity[3]								
Urban..........	— (†)	11.9 (0.73)	13.2 (0.83)	12.2 (0.86)	9.7 (0.83)	9.9 (0.93)	8.0 (0.77)	7.2 (0.76)
Suburban.....	— (†)	12.4 (0.63)	10.7 (0.58)	9.4 (0.52)	9.3 (0.62)	8.3 (0.64)	9.8 (0.71)	6.6 (0.50)
Rural...........	— (†)	12.4 (1.11)	12.2 (1.35)	15.5 (1.74)	11.0 (1.07)	8.1 (1.37)	8.5 (1.00)	5.7 (0.80)
Control of school								
Public.........	— (†)	12.7 (0.51)	11.9 (0.49)	11.6 (0.53)	10.1 (0.46)	8.9 (0.54)	9.3 (0.50)	6.6 (0.41)
Private........	— (†)	8.2 (1.13)	9.7 (1.11)	6.8 (1.18)	6.1 (1.25)	6.6 (1.62)	6.9 (1.29)	6.7 (1.41)
Hate-related graffiti								
Total............	36.3 (0.94)	35.5 (0.75)	36.3 (0.84)	38.4 (0.83)	34.9 (0.89)	29.2 (0.96)	28.4 (0.88)	24.6 (0.88)
Sex								
Male............	33.8 (1.06)	34.9 (0.89)	35.0 (0.97)	37.7 (1.10)	34.4 (1.12)	29.0 (1.26)	28.6 (1.11)	24.1 (1.11)
Female........	38.9 (1.14)	36.1 (0.92)	37.6 (1.06)	39.1 (0.93)	35.4 (1.12)	29.3 (1.09)	28.1 (1.07)	25.1 (1.05)
Race/ethnicity[2]								
White..........	36.4 (1.20)	36.2 (0.95)	35.2 (0.86)	38.5 (0.96)	35.5 (1.05)	28.3 (1.10)	28.2 (1.19)	23.7 (1.20)
Black..........	37.6 (1.71)	33.6 (1.52)	38.1 (1.95)	38.0 (2.29)	33.7 (2.37)	29.0 (2.44)	28.1 (1.90)	26.3 (2.10)
Hispanic......	35.6 (1.46)	35.1 (1.87)	40.3 (2.24)	38.0 (1.78)	34.8 (1.76)	32.2 (1.61)	29.1 (1.33)	25.6 (1.52)
Asian..........	— (†)	— (†)	— (†)	34.5 (3.76)	28.2 (3.01)	31.2 (3.59)	29.9 (4.56)	20.8 (3.22)
Other..........	32.2 (2.53)	32.1 (2.82)	31.4 (2.83)	46.9 (4.68)	38.7 (3.44)	25.8 (4.20)	25.9 (3.79)	28.4 (3.52)
Grade								
6th.............	30.3 (1.82)	34.9 (1.88)	35.7 (1.83)	34.0 (2.24)	35.5 (2.30)	28.1 (2.26)	25.9 (2.13)	21.9 (1.77)
7th.............	34.9 (1.43)	34.9 (1.36)	37.2 (1.41)	37.0 (1.63)	32.3 (1.52)	27.9 (1.88)	26.0 (1.70)	21.7 (1.49)
8th.............	35.6 (1.51)	36.7 (1.40)	34.2 (1.53)	35.7 (1.61)	33.5 (1.81)	30.8 (1.80)	25.9 (1.55)	24.0 (1.80)
9th.............	39.2 (1.55)	35.7 (1.55)	37.0 (1.48)	41.6 (1.64)	34.5 (1.77)	28.1 (1.83)	28.7 (1.69)	27.2 (1.74)
10th...........	38.9 (1.77)	36.2 (1.49)	40.7 (1.67)	40.7 (1.83)	36.4 (1.69)	31.0 (2.03)	33.3 (1.78)	26.0 (1.58)
11th...........	37.0 (1.74)	36.1 (1.76)	36.6 (1.74)	40.2 (1.70)	35.3 (1.81)	27.4 (2.01)	32.1 (1.70)	25.8 (2.03)
12th...........	35.6 (2.04)	33.0 (1.79)	32.2 (1.78)	37.8 (2.34)	37.7 (2.03)	30.4 (2.00)	25.7 (1.51)	24.2 (1.91)
Urbanicity[3]								
Urban..........	37.0 (1.18)	35.7 (1.21)	38.6 (1.27)	40.9 (1.43)	34.4 (1.36)	31.1 (1.56)	27.5 (1.49)	27.8 (1.48)
Suburban.....	37.3 (1.12)	36.0 (0.87)	35.9 (1.16)	38.0 (1.02)	34.2 (1.03)	28.6 (1.15)	29.9 (1.08)	23.7 (1.11)
Rural...........	32.7 (2.60)	33.8 (2.56)	33.9 (1.97)	35.8 (2.40)	37.8 (3.06)	27.7 (2.43)	24.9 (2.25)	21.6 (2.71)
Control of school								
Public.........	38.0 (0.97)	37.3 (0.80)	37.9 (0.90)	40.0 (0.87)	36.4 (0.93)	30.7 (1.01)	29.7 (0.95)	25.6 (0.94)
Private........	20.7 (1.85)	16.8 (1.34)	19.5 (1.75)	18.6 (1.97)	18.5 (2.07)	11.8 (1.93)	13.4 (1.56)	12.6 (1.74)

—Not available.
†Not applicable.
[1]Starting in 2007, the reference period was the school year, whereas in prior survey years the reference period was the previous 6 months. Cognitive testing showed that estimates from 2007 onward are comparable to previous years.
[2]Race categories exclude persons of Hispanic ethnicity. "Other" includes American Indians/Alaska Natives, Asians (prior to 2005), Pacific Islanders, and, from 2003 onward, persons of Two or more races. Due to changes in racial/ethnic categories, comparisons of race/ethnicity across years should be made with caution.
[3]Refers to the Standard Metropolitan Statistical Area (MSA) status of the respondent's household as defined in 2000 by the U.S. Census Bureau. Categories include "central city of an MSA (Urban)," "in MSA but not in central city (Suburban)," and "not MSA (Rural)."
NOTE: "At school" includes in the school building, on school property, on a school bus, and, from 2001 onward, going to and from school. "Hate-related" refers to derogatory terms used by others in reference to students' personal characteristics.
SOURCE: U.S. Department of Justice, Bureau of Justice Statistics, School Crime Supplement (SCS) to the National Crime Victimization Survey, selected years, 1999 through 2013. (This table was prepared August 2014.)

Table 230.35. Percentage of students ages 12–18 who reported being the target of hate-related words at school, by type of hate-related word and selected student and school characteristics: 2013

[Standard errors appear in parentheses]

Student or school characteristic	Total[1]		Hate-related words related to student's characteristic											
			Race		Ethnicity		Religion		Disability		Gender		Sexual orientation	
1	2		3		4		5		6		7		8	
Total............................	6.6	(0.40)	3.3	(0.31)	1.9	(0.21)	1.2	(0.15)	0.8	(0.14)	1.0	(0.14)	1.1	(0.13)
Sex														
Male..........................	6.6	(0.51)	3.5	(0.41)	1.9	(0.27)	1.0	(0.19)	0.7	(0.16)	0.3	(0.09)	0.9	(0.16)
Female.......................	6.7	(0.53)	3.1	(0.40)	1.9	(0.30)	1.4	(0.22)	0.9	(0.21)	1.7	(0.29)	1.3	(0.22)
Race/ethnicity[2]														
White........................	5.3	(0.43)	1.6	(0.25)	0.8	(0.18)	1.2	(0.22)	1.2	(0.22)	1.1	(0.20)	1.3	(0.22)
Black........................	7.8	(1.20)	5.8	(1.03)	1.9	(0.48)	1.0 !	(0.39)	‡	(†)	1.0 !	(0.41)	1.1 !	(0.43)
Hispanic....................	7.4	(0.84)	3.9	(0.64)	3.7	(0.62)	1.0	(0.27)	‡	(†)	0.9	(0.25)	0.8 !	(0.27)
Asian.......................	10.3	(2.19)	8.5	(2.05)	7.1	(2.00)	2.1 !	(0.87)	‡	(†)	‡	(†)	‡	(†)
Other........................	11.2	(2.47)	8.3	(2.10)	‡	(†)	‡	(†)	‡	(†)	‡	(†)	‡	(†)
Grade														
6th...........................	6.7	(1.33)	3.5	(0.98)	1.9 !	(0.67)	1.1 !	(0.52)	‡	(†)	‡	(†)	‡	(†)
7th...........................	7.5	(0.89)	3.6	(0.64)	2.0	(0.46)	0.8 !	(0.32)	1.1 !	(0.35)	1.1 !	(0.36)	0.9 !	(0.35)
8th...........................	7.4	(1.01)	3.3	(0.72)	1.8 !	(0.54)	1.7	(0.48)	1.0 !	(0.33)	1.4	(0.40)	1.4 !	(0.43)
9th...........................	6.6	(0.94)	3.0	(0.68)	2.0	(0.58)	2.1	(0.56)	0.9 !	(0.36)	0.9 !	(0.33)	0.8 !	(0.31)
10th..........................	6.4	(0.97)	3.9	(0.76)	2.0	(0.50)	1.2 !	(0.39)	0.9 !	(0.32)	0.7 !	(0.28)	0.8 !	(0.32)
11th..........................	7.5	(1.01)	3.9	(0.74)	1.9	(0.53)	1.1 !	(0.40)	‡	(†)	1.4 !	(0.45)	2.3	(0.48)
12th..........................	4.1	(0.78)	1.8	(0.55)	1.9	(0.53)	‡	(†)	‡	(†)	0.6 !	(0.32)	0.8 !	(0.36)
Urbanicity[3]														
Urban........................	7.2	(0.76)	4.2	(0.65)	2.2	(0.37)	0.9	(0.21)	0.6 !	(0.23)	0.8	(0.23)	1.2	(0.25)
Suburban....................	6.6	(0.50)	3.1	(0.39)	1.9	(0.29)	1.3	(0.21)	0.8	(0.19)	1.0	(0.18)	0.9	(0.18)
Rural........................	5.7	(0.80)	2.3	(0.56)	1.5 !	(0.49)	1.5 !	(0.45)	1.2 !	(0.44)	1.4 !	(0.46)	1.4	(0.39)
Control of school														
Public.......................	6.6	(0.41)	3.3	(0.30)	1.9	(0.21)	1.2	(0.15)	0.8	(0.14)	1.0	(0.15)	1.1	(0.13)
Private......................	6.7	(1.41)	3.7	(1.08)	1.9 !	(0.79)	‡	(†)	‡	(†)	1.2 !	(0.55)	‡	(†)

†Not applicable.

!Interpret data with caution. The coefficient of variation (CV) for this estimate is between 30 and 50 percent.

‡Reporting standards not met. Either there are too few cases for a reliable estimate or the coefficient of variation (CV) is 50 percent or greater.

[1]Students who indicated that they had been called a hate-related word were asked to choose the specific characteristics that the hate-related word or words targeted. Students were allowed to choose more than one characteristic. If a student chose more than one characteristic, he or she is counted only once in the total percentage of students who reported being called a hate-related word; therefore, the total is less than the sum of the students' individual characteristics.

[2]Race categories exclude persons of Hispanic ethnicity. "Other" includes American Indians/

Alaska Natives, Pacific Islanders, and persons of Two or more races.

[3]Refers to the Standard Metropolitan Statistical Area (MSA) status of the respondent's household as defined in 2000 by the U.S. Census Bureau. Categories include "central city of an MSA (Urban)," "in MSA but not in central city (Suburban)," "and not MSA (Rural)."

NOTE: "At school" includes in the school building, on school property, on a school bus, or going to and from school. "Hate-related" refers to derogatory terms used by others in reference to students' personal characteristics. Detail may not sum to totals because of rounding and because students may have reported being targets of hate-related words related to more than one student characteristic.

SOURCE: U.S. Department of Justice, Bureau of Justice Statistics, School Crime Supplement (SCS) to the National Crime Victimization Survey, 2013. (This table was prepared August 2014.)

Table 230.40. Percentage of students ages 12–18 who reported being bullied at school or cyber-bullied anywhere during the school year, by type of bullying at school, reports of injury, and selected student and school characteristics: 2013

[Standard errors appear in parentheses]

Student or school characteristic	Bullied at school or cyber-bullied anywhere			Type of bullying at school							Of students who were pushed, shoved, tripped, or spit on, percent reporting injury[1]
	Total bullied at school or cyber-bullied anywhere[2]	Total cyber-bullied anywhere[3]	Total bullied at school[4]	Made fun of, called names, or insulted	Subject of rumors	Threatened with harm	Tried to make do things did not want to do	Excluded from activities on purpose	Property destroyed on purpose	Pushed, shoved, tripped, or spit on	
1	2	3	4	5	6	7	8	9	10	11	12
Total	23.1 (0.67)	6.9 (0.42)	21.5 (0.66)	13.6 (0.51)	13.2 (0.50)	3.9 (0.27)	2.2 (0.21)	4.5 (0.30)	1.6 (0.20)	6.0 (0.39)	20.8 (2.48)
Sex											
Male	21.1 (0.84)	5.2 (0.43)	19.5 (0.81)	12.6 (0.70)	9.6 (0.60)	4.1 (0.38)	2.4 (0.30)	3.5 (0.34)	1.8 (0.28)	7.4 (0.59)	20.6 (3.21)
Female	25.2 (0.99)	8.6 (0.63)	23.7 (0.98)	14.7 (0.75)	17.0 (0.80)	3.7 (0.37)	1.9 (0.27)	5.5 (0.47)	1.3 (0.25)	4.6 (0.42)	21.1 (3.63)
Race/ethnicity[5]											
White	25.3 (0.94)	7.6 (0.57)	23.7 (0.93)	15.6 (0.74)	14.6 (0.76)	4.4 (0.40)	2.0 (0.28)	5.4 (0.46)	1.5 (0.24)	6.1 (0.49)	22.3 (3.39)
Black	21.2 (1.85)	4.5 (0.94)	20.3 (1.81)	10.5 (1.22)	12.7 (1.40)	3.2 (0.68)	2.7 (0.59)	2.7 (0.71)	2.0 (0.54)	6.0 (0.97)	15.6! (6.04)
Hispanic	20.5 (1.32)	5.8 (0.78)	19.2 (1.30)	12.1 (1.13)	11.5 (1.02)	4.0 (0.58)	1.6 (0.32)	3.5 (0.53)	1.4 (0.38)	6.3 (0.79)	18.3 (4.15)
Asian	11.8 (2.02)	5.8 (1.67)	9.2 (1.67)	7.5 (1.63)	3.7 (0.95)	‡ (†)	3.8! (1.32)	2.2! (0.71)	1.6! (0.78)	2.0! (0.85)	‡ (†)
Other	29.7 (3.83)	13.4 (2.43)	25.2 (3.60)	16.5 (2.99)	17.3 (3.05)	4.3! (1.56)	4.0! (1.38)	6.5 (1.85)	2.1! (1.00)	8.5 (1.90)	‡ (†)
Grade											
6th	29.9 (2.31)	5.9 (1.20)	27.8 (2.31)	21.3 (2.15)	16.1 (1.61)	5.9 (1.13)	3.4 (0.88)	6.5 (1.20)	3.1 (0.77)	11.0 (1.46)	26.8 (6.90)
7th	27.3 (1.65)	7.0 (0.91)	26.4 (1.65)	17.9 (1.35)	15.5 (1.35)	6.1 (0.88)	3.0 (0.52)	6.3 (0.86)	2.2 (0.52)	11.6 (1.12)	24.0 (4.11)
8th	22.7 (1.43)	6.4 (0.86)	21.7 (1.42)	14.5 (1.23)	12.7 (1.11)	3.9 (0.68)	2.3 (0.54)	5.2 (0.80)	1.5 (0.45)	6.5 (0.85)	20.8 (5.92)
9th	24.4 (1.46)	6.7 (0.97)	23.0 (1.42)	13.7 (1.16)	13.8 (1.22)	3.6 (0.61)	2.6 (0.58)	4.3 (0.70)	1.2! (0.40)	4.9 (0.83)	18.2! (7.32)
10th	21.4 (1.52)	8.6 (1.16)	19.5 (1.48)	12.9 (1.21)	12.9 (1.28)	4.3 (0.73)	1.7 (0.47)	4.6 (0.72)	1.3 (0.37)	3.7 (0.68)	21.2! (7.78)
11th	22.4 (1.50)	6.8 (0.87)	20.0 (1.50)	11.2 (1.20)	12.5 (1.31)	3.0 (0.60)	1.5 (0.45)	2.4 (0.61)	1.6! (0.50)	3.4 (0.72)	‡ (†)
12th	15.4 (1.45)	5.9 (0.93)	14.1 (1.51)	6.4 (1.04)	9.7 (1.15)	1.0! (0.43)	1.3! (0.48)	2.5 (0.67)	0.7! (0.31)	3.0 (0.71)	‡ (†)
Urbanicity[6]											
Urban	22.6 (1.10)	7.1 (0.73)	20.7 (1.10)	12.8 (0.80)	12.7 (0.87)	3.9 (0.47)	2.7 (0.45)	4.1 (0.51)	1.4 (0.27)	5.6 (0.60)	20.9 (4.99)
Suburban	23.5 (0.93)	7.0 (0.61)	22.0 (0.90)	14.2 (0.69)	13.4 (0.71)	3.9 (0.39)	2.0 (0.28)	4.7 (0.43)	1.3 (0.24)	6.4 (0.52)	21.8 (3.31)
Rural	22.7 (1.87)	5.9 (1.02)	21.4 (1.86)	13.2 (1.49)	13.3 (1.45)	4.1 (0.67)	1.7 (0.42)	4.2 (0.73)	2.8 (0.66)	5.8 (0.88)	16.7! (5.31)
Control of school											
Public	23.0 (0.69)	6.9 (0.45)	21.5 (0.67)	13.5 (0.53)	13.2 (0.52)	3.9 (0.28)	2.2 (0.22)	4.3 (0.31)	1.6 (0.19)	6.1 (0.41)	20.3 (2.57)
Private	23.8 (2.79)	6.4 (1.44)	22.4 (2.71)	15.3 (2.01)	13.4 (2.20)	3.9 (1.14)	2.7! (0.82)	6.7 (1.31)	1.3! (0.60)	5.2 (1.24)	‡ (†)

†Not applicable.
‡Reporting standards not met. Either there are too few cases for a reliable estimate or the coefficient of variation (CV) is 50 percent or greater.
!Interpret data with caution. The coefficient of variation (CV) for this estimate is between 30 and 50 percent.
[1]Only students who reported that they were pushed, shoved, tripped, or spit on were asked if they suffered injuries as a result of the incident.
[2]Students who reported that they were both bullied at school and cyber-bullied anywhere were counted only once in the total for students bullied at school or cyber-bullied anywhere.
[3]Students who reported being cyber-bullied are those who responded that another student had done one or more of the following: posted hurtful information about them on the Internet; purposely shared private information about them on the Internet; threatened or insulted them through instant messaging; threatened or insulted them through text messaging; threatened or insulted them through e-mail; threatened or insulted them while gaming; or excluded them online. Students who reported more than one of these types of cyber-bullying were counted only once in the total for students cyber-bullied anywhere.
[4]Students who reported experiencing more than one type of bullying at school were counted only once in the total for students bullied at school.
[5]Race categories exclude persons of Hispanic ethnicity. "Other" includes American Indians/Alaska Natives, Pacific Islanders, and persons of Two or more races.
[6]Refers to the Standard Metropolitan Statistical Area (MSA) status of the respondent's household as defined in 2000 by the U.S. Census Bureau. Categories include "central city of an MSA (Urban)," "in MSA but not in central city (Suburban)," and "not MSA (Rural)."
NOTE: "At school" includes the school building, on school property, on a school bus, or going to and from school. Bullying types do not sum to totals because students could have experienced more than one type of bullying.
SOURCE: U.S. Department of Justice, Bureau of Justice Statistics, School Crime Supplement (SCS) to the National Crime Victimization Survey, 2013. (This table was prepared August 2014.)

Table 230.45. Percentage of students ages 12–18 who reported being bullied at school during the school year, by type of bullying and selected student and school characteristics: Selected years, 2005 through 2013

[Standard errors appear in parentheses]

Year and student or school characteristic	Total bullied at school		Type of bullying at school												
			Made fun of, called names, or insulted		Subject of rumors		Threatened with harm		Tried to make do things did not want to do		Excluded from activities on purpose		Property destroyed on purpose		Pushed, shoved, tripped, or spit on	
1	2		3		4		5		6		7		8		9	
2005																
Total	28.1	(0.70)	18.7	(0.58)	14.7	(0.53)	4.8	(0.31)	3.5	(0.27)	4.6	(0.30)	3.4	(0.29)	9.0	(0.45)
Sex																
Male	27.1	(0.90)	18.5	(0.73)	11.0	(0.64)	5.2	(0.51)	3.9	(0.39)	4.1	(0.40)	3.5	(0.41)	10.9	(0.70)
Female	29.2	(0.84)	19.0	(0.79)	18.5	(0.74)	4.4	(0.37)	3.1	(0.32)	5.2	(0.40)	3.3	(0.35)	7.1	(0.50)
Race/ethnicity[1]																
White	30.0	(0.84)	20.1	(0.72)	15.8	(0.66)	5.1	(0.47)	3.6	(0.35)	5.3	(0.36)	3.4	(0.35)	9.7	(0.62)
Black	28.5	(2.21)	18.5	(1.72)	14.2	(1.36)	4.9	(0.76)	4.7	(1.00)	4.5	(0.91)	4.6	(0.89)	8.9	(1.14)
Hispanic	22.3	(1.28)	14.7	(1.11)	12.4	(1.00)	4.6	(0.64)	2.6	(0.55)	3.0	(0.53)	2.7	(0.49)	7.6	(0.94)
Asian	—	(†)	—	(†)	—	(†)	—	(†)	—	(†)	—	(†)	—	(†)	—	(†)
Other	24.6	(2.06)	16.3	(1.82)	11.6	(1.71)	2.1	(0.59)	2.1 !	(0.74)	2.5 !	(0.79)	2.5 !	(0.77)	6.8	(1.19)
Grade																
6th	36.6	(1.99)	26.3	(2.05)	16.4	(1.60)	6.4	(1.18)	4.4	(0.92)	7.4	(1.19)	3.9	(0.91)	15.1	(1.75)
7th	35.0	(1.72)	25.2	(1.57)	18.9	(1.27)	6.3	(0.80)	4.7	(0.83)	7.1	(0.85)	4.6	(0.79)	15.4	(1.25)
8th	30.4	(1.50)	20.4	(1.30)	14.3	(1.10)	4.3	(0.64)	3.8	(0.71)	5.4	(0.68)	4.5	(0.75)	11.3	(1.23)
9th	28.1	(1.57)	18.9	(1.33)	13.8	(1.23)	5.3	(0.67)	3.2	(0.58)	3.8	(0.63)	2.7	(0.53)	8.2	(0.91)
10th	24.9	(1.43)	15.5	(1.14)	13.6	(1.19)	4.9	(0.82)	3.6	(0.64)	3.6	(0.63)	2.9	(0.64)	6.8	(0.78)
11th	23.0	(1.58)	14.7	(1.32)	13.4	(1.29)	3.2	(0.61)	2.8	(0.59)	3.3	(0.61)	2.6	(0.56)	4.2	(0.69)
12th	19.9	(1.75)	11.3	(1.52)	12.5	(1.54)	3.5	(0.71)	1.8	(0.51)	2.2 !	(0.72)	2.4	(0.63)	2.9	(0.66)
Urbanicity[2]																
Urban	26.0	(1.29)	17.7	(0.95)	13.3	(1.07)	5.5	(0.49)	4.1	(0.53)	4.9	(0.63)	3.9	(0.58)	8.5	(0.73)
Suburban	28.9	(0.81)	18.9	(0.75)	14.6	(0.64)	4.4	(0.42)	3.1	(0.33)	4.5	(0.37)	3.0	(0.32)	9.0	(0.56)
Rural	29.0	(1.96)	19.8	(1.76)	17.2	(1.32)	5.0	(1.10)	3.7	(0.74)	4.5	(0.88)	3.8	(0.87)	9.9	(1.23)
Control of school[3]																
Public	28.6	(0.74)	19.0	(0.61)	14.9	(0.55)	5.1	(0.33)	3.5	(0.27)	4.5	(0.30)	3.5	(0.31)	9.3	(0.48)
Private	22.7	(2.09)	15.3	(1.67)	12.4	(1.66)	0.9 !	(0.40)	3.0 !	(0.90)	6.2	(1.06)	2.0 !	(0.70)	5.5	(1.03)
2007																
Total	31.7	(0.74)	21.0	(0.62)	18.1	(0.61)	5.8	(0.35)	4.1	(0.27)	5.2	(0.30)	4.2	(0.28)	11.0	(0.42)
Sex																
Male	30.3	(0.96)	20.3	(0.83)	13.5	(0.73)	6.0	(0.50)	4.8	(0.43)	4.6	(0.40)	4.0	(0.35)	12.2	(0.58)
Female	33.2	(0.99)	21.7	(0.89)	22.8	(0.91)	5.6	(0.45)	3.4	(0.32)	5.8	(0.43)	4.4	(0.41)	9.7	(0.59)
Race/ethnicity[1]																
White	34.1	(0.97)	23.5	(0.84)	20.3	(0.84)	6.3	(0.47)	4.8	(0.36)	6.1	(0.44)	4.2	(0.35)	11.5	(0.56)
Black	30.4	(2.18)	19.5	(1.71)	15.7	(1.51)	5.8	(0.89)	3.2	(0.69)	3.7	(0.72)	5.6	(0.96)	11.3	(1.42)
Hispanic	27.3	(1.53)	16.1	(1.25)	14.4	(1.27)	4.9	(0.75)	3.0	(0.71)	4.0	(0.60)	3.6	(0.67)	9.9	(1.05)
Asian	18.1	(2.60)	10.6	(2.19)	8.2	(1.93)	‡	(†)	‡	(†)	‡	(†)	1.8 !	(0.89)	3.8 !	(1.25)
Other	34.1	(3.03)	20.1	(3.12)	20.8	(2.98)	7.7	(2.01)	3.1 !	(1.23)	7.7	(2.08)	3.4 !	(1.30)	14.4	(2.73)
Grade																
6th	42.7	(2.23)	31.2	(2.00)	21.3	(1.84)	7.0	(1.13)	5.4	(0.98)	7.4	(1.20)	5.2	(0.98)	17.6	(1.56)
7th	35.6	(1.78)	27.6	(1.58)	20.2	(1.33)	7.4	(0.92)	4.1	(0.64)	7.7	(0.92)	6.0	(0.81)	15.8	(1.28)
8th	36.9	(1.84)	25.1	(1.65)	19.7	(1.41)	6.9	(0.84)	3.6	(0.64)	5.4	(0.77)	4.6	(0.79)	14.2	(1.23)
9th	30.6	(1.72)	20.3	(1.39)	18.1	(1.45)	4.6	(0.77)	5.1	(0.67)	4.5	(0.69)	3.5	(0.63)	11.4	(1.13)
10th	27.7	(1.44)	17.7	(1.22)	15.0	(1.13)	5.8	(0.81)	4.6	(0.68)	4.6	(0.74)	3.4	(0.59)	8.6	(0.89)
11th	28.5	(1.48)	15.3	(1.25)	18.7	(1.40)	4.9	(0.80)	4.2	(0.73)	3.9	(0.68)	4.4	(0.78)	6.5	(0.92)
12th	23.0	(1.60)	12.1	(1.36)	14.1	(1.38)	4.3	(0.83)	2.1	(0.53)	3.5	(0.75)	2.4	(0.61)	4.1	(0.81)
Urbanicity[2]																
Urban	30.7	(1.36)	20.0	(1.09)	15.5	(1.02)	5.2	(0.54)	3.6	(0.46)	4.9	(0.57)	4.2	(0.59)	9.2	(0.76)
Suburban	31.2	(1.07)	21.1	(0.84)	17.4	(0.87)	5.7	(0.48)	4.1	(0.37)	5.0	(0.42)	4.0	(0.38)	11.2	(0.60)
Rural	35.2	(1.73)	22.1	(1.43)	24.1	(1.42)	7.0	(0.78)	5.1	(0.69)	6.3	(0.79)	4.9	(0.63)	13.1	(0.98)
Control of school[3]																
Public	32.0	(0.76)	21.1	(0.65)	18.3	(0.64)	6.2	(0.38)	4.2	(0.28)	5.2	(0.32)	4.1	(0.28)	11.4	(0.45)
Private	29.1	(2.10)	20.1	(1.79)	16.0	(1.76)	1.3 !	(0.50)	3.6	(0.92)	5.9	(1.11)	5.0	(1.11)	6.5	(1.14)
2009																
Total	28.0	(0.83)	18.8	(0.65)	16.5	(0.66)	5.7	(0.34)	3.6	(0.28)	4.7	(0.34)	3.3	(0.28)	9.0	(0.48)
Sex																
Male	26.6	(1.04)	18.4	(0.89)	12.8	(0.79)	5.6	(0.50)	4.0	(0.43)	3.8	(0.39)	3.4	(0.40)	10.1	(0.65)
Female	29.5	(1.08)	19.2	(0.95)	20.3	(0.92)	5.8	(0.50)	3.2	(0.37)	5.7	(0.52)	3.2	(0.39)	7.9	(0.64)
Race/ethnicity[1]																
White	29.3	(1.03)	20.5	(0.89)	17.4	(0.86)	5.4	(0.40)	3.7	(0.38)	5.2	(0.44)	3.3	(0.32)	9.1	(0.61)
Black	29.1	(2.29)	18.4	(1.78)	17.7	(1.60)	7.8	(1.20)	4.8	(0.92)	4.6	(0.97)	4.6	(0.99)	9.9	(1.55)
Hispanic	25.5	(1.71)	15.8	(1.34)	14.8	(1.44)	5.8	(0.87)	2.7	(0.59)	3.6	(0.68)	2.6	(0.55)	9.1	(0.97)
Asian	17.3	(3.01)	9.6	(2.38)	8.1	(2.11)	‡	(†)	‡	(†)	3.4 !	(1.41)	‡	(†)	5.5 !	(1.75)
Other	26.7	(4.61)	17.4	(3.83)	12.9	(3.21)	9.7 !	(3.01)	4.5 !	(1.97)	4.5 !	(1.85)	3.8 !	(1.67)	7.1 !	(2.39)
Grade																
6th	39.4	(2.60)	30.6	(2.32)	21.4	(2.20)	9.3	(1.34)	4.2 !	(1.27)	6.6	(1.31)	4.0	(1.00)	14.5	(1.89)
7th	33.1	(1.87)	23.6	(1.76)	17.3	(1.58)	5.7	(1.00)	4.6	(0.82)	5.6	(0.95)	4.6	(0.85)	13.1	(1.34)
8th	31.7	(1.85)	22.8	(1.64)	18.1	(1.50)	6.8	(0.94)	5.4	(0.91)	6.9	(1.04)	6.1	(0.92)	12.8	(1.29)
9th	28.0	(1.90)	19.2	(1.66)	16.6	(1.53)	7.1	(1.00)	4.0	(0.74)	4.5	(0.78)	2.9	(0.71)	9.7	(1.24)
10th	26.6	(1.71)	15.0	(1.41)	17.0	(1.32)	5.8	(0.91)	3.1	(0.63)	4.0	(0.76)	2.9	(0.63)	7.3	(1.03)
11th	21.1	(1.69)	13.9	(1.42)	13.9	(1.42)	4.8	(0.84)	2.5	(0.63)	3.6	(0.76)	1.5 !	(0.49)	4.4	(0.84)
12th	20.4	(1.63)	11.1	(1.20)	13.1	(1.32)	2.0	(0.57)	1.7 !	(0.52)	2.6	(0.64)	1.3 !	(0.46)	3.0	(0.65)
Urbanicity[2]																
Urban	27.4	(1.25)	17.0	(1.00)	16.5	(1.01)	6.6	(0.67)	4.2	(0.59)	4.0	(0.57)	4.2	(0.63)	9.0	(0.98)
Suburban	27.5	(1.06)	19.3	(0.87)	15.5	(0.97)	5.2	(0.44)	3.2	(0.33)	5.0	(0.46)	2.9	(0.34)	8.9	(0.56)
Rural	30.7	(1.99)	20.2	(1.60)	19.9	(1.56)	6.1	(0.79)	4.1	(0.80)	5.2	(0.85)	3.3	(0.64)	9.5	(1.27)
Control of school[3]																
Public	28.8	(0.88)	19.3	(0.68)	16.9	(0.69)	5.9	(0.37)	3.8	(0.30)	4.7	(0.36)	3.4	(0.29)	9.4	(0.52)
Private	18.9	(2.16)	13.3	(1.87)	11.6	(1.75)	4.4	(1.12)	1.9 !	(0.76)	4.9	(1.16)	1.8 !	(0.68)	4.5	(1.14)

See notes at end of table.

Table 230.45. Percentage of students ages 12–18 who reported being bullied at school during the school year, by type of bullying and selected student and school characteristics: Selected years, 2005 through 2013—Continued

[Standard errors appear in parentheses]

Year and student or school characteristic	Total bullied at school		Type of bullying at school											
			Made fun of, called names, or insulted		Subject of rumors		Threatened with harm		Tried to make do things did not want to do		Excluded from activities on purpose		Property destroyed on purpose		Pushed, shoved, tripped, or spit on	
1	2		3		4		5		6		7		8		9	
2011																
Total	27.8	(0.76)	17.6	(0.62)	18.3	(0.61)	5.0	(0.30)	3.3	(0.26)	5.6	(0.34)	2.8	(0.23)	7.9	(0.38)
Sex																
Male	24.5	(0.91)	16.2	(0.73)	13.2	(0.66)	5.0	(0.44)	3.6	(0.34)	4.8	(0.41)	3.3	(0.34)	8.9	(0.57)
Female	31.4	(0.99)	19.1	(0.84)	23.8	(0.93)	5.1	(0.41)	3.0	(0.36)	6.4	(0.49)	2.3	(0.30)	6.8	(0.49)
Race/ethnicity[1]																
White	31.5	(1.07)	20.6	(0.89)	20.3	(0.81)	5.8	(0.44)	3.3	(0.35)	7.1	(0.51)	3.1	(0.33)	8.6	(0.55)
Black	27.2	(1.97)	16.4	(1.45)	18.6	(1.79)	5.5	(0.83)	4.3	(0.79)	4.7	(0.90)	3.3	(0.72)	9.3	(1.00)
Hispanic	21.9	(1.07)	12.7	(0.93)	15.1	(0.87)	3.3	(0.53)	2.9	(0.46)	2.8	(0.52)	2.4	(0.52)	6.2	(0.75)
Asian	14.9	(2.70)	9.0	(2.04)	7.7	(2.03)	‡	(†)	2.7 !	(1.10)	2.9 !	(1.13)	‡	(†)	2.1 !	(0.95)
Other	23.7	(3.38)	15.0	(2.47)	17.0	(2.94)	6.5	(1.73)	‡	(†)	5.0 !	(1.62)	‡	(†)	7.2	(1.81)
Grade																
6th	37.0	(2.17)	27.0	(2.03)	23.1	(1.90)	4.9	(0.94)	3.9	(0.85)	6.6	(1.19)	3.7	(0.87)	12.7	(1.56)
7th	30.3	(1.64)	22.4	(1.35)	18.3	(1.31)	6.9	(0.89)	4.5	(0.72)	7.8	(0.95)	4.0	(0.68)	12.6	(1.16)
8th	30.7	(1.68)	20.7	(1.51)	19.0	(1.40)	5.3	(0.75)	2.9	(0.56)	6.4	(0.80)	4.0	(0.73)	10.8	(1.07)
9th	26.5	(1.66)	16.4	(1.28)	16.3	(1.38)	5.4	(0.73)	3.3	(0.64)	4.1	(0.87)	2.5	(0.60)	7.3	(0.85)
10th	28.0	(1.56)	16.9	(1.26)	19.6	(1.24)	5.1	(0.75)	3.9	(0.65)	5.3	(0.71)	2.2	(0.48)	6.7	(0.82)
11th	23.8	(1.72)	12.7	(1.17)	17.1	(1.48)	4.0	(0.68)	2.4	(0.60)	4.7	(0.71)	1.8	(0.50)	3.9	(0.73)
12th	22.0	(1.34)	10.6	(1.12)	16.7	(1.23)	3.5	(0.65)	2.3	(0.55)	4.3	(0.75)	1.9	(0.51)	2.7	(0.59)
Urbanicity[2]																
Urban	24.8	(1.28)	15.9	(1.07)	16.1	(1.05)	4.4	(0.49)	3.1	(0.38)	4.6	(0.50)	2.5	(0.38)	7.6	(0.66)
Suburban	29.0	(1.07)	18.4	(0.85)	18.7	(0.86)	5.0	(0.47)	3.2	(0.33)	6.0	(0.46)	3.0	(0.35)	8.2	(0.56)
Rural	29.7	(1.82)	18.4	(1.33)	21.4	(1.47)	6.3	(0.69)	3.9	(0.80)	5.8	(0.89)	3.0	(0.54)	7.3	(0.78)
Control of school[3]																
Public	28.4	(0.82)	17.9	(0.66)	18.8	(0.65)	5.3	(0.33)	3.3	(0.28)	5.5	(0.37)	2.9	(0.24)	8.1	(0.42)
Private	21.5	(1.91)	13.9	(1.68)	12.6	(1.59)	1.6 !	(0.62)	2.9	(0.76)	5.6	(1.07)	2.1 !	(0.71)	4.7	(1.03)
2013																
Total	21.5	(0.66)	13.6	(0.51)	13.2	(0.50)	3.9	(0.27)	2.2	(0.21)	4.5	(0.30)	1.6	(0.20)	6.0	(0.39)
Sex																
Male	19.5	(0.81)	12.6	(0.70)	9.6	(0.60)	4.1	(0.38)	2.4	(0.30)	3.5	(0.34)	1.8	(0.28)	7.4	(0.59)
Female	23.7	(0.98)	14.7	(0.75)	17.0	(0.80)	3.7	(0.37)	1.9	(0.27)	5.5	(0.47)	1.3	(0.25)	4.6	(0.42)
Race/ethnicity[1]																
White	23.7	(0.93)	15.6	(0.74)	14.6	(0.76)	4.4	(0.40)	2.0	(0.28)	5.4	(0.46)	1.5	(0.24)	6.1	(0.49)
Black	20.3	(1.81)	10.5	(1.22)	12.7	(1.40)	3.2	(0.68)	2.7	(0.59)	2.7	(0.71)	2.0	(0.54)	6.0	(0.97)
Hispanic	19.2	(1.30)	12.1	(1.13)	11.5	(1.02)	4.0	(0.58)	1.6	(0.32)	3.5	(0.53)	1.4	(0.38)	6.3	(0.79)
Asian	9.2	(1.67)	7.5	(1.63)	3.7	(0.95)	‡	(†)	3.8 !	(1.32)	2.2 !	(0.71)	1.6 !	(0.78)	2.0 !	(0.85)
Other	25.2	(3.60)	16.5	(2.99)	17.3	(3.05)	4.3 !	(1.56)	4.0 !	(1.38)	6.5	(1.85)	2.1 !	(1.00)	8.5	(1.90)
Grade																
6th	27.8	(2.31)	21.3	(2.15)	16.1	(1.61)	5.9	(1.13)	3.4	(0.88)	6.5	(1.20)	3.1	(0.77)	11.0	(1.46)
7th	26.4	(1.65)	17.9	(1.35)	15.5	(1.35)	6.1	(0.88)	3.0	(0.52)	6.3	(0.86)	2.2	(0.52)	11.6	(1.12)
8th	21.7	(1.42)	14.5	(1.23)	12.7	(1.11)	3.9	(0.68)	2.3	(0.54)	5.2	(0.80)	1.5 !	(0.45)	6.5	(0.85)
9th	23.0	(1.42)	13.7	(1.16)	13.8	(1.22)	3.6	(0.61)	2.6	(0.58)	4.3	(0.70)	1.2 !	(0.40)	4.9	(0.83)
10th	19.5	(1.48)	12.9	(1.21)	12.9	(1.28)	4.3	(0.73)	1.7	(0.47)	4.6	(0.72)	1.3	(0.37)	3.7	(0.68)
11th	20.0	(1.50)	11.2	(1.20)	12.5	(1.31)	3.0	(0.60)	1.5	(0.45)	2.4	(0.61)	1.6 !	(0.50)	3.4	(0.72)
12th	14.1	(1.51)	6.4	(1.04)	9.7	(1.15)	1.0 !	(0.43)	1.3 !	(0.48)	2.5	(0.67)	0.7 !	(0.31)	3.0	(0.71)
Urbanicity[2]																
Urban	20.7	(1.10)	12.8	(0.80)	12.7	(0.87)	3.9	(0.47)	2.7	(0.45)	4.1	(0.51)	1.4	(0.27)	5.6	(0.60)
Suburban	22.0	(0.90)	14.2	(0.69)	13.4	(0.71)	3.9	(0.39)	2.0	(0.28)	4.7	(0.43)	1.3	(0.24)	6.4	(0.52)
Rural	21.4	(1.86)	13.2	(1.49)	13.3	(1.45)	4.1	(0.67)	1.7	(0.42)	4.2	(0.73)	2.8	(0.66)	5.8	(0.88)
Control of school[3]																
Public	21.5	(0.67)	13.5	(0.53)	13.2	(0.52)	3.9	(0.28)	2.2	(0.22)	4.3	(0.31)	1.6	(0.19)	6.1	(0.41)
Private	22.4	(2.71)	15.3	(2.01)	13.4	(2.20)	3.9	(1.14)	2.7 !	(0.82)	6.7	(1.31)	1.3 !	(0.60)	5.2	(1.24)

—Not available.
†Not applicable.
!Interpret data with caution. The coefficient of variation (CV) for this estimate is between 30 and 50 percent.
‡Reporting standards not met. Either there are too few cases for a reliable estimate or the coefficient of variation (CV) is 50 percent or greater.
[1]Race categories exclude persons of Hispanic ethnicity. "Other" includes American Indians/ Alaska Natives, Pacific Islanders, and persons of Two or more races.
[2]Refers to the Standard Metropolitan Statistical Area (MSA) status of the respondent's household as defined in 2000 by the U.S. Census Bureau. Categories include "central city of an MSA (Urban)," "in MSA but not in central city (Suburban)," and "not MSA (Rural)." These data by metropolitan status were based on the location of households and differ from those published in *Student Reports of Bullying and Cyber-Bullying: Results from the 2011 School Crime Supplement to the National Crime Victimization Survey*, which were based on the urban-centric measure of the location of the school that the child attended.
[3]Control of school as reported by the respondent. These data differ from those based on a matching of the respondent-reported school name to the Common Core of Data's Public Elementary/Secondary School Universe Survey or the Private School Survey, as reported in *Student Reports of Bullying and Cyber-Bullying: Results from the 2011 School Crime Supplement to the National Crime Victimization Survey*.
NOTE: "At school" includes the school building, on school property, on a school bus, or going to and from school. Bullying types do not sum to totals because students could have experienced more than one type of bullying.
SOURCE: U.S. Department of Justice, Bureau of Justice Statistics, School Crime Supplement (SCS) to the National Crime Victimization Survey, selected years, 2005 through 2013. (This table was prepared August 2014.)

Table 230.50. Percentage of students ages 12–18 who reported being bullied at school during the school year and, among bullied students, percentage who reported being bullied in various locations, by selected student and school characteristics: 2013

[Standard errors appear in parentheses]

Student or school characteristic	Total		Among students who were bullied, percent by location[1]												
			Inside classroom		In hallway or stairwell		In bathroom or locker room		Cafeteria		Somewhere else in school building		Outside on school grounds		On school bus	
1	2		3		4		5		6		7		8		9	
Total...............	21.5	(0.66)	33.6	(1.54)	45.6	(1.73)	9.1	(0.84)	18.9	(1.17)	0.8 !	(0.30)	22.9	(1.44)	7.8	(0.86)
Sex																
Male...............	19.5	(0.81)	31.1	(2.13)	45.8	(2.37)	11.6	(1.46)	17.9	(1.76)	‡	(†)	22.3	(1.85)	8.9	(1.41)
Female...............	23.7	(0.98)	35.8	(2.03)	45.3	(2.37)	7.0	(1.01)	19.7	(1.69)	1.2 !	(0.54)	23.4	(1.92)	6.9	(1.12)
Race/ethnicity[2]																
White...............	23.7	(0.93)	33.9	(2.08)	46.9	(2.09)	11.0	(1.24)	19.8	(1.53)	0.8 !	(0.34)	22.9	(1.89)	9.6	(1.18)
Black...............	20.3	(1.81)	28.7	(4.03)	39.5	(4.27)	5.1 !	(2.00)	19.2	(3.36)	‡	(†)	18.7	(3.10)	6.4 !	(2.15)
Hispanic...............	19.2	(1.30)	35.6	(3.02)	44.8	(3.47)	7.1	(1.66)	15.5	(2.45)	‡	(†)	26.4	(3.08)	2.3 !	(1.00)
Asian...............	9.2	(1.67)	‡	(†)	‡	(†)	‡	(†)	‡	(†)	‡	(†)	‡	(†)	‡	(†)
Other...............	25.2	(3.60)	31.9	(5.92)	48.3	(7.19)	‡	(†)	14.3 !	(5.14)	‡	(†)	25.1	(5.03)	17.0 !	(5.47)
Grade																
6th...............	27.8	(2.31)	34.9	(4.23)	40.9	(4.91)	7.3 !	(2.57)	11.6	(2.98)	‡	(†)	36.4	(4.37)	17.1	(3.61)
7th...............	26.4	(1.65)	32.4	(2.88)	43.6	(3.35)	12.9	(2.25)	20.8	(2.63)	‡	(†)	26.8	(3.03)	10.2	(1.92)
8th...............	21.7	(1.42)	38.0	(4.12)	41.2	(4.00)	7.7	(2.06)	18.0	(2.97)	‡	(†)	26.1	(3.53)	8.7	(2.40)
9th...............	23.0	(1.42)	29.9	(3.44)	42.0	(3.61)	9.5	(2.01)	23.9	(3.22)	‡	(†)	19.0	(2.76)	5.7 !	(1.80)
10th...............	19.5	(1.48)	40.1	(4.32)	52.6	(4.63)	9.0	(2.24)	19.2	(3.15)	‡	(†)	20.0	(3.79)	7.9	(2.17)
11th...............	20.0	(1.50)	29.5	(3.66)	52.2	(4.05)	8.2	(2.43)	18.8	(3.35)	‡	(†)	16.6	(3.52)	‡	(†)
12th...............	14.1	(1.51)	30.1	(5.29)	47.4	(5.92)	6.2 !	(2.47)	14.9	(4.18)	‡	(†)	14.1	(3.80)	‡	(†)
Urbanicity[3]																
Urban...............	20.7	(1.10)	34.3	(3.05)	42.2	(3.07)	7.9	(1.59)	21.5	(2.35)	‡	(†)	26.2	(2.86)	4.8	(1.29)
Suburban...............	22.0	(0.90)	32.9	(2.01)	48.3	(2.18)	9.5	(1.12)	18.0	(1.61)	‡	(†)	22.3	(1.89)	9.0	(1.25)
Rural...............	21.4	(1.86)	35.1	(4.17)	41.9	(3.93)	10.2	(2.07)	17.0	(2.79)	‡	(†)	18.7	(3.57)	9.2	(1.84)
Control of school																
Public...............	21.5	(0.67)	33.3	(1.61)	46.1	(1.80)	9.3	(0.90)	18.7	(1.22)	0.8 !	(0.33)	22.3	(1.47)	8.2	(0.91)
Private...............	22.4	(2.71)	36.7	(5.32)	39.2	(5.26)	6.7 !	(2.64)	20.5	(4.47)	‡	(†)	30.1	(5.17)	‡	(†)

†Not applicable.

!Interpret data with caution. The coefficient of variation (CV) for this estimate is between 30 and 50 percent.

‡Reporting standards not met. Either there are too few cases for a reliable estimate or the coefficient of variation (CV) is 50 percent or greater.

[1]Includes only students who indicated the location of bullying. Excludes students who indicated that they were bullied but did not answer the question about where the bullying occurred.

[2]Race categories exclude persons of Hispanic ethnicity. "Other" includes American Indians/Alaska Natives, Pacific Islanders, and persons of Two or more races.

[3]Refers to the Standard Metropolitan Statistical Area (MSA) status of the respondent's household as defined in 2000 by the U.S. Census Bureau. Categories include "central city of an MSA (Urban)," "in MSA but not in central city (Suburban)," and "not MSA (Rural)."

NOTE: "At school" includes the school building, on school property, on a school bus, or going to and from school. Location totals may sum to more than 100 percent because students could have been bullied in more than one location.

SOURCE: U.S. Department of Justice, Bureau of Justice Statistics, School Crime Supplement (SCS) to the National Crime Victimization Survey, 2013. (This table was prepared August 2014.)

Table 230.55. Percentage of students ages 12–18 who reported being cyber-bullied anywhere during the school year, by type of cyber-bullying and selected student and school characteristics: 2013

[Standard errors appear in parentheses]

Student or school characteristic	Total cyber-bullying[1]		Type of cyber-bullying												
			Hurtful information on Internet		Private information purposely shared on Internet		Subject of harassing instant messages		Subject of harassing text messages		Subject of harassing e-mails		Subject of harassment while gaming		Excluded online	
1	2		3		4		5		6		7		8		9	
Total	6.9	(0.42)	2.8	(0.24)	0.9	(0.15)	2.1	(0.22)	3.2	(0.28)	0.9	(0.15)	1.5	(0.18)	0.9	(0.13)
Sex																
Male	5.2	(0.43)	1.2	(0.22)	0.4	(0.12)	1.0	(0.19)	1.6	(0.25)	0.2 !	(0.09)	2.5	(0.31)	0.9	(0.18)
Female	8.6	(0.63)	4.5	(0.42)	1.5	(0.27)	3.4	(0.39)	4.9	(0.51)	1.7	(0.30)	0.4 !	(0.14)	0.9	(0.18)
Race/ethnicity[2]																
White	7.6	(0.57)	2.9	(0.35)	1.0	(0.22)	2.2	(0.27)	3.8	(0.42)	0.8	(0.19)	1.8	(0.26)	1.0	(0.18)
Black	4.5	(0.94)	2.2	(0.63)	‡	(†)	1.8 !	(0.57)	1.9	(0.49)	0.8 !	(0.35)	‡	(†)	‡	(†)
Hispanic	5.8	(0.78)	2.6	(0.52)	1.0 !	(0.34)	1.9	(0.41)	2.6	(0.52)	0.8 !	(0.28)	0.9 !	(0.30)	1.0	(0.29)
Asian	5.8	(1.67)	1.8 !	(0.85)	‡	(†)	‡	(†)	‡	(†)	‡	(†)	3.1 !	(1.20)	‡	(†)
Other	13.4	(2.43)	6.9	(1.86)	1.9 !	(0.96)	4.9 !	(1.63)	6.2	(1.69)	4.7 !	(1.62)	3.2 !	(1.30)	‡	(†)
Grade																
6th	5.9	(1.20)	1.4 !	(0.58)	‡	(†)	1.2 !	(0.54)	2.3 !	(0.78)	‡	(†)	1.5 !	(0.61)	‡	(†)
7th	7.0	(0.91)	2.1	(0.53)	1.1 !	(0.36)	2.3	(0.51)	3.8	(0.74)	1.0 !	(0.35)	1.8	(0.44)	0.8 !	(0.30)
8th	6.4	(0.86)	3.1	(0.59)	0.9 !	(0.26)	2.3	(0.55)	3.2	(0.64)	1.5 !	(0.48)	1.7	(0.50)	1.5 !	(0.46)
9th	6.7	(0.97)	2.0	(0.49)	‡	(†)	2.9	(0.58)	2.8	(0.62)	‡	(†)	1.6	(0.48)	1.4 !	(0.43)
10th	8.6	(1.16)	4.1	(0.84)	1.2 !	(0.41)	2.8	(0.61)	4.5	(0.81)	1.4 !	(0.41)	1.0 !	(0.35)	1.0 !	(0.34)
11th	6.8	(0.87)	3.9	(0.71)	1.3 !	(0.41)	1.1 !	(0.43)	2.7	(0.55)	‡	(†)	1.3	(0.39)	‡	(†)
12th	5.9	(0.93)	2.6	(0.67)	‡	(†)	1.9	(0.55)	2.3	(0.59)	1.1 !	(0.40)	1.4 !	(0.51)	‡	(†)
Urbanicity[3]																
Urban	7.1	(0.73)	3.4	(0.50)	1.1	(0.32)	2.4	(0.45)	3.1	(0.50)	1.4	(0.34)	1.5	(0.25)	1.2	(0.33)
Suburban	7.0	(0.61)	2.7	(0.35)	0.9	(0.20)	2.0	(0.27)	3.3	(0.40)	0.8	(0.18)	1.6	(0.27)	0.9	(0.17)
Rural	5.9	(1.02)	2.2	(0.43)	0.8 !	(0.29)	2.0 !	(0.62)	2.9	(0.72)	0.7 !	(0.31)	1.0 !	(0.48)	‡	(†)
Control of school																
Public	6.9	(0.45)	2.9	(0.26)	0.9	(0.16)	2.2	(0.23)	3.2	(0.30)	0.9	(0.16)	1.5	(0.19)	0.9	(0.14)
Private	6.4	(1.44)	2.0 !	(0.76)	1.2 !	(0.54)	‡	(†)	2.9 !	(0.98)	‡	(†)	‡	(†)	‡	(†)

†Not applicable.
!Interpret data with caution. The coefficient of variation (CV) for this estimate is between 30 and 50 percent.
‡Reporting standards not met. Either there are too few cases for a reliable estimate or the coefficient of variation (CV) is 50 percent or greater.
[1]Students who reported experiencing more than one type of cyber-bullying were counted only once in the total for students cyber-bullied.
[2]Race categories exclude persons of Hispanic ethnicity. "Other" includes American Indians/Alaska Natives, Pacific Islanders, and persons of Two or more races.

[3]Refers to the Standard Metropolitan Statistical Area (MSA) status of the respondent's household as defined in 2000 by the U.S. Census Bureau. Categories include "central city of an MSA (Urban)," "in MSA but not in central city (Suburban)," and "not MSA (Rural)."
NOTE: Detail may not sum to totals because of rounding and because students could have experienced more than one type of cyber-bullying.
SOURCE: U.S. Department of Justice, Bureau of Justice Statistics, School Crime Supplement (SCS) to the National Crime Victimization Survey, 2013. (This table was prepared August 2014.)

Table 230.60. Among students ages 12–18 who reported being bullied at school or cyber-bullied anywhere during the school year, percentage reporting various frequencies of bullying and the notification of an adult at school, by selected student and school characteristics: 2013

[Standard errors appear in parentheses]

Student or school characteristic	Among students who reported being bullied at school					Among students who reported being cyber-bullied anywhere[1]				
	Once or twice in the school year	Frequency of bullying			Adult at school was notified[2]	Once or twice in the school year	Frequency of cyber-bullying			Adult at school was notified[2]
		Once or twice a month	Once or twice a week	Almost every day			Once or twice a month	Once or twice a week	Almost every day	
1	2	3	4	5	6	7	8	9	10	11
Total	67.3 (1.53)	19.4 (1.32)	7.6 (0.78)	5.7 (0.71)	38.9 (1.45)	73.2 (2.72)	15.0 (2.08)	7.9 (1.46)	3.8 (1.05)	23.3 (2.55)
Sex										
Male	68.0 (2.19)	19.2 (1.98)	7.4 (1.09)	5.5 (1.01)	38.5 (2.01)	75.2 (3.80)	9.3 (2.62)	8.1 (2.24)	7.4! (2.23)	10.5 (2.53)
Female	66.6 (2.13)	19.6 (1.89)	7.8 (1.11)	6.0 (0.94)	39.3 (2.20)	71.9 (3.40)	18.8 (2.90)	7.9 (1.82)	‡ (†)	31.6 (3.54)
Race/ethnicity[3]										
White	64.6 (2.04)	20.6 (1.70)	9.1 (1.20)	5.7 (0.87)	40.5 (2.04)	76.9 (3.27)	15.2 (2.80)	4.6! (1.53)	3.3! (1.23)	24.4 (3.08)
Black	70.2 (3.93)	18.0 (3.40)	5.6! (2.07)	6.2! (2.13)	40.0 (3.44)	68.2 (7.99)	18.9! (6.71)	‡ (†)	‡ (†)	24.5! (10.44)
Hispanic	73.8 (3.24)	17.9 (2.88)	4.4 (1.30)	4.0! (1.26)	37.5 (3.15)	73.5 (6.28)	8.9! (3.78)	12.5! (4.48)	‡ (†)	23.7 (4.92)
Asian	‡ (†)	‡ (†)	‡ (†)	‡ (†)	‡ (†)	‡ (†)	‡ (†)	‡ (†)	‡ (†)	‡ (†)
Other	66.9 (7.42)	15.2! (5.49)	‡ (†)	12.8! (5.30)	36.8 (6.34)	‡ (†)	‡ (†)	‡ (†)	‡ (†)	‡ (†)
Grade										
6th	62.4 (4.19)	22.7 (3.64)	6.5! (2.00)	8.4! (3.10)	58.3 (4.71)	65.5 (6.74)	24.9 (6.48)	‡ (†)	‡ (†)	28.0 (5.87)
7th	63.8 (2.92)	17.3 (2.60)	11.4 (2.18)	7.5 (1.69)	52.3 (3.53)	70.5 (6.04)	17.1! (5.69)	‡ (†)	‡ (†)	30.4 (6.05)
8th	64.0 (3.74)	19.1 (3.05)	7.9 (2.12)	9.1 (2.30)	38.1 (3.82)	79.6 (5.43)	7.7! (3.68)	8.6! (3.16)	‡ (†)	12.4! (4.90)
9th	67.4 (3.49)	24.7 (3.48)	3.7! (1.41)	4.2! (1.59)	35.2 (3.89)	73.8 (5.76)	16.7! (5.09)	9.2! (3.89)	‡ (†)	23.9 (5.47)
10th	65.6 (4.11)	21.5 (3.56)	7.8 (2.29)	5.0! (1.79)	34.6 (3.84)	‡ (†)	‡ (†)	6.7! (3.30)	‡ (†)	26.7 (6.87)
11th	75.8 (3.60)	12.9 (2.83)	8.2 (2.09)	3.2! (1.41)	25.8 (3.37)	71.4 (7.36)	14.2! (5.62)	12.3! (5.36)	‡ (†)	21.0! (6.70)
12th	75.2 (5.35)	17.4 (4.42)	6.1! (2.63)	‡ (†)	22.4 (4.32)	74.6 (7.15)	13.3! (5.46)	‡ (†)	‡ (†)	‡ (†)
Urbanicity[4]										
Urban	71.8 (2.86)	14.9 (2.21)	7.0 (1.36)	6.3 (1.46)	36.6 (2.64)	68.4 (4.76)	15.1 (3.76)	11.9 (3.17)	4.6! (1.99)	21.7 (4.81)
Suburban	67.0 (1.94)	20.6 (1.64)	7.1 (1.09)	5.2 (0.85)	40.7 (2.01)	77.9 (3.29)	13.2 (2.67)	5.0! (1.59)	3.9! (1.48)	24.1 (3.25)
Rural	59.7 (4.96)	23.4 (3.83)	10.2 (2.51)	6.6 (1.66)	36.9 (4.03)	65.2 (8.87)	22.2 (5.79)	10.8! (4.91)	‡ (†)	24.1 (5.37)
Control of school										
Public	67.2 (1.63)	19.7 (1.40)	7.4 (0.81)	5.7 (0.74)	38.9 (1.48)	72.0 (2.78)	16.1 (2.20)	7.8 (1.48)	4.1 (1.13)	22.5 (2.61)
Private	67.9 (5.01)	16.7 (3.74)	9.6! (2.96)	5.8! (2.09)	39.5 (5.50)	‡ (†)	‡ (†)	‡ (†)	‡ (†)	‡ (†)
Total indicating adult at school notified,[2] by frequency of bullying	36.9 (1.86)	38.3 (3.29)	55.0 (5.81)	50.0 (6.95)	† (†)	20.2 (2.57)	21.6 (6.11)	‡ (†)	‡ (†)	† (†)
Males indicating adult notified	39.4 (2.55)	31.8 (4.54)	45.9 (9.12)	‡ (†)	† (†)	8.6! (2.75)	‡ (†)	‡ (†)	‡ (†)	† (†)
Females indicating adult notified	34.7 (2.64)	43.8 (4.83)	62.5 (7.39)	43.7 (8.65)	† (†)	28.2 (4.02)	28.6 (7.67)	‡ (†)	‡ (†)	† (†)

†Not applicable.
!Interpret data with caution. The coefficient of variation (CV) for this estimate is between 30 and 50 percent.
‡Reporting standards not met. Either there are too few cases for a reliable estimate or the coefficient of variation (CV) is 50 percent or greater.
[1]Students who reported being cyber-bullied are those who responded that another student had done one or more of the following: posted hurtful information about them on the Internet; purposely shared private information about them on the Internet; threatened or insulted them through instant messaging; threatened or insulted them through text messaging; threatened or insulted them through e-mail; threatened or insulted them while gaming; or excluded them online.
[2]Teacher or other adult at school notified.

[3]Race categories exclude persons of Hispanic ethnicity. "Other" includes American Indians/Alaska Natives, Pacific Islanders, and persons of Two or more races.
[4]Refers to the Standard Metropolitan Statistical Area (MSA) status of the respondent's household as defined in 2000 by the U.S. Census Bureau. Categories include "central city of an MSA (Urban)," "in MSA but not in central city (Suburban)," and "not MSA (Rural)."
NOTE: "At school" includes the school building, on school property, on a school bus, or going to and from school. Detail may not sum to totals because of rounding.
SOURCE: U.S. Department of Justice, Bureau of Justice Statistics, School Crime Supplement (SCS) to the National Crime Victimization Survey, 2013. (This table was prepared September 2014.)

Table 230.62. Percentage of public school students in grades 9–12 who reported having been bullied on school property or electronically bullied during the previous 12 months, by state: Selected years, 2009 through 2013

[Standard errors appear in parentheses]

State	Bullied on school property[1]						Electronically bullied[2]					
	2009		2011		2013		2009		2011		2013	
1	2		3		4		5		6		7	
United States[3]	19.9	(0.58)	20.1	(0.68)	19.6	(0.55)	—	(†)	16.2	(0.45)	14.8	(0.54)
Alabama	19.3	(1.45)	14.1	(1.22)	20.8	(1.28)	—	(†)	12.3	(1.64)	13.5	(0.95)
Alaska	20.7	(1.29)	23.0	(1.32)	20.7	(1.35)	—	(†)	15.3	(1.04)	14.7	(1.10)
Arizona	—	(†)	—	(†)	—	(†)	—	(†)	—	(†)	—	(†)
Arkansas	—	(†)	21.9	(1.74)	25.0	(1.51)	—	(†)	16.7	(1.48)	17.6	(1.05)
California	—	(†)	—	(†)	—	(†)	—	(†)	—	(†)	—	(†)
Colorado	18.8	(1.60)	19.3	(1.33)	—	(†)	—	(†)	14.4	(1.09)	—	(†)
Connecticut	—	(†)	21.6	(1.09)	21.9	(0.96)	—	(†)	16.3	(0.81)	17.5	(1.23)
Delaware	15.9	(1.11)	16.5	(1.03)	18.5	(0.96)	—	(†)	—	(†)	13.4	(0.78)
District of Columbia	—	(†)	—	(†)	—	(†)	—	(†)	—	(†)	—	(†)
Florida	13.4	(0.51)	14.0	(0.54)	15.7	(0.50)	—	(†)	12.4	(0.53)	12.3	(0.54)
Georgia	—	(†)	19.1	(1.66)	19.5	(1.36)	—	(†)	13.6	(1.09)	13.9	(0.93)
Hawaii	—	(†)	20.3	(1.29)	18.7	(1.00)	—	(†)	14.9	(0.80)	15.6	(0.98)
Idaho	22.3	(1.03)	22.8	(1.76)	25.4	(1.12)	—	(†)	17.0	(1.18)	18.8	(1.18)
Illinois	19.6	(1.46)	19.3	(1.31)	22.2	(1.00)	—	(†)	16.0	(1.38)	16.9	(0.77)
Indiana	22.8	(1.69)	25.0	(1.38)	—	(†)	—	(†)	18.7	(1.15)	—	(†)
Iowa	—	(†)	22.5	(1.47)	—	(†)	—	(†)	16.8	(0.97)	—	(†)
Kansas	18.5	(1.21)	20.5	(1.31)	22.1	(1.57)	—	(†)	15.5	(0.88)	16.9	(0.97)
Kentucky	20.8	(1.30)	18.9	(1.24)	21.4	(1.41)	—	(†)	17.4	(1.14)	13.2	(1.06)
Louisiana	15.9	(1.88)	19.2	(1.40)	24.2	(1.64)	—	(†)	18.0	(1.53)	16.9	(1.91)
Maine	22.4	(0.49)	22.4	(0.43)	24.2	(0.66)	—	(†)	19.7	(0.55)	20.6	(0.61)
Maryland	20.9	(0.96)	21.2	(1.28)	19.6	(0.25)	—	(†)	14.2	(0.78)	14.0	(0.22)
Massachusetts	19.4	(0.89)	18.1	(1.04)	16.6	(0.98)	—	(†)	—	(†)	13.8	(0.79)
Michigan	24.0	(1.77)	22.7	(1.40)	25.3	(1.47)	—	(†)	18.0	(0.91)	18.8	(1.20)
Minnesota	—	(†)	—	(†)	—	(†)	—	(†)	—	(†)	—	(†)
Mississippi	16.0	(1.04)	15.6	(1.32)	19.2	(0.93)	—	(†)	12.5	(0.93)	11.9	(0.74)
Missouri	22.8	(1.74)	—	(†)	25.2	(1.72)	—	(†)	—	(†)	—	(†)
Montana	23.1	(1.32)	26.0	(1.06)	26.3	(0.68)	—	(†)	19.2	(0.92)	18.1	(0.62)
Nebraska	—	(†)	22.9	(0.85)	20.8	(1.10)	—	(†)	15.8	(0.81)	15.7	(0.91)
Nevada	—	(†)	—	(†)	19.7	(1.09)	—	(†)	—	(†)	15.0	(1.28)
New Hampshire	22.1	(1.53)	25.3	(1.21)	22.8	(1.05)	—	(†)	21.6	(1.27)	18.1	(1.02)
New Jersey	20.7	(1.44)	20.0	(1.57)	21.3	(1.12)	—	(†)	15.6	(1.65)	14.8	(1.25)
New Mexico	19.5	(0.80)	18.7	(0.72)	18.2	(0.95)	—	(†)	13.2	(0.66)	13.1	(0.67)
New York	18.2	(1.01)	17.7	(0.66)	19.7	(1.43)	—	(†)	16.2	(0.68)	15.3	(0.89)
North Carolina	16.6	(1.00)	20.5	(1.34)	19.2	(0.94)	—	(†)	15.7	(0.83)	12.5	(1.11)
North Dakota	21.1	(1.29)	24.9	(1.24)	25.4	(1.28)	—	(†)	17.4	(1.15)	17.1	(0.82)
Ohio[4]	—	(†)	22.7	(1.83)	20.8	(1.40)	—	(†)	14.7	(1.08)	15.1	(1.31)
Oklahoma	17.5	(1.25)	16.7	(1.27)	18.6	(1.08)	—	(†)	15.6	(1.21)	14.3	(1.33)
Oregon	—	(†)	—	(†)	—	(†)	—	(†)	—	(†)	—	(†)
Pennsylvania	19.2	(1.18)	—	(†)	—	(†)	—	(†)	—	(†)	—	(†)
Rhode Island	16.3	(0.85)	19.1	(1.74)	18.1	(1.00)	—	(†)	15.3	(1.14)	14.3	(1.11)
South Carolina	15.1	(1.53)	18.3	(1.36)	20.2	(1.33)	—	(†)	15.6	(1.44)	13.8	(1.00)
South Dakota[4]	—	(†)	26.7	(1.25)	24.3	(2.05)	—	(†)	19.6	(0.94)	17.8	(1.05)
Tennessee	17.3	(1.24)	17.5	(0.88)	21.1	(1.22)	—	(†)	13.9	(0.69)	15.5	(0.94)
Texas	18.7	(1.06)	16.5	(0.73)	19.1	(1.06)	—	(†)	13.0	(0.66)	13.8	(1.04)
Utah	18.8	(1.05)	21.7	(0.97)	21.8	(0.99)	—	(†)	16.6	(1.12)	16.9	(0.87)
Vermont	—	(†)	—	(†)	—	(†)	—	(†)	15.2	(0.54)	18.0	(0.32)
Virginia	—	(†)	20.3	(1.37)	21.9	(0.87)	—	(†)	14.8	(1.49)	14.5	(0.61)
Washington	—	(†)	—	(†)	—	(†)	—	(†)	—	(†)	—	(†)
West Virginia	23.5	(1.33)	18.6	(1.71)	22.1	(1.72)	—	(†)	15.5	(1.18)	17.2	(0.89)
Wisconsin	22.5	(1.28)	24.0	(1.35)	22.7	(1.23)	—	(†)	16.6	(0.74)	17.6	(0.86)
Wyoming	24.4	(0.93)	25.0	(0.98)	23.3	(0.82)	—	(†)	18.7	(0.80)	16.1	(0.71)

—Not available.
†Not applicable.
[1]Bullying was defined for respondents as "when one or more students tease, threaten, spread rumors about, hit, shove, or hurt another student over and over again." "On school property" was not defined for survey respondents.
[2]Survey respondents were asked about being electronically bullied ("being bullied through e-mail, chat rooms, instant messaging, websites, or texting"). Data on electronic bullying were not collected in 2009.
[3]Data for the U.S. total include both public and private schools and were collected through a national survey representing the entire country.
[4]Data include both public and private schools.

NOTE: State-level data include public schools only, with the exception of data for Ohio and South Dakota. Data for the U.S. total, Ohio, and South Dakota include both public and private schools. For specific states, a given year's data may be unavailable (1) because the state did not participate in the survey that year; (2) because the state omitted this particular survey item from the state-level questionnaire; or (3) because the state had an overall response rate of less than 60 percent (the overall response rate is the school response rate multiplied by the student response rate).
SOURCE: Centers for Disease Control and Prevention, Division of Adolescent and School Health, Youth Risk Behavior Surveillance System (YRBSS), 2009 through 2013. (This table was prepared September 2014.)

Table 230.65. Percentage of public schools reporting selected types of cyber-bullying problems occurring at school or away from school at least once a week, by selected school characteristics: 2009–10

[Standard errors appear in parentheses]

School characteristic	Cyber-bullying among students		School environment is affected by cyber-bullying		Staff resources are used to deal with cyber-bullying	
1	2		3		4	
All public schools	7.9	(0.49)	4.4	(0.34)	3.8	(0.39)
School level[1]						
Primary	1.5	(0.43)	0.9 !	(0.38)	0.9 !	(0.34)
Middle	18.6	(1.48)	9.8	(1.07)	8.5	(1.01)
High school	17.6	(1.11)	9.9	(0.85)	8.6	(0.81)
Combined	12.6	(3.34)	7.4 !	(2.64)	‡	(†)
Enrollment size						
Less than 300	4.8	(1.21)	3.2 !	(1.05)	2.9 !	(0.89)
300–499	4.6	(0.74)	2.8	(0.57)	2.7	(0.64)
500–999	9.3	(0.63)	4.6	(0.57)	3.7	(0.58)
1,000 or more	19.2	(1.42)	10.7	(1.26)	9.4	(0.96)
Locale						
City	5.7	(0.62)	3.8	(0.57)	3.6	(0.70)
Suburban	8.5	(0.85)	4.0	(0.48)	3.7	(0.46)
Town	9.6	(1.45)	5.8	(1.15)	4.1	(1.06)
Rural	8.4	(1.07)	4.5	(0.89)	4.0	(0.82)
Percent combined enrollment of Black, Hispanic, Asian/Pacific Islander, and American Indian/Alaska Native students						
Less than 5 percent	12.8	(2.05)	7.7	(1.66)	4.7	(1.32)
5 percent to less than 20 percent	10.1	(0.90)	5.1	(0.59)	4.7	(0.72)
20 percent to less than 50 percent	6.7	(0.77)	3.6	(0.67)	3.9	(0.74)
50 percent or more	5.3	(0.60)	3.1	(0.41)	2.8	(0.54)
Percent of students eligible for free or reduced-price lunch						
0–25	10.8	(1.08)	5.0	(0.62)	4.9	(0.72)
26–50	9.7	(1.14)	4.3	(0.55)	3.4	(0.48)
51–75	6.8	(0.83)	4.9	(0.78)	4.1	(0.78)
76–100	4.5	(0.96)	3.3	(0.91)	3.0	(0.73)
Student/teacher ratio[2]						
Less than 12	6.8	(1.36)	4.1	(1.20)	3.5	(1.02)
12–16	7.4	(0.71)	4.0	(0.48)	3.8	(0.66)
More than 16	8.7	(0.75)	4.8	(0.60)	3.9	(0.56)
Prevalence of violent incidents[3]						
No violent incidents	2.4 !	(0.90)	‡	(†)	‡	(†)
Any violent incidents	9.9	(0.53)	5.6	(0.40)	5.1	(0.53)

†Not applicable.
!Interpret data with caution. The coefficient of variation (CV) for this estimate is between 30 and 50 percent.
‡Reporting standards not met. Either there are too few cases for a reliable estimate or the coefficient of variation (CV) is 50 percent or greater.
[1]Primary schools are defined as schools in which the lowest grade is not higher than grade 3 and the highest grade is not higher than grade 8. Middle schools are defined as schools in which the lowest grade is not lower than grade 4 and the highest grade is not higher than grade 9. High schools are defined as schools in which the lowest grade is not lower than grade 9 and the highest grade is not higher than grade 12. Combined schools include all other combinations of grades, including K–12 schools.
[2]Student/teacher ratio was calculated by dividing the total number of students enrolled in the school by the total number of full-time-equivalent (FTE) teachers. Information regarding the total number of FTE teachers was obtained from the Common Core of Data (CCD), the sampling frame for SSOCS.

[3]"Violent incidents" include rape or attempted rape, sexual battery other than rape, physical attack or fight with or without a weapon, threat of physical attack or fight with or without a weapon, and robbery with or without a weapon. "At school" was defined for respondents to include activities that happen in school buildings, on school grounds, on school buses, and at places that hold school-sponsored events or activities. Respondents were instructed to respond only for those times that were during normal school hours or when school activities and events were in session.
NOTE: Includes schools reporting that cyber-bullying happens either "daily" or "at least once a week." "Cyber-bullying" was defined for respondents as occurring "when willful and repeated harm is inflicted through the use of computers, cell phones, or other electronic devices." Responses were provided by the principal or the person most knowledgeable about crime and safety issues at the school. Respondents were instructed to include cyber-bullying "problems that can occur anywhere (both at your school and away from school)."
SOURCE: U.S. Department of Education, National Center for Education Statistics, 2009–10 School Survey on Crime and Safety (SSOCS), 2010. (This table was prepared September 2013.)

Table 230.70. Percentage of students ages 12–18 who reported being afraid of attack or harm, by location and selected student and school characteristics: Selected years, 1995 through 2013

[Standard errors appear in parentheses]

Student or school characteristic	1995		1999		2001		2003		2005		2007[1]		2009[1]		2011[1]		2013[1]	
1	2		3		4		5		6		7		8		9		10	
At school																		
Total	11.8	(0.39)	7.3	(0.37)	6.4	(0.31)	6.1	(0.31)	6.4	(0.39)	5.3	(0.33)	4.2	(0.33)	3.7	(0.28)	3.5	(0.33)
Sex																		
Male	10.8	(0.51)	6.5	(0.44)	6.4	(0.38)	5.3	(0.34)	6.1	(0.56)	4.6	(0.42)	3.7	(0.38)	3.7	(0.41)	3.1	(0.38)
Female	12.8	(0.58)	8.2	(0.53)	6.4	(0.43)	6.9	(0.48)	6.7	(0.47)	6.0	(0.45)	4.8	(0.51)	3.8	(0.36)	4.0	(0.48)
Race/ethnicity[2]																		
White	8.1	(0.36)	5.0	(0.32)	4.9	(0.35)	4.1	(0.35)	4.6	(0.39)	4.2	(0.37)	3.3	(0.35)	3.0	(0.31)	2.6	(0.33)
Black	20.3	(1.31)	13.5	(1.27)	8.9	(0.87)	10.7	(1.22)	9.2	(1.19)	8.6	(1.18)	7.0	(1.12)	4.9	(1.03)	4.6	(0.85)
Hispanic	20.9	(1.27)	11.7	(1.20)	10.6	(1.07)	9.5	(0.65)	10.3	(1.16)	7.1	(0.88)	4.9	(0.89)	4.8	(0.59)	4.9	(0.78)
Asian	—	(†)	—	(†)	—	(†)	—	(†)	6.2 !	(2.09)	2.3 !	(1.05)	5.9 !	(2.25)	4.2 !	(1.52)	3.1 !	(1.09)
Other	13.5	(1.58)	6.7	(1.09)	6.4	(1.11)	5.0	(1.31)	5.7	(1.63)	3.3 !	(1.09)	‡	(†)	4.1 !	(1.31)	3.8 !	(1.44)
Grade																		
6th	14.3	(1.13)	10.9	(1.37)	10.6	(1.26)	10.0	(1.35)	9.5	(1.14)	9.9	(1.33)	6.4	(1.20)	5.6	(1.08)	4.7	(1.01)
7th	15.3	(1.02)	9.5	(0.79)	9.2	(0.95)	8.2	(0.86)	9.1	(1.04)	6.7	(0.86)	6.2	(1.06)	4.5	(0.69)	4.3	(0.69)
8th	13.0	(0.84)	8.1	(0.74)	7.6	(0.69)	6.3	(0.68)	7.1	(0.95)	4.6	(0.71)	3.5	(0.75)	4.6	(0.71)	3.3	(0.78)
9th	11.6	(0.82)	7.1	(0.74)	5.5	(0.63)	6.3	(0.61)	5.9	(0.71)	5.5	(0.87)	4.6	(0.75)	4.2	(0.66)	3.4	(0.71)
10th	11.0	(0.82)	7.1	(0.77)	5.0	(0.71)	4.4	(0.67)	5.5	(0.89)	5.2	(0.87)	4.6	(0.79)	3.9	(0.63)	4.4	(0.75)
11th	8.9	(0.80)	4.8	(0.68)	4.8	(0.65)	4.7	(0.66)	4.6	(0.73)	3.1	(0.63)	3.3	(0.74)	1.8	(0.48)	2.6	(0.55)
12th	7.8	(0.94)	4.8	(0.88)	2.9	(0.55)	3.7	(0.53)	3.3	(0.69)	3.1	(0.65)	1.9 !	(0.57)	2.2	(0.57)	2.0	(0.56)
Urbanicity[3]																		
Urban	18.4	(0.84)	11.6	(0.81)	9.7	(0.59)	9.5	(0.68)	10.5	(0.92)	7.1	(0.81)	6.9	(0.84)	5.2	(0.60)	4.5	(0.60)
Suburban	9.8	(0.49)	6.2	(0.42)	4.8	(0.33)	4.8	(0.30)	4.7	(0.41)	4.4	(0.41)	3.0	(0.33)	3.1	(0.39)	3.0	(0.38)
Rural	8.6	(0.80)	4.8	(0.70)	6.0	(0.97)	4.7	(0.93)	5.1	(0.97)	4.9	(0.59)	3.9	(0.63)	3.0	(0.63)	3.3	(0.62)
Control of school																		
Public	12.2	(0.43)	7.7	(0.38)	6.6	(0.33)	6.4	(0.34)	6.6	(0.42)	5.5	(0.34)	4.4	(0.35)	3.9	(0.30)	3.5	(0.35)
Private	7.3	(1.01)	3.6	(0.81)	4.6	(0.92)	3.0	(0.73)	3.8	(0.82)	2.5 !	(0.89)	1.9 !	(0.74)	1.5 !	(0.64)	2.6 !	(0.83)
Away from school																		
Total	—	(†)	5.7	(0.32)	4.6	(0.28)	5.4	(0.29)	5.2	(0.33)	3.5	(0.29)	3.3	(0.32)	2.4	(0.23)	2.7	(0.35)
Sex																		
Male	—	(†)	4.1	(0.34)	3.7	(0.31)	4.0	(0.30)	4.6	(0.42)	2.4	(0.31)	2.5	(0.34)	2.0	(0.27)	2.4	(0.40)
Female	—	(†)	7.4	(0.49)	5.6	(0.42)	6.8	(0.48)	5.8	(0.48)	4.5	(0.40)	4.1	(0.51)	2.7	(0.30)	3.0	(0.44)
Race/ethnicity[2]																		
White	—	(†)	4.3	(0.32)	3.7	(0.29)	3.8	(0.31)	4.2	(0.40)	2.5	(0.28)	2.2	(0.28)	1.6	(0.24)	1.6	(0.30)
Black	—	(†)	8.7	(1.00)	6.3	(0.87)	10.0	(1.13)	7.3	(0.96)	4.9	(0.73)	5.7	(1.10)	3.5	(0.86)	3.6	(0.78)
Hispanic	—	(†)	8.9	(1.03)	6.5	(0.75)	7.4	(0.80)	6.2	(0.84)	5.9	(0.80)	3.9	(0.70)	3.3	(0.50)	4.5	(0.86)
Asian	—	(†)	—	(†)	—	(†)	—	(†)	7.4 !	(2.89)	‡	(†)	7.1 !	(2.50)	3.2 !	(1.15)	2.9 !	(1.03)
Other	—	(†)	5.4	(1.04)	6.6	(1.32)	3.9	(1.02)	3.1 !	(1.28)	‡	(†)	4.0 !	(1.79)	2.5 !	(1.05)	3.2 !	(1.42)
Grade																		
6th	—	(†)	7.8	(1.11)	6.3	(1.15)	6.8	(1.01)	5.6	(0.99)	5.9	(1.20)	3.3	(0.89)	3.0	(0.86)	3.9	(0.88)
7th	—	(†)	6.1	(0.72)	5.5	(0.80)	6.7	(0.80)	7.5	(0.89)	3.0	(0.55)	4.0	(0.78)	2.7	(0.58)	2.2	(0.54)
8th	—	(†)	5.5	(0.66)	4.4	(0.61)	5.3	(0.71)	5.0	(0.72)	3.6	(0.65)	3.3	(0.72)	2.1	(0.43)	2.4 !	(0.80)
9th	—	(†)	4.6	(0.63)	4.5	(0.62)	4.3	(0.55)	3.8	(0.61)	4.0	(0.75)	2.6	(0.62)	3.5	(0.65)	2.8	(0.59)
10th	—	(†)	4.8	(0.63)	4.2	(0.63)	5.3	(0.67)	4.7	(0.66)	3.0	(0.60)	5.5	(0.96)	1.7	(0.46)	4.4	(0.83)
11th	—	(†)	5.9	(0.72)	4.7	(0.62)	4.7	(0.69)	4.2	(0.74)	2.3	(0.56)	2.2	(0.56)	2.9	(0.70)	2.2	(0.47)
12th	—	(†)	6.1	(0.86)	3.3	(0.62)	4.9	(0.72)	5.4	(0.98)	3.2	(0.61)	2.1	(0.63)	1.0 !	(0.37)	1.3 !	(0.46)
Urbanicity[3]																		
Urban	—	(†)	9.1	(0.82)	7.4	(0.68)	8.1	(0.60)	6.7	(0.61)	5.3	(0.67)	5.8	(0.87)	3.4	(0.42)	4.0	(0.54)
Suburban	—	(†)	5.0	(0.31)	3.8	(0.33)	4.4	(0.34)	4.6	(0.43)	2.7	(0.36)	2.5	(0.33)	2.2	(0.30)	2.2	(0.42)
Rural	—	(†)	3.0	(0.71)	3.0	(0.59)	4.0	(0.69)	4.7	(0.98)	2.8	(0.54)	1.9	(0.48)	1.0 !	(0.35)	1.7	(0.49)
Control of school																		
Public	—	(†)	5.8	(0.32)	4.6	(0.30)	5.4	(0.31)	5.2	(0.34)	3.6	(0.30)	3.5	(0.33)	2.4	(0.23)	2.7	(0.36)
Private	—	(†)	5.0	(0.92)	5.1	(1.08)	4.7	(0.89)	4.9	(1.41)	2.1 !	(0.72)	1.8 !	(0.71)	1.6 !	(0.68)	2.0 !	(0.70)

—Not available.
†Not applicable.
!Interpret data with caution. The coefficient of variation (CV) for this estimate is between 30 and 50 percent.
‡Reporting standards not met. Either there are too few cases for a reliable estimate or the coefficient of variation (CV) is 50 percent or greater.
[1]Starting in 2007, the reference period was the school year, whereas in prior survey years the reference period was the previous 6 months. Cognitive testing showed that estimates from 2007 onward are comparable to previous years.
[2]Race categories exclude persons of Hispanic ethnicity. "Other" includes American Indians/Alaska Natives, Asians (prior to 2005), Pacific Islanders, and, from 2003 onward, persons of Two or more races. Due to changes in racial/ethnic categories, comparisons of race/ethnicity across years should be made with caution.

[3]Refers to the Standard Metropolitan Statistical Area (MSA) status of the respondent's household as defined in 2000 by the U.S. Census Bureau. Categories include "central city of an MSA (Urban)," "in MSA but not in central city (Suburban)," and "not MSA (Rural)."
NOTE: "At school" includes the school building, on school property, on a school bus, and, from 2001 onward, going to and from school. Students were asked if they "never," "almost never," "sometimes," or "most of the time" feared that someone would attack or harm them at school or away from school. Students responding "sometimes" or "most of the time" were considered fearful. For the 2001 survey only, the wording was changed from "attack or harm" to "attack or threaten to attack."
SOURCE: U.S. Department of Justice, Bureau of Justice Statistics, School Crime Supplement (SCS) to the National Crime Victimization Survey, selected years, 1995 through 2013. (This table was prepared September 2014.)

Table 230.80. Percentage of students ages 12–18 who reported avoiding one or more places in school or avoiding school activities or classes because of fear of attack or harm, by selected student and school characteristics: Selected years, 1995 through 2013

[Standard errors appear in parentheses]

Type of avoidance and student or school characteristic	1995		1999		2001		2003		2005		2007[1]		2009[1]		2011[1]		2013[1]	
1	2		3		4		5		6		7		8		9		10	
Total, any avoidance	—	(†)	6.9	(0.34)	6.1	(0.32)	5.0	(0.30)	5.5	(0.32)	7.2	(0.36)	5.0	(0.35)	5.5	(0.34)	4.7	(0.31)
Avoided one or more places in school																		
Total	8.7	(0.29)	4.6	(0.29)	4.7	(0.27)	4.0	(0.27)	4.5	(0.28)	5.8	(0.31)	4.0	(0.32)	4.7	(0.30)	3.7	(0.27)
Entrance to the school	2.1	(0.15)	1.1	(0.14)	1.2	(0.11)	1.2	(0.11)	1.0	(0.14)	1.5	(0.15)	0.9	(0.15)	0.9	(0.13)	0.8	(0.14)
Hallways or stairs in school	4.2	(0.21)	2.1	(0.17)	2.1	(0.18)	1.7	(0.17)	2.1	(0.21)	2.6	(0.21)	2.2	(0.23)	2.5	(0.21)	1.7	(0.18)
Parts of the school cafeteria	2.5	(0.18)	1.3	(0.15)	1.4	(0.16)	1.2	(0.13)	1.8	(0.16)	1.9	(0.19)	1.1	(0.17)	1.8	(0.18)	1.4	(0.19)
Any school restrooms	4.4	(0.22)	2.1	(0.19)	2.2	(0.19)	2.0	(0.16)	2.1	(0.20)	2.6	(0.24)	1.4	(0.19)	1.7	(0.19)	1.3	(0.16)
Other places inside the school building	2.5	(0.18)	1.4	(0.17)	1.4	(0.14)	1.2	(0.14)	1.4	(0.18)	1.5	(0.17)	1.0	(0.16)	1.1	(0.15)	0.8	(0.13)
Sex																		
Male	8.8	(0.43)	4.6	(0.35)	4.7	(0.40)	3.9	(0.34)	4.9	(0.46)	6.1	(0.47)	3.9	(0.45)	3.9	(0.42)	3.4	(0.34)
Female	8.5	(0.46)	4.6	(0.39)	4.6	(0.35)	4.1	(0.37)	4.1	(0.40)	5.5	(0.41)	4.0	(0.42)	5.5	(0.40)	3.9	(0.43)
Race/ethnicity[2]																		
White	7.1	(0.32)	3.8	(0.27)	3.9	(0.30)	3.0	(0.27)	3.6	(0.30)	5.3	(0.36)	3.3	(0.38)	4.4	(0.38)	3.0	(0.34)
Black	12.1	(1.01)	6.7	(0.90)	6.6	(0.75)	5.1	(0.79)	7.2	(0.98)	8.3	(1.02)	6.1	(1.04)	4.5	(0.80)	3.3	(0.79)
Hispanic	12.9	(0.97)	6.2	(0.73)	5.5	(0.71)	6.3	(0.70)	6.0	(0.80)	6.8	(0.82)	4.8	(0.86)	6.0	(0.68)	4.9	(0.63)
Asian	—	(†)	—	(†)	—	(†)	—	(†)	2.5 !	(0.87)	‡	(†)	3.7 !	(1.53)	2.7 !	(1.06)	3.8 !	(1.26)
Other	11.1	(1.61)	5.4	(0.99)	6.2	(1.16)	4.4	(1.02)	4.3 !	(1.86)	3.5 !	(1.22)	‡	(†)	3.3 !	(1.04)	5.9	(1.72)
Grade																		
6th	11.6	(0.99)	5.9	(0.92)	6.8	(0.93)	5.6	(0.94)	7.9	(1.27)	7.8	(1.20)	7.1	(1.13)	6.9	(0.99)	4.4	(0.92)
7th	11.8	(0.89)	6.1	(0.72)	6.2	(0.79)	5.7	(0.73)	5.8	(0.93)	7.5	(0.86)	5.5	(0.86)	5.1	(0.76)	4.6	(0.72)
8th	8.8	(0.77)	5.5	(0.70)	5.2	(0.62)	4.7	(0.63)	4.5	(0.67)	5.9	(0.84)	4.8	(0.93)	5.2	(0.75)	2.7	(0.62)
9th	9.5	(0.71)	5.3	(0.63)	5.0	(0.61)	5.1	(0.62)	5.2	(0.78)	6.7	(0.81)	4.5	(0.89)	3.7	(0.67)	5.1	(0.78)
10th	7.8	(0.75)	4.7	(0.61)	4.2	(0.64)	3.1	(0.54)	4.2	(0.65)	5.5	(0.80)	4.2	(0.88)	5.4	(0.72)	4.0	(0.72)
11th	6.9	(0.64)	2.5	(0.46)	2.8	(0.43)	2.5	(0.53)	3.3	(0.58)	4.2	(0.70)	1.2 !	(0.44)	3.6	(0.65)	2.5	(0.61)
12th	4.1	(0.74)	2.4	(0.51)	3.0	(0.64)	1.2 !	(0.41)	1.3 !	(0.41)	3.2	(0.71)	1.6 !	(0.50)	3.7	(0.71)	2.3	(0.62)
Urbanicity[3]																		
Urban	11.7	(0.73)	5.8	(0.48)	6.0	(0.52)	5.7	(0.59)	6.3	(0.67)	6.1	(0.65)	5.5	(0.69)	5.3	(0.61)	4.3	(0.54)
Suburban	7.9	(0.40)	4.7	(0.38)	4.3	(0.38)	3.5	(0.30)	3.8	(0.36)	5.2	(0.38)	3.1	(0.38)	4.6	(0.36)	3.3	(0.33)
Rural	7.0	(0.65)	3.0	(0.56)	3.9	(0.70)	2.8	(0.53)	4.2	(0.74)	6.9	(0.69)	4.3	(0.80)	3.5	(0.54)	3.5	(0.68)
School control																		
Public	9.3	(0.33)	5.0	(0.31)	4.9	(0.29)	4.2	(0.29)	4.8	(0.30)	6.2	(0.35)	4.2	(0.34)	4.9	(0.32)	3.9	(0.29)
Private	2.2	(0.47)	1.6	(0.45)	2.0 !	(0.69)	1.5 !	(0.49)	1.4 !	(0.55)	1.4 !	(0.54)	1.8 !	(0.73)	2.1 !	(0.70)	1.0 !	(0.49)
Avoided school activities or classes																		
Total	—	(†)	3.2	(0.22)	2.3	(0.18)	1.9	(0.18)	2.1	(0.23)	2.6	(0.23)	2.1	(0.25)	2.0	(0.20)	2.0	(0.21)
Any activities[4]	1.7	(0.15)	0.8	(0.10)	1.1	(0.12)	1.0	(0.11)	1.0	(0.16)	1.8	(0.20)	1.3	(0.20)	1.2	(0.16)	1.0	(0.13)
Any classes	—	(†)	0.6	(0.09)	0.6	(0.09)	0.6	(0.10)	0.7	(0.13)	0.7	(0.12)	0.6	(0.13)	0.7	(0.10)	0.5	(0.10)
Stayed home from school	—	(†)	2.3	(0.19)	1.1	(0.13)	0.8	(0.11)	0.7	(0.11)	0.8	(0.13)	0.6	(0.14)	0.8	(0.12)	0.9	(0.13)

—Not available.
†Not applicable.
!Interpret data with caution. The coefficient of variation (CV) for this estimate is between 30 and 50 percent.
‡Reporting standards not met. Either there are too few cases for a reliable estimate or the coefficient of variation (CV) is 50 percent or greater.
[1]Starting in 2007, the reference period was the school year, whereas in prior survey years the reference period was the previous 6 months. Cognitive testing showed that estimates from 2007 onward are comparable to previous years.
[2]Race categories exclude persons of Hispanic ethnicity. "Other" includes American Indians/Alaska Natives, Asians (prior to 2005), Pacific Islanders, and, from 2003 onward, persons of Two or more races. Due to changes in racial/ethnic categories, comparisons of race/ethnicity across years should be made with caution.

[3]Refers to the Standard Metropolitan Statistical Area (MSA) status of the respondent's household as defined in 2000 by the U.S. Census Bureau. Categories include "central city of an MSA (Urban)," "in MSA but not in central city (Suburban)," and "not MSA (Rural)."
[4]Before 2007, students were asked whether they avoided "any extracurricular activities." Starting in 2007, the survey wording was changed to "any activities."
NOTE: Students were asked whether they avoided places or activities because they thought that someone might attack or harm them. For the 2001 survey only, the wording was changed from "attack or harm" to "attack or threaten to attack." Detail may not sum to totals because of rounding and because students reporting more than one type of avoidance were counted only once in the totals.
SOURCE: U.S. Department of Justice, Bureau of Justice Statistics, School Crime Supplement (SCS) to the National Crime Victimization Survey, selected years, 1995 through 2013. (This table was prepared September 2014.)

Table 230.90. Percentage of public and private school teachers who agreed that student misbehavior and student tardiness and class cutting interfered with their teaching, by selected teacher and school characteristics: Selected years, 1987–88 through 2011–12

[Standard errors appear in parentheses]

Teacher or school characteristic	Student misbehavior interfered with teaching							Student tardiness and class cutting interfered with teaching						
	1987–88	1990–91	1993–94	1999–2000	2003–04	2007–08	2011–12	1987–88	1990–91	1993–94	1999–2000	2003–04	2007–08	2011–12
1	2	3	4	5	6	7	8	9	10	11	12	13	14	15
Total	40.2 (0.33)	33.8 (0.31)	41.3 (0.34)	38.6 (0.39)	35.1 (0.58)	34.1 (0.50)	38.5 (0.61)	32.6 (0.28)	—	25.4 (0.28)	29.3 (0.30)	31.3 (0.44)	31.5 (0.60)	35.3 (0.46)
Years of teaching experience														
3 or fewer	42.1 (0.95)	35.5 (0.75)	44.8 (0.98)	41.5 (0.79)	39.2 (2.15)	37.3 (1.00)	43.2 (1.21)	34.6 (0.89)	(†)	27.8 (0.71)	32.3 (0.73)	34.0 (1.20)	34.3 (1.01)	38.5 (1.28)
4 to 9	40.1 (0.65)	33.6 (0.69)	41.9 (0.61)	40.5 (0.66)	36.2 (0.75)	35.1 (1.02)	39.8 (1.05)	31.4 (0.50)	(†)	25.5 (0.59)	30.1 (0.55)	32.0 (0.70)	32.6 (1.01)	36.0 (0.96)
10 to 19	39.5 (0.41)	33.0 (0.52)	40.7 (0.57)	36.4 (0.65)	34.0 (0.83)	33.6 (0.83)	38.0 (0.92)	31.7 (0.35)	(†)	24.3 (0.48)	26.7 (0.55)	30.7 (0.75)	30.9 (1.04)	35.3 (0.93)
20 or more	40.7 (0.73)	34.1 (0.70)	40.1 (0.53)	37.6 (0.57)	32.8 (0.68)	31.5 (0.82)	35.4 (0.97)	34.3 (0.61)	(†)	25.5 (0.35)	29.3 (0.51)	29.7 (0.67)	29.1 (0.90)	33.0 (0.95)
School level[1]														
Elementary	39.2 (0.53)	34.1 (0.45)	40.9 (0.54)	39.1 (0.57)	33.8 (0.74)	32.6 (0.73)	38.6 (0.92)	22.6 (0.35)	(†)	17.2 (0.41)	24.2 (0.42)	26.5 (0.57)	25.6 (0.76)	31.0 (0.71)
Secondary	43.2 (0.43)	34.9 (0.43)	43.7 (0.35)	39.5 (0.42)	40.0 (0.60)	38.8 (0.74)	40.5 (0.80)	49.9 (0.45)	(†)	43.0 (0.37)	41.5 (0.46)	43.8 (0.65)	45.4 (0.81)	45.3 (0.69)
School control														
Public[2]	42.3 (0.36)	35.7 (0.34)	44.1 (0.40)	40.8 (0.42)	37.2 (0.52)	36.0 (0.57)	40.7 (0.65)	34.7 (0.29)	(†)	27.9 (0.32)	31.5 (0.35)	33.4 (0.45)	33.4 (0.64)	37.6 (0.51)
Private	24.2 (0.95)	20.0 (0.63)	22.4 (0.43)	24.1 (0.61)	20.7 (2.47)	20.6 (0.72)	22.0 (1.05)	17.2 (0.73)	(†)	8.6 (0.42)	15.0 (0.43)	16.9 (1.11)	17.9 (0.72)	18.8 (1.06)
School enrollment														
Under 200	31.9 (0.89)	25.0 (0.82)	31.1 (0.72)	32.5 (0.93)	29.4 (2.44)	29.9 (1.10)	33.9 (1.27)	24.5 (0.94)	(†)	14.7 (0.51)	21.7 (0.71)	24.9 (1.52)	26.1 (0.91)	29.4 (1.03)
200 to 499	36.6 (0.52)	30.6 (0.60)	36.9 (0.72)	36.4 (0.57)	30.7 (0.91)	32.9 (0.87)	37.3 (0.87)	23.9 (0.37)	(†)	16.9 (0.52)	25.0 (0.60)	26.2 (0.73)	27.4 (0.94)	32.1 (0.92)
500 to 749	41.2 (0.63)	34.9 (0.64)	41.9 (0.74)	40.0 (0.82)	34.0 (0.94)	34.4 (1.28)	37.4 (1.38)	29.0 (0.66)	(†)	21.2 (0.67)	27.1 (0.63)	28.2 (0.83)	28.4 (1.25)	32.5 (1.02)
750 to 999	44.6 (1.10)	39.3 (1.03)	47.6 (0.85)	39.8 (1.32)	37.2 (1.45)	32.4 (1.34)	41.9 (1.82)	35.6 (1.05)	(†)	30.2 (1.19)	27.7 (1.00)	31.0 (1.15)	29.6 (1.24)	36.7 (1.87)
1,000 or more	47.0 (0.75)	38.8 (0.76)	48.0 (0.69)	41.9 (0.65)	43.7 (0.85)	37.9 (1.01)	40.9 (0.97)	54.2 (0.72)	(†)	46.8 (0.70)	41.7 (0.77)	44.9 (0.97)	43.1 (1.13)	44.2 (0.92)
Locale[3]														
City	—	(†)	(†)	(†)	41.8 (1.14)	39.9 (1.08)	‡	—	(†)	(†)	(†)	37.3 (0.89)	38.5 (0.95)	‡
Suburban	—	(†)	(†)	(†)	32.3 (0.77)	31.7 (0.78)	‡	—	(†)	(†)	(†)	28.5 (0.74)	28.8 (0.86)	‡
Town	—	(†)	(†)	(†)	34.7 (1.32)	34.7 (1.32)	‡	—	(†)	(†)	(†)	31.7 (1.12)	34.0 (1.68)	‡
Rural	—	(†)	(†)	(†)	31.1 (1.31)	30.8 (0.97)	‡	—	(†)	(†)	(†)	27.9 (0.88)	26.4 (0.92)	‡

—Not available.
†Not applicable.
‡Reporting standards not met. Data may be suppressed because the response rate is under 50 percent, there are too few cases for a reliable estimate, or the coefficient of variation (CV) is 50 percent or greater.
[1]Elementary schools are those with any of grades kindergarten through grade 6 and none of grades 7 through 12. Secondary schools have any of grades 7 through 12 and none of grades kindergarten through grade 6. Combined elementary/secondary schools are included in totals but are not shown separately.
[2]Includes traditional public and public charter schools.

[3]Substantial improvements in geocoding technology and changes in the Office of Management and Budget's definition of metropolitan and nonmetropolitan areas allow for more precision in describing an area as of 2003–04. Comparisons with earlier years are not possible.
NOTE: Teachers who taught only prekindergarten students are excluded. Includes both teachers who "strongly" agreed and those who "somewhat" agreed that student misbehavior or student tardiness and class cutting interfered with their teaching. Some data have been revised from previously published figures.
SOURCE: U.S. Department of Education, National Center for Education Statistics, Schools and Staffing Survey (SASS), "Public School Teacher Data File," and "Private School Teacher Data File," 1987–88, 1990–91, 1993–94, 1999–2000, 2003–04, 2007–08, and 2011–12; and "Charter School Teacher Data File," 1999–2000. (This table was prepared October 2013.)

Table 230.92. Percentage of public and private school teachers who agreed that other teachers and the principal enforced school rules, by selected teacher and school characteristics: Selected years, 1987–88 through 2011–12

[Standard errors appear in parentheses]

Teacher or school characteristic	Other teachers enforced school rules[1]							Principal enforced school rules[2]						
	1987–88	1990–91	1993–94	1999–2000	2003–04	2007–08	2011–12	1987–88	1990–91	1993–94	1999–2000	2003–04	2007–08	2011–12
1	2	3	4	5	6	7	8	9	10	11	12	13	14	15
Total	65.1 (0.30)	73.4 (0.34)	63.8 (0.36)	64.4 (0.35)	72.4 (0.41)	71.8 (0.47)	68.8 (0.48)	83.7 (0.22)	87.4 (0.26)	81.8 (0.31)	83.0 (0.28)	87.8 (0.30)	88.5 (0.34)	84.4 (0.41)
Years of teaching experience														
3 or fewer	68.6 (0.93)	76.1 (0.88)	68.8 (0.92)	69.4 (0.71)	76.6 (0.91)	73.6 (1.07)	70.2 (1.27)	85.0 (0.52)	88.1 (0.49)	85.1 (0.59)	84.5 (0.52)	88.6 (0.66)	89.9 (0.68)	86.6 (1.15)
4 to 9	65.3 (0.71)	72.7 (0.69)	63.0 (0.78)	61.6 (0.62)	70.6 (0.70)	69.5 (0.88)	66.6 (0.88)	84.1 (0.45)	87.4 (0.55)	80.7 (0.63)	82.7 (0.49)	86.9 (0.57)	88.2 (0.61)	84.6 (0.72)
10 to 19	64.3 (0.49)	72.9 (0.48)	63.1 (0.55)	64.6 (0.65)	71.4 (0.76)	71.0 (0.73)	68.3 (0.86)	83.9 (0.35)	87.5 (0.43)	82.4 (0.41)	83.1 (0.49)	87.8 (0.53)	87.2 (0.62)	82.3 (0.74)
20 or more	64.9 (0.58)	73.5 (0.57)	63.1 (0.58)	63.6 (0.59)	72.5 (0.64)	73.8 (0.80)	71.1 (0.84)	82.8 (0.56)	86.9 (0.41)	80.6 (0.38)	82.4 (0.41)	88.3 (0.43)	89.4 (0.55)	85.9 (0.79)
School level[3]														
Elementary	74.2 (0.41)	80.5 (0.52)	72.2 (0.48)	72.2 (0.49)	79.5 (0.54)	79.4 (0.61)	75.6 (0.71)	85.1 (0.36)	88.0 (0.41)	82.8 (0.45)	84.2 (0.41)	88.3 (0.45)	89.5 (0.44)	85.0 (0.60)
Secondary	49.9 (0.60)	60.2 (0.43)	47.0 (0.34)	47.2 (0.46)	55.7 (0.55)	56.1 (0.64)	54.4 (0.69)	81.5 (0.37)	85.8 (0.37)	79.0 (0.31)	80.0 (0.39)	86.2 (0.41)	86.3 (0.48)	82.5 (0.56)
School control														
Public[4]	63.8 (0.31)	71.9 (0.36)	61.8 (0.42)	62.6 (0.39)	71.1 (0.46)	70.6 (0.55)	67.6 (0.51)	83.1 (0.22)	86.7 (0.29)	80.8 (0.35)	82.2 (0.33)	87.2 (0.34)	88.0 (0.37)	83.7 (0.43)
Private	75.4 (0.98)	84.3 (0.61)	77.6 (0.50)	75.9 (0.51)	81.0 (1.52)	80.1 (0.81)	77.4 (1.49)	88.6 (0.57)	92.0 (0.42)	88.4 (0.41)	88.3 (0.39)	92.2 (0.75)	92.2 (0.57)	89.4 (0.98)
School enrollment														
Under 200	76.1 (0.90)	83.7 (0.60)	76.5 (0.84)	75.4 (0.81)	84.0 (1.54)	81.0 (0.85)	78.7 (0.91)	86.6 (0.54)	89.3 (0.54)	85.2 (0.61)	87.1 (0.48)	90.9 (0.86)	90.8 (0.60)	88.7 (0.84)
200 to 499	72.6 (0.42)	79.4 (0.55)	71.2 (0.65)	71.6 (0.58)	78.9 (0.62)	78.6 (0.71)	74.2 (1.00)	84.6 (0.38)	88.1 (0.42)	83.5 (0.47)	84.2 (0.46)	89.3 (0.48)	89.4 (0.60)	84.7 (0.87)
500 to 749	66.6 (0.74)	75.8 (0.74)	66.8 (0.81)	67.7 (0.66)	75.8 (0.68)	74.1 (1.04)	72.2 (1.06)	84.4 (0.55)	88.5 (0.53)	82.3 (0.76)	83.5 (0.55)	87.7 (0.66)	88.6 (0.68)	85.2 (0.75)
750 to 999	59.8 (1.00)	68.5 (1.01)	58.6 (1.10)	63.0 (0.97)	69.4 (1.32)	71.7 (1.50)	66.0 (1.33)	83.0 (0.80)	85.7 (0.81)	79.6 (0.87)	82.5 (0.83)	86.0 (1.14)	88.4 (0.89)	82.7 (1.30)
1,000 or more	48.1 (0.89)	57.5 (0.67)	45.8 (0.77)	47.3 (0.75)	56.3 (0.88)	57.1 (1.17)	55.4 (1.04)	80.7 (0.62)	84.9 (0.66)	78.0 (0.58)	79.4 (0.57)	85.8 (0.63)	86.5 (0.73)	82.3 (0.81)
Locale[5]														
City	— (†)	— (†)	— (†)	— (†)	69.6 (0.86)	69.4 (0.98)	‡ (†)	— (†)	— (†)	— (†)	— (†)	85.5 (0.60)	86.5 (0.72)	‡ (†)
Suburban	— (†)	— (†)	— (†)	— (†)	73.5 (0.70)	72.6 (0.76)	‡ (†)	— (†)	— (†)	— (†)	— (†)	89.1 (0.47)	89.7 (0.53)	‡ (†)
Town	— (†)	— (†)	— (†)	— (†)	72.4 (1.03)	71.7 (1.32)	‡ (†)	— (†)	— (†)	— (†)	— (†)	88.9 (0.71)	87.5 (1.26)	‡ (†)
Rural	— (†)	— (†)	— (†)	— (†)	74.3 (0.74)	73.6 (0.81)	‡ (†)	— (†)	— (†)	— (†)	— (†)	88.5 (0.61)	89.5 (0.58)	‡ (†)

—Not available.
†Not applicable.
‡Reporting standards not met. Data may be suppressed because the response rate is under 50 percent, there are too few cases for a reliable estimate, or the coefficient of variation (CV) is 50 percent or greater.
[1]Respondents were asked whether "rules for student behavior are consistently enforced by teachers in this school, even for students not in their classes."
[2]Respondents were asked whether their "principal enforces school rules for student conduct and backs me up when I need it."
[3]Elementary schools are those with any of grades kindergarten through grade 6 and none of grades 9 through 12. Secondary schools have any of grades 7 through 12 and none of grades kindergarten through grade 6. Combined elementary/secondary schools are included in totals but are not shown separately.

[4]Includes traditional public and public charter schools.
[5]Substantial improvements in geocoding technology and changes in the Office of Management and Budget's definition of metropolitan and nonmetropolitan areas allow for more precision in describing an area as of 2003–04. Comparisons with earlier years are not possible.
NOTE: Teachers who taught only prekindergarten students are excluded. Includes both teachers who "strongly" agreed and those who "somewhat" agreed that rules were enforced by other teachers and the principal. Some data have been revised from previously published figures.
SOURCE: U.S. Department of Education, National Center for Education Statistics, Schools and Staffing Survey (SASS), "Public School Teacher Data File" and "Private School Teacher Data File," 1987–88, 1990–91, 1993–94, 1999–2000, 2003–04, 2007–08, and 2011–12; and "Charter School Teacher Data File," 1999–2000. (This table was prepared October 2013.)

Table 230.95. Percentage of public school teachers who agreed that student misbehavior and student tardiness and class cutting interfered with their teaching and that other teachers and the principal enforced school rules, by state: 2011–12

[Standard errors appear in parentheses]

State	Interfered with teaching				Enforced school rules			
	Student misbehavior		Student tardiness and class cutting		Other teachers[1]		Principal[2]	
1	2		3		4		5	
United States...............	40.7	(0.65)	37.6	(0.51)	67.6	(0.51)	83.7	(0.43)
Alabama.........................	40.9	(3.36)	38.6	(2.82)	71.8	(2.84)	86.8	(2.26)
Alaska..........................	35.8	(5.73)	56.8	(6.73)	72.2	(4.41)	83.2	(5.16)
Arizona	41.3	(2.56)	44.5	(2.67)	67.9	(2.72)	83.4	(2.06)
Arkansas.......................	39.5	(3.56)	38.5	(3.80)	74.0	(2.60)	90.0	(2.16)
California.......................	38.9	(2.47)	39.7	(2.36)	69.7	(1.83)	83.0	(1.63)
Colorado	45.5	(3.54)	47.6	(4.02)	61.7	(3.39)	80.6	(3.28)
Connecticut....................	37.2	(2.35)	28.6	(3.81)	61.7	(3.91)	80.7	(2.98)
Delaware.......................	46.7	(4.47)	35.2	(4.58)	68.7	(3.58)	82.9	(3.32)
District of Columbia	‡	(†)	‡	(†)	‡	(†)	‡	(†)
Florida...........................	‡	(†)	‡	(†)	‡	(†)	‡	(†)
Georgia.........................	38.2	(3.56)	32.1	(3.36)	71.9	(2.64)	85.5	(2.29)
Hawaii...........................	‡	(†)	‡	(†)	‡	(†)	‡	(†)
Idaho.............................	34.6	(3.54)	36.1	(3.08)	74.7	(2.48)	87.9	(2.18)
Illinois...........................	40.0	(2.96)	33.9	(3.07)	66.0	(3.18)	83.6	(2.31)
Indiana..........................	38.8	(3.33)	41.0	(2.95)	68.4	(2.47)	81.8	(2.99)
Iowa..............................	37.9	(3.12)	34.6	(3.18)	68.5	(2.77)	81.8	(2.40)
Kansas..........................	32.0	(3.57)	24.9	(2.34)	70.9	(3.29)	91.8	(1.61)
Kentucky	42.8	(3.06)	32.8	(2.92)	67.4	(2.80)	86.9	(2.47)
Louisiana	55.1	(3.92)	36.1	(3.60)	62.5	(3.19)	82.1	(3.89)
Maine............................	39.1	(3.00)	39.2	(3.02)	62.9	(2.90)	83.2	(3.06)
Maryland........................	‡	(†)	‡	(†)	‡	(†)	‡	(†)
Massachusetts.................	37.2	(3.07)	32.0	(2.74)	66.6	(3.04)	83.1	(2.80)
Michigan	46.6	(2.87)	40.9	(2.63)	67.6	(2.12)	84.4	(2.08)
Minnesota	43.7	(2.49)	37.3	(2.50)	68.7	(1.88)	84.5	(1.84)
Mississippi	37.4	(3.30)	35.6	(3.40)	72.4	(2.96)	84.5	(2.51)
Missouri	33.2	(2.10)	33.6	(2.87)	68.9	(2.17)	86.6	(1.76)
Montana.........................	41.3	(3.43)	45.3	(4.08)	66.5	(3.65)	83.1	(2.97)
Nebraska	38.2	(3.01)	33.6	(2.81)	70.9	(2.73)	86.7	(1.66)
Nevada	45.5	(3.77)	42.3	(4.86)	65.5	(3.42)	79.3	(3.22)
New Hampshire	38.3	(4.36)	30.9	(3.11)	62.0	(3.93)	83.2	(2.66)
New Jersey	35.9	(2.36)	29.9	(2.29)	66.8	(2.06)	84.4	(1.70)
New Mexico	39.0	(4.55)	54.5	(5.87)	64.2	(3.80)	78.7	(4.23)
New York........................	40.3	(2.91)	45.3	(3.06)	65.9	(2.47)	80.7	(2.46)
North Carolina	41.9	(3.13)	37.0	(2.94)	69.0	(2.58)	84.0	(2.34)
North Dakota	34.6	(3.26)	33.5	(3.52)	70.4	(2.77)	86.7	(2.45)
Ohio..............................	41.8	(1.95)	38.8	(1.96)	66.4	(1.73)	84.7	(1.55)
Oklahoma	40.1	(2.74)	40.8	(2.87)	72.5	(2.47)	86.5	(2.12)
Oregon..........................	33.1	(3.24)	35.6	(3.73)	77.3	(2.90)	88.1	(1.77)
Pennsylvania..................	40.0	(2.64)	33.4	(2.55)	65.2	(2.18)	82.5	(1.88)
Rhode Island	‡	(†)	‡	(†)	‡	(†)	‡	(†)
South Carolina................	40.9	(3.22)	33.7	(3.40)	71.8	(3.23)	86.8	(2.15)
South Dakota..................	40.1	(3.10)	37.2	(3.92)	73.2	(2.91)	84.8	(2.53)
Tennessee	41.5	(3.56)	40.0	(3.56)	71.4	(3.14)	88.7	(2.14)
Texas............................	45.6	(2.29)	35.1	(2.13)	65.8	(2.56)	81.8	(1.99)
Utah..............................	39.7	(3.67)	45.1	(4.30)	75.8	(3.56)	89.9	(2.27)
Vermont	39.9	(2.61)	36.2	(2.62)	59.2	(2.59)	80.5	(2.28)
Virginia..........................	40.8	(3.46)	35.6	(3.06)	64.9	(2.87)	82.5	(2.52)
Washington.....................	39.2	(2.89)	39.5	(3.16)	73.1	(2.60)	85.6	(2.18)
West Virginia...................	43.9	(3.87)	42.4	(4.09)	73.4	(2.90)	90.4	(2.58)
Wisconsin	42.7	(2.70)	34.2	(3.07)	69.5	(2.87)	85.8	(1.70)
Wyoming........................	30.7	(4.76)	40.0	(4.78)	73.9	(3.55)	89.1	(3.41)

†Not applicable.
‡Reporting standards not met. Data may be suppressed because the response rate is under 50 percent, there are too few cases for a reliable estimate, or the coefficient of variation (CV) is 50 percent or greater.
[1]Respondents were asked whether "rules for student behavior are consistently enforced by teachers in this school, even for students not in their classes."
[2]Respondents were asked whether their "principal enforces school rules for student conduct and backs me up when I need it."
NOTE: Teachers who taught only prekindergarten students are excluded. Includes traditional public and public charter school teachers. Includes both teachers who "strongly" agreed and those who "somewhat" agreed.
SOURCE: U.S. Department of Education, National Center for Education Statistics, Schools and Staffing Survey (SASS), "Public School Teacher Data File," 2011–12. (This table was prepared July 2013.)

Table 231.10. Percentage of students in grades 9–12 who reported having been in a physical fight at least one time during the previous 12 months, by location and selected student characteristics: Selected years, 1993 through 2013

[Standard errors appear in parentheses]

Location and student characteristic	1993	1995	1997	1999	2001	2003	2005	2007	2009	2011	2013
1	2	3	4	5	6	7	8	9	10	11	12
Anywhere (including on school property)[1]											
Total	41.8 (0.99)	38.7 (1.14)	36.6 (1.01)	35.7 (1.17)	33.2 (0.71)	33.0 (0.99)	35.9 (0.77)	35.5 (0.77)	31.5 (0.70)	32.8 (0.65)	24.7 (0.74)
Sex											
Male	51.2 (1.05)	46.1 (1.09)	45.5 (1.07)	44.0 (1.27)	43.1 (0.84)	40.5 (1.32)	43.4 (1.01)	44.4 (0.89)	39.3 (1.20)	40.7 (0.74)	30.2 (1.10)
Female	31.7 (1.19)	30.6 (1.49)	26.0 (1.26)	27.3 (1.70)	23.9 (0.95)	25.1 (0.85)	28.1 (0.94)	26.5 (0.99)	22.9 (0.74)	24.4 (0.92)	19.2 (0.72)
Race/ethnicity[2]											
White	40.3 (1.13)	36.0 (1.06)	33.7 (1.29)	33.1 (1.45)	32.2 (0.95)	30.5 (1.11)	33.1 (0.88)	31.7 (0.96)	27.8 (0.88)	29.4 (0.74)	20.9 (0.70)
Black	49.5 (1.82)	41.6 (1.99)	43.0 (1.92)	41.4 (3.12)	36.5 (1.60)	39.7 (1.23)	43.1 (1.74)	44.7 (1.33)	41.1 (1.71)	39.1 (1.52)	34.7 (1.67)
Hispanic	43.2 (1.58)	47.9 (2.69)	40.7 (1.68)	39.9 (1.65)	35.8 (0.91)	36.1 (0.98)	41.0 (1.64)	40.4 (1.25)	36.2 (0.95)	36.8 (1.44)	28.4 (1.15)
Asian[3]	— (†)	— (†)	— (†)	22.7 (2.71)	22.3 (2.73)	25.9 (2.99)	21.6 (2.43)	24.3 (3.50)	18.9 (1.72)	18.4 (1.87)	16.1 (1.87)
Pacific Islander[3]	— (†)	— (†)	— (†)	50.7 (3.42)	51.7 (6.25)	30.0 (5.21)	34.4 (5.58)	42.6 (7.74)	32.6 (3.50)	43.0 (5.14)	22.0 (4.95)
American Indian/Alaska Native	49.8 (4.79)	47.2 (6.44)	54.7 (5.75)	48.7 (6.78)	49.2 (6.58)	46.6 (6.53)	44.2 (3.40)	36.0 (1.49)	42.4 (5.23)	42.4 (2.12)	32.1 (7.39)
Two or more races[3]	— (†)	—	—	40.2 (2.76)	39.6 (2.85)	38.2 (3.64)	46.9 (4.16)	47.8 (3.30)	34.2 (3.51)	45.0 (2.60)	28.5 (2.31)
Grade											
9th	50.4 (1.54)	47.3 (2.22)	44.8 (1.98)	41.1 (1.96)	39.5 (1.27)	38.6 (1.38)	43.5 (1.15)	40.9 (1.16)	37.0 (1.21)	37.7 (1.11)	28.3 (1.17)
10th	42.2 (1.45)	40.4 (1.49)	40.2 (1.91)	37.7 (2.11)	34.7 (1.37)	33.5 (1.20)	36.6 (1.09)	36.2 (1.34)	33.5 (1.19)	35.3 (1.35)	26.4 (1.42)
11th	40.5 (1.52)	36.9 (1.48)	34.2 (1.72)	31.3 (1.55)	29.1 (1.10)	30.9 (1.38)	31.6 (1.44)	34.8 (1.36)	28.6 (0.93)	29.7 (1.14)	24.0 (1.04)
12th	34.8 (1.56)	31.0 (1.71)	28.8 (1.36)	30.4 (1.91)	26.5 (1.01)	26.5 (1.08)	29.1 (1.26)	28.0 (1.42)	24.9 (0.99)	26.9 (0.95)	18.8 (1.19)
Urbanicity[4]											
Urban	— (†)	— (†)	38.1 (2.00)	37.0 (2.66)	36.8 (1.53)	35.5 (2.17)	— (†)	— (†)	— (†)	— (†)	— (†)
Suburban	— (†)	— (†)	36.7 (1.59)	35.0 (1.56)	31.3 (0.80)	33.1 (1.23)	— (†)	— (†)	— (†)	— (†)	— (†)
Rural	— (†)	— (†)	32.9 (2.91)	36.6 (2.14)	33.8 (2.58)	29.7 (1.61)	— (†)	— (†)	— (†)	— (†)	— (†)
On school property[5]											
Total	16.2 (0.59)	15.5 (0.79)	14.8 (0.64)	14.2 (0.62)	12.5 (0.49)	12.8 (0.76)	13.6 (0.56)	12.4 (0.48)	11.1 (0.54)	12.0 (0.39)	8.1 (0.35)
Sex											
Male	23.5 (0.71)	21.0 (0.90)	20.0 (1.04)	18.5 (0.66)	18.0 (0.74)	17.1 (0.92)	18.2 (0.93)	16.3 (0.60)	15.1 (1.05)	16.0 (0.58)	10.7 (0.55)
Female	8.6 (0.73)	9.5 (1.03)	8.6 (0.78)	9.8 (0.95)	7.2 (0.47)	8.0 (0.70)	8.8 (0.52)	8.5 (0.62)	6.7 (0.42)	7.8 (0.43)	5.6 (0.38)
Race/ethnicity[2]											
White	15.0 (0.68)	12.9 (0.62)	13.3 (0.84)	12.3 (0.86)	11.2 (0.60)	10.0 (0.73)	11.6 (0.66)	10.2 (0.56)	8.6 (0.58)	9.9 (0.51)	6.4 (0.45)
Black	22.0 (1.39)	20.3 (1.25)	20.7 (1.20)	18.7 (1.51)	16.8 (1.26)	17.1 (1.30)	16.9 (1.39)	17.6 (1.10)	17.4 (0.99)	16.4 (0.89)	12.8 (0.84)
Hispanic	17.9 (1.75)	21.1 (1.68)	19.0 (1.50)	15.7 (0.91)	14.1 (0.89)	16.7 (1.14)	18.3 (1.62)	15.5 (0.81)	13.5 (0.82)	14.4 (0.79)	9.4 (0.44)
Asian[3]	— (†)	— (†)	— (†)	10.4 (0.95)	10.8 (1.92)	13.1 (2.26)	5.9 (1.53)	8.5 (1.99)	7.7 (1.09)	6.2 (1.06)	5.5 (1.39)
Pacific Islander[3]	— (†)	— (†)	— (†)	25.3 (4.60)	29.1 (7.63)	22.2 (4.82)	24.5 (5.60)	9.6 ! (3.47)	14.8 (2.37)	20.9 (4.41)	7.1 ! (2.58)
American Indian/Alaska Native	18.6 (2.74)	31.4 (5.58)	18.9 (5.55)	16.2 ! (5.23)	18.2 (4.41)	24.2 (5.03)	22.0 (3.16)	15.0 (1.12)	20.7 (3.73)	12.0 (1.77)	10.7 (3.13)
Two or more races[3]	— (†)	—	—	16.9 (2.40)	14.7 (1.97)	20.2 (3.83)	15.8 (2.61)	19.6 (2.39)	12.4 (2.19)	16.6 (1.41)	10.0 (1.04)
Grade											
9th	23.1 (1.55)	21.6 (1.79)	21.3 (1.29)	18.6 (1.02)	17.3 (0.77)	18.0 (1.24)	18.9 (0.93)	17.0 (0.67)	14.9 (0.98)	16.2 (0.77)	10.9 (0.78)
10th	17.2 (1.07)	16.5 (1.57)	17.0 (1.67)	17.2 (1.23)	13.5 (0.88)	12.8 (0.89)	14.4 (1.08)	11.7 (0.86)	12.1 (0.83)	12.8 (0.86)	8.3 (0.61)
11th	13.8 (1.27)	13.6 (1.00)	12.5 (0.87)	10.8 (1.01)	9.4 (0.71)	10.4 (0.89)	10.4 (0.75)	11.0 (0.73)	9.5 (0.63)	9.2 (0.55)	7.5 (0.53)
12th	11.4 (0.66)	10.6 (0.73)	9.5 (0.73)	8.1 (1.00)	7.5 (0.56)	7.3 (0.70)	8.5 (0.70)	8.6 (0.62)	6.6 (0.59)	8.8 (0.69)	4.9 (0.63)
Urbanicity[4]											
Urban	— (†)	— (†)	— (†)	— (†)	— (†)	— (†)	— (†)	— (†)	— (†)	— (†)	— (†)
Suburban	— (†)	— (†)	— (†)	— (†)	— (†)	— (†)	— (†)	— (†)	— (†)	— (†)	— (†)
Rural	— (†)	— (†)	— (†)	— (†)	— (†)	— (†)	— (†)	— (†)	— (†)	— (†)	— (†)

—Not available.
†Not applicable.
!Interpret data with caution. The coefficient of variation (CV) for this estimate is between 30 and 50 percent.
[1]The term "anywhere" is not used in the Youth Risk Behavior Survey (YRBS) questionnaire; students were simply asked how many times in the past 12 months they had been in a physical fight.
[2]Race categories exclude persons of Hispanic ethnicity.

[3]Before 1999, Asian students and Pacific Islander students were not categorized separately, and students could not be classified as Two or more races. Because the response categories changed in 1999, caution should be used in comparing data on race from 1993, 1995, and 1997 with data from later years.
[4]Refers to the Standard Metropolitan Statistical Area (MSA) status of the respondent's household as defined in 2000 by the U.S. Census Bureau. Categories include "central city of an MSA (Urban)," "in MSA but not in central city (Suburban)," and "not MSA (Rural)."
[5]In the question asking students about physical fights at school, "on school property" was not defined for survey respondents.
SOURCE: Centers for Disease Control and Prevention, Division of Adolescent and School Health, Youth Risk Behavior Surveillance System (YRBSS), 1993 through 2013. (This table was prepared June 2014.)

Table 231.20. Percentage distribution of students in grades 9–12, by number of times they reported having been in a physical fight anywhere or on school property during the previous 12 months and selected student characteristics: 2013

[Standard errors appear in parentheses]

Student characteristic	Anywhere (including on school property)[1]								On school property[2]							
	0 times		1 to 3 times		4 to 11 times		12 or more times		0 times		1 to 3 times		4 to 11 times		12 or more times	
1	2		3		4		5		6		7		8		9	
Total	75.3	(0.74)	18.8	(0.59)	4.0	(0.26)	1.9	(0.18)	91.9	(0.35)	7.1	(0.34)	0.6	(0.08)	0.5	(0.07)
Sex																
Male	69.8	(1.10)	22.1	(0.82)	5.4	(0.43)	2.7	(0.30)	89.3	(0.55)	9.1	(0.48)	0.8	(0.15)	0.7	(0.12)
Female	80.8	(0.72)	15.6	(0.64)	2.6	(0.21)	1.0	(0.17)	94.4	(0.38)	5.1	(0.38)	0.3 !	(0.09)	0.3	(0.07)
Race/ethnicity[3]																
White	79.1	(0.70)	16.5	(0.61)	3.2	(0.30)	1.2	(0.18)	93.6	(0.45)	5.7	(0.44)	0.4	(0.11)	0.3	(0.08)
Black	65.3	(1.67)	26.3	(1.49)	5.9	(0.66)	2.5	(0.31)	87.2	(0.84)	11.1	(0.90)	1.2	(0.30)	0.5	(0.13)
Hispanic	71.6	(1.15)	20.4	(1.30)	5.2	(0.55)	2.8	(0.44)	90.6	(0.44)	7.9	(0.41)	0.7	(0.17)	0.7	(0.14)
Asian	83.9	(1.87)	10.4	(1.55)	2.1 !	(0.80)	3.7 !	(1.28)	94.5	(1.39)	3.1 !	(0.94)	‡	(†)	‡	(†)
Pacific Islander	78.0	(4.95)	19.9	(3.98)	‡	(†)	‡	(†)	92.9	(2.58)	7.1 !	(2.58)	‡	(†)	‡	(†)
American Indian/Alaska Native	67.9	(7.39)	23.0	(5.74)	‡	(†)	‡	(†)	89.3	(3.13)	9.1 !	(3.14)	‡	(†)	‡	(†)
Two or more races	71.5	(2.31)	22.3	(2.03)	3.7	(0.83)	2.6 !	(0.81)	90.0	(1.04)	9.1	(1.03)	‡	(†)	‡	(†)
Grade																
9th	71.7	(1.17)	20.8	(1.02)	5.1	(0.38)	2.4	(0.35)	89.1	(0.78)	9.5	(0.77)	0.9	(0.24)	0.5	(0.12)
10th	73.6	(1.42)	20.8	(1.21)	3.8	(0.46)	1.8	(0.31)	91.7	(0.61)	7.4	(0.59)	0.4	(0.10)	0.5	(0.14)
11th	76.0	(1.04)	18.7	(0.82)	3.4	(0.46)	1.9	(0.31)	92.5	(0.53)	6.4	(0.52)	0.4 !	(0.15)	0.6	(0.17)
12th	81.2	(1.19)	14.5	(0.91)	3.1	(0.45)	1.1	(0.19)	95.1	(0.63)	4.1	(0.54)	0.5 !	(0.14)	0.4	(0.10)

†Not applicable.
!Interpret data with caution. The coefficient of variation (CV) for this estimate is between 30 and 50 percent.
‡Reporting standards not met. Either there are too few cases for a reliable estimate or the coefficient of variation (CV) is 50 percent or greater.
[1]The term "anywhere" is not used in the Youth Risk Behavior Survey (YRBS) questionnaire; students were simply asked how many times in the past 12 months they had been in a physical fight.

[2]In the question asking students about physical fights at school, "on school property" was not defined for respondents.
[3]Race categories exclude persons of Hispanic ethnicity.
NOTE: Detail may not sum to totals because of rounding.
SOURCE: Centers for Disease Control and Prevention, Division of Adolescent and School Health, Youth Risk Behavior Surveillance System (YRBSS), 2013. (This table was prepared June 2014.)

Table 231.30. Percentage of public school students in grades 9–12 who reported having been in a physical fight at least one time during the previous 12 months, by location and state: Selected years, 2003 through 2013

[Standard errors appear in parentheses]

State	Anywhere (including on school property)[1]						On school property[2]					
	2003	2005	2007	2009	2011	2013	2003	2005	2007	2009	2011	2013
1	2	3	4	5	6	7	8	9	10	11	12	13
United States[3]	33.0 (0.99)	35.9 (0.77)	35.5 (0.77)	31.5 (0.70)	32.8 (0.65)	24.7 (0.74)	12.8 (0.76)	13.6 (0.56)	12.4 (0.48)	11.1 (0.54)	12.0 (0.39)	8.1 (0.35)
Alabama	30.0 (1.78)	31.7 (1.84)	— (†)	31.7 (2.44)	28.4 (1.79)	29.2 (2.32)	12.9 (1.21)	14.6 (1.29)	— (†)	13.1 (1.41)	11.8 (1.30)	10.9 (0.93)
Alaska	27.1 (1.55)	— (†)	29.2 (1.77)	27.8 (1.52)	23.7 (1.17)	22.7 (1.64)	8.6 (0.92)	— (†)	10.4 (1.17)	9.8 (1.04)	7.7 (0.90)	— (†)
Arizona	32.4 (1.79)	32.4 (1.43)	31.3 (1.54)	35.9 (1.83)	27.7 (1.41)	23.9 (1.48)	11.4 (0.86)	11.7 (0.87)	11.3 (0.72)	12.0 (0.82)	10.8 (0.78)	8.8 (0.94)
Arkansas	— (†)	32.1 (1.67)	32.8 (1.79)	34.7 (2.08)	29.1 (1.76)	27.0 (1.30)	— (†)	13.9 (1.33)	13.0 (1.03)	14.8 (1.30)	11.0 (1.36)	11.4 (0.89)
California	— (†)	— (†)	— (†)	— (†)	— (†)	— (†)	— (†)	— (†)	— (†)	— (†)	— (†)	— (†)
Colorado	— (†)	32.2 (1.54)	— (†)	32.0 (1.51)	24.9 (1.69)	— (†)	— (†)	12.1 (0.89)	— (†)	10.7 (0.83)	— (†)	— (†)
Connecticut	— (†)	32.7 (1.45)	31.4 (1.39)	28.3 (1.26)	25.1 (1.53)	22.4 (1.23)	— (†)	10.5 (0.72)	10.5 (0.83)	9.6 (0.79)	8.7 (0.84)	— (†)
Delaware	34.9 (1.15)	30.3 (1.38)	33.0 (1.31)	30.4 (1.22)	28.0 (1.59)	25.1 (1.24)	11.4 (0.70)	9.8 (0.82)	10.5 (0.72)	8.6 (0.72)	8.8 (1.02)	9.3 (0.82)
District of Columbia	38.0 (1.61)	36.3 (1.26)	43.0 (1.45)	— (†)	37.9 (1.71)	— (†)	15.2 (1.07)	16.4 (0.88)	19.8 (1.21)	— (†)	15.8 (1.55)	— (†)
Florida	32.1 (0.74)	30.0 (0.94)	32.3 (1.24)	29.8 (0.83)	28.0 (0.72)	22.0 (0.77)	13.3 (0.65)	11.5 (0.77)	12.5 (0.84)	10.5 (0.47)	10.2 (0.44)	8.1 (0.52)
Georgia	31.4 (1.20)	33.8 (1.40)	34.0 (1.26)	32.3 (1.76)	33.1 (1.65)	21.4 (1.24)	11.1 (0.74)	12.1 (1.01)	13.1 (1.07)	11.7 (1.21)	11.9 (1.07)	10.3 (1.37)
Hawaii	— (†)	27.0 (1.37)	28.6 (2.20)	29.5 (1.92)	22.3 (1.11)	16.7 (0.87)	— (†)	10.0 (1.01)	7.0 (0.78)	10.2 (0.99)	8.2 (0.75)	— (†)
Idaho	28.3 (2.00)	32.3 (1.38)	30.0 (1.39)	29.0 (1.08)	26.4 (1.45)	21.6 (1.18)	11.7 (1.20)	12.1 (1.14)	12.3 (0.98)	10.2 (0.79)	9.4 (0.81)	7.3 (0.75)
Illinois	— (†)	— (†)	33.9 (1.91)	33.0 (1.38)	29.5 (1.41)	24.6 (1.67)	— (†)	— (†)	11.3 (1.11)	11.5 (0.82)	9.8 (0.69)	8.2 (0.66)
Indiana	30.6 (2.01)	29.3 (1.51)	29.5 (1.35)	29.1 (1.51)	29.0 (1.34)	— (†)	10.9 (1.14)	11.2 (0.98)	11.5 (0.92)	9.5 (1.18)	8.9 (0.80)	— (†)
Iowa	— (†)	28.3 (1.61)	24.0 (1.39)	— (†)	24.4 (1.87)	— (†)	— (†)	11.3 (1.12)	9.1 (0.96)	— (†)	9.6 (0.89)	— (†)
Kansas	— (†)	27.9 (1.51)	30.3 (1.62)	27.8 (1.37)	22.4 (1.40)	20.4 (1.21)	— (†)	10.1 (0.92)	10.6 (1.04)	9.0 (0.81)	7.8 (0.84)	7.2 (0.72)
Kentucky	26.4 (1.66)	29.6 (1.17)	27.0 (0.98)	28.7 (1.66)	28.7 (1.65)	21.2 (1.20)	10.1 (1.05)	12.7 (0.81)	10.6 (0.65)	9.5 (0.93)	11.4 (0.93)	6.0 (0.94)
Louisiana	— (†)	— (†)	— (†)	36.1 (1.60)	36.0 (2.72)	30.8 (2.59)	— (†)	— (†)	— (†)	13.7 (1.28)	15.8 (2.17)	12.0 (1.68)
Maine	26.5 (1.39)	28.2 (1.11)	26.5 (1.93)	22.8 (0.55)	19.5 (0.46)	17.0 (0.40)	9.1 (1.01)	10.0 (1.03)	10.1 (1.09)	9.1 (0.33)	7.9 (0.27)	5.7 (0.29)
Maryland	— (†)	36.6 (1.83)	35.7 (2.62)	32.5 (2.23)	29.1 (1.80)	— (†)	— (†)	14.9 (1.33)	12.4 (1.69)	11.2 (1.30)	11.1 (1.24)	14.3 (0.32)
Massachusetts	30.7 (1.05)	28.6 (1.33)	27.5 (1.34)	29.2 (1.24)	25.4 (0.92)	20.3 (0.91)	10.2 (0.67)	10.2 (0.67)	9.1 (0.81)	8.7 (0.68)	7.1 (0.65)	4.6 (0.49)
Michigan	30.8 (1.51)	30.1 (2.02)	30.7 (1.89)	31.6 (1.72)	27.4 (1.22)	21.6 (0.88)	12.2 (1.02)	11.4 (1.11)	11.4 (0.89)	11.3 (1.02)	9.1 (0.68)	6.9 (0.55)
Minnesota	— (†)	— (†)	— (†)	— (†)	— (†)	— (†)	— (†)	— (†)	— (†)	— (†)	— (†)	— (†)
Mississippi	30.6 (1.66)	— (†)	30.6 (1.43)	34.1 (1.73)	29.3 (1.72)	31.0 (1.84)	10.2 (1.26)	— (†)	11.9 (0.96)	12.6 (1.02)	12.3 (1.06)	13.6 (1.40)
Missouri	28.2 (2.07)	29.8 (2.12)	30.9 (2.18)	28.7 (1.34)	— (†)	— (†)	9.8 (0.95)	10.2 (1.31)	10.7 (1.21)	9.0 (0.97)	— (†)	— (†)
Montana	28.6 (1.16)	30.5 (1.19)	32.8 (1.08)	31.7 (2.25)	25.4 (0.73)	22.8 (0.90)	10.3 (0.68)	10.9 (0.67)	12.0 (0.75)	10.8 (1.33)	9.1 (0.51)	7.3 (0.37)
Nebraska	29.6 (1.14)	28.5 (1.02)	— (†)	— (†)	26.7 (1.09)	20.1 (1.22)	10.6 (0.81)	9.3 (0.60)	— (†)	— (†)	7.4 (0.68)	5.7 (0.70)
Nevada	35.0 (1.56)	34.5 (1.78)	31.6 (1.53)	35.0 (1.45)	— (†)	23.6 (1.93)	12.6 (1.01)	14.2 (1.32)	11.3 (1.10)	10.0 (0.82)	— (†)	6.8 (1.12)
New Hampshire	30.5 (1.84)	26.4 (1.84)	27.0 (1.40)	25.9 (1.59)	23.8 (1.27)	— (†)	11.6 (1.20)	10.7 (1.06)	11.3 (0.70)	9.1 (0.87)	9.9 (0.89)	6.9 (0.81)
New Jersey	— (†)	30.7 (2.18)	— (†)	27.5 (1.46)	23.9 (1.56)	21.8 (1.34)	— (†)	10.1 (1.31)	— (†)	— (†)	— (†)	— (†)
New Mexico	— (†)	36.7 (1.47)	37.1 (1.06)	37.3 (1.07)	31.5 (1.02)	27.2 (1.27)	— (†)	15.6 (1.19)	16.9 (0.70)	15.0 (0.85)	11.3 (0.78)	9.7 (0.61)
New York	32.1 (0.82)	32.1 (1.07)	31.7 (1.08)	29.6 (1.23)	27.0 (1.25)	22.8 (1.10)	14.6 (0.73)	12.5 (0.74)	12.2 (0.91)	11.4 (0.91)	— (†)	— (†)
North Carolina	30.9 (1.41)	29.9 (1.41)	30.1 (1.54)	28.6 (0.96)	27.6 (1.37)	24.1 (1.49)	10.7 (1.00)	11.6 (0.85)	10.4 (0.84)	9.4 (0.43)	10.6 (1.01)	7.6 (0.94)
North Dakota	27.2 (1.60)	— (†)	— (†)	— (†)	— (†)	— (†)	8.6 (0.96)	10.7 (1.13)	9.6 (0.79)	7.4 (0.78)	8.2 (0.73)	8.8 (0.75)
Ohio[4]	31.5 (2.83)	30.2 (1.95)	30.4 (1.57)	— (†)	31.2 (1.58)	19.8 (1.49)	11.3 (1.67)	10.2 (1.17)	9.4 (0.82)	— (†)	8.8 (0.68)	6.2 (0.88)
Oklahoma	28.4 (2.61)	31.1 (1.63)	29.2 (1.37)	30.8 (2.10)	28.5 (1.96)	25.1 (1.79)	11.4 (1.15)	12.1 (1.13)	10.6 (0.81)	12.8 (1.43)	9.4 (1.25)	7.2 (1.05)
Oregon	— (†)	— (†)	— (†)	— (†)	— (†)	— (†)	— (†)	— (†)	— (†)	— (†)	— (†)	— (†)
Pennsylvania	— (†)	— (†)	— (†)	29.6 (1.76)	— (†)	— (†)	— (†)	— (†)	— (†)	9.9 (1.01)	— (†)	— (†)
Rhode Island	27.6 (1.59)	28.4 (1.34)	26.3 (1.61)	25.1 (0.83)	23.5 (0.81)	18.8 (1.12)	11.4 (1.18)	11.2 (0.80)	9.6 (0.93)	9.1 (0.73)	7.8 (0.52)	6.4 (0.52)
South Carolina	— (†)	31.3 (1.68)	29.1 (1.37)	36.4 (2.06)	32.6 (2.04)	26.7 (1.42)	— (†)	12.7 (1.18)	10.8 (0.86)	12.1 (1.43)	12.2 (1.48)	9.6 (1.17)
South Dakota[4]	27.0 (2.72)	26.5 (2.86)	29.8 (2.00)	27.1 (1.36)	24.5 (2.22)	24.2 (0.52)	9.0 (1.12)	8.4 (1.56)	9.3 (1.32)	8.3 (0.52)	8.2 (0.92)	6.6 (0.52)
Tennessee	28.3 (1.94)	30.9 (1.66)	31.8 (1.55)	32.3 (1.31)	30.8 (1.24)	25.7 (1.69)	12.2 (1.33)	10.9 (1.00)	12.4 (1.13)	11.3 (0.96)	10.5 (0.83)	10.4 (1.02)
Texas	— (†)	34.2 (1.57)	34.9 (1.17)	33.3 (1.05)	34.1 (0.92)	25.4 (1.33)	— (†)	14.5 (0.94)	13.9 (0.90)	13.2 (0.67)	12.5 (0.65)	9.1 (0.79)
Utah	28.7 (2.74)	25.9 (1.84)	30.1 (2.01)	28.2 (1.61)	23.9 (1.88)	21.3 (1.16)	11.9 (1.80)	10.4 (1.57)	11.6 (1.36)	10.6 (0.84)	8.1 (1.18)	6.9 (0.65)
Vermont	26.9 (0.92)	24.3 (1.36)	26.0 (1.44)	25.6 (0.71)	23.1 (1.42)	— (†)	12.2 (0.71)	12.2 (0.98)	11.5 (0.88)	11.0 (0.36)	8.8 (0.72)	9.4 (0.50)
Virginia	— (†)	— (†)	— (†)	— (†)	24.9 (1.71)	23.5 (0.90)	— (†)	— (†)	— (†)	— (†)	7.9 (0.93)	— (†)
Washington	— (†)	— (†)	— (†)	— (†)	— (†)	— (†)	— (†)	— (†)	— (†)	— (†)	— (†)	— (†)
West Virginia	26.5 (1.62)	29.1 (1.88)	29.9 (2.39)	31.7 (1.96)	25.7 (1.66)	25.2 (1.84)	10.3 (1.39)	12.1 (1.41)	12.9 (1.70)	11.3 (1.07)	10.3 (1.02)	9.1 (1.08)
Wisconsin	31.4 (1.68)	32.6 (1.51)	31.2 (1.46)	25.8 (1.52)	25.3 (1.72)	22.4 (1.46)	11.6 (0.92)	12.2 (1.03)	11.4 (0.97)	9.6 (0.87)	9.1 (0.95)	6.8 (0.69)
Wyoming	31.2 (1.23)	30.4 (1.08)	27.9 (1.12)	30.9 (1.17)	26.5 (1.08)	24.3 (1.11)	12.7 (0.93)	12.2 (0.72)	11.6 (0.83)	12.6 (0.73)	11.3 (0.65)	8.9 (0.60)

—Not available.
†Not applicable.
[1]The term "anywhere" is not used in the Youth Risk Behavior Survey (YRBS) questionnaire; students were simply asked how many times in the past 12 months they had been in a physical fight.
[2]In the question asking students about physical fights at school, "on school property" was not defined for survey respondents.
[3]Data for the U.S. total include both public and private schools and were collected through a national survey representing the entire country.
[4]Data include both public and private schools.

NOTE: State-level data include public schools only, with the exception of data for Ohio and South Dakota. Data for the U.S. total, Ohio, and South Dakota include both public and private schools. For specific states, a given year's data may be unavailable (1) because the state did not participate in the survey that year; (2) because the state omitted this particular survey item from the state-level questionnaire; or (3) because the state had an overall response rate of less than 60 percent (the overall response rate is the school response rate multiplied by the student response rate).
SOURCE: Centers for Disease Control and Prevention, Division of Adolescent and School Health, Youth Risk Behavior Surveillance System (YRBSS), 2003 through 2013. (This table was prepared June 2014.)

Table 231.40. Percentage of students in grades 9–12 who reported carrying a weapon at least 1 day during the previous 30 days, by location and selected student characteristics: Selected years, 1993 through 2013

[Standard errors appear in parentheses]

Location and student characteristic	1993		1995		1997		1999		2001		2003		2005		2007		2009		2011		2013	
1	2		3		4		5		6		7		8		9		10		11		12	
Anywhere (including on school property)[1]																						
Total	22.1	(1.18)	20.0	(0.66)	18.3	(0.91)	17.3	(0.97)	17.4	(0.99)	17.1	(0.90)	18.5	(0.80)	18.0	(0.87)	17.5	(0.73)	16.6	(0.65)	17.9	(0.73)
Sex																						
Male	34.3	(1.68)	31.1	(1.03)	27.7	(1.57)	28.6	(1.71)	29.3	(1.67)	26.9	(1.31)	29.8	(1.35)	28.5	(1.41)	27.1	(1.45)	25.9	(1.07)	28.1	(1.31)
Female	9.2	(0.85)	8.3	(0.72)	7.0	(0.54)	6.0	(0.56)	6.2	(0.41)	6.7	(0.60)	7.1	(0.43)	7.5	(0.66)	7.1	(0.38)	6.8	(0.41)	7.9	(0.56)
Race/ethnicity[2]																						
White	20.6	(1.43)	18.9	(0.93)	17.0	(1.29)	16.4	(1.36)	17.9	(1.30)	16.7	(0.95)	18.7	(1.13)	18.2	(1.28)	18.6	(1.16)	17.0	(1.05)	20.8	(0.90)
Black	28.5	(1.24)	21.8	(2.03)	21.7	(1.99)	17.2	(2.68)	15.2	(1.23)	17.3	(1.77)	16.4	(0.81)	17.2	(1.05)	14.4	(1.33)	14.2	(0.85)	12.5	(0.96)
Hispanic	24.4	(1.35)	24.7	(1.87)	23.3	(1.44)	18.7	(1.35)	16.5	(0.78)	16.5	(1.31)	19.0	(1.10)	18.5	(1.21)	17.2	(0.94)	16.2	(0.82)	15.5	(0.95)
Asian[3]	—		—		—	(†)	13.0	(2.01)	10.6	(2.10)	11.6	(2.67)	7.0	(1.70)	7.8	(1.41)	8.4	(1.28)	9.1	(1.57)	8.7	(1.79)
Pacific Islander[3]	—		—	(†)	—	(†)	25.3	(5.02)	17.4	(4.35)	16.3 !	(6.37)	20.0 !	(6.52)	25.5	(4.35)	20.3	(3.40)	20.7	(5.00)	12.6 !	(3.98)
American Indian/Alaska Native[3]	34.2	(8.06)	32.0	(5.69)	26.2	(3.65)	21.8	(5.68)	31.2	(5.52)	29.3	(4.58)	25.6	(3.79)	20.6	(3.02)	20.7	(3.40)	27.6	(2.41)	17.8	(4.01)
Two or more races[3]	—		—		—		22.2	(3.34)	25.2	(3.41)	29.8	(5.03)	26.7	(3.11)	19.0	(2.46)	17.9	(1.61)	23.7	(2.58)	18.8	(2.09)
Grade																						
9th	25.5	(1.42)	22.6	(1.24)	22.6	(1.34)	17.6	(1.58)	19.8	(1.44)	18.0	(1.81)	19.9	(1.21)	20.1	(1.41)	18.0	(0.87)	17.3	(1.07)	17.5	(0.99)
10th	21.4	(1.11)	21.1	(0.94)	17.4	(1.33)	18.7	(1.31)	16.7	(1.11)	15.9	(1.14)	19.4	(1.19)	18.8	(1.21)	18.4	(1.51)	16.6	(0.89)	17.8	(1.09)
11th	21.5	(1.66)	20.3	(1.40)	18.2	(1.69)	16.1	(1.31)	16.8	(1.26)	18.2	(1.21)	17.1	(1.13)	16.7	(1.08)	16.2	(0.93)	16.2	(0.84)	17.9	(1.43)
12th	19.9	(1.46)	16.1	(0.93)	15.4	(1.65)	15.9	(1.44)	15.1	(1.28)	15.5	(1.06)	16.9	(0.95)	15.5	(1.28)	16.6	(0.85)	15.8	(0.90)	18.3	(1.17)
Urbanicity[4]																						
Urban	—		—		18.7	(1.34)	15.8	(0.85)	15.3	(0.99)	17.0	(1.32)	—	(†)	—	(†)	—	(†)	—	(†)	—	(†)
Suburban	—		—		16.8	(1.02)	17.0	(1.34)	17.4	(1.39)	16.5	(1.36)	—	(†)	—	(†)	—	(†)	—	(†)	—	(†)
Rural	—		—		22.3	(2.12)	22.3	(2.19)	23.0	(1.86)	18.9	(1.91)	—	(†)	—	(†)	—	(†)	—	(†)	—	(†)
On school property[5]																						
Total	11.8	(0.73)	9.8	(0.45)	8.5	(0.79)	6.9	(0.60)	6.4	(0.52)	6.1	(0.57)	6.5	(0.46)	5.9	(0.37)	5.6	(0.32)	5.4	(0.35)	5.2	(0.44)
Sex																						
Male	17.9	(0.96)	14.3	(0.76)	12.5	(1.50)	11.0	(1.07)	10.2	(0.88)	8.9	(0.74)	10.2	(0.83)	9.0	(0.65)	8.0	(0.52)	8.2	(0.59)	7.6	(0.70)
Female	5.1	(0.65)	4.9	(0.53)	3.7	(0.37)	2.8	(0.38)	2.9	(0.27)	3.1	(0.50)	2.6	(0.30)	2.7	(0.33)	2.9	(0.24)	2.3	(0.19)	3.0	(0.40)
Race/ethnicity[2]																						
White	10.9	(0.86)	9.0	(0.65)	7.8	(1.16)	6.4	(0.87)	6.1	(0.62)	5.5	(0.57)	6.1	(0.66)	5.3	(0.55)	5.6	(0.44)	5.1	(0.40)	5.7	(0.65)
Black	15.0	(0.85)	10.3	(1.13)	9.2	(0.98)	5.0	(0.50)	6.3	(0.92)	6.9	(0.96)	5.1	(0.66)	6.0	(0.46)	5.3	(0.74)	4.6	(0.67)	3.9	(0.42)
Hispanic	13.3	(1.09)	14.1	(1.63)	10.4	(0.99)	7.9	(0.73)	6.4	(0.53)	6.0	(0.56)	8.2	(0.91)	7.3	(0.82)	5.8	(0.58)	5.8	(0.70)	4.7	(0.61)
Asian[3]	—		—		—	(†)	6.5	(1.44)	7.2	(2.05)	6.6 !	(2.44)	2.8 !	(1.24)	4.1	(1.01)	3.6	(0.84)	4.3 !	(1.66)	3.8	(1.13)
Pacific Islander[3]	—		—	(†)	—	(†)	9.3	(2.66)	10.0 !	(3.05)	4.9 !	(2.05)	15.4 !	(6.10)	9.5 !	(3.40)	9.8	(2.33)	10.9 !	(3.73)	4.0 !	(1.95)
American Indian/Alaska Native[3]	17.6 !	(5.70)	13.0 !	(4.35)	15.9	(3.68)	11.6 !	(5.13)	16.4	(4.02)	12.9	(3.40)	7.2	(1.60)	7.7	(2.08)	4.2 !	(1.50)	7.5	(1.62)	7.0 !	(3.22)
Two or more races[3]	—		—		—		11.4	(2.76)	13.2	(3.61)	13.3 !	(4.10)	11.9	(2.99)	5.0	(1.11)	5.8	(1.35)	7.5	(1.87)	6.3	(1.58)
Grade																						
9th	12.6	(0.73)	10.7	(0.76)	10.2	(0.90)	7.2	(1.07)	6.7	(0.66)	5.3	(1.13)	6.4	(0.75)	6.0	(0.59)	4.9	(0.46)	4.8	(0.50)	4.8	(0.69)
10th	11.5	(0.97)	10.4	(0.78)	7.7	(0.99)	6.6	(0.83)	6.7	(0.60)	6.0	(0.53)	6.9	(0.70)	5.8	(0.61)	6.1	(0.57)	6.1	(0.72)	4.8	(0.58)
11th	11.9	(1.41)	10.2	(0.94)	9.4	(1.33)	7.0	(0.60)	6.1	(0.74)	6.6	(0.80)	5.9	(0.71)	5.5	(0.68)	5.2	(0.44)	4.7	(0.44)	5.9	(1.19)
12th	10.8	(0.83)	7.6	(0.68)	7.0	(0.91)	6.2	(0.78)	6.1	(0.71)	6.4	(0.64)	6.7	(0.64)	6.0	(0.58)	6.0	(0.57)	5.6	(0.51)	5.3	(0.88)
Urbanicity[4]																						
Urban	—		—		7.0	(0.67)	7.2	(1.09)	6.0	(0.67)	5.6	(0.81)	—	(†)	—	(†)	—	(†)	—	(†)	—	(†)
Suburban	—		—		8.7	(0.68)	6.2	(0.74)	6.3	(0.68)	6.4	(1.01)	—	(†)	—	(†)	—	(†)	—	(†)	—	(†)
Rural	—		—		11.2	(2.19)	9.6	(1.61)	8.3	(1.48)	6.3	(0.67)	—	(†)	—	(†)	—	(†)	—	(†)	—	(†)

—Not available.
†Not applicable.
! Interpret data with caution. The coefficient of variation (CV) for this estimate is between 30 and 50 percent.
[1] The term "anywhere" is not used in the Youth Risk Behavior Survey (YRBS) questionnaire; students were simply asked how many days they carried a weapon during the past 30 days.
[2] Race categories exclude persons of Hispanic ethnicity.
[3] Before 1999, Asian students and Pacific Islander students were not categorized separately, and students could not be classified as Two or more races. Because the response categories changed in 1999, caution should be used in comparing data on race from 1993, 1995, and 1997 with data from later years.

[4] Refers to the Standard Metropolitan Statistical Area (MSA) status of the respondent's household as defined in 2000 by the U.S. Census Bureau. Categories include "central city of an MSA (Urban)," "in MSA but not in central city (Suburban)," and "not MSA (Rural)."
[5] In the question asking students about carrying a weapon at school, "on school property" was not defined for survey respondents.
NOTE: Respondents were asked about carrying "a weapon such as a gun, knife, or club."
SOURCE: Centers for Disease Control and Prevention, Division of Adolescent and School Health, Youth Risk Behavior Surveillance System (YRBSS), 1993 through 2013. (This table was prepared June 2014.)

Table 231.50. Percentage distribution of students in grades 9–12, by number of days they reported carrying a weapon anywhere or on school property during the previous 30 days and selected student characteristics: 2013

[Standard errors appear in parentheses]

Student characteristic	Anywhere (including on school property)[1]								On school property[2]							
	0 days		1 day		2 to 5 days		6 or more days		0 days		1 day		2 to 5 days		6 or more days	
1	2		3		4		5		6		7		8		9	
Total..................................	82.1	(0.73)	3.4	(0.19)	5.5	(0.22)	9.0	(0.67)	94.8	(0.44)	1.4	(0.14)	1.2	(0.13)	2.6	(0.42)
Sex																
Male...........................	71.9	(1.31)	5.0	(0.31)	8.9	(0.45)	14.2	(1.23)	92.4	(0.70)	2.0	(0.23)	1.9	(0.23)	3.7	(0.64)
Female.......................	92.1	(0.56)	1.8	(0.20)	2.2	(0.19)	3.8	(0.39)	97.0	(0.40)	0.8	(0.15)	0.5	(0.14)	1.6	(0.33)
Race/ethnicity[3]																
White.........................	79.2	(0.90)	3.4	(0.31)	6.1	(0.30)	11.3	(0.97)	94.3	(0.65)	1.3	(0.19)	1.1	(0.15)	3.3	(0.67)
Black.........................	87.5	(0.96)	2.8	(0.42)	4.2	(0.63)	5.5	(0.57)	96.1	(0.42)	1.6	(0.29)	1.4	(0.31)	0.9	(0.18)
Hispanic....................	84.5	(0.95)	4.0	(0.37)	5.1	(0.46)	6.4	(0.59)	95.3	(0.61)	1.5	(0.33)	1.3	(0.28)	1.9	(0.29)
Asian.........................	91.3	(1.79)	1.5 !	(0.55)	2.5 !	(0.76)	4.7 !	(1.49)	96.2	(1.13)	0.8 !	(0.41)	‡	(†)	2.4 !	(1.01)
Pacific Islander.........	87.4	(3.98)	‡	(†)	6.8	(1.95)	4.5 !	(1.99)	96.0	(1.95)	‡	(†)	‡	(†)	‡	(†)
American Indian/Alaska Native.................	82.2	(4.01)	‡	(†)	‡	(†)	9.9	(2.12)	93.0	(3.22)	‡	(†)	‡	(†)	2.7 !	(1.31)
Two or more races.....	81.2	(2.09)	5.3	(1.26)	6.8	(1.14)	6.6	(1.08)	93.7	(1.58)	2.4 !	(0.93)	‡	(†)	2.6	(0.69)
Grade																
9th.............................	82.5	(0.99)	4.0	(0.37)	5.7	(0.69)	7.8	(0.69)	95.2	(0.69)	1.6	(0.28)	1.1	(0.28)	2.1	(0.38)
10th...........................	82.2	(1.09)	3.8	(0.42)	5.9	(0.72)	8.0	(0.64)	95.2	(0.58)	1.7	(0.26)	1.0	(0.21)	2.1	(0.44)
11th...........................	82.1	(1.43)	2.8	(0.34)	5.5	(0.49)	9.6	(1.29)	94.1	(1.19)	1.3	(0.34)	1.4	(0.25)	3.3 !	(1.10)
12th...........................	81.7	(1.17)	2.9	(0.37)	4.9	(0.60)	10.5	(0.86)	94.7	(0.88)	0.9	(0.18)	1.4	(0.37)	3.1	(0.60)

†Not applicable.
!Interpret data with caution. The coefficient of variation (CV) for this estimate is between 30 and 50 percent.
‡Reporting standards not met. Either there are too few cases for a reliable estimate or the coefficient of variation (CV) is 50 percent or greater.
[1]The term "anywhere" is not used in the Youth Risk Behavior Survey (YRBS) questionnaire; students were simply asked how many days they carried a weapon during the past 30 days.

[2]In the question asking students about carrying a weapon at school, "on school property" was not defined for survey respondents.
[3]Race categories exclude persons of Hispanic ethnicity.
NOTE: Respondents were asked about carrying "a weapon such as a gun, knife, or club." Detail may not sum to totals because of rounding.
SOURCE: Centers for Disease Control and Prevention, Division of Adolescent and School Health, Youth Risk Behavior Surveillance System (YRBSS), 2013. (This table was prepared June 2014.)

Table 231.60. Percentage of public school students in grades 9–12 who reported carrying a weapon at least 1 day during the previous 30 days, by location and state: Selected years, 2003 through 2013

[Standard errors appear in parentheses]

State	Anywhere (including on school property)[1]						On school property[2]					
	2003	2005	2007	2009	2011	2013	2003	2005	2007	2009	2011	2013
1	2	3	4	5	6	7	8	9	10	11	12	13
United States[3]	17.1 (0.90)	18.5 (0.80)	18.0 (0.87)	17.5 (0.73)	16.6 (0.65)	17.9 (0.73)	6.1 (0.57)	6.5 (0.46)	5.9 (0.37)	5.6 (0.32)	5.4 (0.35)	5.2 (0.44)
Alabama	19.9 (1.44)	21.0 (1.72)	— (†)	22.9 (2.27)	21.5 (1.54)	23.1 (1.55)	7.3 (1.35)	8.4 (1.44)	— (†)	8.7 (1.42)	8.2 (1.02)	5.5 (0.56)
Alaska	18.4 (1.14)	— (†)	24.4 (1.61)	20.0 (1.30)	19.0 (1.19)	19.2 (1.31)	7.1 (0.81)	— (†)	8.4 (1.07)	7.8 (0.83)	5.7 (0.72)	6.1 (0.80)
Arizona	18.4 (0.82)	20.6 (0.84)	20.5 (0.91)	19.9 (1.25)	17.5 (1.17)	17.5 (1.17)	5.8 (0.68)	7.4 (0.53)	7.0 (0.75)	6.5 (0.64)	5.7 (0.59)	4.8 (0.86)
Arkansas	— (†)	25.9 (1.15)	20.7 (1.36)	22.9 (1.82)	21.1 (1.76)	27.1 (1.76)	— (†)	10.5 (1.10)	6.8 (0.85)	8.4 (1.02)	6.5 (0.95)	9.1 (1.10)
California	— (†)	— (†)	— (†)	— (†)	— (†)	— (†)	— (†)	— (†)	— (†)	— (†)	— (†)	— (†)
Colorado	— (†)	17.0 (1.57)	— (†)	16.7 (1.27)	15.5 (1.31)	— (†)	— (†)	5.4 (0.81)	— (†)	5.5 (0.90)	5.5 (0.69)	— (†)
Connecticut	— (†)	16.3 (1.30)	17.2 (1.72)	12.4 (0.89)	— (†)	— (†)	— (†)	6.4 (0.83)	5.5 (1.03)	3.9 (0.45)	6.6 (0.67)	6.6 (0.82)
Delaware	16.0 (0.88)	16.6 (1.04)	17.1 (1.00)	18.5 (0.92)	13.5 (0.88)	14.4 (0.80)	5.0 (0.47)	5.7 (0.54)	5.4 (0.55)	5.1 (0.59)	5.2 (0.57)	3.1 (0.34)
District of Columbia	25.0 (1.40)	17.2 (1.11)	21.3 (1.45)	— (†)	18.9 (1.34)	— (†)	10.6 (0.96)	6.7 (0.60)	7.4 (0.76)	— (†)	5.5 (0.88)	— (†)
Florida	17.2 (0.76)	15.2 (0.68)	18.0 (0.93)	17.3 (0.60)	15.6 (0.65)	15.7 (0.67)	5.3 (0.38)	4.7 (0.41)	5.6 (0.41)	4.7 (0.35)	— (†)	— (†)
Georgia	18.7 (1.17)	22.1 (1.99)	19.5 (0.96)	18.8 (1.11)	22.8 (2.25)	18.5 (1.51)	5.0 (0.52)	7.5 (1.50)	5.3 (0.48)	6.0 (0.90)	8.6 (1.80)	4.2 (0.66)
Hawaii	— (†)	13.3 (1.03)	14.8 (1.56)	15.9 (2.06)	13.9 (0.81)	10.5 (0.87)	— (†)	4.9 (0.72)	3.7 (0.92)	4.7 (0.63)	4.2 (0.45)	— (†)
Idaho	— (†)	23.9 (1.45)	23.6 (1.35)	21.8 (1.15)	22.8 (1.30)	27.1 (1.31)	7.7 (0.90)	— (†)	8.9 (0.96)	6.7 (0.59)	6.3 (0.78)	6.5 (0.92)
Illinois	— (†)	— (†)	14.3 (1.01)	16.0 (1.04)	12.6 (0.91)	15.8 (1.22)	— (†)	— (†)	3.7 (0.67)	4.8 (0.59)	3.9 (0.53)	4.7 (0.57)
Indiana	17.8 (1.93)	19.2 (1.25)	20.9 (0.80)	18.1 (1.58)	17.0 (1.46)	— (†)	6.2 (0.91)	5.8 (0.71)	6.9 (0.64)	5.7 (0.80)	3.7 (0.46)	— (†)
Iowa	— (†)	15.7 (1.49)	12.8 (1.13)	— (†)	15.8 (1.26)	— (†)	— (†)	4.3 (0.70)	4.4 (0.61)	— (†)	4.5 (0.76)	— (†)
Kansas	— (†)	16.2 (1.37)	18.4 (1.19)	16.0 (1.26)	— (†)	16.1 (0.87)	— (†)	4.9 (0.85)	5.7 (0.75)	5.1 (0.65)	5.2 (0.72)	— (†)
Kentucky	18.5 (1.20)	23.1 (1.49)	24.4 (1.08)	21.7 (1.72)	22.8 (1.72)	20.7 (1.35)	7.4 (0.86)	6.8 (0.72)	8.0 (0.59)	6.5 (0.77)	7.4 (1.25)	6.4 (0.73)
Louisiana	— (†)	— (†)	— (†)	19.6 (1.73)	22.2 (0.98)	22.8 (2.78)	— (†)	— (†)	— (†)	5.8 (1.12)	4.2 (1.01)	7.0 (1.37)
Maine	16.5 (1.20)	18.3 (2.00)	15.0 (1.47)	— (†)	— (†)	— (†)	6.6 (0.91)	5.9 (1.03)	4.9 (0.70)	— (†)	8.0 (0.45)	7.1 (0.46)
Maryland	— (†)	19.1 (1.59)	19.3 (1.51)	16.6 (1.19)	15.9 (1.10)	15.8 (0.27)	— (†)	6.9 (0.88)	5.9 (0.81)	4.6 (0.58)	5.3 (0.55)	4.8 (0.13)
Massachusetts	13.5 (0.89)	15.2 (0.88)	14.9 (0.88)	12.8 (1.00)	12.3 (0.95)	11.6 (0.83)	5.0 (0.50)	5.8 (0.59)	5.0 (0.48)	4.4 (0.58)	3.7 (0.46)	3.1 (0.50)
Michigan	15.2 (0.89)	15.8 (1.49)	17.9 (1.30)	16.6 (0.69)	15.7 (0.94)	15.5 (1.06)	5.1 (0.66)	4.7 (0.54)	5.0 (0.66)	5.4 (0.33)	3.5 (0.37)	3.8 (0.35)
Minnesota	— (†)	— (†)	— (†)	— (†)	— (†)	— (†)	— (†)	— (†)	— (†)	— (†)	— (†)	— (†)
Mississippi	20.0 (1.78)	— (†)	17.3 (1.33)	17.2 (1.02)	18.0 (1.39)	19.1 (1.56)	5.2 (0.78)	— (†)	4.8 (0.60)	4.5 (0.48)	4.2 (0.76)	4.1 (0.66)
Missouri	16.8 (1.87)	19.4 (1.79)	18.6 (1.48)	16.0 (1.44)	— (†)	22.2 (1.93)	5.5 (1.04)	7.3 (0.99)	4.6 (0.83)	5.3 (1.02)	— (†)	— (†)
Montana	19.4 (0.88)	21.4 (1.20)	22.1 (0.76)	23.0 (1.07)	23.5 (0.96)	25.7 (0.84)	7.2 (0.56)	10.2 (0.89)	9.7 (0.57)	7.9 (0.67)	9.3 (0.69)	9.9 (0.58)
Nebraska	16.0 (1.06)	17.9 (0.89)	— (†)	— (†)	18.6 (0.90)	— (†)	5.0 (0.53)	4.8 (0.48)	— (†)	— (†)	3.8 (0.45)	— (†)
Nevada	14.9 (1.09)	18.4 (1.32)	14.5 (1.08)	19.1 (1.08)	— (†)	16.0 (1.50)	6.3 (0.67)	6.8 (0.91)	4.7 (0.61)	6.2 (0.62)	— (†)	3.3 (0.64)
New Hampshire	15.1 (1.59)	16.2 (1.26)	18.1 (1.46)	— (†)	14.5 (1.04)	— (†)	5.8 (1.00)	6.5 (0.93)	5.8 (0.61)	8.8 (1.00)	— (†)	— (†)
New Jersey	— (†)	10.5 (0.95)	— (†)	9.6 (0.81)	9.6 (1.17)	10.2 (1.08)	— (†)	3.1 (0.53)	— (†)	3.1 (0.45)	— (†)	2.7 (0.34)
New Mexico	— (†)	24.5 (1.44)	27.5 (1.20)	27.4 (0.90)	22.8 (0.93)	22.2 (0.88)	— (†)	8.0 (0.29)	9.3 (0.66)	8.1 (0.59)	6.5 (0.51)	5.4 (0.42)
New York	13.5 (1.01)	14.3 (0.74)	14.2 (0.76)	13.9 (0.98)	12.6 (0.76)	12.8 (0.82)	5.2 (0.51)	5.2 (0.42)	4.7 (0.41)	4.8 (0.64)	4.2 (0.32)	4.0 (0.38)
North Carolina	19.2 (1.49)	21.5 (1.35)	21.2 (1.19)	19.6 (0.95)	20.8 (1.24)	20.6 (1.34)	6.3 (0.79)	6.4 (0.94)	6.8 (0.94)	4.7 (0.57)	6.1 (0.64)	4.5 (0.67)
North Dakota	— (†)	— (†)	— (†)	— (†)	— (†)	— (†)	5.7 (0.98)	6.0 (0.74)	5.0 (0.57)	5.4 (0.64)	5.7 (0.73)	6.4 (0.75)
Ohio[4]	12.5 (1.40)	15.2 (1.27)	16.6 (1.42)	— (†)	16.4 (1.37)	14.2 (1.61)	3.6 (0.75)	4.4 (0.63)	4.1 (0.51)	— (†)	— (†)	— (†)
Oklahoma	21.8 (1.72)	18.9 (1.38)	22.3 (1.65)	19.0 (1.44)	19.4 (1.86)	19.9 (1.41)	8.0 (1.01)	7.0 (0.77)	9.0 (1.43)	5.6 (0.79)	6.1 (1.14)	6.0 (0.77)
Oregon	— (†)	— (†)	— (†)	— (†)	— (†)	— (†)	— (†)	— (†)	— (†)	— (†)	— (†)	— (†)
Pennsylvania	— (†)	— (†)	— (†)	14.8 (1.28)	— (†)	— (†)	— (†)	— (†)	— (†)	3.3 (0.47)	— (†)	— (†)
Rhode Island	12.3 (1.01)	12.4 (0.90)	12.0 (0.74)	10.4 (0.50)	11.2 (0.82)	— (†)	5.9 (0.85)	4.9 (0.41)	4.9 (0.63)	4.0 (0.33)	4.0 (0.39)	5.0 (0.78)
South Carolina	— (†)	20.5 (1.42)	19.8 (1.69)	20.4 (2.22)	23.4 (1.86)	21.2 (1.25)	— (†)	6.7 (0.82)	4.8 (0.79)	4.6 (0.67)	6.3 (0.89)	3.7 (0.48)
South Dakota[4]	— (†)	— (†)	— (†)	— (†)	— (†)	— (†)	7.1 (0.73)	8.3 (0.72)	6.3 (0.80)	9.2 (0.76)	5.7 (0.52)	6.8 (0.87)
Tennessee	21.3 (2.06)	24.1 (1.58)	22.6 (1.41)	20.5 (1.64)	21.1 (1.34)	19.2 (1.70)	5.4 (0.80)	8.1 (0.92)	5.6 (0.70)	5.1 (0.70)	5.2 (0.80)	5.4 (0.79)
Texas	— (†)	19.3 (0.93)	18.8 (0.71)	18.2 (0.89)	17.6 (0.73)	18.4 (1.33)	— (†)	7.9 (0.63)	6.8 (0.55)	6.4 (0.76)	4.9 (0.45)	5.6 (0.68)
Utah	15.3 (1.80)	17.7 (1.70)	17.1 (1.38)	16.0 (1.40)	16.8 (1.48)	17.2 (1.19)	5.6 (1.24)	7.0 (1.03)	7.5 (1.00)	4.6 (0.63)	5.9 (1.01)	5.0 (0.57)
Vermont	— (†)	— (†)	— (†)	— (†)	— (†)	— (†)	8.3 (0.31)	9.1 (0.90)	9.6 (1.05)	9.0 (0.61)	9.1 (0.73)	10.4 (1.28)
Virginia	— (†)	— (†)	— (†)	— (†)	20.4 (1.26)	15.8 (0.69)	— (†)	— (†)	— (†)	— (†)	5.7 (0.64)	— (†)
Washington	— (†)	— (†)	— (†)	— (†)	— (†)	— (†)	— (†)	— (†)	— (†)	— (†)	— (†)	— (†)
West Virginia	20.7 (1.37)	22.3 (1.32)	21.3 (1.52)	24.4 (1.05)	20.7 (1.64)	24.3 (2.16)	6.6 (1.25)	8.5 (1.00)	6.9 (0.89)	6.5 (0.72)	5.5 (0.75)	5.5 (0.99)
Wisconsin	13.2 (0.81)	15.8 (1.19)	12.7 (0.76)	10.9 (0.81)	10.4 (0.66)	14.4 (1.32)	3.2 (0.43)	3.9 (0.54)	3.6 (0.49)	3.4 (0.50)	3.1 (0.41)	3.2 (0.52)
Wyoming	24.6 (1.49)	28.0 (1.17)	26.8 (1.28)	26.0 (1.04)	27.1 (1.19)	28.8 (0.95)	10.1 (0.91)	10.0 (0.71)	11.4 (0.76)	11.5 (0.81)	10.5 (0.71)	9.9 (0.62)

—Not available.

†Not applicable.

[1]The term "anywhere" is not used in the Youth Risk Behavior Survey (YRBS) questionnaire; students were simply asked how many days they carried a weapon during the past 30 days.

[2]In the question asking students about carrying a weapon at school, "on school property" was not defined for survey respondents.

[3]Data for the U.S. total include both public and private schools and were collected through a national survey representing the entire country.

[4]Data include both public and private schools.

NOTE: Respondents were asked about carrying "a weapon such as a gun, knife, or club." State-level data include public schools only, with the exception of data for Ohio and South Dakota. Data for the U.S. total, Ohio, and South Dakota include both public and private schools. For specific states, a given year's data may be unavailable (1) because the state did not participate in the survey that year; (2) because the state omitted this particular survey item from the state-level questionnaire; or (3) because the state had an overall response rate of less than 60 percent (the overall response rate is the school response rate multiplied by the student response rate).

SOURCE: Centers for Disease Control and Prevention, Division of Adolescent and School Health, Youth Risk Behavior Surveillance System (YRBSS), 2003 through 2013. (This table was prepared June 2014.)

Table 231.65. Number of incidents of students bringing firearms to or possessing firearms at a public school and rate of incidents per 100,000 students, by state: 2009–10 through 2013–14

State	Number of firearm incidents					Rate of firearm incidents per 100,000 students				
	2009–10	2010–11	2011–12	2012–13	2013–14	2009–10	2010–11	2011–12	2012–13	2013–14
1	2	3	4	5	6	7	8	9	10	11
United States	1,749	1,685	1,333	1,556	1,501	3.5	3.4	2.7	3.1	3.0
Alabama........................	23	15	5	46	29	3.1	2.0	0.7	6.2	3.9
Alaska..........................	7	3	5	5	4	5.3	2.3	3.8	3.8	3.1
Arizona.........................	18	7	22	18	17	1.7	0.7	2.0	1.7	1.5
Arkansas.......................	32	45	50	65	51	6.7	9.3	10.3	13.4	10.4
California	267	220	79	129	92	4.3	3.5	1.3	2.0	1.5
Colorado.......................	23	19	17	23	21	2.8	2.3	2.0	2.7	2.4
Connecticut....................	29	12	21	19	7	5.1	2.1	3.8	3.4	1.3
Delaware.......................	7	2	1	2	5	5.5	1.5	0.8	1.6	3.8
District of Columbia	2	2	2	0	2	2.9	2.8	2.7	0.0	2.6
Florida..........................	66	63	51	62	71	2.5	2.4	1.9	2.3	2.6
Georgia.........................	132	154	104	118	83	7.9	9.2	6.2	6.9	4.8
Hawaii..........................	1	2	1	0	0	0.6	1.1	0.5	0.0	0.0
Idaho...........................	12	—	10	5	4	4.3	—	3.6	1.8	1.3
Illinois..........................	21	5	5	9	4	1.0	0.2	0.2	0.4	0.2
Indiana.........................	42	28	26	27	25	4.0	2.7	2.5	2.6	2.4
Iowa............................	5	2	2	3	3	1.0	0.4	0.4	0.6	0.6
Kansas..........................	32	20	9	28	19	6.7	4.1	1.9	5.7	3.8
Kentucky	12	15	23	20	43	1.8	2.2	3.4	2.9	6.3
Louisiana	50	49	43	66	80	7.2	7.0	6.1	9.3	11.2
Maine...........................	2	2	4	2	0	1.1	1.1	2.1	1.1	0.0
Maryland.......................	8	8	10	11	7	0.9	0.9	1.2	1.3	0.8
Massachusetts.................	11	12	7	10	19	1.1	1.3	0.7	1.0	2.0
Michigan	37	80	60	70	41	2.2	5.0	3.8	4.5	2.6
Minnesota......................	21	23	10	19	22	2.5	2.7	1.2	2.2	2.6
Mississippi	42	32	32	38	49	8.5	6.5	6.5	7.7	9.9
Missouri........................	104	120	81	110	88	11.3	13.1	8.8	12.0	9.6
Montana........................	14	11	9	8	8	9.9	7.8	6.3	5.6	5.6
Nebraska	8	13	10	16	14	2.7	4.4	3.3	5.3	4.6
Nevada	18	14	14	8	29	4.2	3.2	3.2	1.8	6.4
New Hampshire	2	5	6	4	9	1.0	2.6	3.1	2.1	4.8
New Jersey.....................	5	5	6	5	5	0.4	0.4	0.4	0.4	0.4
New Mexico	18	25	18	13	15	5.4	7.4	5.3	3.8	4.4
New York........................	17 [1]	18 [1]	46	28	45	0.6 [1]	0.7 [1]	1.7	1.0	1.6
North Carolina	23	9	9	11	19	1.6	0.6	0.6	0.7	1.2
North Dakota	2	11	2	5	6	2.1	11.4	2.0	4.9	5.8
Ohio.............................	103	91	76	71	102	5.8	5.2	4.4	4.1	5.9
Oklahoma.......................	37	22	27	39	21	5.7	3.3	4.1	5.8	3.1
Oregon..........................	14	17	19	16	15	2.4	3.0	3.3	2.7	2.5
Pennsylvania...................	27	24	23	34	23	1.5	1.3	1.3	1.9	1.3
Rhode Island	3	7	1	0	2	2.1	4.9	0.7	0.0	1.4
South Carolina.................	32	8	26	49	51	4.4	1.1	3.6	6.7	6.8
South Dakota...................	8	2	10	9	4	6.5	1.6	7.8	6.9	3.1
Tennessee	79	43	82	64	57	8.1	4.4	8.2	6.4	5.7
Texas	103	93	85	100	103	2.1	1.9	1.7	2.0	2.0
Utah.............................	5	76	99 [2]	49	45	0.9	13.0	16.5 [2]	8.0	7.2
Vermont.........................	1	3	1	2	9	1.1	3.1	1.1	2.2	10.1
Virginia..........................	34	30	32	31	22	2.7	2.4	2.5	2.4	1.7
Washington.....................	162	173	26	33	46	15.6	16.6	2.5	3.1	4.3
West Virginia...................	4	3	14	1	16	1.4	1.1	4.9	0.4	5.7
Wisconsin	19	33	8	37	40	2.2	3.8	0.9	4.2	4.6
Wyoming........................	5	9	4	18	9	5.7	10.1	4.4	19.7	9.7

—Not available.

[1] Data for New York City Public Schools were not reported.

[2] The state reported a total state-level firearm incident count that was less than the sum of its reported district-level counts. The sum of the district-level firearm incident counts is displayed instead of the reported state-level count.

NOTE: Separate counts were collected for incidents involving handguns, rifles/shotguns, other firearms, and multiple types of firearms. The counts reported here exclude the "other firearms" category.

SOURCE: U.S. Department of Education, National Center for Education Statistics, EDFacts file 094, Data Group 601, extracted September 23, 2015, from the EDFacts Data Warehouse (internal U.S. Department of Education source); Common Core of Data (CCD), "State Nonfiscal Survey of Public Elementary and Secondary Education," 2009–10 through 2013–14. (This table was prepared September 2015.)

Table 231.70. Percentage of students ages 12–18 who reported having access to a loaded gun, without adult permission, at school or away from school during the school year, by selected student and school characteristics: Selected years, 2007 through 2013

[Standard errors appear in parentheses]

Student or school characteristic	2007		2009		2011		2013	
1	2		3		4		5	
Total...........................	6.7	(0.40)	5.5	(0.47)	4.7	(0.43)	3.7	(0.38)
Sex								
Male..........................	8.4	(0.56)	7.6	(0.72)	5.6	(0.59)	3.9	(0.56)
Female.......................	5.0	(0.47)	3.4	(0.44)	3.6	(0.44)	3.4	(0.35)
Race/ethnicity[1]								
White...........................	7.7	(0.55)	6.4	(0.60)	5.3	(0.50)	4.2	(0.45)
Black..........................	6.2	(0.98)	3.9	(0.92)	4.1	(0.86)	3.4	(0.78)
Hispanic	4.8	(0.79)	4.9	(0.90)	4.1	(0.89)	3.0	(0.71)
Asian..........................	‡	(†)	‡	(†)	‡	(†)	‡	(†)
Other..........................	9.3	(2.30)	5.4 !	(2.40)	‡	(†)	4.7 !	(1.79)
Grade								
6th..............................	2.4	(0.64)	0.8 !	(0.40)	2.0 !	(0.89)	‡	(†)
7th..............................	2.6	(0.56)	3.6	(0.84)	3.0	(0.63)	2.0	(0.50)
8th..............................	3.2	(0.63)	3.2	(0.63)	2.9	(0.60)	2.4	(0.62)
9th..............................	6.8	(0.98)	4.4	(0.80)	4.0	(0.75)	3.3	(0.80)
10th............................	9.2	(1.13)	7.3	(1.02)	5.3	(0.70)	4.7	(0.80)
11th............................	9.9	(1.00)	7.6	(1.16)	6.4	(1.06)	5.9	(0.99)
12th............................	12.3	(1.33)	9.8	(1.44)	8.2	(1.06)	5.8	(0.99)
Urbanicity[2]								
Urban..........................	5.8	(0.67)	4.7	(0.72)	4.1	(0.61)	3.2	(0.54)
Suburban.....................	6.4	(0.59)	5.5	(0.57)	4.9	(0.55)	3.7	(0.46)
Rural..........................	9.1	(1.04)	7.1	(1.39)	4.9	(0.92)	4.6	(0.91)
Control of school								
Public.........................	6.9	(0.44)	5.8	(0.49)	4.8	(0.42)	3.7	(0.40)
Private........................	4.5	(0.88)	2.3 !	(0.83)	3.2 !	(0.98)	3.6	(1.01)

†Not applicable.
!Interpret data with caution. The coefficient of variation (CV) for this estimate is between 30 and 50 percent.
‡Reporting standards not met. Either there are too few cases for a reliable estimate or the coefficient of variation (CV) is 50 percent or greater.
[1]Race categories exclude persons of Hispanic ethnicity. "Other" includes American Indians/Alaska Natives, Pacific Islanders, and persons reporting that they are of Two or more races.

[2]Refers to the Standard Metropolitan Statistical Area (MSA) status of the respondent's household as defined in 2000 by the U.S. Census Bureau. Categories include "central city of an MSA (Urban)," "in MSA but not in central city (Suburban)," and "not MSA (Rural)."
SOURCE: U.S. Department of Justice, Bureau of Justice Statistics, School Crime Supplement (SCS) to the National Crime Victimization Survey, 2007 through 2013. (This table was prepared October 2014.)

Table 232.10. Percentage of students in grades 9–12 who reported using alcohol at least 1 day during the previous 30 days, by location and selected student characteristics: Selected years, 1993 through 2013

[Standard errors appear in parentheses]

Location and student characteristic	1993	1995	1997	1999	2001	2003	2005	2007	2009	2011	2013
	2	3	4	5	6	7	8	9	10	11	12
Anywhere (including on school property)[1]											
Total	48.0 (1.06)	51.6 (1.19)	50.8 (1.43)	50.0 (1.30)	47.1 (1.11)	44.9 (1.21)	43.3 (1.38)	44.7 (1.15)	41.8 (0.80)	38.7 (0.75)	34.9 (1.08)
Sex											
Male	50.1 (1.23)	53.2 (1.33)	53.3 (1.22)	52.3 (1.47)	49.2 (1.42)	43.8 (1.31)	43.8 (1.40)	44.7 (1.39)	40.8 (1.11)	39.5 (0.93)	34.4 (1.30)
Female	45.9 (1.32)	49.9 (1.79)	47.8 (1.99)	47.7 (1.45)	45.0 (1.11)	45.8 (1.29)	42.8 (1.56)	44.6 (1.42)	42.9 (0.85)	37.9 (0.91)	35.5 (1.39)
Race/ethnicity[2]											
White	49.9 (1.26)	54.1 (1.77)	54.0 (1.51)	52.5 (1.62)	50.4 (1.12)	47.1 (1.51)	46.4 (1.84)	47.3 (1.67)	44.7 (1.16)	40.3 (0.97)	36.3 (1.63)
Black	42.5 (1.82)	42.0 (2.24)	36.9 (1.46)	39.9 (4.07)	32.7 (2.33)	37.4 (1.67)	31.2 (1.05)	34.5 (1.65)	33.4 (1.45)	30.5 (1.40)	29.6 (1.65)
Hispanic	50.8 (2.82)	54.7 (2.56)	53.9 (1.96)	52.8 (2.41)	49.2 (1.52)	45.6 (1.39)	46.8 (1.39)	47.6 (1.80)	42.9 (1.43)	42.3 (1.38)	37.5 (2.11)
Asian[3]	— (†)	— (†)	— (†)	25.7 (2.24)	28.4 (3.22)	27.5 (3.47)	21.5 (1.98)	25.4 (2.17)	18.3 (1.60)	25.6 (2.90)	21.7 (1.80)
Pacific Islander[3]	— (†)	— (†)	57.6 (3.79)	60.8 (5.11)	52.3 (8.54)	40.0 (7.04)	38.7 (8.43)	48.8 (6.58)	34.8 (4.36)	38.4 (6.40)	26.8 (5.84)
American Indian/Alaska Native	45.3 (7.18)	51.4 (7.18)	— (†)	49.4 (6.43)	51.4 (3.97)	51.9 (5.29)	57.4 (4.13)	34.5 (1.77)	42.8 (5.43)	44.9 (2.26)	33.4 (5.13)
Two or more races[3]	— (†)	— (†)	— (†)	51.1 (3.98)	45.4 (4.11)	47.1 (3.59)	39.0 (3.59)	46.2 (2.89)	44.3 (2.42)	36.9 (3.08)	36.1 (2.87)
Grade											
9th	40.5 (1.79)	45.6 (1.87)	44.2 (3.12)	40.6 (2.17)	41.1 (1.82)	36.2 (1.43)	36.2 (1.23)	35.7 (1.15)	31.5 (1.28)	29.8 (1.35)	24.4 (1.13)
10th	44.0 (2.00)	49.5 (2.38)	47.2 (2.19)	49.7 (1.89)	45.2 (1.29)	43.5 (1.66)	42.0 (1.95)	41.8 (1.68)	40.6 (1.42)	35.7 (1.37)	30.9 (1.84)
11th	49.7 (1.73)	53.7 (1.51)	53.2 (1.49)	50.9 (1.98)	49.3 (1.70)	47.0 (2.08)	46.0 (1.98)	49.0 (1.83)	45.7 (2.05)	42.7 (1.28)	39.2 (1.52)
12th	56.4 (1.35)	56.5 (1.64)	57.3 (2.50)	61.7 (2.25)	55.2 (1.53)	55.9 (1.65)	50.8 (2.12)	54.9 (2.09)	51.7 (1.37)	48.4 (1.29)	46.8 (1.85)
Urbanicity[4]											
Urban	— (†)	— (†)	48.9 (2.07)	46.5 (2.75)	45.2 (1.97)	41.5 (1.48)	— (†)	— (†)	— (†)	— (†)	— (†)
Suburban	— (†)	— (†)	50.5 (2.11)	51.4 (1.32)	47.6 (1.26)	46.5 (2.10)	— (†)	— (†)	— (†)	— (†)	— (†)
Rural	— (†)	— (†)	55.4 (5.36)	52.2 (4.51)	50.2 (1.91)	45.3 (2.35)	— (†)	— (†)	— (†)	— (†)	— (†)
On school property[5]											
Total	5.2 (0.39)	6.3 (0.45)	5.6 (0.34)	4.9 (0.39)	4.9 (0.28)	5.2 (0.46)	4.3 (0.30)	4.1 (0.32)	4.5 (0.29)	5.1 (0.33)	— (†)
Sex											
Male	6.2 (0.39)	7.2 (0.50)	7.2 (0.66)	6.1 (0.54)	6.1 (0.43)	6.0 (0.61)	5.3 (0.39)	4.6 (0.35)	5.3 (0.41)	5.4 (0.43)	— (†)
Female	4.2 (0.54)	5.3 (0.70)	3.6 (0.37)	3.6 (0.39)	3.8 (0.39)	4.2 (0.41)	3.3 (0.32)	3.6 (0.37)	3.6 (0.34)	4.7 (0.35)	— (†)
Race/ethnicity[2]											
White	4.6 (0.44)	5.6 (0.62)	4.8 (0.42)	4.8 (0.55)	4.2 (0.26)	3.9 (0.45)	3.8 (0.38)	3.2 (0.35)	3.3 (0.27)	4.0 (0.38)	— (†)
Black	6.9 (0.98)	7.6 (0.87)	5.6 (0.72)	4.3 (0.52)	5.3 (0.65)	5.8 (0.80)	3.2 (0.45)	3.4 (0.63)	5.4 (0.59)	5.1 (0.50)	— (†)
Hispanic	6.8 (0.84)	9.6 (1.73)	8.2 (0.96)	7.0 (0.88)	7.0 (0.71)	7.6 (1.08)	7.7 (1.04)	7.5 (0.86)	6.9 (0.70)	7.3 (0.68)	— (†)
Asian[3]	— (†)	— (†)	— (†)	2.0 (0.42)	6.8 (1.42)	5.6 (1.55)	1.3! (0.62)	4.4 (1.17)	2.9 (0.65)	3.5! (1.21)	— (†)
Pacific Islander[3]	— (†)	— (†)	8.6! (4.15)	6.7 (1.59)	12.4 (3.50)	8.5! (3.29)	‡ (†)	‡ (†)	10.0 (2.34)	8.3! (3.61)	— (†)
American Indian/Alaska Native	6.7! (3.06)	8.1! (3.30)	— (†)	‡ (†)	8.2 (1.69)	7.1! (2.61)	6.2! (2.05)	5.0 (0.89)	4.3! (1.58)	20.9 (4.15)	— (†)
Two or more races[3]	— (†)	— (†)	— (†)	5.2 (1.09)	7.0! (2.36)	13.3 (2.93)	3.5 (1.02)	5.4 (1.25)	6.7 (1.37)	5.8 (1.32)	— (†)
Grade											
9th	5.2 (0.38)	7.5 (0.90)	5.9 (0.83)	4.4 (0.60)	5.3 (0.47)	5.1 (0.69)	3.7 (0.48)	3.4 (0.43)	4.4 (0.37)	5.4 (0.56)	— (†)
10th	4.7 (0.43)	5.9 (0.88)	4.6 (0.71)	5.0 (0.67)	5.1 (0.45)	5.6 (0.60)	4.5 (0.45)	4.1 (0.50)	4.8 (0.46)	4.4 (0.51)	— (†)
11th	5.2 (0.80)	5.7 (0.86)	6.0 (0.86)	4.7 (0.57)	4.7 (0.45)	5.0 (0.57)	4.0 (0.47)	4.2 (0.54)	4.6 (0.44)	5.2 (0.56)	— (†)
12th	5.5 (0.64)	6.2 (0.58)	5.9 (0.66)	5.0 (0.89)	4.3 (0.44)	4.5 (0.68)	4.8 (0.57)	4.8 (0.55)	4.1 (0.44)	5.1 (0.48)	— (†)
Urbanicity[4]											
Urban	— (†)	— (†)	— (†)	— (†)	— (†)	— (†)	— (†)	— (†)	— (†)	— (†)	— (†)
Suburban	— (†)	— (†)	— (†)	— (†)	— (†)	— (†)	— (†)	— (†)	— (†)	— (†)	— (†)
Rural	— (†)	— (†)	— (†)	— (†)	— (†)	— (†)	— (†)	— (†)	— (†)	— (†)	— (†)

—Not available.
†Not applicable.
!Interpret data with caution. The coefficient of variation (CV) for this estimate is between 30 and 50 percent.
‡Reporting standards not met. The coefficient of variation (CV) for this estimate is 50 percent or greater.
[1]The term "anywhere" is not used in the Youth Risk Behavior Survey (YRBS) questionnaire; students were simply asked how many days during the previous 30 days they had at least one drink of alcohol.
[2]Race categories exclude persons of Hispanic ethnicity.
[3]Before 1999, Asian students and Pacific Islander students were not categorized separately, and students could not be classified as Two or more races. Because the response categories changed in 1999, caution should be used in comparing data on race from 1993, 1995, and 1997 with data from later years.
[4]Refers to the Standard Metropolitan Statistical Area (MSA) status of the respondent's household as defined in 2000 by the U.S. Census Bureau. Categories include "central city of an MSA (Urban)," "in MSA but not in central city (Suburban)," and "not MSA (Rural)."
[5]In the question about drinking alcohol at school, "on school property" was not defined for survey respondents. Data on alcohol use at school were not collected in 2013.
SOURCE: Centers for Disease Control and Prevention, Division of Adolescent and School Health, Youth Risk Behavior Surveillance System (YRBSS), 1993 through 2013. (This table was prepared June 2014.)

Table 232.20. Percentage distribution of students in grades 9–12, by number of days they reported using alcohol anywhere or on school property during the previous 30 days and selected student characteristics: Selected years, 2009 through 2013

[Standard errors appear in parentheses]

Year and student characteristic	Anywhere (including on school property)[1] 0 days		1 or 2 days		3 to 29 days		All 30 days		On school property[2] 0 days		1 or 2 days		3 to 29 days		All 30 days	
1	2		3		4		5		6		7		8		9	
2009																
Total	58.2	(0.80)	20.5	(0.40)	20.5	(0.73)	0.8	(0.09)	95.5	(0.29)	2.8	(0.21)	1.3	(0.14)	0.4	(0.07)
Sex																
Male	59.2	(1.11)	17.9	(0.59)	21.7	(0.90)	1.3	(0.19)	94.7	(0.41)	3.0	(0.27)	1.7	(0.20)	0.6	(0.14)
Female	57.1	(0.85)	23.4	(0.73)	19.2	(0.74)	0.3	(0.05)	96.4	(0.34)	2.6	(0.26)	0.9	(0.16)	0.1 !	(0.03)
Race/ethnicity[3]																
White	55.3	(1.16)	20.9	(0.50)	23.2	(1.10)	0.6	(0.10)	96.7	(0.27)	2.0	(0.20)	1.0	(0.14)	0.2	(0.06)
Black	66.6	(1.45)	18.5	(0.80)	14.0	(1.04)	0.9	(0.25)	94.6	(0.59)	3.0	(0.36)	1.8	(0.32)	0.5 !	(0.22)
Hispanic	57.1	(1.43)	21.9	(0.82)	19.6	(1.12)	1.3	(0.22)	93.1	(0.70)	4.4	(0.46)	1.9	(0.37)	0.6	(0.16)
Asian	81.7	(1.60)	11.5	(1.90)	5.9	(1.22)	0.9 !	(0.44)	97.1	(0.65)	1.4 !	(0.47)	0.9 !	(0.43)	‡	(†)
Pacific Islander	65.2	(4.36)	12.4	(2.86)	22.0	(3.42)	‡	(†)	90.0	(2.34)	5.9	(1.68)	3.8 !	(1.56)	‡	(†)
American Indian/Alaska Native	57.2	(5.43)	17.0 !	(5.28)	24.7	(5.33)	‡	(†)	95.7	(1.58)	3.5 !	(1.45)	‡	(†)	#	(†)
Two or more races	55.7	(2.42)	26.8	(2.58)	16.1	(1.90)	1.4 !	(0.56)	93.3	(1.37)	4.7	(0.98)	1.6 !	(0.64)	‡	(†)
Grade																
9th	68.5	(1.28)	17.9	(1.00)	12.9	(0.64)	0.7	(0.16)	95.6	(0.37)	3.0	(0.28)	1.0	(0.17)	0.4 !	(0.13)
10th	59.4	(1.42)	19.5	(0.79)	20.3	(1.27)	0.8	(0.21)	95.2	(0.46)	2.9	(0.35)	1.5	(0.25)	0.4 !	(0.15)
11th	54.3	(2.05)	21.7	(1.41)	23.2	(1.36)	0.8	(0.13)	95.4	(0.44)	2.9	(0.40)	1.4	(0.24)	0.3	(0.09)
12th	48.3	(1.37)	23.6	(0.95)	27.3	(1.55)	0.8	(0.19)	95.9	(0.44)	2.3	(0.29)	1.5	(0.25)	0.3 !	(0.12)
2011																
Total	61.3	(0.75)	19.4	(0.62)	18.3	(0.47)	0.9	(0.11)	94.9	(0.33)	3.3	(0.23)	1.3	(0.15)	0.5	(0.07)
Sex																
Male	60.5	(0.93)	18.5	(0.68)	19.5	(0.65)	1.5	(0.19)	94.6	(0.43)	3.1	(0.26)	1.5	(0.21)	0.8	(0.14)
Female	62.1	(0.91)	20.5	(0.74)	17.1	(0.63)	0.3	(0.08)	95.3	(0.35)	3.4	(0.29)	1.1	(0.16)	0.1 !	(0.04)
Race/ethnicity[3]																
White	59.7	(0.97)	19.5	(0.83)	20.1	(0.62)	0.7	(0.13)	96.0	(0.38)	2.8	(0.29)	0.9	(0.12)	0.3	(0.06)
Black	69.5	(1.40)	17.5	(1.06)	12.1	(0.97)	0.9	(0.21)	94.9	(0.50)	3.2	(0.41)	1.4	(0.28)	0.5 !	(0.18)
Hispanic	57.7	(1.38)	21.5	(0.75)	19.4	(0.94)	1.4	(0.25)	92.7	(0.68)	4.3	(0.31)	2.2	(0.45)	0.7	(0.17)
Asian	74.4	(2.90)	16.7	(2.86)	7.3	(1.42)	1.6 !	(0.73)	96.5	(1.21)	2.2 !	(0.96)	‡	(†)	‡	(†)
Pacific Islander	61.6	(6.40)	15.6	(3.98)	21.9	(4.87)	‡	(†)	91.7	(3.61)	3.6 !	(1.62)	‡	(†)	‡	(†)
American Indian/Alaska Native	55.1	(2.26)	23.8	(2.23)	20.1	(1.51)	‡	(†)	79.1	(4.15)	15.0	(3.14)	5.3	(0.96)	‡	(†)
Two or more races	63.1	(3.08)	19.6	(2.94)	15.0	(1.88)	2.3 !	(0.96)	94.2	(1.32)	3.3	(0.86)	‡	(†)	1.6 !	(0.74)
Grade																
9th	70.2	(1.35)	17.8	(0.99)	11.2	(0.95)	0.7	(0.18)	94.6	(0.56)	3.7	(0.41)	1.4	(0.31)	0.4	(0.09)
10th	64.3	(1.37)	19.2	(1.11)	15.8	(0.66)	0.6	(0.15)	95.6	(0.51)	2.8	(0.40)	1.2	(0.24)	0.4	(0.11)
11th	57.3	(1.28)	21.1	(0.87)	20.6	(1.31)	1.1	(0.21)	94.8	(0.56)	3.2	(0.39)	1.3	(0.26)	0.7	(0.16)
12th	51.6	(1.29)	20.1	(0.93)	27.1	(1.25)	1.1	(0.24)	94.9	(0.48)	3.5	(0.38)	1.3	(0.26)	0.3 !	(0.10)
2013[4]																
Total	65.1	(1.08)	17.3	(0.56)	16.9	(0.78)	0.8	(0.12)	—	(†)	—	(†)	—	(†)	—	(†)
Sex																
Male	65.6	(1.30)	15.7	(0.75)	17.4	(0.90)	1.2	(0.19)	—	(†)	—	(†)	—	(†)	—	(†)
Female	64.5	(1.39)	18.8	(0.98)	16.3	(0.88)	0.3	(0.09)	—	(†)	—	(†)	—	(†)	—	(†)
Race/ethnicity[3]																
White	63.7	(1.63)	17.6	(0.87)	18.0	(1.11)	0.6	(0.13)	—	(†)	—	(†)	—	(†)	—	(†)
Black	70.4	(1.65)	15.5	(0.90)	13.6	(1.46)	0.6	(0.16)	—	(†)	—	(†)	—	(†)	—	(†)
Hispanic	62.5	(2.11)	18.0	(1.30)	18.3	(1.27)	1.2	(0.35)	—	(†)	—	(†)	—	(†)	—	(†)
Asian	78.3	(1.80)	14.8	(2.26)	6.3	(1.27)	‡	(†)	—	(†)	—	(†)	—	(†)	—	(†)
Pacific Islander	73.2	(5.84)	18.2	(4.71)	7.5	(2.24)	‡	(†)	—	(†)	—	(†)	—	(†)	—	(†)
American Indian/Alaska Native	66.6	(5.13)	14.8	(4.41)	17.4 !	(5.62)	‡	(†)	—	(†)	—	(†)	—	(†)	—	(†)
Two or more races	63.9	(2.87)	18.7	(1.71)	16.4	(2.12)	1.0 !	(0.42)	—	(†)	—	(†)	—	(†)	—	(†)
Grade																
9th	75.6	(1.13)	13.6	(0.89)	10.0	(0.85)	0.7	(0.22)	—	(†)	—	(†)	—	(†)	—	(†)
10th	69.1	(1.84)	15.9	(1.17)	14.5	(1.22)	0.6	(0.16)	—	(†)	—	(†)	—	(†)	—	(†)
11th	60.8	(1.52)	18.6	(1.01)	19.7	(1.26)	0.9	(0.23)	—	(†)	—	(†)	—	(†)	—	(†)
12th	53.2	(1.85)	21.5	(0.93)	24.6	(1.31)	0.7	(0.17)	—	(†)	—	(†)	—	(†)	—	(†)

—Not available.
†Not applicable.
#Rounds to zero.
!Interpret data with caution. The coefficient of variation (CV) for this estimate is between 30 and 50 percent.
‡Reporting standards not met. Either there are too few cases for a reliable estimate or the coefficient of variation (CV) is 50 percent or greater.
[1]The term "anywhere" is not used in the Youth Risk Behavior Survey (YRBS) questionnaire; students were simply asked how many days during the previous 30 days they had at least one drink of alcohol.

[2]In the question about drinking alcohol at school, "on school property" was not defined for survey respondents.
[3]Race categories exclude persons of Hispanic ethnicity.
[4]Data on alcohol use at school were not collected in 2013.
NOTE: Detail may not sum to totals because of rounding.
SOURCE: Centers for Disease Control and Prevention, Division of Adolescent and School Health, Youth Risk Behavior Surveillance System (YRBSS), 2009 through 2013. (This table was prepared September 2014.)

Table 232.30. Percentage of public school students in grades 9–12 who reported using alcohol at least 1 day during the previous 30 days, by location and state: Selected years, 2003 through 2013

[Standard errors appear in parentheses]

State	Anywhere (including on school property)[1]						On school property[2]					
	2003	2005	2007	2009	2011	2013	2003	2005	2007	2009	2011	2013
1	2	3	4	5	6	7	8	9	10	11	12	13
United States[3]	44.9 (1.21)	43.3 (1.38)	44.7 (1.15)	41.8 (0.80)	38.7 (0.75)	34.9 (1.08)	5.2 (0.46)	4.3 (0.30)	4.1 (0.32)	4.5 (0.29)	5.1 (0.33)	— (†)
Alabama	40.2 (2.04)	39.4 (2.55)	— (†)	39.5 (2.22)	35.6 (1.99)	35.0 (2.45)	4.1 (0.82)	4.5 (0.59)	— (†)	5.4 (0.76)	5.7 (1.08)	— (†)
Alaska	38.7 (2.05)	— (†)	39.7 (2.11)	33.2 (1.66)	28.6 (1.95)	22.5 (1.69)	4.9 (0.81)	— (†)	4.1 (0.58)	3.0 (0.48)	3.4 (0.52)	— (†)
Arizona	51.8 (1.93)	47.1 (1.73)	45.6 (1.73)	44.5 (1.67)	43.8 (1.47)	36.0 (2.25)	7.1 (0.67)	7.5 (0.88)	6.0 (0.54)	5.9 (0.61)	6.2 (0.55)	— (†)
Arkansas	— (†)	43.1 (1.99)	42.2 (1.75)	39.7 (1.91)	33.9 (1.81)	36.3 (1.97)	— (†)	5.2 (0.62)	5.1 (0.65)	6.1 (0.89)	4.2 (0.68)	— (†)
California	— (†)	— (†)	— (†)	— (†)	— (†)	— (†)	— (†)	— (†)	— (†)	— (†)	— (†)	— (†)
Colorado	— (†)	47.4 (4.42)	— (†)	40.8 (2.44)	36.4 (2.29)	— (†)	— (†)	5.9 (1.08)	— (†)	4.1 (0.61)	5.3 (0.87)	— (†)
Connecticut	— (†)	45.3 (2.16)	46.0 (2.13)	43.5 (2.22)	41.5 (1.90)	36.7 (2.02)	— (†)	6.6 (0.71)	5.6 (0.99)	5.0 (0.47)	4.6 (0.61)	— (†)
Delaware	45.4 (1.30)	43.1 (1.16)	45.2 (1.40)	43.7 (1.65)	40.4 (1.55)	36.3 (1.34)	4.8 (0.44)	5.5 (0.66)	4.5 (0.48)	5.0 (0.73)	5.0 (0.50)	— (†)
District of Columbia	33.8 (1.72)	23.1 (1.40)	32.6 (1.47)	— (†)	32.8 (1.89)	— (†)	4.9 (0.64)	4.6 (0.55)	6.1 (0.92)	— (†)	6.8 (0.91)	— (†)
Florida	42.7 (1.10)	39.7 (1.43)	42.3 (1.30)	40.5 (1.03)	37.0 (0.98)	34.9 (0.87)	5.1 (0.36)	4.5 (0.30)	5.3 (0.31)	4.9 (0.26)	5.1 (0.29)	— (†)
Georgia	37.7 (1.41)	39.9 (2.12)	37.7 (1.52)	34.3 (1.65)	34.6 (1.93)	27.9 (2.04)	3.7 (0.55)	4.3 (0.67)	4.4 (0.58)	4.2 (0.48)	5.4 (0.80)	— (†)
Hawaii	— (†)	34.8 (2.05)	29.1 (2.93)	37.8 (3.02)	29.1 (1.64)	25.2 (1.75)	— (†)	8.8 (0.93)	6.0 (0.93)	7.9 (1.31)	5.0 (0.42)	— (†)
Idaho	34.8 (2.44)	39.8 (2.62)	42.5 (2.73)	34.2 (1.97)	36.2 (2.28)	28.3 (2.23)	3.8 (0.56)	4.3 (0.69)	6.2 (0.81)	3.5 (0.53)	4.1 (0.50)	— (†)
Illinois	— (†)	— (†)	43.7 (2.72)	39.8 (1.91)	37.8 (1.87)	36.6 (2.41)	— (†)	— (†)	5.5 (0.75)	4.4 (0.64)	3.3 (0.40)	— (†)
Indiana	44.9 (1.57)	41.4 (2.12)	43.9 (2.24)	38.5 (2.13)	33.5 (1.65)	— (†)	3.9 (0.57)	3.4 (0.64)	4.1 (0.47)	3.5 (0.52)	2.0 (0.36)	— (†)
Iowa	— (†)	43.8 (2.56)	41.0 (2.36)	— (†)	37.1 (2.58)	— (†)	— (†)	4.6 (0.89)	3.4 (0.78)	— (†)	2.3 (0.41)	— (†)
Kansas	— (†)	43.9 (1.74)	42.4 (1.69)	38.7 (1.93)	32.6 (1.53)	27.6 (1.02)	— (†)	5.1 (0.74)	4.8 (0.66)	3.2 (0.55)	2.9 (0.45)	— (†)
Kentucky	45.1 (1.87)	37.4 (1.77)	40.6 (1.25)	37.8 (1.30)	34.6 (1.56)	30.4 (1.37)	4.8 (0.69)	3.5 (0.37)	4.7 (0.47)	5.2 (0.87)	4.1 (0.53)	— (†)
Louisiana	— (†)	— (†)	— (†)	47.5 (2.80)	44.4 (2.00)	38.6 (2.75)	— (†)	— (†)	— (†)	5.6 (1.33)	6.0 (1.36)	— (†)
Maine	42.2 (1.78)	43.0 (2.15)	39.3 (2.29)	32.2 (0.66)	28.7 (0.69)	26.6 (0.90)	3.7 (0.48)	3.9 (0.44)	5.6 (0.89)	4.0 (0.23)	3.1 (0.21)	— (†)
Maryland	— (†)	39.8 (2.17)	42.9 (3.13)	37.0 (1.44)	34.8 (1.98)	31.2 (0.45)	— (†)	3.2 (0.42)	6.2 (1.10)	4.8 (0.67)	5.4 (0.63)	— (†)
Massachusetts	45.7 (1.19)	47.8 (1.36)	46.2 (1.57)	43.6 (1.28)	40.1 (1.54)	35.6 (1.14)	5.3 (0.50)	4.2 (0.32)	4.7 (0.45)	3.8 (0.48)	3.6 (0.44)	— (†)
Michigan	44.0 (1.40)	38.1 (1.73)	42.8 (1.70)	37.0 (1.28)	30.6 (1.64)	28.3 (1.81)	4.6 (0.33)	3.6 (0.46)	3.6 (0.51)	3.7 (0.40)	2.7 (0.37)	— (†)
Minnesota	— (†)	— (†)	— (†)	— (†)	— (†)	— (†)	— (†)	— (†)	— (†)	— (†)	— (†)	— (†)
Mississippi	41.8 (1.74)	— (†)	40.6 (1.57)	39.2 (1.43)	36.2 (2.07)	32.9 (2.09)	4.9 (0.70)	— (†)	5.1 (0.71)	4.3 (0.45)	4.6 (0.67)	— (†)
Missouri	49.2 (2.16)	40.8 (2.04)	44.4 (2.35)	39.3 (2.71)	— (†)	35.6 (1.33)	2.6 (0.58)	3.3 (0.57)	3.4 (0.74)	3.0 (0.55)	— (†)	— (†)
Montana	49.5 (1.68)	48.6 (1.50)	46.5 (1.39)	42.8 (1.81)	38.3 (1.08)	37.1 (1.20)	6.7 (0.70)	6.4 (0.73)	5.7 (0.47)	5.1 (0.69)	3.5 (0.35)	— (†)
Nebraska	46.5 (1.29)	42.9 (1.27)	— (†)	— (†)	26.6 (1.24)	22.1 (1.46)	4.6 (0.61)	3.6 (0.42)	— (†)	— (†)	3.0 (0.41)	— (†)
Nevada	43.4 (1.51)	41.4 (1.73)	37.0 (1.52)	38.6 (1.66)	— (†)	34.0 (2.11)	7.4 (0.74)	6.8 (0.92)	4.4 (0.58)	4.4 (0.52)	— (†)	— (†)
New Hampshire	47.1 (2.70)	44.0 (2.31)	44.8 (1.83)	39.3 (2.18)	38.4 (1.83)	32.9 (1.71)	4.0 (0.79)	— (†)	5.1 (0.73)	4.3 (0.68)	5.6 (0.70)	— (†)
New Jersey	— (†)	46.5 (2.65)	— (†)	45.2 (2.21)	42.9 (2.46)	39.3 (1.92)	— (†)	3.7 (0.42)	— (†)	— (†)	— (†)	— (†)
New Mexico	— (†)	42.3 (1.93)	43.2 (1.07)	40.5 (1.41)	36.9 (1.40)	28.9 (1.25)	— (†)	7.6 (0.87)	8.7 (1.35)	8.0 (0.90)	6.4 (0.54)	— (†)
New York	44.2 (1.53)	43.4 (1.47)	43.7 (1.41)	41.4 (1.38)	38.4 (1.96)	32.5 (1.36)	5.2 (0.39)	4.1 (0.45)	5.1 (0.58)	— (†)	— (†)	— (†)
North Carolina	39.4 (2.68)	42.3 (2.16)	37.7 (1.36)	35.0 (2.43)	34.3 (1.41)	32.2 (1.27)	3.6 (0.47)	5.4 (0.74)	4.7 (0.65)	4.1 (0.57)	5.5 (0.77)	— (†)
North Dakota	54.2 (1.74)	49.0 (1.89)	46.1 (1.82)	43.3 (1.79)	38.8 (1.67)	35.3 (1.59)	5.1 (0.79)	3.6 (0.52)	4.4 (0.65)	4.2 (0.53)	3.1 (0.51)	— (†)
Ohio[4]	42.2 (2.40)	42.4 (1.96)	45.7 (1.70)	— (†)	38.0 (2.94)	29.5 (2.21)	3.9 (0.69)	3.2 (0.59)	3.2 (0.50)	— (†)	— (†)	— (†)
Oklahoma	47.8 (1.41)	40.5 (1.62)	43.1 (1.88)	39.0 (1.97)	38.3 (1.75)	33.4 (1.91)	3.2 (0.64)	3.8 (0.49)	5.0 (0.59)	3.9 (0.55)	2.6 (0.65)	— (†)
Oregon	— (†)	— (†)	— (†)	— (†)	— (†)	— (†)	— (†)	— (†)	— (†)	— (†)	— (†)	— (†)
Pennsylvania	— (†)	— (†)	— (†)	38.4 (2.10)	— (†)	— (†)	— (†)	— (†)	— (†)	2.8 (0.50)	— (†)	— (†)
Rhode Island	44.5 (1.92)	42.7 (1.15)	42.9 (1.76)	34.0 (2.01)	34.0 (1.25)	30.9 (1.78)	4.6 (0.73)	5.3 (0.66)	4.8 (0.54)	3.2 (0.50)	— (†)	— (†)
South Carolina	— (†)	43.2 (1.64)	36.8 (2.31)	35.2 (2.80)	39.7 (1.72)	28.9 (1.34)	— (†)	6.0 (0.96)	4.7 (0.73)	3.6 (0.79)	5.9 (0.90)	— (†)
South Dakota[4]	50.2 (2.58)	46.6 (2.12)	44.5 (1.80)	40.1 (1.54)	39.3 (2.14)	30.8 (1.45)	5.4 (1.13)	4.0 (0.70)	3.6 (0.92)	— (†)	— (†)	— (†)
Tennessee	41.1 (2.04)	41.8 (1.90)	36.7 (1.90)	33.5 (1.71)	33.3 (1.39)	28.4 (1.35)	4.2 (0.48)	3.7 (0.66)	4.1 (0.54)	3.0 (0.38)	3.2 (0.34)	— (†)
Texas	— (†)	47.3 (1.93)	48.3 (1.64)	44.8 (1.25)	39.7 (1.15)	36.1 (1.75)	— (†)	5.7 (0.56)	4.9 (0.57)	4.7 (0.36)	3.9 (0.35)	— (†)
Utah	21.3 (2.19)	15.8 (1.92)	17.0 (1.88)	18.2 (2.72)	15.1 (1.54)	11.0 (0.90)	3.8 (0.74)	2.1 (0.39)	4.7 ! (1.69)	2.7 (0.45)	2.7 (0.54)	— (†)
Vermont	43.5 (1.48)	41.8 (1.53)	42.6 (1.04)	39.0 (1.57)	35.3 (1.10)	— (†)	5.3 (0.60)	4.8 (0.54)	4.6 (0.40)	3.3 (0.28)	3.3 (0.50)	— (†)
Virginia	— (†)	— (†)	— (†)	— (†)	30.5 (2.49)	27.3 (1.22)	— (†)	— (†)	— (†)	— (†)	3.3 (0.59)	— (†)
Washington	— (†)	— (†)	— (†)	— (†)	— (†)	— (†)	— (†)	— (†)	— (†)	— (†)	— (†)	— (†)
West Virginia	44.4 (1.81)	41.5 (1.41)	43.5 (1.45)	40.4 (1.10)	34.3 (2.40)	37.1 (2.04)	4.1 (0.84)	6.4 (1.08)	5.5 (0.89)	5.7 (0.61)	4.2 (0.67)	— (†)
Wisconsin	47.3 (1.63)	49.2 (1.51)	48.9 (1.56)	41.3 (1.83)	39.2 (1.35)	32.7 (1.21)	— (†)	— (†)	— (†)	— (†)	— (†)	— (†)
Wyoming	49.0 (2.16)	45.4 (1.47)	42.4 (1.22)	41.7 (1.36)	36.1 (1.34)	34.4 (1.14)	6.2 (0.75)	6.2 (0.56)	6.9 (0.63)	6.4 (0.50)	5.1 (0.48)	— (†)

—Not available.
†Not applicable.
!Interpret data with caution. The coefficient of variation (CV) for this estimate is between 30 and 50 percent.
[1]The term "anywhere" is not used in the Youth Risk Behavior Survey (YRBS) questionnaire; students were simply asked how many days during the previous 30 days they had at least one drink of alcohol.
[2]In the question about drinking alcohol at school, "on school property" was not defined for survey respondents. Data on alcohol use at school were not collected in 2013.
[3]Data for the U.S. total include both public and private schools and were collected through a national survey representing the entire country.

[4]Data include both public and private schools.
NOTE: State-level data include public schools only, with the exception of data for Ohio and South Dakota. Data for the U.S. total, Ohio, and South Dakota include both public and private schools. For specific states, a given year's data may be unavailable (1) because the state did not participate in the survey that year; (2) because the state omitted this particular survey item from the state-level questionnaire; or (3) because the state had an overall response rate of less than 60 percent (the overall response rate is the school response rate multiplied by the student response rate).
SOURCE: Centers for Disease Control and Prevention, Division of Adolescent and School Health, Youth Risk Behavior Surveillance System (YRBSS), 2003 through 2013. (This table was prepared June 2014.)

Table 232.40. Percentage of students in grades 9–12 who reported using marijuana at least one time during the previous 30 days, by location and selected student characteristics: Selected years, 1993 through 2013

[Standard errors appear in parentheses]

Location and student characteristic	1993	1995	1997	1999	2001	2003	2005	2007	2009	2011	2013
	2	3	4	5	6	7	8	9	10	11	12
Anywhere (including on school property)[1]											
Total	17.7 (1.22)	25.3 (1.03)	26.2 (1.11)	26.7 (1.30)	23.9 (0.77)	22.4 (1.09)	20.2 (0.84)	19.7 (0.97)	20.8 (0.70)	23.1 (0.80)	23.4 (1.08)
Sex											
Male	20.6 (1.61)	28.4 (1.08)	30.2 (1.46)	30.8 (1.92)	27.9 (0.81)	25.1 (1.25)	22.1 (0.98)	22.4 (1.02)	23.4 (0.80)	25.9 (1.01)	25.0 (1.14)
Female	14.6 (1.02)	22.0 (1.44)	21.4 (1.04)	22.6 (0.96)	20.0 (0.87)	19.3 (0.96)	18.2 (0.99)	17.0 (1.13)	17.9 (0.87)	20.1 (0.95)	21.9 (1.28)
Race/ethnicity[2]											
White	17.3 (1.41)	24.5 (1.49)	25.0 (1.56)	26.4 (1.59)	24.4 (1.04)	21.7 (1.20)	20.3 (1.11)	19.9 (1.28)	20.7 (0.93)	21.7 (1.09)	20.4 (1.36)
Black	18.6 (1.84)	28.6 (2.62)	28.2 (1.67)	26.4 (3.49)	21.8 (2.12)	23.9 (1.58)	20.4 (1.11)	21.5 (1.64)	22.2 (1.44)	25.1 (1.35)	28.9 (1.30)
Hispanic	19.4 (1.33)	27.8 (2.92)	28.6 (2.06)	28.2 (2.29)	24.6 (0.81)	23.8 (1.16)	23.0 (1.22)	18.5 (1.41)	21.6 (1.04)	24.4 (1.27)	27.6 (1.50)
Asian[3]	— (†)	— (†)	— (†)	13.5 (2.04)	10.9 (2.12)	9.5 (2.21)	6.7 (1.64)	9.4 (1.63)	7.5 (1.40)	13.6 (3.75)	16.4 (2.99)
Pacific Islander[3]	— (†)	— (†)	— (†)	33.8 (4.11)	21.9 (4.07)	28.1 (6.47)	12.4 ! (3.87)	28.7 (6.14)	24.8 (5.50)	31.1 (7.08)	23.4 ! (7.35)
American Indian/Alaska Native	17.4 (4.77)	28.0 (5.72)	44.2 (4.31)	36.2 (6.55)	36.4 (5.48)	32.8 (5.29)	30.3 (4.36)	27.4 (3.50)	31.6 (5.26)	47.4 (3.20)	35.5 (6.37)
Two or more races[3]	— (†)	— (†)	— (†)	29.1 (4.00)	31.8 (3.22)	28.3 (5.57)	16.9 (2.43)	20.5 (2.73)	21.7 (2.33)	26.8 (2.10)	28.8 (2.55)
Grade											
9th	13.2 (1.10)	20.9 (1.83)	23.6 (1.95)	21.7 (1.84)	19.4 (1.25)	18.5 (1.52)	17.4 (1.16)	14.7 (1.02)	15.5 (0.97)	18.0 (1.11)	17.7 (1.13)
10th	16.5 (1.79)	25.5 (1.89)	25.0 (1.29)	27.8 (2.21)	24.8 (1.12)	22.0 (1.47)	20.2 (1.27)	19.3 (1.12)	21.1 (1.11)	21.6 (1.15)	23.5 (1.89)
11th	18.4 (1.77)	27.6 (1.35)	29.3 (1.81)	26.7 (2.47)	25.8 (1.33)	24.1 (1.56)	21.0 (1.24)	21.4 (1.49)	23.2 (1.52)	25.5 (1.44)	25.5 (1.37)
12th	22.0 (1.40)	26.2 (2.35)	26.6 (2.09)	31.5 (2.81)	26.9 (1.77)	25.8 (1.19)	22.8 (1.23)	25.1 (1.96)	24.6 (1.49)	28.0 (1.08)	27.7 (1.58)
Urbanicity[4]											
Urban	— (†)	— (†)	26.8 (1.50)	27.5 (2.32)	25.6 (1.23)	23.4 (1.65)	— (†)	— (†)	— (†)	—	— (†)
Suburban	— (†)	— (†)	27.0 (1.05)	26.1 (1.60)	22.5 (0.96)	22.8 (1.90)	— (†)	— (†)	— (†)	—	— (†)
Rural	— (†)	— (†)	21.9 (3.23)	28.0 (4.36)	26.2 (2.49)	19.9 (2.80)	— (†)	— (†)	— (†)	—	— (†)
On school property[5]											
Total	5.6 (0.65)	8.8 (0.59)	7.0 (0.52)	7.2 (0.73)	5.4 (0.37)	5.8 (0.68)	4.5 (0.32)	4.5 (0.46)	4.6 (0.35)	5.9 (0.39)	(†)
Sex											
Male	7.8 (0.83)	11.9 (0.85)	9.0 (0.68)	10.1 (1.30)	8.0 (0.54)	7.6 (0.88)	6.0 (0.44)	5.9 (0.61)	6.3 (0.54)	7.5 (0.56)	(†)
Female	3.3 (0.48)	5.5 (0.72)	4.6 (0.56)	4.4 (0.40)	2.9 (0.28)	3.7 (0.48)	3.0 (0.31)	3.0 (0.39)	2.8 (0.32)	4.1 (0.32)	(†)
Race/ethnicity[2]											
White	5.0 (0.72)	7.1 (0.62)	5.8 (0.69)	6.5 (0.84)	4.8 (0.45)	4.5 (0.66)	3.8 (0.41)	4.0 (0.63)	3.8 (0.38)	4.5 (0.42)	(†)
Black	7.3 (1.23)	12.3 (1.88)	9.1 (1.07)	7.2 (1.10)	6.1 (0.60)	6.6 (0.89)	4.9 (0.65)	5.0 (0.73)	5.6 (0.64)	6.7 (0.77)	(†)
Hispanic	7.5 (1.10)	12.9 (2.20)	10.4 (1.03)	10.7 (1.21)	7.4 (0.58)	8.2 (0.72)	7.7 (0.76)	5.4 (0.80)	6.5 (0.76)	7.7 (0.54)	(†)
Asian[3]	— (†)	— (†)	— (†)	4.3 (0.71)	4.7 ! (1.56)	4.3 ! (1.38)	‡	2.7 ! (1.06)	2.0 (0.54)	4.5 (1.34)	(†)
Pacific Islander[3]	— (†)	— (†)	16.2 ! (5.56)	11.0 (3.21)	6.4 ! (2.46)	9.1 ! (3.17)	‡	13.4 ! (5.38)	9.0 (2.40)	12.5 ! (4.94)	(†)
American Indian/Alaska Native	‡	10.1 ! (3.39)	—	‡	21.5 ! (6.55)	11.4 ! (4.42)	9.2 (1.85)	8.2 (2.30)	2.9 ! (1.25)	20.9 (4.05)	(†)
Two or more races[3]	— (†)	— (†)	—	7.8 (1.81)	5.2 (1.24)	11.4 ! (5.49)	3.6 (0.91)	3.6 ! (1.08)	5.4 (1.34)	8.1 (1.79)	(†)
Grade											
9th	4.4 (0.40)	8.7 (1.38)	8.1 (0.90)	6.6 (0.97)	5.5 (0.62)	6.6 (1.03)	5.0 (0.59)	4.0 (0.52)	4.3 (0.38)	5.4 (0.65)	(†)
10th	6.5 (0.94)	9.8 (0.87)	6.4 (0.73)	7.6 (1.14)	5.8 (0.51)	5.2 (0.70)	4.6 (0.54)	4.8 (0.60)	4.6 (0.50)	6.2 (0.63)	(†)
11th	6.5 (1.07)	8.6 (0.62)	7.9 (1.17)	7.0 (0.72)	5.1 (0.48)	5.6 (0.71)	4.1 (0.49)	4.1 (0.73)	5.0 (0.55)	6.2 (0.70)	(†)
12th	5.1 (0.78)	8.0 (1.15)	5.7 (0.61)	7.3 (1.14)	4.9 (0.71)	5.0 (0.75)	4.1 (0.45)	5.1 (0.73)	4.6 (0.49)	5.4 (0.39)	(†)
Urbanicity[4]											
Urban	— (†)	— (†)	8.0 (1.11)	8.5 (1.03)	6.8 (0.56)	6.8 (1.05)	— (†)	— (†)	— (†)	—	— (†)
Suburban	— (†)	— (†)	7.0 (0.67)	6.4 (1.03)	4.7 (0.46)	6.0 (1.03)	— (†)	— (†)	— (†)	—	— (†)
Rural	— (†)	— (†)	4.9 ! (2.02)	8.1 (1.57)	5.3 (0.93)	3.9 (0.64)	— (†)	— (†)	— (†)	—	— (†)

—Not available.
†Not applicable.
!Interpret data with caution. The coefficient of variation (CV) for this estimate is between 30 and 50 percent.
‡Reporting standards not met. The coefficient of variation (CV) for this estimate is 50 percent or greater.
[1]The term "anywhere" is not used in the Youth Risk Behavior Survey (YRBS) questionnaire; students were simply asked how many times during the previous 30 days they had used marijuana.
[2]Race categories exclude persons of Hispanic ethnicity.
[3]Before 1999, Asian students and Pacific Islander students were not classified as Two or more races. Because the response categories changed in 1999, caution should be used in comparing data on race from 1993, 1995, and 1997 with data from later years.
[4]Refers to the Standard Metropolitan Statistical Area (MSA) status of the respondent's household as defined in 2000 by the U.S. Census Bureau. Categories include "central city of an MSA (Urban)," "in MSA but not in central city (Suburban)," and "not MSA (Rural)."
[5]In the question about using marijuana at school, "on school property" was not defined for survey respondents. Data on marijuana use at school were not collected in 2013.
SOURCE: Centers for Disease Control and Prevention, Division of Adolescent and School Health, Youth Risk Behavior Surveillance System (YRBSS), 1993 through 2013. (This table was prepared June 2014.)

Table 232.50. Percentage distribution of students in grades 9–12, by number of times they reported using marijuana anywhere or on school property during the previous 30 days and selected student characteristics: Selected years, 2009 through 2013

[Standard errors appear in parentheses]

Year and student characteristic	Anywhere (including on school property)[1]								On school property[2]							
	0 times		1 or 2 times		3 to 39 times		40 or more times		0 times		1 or 2 times		3 to 39 times		40 or more times	
1	2		3		4		5		6		7		8		9	
2009																
Total	79.2	(0.70)	7.2	(0.30)	9.7	(0.37)	3.8	(0.27)	95.4	(0.35)	2.1	(0.16)	1.8	(0.18)	0.7	(0.10)
Sex																
Male	76.6	(0.80)	6.8	(0.38)	10.8	(0.48)	5.8	(0.46)	93.7	(0.54)	2.6	(0.24)	2.6	(0.27)	1.1	(0.18)
Female	82.1	(0.87)	7.7	(0.39)	8.5	(0.56)	1.7	(0.20)	97.2	(0.32)	1.7	(0.19)	1.0	(0.21)	0.2	(0.06)
Race/ethnicity[3]																
White	79.3	(0.93)	7.4	(0.43)	9.6	(0.49)	3.7	(0.38)	96.2	(0.38)	1.9	(0.21)	1.4	(0.18)	0.5	(0.10)
Black	77.8	(1.44)	6.7	(0.62)	10.9	(0.90)	4.6	(0.68)	94.4	(0.64)	2.2	(0.31)	2.8	(0.44)	0.6 !	(0.24)
Hispanic	78.4	(1.04)	8.2	(0.57)	9.8	(0.71)	3.6	(0.37)	93.5	(0.76)	3.2	(0.43)	2.3	(0.39)	1.0	(0.22)
Asian	92.5	(1.40)	3.0	(0.69)	3.3	(0.85)	1.2 !	(0.55)	98.0	(0.54)	‡	(†)	1.1 !	(0.50)	‡	(†)
Pacific Islander	75.2	(5.50)	5.0 !	(1.61)	13.0	(2.95)	6.8 !	(2.56)	91.0	(2.40)	4.4 !	(1.59)	3.7 !	(1.58)	‡	(†)
American Indian/Alaska Native	68.4	(5.26)	6.7 !	(2.47)	19.6	(3.43)	5.3 !	(2.11)	97.1	(1.25)	‡	(†)	‡	(†)	#	(†)
Two or more races	78.3	(2.33)	7.8	(1.40)	9.8	(1.51)	4.1 !	(1.27)	94.6	(1.34)	1.4 !	(0.51)	2.2 !	(0.90)	1.8 !	(0.66)
Grade																
9th	84.5	(0.97)	5.8	(0.55)	7.6	(0.55)	2.1	(0.29)	95.7	(0.38)	2.3	(0.22)	1.4	(0.21)	0.6	(0.15)
10th	78.9	(1.11)	7.9	(0.59)	9.6	(0.64)	3.6	(0.44)	95.4	(0.50)	1.9	(0.28)	2.1	(0.35)	0.6	(0.12)
11th	76.8	(1.52)	7.9	(0.66)	11.2	(0.89)	4.1	(0.42)	95.0	(0.55)	2.5	(0.37)	2.0	(0.31)	0.5	(0.12)
12th	75.4	(1.49)	7.7	(0.60)	10.9	(0.86)	6.0	(0.64)	95.4	(0.49)	1.9	(0.30)	1.9	(0.27)	0.8	(0.23)
2011																
Total	76.9	(0.80)	7.4	(0.30)	10.9	(0.42)	4.8	(0.30)	94.1	(0.39)	2.8	(0.22)	2.3	(0.21)	0.7	(0.09)
Sex																
Male	74.1	(1.01)	7.1	(0.40)	11.8	(0.57)	7.0	(0.47)	92.5	(0.56)	3.1	(0.28)	3.2	(0.31)	1.2	(0.17)
Female	79.9	(0.95)	7.7	(0.48)	9.9	(0.56)	2.4	(0.26)	95.9	(0.32)	2.5	(0.21)	1.4	(0.19)	0.2	(0.04)
Race/ethnicity[3]																
White	78.3	(1.09)	6.9	(0.42)	10.2	(0.59)	4.6	(0.44)	95.5	(0.42)	2.2	(0.26)	1.9	(0.23)	0.4	(0.09)
Black	74.9	(1.35)	7.9	(0.69)	12.5	(0.81)	4.7	(0.63)	93.3	(0.77)	3.2	(0.43)	2.8	(0.52)	0.7	(0.18)
Hispanic	75.6	(1.27)	8.3	(0.59)	11.5	(0.67)	4.7	(0.46)	92.3	(0.54)	3.6	(0.26)	3.1	(0.40)	1.0	(0.21)
Asian	86.4	(3.75)	‡	(†)	5.5	(0.96)	3.2 !	(1.34)	95.5	(1.34)	2.4 !	(1.15)	‡	(†)	1.5 !	(0.70)
Pacific Islander	68.9	(7.08)	11.3	(3.34)	13.2 !	(5.20)	6.6 !	(2.27)	87.5	(4.94)	5.6 !	(2.24)	‡	(†)	‡	(†)
American Indian/Alaska Native	52.6	(3.20)	10.5	(2.82)	23.6	(2.57)	13.2	(1.81)	79.1	(4.05)	8.6	(2.18)	9.8	(1.79)	2.5	(0.67)
Two or more races	73.2	(2.10)	7.2	(1.20)	12.9	(1.44)	6.7	(1.33)	91.9	(1.79)	3.7	(0.98)	2.4 !	(0.86)	2.0 !	(0.69)
Grade																
9th	82.0	(1.11)	6.2	(0.47)	8.2	(0.63)	3.6	(0.42)	94.6	(0.65)	2.7	(0.41)	2.2	(0.33)	0.5	(0.11)
10th	78.4	(1.15)	7.4	(0.60)	10.0	(0.65)	4.3	(0.50)	93.8	(0.63)	3.2	(0.38)	2.3	(0.40)	0.7	(0.16)
11th	74.5	(1.44)	8.0	(0.59)	12.9	(0.82)	4.5	(0.50)	93.8	(0.70)	3.2	(0.47)	2.3	(0.35)	0.7	(0.16)
12th	72.0	(1.08)	8.3	(0.59)	13.0	(0.69)	6.7	(0.53)	94.6	(0.39)	2.2	(0.30)	2.4	(0.30)	0.8	(0.18)
2013[4]																
Total	76.6	(1.08)	7.1	(0.42)	11.3	(0.68)	5.0	(0.39)	—	(†)	—	(†)	—	(†)	—	(†)
Sex																
Male	75.0	(1.14)	6.5	(0.42)	12.0	(0.72)	6.5	(0.53)	—	(†)	—	(†)	—	(†)	—	(†)
Female	78.1	(1.28)	7.8	(0.59)	10.7	(0.77)	3.4	(0.36)	—	(†)	—	(†)	—	(†)	—	(†)
Race/ethnicity[3]																
White	79.6	(1.36)	6.3	(0.63)	9.7	(0.75)	4.4	(0.42)	—	(†)	—	(†)	—	(†)	—	(†)
Black	71.1	(1.30)	8.2	(0.52)	14.3	(0.90)	6.3	(0.71)	—	(†)	—	(†)	—	(†)	—	(†)
Hispanic	72.4	(1.50)	8.6	(0.52)	13.4	(1.22)	5.6	(0.70)	—	(†)	—	(†)	—	(†)	—	(†)
Asian	83.6	(2.99)	4.1	(1.02)	7.6	(1.32)	4.7 !	(2.03)	—	(†)	—	(†)	—	(†)	—	(†)
Pacific Islander	76.6	(7.35)	4.9 !	(2.31)	17.1 !	(5.82)	‡	(†)	—	(†)	—	(†)	—	(†)	—	(†)
American Indian/Alaska Native	64.5	(6.37)	8.8 !	(2.70)	18.9	(4.54)	7.9 !	(2.77)	—	(†)	—	(†)	—	(†)	—	(†)
Two or more races	71.2	(2.55)	9.7	(1.36)	12.4	(1.45)	6.7	(1.29)	—	(†)	—	(†)	—	(†)	—	(†)
Grade																
9th	82.3	(1.13)	6.3	(0.59)	8.6	(0.70)	2.8	(0.38)	—	(†)	—	(†)	—	(†)	—	(†)
10th	76.5	(1.89)	7.2	(0.65)	11.3	(1.35)	5.0	(0.81)	—	(†)	—	(†)	—	(†)	—	(†)
11th	74.5	(1.37)	7.6	(0.68)	12.0	(0.85)	6.0	(0.56)	—	(†)	—	(†)	—	(†)	—	(†)
12th	72.3	(1.58)	7.6	(0.68)	13.8	(1.00)	6.4	(0.63)	—	(†)	—	(†)	—	(†)	—	(†)

—Not available.
†Not applicable.
#Rounds to zero.
!Interpret data with caution. The coefficient of variation (CV) for this estimate is between 30 and 50 percent.
‡Reporting standards not met. Either there are too few cases for a reliable estimate or the coefficient of variation (CV) is 50 percent or greater.
[1]The term "anywhere" is not used in the Youth Risk Behavior Survey (YRBS) questionnaire; students were simply asked how many times during the previous 30 days they had used marijuana.

[2]In the question about using marijuana at school, "on school property" was not defined for survey respondents.
[3]Race categories exclude persons of Hispanic ethnicity.
[4]Data on marijuana use at school were not collected in 2013.
NOTE: Detail may not sum to totals because of rounding.
SOURCE: Centers for Disease Control and Prevention, Division of Adolescent and School Health, Youth Risk Behavior Surveillance System (YRBSS), 2009 through 2013. (This table was prepared September 2014.)

Table 232.60. Percentage of public school students in grades 9–12 who reported using marijuana at least one time during the previous 30 days, by location and state: Selected years, 2003 through 2013

[Standard errors appear in parentheses]

State	Anywhere (including on school property)[1]						On school property[2]					
	2003	2005	2007	2009	2011	2013	2003	2005	2007	2009	2011	2013
1	2	3	4	5	6	7	8	9	10	11	12	13
United States[3]	22.4 (1.09)	20.2 (0.84)	19.7 (0.97)	20.8 (0.70)	23.1 (0.80)	23.4 (1.08)	5.8 (0.68)	4.5 (0.32)	4.5 (0.46)	4.6 (0.35)	5.9 (0.39)	— (†)
Alabama	17.7 (1.38)	18.5 (1.49)	— (†)	16.2 (1.28)	20.8 (1.62)	19.2 (1.46)	2.6 (0.54)	3.5 (0.80)	— (†)	4.6 (0.81)	4.0 (0.68)	— (†)
Alaska	23.9 (1.29)	— (†)	20.5 (1.47)	22.7 (1.65)	21.2 (1.68)	19.7 (1.35)	6.5 (0.80)	— (†)	5.9 (0.70)	5.9 (0.69)	4.3 (0.59)	— (†)
Arizona	25.6 (1.08)	20.0 (1.08)	22.0 (1.38)	23.7 (1.90)	22.9 (1.59)	23.5 (1.75)	6.5 (0.52)	5.1 (0.63)	6.1 (0.68)	6.4 (0.74)	5.6 (0.75)	— (†)
Arkansas	— (†)	18.9 (1.70)	16.4 (1.08)	17.8 (1.24)	16.8 (1.72)	19.0 (0.98)	— (†)	4.1 (0.61)	2.8 (0.50)	4.5 (1.02)	3.9 (0.78)	— (†)
California	— (†)	— (†)	— (†)	— (†)	— (†)	— (†)	— (†)	— (†)	— (†)	— (†)	— (†)	— (†)
Colorado	— (†)	22.7 (2.99)	— (†)	24.8 (2.22)	22.0 (1.16)	— (†)	— (†)	6.0 (0.88)	— (†)	6.1 (0.89)	6.0 (0.77)	— (†)
Connecticut	— (†)	23.1 (1.37)	23.2 (1.35)	21.8 (1.52)	24.2 (1.44)	26.1 (1.44)	— (†)	5.1 (0.49)	5.9 (0.77)	6.2 (0.76)	5.2 (0.68)	— (†)
Delaware	27.3 (1.13)	22.8 (1.12)	25.1 (1.03)	25.8 (1.30)	27.6 (1.37)	25.6 (1.17)	6.0 (0.54)	5.6 (0.57)	5.4 (0.53)	5.6 (0.71)	6.1 (0.65)	— (†)
District of Columbia	23.5 (1.23)	14.5 (1.08)	20.8 (1.33)	— (†)	26.1 (1.29)	— (†)	7.5 (0.88)	4.8 (0.62)	5.8 (0.66)	— (†)	7.9 (0.91)	— (†)
Florida	21.4 (0.89)	16.8 (0.86)	18.9 (0.88)	21.4 (0.72)	22.5 (0.86)	22.0 (0.81)	4.9 (0.41)	4.0 (0.31)	4.7 (0.40)	5.2 (0.39)	6.3 (0.39)	— (†)
Georgia	19.5 (0.94)	18.9 (1.59)	19.6 (0.96)	18.3 (1.02)	21.2 (1.23)	20.3 (1.64)	3.2 (0.45)	3.3 (0.58)	3.6 (0.58)	3.4 (0.62)	5.6 (0.70)	— (†)
Hawaii	— (†)	17.2 (1.73)	15.7 (1.78)	22.1 (2.03)	22.0 (1.32)	18.9 (1.54)	— (†)	7.2 (1.14)	5.7 (0.85)	8.3 (1.86)	7.6 (0.67)	— (†)
Idaho	14.7 (1.56)	17.1 (1.32)	17.9 (1.73)	13.7 (1.07)	18.8 (1.76)	15.3 (1.10)	2.7 (0.55)	3.9 (0.61)	4.7 (0.80)	3.0 (0.44)	4.9 (0.73)	— (†)
Illinois	— (†)	— (†)	20.3 (1.38)	21.0 (1.53)	23.1 (1.59)	24.0 (1.70)	— (†)	— (†)	4.2 (0.76)	5.0 (0.77)	4.7 (0.50)	— (†)
Indiana	22.1 (1.19)	18.9 (1.38)	18.9 (1.19)	20.9 (1.83)	20.0 (1.13)	— (†)	3.8 (0.67)	3.4 (0.57)	4.1 (0.45)	4.4 (0.62)	3.3 (0.66)	— (†)
Iowa	— (†)	15.6 (1.74)	11.5 (1.53)	— (†)	14.6 (1.99)	— (†)	— (†)	2.7 (0.64)	2.5 (0.66)	— (†)	3.4 (0.88)	— (†)
Kansas	— (†)	15.6 (1.46)	15.3 (0.93)	14.7 (1.19)	16.8 (0.87)	14.3 (1.19)	— (†)	3.2 (0.51)	3.8 (0.53)	2.7 (0.35)	2.9 (0.53)	— (†)
Kentucky	21.1 (1.09)	15.8 (1.19)	16.4 (1.07)	16.1 (1.15)	19.2 (1.47)	17.7 (1.50)	4.3 (0.55)	3.2 (0.45)	3.9 (0.44)	3.1 (0.54)	4.2 (0.65)	— (†)
Louisiana	— (†)	— (†)	— (†)	16.3 (1.29)	16.8 (1.02)	17.5 (1.38)	— (†)	— (†)	— (†)	3.6 (0.89)	4.1 (0.59)	— (†)
Maine	26.4 (1.69)	22.2 (2.13)	22.0 (1.55)	20.5 (0.57)	21.2 (0.72)	21.3 (0.89)	6.3 (0.76)	4.6 (0.72)	5.2 (0.65)	— (†)	— (†)	— (†)
Maryland	— (†)	18.5 (2.25)	19.4 (1.91)	21.9 (1.57)	23.2 (1.51)	19.8 (0.36)	— (†)	3.7 (0.82)	4.7 (1.13)	5.0 (0.65)	5.7 (0.70)	— (†)
Massachusetts	27.7 (1.39)	26.2 (1.22)	24.6 (1.43)	27.1 (1.24)	27.9 (1.31)	24.8 (0.92)	6.3 (0.44)	5.3 (0.54)	4.8 (0.44)	5.9 (0.79)	6.3 (0.51)	— (†)
Michigan	24.0 (1.96)	18.8 (1.29)	18.0 (1.10)	20.7 (0.91)	18.6 (1.15)	18.2 (0.73)	7.0 (1.20)	3.7 (0.50)	4.0 (0.57)	4.8 (0.59)	3.3 (0.44)	— (†)
Minnesota	— (†)	— (†)	— (†)	— (†)	— (†)	— (†)	— (†)	— (†)	— (†)	— (†)	— (†)	— (†)
Mississippi	20.6 (1.57)	— (†)	16.7 (1.02)	17.7 (1.21)	17.5 (1.18)	17.7 (1.28)	4.4 (0.90)	— (†)	2.7 (0.35)	2.5 (0.46)	3.2 (0.58)	— (†)
Missouri	21.8 (1.37)	18.1 (2.23)	19.0 (1.23)	20.6 (2.02)	— (†)	20.5 (1.69)	3.0 (0.58)	4.0 (0.82)	3.6 (0.63)	3.4 (0.48)	— (†)	— (†)
Montana	23.1 (1.45)	22.3 (1.43)	21.0 (1.44)	23.1 (1.58)	21.2 (1.50)	21.0 (1.18)	6.4 (0.70)	6.1 (0.70)	5.0 (0.49)	5.8 (0.67)	5.5 (0.59)	— (†)
Nebraska	18.3 (1.23)	17.5 (1.05)	— (†)	— (†)	12.7 (1.06)	11.7 (1.10)	3.9 (0.51)	3.1 (0.41)	— (†)	— (†)	2.7 (0.43)	— (†)
Nevada	22.3 (1.31)	17.3 (1.34)	15.5 (1.07)	20.0 (1.36)	— (†)	18.7 (1.57)	5.3 (0.69)	5.7 (0.81)	3.6 (0.55)	4.9 (0.53)	— (†)	— (†)
New Hampshire	30.6 (2.51)	25.9 (1.69)	22.9 (1.39)	25.6 (1.86)	28.4 (1.82)	24.4 (1.36)	6.6 (0.86)	— (†)	4.7 (0.64)	6.8 (0.78)	7.3 (0.87)	— (†)
New Jersey	— (†)	19.9 (2.18)	— (†)	20.3 (1.53)	21.1 (1.33)	21.0 (1.20)	— (†)	3.4 (0.67)	— (†)	— (†)	— (†)	— (†)
New Mexico	— (†)	26.2 (2.00)	25.0 (2.07)	28.0 (1.52)	27.6 (1.58)	27.8 (1.70)	— (†)	8.4 (0.98)	7.9 (0.86)	9.7 (1.06)	9.7 (0.84)	— (†)
New York	20.7 (1.05)	18.3 (1.13)	18.6 (0.78)	20.9 (1.32)	20.6 (1.07)	21.4 (1.04)	4.5 (0.41)	3.6 (0.41)	4.1 (0.44)	— (†)	— (†)	— (†)
North Carolina	24.3 (1.99)	21.4 (1.61)	19.1 (1.27)	19.8 (1.67)	24.2 (1.25)	23.2 (1.83)	3.5 (0.71)	4.1 (0.65)	4.3 (0.54)	4.0 (0.63)	5.2 (0.91)	— (†)
North Dakota	20.6 (1.58)	15.5 (1.62)	14.8 (1.18)	16.9 (1.55)	15.3 (1.52)	15.9 (1.26)	6.3 (0.98)	4.0 (0.71)	2.7 (0.43)	3.8 (0.59)	3.4 (0.45)	— (†)
Ohio[4]	21.4 (2.33)	20.9 (1.79)	17.7 (1.50)	— (†)	23.6 (1.95)	20.7 (2.30)	4.2 (0.96)	4.3 (0.62)	3.7 (0.67)	— (†)	— (†)	— (†)
Oklahoma	22.0 (2.20)	18.7 (1.12)	15.9 (1.37)	17.2 (2.04)	19.1 (1.90)	16.3 (1.57)	4.3 (0.70)	3.0 (0.38)	2.6 (0.40)	2.9 (0.70)	2.4 (0.58)	— (†)
Oregon	— (†)	— (†)	— (†)	— (†)	— (†)	— (†)	— (†)	— (†)	— (†)	— (†)	— (†)	— (†)
Pennsylvania	— (†)	— (†)	— (†)	19.3 (1.43)	— (†)	— (†)	— (†)	— (†)	— (†)	3.5 (0.58)	— (†)	— (†)
Rhode Island	27.6 (1.11)	25.0 (1.16)	23.2 (1.85)	26.3 (1.33)	26.3 (1.35)	23.9 (1.92)	7.4 (0.70)	7.2 (0.65)	6.5 (0.93)	5.1 (0.60)	— (†)	— (†)
South Carolina	— (†)	19.0 (1.24)	18.6 (1.44)	20.4 (1.56)	24.1 (1.99)	19.7 (1.22)	— (†)	4.6 (0.64)	3.3 (0.52)	3.7 (0.63)	5.2 (0.75)	— (†)
South Dakota[4]	21.5 (3.35)	16.8 (1.87)	17.7 (3.72)	15.2 (1.36)	17.8 (3.57)	16.1 (3.01)	4.5 ! (1.50)	2.9 (0.73)	5.0 ! (2.41)	2.9 (0.49)	— (†)	— (†)
Tennessee	23.6 (2.10)	19.5 (1.38)	19.4 (1.29)	20.1 (1.31)	20.6 (0.96)	21.4 (1.70)	4.1 (0.86)	3.5 (0.67)	4.1 (0.60)	3.8 (0.65)	3.6 (0.40)	— (†)
Texas	— (†)	21.7 (0.99)	19.3 (1.01)	19.5 (0.71)	20.8 (1.30)	20.5 (1.26)	— (†)	3.8 (0.52)	3.6 (0.30)	4.6 (0.51)	4.8 (0.47)	— (†)
Utah	11.4 (1.28)	7.6 (1.18)	8.7 (2.00)	10.0 (1.53)	9.6 (1.26)	7.6 (0.79)	3.7 (0.59)	1.7 (0.42)	3.8 ! (1.24)	2.5 (0.48)	4.0 (0.72)	— (†)
Vermont	28.2 (1.58)	25.3 (1.59)	24.1 (0.88)	24.6 (1.14)	24.4 (1.43)	25.7 (0.83)	8.0 (0.44)	7.0 (0.80)	6.3 (0.63)	6.3 (0.57)	6.0 (0.84)	— (†)
Virginia	— (†)	— (†)	— (†)	— (†)	18.0 (1.79)	17.9 (0.85)	— (†)	— (†)	— (†)	— (†)	3.5 (0.70)	— (†)
Washington	— (†)	— (†)	— (†)	— (†)	— (†)	— (†)	— (†)	— (†)	— (†)	— (†)	— (†)	— (†)
West Virginia	23.1 (2.13)	19.6 (1.70)	23.5 (1.05)	20.3 (1.73)	19.7 (1.61)	18.9 (1.39)	4.5 (0.72)	4.9 (0.85)	5.8 (0.97)	3.9 (0.37)	3.0 (0.45)	— (†)
Wisconsin	21.8 (1.18)	15.9 (1.07)	20.3 (1.30)	18.9 (1.64)	21.6 (1.78)	17.3 (1.12)	— (†)	— (†)	— (†)	— (†)	— (†)	— (†)
Wyoming	20.4 (1.56)	17.8 (1.05)	14.4 (0.79)	16.9 (0.91)	18.5 (1.23)	17.8 (0.81)	5.1 (0.66)	4.0 (0.43)	4.7 (0.52)	5.3 (0.45)	4.7 (0.44)	— (†)

—Not available.
†Not applicable.
!Interpret data with caution. The coefficient of variation (CV) for this estimate is between 30 and 50 percent.
[1]The term "anywhere" is not used in the Youth Risk Behavior Survey (YRBS) questionnaire; students were simply asked how many times during the previous 30 days they had used marijuana.
[2]In the question about using marijuana at school, "on school property" was not defined for survey respondents. Data on marijuana use at school were not collected in 2013.
[3]Data for the U.S. total include both public and private schools and were collected through a national survey representing the entire country.

[4]Data include both public and private schools.
NOTE: State-level data include public schools only, with the exception of data for Ohio and South Dakota. Data for the U.S. total, Ohio, and South Dakota include both public and private schools. For specific states, a given year's data may be unavailable (1) because the state did not participate in the survey that year; (2) because the state omitted this particular survey item from the state-level questionnaire; or (3) because the state had an overall response rate of less than 60 percent (the overall response rate is the school response rate multiplied by the student response rate).
SOURCE: Centers for Disease Control and Prevention, Division of Adolescent and School Health, Youth Risk Behavior Surveillance System (YRBSS), 2003 through 2013. (This table was prepared June 2014.)

Table 232.70. Percentage of students in grades 9–12 who reported that illegal drugs were made available to them on school property during the previous 12 months, by selected student characteristics: Selected years, 1993 through 2013

[Standard errors appear in parentheses]

Student characteristic	1993		1995		1997		1999		2001		2003		2005		2007		2009		2011		2013	
1	2		3		4		5		6		7		8		9		10		11		12	
Total	24.0	(1.33)	32.1	(1.55)	31.7	(0.90)	30.2	(1.23)	28.5	(1.01)	28.7	(1.95)	25.4	(1.05)	22.3	(1.04)	22.7	(1.04)	25.6	(0.99)	22.1	(0.96)
Sex																						
Male	28.5	(1.50)	38.8	(1.73)	37.4	(1.19)	34.7	(1.69)	34.6	(1.20)	31.9	(2.07)	28.8	(1.23)	25.7	(1.15)	25.9	(1.36)	29.2	(1.10)	24.5	(1.21)
Female	19.1	(1.31)	24.8	(1.43)	24.7	(1.22)	25.7	(1.26)	22.7	(1.03)	25.0	(1.92)	21.8	(1.03)	18.7	(1.16)	19.3	(1.01)	21.7	(1.17)	19.7	(0.89)
Race/ethnicity[1]																						
White	24.1	(1.69)	31.7	(2.24)	31.0	(1.36)	28.8	(1.50)	28.3	(1.31)	27.5	(2.68)	23.6	(1.32)	20.8	(1.23)	19.8	(1.13)	22.7	(0.96)	20.4	(1.11)
Black	17.5	(1.49)	28.5	(1.98)	25.4	(1.69)	25.3	(2.03)	21.9	(1.72)	23.1	(1.42)	23.9	(2.22)	19.2	(1.36)	22.2	(1.42)	22.8	(1.82)	18.6	(1.11)
Hispanic	34.1	(1.58)	40.7	(2.45)	41.1	(2.04)	36.9	(2.10)	34.2	(1.17)	36.5	(1.91)	33.5	(1.18)	29.1	(1.94)	31.2	(1.53)	33.2	(1.70)	27.4	(1.42)
Asian[2]	—	(†)	—	(†)	—	(†)	25.7	(2.65)	25.7	(2.92)	22.5	(3.71)	15.9	(2.68)	21.0	(2.78)	18.3	(2.03)	23.3	(2.46)	22.6	(2.57)
Pacific Islander[2]	—	(†)	—	(†)	—	(†)	46.9	(4.33)	50.2	(5.73)	34.7	(6.19)	41.3	(5.75)	38.5	(5.45)	27.6	(5.10)	38.9	(5.01)	27.7	(3.68)
American Indian/Alaska Native[2]	20.9	(4.55)	22.8	(4.78)	30.1	(4.54)	30.6	(5.90)	34.5	(5.15)	31.3	(5.64)	24.4	(3.57)	25.1	(2.04)	34.0	(4.81)	40.5	(2.80)	25.5	(4.10)
Two or more races[2]	—	(†)	—	(†)	—	(†)	36.0	(2.72)	34.5	(3.22)	36.6	(3.99)	31.6	(3.13)	24.6	(3.55)	26.9	(2.62)	33.3	(2.79)	26.4	(2.67)
Grade																						
9th	21.8	(1.24)	31.1	(1.69)	31.4	(2.33)	27.6	(2.51)	29.0	(1.59)	29.5	(2.39)	24.0	(1.21)	21.2	(1.23)	22.0	(1.32)	23.7	(1.22)	22.4	(1.15)
10th	23.7	(1.86)	35.0	(1.54)	33.4	(1.71)	32.1	(1.94)	29.0	(1.39)	29.2	(2.02)	27.5	(1.68)	25.3	(1.29)	23.7	(1.11)	27.8	(1.21)	23.2	(1.54)
11th	27.5	(1.61)	32.8	(1.88)	33.2	(1.42)	31.1	(2.16)	28.7	(1.39)	29.9	(2.33)	24.9	(1.03)	22.8	(1.42)	24.3	(1.44)	27.0	(1.51)	23.2	(1.32)
12th	23.0	(1.82)	29.1	(2.63)	29.0	(1.80)	30.5	(1.11)	26.9	(1.30)	24.9	(2.24)	24.9	(1.40)	19.6	(1.26)	20.6	(1.21)	23.8	(1.13)	18.8	(1.11)
Urbanicity[3]																						
Urban	—		—		31.2	(1.11)	30.3	(1.50)	32.0	(1.36)	31.1	(2.12)	—	(†)	—	(†)	—	(†)	—	(†)	—	(†)
Suburban	—		—		34.2	(0.94)	29.7	(1.87)	26.6	(1.34)	28.4	(2.16)	—	(†)	—	(†)	—	(†)	—	(†)	—	(†)
Rural	—		—		22.7	(1.91)	32.1	(5.76)	28.2	(3.10)	26.2	(5.08)	—	(†)	—	(†)	—	(†)	—	(†)	—	(†)

—Not available.
†Not applicable.
[1]Race categories exclude persons of Hispanic ethnicity.
[2]Before 1999, Asian students and Pacific Islander students were not categorized separately, and students were not given the option of choosing Two or more races. Because the response categories changed in 1999, caution should be used in comparing data on race from 1993, 1995, and 1997 with data from later years.
[3]Refers to the Standard Metropolitan Statistical Area (MSA) status of the respondent's household as defined in 2000 by the U.S. Census Bureau. Categories include "central city of an MSA (Urban)," "in MSA but not in central city (Suburban)," and "not MSA (Rural)."
NOTE: "On school property" was not defined for survey respondents.
SOURCE: Centers for Disease Control and Prevention, Division of Adolescent and School Health, Youth Risk Behavior Surveillance System (YRBSS), 1993 through 2013. (This table was prepared June 2014.)

Table 232.80. Percentage of public school students in grades 9–12 who reported that illegal drugs were made available to them on school property during the previous 12 months, by state: Selected years, 2003 through 2013

[Standard errors appear in parentheses]

State	2003		2005		2007		2009		2011		2013	
1	2		3		4		5		6		7	
United States[1]	28.7	(1.95)	25.4	(1.05)	22.3	(1.04)	22.7	(1.04)	25.6	(0.99)	22.1	(0.96)
Alabama	26.0	(1.78)	26.2	(1.90)	—	(†)	27.6	(1.30)	20.3	(1.32)	25.3	(1.11)
Alaska	28.4	(1.24)	—	(†)	25.1	(1.36)	24.8	(1.25)	23.2	(0.98)	—	(†)
Arizona	28.6	(1.23)	38.7	(1.18)	37.1	(1.45)	34.6	(1.43)	34.6	(1.55)	31.3	(1.46)
Arkansas	—	(†)	29.2	(1.35)	28.1	(1.28)	31.4	(1.56)	26.1	(1.30)	27.4	(1.28)
California	—	(†)	—	(†)	—	(†)	—	(†)	—	(†)	—	(†)
Colorado	—	(†)	21.2	(1.81)	—	(†)	22.7	(1.52)	17.2	(1.28)	—	(†)
Connecticut	—	(†)	31.5	(0.90)	30.5	(1.52)	28.9	(1.25)	27.8	(1.43)	27.1	(0.85)
Delaware	27.9	(0.90)	26.1	(1.05)	22.9	(0.99)	20.9	(0.87)	23.1	(1.20)	19.1	(0.83)
District of Columbia	30.2	(1.46)	20.3	(1.18)	25.7	(1.20)	—	(†)	22.6	(1.53)	—	(†)
Florida	25.7	(0.81)	23.2	(0.85)	19.0	(0.80)	21.8	(0.72)	22.9	(0.84)	20.0	(0.64)
Georgia	33.3	(1.00)	30.7	(1.25)	32.0	(1.23)	32.9	(1.22)	32.1	(1.34)	26.5	(1.32)
Hawaii	—	(†)	32.7	(1.74)	36.2	(2.46)	36.1	(1.51)	31.7	(1.48)	31.2	(0.99)
Idaho	19.6	(1.26)	24.8	(1.52)	25.1	(1.63)	22.7	(1.39)	24.4	(1.56)	22.1	(1.31)
Illinois	—	(†)	—	(†)	21.2	(1.18)	27.5	(1.97)	27.3	(1.46)	27.2	(1.06)
Indiana	28.3	(1.55)	28.9	(1.33)	20.5	(1.02)	25.5	(1.24)	28.3	(1.33)	—	(†)
Iowa	—	(†)	15.5	(1.37)	10.1	(1.08)	—	(†)	11.9	(1.16)	—	(†)
Kansas	—	(†)	16.7	(1.27)	15.0	(1.24)	15.1	(0.78)	24.9	(1.19)	19.4	(1.06)
Kentucky	30.4	(1.51)	19.8	(1.23)	27.0	(1.11)	25.6	(1.49)	24.4	(1.40)	20.6	(1.15)
Louisiana	—	(†)	—	(†)	—	(†)	22.8	(1.66)	25.1	(1.82)	—	(†)
Maine	32.6	(1.73)	33.5	(1.89)	29.1	(1.67)	21.2	(0.51)	21.7	(0.80)	18.4	(0.87)
Maryland	—	(†)	28.9	(2.04)	27.4	(1.46)	29.3	(1.35)	30.4	(1.99)	29.1	(0.37)
Massachusetts	31.9	(1.08)	29.9	(1.09)	27.3	(1.06)	26.1	(1.34)	27.1	(1.04)	23.0	(0.90)
Michigan	31.3	(1.50)	28.8	(1.37)	29.1	(1.07)	29.5	(0.90)	25.4	(0.90)	23.8	(0.94)
Minnesota	—	(†)	—	(†)	—	(†)	—	(†)	—	(†)	—	(†)
Mississippi	22.3	(1.31)	—	(†)	15.6	(1.53)	18.0	(1.07)	15.9	(0.89)	12.1	(1.00)
Missouri	21.6	(2.09)	18.2	(1.92)	17.8	(1.49)	17.3	(1.32)	—	(†)	—	(†)
Montana	26.9	(1.23)	25.3	(1.09)	24.9	(0.83)	20.7	(1.10)	25.2	(0.93)	22.8	(0.71)
Nebraska	23.3	(1.04)	22.0	(0.82)	—	(†)	—	(†)	20.3	(1.01)	19.2	(1.15)
Nevada	34.5	(1.30)	32.6	(1.53)	28.8	(1.39)	35.6	(1.30)	—	(†)	31.2	(1.90)
New Hampshire	28.2	(1.87)	26.9	(1.40)	22.5	(1.25)	22.1	(1.44)	23.2	(1.44)	20.1	(1.03)
New Jersey	—	(†)	32.6	(1.32)	—	(†)	32.2	(1.38)	27.3	(1.41)	30.7	(1.70)
New Mexico	—	(†)	33.5	(1.37)	31.3	(1.39)	30.9	(1.54)	34.5	(1.24)	32.8	(1.04)
New York	23.0	(0.97)	23.7	(0.76)	26.6	(1.09)	24.0	(1.05)	—	(†)	—	(†)
North Carolina	31.9	(1.74)	27.4	(1.66)	28.5	(1.37)	30.2	(1.51)	29.8	(1.87)	23.6	(1.61)
North Dakota	21.3	(1.07)	19.6	(1.10)	18.7	(1.05)	19.5	(1.16)	20.8	(1.03)	14.1	(0.79)
Ohio[2]	31.1	(1.68)	30.9	(1.88)	26.7	(1.26)	—	(†)	24.3	(1.70)	19.9	(1.41)
Oklahoma	22.2	(1.23)	18.4	(1.49)	19.1	(1.12)	16.8	(1.50)	17.2	(1.36)	14.0	(1.07)
Oregon	—	(†)	—	(†)	—	(†)	—	(†)	—	(†)	—	(†)
Pennsylvania	—	(†)	—	(†)	—	(†)	16.1	(1.07)	—	(†)	—	(†)
Rhode Island	26.0	(1.26)	24.1	(1.11)	25.3	(1.33)	25.2	(1.52)	22.4	(0.95)	22.6	(1.16)
South Carolina	—	(†)	29.1	(1.45)	26.6	(1.58)	27.6	(1.74)	29.3	(1.83)	24.5	(1.43)
South Dakota[2]	22.1	(1.25)	20.9	(2.30)	21.1	(1.98)	17.7	(0.64)	16.0	(1.81)	15.4	(1.70)
Tennessee	24.3	(2.25)	26.6	(1.21)	21.6	(1.35)	18.8	(1.06)	16.6	(0.88)	24.8	(1.57)
Texas	—	(†)	30.7	(1.73)	26.5	(0.83)	25.9	(1.25)	29.4	(1.34)	26.4	(1.24)
Utah	24.7	(2.04)	20.6	(1.36)	23.2	(1.83)	19.7	(1.52)	21.4	(1.55)	20.0	(1.57)
Vermont	29.4	(1.67)	23.1	(1.59)	22.0	(0.99)	21.1	(1.21)	17.6	(1.51)	—	(†)
Virginia	—	(†)	—	(†)	—	(†)	—	(†)	24.0	(1.67)	—	(†)
Washington	—	(†)	—	(†)	—	(†)	—	(†)	—	(†)	—	(†)
West Virginia	26.5	(2.06)	24.8	(1.36)	28.6	(2.76)	28.0	(1.27)	17.3	(1.04)	17.1	(1.16)
Wisconsin	26.3	(1.18)	21.7	(1.18)	22.7	(1.34)	20.5	(1.03)	20.9	(1.29)	18.3	(1.01)
Wyoming	18.1	(0.99)	22.7	(0.97)	24.7	(1.08)	23.7	(0.93)	25.2	(0.97)	20.2	(0.74)

— Not available.
†Not applicable.
[1]Data for the U.S. total include both public and private schools and were collected through a national survey representing the entire country.
[2]Data include both public and private schools.
NOTE: "On school property" was not defined for survey respondents. State-level data include public schools only, with the exception of data for Ohio and South Dakota. Data for the U.S. total, Ohio, and South Dakota include both public and private schools. For specific states, a given year's data may be unavailable (1) because the state did not participate in the survey that year; (2) because the state omitted this particular survey item from the state-level questionnaire; or (3) because the state had an overall response rate of less than 60 percent (the overall response rate is the school response rate multiplied by the student response rate).
SOURCE: Centers for Disease Control and Prevention, Division of Adolescent and School Health, Youth Risk Behavior Surveillance System (YRBSS), 2003 through 2013. (This table was prepared June 2014.)

Table 232.90. Percentage of high school seniors reporting use of alcohol and illicit drugs, by frequency of use and substance used: Selected years, 1975 through 2015

[Standard errors appear in parentheses]

Frequency of use and substance used	1975	1980	1985	1990	1995	2000	2005	2009	2010	2011	2012	2013	2014	2015
1	2	3	4	5	6	7	8	9	10	11	12	13	14	15
Ever used														
Alcohol[1]	90.4 (0.69)	93.2 (0.46)	92.2 (0.48)	89.5 (0.57)	80.7 (0.73)	80.3 (0.80)	75.1 (0.81)	72.3 (0.85)	71.0 (0.84)	70.0 (0.88)	69.4 (0.90)	68.2 (0.95)	66.0 (0.95)	64.0 (0.94)
Any illicit drug	55.2 (1.68)	65.4 (1.23)	60.6 (1.26)	47.9 (1.33)	48.4 (1.32)	54.0 (1.44)	50.4 (1.35)	46.7 (1.36)	48.2 (1.33)	49.9 (1.38)	49.1 (1.40)	49.8 (1.46)	49.1 (1.43)	48.9 (1.40)
Marijuana only	19.0 (1.32)	26.7 (1.15)	20.9 (1.05)	18.5 (1.03)	20.3 (1.06)	25.0 (1.25)	23.0 (1.14)	22.7 (1.15)	23.5 (1.13)	25.0 (1.19)	25.0 (1.21)	25.0 (1.26)	26.5 (1.27)	27.8 (1.25)
Any illicit drug other than marijuana[2]	36.2 (1.33)	38.7 (1.04)	39.7 (1.04)	29.4 (0.99)	28.1 (0.97)	29.0 (1.08)	27.4 (0.99)	24.0 (0.96)	24.7 (0.94)	24.9 (0.98)	24.1 (0.98)	24.8 (1.03)	22.6 (0.98)	21.1 (0.94)
Selected drugs														
Cocaine	9.0 (0.73)	15.7 (0.72)	17.3 (0.74)	9.4 (0.59)	6.0 (0.48)	8.6 (0.62)	8.0 (0.56)	6.0 (0.49)	5.5 (0.46)	5.2 (0.47)	4.9 (0.46)	4.5 (0.46)	4.6 (0.46)	4.0 (0.42)
Heroin	2.2 (0.21)	1.1 (0.12)	1.2 (0.12)	1.3 (0.13)	1.6 (0.14)	2.4 (0.19)	1.5 (0.14)	1.2 (0.13)	1.6 (0.14)	1.4 (0.14)	1.1 (0.13)	1.0 (0.13)	1.0 (0.12)	0.8 (0.11)
LSD	11.3 (0.81)	9.3 (0.57)	7.5 (0.52)	8.7 (0.57)	11.7 (0.64)	11.1 (0.69)	3.5 (0.38)	3.1 (0.36)	4.0 (0.40)	4.0 (0.41)	3.8 (0.41)	3.9 (0.43)	3.7 (0.41)	4.3 (0.43)
Marijuana/hashish	47.3 (1.68)	60.3 (1.27)	54.2 (1.83)	40.7 (1.30)	41.7 (1.30)	48.8 (1.45)	44.8 (1.34)	42.0 (1.35)	43.8 (1.32)	45.5 (1.37)	45.2 (1.39)	45.5 (1.45)	44.4 (1.43)	44.7 (1.39)
PCP	— (†)	9.6 (0.33)	4.9 (0.24)	2.8 (0.19)	2.7 (0.18)	3.4 (0.23)	2.4 (0.18)	1.7 (0.15)	1.8 (0.15)	2.3 (0.18)	1.6 (0.15)	1.3 (0.14)	— (†)	— (†)
Used during past 12 months														
Alcohol[1]	84.8 (0.84)	87.9 (0.59)	85.6 (0.63)	80.6 (0.73)	73.7 (0.81)	73.2 (0.89)	68.6 (0.87)	66.2 (0.90)	65.2 (0.88)	63.5 (0.92)	63.5 (0.94)	62.0 (0.99)	60.2 (0.98)	58.2 (0.96)
Any illicit drug	45.0 (1.64)	53.1 (1.26)	46.3 (1.26)	32.5 (1.21)	39.0 (1.26)	40.9 (1.39)	38.4 (1.28)	36.5 (1.29)	38.3 (1.26)	40.0 (1.32)	39.7 (1.34)	40.1 (1.39)	38.7 (1.36)	38.6 (1.33)
Marijuana only	18.8 (1.29)	22.7 (1.06)	18.9 (0.99)	14.6 (0.91)	19.6 (1.02)	20.5 (1.14)	18.8 (1.03)	19.5 (1.06)	21.0 (1.06)	22.4 (1.12)	22.7 (1.14)	22.3 (1.18)	22.8 (1.18)	23.4 (1.16)
Any illicit drug other than marijuana[2]	26.2 (1.15)	30.4 (0.92)	27.4 (0.89)	17.9 (0.79)	19.4 (0.81)	20.4 (0.90)	19.7 (0.83)	17.0 (0.79)	17.3 (0.78)	17.6 (0.81)	17.0 (0.81)	17.8 (0.86)	15.9 (0.81)	15.2 (0.78)
Selected drugs														
Cocaine	5.6 (0.52)	12.3 (0.58)	13.1 (0.59)	5.3 (0.40)	4.0 (0.35)	5.0 (0.43)	5.1 (0.40)	3.4 (0.34)	2.9 (0.30)	2.9 (0.31)	2.7 (0.31)	2.6 (0.31)	2.6 (0.31)	2.5 (0.30)
Heroin	1.0 (0.13)	0.5 (0.07)	0.6 (0.07)	0.5 (0.07)	1.1 (0.10)	1.5 (0.13)	0.8 (0.09)	0.7 (0.09)	0.9 (0.09)	0.8 (0.09)	0.6 (0.08)	0.6 (0.08)	0.6 (0.08)	0.5 (0.07)
LSD	7.2 (0.59)	6.5 (0.43)	4.4 (0.36)	5.4 (0.41)	8.4 (0.49)	6.6 (0.49)	1.8 (0.24)	1.9 (0.25)	2.6 (0.29)	2.7 (0.30)	2.4 (0.29)	2.2 (0.29)	2.5 (0.30)	2.9 (0.32)
Marijuana/hashish	40.0 (1.61)	48.8 (1.27)	40.6 (1.24)	27.0 (1.15)	34.7 (1.23)	36.5 (1.36)	33.6 (1.24)	32.8 (1.25)	34.8 (1.24)	36.4 (1.29)	36.4 (1.31)	36.4 (1.37)	35.1 (1.34)	34.9 (1.30)
PCP	— (†)	4.4 (0.20)	2.9 (0.16)	1.2 (0.11)	1.8 (0.13)	2.3 (0.16)	1.3 (0.11)	1.0 (0.10)	1.0 (0.10)	1.3 (0.12)	0.9 (0.10)	0.7 (0.09)	0.8 (0.10)	1.4 (0.12)
Used during past 30 days														
Alcohol[1]	68.2 (1.10)	72.0 (0.81)	65.9 (0.85)	57.1 (0.92)	51.3 (0.92)	50.0 (1.01)	47.0 (0.94)	43.5 (0.95)	41.2 (0.91)	40.0 (0.94)	41.5 (0.96)	39.2 (0.99)	37.4 (0.97)	35.3 (0.93)
Any illicit drug	30.7 (1.35)	37.2 (1.09)	29.7 (1.03)	17.2 (0.87)	23.8 (0.98)	24.9 (1.09)	23.1 (0.99)	23.3 (1.01)	23.8 (0.99)	25.2 (1.04)	25.2 (1.06)	25.2 (1.10)	23.7 (1.06)	23.6 (1.03)
Marijuana only	15.3 (1.06)	18.8 (0.88)	14.8 (0.80)	9.2 (0.67)	13.8 (0.79)	14.5 (0.89)	12.8 (0.78)	14.7 (0.84)	15.2 (0.83)	16.3 (0.89)	16.8 (0.91)	17.0 (0.95)	16.0 (0.92)	16.0 (0.89)
Any illicit drug other than marijuana[2]	15.4 (0.80)	18.4 (0.66)	14.9 (0.60)	8.0 (0.47)	10.0 (0.52)	10.4 (0.58)	10.3 (0.54)	8.6 (0.50)	8.6 (0.49)	8.9 (0.51)	8.4 (0.51)	8.2 (0.52)	7.7 (0.50)	7.6 (0.49)
Selected drugs														
Cocaine	1.9 (0.25)	5.2 (0.31)	6.7 (0.35)	1.9 (0.20)	1.8 (0.19)	2.1 (0.23)	2.3 (0.22)	1.3 (0.17)	1.3 (0.16)	1.1 (0.16)	1.1 (0.16)	1.1 (0.17)	1.0 (0.16)	1.1 (0.16)
Heroin	0.4 (0.08)	0.2 (0.04)	0.3 (0.05)	0.2 (0.04)	0.6 (0.08)	0.7 (0.09)	0.5 (0.07)	0.4 (0.06)	0.4 (0.06)	0.4 (0.07)	0.3 (0.06)	0.3 (0.06)	0.4 (0.07)	0.3 (0.06)
LSD	2.3 (0.28)	2.3 (0.21)	1.6 (0.18)	1.9 (0.20)	4.0 (0.28)	1.6 (0.20)	0.7 (0.12)	0.5 (0.11)	0.8 (0.13)	0.8 (0.13)	0.8 (0.14)	0.8 (0.14)	1.0 (0.16)	1.1 (0.16)
Marijuana/hashish	27.1 (1.30)	33.7 (1.07)	25.7 (0.98)	14.0 (0.80)	21.2 (0.94)	21.6 (1.04)	19.8 (0.94)	20.6 (0.96)	21.4 (0.95)	22.6 (1.00)	22.9 (1.02)	22.7 (1.06)	21.2 (1.02)	21.3 (1.00)
PCP	— (†)	1.4 (0.11)	1.6 (0.12)	0.4 (0.06)	0.6 (0.08)	0.9 (0.10)	0.7 (0.08)	0.5 (0.07)	0.8 (0.09)	0.8 (0.09)	0.5 (0.07)	0.4 (0.07)	— (†)	— (†)

—Not available.
†Not applicable.
[1]Survey question changed in 1993; later data are not comparable to figures for earlier years.
[2]Other illicit drugs include any use of LSD or other hallucinogens, crack or other cocaine, or heroin, or any use of other narcotics, amphetamines, barbiturates, or tranquilizers not under a doctor's orders.

NOTE: Detail may not sum to totals because of rounding. Standard errors were calculated from formulas to perform trend analysis over an interval greater than 1 year (for example, a comparison between 1975 and 1990). A revised questionnaire was used in 1982 and later years to reduce the inappropriate reporting of nonprescription stimulants. This slightly reduced the positive responses for some types of drug abuse.
SOURCE: University of Michigan, Institute for Social Research, Monitoring the Future, selected years, 1975 through 2015, retrieved January 29, 2016, from http://monitoringthefuture.org/data/data.html. (This table was prepared February 2016.)

Table 232.95. Percentage of 12- to 17-year-olds reporting use of illicit drugs, alcohol, and cigarettes during the past 30 days and the past year, by substance used, sex, and race/ethnicity: Selected years, 1985 through 2014

[Standard errors appear in parentheses]

Year, sex, and race/ethnicity	Percent reporting use during past 30 days					Percent reporting use during past year				
	Illicit drugs			Alcohol	Cigarettes	Illicit drugs			Alcohol	Cigarettes
	Any[1]	Marijuana	Cocaine			Any[1]	Marijuana	Cocaine		
1	2	3	4	5	6	7	8	9	10	11
1985	13.2 (—)	10.2 (—)	1.5 (—)	41.2 (—)	29.4 (—)	20.7 (—)	16.7 (—)	3.4 (—)	52.7 (—)	29.9 (—)
1990	7.1 (—)	4.4 (—)	0.6 (—)	32.5 (—)	22.4 (—)	14.1 (—)	9.6 (—)	1.9 (—)	41.8 (—)	26.2 (—)
1995	10.9 (—)	8.2 (—)	0.8 (—)	21.1 (—)	20.2 (—)	18.0 (—)	14.2 (—)	1.7 (—)	35.1 (—)	26.6 (—)
1999	9.8 (0.23)	7.2 (0.20)	0.5 (0.06)	16.5 (0.30)	14.9 (0.31)	19.8 (0.32)	14.2 (0.29)	1.6 (0.10)	34.1 (0.41)	23.4 (0.37)
2000	9.7 (0.24)	7.2 (0.21)	0.6 (0.07)	16.4 (0.29)	13.4 (0.28)	18.6 (0.31)	13.4 (0.27)	1.7 (0.12)	33.0 (0.39)	20.8 (0.34)
2001	10.8 (0.26)	8.0 (0.24)	0.4 (0.06)	17.3 (0.33)	13.0 (0.28)	20.8 (0.36)	15.2 (0.32)	1.5 (0.10)	33.9 (0.39)	20.0 (0.35)
2002	11.6 (0.29)	8.2 (0.24)	0.6 (0.07)	17.6 (0.32)	13.0 (0.30)	22.2 (0.38)	15.8 (0.32)	2.1 (0.13)	34.6 (0.42)	20.3 (0.35)
2003	11.2 (0.27)	7.9 (0.24)	0.6 (0.06)	17.7 (0.33)	12.2 (0.29)	21.8 (0.36)	15.0 (0.31)	1.8 (0.11)	34.3 (0.42)	19.0 (0.36)
2004	10.6 (0.27)	7.6 (0.23)	0.5 (0.06)	17.6 (0.32)	11.9 (0.30)	21.0 (0.34)	14.5 (0.31)	1.6 (0.11)	33.9 (0.41)	18.4 (0.35)
2005	9.9 (0.25)	6.8 (0.22)	0.6 (0.06)	16.5 (0.32)	10.8 (0.28)	19.9 (0.35)	13.3 (0.30)	1.7 (0.11)	33.3 (0.41)	17.3 (0.36)
2006	9.8 (0.27)	6.7 (0.21)	0.4 (0.05)	16.6 (0.32)	10.4 (0.26)	19.6 (0.37)	13.2 (0.31)	1.6 (0.11)	32.9 (0.42)	17.0 (0.35)
2007	9.5 (0.27)	6.7 (0.22)	0.4 (0.05)	15.9 (0.34)	9.8 (0.26)	18.7 (0.35)	12.5 (0.30)	1.5 (0.11)	31.8 (0.42)	15.7 (0.34)
2008	9.3 (0.24)	6.7 (0.22)	0.4 (0.05)	14.6 (0.31)	9.1 (0.24)	19.0 (0.35)	13.0 (0.29)	1.2 (0.10)	30.8 (0.40)	15.0 (0.31)
2009	10.0 (0.27)	7.3 (0.24)	0.3 (0.05)	14.7 (0.32)	8.9 (0.26)	19.5 (0.36)	13.6 (0.31)	1.0 (0.09)	30.3 (0.42)	15.0 (0.33)
2010	10.1 (0.29)	7.4 (0.25)	0.2 (0.05)	13.6 (0.33)	8.4 (0.26)	19.5 (0.38)	14.0 (0.34)	1.0 (0.09)	28.7 (0.43)	14.2 (0.34)
2011	10.1 (0.27)	7.9 (0.24)	0.3 (0.05)	13.3 (0.31)	7.8 (0.24)	19.0 (0.37)	14.2 (0.33)	0.9 (0.08)	27.8 (0.43)	13.2 (0.31)
2012	9.5 (0.25)	7.2 (0.22)	0.1 ! (0.03)	12.9 (0.31)	6.6 (0.22)	17.9 (0.33)	13.5 (0.30)	0.7 (0.08)	26.3 (0.42)	11.8 (0.29)
2013	8.8 (0.25)	7.1 (0.23)	0.2 (0.04)	11.6 (0.29)	5.6 (0.20)	17.2 (0.35)	13.4 (0.31)	0.5 (0.06)	24.6 (0.40)	10.3 (0.27)
Sex										
Male	9.6 (0.36)	7.9 (0.33)	0.2 (0.05)	11.2 (0.41)	5.7 (0.28)	17.8 (0.51)	14.1 (0.45)	0.6 (0.09)	23.5 (0.56)	10.3 (0.37)
Female	8.0 (0.34)	6.2 (0.30)	0.2 ! (0.06)	11.9 (0.43)	5.5 (0.30)	16.6 (0.50)	12.8 (0.44)	0.5 (0.09)	25.8 (0.58)	10.3 (0.40)
Race/ethnicity										
White	8.8 (0.32)	7.1 (0.29)	0.2 (0.05)	12.9 (0.40)	7.2 (0.31)	17.0 (0.43)	13.5 (0.40)	0.6 (0.09)	27.1 (0.52)	12.2 (0.38)
Black	10.5 (0.73)	7.4 (0.59)	‡ (†)	9.7 (0.71)	3.2 (0.39)	20.1 (0.90)	14.7 (0.83)	‡ (†)	21.6 (0.97)	6.4 (0.57)
Hispanic	8.7 (0.58)	7.2 (0.52)	0.3 (0.08)	10.7 (0.66)	3.7 (0.37)	17.2 (0.83)	13.5 (0.76)	0.6 (0.13)	23.2 (0.91)	9.0 (0.60)
Asian	3.8 (0.91)	3.6 (0.90)	‡ (†)	8.0 (1.48)	2.5 (0.71)	9.1 (1.37)	7.1 (1.26)	‡ (†)	15.8 (2.25)	5.1 (1.12)
Pacific Islander	‡ (†)	‡ (†)	‡ (†)	8.2 ! (2.90)	3.6 ! (1.48)	‡ (†)	‡ (†)	‡ (†)	‡ (†)	6.0 ! (2.52)
American Indian/Alaska Native	‡ (†)	9.1 (2.58)	‡ (†)	9.3 (2.39)	7.5 (1.95)	27.8 (4.94)	20.1 (3.52)	‡ (†)	20.3 (3.90)	16.1 (3.13)
Two or more races	10.3 (1.25)	8.6 (1.15)	‡ (†)	9.0 (1.10)	7.0 (1.18)	19.0 (1.73)	15.5 (1.59)	‡ (†)	21.8 (1.79)	10.3 (1.36)
2014	9.4 (0.30)	7.4 (0.27)	0.2 (0.04)	11.5 (0.33)	4.9 (0.21)	17.4 (0.38)	13.1 (0.33)	0.7 (0.09)	24.0 (0.42)	8.9 (0.29)
Sex										
Male	9.6 (0.41)	7.9 (0.38)	‡ (†)	10.8 (0.42)	5.1 (0.28)	16.7 (0.52)	13.2 (0.46)	0.7 (0.13)	22.0 (0.56)	9.1 (0.41)
Female	9.1 (0.41)	6.8 (0.35)	0.2 ! (0.06)	12.3 (0.47)	4.6 (0.28)	18.2 (0.53)	13.0 (0.46)	0.7 (0.13)	26.1 (0.61)	8.7 (0.38)
Race/ethnicity										
White	9.3 (0.41)	7.7 (0.37)	‡ (†)	13.2 (0.47)	6.3 (0.31)	17.0 (0.51)	13.2 (0.45)	0.7 (0.12)	26.7 (0.57)	10.6 (0.39)
Black	9.8 (0.76)	6.9 (0.65)	‡ (†)	8.6 (0.71)	2.2 (0.31)	19.2 (0.94)	13.6 (0.83)	‡ (†)	18.7 (0.97)	4.4 (0.44)
Hispanic	10.5 (0.69)	7.9 (0.62)	0.4 ! (0.14)	11.2 (0.71)	3.8 (0.42)	18.9 (0.85)	14.1 (0.74)	1.2 (0.27)	23.9 (0.97)	8.4 (0.63)
Asian	3.5 (0.84)	2.5 (0.69)	‡ (†)	4.5 (0.97)	1.3 ! (0.55)	9.1 (1.40)	6.2 (1.15)	‡ (†)	12.3 (1.57)	3.4 (0.88)
Pacific Islander	‡ (†)	‡ (†)	‡ (†)	‡ (†)	‡ (†)	‡ (†)	‡ (†)	‡ (†)	‡ (†)	‡ (†)
American Indian/Alaska Native	10.6 (2.78)	9.4 (2.78)	‡ (†)	‡ (†)	8.6 ! (2.83)	23.2 (4.29)	20.2 (4.28)	‡ (†)	22.3 (5.06)	17.5 (4.55)
Two or more races	10.0 (1.29)	6.9 (1.05)	‡ (†)	9.7 (1.35)	4.4 (0.87)	19.3 (1.79)	13.0 (1.43)	‡ (†)	22.1 (1.92)	9.3 (1.31)

—Not available.
†Not applicable.
!Interpret data with caution. The coefficient of variation (CV) for this estimate is between 30 and 50 percent.
‡Reporting standards not met. Either there are too few cases for a reliable estimate or the coefficient of variation (CV) is 50 percent or greater.
[1]Includes other illegal drug use not shown separately—specifically, the use of heroin, hallucinogens, and inhalants, as well as the nonmedical use of prescription-type pain relievers, tranquilizers, stimulants, and sedatives.

NOTE: Marijuana includes hashish usage. Data for 1999 and later years were gathered using Computer Assisted Interviewing (CAI) and may not be directly comparable to previous years. Because of survey improvements in 2002, the 2002 data constitute a new baseline for tracking trends. Valid trend comparisons can be made for 1985 through 1995, 1999 through 2001, and 2002 through 2014. Race categories exclude persons of Hispanic ethnicity.
SOURCE: U.S. Department of Health and Human Services, Substance Abuse and Mental Health Services Administration, *National Household Survey on Drug Abuse: Main Findings*, selected years, 1985 through 2001, and National Survey on Drug Use and Health, 2002 through 2014. Retrieved March 4, 2016, from http://www.samhsa.gov/data/population-data-nsduh/reports?tab=38. (This table was prepared March 2016.)

Table 233.10. Number and percentage of public schools that took a serious disciplinary action in response to specific offenses, number of serious actions taken, and percentage distribution of actions, by type of offense, school level, and type of action: Selected years, 1999–2000 through 2009–10

[Standard errors appear in parentheses]

Year, school level, and type of serious disciplinary action	Total	Physical attacks or fights	Insubordination	Distribution, possession, or use of alcohol	Distribution, possession, or use of illegal drugs	Use or possession of a firearm or explosive device	Use or possession of a weapon other than a firearm or explosive device[1]
1	2	3	4	5	6	7	8
Number of schools taking at least one action							
2009–10	32,300 (940)	24,000 (770)	— (†)	7,600 (320)	16,100 (400)	2,500 (340)	11,200 (650)
Percent of schools taking at least one action							
1999–2000[2]	— (†)	35.4 (1.02)	18.3 (0.79)	— (†)	— (†)	— (†)	— (†)
2003–04	45.7 (1.15)	32.0 (0.94)	21.6 (0.85)	9.2 (0.50)	21.2 (0.58)	3.9 (0.40)	16.8 (0.84)
2005–06	48.0 (1.18)	31.5 (1.02)	21.2 (0.85)	10.2 (0.47)	20.8 (0.61)	4.5 (0.35)	19.3 (0.91)
2007–08	46.4 (1.16)	31.5 (0.89)	21.4 (0.95)	9.8 (0.48)	19.3 (0.53)	2.8 (0.26)	15.3 (0.77)
2009–10[3]	39.1 (1.14)	29.0 (0.94)	— (†)	9.2 (0.39)	19.5 (0.48)	3.0 (0.41)	13.5 (0.78)
Primary school[4]	18.1 (1.51)	13.2 (1.26)	— (†)	1.0! (0.33)	2.0 (0.47)	1.7! (0.57)	6.4 (0.93)
Middle school[4]	67.0 (1.68)	49.7 (1.87)	— (†)	13.6 (1.17)	36.9 (1.19)	4.1 (0.65)	25.1 (1.70)
High school[4]	82.7 (1.57)	62.6 (1.63)	— (†)	36.1 (1.47)	66.1 (1.39)	7.3 (1.05)	28.9 (1.39)
Combined school[4]	49.2 (5.31)	35.6 (4.26)	— (†)	9.9 (2.54)	22.7 (3.57)	‡ (†)	10.9 (2.72)
Number of actions taken							
1999–2000[2]	— (†)	332,500 (27,420)	253,500 (27,720)	— (†)	— (†)	— (†)	— (†)
2003–04	655,700 (29,160)	273,500 (14,450)	220,400 (16,990)	25,500 (1,600)	91,100 (3,410)	9,900! (4,300)	35,400 (1,470)
2005–06	830,700 (45,710)	323,900 (16,690)	309,000 (33,840)	30,100 (1,880)	106,800 (4,950)	14,300 (2,690)	46,600 (2,040)
2007–08	767,900 (44,010)	271,800 (15,180)	327,100 (38,470)	28,400 (1,470)	98,700 (5,780)	5,200 (910)	36,800 (2,630)
2009–10[3]	433,800 (22,880)	265,100 (22,170)	— (†)	28,700 (1,920)	105,400 (4,070)	5,800 (1,360)	28,800 (1,580)
Percentage distribution of actions, 2009–10	100.0 (†)	100.0 (†)	— (†)	100.0 (2.23)	100.0 (†)	100.0 (†)	100.0 (†)
Out-of-school suspensions lasting 5 days or more	73.9 (1.79)	81.2 (2.18)	— (†)	74.3 (2.23)	59.6 (1.70)	55.5 (9.64)	62.2 (2.44)
Removal with no services for remainder of school year	6.1 (0.86)	5.0 (1.22)	— (†)	4.0 (0.92)	8.0 (0.94)	22.2 (4.96)	8.8 (1.31)
Transfer to specialized schools	20.0 (1.36)	13.9 (1.57)	— (†)	21.7 (2.27)	32.4 (1.57)	22.3! (7.91)	29.0 (2.32)

—Not available.
†Not applicable.
!Interpret data with caution. The coefficient of variation (CV) for this estimate is between 30 and 50 percent.
‡Reporting standards not met. Either there are too few cases for a reliable estimate or the coefficient of variation (CV) is 50 percent or greater.
[1]Prior to 2005–06, the questionnaire wording was simply "a weapon other than a firearm" (instead of "a weapon other than a firearm or explosive device").
[2]In the 1999–2000 questionnaire, only two items are the same as in questionnaires for later years—the item on physical attacks or fights and the item on insubordination. There are no comparable 1999–2000 data for serious disciplinary actions taken in response to the other specific offenses listed in this table, nor for total actions taken in response to all the listed offenses.
[3]Totals for 2009–10 are not comparable to totals for other years, because the 2009–10 questionnaire did not include an item on insubordination.
[4]Primary schools are defined as schools in which the lowest grade is not higher than grade 3 and the highest grade is not higher than grade 8. Middle schools are defined as schools in which the lowest grade is not lower than grade 4 and the highest grade is not higher than grade 9. High schools are defined as schools in which the lowest grade is not lower than grade 9 and the highest grade is not higher than grade 12. Combined schools include all other combinations of grades, including K–12 schools.
NOTE: Serious disciplinary actions include out-of-school suspensions lasting 5 or more days, but less than the remainder of the school year; removals with no continuing services for at least the remainder of the school year; and transfers to specialized schools for disciplinary reasons. Responses were provided by the principal or the person most knowledgeable about crime and safety issues at the school. Respondents were instructed to respond only for those times that were during normal school hours or when school activities or events were in session, unless the survey specified otherwise. Detail may not sum to totals because of rounding and because schools that reported serious disciplinary actions in response to more than one type of offense were counted only once in the total number or percentage of schools.
SOURCE: U.S. Department of Education, National Center for Education Statistics, 1999–2000, 2003–04, 2005–06, 2007–08, and 2009–10 School Survey on Crime and Safety (SSOCS), 2000, 2004, 2006, 2008, and 2010. (This table was prepared September 2013.)

Table 233.20. Percentage of public school students in grades 6 through 12 who had ever been suspended or expelled, by sex and race/ethnicity: 2003, 2007, and 2012

[Standard errors appear in parentheses]

Race/ethnicity	2003						2007						2012					
	Total		Male		Female		Total		Male		Female		Total		Male		Female	
1	2		3		4		5		6		7		8		9		10	
Ever suspended																		
Total	17.1	(0.58)	22.1	(1.01)	11.8	(0.70)	21.6	(0.98)	27.9	(1.48)	14.9	(1.02)	19.6	(0.57)	25.7	(0.89)	13.2	(0.78)
White	14.3	(0.71)	19.8	(1.16)	8.4	(0.78)	15.6	(0.99)	21.3	(1.43)	9.7	(1.02)	15.6	(0.70)	21.4	(1.07)	9.4	(0.90)
Black	27.5	(1.94)	31.2	(2.86)	23.9	(2.36)	42.8	(3.16)	49.5	(4.52)	34.7	(3.40)	38.8	(2.21)	48.3	(3.40)	29.0	(2.94)
Hispanic	17.7	(1.40)	22.8	(2.04)	11.9	(1.86)	21.9	(2.24)	29.7	(3.64)	14.1	(2.36)	17.3	(1.29)	22.6	(2.21)	11.8	(1.60)
Asian/Pacific Islander	11.9 !	(4.78)	18.6 !	(7.37)	‡	(†)	11.6 !	(4.57)	‡	(†)	9.3 !	(4.17)	9.5	(2.58)	11.2 !	(3.94)	7.9 !	(3.86)
Asian	—	(†)	—	(†)	—	(†)	10.8 !	(5.03)	‡	(†)	‡	(†)	8.6 !	(2.73)	9.5 !	(4.04)	‡	(†)
Pacific Islander	—	(†)	—	(†)	—	(†)	‡	(†)	‡	(†)	‡	(†)	‡	(†)	‡	(†)	‡	(†)
American Indian/Alaska Native	‡	(†)	‡	(†)	‡	(†)	14.2 !	(5.34)	‡	(†)	‡	(†)	22.9 !	(7.30)	‡	(†)	‡	(†)
Other	24.4	(3.91)	25.8	(5.19)	22.6	(5.40)	24.9	(4.37)	28.6	(6.67)	20.3	(5.32)	27.2	(4.30)	35.7	(7.26)	16.9	(3.49)
Ever expelled																		
Total	3.2	(0.28)	4.4	(0.48)	1.8	(0.29)	3.4	(0.54)	4.5	(0.84)	2.3	(0.52)	2.2	(0.26)	2.9	(0.46)	1.3	(0.20)
White	2.4	(0.30)	3.6	(0.50)	1.0 !	(0.38)	1.0	(0.19)	1.3	(0.30)	0.7 !	(0.26)	1.8	(0.21)	2.6	(0.39)	1.0	(0.21)
Black	7.1	(0.98)	9.1	(1.79)	5.1	(1.01)	12.8	(2.85)	16.6	(4.29)	8.2	(2.20)	4.6	(1.26)	6.9 !	(2.39)	2.2 !	(0.74)
Hispanic	2.6	(0.60)	3.6	(1.02)	1.5 !	(0.53)	3.0 !	(0.96)	3.1 !	(1.01)	‡	(†)	1.9	(0.40)	2.0	(0.58)	1.7 !	(0.56)
Asian/Pacific Islander	‡	(†)	‡	(†)	‡	(†)	‡	(†)	‡	(†)	‡	(†)	‡	(†)	‡	(†)	‡	(†)
Asian	—	(†)	—	(†)	—	(†)	‡	(†)	‡	(†)	‡	(†)	‡	(†)	‡	(†)	‡	(†)
Pacific Islander	—	(†)	—	(†)	—	(†)	‡	(†)	‡	(†)	‡	(†)	‡	(†)	‡	(†)	‡	(†)
American Indian/Alaska Native	‡	(†)	‡	(†)	‡	(†)	‡	(†)	‡	(†)	‡	(†)	‡	(†)	‡	(†)	‡	(†)
Other	3.0 !	(1.48)	‡	(†)	‡	(†)	3.5 !	(1.67)	6.1 !	(3.02)	‡	(†)	2.0 !	(0.65)	1.8 !	(0.77)	‡	(†)

—Not available.
†Not applicable.
!Interpret data with caution. The coefficient of variation (CV) for this estimate is between 30 and 50 percent.
‡Reporting standards not met. Either there are too few cases for a reliable estimate or the coefficient of variation (CV) is 50 percent or greater.
NOTE: While National Household Education Surveys Program (NHES) administrations prior to 2012 were administered via telephone with an interviewer, NHES:2012 used self-administered paper-and-pencil questionnaires that were mailed to respondents. Measur-

able differences in estimates between 2012 and prior years could reflect actual changes in the population, or the changes could be due to the mode change from telephone to mail. Includes both in-school and out-of-school suspensions. All information is based on parent reports. Excludes homeschooled children. Race categories exclude persons of Hispanic ethnicity. Asian and Pacific Islander data were not collected separately prior to 2007.
SOURCE: U.S. Department of Education, National Center for Education Statistics, Parent and Family Involvement in Education Survey of the National Household Education Surveys Program (PFI-NHES:2003, 2007, and 2012). (This table was prepared July 2015.)

Table 233.25. Number and percentage of fall 2009 ninth-graders who were ever suspended or expelled through spring 2012, by when student was suspended or expelled and selected student characteristics: 2013

[Standard errors appear in parentheses]

Selected student characteristic	Number of fall 2009 ninth-graders		Percentage distribution of fall 2009 ninth-graders		Percent ever suspended or expelled			
	Total, all students[1]	Total, ever suspended or expelled	All students	Ever suspended or expelled	Total	When suspended or expelled		
						Only before fall of 2009	Only between fall 2009 and spring 2012	Both before fall 2009 and between fall 2009 and spring 2012
1	2	3	4	5	6	7	8	9
Total, all students	3,776,000 (38,600)	734,000 (35,400)	100.0 (†)	100.0 (†)	19.4 (0.91)	7.2 (0.72)	6.6 (0.54)	5.7 (0.65)
High school completion status in 2013								
Less than high school completion	213,000 (26,600)	116,000 (18,500)	5.8 (0.72)	16.7 (2.52)	54.5 (5.05)	13.8 (3.76)	17.5 (3.69)	23.2 (4.45)
High school completion	3,456,000 (44,300)	578,000 (31,600)	94.2 (0.72)	83.3 (2.52)	16.7 (0.88)	6.6 (0.74)	5.8 (0.46)	4.4 (0.63)
Sex								
Male	1,906,000 (20,000)	498,000 (26,200)	50.5 (0.42)	67.8 (2.34)	26.1 (1.35)	8.9 (1.22)	8.5 (0.88)	8.7 (1.20)
Female	1,869,000 (29,100)	236,000 (22,200)	49.5 (0.42)	32.2 (2.34)	12.6 (1.17)	5.5 (0.89)	4.6 (0.62)	2.6 (0.55)
Race/ethnicity								
White	2,001,000 (39,400)	288,000 (19,400)	53.0 (1.00)	39.3 (2.37)	14.4 (0.93)	4.3 (0.51)	6.7 (0.65)	3.4 (0.38)
Black	478,000 (25,400)	170,000 (18,300)	12.7 (0.68)	23.2 (2.63)	35.6 (3.42)	14.8 (2.47)	6.9 (1.60)	13.9 (3.17)
Hispanic	819,000 (39,200)	175,000 (29,700)	21.7 (0.96)	23.8 (3.66)	21.3 (3.21)	10.1 (2.77)	7.0 (1.38)	4.3 (0.95)
Asian	129,000 (9,800)	‡ (†)	3.4 (0.26)	1.1 ! (0.42)	6.4 ! (2.38)	‡ (†)	1.2 ! (0.54)	‡ (†)
Pacific Islander	15,000 (5,400)	‡ (†)	0.4 ! (0.14)	‡ (†)	‡ (†)	‡ (†)	‡ (†)	‡ (†)
American Indian/Alaska Native	30,000 (8,100)	‡ (†)	0.8 (0.21)	1.6 ! (0.66)	40.6 ! (14.16)	‡ (†)	‡ (†)	‡ (†)
Two or more races	304,000 (20,700)	78,000 (14,100)	8.1 (0.54)	10.6 (1.84)	25.6 (4.07)	6.7 (1.84)	5.8 ! (1.76)	13.1 ! (4.09)
Highest education of parents in 2012								
High school completion or less	1,456,000 (67,800)	398,000 (38,100)	38.6 (1.76)	54.2 (3.91)	27.3 (1.92)	10.6 (1.55)	8.6 (1.00)	8.1 (1.57)
Some college	745,000 (35,200)	152,000 (19,800)	19.7 (0.92)	20.8 (2.76)	20.5 (2.20)	7.1 (1.62)	6.6 (1.20)	6.8 (1.30)
Bachelor's degree	881,000 (41,200)	118,000 (12,300)	23.3 (1.06)	16.0 (1.71)	13.4 (1.20)	4.3 (0.84)	5.8 (0.99)	3.3 (0.72)
Master's or higher degree	693,000 (37,700)	66,000 (10,500)	18.4 (0.98)	9.0 (1.44)	9.5 (1.41)	3.9 (0.94)	3.1 (0.57)	2.5 ! (0.80)
Socioeconomic status of parents in 2012[2]								
Lowest two fifths	1,391,000 (62,200)	400,000 (35,300)	36.8 (1.60)	54.5 (3.39)	28.8 (1.88)	10.7 (1.57)	8.8 (1.00)	9.3 (1.62)
Middle two fifths	1,381,000 (44,500)	241,000 (19,800)	36.6 (1.14)	32.8 (2.68)	17.4 (1.41)	6.6 (1.02)	6.0 (0.88)	4.8 (0.76)
Highest fifth	1,004,000 (45,700)	93,000 (12,400)	26.6 (1.18)	12.7 (1.74)	9.3 (1.10)	3.2 (0.69)	4.2 (0.66)	1.9 ! (0.59)
Cumulative high school grade point average								
0.00–1.99	601,000 (42,500)	279,000 (27,500)	16.7 (1.15)	40.2 (3.50)	46.4 (3.31)	11.3 (1.82)	13.7 (2.06)	21.4 (3.44)
2.00–2.49	655,000 (43,100)	186,000 (23,200)	18.2 (1.11)	26.9 (3.22)	28.5 (2.49)	12.5 (2.73)	9.6 (1.65)	6.4 (1.11)
2.50–2.99	752,000 (37,400)	136,000 (15,300)	20.9 (1.01)	19.6 (2.02)	18.1 (1.99)	7.0 (1.30)	7.3 (1.22)	3.7 (0.76)
3.00–3.49	845,000 (33,800)	72,000 (11,800)	23.5 (0.98)	10.3 (1.56)	8.5 (1.33)	4.7 (1.11)	3.0 (0.57)	‡ (†)
3.50 or higher	743,000 (29,900)	21,000 (4,500)	20.7 (0.78)	3.0 (0.65)	2.8 (0.60)	1.0 ! (0.33)	1.5 (0.45)	‡ (†)
School engagement in 2009[3]								
Low	794,000 (43,700)	222,000 (22,200)	21.8 (1.12)	31.9 (2.77)	28.0 (2.40)	9.1 (1.46)	7.8 (1.34)	11.1 (1.71)
Middle	1,923,000 (43,900)	395,000 (26,200)	52.8 (1.16)	56.6 (2.99)	20.5 (1.34)	8.2 (1.25)	7.6 (0.82)	4.7 (0.77)
High	922,000 (34,200)	81,000 (14,400)	25.3 (0.94)	11.6 (1.97)	8.8 (1.50)	3.5 (0.85)	2.4 (0.49)	2.8 ! (1.21)
Sense of school belonging in 2009[4]								
Low	854,000 (40,600)	243,000 (24,200)	23.7 (1.13)	35.4 (3.07)	28.5 (2.22)	9.6 (1.54)	9.2 (1.04)	9.7 (1.57)
Middle	1,850,000 (46,700)	304,000 (28,000)	51.2 (1.12)	44.2 (3.57)	16.4 (1.36)	5.8 (0.73)	6.4 (0.78)	4.2 (0.69)
High	907,000 (40,600)	140,000 (21,600)	25.1 (1.08)	20.4 (3.03)	15.5 (2.13)	7.4 (2.14)	3.6 (0.71)	4.5 (1.30)

†Not applicable.
!Interpret data with caution. The coefficient of variation (CV) for this estimate is between 30 and 50 percent.
‡Reporting standards not met. Either there are too few cases for a reliable estimate or the coefficient of variation (CV) is 50 percent or greater.
[1]The total includes all students whose parents provided a response about their child's suspension and expulsion status both on the base-year (2009) questionnaire and on the first follow-up (2012) questionnaire.
[2]Socioeconomic status (SES) was measured by a composite score on parental education and occupations, and family income.
[3]A school engagement scale was constructed based on students' responses to questions about how frequently they went to class without homework done, without pencil or paper, without books, or late. Students' school engagement is considered low if they were in the bottom quarter of the scale distribution, middle if they were in the middle two quarters, and high if they were in the highest quarter.

[4]A school belonging scale was constructed based on the extent to which students agreed or disagreed that they felt safe at school, that they felt proud of being part of the school, that there were always teachers or other adults at school they could talk to if they had a problem, that school was often a waste of time, and that getting good grades was important to them. Students' sense of school belonging is considered low if they were in the bottom quarter of the scale distribution, middle if they were in the middle two quarters, and high if they were in the highest quarter.
NOTE: Estimates weighted by W2W1PAR. Race categories exclude persons of Hispanic ethnicity. Detail may not sum to totals because of rounding and survey item nonresponse.
SOURCE: U.S. Department of Education, National Center for Education Statistics, High School Longitudinal Study of 2009 (HSLS:2009), 2013 Update and High School Transcripts Public-Use Data File. (This table was prepared October 2015.)

Table 233.27. Number of students receiving selected disciplinary actions in public elementary and secondary schools, by type of disciplinary action, disability status, sex, and race/ethnicity: 2011–12

Disability status, sex, and race/ethnicity	Corporal punishment[1]	One or more in-school suspension[2]	Out-of-school suspensions[3] Total	Only one	More than one	Expulsions[4] Total[7] All expulsions	Under zero-tolerance policies[8]	With educational services	Without educational services	Referral to law enforcement[5]	School-related arrest[6]
1	2	3	4	5	6	7	8	9	10	11	12
All students											
Total	166,807	3,385,868	3,172,403	1,752,997	1,419,690	111,018	29,677	69,995	40,989	249,752	64,218
Sex											
Male	130,591	2,271,265	2,215,608	1,193,437	1,022,224	83,283	22,310	52,937	30,343	178,132	45,802
Female	36,216	1,114,603	956,795	559,560	397,466	27,735	7,367	17,058	10,646	71,620	18,416
Race/ethnicity[9]											
White	87,607	1,381,239	1,084,048	639,584	444,670	39,766	11,597	24,812	14,947	104,484	25,113
Black	57,215	1,045,021	1,200,401	596,261	604,181	39,443	6,924	22,544	16,895	67,907	19,149
Hispanic	14,085	756,254	688,774	400,155	288,672	23,696	8,746	17,551	6,130	60,187	15,426
Asian	439	34,539	34,526	24,510	9,999	1,096	372	816	282	3,343	728
Pacific Islander	87	5,541	8,258	5,219	3,045	266	229	179	87	513	201
American Indian/Alaska Native	3,922	43,686	44,549	26,035	18,492	2,443	523	1,340	1,104	5,588	1,357
Two or more races	2,087	80,418	80,738	43,667	37,087	2,845	846	1,623	1,224	5,565	1,586
Race/ethnicity by sex[9]											
Male											
White	71,152	977,726	807,781	465,059	342,736	30,700	8,778	19,261	11,452	76,763	18,413
Black	42,211	650,932	776,082	371,985	404,088	27,985	5,285	16,136	11,844	45,689	12,906
Hispanic	11,017	502,718	487,822	273,471	214,426	18,508	6,408	13,655	4,849	43,214	11,262
Asian	361	25,395	27,045	18,970	8,064	887	291	648	239	2,626	575
Pacific Islander	65	3,842	5,931	3,668	2,263	197	186	146	50	370	144
American Indian/Alaska Native	3,054	28,552	30,389	17,259	13,126	1,745	385	977	771	3,884	934
Two or more races	1,642	52,641	56,314	29,668	26,644	2,056	636	1,191	866	3,880	1,060
Female											
White	16,455	403,513	276,267	174,525	101,934	9,066	2,819	5,551	3,495	27,721	6,700
Black	15,004	394,089	424,319	224,276	200,093	11,458	1,639	6,408	5,051	22,218	6,243
Hispanic	3,068	253,536	200,952	126,684	74,246	5,188	2,338	3,896	1,281	16,973	4,164
Asian	78	9,144	7,481	5,540	1,935	209	81	168	43	717	153
Pacific Islander	22	1,699	2,327	1,551	782	69	43	33	37	143	57
American Indian/Alaska Native	868	15,134	14,160	8,776	5,366	698	138	363	333	1,704	423
Two or more races	445	27,777	24,424	13,999	10,443	789	210	432	358	1,685	526
Students with disabilities											
Total	25,668	666,499	720,928	361,018	360,049	23,032	6,260	17,444	5,577	58,805	16,576
Sex											
Male	21,525	510,812	569,752	278,742	291,093	18,917	5,121	14,355	4,563	46,884	13,049
Female	4,143	155,687	151,176	82,276	68,956	4,115	1,139	3,089	1,014	11,921	3,527
Race/ethnicity[9]											
White	13,390	281,208	275,051	144,286	130,825	8,448	2,501	6,499	1,953	25,399	6,317
Black	7,824	192,218	237,998	110,605	127,491	7,547	1,349	5,606	1,938	15,735	5,005
Hispanic	1,968	124,261	138,982	68,749	70,217	4,157	1,385	3,265	889	12,415	3,553
Asian	36	3,582	4,971	3,102	1,863	133	74	104	29	447	145
Pacific Islander	10	1,101	2,389	1,371	1,018	47	169	35	12	88	107
American Indian/Alaska Native	703	9,193	10,812	5,906	4,900	615	112	405	212	1,242	329
Two or more races	372	15,766	19,616	9,433	10,191	622	230	400	224	1,314	462
Race/ethnicity by sex[9]											
Male											
White	11,453	221,833	225,121	115,240	109,887	6,976	2,061	5,379	1,608	20,631	5,069
Black	6,429	142,039	180,611	81,592	99,093	6,041	1,121	4,488	1,552	12,207	3,807
Hispanic	1,631	94,865	109,707	53,127	56,596	3,540	1,121	2,780	757	9,882	2,846
Asian	28	2,889	4,208	2,602	1,600	115	60	90	24	378	113
Pacific Islander	8	881	1,908	1,069	839	37	139	29	8	65	75
American Indian/Alaska Native	574	6,918	8,406	4,471	3,936	494	94	328	169	971	260
Two or more races	313	11,928	15,547	7,284	8,265	509	184	338	173	1,044	371
Female											
White	1,937	59,375	49,930	29,046	20,938	1,472	440	1,120	345	4,768	1,248
Black	1,395	50,179	57,387	29,013	28,398	1,506	228	1,118	386	3,528	1,198
Hispanic	337	29,396	29,275	15,622	13,621	617	264	485	132	2,533	707
Asian	8	693	763	500	263	18	14	14	5	69	32
Pacific Islander	1-3	220	481	302	179	10	30	6	4	23	32
American Indian/Alaska Native	129	2,275	2,406	1,435	964	121	18	77	43	271	69
Two or more races	59	3,838	4,069	2,149	1,926	113	46	62	51	270	91

[1]Corporal punishment is paddling, spanking, or other forms of physical punishment imposed on a student.

[2]An in-school suspension is an instance in which a student is temporarily removed from his or her regular classroom(s) for at least half a day but remains under the direct supervision of school personnel.

[3]For students without disabilities and students with disabilities served only under Section 504 of the Rehabilitation Act, out-of-school suspensions are instances in which a student is excluded from school for disciplinary reasons for 1 school day or longer. This does not include students who served their suspension in the school. For students with disabilities served under the Individuals with Disabilities Education Act (IDEA), out-of-school suspensions are instances in which a student is temporarily removed from his or her regular school for disciplinary purposes to another setting (e.g., home, behavior center). This includes both removals in which no Individualized Education Program (IEP) services are provided because the removal is 10 days or less and removals in which IEP services continue to be provided.

[4]Expulsions are actions taken by a local education agency that result in the removal of a student from his or her regular school for disciplinary purposes for the remainder of the school year or longer in accordance with local education agency policy. Expulsions also include removals resulting from violations of the Gun Free Schools Act that are modified to less than 365 days.

[5]Referral to law enforcement is an action by which a student is reported to any law enforcement agency or official, including a school police unit, for an incident that occurs on school grounds, during school-related events, or while taking school transportation, regardless of whether official action is taken.

[6]A school-related arrest is an arrest of a student for any activity conducted on school grounds, during off-campus school activities (including while taking school transportation), or due to a referral by any school official.

[7]Totals include expulsions with and without educational services.

[8]Includes all expulsions under zero-tolerance policies, including expulsions with and without educational services. A zero-tolerance policy results in mandatory expulsion of any student who commits one or more specified offenses (for example, offenses involving guns, other weapons, violence, or similar factors, or combinations of these factors). A policy is considered zero tolerance even if there are some exceptions to the mandatory aspect of the expulsion, such as allowing the chief administering officer of a local education agency to modify the expulsion on a case-by-case basis.

[9]Data by race/ethnicity exclude data for students with disabilities served only under Section 504 (not receiving services under IDEA).

NOTE: Student counts between 1 and 3 are displayed as 1-3 to protect student privacy. Detail may not sum to totals because of privacy protection routines applied to the data. Race categories exclude persons of Hispanic ethnicity.

SOURCE: U.S. Department of Education, Office for Civil Rights, Civil Rights Data Collection, "2011–12 Discipline Estimations by State." (This table was prepared November 2015.)

Table 233.28. Percentage of students receiving selected disciplinary actions in public elementary and secondary schools, by type of disciplinary action, disability status, sex, and race/ethnicity: 2011–12

Disability status, sex, and race/ethnicity	Corporal punishment[1]	One or more in-school suspension[2]	Out-of-school suspensions[3]			Expulsions[4] Total[7]				Referral to law enforcement[5]	School-related arrest[6]
			Total	Only one	More than one	All expulsions	Under zero-tolerance policies[8]	With educational services	Without educational services		
1	2	3	4	5	6	7	8	9	10	11	12
All students											
Total	0.34	6.83	6.40	3.53	2.86	0.22	0.06	0.14	0.08	0.50	0.13
Sex											
Male	0.51	8.91	8.69	4.68	4.01	0.33	0.09	0.21	0.12	0.70	0.18
Female	0.15	4.62	3.97	2.32	1.65	0.12	0.03	0.07	0.04	0.30	0.08
Race/ethnicity[9]											
White	0.35	5.49	4.31	2.54	1.77	0.16	0.05	0.10	0.06	0.42	0.10
Black	0.74	13.43	15.43	7.66	7.76	0.51	0.09	0.29	0.22	0.87	0.25
Hispanic	0.12	6.53	5.95	3.46	2.49	0.20	0.08	0.15	0.05	0.52	0.13
Asian	0.02	1.50	1.50	1.06	0.43	0.05	0.02	0.04	0.01	0.15	0.03
Pacific Islander	0.04	2.52	3.75	2.37	1.38	0.12	0.10	0.08	0.04	0.23	0.09
American Indian/Alaska Native	0.69	7.70	7.85	4.59	3.26	0.43	0.09	0.24	0.19	0.98	0.24
Two or more races	0.16	6.34	6.37	3.44	2.92	0.22	0.07	0.13	0.10	0.44	0.13
Race/ethnicity by sex[9]											
Male											
White	0.55	7.56	6.24	3.60	2.65	0.24	0.07	0.15	0.09	0.59	0.14
Black	1.06	16.42	19.57	9.38	10.19	0.71	0.13	0.41	0.30	1.15	0.33
Hispanic	0.19	8.49	8.24	4.62	3.62	0.31	0.11	0.23	0.08	0.73	0.19
Asian	0.03	2.17	2.31	1.62	0.69	0.08	0.02	0.06	0.02	0.22	0.05
Pacific Islander	0.06	3.38	5.22	3.23	1.99	0.17	0.16	0.13	0.04	0.33	0.13
American Indian/Alaska Native	1.05	9.82	10.46	5.94	4.52	0.60	0.13	0.34	0.27	1.34	0.32
Two or more races	0.26	8.24	8.81	4.64	4.17	0.32	0.10	0.19	0.14	0.61	0.17
Female											
White	0.13	3.30	2.26	1.43	0.83	0.07	0.02	0.05	0.03	0.23	0.05
Black	0.39	10.33	11.12	5.88	5.24	0.30	0.04	0.17	0.13	0.58	0.16
Hispanic	0.05	4.48	3.55	2.24	1.31	0.09	0.04	0.07	0.02	0.30	0.07
Asian	0.01	0.81	0.66	0.49	0.17	0.02	0.01	0.01	0.00	0.06	0.01
Pacific Islander	0.02	1.60	2.19	1.46	0.73	0.06	0.04	0.03	0.03	0.13	0.05
American Indian/Alaska Native	0.31	5.46	5.11	3.17	1.94	0.25	0.05	0.13	0.12	0.62	0.15
Two or more races	0.07	4.41	3.88	2.22	1.66	0.13	0.03	0.07	0.06	0.27	0.08
Students with disabilities											
Total	0.42	10.95	11.84	5.93	5.92	0.38	0.10	0.29	0.09	0.97	0.27
Sex											
Male	0.53	12.59	14.04	6.87	7.17	0.47	0.13	0.35	0.11	1.16	0.32
Female	0.20	7.67	7.45	4.05	3.40	0.20	0.06	0.15	0.05	0.59	0.17
Race/ethnicity[9]											
White	0.41	8.71	8.51	4.47	4.05	0.26	0.08	0.20	0.06	0.79	0.20
Black	0.67	16.57	20.52	9.54	10.99	0.65	0.12	0.48	0.17	1.36	0.43
Hispanic	0.15	9.57	10.70	5.29	5.41	0.32	0.11	0.25	0.07	0.96	0.27
Asian	0.03	2.61	3.62	2.26	1.36	0.10	0.05	0.08	0.02	0.33	0.11
Pacific Islander	0.04	4.74	10.28	5.90	4.38	0.20	0.73	0.15	0.05	0.38	0.46
American Indian/Alaska Native	0.79	10.32	12.14	6.63	5.50	0.69	0.13	0.45	0.24	1.39	0.37
Two or more races	0.25	10.64	13.24	6.37	6.88	0.42	0.16	0.27	0.15	0.89	0.31
Race/ethnicity by sex[9]											
Male											
White	0.53	10.32	10.48	5.36	5.11	0.32	0.10	0.25	0.07	0.96	0.24
Black	0.83	18.24	23.19	10.48	12.72	0.78	0.14	0.58	0.20	1.57	0.49
Hispanic	0.19	10.98	12.70	6.15	6.55	0.41	0.13	0.32	0.09	1.14	0.33
Asian	0.03	3.10	4.52	2.80	1.72	0.12	0.06	0.10	0.03	0.41	0.12
Pacific Islander	0.05	5.55	12.01	6.73	5.28	0.23	0.87	0.18	0.05	0.41	0.47
American Indian/Alaska Native	0.98	11.85	14.40	7.66	6.74	0.85	0.16	0.56	0.29	1.66	0.45
Two or more races	0.32	12.12	15.79	7.40	8.40	0.52	0.19	0.34	0.18	1.06	0.38
Female											
White	0.18	5.49	4.62	2.69	1.94	0.14	0.04	0.10	0.03	0.44	0.12
Black	0.37	13.17	15.06	7.61	7.45	0.40	0.06	0.29	0.10	0.93	0.31
Hispanic	0.08	6.76	6.73	3.59	3.13	0.14	0.06	0.11	0.03	0.58	0.16
Asian	0.02	1.57	1.73	1.13	0.60	0.04	0.03	0.03	0.01	0.16	0.07
Pacific Islander	‡	2.99	6.55	4.11	2.44	0.14	0.41	0.08	0.05	0.31	0.44
American Indian/Alaska Native	0.42	7.42	7.84	4.68	3.14	0.39	0.06	0.25	0.14	0.88	0.22
Two or more races	0.12	7.73	8.19	4.33	3.88	0.23	0.09	0.12	0.10	0.54	0.18

‡Reporting standards not met (too few cases).

[1]Corporal punishment is paddling, spanking, or other forms of physical punishment imposed on a student.

[2]An in-school suspension is an instance in which a student is temporarily removed from his or her regular classroom(s) for at least half a day but remains under the direct supervision of school personnel.

[3]For students without disabilities and students with disabilities served only under Section 504 of the Rehabilitation Act, out-of-school suspensions are instances in which a student is excluded from school for disciplinary reasons for 1 school day or longer. This does not include students who served their suspension in the school. For students with disabilities served under the Individuals with Disabilities Education Act (IDEA), out-of-school suspensions are instances in which a student is temporarily removed from his or her regular school for disciplinary purposes to another setting (e.g., home, behavior center). This includes both removals in which no Individualized Education Program (IEP) services are provided because the removal is 10 days or less and removals in which IEP services continue to be provided.

[4]Expulsions are actions taken by a local education agency that result in the removal of a student from his or her regular school for disciplinary purposes for the remainder of the school year or longer in accordance with local education agency policy. Expulsions also include removals resulting from violations of the Gun Free Schools Act that are modified to less than 365 days.

[5]Referral to law enforcement is an action by which a student is reported to any law enforcement agency or official, including a school police unit, for an incident that occurs on school grounds, during school-related events, or while taking school transportation, regardless of whether official action is taken.

[6]A school-related arrest is an arrest of a student for any activity conducted on school grounds, during off-campus school activities (including while taking school transportation), or due to a referral by any school official.

[7]Totals include expulsions with and without educational services.

[8]Includes all expulsions under zero-tolerance policies, including expulsions with and without educational services. A zero-tolerance policy results in mandatory expulsion of any student who commits one or more specified offenses (for example, offenses involving guns, other weapons, violence, or similar factors, or combinations of these factors). A policy is considered zero tolerance even if there are some exceptions to the mandatory aspect of the expulsion, such as allowing the chief administering officer of a local education agency to modify the expulsion on a case-by-case basis.

[9]Data by race/ethnicity exclude data for students with disabilities served only under Section 504 (not receiving services under IDEA).

NOTE: The percentage of students receiving a disciplinary action is calculated by dividing the cumulative number of students receiving that type of disciplinary action for the entire 2011–12 school year by the student enrollment based on a count of students taken on a single day between September 27 and December 31. Race categories exclude persons of Hispanic ethnicity.

SOURCE: U.S. Department of Education, Office for Civil Rights, Civil Rights Data Collection, "2011–12 Discipline Estimations by State" and "2011–12 Estimations for Enrollment." (This table was prepared November 2015.)

Table 233.30. Number of students suspended and expelled from public elementary and secondary schools, by sex, race/ethnicity, and state: 2011–12

| State | Total | Sex | | Race/ethnicity[3] | | | | | | |
		Male	Female	White	Black	Hispanic	Asian	Pacific Islander	American Indian/Alaska Native	Two or more races
1	2	3	4	5	6	7	8	9	10	11
United States	3,172,403	2,215,608	956,795	1,084,048	1,200,401	688,774	34,526	8,258	44,549	80,738
Alabama	71,851	47,658	24,193	23,638	45,750	1,294	189	22	394	430
Alaska	6,677	4,917	1,760	2,474	422	389	165	191	2,511	477
Arizona	66,746	48,821	17,925	21,371	7,183	29,877	615	188	5,766	1,327
Arkansas	36,461	25,160	11,301	14,912	18,185	2,302	138	162	147	291
California	360,158	261,540	98,618	78,290	59,639	190,473	12,449	2,996	5,089	8,112
Colorado	42,071	30,394	11,677	16,574	4,605	18,119	564	76	618	1,298
Connecticut	25,890	17,273	8,617	7,284	8,709	8,587	206	18	135	540
Delaware	13,683	9,159	4,524	3,824	7,903	1,414	90	6	34	147
District of Columbia	9,610	5,979	3,631	49	9,047	459	17	1-3	4	20
Florida	309,927	217,352	92,575	99,330	121,468	75,768	1,390	205	1,126	10,067
Georgia	151,879	101,574	50,305	33,081	101,813	11,353	1,131	151	255	3,633
Hawaii	2,510	2,039	471	296	66	178	280	1,245	17	164
Idaho	9,301	7,191	2,110	6,547	183	1,916	48	38	258	165
Illinois	122,860	81,884	40,976	35,786	57,246	24,281	993	70	314	3,371
Indiana	77,747	54,141	23,606	39,672	25,775	6,739	353	38	210	4,540
Iowa	17,999	12,792	5,207	10,626	3,997	2,335	144	26	125	696
Kansas	19,332	14,085	5,247	9,052	4,588	4,133	196	19	322	959
Kentucky	36,842	26,070	10,772	24,706	9,656	1,103	126	11	44	914
Louisiana	65,595	44,085	21,510	18,025	41,689	1,388	215	15	457	480
Maine	7,176	5,315	1,861	6,298	445	137	44	6	62	79
Maryland	48,316	32,661	15,655	11,706	29,795	3,631	521	199	160	1,538
Massachusetts	47,595	33,193	14,402	21,251	8,701	13,322	854	38	188	2,154
Michigan	132,949	91,547	41,402	59,552	60,728	7,218	871	50	1,134	2,795
Minnesota	31,880	22,801	9,079	14,005	11,393	2,951	913	18	1,709	778
Mississippi	51,030	34,216	16,814	12,375	37,897	546	122	15	46	14
Missouri	65,463	45,667	19,796	30,273	30,767	2,412	341	69	285	1,041
Montana	6,187	4,584	1,603	3,767	81	207	18	13	2,015	68
Nebraska	14,002	9,949	4,053	6,733	3,711	2,401	141	14	476	490
Nevada	24,573	17,628	6,945	6,970	5,274	10,071	443	260	387	1,157
New Hampshire	10,011	7,264	2,747	8,360	507	543	98	4	27	69
New Jersey	63,780	44,090	19,690	19,342	25,481	16,737	1,221	68	71	517
New Mexico	23,577	15,818	7,759	4,108	735	15,477	101	9	2,796	293
New York	94,191	65,760	28,431	40,213	34,129	15,413	1,202	51	697	1,073
North Carolina	129,068	90,643	38,425	40,904	65,897	12,837	632	82	3,228	4,682
North Dakota	1,951	1,389	562	1,117	86	66	5	8	650	1-3
Ohio	121,658	84,844	36,814	57,275	51,261	4,474	479	47	153	6,650
Oklahoma	39,013	27,309	11,704	16,452	9,679	6,329	243	90	5,144	984
Oregon	29,337	21,769	7,568	17,499	1,713	6,921	385	201	859	1,506
Pennsylvania	106,859	73,220	33,639	43,092	45,520	14,166	822	39	129	2,509
Rhode Island	12,035	8,298	3,737	5,503	1,898	3,773	192	19	138	447
South Carolina	76,560	52,456	24,104	25,116	45,494	2,992	226	66	245	1,598
South Dakota	4,327	3,062	1,265	2,220	277	236	44	4	1,454	84
Tennessee	77,603	52,282	25,321	29,288	44,498	2,432	377	38	115	439
Texas	269,760	188,832	80,928	41,336	82,231	132,040	2,054	253	926	3,868
Utah	14,644	11,029	3,615	9,111	548	3,743	159	335	443	245
Vermont	3,603	2,605	998	3,139	123	46	13	4	66	42
Virginia	86,196	60,615	25,581	31,465	42,999	6,467	793	71	282	2,961
Washington	57,230	42,438	14,792	29,360	5,906	13,102	1,408	700	1,591	3,738
West Virginia	24,057	17,195	6,862	20,856	2,570	225	37	4	12	263
Wisconsin	47,231	32,479	14,752	17,354	22,023	5,220	446	20	1,011	954
Wyoming	3,416	2,546	870	2,471	111	531	10	4	224	65

See notes at end of table.

Table 233.30. Number of students suspended and expelled from public elementary and secondary schools, by sex, race/ethnicity, and state: 2011–12—Continued

State	Number expelled[2]									
		Sex		Race/ethnicity[3]						
	Total	Male	Female	White	Black	Hispanic	Asian	Pacific Islander	American Indian/Alaska Native	Two or more races
1	12	13	14	15	16	17	18	19	20	21
United States	111,018	83,283	27,735	39,766	39,443	23,696	1,096	266	2,443	2,845
Alabama	1,062	776	286	402	608	21	4	4	4	15
Alaska	96	76	20	35	12	9	4	6	20	6
Arizona	710	547	163	245	52	259	4	0	134	9
Arkansas	728	563	165	411	231	46	4	4	7	7
California	15,537	12,350	3,187	3,816	2,344	7,906	570	120	262	390
Colorado	2,185	1,782	403	844	277	895	25	8	52	67
Connecticut	1,347	1,024	323	524	385	383	10	0	6	22
Delaware	185	139	46	65	98	10	1-3	0	6	1-3
District of Columbia	164	111	53	1-3	156	4	0	0	0	0
Florida	982	752	230	414	270	222	4	1-3	6	48
Georgia	4,391	3,298	1,093	1,218	2,786	225	10	6	5	130
Hawaii	22	18	4	4	0	4	1-3	10	0	0
Idaho	433	341	92	263	4	133	4	1-3	14	1-3
Illinois	3,712	2,662	1,050	1,311	1,606	622	12	0	17	117
Indiana	6,210	4,461	1,749	3,236	2,086	527	15	0	15	294
Iowa	185	161	24	127	22	22	6	0	1-3	6
Kansas	679	551	128	390	122	91	9	1-3	24	37
Kentucky	254	200	54	207	33	8	0	0	0	6
Louisiana	5,752	4,202	1,550	1,372	3,897	92	12	0	55	25
Maine	111	97	14	95	6	4	1-3	0	0	1-3
Maryland	1,476	1,033	443	204	1,156	50	11	0	9	34
Massachusetts	375	312	63	146	94	100	14	0	6	7
Michigan	3,279	2,464	815	1,823	1,123	195	16	0	47	58
Minnesota	1,609	973	636	473	927	115	9	0	56	21
Mississippi	1,062	837	225	282	763	9	4	0	0	4
Missouri	1,514	1,119	395	1,154	247	53	6	0	23	27
Montana	160	114	46	72	1-3	4	0	1-3	78	1-3
Nebraska	659	475	184	320	175	106	8	1-3	17	29
Nevada	79	65	14	53	0	11	1-3	0	7	4
New Hampshire	57	43	14	45	4	6	1-3	0	0	0
New Jersey	505	345	160	90	279	128	0	0	0	6
New Mexico	713	550	163	81	20	369	6	0	221	14
New York	2,411	1,806	605	1,309	722	234	22	4	37	51
North Carolina	647	497	150	294	244	58	1-3	1-3	21	22
North Dakota	66	53	13	41	1-3	0	0	0	23	0
Ohio	5,706	4,176	1,530	2,423	2,754	220	14	6	4	236
Oklahoma	6,840	4,677	2,163	2,077	2,562	866	31	13	890	391
Oregon	1,996	1,529	467	1,188	91	492	12	16	84	89
Pennsylvania	4,253	3,070	1,183	1,860	1,557	701	19	4	4	49
Rhode Island	8	8	0	6	0	0	0	0	1-3	0
South Carolina	2,995	2,359	636	968	1,842	82	1-3	1-3	14	58
South Dakota	58	54	4	33	1-3	4	0	0	17	1-3
Tennessee	7,911	5,738	2,173	2,074	5,559	179	24	4	10	25
Texas	13,787	10,559	3,228	3,119	3,007	6,826	82	13	55	271
Utah	185	141	44	126	6	28	0	4	13	4
Vermont	54	50	4	52	0	0	0	0	0	0
Virginia	1,402	1,166	236	551	568	186	38	1-3	4	39
Washington	3,683	2,880	803	1,914	221	979	71	42	133	191
West Virginia	673	517	156	603	54	8	1-3	0	0	4
Wisconsin	2,019	1,449	570	1,290	463	173	13	4	41	33
Wyoming	179	144	35	118	6	40	1-3	0	11	1-3

[1]For students without disabilities and students with disabilities served only under Section 504 of the Rehabilitation Act, out-of-school suspensions are instances in which a student is excluded from school for disciplinary reasons for 1 school day or longer. This does not include students who served their suspension in the school. For students with disabilities served under the Individuals with Disabilities Education Act (IDEA), out-of-school suspensions are instances in which a student is temporarily removed from his or her regular school for disciplinary purposes to another setting (e.g., home, behavior center). This includes both removals in which no Individualized Education Program (IEP) services are provided because the removal is 10 days or less and removals in which IEP services continue to be provided.

[2]Expulsions are actions taken by a local education agency that result in the removal of a student from his or her regular school for disciplinary purposes, with or without the continu-ation of educational services, for the remainder of the school year or longer in accordance with local education agency policy. Expulsions also include removals resulting from violations of the Gun Free Schools Act that are modified to less than 365 days.

[3]Data by race/ethnicity exclude students with disabilities served only under Section 504 (not receiving services under IDEA).

NOTE: Student counts between 1 and 3 are displayed as 1-3 to protect student privacy. Detail may not sum to totals because of privacy protection routines applied to the data. Race categories exclude persons of Hispanic ethnicity.

SOURCE: U.S. Department of Education, Office for Civil Rights, Civil Rights Data Collection, "2011–12 Discipline Estimations by State." (This table was prepared November 2015.)

Table 233.40. Percentage of students suspended and expelled from public elementary and secondary schools, by sex, race/ethnicity, and state: 2011–12

State	Percent receiving out-of-school suspensions[1]										Percent expelled[2]									
	Total	Sex		Race/ethnicity[3]							Total	Sex		Race/ethnicity[3]						
		Male	Female	White	Black	Hispanic	Asian	Pacific Islander	American Indian/ Alaska Native	Two or more races		Male	Female	White	Black	Hispanic	Asian	Pacific Islander	American Indian/ Alaska Native	Two or more races
1	2	3	4	5	6	7	8	9	10	11	12	13	14	15	16	17	18	19	20	21
United States	**6.40**	**8.69**	**3.97**	**4.31**	**15.43**	**5.95**	**1.50**	**3.75**	**7.85**	**6.37**	**0.22**	**0.33**	**0.12**	**0.16**	**0.51**	**0.20**	**0.05**	**0.12**	**0.43**	**0.22**
Alabama	9.63	12.44	6.67	5.52	18.02	3.77	1.94	4.79	6.32	5.95	0.14	0.20	0.08	0.09	0.24	0.06	0.04	0.87	0.06	0.21
Alaska	4.99	7.10	2.72	3.69	8.69	4.61	1.93	6.41	8.30	4.60	0.07	0.11	0.03	0.05	0.25	0.11	0.05	0.20	0.07	0.06
Arizona	6.08	8.66	3.36	4.62	12.43	6.51	1.99	5.07	10.37	7.52	0.06	0.10	0.03	0.05	0.09	0.06	0.01	‡	0.24	0.05
Arkansas	7.66	10.34	4.85	4.98	17.47	4.88	1.91	6.91	5.28	4.60	0.15	0.23	0.07	0.07	0.23	0.10	0.06	0.17	0.19	0.11
California	5.75	8.13	3.24	4.88	14.56	5.86	1.87	5.40	9.20	4.60	0.25	0.38	0.10	0.24	0.57	0.24	0.09	0.22	0.47	0.22
Colorado	4.87	6.87	2.77	3.46	11.18	6.64	2.10	4.13	8.24	5.00	0.25	0.40	0.10	0.18	0.67	0.33	0.09	0.43	0.69	0.26
Connecticut	4.61	5.97	3.17	2.20	12.40	8.18	0.84	3.78	5.94	5.94	0.24	0.35	0.13	0.16	0.55	0.36	0.04	‡	0.26	0.20
Delaware	10.30	13.39	7.02	5.98	16.72	8.33	2.02	6.59	5.28	6.46	0.14	0.20	0.07	0.10	0.23	0.06	‡	‡	0.93	‡
District of Columbia	10.30	16.38	9.95	0.88	18.42	4.84	1.70	‡	1.80	12.85	0.22	0.30	0.15	0.04	0.28	0.04	0.01	‡	‡	‡
Florida	11.64	15.88	7.15	9.04	20.16	10.07	2.07	6.92	11.68	10.10	0.04	0.05	0.02	†	0.04	0.03	0.01	†	0.06	0.06
Georgia	8.94	11.67	6.07	4.50	16.17	5.55	1.98	8.20	6.60	7.19	0.26	0.38	0.13	0.17	0.44	0.11	0.02	0.33	0.13	0.26
Hawaii	2.13	2.13	1.63	1.17	1.56	1.45	0.45	2.04	1.78	2.95	0.02	0.03	#	0.02	0.13	0.03	0.10	0.02	0.33	‡
Idaho	3.27	4.90	1.53	3.00	5.99	4.40	1.24	3.38	6.05	2.95	0.15	0.25	0.07	0.12	0.44	0.13	0.10	‡	0.27	0.20
Illinois	5.94	7.71	4.07	3.47	15.54	5.00	1.14	3.50	6.93	10.10	0.15	0.25	0.10	0.13	0.44	0.13	0.01	‡	0.49	0.20
Indiana	7.44	10.10	4.64	5.29	20.72	7.26	1.93	5.00	6.93	10.10	0.59	0.83	0.34	0.43	1.68	0.57	0.08	‡	0.49	0.65
Iowa	3.64	5.02	2.17	2.68	15.30	5.54	1.35	3.37	5.17	5.76	0.04	0.06	0.01	0.03	0.08	0.05	0.06	‡	0.36	0.05
Kansas	4.01	5.67	2.25	2.82	12.91	5.11	1.56	2.36	4.85	4.69	0.14	0.22	0.05	0.12	0.34	0.07	0.07	‡	0.26	0.18
Kentucky	5.35	7.34	3.23	4.48	13.14	3.70	1.33	1.68	4.72	5.35	0.04	0.06	0.02	0.03	0.04	0.03	‡	‡	1.05	0.04
Louisiana	9.49	12.43	6.39	5.68	13.99	5.17	2.10	3.92	8.72	6.35	0.83	1.18	0.46	0.43	1.31	0.34	0.12	‡	1.05	0.33
Maine	4.01	5.75	2.15	3.95	8.17	4.94	1.93	2.60	4.88	4.08	0.06	0.10	0.02	0.06	0.11	0.14	‡	‡	‡	1.27
Maryland	5.63	7.41	3.75	3.85	9.12	3.49	1.04	4.00	5.60	5.04	0.17	0.23	0.11	0.07	0.35	0.05	0.02	0.04	0.32	0.11
Massachusetts	5.00	6.80	3.11	3.51	10.82	8.89	1.58	3.63	8.10	4.69	0.04	0.06	0.01	0.03	0.39	0.07	0.03	‡	0.26	0.02
Michigan	8.39	11.21	5.39	5.45	20.86	7.72	2.01	3.26	8.58	5.89	0.21	0.30	0.13	0.17	1.11	0.21	0.02	0.13	0.36	0.11
Minnesota	3.64	5.08	2.13	2.23	13.64	4.57	1.68	1.85	10.41	4.22	0.18	0.26	0.15	0.12	1.11	0.18	0.02	‡	0.34	0.11
Mississippi	10.31	13.51	6.96	3.95	15.54	4.94	2.46	2.60	4.39	4.08	0.21	0.10	0.09	0.06	0.31	0.07	0.08	‡	‡	1.27
Missouri	7.11	9.61	4.44	4.45	20.64	5.60	1.99	4.00	6.69	6.77	0.16	0.24	0.09	0.17	0.17	0.12	0.04	‡	0.54	0.18
Montana	4.39	6.33	2.34	3.34	10.56	4.86	1.45	3.63	11.96	3.62	0.11	0.16	0.07	0.06	0.87	0.21	0.13	‡	0.45	0.32
Nebraska	4.64	6.98	2.78	3.21	18.34	4.96	2.25	3.57	8.77	5.47	0.22	0.30	0.13	0.15	1.11	0.21	0.02	‡	0.31	0.02
Nevada	5.56	7.73	3.25	4.28	12.51	5.77	1.79	4.74	7.69	5.05	0.03	0.05	0.01	0.03	0.11	0.08	0.02	‡	0.14	0.02
New Hampshire	5.42	7.64	3.07	5.37	13.71	7.31	1.83	2.38	7.81	2.71	0.03	0.05	0.02	0.03	0.11	0.08	‡	0.08	‡	‡
New Jersey	4.68	6.31	2.97	2.85	11.54	5.71	1.00	2.50	4.21	3.43	0.04	0.05	0.02	0.01	0.13	0.04	‡	‡	0.66	0.04
New Mexico	7.25	9.49	4.89	4.93	10.87	8.07	2.48	2.63	8.31	7.23	0.22	0.33	0.10	0.10	0.30	0.19	0.15	‡	0.25	0.35
New York	3.43	4.66	2.13	3.12	6.77	2.45	0.53	1.62	4.65	4.17	0.09	0.13	0.05	0.04	0.14	0.04	0.01	‡	0.09	0.20
North Carolina	8.64	11.84	5.27	4.28	17.19	6.50	1.64	4.62	14.14	9.03	0.04	0.06	0.03	0.04	0.06	0.03	‡	0.08	0.09	0.04
North Dakota	1.94	2.67	1.15	1.37	2.88	2.29	0.41	3.38	6.76	9.03	0.07	0.10	0.03	0.05	‡	‡	‡	‡	0.24	0.04
Ohio	6.84	9.25	4.27	4.38	18.51	6.82	1.55	5.53	6.30	8.89	0.32	0.46	0.18	0.19	0.99	0.34	0.05	0.71	0.16	0.32
Oklahoma	5.96	8.10	3.68	4.74	18.50	7.29	1.97	5.14	4.79	3.03	1.04	1.39	0.68	0.60	4.02	1.00	0.25	0.74	0.83	1.20
Oregon	5.25	7.58	2.78	4.86	12.03	5.97	1.75	5.22	8.05	5.86	0.36	0.53	0.17	0.33	0.64	0.42	0.05	0.42	0.79	0.35
Pennsylvania	6.11	8.15	3.95	3.53	17.25	9.85	1.46	2.60	4.23	7.15	0.24	0.34	0.14	0.15	0.59	0.49	0.03	0.27	0.13	0.14
Rhode Island	8.77	11.69	5.64	6.59	16.43	12.74	4.85	9.95	14.24	8.82	0.01	0.01	#	0.01	‡	‡	‡	‡	‡	‡
South Carolina	10.31	13.70	6.71	6.47	17.18	6.17	2.22	6.73	10.50	8.38	0.40	0.62	0.18	0.25	0.70	0.17	0.05	‡	0.60	0.30
South Dakota	7.92	10.38	5.32	4.61	8.10	4.68	2.24	3.33	10.72	3.42	0.05	0.08	0.01	0.03	2.43	0.08	0.25	0.74	0.13	‡
Tennessee	5.39	10.38	3.32	4.42	19.48	4.76	2.23	3.84	5.57	4.76	0.81	1.14	0.46	0.31	2.43	0.35	0.14	0.35	0.48	0.27
Texas	2.45	3.59	1.25	2.83	13.13	5.30	1.16	3.70	5.89	4.47	0.28	0.41	0.13	0.21	0.48	0.27	0.05	0.04	0.23	0.31
Utah	2.45	3.59	1.25	1.99	6.61	4.12	1.48	3.70	5.89	2.66	0.03	0.05	0.02	0.03	0.07	0.03	‡	0.04	0.17	0.04
Vermont	4.53	6.34	2.60	4.51	6.99	5.40	0.83	4.49	10.71	3.41	0.07	0.12	0.01	0.07	0.19	0.12	0.05	‡	0.60	0.08
Virginia	6.78	9.24	4.15	4.69	14.26	4.33	1.04	3.92	6.95	5.75	0.11	0.18	0.04	0.08	0.14	0.47	0.09	‡	0.83	0.31
Washington	5.40	7.78	2.87	4.71	13.88	4.87	1.87	7.42	9.95	6.05	0.35	0.53	0.16	0.31	0.44	0.20	‡	0.45	‡	‡
West Virginia	8.43	11.62	5.00	8.08	17.68	6.58	1.85	3.64	3.68	6.05	0.24	0.35	0.13	0.23	0.37	0.23	0.04	0.53	0.36	0.21
Wisconsin	5.41	7.23	3.48	2.71	25.72	6.76	1.45	2.64	8.98	5.93	0.23	0.32	0.11	0.20	0.54	0.20	0.04	‡	‡	‡
Wyoming	3.65	5.28	1.92	3.33	8.55	4.74	1.14	1.46	6.56	4.79	0.19	0.30	0.08	0.16	0.46	0.36	‡	‡	0.32	‡

#Rounds to zero.
‡Reporting standards not met (too few cases).
[1]For students without disabilities and students with disabilities served only under Section 504 of the Rehabilitation Act, out-of-school suspensions are instances in which a student is excluded from school for disciplinary reasons for 1 school day or longer. This does not include students who served their suspension in the school. For students with disabilities served under the Individuals with Disabilities Education Act (IDEA), out-of-school suspensions are instances in which a student is temporarily removed from his or her regular school for disciplinary purposes to another setting (e.g., home, behavior center). This includes both removals in which no Individualized Education Program (IEP) services are provided because the removal is 10 days or less and removals in which IEP services continue to be provided.

[2]Expulsions are actions taken by a local education agency that result in the removal of a student from his or her regular school for disciplinary purposes, with or without the continuation of educational services, for the remainder of the school year or longer in accordance with local education agency policy. Expulsions also include removals resulting from violations of the Gun Free Schools Act that are modified to less than 365 days.
[3]Data by race/ethnicity exclude students with disabilities served only under Section 504 (not receiving services under IDEA).
NOTE: The percentage of students receiving a disciplinary action is calculated by dividing the cumulative number of students receiving that type of disciplinary action for the entire 2011–12 school year by the student enrollment based on a count of students taken on a single day between September 27 and December 31. Race categories exclude persons of Hispanic ethnicity.
SOURCE: U.S. Department of Education, Office for Civil Rights, Civil Rights Data Collection, "2011–12 Discipline Estimations by State" and "2011–12 Estimations for Enrollment." (This table was prepared November 2015.)

Table 233.45. Number of discipline incidents resulting in removal of a student from a regular education program for at least an entire school day and rate of incidents per 100,000 students, by discipline reason and state: 2013–14

State	Number of discipline incidents					Rate of discipline incidents per 100,000 students				
	Total	Alcohol	Illicit drug	Violent incident[1]	Weapons possession	Total	Alcohol	Illicit drug	Violent incident[1]	Weapons possession
1	2	3	4	5	6	7	8	9	10	11
United States	1,308,568	24,015	197,171	1,020,894	66,488	2,615	48	394	2,040	133
Alabama	41,991	560	5,931	33,808	1,692	5,627	75	795	4,531	227
Alaska	2,755	116	580	1,915	144	2,104	89	443	1,462	110
Arizona	30,463	816	3,774	25,050	823	2,763	74	342	2,272	75
Arkansas	20,890	410	1,894	17,743	843	4,263	84	387	3,621	172
California	285,039	—[2]	46,425[2]	224,727	13,887	4,515	—[2]	735[2]	3,560	220
Colorado	61,546	711	6,866	53,262	707	7,018	81	783	6,073	81
Connecticut	25,670	418	1,379	22,643	1,230	4,700	77	252	4,146	225
Delaware	597	56	315	63	163	453	43	239	48	124
District of Columbia	7,088	33	198	6,655	202	9,069	42	253	8,515	258
Florida	16,755	992	10,642	3,605	1,516	616	36	391	133	56
Georgia	67,772	725	10,145	53,974	2,928	3,931	42	588	3,131	170
Hawaii	1,956	155	610	946	245	1,047	83	327	506	131
Idaho	946	62	481	233	170	319	21	162	79	57
Illinois	16,502	1,106	6,043	4,795	4,558	798	54	292	232	221
Indiana	42,221	931	3,229	36,447	1,614	4,031	89	308	3,480	154
Iowa	12,410	301	2,000	9,336	773	2,467	60	398	1,856	154
Kansas	11,106	237	2,068	8,186	615	2,237	48	417	1,649	124
Kentucky	44,472	649	9,521	33,947	355	6,565	96	1,406	5,011	52
Louisiana	47,602	340	5,339	40,574	1,349	6,690	48	750	5,703	190
Maine	3,257	110	595	2,381	171	1,770	60	323	1,294	93
Maryland	33,586	584	3,077	28,215	1,710	3,878	67	355	3,257	197
Massachusetts[3]	24,272	542	2,727	19,795	1,208	2,540	57	285	2,071	126
Michigan	11,677	245	1,450	9,101	881	754	16	94	588	57
Minnesota[3]	21,097	478	4,045	15,511	1,063	2,479	56	475	1,823	125
Mississippi	15,040	304	803	13,276	657	3,053	62	163	2,695	133
Missouri	19,993	917	6,732	10,904	1,440	2,177	100	733	1,187	157
Montana	4,768	162	1,030	3,334	242	3,308	112	715	2,313	168
Nebraska	8,229	169	1,307	6,305	448	2,675	55	425	2,049	146
Nevada	10,015	278	1,968	7,317	452	2,217	62	436	1,619	100
New Hampshire	5,022	124	701	3,855	342	2,696	67	376	2,069	184
New Jersey	12,026	371	2,320	8,541	794	878	27	169	623	58
New Mexico	13,878	303	3,619	9,117	839	4,091	89	1,067	2,687	247
New York	18,625	1,373	5,160	7,037	5,055	682	50	189	258	185
North Carolina	65,259	858	10,413	51,417	2,571	4,263	56	680	3,359	168
North Dakota	1,460	58	432	899	71	1,405	56	416	865	68
Ohio	76,271	1,047	8,175	64,108	2,941	4,424	61	474	3,718	171
Oklahoma	14,483	418	2,199	10,702	1,164	2,124	61	323	1,570	171
Oregon	15,104	379	2,850	11,332	543	2,547	64	481	1,911	92
Pennsylvania	39,744	698	2,793	33,741	2,512	2,264	40	159	1,922	143
Rhode Island	14,735	60	834	13,603	238	10,376	42	587	9,579	168
South Carolina	21,622	403	1,631	19,271	317	2,900	54	219	2,584	43
South Dakota[3]	3,297	100	827	2,154	216	2,519	76	632	1,646	165
Tennessee	36,335	2,643	525	33,075	92	3,657	266	53	3,329	9
Texas	2,468	37	1,422	517	492	48	1	28	10	10
Utah[3]	6,162	112	1,732	3,899	419	985	18	277	623	67
Vermont	—	—	—	—	—	—	—	—	—	—
Virginia	21,210	856	937	17,336	2,081	1,665	67	74	1,361	163
Washington	23,172	1,187	6,177	13,472	2,336	2,188	112	583	1,272	221
West Virginia	3,213	42	507	2,604	60	1,144	15	180	927	21
Wisconsin	24,116	535	2,735	19,797	1,049	2,758	61	313	2,264	120
Wyoming	651	4	8	369	270	702	4	9	398	291

—Not available.
[1] Includes violent incidents with and without physical injury.
[2] Alcohol incidents were reported in the illicit drug category.
[3] This state did not report state-level counts of discipline incidents, but did report school-level counts. The sums of the school-level counts are displayed in place of the unreported state-level counts.

SOURCE: U.S. Department of Education, National Center for Education Statistics, EDFacts file 030, Data Group 523, extracted October 14, 2015, from the EDFacts Data Warehouse (internal U.S. Department of Education source); Common Core of Data (CCD), "State Nonfiscal Survey of Public Elementary and Secondary Education," 2013–14. (This table was prepared October 2015.)

Table 233.50. Percentage of public schools with various safety and security measures: Selected years, 1999–2000 through 2013–14

[Standard errors appear in parentheses]

School safety and security measures	1999–2000		2003–04		2005–06		2007–08		2009–10		2013–14[1]	
1	2		3		4		5		6		7	
Controlled access during school hours												
Buildings (e.g., locked or monitored doors)	74.6	(1.35)	83.0	(1.04)	84.9	(0.89)	89.5	(0.80)	91.7	(0.80)	93.3	(0.95)
Grounds (e.g., locked or monitored gates)	33.7	(1.26)	36.2	(1.08)	41.1	(1.25)	42.6	(1.41)	46.0	(1.26)	42.7	(1.53)
Visitors required to sign or check in	96.6	(0.54)	98.3	(0.40)	97.6	(0.42)	98.7	(0.37)	99.3	(0.27)	98.6	(0.49)
Campus closed for most students during lunch	64.6	(1.48)	66.0	(1.08)	66.1	(1.19)	65.0	(1.34)	66.9	(0.88)	92.6	(0.80)
Student dress, IDs, and school supplies												
Required students to wear uniforms	11.8	(0.82)	13.8	(0.85)	13.8	(0.78)	17.5	(0.70)	18.9	(1.02)	20.4	(1.27)
Enforced a strict dress code	47.4	(1.50)	55.1	(1.24)	55.3	(1.18)	54.8	(1.20)	56.9	(1.56)	58.5	(1.60)
Required students to wear badges or picture IDs	3.9	(0.32)	6.4	(0.64)	6.2	(0.47)	7.6	(0.60)	6.9	(0.57)	8.9	(0.81)
Required faculty and staff to wear badges or picture IDs	25.4	(1.39)	48.0	(1.21)	47.9	(1.12)	58.3	(1.37)	62.9	(1.14)	68.0	(1.65)
Required clear book bags or banned book bags on school grounds	5.9	(0.50)	6.2	(0.63)	6.4	(0.43)	6.0	(0.48)	5.5	(0.53)	6.3	(0.81)
Provided school lockers to students	46.5	(1.07)	49.5	(1.24)	50.5	(1.08)	48.9	(1.17)	52.1	(1.10)	49.9	(1.35)
Drug testing												
Athletes	—	(†)	4.2	(0.44)	5.0	(0.46)	6.4	(0.48)	6.0	(0.52)	6.6	(0.59)
Students in extracurricular activities (other than athletes)	—	(†)	2.6	(0.37)	3.4	(0.32)	4.5	(0.51)	4.6	(0.47)	4.3	(0.47)
Any other students	—	(†)	—	(†)	3.0	(0.34)	3.0	(0.42)	3.0	(0.26)	3.5	(0.44)
Metal detectors, dogs, and sweeps												
Random metal detector checks on students	7.2	(0.54)	5.6	(0.55)	4.9	(0.40)	5.3	(0.37)	5.2	(0.42)	4.2	(0.48)
Students required to pass through metal detectors daily	0.9	(0.16)	1.1	(0.16)	1.1	(0.18)	1.3	(0.20)	1.4	(0.24)	2.0	(0.40)
Random dog sniffs to check for drugs	20.6	(0.75)	21.3	(0.77)	23.0	(0.79)	21.5	(0.59)	22.9	(0.71)	24.1	(0.97)
Random sweeps[2] for contraband (e.g., drugs or weapons)	11.8	(0.54)	12.8	(0.58)	13.1	(0.76)	11.4	(0.71)	12.1	(0.68)	11.4	(0.86)
Communication systems and technology												
Provided telephones in most classrooms	44.6	(1.80)	60.8	(1.48)	66.9	(1.30)	71.6	(1.16)	74.0	(1.13)	78.7	(1.34)
Provided electronic notification system for schoolwide emergency	—	(†)	—	(†)	—	(†)	43.2	(1.26)	63.1	(1.40)	81.6	(1.12)
Provided structured anonymous threat reporting system[3]	—	(†)	—	(†)	—	(†)	31.2	(1.22)	35.9	(1.19)	46.5	(1.63)
Used security cameras to monitor the school	19.4	(0.88)	36.0	(1.28)	42.8	(1.29)	55.0	(1.37)	61.1	(1.16)	75.1	(1.31)
Provided two-way radios to any staff	—	(†)	71.2	(1.18)	70.9	(1.22)	73.1	(1.15)	73.3	(1.33)	74.2	(1.42)
Limited access to social networking sites from school computers	—	(†)	—	(†)	—	(†)	—	(†)	93.4	(0.59)	91.9	(0.80)
Prohibited use of cell phones and text messaging devices	—	(†)	—	(†)	—	(†)	—	(†)	90.9	(0.67)	75.9	(1.07)

—Not available.
†Not applicable.
[1]Data for 2013–14 were collected using the Fast Response Survey System, while data for earlier years were collected using the School Survey on Crime and Safety (SSOCS). The 2013–14 survey was designed to allow comparisons with SSOCS data. However, respondents to the 2013–14 survey could choose either to complete the survey on paper (and mail it back) or to complete the survey online, whereas respondents to SSOCS did not have the option of completing the survey online. The 2013–14 survey also relied on a smaller sample. The smaller sample size and change in survey administration may have impacted 2013–14 results.

[2]Does not include random dog sniffs.
[3]For example, a system for reporting threats through online submission, telephone hotline, or written submission via drop box.
NOTE: Responses were provided by the principal or the person most knowledgeable about crime and safety issues at the school.
SOURCE: U.S. Department of Education, National Center for Education Statistics, 1999–2000, 2003–04, 2005–06, 2007–08, and 2009–10 School Survey on Crime and Safety (SSOCS), 2000, 2004, 2006, 2008, and 2010; Fast Response Survey System (FRSS), "School Safety and Discipline: 2013–14," FRSS 106, 2014. (This table was prepared September 2015.)

Table 233.60. Percentage of public schools with various safety and security measures, by selected school characteristics: 2013–14

[Standard errors appear in parentheses]

School characteristic	Total schools — Number	Total schools — Percentage distribution	Controlled access — School buildings[1]	Controlled access — School grounds[2]	Student dress, IDs, and school supplies — School uniforms required	Student dress, IDs, and school supplies — Strict dress code enforced	Student dress, IDs, and school supplies — Student badges or picture IDs required	Student dress, IDs, and school supplies — Faculty/staff badges or picture IDs required	Student dress, IDs, and school supplies — Bookbags must be clear or are banned	Metal detectors, dogs, and sweeps — Random metal detector checks	Metal detectors, dogs, and sweeps — Daily metal detector checks[3]	Metal detectors, dogs, and sweeps — Random dog sniffs for drugs	Metal detectors, dogs, and sweeps — Random sweeps for contraband[4]	Used security cameras to monitor the school
	2	3	4	5	6	7	8	9	10	11	12	13	14	15
Total	84,100 (840)	100.0 (†)	93.3 (0.95)	42.7 (1.53)	20.4 (1.27)	58.5 (1.60)	8.9 (0.81)	66.0 (1.65)	6.3 (0.81)	4.2 (0.48)	2.0 (0.40)	24.1 (0.97)	11.4 (0.86)	75.1 (1.31)
School level[5]														
Primary	49,700 (800)	59.1 (0.47)	94.5 (1.27)	47.3 (2.36)	22.7 (1.99)	52.6 (2.49)	4.1 (0.98)	72.8 (2.35)	4.5 (1.20)	1.4! (0.52)	1.0! (0.45)	5.5 (1.17)	3.3 (0.95)	67.2 (2.07)
Middle	16,100 (250)	19.1 (0.33)	94.9 (1.21)	36.2 (2.43)	19.7 (2.03)	70.5 (2.61)	16.0 (1.96)	68.5 (2.61)	9.9 (1.58)	7.6 (1.23)	2.4! (0.76)	44.2 (2.46)	19.9 (2.06)	83.7 (1.96)
High school/combined	18,400 (330)	21.8 (0.40)	88.8 (1.60)	35.9 (2.47)	14.8 (1.66)	63.8 (2.55)	15.6 (1.72)	54.4 (2.55)	8.1 (1.53)	8.7 (1.48)	4.3 (0.96)	57.0 (2.39)	26.1 (2.36)	89.2 (1.65)
Enrollment size														
Less than 300	19,500 (1,540)	23.2 (1.63)	87.1 (2.98)	24.9 (3.65)	14.8 (2.54)	56.3 (3.96)	5.6! (1.95)	46.1 (4.25)	8.5 (2.04)	2.0! (0.88)	‡ (†)	28.8 (3.39)	14.3 (2.40)	73.2 (3.57)
300–499	25,400 (1,250)	30.1 (1.62)	96.9 (0.96)	43.5 (2.95)	20.3 (2.26)	56.6 (2.97)	8.0 (1.65)	71.0 (2.75)	5.4 (1.24)	4.6 (1.14)	2.1! (0.78)	15.1 (1.50)	8.3 (1.34)	74.8 (2.50)
500–999	30,700 (950)	36.5 (1.22)	94.7 (1.04)	50.4 (2.46)	25.1 (2.23)	59.8 (2.30)	7.9 (1.08)	76.6 (2.06)	5.6 (0.97)	3.7 (0.71)	2.1! (0.66)	22.1 (1.31)	10.1 (1.02)	72.8 (2.04)
1,000 or more	8,500 (300)	10.1 (0.38)	92.1 (1.38)	53.2 (2.92)	16.3 (2.39)	64.3 (3.03)	22.6 (2.46)	78.2 (2.43)	6.5 (1.35)	9.6 (1.55)	3.8 (1.05)	47.5 (3.06)	19.2 (2.27)	89.1 (2.11)
Locale														
City	21,100 (570)	25.1 (0.56)	94.0 (1.30)	56.0 (3.14)	41.2 (3.24)	66.1 (2.99)	13.0 (1.73)	66.9 (3.06)	8.8 (1.78)	9.9 (1.48)	5.0 (1.14)	10.7 (1.01)	10.8 (1.28)	68.4 (3.07)
Suburban	23,500 (630)	28.0 (0.86)	96.6 (1.05)	44.9 (3.30)	17.0 (2.57)	56.2 (2.95)	9.9 (1.52)	79.1 (2.43)	3.1! (1.20)	2.5! (0.77)	‡ (†)	18.9 (1.72)	8.3 (1.52)	78.3 (2.37)
Town	10,800 (750)	12.9 (0.93)	95.8 (1.45)	40.0 (4.37)	13.9 (2.92)	53.1 (4.39)	4.3! (1.54)	67.4 (4.02)	9.5 (2.18)	3.9! (1.47)	‡ (†)	31.9 (2.56)	14.0 (2.36)	75.8 (3.88)
Rural	28,600 (1,030)	34.1 (0.97)	89.3 (2.18)	32.1 (2.87)	10.3 (1.63)	56.8 (2.80)	6.8 (1.40)	59.9 (3.17)	5.9 (1.13)	1.4! (0.43)	‡ (†)	35.4 (2.19)	13.5 (1.75)	77.3 (2.87)
Percent combined enrollment of Black, Hispanic, Asian/Pacific Islander, and American Indian/Alaska Native students														
Less than 5 percent	7,300 (920)	8.7 (1.07)	91.3 (3.88)	22.2 (5.42)	‡ (†)	46.3 (5.44)	‡ (†)	63.8 (5.81)	‡ (†)	‡ (†)	‡ (†)	26.2 (4.19)	12.1! (4.21)	77.0 (5.80)
5 percent to less than 20 percent	22,800 (1,130)	27.1 (1.32)	93.8 (1.76)	25.3 (2.72)	2.5! (0.82)	48.4 (3.38)	3.7! (1.15)	68.8 (3.23)	5.6 (1.16)	‡ (†)	‡ (†)	33.3 (2.85)	9.7 (1.49)	81.1 (2.58)
20 percent to less than 50 percent	22,700 (1,290)	27.0 (1.51)	93.6 (1.59)	41.3 (3.19)	12.3 (2.30)	56.9 (3.33)	6.2 (1.19)	73.2 (2.96)	4.8 (1.30)	2.9 (0.86)	‡ (†)	24.9 (1.89)	10.2 (1.58)	75.9 (2.72)
50 percent or more	31,300 (1,120)	37.2 (1.35)	93.4 (1.43)	61.0 (2.75)	43.8 (2.84)	69.8 (2.18)	16.0 (1.80)	64.6 (2.60)	8.1 (1.45)	8.2 (1.05)	3.8 (0.82)	16.4 (1.32)	13.5 (1.45)	69.9 (2.14)
Percent of students eligible for free or reduced-price lunch[6]														
0–25	15,100 (1,090)	18.0 (1.30)	93.7 (1.97)	38.4 (3.25)	4.1! (1.80)	40.8 (3.59)	6.2! (1.89)	81.9 (3.59)	2.9! (1.89)	‡ (†)	‡ (†)	22.9 (2.97)	4.5 (1.26)	73.9 (3.45)
26–50	22,900 (1,290)	27.3 (1.48)	91.6 (2.13)	34.4 (2.92)	5.6 (1.19)	52.9 (3.46)	6.1 (1.33)	69.2 (3.13)	3.2 (0.84)	2.3! (0.71)	‡ (†)	28.2 (2.11)	10.9 (1.46)	76.8 (2.57)
51–75	23,200 (1,200)	27.6 (1.43)	91.7 (1.89)	39.6 (3.19)	17.7 (2.24)	63.0 (3.30)	9.2 (1.41)	60.4 (3.09)	7.0 (1.30)	4.1 (1.0)	2.0! (0.7)	30.5 (2.19)	14.5 (2.15)	78.2 (2.68)
76–100	19,800 (1,100)	23.5 (1.28)	95.9 (1.34)	59.1 (3.66)	53.2 (3.12)	74.4 (2.63)	14.7 (1.89)	65.3 (3.10)	10.9 (2.09)	8.3 (1.3)	4.3 (1.17)	14.0 (1.91)	14.1 (1.95)	71.0 (3.04)

†Not applicable.

!Interpret data with caution. The coefficient of variation (CV) for this estimate is between 30 and 50 percent.

‡Reporting standards not met. Either there are too few cases for a reliable estimate or the coefficient of variation (CV) is 50 percent or greater.

[1]Access to buildings is controlled during school hours (e.g., by locked or monitored doors).

[2]Access to grounds is controlled during school hours (e.g., by locked or monitored gates).

[3]All students must pass through a metal detector each day.

[4]Examples of contraband include drugs and weapons. The "sweeps" category does not include dog sniffs.

[5]Primary schools are defined as schools in which the lowest grade is not higher than grade 3 and the highest grade is not higher than grade 8. Middle schools are defined as schools in which the lowest grade is not lower than grade 4 and the highest grade is not higher than grade 9. High schools are defined as schools in which the lowest grade is not lower than grade 9 and the highest grade is not higher than grade 12. Combined schools include all other combinations of grades, including K–12 schools. Separate data on high schools and combined schools are not available.

[6]The classification of schools by the percentage of students eligible for free or reduced-price lunch was computed based on data obtained from the Common Core of Data.

NOTE: Responses were provided by the principal or the person most knowledgeable about crime and safety issues at the school. Detail may not sum to totals because of rounding.

SOURCE: U.S. Department of Education, National Center for Education Statistics, Fast Response Survey System (FRSS), "School Safety and Discipline: 2013–14," FRSS 106, 2014; and Common Core of Data (CCD), "Public Elementary/Secondary School Universe Survey," 2013–14. (This table was prepared September 2015.)

Table 233.65. Percentage of public schools with a written plan for procedures to be performed in selected crises and percentage that have drilled students on the use of a plan, by selected school characteristics: Selected years, 2003–04 through 2013–14

[Standard errors appear in parentheses]

Year and school characteristic	Percent with a written plan that describes procedures to be performed in selected crises								Percent that have drilled students during the current school year on the use of a plan in selected crises[1]				
	Shootings	Natural disasters[2]	Hostages	Bomb threats or incidents	Chemical, biological, or radiological threats or incidents[3]	Suicide threat or incident	Severe risk of terrorist attack[4]	Pandemic flu	Shootings	Natural disasters[2]	Hostages	Bomb threats or incidents	Chemical, biological, or radiological threats or incidents[3]
1	2	3	4	5	6	7	8	9	10	11	12	13	14
2003–04[5]													
All public schools	78.5 (1.17)	96.0 (0.52)	73.5 (1.12)	94.0 (0.71)	69.2 (1.15)	— (†)	— (†)	— (†)	46.5 (1.19)	84.0 (1.02)	43.0 (1.40)	55.4 (1.40)	39.2 (1.66)
School level[6]													
Primary	75.5 (1.87)	96.9 (0.73)	73.0 (1.62)	94.5 (0.95)	70.6 (1.73)	(†)	(†)	(†)	47.9 (2.14)	85.0 (1.51)	44.8 (2.36)	55.6 (2.20)	40.4 (2.32)
Middle	86.1 (1.20)	96.9 (0.53)	77.6 (1.25)	95.6 (0.66)	70.3 (1.49)	(†)	(†)	(†)	47.9 (2.08)	81.9 (1.29)	43.4 (1.83)	58.1 (1.77)	38.7 (2.05)
High school	85.7 (1.29)	95.4 (0.82)	78.9 (1.60)	96.1 (0.84)	72.5 (1.60)	(†)	(†)	(†)	44.4 (1.89)	81.6 (1.35)	39.8 (1.84)	59.3 (1.67)	34.4 (2.19)
Combined	72.0 (4.69)	88.5 (3.62)	58.3 (4.58)	82.6 (4.39)	51.2 (4.88)	(†)	(†)	(†)	36.4 (7.07)	85.2 (3.89)	32.5 (7.42)	38.9 (6.66)	39.3 (8.30)
Enrollment size													
Less than 300	69.4 (3.06)	91.8 (1.84)	63.5 (3.06)	88.2 (2.37)	58.4 (3.18)	(†)	(†)	(†)	38.7 (4.06)	76.4 (3.39)	34.1 (4.55)	44.1 (4.05)	32.8 (4.45)
300–499	79.7 (2.25)	97.3 (0.78)	74.7 (2.23)	94.1 (1.20)	72.4 (2.23)	(†)	(†)	(†)	45.2 (2.32)	86.8 (1.72)	42.2 (2.54)	52.8 (2.43)	38.0 (2.73)
500–999	81.5 (1.46)	97.5 (0.59)	76.6 (1.58)	96.8 (0.67)	72.3 (1.68)	(†)	(†)	(†)	49.5 (1.93)	86.1 (1.36)	45.8 (1.94)	59.7 (2.20)	40.7 (2.19)
1,000 or more	85.3 (1.67)	96.8 (0.77)	81.4 (1.85)	96.7 (0.98)	73.8 (2.03)	(†)	(†)	(†)	54.2 (2.14)	85.0 (1.56)	51.2 (2.42)	69.7 (1.95)	48.0 (2.37)
Locale													
City	74.0 (2.71)	95.8 (0.96)	67.4 (2.92)	92.9 (1.43)	70.7 (2.62)	(†)	(†)	(†)	50.7 (2.79)	86.1 (1.90)	48.1 (3.21)	64.7 (2.44)	44.0 (3.17)
Suburb	80.9 (1.65)	97.1 (0.95)	78.5 (1.74)	96.7 (0.73)	74.3 (1.86)	(†)	(†)	(†)	54.2 (2.67)	84.4 (1.46)	49.1 (2.36)	63.2 (1.90)	45.8 (2.61)
Town	80.5 (2.85)	96.6 (1.39)	75.4 (3.36)	95.3 (1.28)	65.1 (3.10)	(†)	(†)	(†)	39.9 (3.68)	81.7 (3.34)	38.9 (4.18)	40.7 (3.82)	25.6 (4.65)
Rural	78.8 (2.15)	94.8 (1.10)	72.2 (2.36)	91.3 (1.57)	64.2 (2.63)	(†)	(†)	(†)	37.3 (2.51)	82.7 (2.39)	33.5 (2.15)	44.5 (2.98)	31.7 (3.36)
Percent combined enrollment of Black, Hispanic, Asian/Pacific Islander, and American Indian/Alaska Native students													
Less than 5 percent	84.6 (2.40)	97.1 (0.86)	75.7 (2.32)	94.9 (1.27)	70.4 (2.57)	(†)	(†)	(†)	35.1 (2.82)	79.0 (2.48)	33.8 (3.02)	40.8 (3.12)	30.6 (3.37)
5 percent to less than 20 percent	79.9 (3.09)	95.1 (1.26)	77.9 (2.45)	96.2 (0.93)	69.2 (3.05)	(†)	(†)	(†)	52.0 (3.34)	87.6 (1.62)	46.4 (3.02)	56.0 (3.11)	38.0 (2.99)
20 percent to less than 50 percent	74.6 (2.92)	98.1 (0.73)	72.5 (2.77)	92.5 (1.48)	68.6 (2.54)	(†)	(†)	(†)	46.4 (2.77)	85.8 (1.81)	44.1 (2.58)	57.9 (2.69)	42.6 (3.25)
50 percent or more	75.7 (2.44)	94.3 (1.05)	68.2 (2.57)	92.7 (1.67)	69.4 (2.35)	(†)	(†)	(†)	49.4 (2.66)	82.2 (1.71)	44.2 (2.91)	61.5 (2.47)	43.0 (2.53)
Percent of students eligible for free or reduced-price lunch													
0–25	80.9 (1.77)	96.7 (0.85)	76.5 (1.69)	95.2 (1.13)	72.9 (1.95)	(†)	(†)	(†)	49.6 (2.52)	85.2 (1.70)	45.4 (2.49)	56.2 (2.11)	40.4 (2.79)
26–50	81.5 (1.98)	96.9 (0.76)	78.4 (1.75)	95.4 (0.98)	71.4 (2.05)	(†)	(†)	(†)	44.1 (2.45)	83.3 (1.87)	39.9 (2.35)	52.3 (2.51)	34.6 (2.98)
51–75	77.4 (2.45)	95.9 (1.23)	69.7 (2.84)	93.8 (1.48)	66.2 (3.17)	(†)	(†)	(†)	43.1 (3.27)	86.3 (2.05)	40.5 (2.74)	52.2 (2.72)	38.9 (3.55)
76–100	71.7 (3.38)	93.8 (1.61)	65.9 (3.38)	90.2 (2.45)	63.8 (3.23)	(†)	(†)	(†)	49.3 (3.57)	80.7 (2.69)	47.2 (4.16)	62.4 (3.30)	44.9 (3.70)
2005–06[5]													
All public schools	79.3 (1.31)	95.0 (0.65)	73.1 (1.12)	94.5 (0.65)	70.5 (1.04)	— (†)	— (†)	— (†)	50.0 (1.47)	87.8 (0.78)	45.8 (1.52)	58.1 (1.36)	39.7 (1.33)
School level[6]													
Primary	74.5 (2.16)	94.6 (1.09)	71.1 (1.98)	93.5 (1.02)	68.9 (1.73)	(†)	(†)	(†)	51.8 (2.08)	89.6 (1.11)	47.4 (2.24)	58.9 (1.85)	41.7 (2.18)
Middle	84.2 (1.27)	96.6 (0.61)	75.4 (1.53)	96.7 (0.55)	73.9 (1.68)	(†)	(†)	(†)	51.9 (1.93)	87.8 (1.28)	45.5 (2.05)	60.3 (1.73)	40.2 (1.64)
High school	86.9 (1.39)	95.5 (0.76)	77.2 (1.44)	96.6 (0.88)	71.8 (1.40)	(†)	(†)	(†)	44.6 (1.78)	81.5 (1.48)	40.1 (2.25)	56.0 (1.65)	32.6 (2.20)
Combined	88.4 (3.53)	93.4 (2.32)	75.0 (3.28)	92.9 (2.31)	71.9 (3.58)	(†)	(†)	(†)	44.5 (4.68)	85.4 (3.53)	45.3 (5.94)	51.4 (5.54)	36.8 (5.90)
Enrollment size													
Less than 300	74.0 (3.44)	89.5 (2.16)	67.8 (3.05)	89.1 (2.36)	67.9 (2.44)	(†)	(†)	(†)	39.6 (3.28)	87.1 (1.88)	37.9 (3.59)	51.1 (3.34)	37.9 (3.31)
300–499	77.8 (2.05)	96.5 (0.81)	76.0 (2.13)	96.1 (0.99)	69.5 (2.48)	(†)	(†)	(†)	48.2 (2.99)	88.2 (1.51)	45.9 (3.04)	54.4 (2.72)	36.2 (2.75)
500–999	82.0 (1.42)	97.1 (0.52)	72.9 (1.85)	96.4 (0.69)	72.5 (1.77)	(†)	(†)	(†)	55.5 (2.18)	88.3 (1.11)	49.1 (2.24)	61.9 (1.94)	42.3 (2.27)
1,000 or more	86.3 (1.67)	95.6 (0.95)	78.3 (1.77)	97.0 (0.95)	72.6 (2.09)	(†)	(†)	(†)	57.8 (2.18)	86.3 (1.39)	50.8 (2.60)	69.4 (2.12)	43.5 (2.39)
Locale													
City	76.3 (2.34)	93.9 (1.24)	66.3 (2.12)	94.4 (1.13)	68.7 (2.24)	(†)	(†)	(†)	54.9 (2.46)	89.5 (1.53)	50.4 (2.74)	66.2 (2.30)	48.0 (2.58)
Suburb	81.2 (1.63)	96.5 (0.82)	77.3 (1.58)	97.1 (0.73)	75.7 (1.70)	(†)	(†)	(†)	54.9 (2.27)	84.8 (1.42)	48.6 (2.55)	60.1 (2.18)	46.2 (2.74)
Town	81.4 (3.39)	95.0 (2.05)	69.1 (3.58)	95.8 (1.83)	64.6 (4.11)	(†)	(†)	(†)	49.1 (4.40)	88.3 (2.35)	43.3 (4.56)	54.1 (4.10)	28.9 (4.19)
Rural	79.1 (2.31)	94.2 (1.22)	75.4 (2.14)	91.5 (1.70)	68.4 (2.09)	(†)	(†)	(†)	41.2 (2.45)	89.3 (1.33)	40.2 (2.50)	50.4 (2.35)	28.6 (2.40)

See notes at end of table.

Table 233.65. Percentage of public schools with a written plan for procedures to be performed in selected crises and percentage that have drilled students on the use of a plan, by selected school characteristics: Selected years, 2003–04 through 2013–14—Continued

[Standard errors appear in parentheses]

Year and school characteristic	Shootings	Natural disasters[2]	Hostages	Bomb threats or incidents	Chemical, biological, or radiological threats or incidents[3]	Suicide threat or incident	Severe risk of terrorist attack[4]	Pandemic flu	Shootings	Natural disasters[2]	Hostages	Bomb threats or incidents	Chemical, biological, or radiological threats or incidents[3]
	2	3	4	5	6	7	8	9	10	11	12	13	14
Percent combined enrollment of Black, Hispanic, Asian/Pacific Islander, and American Indian/Alaska Native students													
Less than 5 percent	77.0 (2.99)	92.2 (1.98)	74.5 (3.00)	93.5 (1.92)	75.9 (2.40)	— (†)	— (†)	— (†)	37.7 (3.44)	89.3 (1.74)	37.5 (3.53)	47.6 (3.43)	31.4 (3.17)
5 percent to less than 20 percent	82.4 (2.05)	95.6 (0.99)	78.6 (2.12)	95.4 (1.22)	72.8 (2.72)	— (†)	— (†)	— (†)	50.4 (2.40)	85.4 (1.55)	47.8 (2.63)	56.1 (2.54)	36.3 (2.97)
20 percent to less than 50 percent	82.3 (1.95)	97.0 (0.96)	75.9 (1.82)	95.9 (1.09)	71.3 (2.12)	— (†)	— (†)	— (†)	54.3 (3.23)	88.9 (1.85)	49.3 (2.93)	61.9 (3.18)	42.5 (2.93)
50 percent or more	75.5 (1.96)	94.4 (1.16)	65.0 (1.82)	93.1 (1.10)	65.9 (2.08)	— (†)	— (†)	— (†)	55.4 (2.77)	87.1 (1.47)	47.0 (2.73)	64.0 (2.24)	47.6 (2.28)
Percent of students eligible for free or reduced-price lunch													
0–25	82.1 (1.87)	96.2 (0.89)	76.3 (1.50)	95.3 (1.20)	75.5 (1.66)	— (†)	— (†)	— (†)	48.5 (2.25)	83.5 (1.51)	44.2 (2.34)	51.7 (2.16)	34.9 (2.53)
26–50	80.6 (2.06)	95.7 (1.02)	75.8 (2.20)	96.7 (1.03)	72.7 (2.21)	— (†)	— (†)	— (†)	49.0 (2.45)	91.3 (1.20)	48.3 (2.46)	58.3 (2.55)	41.0 (2.47)
51–75	81.8 (2.23)	95.1 (1.43)	73.7 (2.25)	94.3 (1.29)	71.3 (2.55)	— (†)	— (†)	— (†)	51.4 (2.99)	90.4 (1.47)	47.7 (2.86)	63.0 (2.05)	41.1 (2.59)
76–100	69.8 (2.68)	91.8 (2.07)	63.5 (2.67)	90.2 (1.95)	58.7 (3.25)	— (†)	— (†)	— (†)	52.3 (3.36)	85.6 (2.20)	41.3 (3.96)	61.2 (3.21)	44.2 (3.91)
2007–08													
All public schools	83.0 (1.31)	95.8 (0.48)	71.3 (1.26)	93.8 (0.65)	71.5 (1.16)	74.1 (1.33)	40.0 (1.26)	36.1 (1.10)	63.2 (1.20)	86.7 (0.86)	54.0 (1.54)	62.3 (1.25)	39.7 (1.67)
School level[6]													
Primary	79.9 (2.07)	96.3 (0.75)	69.8 (2.06)	93.4 (0.97)	71.5 (1.83)	69.7 (1.91)	41.2 (1.93)	34.7 (1.57)	61.6 (1.98)	87.8 (1.28)	56.7 (2.38)	62.4 (1.84)	39.1 (2.48)
Middle	88.3 (1.21)	96.1 (0.79)	76.3 (1.41)	96.7 (0.67)	73.2 (1.83)	80.8 (1.47)	39.4 (1.63)	39.7 (1.57)	71.0 (1.76)	85.8 (1.31)	54.1 (2.12)	63.1 (1.59)	42.2 (1.97)
High school	90.6 (1.07)	94.3 (0.79)	76.0 (1.56)	96.0 (0.90)	73.0 (1.82)	84.2 (1.40)	40.5 (1.80)	38.3 (1.81)	62.8 (1.64)	84.5 (1.38)	51.5 (2.09)	64.8 (1.89)	39.3 (1.88)
Combined	80.1 (4.55)	94.6 (2.18)	62.7 (5.31)	86.3 (4.22)	65.8 (5.30)	72.8 (5.05)	31.8 (4.65)	34.3 (4.64)	56.1 (5.32)	83.8 (3.92)	37.1 (6.03)	54.2 (4.81)	38.9 (5.43)
Enrollment size													
Less than 300	75.7 (3.40)	93.6 (1.74)	61.5 (3.81)	88.3 (2.47)	61.2 (3.15)	68.0 (4.18)	35.8 (3.25)	34.0 (3.61)	62.5 (3.51)	88.9 (1.99)	47.9 (3.70)	58.8 (3.32)	37.7 (5.20)
300–499	81.1 (2.27)	96.3 (0.95)	70.6 (2.54)	93.7 (1.62)	72.6 (2.59)	73.0 (2.08)	36.8 (2.53)	36.0 (2.68)	62.8 (3.41)	85.0 (2.17)	54.3 (3.37)	60.6 (2.76)	37.6 (3.39)
500–999	87.0 (1.36)	96.9 (0.65)	76.5 (1.80)	96.9 (0.72)	76.1 (1.70)	76.1 (1.75)	44.2 (1.88)	37.2 (1.79)	61.5 (2.34)	86.6 (1.21)	55.0 (2.60)	62.7 (2.03)	39.5 (2.29)
1,000 or more	90.3 (1.44)	95.6 (0.87)	76.7 (2.10)	95.6 (1.03)	75.4 (2.20)	82.8 (1.93)	43.6 (2.19)	37.0 (2.17)	70.8 (2.28)	86.8 (1.40)	60.2 (2.58)	71.7 (2.07)	48.8 (2.59)
Locale													
City	83.0 (2.03)	95.1 (1.16)	69.4 (2.64)	94.9 (1.17)	73.9 (2.30)	75.5 (2.23)	49.3 (2.42)	32.1 (2.71)	61.3 (3.06)	81.6 (2.00)	51.4 (3.60)	61.5 (2.49)	39.8 (3.05)
Suburb	84.9 (1.88)	96.3 (0.93)	74.7 (1.91)	96.9 (0.82)	76.0 (1.82)	76.3 (2.38)	43.4 (2.24)	36.8 (2.19)	67.7 (2.78)	84.4 (1.41)	62.4 (2.46)	69.6 (2.26)	46.4 (2.66)
Town	85.3 (2.56)	96.8 (1.27)	73.9 (3.00)	94.4 (1.89)	70.3 (2.97)	73.3 (3.26)	30.6 (2.94)	38.7 (3.06)	61.9 (3.22)	86.9 (2.56)	51.3 (4.15)	57.0 (3.24)	31.6 (3.66)
Rural	80.3 (2.70)	95.7 (1.11)	68.7 (2.44)	89.8 (1.78)	66.1 (2.23)	71.3 (2.22)	33.6 (2.32)	37.5 (2.54)	61.0 (2.27)	89.1 (1.31)	49.1 (3.15)	58.2 (2.95)	36.4 (3.32)
Percent combined enrollment of Black, Hispanic, Asian/Pacific Islander, and American Indian/Alaska Native students													
Less than 5 percent	80.6 (3.20)	95.0 (1.51)	75.5 (2.94)	94.4 (1.77)	68.2 (3.03)	75.7 (3.67)	36.4 (3.41)	42.8 (3.13)	56.7 (3.95)	87.7 (2.19)	48.2 (4.46)	58.7 (3.81)	34.3 (3.81)
5 percent to less than 20 percent	87.8 (2.07)	96.9 (0.91)	71.9 (2.16)	93.9 (1.45)	74.6 (2.16)	80.0 (2.08)	36.2 (2.36)	41.4 (2.97)	66.0 (2.66)	88.7 (1.31)	56.4 (2.45)	62.9 (2.74)	35.9 (2.96)
20 percent to less than 50 percent	84.5 (1.98)	96.1 (1.13)	73.1 (2.79)	95.9 (1.10)	74.3 (2.43)	70.4 (2.46)	40.1 (2.36)	34.3 (2.31)	61.7 (2.56)	87.3 (1.72)	56.5 (2.79)	62.9 (2.95)	41.5 (2.99)
50 percent or more	79.4 (2.01)	95.3 (0.91)	67.6 (2.29)	91.9 (1.30)	68.8 (2.19)	71.5 (2.04)	44.7 (2.52)	30.0 (2.19)	65.3 (2.49)	84.2 (1.77)	53.3 (2.55)	63.2 (2.28)	44.1 (2.59)
Percent of students eligible for free or reduced-price lunch													
0–25	86.9 (1.91)	95.8 (0.95)	75.2 (2.25)	96.8 (0.89)	76.8 (1.78)	78.4 (2.02)	40.8 (2.27)	39.6 (2.71)	62.3 (2.48)	84.5 (1.73)	57.6 (2.75)	64.7 (2.30)	42.7 (2.69)
26–50	85.3 (2.02)	97.0 (0.93)	71.7 (2.40)	94.2 (1.37)	72.7 (2.29)	73.9 (2.39)	37.8 (2.27)	39.1 (2.33)	64.0 (2.36)	89.3 (1.24)	52.2 (2.71)	60.4 (2.55)	39.8 (2.68)
51–75	79.3 (2.55)	96.2 (1.10)	71.2 (2.79)	92.8 (1.51)	67.5 (2.56)	71.7 (3.05)	38.8 (2.65)	32.9 (2.76)	61.3 (2.87)	87.1 (1.76)	54.2 (3.05)	63.0 (2.91)	35.6 (3.04)
76–100	78.6 (2.90)	93.6 (1.53)	65.9 (3.72)	90.3 (2.00)	67.5 (2.92)	71.5 (2.71)	43.9 (3.69)	30.3 (2.98)	65.5 (3.29)	84.9 (2.11)	51.5 (3.40)	60.9 (2.85)	39.8 (3.46)

See notes at end of table.

Table 233.65. Percentage of public schools with a written plan for procedures to be performed in selected crises and percentage that have drilled students on the use of a plan, by selected school characteristics: Selected years, 2003–04 through 2013–14—Continued

[Standard errors appear in parentheses]

Year and school characteristic	Percent with a written plan that describes procedures to be performed in selected crises								Percent that have drilled students during the current school year on the use of a plan in selected crises[1]				
	Shootings	Natural disasters[2]	Hostages	Bomb threats or incidents	Chemical, biological, or radiological threats or incidents[3]	Suicide threat or incident	Severe risk of terrorist attack[4]	Pandemic flu	Shootings	Natural disasters[2]	Hostages	Bomb threats or incidents	Chemical, biological, or radiological threats or incidents[3]
1	2	3	4	5	6	7	8	9	10	11	12	13	14
2009–10													
All public schools	84.3 (1.10)	95.1 (0.54)	74.3 (1.20)	93.5 (0.66)	71.1 (1.28)	74.9 (1.30)	41.3 (1.23)	69.4 (1.34)	61.6 (1.28)	86.5 (0.93)	55.7 (1.37)	62.6 (1.43)	43.2 (1.67)
School level[6]													
Primary	80.6 (1.68)	95.1 (0.82)	72.4 (1.78)	92.4 (1.04)	69.3 (1.78)	69.9 (1.88)	42.5 (1.95)	67.1 (1.96)	62.2 (2.32)	87.4 (1.46)	59.6 (2.24)	63.1 (2.06)	46.5 (2.51)
Middle	88.1 (1.06)	95.7 (0.94)	77.0 (1.37)	95.5 (0.78)	74.7 (1.98)	83.7 (1.21)	41.0 (1.88)	71.8 (1.45)	63.9 (1.90)	83.3 (0.91)	53.3 (1.65)	61.8 (1.67)	37.7 (1.86)
High school	91.4 (1.16)	94.6 (0.92)	77.4 (1.69)	96.5 (1.06)	76.8 (1.66)	83.1 (1.30)	43.7 (1.97)	75.6 (1.49)	62.4 (1.76)	80.6 (1.38)	50.7 (1.89)	62.4 (1.54)	40.1 (1.54)
Combined	89.2 (4.16)	94.8 (2.53)	76.4 (4.41)	91.8 (2.95)	65.1 (5.04)	77.0 (4.38)	28.0 (5.10)	69.5 (5.15)	50.7 (5.67)	87.1 (3.87)	42.4 (5.44)	61.8 (5.62)	39.1 (6.98)
Enrollment size													
Less than 300	83.3 (2.71)	93.3 (1.71)	74.2 (2.83)	90.4 (1.82)	64.9 (3.45)	70.1 (3.43)	37.8 (3.40)	64.9 (3.17)	51.8 (3.84)	82.0 (2.80)	50.3 (4.48)	58.6 (3.89)	39.0 (4.15)
300–499	81.1 (2.25)	96.6 (0.80)	72.5 (2.41)	94.7 (1.09)	70.0 (2.12)	74.3 (2.39)	42.9 (2.45)	72.4 (2.31)	63.8 (2.91)	86.6 (1.57)	57.2 (2.79)	63.0 (2.27)	45.2 (2.74)
500–999	86.0 (1.33)	94.6 (0.87)	75.2 (1.49)	96.5 (0.89)	74.2 (1.59)	76.0 (1.58)	41.5 (1.56)	69.2 (1.58)	64.2 (2.18)	89.4 (1.23)	57.6 (2.35)	64.1 (2.00)	42.8 (2.46)
1,000 or more	89.4 (1.53)	96.2 (0.86)	76.3 (2.09)	95.4 (1.13)	77.2 (1.94)	83.6 (1.68)	43.2 (2.06)	70.9 (1.70)	67.3 (1.80)	86.1 (1.35)	56.4 (2.28)	65.2 (2.16)	47.1 (2.08)
Locale													
City	81.0 (2.48)	93.5 (1.09)	71.7 (2.55)	92.8 (1.37)	68.8 (2.45)	74.9 (2.64)	44.4 (2.95)	68.7 (2.33)	60.1 (2.70)	86.0 (1.64)	58.8 (2.75)	63.4 (2.71)	47.9 (3.00)
Suburb	83.4 (1.94)	94.0 (1.12)	73.7 (2.11)	93.7 (1.38)	73.0 (2.25)	72.6 (2.52)	45.6 (2.05)	70.9 (1.90)	69.7 (2.53)	88.2 (1.45)	57.9 (2.31)	64.2 (2.71)	50.1 (2.98)
Town	86.5 (2.77)	98.2 (0.67)	77.9 (3.06)	96.0 (1.73)	73.5 (3.44)	76.4 (3.34)	36.3 (3.15)	69.2 (3.34)	61.1 (3.55)	86.9 (2.40)	55.0 (3.51)	59.5 (3.12)	33.4 (4.15)
Rural	86.8 (2.03)	96.1 (1.11)	75.3 (2.68)	92.9 (1.41)	70.2 (2.61)	76.6 (2.30)	36.9 (2.38)	68.6 (2.59)	55.8 (2.69)	85.4 (1.80)	51.4 (2.98)	62.1 (2.41)	37.4 (3.35)
Percent combined enrollment of Black, Hispanic, Asian/Pacific Islander, and American Indian/Alaska Native students													
Less than 5 percent	86.8 (2.99)	97.7 (0.94)	74.9 (3.03)	94.2 (1.88)	74.5 (2.94)	83.5 (2.61)	40.0 (3.15)	70.6 (3.46)	58.7 (3.60)	83.0 (2.94)	48.1 (4.06)	60.1 (3.88)	45.3 (4.25)
5 percent to less than 20 percent	85.3 (2.52)	95.8 (1.11)	75.2 (2.40)	93.9 (1.49)	70.0 (3.06)	76.5 (2.39)	36.7 (2.63)	69.8 (2.80)	61.2 (2.64)	84.5 (2.21)	56.0 (3.35)	60.2 (2.83)	34.7 (2.43)
20 percent to less than 50 percent	87.2 (1.55)	93.2 (1.42)	78.4 (1.96)	95.7 (0.99)	75.1 (2.20)	74.3 (2.43)	42.1 (2.30)	75.4 (1.88)	61.3 (2.69)	89.7 (1.64)	56.8 (2.88)	63.8 (3.02)	43.6 (3.33)
50 percent or more	80.6 (2.00)	94.8 (0.94)	70.6 (2.04)	91.6 (1.05)	68.0 (2.34)	70.9 (2.16)	44.4 (2.32)	64.6 (2.33)	63.5 (1.93)	87.4 (1.31)	57.8 (2.51)	64.7 (1.94)	48.1 (2.54)
Percent of students eligible for free or reduced-price lunch													
0–25	83.7 (2.44)	95.5 (1.07)	74.2 (2.42)	94.6 (1.26)	74.6 (2.47)	81.3 (2.22)	43.9 (2.85)	72.8 (2.70)	64.1 (2.70)	83.1 (2.05)	58.2 (3.12)	62.9 (3.02)	41.7 (2.83)
26–50	85.8 (1.98)	95.1 (1.06)	77.7 (2.16)	94.9 (1.35)	76.8 (2.08)	77.7 (1.98)	41.6 (2.35)	74.3 (2.04)	58.9 (2.08)	88.4 (1.67)	53.1 (2.44)	60.1 (2.48)	41.7 (2.38)
51–75	85.4 (1.81)	95.5 (1.08)	74.6 (2.00)	93.2 (1.22)	67.7 (2.79)	71.8 (2.53)	38.8 (2.26)	68.2 (2.98)	60.7 (2.62)	88.4 (1.75)	53.6 (3.06)	62.0 (2.62)	42.5 (3.46)
76–100	81.5 (2.12)	94.3 (1.16)	69.9 (2.72)	91.3 (1.50)	65.5 (2.78)	69.9 (2.95)	41.6 (3.03)	62.0 (2.92)	64.1 (3.08)	85.0 (2.21)	59.5 (3.01)	66.4 (2.39)	47.8 (3.61)
2013–14[7]													
All public schools	88.3 (1.02)	93.8 (0.79)	50.2 (1.64)	87.6 (0.99)	59.5 (1.47)	71.7 (1.43)	46.8 (1.69)	36.4 (1.61)	70.3 (1.59)	82.6 (1.16)	21.7 (1.27)	49.2 (1.47)	21.9 (1.25)
School level[6]													
Primary	87.2 (1.52)	94.2 (1.04)	46.7 (2.35)	85.8 (1.53)	57.6 (2.20)	66.9 (2.20)	43.0 (2.79)	34.2 (2.22)	70.5 (2.31)	84.2 (1.76)	21.3 (1.98)	48.6 (2.28)	22.1 (1.94)
Middle	91.2 (1.53)	94.5 (1.29)	55.3 (2.71)	92.3 (1.43)	61.0 (2.37)	80.0 (2.15)	55.6 (2.47)	40.8 (2.63)	72.7 (2.36)	82.5 (1.94)	25.1 (2.33)	50.6 (2.77)	22.7 (2.16)
High school/combined	88.7 (1.71)	92.1 (1.55)	55.2 (2.40)	88.2 (1.68)	63.6 (2.35)	77.5 (2.10)	49.4 (2.18)	38.7 (2.52)	67.6 (2.23)	78.3 (2.02)	19.9 (1.84)	49.6 (2.48)	20.6 (1.83)
Enrollment size													
Less than 300	87.2 (2.59)	91.0 (2.20)	48.1 (4.00)	85.3 (2.60)	53.9 (3.74)	66.0 (3.44)	41.8 (3.53)	34.2 (4.15)	64.3 (4.03)	78.9 (3.25)	19.1 (2.81)	40.7 (3.55)	15.1 (2.91)
300–499	86.2 (2.03)	93.2 (1.41)	45.9 (2.78)	85.1 (2.08)	55.1 (3.17)	67.8 (2.79)	43.9 (2.92)	34.8 (2.86)	71.8 (2.79)	85.7 (2.10)	21.4 (2.56)	51.5 (3.16)	25.6 (2.59)
500–999	90.2 (1.59)	95.9 (1.00)	54.1 (2.54)	89.5 (1.47)	64.3 (2.30)	76.0 (2.09)	50.1 (2.42)	38.4 (2.29)	72.1 (2.15)	82.7 (1.83)	23.8 (2.10)	50.7 (2.47)	22.3 (1.91)
1,000 or more	90.2 (1.93)	94.4 (1.85)	53.7 (2.84)	93.5 (1.47)	68.6 (2.91)	81.0 (2.60)	55.5 (3.10)	39.3 (2.78)	73.1 (2.41)	81.4 (2.58)	21.0 (2.52)	55.8 (3.08)	25.3 (2.54)
Locale													
City	85.0 (2.24)	91.9 (1.72)	46.0 (3.55)	82.1 (2.47)	57.9 (3.56)	67.0 (2.96)	49.2 (3.49)	35.4 (3.42)	70.9 (3.02)	83.4 (2.28)	29.2 (3.10)	57.1 (3.17)	26.7 (3.11)
Suburb	90.8 (1.67)	95.2 (1.49)	49.0 (3.23)	88.3 (1.89)	60.6 (2.78)	74.8 (2.79)	47.1 (2.96)	38.1 (3.05)	75.1 (2.60)	81.6 (2.26)	20.8 (2.34)	52.1 (2.85)	24.1 (2.34)
Town	90.7 (2.30)	93.8 (2.14)	49.7 (4.47)	92.1 (2.31)	62.2 (3.97)	71.7 (3.81)	48.5 (4.20)	39.1 (4.34)	72.7 (3.46)	83.2 (3.09)	18.1 (2.88)	48.7 (4.59)	24.0 (3.85)
Rural	87.9 (1.89)	94.0 (1.35)	54.5 (2.60)	89.2 (1.79)	56.6 (2.67)	72.6 (2.62)	44.2 (2.76)	34.8 (2.43)	65.0 (3.16)	82.6 (2.33)	18.3 (2.15)	41.1 (2.65)	15.9 (2.20)

See notes at end of table.

Table 233.65. Percentage of public schools with a written plan for procedures to be performed in selected crises and percentage that have drilled students on the use of a plan, by selected school characteristics: Selected years, 2003–04 through 2013–14—Continued

[Standard errors appear in parentheses]

Year and school characteristic	Percent with a written plan that describes procedures to be performed in selected crises							Percent that have drilled students during the current school year on the use of a plan in selected crises[1]					
	Shootings	Natural disasters[2]	Hostages	Bomb threats or incidents	Chemical, biological, or radiological threats or incidents[3]	Suicide threat or incident	Severe risk of terrorist attack[4]	Pandemic flu	Shootings	Natural disasters[2]	Hostages	Bomb threats or incidents	Chemical, biological, or radiological threats or incidents[3]
1	2	3	4	5	6	7	8	9	10	11	12	13	14
Percent combined enrollment of Black, Hispanic, Asian/Pacific Islander, and American Indian/Alaska Native students													
Less than 5 percent	86.9 (3.93)	91.8 (3.74)	61.7 (5.80)	91.2 (4.21)	67.7 (6.32)	75.6 (4.89)	47.4 (5.71)	37.9 (6.10)	69.6 (5.34)	80.9 (5.42)	15.1 (4.00)	39.2 (6.14)	16.0 (3.68)
5 percent to less than 20 percent	90.4 (1.98)	96.2 (1.21)	48.4 (2.92)	90.3 (1.81)	58.0 (2.81)	72.4 (2.72)	46.0 (2.93)	34.0 (2.77)	67.6 (2.93)	81.8 (2.21)	16.0 (2.20)	44.2 (3.21)	19.0 (2.36)
20 percent to less than 50 percent	90.9 (1.68)	93.1 (1.53)	50.0 (3.07)	89.6 (1.88)	60.6 (2.91)	71.6 (2.64)	46.8 (3.08)	40.9 (3.10)	72.6 (2.65)	82.8 (2.16)	22.6 (2.79)	48.6 (2.69)	21.0 (2.37)
50 percent or more	85.2 (1.94)	93.0 (1.31)	49.0 (2.51)	83.2 (1.91)	58.0 (2.50)	70.5 (2.15)	47.4 (2.40)	34.5 (2.44)	70.7 (2.48)	83.3 (1.82)	26.7 (2.26)	55.5 (2.47)	26.1 (2.06)
Percent of students eligible for free or reduced-price lunch[8]													
0–25	90.8 (2.38)	94.5 (1.75)	50.2 (3.98)	84.6 (3.03)	61.7 (3.78)	76.4 (3.54)	47.7 (3.92)	38.5 (3.68)	71.3 (3.17)	78.4 (3.07)	18.9 (2.95)	45.9 (3.81)	24.2 (3.15)
26–50	88.9 (1.80)	92.5 (1.59)	47.0 (3.05)	88.6 (2.05)	60.2 (2.92)	71.9 (2.68)	46.6 (3.27)	35.1 (2.57)	67.7 (3.28)	82.1 (1.99)	16.1 (2.00)	47.5 (3.03)	19.4 (2.54)
51–75	89.4 (2.00)	95.3 (1.34)	52.3 (3.03)	89.3 (1.78)	60.4 (3.10)	71.1 (2.61)	47.0 (3.23)	38.3 (3.12)	71.7 (2.54)	86.7 (2.11)	22.6 (2.30)	47.3 (2.85)	23.1 (2.81)
76–100	85.5 (2.38)	93.8 (1.62)	50.6 (3.52)	86.7 (2.14)	54.7 (3.29)	68.0 (3.34)	45.9 (3.43)	31.1 (3.39)	71.3 (3.27)	84.0 (2.65)	29.4 (3.23)	56.6 (3.25)	22.1 (2.78)

—Not available.
†Not applicable.
[1]Schools were not asked whether they had drilled students on the use of a plan for suicide threat or incident, severe risk of terrorist attack, and pandemic flu.
[2]For example, earthquakes or tornadoes.
[3]For example, release of mustard gas, anthrax, smallpox, or radioactive materials.
[4]In 2007–08 and 2009–10, schools were asked whether they had a plan for procedures to be performed if the U.S. national threat level were changed to Red (Severe Risk of Terrorist Attack) by the Department of Homeland Security. In 2013–14, schools were asked whether they had a plan for procedures to be performed if an "imminent threat alert" were issued by the Department of Homeland Security's National Terrorism Advisory System.
[5]Data on suicide threat or incident, severe risk of terrorist attack, and pandemic flu were not collected in 2003–04 and 2005–06.
[6]Primary schools are defined as schools in which the lowest grade is not higher than grade 3 and the highest grade is not higher than grade 8. Middle schools are defined as schools in which the lowest grade is not lower than grade 4 and the highest grade is not higher than grade 9. High schools are defined as schools in which the lowest grade is not lower than grade 9 and the highest grade

is not higher than grade 12. Combined schools include all other combinations of grades, including K–12 schools. Separate data on high schools and combined schools are not available for 2013–14.
[7]Data for 2013–14 were collected using the Fast Response Survey System, while data for earlier years were collected using the School Survey on Crime and Safety (SSOCS). The 2013–14 survey was designed to allow comparisons with SSOCS data. However, respondents to the 2013–14 survey could choose either to complete the survey on paper (and mail it back) or to complete the survey online, whereas respondents to SSOCS did not have the option of completing the survey online. The 2013–14 survey also relied on a smaller sample. The smaller sample size and change in survey administration may have impacted 2013–14 results.
[8]Because the 2013–14 survey did not collect data on the percentage of students eligible for free or reduced-price lunch, the classification of schools by the percentage of students eligible for free or reduced-price lunch was computed based on data obtained from the Common Core of Data.
NOTE: Responses were provided by the principal or the person most knowledgeable about crime and safety issues at the school.
SOURCE: U.S. Department of Education, National Center for Education Statistics, 2003–04, 2005–06, 2007–08, and 2009–10 School Survey on Crime and Safety (SSOCS), 2004, 2006, 2008, and 2010; Fast Response Survey System (FRSS), "School Safety and Discipline: 2013–14," FRSS 106, 2014; and Common Core of Data (CCD), "Public Elementary/Secondary School Universe Survey," 2013–14. (This table was prepared September 2015.)

Table 233.70. Percentage of public schools with one or more full-time or part-time security staff present at least once a week, by selected school characteristics: 2005–06 through 2013–14

[Standard errors appear in parentheses]

Percent with one or more security guards, security personnel, School Resource Officers (SROs), or sworn law enforcement officers who are not SROs[1]

School characteristic	Total				Full-time				Part-time only			
	2005–06	2007–08	2009–10	2013–14[2]	2005–06	2007–08	2009–10	2013–14[2]	2005–06	2007–08	2009–10	2013–14[2]
1	2	3	4	5	6	7	8	9	10	11	12	13
All public schools	41.7 (1.28)	46.3 (1.29)	42.8 (1.07)	43.0 (1.48)	27.0 (0.88)	30.4 (0.98)	28.7 (0.97)	23.7 (1.10)	14.6 (1.06)	15.9 (0.89)	14.1 (0.66)	19.3 (1.18)
School level[3]												
Primary	26.2 (1.87)	33.1 (2.04)	27.7 (1.50)	28.6 (2.15)	12.5 (1.32)	17.8 (1.37)	15.7 (1.43)	10.4 (1.46)	13.7 (1.59)	15.3 (1.31)	12.1 (0.89)	18.2 (1.73)
Middle	63.7 (1.30)	65.5 (1.59)	66.4 (1.45)	63.3 (2.15)	44.5 (1.17)	44.9 (1.55)	45.8 (1.39)	36.9 (2.21)	19.2 (1.18)	20.7 (1.17)	20.6 (1.32)	26.4 (2.17)
High school/combined	— (†)	— (†)	— (†)	64.1 (2.44)	— (†)	— (†)	— (†)	48.1 (2.25)	— (†)	— (†)	— (†)	16.1 (1.98)
High school	75.2 (1.66)	79.6 (1.47)	76.4 (1.45)	— (†)	64.0 (1.53)	66.1 (1.48)	62.0 (1.56)	— (†)	11.2 (1.14)	13.5 (1.42)	14.5 (1.50)	— (†)
Combined	43.5 (5.25)	39.9 (5.59)	36.6 (4.89)	— (†)	26.8 (4.44)	26.2 (4.79)	24.0 (4.49)	— (†)	16.7 (4.13)	13.6 ! (4.15)	12.7 (3.56)	— (†)
Enrollment size												
Less than 300	22.7 (2.65)	27.6 (2.55)	25.6 (2.91)	21.7 (3.05)	10.8 (1.58)	15.1 (2.09)	15.1 (2.29)	6.8 (1.72)	11.9 (2.07)	12.5 (2.07)	10.5 (2.20)	14.9 (2.81)
300–499	29.8 (2.29)	36.1 (2.66)	33.5 (2.26)	35.4 (2.90)	16.7 (1.93)	19.4 (1.84)	18.0 (1.96)	15.4 (2.12)	13.0 (1.64)	16.8 (2.05)	15.5 (1.76)	20.0 (2.28)
500–999	50.5 (1.90)	52.7 (1.99)	47.3 (1.60)	50.6 (2.37)	31.0 (1.27)	34.0 (1.52)	31.2 (1.34)	26.4 (1.79)	19.5 (1.62)	18.8 (1.53)	16.1 (1.08)	24.2 (1.91)
1,000 or more	86.9 (1.39)	90.6 (1.59)	90.0 (1.37)	87.2 (2.27)	77.3 (1.61)	79.5 (1.65)	79.3 (1.82)	77.5 (2.66)	9.7 (1.40)	11.1 (1.83)	10.7 (1.50)	9.8 (2.06)
Locale												
City	49.1 (2.57)	57.3 (3.05)	50.9 (2.51)	45.5 (3.13)	37.7 (2.04)	45.3 (2.24)	39.7 (2.19)	35.0 (2.71)	11.4 (1.59)	12.0 (1.97)	11.2 (1.69)	10.4 (2.13)
Suburb	42.7 (1.67)	45.4 (2.08)	45.4 (1.90)	47.7 (2.70)	27.1 (1.41)	30.0 (1.64)	31.3 (1.58)	26.2 (1.97)	15.6 (1.44)	15.4 (1.59)	14.1 (1.50)	21.5 (2.23)
Town	44.4 (3.86)	51.1 (3.50)	39.0 (3.11)	48.0 (4.08)	26.3 (2.88)	26.9 (2.32)	21.2 (2.15)	18.4 (2.63)	18.1 (2.90)	24.2 (2.75)	17.8 (2.39)	29.6 (3.88)
Rural	33.8 (1.87)	36.0 (1.98)	35.2 (2.20)	35.5 (2.33)	18.6 (1.39)	20.2 (1.67)	20.5 (1.83)	15.3 (1.42)	15.2 (1.87)	15.7 (1.70)	14.7 (1.51)	20.2 (2.26)
Percent combined enrollment of Black, Hispanic, Asian/Pacific Islander, and American Indian/Alaska Native students												
Less than 5 percent	28.3 (1.96)	35.6 (3.23)	30.4 (2.69)	35.6 (5.44)	12.4 (1.60)	16.9 (2.70)	13.6 (2.41)	8.7 ! (2.72)	16.0 (1.81)	18.7 (2.56)	16.8 (2.51)	26.9 (5.40)
5 percent to less than 20 percent	38.9 (2.54)	42.9 (2.19)	36.5 (2.91)	34.9 (2.93)	23.9 (1.73)	23.1 (1.63)	19.9 (2.26)	13.7 (1.66)	15.0 (1.98)	19.9 (1.93)	16.6 (1.71)	21.2 (2.41)
20 percent to less than 50 percent	41.6 (2.32)	44.7 (2.76)	41.9 (1.93)	46.7 (3.26)	28.3 (1.94)	29.1 (2.21)	27.8 (1.69)	25.3 (2.28)	13.3 (1.75)	15.5 (1.93)	14.1 (1.50)	21.5 (2.48)
50 percent or more	51.3 (2.46)	55.4 (2.71)	52.5 (2.04)	48.0 (2.24)	37.3 (1.91)	43.8 (2.16)	41.3 (2.09)	33.3 (2.09)	14.0 (1.81)	11.6 (1.68)	11.2 (1.33)	14.6 (1.73)
Percent of students eligible for free or reduced-price lunch[4]												
0–25	37.9 (2.14)	46.5 (2.33)	39.2 (2.44)	41.6 (3.81)	24.9 (1.70)	29.7 (2.01)	27.9 (2.17)	21.0 (2.20)	13.0 (1.33)	16.8 (1.52)	11.3 (1.21)	20.6 (3.01)
26–50	42.1 (2.08)	40.8 (2.52)	40.0 (1.68)	39.6 (3.10)	26.4 (1.63)	24.2 (2.01)	21.5 (1.52)	17.7 (1.87)	15.7 (2.01)	16.6 (1.65)	18.5 (1.37)	21.8 (2.64)
51–75	39.3 (2.21)	46.1 (2.83)	42.3 (2.60)	44.4 (2.71)	25.7 (1.85)	29.7 (2.34)	29.0 (2.04)	24.3 (2.00)	13.7 (1.90)	16.4 (2.34)	13.3 (1.45)	20.2 (2.38)
76–100	49.8 (2.73)	55.0 (3.68)	49.8 (2.76)	45.8 (3.24)	33.0 (2.49)	42.1 (3.17)	37.6 (2.66)	31.3 (2.86)	16.8 (2.07)	12.9 (2.17)	12.2 (1.84)	14.6 (2.37)

—Not available.
†Not applicable.
!Interpret data with caution. The coefficient of variation (CV) for this estimate is between 30 and 50 percent.
[1]"Security guards" and "security personnel" do not include law enforcement. School Resource Officers include all career law enforcement officers with arrest authority who have specialized training and are assigned to work in collaboration with school organizations.
[2]Data for 2013–14 were collected using the Fast Response Survey System, while data for earlier years were collected using the School Survey on Crime and Safety (SSOCS). The 2013–14 survey was designed to allow comparisons with SSOCS data. However, respondents to the 2013–14 survey could choose either to complete the survey on paper (and mail it back) or to complete the survey online, whereas respondents to SSOCS did not have the option of completing the survey online. The 2013–14 survey also relied on a smaller sample. The smaller sample size and change in survey administration may have impacted 2013–14 results.
[3]Primary schools are defined as schools in which the lowest grade is not higher than grade 3 and the highest grade is not higher than grade 4 and the highest grade is not

higher than grade 9. High schools are defined as schools in which the lowest grade is not lower than grade 9 and the highest grade is not higher than grade 12. Combined schools include all other combinations of grades, including K–12 schools. Separate data on high schools and combined schools are not available for 2013–14.
[4]For 2013–14, the questionnaire did not include a question about the percentage of students eligible for free or reduced-price lunch, so the classification of schools by the percentage of eligible students was computed based on data obtained from the Common Core of Data.
NOTE: Responses were provided by the principal or the person most knowledgeable about crime and safety issues at the school. Detail may not sum to totals because of rounding.
SOURCE: U.S. Department of Education, National Center for Education Statistics, 2005–06, 2007–08, and 2009–10 School Survey on Crime and Safety (SSOCS), 2006, 2008, and 2010; Fast Response Survey System (FRSS), "School Safety and Discipline: 2013–14," FRSS 106, 2014; and Common Core of Data (CCD), "Public Elementary/Secondary School Universe Survey," 2013–14. (This table was prepared September 2015.)

Table 233.80. Percentage of students ages 12–18 who reported various security measures at school: Selected years, 1999 through 2013

[Standard errors appear in parentheses]

Security measure	1999		2001		2003		2005		2007		2009		2011		2013	
1	2		3		4		5		6		7		8		9	
Total, at least one of the listed security measures	—	(†)	99.4	(0.09)	99.3	(0.12)	99.6	(0.10)	99.8	(0.06)	99.3	(0.10)	99.6	(0.08)	99.6	(0.07)
Metal detectors	9.0	(0.51)	8.7	(0.61)	10.1	(0.84)	10.7	(0.74)	10.1	(0.51)	10.6	(0.76)	11.2	(0.64)	11.0	(0.72)
Locker checks...	53.3	(0.83)	53.5	(0.92)	53.0	(0.91)	53.2	(0.90)	53.6	(0.95)	53.8	(1.17)	53.0	(0.99)	52.0	(1.13)
One or more security cameras to monitor the school............................	—	(†)	38.5	(1.13)	47.9	(1.16)	57.9	(1.35)	66.0	(0.99)	70.0	(1.05)	76.7	(0.83)	76.7	(1.06)
Security guards and/or assigned police officers...................................	54.1	(1.36)	63.6	(1.25)	69.6	(0.91)	68.3	(1.13)	68.8	(0.98)	68.1	(1.05)	69.8	(1.01)	70.4	(1.04)
Other school staff or other adults supervising the hallway	85.4	(0.54)	88.3	(0.45)	90.6	(0.39)	90.1	(0.42)	90.0	(0.50)	90.6	(0.46)	88.9	(0.46)	90.5	(0.51)
A requirement that students wear badges or picture identification	—	(†)	21.2	(0.99)	22.5	(1.11)	24.9	(1.20)	24.3	(1.00)	23.4	(1.14)	24.8	(1.02)	26.2	(1.02)
A written code of student conduct	—	(†)	95.1	(0.34)	95.3	(0.37)	95.5	(0.36)	95.9	(0.29)	95.6	(0.39)	95.7	(0.30)	95.9	(0.30)
Locked entrance or exit doors during the day...	38.1	(0.97)	48.8	(1.12)	52.8	(1.16)	54.3	(1.06)	60.9	(1.07)	64.3	(1.27)	64.5	(1.02)	75.8	(1.10)
A requirement that visitors sign in	87.1	(0.62)	90.2	(0.58)	91.7	(0.48)	93.0	(0.49)	94.3	(0.38)	94.3	(0.52)	94.9	(0.37)	95.8	(0.37)

—Not available.
†Not applicable.
NOTE: "At school" includes the school building, on school property, on a school bus, and, from 2001 onward, going to and from school.

SOURCE: U.S. Department of Justice, Bureau of Justice Statistics, School Crime Supplement (SCS) to the National Crime Victimization Survey, selected years, 1999 through 2013. (This table was prepared September 2014.)

Table 233.90. Number of juvenile offenders in residential placement facilities, by selected juvenile and facility characteristics: Selected years, 1997 through 2013

Juvenile or facility characteristic	1997	1999	2001	2003	2006	2007	2010	2011	2013
1	2	3	4	5	6	7	8	9	10
Total	105,055	107,493	104,219	96,531	92,721	86,814	70,793	61,423	54,148
Juvenile characteristics									
Sex									
Male	90,771	92,985	89,115	81,975	78,998	75,017	61,359	53,079	46,421
Female	14,284	14,508	15,104	14,556	13,723	11,797	9,434	8,344	7,727
Race/ethnicity									
White	39,445	40,911	41,324	37,307	32,490	29,534	22,947	19,927	17,563
Black	41,896	42,344	40,742	36,733	37,334	35,447	28,977	24,574	21,550
Hispanic	19,322	19,580	18,011	18,405	19,027	18,056	15,590	13,973	12,291
Asian	1,927	1,873	1,193	1,153	924	754	516	417	338
Pacific Islander	288	256	317	308	231	281	212	149	138
American Indian/Alaska Native	1,615	1,879	2,011	1,712	1,703	1,464	1,236	1,191	1,078
Other[1]	562	650	621	913	1,012	1,278	1,315	1,192	1,190
Race/ethnicity by sex									
Male									
White	32,425	34,071	34,245	30,766	26,578	24,579	19,273	16,659	14,579
Black	37,135	37,282	35,433	31,611	32,580	31,291	25,542	21,686	18,977
Hispanic	17,503	17,713	16,006	16,254	16,754	16,103	13,928	12,411	10,723
Asian	1,759	1,690	1,050	1,012	829	663	456	360	299
Pacific Islander	248	208	268	251	195	231	178	121	114
American Indian/Alaska Native	1,273	1,498	1,645	1,361	1,266	1,108	924	896	812
Other[1]	428	523	468	720	796	1,042	1,058	946	917
Female									
White	7,020	6,840	7,079	6,541	5,912	4,955	3,674	3,268	2,984
Black	4,761	5,062	5,309	5,122	4,754	4,156	3,435	2,888	2,573
Hispanic	1,819	1,867	2,005	2,151	2,273	1,953	1,662	1,562	1,568
Asian	168	183	143	141	95	91	60	57	39
Pacific Islander	40	48	49	57	36	50	34	28	24
American Indian/Alaska Native	342	381	366	351	437	356	312	295	266
Other[1]	134	127	153	193	216	236	257	246	273
Age									
12 or younger	2,178	3,914	1,844	1,662	1,206	979	693	764	706
13	4,648	6,445	4,429	4,079	3,419	2,844	2,079	1,999	1,957
14	11,578	13,010	10,470	9,871	9,113	7,621	5,955	5,276	4,717
15	21,237	20,924	19,519	18,335	17,552	15,565	12,604	10,589	9,473
16	28,201	26,144	26,945	24,786	24,606	23,091	19,540	16,473	14,108
17	24,564	23,627	24,948	23,963	23,716	23,193	19,990	17,447	15,100
18 to 20	12,649	13,429	16,064	13,835	13,109	13,521	9,932	8,875	8,087
Most serious offense[2]									
Person offense	35,138	37,367	34,885	33,170	31,674	31,140	26,011	22,964	19,922
Property offense	31,907	31,432	29,341	26,813	23,152	21,076	17,037	14,705	12,768
Drug offense	9,071	9,645	9,076	7,988	7,985	7,095	4,986	4,315	3,533
Public order offense	10,287	10,848	10,806	9,949	10,015	11,000	8,139	7,317	6,085
Technical violation	12,410	13,909	15,413	14,102	15,280	13,093	11,604	9,883	9,316
Status offense	6,242	4,292	4,698	4,509	4,615	3,410	3,016	2,239	2,524
Facility characteristics									
Facility size									
1 to 10 residents	5,511	5,110	5,253	4,808	4,215	4,085	3,865	3,468	3,469
11 to 20 residents	7,443	7,214	7,445	6,935	7,044	7,320	6,304	6,337	5,782
21 to 50 residents	17,934	19,721	20,932	20,646	18,988	18,400	17,534	15,104	14,700
51 to 150 residents	29,789	33,045	32,211	31,232	31,417	30,505	25,605	22,947	19,669
151 to 200 residents	7,781	9,525	7,677	6,635	8,757	6,810	5,244	3,942	3,333
201 or more residents	36,597	32,878	30,701	26,275	22,300	19,694	12,241	9,625	7,195
Facility operation									
State	46,516	47,347	43,669	37,335	34,658	31,539	24,881	20,783	17,532
Local	29,084	28,875	29,659	28,875	29,505	29,085	24,231	21,801	19,298
Private[3]	29,455	31,271	30,891	30,321	28,558	26,190	21,681	18,839	17,318
Facility self-classification[4]									
Detention center	29,057	34,840	38,741	29,755	30,929	29,618	24,119	21,090	19,407
Shelter	2,880	2,717	2,700	1,375	1,134	982	1,052	1,313	1,103
Reception/diagnostic center	2,999	4,988	6,038	1,229	1,820	1,391	1,476	1,027	422
Group home	18,326	15,722	13,744	7,120	6,708	6,397	7,320	4,800	4,590
Boot camp	3,811	1,615	2,906	2,111	1,736	1,391	526	524	320
Ranch/wilderness camp	7,338	10,620	7,737	4,375	2,721	3,038	2,441	2,224	1,308
Residential treatment center[5]	—	—	—	18,522	20,355	18,289	15,565	13,783	12,416
Long-term secure facility	40,317	36,991	32,353	32,044	27,318	25,708	18,294	16,662	14,582

—Not available.

[1]For 2006 and later years, includes the "Two or more races" category, which did not appear on earlier questionnaires. For 2003 and earlier years, includes an "Other" category. Respondents who selected "Other" were instructed to specify what this meant. Examination of these written-in responses, which account for less than 1 percent of the records, indicates that the majority refer to individuals of mixed racial/ethnic identity.

[2]Delinquent/criminal offenses range from those committed against persons (e.g., assault) to technical violations, which include violations of probation, parole, or valid court orders. A "status" offense is illegal for underage persons, but not for adults (e.g., truancy or underage drinking).

[3]Private facilities are operated by private nonprofit or for-profit corporations or organizations.

[4]Although respondents may select more than one type for their facility, this table assigns each facility to a single primary type based on an analysis that applies a hierarchy rule. For 1997, the facility type data exclude 327 juveniles who were in facilities identified only as "Other."

[5]Prior to 2003, residential treatment centers were included in the "Group home" category.

NOTE: Data are from a biennial survey of all secure and nonsecure residential placement facilities that house juvenile offenders, defined as persons younger than 21 who are held in a residential setting as a result of some contact with the justice system (they are charged with or adjudicated for an offense). Data do not include adult prisons, jails, federal facilities, or facilities exclusively for drug or mental health treatment or for abused or neglected youth. The data provide 1-day population counts of juveniles in residential placement facilities; 1-day counts differ substantially from the annual admission and release data used to measure facility population flow. For definitions of specific terms, see http://www.ojjdp.gov/ojstatbb/ezacjrp/asp/glossary.asp.

SOURCE: U.S. Department of Justice, Office of Juvenile Justice and Delinquency Prevention, Census of Juveniles in Residential Placement (CJRP), retrieved September 25, 2015, from http://www.ojjdp.gov/ojstatbb/ezacjrp/. (This table was prepared October 2015.)

Table 233.92. Residential placement rate (number of juvenile offenders in residential facilities) per 100,000 juveniles, by sex and race/ethnicity: Selected years, 1997 through 2013

Sex and race/ethnicity	1997	1999	2001	2003	2006	2007	2010	2011	2013
1	2	3	4	5	6	7	8	9	10
Total...	356	355	334	303	289	272	225	196	173
Sex									
Male..	599	599	556	502	479	458	380	330	290
Female...	99	99	99	94	88	76	61	54	50
Race/ethnicity									
White...	201	208	208	189	170	157	128	112	100
Black...	968	937	857	742	743	714	606	520	464
Hispanic.......................................	468	435	360	335	309	284	228	202	173
Asian/Pacific Islander...................	195	178	119	110	80	71	47	35	28
American Indian/Alaska Native...........	490	542	556	468	476	416	369	361	334
Other[1]...	—	—	—	—	—	—	—	—	—
Race/ethnicity by sex									
Male									
White...	322	337	336	304	270	254	209	182	162
Black...	1,688	1,623	1,466	1,256	1,275	1,238	1,049	902	804
Hispanic.......................................	823	764	622	577	530	494	398	351	296
Asian/Pacific Islander...................	346	309	203	185	139	119	80	60	49
American Indian/Alaska Native...........	759	849	894	732	698	621	544	535	496
Other[1]...	—	—	—	—	—	—	—	—	—
Female									
White...	74	72	73	68	64	54	42	38	35
Black...	224	228	227	210	193	170	146	124	113
Hispanic.......................................	91	86	83	81	76	63	50	46	45
Asian/Pacific Islander...................	38	40	31	31	19	20	12	11	8
American Indian/Alaska Native...........	211	224	206	195	248	205	190	182	167
Other[1]...	—	—	—	—	—	—	—	—	—

—Not available.
[1]For 2006 and later years, includes the "Two or more races" category, which did not appear on earlier questionnaires. For 2003 and earlier years, includes an "Other" category. Respondents who selected "Other" were instructed to specify what this meant. Examination of these written-in responses, which account for less than 1 percent of the records, indicates that the majority refer to individuals of mixed racial/ethnic identity.
NOTE: Residential placement rate calculated per 100,000 persons age 10 through the upper age at which those charged with a criminal law violation were under original jurisdiction of the juvenile courts in each state in the given year (through age 17 in most states); for more information, see http://www.ojjdp.gov/ojstatbb/structure_process/qa04101.asp?qaDate=2013. Data are

from a biennial survey of all secure and nonsecure residential placement facilities that house juvenile offenders, defined as persons younger than 21 who are held in a residential setting as a result of some contact with the justice system (they are charged with or adjudicated for an offense). Data do not include adult prisons, jails, federal facilities, or facilities exclusively for drug or mental health treatment or for abused or neglected youth. The data provide 1-day population counts of juveniles in residential placement facilities; 1-day counts differ substantially from the annual admission and release data used to measure facility population flow.
SOURCE: U.S. Department of Justice, Office of Juvenile Justice and Delinquency Prevention, Census of Juveniles in Residential Placement (CJRP), retrieved October 20, 2015, from http://www.ojjdp.gov/ojstatbb/ezacjrp/. (This table was prepared October 2015.)

Table 234.10. Age range for compulsory school attendance and special education services, and policies on year-round schools and kindergarten programs, by state: Selected years, 2000 through 2014

State	Compulsory attendance							Compulsory special education services, 2004[1]	Year-round schools, 2008		Kindergarten programs, 2014		
	2000	2002	2004	2006	2008	2010	2014		Has policy on year-round schools	Has districts with year-round schools	School districts required to offer		Attendance required
											Program	Full-day program	
1	2	3	4	5	6	7	8	9	10	11	12	13	14
Alabama	7 to 16	7 to 16	7 to 16[2]	7 to 16	7 to 16	7 to 17	6 to 17[3]	6 to 21		Yes	X	X	
Alaska	7 to 16	7 to 16	7 to 16[2]	7 to 16	7 to 16	7 to 16	7 to 16[2]	3 to 22		Yes			
Arizona	6 to 16[2]	6 to 16[2]	6 to 16[2]	6 to 16[2]	6 to 16[2]	6 to 16[2]	6 to 16[2]	3 to 21	—	—	X		
Arkansas	5 to 17[2,3]	5 to 17[2,3]	5 to 17[2,3]	5 to 17[2,3]	5 to 17[2,3]	5 to 17[2,3]	5 to 18	5 to 21	X	Yes	X	X	X
California	6 to 18[2]	6 to 18	6 to 18	6 to 18	6 to 18	6 to 18	6 to 18	Birth to 21[4]	X	Yes	X		
Colorado	—	—	7 to 16	7 to 16	6 to 17	6 to 17	6 to 17	3 to 21		Yes	X		
Connecticut	7 to 16	7 to 16[2]	7 to 18[2]	5 to 18[3]	5 to 18[3]	5 to 18[3]	5 to 18[3]	3 to 21		—	X		X
Delaware	5 to 16	5 to 16	5 to 16[2]	5 to 16	5 to 16	5 to 16	5 to 16	Birth to 20		Yes	X	X	X
District of Columbia	—	5 to 18[5]	5 to 18	5 to 18	5 to 18	5 to 18	5 to 18	—	—	—	X	X	X
Florida	6 to 16[5]	6 to 16[5]	6 to 16[5]	6 to 16[5]	6 to 16[5]	6 to 16[5]	6 to 16	3 to 21	X	Yes	X		
Georgia	6 to 16	6 to 16	6 to 16	6 to 16	6 to 16	6 to 16	6 to 16	Birth to 21[6]		Yes	X		
Hawaii	6 to 18	6 to 18	6 to 18	6 to 18	6 to 18	6 to 18	5 to 18	Birth to 19		[7]	X		
Idaho	7 to 16	7 to 16	7 to 16	7 to 16	7 to 16	7 to 16	7 to 16	3 to 21		Yes			
Illinois	7 to 16	7 to 16	7 to 17	7 to 17	7 to 17	7 to 17	6 to 17	3 to 21	X	Yes	X		
Indiana	7 to 16	7 to 16	7 to 16	7 to 18[2]	7 to 18[2]	7 to 18[2]	7 to 18	3 to 22		Yes	X		
Iowa	6 to 16[2]	6 to 16[2]	6 to 16	6 to 16	6 to 16	6 to 16	6 to 16[8]	Birth to 21	X	Yes	X		
Kansas	7 to 18[2]	7 to 18[2]	7 to 18[2]	7 to 18[2]	7 to 18[2]	7 to 18[2]	7 to 18[2]	3 to 21[9]		—	X		
Kentucky	6 to 16	6 to 16	6 to 16[2]	6 to 16	6 to 16	6 to 16	6 to 18[10]	Birth to 21		Yes	X		
Louisiana	7 to 17	7 to 17	7 to 17[2]	7 to 18[2]	7 to 18[2]	7 to 18[2]	7 to 18	3 to 21[11]		Yes	X	X	X
Maine	7 to 17	7 to 17	7 to 17[2]	7 to 17[2]	7 to 17[2]	7 to 17[2]	7 to 17	5 to 19[11,12]		—	X		
Maryland	5 to 16	5 to 16	5 to 16	5 to 16	5 to 16	5 to 16[3]	5 to 17	Birth to 21	X	—	X	X	X
Massachusetts	6 to 16	6 to 16	6 to 16[2]	6 to 16[2]	6 to 16[2]	6 to 16[2]	6 to 16	3 to 21[6]	X[13]		X		
Michigan	6 to 16	6 to 16	6 to 16	6 to 16	6 to 16	6 to 18	6 to 18	Birth to 25	X	Yes	X		
Minnesota	7 to 18[2]	7 to 18[2]	7 to 16	7 to 16[2]	7 to 16[2]	7 to 16[2]	7 to 17	Birth to 21	X	Yes	X		
Mississippi	6 to 17	6 to 17	6 to 16	6 to 16	6 to 17	6 to 17	6 to 17	Birth to 20		—	X	X	
Missouri	7 to 16	7 to 16	7 to 16	7 to 16	7 to 16	7 to 17	7 to 17[2,3]	Birth to 20		Yes[14]	X		
Montana	7 to 16[2]	7 to 16[2]	7 to 16[2]	7 to 16[2]	7 to 16[2]	7 to 16[2]	7 to 16[2]	3 to 18[11]		—	X		
Nebraska	7 to 16	7 to 16	7 to 16	6 to 18	6 to 18	6 to 18	6 to 18	Birth to 20		Yes	X		
Nevada	7 to 17	7 to 17	7 to 17	7 to 17	7 to 18[2]	7 to 18[2]	7 to 18	Birth to 21[4]		Yes	X	[15]	X
New Hampshire	6 to 16	6 to 16	6 to 16	6 to 16	6 to 16	6 to 18	6 to 18	3 to 21		—	X		
New Jersey	6 to 16	6 to 16	6 to 16	6 to 16	6 to 16	6 to 16	6 to 16	5 to 21		—	X	[16]	
New Mexico	5 to 18	5 to 18	5 to 18[2]	5 to 18[2]	5 to 18[2]	5 to 18	5 to 18	3 to 21	X	Yes	X		
New York	6 to 16[2]	6 to 16	6 to 16	6 to 16[17]	6 to 16[17]	6 to 16[17]	6 to 16[17]	Birth to 20		—	X		
North Carolina	7 to 16	7 to 16	7 to 16	7 to 16	7 to 16	7 to 16	7 to 16	5 to 20	X	Yes	X	X	
North Dakota	7 to 16	7 to 16	7 to 16	7 to 16	7 to 16	7 to 16	7 to 16	3 to 21		No	X		
Ohio	6 to 18	6 to 18	6 to 18	6 to 18	6 to 18	6 to 18	6 to 18	3 to 21	X		X		X
Oklahoma	5 to 18	5 to 18	5 to 18	5 to 18	5 to 18	5 to 18	5 to 18	Birth to 21[11]		Yes	X	X	X
Oregon	7 to 18	7 to 18	7 to 18[2]	7 to 18[2]	7 to 18[2]	7 to 18[2]	7 to 18	3 to 20		Yes	X		
Pennsylvania	8 to 17	8 to 17	8 to 17[2]	8 to 17[2]	8 to 17[2]	8 to 17[2]	8 to 17	6 to 21	X[14]	—[14]	X		
Rhode Island	6 to 16	6 to 16	6 to 16	6 to 16	6 to 16	6 to 16	6 to 18[2]	3 to 21			X		X
South Carolina	5 to 16	5 to 16	5 to 16	5 to 17[3]	5 to 17[3]	5 to 17[3]	5 to 17	3 to 21[18]		—	X	X	X
South Dakota	6 to 16	6 to 16	6 to 16	6 to 16	6 to 16	6 to 18[2]	6 to 18[2]	Birth to 21	X	—	X		X[19]
Tennessee	6 to 17	6 to 17	6 to 17	6 to 17[3]	6 to 17[3]	6 to 17[3]	5 to 17	3 to 21[4]	X	Yes	X	X	X
Texas	6 to 18	6 to 18	6 to 18	6 to 18	6 to 18	6 to 18	6 to 18	3 to 21	X	Yes	X		
Utah	6 to 18	6 to 18	6 to 18	6 to 18	6 to 18	6 to 18	6 to 18	3 to 22		Yes	X		
Vermont	7 to 16	7 to 16	7 to 16	6 to 16[2]	6 to 16[2]	6 to 16[2]	6 to 16[2]	3 to 21		—[14]	X		
Virginia	5 to 18	5 to 18	5 to 18	5 to 18[2]	5 to 18[2]	5 to 18[2,3]	5 to 18	2 to 21	X	Yes	X		X
Washington	8 to 17[2]	8 to 17[2]	8 to 16[2]	8 to 18	8 to 18	8 to 18	8 to 18	3 to 21[18]		Yes	X	[20]	
West Virginia	6 to 16	6 to 16	6 to 16	6 to 16	6 to 16	6 to 17	6 to 17	5 to 21[21]	X	Yes	X	X	X
Wisconsin	6 to 18	6 to 18	6 to 18	6 to 18	6 to 18	6 to 18	6 to 18	3 to 21		Yes	X		
Wyoming	6 to 16[2]	6 to 16[2]	7 to 16[2]	7 to 16[2]	7 to 16[2]	7 to 16[2]	7 to 16[2]	3 to 21		—	X	[22]	

—Not available.

X Denotes that the state has a policy. A blank denotes that the state does not have a policy.

[1]Most states have a provision whereby education is provided up to a certain age or completion of secondary school, whichever comes first.

[2]Child may be exempted from compulsory attendance if he/she meets state requirements for early withdrawal with or without meeting conditions for a diploma or equivalency.

[3]Parent/guardian may delay child's entry until a later age per state law/regulation.

[4]Student may continue in the program if 22nd birthday falls before the end of the school year.

[5]Attendance is compulsory until age 18 for Manatee County students, unless they earn a high school diploma prior to reaching their 18th birthday.

[6]Through age 21 or until child graduates with a high school or special education diploma or equivalent.

[7]Some schools operate on a multitrack system; the schools are open year-round, but different cohorts start and end at different times.

[8]Children enrolled in preschool programs (4 years old on or before September 15) are considered to be of compulsory school attendance age.

[9]To be determined by rules and regulations adopted by the state board.

[10]All districts have adopted a policy to raise the upper compulsory school age from 16 to 18. The policy will take effect for most districts in the 2015–16 school year.

[11]Children from birth through age 2 are eligible for additional services.

[12]Must be age 5 before October 15, and not age 20 before start of school year.

[13]Policies about year-round schools are decided locally.

[14]State did not participate in 2008 online survey. Data are from 2006.

[15]In certain school districts in Nevada, the lowest performing schools with the highest numbers of limited English proficient students will start offering full-day kindergarten programs.

[16]The Abbott District is required to offer full-day kindergarten.

[17]Local boards of education can require school attendance until age 17 unless employed. The boards of education of Syracuse, New York City, Rochester, Utica, and Buffalo are authorized to require kindergarten attendance at age 5 unless the parents elect not to enroll their child until the following September or the child is enrolled in nonpublic school or in home instruction.

[18]Student may complete school year if 21st birthday occurs while attending school.

[19]All children must attend kindergarten before age 7.

[20]Full-day kindergarten is being phased in beginning in the 2012–13 school year, starting with the highest poverty schools. Statewide implementation will be achieved by 2017–18.

[21]Children with severe disabilities may begin receiving services at age 3.

[22]Statute requires one full-day program per district.

NOTE: The Education of the Handicapped Act (EHA) Amendments of 1986 make it mandatory for all states receiving EHA funds to serve all 3- to 18-year-old disabled children.

SOURCE: Council of Chief State School Officers, *Key State Education Policies on PK–12 Education*, 2000, 2002, 2004, and 2008; Education Commission of the States (ECS), ECS StateNotes, *Compulsory School Age Requirements*, retrieved August 9, 2010, from http://www.ecs.org/clearinghouse/86/62/8662.pdf; ECS StateNotes, *Special Education: State Special Education Definitions, Ages Served*, retrieved August 9, 2010, from http://www.ecs.org/clearinghouse/52/29/5229.pdf; ECS StateNotes, *Compulsory School Age Requirements*, retrieved May 19, 2015, from http://www.ecs.org/clearinghouse/01/18/68/11868.pdf; ECS StateNotes, *District Must Offer Kindergarten*, retrieved April 18, 2014, from http://ecs.force.com/mbdata/mbquestRT?rep=Kq1416; ECS StateNotes, *Child Must Attend Kindergarten*, retrieved April 18, 2014, from http://ecs.force.com/mbdata/mbquestRT?rep=Kq1403; and supplemental information retrieved from various state websites. (This table was prepared May 2015.)

Table 234.20. Minimum amount of instructional time per year and policies on textbooks, by state: Selected years, 2000 through 2014

State	Minimum amount of instructional time per year — In days — 2000	2006	2011	2014	In hours — 2014	Policies on textbooks, 2014 — Textbook selection level — State	Local education agency	Free textbooks provided to students
1	2	3	4	5	6	7	8	9
Alabama	175	175	180	180[1]	†	X	X	X
Alaska	180	180	170[2]	180[3]	740 (K–3); 900 (4–12)		X	X
Arizona	—	180	180[1]	180[1]	356 (K); 712 (1–3); 890 (4–6); 1,000 (7–8); 720[9] (9–12)		X[6]	X[5]
Arkansas	178	178	178[2]	178[3]	†		X	X
California	175	180	180/175[7]	180/175[7]	600 (K); 840 (1–3); 900 (4–8); 1,080 (9–12)	X[8]		X
Colorado	[9]	160	160	160	435/870[2] (K); 968[2] (1–5); 1,056[2] (6–12)		X	X
Connecticut	180	180	180	180	450/900 (K); 900 (1–12)		X	X
Delaware	[9]	†	†	†	1,060 (K–11); 1,032 (12)		X	X
District of Columbia	180[10]	180	178	180	†			X
Florida	180	180	180	180	720[11] (K–3); 900[11] (4–12)	X		X
Georgia	180[10]	180	180	180	810 (K–3); 900 (4–5); 990 (6–12)	X		X[14]
Hawaii	184	179	180[12]	180[12]	915 (K–6)[12,13]; 990 (7–12)[12,13]	X		X
Idaho	180[16]	†	†	†	450[3] (K); 810[3] (1–3); 900[3] (4–8); 990[3,15] (9–12)	X		X[17]
Illinois	180[16]	176	176	180[3]	†		X	
Indiana	180	180	180	180	†		X	
Iowa	180	180	180	180	1,080		X	
Kansas	186	186 (K–11); 181 (12)	186 (K–11); 181 (12)	186 (K–11); 181 (12)	465 (K); 1,116 (1–11); 1,086 (12)	X	X	X[18]
Kentucky	175	175	175[2]	170[2]	1,062	X		X
Louisiana	175	177	177[2]	177[2,15]	1,062			X
Maine	175	175	175[2]	175[2]	†		X	X
Maryland	180	180	180	180	1,080; 1,170 (8–12)		X	X
Massachusetts	180	180	180	180	425 (K); 900 (1–5); 990 (6–12)		X	X
Michigan	180	†	165	175	1,098		X	X[19]
Minnesota	[9]	[9]	†	†	425/850 (K); 935 (1–6); 1,020 (7–12)		X	X
Mississippi	180	180	180	180	†	X		X
Missouri	174	174	174/142[20]	174/142[20]	1,044		X	X
Montana	180	†	†	†	360/720[3] (K); 720[3] (1–3); 1,080[3,15] (4–12)		X	X
Nebraska	[9]	180	180	180	400 (K); 1,032 (1–8); 1,080 (9–12)			X[14]
Nevada	180	180	180	180	—	X	X	X
New Hampshire	180	180	180	180	450 (K); 945 (1–5); 990[15] (6–12)		X	X
New Jersey	180	180	180	180	†		X	X
New Mexico	180	180	180	180	450/990 (K); 990 (1–6); 1,080 (7–12)	X	X	X
New York	180[10]	180	180	180	—		X	X[19]
North Carolina	180	180	180	185	1,025	X		X
North Dakota	173	173	175[2]	175[2]	951.5 (K–8); 1,038 (9–12)		X	X
Ohio	182	182	182[3]	180	455/910[3] (K); 910[3] (1–6); 1,001[3] (7–12)	X	X	X
Oklahoma	180	180	180[3]	180	1,083[3]			X
Oregon	[9]	†	†	†	405 (K); 810 (1–3); 900 (4–8); 990[15] (9–12)	X	X	X
Pennsylvania	180	180	180	180	450 (K); 900 (1–8); 990 (9–12)	X	X	X[19]
Rhode Island	180	180	180	180	1,080			X
South Carolina	180	180	180[2]	180[2]	—	X		X
South Dakota	—	†	†	†	437.5 (K); 875 (1–5); 962.5[15] (6–12)		X	X
Tennessee	[9]	180	180[2]	180[2]	†	X		X
Texas	187	180	180	180	—	X	X	X
Utah	180	180	180	180	450 (K); 810 (1); 990 (2–12)	X	(21)	X

See notes at end of table.

Table 234.20. Minimum amount of instructional time per year and policies on textbooks, by state: Selected years, 2000 through 2014—Continued

State	Minimum amount of instructional time per year					Policies on textbooks, 2014		
	In days				In hours	Textbook selection level		Free textbooks provided to students
	2000	2006	2011	2014	2014	State	Local education agency	
1	2	3	4	5	6	7	8	9
Vermont	175	175	175	175	†		X	X
Virginia	180	180	180	180	540 (K); 990 (1–12)	X		X
Washington	180[16]	180	180	180	450[22] (K); 1,000[22] (1–12)	X	X	(23)
West Virginia	180	180	180	180	†			X
Wisconsin	180	180	180	†	437/1,050[2] (K); 1,050[2] (1–6); 1,137[2] (7–12)		X	
Wyoming	175	175	180	175	450 (K); 900 (Elementary); 1,050 (Middle/Jr. High); 1,100 (Secondary)		X	X

—Not available.
†Not applicable.
X Denotes that the state has a policy. A blank denotes that the state does not have a policy.
[1]Or an equivalent number of hours or minutes of instruction per year.
[2]Does not include time for in-service or staff development or parent-teacher conferences.
[3]Includes time for in-service or staff development or parent-teacher conferences.
[4]Students must enroll in at least 4 subjects that meet at least 720 hours.
[5]Fees permitted at the high school level for nonrequired or supplementary textbooks.
[6]State Department of Education prepares a list of suggestions, but the districts choose.
[7]Through 2014–15, districts are allowed to shorten the 180-day instructional year to 175 days without fiscal penalty.
[8]Statewide textbook adoption is only at the elementary level. Adoption practices have been suspended until the 2015–16 school year.
[9]No statewide policy; varies by district.
[10]1996 data.
[11]For schools on double-session or approved experimental calendar: 630 (K–3); 810 (4–12).
[12]Does not apply to charter and multitrack schools.
[13]For the 2014–15 and 2015–16 school years.
[14]Fees for lost or damaged books permitted.
[15]Instructional time for graduating seniors may be reduced.
[16]1998 data.

[17]Fees permitted, but if 5 percent or more of the voters in a district petition the school board, a majority of the district's voters may decide to furnish free textbooks to students.
[18]Fees permitted for students in grades 9–12, but students who qualify for free or reduced-price lunch are exempted.
[19]Refundable or security deposits permitted.
[20]174 days required for a 5-day week; 142 days required for a 4-day week.
[21]Local districts may select textbooks not on the state recommended list provided the textbooks meet specific criteria and the selection is based on recommendations by the district's curriculum materials review committee.
[22]Starting in the 2015–16 school year, grades 9 through 12 will transition to 1,080 hours and kindergarten will transition to 1,000 hours statewide by the 2017–18 school year.
[23]A district may provide free textbooks to students when, in its judgment, the best interests of the district will be served.
NOTE: Minimum number of instructional days refers to the actual number of days that pupils have contact with a teacher. Some states allow for different types of school calendars by setting instructional time in both days and hours, while others use only days or only hours. For states in which the number of days or hours varies by grade, the relevant grade(s) appear in parentheses.
SOURCE: Council of Chief State School Officers, Key State Education Policies on PK-12 Education, 2000 and 2006; Education Commission of the States, StateNotes, Number of Instructional Days/Hours in the School Year (October 2014 revision), retrieved May 19, 2015, from http://www.ecs.org/clearinghouse/01/15/05/11505.pdf; State Textbook Adoption (September 2013 edition), retrieved May 19, 2015, from http://www.ecs.org/clearinghouse/01/09/23/10923.pdf; and supplemental information retrieved from various state websites. (This table was prepared May 2015.)

Table 234.30. Course credit requirements and exit exam requirements for a standard high school diploma and the use of other high school completion credentials, by state: 2013

State	Course credits (in Carnegie units)						High school exit exams				Other completion credentials	
	Total required credits for standard diploma, all courses	Required credits in selected subject areas					Exit exam required for standard diploma	Characteristics of required exams			Advanced recognition for exceeding standard requirements	Alternative credential for not meeting all standard requirements[2]
		English/ language arts	Social studies	Science	Mathematics	Other credits		Subjects tested[1]	Exam based on standards for 10th grade or higher	Appeals or alternative route to standard diploma if exam failed		
1	2	3	4	5	6	7	8	9	10	11	12	13
Alabama	24.0	4.0	4.0	4.0	4.0	8.0	Yes	EMSH	Yes	Yes	Yes	Yes
Alaska	21.0	4.0	3.0	2.0	2.0	10.0	Yes	EM	Yes	Yes	No	Yes
Arizona	22.0	4.0	3.0	3.0	4.0	8.0	Yes	EM	Yes	Yes	Yes	No
Arkansas	22.0	4.0	3.0	3.0	4.0	8.0	Yes	M	No	Yes	Yes	No
California	13.0	3.0	3.0	2.0	2.0	3.0	Yes	EM	Yes	Yes	Yes	Yes
Colorado	—	—	0.5	—	—	—	No	†	†	†	No	No
Connecticut	20.0	4.0	3.0	2.0	3.0	8.0	No [3]	†	†	†	No	No
Delaware	22.0	4.0	3.0	3.0	4.0	8.0	No	†	†	†	No	Yes
District of Columbia	24.0	4.0	4.0	4.0	4.0	8.0	No	†	†	†	No	Yes
Florida	24.0	4.0	3.0	3.0	4.0	10.0	Yes	EM	Yes	Yes	No	Yes
Georgia	23.0	4.0	3.0	4.0	4.0	8.0	Yes	EMSH	Yes	Yes	No	Yes
Hawaii	24.0	4.0	4.0	3.0	3.0	10.0	No	†	†	†	Yes	Yes
Idaho	23.0	4.5	2.5	3.0	3.0	10.0	Yes	EM	Yes	Yes	No	No
Illinois	16.0	4.0	2.0	2.0	3.0	5.0	No	†	†	†	No	No
Indiana	20.0	4.0	3.0	3.0	3.0	7.0	Yes	EM	Yes	Yes	Yes	Yes
Iowa	14.0	4.0	3.0	3.0	3.0	1.0	No	†	†	†	Yes	Yes
Kansas	21.0	4.0	3.0	3.0	3.0	8.0	No	†	†	†	No	No
Kentucky	22.0	4.0	3.0	3.0	3.0	9.0	No	†	†	†	Yes	Yes
Louisiana	24.0	4.0	4.0	4.0	4.0	8.0	Yes	EMSH [4]	Yes	Yes	Yes	Yes
Maine	16.0	4.0	2.0	2.0	2.0	6.0	No	†	†	†	No	Yes
Maryland	21.0	4.0	3.0	3.0	3.0	8.0	Yes	EMS	Yes	Yes	Yes	Yes
Massachusetts	—	—	—	—	—	—	Yes	EMS	Yes	Yes	No	No
Michigan	16.0	4.0	3.0	3.0	4.0	2.0	No	†	†	†	No	No
Minnesota	21.5	4.0	3.5	3.0	3.0	8.0	Yes	EM [5]	Yes	Yes	No	No
Mississippi	24.0	4.0	4.0	4.0	4.0	8.0	Yes	EMSH	Yes	Yes	No	Yes
Missouri	24.0	4.0	3.0	3.0	3.0	11.0	No	†	†	†	No	No
Montana	20.0	4.0	2.0	2.0	2.0	10.0	No	†	†	†	No	No
Nebraska	200.0 [6]	—	—	—	—	—	No	†	†	†	No	No
Nevada	22.5	4.0	2.0	2.0	3.0	11.5	Yes	EMS	Yes	Yes	Yes	Yes
New Hampshire	20.0	4.0	2.5	2.0	3.0	8.5	No	†	†	†	Yes	Yes
New Jersey	24.0	4.0	3.0	3.0	3.0	11.0	Yes	EM	Yes	Yes	No	No
New Mexico	24.0	4.0	3.5	3.0	4.0	9.5	Yes	EMSH	Yes	Yes	No	Yes
New York	22.0	4.0	4.0	3.0	3.0	8.0	Yes	EMSH	Yes	Yes	Yes	Yes
North Carolina	21.0	4.0	3.0	3.0	4.0	7.0	No	†	†	†	Yes	Yes
North Dakota	22.0	4.0	3.0	3.0	3.0	9.0	No	†	†	†	No	No
Ohio	20.0	4.0	3.0	3.0	3.0	7.0	Yes	EMSH	Yes	Yes	Yes	No
Oklahoma	23.0	4.0	3.0	3.0	3.0	10.0	Yes	EMSH [7]	Yes	Yes	Yes	No
Oregon	24.0	4.0	3.0	3.0	3.0	11.0	No	†	†	†	No	Yes
Pennsylvania	—	—	—	—	—	—	No	†	†	†	No	No
Rhode Island	20.0	4.0	3.0	3.0	4.0	6.0	No [8]	†	†	†	No	No
South Carolina	24.0	4.0	3.0	3.0	4.0	10.0	Yes	EM	Yes	No	Yes	Yes
South Dakota	22.0	4.0	3.0	3.0	3.0	9.0	No	†	†	†	Yes	No
Tennessee	22.0	4.0	3.0	3.0	4.0	8.0	No	†	†	No	Yes	Yes
Texas	26.0	4.0	4.0	4.0	4.0	10.0	Yes	EMSH	Yes	Yes	Yes	Yes
Utah	24.0	4.0	3.0	3.0	3.0	11.0	No	†	†	†	No	Yes
Vermont	20.0	4.0	3.0	3.0	3.0	7.0	No	†	†	†	No	No
Virginia	22.0	4.0	3.0	3.0	3.0	9.0	Yes	EMSH [9]	Yes	Yes	Yes	Yes
Washington	20.0	3.0	2.5	2.0	3.0	9.5	Yes	EM	Yes	Yes	No	No
West Virginia	24.0	4.0	4.0	3.0	4.0	9.0	No	†	†	†	Yes	Yes
Wisconsin	13.0	4.0	3.0	2.0	2.0	2.0	No	†	†	†	No	Yes
Wyoming	13.0	4.0	3.0	3.0	3.0	0.0	No	†	†	†	Yes	No

—Not available.
†Not applicable.
[1]Exit exam subjects tested: E = English (including writing), M = Mathematics, S = Science, and H = History/social studies.
[2]A certificate of attendance is an example of an alternative credential for students who do not meet all requirements for a standard diploma. Depending on an individual state's policies, alternative credentials may be offered to students with disabilities, students who fail exit exams, or other students who do not meet all requirements.
[3]Requirement takes effect for class of 2020.
[4]Students must pass either the science or social studies components of the Graduation Exit Examination (GEE) to receive a standard diploma.
[5]Students can graduate by passing statewide reading and writing assessments and either passing mathematics assessments or meeting other requirements.

[6]Expressed in semester credits instead of Carnegie units.
[7]To receive the standard diploma, students must pass tests in algebra 1, English 2, and two of the following five subjects: algebra 2, biology 1, English 3, geometry, and U.S. history.
[8]Requirement takes effect for class of 2014.
[9]To receive the standard diploma, students must earn at least six verified credits by passing end-of-course assessments. One of those credits may be earned by passing a student-selected test in computer science, technology, career and technical education, or other areas.
NOTE: Local school districts frequently have other graduation requirements in addition to state requirements. The Carnegie unit is a standard of measurement that represents one credit for the completion of a 1-year course.
SOURCE: Editorial Projects in Education Research Center, custom table, retrieved August 27, 2013, from Education Counts database (http://www.edcounts.org/createtable/step1.php). (This table was prepared August 2013.)

Table 234.40. States that use criterion-referenced tests (CRTs) aligned to state standards, by subject area and level: 2006–07

State	Aligned to state standards		Off-the-shelf/ norm-referenced test (NRT)[1]	CRTs,[2] by subject area and level			
	CRT[2]	Augmented or hybrid test[3]		English/ language arts	Mathematics	Science	Social studies/ history
1	2	3	4	5	6	7	8
Alabama	X		X	ES, MS, HS	ES, MS, HS	HS	HS
Alaska	X		X	ES, MS, HS	ES, MS, HS		
Arizona	X	X	X	ES, MS, HS	ES, MS, HS		
Arkansas	X		X	ES, MS, HS	ES, MS, HS	ES, MS	
California	X		X	ES, MS, HS	ES, MS, HS	ES, MS, HS	MS, HS
Colorado	X		X	ES, MS, HS	ES, MS, HS	ES, MS, HS	
Connecticut	X			ES, MS, HS	ES, MS, HS	HS	
Delaware		X		ES, MS, HS	ES, MS, HS	ES, MS, HS	ES, MS, HS
District of Columbia	X			ES, MS, HS	ES, MS, HS		
Florida	X		X	ES, MS, HS	ES, MS, HS	ES, MS, HS	
Georgia	X		X	ES, MS, HS	ES, MS, HS	ES, MS, HS	ES, MS, HS
Hawaii		X		ES, MS, HS	ES, MS, HS		
Idaho	X			ES, MS, HS	ES, MS, HS		
Illinois	X	X		ES, MS, HS	ES, MS, HS	HS	
Indiana	X			ES, MS, HS	ES, MS, HS	ES, MS	
Iowa			X	ES, MS, HS	ES, MS, HS	ES, MS, HS	
Kansas	X			ES, MS, HS	ES, MS, HS		
Kentucky	X		X	ES, MS, HS	ES, MS, HS	ES, MS, HS	ES, MS, HS
Louisiana	X	X		ES, MS, HS	ES, MS, HS	ES, MS, HS	ES, MS, HS
Maine	X		X	ES, MS, HS	ES, MS, HS	ES, MS	
Maryland	X	X		ES, MS, HS	ES, MS, HS	HS	HS
Massachusetts	X			ES, MS, HS	ES, MS, HS	ES, MS, HS	
Michigan	X		X	ES, MS, HS	ES, MS, HS	ES, MS, HS	MS, HS
Minnesota	X			ES, MS, HS	ES, MS, HS		
Mississippi	X		X	ES, MS, HS	ES, MS, HS	ES, MS, HS	HS
Missouri		X		ES, MS, HS	ES, MS, HS		
Montana	X		X	ES, MS, HS	ES, MS, HS		
Nebraska	X			ES, MS, HS			
Nevada	X		X	ES, MS, HS	ES, MS, HS		
New Hampshire	X			ES, MS	ES, MS		
New Jersey	X			ES, HS	ES, MS, HS	ES, MS	
New Mexico	X		X	ES, MS, HS	ES, MS, HS	ES, MS, HS	
New York	X			ES, MS, HS	ES, MS, HS	ES, MS, HS	ES, MS, HS
North Carolina	X			ES, MS, HS	ES, MS, HS	HS	HS
North Dakota	X			ES, MS, HS	ES, MS, HS	ES, MS, HS	
Ohio	X			ES, MS, HS	ES, MS, HS	ES, MS, HS	ES, MS, HS
Oklahoma	X			ES, MS, HS	ES, MS, HS	ES, MS, HS	ES, MS, HS
Oregon	X			ES, MS, HS	ES, MS, HS	MS, HS	
Pennsylvania	X			ES, MS, HS	ES, MS		
Rhode Island	X	X		ES, MS, HS	ES, MS, HS		
South Carolina	X			ES, MS, HS	ES, MS, HS	ES, MS, HS	ES, MS, HS
South Dakota		X	X	ES, MS, HS	ES, MS, HS	ES, MS, HS	
Tennessee	X			ES, MS, HS	ES, MS, HS	ES, MS, HS	ES, MS, HS
Texas	X			ES, MS, HS	ES, MS, HS	ES, MS, HS	MS, HS
Utah	X		X	ES, MS, HS	ES, MS, HS	ES, MS, HS	
Vermont	X			ES, MS	ES, MS		
Virginia	X			ES, MS, HS	ES, MS, HS	ES, MS, HS	ES, MS, HS
Washington	X			ES, MS, HS	ES, MS, HS	ES, MS, HS	
West Virginia	X		X	ES, MS, HS	ES, MS, HS	ES, MS, HS	ES, MS
Wisconsin		X		ES, MS, HS	ES, MS, HS	ES, MS, HS	ES, MS, HS
Wyoming	X			ES, MS, HS	ES, MS, HS		

X State has a test. A blank denotes that the state does not have this type of test.
[1]Off-the-shelf/norm-referenced tests (NRTs) are commercially developed tests that have not been modified to reflect state content standards.
[2]Criterion-referenced tests (CRTs) are custom-developed and explicitly designed to measure state content standards.

[3]Augmented or hybrid tests incorporate elements of both NRTs and CRTs. These tests include NRTs that have been augmented or modified to reflect state standards.
NOTE: ES = elementary school, MS = middle school, and HS = high school.
SOURCE: Quality Counts 2007, Cradle to Career, *Education Week*, 2007. (This table was prepared September 2008.)

Table 234.50.   Required testing for initial certification of elementary and secondary school teachers, by type of assessment and state: 2014 and 2015

State	Assessment for certification, 2014				Assessment for certification, 2015			
	Basic skills exam	Subject-matter exam	Knowledge of teaching exam	Assessment of teaching performance	Basic skills exam	Subject-matter exam	Knowledge of teaching exam	Assessment of teaching performance
1	2	3	4	5	6	7	8	9
Alabama	X	X	X	X	X	X	X	X
Alaska	X				X			
Arizona		X	X			X	X	
Arkansas	X	X	X	X	X	X	X	
California	X	—		X	X	—		X
Colorado		X				X		
Connecticut	X	X	—	—	X	X	—	—
Delaware	X	X			X	X		
District of Columbia	X	X	X		X	X	X	
Florida	X			X	X			X
Georgia	X	X			X	X		
Hawaii	X	X	—		X	X		
Idaho		X		X		X		X
Illinois	X	X	X		X	X	X	X[1]
Indiana	X	X		X	X	X		X
Iowa						X	X	
Kansas		X	X			X	X	
Kentucky	X	X	X	X	X	X	X	X
Louisiana	X	X	X	X	X	X	X	X
Maine	—	—	—	—	X	X	X	
Maryland	X	X	X	X	X	X	X	
Massachusetts	X	X		X	X	X		X
Michigan	X	X		X	X	X		X
Minnesota	X	X	X		X	X	X	
Mississippi	—	—	—	—	X	X	X	X
Missouri	X	X		X	X	X	X	X
Montana								
Nebraska	X				X			
Nevada	—	X	—	—	X	X		
New Hampshire	X	X			X			
New Jersey	—	—	—	—	X	X		
New Mexico	X	X	X	X	X	X	X	X
New York		X	X		X	X	X	X
North Carolina	—	—	—	—	X	X	X	X
North Dakota	—	X	—	—	X	X	X	X
Ohio		X	X	X		X	X	X
Oklahoma	—	—	—	—	—	—	—	—
Oregon	X	X		X	X	X		X
Pennsylvania	X	X	X	X	X	X		X
Rhode Island			X	X	X	X	X	X
South Carolina		X	X			X	X	
South Dakota	X	X	X	X	X	X	X	X
Tennessee	X	X	X		X	X	X	
Texas	X	X	X	X	X	X	X	X
Utah		X		X		X		X
Vermont	X	X			X			
Virginia	X	X	X		X	X	X	
Washington	X	X		X	X	X		X
West Virginia	X	X	X	X	X	X	X	X
Wisconsin	X	X			X	X		X
Wyoming	—		—					

—Not available.
X Denotes that the state requires testing. A blank denotes that the state does not require testing.
[1]Beginning September 1, 2015.

SOURCE: National Association of State Directors of Teacher Education and Certification (NAS-DTEC), NASDTEC Knowledgebase, retrieved July 9, 2015, from https://www.nasdtec.net/. (This table was prepared July 2015.)

Table 235.10. Revenues for public elementary and secondary schools, by source of funds: Selected years, 1919–20 through 2012–13

	Revenues (in thousands)							Revenues per pupil						
				Local (including intermediate sources below the state level)							Local (including intermediate sources below the state level)			
School year	Total	Federal	State	Total	Property taxes	Other public revenue	Private[1]	Total	Federal	State	Total	Property taxes	Other public revenue	Private[1]
1	2	3	4	5	6	7	8	9	10	11	12	13	14	15
							Current dollars							
1919–20	$970,121	$2,475	$160,085	$807,561	—	—	—	$45	#	$7	$37	—	—	—
1929–30	2,088,557	7,334	353,670	1,727,553	—	—	—	81	#	14	67	—	—	—
1939–40	2,260,527	39,810	684,354	1,536,363	—	—	—	89	$2	27	60	—	—	—
1949–50	5,437,044	155,848	2,165,689	3,115,507	—	—	—	217	6	86	124	—	—	—
1959–60	14,746,618	651,639	5,768,047	8,326,932	—	—	—	419	19	164	237	—	—	—
1969–70	40,266,922	3,219,557	16,062,776	20,984,589	—	—	—	884	71	353	461	—	—	—
1979–80	96,881,164	9,503,537	45,348,814	42,028,813	—	—	—	2,326	228	1,089	1,009	—	—	—
1989–90	208,547,573	12,700,784	98,238,633	97,608,157	$74,867,627	$17,084,494	$5,656,036	5,144	313	2,423	2,408	$1,847	$421	$140
1991–92	234,581,384	15,493,330	108,783,449	110,304,605	85,874,700	18,213,748	6,216,157	5,579	368	2,587	2,623	2,042	433	148
1992–93	247,626,168	17,261,252	113,403,436	116,961,481	87,143,955	23,116,567	6,700,958	5,783	403	2,648	2,731	2,035	540	156
1993–94	260,159,468	18,341,483	117,474,209	124,343,776	97,762,990	19,661,128	6,919,657	5,986	422	2,703	2,861	2,249	452	159
1994–95	273,149,449	18,582,157	127,729,576	126,837,717	97,978,129	21,560,162	7,299,425	6,192	421	2,896	2,875	2,221	489	165
1995–96	287,702,844	19,104,019	136,670,754	131,928,071	101,785,858	22,522,345	7,619,869	6,416	426	3,048	2,942	2,270	502	170
1996–97	305,065,192	20,081,287	146,435,584	138,548,321	106,545,881	24,288,693	7,713,747	6,688	440	3,211	3,038	2,336	533	169
1997–98	325,925,708	22,201,965	157,645,372	146,078,370	111,184,150	26,676,244	8,217,977	7,066	481	3,418	3,167	2,410	578	178
1998–99	347,377,993	24,521,817	169,298,232	153,557,944	119,483,487	25,348,879	8,725,578	7,446	527	3,638	3,300	2,567	545	187
1999–2000	372,943,802	27,097,866	184,613,352	161,232,584	124,735,516	27,628,923	8,868,145	7,959	578	3,940	3,441	2,662	590	189
2000–01	401,356,120	29,100,183	199,583,097	172,672,840	132,575,925	30,889,273	9,207,643	8,503	616	4,228	3,658	2,809	654	195
2001–02	419,501,976	33,144,633	206,541,793	179,815,551	141,095,685	28,924,825	9,795,041	8,800	695	4,333	3,772	2,960	607	205
2002–03	440,111,653	37,515,909	214,277,407	188,318,337	148,511,786	29,579,240	10,227,310	9,134	779	4,447	3,908	3,082	614	212
2003–04	462,026,099	41,923,435	217,384,191	202,718,474	160,602,055	31,651,489	10,464,930	9,518	864	4,478	4,176	3,309	652	216
2004–05	487,753,525	44,809,532	228,553,579	214,390,414	167,909,883	35,433,486	11,047,044	9,996	918	4,684	4,394	3,441	726	226
2005–06	520,621,788	47,553,778	242,151,076	230,916,934	178,279,408	41,111,066	11,526,460	10,600	968	4,930	4,702	3,630	837	235
2006–07	555,710,762	47,150,608	263,608,741	244,951,413	188,287,298	44,806,422	11,857,694	11,281	957	5,351	4,972	3,822	910	241
2007–08	584,683,686	47,788,467	282,622,523	254,272,697	196,521,569	45,314,965	12,436,163	11,879	971	5,742	5,166	3,993	921	253
2008–09	592,422,033	56,670,261	276,525,603	259,226,169	205,821,844	41,195,313	12,209,012	12,032	1,151	5,616	5,265	4,180	837	248
2009–10	596,390,664	75,997,858	258,863,973	261,528,833	210,837,095	38,771,186	11,920,551	12,088	1,540	5,247	5,301	4,274	786	242
2010–11	604,228,585	75,549,471	266,786,402	261,892,711	211,649,523	38,558,755	11,684,433	12,218	1,528	5,395	5,296	4,280	780	236
2011–12[2]	597,885,111	60,921,462	269,043,077	267,920,572	215,830,316	40,290,007	11,800,249	12,075	1,230	5,434	5,411	4,359	814	238
2012–13[2]	603,686,987	55,862,552	273,101,724	274,722,710	221,961,238	41,141,278	11,620,194	12,130	1,122	5,487	5,520	4,460	827	233
							Constant 2014–15 dollars[3]							
1919–20	$12,047,714	$30,736	$1,988,059	$10,028,918	—	—	—	$558	$1	$92	$465	—	—	—
1929–30	28,878,507	101,407	4,890,200	23,886,900	—	—	—	1,125	4	190	930	—	—	—
1939–40	38,283,703	674,212	11,590,043	26,019,448	—	—	—	1,505	27	456	1,023	—	—	—
1949–50	54,335,315	1,557,473	21,642,899	31,134,943	—	—	—	2,164	62	862	1,240	—	—	—
1959–60	118,782,470	5,248,884	46,461,017	67,072,569	—	—	—	3,376	149	1,321	1,906	—	—	—
1969–70	252,289,988	20,171,942	100,640,361	131,477,686	—	—	—	5,539	443	2,209	2,886	—	—	—
1979–80	295,358,201	28,973,099	138,253,336	128,131,766	—	—	—	7,091	696	3,319	3,076	—	—	—
1989–90	388,725,450	23,673,821	183,113,407	181,938,222	$139,550,663	$31,844,906	$10,542,654	9,588	584	4,517	4,488	$3,442	$785	$260
1991–92	401,713,492	26,531,857	186,288,351	188,893,284	147,057,815	31,190,490	10,644,980	9,554	631	4,430	4,492	3,497	742	253
1992–93	411,207,989	28,664,033	188,317,734	194,226,222	144,711,243	38,387,369	11,207,610	9,602	669	4,398	4,536	3,379	896	260
1993–94	421,112,199	29,688,800	190,151,920	201,271,479	158,245,971	31,824,869	11,200,638	9,689	683	4,375	4,631	3,641	732	258
1994–95	429,818,841	29,240,261	200,990,990	199,587,590	154,175,108	33,926,351	11,486,131	9,744	663	4,556	4,525	3,495	769	260
1995–96	440,729,100	29,265,255	209,364,556	202,099,289	155,924,735	34,501,754	11,672,800	9,829	653	4,669	4,507	3,477	769	260
1996–97	454,362,992	29,908,996	218,100,628	206,353,368	158,689,049	36,175,491	11,488,827	9,962	656	4,782	4,524	3,479	793	252
1997–98	476,926,950	32,488,126	230,682,406	213,756,417	162,695,719	39,035,336	12,025,362	10,339	704	5,001	4,634	3,527	846	261
1998–99	499,668,056	35,272,150	243,518,357	220,877,548	171,864,893	36,461,795	12,550,860	10,737	758	5,233	4,746	3,693	783	270
1999–2000	521,390,379	37,883,903	258,096,864	225,409,613	174,385,250	38,626,341	12,398,022	11,127	808	5,508	4,811	3,722	824	265
2000–01	542,524,858	39,335,572	269,782,336	233,406,950	179,206,772	41,753,937	12,446,241	11,493	833	5,715	4,945	3,796	885	264

See notes at end of table.

Table 235.10. Revenues for public elementary and secondary schools, by source of funds: Selected years, 1919–20 through 2012–13—Continued

In the tables below, columns 2–8 are **Revenues (in thousands)** and columns 9–15 are **Revenues per pupil**. Within each group, "Local" refers to *Local (including intermediate sources below the state level)*.

Dollar amounts

School year	Revenues (in thousands) Total	Federal	State	Local: Total	Local: Property taxes	Local: Other public revenue	Local: Private[1]	Revenues per pupil Total	Federal	State	Local: Total	Local: Property taxes	Local: Other public revenue	Local: Private[1]
1	2	3	4	5	6	7	8	9	10	11	12	13	14	15
2001–02	557,188,141	44,023,145	274,331,574	238,833,422	187,405,178	38,418,340	13,009,904	11,688	923	5,755	5,010	3,931	806	273
2002–03	571,991,926	48,757,621	278,486,029	244,748,276	193,013,619	38,442,715	13,291,942	11,871	1,012	5,780	5,080	4,006	798	276
2003–04	587,617,690	53,319,395	276,475,281	257,823,014	204,258,176	40,255,248	13,309,590	12,106	1,098	5,696	5,312	4,208	829	274
2004–05	602,216,288	55,325,134	282,189,008	264,702,126	207,313,855	43,748,780	13,639,491	12,342	1,134	5,783	5,425	4,249	897	280
2005–06	619,216,867	56,559,487	288,009,519	274,647,861	212,041,868	48,896,658	13,709,335	12,608	1,152	5,864	5,592	4,317	996	279
2006–07	644,289,432	54,666,277	305,627,203	283,995,952	218,299,742	51,948,434	13,747,776	13,079	1,110	6,204	5,765	4,431	1,055	279
2007–08	653,660,243	53,426,188	315,964,189	284,269,865	219,705,696	50,660,882	13,903,288	13,280	1,085	6,419	5,775	4,464	1,029	282
2008–09	653,190,980	62,483,333	304,890,804	285,816,843	226,934,457	45,421,009	13,461,377	13,267	1,269	6,193	5,805	4,609	923	273
2009–10	651,265,154	82,990,496	282,682,301	285,592,357	230,236,423	42,338,561	13,017,373	13,201	1,682	5,730	5,789	4,667	858	264
2010–11	646,835,901	80,876,859	285,598,906	280,360,136	226,574,037	42,277,735	12,508,364	13,080	1,635	5,775	5,669	4,582	835	253
2011–12[2]	621,825,212	63,360,837	279,815,914	278,648,462	224,472,444	41,903,271	12,272,746	12,559	1,280	5,651	5,628	4,534	846	248
2012–13	617,581,975	57,148,334	279,387,672	281,045,969	227,070,092	42,088,222	11,887,655	12,409	1,148	5,614	5,647	4,562	846	239

Percentage distribution

(Values are identical for Revenues in thousands, columns 2–8, and Revenues per pupil, columns 9–15.)

School year	Total	Federal	State	Local: Total	Local: Property taxes	Local: Other public revenue	Local: Private[1]
1919–20	100.0	0.3	16.5	83.2	—	—	—
1929–30	100.0	0.4	16.9	82.7	—	—	—
1939–40	100.0	1.8	30.3	68.0	—	—	—
1949–50	100.0	2.9	39.8	57.3	—	—	—
1959–60	100.0	4.4	39.1	56.5	—	—	—
1969–70	100.0	8.0	39.9	52.1	—	—	—
1979–80	100.0	9.8	46.8	43.4	—	—	—
1989–90	100.0	6.1	47.1	46.8	35.9	8.2	2.7
1991–92	100.0	6.6	46.4	47.0	36.6	7.8	2.6
1992–93	100.0	7.0	45.8	47.2	35.2	9.3	2.7
1993–94	100.0	7.1	45.2	47.8	37.6	7.6	2.7
1994–95	100.0	6.8	46.8	46.4	35.9	7.9	2.7
1995–96	100.0	6.6	47.5	45.9	35.4	7.8	2.6
1996–97	100.0	6.6	48.0	45.4	34.9	8.0	2.5
1997–98	100.0	6.8	48.4	44.8	34.1	8.2	2.5
1998–99	100.0	7.1	48.7	44.2	34.4	7.3	2.5
1999–2000	100.0	7.3	49.5	43.2	33.4	7.4	2.4
2000–01	100.0	7.3	49.7	43.0	33.0	7.7	2.3
2001–02	100.0	7.9	49.2	42.9	33.6	6.9	2.3
2002–03	100.0	8.5	48.7	42.8	33.7	6.7	2.3
2003–04	100.0	9.1	47.1	43.9	34.8	6.9	2.3
2004–05	100.0	9.2	46.9	44.0	34.4	7.3	2.3
2005–06	100.0	9.1	46.5	44.4	34.2	7.9	2.2
2006–07	100.0	8.5	47.4	44.1	33.9	8.1	2.1
2007–08	100.0	8.2	48.3	43.5	33.6	7.8	2.1
2008–09	100.0	9.6	46.7	43.8	34.7	7.0	2.1
2009–10	100.0	12.7	43.4	43.9	35.4	6.5	2.0
2010–11	100.0	12.5	44.2	43.3	35.0	6.4	1.9
2011–12[2]	100.0	10.2	45.0	44.8	36.1	6.7	2.0
2012–13	100.0	9.3	45.2	45.5	36.8	6.8	1.9

—Not available.
#Rounds to zero.
[1]Includes revenues from gifts, and tuition and fees from patrons.
[2]Data have been revised from previously published figures.
[3]Constant dollars based on the Consumer Price Index, prepared by the Bureau of Labor Statistics, U.S. Department of Labor, adjusted to a school-year basis.

NOTE: Beginning in 1989–90, revenues for state education agencies were excluded and new survey collection procedures were initiated; data may not be entirely comparable with figures for earlier years. Detail may not sum to totals because of rounding.
SOURCE: U.S. Department of Education, National Center for Education Statistics, *Biennial Survey of Education in the United States,* 1919–20 through 1949–50; *Statistics of State School Systems,* 1959–60 and 1969–70; *Revenues and Expenditures for Public Elementary and Secondary Education,* 1979–80; and Common Core of Data (CCD), "National Public Education Financial Survey," 1989–90 through 2012–13. (This table was prepared September 2015.)

Table 235.20. Revenues for public elementary and secondary schools, by source of funds and state or jurisdiction: 2012–13

[In current dollars]

State or jurisdiction	Total (in thousands)	Federal Amount (in thousands)	Federal Per pupil	Federal Percent of total	State Amount (in thousands)	State Percent of total	Local Amount (in thousands)[1]	Local Percent of total	Property taxes Amount (in thousands)	Property taxes Percent of total	Private[2] Amount (in thousands)	Private Percent of total
1	2	3	4	5	6	7	8	9	10	11	12	13
United States	$603,686,987	$55,862,552	$1,128	9.3	$273,101,724	45.2	$274,722,710	45.5	$221,961,238	36.8	$11,620,194	1.9
Alabama	7,188,210	850,523	1,142	11.8	3,936,486	54.8	2,401,201	33.4	1,099,433	15.3	321,517	4.5
Alaska	2,670,758	324,045	2,464	12.1	1,830,051	68.5	516,661	19.3	299,136	11.2	19,536	0.7
Arizona	9,385,733	1,278,835	1,174	13.6	3,965,426	42.2	4,141,471	44.1	3,013,964	32.1	228,247	2.4
Arkansas	5,051,804	612,256	1,259	12.1	2,624,126	51.9	1,815,421	35.9	1,568,431	31.0	148,938	2.9
California	66,026,445	7,388,302	1,173	11.2	35,878,654	54.3	22,759,489	34.5	18,324,216	27.8	402,845	0.6
Colorado	8,905,156	702,772	814	7.9	3,765,335	42.3	4,437,048	49.8	3,599,102	40.4	340,019	3.8
Connecticut	10,549,973	461,506	838	4.4	4,163,960	39.5	5,924,506	56.2	5,757,213	54.6	109,174	1.0
Delaware	1,909,503	192,422	1,491	10.1	1,123,567	58.8	593,514	31.1	506,397	26.5	15,084	0.8
District of Columbia	2,094,445	200,097	2,628	9.6	†	†	1,894,347	90.4	611,079	29.2	10,909	0.5
Florida	24,506,837	3,087,261	1,147	12.6	9,455,551	38.6	11,964,026	48.8	9,907,489	40.4	1,020,457	4.2
Georgia	17,492,816	1,864,121	1,094	10.7	7,620,092	43.6	8,008,603	45.8	5,396,960	30.9	468,040	2.7
Hawaii	2,331,839	310,777	1,682	13.3	1,962,993	84.2	58,069	2.5	0	0.0	31,653	1.4
Idaho	2,103,804	251,215	882	11.9	1,347,311	64.0	505,278	24.0	426,539	20.3	35,519	1.7
Illinois	26,879,107	2,313,498	1,116	8.6	7,003,524	26.1	17,562,085	65.3	15,453,409	57.5	499,742	1.9
Indiana	11,887,836	1,036,984	996	8.7	6,654,115	56.0	4,196,737	35.3	2,825,697	23.8	320,866	2.7
Iowa	6,033,012	472,925	946	7.8	3,118,397	51.7	2,441,689	40.5	1,988,380	33.0	138,259	2.3
Kansas	5,866,415	502,059	1,027	8.6	3,229,626	55.1	2,134,730	36.4	1,604,032	27.3	136,348	2.3
Kentucky	7,120,960	875,760	1,278	12.3	3,878,756	54.5	2,366,445	33.2	1,711,443	24.0	99,046	1.4
Louisiana	8,439,545	1,280,583	1,801	15.2	3,651,777	43.3	3,507,185	41.6	1,510,093	17.9	65,839	0.8
Maine	2,584,962	196,780	1,059	7.6	1,032,121	39.9	1,356,060	52.5	1,288,470	49.8	38,403	1.5
Maryland	13,800,320	831,092	967	6.0	6,093,647	44.2	6,875,581	49.8	3,349,654	24.3	118,938	0.9
Massachusetts	16,436,188	936,545	981	5.7	6,479,966	39.4	9,019,677	54.9	8,433,566	51.3	215,274	1.3
Michigan	18,632,336	1,819,682	1,170	9.8	10,938,995	58.7	5,873,659	31.5	4,950,705	26.6	275,054	1.5
Minnesota	11,215,788	709,817	840	6.3	7,233,164	64.5	3,272,807	29.2	2,104,741	18.8	331,571	3.0
Mississippi	4,394,942	707,620	1,433	16.1	2,213,480	50.4	1,473,842	33.5	1,216,479	27.7	108,453	2.5
Missouri	10,311,473	927,013	1,010	9.0	3,382,862	32.8	6,001,597	58.2	4,730,986	45.9	345,634	3.4
Montana	1,657,908	213,213	1,492	12.9	797,417	48.1	647,279	39.0	409,351	24.7	58,990	3.6
Nebraska	3,800,737	358,790	1,182	9.4	1,217,700	32.0	2,224,247	58.5	1,969,368	51.8	143,380	3.8
Nevada	4,140,625	401,968	902	9.7	1,397,295	33.7	2,341,362	56.5	1,080,253	26.1	40,006	1.0
New Hampshire	2,875,406	164,398	870	5.7	1,020,239	35.5	1,690,769	58.8	1,616,304	56.2	45,830	1.6
New Jersey	27,087,144	1,184,706	863	4.4	11,052,695	40.8	14,849,743	54.8	14,002,457	51.7	540,858	2.0
New Mexico	3,695,203	561,650	1,661	15.2	2,535,796	68.6	597,756	16.2	483,289	13.1	54,107	1.5
New York	59,007,178	3,234,775	1,193	5.5	23,665,880	40.1	32,106,522	54.4	28,771,765	48.8	325,359	0.6
North Carolina	13,107,879	1,652,625	1,088	12.6	8,150,584	62.2	3,304,670	25.2	2,754,510	21.0	220,079	1.7
North Dakota	1,354,505	159,520	1,578	11.8	690,150	51.0	504,835	37.3	377,577	27.9	59,087	4.4
Ohio	22,609,388	1,944,765	1,124	8.6	9,830,868	43.5	10,833,755	47.9	8,917,668	39.4	653,040	2.9
Oklahoma	5,912,975	732,453	1,088	12.4	2,906,491	49.2	2,274,031	38.5	1,650,554	27.9	266,078	4.5
Oregon	6,160,158	569,756	970	9.2	3,041,818	49.4	2,548,584	41.4	2,056,350	33.4	152,807	2.5
Pennsylvania	27,446,614	2,186,130	1,240	8.0	9,841,441	35.9	15,419,043	56.2	12,199,033	44.4	424,679	1.5
Rhode Island	2,336,776	202,770	1,423	8.7	909,689	38.9	1,224,317	52.4	1,194,407	51.1	19,658	0.8
South Carolina	8,414,913	845,279	1,148	10.0	3,904,090	46.4	3,665,545	43.6	2,693,565	32.0	244,930	2.9
South Dakota	1,323,242	198,333	1,520	15.0	413,443	31.2	711,466	53.8	585,913	44.3	38,339	2.9
Tennessee	9,084,504	1,182,985	1,191	13.0	4,151,138	45.7	3,750,381	41.3	1,828,701	20.1	435,060	4.8
Texas	50,053,709	5,872,123	1,156	11.7	20,134,113	40.2	24,047,473	48.0	21,886,177	43.7	985,247	2.0
Utah	4,860,217	449,443	733	9.2	2,527,828	52.0	1,882,946	38.7	1,466,486	30.2	204,466	4.2
Vermont	1,641,315	116,847	1,304	7.1	1,459,459	88.9	65,009	4.0	956	0.1	23,197	1.4
Virginia	15,106,627	1,108,890	876	7.3	5,880,122	38.9	8,117,614	53.7	4,899,822	32.4	256,811	1.7
Washington	12,142,892	1,042,169	991	8.6	7,160,382	59.0	3,940,341	32.4	3,326,713	27.4	322,510	2.7
West Virginia	3,543,326	380,192	1,343	10.7	2,089,304	59.0	1,073,830	30.3	957,233	27.0	25,682	0.7
Wisconsin	10,809,097	850,329	975	7.9	4,858,710	45.0	5,100,059	47.2	4,673,928	43.2	216,894	2.0
Wyoming	1,694,441	113,949	1,252	6.7	881,087	52.0	699,405	41.3	481,248	28.4	17,734	1.0
Other jurisdictions												
American Samoa	64,420	54,272	—	84.2	9,890	15.4	258	0.4	0	0.0	36	0.1
Guam	290,408	69,078	2,215	23.8	0	0.0	221,330	76.2	0	0.0	554	0.2
Northern Marianas	61,275	28,024	2,632	45.7	33,251	54.3	0	0.0	0	0.0	0	0.0
Puerto Rico	3,577,365	1,234,613	2,841	34.5	2,342,270	65.5	481	#	0	0.0	481	#
U.S. Virgin Islands	206,300	35,112	2,311	17.0	0	0.0	171,188	83.0	0	0.0	24	#

—Not available.
†Not applicable.
#Rounds to zero.
[1]Includes other categories of revenue not separately shown.
[2]Includes revenues from gifts, and tuition and fees from patrons.

NOTE: Excludes revenues for state education agencies. Detail may not sum to totals because of rounding.
SOURCE: U.S. Department of Education, National Center for Education Statistics, Common Core of Data (CCD), "National Public Education Financial Survey," 2012–13. (This table was prepared August 2015.)

Table 235.30. Revenues for public elementary and secondary schools, by source of funds and state or jurisdiction: 2011–12

[In current dollars]

State or jurisdiction	Total (in thousands)	Federal Amount (in thousands)	Federal Per pupil	Federal Percent of total	State Amount (in thousands)	State Percent of total	Local Amount (in thousands)[1]	Local Percent of total	Property taxes Amount (in thousands)	Property taxes Percent of total	Private[2] Amount (in thousands)	Private[2] Percent of total
1	2	3	4	5	6	7	8	9	10	11	12	13
United States	$597,885,111	$60,921,462	$1,230	10.2	$269,043,077	45.0	$267,920,572	44.8	$215,830,316	36.1	$11,800,249	2.0
Alabama	7,099,553	838,285	1,126	11.8	3,934,577	55.4	2,326,690	32.8	1,088,896	15.3	314,693	4.4
Alaska	2,496,679	353,993	2,699	14.2	1,618,975	64.8	523,711	21.0	297,730	11.9	21,069	0.8
Arizona	9,247,003	1,316,434	1,219	14.2	3,804,900	41.1	4,125,669	44.6	3,007,906	32.5	235,016	2.5
Arkansas	5,284,555	698,938	1,447	13.2	2,723,740	51.5	1,861,878	35.2	1,608,527	30.4	148,872	2.8
California	65,808,329	8,260,861	1,314	12.6	37,079,384	56.3	20,468,083	31.1	16,065,320	24.4	427,487	0.6
Colorado	8,698,810	722,810	846	8.3	3,765,940	43.3	4,210,060	48.4	3,412,026	39.2	339,720	3.9
Connecticut	10,274,602	535,208	965	5.2	3,978,525	38.7	5,760,869	56.1	5,607,191	54.6	109,351	1.1
Delaware	1,871,464	235,905	1,829	12.6	1,096,243	58.6	539,316	28.8	464,458	24.8	16,067	0.9
District of Columbia	2,073,564	208,249	2,818	10.0	†	†	1,865,315	90.0	583,315	28.1	11,295	0.5
Florida	23,988,519	3,122,488	1,170	13.0	8,702,310	36.3	12,163,720	50.7	10,191,658	42.5	999,689	4.2
Georgia	17,620,300	1,920,092	1,140	10.9	7,533,980	42.8	8,166,229	46.3	5,576,107	31.6	487,664	2.8
Hawaii	2,535,039	318,728	1,744	12.6	2,161,254	85.3	55,057	2.2	0	0.0	32,842	1.3
Idaho	2,062,254	278,914	997	13.5	1,302,949	63.2	480,391	23.3	399,952	19.4	35,389	1.7
Illinois	26,764,139	2,406,643	1,156	9.0	6,984,396	26.1	17,373,101	64.9	15,347,696	57.3	489,205	1.8
Indiana	11,940,988	1,149,521	1,104	9.6	6,510,737	54.5	4,280,730	35.8	2,886,835	24.2	338,359	2.8
Iowa	6,038,962	526,409	1,062	8.7	2,681,029	44.4	2,831,524	46.9	1,977,465	32.7	141,451	2.3
Kansas	5,796,537	485,235	998	8.4	3,209,527	55.4	2,101,775	36.3	1,584,595	27.3	140,899	2.4
Kentucky	7,086,717	971,266	1,424	13.7	3,841,443	54.2	2,274,008	32.1	1,632,734	23.0	108,175	1.5
Louisiana	8,412,167	1,458,572	2,074	17.3	3,602,717	42.8	3,350,878	39.8	1,404,203	16.7	68,960	0.8
Maine	2,556,186	233,761	1,237	9.1	1,022,269	40.0	1,300,156	50.9	1,231,367	48.2	39,813	1.6
Maryland	13,744,621	859,635	1,006	6.3	5,980,909	43.5	6,904,078	50.2	3,354,919	24.4	128,061	0.9
Massachusetts	15,835,037	1,059,639	1,111	6.7	6,206,699	39.2	8,568,699	54.1	8,060,794	50.9	214,459	1.4
Michigan	18,751,262	2,031,233	1,291	10.8	10,700,372	57.1	6,019,657	32.1	5,061,587	27.0	287,267	1.5
Minnesota	10,989,685	797,917	950	7.3	7,044,954	64.1	3,146,814	28.6	2,013,840	18.3	330,096	3.0
Mississippi	4,441,163	795,121	1,621	17.9	2,195,730	49.4	1,450,312	32.7	1,169,902	26.3	112,490	2.5
Missouri	10,221,689	1,034,047	1,128	10.1	3,275,438	32.0	5,912,203	57.8	4,623,345	45.2	349,994	3.4
Montana	1,622,721	218,297	1,534	13.5	770,180	47.5	634,244	39.1	402,736	24.8	59,287	3.7
Nebraska	3,634,647	295,392	980	8.1	1,168,027	32.1	2,171,228	59.7	1,918,003	52.8	144,822	4.0
Nevada	4,137,704	413,861	941	10.0	1,366,314	33.0	2,357,529	57.0	1,133,785	27.4	41,808	1.0
New Hampshire	2,864,747	188,927	985	6.6	1,031,778	36.0	1,644,043	57.4	1,571,664	54.9	48,682	1.7
New Jersey	26,581,734	1,425,761	1,051	5.4	10,499,156	39.5	14,656,818	55.1	13,818,756	52.0	561,254	2.1
New Mexico	3,611,545	540,071	1,602	15.0	2,455,787	68.0	615,688	17.0	493,780	13.7	53,220	1.5
New York	58,645,470	3,956,260	1,463	6.7	23,131,272	39.4	31,557,937	53.8	28,290,435	48.2	351,068	0.6
North Carolina	13,113,012	1,878,905	1,246	14.3	7,877,949	60.1	3,356,157	25.6	2,781,052	21.2	235,542	1.8
North Dakota	1,296,813	170,085	1,742	13.1	653,842	50.4	472,886	36.5	351,001	27.1	54,046	4.2
Ohio	22,886,511	2,186,000	1,256	9.6	10,132,936	44.3	10,567,575	46.2	8,702,819	38.0	676,160	3.0
Oklahoma	5,862,837	794,080	1,192	13.5	2,882,879	49.2	2,185,878	37.3	1,591,425	27.1	260,466	4.4
Oregon	6,172,422	618,981	1,089	10.0	3,038,044	49.2	2,515,397	40.8	2,034,939	33.0	153,561	2.5
Pennsylvania	26,807,485	2,201,593	1,243	8.2	9,594,823	35.8	15,011,068	56.0	11,973,510	44.7	434,758	1.6
Rhode Island	2,278,095	217,363	1,522	9.5	846,435	37.2	1,214,297	53.3	1,181,575	51.9	20,379	0.9
South Carolina	8,041,045	871,480	1,198	10.8	3,670,717	45.6	3,498,848	43.5	2,628,375	32.7	242,015	3.0
South Dakota	1,303,055	215,937	1,687	16.6	400,362	30.7	686,756	52.7	568,577	43.6	38,621	3.0
Tennessee	8,988,710	1,263,157	1,264	14.1	4,059,869	45.2	3,665,684	40.8	1,750,319	19.5	437,852	4.9
Texas	49,533,579	6,311,758	1,262	12.7	20,341,491	41.1	22,880,330	46.2	20,766,669	41.9	972,423	2.0
Utah	4,619,102	461,333	770	10.0	2,418,166	52.4	1,739,603	37.7	1,308,562	28.3	198,911	4.3
Vermont	1,644,282	127,644	1,420	7.8	1,451,850	88.3	64,787	3.9	961	0.1	21,862	1.3
Virginia	14,659,153	1,356,037	1,078	9.3	5,564,497	38.0	7,738,618	52.8	4,648,724	31.7	271,223	1.9
Washington	11,844,779	1,057,047	1,011	8.9	7,001,099	59.1	3,786,633	32.0	3,209,638	27.1	319,128	2.7
West Virginia	3,556,656	433,205	1,531	12.2	2,069,942	58.2	1,053,510	29.6	934,089	26.3	31,316	0.9
Wisconsin	10,879,541	953,230	1,103	8.8	4,806,328	44.2	5,119,983	47.1	4,665,016	42.9	224,611	2.1
Wyoming	1,659,641	145,148	1,620	8.7	850,339	51.2	664,154	40.0	451,537	27.2	18,852	1.1
Other jurisdictions												
American Samoa	99,334	88,536	—	89.1	10,528	10.6	271	0.3	0	0.0	58	0.1
Guam	305,415	74,850	2,396	24.5	0	0.0	230,565	75.5	0	0.0	677	0.2
Northern Marianas	65,214	33,334	3,027	51.1	31,880	48.9	0	0.0	0	0.0	0	0.0
Puerto Rico	3,374,611	1,153,166	2,547	34.2	2,221,384	65.8	62	#	0	0.0	62	#
U.S. Virgin Islands	221,673	37,899	2,412	17.1	0	0.0	183,774	82.9	0	0.0	36	#

—Not available.
†Not applicable.
#Rounds to zero.
[1]Includes other categories of revenue not separately shown.
[2]Includes revenues from gifts, and tuition and fees from patrons.

NOTE: Excludes revenues for state education agencies. Some data have been revised from previously published figures. Detail may not sum to totals because of rounding.
SOURCE: U.S. Department of Education, National Center for Education Statistics, Common Core of Data (CCD), "National Public Education Financial Survey," 2011–12. (This table was prepared August 2015.)

Table 235.40. Public elementary and secondary revenues and expenditures, by locale, source of revenue, and purpose of expenditure: 2012–13

Source of revenue and purpose of expenditure	Total	City, large[1]	City, midsize[2]	City, small[3]	Suburban, large[4]	Suburban, midsize[5]	Suburban, small[6]	Town, fringe[7]	Town, distant[8]	Town, remote[9]	Rural, fringe[10]	Rural, distant[11]	Rural, remote[12]
1	2	3	4	5	6	7	8	9	10	11	12	13	14
Revenue amounts (in millions of current dollars)													
Total revenue[13]	$606,778	$83,757	$28,720	$35,386	$189,618	$17,923	$8,362	$12,447	$24,745	$17,814	$37,849	$29,026	$11,289
Federal	55,104	9,596	3,383	3,465	12,127	1,376	667	978	2,471	2,082	3,136	2,530	1,266
Title I	14,213	3,228	959	903	2,600	323	146	212	627	545	685	628	328
Child Nutrition Act	14,020	2,269	837	863	3,238	392	169	262	677	492	853	715	277
Children with disabilities (IDEA)	11,249	1,341	559	686	3,242	310	165	215	470	356	686	440	162
Impact aid	1,522	108	83	65	195	26	3	63	35	120	118	72	170
Bilingual education	361	37	15	17	63	3	1	2	4	5	9	3	1
Indian education	107	5	2	3	6	1	0	2	8	12	5	7	10
Math, science, and professional development	1,577	230	95	95	253	38	18	26	75	78	87	78	45
Safe and drug-free schools	141	7	11	12	23	1	2	2	9	7	12	5	5
Vocational and technical education	555	89	32	35	137	15	9	9	29	26	40	19	8
Other and unclassified	11,361	2,283	789	786	2,371	267	152	184	537	440	640	563	258
State	274,732	34,269	13,383	17,304	74,286	8,711	3,920	6,307	12,905	9,084	18,487	15,529	5,386
Special education programs	18,323	2,460	808	1,043	6,001	485	251	392	698	433	963	710	249
Compensatory and basic skills	5,610	659	177	415	1,635	195	43	83	182	102	278	184	81
Bilingual education	893	49	33	54	592	52	6	5	23	7	30	7	3
Gifted and talented	935	24	55	62	585	33	7	12	32	9	73	26	7
Vocational education	988	25	52	65	342	35	23	22	77	59	115	78	29
Other	247,982	31,052	12,257	15,666	65,132	7,911	3,591	5,794	11,892	8,474	17,028	14,525	5,017
Local[13]	276,942	39,892	11,955	14,617	103,205	7,836	3,775	5,162	9,369	6,648	16,226	10,967	4,638
Property tax[14]	176,222	16,779	7,352	9,731	72,452	4,623	2,861	3,834	6,708	4,938	10,642	7,833	3,527
Parent government contribution[14]	48,335	14,845	2,199	2,189	16,167	1,808	148	249	661	151	2,342	874	166
Private (fees from individuals)	14,052	979	629	718	5,279	562	203	354	633	414	1,061	737	306
Other[13]	38,333	7,289	1,776	1,979	9,306	843	563	725	1,367	1,145	2,182	1,523	638
Percentage distribution of revenue													
Total revenue	100.0	100.0	100.0	100.0	100.0	100.0	100.0	100.0	100.0	100.0	100.0	100.0	100.0
Federal	9.1	11.5	11.8	9.8	6.4	7.7	8.0	7.9	10.0	11.7	8.3	8.7	11.2
State	45.3	40.9	46.6	48.9	39.2	48.6	46.9	50.7	52.2	51.0	48.8	53.5	47.7
Local	45.6	47.6	41.6	41.3	54.4	43.7	45.1	41.5	37.9	37.3	42.9	37.8	41.1
Expenditure amounts (in millions of current dollars)													
Total expenditures	$618,331	$88,215	$28,979	$36,218	$190,912	$17,940	$8,617	$12,802	$25,154	$18,108	$38,076	$29,063	$11,467
Current expenditures for schools	526,937	72,281	24,946	30,913	164,730	15,638	7,410	10,881	21,720	15,583	33,164	25,359	9,734
Instruction	319,544	45,795	14,673	18,712	100,943	9,468	4,461	6,584	13,045	9,348	19,843	15,057	5,719
Support services, students	29,395	2,999	1,598	1,922	10,180	900	471	590	1,123	853	1,828	1,143	409
Support services, instructional staff	24,563	3,026	1,479	1,571	7,367	733	307	449	1,024	673	1,436	1,000	337
Administration	39,620	4,804	1,827	2,194	11,951	1,098	554	870	1,778	1,325	2,606	2,297	971
Operation and maintenance	49,918	7,023	2,249	2,871	15,331	1,484	672	996	2,010	1,503	3,111	2,398	962
Transportation	23,692	3,187	1,033	1,205	7,958	737	387	549	1,001	650	1,870	1,509	561
Food service	21,400	2,783	1,105	1,264	5,792	676	306	467	1,052	782	1,455	1,228	487
Other	18,804	2,664	981	1,175	5,208	542	252	377	686	449	1,014	728	287
Other current expenditures	22,478	2,828	1,135	1,324	6,172	708	321	483	1,076	811	1,540	1,263	525
Interest on school debt	17,067	2,680	714	923	5,458	471	205	403	585	336	1,014	613	168
Capital outlay	47,281	7,551	2,323	3,028	12,885	1,235	611	1,034	1,986	1,663	2,527	1,997	964
Percentage distribution of current expenditures for schools													
All current expenditures for schools	100.0	100.0	100.0	100.0	100.0	100.0	100.0	100.0	100.0	100.0	100.0	100.0	100.0
Instruction	60.6	63.4	58.8	60.5	61.3	60.5	60.2	60.5	60.1	60.0	59.8	59.4	58.8
Support services	10.2	8.3	12.3	11.3	10.7	10.4	10.5	9.5	9.9	9.8	9.8	8.5	7.7
Administration	7.5	6.6	7.3	7.1	7.3	7.0	7.5	8.0	8.2	8.5	7.9	9.1	10.0
Operation and maintenance	9.5	9.7	9.0	9.3	9.3	9.5	9.1	9.1	9.3	9.6	9.4	9.5	9.9
Transportation	4.5	4.4	4.1	3.9	4.8	4.7	5.2	5.0	4.6	4.2	5.6	5.9	5.8
Food service and other	7.6	7.5	8.4	7.9	6.7	7.8	7.5	7.8	8.0	7.9	7.4	7.7	8.0
Per student amounts (in current dollars)													
Current expenditure per student	$10,628	$12,169	$10,052	$10,803	$11,233	$10,115	$10,837	$10,178	$9,988	$9,836	$10,355	$10,334	$11,402
Instruction expenditure per student	6,445	7,710	5,913	6,539	6,884	6,124	6,523	6,158	5,999	5,901	6,196	6,136	6,699

[1]Located inside an urbanized area and inside a principal city with a population of at least 250,000.

[2]Located inside an urbanized area and inside a principal city with a population of at least 100,000, but less than 250,000.

[3]Located inside an urbanized area and inside a principal city with a population less than 100,000.

[4]Located inside an urbanized area and outside a principal city with a population of 250,000 or more.

[5]Located inside an urbanized area and outside a principal city with a population of at least 100,000, but less than 250,000.

[6]Located inside an urbanized area and outside a principal city with a population less than 100,000.

[7]Located inside an urban cluster that is 10 miles or less from an urbanized area.

[8]Located inside an urban cluster that is more than 10 but less than or equal to 35 miles from an urbanized area.

[9]Located inside an urban cluster that is more than 35 miles from an urbanized area.

[10]Located outside any urbanized area or urban cluster, but 5 miles or less from an urbanized area or 2.5 miles or less from an urban cluster.

[11]Located outside any urbanized area or urban cluster and more than 5 miles but less than or equal to 25 miles from an urbanized area, or more than 2.5 miles but less than or equal to 10 miles from an urban cluster.

[12]Located outside any urbanized area or urban cluster, more than 25 miles from an urbanized area, and more than 10 miles from an urban cluster.

[13]Excludes revenues from other in-state school systems.

[14]Property tax and parent government contributions are determined on the basis of independence or dependence of the local school system and are mutually exclusive.

NOTE: Total includes data for some school districts not identified by locale. Detail may not sum to totals because of rounding.

SOURCE: U.S. Department of Education, National Center for Education Statistics, Common Core of Data (CCD), "Local Education Agency (School District) Finance Survey (F33)," 2012–13. (This table was prepared January 2016.)

Table 236.10. Summary of expenditures for public elementary and secondary education and other related programs, by purpose: Selected years, 1919–20 through 2012–13

School year	Total expenditures	Current expenditures for public elementary and secondary education								Current expenditures for other programs[1]	Capital outlay[2]	Interest on school debt
		Total	Administration	Instruction	Plant operation	Plant maintenance	Fixed charges	Other school services[3]				
1	2	3	4	5	6	7	8	9		10	11	12
Amounts in thousands of current dollars												
1919–20	$1,036,151	$861,120	$36,752	$632,556	$115,707	$30,432	$9,286	$36,387		$3,277	$153,543	$18,212
1929–30	2,316,790	1,843,552	78,680	1,317,727	216,072	78,810	50,270	101,993		9,825	370,878	92,536
1939–40	2,344,049	1,941,799	91,571	1,403,285	194,365	73,321	50,116	129,141		13,367	257,974	130,909
1949–50	5,837,643	4,687,274	220,050	3,112,340	427,587	214,164	261,469	451,663		35,614	1,014,176	100,578
1959–60	15,613,254	12,329,388	528,408	8,350,738	1,085,036	422,586	909,323	1,033,297		132,566	2,661,786	489,514
1969–70	40,683,429	34,217,773	1,606,646	23,270,158	2,537,257	974,941	3,266,920	2,561,856		635,803	4,659,072	1,170,782
1979–80	95,961,561	86,984,142	4,263,757	53,257,937	9,744,785	(4)	11,793,934	7,923,729		597,585	6,506,167	1,873,666
1989–90	212,769,564	188,229,359	16,346,991 [5]	113,550,405 [5]	20,261,415 [5]	(4)	—	38,070,548 [5]		2,982,543	17,781,342	3,776,321
1999–2000	381,838,155	323,888,508	25,079,298 [5]	199,968,138 [5]	31,190,295 [5]	(4)	—	67,650,776 [5]		5,457,015	43,357,186	9,135,445
2002–03	454,906,912	387,593,617	29,751,958 [5]	237,731,734 [5]	36,830,517 [5]	(4)	—	83,279,408 [5]		6,873,762	48,940,374	11,499,160
2003–04	474,241,531	403,390,369	30,864,875 [5]	247,444,620 [5]	38,720,429 [5]	(4)	—	86,360,444 [5]		6,927,551	50,842,973	13,080,638
2004–05	499,568,736	425,047,565	32,666,223 [5]	260,046,266 [5]	40,926,881 [5]	(4)	—	91,408,195 [5]		7,691,468	53,528,382	13,301,322
2005–06	528,268,772	449,131,342	34,197,083 [5]	273,760,798 [5]	44,313,835 [5]	(4)	—	96,859,626 [5]		7,415,575	57,375,299	14,346,556
2006–07	562,194,807	476,814,206	36,213,814 [5]	290,678,482 [5]	46,828,916 [5]	(4)	—	103,092,995 [5]		7,804,253	62,863,465	14,712,882
2007–08	597,313,726	506,884,219	38,203,341 [5]	308,238,664 [5]	49,362,661 [5]	(4)	—	111,079,554 [5]		8,307,720	66,426,299	15,695,488
2008–09	610,326,007	518,922,842	38,811,325 [5]	316,075,710 [5]	50,559,027 [5]	(4)	—	113,476,779 [5]		8,463,793	65,890,367	17,049,004
2009–10	607,018,292	524,715,242	38,972,700 [5]	321,213,401 [5]	50,023,919 [5]	(4)	—	114,505,223 [5]		8,355,761	56,714,992	17,232,297
2010–11	604,355,852	527,291,339	39,154,833 [5]	322,536,983 [5]	50,214,709 [5]	(4)	—	115,384,813 [5]		8,161,474	50,968,815	17,934,224
2011–12[6]	601,993,584	527,207,246	39,491,926 [5]	320,994,474 [5]	49,834,165 [5]	(4)	—	116,886,681 [5]		8,188,640	48,793,436	17,804,262
2012–13	606,490,475	535,665,075	40,310,695 [5]	325,628,793 [5]	50,656,312 [5]	(4)	—	119,069,275 [5]		8,103,477	45,474,445	17,247,479
Amounts in thousands of constant 2014–15 dollars[7]												
1919–20	$12,867,725	$10,694,055	$456,415	$7,855,570	$1,436,939	$377,928	$115,321	$451,882		$40,696	$1,906,816	$226,171
1929–30	32,034,288	25,490,819	1,087,909	18,220,230	2,987,631	1,089,707	695,084	1,410,259		135,850	5,128,135	1,279,497
1939–40	39,698,210	32,885,808	1,550,823	23,765,673	3,291,716	1,241,746	848,752	2,187,099		226,380	4,368,981	2,217,041
1949–50	58,338,717	46,842,449	2,199,078	31,103,293	4,273,108	2,140,256	2,613,001	4,513,712		355,910	10,135,208	1,005,130
1959–60	125,763,132	99,311,934	4,256,271	67,264,324	8,739,852	3,403,886	7,324,502	8,323,100		1,067,805	21,440,409	3,942,984
1969–70	254,899,588	214,389,439	10,066,344	145,797,781	15,897,032	6,108,434	20,468,692	16,051,155		3,983,586	29,191,137	7,335,464
1979–80	292,554,640	265,185,498	12,998,766	162,365,602	29,708,584	(4)	35,955,752	24,156,794		1,821,836	19,835,123	5,712,180
1989–90	396,595,094	350,853,003	30,470,225 [5]	211,654,020 [5]	37,766,575 [5]	(4)	—	70,962,182 [5]		5,559,357	33,143,805	7,038,931
1999–2000	533,825,041	452,809,113	35,061,864 [5]	279,563,470 [5]	43,605,282 [5]	(4)	—	94,578,496 [5]		7,629,126	60,615,084	12,771,719
2002–03	591,220,612	503,736,763	38,667,188 [5]	308,968,489 [5]	47,866,849 [5]	(4)	—	108,234,237 [5]		8,933,497	63,605,448	14,944,904
2003–04	603,153,617	513,043,131	39,254,810 [5]	314,706,975 [5]	49,245,722 [5]	(4)	—	109,835,624 [5]		8,810,653	64,663,513	16,636,321
2004–05	616,804,195	524,794,893	40,332,114 [5]	321,072,189 [5]	50,501,328 [5]	(4)	—	112,859,261 [5]		9,496,450	66,090,065	16,422,787
2005–06	628,312,033	534,187,599	40,673,309 [5]	325,605,474 [5]	52,705,965 [5]	(4)	—	115,202,851 [5]		8,819,933	68,241,002	17,063,499
2006–07	651,807,014	552,816,996	41,986,190 [5]	337,011,781 [5]	54,293,308 [5]	(4)	—	119,525,716 [5]		9,048,229	72,883,717	17,058,073
2007–08	667,780,279	566,682,584	42,710,282 [5]	344,602,329 [5]	55,186,094 [5]	(4)	—	124,183,879 [5]		9,287,802	74,262,771	17,547,123
2008–09	672,931,492	572,152,454	42,792,479 [5]	348,497,847 [5]	55,745,227 [5]	(4)	—	125,116,901 [5]		9,331,985	72,649,211	18,797,842
2009–10	662,870,640	572,994,806	42,558,616 [5]	350,768,561 [5]	54,626,668 [5]	(4)	—	125,040,961 [5]		9,124,583	61,933,394	18,817,858
2010–11	646,972,142	564,473,407	41,915,845 [5]	345,280,752 [5]	53,755,611 [5]	(4)	—	123,521,200 [5]		8,736,982	54,562,892	19,198,860
2011–12[6]	626,098,194	548,317,313	41,073,234 [5]	333,847,513 [5]	51,829,590 [5]	(4)	—	121,566,976 [5]		8,516,523	50,747,189	18,517,168
2012–13	620,449,991	547,994,411	41,238,521 [5]	333,123,750 [5]	51,822,262 [5]	(4)	—	121,809,878 [5]		8,289,993	46,521,125	17,644,462
Percentage distribution												
1919–20	100.0	83.1	3.5	61.0	11.2	2.9	0.9	3.5		0.3	14.8	1.8
1929–30	100.0	79.6	3.4	56.9	9.3	3.4	2.2	4.4		0.4	16.0	4.0
1939–40	100.0	82.8	3.9	59.9	8.3	3.1	2.1	5.5		0.6	11.0	5.6
1949–50	100.0	80.3	3.8	53.3	7.3	3.7	4.5	7.7		0.6	17.4	1.7
1959–60	100.0	79.0	3.4	53.5	6.9	2.7	5.8	6.6		0.8	17.0	3.1
1969–70	100.0	84.1	3.9	57.2	6.2	2.4	8.0	6.3		1.6	11.5	2.9
1979–80	100.0	90.6	4.4	55.5	10.2	(4)	12.3	8.3		0.6	6.8	2.0
1989–90	100.0	88.5	7.7 [5]	53.4 [5]	9.5 [5]	(4)	—	17.9 [5]		1.4	8.4	1.8
1999–2000	100.0	84.8	6.6 [5]	52.4 [5]	8.2 [5]	(4)	—	17.7 [5]		1.4	11.4	2.4
2002–03	100.0	85.2	6.5 [5]	52.3 [5]	8.1 [5]	(4)	—	18.3 [5]		1.5	10.8	2.5
2003–04	100.0	85.1	6.5 [5]	52.2 [5]	8.2 [5]	(4)	—	18.2 [5]		1.5	10.7	2.8
2004–05	100.0	85.1	6.5 [5]	52.1 [5]	8.2 [5]	(4)	—	18.3 [5]		1.5	10.7	2.7
2005–06	100.0	85.0	6.5 [5]	51.8 [5]	8.4 [5]	(4)	—	18.3 [5]		1.4	10.9	2.7
2006–07	100.0	84.8	6.4 [5]	51.7 [5]	8.3 [5]	(4)	—	18.3 [5]		1.4	11.2	2.6
2007–08	100.0	84.9	6.4 [5]	51.6 [5]	8.3 [5]	(4)	—	18.6 [5]		1.4	11.1	2.6
2008–09	100.0	85.0	6.4 [5]	51.8 [5]	8.3 [5]	(4)	—	18.6 [5]		1.4	10.8	2.8
2009–10	100.0	86.4	6.4 [5]	52.9 [5]	8.2 [5]	(4)	—	18.9 [5]		1.4	9.3	2.8
2010–11	100.0	87.2	6.5 [5]	53.4 [5]	8.3 [5]	(4)	—	19.1 [5]		1.4	8.4	3.0
2011–12[6]	100.0	87.6	6.6 [5]	53.3 [5]	8.3 [5]	(4)	—	19.4 [5]		1.4	8.1	3.0
2012–13	100.0	88.3	6.6 [5]	53.7 [5]	8.4 [5]	(4)	—	19.6 [5]		1.3	7.5	2.8

—Not available.
[1] Includes expenditures for summer schools, adult education, community colleges, and community services.
[2] Prior to 1969–70, excludes capital outlay by state and local school housing authorities.
[3] Prior to 1959–60, items included under "other school services" were listed under "auxiliary services," a more comprehensive classification that also included community services.
[4] Plant operation also includes plant maintenance.
[5] Data not comparable to figures prior to 1989–90.
[6] Data have been revised from previously published figures.
[7] Constant dollars based on the Consumer Price Index, prepared by the Bureau of Labor Statistics, U.S. Department of Labor, adjusted to a school-year basis.

NOTE: Beginning in 1959–60, includes Alaska and Hawaii. Beginning in 1989–90, state administration expenditures were excluded from both "total" and "current" expenditures. Beginning in 1989–90, extensive changes were made in the data collection procedures. Detail may not sum to totals because of rounding.
SOURCE: U.S. Department of Education, National Center for Education Statistics, *Biennial Survey of Education in the United States*, 1919–20 through 1949–50; *Statistics of State School Systems*, 1959–60 and 1969–70; *Revenues and Expenditures for Public Elementary and Secondary Education, 1979–80*; and Common Core of Data (CCD), "National Public Education Financial Survey," 1989–90 through 2012–13. (This table was prepared September 2015.)

Table 236.15. **Current expenditures and current expenditures per pupil in public elementary and secondary schools: 1989–90 through 2025–26**

School year	Current expenditures in unadjusted dollars[1]			Current expenditures in constant 2014–15 dollars[2]					
				Total current expenditures		Per pupil in fall enrollment		Per pupil in average daily attendance (ADA)	
	Total, in billions	Per pupil in fall enrollment	Per pupil in average daily attendance (ADA)	In billions	Annual percentage change	Per pupil enrolled	Annual percentage change	Per pupil in ADA	Annual percentage change
1	2	3	4	5	6	7	8	9	10
1989–90	$188.2	$4,643	$4,980	$350.9	3.8	$8,654	2.9	$9,282	2.3
1990–91	202.0	4,902	5,258	357.1	1.8	8,663	0.1	9,292	0.1
1991–92	211.2	5,023	5,421	361.7	1.3	8,602	-0.7	9,283	-0.1
1992–93	220.9	5,160	5,584	366.9	1.4	8,568	-0.4	9,272	-0.1
1993–94	231.5	5,327	5,767	374.8	2.1	8,623	0.6	9,336	0.7
1994–95	243.9	5,529	5,989	383.8	2.4	8,700	0.9	9,424	0.9
1995–96	255.1	5,689	6,147	390.8	1.8	8,715	0.2	9,416	-0.1
1996–97	270.2	5,923	6,393	402.4	3.0	8,822	1.2	9,521	1.1
1997–98	285.5	6,189	6,676	417.8	3.8	9,057	2.7	9,768	2.6
1998–99	302.9	6,508	7,013	435.7	4.3	9,361	3.4	10,088	3.3
1999–2000	323.9	6,912	7,394	452.8	3.9	9,664	3.2	10,337	2.5
2000–01	348.4	7,380	7,904	470.9	4.0	9,976	3.2	10,684	3.4
2001–02	368.4	7,727	8,259	489.3	3.9	10,264	2.9	10,969	2.7
2002–03	387.6	8,044	8,610	503.7	3.0	10,455	1.9	11,190	2.0
2003–04	403.4	8,310	8,900	513.0	1.8	10,569	1.1	11,319	1.2
2004–05	425.0	8,711	9,316	524.8	2.3	10,755	1.8	11,502	1.6
2005–06	449.1	9,145	9,778	534.2	1.8	10,877	1.1	11,630	1.1
2006–07	476.8	9,679	10,336	552.8	3.5	11,222	3.2	11,983	3.0
2007–08	506.9	10,298	10,982	566.7	2.5	11,513	2.6	12,278	2.5
2008–09	518.9	10,540	11,239	572.2	1.0	11,621	0.9	12,391	0.9
2009–10	524.7	10,636	11,427	573.0	0.1	11,615	-0.1	12,478	0.7
2010–11	527.3	10,663	11,433	564.5	-1.5	11,414	-1.7	12,240	-1.9
2011–12	527.2	10,648	11,362	548.3	-2.9	11,074	-3.0	11,817	-3.5
2012–13	535.7	10,763	11,503	548.0	-0.1	11,011	-0.6	11,768	-0.4
2013–14[3]	530.0	10,590	11,330	533.9	-2.6	10,667	-3.1	11,410	-3.0
2014–15[3]	544.9	10,870	11,630	544.9	2.1	10,870	1.9	11,630	1.9
2015–16[3]	560.5	11,150	11,930	557.4	2.3	11,090	2.0	11,860	2.0
2016–17[3]	584.4	11,600	12,410	567.1	1.7	11,260	1.5	12,040	1.5
2017–18[3]	611.9	12,120	12,970	578.8	2.1	11,470	1.9	12,270	1.9
2018–19[3]	637.8	12,620	13,500	589.6	1.9	11,670	1.8	12,480	1.8
2019–20[3]	663.6	13,110	14,020	599.0	1.6	11,830	1.4	12,660	1.4
2020–21[3]	690.7	13,600	14,550	608.3	1.5	11,980	1.2	12,820	1.2
2021–22[3]	718.5	14,110	15,090	616.3	1.3	12,100	1.0	12,950	1.0
2022–23[3]	747.0	14,620	15,640	623.8	1.2	12,210	0.9	13,060	0.9
2023–24[3]	775.5	15,140	16,190	630.9	1.1	12,320	0.9	13,180	0.9
2024–25[3]	803.2	15,640	16,740	637.8	1.1	12,420	0.9	13,290	0.9
2025–26[3]	822.8	16,000	17,120	642.2	0.7	12,490	0.5	13,360	0.5

[1]Unadjusted (or "current") dollars have not been adjusted to compensate for inflation.
[2]Constant dollars based on the Consumer Price Index, prepared by the Bureau of Labor Statistics, U.S. Department of Labor, adjusted to a school-year basis.
[3]Projected.
NOTE: Current expenditures include instruction, support services, food services, and enterprise operations. Some data have been revised from previously published figures.

SOURCE: U.S. Department of Education, National Center for Education Statistics, Common Core of Data (CCD), "National Public Education Financial Survey," 1989–90 through 2012–13; National Elementary and Secondary Enrollment Projection Model, 1972 through 2025; and Public Elementary and Secondary Education Current Expenditure Projection Model, 1973–74 through 2025–26. (This table was prepared April 2016.)

Table 236.20. Total expenditures for public elementary and secondary education and other related programs, by function and subfunction: Selected years, 1990–91 through 2012–13

Function and subfunction	Expenditures (in thousands of current dollars)								Percentage distribution of current expenditures for public schools							
1	1990–91	2000–01	2002–03	2008–09	2009–10	2010–11	2011–12[1]	2012–13[1]	1990–91	2000–01	2002–03	2008–09	2009–10	2010–11	2011–12[1]	2012–13[1]
	2	3	4	5	6	7	8	9	10	11	12	13	14	15	16	17
Total expenditures	$229,429,715	$410,811,185	$454,906,912	$610,326,007	$607,018,292	$604,355,852	$601,993,584	$606,490,475	†	†	†	†	†	†	†	†
Current expenditures for public schools	202,037,752	348,360,841	387,593,617	518,922,842	524,715,242	527,291,339	527,207,246	535,665,075	100.00	100.00	100.00	100.00	100.00	100.00	100.00	100.00
Salaries	132,730,931[2]	224,305,806	246,349,926	312,552,150	314,037,286	311,541,792	308,593,027	311,614,921	65.70	64.39	63.56	60.23	59.85	59.08	58.53	58.17
Employee benefits	33,954,456[2]	57,976,490	68,137,020	105,667,462	108,475,595	111,750,200	114,335,598	117,831,435	16.81	16.64	17.58	20.36	20.67	21.19	21.69	22.00
Purchased services	16,380,643[2]	31,778,754	35,325,876	50,715,562	51,969,406	53,498,786	54,335,285	55,738,664	8.11	9.12	9.11	9.77	9.90	10.15	10.31	10.41
Tuition	1,192,505[2]	2,458,366	3,298,588	4,492,060	4,749,301	4,988,203	5,013,317	5,097,362	0.59	0.71	0.85	0.87	0.91	0.95	0.95	0.95
Supplies	14,805,956[2]	28,262,078	30,528,970	40,629,203	40,334,985	40,417,163	40,076,526	40,656,514	7.33	8.11	7.88	7.83	7.69	7.67	7.60	7.59
Other	2,973,261[2]	3,579,347	3,953,237	4,866,404	5,148,668	5,095,195	4,853,493	4,726,179	1.47	1.03	1.02	0.94	0.98	0.97	0.92	0.88
Instruction	122,223,362	214,333,003	237,731,734	316,075,710	321,213,401	322,536,983	320,994,474	325,628,793	60.50	61.53	61.34	60.91	61.22	61.17	60.89	60.79
Salaries	90,742,284	154,512,089	168,828,934	212,963,123	214,435,825	212,998,609	210,735,097	212,545,500	44.91	44.35	43.56	41.04	40.87	40.39	39.97	39.68
Employee benefits	22,347,524	39,522,678	45,947,180	71,029,220	73,051,571	75,248,811	76,950,048	79,416,636	11.06	11.35	11.85	13.69	13.92	14.27	14.60	14.83
Purchased services	2,722,639	6,430,708	7,289,623	12,782,555	13,843,875	14,694,620	14,537,511	14,773,355	1.35	1.85	1.88	2.46	2.64	2.79	2.76	2.76
Tuition	1,192,505	2,458,366	3,298,588	4,492,060	4,749,301	4,988,203	5,013,317	5,097,362	0.59	0.71	0.85	0.87	0.91	0.95	0.95	0.95
Supplies	4,584,754	10,377,554	11,294,271	13,421,846	13,689,672	13,135,284	12,433,973	12,421,155	2.27	2.98	2.91	2.59	2.61	2.49	2.36	2.32
Textbooks	—	—	—	2,934,200	2,547,273	2,324,846	2,167,152	2,129,571	—	—	—	0.57	0.49	0.44	0.41	0.40
Other	633,656	1,031,608	1,073,139	1,386,906	1,443,155	1,471,457	1,324,530	1,374,785	0.31	0.30	0.28	0.27	0.28	0.28	0.25	0.26
Student support[3]	8,926,010	17,292,756	19,992,229	28,533,413	29,134,124	29,368,646	29,173,107	29,863,845	4.42	4.96	5.16	5.50	5.55	5.57	5.53	5.58
Salaries	6,565,965	12,354,464	14,030,739	19,109,617	19,397,151	19,367,865	18,987,262	19,315,653	3.25	3.55	3.62	3.68	3.70	3.67	3.60	3.61
Employee benefits	1,660,082	3,036,037	3,678,398	6,145,103	6,337,026	6,533,691	6,787,639	7,043,849	0.82	0.87	0.95	1.18	1.21	1.24	1.29	1.31
Purchased services	455,996	1,328,600	1,666,297	2,414,847	2,490,533	2,583,714	2,681,311	2,771,134	0.23	0.38	0.42	0.47	0.47	0.49	0.51	0.52
Supplies	191,482	421,838	470,505	525,459	544,965	521,729	510,364	533,491	0.09	0.12	0.12	0.10	0.10	0.10	0.10	0.10
Other	52,485	151,817	166,291	338,387	364,449	361,647	206,531	199,717	0.03	0.04	0.04	0.07	0.07	0.07	0.04	0.04
Instructional staff services[4]	8,467,142	15,926,856	18,568,413	25,018,199	25,108,146	24,893,140	24,647,377	24,954,839	4.19	4.57	4.79	4.82	4.79	4.72	4.68	4.66
Salaries	5,560,129	9,790,767	11,312,220	14,962,194	14,827,754	14,490,521	14,333,780	14,476,325	2.75	2.81	2.92	2.88	2.83	2.75	2.72	2.70
Employee benefits	1,408,217	2,356,440	2,909,834	4,746,650	4,835,699	4,933,118	4,973,417	5,092,704	0.70	0.68	0.75	0.91	0.92	0.94	0.94	0.95
Purchased services	622,487	2,003,598	2,332,965	3,256,725	3,379,483	3,438,979	3,413,606	3,491,664	0.31	0.58	0.60	0.63	0.64	0.65	0.65	0.65
Supplies	776,863	1,566,954	1,792,008	1,834,852	1,838,108	1,810,950	1,708,502	1,666,409	0.38	0.45	0.46	0.35	0.35	0.34	0.32	0.31
Other	99,445	209,097	221,387	217,778	227,101	219,573	218,072	227,737	0.05	0.06	0.06	0.04	0.04	0.04	0.04	0.04
General administration	5,791,253	7,108,291	7,960,378	10,202,846	10,421,207	10,494,526	10,569,141	10,786,389	2.87	2.04	2.05	1.97	1.99	1.99	2.00	2.01
Salaries	2,603,562	3,351,554	3,680,522	4,420,788	4,452,059	4,401,697	4,377,224	4,473,350	1.29	0.96	0.95	0.85	0.85	0.83	0.83	0.84
Employee benefits	777,381	1,000,698	1,166,775	1,747,378	1,801,413	1,856,221	1,920,231	1,950,527	0.38	0.29	0.30	0.34	0.34	0.35	0.36	0.36
Purchased services	1,482,427	2,099,032	2,384,109	3,174,832	3,145,503	3,236,857	3,305,165	3,396,437	0.73	0.60	0.62	0.61	0.60	0.61	0.63	0.63
Supplies	172,898	206,137	223,696	230,822	233,729	228,417	239,097	233,312	0.09	0.06	0.06	0.04	0.04	0.04	0.05	0.04
Other	754,985	450,870	505,276	629,025	788,501	771,334	727,423	732,763	0.37	0.13	0.13	0.12	0.15	0.15	0.14	0.14
School administration	11,695,344	19,580,890	21,791,580	28,608,480	28,551,493	28,660,307	28,922,785	29,524,306	5.79	5.62	5.62	5.51	5.44	5.44	5.49	5.51
Salaries	8,935,903	14,817,213	16,206,443	20,521,736	20,351,317	20,191,545	20,198,660	20,577,846	4.42	4.25	4.18	3.95	3.88	3.83	3.83	3.84
Employee benefits	2,257,783	3,689,689	4,341,364	6,600,069	6,722,417	6,972,708	7,167,104	7,418,614	1.12	1.06	1.12	1.27	1.28	1.32	1.36	1.38
Purchased services	247,750	611,638	718,442	934,243	931,494	931,765	976,085	943,880	0.12	0.18	0.19	0.18	0.18	0.18	0.19	0.18
Supplies	189,711	369,257	416,265	430,083	419,531	426,864	423,318	433,589	0.09	0.11	0.11	0.08	0.08	0.08	0.08	0.08
Other	64,197	93,093	109,066	122,349	126,734	137,426	157,618	150,377	0.03	0.03	0.03	0.02	0.02	0.03	0.03	0.03
Operation and maintenance	21,290,655	34,034,158	36,830,517	50,559,027	50,023,919	50,214,709	49,834,165	50,656,312	10.54	9.77	9.50	9.74	9.53	9.52	9.45	9.46
Salaries	8,849,559	13,461,242	14,596,762	18,045,474	17,956,826	17,604,634	17,434,337	17,466,366	4.38	3.86	3.77	3.48	3.42	3.34	3.31	3.26
Employee benefits	2,633,075	3,778,520	4,476,354	6,881,875	7,040,412	7,195,927	7,327,835	7,463,766	1.30	1.08	1.15	1.33	1.34	1.36	1.39	1.39
Purchased services	5,721,125	9,642,217	9,866,874	13,150,025	13,095,871	13,351,922	13,436,115	14,017,078	2.83	2.77	2.55	2.53	2.50	2.53	2.55	2.62
Supplies	3,761,738	6,871,845	7,543,937	12,043,690	11,483,968	11,638,187	11,242,771	11,339,612	1.86	1.97	1.95	2.32	2.19	2.21	2.13	2.12
Other	325,157	280,334	346,590	437,964	446,842	424,039	393,107	369,490	0.16	0.08	0.09	0.08	0.09	0.08	0.07	0.07

See notes at end of table.

Table 236.20. Total expenditures for public elementary and secondary education and other related programs, by function and subfunction: Selected years, 1990–91 through 2012–13—Continued

Function and subfunction	Expenditures (in thousands of current dollars)								Percentage distribution of current expenditures for public schools							
	1990–91	2000–01	2002–03	2008–09	2009–10	2010–11	2011–12[1]	2012–13[1]	1990–91	2000–01	2002–03	2008–09	2009–10	2010–11	2011–12[1]	2012–13[1]
1	2	3	4	5	6	7	8	9	10	11	12	13	14	15	16	17
Student transportation	8,678,954	14,052,654	15,648,821	21,679,876	21,819,304	22,370,807	22,926,700	23,233,698	4.30	4.03	4.04	4.18	4.16	4.24	4.35	4.34
Salaries	3,285,127	5,406,092	5,974,787	7,591,289	7,633,213	7,527,611	7,483,297	7,525,390	1.63	1.55	1.54	1.46	1.45	1.43	1.42	1.40
Employee benefits	892,985	1,592,127	1,905,504	2,933,989	3,048,962	3,124,937	3,182,346	3,245,727	0.44	0.46	0.49	0.57	0.58	0.59	0.60	0.61
Purchased services	3,345,232	5,767,462	6,450,377	9,001,837	8,982,432	9,153,621	9,409,711	9,581,784	1.66	1.66	1.66	1.73	1.71	1.74	1.78	1.79
Supplies	961,447	1,159,350	1,130,478	1,983,454	1,967,717	2,370,182	2,625,741	2,656,197	0.48	0.33	0.29	0.38	0.38	0.45	0.50	0.50
Other	194,163	127,623	187,675	169,307	186,979	194,456	225,605	224,599	0.10	0.04	0.05	0.03	0.04	0.04	0.04	0.04
Other support services[5]	5,587,837	11,439,134	13,231,082	17,187,109	17,189,474	17,246,807	17,850,135	18,050,864	2.77	3.28	3.41	3.31	3.28	3.27	3.39	3.37
Salaries	2,900,394	5,521,381	6,234,410	8,091,102	8,162,557	8,139,084	8,178,386	8,323,115	1.44	1.58	1.61	1.56	1.56	1.54	1.55	1.55
Employee benefits	980,859	1,594,540	2,019,058	3,148,252	3,136,979	3,295,052	3,395,915	3,493,682	0.49	0.46	0.52	0.61	0.60	0.62	0.64	0.65
Purchased services	798,922	2,783,176	3,283,907	3,928,346	3,915,823	3,876,650	4,221,440	4,317,745	0.40	0.80	0.85	0.76	0.75	0.74	0.80	0.81
Supplies	294,527	626,889	717,844	884,381	852,467	876,293	916,214	964,936	0.15	0.18	0.19	0.17	0.16	0.17	0.17	0.18
Other	613,135	913,148	975,863	1,135,027	1,121,648	1,059,728	1,138,181	951,386	0.30	0.26	0.25	0.22	0.21	0.20	0.22	0.18
Food services	8,430,490	13,816,635	14,930,942	19,794,945	19,996,995	20,394,768	21,198,367	21,862,081	4.17	3.97	3.85	3.81	3.81	3.87	4.02	4.08
Salaries	—	4,966,092	5,325,744	6,505,821	6,483,443	6,482,085	6,563,700	6,607,701	—	1.43	1.37	1.25	1.24	1.23	1.24	1.23
Employee benefits	—	1,381,923	1,636,523	2,343,119	2,409,983	2,492,673	2,529,156	2,603,230	—	0.40	0.42	0.45	0.46	0.47	0.48	0.49
Purchased services	—	923,091	1,155,396	1,815,966	1,926,821	2,058,018	2,177,107	2,267,341	—	0.26	0.30	0.35	0.37	0.39	0.41	0.42
Supplies	—	6,420,201	6,641,477	8,908,841	8,943,177	9,118,886	9,681,540	10,110,833	—	1.84	1.71	1.72	1.70	1.73	1.84	1.89
Other	—	125,327	171,801	221,198	233,573	243,105	246,864	272,976	—	0.04	0.04	0.04	0.04	0.05	0.05	0.05
Enterprise operations[6]	946,705	776,463	907,921	1,263,238	1,257,180	1,110,646	1,090,995	1,103,949	0.47	0.22	0.23	0.24	0.24	0.21	0.21	0.21
Salaries	—	124,913	159,366	341,007	337,140	338,141	301,285	303,674	—	0.04	0.04	0.07	0.06	0.06	0.06	0.06
Employee benefits	—	23,837	56,031	91,807	91,133	97,063	101,907	102,699	—	0.01	0.01	0.02	0.02	0.02	0.02	0.02
Purchased services	—	189,230	197,885	256,186	257,570	172,641	177,234	178,246	—	0.05	0.05	0.05	0.05	0.03	0.03	0.03
Supplies	—	242,052	298,489	365,775	361,651	290,372	295,006	296,981	—	0.07	0.08	0.07	0.07	0.06	0.06	0.06
Other	—	196,430	196,150	208,463	209,686	212,430	215,563	222,349	—	0.06	0.05	0.04	0.04	0.04	0.04	0.04
Current expenditures for other programs	3,295,717	6,063,700	6,873,762	8,463,793	8,355,761	8,161,474	8,188,640	8,103,477	†	†	†	†	†	†	†	†
Community services	964,370	2,426,189	2,695,832	3,364,620	3,398,025	3,269,802	3,209,484	3,132,483	†	†	†	†	†	†	†	†
Private school programs	527,609	1,026,695	1,161,470	1,541,922	1,423,681	1,427,539	1,441,688	1,471,013	†	†	†	†	†	†	†	†
Adult education	1,365,523	1,838,265	2,005,813	2,187,628	2,084,477	2,013,156	1,931,449	1,829,564	†	†	†	†	†	†	†	†
Community colleges	5,356	351	460	33,303	33,274	34,045	29,488	30,107	†	†	†	†	†	†	†	†
Other	432,858	772,200	1,010,187	1,336,321	1,416,305	1,416,931	1,576,530	1,640,310	†	†	†	†	†	†	†	†
Capital outlay[7]	19,771,478	46,220,704	48,940,374	65,890,367	56,714,992	50,968,815	48,793,436	45,474,445	†	†	†	†	†	†	†	†
Public schools	19,655,496	46,078,494	48,833,138	65,799,088	56,621,337	50,888,951	48,717,033	45,309,336	†	†	†	†	†	†	†	†
Other current expenditures	115,982	142,210	107,236	91,279	93,655	79,864	76,403	165,109	†	†	†	†	†	†	†	†
Interest on school debt	4,324,768	10,165,940	11,499,160	17,049,004	17,232,297	17,934,224	17,804,262	17,247,479	†	†	†	†	†	†	†	†

—Not available.
†Not applicable.
[1]Data have been revised from previously published figures.
[2]Includes estimated data for subfunctions of food services and enterprise operations.
[3]Includes expenditures for guidance, health, attendance, and speech pathology services.
[4]Includes expenditures for curriculum development, staff training, libraries, and media and computer centers.
[5]Includes business support services concerned with paying, transporting, exchanging, and maintaining goods and services for local education agencies; central support services, including planning, research, evaluation, information, staff, and data processing services; and other support services.

[6]Includes expenditures for operations funded by sales of products or services (e.g., school bookstore or computer time). Includes very small amounts for direct program support made by state education agencies for local school districts.
[7]Includes expenditures for property and for buildings and alterations completed by school district staff or contractors.
NOTE: Excludes expenditures for state education agencies. Detail may not sum to totals because of rounding.
SOURCE: U.S. Department of Education, National Center for Education Statistics, Common Core of Data (CCD), "National Public Education Financial Survey," 1990–91 through 2012–13. (This table was prepared August 2015.)

Table 236.25. Current expenditures for public elementary and secondary education, by state or jurisdiction: Selected years, 1969–70 through 2012–13

[In thousands of current dollars]

State or jurisdiction	1969–70	1979–80	1989–90	1999–2000	2001–02	2002–03	2003–04	2004–05	2005–06	2006–07	2007–08	2008–09	2009–10	2010–11	2011–12¹	2012–13
1	2	3	4	5	6	7	8	9	10	11	12	13	14	15	16	17
United States	$34,217,773	$86,984,142	$188,229,359	$323,888,508	$368,378,006	$387,593,617	$403,390,369	$425,047,565	$449,131,342	$476,814,206	$506,884,219	$518,922,842	$524,715,242	$527,291,339	$527,207,246	$535,665,075
Alabama	422,730	1,146,713	2,275,233	4,176,082	4,444,390	4,657,643	4,812,479	5,164,406	5,699,076	6,245,031	6,832,439	6,683,843	6,670,517	6,592,925	6,386,517	6,532,358
Alaska	81,374	377,947	828,051	1,183,499	1,204,854	1,326,226	1,354,846	1,442,289	1,529,645	1,634,316	1,918,375	2,007,319	2,084,019	2,201,270	2,292,205	2,395,354
Arizona	281,941	949,753	2,258,660	4,288,739	5,395,814	5,892,227	6,071,785	6,579,957	7,130,341	7,815,720	8,403,221	8,726,755	8,482,552	8,340,211	7,976,089	8,164,529
Arkansas	235,083	666,949	1,404,545	2,380,331	2,822,877	2,923,401	3,109,644	3,546,999	3,808,011	3,997,701	4,156,368	4,240,839	4,459,910	4,578,136	4,606,995	4,637,169
California	3,831,595	9,172,158	21,485,782	38,129,479	46,265,544	47,983,402	49,215,866	50,918,654	53,436,103	57,352,599	61,570,555	60,080,929	58,248,662	57,526,835	57,975,189	58,323,458
Colorado	369,218	1,243,049	2,451,833	4,401,010	5,151,003	5,551,506	5,666,191	5,994,440	6,368,289	6,579,053	7,338,766	7,187,267	7,429,302	7,409,462	7,341,585	7,506,978
Connecticut	588,710	1,227,892	3,444,520	5,402,836	6,031,062	6,302,988	6,600,767	7,080,396	7,517,025	7,855,459	8,336,789	8,708,294	8,853,337	9,094,036	9,344,999	9,543,010
Delaware	108,747	269,108	520,953	937,630	1,072,875	1,127,745	1,201,631	1,299,349	1,405,465	1,437,707	1,489,594	1,518,786	1,549,812	1,613,304	1,751,143	1,761,559
District of Columbia	141,138	298,448	639,983	780,192	912,432	902,318	1,011,536	1,067,500	1,057,166	1,130,006	1,282,437	1,352,905	1,451,870	1,482,202	1,466,888	1,563,148
Florida	961,273	2,766,468	8,228,531	13,885,988	15,535,864	16,355,123	17,578,884	19,042,877	20,897,327	22,887,024	24,224,114	23,328,028	23,349,314	23,870,090	22,732,752	23,214,634
Georgia	599,371	1,608,028	4,505,962	9,158,624	10,853,496	11,630,576	11,788,616	12,528,856	13,739,263	14,828,715	16,030,039	15,976,945	15,730,409	15,527,907	15,623,633	15,536,733
Hawaii	141,324	351,889	700,012	1,213,695	1,348,381	1,489,092	1,566,792	1,648,086	1,805,521	2,045,198	2,122,779	2,225,438	2,136,144	2,141,561	2,187,480	2,169,636
Idaho	103,107	313,927	627,794	1,302,817	1,481,803	1,511,862	1,555,006	1,618,215	1,694,827	1,777,491	1,891,505	1,957,740	1,961,857	1,881,746	1,854,556	1,925,676
Illinois	1,896,067	4,579,355	8,125,493	14,462,773	16,480,787	17,271,301	18,081,827	18,658,428	19,244,908	20,326,591	21,874,484	23,495,271	24,695,773	24,554,467	25,012,915	25,783,911
Indiana	809,105	1,851,292	4,074,578	7,110,930	7,704,547	8,088,684	8,524,980	9,108,931	9,241,986	9,497,077	9,281,709	9,680,895	9,921,243	9,687,949	9,978,491	9,811,166
Iowa	527,086	1,186,659	2,004,742	3,264,336	3,565,796	3,652,022	3,669,797	3,808,200	4,039,389	4,231,932	4,499,236	4,731,463	4,794,308	4,855,871	4,971,944	5,143,771
Kansas	362,593	830,133	1,848,302	2,971,814	3,450,923	3,510,675	3,658,421	3,718,153	4,039,417	4,339,477	4,633,517	4,806,603	4,731,676	4,741,372	4,871,381	4,895,863
Kentucky	353,265	1,054,459	2,134,011	3,837,794	4,268,608	4,401,627	4,553,382	4,812,591	5,213,620	5,424,621	5,822,550	5,886,890	6,091,814	6,211,453	6,360,799	6,354,306
Louisiana	503,217	1,303,902	2,838,283	4,391,189	4,802,565	5,056,583	5,290,964	5,554,766	5,554,278	6,040,368	6,814,455	7,276,651	7,393,452	7,522,098	7,544,782	7,492,134
Maine	155,907	385,492	1,048,195	1,604,438	1,812,798	1,909,268	1,969,497	2,056,266	2,119,408	2,258,764	2,308,071	2,350,447	2,370,085	2,377,878	2,330,842	2,350,469
Maryland	721,794	1,783,056	3,894,644	6,545,135	7,480,723	7,933,055	8,198,454	8,682,586	9,381,613	10,210,303	11,211,176	11,591,965	11,883,677	11,885,333	11,850,634	12,108,546
Massachusetts	907,341	2,638,734	4,760,390	8,564,039	9,957,292	10,281,820	10,799,765	11,357,857	11,747,010	12,383,447	13,182,987	13,937,097	13,356,373	13,962,366	14,151,659	14,627,898
Michigan	1,799,945	4,642,847	8,025,621	13,994,294	14,975,150	15,674,698	15,983,044	16,353,921	16,681,981	17,013,259	17,053,521	17,217,584	17,227,515	16,786,444	16,485,178	16,354,807
Minnesota	781,243	1,786,768	3,474,398	6,140,442	6,586,559	6,867,403	7,084,005	7,310,284	7,686,638	8,060,410	8,426,264	9,182,281	8,927,288	8,944,867	9,053,021	9,354,376
Mississippi	262,760	756,018	1,472,710	2,510,376	2,642,116	2,853,531	3,059,569	3,243,888	3,550,261	3,692,358	3,898,401	3,967,232	3,990,876	3,887,981	3,972,787	4,006,798
Missouri	642,030	1,504,988	3,288,738	5,655,531	6,491,885	6,793,957	6,832,454	7,115,207	7,592,485	7,957,705	8,526,641	8,827,224	8,923,448	8,691,887	8,719,925	8,905,756
Montana	127,176	358,118	641,345	994,770	1,073,005	1,124,291	1,160,838	1,193,182	1,254,360	1,320,112	1,392,449	1,436,062	1,498,252	1,518,818	1,504,531	1,523,696
Nebraska	231,612	581,615	1,233,431	1,926,500	2,206,946	2,304,223	2,413,404	2,512,914	2,672,629	2,825,608	2,970,323	3,053,575	3,213,646	3,345,530	3,462,575	3,563,939
Nevada	87,273	281,901	712,898	1,875,467	2,169,000	2,251,044	2,470,581	2,722,264	2,959,728	3,311,471	3,515,004	3,606,035	3,592,994	3,676,997	3,574,233	3,577,346
New Hampshire	101,370	295,400	821,671	1,418,503	1,641,378	1,781,594	1,900,240	2,021,144	2,139,113	2,246,692	2,399,330	2,490,623	2,576,956	2,637,911	2,643,256	2,655,077
New Jersey	1,343,564	3,638,533	8,119,336	13,327,645	15,822,609	17,185,966	18,416,695	19,669,576	20,869,993	22,448,262	24,357,079	23,446,911	24,261,392	23,639,281	24,391,278	25,417,320
New Mexico	183,736	515,451	1,020,148	1,890,274	2,204,165	2,281,608	2,446,115	2,554,638	2,729,707	2,904,474	3,057,061	3,186,252	3,217,328	3,127,463	3,039,461	3,099,308
New York	4,111,839	8,760,500	18,090,978	28,433,240	32,218,975	34,546,965	36,205,111	38,866,853	41,149,457	43,679,908	46,443,426	48,635,363	50,251,461	51,574,134	52,460,494	52,938,586
North Carolina	676,193	1,880,862	4,342,826	7,713,293	8,543,290	8,766,968	8,994,620	9,835,550	10,476,056	11,248,336	11,482,912	12,598,382	12,200,362	12,322,555	12,303,426	12,666,607
North Dakota	97,895	228,483	459,391	638,946	711,437	716,007	749,697	832,157	857,774	838,221	886,317	928,528	1,000,095	1,049,772	1,098,090	1,174,364
Ohio	1,639,805	3,836,576	7,994,379	12,974,575	14,774,065	15,868,494	16,662,985	17,167,866	17,829,599	18,251,361	18,892,374	19,387,318	19,801,670	19,988,921	19,701,810	19,506,123
Oklahoma	339,105	1,055,844	1,905,332	3,382,581	3,875,547	3,804,570	3,853,308	4,161,024	4,406,002	4,750,536	4,932,913	5,082,062	5,192,124	5,036,031	5,170,978	5,329,897
Oregon	403,844	1,126,812	2,297,944	3,896,287	4,214,512	4,150,747	4,199,485	4,458,028	4,773,751	5,039,632	5,409,630	5,529,831	5,401,667	5,430,888	5,389,273	5,395,742
Pennsylvania	1,912,644	4,584,320	9,496,788	14,120,112	15,550,975	16,344,439	17,680,332	18,711,100	19,631,006	20,404,304	21,157,430	21,831,816	22,733,518	23,485,203	23,190,198	23,712,931
Rhode Island	145,443	362,046	801,908	1,393,143	1,533,455	1,647,587	1,765,585	1,825,900	1,934,429	2,039,633	2,134,609	2,139,317	2,136,582	2,149,366	2,167,450	2,121,403
South Carolina	367,689	997,984	2,322,618	4,087,355	4,744,809	4,888,250	5,017,833	5,312,739	5,696,629	6,023,043	6,453,817	6,626,763	6,566,165	6,465,486	6,619,072	6,950,410
South Dakota	109,375	238,332	447,074	737,998	819,296	851,429	887,328	916,563	948,671	977,006	1,037,875	1,080,054	1,115,861	1,126,503	1,100,100	1,125,929
Tennessee	473,226	1,319,303	2,790,808	4,931,734	5,501,029	5,674,773	6,056,657	6,446,691	6,681,445	6,975,099	7,540,306	7,768,063	7,894,661	8,225,374	8,345,584	8,531,675
Texas	1,518,181	4,997,689	12,763,954	25,098,703	28,191,128	30,399,603	30,974,890	31,919,107	33,851,773	36,105,784	39,033,235	40,688,181	42,621,886	42,864,291	41,067,619	41,947,639
Utah	179,981	518,251	1,130,135	2,102,655	2,374,702	2,366,897	2,475,550	2,627,022	2,778,236	2,987,810	3,444,936	3,638,775	3,635,085	3,704,133	3,779,760	3,944,736

See notes at end of table.

Table 236.25. Current expenditures for public elementary and secondary education, by state or jurisdiction: Selected years, 1969–70 through 2012–13—Continued

[In thousands of current dollars]

State or jurisdiction	1969-70	1979-80	1989-90	1999-2000	2001-02	2002-03	2003-04	2004-05	2005-06	2006-07	2007-08	2008-09	2009-10	2010-11	2011-12[1]	2012-13
1	2	3	4	5	6	7	8	9	10	11	12	13	14	15	16	17
Vermont	78,921	189,811	546,901	870,198	992,149	1,045,213	1,111,029	1,177,478	1,237,442	1,300,149	1,356,165	1,413,329	1,432,683	1,424,507	1,497,093	1,549,228
Virginia	704,677	1,881,519	4,621,071	7,757,598	8,718,554	9,208,329	9,798,239	10,705,162	11,470,735	12,465,858	13,125,666	13,505,290	13,193,633	12,968,457	13,403,576	13,868,587
Washington	699,984	1,825,782	3,550,819	6,399,885	7,103,817	7,359,566	7,549,235	7,870,979	8,239,716	8,752,007	9,331,539	9,940,325	9,832,913	10,040,312	10,040,607	10,216,676
West Virginia	249,404	678,386	1,316,637	2,086,937	2,219,013	2,349,833	2,415,043	2,527,767	2,651,491	2,742,344	2,841,962	2,998,657	3,328,177	3,388,294	3,275,246	3,186,121
Wisconsin	777,288	1,908,523	3,929,920	6,852,178	7,592,176	7,934,755	8,131,276	8,435,359	8,745,195	9,029,660	9,366,134	9,696,228	9,966,244	10,333,016	9,704,932	9,758,650
Wyoming	69,584	226,067	509,084	683,918	761,830	791,732	814,092	863,423	965,350	1,124,564	1,191,736	1,268,407	1,334,655	1,398,444	1,432,216	1,439,041
Other jurisdictions																
American Samoa	—	16,652	21,838	42,395	46,192	47,566	55,519	58,163	58,539	57,093	63,105	65,436	70,305	75,355	80,105	65,039
Guam	—	—	101,130	—	—	—	182,506	—	210,119	219,881	229,243	235,711	235,639	266,952	290,575	279,077
Northern Marianas	—	—	20,476	49,832	46,508	50,843	47,681	58,400	57,694	55,048	51,241	62,787	62,210	84,657	68,775	61,029
Puerto Rico	—	—	1,045,407	2,086,414	2,152,724	2,541,385	2,425,372	2,865,945	3,082,295	3,268,200	3,433,229	3,502,757	3,464,044	3,519,547	3,351,423	3,468,812
U.S. Virgin Islands	—	—	128,065	135,174	107,343	125,405	128,250	137,793	146,872	157,446	196,533	201,326	220,234	204,932	183,333	161,955

—Not available.

[1]Data have been revised from previously published figures.

NOTE: Current expenditures include instruction, support services, food services, and enterprise operations. Beginning in 1989–90, expenditures for state administration are excluded. Data are not adjusted for changes in the purchasing power of the dollar due to inflation. Detail may not sum to totals because of rounding.

SOURCE: U.S. Department of Education, National Center for Education Statistics, *Statistics of State School Systems, 1969–70; Revenues and Expenditures for Public Elementary and Secondary Education*, 1979–80; and Common Core of Data (CCD), "National Public Education Financial Survey," 1989–90 through 2012–13. (This table was prepared September 2015.)

Table 236.30. Total expenditures for public elementary and secondary education and other related programs, by function and state or jurisdiction: 2012–13

[In thousands of current dollars]

State or jurisdiction	Total expenditures	Current expenditures for elementary and secondary programs													Current expenditures for other programs[1]	Capital outlay[2]	Interest on school debt[2]
		Elementary/ secondary current expenditures, total	Instruction	Support services								Food services	Enterprise operations[3]				
				Total	Student support[4]	Instructional staff[5]	General administration[6]	School administration	Operation and maintenance	Student transportation	Other support services					
1	2	3	4	5	6	7	8	9	10	11	12	13	14	15	16	17
United States	$606,490,475	$535,665,075	$325,628,793	$187,070,253	$29,863,845	$24,954,839	$10,786,389	$29,524,306	$50,656,312	$23,233,698	$18,050,864	$21,862,081	$1,103,949	$8,103,477	$45,474,445	$17,247,479
Alabama	7,438,872	6,532,358	3,752,483	2,323,869	374,954	297,807	148,147	401,428	619,376	340,284	141,873	456,007	0	123,541	645,701	137,271
Alaska	2,693,661	2,395,354	1,330,026	989,472	199,963	165,682	34,113	146,390	282,542	73,116	87,665	66,895	8,962	11,678	248,746	37,882
Arizona	9,358,343	8,164,529	4,445,724	3,296,728	588,893	421,054	139,403	434,540	1,012,028	361,902	338,908	420,278	1,798	46,901	913,055	233,857
Arkansas	5,332,363	4,637,169	2,606,371	1,751,185	238,029	391,543	112,785	236,667	451,891	183,294	136,976	274,051	5,562	29,261	539,361	126,572
California	67,627,778	58,323,458	34,815,539	20,869,548	3,141,349	3,410,838	609,854	3,863,628	5,913,612	1,373,984	2,556,282	2,489,896	148,476	742,823	6,108,855	2,452,642
Colorado	8,782,678	7,506,978	4,350,747	2,842,586	367,098	405,485	121,553	523,746	693,535	227,315	503,855	275,661	37,983	66,285	763,570	445,844
Connecticut	10,501,618	9,543,010	6,041,142	3,194,582	601,860	284,419	199,491	555,515	844,379	488,025	220,893	227,116	80,170	144,345	684,955	129,308
Delaware	1,993,275	1,761,559	1,093,785	608,144	76,482	33,129	24,031	94,547	188,335	93,642	97,977	59,630	0	46,231	162,010	23,475
District of Columbia	2,058,766	1,563,148	854,994	616,969	60,157	79,664	87,738	121,702	133,570	100,358	33,781	87,400	3,785	27,234	430,681	37,703
Florida	25,860,890	23,214,634	14,229,515	7,840,584	1,001,065	1,440,774	206,317	1,289,470	2,374,973	945,113	582,873	1,144,535	0	544,881	1,411,457	689,919
Georgia	17,433,263	15,536,733	9,634,374	4,995,146	722,536	798,731	198,154	947,717	1,148,949	717,483	461,576	861,914	45,299	28,498	1,633,451	234,581
Hawaii	2,331,160	2,169,636	1,278,215	762,005	200,606	83,457	11,573	135,230	207,665	68,883	54,390	129,416	0	14,868	146,656	0
Idaho	2,128,510	1,925,676	1,159,685	661,512	107,881	81,597	44,360	108,543	175,298	94,332	49,481	104,314	164	5,007	143,634	54,193
Illinois	28,921,291	25,783,911	15,563,587	9,423,076	1,732,959	1,032,544	1,040,726	1,309,178	2,212,007	1,204,893	890,770	797,248	0	157,765	2,089,654	889,962
Indiana	11,190,695	9,811,166	5,704,772	3,643,097	480,249	378,797	248,527	597,412	1,085,645	607,172	245,296	463,298	0	144,525	902,224	332,780
Iowa	6,085,190	5,143,771	3,157,493	1,744,997	291,722	247,002	129,495	295,057	438,411	191,291	152,020	236,548	4,733	32,144	790,085	119,189
Kansas	5,727,345	4,895,863	2,955,218	1,701,553	290,282	200,445	138,527	280,151	460,326	196,297	135,525	239,092	4,022	4,022	635,863	191,597
Kentucky	7,350,748	6,354,306	3,646,894	2,298,416	293,737	347,606	145,771	367,483	574,776	401,540	167,504	393,283	15,713	77,674	714,091	204,676
Louisiana	8,326,654	7,492,134	4,237,230	2,844,910	460,358	378,831	188,696	453,223	697,110	445,702	220,990	409,591	401	45,734	674,546	114,240
Maine	2,529,405	2,350,469	1,397,481	870,922	147,741	120,036	78,751	130,512	243,620	121,301	28,960	81,556	510	27,137	99,996	51,803
Maryland	13,284,124	12,108,546	7,526,965	4,245,916	543,726	648,911	98,526	839,948	1,096,680	664,270	353,856	335,665	0	25,567	985,050	164,962
Massachusetts	15,799,036	14,627,898	9,424,639	4,804,571	1,042,746	651,219	229,862	613,796	1,287,892	622,931	356,125	398,688	0	61,059	868,910	241,168
Michigan	18,665,271	16,354,807	9,454,619	6,288,969	1,250,569	801,702	343,287	901,874	1,478,909	686,116	826,512	611,219	0	293,833	1,146,632	869,999
Minnesota	11,214,813	9,354,376	6,110,992	2,804,835	250,351	407,333	295,024	373,423	674,104	530,609	273,992	411,083	27,465	435,817	1,047,441	377,178
Mississippi	4,290,456	4,006,798	2,280,841	1,473,992	197,598	201,142	128,000	237,981	411,497	202,333	95,440	251,585	380	26,666	199,275	57,717
Missouri	10,287,818	8,905,756	5,280,589	3,201,459	417,270	389,155	298,748	519,511	891,682	466,349	218,746	423,708	0	203,180	858,599	320,284
Montana	1,665,435	1,523,696	907,914	548,500	97,206	58,345	47,170	83,810	150,952	75,079	35,939	65,060	2,223	10,822	114,730	16,188
Nebraska	3,968,149	3,563,939	2,267,067	1,058,381	155,033	116,199	113,048	166,210	297,764	111,453	98,673	147,950	90,542	1,939	298,806	103,465
Nevada	4,031,661	3,577,346	2,056,074	1,378,092	191,508	214,612	45,920	262,911	376,978	152,647	133,517	142,805	375	21,514	222,214	210,587
New Hampshire	2,777,539	2,655,077	1,705,115	879,389	198,333	82,077	88,966	145,276	218,816	116,019	29,902	70,572	0	6,382	72,624	43,456
New Jersey	27,096,459	25,417,320	15,240,168	9,369,401	2,540,290	815,726	506,164	1,199,643	2,473,388	1,258,998	575,191	552,844	254,907	146,693	916,286	616,160
New Mexico	3,523,693	3,099,308	1,779,552	1,170,061	313,995	84,015	67,208	185,735	321,395	103,208	94,546	147,677	2,019	2,915	421,438	32
New York	58,251,602	52,938,586	36,702,703	15,150,218	1,808,017	1,345,664	1,014,091	2,069,642	4,631,538	2,762,525	1,518,741	1,085,665	0	2,303,383	1,896,908	1,112,725
North Carolina	13,342,009	12,666,607	7,857,027	4,091,096	599,379	444,926	197,597	801,161	1,088,307	560,171	399,555	718,484	0	62,664	603,732	9,006
North Dakota	1,422,121	1,174,364	779,292	397,593	50,299	42,329	52,595	59,864	109,404	51,448	31,655	62,293	35,187	4,331	224,239	19,187
Ohio	22,671,054	19,506,123	11,136,934	7,695,613	1,260,380	1,203,613	588,230	1,065,850	1,714,718	947,720	915,101	672,079	1,497	479,265	2,028,350	657,317
Oklahoma	5,960,692	5,329,897	2,948,307	1,983,439	356,192	231,364	175,504	290,315	576,283	183,122	170,660	343,581	54,571	25,090	557,951	47,754
Oregon	6,120,543	5,395,742	3,126,634	2,065,950	385,041	197,469	71,081	346,961	448,101	261,552	355,745	200,910	2,248	24,730	343,353	356,718
Pennsylvania	26,904,492	23,712,931	14,595,921	8,204,818	1,262,977	813,988	711,081	1,076,176	2,294,328	1,188,796	857,291	802,887	109,305	562,868	1,624,973	1,003,720
Rhode Island	2,345,057	2,121,403	1,311,364	753,756	221,290	69,477	29,982	100,184	165,748	87,096	79,980	55,595	689	67,833	109,485	46,336
South Carolina	8,231,823	6,950,410	3,924,756	2,634,902	520,192	415,255	71,560	434,987	669,227	285,018	238,663	371,462	19,290	68,364	845,819	367,230
South Dakota	1,340,137	1,125,929	659,857	398,504	61,570	44,902	37,573	54,970	115,854	41,913	41,722	62,504	5,065	6,065	180,112	28,031
Tennessee	9,352,109	8,531,675	5,256,131	2,808,875	360,017	542,995	202,166	501,295	719,616	321,523	161,263	466,669	0	75,136	545,873	199,425
Texas	50,714,696	41,947,639	24,745,576	14,721,919	2,053,944	2,114,729	638,355	2,411,269	4,599,859	1,235,216	1,668,547	2,480,145	0	325,576	5,472,069	2,969,412
Utah	4,934,014	3,944,736	2,494,567	1,214,914	148,654	157,245	38,293	250,339	378,445	126,966	114,971	219,102	16,152	83,912	767,890	137,476

See notes at end of table.

Table 236.30. Total expenditures for public elementary and secondary education and other related programs, by function and state or jurisdiction: 2012–13—Continued
[In thousands of current dollars]

		Total expenditures														
State or jurisdiction	Total	Current expenditures for elementary and secondary programs												Current expenditures for other programs[1]	Capital outlay[2]	Interest on school debt
		Elementary/ secondary current expenditures, total	Instruction	Support services												
				Total	Student support	Instructional staff[4]	General administration	School administration	Operation and maintenance	Student transportation	Other support services	Food services	Enterprise operations[3]			
1	2	3	4	5	6	7	8	9	10	11	12	13	14	15	16	17
Vermont	1,629,270	1,549,228	976,324	527,714	117,572	65,806	34,551	96,503	127,402	50,105	35,776	43,881	1,309	12,425	55,963	11,653
Virginia	15,210,959	13,868,587	8,445,798	4,874,084	687,633	890,139	215,168	813,121	1,305,271	744,280	218,473	546,214	2,491	77,377	1,094,943	170,052
Washington	12,086,119	10,216,676	5,920,699	3,820,789	683,841	618,475	184,350	601,884	915,179	420,763	396,298	351,189	123,999	37,878	1,438,049	393,516
West Virginia	3,310,960	3,186,121	1,850,693	1,145,565	156,882	129,848	61,573	171,524	328,444	241,477	55,818	189,863	0	45,570	58,326	20,942
Wisconsin	10,722,534	9,758,650	5,857,523	3,531,209	468,935	471,508	263,928	477,192	888,325	426,854	534,468	369,828	90	275,805	521,892	166,186
Wyoming	1,663,326	1,439,041	848,877	546,427	84,528	85,231	28,581	78,811	141,956	71,216	56,104	43,147	590	8,265	213,918	2,102
Other jurisdictions																
American Samoa	69,796	65,039	32,595	17,330	75	6,852	892	4,792	2,340	1,082	1,295	15,114	0	1,284	3,474	0
Guam	340,792	279,077	144,205	118,807	26,204	5,113	2,217	16,864	44,768	7,371	16,270	16,065	0	0	59,445	2,270
Northern Marianas	63,233	61,029	28,238	23,914	4,572	5,477	2,439	4,085	4,919	1,592	831	8,877	0	1,965	240	0
Puerto Rico	3,622,986	3,468,812	1,530,559	1,446,191	233,613	175,155	58,046	161,770	321,757	138,472	357,379	492,062	0	90,766	63,408	0
U.S. Virgin Islands	163,959	161,955	81,963	71,291	13,564	5,129	7,366	8,589	11,418	7,056	18,168	8,454	247	1,911	92	0

[1]Includes expenditures for adult education, community colleges, private school programs funded by local and state education agencies, and community services.
[2]Includes expenditures for property and for buildings and alterations completed by school district staff or contractors.
[3]Includes expenditures for operations funded by sales of products or services (e.g., school bookstore or computer time). Also includes small amounts for direct program support made by state education agencies for local school districts.

[4]Includes expenditures for guidance, health, attendance, and speech pathology services.
[5]Includes expenditures for curriculum development, staff training, libraries, and media and computer centers.
NOTE: Excludes expenditures for state education agencies. Detail may not sum to totals because of rounding.
SOURCE: U.S. Department of Education, National Center for Education Statistics, Common Core of Data (CCD), "National Public Education Financial Survey," 2012–13. (This table was prepared August 2015.)

Table 236.40. Total expenditures for public elementary and secondary education and other related programs, by function and state or jurisdiction: 2011–12

[In thousands of current dollars]

State or jurisdiction	Total	Elementary/ secondary current expenditures, total	Instruction	Total	Student support[4]	Instructional staff[5]	General administration	School administration	Operation and maintenance	Student transportation	Other support services	Food services	Enterprise operations[3]	Current expenditures for other programs[1]	Capital outlay[2]	Interest on school debt
1	2	3	4	5	6	7	8	9	10	11	12	13	14	15	16	17
United States	$601,993,584	$527,207,246	$320,994,474	$183,923,409	$29,173,107	$24,647,377	$10,569,141	$28,922,785	$49,834,165	$22,926,700	$17,850,135	$21,198,367	$1,090,995	$8,188,640	$48,793,436	$17,804,262
Alabama	7,229,299	6,386,517	3,698,119	2,245,315	368,382	288,628	145,490	393,961	581,679	329,498	137,677	443,083	0	118,530	582,173	142,079
Alaska	2,486,951	2,292,205	1,265,045	955,644	192,256	150,609	33,339	138,799	284,072	69,594	86,933	62,573	8,943	11,357	145,341	38,048
Arizona	9,173,201	7,976,089	4,359,393	3,210,298	574,402	409,195	134,032	417,604	1,001,889	354,235	318,940	404,875	1,522	48,342	922,249	226,521
Arkansas	5,393,330	4,606,995	2,606,990	1,732,433	296,339	385,799	113,873	292,152	450,651	179,815	133,804	262,041	5,531	30,470	625,078	130,787
California	67,933,295	57,775,189	34,834,633	20,615,172	3,069,455	3,451,830	557,468	3,831,331	5,775,903	1,406,656	2,522,529	2,377,552	147,832	849,005	6,693,286	2,415,815
Colorado	8,548,413	7,341,585	4,226,623	2,816,186	360,503	405,398	124,477	498,026	702,106	220,549	505,126	262,291	36,486	66,505	706,236	434,087
Connecticut	10,305,815	9,344,999	5,909,965	3,132,730	592,808	278,470	188,712	540,966	841,833	472,697	217,243	225,988	76,316	145,832	680,346	134,638
Delaware	1,978,562	1,751,143	1,116,490	575,915	74,118	31,668	25,377	91,724	182,906	87,655	82,466	58,738	3,172	43,176	160,864	23,380
District of Columbia	1,880,846	1,466,888	835,297	570,575	52,176	55,291	77,610	128,782	128,651	95,733	32,381	57,844	0	29,242	350,947	33,390
Florida	25,827,411	22,732,752	13,863,360	7,778,213	988,122	1,444,964	200,665	1,262,173	2,366,281	943,642	572,365	1,091,180	0	531,446	1,837,262	725,950
Georgia	17,465,095	15,623,633	9,661,561	5,069,710	721,257	804,370	205,132	938,987	1,162,751	702,706	534,508	847,025	45,336	28,718	1,566,185	246,559
Hawaii	2,431,422	2,187,480	1,253,486	809,606	205,572	77,727	10,622	133,574	251,251	75,894	54,965	124,388	0	18,339	124,096	101,508
Idaho	2,052,295	1,854,556	1,118,508	635,933	103,651	73,963	42,845	104,940	171,375	92,810	46,349	99,904	210	4,818	135,343	57,578
Illinois	28,197,052	25,012,915	15,062,473	9,173,619	1,670,799	1,004,347	1,035,931	1,270,844	2,163,144	1,177,291	851,264	776,822	0	147,857	2,169,707	866,573
Indiana	11,412,416	9,978,491	5,869,436	3,660,416	477,217	379,746	252,792	584,868	1,110,673	605,250	249,869	448,640	0	143,578	943,637	346,710
Iowa	6,021,744	4,971,944	3,056,382	1,684,665	277,615	238,874	126,418	286,572	423,592	185,378	146,216	226,252	4,645	32,354	905,980	111,467
Kansas	5,759,773	4,871,381	2,960,225	1,680,456	288,453	203,500	144,033	280,207	456,009	191,668	116,586	230,700	4,325	4,325	682,546	201,522
Kentucky	7,394,709	6,360,799	3,683,142	2,282,369	291,664	347,964	142,037	361,259	581,667	395,751	162,027	379,094	16,194	82,974	770,827	180,110
Louisiana	8,457,692	7,544,782	4,296,513	2,835,500	454,281	398,623	185,249	453,378	683,208	443,255	217,505	412,389	380	49,166	744,610	119,135
Maine	2,536,202	2,330,842	1,393,423	857,340	152,289	117,581	72,257	126,668	240,166	119,519	28,859	79,839	240	27,586	121,421	56,354
Maryland	13,208,730	11,850,634	7,362,229	4,167,836	536,147	640,551	106,627	848,596	1,008,194	635,115	392,606	320,569	0	23,329	1,166,856	167,911
Massachusetts	15,572,302	14,151,659	9,156,777	4,611,079	1,000,934	648,571	196,699	576,269	1,238,278	604,424	345,904	383,803	0	57,753	1,117,722	245,167
Michigan	19,056,799	16,485,178	9,569,531	6,313,528	1,258,620	812,118	339,716	897,935	1,473,648	702,868	828,624	602,119	0	311,414	1,376,616	883,591
Minnesota	10,938,012	9,053,021	5,936,623	2,694,668	241,917	389,865	280,590	360,455	641,585	512,952	267,305	396,582	25,148	425,508	1,069,044	390,439
Mississippi	4,341,018	3,972,787	2,266,650	1,459,137	193,147	205,228	126,294	230,737	417,379	195,478	90,874	246,687	314	29,067	270,440	68,724
Missouri	10,184,551	8,719,925	5,197,338	3,106,738	407,036	377,844	281,381	505,252	871,532	456,838	206,856	415,850	0	202,882	905,554	356,189
Montana	1,654,625	1,504,531	895,081	542,398	93,009	57,111	46,197	82,345	152,916	74,246	36,574	64,452	2,599	12,147	120,771	17,177
Nebraska	4,032,298	3,462,575	2,204,031	1,022,843	149,831	110,451	107,628	163,981	290,413	106,081	94,458	145,628	90,072	5,423	376,182	188,118
Nevada	4,164,339	3,574,233	2,094,490	1,343,876	191,677	179,804	53,452	267,375	379,003	146,186	126,380	135,504	363	22,486	327,173	240,447
New Hampshire	2,856,080	2,643,256	1,703,049	868,500	196,953	79,849	88,636	144,574	217,501	113,241	27,745	71,707	0	7,357	159,998	45,469
New Jersey	26,131,462	24,391,278	14,621,161	8,962,705	2,417,153	757,081	494,351	1,152,284	2,383,511	1,216,595	541,731	546,146	261,266	145,630	912,022	682,532
New Mexico	3,559,744	3,039,461	1,737,157	1,157,041	312,821	85,237	67,783	181,676	316,282	100,818	92,424	143,476	1,788	4,191	516,030	62
New York	58,096,880	52,460,494	36,402,730	14,954,302	1,760,925	1,318,950	999,411	2,019,007	4,555,669	2,784,794	1,515,546	1,103,462	0	2,324,980	2,097,414	1,213,993
North Carolina	13,060,157	12,303,426	7,670,507	3,945,148	579,241	435,298	190,431	769,521	1,044,027	545,327	381,302	687,771	0	64,190	683,545	8,996
North Dakota	1,280,669	1,098,090	641,580	364,739	47,135	39,380	49,409	55,404	99,354	47,199	26,859	57,503	34,268	8,589	160,058	13,932
Ohio	23,186,166	19,701,810	11,213,502	7,818,594	1,252,066	1,287,265	599,478	1,121,867	1,722,344	952,381	883,193	668,572	1,143	419,786	2,467,639	596,930
Oklahoma	5,748,976	5,170,978	2,876,200	1,917,119	352,443	213,457	165,841	275,679	571,120	179,111	159,468	326,066	51,583	26,462	496,205	55,341
Oregon	6,178,860	5,389,273	3,130,150	2,056,269	382,606	200,455	72,074	342,400	444,810	256,779	357,145	200,953	1,901	25,275	448,212	316,100
Pennsylvania	26,596,835	23,190,198	14,158,464	8,125,146	1,228,638	795,160	717,818	1,065,797	2,250,183	1,188,792	878,759	800,030	106,557	554,665	1,822,156	1,029,815
Rhode Island	2,317,889	2,167,450	1,343,508	767,921	223,902	76,246	30,517	105,644	171,275	83,893	76,444	55,197	824	68,570	36,926	44,943
South Carolina	7,955,526	6,619,072	3,741,969	2,504,442	492,122	398,350	71,022	399,056	631,459	291,507	220,925	354,171	18,491	66,542	871,103	398,809
South Dakota	1,302,875	1,100,100	646,885	385,880	60,231	44,018	36,716	53,656	111,350	41,049	38,859	60,524	6,811	2,894	172,738	27,142
Tennessee	9,289,770	8,345,584	5,187,805	2,712,515	359,656	522,641	175,728	477,465	714,723	312,548	149,754	445,264	0	75,695	664,129	204,361
Texas	49,991,336	41,067,619	24,235,087	14,453,152	1,996,385	2,055,843	618,148	2,330,464	4,547,753	1,185,258	1,719,301	2,363,381	0	340,085	5,536,572	3,047,060
Utah	4,790,073	3,779,760	2,406,489	1,143,856	147,162	153,201	44,775	234,966	343,867	120,566	99,319	212,909	16,506	111,616	746,262	152,435

See notes at end of table.

..

Table 236.40. Total expenditures for public elementary and secondary education and other related programs, by function and state or jurisdiction: 2011–12—Continued
[In thousands of current dollars]

State or jurisdiction	Total	Elementary/ secondary current expenditures, total	Total expenditures — Current expenditures for elementary and secondary programs									Food services	Enterprise operations[3]	Current expenditures for other programs[1]	Capital outlay[2]	Interest on school debt
			Instruction	Support services												
				Total	Student support[4]	Instructional staff	General administration	School administration	Operation and maintenance	Student transportation	Other support services					
1	2	3	4	5	6	7	8	9	10	11	12	13	14	15	16	17
Vermont	1,568,294	1,497,093	938,085	516,635	114,891	63,152	30,641	97,006	125,004	49,290	36,651	41,333	1,040	12,479	46,009	12,713
Virginia	14,730,695	13,403,576	8,123,189	4,744,409	652,507	888,941	207,325	775,363	1,282,360	726,330	211,583	533,759	2,218	75,794	1,078,786	172,540
Washington	12,039,428	10,040,607	5,850,029	3,723,294	670,533	581,359	187,088	582,827	904,239	414,602	382,645	346,975	120,310	35,983	1,545,989	416,850
West Virginia	3,409,105	3,275,246	1,919,623	1,170,981	155,961	135,590	64,988	174,123	339,632	243,898	56,789	184,643	0	47,168	69,611	17,079
Wisconsin	10,609,035	9,704,932	5,830,090	3,506,067	462,397	458,211	270,244	477,135	887,149	419,844	531,086	368,643	133	258,100	450,303	195,700
Wyoming	1,655,911	1,432,216	847,393	540,500	83,700	87,601	29,735	77,161	137,797	69,092	55,413	43,469	854	8,968	213,240	1,487
Other jurisdictions																
American Samoa	95,015	80,105	35,110	26,735	37	9,009	3,987	4,587	6,529	1,134	1,451	18,260	0	1,888	13,022	0
Guam	307,068	290,575	142,979	136,193	26,092	4,855	1,749	16,840	46,928	5,626	34,102	11,403	0	0	13,369	3,124
Northern Marianas	71,875	68,775	29,685	29,802	6,600	5,517	2,514	5,415	4,578	3,048	2,131	9,288	0	1,913	1,186	0
Puerto Rico	3,500,379	3,351,423	1,478,763	1,397,250	225,707	169,227	56,082	156,295	310,868	133,786	345,285	475,410	0	87,694	61,262	0
U.S. Virgin Islands	185,853	183,333	95,711	76,567	14,395	5,162	7,245	9,332	13,000	7,038	20,396	10,700	356	2,434	86	0

[1]Includes expenditures for adult education, community colleges, private school programs funded by local and state education agencies, and community services.
[2]Includes expenditures for property and for buildings and alterations completed by school district staff or contractors.
[3]Includes expenditures for operations funded by sales of products or services (e.g., school bookstore or computer time). Also includes small amounts for direct program support made by state education agencies for local school districts.
[4]Includes expenditures for guidance, health, attendance, and speech pathology services.

[5]Includes expenditures for curriculum development, staff training, libraries, and media and computer centers.
NOTE: Excludes expenditures for state education agencies. Detail may not sum to totals because of rounding. Some data have been revised from previously published figures.
SOURCE: U.S. Department of Education, National Center for Education Statistics, Common Core of Data (CCD), "National Public Education Financial Survey," 2011–12. (This table was prepared August 2015.)

Table 236.50. Expenditures for instruction in public elementary and secondary schools, by subfunction and state or jurisdiction: 2011–12 and 2012–13

[In thousands of current dollars]

State or jurisdiction	2011–12[1]						2012–13					
	Total	Salaries	Employee benefits	Purchased services[2]	Supplies	Tuition and other	Total	Salaries	Employee benefits	Purchased services[2]	Supplies	Tuition and other
1	2	3	4	5	6	7	8	9	10	11	12	13
United States	$320,994,474	$210,735,097	$76,950,048	$14,537,511	$12,433,973	$6,337,847	$325,628,793	$212,545,500	$79,416,636	$14,773,355	$12,421,155	$6,472,147
Alabama...............	3,698,119	2,442,365	872,821	120,379	246,710	15,844	3,752,483	2,454,717	879,398	127,499	274,715	16,153
Alaska..................	1,265,045	673,082	460,009	56,675	65,145	10,136	1,330,026	682,496	520,603	57,637	59,502	9,788
Arizona	4,359,393	3,027,595	861,742	269,410	173,792	26,856	4,445,724	3,070,787	898,038	272,990	178,046	25,863
Arkansas..............	2,606,990	1,791,543	490,983	95,351	198,824	30,288	2,606,371	1,803,661	492,677	94,156	183,501	32,375
California	34,834,633	22,845,108	8,250,199	1,724,400	1,254,825	760,100	34,815,539	22,901,587	8,228,479	1,743,564	1,180,926	760,982
Colorado..............	4,226,623	2,987,372	762,688	114,592	253,575	108,397	4,350,747	3,034,027	819,270	113,518	272,730	111,202
Connecticut..........	5,909,965	3,597,321	1,602,150	200,190	104,888	405,415	6,041,142	3,671,908	1,633,961	204,248	109,301	421,724
Delaware..............	1,116,490	675,131	334,281	14,835	56,812	35,431	1,093,785	661,954	342,146	13,071	42,208	34,407
District of Columbia	835,297	565,156	71,658	39,238	17,088	142,158	854,994	562,914	80,106	69,214	20,038	122,723
Florida..................	13,863,360	8,614,099	2,328,432	2,295,047	524,711	101,072	14,229,515	8,687,300	2,395,363	2,483,441	551,247	112,163
Georgia................	9,661,561	6,626,114	2,231,871	235,960	521,023	46,593	9,634,374	6,489,863	2,294,937	291,889	508,893	48,792
Hawaii..................	1,253,486	814,926	284,553	63,248	73,373	17,386	1,278,215	822,899	304,591	59,614	69,796	21,316
Idaho...................	1,118,508	776,701	261,534	38,478	40,443	1,352	1,159,685	811,855	269,183	38,325	39,029	1,294
Illinois..................	15,062,473	9,543,026	4,086,127	723,338	390,371	319,612	15,563,587	9,727,147	4,298,568	780,428	412,657	344,786
Indiana................	5,869,436	3,642,956	1,896,207	94,510	225,786	9,977	5,704,772	3,591,802	1,847,374	86,936	169,484	9,176
Iowa....................	3,056,382	2,136,793	701,068	80,257	105,506	32,757	3,157,493	2,206,410	729,091	84,706	102,122	35,164
Kansas.................	2,960,225	2,082,098	632,726	84,449	138,981	21,971	2,955,218	2,087,915	619,997	88,692	137,014	21,599
Kentucky..............	3,683,142	2,597,859	889,303	68,085	115,498	12,396	3,646,894	2,583,238	892,010	59,655	100,084	11,909
Louisiana	4,296,513	2,742,735	1,226,052	99,045	212,088	16,593	4,237,230	2,681,985	1,203,730	104,179	217,081	30,256
Maine...................	1,393,423	905,608	355,106	27,509	34,722	70,478	1,397,481	908,537	361,132	26,541	31,847	69,424
Maryland..............	7,362,229	4,632,076	2,070,610	205,132	190,263	264,149	7,526,965	4,694,571	2,141,072	228,241	197,632	265,449
Massachusetts...........	9,156,777	5,877,769	2,307,285	63,400	223,619	684,704	9,424,639	6,068,435	2,305,486	73,703	254,791	722,224
Michigan	9,569,531	5,565,714	2,945,017	789,381	249,001	20,417	9,454,619	5,432,104	2,946,983	801,473	252,608	21,451
Minnesota	5,936,623	4,058,508	1,294,397	318,001	185,373	80,343	6,110,992	4,184,253	1,347,793	310,968	190,756	77,222
Mississippi	2,266,650	1,577,427	482,207	64,024	127,490	15,504	2,280,841	1,579,059	509,264	62,112	113,760	16,646
Missouri...............	5,197,338	3,619,733	1,045,107	162,013	339,844	30,642	5,280,589	3,679,534	1,075,316	154,578	342,050	29,111
Montana...............	895,081	593,487	173,388	58,350	64,519	5,338	907,914	606,371	179,624	54,428	62,705	4,787
Nebraska	2,204,031	1,477,376	481,153	129,679	96,671	19,152	2,267,067	1,505,035	517,892	123,921	101,912	18,307
Nevada	2,094,490	1,381,696	537,318	59,790	111,032	4,654	2,056,074	1,353,136	531,836	46,779	120,796	3,527
New Hampshire	1,703,049	1,035,563	447,494	45,673	38,356	135,963	1,705,115	1,042,545	447,437	44,897	35,922	134,315
New Jersey	14,621,161	9,110,277	3,839,863	512,220	448,775	710,025	15,240,168	9,329,281	4,168,394	548,056	469,672	724,765
New Mexico	1,737,157	1,212,444	361,826	66,333	96,389	165	1,779,552	1,220,166	386,398	60,839	111,963	186
New York	36,402,730	22,224,345	10,879,678	1,947,269	629,095	722,344	36,702,703	22,291,799	11,327,198	1,720,171	653,663	709,872
North Carolina	7,670,507	5,318,475	1,658,938	263,158	429,912	24	7,857,027	5,405,041	1,759,958	243,293	448,487	248
North Dakota	641,580	446,277	142,380	19,344	26,894	6,684	679,292	470,450	159,741	18,492	26,614	3,994
Ohio....................	11,213,502	7,295,354	2,544,023	588,716	389,687	395,722	11,136,934	7,168,926	2,534,373	626,853	398,156	408,626
Oklahoma.............	2,876,209	2,036,896	621,640	53,612	152,807	11,254	2,948,307	2,073,159	636,947	54,338	171,857	12,006
Oregon.................	3,130,150	1,836,484	996,077	112,237	148,930	36,422	3,126,634	1,832,779	1,001,104	112,389	144,572	35,789
Pennsylvania...........	14,158,464	9,045,636	3,633,493	719,952	468,636	290,746	14,595,921	9,035,398	4,037,638	741,697	482,111	299,077
Rhode Island	1,343,508	860,983	368,579	11,330	19,188	83,428	1,311,364	831,416	373,798	9,411	20,873	75,866
South Carolina...........	3,741,969	2,571,505	821,616	126,537	200,712	21,598	3,924,756	2,693,306	900,260	128,341	180,009	22,839
South Dakota	646,885	433,855	129,205	31,170	42,887	9,768	659,857	441,855	133,453	28,022	45,163	11,364
Tennessee	5,187,805	3,483,791	1,144,100	101,288	444,156	14,470	5,256,131	3,545,257	1,160,143	98,844	437,709	14,179
Texas	24,251,087	18,848,805	2,844,914	828,320	1,445,811	283,237	24,745,576	19,297,810	2,869,785	888,577	1,401,264	288,140
Utah....................	2,406,489	1,514,906	637,549	79,258	166,169	8,606	2,494,567	1,551,598	674,940	88,612	170,447	8,971
Vermont	938,085	569,351	226,734	50,935	20,910	70,155	976,324	581,610	245,435	56,856	20,790	71,634
Virginia................	8,123,189	5,651,526	1,903,355	195,852	360,645	11,812	8,445,798	5,739,910	2,161,327	185,968	345,609	12,984
Washington...........	5,850,029	3,962,433	1,324,490	314,111	211,497	37,499	5,920,699	4,025,955	1,339,190	307,061	209,302	39,191
West Virginia..............	1,919,623	1,146,316	613,799	40,563	114,884	4,061	1,850,693	1,132,541	565,745	38,033	110,489	3,886
Wisconsin	5,830,090	3,707,668	1,651,212	106,133	193,774	171,303	5,857,523	3,733,733	1,641,083	87,953	203,507	191,247
Wyoming..............	847,393	550,836	223,093	28,730	41,885	2,849	848,877	555,467	226,367	28,148	35,746	3,149
Other jurisdictions												
American Samoa	35,110	20,798	3,374	1,576	4,751	4,612	32,595	21,651	3,478	1,611	1,359	4,495
Guam..................	142,979	101,797	34,873	4,443	1,773	92	144,205	101,120	36,416	4,176	1,709	784
Northern Marianas...	29,685	22,581	4,948	708	696	752	28,238	20,038	5,224	2,229	146	600
Puerto Rico............	1,478,763	1,017,564	216,619	221,632	21,806	1,143	1,530,559	1,053,205	224,206	229,395	22,570	1,183
U.S. Virgin Islands....	95,711	66,584	25,302	1,861	1,964	0	81,963	56,106	21,320	1,913	2,623	0

[1]Data have been revised from previously published figures.
[2]Includes purchased professional services of teachers or others who provide instruction for students.
NOTE: Excludes expenditures for state education agencies. Detail may not sum to totals because of rounding.

SOURCE: U.S. Department of Education, National Center for Education Statistics, Common Core of Data (CCD), "National Public Education Financial Survey," 2011–12 and 2012–13. (This table was prepared September 2015.)

Table 236.55. Total and current expenditures per pupil in public elementary and secondary schools: Selected years, 1919–20 through 2012–13

School year	Expenditure per pupil in average daily attendance				Expenditure per pupil in fall enrollment[1]				
	Unadjusted dollars[2]		Constant 2014–15 dollars[3]		Unadjusted dollars[2]		Constant 2014–15 dollars[3]		
	Total expenditure[4]	Current expenditure	Total expenditure[4]	Current expenditure	Total expenditure[4]	Current expenditure	Total expenditure[4]	Current expenditure	Annual percent change in current expenditure
1	2	3	4	5	6	7	8	9	10
1919–20	$64	$53	$794	$662	$48	$40	$594	$496	—
1929–30	108	87	1,500	1,199	90	72	1,242	993	—
1931–32	97	81	1,590	1,331	82	69	1,346	1,127	—
1933–34	76	67	1,362	1,206	65	57	1,157	1,025	—
1935–36	88	74	1,515	1,280	74	63	1,281	1,082	—
1937–38	100	84	1,647	1,386	86	72	1,414	1,190	—
1939–40	106	88	1,791	1,492	92	76	1,552	1,293	—
1941–42	110	98	1,670	1,492	94	84	1,430	1,278	—
1943–44	125	117	1,693	1,589	105	99	1,427	1,339	—
1945–46	146	136	1,893	1,770	124	116	1,612	1,508	—
1947–48	205	181	2,081	1,843	179	158	1,817	1,610	—
1949–50	260	210	2,602	2,102	231	187	2,309	1,865	—
1951–52	314	246	2,832	2,216	275	215	2,479	1,940	—
1953–54	351	265	3,089	2,331	312	236	2,747	2,073	—
1955–56	387	294	3,407	2,590	354	269	3,115	2,368	—
1957–58	447	341	3,708	2,827	408	311	3,382	2,578	—
1959–60	471	375	3,794	3,022	440	350	3,544	2,823	—
1961–62	517	419	4,072	3,299	485	393	3,821	3,096	—
1963–64	559	460	4,287	3,532	520	428	3,990	3,288	—
1965–66	654	538	4,850	3,988	607	499	4,502	3,703	—
1967–68	786	658	5,474	4,581	732	612	5,091	4,262	—
1969–70	955	816	5,984	5,112	879	751	5,509	4,707	—
1970–71	1,049	911	6,253	5,428	970	842	5,780	5,018	6.6
1971–72	1,128	990	6,487	5,692	1,034	908	5,949	5,221	4.0
1972–73	1,211	1,077	6,693	5,954	1,117	993	6,174	5,492	5.2
1973–74	1,364	1,207	6,923	6,128	1,244	1,101	6,313	5,588	1.7
1974–75	1,545	1,365	7,059	6,236	1,423	1,257	6,503	5,745	2.8
1975–76	1,697	1,504	7,244	6,417	1,563	1,385	6,670	5,909	2.9
1976–77	1,816	1,638	7,324	6,603	1,674	1,509	6,749	6,085	3.0
1977–78	2,002	1,823	7,567	6,888	1,842	1,677	6,959	6,335	4.1
1978–79	2,210	2,020	7,636	6,981	2,029	1,855	7,012	6,411	1.2
1979–80	2,491	2,272	7,593	6,926	2,290	2,088	6,980	6,367	-0.7
1980–81	2,742[5]	2,502	7,493[5]	6,835	2,529[5]	2,307	6,911[5]	6,304	-1.0
1981–82	2,973[5]	2,726	7,478[5]	6,855	2,754[5]	2,525	6,927[5]	6,350	0.7
1982–83	3,203[5]	2,955	7,725[5]	7,126	2,966[5]	2,736	7,153[5]	6,599	3.9
1983–84	3,471[5]	3,173	8,072[5]	7,379	3,216[5]	2,940	7,478[5]	6,836	3.6
1984–85	3,722[5]	3,470	8,329[5]	7,766	3,456[5]	3,222	7,733[5]	7,210	5.5
1985–86	4,020[5]	3,756	8,743[5]	8,168	3,724[5]	3,479	8,100[5]	7,568	5.0
1986–87	4,308[5]	3,970	9,166[5]	8,448	3,995[5]	3,682	8,500[5]	7,834	3.5
1987–88	4,654[5]	4,240	9,509[5]	8,663	4,310[5]	3,927	8,806[5]	8,023	2.4
1988–89	5,108	4,645	9,975	9,071	4,737	4,307	9,250	8,411	4.8
1989–90	5,547	4,980	10,339	9,282	5,172	4,643	9,640	8,654	2.9
1990–91	5,882	5,258	10,395	9,292	5,484	4,902	9,691	8,663	0.1
1991–92	6,072	5,421	10,398	9,283	5,626	5,023	9,635	8,602	-0.7
1992–93	6,279	5,584	10,428	9,272	5,802	5,160	9,635	8,568	-0.4
1993–94	6,489	5,767	10,504	9,336	5,994	5,327	9,702	8,623	0.6
1994–95	6,723	5,989	10,579	9,424	6,206	5,529	9,766	8,700	0.9
1995–96	6,959	6,147	10,661	9,416	6,441	5,689	9,867	8,715	0.2
1996–97	7,297	6,393	10,868	9,521	6,761	5,923	10,070	8,822	1.2
1997–98	7,701	6,676	11,268	9,768	7,139	6,189	10,447	9,057	2.7
1998–99	8,115	7,013	11,673	10,088	7,531	6,508	10,833	9,361	3.4
1999–2000	8,589	7,394	12,008	10,337	8,030	6,912	11,226	9,664	3.2
2000–01	9,180	7,904	12,409	10,684	8,572	7,380	11,586	9,976	3.2
2001–02	9,611	8,259	12,766	10,969	8,993	7,727	11,944	10,264	2.9
2002–03	9,950	8,610	12,932	11,190	9,296	8,044	12,082	10,455	1.9
2003–04	10,308	8,900	13,110	11,319	9,625	8,310	12,241	10,569	1.1
2004–05	10,779	9,316	13,308	11,502	10,078	8,711	12,444	10,755	1.8
2005–06	11,338	9,778	13,485	11,630	10,603	9,145	12,611	10,877	1.1
2006–07	12,015	10,336	13,930	11,983	11,252	9,679	13,045	11,222	3.2
2007–08	12,759	10,982	14,264	12,278	11,965	10,298	13,376	11,513	2.6
2008–09	13,033	11,239	14,370	12,391	12,222	10,540	13,476	11,621	0.9
2009–10	13,035	11,427	14,235	12,478	12,133	10,636	13,249	11,615	-0.1
2010–11	12,926	11,433	13,837	12,240	12,054	10,663	12,904	11,414	-1.7
2011–12[6]	12,796	11,362	13,308	11,817	11,991	10,648	12,471	11,074	-3.0
2012–13	12,846	11,503	13,142	11,768	12,020	10,763	12,296	11,011	-0.6

—Not available.

[1]Data for 1919–20 to 1953–54 are based on school-year enrollment.
[2]Unadjusted (or "current") dollars have not been adjusted to compensate for inflation.
[3]Constant dollars based on the Consumer Price Index, prepared by the Bureau of Labor Statistics, U.S. Department of Labor, adjusted to a school-year basis.
[4]Excludes "Other current expenditures," such as community services, private school programs, adult education, and other programs not allocable to expenditures per student at public schools.
[5]Estimated.
[6]Revised from previously published figures.

NOTE: Beginning in 1980–81, state administration expenditures are excluded from both "total" and "current" expenditures. Current expenditures include instruction, support services, food services, and enterprise operations. Total expenditures include current expenditures, capital outlay, and interest on debt. Beginning in 1988–89, extensive changes were made in the data collection procedures.
SOURCE: U.S. Department of Education, National Center for Education Statistics, *Biennial Survey of Education in the United States*, 1919–20 through 1955–56; *Statistics of State School Systems*, 1957–58 through 1969–70; *Revenues and Expenditures for Public Elementary and Secondary Education*, 1970–71 through 1986–87; and Common Core of Data (CCD), "National Public Education Financial Survey," 1987–88 through 2012–13. (This table was prepared September 2015.)

Table 236.60. Total and current expenditures per pupil in fall enrollment in public elementary and secondary schools, by function and subfunction: Selected years, 1990–91 through 2012–13

Function and subfunction	Expenditures per pupil in current dollars									Expenditures per pupil in constant 2014–15 dollars[1]								
	1990–91	2000–01	2002–03	2007–08	2008–09	2009–10	2010–11	2011–12[2]	2012–13	1990–91	2000–01	2002–03	2007–08	2008–09	2009–10	2010–11	2011–12[2]	2012–13
1	2	3	4	5	6	7	8	9	10	11	12	13	14	15	16	17	18	19
Total expenditures	$5,484	$8,572	$9,296	$11,965	$12,222	$12,133	$12,054	$11,991	$12,020	$9,691	$11,586	$12,082	$13,376	$13,476	$13,249	$12,904	$12,471	$12,296
Current expenditures for public schools	4,902	7,380	8,044	10,298	10,540	10,636	10,663	10,648	10,763	8,663	9,976	10,455	11,513	11,621	11,615	11,414	11,074	11,011
Salaries	3,220[3]	4,752	5,113	6,177	6,348	6,366	6,300	6,233	6,261	5,691[3]	6,423	6,645	6,905	6,999	6,951	6,744	6,482	6,405
Employee benefits	824[3]	1,228	1,414	2,093	2,146	2,199	2,260	2,309	2,368	1,456[3]	1,660	1,838	2,340	2,366	2,401	2,419	2,402	2,422
Purchased services	397[3]	673	733	1,000	1,030	1,053	1,082	1,097	1,120	702[3]	910	953	1,118	1,136	1,150	1,158	1,141	1,146
Tuition	29[3]	52	68	93	91	96	101	101	102	51[3]	70	89	104	101	105	108	105	105
Supplies	359[3]	599	634	840	825	818	817	809	817	635[3]	809	823	939	910	893	875	842	836
Other	72[3]	76	82	96	99	104	103	98	95	127[3]	102	107	107	109	114	110	102	97
Instruction	2,965	4,541	4,934	6,262	6,420	6,511	6,522	6,483	6,543	5,241	6,138	6,412	7,001	7,078	7,110	6,982	6,743	6,693
Salaries	2,202	3,273	3,504	4,199	4,325	4,347	4,307	4,256	4,271	3,891	4,425	4,554	4,695	4,769	4,747	4,611	4,427	4,369
Employee benefits	542	837	954	1,407	1,443	1,481	1,522	1,554	1,596	958	1,132	1,239	1,573	1,591	1,617	1,629	1,616	1,632
Purchased services	66	136	151	249	260	281	297	294	297	117	184	197	278	286	306	318	305	304
Tuition	29	52	68	93	91	96	101	101	102	51	70	89	104	101	105	108	105	105
Supplies	111	220	234	287	273	277	266	251	250	197	297	305	321	301	303	284	261	255
Textbooks	—	—	—	55	60	52	47	44	43	—	—	—	62	66	56	50	46	44
Other	15	22	22	27	28	29	30	27	28	27	30	29	30	31	32	32	28	28
Student support[4]	217	366	415	559	580	591	594	589	600	383	495	539	624	639	645	636	613	614
Salaries	159	262	291	372	388	393	392	383	388	282	354	378	416	428	429	419	399	397
Employee benefits	40	64	76	120	125	128	132	137	142	71	87	99	134	138	140	141	143	145
Purchased services	11	28	34	48	49	50	52	54	56	20	38	44	54	54	55	56	56	57
Supplies	5	9	10	11	11	11	11	10	11	8	12	13	12	12	12	11	11	11
Other	1	3	3	7	7	7	7	4	4	2	4	4	8	8	8	8	4	4
Instructional staff services[5]	205	337	385	515	508	509	503	498	501	363	456	501	576	560	556	539	518	513
Salaries	135	207	235	309	304	301	293	289	291	238	280	305	346	335	328	314	301	298
Employee benefits	34	50	60	95	96	98	100	100	102	60	67	78	106	106	107	107	104	105
Purchased services	15	42	48	67	66	69	70	69	70	27	57	63	75	73	75	74	72	72
Supplies	19	33	37	40	37	37	37	35	33	33	45	48	44	41	41	39	36	34
Other	2	4	5	4	4	4	4	4	5	4	6	6	5	5	5	5	4	5
General administration	141	151	165	200	207	211	212	213	217	248	204	215	224	228	231	227	222	222
Salaries	63	71	76	87	90	90	89	88	90	112	96	99	98	99	99	95	92	92
Employee benefits	19	21	24	34	35	37	38	39	39	33	29	31	38	39	40	40	40	40
Purchased services	36	44	49	60	64	64	65	67	68	64	60	64	68	71	70	70	69	70
Supplies	4	4	5	5	5	5	5	5	5	7	6	6	5	5	5	5	5	5
Other	18	10	10	14	13	16	16	15	15	32	13	14	15	14	17	17	15	15
School administration	284	415	452	576	581	579	580	584	593	501	561	588	644	641	632	620	608	607
Salaries	217	314	336	410	417	413	408	408	413	383	424	437	458	460	450	437	424	423
Employee benefits	55	78	90	133	134	136	141	145	149	97	106	117	149	148	149	151	151	149
Purchased services	6	13	15	20	19	19	19	20	19	11	18	19	22	21	21	20	21	19
Supplies	5	8	9	10	9	9	9	9	9	8	11	11	11	10	9	9	9	9
Other	2	2	2	3	2	3	3	3	3	3	3	3	3	3	3	3	3	3
Operation and maintenance	517	721	764	1,003	1,027	1,014	1,015	1,006	1,018	913	975	993	1,121	1,132	1,107	1,087	1,047	1,041
Salaries	215	285	303	359	367	364	356	352	351	379	385	394	401	404	397	381	366	359
Employee benefits	64	80	93	136	140	143	146	148	150	113	108	121	152	154	156	156	154	153
Purchased services	139	204	205	265	267	265	270	271	282	245	276	266	296	294	290	289	282	288
Supplies	91	146	157	234	245	233	235	227	228	161	197	203	261	270	254	252	236	233
Other	8	6	7	9	9	9	9	8	7	14	8	9	10	10	10	9	8	8
Student transportation	211	298	325	438	440	442	452	463	467	372	402	422	489	485	483	484	482	478
Salaries	80	115	124	153	154	155	152	151	151	141	155	161	171	170	169	163	157	155
Employee benefits	22	34	40	58	60	62	63	64	65	38	46	51	65	66	67	68	67	67
Purchased services	81	122	134	174	183	182	185	190	193	143	165	174	194	202	198	198	198	197
Supplies	23	25	23	49	40	40	48	53	53	41	33	30	55	44	44	51	55	53
Other	5	3	4	4	3	4	4	5	5	8	4	5	4	4	4	4	5	5

See notes at end of table.

Table 236.60. Total and current expenditures per pupil in fall enrollment in public elementary and secondary schools, by function and subfunction: Selected years, 1990–91 through 2012–13—Continued

Function and subfunction	Expenditures per pupil in current dollars									Expenditures per pupil in constant 2014–15 dollars[1]								
	1990–91	2000–01	2002–03	2007–08	2008–09	2009–10	2010–11	2011–12[2]	2012–13	1990–91	2000–01	2002–03	2007–08	2008–09	2009–10	2010–11	2011–12[2]	2012–13
	2	3	4	5	6	7	8	9	10	11	12	13	14	15	16	17	18	19
Other support services[6]	136	242	275	331	349	348	349	361	363	240	328	357	370	385	380	373	375	371
Salaries	70	117	129	153	164	165	165	165	167	124	158	168	171	181	181	176	172	171
Employee benefits	24	34	42	61	64	64	67	69	70	42	46	54	68	71	69	71	71	72
Purchased services	19	59	68	77	80	79	78	85	87	34	80	89	86	88	87	84	89	89
Supplies	7	13	15	20	18	17	18	19	19	13	18	19	22	20	19	19	19	20
Other	15	19	20	21	23	23	21	23	19	26	26	26	24	25	25	23	24	20
Food services	205	293	310	390	402	405	412	428	439	361	396	403	436	443	443	441	445	449
Salaries	—	105	111	129	132	131	131	133	133	—	142	144	144	146	144	140	138	136
Employee benefits	—	29	34	46	48	49	50	51	52	—	40	44	51	52	53	54	53	54
Purchased services	—	20	24	35	37	39	42	44	46	—	26	31	39	41	43	45	46	47
Supplies	—	136	138	177	181	181	184	196	203	—	184	179	198	200	198	197	203	208
Other	—	3	4	3	4	5	5	5	5	—	4	5	4	5	5	5	5	6
Enterprise operations[7]	23	16	19	24	26	25	22	22	22	41	22	24	27	28	28	24	23	23
Salaries	—	3	3	6	6	7	7	6	6	—	4	4	7	8	7	7	6	6
Employee benefits	—	1	1	2	2	2	2	2	2	—	1	2	2	2	2	2	2	2
Purchased services	—	4	4	5	5	5	3	4	4	—	5	5	6	6	6	4	4	4
Supplies	—	5	6	7	7	7	6	6	6	—	7	8	8	8	8	6	6	6
Other	—	4	4	4	4	4	4	4	4	—	6	5	5	5	5	5	5	5
Capital outlay[8]	477	976	1,013	1,348	1,336	1,148	1,029	984	910	843	1,320	1,317	1,507	1,474	1,253	1,102	1,023	931
Interest on school debt	105	215	239	319	346	349	363	360	347	185	291	310	356	382	381	388	374	355

—Not available.
[1]Constant dollars based on the Consumer Price Index, prepared by the Bureau of Labor Statistics, U.S. Department of Labor, adjusted to a school-year basis.
[2]Data have been revised from previously published figures.
[3]Includes estimated data for subfunctions of food services and enterprise operations.
[4]Includes expenditures for guidance, health, attendance, and speech pathology services.
[5]Includes expenditures for curriculum development, staff training, libraries, and media and computer centers.
[6]Includes business support services concerned with paying, transporting, exchanging, and maintaining goods and services for local education agencies; central support services, including planning, research, evaluation, information, staff, and data processing services; and other support services.
[7]Includes expenditures for operations funded by sales of products or services (e.g., school bookstore or computer time).
[8]Includes expenditures for property and for buildings and alterations completed by school district staff or contractors.
NOTE: Excludes expenditures for state education agencies. Detail may not sum to totals because of rounding.
SOURCE: U.S. Department of Education, National Center for Education Statistics, Common Core of Data (CCD), "National Public Education Financial Survey," 1990–91 through 2012–13. (This table was prepared September 2015.)

Table 236.65. Current expenditure per pupil in fall enrollment in public elementary and secondary schools, by state or jurisdiction: Selected years, 1969–70 through 2012–13

State or jurisdiction	Unadjusted dollars[1]														
	1969–70	1979–80	1989–90	1999–2000	2002–03	2003–04	2004–05	2005–06	2006–07	2007–08	2008–09	2009–10	2010–11	2011–12	2012–13
1	2	3	4	5	6	7	8	9	10	11	12	13	14	15	16
United States	$751	$2,088	$4,643	$6,912	$8,044	$8,310	$8,711	$9,145	$9,679	$10,298	$10,540	$10,636	$10,663	$10,648	$10,763
Alabama	512	1,520	3,144	5,638	6,300	6,581	7,073	7,683	8,398	9,197	8,964	8,907	8,726	8,577	8,773
Alaska	1,059	4,267	7,577	8,806	9,870	10,116	10,847	11,476	12,324	14,641	15,363	15,829	16,663	17,475	18,217
Arizona	674	1,865	3,717	5,030	6,283	5,999	6,307	6,515	7,316	7,727	8,022	7,870	7,782	7,383	7,495
Arkansas	511	1,472	3,229	5,277	6,482	6,842	7,659	8,030	8,391	8,677	8,854	9,281	9,496	9,536	9,538
California	833	2,227	4,502	6,314	7,552	7,673	7,905	8,301	8,952	9,706	9,503	9,300	9,146	9,220	9,258
Colorado	686	2,258	4,357	6,215	7,384	7,478	7,826	8,166	8,286	9,152	8,782	8,926	8,786	8,594	8,693
Connecticut	911	2,167	7,463	9,753	11,057	11,436	12,263	13,072	13,659	14,610	15,353	15,698	16,224	16,855	17,321
Delaware	833	2,587	5,326	8,310	9,693	10,212	10,911	11,621	11,760	12,153	12,109	12,222	12,467	13,580	13,653
District of Columbia	947	2,811	7,872	10,107	11,847	12,959	13,915	13,752	15,511	16,353	19,698	20,910	20,793	19,847	20,530
Florida	683	1,834	4,597	5,831	6,439	6,793	7,215	7,812	8,567	9,084	8,867	8,863	9,030	8,520	8,623
Georgia	539	1,491	4,000	6,437	7,774	7,742	8,065	8,595	9,102	9,718	9,649	9,432	9,259	9,272	9,121
Hawaii	792	2,086	4,130	6,530	8,100	8,533	8,997	9,876	11,316	11,800	12,400	11,855	11,924	11,973	11,743
Idaho	573	1,548	2,921	5,315	6,081	6,168	6,319	6,469	6,648	6,951	7,118	7,100	6,821	6,626	6,761
Illinois	816	2,241	4,521	7,133	8,287	8,606	8,896	9,113	9,596	10,353	11,097	11,739	11,742	12,011	12,443
Indiana	661	1,708	4,270	7,192	8,057	8,431	8,919	8,929	9,080	8,867	9,254	9,479	9,251	9,588	9,421
Iowa	798	2,164	4,190	6,564	7,574	7,626	7,962	8,355	8,791	9,520	9,704	9,748	9,795	10,027	10,291
Kansas	699	1,963	4,290	6,294	7,454	7,776	7,926	8,640	9,243	9,894	10,204	9,972	9,802	10,021	10,011
Kentucky	502	1,557	3,384	5,921	6,661	6,864	7,132	7,668	7,941	8,740	8,786	8,957	9,228	9,327	9,274
Louisiana	589	1,629	3,625	5,804	6,922	7,271	7,669	8,486	8,937	10,006	10,625	10,701	10,799	10,726	10,539
Maine	649	1,692	4,903	7,667	9,344	9,746	10,342	10,841	11,644	11,761	12,183	12,525	12,576	12,335	12,655
Maryland	809	2,293	5,573	7,731	9,153	9,433	10,031	10,909	11,989	13,257	13,737	14,007	13,946	13,875	14,086
Massachusetts	791	2,548	5,766	8,816	10,460	11,015	11,642	12,087	12,784	13,690	14,534	13,956	14,612	14,844	15,321
Michigan	841	2,495	5,090	8,110	8,781	9,094	9,338	9,575	9,876	10,075	10,373	10,447	10,577	10,477	10,515
Minnesota	855	2,296	4,698	7,190	8,109	8,405	8,718	9,159	9,589	10,060	10,983	10,665	10,674	10,781	11,065
Mississippi	457	1,568	2,934	5,014	5,792	6,199	6,548	7,173	7,459	7,890	8,064	8,104	7,926	8,097	8,117
Missouri	596	1,724	4,071	6,187	7,495	7,542	7,858	8,273	8,848	9,532	9,617	9,721	9,461	9,514	9,702
Montana	728	2,264	4,240	6,314	7,496	7,825	8,133	8,626	9,191	9,786	10,120	10,565	10,719	10,569	10,662
Nebraska	700	2,025	4,553	6,683	8,074	8,452	8,794	9,324	10,068	10,565	10,846	11,339	11,704	11,492	11,743
Nevada	706	1,908	3,816	5,760	6,092	6,410	6,804	7,177	7,796	8,187	8,321	8,376	8,411	8,130	8,026
New Hampshire	666	1,732	4,786	6,860	8,579	9,161	9,771	10,396	11,036	11,951	12,583	13,072	13,548	13,774	14,050
New Jersey	924	2,825	7,546	10,337	12,568	13,338	14,117	14,954	16,163	17,620	16,973	17,379	16,855	17,982	18,523
New Mexico	665	1,870	3,446	5,825	7,125	7,572	7,834	8,354	8,849	9,291	9,648	9,621	9,250	9,013	9,164
New York	1,194	2,950	7,051	9,846	11,961	12,638	13,703	14,615	15,546	16,794	17,746	18,167	18,857	19,396	19,529
North Carolina	570	1,635	4,018	6,045	6,562	6,613	7,098	7,396	7,878	7,798	8,463	8,225	8,267	8,160	8,342
North Dakota	662	1,941	3,899	5,667	6,870	7,333	8,279	8,728	8,671	9,324	9,802	10,519	10,898	11,246	11,615
Ohio	677	1,894	4,531	7,065	8,632	9,029	9,330	9,692	9,937	10,340	10,669	11,224	11,395	11,323	11,276
Oklahoma	554	1,810	3,293	5,395	6,092	6,154	6,610	6,941	7,430	7,683	7,878	7,929	7,631	7,763	7,914
Oregon	843	2,412	4,864	7,149	7,491	7,618	8,069	8,645	8,958	9,565	9,611	9,268	9,516	9,485	9,183
Pennsylvania	815	2,328	5,737	7,772	8,997	9,708	10,235	10,723	10,905	11,741	12,299	12,729	13,096	13,091	13,445
Rhode Island	807	2,340	5,908	8,904	10,349	11,078	11,667	12,609	13,453	14,459	14,719	14,723	14,948	15,172	14,889
South Carolina	567	1,597	3,769	6,130	7,040	7,177	7,549	8,120	8,507	9,060	9,228	9,080	8,908	9,102	9,444
South Dakota	656	1,781	3,511	5,632	6,547	7,068	7,464	7,775	8,064	8,535	8,543	9,020	8,931	8,593	8,630
Tennessee	531	1,523	3,405	5,383	6,118	6,466	6,850	7,004	7,129	7,820	7,992	8,117	8,330	8,348	8,588
Texas	551	1,740	3,835	6,288	7,136	7,151	7,246	7,480	7,850	8,350	8,562	8,788	8,685	8,213	8,261
Utah	595	1,556	2,577	4,378	4,838	4,991	5,216	5,464	5,709	5,978	6,612	6,452	6,440	6,312	6,432
Vermont	790	1,930	5,770	8,323	10,454	11,211	11,972	12,805	13,629	14,421	15,096	15,666	14,707	16,651	17,286
Virginia	654	1,824	4,690	6,841	7,822	8,219	8,886	9,452	10,214	10,664	10,928	10,594	10,363	10,656	10,960
Washington	853	2,387	4,382	6,376	7,252	7,391	7,717	7,984	8,524	9,058	9,585	9,497	9,619	9,604	9,714
West Virginia	621	1,749	4,020	7,152	8,319	8,588	9,024	9,440	9,727	10,059	10,606	11,774	11,978	11,579	11,257
Wisconsin	793	2,225	5,020	7,806	9,004	9,240	9,755	9,993	10,372	10,791	11,183	11,507	11,947	11,233	11,186
Wyoming	805	2,369	5,239	7,425	8,985	9,308	10,190	11,437	13,266	13,856	14,628	15,232	15,815	15,988	15,815
Other jurisdictions															
American Samoa	—	—	1,781	2,739	2,976	3,493	3,607	3,561	3,481	—	—	—	—	—	—
Guam	766	—	3,817	—	5,781	—	6,781	—	—	—	—	8,443	9,300	8,949
Northern Marianas	—	—	3,356	5,120	4,519	4,241	5,034	4,924	4,707	4,535	5,753	5,676	7,623	6,246	5,733
Puerto Rico	—	—	1,605	3,404	4,260	4,147	4,979	5,470	6,006	6,520	6,955	7,021	7,429	7,403	7,981
U.S. Virgin Islands	—	—	6,043	6,478	6,840	7,239	8,387	8,768	9,669	12,358	12,768	14,215	13,226	11,669	10,661

See notes at end of table.

Table 236.65. Current expenditure per pupil in fall enrollment in public elementary and secondary schools, by state or jurisdiction: Selected years, 1969–70 through 2012–13—Continued

State or jurisdiction	Constant 2014–15 dollars[2]														
	1969–70	1979–80	1989–90	1999–2000	2002–03	2003–04	2004–05	2005–06	2006–07	2007–08	2008–09	2009–10	2010–11	2011–12	2012–13
1	17	18	19	20	21	22	23	24	25	26	27	28	29	30	31
United States	$4,707	$6,367	$8,654	$9,664	$10,455	$10,569	$10,755	$10,877	$11,222	$11,513	$11,621	$11,615	$11,414	$11,074	$11,011
Alabama	3,206	4,635	5,860	7,882	8,187	8,370	8,733	9,138	9,737	10,282	9,883	9,727	9,341	8,920	8,974
Alaska.........................	6,636	13,009	14,124	12,312	12,828	12,866	13,392	13,650	14,289	16,368	16,939	17,285	17,838	18,175	18,636
Arizona	4,225	5,686	6,929	7,032	8,166	7,630	7,787	7,749	8,483	8,639	8,845	8,594	8,331	7,679	7,667
Arkansas.....................	3,201	4,487	6,019	7,378	8,425	8,701	9,456	9,551	9,729	9,701	9,762	10,135	10,166	9,918	9,758
California	5,221	6,788	8,392	8,828	9,815	9,759	9,760	9,873	10,379	10,851	10,477	10,155	9,791	9,589	9,472
Colorado	4,298	6,884	8,121	8,689	9,596	9,511	9,662	9,713	9,606	10,232	9,682	9,747	9,406	8,938	8,893
Connecticut..................	5,706	6,606	13,910	13,634	14,371	14,544	15,141	15,547	15,837	16,333	16,928	17,143	17,368	17,530	17,720
Delaware.....................	5,222	7,886	9,928	11,617	12,598	12,988	13,471	13,822	13,635	13,586	13,351	13,347	13,346	14,124	13,967
District of Columbia	5,933	8,571	14,673	14,130	15,397	16,482	17,181	16,356	17,984	18,282	21,719	22,834	22,259	20,641	21,002
Florida........................	4,277	5,592	8,569	8,152	8,369	8,640	8,908	9,291	9,933	10,155	9,776	9,678	9,667	8,861	8,822
Georgia.......................	3,376	4,546	7,456	8,999	10,104	9,847	9,958	10,223	10,553	10,864	10,639	10,300	9,912	9,643	9,331
Hawaii.........................	4,962	6,361	7,698	9,129	10,528	10,853	11,108	11,746	13,120	13,192	13,671	12,945	12,765	12,452	12,013
Idaho..........................	3,591	4,720	5,444	7,430	7,904	7,844	7,802	7,694	7,707	7,771	7,848	7,754	7,302	6,892	6,916
Illinois........................	5,111	6,833	8,427	9,972	10,770	10,946	10,983	10,839	11,125	11,575	12,235	12,819	12,570	12,492	12,730
Indiana........................	4,143	5,207	7,960	10,055	10,472	10,723	11,011	10,620	10,527	9,913	10,203	10,351	9,903	9,972	9,638
Iowa	5,001	6,598	7,810	9,177	9,843	9,699	9,830	9,937	10,193	10,643	10,700	10,645	10,485	10,428	10,528
Kansas........................	4,378	5,984	7,996	8,799	9,688	9,889	9,785	10,276	10,716	11,062	11,250	10,890	10,493	10,422	10,242
Kentucky......................	3,145	4,748	6,307	8,278	8,657	8,730	8,806	9,121	9,206	9,771	9,687	9,782	9,878	9,700	9,488
Louisiana.....................	3,693	4,966	6,756	8,114	8,997	9,247	9,469	10,093	10,362	11,186	11,715	11,686	11,560	11,156	10,781
Maine	4,067	5,159	9,140	10,719	12,144	12,395	12,769	12,894	13,500	13,149	13,432	13,678	13,463	12,828	12,946
Maryland......................	5,070	6,990	10,388	10,809	11,895	11,997	12,385	12,974	13,900	14,821	15,146	15,296	14,930	14,431	14,410
Massachusetts...............	4,954	7,767	10,748	12,325	13,594	14,009	14,374	14,375	14,822	15,305	16,025	15,240	15,642	15,438	15,673
Michigan......................	5,272	7,608	9,487	11,338	11,412	11,566	11,530	11,388	11,450	11,263	11,437	11,408	11,323	10,896	10,757
Minnesota....................	5,356	7,001	8,757	10,052	10,539	10,689	10,764	10,894	11,118	11,247	12,110	11,646	11,426	11,212	11,320
Mississippi	2,862	4,781	5,468	7,009	7,528	7,884	8,085	8,531	8,648	8,820	8,891	8,849	8,485	8,422	8,303
Missouri......................	3,734	5,256	7,587	8,650	9,741	9,592	9,702	9,840	10,258	10,657	10,604	10,615	10,128	9,894	9,926
Montana.......................	4,559	6,901	7,903	8,827	9,742	9,952	10,042	10,260	10,657	10,941	11,158	11,538	11,475	10,993	10,907
Nebraska.....................	4,384	6,172	8,486	9,343	10,493	10,750	10,857	11,090	11,673	11,811	11,958	12,382	12,529	11,952	12,013
Nevada	4,422	5,817	7,112	8,053	7,918	8,153	8,401	8,536	9,039	9,152	9,174	9,147	9,004	8,456	8,211
New Hampshire	4,173	5,281	8,920	9,590	11,150	11,652	12,064	12,365	12,796	13,360	13,874	14,274	14,503	14,326	14,373
New Jersey	5,788	8,614	14,065	14,452	16,334	16,964	17,430	17,786	18,740	19,699	18,714	18,978	18,443	18,702	18,949
New Mexico	4,167	5,702	6,423	8,144	9,260	9,630	9,672	9,936	10,260	10,387	10,638	10,506	9,902	9,374	9,375
New York......................	7,483	8,995	13,142	13,765	15,546	16,073	16,919	17,383	18,024	18,776	19,567	19,839	20,187	20,173	19,979
North Carolina	3,573	4,986	7,490	8,452	8,529	8,410	8,763	8,797	9,133	8,718	9,331	8,981	8,850	8,486	8,534
North Dakota	4,150	5,919	7,268	7,923	8,928	9,327	10,222	10,380	10,053	10,424	10,808	11,487	11,667	11,696	11,882
Ohio...........................	4,239	5,775	8,445	9,877	11,219	11,484	11,520	11,527	11,521	11,559	11,763	12,256	12,198	11,776	11,535
Oklahoma.....................	3,470	5,517	6,138	7,542	7,917	7,827	8,162	8,256	8,614	8,589	8,686	8,659	8,170	8,074	8,096
Oregon........................	5,283	7,354	9,067	9,994	9,736	9,689	9,962	10,282	10,386	10,693	10,596	10,121	10,187	9,864	9,395
Pennsylvania.................	5,108	7,099	10,694	10,866	11,692	12,347	12,637	12,754	12,643	13,126	13,561	13,900	14,020	13,616	13,755
Rhode Island	5,055	7,135	11,013	12,449	13,450	14,090	14,405	14,996	15,597	16,165	16,229	16,078	16,002	15,780	15,232
South Carolina...............	3,554	4,870	7,026	8,570	9,149	9,127	9,321	9,658	9,863	10,129	10,175	9,916	9,536	9,467	9,661
South Dakota.................	4,111	5,429	6,545	7,874	8,509	8,990	9,216	9,248	9,349	9,542	9,419	9,850	9,561	8,938	8,828
Tennessee	3,326	4,644	6,346	7,525	7,951	8,224	8,458	8,331	8,266	8,742	8,812	8,864	8,918	8,682	8,785
Texas..........................	3,453	5,304	7,148	8,790	9,275	9,094	8,964	8,897	9,101	9,335	9,440	9,596	9,297	8,542	8,451
Utah	3,729	4,744	4,803	6,121	6,287	6,348	6,441	6,499	6,619	6,684	7,291	7,046	6,894	6,565	6,580
Vermont.......................	4,947	5,885	10,756	11,635	13,587	14,258	14,782	15,230	15,801	16,123	16,644	17,108	15,744	17,318	17,684
Virginia........................	4,100	5,561	8,742	9,564	10,166	10,454	10,971	11,242	11,842	11,922	12,049	11,569	11,094	11,082	11,212
Washington...................	5,345	7,277	8,169	8,914	9,425	9,401	9,527	9,496	9,882	10,126	10,569	10,371	10,297	9,989	9,938
West Virginia.................	3,893	5,331	7,493	9,998	10,812	10,922	11,141	11,228	11,277	11,245	11,694	12,858	12,823	12,042	11,516
Wisconsin.....................	4,969	6,783	9,356	10,914	11,702	11,751	12,044	11,885	12,025	12,064	12,330	12,566	12,790	11,683	11,443
Wyoming......................	5,044	7,223	9,765	10,381	11,678	11,838	12,581	13,602	15,381	15,491	16,129	16,634	16,930	16,628	16,179
Other jurisdictions															
American Samoa	—	—	3,321	3,830	3,868	4,443	4,453	4,236	4,036	—	—	—	—	—	—
Guam..........................	4,802	—	7,115	—	—	7,352	—	8,065	—	—	—	—	9,038	9,673	9,155
Northern Marianas............	—	—	6,256	7,159	5,873	5,393	6,215	5,856	5,457	5,070	6,344	6,198	8,161	6,496	5,864
Puerto Rico	—	—	2,992	4,758	5,537	5,274	6,147	6,506	6,964	7,289	7,668	7,667	7,953	7,699	8,165
U.S. Virgin Islands............	—	—	11,264	9,057	8,890	9,207	10,355	10,429	11,210	13,816	14,078	15,523	14,158	12,136	10,906

—Not available.
[1]Unadjusted (or "current") dollars have not been adjusted to compensate for inflation.
[2]Constant dollars based on the Consumer Price Index (CPI), prepared by the Bureau of Labor Statistics, U.S. Department of Labor, adjusted to a school-year basis. The CPI does not account for differences in inflation rates from state to state.
NOTE: Current expenditures include instruction, support services, food services, and enterprise operations. Expenditures for state administration are excluded in all years except

1969–70 and 1979–80. Beginning in 1989–90, extensive changes were made in the data collection procedures. Some data have been revised from previously published figures.
SOURCE: U.S. Department of Education, National Center for Education Statistics, *Statistics of State School Systems*, 1969–70; *Revenues and Expenditures for Public Elementary and Secondary Schools*, 1979–80; and Common Core of Data (CCD), "National Public Education Financial Survey," 1989–90 through 2012–13. (This table was prepared September 2015.)

Table 236.70. Current expenditure per pupil in average daily attendance in public elementary and secondary schools, by state or jurisdiction: Selected years, 1969–70 through 2012–13

State or jurisdiction	1969–70	1979–80	1989–90	1999–2000	2002–03	2003–04	2004–05	2005–06	2006–07	2007–08	2008–09	2009–10	2010–11	2011–12	2012–13
1	2	3	4	5	6	7	8	9	10	11	12	13	14	15	16
United States	$816	$2,272	$4,980	$7,394	$8,610	$8,900	$9,316	$9,778	$10,336	$10,982	$11,239	$11,427	$11,433	$11,362	$11,503
Alabama	544	1,612	3,327	5,758	6,642	6,812	7,309	7,980	8,743	9,345	9,385	9,554	9,296	8,927	9,486
Alaska	1,123	4,728	8,431	9,668	10,770	11,074	11,851	12,537	13,508	16,002	16,822	17,350	18,352	19,134	19,982
Arizona	720	1,971	4,053	5,478	6,784	6,908	7,218	7,637	8,038	8,630	8,732	8,756	8,646	8,224	8,388
Arkansas	568	1,574	3,485	5,628	6,981	7,307	8,243	8,748	9,152	9,460	9,651	10,237	10,332	10,397	9,853
California	867	2,268	4,391	6,401	7,601	7,708	7,989	8,416	9,029	9,673	9,439	9,680	9,540	9,608	9,686
Colorado	738	2,421	4,720	6,702	7,826	8,416	8,558	8,938	9,110	9,977	9,611	9,747	9,709	9,415	9,572
Connecticut	951	2,420	7,837	10,122	11,302	11,755	12,655	13,461	14,143	15,063	15,840	16,133	16,932	17,472	17,859
Delaware	900	2,861	5,799	8,809	10,257	11,049	11,770	12,330	12,612	12,789	12,753	12,928	13,228	14,253	14,129
District of Columbia	1,018	3,259	8,955	11,935	14,735	15,414	15,074	17,877	18,285	20,807	19,766	21,283	21,304	20,399	20,437
Florida	732	1,889	4,997	6,383	6,922	7,269	7,731	8,376	9,055	9,711	9,452	9,363	9,394	8,825	8,925
Georgia	588	1,625	4,275	6,903	8,308	8,278	8,577	9,164	9,615	10,263	10,178	9,855	9,577	9,492	9,437
Hawaii	841	2,322	4,448	7,090	8,770	9,341	9,705	10,747	12,364	12,774	13,397	12,887	12,603	12,735	12,535
Idaho	603	1,659	3,078	5,644	6,454	6,559	6,698	6,861	7,074	7,402	7,567	7,481	7,155	7,041	7,273
Illinois	909	2,587	5,118	8,084	9,309	9,710	10,020	10,282	10,816	11,624	12,489	13,083	13,180	13,459	13,808
Indiana	728	1,882	4,606	7,652	8,582	9,033	9,640	9,558	9,727	9,569	9,946	10,160	9,924	10,220	10,037
Iowa	844	2,326	4,453	6,925	7,943	8,017	8,341	8,460	8,789	9,128	10,482	10,524	10,565	10,748	10,915
Kansas	771	2,173	4,752	6,962	8,373	8,804	9,037	9,905	10,280	11,065	11,485	10,859	10,700	10,712	10,789
Kentucky	545	1,701	3,745	6,784	7,728	7,976	8,379	8,975	9,303	9,940	10,054	10,376	10,469	10,700	10,269
Louisiana	648	1,792	3,903	6,256	7,492	7,846	8,288	8,568	9,650	10,797	11,410	11,492	11,500	11,352	11,121
Maine	692	1,824	5,373	8,247	10,114	10,504	11,153	11,760	12,628	13,177	13,558	14,090	14,406	14,000	14,303
Maryland	918	2,598	6,275	8,273	9,801	10,140	10,790	11,719	12,836	14,122	14,612	14,937	14,876	14,746	15,010
Massachusetts	859	2,819	6,237	9,375	11,161	11,583	12,208	12,629	13,263	14,373	15,249	14,632	15,334	15,607	16,111
Michigan	904	2,640	5,546	8,886	9,847	10,049	10,328	10,598	10,932	11,155	11,493	11,661	11,560	11,462	11,495
Minnesota	904	2,387	4,971	7,499	8,440	8,934	9,273	9,761	10,185	10,663	11,602	11,366	11,368	11,424	11,754
Mississippi	501	1,664	3,094	5,356	6,186	6,601	6,994	7,699	7,988	8,448	8,610	8,670	8,436	8,623	8,685
Missouri	709	1,936	4,507	6,764	8,002	8,022	8,360	8,834	9,266	10,007	10,341	10,468	10,348	10,370	10,555
Montana	782	2,476	4,736	6,990	8,391	8,771	9,108	9,653	10,244	10,541	10,881	11,463	11,599	11,290	11,493
Nebraska	736	2,150	4,842	7,360	8,550	9,270	9,638	10,170	10,711	11,217	11,457	11,920	12,324	12,114	12,374
Nevada	769	2,088	4,117	6,148	6,496	6,780	7,198	7,720	8,372	8,891	8,865	8,869	9,035	8,677	8,525
New Hampshire	723	1,916	5,304	7,082	8,900	9,391	10,043	10,698	11,347	12,280	12,912	13,424	13,964	14,215	14,463
New Jersey	1,016	3,191	8,139	10,903	13,093	13,776	14,666	15,362	16,650	18,174	17,466	18,060	17,654	18,197	19,020
New Mexico	707	2,034	3,515	5,835	7,126	7,653	7,933	8,426	8,876	9,377	9,727	9,716	9,356	9,069	9,230
New York	1,327	3,462	8,062	10,957	13,211	13,926	15,054	16,095	17,182	18,423	19,373	19,965	20,517	20,881	21,172
North Carolina	612	1,754	4,290	6,505	7,057	7,114	7,628	7,940	8,373	8,415	9,167	8,930	8,943	8,828	9,041
North Dakota	690	1,920	4,189	6,078	7,315	7,791	8,776	9,239	9,203	9,637	10,113	10,976	11,356	11,643	12,090
Ohio	730	2,075	5,045	7,816	9,427	9,799	9,984	10,306	10,792	11,374	11,905	12,307	12,484	12,271	12,284
Oklahoma	604	1,926	3,508	5,770	6,540	6,599	7,086	7,449	7,968	8,270	8,423	8,511	8,165	8,281	8,450
Oregon	925	2,692	5,474	8,129	8,514	8,640	8,799	9,294	9,762	10,487	10,673	10,476	10,497	10,386	10,370
Pennsylvania	882	2,535	6,228	8,380	9,648	10,393	11,014	11,530	11,995	12,493	12,989	13,678	14,072	13,973	14,378
Rhode Island	891	2,601	6,368	9,646	11,377	12,279	12,685	13,917	14,674	15,843	16,211	16,243	16,346	16,498	15,208
South Carolina	613	1,752	4,082	6,545	7,759	7,893	8,302	8,795	9,226	9,823	10,007	9,887	9,735	9,823	10,200
South Dakota	690	1,908	3,731	6,037	7,192	7,607	7,960	8,273	8,506	9,047	9,457	9,683	9,431	9,095	9,138
Tennessee	566	1,635	3,664	5,837	6,674	7,047	7,426	7,580	7,843	8,459	8,676	8,810	9,146	9,235	9,370
Texas	624	1,916	4,150	6,771	7,714	7,711	7,814	8,085	8,484	9,029	9,260	9,528	9,418	8,862	8,926
Utah	626	1,657	2,764	4,692	5,247	5,427	5,654	5,809	6,116	6,841	7,081	6,877	6,851	6,787	6,950
Vermont	807	1,997	6,227	8,799	10,903	11,675	12,579	13,377	14,219	15,089	16,073	16,586	16,661	17,575	18,372
Virginia	708	1,970	4,672	6,491	8,300	8,761	9,441	10,046	10,913	11,410	11,696	11,383	11,123	11,385	11,748
Washington	915	2,568	4,702	6,914	7,882	8,051	8,362	8,702	9,233	9,846	10,423	10,242	10,402	10,413	10,553
West Virginia	670	1,920	4,360	7,637	9,025	9,076	9,321	9,756	10,080	10,605	11,122	12,378	12,505	11,982	11,658
Wisconsin	883	2,477	5,524	8,299	9,538	9,834	10,141	10,484	10,813	11,370	11,773	12,194	12,515	11,750	11,768
Wyoming	856	2,527	5,577	7,944	9,906	10,351	11,087	12,415	14,219	14,936	15,658	16,535	17,126	17,228	17,135
Other jurisdictions															
American Samoa	—	—	1,908	2,807	3,121	3,671	3,801	3,842	3,909	4,309	4,468	4,881	4,877	5,154	4,870
Guam	820	—	4,234	—	—	6,449	—	7,095	7,450	8,084	8,264	8,393	9,280	10,112	9,431
Northern Marianas	—	—	3,007	5,720	5,221	4,746	5,669	5,307	5,356	5,162	6,397	6,284	8,495	7,068	6,381
Puerto Rico	—	—	1,750	3,859	4,743	4,534	5,304	5,897	6,152	6,937	7,329	7,426	8,560	7,798	8,209
U.S. Virgin Islands	—	—	6,767	7,238	7,747	8,077	8,698	9,637	10,548	12,358	12,768	14,215	13,014	11,669	10,661

See notes at end of table.

Table 236.70. Current expenditure per pupil in average daily attendance in public elementary and secondary schools, by state or jurisdiction: Selected years, 1969–70 through 2012–13—Continued

State or jurisdiction	Constant 2014–15 dollars[2]														
	1969–70	1979–80	1989–90	1999–2000	2002–03	2003–04	2004–05	2005–06	2006–07	2007–08	2008–09	2009–10	2010–11	2011–12	2012–13
1	17	18	19	20	21	22	23	24	25	26	27	28	29	30	31
United States	$5,112	$6,926	$9,282	$10,337	$11,190	$11,319	$11,502	$11,630	$11,983	$12,278	$12,391	$12,478	$12,240	$11,817	$11,768
Alabama	3,408	4,914	6,202	8,051	8,632	8,664	9,024	9,491	10,136	10,447	10,348	10,433	9,951	9,285	9,705
Alaska........................	7,033	14,413	15,715	13,516	13,997	14,085	14,632	14,911	15,661	17,890	18,547	18,946	19,646	19,900	20,442
Arizona......................	4,512	6,008	7,555	7,659	8,817	8,786	8,912	9,083	9,319	9,648	9,628	9,562	9,255	8,554	8,581
Arkansas....................	3,556	4,800	6,496	7,868	9,073	9,293	10,178	10,405	10,611	10,576	10,641	11,179	11,060	10,813	10,080
California	5,433	6,913	8,184	8,948	9,879	9,803	9,863	10,010	10,469	10,814	10,407	10,571	10,213	9,992	9,909
Colorado	4,623	7,380	8,799	9,369	10,171	10,703	10,566	10,631	10,562	11,154	10,596	10,644	10,394	9,792	9,793
Connecticut................	5,960	7,378	14,608	14,151	14,688	14,950	15,625	16,010	16,397	16,841	17,465	17,617	18,126	18,172	18,270
Delaware....................	5,639	8,722	10,809	12,315	13,331	14,053	14,532	14,665	14,623	14,298	14,061	14,118	14,161	14,823	14,454
District of Columbia	6,380	9,936	16,691	16,685	19,150	19,604	18,612	21,262	21,200	23,261	21,793	23,241	22,806	21,216	20,907
Florida.......................	4,588	5,759	9,315	8,924	8,996	9,245	9,545	9,963	10,499	10,857	10,422	10,225	10,056	9,179	9,131
Georgia......................	3,684	4,955	7,968	9,651	10,797	10,529	10,590	10,899	11,147	11,474	11,222	10,762	10,252	9,872	9,654
Hawaii	5,266	7,078	8,292	9,912	11,398	11,880	11,982	12,782	14,335	14,281	14,771	14,072	13,492	13,245	12,823
Idaho.........................	3,780	5,058	5,737	7,891	8,388	8,341	8,270	8,161	8,201	8,276	8,343	8,170	7,659	7,323	7,440
Illinois.......................	5,698	7,886	9,539	11,302	12,098	12,349	12,372	12,230	12,540	12,996	13,770	14,287	14,109	13,998	14,126
Indiana......................	4,561	5,739	8,586	10,698	11,154	11,489	11,902	11,368	11,277	10,698	10,966	11,095	10,624	10,630	10,268
Iowa..........................	5,289	7,092	8,300	9,681	10,324	10,196	10,299	10,062	10,189	10,204	11,557	11,492	11,310	11,179	11,166
Kansas.......................	4,831	6,625	8,857	9,733	10,882	11,197	11,157	11,781	11,918	12,370	12,664	11,858	11,454	11,141	11,037
Kentucky....................	3,416	5,186	6,981	9,485	10,044	10,144	10,345	10,674	10,786	11,113	11,085	11,331	11,207	11,129	10,506
Louisiana	4,060	5,463	7,276	8,746	9,737	9,979	10,233	10,191	11,189	12,070	12,580	12,549	12,311	11,806	11,376
Maine	4,339	5,559	10,015	11,529	13,145	13,360	13,770	13,987	14,641	14,731	14,949	15,386	15,421	14,561	14,632
Maryland....................	5,754	7,920	11,697	11,566	12,738	12,896	13,322	13,938	14,881	15,788	16,111	16,312	15,925	15,336	15,356
Massachusetts............	5,382	8,595	11,626	13,107	14,506	14,731	15,073	15,021	15,377	16,069	16,813	15,979	16,415	16,232	16,482
Michigan....................	5,664	8,050	10,338	12,423	12,797	12,780	12,751	12,605	12,674	12,471	12,672	12,734	12,375	11,921	11,759
Minnesota..................	5,661	7,277	9,265	10,484	10,969	11,363	11,449	11,609	11,808	11,921	12,792	12,412	12,170	11,882	12,025
Mississippi.................	3,138	5,072	5,766	7,487	8,040	8,396	8,635	9,157	9,261	9,445	9,493	9,467	9,031	8,969	8,885
Missouri.....................	4,439	5,903	8,401	9,457	10,400	10,202	10,322	10,507	10,743	11,187	11,402	11,431	11,077	10,785	10,798
Montana.....................	4,899	7,550	8,829	9,772	10,905	11,155	11,246	11,481	11,876	11,784	11,997	12,518	12,416	11,742	11,757
Nebraska....................	4,614	6,554	9,025	10,289	11,112	11,790	11,900	12,096	12,419	12,540	12,632	13,017	13,193	12,599	12,659
Nevada	4,821	6,366	7,674	8,595	8,443	8,623	8,887	9,182	9,707	9,940	9,774	9,686	9,672	9,024	8,721
New Hampshire	4,530	5,841	9,886	9,902	11,567	11,943	12,400	12,724	13,155	13,729	14,237	14,659	14,948	14,784	14,796
New Jersey.................	6,367	9,729	15,171	15,242	17,016	17,521	18,108	18,271	19,303	20,318	19,258	19,721	18,899	18,926	19,458
New Mexico	4,430	6,200	6,551	8,157	9,261	9,733	9,794	10,022	10,290	10,483	10,725	10,610	10,016	9,432	9,443
New York....................	8,313	10,555	15,026	15,318	17,170	17,711	18,587	19,143	19,920	20,597	21,360	21,802	21,963	21,717	21,660
North Carolina	3,837	5,348	7,997	9,094	9,172	9,048	9,418	9,444	9,708	9,408	10,108	9,752	9,574	9,182	9,249
North Dakota	4,321	5,854	7,809	8,497	9,507	9,408	10,835	10,989	10,670	10,774	11,150	11,986	12,157	12,110	12,368
Ohio..........................	4,574	6,325	9,403	10,928	12,252	12,462	12,327	12,257	12,512	12,716	13,126	13,439	13,364	12,762	12,567
Oklahoma	3,787	5,873	6,538	8,066	8,499	8,393	8,749	8,860	9,239	9,246	9,287	9,295	8,741	8,613	8,644
Oregon......................	5,794	8,207	10,204	11,364	11,065	10,988	10,864	11,054	11,318	11,724	11,768	11,439	11,237	10,802	10,609
Pennsylvania..............	5,524	7,727	11,609	11,716	12,539	13,219	13,599	13,714	13,907	13,967	14,322	14,937	15,064	14,533	14,709
Rhode Island..............	5,584	7,930	11,869	13,486	14,787	15,616	15,662	16,552	17,013	17,712	17,874	17,738	17,498	17,158	15,558
South Carolina	3,838	5,341	7,608	9,151	10,084	10,038	10,250	10,461	10,697	10,982	11,033	10,796	10,422	10,216	10,435
South Dakota	4,322	5,816	6,955	8,440	9,347	9,674	9,828	9,840	9,862	10,114	10,427	10,574	10,096	9,460	9,348
Tennessee	3,547	4,986	6,829	8,161	8,673	8,962	9,169	9,016	9,093	9,457	9,566	9,620	9,790	9,605	9,586
Texas........................	3,911	5,840	7,736	9,467	10,026	9,808	9,648	9,617	9,836	10,094	10,210	10,405	10,083	9,217	9,132
Utah..........................	3,924	5,051	5,151	6,560	6,820	6,902	6,981	6,910	7,091	7,648	7,807	7,509	7,334	7,059	7,110
Vermont	5,057	6,088	11,606	12,302	14,170	14,849	15,531	15,910	16,486	16,869	17,722	18,112	17,836	18,279	18,795
Virginia......................	4,435	6,006	8,708	9,075	10,787	11,142	11,657	11,949	12,652	12,757	12,896	12,430	11,907	11,841	12,018
Washington................	5,735	7,829	8,765	9,665	10,244	10,240	10,325	10,351	10,705	11,007	11,492	11,184	11,136	10,830	10,796
West Virginia..............	4,197	5,854	8,128	10,676	11,730	11,544	11,508	11,604	11,687	11,856	12,262	13,517	13,387	12,461	11,926
Wisconsin	5,530	7,551	10,296	11,602	12,396	12,507	12,521	12,469	12,537	12,711	12,981	13,316	13,398	12,221	12,039
Wyoming....................	5,363	7,703	10,396	11,106	12,875	13,164	13,689	14,766	16,485	16,698	17,264	18,056	18,334	17,918	17,529
Other jurisdictions															
American Samoa	—	—	3,556	3,925	4,056	4,669	4,693	4,569	4,532	4,817	4,926	5,330	5,221	5,361	4,982
Guam	5,136	—	7,893	—	8,202	—	8,438	8,637	9,038	9,112	9,165	9,935	10,517	9,648
Northern Marianas.........	—	—	5,605	7,997	6,785	6,036	7,000	6,312	6,210	5,771	7,053	6,862	9,094	7,351	6,528
Puerto Rico..................	—	—	3,262	5,395	6,164	5,766	6,548	7,014	7,132	7,756	8,081	8,109	9,164	8,110	8,398
U.S. Virgin Islands..........	—	—	12,614	10,119	10,069	10,273	10,740	11,462	12,229	13,816	14,078	15,523	13,932	12,136	10,906

—Not available.

[1]Unadjusted (or "current") dollars have not been adjusted to compensate for inflation.
[2]Constant dollars based on the Consumer Price Index (CPI), prepared by the Bureau of Labor Statistics, U.S. Department of Labor, adjusted to a school-year basis. The CPI does not account for differences in inflation rates from state to state.
NOTE: Current expenditures include instruction, support services, food services, and enterprise operations. Expenditures for state administration are excluded in all years except

1969–70 and 1979–80. Beginning in 1989–90, extensive changes were made in the data collection procedures. There are discrepancies in average daily attendance reporting practices from state to state. Some data have been revised from previously published figures.
SOURCE: U.S. Department of Education, National Center for Education Statistics, *Statistics of State School Systems*, 1969–70; *Revenues and Expenditures for Public Elementary and Secondary Education*, 1979–80; and Common Core of Data (CCD), "National Public Education Financial Survey," 1989–90 through 2012–13. (This table was prepared September 2015.)

Table 236.75. Total and current expenditures per pupil in fall enrollment in public elementary and secondary education, by function and state or jurisdiction: 2012–13

State or jurisdiction	Total[1]	Total	Instruction	Total	Student support[4]	Instructional staff[5]	General administration	School administration	Operation and maintenance	Student transportation	Other support services	Food services	Enterprise operations[3]	Capital outlay[2]	Interest on school debt
1	2	3	4	5	6	7	8	9	10	11	12	13	14	15	16
United States	$12,020	$10,763	$6,543	$3,759	$600	$501	$217	$593	$1,018	$467	$363	$439	$22	$910	$347
Alabama	9,824	8,773	5,039	3,121	504	400	199	539	832	457	191	612	0	867	184
Alaska	20,397	18,217	10,115	7,525	1,521	1,260	259	1,113	2,149	556	667	509	68	1,891	288
Arizona	8,546	7,495	4,081	3,026	541	387	128	399	929	332	311	386	2	837	215
Arkansas	10,908	9,538	5,361	3,602	490	805	232	487	930	377	282	564	11	1,109	260
California	10,617	9,258	5,527	3,313	499	541	97	613	939	218	406	395	24	970	389
Colorado	10,092	8,693	5,038	3,292	425	470	141	606	803	263	583	319	44	883	516
Connecticut................	18,797	17,321	10,965	5,798	1,092	516	362	1,008	1,533	886	401	412	146	1,242	235
Delaware....................	15,090	13,653	8,477	4,713	593	257	186	733	1,460	726	759	462	0	1,256	182
District of Columbia	26,670	20,530	11,229	8,103	790	1,046	1,152	1,598	1,754	1,318	444	1,148	50	5,645	495
Florida........................	9,403	8,623	5,286	2,912	372	535	77	479	882	351	217	425	0	524	256
Georgia......................	10,218	9,121	5,656	2,933	424	469	116	556	675	421	271	506	27	959	138
Hawaii........................	12,536	11,743	6,918	4,124	1,086	452	63	732	1,125	373	294	700	0	793	0
Idaho..........................	7,455	6,761	4,071	2,322	379	286	156	381	615	331	174	366	1	504	190
Illinois........................	13,880	12,443	7,511	4,548	836	498	502	632	1,068	581	430	385	0	1,007	429
Indiana.......................	10,605	9,421	5,478	3,498	461	364	239	574	1,043	583	236	445	0	864	320
Iowa...........................	12,110	10,291	6,317	3,491	584	494	259	590	877	383	304	473	9	1,580	238
Kansas.......................	11,703	10,011	6,043	3,479	594	410	283	573	941	401	277	489	0	1,300	392
Kentucky....................	10,614	9,274	5,323	3,355	429	507	213	536	839	586	244	574	23	1,041	299
Louisiana...................	11,648	10,539	5,960	4,002	648	533	265	638	981	627	311	576	1	949	161
Maine.........................	13,471	12,655	7,524	4,689	795	646	424	703	1,312	653	156	439	3	537	279
Maryland.....................	15,423	14,086	8,756	4,939	633	755	115	977	1,276	773	412	390	0	1,145	192
Massachusetts............	16,483	15,321	9,871	5,032	1,092	682	241	643	1,349	652	373	418	0	910	253
Michigan	11,810	10,515	6,079	4,043	804	515	221	580	951	441	531	393	0	736	559
Minnesota..................	12,746	11,065	7,228	3,318	296	482	349	442	797	628	324	486	32	1,234	446
Mississippi	8,637	8,117	4,620	2,986	400	407	259	482	834	410	193	510	1	403	117
Missouri.....................	10,975	9,702	5,753	3,488	455	424	325	566	971	508	238	462	0	924	349
Montana.....................	11,577	10,662	6,353	3,838	680	408	330	586	1,056	525	251	455	16	801	113
Nebraska	13,068	11,743	7,470	3,487	511	383	372	548	981	367	325	487	298	984	341
Nevada	8,997	8,026	4,613	3,092	430	482	103	590	846	342	300	320	1	498	472
New Hampshire	14,663	14,050	9,023	4,653	1,050	434	471	769	1,158	614	158	373	0	383	230
New Jersey.................	19,639	18,523	11,106	6,828	1,851	594	369	874	1,802	918	419	403	186	667	449
New Mexico	10,410	9,164	5,262	3,459	928	248	199	549	950	305	280	437	6	1,246	0
New York....................	20,636	19,529	13,540	5,589	667	496	374	764	1,709	1,019	560	401	0	696	410
North Carolina	8,745	8,342	5,174	2,694	395	293	130	528	717	369	263	473	0	398	6
North Dakota	14,022	11,615	6,718	3,932	497	419	520	592	1,082	509	313	616	348	2,218	190
Ohio...........................	12,807	11,276	6,438	4,449	729	696	340	616	991	548	529	389	1	1,151	380
Oklahoma...................	8,813	7,914	4,378	2,945	529	344	261	431	856	272	253	510	81	828	71
Oregon.......................	10,375	9,183	5,321	3,516	655	336	121	591	763	445	605	342	4	584	607
Pennsylvania..............	14,934	13,445	8,276	4,652	716	462	403	610	1,301	674	486	455	62	919	569
Rhode Island	15,476	14,889	9,204	5,290	1,553	488	210	703	1,163	611	561	390	5	262	325
South Carolina	11,091	9,444	5,333	3,580	707	564	97	591	909	387	324	505	26	1,149	499
South Dakota...............	10,225	8,630	5,057	3,054	472	344	288	421	888	321	320	479	39	1,380	215
Tennessee	9,336	8,588	5,291	2,827	362	547	203	505	724	324	162	470	0	548	201
Texas	9,923	8,261	4,873	2,899	405	416	126	475	906	243	329	488	0	1,077	585
Utah	7,905	6,432	4,068	1,981	242	256	62	408	617	207	187	357	26	1,248	224
Vermont	18,038	17,286	10,894	5,888	1,312	734	386	1,077	1,422	559	399	490	15	622	130
Virginia......................	11,959	10,960	6,674	3,852	543	703	170	643	1,031	588	173	432	2	865	134
Washington................	11,456	9,714	5,630	3,633	650	588	175	572	870	400	377	334	118	1,367	374
West Virginia..............	11,536	11,257	6,539	4,047	554	459	218	606	1,160	853	197	671	0	205	74
Wisconsin	11,972	11,186	6,714	4,048	538	540	303	547	1,018	489	613	424	0	596	190
Wyoming.....................	18,187	15,815	9,329	6,005	929	937	314	866	1,560	783	617	474	6	2,350	23
Other jurisdictions															
American Samoa	—	—	—	—	—	—	—	—	—	—	—	—	—	—	—
Guam......................	10,928	8,949	4,624	3,810	840	164	71	541	1,436	236	522	515	0	1,906	73
Northern Marianas........	5,755	5,733	2,652	2,246	429	514	229	384	462	150	78	834	0	23	0
Puerto Rico...................	8,125	7,981	3,522	3,328	538	403	134	372	740	319	822	1,132	0	143	0
U.S. Virgin Islands..........	10,667	10,661	5,395	4,693	893	338	485	565	752	464	1,196	556	16	6	0

—Not available.
[1]Excludes "Other current expenditures," such as community services, private school programs, adult education, and other programs not allocable to expenditures per pupil in public schools.
[2]Includes expenditures for property and for buildings and alterations completed by school district staff or contractors.
[3]Includes expenditures for operations funded by sales of products or services (e.g., school bookstore or computer time).

[4]Includes expenditures for guidance, health, attendance, and speech pathology services.
[5]Includes expenditures for curriculum development, staff training, libraries, and media and computer centers.
NOTE: Excludes expenditures for state education agencies. "0" indicates none or less than $0.50. Detail may not sum to totals because of rounding.
SOURCE: U.S. Department of Education, National Center for Education Statistics, Common Core of Data (CCD), "National Public Education Financial Survey," 2012–13. (This table was prepared September 2015.)

Table 236.80. Total and current expenditures per pupil in fall enrollment in public elementary and secondary education, by function and state or jurisdiction: 2011–12

State or jurisdiction	Current expenditures, capital expenditures, and interest on school debt per pupil															
	Total[1]	Current expenditures												Capital outlay[2]	Interest on school debt
		Total	Instruction	Support services									Food services	Enterprise operations[3]		
				Total	Student support[4]	Instructional staff[5]	General administration	School administration	Operation and maintenance	Student transportation	Other support services				
1	2	3	4	5	6	7	8	9	10	11	12	13	14	15	16
United States	$11,991	$10,648	$6,483	$3,715	$589	$498	$213	$584	$1,006	$463	$361	$428	$22	$984	$360
Alabama	9,549	8,577	4,966	3,015	495	388	195	529	781	443	185	595	0	782	191
Alaska	18,873	17,475	9,645	7,286	1,466	1,148	254	1,058	2,166	531	663	477	68	1,108	290
Arizona	8,445	7,383	4,035	2,972	532	379	124	387	927	328	295	375	1	852	210
Arkansas....................	11,100	9,536	5,396	3,586	489	799	236	481	933	372	277	542	11	1,293	271
California	10,669	9,220	5,540	3,279	488	549	89	609	919	224	401	378	24	1,064	384
Colorado	9,928	8,594	4,948	3,297	422	475	146	583	822	258	591	307	43	826	508
Connecticut.................	18,324	16,855	10,659	5,650	1,069	502	340	976	1,518	853	392	408	138	1,226	243
Delaware....................	15,009	13,580	8,659	4,466	575	246	197	711	1,418	680	640	456	0	1,248	181
District of Columbia	25,038	19,847	11,301	7,720	706	748	1,050	1,742	1,741	1,295	438	783	43	4,740	452
Florida.......................	9,480	8,520	5,196	2,915	370	542	75	473	887	354	215	409	0	688	272
Georgia	10,348	9,272	5,734	3,009	428	477	122	557	690	417	317	503	27	929	146
Hawaii	13,206	11,973	6,861	4,431	1,125	425	58	731	1,375	415	301	681	0	678	556
Idaho	7,316	6,626	3,996	2,272	370	264	153	375	612	332	166	357	1	483	206
Illinois	13,468	12,011	7,233	4,405	802	482	497	610	1,039	565	409	373	0	1,041	416
Indiana	10,825	9,588	5,640	3,517	459	365	243	562	1,067	582	240	431	0	905	333
Iowa..........................	12,078	10,027	6,164	3,397	560	482	255	578	854	374	295	456	9	1,826	225
Kansas	11,840	10,021	6,090	3,457	593	419	296	576	938	394	240	475	0	1,404	415
Kentucky	10,720	9,327	5,401	3,347	428	510	208	530	853	580	238	556	24	1,129	264
Louisiana	11,954	10,726	6,108	4,031	646	567	263	645	971	630	309	586	1	1,059	169
Maine........................	13,274	12,335	7,374	4,537	806	622	382	670	1,271	632	153	422	1	641	298
Maryland	15,438	13,875	8,620	4,880	628	750	125	994	1,180	744	460	375	0	1,366	197
Massachusetts..................	16,273	14,844	9,605	4,837	1,050	680	206	604	1,299	634	363	403	0	1,172	257
Michigan	11,911	10,477	6,082	4,012	800	516	216	571	937	447	527	383	0	873	562
Minnesota	12,515	10,781	7,070	3,209	288	464	334	429	764	611	318	472	30	1,269	465
Mississippi	8,788	8,097	4,620	2,974	394	418	257	470	851	398	185	503	1	550	140
Missouri	10,888	9,514	5,670	3,389	444	412	307	551	951	498	226	454	0	986	389
Montana.....................	11,537	10,569	6,288	3,810	653	401	325	578	1,074	522	257	453	18	847	121
Nebraska	13,365	11,492	7,315	3,395	497	367	357	544	964	352	314	483	299	1,248	624
Nevada	9,421	8,130	4,764	3,057	436	409	122	608	862	333	287	308	1	744	547
New Hampshire	14,844	13,774	8,875	4,526	1,026	416	462	753	1,133	590	145	374	0	833	237
New Jersey	19,156	17,982	10,779	6,608	1,782	558	364	849	1,757	897	399	403	193	671	503
New Mexico	10,544	9,013	5,151	3,431	928	253	201	539	938	299	274	425	5	1,530	0
New York.....................	20,617	19,396	13,459	5,529	651	488	370	746	1,684	1,030	560	408	0	772	449
North Carolina	8,619	8,160	5,087	2,616	384	289	126	510	692	362	253	456	0	453	6
North Dakota	13,026	11,246	6,570	3,735	483	403	506	567	1,017	483	275	589	351	1,637	143
Ohio..........................	13,066	11,323	6,444	4,493	720	740	345	645	990	547	508	384	1	1,401	343
Oklahoma...................	8,591	7,763	4,318	2,878	529	320	249	414	857	269	239	490	77	745	83
Oregon.......................	10,830	9,485	5,509	3,619	673	353	127	603	783	452	629	354	3	789	556
Pennsylvania................	14,699	13,091	7,993	4,587	694	449	405	602	1,270	671	496	452	60	1,027	581
Rhode Island	15,745	15,172	9,405	5,376	1,567	534	214	740	1,199	587	535	386	6	257	315
South Carolina.................	10,848	9,102	5,146	3,444	677	548	98	549	868	401	304	487	25	1,197	548
South Dakota	10,155	8,593	5,053	3,014	470	344	287	419	870	321	304	473	53	1,349	212
Tennessee	9,216	8,348	5,189	2,713	360	523	176	478	715	313	150	445	0	663	204
Texas	9,929	8,213	4,850	2,890	399	411	124	466	909	237	344	473	0	1,107	609
Utah..........................	7,810	6,312	4,019	1,910	246	256	75	392	574	201	166	356	28	1,244	255
Vermont	17,303	16,651	10,434	5,746	1,278	702	341	1,079	1,390	548	408	460	12	511	141
Virginia.......................	11,650	10,656	6,458	3,772	519	707	165	616	1,019	577	168	424	2	857	137
Washington..................	11,481	9,604	5,596	3,561	641	556	179	557	865	397	366	332	115	1,478	399
West Virginia................	11,884	11,579	6,786	4,140	551	479	230	616	1,201	862	201	653	0	245	60
Wisconsin	11,979	11,233	6,748	4,058	535	530	313	552	1,027	486	615	427	0	519	227
Wyoming.....................	18,382	15,988	9,460	6,034	934	978	332	861	1,538	771	619	485	10	2,378	17
Other jurisdictions															
American Samoa	—	—	—	—	—	—	—	—	—	—	—	—	—	—	—
Guam......................	9,828	9,300	4,576	4,359	835	155	56	539	1,502	180	1,092	365	0	428	100
Northern Marianas........	6,354	6,246	2,696	2,707	599	501	228	492	416	277	194	844	0	108	0
Puerto Rico.................	7,536	7,403	3,266	3,086	499	374	124	345	687	296	763	1,050	0	133	0
U.S. Virgin Islands.........	11,675	11,669	6,092	4,873	916	329	461	594	827	448	1,298	681	23	5	0

—Not available.

[1]Excludes "Other current expenditures," such as community services, private school programs, adult education, and other programs not allocable to expenditures per pupil in public schools.

[2]Includes expenditures for property and for buildings and alterations completed by school district staff or contractors.

[3]Includes expenditures for operations funded by sales of products or services (e.g., school bookstore or computer time).

[4]Includes expenditures for guidance, health, attendance, and speech pathology services.

[5]Includes expenditures for curriculum development, staff training, libraries, and media and computer centers.

NOTE: Excludes expenditures for state education agencies. "0" indicates none or less than $0.50. Some data have been revised from previously published figures. Detail may not sum to totals because of rounding.

SOURCE: U.S. Department of Education, National Center for Education Statistics, Common Core of Data (CCD), "National Public Education Financial Survey," 2011–12. (This table was prepared September 2015.)

Table 236.90. Students transported at public expense and current expenditures for transportation: Selected years, 1929–30 through 2012–13

| School year | Average daily attendance, all students | Students transported at public expense | | Expenditures for transportation (in unadjusted dollars)[1] | | Expenditures for transportation (in constant 2014–15 dollars)[2] | |
		Number	Percent of total	Total[3] (in thousands)	Average per student transported	Total[3] (in thousands)	Average per student transported
1	2	3	4	5	6	7	8
1929–30	21,265,000	1,902,826	8.9	$54,823	$29	$758,038	$398
1931–32	22,245,000	2,419,173	10.9	58,078	24	953,439	394
1933–34	22,458,000	2,794,724	12.4	53,908	19	963,509	345
1935–36	22,299,000	3,250,658	14.6	62,653	19	1,079,066	332
1937–38	22,298,000	3,769,242	16.9	75,637	20	1,249,671	332
1939–40	22,042,000	4,144,161	18.8	83,283	20	1,410,459	340
1941–42	21,031,000	4,503,081	21.4	92,922	21	1,410,499	313
1943–44	19,603,000	4,512,412	23.0	107,754	24	1,463,581	324
1945–46	19,849,000	5,056,966	25.5	129,756	26	1,683,492	333
1947–48	20,910,000	5,854,041	28.0	176,265	30	1,790,467	306
1949–50	22,284,000	6,947,384	31.2	214,504	31	2,143,654	309
1951–52	23,257,000	7,697,130	33.1	268,827	35	2,420,773	315
1953–54	25,643,871	8,411,719	32.8	307,437	37	2,705,759	322
1955–56	27,740,149	9,695,819	35.0	353,972	37	3,116,357	321
1957–58	29,722,275	10,861,689	36.5	416,491	38	3,451,707	318
1959–60	32,477,440	12,225,142	37.6	486,338	40	3,917,402	320
1961–62	34,682,340	13,222,667	38.1	576,361	44	4,538,272	343
1963–64	37,405,058	14,475,778	38.7	673,845	47	5,170,988	357
1965–66	39,154,497	15,536,567	39.7	787,358	51	5,840,213	376
1967–68	40,827,965	17,130,873	42.0	981,006	57	6,827,263	399
1969–70	41,934,376	18,198,577	43.4	1,218,557	67	7,634,796	420
1971–72	42,254,272	19,474,355	46.1	1,507,830	77	8,672,386	445
1973–74	41,438,054	21,347,039	51.5	1,858,141	87	9,432,262	442
1975–76	41,269,720	21,772,483	52.8	2,377,313	109	10,145,611	466
1977–78	40,079,590	21,800,000 [4]	54.4	2,731,041	125 [4]	10,320,032	473 [4]
1979–80	38,288,911	21,713,515	56.7	3,833,145	177	11,685,975	538
1980–81	37,703,744	22,272,000 [4]	59.1	4,408,000 [4]	198 [4]	12,043,547 [4]	541 [4]
1981–82	37,094,652	22,246,000 [4]	60.0	4,793,000 [4]	215 [4]	12,054,160 [4]	542 [4]
1982–83	36,635,868	22,199,000 [4]	60.6	5,000,000 [4]	225 [4]	12,056,903 [4]	543 [4]
1983–84	36,362,978	22,031,000 [4]	60.6	5,284,000 [4]	240 [4]	12,286,937 [4]	558 [4]
1984–85	36,404,261	22,320,000 [4]	61.3	5,722,000 [4]	256 [4]	12,804,238 [4]	574 [4]
1985–86	36,523,103	22,041,000 [4]	60.3	6,123,000 [4]	278 [4]	13,317,526 [4]	604 [4]
1986–87	36,863,867	22,397,000 [4]	60.8	6,551,000 [4]	292 [4]	13,938,948 [4]	622 [4]
1987–88	37,050,707	22,158,000 [4]	59.8	6,888,000 [4]	311 [4]	14,072,885 [4]	635 [4]
1988–89	37,268,072	22,635,000 [4]	60.7	7,550,000 [4]	334 [4]	14,744,466 [4]	651 [4]
1989–90	37,799,296	22,459,000 [4]	59.4	8,030,990	358 [4]	14,969,488	667 [4]
1990–91	38,426,543	22,000,000 [4]	57.3	8,678,954	394 [4]	15,338,672	697 [4]
1991–92	38,960,783	23,165,000 [4]	59.5	8,769,754	379 [4]	15,017,937	648 [4]
1992–93	39,570,462	23,439,000 [4]	59.2	9,252,300	395 [4]	15,364,369	656 [4]
1993–94	40,146,393	23,858,000 [4]	59.4	9,627,155	404 [4]	15,583,182	653 [4]
1994–95	40,720,763	23,693,000 [4]	58.2	9,889,034	417 [4]	15,561,053	657 [4]
1995–96	41,501,596	24,155,000 [4]	58.2	10,396,426	430 [4]	15,926,180	659 [4]
1996–97	42,262,004	24,090,000 [4]	57.0	10,989,809	456 [4]	16,368,182	679 [4]
1997–98	42,765,774	24,342,000 [4]	56.9	11,465,658	471 [4]	16,777,693	689 [4]
1998–99	43,186,715	24,898,000 [4]		12,224,454	491 [4]	17,583,639	706 [4]
1999–2000	43,806,726	24,951,000 [4]	57.0	13,007,625	521 [4]	18,185,182	729 [4]
2000–01	44,075,930	24,471,000 [4]	55.5	14,052,654	574 [4]	18,995,386	776 [4]
2001–02	44,604,592	24,529,000 [5]	55.0	14,799,365	603 [5]	19,656,715	801 [5]
2002–03	45,017,360	24,621,000 [5]	54.7	15,648,821	636 [5]	20,338,019	826 [5]
2003–04	45,325,731	25,159,000 [5]	55.5	16,348,784	650 [5]	20,792,839	826 [5]
2004–05	45,625,458	25,318,000 [5]	55.5	17,459,659	690 [5]	21,556,975	851 [5]
2005–06	45,931,617	25,252,000 [5]	55.0	18,850,234	746 [5]	22,420,081	888 [5]
2006–07	46,132,663	25,285,000 [5]	54.8	19,979,068	790 [5]	23,163,673	916 [5]
2007–08	46,155,880	25,221,000 [5]	54.6	21,536,978	854 [4]	24,077,748	955 [4]
2008–09	46,173,477	—	—	21,679,876	860 [4]	23,903,735	948 [4]
2009–10	45,919,206	—	—	21,819,304	870 [4]	23,826,919	950 [4]
2010–11	46,118,737	—	—	22,370,807	888 [4]	24,429,167	970 [4]
2011–12	46,400,465	—	—	22,926,700	905 [4]	24,543,381	969 [4]
2012–13	46,567,834	—	—	23,233,698	914 [4]	24,164,005	950 [4]

—Not available.
[1]Unadjusted (or "current") dollars have not been adjusted to compensate for inflation.
[2]Constant dollars based on the Consumer Price Index, prepared by the Bureau of Labor Statistics, U.S. Department of Labor, adjusted to a school-year basis.
[3]Excludes capital outlay for years through 1979–80, and 1989–90 to the latest year. From 1980–81 to 1988–89, total transportation figures include capital outlay.
[4]Estimate based on data appearing in January issues of *School Bus Fleet.*
[5]Estimate based on data reported by *School Transportation News.*
NOTE: Some data have been revised from previously published figures.

SOURCE: U.S. Department of Education, National Center for Education Statistics, *Statistics of State School Systems,* 1929–30 through 1975–76; *Revenues and Expenditures for Public Elementary and Secondary Education,* 1977–78 and 1979–80; Common Core of Data (CCD), "National Public Education Financial Survey," 1987–88 through 2012–13; Bobit Publishing Co., *School Bus Fleet,* "School Transportation: 2000–2001 School Year" and "2010 Fact Book"; *School Transportation News,* "K–12 Enrollment/Transportation Data," 2001–02 through 2007–08; and unpublished data. (This table was prepared September 2015.)

CHAPTER 3
Postsecondary Education

Postsecondary education includes academic, career and technical, and continuing professional education programs after high school. American colleges and universities and career/technical institutions offer a diverse array of postsecondary educational experiences. For example, a community college normally offers the first 2 years of a standard college curriculum as well as a selection of terminal career and technical education programs. A university typically offers a full undergraduate course of study leading to a bachelor's degree, as well as programs leading to advanced degrees. A specialized career/technical institution offers training programs of varying lengths that are designed to prepare students for specific careers.

This chapter provides an overview of the latest statistics on postsecondary education, including data on various types of postsecondary institutions and programs. However, to maintain comparability over time, most of the data in the *Digest* are for degree-granting institutions, which are defined as postsecondary institutions that grant an associate's or higher degree and whose students are eligible to participate in Title IV federal financial aid programs.[1] Degree-granting institutions include almost all 2- and 4-year colleges and universities; they exclude institutions offering only career and technical programs of less than 2 years' duration and continuing education programs. The degree-granting institution classification currently used by the National Center for Education Statistics (NCES) includes approximately the same set of institutions as the higher education institution classification that was used by NCES prior to 1996–97.[2] This chapter highlights historical data that enable the reader to observe long-range trends in college education in America.

Other chapters provide related information on postsecondary education. Data on price indexes and on the number of degrees held by the general population are shown in chapter 1. Chapter 4 contains tabulations on federal funding for postsecondary education. Information on employment outcomes for college graduates is shown in chapter 5. Chapter 7 contains data on college libraries. Further information on survey methodologies is presented in Appendix A: Guide to Sources and in the publications cited in the table source notes. See chapter 5 for information on adults' participation in nonpostsecondary education, such as adult secondary education classes (e.g., to prepare for the GED test) or English as a Second Language (ESL) classes.

Enrollment

Fall enrollment in degree-granting postsecondary institutions increased by 21 percent between 1994 and 2004 (table 303.10 and figure 12). Between 2004 and 2014, enrollment increased 17 percent, from 17.3 million to 20.2 million. The number of full-time students rose 17 percent between 2004 and 2014, while the number of part-time students rose 16 percent. During the same period, the number of female students rose 15 percent, while the number of male students rose 19 percent. Although male enrollment increased by a larger percentage than female enrollment between 2004 and 2014, the majority (56 percent) of students in 2014 were female. During the most recent part of this period, between 2010 and 2014, enrollment decreased by 4 percent, reflecting decreases for both males (3 percent) and females (5 percent). In addition to enrollment in degree-granting institutions, about 456,000 students attended non-degree-granting, Title IV eligible, postsecondary institutions in fall 2014 (table 303.20). These institutions are postsecondary institutions that do not award associate's or higher degrees; they include, for example, institutions that offer only career and technical programs of less than 2 years' duration.

Enrollment trends can be affected both by changes in population and by changing rates of enrollment. Between 2004 and 2014, the number of 18- to 24-year-olds in the population rose from 29.3 million to 31.5 million, an increase of 7 percent (table 101.10), and the percentage of 18- to 24-year-olds enrolled in degree-granting postsecondary institutions rose from 38 percent in 2004 to 40 percent in 2014 (table 302.60). During this period, the enrollment rate for males in the 18- to 24-year-old age group increased from 35 to 37 percent. There

---

[1] Title IV programs, which are administered by the U.S. Department of Education, provide financial aid to postsecondary students.

[2] Included in the current degree-granting classification are some institutions (primarily 2-year colleges) that were not previously designated as higher education institutions. Excluded from the current degree-granting classification are a few institutions that were previously designated as higher education institutions even though they did not award an associate's or higher degree. The former higher education classification was defined as including institutions that were accredited by an agency or association that was recognized by the U.S. Department of Education, or recognized directly by the Secretary of Education. The former higher education institutions offered courses that led to an associate's or higher degree, or were accepted for credit towards a degree.

was no measurable change in the enrollment rate for females in this age group between 2004 and 2014. The enrollment rate for 18- to 24-year-old Hispanics rose from 25 percent in 2004 to 35 percent in 2014. In 2014, the enrollment rate for Whites in the same age group was 42 percent, and the enrollment rate for Blacks was 33 percent; neither of these rates was measurably different from the corresponding rate in 2004.

Like enrollment in degree-granting institutions for the United States as a whole, the number of students enrolled in degree-granting institutions located within individual states generally has been lower in recent years (table 304.10 and figure 13). Overall, fall enrollment in degree-granting institutions declined 0.5 percent between 2009 and 2014. Similarly, fall 2014 enrollment was lower than fall 2009 enrollment in the majority of states (27) and the District of Columbia. The District of Columbia's enrollment was 34 percent lower in 2014 than in 2009, Iowa's was 20 percent lower, and Michigan's was 10 percent lower. In contrast, enrollment was higher in 2014 than in 2009 in 23 states. The largest increase was in New Hampshire (44 percent), followed by Idaho (41 percent), Utah (16 percent), Delaware (10 percent), and West Virginia (10 percent).

Between fall 2004 and fall 2014, the percentage increase in the number of students enrolled in degree-granting institutions was higher for students under age 25 than for older students; however, the rate of increase is expected to be lower for students under age 25 than for older students in the coming years (table 303.40 and figure 14). The enrollment of students under age 25 increased by 18 percent from 2004 to 2014, while the enrollment of those age 25 and over increased by 16 percent. From 2014 to 2025, however, NCES projects the increase for students under age 25 to be 13 percent, compared with 18 percent for students age 25 and over.

Enrollment trends have differed at the undergraduate and postbaccalaureate levels. Undergraduate enrollment increased 47 percent between fall 1970 and fall 1983, when it reached 10.8 million (table 303.70). Undergraduate enrollment dipped to 10.6 million in 1984 and 1985, but then increased each year from 1985 to 1992, rising 18 percent before stabilizing between 1992 and 1998. Between 2004 and 2014, undergraduate enrollment rose 17 percent overall, from 14.8 million to 17.3 million; however, undergraduate enrollment in 2014 was lower than in 2010 (18.1 million). Postbaccalaureate enrollment increased 34 percent between 1970 and 1984, with most of this increase occurring in the early and mid-1970s (table 303.80). Postbaccalaureate enrollment increased from 1985 to 2014, rising a total of 77 percent. During the last decade of this period, between 2004 and 2014, postbaccalaureate enrollment rose 17 percent, from 2.4 million to 2.9 million.

Since fall 1988, the number of females in postbaccalaureate programs has exceeded the number of males. Between 2004 and 2014, the number of full-time male postbaccalaureate students increased by 24 percent, compared with a 28 percent increase in the number of full-time female postbaccalaureate students. Among part-time postbaccalaureate students, the number of males increased by 5 percent and the number of females increased by 8 percent.

Eleven percent of undergraduates in both 2007–08 and 2011–12 reported having a disability (table 311.10). In 2011–12, the percentage of undergraduates who reported having a disability was 11 percent for both males and females. However, there were some differences in the percentages of undergraduates with disabilities by characteristics such as veteran status, age, dependency status, and race/ethnicity. For example, 21 percent of undergraduates who were veterans reported having a disability, compared with 11 percent of undergraduates who were not veterans. The percentage of undergraduates having a disability was higher among those age 30 and over (16 percent) than among 15- to 23-year-olds (9 percent) and 24- to 29-year-olds (11 percent). Among dependent undergraduates, 9 percent reported having a disability, which was lower than the percentages for independent undergraduates who were married (13 percent) or unmarried (14 percent). Compared to undergraduates of other racial/ethnic groups, a lower percentage of Asian undergraduates (8 percent) had a disability. The percentage of postbaccalaureate students who reported having a disability in 2011–12 (5 percent) was lower than the percentage for undergraduates (11 percent).

The percentage of American college students who are Hispanic, Asian/Pacific Islander, Black, and American Indian/Alaska Native has been increasing (table 306.10). From fall 1976 to fall 2014, the percentage of Hispanic students rose from 4 percent to 17 percent, the percentage of Asian/Pacific Islander students rose from 2 percent to 7 percent, the percentage of Black students rose from 10 percent to 14 percent, and the percentage of American Indian/Alaska Native students rose from 0.7 percent to 0.8 percent. During the same period, the percentage of White students fell from 84 percent to 58 percent. Nonresident aliens, for whom race/ethnicity is not reported, made up 5 percent of college students in 2014.

Of the 20.2 million students enrolled in fall 2014, some 14 percent took at least one distance education course as part of their program that included a mix of in-person and distance education courses (table 311.15). In addition, 14 percent of students took their college program exclusively through distance education courses. The remaining 72 percent of students took no distance education courses. About 9 percent of students at public institutions took their coursework exclusively through distance education courses, in comparison to 15 percent of students at private nonprofit institutions and 54 percent of students at private for-profit institutions. About 12 percent of undergraduates took their coursework exclusively through distance education courses, compared to 25 percent of postbaccalaureate students.

Despite the sizable numbers of small degree-granting colleges, most students attend larger colleges and universities. In fall 2014, some 44 percent of institutions had fewer than 1,000 students; however, these campuses enrolled 4 percent of all college students (table 317.40). While 12 percent of campuses enrolled 10,000 or more students, they accounted for 60 percent of total college enrollment.

In fall 2014, the five postsecondary institutions with the highest enrollment were University of Phoenix, with 195,100 students; Ivy Tech Community College, with 91,200 students; Liberty University, with 81,500 students; Lone Star College System, with 69,400 students; and Miami Dade College, with 66,000 students (table 312.10).

Faculty, Staff, and Salaries

Approximately 3.9 million people were employed in degree-granting postsecondary institutions in fall 2013, including 1.5 million faculty, 0.4 million graduate assistants, and 2.0 million other staff (table 314.20). Out of the 1.5 million faculty in 2013, 0.8 million were full-time and 0.8 million were part-time faculty. From 2003 to 2013, the proportion of staff who were faculty rose from 37 percent to 40 percent. The proportion of other staff not engaged in teaching decreased from 54 percent in 2003 to 51 percent in 2013. The proportion of graduate assistants was 9 percent in both 2003 and 2013. The full-time-equivalent (FTE) student/FTE staff ratio at degree-granting institutions was 5.2 in both 2003 and 2013 (table 314.10 and figure 15). The FTE student/FTE faculty ratio was lower in 2013 (14.8) than in 2003 (15.6).

Colleges and universities differ in their practices of employing part-time and full-time staff. In fall 2013, some 47 percent of the employees at public 2-year colleges were employed full time, compared with 67 percent at public 4-year colleges and universities, 69 percent at private nonprofit 4-year colleges and universities, and 60 percent at private nonprofit 2-year colleges (table 314.30). A higher percentage of the faculty at public 4-year colleges and universities were employed full time (67 percent) than at private nonprofit 4-year colleges and universities (56 percent), private for-profit 4-year colleges and universities (15 percent), private nonprofit 2-year colleges (43 percent), private for-profit 2-year colleges (41 percent), or public 2-year colleges (30 percent). In general, the number of full-time staff has been growing at a slower rate than the number of part-time staff (table 314.20). Between 2003 and 2013, the number of full-time staff increased by 19 percent, compared to an increase of 29 percent in the number of part-time staff. Most of the increase in part-time staff was due to the increase in the number of part-time faculty (39 percent) and graduate assistants (24 percent) during this time period.

In fall 2013, some 7 percent of college and university faculty were Black (based on a faculty count that excludes persons whose race/ethnicity was unknown), 7 percent were Asian, 5 percent were Hispanic, 1 percent were American Indian/Alaska Native, 1 percent were of Two or more races, and less than 0.5 percent were Pacific Islander (table 314.40). About 79 percent of all faculty with known race/ethnicity were White; 41 percent were White males and 38 percent were White females. Staff who were Black, Hispanic, Asian, Pacific Islander, American Indian/Alaska Native, or of Two or more races made up 26 percent of graduate assistants and 29 percent of other staff in nonfaculty positions in 2013. The proportion of total staff made up of

Blacks, Hispanics, Asians, Pacific Islanders, American Indians/Alaska Natives, and persons of Two or more races was similar at public 4-year colleges (26 percent), private nonprofit 4-year colleges (24 percent), public 2-year colleges (25 percent), and private nonprofit 2-year colleges (26 percent), but the proportion was higher at private for-profit 4-year colleges (31 percent) and at private for-profit 2-year colleges (38 percent).

On average, full-time faculty and instructional staff spent 58 percent of their time teaching in 2003 (table 315.30). Research and scholarship accounted for 20 percent of their time, and 22 percent was spent on other activities (administration, professional growth, etc.).

Faculty salaries generally lost purchasing power during the 1970s. In constant 2014–15 dollars, average salaries for faculty on 9-month contracts declined by 16 percent during the period from 1970–71 ($75,700) to 1980–81 ($63,700) (table 316.10). During the 1980s, average salaries rose and recouped most of the losses. Between 1990–91 and 2014–15, there was a further increase in average faculty salaries, resulting in an average salary in 2014–15 ($80,200) that was 6 percent higher than the average salary in 1970–71. The average salary for males was higher than the average salary for females in all years for which data are available. The average salary for males in 2014–15 ($87,200) was slightly higher than in 2004–05 ($85,600 in constant 2014–15 dollars). For females, the average salary in 2014–15 ($71,900) also was slightly higher than the salary in 2004–05 ($70,300). In 2014–15, average salaries for males were 21 percent higher than for females, compared to 22 percent higher in 2004–05.

The percentage of faculty with tenure has declined. Of those faculty at institutions with tenure systems, 48 percent of full-time faculty had tenure in 2013–14, compared with 56 percent in 1993–94 (table 316.80). Also, the percentage of institutions with tenure systems decreased between 1993–94 (63 percent) and 2013–14 (49 percent). Part of this change was due to the expansion in the number of for-profit institutions (table 317.10), relatively few of which have tenure systems (1.2 percent in 2013–14) (table 316.80). At institutions with tenure systems, there were differences between males and females in the percentage of full-time instructional faculty having tenure. Fifty-seven percent of males had tenure in 2013–14, compared with 43 percent of females. In 2013–14, about 53 percent of full-time instructional faculty had tenure at public institutions with tenure systems, compared with 46 percent at private nonprofit institutions with tenure systems and 20 percent at private for-profit institutions with tenure systems.

Degrees

During the 2014–15 academic year, 4,627 accredited institutions offered degrees at the associate's degree level or above (table 317.10). These included 1,621 public institutions, 1,672 private nonprofit institutions, and 1,334 private for-profit institutions. Of the 4,627 institutions, 3,011 were 4-year institutions that awarded degrees at the bachelor's or higher level, and 1,616 were 2-year institutions that offered associate's degrees as their highest award. In 2013–14, associate's degrees were awarded by 3,006 institutions, bachelor's degrees by 2,588 institutions, master's degrees by 1,902 institutions, and doctor's degrees by 939 institutions (table 318.60).

Growing numbers of people are completing college degrees. Between 2003–04 and 2013–14, the number of associate's, bachelor's, master's, and doctor's degrees that were conferred rose (table 318.10). The doctor's degree total includes most degrees formerly classified as first-professional, such as M.D. (medical), D.D.S. (dental), and J.D. (law) degrees. During this period, the number of associate's degrees increased by 51 percent, the number of bachelor's degrees increased by 34 percent, the number of master's degrees increased by 34 percent, and the number of doctor's degrees increased by 41 percent. Since the mid-1980s, more females than males have earned associate's, bachelor's, and master's degrees. Beginning in 2005–06, the number of females earning doctor's degrees has exceeded the number of males. Also, the number of associate's, master's, and doctor's degrees awarded to females has increased at a faster rate than the number awarded to males. Between 2003–04 and 2013–14, the number of associate's degrees awarded to females increased by 51 percent, while the number awarded to males increased by 50 percent. The number of females earning master's degrees rose 36 percent during this period, while the number of males earning master's degrees rose 30 percent. The number of females earning doctor's degrees increased 48 percent, while the number of males earning doctor's degrees increased 34 percent. Between 2003–04 and 2013–14, the number of bachelor's degrees awarded to males increased by 35 percent and the number awarded to females increased by 33 percent. In addition to degrees awarded at the associate's and higher levels, 969,000 certificates were awarded by postsecondary institutions participating in federal Title IV financial aid programs in 2013–14 (table 320.20).

Of the 1,870,000 bachelor's degrees conferred in 2013–14, the greatest numbers of degrees were conferred in the fields of business (358,000), health professions and related programs (199,000), social sciences and history (173,000), psychology (117,000), biological and biomedical sciences (105,000), and education (99,000) (table 322.10). At the master's degree level, the greatest numbers of degrees were conferred in the fields of business (189,000), education (155,000), and health professions and related programs (97,000) (table 323.10). At the doctor's degree level, the greatest numbers of degrees were conferred in the fields of health professions and related programs (67,400), legal professions and studies (44,200), education (10,900), engineering (10,000), biological and biomedical sciences (8,300), psychology (6,600), and physical sciences and science technologies (5,800) (table 324.10).

In recent years, the numbers of bachelor's degrees conferred have followed patterns that differed significantly by field of study. While the number of degrees conferred increased by 34 percent overall between 2003–04 and 2013–14, there was substantial variation among the different fields of study, as well as shifts in the patterns of change during this time period (table 322.10 and figure 16). For example, the number of degrees conferred in computer and information sciences decreased 36 percent between 2003–04 and 2008–09, but then increased 46 percent between 2008–09 and 2013–14. In contrast, the number of bachelor's degrees conferred in the combined fields of engineering and engineering technologies increased 8 percent between 2003–04 and 2008–09, and then increased a further 29 percent between 2008–09 and 2013–14. In a number of other major fields, the number of bachelor's degrees also increased by higher percentages in the second half of the 10-year period than in the first half. For example, the number of degrees conferred in agriculture and natural resources increased by 9 percent between 2003–04 and 2008–09 and then by 41 percent between 2008–09 and 2013–14. The number of degrees conferred in health professions and related programs increased by 63 percent between 2003–04 and 2008–09 and then by 65 percent between 2008–09 and 2013–14. Also, the number of degrees conferred in public administration and social services increased by 16 percent between 2003–04 and 2008–09 and then by 40 percent between 2008–09 and 2013–14. Other fields with sizable numbers of degrees (over 5,000 in 2013–14) that showed increases of 30 percent or more between 2008–09 and 2013–14 included homeland security, law enforcement, and firefighting (49 percent); parks, recreation, leisure, and fitness studies (45 percent); multi/interdisciplinary studies (37 percent); and mathematics and statistics (35 percent). Some fields with sizable numbers of degrees did not have increases during the 2008–09 to 2013–14 period. The number of degrees in education was 3 percent lower in 2013–14 than in 2008–09. Also, the number of degrees in foreign languages, literatures, and linguistics was 4 percent lower in 2013–14 than in 2008–09; and the number of degrees in philosophy and religious studies was also 4 percent lower.

Among first-time students who were seeking a bachelor's degree or its equivalent and attending a 4-year institution full time in 2008, about 40 percent completed a bachelor's degree or its equivalent at that institution within 4 years, while 55 percent did so within 5 years, and 60 percent did so within 6 years (table 326.10). These graduation rates were calculated as the total number of completers within the specified time to degree attainment divided by the cohort of students who first enrolled at that institution in 2008. Graduation rates were higher at private nonprofit institutions than at public or private for-profit institutions. For example, the 6-year graduation rate for the 2008 cohort at private nonprofit institutions was 65 percent, compared with 58 percent at public institutions and 27 percent at private for-profit institutions. Graduation rates also varied by race/ethnicity. At 4-year institutions overall, the 6-year graduation rate for Asians in the 2008 cohort was 71 percent, compared with 65 percent for students of Two or more races, 63 percent for Whites, 54 percent for Hispanics, 50 percent for Pacific Islanders, 41 percent for Blacks, and 41 percent for American Indians/Alaska Natives.

Finances and Financial Aid

For the 2014–15 academic year, annual current dollar prices for undergraduate tuition, fees, room, and board were estimated to be $16,188 at public institutions, $41,970 at private nonprofit institutions, and $23,372 at private for-profit institutions (table 330.10). Between 2004–05 and 2014–15, prices for undergraduate tuition, fees, room, and board at public institutions rose 33 percent, and prices at private nonprofit institutions rose 26 percent, after adjustment for inflation. The price for undergraduate tuition, fees, room, and board at private for-profit institutions decreased 18 percent between 2004–05 and 2014–15, after adjustment for inflation.

In 2011–12, about 84 percent of full-time undergraduate students received financial aid (grants, loans, work-study, or aid of multiple types) (table 331.10). About 73 percent of full-time undergraduates received federal financial aid in 2011–12, and 57 percent received aid from nonfederal sources. (Some students receive aid from both federal and nonfederal sources.) Section 484(r) of the Higher Education Act of 1965, as amended, suspends a student's eligibility for Title IV federal financial aid if the student is convicted of certain drug-related offenses that were committed while the student was receiving Title IV aid. For 2013–14, less than 0.01 percent of postsecondary students had their eligibility to receive aid suspended due to a conviction (table C).

Table C. Suspension of eligibility for Title IV federal student financial aid due to a drug-related conviction or failure to report conviction status on aid application form: 2007–08 through 2013–14

| | | Suspension of eligibility | | |
| | No suspension of eligibility | For part of award year | For full award year | |
Award year			Due to conviction	Due to failure to report
2007–08				
Number..........	14,610,371	361	2,832	2,433
Percent..........	99.96	#	0.02	0.02
2008–09				
Number..........	16,410,285	398	1,064	724
Percent..........	99.99	#	0.01	#
2009–10				
Number..........	19,487,370	666	1,751	879
Percent..........	99.98	#	0.01	#
2010–11				
Number..........	21,114,404	606	1,284	406
Percent..........	99.99	#	0.01	#
2011–12				
Number..........	21,947,204	404	968	732
Percent..........	99.99	#	#	#
2012–13				
Number..........	21,803,176	322	778	432
Percent..........	99.99	#	#	#
2013–14				
Number..........	21,192,389	257	572	535
Percent..........	99.99	#	#	#

#Rounds to zero.
NOTE: It is not possible to determine whether a student who lost eligibility due to a drug conviction otherwise would have received Title IV aid, since there are other reasons why an applicant may not receive aid. Detail may not sum to totals because of rounding.
SOURCE: U.S. Department of Education, Federal Student Aid, Free Application for Federal Student Aid (FAFSA), unpublished data.

In 2013–14, total revenue was $353 billion at public institutions, $229 billion at private nonprofit institutions, and $23 billion at private for-profit institutions (tables 333.10, 333.40, and 333.55 and figures 17, 18, and 19). The category of student tuition and fees typically accounts for a significant percentage of total revenue and was the largest single revenue source at both private nonprofit and for-profit institutions in 2013–14 (30 and 90 percent, respectively). Tuition and fees accounted for 20 percent of revenue at public institutions in 2013–14. Public institutions typically report Pell grants as revenue from federal grants, while private institutions report Pell grants as revenue from tuition and fees; this difference in reporting contributes to the smaller percentage of revenue reported as tuition and fees at public institutions compared to private institutions. At public institutions, the share of revenue from tuition and fees in 2013–14 (20 percent) was higher than the share from state appropriations (18 percent), while the share from state appropriations in 2007–08 (25 percent) was higher than that from tuition and fees (18 percent) (table 333.10). In 2013–14, tuition and fees constituted the largest revenue category at private nonprofit 2- and 4-year institutions, private for-profit 2- and 4-year institutions, and public 4-year institutions (tables 333.10, 333.40, and 333.55). At public 2-year institutions, tuition and fees constituted the fourth largest revenue category.

Average total expenditures of institutions per full-time-equivalent (FTE) student in 2013–14—shown in constant 2014–15 dollars throughout this paragraph—varied by institution control and level, as did changes in average total expenditures per FTE student between 2008–09 and 2013–14 (after adjustment for inflation). In 2013–14, average total expenditures per full-time-equivalent (FTE) student at public degree-granting colleges were $30,500 (table 334.10). The 2013–14 total expenditures per FTE student were 2 percent higher than in 2008–09. In 2013–14, public 4-year colleges had average total expenditures per FTE student of $40,000, compared with $13,900 at public 2-year colleges. At private nonprofit institutions, total expenditures per FTE student in 2013–14 were 2 percent higher than in 2008–09 (table 334.30). In 2013–14, total expenditures per FTE student at private nonprofit institutions averaged $52,000 at 4-year colleges and $20,800 at 2-year colleges. The expenditures per FTE student at private for-profit institutions in 2013–14 ($19,700) were 39 percent higher than in 2008–09 (table 334.50). In 2013–14, total expenditures per FTE student at private for-profit institutions averaged $20,700 at 4-year colleges and $16,600 at 2-year colleges. This difference in expenditures per FTE student between 4-year and 2-year for-profit colleges was relatively small compared to the differences between 4-year and 2-year public and private nonprofit colleges.

At the end of fiscal year 2014, the market value of the endowment funds of colleges and universities was $535 billion, reflecting an increase of 15 percent compared to the beginning of the fiscal year, when the total was $466 billion (table 333.90). At the end of fiscal year 2014, the 120 colleges with the largest endowments accounted for $399 billion, or about three-fourths of the national total. The five colleges with the largest endowments in 2014 were Harvard University ($36 billion), the University of Texas System ($25 billion), Yale University ($24 billion), Stanford University ($21 billion), and Princeton University ($21 billion).

Figure 12. Enrollment, degrees conferred, and expenditures in degree-granting postsecondary institutions: 1960–61 through 2014–15

Fall enrollment, in millions

Degrees, in millions

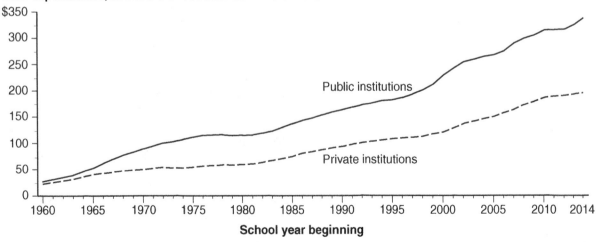

Total expenditures, in billions of constant 2014–15 dollars

NOTE: Expenditure data for the school year beginning in 2014 (2014–15) are estimated. Degree data for the school year beginning in 2014 are projected. Doctor's degrees include Ph.D., Ed.D., and comparable degrees at the doctoral level, as well as such degrees as M.D., D.D.S., and law degrees that were formerly classified as first-professional degrees.

SOURCE: U.S. Department of Education, National Center for Education Statistics, *Opening Fall Enrollment in Higher Education*, 1960 through 1965; *Financial Statistics of Higher Education*, 1959–60 through 1964–65; *Earned Degrees Conferred*, 1959–60 through 1964–65; Degrees Conferred Projection Model, 1980–81 through 2025–26; Higher Education General Information Survey (HEGIS), "Fall Enrollment in Institutions of Higher Education," "Degrees and Other Formal Awards Conferred," and "Financial Statistics of Institutions of Higher Education" surveys, 1965–66 through 1985–86; Integrated Postsecondary Education Data System (IPEDS), "Fall Enrollment Survey" (IPEDS-EF:86–99), "Completions Survey" (IPEDS-C:87–99), and "Finance Survey" (IPEDS-F:FY87–99); IPEDS Fall 2000 through Fall 2014, Completions component; and IPEDS Spring 2001 through Spring 2015, Fall Enrollment and Finance components.

Figure 13. Percentage change in total enrollment in degree-granting postsecondary institutions, by state: Fall 2009 to fall 2014

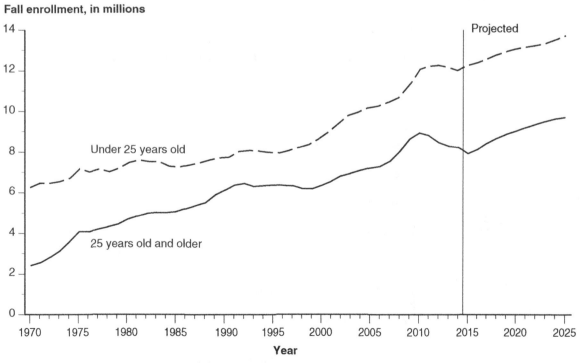

Percent change

Increase of 5 percent or more (11 states)

Increase of less than 5 percent (12 states)

Decrease of less than 5 percent (23 states)

Decrease of 5 percent or more (4 states & DC)

SOURCE: U.S. Department of Education, National Center for Education Statistics, Integrated Postsecondary Education Data System (IPEDS), Spring 2010 and Spring 2015, Fall enrollment component.

Figure 14. Enrollment in degree-granting postsecondary institutions, by age: Fall 1970 through fall 2025

Fall enrollment, in millions

Projected

Under 25 years old

25 years old and older

SOURCE: U.S. Department of Education, National Center for Education Statistics, Higher Education General Information Survey (HEGIS), "Fall Enrollment in Colleges and Universities" surveys, 1970 through 1985; Integrated Postsecondary Education Data System (IPEDS), "Fall Enrollment Survey" (IPEDS-EF:86–99); IPEDS Spring 2001 through Spring 2015, Fall Enrollment component; and Enrollment in Degree-Granting Institutions Projection Model, 1980 through 2025. U.S. Department of Commerce, Census Bureau, Current Population Survey (CPS), October, selected years, 1970 through 2014.

Figure 15. Ratio of full-time-equivalent (FTE) students to total FTE staff and to FTE faculty in degree-granting postsecondary institutions, by control of institution: 1993, 2003, and 2013

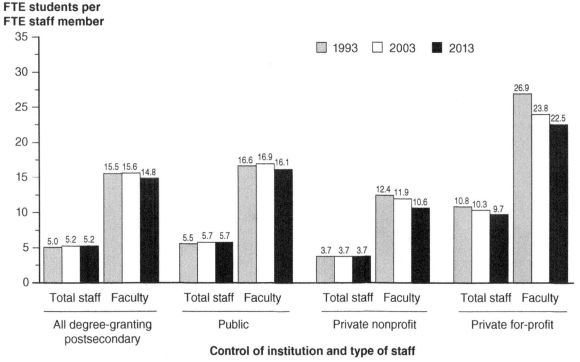

SOURCE: U.S. Department of Education, National Center for Education Statistics, Integrated Postsecondary Education Data System (IPEDS), "Fall Enrollment Survey" (IPEDS-EF:93) and "Fall Staff Survey" (IPEDS-S:93); IPEDS Spring 2003 and 2013, Enrollment component; and IPEDS Winter 2003–04 and Spring 2014, Human Resources component, Fall Staff section.

Figure 16. Bachelor's degrees conferred by postsecondary institutions in selected fields of study: 2003–04, 2008–09, and 2013–14

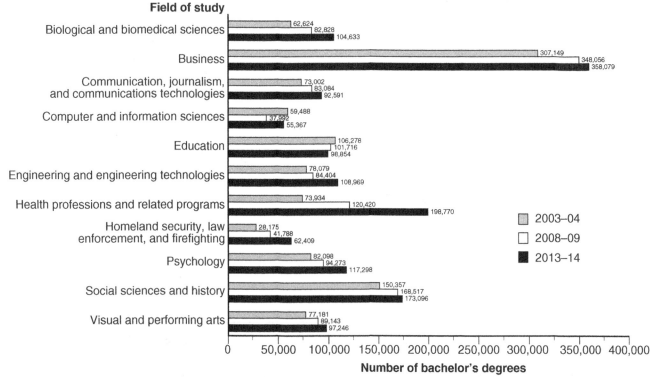

SOURCE: U.S. Department of Education, National Center for Education Statistics, Integrated Postsecondary Education Data System (IPEDS), Fall 2004, Fall 2009, and Fall 2014, Completions component.

Figure 17. Percentage distribution of total revenues of public degree-granting postsecondary institutions, by source of funds: 2013–14

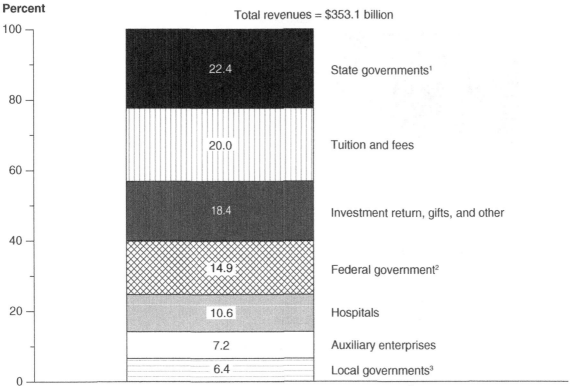

Total revenues = $353.1 billion

State governments[1] — 22.4

Tuition and fees — 20.0

Investment return, gifts, and other — 18.4

Federal government[2] — 14.9

Hospitals — 10.6

Auxiliary enterprises — 7.2

Local governments[3] — 6.4

Source of funds

[1]Revenues from state governments include operating grants and contracts, nonoperating revenue appropriations, nonoperating grants, and capital appropriations.
[2]Revenues from the federal government include operating grants and contracts, funds for independent operations, nonoperating revenue appropriations, and nonoperating grants.
[3]Revenues from local governments include operating grants and contracts, private grants and contracts, nonoperating revenue appropriations, and nonoperating grants.
NOTE: Detail may not sum to totals because of rounding.
SOURCE: U.S. Department of Education, National Center for Education Statistics, Integrated Postsecondary Education Data System (IPEDS), Spring 2015, Finance component.

Figure 18. Percentage distribution of total revenues of private nonprofit degree-granting postsecondary institutions, by source of funds: 2013–14

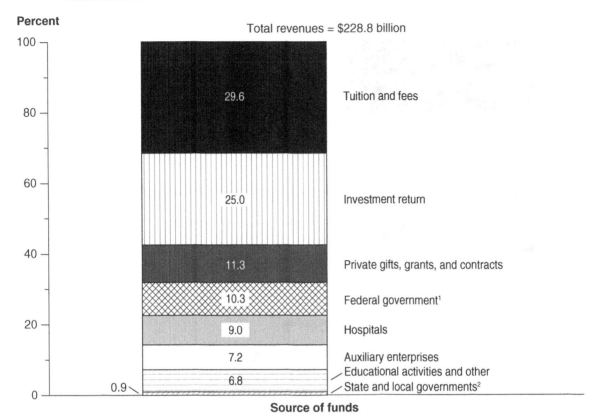

Percent

Total revenues = $228.8 billion

29.6	Tuition and fees
25.0	Investment return
11.3	Private gifts, grants, and contracts
10.3	Federal government[1]
9.0	Hospitals
7.2	Auxiliary enterprises
6.8	Educational activities and other
0.9	State and local governments[2]

Source of funds

[1]Includes appropriations, grants, contracts, and independent operations.
[2]Includes appropriations, grants, and contracts.
NOTE: Detail may not sum to totals because of rounding.
SOURCE: U.S. Department of Education, National Center for Education Statistics, Integrated Postsecondary Education Data System (IPEDS), Spring 2015, Finance component.

Figure 19. Percentage distribution of total revenues of private for-profit degree-granting postsecondary institutions, by source of funds: 2013–14

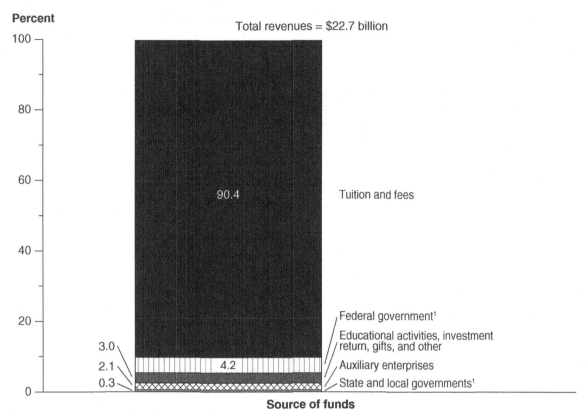

¹Includes appropriations, grants, and contracts.
NOTE: Detail may not sum to totals because of rounding.
SOURCE: U.S. Department of Education, National Center for Education Statistics, Integrated Postsecondary Education Data System (IPEDS), Spring 2015, Finance component.

Table 301.10. Enrollment, staff, and degrees/certificates conferred in degree-granting and non-degree-granting postsecondary institutions, by control and level of institution, sex of student, type of staff, and level of degree: Fall 2013, fall 2014, and 2013–14

Level of institution, sex of student, type of staff, and level of degree	Total[1]	Degree-granting institutions					Non-degree-granting institutions				
		Total	Public	Private			Total	Public	Private		
				Total	Nonprofit	For-profit			Total	Nonprofit	For-profit
1	2	3	4	5	6	7	8	9	10	11	12
Enrollment, fall 2014											
Total	20,663,464	20,207,369	14,655,015	5,552,354	3,996,089	1,556,265	456,095	110,858	345,237	19,005	326,232
4-year institutions	13,493,388	13,492,884	8,257,250	5,235,634	3,965,724	1,269,910	504	0	504	504	0
Males	5,903,390	5,903,282	3,747,975	2,155,307	1,692,461	462,846	108	0	108	108	0
Females	7,589,998	7,589,602	4,509,275	3,080,327	2,273,263	807,064	396	0	396	396	0
2-year institutions	6,845,040	6,714,485	6,397,765	316,720	30,365	286,355	130,555	59,967	70,588	8,922	61,666
Males	2,955,965	2,893,779	2,790,959	102,820	11,264	91,556	62,186	33,635	28,551	2,397	26,154
Females	3,889,075	3,820,706	3,606,806	213,900	19,101	194,799	68,369	26,332	42,037	6,525	35,512
Less-than-2-year institutions	325,036	†	†	†	†	†	325,036	50,891	274,145	9,579	264,566
Males	90,670	†	†	†	†	†	90,670	23,811	66,859	3,853	63,006
Females	234,366	†	†	†	†	†	234,366	27,080	207,286	5,726	201,560
Staff, fall 2013											
Total	3,969,226	3,896,053	2,527,284	1,368,769	1,156,998	211,771	73,173	22,452	50,721	4,394	46,327
Faculty (instruction/research/ public service)	1,582,360	1,545,381	968,734	576,647	449,072	127,575	36,979	11,606	25,373	2,015	23,358
Instruction	1,474,768	1,437,789	899,741	538,048	410,675	127,373	36,979	11,606	25,373	2,015	23,358
Research	81,670	81,670	51,478	30,192	30,080	112	†	†	†	†	†
Public service	25,922	25,922	17,515	8,407	8,317	90	†	†	†	†	†
Graduate assistants	363,416	363,416	287,852	75,564	75,113	451	†	†	†	†	†
Librarians, curators, and archivists	44,906	44,677	24,759	19,918	18,318	1,600	229	79	150	42	108
Student and academic affairs and other education services	165,006	158,653	105,772	52,881	39,793	13,088	6,353	2,640	3,713	438	3,275
Management	259,646	252,615	139,745	112,870	96,421	16,449	7,031	1,305	5,726	468	5,258
Business and financial operations	196,073	193,065	127,211	65,854	58,637	7,217	3,008	461	2,547	137	2,410
Computer, engineering, and science	232,338	231,714	158,570	73,144	70,416	2,728	624	340	284	25	259
Community, social service, legal, arts, design, entertainment, sports, and media	167,955	167,466	101,142	66,324	58,422	7,902	489	314	175	42	133
Healthcare practitioners and technicians	118,310	117,576	76,793	40,783	40,530	253	734	450	284	130	154
Service occupations	244,521	241,064	160,420	80,644	78,358	2,286	3,457	1,636	1,821	491	1,330
Sales and related occupations	17,813	15,400	4,994	10,406	4,540	5,866	2,413	32	2,381	37	2,344
Office and administrative support	480,789	470,167	301,625	168,542	142,976	25,566	10,622	2,901	7,721	526	7,195
Natural resources, construction, and maintenance	76,412	75,401	55,470	19,931	19,404	527	1,011	509	502	33	469
Production, transportation, and material moving	19,681	19,458	14,197	5,261	4,998	263	223	179	44	10	34
Degrees/certificates conferred, 2013–14											
Total	4,774,644	4,470,351	2,925,339	1,545,012	1,030,018	514,994	304,293	65,501	238,792	12,526	226,266
Less-than-1-year and 1- to less-than-4-year certificates	969,353	665,118	510,757	154,361	18,204	136,157	304,235	65,501	238,734	12,526	226,208
4-year institutions	104,754	104,690	61,227	43,463	12,637	30,826	64	0	64	64	0
Males	42,457	42,450	29,169	13,281	5,044	8,237	7	0	7	7	0
Females	62,297	62,240	32,058	30,182	7,593	22,589	57	0	57	57	0
2-year institutions	632,683	560,428	449,530	110,898	5,567	105,331	72,255	33,198	39,057	4,198	34,859
Males	282,548	251,434	216,893	34,541	1,918	32,623	31,114	15,938	15,176	1,280	13,896
Females	350,135	308,994	232,637	76,357	3,649	72,708	41,141	17,260	23,881	2,918	20,963
Less-than-2-year institutions	231,916	†	†	†	†	†	231,916	32,303	199,613	8,264	191,349
Males	65,789	†	†	†	†	†	65,789	13,727	52,062	3,608	48,454
Females	166,127	†	†	†	†	†	166,127	18,576	147,551	4,656	142,895
Associate's degrees	1,003,422	1,003,364	793,180	210,184	53,127	157,057	58	0	58	0	58
4-year institutions	287,076	287,076	140,109	146,967	46,679	100,288	0	0	0	0	0
Males	111,085	111,085	55,701	55,384	17,323	38,061	0	0	0	0	0
Females	175,991	175,991	84,408	91,583	29,356	62,227	0	0	0	0	0
2-year institutions	716,290	716,288	653,071	63,217	6,448	56,769	2	0	2	0	2
Males	279,721	279,720	257,568	22,152	2,356	19,796	1	0	1	0	1
Females	436,569	436,568	395,503	41,065	4,092	36,973	1	0	1	0	1
Less-than-2-year institutions	56	†	†	†	†	†	56	0	56	0	56
Males	14	†	†	†	†	†	14	0	14	0	14
Females	42	†	†	†	†	†	42	0	42	0	42
Bachelor's degrees	1,869,814	1,869,814	1,186,397	683,417	544,213	139,204	0	0	0	0	0
Males	801,692	801,692	522,295	279,397	223,439	55,958	0	0	0	0	0
Females	1,068,122	1,068,122	664,102	404,020	320,774	83,246	0	0	0	0	0
Master's degrees	754,475	754,475	346,101	408,374	333,580	74,794	0	0	0	0	0
Males	302,807	302,807	142,365	160,442	134,906	25,536	0	0	0	0	0
Females	451,668	451,668	203,736	247,932	198,674	49,258	0	0	0	0	0
Doctor's degrees	177,580	177,580	88,904	88,676	80,894	7,782	0	0	0	0	0
Males	85,587	85,587	43,737	41,850	38,927	2,923	0	0	0	0	0
Females	91,993	91,993	45,167	46,826	41,967	4,859	0	0	0	0	0

†Not applicable.

[1]Includes both degree-granting and non-degree-granting institutions.

NOTE: Data are for postsecondary institutions participating in Title IV federal financial aid programs. Degree-granting institutions grant degrees at the associate's or higher level, while non-degree-granting institutions grant only awards below that level. The non-degree-granting classification includes some institutions transitioning to higher level program offerings, though still classified at a lower level; therefore, a small number of associate's degrees are shown as awarded by non-degree-granting institutions. Some data have been revised from previously published figures.

SOURCE: U.S. Department of Education, National Center for Education Statistics, Integrated Postsecondary Education Data System (IPEDS), Spring 2014, Human Resources component; Spring 2015, Fall Enrollment component; and Fall 2014, Completions component. (This table was prepared April 2016.)

Table 301.20. Historical summary of faculty, enrollment, degrees conferred, and finances in degree-granting postsecondary institutions: Selected years, 1869–70 through 2013–14

Selected characteristic	1869–70	1879–80	1889–90	1899–1900	1909–10	1919–20	1929–30	1939–40	1949–50	1959–60	1969–70	1979–80	1989–90	1999–2000	2009–10	2013–14
	2	3	4	5	6	7	8	9	10	11	12	13	14	15	16	17
Total institutions[1]	563	811	998	977	951	1,041	1,409	1,708	1,851	2,004	2,525	3,152	3,535	4,084	4,495	4,724
Total faculty[2]	5,553[3]	11,522[3]	15,809	23,868	36,480	48,615	82,386	146,929	246,722	380,554	450,000[4]	675,000[4]	824,220[5]	1,027,830[5]	1,439,144[5]	1,544,060
Males	4,887[3]	7,328[3]	12,704[3]	19,151	29,132	35,807	60,017	106,328	186,189	296,773	346,000[4]	479,000[4]	534,254[5]	602,469[5]	761,035[5]	791,310
Females	666[3]	4,194[3]	3,105[3]	4,717	7,348	12,808	22,369	40,601	60,533	83,781	104,000[4]	196,000[4]	289,966[5]	425,361[5]	678,109[5]	752,750
Total fall enrollment[6]	52,286[3]	115,817	156,756	237,592	355,213	597,880	1,100,737	1,494,203	2,444,900	3,639,847	8,004,660	11,569,899	13,538,560	14,791,224	20,313,594	20,375,789
Males	41,160[3]	77,972[3]	100,453[3]	152,254	214,648[3]	314,938	619,935	893,250	1,721,572	2,332,617	4,746,201	5,682,877	6,190,015	6,490,646	8,732,953	8,860,786
Females	11,126[3]	37,845[3]	56,303[3]	85,338	140,565[3]	282,942	480,802	600,953	723,328	1,307,230	3,258,459	5,887,022	7,348,545	8,300,578	11,580,641	11,515,003
Degrees conferred																
Associate's, total	—	—	—	—	—	—	—	—	—	—	206,023	400,910	455,102	564,933	848,856	1,003,364
Males	—	—	—	—	—	—	—	—	—	—	117,432	183,737	191,195	224,721	322,747	390,805
Females	—	—	—	—	—	—	—	—	—	—	88,591	217,173	263,907	340,212	526,109	612,559
Bachelor's, total[7]	9,371	12,896	15,539	27,410	37,199	48,622	122,484	186,500	432,058	392,440	792,316	929,417	1,051,344	1,237,875	1,649,919	1,869,814
Males	7,993	10,411	12,857	22,173	28,762	31,980	73,615	109,546	328,841	254,063	451,097	473,611	491,696	530,367	706,660	801,692
Females	1,378	2,485	2,682	5,237	8,437	16,642	48,869	76,954	103,217	138,377	341,219	455,806	559,648	707,508	943,259	1,068,122
Master's, total[8]	0	879	1,015	1,583	2,113	4,279	14,969	26,731	58,183	74,435	213,589	305,196	330,152	463,185	693,313	754,475
Males	0	868	821	1,280	1,555	2,985	8,925	16,508	41,220	50,898	130,799	156,882	158,052	196,129	275,317	302,807
Females	0	11	194	303	558	1,294	6,044	10,223	16,963	23,537	82,790	148,314	172,100	267,056	417,996	451,668
Doctor's, total[9]	1	54	149	382	443	615	2,299	3,290	6,420	9,829	59,486	95,631	103,508	118,736	158,590	177,580
Males	1	51	147	359	399	522	1,946	2,861	5,804	8,801	53,792	69,526	63,963	64,930	76,610	85,587
Females	0	3	2	23	44	93	353	429	616	1,028	5,694	26,105	39,545	53,806	81,990	91,993
Finances							*In thousands of current dollars*									
Current-fund revenue... Educational and general income[10]	—	—	$21,464	$35,084	$76,883	$199,922	$554,511	$715,211	$2,374,645	$5,785,537	$21,515,242	$58,519,982	$139,635,477	$236,784,000	$446,479,000	$517,095,000
	—	—	—	—	—	—	483,065	571,288	1,833,845	4,688,362	16,486,177	—	—	—	—	—
Expenditures[10]	—	—	—	—	67,917	172,929	507,142	674,688	2,245,661	5,601,376	21,043,113	56,913,588	134,655,571	—	355,910,203	535,186,040
Value of physical property	—	—	95,426	253,599	457,594	747,333	2,065,049	2,753,780[11]	4,799,964	13,548,548	42,093,580	83,733,387	164,635,000	—	—	—
Market value of endowment funds	—	—	78,788[12]	194,998[12]	323,661[12]	569,071[12]	1,372,068[12]	1,686,283[12]	2,601,223[12]	5,322,080[12]	11,206,632	20,743,045	67,978,726	—	—	—
Finances							*In thousands of constant 2014–15 dollars[13]*									
Current-fund revenue... Educational and general income[10]							$7,667,231	$12,112,629	$23,731,109	$46,601,897	$134,802,460	$178,407,813	$260,275,690	$331,034,000	$487,560,000	$520,860,000
							6,679,347	9,675,186	18,326,603	37,764,186	103,293,155	—	—	—	—	—
Expenditures[10]							7,012,260	11,426,342	22,442,102	45,118,499	131,844,364	173,510,456	250,993,318	—	388,657,850	539,083,214
Value of physical property							28,553,462	46,637,309[11]	47,968,631	109,132,141	263,734,804	255,275,036	306,873,935	—	—	—
Market value of endowment funds							18,971,604[12]	28,558,454[12]	25,995,425[12]	42,868,799[12]	70,214,482	63,238,593	126,709,990	—	—	—

—Not available.
[1] Prior to 1979–80, excludes branch campuses.
[2] Total number of different individuals (not reduced to full-time equivalent). Beginning in 1959–60, data are for the first term of the academic year.
[3] Estimated.
[4] Estimated number of senior instructional staff based on actual enrollment data for the designated year and enrollment/staff ratios for the prior staff survey. Excludes graduate assistants.
[5] Because of revised survey procedures, data may not be directly comparable with figures prior to 1989–90. Excludes graduate assistants.
[6] Data for 1869–70 to 1939–40 are for resident degree-credit students who enrolled at any time during the academic year.
[7] From 1869–70 to 1959–60, bachelor's degrees include degrees formerly classified as first-professional, such as M.D., D.D.S., and law degrees.
[8] Figures for years prior to 1969–70 are not precisely comparable with later data.
[9] Includes Ph.D., Ed.D., and comparable degrees at the doctoral level. Includes most degrees formerly classified as first-professional, such as M.D., D.D.S., and law degrees.
[10] Data for 1929–30 and 1939–40 include current-fund expenditures only. Data for 1949–50 through 1989–90 include current-fund expenditures and additions to plant value. Data for 1999–2000 include total expenditures for private institutions and current-fund expenditures for public institutions. Data for later years are for total expenditures.
[11] Includes unexpended plant funds.
[12] Book value. Includes other nonexpendable funds.
[13] Constant dollars based on the Consumer Price Index, prepared by the Bureau of Labor Statistics, U.S. Department of Labor, adjusted to a school-year basis.

NOTE: Data through 1989–90 are for institutions of higher education, while later data are for degree-granting institutions. Degree-granting institutions grant associate's or higher degrees and participate in Title IV federal financial aid programs. The degree-granting classification is very similar to the earlier higher education classification, but it includes more 2-year colleges and excludes a few higher education institutions that did not grant degrees. Detail may not sum to totals because of rounding.

SOURCE: U.S. Department of Education, National Center for Education Statistics, Biennial Survey of Education in the United States; Education Directory, Colleges and Universities; Faculty and Other Professional Staff in Institutions of Higher Education; Fall Enrollment in Colleges and Universities; Earned Degrees Conferred; Financial Statistics of Institutions of Higher Education; Higher Education General Information Survey (HEGIS), "Fall Enrollment in Institutions of Higher Education," "Degrees and Other Formal Awards Conferred," and "Financial Statistics of Institutions of Higher Education" surveys; Integrated Postsecondary Education Data System (IPEDS), "Fall Enrollment Survey" (IPEDS-EF:89–99), "Fall Staff Survey" (IPEDS-S:89–99), "Finance Survey" (IPEDS-F:FY90–00), "Completions Survey" (IPEDS-C:90–00), and "Institutional Characteristics Survey" (IPEDS-IC:89–99); IPEDS Winter 2009–10 and Spring 2014, Human Resources component, Fall Staff section; IPEDS Spring 2010 and Spring 2014, Fall Enrollment component; IPEDS Fall 2010 and Fall 2014, Completions component; and IPEDS Spring 2011 and Spring 2015, Finance component. (This table was prepared February 2016.)

Table 302.10. Recent high school completers and their enrollment in 2-year and 4-year colleges, by sex: 1960 through 2014
[Standard errors appear in parentheses]

Year	Number of high school completers[1] (in thousands)			Percent of recent high school completers[1] enrolled in college[2]								
				Total			Males			Females		
	Total	Males	Females	Total	2-year	4-year	Total	2-year	4-year	Total	2-year	4-year
1	2	3	4	5	6	7	8	9	10	11	12	13
1960	1,679 (43.8)	756 (31.8)	923 (29.6)	45.1 (2.13)	— (†)	— (†)	54.0 (3.18)	— (†)	— (†)	37.9 (2.80)	— (†)	— (†)
1961	1,763 (46.0)	790 (33.2)	973 (31.3)	48.0 (2.09)	— (†)	— (†)	56.3 (3.10)	— (†)	— (†)	41.3 (2.77)	— (†)	— (†)
1962	1,838 (43.6)	872 (31.5)	966 (30.0)	49.0 (2.05)	— (†)	— (†)	55.0 (2.96)	— (†)	— (†)	43.5 (2.80)	— (†)	— (†)
1963	1,741 (44.2)	794 (32.1)	947 (30.0)	45.0 (2.09)	— (†)	— (†)	52.3 (3.11)	— (†)	— (†)	39.0 (2.78)	— (†)	— (†)
1964	2,145 (43.0)	997 (31.9)	1,148 (28.5)	48.3 (1.89)	— (†)	— (†)	57.2 (2.75)	— (†)	— (†)	40.7 (2.54)	— (†)	— (†)
1965	2,659 (47.7)	1,254 (35.1)	1,405 (32.0)	50.9 (1.70)	— (†)	— (†)	57.3 (2.45)	— (†)	— (†)	45.3 (2.33)	— (†)	— (†)
1966	2,612 (45.0)	1,207 (33.8)	1,405 (29.0)	50.1 (1.72)	— (†)	— (†)	58.7 (2.49)	— (†)	— (†)	42.7 (2.32)	— (†)	— (†)
1967	2,525 (37.9)	1,142 (28.4)	1,383 (24.3)	51.9 (1.42)	— (†)	— (†)	57.6 (2.09)	— (†)	— (†)	47.2 (1.92)	— (†)	— (†)
1968	2,606 (37.3)	1,184 (28.2)	1,422 (23.8)	55.4 (1.39)	— (†)	— (†)	63.2 (2.00)	— (†)	— (†)	48.9 (1.89)	— (†)	— (†)
1969	2,842 (36.0)	1,352 (26.8)	1,490 (23.7)	53.3 (1.34)	— (†)	— (†)	60.1 (1.90)	— (†)	— (†)	47.2 (1.85)	— (†)	— (†)
1970	2,758 (37.4)	1,343 (26.1)	1,415 (26.8)	51.7 (1.36)	— (†)	— (†)	55.2 (1.94)	— (†)	— (†)	48.5 (1.90)	— (†)	— (†)
1971	2,875 (38.0)	1,371 (26.6)	1,504 (27.1)	53.5 (1.33)	— (†)	— (†)	57.6 (1.90)	— (†)	— (†)	49.8 (1.84)	— (†)	— (†)
1972	2,964 (37.8)	1,423 (27.0)	1,542 (26.4)	49.2 (1.31)	— (†)	— (†)	52.7 (1.89)	— (†)	— (†)	46.0 (1.81)	— (†)	— (†)
1973	3,058 (37.1)	1,460 (27.6)	1,599 (24.6)	46.6 (1.29)	14.9 (0.92)	31.6 (1.20)	50.0 (1.87)	14.6 (1.32)	35.4 (1.79)	43.4 (1.77)	15.2 (1.28)	28.2 (1.61)
1974	3,101 (38.6)	1,491 (27.8)	1,611 (26.8)	47.6 (1.28)	15.2 (0.92)	32.4 (1.20)	49.4 (1.85)	16.6 (1.37)	32.8 (1.74)	45.9 (1.77)	13.9 (1.23)	32.0 (1.66)
1975	3,185 (38.6)	1,513 (27.3)	1,672 (27.2)	50.7 (1.26)	18.2 (0.98)	32.6 (1.19)	52.6 (1.83)	19.0 (1.44)	33.6 (1.73)	49.0 (1.75)	17.4 (1.32)	31.6 (1.62)
1976	2,986 (39.8)	1,451 (28.9)	1,535 (27.3)	48.8 (1.31)	15.6 (0.95)	33.3 (1.23)	47.2 (1.87)	14.5 (1.32)	32.7 (1.76)	50.3 (1.82)	16.6 (1.35)	33.8 (1.72)
1977	3,141 (40.7)	1,483 (29.7)	1,659 (27.7)	50.6 (1.29)	17.5 (0.98)	33.1 (1.21)	52.1 (1.87)	17.2 (1.41)	35.0 (1.79)	49.3 (1.77)	17.8 (1.36)	31.5 (1.65)
1978	3,163 (39.7)	1,485 (29.3)	1,677 (26.7)	50.1 (1.28)	17.0 (0.96)	33.1 (1.21)	51.1 (1.87)	15.6 (1.36)	35.5 (1.79)	49.3 (1.76)	18.3 (1.36)	31.0 (1.63)
1979	3,160 (40.0)	1,475 (29.2)	1,685 (27.2)	49.3 (1.28)	17.5 (0.98)	31.8 (1.20)	50.4 (1.88)	16.9 (1.41)	33.5 (1.78)	48.4 (1.76)	18.1 (1.35)	30.3 (1.62)
1980	3,088 (39.4)	1,498 (28.4)	1,589 (27.3)	49.3 (1.30)	19.4 (1.03)	29.9 (1.19)	46.7 (1.86)	17.1 (1.40)	29.7 (1.70)	51.8 (1.81)	21.6 (1.49)	30.2 (1.66)
1981	3,056 (42.2)	1,491 (30.4)	1,565 (29.1)	53.9 (1.30)	20.5 (1.05)	33.5 (1.23)	54.8 (1.86)	20.9 (1.52)	33.9 (1.77)	53.1 (1.82)	20.1 (1.46)	33.0 (1.72)
1982	3,100 (40.4)	1,509 (29.0)	1,592 (28.2)	50.6 (1.36)	19.1 (1.07)	31.5 (1.26)	49.1 (1.95)	17.5 (1.48)	31.6 (1.81)	52.0 (1.90)	20.6 (1.54)	31.4 (1.76)
1983	2,963 (41.6)	1,389 (30.4)	1,573 (28.2)	52.7 (1.39)	19.2 (1.10)	33.5 (1.31)	51.9 (2.03)	20.2 (1.63)	31.7 (1.89)	53.4 (1.91)	18.4 (1.48)	35.1 (1.82)
1984	3,012 (36.5)	1,429 (28.7)	1,584 (21.9)	55.2 (1.37)	19.4 (1.09)	35.8 (1.32)	56.0 (1.99)	17.7 (1.53)	38.4 (1.95)	54.5 (1.90)	21.0 (1.55)	33.5 (1.80)
1985	2,668 (40.1)	1,287 (28.7)	1,381 (27.9)	57.7 (1.45)	19.6 (1.16)	38.1 (1.43)	58.6 (2.08)	19.9 (1.69)	38.8 (2.06)	56.8 (2.02)	19.3 (1.61)	37.5 (1.97)
1986	2,786 (38.6)	1,332 (28.5)	1,454 (26.0)	53.8 (1.43)	19.2 (1.13)	34.5 (1.37)	55.8 (2.06)	21.3 (1.70)	34.5 (1.97)	51.9 (1.99)	17.3 (1.50)	34.6 (1.89)
1987	2,647 (40.9)	1,278 (29.8)	1,369 (28.0)	56.8 (1.46)	18.9 (1.15)	37.9 (1.43)	58.3 (2.09)	17.3 (1.60)	41.0 (2.09)	55.3 (2.04)	20.3 (1.65)	35.0 (1.95)
1988	2,673 (47.0)	1,334 (34.1)	1,339 (32.3)	58.9 (1.57)	21.9 (1.32)	37.1 (1.54)	57.1 (2.24)	21.3 (1.85)	35.8 (2.17)	60.7 (2.20)	22.4 (1.88)	38.3 (2.19)
1989	2,450 (46.5)	1,204 (32.9)	1,246 (32.8)	59.6 (1.64)	20.7 (1.35)	38.9 (1.63)	57.6 (2.35)	18.3 (1.84)	39.3 (2.32)	61.6 (2.27)	23.1 (1.97)	38.5 (2.28)
1990	2,362 (43.0)	1,173 (30.6)	1,189 (30.2)	60.1 (1.60)	20.1 (1.31)	40.0 (1.60)	58.0 (2.29)	19.6 (1.85)	38.4 (2.26)	62.2 (2.24)	20.6 (1.87)	41.6 (2.28)
1991	2,276 (41.0)	1,140 (29.0)	1,136 (29.0)	62.5 (1.62)	24.9 (1.44)	37.7 (1.62)	57.9 (2.33)	22.9 (1.98)	35.0 (2.25)	67.1 (2.22)	26.8 (2.09)	40.3 (2.32)
1992	2,397 (40.4)	1,216 (29.1)	1,180 (28.1)	61.9 (1.58)	23.0 (1.37)	38.9 (1.59)	60.0 (2.24)	22.1 (1.89)	37.8 (2.21)	63.8 (2.23)	23.9 (1.98)	40.0 (2.27)
1993	2,342 (41.4)	1,120 (30.6)	1,223 (27.8)	62.6 (1.59)	22.8 (1.38)	39.8 (1.61)	59.9 (2.33)	22.9 (2.00)	37.0 (2.30)	65.2 (2.17)	22.7 (1.92)	42.4 (2.25)
1994	2,517 (38.1)	1,244 (27.9)	1,273 (25.9)	61.9 (1.43)	21.0 (1.20)	40.9 (1.45)	60.6 (2.05)	23.0 (1.76)	37.5 (2.03)	63.2 (1.99)	19.1 (1.63)	44.1 (2.05)
1995	2,599 (40.9)	1,238 (29.9)	1,361 (27.7)	61.9 (1.41)	21.5 (1.19)	40.4 (1.42)	62.6 (2.03)	25.3 (1.82)	37.4 (2.03)	61.3 (1.95)	18.1 (1.54)	43.2 (1.98)
1996	2,660 (40.5)	1,297 (29.5)	1,363 (27.7)	65.0 (1.42)	23.1 (1.26)	41.9 (1.47)	60.1 (2.09)	21.5 (1.76)	38.5 (2.08)	69.7 (1.92)	24.6 (1.80)	45.1 (2.07)
1997	2,769 (41.8)	1,354 (31.0)	1,415 (27.9)	67.0 (1.38)	22.8 (1.23)	44.3 (1.45)	63.6 (2.01)	21.4 (1.71)	42.2 (2.07)	70.3 (1.87)	24.1 (1.75)	46.2 (2.04)
1998	2,810 (43.9)	1,452 (31.0)	1,358 (31.0)	65.6 (1.38)	24.4 (1.25)	41.3 (1.43)	62.4 (1.96)	24.4 (1.74)	38.0 (1.96)	69.1 (1.93)	24.3 (1.79)	44.8 (2.08)
1999	2,897 (41.5)	1,474 (29.9)	1,423 (28.8)	62.9 (1.38)	21.0 (1.17)	41.9 (1.41)	61.4 (1.95)	21.0 (1.63)	40.5 (1.97)	64.4 (1.95)	21.1 (1.67)	43.3 (2.02)
2000	2,756 (45.3)	1,251 (33.6)	1,505 (29.7)	63.3 (1.41)	21.4 (1.20)	41.9 (1.45)	59.9 (2.13)	23.1 (1.83)	36.8 (2.10)	66.2 (1.88)	20.0 (1.59)	46.2 (1.98)
2001	2,549 (46.5)	1,277 (33.7)	1,273 (32.0)	61.8 (1.48)	19.6 (1.21)	42.1 (1.51)	60.1 (2.11)	18.6 (1.68)	41.4 (2.12)	63.5 (2.08)	20.6 (1.75)	42.8 (2.13)
2002	2,796 (42.7)	1,412 (31.3)	1,384 (29.0)	65.2 (1.31)	21.6 (1.14)	43.6 (1.37)	62.1 (1.88)	20.4 (1.57)	41.7 (1.92)	68.4 (1.82)	22.8 (1.65)	45.6 (1.95)
2003	2,677 (42.2)	1,306 (29.9)	1,372 (29.7)	63.9 (1.35)	21.5 (1.16)	42.5 (1.39)	61.2 (1.97)	21.9 (1.67)	39.3 (1.97)	66.5 (1.86)	21.0 (1.61)	45.5 (1.96)
2004	2,752 (40.0)	1,327 (29.1)	1,425 (27.3)	66.7 (1.31)	22.4 (1.16)	44.2 (1.38)	61.4 (1.95)	21.8 (1.65)	39.6 (1.96)	71.5 (1.74)	23.1 (1.63)	48.5 (1.93)
2005	2,675 (40.8)	1,262 (31.5)	1,414 (24.9)	68.6 (1.31)	24.0 (1.21)	44.6 (1.40)	66.5 (1.94)	24.7 (1.77)	41.8 (2.03)	70.4 (1.77)	23.4 (1.64)	47.0 (1.94)
2006	2,692 (44.6)	1,328 (32.7)	1,363 (30.1)	66.0 (1.33)	24.7 (1.21)	41.3 (1.39)	65.8 (1.90)	24.9 (1.73)	40.9 (1.97)	66.1 (1.87)	24.5 (1.70)	41.7 (1.95)
2007	2,955 (42.6)	1,511 (30.0)	1,444 (30.3)	67.2 (1.26)	24.1 (1.15)	43.1 (1.33)	66.1 (1.78)	22.7 (1.57)	43.4 (1.86)	68.3 (1.79)	25.5 (1.67)	42.8 (1.90)
2008	3,151 (42.8)	1,640 (29.6)	1,511 (30.9)	68.6 (1.21)	27.7 (1.16)	40.9 (1.28)	65.9 (1.71)	24.9 (1.56)	41.0 (1.77)	71.6 (1.69)	30.6 (1.73)	40.9 (1.85)
2009	2,937 (45.0)	1,407 (32.8)	1,531 (30.6)	70.1 (1.23)	27.7 (1.21)	42.4 (1.33)	66.0 (1.84)	25.1 (1.69)	40.9 (1.91)	73.8 (1.64)	30.1 (1.71)	43.8 (1.85)
2010[3]	3,160 (91.8)	1,679 (64.6)	1,482 (58.4)	68.1 (1.49)	26.7 (1.52)	41.4 (1.61)	62.8 (1.88)	28.5 (2.03)	34.3 (1.97)	74.0 (2.31)	24.6 (2.32)	49.5 (2.59)
2011[3]	3,079 (88.3)	1,611 (60.6)	1,468 (58.4)	68.2 (1.45)	25.9 (1.49)	42.3 (1.44)	64.7 (2.16)	24.7 (1.79)	40.0 (2.10)	72.2 (1.98)	27.3 (2.17)	44.9 (2.37)
2012[3]	3,203 (96.2)	1,622 (70.1)	1,581 (54.0)	66.2 (1.59)	28.8 (1.57)	37.5 (1.60)	61.3 (2.17)	26.9 (2.20)	34.4 (2.15)	71.3 (2.11)	30.7 (2.09)	40.6 (2.21)
2013[3]	2,977 (84.4)	1,524 (62.9)	1,453 (57.0)	65.9 (1.58)	23.8 (1.44)	42.1 (1.76)	63.5 (2.20)	24.5 (2.14)	39.0 (2.48)	68.4 (2.17)	23.0 (2.15)	45.3 (2.21)
2014[3]	2,868 (78.5)	1,423 (58.1)	1,445 (57.5)	68.4 (1.67)	24.6 (1.56)	43.7 (1.81)	64.0 (2.32)	21.2 (2.07)	42.8 (2.69)	72.6 (2.50)	28.0 (2.35)	44.6 (2.57)

—Not available.
†Not applicable.
[1]Individuals ages 16 to 24 who graduated from high school or completed a GED during the calendar year.
[2]Enrollment in college as of October of each year for individuals ages 16 to 24 who completed high school during the calendar year.
[3]Beginning in 2010, standard errors were computed using replicate weights, which produced more precise values than the generalized variance function methodology used in prior years.

NOTE: Data are based on sample surveys of the civilian noninstitutionalized population. High school completion data in this table differ from figures appearing in other tables because of varying survey procedures and coverage. High school completers include GED recipients. Detail may not sum to totals because of rounding.
SOURCE: American College Testing Program, unpublished tabulations, derived from statistics collected by the Census Bureau, 1960 through 1969. U.S. Department of Commerce, Census Bureau, Current Population Survey (CPS), October, 1970 through 2014. (This table was prepared August 2015.)

Table 302.20. Percentage of recent high school completers enrolled in 2- and 4-year colleges, by race/ethnicity: 1960 through 2014
[Standard errors appear in parentheses]

Year	Percent of recent high school completers[1] enrolled in college[2] (annual data)					3-year moving averages[3]							
						Percent of recent high school completers[1] enrolled in college[2]					Difference between percent enrolled		
	Total	White	Black	Hispanic	Asian	Total	White	Black	Hispanic	Asian	White-Black	White-Hispanic	White-Asian
1	2	3	4	5	6	7	8	9	10	11	12	13	14
1960[4]	45.1 (2.13)	45.8 (2.21)	— (†)	— (†)	— (†)	46.6 (1.49)	47.7 (1.56)	— (†)	— (†)	— (†)	— (†)	— (†)	— (†)
1961[4]	48.0 (2.09)	49.5 (2.19)	— (†)	— (†)	— (†)	47.4 (1.21)	48.7 (1.26)	— (†)	— (†)	— (†)	— (†)	— (†)	— (†)
1962[4]	49.0 (2.05)	50.6 (2.15)	— (†)	— (†)	— (†)	47.4 (1.20)	48.6 (1.25)	— (†)	— (†)	— (†)	— (†)	— (†)	— (†)
1963[4]	45.0 (2.09)	45.6 (2.17)	— (†)	— (†)	— (†)	47.5 (1.16)	48.5 (1.21)	— (†)	— (†)	— (†)	— (†)	— (†)	— (†)
1964[4]	48.3 (1.89)	49.2 (1.98)	— (†)	— (†)	— (†)	48.5 (1.08)	49.2 (1.13)	— (†)	— (†)	— (†)	— (†)	— (†)	— (†)
1965[4]	50.9 (1.70)	51.7 (1.78)	— (†)	— (†)	— (†)	49.9 (1.02)	51.0 (1.07)	— (†)	— (†)	— (†)	— (†)	— (†)	— (†)
1966[4]	50.1 (1.72)	51.7 (1.79)	— (†)	— (†)	— (†)	51.0 (0.99)	52.1 (1.04)	— (†)	— (†)	— (†)	— (†)	— (†)	— (†)
1967[4]	51.9 (1.42)	53.0 (1.50)	— (†)	— (†)	— (†)	52.5 (0.81)	53.8 (0.85)	— (†)	— (†)	— (†)	— (†)	— (†)	— (†)
1968[4]	55.4 (1.39)	56.6 (1.47)	— (†)	— (†)	— (†)	53.6 (0.80)	55.0 (0.84)	— (†)	— (†)	— (†)	— (†)	— (†)	— (†)
1969[4]	53.3 (1.34)	55.2 (1.41)	— (†)	— (†)	— (†)	53.5 (0.79)	54.6 (0.83)	— (†)	— (†)	— (†)	— (†)	— (†)	— (†)
1970[4]	51.7 (1.36)	52.0 (1.44)	— (†)	— (†)	— (†)	52.9 (0.77)	53.8 (0.82)	— (†)	— (†)	— (†)	— (†)	— (†)	— (†)
1971[4]	53.5 (1.33)	54.0 (1.40)	— (†)	— (†)	— (†)	51.5 (0.77)	51.9 (0.82)	— (†)	— (†)	— (†)	— (†)	— (†)	— (†)
1972	49.2 (1.31)	49.7 (1.42)	44.6 (4.62)	45.0 (9.74)	— (†)	49.7 (0.76)	50.5 (0.81)	38.4 (3.18)	49.9 (6.64)	— (†)	12.1 (3.28)	‡ (†)	— (†)
1973	46.6 (1.29)	47.8 (1.40)	32.5 (4.30)	54.1 (9.01)	— (†)	47.8 (0.75)	48.2 (0.81)	41.4 (2.62)	48.8 (5.33)	— (†)	6.8 ! (2.74)	‡ (†)	— (†)
1974	47.6 (1.28)	47.2 (1.39)	47.2 (4.58)	46.9 (8.94)	— (†)	48.3 (0.74)	48.7 (0.80)	40.5 (2.63)	53.1 (5.09)	— (†)	8.3 ! (2.75)	‡ (†)	— (†)
1975	50.7 (1.26)	51.1 (1.37)	41.7 (3.97)	58.0 (8.44)	— (†)	49.1 (0.74)	49.1 (0.81)	44.5 (2.29)	52.7 (4.88)	— (†)	‡ (†)	‡ (†)	— (†)
1976	48.8 (1.31)	48.8 (1.43)	44.4 (4.08)	52.7 (7.97)	— (†)	50.1 (0.74)	50.3 (0.81)	45.3 (2.30)	53.6 (4.68)	— (†)	5.0 ! (2.44)	‡ (†)	— (†)
1977	50.6 (1.29)	50.8 (1.41)	49.5 (4.65)	50.8 (7.96)	— (†)	49.9 (0.75)	50.1 (0.82)	46.8 (2.70)	48.8 (4.72)	— (†)	‡ (†)	‡ (†)	— (†)
1978	50.1 (1.28)	50.5 (1.41)	46.4 (4.51)	42.0 (8.44)	— (†)	50.0 (0.74)	50.4 (0.81)	47.5 (2.67)	46.1 (4.69)	— (†)	‡ (†)	‡ (†)	— (†)
1979	49.3 (1.28)	49.9 (1.41)	46.7 (4.69)	45.0 (7.92)	— (†)	49.6 (0.74)	50.1 (0.82)	45.2 (2.62)	46.3 (4.83)	— (†)	‡ (†)	‡ (†)	— (†)
1980	49.3 (1.30)	49.8 (1.43)	42.7 (4.44)	52.3 (8.70)	— (†)	50.8 (0.75)	51.5 (0.82)	44.0 (2.61)	49.6 (4.78)	— (†)	7.5 ! (2.74)	‡ (†)	— (†)
1981	53.9 (1.30)	54.9 (1.44)	42.7 (4.44)	52.1 (8.19)	— (†)	51.3 (0.75)	52.4 (0.83)	40.3 (2.50)	48.7 (4.68)	— (†)	12.2 (2.64)	‡ (†)	— (†)
1982	50.6 (1.36)	52.7 (1.52)	35.8 (4.33)	43.2 (7.96)	— (†)	52.4 (0.79)	54.2 (0.84)	38.8 (2.57)	49.4 (4.94)	— (†)	15.4 (2.70)	‡ (†)	— (†)
1983	52.7 (1.39)	55.0 (1.55)	38.2 (4.34)	54.2 (8.96)	— (†)	52.8 (0.80)	55.5 (0.89)	38.0 (2.47)	46.7 (4.72)	— (†)	17.5 (2.62)	‡ (†)	— (†)
1984	55.2 (1.37)	59.0 (1.54)	39.8 (4.15)	44.3 (7.67)	— (†)	55.1 (0.81)	57.9 (0.91)	39.9 (2.54)	49.3 (4.89)	— (†)	18.0 (2.70)	‡ (†)	— (†)
1985	57.7 (1.45)	60.1 (1.62)	42.2 (4.78)	51.0 (9.76)	— (†)	55.5 (0.82)	58.6 (0.92)	39.5 (2.55)	46.1 (5.18)	— (†)	19.1 (2.71)	12.5 ! (5.27)	— (†)
1986	53.8 (1.43)	56.8 (1.62)	36.9 (4.38)	44.0 (8.85)	— (†)	56.1 (0.84)	58.5 (0.94)	43.5 (2.71)	42.3 (5.20)	— (†)	15.0 (2.87)	16.2 ! (5.28)	— (†)
1987	56.8 (1.46)	58.6 (1.65)	52.2 (4.82)	33.5 (8.25)	— (†)	56.5 (0.83)	58.8 (0.95)	44.2 (2.65)	45.0 (5.04)	— (†)	14.6 (2.82)	13.8 ! (5.13)	— (†)
1988	58.9 (1.57)	61.1 (1.79)	44.4 (4.91)	57.1 (10.14)	— (†)	58.4 (0.92)	60.1 (0.96)	49.7 (2.98)	48.5 (5.99)	— (†)	10.4 ! (3.13)	‡ (†)	— (†)
1989	59.6 (1.64)	60.7 (1.85)	53.4 (5.27)	55.1 (10.51)	— (†)	59.5 (0.94)	61.6 (1.06)	48.0 (2.98)	52.7 (6.33)	— (†)	13.6 (3.16)	‡ (†)	— (†)
1990	60.1 (1.60)	63.0 (1.80)	46.8 (5.08)	42.7 (10.82)	— (†)	60.7 (0.92)	63.0 (1.08)	48.9 (2.97)	52.5 (5.70)	— (†)	14.0 (3.16)	‡ (†)	— (†)
1991	62.5 (1.62)	65.4 (1.82)	46.4 (5.25)	57.2 (9.58)	— (†)	61.5 (0.92)	64.2 (1.05)	47.2 (2.93)	52.6 (5.52)	— (†)	17.0 (3.11)	11.7 ! (5.62)	— (†)
1992	61.9 (1.58)	64.3 (1.84)	48.2 (4.92)	55.0 (8.50)	— (†)	62.3 (0.92)	64.2 (1.06)	50.0 (2.98)	58.2 (5.04)	— (†)	14.2 (3.16)	‡ (†)	— (†)
1993	62.6 (1.59)	62.9 (1.85)	55.6 (5.26)	62.2 (8.22)	— (†)	62.1 (0.91)	63.9 (1.04)	51.3 (2.97)	55.7 (4.97)	— (†)	12.6 (3.14)	‡ (†)	— (†)
1994	61.9 (1.43)	64.5 (1.61)	50.8 (4.42)	49.1 (6.28)	— (†)	62.1 (0.83)	64.0 (1.03)	52.4 (2.52)	55.0 (3.23)	— (†)	11.5 (2.72)	8.9 ! (3.39)	— (†)
1995	61.9 (1.41)	64.3 (1.64)	51.2 (4.20)	53.7 (4.92)	— (†)	63.0 (0.81)	65.4 (0.93)	52.9 (2.40)	51.6 (3.18)	— (†)	12.5 (2.57)	13.8 (3.31)	— (†)
1996	65.0 (1.42)	67.4 (1.67)	56.0 (4.03)	50.8 (5.79)	— (†)	64.7 (0.82)	66.6 (0.93)	55.4 (2.41)	57.6 (2.96)	— (†)	11.3 (2.58)	9.0 ! (3.10)	— (†)
1997	67.0 (1.38)	68.2 (1.64)	58.5 (4.12)	65.6 (4.53)	— (†)	65.9 (0.80)	68.1 (0.95)	58.8 (2.35)	55.3 (2.93)	— (†)	9.3 (2.53)	12.8 (3.08)	— (†)
1998	65.6 (1.38)	68.5 (1.61)	61.9 (4.05)	47.4 (4.92)	— (†)	65.2 (0.80)	67.7 (0.94)	59.8 (2.31)	51.9 (2.79)	— (†)	7.9 ! (2.50)	15.7 (2.94)	— (†)
1999	62.9 (1.38)	66.3 (1.64)	58.9 (3.86)	42.3 (4.76)	— (†)	64.0 (0.80)	66.8 (0.94)	58.6 (2.31)	47.4 (2.84)	— (†)	8.3 ! (2.50)	19.5 (2.99)	— (†)
2000	63.3 (1.41)	65.7 (1.66)	54.9 (4.11)	52.9 (5.03)	— (†)	62.7 (0.82)	65.4 (0.97)	56.4 (2.33)	48.6 (2.96)	— (†)	9.1 (2.53)	16.9 (3.11)	— (†)
2001	61.8 (1.48)	64.3 (1.72)	55.0 (4.17)	51.7 (5.63)	— (†)	63.5 (0.82)	66.3 (0.97)	56.4 (2.39)	52.8 (2.93)	— (†)	10.0 (2.58)	13.5 (3.09)	— (†)
2002	65.2 (1.31)	69.1 (1.55)	59.4 (3.90)	53.6 (4.46)	— (†)	63.7 (0.78)	66.5 (0.97)	57.3 (2.33)	54.8 (2.75)	— (†)	9.3 (2.52)	11.7 (2.92)	— (†)
2003[5]	63.9 (1.35)	66.2 (1.61)	57.5 (4.25)	58.6 (4.61)	84.1 (5.10)	65.3 (0.77)	68.0 (0.91)	59.9 (2.29)	57.7 (2.66)	80.0 (3.99)	8.1 ! (2.46)	10.3 (2.81)	-11.9 ! (4.10)
2004[5]	66.7 (1.31)	68.8 (1.57)	62.5 (3.77)	61.8 (4.76)	75.6 (6.13)	66.4 (0.77)	69.4 (0.91)	58.8 (2.34)	57.7 (2.60)	81.6 (3.37)	10.6 (2.51)	11.7 (2.75)	-12.2 (3.49)
2005[5]	68.6 (1.31)	73.2 (1.52)	55.7 (4.15)	54.0 (4.18)	86.7 (5.99)	67.1 (0.76)	70.2 (0.90)	58.2 (2.35)	57.5 (2.52)	80.9 (3.64)	12.0 (2.52)	12.6 (2.67)	-10.7 ! (3.75)
2006[5]	66.0 (1.33)	68.5 (1.60)	55.5 (4.33)	57.9 (4.18)	82.3 (5.32)	67.2 (0.75)	70.4 (0.89)	55.6 (2.35)	58.5 (2.43)	85.1 (3.64)	14.7 (2.51)	11.9 (2.59)	-14.7 (3.74)
2007[5]	67.2 (1.26)	69.5 (1.49)	55.7 (3.78)	64.0 (4.22)	88.8 (6.26)	67.3 (0.73)	70.0 (0.87)	55.7 (2.27)	62.0 (2.33)	85.8 (3.45)	14.3 (2.43)	8.0 ! (2.48)	-15.8 (3.56)
2008[5]	68.6 (1.21)	71.7 (1.44)	55.7 (3.78)	63.9 (3.72)	88.4 (5.08)	68.6 (0.71)	70.8 (0.86)	60.3 (2.15)	62.3 (2.25)	90.1 (3.01)	10.5 (2.31)	8.6 (2.41)	-19.2 (3.13)
2009[5]	70.1 (1.23)	71.3 (1.53)	69.5 (3.51)	59.3 (3.80)	92.1 (3.90)	68.9 (0.70)	71.2 (0.86)	62.4 (2.09)	60.9 (2.14)	88.1 (2.85)	8.8 (2.26)	10.3 (2.31)	-16.9 (2.98)
2010[5,6]	68.1 (1.49)	70.5 (1.68)	62.0 (4.81)	59.7 (4.18)	84.7 (5.27)	68.8 (0.71)	70.1 (0.90)	66.1 (2.01)	62.3 (2.01)	87.4 (2.78)	‡ (†)	7.8 (2.21)	-17.3 (2.92)
2011[5,6]	68.2 (1.45)	68.3 (1.86)	67.1 (4.01)	66.6 (3.50)	86.1 (4.25)	67.5 (0.89)	68.2 (1.03)	62.1 (2.86)	66.1 (2.17)	83.9 (2.79)	6.1 ! (3.04)	‡ (†)	-15.7 (2.97)
2012[5,6]	66.2 (1.59)	65.7 (1.94)	56.4 (4.84)	70.3 (3.22)	81.5 (5.15)	67.6 (1.12)	67.6 (1.12)	60.5 (2.64)	65.9 (1.99)	82.3 (3.59)	7.1 ! (2.87)	‡ (†)	-14.7 (3.76)
2013[5,6]	65.9 (1.58)	68.8 (1.90)	56.7 (5.59)	59.8 (3.62)	80.1 (6.52)	66.8 (0.98)	67.4 (1.26)	60.7 (3.09)	65.5 (2.06)	83.6 (3.20)	6.7 ! (3.34)	‡ (†)	-16.2 (3.44)
2014[5,6]	68.4 (1.67)	67.7 (2.25)	70.2 (4.56)	65.2 (4.08)	90.9 (3.91)	67.1 (1.30)	68.3 (1.58)	63.1 (4.17)	62.5 (2.91)	84.8 (4.01)	‡ (†)	‡ (†)	-16.5 (4.31)

—Not available.
†Not applicable.
!Interpret data with caution. The coefficient of variation (CV) for this estimate is between 30 and 50 percent.
‡Reporting standards not met. The coefficient of variation (CV) for this estimate is 50 percent or greater.
[1]Individuals ages 16 to 24 who graduated from high school or completed a GED during the calendar year.
[2]Enrollment in college as of October of each year for individuals ages 16 to 24 who completed high school during the calendar year.
[3]A 3-year moving average is a weighted average of the year indicated, the year immediately preceding, and the year immediately following. For the first and final years of available data, a 2-year moving average is used: The moving average for 1960 reflects an average of 1960 and 1961; for Black and Hispanic data, the moving average for 1972 reflects an average of 1972 and 1973; for Asian data, the moving average for 2003 reflects an average of 2003 and 2004; and the moving average for 2014 reflects an average of 2013 and 2014. Moving averages are used to produce more stable estimates.
[4]Prior to 1972, White data include persons of Hispanic ethnicity.
[5]White, Black, and Asian data exclude persons of Two or more races.
[6]Beginning in 2010, standard errors were computed using replicate weights, which produced more precise values than the generalized variance function methodology used in prior years.
NOTE: Data are based on sample surveys of the civilian noninstitutionalized population. Race categories exclude persons of Hispanic ethnicity except where otherwise noted. Total includes persons of other racial/ethnic groups not separately shown.
SOURCE: American College Testing Program, unpublished tabulations, derived from statistics collected by the Census Bureau, 1960 through 1969. U.S. Department of Commerce, Census Bureau, Current Population Survey (CPS), October, 1970 through 2014. (This table was prepared August 2015.)

Table 302.30. Percentage of recent high school completers enrolled in 2-year and 4-year colleges, by income level: 1975 through 2014

[Standard errors appear in parentheses]

Year	Percent of recent high school completers[1] enrolled in college[2] (annual data)				3-year moving averages[3]						
					Percent of recent high school completers[1] enrolled in college[2]				Difference between percent enrolled	
	Total	Low income	Middle income	High income	Total	Low income	Middle income	High income	High-low income	High-middle income
1	2	3	4	5	6	7	8	9	10	11
1975	50.7 (1.26)	31.2 (3.59)	46.2 (1.69)	64.5 (2.09)	49.1 (0.74)	34.7 (2.74)	43.5 (1.22)	63.7 (1.47)	29.0 (3.11)	20.2 (1.91)
1976	48.8 (1.31)	39.1 (4.20)	40.5 (1.76)	63.0 (2.06)	50.1 (0.74)	32.3 (2.17)	43.8 (1.00)	64.6 (1.18)	32.3 (2.47)	20.8 (1.55)
1977	50.6 (1.29)	27.7 (3.54)	44.2 (1.76)	66.3 (2.01)	49.9 (0.75)	32.4 (2.22)	43.1 (1.02)	64.4 (1.18)	32.1 (2.51)	21.4 (1.56)
1978	50.1 (1.28)	31.4 (3.74)	44.3 (1.74)	64.0 (2.05)	50.0 (0.74)	29.8 (2.13)	43.9 (1.01)	64.5 (1.17)	34.6 (2.43)	20.5 (1.55)
1979	49.3 (1.28)	30.5 (3.78)	43.2 (1.74)	63.2 (2.04)	49.6 (0.74)	31.6 (2.11)	43.4 (1.01)	64.1 (1.19)	32.6 (2.42)	20.8 (1.56)
1980	49.3 (1.30)	32.5 (3.47)	42.5 (1.78)	65.2 (2.08)	50.8 (0.75)	32.2 (2.14)	45.0 (1.02)	65.3 (1.20)	33.0 (2.45)	20.2 (1.57)
1981	53.9 (1.30)	33.6 (3.90)	49.2 (1.75)	67.6 (2.09)	51.3 (0.75)	32.9 (2.11)	44.5 (1.01)	67.9 (1.19)	34.9 (2.42)	23.4 (1.57)
1982	50.6 (1.36)	32.8 (3.81)	41.7 (1.81)	70.9 (2.13)	52.4 (0.79)	33.6 (2.29)	45.4 (1.06)	69.6 (1.25)	36.0 (2.61)	24.2 (1.64)
1983	52.7 (1.39)	34.6 (4.02)	45.2 (1.88)	70.3 (2.17)	52.8 (0.79)	34.0 (2.20)	45.1 (1.08)	71.7 (1.23)	37.8 (2.52)	26.7 (1.63)
1984	55.2 (1.37)	34.5 (3.62)	48.4 (1.89)	74.0 (2.09)	55.1 (0.81)	36.3 (2.26)	48.0 (1.11)	72.9 (1.24)	36.6 (2.58)	24.9 (1.66)
1985	57.7 (1.45)	40.2 (4.14)	50.6 (2.02)	74.6 (2.16)	55.5 (0.82)	35.9 (2.18)	49.1 (1.13)	73.2 (1.26)	37.3 (2.51)	24.1 (1.69)
1986	53.8 (1.43)	33.9 (3.59)	48.5 (1.97)	71.0 (2.28)	56.1 (0.84)	36.8 (2.23)	49.6 (1.17)	73.2 (1.27)	36.4 (2.57)	23.5 (1.72)
1987	56.8 (1.46)	36.9 (3.88)	50.0 (2.07)	73.8 (2.16)	56.5 (0.83)	37.6 (2.21)	51.1 (1.16)	72.6 (1.30)	35.0 (2.57)	21.5 (1.74)
1988	58.9 (1.57)	42.5 (4.39)	54.7 (2.14)	72.8 (2.52)	58.4 (0.92)	42.4 (2.54)	53.4 (1.28)	72.5 (1.44)	30.2 (2.92)	19.1 (1.93)
1989	59.6 (1.64)	48.1 (4.56)	55.4 (2.28)	70.7 (2.61)	59.5 (0.94)	45.6 (2.66)	54.9 (1.28)	73.2 (1.50)	27.6 (3.06)	18.4 (1.97)
1990	60.1 (1.60)	46.7 (4.76)	54.4 (2.14)	76.6 (2.54)	60.7 (0.92)	44.8 (2.63)	56.0 (1.27)	75.0 (1.44)	30.2 (3.00)	19.0 (1.92)
1991	62.5 (1.62)	39.5 (4.50)	58.4 (2.25)	78.2 (2.39)	61.5 (0.92)	42.2 (2.62)	56.5 (1.26)	78.0 (1.40)	35.8 (2.97)	21.4 (1.88)
1992	61.9 (1.58)	40.9 (4.37)	57.0 (2.18)	79.0 (2.35)	62.3 (0.92)	43.6 (2.60)	57.4 (1.26)	78.8 (1.38)	35.3 (2.94)	21.4 (1.87)
1993	62.6 (1.59)	50.4 (4.56)	56.9 (2.15)	79.3 (2.46)	62.1 (0.91)	44.7 (2.55)	57.3 (1.23)	78.7 (1.39)	34.0 (2.90)	21.5 (1.86)
1994	61.9 (1.43)	43.3 (3.96)	57.8 (1.94)	77.9 (2.22)	62.1 (0.83)	42.0 (2.27)	57.0 (1.14)	80.4 (1.22)	38.4 (2.57)	23.4 (1.67)
1995	61.9 (1.41)	34.2 (3.56)	56.0 (2.00)	83.5 (1.86)	63.0 (0.81)	42.1 (2.16)	58.9 (1.12)	79.9 (1.20)	37.8 (2.47)	21.0 (1.64)
1996	65.0 (1.42)	48.6 (3.78)	62.7 (1.95)	78.0 (2.27)	64.7 (0.82)	47.1 (2.18)	59.9 (1.16)	81.3 (1.19)	34.3 (2.49)	21.4 (1.66)
1997	67.0 (1.38)	57.0 (3.66)	60.7 (1.97)	82.2 (1.98)	65.9 (0.80)	50.6 (2.14)	62.7 (1.12)	79.3 (1.24)	28.7 (2.47)	16.6 (1.67)
1998	65.6 (1.38)	46.4 (3.62)	64.7 (1.89)	77.5 (2.21)	65.2 (0.80)	50.3 (2.14)	61.9 (1.10)	78.4 (1.24)	28.1 (2.47)	16.6 (1.66)
1999	62.9 (1.38)	47.6 (3.77)	60.2 (1.87)	75.4 (2.26)	64.0 (0.80)	47.9 (2.13)	61.5 (1.10)	76.6 (1.29)	28.7 (2.49)	15.1 (1.70)
2000	63.3 (1.41)	49.7 (3.67)	59.5 (1.97)	76.9 (2.22)	62.7 (0.82)	47.1 (2.17)	58.8 (1.14)	77.4 (1.29)	30.3 (2.52)	18.6 (1.72)
2001	61.8 (1.48)	43.8 (3.81)	56.4 (2.07)	80.0 (2.19)	63.5 (0.82)	49.9 (2.19)	59.1 (1.14)	78.3 (1.28)	28.4 (2.53)	19.3 (1.71)
2002	65.2 (1.31)	56.3 (3.64)	60.9 (1.78)	78.2 (2.12)	63.7 (0.78)	50.9 (2.14)	58.4 (1.08)	79.5 (1.20)	28.6 (2.45)	21.0 (1.61)
2003	63.9 (1.35)	52.8 (3.83)	57.6 (1.87)	80.1 (2.02)	65.3 (0.77)	52.5 (2.20)	60.6 (1.05)	79.5 (1.18)	27.0 (2.49)	18.9 (1.58)
2004	66.7 (1.31)	47.8 (3.95)	63.3 (1.79)	80.1 (1.98)	66.4 (0.77)	51.4 (2.24)	62.0 (1.05)	80.5 (1.15)	29.0 (2.52)	18.5 (1.56)
2005	68.6 (1.31)	53.5 (3.86)	65.1 (1.81)	81.2 (1.98)	67.1 (0.76)	50.8 (2.26)	63.3 (1.04)	80.7 (1.15)	29.9 (2.53)	17.4 (1.55)
2006	66.0 (1.33)	50.9 (3.92)	61.4 (1.82)	80.7 (2.01)	67.2 (0.75)	54.5 (2.18)	63.3 (1.03)	80.0 (1.15)	25.5 (2.47)	16.7 (1.55)
2007	67.2 (1.26)	58.4 (3.57)	63.3 (1.73)	78.2 (2.01)	67.3 (0.73)	55.3 (2.11)	63.5 (0.99)	80.2 (1.14)	24.9 (2.40)	16.8 (1.51)
2008	68.6 (1.21)	55.9 (3.50)	65.2 (1.62)	81.9 (1.90)	68.6 (0.71)	56.1 (2.08)	65.1 (0.96)	81.4 (1.11)	25.3 (2.36)	16.2 (1.47)
2009	70.1 (1.23)	53.9 (3.75)	66.7 (1.66)	84.2 (1.84)	68.9 (0.70)	53.3 (2.02)	66.2 (0.94)	82.8 (1.10)	29.5 (2.30)	16.6 (1.44)
2010[4]	68.1 (1.49)	50.7 (3.88)	66.7 (2.03)	82.2 (2.34)	68.8 (0.71)	52.6 (1.97)	66.5 (0.94)	83.0 (1.12)	30.4 (2.27)	16.4 (1.46)
2011[4]	68.2 (1.45)	53.5 (4.25)	66.2 (1.94)	82.4 (2.46)	67.5 (0.89)	51.6 (2.47)	65.9 (1.11)	81.7 (1.42)	30.1 (2.85)	15.9 (1.81)
2012[4]	66.2 (1.59)	50.9 (4.39)	64.7 (2.10)	80.7 (2.54)	66.8 (0.94)	50.3 (2.63)	64.9 (1.26)	80.4 (1.59)	30.1 (3.07)	15.5 (2.03)
2013[4]	65.9 (1.58)	45.5 (4.31)	63.8 (2.32)	78.5 (2.68)	66.8 (0.98)	51.6 (2.74)	64.0 (1.36)	80.8 (1.46)	29.2 (3.10)	16.8 (2.00)
2014[4]	68.4 (1.67)	57.8 (4.42)	63.6 (2.31)	83.6 (2.17)	67.1 (1.30)	52.1 (3.19)	63.7 (1.80)	80.9 (1.81)	28.8 (3.66)	17.2 (2.55)

[1]Individuals ages 16 to 24 who graduated from high school or completed a GED during the calendar year.
[2]Enrollment in college as of October of each year for individuals ages 16 to 24 who completed high school during the calendar year.
[3]A 3-year moving average is a weighted average of the year indicated, the year immediately preceding, and the year immediately following. For 1975 and 2014, a 2-year moving average is used: The moving average for income groups in 1975 reflects an average of 1975 and 1976, and the moving average for 2014 reflects an average of 2013 and 2014. Moving averages are used to produce more stable estimates.

[4]Beginning in 2010, standard errors were computed using replicate weights, which produced more precise values than the generalized variance function methodology used in prior years.
NOTE: Data are based on sample surveys of the civilian noninstitutionalized population. Low income refers to the bottom 20 percent of all family incomes, high income refers to the top 20 percent of all family incomes, and middle income refers to the 60 percent in between.
SOURCE: U.S. Department of Commerce, Census Bureau, Current Population Survey (CPS), October, 1975 through 2014. (This table was prepared August 2015.)

Table 302.40. Number of high schools with 12th-graders and percentage of high school graduates attending 4-year colleges, by selected high school characteristics: Selected years, 1998–99 through 2011–12

[Standard errors appear in parentheses]

Selected high school characteristic	Number of high schools with 12th-graders				Graduation rate of 12th-graders in 2010–11[1]	Percent of graduates attending 4-year colleges			
	1998–99	2002–03	2006–07	2010–11		1998–99 graduates attending in 1999–2000	2002–03 graduates attending in 2003–04	2006–07 graduates attending in 2007–08	2010–11 graduates attending in 2011–12
1	2	3	4	5	6	7	8	9	10
Public high schools	20,000 (230)	22,500 (400)	24,100 (540)	23,300 (330)	88.7 (0.90)	35.4 (0.43)	35.0 (0.61)	39.5 (0.91)	39.4 (0.59)
Percent of students who are Black, Hispanic, Asian, Pacific Islander, American Indian/Alaska Native, or Two or more races									
Less than 5 percent	6,400 (170)	6,100 (220)	5,200 (270)	3,600 (140)	94.7 (1.19)	41.3 (0.67)	42.6 (0.96)	46.8 (1.54)	43.9 (1.40)
5 to 19 percent	4,800 (180)	5,200 (270)	5,400 (320)	5,700 (310)	92.4 (2.55)	36.6 (0.88)	38.0 (1.77)	48.4 (2.06)	44.9 (1.02)
20 to 49 percent	4,000 (170)	4,700 (180)	6,200 (440)	5,900 (270)	91.2 (1.14)	32.5 (0.92)	34.1 (1.27)	35.0 (1.89)	39.6 (1.31)
50 percent or more	4,800 (150)	6,500 (280)	7,300 (430)	8,100 (320)	81.7 (1.58)	28.7 (0.89)	25.8 (1.43)	30.8 (2.00)	33.0 (1.17)
Percent of students approved for free or reduced-price lunch									
School does not participate	2,400 (130)	2,400 (230)	2,800 (320)	1,900 (250)	72.8 (7.11)	30.0 (1.75)	23.2 (2.26)	25.4 (4.12)	27.6 (5.24)
0 to 25 percent	8,600 (180)	6,800 (230)	6,700 (360)	5,100 (220)	93.3 (1.02)	42.6 (0.67)	46.9 (0.78)	52.1 (1.63)	50.7 (1.42)
26 to 50 percent	4,800 (160)	6,700 (220)	7,300 (350)	6,800 (230)	92.8 (0.91)	33.4 (0.81)	36.7 (1.08)	41.5 (1.44)	42.5 (1.00)
51 to 75 percent	2,300 (140)	4,000 (270)	4,100 (290)	5,100 (260)	90.3 (1.06)	29.1 (1.57)	27.3 (1.58)	33.2 (1.91)	35.8 (1.35)
76 to 100 percent	2,000 (100)	2,600 (260)	3,300 (360)	4,300 (230)	82.3 (1.93)	22.2 (1.35)	20.7 (2.79)	26.0 (2.93)	29.1 (1.66)
School locale									
City	— (†)	4,500 (240)	4,800 (300)	5,100 (220)	81.3 (3.11)	— (†)	32.5 (1.61)	36.1 (2.73)	38.6 (1.53)
Suburb	— (†)	4,800 (200)	5,400 (360)	4,800 (160)	86.1 (1.50)	— (†)	40.3 (1.11)	41.2 (2.35)	42.2 (1.42)
Town	— (†)	3,700 (200)	3,900 (310)	3,300 (260)	89.9 (2.21)	— (†)	31.1 (1.65)	35.2 (2.28)	35.3 (1.76)
Rural	— (†)	9,500 (390)	10,000 (460)	10,100 (260)	93.4 (0.67)	— (†)	35.2 (1.28)	41.9 (1.47)	39.8 (0.88)
Private high schools	7,600 (240)	8,200 (260)	8,900 (280)	8,900 (310)	92.4 (1.34)	55.6 (1.74)	56.2 (1.77)	66.5 (1.57)	64.3 (2.10)
Percent of students who are Black, Hispanic, Asian, Pacific Islander, American Indian/Alaska Native, or Two or more races									
Less than 5 percent	2,700 (150)	2,500 (180)	2,100 (160)	1,600 (190)	96.1 (1.72)	53.3 (2.85)	54.4 (3.71)	68.2 (3.81)	58.0 (6.31)
5 to 19 percent	2,500 (130)	2,900 (170)	3,500 (200)	3,100 (230)	95.1 (1.90)	63.6 (2.37)	64.2 (2.71)	70.3 (2.24)	67.9 (3.40)
20 to 49 percent	1,400 (100)	1,700 (140)	2,000 (190)	2,200 (200)	90.4 (2.33)	55.3 (3.29)	56.7 (3.70)	58.7 (3.39)	69.4 (3.89)
50 percent or more	1,000 (110)	1,100 (140)	1,400 (130)	1,900 (190)	87.1 (3.49)	41.6 (5.34)	38.3 (4.52)	65.3 (3.37)	57.6 (5.18)
Percent of students approved for free or reduced-price lunch									
School does not participate	6,700 (230)	7,100 (250)	7,300 (280)	7,400 (280)	93.3 (1.27)	57.0 (1.74)	56.2 (2.00)	68.3 (1.77)	66.5 (2.29)
0 to 25 percent	700 (70)	600 (80)	700 (100)	600 (80)	96.8 (2.45)	53.8 (5.69)	66.2 (4.35)	73.2 (4.64)	74.6 (5.23)
26 to 100 percent	‡ (†)	400 (80)	1,000 (130)	900 (140)	83.0 (5.65)	‡ (†)	38.9 (6.70)	46.7 (6.86)	37.8 (8.06)
School locale									
City	— (†)	— (†)	3,100 (170)	3,100 (190)	‡ (†)	—	—	71.8 (2.62)	‡ (†)
Suburb	— (†)	— (†)	2,800 (180)	2,800 (230)	‡ (†)	—	—	67.0 (2.99)	‡ (†)
Town	— (†)	— (†)	1,000 (150)	1,000 (200)	‡ (†)	—	—	63.8 (5.02)	‡ (†)
Rural	— (†)	— (†)	2,000 (190)	1,900 (190)	‡ (†)	—	—	58.9 (3.54)	‡ (†)

—Not available.
†Not applicable.
‡Reporting standards not met. Data may be suppressed because the response rate is under 50 percent, there are too few cases for a reliable estimate, or the coefficient of variation (CV) is 50 percent or greater.
[1]The 12th-grade graduation rate is the number of students who graduated from grade 12 with a diploma during the 2010–11 school year divided by 12th-grade enrollment in October 2010.

NOTE: Data are based on a sample survey and may not be strictly comparable with data reported elsewhere. Includes all schools, including combined schools, with students enrolled in the 12th grade. Some data have been revised from previously published figures. Detail may not sum to totals because of rounding.
SOURCE: U.S. Department of Education, National Center for Education Statistics, Schools and Staffing Survey (SASS), "Public School Teacher Data File" and "Private School Teacher Data File," 1999–2000, 2003–04, 2007–08, and 2011–12; and "Charter School Teacher Data File," 1999–2000. (This table was prepared April 2014.)

Table 302.43. Percentage distribution of fall 2009 ninth-graders who had completed high school, by postsecondary enrollment status in fall 2013, and selected measures of their high school achievement and selected student characteristics: 2013

[Standard errors appear in parentheses]

Selected student characteristic	All students who had completed high school	Students not enrolled in a postsecondary institution	Total enrolled in a postsecondary institution	Students enrolled in a postsecondary institution — Enrolled in a degree or certificate program — Total, all programs	Occupational certificate program[1]	Associate's degree program	Bachelor's degree program	Taking classes only, not enrolled in program
1	2	3	4	5	6	7	8	9
				Percentage distribution				
Total	100.0 (†)	25.5 (0.85)	74.5 (0.85)	60.1 (0.88)	3.3 (0.27)	25.0 (0.60)	31.8 (0.85)	14.5 (0.56)
Sex								
Male	100.0 (†)	30.0 (1.22)	70.0 (1.22)	56.6 (1.32)	3.4 (0.41)	23.1 (0.84)	30.1 (1.07)	13.4 (0.76)
Female	100.0 (†)	21.0 (0.92)	79.0 (0.92)	63.5 (0.96)	3.3 (0.34)	26.8 (0.80)	33.4 (0.97)	15.5 (0.77)
Race/ethnicity								
White	100.0 (†)	23.4 (0.81)	76.6 (0.81)	65.1 (0.83)	3.1 (0.33)	23.3 (0.75)	38.7 (1.01)	11.6 (0.54)
Black	100.0 (†)	28.8 (2.11)	71.2 (2.11)	52.9 (2.73)	3.3 (0.78)	25.9 (1.93)	23.8 (2.37)	18.3 (1.97)
Hispanic	100.0 (†)	30.0 (2.36)	70.0 (2.36)	51.5 (2.07)	4.1 (0.74)	29.1 (1.74)	18.3 (1.38)	18.4 (1.59)
Asian	100.0 (†)	10.2 (2.38)	89.8 (2.38)	73.6 (2.74)	0.9 ! (0.37)	22.5 (2.46)	50.1 (3.57)	16.2 (2.21)
Pacific Islander	100.0 (†)	‡ (†)	80.2 (10.01)	39.9 ! (13.24)	‡ (†)	‡ (†)	17.7 ! (7.74)	40.3 ! (15.26)
American Indian/Alaska Native	100.0 (†)	27.5 (7.09)	72.5 (7.09)	60.6 (6.79)	16.1 ! (7.64)	22.0 ! (7.58)	22.5 ! (10.09)	11.9 ! (5.06)
Two or more races	100.0 (†)	28.8 (2.52)	71.2 (2.52)	56.4 (2.44)	3.2 ! (1.08)	25.2 (1.97)	28.0 (2.18)	14.8 (1.89)
Socioeconomic status (SES)[2]								
Low SES	100.0 (†)	41.1 (1.89)	58.9 (1.89)	40.8 (2.11)	5.3 (0.80)	23.1 (1.57)	12.3 (1.39)	18.2 (1.68)
Middle SES	100.0 (†)	26.7 (1.00)	73.3 (1.00)	58.4 (1.04)	3.4 (0.36)	27.4 (0.79)	27.6 (0.92)	14.9 (0.67)
High SES	100.0 (†)	8.4 (0.67)	91.6 (0.67)	81.5 (1.01)	1.4 (0.36)	19.8 (0.98)	60.4 (1.36)	10.1 (0.82)
Highest mathematics course completed in high school								
Algebra I or below	100.0 (†)	56.2 (3.79)	43.8 (3.79)	28.7 (3.01)	9.5 (1.93)	15.5 (2.23)	3.7 ! (1.33)	15.0 (2.67)
Geometry	100.0 (†)	53.5 (3.39)	46.5 (3.39)	30.5 (2.57)	5.0 (1.17)	21.5 (2.58)	4.0 (0.87)	16.0 (2.34)
Algebra II/trigonometry	100.0 (†)	31.2 (1.39)	68.8 (1.39)	52.2 (1.37)	4.6 (0.69)	29.7 (1.31)	17.9 (1.23)	16.6 (1.05)
Other math[3]	100.0 (†)	25.5 (1.77)	74.5 (1.77)	60.3 (1.82)	3.2 (0.48)	29.7 (1.58)	27.5 (1.54)	14.2 (1.18)
Precalculus	100.0 (†)	11.7 (1.07)	88.3 (1.07)	72.8 (1.28)	1.5 (0.31)	24.7 (1.15)	46.6 (1.47)	15.5 (0.96)
Calculus[4]	100.0 (†)	5.1 (0.89)	94.9 (0.89)	86.7 (1.44)	0.6 ! (0.26)	16.4 (1.34)	69.8 (1.72)	8.2 (1.04)
Ever took dual enrollment course(s) in high school	100.0 (†)	9.3 (0.93)	90.7 (0.93)	79.9 (1.27)	1.8 (0.39)	29.2 (1.33)	48.9 (1.44)	10.8 (0.96)
As 9th-grader, expected to complete								
High school or less	100.0 (†)	47.0 (2.49)	53.0 (2.49)	36.4 (2.29)	4.8 (1.24)	21.7 (1.83)	9.9 (2.15)	16.6 (2.00)
Some college	100.0 (†)	33.0 (2.66)	67.0 (2.66)	49.9 (3.28)	7.1 (1.17)	29.0 (2.89)	13.8 (1.82)	17.1 (2.33)
Bachelor's or graduate/professional degree	100.0 (†)	17.1 (0.75)	82.9 (0.75)	69.7 (0.90)	2.3 (0.28)	25.9 (0.75)	41.6 (0.94)	13.1 (0.60)
Bachelor's degree	100.0 (†)	41.7 (1.92)	58.3 (1.92)	41.5 (1.84)	5.7 (0.83)	24.5 (1.53)	11.4 (1.39)	16.8 (1.38)
Graduate or professional degree	100.0 (†)	20.2 (1.23)	79.8 (1.23)	65.8 (1.72)	2.1 (0.41)	26.6 (1.46)	37.1 (1.72)	14.0 (1.40)
Don't know	100.0 (†)	15.8 (0.89)	84.2 (0.89)	71.4 (1.02)	2.3 (0.35)	25.5 (0.93)	43.5 (1.22)	12.8 (0.72)
As of spring of 11th grade, had taken the following at least once								
PSAT or PLAN	100.0 (†)	18.5 (0.81)	81.5 (0.81)	68.1 (0.91)	2.4 (0.27)	24.3 (0.74)	41.4 (0.99)	13.4 (0.66)
SAT or ACT	100.0 (†)	19.0 (1.12)	81.0 (1.12)	68.0 (1.27)	3.3 (0.47)	21.8 (0.94)	42.9 (1.34)	13.0 (0.86)
Any Advanced Placement (AP) test	100.0 (†)	15.8 (1.24)	84.2 (1.24)	71.0 (1.42)	3.1 (0.71)	21.8 (1.22)	46.1 (1.60)	13.2 (1.13)
Any International Baccalaureate (IB) test	100.0 (†)	18.8 (3.72)	81.2 (3.72)	63.9 (5.05)	‡ (†)	21.1 (5.01)	31.2 (5.85)	17.3 (3.95)
As 11th-grader, thought would qualify for this type of financial aid								
Aid based on financial need	100.0 (†)	26.8 (1.03)	73.2 (1.03)	57.2 (1.13)	3.6 (0.35)	28.2 (0.97)	25.4 (0.90)	16.0 (0.91)
Aid based on academic achievement such as good grades or college admission test scores	100.0 (†)	17.0 (0.73)	83.0 (0.73)	69.3 (0.97)	2.3 (0.28)	25.4 (0.81)	41.6 (0.94)	13.7 (0.69)
Aid through an athletic scholarship	100.0 (†)	23.3 (1.57)	76.7 (1.57)	62.0 (1.84)	2.8 (0.58)	26.9 (1.66)	32.4 (1.67)	14.7 (1.29)
Federal or state loans	100.0 (†)	24.0 (1.09)	76.0 (1.09)	60.4 (1.14)	3.8 (0.43)	27.4 (0.98)	29.3 (0.97)	15.6 (0.90)
Private loans	100.0 (†)	21.9 (1.25)	78.1 (1.25)	64.0 (1.42)	3.0 (0.50)	26.3 (1.35)	34.7 (1.40)	14.2 (1.04)
Completed a Free Application for Federal Student Aid (FAFSA)	100.0 (†)	11.1 (0.62)	88.9 (0.62)	74.8 (0.84)	3.4 (0.35)	30.4 (0.72)	41.0 (1.01)	14.0 (0.66)

See notes at end of table.

Table 302.43. Percentage distribution of fall 2009 ninth-graders who had completed high school, by postsecondary enrollment status in fall 2013, and selected measures of their high school achievement and selected student characteristics: 2013—Continued

[Standard errors appear in parentheses]

Selected student characteristic	All students who had completed high school	Students not enrolled in a postsecondary institution	Total enrolled in a postsecondary institution	Students enrolled in a postsecondary institution					Taking classes only, not enrolled in program
				Enrolled in a degree or certificate program					
				Total, all programs	Occupational certificate program[1]	Associate's degree program	Bachelor's degree program		
1	2	3	4	5	6	7	8		9
For students who did not complete a FAFSA, did not do so because student or family									
Did not want to take on debt	100.0 (†)	47.2 (3.04)	52.8 (3.04)	38.4 (2.95)	4.8 ! (1.47)	15.6 (1.90)	18.0 (2.02)		14.4 (2.18)
Can afford without financial aid	100.0 (†)	31.3 (2.35)	68.7 (2.35)	55.0 (2.72)	2.6 ! (0.94)	21.6 (2.01)	30.7 (2.64)		13.8 (1.96)
Thought may be ineligible or not qualify	100.0 (†)	32.9 (2.67)	67.1 (2.67)	53.2 (2.57)	2.8 ! (0.92)	20.6 (2.05)	29.8 (2.26)		13.9 (1.82)
Thought would not qualify because									
Other family member didn't qualify	100.0 (†)	33.1 (6.16)	66.9 (6.16)	52.5 (5.61)	‡ (†)	22.6 (3.88)	28.3 (4.88)		14.4 (4.25)
Concerns about credit score	100.0 (†)	64.6 (7.70)	35.4 (7.70)	21.1 (5.01)	‡ (†)	17.2 (4.90)	‡ (†)		14.3 ! (6.15)
Family income too high	100.0 (†)	16.4 (2.42)	83.6 (2.42)	69.9 (2.79)	1.6 ! (0.64)	24.5 (2.66)	43.8 (2.85)		13.6 (2.09)
Grades or test scores too low	100.0 (†)	60.7 (5.31)	39.3 (5.31)	22.7 (4.18)	‡ (†)	15.1 (3.96)	5.0 ! (2.04)		16.5 (3.55)
Part-time postsecondary enrollment	100.0 (†)	70.2 (5.94)	29.8 (5.94)	13.2 ! (4.69)	‡ (†)	10.6 ! (4.62)	‡ (†)		16.6 (4.91)
Did not have enough information about how to complete a FAFSA	100.0 (†)	56.2 (3.42)	43.8 (3.42)	29.3 (2.90)	4.5 (1.30)	18.2 (2.58)	6.7 (1.28)		14.5 (2.55)
Thought FAFSA forms too much work or too time-consuming	100.0 (†)	43.2 (4.83)	56.8 (4.83)	42.2 (4.67)	‡ (†)	18.6 (4.42)	19.5 (2.79)		14.7 (3.23)
Did not know you could complete a FAFSA	100.0 (†)	59.5 (4.12)	40.5 (4.12)	24.1 (3.29)	4.9 ! (1.86)	14.0 (2.44)	5.2 (1.45)		16.3 (3.32)
Not planning to continue education after high school	100.0 (†)	93.4 (1.89)	6.6 (1.89)	3.2 ! (0.97)	‡ (†)	1.8 ! (0.81)	‡ (†)		3.4 ! (1.61)
Selected measures of high school achievement									
Total number of credits earned in high school[5]	25.8 (0.12)	23.9 (0.21)	26.4 (0.13)	26.6 (0.14)	24.2 (0.54)	26.1 (0.18)	27.3 (0.20)		25.6 (0.28)
Overall GPA earned in high school[6]	2.8 (0.01)	2.3 (0.02)	3.0 (0.01)	3.0 (0.01)	2.4 (0.06)	2.8 (0.02)	3.3 (0.01)		2.6 (0.03)
Average SAT/ACT score (standardized to SAT)[7]	988 (6.5)	854 (10.4)	1008 (6.4)	1023 (5.9)	811 (29.7)	936 (7.3)	1083 (6.4)		922 (14.1)

†Not applicable.
!Interpret data with caution. The coefficient of variation (CV) for this estimate is between 30 and 50 percent.
‡Reporting standards not met. Either there are too few cases for a reliable estimate or the coefficient of variation (CV) is 50 percent or greater.
[1]A certificate or diploma program at a school that provides occupational training. Such a program usually takes 2 years or less to complete and often leads to a license, such as cosmetology.
[2]SES was measured by a composite score based on parental education and occupations, family income, and school urbanicity in the student's 11th-grade year. The weighted SES distribution (weighted by W2STUDENT) was divided into five equal groups. Low SES corresponds to the lowest one-fifth of the population, and high SES corresponds to the highest one-fifth of the population. The three fifths in the middle were combined to form the middle SES category.
[3]Includes integrated math, algebra III, probability and statistics, and non-calculus Advanced Placement (AP) or International Baccalaureate (IB) courses.

[4]Includes AP/IB calculus.
[5]Ranges from 0 to 59.
[6]Includes all courses and ranges from 0 to 4.
[7]The average applies to all students who took the SAT or ACT. For those who took the SAT, the combined critical reading and mathematics score was used. For those who took the ACT, scores were converted to the equivalent of the SAT combined score. Scale ranges from 400 to 1600.
NOTE: Includes students who completed high school by September 2013. Estimates weighted by W3W1W2STUTR. Race categories exclude persons of Hispanic ethnicity. Detail may not sum to totals because of rounding.
SOURCE: U.S. Department of Education, National Center for Education Statistics, High School Longitudinal Study of 2009 (HSLS:09), Base-Year, First Follow-up, 2013 Update, and High School Transcripts Restricted-Use Data File. (This table was prepared January 2016.)

Table 302.50. Estimated rate of 2011–12 high school graduates attending degree-granting postsecondary institutions, by state: 2012

State	Number of graduates from high schools located in the state			Number of fall 2012 first-time freshmen graduating from high school in the previous 12 months		Estimated rate of high school graduates going to college	
	Total[1]	Public, 2011–12	Private, 2012–13	State residents enrolled in institutions in any state[2]	State residents enrolled in institutions in their home state[3]	In any state	In their home state
1	2	3	4	5	6	7	8
United States	3,457,955	3,149,185	308,770	2,132,264 [4]	1,729,792	61.7	50.0
Alabama	50,164	45,394	4,770	29,728	26,567	59.3	53.0
Alaska	8,189	7,989	200	3,732	2,413	45.6	29.5
Arizona	66,218	63,208	3,010	35,181	31,132	53.1	47.0
Arkansas	30,019	28,419	1,600	20,185	18,244	67.2	60.8
California	451,364	418,664	32,700	263,843	231,215	58.5	51.2
Colorado	52,607	50,087	2,520	31,139	23,268	59.2	44.2
Connecticut	44,751	38,681	6,070	31,662	17,396	70.8	38.9
Delaware	10,037	8,247	1,790	6,500	4,632	64.8	46.1
District of Columbia[5]	5,680	3,860	1,820	2,463	450	43.4	7.9
Florida	171,404	151,964	19,440	107,716	94,985	62.8	55.4
Georgia	99,952	90,582	9,370	66,494	55,399	66.5	55.4
Hawaii	13,970	11,360	2,610	9,040	6,091	64.7	43.6
Idaho	18,238	17,568	670	8,782	6,179	48.2	33.9
Illinois	153,605	139,575	14,030	92,394	63,610	60.2	41.4
Indiana	70,767	65,667	5,100	44,612	38,812	63.0	54.8
Iowa	41,550	33,230	2,400	23,488	20,340	56.5	49.0
Kansas	34,078	31,898	2,180	22,239	19,058	65.3	55.9
Kentucky	47,442	42,642	4,800	29,830	26,624	62.9	56.1
Louisiana	44,575	36,675	7,900	28,831	26,024	64.7	58.4
Maine	16,103	13,473	2,630	8,681	5,829	53.9	36.2
Maryland	67,781	58,811	8,970	41,033	25,773	60.5	38.0
Massachusetts	76,177	65,157	11,020	53,836	36,132	70.7	47.4
Michigan	115,256	105,446	9,810	70,843	63,296	61.5	54.9
Minnesota	61,891	57,501	4,390	43,264	30,237	69.9	48.9
Mississippi	29,748	26,158	3,590	23,436	21,752	78.8	73.1
Missouri	69,053	61,313	7,740	42,762	35,648	61.9	51.6
Montana	10,140	9,750	390	5,907	4,598	58.3	45.3
Nebraska	22,844	20,464	2,380	14,750	11,969	64.6	52.4
Nevada	22,731	21,891	840	12,288	9,310	54.1	41.0
New Hampshire	16,886	14,426	2,460	10,418	5,618	61.7	33.3
New Jersey	106,919	93,819	13,100	72,631	41,204	67.9	38.5
New Mexico	21,375	20,315	1,060	14,831	12,903	69.4	60.4
New York	209,216	180,806	28,410	146,458	117,960	70.0	56.4
North Carolina	101,097	93,977	7,120	62,531	55,578	61.9	55.0
North Dakota	7,322	6,942	380	4,751	3,527	64.9	48.2
Ohio	135,885	123,135	12,750	81,428	69,039	59.9	50.8
Oklahoma	39,295	37,305	1,990	22,667	20,207	57.7	51.4
Oregon	37,301	34,261	3,040	17,509	13,343	46.9	35.8
Pennsylvania	146,493	131,733	14,760	87,075	70,625	59.4	48.2
Rhode Island	11,501	9,751	1,750	7,715	5,056	67.1	44.0
South Carolina	44,452	41,442	3,010	29,023	26,154	65.3	58.8
South Dakota	8,456	8,196	260	5,825	4,443	68.9	52.5
Tennessee	67,964	62,454	5,510	41,027	34,318	60.4	50.5
Texas	306,591	292,531	14,060	176,871	156,566	57.7	51.1
Utah	32,757	31,157	1,600	16,650	15,101	50.8	46.1
Vermont	7,789	6,859	930	4,142	2,040	53.2	26.2
Virginia	89,866	83,336	6,530	58,035	47,582	64.6	52.9
Washington	71,165	65,205	5,960	34,168	25,854	48.0	36.3
West Virginia	18,383	17,603	780	10,241	9,110	55.7	49.6
Wisconsin	71,225	62,705	8,520	41,715	33,972	58.6	47.7
Wyoming	5,603	5,553	50	3,170	2,426	56.6	43.3

[1]Total includes public high school graduates for 2011–12 and private high school graduates for 2012–13. Data on private high school graduates are not available for 2011–12.
[2]All U.S. resident students living in a particular state when admitted to an institution in any state. Students may be enrolled in any state.
[3]Students who attend institutions in their home state. Total includes 183 students attending U.S. Service Academies in their home state, not shown separately.
[4]U.S. total includes some U.S. residents whose home state is unknown.
[5]A percentage of the private high school graduates are not residents of the District of Columbia.

NOTE: Degree-granting institutions grant associate's or higher degrees and participate in Title IV federal financial aid programs. Detail may not sum to totals because of rounding.
SOURCE: U.S. Department of Education, National Center for Education Statistics, Common Core of Data (CCD), "NCES Common Core of Data State Dropout and Completion Data File," 2011–12; Private School Universe Survey (PSS), 2013–14; and Integrated Postsecondary Education Data System (IPEDS), Spring 2013, Fall Enrollment component. (This table was prepared January 2016.)

Table 302.60. Percentage of 18- to 24-year-olds enrolled in degree-granting postsecondary institutions, by level of institution and sex and race/ethnicity of student: 1970 through 2014

[Standard errors appear in parentheses]

Year	Total, all students	Level of institution		Sex		Race/ethnicity							Race/ethnicity by sex					
											American Indian/		White		Black		Hispanic	
		2-year	4-year	Male	Female	White	Black	Hispanic	Asian	Pacific Islander	Alaska Native	Two or more races	Male	Female	Male	Female	Male	Female
1	2	3	4	5	6	7	8	9	10	11	12	13	14	15	16	17	18	19
1970[1]	25.7 (0.42)	—	—	32.1 (0.63)	20.3 (0.52)	27.1 (0.45)	15.5 (1.15)	—	‡	‡	‡	‡	—	—	‡	—	‡	—
1971	26.2 (0.41)	—	—	32.5 (0.61)	20.8 (0.52)	27.2 (0.44)	18.2 (1.19)	—	‡	‡	‡	‡	—	—	‡	—	‡	—
1972	25.5 (0.37)	—	—	30.2 (0.56)	21.2 (0.47)	27.2 (0.41)	18.3 (1.18)	13.4 (1.63)	‡	‡	‡	‡	32.3 (0.63)	22.5 (0.54)	21.1 (1.83)	15.9 (1.51)	15.1 (2.85)	12.0 (2.37)
1973	24.0 (0.35)	6.9 (0.21)	17.1 (0.31)	27.7 (0.54)	20.5 (0.46)	25.5 (0.40)	15.9 (1.09)	16.1 (2.02)	‡	‡	‡	‡	29.6 (0.60)	21.8 (0.53)	18.7 (1.77)	13.5 (1.38)	16.7 (2.94)	15.5 (2.77)
1974	24.6 (0.35)	7.6 (0.22)	17.0 (0.31)	27.7 (0.53)	21.7 (0.47)	25.8 (0.40)	18.0 (1.14)	18.0 (1.95)	‡	‡	‡	‡	28.9 (0.60)	22.9 (0.53)	19.8 (1.77)	15.9 (1.47)	19.7 (2.92)	16.5 (2.60)
1975	26.3 (0.36)	9.0 (0.23)	17.3 (0.31)	29.0 (0.53)	23.7 (0.48)	27.4 (0.40)	20.4 (1.18)	20.4 (2.09)	‡	‡	‡	‡	30.7 (0.59)	24.3 (0.54)	19.9 (1.74)	20.8 (1.61)	21.4 (3.10)	19.5 (2.81)
1976	26.7 (0.35)	6.4 (0.20)	20.2 (0.32)	28.2 (0.52)	25.2 (0.48)	27.6 (0.40)	22.5 (1.20)	20.0 (2.00)	‡	‡	‡	‡	29.3 (0.58)	26.1 (0.55)	22.0 (1.77)	22.9 (1.64)	21.3 (3.05)	18.8 (2.64)
1977	26.1 (0.35)	6.8 (0.22)	19.4 (0.35)	28.1 (0.56)	24.3 (0.50)	27.2 (0.43)	21.1 (1.18)	17.2 (1.87)	‡	‡	‡	‡	29.4 (0.64)	25.1 (0.59)	20.3 (1.79)	21.6 (1.61)	18.3 (2.80)	16.3 (2.50)
1978	25.3 (0.38)	6.6 (0.22)	18.7 (0.34)	27.1 (0.55)	23.6 (0.51)	26.5 (0.43)	20.1 (1.15)	15.2 (1.74)	‡	‡	‡	‡	28.4 (0.63)	24.6 (0.59)	19.7 (1.70)	20.4 (1.56)	16.1 (2.61)	14.3 (2.33)
1979	25.0 (0.37)	6.3 (0.21)	18.7 (0.34)	25.9 (0.54)	24.2 (0.52)	26.3 (0.43)	19.8 (1.13)	16.7 (1.77)	‡	‡	‡	‡	27.1 (0.61)	25.5 (0.59)	19.1 (1.67)	20.3 (1.54)	18.3 (2.65)	15.2 (2.35)
1980	25.7 (0.38)	7.1 (0.22)	18.6 (0.33)	26.4 (0.54)	25.0 (0.52)	27.3 (0.43)	19.4 (1.09)	16.1 (1.64)	‡	‡	‡	‡	28.4 (0.63)	26.3 (0.60)	17.5 (1.60)	20.9 (1.55)	15.9 (2.33)	16.2 (2.32)
1981	26.1 (0.37)	7.5 (0.22)	18.6 (0.33)	27.1 (0.54)	25.2 (0.51)	27.7 (0.43)	19.9 (1.09)	16.6 (1.63)	‡	‡	‡	‡	28.7 (0.63)	26.6 (0.60)	18.9 (1.58)	20.7 (1.51)	16.6 (2.35)	16.7 (2.27)
1982	26.6 (0.39)	7.7 (0.24)	18.9 (0.35)	27.2 (0.57)	26.0 (0.55)	28.1 (0.46)	19.9 (1.14)	16.8 (1.77)	‡	‡	‡	‡	28.9 (0.66)	27.4 (0.64)	18.7 (1.64)	21.0 (1.59)	14.9 (2.45)	18.6 (2.52)
1983	26.2 (0.39)	7.4 (0.23)	18.8 (0.35)	27.3 (0.58)	25.1 (0.54)	27.9 (0.46)	19.2 (1.12)	17.3 (1.77)	‡	‡	‡	‡	29.0 (0.66)	26.5 (0.64)	18.1 (1.63)	20.1 (1.56)	15.6 (2.46)	18.8 (2.54)
1984	27.1 (0.40)	7.3 (0.24)	19.8 (0.36)	28.6 (0.58)	25.6 (0.55)	28.9 (0.47)	20.3 (1.15)	17.9 (1.80)	‡	‡	‡	‡	30.8 (0.68)	27.1 (0.65)	20.3 (1.67)	20.3 (1.57)	16.1 (2.51)	19.6 (2.57)
1985	27.8 (0.41)	7.4 (0.24)	20.4 (0.37)	28.4 (0.60)	27.2 (0.57)	30.0 (0.49)	19.6 (1.16)	16.9 (1.84)	‡	‡	‡	‡	30.9 (0.70)	29.2 (0.67)	20.2 (1.72)	19.1 (1.56)	14.9 (2.46)	18.9 (2.75)
1986	27.9 (0.42)	7.6 (0.25)	20.3 (0.37)	28.2 (0.60)	27.6 (0.58)	29.7 (0.50)	21.9 (1.21)	17.6 (1.76)	‡	‡	‡	‡	30.6 (0.72)	28.8 (0.68)	20.0 (1.72)	23.4 (1.69)	16.7 (2.36)	18.7 (2.64)
1987	29.6 (0.43)	8.1 (0.29)	21.5 (0.42)	30.6 (0.62)	28.7 (0.59)	31.9 (0.57)	22.8 (1.25)	17.5 (1.73)	‡	‡	‡	‡	33.0 (0.74)	30.8 (0.71)	22.6 (1.83)	22.9 (1.70)	18.5 (2.46)	16.5 (2.43)
1988	30.3 (0.47)	8.8 (0.29)	21.5 (0.42)	30.2 (0.68)	30.4 (0.66)	33.2 (0.57)	21.2 (1.33)	17.0 (2.00)	‡	‡	‡	‡	33.4 (0.82)	33.0 (0.79)	18.5 (1.87)	23.5 (1.88)	17.4 (2.74)	17.6 (2.93)
1989	30.9 (0.48)	8.0 (0.28)	22.9 (0.44)	30.2 (0.68)	31.6 (0.67)	34.2 (0.58)	23.4 (1.38)	16.1 (1.90)	46.1 (3.92)	‡	15.7! (5.33)	‡	34.1 (0.83)	34.4 (0.81)	19.7 (1.89)	26.7 (1.97)	14.6 (2.55)	17.6 (2.81)
1990	32.0 (0.47)	8.7 (0.28)	23.3 (0.43)	32.3 (0.68)	31.8 (0.66)	35.1 (0.57)	25.4 (1.37)	15.8 (1.67)	56.9 (3.56)	‡	15.8 (5.08)	‡	35.5 (0.82)	34.7 (0.80)	26.0 (2.03)	24.8 (1.86)	15.3 (2.31)	16.4 (2.42)
1991	33.3 (0.48)	9.7 (0.30)	23.6 (0.44)	32.8 (0.68)	33.6 (0.67)	35.5 (0.58)	23.5 (1.34)	17.9 (1.72)	57.1 (3.19)	‡	15.9 (5.45)	‡	36.5 (0.84)	37.0 (0.84)	23.6 (1.95)	23.8 (1.84)	14.0 (2.15)	22.2 (2.70)
1992	34.4 (0.49)	9.9 (0.31)	24.4 (0.44)	32.7 (0.69)	36.0 (0.69)	37.3 (0.59)	25.2 (1.35)	21.3 (1.87)	58.4 (3.28)	‡	18.5! (6.18)	‡	36.2 (0.84)	38.3 (0.83)	21.3 (1.87)	28.8 (1.96)	19.8 (2.47)	24.7 (2.80)
1993	34.0 (0.49)	9.8 (0.30)	24.2 (0.44)	33.6 (0.69)	34.4 (0.68)	36.8 (0.59)	24.5 (1.35)	21.8 (1.88)	61.2 (3.27)	‡	18.9 (5.66)	‡	36.5 (0.84)	37.1 (0.83)	22.9 (1.92)	26.0 (1.90)	19.7 (2.60)	23.7 (2.71)
1994	34.6 (0.42)	9.1 (0.36)	25.5 (0.39)	33.1 (0.59)	36.0 (0.60)	38.1 (0.53)	27.7 (1.17)	18.8 (1.10)	62.7 (2.81)	‡	29.4 (5.64)	‡	37.0 (0.74)	39.2 (0.74)	25.6 (1.66)	29.5 (1.64)	16.5 (1.43)	21.5 (1.71)
1995	34.3 (0.44)	8.9 (0.27)	25.4 (0.41)	33.1 (0.63)	35.5 (0.63)	37.9 (0.55)	27.5 (1.18)	20.7 (1.13)	54.6 (3.10)	‡	27.6 (6.14)	‡	37.0 (0.78)	38.8 (0.78)	26.0 (1.71)	28.7 (1.62)	18.7 (1.49)	23.0 (1.71)
1996	35.5 (0.47)	9.5 (0.29)	26.1 (0.43)	34.1 (0.66)	37.0 (0.67)	39.5 (0.59)	27.4 (1.23)	20.1 (1.18)	53.9 (2.47)	‡	30.3 (5.25)	‡	38.3 (0.83)	40.6 (0.84)	25.7 (1.75)	28.8 (1.70)	16.5 (1.52)	24.0 (1.81)
1997	36.8 (0.46)	9.7 (0.29)	27.0 (0.43)	35.0 (0.66)	38.7 (0.67)	40.6 (0.59)	29.8 (1.25)	22.4 (1.21)	55.1 (2.60)	‡	27.1 (4.63)	‡	39.3 (0.82)	41.8 (0.84)	25.4 (1.76)	33.7 (1.77)	19.2 (1.56)	26.1 (1.88)
1998	36.5 (0.46)	10.2 (0.29)	26.3 (0.42)	34.5 (0.65)	38.6 (0.66)	40.6 (0.58)	29.8 (1.24)	20.4 (1.21)	60.4 (2.49)	‡	20.3 (4.91)	‡	39.4 (0.82)	41.9 (0.84)	26.1 (1.76)	32.9 (1.73)	16.4 (1.56)	24.9 (1.73)
1999	35.6 (0.46)	9.1 (0.27)	26.5 (0.42)	34.1 (0.64)	37.0 (0.65)	39.4 (0.58)	30.4 (1.24)	18.7 (1.08)	55.7 (2.42)	‡	19.5 (4.71)	‡	38.3 (0.81)	40.6 (0.82)	28.9 (1.81)	31.6 (1.70)	15.8 (1.41)	21.9 (1.65)
2000	35.5 (0.45)	9.4 (0.28)	26.0 (0.41)	32.6 (0.63)	38.4 (0.65)	38.7 (0.57)	30.5 (1.21)	21.7 (1.12)	55.9 (2.42)	‡	15.9 (4.30)	‡	36.2 (0.79)	41.3 (0.81)	25.1 (1.67)	35.2 (1.72)	18.5 (1.45)	25.4 (1.72)
2001	36.3 (0.45)	9.8 (0.28)	26.6 (0.41)	33.6 (0.63)	39.0 (0.64)	39.5 (0.57)	31.4 (1.22)	21.7 (1.10)	61.3 (2.35)	‡	23.3 (4.29)	‡	37.2 (0.79)	41.9 (0.82)	26.7 (1.63)	35.5 (1.71)	17.4 (1.42)	26.1 (1.67)
2002[2]	36.7 (0.43)	9.7 (0.26)	27.0 (0.39)	33.7 (0.59)	39.7 (0.61)	40.9 (0.55)	31.9 (1.18)	19.9 (0.94)	60.9 (2.10)	‡	23.6 (3.96)	‡	38.9 (0.77)	42.8 (0.78)	26.3 (1.63)	36.9 (1.68)	16.2 (1.17)	24.4 (1.51)
2003[2]	37.8 (0.43)	10.2 (0.27)	27.7 (0.39)	34.3 (0.59)	41.3 (0.61)	41.6 (0.55)	32.3 (1.20)	23.5 (1.02)	61.2 (2.27)	43.3 (9.97)	17.7 (4.45)	41.6 (3.58)	38.5 (0.77)	44.5 (0.78)	28.2 (1.65)	36.0 (1.69)	18.3 (1.27)	29.4 (1.60)
2004[2]	38.0 (0.42)	9.4 (0.25)	28.6 (0.39)	34.7 (0.59)	41.2 (0.61)	41.7 (0.55)	31.8 (1.18)	24.7 (1.02)	60.6 (2.24)	55.8 (8.99)	24.4 (4.52)	36.8 (3.44)	38.4 (0.76)	45.0 (0.78)	26.5 (1.63)	36.6 (1.67)	21.7 (1.33)	28.2 (1.56)
2005[2,3]	38.9 (0.43)	9.6 (0.26)	29.2 (0.40)	35.3 (0.59)	42.5 (0.61)	42.8 (0.55)	33.1 (1.18)	24.8 (1.02)	61.0 (2.26)	50.6 (10.95)	27.8 (4.88)	41.8 (3.48)	39.4 (0.76)	46.1 (0.79)	28.2 (1.64)	37.6 (1.69)	20.7 (1.31)	29.5 (1.58)
2006[2,3]	37.3 (0.42)	9.6 (0.25)	27.8 (0.39)	34.1 (0.58)	40.6 (0.60)	41.0 (0.54)	32.6 (1.16)	23.6 (0.99)	58.3 (2.28)	39.1 (8.36)	26.2 (5.18)	38.5 (3.51)	37.9 (0.75)	44.1 (0.78)	28.1 (1.60)	36.9 (1.65)	20.7 (1.29)	27.6 (1.52)
2007[2,3]	38.8 (0.42)	10.9 (0.27)	27.9 (0.38)	35.5 (0.58)	42.1 (0.60)	42.6 (0.54)	33.1 (1.15)	26.7 (1.02)	57.2 (2.36)	37.1 (9.07)	24.7 (4.63)	39.2 (3.48)	39.6 (0.76)	45.7 (0.78)	32.2 (1.63)	34.0 (1.61)	20.7 (1.35)	33.0 (1.57)
2008[2,3]	39.6 (0.42)	11.8 (0.28)	27.8 (0.38)	35.0 (0.59)	42.3 (0.60)	44.2 (0.54)	32.1 (1.13)	25.8 (1.01)	59.3 (2.17)	27.3! (8.92)	21.9 (4.22)	45.7 (3.55)	41.7 (0.76)	46.9 (0.78)	29.7 (1.61)	34.2 (1.59)	23.0 (1.35)	28.9 (1.50)
2009[2,3]	41.3 (0.42)	11.7 (0.27)	29.6 (0.39)	38.4 (0.59)	44.2 (0.60)	45.0 (0.54)	37.7 (1.17)	25.5 (1.01)	65.2 (2.37)	33.4 (7.45)	29.8 (5.10)	39.3 (3.32)	42.3 (0.76)	47.7 (0.77)	33.2 (1.64)	41.9 (1.64)	24.2 (1.64)	31.0 (1.50)
2010[2,3]	41.2 (0.57)	12.9 (0.36)	28.2 (0.53)	38.3 (0.78)	44.1 (0.84)	43.3 (0.81)	38.4 (1.66)	31.9 (1.15)	63.6 (2.70)	36.0 (8.36)	41.4 (6.60)	38.3 (4.38)	40.6 (1.00)	46.1 (1.17)	35.2 (2.13)	41.4 (2.16)	27.9 (1.57)	36.1 (1.60)
2011[2,3]	42.0 (0.59)	12.0 (0.35)	30.0 (0.58)	39.1 (0.80)	44.9 (0.80)	44.7 (0.77)	37.1 (1.53)	34.8 (1.20)	60.1 (2.45)	37.8 (7.93)	23.5 (5.30)	38.8 (3.60)	42.4 (0.96)	47.1 (1.08)	34.0 (2.29)	39.9 (1.90)	31.0 (1.63)	39.4 (1.58)
2012[2,3]	41.0 (0.60)	12.7 (0.38)	28.3 (0.58)	37.6 (0.79)	44.5 (0.86)	42.1 (0.83)	36.4 (1.53)	37.5 (1.18)	59.8 (2.61)	50.3 (9.60)	27.8 (4.43)	39.4 (3.64)	38.1 (1.06)	46.0 (1.08)	33.9 (2.13)	38.7 (2.33)	33.5 (1.72)	41.7 (1.73)
2013[2,3]	39.9 (0.63)	11.6 (0.36)	28.3 (0.57)	36.6 (0.85)	43.3 (0.80)	41.6 (0.90)	34.2 (1.58)	35.8 (1.24)	62.3 (2.82)	32.9 (8.26)	31.8 (5.58)	44.7 (3.48)	38.1 (1.11)	45.3 (1.11)	30.6 (2.13)	37.6 (2.18)	29.1 (1.72)	38.8 (1.58)
2014[2,3]	40.0 (0.65)	10.6 (0.40)	29.4 (0.61)	37.3 (0.89)	42.8 (0.79)	42.2 (0.87)	32.6 (1.48)	34.7 (1.21)	65.2 (2.27)	41.0 (11.29)	35.4 (4.63)	31.6 (3.20)	40.2 (1.28)	44.2 (0.99)	28.5 (1.95)	36.6 (2.04)	30.3 (1.65)	39.4 (1.70)

—Not available.
†Not applicable.
‡Reporting standards not met.
!Interpret data with caution. The coefficient of variation (CV) for this estimate is between 30 and 50 percent.
[1]Prior to 1972, White and Black data include persons of Hispanic ethnicity.
[2]After 2002, data for individual race categories exclude persons of Two or more races. (This

[3]Beginning in 2010, standard errors were computed using replicate weights, which produced more precise values than the generalized variance function methodology used in prior years.
NOTE: Data are based on sample surveys of the civilian noninstitutionalized population. Totals include other racial/ethnic groups not separately shown. Race categories exclude persons of Hispanic ethnicity except where otherwise noted.
SOURCE: U.S. Department of Commerce, Census Bureau, Current Population Survey (CPS), October, 1970 through 2014. (This table was prepared August 2015.)

Table 302.62. Percentage of 18- to 24-year-olds enrolled in degree-granting postsecondary institutions and percentage distribution of those enrolled, by sex, race/ethnicity, and selected racial/ethnic subgroups: 2009 and 2014

[Standard errors appear in parentheses]

Race/ethnicity	2009 Total		2009 Male		2009 Female		2014 Total		2014 Male		2014 Female	
1	2		3		4		5		6		7	
Percent enrolled												
Total[1]	41.7	(0.12)	37.3	(0.19)	46.3	(0.17)	42.1	(0.13)	38.2	(0.18)	46.3	(0.17)
White	45.7	(0.15)	41.6	(0.23)	50.0	(0.22)	44.4	(0.17)	40.7	(0.23)	48.4	(0.24)
Black	35.3	(0.34)	29.6	(0.52)	41.2	(0.57)	35.6	(0.34)	30.4	(0.46)	41.0	(0.46)
Hispanic	29.1	(0.29)	24.5	(0.35)	34.4	(0.41)	35.4	(0.28)	30.8	(0.35)	40.4	(0.37)
Cuban	45.5	(1.67)	43.1	(2.25)	48.1	(2.59)	45.7	(1.53)	41.8	(2.27)	50.2	(2.04)
Dominican	37.0	(1.66)	32.9	(2.02)	41.2	(2.79)	41.0	(1.49)	33.2	(1.62)	49.2	(2.21)
Mexican	26.2	(0.32)	21.7	(0.41)	31.3	(0.49)	33.4	(0.36)	29.0	(0.44)	38.1	(0.47)
Puerto Rican	29.9	(0.75)	24.6	(1.10)	35.2	(1.03)	32.7	(0.84)	28.6	(1.01)	37.0	(1.26)
Spaniard	43.6	(3.18)	38.3	(4.44)	48.5	(4.35)	47.9	(2.45)	41.6	(3.64)	54.8	(3.88)
Central American[2]	26.8	(0.81)	22.3	(1.05)	33.0	(1.39)	32.9	(0.83)	27.7	(1.15)	39.4	(1.12)
Costa Rican	39.6	(5.44)	41.1	(6.90)	37.1	(9.08)	55.1	(5.75)	50.8	(8.69)	58.9	(6.87)
Guatemalan	18.8	(1.40)	14.1	(1.55)	27.7	(2.72)	27.2	(1.44)	20.0	(1.80)	38.9	(2.19)
Honduran	20.0	(1.87)	13.8	(2.27)	28.5	(2.97)	27.0	(2.00)	25.1	(2.88)	29.3	(3.22)
Nicaraguan	43.4	(3.34)	41.7	(4.61)	45.0	(4.46)	51.5	(2.87)	46.4	(4.53)	56.3	(4.45)
Panamanian	53.1	(4.54)	41.5	(6.75)	63.8	(5.46)	50.3	(4.23)	42.9	(6.62)	57.0	(5.67)
Salvadoran	28.4	(1.37)	26.0	(1.63)	31.3	(1.98)	32.5	(1.27)	29.1	(1.64)	36.5	(1.61)
South American	49.4	(1.38)	45.6	(1.75)	53.3	(1.93)	54.7	(1.17)	50.6	(1.69)	58.9	(1.60)
Chilean	56.1	(4.70)	45.5	(6.99)	68.3	(7.22)	47.1	(6.62)	37.9	(7.19)	56.1	(9.33)
Colombian	50.0	(2.11)	45.4	(2.77)	55.2	(3.00)	57.9	(2.44)	53.7	(3.71)	61.9	(2.47)
Ecuadorian	42.4	(2.80)	34.9	(3.51)	50.0	(4.14)	48.2	(2.32)	44.8	(3.64)	51.9	(3.65)
Peruvian	54.3	(2.92)	50.8	(3.89)	57.7	(4.15)	54.9	(3.16)	50.7	(3.98)	59.7	(3.92)
Venezuelan	57.5	(4.66)	62.3	(7.00)	52.2	(6.32)	58.3	(3.45)	56.8	(6.10)	59.9	(5.05)
Other South American	45.8	(3.87)	48.2	(5.57)	43.4	(4.87)	55.8	(3.26)	51.2	(4.11)	60.3	(4.31)
Other Hispanic	37.0	(1.49)	30.6	(1.76)	43.2	(1.92)	40.1	(1.27)	34.9	(1.75)	45.8	(1.91)
Asian	64.6	(0.56)	64.3	(0.78)	64.9	(0.77)	65.3	(0.44)	65.1	(0.60)	65.5	(0.67)
Chinese[3]	75.5	(0.96)	75.8	(1.39)	75.1	(1.38)	75.5	(0.72)	75.1	(1.03)	76.0	(0.99)
Filipino	55.3	(1.26)	52.5	(1.72)	58.1	(2.03)	55.1	(1.34)	54.7	(1.84)	55.5	(2.04)
Japanese	65.8	(2.92)	66.6	(3.80)	65.2	(3.81)	71.4	(3.00)	67.8	(4.74)	74.4	(3.49)
Korean	67.7	(1.47)	64.2	(2.42)	70.9	(2.10)	68.7	(1.60)	67.5	(2.16)	69.8	(2.56)
South Asian[4]	66.3	(1.18)	68.3	(1.63)	63.9	(1.64)	64.3	(0.97)	65.8	(1.30)	62.7	(1.46)
Asian Indian	66.4	(1.22)	68.8	(1.74)	63.5	(1.76)	67.0	(1.05)	68.2	(1.36)	65.7	(1.69)
Bangladeshi	57.2	(6.29)	52.3	(8.74)	63.9	(8.10)	62.4	(5.41)	79.6	(5.46)	47.4	(8.07)
Bhutanese	—	(†)	—	(†)	—	(†)	‡	(†)	‡	(†)	‡	(†)
Nepalese	—	(†)	—	(†)	—	(†)	45.5	(6.44)	45.6	(8.34)	45.4	(8.11)
Pakistani	67.4	(3.72)	69.1	(4.67)	65.5	(4.49)	58.7	(2.62)	60.5	(4.02)	56.9	(3.73)
Southeast Asian	54.9	(1.26)	53.9	(1.57)	55.8	(1.81)	56.5	(1.21)	54.8	(1.59)	58.1	(1.73)
Burmese	—	(†)	—	(†)	—	(†)	27.5	(5.10)	29.5	(6.79)	25.2	(5.60)
Cambodian	36.2	(3.56)	29.8	(4.34)	43.3	(4.91)	39.9	(3.67)	31.0	(5.18)	46.8	(4.83)
Hmong	40.2	(2.64)	38.7	(4.04)	42.0	(4.52)	43.1	(3.33)	37.9	(4.88)	48.2	(4.51)
Laotian	40.3	(4.69)	37.7	(6.40)	42.5	(5.90)	36.1	(4.67)	24.8	(5.89)	45.4	(6.32)
Thai	61.6	(5.06)	68.6	(7.04)	57.6	(7.13)	50.2	(5.59)	52.6	(7.76)	47.8	(7.74)
Vietnamese	65.1	(1.65)	65.6	(2.09)	64.6	(2.17)	66.9	(1.56)	65.9	(1.95)	67.9	(2.19)
Other Southeast Asian[5]	80.9	(6.16)	83.2	(7.52)	78.6	(7.74)	71.5	(6.19)	84.6	(6.73)	58.4	(10.66)
Other Asian	63.1	(2.35)	63.1	(3.15)	63.1	(3.14)	66.1	(2.27)	67.4	(3.08)	64.8	(3.16)
Pacific Islander	33.2	(2.82)	30.3	(3.50)	36.6	(3.81)	30.5	(2.59)	30.7	(3.95)	30.3	(3.65)
American Indian/Alaska Native	24.8	(0.99)	21.0	(1.41)	28.7	(1.68)	24.9	(0.96)	20.1	(1.42)	29.7	(1.68)
Two or more races	42.1	(0.82)	37.0	(1.29)	47.1	(1.00)	44.5	(0.65)	41.3	(0.91)	47.8	(0.86)
White and Black	40.8	(1.58)	35.6	(2.39)	45.7	(2.26)	38.6	(1.17)	34.1	(1.73)	43.2	(1.50)
White and Asian	54.7	(1.57)	49.9	(2.44)	59.5	(2.05)	57.1	(1.65)	56.4	(1.97)	57.8	(2.20)
White and American Indian/ Alaska Native	34.3	(1.56)	28.2	(2.41)	40.7	(2.18)	33.8	(1.52)	29.3	(1.86)	39.0	(2.28)
Other Two or more races	40.4	(1.69)	36.4	(1.89)	44.3	(2.89)	48.4	(1.55)	46.1	(2.06)	50.6	(1.92)
Percentage distribution of those enrolled												
Total[1]	100.0	(†)	46.1	(0.18)	53.9	(0.18)	100.0	(†)	46.5	(0.14)	53.5	(0.14)
White	100.0	(†)	46.7	(0.20)	53.3	(0.20)	100.0	(†)	47.0	(0.18)	53.0	(0.18)
Black	100.0	(†)	42.8	(0.62)	57.2	(0.62)	100.0	(†)	43.4	(0.45)	56.6	(0.45)
Hispanic	100.0	(†)	44.6	(0.44)	55.4	(0.44)	100.0	(†)	45.2	(0.36)	54.8	(0.36)
Cuban	100.0	(†)	48.7	(2.27)	51.3	(2.27)	100.0	(†)	48.7	(2.02)	51.3	(2.02)
Dominican	100.0	(†)	45.6	(2.88)	54.4	(2.88)	100.0	(†)	41.3	(1.72)	58.7	(1.72)
Mexican	100.0	(†)	44.2	(0.61)	55.8	(0.61)	100.0	(†)	44.9	(0.47)	55.1	(0.47)
Puerto Rican	100.0	(†)	41.8	(1.45)	58.2	(1.45)	100.0	(†)	44.8	(1.49)	55.2	(1.49)
Spaniard	100.0	(†)	42.5	(4.96)	57.5	(4.96)	100.0	(†)	45.7	(4.17)	54.3	(4.17)
Central American[2]	100.0	(†)	48.0	(1.94)	52.0	(1.94)	100.0	(†)	46.7	(1.53)	53.3	(1.53)
Costa Rican	100.0	(†)	65.8	(8.03)	34.2	(8.03)	100.0	(†)	43.6	(8.07)	56.4	(8.07)
Guatemalan	100.0	(†)	49.3	(3.59)	50.7	(3.59)	100.0	(†)	45.6	(3.13)	54.4	(3.13)
Honduran	100.0	(†)	40.0	(5.16)	60.0	(5.16)	100.0	(†)	52.1	(5.21)	47.9	(5.21)
Nicaraguan	100.0	(†)	48.2	(5.09)	51.8	(5.09)	100.0	(†)	43.9	(4.59)	56.1	(4.59)
Panamanian	100.0	(†)	37.5	(6.74)	62.5	(6.74)	100.0	(†)	40.4	(5.44)	59.6	(5.44)
Salvadoran	100.0	(†)	49.7	(2.53)	50.3	(2.53)	100.0	(†)	47.9	(1.75)	52.1	(1.75)

See notes at end of table.

Table 302.62. Percentage of 18- to 24-year-olds enrolled in degree-granting postsecondary institutions and percentage distribution of those enrolled, by sex, race/ethnicity, and selected racial/ethnic subgroups: 2009 and 2014—Continued

[Standard errors appear in parentheses]

Race/ethnicity	2009 Total		2009 Male		2009 Female		2014 Total		2014 Male		2014 Female	
1	2		3		4		5		6		7	
South American	100.0	(†)	47.1	(1.73)	52.9	(1.73)	100.0	(†)	46.7	(1.47)	53.3	(1.47)
Chilean	100.0	(†)	43.3	(7.82)	56.7	(7.82)	100.0	(†)	39.7	(7.55)	60.3	(7.55)
Colombian	100.0	(†)	47.7	(2.73)	52.3	(2.73)	100.0	(†)	45.4	(2.40)	54.6	(2.40)
Ecuadorian	100.0	(†)	41.4	(3.84)	58.6	(3.84)	100.0	(†)	48.4	(3.62)	51.6	(3.62)
Peruvian	100.0	(†)	45.8	(3.37)	54.2	(3.37)	100.0	(†)	49.2	(3.38)	50.8	(3.38)
Venezuelan	100.0	(†)	57.4	(5.57)	42.6	(5.57)	100.0	(†)	49.2	(4.82)	50.8	(4.82)
Other South American	100.0	(†)	52.2	(4.60)	47.8	(4.60)	100.0	(†)	44.7	(4.22)	55.3	(4.22)
Other Hispanic	100.0	(†)	40.6	(2.00)	59.4	(2.00)	100.0	(†)	45.0	(2.24)	55.0	(2.24)
Asian	100.0	(†)	50.8	(0.58)	49.2	(0.58)	100.0	(†)	50.4	(0.52)	49.6	(0.52)
Chinese[3]	100.0	(†)	52.3	(1.12)	47.7	(1.12)	100.0	(†)	51.0	(0.94)	49.0	(0.94)
Filipino	100.0	(†)	46.7	(1.66)	53.3	(1.66)	100.0	(†)	50.4	(1.79)	49.6	(1.79)
Japanese	100.0	(†)	49.4	(3.33)	50.6	(3.33)	100.0	(†)	42.9	(3.64)	57.1	(3.64)
Korean	100.0	(†)	45.7	(1.89)	54.3	(1.89)	100.0	(†)	49.4	(1.91)	50.6	(1.91)
South Asian[4]	100.0	(†)	55.7	(1.45)	44.3	(1.45)	100.0	(†)	52.5	(1.22)	47.5	(1.22)
Asian Indian	100.0	(†)	56.0	(1.75)	44.0	(1.75)	100.0	(†)	52.7	(1.40)	47.3	(1.40)
Bangladeshi	100.0	(†)	52.9	(8.16)	47.1	(8.16)	100.0	(†)	59.3	(5.98)	40.7	(5.98)
Bhutanese	—	(†)	—	(†)	—	(†)	100.0	(†)	‡	(†)	‡	(†)
Nepalese	—	(†)	—	(†)	—	(†)	100.0	(†)	56.8	(7.26)	43.2	(7.26)
Pakistani	100.0	(†)	56.0	(3.25)	44.0	(3.25)	100.0	(†)	51.4	(3.70)	48.6	(3.70)
Southeast Asian	100.0	(†)	49.7	(1.54)	50.3	(1.54)	100.0	(†)	47.4	(1.57)	52.6	(1.57)
Burmese	—	(†)	—	(†)	—	(†)	100.0	(†)	58.3	(7.22)	41.7	(7.22)
Cambodian	100.0	(†)	43.0	(4.59)	57.0	(4.59)	100.0	(†)	33.7	(5.85)	66.3	(5.85)
Hmong	100.0	(†)	52.2	(4.45)	47.8	(4.45)	100.0	(†)	43.7	(4.11)	56.3	(4.11)
Laotian	100.0	(†)	42.4	(6.18)	57.6	(6.18)	100.0	(†)	31.0	(6.44)	69.0	(6.44)
Thai	100.0	(†)	41.1	(6.71)	58.9	(6.71)	100.0	(†)	51.8	(6.84)	48.2	(6.84)
Vietnamese	100.0	(†)	52.0	(1.95)	48.0	(1.95)	100.0	(†)	48.7	(1.69)	51.3	(1.69)
Other Southeast Asian[5]	100.0	(†)	50.9	(6.39)	49.1	(6.39)	100.0	(†)	59.2	(9.89)	40.8	(9.89)
Other Asian	100.0	(†)	49.6	(3.34)	50.4	(3.34)	100.0	(†)	53.2	(3.09)	46.8	(3.09)
Pacific Islander	100.0	(†)	48.9	(4.53)	51.1	(4.53)	100.0	(†)	54.4	(5.58)	45.6	(5.58)
American Indian/Alaska Native	100.0	(†)	42.2	(2.75)	57.8	(2.75)	100.0	(†)	39.9	(2.55)	60.1	(2.55)
Two or more races	100.0	(†)	44.0	(1.38)	56.0	(1.38)	100.0	(†)	47.1	(0.87)	52.9	(0.87)
White and Black	100.0	(†)	42.6	(2.70)	57.4	(2.70)	100.0	(†)	44.3	(2.05)	55.7	(2.05)
White and Asian	100.0	(†)	45.8	(2.38)	54.2	(2.38)	100.0	(†)	50.0	(1.73)	50.0	(1.73)
White and American Indian/ Alaska Native	100.0	(†)	42.6	(3.12)	57.4	(3.12)	100.0	(†)	46.7	(2.49)	53.3	(2.49)
Other Two or more races	100.0	(†)	44.8	(2.87)	55.2	(2.87)	100.0	(†)	47.1	(1.88)	52.9	(1.88)

—Not available.
†Not applicable.
‡Reporting standards not met (too few cases for a reliable estimate).
[1]Total includes other racial/ethnic groups not shown separately.
[2]Includes other Central American subgroups not shown separately.
[3]Includes Taiwanese.
[4]In addition to the subgroups shown, also includes Sri Lankan.
[5]Consists of Indonesian and Malaysian.

NOTE: Data are based on sample surveys of the entire population in the indicated age range, including persons living in households, noninstitutionalized group quarters (such as college or military housing), and institutionalized group quarters (such as correctional or nursing facilities). Enrollment data in this table may differ from data in tables based on the Current Population Survey (CPS) because of differences in survey design and target populations. Race categories exclude persons of Hispanic ethnicity. Detail may not sum to totals because of rounding.
SOURCE: U.S. Department of Commerce, Census Bureau, American Community Survey (ACS), 2009 and 2014. (This table was prepared April 2016.)

Table 303.10. Total fall enrollment in degree-granting postsecondary institutions, by attendance status, sex of student, and control of institution: Selected years, 1947 through 2025

Year	Total enrollment	Attendance status			Sex of student			Control of institution			
		Full-time	Part-time	Percent part-time	Male	Female	Percent female	Public	Private		
									Total	Nonprofit	For-profit
1	2	3	4	5	6	7	8	9	10	11	12
1947[1]	2,338,226	—	—	—	1,659,249	678,977	29.0	1,152,377	1,185,849	—	—
1948[1]	2,403,396	—	—	—	1,709,367	694,029	28.9	1,185,588	1,217,808	—	—
1949[1]	2,444,900	—	—	—	1,721,572	723,328	29.6	1,207,151	1,237,749	—	—
1950[1]	2,281,298	—	—	—	1,560,392	720,906	31.6	1,139,699	1,141,599	—	—
1951[1]	2,101,962	—	—	—	1,390,740	711,222	33.8	1,037,938	1,064,024	—	—
1952[1]	2,134,242	—	—	—	1,380,357	753,885	35.3	1,101,240	1,033,002	—	—
1953[1]	2,231,054	—	—	—	1,422,598	808,456	36.2	1,185,876	1,045,178	—	—
1954[1]	2,446,693	—	—	—	1,563,382	883,311	36.1	1,353,531	1,093,162	—	—
1955[1]	2,653,034	—	—	—	1,733,184	919,850	34.7	1,476,282	1,176,752	—	—
1956[1]	2,918,212	—	—	—	1,911,458	1,006,754	34.5	1,656,402	1,261,810	—	—
1957	3,323,783	—	—	—	2,170,765	1,153,018	34.7	1,972,673	1,351,110	—	—
1959	3,639,847	2,421,016	1,218,831[2]	33.5	2,332,617	1,307,230	35.9	2,180,982	1,458,865	—	—
1961	4,145,065	2,785,133	1,359,932[2]	32.8	2,585,821	1,559,244	37.6	2,561,447	1,583,618	—	—
1963	4,779,609	3,183,833	1,595,776[2]	33.4	2,961,540	1,818,069	38.0	3,081,279	1,698,330	—	—
1964	5,280,020	3,573,238	1,706,782[2]	32.3	3,248,713	2,031,307	38.5	3,467,708	1,812,312	—	—
1965	5,920,864	4,095,728	1,825,136[2]	30.8	3,630,020	2,290,844	38.7	3,969,596	1,951,268	—	—
1966	6,389,872	4,438,606	1,951,266[2]	30.5	3,856,216	2,533,656	39.7	4,348,917	2,040,955	—	—
1967	6,911,748	4,793,128	2,118,620[2]	30.7	4,132,800	2,778,948	40.2	4,816,028	2,095,720	2,074,041	21,679
1968	7,513,091	5,210,155	2,302,936	30.7	4,477,649	3,035,442	40.4	5,430,652	2,082,439	2,061,211	21,228
1969	8,004,660	5,498,883	2,505,777	31.3	4,746,201	3,258,459	40.7	5,896,868	2,107,792	2,087,653	20,139
1970	8,580,887	5,816,290	2,764,597	32.2	5,043,642	3,537,245	41.2	6,428,134	2,152,753	2,134,420	18,333
1971	8,948,644	6,077,232	2,871,412	32.1	5,207,004	3,741,640	41.8	6,804,309	2,144,335	2,121,913	22,422
1972	9,214,860	6,072,389	3,142,471	34.1	5,238,757	3,976,103	43.1	7,070,635	2,144,225	2,123,245	20,980
1973	9,602,123	6,189,493	3,412,630	35.5	5,371,052	4,231,071	44.1	7,419,516	2,182,607	2,148,784	33,823
1974	10,223,729	6,370,273	3,853,456	37.7	5,622,429	4,601,300	45.0	7,988,500	2,235,229	2,200,963	34,266
1975	11,184,859	6,841,334	4,343,525	38.8	6,148,997	5,035,862	45.0	8,834,508	2,350,351	2,311,448	38,903
1976	11,012,137	6,717,058	4,295,079	39.0	5,810,828	5,201,309	47.2	8,653,477	2,358,660	2,314,298	44,362
1977	11,285,787	6,792,925	4,492,862	39.8	5,789,016	5,496,771	48.7	8,846,993	2,438,794	2,386,652	52,142
1978	11,260,092	6,667,657	4,592,435	40.8	5,640,998	5,619,094	49.9	8,785,893	2,474,199	2,408,331	65,868
1979	11,569,899	6,794,039	4,775,860	41.3	5,682,877	5,887,022	50.9	9,036,822	2,533,077	2,461,773	71,304
1980	12,096,895	7,097,958	4,998,937	41.3	5,874,374	6,222,521	51.4	9,457,394	2,639,501	2,527,787	111,714[3]
1981	12,371,672	7,181,250	5,190,422	42.0	5,975,056	6,396,616	51.7	9,647,032	2,724,640	2,572,405	152,235[3]
1982	12,425,780	7,220,618	5,205,162	41.9	6,031,384	6,394,396	51.5	9,696,087	2,729,693	2,552,739	176,954[3]
1983	12,464,661	7,261,050	5,203,611	41.7	6,023,725	6,440,936	51.7	9,682,734	2,781,927	2,589,187	192,740
1984	12,241,940	7,098,388	5,143,552	42.0	5,863,574	6,378,366	52.1	9,477,370	2,764,570	2,574,419	190,151
1985	12,247,055	7,075,221	5,171,834	42.2	5,818,450	6,428,605	52.5	9,479,273	2,767,782	2,571,791	195,991
1986	12,503,511	7,119,550	5,383,961	43.1	5,884,515	6,618,996	52.9	9,713,893	2,789,618	2,572,479	217,139[4]
1987	12,766,642	7,231,085	5,535,557	43.4	5,932,056	6,834,586	53.5	9,973,254	2,793,388	2,602,350	191,038[4]
1988	13,055,337	7,436,768	5,618,569	43.0	6,001,896	7,053,441	54.0	10,161,388	2,893,949	2,673,567	220,382
1989	13,538,560	7,660,950	5,877,610	43.4	6,190,015	7,348,545	54.3	10,577,963	2,960,597	2,731,174	229,423
1990	13,818,637	7,820,985	5,997,652	43.4	6,283,909	7,534,728	54.5	10,844,717	2,973,920	2,760,227	213,693
1991	14,358,953	8,115,329	6,243,624	43.5	6,501,844	7,857,109	54.7	11,309,563	3,049,390	2,819,041	230,349
1992	14,487,359	8,162,118	6,325,241	43.7	6,523,989	7,963,370	55.0	11,384,567	3,102,792	2,872,523	230,269
1993	14,304,803	8,127,618	6,177,185	43.2	6,427,450	7,877,353	55.1	11,189,088	3,115,715	2,888,897	226,818
1994	14,278,790	8,137,776	6,141,014	43.0	6,371,898	7,906,892	55.4	11,133,680	3,145,110	2,910,107	235,003
1995	14,261,781	8,128,802	6,132,979	43.0	6,342,539	7,919,242	55.5	11,092,374	3,169,407	2,929,044	240,363
1996	14,367,520	8,302,953	6,064,567	42.2	6,352,825	8,014,695	55.8	11,120,499	3,247,021	2,942,556	304,465
1997	14,502,334	8,438,062	6,064,272	41.8	6,396,028	8,106,306	55.9	11,196,119	3,306,215	2,977,614	328,601
1998	14,506,967	8,563,338	5,943,629	41.0	6,369,265	8,137,702	56.1	11,137,769	3,369,198	3,004,925	364,273
1999	14,849,691	8,803,139	6,046,552	40.7	6,515,164	8,334,527	56.1	11,375,739	3,473,952	3,055,029	418,923
2000	15,312,289	9,009,600	6,302,689	41.2	6,721,769	8,590,520	56.1	11,752,786	3,559,503	3,109,419	450,084
2001	15,927,987	9,447,502	6,480,485	40.7	6,960,815	8,967,172	56.3	12,233,156	3,694,831	3,167,330	527,501
2002	16,611,711	9,946,359	6,665,352	40.1	7,202,116	9,409,595	56.6	12,751,993	3,859,718	3,265,476	594,242
2003	16,911,481	10,326,133	6,585,348	38.9	7,260,264	9,651,217	57.1	12,858,698	4,052,783	3,341,048	711,735
2004	17,272,044	10,610,177	6,661,867	38.6	7,387,262	9,884,782	57.2	12,980,112	4,291,932	3,411,685	880,247
2005	17,487,475	10,797,011	6,690,464	38.3	7,455,925	10,031,550	57.4	13,021,834	4,465,641	3,454,692	1,010,949
2006	17,758,870	10,957,305	6,801,565	38.3	7,574,815	10,184,055	57.3	13,180,133	4,578,737	3,512,866	1,065,871
2007	18,248,128	11,269,892	6,978,236	38.2	7,815,914	10,432,214	57.2	13,490,780	4,757,348	3,571,150	1,186,198
2008	19,102,814	11,747,743	7,355,071	38.5	8,188,895	10,913,919	57.1	13,972,153	5,130,661	3,661,519	1,469,142
2009	20,313,594	12,605,355	7,708,239	37.9	8,732,953	11,580,641	57.0	14,810,768	5,502,826	3,767,672	1,735,154
2010	21,019,438	13,087,182	7,932,256	37.7	9,045,759	11,973,679	57.0	15,142,171	5,877,267	3,854,482	2,022,785
2011	21,010,590	13,002,531	8,008,059	38.1	9,034,256	11,976,334	57.0	15,116,303	5,894,287	3,926,819	1,967,468
2012	20,644,478	12,734,404	7,910,074	38.3	8,919,006	11,725,472	56.8	14,884,667	5,759,811	3,951,388	1,808,423
2013	20,375,789	12,597,112	7,778,677	38.2	8,860,786	11,515,003	56.5	14,745,558	5,630,231	3,974,004	1,656,227
2014	20,207,369	12,453,975	7,753,394	38.2	8,797,061	11,410,308	57.0	14,655,015	5,552,354	3,996,089	1,556,265

See notes at end of table.

Table 303.10. Total fall enrollment in degree-granting postsecondary institutions, by attendance status, sex of student, and control of institution: Selected years, 1947 through 2025—Continued

Year	Total enrollment	Attendance status			Sex of student			Control of institution			
		Full-time	Part-time	Percent part-time	Male	Female	Percent female	Public	Private		
									Total	Nonprofit	For-profit
1	2	3	4	5	6	7	8	9	10	11	12
2015[5]	20,264,000	12,484,000	7,779,000	38.3	8,760,000	11,503,000	57.3	14,789,000	5,475,000	—	—
2016[5]	20,516,000	12,651,000	7,865,000	38.5	8,808,000	11,708,000	57.6	14,964,000	5,552,000	—	—
2017[5]	20,972,000	12,942,000	8,030,000	38.6	8,944,000	12,028,000	57.9	15,287,000	5,686,000	—	—
2018[5]	21,410,000	13,207,000	8,203,000	38.7	9,118,000	12,292,000	58.1	15,604,000	5,807,000	—	—
2019[5]	21,753,000	13,403,000	8,349,000	38.8	9,260,000	12,493,000	58.2	15,852,000	5,900,000	—	—
2020[5]	22,013,000	13,550,000	8,463,000	38.9	9,364,000	12,648,000	58.4	16,038,000	5,975,000	—	—
2021[5]	22,323,000	13,726,000	8,597,000	39.0	9,496,000	12,827,000	58.5	16,261,000	6,062,000	—	—
2022[5]	22,613,000	13,894,000	8,720,000	39.0	9,625,000	12,989,000	58.7	16,471,000	6,143,000	—	—
2023[5]	22,896,000	14,072,000	8,824,000	39.1	9,747,000	13,149,000	58.8	16,673,000	6,223,000	—	—
2024[5]	23,149,000	14,220,000	8,929,000	39.1	9,859,000	13,290,000	58.8	16,858,000	6,291,000	—	—
2025[5]	23,290,000	14,278,000	9,012,000	39.1	9,937,000	13,353,000	58.8	16,967,000	6,323,000	—	—

—Not available.

[1]Degree-credit enrollment only.

[2]Includes part-time resident students and all extension students (students attending courses at sites separate from the primary reporting campus). In later years, part-time student enrollment was collected as a distinct category.

[3]Large increases are due to the addition of schools accredited by the Accrediting Commission of Career Schools and Colleges of Technology.

[4]Because of imputation techniques, data are not consistent with figures for other years.

[5]Projected.

NOTE: Data through 1995 are for institutions of higher education, while later data are for degree-granting institutions. Degree-granting institutions grant associate's or higher degrees and partici-pate in Title IV federal financial aid programs. The degree-granting classification is very similar to the earlier higher education classification, but it includes more 2-year colleges and excludes a few higher education institutions that did not grant degrees. Some data have been revised from previously published figures.

SOURCE: U.S. Department of Education, National Center for Education Statistics, *Biennial Survey of Education in the United States*; *Opening Fall Enrollment in Higher Education*, 1963 through 1965; Higher Education General Information Survey (HEGIS), "Fall Enrollment in Colleges and Universities" surveys, 1966 through 1985; Integrated Postsecondary Education Data System (IPEDS), "Fall Enrollment Survey" (IPEDS-EF:86–99); IPEDS Spring 2001 through Spring 2015, Fall Enrollment component; and Enrollment in Degree-Granting Institutions Projection Model, 1980 through 2025. (This table was prepared February 2016.)

Table 303.20. Total fall enrollment in all postsecondary institutions participating in Title IV programs and annual percentage change in enrollment, by degree-granting status and control of institution: 1995 through 2014

Year	All Title IV institutions[1]				Degree-granting institutions[2]					Non-degree-granting institutions[3]			
			Private				Private					Private	
	Total	Public	Nonprofit	For-profit	Total	Public	Total	Nonprofit	For-profit	Total	Public	Nonprofit	For-profit
1	2	3	4	5	6	7	8	9	10	11	12	13	14
Enrollment													
1995	14,836,338	11,312,491	2,977,794	546,053	14,261,781	11,092,374	3,169,407	2,929,044	240,363	574,557	220,117	48,750	305,690
1996	14,809,897	11,312,775	2,976,850	520,272	14,367,520	11,120,499	3,247,021	2,942,556	304,465	442,377	192,276	34,294	215,807
1997	14,900,416	11,370,755	3,012,106	517,555	14,502,334	11,196,119	3,306,215	2,977,614	328,601	398,082	174,636	34,492	188,954
1998	14,923,839	11,330,811	3,040,251	552,777	14,506,967	11,137,769	3,369,198	3,004,925	364,273	416,872	193,042	35,326	188,504
1999	15,262,888	11,556,731	3,088,233	617,924	14,849,691	11,375,739	3,473,952	3,055,029	418,923	413,197	180,992	33,204	199,001
2000	15,701,409	11,891,450	3,137,108	672,851	15,312,289	11,752,786	3,559,503	3,109,419	450,084	389,120	138,664	27,689	222,767
2001	16,334,134	12,370,079	3,198,354	765,701	15,927,987	12,233,156	3,694,831	3,167,330	527,501	406,147	136,923	31,024	238,200
2002	17,035,027	12,883,071	3,299,094	852,862	16,611,711	12,751,993	3,859,718	3,265,476	594,242	423,316	131,078	33,618	258,620
2003	17,330,775	12,965,502	3,372,647	992,626	16,911,481	12,858,698	4,052,783	3,341,048	711,735	419,294	106,804	31,599	280,891
2004	17,710,798	13,081,358	3,440,559	1,188,881	17,272,044	12,980,112	4,291,932	3,411,685	880,247	438,754	101,246	28,874	308,634
2005	17,921,804	13,115,177	3,484,013	1,322,614	17,487,475	13,021,834	4,465,641	3,454,692	1,010,949	434,329	93,343	29,321	311,665
2006	18,205,474	13,281,664	3,543,455	1,380,355	17,758,870	13,180,133	4,578,737	3,512,866	1,065,871	446,604	101,531	30,589	314,484
2007	18,671,084	13,595,849	3,595,207	1,480,028	18,248,128	13,490,780	4,757,348	3,571,150	1,186,198	422,956	105,069	24,057	293,830
2008	19,574,395	14,092,109	3,684,723	1,797,563	19,102,814	13,972,153	5,130,661	3,661,519	1,469,142	471,581	119,956	23,204	328,421
2009	20,853,423	14,936,402	3,793,751	2,123,270	20,313,594	14,810,768	5,502,826	3,767,672	1,735,154	539,829	125,634	26,079	388,116
2010	21,591,742	15,279,455	3,881,630	2,430,657	21,019,438	15,142,171	5,877,267	3,854,482	2,022,785	572,304	137,284	27,148	407,872
2011	21,573,798	15,251,185	3,954,173	2,368,440	21,010,590	15,116,303	5,894,287	3,926,819	1,967,468	563,208	134,882	27,354	400,972
2012	21,148,181	15,000,302	3,973,422	2,174,457	20,644,478	14,884,667	5,759,811	3,951,388	1,808,423	503,703	115,635	22,034	366,034
2013	20,847,787	14,855,412	3,993,462	1,998,913	20,375,789	14,745,558	5,630,231	3,974,004	1,656,227	471,998	109,854	19,458	342,686
2014	20,663,464	14,765,873	4,015,094	1,882,497	20,207,369	14,655,015	5,552,354	3,996,089	1,556,265	456,095	110,858	19,005	326,232
Annual percentage change													
1995 to 1996	-0.2	#	#	-4.7	0.7	0.3	2.4	0.5	26.7	-23.0	-12.6	-29.7	-29.4
1996 to 1997	0.6	0.5	1.2	-0.5	0.9	0.7	1.8	1.2	7.9	-10.0	-9.2	0.6	-12.4
1997 to 1998	0.2	-0.4	0.9	6.8	#	-0.5	1.9	0.9	10.9	4.7	10.5	2.4	-0.2
1998 to 1999	2.3	2.0	1.6	11.8	2.4	2.1	3.1	1.7	15.0	-0.9	-6.2	-6.0	5.6
1999 to 2000	2.9	2.9	1.6	8.9	3.1	3.3	2.5	1.8	7.4	-5.8	-23.4	-16.6	11.9
2000 to 2001	4.0	4.0	2.0	13.8	4.0	4.1	3.8	1.9	17.2	4.4	-1.3	12.0	6.9
2001 to 2002	4.3	4.1	3.1	11.4	4.3	4.2	4.5	3.1	12.7	4.2	-4.3	8.4	8.6
2002 to 2003	1.7	0.6	2.2	16.4	1.8	0.8	5.0	2.3	19.8	-1.0	-18.5	-6.0	8.6
2003 to 2004	2.2	0.9	2.0	19.8	2.1	0.9	5.9	2.1	23.7	4.6	-5.2	-8.6	9.9
2004 to 2005	1.2	0.3	1.3	11.2	1.2	0.3	4.0	1.3	14.8	-1.0	-7.8	1.5	1.0
2005 to 2006	1.6	1.3	1.7	4.4	1.6	1.2	2.5	1.7	5.4	2.8	8.8	4.3	0.9
2006 to 2007	2.6	2.4	1.5	7.2	2.8	2.4	3.9	1.7	11.3	-5.3	3.5	-21.4	-6.6
2007 to 2008	4.8	3.7	2.5	21.5	4.7	3.6	7.8	2.5	23.9	11.5	14.2	-3.5	11.8
2008 to 2009	6.5	6.0	3.0	18.1	6.3	6.0	7.3	2.9	18.1	14.5	4.7	12.4	18.2
2009 to 2010	3.5	2.3	2.3	14.5	3.5	2.2	6.8	2.3	16.6	6.0	9.3	4.1	5.1
2010 to 2011	-0.1	-0.2	1.9	-2.6	#	-0.2	0.3	1.9	-2.7	-1.6	-1.7	0.8	-1.7
2011 to 2012	-2.0	-1.6	0.5	-8.2	-1.7	-1.5	-2.3	0.6	-8.1	-10.6	-14.3	-19.4	-8.7
2012 to 2013	-1.4	-1.0	0.5	-8.1	-1.3	-0.9	-2.2	0.6	-8.4	-6.3	-5.0	-11.7	-6.4
2013 to 2014	-0.9	-0.6	0.5	-5.8	-0.8	-0.6	-1.4	0.6	-6.0	-3.4	0.9	-2.3	-4.8

#Rounds to zero.
[1]Includes degree-granting and non-degree-granting institutions.
[2]Data for 1995 are for institutions of higher education, while later data are for degree-granting institutions. Degree-granting institutions grant associate's or higher degrees and participate in Title IV federal financial aid programs. The degree-granting classification is very similar to the earlier higher education classification, but it includes more 2-year colleges and excludes a few higher education institutions that did not grant degrees.

[3]Data are for institutions that did not offer accredited 4-year or 2-year programs, but were participating in Title IV federal financial aid programs. Includes some institutions transitioning to higher level offerings, though still classified at a lower level.
NOTE: Some data have been revised from previously published figures.
SOURCE: U.S. Department of Education, National Center for Education Statistics, Integrated Postsecondary Education Data System (IPEDS), "Fall Enrollment Survey" (IPEDS-EF:95–99); and IPEDS Spring 2001 through Spring 2015, Fall Enrollment component. (This table was prepared October 2015.)

Table 303.25. Total fall enrollment in degree-granting postsecondary institutions, by control and level of institution: 1970 through 2014

Year	All institutions			Public institutions			Private institutions								
							All private institutions			Nonprofit			For-profit		
	Total	4-year	2-year	Total	4-year	2-year	Total	4-year	2-year	Total	4-year	2-year	Total	4-year	2-year
1	2	3	4	5	6	7	8	9	10	11	12	13	14	15	16
1970	8,580,887	6,261,502	2,319,385	6,428,134	4,232,722	2,195,412	2,152,753	2,028,780	123,973	2,134,420	2,021,121	113,299	18,333	7,659	10,674
1971	8,948,644	6,369,355	2,579,289	6,804,309	4,346,990	2,457,319	2,144,335	2,022,365	121,970	2,121,913	2,011,682	110,231	22,422	10,683	11,739
1972	9,214,860	6,458,674	2,756,186	7,070,635	4,429,696	2,640,939	2,144,225	2,028,978	115,247	2,123,245	2,019,380	103,865	20,980	9,598	11,382
1973	9,602,123	6,590,023	3,012,100	7,419,516	4,529,895	2,889,621	2,182,607	2,060,128	122,479	2,148,784	2,045,804	102,980	33,823	14,324	19,499
1974	10,223,729	6,819,735	3,403,994	7,988,500	4,703,018	3,285,482	2,235,229	2,116,717	118,512	2,200,963	2,098,599	102,364	34,266	18,118	16,148
1975	11,184,859	7,214,740	3,970,119	8,834,508	4,998,142	3,836,366	2,350,351	2,216,598	133,753	2,311,448	2,198,451	112,997	38,903	18,147	20,756
1976	11,012,137	7,128,816	3,883,321	8,653,477	4,901,691	3,751,786	2,358,660	2,227,125	131,535	2,314,298	2,206,457	107,841	44,362	20,668	23,694
1977	11,285,787	7,242,845	4,042,942	8,846,993	4,945,224	3,901,769	2,438,794	2,297,621	141,173	2,386,652	2,277,072	109,580	52,142	20,549	31,593
1978	11,260,092	7,231,625	4,028,467	8,785,893	4,912,203	3,873,690	2,474,199	2,319,422	154,777	2,408,331	2,299,132	109,199	65,868	20,290	45,578
1979	11,569,899	7,353,233	4,216,666	9,036,822	4,980,012	4,056,810	2,533,077	2,373,221	159,856	2,461,773	2,351,364	110,409	71,304	21,857	49,447
1980	12,096,895	7,570,608	4,526,287	9,457,394	5,128,612	4,328,782	2,639,501	2,441,996	197,505 [1]	2,527,787	2,413,693	114,094	111,714	28,303	83,411 [1]
1981	12,371,672	7,655,461	4,716,211	9,647,032	5,166,324	4,480,708	2,724,640	2,489,137	235,503 [1]	2,572,405	2,453,239	119,166	152,235	35,898	116,337 [1]
1982	12,425,780	7,654,074	4,771,706	9,696,087	5,176,434	4,519,653	2,729,693	2,477,640	252,053 [1]	2,552,739	2,437,763	114,976	176,954	39,877	137,077 [1]
1983	12,464,661	7,741,195	4,723,466	9,682,734	5,223,404	4,459,330	2,781,927	2,517,791	264,136	2,589,187	2,472,894	116,293	192,740	44,897	147,843
1984	12,241,940	7,711,167	4,530,773	9,477,370	5,198,273	4,279,097	2,764,570	2,512,894	251,676	2,574,419	2,466,172	108,247	190,151	46,722	143,429
1985	12,247,055	7,715,978	4,531,077	9,479,273	5,209,540	4,269,733	2,767,782	2,506,438	261,344	2,571,791	2,463,000	108,791	195,991	43,438	152,553
1986	12,503,511	7,823,963	4,679,548	9,713,893	5,300,202	4,413,691	2,789,618	2,523,761	265,857 [2]	2,572,479	2,470,981	101,498	217,139	52,780	164,359 [2]
1987	12,766,642	7,990,420	4,776,222	9,973,254	5,432,200	4,541,054	2,793,388	2,558,220	235,168 [2]	2,602,350	2,512,248	90,102	191,038	45,972	145,066 [2]
1988	13,055,337	8,180,182	4,875,155	10,161,388	5,545,901	4,615,487	2,893,949	2,634,281	259,668	—	—	—	—	—	—
1989	13,538,560	8,387,671	5,150,889	10,577,963	5,694,303	4,883,660	2,960,597	2,693,368	267,229	—	—	—	—	—	—
1990	13,818,637	8,578,554	5,240,083	10,844,717	5,848,242	4,996,475	2,973,920	2,730,312	243,608	2,760,227	2,671,069	89,158	213,693	59,243	154,450
1991	14,358,953	8,707,053	5,651,900	11,309,563	5,904,748	5,404,815	3,049,390	2,802,305	247,085	2,819,041	2,729,752	89,289	230,349	72,553	157,796
1992	14,487,359	8,764,969	5,722,390	11,384,567	5,900,012	5,484,555	3,102,792	2,864,957	237,835	2,872,523	2,789,235	83,288	230,269	75,722	154,547
1993	14,304,803	8,738,936	5,565,867	11,189,088	5,851,760	5,337,328	3,115,715	2,887,176	228,539	2,888,897	2,802,540	86,357	226,818	84,636	142,182
1994	14,278,790	8,749,080	5,529,710	11,133,680	5,825,213	5,308,467	3,145,110	2,923,867	221,243	2,910,107	2,824,500	85,607	235,003	99,367	135,636
1995	14,261,781	8,769,252	5,492,529	11,092,374	5,814,545	5,277,829	3,169,407	2,954,707	214,700	2,929,044	2,853,890	75,154	240,363	100,817	139,546
1996	14,367,520	8,804,193	5,563,327	11,120,499	5,806,036	5,314,463	3,247,021	2,998,157	248,864	2,942,556	2,867,181	75,375	304,465	130,976	173,489
1997	14,502,334	8,896,765	5,605,569	11,196,119	5,835,433	5,360,686	3,306,215	3,061,332	244,883	2,977,614	2,905,820	71,794	328,601	155,512	173,089
1998	14,506,967	9,017,653	5,489,314	11,137,769	5,891,806	5,245,963	3,369,198	3,125,847	243,351	3,004,925	2,939,055	65,870	364,273	186,792	177,481
1999	14,849,691	9,196,160	5,653,531	11,375,739	5,977,678	5,398,061	3,473,952	3,218,482	255,470	3,055,029	2,991,728	63,301	418,923	226,754	192,169
2000	15,312,289	9,363,858	5,948,431	11,752,786	6,055,398	5,697,388	3,559,503	3,308,460	251,043	3,109,419	3,050,575	58,844	450,084	257,885	192,199
2001	15,927,987	9,677,408	6,250,579	12,233,156	6,236,455	5,996,701	3,694,831	3,440,953	253,878	3,167,330	3,119,781	47,549	527,501	321,172	206,329
2002	16,611,711	10,082,332	6,529,379	12,751,993	6,481,613	6,270,380	3,859,718	3,600,719	258,999	3,265,476	3,218,389	47,087	594,242	382,330	211,912
2003	16,911,481	10,417,247	6,494,234	12,858,698	6,649,441	6,209,257	4,052,783	3,767,806	284,977	3,341,048	3,297,180	43,868	711,735	470,626	241,109
2004	17,272,044	10,726,181	6,545,863	12,980,112	6,736,536	6,243,576	4,291,932	3,989,645	302,287	3,411,685	3,369,435	42,250	880,247	620,210	260,037
2005	17,487,475	10,999,420	6,488,055	13,021,834	6,837,605	6,184,229	4,465,641	4,161,815	303,826	3,454,692	3,411,170	43,522	1,010,949	750,645	260,304
2006	17,758,870	11,240,330	6,518,540	13,180,133	6,955,013	6,225,120	4,578,737	4,285,317	293,420	3,512,866	3,473,710	39,156	1,065,871	811,607	254,264
2007	18,248,128	11,630,198	6,617,930	13,490,780	7,166,661	6,324,119	4,757,348	4,463,537	293,811	3,571,150	3,537,664	33,486	1,186,198	925,873	260,325
2008	19,102,814	12,131,436	6,971,378	13,972,153	7,331,809	6,640,344	5,130,661	4,799,627	331,034	3,661,519	3,626,168	35,351	1,469,142	1,173,459	295,683
2009	20,313,594	12,791,012	7,522,582	14,810,768	7,709,198	7,101,570	5,502,826	5,081,814	421,012	3,767,672	3,732,900	34,772	1,735,154	1,348,914	386,240
2010	21,019,438	13,335,841	7,683,597	15,142,171	7,924,108	7,218,063	5,877,267	5,411,733	465,534	3,854,482	3,821,799	32,683	2,022,785	1,589,934	432,851
2011	21,010,590	13,499,440	7,511,150	15,116,303	8,048,145	7,068,158	5,894,287	5,451,295	442,992	3,926,819	3,886,964	39,855	1,967,468	1,564,331	403,137
2012	20,644,478	13,476,638	7,167,840	14,884,667	8,092,602	6,792,065	5,759,811	5,384,036	375,775	3,951,388	3,913,690	37,698	1,808,423	1,470,346	338,077
2013	20,375,789	13,407,050	6,968,739	14,745,558	8,120,417	6,625,141	5,630,231	5,286,633	343,598	3,974,004	3,941,806	32,198	1,656,227	1,344,827	311,400
2014	20,207,369	13,492,884	6,714,485	14,655,015	8,257,250	6,397,765	5,552,354	5,235,634	316,720	3,996,089	3,965,724	30,365	1,556,265	1,269,910	286,355

—Not available.
[1] Large increases are due to the addition of schools accredited by the Accrediting Commission of Career Schools and Colleges of Technology.
[2] Because of imputation techniques, data are not consistent with figures for other years.
NOTE: Data through 1995 are for institutions of higher education, while later data are for degree-granting institutions. Degree-granting institutions grant associate's or higher degrees and participate in Title IV federal financial aid programs. The degree-granting classification is very similar to the earlier higher education classification, but it includes more 2-year colleges and

excludes a few higher education institutions that did not grant degrees. Some data have been revised from previously published figures.
SOURCE: U.S. Department of Education, National Center for Education Statistics, Higher Education General Information Survey (HEGIS), "Fall Enrollment in Institutions of Higher Education" surveys, 1970 through 1985; Integrated Postsecondary Education Data System (IPEDS), "Fall Enrollment Survey" (IPEDS-EF-86-99); and IPEDS Spring 2001 through Spring 2015, Fall Enrollment component. (This table was prepared October 2015.)

Table 303.30. Total fall enrollment in degree-granting postsecondary institutions, by level and control of institution, attendance status, and sex of student: Selected years, 1970 through 2025

Level and control of institution, attendance status, and sex of student	Actual													
	1970	1975	1980[1]	1985	1990	1995	2000	2005	2009	2010	2011	2012	2013	2014
1	2	3	4	5	6	7	8	9	10	11	12	13	14	15
Total	8,580,887	11,184,859	12,096,895	12,247,055	13,818,637	14,261,781	15,312,289	17,487,475	20,313,594	21,019,438	21,010,590	20,644,478	20,375,789	20,207,369
Full-time	5,816,290	6,841,334	7,097,958	7,075,221	7,820,985	8,128,802	9,009,600	10,797,011	12,605,355	13,087,182	13,002,531	12,734,404	12,597,112	12,453,975
Males	3,504,095	3,926,753	3,689,244	3,607,720	3,807,752	3,807,392	4,111,093	4,803,388	5,632,097	5,838,383	5,792,818	5,708,406	5,682,166	5,619,391
Females	2,312,195	2,914,581	3,408,714	3,467,501	4,013,233	4,321,410	4,898,507	5,993,623	6,973,258	7,248,799	7,209,713	7,025,998	6,914,946	6,834,584
Part-time	2,764,597	4,343,525	4,998,937	5,171,834	5,997,652	6,132,979	6,302,689	6,690,464	7,708,239	7,932,256	8,008,059	7,910,074	7,778,677	7,753,394
Males	1,539,547	2,222,244	2,185,130	2,210,730	2,476,157	2,535,147	2,610,676	2,652,537	3,100,856	3,207,376	3,241,438	3,210,600	3,178,620	3,177,670
Females	1,225,050	2,121,281	2,813,807	2,961,104	3,521,495	3,597,832	3,692,013	4,037,927	4,607,383	4,724,880	4,766,621	4,699,474	4,600,057	4,575,724
4-year	6,261,502	7,214,740	7,570,608	7,715,978	8,578,554	8,769,252	9,363,858	10,999,420	12,791,013	13,335,841	13,499,440	13,476,638	13,407,050	13,492,884
Full-time	4,587,379	5,080,256	5,344,163	5,384,614	5,937,023	6,151,755	6,792,551	8,150,209	9,361,404	9,721,803	9,832,324	9,792,607	9,764,196	9,793,247
Males	2,732,796	2,891,192	2,809,528	2,781,412	2,926,360	2,929,177	3,115,252	3,649,622	4,185,726	4,355,153	4,401,635	4,402,749	4,403,914	4,419,286
Females	1,854,583	2,189,064	2,534,635	2,603,202	3,010,663	3,222,578	3,677,299	4,500,587	5,175,678	5,366,650	5,430,689	5,389,858	5,360,282	5,373,961
Part-time	1,674,123	2,134,484	2,226,445	2,331,364	2,641,531	2,617,497	2,571,307	2,849,211	3,429,609	3,614,038	3,667,116	3,684,031	3,642,854	3,699,637
Males	936,189	1,092,461	1,017,813	1,034,804	1,124,780	1,084,753	1,047,917	1,125,935	1,349,890	1,424,721	1,456,818	1,470,164	1,458,956	1,483,996
Females	737,934	1,042,023	1,208,632	1,296,560	1,516,751	1,532,744	1,523,390	1,723,276	2,079,719	2,189,317	2,210,298	2,213,867	2,183,898	2,215,641
Public 4-year	4,232,722	4,998,142	5,128,612	5,209,540	5,848,242	5,814,545	6,055,398	6,837,605	7,709,198	7,924,108	8,048,145	8,092,602	8,120,417	8,257,250
Full-time	3,086,491	3,469,821	3,592,193	3,623,341	4,033,654	4,084,711	4,371,218	5,021,745	5,649,722	5,811,214	5,890,689	5,909,868	5,934,852	6,012,706
Males	1,813,584	1,947,823	1,873,397	1,863,689	1,982,369	1,951,140	2,008,618	2,295,456	2,626,174	2,707,307	2,743,773	2,756,885	2,772,506	2,807,232
Females	1,272,907	1,521,998	1,718,796	1,759,652	2,051,285	2,133,571	2,362,600	2,726,289	3,023,548	3,103,907	3,146,916	3,152,983	3,162,346	3,205,474
Part-time	1,146,231	1,528,321	1,536,419	1,586,199	1,814,588	1,729,834	1,684,180	1,815,860	2,059,476	2,112,894	2,157,456	2,182,734	2,185,565	2,244,544
Males	609,422	760,469	685,051	693,115	764,248	720,402	683,100	724,375	833,155	860,968	885,045	901,212	911,040	940,743
Females	536,809	767,852	851,368	893,084	1,050,340	1,009,432	1,001,080	1,091,485	1,226,321	1,251,926	1,272,411	1,281,522	1,274,525	1,303,801
Private 4-year	2,028,780	2,216,598	2,441,996	2,506,438	2,730,312	2,954,707	3,308,460	4,161,815	5,081,815	5,411,733	5,451,295	5,384,036	5,286,633	5,235,634
Full-time	1,500,888	1,610,435	1,751,970	1,761,273	1,903,369	2,067,044	2,421,333	3,128,464	3,711,682	3,910,589	3,941,635	3,882,739	3,829,344	3,780,541
Males	919,212	943,369	936,131	917,723	943,991	978,037	1,106,634	1,354,166	1,559,552	1,647,846	1,657,862	1,645,864	1,631,408	1,612,054
Females	581,676	667,066	815,839	843,550	959,378	1,089,007	1,314,699	1,774,298	2,152,130	2,262,743	2,283,773	2,236,875	2,197,936	2,168,487
Part-time	527,892	606,163	690,026	745,165	826,943	887,663	887,127	1,033,351	1,370,133	1,501,144	1,509,660	1,501,297	1,457,289	1,455,093
Males	326,767	331,992	332,762	341,689	360,532	364,351	364,817	401,560	516,735	563,753	571,773	568,952	547,916	543,253
Females	201,125	274,171	357,264	403,476	466,411	523,312	522,310	631,791	853,398	937,391	937,887	932,345	909,373	911,840
Nonprofit 4-year	2,021,121	2,198,451	2,413,693	2,463,000	2,671,069	2,853,890	3,050,575	3,411,170	3,732,900	3,821,799	3,886,964	3,913,690	3,941,806	3,965,724
Full-time	1,494,625	1,596,074	1,733,014	1,727,707	1,859,124	1,989,457	2,226,028	2,534,793	2,787,321	2,864,640	2,905,674	2,927,108	2,961,998	2,980,433
Males	914,020	930,842	921,253	894,080	915,100	931,956	996,113	1,109,075	1,223,933	1,259,638	1,275,590	1,288,669	1,303,567	1,313,033
Females	580,605	665,232	811,761	833,627	944,024	1,057,501	1,229,915	1,425,718	1,563,988	1,605,002	1,630,084	1,638,439	1,658,431	1,667,400
Part-time	526,496	602,377	680,679	735,293	811,945	864,433	824,547	876,377	945,579	957,159	981,290	986,582	979,808	985,291
Males	325,693	329,662	327,986	336,168	352,106	351,874	332,814	339,572	363,789	366,735	375,713	377,521	377,480	379,428
Females	200,803	272,715	352,693	399,125	459,839	512,559	491,733	536,805	581,790	590,424	605,577	609,061	602,328	605,863
For-profit 4-year	7,659	18,147	28,303	43,438	59,243	100,817	257,885	750,645	1,348,915	1,589,934	1,564,331	1,470,346	1,344,827	1,269,910
2-year	2,319,385	3,970,119	4,526,287	4,531,077	5,240,083	5,492,529	5,948,431	6,488,055	7,522,581	7,683,597	7,511,150	7,167,840	6,968,739	6,714,485
Full-time	1,228,911	1,761,078	1,753,795	1,690,607	1,883,962	1,977,047	2,217,049	2,646,802	3,243,951	3,365,379	3,170,207	2,941,797	2,832,916	2,660,728
Males	771,299	1,035,561	879,716	826,308	881,392	878,215	995,841	1,153,766	1,446,371	1,483,230	1,391,183	1,305,657	1,278,252	1,200,105
Females	457,612	725,517	874,079	864,299	1,002,570	1,098,832	1,221,208	1,493,036	1,797,580	1,882,149	1,779,024	1,636,140	1,554,664	1,460,623
Part-time	1,090,474	2,209,041	2,772,492	2,840,470	3,356,121	3,515,482	3,731,382	3,841,253	4,278,630	4,318,218	4,340,943	4,226,043	4,135,823	4,053,757
Males	603,358	1,129,783	1,167,317	1,175,926	1,351,377	1,450,394	1,562,759	1,526,602	1,750,966	1,782,655	1,784,620	1,740,436	1,719,664	1,693,674
Females	487,116	1,079,258	1,605,175	1,664,544	2,004,744	2,065,088	2,168,623	2,314,651	2,527,664	2,535,563	2,556,323	2,485,607	2,416,159	2,360,083
Public 2-year	2,195,412	3,836,366	4,328,782	4,269,733	4,996,475	5,277,829	5,697,388	6,184,229	7,101,569	7,218,063	7,068,158	6,792,065	6,625,141	6,397,765
Full-time	1,129,165	1,662,621	1,595,493	1,496,905	1,716,843	1,840,590	2,000,008	2,387,016	2,875,291	2,950,024	2,781,419	2,615,331	2,529,957	2,385,013
Males	720,440	988,701	811,871	742,673	810,664	818,605	891,282	1,055,029	1,315,200	1,340,820	1,260,759	1,197,301	1,176,699	1,107,397
Females	408,725	673,920	783,622	754,232	906,179	1,021,985	1,108,726	1,331,987	1,560,091	1,609,204	1,520,660	1,418,030	1,353,258	1,277,616
Part-time	1,066,247	2,173,745	2,733,289	2,772,828	3,279,632	3,437,239	3,697,380	3,797,213	4,226,278	4,268,039	4,286,739	4,176,734	4,095,184	4,012,752
Males	589,439	1,107,680	1,152,268	1,138,011	1,317,730	1,417,488	1,549,407	1,514,363	1,735,300	1,769,737	1,770,197	1,727,555	1,708,594	1,683,562
Females	476,808	1,066,065	1,581,021	1,634,817	1,961,902	2,019,751	2,147,973	2,282,850	2,490,978	2,498,302	2,516,542	2,449,179	2,386,590	2,329,190
Private 2-year	123,973	133,753	197,505	261,344	243,608	214,700	251,043	303,826	421,012	465,534	442,992	375,775	343,598	316,720
Full-time	99,746	98,457	158,302	193,702	167,119	136,457	217,041	259,786	368,660	415,355	388,788	326,466	302,959	275,715
Males	50,859	46,860	67,845	83,635	70,728	59,610	104,559	98,737	131,171	142,410	130,424	108,356	101,553	92,708
Females	48,887	51,597	90,457	110,067	96,391	76,847	112,482	161,049	237,489	272,945	258,364	218,110	201,406	183,007
Part-time	24,227	35,296	39,203	67,642	76,489	78,243	34,002	44,040	52,352	50,179	54,204	49,309	40,639	41,005
Males	13,919	22,103	15,049	37,915	33,647	32,906	13,352	12,239	15,666	12,918	14,423	12,881	11,070	10,112
Females	10,308	13,193	24,154	29,727	42,842	45,337	20,650	31,801	36,686	37,261	39,781	36,428	29,569	30,893
Nonprofit 2-year	113,299	112,997	114,094	108,791	89,158	75,154	58,844	43,522	34,772	32,683	39,855	37,698	32,198	30,365
Full-time	91,514	82,158	83,009	76,547	62,003	54,033	46,670	28,939	23,488	23,127	30,584	29,384	24,055	22,778
Males	46,030	40,548	34,968	30,878	25,946	23,265	21,950	12,086	9,578	9,944	11,298	10,463	9,470	9,066
Females	45,484	41,610	48,041	45,669	36,057	30,768	24,720	16,853	13,910	13,183	19,286	18,921	14,585	13,712
Part-time	21,785	30,839	31,085	32,244	27,155	21,121	12,174	14,583	11,284	9,556	9,271	8,314	8,143	7,587
Males	12,097	18,929	11,445	10,786	7,970	6,080	4,499	3,566	2,721	2,585	2,540	2,467	2,386	2,198
Females	9,688	11,910	19,640	21,458	19,185	15,041	7,675	11,017	8,563	6,971	6,731	5,847	5,757	5,389
For-profit 2-year	10,674	20,756	83,411	152,553	154,450	139,546	192,199	260,304	386,240	432,851	403,137	338,077	311,400	286,355

See notes at end of table.

Table 303.30. Total fall enrollment in degree-granting postsecondary institutions, by level and control of institution, attendance status, and sex of student: Selected years, 1970 through 2025—Continued

Level and control of institution, attendance status, and sex of student	Projected										
	2015	2016	2017	2018	2019	2020	2021	2022	2023	2024	2025
1	16	17	18	19	20	21	22	23	24	25	26
Total	**20,264,000**	**20,516,000**	**20,972,000**	**21,410,000**	**21,753,000**	**22,013,000**	**22,323,000**	**22,613,000**	**22,896,000**	**23,149,000**	**23,290,000**
Full-time	12,484,000	12,651,000	12,942,000	13,207,000	13,403,000	13,550,000	13,726,000	13,894,000	14,072,000	14,220,000	14,278,000
Males	5,638,000	5,671,000	5,754,000	5,857,000	5,938,000	5,998,000	6,068,000	6,137,000	6,211,000	6,278,000	6,318,000
Females	6,846,000	6,980,000	7,188,000	7,350,000	7,465,000	7,552,000	7,658,000	7,757,000	7,861,000	7,941,000	7,960,000
Part-time	7,779,000	7,865,000	8,030,000	8,203,000	8,349,000	8,463,000	8,597,000	8,720,000	8,824,000	8,929,000	9,012,000
Males	3,122,000	3,137,000	3,190,000	3,261,000	3,322,000	3,367,000	3,428,000	3,488,000	3,536,000	3,581,000	3,619,000
Females	4,657,000	4,728,000	4,840,000	4,942,000	5,028,000	5,097,000	5,169,000	5,232,000	5,288,000	5,349,000	5,393,000
4-year	**13,150,000**	**13,322,000**	**13,627,000**	**13,910,000**	**14,131,000**	**14,307,000**	**14,513,000**	**14,702,000**	**14,889,000**	**15,052,000**	**15,133,000**
Full-time	9,525,000	9,649,000	9,867,000	10,065,000	10,212,000	10,328,000	10,464,000	10,588,000	10,720,000	10,831,000	10,873,000
Males	4,327,000	4,351,000	4,414,000	4,491,000	4,553,000	4,602,000	4,657,000	4,709,000	4,764,000	4,815,000	4,844,000
Females	5,197,000	5,298,000	5,453,000	5,574,000	5,659,000	5,726,000	5,807,000	5,879,000	5,956,000	6,016,000	6,029,000
Part-time	3,625,000	3,673,000	3,759,000	3,845,000	3,919,000	3,979,000	4,049,000	4,114,000	4,169,000	4,221,000	4,260,000
Males	1,409,000	1,419,000	1,447,000	1,483,000	1,514,000	1,538,000	1,571,000	1,602,000	1,628,000	1,651,000	1,669,000
Females	2,216,000	2,254,000	2,312,000	2,363,000	2,406,000	2,441,000	2,478,000	2,512,000	2,541,000	2,570,000	2,590,000
Public 4-year	8,026,000	8,126,000	8,306,000	8,477,000	8,610,000	8,715,000	8,839,000	8,952,000	9,065,000	9,164,000	9,215,000
Full-time	5,839,000	5,911,000	6,040,000	6,160,000	6,249,000	6,319,000	6,401,000	6,475,000	6,554,000	6,623,000	6,650,000
Males	2,740,000	2,754,000	2,793,000	2,840,000	2,879,000	2,909,000	2,944,000	2,976,000	3,010,000	3,042,000	3,061,000
Females	3,099,000	3,157,000	3,248,000	3,319,000	3,370,000	3,410,000	3,457,000	3,499,000	3,544,000	3,581,000	3,589,000
Part-time	2,187,000	2,215,000	2,266,000	2,317,000	2,361,000	2,397,000	2,439,000	2,477,000	2,510,000	2,542,000	2,565,000
Males	887,000	893,000	910,000	932,000	951,000	966,000	986,000	1,006,000	1,021,000	1,035,000	1,047,000
Females	1,300,000	1,322,000	1,356,000	1,385,000	1,410,000	1,431,000	1,453,000	1,472,000	1,489,000	1,506,000	1,518,000
Private 4-year	5,124,000	5,196,000	5,321,000	5,433,000	5,521,000	5,591,000	5,674,000	5,750,000	5,824,000	5,888,000	5,918,000
Full-time	3,686,000	3,738,000	3,827,000	3,905,000	3,963,000	4,009,000	4,064,000	4,113,000	4,166,000	4,209,000	4,224,000
Males	1,587,000	1,597,000	1,622,000	1,651,000	1,674,000	1,692,000	1,714,000	1,734,000	1,754,000	1,773,000	1,784,000
Females	2,099,000	2,141,000	2,205,000	2,254,000	2,289,000	2,317,000	2,350,000	2,380,000	2,411,000	2,435,000	2,440,000
Part-time	1,438,000	1,458,000	1,494,000	1,528,000	1,558,000	1,582,000	1,610,000	1,636,000	1,659,000	1,680,000	1,695,000
Males	522,000	527,000	537,000	551,000	563,000	572,000	585,000	597,000	607,000	615,000	622,000
Females	915,000	932,000	956,000	977,000	995,000	1,010,000	1,026,000	1,040,000	1,052,000	1,064,000	1,072,000
Nonprofit 4-year	—	—	—	—	—	—	—	—	—	—	—
Full-time	—	—	—	—	—	—	—	—	—	—	—
Males	—	—	—	—	—	—	—	—	—	—	—
Females	—	—	—	—	—	—	—	—	—	—	—
Part-time	—	—	—	—	—	—	—	—	—	—	—
Males	—	—	—	—	—	—	—	—	—	—	—
Females	—	—	—	—	—	—	—	—	—	—	—
For-profit 4-year	—	—	—	—	—	—	—	—	—	—	—
2-year	**7,114,000**	**7,194,000**	**7,346,000**	**7,500,000**	**7,622,000**	**7,706,000**	**7,810,000**	**7,912,000**	**8,007,000**	**8,096,000**	**8,157,000**
Full-time	2,960,000	3,002,000	3,075,000	3,142,000	3,191,000	3,222,000	3,262,000	3,306,000	3,351,000	3,388,000	3,405,000
Males	1,311,000	1,320,000	1,340,000	1,365,000	1,385,000	1,396,000	1,411,000	1,428,000	1,446,000	1,463,000	1,474,000
Females	1,649,000	1,682,000	1,735,000	1,777,000	1,806,000	1,826,000	1,851,000	1,878,000	1,905,000	1,925,000	1,931,000
Part-time	4,154,000	4,192,000	4,271,000	4,358,000	4,430,000	4,484,000	4,548,000	4,606,000	4,655,000	4,708,000	4,752,000
Males	1,713,000	1,718,000	1,743,000	1,779,000	1,808,000	1,829,000	1,857,000	1,886,000	1,908,000	1,930,000	1,950,000
Females	2,441,000	2,474,000	2,528,000	2,579,000	2,622,000	2,656,000	2,691,000	2,721,000	2,747,000	2,778,000	2,803,000
Public 2-year	6,763,000	6,838,000	6,981,000	7,127,000	7,243,000	7,323,000	7,422,000	7,519,000	7,608,000	7,693,000	7,752,000
Full-time	2,652,000	2,689,000	2,754,000	2,814,000	2,858,000	2,885,000	2,921,000	2,960,000	3,001,000	3,034,000	3,049,000
Males	1,209,000	1,218,000	1,236,000	1,260,000	1,278,000	1,288,000	1,302,000	1,318,000	1,335,000	1,350,000	1,360,000
Females	1,442,000	1,471,000	1,518,000	1,554,000	1,580,000	1,597,000	1,619,000	1,642,000	1,666,000	1,684,000	1,689,000
Part-time	4,111,000	4,149,000	4,227,000	4,313,000	4,384,000	4,438,000	4,501,000	4,558,000	4,607,000	4,659,000	4,703,000
Males	1,702,000	1,707,000	1,732,000	1,767,000	1,797,000	1,817,000	1,846,000	1,874,000	1,896,000	1,918,000	1,937,000
Females	2,409,000	2,441,000	2,495,000	2,545,000	2,588,000	2,621,000	2,655,000	2,685,000	2,711,000	2,742,000	2,766,000
Private 2-year	351,000	356,000	365,000	373,000	379,000	383,000	388,000	393,000	399,000	403,000	405,000
Full-time	308,000	313,000	321,000	328,000	333,000	337,000	341,000	346,000	350,000	354,000	356,000
Males	101,000	102,000	104,000	105,000	107,000	108,000	109,000	110,000	112,000	113,000	114,000
Females	207,000	211,000	217,000	223,000	226,000	229,000	232,000	235,000	239,000	241,000	242,000
Part-time	43,000	43,000	44,000	45,000	46,000	47,000	47,000	48,000	48,000	49,000	49,000
Males	11,000	11,000	11,000	11,000	11,000	12,000	12,000	12,000	12,000	12,000	12,000
Females	32,000	33,000	33,000	34,000	35,000	35,000	36,000	36,000	36,000	37,000	37,000
Nonprofit 2-year	—	—	—	—	—	—	—	—	—	—	—
Full-time	—	—	—	—	—	—	—	—	—	—	—
Males	—	—	—	—	—	—	—	—	—	—	—
Females	—	—	—	—	—	—	—	—	—	—	—
Part-time	—	—	—	—	—	—	—	—	—	—	—
Males	—	—	—	—	—	—	—	—	—	—	—
Females	—	—	—	—	—	—	—	—	—	—	—
For-profit 2-year	—	—	—	—	—	—	—	—	—	—	—

—Not available.

[1]Large increase in private 2-year institutions in 1980 is due to the addition of schools accredited by the Accrediting Commission of Career Schools and Colleges of Technology.
NOTE: Data through 1995 are for institutions of higher education, while later data are for degree-granting institutions. Degree-granting institutions grant associate's or higher degrees and participate in Title IV federal financial aid programs. The degree-granting classification is very similar to the earlier higher education classification, but it includes more 2-year colleges and excludes a few higher education institutions that did not grant degrees. Some data have been revised from previously published figures.
SOURCE: U.S. Department of Education, National Center for Education Statistics, Higher Education General Information Survey (HEGIS), "Fall Enrollment in Colleges and Universities" surveys, 1970 through 1985; Integrated Postsecondary Education Data System (IPEDS), "Fall Enrollment Survey" (IPEDS-EF:90–99); IPEDS Spring 2001 through Spring 2015, Fall Enrollment component; and Enrollment in Degree-Granting Institutions Projection Model, 1980 through 2025. (This table was prepared April 2016.)

Table 303.40. Total fall enrollment in degree-granting postsecondary institutions, by attendance status, sex, and age: Selected years, 1970 through 2025

[In thousands]

Attendance status, sex, and age	1970	1980	1990	2000	2004	2005	2006	2007	2008	2009	2010	2011	2012	2013	2014	Projected 2015	Projected 2016	Projected 2020	Projected 2025
1	2	3	4	5	6	7	8	9	10	11	12	13	14	15	16	17	18	19	20
All students	8,581	12,097	13,819	15,312	17,272	17,487	17,759	18,248	19,103	20,314	21,019	21,011	20,644	20,376	20,207	20,264	20,516	22,013	23,290
14 to 17 years old	263	257	153	131	166	187	184	200	195	215	202	221	242	256	257	251	256	271	287
18 and 19 years old	2,579	2,852	2,777	3,258	3,367	3,444	3,561	3,690	3,813	4,009	4,057	3,956	3,782	3,720	3,694	3,881	3,929	4,137	4,360
20 and 21 years old	1,885	2,395	2,593	3,005	3,516	3,563	3,573	3,570	3,649	3,916	4,103	4,269	4,235	4,183	4,074	4,292	4,279	4,527	4,689
22 to 24 years old	1,469	1,947	2,202	2,600	3,166	3,114	3,185	3,280	3,443	3,571	3,759	3,793	3,951	3,964	3,990	3,962	3,974	4,083	4,283
25 to 29 years old	1,091	1,843	2,083	2,044	2,418	2,469	2,506	2,651	2,840	3,082	3,254	3,272	3,155	3,050	3,016	2,955	3,066	3,372	3,426
30 to 34 years old	527	1,227	1,384	1,333	1,440	1,438	1,472	1,519	1,609	1,735	1,805	1,788	1,684	1,606	1,552	1,471	1,506	1,706	1,877
35 years old and over	767	1,577	2,627	2,942	3,199	3,272	3,277	3,339	3,554	3,785	3,840	3,712	3,597	3,597	3,625	3,453	3,506	3,917	4,367
Males	5,044	5,874	6,284	6,722	7,387	7,456	7,575	7,816	8,189	8,733	9,046	9,034	8,919	8,861	8,797	8,760	8,808	9,364	9,937
14 to 17 years old	125	106	66	58	62	68	69	88	93	103	94	104	119	125	126	114	116	120	128
18 and 19 years old	1,355	1,368	1,298	1,464	1,475	1,523	1,604	1,669	1,704	1,795	1,820	1,782	1,707	1,661	1,639	1,688	1,704	1,781	1,880
20 and 21 years old	1,064	1,219	1,259	1,411	1,608	1,658	1,628	1,634	1,695	1,866	1,948	1,985	1,960	1,955	1,932	2,034	2,009	2,099	2,158
22 to 24 years old	1,004	1,075	1,129	1,222	1,437	1,410	1,445	1,480	1,555	1,599	1,723	1,769	1,864	1,846	1,803	1,799	1,788	1,811	1,895
25 to 29 years old	796	983	1,024	908	1,039	1,057	1,040	1,148	1,222	1,378	1,410	1,404	1,353	1,356	1,376	1,329	1,373	1,510	1,548
30 to 34 years old	333	564	605	581	619	591	628	638	691	707	731	700	661	634	621	565	576	653	734
35 years old and over	366	559	902	1,077	1,147	1,149	1,160	1,159	1,228	1,285	1,320	1,290	1,255	1,283	1,300	1,231	1,242	1,390	1,593
Females	3,537	6,223	7,535	8,591	9,885	10,032	10,184	10,432	10,914	11,581	11,974	11,976	11,725	11,515	11,410	11,503	11,708	12,648	13,353
14 to 17 years old	137	151	87	73	104	119	115	112	102	113	108	116	123	131	130	137	141	150	159
18 and 19 years old	1,224	1,484	1,479	1,794	1,892	1,920	1,956	2,021	2,109	2,214	2,237	2,173	2,074	2,059	2,055	2,193	2,225	2,356	2,479
20 and 21 years old	821	1,177	1,334	1,593	1,908	1,905	1,945	1,936	1,954	2,050	2,155	2,284	2,276	2,228	2,142	2,258	2,269	2,428	2,532
22 to 24 years old	464	871	1,073	1,378	1,729	1,704	1,740	1,800	1,888	1,972	2,036	2,024	2,087	2,118	2,187	2,163	2,187	2,272	2,388
25 to 29 years old	296	859	1,059	1,136	1,379	1,413	1,466	1,502	1,618	1,704	1,844	1,868	1,802	1,694	1,640	1,625	1,693	1,862	1,878
30 to 34 years old	194	663	779	752	821	847	844	881	918	1,028	1,074	1,088	1,022	972	931	906	930	1,053	1,143
35 years old and over	401	1,018	1,725	1,865	2,052	2,123	2,117	2,180	2,326	2,500	2,520	2,422	2,341	2,314	2,325	2,221	2,264	2,528	2,774
Full-time	5,816	7,098	7,821	9,010	10,610	10,797	10,957	11,270	11,748	12,605	13,087	13,003	12,734	12,597	12,454	12,484	12,651	13,550	14,278
14 to 17 years old	246	231	134	121	138	152	148	169	168	179	170	185	207	210	208	182	187	196	205
18 and 19 years old	2,374	2,544	2,471	2,823	2,960	3,026	3,120	3,244	3,359	3,481	3,496	3,351	3,226	3,199	3,198	3,296	3,343	3,530	3,720
20 and 21 years old	1,649	2,007	2,137	2,452	2,926	2,976	2,972	2,985	3,043	3,241	3,364	3,427	3,386	3,327	3,260	3,277	3,276	3,488	3,625
22 to 24 years old	904	1,181	1,405	1,714	2,143	2,122	2,127	2,205	2,347	2,511	2,585	2,580	2,603	2,650	2,620	2,619	2,638	2,716	2,837
25 to 29 years old	426	641	791	886	1,132	1,174	1,225	1,299	1,369	1,506	1,605	1,600	1,555	1,529	1,527	1,532	1,593	1,771	1,809
30 to 34 years old	113	272	383	418	517	547	571	556	571	657	745	763	711	664	616	575	591	681	758
35 years old and over	104	221	500	596	795	800	794	812	890	1,030	1,122	1,096	1,047	1,019	1,024	1,003	1,023	1,168	1,324
Males	3,504	3,689	3,808	4,111	4,739	4,803	4,879	5,029	5,234	5,632	5,838	5,793	5,708	5,682	5,619	5,638	5,671	5,998	6,318
14 to 17 years old	121	95	55	51	49	53	52	74	73	77	71	85	102	106	106	98	100	104	111
18 and 19 years old	1,261	1,219	1,171	1,252	1,297	1,339	1,404	1,465	1,516	1,570	1,574	1,510	1,461	1,423	1,400	1,392	1,409	1,476	1,560
20 and 21 years old	955	1,046	1,035	1,156	1,360	1,398	1,372	1,366	1,407	1,536	1,586	1,586	1,537	1,542	1,523	1,583	1,564	1,639	1,688
22 to 24 years old	686	717	768	834	1,001	982	992	1,043	1,105	1,169	1,215	1,217	1,254	1,270	1,249	1,261	1,253	1,275	1,337
25 to 29 years old	346	391	433	410	498	506	533	578	597	661	715	727	728	734	744	733	761	842	866
30 to 34 years old	77	142	171	186	231	225	235	231	249	279	301	299	278	257	233	215	221	252	285
35 years old and over	58	80	174	222	302	300	291	273	287	341	376	369	349	351	363	357	363	410	473
Females	2,312	3,409	4,013	4,899	5,871	5,994	6,078	6,240	6,513	6,973	7,249	7,210	7,026	6,915	6,835	6,846	6,980	7,552	7,960
14 to 17 years old	125	136	78	70	89	98	95	95	95	102	99	100	105	104	102	84	87	92	94
18 and 19 years old	1,113	1,325	1,300	1,571	1,662	1,687	1,716	1,779	1,843	1,911	1,922	1,842	1,765	1,776	1,798	1,904	1,935	2,054	2,160
20 and 21 years old	693	961	1,101	1,296	1,566	1,578	1,601	1,619	1,636	1,705	1,778	1,840	1,849	1,785	1,738	1,694	1,712	1,849	1,938
22 to 24 years old	218	464	638	880	1,142	1,140	1,135	1,163	1,242	1,343	1,370	1,364	1,349	1,380	1,371	1,359	1,385	1,442	1,500
25 to 29 years old	80	250	358	476	634	668	692	721	772	845	891	873	827	794	783	798	832	929	943
30 to 34 years old	37	130	212	232	286	322	336	324	322	378	444	464	433	408	383	360	370	429	473
35 years old and over	46	141	326	374	493	500	503	539	603	690	746	727	698	668	661	646	660	758	852
Part-time	2,765	4,999	5,998	6,303	6,662	6,690	6,802	6,978	7,355	7,708	7,932	8,008	7,910	7,779	7,753	7,779	7,865	8,463	9,012
14 to 17 years old	16	26	19	10	28	36	36	31	27	36	32	36	35	47	48	68	70	75	82
18 and 19 years old	205	308	306	435	407	417	440	446	453	528	561	604	556	521	496	585	586	607	639
20 and 21 years old	236	388	456	553	590	586	601	585	606	675	738	842	850	855	814	1,015	1,003	1,040	1,064
22 to 24 years old	564	765	796	886	1,023	992	1,058	1,074	1,096	1,059	1,174	1,212	1,348	1,314	1,370	1,343	1,336	1,366	1,446
25 to 29 years old	665	1,202	1,291	1,158	1,286	1,296	1,282	1,352	1,471	1,576	1,648	1,672	1,600	1,522	1,489	1,423	1,472	1,601	1,618
30 to 34 years old	414	954	1,001	915	923	891	901	963	1,037	1,079	1,060	1,025	973	942	935	896	915	1,025	1,119
35 years old and over	663	1,356	2,127	2,345	2,404	2,472	2,483	2,527	2,664	2,754	2,718	2,616	2,550	2,578	2,600	2,449	2,483	2,749	3,043
Males	1,540	2,185	2,476	2,611	2,648	2,653	2,696	2,786	2,955	3,101	3,207	3,241	3,211	3,179	3,178	3,122	3,137	3,367	3,619
14 to 17 years old	4	12	11	7	13	15	17	14	20	25	23	20	17	20	20	16	16	17	18
18 and 19 years old	94	149	127	212	178	184	200	204	188	226	245	273	246	239	239	297	295	305	320
20 and 21 years old	108	172	224	255	248	260	257	269	289	330	362	398	423	413	409	451	445	460	470
22 to 24 years old	318	359	361	388	436	428	452	438	450	430	508	552	610	576	554	538	535	537	558
25 to 29 years old	450	592	591	498	540	551	507	570	625	718	695	677	625	622	632	596	612	668	682
30 to 34 years old	257	422	435	395	388	365	393	406	442	428	430	401	383	377	387	350	355	401	449
35 years old and over	309	479	728	855	845	850	869	886	941	944	944	921	906	932	936	874	879	980	1,121
Females	1,225	2,814	3,521	3,692	4,014	4,038	4,106	4,192	4,401	4,607	4,725	4,767	4,699	4,600	4,576	4,657	4,728	5,096	5,393
14 to 17 years old	12	14	9	3	15	21	20	17	7	11	9	16	18	27	28	53	54	59	65
18 and 19 years old	112	159	179	223	230	233	240	242	265	303	316	332	310	283	257	288	290	302	319
20 and 21 years old	128	216	233	298	342	327	344	317	318	345	377	444	427	443	405	564	558	580	594
22 to 24 years old	246	407	435	497	588	564	605	637	646	629	666	660	738	738	816	804	802	830	888
25 to 29 years old	216	609	700	660	746	745	774	781	846	859	953	995	975	900	857	827	860	933	935
30 to 34 years old	158	532	567	520	535	526	508	557	595	651	630	624	589	564	548	546	560	624	670
35 years old and over	354	876	1,399	1,491	1,560	1,623	1,614	1,640	1,723	1,810	1,774	1,695	1,643	1,646	1,664	1,575	1,604	1,770	1,922

NOTE: Distributions by age are estimates based on samples of the civilian noninstitutional population from the U.S. Census Bureau's Current Population Survey. Data through 1995 are for institutions of higher education, while later data are for degree-granting institutions. Degree-granting institutions grant associate's or higher degrees and participate in Title IV federal financial aid programs. The degree-granting classification is very similar to the earlier higher education classification, but it includes more 2-year colleges and excludes a few higher education institutions that did not grant degrees. Some data have been revised from previously published figures. Detail may not sum to totals because of rounding.

SOURCE: U.S. Department of Education, National Center for Education Statistics, Higher Education General Information Survey (HEGIS), "Fall Enrollment in Colleges and Universities" surveys, 1970 and 1980; Integrated Postsecondary Education Data System (IPEDS), "Fall Enrollment Survey" (IPEDS-EF:90–99); IPEDS Spring 2001 through Spring 2015, Fall Enrollment component; and Enrollment in Degree-Granting Institutions Projection Model, 1980 through 2025. U.S. Department of Commerce, Census Bureau, Current Population Survey (CPS), October, selected years, 1970 through 2014. (This table was prepared March 2016.)

Table 303.45. Total fall enrollment in degree-granting postsecondary institutions, by level of enrollment, sex, attendance status, and age of student: 2009, 2011, and 2013

Attendance status and age of student	Fall 2009 All levels Total	Fall 2011 All levels Total	Males	Females	Fall 2013 All levels Total	Males	Females	Undergraduate Total	Males	Females	Postbaccalaureate Total	Males	Females
1	2	3	4	5	6	7	8	9	10	11	12	13	14
All students	20,313,594	21,010,590	9,034,256	11,976,334	20,375,789	8,860,786	11,515,003	17,474,835	7,659,626	9,815,209	2,900,954	1,201,160	1,699,794
Under 18	758,719	796,322	330,026	466,296	879,127	363,634	515,493	878,960	363,571	515,389	167	63	104
18 and 19	4,291,786	4,291,189	1,935,116	2,356,073	4,265,853	1,920,939	2,344,914	4,264,764	1,920,536	2,344,228	1,089	403	686
20 and 21	3,995,409	4,161,496	1,874,220	2,287,276	4,085,724	1,852,000	2,233,724	4,051,605	1,839,026	2,212,579	34,119	12,974	21,145
22 to 24	3,300,898	3,434,603	1,574,540	1,860,063	3,430,650	1,580,020	1,850,630	2,812,445	1,331,251	1,481,194	618,205	248,769	369,436
25 to 29	2,934,931	3,045,652	1,329,306	1,716,346	2,857,056	1,259,180	1,597,876	1,949,698	859,923	1,089,775	907,358	399,257	508,101
30 to 34	1,614,852	1,759,975	726,923	1,033,052	1,642,431	695,841	946,590	1,166,637	482,591	684,046	475,794	213,250	262,544
35 to 39	1,113,548	1,125,125	427,973	697,152	1,034,148	403,714	630,434	756,185	288,377	467,808	277,963	115,337	162,626
40 to 49	1,432,883	1,503,908	526,491	977,417	1,346,655	483,480	863,175	988,078	351,076	637,002	358,577	132,404	226,173
50 to 64	728,033	760,089	253,539	506,550	717,300	252,559	464,741	518,914	186,574	332,340	198,386	65,985	132,401
65 and over	69,679	65,122	27,123	37,999	66,161	28,065	38,096	55,195	23,056	32,139	10,966	5,009	5,957
Age unknown	72,856	67,109	28,999	38,110	50,684	21,354	29,330	32,354	13,645	18,709	18,330	7,709	10,621
Full-time	12,605,355	13,002,531	5,792,818	7,209,713	12,597,112	5,682,166	6,914,946	10,938,494	4,949,572	5,988,922	1,658,618	732,594	926,024
Under 18	176,567	181,159	72,371	108,788	185,718	74,583	111,135	185,631	74,555	111,076	87	28	59
18 and 19	3,630,783	3,571,443	1,597,775	1,973,668	3,548,294	1,585,220	1,963,074	3,547,315	1,584,855	1,962,460	979	365	614
20 and 21	3,240,417	3,311,201	1,495,119	1,816,082	3,244,414	1,472,318	1,772,096	3,213,421	1,460,365	1,753,056	30,993	11,953	19,040
22 to 24	2,183,499	2,257,755	1,072,259	1,185,496	2,239,397	1,066,976	1,172,421	1,743,151	861,461	881,690	496,246	205,515	290,731
25 to 29	1,513,822	1,607,135	745,669	861,466	1,499,143	705,540	793,603	923,550	434,039	489,511	575,593	271,501	304,092
30 to 34	705,835	793,229	342,108	451,121	725,416	325,394	400,022	491,630	212,248	279,382	233,786	113,146	120,640
35 to 39	433,345	459,050	176,259	282,791	409,512	164,713	244,799	295,425	114,157	181,268	114,087	50,556	63,531
40 to 49	485,700	550,606	195,769	354,837	484,308	182,654	301,654	355,343	132,126	223,217	128,965	50,528	78,437
50 to 64	201,201	232,693	79,027	153,666	226,606	89,774	136,832	162,457	67,040	95,417	64,149	22,734	41,415
65 and over	6,502	8,387	3,586	4,801	9,133	4,082	5,051	5,931	2,599	3,332	3,202	1,483	1,719
Age unknown	27,684	29,873	12,876	16,997	25,171	10,912	14,259	14,640	6,127	8,513	10,531	4,785	5,746
Part-time	7,708,239	8,008,059	3,241,438	4,766,621	7,778,677	3,178,620	4,600,057	6,536,341	2,710,054	3,826,287	1,242,336	468,566	773,770
Under 18	582,152	615,163	257,655	357,508	693,409	289,051	404,358	693,329	289,016	404,313	80	35	45
18 and 19	661,003	719,746	337,341	382,405	717,559	335,719	381,840	717,449	335,681	381,768	110	38	72
20 and 21	754,992	850,295	379,101	471,194	841,310	379,682	461,628	838,184	378,661	459,523	3,126	1,021	2,105
22 to 24	1,117,399	1,176,848	502,281	674,567	1,191,253	513,044	678,209	1,069,294	469,790	599,504	121,959	43,254	78,705
25 to 29	1,421,109	1,438,517			1,357,913	553,640	804,273	1,026,148	425,884	600,264	331,765	127,756	204,009
30 to 34	909,017	966,746	384,815	581,931	917,015	370,447	546,568	675,007	270,343	404,664	242,008	100,104	141,904
35 to 39	680,203	666,075	251,714	414,361	624,636	239,001	385,635	460,760	174,220	286,540	163,876	64,781	99,095
40 to 49	947,183	953,302	330,722	622,580	862,347	300,826	561,521	632,735	218,950	413,785	229,612	81,876	147,736
50 to 64	526,832	527,396	174,512	352,884	490,694	162,785	327,909	356,457	119,534	236,923	134,237	43,251	90,986
65 and over	63,177	56,735	23,537	33,198	57,028	23,983	33,045	49,264	20,457	28,807	7,764	3,526	4,238
Age unknown	45,172	37,236	16,123	21,113	25,513	10,442	15,071	17,714	7,518	10,196	7,799	2,924	4,875
					Percentage distribution								
All students	100.0	100.0	100.0	100.0	100.0	100.0	100.0	100.0	100.0	100.0	100.0	100.0	100.0
Under 18	3.7	3.8	3.7	3.9	4.3	4.1	4.5	5.0	4.7	5.3	#	#	#
18 and 19	21.1	20.4	21.4	19.7	20.9	21.7	20.4	24.4	25.1	23.9	#	#	#
20 and 21	19.7	19.8	20.7	19.1	20.1	20.9	19.4	23.2	24.0	22.5	1.2	1.1	1.2
22 to 24	16.2	16.3	17.4	15.5	16.8	17.8	16.1	16.1	17.4	15.1	21.3	20.7	21.7
25 to 29	14.4	14.5	14.7	14.3	14.0	14.2	13.9	11.2	11.2	11.1	31.3	33.2	29.9
30 to 34	7.9	8.4	8.0	8.6	8.1	7.9	8.2	6.7	6.3	7.0	16.4	17.8	15.4
35 to 39	5.5	5.4	4.7	5.8	5.1	4.6	5.5	4.3	3.8	4.8	9.6	9.6	9.6
40 to 49	7.1	7.2	5.8	8.2	6.6	5.5	7.5	5.7	4.6	6.5	12.4	11.0	13.3
50 to 64	3.6	3.6	2.8	4.2	3.5	2.9	4.0	3.0	2.4	3.4	6.8	5.5	7.8
65 and over	0.3	0.3	0.3	0.3	0.3	0.3	0.3	0.3	0.3	0.3	0.4	0.4	0.4
Age unknown	0.4	0.3	0.3	0.3	0.2	0.2	0.3	0.2	0.2	0.2	0.6	0.6	0.6
Full-time	100.0	100.0	100.0	100.0	100.0	100.0	100.0	100.0	100.0	100.0	100.0	100.0	100.0
Under 18	1.4	1.4	1.2	1.5	1.5	1.3	1.6	1.7	1.5	1.9	#	#	#
18 and 19	28.8	27.5	27.6	27.4	28.2	27.9	28.4	32.4	32.0	32.8	0.1	#	0.1
20 and 21	25.7	25.5	25.8	25.2	25.8	25.9	25.6	29.4	29.5	29.3	1.9	1.6	2.1
22 to 24	17.3	17.4	18.5	16.4	17.8	18.8	17.0	15.9	17.4	14.7	29.9	28.1	31.4
25 to 29	12.0	12.4	12.9	11.9	11.9	12.4	11.5	8.4	8.8	8.2	34.7	37.1	32.8
30 to 34	5.6	6.1	5.9	6.3	5.8	5.7	5.8	4.5	4.3	4.7	14.1	15.4	13.0
35 to 39	3.4	3.5	3.0	3.9	3.3	2.9	3.5	2.7	2.3	3.0	6.9	6.9	6.9
40 to 49	3.9	4.2	3.4	4.9	3.8	3.2	4.4	3.2	2.7	3.7	7.8	6.9	8.5
50 to 64	1.6	1.8	1.4	2.1	1.8	1.6	2.0	1.5	1.4	1.6	3.9	3.1	4.5
65 and over	0.1	0.1	0.1	0.1	0.1	0.1	0.1	0.1	0.1	0.1	0.2	0.2	0.2
Age unknown	0.2	0.2	0.2	0.2	0.2	0.2	0.2	0.1	0.1	0.1	0.6	0.7	0.6
Part-time	100.0	100.0	100.0	100.0	100.0	100.0	100.0	100.0	100.0	100.0	100.0	100.0	100.0
Under 18	7.6	7.7	7.9	7.5	8.9	9.1	8.8	10.6	10.7	10.6	#	#	#
18 and 19	8.6	9.0	10.4	8.0	9.2	10.6	8.3	11.0	12.4	10.0	#	#	#
20 and 21	9.8	10.6	11.7	9.9	10.8	11.9	10.0	12.8	14.0	12.0	0.3	0.2	0.3
22 to 24	14.5	14.7	15.5	14.2	15.3	16.1	14.7	16.4	17.3	15.7	9.8	9.2	10.2
25 to 29	18.4	18.0	18.0	17.9	17.5	17.4	17.5	15.7	15.7	15.7	26.7	27.3	26.4
30 to 34	11.8	12.1	11.9	12.2	11.8	11.7	11.9	10.3	10.0	10.6	19.5	21.4	18.3
35 to 39	8.8	8.3	7.8	8.7	8.0	7.5	8.4	7.0	6.4	7.5	13.2	13.8	12.8
40 to 49	12.3	11.9	10.2	13.1	11.1	9.5	12.2	9.7	8.1	10.8	18.5	17.5	19.1
50 to 64	6.8	6.6	5.4	7.4	6.3	5.1	7.1	5.5	4.4	6.2	10.8	9.2	11.8
65 and over	0.8	0.7	0.7	0.7	0.7	0.8	0.7	0.8	0.8	0.8	0.6	0.8	0.5
Age unknown	0.6	0.5	0.5	0.4	0.3	0.3	0.3	0.3	0.3	0.3	0.6	0.6	0.6

#Rounds to zero.
NOTE: Degree-granting institutions grant associate's or higher degrees and participate in Title IV federal financial aid programs. Detail may not sum to totals because of rounding. Some data have been revised from previously published figures.

SOURCE: U.S. Department of Education, National Center for Education Statistics, Integrated Postsecondary Education Data System (IPEDS), Spring 2010, 2012, and 2014, Enrollment component. (This table was prepared November 2014.)

Table 303.50. Total fall enrollment in degree-granting postsecondary institutions, by level of enrollment, control and level of institution, attendance status, and age of student: 2013

Attendance status and age of student	Undergraduate										Postbaccalaureate			
	Total	Public			Private, nonprofit			Private, for-profit			Total	Public	Private, nonprofit	Private, for-profit
		Total	4-year	2-year	Total	4-year	2-year	Total	4-year	2-year				
1	2	3	4	5	6	7	8	9	10	11	12	13	14	15
All students	17,474,835	13,347,002	6,721,861	6,625,141	2,757,447	2,725,249	32,198	1,370,386	1,058,986	311,400	2,900,954	1,398,556	1,216,557	285,841
Under 18......................	878,960	784,803	242,293	542,510	87,570	86,484	1,086	6,587	5,324	1,263	167	48	83	36
18 and 19.....................	4,264,764	3,349,245	1,896,915	1,452,330	826,654	820,296	6,358	88,865	54,440	34,425	1,089	461	608	20
20 and 21.....................	4,051,605	3,087,024	1,947,466	1,139,558	826,717	821,161	5,556	137,864	88,292	49,572	34,119	17,077	16,460	582
22 to 24......................	2,812,445	2,240,127	1,284,653	955,474	369,438	364,227	5,211	202,880	144,567	58,313	618,205	338,529	265,056	14,620
25 to 29......................	1,949,698	1,458,960	595,850	863,110	198,958	194,108	4,850	291,780	229,218	62,562	907,358	465,212	390,187	51,959
30 to 34......................	1,166,637	815,017	285,188	529,829	132,642	129,704	2,938	218,978	182,140	36,838	475,794	230,680	192,088	53,026
35 to 39......................	756,185	512,097	165,362	346,735	95,749	93,694	2,055	148,339	124,662	23,677	277,963	123,327	109,698	44,938
40 to 49......................	988,078	664,808	197,606	467,202	136,255	133,669	2,586	187,015	158,318	28,697	358,577	141,825	143,168	73,584
50 to 64......................	518,914	371,772	93,356	278,416	65,567	64,252	1,315	81,575	67,903	13,672	198,386	72,180	81,789	44,417
65 and over..................	55,195	48,830	8,861	39,969	3,805	3,721	84	2,560	2,097	463	10,966	4,063	4,678	2,225
Age unknown................	32,354	14,319	4,311	10,008	14,092	13,933	159	3,943	2,025	1,918	18,330	5,154	12,742	434
Full-time......................	10,938,494	7,685,669	5,155,712	2,529,957	2,261,723	2,237,668	24,055	991,102	712,198	278,904	1,658,618	779,140	724,330	155,148
Under 18......................	185,631	144,552	68,114	76,438	36,463	36,234	229	4,616	3,466	1,150	87	20	44	23
18 and 19.....................	3,547,315	2,664,561	1,768,650	895,911	804,479	798,645	5,834	78,275	45,455	32,820	979	429	540	10
20 and 21.....................	3,213,421	2,304,294	1,759,408	544,886	796,874	792,100	4,774	112,253	66,580	45,673	30,993	15,478	15,140	375
22 to 24......................	1,743,151	1,286,138	958,567	327,571	303,865	299,925	3,940	153,148	100,753	52,395	496,246	270,991	215,711	9,544
25 to 29......................	923,550	593,123	325,284	267,839	119,627	116,184	3,443	210,800	155,170	55,630	575,593	286,545	259,401	29,647
30 to 34......................	491,630	272,350	124,514	147,836	66,912	64,925	1,987	152,368	120,141	32,227	233,786	106,195	99,125	28,466
35 to 39......................	295,425	151,244	61,252	89,992	44,044	42,691	1,353	100,137	79,591	20,546	114,087	43,225	46,799	24,063
40 to 49......................	355,343	174,691	62,740	111,951	57,405	55,833	1,572	123,247	98,467	24,780	128,965	36,942	52,829	39,194
50 to 64......................	162,457	86,358	24,229	62,129	24,143	23,365	778	51,956	40,191	11,765	64,149	14,532	27,111	22,506
65 and over..................	5,931	3,407	891	2,516	986	929	57	1,538	1,159	379	3,202	578	1,549	1,075
Age unknown...............	14,640	4,951	2,063	2,888	6,925	6,837	88	2,764	1,225	1,539	10,531	4,205	6,081	245
Part-time......................	6,536,341	5,661,333	1,566,149	4,095,184	495,724	487,581	8,143	379,284	346,788	32,496	1,242,336	619,416	492,227	130,693
Under 18......................	693,329	640,251	174,179	466,072	51,107	50,250	857	1,971	1,858	113	80	28	39	13
18 and 19.....................	717,449	684,684	128,265	556,419	22,175	21,651	524	10,590	8,985	1,605	110	32	68	10
20 and 21.....................	838,184	782,730	188,058	594,672	29,843	29,061	782	25,611	21,712	3,899	3,126	1,599	1,320	207
22 to 24......................	1,069,294	953,989	326,086	627,903	65,573	64,302	1,271	49,732	43,814	5,918	121,959	67,538	49,345	5,076
25 to 29......................	1,026,148	865,837	270,566	595,271	79,331	77,924	1,407	80,980	74,048	6,932	331,765	178,667	130,786	22,312
30 to 34......................	675,007	542,667	160,674	381,993	65,730	64,779	951	66,610	61,999	4,611	242,008	124,485	92,963	24,560
35 to 39......................	460,760	360,853	104,110	256,743	51,705	51,003	702	48,202	45,071	3,131	163,876	80,102	62,899	20,875
40 to 49......................	632,735	490,117	134,866	355,251	78,850	77,836	1,014	63,768	59,851	3,917	229,612	104,883	90,339	34,390
50 to 64......................	356,457	285,414	69,127	216,287	41,424	40,887	537	29,619	27,712	1,907	134,237	57,648	54,678	21,911
65 and over..................	49,264	45,423	7,970	37,453	2,819	2,792	27	1,022	938	84	7,764	3,485	3,129	1,150
Age unknown...............	17,714	9,368	2,248	7,120	7,167	7,096	71	1,179	800	379	7,799	949	6,661	189
	Percentage distribution													
All students	100.0	100.0	100.0	100.0	100.0	100.0	100.0	100.0	100.0	100.0	100.0	100.0	100.0	100.0
Under 18......................	5.0	5.9	3.6	8.2	3.2	3.2	3.4	0.5	0.5	0.4	#	#	#	#
18 and 19.....................	24.4	25.1	28.2	21.9	30.0	30.1	19.7	6.5	5.1	11.1	#	#	#	#
20 and 21.....................	23.2	23.1	29.0	17.2	30.0	30.1	17.3	10.1	8.3	15.9	1.2	1.2	1.4	0.2
22 to 24......................	16.1	16.8	19.1	14.4	13.4	13.4	16.2	14.8	13.7	18.7	21.3	24.2	21.8	5.1
25 to 29......................	11.2	10.9	8.9	13.0	7.2	7.1	15.1	21.3	21.6	20.1	31.3	33.3	32.1	18.2
30 to 34......................	6.7	6.1	4.2	8.0	4.8	4.8	9.1	16.0	17.2	11.8	16.4	16.5	15.8	18.6
35 to 39......................	4.3	3.8	2.5	5.2	3.5	3.4	6.4	10.8	11.8	7.6	9.6	8.8	9.0	15.7
40 to 49......................	5.7	5.0	2.9	7.1	4.9	4.9	8.0	13.6	14.9	9.2	12.4	10.1	11.8	25.7
50 to 64......................	3.0	2.8	1.4	4.2	2.4	2.4	4.1	6.0	6.4	4.4	6.8	5.2	6.7	15.5
65 and over..................	0.3	0.4	0.1	0.6	0.1	0.1	0.3	0.2	0.2	0.1	0.4	0.3	0.4	0.8
Age unknown................	0.2	0.1	0.1	0.2	0.5	0.5	0.5	0.3	0.2	0.6	0.6	0.4	1.0	0.2
Full-time......................	100.0	100.0	100.0	100.0	100.0	100.0	100.0	100.0	100.0	100.0	100.0	100.0	100.0	100.0
Under 18......................	1.7	1.9	1.3	3.0	1.6	1.6	1.0	0.5	0.5	0.4	#	#	#	#
18 and 19.....................	32.4	34.7	34.3	35.4	35.6	35.7	24.3	7.9	6.4	11.8	0.1	0.1	0.1	#
20 and 21.....................	29.4	30.0	34.1	21.5	35.2	35.4	19.8	11.3	9.3	16.4	1.9	2.0	2.1	0.2
22 to 24......................	15.9	16.7	18.6	12.9	13.4	13.4	16.4	15.5	14.1	18.8	29.9	34.8	29.8	6.2
25 to 29......................	8.4	7.7	6.3	10.6	5.3	5.2	14.3	21.3	21.8	19.9	34.7	36.8	35.8	19.1
30 to 34......................	4.5	3.5	2.4	5.8	3.0	2.9	8.3	15.4	16.9	11.6	14.1	13.6	13.7	18.3
35 to 39......................	2.7	2.0	1.2	3.6	1.9	1.9	5.6	10.1	11.2	7.4	6.9	5.5	6.5	15.5
40 to 49......................	3.2	2.3	1.2	4.4	2.5	2.5	6.5	12.4	13.8	8.9	7.8	4.7	7.3	25.3
50 to 64......................	1.5	1.1	0.5	2.5	1.1	1.0	3.2	5.2	5.6	4.2	3.9	1.9	3.7	14.5
65 and over..................	0.1	#	#	0.1	#	#	0.2	0.2	0.2	0.1	0.2	0.1	0.2	0.7
Age unknown................	0.1	0.1	#	0.1	0.3	0.3	0.4	0.3	0.2	0.6	0.6	0.5	0.8	0.2
Part-time......................	100.0	100.0	100.0	100.0	100.0	100.0	100.0	100.0	100.0	100.0	100.0	100.0	100.0	100.0
Under 18......................	10.6	11.3	11.1	11.4	10.3	10.3	10.5	0.5	0.5	0.3	#	#	#	#
18 and 19.....................	11.0	12.1	8.2	13.6	4.5	4.4	6.4	2.8	2.6	4.9	#	#	#	#
20 and 21.....................	12.8	13.8	12.0	14.5	6.0	6.0	9.6	6.8	6.3	12.0	0.3	0.3	0.3	0.2
22 to 24......................	16.4	16.9	20.8	15.3	13.2	13.2	15.6	13.1	12.6	18.2	9.8	10.9	10.0	3.9
25 to 29......................	15.7	15.3	17.3	14.5	16.0	16.0	17.3	21.4	21.4	21.3	26.7	28.8	26.6	17.1
30 to 34......................	10.3	9.6	10.3	9.3	13.3	13.3	11.7	17.6	17.9	14.2	19.5	20.1	18.9	18.8
35 to 39......................	7.0	6.4	6.6	6.3	10.4	10.5	8.6	12.7	13.0	9.6	13.2	12.9	12.8	16.0
40 to 49......................	9.7	8.7	8.6	8.7	15.9	16.0	12.5	16.8	17.3	12.1	18.5	16.9	18.4	26.3
50 to 64......................	5.5	5.0	4.4	5.3	8.4	8.4	6.6	7.8	8.0	5.9	10.8	9.3	11.1	16.8
65 and over..................	0.8	0.8	0.5	0.9	0.6	0.6	0.3	0.3	0.3	0.3	0.6	0.6	0.6	0.9
Age unknown...............	0.3	0.2	0.1	0.2	1.4	1.5	0.9	0.3	0.2	1.2	0.6	0.2	1.4	0.1

#Rounds to zero.
NOTE: Degree-granting institutions grant associate's or higher degrees and participate in Title IV federal financial aid programs. Detail may not sum to totals because of rounding.

SOURCE: U.S. Department of Education, National Center for Education Statistics, Integrated Postsecondary Education Data System (IPEDS), Spring 2014, Enrollment component. (This table was prepared November 2014.)

Table 303.55. Total fall enrollment in degree-granting postsecondary institutions, by control and level of institution, attendance status, and age of student: 2013

Attendance status and age of student	All institutions			Public institutions			Private (nonprofit and for-profit) institutions						
							Total	Nonprofit institutions			For-profit institutions		
	Total	4-year	2-year	Total	4-year	2-year	Total	Total	4-year	2-year	Total	4-year	2-year
1	2	3	4	5	6	7	8	9	10	11	12	13	14
All students	20,375,789	13,407,050	6,968,739	14,745,558	8,120,417	6,625,141	5,630,231	3,974,004	3,941,806	32,198	1,656,227	1,344,827	311,400
Under 18	879,127	334,268	544,859	784,851	242,341	542,510	94,276	87,653	86,567	1,086	6,623	5,360	1,263
18 and 19	4,265,853	2,772,740	1,493,113	3,349,706	1,897,376	1,452,330	916,147	827,262	820,904	6,358	88,885	54,460	34,425
20 and 21	4,085,724	2,891,038	1,194,686	3,104,101	1,964,543	1,139,558	981,623	843,177	837,621	5,556	138,446	88,874	49,572
22 to 24	3,430,650	2,411,652	1,018,998	2,578,656	1,623,182	955,474	851,994	634,494	629,283	5,211	217,500	159,187	58,313
25 to 29	2,857,056	1,926,534	930,522	1,924,172	1,061,062	863,110	932,884	589,145	584,295	4,850	343,739	281,177	62,562
30 to 34	1,642,431	1,072,826	569,605	1,045,697	515,868	529,829	596,734	324,730	321,792	2,938	272,004	235,166	36,838
35 to 39	1,034,148	661,681	372,467	635,424	288,689	346,735	398,724	205,447	203,392	2,055	193,277	169,600	23,677
40 to 49	1,346,655	848,170	498,485	806,633	339,431	467,202	540,022	279,423	276,837	2,586	260,599	231,902	28,697
50 to 64	717,300	423,897	293,403	443,952	165,536	278,416	273,348	147,356	146,041	1,315	125,992	112,320	13,672
65 and over	66,161	25,645	40,516	52,893	12,924	39,969	13,268	8,483	8,399	84	4,785	4,322	463
Age unknown	50,684	38,599	12,085	19,473	9,465	10,008	31,211	26,834	26,675	159	4,377	2,459	1,918
Full-time	12,597,112	9,764,196	2,832,916	8,464,809	5,934,852	2,529,957	4,132,303	2,986,053	2,961,998	24,055	1,146,250	867,346	278,904
Under 18	185,718	107,901	77,817	144,572	68,134	76,438	41,146	36,507	36,278	229	4,639	3,489	1,150
18 and 19	3,548,294	2,613,729	934,565	2,664,990	1,769,079	895,911	883,304	805,019	799,185	5,834	78,285	45,465	32,820
20 and 21	3,244,414	2,649,081	595,333	2,319,772	1,774,886	544,886	924,642	812,014	807,240	4,774	112,628	66,955	45,673
22 to 24	2,239,397	1,855,491	383,906	1,557,129	1,229,558	327,571	682,268	519,576	515,636	3,940	162,692	110,297	52,395
25 to 29	1,499,143	1,172,231	326,912	879,668	611,829	267,839	619,475	379,028	375,585	3,443	240,447	184,817	55,630
30 to 34	725,416	543,366	182,050	378,545	230,709	147,836	346,871	166,037	164,050	1,987	180,834	148,607	32,227
35 to 39	409,512	297,621	111,891	194,469	104,477	89,992	215,043	90,843	89,490	1,353	124,200	103,654	20,546
40 to 49	484,308	346,005	138,303	211,633	99,682	111,951	272,675	110,234	108,662	1,572	162,441	137,661	24,780
50 to 64	226,606	151,934	74,672	100,890	38,761	62,129	125,716	51,254	50,476	778	74,462	62,697	11,765
65 and over	9,133	6,181	2,952	3,985	1,469	2,516	5,148	2,535	2,478	57	2,613	2,234	379
Age unknown	25,171	20,656	4,515	9,156	6,268	2,888	16,015	13,006	12,918	88	3,009	1,470	1,539
Part-time	7,778,677	3,642,854	4,135,823	6,280,749	2,185,565	4,095,184	1,497,928	987,951	979,808	8,143	509,977	477,481	32,496
Under 18	693,409	226,367	467,042	640,279	174,207	466,072	53,130	51,146	50,289	857	1,984	1,871	113
18 and 19	717,559	159,011	558,548	684,716	128,297	556,419	32,843	22,243	21,719	524	10,600	8,995	1,605
20 and 21	841,310	241,957	599,353	784,329	189,657	594,672	56,981	31,163	30,381	782	25,818	21,919	3,899
22 to 24	1,191,253	556,161	635,092	1,021,527	393,624	627,903	169,726	114,918	113,647	1,271	54,808	48,890	5,918
25 to 29	1,357,913	754,303	603,610	1,044,504	449,233	595,271	313,409	210,117	208,710	1,407	103,292	96,360	6,932
30 to 34	917,015	529,460	387,555	667,152	285,159	381,993	249,863	158,693	157,742	951	91,170	86,559	4,611
35 to 39	624,636	364,060	260,576	440,955	184,212	256,743	183,681	114,604	113,902	702	69,077	65,946	3,131
40 to 49	862,347	502,165	360,182	595,000	239,749	355,251	267,347	169,189	168,175	1,014	98,158	94,241	3,917
50 to 64	490,694	271,963	218,731	343,062	126,775	216,287	147,632	96,102	95,565	537	51,530	49,623	1,907
65 and over	57,028	19,464	37,564	48,908	11,455	37,453	8,120	5,948	5,921	27	2,172	2,088	84
Age unknown	25,513	17,943	7,570	10,317	3,197	7,120	15,196	13,828	13,757	71	1,368	989	379
	Percentage distribution												
All students	100.0	100.0	100.0	100.0	100.0	100.0	100.0	100.0	100.0	100.0	100.0	100.0	100.0
Under 18	4.3	2.5	7.8	5.3	3.0	8.2	1.7	2.2	2.2	3.4	0.4	0.4	0.4
18 and 19	20.9	20.7	21.4	22.7	23.4	21.9	16.3	20.8	20.8	19.7	5.4	4.0	11.1
20 and 21	20.1	21.6	17.1	21.1	24.2	17.2	17.4	21.2	21.2	17.3	8.4	6.6	15.9
22 to 24	16.8	18.0	14.6	17.5	20.0	14.4	15.1	16.0	16.0	16.2	13.1	11.8	18.7
25 to 29	14.0	14.4	13.4	13.0	13.1	13.0	16.6	14.8	14.8	15.1	20.8	20.9	20.1
30 to 34	8.1	8.0	8.2	7.1	6.4	8.0	10.6	8.2	8.2	9.1	16.4	17.5	11.8
35 to 39	5.1	4.9	5.3	4.3	3.6	5.2	7.1	5.2	5.2	6.4	11.7	12.6	7.6
40 to 49	6.6	6.3	7.2	5.5	4.2	7.1	9.6	7.0	7.0	8.0	15.7	17.2	9.2
50 to 64	3.5	3.2	4.2	3.0	2.0	4.2	4.9	3.7	3.7	4.1	7.6	8.4	4.4
65 and over	0.3	0.2	0.6	0.4	0.2	0.6	0.2	0.2	0.2	0.3	0.3	0.3	0.1
Age unknown	0.2	0.3	0.2	0.1	0.1	0.2	0.6	0.7	0.7	0.5	0.3	0.2	0.6
Full-time	100.0	100.0	100.0	100.0	100.0	100.0	100.0	100.0	100.0	100.0	100.0	100.0	100.0
Under 18	1.5	1.1	2.7	1.7	1.1	3.0	1.0	1.2	1.2	1.0	0.4	0.4	0.4
18 and 19	28.2	26.8	33.0	31.5	29.8	35.4	21.4	27.0	27.0	24.3	6.8	5.2	11.8
20 and 21	25.8	27.1	21.0	27.4	29.9	21.5	22.4	27.2	27.3	19.8	9.8	7.7	16.4
22 to 24	17.8	19.0	13.6	18.4	20.7	12.9	16.5	17.4	17.4	16.4	14.2	12.7	18.8
25 to 29	11.9	12.0	11.5	10.4	10.3	10.6	15.0	12.7	12.7	14.3	21.0	21.3	19.9
30 to 34	5.8	5.6	6.4	4.5	3.9	5.8	8.4	5.6	5.5	8.3	15.8	17.1	11.6
35 to 39	3.3	3.0	3.9	2.3	1.8	3.6	5.2	3.0	3.0	5.6	10.8	12.0	7.4
40 to 49	3.8	3.5	4.9	2.5	1.7	4.4	6.6	3.7	3.7	6.5	14.2	15.9	8.9
50 to 64	1.8	1.6	2.6	1.2	0.7	2.5	3.0	1.7	1.7	3.2	6.5	7.2	4.2
65 and over	0.1	0.1	0.1	#	#	0.1	0.1	0.1	0.1	0.2	0.2	0.3	0.1
Age unknown	0.2	0.2	0.2	0.1	0.1	0.1	0.4	0.4	0.4	0.4	0.3	0.2	0.6
Part-time	100.0	100.0	100.0	100.0	100.0	100.0	100.0	100.0	100.0	100.0	100.0	100.0	100.0
Under 18	8.9	6.2	11.3	10.2	8.0	11.4	3.5	5.2	5.1	10.5	0.4	0.4	0.3
18 and 19	9.2	4.4	13.5	10.9	5.9	13.6	2.2	2.3	2.2	6.4	2.1	1.9	4.9
20 and 21	10.8	6.6	14.5	12.5	8.7	14.5	3.8	3.2	3.1	9.6	5.1	4.6	12.0
22 to 24	15.3	15.3	15.4	16.3	18.0	15.3	11.3	11.6	11.6	15.6	10.7	10.2	18.2
25 to 29	17.5	20.7	14.6	16.6	20.6	14.5	20.9	21.3	21.3	17.3	20.3	20.2	21.3
30 to 34	11.8	14.5	9.4	10.6	13.0	9.3	16.7	16.1	16.1	11.7	17.9	18.1	14.2
35 to 39	8.0	10.0	6.3	7.0	8.4	6.3	12.3	11.6	11.6	8.6	13.5	13.8	9.6
40 to 49	11.1	13.8	8.7	9.5	11.0	8.7	17.8	17.1	17.2	12.5	19.2	19.7	12.1
50 to 64	6.3	7.5	5.3	5.5	5.8	5.3	9.9	9.7	9.8	6.6	10.1	10.4	5.9
65 and over	0.7	0.5	0.9	0.8	0.5	0.9	0.5	0.6	0.6	0.3	0.4	0.4	0.3
Age unknown	0.3	0.5	0.2	0.2	0.1	0.2	1.0	1.4	1.4	0.9	0.3	0.2	1.2

#Rounds to zero.
NOTE: Degree-granting institutions grant associate's or higher degrees and participate in Title IV federal financial aid programs. Detail may not sum to totals because of rounding.

SOURCE: U.S. Department of Education, National Center for Education Statistics, Integrated Postsecondary Education Data System (IPEDS), Spring 2014, Enrollment component. (This table was prepared November 2014.)

Table 303.60. Total fall enrollment in degree-granting postsecondary institutions, by level of enrollment, sex of student, and other selected characteristics: 2014

Level and control of institution and attendance status of student	Total			Undergraduate			Postbaccalaureate		
	Total	Males	Females	Total	Males	Females	Total	Males	Females
1	2	3	4	5	6	7	8	9	10
Total	20,207,369	8,797,061	11,410,308	17,292,787	7,585,910	9,706,877	2,914,582	1,211,151	1,703,431
Full-time	12,453,975	5,619,391	6,834,584	10,783,802	4,876,952	5,906,850	1,670,173	742,439	927,734
Part-time	7,753,394	3,177,670	4,575,724	6,508,985	2,708,958	3,800,027	1,244,409	468,712	775,697
4-year	13,492,884	5,903,282	7,589,602	10,578,302	4,692,131	5,886,171	2,914,582	1,211,151	1,703,431
Full-time	9,793,247	4,419,286	5,373,961	8,123,074	3,676,847	4,446,227	1,670,173	742,439	927,734
Part-time	3,699,637	1,483,996	2,215,641	2,455,228	1,015,284	1,439,944	1,244,409	468,712	775,697
2-year	6,714,485	2,893,779	3,820,706	6,714,485	2,893,779	3,820,706	†	†	†
Full-time	2,660,728	1,200,105	1,460,623	2,660,728	1,200,105	1,460,623	†	†	†
Part-time	4,053,757	1,693,674	2,360,083	4,053,757	1,693,674	2,360,083	†	†	†
Public	14,655,015	6,538,934	8,116,081	13,244,837	5,929,887	7,314,950	1,410,178	609,047	801,131
Full-time	8,397,719	3,914,629	4,483,090	7,607,968	3,547,635	4,060,333	789,751	366,994	422,757
Part-time	6,257,296	2,624,305	3,632,991	5,636,869	2,382,252	3,254,617	620,427	242,053	378,374
Public 4-year	8,257,250	3,747,975	4,509,275	6,847,072	3,138,928	3,708,144	1,410,178	609,047	801,131
Full-time	6,012,706	2,807,232	3,205,474	5,222,955	2,440,238	2,782,717	789,751	366,994	422,757
Part-time	2,244,544	940,743	1,303,801	1,624,117	698,690	925,427	620,427	242,053	378,374
Public 2-year	6,397,765	2,790,959	3,606,806	6,397,765	2,790,959	3,606,806	†	†	†
Full-time	2,385,013	1,107,397	1,277,616	2,385,013	1,107,397	1,277,616	†	†	†
Part-time	4,012,752	1,683,562	2,329,190	4,012,752	1,683,562	2,329,190	†	†	†
Private	5,552,354	2,258,127	3,294,227	4,047,950	1,656,023	2,391,927	1,504,404	602,104	902,300
Full-time	4,056,256	1,704,762	2,351,494	3,175,834	1,329,317	1,846,517	880,422	375,445	504,977
Part-time	1,496,098	553,365	942,733	872,116	326,706	545,410	623,982	226,659	397,323
Private 4-year	5,235,634	2,155,307	3,080,327	3,731,230	1,553,203	2,178,027	1,504,404	602,104	902,300
Full-time	3,780,541	1,612,054	2,168,487	2,900,119	1,236,609	1,663,510	880,422	375,445	504,977
Part-time	1,455,093	543,253	911,840	831,111	316,594	514,517	623,982	226,659	397,323
Private 2-year	316,720	102,820	213,900	316,720	102,820	213,900	†	†	†
Full-time	275,715	92,708	183,007	275,715	92,708	183,007	†	†	†
Part-time	41,005	10,112	30,893	41,005	10,112	30,893	†	†	†
Nonprofit	3,996,089	1,703,725	2,292,364	2,771,341	1,189,779	1,581,562	1,224,748	513,946	710,802
Full-time	3,003,211	1,322,099	1,681,112	2,269,597	995,746	1,273,851	733,614	326,353	407,261
Part-time	992,878	381,626	611,252	501,744	194,033	307,711	491,134	187,593	303,541
Nonprofit 4-year	3,965,724	1,692,461	2,273,263	2,740,976	1,178,515	1,562,461	1,224,748	513,946	710,802
Full-time	2,980,433	1,313,033	1,667,400	2,246,819	986,680	1,260,139	733,614	326,353	407,261
Part-time	985,291	379,428	605,863	494,157	191,835	302,322	491,134	187,593	303,541
Nonprofit 2-year	30,365	11,264	19,101	30,365	11,264	19,101	†	†	†
Full-time	22,778	9,066	13,712	22,778	9,066	13,712	†	†	†
Part-time	7,587	2,198	5,389	7,587	2,198	5,389	†	†	†
For-profit	1,556,265	554,402	1,001,863	1,276,609	466,244	810,365	279,656	88,158	191,498
Full-time	1,053,045	382,663	670,382	906,237	333,571	572,666	146,808	49,092	97,716
Part-time	503,220	171,739	331,481	370,372	132,673	237,699	132,848	39,066	93,782
For-profit 4-year	1,269,910	462,846	807,064	990,254	374,688	615,566	279,656	88,158	191,498
Full-time	800,108	299,021	501,087	653,300	249,929	403,371	146,808	49,092	97,716
Part-time	469,802	163,825	305,977	336,954	124,759	212,195	132,848	39,066	93,782
For-profit 2-year	286,355	91,556	194,799	286,355	91,556	194,799	†	†	†
Full-time	252,937	83,642	169,295	252,937	83,642	169,295	†	†	†
Part-time	33,418	7,914	25,504	33,418	7,914	25,504	†	†	†

†Not applicable.
NOTE: Degree-granting institutions grant associate's or higher degrees and participate in Title IV federal financial aid programs.

SOURCE: U.S. Department of Education, National Center for Education Statistics, Integrated Postsecondary Education Data System (IPEDS), Spring 2015, Fall Enrollment component. (This table was prepared October 2015.)

Table 303.65. Total fall enrollment in degree-granting postsecondary institutions, by level of enrollment, sex of student, and other selected characteristics: 2012

Level and control of institution and attendance status of student	Total			Undergraduate			Postbaccalaureate		
	Total	Males	Females	Total	Males	Females	Total	Males	Females
1	2	3	4	5	6	7	8	9	10
Total	**20,644,478**	**8,919,006**	**11,725,472**	**17,735,638**	**7,714,938**	**10,020,700**	**2,908,840**	**1,204,068**	**1,704,772**
Full-time	12,734,404	5,708,406	7,025,998	11,097,092	4,984,389	6,112,703	1,637,312	724,017	913,295
Part-time	7,910,074	3,210,600	4,699,474	6,638,546	2,730,549	3,907,997	1,271,528	480,051	791,477
4-year	**13,476,638**	**5,872,913**	**7,603,725**	**10,567,798**	**4,668,845**	**5,898,953**	**2,908,840**	**1,204,068**	**1,704,772**
Full-time	9,792,607	4,402,749	5,389,858	8,155,295	3,678,732	4,476,563	1,637,312	724,017	913,295
Part-time	3,684,031	1,470,164	2,213,867	2,412,503	990,113	1,422,390	1,271,528	480,051	791,477
2-year	**7,167,840**	**3,046,093**	**4,121,747**	**7,167,840**	**3,046,093**	**4,121,747**	†	†	†
Full-time	2,941,797	1,305,657	1,636,140	2,941,797	1,305,657	1,636,140	†	†	†
Part-time	4,226,043	1,740,436	2,485,607	4,226,043	1,740,436	2,485,607	†	†	†
Public	**14,884,667**	**6,582,953**	**8,301,714**	**13,478,100**	**5,985,106**	**7,492,994**	**1,406,567**	**597,847**	**808,720**
Full-time	8,525,199	3,954,186	4,571,013	7,752,040	3,599,620	4,152,420	773,159	354,566	418,593
Part-time	6,359,468	2,628,767	3,730,701	5,726,060	2,385,486	3,340,574	633,408	243,281	390,127
Public 4-year	8,092,602	3,658,097	4,434,505	6,686,035	3,060,250	3,625,785	1,406,567	597,847	808,720
Full-time	5,909,868	2,756,885	3,152,983	5,136,709	2,402,319	2,734,390	773,159	354,566	418,593
Part-time	2,182,734	901,212	1,281,522	1,549,326	657,931	891,395	633,408	243,281	390,127
Public 2-year	6,792,065	2,924,856	3,867,209	6,792,065	2,924,856	3,867,209	†	†	†
Full-time	2,615,331	1,197,301	1,418,030	2,615,331	1,197,301	1,418,030	†	†	†
Part-time	4,176,734	1,727,555	2,449,179	4,176,734	1,727,555	2,449,179	†	†	†
Private	**5,759,811**	**2,336,053**	**3,423,758**	**4,257,538**	**1,729,832**	**2,527,706**	**1,502,273**	**606,221**	**896,052**
Full-time	4,209,205	1,754,220	2,454,985	3,345,052	1,384,769	1,960,283	864,153	369,451	494,702
Part-time	1,550,606	581,833	968,773	912,486	345,063	567,423	638,120	236,770	401,350
Private 4-year	5,384,036	2,214,816	3,169,220	3,881,763	1,608,595	2,273,168	1,502,273	606,221	896,052
Full-time	3,882,739	1,645,864	2,236,875	3,018,586	1,276,413	1,742,173	864,153	369,451	494,702
Part-time	1,501,297	568,952	932,345	863,177	332,182	530,995	638,120	236,770	401,350
Private 2-year	375,775	121,237	254,538	375,775	121,237	254,538	†	†	†
Full-time	326,466	108,356	218,110	326,466	108,356	218,110	†	†	†
Part-time	49,309	12,881	36,428	49,309	12,881	36,428	†	†	†
Nonprofit	3,951,388	1,679,120	2,272,268	2,744,400	1,169,797	1,574,603	1,206,988	509,323	697,665
Full-time	2,956,492	1,299,132	1,657,360	2,249,833	981,940	1,267,893	706,659	317,192	389,467
Part-time	994,896	379,988	614,908	494,567	187,857	306,710	500,329	192,131	308,198
Nonprofit 4-year	3,913,690	1,666,190	2,247,500	2,706,702	1,156,867	1,549,835	1,206,988	509,323	697,665
Full-time	2,927,108	1,288,669	1,638,439	2,220,449	971,477	1,248,972	706,659	317,192	389,467
Part-time	986,582	377,521	609,061	486,253	185,390	300,863	500,329	192,131	308,198
Nonprofit 2-year	37,698	12,930	24,768	37,698	12,930	24,768	†	†	†
Full-time	29,384	10,463	18,921	29,384	10,463	18,921	†	†	†
Part-time	8,314	2,467	5,847	8,314	2,467	5,847	†	†	†
For-profit	1,808,423	656,933	1,151,490	1,513,138	560,035	953,103	295,285	96,898	198,387
Full-time	1,252,713	455,088	797,625	1,095,219	402,829	692,390	157,494	52,259	105,235
Part-time	555,710	201,845	353,865	417,919	157,206	260,713	137,791	44,639	93,152
For-profit 4-year	1,470,346	548,626	921,720	1,175,061	451,728	723,333	295,285	96,898	198,387
Full-time	955,631	357,195	598,436	798,137	304,936	493,201	157,494	52,259	105,235
Part-time	514,715	191,431	323,284	376,924	146,792	230,132	137,791	44,639	93,152
For-profit 2-year	338,077	108,307	229,770	338,077	108,307	229,770	†	†	†
Full-time	297,082	97,893	199,189	297,082	97,893	199,189	†	†	†
Part-time	40,995	10,414	30,581	40,995	10,414	30,581	†	†	†

†Not applicable.

NOTE: Degree-granting institutions grant associate's or higher degrees and participate in Title IV federal financial aid programs. Some data have been revised from previously published figures.

SOURCE: U.S. Department of Education, National Center for Education Statistics, Integrated Postsecondary Education Data System (IPEDS), Spring 2013, Fall Enrollment component. (This table was prepared October 2015.)

Table 303.70. Total undergraduate fall enrollment in degree-granting postsecondary institutions, by attendance status, sex of student, and control and level of institution: Selected years, 1970 through 2025

Level and year	Total	Full-time	Part-time	Males	Females	Males Full-time	Males Part-time	Females Full-time	Females Part-time	Public	Private Total	Private Nonprofit	Private For-profit
1	2	3	4	5	6	7	8	9	10	11	12	13	14
Total, all levels													
1970	7,368,644	5,280,064	2,088,580	4,249,702	3,118,942	3,096,371	1,153,331	2,183,693	935,249	5,620,255	1,748,389	1,730,133	18,256
1975	9,679,455	6,168,396	3,511,059	5,257,005	4,422,450	3,459,328	1,797,677	2,709,068	1,713,382	7,826,032	1,853,423	1,814,844	38,579
1980	10,475,055	6,361,744	4,113,311	5,000,177	5,474,878	3,226,857	1,773,320	3,134,887	2,339,991	8,441,955	2,033,100	1,926,703	106,397
1981	10,754,522	6,449,068	4,305,454	5,108,271	5,646,251	3,260,473	1,847,798	3,188,595	2,457,656	8,648,363	2,106,159	1,958,848	147,311
1982	10,825,062	6,483,805	4,341,257	5,170,494	5,654,568	3,299,436	1,871,058	3,184,369	2,470,199	8,713,073	2,111,989	1,939,389	172,600
1983	10,845,995	6,514,034	4,331,961	5,158,300	5,687,695	3,304,247	1,854,053	3,209,787	2,477,908	8,697,118	2,148,877	1,961,076	187,801
1984	10,618,071	6,347,653	4,270,418	5,006,813	5,611,258	3,194,930	1,811,883	3,152,723	2,458,535	8,493,491	2,124,580	1,940,310	184,270
1985	10,596,674	6,319,592	4,277,082	4,962,080	5,634,594	3,156,446	1,805,634	3,163,146	2,471,448	8,477,125	2,119,549	1,928,996	190,553
1986	10,797,975	6,352,073	4,445,902	5,017,505	5,780,470	3,146,330	1,871,175	3,205,743	2,574,727	8,660,716	2,137,259	1,928,294	208,965
1987	11,046,235	6,462,549	4,583,686	5,068,457	5,977,778	3,163,676	1,904,781	3,298,873	2,678,905	8,918,589	2,127,646	1,939,942	187,704
1988	11,316,548	6,642,428	4,674,120	5,137,644	6,178,904	3,206,442	1,931,202	3,435,986	2,742,918	9,103,146	2,213,402	—	—
1989	11,742,531	6,840,696	4,901,835	5,310,990	6,431,541	3,278,647	2,032,343	3,562,049	2,869,492	9,487,742	2,254,789	—	—
1990	11,959,106	6,976,030	4,983,076	5,379,759	6,579,347	3,336,535	2,043,224	3,639,495	2,939,852	9,709,596	2,249,510	2,043,407	206,103
1991	12,439,287	7,221,412	5,217,875	5,571,003	6,868,284	3,435,526	2,135,477	3,785,886	3,082,398	10,147,957	2,291,330	2,072,354	218,976
1992	12,537,700	7,244,442	5,293,258	5,582,936	6,954,764	3,424,739	2,158,197	3,819,703	3,135,061	10,216,297	2,321,403	2,101,721	219,682
1993	12,323,959	7,179,482	5,144,477	5,483,682	6,840,277	3,381,997	2,101,685	3,797,485	3,042,792	10,011,787	2,312,172	2,099,197	212,975
1994	12,262,608	7,168,706	5,093,902	5,422,113	6,840,495	3,341,591	2,080,522	3,827,115	3,013,380	9,945,128	2,317,480	2,100,465	217,015
1995	12,231,719	7,145,268	5,086,451	5,401,130	6,830,589	3,296,610	2,104,520	3,848,658	2,981,931	9,903,626	2,328,093	2,104,693	223,400
1996	12,326,948	7,298,839	5,028,109	5,420,672	6,906,276	3,339,108	2,081,564	3,959,731	2,946,545	9,935,283	2,391,665	2,112,318	279,347
1997	12,450,587	7,418,598	5,031,989	5,468,532	6,982,055	3,379,597	2,088,935	4,039,001	2,943,054	10,007,479	2,443,108	2,139,824	303,284
1998	12,436,937	7,538,711	4,898,226	5,446,133	6,990,804	3,428,161	2,017,972	4,110,550	2,880,254	9,950,212	2,486,725	2,152,655	334,070
1999	12,739,445	7,753,548	4,985,897	5,584,234	7,155,211	3,524,586	2,059,648	4,228,962	2,926,249	10,174,228	2,565,217	2,185,290	379,927
2000	13,155,393	7,922,926	5,232,467	5,778,268	7,377,125	3,588,246	2,190,022	4,334,680	3,042,445	10,539,322	2,616,071	2,213,180	402,891
2001	13,715,610	8,327,640	5,387,970	6,004,431	7,711,179	3,768,630	2,235,801	4,559,010	3,152,169	10,985,871	2,729,739	2,257,718	472,021
2002	14,257,077	8,734,252	5,522,825	6,192,390	8,064,687	3,934,168	2,258,222	4,800,084	3,264,603	11,432,855	2,824,222	2,306,091	518,131
2003	14,480,364	9,045,253	5,435,111	6,227,372	8,252,992	4,048,682	2,178,690	4,996,571	3,256,421	11,523,103	2,957,261	2,346,673	610,588
2004	14,780,630	9,284,336	5,496,294	6,340,048	8,440,582	4,140,628	2,199,420	5,143,708	3,296,874	11,650,580	3,130,050	2,389,366	740,684
2005	14,963,964	9,446,430	5,517,534	6,408,871	8,555,093	4,200,863	2,208,008	5,245,567	3,309,526	11,697,730	3,266,234	2,418,368	847,866
2006	15,184,302	9,571,079	5,613,223	6,513,756	8,670,546	4,264,606	2,249,150	5,306,473	3,364,073	11,847,426	3,336,876	2,448,240	888,636
2007	15,603,771	9,840,978	5,762,793	6,727,600	8,876,171	4,396,868	2,330,732	5,444,110	3,432,061	12,137,583	3,466,188	2,470,327	995,861
2008	16,365,738	10,254,930	6,110,808	7,066,623	9,299,115	4,577,431	2,489,192	5,677,499	3,621,616	12,591,217	3,774,521	2,536,532	1,237,989
2009	17,464,179	11,038,275	6,425,904	7,563,176	9,901,003	4,942,120	2,621,056	6,096,155	3,804,848	13,386,375	4,077,804	2,595,171	1,482,633
2010	18,082,427	11,457,040	6,625,387	7,836,282	10,246,145	5,118,975	2,717,307	6,338,065	3,908,080	13,703,000	4,379,427	2,652,993	1,726,434
2011	18,077,303	11,365,175	6,712,128	7,822,992	10,254,311	5,070,553	2,752,439	6,294,622	3,959,689	13,694,899	4,382,404	2,718,923	1,663,481
2012	17,735,638	11,097,092	6,638,546	7,714,938	10,020,700	4,984,389	2,730,549	6,112,703	3,907,997	13,478,100	4,257,538	2,744,400	1,513,138
2013	17,474,835	10,938,494	6,536,341	7,659,626	9,815,209	4,949,572	2,710,054	5,988,922	3,826,287	13,347,002	4,127,833	2,757,447	1,370,386
2014	17,292,787	10,783,802	6,508,985	7,585,910	9,706,877	4,876,952	2,708,958	5,906,850	3,800,027	13,244,837	4,047,950	2,771,341	1,276,609
2015[1]	17,298,000	10,801,000	6,497,000	7,499,000	9,799,000	4,861,000	2,638,000	5,940,000	3,859,000	13,353,000	3,945,000	—	—
2016[1]	17,490,000	10,930,000	6,561,000	7,528,000	9,962,000	4,880,000	2,648,000	6,049,000	3,913,000	13,499,000	3,992,000	—	—
2017[1]	17,853,000	11,164,000	6,689,000	7,634,000	10,219,000	4,945,000	2,689,000	6,219,000	4,000,000	13,777,000	4,076,000	—	—
2018[1]	18,214,000	11,386,000	6,828,000	7,774,000	10,440,000	5,029,000	2,746,000	6,358,000	4,082,000	14,056,000	4,158,000	—	—
2019[1]	18,496,000	11,551,000	6,944,000	7,889,000	10,607,000	5,095,000	2,793,000	6,456,000	4,151,000	14,275,000	4,220,000	—	—
2020[1]	18,704,000	11,670,000	7,034,000	7,970,000	10,734,000	5,142,000	2,828,000	6,528,000	4,206,000	14,436,000	4,268,000	—	—
2021[1]	18,954,000	11,814,000	7,140,000	8,074,000	10,880,000	5,198,000	2,876,000	6,616,000	4,264,000	14,630,000	4,324,000	—	—
2022[1]	19,187,000	11,950,000	7,236,000	8,176,000	11,011,000	5,253,000	2,923,000	6,697,000	4,314,000	14,811,000	4,376,000	—	—
2023[1]	19,417,000	12,098,000	7,318,000	8,274,000	11,143,000	5,313,000	2,960,000	6,785,000	4,358,000	14,988,000	4,429,000	—	—
2024[1]	19,631,000	12,229,000	7,403,000	8,367,000	11,264,000	5,372,000	2,995,000	6,857,000	4,407,000	15,154,000	4,477,000	—	—
2025[1]	19,756,000	12,285,000	7,471,000	8,433,000	11,323,000	5,407,000	3,026,000	6,878,000	4,445,000	15,255,000	4,501,000	—	—
2-year institutions[2]													
1970	2,318,956	1,228,909	1,090,047	1,374,426	944,530	771,298	603,128	457,611	486,919	2,194,983	123,973	113,299	10,674
1975	3,965,726	1,761,009	2,204,717	2,163,604	1,802,122	1,035,531	1,128,073	725,478	1,076,644	3,831,973	133,753	112,997	20,756
1980	4,525,097	1,753,637	2,771,460	2,046,642	2,478,455	879,619	1,167,023	874,018	1,604,437	4,327,592	197,505	114,094	83,411
1981	4,715,403	1,795,858	2,919,545	2,124,136	2,591,267	897,657	1,226,479	898,201	1,693,066	4,479,900	235,503	119,166	116,337
1982	4,770,712	1,839,704	2,931,008	2,169,802	2,600,910	930,606	1,239,196	909,098	1,691,812	4,518,659	252,053	114,976	137,077
1983	4,723,466	1,826,801	2,896,665	2,131,109	2,592,357	914,704	1,216,405	912,097	1,680,260	4,459,330	264,136	116,293	147,843
1984	4,530,337	1,703,786	2,826,551	2,016,463	2,513,874	841,347	1,175,116	862,439	1,651,435	4,278,661	251,676	108,247	143,429
1985	4,531,077	1,690,607	2,840,470	2,002,234	2,528,843	826,308	1,175,926	864,299	1,664,544	4,269,733	261,344	108,791	152,553
1986	4,679,548	1,696,261	2,983,287	2,060,932	2,618,616	824,551	1,236,381	871,710	1,746,906	4,413,691	265,857	101,498	164,359
1987	4,776,222	1,708,669	3,067,553	2,072,823	2,703,399	820,167	1,252,656	888,502	1,814,897	4,541,054	235,168	90,102	145,066
1988	4,875,155	1,743,592	3,131,563	2,089,689	2,785,466	818,593	1,271,096	924,999	1,860,467	4,615,487	259,668	—	—
1989	5,150,889	1,855,701	3,295,188	2,216,800	2,934,089	869,688	1,347,112	986,013	1,948,076	4,883,660	267,229	—	—
1990	5,240,083	1,883,962	3,356,121	2,232,769	3,007,314	881,392	1,351,377	1,002,570	2,004,744	4,996,475	243,608	89,158	154,450
1991	5,651,900	2,074,530	3,577,370	2,401,910	3,249,990	961,397	1,440,513	1,113,133	2,136,857	5,404,815	247,085	89,289	157,796
1992	5,722,349	2,080,005	3,642,344	2,413,266	3,309,083	951,816	1,461,450	1,128,189	2,180,894	5,484,514	237,835	83,288	154,547
1993	5,565,561	2,043,319	3,522,242	2,345,396	3,220,165	928,216	1,417,180	1,115,103	2,105,062	5,337,022	228,539	86,357	142,182
1994	5,529,609	2,031,713	3,497,896	2,323,161	3,206,448	911,589	1,411,572	1,120,124	2,086,324	5,308,366	221,243	85,607	135,636
1995	5,492,098	1,977,046	3,515,052	2,328,500	3,163,598	878,215	1,450,285	1,098,831	2,064,767	5,277,398	214,700	75,154	139,546
1996	5,562,780	2,072,215	3,490,565	2,358,792	3,203,988	916,452	1,442,340	1,155,763	2,048,225	5,314,038	248,742	75,253	173,489
1997	5,605,569	2,095,171	3,510,398	2,389,711	3,215,858	931,394	1,458,317	1,163,777	2,052,081	5,360,686	244,883	71,794	173,089
1998	5,489,314	2,085,906	3,403,408	2,333,334	3,155,980	936,421	1,396,913	1,149,485	2,006,495	5,245,963	243,351	65,870	177,481
1999	5,653,256	2,167,242	3,486,014	2,413,322	3,239,934	979,203	1,434,119	1,188,039	2,051,895	5,397,786	255,470	63,301	192,169
2000	5,948,104	2,217,044	3,731,060	2,558,520	3,389,584	995,839	1,562,681	1,221,205	2,168,379	5,697,061	251,043	58,844	192,199
2001	6,250,529	2,374,490	3,876,039	2,675,193	3,575,336	1,066,281	1,608,912	1,308,209	2,267,127	5,996,651	253,878	47,549	206,329
2002	6,529,198	2,556,032	3,973,166	2,753,405	3,775,793	1,135,669	1,617,736	1,420,363	2,355,430	6,270,199	258,999	47,087	211,912
2003	6,493,862	2,650,337	3,843,525	2,689,928	3,803,934	1,162,555	1,527,373	1,487,782	2,316,152	6,208,885	284,977	43,868	241,109
2004	6,545,570	2,683,489	3,862,081	2,697,507	3,848,063	1,166,554	1,530,953	1,516,935	2,331,128	6,243,344	302,226	42,250	259,976

See notes at end of table.

Table 303.70. Total undergraduate fall enrollment in degree-granting postsecondary institutions, by attendance status, sex of student, and control and level of institution: Selected years, 1970 through 2025—Continued

Level and year	Total	Full-time	Part-time	Males	Females	Males Full-time	Males Part-time	Females Full-time	Females Part-time	Public	Private Total	Private Nonprofit	Private For-profit
1	2	3	4	5	6	7	8	9	10	11	12	13	14
2005	6,487,826	2,646,763	3,841,063	2,680,299	3,807,527	1,153,759	1,526,540	1,493,004	2,314,523	6,184,000	303,826	43,522	260,304
2006	6,518,291	2,643,222	3,875,069	2,704,654	3,813,637	1,159,800	1,544,854	1,483,422	2,330,215	6,224,871	293,420	39,156	254,264
2007	6,617,621	2,692,491	3,925,130	2,770,457	3,847,164	1,190,067	1,580,390	1,502,424	2,344,740	6,323,810	293,811	33,486	260,325
2008	6,971,105	2,832,110	4,138,995	2,935,793	4,035,312	1,249,832	1,685,961	1,582,278	2,453,034	6,640,071	331,034	35,351	295,683
2009	7,522,581	3,243,952	4,278,629	3,197,338	4,325,243	1,446,372	1,750,966	1,797,580	2,527,663	7,101,569	421,012	34,772	386,240
2010	7,683,597	3,365,379	4,318,218	3,265,885	4,417,712	1,483,230	1,782,655	1,882,149	2,535,563	7,218,063	465,534	32,683	432,851
2011	7,511,150	3,170,207	4,340,943	3,175,803	4,335,347	1,391,183	1,784,620	1,779,024	2,556,323	7,068,158	442,992	39,855	403,137
2012	7,167,840	2,941,797	4,226,043	3,046,093	4,121,747	1,305,657	1,740,436	1,636,140	2,485,607	6,792,065	375,775	37,698	338,077
2013	6,968,739	2,832,916	4,135,823	2,997,916	3,970,823	1,278,252	1,719,664	1,554,664	2,416,159	6,625,141	343,598	32,198	311,400
2014	6,714,485	2,660,728	4,053,757	2,893,779	3,820,706	1,200,105	1,693,674	1,460,623	2,360,083	6,397,765	316,720	30,365	286,355
2015[1]	7,114,000	2,960,000	4,154,000	3,024,000	4,090,000	1,311,000	1,713,000	1,649,000	2,441,000	6,763,000	351,000	—	—
2016[1]	7,194,000	3,002,000	4,192,000	3,038,000	4,156,000	1,320,000	1,718,000	1,682,000	2,474,000	6,838,000	356,000	—	—
2017[1]	7,346,000	3,075,000	4,271,000	3,083,000	4,263,000	1,340,000	1,743,000	1,735,000	2,528,000	6,981,000	365,000	—	—
2018[1]	7,500,000	3,142,000	4,358,000	3,144,000	4,356,000	1,365,000	1,779,000	1,777,000	2,579,000	7,127,000	373,000	—	—
2019[1]	7,622,000	3,191,000	4,430,000	3,193,000	4,429,000	1,385,000	1,808,000	1,806,000	2,622,000	7,243,000	379,000	—	—
2020[1]	7,706,000	3,222,000	4,484,000	3,225,000	4,481,000	1,396,000	1,829,000	1,826,000	2,656,000	7,323,000	383,000	—	—
2021[1]	7,810,000	3,262,000	4,548,000	3,268,000	4,542,000	1,411,000	1,857,000	1,851,000	2,691,000	7,422,000	388,000	—	—
2022[1]	7,912,000	3,306,000	4,606,000	3,314,000	4,598,000	1,428,000	1,886,000	1,878,000	2,721,000	7,519,000	393,000	—	—
2023[1]	8,007,000	3,351,000	4,655,000	3,355,000	4,652,000	1,446,000	1,908,000	1,905,000	2,747,000	7,608,000	399,000	—	—
2024[1]	8,096,000	3,388,000	4,708,000	3,393,000	4,704,000	1,463,000	1,930,000	1,925,000	2,778,000	7,693,000	403,000	—	—
2025[1]	8,157,000	3,405,000	4,752,000	3,423,000	4,734,000	1,474,000	1,950,000	1,931,000	2,803,000	7,752,000	405,000	—	—
4-year institutions													
1970	5,049,688	4,051,155	998,533	2,875,276	2,174,412	2,325,073	550,203	1,726,082	448,330	3,425,272	1,624,416	1,616,834	7,582
1975	5,713,729	4,407,387	1,306,342	3,093,401	2,620,328	2,423,797	669,604	1,983,590	636,738	3,994,059	1,719,670	1,701,847	17,823
1980	5,949,958	4,608,107	1,341,851	2,953,535	2,996,423	2,347,238	606,297	2,260,869	735,554	4,114,363	1,835,595	1,812,609	22,986
1981	6,039,119	4,653,210	1,385,909	2,984,135	3,054,984	2,362,816	621,319	2,290,394	764,590	4,168,463	1,870,656	1,839,682	30,974
1982	6,054,350	4,644,101	1,410,249	3,000,692	3,053,658	2,368,830	631,862	2,275,271	778,387	4,194,414	1,859,936	1,824,413	35,523
1983	6,122,529	4,687,233	1,435,296	3,027,191	3,095,338	2,389,543	637,648	2,297,690	797,648	4,237,788	1,884,741	1,844,783	39,958
1984	6,087,734	4,643,867	1,443,867	2,990,350	3,097,384	2,353,583	636,767	2,290,284	807,100	4,214,830	1,872,904	1,832,063	40,841
1985	6,065,597	4,628,985	1,436,612	2,959,846	3,105,751	2,330,138	629,708	2,298,847	806,904	4,207,392	1,858,205	1,820,205	38,000
1986	6,118,427	4,655,812	1,462,615	2,956,573	3,161,854	2,321,779	634,794	2,334,033	827,821	4,247,025	1,871,402	1,826,796	44,606
1987	6,270,013	4,753,880	1,516,133	2,995,634	3,274,379	2,343,509	652,125	2,410,371	864,008	4,377,535	1,892,478	1,849,840	42,638
1988	6,441,393	4,898,836	1,542,557	3,047,955	3,393,438	2,387,849	660,106	2,510,987	882,451	4,487,659	1,953,734	—	—
1989	6,591,642	4,984,995	1,606,647	3,094,190	3,497,452	2,408,959	685,231	2,576,036	921,416	4,604,082	1,987,560	—	—
1990	6,719,023	5,092,068	1,626,955	3,146,990	3,572,033	2,455,143	691,847	2,636,925	935,108	4,713,121	2,005,902	1,954,249	51,653
1991	6,787,387	5,146,882	1,640,505	3,169,093	3,618,294	2,474,129	694,964	2,672,753	945,541	4,743,142	2,044,245	1,983,065	61,180
1992	6,815,351	5,164,437	1,650,914	3,169,670	3,645,681	2,472,923	696,747	2,691,514	954,167	4,731,783	2,083,568	2,018,433	65,135
1993	6,758,398	5,136,163	1,622,235	3,138,286	3,620,112	2,453,781	684,505	2,682,382	937,730	4,674,765	2,083,633	2,012,840	70,793
1994	6,732,999	5,136,993	1,596,006	3,098,952	3,634,047	2,430,002	668,950	2,706,991	927,056	4,636,762	2,096,237	2,014,858	81,379
1995	6,739,621	5,168,222	1,571,399	3,072,630	3,666,991	2,418,395	654,235	2,749,827	917,164	4,626,228	2,113,393	2,029,539	83,854
1996	6,764,168	5,226,624	1,537,544	3,061,880	3,702,288	2,422,656	639,224	2,803,968	898,320	4,621,245	2,142,923	2,037,065	105,858
1997	6,845,018	5,323,427	1,521,591	3,078,821	3,766,197	2,448,203	630,618	2,875,224	890,973	4,646,793	2,198,225	2,068,030	130,195
1998	6,947,623	5,452,805	1,494,818	3,112,799	3,834,824	2,491,740	621,059	2,961,065	873,759	4,704,249	2,243,374	2,086,785	156,589
1999	7,086,189	5,586,306	1,499,883	3,170,912	3,915,277	2,545,383	625,529	3,040,923	874,354	4,776,442	2,309,747	2,121,989	187,758
2000	7,207,289	5,705,882	1,501,407	3,219,748	3,987,541	2,592,407	627,341	3,113,475	874,066	4,842,261	2,365,028	2,154,336	210,692
2001	7,465,081	5,953,150	1,511,931	3,329,238	4,135,843	2,702,349	626,889	3,250,801	885,042	4,989,220	2,475,861	2,210,169	265,692
2002	7,727,879	6,178,220	1,549,659	3,438,985	4,288,894	2,798,499	640,486	3,379,721	909,173	5,162,656	2,565,223	2,259,004	306,219
2003	7,986,502	6,394,916	1,591,586	3,537,444	4,449,058	2,886,127	651,317	3,508,789	940,269	5,314,218	2,672,284	2,302,805	369,479
2004	8,235,060	6,600,847	1,634,213	3,642,541	4,592,519	2,974,074	668,467	3,626,773	965,746	5,407,236	2,827,824	2,347,116	480,708
2005	8,476,138	6,799,667	1,676,471	3,728,572	4,747,566	3,047,104	681,468	3,752,563	995,003	5,513,730	2,962,408	2,374,846	587,562
2006	8,666,011	6,927,857	1,738,154	3,809,102	4,856,909	3,104,806	704,296	3,823,051	1,033,858	5,622,555	3,043,456	2,409,084	634,372
2007	8,986,150	7,148,487	1,837,663	3,957,143	5,029,007	3,206,801	750,342	3,941,686	1,087,321	5,813,773	3,172,377	2,436,841	735,536
2008	9,394,633	7,422,820	1,971,813	4,130,830	5,263,803	3,327,599	803,231	4,095,221	1,168,582	5,951,146	3,443,487	2,501,181	942,306
2009	9,941,598	7,794,323	2,147,275	4,365,838	5,575,760	3,495,748	870,090	4,298,575	1,277,185	6,284,806	3,656,792	2,560,399	1,096,393
2010	10,398,830	8,091,661	2,307,169	4,570,397	5,828,433	3,635,745	934,652	4,455,916	1,372,517	6,484,937	3,913,893	2,620,310	1,293,583
2011	10,566,153	8,194,968	2,371,185	4,647,189	5,918,964	3,679,370	967,819	4,515,598	1,403,366	6,626,741	3,939,412	2,679,068	1,260,344
2012	10,567,798	8,155,295	2,412,503	4,668,845	5,898,953	3,678,732	990,113	4,476,563	1,422,390	6,686,035	3,881,763	2,706,702	1,175,061
2013	10,506,096	8,105,578	2,400,518	4,661,710	5,844,386	3,671,320	990,390	4,434,258	1,410,128	6,721,861	3,784,235	2,725,249	1,058,986
2014	10,578,302	8,123,074	2,455,228	4,692,131	5,886,171	3,676,847	1,015,284	4,446,227	1,439,944	6,847,072	3,731,230	2,740,976	990,254
2015[1]	10,184,000	7,841,000	2,343,000	4,475,000	5,709,000	3,550,000	925,000	4,291,000	1,418,000	6,589,000	3,595,000	—	—
2016[1]	10,296,000	7,928,000	2,369,000	4,491,000	5,806,000	3,561,000	930,000	4,367,000	1,439,000	6,661,000	3,636,000	—	—
2017[1]	10,507,000	8,089,000	2,418,000	4,551,000	5,956,000	3,605,000	946,000	4,484,000	1,472,000	6,796,000	3,711,000	—	—
2018[1]	10,714,000	8,244,000	2,470,000	4,630,000	6,084,000	3,663,000	967,000	4,581,000	1,503,000	6,929,000	3,785,000	—	—
2019[1]	10,874,000	8,360,000	2,514,000	4,695,000	6,178,000	3,710,000	985,000	4,649,000	1,529,000	7,033,000	3,841,000	—	—
2020[1]	10,998,000	8,449,000	2,550,000	4,746,000	6,253,000	3,747,000	999,000	4,702,000	1,550,000	7,113,000	3,885,000	—	—
2021[1]	11,144,000	8,553,000	2,592,000	4,806,000	6,338,000	3,788,000	1,019,000	4,765,000	1,573,000	7,208,000	3,936,000	—	—
2022[1]	11,275,000	8,644,000	2,630,000	4,862,000	6,413,000	3,825,000	1,037,000	4,819,000	1,593,000	7,292,000	3,982,000	—	—
2023[1]	11,410,000	8,747,000	2,663,000	4,919,000	6,491,000	3,867,000	1,052,000	4,880,000	1,611,000	7,380,000	4,030,000	—	—
2024[1]	11,535,000	8,840,000	2,695,000	4,974,000	6,561,000	3,909,000	1,065,000	4,932,000	1,629,000	7,461,000	4,074,000	—	—
2025[1]	11,599,000	8,880,000	2,719,000	5,010,000	6,589,000	3,933,000	1,077,000	4,947,000	1,642,000	7,503,000	4,096,000	—	—

—Not available.
[1]Projected.
[2]Beginning in 1980, 2-year institutions include schools accredited by the Accrediting Commission of Career Schools and Colleges of Technology.
NOTE: Data include unclassified undergraduate students. Data through 1995 are for institutions of higher education, while later data are for degree-granting institutions. Degree-granting institutions grant associate's or higher degrees and participate in Title IV federal financial aid programs. The degree-granting classification is very similar to the earlier higher education classification, but it includes more 2-year colleges and excludes a few

higher education institutions that did not grant degrees. Some data have been revised from previously published figures.
SOURCE: U.S. Department of Education, National Center for Education Statistics, Higher Education General Information Survey (HEGIS), "Fall Enrollment in Colleges and Universities" surveys, 1970 through 1985; Integrated Postsecondary Education Data System (IPEDS), "Fall Enrollment Survey" (IPEDS-EF:86–99); IPEDS Spring 2001 through Spring 2015, Fall Enrollment component; and Enrollment in Degree-Granting Institutions Projection Model, 1980 through 2025. (This table was prepared February 2016.)

Table 303.80. Total postbaccalaureate fall enrollment in degree-granting postsecondary institutions, by attendance status, sex of student, and control of institution: 1967 through 2025

Year	Total	Full-time	Part-time	Males	Females	Males Full-time	Males Part-time	Females Full-time	Females Part-time	Public	Private Total	Private Nonprofit	Private For-profit
1	2	3	4	5	6	7	8	9	10	11	12	13	14
1967	896,065	448,238	447,827	630,701	265,364	354,628	276,073	93,610	171,754	522,623	373,442	373,336	106
1968	1,037,377	469,747	567,630	696,649	340,728	358,686	337,963	111,061	229,667	648,657	388,720	388,681	39
1969	1,120,175	506,833	613,342	738,673	381,502	383,630	355,043	123,203	258,299	738,551	381,624	381,558	66
1970	1,212,243	536,226	676,017	793,940	418,303	407,724	386,216	128,502	289,801	807,879	404,364	404,287	77
1971	1,204,390	564,236	640,154	789,131	415,259	428,167	360,964	136,069	279,190	796,516	407,874	407,804	70
1972	1,272,421	583,299	689,122	810,164	462,257	436,533	373,631	146,766	315,491	848,031	424,390	424,278	112
1973	1,342,452	610,935	731,517	833,453	508,999	444,219	389,234	166,716	342,283	897,104	445,348	445,205	143
1974	1,425,001	643,927	781,074	856,847	568,154	454,706	402,141	189,221	378,933	956,770	468,231	467,950	281
1975	1,505,404	672,938	832,466	891,992	613,412	467,425	424,567	205,513	407,899	1,008,476	496,928	496,604	324
1976	1,577,546	683,825	893,721	904,551	672,995	459,286	445,265	224,539	448,456	1,033,115	544,431	541,064	3,367
1977	1,569,084	698,902	870,182	891,819	677,265	462,038	429,781	236,864	440,401	1,004,013	565,071	561,384	3,687
1978	1,575,693	704,831	870,862	879,931	695,762	458,865	421,066	245,966	449,796	998,608	577,085	573,563	3,522
1979	1,571,922	714,624	857,298	862,754	709,168	456,197	406,557	258,427	450,741	989,991	581,931	578,425	3,506
1980	1,621,840	736,214	885,626	874,197	747,643	462,387	411,810	273,827	473,816	1,015,439	606,401	601,084	5,317
1981	1,617,150	732,182	884,968	866,785	750,365	452,364	414,421	279,818	470,547	998,669	618,481	613,557	4,924
1982	1,600,718	736,813	863,905	860,890	739,828	453,519	407,371	283,294	456,534	983,014	617,704	613,350	4,354
1983	1,618,666	747,016	871,650	865,425	753,241	455,540	409,885	291,476	461,765	985,616	633,050	628,111	4,939
1984	1,623,869	750,735	873,134	856,761	767,108	452,579	404,182	298,156	468,952	983,879	639,990	634,109	5,881
1985	1,650,381	755,629	894,752	856,370	794,011	451,274	405,096	304,355	489,656	1,002,148	648,233	642,795	5,438
1986	1,705,536	767,477	938,059	867,010	838,526	452,717	414,293	314,760	523,766	1,053,177	652,359	644,185	8,174
1987	1,720,407	768,536	951,871	863,599	856,808	447,212	416,387	321,324	535,484	1,054,665	665,742	662,408	3,334
1988	1,738,789	794,340	944,449	864,252	874,537	455,337	408,915	339,003	535,534	1,058,242	680,547	—	—
1989	1,796,029	820,254	975,775	879,025	917,004	461,596	417,429	358,658	558,346	1,090,221	705,808	—	—
1990	1,859,531	844,955	1,014,576	904,150	955,381	471,217	432,933	373,738	581,643	1,135,121	724,410	716,820	7,590
1991	1,919,666	893,917	1,025,749	930,841	988,825	493,849	436,992	400,068	588,757	1,161,606	758,060	746,687	11,373
1992	1,949,659	917,676	1,031,983	941,053	1,008,606	502,166	438,887	415,510	593,096	1,168,270	781,389	770,802	10,587
1993	1,980,844	948,136	1,032,708	943,768	1,037,076	508,574	435,194	439,562	597,514	1,177,301	803,543	789,700	13,843
1994	2,016,182	969,070	1,047,112	949,785	1,066,397	513,592	436,193	455,478	610,919	1,188,552	827,630	809,642	17,988
1995	2,030,062	983,534	1,046,528	941,409	1,088,653	510,782	430,627	472,752	615,901	1,188,748	841,314	824,351	16,963
1996	2,040,572	1,004,114	1,036,458	932,153	1,108,419	512,100	420,053	492,014	616,405	1,185,216	855,356	830,238	25,118
1997	2,051,747	1,019,464	1,032,283	927,496	1,124,251	510,845	416,651	508,619	615,632	1,188,640	863,107	837,790	25,317
1998	2,070,030	1,024,627	1,045,403	923,132	1,146,898	505,492	417,640	519,135	627,763	1,187,557	882,473	852,270	30,203
1999	2,110,246	1,049,591	1,060,655	930,930	1,179,316	508,930	422,000	540,661	638,655	1,201,511	908,735	869,739	38,996
2000	2,156,896	1,086,674	1,070,222	943,501	1,213,395	522,847	420,654	563,827	649,568	1,213,464	943,432	896,239	47,193
2001	2,212,377	1,119,862	1,092,515	956,384	1,255,993	531,260	425,124	588,602	667,391	1,247,285	965,092	909,612	55,480
2002	2,354,634	1,212,107	1,142,527	1,009,726	1,344,908	566,930	442,796	645,177	699,731	1,319,138	1,035,496	959,385	76,111
2003	2,431,117	1,280,880	1,150,237	1,032,892	1,398,225	589,190	443,702	691,690	706,535	1,335,595	1,095,522	994,375	101,147
2004	2,491,414	1,325,841	1,165,573	1,047,214	1,444,200	598,727	448,487	727,114	717,086	1,329,532	1,161,882	1,022,319	139,563
2005	2,523,511	1,350,581	1,172,930	1,047,054	1,476,457	602,525	444,529	748,056	728,401	1,324,104	1,199,407	1,036,324	163,083
2006	2,574,568	1,386,226	1,188,342	1,061,059	1,513,509	614,709	446,350	771,517	741,992	1,332,707	1,241,861	1,064,626	177,235
2007	2,644,357	1,428,914	1,215,443	1,088,314	1,556,043	632,576	455,738	796,338	759,705	1,353,197	1,291,160	1,100,823	190,337
2008	2,737,076	1,492,813	1,244,263	1,122,272	1,614,804	656,926	465,346	835,887	778,917	1,380,936	1,356,140	1,124,987	231,153
2009	2,849,415	1,567,080	1,282,335	1,169,777	1,679,638	689,977	479,800	877,103	802,535	1,424,393	1,425,022	1,172,501	252,521
2010	2,937,011	1,630,142	1,306,869	1,209,477	1,727,534	719,408	490,069	910,734	816,800	1,439,171	1,497,840	1,201,489	296,351
2011	2,933,287	1,637,356	1,295,931	1,211,264	1,722,023	722,265	488,999	915,091	806,932	1,421,404	1,511,883	1,207,896	303,987
2012	2,908,840	1,637,312	1,271,528	1,204,068	1,704,772	724,017	480,051	913,295	791,477	1,406,567	1,502,273	1,206,988	295,285
2013	2,900,954	1,658,618	1,242,336	1,201,160	1,699,794	732,594	468,566	926,024	773,770	1,398,556	1,502,398	1,216,557	285,841
2014	2,914,582	1,670,173	1,244,409	1,211,151	1,703,431	742,439	468,712	927,734	775,697	1,410,178	1,504,404	1,224,748	279,656
2015[1]	2,966,000	1,684,000	1,282,000	1,261,000	1,704,000	777,000	484,000	906,000	798,000	1,436,000	1,529,000	—	—
2016[1]	3,025,000	1,721,000	1,304,000	1,279,000	1,746,000	790,000	489,000	931,000	815,000	1,465,000	1,560,000	—	—
2017[1]	3,119,000	1,778,000	1,341,000	1,311,000	1,809,000	809,000	501,000	969,000	840,000	1,510,000	1,609,000	—	—
2018[1]	3,196,000	1,821,000	1,375,000	1,344,000	1,852,000	828,000	516,000	993,000	860,000	1,547,000	1,649,000	—	—
2019[1]	3,257,000	1,852,000	1,405,000	1,371,000	1,886,000	843,000	528,000	1,009,000	876,000	1,577,000	1,680,000	—	—
2020[1]	3,308,000	1,879,000	1,429,000	1,394,000	1,914,000	855,000	539,000	1,024,000	890,000	1,602,000	1,706,000	—	—
2021[1]	3,369,000	1,912,000	1,457,000	1,422,000	1,947,000	870,000	552,000	1,042,000	905,000	1,631,000	1,738,000	—	—
2022[1]	3,427,000	1,944,000	1,483,000	1,449,000	1,978,000	884,000	565,000	1,060,000	918,000	1,660,000	1,767,000	—	—
2023[1]	3,479,000	1,973,000	1,506,000	1,473,000	2,006,000	897,000	576,000	1,076,000	930,000	1,685,000	1,794,000	—	—
2024[1]	3,517,000	1,991,000	1,526,000	1,492,000	2,026,000	907,000	585,000	1,085,000	941,000	1,704,000	1,814,000	—	—
2025[1]	3,534,000	1,994,000	1,541,000	1,504,000	2,030,000	911,000	593,000	1,082,000	948,000	1,712,000	1,822,000	—	—

—Not available.
[1]Projected.
NOTE: Data include unclassified graduate students. Data through 1995 are for institutions of higher education, while later data are for degree-granting institutions. Degree-granting institutions grant associate's or higher degrees and participate in Title IV federal financial aid programs. The degree-granting classification is very similar to the earlier higher education classification, but it includes more 2-year colleges and excludes a few higher education institutions that did not grant degrees. Some data have been revised from previously published figures.

SOURCE: U.S. Department of Education, National Center for Education Statistics, Higher Education General Information Survey (HEGIS), "Fall Enrollment in Colleges and Universities" surveys, 1967 through 1985; Integrated Postsecondary Education Data System (IPEDS), "Fall Enrollment Survey" (IPEDS-EF:86–99); IPEDS Spring 2001 through Spring 2015, Fall Enrollment component; and Enrollment in Degree-Granting Institutions Projection Model, 1980 through 2025. (This table was prepared February 2016.)

Table 303.90. Fall enrollment and number of degree-granting postsecondary institutions, by control and religious affiliation of institution: Selected years, 1980 through 2014

Control and religious affiliation of institution	Total enrollment						Enrollment, fall 2014					Number of institutions¹				
	Fall 1980	Fall 1990	Fall 2000	Fall 2010	Fall 2012	Fall 2013	Total	Full-time Males	Full-time Females	Part-time Males	Part-time Females	Fall 1980	Fall 1990	Fall 2000	Fall 2010	Fall 2014
1	2	3	4	5	6	7	8	9	10	11	12	13	14	15	16	17
All institutions	12,096,895	13,818,637	15,312,289	21,019,438	20,644,478	20,375,789	20,207,369	5,619,391	6,834,584	3,177,670	4,575,724	3,226	3,501	4,056	4,589	4,614
Public institutions	9,457,394	10,844,717	11,752,786	15,142,171	14,884,667	14,745,558	14,655,015	3,914,629	4,483,090	2,624,305	3,632,991	1,493	1,548	1,676	1,652	1,621
Federal	50,989	50,669	16,917	21,610	20,691	19,802	19,791	13,020	5,103	589	1,079	12	17	12	14	14
State	(²)	7,181,380	9,548,090	12,364,881	12,195,406	12,120,534	12,076,058	3,429,928	3,947,388	1,963,263	2,735,479	(²)	978	1,355	1,331	1,310
Local	(²)	3,508,941	2,078,090	2,542,044	2,457,497	2,398,360	2,355,444	418,894	468,270	624,915	843,365	(²)	523	277	261	257
Other public	9,406,405	103,727	109,689	213,636	211,073	206,862	203,722	52,787	62,329	35,538	53,068	1,481	30	32	46	40
Private institutions	2,639,501	2,973,920	3,559,503	5,877,267	5,759,811	5,630,231	5,552,354	1,704,762	2,351,494	553,365	942,733	1,733	1,953	2,380	2,937	2,993
Independent nonprofit	1,521,614	1,474,818	1,577,242	1,994,900	2,062,099	2,089,266	2,107,949	723,857	873,292	203,291	307,509	795	709	729	736	784
For-profit	111,714	213,693	450,084	2,022,785	1,808,423	1,656,227	1,556,265	382,663	670,382	171,739	331,481	164	322	724	1,310	1,327
Religiously affiliated³	1,006,173	1,285,409	1,532,177	1,859,582	1,889,289	1,884,738	1,888,140	598,242	807,820	178,335	303,743	774	922	927	891	882
Advent Christian Church	143											1				
African Methodist Episcopal Zion Church	1,091	88	34	1,536	1,459	1,541	1,683	864	754	33	32	3	1	1	3	3
African Methodist Episcopal	4,541	3,220	5,980	2,674	2,491	2,700	2,777	1,165	1,385	83	144	6	5	6	5	6
American Baptist	6,131	10,800	15,410	15,120	14,455	13,990	13,917	4,171	5,510	1,411	2,825	11	15	17	18	18
American Evangelical Lutheran Church			743	1,340	1,315	1,341	1,320	594	647	34	45			1	1	1
American Lutheran and Lutheran Church in America	3,092		1,460									3		1		
American Lutheran	21,608											13				
Assemblies of God Church	7,814	8,307	14,272	15,806	15,334	15,953	15,801	5,235	6,682	1,744	2,140	10	11	14	16	14
Baptist	38,231	99,510	107,610	174,538	111,863	111,586	106,897	34,925	46,028	10,363	15,581	33	69	68	69	66
Brethren Church	3,925	958	2,088	8,506	7,979	8,070	7,829	2,103	3,037	1,536	1,153	3	3	3	3	3
Brethren in Christ Church	1,301	2,239	2,797									1	1	1		
Christian and Missionary Alliance Church	1,705	2,519	5,278	6,455	6,688	6,530	6,361	1,987	2,795	651	928	3	4	4	4	4
Christian Church (Disciples of Christ)	14,913	30,397	35,984	52,839	54,855	47,253	47,113	14,617	21,369	4,368	6,759	12	18	16	18	17
Christian Churches and Churches of Christ	1,342	2,263	7,277	10,074	10,700	10,536	10,349	3,933	4,033	1,177	1,206	7	8	18	18	19
Christian Methodist Episcopal	2,486	2,174	1,502	4,817	4,048	4,191	3,857	2,016	1,724	55	62	4	4	1	3	3
Christian Reformed Church	5,408	4,488	5,999	5,625	5,697	5,770	5,743	2,611	2,765	186	181	3	2	3	3	3
Church of Christ (Scientist)	2,773	2,557										6	8			
Church of God of Prophecy		249											1			
Church of God	6,082	5,627	12,540	16,731	17,821	17,977	17,946	5,407	7,902	1,935	2,702	9	9	7	7	9
Church of New Jerusalem	170											1				
Church of the Brethren	8,482	4,463	4,187	6,154	6,261	6,245	6,243	2,518	3,108	234	383	6	5	4	5	6
Church of the Nazarene	11,716	10,779	16,661	21,144	21,401	21,597	21,563	6,167	9,871	2,050	3,475	10	9	12	10	10
Churches of Christ	9,343	14,611	30,140	35,538	35,915	35,281	35,122	11,611	15,280	3,189	5,042	9	19	19	17	17
Cumberland Presbyterian	594	746	1,112	4,652	6,500	6,926	6,508	2,003	2,601	724	1,180	2	2	2	2	2
Episcopal Church, Reformed	67				1,204	1,238	1,221	56	356	93	716	1			2	1
Evangelical Christian	80				74,372	77,338	81,459	16,188	22,115	16,942	26,214	1			5	6
Evangelical Congregational Church		88	148	153	123	113	123	15	17	59	32	1	1	1	1	1
Evangelical Covenant Church of America	1,401	1,035	2,387	3,233	3,141	3,189	3,253	808	1,295	343	807	1	1	1	2	2
Evangelical Free Church of America	833	2,355	4,022	2,926	2,651	2,472	2,495	755	520	755	465	1	2	3	2	2
Evangelical Lutheran Church	743	49,210	49,085	56,162	52,122	51,796	50,905	20,115	25,466	2,027	3,297	3	33	34	33	31
Free Methodist	5,543	5,902	7,323	12,270	12,254	12,372	12,184	3,426	6,204	749	1,805	5	3	4	5	5
Free Will Baptist Church	1,132	1,177	2,378	528	568	570	583	254	191	92	46	4	3	4	3	3
Friends United Meeting	1,109											1				
Friends	5,157	5,844	10,898	13,876	12,921	12,555	12,203	4,562	5,242	930	1,469	5	6	8	7	7
General Baptist							2,086	301	294	605	886					1
General Conference Mennonite Church	820	1,243	1,059	220	209	208	183	129	41	11	2	2	2	1	1	1
Greek Orthodox	204	148	132										1	1		
Interdenominational	1,254	11,103	9,788	33,778	39,376	39,277	39,716	12,972	16,450	4,798	5,496	4	17	14	31	32
Jewish	5,738	12,217	14,182	12,755	14,991	15,390	14,873	9,692	3,127	532	1,522	24	63	62	36	35
Latter-Day Saints	39,172	42,274	44,680	53,514	63,027	63,733	71,901	23,365	22,480	11,307	14,749	4	4	4	4	4

See notes at end of table.

Table 303.90. Fall enrollment and number of degree-granting postsecondary institutions, by control and religious affiliation of institution: Selected years, 1980 through 2014—Continued

Control and religious affiliation of institution	Total enrollment						Enrollment, fall 2014					Number of institutions[1]				
								Full-time		Part-time						
	Fall 1980	Fall 1990	Fall 2000	Fall 2010	Fall 2012	Fall 2013	Total	Males	Females	Males	Females	Fall 1980	Fall 1990	Fall 2000	Fall 2010	Fall 2014
1	2	3	4	5	6	7	8	9	10	11	12	13	14	15	16	17
Lutheran Church—Missouri Synod	11,727	13,827	18,866	28,255	30,332	34,105	36,350	8,172	15,628	4,242	8,308	15	14	13	12	11
Lutheran Church in America	23,877	5,796	4,322	8,240	8,193	8,732	8,702	3,518	4,323	331	530	20	5	2	3	3
Mennonite Brethren Church	1,344	1,864	2,390	4,136	4,121	4,129	4,224	1,130	1,996	324	774	3	3	3	3	2
Mennonite Church	4,008	2,859	3,553	4,263	4,236	4,265	4,223	1,415	1,882	290	636	6	5	5	6	6
Missionary Church Inc.	487	699	1,647	2,152	1,963	1,804	1,792	465	787	178	362	1	1	1	1	1
Moravian Church	2,434	2,511	2,939	3,095	3,075	3,024	3,088	688	1,671	139	590	2	2	2	2	2
Multiple Protestant denominations	5,526	211	4,690	5,350	5,274	5,126	5,013	1,233	1,532	1,349	899	8	1	7	6	6
North American Baptist	155	—	124	120	148	143	195	48	21	72	54	1	—	1	1	1
Original Free Will Baptist	—	—	—	3,855	3,714	3,414	3,456	562	836	598	1,460	—	—	—	1	1
Pentecostal Holiness Church	767	566	976	1,272	1,526	1,653	1,629	684	650	111	184	3	3	2	3	2
Presbyterian	—	—	—	—	—	2,882	2,982	971	1,457	179	375	—	—	—	—	2
Presbyterian U.S.A.	47,144	77,700	78,950	85,719	86,696	83,648	84,303	31,204	40,547	3,881	8,671	57	70	64	58	57
Presbyterian Church in America	—	1,877	4,499	2,071	1,803	1,775	1,714	683	705	198	128	—	1	5	2	2
Protestant Episcopal	5,396	4,559	5,479	5,006	4,202	3,935	3,585	1,661	1,687	126	111	12	9	12	11	8
Protestant, other	4,072	38,136	30,116	13,450	16,182	16,884	17,572	5,083	5,929	2,921	3,639	11	44	34	23	24
Reformed Church in America	2,713	5,525	6,002	6,555	6,502	6,453	6,521	2,554	3,393	226	348	4	4	5	5	5
Reformed Presbyterian Church	2,014	1,556	2,355	2,982	2,700	2,748	2,546	1,079	1,090	228	149	4	2	2	3	3
Reorganized Latter-Day Saints Church	4,274	4,793	3,390	—	—	—	—	—	—	—	—	2	1	2	—	—
Roman Catholic	422,842	530,585	636,336	751,091	747,108	740,576	734,339	220,466	323,378	63,433	127,062	229	239	239	237	234
Russian Orthodox	47	38	106	60	55	81	88	64	10	13	1	1	1	1	1	1
Seventh-Day Adventists	19,168	15,771	19,223	25,430	26,343	25,590	24,918	8,089	11,106	2,060	3,663	11	11	13	14	13
Southern Baptist	85,281	49,493	54,275	49,936	52,627	55,363	55,323	16,489	20,760	7,709	10,365	54	29	32	22	23
Undenominational	—	6,758	23,573	27,748	29,966	32,391	32,811	8,823	12,304	5,013	6,671	—	14	16	16	19
Unitarian Universalist	87	82	132	166	227	174	174	25	68	26	55	2	2	2	2	2
United Brethren Church	545	601	938	1,260	1,204	1,124	1,209	447	621	54	87	1	1	1	1	1
United Church of Christ	14,169	20,175	23,709	20,537	17,480	16,850	16,574	5,305	6,257	1,845	3,167	16	18	18	17	14
United Methodist	127,099	148,851	171,109	206,744	204,482	203,116	203,419	74,393	95,306	12,384	21,336	91	96	100	96	94
Wesleyan Church	3,583	5,311	11,128	20,670	20,160	19,733	19,868	5,903	11,478	874	1,613	5	4	4	6	6
Wisconsin Evangelical Lutheran Synod	808	931	1,660	1,677	1,889	2,002	2,036	788	903	165	180	1	3	2	2	2
Other religiously affiliated	462	5,743	2,534	4,778	5,340	5,280	5,272	1,735	2,206	350	981	1	9	4	11	10

—Not available.
[1]Counts of institutions in this table may be lower than reported in other tables, because counts in this table include only institutions reporting separate enrollment data.
[2]Included under "Other public."
[3]Religious affiliation as reported by institution.
NOTE: Data for 1980 and 1990 are for institutions of higher education, while later data are for degree-granting institutions. Degree-granting institutions grant associate's or higher degrees and participate in Title IV federal financial aid programs. The degree-granting classification is very similar to the earlier higher education classification, but it includes more 2-year colleges and excludes a few higher education institutions that did not grant degrees. Some data have been revised from previously published figures.
SOURCE: U.S. Department of Education, National Center for Education Statistics, Higher Education General Information Survey (HEGIS), "Fall Enrollment in Institutions of Higher Education" and "Institutional Characteristics" surveys, 1980; Integrated Postsecondary Education Data System (IPEDS), "Fall Enrollment Survey" (IPEDS-EF:90) and "Institutional Characteristics Survey" (IPEDS-IC:90); and IPEDS Spring 2001 through Spring 2015, Fall Enrollment component. (This table was prepared February 2016.)

Table 304.10. Total fall enrollment in degree-granting postsecondary institutions, by state or jurisdiction: Selected years, 1970 through 2014

State or jurisdiction	Fall 1970	Fall 1980	Fall 1990	Fall 2000	Fall 2009	Fall 2010	Fall 2011	Fall 2012	Fall 2013	Fall 2014	Percent change, 2009 to 2014
1	2	3	4	5	6	7	8	9	10	11	12
United States	8,580,887	12,096,895	13,818,637	15,312,289	20,313,594	21,019,438	21,010,590	20,644,478	20,375,789	20,207,369	-0.5
Alabama	103,936	164,306	218,589	233,962	311,641	327,606	320,349	310,311	305,712	305,028	-2.1
Alaska	9,471	21,296	29,833	27,953	32,406	34,799	34,932	32,797	34,890	34,331	5.9
Arizona	109,619	202,716	264,148	342,490	738,753	793,871	796,974	736,465	694,123	674,746	-8.7
Arkansas	52,039	77,607	90,425	115,172	168,081	175,848	179,345	176,458	172,224	169,571	0.9
California	1,257,245	1,790,993	1,808,740	2,256,708	2,732,147	2,714,699	2,691,852	2,621,606	2,636,921	2,696,415	-1.3
Colorado	123,395	162,916	227,131	263,872	345,034	369,450	365,939	363,170	358,723	353,827	2.5
Connecticut	124,700	159,632	168,604	161,243	191,790	199,384	201,638	201,658	200,966	201,928	5.3
Delaware	25,260	32,939	42,004	43,897	54,735	55,258	56,547	58,127	59,615	60,368	10.3
District of Columbia	77,158	86,675	79,551	72,689	136,792	91,992	90,245	90,150	89,257	90,053	-34.2
Florida	235,525	411,891	588,086	707,684	1,051,917	1,124,778	1,149,160	1,154,506	1,125,810	1,111,018	5.6
Georgia	126,511	184,159	251,786	346,204	531,510	568,916	565,414	545,360	533,424	531,004	-0.1
Hawaii	36,562	47,181	56,436	60,182	74,668	78,073	79,006	78,456	76,434	73,505	-1.6
Idaho	34,567	43,018	51,881	65,594	84,349	85,201	90,142	108,008	109,318	118,953	41.0
Illinois	452,146	644,245	729,246	743,918	893,207	906,845	892,452	866,893	842,888	824,980	-7.6
Indiana	192,668	247,253	284,832	314,334	441,031	459,493	457,506	447,263	444,364	436,327	-1.1
Iowa	108,902	140,449	170,515	188,974	351,036	381,867	372,146	361,189	339,738	282,482	-19.5
Kansas	102,485	136,605	163,733	179,968	210,819	214,849	216,662	213,855	215,855	226,401	7.4
Kentucky	98,591	143,066	177,852	188,341	277,876	291,104	293,766	281,133	273,073	264,197	-4.9
Louisiana	120,728	160,058	186,840	223,800	251,468	263,676	265,740	258,846	251,887	245,938	-2.2
Maine	34,134	43,264	57,186	58,473	70,183	72,406	72,297	73,095	70,849	72,246	2.9
Maryland	149,607	225,526	259,700	273,745	358,775	377,967	380,097	374,496	363,771	365,597	1.9
Massachusetts	303,809	418,415	417,833	421,142	497,234	507,753	508,546	514,119	514,008	510,912	2.8
Michigan	392,726	520,131	569,803	567,631	685,628	697,765	685,420	663,703	643,592	619,438	-9.7
Minnesota	160,788	206,691	253,789	293,445	442,109	465,449	457,737	451,661	441,491	433,854	-1.9
Mississippi	73,967	102,364	122,883	137,389	173,136	179,995	180,576	176,618	173,634	170,728	-1.4
Missouri	183,930	234,421	289,899	321,348	424,541	444,750	456,994	441,186	438,222	419,900	-1.1
Montana	30,062	35,177	35,876	42,240	51,588	53,282	54,042	53,254	52,777	51,942	0.7
Nebraska	66,915	89,488	112,831	112,117	139,594	144,692	142,875	139,558	137,943	135,825	-2.7
Nevada	13,669	40,455	61,728	87,893	124,896	129,360	121,013	118,300	116,738	119,205	-4.6
New Hampshire	29,400	46,794	59,510	61,718	74,234	75,539	77,436	82,678	92,440	106,984	44.1
New Jersey	216,121	321,610	324,286	335,945	431,978	444,092	443,750	439,966	436,939	436,208	1.0
New Mexico	44,461	58,283	85,500	110,739	153,055	162,552	159,058	156,424	153,455	146,246	-4.4
New York	806,479	992,237	1,048,286	1,043,395	1,290,046	1,305,151	1,318,076	1,309,684	1,304,230	1,299,055	0.7
North Carolina	171,925	287,537	352,138	404,652	567,841	585,792	585,013	578,265	575,198	570,045	0.4
North Dakota	31,495	34,069	37,878	40,248	54,456	56,903	56,482	55,242	55,063	54,048	-0.7
Ohio	376,267	489,145	557,690	549,553	712,192	745,115	735,034	710,379	697,647	680,238	-4.5
Oklahoma	110,155	160,295	173,221	178,016	220,377	230,560	230,176	228,492	220,897	215,349	-2.3
Oregon	122,177	157,458	165,741	183,065	243,271	251,708	259,064	254,926	251,106	245,547	0.9
Pennsylvania	411,044	507,716	604,060	609,521	778,054	804,640	787,960	777,350	765,582	750,651	-3.5
Rhode Island	45,898	66,869	78,273	75,450	84,673	85,110	84,647	83,952	83,460	83,499	-1.4
South Carolina	69,518	132,476	159,302	185,931	246,525	257,064	260,002	259,617	257,844	254,629	3.3
South Dakota	30,639	32,761	34,208	43,221	53,342	58,360	55,899	56,058	55,129	53,963	1.2
Tennessee	135,103	204,581	226,238	263,910	332,555	351,762	350,186	343,478	338,197	326,575	-1.8
Texas	442,225	701,391	901,437	1,033,973	1,447,028	1,535,864	1,564,208	1,544,524	1,541,378	1,555,462	7.5
Utah	81,687	93,987	121,303	163,776	236,204	255,653	264,394	267,309	264,255	274,926	16.4
Vermont	22,209	30,628	36,398	35,489	44,975	45,572	45,143	44,697	43,534	43,983	-2.2
Virginia	151,915	280,504	353,442	381,893	544,665	577,922	589,145	588,708	583,755	577,908	6.1
Washington	183,544	303,603	263,384	320,840	382,613	388,116	372,839	365,529	363,377	365,193	-4.6
West Virginia	63,153	81,973	84,790	87,888	142,492	152,431	162,347	162,182	157,954	157,052	10.2
Wisconsin	202,058	269,086	299,774	307,179	373,307	384,181	376,535	369,738	364,021	358,894	-3.9
Wyoming	15,220	21,147	31,326	30,004	37,019	38,298	38,092	37,812	37,084	35,461	-4.2
U.S. Service Academies[1]	17,079	49,808	48,692	13,475	15,748	15,925	15,692	15,227	14,997	14,734	-6.4
Other jurisdictions	67,237	137,749	164,618	194,633	243,447	264,240	267,159	259,975	254,543	255,843	5.1
American Samoa	0	976	1,219	297	2,189	2,193	2,091	1,795	1,488	1,276	-41.7
Federated States of Micronesia	0	224	975	1,576	3,401	2,699	2,915	2,744	2,446	2,344	-31.1
Guam	2,719	3,217	4,741	5,215	5,755	6,188	6,360	5,955	6,518	6,488	12.7
Marshall Islands	0	0	0	328	847	869	989	1,123	1,000	1,087	28.3
Northern Marianas	0	0	661	1,078	989	1,137	1,046	1,178	1,109	1,186	19.9
Palau	0	0	491	581	651	694	742	680	646	604	-7.2
Puerto Rico	63,073	131,184	154,065	183,290	227,013	247,727	250,402	244,077	239,015	240,578	6.0
U.S. Virgin Islands	1,445	2,148	2,466	2,268	2,602	2,733	2,614	2,423	2,321	2,280	-12.4

[1]Data for 2000 and later years reflect a substantial reduction in the number of Department of Defense institutions included in the IPEDS survey.
NOTE: Data through 1990 are for institutions of higher education, while later data are for degree-granting institutions. Degree-granting institutions grant associate's or higher degrees and participate in Title IV federal financial aid programs. The degree-granting classification is very similar to the earlier higher education classification, but it includes more 2-year colleges

and excludes a few higher education institutions that did not grant degrees. Some data have been revised from previously published figures.
SOURCE: U.S. Department of Education, National Center for Education Statistics, Higher Education General Information Survey (HEGIS), "Fall Enrollment in Colleges and Universities" surveys, 1970 and 1980; Integrated Postsecondary Education Data System (IPEDS), "Fall Enrollment Survey" (IPEDS-EF:90); and IPEDS Spring 2001 through Spring 2015, Fall Enrollment component. (This table was prepared October 2015.)

Table 304.15. Total fall enrollment in public degree-granting postsecondary institutions, by state or jurisdiction: Selected years, 1970 through 2014

State or jurisdiction	Fall 1970	Fall 1980	Fall 1990	Fall 2000	Fall 2009	Fall 2010	Fall 2011	Fall 2012	Fall 2013	Fall 2014	Percent change, 2009 to 2014
1	2	3	4	5	6	7	8	9	10	11	12
United States	6,428,134	9,457,394	10,844,717	11,752,786	14,810,768	15,142,171	15,116,303	14,884,667	14,745,558	14,655,015	-1.1
Alabama	87,884	143,674	195,939	207,435	260,277	267,083	260,523	251,045	248,284	246,989	-5.1
Alaska	8,563	20,561	27,792	26,559	30,493	32,303	32,158	30,595	31,600	29,892	-2.0
Arizona	107,315	194,034	248,213	284,522	350,435	366,976	366,116	359,229	354,462	354,997	1.3
Arkansas	43,599	66,068	78,645	101,775	149,474	155,780	158,824	157,224	153,690	151,399	1.3
California	1,123,529	1,599,838	1,594,710	1,927,771	2,289,427	2,223,163	2,181,675	2,129,152	2,148,147	2,167,444	-5.3
Colorado	108,562	145,598	200,653	217,897	255,438	269,433	269,298	272,444	271,223	268,041	4.9
Connecticut	73,391	97,788	109,556	101,027	123,211	127,194	126,487	124,952	123,093	122,303	-0.7
Delaware	21,151	28,325	34,252	34,194	39,989	39,935	40,729	41,113	40,992	41,012	2.6
District of Columbia	12,194	13,900	11,990	5,499	5,253	5,840	5,312	5,476	5,347	5,115	-2.6
Florida	189,450	334,349	489,081	556,912	759,479	790,027	803,200	804,693	795,860	795,628	4.8
Georgia	101,900	140,158	196,413	271,755	418,037	436,047	428,708	422,189	413,706	413,752	-1.0
Hawaii	32,963	43,269	45,728	44,579	57,945	60,090	60,330	60,295	58,941	57,052	-1.5
Idaho	27,072	34,491	41,315	53,751	63,261	64,204	65,753	78,781	75,910	76,806	21.4
Illinois	315,634	491,274	551,333	534,155	588,741	585,515	577,043	556,890	546,483	529,462	-10.1
Indiana	136,739	189,224	223,953	240,023	325,072	337,705	339,946	333,769	335,923	328,442	1.0
Iowa	68,390	97,454	117,834	135,008	171,283	177,781	178,491	173,558	168,644	169,896	-0.8
Kansas	88,215	121,987	149,117	159,976	182,736	185,623	186,475	183,914	184,075	183,222	0.3
Kentucky	77,240	114,884	147,095	151,973	221,508	229,725	233,427	223,100	218,472	213,043	-3.8
Louisiana	101,127	136,703	158,290	189,213	215,511	224,811	225,210	220,971	215,653	210,943	-2.1
Maine	25,405	31,878	41,500	40,662	49,668	50,903	50,253	50,555	49,602	48,852	-1.6
Maryland	118,988	195,051	220,783	223,797	298,185	309,779	314,383	310,503	301,565	305,156	2.3
Massachusetts	116,127	183,765	186,035	183,248	218,999	224,542	227,006	228,178	228,255	226,158	3.3
Michigan	339,625	454,147	487,359	467,861	553,022	562,448	554,704	540,242	527,740	514,712	-6.9
Minnesota	130,567	162,379	199,211	218,617	270,336	276,176	274,192	272,290	266,440	259,695	-3.9
Mississippi	64,968	90,661	109,038	125,355	155,517	161,493	161,842	157,995	154,916	152,096	-2.2
Missouri	132,540	165,179	200,093	201,509	245,568	256,030	260,585	257,430	254,650	252,980	3.0
Montana	27,287	31,178	31,865	37,387	46,653	48,231	48,912	48,333	47,851	47,024	0.8
Nebraska	51,454	73,509	94,614	88,531	104,149	107,979	106,794	104,166	101,893	99,821	-4.2
Nevada	13,576	40,280	61,242	83,120	112,397	113,103	105,048	103,619	102,538	106,028	-5.7
New Hampshire	15,979	24,119	32,163	35,870	43,507	44,077	43,325	43,289	42,711	43,298	-0.5
New Jersey	145,373	247,028	261,601	266,921	348,934	358,256	359,458	356,457	352,822	351,316	0.7
New Mexico	40,795	55,077	83,403	101,450	143,987	150,844	148,018	146,792	144,381	138,311	-3.9
New York	449,437	563,251	616,884	583,417	712,467	723,500	731,914	722,274	720,934	721,847	1.3
North Carolina	123,761	228,154	285,405	329,422	469,590	475,064	470,989	465,950	460,100	455,178	-3.1
North Dakota	30,192	31,709	34,690	36,014	46,727	48,904	49,578	48,929	48,751	48,292	3.3
Ohio	281,099	381,765	427,613	411,161	522,033	547,551	542,733	524,973	520,039	510,244	-2.3
Oklahoma	91,438	137,188	151,073	153,699	189,953	197,641	197,373	195,118	187,078	182,449	-4.0
Oregon	108,483	140,102	144,427	154,756	201,246	208,001	215,469	212,541	208,317	201,645	0.2
Pennsylvania	232,982	292,499	343,478	339,229	425,979	432,923	428,335	425,890	419,849	413,591	-2.9
Rhode Island	25,527	35,052	42,350	38,458	43,409	43,224	43,254	43,204	42,786	42,765	-1.5
South Carolina	47,101	107,683	131,134	155,519	200,204	205,080	208,302	209,023	207,717	205,756	2.8
South Dakota	23,936	24,328	26,596	34,857	41,674	44,569	43,729	44,185	44,272	44,132	5.9
Tennessee	98,897	156,835	175,049	202,530	231,741	242,486	241,917	235,010	229,302	224,033	-3.3
Texas	365,522	613,552	802,314	896,534	1,258,841	1,334,110	1,366,829	1,352,060	1,349,609	1,365,339	8.5
Utah	49,588	59,598	86,108	123,046	170,921	179,061	179,208	171,001	168,311	167,716	-1.9
Vermont	12,536	17,984	20,910	20,021	27,028	27,524	27,132	26,501	25,852	25,643	-5.1
Virginia	123,279	246,500	291,286	313,780	401,093	409,004	413,761	409,753	405,915	399,359	-0.4
Washington	162,718	276,028	227,632	273,928	328,391	330,853	317,066	311,497	310,192	312,523	-4.8
West Virginia	51,363	71,228	74,108	76,136	94,533	96,104	95,634	93,017	90,782	87,842	-7.1
Wisconsin	170,374	235,179	253,529	249,737	295,090	301,259	296,795	293,416	289,339	286,726	-2.8
Wyoming	15,220	21,121	30,623	28,715	35,608	36,292	36,368	35,859	35,547	34,316	-3.6
U.S. Service Academies[1]	17,079	49,808	48,692	13,475	15,748	15,925	15,692	15,227	14,997	14,734	-6.4
Other jurisdictions	46,680	60,692	66,244	84,464	87,030	83,719	78,928	78,400	78,136	77,716	-10.7
American Samoa	0	976	1,219	297	2,189	2,193	2,091	1,795	1,488	1,276	-41.7
Federated States of Micronesia	0	224	975	1,576	3,401	2,699	2,915	2,744	2,446	2,344	-31.1
Guam	2,719	3,217	4,741	5,215	5,661	6,103	6,274	5,878	6,439	6,416	13.3
Marshall Islands	0	0	0	328	847	869	989	1,123	1,000	1,087	28.3
Northern Marianas	0	0	661	1,078	989	1,137	1,046	1,178	1,109	1,186	19.9
Palau	0	0	491	581	651	694	742	680	646	604	-7.2
Puerto Rico	42,516	54,127	55,691	73,121	70,690	67,291	62,257	62,579	62,687	62,523	-11.6
U.S. Virgin Islands	1,445	2,148	2,466	2,268	2,602	2,733	2,614	2,423	2,321	2,280	-12.4

[1]Data for 2000 and later years reflect a substantial reduction in the number of Department of Defense institutions included in the IPEDS survey.
NOTE: Data through 1990 are for institutions of higher education, while later data are for degree-granting institutions. Degree-granting institutions grant associate's or higher degrees and participate in Title IV federal financial aid programs. The degree-granting classification is very similar to the earlier higher education classification, but it includes more 2-year colleges and excludes a few higher education institutions that did not grant degrees. Some data have been revised from previously published figures.
SOURCE: U.S. Department of Education, National Center for Education Statistics, Higher Education General Information Survey (HEGIS), "Fall Enrollment in Colleges and Universities" surveys, 1970 and 1980; Integrated Postsecondary Education Data System (IPEDS), "Fall Enrollment Survey" (IPEDS-EF:90); and IPEDS Spring 2001 through Spring 2015, Fall Enrollment component. (This table was prepared October 2015.)

Table 304.20. Total fall enrollment in private degree-granting postsecondary institutions, by state or jurisdiction: Selected years, 1970 through 2014

State or jurisdiction	Fall 1970	Fall 1980	Fall 1990	Fall 2000	Fall 2009	Fall 2010	Fall 2011	Fall 2012	Fall 2013	Fall 2014	Percent change, 2009 to 2014
1	2	3	4	5	6	7	8	9	10	11	12
United States	2,152,753	2,639,501	2,973,920	3,559,503	5,502,826	5,877,267	5,894,287	5,759,811	5,630,231	5,552,354	0.9
Alabama	16,052	20,632	22,650	26,527	51,364	60,523	59,826	59,266	57,428	58,039	13.0
Alaska	908	735	2,041	1,394	1,913	2,496	2,774	2,202	3,290	4,439	132.0
Arizona	2,304	8,682	15,935	57,968	388,318	426,895	430,858	377,236	339,661	319,749	-17.7
Arkansas	8,440	11,539	11,780	13,397	18,607	20,068	20,521	19,234	18,534	18,172	-2.3
California	133,716	191,155	214,030	328,937	442,720	491,536	510,177	492,454	488,774	528,971	19.5
Colorado	14,833	17,318	26,478	45,975	89,596	100,017	96,641	90,726	87,500	85,786	-4.3
Connecticut	51,309	61,844	59,048	60,216	68,579	72,190	75,151	76,706	77,873	79,625	16.1
Delaware	4,109	4,614	7,752	9,703	14,746	15,323	15,818	17,014	18,623	19,356	31.3
District of Columbia	64,964	72,775	67,561	67,190	131,539	86,152	84,933	84,674	83,910	84,938	-35.4
Florida	46,075	77,542	99,005	150,772	292,438	334,751	345,960	349,813	329,950	315,390	7.8
Georgia	24,611	44,001	55,373	74,449	113,473	132,869	136,706	123,171	119,718	117,252	3.3
Hawaii	3,599	3,912	10,708	15,603	16,723	17,983	18,676	18,161	17,493	16,453	-1.6
Idaho	7,495	8,527	10,566	11,843	21,088	20,997	24,389	29,227	33,408	42,147	99.9
Illinois	136,512	152,971	177,913	209,763	304,466	321,330	315,409	310,003	296,405	295,518	-2.9
Indiana	55,929	58,029	60,879	74,311	115,959	121,788	117,560	113,494	108,441	107,885	-7.0
Iowa	40,512	42,995	52,681	53,966	179,753	204,086	193,655	187,631	171,094	112,586	-37.4
Kansas	14,270	14,618	14,616	19,992	28,083	29,226	30,187	29,941	31,780	43,179	53.8
Kentucky	21,351	28,182	30,757	36,368	56,368	61,379	60,339	58,033	54,601	51,154	-9.2
Louisiana	19,601	23,355	28,550	34,587	35,957	38,865	40,530	37,875	36,234	34,995	-2.7
Maine	8,729	11,386	15,686	17,811	20,515	21,503	22,044	22,540	21,247	23,394	14.0
Maryland	30,619	30,475	38,917	49,948	60,590	68,188	65,714	63,993	62,206	60,441	-0.2
Massachusetts	187,682	234,650	231,798	237,894	278,235	283,211	281,540	285,941	285,753	284,754	2.3
Michigan	53,101	65,984	82,444	99,770	132,606	135,317	130,716	123,461	115,852	104,726	-21.0
Minnesota	30,221	44,312	54,578	74,828	171,773	189,273	183,545	179,371	175,051	174,159	1.4
Mississippi	8,999	11,703	13,845	12,034	17,619	18,502	18,734	18,623	18,718	18,632	5.7
Missouri	51,390	69,242	89,806	119,839	178,973	188,720	196,409	183,756	183,572	166,920	-6.7
Montana	2,775	3,999	4,011	4,853	4,935	5,051	5,130	4,921	4,926	4,918	-0.3
Nebraska	15,461	15,979	18,217	23,586	35,445	36,713	36,081	35,392	36,050	36,004	1.6
Nevada	93	175	486	4,773	12,499	16,257	15,965	14,681	14,200	13,177	5.4
New Hampshire	13,421	22,675	27,347	25,848	30,727	31,462	34,111	39,389	49,729	63,686	107.3
New Jersey	70,748	74,582	62,685	69,024	83,044	85,836	84,292	83,509	84,117	84,892	2.2
New Mexico	3,666	3,206	2,097	9,289	9,068	11,708	11,040	9,632	9,074	7,935	-12.5
New York	357,042	428,986	431,402	459,978	577,579	581,651	586,162	587,410	583,296	577,208	-0.1
North Carolina	48,164	59,383	66,733	75,230	98,251	110,728	114,024	112,315	115,098	114,867	16.9
North Dakota	1,303	2,360	3,188	4,234	7,729	7,999	6,904	6,313	6,312	5,756	-25.5
Ohio	95,168	107,380	130,077	138,392	190,159	197,564	192,301	185,406	177,608	169,994	-10.6
Oklahoma	18,717	23,107	22,148	24,317	30,424	32,919	32,803	33,374	33,819	32,900	8.1
Oregon	13,694	17,356	21,314	28,309	42,025	43,707	43,595	42,385	42,789	43,902	4.5
Pennsylvania	178,062	215,217	260,582	270,292	352,075	371,717	359,625	351,460	345,733	337,060	-4.3
Rhode Island	20,371	31,817	35,923	36,992	41,264	41,886	41,393	40,748	40,674	40,734	-1.3
South Carolina	22,417	24,793	28,168	30,412	46,321	51,984	51,700	50,594	50,127	48,873	5.5
South Dakota	6,703	8,433	7,612	8,364	11,668	13,791	12,170	11,873	10,857	9,831	-15.7
Tennessee	36,206	47,746	51,189	61,380	100,814	109,276	108,269	108,468	108,895	102,542	1.7
Texas	76,703	87,839	99,123	137,439	188,187	201,754	197,379	192,464	191,769	190,123	1.0
Utah	32,099	34,389	35,195	40,730	65,283	76,592	85,186	96,308	95,944	107,210	64.2
Vermont	9,673	12,644	15,488	15,468	17,947	18,048	18,011	18,196	17,682	18,340	2.2
Virginia	28,636	34,004	62,156	68,113	143,572	168,918	175,384	178,955	177,840	178,549	24.4
Washington	20,826	27,575	35,752	46,912	54,222	57,263	55,773	54,032	53,185	52,670	-2.9
West Virginia	11,790	10,745	10,682	11,752	47,959	56,327	66,713	69,165	67,172	69,210	44.3
Wisconsin	31,684	33,907	46,245	57,442	78,217	82,922	79,740	76,322	74,682	72,168	-7.7
Wyoming	0	26	703	1,289	1,411	2,006	1,724	1,953	1,537	1,145	-18.9
Other jurisdictions	20,557	77,057	98,374	110,169	156,417	180,521	188,231	181,575	176,407	178,127	13.9
American Samoa	0	0	0	0	0	0	0	0	0	0	†
Federated States of Micronesia	0	0	0	0	0	0	0	0	0	0	†
Guam	0	0	0	0	94	85	86	77	79	72	-23.4
Marshall Islands	0	0	0	0	0	0	0	0	0	0	†
Northern Marianas	0	0	0	0	0	0	0	0	0	0	†
Palau	0	0	0	0	0	0	0	0	0	0	†
Puerto Rico	20,557	77,057	98,374	110,169	156,323	180,436	188,145	181,498	176,328	178,055	13.9
U.S. Virgin Islands	0	0	0	0	0	0	0	0	0	0	†

†Not applicable.
NOTE: Data through 1990 are for institutions of higher education, while later data are for degree-granting institutions. Degree-granting institutions grant associate's or higher degrees and participate in Title IV federal financial aid programs. The degree-granting classification is very similar to the earlier higher education classification, but it includes more 2-year colleges and excludes a few higher education institutions that did not grant degrees. Some data have been revised from previously published figures.

SOURCE: U.S. Department of Education, National Center for Education Statistics, Higher Education General Information Survey (HEGIS), "Fall Enrollment in Colleges and Universities" surveys, 1970 and 1980; Integrated Postsecondary Education Data System (IPEDS), "Fall Enrollment Survey" (IPEDS-EF:90); and IPEDS Spring 2001 through Spring 2015, Fall Enrollment component. (This table was prepared October 2015.)

Table 304.30. Total fall enrollment in degree-granting postsecondary institutions, by attendance status, sex, and state or jurisdiction: 2013 and 2014

State or jurisdiction	Fall 2013					Fall 2014					Percent change in total, 2013 to 2014
		Full-time		Part-time			Full-time		Part-time		
	Total	Males	Females	Males	Females	Total	Males	Females	Males	Females	
1	2	3	4	5	6	7	8	9	10	11	12
United States	20,375,789	5,682,166	6,914,946	3,178,620	4,600,057	20,207,369	5,619,391	6,834,584	3,177,670	4,575,724	-0.8
Alabama	305,712	90,022	116,634	40,092	58,964	305,028	90,962	117,246	40,151	56,669	-0.2
Alaska	34,890	7,090	9,311	7,190	11,299	34,331	7,289	9,761	6,619	10,662	-1.6
Arizona	694,123	179,273	280,864	89,686	144,300	674,746	172,819	264,044	90,771	147,112	-2.8
Arkansas	172,224	48,312	62,455	23,371	38,086	169,571	46,773	60,292	24,059	38,447	-1.5
California	2,636,921	658,149	783,689	549,589	645,494	2,696,415	678,452	833,367	544,611	639,985	2.3
Colorado	358,723	97,207	110,187	63,491	87,838	353,827	95,788	107,804	63,095	87,140	-1.4
Connecticut	200,966	58,225	69,394	27,432	45,915	201,928	59,190	69,523	27,376	45,839	0.5
Delaware	59,615	16,025	21,171	8,263	14,156	60,368	16,149	21,369	8,225	14,625	1.3
District of Columbia	89,257	26,553	36,646	10,058	16,000	90,053	26,168	36,613	10,465	16,807	0.9
Florida	1,125,810	285,310	369,326	188,032	283,142	1,111,018	276,382	358,038	188,910	287,688	-1.3
Georgia	533,424	151,280	202,518	66,863	112,763	531,004	148,295	201,928	68,414	112,367	-0.5
Hawaii	76,434	19,192	25,493	13,314	18,435	73,505	18,673	24,862	12,302	17,668	-3.8
Idaho	109,318	29,299	33,350	18,606	28,063	118,953	29,464	32,824	22,563	34,102	8.8
Illinois	842,888	225,063	260,136	142,705	214,984	824,980	219,578	255,549	139,410	210,443	-2.1
Indiana	444,364	131,401	155,023	66,047	91,893	436,327	128,508	152,588	65,375	89,856	-1.8
Iowa	339,738	93,824	130,782	41,146	73,986	282,482	76,051	86,292	43,691	76,448	-16.9
Kansas	215,855	61,637	67,826	35,551	50,841	226,401	65,158	72,182	37,748	51,313	4.9
Kentucky	273,073	74,015	97,800	42,072	59,186	264,197	72,160	94,879	40,149	57,009	-3.3
Louisiana	251,887	71,515	99,225	31,272	49,875	245,938	70,383	96,882	29,808	48,865	-2.4
Maine	70,849	20,489	24,644	9,241	16,475	72,246	20,065	24,554	9,755	17,872	2.0
Maryland	363,771	88,953	104,820	68,778	101,220	365,597	88,890	104,418	70,922	101,367	0.5
Massachusetts	514,008	161,041	192,013	61,751	99,203	510,912	161,331	191,154	60,788	97,639	-0.6
Michigan	643,592	176,077	200,368	109,899	157,248	619,438	170,034	193,265	107,113	149,026	-3.8
Minnesota	441,491	107,181	138,939	69,361	126,010	433,854	103,130	134,136	69,513	127,075	-1.7
Mississippi	173,634	54,536	78,688	14,030	26,380	170,728	53,742	76,407	14,056	26,523	-1.7
Missouri	438,222	123,191	148,389	67,546	99,096	419,900	117,201	141,261	64,762	96,676	-4.2
Montana	52,777	18,898	19,213	5,637	9,029	51,942	18,593	19,179	5,573	8,597	-1.6
Nebraska	137,943	42,041	48,809	19,382	27,711	135,825	41,363	48,730	18,806	26,926	-1.5
Nevada	116,738	27,231	33,413	24,380	31,714	119,205	27,684	34,679	24,383	32,459	2.1
New Hampshire	92,440	26,839	33,198	12,136	20,267	106,984	29,103	35,711	15,542	26,628	15.7
New Jersey	436,939	131,970	144,931	66,932	93,106	436,208	131,777	145,004	67,021	92,406	-0.2
New Mexico	153,455	35,597	44,413	30,544	42,901	146,246	33,091	41,241	29,898	42,016	-4.7
New York	1,304,230	412,687	498,437	155,437	237,669	1,299,055	412,001	494,717	156,923	235,414	-0.4
North Carolina	575,198	160,139	210,027	77,201	127,831	570,045	159,210	207,162	76,883	126,790	-0.9
North Dakota	55,063	19,367	18,442	7,636	9,618	54,048	19,207	18,392	7,457	8,992	-1.8
Ohio	697,647	206,392	239,811	97,694	153,750	680,238	200,487	231,645	97,495	150,611	-2.5
Oklahoma	220,897	65,027	76,578	31,804	47,488	215,349	63,883	75,128	30,575	45,763	-2.5
Oregon	251,106	72,684	84,379	41,058	52,985	245,547	69,945	82,990	40,791	51,821	-2.2
Pennsylvania	765,582	256,235	292,466	82,455	134,426	750,651	253,632	289,674	78,564	128,781	-2.0
Rhode Island	83,460	28,045	33,612	8,379	13,424	83,499	28,059	33,878	8,220	13,342	#
South Carolina	257,844	77,600	99,597	28,075	52,572	254,629	76,448	99,017	28,167	50,997	-1.2
South Dakota	55,129	16,595	17,384	7,601	13,549	53,963	16,173	17,113	7,680	12,997	-2.1
Tennessee	338,197	104,647	133,296	37,748	62,506	326,575	101,396	128,484	37,322	59,373	-3.4
Texas	1,541,378	378,901	448,538	293,708	420,231	1,555,462	381,474	450,415	296,927	426,646	0.9
Utah	264,255	86,006	91,907	41,809	44,533	274,926	90,181	100,068	41,194	43,483	4.0
Vermont	43,534	16,033	16,415	3,885	7,201	43,983	16,313	15,859	4,376	7,435	1.0
Virginia	583,755	159,354	194,623	92,646	137,132	577,908	157,362	194,393	91,413	134,740	-1.0
Washington	363,377	115,712	134,861	47,934	64,870	365,193	115,181	134,645	49,593	65,774	0.5
West Virginia	157,954	38,040	43,252	40,833	35,829	157,052	37,002	41,509	42,752	35,789	-0.6
Wisconsin	364,021	108,999	124,492	51,003	79,527	358,894	105,828	120,918	52,220	79,928	-1.4
Wyoming	37,084	10,375	10,083	7,294	9,332	35,461	9,788	9,658	7,226	8,789	-4.4
U.S. Service Academies	14,997	11,892	3,078	23	4	14,734	11,575	3,137	18	4	-1.8
Other jurisdictions	254,543	86,584	118,101	20,101	29,757	255,843	86,986	118,324	20,450	30,083	0.5
American Samoa	1,488	285	450	291	462	1,276	251	465	219	341	-14.2
Federated States of Micronesia	2,446	778	852	405	411	2,344	717	887	376	364	-4.2
Guam	6,518	1,583	2,288	1,201	1,446	6,488	1,652	2,310	1,137	1,389	-0.5
Marshall Islands	1,000	333	340	180	147	1,087	404	380	143	160	8.7
Northern Marianas	1,109	352	562	77	118	1,186	387	597	85	117	6.9
Palau	646	200	217	102	127	604	188	180	100	136	-6.5
Puerto Rico	239,015	82,604	112,445	17,591	26,375	240,578	82,951	112,528	18,128	26,971	0.7
U.S. Virgin Islands	2,321	449	947	254	671	2,280	436	977	262	605	-1.8

#Rounds to zero.
NOTE: Degree-granting institutions grant associate's or higher degrees and participate in Title IV federal financial aid programs.

SOURCE: U.S. Department of Education, National Center for Education Statistics, Integrated Postsecondary Education Data System (IPEDS), Spring 2014 and Spring 2015, Fall Enrollment component. (This table was prepared October 2015.)

Table 304.35. Total fall enrollment in public degree-granting postsecondary institutions, by attendance status, sex, and state or jurisdiction: 2013 and 2014

State or jurisdiction	Total	Fall 2013 Full-time Males	Full-time Females	Part-time Males	Part-time Females	Total	Fall 2014 Full-time Males	Full-time Females	Part-time Males	Part-time Females	Percent change in total, 2013 to 2014
1	2	3	4	5	6	7	8	9	10	11	12
United States	14,745,558	3,949,205	4,515,604	2,619,634	3,661,115	14,655,015	3,914,629	4,483,090	2,624,305	3,632,991	-0.6
Alabama	248,284	71,809	92,545	32,295	51,635	246,989	72,141	93,383	32,008	49,457	-0.5
Alaska	31,600	6,260	7,222	7,068	11,050	29,892	6,131	6,806	6,517	10,438	-5.4
Arizona	354,462	88,061	92,556	73,416	100,429	354,997	89,015	92,951	73,799	99,232	0.2
Arkansas	153,690	41,480	54,014	22,050	36,146	151,399	39,992	52,200	22,676	36,531	-1.5
California	2,148,147	494,156	563,299	505,112	585,580	2,167,444	502,259	577,649	503,954	583,582	0.9
Colorado	271,223	74,225	76,612	52,217	68,169	268,041	73,434	75,889	51,179	67,539	-1.2
Connecticut	123,093	33,460	37,022	20,680	31,931	122,303	33,432	36,877	20,506	31,488	-0.6
Delaware	40,992	12,775	16,875	4,346	6,996	41,012	12,624	16,815	4,313	7,260	#
District of Columbia	5,347	1,003	1,391	988	1,965	5,115	986	1,296	940	1,893	-4.3
Florida	795,860	183,850	226,339	155,416	230,255	795,628	179,636	223,195	158,411	234,386	#
Georgia	413,706	116,515	144,667	57,758	94,766	413,752	114,063	144,561	59,824	95,304	#
Hawaii	58,941	14,018	17,588	11,261	16,074	57,052	13,705	17,191	10,554	15,602	-3.2
Idaho	75,910	21,044	22,306	12,839	19,721	76,806	20,637	21,284	13,740	21,145	1.2
Illinois	546,483	137,551	147,809	109,238	151,885	529,462	134,021	143,661	106,296	145,484	-3.1
Indiana	335,923	93,707	104,803	58,278	79,135	328,442	90,990	102,029	57,809	77,614	-2.2
Iowa	168,644	52,089	52,774	28,027	35,754	169,896	51,294	51,533	30,511	36,558	0.7
Kansas	184,075	52,481	56,199	31,469	43,926	183,222	52,569	56,118	31,316	43,219	-0.5
Kentucky	218,472	58,768	73,416	37,186	49,102	213,043	58,081	72,669	35,226	47,067	-2.5
Louisiana	215,653	60,722	80,581	29,118	45,232	210,943	60,096	79,129	27,731	43,987	-2.2
Maine	49,602	13,520	14,497	8,073	13,512	48,852	13,016	13,922	8,211	13,703	-1.5
Maryland	301,565	71,090	82,010	60,690	87,775	305,156	71,511	81,809	63,471	88,365	1.2
Massachusetts	228,255	61,064	67,564	38,029	61,598	226,158	60,826	66,823	37,493	61,016	-0.9
Michigan	527,740	145,866	162,494	91,646	127,734	514,712	142,772	158,818	90,466	122,656	-2.5
Minnesota	266,440	73,921	77,286	47,326	67,907	259,695	71,151	74,722	47,014	66,808	-2.5
Mississippi	154,916	49,661	70,748	12,295	22,212	152,096	48,843	68,410	12,457	22,386	-1.8
Missouri	254,650	73,112	85,376	38,054	58,108	252,980	72,860	84,863	38,132	57,125	-0.7
Montana	47,851	17,094	16,850	5,414	8,493	47,024	16,803	16,833	5,388	8,000	-1.7
Nebraska	101,893	30,443	32,406	16,620	22,424	99,821	29,978	32,145	16,090	21,608	-2.0
Nevada	102,538	21,833	26,314	23,573	30,818	106,028	22,778	27,858	23,741	31,651	3.4
New Hampshire	42,711	13,378	15,414	5,423	8,496	43,298	13,597	15,612	5,460	8,629	1.4
New Jersey	352,822	101,666	112,725	58,319	80,112	351,316	100,640	111,752	58,942	79,982	-0.4
New Mexico	144,381	32,928	39,677	30,070	41,706	138,311	30,808	37,245	29,425	40,833	-4.2
New York	720,934	221,114	254,482	99,059	146,279	721,847	220,646	253,264	101,691	146,426	0.1
North Carolina	460,100	120,316	157,466	69,489	112,829	455,178	119,397	154,628	69,329	111,824	-1.1
North Dakota	48,751	17,728	15,710	6,989	8,324	48,292	17,516	15,531	7,034	8,211	-0.9
Ohio	520,039	148,566	164,349	82,222	124,902	510,244	144,262	159,731	82,722	123,529	-1.9
Oklahoma	187,078	51,692	61,309	29,573	44,504	182,449	50,731	60,298	28,540	42,880	-2.5
Oregon	208,317	59,241	62,772	37,941	48,363	201,645	56,677	60,461	37,859	46,648	-3.2
Pennsylvania	419,849	139,030	148,130	52,231	80,458	413,591	137,111	146,193	51,203	79,084	-1.5
Rhode Island	42,786	10,816	14,107	6,606	11,257	42,765	10,844	14,263	6,512	11,146	#
South Carolina	207,717	61,336	75,293	25,067	46,021	205,756	60,592	75,523	25,200	44,441	-0.9
South Dakota	44,272	14,460	14,008	5,904	9,900	44,132	14,088	13,992	6,149	9,903	-0.3
Tennessee	229,302	66,912	81,621	30,771	49,998	224,033	66,074	79,998	30,518	47,443	-2.3
Texas	1,349,609	313,562	363,104	276,100	396,843	1,365,339	316,626	365,466	279,715	403,532	1.2
Utah	168,311	45,721	42,782	38,474	41,334	167,716	46,036	43,159	37,915	40,606	-0.4
Vermont	25,852	7,995	9,151	2,803	5,903	25,643	7,981	8,902	2,839	5,921	-0.8
Virginia	405,915	112,506	130,503	67,608	95,298	399,359	110,903	129,746	66,280	92,430	-1.6
Washington	310,192	98,583	109,261	43,527	58,821	312,523	98,407	109,554	45,259	59,303	0.8
West Virginia	90,782	31,737	35,381	8,838	14,826	87,842	30,716	33,826	8,536	14,764	-3.2
Wisconsin	289,339	87,500	91,745	44,821	65,273	286,726	85,197	89,810	46,160	65,559	-0.9
Wyoming	35,547	8,948	9,973	7,294	9,332	34,316	8,741	9,560	7,226	8,789	-3.5
U.S. Service Academies	14,997	11,892	3,078	23	4	14,734	11,575	3,137	18	4	-1.8
Other jurisdictions	78,136	28,083	37,217	5,490	7,346	77,716	28,239	37,280	5,341	6,856	-0.5
American Samoa	1,488	285	450	291	462	1,276	251	465	219	341	-14.2
Federated States of Micronesia	2,446	778	852	405	411	2,344	717	887	376	364	-4.2
Guam	6,439	1,551	2,263	1,187	1,438	6,416	1,623	2,285	1,127	1,381	-0.4
Marshall Islands	1,000	333	340	180	147	1,087	404	380	143	160	8.7
Northern Marianas	1,109	352	562	77	118	1,186	387	597	85	117	6.9
Palau	646	200	217	102	127	604	188	180	100	136	-6.5
Puerto Rico	62,687	24,135	31,586	2,994	3,972	62,523	24,233	31,509	3,029	3,752	-0.3
U.S. Virgin Islands	2,321	449	947	254	671	2,280	436	977	262	605	-1.8

#Rounds to zero.
NOTE: Degree-granting institutions grant associate's or higher degrees and participate in Title IV federal financial aid programs.

SOURCE: U.S. Department of Education, National Center for Education Statistics, Integrated Postsecondary Education Data System (IPEDS), Spring 2014 and Spring 2015, Fall Enrollment component. (This table was prepared October 2015.)

Table 304.40. Total fall enrollment in private degree-granting postsecondary institutions, by attendance status, sex, and state or jurisdiction: 2013 and 2014

State or jurisdiction	Fall 2013					Fall 2014					Percent change in total, 2013 to 2014
	Total	Full-time		Part-time		Total	Full-time		Part-time		
		Males	Females	Males	Females		Males	Females	Males	Females	
1	2	3	4	5	6	7	8	9	10	11	12
United States	5,630,231	1,732,961	2,399,342	558,986	938,942	5,552,354	1,704,762	2,351,494	553,365	942,733	-1.4
Alabama	57,428	18,213	24,089	7,797	7,329	58,039	18,821	23,863	8,143	7,212	1.1
Alaska	3,290	830	2,089	122	249	4,439	1,158	2,955	102	224	34.9
Arizona	339,661	91,212	188,308	16,270	43,871	319,749	83,804	171,093	16,972	47,880	-5.9
Arkansas	18,534	6,832	8,441	1,321	1,940	18,172	6,781	8,092	1,383	1,916	-2.0
California	488,774	163,993	220,390	44,477	59,914	528,971	176,193	255,718	40,657	56,403	8.2
Colorado	87,500	22,982	33,575	11,274	19,669	85,786	22,354	31,915	11,916	19,601	-2.0
Connecticut	77,873	24,765	32,372	6,752	13,984	79,625	25,758	32,646	6,870	14,351	2.2
Delaware	18,623	3,250	4,296	3,917	7,160	19,356	3,525	4,554	3,912	7,365	3.9
District of Columbia	83,910	25,550	35,255	9,070	14,035	84,938	25,182	35,317	9,525	14,914	1.2
Florida	329,950	101,460	142,987	32,616	52,887	315,390	96,746	134,843	30,499	53,302	-4.4
Georgia	119,718	34,765	57,851	9,105	17,997	117,252	34,232	57,367	8,590	17,063	-2.1
Hawaii	17,493	5,174	7,905	2,053	2,361	16,453	4,968	7,671	1,748	2,066	-5.9
Idaho	33,408	8,255	11,044	5,767	8,342	42,147	8,827	11,540	8,823	12,957	26.2
Illinois	296,405	87,512	112,327	33,467	63,099	295,518	85,557	111,888	33,114	64,959	-0.3
Indiana	108,441	37,694	50,220	7,769	12,758	107,885	37,518	50,559	7,566	12,242	-0.5
Iowa	171,094	41,735	78,008	13,119	38,232	112,586	24,757	34,759	13,180	39,890	-34.2
Kansas	31,780	9,156	11,627	4,082	6,915	43,179	12,589	16,064	6,432	8,094	35.9
Kentucky	54,601	15,247	24,384	4,886	10,084	51,154	14,079	22,210	4,923	9,942	-6.3
Louisiana	36,234	10,793	18,644	2,154	4,643	34,995	10,287	17,753	2,077	4,878	-3.4
Maine	21,247	6,969	10,147	1,168	2,963	23,394	7,049	10,632	1,544	4,169	10.1
Maryland	62,206	17,863	22,810	8,088	13,445	60,441	17,379	22,609	7,451	13,002	-2.8
Massachusetts	285,753	99,977	124,449	23,722	37,605	284,754	100,505	124,331	23,295	36,623	-0.3
Michigan	115,852	30,211	37,874	18,253	29,514	104,726	27,262	34,447	16,647	26,370	-9.6
Minnesota	175,051	33,260	61,653	22,035	58,103	174,159	31,979	59,414	22,499	60,267	-0.5
Mississippi	18,718	4,875	7,940	1,735	4,168	18,632	4,899	7,997	1,599	4,137	-0.5
Missouri	183,572	50,079	63,013	29,492	40,988	166,920	44,341	56,398	26,630	39,551	-9.1
Montana	4,926	1,804	2,363	223	536	4,918	1,790	2,346	185	597	-0.2
Nebraska	36,050	11,598	16,403	2,762	5,287	36,004	11,385	16,585	2,716	5,318	-0.1
Nevada	14,200	5,398	7,099	807	896	13,177	4,906	6,821	642	808	-7.2
New Hampshire	49,729	13,461	17,784	6,713	11,771	63,686	15,506	20,099	10,082	17,999	28.1
New Jersey	84,117	30,304	32,206	8,613	12,994	84,892	31,137	33,252	8,079	12,424	0.9
New Mexico	9,074	2,669	4,736	474	1,195	7,935	2,283	3,996	473	1,183	-12.6
New York	583,296	191,573	243,955	56,378	91,390	577,208	191,535	241,453	55,232	88,988	-1.0
North Carolina	115,098	39,823	52,561	7,712	15,002	114,867	39,813	52,534	7,554	14,966	-0.2
North Dakota	6,312	1,639	2,732	647	1,294	5,756	1,691	2,861	423	781	-8.8
Ohio	177,608	57,826	75,462	15,472	28,848	169,994	56,225	71,914	14,773	27,082	-4.3
Oklahoma	33,819	13,335	15,269	2,231	2,984	32,900	13,152	14,830	2,035	2,883	-2.7
Oregon	42,789	13,443	21,607	3,117	4,622	43,902	13,268	22,529	2,932	5,173	2.6
Pennsylvania	345,733	117,205	144,336	30,224	53,968	337,060	116,521	143,481	27,361	49,697	-2.5
Rhode Island	40,674	17,229	19,505	1,773	2,167	40,734	17,215	19,615	1,708	2,196	0.1
South Carolina	50,127	16,264	24,304	3,008	6,551	48,873	15,856	23,494	2,967	6,556	-2.5
South Dakota	10,857	2,135	3,376	1,697	3,649	9,831	2,085	3,121	1,531	3,094	-9.5
Tennessee	108,895	37,735	51,675	6,977	12,508	102,542	35,322	48,486	6,804	11,930	-5.8
Texas	191,769	65,339	85,434	17,608	23,388	190,123	64,848	84,949	17,212	23,114	-0.9
Utah	95,944	40,285	49,125	3,335	3,199	107,210	44,145	56,909	3,279	2,877	11.7
Vermont	17,682	8,038	7,264	1,082	1,298	18,340	8,332	6,957	1,537	1,514	3.7
Virginia	177,840	46,848	64,120	25,038	41,834	178,549	46,459	64,647	25,133	42,310	0.4
Washington	53,185	17,129	25,600	4,407	6,049	52,670	16,774	25,091	4,334	6,471	-1.0
West Virginia	67,172	6,303	7,871	31,995	21,003	69,210	6,286	7,683	34,216	21,025	3.0
Wisconsin	74,682	21,499	32,747	6,182	14,254	72,168	20,631	31,108	6,060	14,369	-3.4
Wyoming	1,537	1,427	110	0	0	1,145	1,047	98	0	0	-25.5
Other jurisdictions	176,407	58,501	80,884	14,611	22,411	178,127	58,747	81,044	15,109	23,227	1.0
American Samoa	0	0	0	0	0	0	0	0	0	0	†
Federated States of Micronesia	0	0	0	0	0	0	0	0	0	0	†
Guam	79	32	25	14	8	72	29	25	10	8	-8.9
Marshall Islands	0	0	0	0	0	0	0	0	0	0	†
Northern Marianas	0	0	0	0	0	0	0	0	0	0	†
Palau	0	0	0	0	0	0	0	0	0	0	†
Puerto Rico	176,328	58,469	80,859	14,597	22,403	178,055	58,718	81,019	15,099	23,219	1.0
U.S. Virgin Islands	0	0	0	0	0	0	0	0	0	0	†

†Not applicable.
NOTE: Degree-granting institutions grant associate's or higher degrees and participate in Title IV federal financial aid programs.

SOURCE: U.S. Department of Education, National Center for Education Statistics, Integrated Postsecondary Education Data System (IPEDS), Spring 2014 and Spring 2015, Fall Enrollment component. (This table was prepared October 2015.)

Table 304.45. Total fall enrollment in private nonprofit degree-granting postsecondary institutions, by attendance status, sex, and state or jurisdiction: 2013 and 2014

State or jurisdiction	Fall 2013					Fall 2014					Percent change in total, 2013 to 2014
	Total	Full-time		Part-time		Total	Full-time		Part-time		
		Males	Females	Males	Females		Males	Females	Males	Females	
1	2	3	4	5	6	7	8	9	10	11	12
United States	3,974,004	1,313,037	1,673,016	379,866	608,085	3,996,089	1,322,099	1,681,112	381,626	611,252	0.6
Alabama	25,146	9,292	12,303	1,357	2,194	26,032	9,764	12,633	1,420	2,215	3.5
Alaska	764	159	234	122	249	693	141	226	102	224	-9.3
Arizona	9,582	4,275	3,232	986	1,089	9,854	4,403	3,426	918	1,107	2.8
Arkansas	16,919	6,299	7,597	1,231	1,792	16,995	6,401	7,561	1,286	1,747	0.4
California	307,826	101,094	137,146	28,268	41,318	307,471	102,501	137,781	26,879	40,310	-0.1
Colorado	35,112	8,799	12,999	5,278	8,036	34,372	8,677	12,594	5,285	7,816	-2.1
Connecticut	68,717	23,358	29,950	4,625	10,784	70,396	24,370	30,397	4,753	10,876	2.4
Delaware	18,245	3,227	4,266	3,815	6,937	19,021	3,499	4,534	3,825	7,163	4.3
District of Columbia	78,908	24,976	34,506	7,784	11,642	78,502	24,578	34,552	7,743	11,629	-0.5
Florida	180,614	58,492	71,253	22,322	28,547	181,931	59,308	72,443	21,948	28,232	0.7
Georgia	73,394	23,901	36,018	5,067	8,408	73,262	23,972	36,195	4,989	8,106	-0.2
Hawaii	13,087	3,717	5,928	1,700	1,742	11,969	3,390	5,552	1,470	1,557	-8.5
Idaho	31,763	7,806	10,016	5,710	8,231	40,662	8,443	10,608	8,767	12,844	28.0
Illinois	224,127	75,260	94,730	20,358	33,779	222,651	74,475	94,740	20,607	32,829	-0.7
Indiana	88,789	32,351	40,965	5,644	9,829	90,524	32,969	41,757	5,955	9,843	2.0
Iowa	56,283	20,364	25,104	3,541	7,274	56,114	20,405	24,405	3,611	7,693	-0.3
Kansas	26,693	7,620	9,361	3,735	5,977	26,057	7,711	9,092	3,540	5,714	-2.4
Kentucky	39,830	12,005	17,231	3,438	7,156	39,025	11,490	16,333	3,797	7,405	-2.0
Louisiana	28,065	8,722	13,974	1,836	3,533	27,052	8,336	13,349	1,761	3,606	-3.6
Maine	19,766	6,723	9,552	1,025	2,466	21,392	6,807	9,912	1,331	3,342	8.2
Maryland	53,928	15,507	20,580	6,748	11,093	52,822	15,273	20,387	6,372	10,790	-2.1
Massachusetts	280,130	98,097	122,525	23,062	36,446	280,045	98,842	122,715	22,753	35,735	#
Michigan	108,188	27,279	34,898	17,371	28,640	98,367	24,970	31,691	16,049	25,657	-9.1
Minnesota	71,258	22,303	31,289	6,403	11,263	70,910	21,864	31,399	6,461	11,186	-0.5
Mississippi	16,046	4,516	6,467	1,575	3,488	16,376	4,557	6,737	1,484	3,598	2.1
Missouri	152,218	39,420	49,242	26,074	37,482	149,771	38,906	47,902	25,568	37,395	-1.6
Montana	4,926	1,804	2,363	223	536	4,918	1,790	2,346	185	597	-0.2
Nebraska	33,400	10,981	15,184	2,511	4,724	33,707	10,916	15,535	2,482	4,774	0.9
Nevada	3,546	1,490	1,592	126	338	3,762	1,554	1,773	130	305	6.1
New Hampshire	46,681	12,491	16,617	6,426	11,147	61,443	14,658	19,431	9,802	17,552	31.6
New Jersey	73,483	28,048	27,001	7,462	10,972	73,908	28,800	27,584	6,962	10,562	0.6
New Mexico	1,503	380	467	172	484	1,568	400	445	189	534	4.3
New York	532,881	177,267	217,982	53,205	84,427	528,700	177,843	216,513	52,358	81,986	-0.8
North Carolina	96,336	36,092	45,521	5,465	9,258	96,504	36,418	45,454	5,370	9,262	0.2
North Dakota	5,348	1,511	2,334	504	999	4,963	1,587	2,539	328	509	-7.2
Ohio	143,121	50,131	58,175	12,495	22,320	141,046	49,779	57,372	12,593	21,302	-1.4
Oklahoma	25,117	9,782	10,813	1,974	2,548	24,737	9,847	10,545	1,825	2,520	-1.5
Oregon	35,308	11,275	18,053	2,487	3,493	37,256	11,525	19,437	2,389	3,905	5.5
Pennsylvania	294,772	102,786	126,974	22,621	42,391	292,305	102,852	126,372	21,745	41,336	-0.8
Rhode Island	40,674	17,229	19,505	1,773	2,167	40,734	17,215	19,615	1,708	2,196	0.1
South Carolina	34,195	12,310	17,124	1,739	3,022	34,552	12,383	17,225	1,820	3,124	1.0
South Dakota	7,153	1,897	2,885	824	1,547	7,139	1,953	2,799	840	1,547	-0.2
Tennessee	83,909	29,558	40,303	5,337	8,711	83,412	28,688	39,866	5,708	9,150	-0.6
Texas	136,053	47,735	57,232	13,389	17,697	136,670	48,380	58,012	13,029	17,249	0.5
Utah	87,957	37,556	45,337	2,750	2,314	100,548	41,677	53,774	2,891	2,206	14.3
Vermont	17,220	7,847	7,108	1,018	1,247	17,918	8,145	6,806	1,492	1,475	4.1
Virginia	130,794	32,830	46,630	19,564	31,770	134,599	33,596	47,509	20,301	33,193	2.9
Washington	43,222	13,799	20,762	3,407	5,254	43,169	13,553	20,253	3,526	5,837	-0.1
West Virginia	8,505	3,655	3,887	300	663	8,679	3,798	3,934	322	625	2.0
Wisconsin	62,427	18,995	27,752	5,019	10,661	61,526	18,669	27,013	4,957	10,887	-1.4
Wyoming	75	26	49	0	0	60	21	39	0	0	-20.0
Other jurisdictions	134,587	42,658	61,234	12,223	18,472	131,649	41,896	59,236	12,356	18,161	-2.2
American Samoa	0	0	0	0	0	0	0	0	0	0	†
Federated States of Micronesia	0	0	0	0	0	0	0	0	0	0	†
Guam	79	32	25	14	8	72	29	25	10	8	-8.9
Marshall Islands	0	0	0	0	0	0	0	0	0	0	†
Northern Marianas	0	0	0	0	0	0	0	0	0	0	†
Palau	0	0	0	0	0	0	0	0	0	0	†
Puerto Rico	134,508	42,626	61,209	12,209	18,464	131,577	41,867	59,211	12,346	18,153	-2.2
U.S. Virgin Islands	0	0	0	0	0	0	0	0	0	0	†

†Not applicable.
#Rounds to zero.
NOTE: Degree-granting institutions grant associate's or higher degrees and participate in Title IV federal financial aid programs.

SOURCE: U.S. Department of Education, National Center for Education Statistics, Integrated Postsecondary Education Data System (IPEDS), Spring 2014 and Spring 2015, Fall Enrollment component. (This table was prepared October 2015.)

Table 304.50. Total fall enrollment in private for-profit degree-granting postsecondary institutions, by attendance status, sex, and state or jurisdiction: 2013 and 2014

State or jurisdiction		Fall 2013				Fall 2014				Percent change in total, 2013 to 2014
	Total	Full-time		Part-time		Total	Full-time		Part-time		
		Males	Females	Males	Females		Males	Females	Males	Females	
1	2	3	4	5	6	7	8	9	10	11	12
United States	1,656,227	419,924	726,326	179,120	330,857	1,556,265	382,663	670,382	171,739	331,481	-6.0
Alabama	32,282	8,921	11,786	6,440	5,135	32,007	9,057	11,230	6,723	4,997	-0.9
Alaska	2,526	671	1,855	0	0	3,746	1,017	2,729	0	0	48.3
Arizona	330,079	86,937	185,076	15,284	42,782	309,895	79,401	167,667	16,054	46,773	-6.1
Arkansas	1,615	533	844	90	148	1,177	380	531	97	169	-27.1
California	180,948	62,899	83,244	16,209	18,596	221,500	73,692	117,937	13,778	16,093	22.4
Colorado	52,388	14,183	20,576	5,996	11,633	51,414	13,677	19,321	6,631	11,785	-1.9
Connecticut	9,156	1,407	2,422	2,127	3,200	9,229	1,388	2,249	2,117	3,475	0.8
Delaware	378	23	30	102	223	335	26	20	87	202	-11.4
District of Columbia	5,002	574	749	1,286	2,393	6,436	604	765	1,782	3,285	28.7
Florida	149,336	42,968	71,734	10,294	24,340	133,459	37,438	62,400	8,551	25,070	-10.6
Georgia	46,324	10,864	21,833	4,038	9,589	43,990	10,260	21,172	3,601	8,957	-5.0
Hawaii	4,406	1,457	1,977	353	619	4,484	1,578	2,119	278	509	1.8
Idaho	1,645	449	1,028	57	111	1,485	384	932	56	113	-9.7
Illinois	72,278	12,252	17,597	13,109	29,320	72,867	11,082	17,148	12,507	32,130	0.8
Indiana	19,652	5,343	9,255	2,125	2,929	17,361	4,549	8,802	1,611	2,399	-11.7
Iowa	114,811	21,371	52,904	9,578	30,958	56,472	4,352	10,354	9,569	32,197	-50.8
Kansas	5,087	1,536	2,266	347	938	17,122	4,878	6,972	2,892	2,380	236.6
Kentucky	14,771	3,242	7,153	1,448	2,928	12,129	2,589	5,877	1,126	2,537	-17.9
Louisiana	8,169	2,071	4,670	318	1,110	7,943	1,951	4,404	316	1,272	-2.8
Maine	1,481	246	595	143	497	2,002	242	720	213	827	35.2
Maryland	8,278	2,356	2,230	1,340	2,352	7,619	2,106	2,222	1,079	2,212	-8.0
Massachusetts	5,623	1,880	1,924	660	1,159	4,709	1,663	1,616	542	888	-16.3
Michigan	7,664	2,932	2,976	882	874	6,359	2,292	2,756	598	713	-17.0
Minnesota	103,793	10,957	30,364	15,632	46,840	103,249	10,115	28,015	16,038	49,081	-0.5
Mississippi	2,672	359	1,473	160	680	2,256	342	1,260	115	539	-15.6
Missouri	31,354	10,659	13,771	3,418	3,506	17,149	5,435	8,496	1,062	2,156	-45.3
Montana	0	0	0	0	0	0	0	0	0	0	†
Nebraska	2,650	617	1,219	251	563	2,297	469	1,050	234	544	-13.3
Nevada	10,654	3,908	5,507	681	558	9,415	3,352	5,048	512	503	-11.6
New Hampshire	3,048	970	1,167	287	624	2,243	848	668	280	447	-26.4
New Jersey	10,634	2,256	5,205	1,151	2,022	10,984	2,337	5,668	1,117	1,862	3.3
New Mexico	7,571	2,289	4,269	302	711	6,367	1,883	3,551	284	649	-15.9
New York	50,415	14,306	25,973	3,173	6,963	48,508	13,692	24,940	2,874	7,002	-3.8
North Carolina	18,762	3,731	7,040	2,247	5,744	18,363	3,395	7,080	2,184	5,704	-2.1
North Dakota	964	128	398	143	295	793	104	322	95	272	-17.7
Ohio	34,487	7,695	17,287	2,977	6,528	28,948	6,446	14,542	2,180	5,780	-16.1
Oklahoma	8,702	3,553	4,456	257	436	8,163	3,305	4,285	210	363	-6.2
Oregon	7,481	2,168	3,554	630	1,129	6,646	1,743	3,092	543	1,268	-11.2
Pennsylvania	50,961	14,419	17,362	7,603	11,577	44,755	13,669	17,109	5,616	8,361	-12.2
Rhode Island	0	0	0	0	0	0	0	0	0	0	†
South Carolina	15,932	3,954	7,180	1,269	3,529	14,321	3,473	6,269	1,147	3,432	-10.1
South Dakota	3,704	238	491	873	2,102	2,692	132	322	691	1,547	-27.3
Tennessee	24,986	8,177	11,372	1,640	3,797	19,130	6,634	8,620	1,096	2,780	-23.4
Texas	55,716	17,604	28,202	4,219	5,691	53,453	16,468	26,937	4,183	5,865	-4.1
Utah	7,987	2,729	3,788	585	885	6,662	2,468	3,135	388	671	-16.6
Vermont	462	191	156	64	51	422	187	151	45	39	-8.7
Virginia	47,046	14,018	17,490	5,474	10,064	43,950	12,863	17,138	4,832	9,117	-6.6
Washington	9,963	3,330	4,838	1,000	795	9,501	3,221	4,838	808	634	-4.6
West Virginia	58,667	2,648	3,984	31,695	20,340	60,531	2,488	3,749	33,894	20,400	3.2
Wisconsin	12,255	2,504	4,995	1,163	3,593	10,642	1,962	4,095	1,103	3,482	-13.2
Wyoming	1,462	1,401	61	0	0	1,085	1,026	59	0	0	-25.8
Other jurisdictions	41,820	15,843	19,650	2,388	3,939	46,478	16,851	21,808	2,753	5,066	11.1
American Samoa	0	0	0	0	0	0	0	0	0	0	†
Federated States of Micronesia	0	0	0	0	0	0	0	0	0	0	†
Guam	0	0	0	0	0	0	0	0	0	0	†
Marshall Islands	0	0	0	0	0	0	0	0	0	0	†
Northern Marianas	0	0	0	0	0	0	0	0	0	0	†
Palau	0	0	0	0	0	0	0	0	0	0	†
Puerto Rico	41,820	15,843	19,650	2,388	3,939	46,478	16,851	21,808	2,753	5,066	11.1
U.S. Virgin Islands	0	0	0	0	0	0	0	0	0	0	†

†Not applicable.
NOTE: Degree-granting institutions grant associate's or higher degrees and participate in Title IV federal financial aid programs.

SOURCE: U.S. Department of Education, National Center for Education Statistics, Integrated Postsecondary Education Data System (IPEDS), Spring 2014 and Spring 2015, Fall Enrollment component. (This table was prepared October 2015.)

Table 304.60. Total fall enrollment in degree-granting postsecondary institutions, by control and level of institution and state or jurisdiction: 2013 and 2014

State or jurisdiction	Fall 2013						Fall 2014					
	Public 4-year	Public 2-year	Private 4-year Nonprofit	Private 4-year For-profit	Private 2-year Nonprofit	Private 2-year For-profit	Public 4-year	Public 2-year	Private 4-year Nonprofit	Private 4-year For-profit	Private 2-year Nonprofit	Private 2-year For-profit
1	2	3	4	5	6	7	8	9	10	11	12	13
United States	8,120,417	6,625,141	3,941,806	1,344,827	32,198	311,400	8,257,250	6,397,765	3,965,724	1,269,910	30,365	286,355
Alabama	163,660	84,624	24,674	29,338	472	2,944	164,447	82,542	25,514	29,227	518	2,780
Alaska	29,525	2,075	711	2,191	53	335	28,760	1,132	625	3,267	68	479
Arizona	145,409	209,053	9,582	320,062	0	10,017	154,689	200,308	9,854	300,524	0	9,371
Arkansas	97,705	55,985	16,360	1,531	559	84	97,986	53,413	16,339	1,116	656	61
California	685,096	1,463,051	306,233	117,411	1,593	63,537	706,431	1,461,013	305,607	162,707	1,864	58,793
Colorado	177,678	93,545	35,105	42,742	7	9,646	178,889	89,152	34,372	42,026	0	9,388
Connecticut	66,116	56,977	68,717	9,094	0	62	67,149	55,154	70,396	9,229	0	0
Delaware	26,502	14,490	18,049	378	196	0	27,077	13,935	18,836	335	185	0
District of Columbia	5,347	0	78,908	4,822	0	180	5,115	0	78,480	6,221	22	215
Florida	743,237	52,623	178,825	115,425	1,789	33,911	752,959	42,669	180,359	99,701	1,572	33,758
Georgia	273,434	140,272	72,904	37,830	490	8,494	288,473	125,279	72,797	35,721	465	8,269
Hawaii	30,486	28,455	13,087	2,302	0	2,104	29,901	27,151	11,969	2,580	0	1,904
Idaho	51,635	24,275	31,763	1,093	0	552	51,662	25,144	40,662	991	0	494
Illinois	194,913	351,570	223,384	66,458	743	5,820	193,360	336,102	221,916	67,409	735	5,458
Indiana	237,145	98,778	88,365	15,221	424	4,431	237,263	91,179	90,124	13,167	400	4,194
Iowa	74,862	93,782	56,283	114,208	0	603	76,333	93,563	56,114	55,909	0	563
Kansas	100,524	83,551	26,248	3,292	445	1,795	101,889	81,333	25,629	15,371	428	1,751
Kentucky	126,535	91,937	39,830	12,133	0	2,638	126,484	86,559	39,025	10,046	0	2,083
Louisiana	139,717	75,936	27,121	3,222	944	4,947	139,400	71,543	26,416	2,619	636	5,324
Maine	31,383	18,219	19,458	1,017	308	464	30,673	18,179	21,104	1,573	288	429
Maryland	162,722	138,843	53,928	5,593	0	2,685	171,419	133,737	52,822	5,185	0	2,434
Massachusetts	123,892	104,363	279,066	4,219	1,064	1,404	124,575	101,583	278,952	3,504	1,093	1,205
Michigan	305,454	222,286	108,188	6,116	0	1,548	314,512	200,200	98,367	5,318	0	1,041
Minnesota	136,044	130,396	71,198	102,465	60	1,328	134,340	125,355	70,841	102,284	69	965
Mississippi	79,708	75,208	16,046	343	0	2,329	79,112	72,984	16,376	325	0	1,931
Missouri	149,285	105,365	151,006	25,449	1,212	5,905	153,377	99,603	148,633	11,167	1,138	5,982
Montana	39,145	8,706	4,476	0	450	0	38,392	8,632	4,423	0	495	0
Nebraska	59,389	42,504	33,234	2,148	166	502	59,833	39,988	33,558	1,977	149	320
Nevada	91,334	11,204	3,546	5,771	0	4,883	94,922	11,106	3,762	4,658	0	4,757
New Hampshire	28,056	14,655	46,463	3,048	218	0	28,259	15,039	61,299	2,243	144	0
New Jersey	185,242	167,580	73,483	6,639	0	3,995	188,479	162,837	73,908	6,867	0	4,117
New Mexico	64,647	79,734	1,503	5,994	0	1,577	62,714	75,597	1,568	4,889	0	1,478
New York	393,331	327,603	528,920	31,567	3,961	18,848	397,844	324,003	525,903	31,278	2,797	17,230
North Carolina	220,121	239,979	95,658	14,894	678	3,868	221,968	233,210	95,803	15,238	701	3,125
North Dakota	41,729	7,022	5,348	964	0	0	41,450	6,842	4,963	793	0	0
Ohio	334,980	185,059	142,035	20,151	1,086	14,336	334,020	176,224	139,999	16,895	1,047	12,053
Oklahoma	124,596	62,482	25,117	4,632	0	4,070	122,344	60,105	24,737	3,922	0	4,241
Oregon	105,140	103,177	35,308	4,529	0	2,952	104,435	97,210	37,256	4,359	0	2,287
Pennsylvania	280,546	139,303	286,084	21,782	8,688	29,179	279,610	133,981	284,260	18,742	8,045	26,013
Rhode Island	25,087	17,699	40,674	0	0	0	25,212	17,553	40,734	0	0	0
South Carolina	107,733	99,984	33,377	11,472	818	4,460	109,659	96,097	33,759	11,236	793	3,085
South Dakota	37,819	6,453	6,900	3,704	253	0	37,896	6,236	6,915	2,692	224	0
Tennessee	139,579	89,723	83,270	14,644	639	10,342	137,797	86,236	82,654	10,946	758	8,184
Texas	654,008	695,601	133,708	29,081	2,345	26,635	675,047	690,292	134,083	29,411	2,587	24,042
Utah	136,308	32,003	85,921	6,839	2,036	1,148	137,468	30,248	98,542	5,788	2,006	874
Vermont	19,652	6,200	17,220	462	0	0	19,624	6,019	17,918	422	0	0
Virginia	215,370	190,545	130,345	39,029	449	8,017	214,391	184,968	134,178	36,346	421	7,604
Washington	179,895	130,297	43,170	5,793	52	4,170	210,383	102,140	43,108	5,323	61	4,178
West Virginia	70,303	20,479	8,505	56,250	0	2,417	68,721	19,121	8,679	58,266	0	2,265
Wisconsin	180,618	108,721	62,427	11,479	0	776	182,953	103,773	61,526	10,097	0	545
Wyoming	12,778	22,769	75	0	0	1,462	12,820	21,496	60	0	0	1,085
U.S. Service Academies	14,997	0	†	†	†	†	14,734	0	†	†	†	†
Other jurisdictions	68,531	9,605	134,587	13,923	0	27,897	68,615	9,101	130,925	16,264	724	30,214
American Samoa	1,488	0	0	0	0	0	1,276	0	0	0	0	0
Federated States of Micronesia	0	2,446	0	0	0	0	0	2,344	0	0	0	0
Guam	3,836	2,603	79	0	0	0	3,958	2,458	72	0	0	0
Marshall Islands	0	1,000	0	0	0	0	0	1,087	0	0	0	0
Northern Marianas	1,109	0	0	0	0	0	1,186	0	0	0	0	0
Palau	0	646	0	0	0	0	0	604	0	0	0	0
Puerto Rico	59,777	2,910	134,508	13,923	0	27,897	59,915	2,608	130,853	16,264	724	30,214
U.S. Virgin Islands	2,321	0	0	0	0	0	2,280	0	0	0	0	0

†Not applicable.
NOTE: Degree-granting institutions grant associate's or higher degrees and participate in Title IV federal financial aid programs.

SOURCE: U.S. Department of Education, National Center for Education Statistics, Integrated Postsecondary Education Data System (IPEDS), Spring 2014 and Spring 2015, Fall Enrollment component. (This table was prepared October 2015.)

Table 304.70. Total fall enrollment in degree-granting postsecondary institutions, by level of enrollment and state or jurisdiction: Selected years, 2000 through 2014

State or jurisdiction	Undergraduate						Postbaccalaureate					
	Fall 2000	Fall 2010	Fall 2011	Fall 2012	Fall 2013	Fall 2014	Fall 2000	Fall 2010	Fall 2011	Fall 2012	Fall 2013	Fall 2014
1	2	3	4	5	6	7	8	9	10	11	12	13
United States	13,155,393	18,082,427	18,077,303	17,735,638	17,474,835	17,292,787	2,156,896	2,937,011	2,933,287	2,908,840	2,900,954	2,914,582
Alabama	201,389	282,128	274,837	265,917	261,188	259,630	32,573	45,478	45,512	44,394	44,524	45,398
Alaska	26,222	31,925	32,104	30,018	32,097	31,763	1,731	2,874	2,828	2,779	2,793	2,568
Arizona	299,529	672,083	675,028	621,684	580,602	562,449	42,961	121,788	121,946	114,781	113,521	112,297
Arkansas	104,580	156,970	159,973	157,504	153,640	151,132	10,592	18,878	19,372	18,954	18,584	18,439
California	2,012,213	2,444,496	2,424,395	2,359,805	2,371,922	2,426,640	244,495	270,203	267,457	261,801	264,999	269,775
Colorado	220,059	312,099	308,249	305,465	300,452	294,581	43,813	57,351	57,690	57,705	58,271	59,246
Connecticut	127,715	163,291	165,707	166,812	166,181	165,825	33,528	36,093	35,931	34,846	34,785	36,103
Delaware	37,930	45,848	46,973	47,815	48,226	48,390	5,967	9,410	9,574	10,312	11,389	11,978
District of Columbia	40,703	50,330	48,491	47,699	47,187	48,156	31,986	41,662	41,754	42,451	42,070	41,897
Florida	623,071	993,545	1,017,088	1,023,378	997,958	984,355	84,613	131,233	132,072	131,128	127,852	126,663
Georgia	296,980	499,187	495,192	476,815	464,779	460,166	49,224	69,729	70,222	68,545	68,645	70,838
Hawaii	51,783	68,244	69,595	69,272	67,683	65,067	8,399	9,829	9,411	9,184	8,751	8,438
Idaho	58,644	76,998	82,297	99,901	101,162	110,962	6,950	8,203	7,845	8,107	8,156	7,991
Illinois	623,018	748,921	735,155	713,472	694,099	676,251	120,900	157,924	157,297	153,421	148,789	148,729
Indiana	273,198	404,033	401,854	392,626	389,805	380,875	41,136	55,460	55,652	54,637	54,559	55,452
Iowa	165,360	339,036	328,242	315,424	293,677	243,391	23,614	42,831	43,904	45,765	46,061	39,091
Kansas	156,385	188,326	190,125	187,921	189,780	197,869	23,583	26,523	26,537	25,934	26,075	28,532
Kentucky	164,183	256,447	257,828	244,950	237,737	229,067	24,158	34,657	35,938	36,183	35,336	35,130
Louisiana	191,517	230,370	233,374	227,290	221,120	215,289	32,283	33,306	32,366	31,556	30,767	30,649
Maine	50,728	63,599	62,924	63,369	62,062	62,500	7,745	8,807	9,373	9,726	8,787	9,746
Maryland	221,952	305,358	307,345	302,485	294,381	296,683	51,793	72,609	72,752	72,011	69,390	68,914
Massachusetts	320,012	377,241	376,515	381,253	380,870	378,075	101,130	130,512	132,031	132,866	133,138	132,837
Michigan	480,618	605,990	594,842	575,388	557,770	535,000	87,013	91,775	90,578	88,315	85,822	84,438
Minnesota	254,632	346,864	340,621	335,747	326,325	317,968	38,813	118,585	117,116	115,914	115,166	115,886
Mississippi	123,299	159,262	159,627	155,292	152,076	150,179	14,090	20,733	20,949	21,326	21,558	20,549
Missouri	266,802	367,032	378,421	363,123	359,630	341,640	54,546	77,718	78,573	78,063	78,592	78,260
Montana	38,481	48,446	49,143	48,424	47,903	47,128	3,759	4,836	4,899	4,830	4,874	4,814
Nebraska	96,759	121,430	119,310	115,701	113,432	110,813	15,358	23,262	23,565	23,857	24,511	25,012
Nevada	79,053	116,743	108,998	106,854	105,501	107,961	8,840	12,617	12,015	11,446	11,237	11,244
New Hampshire	51,990	62,442	63,412	66,770	72,706	83,945	9,728	13,097	14,024	15,908	19,734	23,039
New Jersey	284,785	380,060	380,081	376,901	374,073	372,616	51,160	64,032	63,669	63,065	62,866	63,592
New Mexico	96,377	147,976	144,287	141,773	138,898	132,120	14,362	14,576	14,771	14,651	14,557	14,126
New York	839,423	1,059,332	1,075,580	1,070,674	1,065,771	1,063,625	203,972	245,819	242,496	239,010	238,459	235,430
North Carolina	358,912	516,254	515,436	508,495	503,532	498,637	45,740	69,538	69,577	69,770	71,666	71,408
North Dakota	36,899	50,003	49,340	48,196	47,592	46,724	3,349	6,900	7,142	7,046	7,471	7,324
Ohio	469,999	650,546	641,780	619,564	606,625	589,426	79,554	94,569	93,254	90,815	91,022	90,812
Oklahoma	157,021	204,217	203,708	202,092	194,723	189,687	20,995	26,343	26,468	26,400	26,174	25,662
Oregon	160,805	221,825	229,389	225,425	219,454	211,529	22,260	29,883	29,675	29,501	31,652	34,018
Pennsylvania	506,948	664,384	651,257	640,440	630,320	614,990	102,573	140,256	136,703	136,910	135,262	135,661
Rhode Island	65,067	73,974	73,952	73,338	73,256	73,452	10,383	11,136	10,695	10,614	10,204	10,047
South Carolina	161,699	231,375	234,149	233,835	232,089	228,594	24,232	25,689	25,853	25,782	25,755	26,035
South Dakota	37,497	50,605	49,205	49,259	48,190	47,234	5,724	7,755	6,694	6,799	6,939	6,729
Tennessee	230,376	302,248	301,406	295,126	290,530	279,962	33,534	49,514	48,780	48,352	47,667	46,613
Texas	905,649	1,360,528	1,386,966	1,367,078	1,364,096	1,369,947	128,324	175,336	177,242	177,446	177,282	185,515
Utah	149,954	231,721	239,189	239,025	234,683	243,521	13,822	23,932	25,205	28,284	29,572	31,405
Vermont	30,809	38,608	38,182	37,792	37,111	37,375	4,680	6,964	6,961	6,905	6,423	6,608
Virginia	325,395	486,820	495,078	492,564	487,858	481,768	56,498	91,102	94,067	96,144	95,897	96,140
Washington	290,292	351,863	336,893	329,638	327,655	328,957	30,548	36,253	35,946	35,891	35,722	36,236
West Virginia	76,556	128,335	137,314	136,166	132,914	132,805	11,332	24,096	25,033	26,016	25,040	24,247
Wisconsin	271,839	341,698	335,447	329,778	324,121	318,591	35,340	42,483	41,088	39,960	39,900	40,303
Wyoming	26,811	35,466	35,330	35,103	34,423	32,765	3,193	2,832	2,762	2,709	2,661	2,696
U.S. Service Academies	13,475	15,905	15,669	15,202	14,970	14,712	0	20	23	25	27	22
Other jurisdictions	174,410	234,281	237,048	231,395	226,152	227,276	20,223	29,959	30,111	28,580	28,391	28,567
American Samoa	297	2,193	2,091	1,795	1,488	1,276	0	0	0	0	0	0
Federated States of Micronesia	1,576	2,699	2,915	2,744	2,446	2,344	0	0	0	0	0	0
Guam	4,746	5,857	6,009	5,662	6,210	6,187	469	331	351	293	308	301
Marshall Islands	328	869	989	1,123	1,000	1,087	0	0	0	0	0	0
Northern Marianas	1,078	1,137	1,046	1,178	1,109	1,186	0	0	0	0	0	0
Palau	581	694	742	680	646	604	0	0	0	0	0	0
Puerto Rico	163,690	218,312	220,857	215,973	211,110	212,482	19,600	29,415	29,545	28,104	27,905	28,096
U.S. Virgin Islands	2,114	2,520	2,399	2,240	2,143	2,110	154	213	215	183	178	170

NOTE: Degree-granting institutions grant associate's or higher degrees and participate in Title IV federal financial aid programs. Some data have been revised from previously published figures.

SOURCE: U.S. Department of Education, National Center for Education Statistics, Integrated Postsecondary Education Data System (IPEDS), Spring 2001 through Spring 2015, Fall Enrollment component. (This table was prepared October 2015.)

Table 304.80. Total fall enrollment in degree-granting postsecondary institutions, by control, level of enrollment, level of institution, and state or jurisdiction: 2014

State or jurisdiction	Public				Private							
	Undergraduate			Post-bacca-laureate	Undergraduate					Postbaccalaureate		
	Total	4-year	2-year		Total	Nonprofit 4-year	For-profit 4-year	Nonprofit 2-year	For-profit 2-year	Total	Nonprofit 4-year	For-profit 4-year
1	2	3	4	5	6	7	8	9	10	11	12	13
United States	13,244,837	6,847,072	6,397,765	1,410,178	4,047,950	2,740,976	990,254	30,365	286,355	1,504,404	1,224,748	279,656
Alabama	212,458	129,916	82,542	34,531	47,172	21,160	22,714	518	2,780	10,867	4,354	6,513
Alaska	27,588	26,456	1,132	2,304	4,175	372	3,256	68	479	264	253	11
Arizona	325,609	125,301	200,308	29,388	236,840	4,569	222,900	0	9,371	82,909	5,285	77,624
Arkansas	135,303	81,890	53,413	16,096	15,829	14,136	976	656	61	2,343	2,203	140
California	2,060,715	599,702	1,461,013	106,729	365,925	169,008	136,260	1,864	58,793	163,046	136,599	26,447
Colorado	232,636	143,484	89,152	35,405	61,945	21,585	30,972	0	9,388	23,841	12,787	11,054
Connecticut	108,641	53,487	55,154	13,662	57,184	48,679	8,505	0	0	22,441	21,717	724
Delaware	36,898	22,963	13,935	4,114	11,492	11,070	237	185	0	7,864	7,766	98
District of Columbia	4,491	4,491	0	624	43,665	39,370	4,058	22	215	41,273	39,110	2,163
Florida	730,317	687,648	42,669	65,311	254,038	127,491	91,217	1,572	33,758	61,352	52,868	8,484
Georgia	372,283	247,004	125,279	41,469	87,883	51,820	27,329	465	8,269	29,369	20,977	8,392
Hawaii	51,109	23,958	27,151	5,943	13,958	10,215	1,839	0	1,904	2,495	1,754	741
Idaho	69,581	44,437	25,144	7,225	41,381	39,913	974	0	494	766	749	17
Illinois	480,483	144,381	336,102	48,979	195,768	136,222	53,353	735	5,458	99,750	85,694	14,056
Indiana	289,939	198,760	91,179	38,503	90,936	73,466	12,876	400	4,194	16,949	16,658	291
Iowa	154,952	61,389	93,563	14,944	88,439	43,737	44,139	0	563	24,147	12,377	11,770
Kansas	161,526	80,193	81,333	21,696	36,343	20,492	13,672	428	1,751	6,836	5,137	1,699
Kentucky	190,092	103,533	86,559	22,951	38,975	28,221	8,671	0	2,083	12,179	10,804	1,375
Louisiana	188,271	116,728	71,543	22,672	27,018	18,677	2,381	636	5,324	7,977	7,739	238
Maine	44,889	26,710	18,179	3,963	17,611	15,392	1,502	288	429	5,783	5,712	71
Maryland	262,022	128,285	133,737	43,134	34,661	28,098	4,129	0	2,434	25,780	24,724	1,056
Massachusetts	199,096	97,513	101,583	27,062	178,979	173,347	3,334	1,093	1,205	105,775	105,605	170
Michigan	449,024	248,824	200,200	65,688	85,976	80,187	4,748	0	1,041	18,750	18,180	570
Minnesota	235,515	110,160	125,355	24,180	82,453	49,566	31,853	69	965	91,706	21,275	70,431
Mississippi	137,021	64,037	72,984	15,075	13,158	11,019	208	0	1,931	5,474	5,357	117
Missouri	224,164	124,561	99,603	28,816	117,476	99,675	10,681	1,138	5,982	49,444	48,958	486
Montana	42,376	33,744	8,632	4,648	4,752	4,257	0	495	0	166	166	0
Nebraska	85,923	45,935	39,988	13,898	24,890	22,551	1,870	149	320	11,114	11,007	107
Nevada	98,191	87,085	11,106	7,837	9,770	858	4,155	0	4,757	3,407	2,904	503
New Hampshire	39,105	24,066	15,039	4,193	44,840	42,537	2,159	144	0	18,846	18,762	84
New Jersey	313,248	150,411	162,837	38,068	59,368	48,824	6,427	0	4,117	25,524	25,084	440
New Mexico	125,373	49,776	75,597	12,938	6,747	706	4,563	0	1,478	1,188	862	326
New York	653,867	329,864	324,003	67,980	409,758	361,372	28,359	2,797	17,230	167,450	164,531	2,919
North Carolina	410,954	177,744	233,210	44,224	87,683	71,893	11,964	701	3,125	27,184	23,910	3,274
North Dakota	41,831	34,989	6,842	6,461	4,893	4,100	793	0	0	863	863	0
Ohio	448,069	271,845	176,224	62,175	141,357	112,060	16,197	1,047	12,053	28,637	27,939	698
Oklahoma	161,766	101,661	60,105	20,683	27,921	19,857	3,823	0	4,241	4,979	4,880	99
Oregon	183,412	86,202	97,210	18,233	28,117	21,728	4,102	0	2,287	15,785	15,528	257
Pennsylvania	366,915	232,934	133,981	46,676	248,075	196,194	17,823	8,045	26,013	88,985	88,066	919
Rhode Island	38,660	21,107	17,553	4,105	34,792	34,792	0	0	0	5,942	5,942	0
South Carolina	185,617	89,520	96,097	20,139	42,977	29,975	9,124	793	3,085	5,896	3,784	2,112
South Dakota	38,323	32,087	6,236	5,809	8,911	6,006	2,681	224	0	920	909	11
Tennessee	200,410	114,174	86,236	23,623	79,552	61,610	9,000	758	8,184	22,990	21,044	1,946
Texas	1,220,003	529,711	690,292	145,336	149,944	97,103	26,212	2,587	24,042	40,179	36,980	3,199
Utah	155,207	124,959	30,248	12,509	88,314	80,850	4,584	2,006	874	18,896	17,692	1,204
Vermont	23,340	17,321	6,019	2,303	14,035	13,613	422	0	0	4,305	4,305	0
Virginia	353,725	168,757	184,968	45,634	128,043	88,815	31,203	421	7,604	50,506	45,363	5,143
Washington	289,241	187,101	102,140	23,282	39,716	30,653	4,824	61	4,178	12,954	12,455	499
West Virginia	75,553	56,432	19,121	12,289	57,252	7,432	47,555	0	2,265	11,958	1,247	10,711
Wisconsin	262,773	159,000	103,773	23,953	55,818	45,643	9,630	0	545	16,350	15,883	467
Wyoming	31,620	10,124	21,496	2,696	1,145	60	0	0	1,085	0	0	0
U.S. Service Academies	14,712	14,712	0	22	†	†	†	†	†	†	†	†
Other jurisdictions	71,140	62,039	9,101	6,576	156,136	109,819	15,379	724	30,214	21,991	21,106	885
American Samoa	1,276	1,276	0	0	0	0	0	0	0	0	0	0
Federated States of Micronesia	2,344	0	2,344	0	0	0	0	0	0	0	0	0
Guam	6,118	3,660	2,458	298	69	69	0	0	0	3	3	0
Marshall Islands	1,087	0	1,087	0	0	0	0	0	0	0	0	0
Northern Marianas	1,186	1,186	0	0	0	0	0	0	0	0	0	0
Palau	604	0	604	0	0	0	0	0	0	0	0	0
Puerto Rico	56,415	53,807	2,608	6,108	156,067	109,750	15,379	724	30,214	21,988	21,103	885
U.S. Virgin Islands	2,110	2,110	0	170	0	0	0	0	0	0	0	0

†Not applicable.
NOTE: Degree-granting institutions grant associate's or higher degrees and participate in Title IV federal financial aid programs.

SOURCE: U.S. Department of Education, National Center for Education Statistics, Integrated Postsecondary Education Data System (IPEDS), Spring 2015, Fall Enrollment component. (This table was prepared October 2015.)

Table 305.10.   Total fall enrollment of first-time degree/certificate-seeking students in degree-granting postsecondary institutions, by attendance status, sex of student, and level and control of institution: 1955 through 2025

Year	Total	Full-time	Part-time	Males Total	Males Full-time	Males Part-time	Females Total	Females Full-time	Females Part-time	4-year Public	4-year Private	2-year Public	2-year Private
1	2	3	4	5	6	7	8	9	10	11	12	13	14
1955[1]	670,013	—	—	415,604	—	—	254,409	—	—	283,084 [2]	246,960 [2]	117,288 [2]	22,681 [2]
1956[1]	717,504	—	—	442,903	—	—	274,601	—	—	292,743 [2]	261,951 [2]	137,406 [2]	25,404 [2]
1957[1]	723,879	—	—	441,969	—	—	281,910	—	—	293,544 [2]	262,695 [2]	140,522 [2]	27,118 [2]
1958[1]	775,308	—	—	465,422	—	—	309,886	—	—	328,242 [2]	272,117 [2]	146,379 [2]	28,570 [2]
1959[1]	821,520	—	—	487,890	—	—	333,630	—	—	348,150 [2]	291,691 [2]	153,393 [2]	28,286 [2]
1960[1]	923,069	—	—	539,512	—	—	383,557	—	—	395,884 [2]	313,209 [2]	181,860 [2]	32,116 [2]
1961[1]	1,018,361	—	—	591,913	—	—	426,448	—	—	438,135 [2]	336,449 [2]	210,101 [2]	33,676 [2]
1962[1]	1,030,554	—	—	598,099	—	—	432,455	—	—	445,191 [2]	324,923 [2]	224,537 [2]	35,903 [2]
1963[1]	1,046,424	—	—	604,282	—	—	442,142	—	—	—	—	—	—
1964[1]	1,224,840	—	—	701,524	—	—	523,316	—	—	539,251 [2]	363,348 [2]	275,413 [2]	46,828 [2]
1965[1]	1,441,822	—	—	829,215	—	—	612,607	—	—	642,233 [2]	398,792 [2]	347,788 [2]	53,009 [2]
1966	1,554,337	—	—	889,516	—	—	664,821	—	—	626,472 [2]	382,889 [2]	478,459 [2]	66,517 [2]
1967	1,640,936	1,335,512	305,424	931,127	761,299	169,828	709,809	574,213	135,596	644,525	368,300	561,488	66,623
1968	1,892,849	1,470,653	422,196	1,082,367	847,005	235,362	810,482	623,648	186,834	724,377	378,052	718,562	71,858
1969	1,967,104	1,525,290	441,814	1,118,269	876,280	241,989	848,835	649,010	199,825	699,167	391,508	814,132	62,297
1970	2,063,397	1,587,072	476,325	1,151,960	896,281	255,679	911,437	690,791	220,646	717,449	395,886	890,703	59,359
1971	2,119,018	1,606,036	512,982	1,170,518	895,715	274,803	948,500	710,321	238,179	704,052	384,695	971,295	58,976
1972	2,152,778	1,574,197	578,581	1,157,501	858,254	299,247	995,277	715,943	279,334	680,337	380,982	1,036,616	54,843
1973	2,226,041	1,607,269	618,772	1,182,173	867,314	314,859	1,043,868	739,955	303,913	698,777	378,994	1,089,182	59,088
1974	2,365,761	1,673,333	692,428	1,243,790	896,077	347,713	1,121,971	777,256	344,715	745,637	386,391	1,175,759	57,974
1975	2,515,155	1,763,296	751,859	1,327,935	942,198	385,737	1,187,220	821,098	366,122	771,725	395,440	1,283,523	64,467
1976	2,347,014	1,662,333	684,681	1,170,326	854,557	315,729	1,176,688	807,736	368,952	717,373	413,961	1,152,944	62,736
1977	2,394,426	1,680,916	713,510	1,155,856	839,848	316,008	1,238,570	841,068	397,502	737,497	404,631	1,185,648	66,650
1978	2,389,627	1,650,848	738,779	1,141,777	817,294	324,483	1,247,850	833,554	414,296	736,703	406,669	1,173,544	72,711
1979	2,502,896	1,706,732	796,164	1,179,846	840,315	339,531	1,323,050	866,417	456,633	760,119	415,126	1,253,854	73,797
1980	2,587,644	1,749,928	837,716	1,218,961	862,458	356,503	1,368,683	887,470	481,213	765,395	417,937	1,313,591	90,721 [3]
1981	2,595,421	1,737,714	857,707	1,217,680	851,833	365,847	1,377,741	885,881	491,860	754,007	419,257	1,318,436	103,721 [3]
1982	2,505,466	1,688,620	816,846	1,199,237	837,223	362,014	1,306,229	851,397	454,832	730,775	404,252	1,254,193	116,246 [3]
1983	2,443,703	1,678,071	765,632	1,159,049	824,609	334,440	1,284,654	853,462	431,192	728,244	403,882	1,189,869	121,708
1984	2,356,898	1,613,185	743,713	1,112,303	786,099	326,204	1,244,595	827,086	417,509	713,790	402,959	1,130,311	109,838
1985	2,292,222	1,602,038	690,184	1,075,736	774,858	300,878	1,216,486	827,180	389,306	717,199	398,556	1,060,275	116,192
1986	2,219,208	1,589,451	629,757	1,046,527	768,856	277,671	1,172,681	820,595	352,086	719,974	391,673	990,973	116,588
1987	2,246,359	1,626,719	619,640	1,046,615	779,226	267,389	1,199,744	847,493	352,251	757,833	405,113	979,820	103,593
1988	2,378,803	1,698,927	679,876	1,100,026	807,319	292,707	1,278,777	891,608	387,169	783,358	425,907	1,048,914	120,624
1989	2,341,035	1,656,594	684,441	1,094,750	791,295	303,455	1,246,285	865,299	380,986	762,217	413,836	1,048,529	116,453
1990	2,256,624	1,617,118	639,506	1,045,191	771,372	273,819	1,211,433	845,746	365,687	727,264	400,120	1,041,097	88,143
1991	2,277,920	1,652,983	624,937	1,068,433	798,043	270,390	1,209,487	854,940	354,547	717,697	392,904	1,070,048	97,271
1992	2,184,113	1,603,737	580,376	1,013,058	760,290	252,768	1,171,055	843,447	327,608	697,393	408,306	993,074	85,340
1993	2,160,710	1,608,274	552,436	1,007,647	762,240	245,407	1,153,063	846,034	307,029	702,273	410,688	973,545	74,204
1994	2,133,205	1,603,106	530,099	984,558	751,081	233,477	1,148,647	852,025	296,622	709,042	405,917	952,468	65,778
1995	2,168,831	1,646,812	522,019	1,001,052	767,185	233,867	1,167,779	879,627	288,152	731,836	419,025	954,595	63,375
1996	2,274,319	1,739,852	534,467	1,046,662	805,982	240,680	1,227,657	933,870	293,787	741,164	427,442	989,536	116,177
1997	2,219,255	1,733,512	485,743	1,026,058	806,054	220,004	1,193,197	927,458	265,739	755,362	442,397	923,954	97,542
1998	2,212,593	1,775,412	437,181	1,022,656	825,577	197,079	1,189,937	949,835	240,102	792,772	460,948	858,417	100,456
1999	2,357,590	1,849,741	507,849	1,094,539	865,545	228,994	1,263,051	984,196	278,855	819,503	474,223	955,499	108,365
2000	2,427,551	1,918,093	509,458	1,123,948	894,432	229,516	1,303,603	1,023,661	279,942	842,228	498,532	952,175	134,616
2001	2,497,078	1,989,179	507,899	1,152,837	926,393	226,444	1,344,241	1,062,786	281,455	866,619	508,030	988,726	133,703
2002	2,570,611	2,053,065	517,546	1,170,609	945,938	224,671	1,400,002	1,107,127	292,875	886,297	517,621	1,037,267	129,426
2003	2,591,754	2,102,394	489,360	1,175,856	965,075	210,781	1,415,898	1,137,319	278,579	918,602	537,726	1,004,428	130,998
2004	2,630,243	2,147,546	482,697	1,190,268	981,591	208,677	1,439,975	1,165,955	274,020	925,249	562,485	1,009,082	133,427
2005	2,657,338	2,189,884	467,454	1,200,055	995,610	204,445	1,457,283	1,194,274	263,009	953,903	606,712	977,224	119,499
2006	2,707,213	2,219,853	487,360	1,228,665	1,015,585	213,080	1,478,548	1,204,268	274,280	990,262	598,412	1,013,080	105,459
2007	2,776,168	2,293,855	482,313	1,267,030	1,052,600	214,430	1,509,138	1,241,255	267,883	1,023,543	633,296	1,016,262	103,067
2008	3,024,723	2,427,740	596,983	1,389,302	1,115,500	273,802	1,635,421	1,312,240	323,181	1,053,838	673,581	1,186,576	110,728
2009	3,156,882	2,534,440	622,442	1,464,424	1,177,119	287,305	1,692,458	1,357,321	335,137	1,090,980	658,808	1,275,974	131,120
2010	3,156,727	2,533,636	623,091	1,461,016	1,171,090	289,926	1,695,711	1,362,546	333,165	1,110,601	674,573	1,238,491	133,062
2011	3,091,496	2,479,155	612,341	1,424,140	1,140,843	283,297	1,667,356	1,338,312	329,044	1,131,091	656,864	1,195,083	108,458
2012	2,994,187	2,408,063	586,124	1,387,316	1,115,266	272,050	1,606,871	1,292,797	314,074	1,128,344	642,716	1,137,927	85,200
2013	2,986,596	2,415,925	570,671	1,384,314	1,117,375	266,939	1,602,282	1,298,550	303,732	1,143,870	633,041	1,128,054	81,631
2014	2,925,026	2,381,676	543,350	1,354,494	1,099,039	255,455	1,570,532	1,282,637	287,895	1,170,274	612,106	1,070,700	71,946
2015[4]	2,926,000	—	—	1,341,000	—	—	1,585,000	—	—	—	—	—	—
2016[4]	2,958,000	—	—	1,346,000	—	—	1,612,000	—	—	—	—	—	—
2017[4]	3,018,000	—	—	1,365,000	—	—	1,653,000	—	—	—	—	—	—
2018[4]	3,079,000	—	—	1,390,000	—	—	1,689,000	—	—	—	—	—	—
2019[4]	3,126,000	—	—	1,410,000	—	—	1,716,000	—	—	—	—	—	—
2020[4]	3,162,000	—	—	1,425,000	—	—	1,737,000	—	—	—	—	—	—
2021[4]	3,204,000	—	—	1,443,000	—	—	1,760,000	—	—	—	—	—	—
2022[4]	3,243,000	—	—	1,462,000	—	—	1,782,000	—	—	—	—	—	—
2023[4]	3,282,000	—	—	1,479,000	—	—	1,803,000	—	—	—	—	—	—
2024[4]	3,318,000	—	—	1,496,000	—	—	1,823,000	—	—	—	—	—	—
2025[4]	3,340,000	—	—	1,508,000	—	—	1,832,000	—	—	—	—	—	—

—Not available.

[1]Excludes first-time degree/certificate-seeking students in occupational programs not creditable towards a bachelor's degree.

[2]Data for 2-year branches of 4-year college systems are aggregated with the 4-year institutions.

[3]Large increases are due to the addition of schools accredited by the Accrediting Commission of Career Schools and Colleges of Technology.

[4]Projected.

NOTE: Data through 1995 are for institutions of higher education, while later data are for degree-granting institutions. Degree-granting institutions grant associate's or higher degrees and participate in Title IV federal financial aid programs. The degree-granting classification is very similar to the earlier higher education classification, but it includes more 2-year colleges and excludes a few higher education institutions that did not grant degrees. Alaska and Hawaii are included in all years. Some data have been revised from previously published figures. SOURCE: U.S. Department of Education, National Center for Education Statistics, *Biennial Survey of Education in the United States; Opening Fall Enrollment in Higher Education*, 1963 through 1965; Higher Education General Information Survey (HEGIS), "Fall Enrollment in Colleges and Universities" surveys, 1966 through 1985; Integrated Postsecondary Education Data System (IPEDS), "Fall Enrollment Survey" (IPEDS-EF:86–99); IPEDS Spring 2001 through Spring 2014, Fall Enrollment component; and First-Time Freshmen Projection Model, 1980 through 2025. (This table was prepared April 2016.)

Table 305.20. Total fall enrollment of first-time degree/certificate-seeking students in degree-granting postsecondary institutions, by attendance status, sex of student, control of institution, and state or jurisdiction: Selected years, 2000 through 2014

State or jurisdiction	Total, fall 2000	Total, fall 2010	Total, fall 2011	Total, fall 2012	Total, fall 2013	Fall 2014 Total	Full-time Total	Full-time Males	Full-time Females	Part-time Total	Part-time Males	Part-time Females	Public	Private
1	2	3	4	5	6	7	8	9	10	11	12	13	14	15
United States	2,427,551	3,156,727	3,091,496	2,994,187	2,986,596	2,925,026	2,381,676	1,099,039	1,282,637	543,350	255,455	287,895	2,240,974	684,052
Alabama	43,411	52,990	50,921	52,065	51,563	51,149	45,383	20,145	25,238	5,766	2,735	3,031	43,501	7,648
Alaska	2,432	5,400	4,891	4,474	4,791	4,562	3,226	1,393	1,833	1,336	805	531	3,838	724
Arizona	46,646	76,832	89,062	79,099	74,559	73,047	56,297	24,493	31,804	16,750	8,018	8,732	53,298	19,749
Arkansas	22,695	29,321	29,366	28,830	27,967	27,407	24,835	11,352	13,483	2,572	1,101	1,471	23,817	3,590
California	246,128	402,832	392,410	373,541	395,033	392,472	264,980	120,784	144,196	127,492	65,447	62,045	341,611	50,861
Colorado	43,201	54,594	51,130	47,335	45,129	44,233	34,662	17,042	17,620	9,571	4,435	5,136	36,242	7,991
Connecticut	24,212	32,719	32,307	32,193	32,204	31,550	26,705	12,334	14,371	4,845	2,124	2,721	19,220	12,330
Delaware	7,636	8,947	10,290	9,655	9,549	9,589	8,395	3,538	4,857	1,194	519	675	8,203	1,386
District of Columbia	9,150	10,747	9,822	9,546	9,606	9,978	8,881	3,448	5,433	1,097	344	753	521	9,457
Florida	109,931	176,040	173,010	165,165	163,741	157,545	120,420	52,389	68,031	37,125	16,447	20,678	119,952	37,593
Georgia	67,616	100,140	91,912	88,463	89,407	84,438	68,968	30,435	38,533	15,470	6,583	8,887	68,369	16,069
Hawaii	8,931	10,740	10,407	10,271	10,123	9,613	7,485	3,107	4,378	2,128	1,023	1,105	7,813	1,800
Idaho	10,669	12,668	13,032	14,238	13,292	12,373	10,504	4,821	5,683	1,869	846	1,023	9,421	2,952
Illinois	107,592	114,467	109,223	105,472	102,217	99,528	83,995	40,004	43,991	15,533	7,414	8,119	68,172	31,356
Indiana	59,320	82,406	74,455	71,921	70,008	67,860	57,557	26,889	30,668	10,303	4,842	5,461	50,063	17,797
Iowa	39,564	47,257	44,514	43,608	43,309	40,657	32,991	16,907	16,084	7,666	2,598	5,068	27,900	12,757
Kansas	31,424	33,544	32,773	33,166	32,171	33,786	29,721	14,280	15,441	4,065	1,938	2,127	27,032	6,754
Kentucky	34,140	43,735	41,506	41,506	39,805	38,848	34,293	15,256	19,037	4,555	2,096	2,459	31,722	7,126
Louisiana	45,383	43,144	44,737	42,204	40,977	40,871	35,831	15,297	20,534	5,040	2,565	2,475	35,129	5,742
Maine	9,231	12,203	12,364	12,433	11,748	11,287	9,886	4,675	5,211	1,401	601	800	7,516	3,771
Maryland	35,552	51,104	49,625	48,002	47,459	46,129	34,455	16,283	18,172	11,674	5,099	6,575	38,810	7,319
Massachusetts	66,044	76,857	76,263	76,146	76,628	75,149	66,419	30,867	35,552	8,730	3,805	4,925	36,333	38,816
Michigan	84,998	101,063	99,576	95,588	91,459	89,195	70,620	33,288	37,332	18,575	8,629	9,946	75,295	13,900
Minnesota	63,893	55,723	51,496	49,875	47,957	46,234	39,092	19,203	19,889	7,142	3,191	3,951	34,604	11,630
Mississippi	30,356	37,034	35,624	34,313	34,885	31,416	28,616	12,716	15,900	2,800	1,175	1,625	28,938	2,478
Missouri	48,639	64,381	63,964	60,989	60,906	57,357	50,145	23,003	27,142	7,212	3,447	3,765	42,274	15,083
Montana	7,771	9,959	9,286	8,918	8,924	8,887	7,826	4,003	3,823	1,061	484	577	7,933	954
Nebraska	19,027	19,284	18,143	18,174	18,789	18,372	16,581	7,982	8,599	1,791	796	995	14,852	3,520
Nevada	10,490	18,572	16,659	15,908	16,388	16,337	11,851	5,300	6,551	4,486	2,043	2,443	14,970	1,367
New Hampshire	13,143	13,613	13,439	13,764	14,009	15,312	12,644	5,786	6,858	2,668	1,123	1,545	8,629	6,683
New Jersey	52,233	71,296	67,420	66,910	67,906	66,903	57,771	27,652	30,119	9,132	4,382	4,750	55,608	11,295
New Mexico	15,261	22,353	20,924	20,094	19,581	17,311	14,058	6,454	7,604	3,253	1,605	1,648	16,297	1,014
New York	168,181	197,849	196,562	192,170	190,713	189,350	179,578	85,417	94,161	9,772	4,717	5,055	114,834	74,516
North Carolina	69,343	92,627	91,893	94,541	94,285	92,343	72,576	32,674	39,902	19,767	8,546	11,221	71,988	20,355
North Dakota	8,929	9,073	9,053	9,066	8,833	8,565	8,281	4,399	3,882	284	120	164	7,538	1,027
Ohio	98,823	123,063	113,892	110,651	107,152	103,213	89,693	42,494	47,199	13,520	6,335	7,185	75,488	27,725
Oklahoma	35,094	39,107	38,221	36,815	36,724	36,051	30,020	14,296	15,724	6,031	2,593	3,438	30,723	5,328
Oregon	26,946	35,442	33,663	32,574	31,638	29,612	23,482	10,797	12,685	6,130	2,997	3,133	23,908	5,704
Pennsylvania	125,578	144,184	138,814	132,469	131,399	131,583	115,618	54,481	61,137	15,965	6,819	9,146	76,810	54,773
Rhode Island	13,789	15,698	15,829	15,454	15,494	15,447	13,846	6,283	7,563	1,601	750	851	7,398	8,049
South Carolina	32,353	47,535	48,443	48,307	47,965	47,164	40,211	17,914	22,297	6,953	3,052	3,901	37,640	9,524
South Dakota	8,597	10,074	9,561	9,316	9,253	8,372	7,730	3,943	3,787	642	241	401	7,147	1,225
Tennessee	43,327	59,279	58,720	54,394	54,610	52,846	47,199	20,850	26,349	5,647	2,454	3,193	37,494	15,352
Texas	181,813	228,503	238,066	231,816	238,255	237,857	174,108	79,048	95,060	63,749	30,116	33,633	203,863	33,994
Utah	24,953	35,126	32,712	30,456	27,283	28,221	23,551	9,310	14,241	4,670	2,327	2,343	21,135	7,086
Vermont	6,810	8,242	7,830	7,889	7,671	7,527	6,825	3,499	3,326	702	252	450	4,272	3,255
Virginia	52,661	83,166	83,000	82,243	83,288	81,470	67,104	30,702	36,402	14,366	6,631	7,735	62,477	18,993
Washington	36,287	41,124	41,529	40,976	41,942	42,543	37,972	17,484	20,488	4,571	2,135	2,436	34,901	7,642
West Virginia	15,659	23,020	26,127	25,076	24,828	22,357	16,347	7,839	8,508	6,010	3,289	2,721	14,431	7,926
Wisconsin	53,662	61,249	57,993	56,567	54,162	52,437	44,251	21,277	22,974	8,186	3,601	4,585	42,660	9,777
Wyoming	4,209	6,042	5,851	5,759	5,075	4,681	4,199	2,149	2,050	482	220	262	4,392	289
U.S. Service Academies	3,818	4,359	4,016	3,782	3,936	3,992	3,992	3,057	935	0	0	0	3,992	†
Other jurisdictions	39,609	52,222	54,788	51,838	50,425	50,781	48,271	21,963	26,308	2,510	1,100	1,410	15,710	35,071
American Samoa	297	657	737	545	438	450	322	117	205	128	56	72	450	0
Federated States of Micronesia .	786	653	742	700	481	558	431	214	217	127	56	71	558	0
Guam	770	1,043	1,063	846	792	813	639	268	371	174	79	95	804	9
Marshall Islands	199	240	372	349	260	342	331	174	157	11	5	6	342	0
Northern Marianas	333	360	287	322	284	302	274	112	162	28	15	13	302	0
Palau	147	114	125	236	216	164	117	68	49	47	30	17	164	0
Puerto Rico	36,773	48,672	51,009	48,441	47,609	47,759	45,802	20,893	24,909	1,957	847	1,110	12,697	35,062
U.S. Virgin Islands	304	483	453	399	345	393	355	117	238	38	12	26	393	0

†Not applicable.
NOTE: Degree-granting institutions grant associate's or higher degrees and participate in Title IV federal financial aid programs. Some data have been revised from previously published figures.

SOURCE: U.S. Department of Education, National Center for Education Statistics, Integrated Postsecondary Education Data System (IPEDS), Spring 2001 through Spring 2015, Fall Enrollment component. (This table was prepared February 2016.)

Table 305.30. Number and percentage of degree-granting postsecondary institutions with first-year undergraduates using various selection criteria for admission, by control and level of institution: Selected years, 2000–01 through 2014–15

Selection criteria	All institutions			Public institutions			Private institutions								
										Nonprofit			For-profit		
	Total	4-year	2-year	Total	4-year	2-year	Total	4-year	2-year	Total	4-year	2-year	Total	4-year	2-year
1	2	3	4	5	6	7	8	9	10	11	12	13	14	15	16
	Number of institutions with first-year undergraduates														
2000–01	3,717	2,034	1,683	1,647	580	1,067	2,070	1,454	616	1,383	1,247	136	687	207	480
2005–06	3,880	2,198	1,682	1,638	588	1,050	2,242	1,610	632	1,351	1,240	111	891	370	521
2010–11	4,208	2,487	1,721	1,614	637	977	2,594	1,850	744	1,320	1,238	82	1,274	612	662
2014–15	4,207	2,603	1,604	1,583	664	919	2,624	1,939	685	1,366	1,283	83	1,258	656	602
	Percent of institutions														
Open admissions															
2000–01	40.2	12.9	73.2	63.8	12.1	91.9	21.4	13.3	40.7	14.0	11.7	34.6	36.5	22.7	42.5
2005–06	44.7	18.3	79.3	66.1	13.6	95.4	29.2	20.1	52.4	15.3	13.1	40.5	50.2	43.5	54.9
2010–11	47.2	22.5	83.0	65.6	17.6	96.9	35.8	24.2	64.7	15.5	13.0	52.4	56.9	46.9	66.2
2014–15	52.2	28.5	90.6	65.1	19.3	98.3	44.4	31.7	80.4	16.9	14.4	55.4	74.3	65.5	83.9
Some admission requirements[1]															
2000–01	58.4	85.8	25.1	35.4	87.4	7.1	76.6	85.2	56.3	84.5	86.8	63.2	60.7	75.4	54.4
2005–06	53.4	80.5	18.0	33.6	86.1	4.3	67.9	78.5	40.8	84.2	86.5	57.7	43.2	51.6	37.2
2010–11	50.1	75.6	13.2	34.4	82.4	3.1	59.9	73.3	26.6	84.2	86.7	47.6	34.7	46.2	24.0
2014–15	47.0	70.8	8.3	34.9	80.7	1.7	54.3	67.4	17.1	81.8	85.0	32.5	24.4	33.1	15.0
Secondary grades															
2000–01	34.6	58.7	5.5	23.9	63.4	2.4	43.0	56.7	10.7	60.1	64.1	23.5	8.7	12.6	7.1
2005–06	34.1	57.1	4.2	25.9	68.4	2.2	40.1	53.0	7.4	62.8	66.2	25.2	5.7	8.6	3.6
2010–11	33.3	54.2	3.2	27.8	67.8	1.7	36.7	49.5	5.1	66.1	68.7	26.8	6.4	10.6	2.4
2014–15	34.4	54.1	2.6	29.6	68.7	1.4	37.3	49.0	4.1	66.4	69.4	20.5	5.7	9.3	1.8
Secondary class rank															
2000–01	13.7	24.3	1.0	10.9	30.3	0.3	16.0	21.9	2.3	23.2	25.1	5.9	1.6	2.4	1.3
2005–06	11.3	19.4	0.7	10.4	28.7	0.2	11.9	16.0	1.6	19.3	20.5	6.3	0.7	0.8	0.6
2010–11	8.4	13.9	0.4	9.2	22.9	0.3	7.8	10.8	0.5	15.0	15.8	3.7	0.4	0.7	0.2
2014–15	7.1	11.3	0.3	8.0	18.8	0.1	6.6	8.8	0.6	10.6	11.1	2.4	2.3	4.1	0.3
Secondary school record															
2000–01	45.8	70.3	16.2	29.4	72.9	5.8	58.7	69.2	34.1	73.2	75.5	52.2	29.5	30.9	29.0
2005–06	48.5	73.3	15.9	30.8	78.2	4.2	61.4	71.6	35.4	77.6	79.7	55.0	36.7	44.3	31.3
2010–11	45.9	70.1	10.8	33.0	78.8	3.1	53.9	67.1	21.0	77.1	79.4	42.7	29.8	42.3	18.3
2014–15	43.9	66.2	7.7	33.7	77.9	1.7	50.0	62.1	15.6	74.7	77.7	28.9	23.1	31.7	13.8
College preparatory program															
2000–01	15.5	27.3	1.2	16.2	44.0	1.1	14.9	20.7	1.3	22.1	24.1	4.4	0.4	0.5	0.4
2005–06	15.2	26.4	0.6	17.4	47.1	0.8	13.6	18.8	0.3	22.4	24.3	1.8	0.2	0.5	0.0
2010–11	14.7	24.4	0.6	18.3	45.4	0.7	12.4	17.1	0.5	24.0	25.4	2.4	0.3	0.3	0.3
2014–15	14.3	22.8	0.5	18.7	43.5	0.8	11.7	15.7	0.1	22.4	23.8	1.2	0.0	0.0	0.0
Recommendations															
2000–01	20.4	34.4	3.5	2.7	7.4	0.2	34.4	45.1	9.3	46.6	49.2	22.8	10.0	20.8	5.4
2005–06	19.2	31.9	2.5	2.9	7.7	0.2	31.1	40.8	6.3	49.1	51.5	23.4	3.7	5.1	2.7
2010–11	18.1	29.2	2.1	3.3	8.3	0.1	27.3	36.3	4.7	51.6	53.3	25.6	2.0	2.0	2.1
2014–15	18.0	28.2	1.6	4.6	10.8	0.1	26.1	34.1	3.6	48.3	50.5	14.5	2.1	2.0	2.2
Demonstration of competencies[2]															
2000–01	8.0	12.1	3.0	2.2	5.0	0.7	12.7	15.0	7.1	12.1	12.7	7.4	13.7	29.0	7.1
2005–06	7.0	9.8	3.3	2.3	6.1	0.2	10.3	11.1	8.4	10.2	10.3	9.0	10.5	13.8	8.3
2010–11	5.8	8.0	2.5	1.8	4.6	0.0	8.2	9.2	5.8	8.9	8.8	9.8	7.6	10.1	5.3
2014–15	4.0	5.6	1.5	1.6	3.8	0.0	5.5	6.2	3.5	7.8	7.8	8.4	3.0	3.2	2.8
Test scores[3]															
2000–01	47.2	72.5	16.7	33.2	83.4	5.8	58.5	68.2	35.6	70.3	73.4	41.9	34.6	36.7	33.8
2005–06	36.5	62.5	2.6	31.1	82.3	2.4	40.5	55.2	3.0	65.7	70.5	12.6	2.2	4.1	1.0
2010–11	31.3	51.6	1.9	30.4	73.9	1.9	31.8	43.9	1.7	61.7	64.9	13.4	0.9	1.6	0.3
2014–15	30.9	49.3	1.1	32.5	75.6	1.3	30.0	40.3	0.9	57.2	60.4	7.2	0.5	0.9	0.0
TOEFL[4]															
2000–01	43.4	71.2	9.9	30.2	77.4	4.6	54.0	68.7	19.2	66.2	70.1	30.9	29.3	60.4	15.8
2005–06	41.5	67.9	7.1	31.0	79.3	3.9	49.3	63.8	12.3	67.0	70.6	27.0	22.4	41.1	9.2
2010–11	38.7	61.9	5.1	29.9	71.6	2.7	44.1	58.6	8.2	66.3	69.1	24.4	21.2	37.4	6.2
2014–15	36.4	57.0	2.9	29.9	69.1	1.5	40.3	52.9	4.7	62.7	65.9	13.3	16.0	27.4	3.5
No admission requirements, only recommendations for admission															
2000–01	1.4	1.2	1.7	0.8	0.5	0.9	1.9	1.5	2.9	1.5	1.4	2.2	2.8	1.9	3.1
2005–06	1.8	1.1	2.7	0.3	0.3	0.3	2.9	1.4	6.8	0.5	0.4	1.8	6.6	4.9	7.9
2010–11	2.6	1.8	3.8	0.0	0.0	0.0	4.3	2.5	8.7	0.3	0.3	0.0	8.4	6.9	9.8
2014–15	0.8	0.7	1.1	0.0	0.0	0.0	1.3	0.9	2.5	1.3	0.6	12.0	1.3	1.4	1.2

[1]Many institutions have more than one admission requirement.
[2]Formal demonstration of competencies (e.g., portfolios, certificates of mastery, assessment instruments).
[3]Includes SAT, ACT, or other admission tests.
[4]Test of English as a Foreign Language.

NOTE: Degree-granting institutions grant associate's or higher degrees and participate in Title IV federal financial aid programs. Excludes institutions not enrolling any first-time degree/certificate-seeking undergraduates. Detail may not sum to totals because of rounding.
SOURCE: U.S. Department of Education, National Center for Education Statistics, Integrated Postsecondary Education Data System (IPEDS), Fall 2000 through Fall 2010, Institutional Characteristics component; and Winter 2014–15, Admissions component. (This table was prepared December 2015.)

Table 305.40. Acceptance rates; number of applications, admissions, and enrollees; and enrollees' SAT and ACT scores for degree-granting postsecondary institutions with first-year undergraduates, by control and level of institution: 2014–15

Acceptance rates, applications, admissions, enrollees, and SAT and ACT scores	All institutions: Total	All institutions: 4-year	All institutions: 2-year	Public: Total	Public: 4-year	Public: 2-year	Private Total	Private 4-year	Private 2-year	Private Nonprofit Total	Private Nonprofit 4-year	Private Nonprofit 2-year	Private For-profit Total	Private For-profit 4-year	Private For-profit 2-year
1	2	3	4	5	6	7	8	9	10	11	12	13	14	15	16
Number of institutions reporting application data[1]	4,193	2,590	1,603	1,583	664	919	2,610	1,926	684	1,353	1,271	82	1,257	655	602
Percentage distribution of institutions by their acceptance of applications	100.0	100.0	100.0	100.0	100.0	100.0	100.0	100.0	100.0	100.0	100.0	100.0	100.0	100.0	99.8
No application criteria	52.4	28.7	90.7	65.1	19.3	98.3	44.7	31.9	80.6	17.1	14.6	56.1	74.4	65.6	83.9
90 percent or more accepted	8.0	10.7	3.7	3.5	7.7	0.4	10.8	11.7	8.2	10.3	10.6	6.1	11.3	13.9	8.5
75.0 to 89.9 percent accepted	11.5	17.3	2.2	10.4	24.7	0.1	12.2	14.7	5.0	16.4	16.9	8.5	7.6	10.5	4.5
50.0 to 74.9 percent accepted	19.5	30.2	2.2	15.1	34.8	0.9	22.1	28.6	3.9	37.5	38.9	15.9	5.5	8.4	2.3
25.0 to 49.9 percent accepted	6.8	10.5	0.9	5.1	12.0	0.1	7.9	10.0	1.9	14.3	14.6	11.0	0.9	1.1	0.7
10.0 to 24.9 percent accepted	1.4	2.1	0.3	0.6	1.2	0.2	1.9	2.4	0.4	3.4	3.5	2.4	0.3	0.0	0.0
Less than 10 percent accepted	0.3	0.5	0.0	0.1	0.3	0.0	0.5	0.6	0.0	0.9	0.9	0.0	0.0	0.0	0.0
Number of applications (in thousands)	9,586	9,518	68	5,292	5,260	33	4,293	4,259	35	4,184	4,170	13	110	88	21
Percentage distribution of applications by institutions' acceptance of applications	100.0	100.0	100.0	100.0	100.0	100.0	100.0	100.0	100.0	100.0	100.0	100.0	100.0	100.0	99.9
No application criteria	†	†	39.3	†	†	44.5	†	†	34.5	†	†	16.8	†	†	†
90 percent or more accepted	3.7	3.4	12.3	4.2	4.0	1.6	3.0	2.7	22.4	2.4	2.4	8.4	23.7	18.4	45.7
75.0 to 89.9 percent accepted	17.8	17.8	31.7	20.1	20.2	42.4	14.9	14.8	21.7	14.5	14.5	31.4	29.6	29.2	31.2
50.0 to 74.9 percent accepted	42.3	42.4	9.8	45.9	45.9	2.9	37.9	38.1	16.3	37.9	37.9	30.3	38.9	44.6	15.5
25.0 to 49.9 percent accepted	25.2	25.3	6.8	25.7	25.8	8.6	24.7	24.8	5.1	25.1	25.1	13.1	7.6	7.6	7.4
10.0 to 24.9 percent accepted	8.0	8.0	0.0	3.5	3.5	0.0	13.6	13.7	0.0	13.9	13.9	0.0	0.1	0.1	0.0
Less than 10 percent accepted	3.0	3.0	0.0	0.6	0.6	0.0	6.0	6.0	0.0	6.1	6.1	0.0	0.0	0.0	0.0
Number of admissions (in thousands)	5,357	5,308	49	3,162	3,138	24	2,195	2,169	26	2,114	2,106	8	81	63	18
Percentage distribution of admissions by institutions' acceptance of applications	100.0	100.0	100.0	100.0	100.0	100.0	100.0	100.0	100.0	100.0	100.0	100.0	100.0	100.0	100.0
No application criteria	†	†	53.2	†	†	61.7	†	†	45.5	†	†	27.7	†	†	†
90 percent or more accepted	6.2	5.8	14.2	6.7	6.2	1.7	5.5	5.1	25.7	4.6	4.5	11.3	30.9	24.6	53.3
75.0 to 89.9 percent accepted	25.7	25.8	25.0	27.3	27.5	32.1	23.3	23.3	18.4	23.0	23.0	33.9	33.1	33.4	32.0
50.0 to 74.9 percent accepted	47.5	47.8	5.5	48.1	48.2	1.6	46.8	47.2	9.1	47.4	47.4	22.7	32.1	37.9	11.6
25.0 to 49.9 percent accepted	17.7	17.8	2.1	16.8	16.9	2.8	19.0	19.1	1.4	19.6	19.6	4.4	3.9	4.2	3.1
10.0 to 24.9 percent accepted	2.4	2.4	0.0	1.0	1.0	0.0	4.5	4.5	0.0	4.6	4.6	0.0	0.0	0.0	0.0
Less than 10 percent accepted	0.4	0.4	0.0	0.1	0.1	0.0	0.8	0.8	0.0	0.9	0.9	0.0	0.0	0.0	0.0
Number of enrollees (in thousands)	1,556	1,528	27	1,028	1,014	14	528	514	13	492	488	4	36	26	10
Percentage distribution of enrollees by institutions' acceptance of applications	100.0	100.0	100.0	100.0	100.0	100.0	100.0	100.0	100.0	100.0	100.0	100.0	100.0	100.0	100.0
No application criteria	†	†	49.3	†	†	57.5	†	†	40.6	†	†	12.6	†	†	†
90 percent or more accepted	7.6	6.8	14.2	7.6	6.9	1.1	7.4	6.6	28.2	5.5	5.5	17.6	33.5	26.9	51.4
75.0 to 89.9 percent accepted	25.8	26.0	27.7	28.4	28.8	36.1	20.6	20.4	18.8	19.6	19.6	38.4	35.1	36.1	32.2
50.0 to 74.9 percent accepted	45.5	45.8	6.4	47.3	47.4	1.9	41.9	42.5	11.1	43.0	43.1	27.0	25.8	31.1	11.3
25.0 to 49.9 percent accepted	16.7	16.8	2.4	15.0	15.2	3.5	19.8	20.1	1.3	20.9	20.8	4.5	5.6	5.9	5.0
10.0 to 24.9 percent accepted	3.6	3.6	0.0	1.4	1.3	0.0	7.9	8.1	0.0	8.5	8.5	0.0	#	#	#
Less than 10 percent accepted	0.9	0.9	0.0	0.2	0.2	0.0	2.3	2.4	0.0	2.5	2.5	0.0	0.0	0.0	0.0
SAT scores of enrollees															
Critical reading, 25th percentile[2]	469	470	393	459	460	415	475	476	360	475	476	360	445	445	‡
Critical reading, 75th percentile[2]	577	579	489	566	568	511	584	585	456	585	586	456	553	553	‡
Mathematics, 25th percentile[2]	476	477	398	472	473	421	479	480	364	480	480	364	437	437	‡
Mathematics, 75th percentile[2]	586	587	498	580	581	515	589	590	473	590	591	473	560	560	‡
ACT scores of enrollees															
Composite, 25th percentile[2]	20.4	20.5	16.2	19.9	19.9	16.6	20.8	20.8	15.0	20.8	20.8	15.0	16.8	16.8	‡
Composite, 75th percentile[2]	25.5	25.6	20.6	24.9	24.9	21.3	26.0	26.0	18.8	26.0	26.0	18.8	24.0	24.0	‡
English, 25th percentile[2]	19.5	19.5	14.3	18.8	18.9	15.0	19.9	19.9	13.0	19.9	20.0	13.0	18.0	18.0	‡
English, 75th percentile[2]	25.8	25.9	20.2	25.0	25.0	21.6	26.3	26.4	17.8	26.4	26.4	17.8	26.0	26.0	‡
Mathematics, 25th percentile[2]	19.4	19.5	15.7	19.0	19.1	16.1	19.7	19.7	15.0	19.7	19.7	15.0	18.8	18.8	‡
Mathematics, 75th percentile[2]	25.4	25.5	20.4	24.9	25.0	21.6	25.7	25.8	18.4	25.7	25.8	18.4	24.8	24.8	‡

†Not applicable.

#Rounds to zero.

‡Reporting standards not met (too few cases).

[1]The total on this table differs slightly from other counts of institutions with first-year undergraduates because approximately 0.3 percent of these institutions did not report application information.

[2]Data are only for institutions that require test scores for admission. Relatively few 2-year institutions require test scores for admission. The SAT Critical reading and Mathematics scales range from 200 to 800. The ACT Composite, English, and Mathematics scales range from 1 to 36.

NOTE: Degree-granting institutions grant associate's or higher degrees and participate in Title IV federal financial aid programs. Excludes institutions not enrolling any first-time degree/certificate-seeking undergraduates. Detail may not sum to totals because of rounding.

SOURCE: U.S. Department of Education, National Center for Education Statistics, Integrated Postsecondary Education Data System (IPEDS), Winter 2014–15, Admissions component. (This table was prepared December 2015.)

Table 306.10. Total fall enrollment in degree-granting postsecondary institutions, by level of enrollment, sex, attendance status, and race/ethnicity of student: Selected years, 1976 through 2014

Level of enrollment, sex, attendance status, and race/ethnicity of student	Fall enrollment (in thousands)											Percentage distribution of U.S. residents										
	1976	1980	1990	2000	2005	2009	2010	2011	2012	2013	2014	1976	1980	1990	2000	2005	2009	2010	2011	2012	2013	2014
1	2	3	4	5	6	7	8	9	10	11	12	13	14	15	16	17	18	19	20	21	22	23
All students, total	10,985.6	12,086.8	13,818.6	15,312.3	17,487.5	20,313.6	21,019.4	21,010.6	20,644.5	20,375.8	20,207.4	100.0	100.0	100.0	100.0	100.0	100.0	100.0	100.0	100.0	100.0	100.0
White	9,076.1	9,833.0	10,722.5	10,462.1	11,495.4	12,668.9	12,720.8	12,401.9	11,982.2	11,590.7	11,237.4	84.3	83.5	79.9	70.8	68.0	64.5	62.6	61.2	60.3	59.3	58.3
Total, selected races/ethnicities	1,690.8	1,948.8	2,704.7	4,321.5	5,407.2	6,962.5	7,591.0	7,868.2	7,878.7	7,944.8	8,051.0	15.7	16.5	20.1	29.2	32.0	35.5	37.4	38.8	39.7	40.7	41.7
Black	1,033.0	1,106.8	1,247.0	1,730.3	2,214.6	2,883.9	3,039.0	3,079.2	2,962.4	2,872.1	2,791.9	9.6	9.4	9.3	11.7	13.1	14.7	15.0	15.2	14.9	14.7	14.5
Hispanic	383.8	471.7	782.4	1,461.8	1,882.0	2,537.4	2,748.8	2,893.0	2,980.3	2,891.1	3,191.7	3.6	4.0	5.8	9.9	11.1	12.9	13.5	14.3	15.0	15.8	16.5
Asian/Pacific Islander	197.9	286.4	572.4	978.2	1,134.4	1,335.3	1,281.6	1,277.0	1,258.2	1,259.6	1,272.4	1.8	2.4	4.3	6.6	6.7	6.8	6.3	6.3	6.3	6.4	6.6
Asian	—	—	—	—	—	—	1,217.6	1,211.0	1,194.7	1,198.5	1,213.6	—	—	—	—	—	—	6.0	6.0	6.0	6.1	6.3
Pacific Islander	—	—	—	—	—	—	64.0	66.0	63.5	61.1	58.8	—	—	—	—	—	—	0.3	0.3	0.3	0.3	0.3
American Indian/Alaska Native	76.1	83.9	102.8	151.2	176.3	205.9	196.2	186.2	173.0	162.6	152.9	0.7	0.7	0.8	1.0	1.0	1.0	1.0	0.9	0.9	0.8	0.8
Two or more races	—	—	—	—	—	—	325.4	432.7	504.8	559.4	642.1	†	†	†	†	†	†	1.6	2.1	2.5	2.9	3.3
Nonresident alien	218.7	305.0	391.5	528.7	584.8	682.2	707.7	740.5	783.6	840.3	918.9											
Male	5,794.4	5,868.1	6,283.9	6,721.8	7,455.9	8,733.0	9,045.8	9,034.3	8,919.0	8,860.8	8,797.1	100.0	100.0	100.0	100.0	100.0	100.0	100.0	100.0	100.0	100.0	100.0
White	4,813.7	4,772.9	4,861.0	4,634.6	5,007.2	5,572.8	5,605.8	5,457.2	5,285.3	5,133.1	4,973.7	85.3	84.4	80.5	72.1	70.1	66.6	64.7	63.2	62.2	61.1	60.0
Total, selected races/ethnicities	826.6	884.4	1,176.6	1,789.8	2,139.2	2,794.6	3,060.3	3,177.9	3,208.6	3,267.6	3,312.9	14.7	15.6	19.5	27.9	29.9	33.4	35.3	36.8	37.8	38.9	40.0
Black	469.9	463.7	484.7	635.3	774.1	1,028.1	1,089.0	1,107.8	1,079.1	1,065.0	1,034.7	8.3	8.0	8.0	9.8	10.8	12.7	12.6	12.7	12.7	12.7	12.5
Hispanic	209.7	231.6	353.9	627.1	774.6	1,063.0	1,157.6	1,215.8	1,254.6	1,306.5	1,347.9	3.7	4.1	5.9	9.8	10.8	12.7	13.4	14.1	14.8	15.6	16.3
Asian/Pacific Islander	108.4	151.3	294.9	465.9	522.0	620.7	600.6	600.7	593.1	594.3	599.2	1.9	2.7	4.9	7.3	7.3	7.4	6.9	7.0	7.0	7.1	7.2
Asian	—	—	—	—	—	—	571.2	571.6	564.7	567.0	573.0	—	—	—	—	—	—	6.6	6.6	6.6	6.7	6.9
Pacific Islander	—	—	—	—	—	—	28.5	29.1	28.4	27.3	26.3	—	—	—	—	—	—	0.3	0.3	0.3	0.3	0.3
American Indian/Alaska Native	38.5	37.8	43.1	61.4	68.4	82.8	78.7	73.8	68.7	64.8	61.3	0.7	0.7	0.7	1.0	1.0	1.0	0.9	0.9	0.8	0.8	0.7
Two or more races	—	—	—	—	—	—	134.4	179.8	213.2	236.9	269.7	†	†	†	†	†	†	1.6	2.1	2.5	2.8	3.3
Nonresident alien	154.1	210.8	246.3	297.3	309.5	365.6	379.6	399.1	425.1	460.1	510.5											
Female	5,191.2	6,218.7	7,534.7	8,590.5	10,031.6	11,580.6	11,973.7	11,976.3	11,725.5	11,515.0	11,410.3	100.0	100.0	100.0	100.0	100.0	100.0	100.0	100.0	100.0	100.0	100.0
White	4,262.4	5,060.1	5,861.5	5,827.5	6,488.2	7,096.1	7,115.0	6,944.6	6,696.8	6,457.6	6,263.7	83.1	82.6	79.3	69.7	66.5	63.0	61.1	59.7	58.9	58.0	56.9
Total, selected races/ethnicities	864.2	1,064.4	1,528.1	2,531.7	3,268.0	4,167.9	4,530.7	4,690.4	4,670.1	4,677.2	4,757.2	16.9	17.4	20.7	30.3	33.5	37.0	38.9	40.3	41.1	42.0	43.1
Black	563.1	643.0	762.3	1,095.0	1,440.4	1,855.8	1,949.9	1,971.4	1,883.3	1,807.1	1,757.2	11.0	10.5	10.3	13.1	14.8	16.5	16.7	16.9	16.6	16.2	16.0
Hispanic	174.1	240.1	428.5	834.7	1,107.3	1,474.4	1,591.2	1,677.2	1,725.7	1,784.6	1,843.8	3.4	3.9	5.8	10.0	11.4	13.1	13.7	14.4	15.2	16.0	16.8
Asian/Pacific Islander	89.4	135.2	277.5	512.3	612.4	714.6	681.0	676.4	665.1	665.3	673.2	1.7	2.2	3.8	6.1	6.3	6.3	5.8	5.8	5.9	6.0	6.1
Asian	—	—	—	—	—	—	645.5	639.4	630.0	631.5	640.6	—	—	—	—	—	—	5.5	5.5	5.5	5.7	5.8
Pacific Islander	—	—	—	—	—	—	35.5	36.9	35.1	33.8	32.6	—	—	—	—	—	—	0.3	0.3	0.3	0.3	0.3
American Indian/Alaska Native	37.6	46.1	59.7	89.7	107.9	123.2	117.5	112.5	104.4	97.7	91.6	0.7	0.8	0.8	1.1	1.1	1.1	1.0	1.0	0.9	0.9	0.8
Two or more races	—	—	—	—	—	—	191.0	253.0	291.6	325.5	372.4	†	†	†	†	†	†	1.6	2.2	2.6	2.9	3.4
Nonresident alien	64.6	94.2	145.2	231.4	275.3	316.6	328.0	341.4	358.5	380.2	408.4											
Full-time	6,703.6	7,089.9	7,821.0	9,009.6	10,797.0	12,605.4	13,087.0	13,002.5	12,734.4	12,597.1	12,454.0	100.0	100.0	100.0	100.0	100.0	100.0	100.0	100.0	100.0	100.0	100.0
White	5,512.6	5,717.0	6,016.5	6,231.1	7,220.5	8,016.2	8,053.5	7,781.2	7,484.4	7,239.2	6,982.4	84.2	83.4	79.9	72.5	69.8	66.4	64.3	62.7	61.9	60.8	59.7
Total, selected races/ethnicities	1,030.9	1,137.5	1,514.9	2,368.5	3,117.1	4,049.6	4,468.5	4,623.1	4,608.1	4,662.5	4,708.5	15.8	16.6	20.1	27.5	30.2	33.6	35.7	37.3	38.1	39.2	40.3
Black	659.2	685.6	718.3	982.6	1,321.7	1,727.6	1,811.3	1,807.3	1,719.9	1,669.3	1,600.0	10.1	10.0	9.5	11.4	12.8	14.3	14.5	14.6	14.2	14.0	13.7
Hispanic	211.1	247.0	394.7	710.3	979.7	1,350.9	1,501.0	1,593.3	1,631.7	1,700.3	1,748.3	3.2	3.6	5.2	8.3	9.5	11.2	12.0	12.8	13.5	14.3	15.0
Asian/Pacific Islander	117.7	162.0	347.4	591.2	710.1	845.9	820.8	822.1	814.6	821.0	832.1	1.8	2.4	4.6	6.9	6.9	7.0	6.6	6.6	6.7	6.9	7.1
Asian	—	—	—	—	—	—	783.0	782.9	777.7	785.5	798.1	—	—	—	—	—	—	6.3	6.3	6.4	6.6	6.8
Pacific Islander	—	—	—	—	—	—	37.8	39.2	36.9	35.7	34.0	—	—	—	—	—	—	0.3	0.3	0.3	0.3	0.3
American Indian/Alaska Native	43.0	43.0	54.4	84.4	105.6	125.2	118.3	110.8	102.1	94.5	88.0	0.7	0.6	0.7	1.0	1.0	1.0	0.9	0.9	0.8	0.8	0.8
Two or more races	—	—	—	—	—	—	217.2	289.6	339.7	377.2	440.1	†	†	†	†	†	†	1.7	2.3	2.8	3.2	3.8
Nonresident alien	160.0	234.4	289.6	410.0	459.4	539.6	565.2	598.2	641.9	695.3	763.1											
Part-time	4,282.1	4,997.9	5,997.7	6,302.7	6,690.5	7,708.2	7,932.3	8,008.1	7,910.1	7,778.7	7,753.4	100.0	100.0	100.0	100.0	100.0	100.0	100.0	100.0	100.0	100.0	100.0
White	3,563.5	4,116.0	4,706.0	4,231.0	4,274.9	4,652.7	4,667.3	4,620.6	4,497.7	4,351.5	4,255.0	84.4	83.5	79.8	68.4	65.1	61.5	59.9	58.7	57.9	57.0	56.0
Total, selected races/ethnicities	659.9	811.3	1,189.8	1,953.0	2,290.1	2,912.9	3,122.5	3,245.2	3,270.6	3,282.2	3,342.6	15.6	16.5	20.2	31.6	34.9	38.5	40.1	41.3	42.1	43.0	44.0
Black	373.8	421.2	528.7	747.7	892.9	1,156.3	1,227.7	1,272.0	1,242.5	1,202.9	1,191.9	8.9	8.5	9.0	12.1	13.6	15.3	15.8	16.2	16.0	15.8	15.7
Hispanic	172.7	224.8	387.7	751.5	902.2	1,186.5	1,247.9	1,299.7	1,348.6	1,390.8	1,443.4	4.1	4.6	6.6	12.2	13.7	15.7	16.0	16.5	17.4	18.2	19.0
Asian/Pacific Islander	80.2	124.4	225.1	387.1	424.3	489.4	460.8	454.9	443.7	438.0	440.3	1.9	2.5	3.8	6.3	6.5	6.5	5.9	5.8	5.7	5.7	5.8
Asian	—	—	—	—	—	—	434.6	428.1	417.0	413.0	415.5	—	—	—	—	—	—	5.6	5.4	5.4	5.4	5.5
Pacific Islander	—	—	—	—	—	—	26.2	26.8	26.7	25.3	24.8	—	—	—	—	—	—	0.3	0.3	0.3	0.3	0.3
American Indian/Alaska Native	33.1	40.9	48.4	66.8	70.7	80.7	78.0	75.4	70.9	68.1	64.9	0.8	0.8	0.7	1.1	1.1	1.1	1.0	1.0	0.9	0.9	0.9
Two or more races	—	—	—	—	—	—	108.2	143.2	165.0	182.1	202.0	†	†	†	†	†	†	1.4	1.8	2.1	2.4	2.7
Nonresident alien	58.7	70.6	101.8	118.7	125.5	142.6	142.5	142.3	141.7	145.0	155.8											

See notes at end of table.

Table 306.10. Total fall enrollment in degree-granting postsecondary institutions, by level of enrollment, sex, attendance status, and race/ethnicity of student: Selected years, 1976 through 2014—Continued

Level of enrollment, sex, attendance status, and race/ethnicity of student	Fall enrollment (in thousands)											Percentage distribution of U.S. residents										
	1976	1980	1990	2000	2005	2009	2010	2011	2012	2013	2014	1976	1980	1990	2000	2005	2009	2010	2011	2012	2013	2014
1	2	3	4	5	6	7	8	9	10	11	12	13	14	15	16	17	18	19	20	21	22	23
Undergraduate, total	9,419.0	10,469.1	11,959.1	13,155.4	14,964.0	17,464.2	18,082.4	18,077.3	17,735.6	17,474.8	17,292.8	100.0	100.0	100.0	100.0	100.0	100.0	100.0	100.0	100.0	100.0	100.0
White	7,740.5	8,480.7	9,272.6	8,983.5	9,828.6	10,859.4	10,895.9	10,618.6	10,249.1	9,899.2	9,581.5	83.4	82.7	79.0	69.8	67.1	63.6	61.6	60.1	59.3	58.3	57.2
Total, selected races/ethnicities	1,535.3	1,778.5	2,467.7	3,884.0	4,820.7	6,228.3	6,788.1	7,036.1	7,036.0	7,092.3	7,180.9	16.6	17.3	21.0	30.2	32.9	36.4	38.4	39.9	40.7	41.7	42.8
Black	943.4	1,018.8	1,147.2	1,548.9	1,955.4	2,545.9	2,677.1	2,708.3	2,593.2	2,504.8	2,425.8	10.2	9.9	9.8	12.0	13.3	14.9	15.1	15.3	15.0	14.7	14.5
Hispanic	352.9	433.1	724.6	1,351.0	1,733.6	2,354.4	2,551.0	2,687.9	2,767.7	2,870.2	2,961.9	3.8	4.2	6.2	10.5	11.8	13.8	14.4	15.2	16.0	16.9	17.7
Asian/Pacific Islander	169.3	248.7	500.5	845.5	971.4	1,140.3	1,087.3	1,079.6	1,062.8	1,064.4	1,075.0	1.8	2.4	4.3	6.6	6.6	6.7	—	—	—	—	—
Asian	—	—	—	—	—	—	1,029.8	1,020.2	1,006.2	1,010.1	1,022.7	—	—	—	—	—	—	5.8	5.8	5.8	5.9	6.1
Pacific Islander	—	—	—	—	—	—	57.5	59.4	56.6	54.2	52.3	—	—	—	—	—	—	0.3	0.3	0.3	0.3	0.3
American Indian/Alaska Native	69.7	77.9	95.5	138.5	160.4	187.6	179.1	170.2	157.6	147.8	138.6	0.8	0.8	0.8	1.1	1.1	1.1	1.0	1.0	0.9	0.9	0.8
Two or more races	—	—	—	—	—	—	293.7	390.2	454.7	505.2	579.5	—	—	—	—	—	—	1.7	2.2	2.6	3.0	3.5
Nonresident alien	143.2	209.9	218.7	288.0	314.7	376.5	398.4	422.6	450.6	483.4	530.4	†	†	†	†	†	†	†	†	†	†	†
Male	4,896.8	4,997.4	5,379.8	5,778.3	6,408.9	7,563.2	7,836.3	7,823.0	7,714.9	7,659.6	7,585.9	100.0	100.0	100.0	100.0	100.0	100.0	100.0	100.0	100.0	100.0	100.0
White	4,052.2	4,054.9	4,184.4	4,010.1	4,330.4	4,840.7	4,861.0	4,725.5	4,572.7	4,439.6	4,298.9	84.4	83.5	79.6	71.3	69.2	65.6	63.7	62.1	61.2	60.0	58.9
Total, selected races/ethnicities	748.2	802.7	1,069.3	1,618.0	1,926.6	2,534.2	2,773.8	2,879.8	2,905.0	2,961.6	2,999.6	15.6	16.5	20.4	28.7	30.8	34.4	36.3	37.9	38.8	40.0	41.1
Black	430.7	428.2	448.0	577.0	697.5	930.4	982.9	998.6	969.4	955.4	924.6	9.0	8.8	8.5	10.3	11.1	12.6	12.9	13.1	13.0	12.9	12.7
Hispanic	191.7	211.2	326.9	582.6	718.5	994.5	1,082.9	1,137.8	1,173.7	1,222.9	1,261.4	4.0	4.3	6.2	10.4	11.5	13.5	14.2	15.0	15.7	16.5	17.3
Asian/Pacific Islander	91.1	128.5	254.5	401.9	448.1	533.4	513.4	512.0	505.3	507.4	511.7	1.9	2.6	4.8	7.1	7.2	7.2	—	—	—	—	—
Asian	—	—	—	—	—	—	487.4	485.5	479.7	482.9	488.1	—	—	—	—	—	—	6.4	6.4	6.4	6.5	6.7
Pacific Islander	—	—	—	—	—	—	26.0	26.5	25.6	24.5	23.6	—	—	—	—	—	—	0.3	0.3	0.3	0.3	0.3
American Indian/Alaska Native	34.8	34.8	39.9	56.4	62.5	75.9	72.3	67.9	63.0	59.5	56.0	0.7	0.7	0.8	1.0	1.0	1.0	0.9	0.9	0.8	0.8	0.8
Two or more races	—	—	—	—	—	—	122.3	163.6	193.6	216.3	245.9	—	—	—	—	—	—	1.6	2.2	2.6	2.9	3.4
Nonresident alien	96.4	139.8	126.1	150.2	151.8	188.3	201.5	217.7	237.2	258.4	287.5	†	†	†	†	†	†	†	†	†	†	†
Female	4,522.1	5,471.7	6,579.3	7,377.1	8,555.1	9,901.0	10,246.1	10,254.3	10,020.7	9,815.2	9,706.9	100.0	100.0	100.0	100.0	100.0	100.0	100.0	100.0	100.0	100.0	100.0
White	3,688.3	4,425.8	5,088.2	4,973.3	5,498.2	6,018.6	6,035.0	5,893.1	5,676.3	5,459.6	5,282.6	82.4	81.9	78.4	68.7	65.5	62.0	60.1	58.6	57.9	56.9	55.8
Total, selected races/ethnicities	787.0	975.8	1,398.5	2,266.0	2,894.0	3,694.1	4,014.3	4,156.4	4,131.0	4,130.6	4,181.3	17.6	18.1	21.6	31.3	34.5	38.0	39.9	41.4	42.1	43.1	44.2
Black	512.7	590.6	699.2	971.9	1,257.8	1,615.5	1,694.2	1,709.7	1,623.8	1,549.4	1,501.3	11.5	10.9	10.8	13.4	15.0	16.6	16.9	17.0	16.6	16.2	15.9
Hispanic	161.2	221.8	397.6	768.4	1,015.0	1,359.9	1,468.1	1,550.1	1,594.0	1,647.2	1,700.5	3.6	4.1	6.1	10.6	12.1	14.0	14.6	15.4	16.3	17.2	18.0
Asian/Pacific Islander	78.2	120.2	246.0	443.6	523.2	607.0	573.9	567.6	557.5	556.9	563.3	1.7	2.2	3.8	6.1	6.2	6.2	—	—	—	—	—
Asian	—	—	—	—	—	—	542.4	534.7	526.5	527.3	534.6	—	—	—	—	—	—	5.4	5.3	5.4	5.5	5.6
Pacific Islander	—	—	—	—	—	—	31.5	32.9	31.0	29.7	28.7	—	—	—	—	—	—	0.3	0.3	0.3	0.3	0.3
American Indian/Alaska Native	34.9	43.1	55.5	82.1	98.0	111.7	106.8	102.3	94.6	88.2	82.5	0.8	0.8	0.9	1.1	1.2	1.2	1.1	1.0	1.0	0.9	0.9
Two or more races	—	—	—	—	—	—	171.3	226.6	261.1	288.8	333.6	—	—	—	—	—	—	1.7	2.3	2.7	3.0	3.5
Nonresident alien	46.8	70.1	92.6	137.8	162.9	188.2	196.9	204.9	213.4	225.0	243.0	†	†	†	†	†	†	†	†	†	†	†
Postbaccalaureate, total	1,566.6	1,617.7	1,859.5	2,156.9	2,523.5	2,849.4	2,937.0	2,933.3	2,908.8	2,901.0	2,914.6	100.0	100.0	100.0	100.0	100.0	100.0	100.0	100.0	100.0	100.0	100.0
White	1,335.6	1,352.4	1,449.8	1,478.6	1,666.8	1,809.5	1,824.9	1,783.3	1,733.1	1,691.5	1,655.9	89.6	88.8	86.0	77.2	74.0	71.1	69.4	68.2	67.3	66.5	65.6
Total, selected races/ethnicities	155.5	170.3	237.0	437.5	586.6	734.2	802.8	832.1	842.8	852.5	870.2	10.4	11.2	14.0	22.8	26.0	28.9	30.6	31.8	32.7	33.5	34.4
Black	89.7	87.9	99.8	181.4	259.2	338.0	361.9	370.9	369.2	367.0	366.0	6.0	5.8	5.9	9.5	11.5	13.3	13.8	14.2	14.3	14.4	14.5
Hispanic	30.9	38.6	57.9	110.8	148.4	183.0	197.8	205.1	212.6	221.0	229.8	2.1	2.5	3.4	5.8	6.6	7.2	7.5	7.8	8.3	8.7	9.1
Asian/Pacific Islander	28.6	37.7	72.0	132.7	163.0	194.9	194.3	197.4	195.4	195.2	197.4	1.9	2.5	4.3	6.9	7.2	7.7	—	—	—	—	—
Asian	—	—	—	—	—	—	187.8	190.8	188.5	188.4	190.9	—	—	—	—	—	—	7.1	7.3	7.3	7.4	7.6
Pacific Islander	—	—	—	—	—	—	6.5	6.7	6.8	6.8	6.5	—	—	—	—	—	—	0.2	0.3	0.3	0.3	0.3
American Indian/Alaska Native	6.4	6.0	7.3	12.6	15.9	18.3	17.1	16.1	15.4	14.8	14.3	0.4	0.4	0.4	0.7	0.7	0.7	0.7	0.6	0.6	0.6	0.6
Two or more races	—	—	—	—	—	—	31.7	42.5	50.1	54.2	62.6	—	—	—	—	—	—	1.2	1.6	1.9	2.1	2.5
Nonresident alien	75.5	95.1	172.7	240.7	270.1	305.7	309.3	317.9	333.0	356.9	388.5	†	†	†	†	†	†	†	†	†	†	†
Male	897.6	870.7	904.2	943.5	1,047.1	1,169.8	1,209.5	1,211.3	1,204.1	1,201.2	1,211.2	100.0	100.0	100.0	100.0	100.0	100.0	100.0	100.0	100.0	100.0	100.0
White	761.6	718.1	676.6	624.5	676.8	732.0	744.9	731.8	712.6	693.5	674.8	90.7	89.8	86.3	78.4	76.1	73.8	72.2	71.1	70.1	69.4	68.3
Total, selected races/ethnicities	78.4	81.7	107.4	171.9	212.5	260.4	286.5	298.1	303.6	306.0	313.3	9.3	10.2	13.7	21.6	23.9	26.2	27.8	28.9	29.9	30.6	31.7
Black	39.2	35.5	36.7	58.3	76.6	97.7	106.1	109.3	109.7	109.6	110.1	4.7	4.4	4.7	7.3	8.6	9.8	10.3	10.6	10.8	11.0	11.1
Hispanic	18.1	20.4	27.0	44.5	56.1	68.6	74.7	78.0	80.9	83.6	86.5	2.2	2.5	3.4	5.6	6.3	6.9	7.2	7.6	8.0	8.4	8.8
Asian/Pacific Islander	17.4	22.8	40.4	64.0	73.9	87.3	84.7	86.1	85.0	86.9	87.5	2.1	2.8	5.2	8.0	8.3	8.8	—	—	—	—	—
Asian	—	—	—	—	—	—	82.2	83.5	82.2	84.2	84.9	—	—	—	—	—	—	8.0	8.1	8.1	8.4	8.6
Pacific Islander	—	—	—	—	—	—	2.5	2.6	2.8	2.7	2.7	—	—	—	—	—	—	0.2	0.3	0.3	0.3	0.3
American Indian/Alaska Native	3.7	3.0	3.2	5.0	5.9	6.8	6.4	5.9	5.7	5.3	5.3	0.4	0.4	0.4	0.7	0.7	0.7	0.6	0.6	0.6	0.5	0.5
Two or more races	—	—	—	—	—	—	12.0	16.2	19.6	20.6	23.8	—	—	—	—	—	—	1.2	1.6	1.9	2.1	2.4
Nonresident alien	57.7	71.0	120.2	147.1	157.7	177.4	178.2	181.4	187.9	201.7	223.0	†	†	†	†	†	†	†	†	†	†	†

See notes at end of table.

Table 306.10. Total fall enrollment in degree-granting postsecondary institutions, by level of enrollment, sex, attendance status, and race/ethnicity of student: Selected years, 1976 through 2014—Continued

Level of enrollment, sex, attendance status, and race/ethnicity of student	Fall enrollment (in thousands)											Percentage distribution of U.S. residents										
	1976	1980	1990	2000	2005	2009	2010	2011	2012	2013	2014	1976	1980	1990	2000	2005	2009	2010	2011	2012	2013	2014
1	2	3	4	5	6	7	8	9	10	11	12	13	14	15	16	17	18	19	20	21	22	23
Female	669.1	747.0	955.4	1,213.4	1,476.5	1,679.6	1,727.5	1,722.0	1,704.8	1,699.8	1,703.4	100.0	100.0	100.0	100.0	100.0	100.0	100.0	100.0	100.0	100.0	100.0
White	574.1	634.3	773.2	854.1	990.0	1,077.5	1,080.0	1,051.5	1,020.5	998.0	981.1	88.1	87.7	85.6	76.3	72.6	69.5	67.7	66.3	65.4	64.6	63.8
Total, selected races/ethnicities	77.2	88.6	129.6	265.7	374.0	473.8	516.4	534.0	539.1	546.5	556.9	11.9	12.3	14.4	23.7	27.4	30.5	32.3	33.7	34.6	35.4	36.2
Black	50.5	52.4	63.1	123.1	182.6	240.3	255.8	261.7	259.5	257.7	255.9	7.7	7.2	7.0	11.0	13.4	15.5	16.0	16.5	16.6	16.7	16.6
Hispanic	12.8	18.3	30.9	66.3	92.3	114.5	123.1	127.1	131.8	137.4	143.3	2.0	2.5	3.4	5.9	6.8	7.4	7.7	8.0	8.4	8.9	9.3
Asian/Pacific Islander	11.2	15.0	31.5	68.7	89.1	107.6	107.0	108.7	107.6	108.4	109.9	1.7	2.1	3.5	6.1	6.5	6.9	6.7	6.9	6.9	7.0	7.1
Asian	—	—	—	—	—	—	103.1	104.7	103.5	104.2	106.0	—	—	—	—	—	—	6.5	6.6	6.6	6.7	6.9
Pacific Islander	—	—	—	—	—	—	3.9	4.0	4.1	4.1	3.9	—	—	—	—	—	—	0.2	0.3	0.3	0.3	0.3
American Indian/Alaska Native	2.7	3.0	4.1	7.6	10.0	11.5	10.7	10.2	9.8	9.5	9.0	0.4	0.4	0.5	0.7	0.7	0.7	0.7	0.6	0.6	0.6	0.6
Two or more races	—	—	—	—	—	—	19.7	26.3	30.5	33.6	38.8	—	—	—	—	—	—	1.2	1.7	2.0	2.2	2.5
Nonresident alien	17.8	24.1	52.5	93.6	112.4	128.3	131.1	136.5	145.1	155.2	165.5	†	†	†	†	†	†	†	†	†	†	†

—Not available.
†Not applicable.
NOTE: Race categories exclude persons of Hispanic ethnicity. Because of underreporting and nonreporting of racial/ethnic data, some figures are slightly lower than corresponding data in other tables. Data through 1990 are for institutions of higher education, while later data are for degree-granting institutions. Degree-granting institutions grant associate's or higher degrees and participate in Title IV federal financial aid programs. The degree-granting classification is very similar to the earlier higher educa-tion classification, but it includes more 2-year colleges and excludes a few higher education institutions that did not grant degrees. Some data have been revised from previously published figures. Detail may not sum to totals because of rounding.
SOURCE: U.S. Department of Education, National Center for Education Statistics, Higher Education General Information Sur-vey (HEGIS), "Fall Enrollment in Colleges and Universities" surveys, 1976 and 1980; Integrated Postsecondary Education Data System (IPEDS), "Fall Enrollment Survey" (IPEDS-EF:90); and IPEDS Spring 2001 through Spring 2015, Fall Enrollment com-ponent. (This table was prepared October 2015.)

Table 306.20. Total fall enrollment in degree-granting postsecondary institutions, by level and control of institution and race/ethnicity of student: Selected years, 1976 through 2014

Level and control of institution and race/ethnicity of student	Fall enrollment (in thousands)											Percentage distribution of U.S. residents										
	1976	1980	1990	2000	2005	2009	2010	2011	2012	2013	2014	1976	1980	1990	2000	2005	2009	2010	2011	2012	2013	2014
	2	3	4	5	6	7	8	9	10	11	12	13	14	15	16	17	18	19	20	21	22	23
All students, total	10,985.6	12,086.8	13,818.6	15,312.3	17,487.5	20,313.6	21,019.4	21,010.6	20,644.5	20,375.8	20,207.4	100.0	100.0	100.0	100.0	100.0	100.0	100.0	100.0	100.0	100.0	100.0
White	9,076.1	9,833.0	10,722.5	10,462.1	11,495.4	12,668.9	12,720.8	12,401.9	11,982.2	11,590.7	11,237.4	84.3	83.5	79.9	70.8	68.0	64.5	62.6	61.2	60.3	59.3	58.3
Total, selected races/ethnicities	1,690.8	1,948.8	2,704.7	4,321.5	5,407.2	6,962.5	7,591.0	7,868.7	7,878.7	7,944.8	8,051.0	15.7	16.5	20.1	29.2	32.0	35.5	37.4	38.8	39.7	40.7	41.7
Black	1,033.0	1,106.8	1,247.0	1,730.3	2,214.6	2,883.9	3,039.0	3,079.2	2,964.4	2,872.1	2,791.9	9.6	9.4	9.3	11.7	13.1	14.7	15.0	15.2	14.9	14.7	14.5
Hispanic	383.8	471.7	782.4	1,461.8	1,882.0	2,537.4	2,748.8	2,893.0	2,980.3	3,091.1	3,191.7	3.6	4.0	5.8	9.9	11.1	12.9	13.5	14.3	15.0	15.8	16.5
Asian/Pacific Islander	197.9	286.4	572.4	978.2	1,134.4	1,335.3	1,281.6	1,277.0	1,258.2	1,259.6	1,272.4	1.8	2.4	4.3	6.6	6.7	6.8	6.3	6.3	6.3	6.4	6.6
Asian	—	—	—	—	—	—	1,217.6	1,211.0	1,194.7	1,198.5	1,213.6	—	—	—	—	—	—	6.0	6.0	6.0	6.1	6.3
Pacific Islander	—	—	—	—	—	—	64.0	66.0	63.5	61.1	58.8	—	—	—	—	—	—	0.3	0.3	0.3	0.3	0.3
American Indian/Alaska Native	76.1	83.9	102.8	151.2	176.3	205.9	196.2	186.2	173.0	162.6	152.9	0.7	0.7	0.8	1.0	1.0	1.0	0.9	0.9	0.9	0.8	0.8
Two or more races	—	—	—	—	—	—	325.4	432.7	504.8	559.4	642.1	—	—	—	—	—	—	1.6	2.1	2.5	2.9	3.3
Nonresident alien	218.7	305.0	391.5	528.7	584.8	682.2	707.7	740.5	783.6	840.3	918.9	†	†	†	†	†	†	†	†	†	†	†
Public	8,641.0	9,456.4	10,844.7	11,752.8	13,021.8	14,810.8	15,142.2	15,116.3	14,884.7	14,745.6	14,655.0	100.0	100.0	100.0	100.0	100.0	100.0	100.0	100.0	100.0	100.0	100.0
White	7,094.5	7,656.1	8,385.4	7,963.4	8,518.2	9,232.4	9,182.1	8,938.2	8,636.4	8,364.1	8,119.5	83.5	82.7	79.2	69.8	67.3	64.2	62.5	61.0	60.0	58.9	57.7
Total, selected races/ethnicities	1,401.2	1,596.2	2,199.2	3,446.3	4,130.8	5,137.5	5,507.1	5,706.0	5,748.8	5,847.0	5,947.3	16.5	17.3	20.8	30.2	32.7	35.8	37.5	39.0	40.0	41.1	42.3
Black	831.2	876.1	976.4	1,319.2	1,580.4	1,936.7	1,988.8	2,014.0	1,937.6	1,886.8	1,839.7	9.8	9.5	9.2	11.6	12.5	13.5	13.5	13.8	13.5	13.3	13.1
Hispanic	336.8	406.2	671.4	1,229.3	1,525.6	2,020.4	2,163.8	2,277.6	2,366.8	2,477.5	2,580.4	4.0	4.4	6.3	10.8	12.1	14.1	14.7	15.6	16.5	17.4	18.3
Asian/Pacific Islander	165.7	239.7	461.0	770.5	881.9	1,018.7	968.7	958.5	942.6	944.8	956.3	2.0	2.6	4.4	6.8	7.0	7.1	6.6	6.5	6.6	6.6	6.8
Asian	—	—	—	—	—	—	924.8	915.5	901.2	905.6	918.6	—	—	—	—	—	—	6.3	6.3	6.3	6.4	6.5
Pacific Islander	—	—	—	—	—	—	43.9	43.0	41.4	39.2	37.7	—	—	—	—	—	—	0.3	0.3	0.3	0.3	0.3
American Indian/Alaska Native	67.5	74.2	90.4	127.3	143.0	161.7	150.8	142.5	131.8	124.6	117.8	0.8	0.8	0.9	1.1	1.1	1.1	1.0	1.0	0.9	0.9	0.8
Two or more races	—	—	—	—	—	—	235.0	313.4	370.0	413.4	453.1	—	—	—	—	—	—	1.6	2.1	2.6	2.9	3.2
Nonresident alien	145.3	204.2	260.0	343.1	372.8	440.9	453.0	472.0	499.5	534.4	588.2	†	†	†	†	†	†	†	†	†	†	†
Private	2,344.6	2,630.4	2,973.9	3,559.5	4,465.6	5,502.8	5,877.3	5,894.3	5,759.8	5,630.2	5,552.4	100.0	100.0	100.0	100.0	100.0	100.0	100.0	100.0	100.0	100.0	100.0
White	1,981.6	2,176.9	2,337.0	2,498.7	2,977.3	3,436.5	3,538.7	3,463.6	3,345.7	3,226.6	3,117.9	87.3	86.1	82.2	74.1	70.0	65.3	62.9	61.6	61.1	60.6	59.7
Total, selected races/ethnicities	289.6	352.7	505.5	875.2	1,276.4	1,825.0	2,083.9	2,162.2	2,130.0	2,097.8	2,103.7	12.7	13.9	17.8	25.9	30.0	34.7	37.1	38.4	38.9	39.4	40.3
Black	201.8	230.7	270.6	411.1	634.2	947.2	1,050.2	1,065.2	1,024.9	985.3	952.2	8.9	9.1	9.5	12.2	14.9	18.0	18.7	18.9	18.5	18.5	18.2
Hispanic	47.0	65.6	111.0	232.5	356.4	517.1	585.0	615.4	613.6	613.6	611.3	2.1	2.6	3.9	6.9	8.4	9.8	10.4	10.9	11.2	11.5	11.7
Asian/Pacific Islander	32.2	46.7	111.5	207.7	252.4	316.5	312.8	318.6	315.6	314.8	316.1	1.4	1.8	3.9	5.9	5.9	6.0	5.6	5.7	5.8	5.9	6.1
Asian	—	—	—	—	—	—	292.7	295.5	293.5	293.0	295.0	—	—	—	—	—	—	5.2	5.3	5.4	5.5	5.7
Pacific Islander	—	—	—	—	—	—	20.1	23.0	22.2	21.9	21.1	—	—	—	—	—	—	0.4	0.4	0.4	0.4	0.4
American Indian/Alaska Native	8.6	9.7	12.4	23.9	33.3	44.3	45.5	43.7	41.3	37.9	35.1	0.4	0.4	0.4	0.7	0.8	0.8	0.8	0.8	0.8	0.7	0.7
Two or more races	—	—	—	—	—	—	90.4	119.3	134.7	146.0	189.0	—	—	—	—	—	—	1.6	2.1	2.5	2.7	3.6
Nonresident alien	73.4	100.8	131.4	185.6	212.0	241.3	254.7	268.5	284.1	305.9	330.7	†	†	†	†	†	†	†	†	†	†	†
4-year, total	7,106.5	7,565.4	8,578.6	9,363.9	10,999.4	12,791.0	13,335.8	13,499.4	13,476.6	13,407.1	13,492.9	100.0	100.0	100.0	100.0	100.0	100.0	100.0	100.0	100.0	100.0	100.0
White	5,999.0	6,274.5	6,768.1	6,658.0	7,496.9	8,296.8	8,399.5	8,309.6	8,143.2	7,954.6	7,827.6	86.6	85.7	82.0	74.6	71.4	68.0	66.0	64.6	63.7	62.8	61.8
Total, selected races/ethnicities	931.0	1,049.9	1,486.1	2,266.1	3,009.5	3,912.2	4,328.0	4,545.2	4,643.5	4,704.2	4,842.5	13.4	14.3	18.0	25.4	28.6	32.0	34.0	35.4	36.3	37.2	38.2
Black	603.7	634.3	722.8	995.4	1,313.4	1,730.9	1,840.0	1,879.7	1,845.6	1,799.1	1,778.2	8.7	8.7	8.8	11.2	12.5	14.2	14.5	14.6	14.4	14.2	14.0
Hispanic	173.6	216.6	358.2	617.9	900.5	1,226.3	1,355.5	1,453.5	1,532.6	1,599.9	1,670.8	2.5	3.0	4.3	6.9	8.6	10.0	10.7	11.3	12.0	12.6	13.2
Asian/Pacific Islander	118.7	162.1	357.2	576.3	700.0	839.3	818.5	831.9	834.3	843.9	864.9	1.7	2.2	4.3	6.5	6.7	6.9	6.4	6.5	6.5	6.7	6.8
Asian	—	—	—	—	—	—	782.5	793.2	795.6	806.2	827.5	—	—	—	—	—	—	6.1	6.2	6.2	6.4	6.5
Pacific Islander	—	—	—	—	—	—	36.0	38.7	38.7	37.7	37.4	—	—	—	—	—	—	0.3	0.3	0.3	0.3	0.3
American Indian/Alaska Native	35.0	36.9	47.9	76.5	95.6	115.7	109.0	105.1	98.1	91.6	87.0	0.5	0.5	0.6	0.9	0.9	0.9	0.9	0.8	0.8	0.7	0.7
Two or more races	—	—	—	—	—	—	204.6	275.0	332.9	369.8	441.6	—	—	—	—	—	—	1.6	2.1	2.6	2.9	3.5
Nonresident alien	176.5	240.9	324.3	439.7	493.1	582.1	608.3	644.6	689.9	748.3	822.7	†	†	†	†	†	†	†	†	†	†	†
Public	4,892.9	5,127.6	5,848.2	6,055.4	6,837.6	7,709.2	7,924.1	8,048.1	8,092.6	8,120.4	8,257.3	100.0	100.0	100.0	100.0	100.0	100.0	100.0	100.0	100.0	100.0	100.0
White	4,120.2	4,243.0	4,605.6	4,311.2	4,678.1	5,057.0	5,069.6	5,028.3	4,952.3	4,866.8	4,833.6	86.1	85.1	81.5	74.4	71.4	68.7	67.0	65.6	64.4	63.4	62.3
Total, selected races/ethnicities	666.7	740.8	1,046.2	1,486.4	1,876.9	2,308.3	2,496.8	2,640.2	2,732.0	2,808.8	2,929.1	13.9	14.9	18.5	25.6	28.6	31.3	33.0	34.4	35.6	36.6	37.7
Black	421.8	438.2	495.1	627.8	754.0	896.7	912.6	931.8	922.5	908.9	914.6	8.8	8.8	8.8	10.8	11.5	12.2	12.1	12.2	12.0	11.8	11.8
Hispanic	129.3	156.4	262.5	420.0	595.6	794.9	869.5	945.5	1,007.0	1,063.6	1,133.3	2.7	3.1	4.6	7.2	9.1	10.8	11.5	12.3	13.1	13.9	14.6
Asian/Pacific Islander	87.5	117.2	250.6	381.3	460.1	540.1	522.8	531.4	535.0	544.7	563.4	1.8	2.4	4.4	6.6	7.0	7.3	6.9	6.9	6.9	7.1	7.3
Asian	—	—	—	—	—	—	504.7	512.3	516.1	526.2	544.6	—	—	—	—	—	—	6.7	6.7	6.7	6.9	7.0
Pacific Islander	—	—	—	—	—	—	18.1	19.0	19.0	18.6	18.9	—	—	—	—	—	—	0.2	0.2	0.2	0.2	0.2
American Indian/Alaska Native	28.2	29.0	38.0	57.2	67.2	76.6	69.5	66.2	61.3	58.1	56.0	0.6	0.6	0.7	1.0	1.0	1.0	0.9	0.9	0.8	0.8	0.7
Two or more races	—	—	—	—	—	—	122.4	165.4	206.2	233.4	261.8	—	—	—	—	—	—	1.6	2.2	2.7	3.0	3.4
Nonresident alien	106.0	143.8	196.4	257.8	282.6	343.9	357.8	379.6	408.2	444.9	494.6	†	†	†	†	†	†	†	†	†	†	†

See notes at end of table.

Table 306.20. Total fall enrollment in degree-granting postsecondary institutions, by level and control of institution and race/ethnicity of student: Selected years, 1976 through 2014—Continued

Level and control of institution and race/ethnicity of student	Fall enrollment (in thousands)											Percentage distribution of U.S. residents										
	1976	1980	1990	2000	2005	2009	2010	2011	2012	2013	2014	1976	1980	1990	2000	2005	2009	2010	2011	2012	2013	2014
1	2	3	4	5	6	7	8	9	10	11	12	13	14	15	16	17	18	19	20	21	22	23
Private	2,213.6	2,437.8	2,730.3	3,308.5	4,161.8	5,081.8	5,411.7	5,451.3	5,384.0	5,286.6	5,235.6	100.0	100.0	100.0	100.0	100.0	100.0	100.0	100.0	100.0	100.0	100.0
White	1,878.8	2,031.5	2,162.5	2,346.9	2,818.8	3,239.8	3,330.0	3,281.2	3,190.9	3,087.8	2,994.0	87.7	86.8	83.1	75.1	71.3	66.9	64.5	63.3	62.5	62.0	61.0
Total, selected races/ethnicities	264.3	309.2	439.8	779.7	1,132.5	1,603.9	1,831.2	1,905.0	1,911.4	1,895.4	1,913.5	12.3	13.2	16.9	24.9	28.7	33.1	35.5	36.7	37.5	38.0	39.0
Black	182.0	196.1	227.7	367.6	559.4	834.2	927.4	947.9	923.1	890.1	863.6	8.5	8.4	8.7	11.8	14.2	17.2	18.0	18.3	18.1	17.9	17.6
Hispanic	44.3	60.2	95.7	197.9	304.9	431.3	486.3	508.0	525.6	536.3	537.5	2.1	2.6	3.7	6.3	7.7	8.9	9.4	9.8	10.3	10.8	11.0
Asian/Pacific Islander	31.2	44.9	106.6	195.0	239.8	299.3	295.7	300.6	299.5	299.1	301.5	1.5	1.9	4.1	6.2	6.1	6.2	5.7	5.8	5.9	6.0	6.1
Asian	—	—	—	—	—	—	277.8	280.8	279.5	280.0	282.9	—	—	—	—	—	—	5.4	5.4	5.5	5.6	5.8
Pacific Islander	—	—	—	—	—	—	17.9	19.7	19.8	19.1	18.6	—	—	—	—	—	—	0.3	0.4	0.4	0.4	0.4
American Indian/Alaska Native	6.8	7.9	9.9	19.3	28.4	39.1	39.6	38.9	36.8	33.5	31.0	0.3	0.3	0.4	0.6	0.7	0.8	0.8	0.8	0.7	0.7	0.6
Two or more races	—	—	—	—	—	—	82.2	109.6	126.7	136.4	179.9	—	—	—	—	—	—	1.6	2.1	2.5	2.7	3.7
Nonresident alien	70.5	97.1	127.9	181.9	210.4	238.1	250.6	265.1	281.7	303.4	328.2	†	†	†	†	†	†	†	†	†	†	†
2-year, total	3,879.1	4,521.4	5,240.1	5,948.4	6,488.1	7,522.6	7,683.6	7,511.2	7,167.8	6,968.7	6,714.5	100.0	100.0	100.0	100.0	100.0	100.0	100.0	100.0	100.0	100.0	100.0
White	3,077.1	3,558.5	3,954.3	3,804.1	3,998.6	4,372.1	4,321.3	4,092.3	3,838.9	3,636.1	3,409.8	80.2	79.8	76.4	64.9	62.5	58.9	57.0	55.2	54.3	52.9	51.5
Total, selected races/ethnicities	759.8	898.9	1,218.6	2,055.4	2,397.1	3,050.3	3,263.0	3,323.0	3,235.3	3,240.6	3,208.5	19.8	20.2	23.6	35.1	37.5	41.1	43.0	44.8	45.7	47.1	48.5
Black	429.3	472.5	524.3	734.9	901.1	1,153.0	1,198.9	1,199.5	1,116.9	1,073.1	1,013.7	11.2	10.6	10.1	12.5	14.1	15.5	15.8	16.2	15.8	15.6	15.3
Hispanic	210.2	255.1	424.2	843.9	981.5	1,311.1	1,393.0	1,439.5	1,447.7	1,491.2	1,520.9	5.5	5.7	8.2	14.4	15.3	17.7	18.4	19.4	20.5	21.7	23.0
Asian/Pacific Islander	79.2	124.3	215.2	401.9	434.4	496.0	463.1	445.1	424.0	415.7	407.5	2.1	2.8	4.2	6.9	6.8	6.7	—	—	—	—	—
Asian	—	—	—	—	—	—	435.1	417.8	399.1	392.3	386.1	—	—	—	—	—	—	5.7	5.6	5.6	5.7	5.8
Pacific Islander	—	—	—	—	—	—	28.0	27.3	24.8	23.4	21.4	—	—	—	—	—	—	0.4	0.4	0.4	0.3	0.3
American Indian/Alaska Native	41.2	47.0	54.9	74.7	80.7	90.2	87.2	81.1	74.9	71.0	65.9	1.1	1.1	1.1	1.3	1.3	1.2	1.1	1.1	1.1	1.0	1.0
Two or more races	—	—	—	—	—	—	120.8	157.7	171.9	189.6	200.5	—	—	—	—	—	—	1.6	2.1	2.4	2.8	3.0
Nonresident alien	42.2	64.1	67.1	89.0	91.8	100.1	99.3	95.9	93.7	92.0	96.2	†	†	†	†	†	†	†	†	†	†	†
Public	3,748.1	4,328.8	4,996.5	5,697.4	6,184.2	7,101.6	7,218.1	7,068.2	6,792.1	6,625.1	6,397.8	100.0	100.0	100.0	100.0	100.0	100.0	100.0	100.0	100.0	100.0	100.0
White	2,974.0	3,413.4	3,779.8	3,652.2	3,840.1	4,175.4	4,112.5	3,909.9	3,684.1	3,497.4	3,285.9	80.2	80.0	76.6	65.1	63.0	59.6	57.7	56.1	55.0	53.5	52.1
Total, selected races/ethnicities	734.5	855.4	1,153.0	1,959.9	2,253.9	2,829.2	3,010.3	3,065.8	3,016.7	3,038.2	3,018.2	19.8	20.0	23.4	34.9	37.0	40.4	42.3	43.9	45.0	46.5	47.9
Black	409.5	437.9	481.4	691.4	826.3	1,040.0	1,076.1	1,082.1	1,015.0	977.9	925.1	11.0	10.3	9.8	12.3	13.6	14.8	15.1	15.5	15.1	15.0	14.7
Hispanic	207.5	249.8	408.9	809.2	930.0	1,225.4	1,294.3	1,332.1	1,359.8	1,413.9	1,447.1	5.6	5.9	8.3	14.4	15.3	17.5	18.2	19.1	20.3	21.6	23.0
Asian/Pacific Islander	78.2	122.5	210.3	389.2	421.8	478.7	445.9	427.1	407.6	400.0	392.9	2.1	2.9	4.3	6.9	6.9	6.8	—	—	—	—	—
Asian	—	—	—	—	—	—	420.2	403.1	385.2	379.4	374.0	—	—	—	—	—	—	5.9	5.8	5.7	5.8	5.9
Pacific Islander	—	—	—	—	—	—	25.7	24.0	22.4	20.6	18.9	—	—	—	—	—	—	0.4	0.3	0.3	0.3	0.3
American Indian/Alaska Native	39.3	45.2	52.4	70.1	75.7	85.1	81.3	76.3	70.4	66.5	61.8	1.1	1.1	1.1	1.2	1.2	1.2	1.1	1.1	1.1	1.0	1.0
Two or more races	—	—	—	—	—	—	112.7	148.0	163.8	180.0	191.3	—	—	—	—	—	—	1.6	2.1	2.4	2.8	3.0
Nonresident alien	39.2	60.3	63.6	85.2	90.2	96.9	95.2	92.5	91.3	89.6	93.6	†	†	†	†	†	†	†	†	†	†	†
Private	131.0	192.6	243.6	251.0	303.8	421.0	465.5	443.0	375.8	343.6	316.7	100.0	100.0	100.0	100.0	100.0	100.0	100.0	100.0	100.0	100.0	100.0
White	102.8	145.4	174.5	151.8	158.4	196.7	208.8	182.4	154.8	138.7	123.9	80.3	77.0	72.7	61.4	52.4	47.1	45.2	41.5	41.5	40.7	39.4
Total, selected races/ethnicities	25.3	43.5	65.6	95.5	143.8	221.2	252.7	257.2	218.5	202.4	190.2	19.7	23.0	27.3	38.6	47.6	52.9	54.8	58.5	58.5	59.3	60.6
Black	19.8	34.6	42.9	43.5	74.8	113.0	122.8	117.3	101.8	95.2	88.6	15.5	18.3	17.9	17.6	24.7	27.0	26.6	26.7	27.3	27.9	28.2
Hispanic	2.6	5.3	15.3	34.7	51.4	85.7	98.7	107.4	87.9	77.3	73.8	2.0	2.8	6.4	14.0	17.0	20.5	21.4	24.4	23.5	22.7	23.5
Asian/Pacific Islander	0.9	1.8	4.9	12.7	12.6	17.3	17.2	18.0	16.4	15.7	14.6	0.7	1.0	2.0	5.1	4.2	4.1	—	—	—	—	—
Asian	—	—	—	—	—	—	14.9	14.7	13.9	12.9	12.1	—	—	—	—	—	—	3.2	3.3	3.7	3.8	3.9
Pacific Islander	—	—	—	—	—	—	2.2	3.3	2.4	2.8	2.5	—	—	—	—	—	—	0.5	0.7	0.6	0.8	0.8
American Indian/Alaska Native	1.8	1.8	2.5	4.5	5.0	5.1	5.9	4.8	4.5	4.5	4.1	1.4	1.0	1.1	1.8	1.6	1.2	1.2	1.1	1.2	1.3	1.3
Two or more races	—	—	—	—	—	—	8.1	9.7	8.0	9.7	9.2	—	—	—	—	—	—	1.8	2.2	2.1	2.8	2.9
Nonresident alien	3.0	3.7	3.5	3.8	1.6	3.2	4.1	3.4	2.4	2.5	2.5	†	†	†	†	†	†	†	†	†	†	†

—Not available.
†Not applicable.
NOTE: Race categories exclude persons of Hispanic ethnicity. Because of underreporting and nonreporting of racial/ethnic data, some figures are slightly lower than corresponding data in other tables. Data through 1990 are for institutions of higher education, while later data are for degree-granting institutions. Degree-granting institutions grant associate's or higher degrees and participate in Title IV federal financial aid programs. The degree-granting classification is very similar to the earlier higher educa-

tion classification, but it includes more 2-year colleges and excludes a few higher education institutions that did not grant degrees. Some data have been revised from previously published figures. Detail may not sum to totals because of rounding.

SOURCE: U.S. Department of Education, National Center for Education Statistics, Higher Education General Information Survey (HEGIS), "Fall Enrollment in Colleges and Universities" surveys, 1976 and 1980; Integrated Postsecondary Education Data System (IPEDS), "Fall Enrollment Survey" (IPEDS-EF:90); and IPEDS Spring 2001 through Spring 2015, Fall Enrollment component. (This table was prepared October 2015.)

Table 306.30. Fall enrollment of U.S. residents in degree-granting postsecondary institutions, by race/ethnicity: Selected years, 1976 through 2025

Year	Enrollment (in thousands)									Percentage distribution								
					Asian/Pacific Islander			American Indian/ Alaska Native	Two or more races					Asian/Pacific Islander			American Indian/ Alaska Native	Two or more races
	Total	White	Black	Hispanic	Total	Asian	Pacific Islander			Total	White	Black	Hispanic	Total	Asian	Pacific Islander		
1	2	3	4	5	6	7	8	9	10	11	12	13	14	15	16	17	18	19
1976	10,767	9,076	1,033	384	198	—	—	76	—	100.0	84.3	9.6	3.6	1.8	—	—	0.7	—
1980	11,782	9,833	1,107	472	286	—	—	84	—	100.0	83.5	9.4	4.0	2.4	—	—	0.7	—
1990	13,427	10,722	1,247	782	572	—	—	103	—	100.0	79.9	9.3	5.8	4.3	—	—	0.8	—
1994	13,823	10,427	1,449	1,046	774	—	—	127	—	100.0	75.4	10.5	7.6	5.6	—	—	0.9	—
1995	13,807	10,311	1,474	1,094	797	—	—	131	—	100.0	74.7	10.7	7.9	5.8	—	—	1.0	—
1996	13,901	10,264	1,506	1,166	828	—	—	138	—	100.0	73.8	10.8	8.4	6.0	—	—	1.0	—
1997	14,037	10,266	1,551	1,218	859	—	—	142	—	100.0	73.1	11.0	8.7	6.1	—	—	1.0	—
1998	14,063	10,179	1,583	1,257	900	—	—	144	—	100.0	72.4	11.3	8.9	6.4	—	—	1.0	—
1999	14,361	10,329	1,649	1,324	914	—	—	146	—	100.0	71.9	11.5	9.2	6.4	—	—	1.0	—
2000	14,784	10,462	1,730	1,462	978	—	—	151	—	100.0	70.8	11.7	9.9	6.6	—	—	1.0	—
2001	15,363	10,775	1,850	1,561	1,019	—	—	158	—	100.0	70.1	12.0	10.2	6.6	—	—	1.0	—
2002	16,021	11,140	1,979	1,662	1,074	—	—	166	—	100.0	69.5	12.4	10.4	6.7	—	—	1.0	—
2003	16,314	11,281	2,068	1,716	1,076	—	—	173	—	100.0	69.1	12.7	10.5	6.6	—	—	1.1	—
2004	16,682	11,423	2,165	1,810	1,109	—	—	176	—	100.0	68.5	13.0	10.8	6.6	—	—	1.1	—
2005	16,903	11,495	2,215	1,882	1,134	—	—	176	—	100.0	68.0	13.1	11.1	6.7	—	—	1.0	—
2006	17,163	11,572	2,280	1,964	1,165	—	—	181	—	100.0	67.4	13.3	11.4	6.8	—	—	1.1	—
2007	17,624	11,756	2,383	2,076	1,218	—	—	190	—	100.0	66.7	13.5	11.8	6.9	—	—	1.1	—
2008	18,442	12,089	2,584	2,273	1,303	—	—	193	—	100.0	65.5	14.0	12.3	7.1	—	—	1.0	—
2009	19,631	12,669	2,884	2,537	1,335	—	—	206	—	100.0	64.5	14.7	12.9	6.8	—	—	1.0	—
2010	20,312	12,721	3,039	2,749	1,282	1,218	64	196	325	100.0	62.6	15.0	13.5	6.3	6.0	0.3	1.0	1.6
2011	20,270	12,402	3,079	2,893	1,277	1,211	66	186	433	100.0	61.2	15.2	14.3	6.3	6.0	0.3	0.9	2.1
2012	19,861	11,982	2,962	2,980	1,258	1,195	64	173	505	100.0	60.3	14.9	15.0	6.3	6.0	0.3	0.9	2.5
2013	19,535	11,591	2,872	3,091	1,260	1,199	61	163	559	100.0	59.3	14.7	15.8	6.4	6.1	0.3	0.8	2.9
2014	19,288	11,237	2,792	3,192	1,272	1,214	59	153	642	100.0	58.3	14.5	16.5	6.6	6.3	0.3	0.8	3.3
2015[1]	19,332	11,195	2,853	3,232	1,238	—	—	150	665	100.0	57.9	14.8	16.7	6.4	—	—	0.8	3.4
2016[1]	19,542	11,177	2,915	3,359	1,255	—	—	149	686	100.0	57.2	14.9	17.2	6.4	—	—	0.8	3.5
2017[1]	19,936	11,300	3,009	3,484	1,286	—	—	150	707	100.0	56.7	15.1	17.5	6.5	—	—	0.8	3.5
2018[1]	20,310	11,425	3,087	3,603	1,316	—	—	151	728	100.0	56.3	15.2	17.7	6.5	—	—	0.7	3.6
2019[1]	20,588	11,498	3,145	3,704	1,341	—	—	151	748	100.0	55.8	15.3	18.0	6.5	—	—	0.7	3.6
2020[1]	20,781	11,517	3,195	3,793	1,360	—	—	151	765	100.0	55.4	15.4	18.3	6.5	—	—	0.7	3.7
2021[1]	21,018	11,557	3,251	3,888	1,386	—	—	152	785	100.0	55.0	15.5	18.5	6.6	—	—	0.7	3.7
2022[1]	21,232	11,586	3,297	3,977	1,412	—	—	152	807	100.0	54.6	15.5	18.7	6.7	—	—	0.7	3.8
2023[1]	21,433	11,602	3,346	4,068	1,436	—	—	152	830	100.0	54.1	15.6	19.0	6.7	—	—	0.7	3.9
2024[1]	21,604	11,598	3,388	4,154	1,458	—	—	152	854	100.0	53.7	15.7	19.2	6.7	—	—	0.7	4.0
2025[1]	21,668	11,539	3,410	4,217	1,472	—	—	151	880	100.0	53.3	15.7	19.5	6.8	—	—	0.7	4.1

—Not available.
[1]Projected.
NOTE: Race categories exclude persons of Hispanic ethnicity. Prior to 2010, institutions were not required to report separate data on Asians, Pacific Islanders, and students of Two or more races. Projections for Asian, Pacific Islander, and Two or more races enrollment are not available due to the limited amount of historical data available upon which to base a projections model. Detail may not sum to totals because of rounding. Some data have been revised from previously published figures.

SOURCE: U.S. Department of Education, National Center for Education Statistics, Higher Education General Information Survey (HEGIS), "Fall Enrollment in Colleges and Universities" surveys, 1976 and 1980; Integrated Postsecondary Education Data System (IPEDS), "Fall Enrollment Survey" (IPEDS-EF:90–99); IPEDS Spring 2001 through Spring 2015, Fall Enrollment component; and Enrollment in Degree-Granting Institutions by Race/Ethnicity Projection Model, 1980 through 2025. (This table was prepared March 2016.)

Table 306.40. Fall enrollment of males and females and specific racial/ethnic groups in degree-granting postsecondary institutions, by control and level of institution and percentage of U.S. resident enrollment in the same racial/ethnic group: 2014

Sex, racial/ethnic group, and percentage of U.S. resident enrollment	Total, all institutions	Public institutions								Nonprofit institutions								For-profit institutions		
		Total	4-year						2-year	Total	4-year						2-year	Total	4-year	2-year
			Research university, very high[1]	Research university, high[2]	Doctoral/research[3]	Master's[4]	Baccalaureate[5]	Special focus[6]			Research university, very high[1]	Research university, high[2]	Doctoral/research[3]	Master's[4]	Baccalaureate[5]	Special focus[6]				
1	2	3	4	5	6	7	8	9	10	11	12	13	14	15	16	17	18	19	20	21
All institutions																				
Total enrollment	20,207,369	14,655,015	2,398,724	1,502,013	420,049	2,682,609	1,166,559	87,296	6,397,765	3,996,089	564,781	305,479	322,680	1,586,703	812,195	373,886	30,365	1,556,265	1,269,910	286,355
Sex																				
Male	8,797,061	6,538,934	1,185,722	705,885	176,619	1,134,505	511,573	33,671	2,790,959	1,703,725	279,558	140,245	130,641	622,022	342,277	177,718	11,264	554,402	462,846	91,556
Female	11,410,308	8,116,081	1,213,002	796,128	243,430	1,548,104	654,986	53,625	3,606,806	2,292,364	285,223	165,234	192,039	964,681	469,918	196,168	19,101	1,001,863	807,064	194,799
Race/ethnicity																				
White	11,237,436	8,119,496	1,415,965	919,512	240,388	1,568,640	639,906	49,192	3,285,893	2,445,026	273,442	181,991	177,367	1,032,968	536,353	228,067	14,838	672,914	563,805	109,109
Black	2,791,865	1,839,659	149,761	148,969	95,261	339,292	173,990	7,298	925,088	489,675	33,109	29,269	38,685	214,045	123,402	43,103	8,062	462,531	381,999	80,532
Hispanic	3,191,699	2,580,389	249,177	193,836	42,294	409,015	231,846	7,105	1,447,116	369,010	48,985	27,737	42,931	155,053	62,139	27,924	4,241	242,300	172,741	69,559
Asian	1,213,616	918,572	243,599	75,910	10,975	156,576	47,376	10,149	373,987	243,530	78,117	20,094	24,724	63,779	23,633	32,245	938	51,514	40,330	11,184
Pacific Islander	58,832	37,743	4,563	2,602	389	6,258	4,919	119	18,893	9,875	607	527	820	4,620	2,098	1,110	93	11,214	8,786	2,428
American Indian/Alaska Native	152,911	117,839	9,672	9,931	1,551	18,592	8,759	7,506	61,828	20,624	1,312	774	1,436	7,941	4,128	4,231	802	14,448	11,195	3,253
Two or more races	642,100	453,089	82,398	47,825	11,404	82,866	35,023	2,259	191,314	110,452	18,667	8,418	8,988	40,103	24,160	9,513	603	78,559	70,005	8,554
Nonresident alien	918,910	588,228	243,589	103,428	17,787	101,370	24,740	3,668	93,646	307,897	110,542	36,669	27,729	68,194	36,282	27,693	788	22,785	21,049	1,736
White enrollment, by percentage White																				
Less than 10.0 percent	41,042	34,687	0	2,519	2,287	4,514	6,521	100	18,746	2,469	0	313	6	571	1,158	333	88	3,886	1,881	2,005
10.0 to 24.9 percent	268,802	226,965	14,021	5,758	4,316	39,117	19,268	92	144,393	9,700	0	0	700	4,958	1,784	1,458	800	32,137	19,969	12,168
25.0 to 49.9 percent	1,570,041	1,114,223	130,580	82,829	11,372	146,817	58,992	4,305	679,328	170,339	15,555	8,589	28,306	71,063	25,454	18,134	3,238	285,479	253,440	32,039
50.0 to 74.9 percent	4,763,098	3,272,782	566,996	350,252	121,052	571,003	288,217	27,144	1,348,118	1,200,348	236,339	95,074	93,666	515,265	140,337	115,608	4,059	289,968	250,018	39,950
75.0 to 89.9 percent	4,032,514	3,042,042	679,047	448,564	101,361	713,845	202,059	17,551	879,615	939,207	21,548	78,015	54,689	409,161	312,643	57,646	5,505	51,265	33,479	17,786
90.0 percent or more	561,939	428,797	25,321	29,590	0	93,344	64,849	0	215,693	122,963	0	0	0	31,950	54,977	34,888	1,148	10,179	5,018	5,161
Black enrollment, by percentage Black																				
Less than 10.0 percent	520,489	385,039	86,600	37,247	7,580	79,771	20,179	3,115	150,547	125,218	29,076	13,462	6,739	43,140	22,772	9,736	293	10,232	5,770	4,462
10.0 to 24.9 percent	950,950	672,265	50,933	81,073	33,503	106,917	74,914	3,697	321,228	158,255	4,033	1,166	18,468	90,990	28,293	13,699	1,606	120,430	107,504	12,926
25.0 to 49.9 percent	814,007	491,579	12,228	22,158	8,955	70,049	51,862	131	326,196	115,856	0	5,829	10,172	67,534	18,931	11,182	2,208	206,572	179,794	26,778
50.0 to 74.9 percent	211,774	101,132	0	0	5,798	13,598	5,616	355	75,765	22,047	0	0	0	5,527	9,252	3,972	3,296	88,595	65,419	23,176
75.0 to 89.9 percent	158,661	117,786	0	0	36,271	28,046	12,293	0	41,176	8,442	0	0	0	1,700	4,635	1,843	264	32,433	20,428	12,005
90.0 percent or more	135,984	71,858	0	8,491	3,154	40,911	9,126	0	10,176	59,857	0	8,812	3,306	5,154	39,519	2,671	395	4,269	3,084	1,185
Hispanic enrollment, by percentage Hispanic																				
Less than 10.0 percent	519,717	347,193	76,735	40,867	16,540	67,328	21,949	2,566	121,208	126,786	18,737	6,961	5,908	55,925	26,921	11,564	770	45,738	41,580	4,158
10.0 to 24.9 percent	785,820	569,616	122,565	70,350	12,678	68,701	57,480	3,552	234,290	148,453	26,428	14,144	24,581	50,074	19,898	12,302	1,026	67,751	57,987	9,764
25.0 to 49.9 percent	1,022,780	878,072	49,877	10,522	5,091	181,153	76,286	987	554,156	71,965	3,820	6,632	6,393	38,090	12,342	3,340	1,348	72,743	48,010	24,733
50.0 to 74.9 percent	638,739	584,230	0	53,611	7,985	55,042	47,286	0	420,306	17,714	0	0	6,049	10,150	602	373	540	36,795	12,697	24,098
75.0 to 89.9 percent	134,031	122,724	0	18,486	0	0	0	0	104,238	1,926	0	0	0	814	977	135	0	9,381	5,467	3,914
90.0 percent or more	90,612	78,554	0	0	0	36,791	28,845	0	12,918	2,166	0	0	0	0	1,399	210	557	9,892	7,000	2,892
Asian enrollment, by percentage Asian																				
Less than 10.0 percent	512,809	382,190	82,665	38,249	10,975	56,696	25,883	1,668	166,054	96,873	3,614	12,821	10,800	44,176	17,029	8,001	432	33,746	28,392	5,354
10.0 to 24.9 percent	466,793	340,237	80,054	32,953	0	59,468	17,951	5,780	144,031	114,420	63,479	7,273	11,719	15,171	5,241	11,147	390	12,136	7,966	4,170
25.0 to 49.9 percent	231,884	196,145	80,880	4,708	0	40,412	3,542	2,701	63,902	30,866	11,024	0	2,205	4,325	1,363	11,833	116	4,873	3,399	1,474
50.0 to 74.9 percent	1,105	0	0	0	0	0	0	0	0	600	0	0	0	0	0	549	0	505	319	186
75.0 to 89.9 percent	456	0	0	0	0	0	0	0	0	456	0	0	0	51	0	456	0	0	0	0
90.0 percent or more	569	0	0	0	0	0	0	0	0	315	0	0	0	56	0	259	0	254	254	0

See notes at end of table.

Table 306.40. Fall enrollment of males and females and specific racial/ethnic groups in degree-granting postsecondary institutions, by control and level of institution and percentage of U.S. resident enrollment in the same racial/ethnic group: 2014—Continued

Sex, racial/ethnic group, and percentage of U.S. resident enrollment	Total, all institutions	Public institutions								Nonprofit institutions								For-profit institutions		
		4-year							2-year	4-year							2-year	Total	4-year	2-year
		Total	Research university, very high[1]	Research university, high[2]	Doctoral/research[3]	Master's[4]	Baccalaureate[5]	Special focus[6]		Total	Research university, very high[1]	Research university, high[2]	Doctoral/research[3]	Master's[4]	Baccalaureate[5]	Special focus[6]				
1	2	3	4	5	6	7	8	9	10	11	12	13	14	15	16	17	18	19	20	21
Pacific Islander enrollment, by percentage Pacific Islander																				
Less than 10.0 percent	55,476	36,585	4,563	2,602	389	6,258	4,121	119	18,533	8,948	607	527	820	4,093	1,716	1,092	93	9,943	7,990	1,953
10.0 to 24.9 percent	2,611	1,158	0	0	0	0	798	0	360	794	0	0	0	527	249	18	0	659	319	340
25.0 to 49.9 percent	268	0	0	0	0	0	0	0	0	133	0	0	0	0	133	0	0	135	0	135
50.0 to 74.9 percent	477	0	0	0	0	0	0	0	0	0	0	0	0	0	0	0	0	477	477	0
75.0 to 89.9 percent	0	0	0	0	0	0	0	0	0	0	0	0	0	0	0	0	0	0	0	0
90.0 percent or more	0	0	0	0	0	0	0	0	0	0	0	0	0	0	0	0	0	0	0	0
American Indian/Alaska Native enrollment, by percentage American Indian/Alaska Native																				
Less than 10.0 percent	116,084	86,052	9,672	8,449	1,551	14,093	6,493	483	45,311	16,915	1,312	774	1,436	7,838	3,798	1,657	100	13,117	10,713	2,404
10.0 to 24.9 percent	14,173	12,722	0	1,482	0	4,499	2,266	0	4,475	120	0	0	0	103	0	17	0	1,331	482	849
25.0 to 49.9 percent	6,560	6,287	0	0	0	0	0	0	6,287	273	0	0	0	0	269	4	0	0	0	0
50.0 to 74.9 percent	1,227	713	0	0	0	0	0	0	713	514	0	0	0	0	61	453	0	0	0	0
75.0 to 89.9 percent	5,990	4,151	0	0	0	0	0	1,181	2,970	1,839	0	0	0	0	0	1,607	232	0	0	0
90.0 percent or more	8,877	7,914	0	0	0	0	0	5,842	2,072	963	0	0	0	0	0	493	470	0	0	0
Two or more races enrollment, by percentage Two or more races																				
Less than 10.0 percent	568,615	430,103	77,943	47,825	11,404	80,718	29,667	2,259	180,287	106,610	18,667	8,418	8,988	38,775	22,987	8,276	499	31,902	24,405	7,497
10.0 to 24.9 percent	61,652	11,539	4,455	0	0	2,148	2,386	0	2,550	3,839	0	0	0	1,328	1,173	1,234	104	46,274	45,600	674
25.0 to 49.9 percent	11,833	11,447	0	0	0	0	2,970	0	8,477	0	0	0	0	0	0	3	0	383	0	383
50.0 to 74.9 percent	0	0	0	0	0	0	0	0	0	0	0	0	0	0	0	0	0	0	0	0
75.0 to 89.9 percent	0	0	0	0	0	0	0	0	0	0	0	0	0	0	0	0	0	0	0	0
90.0 percent or more	0	0	0	0	0	0	0	0	0	0	0	0	0	0	0	0	0	0	0	0
Nonresident alien enrollment, by percentage nonresident alien[7]																				
Less than 10.0 percent	481,664	381,059	95,518	77,004	16,000	83,032	21,068	2,373	86,064	89,618	2,393	8,516	12,386	37,528	22,209	6,422	164	10,987	10,652	335
10.0 to 24.9 percent	367,926	203,606	148,071	26,424	1,787	14,775	3,672	1,295	7,582	160,619	91,105	16,966	8,478	24,013	11,786	7,723	548	3,701	2,747	954
25.0 to 49.9 percent	62,013	3,563	0	0	0	3,563	0	0	0	51,172	17,044	11,187	6,865	4,947	1,750	9,303	76	7,278	7,221	57
50.0 to 74.9 percent	4,593	0	0	0	0	0	0	0	0	4,115	0	0	0	996	537	2,582	0	478	88	390
75.0 to 89.9 percent	890	0	0	0	0	0	0	0	0	710	0	0	0	710	0	0	0	180	180	0
90.0 percent or more	1,824	0	0	0	0	0	0	0	0	1,663	0	0	0	0	0	1,663	0	161	161	0

[1] Research universities with a very high level of research activity.
[2] Research universities with a high level of research activity.
[3] Institutions that award at least 20 doctor's degrees per year, but did not have high levels of research activity.
[4] Institutions that award at least 50 master's degrees per year.
[5] Institutions that primarily emphasize undergraduate education. Also includes institutions classified as 4-year under the IPEDS system, which had been classified as 2-year in the Carnegie system because they primarily award associate's degrees.
[6] Four-year institutions that award degrees primarily in single fields of study, such as medicine, business, fine arts, theology, and engineering.

[7] Nonresident alien enrollment percentages based on total enrollment in the institution, rather than on the U.S. resident enrollment.
NOTE: Relative levels of research activity for research universities were determined by an analysis of research and development expenditures, science and engineering research staffing, and doctoral degrees conferred, by field. Further information on the research index ranking may be obtained from http://carnegieclassifications.iu.edu/. Includes imputed Carnegie system classifications for institutions with missing data. Degree-granting institutions grant associate's or higher degrees and participate in Title IV federal financial aid programs. Race categories exclude persons of Hispanic ethnicity.
SOURCE: U.S. Department of Education, National Center for Education Statistics, Integrated Postsecondary Education Data System (IPEDS), Spring 2015, Fall Enrollment component. (This table was prepared November 2015.)

Table 306.50. Total fall enrollment in degree-granting postsecondary institutions, by control and level of institution, level of enrollment, and race/ethnicity of student: 2014

Level of enrollment and race/ethnicity of student	Total, all institutions	Public institutions Total	Public 4-year Total	Research university, very high[1]	Research university, high[2]	Doctoral/research university[3]	Master's[4]	Baccalaureate[5]	Special focus[6]	2-year	Nonprofit Total	Nonprofit 4-year Total	Research university, very high[1]	Research university, high[2]	Doctoral/research university[3]	Master's[4]	Baccalaureate[5]	Special focus[6]	2-year	For-profit Total	For-profit 4-year	For-profit 2-year
1	2	3	4	5	6	7	8	9	10	11	12	13	14	15	16	17	18	19	20	21	22	23
Fall enrollment																						
All students, total	20,207,369	14,655,015	8,257,250	2,398,724	1,502,013	420,049	2,682,609	1,166,559	87,296	6,397,765	3,996,099	3,965,724	564,781	305,479	322,680	1,586,703	812,195	373,886	30,365	1,556,265	1,269,910	286,355
White	11,237,436	8,119,496	4,833,603	1,415,965	919,512	240,388	1,568,640	639,906	49,192	3,285,893	2,445,026	2,430,188	273,442	181,991	177,367	1,032,968	536,353	228,067	14,838	672,914	563,806	109,109
Black	2,791,885	1,839,659	914,571	149,761	148,969	95,261	339,292	173,990	7,298	925,098	481,675	481,613	33,109	29,289	39,685	214,045	123,402	43,103	8,062	462,531	381,999	80,532
Hispanic	3,191,699	2,580,399	1,133,273	249,177	193,836	42,294	409,015	231,846	7,105	1,447,116	369,010	364,769	48,985	27,737	42,931	155,053	62,139	27,924	4,241	242,300	172,741	69,559
Asian	1,213,616	918,572	544,585	243,599	75,910	10,975	156,576	47,376	10,149	373,987	243,530	242,592	78,187	20,094	24,724	63,779	23,633	32,245	938	51,514	40,330	11,184
Pacific Islander	58,832	37,743	18,850	4,563	2,602	389	6,258	4,919	119	18,893	9,875	9,782	607	527	820	4,620	2,098	1,110	93	11,214	8,786	2,428
American Indian/ Alaska Native	152,911	117,839	56,011	9,672	9,931	1,551	18,592	8,759	7,506	61,828	20,624	19,822	1,312	774	1,436	7,941	4,128	4,231	802	14,448	11,195	3,253
Two or more races	642,100	463,009	261,775	82,398	47,825	11,404	82,866	35,023	2,259	191,314	110,452	109,849	18,657	8,418	8,988	40,103	24,160	9,513	603	78,559	70,006	8,554
Nonresident alien	918,910	588,228	494,582	83,589	103,428	17,787	101,370	24,740	3,668	93,646	307,109	307,109	110,542	36,669	27,729	69,194	36,282	27,693	788	22,785	21,049	1,736
Undergraduate	17,292,787	13,244,837	6,847,072	1,812,148	1,192,939	338,809	2,314,068	1,156,960	32,148	6,397,765	2,771,341	2,740,976	274,257	191,147	200,025	1,124,321	759,419	191,807	30,365	1,276,609	990,254	286,355
White	9,581,495	7,294,171	4,008,278	1,083,689	733,807	195,693	1,344,889	633,500	16,700	3,285,893	1,738,529	1,723,691	136,934	123,093	109,424	738,230	499,447	116,563	14,838	548,795	439,686	109,109
Black	2,425,842	1,712,782	787,694	117,561	124,844	79,517	290,490	172,649	2,633	925,088	348,772	340,710	16,832	15,717	22,374	144,160	116,106	25,521	8,062	364,288	283,756	80,532
Hispanic	2,961,917	2,467,541	1,020,425	211,256	169,423	35,465	370,370	231,331	2,580	1,447,116	276,738	272,497	29,737	16,881	29,751	120,487	59,269	16,372	4,241	217,638	148,079	69,559
Asian	1,022,735	832,847	458,960	200,976	61,915	8,321	139,055	46,858	1,735	373,987	150,445	149,507	45,582	13,267	15,922	41,467	21,734	11,535	938	39,443	28,259	11,184
Pacific Islander	52,302	35,613	16,720	3,667	2,216	343	5,537	4,886	71	18,893	7,332	7,239	239	378	524	3,404	2,026	668	93	9,357	6,929	2,428
American Indian/ Alaska Native	139,563	110,528	48,700	7,208	8,283	1,262	16,136	8,697	7,124	61,828	15,552	15,050	720	536	820	5,678	3,787	3,509	802	12,183	8,930	3,253
Two or more races	579,510	423,838	232,524	69,590	41,522	9,905	75,812	34,772	923	191,314	85,676	85,073	12,284	6,175	6,632	31,834	23,363	4,785	603	69,996	61,442	8,554
Nonresident alien	530,423	367,517	273,871	118,201	50,929	8,313	71,779	24,267	382	93,646	147,997	147,209	31,929	15,100	14,578	39,061	33,687	12,854	788	14,909	13,173	1,736
Postbaccalaureate	2,914,582	1,410,178	1,410,178	586,576	309,074	81,240	368,541	9,599	55,148	†	1,224,748	1,224,748	290,524	114,332	122,655	462,382	52,776	182,079	†	279,656	279,656	†
White	1,655,941	825,325	825,325	332,276	186,706	44,695	223,751	6,406	32,492	†	706,497	706,497	136,508	58,898	67,943	294,738	36,906	111,504	†	124,119	124,119	†
Black	366,023	126,877	126,877	33,200	24,125	15,744	48,802	1,341	4,665	†	140,903	140,903	16,277	13,552	16,311	69,885	7,296	17,582	†	98,243	98,243	†
Hispanic	229,782	112,848	112,848	37,921	24,413	6,829	38,645	515	4,525	†	92,272	92,272	19,248	10,856	13,180	34,566	2,870	11,552	†	24,662	24,662	†
Asian	190,881	85,725	85,725	42,623	13,995	2,654	17,521	518	8,414	†	93,085	93,085	32,535	6,827	8,802	22,312	1,899	20,710	†	12,071	12,071	†
Pacific Islander	6,530	2,130	2,130	896	386	46	721	33	48	†	2,543	2,543	368	149	296	1,216	72	442	†	1,857	1,857	†
American Indian/ Alaska Native	14,348	7,311	7,311	2,464	1,648	299	2,456	62	382	†	4,772	4,772	592	238	616	2,263	341	722	†	2,265	2,265	†
Two or more races	62,590	29,251	29,251	12,808	6,300	1,499	7,054	251	1,336	†	24,776	24,776	6,383	2,243	2,356	8,269	797	4,728	†	8,563	8,563	†
Nonresident alien	388,487	220,711	220,711	125,388	52,499	9,474	29,591	473	3,286	†	159,900	159,900	78,613	21,569	13,151	29,133	2,595	14,839	†	7,876	7,876	†
Percentage distribution of U.S. residents																						
U.S. residents, total	100.0	100.0	100.0	100.0	100.0	100.0	100.0	100.0	100.0	100.0	100.0	100.0	100.0	100.0	100.0	100.0	100.0	100.0	100.0	100.0	100.0	100.0
White	58.3	57.7	62.3	65.7	65.7	59.8	60.8	56.0	58.8	52.1	66.3	66.4	60.2	67.7	60.1	68.0	69.1	65.9	50.2	43.9	45.1	38.3
Black	14.5	13.1	11.8	6.9	10.7	23.7	13.1	15.2	8.7	14.7	13.3	13.2	7.3	10.9	13.1	14.1	15.9	12.5	27.3	30.2	30.6	28.3
Hispanic	16.5	18.3	14.6	11.6	13.9	10.5	15.8	20.3	8.5	23.0	10.0	10.0	10.8	10.3	14.6	10.2	8.0	8.1	14.3	15.8	13.8	24.4
Asian	6.3	6.5	7.0	11.3	5.4	2.7	6.1	4.1	12.1	5.9	6.6	6.6	17.2	7.5	8.4	4.2	3.0	9.3	3.2	3.4	3.2	3.9
Pacific Islander	0.3	0.3	0.2	0.2	0.2	0.1	0.2	0.4	0.1	0.3	0.3	0.3	0.3	0.2	0.3	0.3	0.3	0.3	0.3	0.7	0.7	0.9
American Indian/ Alaska Native	0.8	0.8	0.7	0.4	0.7	0.4	0.7	0.8	9.0	1.0	0.6	0.5	0.3	0.3	0.5	0.5	0.5	1.2	2.7	0.9	0.9	1.1
Two or more races	3.3	3.2	3.4	3.8	3.4	2.8	3.2	3.1	2.7	3.0	3.0	3.0	4.1	3.1	3.0	2.6	3.1	2.7	2.0	5.1	5.6	3.0
Undergraduate	100.0	100.0	100.0	100.0	100.0	100.0	100.0	100.0	100.0	100.0	100.0	100.0	100.0	100.0	100.0	100.0	100.0	100.0	100.0	100.0	100.0	100.0
White	57.2	56.6	61.0	64.0	64.3	59.2	60.0	55.9	52.6	52.1	66.3	66.5	56.5	69.9	59.0	68.0	68.8	65.1	50.2	43.5	45.0	38.3
Black	14.5	13.3	12.0	6.9	10.9	24.1	13.0	15.2	8.3	14.7	13.3	13.1	6.9	8.9	12.1	13.3	16.0	14.3	27.3	28.9	29.0	28.3
Hispanic	17.7	19.2	15.5	12.5	14.8	10.7	16.5	20.4	8.1	23.0	10.5	10.5	12.3	9.6	16.0	11.1	8.2	9.1	14.3	17.2	15.2	24.4
Asian	6.1	6.5	7.0	11.9	5.4	2.5	6.2	4.1	5.5	5.9	5.7	5.8	18.8	7.5	8.6	3.8	3.0	6.4	3.2	3.1	2.9	3.9
Pacific Islander	0.3	0.3	0.3	0.2	0.2	0.1	0.2	0.4	0.2	0.3	0.3	0.3	0.1	0.2	0.3	0.3	0.3	0.4	0.3	0.7	0.7	0.9
American Indian/ Alaska Native	0.8	0.7	0.7	0.4	0.7	0.4	0.7	0.8	22.4	1.0	0.6	0.6	0.3	0.3	0.4	0.5	0.5	2.0	2.7	1.0	0.9	1.1
Two or more races	3.5	3.3	3.5	4.1	3.6	3.0	3.4	3.1	2.9	3.0	3.3	3.3	5.1	3.5	3.6	2.9	3.2	2.7	2.0	5.5	6.3	3.0

See notes at end of table.

Table 306.50. Total fall enrollment in degree-granting postsecondary institutions, by control and level of institution, level of enrollment, and race/ethnicity of student: 2014—Continued

Level of enrollment and race/ethnicity of student	Total, all institutions	Public institutions									Nonprofit institutions									For-profit institutions		
		Total	4-year							2-year	Total	4-year							2-year	Total	4-year	2-year
			Total	Research university, very high[1]	Research university, high[2]	Doctoral/ research university[3]	Master's[4]	Bacca-laureate[5]	Special focus[6]			Total	Research university, very high[1]	Research university, high[2]	Doctoral/ research university[3]	Master's[4]	Bacca-laureate[5]	Special focus[6]				
1	2	3	4	5	6	7	8	9	10	11	12	13	14	15	16	17	18	19	20	21	22	23
Postbaccalaureate	100.0	100.0	100.0	100.0	100.0	100.0	100.0	100.0	100.0	†	100.0	100.0	100.0	100.0	100.0	100.0	100.0	100.0	†	100.0	100.0	†
White	66.6	69.4	69.4	72.0	72.4	62.3	66.0	70.2	62.7	†	66.3	66.3	64.4	63.5	62.0	68.0	73.5	66.7	†	45.7	45.7	†
Black	14.5	10.7	10.7	7.0	9.4	21.9	14.4	14.7	9.0	†	13.2	13.2	7.7	14.6	14.9	16.1	14.5	10.5	†	36.1	36.1	†
Hispanic	9.1	9.5	9.5	8.2	9.5	9.5	11.4	5.6	8.7	†	8.7	8.7	9.1	11.7	12.0	8.0	5.7	6.9	†	9.1	9.1	†
Asian	7.6	7.2	7.2	9.2	5.5	3.7	5.2	5.7	16.2	†	8.7	8.7	15.4	7.4	8.0	5.1	3.8	12.4	†	4.4	4.4	†
Pacific Islander	0.3	0.2	0.2	0.2	0.2	0.1	0.2	0.4	0.1	†	0.2	0.2	0.2	0.2	0.3	0.3	0.1	0.3	†	0.7	0.7	†
American Indian/Alaska Native	0.6	0.6	0.6	0.5	0.6	0.4	0.7	0.7	0.7	†	0.4	0.4	0.3	0.3	0.6	0.5	0.7	0.4	†	0.8	0.8	†
Two or more races	2.5	2.5	2.5	2.8	2.5	2.1	2.1	2.8	2.6	†	2.3	2.3	3.0	2.4	2.2	1.9	1.6	2.8	†	3.2	3.2	†

†Not applicable.
[1]Research universities with a very high level of research activity.
[2]Research universities with a high level of research activity.
[3]Institutions that award at least 20 doctor's degrees per year, but did not have high levels of research activity.
[4]Institutions that award at least 50 master's degrees per year.
[5]Institutions that primarily emphasize undergraduate education. Also includes institutions classified as 4-year under the IPEDS system, which had been classified as 2-year in the Carnegie system because they primarily award associate's degrees.
[6]Four-year institutions that award degrees primarily in single fields of study, such as medicine, business, fine arts, theology, and engineering.

NOTE: Relative levels of research activity for research universities were determined by an analysis of research and development expenditures, science and engineering research staffing, and doctoral degrees conferred, by field. Further information on the research index ranking may be obtained from http://carnegieclassifications.iu.edu/. Includes imputed Carnegie system classifications for institutions with missing data. Degree-granting institutions grant associate's or higher degrees and participate in Title IV federal financial aid programs. Race categories exclude persons of Hispanic ethnicity.
SOURCE: U.S. Department of Education, National Center for Education Statistics, Integrated Postsecondary Education Data System (IPEDS), Spring 2015, Fall Enrollment component. (This table was prepared November 2015.)

Table 306.60. Fall enrollment in degree-granting postsecondary institutions, by race/ethnicity of student and state or jurisdiction: 2014

State or jurisdiction	Number									Percentage distribution of U.S. residents							
	Total	White	Black	Hispanic	Asian	Pacific Islander	American Indian/ Alaska Native	Two or more races	Non-resident alien	Total	White	Black	Hispanic	Asian	Pacific Islander	American Indian/ Alaska Native	Two or more races
1	2	3	4	5	6	7	8	9	10	11	12	13	14	15	16	17	18
United States	20,207,369	11,237,436	2,791,865	3,191,699	1,213,616	58,832	152,911	642,100	918,910	100.0	58.3	14.5	16.5	6.3	0.3	0.8	3.3
Alabama	305,028	187,842	87,348	9,102	5,431	317	2,115	5,276	7,597	100.0	63.2	29.4	3.1	1.8	0.1	0.7	1.8
Alaska	34,331	20,860	1,166	3,234	1,729	437	3,743	2,560	602	100.0	61.8	3.5	9.6	5.1	1.3	11.1	7.6
Arizona	674,746	334,479	91,796	136,065	22,090	3,302	15,430	51,765	19,819	100.0	51.1	14.0	20.8	3.4	0.5	2.4	7.9
Arkansas	169,571	116,719	29,438	9,134	2,702	168	1,418	4,809	5,183	100.0	71.0	17.9	5.6	1.6	0.1	0.9	2.9
California	2,696,415	837,251	195,254	994,357	399,024	14,501	11,906	118,478	125,644	100.0	32.6	7.6	38.7	15.5	0.6	0.5	4.6
Colorado	353,827	232,012	26,629	54,155	12,081	991	3,650	13,145	11,164	100.0	67.7	7.8	15.8	3.5	0.3	1.1	3.8
Connecticut	201,928	122,534	26,079	27,318	9,998	249	510	4,901	10,339	100.0	64.0	13.6	14.3	5.2	0.1	0.3	2.6
Delaware	60,368	35,084	12,932	3,667	2,001	95	278	1,315	4,996	100.0	63.4	23.4	6.6	3.6	0.2	0.5	2.4
District of Columbia	90,053	41,065	23,853	6,670	5,985	157	315	2,358	9,650	100.0	51.1	29.7	8.3	7.4	0.2	0.4	2.9
Florida	1,111,018	511,356	215,541	272,563	35,363	2,656	3,693	29,897	39,949	100.0	47.7	20.1	25.4	3.3	0.2	0.3	2.8
Georgia	531,004	263,948	174,973	33,066	24,500	775	1,557	12,636	19,549	100.0	51.6	34.2	6.5	4.8	0.2	0.3	2.5
Hawaii	73,505	13,284	1,775	7,485	22,468	5,764	216	18,202	4,311	100.0	19.2	2.6	10.8	32.5	8.3	0.3	26.3
Idaho	118,953	92,554	1,426	10,236	1,718	792	1,085	4,200	6,942	100.0	82.6	1.3	9.1	1.5	0.7	1.0	3.7
Illinois	824,980	462,547	118,422	132,356	50,985	1,511	2,124	18,267	38,768	100.0	58.8	15.1	16.8	6.5	0.2	0.3	2.3
Indiana	436,327	317,609	45,382	24,642	10,903	303	1,171	10,837	25,480	100.0	77.3	11.0	6.0	2.7	0.1	0.3	2.6
Iowa	282,482	208,193	29,650	17,798	6,807	762	1,934	4,498	12,840	100.0	77.2	11.0	6.6	2.5	0.3	0.7	1.7
Kansas	226,401	155,150	23,300	18,692	5,903	416	2,894	6,840	13,476	100.0	72.9	10.8	8.8	2.8	0.2	1.4	3.2
Kentucky	264,197	213,094	25,419	7,416	3,839	286	716	6,233	7,194	100.0	82.9	9.9	2.9	1.5	0.1	0.3	2.4
Louisiana	245,938	138,052	76,265	11,213	5,929	232	1,452	5,551	7,244	100.0	57.8	32.0	4.7	2.5	0.1	0.6	2.3
Maine	72,246	62,328	2,425	1,918	1,514	75	759	1,606	1,621	100.0	88.3	3.4	2.7	2.1	0.1	1.1	2.3
Maryland	365,597	176,458	103,545	28,120	25,198	837	1,145	12,186	18,108	100.0	50.8	29.8	8.1	7.3	0.2	0.3	3.5
Massachusetts	510,912	308,982	45,801	52,215	38,913	410	1,145	14,115	49,331	100.0	66.9	9.9	11.3	8.4	0.1	0.3	3.1
Michigan	619,438	435,055	82,971	25,699	22,742	779	4,056	16,210	31,926	100.0	74.1	14.1	4.4	3.9	0.1	0.7	2.8
Minnesota	433,854	297,277	62,531	21,024	21,275	627	3,494	13,215	14,411	100.0	70.9	14.9	5.0	5.1	0.1	0.8	3.2
Mississippi	170,728	93,935	65,262	3,212	1,972	121	759	2,234	3,233	100.0	56.1	39.0	1.9	1.2	0.1	0.5	1.3
Missouri	419,900	302,294	54,717	17,306	12,187	685	2,180	10,920	19,611	100.0	75.5	13.7	4.3	3.0	0.2	0.5	2.7
Montana	51,942	41,765	469	1,744	772	107	3,918	1,381	1,786	100.0	83.3	0.9	3.5	1.5	0.2	7.8	2.8
Nebraska	135,825	104,588	7,783	10,403	3,675	217	915	3,123	5,121	100.0	80.0	6.0	8.0	2.8	0.2	0.7	2.4
Nevada	119,205	57,422	10,032	28,255	11,871	1,567	1,007	6,720	2,331	100.0	49.1	8.6	24.2	10.2	1.3	0.9	5.7
New Hampshire	106,984	83,439	9,049	5,689	3,299	138	747	1,330	3,293	100.0	80.5	8.7	5.5	3.2	0.1	0.7	1.3
New Jersey	436,208	218,909	64,181	84,691	37,768	1,401	1,196	8,523	19,539	100.0	52.5	15.4	20.3	9.1	0.3	0.3	2.0
New Mexico	146,246	51,429	4,423	65,815	2,536	337	13,873	3,010	4,823	100.0	36.4	3.1	46.5	1.8	0.2	9.8	2.1
New York	1,299,055	655,695	181,070	210,671	116,553	3,001	4,487	26,532	101,046	100.0	54.7	15.1	17.6	9.7	0.3	0.4	2.2
North Carolina	570,045	337,852	140,150	35,147	17,200	855	6,442	14,185	18,214	100.0	61.2	25.4	6.4	3.1	0.2	1.2	2.6
North Dakota	54,048	43,738	1,798	1,478	657	83	2,156	1,255	2,883	100.0	85.5	3.5	2.9	1.3	0.2	4.2	2.5
Ohio	680,238	503,557	84,570	22,903	16,303	577	1,955	17,773	32,600	100.0	77.8	13.1	3.5	2.5	0.1	0.3	2.7
Oklahoma	215,349	130,179	20,293	15,378	5,887	372	16,981	15,016	11,243	100.0	63.8	9.9	7.5	2.9	0.2	8.3	7.4
Oregon	245,547	168,484	8,626	26,240	13,302	1,602	3,062	11,889	12,342	100.0	72.2	3.7	11.3	5.7	0.7	1.3	5.1
Pennsylvania	750,651	516,011	87,109	47,504	37,327	924	1,659	17,994	42,123	100.0	72.8	12.3	6.7	5.3	0.1	0.2	2.5
Rhode Island	83,499	55,977	5,832	9,930	3,662	69	334	2,705	4,990	100.0	71.3	7.4	12.6	4.7	0.1	0.4	3.4

See notes at end of table.

Table 306.60. Fall enrollment in degree-granting postsecondary institutions, by race/ethnicity of student and state or jurisdiction: 2014—Continued

State or jurisdiction	Number									Percentage distribution of U.S. residents							
	Total	White	Black	Hispanic	Asian	Pacific Islander	American Indian/Alaska Native	Two or more races	Non-resident alien	Total	White	Black	Hispanic	Asian	Pacific Islander	American Indian/Alaska Native	Two or more races
1	2	3	4	5	6	7	8	9	10	11	12	13	14	15	16	17	18
South Carolina	254,629	159,346	68,880	9,906	4,170	285	994	6,116	4,932	100.0	63.8	27.6	4.0	1.7	0.1	0.4	2.4
South Dakota	53,963	44,141	1,797	1,425	588	128	3,089	1,165	1,630	100.0	84.3	3.4	2.7	1.1	0.2	5.9	2.2
Tennessee	326,575	225,204	63,315	11,606	7,275	307	927	8,630	9,311	100.0	71.0	20.0	3.7	2.3	0.1	0.3	2.7
Texas	1,555,462	611,452	210,679	535,092	85,553	2,750	6,283	36,541	67,112	100.0	41.1	14.2	36.0	5.7	0.2	0.4	2.5
Utah	274,926	211,088	11,209	25,325	7,809	1,949	2,335	7,236	7,975	100.0	79.1	4.2	9.5	2.9	0.7	0.9	2.7
Vermont	43,983	36,542	1,222	1,985	1,045	36	256	1,400	1,497	100.0	86.0	2.9	4.7	2.5	0.1	0.6	3.3
Virginia	577,908	337,383	126,281	39,950	33,935	1,491	2,326	20,239	16,303	100.0	60.1	22.5	7.1	6.0	0.3	0.4	3.6
Washington	365,193	225,854	16,401	39,266	32,726	2,212	4,050	23,009	21,675	100.0	65.7	4.8	11.4	9.5	0.6	1.2	6.7
West Virginia	157,052	117,768	19,055	8,232	2,521	636	751	4,101	3,988	100.0	76.9	12.4	5.4	1.6	0.4	0.5	2.7
Wisconsin	358,894	280,196	22,521	20,003	12,675	388	2,794	8,474	11,843	100.0	80.7	6.5	5.8	3.7	0.1	0.8	2.4
Wyoming	35,461	29,432	463	2,739	389	P89	523	714	1,112	100.0	85.7	1.3	8.0	1.1	0.3	1.5	2.1
U.S. Service Academies	14,734	10,023	1,027	1,659	861	63	106	785	210	100.0	69.0	7.1	11.4	5.9	0.4	0.7	5.4
Other jurisdictions	**255,843**	**879**	**2,031**	**239,546**	**3,220**	**9,270**	**111**	**318**	**468**	**100.0**	**0.3**	**0.8**	**93.8**	**1.3**	**3.6**	**#**	**0.1**
American Samoa	1,276	2	0	0	6	1,176	0	0	92	100.0	0.2	0.0	0.0	0.5	99.3	0.0	0.0
Federated States of Micronesia	2,344	1	0	0	0	2,343	0	0	0	100.0	#	0.0	0.0	0.0	100.0	0.0	0.0
Guam	6,488	178	78	37	2,711	3,427	6	0	51	100.0	2.8	1.2	0.6	42.1	53.2	0.1	0.0
Marshall Islands	1,087	0	0	0	0	1,073	7	0	7	100.0	0.0	0.0	0.0	0.0	99.4	0.6	0.0
Northern Marianas	1,186	19	3	4	347	639	2	88	84	100.0	1.7	0.3	0.4	31.5	58.0	0.2	8.0
Palau	604	0	1	0	2	601	0	0	0	100.0	0.0	0.2	0.0	0.3	99.5	0.0	0.0
Puerto Rico	240,578	520	179	239,326	142	11	92	210	98	100.0	0.2	0.1	99.5	0.1	#	#	0.1
U.S. Virgin Islands	2,280	159	1,770	179	12	0	4	20	136	100.0	7.4	82.6	8.3	0.6	0.0	0.2	0.9

#Rounds to zero.
NOTE: Race categories exclude persons of Hispanic ethnicity. Degree-granting institutions grant associate's or higher degrees and participate in Title IV federal financial aid programs. Detail may not sum to totals because of rounding.

SOURCE: U.S. Department of Education, National Center for Education Statistics, Integrated Postsecondary Education Data System (IPEDS), Spring 2015, Fall Enrollment component. (This table was prepared October 2015.)

Table 306.70. Fall enrollment in degree-granting postsecondary institutions, by race/ethnicity of student and state or jurisdiction: 2012

State or jurisdiction	Number									Percentage distribution of U.S. residents							
	Total	White	Black	Hispanic	Asian	Pacific Islander	American Indian/Alaska Native	Two or more races	Non-resident alien	Total	White	Black	Hispanic	Asian	Pacific Islander	American Indian/Alaska Native	Two or more races
1	2	3	4	5	6	7	8	9	10	11	12	13	14	15	16	17	18
United States	20,644,478	11,982,155	2,962,417	2,980,300	1,194,690	63,543	173,011	504,759	783,603	100.0	60.3	14.9	15.0	6.0	0.3	0.9	2.5
Alabama	310,311	191,652	92,603	8,216	5,130	282	2,341	3,600	6,487	100.0	63.1	30.5	2.7	1.7	0.1	0.8	1.2
Alaska	32,797	20,584	1,109	2,486	1,559	261	3,677	2,406	715	100.0	64.2	3.5	7.7	4.9	0.8	11.5	7.5
Arizona	736,465	403,614	115,297	135,659	22,629	4,007	19,196	18,295	17,768	100.0	56.2	16.0	18.9	3.1	0.6	2.7	2.5
Arkansas	176,468	122,860	32,690	7,571	2,736	179	1,558	3,979	4,885	100.0	71.6	19.1	4.4	1.6	0.1	0.9	2.3
California	2,621,606	890,578	187,712	906,010	408,671	16,199	12,867	99,626	99,943	100.0	35.3	7.4	35.9	16.2	0.6	0.5	4.0
Colorado	363,170	244,482	27,687	53,278	12,047	933	3,885	11,600	9,258	100.0	69.1	7.8	15.1	3.4	0.3	1.1	3.3
Connecticut	201,658	128,581	25,222	25,370	9,349	261	586	4,054	8,235	100.0	66.5	13.0	13.1	4.8	0.1	0.3	2.1
Delaware	58,127	35,573	12,691	3,306	2,164	71	189	1,205	2,928	100.0	64.4	23.0	6.0	3.9	0.1	0.3	2.2
District of Columbia	90,150	43,022	24,175	6,322	5,927	174	422	1,924	8,184	100.0	52.5	29.5	7.7	7.2	0.2	0.5	2.3
Florida	1,154,506	554,539	231,005	267,048	36,000	2,477	4,720	26,425	32,292	100.0	49.4	20.6	23.8	3.2	0.2	0.4	2.4
Georgia	545,360	278,142	186,086	28,716	22,881	808	1,734	10,654	16,339	100.0	52.6	35.2	5.4	4.3	0.2	0.3	2.0
Hawaii	78,456	15,103	1,760	7,602	24,506	6,935	268	17,524	4,758	100.0	20.5	2.4	10.3	33.3	9.4	0.4	23.8
Idaho	108,008	88,425	1,284	9,628	1,752	769	1,263	1,577	3,310	100.0	84.5	1.2	9.2	1.7	0.7	1.2	1.5
Illinois	866,893	506,514	132,429	125,650	49,494	2,089	2,575	15,685	32,457	100.0	60.7	15.9	15.1	5.9	0.3	0.3	1.9
Indiana	447,263	335,380	47,901	21,455	9,802	320	1,397	8,536	22,472	100.0	79.0	11.3	5.1	2.3	0.1	0.3	2.0
Iowa	361,189	255,718	55,444	22,328	7,176	1,107	2,787	5,527	11,102	100.0	73.0	15.8	6.4	2.0	0.3	0.8	1.6
Kansas	213,855	155,231	16,184	15,689	5,307	323	2,975	5,180	12,966	100.0	77.3	8.1	7.8	2.6	0.2	1.5	2.6
Kentucky	281,133	230,315	28,363	6,639	3,863	304	823	5,051	5,775	100.0	83.6	10.3	2.4	1.4	0.1	0.3	1.8
Louisiana	258,846	147,316	82,198	10,948	5,862	226	1,498	4,139	6,659	100.0	58.4	32.6	4.3	2.3	0.1	0.6	1.6
Maine	73,095	64,502	2,016	1,554	1,391	206	799	1,278	1,349	100.0	89.9	2.8	2.2	1.9	0.3	1.1	1.8
Maryland	374,496	188,836	108,182	24,378	24,308	736	1,169	9,519	17,368	100.0	52.9	30.3	6.8	6.8	0.2	0.3	2.7
Massachusetts	514,119	327,343	44,186	48,238	36,865	526	1,315	13,002	42,644	100.0	69.4	9.4	10.2	7.8	0.1	0.3	2.8
Michigan	663,703	472,672	97,815	23,590	22,306	882	4,749	13,585	28,104	100.0	74.4	15.4	3.7	3.5	0.1	0.7	2.1
Minnesota	451,661	319,361	63,035	18,865	19,926	635	3,883	12,714	13,242	100.0	72.8	14.4	4.3	4.5	0.1	0.9	2.9
Mississippi	176,618	97,542	69,633	2,857	1,901	138	738	1,458	2,351	100.0	56.0	40.0	1.6	1.1	0.1	0.4	0.8
Missouri	441,186	322,127	62,895	17,132	11,615	738	2,465	8,972	15,242	100.0	75.6	14.8	4.0	2.7	0.2	0.6	2.1
Montana	53,254	43,460	409	1,622	662	100	4,352	1,170	1,479	100.0	83.9	0.8	3.1	1.3	0.2	8.4	2.3
Nebraska	139,558	111,315	8,159	8,921	3,447	254	1,161	1,929	4,372	100.0	82.3	6.0	6.6	2.5	0.2	0.9	1.4
Nevada	118,300	60,974	10,014	24,837	11,640	1,771	1,179	5,560	2,325	100.0	52.6	8.6	21.4	10.0	1.5	1.0	4.8
New Hampshire	82,678	67,885	3,334	4,250	2,719	71	474	1,181	2,764	100.0	84.9	4.2	5.3	3.4	0.1	0.6	1.5
New Jersey	439,966	231,499	64,340	79,765	36,732	1,758	1,655	7,245	16,972	100.0	54.7	15.2	18.9	8.7	0.4	0.4	1.7
New Mexico	156,424	57,146	4,801	69,861	2,572	404	14,469	2,775	4,396	100.0	37.6	3.2	46.0	1.7	0.3	9.5	1.8
New York	1,309,684	702,689	183,059	193,518	113,006	2,767	4,719	20,983	88,943	100.0	57.6	15.0	15.9	9.3	0.2	0.4	1.7
North Carolina	578,265	351,102	148,380	28,973	15,548	725	6,900	9,844	16,793	100.0	62.5	26.4	5.2	2.8	0.1	1.2	1.8
North Dakota	55,242	45,133	1,548	1,296	655	74	2,585	976	2,975	100.0	86.4	3.0	2.5	1.3	0.1	4.9	1.9
Ohio	710,379	533,319	97,007	21,787	15,337	542	2,518	12,911	26,958	100.0	78.0	14.2	3.2	2.2	0.1	0.4	1.9
Oklahoma	228,492	144,474	23,222	13,809	5,665	364	19,839	11,753	9,366	100.0	65.9	10.6	6.3	2.6	0.2	9.1	5.4
Oregon	254,926	185,144	7,928	23,437	13,293	1,731	3,665	9,467	10,261	100.0	75.7	3.2	9.6	5.4	0.7	1.5	3.9
Pennsylvania	777,350	557,659	90,841	42,322	34,759	985	2,039	14,050	34,695	100.0	75.1	12.2	5.7	4.7	0.1	0.3	1.9
Rhode Island	83,952	59,026	5,788	8,855	3,553	60	325	1,732	4,613	100.0	74.4	7.3	11.2	4.5	0.1	0.4	2.2

See notes at end of table.

Table 306.70. Fall enrollment in degree-granting postsecondary institutions, by race/ethnicity of student and state or jurisdiction: 2012—Continued

State or jurisdiction	Number									Percentage distribution of U.S. residents							
	Total	White	Black	Hispanic	Asian	Pacific Islander	American Indian/ Alaska Native	Two or more races	Non-resident alien	Total	White	Black	Hispanic	Asian	Pacific Islander	American Indian/ Alaska Native	Two or more races
1	2	3	4	5	6	7	8	9	10	11	12	13	14	15	16	17	18
South Carolina	259,617	162,624	73,900	8,332	3,979	348	1,073	4,726	4,635	100.0	63.8	29.0	3.3	1.6	0.1	0.4	1.9
South Dakota	56,058	46,143	1,854	1,351	532	94	3,509	1,176	1,399	100.0	84.4	3.4	2.5	1.0	0.2	6.4	2.2
Tennessee	343,478	239,288	70,184	10,786	6,722	290	1,118	7,485	7,605	100.0	71.2	20.9	3.2	2.0	0.1	0.3	2.2
Texas	1,544,524	646,407	211,752	511,220	80,343	2,525	6,788	27,892	57,597	100.0	43.5	14.2	34.4	5.4	0.2	0.5	1.9
Utah	267,309	210,935	9,146	21,584	6,835	2,006	2,420	6,255	8,128	100.0	81.4	3.5	8.3	2.6	0.8	0.9	2.4
Vermont	44,697	38,180	1,212	1,832	1,072	40	234	1,121	1,006	100.0	87.4	2.8	4.2	2.5	0.1	0.5	2.6
Virginia	588,708	348,387	133,462	37,477	32,735	1,581	2,420	16,369	16,277	100.0	60.9	23.3	6.5	5.7	0.3	0.4	2.9
Washington	365,529	238,195	17,109	33,879	32,018	2,159	4,902	18,753	18,514	100.0	68.6	4.9	9.8	9.2	0.6	1.4	5.4
West Virginia	162,182	123,380	19,872	8,081	2,607	744	780	3,493	3,225	100.0	77.6	12.5	5.1	1.6	0.5	0.5	2.2
Wisconsin	369,738	295,033	24,020	17,720	11,989	408	3,284	7,016	10,268	100.0	82.1	6.7	4.9	3.3	0.1	0.9	2.0
Wyoming	37,812	31,992	561	2,669	341	78	637	539	995	100.0	86.9	1.5	7.2	0.9	0.2	1.7	1.5
U.S. Service Academies	15,227	10,754	913	1,581	762	78	87	843	209	100.0	71.6	6.1	10.5	5.1	0.5	0.6	5.6
Other jurisdictions	**259,975**	**1,026**	**2,290**	**242,673**	**2,899**	**9,987**	**115**	**371**	**614**	**100.0**	**0.4**	**0.9**	**93.6**	**1.1**	**3.9**	**#**	**0.1**
American Samoa	1,795	2	0	0	16	1,639	0	0	138	100.0	0.1	0.0	0.0	1.0	98.9	0.0	0.0
Federated States of Micronesia	2,744	4	0	0	2	2,738	0	0	0	100.0	0.1	0.0	0.0	0.1	99.8	0.0	0.0
Guam	5,955	204	25	38	2,411	3,190	8	24	55	100.0	3.5	0.4	0.6	40.9	54.1	0.1	0.4
Marshall Islands	1,123	0	0	0	0	1,109	0	0	14	100.0	0.0	0.0	0.0	0.0	100.0	0.0	0.0
Northern Marianas	1,178	15	3	2	319	625	1	68	145	100.0	1.5	0.3	0.2	30.9	60.5	0.1	6.6
Palau	680	1	1	0	6	672	0	0	0	100.0	0.1	0.1	0.0	0.9	98.8	0.0	0.0
Puerto Rico	244,077	663	265	242,487	139	14	105	279	125	100.0	0.3	0.1	99.4	0.1	#	#	0.1
U.S. Virgin Islands	2,423	137	1,996	146	6	0	1	0	137	100.0	6.0	87.3	6.4	0.3	0.0	#	0.0

#Rounds to zero.
NOTE: Race categories exclude persons of Hispanic ethnicity. Degree-granting institutions grant associate's or higher degrees and participate in Title IV federal financial aid programs. Detail may not sum to totals because of rounding. Some data have been revised from previously published figures.

SOURCE: U.S. Department of Education, National Center for Education Statistics, Integrated Postsecondary Education Data System (IPEDS), Spring 2013, Fall Enrollment component. (This table was prepared October 2015.)

Table 307.10. Full-time-equivalent fall enrollment in degree-granting postsecondary institutions, by control and level of institution: 1967 through 2025

Year	All institutions			Public institutions			Private institutions						
							Total	4-year			2-year		
	Total	4-year	2-year	Total	4-year	2-year		Total	Nonprofit	For-profit	Total	Nonprofit	For-profit
1	2	3	4	5	6	7	8	9	10	11	12	13	14
1967	5,499,360	4,448,302	1,051,058	3,777,701	2,850,432	927,269	1,721,659	1,597,870	—	—	123,789	—	—
1968	5,977,768	4,729,522	1,248,246	4,248,639	3,128,057	1,120,582	1,729,129	1,601,465	—	—	127,664	—	—
1969	6,333,357	4,899,034	1,434,323	4,577,353	3,259,323	1,318,030	1,756,004	1,639,711	—	—	116,293	—	—
1970	6,737,819	5,145,422	1,592,397	4,953,144	3,468,569	1,484,575	1,784,675	1,676,853	—	—	107,822	—	—
1971	7,148,558	5,357,647	1,790,911	5,344,402	3,660,626	1,683,776	1,804,156	1,697,021	—	—	107,135	—	—
1972	7,253,757	5,406,833	1,846,924	5,452,854	3,706,238	1,746,616	1,800,903	1,700,595	—	—	100,308	—	—
1973	7,453,463	5,439,230	2,014,233	5,629,563	3,721,037	1,908,526	1,823,900	1,718,193	—	—	105,707	—	—
1974	7,805,452	5,606,247	2,199,205	5,944,799	3,847,543	2,097,256	1,860,653	1,758,704	—	—	101,949	—	—
1975	8,479,698	5,900,408	2,579,290	6,522,319	4,056,502	2,465,817	1,957,379	1,843,906	—	—	113,473	—	—
1976	8,312,502	5,848,001	2,464,501	6,349,903	3,998,450	2,351,453	1,962,599	1,849,551	—	—	113,048	—	—
1977	8,415,339	5,935,076	2,480,263	6,396,476	4,039,071	2,357,405	2,018,863	1,896,005	—	—	122,858	—	—
1978	8,348,482	5,932,357	2,416,125	6,279,199	3,996,126	2,283,073	2,069,283	1,936,231	—	—	133,052	—	—
1979	8,487,317	6,016,072	2,471,245	6,392,617	4,059,304	2,333,313	2,094,700	1,956,768	—	—	137,932	—	—
1980	8,819,013	6,161,372	2,657,641	6,642,294	4,158,267	2,484,027	2,176,719	2,003,105	—	—	173,614 [1]	—	—
1981	9,014,521	6,249,847	2,764,674	6,781,300	4,208,506	2,572,794	2,233,221	2,041,341	—	—	191,880 [1]	—	—
1982	9,091,648	6,248,923	2,842,725	6,850,589	4,220,648	2,629,941	2,241,059	2,028,275	—	—	212,784 [1]	—	—
1983	9,166,398	6,325,222	2,841,176	6,881,479	4,265,807	2,615,672	2,284,919	2,059,415	—	—	225,504	—	—
1984	8,951,695	6,292,711	2,658,984	6,684,664	4,237,895	2,446,769	2,267,031	2,054,816	—	—	212,215	—	—
1985	8,943,433	6,294,339	2,649,094	6,667,781	4,239,622	2,428,159	2,275,652	2,054,717	—	—	220,935	—	—
1986	9,064,165	6,360,325	2,703,842	6,778,045	4,295,494	2,482,551	2,286,122	2,064,831	—	—	221,291 [2]	—	—
1987	9,229,736	6,486,504	2,743,230	6,937,690	4,395,728	2,541,961	2,292,045	2,090,776	—	—	201,269 [2]	—	—
1988	9,464,271	6,664,146	2,800,125	7,096,905	4,505,774	2,591,131	2,367,366	2,158,372	—	—	208,994	—	—
1989	9,780,881	6,813,602	2,967,279	7,371,590	4,619,828	2,751,762	2,409,291	2,193,774	—	—	215,517	—	—
1990	9,983,436	6,968,008	3,015,428	7,557,982	4,740,049	2,817,933	2,425,454	2,227,959	2,177,668	50,291	197,495	72,785	124,710
1991	10,360,606	7,081,454	3,279,152	7,862,845	4,795,704	3,067,141	2,497,761	2,285,750	2,223,463	62,287	212,011	72,545	139,466
1992	10,436,776	7,129,379	3,307,397	7,911,701	4,797,884	3,113,817	2,525,075	2,331,495	2,267,373	64,122	193,580	66,647	126,933
1993	10,351,415	7,120,921	3,230,494	7,812,394	4,765,983	3,046,411	2,539,021	2,354,938	2,282,643	72,295	184,083	70,469	113,614
1994	10,348,072	7,137,341	3,210,731	7,784,396	4,749,524	3,034,872	2,563,676	2,387,817	2,301,063	86,754	175,859	69,578	106,281
1995	10,334,956	7,172,844	3,162,112	7,751,815	4,757,223	2,994,592	2,583,141	2,415,621	2,328,730	86,891	167,520	62,416	105,104
1996	10,481,886	7,234,541	3,247,345	7,794,995	4,767,117	3,027,778	2,686,991	2,467,424	2,353,561	113,863	219,567	63,954	155,613
1997	10,615,028	7,338,794	3,276,234	7,869,764	4,813,849	3,055,915	2,745,264	2,524,945	2,389,627	135,318	220,319	61,761	158,558
1998	10,698,775	7,467,828	3,230,947	7,880,135	4,868,857	3,011,278	2,818,640	2,598,971	2,436,188	162,783	219,669	56,834	162,835
1999	10,974,519	7,634,247	3,340,272	8,059,240	4,949,851	3,109,389	2,915,279	2,684,396	2,488,140	196,256	230,883	53,956	176,927
2000	11,267,025	7,795,139	3,471,886	8,266,932	5,025,588	3,241,344	3,000,093	2,769,551	2,549,676	219,875	230,542	51,503	179,039
2001	11,765,945	8,087,980	3,677,965	8,639,154	5,194,035	3,445,119	3,126,791	2,893,945	2,612,833	281,112	232,846	41,037	191,809
2002	12,331,319	8,439,064	3,892,255	9,061,411	5,406,283	3,655,128	3,269,908	3,032,781	2,699,702	333,079	237,127	40,110	197,017
2003	12,687,597	8,744,188	3,943,409	9,240,724	5,557,680	3,683,044	3,446,873	3,186,508	2,776,850	409,658	260,365	36,815	223,550
2004	13,000,994	9,018,024	3,982,970	9,348,081	5,640,650	3,707,431	3,652,913	3,377,374	2,837,251	540,123	275,539	34,202	241,337
2005	13,200,790	9,261,634	3,939,156	9,390,216	5,728,327	3,661,889	3,810,574	3,533,307	2,878,354	654,953	277,267	34,729	242,538
2006	13,403,097	9,456,166	3,946,931	9,503,558	5,824,768	3,678,790	3,899,539	3,631,398	2,936,172	695,226	268,141	31,203	236,938
2007	13,782,702	9,769,560	4,013,142	9,739,709	5,994,230	3,745,479	4,042,993	3,775,330	2,993,729	781,601	267,663	26,134	241,529
2008	14,394,238	10,169,454	4,224,784	10,061,812	6,139,525	3,922,287	4,332,426	4,029,929	3,060,308	969,621	302,497	28,065	274,432
2009	15,379,473	10,695,816	4,683,657	10,746,637	6,452,414	4,294,223	4,632,836	4,243,402	3,153,294	1,090,108	389,434	27,964	361,470
2010	15,947,474	11,129,239	4,818,235	11,018,756	6,635,799	4,382,957	4,928,718	4,493,440	3,235,149	1,258,291	435,278	26,920	408,358
2011	15,892,792	11,261,845	4,630,947	10,954,754	6,734,116	4,220,638	4,938,038	4,527,729	3,285,711	1,242,018	410,309	34,267	376,042
2012	15,593,434	11,229,774	4,363,660	10,781,798	6,764,184	4,017,614	4,811,636	4,465,590	3,309,242	1,156,348	346,046	32,684	313,362
2013	15,409,944	11,185,987	4,223,957	10,695,774	6,790,901	3,904,873	4,714,170	4,395,086	3,341,575	1,053,511	319,084	27,290	291,794
2014	15,262,196	11,237,953	4,024,243	10,624,769	6,892,523	3,732,246	4,637,427	4,345,430	3,362,197	983,233	291,997	25,797	266,200
2015[3]	15,296,000	10,939,000	4,357,000	10,727,000	6,695,000	4,032,000	4,569,000	4,244,000	—	—	325,000	—	—
2016[3]	15,494,000	11,082,000	4,412,000	10,860,000	6,778,000	4,082,000	4,634,000	4,304,000	—	—	330,000	—	—
2017[3]	15,845,000	11,334,000	4,511,000	11,100,000	6,927,000	4,173,000	4,745,000	4,407,000	—	—	338,000	—	—
2018[3]	16,173,000	11,565,000	4,608,000	11,328,000	7,067,000	4,262,000	4,845,000	4,498,000	—	—	346,000	—	—
2019[3]	16,422,000	11,741,000	4,681,000	11,503,000	7,173,000	4,330,000	4,920,000	4,568,000	—	—	352,000	—	—
2020[3]	16,610,000	11,880,000	4,730,000	11,631,000	7,257,000	4,375,000	4,979,000	4,624,000	—	—	355,000	—	—
2021[3]	16,835,000	12,044,000	4,791,000	11,786,000	7,355,000	4,432,000	5,049,000	4,689,000	—	—	360,000	—	—
2022[3]	17,047,000	12,193,000	4,855,000	11,934,000	7,444,000	4,490,000	5,113,000	4,749,000	—	—	365,000	—	—
2023[3]	17,263,000	12,346,000	4,917,000	12,084,000	7,537,000	4,547,000	5,179,000	4,810,000	—	—	370,000	—	—
2024[3]	17,449,000	12,478,000	4,972,000	12,215,000	7,617,000	4,598,000	5,234,000	4,861,000	—	—	374,000	—	—
2025[3]	17,538,000	12,535,000	5,003,000	12,281,000	7,653,000	4,628,000	5,257,000	4,882,000	—	—	375,000	—	—

—Not available.

[1]Large increases are due to the addition of schools accredited by the Accrediting Commission of Career Schools and Colleges of Technology.

[2]Because of imputation techniques, data are not consistent with figures for other years.

[3]Projected.

NOTE: Full-time-equivalent enrollment is the full-time enrollment, plus the full-time equivalent of the part-time students. Data through 1995 are for institutions of higher education, while later data are for degree-granting institutions. Degree-granting institutions grant associate's or higher degrees and participate in Title IV federal financial aid programs. The degree-granting classification is very similar to the earlier higher education classification, but it includes more 2-year colleges and excludes a few higher education institutions that did not grant degrees. Some data have been revised from previously published figures.

SOURCE: U.S. Department of Education, National Center for Education Statistics, Higher Education General Information Survey (HEGIS), "Fall Enrollment in Colleges and Universities" surveys, 1967 through 1985; Integrated Postsecondary Education Data System (IPEDS), "Fall Enrollment Survey" (IPEDS-EF:86–99); IPEDS Spring 2001 through Spring 2015, Fall Enrollment component; and Enrollment in Degree-Granting Institutions Projection Model, 1980 through 2025. (This table was prepared March 2016.)

Table 307.20. Full-time-equivalent fall enrollment in degree-granting postsecondary institutions, by control and level of institution and state or jurisdiction: 2000, 2010, and 2014

State or jurisdiction	Public						Private nonprofit 4-year		Private for-profit			
	4-year			2-year					4-year		2-year	
	2000	2010	2014	2000	2010	2014	2010	2014	2010	2014	2010	2014
1	2	3	4	5	6	7	8	9	10	11	12	13
United States	5,025,588	6,635,799	6,892,523	3,241,344	4,382,957	3,732,246	3,235,149	3,362,197	1,258,291	983,233	408,358	266,200
Alabama	111,322	140,235	139,966	48,545	68,677	55,008	22,982	23,297	23,570	22,376	3,138	2,510
Alaska	16,335	20,618	19,069	473	357	595	529	428	1,764	3,267	0	479
Arizona	87,301	120,269	135,954	85,778	122,717	105,755	7,487	8,610	369,895	262,255	15,622	9,179
Arkansas	57,897	77,384	80,021	21,519	41,223	33,637	14,559	14,538	2,450	953	683	61
California	476,027	582,256	651,289	707,558	858,417	798,755	245,393	264,364	102,012	147,424	78,898	55,901
Colorado	109,844	134,234	144,134	41,322	59,409	48,010	25,447	26,356	49,704	31,109	11,486	9,088
Connecticut	46,826	58,329	57,773	20,934	34,116	30,753	57,013	60,816	3,757	5,830	257	0
Delaware	20,427	23,125	25,302	6,939	9,365	8,183	10,550	12,119	218	159	0	0
District of Columbia	3,364	3,964	3,415	0	0	0	65,755	66,553	3,789	3,126	0	215
Florida	190,472	484,181	532,113	173,433	78,027	26,494	132,201	149,778	100,670	83,122	39,981	29,914
Georgia	136,069	224,448	243,576	66,571	118,307	71,472	63,327	64,790	37,344	28,846	9,268	7,486
Hawaii	17,015	24,136	24,012	14,996	17,786	16,209	11,244	10,126	1,670	2,286	1,459	1,718
Idaho	34,125	40,828	40,386	6,807	9,847	14,356	16,641	27,539	1,951	913	777	470
Illinois	164,592	178,192	169,560	186,533	228,507	194,448	190,040	189,147	58,243	40,847	9,379	4,795
Indiana	155,982	194,407	192,932	28,131	66,664	49,753	79,106	80,542	18,546	10,829	9,168	4,094
Iowa	61,763	64,706	69,339	44,717	71,021	56,521	50,088	49,198	107,172	30,495	533	563
Kansas	74,307	84,156	85,758	39,457	53,257	49,315	17,882	20,015	1,420	12,166	1,989	1,751
Kentucky	86,080	105,252	107,498	32,239	65,402	52,586	31,858	32,162	13,585	8,086	5,478	1,818
Louisiana	126,372	124,062	118,520	27,130	52,670	46,745	23,509	23,133	3,939	2,307	6,608	4,675
Maine	24,678	25,966	23,970	4,797	11,555	10,971	16,928	18,335	0	1,005	1,303	366
Maryland	94,929	125,536	132,712	57,367	85,789	74,837	42,957	42,246	5,403	3,266	4,143	2,350
Massachusetts	78,452	97,474	102,386	47,972	65,041	59,986	238,759	243,494	4,181	2,787	2,108	1,054
Michigan	223,981	257,896	266,887	101,794	155,150	110,395	91,255	72,916	8,772	4,553	1,098	1,009
Minnesota	95,345	114,954	110,128	65,167	89,858	76,165	62,150	60,030	71,988	62,342	2,200	910
Mississippi	56,107	67,989	70,479	47,245	70,356	59,130	13,601	13,258	289	165	2,470	1,694
Missouri	99,187	120,933	127,933	46,793	74,399	64,037	113,252	110,521	17,435	9,451	10,713	5,742
Montana	28,278	32,375	32,874	3,900	7,715	5,760	4,073	3,998	0	0	0	0
Nebraska	44,374	50,013	51,179	20,812	30,680	24,248	27,836	29,128	2,151	1,514	1,037	312
Nevada	27,631	68,001	66,647	20,468	6,571	5,604	3,028	3,493	6,841	4,249	5,151	4,548
New Hampshire	21,064	26,150	25,593	5,442	9,172	8,545	22,449	44,624	3,898	1,801	0	0
New Jersey	111,449	144,174	153,257	79,367	125,787	108,823	63,113	63,154	5,993	5,496	1,891	3,679
New Mexico	39,779	52,191	50,775	29,541	49,580	41,924	1,012	1,122	6,612	4,358	3,316	1,444
New York	269,664	328,542	333,368	168,911	242,030	229,264	440,038	444,536	27,670	26,987	21,686	15,524
North Carolina	140,203	193,970	195,514	96,999	158,480	141,370	83,931	86,856	10,987	10,763	2,694	2,791
North Dakota	24,728	35,435	34,414	6,515	4,572	4,386	4,832	4,451	1,154	570	0	0
Ohio	215,993	292,493	280,090	92,749	131,274	98,011	123,493	119,415	13,682	13,759	29,858	10,363
Oklahoma	79,786	102,471	100,751	34,997	44,842	36,220	20,213	22,081	5,434	3,573	4,539	4,241
Oregon	59,588	82,751	86,884	46,099	69,825	60,305	28,591	33,386	5,530	3,370	3,791	2,176
Pennsylvania	211,132	257,017	252,870	58,759	93,216	76,304	248,139	246,760	17,802	11,962	38,769	24,309
Rhode Island	17,967	21,720	21,921	8,650	10,107	9,395	39,093	38,350	0	0	0	0
South Carolina	74,309	93,512	99,959	41,804	66,813	60,281	31,078	30,749	11,326	8,904	2,621	2,627
South Dakota	23,881	29,247	29,130	4,193	5,746	5,166	7,133	5,575	2,831	1,333	0	0
Tennessee	99,636	125,069	119,980	53,146	64,802	53,810	69,240	73,702	15,154	9,001	12,371	7,768
Texas	358,523	506,279	549,935	268,057	403,005	372,805	110,416	115,728	24,705	24,340	39,172	23,003
Utah	71,982	100,176	103,754	16,454	26,302	15,399	56,824	95,840	11,881	5,258	1,393	760
Vermont	13,581	18,461	17,430	1,845	3,114	2,596	15,710	16,102	615	371	0	0
Virginia	147,370	185,096	191,235	72,913	113,060	104,464	87,912	101,500	37,169	28,600	9,380	6,852
Washington	83,899	143,012	175,851	114,754	109,154	70,870	37,741	37,358	7,050	4,476	5,098	4,146
West Virginia	58,171	64,650	60,650	3,969	15,609	12,426	11,487	8,100	18,867	25,272	2,819	2,185
Wisconsin	130,661	160,463	157,645	56,195	68,908	57,305	53,254	51,818	11,045	7,311	2,134	545
Wyoming	9,665	11,089	10,985	10,588	14,676	12,849	0	60	127	0	1,879	1,085
U.S. Service Academies	13,475	15,912	14,720	0	0	0	†	†	†	†	†	†
Other jurisdictions	66,376	65,847	63,120	7,200	8,758	7,066	113,458	112,325	9,417	12,591	30,467	29,144
American Samoa	0	0	942	214	1,275	0	0	0	0	0	0	0
Federated States of Micronesia	0	0	0	1,308	2,243	1,852	0	0	0	0	0	0
Guam	2,802	3,074	3,331	777	1,424	1,482	73	61	0	0	0	0
Marshall Islands	0	0	0	166	739	886	0	0	0	0	0	0
Northern Marianas	0	1,031	1,066	707	0	0	0	0	0	0	0	0
Palau	0	0	0	450	541	447	0	0	0	0	0	0
Puerto Rico	61,987	59,658	56,023	3,578	2,536	2,399	113,385	112,264	9,417	12,591	30,467	29,144
U.S. Virgin Islands	1,587	2,084	1,758	0	0	0	0	0	0	0	0	0

†Not applicable.
NOTE: Full-time-equivalent enrollment is the full-time enrollment, plus the full-time equivalent of the part-time students. Degree-granting institutions grant associate's or higher degrees and participate in Title IV federal financial aid programs.

SOURCE: U.S. Department of Education, National Center for Education Statistics, Integrated Postsecondary Education Data System (IPEDS), Spring 2001, 2011, and 2015, Fall Enrollment component. (This table was prepared October 2015.)

Table 307.30. Full-time-equivalent fall enrollment in degree-granting postsecondary institutions, by control of institution and state or jurisdiction: 2000, 2010, and 2014

State or jurisdiction	Total			Public			Private nonprofit			Private for-profit		
	2000	2010	2014	2000	2010	2014	2000	2010	2014	2000	2010	2014
1	2	3	4	5	6	7	8	9	10	11	12	13
United States	11,267,025	15,947,474	15,262,196	8,266,932	11,018,756	10,624,769	2,601,179	3,262,069	3,387,994	398,914	1,666,649	1,249,433
Alabama	184,031	258,602	243,675	159,867	208,912	194,974	20,605	22,982	23,815	3,559	26,708	24,886
Alaska	17,787	23,268	23,903	16,808	20,975	19,664	672	529	493	307	1,764	3,746
Arizona	225,396	635,990	521,753	173,079	242,986	241,709	8,079	7,487	8,610	44,238	385,517	271,434
Arkansas	91,886	136,299	129,812	79,416	118,607	113,658	11,713	14,559	15,140	757	3,133	1,014
California	1,468,486	1,868,187	1,919,584	1,183,585	1,440,673	1,450,044	214,444	246,604	266,215	70,457	180,910	203,325
Colorado	188,117	280,408	258,697	151,166	193,643	192,144	20,991	25,575	26,356	15,960	61,190	40,197
Connecticut	117,954	153,746	155,172	67,760	92,445	88,526	48,648	57,287	60,816	1,546	4,014	5,830
Delaware	34,057	43,470	45,937	27,366	32,490	33,485	6,691	10,762	12,293	0	218	159
District of Columbia	59,560	73,508	73,318	3,364	3,964	3,415	54,177	65,755	66,562	2,019	3,789	3,341
Florida	486,818	835,295	822,870	363,905	562,208	558,607	90,530	132,436	151,227	32,383	140,651	113,036
Georgia	268,707	453,209	416,630	202,640	342,755	315,048	57,444	63,842	65,250	8,623	46,612	36,332
Hawaii	45,329	56,295	54,351	32,011	41,922	40,221	11,521	11,244	10,126	1,797	3,129	4,004
Idaho	52,353	70,044	83,664	40,932	50,675	54,742	10,751	16,641	27,539	670	2,728	1,383
Illinois	520,087	665,347	599,459	351,125	406,699	364,008	150,578	191,026	189,809	18,384	67,622	45,642
Indiana	250,998	368,373	338,494	184,113	261,071	242,685	60,387	79,588	80,886	6,498	27,714	14,923
Iowa	152,505	293,680	206,116	106,480	135,727	125,860	43,735	50,248	49,198	2,290	107,705	31,058
Kansas	129,839	160,434	169,393	113,764	137,413	135,073	15,605	19,612	20,403	470	3,409	13,917
Kentucky	149,395	221,575	202,150	118,319	170,654	160,084	23,859	31,858	32,162	7,217	19,063	9,904
Louisiana	183,661	210,788	196,016	153,502	176,732	165,265	25,646	23,509	23,769	4,513	10,547	6,982
Maine	43,384	55,950	54,844	29,475	37,521	34,941	13,020	17,126	18,532	889	1,303	1,371
Maryland	188,887	263,828	255,411	152,296	211,325	207,549	34,445	42,957	42,246	2,146	9,546	5,616
Massachusetts	327,984	408,300	410,319	126,424	162,515	162,372	199,745	239,496	244,106	1,815	6,289	3,841
Michigan	402,019	514,171	455,760	325,775	413,046	377,282	73,144	91,255	72,916	3,100	9,870	5,562
Minnesota	223,232	341,248	309,631	160,512	204,812	186,293	52,974	62,248	60,086	9,746	74,188	63,252
Mississippi	113,804	154,705	144,726	103,352	138,345	129,609	10,073	13,601	13,258	379	2,759	1,859
Missouri	237,161	337,846	318,425	145,980	195,332	191,970	82,425	114,366	111,262	8,756	28,148	15,193
Montana	36,005	44,605	43,077	32,178	40,090	38,634	3,827	4,515	4,443	0	0	0
Nebraska	85,993	111,869	106,512	65,186	80,693	75,427	18,956	27,998	29,259	1,851	3,188	1,826
Nevada	52,577	89,592	84,541	48,099	74,572	72,251	455	3,028	3,493	4,023	11,992	8,797
New Hampshire	48,230	61,919	80,658	26,506	35,322	34,138	18,732	22,699	44,719	2,992	3,898	1,801
New Jersey	245,447	340,958	334,409	190,816	269,961	262,080	48,751	63,113	63,154	5,880	7,884	9,175
New Mexico	77,415	112,711	99,623	69,320	101,771	92,699	3,274	1,012	1,122	4,821	9,928	5,802
New York	826,078	1,063,531	1,051,670	438,515	570,572	562,632	355,832	443,603	446,527	31,671	49,356	42,511
North Carolina	305,805	450,726	437,990	237,202	352,450	336,884	68,127	84,595	87,552	476	13,681	13,554
North Dakota	35,230	46,556	43,821	31,243	40,007	38,800	3,876	5,395	4,451	111	1,154	570
Ohio	426,080	591,980	522,565	308,742	423,767	378,101	105,004	124,673	120,342	12,334	43,540	24,122
Oklahoma	136,833	177,499	166,866	114,783	147,313	136,971	18,827	20,213	22,081	3,223	9,973	7,814
Oregon	130,705	190,488	186,121	105,687	152,576	147,189	22,079	28,591	33,386	2,939	9,321	5,546
Pennsylvania	499,729	661,592	619,066	269,891	350,233	329,174	201,136	254,788	253,621	28,702	56,571	36,271
Rhode Island	59,639	70,920	69,666	26,617	31,827	31,316	32,813	39,093	38,350	209	0	0
South Carolina	143,343	206,261	203,303	116,113	160,325	160,240	26,504	31,989	31,532	726	13,947	11,531
South Dakota	34,876	45,155	41,311	28,074	34,993	34,296	4,751	7,331	5,682	2,051	2,831	1,333
Tennessee	209,100	286,834	264,881	152,782	189,871	173,790	50,967	69,438	74,322	5,351	27,525	16,769
Texas	741,012	1,085,155	1,088,195	626,580	909,284	922,740	98,445	111,994	118,112	15,987	63,877	47,343
Utah	125,622	198,079	222,610	88,436	126,478	119,153	32,727	58,327	97,439	4,459	13,274	6,018
Vermont	29,099	38,387	36,499	15,426	21,575	20,026	13,336	16,197	16,102	337	615	371
Virginia	277,270	432,617	432,984	220,283	298,156	295,699	44,825	87,912	101,833	12,162	46,549	35,452
Washington	236,609	302,113	292,762	198,653	252,166	246,721	32,726	37,799	37,419	5,230	12,148	8,622
West Virginia	72,962	113,432	108,633	62,140	80,259	73,076	8,891	11,487	8,100	1,931	21,686	27,457
Wisconsin	232,912	296,246	274,624	186,856	229,371	214,950	44,416	53,696	51,818	1,640	13,179	7,856
Wyoming	21,542	27,771	24,979	20,253	25,765	23,834	0	0	60	1,289	2,006	1,085
U.S. Service Academies	13,475	15,912	14,720	13,475	15,912	14,720	†	†	†	†	†	†
Other jurisdictions	166,039	232,204	224,956	73,576	74,605	70,186	81,642	117,715	113,035	10,821	39,884	41,735
American Samoa	214	1,275	942	214	1,275	942	0	0	0	0	0	0
Federated States of Micronesia	1,308	2,243	1,852	1,308	2,243	1,852	0	0	0	0	0	0
Guam	3,579	4,571	4,874	3,579	4,498	4,813	0	73	61	0	0	0
Marshall Islands	166	739	886	166	739	886	0	0	0	0	0	0
Northern Marianas	707	1,031	1,066	707	1,031	1,066	0	0	0	0	0	0
Palau	450	541	447	450	541	447	0	0	0	0	0	0
Puerto Rico	158,028	219,720	213,131	65,565	62,194	58,422	81,642	117,642	112,974	10,821	39,884	41,735
U.S. Virgin Islands	1,587	2,084	1,758	1,587	2,084	1,758	0	0	0	0	0	0

†Not applicable.
NOTE: Full-time-equivalent enrollment is the full-time enrollment, plus the full-time equivalent of the part-time students. Degree-granting institutions grant associate's or higher degrees and participate in Title IV federal financial aid programs.

SOURCE: U.S. Department of Education, National Center for Education Statistics, Integrated Postsecondary Education Data System (IPEDS), Spring 2001, 2011, and 2015, Fall Enrollment component. (This table was prepared October 2015.)

Table 308.10. Total 12-month enrollment in degree-granting postsecondary institutions, by control and level of institution and state or jurisdiction: 2012–13 and 2013–14

State or jurisdiction	2012–13							2013–14						
	Total	Public 4-year	Public 2-year	Private 4-year		Private 2-year		Total	Public 4-year	Public 2-year	Private 4-year		Private 2-year	
				Nonprofit	For-profit	Nonprofit	For-profit				Nonprofit	For-profit	Nonprofit	For-profit
1	2	3	4	5	6	7	8	9	10	11	12	13	14	15
United States	27,517,468	9,675,774	10,124,629	4,807,325	2,311,768	47,807	550,165	27,083,555	9,760,034	9,798,621	4,819,155	2,159,520	46,513	499,712
Alabama	409,372	192,373	125,477	29,309	55,664	945	5,604	402,409	189,636	124,541	28,968	53,341	881	5,042
Alaska........................	56,900	48,540	3,812	1,001	2,983	56	508	55,691	48,249	2,194	952	3,738	72	486
Arizona	1,074,585	160,382	352,226	12,085	533,490	0	16,402	1,009,011	165,753	335,152	11,504	481,443	0	15,159
Arkansas...................	223,954	115,715	85,556	18,959	2,765	710	249	217,304	114,955	80,369	18,353	2,287	1,105	235
California	3,451,568	712,174	2,082,862	360,136	182,479	2,548	111,369	3,604,116	732,645	2,104,251	368,746	294,862	2,431	101,181
Colorado	504,450	216,149	153,144	43,078	73,985	131	17,963	498,687	219,442	144,908	44,189	72,736	0	17,412
Connecticut...............	256,040	77,314	82,416	79,687	16,344	0	279	254,973	77,027	80,037	81,465	16,444	0	0
Delaware...................	72,787	28,197	20,364	23,329	659	238	0	73,174	28,392	19,421	24,613	541	207	0
District of Columbia	107,907	7,277	0	90,009	10,144	0	477	108,922	6,828	0	88,925	12,357	43	769
Florida......................	1,579,136	998,241	77,144	244,494	196,085	2,220	60,952	1,537,821	999,035	60,146	245,208	176,161	2,600	54,671
Georgia.....................	710,577	326,970	218,850	83,118	66,556	561	14,522	693,775	340,045	196,133	83,304	59,810	561	13,922
Hawaii	100,042	36,729	39,645	17,586	2,943	0	3,139	97,917	36,268	38,812	16,348	3,427	0	3,062
Idaho........................	151,014	68,335	35,223	44,597	2,100	0	759	153,673	65,688	35,366	49,946	1,896	0	777
Illinois......................	1,315,277	224,845	687,396	276,013	113,534	1,104	12,385	1,269,341	220,034	659,501	269,572	110,326	1,138	8,770
Indiana......................	603,925	274,993	180,464	105,984	33,616	531	8,337	600,445	277,082	179,191	106,330	29,703	515	7,624
Iowa.........................	529,741	84,594	145,389	69,685	228,822	0	1,251	385,850	85,534	141,621	69,657	87,938	0	1,100
Kansas......................	308,407	118,754	141,720	38,206	5,517	488	3,722	319,361	116,656	135,496	39,113	24,387	478	3,231
Kentucky...................	357,839	146,461	136,143	47,178	22,519	0	5,538	338,900	145,171	127,441	43,578	19,044	0	3,666
Louisiana..................	328,441	165,735	113,798	31,927	5,721	1,985	9,275	321,844	161,817	113,295	31,227	4,949	1,132	9,424
Maine.......................	94,708	39,646	25,649	26,852	1,434	355	772	95,304	38,628	25,388	27,739	2,317	434	798
Maryland...................	486,259	205,683	200,337	65,746	10,029	0	4,464	471,867	202,547	191,784	64,426	8,874	0	4,236
Massachusetts...............	646,639	157,202	146,222	333,258	5,966	1,282	2,709	648,103	158,104	146,503	334,192	5,744	1,631	1,929
Michigan...................	863,352	352,632	346,521	148,958	11,238	0	4,003	820,146	361,792	309,772	135,617	10,319	0	2,646
Minnesota.................	604,829	164,666	190,779	84,642	162,109	114	2,519	591,700	163,827	183,567	84,781	158,091	86	1,348
Mississippi................	225,199	92,676	106,355	20,542	743	0	4,883	221,006	92,234	102,788	20,863	583	0	4,538
Missouri....................	585,495	175,326	152,523	203,154	41,929	1,502	11,061	552,705	176,704	145,891	196,799	21,608	1,493	10,210
Montana....................	66,874	46,648	14,429	5,188	0	609	0	65,739	46,184	13,817	5,040	0	698	0
Nebraska...................	200,724	68,773	85,245	41,856	3,517	271	1,062	195,515	69,592	78,932	42,430	3,525	251	785
Nevada.....................	159,029	121,603	16,722	3,757	9,351	0	7,596	158,910	122,991	16,017	4,019	8,234	0	7,649
New Hampshire	113,097	34,034	22,231	51,869	4,555	408	0	137,068	33,824	22,999	76,303	3,717	225	0
New Jersey.................	549,933	202,230	249,637	83,090	8,733	0	6,243	552,572	212,434	240,149	83,284	10,071	0	6,634
New Mexico	212,166	78,507	120,342	1,689	9,152	0	2,476	208,313	78,111	117,063	1,926	8,695	0	2,518
New York...................	1,659,415	479,477	466,869	625,245	49,473	6,255	32,096	1,646,123	479,135	459,157	621,719	49,807	5,682	30,623
North Carolina.............	748,797	252,618	353,984	109,908	24,281	782	7,224	742,578	251,272	349,357	108,966	25,156	804	7,023
North Dakota	69,180	51,110	9,435	7,025	1,610	0	0	70,545	51,298	9,455	8,313	1,479	0	0
Ohio.........................	918,553	400,311	279,264	174,411	36,436	2,019	26,112	903,678	400,684	278,816	170,011	30,944	1,699	21,524
Oklahoma..................	295,124	151,633	99,854	29,043	7,885	0	6,709	281,592	148,348	89,263	29,880	7,288	0	6,813
Oregon......................	369,740	131,871	182,545	41,805	7,990	0	5,529	361,135	132,206	171,692	45,619	7,135	0	4,483
Pennsylvania..............	966,588	319,211	212,655	334,888	38,136	12,371	49,327	946,369	319,915	204,711	332,365	32,430	12,341	44,607
Rhode Island	99,627	29,655	24,252	45,720	0	0	0	98,253	29,338	23,464	45,451	0	0	0
South Carolina..............	333,102	123,322	141,342	41,949	17,557	866	8,066	329,072	125,423	136,413	41,764	18,603	865	6,004
South Dakota..............	73,881	49,336	8,064	9,244	6,711	526	0	72,511	49,490	8,070	9,511	5,059	381	0
Tennessee	431,373	163,915	127,151	96,629	24,214	993	18,471	416,118	160,593	123,109	96,767	19,165	975	15,509
Texas	2,096,855	766,405	1,078,570	157,787	45,780	4,387	43,926	2,083,964	775,979	1,058,043	157,073	46,621	4,415	41,833
Utah.........................	356,805	179,494	47,599	112,971	11,749	2,901	2,091	357,258	175,521	46,857	120,077	10,587	2,711	1,505
Vermont.....................	59,583	24,347	10,429	24,142	665	0	0	58,159	23,521	10,794	23,282	562	0	0
Virginia.....................	785,052	253,282	281,976	168,495	66,161	595	14,543	775,300	252,310	274,858	170,196	62,811	588	14,537
Washington................	506,467	228,878	212,018	49,088	9,196	54	7,233	504,616	275,962	163,273	49,131	8,434	71	7,745
West Virginia..............	246,174	84,684	29,216	9,571	118,516	0	4,187	237,356	82,807	23,557	9,966	116,513	0	4,513
Wisconsin..................	483,032	212,697	165,928	82,322	20,726	0	1,359	471,155	209,279	161,588	79,536	19,758	0	994
Wyoming...................	52,524	14,794	34,857	100	0	0	2,773	50,546	14,659	33,599	111	0	0	2,177
U.S. Service Academies ..	15,330	15,330	†	†	†	†	†	15,065	15,065	†	†	†	†	†
Other jurisdictions .	308,174	75,172	14,076	160,275	17,194	0	41,457	306,999	74,910	14,979	155,086	22,289	1,101	38,634
American Samoa............	2,464	2,464	0	0	0	0	0	2,110	2,110	0	0	0	0	0
Federated States of Micronesia	5,082	0	5,082	0	0	0	0	5,536	0	5,536	0	0	0	0
Guam........................	8,345	4,785	3,481	79	0	0	0	8,650	4,890	3,669	91	0	0	0
Marshall Islands..............	1,411	0	1,411	0	0	0	0	1,398	0	1,398	0	0	0	0
Northern Marianas	1,445	1,445	0	0	0	0	0	1,367	1,367	0	0	0	0	0
Palau.........................	897	0	897	0	0	0	0	835	0	835	0	0	0	0
Puerto Rico..................	285,373	63,321	3,205	160,196	17,194	0	41,457	284,274	63,714	3,541	154,995	22,289	1,101	38,634
U.S. Virgin Islands	3,157	3,157	0	0	0	0	0	2,829	2,829	0	0	0	0	0

†Not applicable.
NOTE: Includes students who enrolled at any point during a 12-month period ending during the summer of the academic year indicated. Degree-granting institutions grant associate's or higher degrees and participate in Title IV federal financial aid programs. Some data have been revised from previously published figures.

SOURCE: U.S. Department of Education, National Center for Education Statistics, Integrated Postsecondary Education Data System (IPEDS), Fall 2013 and Fall 2014, 12-Month Enrollment component. (This table was prepared April 2016.)

Table 308.20. Total 12-month enrollment in degree-granting postsecondary institutions, by control of institution and state or jurisdiction: Selected years, 2004–05 through 2013–14

State or jurisdiction	Total					Public			Private nonprofit			Private for-profit		
	2004–05	2010–11	2011–12	2012–13	2013–14	2004–05	2010–11	2013–14	2004–05	2010–11	2013–14	2004–05	2010–11	2013–14
1	2	3	4	5	6	7	8	9	10	11	12	13	14	15
United States	23,798,595	28,561,503	28,172,198	27,517,468	27,083,555	18,058,078	20,516,945	19,558,655	4,222,755	4,761,799	4,865,668	1,517,762	3,282,759	2,659,232
Alabama	349,783	431,219	423,697	409,372	402,409	310,878	341,757	314,177	28,847	30,152	29,849	10,058	59,310	58,383
Alaska	53,786	58,668	60,103	56,900	55,691	51,689	53,841	50,443	1,253	998	1,024	844	3,829	4,224
Arizona	821,240	1,238,668	1,161,102	1,074,585	1,009,011	499,192	544,922	500,905	13,162	11,438	11,504	308,886	682,308	496,602
Arkansas	182,497	228,659	230,899	223,954	217,304	164,751	204,632	195,324	15,260	19,536	19,458	2,486	4,491	2,522
California	3,341,107	3,748,013	3,580,417	3,451,568	3,604,116	2,843,929	3,070,257	2,836,896	327,661	344,961	371,177	169,517	332,795	396,043
Colorado	428,215	519,811	524,887	504,450	498,687	333,100	364,905	364,350	40,144	41,959	44,189	54,971	112,947	90,148
Connecticut	219,327	251,521	254,715	256,040	254,973	144,681	162,795	157,064	71,235	78,212	81,465	3,411	10,514	16,444
Delaware	63,817	70,098	70,454	72,787	73,174	47,148	48,991	47,813	16,669	20,408	24,820	0	699	541
District of Columbia	129,349	114,264	106,523	107,907	108,922	10,095	12,786	6,828	81,718	89,433	88,968	37,536	12,045	13,126
Florida	1,232,578	1,585,959	1,612,394	1,579,136	1,537,821	912,150	1,080,517	1,059,181	191,789	251,966	247,808	128,639	253,476	230,832
Georgia	569,805	776,316	730,684	710,577	693,775	466,589	584,787	536,178	70,449	82,614	83,865	32,767	108,915	73,732
Hawaii	92,643	101,719	101,481	100,042	97,917	67,835	76,929	75,080	20,749	19,182	16,348	4,059	5,608	6,489
Idaho	108,415	126,866	142,195	151,014	153,673	84,627	92,865	101,054	20,802	28,421	49,946	2,986	5,580	2,673
Illinois	1,293,156	1,374,177	1,350,322	1,315,277	1,269,341	933,506	948,489	879,535	257,053	280,649	270,710	102,597	145,039	119,096
Indiana	488,374	621,156	609,700	603,925	600,445	363,817	455,107	456,273	103,295	107,813	106,845	21,262	58,236	37,327
Iowa	309,318	573,112	557,823	529,741	385,850	200,039	236,600	227,155	72,538	78,103	69,657	36,741	258,409	89,038
Kansas	276,293	302,966	298,578	308,407	319,361	241,778	259,654	252,152	32,480	36,532	39,591	2,035	6,780	27,618
Kentucky	303,785	374,660	374,000	357,839	338,900	248,402	293,292	272,612	33,565	44,135	43,578	21,818	37,233	22,710
Louisiana	323,630	338,898	338,468	328,441	321,844	276,599	288,958	275,112	34,050	34,127	32,359	12,981	15,813	14,373
Maine	88,644	92,858	94,341	94,708	95,304	64,380	66,013	64,016	22,474	24,233	28,173	1,790	2,612	3,115
Maryland	412,867	490,738	496,859	486,259	471,867	340,538	404,916	394,331	64,377	66,660	64,426	7,952	19,162	13,110
Massachusetts	565,872	640,116	644,103	646,639	648,103	266,316	301,999	304,607	293,677	327,569	335,823	5,879	10,548	7,673
Michigan	844,731	911,818	889,359	863,352	820,146	690,014	734,343	671,564	141,670	159,624	135,617	13,047	17,851	12,965
Minnesota	469,986	625,540	614,033	604,829	591,700	318,448	361,582	347,394	83,577	88,876	84,867	67,961	175,082	159,439
Mississippi	206,917	235,071	233,236	225,199	221,006	187,594	209,115	195,022	17,299	20,162	20,863	2,024	5,794	5,121
Missouri	504,860	615,010	609,945	585,495	552,705	289,162	336,606	322,595	187,886	209,055	198,292	27,812	69,349	31,818
Montana	60,259	68,083	68,163	66,874	65,739	53,889	61,911	60,001	6,370	6,172	5,738	0	0	0
Nebraska	178,595	205,496	202,876	200,724	195,515	140,544	156,586	148,524	34,369	43,617	42,681	3,682	5,293	4,310
Nevada	153,540	178,375	165,857	159,029	158,910	136,158	154,792	139,008	1,087	4,332	4,019	16,295	19,251	15,883
New Hampshire	92,067	98,788	101,835	113,097	137,068	52,671	58,196	56,823	31,809	34,560	76,528	7,587	6,032	3,717
New Jersey	484,892	569,225	566,181	549,933	552,572	395,088	467,558	452,583	80,936	87,569	83,284	8,868	14,098	16,705
New Mexico	190,031	220,705	216,076	212,166	208,313	175,425	204,209	195,174	5,007	1,386	1,926	9,599	15,110	11,213
New York	1,457,951	1,657,093	1,674,438	1,659,415	1,646,123	820,849	950,505	938,292	560,583	622,623	627,401	76,519	83,965	80,430
North Carolina	637,309	757,889	751,635	748,797	742,578	537,735	620,890	600,629	94,361	106,129	109,770	5,213	30,870	32,179
North Dakota	62,743	70,185	70,816	69,180	70,545	54,671	59,830	60,753	7,090	7,667	8,313	982	2,688	1,479
Ohio	809,712	992,062	966,766	918,553	903,678	601,853	726,472	679,500	167,235	179,987	171,710	40,624	85,603	52,468
Oklahoma	276,437	299,365	300,108	295,124	281,592	238,444	257,400	237,611	27,920	26,726	29,880	10,073	15,239	14,101
Oregon	296,574	374,342	377,098	369,740	361,135	251,800	320,026	303,898	31,580	39,258	45,619	13,194	15,058	11,618
Pennsylvania	868,185	1,019,990	996,327	966,588	946,369	493,773	548,169	524,626	307,862	351,503	344,706	66,550	120,318	77,037
Rhode Island	99,103	101,610	100,938	99,627	98,253	52,263	54,535	52,802	45,906	47,075	45,451	934	0	0
South Carolina	268,590	331,280	335,091	333,102	329,072	221,632	262,422	261,836	43,450	43,306	42,629	3,508	25,552	24,607
South Dakota	63,989	74,210	73,936	73,881	72,511	48,570	56,861	57,560	9,858	9,783	9,892	5,561	7,566	5,059
Tennessee	353,167	438,901	435,377	431,373	416,118	254,104	299,545	283,702	72,505	92,761	97,742	26,558	46,595	34,674
Texas	1,695,267	2,107,654	2,119,327	2,096,855	2,083,964	1,492,623	1,843,574	1,834,022	148,812	160,405	161,488	53,832	103,675	88,454
Utah	278,798	340,784	350,906	356,805	357,258	213,428	236,332	222,378	50,268	80,445	122,788	15,102	24,007	12,092
Vermont	51,313	59,997	60,059	59,583	58,159	31,099	36,594	34,315	19,771	22,623	23,282	443	780	562
Virginia	583,958	783,117	798,893	785,052	775,300	462,958	541,978	527,168	80,805	141,580	170,784	40,195	99,559	77,348
Washington	520,108	554,551	525,030	506,467	504,616	451,410	483,491	439,235	52,896	50,395	49,202	15,802	20,665	16,179
West Virginia	126,082	231,331	242,223	246,174	237,356	104,704	119,247	106,364	15,416	16,749	9,966	5,962	95,335	121,026
Wisconsin	444,120	507,252	492,758	483,032	471,155	353,215	390,899	370,867	83,180	88,330	79,536	7,725	28,023	20,752
Wyoming	48,651	53,987	53,384	52,524	50,546	45,756	50,935	48,258	0	0	111	2,895	3,052	2,177
U.S. Service Academies	16,159	17,330	15,782	15,330	15,065	16,159	17,330	15,065	†	†	†	†	†	†
Other jurisdictions	258,744	316,672	317,210	308,174	306,999	95,808	94,233	89,889	136,708	163,515	156,187	26,228	58,924	60,923
American Samoa	2,299	2,744	2,621	2,464	2,110	2,299	2,744	2,110	0	0	0	0	0	0
Federated States of Micronesia	3,570	5,097	5,457	5,082	5,536	3,570	5,097	5,536	0	0	0	0	0	0
Guam	7,125	8,105	8,005	8,345	8,650	6,936	8,001	8,559	189	104	91	0	0	0
Marshall Islands	466	1,176	1,310	1,411	1,398	466	1,176	1,398	0	0	0	0	0	0
Northern Marianas	1,590	1,388	1,332	1,445	1,367	1,590	1,388	1,367	0	0	0	0	0	0
Palau	987	922	981	897	835	987	922	835	0	0	0	0	0	0
Puerto Rico	239,442	293,820	294,259	285,373	284,274	76,695	71,485	67,255	136,519	163,411	156,096	26,228	58,924	60,923
U.S. Virgin Islands	3,265	3,420	3,245	3,157	2,829	3,265	3,420	2,829	0	0	0	0	0	0

†Not applicable.
NOTE: Includes students who enrolled at any point during a 12-month period ending during the summer of the academic year indicated. Degree-granting institutions grant associate's or higher degrees and participate in Title IV federal financial aid programs. Some data have been revised from previously published figures.

SOURCE: U.S. Department of Education, National Center for Education Statistics, Integrated Postsecondary Education Data System (IPEDS), Fall 2005 through Fall 2014, 12-Month Enrollment component. (This table was prepared April 2016.)

Table 309.10. Residence and migration of all first-time degree/certificate-seeking undergraduates in degree-granting postsecondary institutions, by state or jurisdiction: Fall 2014

State or jurisdiction	Total first-time enrollment in institutions located in the state	State residents enrolled in institutions		Ratio of in-state students		Migration of students		
		In any state[1]	In their home state	To first-time enrollment (col. 4/col. 2)	To residents enrolled in any state (col. 4/col. 3)	Out of state (col. 3 - col. 4)	Into state[2] (col. 2 - col. 4)	Net (col. 8 - col. 7)
1	2	3	4	5	6	7	8	9
United States	2,925,026	2,829,818	2,314,473	0.79	0.82	515,345	610,553	95,208
Alabama	51,149	42,288	36,878	0.72	0.87	5,410	14,271	8,861
Alaska	4,562	5,558	3,941	0.86	0.71	1,617	621	-996
Arizona	73,047	52,506	46,659	0.64	0.89	5,847	26,388	20,541
Arkansas	27,407	24,743	21,535	0.79	0.87	3,208	5,872	2,664
California	392,472	388,315	346,495	0.88	0.89	41,820	45,977	4,157
Colorado	44,233	43,669	33,532	0.76	0.77	10,137	10,701	564
Connecticut	31,550	36,799	21,080	0.67	0.57	15,719	10,470	-5,249
Delaware	9,589	7,906	5,383	0.56	0.68	2,523	4,206	1,683
District of Columbia	9,978	3,694	875	0.09	0.24	2,819	9,103	6,284
Florida	157,545	151,349	132,592	0.84	0.88	18,757	24,953	6,196
Georgia	84,438	89,590	71,840	0.85	0.80	17,750	12,598	-5,152
Hawaii	9,613	11,127	7,395	0.77	0.66	3,732	2,218	-1,514
Idaho	12,373	11,357	8,000	0.65	0.70	3,357	4,373	1,016
Illinois	99,528	116,151	82,455	0.83	0.71	33,696	17,073	-16,623
Indiana	67,860	59,133	51,277	0.76	0.87	7,856	16,583	8,727
Iowa	40,657	28,118	24,315	0.60	0.86	3,803	16,342	12,539
Kansas	33,786	28,032	23,943	0.71	0.85	4,089	9,843	5,754
Kentucky	38,848	35,488	30,672	0.79	0.86	4,816	8,176	3,360
Louisiana	40,871	39,982	35,370	0.87	0.88	4,612	5,501	889
Maine	11,287	10,717	7,535	0.67	0.70	3,182	3,752	570
Maryland	46,129	54,551	36,329	0.79	0.67	18,222	9,800	-8,422
Massachusetts	75,149	66,060	45,933	0.61	0.70	20,127	29,216	9,089
Michigan	89,195	88,711	78,130	0.88	0.88	10,581	11,065	484
Minnesota	46,234	50,747	36,350	0.79	0.72	14,397	9,884	-4,513
Mississippi	31,416	28,881	24,867	0.79	0.86	4,014	6,549	2,535
Missouri	57,357	53,072	44,044	0.77	0.83	9,028	13,313	4,285
Montana	8,887	7,605	6,051	0.68	0.80	1,554	2,836	1,282
Nebraska	18,372	17,310	14,142	0.77	0.82	3,168	4,230	1,062
Nevada	16,337	18,372	14,257	0.87	0.78	4,115	2,080	-2,035
New Hampshire	15,312	11,874	6,555	0.43	0.55	5,319	8,757	3,438
New Jersey	66,903	96,004	61,191	0.91	0.64	34,813	5,712	-29,101
New Mexico	17,311	17,215	14,337	0.83	0.83	2,878	2,974	96
New York	189,350	182,220	149,170	0.79	0.82	33,050	40,180	7,130
North Carolina	92,343	87,968	76,324	0.83	0.87	11,644	16,019	4,375
North Dakota	8,565	5,762	4,297	0.50	0.75	1,465	4,268	2,803
Ohio	103,213	98,602	83,518	0.81	0.85	15,084	19,695	4,611
Oklahoma	36,051	31,014	27,438	0.76	0.88	3,576	8,613	5,037
Oregon	29,612	25,150	20,420	0.69	0.81	4,730	9,192	4,462
Pennsylvania	131,583	114,624	95,069	0.72	0.83	19,555	36,514	16,959
Rhode Island	15,447	9,303	6,231	0.40	0.67	3,072	9,216	6,144
South Carolina	47,164	41,349	36,219	0.77	0.88	5,130	10,945	5,815
South Dakota	8,372	7,019	5,354	0.64	0.76	1,665	3,018	1,353
Tennessee	52,846	51,884	42,999	0.81	0.83	8,885	9,847	962
Texas	237,857	246,012	219,497	0.92	0.89	26,515	18,360	-8,155
Utah	28,221	21,173	19,124	0.68	0.90	2,049	9,097	7,048
Vermont	7,527	4,719	2,459	0.33	0.52	2,260	5,068	2,808
Virginia	81,470	75,257	61,919	0.76	0.82	13,338	19,551	6,213
Washington	42,543	45,774	35,117	0.83	0.77	10,657	7,426	-3,231
West Virginia	22,357	12,961	11,247	0.50	0.87	1,714	11,110	9,396
Wisconsin	52,437	49,834	40,817	0.78	0.82	9,017	11,620	2,603
Wyoming	4,681	3,917	2,916	0.62	0.74	1,001	1,765	764
U.S. Service Academies	3,992	†	380 [3]	0.10	†	-380	3,612	3,992
State unknown[4]	†	18,352	†	†	†	18,352	†	-18,352
Other jurisdictions	50,781	52,222	50,189	0.99	0.96	2,033	592	-1,441
American Samoa	450	553	450	1.00	0.81	103	0	-103
Federated States of Micronesia	558	657	558	1.00	0.85	99	0	-99
Guam	813	970	746	0.92	0.77	224	67	-157
Marshall Islands	342	349	327	0.96	0.94	22	15	-7
Northern Marianas	302	390	301	1.00	0.77	89	1	-88
Palau	164	150	124	0.76	0.83	26	40	14
Puerto Rico	47,759	48,430	47,320	0.99	0.98	1,110	439	-671
U.S. Virgin Islands	393	723	363	0.92	0.50	360	30	-330
Foreign countries	†	83,392	†	†	†	83,392	†	-83,392
Residence unknown	†	10,375	†	†	†	10,375	†	-10,375

†Not applicable.
[1]Students residing in a particular state when admitted to an institution anywhere—either in their home state or another state.
[2]Includes students coming to U.S. colleges from foreign countries and other jurisdictions.
[3]Students whose residence is in the same state as the service academy.
[4]Institution unable to determine student's home state.

NOTE: Includes all first-time postsecondary students enrolled at reporting institutions. Degree-granting institutions grant associate's or higher degrees and participate in Title IV federal financial aid programs.
SOURCE: U.S. Department of Education, National Center for Education Statistics, Integrated Postsecondary Education Data System (IPEDS), Spring 2015, Fall Enrollment component. (This table was prepared October 2015.)

Table 309.20. Residence and migration of all first-time degree/certificate-seeking undergraduates in degree-granting postsecondary institutions who graduated from high school in the previous 12 months, by state or jurisdiction: Fall 2014

State or jurisdiction	Total first-time enrollment in institutions located in the state	State residents enrolled in institutions		Ratio of in-state students		Migration of students		
		In any state[1]	In their home state	To first-time enrollment (col. 4/col. 2)	To residents enrolled in any state (col. 4/col. 3)	Out of state (col. 3 - col. 4)	Into state[2] (col. 2 - col. 4)	Net (col. 8 - col. 7)
1	2	3	4	5	6	7	8	9
United States	2,199,644	2,147,954	1,732,117	0.79	0.81	415,837	467,527	51,690
Alabama...............................	38,651	30,563	27,183	0.70	0.89	3,380	11,468	8,088
Alaska.................................	2,578	3,496	2,298	0.89	0.66	1,198	280	-918
Arizona................................	42,765	35,563	30,986	0.72	0.87	4,577	11,779	7,202
Arkansas.............................	22,927	19,614	17,610	0.77	0.90	2,004	5,317	3,313
California.............................	260,666	273,101	236,753	0.91	0.87	36,348	23,913	-12,435
Colorado..............................	30,470	31,634	22,770	0.75	0.72	8,864	7,700	-1,164
Connecticut.........................	26,077	31,501	16,965	0.65	0.54	14,536	9,112	-5,424
Delaware..............................	7,917	6,200	4,131	0.52	0.67	2,069	3,786	1,717
District of Columbia	8,592	2,461	447	0.05	0.18	2,014	8,145	6,131
Florida.................................	112,570	111,753	97,704	0.87	0.87	14,049	14,866	817
Georgia...............................	63,611	65,133	53,787	0.85	0.83	11,346	9,824	-1,522
Hawaii.................................	7,037	8,550	5,300	0.75	0.62	3,250	1,737	-1,513
Idaho...................................	9,104	8,396	5,807	0.64	0.69	2,589	3,297	708
Illinois.................................	74,124	91,562	61,242	0.83	0.67	30,320	12,882	-17,438
Indiana................................	52,561	44,909	38,817	0.74	0.86	6,092	13,744	7,652
Iowa....................................	31,007	23,136	19,914	0.64	0.86	3,222	11,093	7,871
Kansas................................	25,435	22,284	19,004	0.75	0.85	3,280	6,431	3,151
Kentucky.............................	33,720	29,623	26,570	0.79	0.90	3,053	7,150	4,097
Louisiana.............................	33,137	31,419	28,431	0.86	0.90	2,988	4,706	1,718
Maine..................................	8,908	8,290	5,562	0.62	0.67	2,728	3,346	618
Maryland..............................	33,640	42,072	26,300	0.78	0.63	15,772	7,340	-8,432
Massachusetts.....................	63,849	55,571	36,865	0.58	0.66	18,706	26,984	8,278
Michigan..............................	71,194	69,884	61,800	0.87	0.88	8,084	9,394	1,310
Minnesota............................	37,434	42,426	29,189	0.78	0.69	13,237	8,245	-4,992
Mississippi..........................	25,518	21,370	19,773	0.77	0.93	1,597	5,745	4,148
Missouri..............................	45,743	42,284	35,001	0.77	0.83	7,283	10,742	3,459
Montana..............................	6,985	5,762	4,503	0.64	0.78	1,259	2,482	1,223
Nebraska.............................	15,048	14,166	11,486	0.76	0.81	2,680	3,562	882
Nevada................................	11,502	12,775	9,605	0.84	0.75	3,170	1,897	-1,273
New Hampshire	11,196	10,015	5,204	0.46	0.52	4,811	5,992	1,181
New Jersey..........................	46,679	74,184	42,196	0.90	0.57	31,988	4,483	-27,505
New Mexico.........................	12,684	12,575	10,606	0.84	0.84	1,969	2,078	109
New York.............................	151,801	146,744	117,490	0.77	0.80	29,254	34,311	5,057
North Carolina	70,314	64,036	56,486	0.80	0.88	7,550	13,828	6,278
North Dakota	7,454	4,825	3,681	0.49	0.76	1,144	3,773	2,629
Ohio....................................	83,059	77,755	66,011	0.79	0.85	11,744	17,048	5,304
Oklahoma............................	27,739	23,137	20,621	0.74	0.89	2,516	7,118	4,602
Oregon................................	21,566	17,807	13,835	0.64	0.78	3,972	7,731	3,759
Pennsylvania.......................	103,169	88,109	71,774	0.70	0.81	16,335	31,395	15,060
Rhode Island.......................	13,059	7,272	4,522	0.35	0.62	2,750	8,537	5,787
South Carolina....................	36,412	29,899	26,876	0.74	0.90	3,023	9,536	6,513
South Dakota......................	6,937	5,712	4,279	0.62	0.75	1,433	2,658	1,225
Tennessee	43,437	41,708	35,044	0.81	0.84	6,664	8,393	1,729
Texas..................................	174,430	184,031	163,206	0.94	0.89	20,825	11,224	-9,601
Utah....................................	19,856	14,867	13,294	0.67	0.89	1,573	6,562	4,989
Vermont...............................	6,649	3,863	1,859	0.28	0.48	2,004	4,790	2,786
Virginia................................	64,096	59,879	49,155	0.77	0.82	10,724	14,941	4,217
Washington..........................	32,815	34,951	26,349	0.80	0.75	8,602	6,466	-2,136
West Virginia.......................	13,929	9,739	8,649	0.62	0.89	1,090	5,280	4,190
Wisconsin............................	42,827	40,209	32,563	0.76	0.81	7,646	10,264	2,618
Wyoming..............................	3,667	3,058	2,289	0.62	0.75	769	1,378	609
U.S. Service Academies	3,099	†	325 [3]	0.10	†	-325	2,774	3,099
State unknown[4]................	†	8,081	†	†	†	8,081	†	-8,081
Other jurisdictions	40,039	41,432	39,766	0.99	0.96	1,666	273	-1,393
American Samoa..................	349	430	349	1.00	0.81	81	0	-81
Federated States of Micronesia	558	626	558	†	†	68	0	-68
Guam...................................	661	788	606	0.92	0.77	182	55	-127
Marshall Islands..................	0	18	0	†	†	18	0	-18
Northern Marianas	225	299	224	1.00	0.75	75	1	-74
Palau...................................	134	126	104	0.78	0.83	22	30	8
Puerto Rico.........................	37,836	38,593	37,669	1.00	0.98	924	167	-757
U.S. Virgin Islands	276	552	256	0.93	0.46	296	20	-276
Foreign countries................	†	50,297	†	†	†	50,297	†	-50,297
Residence unknown	†	†	†	†	†	†	†	†

†Not applicable.
[1]Students residing in a particular state when admitted to an institution anywhere—either in their home state or another state.
[2]Includes students coming to U.S. colleges from foreign countries and other jurisdictions.
[3]Students whose residence is in the same state as the service academy.
[4]Institution unable to determine student's home state.

NOTE: Includes all first-time postsecondary students who graduated from high school in the previous 12 months and were enrolled at reporting institutions. Degree-granting institutions grant associate's or higher degrees and participate in Title IV federal financial aid programs. SOURCE: U.S. Department of Education, National Center for Education Statistics, Integrated Postsecondary Education Data System (IPEDS), Spring 2015, Fall Enrollment component. (This table was prepared October 2015.)

Table 309.30. Residence and migration of all first-time degree/certificate-seeking undergraduates in 4-year degree-granting postsecondary institutions who graduated from high school in the previous 12 months, by state or jurisdiction: Fall 2014

State or jurisdiction	Total first-time enrollment in institutions located in the state	State residents enrolled in institutions		Ratio of in-state students		Migration of students		
		In any state[1]	In their home state	To first-time enrollment (col. 4/col. 2)	To residents enrolled in any state (col. 4/col. 3)	Out of state (col. 3 - col. 4)	Into state[2] (col. 2 - col. 4)	Net (col. 8 - col. 7)
1	2	3	4	5	6	7	8	9
United States	**1,545,535**	**1,497,499**	**1,105,035**	**0.71**	**0.74**	**392,464**	**440,500**	**48,036**
Alabama	25,181	17,640	14,645	0.58	0.83	2,995	10,536	7,541
Alaska	2,434	3,251	2,156	0.89	0.66	1,095	278	-817
Arizona	25,996	19,263	14,921	0.57	0.77	4,342	11,075	6,733
Arkansas	17,079	13,621	11,925	0.70	0.88	1,696	5,154	3,458
California	133,112	148,079	112,619	0.85	0.76	35,460	20,493	-14,967
Colorado	24,081	25,037	16,744	0.70	0.67	8,293	7,337	-956
Connecticut	19,450	24,725	10,370	0.53	0.42	14,355	9,080	-5,275
Delaware	5,930	4,227	2,253	0.38	0.53	1,974	3,677	1,703
District of Columbia	8,564	2,220	419	0.05	0.19	1,801	8,145	6,344
Florida	106,116	104,559	91,488	0.86	0.87	13,071	14,628	1,557
Georgia	52,526	53,852	43,267	0.82	0.80	10,585	9,259	-1,326
Hawaii	4,034	5,551	2,473	0.61	0.45	3,078	1,561	-1,517
Idaho	7,321	6,410	4,197	0.57	0.65	2,213	3,124	911
Illinois	48,510	65,573	36,023	0.74	0.55	29,550	12,487	-17,063
Indiana	45,808	37,839	32,210	0.70	0.85	5,629	13,598	7,969
Iowa	20,223	13,527	10,570	0.52	0.78	2,957	9,653	6,696
Kansas	15,577	13,726	10,654	0.68	0.78	3,072	4,923	1,851
Kentucky	24,088	20,178	17,310	0.72	0.86	2,868	6,778	3,910
Louisiana	23,470	21,528	18,938	0.81	0.88	2,590	4,532	1,942
Maine	7,000	6,461	3,785	0.54	0.59	2,676	3,215	539
Maryland	18,390	27,280	11,954	0.65	0.44	15,326	6,436	-8,890
Massachusetts	51,799	43,786	25,332	0.49	0.58	18,454	26,467	8,013
Michigan	51,500	50,082	42,418	0.82	0.85	7,664	9,082	1,418
Minnesota	25,208	30,495	17,905	0.71	0.59	12,590	7,303	-5,287
Mississippi	12,342	8,653	7,180	0.58	0.83	1,473	5,162	3,689
Missouri	30,048	26,308	19,719	0.66	0.75	6,589	10,329	3,740
Montana	6,115	4,729	3,703	0.61	0.78	1,026	2,412	1,386
Nebraska	11,478	10,353	8,241	0.72	0.80	2,112	3,237	1,125
Nevada	10,290	11,321	8,419	0.82	0.74	2,902	1,871	-1,031
New Hampshire	8,929	7,471	3,020	0.34	0.40	4,451	5,909	1,458
New Jersey	28,740	55,919	24,400	0.85	0.44	31,519	4,340	-27,179
New Mexico	6,802	6,979	5,305	0.78	0.76	1,674	1,497	-177
New York	106,977	102,537	73,731	0.69	0.72	28,806	33,246	4,440
North Carolina	47,250	41,415	34,266	0.73	0.83	7,149	12,984	5,835
North Dakota	6,502	3,919	3,105	0.48	0.79	814	3,397	2,583
Ohio	68,579	63,258	52,078	0.76	0.82	11,180	16,501	5,321
Oklahoma	19,469	15,384	13,252	0.68	0.86	2,132	6,217	4,085
Oregon	15,693	12,331	8,590	0.55	0.70	3,741	7,103	3,362
Pennsylvania	82,947	68,017	52,369	0.63	0.77	15,648	30,578	14,930
Rhode Island	11,205	5,403	2,751	0.25	0.51	2,652	8,454	5,802
South Carolina	24,236	17,934	15,129	0.62	0.84	2,805	9,107	6,302
South Dakota	5,850	4,629	3,366	0.58	0.73	1,263	2,484	1,221
Tennessee	30,051	28,284	22,031	0.73	0.78	6,253	8,020	1,767
Texas	102,409	113,338	93,435	0.91	0.82	19,903	8,974	-10,929
Utah	18,321	13,289	11,921	0.65	0.90	1,368	6,400	5,032
Vermont	6,273	3,422	1,507	0.24	0.44	1,915	4,766	2,851
Virginia	43,326	39,719	29,548	0.68	0.74	10,171	13,778	3,607
Washington	26,452	28,390	20,189	0.76	0.71	8,201	6,263	-1,938
West Virginia	12,119	7,834	6,954	0.57	0.89	880	5,165	4,285
Wisconsin	35,148	32,242	25,148	0.72	0.78	7,094	10,000	2,906
Wyoming	1,488	1,428	777	0.52	0.54	651	711	60
U.S. Service Academies	3,099	†	325 [3]	0.10	†	-325	2,774	3,099
State unknown[4]	†	4,083	†	†	†	4,083	†	-4,083
Other jurisdictions	**31,432**	**32,710**	**31,218**	**0.99**	**0.95**	**1,492**	**214**	**-1,278**
American Samoa	349	406	349	1.00	0.86	57	0	-57
Federated States of Micronesia	†	34	†	†	†	34	0	-34
Guam	572	691	519	0.91	0.75	172	53	-119
Marshall Islands	†	14	†	†	†	14	0	-14
Northern Marianas	225	292	224	1.00	0.77	68	1	-67
Palau	†	18	†	†	†	18	0	-18
Puerto Rico	30,010	30,717	29,870	1.00	0.97	847	140	-707
U.S. Virgin Islands	276	538	256	0.93	0.48	282	20	-262
Foreign countries	†	46,758	†	†	†	46,758	†	-46,758
Residence unknown	†	†	†	†	†	†	†	†

†Not applicable.
[1]Students residing in a particular state when admitted to an institution anywhere—either in their home state or another state.
[2]Includes students coming to U.S. colleges from foreign countries and other jurisdictions.
[3]Students whose residence is in the same state as the service academy.
[4]Institution unable to determine student's home state.

NOTE: Includes all first-time postsecondary students who graduated from high school in the previous 12 months and were enrolled at reporting institutions. Degree-granting institutions grant associate's or higher degrees and participate in Title IV federal financial aid programs.
SOURCE: U.S. Department of Education, National Center for Education Statistics, Integrated Postsecondary Education Data System (IPEDS), Spring 2015, Fall Enrollment component. (This table was prepared October 2015.)

Table 310.10. Number of U.S. students studying abroad and percentage distribution, by sex, race/ethnicity, and other selected characteristics: Selected years, 2000–01 through 2013–14

Sex, race/ethnicity, and other selected characteristics	2000–01	2003–04	2004–05	2005–06	2006–07	2007–08	2008–09	2009–10	2010–11	2011–12	2012–13	2013–14	From 2003–04 to 2013–14
1	2	3	4	5	6	7	8	9	10	11	12	13	14
						Number of students							Percent change in number of students
Total	154,168	191,231	205,983	223,534	241,791	262,416	260,327	270,604	273,996	283,332	289,408	304,467	59.2
						Percentage distribution of students							Percentage-point change in student distribution
Sex.................................	100.0	100.0	100.0	100.0	100.0	100.0	100.0	100.0	100.0	100.0	100.0	100.0	†
Male	35.0	34.4	34.5	34.5	34.9	34.9	35.8	36.5	35.6	35.2	34.7	34.7	0.3
Female	65.0	65.6	65.5	65.5	65.1	65.1	64.2	63.5	64.4	64.8	65.3	65.3	-0.3
Race/ethnicity	100.0	100.0	100.0	100.0	100.0	100.0	100.0	100.0	100.0	100.0	100.0	100.0	†
White.............................	84.3	83.7	83.0	83.0	81.9	81.8	80.5	78.7	77.8	76.4	76.3	74.3	-9.4
Black	3.5	3.4	3.5	3.5	3.8	4.0	4.2	4.7	4.8	5.3	5.3	5.6	2.2
Hispanic	5.4	5.0	5.6	5.4	6.0	5.9	6.0	6.4	6.9	7.6	7.6	8.3	3.3
Asian/Pacific Islander.....	5.4	6.1	6.3	6.3	6.7	6.6	7.3	7.9	7.9	7.7	7.3	7.7	1.6
American Indian/ Alaska Native	0.5	0.5	0.4	0.6	0.5	0.5	0.5	0.5	0.5	0.5	0.5	0.5	#
Two or more races	0.9	1.3	1.2	1.2	1.2	1.2	1.6	1.9	2.1	2.5	3.0	3.6	2.3
Academic level..................	100.0	100.0	100.0	100.0	100.0	100.0	100.0	100.0	100.0	100.0	100.0	100.0	†
Freshman......................	3.1	3.0	3.1	3.7	3.3	3.5	3.4	3.5	3.3	3.3	3.8	3.9	0.9
Sophomore	14.0	12.0	12.2	12.8	12.9	13.1	13.9	13.2	12.6	13.0	13.7	13.1	1.1
Junior	38.9	34.7	35.8	34.2	36.6	35.9	36.8	35.8	35.8	36.0	34.7	33.9	-0.8
Senior	20.0	19.3	19.6	19.8	21.3	21.3	21.6	21.8	23.4	24.4	24.7	25.3	6.0
Associate's students	0.9	1.6	2.7	2.7	2.7	2.2	1.1	0.1	0.2	1.1	1.1	1.7	0.1
Bachelor's, unspecified ..	13.5	16.3	15.2	14.9	12.5	13.4	11.3	11.0	10.3	8.4	8.4	9.1	-7.2
Master's level or higher ..	8.3	8.6	8.9	10.0	10.5	10.5	11.8	14.0	13.5	13.5	13.5	12.7	4.1
Other academic level	1.1	4.2	2.5	1.9	#	0.1	#	1.0	0.9	0.3	0.1	0.3	-3.9
Host region	100.0	100.0	100.0	100.0	100.0	100.0	100.0	100.0	100.0	100.0	100.0	100.0	†
Sub-Saharan Africa[1]	2.5	2.5	2.9	3.1	3.5	3.6	4.2	4.2	4.3	4.5	4.6	4.4	1.9
Asia[2]............................	6.0	6.9	8.0	9.3	10.3	11.1	11.4	12.0	11.7	12.4	12.4	11.9	5.0
Europe[3]........................	63.3	61.0	60.3	58.3	57.4	56.3	54.5	53.5	54.6	53.3	53.3	53.3	-7.7
Latin America[4]	14.5	15.2	14.4	15.2	15.0	15.3	15.4	15.0	14.6	15.8	15.7	16.2	1.0
Middle East and North Africa[1,3]	1.6	1.0	1.5	1.8	1.8	2.2	2.5	3.1	2.6	2.5	2.2	2.1	1.1
North America[4,5]	0.7	0.6	0.5	0.5	0.6	0.4	0.5	0.7	0.5	0.6	0.5	0.5	-0.1
Oceania	6.0	7.4	6.7	6.3	5.7	5.3	5.5	5.0	4.8	4.5	4.0	3.9	-3.5
Multiple destinations	5.6	5.5	5.6	5.5	5.6	5.7	6.0	6.5	6.8	6.4	7.3	7.7	2.2
Duration of stay................	100.0	100.0	100.0	100.0	100.0	100.0	100.0	100.0	100.0	100.0	100.0	100.0	†
Summer term.................	33.7	37.0	37.2	37.2	38.7	38.1	35.8	37.8	37.7	37.1	37.8	38.1	1.1
One semester	38.5	38.1	37.5	36.9	36.3	35.5	37.3	35.8	34.5	35.0	33.6	31.9	-6.2
8 weeks or less during academic year.........	7.4	8.9	8.0	9.5	9.8	11.0	11.7	11.9	13.3	14.4	15.3	16.5	7.6
January term.................	7.0	5.7	6.0	5.4	6.8	7.2	7.0	6.9	7.1	7.0	7.1	7.5	1.8
Academic year	7.3	6.0	6.0	5.3	4.3	4.1	4.1	3.8	3.7	3.2	3.1	2.9	-3.1
One quarter	4.1	3.3	3.3	3.3	3.4	3.4	3.3	3.1	3.0	2.5	2.4	2.4	-0.9
Two quarters	0.6	0.5	1.3	0.9	0.5	0.6	0.5	0.4	0.5	0.4	0.3	0.6	0.1
Calendar year	0.6	0.2	0.2	0.2	0.1	0.1	0.1	0.1	0.1	0.1	0.1	0.1	-0.1
Other............................	0.8	0.3	0.5	1.3	0.1	#	0.2	0.1	0.1	0.3	0.3	#	-0.3

†Not applicable.
#Rounds to zero.
[1]North Africa was combined with the Middle East to create the "Middle East and North Africa" category as of 2011–12, and the former "Africa" category was replaced by "Sub-Saharan Africa" (which excludes North Africa). Data for years prior to 2011–12 have been revised for comparability.
[2]Asia excludes the Middle Eastern countries (Bahrain, Iran, Iraq, Israel, Jordan, Kuwait, Lebanon, Oman, the Palestinian Authority, Qatar, Saudi Arabia, Syria, the United Arab Emirates, and Yemen).

[3]Cyprus and Turkey were classified as being in the Middle East prior to 2004–05, but in Europe for 2004–05 and later years. Data for years prior to 2004–05 have been revised for comparability.
[4]Mexico and Central America are included in Latin America, not in North America.
[5]Includes Antarctica from 2002–03 onward.
NOTE: Detail may not sum to totals because of rounding.
SOURCE: Institute of International Education, *Open Doors: Report on International Educational Exchange*, 2014 and 2015. (This table was prepared March 2016.)

Table 310.20. Foreign students enrolled in institutions of higher education in the United States, by continent, region, and selected countries of origin: Selected years, 1980-81 through 2014-15

Continent, region, and selected countries of origin	1980-81		1985-86		1990-91		1995-96		2000-01		2005-06		2010-11		2012-13		2013-14		2014-15	
	Number	Percent	Number	Percent	Number	Percent	Number	Percent	Number	Percent	Number	Percent	Number	Percent	Number	Percent	Number	Percent	Number	Percent
1	2	3	4	5	6	7	8	9	10	11	12	13	14	15	16	17	18	19	20	21
Total	311,880	100.0	343,780	100.0	407,272	100.0	453,787	100.0	547,873	100.0	564,766	100.0	723,277	100.0	819,644	100.0	886,052	100.0	974,926	100.0
Sub-Saharan Africa[1]	30,870	9.9	28,210	8.2	19,262	4.7	17,422	3.8	29,033	5.3	32,538	5.8	31,470	4.4	30,585	3.5	31,113	3.5	33,593	3.4
East Africa	6,260	2.0	6,730	2.0	7,592	1.9	7,596	1.7	13,516	2.5	13,635	2.4	8,863	1.2	7,761	0.9	7,549	0.9	7,560	0.8
Kenya	1,990	0.6	1,720	0.5	2,357	0.6	2,934	0.6	6,229	1.1	6,559	1.2	4,666	0.6	3,516	0.4	3,201	0.4	3,072	0.3
Central Africa	1,130	0.4	1,540	0.4	1,647	0.4	1,346	0.3	1,859	0.3	2,825	0.5	2,831	0.4	2,861	0.3	2,883	0.3	3,032	0.3
Southern Africa	1,480	0.5	2,360	0.7	2,835	0.7	2,657	0.6	3,304	0.6	2,232	0.4	5,330	0.7	5,511	0.7	5,683	0.6	6,043	0.6
West Africa	22,000	7.1	17,580	5.1	7,178	1.8	5,818	1.3	10,346	1.9	13,846	2.5	14,446	2.0	14,452	1.8	14,998	1.7	16,958	1.7
Nigeria	17,350	5.6	13,710	4.0	3,714	0.9	2,093	0.5	3,820	0.7	6,192	1.1	7,148	1.0	7,316	0.9	7,921	0.9	9,494	1.0
Asia	94,640	30.3	156,830	45.6	229,825	56.4	259,893	57.3	302,058	55.1	327,785	58.0	461,903	63.9	525,849	64.2	568,510	64.2	627,306	64.3
East Asia	51,650	16.6	80,720	23.5	146,017	35.9	166,717	36.7	189,371	34.6	197,576	35.0	286,925	39.7	357,596	43.6	393,205	44.4	417,881	42.9
China	2,770	0.9	13,980	4.1	39,597	9.7	39,613	8.7	59,939	10.9	62,582	11.1	157,558	21.8	235,597	28.7	274,439	31.0	304,040	31.2
Hong Kong	9,660	3.1	10,710	3.1	12,625	3.1	12,018	2.6	7,627	1.4	7,849	1.4	8,136	1.1	8,026	1.0	8,104	0.9	8,012	0.8
Japan	13,500	4.3	13,360	3.9	36,611	9.0	45,531	10.0	46,497	8.5	38,712	6.9	21,290	2.9	19,568	2.4	19,334	2.2	19,064	2.0
South Korea	6,150	2.0	18,660	5.4	23,362	5.7	36,231	8.0	45,685	8.3	59,022	10.5	73,351	10.1	70,627	8.6	68,047	7.7	63,710	6.5
Taiwan	19,460	6.2	23,770	6.9	33,531	8.2	32,702	7.2	28,566	5.2	27,876	4.9	24,818	3.4	21,897	2.7	21,266	2.4	20,993	2.2
South and Central Asia	14,540	4.7	25,800	7.5	42,366	10.4	45,401	10.0	54,664	10.0	94,965	16.8	129,058	17.8	121,100	14.8	127,301	14.4	158,560	16.3
India	9,250	3.0	16,070	4.7	28,857	7.1	31,743	7.0	42,337	7.7	76,503	13.5	103,895	14.4	96,754	11.8	102,673	11.6	132,888	13.6
Nepal	250	0.1	390	0.1	670	0.2	1,219	0.3	2,618	0.5	6,061	1.1	10,301	1.4	8,920	1.1	8,155	0.9	8,158	0.8
Pakistan	2,990	1.0	5,440	1.6	7,725	1.9	6,427	1.4	6,948	1.3	5,759	1.0	5,045	0.7	4,772	0.6	4,935	0.6	5,354	0.6
Southeast Asia	28,450	9.1	50,310	14.6	41,441	10.2	47,774	10.5	40,916	7.5	35,244	6.2	46,020	6.4	47,152	5.8	48,004	5.4	50,865	5.2
Indonesia	3,250	1.0	8,210	2.4	9,524	2.3	12,820	2.8	11,625	2.1	7,575	1.3	6,942	1.0	7,670	0.9	7,920	0.9	8,188	0.8
Malaysia	6,010	1.9	23,020	6.7	13,606	3.3	14,015	3.1	7,795	1.4	5,515	1.0	6,735	0.9	6,791	0.8	6,822	0.8	7,231	0.7
Philippines	3,390	1.1	3,930	1.1	4,273	1.0	3,127	0.7	3,139	0.6	3,758	0.7	3,604	0.5	3,215	0.4	3,112	0.4	3,026	0.3
Singapore	1,320	0.4	3,930	1.1	4,495	1.1	4,098	0.9	4,166	0.8	3,909	0.7	4,316	0.6	4,558	0.6	4,592	0.5	4,727	0.5
Thailand	6,550	2.1	6,940	2.0	7,092	1.7	12,165	2.7	11,187	2.0	8,765	1.6	8,236	1.1	7,314	0.9	7,341	0.8	7,217	0.7
Vietnam	6,490	2.1	3,270	1.0	1,396	0.3	922	0.2	2,022	0.4	4,597	0.8	14,888	2.1	16,098	2.0	16,579	1.9	18,722	1.9
Europe[2]	28,650	9.2	38,910	11.3	55,422	13.6	76,855	16.9	93,784	17.1	84,697	15.0	84,296	11.7	85,823	10.5	86,885	9.8	90,625	9.3
Cyprus[2]	720	0.2	2,140	0.6	1,710	0.4	1,810	0.4	2,217	0.4	1,111	0.2	470	0.1	425	0.1	419	#	417	#
France	2,570	0.8	3,680	1.1	5,633	1.4	5,710	1.3	7,273	1.3	6,640	1.2	8,098	1.1	8,297	1.0	8,302	0.9	8,743	0.9
Germany[3]	3,310	1.1	4,730	1.4	7,003	1.7	9,017	2.0	10,128	1.8	8,829	1.6	9,458	1.3	9,819	1.2	10,160	1.1	10,193	1.0
Greece	3,750	1.2	4,440	1.3	4,304	1.1	3,365	0.7	2,768	0.5	2,088	0.4	1,874	0.3	2,046	0.2	2,170	0.2	2,147	0.2
Spain	950	0.3	1,740	0.5	4,078	1.0	4,809	1.1	4,156	0.8	3,455	0.6	4,330	0.6	5,033	0.6	5,350	0.6	6,143	0.6
Turkey[2]	2,600	0.8	2,460	0.7	4,078	1.0	7,678	1.7	10,983	2.0	11,622	2.1	12,184	1.7	11,278	1.4	10,821	1.2	10,724	1.1
United Kingdom	4,440	1.4	5,940	1.7	7,298	1.8	7,799	1.7	8,139	1.5	8,274	1.5	8,947	1.2	9,467	1.2	10,191	1.2	10,743	1.1
Latin America	49,810	16.0	45,480	13.2	47,318	11.6	47,253	10.4	63,634	11.6	64,769	11.5	64,169	8.9	66,864	8.2	72,318	8.2	86,378	8.9
Caribbean	10,650	3.4	11,100	3.2	12,349	3.0	10,737	2.4	14,423	2.6	13,855	2.5	11,644	1.6	11,100	1.4	10,879	1.2	10,478	1.1
Central America	12,970	4.2	12,740	3.7	15,949	3.9	14,220	3.1	16,764	3.1	19,709	3.5	20,361	2.8	21,072	2.6	22,276	2.5	24,709	2.5
Mexico	6,730	2.1	5,460	1.6	6,739	1.7	8,687	1.9	10,670	1.9	13,931	2.5	13,713	1.9	14,199	1.7	14,779	1.7	17,052	1.7
South America	26,190	8.4	21,640	6.3	19,019	4.7	22,296	4.9	32,447	5.9	31,205	5.5	32,164	4.4	34,692	4.2	39,163	4.4	51,191	5.3
Brazil	2,870	0.9	2,840	0.8	3,898	1.0	5,497	1.2	8,846	1.6	7,009	1.2	8,777	1.2	10,868	1.3	13,286	1.5	23,675	2.4
Colombia	6,770	2.2	4,010	1.2	3,183	0.8	3,462	0.8	6,765	1.2	6,835	1.2	6,456	0.9	6,543	0.8	7,083	0.8	7,169	0.7
Venezuela	11,750	3.8	7,040	2.0	2,894	0.7	4,456	1.0	5,217	1.0	4,792	0.8	5,491	0.8	6,158	0.8	7,022	0.8	7,890	0.8
Middle East and North Africa[1]	88,700	28.4	54,100	15.7	32,177	7.9	24,488	5.4	28,842	5.3	21,576	3.8	47,963	6.6	77,049	9.4	92,618	10.5	103,307	10.6
Middle East[1]	81,390	26.1	48,120	14.0	27,636	6.8	21,066	4.6	23,658	4.3	17,806	3.2	42,543	5.9	71,170	8.7	86,372	9.7	96,615	9.9
Iran	47,550	15.2	14,210	4.1	6,262	1.5	2,637	0.6	1,844	0.3	2,420	0.4	5,626	0.8	8,744	1.1	10,194	1.2	11,338	1.2
Israel	2,710	0.9	2,600	0.8	2,977	0.7	2,222	0.5	3,402	0.6	3,419	0.6	2,701	0.4	2,430	0.3	2,457	0.3	2,370	0.2
Jordan	6,140	2.0	6,590	1.9	4,321	1.1	3,035	0.7	3,045	0.6	1,733	0.3	2,002	0.3	2,109	0.3	2,148	0.2	2,215	0.2
Kuwait	2,990	1.0	3,810	1.1	1,624	0.4	1,554	0.3	2,005	0.4	1,950	0.3	2,998	0.4	5,115	0.6	7,288	0.8	9,034	0.9
Lebanon	6,770	2.2	6,900	2.0	3,899	1.0	4,191	0.9	2,005	0.4	1,950	0.3	1,462	0.2	1,266	0.2	1,387	0.2	1,416	0.1
Saudi Arabia	10,440	3.3	7,090	2.1	3,584	0.9	3,899	0.9	5,273	1.0	3,448	0.6	22,104	3.1	44,566	5.4	53,919	6.1	59,945	6.1
North Africa[1]	7,310	2.3	5,980	1.7	4,541	1.1	3,422	0.8	5,184	0.9	3,770	0.7	5,420	0.7	5,879	0.7	6,246	0.7	6,692	0.7
North America[4]	14,790	4.7	16,030	4.7	18,949	4.7	23,644	5.2	25,888	4.7	28,699	5.1	27,941	3.9	27,357	3.3	28,304	3.2	27,240	2.8
Canada	14,320	4.6	15,410	4.5	18,350	4.5	23,005	5.1	25,279	4.6	28,202	5.0	27,546	3.8	27,357	3.3	28,304	3.2	27,240	2.8
Oceania	4,180	1.3	4,030	1.2	4,230	1.0	4,202	0.9	4,624	0.8	4,702	0.8	5,610	0.8	6,104	0.7	6,292	0.7	6,471	0.7
Australia	1,530	0.5	1,530	0.4	1,906	0.5	2,244	0.5	2,645	0.5	2,806	0.5	3,777	0.5	4,121	0.5	4,377	0.5	4,511	0.5
Unidentified[5]	240	0.1	190	0.1	89	#	30	#	10	#	#	#	10	#	13	#	12	#	6	#

#Rounds to zero.
[1]North Africa was combined with the Middle East to create the "Middle East and North Africa" category as of 2012-13, and the former "Africa" category was replaced by "Sub-Saharan Africa" (which excludes North Africa). Data for years prior to 2012-13 have been revised for comparability.
[2]Cyprus and Turkey were classified as Asian prior to 2004-05, but in Europe for 2004-05 and later years. Data for years prior to 2004-05 have been revised for comparability.
[3]Data for 1980-81 and 1985-86 are for West Germany (Federal Republic of Germany before unification).
[4]Excludes Mexico and Central America, which are included in Latin America.
[5]Place of origin unknown or undeclared.
NOTE: Includes foreign students enrolled in American Samoa, Guam, Puerto Rico, and the U.S. Virgin Islands. Totals and subtotals include other countries not shown separately. Region totals may not sum to continent totals, because some continent totals include students who are not classified by country or region. Data are for "nonimmigrants" (i.e., students who have not migrated to the United States). Detail may not sum to totals because of rounding.
SOURCE: Institute of International Education, Open Doors: Report on International Educational Exchange, selected years, 1981 through 2015. (This table was prepared March 2016.)

Table 311.10. Number and percentage distribution of students enrolled in postsecondary institutions, by level, disability status, and selected student characteristics: 2007–08 and 2011–12

[Standard errors appear in parentheses]

Selected student characteristic	Undergraduate									Postbaccalaureate, 2011–12					
	2007–08						2011–12											
	All students		Students with disabilities[1]		Nondisabled students		All students		Students with disabilities[1]		Nondisabled students		All students		Students with disabilities[1]		Nondisabled students	
1	2		3		4		5		6		7		8		9		10	
Number of students (in thousands)	20,511	(—)	2,243	(—)	18,268	(—)	23,055	(—)	2,563	(—)	20,493	(—)	3,682	(—)	195	(—)	3,487	(—)
Percentage distribution of students																		
Total	100.0	(†)	10.9	(0.19)	89.1	(0.19)	100.0	(†)	11.1	(0.17)	88.9	(0.17)	100.0	(†)	5.3	(0.36)	94.7	(0.36)
Sex																		
Male	100.0	(†)	10.9	(0.26)	89.1	(0.26)	100.0	(†)	11.3	(0.27)	88.7	(0.27)	100.0	(†)	4.8	(0.40)	95.2	(0.40)
Female	100.0	(†)	11.0	(0.23)	89.0	(0.23)	100.0	(†)	11.0	(0.23)	89.0	(0.23)	100.0	(†)	5.6	(0.50)	94.4	(0.50)
Race/ethnicity of student																		
White.................................	100.0	(†)	11.7	(0.23)	88.3	(0.23)	100.0	(†)	11.1	(0.24)	88.9	(0.24)	100.0	(†)	5.0	(0.39)	95.0	(0.39)
Black.................................	100.0	(†)	9.9	(0.44)	90.1	(0.44)	100.0	(†)	12.2	(0.38)	87.8	(0.38)	100.0	(†)	6.9	(1.19)	93.1	(1.19)
Hispanic............................	100.0	(†)	9.4	(0.42)	90.6	(0.42)	100.0	(†)	10.4	(0.41)	89.7	(0.41)	100.0	(†)	6.4	(1.40)	93.7	(1.40)
Asian.................................	100.0	(†)	8.0	(0.66)	92.0	(0.66)	100.0	(†)	8.0	(0.64)	92.0	(0.64)	100.0	(†)	4.3	(0.86)	95.7	(0.86)
Pacific Islander..................	100.0	(†)	7.6	(1.25)	92.4	(1.25)	100.0	(†)	14.9	(2.97)	85.1	(2.97)	‡	(†)	‡	(†)	‡	(†)
American Indian/Alaska Native....................	100.0	(†)	10.0	(1.42)	90.0	(1.42)	100.0	(†)	14.4	(2.32)	85.6	(2.32)	‡	(†)	‡	(†)	‡	(†)
Two or more races	100.0	(†)	13.5	(1.11)	86.5	(1.11)	100.0	(†)	13.6	(0.98)	86.4	(0.98)	100.0	(†)	6.4	(1.84)	93.6	(1.84)
Other.................................	100.0	(†)	11.3	(2.63)	88.7	(2.63)	—	(†)	—	(†)	—	(†)	—	(†)	—	(†)	—	(†)
Age																		
15 to 23.............................	100.0	(†)	9.8	(0.19)	90.2	(0.19)	100.0	(†)	9.0	(0.22)	91.0	(0.22)	100.0	(†)	3.9	(0.70)	96.1	(0.70)
24 to 29.............................	100.0	(†)	12.8	(0.48)	87.2	(0.48)	100.0	(†)	11.3	(0.38)	88.7	(0.38)	100.0	(†)	4.6	(0.50)	95.4	(0.50)
30 or older........................	100.0	(†)	12.4	(0.39)	87.7	(0.39)	100.0	(†)	15.7	(0.44)	84.3	(0.44)	100.0	(†)	6.2	(0.57)	93.8	(0.57)
Attendance status																		
Full-time, full-year	100.0	(†)	9.5	(0.19)	90.5	(0.19)	100.0	(†)	9.5	(0.22)	90.5	(0.22)	100.0	(†)	5.4	(0.47)	94.6	(0.47)
Part-time or part-year........	100.0	(†)	11.7	(0.27)	88.3	(0.27)	100.0	(†)	12.1	(0.24)	87.9	(0.24)	100.0	(†)	5.3	(0.45)	94.7	(0.45)
Student housing status																		
On-campus.........................	100.0	(†)	8.6	(0.34)	91.4	(0.34)	100.0	(†)	8.6	(0.37)	91.4	(0.37)	—	(†)	—	(†)	—	(†)
Off-campus........................	100.0	(†)	11.4	(0.25)	88.6	(0.25)	100.0	(†)	11.8	(0.27)	88.2	(0.27)	—	(†)	—	(†)	—	(†)
With parents or relatives	100.0	(†)	11.2	(0.33)	88.8	(0.33)	100.0	(†)	11.3	(0.30)	88.7	(0.30)	—	(†)	—	(†)	—	(†)
Attended more than one institution	100.0	(†)	10.8	(0.43)	89.3	(0.43)	100.0	(†)	10.0	(0.42)	90.0	(0.42)	—	(†)	—	(†)	—	(†)
Dependency status																		
Dependent	100.0	(†)	9.6	(0.19)	90.4	(0.19)	100.0	(†)	8.6	(0.21)	91.4	(0.21)	—	(†)	—	(†)	—	(†)
Independent, unmarried..........	100.0	(†)	14.1	(0.51)	85.9	(0.51)	100.0	(†)	14.3	(0.44)	85.7	(0.44)	100.0	(†)	5.6	(0.47)	94.4	(0.47)
Independent, married..........	100.0	(†)	12.0	(0.80)	88.0	(0.80)	100.0	(†)	13.3	(0.74)	86.7	(0.74)	100.0	(†)	4.2	(0.85)	95.8	(0.85)
Independent with dependents..........	100.0	(†)	11.5	(0.34)	88.5	(0.34)	100.0	(†)	13.1	(0.39)	86.9	(0.39)	100.0	(†)	5.3	(0.58)	94.7	(0.58)
Veteran status																		
Veteran.............................	100.0	(†)	15.0	(1.10)	85.0	(1.10)	100.0	(†)	20.6	(1.35)	79.4	(1.35)	100.0	(†)	7.9	(1.70)	92.1	(1.70)
Not veteran	100.0	(†)	10.8	(0.18)	89.2	(0.18)	100.0	(†)	10.8	(0.17)	89.3	(0.17)	100.0	(†)	5.2	(0.36)	94.8	(0.36)
Field of study																		
Business/management	100.0	(†)	10.0	(0.43)	90.0	(0.43)	100.0	(†)	10.0	(0.42)	90.0	(0.42)	100.0	(†)	5.9	(1.60)	94.2	(1.60)
Education............................	100.0	(†)	10.0	(0.56)	90.0	(0.56)	100.0	(†)	10.1	(0.75)	89.9	(0.75)	100.0	(†)	5.6	(0.88)	94.4	(0.88)
Engineering/computer science/mathematics.	100.0	(†)	10.6	(0.76)	89.4	(0.76)	100.0	(†)	10.6	(0.63)	89.4	(0.63)	100.0	(†)	4.8	(1.04)	95.2	(1.04)
Health................................	100.0	(†)	11.2	(0.45)	88.8	(0.45)	100.0	(†)	10.8	(0.38)	89.2	(0.38)	100.0	(†)	4.6	(0.68)	95.4	(0.68)
Humanities........................	100.0	(†)	12.2	(0.41)	87.8	(0.41)	100.0	(†)	12.2	(0.49)	87.8	(0.49)	100.0	(†)	5.9	(1.12)	94.1	(1.12)
Law	—	(†)	—	(†)	—	(†)	—	(†)	—	(†)	—	(†)	100.0	(†)	7.7	(1.17)	92.3	(1.17)
Life/physical sciences	100.0	(†)	9.8	(0.55)	90.2	(0.55)	100.0	(†)	9.2	(0.54)	90.8	(0.54)	100.0	(†)	3.8	(0.67)	96.2	(0.67)
Social/behavioral sciences.........	100.0	(†)	10.8	(0.65)	89.2	(0.65)	100.0	(†)	11.8	(0.76)	88.2	(0.76)	100.0	(†)	5.8	(0.79)	94.2	(0.79)
Vocational/technical	100.0	(†)	11.2	(0.99)	88.8	(0.99)	100.0	(†)	14.5	(1.09)	85.5	(1.09)	—	(†)	—	(†)	—	(†)
Undeclared	100.0	(†)	11.1	(0.56)	88.9	(0.56)	100.0	(†)	11.8	(0.91)	88.2	(0.91)	100.0	(†)	4.2 !	(1.72)	95.8	(1.72)
Other.................................	100.0	(†)	11.2	(0.45)	88.8	(0.45)	100.0	(†)	11.8	(0.44)	88.2	(0.44)	100.0	(†)	4.8	(0.80)	95.2	(0.80)

—Not available.
†Not applicable.
!Interpret data with caution. The coefficient of variation (CV) for this estimate is between 30 and 50 percent.
‡Reporting standards not met. Either there are too few cases for a reliable estimate or the coefficient of variation (CV) is 50 percent or greater.
[1]Students with disabilities are those who reported that they had one or more of the following conditions: a specific learning disability, a visual impairment, hard of hearing, deafness, a speech impairment, an orthopedic impairment, or a health impairment.

NOTE: Data are based on a sample survey of students who enrolled at any time during the school year. Data exclude Puerto Rico. Detail may not sum to totals because of rounding. Race categories exclude persons of Hispanic ethnicity. Some data have been revised from previously published figures.
SOURCE: U.S. Department of Education, National Center for Education Statistics, 2007–08 and 2011–12 National Postsecondary Student Aid Study (NPSAS:08 and NPSAS:12). (This table was prepared August 2014.)

Table 311.15. Number and percentage of students enrolled in degree-granting postsecondary institutions, by distance education participation, location of student, level of enrollment, and control and level of institution: Fall 2013 and fall 2014

Year, level of enrollment, and control and level of institution	Number of students										Percent of students									
			Taking any distance education course(s)										Taking any distance education course(s)							
					Exclusively distance education courses by location of student										Exclusively distance education courses by location of student					
	Total	No distance education courses	Total, any distance education course(s)	At least one, but not all, of student's courses	Total	Same state	Different state	State not known	Outside of the United States	Location unknown	Total	No distance education courses	Total, any distance education course(s)	At least one, but not all, of student's courses	Total	Same state	Different state	State not known	Outside of the United States	Location unknown
1	2	3	4	5	6	7	8	9	10	11	12	13	14	15	16	17	18	19	20	21
Fall 2013																				
All students, total	20,375,789	14,853,595	5,522,194	2,862,991	2,659,203	1,388,195	1,119,577	30,244	35,767	85,420	100.0	72.9	27.1	14.1	13.1	6.8	5.5	0.1	0.2	0.4
Public	14,745,558	11,001,316	3,744,242	2,462,362	1,281,880	1,065,214	159,637	24,401	12,718	19,910	100.0	74.6	25.4	16.7	8.7	7.2	1.1	0.2	0.1	0.1
Private	5,630,231	3,852,279	1,777,952	400,629	1,377,323	322,981	959,940	5,843	23,049	65,510	100.0	68.4	31.6	7.1	24.5	5.7	17.0	0.1	0.4	1.2
Nonprofit	3,974,004	3,178,594	795,410	275,020	520,390	205,897	289,967	2,349	9,435	12,742	100.0	80.0	20.0	6.9	13.1	5.2	7.3	0.1	0.2	0.3
For-profit	1,656,227	673,685	982,542	125,609	856,953	117,084	669,973	3,494	13,614	52,768	100.0	40.7	59.3	7.6	51.7	7.1	40.5	0.2	0.8	3.2
Fall 2014																				
All students, total	20,207,369	14,456,952	5,750,417	2,926,083	2,824,334	1,510,779	1,154,608	31,676	37,071	90,200	100.0	71.5	28.5	14.5	14.0	7.5	5.7	0.2	0.2	0.4
4-year	13,492,884	9,614,081	3,878,803	1,765,814	2,112,989	869,143	1,104,141	20,991	34,111	84,603	100.0	71.3	28.7	13.1	15.7	6.4	8.2	0.2	0.3	0.6
2-year	6,714,485	4,842,871	1,871,614	1,160,269	711,345	641,636	50,467	10,685	2,960	5,597	100.0	72.1	27.9	17.3	10.6	9.6	0.8	0.2	#	0.1
Public	14,655,015	10,759,400	3,895,615	2,513,718	1,381,897	1,155,511	189,713	9,343	12,291	15,039	100.0	73.4	26.6	17.2	9.4	7.9	1.3	0.1	0.1	0.1
4-year	8,257,250	6,193,691	2,063,559	1,371,848	691,711	519,288	144,035	6,490	9,349	12,549	100.0	75.0	25.0	16.6	8.4	6.3	1.7	0.1	0.1	0.2
2-year	6,397,765	4,565,709	1,832,056	1,141,870	690,186	636,223	45,678	2,853	2,942	2,490	100.0	71.4	28.6	17.8	10.8	9.9	0.7	#	#	#
Private	5,552,354	3,697,552	1,854,802	412,365	1,442,437	355,268	964,895	22,333	24,780	75,161	100.0	66.6	33.4	7.4	26.0	6.4	17.4	0.4	0.4	1.4
Nonprofit	3,996,089	3,096,278	899,811	295,593	604,218	230,083	332,355	11,938	10,878	18,964	100.0	77.5	22.5	7.4	15.1	5.8	8.3	0.3	0.3	0.5
4-year	3,965,724	3,068,453	897,271	293,855	603,416	229,674	331,970	11,938	10,878	18,956	100.0	77.4	22.6	7.4	15.2	5.8	8.4	0.3	0.3	0.5
2-year	30,365	27,825	2,540	1,738	802	409	385	0	0	8	100.0	91.6	8.4	5.7	2.6	1.3	1.3	0.0	0.0	#
For-profit	1,556,265	601,274	954,991	116,772	838,219	125,185	632,540	10,395	13,902	56,197	100.0	38.6	61.4	7.5	53.9	8.0	40.6	0.7	0.9	3.6
4-year	1,269,910	351,937	917,973	100,111	817,862	120,181	628,136	2,563	13,884	53,098	100.0	27.7	72.3	7.9	64.4	9.5	49.5	0.2	1.1	4.2
2-year	286,355	249,337	37,018	16,661	20,357	5,004	4,404	7,832	18	3,099	100.0	87.1	12.9	5.8	7.1	1.7	1.5	2.7	#	1.1
Undergraduate	17,292,787	12,495,754	4,797,033	2,698,612	2,098,612	1,212,694	771,385	26,851	21,844	65,838	100.0	72.3	27.7	15.6	12.1	7.0	4.5	0.2	0.1	0.4
4-year	10,578,302	7,652,883	2,925,419	1,538,152	1,387,267	571,058	720,918	16,166	18,884	60,241	100.0	72.3	27.7	14.5	13.1	5.4	6.8	0.2	0.2	0.6
2-year	6,714,485	4,842,871	1,871,614	1,160,269	711,345	641,636	50,467	10,685	2,960	5,597	100.0	72.1	27.9	17.3	10.6	9.6	0.8	0.2	#	0.1
Public	13,244,837	9,720,733	3,524,104	2,385,617	1,138,487	993,049	120,767	6,421	8,360	9,890	100.0	73.4	26.6	18.0	8.6	7.5	0.9	#	0.1	0.1
4-year	6,847,072	5,155,024	1,692,048	1,243,747	448,301	356,826	75,089	3,568	5,418	7,400	100.0	75.3	24.7	18.2	6.5	5.2	1.1	0.1	0.1	0.1
2-year	6,397,765	4,565,709	1,832,056	1,141,870	690,186	636,223	45,678	2,853	2,942	2,490	100.0	71.4	28.6	17.8	10.8	9.9	0.7	#	#	#
Private	4,047,950	2,775,021	1,272,929	312,804	960,125	219,645	650,618	20,430	13,484	55,948	100.0	68.6	31.4	7.7	23.7	5.4	16.1	0.5	0.3	1.4
Nonprofit	2,771,341	2,215,678	555,663	208,322	347,341	122,516	197,209	10,793	5,530	11,293	100.0	79.9	20.1	7.5	12.5	4.4	7.1	0.4	0.2	0.4
4-year	2,740,976	2,187,853	553,123	206,584	346,539	122,107	196,824	10,793	5,530	11,285	100.0	79.8	20.2	7.5	12.6	4.5	7.2	0.4	0.2	0.4
2-year	30,365	27,825	2,540	1,738	802	409	385	0	0	8	100.0	91.6	8.4	5.7	2.6	1.3	1.3	0.0	0.0	#
For-profit	1,276,609	559,343	717,266	104,482	612,784	97,129	453,409	9,637	7,954	44,655	100.0	43.8	56.2	8.2	48.0	7.6	35.5	0.8	0.6	3.5
4-year	990,254	310,006	680,248	87,821	592,427	92,125	449,005	1,805	7,936	41,556	100.0	31.3	68.7	8.9	59.8	9.3	45.3	0.2	0.8	4.2
2-year	286,355	249,337	37,018	16,661	20,357	5,004	4,404	7,832	18	3,099	100.0	87.1	12.9	5.8	7.1	1.7	1.5	2.7	#	1.1
Postbaccalaureate	2,914,582	1,961,198	953,384	227,662	725,722	298,085	383,223	4,825	15,227	24,362	100.0	67.3	32.7	7.8	24.9	10.2	13.1	0.2	0.5	0.8
Public	1,410,178	1,038,667	371,511	128,101	243,410	162,462	68,946	2,922	3,931	5,149	100.0	73.7	26.3	9.1	17.3	11.5	4.9	0.2	0.3	0.4
Private	1,504,404	922,531	581,873	99,561	482,312	135,623	314,277	1,903	11,296	19,213	100.0	61.3	38.7	6.6	32.1	9.0	20.9	0.1	0.8	1.3
Nonprofit	1,224,748	880,600	344,148	87,271	256,877	107,567	135,146	1,145	5,348	7,671	100.0	71.9	28.1	7.1	21.0	8.8	11.0	0.1	0.4	0.6
For-profit	279,656	41,931	237,725	12,290	225,435	28,056	179,131	758	5,948	11,542	100.0	15.0	85.0	4.4	80.6	10.0	64.1	0.3	2.1	4.1

#Rounds to zero.
NOTE: Degree-granting institutions grant associate's or higher degrees and participate in Title IV federal financial aid programs.
SOURCE: U.S. Department of Education, National Center for Education Statistics, Integrated Postsecondary Education Data System (IPEDS), Spring 2014 and Spring 2015, Fall Enrollment component. (This table was prepared December 2015.)

Table 311.20. Number and percentage of undergraduate students taking night, weekend, or online classes, by selected characteristics: 2011–12

[Standard errors appear in parentheses]

Selected characteristic	Number of students (in thousands)	Total taking any night, weekend, or online classes[1] — Percent of students	Night classes — Any night classes	Night classes — Exclusively night classes	Weekend classes — Any weekend classes	Weekend classes — Exclusively weekend classes	Online classes — Any online classes	Online classes — Exclusively online classes	Percent of students whose entire degree program is online[2]
1	2	3	4	5	6	7	8	9	10
Total	**11,917**	**51.7** (0.33)	**32.4** (0.29)	**5.2** (0.14)	**7.0** (0.17)	**0.3** (0.03)	**32.0** (0.33)	**8.4** (0.20)	**6.5** (0.18)
Sex									
Male	4,865	49.0 (0.46)	32.0 (0.40)	5.1 (0.18)	6.7 (0.22)	0.3 (0.05)	28.5 (0.45)	6.5 (0.25)	4.9 (0.24)
Female	7,052	53.7 (0.40)	32.7 (0.39)	5.3 (0.19)	7.2 (0.22)	0.3 (0.04)	34.5 (0.39)	9.8 (0.24)	7.7 (0.21)
Race/ethnicity									
White	7,019	52.6 (0.45)	32.5 (0.39)	4.9 (0.18)	6.3 (0.20)	0.2 (0.04)	33.5 (0.41)	9.0 (0.24)	6.8 (0.21)
Black	1,930	52.0 (0.68)	30.8 (0.59)	6.0 (0.28)	7.8 (0.41)	0.5 (0.10)	32.7 (0.70)	10.7 (0.57)	9.1 (0.56)
Hispanic	1,863	50.4 (0.64)	33.9 (0.61)	6.3 (0.40)	8.3 (0.36)	0.4 (0.08)	27.9 (0.57)	5.5 (0.29)	4.3 (0.24)
Asian	588	45.5 (1.22)	31.0 (1.18)	3.3 (0.41)	7.4 (0.62)	† (†)	26.0 (1.06)	4.2 (0.45)	2.9 (0.35)
Pacific Islander	64	54.4 (3.80)	45.8 (3.84)	4.6 ! (1.46)	11.2 (2.40)	# (†)	29.9 (3.18)	3.5 ! (1.33)	3.1 ! (1.29)
American Indian/Alaska Native	107	51.2 (2.75)	31.8 (2.44)	6.6 (1.56)	6.7 (1.38)	‡ (†)	32.6 (2.56)	9.1 (1.60)	7.0 (1.43)
Two or more races	346	50.5 (1.63)	31.9 (1.48)	4.9 (0.83)	7.4 (0.76)	0.3 ! (0.15)	30.6 (1.48)	8.3 (0.93)	5.5 (0.69)
Age									
15 through 23	5,884	45.4 (0.38)	29.8 (0.32)	3.0 (0.11)	5.2 (0.17)	0.2 (0.02)	26.5 (0.36)	4.5 (0.16)	3.2 (0.13)
24 through 29	2,474	58.2 (0.71)	36.6 (0.70)	7.7 (0.40)	9.0 (0.38)	0.3 (0.06)	36.5 (0.67)	10.4 (0.43)	8.0 (0.41)
30 or older	3,559	60.9 (0.63)	35.3 (0.69)	8.5 (0.34)	9.5 (0.34)	0.6 (0.10)	40.9 (0.64)	15.6 (0.51)	13.0 (0.50)
Attendance status									
Exclusively full-time	5,579	48.0 (0.43)	30.3 (0.35)	3.9 (0.16)	6.0 (0.20)	0.2 (0.03)	28.8 (0.41)	7.6 (0.22)	6.5 (0.20)
Exclusively part-time	4,136	56.6 (0.62)	34.8 (0.57)	8.3 (0.32)	8.3 (0.31)	0.5 (0.09)	35.3 (0.62)	10.7 (0.42)	7.4 (0.38)
Mixed full-time and part-time	2,203	53.5 (0.60)	34.3 (0.54)	3.3 (0.19)	7.3 (0.33)	0.2 (0.04)	35.0 (0.62)	6.4 (0.31)	5.0 (0.28)
Had job during academic year[3]									
Yes	8,219	57.2 (0.40)	35.9 (0.35)	6.1 (0.19)	7.9 (0.21)	0.3 (0.04)	36.2 (0.42)	9.8 (0.26)	7.6 (0.24)
No	3,699	42.5 (0.45)	26.7 (0.38)	3.9 (0.19)	5.5 (0.24)	0.2 (0.04)	24.9 (0.42)	6.1 (0.25)	4.8 (0.20)
Dependency status									
Dependent	4,994	44.5 (0.39)	29.5 (0.34)	2.6 (0.11)	4.9 (0.18)	0.1 (0.02)	25.5 (0.36)	3.9 (0.16)	2.7 (0.12)
Independent, no dependents, not married[4]	2,331	55.1 (0.71)	35.5 (0.69)	7.5 (0.42)	8.2 (0.34)	0.3 (0.07)	33.6 (0.63)	8.9 (0.38)	6.7 (0.33)
Independent, no dependents, married	736	58.8 (1.27)	36.5 (1.28)	7.8 (0.76)	8.3 (0.70)	0.5 ! (0.17)	37.4 (1.22)	11.7 (0.75)	10.1 (0.72)
Independent, with dependents, not married[4]	2,040	58.2 (0.72)	34.3 (0.79)	8.2 (0.41)	9.4 (0.39)	0.5 (0.10)	38.2 (0.67)	12.7 (0.48)	10.7 (0.45)
Independent, with dependents, married	1,817	64.0 (0.84)	35.2 (0.84)	7.7 (0.50)	9.8 (0.50)	0.6 (0.15)	44.9 (0.92)	18.8 (0.77)	14.7 (0.75)
Control of institution									
Public	8,796	52.0 (0.38)	33.0 (0.32)	4.3 (0.15)	6.6 (0.19)	0.3 (0.04)	33.2 (0.39)	6.3 (0.21)	4.0 (0.16)
Private nonprofit	1,291	42.9 (0.91)	30.6 (0.90)	3.8 (0.38)	5.2 (0.41)	0.2 ! (0.07)	21.0 (0.85)	5.8 (0.61)	4.5 (0.57)
Private for-profit	1,830	58.7 (0.74)	31.2 (0.71)	11.7 (0.48)	10.9 (0.50)	0.6 (0.09)	35.5 (0.83)	22.2 (0.79)	21.6 (0.82)

†Not applicable.
#Rounds to zero.
!Interpret data with caution. The coefficient of variation (CV) for this estimate is between 30 and 50 percent.
‡Reporting standards not met. Either there are too few cases for a reliable estimate or the coefficient of variation (CV) is 50 percent or greater.
[1]Students who reported taking more than one type of class (e.g., night classes and online classes) are counted only once in the total.
[2]Excludes students not in a degree or certificate program.
[3]Excludes work-study/assistantships.
[4]Includes separated.
NOTE: Night classes start after 6:00 p.m. on Monday through Thursday nights; weekend classes start after 6:00 p.m. on Friday or take place any time on Saturday or Sunday; and online classes are taught only online. Detail may not sum to totals because of rounding. Race categories exclude persons of Hispanic ethnicity.
SOURCE: U.S. Department of Education, National Center for Education Statistics, 2011–12 National Postsecondary Student Aid Study (NPSAS:12). (This table was prepared March 2014.)

Table 311.22. **Number and percentage of undergraduate students taking distance education or online classes and degree programs, by selected characteristics: Selected years, 2003–04 through 2011–12**

[Standard errors appear in parentheses]

Selected characteristic	Percent of undergraduate students taking distance education classes				2011–12				
	2003–04		2007–08		Number of undergraduate students (in thousands)		Percent of undergraduate students taking online classes		
	Total, any distance education classes	Entire degree program through distance education[1]	Total, any distance education classes	Entire degree program through distance education[1]	Total, all students	Number taking any online classes	Total, any online classes	Exclusively online classes	Entire degree program is online[1]
1	2	3	4	5	6	7	8	9	10
Total	**15.6 (0.29)**	**4.9 (0.17)**	**20.6 (0.23)**	**3.8 (0.16)**	**23,055**	**7,368**	**32.0 (0.33)**	**8.4 (0.20)**	**6.5 (0.18)**
Sex									
Male	13.6 (0.31)	4.3 (0.19)	18.8 (0.31)	3.4 (0.16)	9,921	2,831	28.5 (0.45)	6.5 (0.25)	4.9 (0.24)
Female	17.0 (0.40)	5.4 (0.23)	21.9 (0.28)	4.2 (0.22)	13,135	4,537	34.5 (0.39)	9.8 (0.24)	7.7 (0.21)
Race/ethnicity									
White	16.2 (0.33)	5.0 (0.19)	21.9 (0.29)	3.9 (0.19)	13,345	4,472	33.5 (0.41)	9.0 (0.24)	6.8 (0.21)
Black	14.9 (0.59)	4.9 (0.37)	19.9 (0.66)	5.1 (0.48)	3,709	1,214	32.7 (0.70)	10.7 (0.57)	9.1 (0.56)
Hispanic	13.4 (0.54)	4.1 (0.27)	16.5 (0.53)	2.7 (0.23)	3,696	1,032	27.9 (0.57)	5.5 (0.29)	4.3 (0.24)
Asian	14.0 (0.92)	5.2 (0.58)	18.1 (0.86)	2.9 (0.40)	1,292	336	26.0 (1.06)	4.2 (0.45)	2.9 (0.35)
Pacific Islander	19.1 (2.37)	6.9 (1.69)	17.0 (1.89)	1.2 ! (0.53)	119	35	29.9 (3.18)	3.5 ! (1.33)	3.1 ! (1.29)
American Indian/Alaska Native	15.5 (1.85)	6.2 (1.41)	21.9 (2.41)	1.8 ! (0.55)	209	68	32.6 (2.56)	9.1 (1.60)	7.0 (1.43)
Two or more races	16.5 (1.33)	5.1 (1.16)	20.4 (1.08)	3.6 (0.86)	686	210	30.6 (1.48)	8.3 (0.93)	5.5 (0.69)
Age									
15 through 23	11.7 (0.26)	3.1 (0.13)	15.2 (0.22)	1.4 (0.09)	12,956	3,429	26.5 (0.36)	4.5 (0.16)	3.2 (0.13)
24 through 29	18.4 (0.46)	6.7 (0.41)	25.7 (0.56)	5.6 (0.45)	4,253	1,551	36.5 (0.67)	10.4 (0.43)	8.0 (0.41)
30 or older	22.4 (0.65)	8.3 (0.42)	30.0 (0.55)	9.0 (0.40)	5,846	2,388	40.9 (0.64)	15.6 (0.51)	13.0 (0.50)
Attendance status									
Exclusively full-time	12.7 (0.32)	3.8 (0.20)	16.7 (0.33)	3.2 (0.29)	11,632	3,346	28.8 (0.41)	7.6 (0.22)	6.5 (0.20)
Exclusively part-time	18.7 (0.46)	6.9 (0.32)	24.8 (0.39)	5.2 (0.22)	7,308	2,583	35.3 (0.62)	10.7 (0.42)	7.4 (0.38)
Mixed full-time and part-time	17.4 (0.53)	4.7 (0.23)	22.5 (0.42)	2.9 (0.20)	4,116	1,440	35.0 (0.62)	6.4 (0.31)	5.0 (0.28)
Undergraduate field of study									
Business/management	18.7 (0.58)	7.0 (0.43)	24.2 (0.55)	6.4 (0.45)	3,487	1,371	39.3 (0.75)	13.1 (0.48)	11.4 (0.45)
Computer/information science	19.5 (0.96)	7.2 (0.71)	26.9 (1.53)	8.4 (1.17)	942	385	40.8 (1.37)	11.6 (0.90)	9.8 (0.81)
Education	17.1 (0.89)	4.6 (0.45)	22.8 (0.81)	3.2 (0.33)	1,175	397	33.8 (1.17)	8.4 (0.71)	6.4 (0.59)
Engineering	12.1 (0.83)	3.3 (0.40)	16.1 (0.77)	2.3 (0.36)	1,087	252	23.2 (0.93)	3.8 (0.54)	2.3 (0.48)
Health	17.4 (0.48)	5.6 (0.30)	21.9 (0.60)	4.2 (0.33)	4,271	1,420	33.3 (0.67)	8.5 (0.48)	6.7 (0.43)
Humanities	14.0 (0.53)	3.9 (0.26)	19.7 (0.53)	2.6 (0.22)	3,817	1,175	30.8 (0.65)	5.8 (0.41)	4.1 (0.33)
Life sciences	11.0 (0.81)	2.7 (0.39)	15.8 (0.68)	1.8 (0.21)	1,448	386	26.7 (0.92)	4.5 (0.44)	3.3 (0.37)
Mathematics	12.8 (2.48)	3.8 ! (1.42)	15.1 (2.51)	‡ (†)	111	23	20.4 (3.02)	4.1 ! (1.32)	2.2 ! (1.05)
Physical sciences	9.8 (2.02)	0.9 ! (0.41)	12.8 (1.56)	0.3 ! (0.16)	207	46	22.1 (1.93)	1.5 ! (0.51)	1.2 ! (0.46)
Social/behavioral sciences	12.5 (0.63)	3.4 (0.33)	17.1 (0.68)	2.3 (0.31)	1,568	499	31.8 (0.93)	8.9 (0.59)	7.0 (0.48)
Vocational/technical	13.1 (0.96)	4.2 (0.60)	18.5 (1.26)	3.3 (0.50)	718	160	22.3 (1.54)	4.1 (0.77)	2.8 (0.59)
Undeclared/no major	15.0 (0.61)	4.6 (0.34)	20.5 (0.56)	3.1 (0.45)	1,232	340	27.6 (1.16)	12.0 (0.96)	5.2 (0.81)
Other	14.4 (0.68)	4.3 (0.29)	19.0 (0.69)	3.9 (0.38)	2,992	913	30.5 (0.83)	8.6 (0.53)	6.9 (0.50)
Had job during academic year[2]									
Yes	16.8 (0.34)	5.5 (0.22)	22.2 (0.25)	4.2 (0.16)	14,363	5,204	36.2 (0.42)	9.8 (0.26)	7.6 (0.24)
No	11.9 (0.32)	3.3 (0.17)	15.8 (0.37)	2.8 (0.25)	8,693	2,163	24.9 (0.42)	6.1 (0.25)	4.8 (0.20)
Dependency status									
Dependent	11.1 (0.24)	2.9 (0.13)	14.4 (0.24)	1.0 (0.08)	11,231	2,865	25.5 (0.36)	3.9 (0.17)	2.7 (0.12)
Independent, no dependents, not married[3]	15.6 (0.50)	5.1 (0.37)	23.6 (0.56)	4.8 (0.30)	4,233	1,421	33.6 (0.64)	8.9 (0.38)	6.7 (0.33)
Independent, no dependents, married	19.6 (0.78)	6.9 (0.52)	28.6 (0.96)	7.2 (0.84)	1,250	468	37.4 (1.22)	11.7 (0.75)	10.1 (0.72)
Independent, with dependents, not married[3]	20.5 (0.70)	6.9 (0.49)	25.3 (0.61)	7.4 (0.52)	3,504	1,340	38.2 (0.67)	12.7 (0.48)	10.7 (0.45)
Independent, with dependents, married	25.1 (0.79)	9.7 (0.53)	32.9 (0.71)	9.4 (0.51)	2,837	1,273	44.9 (0.92)	18.8 (0.77)	14.7 (0.75)
Control and level of institution									
Public	16.2 (0.35)	4.7 (0.18)	21.5 (0.25)	2.7 (0.11)	16,926	5,627	33.2 (0.39)	6.3 (0.21)	4.0 (0.16)
4-year	13.5 (0.54)	3.8 (0.23)	18.4 (0.41)	2.2 (0.19)	7,214	2,356	32.7 (0.51)	5.7 (0.27)	4.3 (0.24)
2-year	18.2 (0.43)	5.4 (0.25)	23.9 (0.33)	3.1 (0.16)	9,624	3,262	33.9 (0.54)	6.8 (0.31)	3.8 (0.24)
Less-than-2-year	11.8 (1.19)	3.0 (0.66)	8.1 (1.66)	1.9 ! (0.73)	87	10	11.3 (2.24)	7.7 ! (2.32)	‡ (†)
Private nonprofit	12.3 (0.79)	4.1 (0.46)	14.3 (0.43)	2.9 (0.23)	3,010	633	21.0 (0.85)	5.8 (0.61)	4.5 (0.57)
4-year	12.3 (0.83)	4.1 (0.48)	14.2 (0.44)	2.8 (0.23)	2,923	622	21.3 (0.87)	5.9 (0.63)	4.6 (0.59)
2-year	11.2 (2.20)	3.1 ! (1.11)	19.4 (2.30)	5.9 (1.02)	79	10	12.7 (3.26)	‡ (†)	0.5 ! (0.22)
Less-than-2-year	17.2 (2.63)	8.1 (1.35)	15.6 ! (4.69)	2.7 (0.66)	7	1	13.6 ! (5.68)	# (†)	# (†)
Private for-profit	15.3 (1.08)	8.6 (1.06)	21.7 (1.18)	12.8 (1.24)	3,120	1,108	35.5 (0.83)	22.2 (0.79)	21.6 (0.82)
4-year	26.3 (2.25)	15.6 (2.26)	29.1 (1.95)	19.1 (1.92)	1,943	1,030	53.0 (1.26)	34.1 (1.25)	33.3 (1.30)
2-year	12.1 (1.64)	6.3 (1.25)	17.6 (1.49)	8.0 (1.34)	707	60	8.4 (1.28)	3.8 (1.09)	2.9 ! (1.01)
Less-than-2-year	5.4 (0.26)	1.9 (0.13)	6.2 (0.40)	1.8 (0.28)	470	18	3.9 (0.77)	1.0 ! (0.34)	‡ (†)

†Not applicable.
#Rounds to zero.
!Interpret data with caution. The coefficient of variation (CV) for this estimate is between 30 and 50 percent.
‡Reporting standards not met. Either there are too few cases for a reliable estimate or the coefficient of variation (CV) is 50 percent or greater.
[1]Excludes students not in a degree or certificate program.
[2]Excludes work-study/assistantships.
[3]Includes separated.
NOTE: In 2011–12, students were asked whether they took classes that were "taught only online" and, if so, whether their entire degree program was online. In 2003–04 and 2007–08, students were asked about distance education, which was defined in 2007–08 as "primarily delivered using live, interactive audio or videoconferencing, pre-recorded instructional videos, webcasts, CD-ROM, or DVD, or computer-based systems delivered over the Internet." The 2003–04 definition was very similar, with only minor differences in wording. In both years, distance education did not include correspondence courses. Data exclude Puerto Rico. Detail may not sum to totals because of rounding. Race categories exclude persons of Hispanic ethnicity.
SOURCE: U.S. Department of Education, National Center for Education Statistics, 2003–04, 2007–08, and 2011–12 National Postsecondary Student Aid Study (NPSAS:04, NPSAS:08, and NPSAS:12). (This table was prepared October 2014.)

Table 311.30. Number and percentage of graduate students taking night, weekend, or online classes, by selected characteristics: 2011–12
[Standard errors appear in parentheses]

Selected characteristic	Total taking any night, weekend, or online classes[1]		Percent of students taking night, weekend, or online classes					
	Number of students (in thousands)	Percent of students	Night classes		Weekend classes		Online classes	
			Any night classes	Exclusively night classes	Any weekend classes	Exclusively weekend classes	Any online classes	Exclusively online classes
1	2	3	4	5	6	7	8	9
Total	**2,309**	**62.7** (0.75)	**33.6** (0.70)	**9.4** (0.43)	**11.8** (0.49)	**2.0** (0.24)	**36.0** (0.74)	**20.1** (0.64)
Sex								
Male	849	58.0 (1.29)	33.4 (1.20)	9.6 (0.73)	10.9 (0.86)	1.6 (0.31)	31.5 (1.17)	17.8 (1.03)
Female	1,460	65.8 (0.94)	33.8 (0.85)	9.3 (0.52)	12.4 (0.68)	2.3 (0.34)	39.0 (0.97)	21.7 (0.84)
Race/ethnicity								
White	1,483	63.4 (0.92)	33.6 (0.82)	9.1 (0.56)	11.4 (0.61)	1.8 (0.26)	36.9 (0.98)	20.2 (0.92)
Black	319	73.6 (1.66)	33.7 (1.94)	10.8 (1.23)	10.8 (1.06)	2.2 (0.54)	48.8 (2.12)	33.0 (1.75)
Hispanic	221	68.6 (2.24)	38.8 (2.56)	14.3 (2.05)	14.2 (1.77)	3.8 ! (1.27)	34.6 (2.73)	19.3 (2.51)
Asian	211	44.5 (1.92)	30.4 (1.99)	7.0 (1.16)	12.3 (1.61)	2.0 ! (0.70)	19.4 (1.67)	7.5 (1.28)
Pacific Islander	14	70.8 (11.38)	29.9 ! (12.43)	‡ (†)	18.9 ! (8.14)	‡ (†)	44.2 (11.10)	20.3 ! (9.95)
American Indian/Alaska Native	12	75.0 (10.31)	28.7 ! (10.01)	16.6 ! (7.55)	‡ (†)	‡ (†)	55.1 (12.39)	42.5 ! (15.09)
Two or more races	48	63.5 (4.17)	36.6 (4.48)	5.4 ! (2.02)	15.8 ! (4.78)	‡ (†)	40.4 (4.24)	20.9 (3.82)
Age								
15 through 23	196	46.8 (1.94)	36.3 (1.93)	8.4 (1.11)	8.1 (1.18)	0.7 ! (0.33)	19.5 (1.45)	4.5 (0.74)
24 through 29	852	57.4 (1.20)	33.4 (1.07)	8.7 (0.58)	10.6 (0.68)	1.6 (0.32)	30.8 (1.05)	15.8 (0.95)
30 or older	1,261	70.8 (0.95)	33.3 (1.09)	10.3 (0.65)	13.6 (0.82)	2.7 (0.40)	44.3 (1.21)	27.4 (1.07)
Attendance status								
Exclusively full-time	910	53.1 (1.11)	27.5 (0.96)	6.0 (0.51)	8.9 (0.58)	1.3 (0.30)	31.7 (1.16)	18.4 (1.04)
Exclusively part-time	1,013	72.6 (1.08)	39.0 (1.24)	13.5 (0.89)	14.4 (0.91)	2.8 (0.43)	41.0 (1.21)	22.7 (1.19)
Mixed full-time and part-time	386	67.3 (1.75)	39.2 (1.60)	9.9 (1.19)	14.1 (1.28)	2.1 (0.41)	36.9 (1.98)	19.1 (1.69)
Had job during academic year[2]								
Yes	1,837	73.7 (0.87)	37.8 (0.86)	11.4 (0.57)	13.6 (0.65)	2.7 (0.32)	43.7 (0.91)	26.3 (0.79)
No	472	39.7 (1.22)	25.0 (1.11)	5.2 (0.50)	7.9 (0.73)	0.7 ! (0.24)	19.9 (1.12)	7.2 (0.82)
Dependency status								
Dependent	—	(†)	(†)	(†)	(†)	(†)	— (†)	— (†)
Independent, no dependents, not married[3]	1,025	55.5 (1.03)	34.0 (0.98)	8.5 (0.52)	11.1 (0.64)	1.5 (0.31)	28.1 (0.88)	13.2 (0.74)
Independent, no dependents, married	345	62.6 (1.89)	32.7 (1.68)	9.2 (1.21)	11.3 (1.37)	2.1 ! (0.67)	36.1 (1.75)	21.0 (1.63)
Independent, with dependents, not married[3]	284	79.3 (1.71)	35.1 (2.57)	10.2 (1.55)	14.9 (1.68)	3.7 (1.02)	52.0 (2.49)	33.4 (2.48)
Independent, with dependents, married	654	70.8 (1.52)	33.0 (1.42)	11.0 (0.96)	12.3 (1.13)	2.4 (0.49)	45.6 (1.60)	28.3 (1.55)
Control of institution								
Public	1,002	57.4 (0.95)	34.3 (0.97)	7.6 (0.51)	9.9 (0.63)	2.0 (0.29)	32.8 (0.93)	14.1 (0.72)
Private nonprofit	924	61.8 (1.14)	38.1 (1.17)	12.8 (0.84)	15.2 (0.88)	2.3 (0.42)	28.5 (1.16)	13.8 (1.08)
Private for-profit	382	86.7 (2.12)	16.1 (1.70)	5.0 (0.79)	8.0 (1.08)	1.1 ! (0.37)	74.1 (2.09)	65.3 (2.58)

—Not available.
†Not applicable.
!Interpret data with caution. The coefficient of variation (CV) for this estimate is between 30 and 50 percent. The coefficient of variation (CV) for this estimate is 50 percent or greater.
‡Reporting standards not met.
[1]Students who reported taking more than one type of class (e.g., night classes and online classes) are counted only once in the total.
[2]Excludes work-study/assistantships.
[3]Includes separated.

NOTE: Night classes start after 6:00 p.m. on Monday through Thursday nights; weekend classes start after 6:00 p.m. on Friday or take place any time on Saturday or Sunday; and online classes are taught only online. Detail may not sum to totals because of rounding. Race categories exclude persons of Hispanic ethnicity.
SOURCE: U.S. Department of Education, National Center for Education Statistics, 2011–12 National Postsecondary Student Aid Study (NPSAS:12). (This table was prepared March 2014.)

Table 311.32. Number and percentage of graduate students taking distance education or online classes and degree programs, by selected characteristics: Selected years, 2003–04 through 2011–12

[Standard errors appear in parentheses]

Selected characteristic	Percent of graduate students taking distance education classes								2011–12							
	2003–04				2007–08				Number of graduate students (in thousands)		Percent of graduate students taking online classes					
	Total, any distance education classes		Entire degree program through distance education[1]		Total, any distance education classes		Entire degree program through distance education[1]		Total, all graduate students	Number taking any online classes	Total, any online classes		Exclusively online classes		Entire degree program is online[1]	
1	2		3		4		5		6	7	8		9		10	
Total...	16.5	(0.76)	6.1	(0.58)	22.8	(0.76)	9.5	(0.68)	3,682	1,326	36.0	(0.74)	20.1	(0.64)	18.2	(0.63)
Sex																
Male	15.4	(1.17)	4.9	(0.74)	20.6	(1.17)	7.8	(1.07)	1,463	461	31.5	(1.17)	17.8	(1.03)	15.9	(1.06)
Female	17.3	(1.00)	7.0	(0.74)	24.2	(0.99)	10.6	(0.77)	2,219	865	39.0	(0.97)	21.7	(0.84)	19.8	(0.78)
Race/ethnicity																
White	17.7	(0.88)	6.7	(0.74)	23.6	(0.99)	9.6	(0.95)	2,341	864	36.9	(0.98)	20.2	(0.92)	18.2	(0.88)
Black	19.2	(2.44)	7.5	(1.72)	25.8	(2.94)	11.5	(2.11)	434	212	48.8	(2.12)	33.0	(1.75)	31.4	(1.66)
Hispanic	13.1	(1.81)	5.0	(1.26)	23.7	(3.09)	9.4 !	(2.85)	321	111	34.6	(2.73)	19.3	(2.51)	17.9	(2.53)
Asian	9.4	(1.40)	3.0 !	(1.01)	12.8	(1.10)	4.5	(0.68)	474	92	19.4	(1.67)	7.5	(1.28)	6.0	(1.13)
Pacific Islander..........................	‡	(†)	‡	(†)	31.1 !	(9.43)	13.5 !	(6.20)	20	9	44.2	(11.10)	20.3 !	(9.95)	‡	(†)
American Indian/Alaska Native	8.7 !	(3.54)	‡	(†)	16.7 !	(6.78)	‡	(†)	16	‡	55.1	(12.39)	42.5 !	(15.09)	43.4 !	(15.26)
Two or more races	17.1	(4.46)	4.8 !	(2.33)	27.7 !	(8.38)	21.3 !	(9.56)	75	30	40.4	(4.24)	20.9	(3.82)	18.4	(3.84)
Age																
15 through 23.............................	11.1	(1.73)	3.7	(0.77)	16.6	(2.64)	1.6	(0.40)	419	82	19.5	(1.45)	4.5	(0.74)	4.3	(0.76)
24 through 29.............................	13.6	(0.82)	3.6	(0.43)	16.1	(0.79)	5.7	(0.54)	1,483	456	30.8	(1.05)	15.8	(0.95)	14.4	(0.91)
30 or older.................................	20.2	(1.21)	9.0	(1.06)	29.5	(1.39)	14.5	(1.31)	1,781	788	44.3	(1.21)	27.4	(1.07)	24.9	(1.01)
Attendance status																
Exclusively full-time	12.0	(1.00)	3.4	(0.72)	16.4	(1.35)	6.5	(1.24)	1,713	543	31.7	(1.16)	18.4	(1.04)	17.4	(0.98)
Exclusively part-time..................	20.0	(1.01)	8.8	(0.97)	28.1	(1.17)	13.3	(1.07)	1,396	572	41.0	(1.21)	22.7	(1.19)	19.5	(1.21)
Mixed full-time and part-time	15.6	(1.89)	4.1	(0.71)	23.6	(2.15)	6.8	(0.95)	573	212	36.9	(1.98)	19.1	(1.69)	17.9	(1.66)
Graduate field of study																
Business/management..................	22.6	(2.30)	10.3	(1.98)	27.6	(2.90)	13.9	(2.68)	615	246	40.0	(2.09)	26.8	(2.00)	25.1	(1.82)
Education....................................	20.7	(1.74)	8.2	(1.29)	28.3	(1.67)	9.9	(1.36)	775	379	48.9	(1.65)	26.1	(1.56)	23.7	(1.47)
Health..	12.6	(1.23)	3.9	(0.79)	22.0	(1.59)	8.9	(1.33)	679	248	36.5	(1.42)	18.9	(1.04)	16.5	(1.00)
Humanities.................................	12.9	(2.43)	2.9 !	(0.87)	15.7	(1.72)	3.1	(0.65)	290	81	28.1	(3.13)	14.1	(2.87)	12.1	(2.88)
Law...	5.6	(1.15)	‡	(†)	6.1	(0.87)	1.7 !	(0.54)	146	15	10.3	(1.46)	2.9	(0.72)	2.5	(0.65)
Life and physical sciences..........	—	(†)	—	(†)	—	(†)	—	(†)	208	29	13.9	(1.49)	7.3	(1.36)	5.3	(1.21)
Life sciences..............................	12.4	(2.51)	6.9 !	(2.14)	14.0	(2.15)	4.3	(1.14)	—	—	—	(†)	—	(†)	—	(†)
Mathematics, engineering, and computer science	12.0	(2.03)	4.6 !	(1.48)	19.7	(3.06)	9.4 !	(2.96)	315	80	25.5	(1.78)	14.6	(1.44)	13.3	(1.42)
Social/behavioral sciences	8.5	(1.42)	3.4 !	(1.11)	21.3	(3.66)	12.7	(3.68)	223	82	36.6	(2.22)	22.6	(1.84)	21.7	(1.89)
Other[2]......................................	19.0	(1.56)	4.6	(1.08)	22.2	(1.49)	9.4	(1.49)	430	166	38.6	(2.03)	20.5	(2.19)	19.2	(2.29)
Had job during academic year[3]																
Yes	19.6	(0.97)	7.7	(0.78)	27.2	(0.89)	11.9	(0.79)	2,494	1,090	43.7	(0.91)	26.3	(0.79)	24.1	(0.79)
No	9.0	(0.81)	2.7	(0.41)	10.0	(1.36)	2.8 !	(1.27)	1,188	236	19.9	(1.12)	7.2	(0.82)	6.2	(0.78)
Dependency status																
Dependent..................................	—	(†)	—	(†)	—	(†)	—	(†)	—	—	—	(†)	—	(†)	—	(†)
Independent, no dependents, not married[4]...................................	12.1	(0.75)	3.7	(0.39)	16.6	(0.90)	5.2	(0.59)	1,848	520	28.1	(0.88)	13.2	(0.74)	11.8	(0.67)
Independent, no dependents, married....	15.5	(1.22)	5.0	(0.77)	22.3	(1.67)	10.1	(1.56)	551	199	36.1	(1.75)	21.0	(1.63)	19.5	(1.64)
Independent, with dependents, not married[4]...................................	21.3	(3.18)	9.4	(2.21)	26.8	(3.23)	10.8	(1.86)	359	187	52.0	(2.49)	33.4	(2.48)	32.5	(2.54)
Independent, with dependents, married..	24.2	(1.72)	10.8	(1.46)	34.2	(1.76)	17.5	(2.14)	923	421	45.6	(1.60)	28.3	(1.55)	25.1	(1.52)
Control of institution																
Public	15.2	(0.68)	4.8	(0.39)	23.1	(0.99)	8.9	(0.95)	1,745	573	32.8	(0.93)	14.1	(0.72)	11.8	(0.69)
Private nonprofit.........................	16.3	(1.25)	6.7	(1.03)	18.5	(0.74)	6.0	(0.41)	1,496	426	28.5	(1.16)	13.8	(1.08)	12.3	(1.03)
Private for-profit	35.3	(8.12)	18.6 !	(6.64)	41.6	(5.47)	29.9	(5.89)	440	327	74.1	(2.09)	65.3	(2.58)	62.5	(2.49)

—Not available.
†Not applicable.
!Interpret data with caution. The coefficient of variation (CV) for this estimate is between 30 and 50 percent.
‡Reporting standards not met. Either there are too few cases for a reliable estimate or the coefficient of variation (CV) is 50 percent or greater.
[1]Excludes students not in a degree or certificate program.
[2]Includes students who are not in a degree program or have not declared a major. For 2003–04 and 2007–08, includes physical sciences.
[3]Excludes work-study/assistantships.
[4]Includes separated.

NOTE: In 2011–12, students were asked whether they took classes that were "taught only online" and, if so, whether their entire degree program was online. In 2003–04 and 2007–08, students were asked about distance education, which was defined in 2007–08 as "primarily delivered using live, interactive audio or videoconferencing, pre-recorded instructional videos, webcasts, CD-ROM, or DVD, or computer-based systems delivered over the Internet." The 2003–04 definition was very similar, with only minor differences in wording. In both years, distance education did not include correspondence courses. Data exclude Puerto Rico. Detail may not sum to totals because of rounding. Race categories exclude persons of Hispanic ethnicity.
SOURCE: U.S. Department of Education, National Center for Education Statistics, 2003–04, 2007–08, and 2011–12 National Postsecondary Student Aid Study (NPSAS:04, NPSAS:08, and NPSAS:12). (This table was prepared October 2014.)

Table 311.33. Selected statistics for degree-granting postsecondary institutions that primarily offer online programs, by control of institution and selected characteristics: 2014

Selected characteristic	All institutions	Primarily online institutions[1]					Other institutions[1]			
		Total	Percent of all institutions	Public	Nonprofit	For-profit	Total	Public	Nonprofit	For-profit
1	2	3	4	5	6	7	8	9	10	11
Number of institutions, fall 2014[2]	**4,614**	**68**	**1.5**	**6**	**17**	**45**	**4,546**	**1,615**	**1,649**	**1,282**
Fall 2014 enrollment										
Total enrollment	20,207,369	802,835	4.0	58,317	121,417	623,101	19,404,534	14,596,698	3,874,672	933,164
Full-time	12,453,975	483,622	3.9	11,928	71,736	399,958	11,970,353	8,385,791	2,931,475	653,087
Males	5,619,391	157,233	2.8	4,944	27,465	124,824	5,462,158	3,909,685	1,294,634	257,839
Females	6,834,584	326,389	4.8	6,984	44,271	275,134	6,508,195	4,476,106	1,636,841	395,248
Part-time	7,753,394	319,213	4.1	46,389	49,681	223,143	7,434,181	6,210,907	943,197	280,077
Males	3,177,670	127,992	4.0	22,448	22,246	83,298	3,049,678	2,601,857	359,380	88,441
Females	4,575,724	191,221	4.2	23,941	27,435	139,845	4,384,503	3,609,050	583,817	191,636
Undergraduate	17,292,787	594,132	3.4	47,457	99,683	446,992	16,698,655	13,197,380	2,671,658	829,617
Full-time	10,783,802	359,220	3.3	10,513	56,178	292,529	10,424,582	7,597,455	2,213,419	613,708
Part-time	6,508,985	234,912	3.6	36,944	43,505	154,463	6,274,073	5,599,925	458,239	215,909
Postbaccalaureate	2,914,582	208,703	7.2	10,860	21,734	176,109	2,705,879	1,399,318	1,203,014	103,547
Full-time	1,670,173	124,402	7.4	1,415	15,558	107,429	1,545,771	788,336	718,056	39,379
Part-time	1,244,409	84,301	6.8	9,445	6,176	68,680	1,160,108	610,982	484,958	64,168
White	11,237,436	412,654	3.7	39,630	79,414	293,610	10,824,782	8,079,866	2,365,612	379,304
Black	2,791,865	227,805	8.2	6,679	23,358	197,768	2,564,060	1,832,980	466,317	264,763
Hispanic	3,191,699	73,422	2.3	7,008	9,624	56,790	3,118,277	2,573,381	359,386	185,510
Asian	1,213,616	17,772	1.5	2,301	3,872	11,599	1,195,844	916,271	239,658	39,915
Pacific Islander	58,832	5,027	8.5	298	611	4,118	53,805	37,445	9,264	7,096
American Indian/Alaska Native	152,911	6,862	4.5	466	811	5,585	146,049	117,373	19,813	8,863
Two or more races	642,100	53,035	8.3	1,319	3,252	48,464	589,065	451,770	107,200	30,095
Nonresident alien	918,910	6,258	0.7	616	475	5,167	912,652	587,612	307,422	17,618
4-year institutions	13,492,884	789,999	5.9	58,317	121,417	610,265	12,702,885	8,198,933	3,844,307	659,645
Full-time	9,793,247	475,756	4.9	11,928	71,736	392,092	9,317,491	6,000,778	2,908,697	408,016
Part-time	3,699,637	314,243	8.5	46,389	49,681	218,173	3,385,394	2,198,155	935,610	251,629
2-year institutions	6,714,485	12,836	0.2	0	0	12,836	6,701,649	6,397,765	30,365	273,519
Full-time	2,660,728	7,866	0.3	0	0	7,866	2,652,862	2,385,013	22,778	245,071
Part-time	4,053,757	4,970	0.1	0	0	4,970	4,048,787	4,012,752	7,587	28,448
Earned degrees conferred, 2013–14										
Associate's	1,003,364	43,002	4.3	823	2,289	39,890	960,362	792,357	50,838	117,167
Males	390,805	14,162	3.6	539	981	12,642	376,643	312,730	18,698	45,215
Females	612,559	28,840	4.7	284	1,308	27,248	583,719	479,627	32,140	71,952
Bachelor's	1,869,814	80,119	4.3	6,092	10,922	63,105	1,789,695	1,180,305	533,291	76,099
Males	801,692	30,465	3.8	2,644	4,496	23,325	771,227	519,651	218,943	32,633
Females	1,068,122	49,654	4.6	3,448	6,426	39,780	1,018,468	660,654	314,348	43,466
Master's	754,475	53,646	7.1	2,265	6,316	45,065	700,829	343,836	327,264	29,729
Males	302,807	18,368	6.1	1,023	2,357	14,988	284,439	141,342	132,549	10,548
Females	451,668	35,278	7.8	1,242	3,959	30,077	416,390	202,494	194,715	19,181
Doctor's[3]	177,580	3,685	2.1	35	111	3,539	173,895	88,869	80,783	4,243
Males	85,587	1,257	1.5	1	40	1,216	84,330	43,736	38,887	1,707
Females	91,993	2,428	2.6	34	71	2,323	89,565	45,133	41,896	2,536
First-time students' rates of graduation from and retention at first institution attended										
Among full-time bachelor's degree-seekers starting at 4-year institutions in 2008, percent earning bachelor's degree										
Within 4 years after start	39.8	8.7	†	‡	20.8	6.3	39.9	34.4	52.8	19.2
Within 5 years after start	55.3	15.5	†	‡	32.9	12.0	55.5	53.1	63.3	24.6
Within 6 years after start	59.6	18.1	†	‡	37.7	14.1	59.9	58.5	65.5	28.4
Among full-time degree/certificate-seekers starting at 2-year institutions in 2011, percent completing credential within 150 percent of normal time	27.9	‡	†	‡	‡	‡	27.9	20.0	51.9	58.5
Among degree-seekers starting in 2013, percent returning in 2014										
Full-time entrants	73.9	46.5	†	‡	57.8	41.5	74.1	72.5	81.2	64.8
Part-time entrants	43.6	38.3	†	44.6	38.3	38.0	43.6	43.8	41.6	37.6

†Not applicable.
‡Reporting standards not met (too few cases for a reliable estimate).
[1]Primarily online institutions have more than 90 percent of their students attending classes exclusively online. Other institutions may have some online offerings, but they are not primarily online.
[2]Includes only institutions reporting enrollment data in fall 2014.
[3]Includes Ph.D., Ed.D., and comparable degrees at the doctoral level. Includes most degrees formerly classified as first-professional, such as M.D., D.D.S., and law degrees.

NOTE: Degree-granting institutions grant associate's or higher degrees and participate in Title IV federal financial aid programs. Race categories exclude persons of Hispanic ethnicity. SOURCE: U.S. Department of Education, National Center for Education Statistics, Integrated Postsecondary Education Data System (IPEDS), Spring 2015, Fall Enrollment component; IPEDS, Fall 2014, Completions component; and IPEDS, Spring 2015, Graduation Rates component. (This table was prepared February 2016.)

Table 311.40. **Percentage of first-year undergraduate students who reported taking remedial education courses, by selected student and institution characteristics: 2003–04, 2007–08, and 2011–12**

[Standard errors appear in parentheses]

Selected student or institution characteristic	2003–04 first-year undergraduates[1]											2007–08 first-year undergraduates[1]			
	Percent who took any remedial courses				Percent who took specific remedial courses in 2003–04								Percent who took any remedial courses			
	Ever		In 2003–04		English		Mathematics		Reading		Writing		Ever		In 2007–08	
1	2		3		4		5		6		7		8		9	
Total	34.8	(0.36)	19.2	(0.30)	5.7	(0.21)	14.6	(0.26)	5.6	(0.17)	6.9	(0.18)	36.2	(0.38)	20.0	(0.35)
Sex																
Male	33.0	(0.53)	18.4	(0.46)	5.6	(0.29)	13.9	(0.41)	5.2	(0.22)	6.6	(0.27)	33.0	(0.53)	19.3	(0.51)
Female	36.2	(0.54)	19.8	(0.39)	5.8	(0.23)	15.1	(0.34)	5.8	(0.24)	7.1	(0.26)	38.7	(0.51)	20.6	(0.46)
Race/ethnicity of student																
White	31.7	(0.42)	17.8	(0.35)	4.9	(0.21)	13.5	(0.32)	4.4	(0.18)	6.4	(0.22)	31.3	(0.46)	17.7	(0.41)
Black	41.2	(1.00)	22.4	(0.76)	7.5	(0.52)	17.1	(0.66)	7.8	(0.49)	6.9	(0.44)	45.1	(0.99)	24.4	(0.86)
Hispanic	38.5	(0.91)	21.5	(0.72)	6.6	(0.52)	17.0	(0.66)	7.1	(0.48)	8.3	(0.47)	43.7	(1.12)	23.3	(0.84)
Asian	39.6	(1.72)	17.6	(1.56)	8.2	(1.09)	10.9	(1.19)	7.0	(0.83)	8.4	(0.93)	38.9	(2.05)	20.0	(1.90)
Pacific Islander	40.8	(5.11)	22.4	(4.55)	10.2 !	(4.18)	19.8	(4.64)	10.1 !	(4.07)	11.3 !	(4.00)	39.9	(4.63)	19.1	(3.90)
American Indian/Alaska Native	44.8	(4.34)	23.7	(3.10)	3.4	(1.0)	17.3	(2.80)	8.4	(2.28)	8.1	(2.35)	47.9	(4.66)	29.7	(3.88)
Two or more races	33.9	(2.02)	20.9	(1.80)	4.7	(0.90)	14.8	(1.48)	4.9	(0.98)	6.5	(1.12)	32.3	(2.29)	20.4	(2.06)
Other	31.1	(2.78)	17.3	(2.34)	5.0	(1.35)	14.3	(2.12)	6.1	(1.30)	6.9	(1.63)	35.2	(6.00)	21.7	(5.11)
Age																
15 to 23	33.7	(0.41)	21.5	(0.39)	6.6	(0.28)	16.1	(0.35)	6.4	(0.22)	8.2	(0.22)	34.5	(0.46)	22.0	(0.43)
24 to 29	35.0	(0.99)	16.0	(0.78)	4.3	(0.41)	12.8	(0.65)	4.0	(0.40)	5.0	(0.55)	39.7	(0.98)	19.5	(0.86)
30 or older	37.6	(0.87)	15.6	(0.52)	4.5	(0.35)	12.1	(0.51)	4.4	(0.32)	4.7	(0.31)	38.1	(0.84)	15.2	(0.68)
Attendance status																
Exclusively full-time	31.4	(0.45)	19.1	(0.37)	5.7	(0.22)	14.1	(0.35)	5.6	(0.23)	7.5	(0.24)	31.4	(0.52)	19.4	(0.46)
Exclusively part-time	37.5	(0.65)	17.9	(0.51)	5.3	(0.31)	14.0	(0.47)	5.0	(0.28)	5.6	(0.28)	39.8	(0.71)	19.0	(0.59)
Mixed full- and part-time	41.1	(0.97)	23.7	(0.85)	7.1	(0.56)	18.7	(0.81)	7.1	(0.48)	8.3	(0.45)	42.6	(0.98)	26.3	(0.93)
Student housing status																
On-campus	24.5	(0.70)	16.8	(0.56)	4.8	(0.31)	11.3	(0.49)	4.8	(0.31)	8.2	(0.40)	23.2	(0.84)	17.1	(0.76)
Off-campus	35.9	(0.58)	17.0	(0.40)	5.1	(0.30)	13.4	(0.35)	4.6	(0.22)	5.5	(0.28)	37.2	(0.57)	17.8	(0.49)
With parents or relatives	37.9	(0.59)	24.5	(0.61)	7.1	(0.36)	18.5	(0.53)	7.7	(0.35)	8.7	(0.37)	39.6	(0.78)	25.2	(0.66)
Attended more than one institution	36.5	(1.18)	18.3	(0.98)	6.4	(0.59)	14.5	(0.98)	5.0	(0.48)	6.2	(0.48)	36.1	(1.11)	20.2	(0.97)
Dependency status																
Dependent	33.4	(0.45)	22.1	(0.41)	6.6	(0.27)	16.4	(0.36)	6.5	(0.24)	8.6	(0.23)	34.4	(0.51)	22.8	(0.46)
Independent	36.4	(0.61)	16.1	(0.39)	4.8	(0.27)	12.7	(0.37)	4.5	(0.23)	5.0	(0.26)	38.1	(0.59)	17.1	(0.51)
Veteran status																
Veteran	35.9	(2.33)	13.2	(1.52)	1.9	(0.51)	9.9	(1.40)	3.2	(0.68)	4.3	(0.84)	35.8	(2.36)	17.1	(2.08)
Not veteran	34.8	(0.38)	19.4	(0.31)	5.8	(0.22)	14.8	(0.27)	5.7	(0.18)	7.0	(0.18)	36.2	(0.38)	20.1	(0.36)
Field of study																
Business/management	36.4	(1.00)	19.6	(0.97)	5.5	(0.41)	14.7	(1.01)	6.0	(0.44)	7.3	(0.61)	37.0	(1.13)	21.7	(1.06)
Computer science	33.7	(1.59)	19.2	(1.39)	4.7	(0.67)	14.7	(1.27)	5.3	(0.82)	5.6	(0.73)	34.7	(2.28)	19.8	(1.77)
Education	41.5	(1.61)	23.1	(1.14)	6.3	(0.74)	17.6	(1.03)	6.4	(0.72)	8.8	(0.86)	40.3	(1.90)	23.0	(1.48)
Engineering	30.9	(1.79)	16.6	(1.41)	5.6	(0.77)	12.9	(1.26)	4.8	(0.77)	6.8	(0.91)	33.0	(1.81)	19.0	(1.57)
Health	37.0	(0.83)	19.7	(0.68)	6.1	(0.48)	15.5	(0.63)	5.7	(0.43)	6.2	(0.50)	38.6	(2.49)	18.9	(4.49)
Humanities	34.0	(1.29)	18.8	(0.94)	5.6	(0.46)	14.2	(0.87)	5.0	(0.52)	7.3	(0.52)	31.2	(1.94)	20.5	(1.77)
Life sciences	31.2	(1.81)	19.7	(1.72)	5.7	(1.29)	14.6	(1.47)	5.4	(1.21)	7.9	(1.20)	31.2	(6.21)	20.5 !	(8.64)
Mathematics	23.0	(5.55)	11.0 !	(4.43)	‡	(†)	9.3 !	(4.26)	‡	(†)	‡	(†)	41.1	(6.31)	15.6 !	(5.20)
Physical sciences	24.0	(4.39)	12.9	(3.49)	7.5 !	(2.85)	5.3 !	(2.13)	6.4 !	(3.05)	‡	(†)	24.5	(4.31)	15.7	(3.92)
Social/behavioral sciences	33.2	(2.08)	19.4	(1.57)	5.5	(0.90)	14.5	(1.39)	6.5	(1.01)	8.7	(1.05)	35.0	(2.16)	23.4	(1.94)
Vocational/technical	38.5	(2.11)	18.3	(1.60)	5.0	(0.86)	14.5	(1.40)	5.6	(1.0)	4.7	(0.61)	31.1	(1.93)	15.7	(1.78)
Undeclared	33.6	(0.67)	19.2	(0.59)	6.0	(0.38)	14.5	(0.49)	5.2	(0.33)	7.2	(0.38)	35.8	(1.29)	20.0	(1.14)
Other	33.3	(1.49)	18.0	(1.06)	5.3	(0.67)	13.6	(0.94)	6.2	(0.57)	5.9	(0.56)	34.6	(1.23)	18.5	(0.97)
Type of institution																
Public less-than-2-year	30.6	(1.85)	10.9	(1.09)	4.8	(0.80)	9.3	(1.05)	4.0	(0.86)	3.9	(0.90)	31.9	(1.99)	9.0	(0.89)
Public 2-year	41.4	(0.59)	23.0	(0.47)	6.9	(0.33)	18.3	(0.42)	7.1	(0.28)	7.2	(0.27)	41.8	(0.54)	23.7	(0.48)
Public 4-year nondoctorate	34.2	(1.77)	21.4	(1.12)	5.3	(0.61)	16.3	(1.05)	5.2	(0.56)	8.5	(0.63)	38.9	(1.24)	25.4	(1.14)
Public 4-year doctorate	25.7	(1.11)	16.3	(0.64)	4.4	(0.34)	11.7	(0.60)	3.9	(0.39)	8.1	(0.42)	25.0	(1.03)	17.8	(0.86)
Private nonprofit less-than-4-year	31.3	(2.06)	12.9	(1.89)	4.5	(1.03)	10.2	(1.49)	2.8	(0.82)	5.0	(1.27)	30.3	(3.75)	10.2	(2.81)
Private nonprofit 4-year nondoctorate	26.0	(1.16)	14.7	(0.78)	5.3	(0.68)	9.5	(0.58)	4.0	(0.41)	6.7	(0.76)	25.5	(1.74)	16.6	(1.46)
Private nonprofit 4-year doctorate	18.3	(1.67)	11.6	(1.39)	2.4	(0.54)	7.4	(1.37)	2.9	(0.57)	6.3	(0.91)	22.1	(1.70)	12.6	(1.38)
Private for-profit less-than-2-year	24.1	(0.50)	7.8	(0.23)	3.1	(0.18)	4.6	(0.16)	2.2	(0.19)	3.5	(0.22)	26.5	(1.02)	5.5	(0.51)
Private for-profit 2 years or more	25.4	(1.63)	11.7	(1.04)	4.1	(0.51)	7.5	(0.75)	3.3	(0.45)	4.9	(0.71)	28.8	(1.46)	11.3	(1.20)

See notes at end of table.

Table 311.40. Percentage of first-year undergraduate students who reported taking remedial education courses, by selected student and institution characteristics: 2003–04, 2007–08, and 2011–12—Continued

[Standard errors appear in parentheses]

Selected student or institution characteristic	2011–12 first-year undergraduates[1]												
	Total number of students (in thousands)	Students who took any remedial courses				Percent who took specific remedial courses in 2011–12							
		Percent who ever took	Number who took in 2011–12 (in thousands)	Percent who took in 2011–12		English		Mathematics		Reading		Writing	
1	10	11	12	13		14		15		16		17	
Total	9,437	32.6	(0.42)	1,864	19.7	(0.36)	10.0	(0.25)	16.2	(0.34)	7.4	(0.23)	7.5	(0.25)
Sex													
Male	4,079	30.8	(0.61)	811	19.9	(0.55)	10.4	(0.37)	16.0	(0.49)	7.2	(0.32)	7.6	(0.36)
Female	5,359	34.0	(0.52)	1,053	19.7	(0.46)	9.7	(0.35)	16.3	(0.43)	7.5	(0.29)	7.4	(0.26)
Race/ethnicity of student													
White	4,997	29.4	(0.51)	885	17.7	(0.47)	8.1	(0.33)	14.7	(0.43)	5.8	(0.29)	6.3	(0.29)
Black	1,871	37.6	(0.89)	416	22.2	(0.75)	12.8	(0.54)	18.2	(0.72)	10.1	(0.53)	9.2	(0.55)
Hispanic	1,728	35.8	(0.99)	388	22.4	(0.81)	11.5	(0.56)	18.7	(0.76)	8.4	(0.46)	8.5	(0.48)
Asian	410	37.6	(2.25)	94	23.0	(1.75)	14.6	(1.53)	15.2	(1.19)	11.1	(1.57)	11.5	(1.52)
Pacific Islander	46	33.4	(5.16)	7	15.2	(3.50)	9.6 !	(3.15)	11.9	(3.11)	4.2	(1.25)	5.5 !	(1.65)
American Indian/Alaska Native	106	34.9	(4.11)	21	19.8	(2.79)	10.2	(2.03)	17.4	(2.79)	9.0	(2.03)	7.1	(1.71)
Two or more races	280	29.8	(2.02)	53	19.0	(1.68)	9.8	(1.56)	15.4	(1.58)	5.5	(1.01)	5.7	(0.91)
Other	—	—	(†)	—	—	(†)	—	(†)	—	(†)	—	(†)	—	(†)
Age													
15 to 23	5,549	31.0	(0.49)	1,169	21.1	(0.38)	10.6	(0.30)	17.3	(0.36)	7.6	(0.24)	7.7	(0.28)
24 to 29	1,618	34.4	(1.12)	278	17.2	(0.91)	8.3	(0.61)	14.2	(0.86)	6.4	(0.55)	6.4	(0.52)
30 or older	2,270	35.4	(0.94)	417	18.4	(0.82)	9.7	(0.53)	14.9	(0.73)	7.6	(0.57)	7.7	(0.56)
Attendance status													
Exclusively full-time	4,774	28.1	(0.48)	840	17.6	(0.41)	9.1	(0.28)	14.2	(0.41)	6.6	(0.27)	6.7	(0.26)
Exclusively part-time	3,280	37.4	(0.81)	699	21.3	(0.78)	10.3	(0.50)	17.7	(0.71)	7.7	(0.43)	7.9	(0.50)
Mixed full- and part-time	1,383	37.0	(0.95)	324	23.4	(0.74)	12.2	(0.57)	19.5	(0.71)	9.3	(0.53)	9.1	(0.50)
Student housing status													
On-campus	1,055	17.9	(0.78)	148	14.1	(0.67)	6.5	(0.48)	10.9	(0.58)	3.9	(0.37)	5.0	(0.46)
Off-campus	4,326	34.0	(0.65)	846	19.6	(0.63)	9.7	(0.41)	15.9	(0.58)	7.8	(0.41)	7.8	(0.43)
With parents or relatives	3,462	35.3	(0.78)	768	22.2	(0.61)	11.6	(0.43)	18.5	(0.56)	8.2	(0.37)	8.1	(0.42)
Attended more than one institution	594	32.7	(1.09)	101	17.0	(0.95)	8.9	(0.77)	14.1	(0.86)	5.7	(0.56)	6.3	(0.62)
Dependency status													
Dependent	4,543	31.2	(0.53)	1,001	22.0	(0.42)	11.0	(0.34)	17.9	(0.41)	8.0	(0.27)	8.1	(0.31)
Independent	4,894	33.9	(0.57)	863	17.6	(0.52)	9.0	(0.34)	14.5	(0.50)	6.8	(0.34)	6.9	(0.30)
Veteran status													
Veteran	310	31.4	(2.21)	54	17.4	(1.74)	8.5	(1.22)	15.9	(1.67)	3.3	(0.68)	5.2	(0.97)
Not veteran	9,127	32.7	(0.42)	1,809	19.8	(0.37)	10.1	(0.26)	16.2	(0.35)	7.5	(0.24)	7.6	(0.25)
Field of study													
Business/management	1,203	32.7	(1.11)	238	19.8	(0.85)	10.5	(0.72)	15.3	(0.75)	8.7	(0.66)	8.2	(0.60)
Computer science	402	29.3	(1.69)	70	17.4	(1.40)	8.9	(1.14)	14.0	(1.29)	6.2	(1.02)	6.8	(1.16)
Education	387	36.0	(1.84)	84	21.6	(1.53)	10.6	(1.08)	16.4	(1.23)	7.9	(1.03)	7.2	(0.90)
Engineering	409	33.1	(1.88)	86	20.9	(1.63)	11.0	(1.22)	15.4	(1.33)	7.9	(1.23)	9.1	(1.22)
Health	2,023	34.6	(0.74)	381	18.8	(0.70)	9.1	(0.55)	16.7	(0.67)	6.7	(0.45)	6.7	(0.39)
Humanities	1,776	36.6	(1.03)	424	23.9	(0.91)	11.7	(0.60)	19.6	(0.80)	8.9	(0.62)	8.9	(0.60)
Life sciences	416	26.7	(1.71)	75	17.9	(1.11)	9.1	(0.92)	14.2	(1.01)	6.4	(0.89)	7.1	(0.82)
Mathematics	24	14.3 !	(4.57)	‡	8.4 !	(2.81)	4.6 !	(2.26)	7.6 !	(2.67)	‡	(†)	6.2 !	(2.51)
Physical sciences	58	29.2	(4.72)	14	24.7	(4.59)	17.2	(4.25)	20.8	(4.24)	8.9 !	(3.16)	13.6	(3.98)
Social/behavioral sciences	392	27.7	(1.87)	78	19.8	(1.38)	9.1	(0.87)	16.6	(1.37)	6.0	(0.88)	7.6	(0.79)
Vocational/technical	431	26.9	(1.94)	68	15.7	(1.59)	7.6	(1.12)	13.0	(1.56)	5.9	(0.85)	5.7	(1.02)
Undeclared	299	31.8	(2.10)	66	22.0	(1.86)	10.7	(1.53)	17.4	(1.68)	7.9	(1.41)	6.6	(1.13)
Other	1,350	29.3	(0.94)	225	16.7	(0.77)	9.4	(0.64)	13.9	(0.70)	6.4	(0.52)	6.7	(0.56)
Type of institution													
Public less-than-2-year	58	30.2	(6.13)	7	12.2 !	(3.86)	8.5 !	(4.11)	10.5 !	(3.34)	6.5 !	(3.19)	1.6 !	(0.75)
Public 2-year	5,038	40.3	(0.67)	1,289	25.6	(0.64)	13.2	(0.43)	21.0	(0.60)	10.3	(0.38)	9.7	(0.41)
Public 4-year nondoctorate	817	37.8	(2.12)	198	24.3	(1.30)	10.2	(0.79)	20.4	(1.25)	6.9	(0.78)	7.9	(0.88)
Public 4-year doctorate	893	21.9	(0.84)	139	15.6	(0.80)	6.8	(0.47)	12.8	(0.71)	3.5	(0.33)	4.5	(0.45)
Private nonprofit less-than-4-year	58	22.3	(4.25)	6	9.4 !	(3.42)	5.9	(1.73)	8.1 !	(2.86)	‡	(†)	3.5 !	(1.64)
Private nonprofit 4-year nondoctorate	375	24.4	(1.66)	58	15.3	(1.23)	7.8	(1.04)	10.9	(1.06)	4.9	(0.77)	7.0	(0.97)
Private nonprofit 4-year doctorate	356	14.6	(1.85)	34	9.6	(1.24)	4.0	(0.65)	7.3	(1.26)	3.4 !	(1.03)	4.2	(0.70)
Private for-profit less-than-2-year	402	16.7	(0.74)	15	3.8	(0.56)	2.2	(0.39)	3.4	(0.57)	1.9	(0.46)	1.7	(0.39)
Private for-profit 2 years or more	1,439	20.9	(0.74)	118	8.2	(0.37)	5.2	(0.34)	6.6	(0.36)	3.2	(0.24)	4.3	(0.29)

—Not available.
†Not applicable.
!Interpret data with caution. The coefficient of variation (CV) for this estimate is between 30 and 50 percent.
‡Reporting standards not met. The coefficient of variation (CV) is 50 percent or greater.
[1]Student status was determined by accumulation of credits. Students attending postsecondary education part time, or not completing the credit accumulation requirements for second-year status, could be considered first-year students for more than one year.

NOTE: Data are based on a sample survey of students who enrolled at any time during the school year. Percentages of students who took remedial courses are based on student reports. Data exclude Puerto Rico. Detail may not sum to totals because of survey item nonresponse and rounding. Race categories exclude persons of Hispanic ethnicity. Some data have been revised from previously published figures.
SOURCE: U.S. Department of Education, National Center for Education Statistics, 2003–04, 2007–08, and 2011–12 National Postsecondary Student Aid Study (NPSAS:04, NPSAS:08, and NPSAS:12). (This table was prepared August 2014.)

Table 311.50. Percentage of degree-granting postsecondary institutions with first-year undergraduates offering remedial services, by control and level of institution: 1989–90 through 2014–15

Year	Public and private			Public			Private								
							Total			Nonprofit			For-profit		
	Total	4-year	2-year	Total	4-year	2-year	Total	4-year	2-year	Total	4-year	2-year	Total	4-year	2-year
1	2	3	4	5	6	7	8	9	10	11	12	13	14	15	16
1989–90	76.6	69.6	87.2	92.4	82.9	98.2	64.1	64.5	63.0	65.0	64.2	71.8	59.5	71.7	57.0
1990–91	77.7	70.6	88.4	93.0	83.5	98.9	65.6	65.6	65.5	65.6	64.9	71.3	65.6	81.3	62.0
1991–92	78.6	71.4	89.2	93.9	84.5	99.6	66.3	66.4	65.8	66.2	65.8	69.9	66.6	79.2	63.2
1992–93	78.5	71.5	88.8	93.5	84.5	98.8	66.4	66.5	65.8	66.7	66.2	71.5	64.6	73.7	62.0
1993–94	79.0	72.2	89.5	93.5	84.6	98.7	67.4	67.5	67.0	67.7	67.0	73.5	65.6	76.3	62.1
1994–95	79.8	73.6	89.1	93.7	85.3	98.6	68.6	69.2	66.6	69.3	68.7	74.0	65.2	76.0	60.8
1995–96	79.5	73.0	89.4	93.7	85.4	98.6	68.0	68.4	66.3	68.9	68.3	73.3	63.5	69.2	60.5
1996–97	80.0	73.1	91.0	94.0	85.1	99.2	68.6	68.6	68.4	69.2	68.3	77.3	65.2	72.7	60.8
1997–98	76.7	72.5	82.2	93.8	85.2	98.7	64.2	67.8	55.1	69.0	68.3	75.4	51.7	63.9	47.5
1998–99	76.1	72.0	81.5	93.6	84.2	99.0	63.6	67.7	52.8	68.6	68.3	71.6	51.1	63.4	46.2
1999–2000	76.1	71.6	82.2	93.5	83.6	99.2	63.9	67.4	54.4	69.2	68.5	76.7	51.5	60.1	47.7
2000–01	75.1	71.4	80.4	93.1	81.7	99.7	62.8	67.9	48.8	67.6	67.0	73.6	52.7	72.9	41.8
2001–02	73.3	69.0	79.5	92.3	79.9	99.4	60.2	65.3	45.0	66.1	65.5	72.6	48.0	64.5	37.3
2002–03	72.5	67.6	79.5	91.7	78.4	99.4	59.0	63.9	44.8	65.4	64.7	74.0	45.6	59.6	37.2
2003–04	72.1	67.1	79.7	91.3	77.3	99.5	59.0	63.7	44.8	65.0	64.0	77.1	47.4	62.0	37.3
2004–05	72.6	67.4	80.3	90.6	75.6	99.6	60.4	64.7	47.4	63.1	62.5	71.4	55.4	73.7	42.2
2005–06	72.2	66.9	80.2	90.2	75.2	99.3	60.4	64.2	48.8	62.2	61.3	74.3	57.2	75.0	43.4
2006–07	72.8	67.5	80.9	90.4	75.6	99.5	61.4	64.9	50.6	62.2	61.3	74.8	60.1	77.0	45.8
2007–08	72.4	67.2	80.9	89.7	74.1	99.5	61.6	64.9	51.0	61.4	60.6	73.9	61.8	78.4	47.2
2008–09	72.6	67.9	80.2	89.9	74.5	99.6	62.1	65.8	50.5	61.4	60.8	70.7	63.1	80.4	47.2
2009–10	72.7	68.3	79.7	89.8	75.3	99.6	62.5	66.1	52.1	61.2	60.6	72.9	64.3	81.2	49.4
2010–11	72.0	69.1	76.7	89.6	75.5	99.4	62.1	67.2	47.3	61.2	60.6	71.3	63.2	82.7	44.1
2011–12	70.4	67.1	75.9	89.6	75.7	99.5	60.0	64.6	46.3	60.2	60.3	59.0	59.8	73.8	44.4
2012–13	70.7	67.8	75.8	89.3	75.5	99.5	60.9	65.5	46.9	60.3	60.5	56.7	61.6	75.4	45.4
2013–14	70.0	66.4	76.4	89.0	74.8	99.5	60.0	64.0	47.7	59.9	59.9	60.2	60.1	72.4	46.0
2014–15	70.5	67.4	76.5	88.7	74.8	99.3	60.7	65.1	46.3	59.7	59.6	62.5	62.0	77.1	43.9
Change in percentage points															
1994–95 to 2004–05	-7.2	-6.2	-8.8	-3.1	-9.7	1.0	-8.2	-4.5	-19.2	-6.2	-6.2	-2.5	-9.8	-2.3	-18.7
2004–05 to 2014–15	-2.0	-0.1	-3.8	-1.9	-0.8	-0.3	0.3	0.4	-1.2	-3.4	-2.9	-8.9	6.6	3.4	1.8

NOTE: Remedial services are instructional activities designed for students deficient in the general competencies necessary for a regular postsecondary curriculum and educational setting. Data through 1995–96 are for institutions of higher education, while later data are for degree-granting institutions. Degree-granting institutions grant associate's or higher degrees and participate in Title IV federal financial aid programs. Excludes institutions not enrolling any first-time degree/certificate-seeking undergraduates.

SOURCE: U.S. Department of Education, National Center for Education Statistics, Integrated Postsecondary Education Data System (IPEDS), "Institutional Characteristics Survey" (IPEDS-IC:89–99); Fall 2000 through Fall 2013, Institutional Characteristics component; and Winter 2014–15, Admissions component. (This table was prepared December 2015.)

Table 311.60. Enrollment in postsecondary education, by level of enrollment, level of institution, student age, and major field of study: 2011–12

[Standard errors appear in parentheses]

Major field of study[1]	All students Total (in thousands)	Under 25	25 to 35	Over 35	Undergraduate 2-year and less-than-2-year institutions[2] Total (in thousands)	Under 25	25 to 35	Over 35	4-year institutions Total (in thousands)	Under 25	25 to 35	Over 35	Post-baccalaureate Total (in thousands)
1	2	3	4	5	6	7	8	9	10	11	12	13	14
Total	23,055	60.5 (0.31)	23.9 (0.25)	15.5 (0.28)	11,990	55.3 (0.42)	26.9 (0.38)	17.8 (0.33)	11,065	66.2 (0.46)	20.8 (0.34)	13.1 (0.39)	3,682
Agriculture and related sciences	132	68.0 (3.71)	15.0 (2.48)	17.0 (3.37)	60	51.5 (5.55)	18.7 (3.94)	29.8 (5.62)	72	81.7 (3.83)	12.0 (3.00)	6.3! (3.05)	12
Anthropology	55	78.8 (4.20)	20.5 (4.12)	‡ (†)	11	67.2 (10.91)	32.8! (10.91)	# (†)	45	81.5 (4.65)	17.6 (4.50)	‡ (†)	12
Architecture and related services	88	73.2 (3.97)	19.4 (3.47)	7.4! (2.47)	32	58.9 (7.86)	24.5! (7.86)	16.6! (5.88)	56	81.2 (3.42)	16.6 (3.36)	‡ (†)	27
Area, ethnic, and gender studies	40	74.6 (4.86)	14.2 (3.78)	11.2! (3.80)	10	66.8 (10.87)	22.1! (9.91)	‡ (†)	30	77.2 (5.43)	11.6! (3.99)	11.2! (4.75)	8
Biological and biomedical sciences	719	86.2 (0.98)	11.8 (0.90)	2.0 (0.49)	223	79.1 (2.05)	17.4 (1.93)	3.5! (1.18)	496	89.4 (1.14)	9.3 (1.04)	1.3! (0.48)	100
Business, management, and marketing	3,487	54.3 (0.68)	26.7 (0.59)	19.0 (0.60)	1,399	53.7 (1.04)	27.4 (1.00)	18.9 (1.09)	2,089	54.7 (0.99)	26.3 (0.87)	19.0 (0.77)	615
Communication and journalism	425	83.8 (1.38)	11.5 (1.13)	4.7 (0.86)	96	77.9 (3.26)	14.0 (2.35)	8.0 (2.32)	329	85.5 (1.46)	10.8 (1.23)	3.7 (0.82)	32
Communications technologies/technicians	99	63.2 (3.88)	24.0 (3.49)	12.9 (2.32)	53	59.6 (4.72)	25.0 (4.44)	15.4 (3.81)	46	67.3 (6.18)	22.8 (5.43)	10.0 (2.79)	‡
Computer and information sciences	942	47.5 (1.39)	32.3 (1.30)	20.2 (1.14)	467	47.0 (2.19)	30.7 (1.85)	22.3 (1.75)	475	48.0 (1.69)	33.9 (1.84)	18.1 (1.42)	104
Construction trades	86	53.9 (3.63)	25.3 (3.22)	20.7 (3.98)	78	52.5 (3.91)	25.9 (3.55)	21.6 (4.25)	8	66.7 (10.97)	20.1! (6.75)	‡ (†)	‡
Criminology	39	73.5 (4.96)	14.9 (3.82)	11.6! (4.15)	10	66.2 (10.90)	‡ (†)	‡ (†)	29	76.1 (4.99)	16.1 (4.44)	7.8! (3.50)	‡
Economics	118	86.0 (3.23)	13.2 (3.19)	‡ (†)	14	67.0 (12.45)	‡ (12.52)	‡ (†)	104	88.6 (3.28)	10.9 (3.23)	‡ (†)	18
Education	1,175	65.4 (1.12)	19.2 (0.84)	15.4 (1.03)	495	57.1 (1.79)	23.7 (1.49)	19.2 (1.77)	679	71.5 (1.39)	15.9 (0.90)	12.6 (1.14)	775
Engineering	697	79.5 (1.21)	15.9 (1.16)	4.6 (0.70)	238	67.2 (2.36)	23.6 (2.48)	9.2 (1.72)	459	85.9 (1.18)	11.9 (1.15)	2.2 (0.47)	176
Engineering technologies/technicians	390	50.3 (2.14)	29.5 (1.91)	20.2 (1.83)	254	44.5 (2.58)	30.5 (2.63)	25.0 (2.44)	136	61.3 (3.80)	27.6 (2.83)	11.1 (2.46)	11
English language and literature/letters	282	77.2 (2.18)	12.5 (1.46)	10.3 (1.57)	82	65.4 (5.02)	14.0 (2.91)	20.6 (4.17)	201	82.1 (2.16)	11.9 (1.87)	6.1 (1.33)	55
Family and consumer/human sciences	225	60.8 (2.69)	17.9 (2.20)	21.3 (2.29)	117	55.9 (4.11)	19.1 (3.37)	25.1 (3.63)	108	66.1 (4.12)	16.6 (2.64)	17.3 (3.08)	11
Foreign languages and literatures	96	71.5 (3.80)	20.7 (3.28)	7.8 (2.02)	27	60.4 (7.53)	23.4 (6.66)	16.2! (5.00)	69	76.0 (4.11)	19.6 (3.88)	4.5! (2.04)	26
Geography	17	59.4 (10.54)	24.6! (7.87)	‡ (†)	‡	‡ (†)	‡ (†)	‡ (†)	‡	‡ (†)	‡ (†)	‡ (†)	‡
Health professions and related sciences	4,271	48.5 (0.73)	30.8 (0.70)	20.7 (0.62)	2,790	45.6 (0.88)	33.5 (0.80)	20.9 (0.75)	1,482	54.0 (1.10)	25.7 (1.04)	20.3 (0.97)	679
History	206	77.7 (2.83)	16.4 (2.24)	5.9 (1.59)	43	78.5 (5.39)	17.3! (5.28)	‡ (†)	163	77.5 (3.35)	16.2 (2.61)	6.3 (1.86)	26
International relations and affairs	40	86.4 (5.51)	13.6! (5.51)	# (†)	‡	‡ (†)	‡ (†)	‡ (†)	33	87.2 (5.48)	12.8! (5.48)	# (†)	15
Legal professions and studies	177	45.7 (3.46)	30.5 (2.44)	23.8 (2.75)	96	45.7 (5.02)	27.1 (3.40)	27.1 (4.04)	80	45.6 (4.17)	34.6 (3.91)	19.8 (3.22)	146
Liberal arts, sciences and humanities	2,341	62.6 (0.89)	23.7 (0.75)	13.7 (0.68)	1,857	63.0 (0.93)	24.0 (0.86)	13.0 (0.76)	484	61.0 (2.43)	22.6 (1.63)	16.4 (1.79)	17
Library science	‡	‡ (†)	‡ (†)	‡ (†)	‡	‡ (†)	‡ (†)	‡ (†)	‡	‡ (†)	‡ (†)	‡ (†)	21
Mathematics and statistics	111	86.2 (2.28)	10.8 (2.22)	3.0! (1.13)	28	70.9 (6.04)	25.1 (6.26)	‡ (†)	82	91.5 (2.17)	5.8! (1.84)	2.6! (1.22)	25
Mechanic and repair technologies	376	54.7 (2.43)	27.8 (1.93)	17.5 (1.72)	341	54.0 (2.43)	29.1 (1.94)	17.0 (1.80)	35	62.3 (8.37)	15.0! (5.50)	22.7 (6.78)	‡
Military technologies	‡	‡ (†)	‡ (†)	‡ (†)	‡	‡ (†)	‡ (†)	‡ (†)	‡	‡ (†)	‡ (†)	‡ (†)	‡
Multi/interdisciplinary studies	283	61.4 (2.35)	24.7 (2.04)	13.9 (1.91)	117	60.7 (3.66)	26.1 (3.46)	13.3 (2.89)	166	61.9 (2.99)	23.8 (2.44)	14.3 (2.63)	36
Natural resources and conservation	121	79.3 (3.13)	11.7 (1.92)	9.0 (2.52)	39	79.1 (5.64)	11.6 (3.02)	9.3! (4.51)	82	79.4 (3.42)	11.7 (2.28)	8.8! (2.81)	22
Parks, recreation, and fitness studies	253	85.8 (1.65)	10.1 (1.50)	4.1 (1.22)	67	74.9 (3.95)	17.2 (3.73)	7.9! (3.17)	186	89.7 (1.71)	7.6 (1.36)	2.7! (1.28)	17
Personal and culinary services	562	57.2 (2.01)	27.3 (1.44)	15.5 (1.53)	500	57.3 (2.16)	27.1 (1.40)	15.5 (1.59)	63	56.6 (5.75)	28.3 (5.93)	15.0 (4.41)	‡
Philosophy and religious studies	64	71.6 (6.19)	22.4 (5.96)	6.1! (2.67)	13	82.3 (10.84)	‡ (†)	‡ (†)	51	68.9 (6.93)	26.7 (6.92)	4.0! (1.62)	20
Physical sciences	207	80.4 (2.65)	13.3 (1.90)	6.4 (1.75)	67	69.8 (5.11)	19.0 (3.14)	11.2! (4.37)	140	85.5 (2.97)	10.5 (2.38)	4.0! (1.62)	61
Political science and government	175	87.7 (2.11)	9.6 (1.79)	2.7! (1.01)	35	74.2 (8.12)	20.9! (7.21)	‡ (†)	140	91.2 (1.67)	6.7 (1.38)	2.1! (0.96)	17
Precision production	103	50.9 (4.64)	24.7 (4.13)	24.4 (3.88)	99	50.4 (4.75)	25.4 (4.26)	24.2 (3.84)	‡	‡ (†)	‡ (†)	‡ (†)	‡
Psychology	794	69.0 (1.49)	20.3 (1.24)	10.7 (0.92)	210	66.6 (2.95)	23.1 (2.53)	10.3 (1.88)	584	69.9 (1.60)	19.3 (1.39)	10.8 (1.08)	150
Public administration and social services	305	46.0 (2.14)	29.5 (2.23)	24.4 (2.08)	131	45.2 (3.54)	27.2 (3.13)	27.5 (3.34)	174	46.7 (2.76)	31.2 (3.14)	22.1 (2.48)	124
Science technologies/technicians	41	49.2 (6.78)	28.2 (6.33)	22.5 (5.67)	32	43.7 (7.27)	29.3 (7.59)	27.1 (7.12)	‡	‡ (†)	‡ (†)	‡ (†)	‡
Security and protective services	970	59.5 (1.76)	26.9 (1.13)	13.7 (1.37)	476	66.5 (1.76)	25.6 (1.61)	7.9 (0.93)	494	52.6 (2.70)	28.1 (1.53)	19.2 (2.36)	43

See notes at end of table.

Table 311.60. Enrollment in postsecondary education, by level of enrollment, level of institution, student age, and major field of study: 2011–12—Continued

[Standard errors appear in parentheses]

	All students				Undergraduate									Post-baccalaureate
					2-year and less-than-2-year institutions[2]				4-year institutions					
	Total (in thousands)	Percentage distribution, by age			Total (in thousands)	Percentage distribution, by age			Total (in thousands)	Percentage distribution, by age			Total (in thousands)
Major field of study[1]		Under 25	25 to 35	Over 35		Under 25	25 to 35	Over 35		Under 25	25 to 35	Over 35	
1	2	3	4	5	6	7	8	9	10	11	12	13	14
Social sciences, other	87	47.4 (4.78)	27.6 (4.39)	25.1 (4.58)	42	50.5 (6.73)	31.3 (6.59)	18.1 (4.77)	45	44.4 (8.26)	24.1 (5.33)	31.5 (8.37)	8
Sociology	149	68.0 (3.15)	21.5 (2.56)	10.5 (2.16)	40	57.2 (7.22)	24.4 (5.75)	18.4 ! (5.65)	109	72.0 (3.46)	20.4 (2.98)	7.6 (2.02)	9
Theology and religious vocations	50	60.5 (14.01)	14.7 (4.26)	24.8 ! (11.18)	‡	‡ (†)	‡ (†)	‡ (†)	46	59.3 (15.13)	14.1 ! (4.45)	26.6 ! (12.09)	63
Transportation and materials moving	72	40.8 (6.18)	39.4 (6.63)	19.8 (4.76)	43	25.5 (5.06)	45.6 (6.33)	28.9 (7.16)	30	62.9 (12.40)	30.4 ! (12.38)	‡ (†)	‡
Visual and performing arts	944	75.2 (1.70)	16.2 (1.14)	8.6 (1.02)	341	65.3 (2.30)	20.2 (1.89)	14.5 (1.80)	604	80.7 (2.39)	13.9 (1.51)	5.4 (1.20)	76
Undecided	465	76.8 (1.68)	15.4 (1.43)	7.8 (1.10)	278	70.6 (2.35)	18.0 (1.99)	11.4 (1.68)	187	86.0 (2.07)	11.7 (1.83)	2.3 ! (1.02)	†

†Not applicable.
#Rounds to zero.
!Interpret data with caution. The coefficient of variation (CV) for this estimate is between 30 and 50 percent.
‡Reporting standards not met. Either there are too few cases for a reliable estimate or the coefficient of variation (CV) is 50 percent or greater.
[1]For undergraduate students, the field of study categories include students who had already declared a major as well as students who had decided on, but not yet declared, an intended major. The "Undecided" category consists of undergraduate students who had neither declared nor decided on a major.

[2]Also includes students attending more than one institution.
NOTE: Because of different survey editing and processing procedures, enrollment data in this table may differ from those appearing in other tables. Includes students who enrolled at any time during the 2011–12 academic year. Data exclude Puerto Rico. Data have been revised from previously published figures. Detail may not sum to totals because of rounding.
SOURCE: U.S. Department of Education, National Center for Education Statistics, 2011–12 National Postsecondary Student Aid Study (NPSAS:12). (This table was prepared March 2014.)

Table 311.70. Course enrollments in languages other than English compared with total enrollment at degree-granting postsecondary institutions, by enrollment level, institution level, and language: Selected years, 1965 through 2013

Enrollment level, institution level, and language	1965	1970	1974	1980	1986	1990	1995	2002	2006	2009	2013	Percent change 1965 to 1974	1974 to 1986	1986 to 1995	1995 to 2006	2006 to 2013
1	2	3	4	5	6	7	8	9	10	11	12	13	14	15	16	17
Number of language course enrollments																
All levels, institutions, and languages	1,034,651	1,153,239	946,310	924,337	1,003,173	1,185,465	1,138,772	1,395,807	1,575,715	1,673,543	1,562,179	-8.5	6.0	13.5	38.4	-0.9
Undergraduate	—	—	904,419	892,275	970,007	1,149,634	1,100,103	1,359,145	1,534,590	1,636,016	1,527,415	†	7.3	13.4	39.5	-0.5
2-year institutions	—	—	154,713	162,716	161,683	227,625	233,123	337,304	364,857	393,060	343,367	†	4.5	44.2	56.5	-5.9
4-year institutions	—	—	749,706	729,559	808,324	922,009	866,980	1,021,841	1,169,733	1,242,956	1,184,048	†	7.8	7.3	34.9	1.2
Graduate	—	—	41,891	32,062	33,166	35,831	38,669	36,662	41,125	37,527	34,764	†	-20.8	16.6	6.4	-15.5
American Sign Language	—	—	—	—	—	1,602	4,304	60,781	79,708	92,072	109,577	†	†	†	1,752.0	37.5
Arabic	911	1,324	2,034	3,471	3,417	3,683	4,444	10,584	23,987	34,908	32,859	123.3	68.0	30.1	439.8	37.0
Chinese[1]	3,359	6,265	10,662	11,405	17,002	19,510	26,504	34,333	51,559	61,797	62,251	217.4	59.5	55.9	94.5	20.7
French	371,747	358,494	253,135	248,303	275,132	273,116	205,351	201,985	206,014	215,244	197,757	-31.9	8.7	-25.4	0.3	-4.0
German	213,909	201,766	152,113	127,015	120,920	133,594	96,263	91,100	94,147	95,628	86,700	-28.9	-20.5	-20.4	-2.2	-7.9
Greek, Ancient[2]	19,495	16,543	24,283	22,132	17,806	16,414	16,272	20,376	22,831	20,040	12,917	24.6	-26.7	-8.6	40.3	-43.4
Hebrew[3]	8,093	16,567	22,371	19,290	15,669	12,966	13,083	22,774	23,739	22,656	19,824	176.4	-30.0	-16.5	81.4	-16.5
Italian	22,950	34,236	33,048	34,793	40,904	49,824	43,760	63,899	78,176	80,322	71,285	44.0	23.8	7.0	78.6	-8.8
Japanese	3,505	6,620	9,604	11,516	23,454	45,830	44,723	52,238	65,403	72,359	66,740	174.0	144.2	90.7	46.2	2.0
Korean	82	101	87	365	875	2,375	3,343	5,211	7,146	8,449	12,229	6.1	905.7	282.1	113.8	71.1
Latin	38,043	28,422	25,167	25,019	25,038	28,178	25,897	29,841	32,164	32,444	27,192	-33.8	-0.5	3.4	24.2	-15.5
Portuguese	3,040	5,065	5,072	4,894	5,071	6,118	6,531	8,385	10,310	11,273	12,415	66.8	#	28.8	57.9	20.4
Russian	33,818	36,369	32,522	23,987	33,945	44,476	24,729	23,921	24,770	26,753	21,962	-3.8	4.4	-27.1	0.2	-11.3
Spanish	310,012	386,617	361,911	378,952	411,376	534,143	606,286	745,215	822,094	861,008	790,756	16.7	13.7	47.4	35.6	-3.8
Other languages	5,687	54,850	14,301	13,195	12,564	13,636	17,282	25,164	33,667	38,590	37,715	151.5	-12.1	37.6	94.8	12.0
Total enrollment at degree-granting institutions																
All levels	5,920,864	8,580,887	10,223,729	12,096,895	12,503,511	13,818,637	14,261,781	16,611,711	17,758,870	20,313,594	20,375,789	72.7	22.3	14.1	42.0	14.7
Undergraduate	—	7,368,644	8,798,728	10,475,055	10,797,975	11,959,106	12,231,719	14,257,077	15,184,302	17,464,179	17,474,835	†	22.7	13.3	40.6	15.1
2-year institutions	—	2,318,956	3,402,732	4,525,097	4,679,548	5,240,083	5,492,098	6,529,198	6,518,291	7,522,581	6,968,739	†	37.5	17.4	39.3	6.9
4-year institutions	—	5,049,688	5,395,996	5,949,958	6,118,427	6,719,023	6,739,621	7,727,879	8,666,011	9,941,598	10,506,096	†	13.4	10.2	41.6	21.2
Graduate	—	1,212,243	1,425,001	1,621,840	1,705,536	1,859,531	2,030,062	2,354,634	2,574,568	2,849,415	2,900,954	†	19.7	19.0	51.0	12.7
												Change in percentage points				
Number of language course enrollments per 100 students enrolled																
All levels	17.5	13.4	9.3	7.6	8.0	8.6	8.0	8.4	8.9	8.2	7.7	-8.2	-1.2	#	0.9	-1.2
Undergraduate	—	—	10.3	8.5	9.0	9.6	9.0	9.5	10.1	9.4	8.7	†	-1.3	#	1.1	-1.4
2-year institutions	—	—	4.5	3.6	3.5	4.3	4.2	5.2	5.6	5.2	4.9	†	-1.1	0.8	1.4	-0.7
4-year institutions	—	—	13.9	12.3	13.2	13.7	12.9	13.2	13.5	12.5	11.3	†	-0.7	-0.3	0.6	-2.2
Graduate	—	—	2.9	2.0	1.9	1.9	1.9	1.6	1.6	1.3	1.2	†	-1.0	#	-0.3	-0.4

—Not available.
†Not applicable.
#Rounds to zero.
[1]Includes Cantonese and Mandarin.
[2]The apparent drop in Ancient Greek from 2006 to 2009 may be attributed to changes in reporting. Some premodern Greek language categories, such as Koine Greek and Old Testament Greek, were reported for the first time in 2009. In previous surveys, these languages may have been reported under the category Ancient Greek.
[3]For 1986 and later years, includes Hebrew, Modern Hebrew, and Biblical Hebrew; other reported categories of Hebrew courses are excluded.
NOTE: The number of course enrollments is not the same as the number of students studying a given language; a single student majoring in a language may be enrolled in more than one class in that language. Unless otherwise noted, enrollments do not include those in classical, religious, or regional dialects of the language. Data through 1995 are for institutions of higher education, while later data are for degree-granting institutions. Degree-granting institutions grant associate's or higher degrees and participate in Title IV federal financial aid programs. The degree-granting classification is very similar to the earlier higher education classification, but it includes more 2-year colleges and excludes a few higher education institutions that did not grant degrees. Some data have been revised from previously published figures.
SOURCE: The Modern Language Association of America, *Enrollments in Languages Other Than English in United States Institutions of Higher Education, Fall 2013*, Table 2d; and MLA historical enrollment data, selected years, 1965 through 2013, retrieved April 14, 2016, from http://www.mla.org/about_search_flsurvey. U.S. Department of Education, National Center for Education Statistics, *Opening Fall Enrollment in Higher Education, 1965*; Higher Education General Information Survey (HEGIS), "Fall Enrollment in Institutions of Higher Education" surveys, 1970 through 1980; Integrated Postsecondary Education Data System (IPEDS), "Fall Enrollment Survey" (IPEDS-EF:86-95); and IPEDS Spring 2003 through Spring 2015, Fall Enrollment component. (This table was prepared April 2016.)

Table 311.80. Number and percentage distribution of course enrollments in languages other than English at degree-granting postsecondary institutions, by language and enrollment level: Selected years, 2002 through 2013

Enrollment and year	Total, all languages	American Sign Language	Arabic	Chinese[1]	French	German	Greek, Ancient[2]	Hebrew[3]	Italian	Japanese	Korean	Latin	Portuguese	Russian	Spanish	Other languages
1	2	3	4	5	6	7	8	9	10	11	12	13	14	15	16	17
All levels																
Number of enrollments																
2002	1,395,807	60,781	10,584	34,333	201,985	91,100	20,376	22,774	63,899	52,238	5,211	29,841	8,385	23,921	745,215	25,164
2006	1,575,715	79,708	23,987	51,559	206,014	94,147	22,831	23,739	78,176	65,403	7,146	32,164	10,310	24,770	822,094	33,667
2009	1,673,543	92,072	34,908	61,797	215,244	95,628	20,040	22,656	80,322	72,359	8,449	32,444	11,273	26,753	861,008	38,590
2013	1,562,179	109,577	32,859	62,251	197,757	86,700	12,917	19,824	71,285	66,740	12,229	27,192	12,415	21,962	790,756	37,715
Percent change in enrollments, 2009 to 2013	-6.7	19.0	-5.9	0.7	-8.1	-9.3	-35.5	-12.5	-11.3	-7.8	44.7	-16.2	10.1	-17.9	-8.2	-2.3
Percentage distribution of enrollments																
2002	100.0	4.4	0.8	2.5	14.5	6.5	1.5	1.6	4.6	3.7	0.4	2.1	0.6	1.7	53.4	1.8
2006	100.0	5.1	1.5	3.3	13.1	6.0	1.4	1.5	5.0	4.2	0.5	2.0	0.7	1.6	52.2	2.1
2009	100.0	5.5	2.1	3.7	12.9	5.7	1.2	1.4	4.8	4.3	0.5	1.9	0.7	1.6	51.4	2.3
2013	100.0	7.0	2.1	4.0	12.7	5.5	0.8	1.3	4.6	4.3	0.8	1.7	0.8	1.4	50.6	2.4
Undergraduate level																
Number of enrollments																
2002	1,359,145	60,660	10,053	33,394	197,385	88,301	14,343	17,245	62,860	51,308	5,100	28,796	7,898	23,151	735,265	23,386
2006	1,534,590	78,940	23,044	50,355	201,304	91,079	16,408	17,473	77,182	64,561	6,909	31,125	9,833	24,016	811,134	31,227
2009	1,636,016	91,237	34,131	60,632	211,077	93,162	15,401	17,053	79,567	71,696	8,097	31,397	10,839	26,149	849,540	36,038
2013 Introductory courses[4]	1,527,415	106,936	32,217	60,968	194,620	84,841	9,994	14,816	70,640	66,180	11,572	26,255	11,901	21,353	781,634	33,488
Advanced courses[4]	254,487	11,028	4,181	13,276	35,017	14,765	1,961	5,772	6,031	11,534	2,184	3,246	2,701	5,444	132,409	4,938
Percent change in enrollments, 2009 to 2013	-6.6	17.2	-5.6	0.6	-7.8	-8.9	-35.1	-13.1	-11.2	-7.7	42.9	-16.4	9.8	-18.3	-8.0	-7.1
Percentage distribution of enrollments																
2002	100.0	4.5	0.7	2.5	14.5	6.5	1.1	1.3	4.6	3.8	0.4	2.1	0.6	1.7	54.1	1.7
2006	100.0	5.1	1.5	3.3	13.1	5.9	1.1	1.1	5.0	4.2	0.5	2.0	0.6	1.6	52.9	2.0
2009	100.0	5.6	2.1	3.7	12.9	5.7	0.9	1.0	4.9	4.4	0.5	1.9	0.7	1.6	51.9	2.2
2013	100.0	7.0	2.1	4.0	12.7	5.6	0.7	1.0	4.6	4.3	0.8	1.7	0.8	1.4	51.2	2.2
Graduate level																
Number of enrollments																
2002	36,662	121	531	939	4,600	2,799	6,033	5,529	1,039	930	111	1,045	487	770	9,950	1,778
2006	41,125	768	943	1,204	4,710	3,068	6,423	6,266	994	842	237	1,039	477	754	10,960	2,440
2009	37,527	835	777	1,165	4,167	2,466	4,639	5,603	755	663	352	1,047	434	604	11,468	2,552
2013	34,764	2,641	642	1,283	3,137	1,859	2,923	5,008	645	560	657	937	514	609	9,122	4,227
Percent change in enrollments, 2009 to 2013	-7.4	216.3	-17.4	10.1	-24.7	-24.6	-37.0	-10.6	-14.6	-15.5	86.6	-10.5	18.4	0.8	-20.5	65.6
Percentage distribution of enrollments																
2002	100.0	0.3	1.4	2.6	12.5	7.6	16.5	15.1	2.8	2.5	0.3	2.9	1.3	2.1	27.1	4.8
2006	100.0	1.9	2.3	2.9	11.5	7.5	15.6	15.2	2.4	2.0	0.6	2.5	1.2	1.8	26.7	5.9
2009	100.0	2.2	2.1	3.1	11.1	6.6	12.4	14.9	2.0	1.8	0.9	2.8	1.2	1.8	30.6	6.8
2013	100.0	7.6	1.8	3.7	9.0	5.3	8.4	14.4	1.9	1.6	1.9	2.7	1.5	1.8	26.2	12.2

[1]Includes Cantonese and Mandarin.
[2]The apparent drop in Ancient Greek from 2006 to 2009 may be attributed to changes in reporting. Some premodern Greek language categories, such as Koine Greek and Old Testament Greek, were reported for the first time in 2009. In previous surveys, these languages may have been reported under the category Ancient Greek.
[3]Includes Hebrew, Modern Hebrew, and Biblical Hebrew; other reported categories of Hebrew courses are excluded.
[4]Introductory courses are first- and second-year courses. Advanced courses are third- and fourth-year courses.

NOTE: This table shows course enrollments, not the number of students studying a given language; a single student majoring in a language may be enrolled in more than one class in that language. Unless otherwise indicated, totals for specific languages do not include classical, religious, or regional dialects. Degree-granting institutions grant associate's or higher degrees and participate in Title IV federal financial aid programs. Some data have been revised from previously published figures.
SOURCE: The Modern Language Association of America, MLA historical enrollment data, selected years, 2002 through 2013, retrieved April 4, 2016, from http://www.mla.org/about_search_flsurvey. (This table was prepared April 2016.)

Table 311.90. Graduate enrollment in programs in engineering, physical and biological sciences, mathematical and computer sciences, social sciences, and research-based health fields in degree-granting postsecondary institutions, by discipline: Fall 2007 through fall 2014

Discipline	2007	2008	2009	2010	2011	2012	2013	2014[1]
1	2	3	4	5	6	7	8	9
Total, all surveyed disciplines	619,499	631,489	631,645	632,652	626,820	627,243	633,010	666,586
Engineering	131,676	137,856	144,677	149,241	146,501	148,385	153,049	164,488
Aerospace	4,616	4,902	5,266	5,540	5,691	5,069	5,181	5,116
Agricultural	1,126	1,233	1,303	1,457	1,656	1,552	1,642	1,740
Architecture	4,601	5,905	6,804	6,795	3,111	2,363	2,176	1,817
Biomedical	6,904	7,339	7,904	8,497	9,175	9,157	9,198	9,510
Chemical	7,584	7,892	8,188	8,668	8,828	9,222	9,698	9,870
Civil	16,071	16,931	18,638	19,559	19,596	19,922	20,110	20,789
Electrical	40,588	41,164	41,218	41,336	41,580	42,347	45,562	51,909
Engineering science	1,806	2,099	2,168	2,071	2,101	2,227	2,142	2,162
Industrial/manufacturing	14,474	15,692	15,825	15,205	14,494	14,469	14,363	14,845
Mechanical	18,347	19,585	21,243	22,509	21,883	23,088	24,087	25,651
Metallurgical/materials	5,314	5,539	5,863	6,274	6,649	6,985	7,144	7,518
Mining	222	290	312	419	500	356	357	396
Nuclear	1,180	1,201	1,243	1,459	1,499	1,513	1,459	1,467
Petroleum	1,014	1,009	1,190	1,295	1,301	1,525	1,609	2,056
Other engineering	7,829	7,075	7,512	8,157	8,437	8,590	8,321	9,642
Physical sciences	36,824	37,319	38,149	38,973	39,694	39,928	40,019	40,332
Astronomy	1,232	1,275	1,409	1,331	1,345	1,278	1,250	1,241
Chemistry	21,298	21,574	22,094	22,436	22,802	23,117	22,949	22,936
Physics	13,816	13,862	14,060	14,507	14,829	14,940	15,239	15,564
Other physical sciences	478	608	586	699	718	593	581	591
Earth, atmospheric, and ocean sciences	14,100	14,389	14,839	15,655	15,820	16,069	15,816	15,710
Atmospheric sciences	1,178	1,400	1,355	1,455	1,513	1,546	1,534	1,466
Geosciences	7,020	7,089	7,539	8,251	8,361	8,659	8,754	8,821
Oceanography	2,615	2,634	2,633	2,556	2,680	2,642	2,682	2,666
Other earth, atmospheric, and ocean sciences	3,287	3,266	3,312	3,393	3,266	3,222	2,846	2,757
Family and consumer science/human science	2,780	3,549	3,794	4,191	4,509	4,110	4,014	4,302
Mathematical sciences	20,975	21,400	22,226	23,136	23,801	24,575	24,804	25,874
Mathematics and applied mathematics	16,528	16,449	17,204	17,589	18,157	18,577	18,323	18,863
Statistics	4,447	4,951	5,022	5,547	5,644	5,998	6,481	7,011
Multidisciplinary/interdisciplinary studies	4,484	5,559	6,557	7,944	6,537	6,038	5,892	7,196
Neuroscience	1,584	2,012	2,356	2,798	4,117	4,547	4,795	4,923
Communication	7,303	8,444	9,418	9,825	11,029	11,010	11,114	11,942
Computer sciences	48,246	49,553	51,161	51,546	51,234	51,789	56,339	76,546
Life sciences	188,760	189,033	174,464	166,704	157,431	158,506	155,788	160,698
Agricultural sciences	13,528	14,153	15,200	15,656	16,129	16,234	16,429	17,505
Biological sciences	71,932	72,666	73,304	74,928	75,423	76,447	76,649	78,490
Anatomy	867	764	833	849	762	700	527	554
Biochemistry	5,853	5,473	5,271	5,308	5,183	5,245	4,970	5,025
Biology	15,898	16,514	16,840	17,210	16,911	16,321	16,004	16,697
Biometry/epidemiology	5,694	5,971	5,739	6,398	6,786	7,800	8,478	8,326
Biophysics	1,193	1,084	1,042	1,072	1,016	976	952	877
Botany	1,821	1,803	1,831	1,863	1,915	1,852	1,878	1,877
Cell biology	6,839	7,096	7,153	7,047	6,905	6,799	6,543	6,214
Ecology	2,026	2,026	1,746	1,828	1,713	1,667	1,437	1,416
Entomology/parasitology	1,078	1,079	1,079	1,116	1,119	1,187	1,278	1,304
Genetics	2,120	2,120	2,242	2,333	2,403	2,342	2,315	2,411
Microbiology, immunology, and virology	5,212	5,054	4,968	4,896	5,031	4,950	4,961	4,670
Nutrition	4,890	5,177	5,330	5,548	5,345	5,336	5,387	5,868
Pathology	1,580	1,618	1,450	1,376	1,313	1,196	1,112	1,036
Pharmacology	3,013	3,005	3,163	3,101	3,053	3,088	2,979	2,916
Physiology	2,738	2,863	2,866	2,879	3,000	3,046	3,224	3,415
Zoology	1,108	925	875	896	1,060	1,083	1,188	1,093
Other biosciences	10,002	10,094	10,876	11,208	11,908	12,859	13,416	14,791
Health fields[2]	103,300	102,214	85,960	76,120	65,879	65,825	62,710	64,703
Clinical medicine fields	22,751	23,939	24,125	25,699	26,634	26,798	26,362	27,048
Other health fields[3]	80,549	78,275	61,835	50,421	39,245	39,027	36,348	37,655
Psychology[3]	59,617	58,991	56,184	53,419	54,486	54,117	54,102	48,833
Social sciences	103,150	103,384	107,820	109,220	111,661	108,169	107,278	105,742
Agricultural economics	1,989	2,132	2,222	2,180	2,095	2,045	1,916	1,931
Economics (except agricultural)	12,597	12,971	13,993	14,317	14,920	14,959	14,819	14,604
Geography	4,660	4,745	4,810	5,059	5,188	5,016	4,891	4,810
Linguistics	2,879	3,095	3,170	3,132	3,219	3,256	3,509	3,489
Political science	41,349	40,871	43,919	45,045	49,660	48,855	48,411	47,370
Sociology and anthropology	18,453	18,988	18,666	18,740	18,365	17,404	17,360	16,789
Other social sciences	21,223	20,582	21,040	20,747	18,214	16,634	16,372	16,378

[1]In 2014, the survey frame was updated following a comprehensive frame evaluation study. The study identified potentially eligible but not previously surveyed academic institutions in the United States with master's- or doctorate-granting programs in science, engineering, or health. A total of 151 newly eligible institutions were added, and 2 institutions offering mostly practitioner-based graduate degrees were determined to be ineligible.

[2]Excludes enrollments in practitioner-oriented programs, which have the primary purpose of providing the knowledge and skills required for credentials or licensure to practice in a medical or other health field.

[3]For 2008 and later years, enrollment declines in psychology and in other health fields such as nursing may be due to more rigorous follow-up with institutions to exclude enrollments in

practitioner-oriented graduate degree programs. Examples of excluded programs are those leading to DNP, PsyD, and DPT degrees.

NOTE: The survey on which this table is based includes all institutions in the United States and its territories (Guam and Puerto Rico) that grant research-based master's degrees or doctorates in science, engineering, and selected health fields.

SOURCE: National Science Foundation, National Center for Science and Engineering Statistics, NSF-NIH Survey of Graduate Students and Postdoctorates in Science and Engineering, 2007 through 2014. (This table was prepared April 2016.)

Table 312.10. Enrollment of the 120 largest degree-granting college and university campuses, by selected characteristics and institution: Fall 2014

Institution	State	Rank[1]	Control[2]	Level	Total enroll-ment	Institution	State	Rank[1]	Control[2]	Level	Total enroll-ment
1	2	3	4	5	6	1	2	3	4	5	6
University of Phoenix, Arizona[3]	AZ	1	PrivFp	4-year	195,059	Texas Tech University	TX	61	Public	4-year	35,158
Ivy Tech Community College	IN	2	Public	2-year	91,179	Capella University	MN	62	PrivFp	4-year	35,061
Liberty University	VA	3	PrivNp	4-year	81,459	University of California, Davis	CA	63	Public	4-year	34,508
Lone Star College System	TX	4	Public	2-year	69,395	Iowa State University	IA	64	Public	4-year	34,435
Miami Dade College	FL	5	Public	4-year	66,046	North Carolina State University at Raleigh	NC	65	Public	4-year	33,989
Grand Canyon University	AZ	6	PrivFp	4-year	62,304	George Mason University	VA	66	Public	4-year	33,729
Texas A & M University, College Station	TX	7	Public	4-year	61,642	San Diego State University	CA	67	Public	4-year	33,483
University of Central Florida	FL	8	Public	4-year	60,767	University of South Carolina, Columbia	SC	68	Public	4-year	32,971
Ohio State University, Main Campus	OH	9	Public	4-year	58,322	San Jose State University	CA	69	Public	4-year	32,713
Houston Community College	TX	10	Public	2-year	58,276	Saint Petersburg College	FL	70	Public	4-year	32,681
Western Governors University	UT	11	PrivNp	4-year	57,821	Georgia State University	GA	71	Public	4-year	32,556
American Public University System	WV	12	PrivFp	4-year	57,539	University of Colorado, Boulder	CO	72	Public	4-year	32,432
Walden University	MN	13	PrivFp	4-year	52,188	Boston University	MA	73	PrivNp	4-year	32,112
Kaplan University, Davenport Campus	IA	14	PrivFp	4-year	52,018	University of Utah	UT	74	Public	4-year	31,515
Northern Virginia Community College	VA	15	Public	2-year	51,487	Colorado State University, Fort Collins	CO	75	Public	4-year	31,354
University of Texas at Austin	TX	16	Public	4-year	51,313	Utah Valley University	UT	76	Public	4-year	31,332
Ashford University	CA	17	PrivFp	4-year	51,237	Virginia Polytechnic Institute and State University	VA	77	Public	4-year	31,224
University of Minnesota, Twin Cities	MN	18	Public	4-year	51,147	Louisiana State U. and Agricultural & Mechanical	LA	78	Public	4-year	31,044
Tarrant County College District	TX	19	Public	2-year	50,595	Portland Community College	OR	79	Public	2-year	30,929
Arizona State University, Tempe	AZ	20	Public	4-year	50,320	Virginia Commonwealth University	VA	80	Public	4-year	30,848
Michigan State University	MI	21	Public	4-year	50,081	University of California, San Diego	CA	81	Public	4-year	30,709
Florida International University	FL	22	Public	4-year	49,610	Indiana University-Purdue University, Indianapolis	IN	82	Public	4-year	30,690
University of Florida	FL	23	Public	4-year	49,459	Brigham Young University, Provo	UT	83	PrivNp	4-year	30,484
New York University	NY	24	PrivNp	4-year	49,274	University of Tennessee, Knoxville	TN	84	Public	4-year	30,386
Rutgers University, New Brunswick	NJ	25	Public	4-year	48,378	Florida Atlantic University	FL	85	Public	4-year	30,297
University of Maryland, University College	MD	26	Public	4-year	47,906	Salt Lake Community College	UT	86	Public	2-year	30,248
Pennsylvania State University, Main Campus	PA	27	Public	4-year	47,040	South Texas College	TX	87	Public	4-year	30,180
Indiana University, Bloomington	IN	28	Public	4-year	46,416	Santa Monica College	CA	88	Public	2-year	30,158
University of Illinois at Urbana-Champaign	IL	29	Public	4-year	45,140	University of California, Irvine	CA	89	Public	4-year	30,051
University of Washington, Seattle Campus	WA	30	Public	4-year	44,784	University at Buffalo	NY	90	Public	4-year	29,995
Broward College	FL	31	Public	4-year	44,119	University of Iowa	IA	91	Public	4-year	29,970
University of Michigan, Ann Arbor	MI	32	Public	4-year	43,625	Santa Ana College	CA	92	Public	2-year	29,590
Southern New Hampshire University	NH	33	PrivNp	4-year	43,274	Kent State University at Kent	OH	93	Public	4-year	29,477
Valencia College	FL	34	Public	4-year	43,217	College of DuPage	IL	94	Public	2-year	29,476
University of Wisconsin, Madison	WI	35	Public	4-year	42,598	San Francisco State University	CA	95	Public	4-year	29,465
University of Southern California	CA	36	PrivNp	4-year	42,453	California State University, Sacramento	CA	96	Public	4-year	29,349
University of Arizona	AZ	37	Public	4-year	42,236	Ohio University, Main Campus	OH	97	Public	4-year	29,217
University of South Florida, Main Campus	FL	38	Public	4-year	41,938	University of Kentucky	KY	98	Public	4-year	29,203
University of California, Los Angeles	CA	39	Public	4-year	41,845	West Virginia University	WV	99	Public	4-year	29,175
Excelsior College	NY	40	PrivNp	4-year	41,527	University of North Carolina at Chapel Hill	NC	100	Public	4-year	29,135
Florida State University	FL	41	Public	4-year	41,226	American River College	CA	101	Public	2-year	29,133
Austin Community College District	TX	42	Public	2-year	40,949	Mount San Antonio College	CA	102	Public	2-year	29,045
University of Houston	TX	43	Public	4-year	40,914	Oregon State University	OR	103	Public	4-year	28,886
California State University, Northridge	CA	44	Public	4-year	40,131	Harvard University	MA	104	PrivNp	4-year	28,791
Purdue University, Main Campus	IN	45	Public	4-year	39,752	Washington State University	WA	105	Public	4-year	28,686
University of Texas at Arlington	TX	46	Public	4-year	39,740	University of Massachusetts, Amherst	MA	106	Public	4-year	28,635
California State University, Fullerton	CA	47	Public	4-year	38,128	University of Texas at San Antonio	TX	107	Public	4-year	28,628
University of Maryland, College Park	MD	48	Public	4-year	37,610	University of Pittsburgh, Pittsburgh Campus	PA	108	Public	4-year	28,617
University of California, Berkeley	CA	49	Public	4-year	37,565	Palm Beach State College	FL	109	Public	4-year	28,517
Temple University	PA	50	Public	4-year	37,485	University of Nevada, Las Vegas	NV	110	Public	4-year	28,515
California State University, Long Beach	CA	51	Public	4-year	36,809	El Paso Community College	TX	111	Public	2-year	28,308
Texas State University	TX	52	Public	4-year	36,739	Pima Community College	AZ	112	Public	2-year	28,070
Brigham Young University, Idaho	ID	53	PrivNp	4-year	36,624	Collin County Community College District	TX	113	Public	2-year	27,991
University of North Texas	TX	54	Public	4-year	36,486	University of Illinois at Chicago	IL	114	Public	4-year	27,969
University of Alabama	AL	55	Public	4-year	36,047	San Jacinto Community College	TX	115	Public	2-year	27,911
East Los Angeles College	CA	56	Public	2-year	36,012	University of New Mexico, Main Campus	NM	116	Public	4-year	27,844
College of Southern Nevada	NV	57	Public	4-year	35,943	Northern Arizona University	AZ	117	Public	4-year	27,705
University of Missouri, Columbia	MO	58	Public	4-year	35,425	Portland State University	OR	118	Public	4-year	27,696
University of Cincinnati, Main Campus	OH	59	Public	4-year	35,313	Utah State University	UT	119	Public	4-year	27,662
University of Georgia	GA	60	Public	4-year	35,197	Tidewater Community College	VA	120	Public	2-year	27,646

[1]College and university campuses ranked by fall 2014 enrollment data.
[2]"PrivNp" stands for private nonprofit. "PrivFp" stands for private for-profit.
[3]Enrollment data for University of Phoenix, Arizona, include three campuses previously reported separately: Online, Phoenix, and Southern Arizona.

NOTE: Degree-granting institutions grant associate's or higher degrees and participate in Title IV federal financial aid programs. Includes online and distance education courses.
SOURCE: U.S. Department of Education, National Center for Education Statistics, Integrated Postsecondary Education Data System (IPEDS), Spring 2015, Fall Enrollment component. (This table was prepared March 2016.)

Table 312.20. Selected statistics for degree-granting postsecondary institutions enrolling more than 15,000 students in 2014, by selected institution and student characteristics: Selected years, 1990 through 2013–14

Line number	Institution	State	Con-trol[1]	Level	Total fall enrollment					Fall enrollment, 2014		
										Total	Sex	
					Fall 1990	Fall 2000	Fall 2010	Fall 2012	Fall 2013		Male	Female
1	2	3	4	5	6	7	8	9	10	11	12	13
i	United States, all institutions[6]	†	†	†	13,818,637	15,312,289	21,019,438	20,644,478	20,375,789	20,207,369	8,797,061	11,410,308
ii	Colleges with enrollment over 15,000	†	†	†	6,161,327	6,613,975	9,134,914	9,322,810	9,281,958	9,343,214	4,234,111	5,109,103
1	Auburn University	AL	Public	4-year	21,537	21,860	25,078	25,134	24,864	25,912	13,114	12,798
2	Columbia Southern University	AL	PrivFp	4-year	†	†	17,695	19,933	20,185	21,359	12,953	8,406
3	Troy University	AL	Public	4-year	5,024	12,541	28,322	22,554	20,573	19,041	7,093	11,948
4	University of Alabama	AL	Public	4-year	19,794	19,277	30,127	33,503	34,752	36,047	16,231	19,816
5	University of Alabama at Birmingham	AL	Public	4-year	15,356	14,951	17,543	17,999	18,568	18,698	7,410	11,288
6	University of South Alabama	AL	Public	4-year	11,584	11,673	14,776	14,636	15,065	15,805	6,105	9,700
7	University of Alaska, Anchorage	AK	Public	4-year	17,490	14,794	18,154	17,497	17,363	17,151	7,142	10,009
8	Arizona State University, Tempe[7]	AZ	Public	4-year	42,936	44,126	70,440	73,378	48,702	50,320	28,706	21,614
9	Glendale Community College	AZ	Public	2-year	18,512	20,091	21,373	21,361	20,872	20,506	9,581	10,925
10	Grand Canyon University	AZ	PrivFp	4-year	1,813	3,615	37,440	48,650	55,497	62,304	15,657	46,647
11	Mesa Community College	AZ	Public	2-year	19,818	22,821	26,408	25,024	23,678	22,711	11,197	11,514
12	Northern Arizona University	AZ	Public	4-year	16,992	19,964	25,197	25,991	26,594	27,705	11,389	16,316
13	Pima Community College	AZ	Public	2-year	28,766	28,078	36,823	32,988	30,082	28,070	13,067	15,003
14	Rio Salado College	AZ	Public	2-year	10,480	11,275	25,266	24,342	21,472	20,215	7,718	12,497
15	University of Arizona	AZ	Public	4-year	35,729	34,488	39,086	40,223	40,621	42,236	20,345	21,891
16	University of Phoenix, Arizona[8]	AZ	PrivFp	4-year	4,149	23,935	316,250	264,073	218,373	195,059	60,337	134,722
17	University of Arkansas	AR	Public	4-year	14,732	15,346	21,405	24,537	25,341	26,237	12,842	13,395
18	Academy of Art University	CA	PrivFp	4-year	1,767	5,995	17,695	17,871	16,001	15,212	6,397	8,815
19	American River College	CA	Public	2-year	18,716	28,420	33,440	31,088	29,701	29,133	13,374	15,759
20	Ashford University	CA	PrivFp	4-year	311	616	63,096	77,734	58,104	51,237	15,121	36,116
21	Bakersfield College	CA	Public	2-year	10,776	14,466	19,569	17,344	17,770	18,698	8,212	10,486
22	California Polytechnic State U., San Luis Obispo	CA	Public	4-year	17,751	16,877	18,360	18,679	19,703	20,186	10,888	9,298
23	California State Polytechnic University, Pomona	CA	Public	4-year	19,468	18,424	20,747	22,156	22,501	23,966	13,335	10,631
24	California State University, Chico	CA	Public	4-year	16,633	15,912	15,989	16,470	16,356	17,287	8,107	9,180
25	California State University, Fresno	CA	Public	4-year	19,960	19,056	20,932	22,565	23,060	23,179	9,699	13,480
26	California State University, Fullerton	CA	Public	4-year	25,592	28,381	35,590	37,677	38,325	38,128	16,966	21,162
27	California State University, Long Beach	CA	Public	4-year	33,987	30,918	33,416	36,279	35,586	36,809	15,820	20,989
28	California State University, Los Angeles	CA	Public	4-year	21,597	19,593	20,142	21,755	23,258	24,488	10,219	14,269
29	California State University, Northridge	CA	Public	4-year	31,167	29,066	35,272	36,164	38,310	40,131	17,998	22,133
30	California State University, Sacramento	CA	Public	4-year	26,336	25,714	27,033	28,539	28,811	29,349	12,606	16,743
31	California State University, San Bernardino	CA	Public	4-year	11,923	14,909	16,400	18,234	18,398	18,952	7,267	11,685
32	Cerritos College	CA	Public	2-year	15,886	24,536	22,142	20,719	21,404	21,774	9,868	11,906
33	Chaffey College	CA	Public	2-year	10,985	15,220	19,469	17,804	19,211	19,557	8,251	11,306
34	City College of San Francisco	CA	Public	2-year	24,408	39,386	32,966	30,106	26,706	23,610	11,130	12,480
35	College of the Canyons	CA	Public	2-year	4,815	10,528	23,332	15,177	18,508	17,148	8,403	8,745
36	Cypress College	CA	Public	2-year	11,917	21,361	16,153	15,144	15,881	15,816	7,002	8,814
37	De Anza College	CA	Public	2-year	21,948	22,770	23,630	23,833	23,261	23,104	11,917	11,187
38	Diablo Valley College	CA	Public	2-year	20,255	21,581	20,703	20,329	20,286	20,089	9,804	10,285
39	East Los Angeles College	CA	Public	2-year	12,447	27,199	35,100	37,055	36,606	36,012	18,306	17,706
40	El Camino Community College District	CA	Public	2-year	25,789	24,067	24,756	23,405	23,996	24,207	11,720	12,487
41	Foothill College	CA	Public	2-year	12,811	14,193	17,474	15,067	14,814	15,030	7,699	7,331
42	Fresno City College	CA	Public	2-year	14,710	19,351	23,902	21,630	21,344	22,307	10,654	11,653
43	Fullerton College	CA	Public	2-year	17,548	19,993	22,562	19,624	24,301	25,051	12,199	12,852
44	Glendale Community College	CA	Public	2-year	12,072	15,596	16,876	15,978	15,744	15,112	6,814	8,298
45	Grossmont College	CA	Public	2-year	15,357	16,309	19,659	17,758	18,618	18,040	7,977	10,063
46	Long Beach City College	CA	Public	2-year	18,378	20,926	26,517	24,839	24,020	24,403	11,100	13,303
47	Los Angeles City College	CA	Public	2-year	14,479	15,174	20,430	20,385	19,635	18,756	8,236	10,520
48	Los Angeles Pierce College	CA	Public	2-year	16,970	16,111	21,368	19,938	20,080	21,034	9,677	11,357
49	Los Angeles Valley College	CA	Public	2-year	16,457	17,393	20,667	18,640	18,762	18,641	8,099	10,542
50	Modesto Junior College	CA	Public	2-year	11,300	15,158	18,492	16,985	17,084	17,578	7,416	10,162
51	Mount San Antonio College	CA	Public	2-year	20,563	28,329	29,064	28,036	28,481	29,045	14,101	14,944
52	National University	CA	PrivNp	4-year	8,836	16,848	16,249	17,898	18,207	17,608	6,928	10,680
53	Orange Coast College	CA	Public	2-year	22,365	23,315	24,239	21,088	21,886	21,775	11,381	10,394
54	Palomar College	CA	Public	2-year	16,707	21,062	26,231	24,626	24,665	24,914	13,708	11,206
55	Pasadena City College	CA	Public	2-year	19,581	22,948	27,023	22,859	25,268	26,611	12,762	13,849
56	Rio Hondo College	CA	Public	2-year	12,048	19,506	21,782	17,643	16,548	16,263	8,595	7,668
57	Riverside City College	CA	Public	2-year	15,683	22,107	20,585	17,218	18,165	18,547	8,177	10,370
58	Sacramento City College	CA	Public	2-year	14,474	20,878	25,039	24,381	23,509	23,317	10,116	13,201
59	Saddleback College	CA	Public	2-year	14,527	18,563	24,793	21,728	20,871	20,007	9,191	10,816
60	San Diego City College	CA	Public	2-year	13,737	27,165	18,549	16,797	16,310	16,298	7,791	8,507
61	San Diego Mesa College	CA	Public	2-year	23,410	21,233	25,972	24,943	24,251	24,159	11,662	12,497
62	San Diego State University	CA	Public	4-year	35,493	31,609	29,187	30,843	31,899	33,483	14,822	18,661
63	San Francisco State University	CA	Public	4-year	29,343	26,826	29,718	30,500	29,905	29,465	12,560	16,905
64	San Joaquin Delta College	CA	Public	2-year	14,792	16,973	18,610	17,002	17,629	18,572	8,051	10,521
65	San Jose State University	CA	Public	4-year	30,334	26,698	29,076	30,448	31,278	32,713	16,475	16,238
66	Santa Ana College	CA	Public	2-year	20,532	27,571	31,377	32,354	28,598	29,590	18,339	11,251
67	Santa Barbara City College	CA	Public	2-year	11,031	13,834	18,827	19,265	19,331	17,927	8,402	9,525
68	Santa Monica College	CA	Public	2-year	18,108	27,868	31,118	30,254	29,999	30,158	14,340	15,818
69	Santa Rosa Junior College	CA	Public	2-year	20,475	27,200	24,879	22,823	22,094	23,144	10,446	12,698
70	Sierra College	CA	Public	2-year	11,637	17,517	19,986	18,247	18,374	18,565	8,547	10,018
71	Southwestern College	CA	Public	2-year	13,010	17,994	19,476	18,362	19,591	19,000	8,864	10,136
72	Stanford University	CA	PrivNp	4-year	14,724	18,549	19,535	18,519	18,346	16,963	9,929	7,034
73	University of California, Berkeley	CA	Public	4-year	30,634	31,277	35,833	35,893	36,198	37,565	18,714	18,851
74	University of California, Davis	CA	Public	4-year	23,890	26,094	31,392	32,354	33,307	34,508	15,000	19,508
75	University of California, Irvine	CA	Public	4-year	16,808	20,211	26,994	27,479	28,895	30,051	14,493	15,558
76	University of California, Los Angeles	CA	Public	4-year	36,420	36,890	38,157	39,945	40,795	41,845	19,739	22,106
77	University of California, Riverside	CA	Public	4-year	8,708	13,015	20,692	20,947	21,207	21,498	10,562	10,936

See notes at end of table.

Table 312.20. Selected statistics for degree-granting postsecondary institutions enrolling more than 15,000 students in 2014, by selected institution and student characteristics: Selected years, 1990 through 2013–14—Continued

Full-time	Part-time	Percent minority[3]	Under-graduate	Postbacca-laureate	Fall 2013	Fall 2014	Certificates[4]	Associate's	Bachelor's	Master's	Doctor's[5]	Total expenditures and deductions, 2013–14 (in thousands)[2]	Line number
14	15	16	17	18	19	20	21	22	23	24	25	26	27
12,453,975	7,753,394	41.7	17,292,787	2,914,582	15,409,944	15,262,196	665,118	1,003,364	1,869,814	754,475	177,580	$517,094,937	i
5,844,741	3,498,473	45.1	7,770,779	1,572,435	7,085,955	7,124,241	157,884	329,221	978,455	403,991	96,524	270,545,122	ii
22,035	3,877	13.5	20,629	5,283	22,532	23,512	0	0	4,485	1,108	490	855,378	1
12,971	8,388	40.7	15,482	5,877	15,437	16,266	150	1,945	3,057	1,693	6	65,230	2
10,202	8,839	47.2	15,114	3,927	14,337	13,654	0	395	2,479	1,224	17	248,928	3
31,023	5,024	19.7	30,752	5,295	31,519	32,967	0	0	5,408	1,645	501	871,630	4
12,334	6,364	33.5	11,679	7,019	14,482	14,770	21	0	2,042	1,597	538	2,419,150	5
12,922	2,883	31.6	11,479	4,326	13,233	14,065	154	0	1,848	747	193	658,614	6
7,711	9,440	36.0	16,291	860	11,689	11,494	223	905	1,131	268	3	308,752	7
43,945	6,375	37.6	39,961	10,359	44,899	46,406	756	0	9,319	2,956	650	1,859,121	8
6,951	13,555	50.9	20,506	†	11,806	11,502	2,135	1,816	†	†	†	113,293	9
10,488	51,816	49.1	39,400	22,904	26,455	30,597	0	0	6,916	5,628	61	513,487	10
7,272	15,439	43.9	22,711	†	12,965	12,455	2,393	2,253	†	†	†	129,223	11
21,173	6,532	34.1	23,328	4,377	22,875	23,710	491	0	4,960	1,345	115	485,958	12
9,303	18,767	56.1	28,070	†	17,258	15,604	3,021	2,633	†	†	†	200,678	13
2,595	17,620	36.7	20,215	†	9,238	8,511	4,621	662	†	†	†	104,277	14
36,580	5,656	41.0	32,987	9,249	37,417	38,770	0	0	6,370	1,702	870	1,753,337	15
195,059	0	56.5	155,872	39,187	218,373	195,059	1,012	19,558	25,268	12,381	409	1,450,755	16
21,047	5,190	19.4	21,836	4,401	22,276	23,032	0	0	3,906	1,088	280	738,381	17
8,843	6,369	53.2	10,044	5,168	11,750	11,324	0	251	1,233	1,167	0	300,707	18
7,120	22,013	51.4	29,133	†	14,994	14,511	4,521	2,435	†	†	†	159,772	19
51,213	24	53.0	45,348	5,889	58,088	51,222	0	1,561	11,850	4,450	0	570,733	20
5,940	12,758	77.6	18,698	†	9,696	10,223	1,016	1,023	†	†	†	128,407	21
19,306	880	37.1	19,246	940	19,139	19,653	0	0	3,830	428	0	389,215	22
20,321	3,645	76.7	22,395	1,571	20,370	21,752	0	0	4,104	414	0	293,925	23
15,771	1,516	43.6	16,081	1,206	15,510	16,369	0	0	3,415	341	0	246,765	24
19,644	3,535	72.6	20,511	2,668	20,908	21,038	0	0	4,267	801	64	306,481	25
29,224	8,904	71.6	32,726	5,402	32,656	32,694	0	0	7,451	1,476	59	496,728	26
30,092	6,717	76.2	31,643	5,166	31,225	32,706	0	0	7,142	1,696	27	458,859	27
19,557	4,931	89.5	20,681	3,807	20,106	21,464	0	0	3,424	1,083	8	293,267	28
31,637	8,494	69.4	35,616	4,515	33,509	34,972	0	0	7,042	1,992	11	508,913	29
22,940	6,409	65.4	26,739	2,610	25,142	25,484	0	0	5,787	968	15	384,403	30
15,758	3,194	80.2	16,743	2,209	16,445	16,995	0	0	3,343	610	10	253,418	31
7,254	14,520	92.2	21,774	†	11,808	12,129	706	1,106	†	†	†	162,886	32
5,385	14,172	81.6	19,557	†	10,212	10,143	859	1,905	†	†	†	142,599	33
7,385	16,225	75.7	23,610	†	15,076	12,832	2,545	987	†	†	†	314,505	34
6,227	10,921	63.9	17,148	†	10,496	9,894	821	1,354	†	†	†	134,284	35
5,085	10,731	78.7	15,816	†	8,706	8,688	888	963	†	†	†	103,619	36
11,086	12,018	77.0	23,104	†	14,966	15,121	528	1,511	†	†	†	163,004	37
7,503	12,586	57.6	20,089	†	11,919	11,729	1,405	1,233	†	†	†	124,112	38
7,739	28,273	92.1	36,012	†	17,000	17,231	2,095	1,645	†	†	†	171,710	39
8,298	15,909	86.3	24,207	†	13,281	13,639	460	1,983	†	†	†	205,560	40
5,255	9,775	62.9	15,030	†	8,472	8,537	533	706	†	†	†	119,475	41
7,820	14,487	76.8	22,307	†	12,357	12,684	415	1,130	†	†	†	146,457	42
8,828	16,223	76.1	25,051	†	13,765	14,275	264	1,612	†	†	†	176,433	43
6,865	8,247	49.8	15,112	†	10,045	9,634	309	453	†	†	†	139,260	44
6,471	11,569	56.8	18,040	†	10,671	10,355	1,126	1,713	†	†	†	89,203	45
9,780	14,623	85.2	24,403	†	14,395	14,689	1,120	1,032	†	†	†	200,193	46
5,072	13,684	81.3	18,756	†	9,556	9,666	779	496	†	†	†	121,619	47
5,812	15,222	69.8	21,034	†	9,723	10,923	656	1,171	†	†	†	119,250	48
4,522	14,119	69.1	18,641	†	9,306	9,262	886	791	†	†	†	111,222	49
6,279	11,299	60.1	17,578	†	9,881	10,072	548	1,286	†	†	†	95,293	50
10,501	18,544	87.6	29,045	†	16,536	16,727	1,368	1,934	†	†	†	246,997	51
8,679	8,929	55.0	9,721	7,887	12,511	12,154	39	133	1,928	3,498	0	210,031	52
8,589	13,186	64.0	21,775	†	12,992	13,016	484	1,782	†	†	†	143,827	53
8,192	16,722	56.3	24,914	†	13,762	13,806	2,120	1,978	†	†	†	190,223	54
10,401	16,210	90.3	26,611	†	14,769	15,843	655	2,589	†	†	†	203,166	55
3,800	12,463	92.1	16,263	†	8,471	7,984	271	989	†	†	†	113,079	56
5,135	13,412	78.3	18,547	†	9,329	9,638	855	1,550	†	†	†	134,893	57
6,063	17,254	71.6	23,317	†	11,974	11,856	486	1,645	†	†	†	126,361	58
6,015	13,992	43.8	20,007	†	11,215	10,713	1,646	1,112	†	†	†	117,988	59
3,666	12,632	76.2	16,298	†	8,019	7,907	549	672	†	†	†	108,536	60
5,874	18,285	65.9	24,159	†	12,399	12,013	374	1,009	†	†	†	112,896	61
28,141	5,342	59.6	28,394	5,089	28,810	30,211	0	0	6,565	1,746	95	502,813	62
23,907	5,558	71.8	25,938	3,527	26,574	26,094	0	0	6,211	1,225	49	475,747	63
7,526	11,046	76.9	18,572	†	10,610	11,235	497	2,513	†	†	†	164,216	64
25,385	7,328	74.2	26,664	6,049	26,967	28,258	0		5,431	2,264	0	409,650	65
4,948	24,642	74.2	29,590	†	11,883	13,221	1,498	1,821	†	†	†	117,993	66
8,356	9,571	53.0	17,927	†	12,147	11,569	1,348	1,755	†	†	†	160,024	67
10,861	19,297	70.8	30,158	†	17,193	17,340	1,528	1,434	†	†	†	236,874	68
7,125	16,019	44.5	23,144	†	11,876	12,503	2,832	1,891	†	†	†	161,116	69
6,828	11,737	40.1	18,565	†	10,786	10,769	453	2,422	†	†	†	132,223	70
7,642	11,358	72.5	19,000	†	11,674	11,455	257	1,062	†	†	†	143,389	71
15,751	1,212	50.0	7,019	9,944	16,643	16,214	0	0	1,651	2,283	1,003	4,291,840	72
35,481	2,084	60.9	27,126	10,439	35,256	36,268	0	0	7,565	2,253	1,288	2,546,190	73
33,153	1,355	61.9	27,565	6,943	32,493	33,675	0	0	6,765	1,028	901	3,799,900	74
29,273	778	75.9	24,489	5,562	28,370	29,569	0	0	5,997	1,210	603	2,416,243	75
40,538	1,307	62.6	29,633	12,212	40,181	41,036	0	0	7,331	2,963	1,432	5,858,971	76
21,020	478	81.6	18,790	2,708	20,871	21,207	0	0	4,576	559	264	717,217	77

See notes at end of table.

Table 312.20. Selected statistics for degree-granting postsecondary institutions enrolling more than 15,000 students in 2014, by selected institution and student characteristics: Selected years, 1990 through 2013–14—Continued

Line number	Institution	State	Con-trol[1]	Level	Total fall enrollment					Fall enrollment, 2014		
					Fall 1990	Fall 2000	Fall 2010	Fall 2012	Fall 2013	Total	Sex	
											Male	Female
1	2	3	4	5	6	7	8	9	10	11	12	13
78	University of California, San Diego	CA	Public	4-year	17,790	20,197	29,176	28,294	29,517	30,709	16,607	14,102
79	University of California, Santa Barbara	CA	Public	4-year	18,385	19,962	22,218	21,927	22,225	23,051	11,173	11,878
80	University of California, Santa Cruz	CA	Public	4-year	10,054	12,144	17,187	17,404	17,203	17,866	8,565	9,301
81	University of Phoenix, California[8]	CA	PrivFp	4-year	†	18,075	24,914	25,930	23,877	23,257	11,319	11,938
82	University of Southern California	CA	PrivNp	4-year	28,374	29,194	36,896	39,958	41,368	42,453	20,341	22,112
83	Colorado State University, Fort Collins	CO	Public	4-year	26,828	26,807	30,155	30,659	31,186	31,354	15,218	16,136
84	Colorado Technical University, Online	CO	PrivFp	4-year	†	†	29,588	22,608	20,826	21,558	7,989	13,569
85	Front Range Community College	CO	Public	2-year	9,706	12,962	20,092	20,527	19,619	18,761	7,992	10,769
86	Metropolitan State University of Denver	CO	Public	4-year	17,400	17,688	23,948	23,381	22,752	21,674	9,969	11,705
87	University of Colorado, Boulder	CO	Public	4-year	28,600	29,352	32,697	31,945	32,017	32,432	18,122	14,310
88	University of Colorado, Denver	CO	Public	4-year	11,512	13,737	24,108	22,396	22,206	22,791	9,893	12,898
89	University of Connecticut	CT	Public	4-year	25,497	19,393	25,498	25,483	25,911	26,541	13,182	13,359
90	University of Delaware	DE	Public	4-year	20,818	19,072	21,177	21,856	22,166	22,680	9,923	12,757
91	George Washington University	DC	PrivNp	4-year	19,103	20,527	25,135	25,653	25,264	25,613	11,010	14,603
92	Georgetown University	DC	PrivNp	4-year	11,525	12,427	16,937	17,357	17,849	17,858	8,285	9,573
93	Broward College	FL	Public	4-year	24,365	27,389	40,375	42,309	43,883	44,119	18,131	25,988
94	Eastern Florida State College	FL	Public	4-year	14,319	13,265	18,096	17,202	16,711	15,931	6,553	9,378
95	Everest University, South Orlando	FL	PrivFp	4-year	†	938	15,189	33,852	29,693	22,535	4,901	17,634
96	Florida Atlantic University	FL	Public	4-year	12,767	21,046	28,270	29,994	30,759	30,297	13,020	17,277
97	Florida International University	FL	Public	4-year	22,466	31,945	42,197	46,171	47,663	49,610	21,853	27,757
98	Florida SouthWestern State College	FL	Public	4-year	8,919	8,919	16,951	15,731	15,423	15,389	6,040	9,349
99	Florida State College at Jacksonville	FL	Public	4-year	20,974	20,838	28,642	30,053	28,134	25,514	10,234	15,280
100	Florida State University	FL	Public	4-year	28,170	33,971	40,416	40,695	40,909	41,226	18,581	22,645
101	Full Sail University	FL	PrivFp	4-year	†	1,910	15,695	23,497	20,949	19,285	13,818	5,467
102	Hillsborough Community College	FL	Public	2-year	19,134	18,497	27,955	27,754	26,590	27,298	11,739	15,559
103	Indian River State College	FL	Public	4-year	12,774	13,186	17,511	17,816	17,248	17,665	7,013	10,652
104	Keiser University, Fort Lauderdale	FL	PrivNp	4-year	104	3,086	16,968	16,713	17,129	19,110	5,850	13,260
105	Miami Dade College	FL	Public	4-year	50,078	46,834	61,674	66,701	66,298	66,046	27,723	38,323
106	Nova Southeastern University	FL	PrivNp	4-year	9,562	18,587	28,741	26,808	25,670	24,148	7,312	16,836
107	Palm Beach State College	FL	Public	4-year	18,392	17,326	29,534	29,974	29,763	28,517	12,384	16,133
108	Saint Leo University	FL	PrivNp	4-year	5,308	8,720	15,565	15,986	16,275	16,349	6,817	9,532
109	Saint Petersburg College	FL	Public	4-year	20,012	19,900	31,793	32,612	31,820	32,681	12,952	19,729
110	Santa Fe College	FL	Public	4-year	11,053	12,464	15,745	15,362	15,113	15,055	6,738	8,317
111	Seminole State College of Florida	FL	Public	4-year	7,799	9,042	18,028	19,450	18,427	18,399	8,104	10,295
112	University of Central Florida	FL	Public	4-year	21,541	33,713	56,106	59,601	59,589	60,767	27,285	33,482
113	University of Florida	FL	Public	4-year	35,477	45,114	49,827	49,913	49,878	49,459	22,639	26,820
114	University of Miami	FL	PrivNp	4-year	13,841	13,963	15,657	16,172	16,935	16,674	8,153	8,521
115	University of North Florida	FL	Public	4-year	8,021	12,550	16,153	16,201	16,083	15,984	7,007	8,977
116	University of South Florida, Main Campus	FL	Public	4-year	32,326	35,561	40,431	41,116	41,428	41,938	18,556	23,382
117	Valencia College	FL	Public	4-year	18,438	27,565	41,583	42,915	42,180	43,217	19,333	23,884
118	Georgia Institute of Technology, Main Campus	GA	Public	4-year	12,241	14,805	20,720	21,557	21,471	23,109	16,140	6,969
119	Georgia Perimeter College	GA	Public	2-year	13,944	13,708	25,113	23,619	21,123	21,371	8,913	12,458
120	Georgia Southern University	GA	Public	4-year	12,249	14,184	19,691	20,574	20,517	20,517	9,801	10,716
121	Georgia State University	GA	Public	4-year	23,336	23,625	31,533	32,087	32,165	32,556	13,348	19,208
122	Kennesaw State University	GA	Public	4-year	10,018	13,360	23,452	24,604	24,629	25,714	10,781	14,933
123	University of Georgia	GA	Public	4-year	28,395	31,288	34,677	34,519	34,536	35,197	14,921	20,276
124	University of North Georgia	GA	Public	4-year	†	†	†	†	15,455	16,064	7,141	8,923
125	University of Hawaii at Manoa	HI	Public	4-year	18,799	17,263	20,337	20,426	20,006	19,507	8,526	10,981
126	Boise State University	ID	Public	4-year	13,367	16,287	19,992	22,344	21,981	22,227	10,107	12,120
127	Brigham Young University, Idaho	ID	PrivNp	4-year	7,795	8,949	14,933	23,261	27,692	36,624	15,488	21,136
128	Chamberlain College of Nursing, Illinois	IL	PrivFp	4-year	†	†	1,505	11,898	13,720	18,665	1,677	16,988
129	College of DuPage	IL	Public	2-year	29,185	28,862	26,722	26,156	28,627	29,476	13,746	15,730
130	College of Lake County	IL	Public	2-year	13,526	14,441	18,091	17,577	17,685	15,410	6,972	8,438
131	DePaul University	IL	PrivNp	4-year	15,711	20,548	25,145	24,966	24,414	23,799	11,149	12,650
132	DeVry University, Illinois	IL	PrivFp	4-year	†	†	†	†	26,851	24,220	10,955	13,265
133	Illinois State University	IL	Public	4-year	22,662	20,755	21,134	20,706	20,272	20,615	9,066	11,549
134	Joliet Junior College	IL	Public	2-year	9,645	11,334	15,676	15,589	16,869	15,776	7,212	8,564
135	Loyola University Chicago	IL	PrivNp	4-year	14,780	12,605	15,951	15,720	15,957	15,902	5,687	10,215
136	Moraine Valley Community College	IL	Public	2-year	13,601	12,972	17,387	16,650	16,106	15,286	7,187	8,099
137	Northern Illinois University	IL	Public	4-year	24,509	23,248	23,850	21,869	21,138	20,611	10,169	10,442
138	Northwestern University	IL	PrivNp	4-year	17,041	16,952	20,481	21,215	21,592	21,554	11,445	10,109
139	Southern Illinois University, Carbondale	IL	Public	4-year	24,078	22,552	20,037	18,847	17,964	17,989	9,671	8,318
140	University of Chicago	IL	PrivNp	4-year	10,867	12,531	15,152	15,245	15,048	15,097	8,756	6,341
141	University of Illinois at Chicago	IL	Public	4-year	24,959	24,942	27,850	27,875	28,038	27,969	12,959	15,010
142	University of Illinois at Urbana-Champaign	IL	Public	4-year	38,163	38,465	43,862	44,520	44,942	45,140	24,869	20,271
143	Ball State University	IN	Public	4-year	20,343	19,004	22,083	21,053	20,503	20,655	8,117	12,538
144	Indiana University, Bloomington	IN	Public	4-year	35,451	37,076	42,464	42,133	46,817	46,416	23,099	23,317
145	Indiana University-Purdue University, Indianapolis	IN	Public	4-year	27,517	27,525	30,566	30,451	30,488	30,690	13,455	17,235
146	Ivy Tech Community College	IN	Public	2-year	4,871	6,748	20,847	100,272	98,778	91,179	37,703	53,476
147	Purdue University, Main Campus	IN	Public	4-year	37,588	39,667	41,063	40,393	39,794	39,752	23,204	16,548
148	Vincennes University	IN	Public	4-year	9,162	9,169	16,595	17,530	18,383	19,205	10,496	8,709
149	Des Moines Area Community College	IA	Public	2-year	10,553	10,998	24,658	23,685	20,167	23,526	11,063	12,463
150	Iowa State University	IA	Public	4-year	25,741	26,845	28,682	30,748	32,955	34,435	19,290	15,145
151	Kaplan University, Davenport Campus	IA	PrivFp	4-year	641	376	77,966	48,865	52,407	52,018	12,166	39,852
152	University of Iowa	IA	Public	4-year	28,785	28,311	29,518	30,129	29,748	29,970	14,509	15,461

See notes at end of table.

Table 312.20. Selected statistics for degree-granting postsecondary institutions enrolling more than 15,000 students in 2014, by selected institution and student characteristics: Selected years, 1990 through 2013–14—Continued

Fall enrollment, 2014					Full-time-equivalent enrollment		Earned degrees/certificates conferred, 2013–14					Total expenditures and deductions, 2013–14 (in thousands)[2]	Line number
Attendance status			Student level										
Full-time	Part-time	Percent minority[3]	Under-graduate	Postbacca-laureate	Fall 2013	Fall 2014	Certificates[4]	Associate's	Bachelor's	Master's	Doctor's[5]		
14	15	16	17	18	19	20	21	22	23	24	25	26	27
29,766	943	68.2	24,810	5,899	28,963	30,135	0	0	6,148	1,214	675	3,884,467	78
22,533	518	56.9	20,238	2,813	21,947	22,734	0	0	4,871	554	360	919,277	79
17,354	512	61.8	16,277	1,589	16,932	17,558	0	0	3,766	252	179	641,157	80
23,257	0	74.6	19,688	3,569	23,877	23,257	10	2	6,119	1,444	0	199,306	81
36,452	6,001	54.8	18,739	23,714	37,993	38,752	0	0	4,932	7,089	1,481	3,682,731	82
23,610	7,744	19.3	23,598	7,756	26,329	26,543	0	0	4,808	1,600	368	928,361	83
12,649	8,909	52.6	18,669	2,889	15,938	16,147	0	1,722	2,376	1,475	6	248,137	84
5,575	13,186	24.9	18,761	†	10,652	10,002	1,990	1,591	†	†	†	107,870	85
13,010	8,664	36.8	21,196	478	17,232	16,498	0	0	3,272	176	0	172,481	86
26,675	5,757	22.2	26,557	5,875	28,421	28,850	0	0	5,415	1,171	552	1,201,563	87
12,147	10,644	34.4	13,509	9,282	15,783	16,228	0	0	2,189	1,876	647	1,589,179	88
23,199	3,342	28.6	18,395	8,146	23,756	24,438	0	21	5,200	1,671	762	2,090,819	89
20,389	2,291	21.3	18,951	3,729	20,651	21,280	0	281	3,749	762	239	864,888	90
17,266	8,347	33.5	10,740	14,873	20,233	20,464	480	232	2,482	4,376	1,091	1,190,681	91
14,416	3,442	30.3	7,595	10,263	15,726	15,735	21	0	1,794	3,209	955	1,119,227	92
12,891	31,228	77.9	44,119	0	25,667	25,493	3,283	5,780	468	0	0	278,975	93
5,650	10,281	30.3	15,931	0	10,280	9,799	1,084	2,796	0	0	0	111,338	94
11,546	10,989	63.3	22,340	195	21,036	15,862	285	2,883	405	28	0	212,632	95
17,607	12,690	52.1	25,476	4,821	22,888	22,612	0	353	5,017	1,355	128	464,023	96
31,766	17,844	87.5	41,009	8,601	38,174	38,863	0	45	8,069	3,159	414	859,364	97
5,116	10,273	44.0	15,389	0	9,230	9,262	222	2,197	328	0	0	91,970	98
7,819	17,695	44.2	25,514	0	16,851	14,960	2,607	4,764	588	0	0	196,888	99
35,181	6,045	31.6	32,948	8,278	37,213	37,524	0	192	8,105	2,065	813	1,088,620	100
19,285	0	49.3	17,318	1,967	20,949	19,285	294	146	3,157	1,060	0	310,866	101
11,391	15,907	57.5	27,298	†	16,588	16,732	1,583	3,374	†	†	†	180,985	102
5,950	11,715	40.6	17,665	0	10,503	10,678	987	2,464	501	0	0	124,101	103
13,649	5,461	60.6	18,101	1,009	14,166	15,786	1	3,557	851	216	17	315,817	104
26,157	39,889	93.1	66,046	0	42,607	42,254	1,885	9,941	1,005	0	0	462,373	105
12,631	11,517	62.9	4,699	19,449	18,100	17,048	0	4	1,376	3,973	1,739	598,195	106
7,732	20,785	59.3	28,517	0	17,653	16,120	1,547	4,127	237	0	0	164,156	107
12,214	4,135	55.8	12,581	3,768	13,817	13,837	28	858	2,723	1,298	0	152,884	108
9,123	23,558	32.1	32,681	0	18,279	18,630	827	3,953	1,083	0	0	209,282	109
6,192	8,863	38.4	15,055	0	9,713	9,769	421	2,718	126	0	0	106,863	110
6,322	12,077	47.1	18,399	0	11,543	11,196	2,798	2,831	183	0	0	116,519	111
40,307	20,460	42.7	52,671	8,096	47,696	48,385	0	478	12,372	2,539	356	868,850	112
41,914	7,545	37.3	32,829	16,630	45,282	44,765	0	446	8,515	4,173	1,994	2,473,160	113
15,415	1,259	47.4	11,175	5,499	16,116	15,902	10	0	2,633	1,045	815	2,544,030	114
10,716	5,268	29.0	14,121	1,863	12,904	12,798	0	261	3,177	547	43	247,986	115
29,724	12,214	41.8	31,067	10,871	34,082	34,446	0	170	8,079	2,630	546	1,097,029	116
16,437	26,780	64.0	43,217	0	26,877	27,244	4,644	7,384	25	0	0	245,886	117
19,084	4,025	38.3	14,682	8,427	19,782	20,600	0	0	3,267	1,988	553	1,357,611	118
7,987	13,384	67.2	21,371	†	12,499	12,481	2	1,880	†	†	†	148,636	119
16,905	3,612	36.7	18,004	2,513	18,213	18,302	0	0	2,973	722	61	338,667	120
24,200	8,356	64.1	25,328	7,228	27,017	27,488	73	0	4,741	2,118	435	636,290	121
18,522	7,192	35.6	23,592	2,122	20,440	21,369	58	0	3,599	730	31	330,928	122
31,868	3,329	25.5	26,882	8,315	32,575	33,136	0	0	6,609	1,623	948	1,271,453	123
10,897	5,167	19.3	15,507	557	12,306	12,965	29	952	1,137	147	28	170,376	124
14,526	4,981	77.3	14,126	5,381	16,787	16,427	0	0	3,378	1,121	384	994,201	125
13,038	9,189	18.4	19,333	2,894	16,692	16,662	0	137	2,797	640	34	344,131	126
15,609	21,015	15.0	36,624	0	19,607	23,865	0	1,639	3,543	0	0	232,495	127
3,136	15,529	34.9	13,279	5,386	6,871	9,182	0	0	4,288	656	2	104,352	128
10,022	19,454	43.3	29,476	†	16,193	16,553	1,951	2,448	†	†	†	231,405	129
4,303	11,107	51.2	15,410	†	9,102	8,032	2,208	1,390	†	†	†	146,046	130
18,501	5,298	38.6	16,153	7,646	20,917	20,552	27	0	3,748	2,549	317	560,970	131
6,905	17,315	46.7	18,264	5,956	15,088	13,654	0	1,009	2,691	2,427	0	195,824	132
18,219	2,396	20.5	18,155	2,460	18,779	19,132	0	0	4,313	689	61	550,161	133
5,562	10,214	39.3	15,776	†	9,549	8,991	507	1,602	†	†	†	137,166	134
13,431	2,471	33.7	10,322	5,580	14,425	14,385	72	0	2,287	1,526	523	505,279	135
6,624	8,662	39.2	15,286	†	9,900	9,532	1,309	1,774	†	†	†	126,507	136
15,857	4,754	36.1	15,435	5,176	17,975	17,658	0	0	3,675	1,347	259	604,398	137
17,022	4,532	37.5	9,048	12,506	18,880	18,760	328	0	2,229	3,610	986	1,973,028	138
14,621	3,368	32.0	13,461	4,528	15,802	15,906	0	79	3,643	995	345	796,741	139
12,658	2,439	37.4	5,738	9,359	13,690	13,590	0	0	1,385	2,621	711	3,288,221	140
23,263	4,706	54.7	16,718	11,251	25,028	25,018	0	0	3,756	2,264	969	2,606,519	141
41,414	3,726	37.0	32,959	12,181	42,551	42,813	7	0	7,660	3,410	1,118	2,472,502	142
16,455	4,200	14.3	16,415	4,240	18,053	18,033	8	68	3,450	1,617	79	453,264	143
37,670	8,746	18.6	36,419	9,997	41,092	41,044	161	10	6,815	2,435	761	1,460,882	144
21,758	8,932	23.9	22,525	8,165	24,730	25,209	479	137	3,807	1,711	772	1,163,356	145
28,815	62,364	25.3	91,179	†	55,889	49,753	9,731	9,453	†	†	†	614,894	146
34,653	5,099	19.0	30,237	9,515	36,726	36,574	369	73	7,055	1,783	965	1,656,273	147
6,175	13,030	20.1	19,205	0	11,026	11,433	819	1,813	101	0	0	120,457	148
7,566	15,960	20.0	23,526	†	11,909	12,924	1,049	2,411	†	†	†	145,793	149
30,888	3,547	14.1	28,893	5,542	30,747	32,231	0	0	5,384	837	494	1,089,037	150
11,390	40,628	48.5	40,477	11,541	28,382	27,296	63	3,250	4,771	2,852	118	492,910	151
24,424	5,546	17.7	22,354	7,616	26,369	26,547	50	0	4,753	1,375	1,000	2,792,543	152

See notes at end of table.

Table 312.20. Selected statistics for degree-granting postsecondary institutions enrolling more than 15,000 students in 2014, by selected institution and student characteristics: Selected years, 1990 through 2013–14—Continued

Line number	Institution	State	Con-trol[1]	Level	Total fall enrollment					Fall enrollment, 2014		
											Sex	
					Fall 1990	Fall 2000	Fall 2010	Fall 2012	Fall 2013	Total	Male	Female
1	2	3	4	5	6	7	8	9	10	11	12	13
153	Johnson County Community College	KS	Public	2-year	13,740	16,383	20,865	20,421	19,672	19,429	9,210	10,219
154	Kansas State University	KS	Public	4-year	21,137	21,929	23,588	24,378	24,581	24,766	12,550	12,216
155	University of Kansas	KS	Public	4-year	26,434	25,920	28,697	27,135	26,968	27,180	13,230	13,950
156	Eastern Kentucky University	KY	Public	4-year	15,290	13,285	16,567	15,968	16,111	16,305	6,932	9,373
157	Northern Kentucky University	KY	Public	4-year	11,254	12,080	15,716	15,634	15,263	15,090	6,638	8,452
158	University of Kentucky	KY	Public	4-year	22,538	23,114	27,108	28,034	28,435	29,203	13,783	15,420
159	University of Louisville	KY	Public	4-year	22,979	19,771	21,234	21,239	21,444	21,561	10,443	11,118
160	Western Kentucky University	KY	Public	4-year	15,170	15,481	20,897	21,110	20,448	20,171	8,461	11,710
161	Delgado Community College	LA	Public	2-year	11,614	12,784	18,767	18,096	18,698	17,152	5,683	11,469
162	Louisiana State U. and Agricultural & Mechanical	LA	Public	4-year	26,112	31,527	29,451	30,225	30,478	31,044	15,075	15,969
163	University of Louisiana at Lafayette	LA	Public	4-year	15,764	15,742	16,763	16,688	16,646	17,195	7,594	9,601
164	Anne Arundel Community College	MD	Public	2-year	12,148	11,761	17,665	17,650	16,463	15,274	6,181	9,093
165	Community College of Baltimore County	MD	Public	2-year	†	18,168	26,425	25,188	23,981	22,887	9,020	13,867
166	Johns Hopkins University	MD	PrivNp	4-year	13,363	17,774	20,977	20,871	20,918	21,372	10,263	11,109
167	Montgomery College	MD	Public	4-year	14,361	20,923	26,015	27,453	26,155	25,517	12,062	13,455
168	Towson University	MD	Public	4-year	15,035	16,729	21,840	21,960	22,499	22,285	8,472	13,813
169	University of Maryland, College Park	MD	Public	4-year	34,829	33,189	37,641	37,248	37,272	37,610	20,030	17,580
170	University of Maryland, University College	MD	Public	4-year	14,476	18,276	39,577	42,268	39,557	47,906	24,668	23,238
171	Boston University	MA	PrivNp	4-year	27,996	28,318	32,179	32,603	32,411	32,112	13,347	18,765
172	Harvard University	MA	PrivNp	4-year	22,851	24,279	27,594	28,006	28,297	28,791	14,822	13,969
173	Northeastern University	MA	PrivNp	4-year	30,510	23,897	29,519	27,694	20,053	19,798	10,034	9,764
174	University of Massachusetts, Amherst	MA	Public	4-year	26,025	24,416	27,569	28,236	28,518	28,635	14,487	14,148
175	University of Massachusetts, Boston	MA	Public	4-year	13,723	13,346	15,454	15,874	16,277	16,756	6,975	9,781
176	University of Massachusetts, Lowell	MA	Public	4-year	14,259	12,189	14,702	16,294	16,932	17,179	10,348	6,831
177	Central Michigan University	MI	Public	4-year	18,286	26,845	28,292	27,626	26,841	26,879	11,572	15,307
178	Eastern Michigan University	MI	Public	4-year	25,011	23,561	23,565	23,518	23,447	22,401	9,039	13,362
179	Grand Rapids Community College	MI	Public	2-year	12,054	13,400	17,870	17,448	16,590	15,668	7,673	7,995
180	Grand Valley State University	MI	Public	4-year	11,725	18,569	24,541	24,654	24,477	25,094	10,133	14,961
181	Lansing Community College	MI	Public	2-year	22,343	16,011	21,969	19,082	17,562	16,031	7,431	8,600
182	Macomb Community College	MI	Public	2-year	31,538	22,001	24,468	23,729	23,446	22,914	10,775	12,139
183	Michigan State University	MI	Public	4-year	44,307	43,366	46,985	48,783	49,317	50,081	24,314	25,767
184	Oakland Community College	MI	Public	2-year	28,069	23,188	28,925	27,296	26,405	24,031	10,447	13,584
185	Oakland University	MI	Public	4-year	12,400	15,235	19,053	19,740	20,169	20,519	8,592	11,927
186	University of Michigan, Ann Arbor	MI	Public	4-year	36,391	38,103	41,924	43,426	43,710	43,625	22,739	20,886
187	Wayne County Community College District	MI	Public	2-year	11,986	9,008	21,198	18,176	18,119	16,310	5,592	10,718
188	Wayne State University	MI	Public	4-year	33,872	30,408	31,505	28,938	27,897	27,578	12,169	15,409
189	Western Michigan University	MI	Public	4-year	26,989	28,657	25,045	24,598	24,294	23,914	11,700	12,214
190	Capella University	MN	PrivFp	4-year	†	36	39,457	35,754	34,007	35,061	8,629	26,432
191	Minnesota State University, Mankato	MN	Public	4-year	16,575	12,842	15,435	15,441	15,426	15,387	7,207	8,180
192	Saint Cloud State University	MN	Public	4-year	17,075	15,181	18,650	16,922	16,765	16,076	7,569	8,507
193	University of Minnesota, Twin Cities	MN	Public	4-year	57,168	45,481	51,721	51,853	51,526	51,147	24,723	26,424
194	Walden University	MN	PrivFp	4-year	422	1,544	47,456	50,209	51,016	52,188	12,317	39,871
195	Mississippi State University	MS	Public	4-year	14,391	16,561	19,644	20,365	20,161	20,138	10,352	9,786
196	University of Mississippi	MS	Public	4-year	11,288	12,118	17,085	18,794	19,431	22,503	9,878	12,625
197	Columbia College	MO	PrivNp	4-year	4,214	7,948	16,962	17,830	16,946	16,567	6,800	9,767
198	Metropolitan Community College, Kansas City	MO	Public	2-year	9,625	8,117	6,539	20,141	19,234	18,222	7,826	10,396
199	Missouri State University, Springfield	MO	Public	4-year	19,480	17,703	20,383	20,629	21,271	21,816	9,084	12,732
200	Saint Louis Community College	MO	Public	2-year	32,347	6,749	8,716	26,603	24,005	21,218	8,640	12,578
201	Saint Louis University	MO	PrivNp	4-year	12,891	13,847	17,709	17,640	17,343	17,052	7,048	10,004
202	University of Missouri, Columbia	MO	Public	4-year	25,058	23,309	32,341	34,704	34,616	35,425	16,708	18,717
203	University of Missouri, Kansas City	MO	Public	4-year	11,263	12,762	15,259	15,990	15,718	16,146	7,195	8,951
204	University of Missouri, Saint Louis	MO	Public	4-year	15,393	15,397	16,791	16,705	16,809	17,072	6,870	10,202
205	Webster University	MO	PrivNp	4-year	8,745	13,783	19,342	18,456	17,904	16,769	7,306	9,463
206	University of Nebraska, Lincoln	NE	Public	4-year	24,453	22,268	24,610	24,207	24,445	25,006	13,062	11,944
207	University of Nebraska, Omaha	NE	Public	4-year	15,804	13,479	14,665	14,786	15,227	15,227	7,220	8,007
208	College of Southern Nevada	NV	Public	4-year	14,161	29,905	42,747	35,678	34,177	35,943	15,882	20,061
209	University of Nevada, Las Vegas	NV	Public	4-year	17,937	22,041	28,203	27,389	27,848	28,515	12,711	15,804
210	University of Nevada, Reno	NV	Public	4-year	11,487	13,149	17,680	18,227	18,776	19,934	9,445	10,489
211	Southern New Hampshire University	NH	PrivNp	4-year	6,403	4,584	8,034	17,454	28,389	43,274	16,981	26,293
212	University of New Hampshire, Main Campus	NH	Public	4-year	13,260	14,689	15,095	15,267	14,913	15,117	6,840	8,277
213	Bergen Community College	NJ	Public	2-year	12,119	11,993	17,197	17,015	15,882	15,651	8,120	7,531
214	Montclair State University	NJ	Public	4-year	13,067	13,502	18,402	18,382	19,464	20,022	7,368	12,654
215	Rutgers University, New Brunswick	NJ	Public	4-year	33,016	35,236	38,912	40,434	48,036	48,378	22,500	25,878
216	Thomas Edison State College	NJ	Public	4-year	7,813	8,137	18,736	20,606	20,877	21,495	11,065	10,430
217	Central New Mexico Community College	NM	Public	2-year	9,739	17,265	29,948	28,323	28,891	26,771	11,690	15,081
218	New Mexico State University, Main Campus	NM	Public	4-year	14,812	14,958	18,600	17,651	16,765	15,829	7,331	8,498
219	University of New Mexico, Main Campus	NM	Public	4-year	23,950	23,670	28,688	29,033	28,592	27,844	12,469	15,375
220	Columbia University in the City of New York	NY	PrivNp	4-year	18,242	19,639	25,208	26,471	26,957	27,589	13,596	13,993
221	Cornell University	NY	PrivNp	4-year	11,533	12,043	20,939	21,424	21,593	21,679	11,172	10,507
222	CUNY Bernard M. Baruch College	NY	Public	4-year	15,849	15,698	17,063	17,373	17,505	18,090	9,140	8,950
223	CUNY Borough of Manhattan Community College	NY	Public	2-year	14,819	15,875	22,534	24,537	24,186	26,606	11,395	15,211
224	CUNY Brooklyn College	NY	Public	4-year	16,605	15,039	16,912	16,523	17,004	17,390	6,904	10,486
225	CUNY City College	NY	Public	4-year	14,085	11,055	15,416	16,023	15,331	15,579	7,447	8,132
226	CUNY Hunter College	NY	Public	4-year	19,639	20,011	22,407	23,005	23,019	23,112	7,464	15,648

See notes at end of table.

Table 312.20. Selected statistics for degree-granting postsecondary institutions enrolling more than 15,000 students in 2014, by selected institution and student characteristics: Selected years, 1990 through 2013–14—Continued

Fall enrollment, 2014					Full-time-equivalent enrollment		Earned degrees/certificates conferred, 2013–14					Total expenditures and deductions, 2013–14 (in thousands)[2]	Line number
Attendance status		Percent minority[3]	Student level										
Full-time	Part-time		Under-graduate	Postbacca-laureate	Fall 2013	Fall 2014	Certificates[4]	Associate's	Bachelor's	Master's	Doctor's[5]		
14	15	16	17	18	19	20	21	22	23	24	25	26	27
6,332	13,097	23.5	19,429	†	10,810	10,729	1,357	1,756	†	†	†	180,711	153
20,741	4,025	16.2	20,327	4,439	22,094	22,283	99	44	3,748	1,031	274	761,439	154
23,183	3,997	20.8	19,343	7,837	24,542	24,712	10	0	4,091	1,593	847	1,171,515	155
11,950	4,355	12.0	13,939	2,366	13,386	13,641	15	219	2,507	701	21	278,010	156
10,204	4,886	12.9	12,809	2,281	12,413	12,112	8	89	2,143	515	172	223,976	157
26,469	2,734	17.6	22,223	6,980	26,727	27,522	8	0	3,988	1,263	870	2,473,108	158
16,459	5,102	22.2	15,961	5,600	18,349	18,449	36	19	2,821	1,216	542	881,611	159
14,228	5,943	17.1	17,452	2,719	16,706	16,552	78	259	2,751	905	23	327,928	160
6,965	10,187	64.8	17,152	†	11,529	10,385	2,478	1,368	†	†	†	128,282	161
27,462	3,582	24.0	25,572	5,472	28,456	28,857	0	0	4,692	1,114	648	1,040,456	162
13,453	3,742	28.5	15,574	1,621	14,575	14,935	0	0	2,493	405	51	262,853	163
4,442	10,832	33.2	15,274	†	8,809	8,079	1,080	1,800	†	†	†	147,771	164
7,301	15,586	54.6	22,887	†	13,354	12,534	1,199	2,020	†	†	†	213,271	165
13,407	7,965	39.2	6,357	15,015	16,186	16,453	0	0	1,682	4,694	619	4,901,327	166
8,931	16,586	70.8	25,517	†	14,919	14,500	340	2,374	†	†	†	311,277	167
17,690	4,595	31.8	18,807	3,478	19,582	19,446	0	0	4,291	1,114	20	370,418	168
32,938	4,672	41.7	27,056	10,554	34,123	34,713	63	0	7,308	2,770	655	1,711,661	169
8,429	39,477	54.8	35,154	12,752	19,093	23,833	426	527	4,188	3,649	49	362,887	170
25,851	6,261	34.9	18,017	14,095	28,341	28,258	359	0	4,426	4,290	1,107	1,641,418	171
20,430	8,361	40.8	10,338	18,453	23,434	23,658	0	5	1,822	3,805	1,535	4,405,997	172
18,622	1,176	31.5	13,510	6,288	18,758	19,071	0	0	3,393	2,119	660	928,762	173
22,946	5,689	22.4	22,252	6,383	24,941	25,070	238	59	5,674	1,409	306	1,023,256	174
10,543	6,213	45.4	12,700	4,056	12,421	12,937	13	0	2,366	923	71	351,886	175
10,797	6,382	27.3	12,983	4,196	12,868	13,254	116	37	2,228	879	100	353,367	176
19,923	6,956	20.5	20,671	6,208	22,364	22,552	0	0	4,078	1,861	129	444,945	177
14,116	8,285	29.5	18,340	4,061	17,968	17,332	0	0	3,249	1,283	26	348,671	178
5,021	10,647	27.4	15,668	†	9,336	8,596	193	1,734	†	†	†	136,709	179
20,461	4,633	15.1	21,636	3,458	21,633	22,244	36	0	4,259	962	50	413,497	180
5,859	10,172	26.5	16,031	†	10,272	9,274	1,678	1,804	†	†	†	133,772	181
7,514	15,400	22.4	22,914	†	12,859	12,684	602	2,719	†	†	†	151,194	182
43,708	6,373	20.7	38,786	11,295	45,593	46,157	92	0	7,924	2,388	1,172	2,109,938	183
7,012	17,019	36.5	24,031	†	14,218	12,726	370	2,589	†	†	†	203,047	184
14,083	6,436	19.6	16,935	3,584	16,325	16,598	0	0	2,817	760	107	286,998	185
41,101	2,524	28.7	28,395	15,230	42,117	42,056	0	0	7,076	4,297	1,636	6,202,947	186
3,186	13,124	83.2	16,310	†	8,649	7,592	1,429	1,832	†	†	†	144,668	187
17,837	9,741	36.8	18,347	9,231	21,908	21,624	2	0	3,047	2,000	807	838,222	188
16,959	6,955	22.7	18,889	5,025	19,804	19,608	0	0	3,823	1,313	126	561,801	189
2,589	32,472	53.6	8,750	26,311	14,367	15,072	0	0	1,030	4,181	1,189	353,350	190
11,900	3,487	15.0	13,395	1,992	13,386	13,253	50	75	2,386	546	11	209,786	191
9,926	6,150	17.0	14,377	1,699	12,953	12,363	9	151	2,199	490	11	205,606	192
38,623	12,524	20.8	34,351	16,796	43,612	43,381	237	0	7,594	3,269	1,795	3,027,768	193
27,467	24,721	54.9	8,960	43,228	37,761	37,000	0	0	1,457	7,303	1,038	488,186	194
17,004	3,134	25.9	16,536	3,602	18,168	18,196	0	0	3,255	815	218	609,071	195
19,925	2,578	22.0	18,101	4,402	18,314	20,917	0	0	3,395	840	573	1,683,786	196
9,311	7,256	39.7	15,639	928	12,461	12,153	15	1,503	2,639	282	0	91,646	197
6,983	11,239	34.9	18,222	†	11,595	10,756	576	2,046	†	†	†	132,623	198
15,703	6,113	12.9	18,517	3,299	17,705	18,099	34	0	2,890	1,124	40	287,140	199
8,682	12,536	43.8	21,218	†	14,681	12,891	422	2,092	†	†	†	200,264	200
10,416	6,636	22.3	12,374	4,678	13,186	13,008	53	0	1,850	904	723	728,582	201
30,962	4,463	16.8	27,642	7,783	31,943	32,651	0	0	5,769	1,580	729	2,019,683	202
10,239	5,907	30.5	10,453	5,693	12,158	12,527	0	0	1,803	1,028	575	379,587	203
7,015	10,057	24.8	13,874	3,198	10,855	10,979	20	0	2,020	854	103	221,096	204
5,360	11,409	53.2	3,459	13,310	10,424	9,729	72	0	824	5,481	8	198,777	205
21,364	3,642	13.6	19,979	5,027	22,223	22,736	0	5	3,864	852	445	938,320	206
10,371	4,856	23.4	12,221	3,006	12,248	12,245	0	0	2,410	698	29	228,434	207
9,289	26,654	60.5	35,943	0	19,102	20,045	1,963	2,623	22	0	0	202,950	208
19,781	8,734	57.6	23,803	4,712	22,345	23,206	1	0	3,764	928	340	535,359	209
15,266	4,668	35.0	16,839	3,095	15,976	17,073	0	0	2,743	612	173	578,439	210
18,214	25,060	27.5	29,353	13,921	19,084	27,953	49	322	1,997	1,696	8	271,321	211
13,593	1,524	9.0	12,831	2,286	13,926	14,163	0	125	2,706	743	75	517,166	212
8,976	6,675	55.1	15,651	†	11,234	11,217	91	2,519	†	†	†	126,995	213
15,253	4,769	45.8	15,885	4,137	16,511	17,062	138	0	3,197	1,095	31	364,004	214
40,970	7,408	50.8	34,544	13,834	43,201	43,739	41	72	7,629	2,708	1,265	2,991,271	215
154	21,341	34.9	20,143	1,352	8,453	8,709	16	581	2,654	182	0	68,476	216
8,292	18,479	66.6	26,771	†	16,041	14,496	3,521	3,179	†	†	†	182,469	217
12,267	3,562	64.2	12,784	3,045	14,461	13,644	0	18	2,714	807	114	452,379	218
19,992	7,852	58.5	21,792	6,052	23,757	23,055	0	0	3,692	1,308	519	1,850,846	219
11,609	6,481	67.4	14,857	3,233	13,648	14,120	0	0	3,082	1,467	0	261,849	220
17,131	9,475	89.9	26,606	†	18,675	20,312	0	3,242	†	†	†	264,580	221
10,386	7,004	62.2	14,115	3,275	12,742	13,096	2	0	2,444	962	0	256,720	222
9,845	5,734	79.2	12,893	2,686	11,885	12,063	0	0	2,118	954	17	393,256	223
13,532	9,580	60.9	16,879	6,233	16,886	17,196	11	0	2,869	2,055	0	353,302	224
10,571	4,474	76.5	13,305	1,740	12,418	12,318	36	46	2,580	535	0	258,123	225
10,300	7,458	67.1	17,758	†	13,386	12,804	4	2,827	†	†	†	183,930	226

See notes at end of table.

Table 312.20. Selected statistics for degree-granting postsecondary institutions enrolling more than 15,000 students in 2014, by selected institution and student characteristics: Selected years, 1990 through 2013–14—Continued

Line number	Institution	State	Control[1]	Level	Total fall enrollment					Fall enrollment, 2014		
											Sex	
					Fall 1990	Fall 2000	Fall 2010	Fall 2012	Fall 2013	Total	Male	Female
1	2	3	4	5	6	7	8	9	10	11	12	13
227	CUNY John Jay College of Criminal Justice	NY	Public	4-year	8,665	10,612	15,206	14,996	15,010	15,045	6,415	8,630
228	CUNY Kingsborough Community College	NY	Public	2-year	13,809	14,801	18,606	18,934	18,634	17,758	8,116	9,642
229	CUNY LaGuardia Community College	NY	Public	2-year	9,167	11,778	17,569	19,287	19,564	20,231	8,676	11,555
230	CUNY New York City College of Technology	NY	Public	4-year	10,908	11,028	15,366	16,207	16,860	17,374	9,718	7,656
231	CUNY Queens College	NY	Public	4-year	18,072	15,061	20,906	20,100	18,974	19,310	7,996	11,314
232	CUNY Queensborough Community College	NY	Public	2-year	12,184	10,598	15,316	15,711	16,291	16,182	7,514	8,668
233	Excelsior College	NY	PrivNp	4-year	13,303	18,067	32,029	39,728	39,897	41,527	18,820	22,707
234	Fordham University	NY	PrivNp	4-year	13,158	13,650	15,158	15,170	15,097	15,231	6,328	8,903
235	Monroe Community College	NY	Public	2-year	13,545	15,315	18,995	17,296	16,458	15,335	7,189	8,146
236	Nassau Community College	NY	Public	2-year	21,537	19,621	23,767	23,340	23,318	22,374	11,098	11,276
237	New York University	NY	PrivNp	4-year	32,813	37,150	43,797	44,516	44,599	49,274	22,121	27,153
238	Rochester Institute of Technology	NY	PrivNp	4-year	12,391	14,106	15,792	16,357	16,583	16,310	11,009	5,301
239	Saint John's University, New York	NY	PrivNp	4-year	19,105	18,621	21,354	21,087	20,729	20,445	8,834	11,611
240	State University of New York at Albany	NY	Public	4-year	17,400	16,751	17,615	17,312	17,338	17,273	8,378	8,895
241	State University of New York at Binghamton	NY	Public	4-year	12,202	12,473	14,895	15,308	16,077	16,695	8,743	7,952
242	Stony Brook University	NY	Public	4-year	17,624	19,924	24,363	23,946	24,143	24,607	12,585	12,022
243	Suffolk County Community College	NY	Public	2-year	†	†	26,719	26,219	26,711	26,600	12,542	14,058
244	Syracuse University	NY	PrivNp	4-year	21,900	18,186	20,407	21,029	21,267	21,492	9,900	11,592
245	University at Buffalo	NY	Public	4-year	27,638	24,830	29,117	28,952	29,850	29,995	15,879	14,116
246	Appalachian State University	NC	Public	4-year	11,931	13,227	17,222	17,589	17,838	18,026	8,052	9,974
247	Central Piedmont Community College	NC	Public	2-year	16,311	14,908	19,921	19,498	20,198	19,957	8,792	11,165
248	Duke University	NC	PrivNp	4-year	11,293	12,192	15,016	15,386	15,467	15,856	7,965	7,891
249	East Carolina University	NC	Public	4-year	17,564	18,750	27,783	26,947	26,887	27,511	11,060	16,451
250	North Carolina State University at Raleigh	NC	Public	4-year	27,199	28,619	34,376	34,340	34,009	33,989	18,945	15,044
251	University of North Carolina at Chapel Hill	NC	Public	4-year	23,878	24,892	29,390	29,278	29,127	29,135	12,654	16,481
252	University of North Carolina at Charlotte	NC	Public	4-year	14,699	17,241	25,063	26,232	26,571	27,238	13,761	13,477
253	University of North Carolina at Greensboro	NC	Public	4-year	12,882	13,125	18,771	18,516	18,074	18,647	6,304	12,343
254	Wake Technical Community College	NC	Public	2-year	6,129	9,654	17,071	20,440	19,160	21,384	9,571	11,813
255	Bowling Green State University, Main Campus	OH	Public	4-year	18,657	18,096	17,706	17,286	16,958	16,554	7,166	9,388
256	Cleveland State University	OH	Public	4-year	19,214	15,294	17,386	17,278	17,497	16,936	7,625	9,311
257	Columbus State Community College	OH	Public	2-year	13,290	18,094	30,513	25,863	25,249	24,448	11,298	13,150
258	Cuyahoga Community College District	OH	Public	2-year	23,157	19,518	31,250	29,701	27,910	27,084	10,794	16,290
259	Kent State University at Kent	OH	Public	4-year	24,434	21,924	26,589	28,602	28,998	29,477	11,836	17,641
260	Miami University, Oxford	OH	Public	4-year	15,835	16,757	17,472	17,683	17,901	18,620	8,617	10,003
261	Ohio State University, Main Campus	OH	Public	4-year	54,087	47,952	56,064	56,387	57,466	58,322	29,664	28,658
262	Ohio University, Main Campus	OH	Public	4-year	18,505	19,920	25,108	27,402	28,786	29,217	12,252	16,965
263	Sinclair Community College	OH	Public	2-year	16,367	19,026	21,993	19,537	19,176	19,093	8,238	10,855
264	University of Akron, Main Campus	OH	Public	4-year	28,801	21,363	27,076	26,581	24,932	23,962	12,265	11,697
265	University of Cincinnati, Main Campus	OH	Public	4-year	31,013	27,327	32,283	33,347	34,379	35,313	16,403	18,910
266	University of Toledo	OH	Public	4-year	24,691	19,491	23,085	21,453	20,743	20,626	10,331	10,295
267	Wright State University, Main Campus	OH	Public	4-year	16,393	13,964	18,447	16,780	16,656	16,842	8,155	8,687
268	Oklahoma State University, Main Campus	OK	Public	4-year	19,827	18,676	23,667	25,708	26,073	25,962	13,385	12,577
269	Tulsa Community College	OK	Public	2-year	17,955	16,270	20,577	19,557	18,640	17,861	7,125	10,736
270	University of Central Oklahoma	OK	Public	4-year	14,232	14,099	17,101	17,211	17,220	16,840	6,893	9,947
271	University of Oklahoma, Norman Campus	OK	Public	4-year	20,774	24,205	26,476	27,507	27,292	27,261	13,938	13,323
272	Oregon State University	OR	Public	4-year	16,361	16,758	23,753	26,363	27,902	28,886	15,466	13,420
273	Portland Community College	OR	Public	2-year	21,888	24,209	32,013	33,767	32,411	30,929	14,305	16,624
274	Portland State University	OR	Public	4-year	16,921	18,889	28,035	28,287	28,260	27,696	12,885	14,811
275	University of Oregon	OR	Public	4-year	18,840	17,801	23,342	24,518	24,473	24,096	11,499	12,597
276	Community College of Allegheny County	PA	Public	2-year	20,553	15,556	20,706	19,567	18,229	17,153	7,238	9,915
277	Community College of Philadelphia	PA	Public	2-year	15,151	15,953	19,503	18,920	19,063	19,119	7,163	11,956
278	Drexel University	PA	PrivNp	4-year	11,926	13,128	23,637	25,500	26,132	26,359	12,526	13,833
279	Harrisburg Area Community College, Harrisburg	PA	Public	2-year	8,355	7,572	23,210	21,945	20,780	20,230	7,560	12,670
280	Pennsylvania State University, Main Campus	PA	Public	4-year	38,864	40,571	45,233	45,783	46,615	47,040	25,341	21,699
281	Temple University	PA	Public	4-year	29,714	28,355	37,367	36,744	37,270	37,485	18,009	19,476
282	University of Pennsylvania	PA	PrivNp	4-year	21,868	21,853	25,007	24,725	24,630	24,806	11,739	13,067
283	University of Pittsburgh, Pittsburgh Campus	PA	Public	4-year	28,120	26,329	28,823	28,769	28,649	28,617	13,715	14,902
284	West Chester University of Pennsylvania	PA	Public	4-year	12,076	12,272	14,490	15,411	15,845	16,086	6,268	9,818
285	Community College of Rhode Island	RI	Public	2-year	16,620	15,583	17,775	17,884	17,699	17,553	7,182	10,371
286	University of Rhode Island	RI	Public	4-year	16,047	14,362	16,294	16,451	16,387	16,571	7,494	9,077
287	Clemson University	SC	Public	4-year	15,714	17,465	19,453	20,768	21,303	21,857	11,697	10,160
288	Trident Technical College	SC	Public	2-year	6,939	10,246	15,790	17,224	17,489	16,136	6,210	9,926
289	University of South Carolina, Columbia	SC	Public	4-year	25,613	23,728	29,599	31,288	31,964	32,971	14,773	18,198
290	Middle Tennessee State University	TN	Public	4-year	14,865	19,121	26,430	25,394	23,881	22,729	10,402	12,327
291	University of Memphis	TN	Public	4-year	20,681	19,986	22,420	22,139	21,480	21,059	8,487	12,572
292	University of Tennessee, Knoxville	TN	Public	4-year	26,055	25,890	30,300	29,833	30,030	30,386	14,971	15,415
293	Austin Community College District	TX	Public	2-year	24,251	25,735	44,100	43,315	41,627	40,949	18,171	22,778
294	Baylor University	TX	PrivNp	4-year	12,014	13,719	14,900	15,364	15,616	16,263	7,111	9,152
295	Blinn College	TX	Public	2-year	6,849	11,588	17,755	17,839	18,561	18,850	9,060	9,790
296	Central Texas College	TX	Public	2-year	4,815	14,636	26,055	22,443	21,647	20,547	10,750	9,797
297	Collin County Community College District	TX	Public	2-year	9,059	12,996	27,069	27,424	27,972	27,991	12,371	15,620
298	Eastfield College	TX	Public	2-year	9,525	7,873	12,919	14,178	14,529	15,112	6,066	9,046
299	El Paso Community College	TX	Public	2-year	17,081	18,001	29,909	32,127	30,468	28,308	12,211	16,097
300	Houston Community College	TX	Public	2-year	36,437	40,929	60,303	58,476	57,978	58,276	24,269	34,007
301	Lone Star College System	TX	Public	2-year	15,653	24,554	54,412	64,872	64,072	69,395	28,127	41,268
302	Northwest Vista College	TX	Public	2-year	†	3,893	15,921	15,992	15,965	15,797	7,189	8,608
303	Richland College	TX	Public	2-year	12,567	12,537	19,201	19,552	19,287	19,343	8,732	10,611

See notes at end of table.

Table 312.20. Selected statistics for degree-granting postsecondary institutions enrolling more than 15,000 students in 2014, by selected institution and student characteristics: Selected years, 1990 through 2013–14—Continued

Fall enrollment, 2014					Full-time-equivalent enrollment		Earned degrees/certificates conferred, 2013–14					Total expenditures and deductions, 2013–14 (in thousands)[2]	Line number
Attendance status			Student level										
Full-time	Part-time	Percent minority[3]	Under-graduate	Postbacca-laureate	Fall 2013	Fall 2014	Certificates[4]	Associate's	Bachelor's	Master's	Doctor's[5]		
14	15	16	17	18	19	20	21	22	23	24	25	26	27
10,922	9,309	87.8	20,231	†	13,513	14,047	71	2,379	†	†	†	222,401	227
10,587	6,787	87.3	17,374	0	12,958	13,326	3	1,038	1,054	0	0	195,374	228
11,561	7,749	62.7	15,773	3,537	14,235	14,560	0	0	3,149	1,181	0	288,576	229
9,551	6,631	84.1	16,182	†	11,864	11,777	24	1,949	†	†	†	154,286	230
23,268	4,321	45.0	8,100	19,489	24,352	24,925	0	0	2,061	7,162	1,397	3,605,779	231
21,602	77	45.0	14,282	7,397	21,553	21,631	0	0	3,570	2,328	781	1,834,268	232
0	41,527	38.8	38,426	3,101	15,648	16,281	31	1,729	2,689	296	0	86,740	233
12,233	2,998	34.8	8,633	6,598	13,200	13,385	0	0	1,938	2,289	580	534,326	234
9,374	5,961	37.5	15,335	†	12,341	11,375	235	2,482	†	†	†	164,910	235
13,541	8,833	56.0	22,374	†	17,267	16,507	86	3,133	†	†	†	240,475	236
39,898	9,376	46.6	24,985	24,289	38,740	43,494	26	62	5,596	8,304	1,507	4,607,555	237
14,421	1,889	23.7	13,460	2,850	15,080	15,157	23	134	2,364	1,100	29	514,877	238
13,349	7,096	51.0	15,762	4,683	16,450	16,115	61	22	2,056	1,367	583	507,026	239
14,409	2,864	38.7	12,929	4,344	15,494	15,476	0	0	2,837	1,214	186	837,696	240
14,852	1,843	34.8	13,412	3,283	15,014	15,539	0	0	3,064	843	178	475,298	241
20,640	3,967	47.5	16,480	8,127	21,573	22,121	0	0	3,890	1,783	576	2,161,645	242
14,318	12,282	35.6	26,600	†	18,820	18,442	82	3,704	†	†	†	271,198	243
19,356	2,136	32.7	15,224	6,268	19,930	20,180	11	10	3,330	2,077	385	838,167	244
24,588	5,407	33.0	19,882	10,113	26,709	26,615	20	0	4,685	2,163	957	996,806	245
16,165	1,861	11.7	16,255	1,771	16,716	16,878	0	0	3,378	711	10	374,652	246
6,788	13,169	53.5	19,957	†	11,524	11,209	563	1,695	†	†	†	181,206	247
15,130	726	37.4	6,626	9,230	15,113	15,408	0	0	1,886	2,265	1,140	4,897,473	248
21,352	6,159	28.6	22,252	5,259	23,237	23,719	0	0	4,137	1,506	163	833,909	249
26,965	7,024	21.9	24,473	9,516	29,517	29,634	0	155	5,541	2,452	575	1,297,220	250
24,275	4,860	30.5	18,350	10,785	26,137	26,066	8	0	4,566	2,090	1,229	2,748,815	251
21,267	5,971	35.1	22,216	5,022	22,789	23,562	0	0	4,362	1,413	123	527,915	252
14,113	4,534	40.9	15,313	3,334	15,479	15,859	0	0	3,037	881	131	374,116	253
7,612	13,772	43.8	21,384	†	10,409	12,236	1,301	1,840	†	†	†	151,585	254
14,337	2,217	18.2	14,099	2,455	15,603	15,185	0	0	2,959	764	106	355,147	255
10,491	6,445	30.7	11,826	5,110	13,369	12,954	0	0	2,252	1,356	230	309,756	256
7,930	16,518	32.9	24,448	†	14,334	13,476	2,628	2,528	†	†	†	178,220	257
9,073	18,011	43.1	27,084	†	15,698	15,120	606	3,045	†	†	†	307,453	258
22,288	7,189	17.2	23,328	6,149	24,549	25,075	72	0	4,669	1,583	259	543,990	259
16,337	2,283	13.0	15,813	2,807	16,731	17,184	82	180	3,989	655	61	485,423	260
50,624	7,698	20.1	44,741	13,581	52,883	53,581	2	2	9,852	2,595	1,604	4,990,173	261
19,869	9,348	13.0	23,571	5,646	23,108	23,524	274	217	6,341	1,329	298	618,478	262
5,211	13,882	25.3	19,093	†	10,938	9,872	1,893	1,537	†	†	†	168,042	263
18,035	5,927	21.4	19,710	4,252	20,917	20,354	213	749	3,032	1,171	252	490,201	264
26,276	9,037	18.1	24,300	11,013	29,091	29,696	272	73	4,817	2,871	768	1,006,659	265
15,903	4,723	24.2	16,090	4,536	17,960	17,748	0	61	2,878	1,026	571	860,194	266
11,553	5,289	23.4	12,682	4,160	14,377	13,581	168	0	2,191	1,036	177	378,223	267
20,129	5,833	25.4	20,952	5,010	22,290	22,354	14	0	4,102	1,219	331	825,301	268
5,964	11,897	37.2	17,861	†	10,488	9,958	368	2,262	†	†	†	150,602	269
11,383	5,457	34.9	14,998	1,842	13,838	13,536	0	81	2,528	553	0	192,506	270
21,089	6,172	32.3	21,011	6,250	23,182	23,448	0	0	3,913	1,693	351	865,092	271
22,052	6,834	25.4	23,903	4,983	24,304	24,751	0	0	4,702	848	341	945,928	272
12,564	18,365	33.0	30,929	†	19,902	18,730	1,920	3,556	†	†	†	297,696	273
17,330	10,366	31.0	22,136	5,560	21,615	21,397	0	0	4,375	1,579	86	488,846	274
21,585	2,511	26.3	20,559	3,537	22,923	22,572	0	0	4,654	891	339	829,403	275
6,012	11,141	28.1	17,153	†	10,316	9,752	715	2,069	†	†	†	133,897	276
4,832	14,287	74.9	19,119	†	9,771	9,629	335	1,882	†	†	†	170,414	277
19,202	7,157	33.6	16,896	9,463	21,697	21,963	73	19	3,083	2,494	644	976,654	278
6,136	14,094	28.0	20,230	†	11,298	10,868	344	1,995	†	†	†	179,049	279
45,191	1,849	20.4	40,541	6,499	45,406	45,910	104	29	11,390	1,347	761	4,580,380	280
31,807	5,678	35.2	28,287	9,198	33,686	33,998	168	1	6,013	1,473	1,146	2,686,982	281
21,441	3,365	40.7	11,548	13,258	22,613	22,739	0	0	2,739	3,713	1,244	6,348,798	282
25,283	3,334	20.9	18,757	9,860	26,411	26,533	999	0	4,346	2,367	1,135	1,778,874	283
13,403	2,683	20.0	13,844	2,242	14,241	14,427	0	0	2,975	691	0	250,052	284
5,272	12,281	38.3	17,553	†	9,568	9,395	303	1,708	†	†	†	120,675	285
14,024	2,547	21.3	13,589	2,982	14,711	15,006	0	0	2,798	544	230	484,654	286
19,462	2,395	14.4	17,260	4,597	19,847	20,357	69	0	3,708	1,135	216	782,075	287
7,183	8,953	40.8	16,136	†	10,868	10,189	1,686	1,612	†	†	†	142,702	288
28,903	4,068	21.8	24,866	8,105	29,517	30,445	15	4	4,928	1,660	719	917,962	289
17,487	5,242	30.8	20,262	2,467	20,464	19,535	0	0	4,012	794	32	360,306	290
14,372	6,687	45.8	17,073	3,986	17,156	16,987	0	0	2,991	1,060	260	426,525	291
26,728	3,658	17.4	21,664	8,722	27,696	28,107	0	0	4,410	1,811	1,054	1,717,925	292
9,040	31,909	50.3	40,949	†	20,270	19,753	617	2,049	†	†	†	298,690	293
15,624	639	32.2	13,859	2,404	15,248	15,871	0	0	2,848	652	284	547,391	294
9,865	8,985	34.8	18,850	†	12,544	12,882	366	1,221	†	†	†	97,736	295
4,789	15,758	57.9	20,547	†	9,761	10,080	885	3,042	†	†	†	123,655	296
9,899	18,092	45.0	27,991	†	15,721	15,973	397	1,944	†	†	†	153,600	297
3,358	11,754	74.7	15,112	†	7,095	7,304	705	1,072	†	†	†	63,103	298
9,329	18,979	91.9	28,308	†	16,734	15,701	885	3,422	†	†	†	169,570	299
17,288	40,988	83.9	58,276	†	31,241	31,049	1,237	4,672	†	†	†	400,773	300
19,234	50,161	64.1	69,395	†	34,674	36,075	2,224	4,409	†	†	†	422,333	301
3,952	11,845	71.6	15,797	†	7,952	7,929	151	1,015	†	†	†	68,954	302
4,591	14,752	70.8	19,343	†	9,540	9,544	237	1,608	†	†	†	86,317	303

See notes at end of table.

Table 312.20. Selected statistics for degree-granting postsecondary institutions enrolling more than 15,000 students in 2014, by selected institution and student characteristics: Selected years, 1990 through 2013–14—Continued

Line number	Institution	State	Control[1]	Level	Total fall enrollment					Fall enrollment, 2014		
											Sex	
					Fall 1990	Fall 2000	Fall 2010	Fall 2012	Fall 2013	Total	Male	Female
1	2	3	4	5	6	7	8	9	10	11	12	13
304	Sam Houston State University	TX	Public	4-year	12,753	12,358	17,291	18,461	19,210	19,573	7,710	11,863
305	San Antonio College	TX	Public	2-year	20,083	19,253	25,269	23,134	23,004	21,280	8,830	12,450
306	San Jacinto Community College	TX	Public	2-year	9,424	10,507	28,549	28,721	28,385	27,911	12,350	15,561
307	South Texas College	TX	Public	4-year	†	11,319	27,692	30,824	31,232	30,180	13,050	17,130
308	Tarrant County College District	TX	Public	2-year	28,161	26,868	49,108	50,439	50,771	50,595	21,176	29,419
309	Texas A & M University, College Station	TX	Public	4-year	41,171	44,026	49,129	50,627	55,697	61,642	32,365	29,277
310	Texas State University	TX	Public	4-year	20,940	22,423	32,572	34,225	35,546	36,739	15,887	20,852
311	Texas Tech University	TX	Public	4-year	25,363	24,558	31,637	32,467	33,111	35,158	19,006	16,152
312	Texas Woman's University	TX	Public	4-year	9,850	8,404	14,180	15,168	15,058	15,071	1,750	13,321
313	University of Houston	TX	Public	4-year	33,115	32,123	38,752	40,747	39,540	40,914	20,730	20,184
314	University of North Texas	TX	Public	4-year	27,160	27,054	36,305	37,950	38,315	36,486	17,189	19,297
315	University of Texas at Arlington	TX	Public	4-year	24,782	20,424	32,975	33,239	33,329	39,740	16,007	23,733
316	University of Texas at Austin	TX	Public	4-year	49,617	49,996	51,195	52,186	52,059	51,313	25,249	26,064
317	University of Texas at Dallas	TX	Public	4-year	8,558	10,945	17,128	19,727	21,193	23,095	13,104	9,991
318	University of Texas at El Paso	TX	Public	4-year	16,524	15,224	22,106	22,749	23,003	23,079	10,622	12,457
319	University of Texas at San Antonio	TX	Public	4-year	15,489	18,830	30,258	30,474	28,623	28,628	14,537	14,091
320	University of Texas, Pan American	TX	Public	4-year	12,337	12,759	18,744	19,302	20,053	21,015	9,149	11,866
321	Brigham Young University, Provo	UT	PrivNp	4-year	31,662	32,554	33,841	34,409	31,123	30,484	16,804	13,680
322	Salt Lake Community College	UT	Public	2-year	13,344	21,596	34,654	29,997	32,003	30,248	14,753	15,495
323	University of Utah	UT	Public	4-year	24,922	24,948	30,819	32,388	32,077	31,515	17,487	14,028
324	Utah State University	UT	Public	4-year	15,155	21,490	16,472	28,786	27,812	27,662	12,704	14,958
325	Utah Valley University	UT	Public	4-year	7,879	20,946	32,670	31,562	30,564	31,332	17,359	13,973
326	Weber State University	UT	Public	4-year	13,449	16,050	24,048	26,532	25,155	25,954	12,088	13,866
327	Western Governors University	UT	PrivNp	4-year	†	205	22,497	41,369	46,733	57,821	22,797	35,024
328	George Mason University	VA	Public	4-year	20,308	23,408	32,562	32,961	33,917	33,729	15,606	18,123
329	James Madison University	VA	Public	4-year	11,251	15,326	19,434	19,927	20,181	20,855	8,427	12,428
330	Liberty University	VA	PrivNp	4-year	18,533	6,192	56,625	74,372	77,338	81,459	33,130	48,329
331	Northern Virginia Community College	VA	Public	2-year	35,194	37,073	48,996	51,864	51,803	51,487	24,981	26,506
332	Old Dominion University	VA	Public	4-year	16,729	18,969	24,466	24,670	24,828	24,932	11,214	13,718
333	Tidewater Community College	VA	Public	2-year	17,726	20,184	31,308	30,134	28,999	27,646	11,211	16,435
334	University of Virginia, Main Campus	VA	Public	4-year	21,110	22,411	24,391	23,907	23,464	23,732	10,907	12,825
335	Virginia Commonwealth University	VA	Public	4-year	21,764	24,066	32,027	31,445	30,974	30,848	12,985	17,863
336	Virginia Polytechnic Institute and State University	VA	Public	4-year	25,568	27,869	31,006	31,087	31,205	31,224	17,983	13,241
337	University of Washington, Seattle Campus	WA	Public	4-year	33,854	36,139	42,451	43,485	43,762	44,784	21,415	23,369
338	Washington State University	WA	Public	4-year	18,412	20,492	26,287	27,679	27,642	28,686	13,958	14,728
339	Western Washington University	WA	Public	4-year	9,730	12,307	14,979	14,833	14,950	15,060	6,692	8,368
340	American Public University System	WV	PrivFp	4-year	†	†	39,296	58,115	55,422	57,539	35,530	22,009
341	West Virginia University	WV	Public	4-year	20,854	21,987	29,306	29,707	29,466	29,175	15,099	14,076
342	Madison Area Technical College	WI	Public	4-year	12,410	14,474	17,463	16,139	15,402	16,759	7,582	9,177
343	Milwaukee Area Technical College	WI	Public	2-year	21,600	14,296	19,827	18,118	17,961	16,712	7,330	9,382
344	University of Wisconsin, Madison	WI	Public	4-year	43,209	40,658	42,180	42,269	42,677	42,598	20,987	21,611
345	University of Wisconsin, Milwaukee	WI	Public	4-year	26,020	23,578	30,470	28,712	27,416	27,596	13,021	14,575

†Not applicable.

[1]"PrivNp" stands for private nonprofit. "PrivFp" stands for private for-profit.

[2]Includes private and some public institutions reporting total expenses and deductions under Financial Accounting Standards Board (FASB) reporting standards and public institutions reporting total expenses and deductions under Governmental Accounting Standards Board (GASB) 34/35 reporting standards.

[3]Combined enrollment of Black, Hispanic, Asian/Pacific Islander, American Indian/Alaska Native, and Two or more races students who are U.S. citizens or resident aliens as a percentage of total enrollment, excluding nonresident aliens.

[4]Includes less-than-1-year awards and 1- to less-than-4-year awards (excluding associate's degrees) conferred by degree-granting institutions.

Table 312.20. Selected statistics for degree-granting postsecondary institutions enrolling more than 15,000 students in 2014, by selected institution and student characteristics: Selected years, 1990 through 2013–14—Continued

Fall enrollment, 2014					Full-time-equivalent enrollment		Earned degrees/certificates conferred, 2013–14					Total expenditures and deductions, 2013–14 (in thousands)[2]	Line number
Attendance status		Percent minority[3]	Student level										
Full-time	Part-time		Under-graduate	Postbacca-laureate	Fall 2013	Fall 2014	Certificates[4]	Associate's	Bachelor's	Master's	Doctor's[5]		
14	15	16	17	18	19	20	21	22	23	24	25	26	27
14,265	5,308	42.9	16,819	2,754	16,090	16,321	0	0	3,310	900	56	295,006	304
4,659	16,621	71.9	21,280	†	11,491	10,239	449	1,579	†	†	†	151,368	305
7,087	20,824	69.9	27,911	†	14,615	14,078	1,898	2,944	†	†	†	215,909	306
9,650	20,530	97.1	30,180	0	18,776	17,935	2,008	2,919	130	0	0	160,108	307
15,764	34,831	57.3	50,595	†	28,617	27,458	2,156	4,771	†	†	†	374,426	308
53,817	7,825	33.1	47,093	14,549	51,467	56,855	0	0	9,847	2,478	1,439	2,545,468	309
28,860	7,879	46.7	32,177	4,562	31,071	31,958	0	0	6,013	1,265	89	564,061	310
29,850	5,308	34.7	28,632	6,526	30,145	31,897	31	0	5,222	1,353	528	758,510	311
8,832	6,239	53.4	9,680	5,391	10,943	11,210	6	0	1,967	1,759	202	191,112	312
29,743	11,171	67.5	33,037	7,877	32,855	34,162	0	0	6,372	2,081	755	985,826	313
26,798	9,688	47.1	29,758	6,728	31,570	30,553	0	0	6,315	1,633	277	599,078	314
19,941	19,799	53.8	29,883	9,857	24,793	27,685	69	0	6,737	2,586	220	546,203	315
46,993	4,320	47.5	39,523	11,790	49,432	48,690	1,037	0	9,398	3,095	1,378	2,506,218	316
17,592	5,503	55.3	14,300	8,795	17,983	19,694	0	0	2,799	2,937	181	526,115	317
14,392	8,687	90.7	19,817	3,262	17,692	17,815	0	0	3,181	993	142	408,220	318
22,230	6,398	70.3	24,285	4,343	24,540	24,713	0	0	4,537	1,219	106	502,587	319
14,600	6,415	96.2	17,858	3,157	16,450	17,105	0	0	2,758	715	20	277,247	320
26,476	4,008	12.9	27,163	3,321	28,674	28,036	0	0	6,492	1,036	225	984,399	321
7,894	22,354	26.9	30,248	†	16,506	15,399	646	3,782	†	†	†	206,562	322
22,994	8,521	21.7	23,907	7,608	26,637	26,359	0	0	5,092	1,823	711	3,451,261	323
16,953	10,709	12.3	24,271	3,391	20,932	21,180	59	1,000	3,548	927	115	596,696	324
16,296	15,036	16.3	31,163	169	21,723	22,358	85	2,280	2,825	52	0	267,943	325
11,330	14,624	25.6	25,316	638	16,789	17,215	58	1,999	2,356	272	0	217,240	326
57,821	0	25.4	44,499	13,322	46,733	57,821	0	0	6,312	4,284	0	272,948	327
21,962	11,767	43.9	22,349	11,380	26,138	26,407	0	0	4,967	2,988	441	767,009	328
19,123	1,732	18.1	19,144	1,711	19,226	19,795	0	0	4,027	820	24	458,816	329
38,303	43,156	33.2	49,744	31,715	52,244	55,032	188	996	7,275	7,423	333	539,232	330
18,742	32,745	59.0	51,487	†	30,478	29,736	1,796	5,578	†	†	†	318,462	331
16,977	7,955	43.5	20,115	4,817	20,002	20,058	0	0	3,944	1,084	190	412,745	332
10,491	17,155	51.5	27,646	†	17,375	16,251	1,129	2,946	†	†	†	188,367	333
21,640	2,092	28.6	16,483	7,249	21,988	22,432	22	0	3,697	1,651	919	2,523,244	334
25,031	5,817	42.1	23,661	7,187	27,186	27,286	34	0	4,741	1,605	749	953,830	335
28,504	2,720	23.9	24,247	6,977	29,453	29,512	0	49	5,732	1,573	590	1,249,337	336
39,171	5,613	42.3	30,672	14,112	40,406	41,323	0	0	7,549	3,436	1,328	4,475,911	337
24,243	4,443	29.5	23,867	4,819	25,180	25,976	167	0	5,054	731	438	1,017,526	338
13,565	1,495	24.0	14,152	908	14,042	14,152	66	0	3,170	267	0	272,310	339
3,551	53,988	39.9	46,997	10,542	23,953	24,652	322	1,906	4,898	3,740	0	254,554	340
25,612	3,563	13.5	22,563	6,612	27,196	26,972	0	0	4,268	1,533	566	979,127	341
4,983	11,776	23.8	16,698	61	9,291	9,733	2,105	1,372	0	0	0	210,765	342
5,261	11,451	54.3	16,712	†	9,837	9,106	1,271	1,523	†	†	†	265,772	343
38,149	4,449	17.1	30,694	11,904	40,056	39,858	0	0	6,700	2,025	1,497	2,545,739	344
21,421	6,175	26.5	22,674	4,922	23,826	23,817	0	0	3,960	1,227	228	532,329	345

[5]Includes Ph.D., Ed.D., and comparable degrees at the doctoral level, as well as such degrees as M.D., D.D.S., and law degrees that were formerly classified as first-professional degrees.
[6]Data for total enrollment in 1990 are for institutions of higher education, rather than degree-granting institutions.
[7]Beginning with enrollment data for fall 2013, totals for Arizona State University are for the Tempe campus and exclude data for the following four branch campuses, which are now reported separately: Downtown Phoenix, Skysong, West, and Polytechnic.

[8]Data for University of Phoenix, Arizona, and for University of Phoenix, California, include branch campuses previously reported separately.
NOTE: Degree-granting institutions grant associate's or higher degrees and participate in Title IV federal financial aid programs. Includes online and distance education courses.
SOURCE: U.S. Department of Education, National Center for Education Statistics, Integrated Postsecondary Education Data System (IPEDS), "Fall Enrollment Survey" (IPEDS-EF:90); Spring 2001 through Spring 2015, Fall Enrollment and Finance components; and Fall 2014, Completions component. (This table was prepared March 2016.)

Table 312.30. Enrollment and degrees conferred in degree-granting women's colleges, by selected characteristics and institution: Fall 2014 and 2013–14

Institution[1]	State	Enrollment, fall 2014							Degrees awarded to females, 2013–14			
		Total	Females	Percent female	Males, full-time	Females, full-time	Males, part-time	Females, part-time	Associate's	Bachelor's	Master's	Doctor's
1	2	3	4	5	6	7	8	9	10	11	12	13
Total................................	†	73,041	68,559	93.9	2,106	51,525	2,376	17,034	790	12,014	5,624	334
Judson College.....................	AL	378	366	96.8	2	264	10	102	15	45	†	†
Mills College	CA	1,542	1,402	90.9	120	1,262	20	140	†	249	215	13
Mount Saint Mary's University.	CA	3,292	2,968	90.2	205	2,304	119	664	180	503	181	28
Scripps College	CA	988	982	99.4	6	972	0	10	†	235	†	†
University of Saint Joseph	CT	2,565	2,284	89.0	120	1,151	161	1,133	†	256	470	55
Trinity Washington University....	DC	2,267	2,106	92.9	23	1,151	138	955	16	266	269	†
Agnes Scott College	GA	873	867	99.3	2	845	4	22	†	214	†	†
Brenau University	GA	2,789	2,418	86.7	187	1,458	184	960	2	373	313	5
Spelman College	GA	2,135	2,135	100.0	0	2,072	0	63	†	464	†	†
Wesleyan College	GA	711	687	96.6	7	533	17	154	†	98	47	†
Saint Mary's College	IN	1,519	1,518	99.9	0	1,501	1	17	†	284	†	†
Midway College	KY	1,140	948	83.2	134	717	58	231	143	218	50	†
Notre Dame of Maryland University......................	MD	2,764	2,388	86.4	92	802	284	1,586	†	323	318	66
Bay Path University...............	MA	2,587	2,460	95.1	63	1,683	64	777	49	372	377	†
Mount Holyoke College..........	MA	2,255	2,245	99.6	6	2,192	4	53	†	578	12	†
Simmons College..................	MA	4,802	4,408	91.8	82	2,216	312	2,192	†	477	964	76
Smith College	MA	2,989	2,927	97.9	45	2,846	17	81	†	670	143	9
Wellesley College	MA	2,323	2,262	97.4	0	2,177	61	85	†	605	†	†
College of Saint Benedict	MN	2,020	2,020	100.0	0	1,992	0	28	†	495	†	†
Saint Catherine University	MN	5,055	4,761	94.2	139	3,109	155	1,652	223	584	431	43
Cottey College	MO	269	269	100.0	0	267	0	2	101	19	†	†
Stephens College	MO	862	831	96.4	22	690	9	141	0	135	59	†
College of Saint Mary	NE	1,018	995	97.7	9	835	14	160	58	132	77	2
College of Saint Elizabeth	NJ	1,411	1,259	89.2	37	661	115	598	†	240	172	12
Barnard College...................	NY	2,573	2,568	99.8	0	2,537	5	31	†	583	†	†
College of New Rochelle..........	NY	3,740	3,323	88.9	296	2,460	121	863	†	691	252	†
Bennett College	NC	633	633	100.0	0	545	0	88	†	105	†	†
Meredith College	NC	1,886	1,856	98.4	18	1,684	12	172	†	344	105	†
Salem College	NC	1,118	1,062	95.0	21	781	35	281	†	193	51	†
Ursuline College	OH	1,236	1,129	91.3	35	533	72	596	†	200	212	3
Bryn Mawr College................	PA	1,709	1,629	95.3	68	1,561	12	68	†	317	103	18
Cedar Crest College..............	PA	1,531	1,417	92.6	45	719	69	698	†	253	30	†
Moore College of Art and Design	PA	453	450	99.3	2	417	1	33	†	98	14	†
Columbia College	SC	1,221	1,054	86.3	109	782	58	272	†	226	122	†
Converse College	SC	1,389	1,273	91.6	23	850	93	423	†	128	115	†
Hollins University	VA	770	730	94.8	12	616	28	114	†	127	85	†
Mary Baldwin College...........	VA	1,754	1,607	91.6	64	1,098	83	509	†	259	113	†
Sweet Briar College..............	VA	700	675	96.4	23	648	2	27	†	116	7	†
Alverno College	WI	2,389	2,314	96.9	57	1,615	18	699	3	346	153	†
Mount Mary University...........	WI	1,385	1,333	96.2	32	979	20	354	†	193	164	4

†Not applicable.

[1]Data are for colleges and universities identified by the Women's College Coalition as women's colleges in 2016. Excludes women's colleges whose IPEDS data are reported together with a coed institution or coordinate men's college. The following institutions were excluded for this reason: the Colorado Women's College of the University of Denver; Douglass Residential College of Rutgers University; and Russell Sage College of the Sage Colleges.

NOTE: The institutions in this table are all 4-year private nonprofit institutions. Degree-granting institutions grant associate's or higher degrees and participate in Title IV federal financial aid programs.
SOURCE: U.S. Department of Education, National Center for Education Statistics, Integrated Postsecondary Education Data System (IPEDS), Spring 2015, Fall Enrollment component; and Fall 2014, Completions component. (This table was prepared March 2016.)

Table 312.40. Enrollment and degrees conferred in degree-granting postsecondary institutions that serve large proportions of Hispanic undergraduate students, by institution level and control, percentage Hispanic, degree level, and other selected characteristics: Fall 2013 and 2012–13

State and institution	Level and control[1]	Total, all enrollment[2,3]	Enrollment, fall 2013 U.S. citizens and permanent residents only Total[3]	Hispanic[3]	Percent Hispanic[4]	Hispanic undergraduate	Hispanic postbaccalaureate	Degrees awarded to Hispanics, 2012–13 Associate's	Bachelor's	Master's	Doctor's[5]
1	2	3	4	5	6	7	8	9	10	11	12
Total, 50 states and District of Columbia...........	†	4,343,755	4,213,775	1,818,633	43.2	1,745,615	73,018	101,648	75,783	17,804	1,817
Total, 50 states, District of Columbia, and Puerto Rico...........	†	4,580,350	4,450,223	2,053,191	46.1	1,955,079	98,112	108,866	95,248	22,531	2,770
Alaska											
Charter College, Anchorage	5	2,191	2,191	730	33.3	730	†	137	3	†	†
Arizona											
Argosy University, Phoenix	5	743	743	137	18.4	60	77	0	7	17	7
Arizona College, Glendale...............	6	937	937	371	39.6	371	†	36	†	†	†
Arizona College, Mesa...............	5	162	162	61	37.7	61	†	0	0	†	†
Arizona State University, Downtown Phoenix	1	10,400	10,193	2,610	25.6	2,326	284	†	454	125	3
Arizona State University, West...............	1	3,661	3,596	941	26.2	880	61	†	200	26	5
Arizona Western College	2	8,000	7,450	5,264	70.7	5,264	†	340	†	†	†
Art Institute of Phoenix	5	1,045	1,045	488	46.7	488	†	12	30	†	†
Art Institute of Tucson	5	426	425	230	54.1	230	†	16	14	†	†
Brookline College, Phoenix	5	844	825	225	27.3	225	0	32	12	†	†
Brookline College, Tempe...............	6	223	222	80	36.0	80	†	10	†	†	†
Brookline College, Tucson	5	420	415	218	52.5	218	†	47	4	†	†
Brown Mackie College, Phoenix	5	637	637	204	32.0	204	†	38	1	†	†
Brown Mackie College, Tucson...............	5	684	684	288	42.1	288	†	94	5	†	†
Bryman School of Arizona	6	594	594	238	40.1	238	†	23	†	†	†
Carrington College, Mesa...............	6	691	691	234	33.9	234	†	9	†	†	†
Carrington College, Phoenix	5	676	676	375	55.5	375	†	2	1	†	†
Carrington College, Phoenix Westside	6	513	513	144	28.1	144	†	54	†	†	†
Carrington College, Tucson...............	6	440	440	278	63.2	278	†	6	†	†	†
Central Arizona College...............	2	6,445	6,427	1,979	30.8	1,979	†	130	†	†	†
Cochise College	2	4,453	4,426	1,904	43.0	1,904	†	430	†	†	†
College America, Phoenix	3	451	451	166	36.8	166	†	42	4	†	†
DeVry University, Arizona	5	1,565	1,546	372	24.1	319	53	7	70	18	†
Estrella Mountain Community College	2	8,832	8,801	4,265	48.5	4,265	†	269	†	†	†
Everest College, Mesa...............	5	367	367	106	28.9	106	†	8	1	†	†
Fortis College, Phoenix	6	271	271	102	37.6	102	†	2	†	†	†
GateWay Community College...............	2	6,440	6,291	2,176	34.6	2,176	†	121	†	†	†
Glendale Community College...............	2	20,872	20,530	6,759	32.9	6,759	†	351	†	†	†
ITT Technical Institute, Phoenix West...............	5	262	262	119	45.4	119	†	16	0	†	†
ITT Technical Institute, Tucson...............	5	409	409	159	38.9	159	†	47	18	†	†
Kaplan College, Phoenix	6	93	93	35	37.6	35	†	18	†	†	†
Phoenix College	2	12,676	12,617	5,839	46.3	5,839	†	412	†	†	†
Pima Community College...............	2	30,082	29,843	12,338	41.3	12,338	†	878	†	†	†
Pima Medical Institute, East Valley...............	6	511	511	146	28.6	146	†	2	†	†	†
Pima Medical Institute, Mesa...............	6	1,146	1,146	340	29.7	340	†	43	†	†	†
Pima Medical Institute, Tucson...............	5	1,726	1,722	685	39.8	685	†	79	15	†	†
Refrigeration School Inc.	6	621	620	178	28.7	178	†	8	†	†	†
South Mountain Community College	2	4,718	4,695	2,274	48.4	2,274	†	250	†	†	†
Southwest University of Visual Arts, Tucson...............	5	221	221	66	29.9	66	0	†	15	0	†
University of Arizona...............	1	40,621	37,257	8,871	23.8	7,801	1,070	†	1,163	172	53
University of Phoenix, Phoenix	5	4,480	4,361	1,144	26.2	893	251	0	105	71	†
University of Phoenix, Southern Arizona...............	5	1,849	1,794	857	47.8	734	123	†	74	38	†
Arkansas											
Bryan University	6	84	84	27	32.1	27	†	13	†	†	†
California											
Academy of Couture Art	5	21	16	4	25.0	4	†	0	1	†	†
Advanced College...............	6	227	227	159	70.0	159	†	9	†	†	†
Allan Hancock College...............	2	10,885	10,863	5,547	51.1	5,547	†	428	†	†	†
Alliant International University	3	4,201	3,981	1,224	30.7	630	594	†	10	75	56
American Career College, Anaheim	6	1,565	1,565	769	49.1	769	†	60	†	†	†
American Career College, Los Angeles	6	1,770	1,770	1,141	64.5	1,141	†	26	†	†	†
American Career College, Ontario	6	1,634	1,634	948	58.0	948	†	49	†	†	†
Angeles College	5	145	145	39	26.9	39	†	†	†	†	†
Antelope Valley College...............	2	14,262	14,245	6,421	45.1	6,421	†	345	†	†	†
Antioch University, Los Angeles...............	3	986	963	221	22.9	132	89	†	6	32	†
Antioch University, Santa Barbara	3	375	369	106	28.7	43	63	†	17	27	4
Argosy University, Inland Empire	5	704	704	280	39.8	175	105	0	11	21	4
Argosy University, Los Angeles	5	620	620	207	33.4	132	75	0	7	17	2
Argosy University, Orange County...............	5	673	673	214	31.8	119	95	0	12	18	10
Argosy University, San Diego	5	487	487	125	25.7	82	43	0	6	21	3
Art Institute of California, Argosy U., Hollywood...............	5	1,906	1,906	942	49.4	942	†	53	66	†	†
Art Institute of California, Argosy U., Inland Empire	5	2,307	2,307	1,315	57.0	1,315	†	139	77	†	†
Art Institute of California, Argosy U., Los Angeles...............	5	1,808	1,808	1,301	72.0	1,301	†	68	94	†	†
Art Institute of California, Argosy U., Orange County	5	1,761	1,761	1,020	57.9	1,020	†	58	54	†	†

See notes at end of table.

Table 312.40. Enrollment and degrees conferred in degree-granting postsecondary institutions that serve large proportions of Hispanic undergraduate students, by institution level and control, percentage Hispanic, degree level, and other selected characteristics: Fall 2013 and 2012–13—Continued

State and institution	Level and control[1]	Total, all enrollment[2,3]	Enrollment, fall 2013 — U.S. citizens and permanent residents only — Total[3]	Hispanic[3]	Percent Hispanic[4]	Hispanic under-graduate	Hispanic postbacca-laureate	Degrees awarded to Hispanics, 2012–13 — Associate's	Bachelor's	Master's	Doctor's[5]
1	2	3	4	5	6	7	8	9	10	11	12
Art Institute of California, Argosy U., Sacramento	5	1,185	1,184	474	40.0	474	†	21	22	†	†
Art Institute of California, Argosy U., San Diego	5	1,869	1,864	1,620	86.9	1,620	†	79	88	†	†
Art Institute of California, Argosy U., San Francisco	5	1,317	1,317	726	55.1	725	1	23	49	0	†
Art Institute of California, Argosy U., Silicon Valley	5	570	570	257	45.1	257	†	25	12	†	†
Ashdown College of Health Sciences	6	41	41	11	26.8	11	†	11	†	†	†
Azusa Pacific Online University	3	726	726	241	33.2	241	†	1	0	†	†
Bakersfield College	2	17,770	17,740	11,061	62.4	11,061	†	415	†	†	†
Barstow Community College	2	3,211	3,209	1,237	38.5	1,237	†	76	†	†	†
Berkeley City College	2	6,471	6,198	1,608	25.9	1,608	†	21	†	†	†
Bethesda University of California	3	353	174	78	44.8	77	1	†	11	0	†
Brandman University	3	7,746	7,739	1,923	24.8	1,132	791	16	289	216	1
Bristol University	5	82	82	21	25.6	20	1	2	0	0	†
Cabrillo College	2	13,666	13,602	5,229	38.4	5,229	†	415	†	†	†
California Baptist University	3	7,144	7,001	2,236	31.9	1,844	392	†	195	100	†
California Christian College	3	30	29	7	24.1	7	†	1	1	†	†
California College San Diego	3	762	762	214	28.1	214	†	117	26	†	†
California College San Diego, National City	3	203	203	104	51.2	104	†	10	0	†	†
California College San Diego, San Marcos	3	269	269	116	43.1	116	†	3	0	†	†
California Lutheran University	3	4,282	3,776	1,021	27.0	758	263	†	154	94	3
California State Polytechnic University, Pomona	1	22,501	21,451	8,621	40.2	8,137	484	†	1,262	79	†
California State University, Bakersfield	1	8,371	8,162	4,493	55.0	4,077	416	†	596	120	†
California State University, Channel Islands	1	5,140	5,132	2,254	43.9	2,206	48	†	372	19	†
California State University, Chico	1	16,356	15,693	3,951	25.2	3,792	159	†	479	37	†
California State University, Dominguez Hills	1	14,670	14,316	7,765	54.2	6,978	787	†	1,098	187	†
California State University, East Bay	1	14,526	13,247	3,667	27.7	3,319	348	†	461	96	0
California State University, Fresno	1	23,060	22,165	9,990	45.1	9,027	963	†	1,284	228	12
California State University, Fullerton	1	38,325	36,123	14,172	39.2	12,920	1,252	†	2,219	249	6
California State University, Long Beach	1	35,586	33,313	13,069	39.2	11,715	1,354	†	1,850	386	1
California State University, Los Angeles	1	23,258	21,841	13,708	62.8	12,220	1,488	†	1,552	356	2
California State University, Monterey Bay	1	5,732	5,584	2,402	43.0	2,273	129	†	373	35	†
California State University, Northridge	1	38,310	35,310	15,528	44.0	14,372	1,156	†	1,910	285	1
California State University, Sacramento	1	28,811	28,171	7,632	27.1	7,119	513	†	983	137	9
California State University, San Bernardino	1	18,398	17,243	10,260	59.5	9,381	879	†	1,360	156	4
California State University, San Marcos	1	11,300	11,043	4,363	39.5	4,218	145	†	482	35	†
California State University, Stanislaus	1	8,917	8,727	4,204	48.2	3,714	490	†	532	79	1
Cambridge Junior College, Yuba City	6	167	167	66	39.5	66	†	3	†	†	†
Canada College	2	6,620	6,558	3,327	50.7	3,327	†	171	†	†	†
Career Networks Institute	6	561	561	247	44.0	247	†	0	†	†	†
Carrington College California, Pleasant Hill	6	589	587	169	28.8	169	†	17	†	†	†
Carrington College California, Pomona	6	301	300	185	61.7	185	†	19	†	†	†
Carrington College California, San Jose	6	693	689	311	45.1	311	†	64	†	†	†
Carrington College California, San Leandro	6	521	520	215	41.3	215	†	28	†	†	†
Carrington College California, Stockton	6	465	465	197	42.4	197	†	27	†	†	†
Casa Loma College, Van Nuys	4	606	606	270	44.6	270	†	10	†	†	†
CBD College	4	230	230	89	38.7	89	†	4	†	†	†
Cerritos College	2	21,404	21,215	14,732	69.4	14,732	†	610	†	†	†
Cerro Coso Community College	2	4,523	4,515	1,524	33.8	1,524	†	38	†	†	†
Chabot College	2	13,142	13,073	4,718	36.1	4,718	†	199	†	†	†
Chaffey College	2	19,211	19,030	11,567	60.8	11,567	†	765	†	†	†
Charles R. Drew University of Medicine and Science	3	515	511	74	14.5	18	56	4	1	9	†
Charter College, Canyon Country	6	1,317	1,317	666	50.6	666	†	†	†	†	†
Citrus College	2	12,920	12,503	7,770	62.1	7,770	†	690	†	†	†
College of San Mateo	2	9,377	9,180	2,881	31.4	2,881	†	158	†	†	†
College of the Canyons	2	18,508	18,398	7,954	43.2	7,954	†	256	†	†	†
College of the Desert	2	9,259	9,066	6,196	68.3	6,196	†	361	†	†	†
College of the Sequoias	2	10,720	10,701	6,504	60.8	6,504	†	485	†	†	†
Community Christian College	4	60	59	28	47.5	28	†	4	†	†	†
Concorde Career College, Garden Grove	6	898	898	269	30.0	269	†	30	†	†	†
Concorde Career College, North Hollywood	6	925	925	503	54.4	503	†	29	†	†	†
Concorde Career College, San Bernardino	6	753	753	242	32.1	242	†	34	†	†	†
Concorde Career College, San Diego	6	895	895	276	30.8	276	†	21	†	†	†
Contra Costa College	2	6,865	6,723	2,596	38.6	2,596	†	171	†	†	†
Crafton Hills College	2	5,697	5,689	2,438	42.9	2,438	†	145	†	†	†
Cuesta College	2	9,256	9,220	2,657	28.8	2,657	†	128	†	†	†
Cuyamaca College	2	8,859	8,810	2,834	32.2	2,834	†	147	†	†	†
Cypress College	2	15,881	15,718	7,066	45.0	7,066	†	277	†	†	†
De Anza College	2	23,261	21,209	5,812	27.4	5,812	†	335	†	†	†
DeVry University, California	5	9,156	8,859	3,280	37.0	2,923	357	83	384	117	†
Dominican University of California	3	2,147	2,093	505	24.1	429	76	†	53	16	†
East Los Angeles College	2	36,606	35,887	25,866	72.1	25,866	†	1,141	†	†	†

See notes at end of table.

Table 312.40. Enrollment and degrees conferred in degree-granting postsecondary institutions that serve large proportions of Hispanic undergraduate students, by institution level and control, percentage Hispanic, degree level, and other selected characteristics: Fall 2013 and 2012–13—Continued

State and institution	Level and control[1]	Total, all enrollment[2,3]	Enrollment, fall 2013					Degrees awarded to Hispanics, 2012–13			
			U.S. citizens and permanent residents only								
			Total[3]	Hispanic[3]	Percent Hispanic[4]	Hispanic under-graduate	Hispanic postbacca-laureate	Associate's	Bachelor's	Master's	Doctor's[5]
1	2	3	4	5	6	7	8	9	10	11	12
El Camino College, Compton Center	2	7,693	7,677	3,784	49.3	3,784	†	137	†	†	†
El Camino Community College District	2	23,996	23,419	11,572	49.4	11,572	†	775	†	†	†
Empire College School of Business	6	419	419	159	37.9	159	†	32	†	†	†
Everest College, Anaheim	6	574	574	375	65.3	375	†	37	†	†	†
Everest College, City of Industry	6	1,029	1,028	835	81.2	835	†	9	†	†	†
Everest College, Los Angeles, Wilshire	6	232	232	124	53.4	124	†	6	†	†	†
Everest College, Ontario Metro	5	962	962	610	63.4	610	†	167	39	†	†
Everest College, Reseda	6	696	696	459	65.9	459	†	11	†	†	†
Everest College, San Bernardino	6	747	747	413	55.3	413	†	38	†	†	†
Everest College, West Los Angeles	6	422	422	218	51.7	218	†	32	†	†	†
Evergreen Valley College	2	9,211	9,180	3,903	42.5	3,903	†	202	†	†	†
Fashion Institute of Design & Merchandising, Los Angeles	5	3,459	3,014	858	28.5	858	†	418	33	†	†
Fashion Institute of Design & Merchandising, Orange County	6	214	206	65	31.6	65	†	†	†	†	†
Fashion Institute of Design & Merchandising, San Diego	6	169	163	63	38.7	63	†	10	†	†	†
Foothill College	2	14,814	13,612	3,421	25.1	3,421	†	122	†	†	†
Four-D College	6	641	641	233	36.3	233	†	†	†	†	†
Fremont College	5	344	344	203	59.0	203	†	78	6	†	†
Fresno City College	2	21,344	21,337	10,867	50.9	10,867	†	452	†	†	†
Fresno Pacific University	3	3,393	3,339	1,363	40.8	1,108	255	0	305	56	†
Fullerton College	2	24,301	24,021	12,709	52.9	12,709	†	632	†	†	†
Gavilan College	2	5,834	5,830	3,190	54.7	3,190	†	218	†	†	†
Glendale Community College	2	15,744	15,122	4,921	32.5	4,921	†	98	†	†	†
Golden West College	2	12,717	12,526	3,942	31.5	3,942	†	205	†	†	†
Grossmont College	2	18,618	18,045	5,887	32.6	5,887	†	273	†	†	†
Hartnell College	2	9,439	9,434	7,012	74.3	7,012	†	411	†	†	†
Heald College, Concord	6	1,503	1,503	443	29.5	443	†	117	†	†	†
Heald College, Fresno	6	1,791	1,791	1,144	63.9	1,144	†	190	†	†	†
Heald College, Hayward	6	1,249	1,249	504	40.4	504	†	230	†	†	†
Heald College, Modesto	6	1,091	1,091	550	50.4	550	†	97	†	†	†
Heald College, Salinas	6	1,076	1,068	680	63.7	680	†	233	†	†	†
Heald College, San Francisco	6	1,074	1,074	341	31.8	341	†	115	†	†	†
Heald College, San Jose	6	1,671	1,671	846	50.6	846	†	217	†	†	†
Heald College, Stockton	6	1,418	1,418	632	44.6	632	†	91	†	†	†
Holy Names University	3	1,343	1,311	347	26.5	263	84	†	36	16	†
Humboldt State University	1	8,293	8,206	2,302	28.1	2,232	70	†	235	11	†
Humphreys College, Stockton and Modesto	3	990	990	437	44.1	363	74	33	38	1	5
Imperial Valley College	2	7,701	7,696	7,443	96.7	7,443	†	639	†	†	†
Institute of Technology Inc.	6	1,989	1,989	739	37.2	739	†	166	†	†	†
InterCoast Colleges, Fairfield	6	118	118	32	27.1	32	†	†	†	†	†
InterCoast Colleges, Orange	6	134	134	53	39.6	53	†	22	†	†	†
Irvine Valley College	2	13,362	12,667	3,242	25.6	3,242	†	129	†	†	†
ITT Technical Institute, Clovis	5	439	439	223	50.8	223	†	81	19	†	†
ITT Technical Institute, Concord	5	258	258	65	25.2	65	†	33	3	†	†
ITT Technical Institute, Corona	5	479	479	202	42.2	202	†	64	0	†	†
ITT Technical Institute, Culver City	5	319	319	172	53.9	172	†	45	0	†	†
ITT Technical Institute, Lathrop	5	492	492	204	41.5	204	†	56	24	†	†
ITT Technical Institute, National City	5	1,209	1,209	397	32.8	397	†	145	26	†	†
ITT Technical Institute, Oakland	5	169	169	50	29.6	50	†	5	0	†	†
ITT Technical Institute, Orange	5	823	823	414	50.3	414	†	159	62	†	†
ITT Technical Institute, Oxnard	5	312	312	144	46.2	144	†	77	26	†	†
ITT Technical Institute, San Bernardino	5	730	730	349	47.8	349	†	150	57	†	†
ITT Technical Institute, San Dimas	5	534	534	313	58.6	313	†	78	40	†	†
ITT Technical Institute, Sylmar	5	557	557	303	54.4	303	†	120	42	†	†
ITT Technical Institute, Torrance	5	457	457	224	49.0	224	†	89	50	†	†
ITT Technical Institute, West Covina	5	148	148	104	70.3	104	†	105	4	†	†
Kaplan College, Bakersfield	6	512	511	402	78.7	402	†	36	†	†	†
Kaplan College, Chula Vista	6	299	299	225	75.3	225	†	28	†	†	†
Kaplan College, Fresno	6	312	312	224	71.8	224	†	36	†	†	†
Kaplan College, Modesto	6	490	490	271	55.3	271	†	21	†	†	†
Kaplan College, North Hollywood	6	792	791	400	50.6	400	†	0	†	†	†
Kaplan College, Palm Springs	6	362	362	250	69.1	250	†	20	†	†	†
Kaplan College, Riverside	6	234	234	148	63.2	148	†	12	†	†	†
Kaplan College, Sacramento	6	547	546	171	31.3	171	†	5	†	†	†
Kaplan College, San Diego	6	1,354	1,354	414	30.6	414	†	35	†	†	†
Kaplan College, Vista	6	896	896	378	42.2	378	†	10	†	†	†
La Sierra University	3	2,440	2,055	935	45.5	876	59	†	61	15	2
Las Positas College	2	8,631	8,497	2,401	28.3	2,401	†	111	†	†	†
Loma Linda University	3	4,693	4,259	796	18.7	366	430	28	71	76	44
Long Beach City College	2	24,020	23,864	12,624	52.9	12,624	†	310	†	†	†
Los Angeles City College	2	19,635	19,201	10,043	52.3	10,043	†	219	†	†	†

See notes at end of table.

Table 312.40. Enrollment and degrees conferred in degree-granting postsecondary institutions that serve large proportions of Hispanic undergraduate students, by institution level and control, percentage Hispanic, degree level, and other selected characteristics: Fall 2013 and 2012–13—Continued

State and institution	Level and control[1]	Total, all enrollment[2,3]	Enrollment, fall 2013					Degrees awarded to Hispanics, 2012–13			
			U.S. citizens and permanent residents only								
			Total[3]	Hispanic[3]	Percent Hispanic[4]	Hispanic under-graduate	Hispanic postbacca-laureate	Associate's	Bachelor's	Master's	Doctor's[5]
1	2	3	4	5	6	7	8	9	10	11	12
Los Angeles Co. College of Nursing and Allied Health....	2	185	185	71	38.4	71	†	35	†	†	†
Los Angeles Film School...	5	2,218	2,166	622	28.7	622	†	193	0	†	†
Los Angeles Harbor College.......................................	2	10,098	10,043	5,928	59.0	5,928	†	280	†	†	†
Los Angeles Mission College......................................	2	8,990	8,889	6,944	78.1	6,944	†	503	†	†	†
Los Angeles Music Academy......................................	6	148	107	31	29.0	31	†	3	†	†	†
Los Angeles Pierce College..	2	20,080	19,921	9,495	47.7	9,495	†	351	†	†	†
Los Angeles Southwest College..................................	2	7,864	7,847	2,985	38.0	2,985	†	83	†	†	†
Los Angeles Trade Technical College..........................	2	13,879	13,795	8,442	61.2	8,442	†	194	†	†	†
Los Angeles Valley College..	2	18,762	18,669	9,623	51.5	9,623	†	289	†	†	†
Los Medanos College...	2	8,525	8,489	3,161	37.2	3,161	†	242	†	†	†
Marymount California University...................................	3	1,037	892	402	45.1	401	1	27	12	†	†
Mayfield College..	6	329	329	203	61.7	203	†	†	†	†	†
Mendocino College...	2	3,729	3,729	915	24.5	915	†	77	†	†	†
Menlo College..	3	745	650	174	26.8	174	†	†	23	†	†
Merced College..	2	10,205	10,142	5,777	57.0	5,777	†	356	†	†	†
Merritt College...	2	5,887	5,823	1,554	26.7	1,554	†	61	†	†	†
MiraCosta College..	2	14,537	14,391	4,756	33.0	4,756	†	319	†	†	†
Modesto Junior College..	2	17,084	17,079	7,592	44.5	7,592	†	397	†	†	†
Monterey Peninsula College..	2	9,519	9,478	3,079	32.5	3,079	†	122	†	†	†
Moorpark College...	2	14,206	14,134	4,214	29.8	4,214	†	258	†	†	†
Moreno Valley College..	2	8,420	8,407	4,794	57.0	4,794	†	286	†	†	†
Mount Saint Mary's College..	3	3,274	3,252	1,852	56.9	1,593	259	81	186	68	1
Mount San Antonio College..	2	28,481	28,030	16,989	60.6	16,989	†	1,002	†	†	†
Mount San Jacinto Community College District..............	2	14,170	14,170	6,219	43.9	6,219	†	579	†	†	†
Mount Sierra College...	5	538	533	290	54.4	290	†	†	11	†	†
Napa Valley College	2	6,308	6,299	2,462	39.1	2,462	†	168	†	†	†
National Career College	6	43	43	21	48.8	21	†	0	†	†	†
National Hispanic University	5	813	809	469	58.0	265	204	1	33	7	†
National University	3	18,207	17,725	4,552	25.7	2,671	1,881	28	320	615	†
Newschool of Architecture and Design.........................	5	514	442	174	39.4	144	30	†	9	7	†
Norco College..	2	9,648	9,612	5,312	55.3	5,312	†	330	†	†	†
Notre Dame de Namur University	3	2,030	1,934	614	31.7	461	153	†	60	24	†
Orange Coast College	2	21,886	21,115	7,279	34.5	7,279	†	387	†	†	†
Oxnard College..	2	6,939	6,934	4,923	71.0	4,923	†	418	†	†	†
Pacific College..	5	277	277	152	54.9	152	†	6	0	†	†
Pacific Oaks College..	3	1,072	1,066	511	47.9	235	276	†	60	56	†
Pacific Union College...	3	1,647	1,621	486	30.0	486	0	31	33	0	†
Palo Alto University..	3	948	931	144	15.5	52	92	†	10	9	7
Palo Verde College	2	3,253	3,251	1,101	33.9	1,101	†	50	†	†	†
Palomar College...	2	24,665	24,424	9,301	38.1	9,301	†	522	†	†	†
Pasadena City College..	2	25,268	24,226	11,984	49.5	11,984	†	543	†	†	†
Pima Medical Institute, Chula Vista.............................	6	927	927	448	48.3	448	†	56	†	†	†
Pinnacle College..	6	147	147	48	32.7	48	†	0	†	†	†
Platt College, Los Angeles	5	608	608	425	69.9	425	†	162	20	†	†
Platt College, Ontario...	5	467	466	268	57.5	268	†	156	26	†	†
Platt College, Riverside	5	334	334	209	62.6	209	†	19	0	†	†
Platt College, San Diego	5	370	365	102	27.9	102	†	23	19	†	†
Porterville College	2	3,810	3,806	2,709	71.2	2,709	†	176	†	†	†
Reedley College...	2	13,807	13,806	7,904	57.3	7,904	†	346	†	†	†
Rio Hondo College	2	16,548	16,528	13,361	80.8	13,361	†	636	†	†	†
Riverside City College	2	18,165	17,875	10,162	56.9	10,162	†	626	†	†	†
Sacramento City College...	2	23,509	23,358	6,676	28.6	6,676	†	349	†	†	†
Saddleback College..	2	20,871	20,454	5,058	24.7	5,058	†	205	†	†	†
Sage College..	6	447	447	143	32.0	143	†	8	†	†	†
Saint Mary's College of California................................	3	4,257	4,181	1,021	24.4	798	223	1	144	35	0
San Bernardino Valley College....................................	2	12,329	12,300	7,816	63.5	7,816	†	453	†	†	†
San Diego City College...	2	16,310	16,157	7,763	48.0	7,763	†	252	†	†	†
San Diego Mesa College...	2	24,251	23,833	8,081	33.9	8,081	†	229	†	†	†
San Diego State University...	1	31,899	30,001	9,396	31.3	8,377	1,019	†	1,580	256	15
San Diego State University, Imperial Valley...................	1	883	879	831	94.5	697	134	†	193	12	†
San Francisco State University.....................................	1	29,905	27,538	7,236	26.3	6,668	568	†	1,163	188	4
San Joaquin Delta College	2	17,629	17,593	7,288	41.4	7,288	†	908	†	†	†
San Joaquin Valley College, Bakersfield	6	642	621	390	62.8	390	†	212	†	†	†
San Joaquin Valley College, Fresno	6	686	676	429	63.5	429	†	219	†	†	†
San Joaquin Valley College, Fresno Aviation	6	87	84	28	33.3	28	†	10	†	†	†
San Joaquin Valley College, Hesperia..........................	6	578	572	312	54.5	312	†	187	†	†	†
San Joaquin Valley College, Lancaster.........................	6	167	165	83	50.3	83	†	0	†	†	†
San Joaquin Valley College, Modesto	6	318	305	157	51.5	157	†	74	†	†	†
San Joaquin Valley College, Ontario	6	698	682	437	64.1	437	†	212	†	†	†
San Joaquin Valley College, Temecula.........................	6	393	370	153	41.4	153	†	62	†	†	†

See notes at end of table.

Table 312.40. Enrollment and degrees conferred in degree-granting postsecondary institutions that serve large proportions of Hispanic undergraduate students, by institution level and control, percentage Hispanic, degree level, and other selected characteristics: Fall 2013 and 2012–13—Continued

			Enrollment, fall 2013					Degrees awarded to Hispanics, 2012–13			
			U.S. citizens and permanent residents only								
State and institution	Level and control[1]	Total, all enrollment[2,3]	Total[3]	Hispanic[3]	Percent Hispanic[4]	Hispanic under-graduate	Hispanic postbacca-laureate	Associate's	Bachelor's	Master's	Doctor's[5]
1	2	3	4	5	6	7	8	9	10	11	12
San Joaquin Valley College, Visalia	6	1,616	1,574	696	44.2	696	†	298	†	†	†
San Jose City College	2	9,446	9,412	3,914	41.6	3,914	†	216	†	†	†
San Jose State University	1	31,278	28,585	7,186	25.1	6,391	795	†	1,105	304	†
Santa Ana College	2	28,598	28,390	15,801	55.7	15,801	†	989	†	†	†
Santa Barbara Business College, Bakersfield	5	543	542	412	76.0	412	†	153	0	†	†
Santa Barbara Business College, Santa Maria	5	188	188	142	75.5	142	†	43	0	†	†
Santa Barbara Business College, Ventura	5	349	341	202	59.2	201	1	65	1	0	†
Santa Barbara City College	2	19,331	17,855	6,573	36.8	6,573	†	497	†	†	†
Santa Monica College	2	29,999	26,746	11,389	42.6	11,389	†	362	†	†	†
Santa Rosa Junior College	2	22,094	22,058	6,608	30.0	6,608	†	416	†	†	†
Santiago Canyon College	2	10,939	10,900	5,175	47.5	5,175	†	417	†	†	†
Sierra College	2	18,374	18,212	4,575	25.1	4,575	†	377	†	†	†
Skyline College	2	10,067	9,952	2,959	29.7	2,959	†	162	†	†	†
Solano Community College	2	9,583	9,553	2,447	25.6	2,447	†	249	†	†	†
Sonoma State University	1	9,120	8,968	2,232	24.9	2,144	88	†	237	25	†
South Coast College	6	374	372	132	35.5	132	†	8	†	†	†
Southern California Institute of Architecture	3	493	279	63	22.6	44	19	†	13	7	†
Southern California Institute of Technology	5	496	496	245	49.4	245	†	0	18	†	†
Southwestern College	2	19,591	19,547	10,471	53.6	10,471	†	479	†	†	†
Stanbridge College	5	963	963	312	32.4	312	†	23	0	0	†
Taft College	2	5,444	5,440	2,774	51.0	2,774	†	166	†	†	†
United Education Institute, Huntington Park	6	2,732	2,729	1,917	70.2	1,917	†	24	†	†	†
United States University	5	282	275	155	56.4	94	61	†	33	9	†
University of Antelope Valley	5	804	804	369	45.9	363	6	49	12	1	†
University of California, Merced	1	6,195	5,927	2,646	44.6	2,598	48	†	274	2	3
University of California, Riverside	1	21,207	19,818	7,098	35.8	6,785	313	†	1,319	57	13
University of California, Santa Barbara	1	22,225	20,859	5,235	25.1	4,968	267	†	1,190	51	29
University of California, Santa Cruz	1	17,203	16,801	5,025	29.9	4,839	186	†	797	36	14
University of La Verne	3	8,796	7,898	3,912	49.5	2,724	1,188	0	478	272	38
University of Phoenix, Bay Area Campus	5	1,655	1,616	420	26.0	364	56	†	25	13	†
University of Phoenix, Central Valley	5	2,725	2,674	1,283	48.0	1,141	142	†	101	41	†
University of Phoenix, Sacramento Valley Campus	5	3,421	3,342	801	24.0	684	117	†	64	27	†
University of Phoenix, San Diego	5	6,122	6,034	2,527	41.9	2,270	257	0	194	55	†
University of Phoenix, Southern California	5	9,954	9,744	4,285	44.0	3,760	525	†	443	117	†
University of Redlands	3	5,147	5,083	1,516	29.8	1,033	483	†	130	114	1
University of the West	3	362	146	48	32.9	39	9	†	2	1	0
Vanguard University of Southern California	3	2,415	2,398	818	34.1	760	58	0	103	13	†
Ventura College	2	12,908	12,881	7,169	55.7	7,169	†	531	†	†	†
Victor Valley College	2	11,504	11,498	5,436	47.3	5,436	†	404	†	†	†
West Coast Ultrasound Institute	6	796	796	309	38.8	309	†	0	†	†	†
West Hills College, Coalinga	2	3,055	2,997	1,843	61.5	1,843	†	130	†	†	†
West Hills College, Lemoore	2	4,102	4,088	2,264	55.4	2,264	†	145	†	†	†
West Los Angeles College	2	10,767	10,637	4,567	42.9	4,567	†	128	†	†	†
West Valley College	2	9,636	9,566	2,299	24.0	2,299	†	136	†	†	†
Westwood College, Anaheim	5	772	772	267	34.6	267	†	11	157	†	†
Westwood College, Inland Empire	5	979	974	439	45.1	439	†	12	154	†	†
Westwood College, Los Angeles	5	672	672	228	33.9	228	0	16	144	8	†
Westwood College, South Bay	5	571	571	184	32.2	184	†	6	84	†	†
Whittier College	3	2,339	2,259	905	40.1	705	200	†	125	23	30
Woodbury University	3	1,607	1,317	441	33.5	397	44	†	72	39	†
Woodland Community College	2	2,641	2,640	1,309	49.6	1,309	†	69	†	†	†
Wyotech, Fremont	6	1,199	1,198	435	36.3	435	†	9	†	†	†
Wyotech, Long Beach	6	1,400	1,400	836	59.7	836	†	19	†	†	†
Yuba College	2	6,874	6,873	2,057	29.9	2,057	†	125	†	†	†
Colorado											
Academy of Natural Therapy Inc.	6	69	69	27	39.1	27	†	1	†	†	†
Adams State University	1	3,211	3,211	862	26.8	727	135	33	92	35	†
Aims Community College	2	4,955	4,947	1,548	31.3	1,548	†	128	†	†	†
Anthem College, Denver	6	207	207	52	25.1	52	†	19	†	†	†
Art Institute of Colorado	5	1,794	1,794	457	25.5	457	†	24	37	†	†
CollegeAmerica, Denver	3	497	497	165	33.2	165	†	33	5	†	†
CollegeAmerica, Fort Collins	3	159	159	44	27.7	44	†	10	3	†	†
CollegeAmerica, Colorado Springs South	3	31	31	9	29.0	9	†	0	0	†	†
Colorado Heights University	3	375	192	99	51.6	98	1	†	5	0	†
Colorado State University, Pueblo	1	7,089	6,964	1,724	24.8	1,625	99	†	196	19	†
Community College of Denver	2	10,432	9,904	3,140	31.7	3,140	†	121	†	†	†
Everest College, Aurora	6	383	383	135	35.2	135	†	12	†	†	†
Everest College, Thornton	6	371	371	167	45.0	167	†	17	†	†	†
Heritage College, Denver	6	466	466	168	36.1	168	†	111	†	†	†

See notes at end of table.

Table 312.40. Enrollment and degrees conferred in degree-granting postsecondary institutions that serve large proportions of Hispanic undergraduate students, by institution level and control, percentage Hispanic, degree level, and other selected characteristics: Fall 2013 and 2012–13—Continued

| | | | Enrollment, fall 2013 | | | | | Degrees awarded to Hispanics, 2012–13 | | | |
| | | | U.S. citizens and permanent residents only | | | | | | | | |
State and institution	Level and control[1]	Total, all enrollment[2,3]	Total[3]	Hispanic[3]	Percent Hispanic[4]	Hispanic under-graduate	Hispanic postbacca-laureate	Associate's	Bachelor's	Master's	Doctor's[5]
1	2	3	4	5	6	7	8	9	10	11	12
Institute of Business and Medical Careers	6	258	258	84	32.6	84	†	32	†	†	†
Intellitec College, Grand Junction	6	536	536	172	32.1	172	†	61	†	†	†
ITT Technical Institute, Westminster	5	218	218	58	26.6	58	†	26	6	†	†
Lamar Community College	2	902	867	242	27.9	242	†	16	†	†	†
Lincoln College of Technology, Denver	6	1,262	1,262	390	30.9	390	†	44	†	†	†
Otero Junior College	2	1,449	1,404	440	31.3	440	†	59	†	†	†
Pima Medical Institute, Denver	6	951	951	381	40.1	381	†	17	†	†	†
Pima Medical Institute, South Denver	6	211	211	92	43.6	92	†	0	†	†	†
Pueblo Community College	2	6,718	6,692	2,011	30.1	2,011	†	213	†	†	†
Trinidad State Junior College	2	1,791	1,768	743	42.0	743	†	81	†	†	†
Connecticut											
Capital Community College	2	4,168	4,164	1,272	30.5	1,272	†	117	†	†	†
Housatonic Community College	2	5,813	5,795	1,600	27.6	1,600	†	132	†	†	†
Norwalk Community College	2	6,556	6,414	2,220	34.6	2,220	†	140	†	†	†
Sanford-Brown College, Farmington	6	62	62	18	29.0	18	†	18	†	†	†
Florida											
Acupuncture and Massage College	5	173	167	94	56.3	19	75	†	16	16	†
Adventist University of Health Sciences	3	2,293	2,282	518	22.7	497	21	56	44	1	†
AI Miami International University of Art and Design	5	3,208	3,204	2,740	85.5	2,699	41	84	278	16	†
American Institute	5	269	269	122	45.4	122	†	19	0	†	†
American InterContinental University, South Florida	5	164	164	53	32.3	51	2	6	46	18	†
American Medical Academy	6	343	343	278	81.0	278	†	21	†	†	†
Anthem College, Orlando	6	491	491	248	50.5	248	†	11	†	†	†
Art Institute of Fort Lauderdale	5	1,924	1,922	898	46.7	898	†	119	112	†	†
Atlantic Institute of Oriental Medicine	3	142	142	49	34.5	11	38	†	6	6	†
Barry University	3	9,030	8,517	2,684	31.5	1,389	1,295	†	297	253	40
Broward College	1	43,883	42,699	15,380	36.0	15,380	†	1,935	80	†	†
Brown Mackie College, Miami	5	953	953	274	28.8	274	†	74	10	†	†
Carlos Albizu University, Miami	3	991	948	783	82.6	250	533	†	94	139	19
CBT College, Cutler Bay	6	174	174	99	56.9	99	†	36	†	†	†
Chamberlain College of Nursing, Florida	5	649	633	195	30.8	195	†	†	5	†	†
City College, Altamonte Springs	4	425	425	133	31.3	133	†	19	†	†	†
City College, Hollywood	4	126	126	40	31.7	40	†	0	†	†	†
City College, Miami	3	283	283	175	61.8	175	†	70	9	†	†
College of Business and Technology, Flagler	6	323	323	322	99.7	322	†	50	†	†	†
College of Business and Technology, Hialeah	6	178	178	176	98.9	176	†	60	†	†	†
College of Business and Technology, Kendall	5	127	125	109	87.2	109	†	34	0	†	†
College of Business and Technology, Miami Gardens	5	54	54	46	85.2	46	†	3	0	†	†
Concorde Career Institute, Tampa	6	454	454	126	27.8	126	†	7	†	†	†
Dade Medical College, Hollywood	6	303	303	85	28.1	85	†	22	†	†	†
Dade Medical College, Homestead	6	309	309	230	74.4	230	†	76	†	†	†
Dade Medical College, Miami	5	1,083	1,083	950	87.7	950	†	200	0	†	†
Dade Medical College, Miami Lakes	6	607	607	397	65.4	397	†	129	†	†	†
DeVry University, Florida	5	3,252	3,143	1,064	33.9	806	258	24	162	99	†
Digital Media Arts College	5	300	300	79	26.3	75	4	†	2	1	†
Edison State College	1	15,423	15,192	3,920	25.8	3,920	†	479	50	†	†
Everest Institute, Kendall	6	461	461	322	69.8	322	†	37	†	†	†
Everest Institute, North Miami	6	768	768	233	30.3	233	†	8	†	†	†
Everest University, Tampa	5	770	770	254	33.0	249	5	43	11	4	†
Florida Career College, Miami	5	5,818	5,818	1,923	33.1	1,923	†	181	29	†	†
Florida College of Natural Health, Miami	6	201	198	137	69.2	137	†	32	†	†	†
Florida College of Natural Health, Pompano Beach	6	262	262	88	33.6	88	†	13	†	†	†
Florida International University	1	47,663	44,283	30,223	68.2	26,578	3,645	55	5,007	1,333	128
Florida National University, Main Campus	5	2,448	2,322	2,182	94.0	2,157	25	399	91	5	†
Florida Technical College	5	4,330	4,328	2,399	55.4	2,399	†	153	0	†	†
Fortis College, Cutler Bay	5	203	203	106	52.2	106	†	0	†	†	†
Fortis College, Miami	6	88	88	84	95.5	84	†	74	†	†	†
Fortis Institute, Miami	6	130	130	103	79.2	103	†	12	†	†	†
Heritage Institute, Fort Myers	6	614	614	165	26.9	165	†	97	†	†	†
Hillsborough Community College	2	26,590	25,876	7,608	29.4	7,608	†	829	†	†	†
Hodges University	3	2,078	2,078	713	34.3	661	52	81	69	17	†
Institute of Technical Arts	6	263	263	96	36.5	96	†	†	†	†	†
International Academy of Design and Technology, Orlando	5	348	348	121	34.8	121	†	9	52	†	†
ITT Technical Institute, Fort Lauderdale	5	531	531	140	26.4	140	†	56	14	†	†
ITT Technical Institute, Miami	5	417	417	301	72.2	301	†	125	57	†	†
ITT Technical Institute, Orlando	5	377	377	131	34.7	131	†	15	0	†	†
ITT Technical Institute, Tampa	5	463	463	120	25.9	120	†	37	6	†	†
Johnson & Wales University, North Miami	3	1,952	1,710	544	31.8	544	†	64	52	†	†
Jose Maria Vargas University	5	159	155	155	100.0	151	4	0	0	5	†

See notes at end of table.

Table 312.40. Enrollment and degrees conferred in degree-granting postsecondary institutions that serve large proportions of Hispanic undergraduate students, by institution level and control, percentage Hispanic, degree level, and other selected characteristics: Fall 2013 and 2012–13—Continued

State and institution	Level and control[1]	Total, all enrollment[2,3]	Enrollment, fall 2013 U.S. citizens and permanent residents only — Total[3]	Hispanic[3]	Percent Hispanic[4]	Hispanic undergraduate	Hispanic postbaccalaureate	Degrees awarded to Hispanics, 2012–13 — Associate's	Bachelor's	Master's	Doctor's[5]
1	2	3	4	5	6	7	8	9	10	11	12
Keiser University, Fort Lauderdale	3	17,129	17,050	5,265	30.9	5,033	232	953	192	47	1
Le Cordon Bleu College of Culinary Arts, Miami	6	721	721	311	43.1	311	†	258	†	†	†
Lincoln Technical Institute, Fern Park	6	231	231	64	27.7	64	†	0	†	†	†
Management Resources Institute	6	822	819	729	89.0	729	†	55	†	†	†
Medvance Institute, West Palm	6	365	365	97	26.6	97	†	10	†	†	†
Miami Dade College	1	66,298	62,610	45,853	73.2	45,853	†	7,074	495	†	†
Millennia Atlantic University	5	112	55	47	85.5	28	19	1	4	14	†
Northwood University, Florida	3	646	454	117	25.8	117	0	0	18	2	†
Nova Southeastern University	3	25,670	24,747	6,586	26.6	1,693	4,893	0	482	818	299
Palm Beach State College	1	29,763	29,297	7,951	27.1	7,951	†	1,044	41	†	†
Polytechnic University of Puerto Rico, Miami	3	120	120	119	99.2	62	57	†	14	25	†
Polytechnic University of Puerto Rico, Orlando	3	125	125	123	98.4	80	43	†	19	14	†
Professional Hands Institute	6	38	38	38	100.0	38	†	†	†	†	†
Professional Training Centers	5	801	801	766	95.6	766	†	160	0	†	†
Remington College, Tampa	3	189	189	59	31.2	59	†	4	1	†	†
SABER College	4	544	544	483	88.8	483	†	132	†	†	†
Saint John Vianney College Seminary	3	94	78	31	39.7	28	3	†	7	†	†
Saint Thomas University	3	2,315	1,996	1,036	51.9	472	564	†	123	77	96
Sanford-Brown Institute, Orlando	6	107	106	44	41.5	44	†	25	†	†	†
South Florida State College	1	2,699	2,669	794	29.7	794	†	81	0	†	†
South University, Tampa	5	983	983	240	24.4	183	57	10	18	14	†
Southeastern College, Greenacres	6	1,157	1,157	326	28.2	326	†	80	†	†	†
Southern Technical College	6	1,502	1,502	408	27.2	408	†	140	†	†	†
Strayer University, Florida	5	2,973	2,945	747	25.4	522	225	17	47	32	†
Trinity International University, Florida	3	347	346	158	45.7	126	32	†	12	9	†
University of Miami	3	16,935	14,305	3,790	26.5	2,637	1,153	†	621	235	131
University of Phoenix, Central Florida	5	1,560	1,524	392	25.7	342	50	†	43	19	†
University of Phoenix, South Florida	5	1,364	1,251	503	40.2	405	98	†	60	26	†
University of Southernmost Florida	5	103	103	74	71.8	71	3	4	†	†	†
Valencia College	1	42,180	41,545	14,678	35.3	14,678	†	2,017	2	†	†
Georgia											
Interactive College of Technology, Gainesville	6	39	39	23	59.0	23	†	0	†	†	†
Illinois											
City Colleges of Chicago, Harold Washington College	2	9,036	9,002	3,489	38.8	3,489	†	222	†	†	†
City Colleges of Chicago, Harry S Truman College	2	11,800	11,797	4,936	41.8	4,936	†	134	†	†	†
City Colleges of Chicago, Richard J. Daley College	2	9,384	9,383	6,724	71.7	6,724	†	229	†	†	†
City Colleges of Chicago, Wilbur Wright College	2	12,640	12,623	7,172	56.8	7,172	†	381	†	†	†
College of Lake County	2	17,685	17,685	6,114	34.6	6,114	†	256	†	†	†
Coyne College	6	590	590	173	29.3	173	†	25	†	†	†
Dominican University	3	3,470	3,386	1,035	30.6	833	202	†	109	59	0
Elgin Community College	2	11,285	11,237	4,318	38.4	4,318	†	243	†	†	†
Fox College	6	387	387	145	37.5	145	†	71	†	†	†
Illinois Institute of Art, Chicago	5	2,322	2,286	1,033	45.2	1,033	†	26	51	†	†
Illinois Institute of Art, Schaumburg	5	1,066	1,051	330	31.4	330	†	2	28	†	†
ITT Technical Institute, Arlington Heights	5	248	248	72	29.0	72	†	28	9	†	†
ITT Technical Institute, Oak Brook	5	336	336	114	33.9	114	†	36	13	†	†
Lexington College	3	55	54	16	29.6	16	†	1	6	†	†
Lincoln College of Technology, Melrose Park	6	617	617	302	48.9	302	†	123	†	†	†
Morton College	2	4,886	4,886	4,179	85.5	4,179	†	303	†	†	†
National Louis University	3	4,814	4,800	746	15.5	383	363	†	81	121	5
Northeastern Illinois University	1	10,821	10,364	3,489	33.7	3,202	287	†	404	67	†
Northwestern College, Chicago	6	430	430	118	27.4	118	†	35	†	†	†
Northwestern College, Southwestern	6	756	756	179	23.7	179	†	61	†	†	†
Robert Morris University, Illinois	3	3,233	3,173	831	26.2	762	69	174	175	50	†
Saint Augustine College	3	1,607	1,570	1,480	94.3	1,480	†	277	24	†	†
Saint Xavier University	3	4,252	4,235	832	19.6	712	120	†	87	30	†
Triton College	2	11,225	11,225	4,790	42.7	4,790	†	272	†	†	†
University of Illinois at Chicago	1	28,038	25,670	5,287	20.6	4,208	1,079	†	725	146	79
Waubonsee Community College	2	10,721	10,721	3,723	34.7	3,723	†	232	†	†	†
Indiana											
Calumet College of Saint Joseph	3	1,140	1,139	338	29.7	311	27	8	59	11	†
Kaplan College, Hammond	6	366	365	92	25.2	92	†	4	†	†	†
Kansas											
Dodge City Community College	2	1,785	1,776	629	35.4	629	†	52	†	†	†
Donnelly College	3	474	446	201	45.1	201	†	18	4	†	†
Garden City Community College	2	1,997	1,990	796	40.0	796	†	77	†	†	†
Northwest Kansas Technical College	2	626	621	141	22.7	141	†	15	†	†	†
Seward County Community College and Area Technical School	2	1,857	1,838	902	49.1	902	†	70	†	†	†

See notes at end of table.

Table 312.40. Enrollment and degrees conferred in degree-granting postsecondary institutions that serve large proportions of Hispanic undergraduate students, by institution level and control, percentage Hispanic, degree level, and other selected characteristics: Fall 2013 and 2012–13—Continued

State and institution	Level and control[1]	Total, all enrollment[2,3]	Enrollment, fall 2013 — U.S. citizens and permanent residents only — Total[3]	Hispanic[3]	Percent Hispanic[4]	Hispanic under-graduate	Hispanic postbacca-laureate	Degrees awarded to Hispanics, 2012–13 — Associate's	Bachelor's	Master's	Doctor's[5]
1	2	3	4	5	6	7	8	9	10	11	12
Louisiana											
Saint Joseph Seminary College	3	133	133	42	31.6	42	†	†	7	†	†
Massachusetts											
Benjamin Franklin Institute of Technology	3	482	472	119	25.2	119	†	11	0	†	†
Cambridge College	3	3,114	2,976	591	19.9	299	292	†	68	103	0
New England Institute of Art	5	779	776	274	35.3	274	†	5	34	†	†
Northern Essex Community College	2	7,352	7,300	2,649	36.3	2,649	†	148	†	†	†
Pine Manor College	3	346	254	58	22.8	55	3	0	11	0	†
Salter College, Chicopee	6	70	70	29	41.4	29	†	19	†	†	†
Salter College, West Boylston	6	699	699	212	30.3	212	†	21	†	†	†
Springfield Technical Community College	2	6,792	6,743	1,753	26.0	1,753	†	148	†	†	†
Urban College of Boston	4	762	762	430	56.4	430	†	25	†	†	†
Nevada											
Art Institute of Las Vegas	5	1,097	1,089	720	66.1	720	†	26	23	†	†
College of Southern Nevada	1	34,177	33,767	9,610	28.5	9,610	†	551	1	†	†
Everest College, Henderson	6	915	915	314	34.3	314	†	40	†	†	†
Kaplan College, Las Vegas	6	994	991	278	28.1	278	†	23	†	†	†
Pima Medical Institute, Las Vegas	6	1,018	1,018	315	30.9	315	†	8	†	†	†
University of Phoenix, Las Vegas	5	2,180	2,159	514	23.8	437	77	†	31	18	†
New Jersey											
Bergen Community College	2	15,882	14,736	4,879	33.1	4,879	†	560	†	†	†
Berkeley College, Woodland Park	5	3,671	3,644	1,650	45.3	1,650	†	97	197	†	†
Cumberland County College	2	3,919	3,915	1,070	27.3	1,070	†	98	†	†	†
DeVry University, New Jersey	5	1,725	1,684	464	27.6	412	52	28	40	6	†
Eastern International College, Belleville	6	216	216	93	43.1	93	†	15	†	†	†
Eastern International College, Jersey City	6	222	222	114	51.4	114	†	11	†	†	†
Eastwick College, Hackensack	6	324	324	168	51.9	168	†	†	†	†	†
Essex County College	2	12,175	11,220	3,216	28.7	3,216	†	337	†	†	†
Fairleigh Dickinson University, Metropolitan	3	8,546	7,808	2,220	28.4	1,896	324	38	189	57	0
Felician College	3	1,933	1,891	463	24.5	409	54	2	54	5	0
Hudson County Community College	2	9,036	9,001	5,487	61.0	5,487	†	460	†	†	†
Kean University	1	14,404	14,209	3,559	25.0	3,179	380	†	545	80	0
Middlesex County College	2	12,602	12,339	3,842	31.1	3,842	†	266	†	†	†
Montclair State University	1	19,464	18,931	4,555	24.1	3,947	608	†	656	111	1
New Jersey City University	1	8,442	8,337	2,961	35.5	2,450	511	†	397	87	0
Passaic County Community College	2	9,129	9,068	5,054	55.7	5,054	†	296	†	†	†
Pillar College	3	418	418	132	31.6	132	†	0	12	†	†
Rutgers University, Newark	1	11,212	10,450	2,111	20.2	1,754	357	†	368	61	39
Saint Peter's University	3	3,194	3,131	874	27.9	736	138	4	111	42	†
Union County College	2	11,969	11,607	4,502	38.8	4,502	†	206	†	†	†
University of Phoenix, Jersey City	5	455	436	147	33.7	147	†	†	5	†	†
William Paterson University of New Jersey	1	11,414	11,304	2,777	24.6	2,566	211	†	413	40	0
New Mexico											
Anamarc College, Santa Teresa	5	96	96	92	95.8	92	†	27	0	†	†
Brookline College, Albuquerque	5	272	271	205	75.6	205	†	37	5	†	†
Brown Mackie College, Albuquerque	5	780	780	356	45.6	356	†	90	0	†	†
Carrington College, Albuquerque	6	647	647	341	52.7	341	†	54	†	†	†
Central New Mexico Community College	2	28,891	27,995	13,899	49.6	13,899	†	1,445	†	†	†
Clovis Community College	2	3,596	3,596	1,087	30.2	1,087	†	122	†	†	†
Eastern New Mexico University, Main Campus	1	5,847	5,686	2,065	36.3	1,694	371	5	192	33	†
Eastern New Mexico University, Roswell	2	3,883	3,818	1,854	48.6	1,854	†	138	†	†	†
Eastern New Mexico University, Ruidoso	2	895	893	291	32.6	291	†	6	†	†	†
ITT Technical Institute, Albuquerque	5	476	476	206	43.3	206	†	77	24	†	†
Luna Community College	2	1,657	1,657	1,243	75.0	1,243	†	91	†	†	†
Mesalands Community College	2	697	689	309	44.8	309	†	33	†	†	†
National American University, Albuquerque	5	397	397	149	37.5	149	†	17	12	†	†
National American University, Albuquerque West	5	346	346	134	38.7	134	†	15	11	†	†
New Mexico Highlands University	1	3,690	3,457	2,009	58.1	1,366	643	0	229	163	†
New Mexico Institute of Mining and Technology	1	2,134	2,019	487	24.1	418	69	1	50	19	0
New Mexico Junior College	2	2,320	2,310	1,205	52.2	1,205	†	96	†	†	†
New Mexico State University, Alamogordo	2	2,458	2,409	903	37.5	903	†	83	†	†	†
New Mexico State University, Carlsbad	2	1,861	1,842	984	53.4	984	†	53	†	†	†
New Mexico State University, Dona Ana	2	8,837	8,558	6,394	74.7	6,394	†	720	†	†	†
New Mexico State University, Grants	2	970	959	449	46.8	449	†	43	†	†	†
New Mexico State University, Main Campus	1	16,765	15,629	8,496	54.4	7,315	1,181	15	1,193	249	22
Northern New Mexico College	1	1,681	1,679	1,170	69.7	1,159	11	66	52	†	†
Pima Medical Institute, Albuquerque	6	930	930	504	54.2	504	†	33	†	†	†
Santa Fe Community College	2	6,265	6,255	3,072	49.1	3,072	†	174	†	†	†
Santa Fe University of Art and Design	5	826	634	177	27.9	177	†	†	7	1	†

See notes at end of table.

Table 312.40. Enrollment and degrees conferred in degree-granting postsecondary institutions that serve large proportions of Hispanic undergraduate students, by institution level and control, percentage Hispanic, degree level, and other selected characteristics: Fall 2013 and 2012–13—Continued

State and institution	Level and control[1]	Total, all enrollment[2,3]	Total[3]	Hispanic[3]	Percent Hispanic[4]	Hispanic undergraduate	Hispanic postbacca-laureate	Associate's	Bachelor's	Master's	Doctor's[5]
1	2	3	4	5	6	7	8	9	10	11	12
Southwest University of Visual Arts, Albuquerque...........	5	224	224	105	46.9	105	†	†	6	†	†
University of New Mexico, Los Alamos......................	2	744	741	332	44.8	332	†	34	†	†	†
University of New Mexico, Main Campus.....................	1	28,592	27,529	11,740	42.6	10,011	1,729	†	1,286	326	104
University of New Mexico, Taos	2	1,802	1,796	1,204	67.0	1,204	†	24	†	†	†
University of New Mexico, Valencia County	2	2,245	2,230	1,438	64.5	1,438	†	134	†	†	†
University of Phoenix, Albuquerque........................	5	2,462	2,415	1,836	76.0	1,593	243	†	278	92	†
University of the Southwest	3	923	919	230	25.0	156	74	†	17	9	†
Western New Mexico University	1	3,560	3,507	1,922	54.8	1,691	231	66	92	37	†
New York											
Art Institute of New York City	6	1,158	1,158	727	62.8	727	†	130	†	†	†
ASA College	6	4,706	4,129	2,019	48.9	2,019	†	576	†	†	†
Berkeley College, New York...............................	5	4,596	3,778	1,346	35.6	1,346	†	81	215	†	†
Boricua College	3	1,118	1,118	932	83.4	875	57	143	132	20	†
Cochran School of Nursing...............................	4	79	79	21	26.6	21	†	8	†	†	†
College of Mount Saint Vincent	3	1,938	1,876	663	35.3	591	72	0	100	13	†
College of Westchester	5	1,197	1,197	527	44.0	527	†	89	31	†	†
Concordia College, New York	3	953	817	213	26.1	204	9	1	30	0	†
CUNY, Borough of Manhattan Community College	2	24,186	22,605	10,299	45.6	10,299	†	972	†	†	†
CUNY, Bronx Community College	2	11,368	11,106	7,221	65.0	7,221	†	830	†	†	†
CUNY, City College.....................................	1	15,331	13,999	4,843	34.6	4,165	678	†	656	170	1
CUNY, Hostos Community College........................	2	7,006	6,677	4,467	66.9	4,467	†	466	†	†	†
CUNY, Hunter College...................................	1	23,019	21,707	5,164	23.8	4,115	1,049	†	562	288	0
CUNY, John Jay College of Criminal Justice	1	15,010	14,577	6,082	41.7	5,683	399	43	824	87	†
CUNY, LaGuardia Community College	2	19,564	18,079	8,675	48.0	8,675	†	790	†	†	†
CUNY, Lehman College...................................	1	12,085	11,560	6,021	52.1	5,263	758	†	773	184	†
CUNY, New York City College of Technology...............	1	16,860	16,087	5,175	32.2	5,175	†	324	214	†	†
CUNY, Queens College	1	18,974	18,080	4,831	26.7	4,091	740	†	529	136	†
CUNY, Queensborough Community College	2	16,291	15,365	5,128	33.4	5,128	†	462	†	†	†
DeVry College of New York	5	2,127	1,941	662	34.1	540	122	12	50	32	†
Dominican College of Blauvelt............................	3	1,998	1,998	596	29.8	549	47	1	58	4	0
Globe Institute of Technology	5	557	523	169	32.3	169	†	17	3	†	†
Mandl School, The College of Allied Health	6	782	782	406	51.9	406	†	132	†	†	†
Manhattanville College	3	2,750	2,534	557	22.0	427	130	†	57	18	0
Mercy College..	3	11,648	11,576	3,566	30.8	2,839	727	9	306	191	4
Mildred Elley, New York.................................	6	617	617	185	30.0	185	†	11	†	†	†
Monroe College	5	7,215	6,627	2,985	45.0	2,894	91	598	377	43	†
Nyack College	3	3,082	2,922	823	28.2	514	309	1	74	56	0
Pacific College of Oriental Medicine, New York	5	602	576	73	12.7	40	33	9	0	2	†
Plaza College	5	726	726	227	31.3	227	†	64	19	†	†
Professional Business College	4	884	884	241	27.3	241	†	61	†	†	†
Saint Francis College....................................	3	2,819	2,665	677	25.4	665	12	0	80	2	†
Stella and Charles Guttman Community College	2	493	476	265	55.7	265	†	0	†	†	†
SUNY, Westchester Community College	2	13,781	13,611	4,238	31.1	4,238	†	358	†	†	†
Swedish Institute College of Health Sciences	6	848	846	251	29.7	251	†	34	†	0	†
Technical Career Institutes	6	3,020	3,001	1,210	40.3	1,210	†	370	†	†	†
Vaughn College of Aeronautics and Technology	3	1,741	1,707	644	37.7	641	3	79	46	0	†
Wood Tobe-Coburn School...............................	6	476	476	253	53.2	253	†	127	†	†	†
Ohio											
Union Institute & University................................	3	1,660	1,660	351	21.1	331	20	†	99	6	1
Oregon											
Mount Angel Seminary...................................	3	170	138	42	30.4	24	18	†	2	6	†
Pennsylvania											
Berks Technical Institute	6	976	976	430	44.1	430	†	82	†	†	†
Consolidated School of Business, Lancaster	6	112	112	53	47.3	53	†	12	†	†	†
Lincoln Technical Institute, Allentown	6	568	568	149	26.2	149	†	17	†	†	†
Pace Institute..	6	65	65	43	66.2	43	†	34	†	†	†
Reading Area Community College	2	4,538	4,538	1,304	28.7	1,304	†	72	†	†	†
Tennessee											
Mid-South Christian College..............................	3	29	25	11	44.0	11	†	0	0	†	†
Texas											
Allied Health Careers....................................	6	177	177	90	50.8	90	†	19	†	†	†
Alvin Community College	2	5,118	5,118	1,549	30.3	1,549	†	160	†	†	†
Amarillo College	2	10,873	10,873	3,933	36.2	3,933	†	312	†	†	†
Anamarc College, El Paso Central	6	347	347	299	86.2	299	†	47	†	†	†
Anamarc College, El Paso East..........................	6	269	269	228	84.8	228	†	4	†	†	†
Angelo State University	1	6,536	6,374	1,850	29.0	1,668	182	37	205	48	1
Anthem College, Irving..................................	6	288	288	125	43.4	125	†	4	†	†	†
Art Institute of Austin	5	1,413	1,413	776	54.9	776	†	13	73	†	†
Art Institute of Houston..................................	5	2,338	2,338	1,001	42.8	1,001	†	61	92	†	†

See notes at end of table.

Table 312.40. Enrollment and degrees conferred in degree-granting postsecondary institutions that serve large proportions of Hispanic undergraduate students, by institution level and control, percentage Hispanic, degree level, and other selected characteristics: Fall 2013 and 2012–13—Continued

State and institution	Level and control[1]	Total, all enrollment[2,3]	Enrollment, fall 2013 — U.S. citizens and permanent residents only — Total[3]	Hispanic[3]	Percent Hispanic[4]	Hispanic under-graduate	Hispanic postbacca-laureate	Degrees awarded to Hispanics, 2012–13 — Associate's	Bachelor's	Master's	Doctor's[5]
1	2	3	4	5	6	7	8	9	10	11	12
Art Institute of San Antonio	5	1,115	1,115	607	54.4	607	†	17	11	†	†
Austin Community College District	2	41,627	40,372	12,925	32.0	12,925	†	428	†	†	†
Baptist Health System School of Health Professions	5	444	444	189	42.6	189	†	78	†	†	†
Baptist University of the Americas	3	189	150	129	86.0	129	†	3	17	†	†
Brazosport College	1	4,127	4,127	1,443	35.0	1,443	†	132	3	†	†
Brookhaven College	2	12,319	12,278	4,475	36.4	4,475	†	208	†	†	†
Brown Mackie College, Dallas	5	308	308	85	27.6	85	†	0	0	†	†
Brown Mackie College, San Antonio	5	785	785	432	55.0	432	†	30	0	†	†
Capitol City Careers	6	10	10	5	50.0	5	†	4	†	†	†
Career Point College	5	1,208	1,208	452	37.4	452	†	82	†	†	†
Center for Advanced Legal Studies	5	182	182	46	25.3	37	9	15	†	†	†
Cisco College	2	3,617	3,545	905	25.5	905	†	69	†	†	†
Coastal Bend College	2	3,533	3,533	2,392	67.7	2,392	†	193	†	†	†
College of Biblical Studies, Houston	3	498	498	150	30.1	150	†	11	10	†	†
College of Health Care Professions, Austin	6	223	223	108	48.4	108	†	4	†	†	†
College of Health Care Professions, Dallas	6	134	134	59	44.0	59	†	0	†	†	†
College of Health Care Professions, Fort Worth	6	208	208	71	34.1	71	†	0	†	†	†
College of Health Care Professions, Northwest	6	810	810	341	42.1	341	†	4	†	†	†
College of the Mainland	2	4,188	4,188	1,145	27.3	1,145	†	99	†	†	†
Concorde Career Institute, San Antonio	6	681	681	401	58.9	401	†	16	†	†	†
Culinary Institute Inc.	6	374	374	134	35.8	134	†	30	†	†	†
Del Mar College	2	10,502	10,488	6,727	64.1	6,727	†	528	†	†	†
DeVry University, Texas	5	3,382	3,262	816	25.0	705	111	36	136	54	†
Eastfield College	2	14,529	14,510	5,847	40.3	5,847	†	238	†	†	†
El Centro College	2	10,771	10,745	4,448	41.4	4,448	†	214	†	†	†
El Paso Community College	2	30,468	29,834	26,218	87.9	26,218	†	2,876	†	†	†
Everest College, Arlington	6	643	643	213	33.1	213	†	22	†	†	†
Everest College, Dallas	6	1,071	1,071	354	33.1	354	†	51	†	†	†
Everest College, Fort Worth	6	505	505	180	35.6	180	†	13	†	†	†
Everest College, Fort Worth, South	6	535	535	221	41.3	221	†	2	†	†	†
Galen College of Nursing, San Antonio	6	1,119	1,119	537	48.0	537	†	60	†	†	†
Galveston College	2	2,131	2,117	659	31.1	659	†	72	†	†	†
Hallmark College	3	735	734	378	51.5	376	2	127	11	†	†
Houston Baptist University	3	2,910	2,802	703	25.1	583	120	†	102	26	†
Houston Community College	2	57,978	52,642	18,702	35.5	18,702	†	1,228	†	†	†
Howard College	2	4,130	4,114	1,859	45.2	1,859	†	110	†	†	†
Interactive Learning Systems, North Houston	6	25	25	12	48.0	12	†	0	†	†	†
Interactive Learning Systems, Pasadena	6	30	30	27	90.0	27	†	0	†	†	†
International Academy of Design and Technology, San Antonio	5	356	356	196	55.1	196	†	25	42	†	†
International Business College, El Paso, Cromo	6	196	196	175	89.3	175	†	5	†	†	†
International Business College, El Paso, North Zaragosa Road	6	195	195	163	83.6	163	†	50	†	†	†
ITT Technical Institute, Austin	5	432	432	145	33.6	145	†	57	11	†	†
ITT Technical Institute, Houston North	5	650	650	197	30.3	197	†	105	10	†	†
ITT Technical Institute, Houston West	5	609	609	218	35.8	218	†	103	15	†	†
ITT Technical Institute, San Antonio	5	585	585	319	54.5	319	†	95	19	†	†
ITT Technical Institute, San Antonio East	5	170	170	74	43.5	74	†	0	0	†	†
ITT Technical Institute, Waco	5	231	231	59	25.5	59	†	12	0	†	†
ITT Technical Institute, Webster	5	303	303	100	33.0	100	†	36	8	†	†
Jacksonville College, Main Campus	4	524	517	193	37.3	193	†	3	†	†	†
Kaplan College, Arlington	6	422	422	180	42.7	180	†	18	†	†	†
Kaplan College, Brownsville	6	461	461	454	98.5	454	†	15	†	†	†
Kaplan College, Corpus Christi	6	370	370	299	80.8	299	†	24	†	†	†
Kaplan College, Dallas	6	357	357	150	42.0	150	†	13	†	†	†
Kaplan College, El Paso	6	681	681	590	86.6	590	†	55	†	†	†
Kaplan College, Fort Worth	6	282	282	118	41.8	118	†	3	†	†	†
Kaplan College, Laredo	6	329	329	324	98.5	324	†	5	†	†	†
Kaplan College, Lubbock	6	267	267	171	64.0	171	†	7	†	†	†
Kaplan College, McAllen	6	540	540	534	98.9	534	†	63	†	†	†
Kaplan College, San Antonio	6	625	625	503	80.5	503	†	19	†	†	†
Kaplan College, San Antonio, San Pedro	6	645	645	418	64.8	418	†	36	†	†	†
Laredo Community College	2	8,726	8,717	8,527	97.8	8,527	†	746	†	†	†
Lee College	2	5,911	5,840	2,291	39.2	2,291	†	224	†	†	†
Lincoln College of Technology, Grand Prairie	6	867	867	372	42.9	372	†	5	†	†	†
Lone Star College System	2	64,072	64,072	22,540	35.2	22,540	†	1,157	†	†	†
McLennan Community College	2	8,555	8,544	2,096	24.5	2,096	†	185	†	†	†
Midland College	1	5,233	5,220	2,271	43.5	2,271	†	156	11	†	†
Mountain View College	2	8,797	8,784	4,977	56.7	4,977	†	351	†	†	†
North American University	3	378	207	49	23.7	49	0	†	0	†	†

See notes at end of table.

Table 312.40. Enrollment and degrees conferred in degree-granting postsecondary institutions that serve large proportions of Hispanic undergraduate students, by institution level and control, percentage Hispanic, degree level, and other selected characteristics: Fall 2013 and 2012–13—Continued

State and institution	Level and control[1]	Total, all enrollment[2,3]	Enrollment, fall 2013 U.S. citizens and permanent residents only — Total[3]	Hispanic[3]	Percent Hispanic[4]	Hispanic under-graduate	Hispanic postbacca-laureate	Degrees awarded to Hispanics, 2012–13 — Associate's	Bachelor's	Master's	Doctor's[5]
1	2	3	4	5	6	7	8	9	10	11	12
North Lake College	2	11,365	11,313	4,184	37.0	4,184	†	273	†	†	†
Northwest Vista College	2	15,965	15,932	9,507	59.7	9,507	†	619	†	†	†
Northwood University, Texas	3	713	682	214	31.4	202	12	1	33	3	†
Odessa College	2	5,059	5,003	3,047	60.9	3,047	†	215	†	†	†
Our Lady of the Lake University, San Antonio	3	2,927	2,908	1,936	66.6	1,194	742	†	208	168	16
Palo Alto College	2	8,427	8,420	5,952	70.7	5,952	†	569	†	†	†
Pima Medical Institute, Houston	6	898	898	429	47.8	429	†	14	†	†	†
Quest College	6	355	352	168	47.7	168	†	†	†	†	†
Remington College, Dallas	3	904	904	414	45.8	414	†	52	0	†	†
Remington College, Fort Worth	4	408	408	144	35.3	144	†	6	†	†	†
Remington College, Houston	4	354	354	129	36.4	129	†	17	†	†	†
Remington College, Houston Southeast	4	252	252	104	41.3	104	†	3	†	†	†
Remington College, North Houston	4	474	473	231	48.8	231	†	15	†	†	†
Richland College	2	19,287	19,127	5,893	30.8	5,893	†	356	†	†	†
Saint Edward's University	3	4,861	4,499	1,709	38.0	1,535	174	†	293	65	†
Saint Mary's University	3	3,868	3,567	2,273	63.7	1,785	488	†	340	103	80
Saint Philip's College	2	10,238	10,197	5,382	52.8	5,382	†	393	†	†	†
San Antonio College	2	23,004	22,899	13,197	57.6	13,197	†	1,051	†	†	†
San Jacinto Community College	2	28,385	27,877	13,856	49.7	13,856	†	1,042	†	†	†
Sanford-Brown College, Austin	6	17	17	5	29.4	5	†	0	†	†	†
Sanford-Brown College, Houston	6	756	748	206	27.5	206	†	19	†	†	†
Sanford-Brown College, Houston North Loop	6	81	81	23	28.4	23	†	5	†	†	†
Sanford-Brown College, San Antonio	6	274	274	100	36.5	100	†	16	†	†	†
Schreiner University	3	1,136	1,131	325	28.7	307	18	0	60	9	†
South Plains College	2	9,559	9,488	3,667	38.6	3,667	†	190	†	†	†
South Texas College	1	31,232	31,228	29,935	95.9	29,935	†	2,052	114	†	†
South University, Art Institute of Dallas	5	1,423	1,421	750	52.8	748	2	32	51	1	†
South University, Art Institute of Fort Worth	5	346	346	107	30.9	107	†	2	2	†	†
South University, Austin	5	156	156	34	21.8	34	0	0	0	0	†
Southwest Collegiate Institute for the Deaf	2	149	130	63	48.5	63	†	2	†	†	†
Southwest Institute of Technology	6	10	10	5	50.0	5	†	6	†	†	†
Southwest Texas Junior College	2	5,410	5,410	4,525	83.6	4,525	†	495	†	†	†
Southwest University at El Paso	5	1,296	1,296	1,212	93.5	1,212	†	200	0	†	†
Southwestern Adventist University	3	808	745	335	45.0	331	4	1	35	4	†
Sul Ross State University	1	2,842	2,827	1,773	62.7	1,274	499	0	226	95	†
Tarrant County College District	2	50,771	50,389	13,957	27.7	13,957	†	879	†	†	†
Texas A & M International University	1	7,431	7,208	6,938	96.3	6,238	700	†	739	197	0
Texas A & M University, Corpus Christi	1	10,913	10,398	4,811	46.3	4,274	537	†	592	147	7
Texas A & M University, Kingsville	1	12,229	11,346	7,811	68.8	6,482	1,329	†	1,187	286	13
Texas Lutheran University	3	1,341	1,339	421	31.4	420	1	†	55	3	†
Texas School of Business, Friendswood	6	262	262	92	35.1	92	†	7	†	†	†
Texas School of Business, North	6	436	436	180	41.3	180	†	12	†	†	†
Texas State Technical College, Harlingen	2	5,332	5,328	4,878	91.6	4,878	†	359	†	†	†
Texas State Technical College, West Texas	2	1,281	1,280	356	27.8	356	†	42	†	†	†
Texas State University	1	35,546	35,172	10,929	31.1	9,947	982	†	1,428	276	12
Texas Wesleyan University	3	2,397	1,967	447	22.7	365	82	†	80	21	17
University of Houston	1	39,540	35,807	10,275	28.7	9,429	846	†	1,496	229	80
University of Houston, Clear Lake	1	8,164	7,155	2,133	29.8	1,625	508	†	351	132	4
University of Houston, Downtown	1	13,757	13,055	5,468	41.9	5,392	76	†	855	13	†
University of Houston, Victoria	1	4,491	4,314	1,147	26.6	903	244	†	152	74	†
University of Phoenix, Austin Campus	5	756	745	193	25.9	180	13	†	6	0	†
University of Phoenix, Houston Campus	5	1,841	1,810	429	23.7	399	30	†	41	10	†
University of Phoenix, McAllen	5	139	138	121	87.7	111	10	†	0	†	†
University of Phoenix, San Antonio	5	1,048	1,037	433	41.8	355	78	†	45	19	†
University of Saint Thomas	3	3,525	3,142	1,158	36.9	600	558	†	113	225	1
University of Texas at Arlington	1	33,329	30,241	7,444	24.6	6,583	861	†	1,156	307	4
University of Texas at Brownsville	1	12,285	11,752	10,935	93.0	10,139	796	757	928	186	4
University of Texas at El Paso	1	23,003	21,541	18,360	85.2	16,318	2,042	†	2,552	641	62
University of Texas at San Antonio	1	28,623	26,845	13,508	50.3	11,935	1,573	†	2,059	444	15
University of Texas Health Science Center at San Antonio	1	3,148	3,005	822	27.4	282	540	†	186	73	88
University of Texas of the Permian Basin	1	5,131	5,073	2,152	42.4	1,835	317	†	229	51	†
University of Texas, Pan American	1	20,053	19,530	18,333	93.9	15,925	2,408	†	2,446	604	12
University of the Incarnate Word	3	8,685	8,281	4,962	59.9	4,094	868	2	706	174	38
Vet Tech Institute of Houston	6	196	196	64	32.7	64	†	41	†	†	†
Victoria College	2	4,419	4,417	1,850	41.9	1,850	†	86	†	†	†
Virginia College, Austin	6	642	641	282	44.0	282	†	38	†	†	†
Vista College	6	2,746	2,745	1,419	51.7	1,419	†	93	†	†	†
Wayland Baptist University	3	6,222	6,172	1,569	25.4	1,236	333	38	310	120	†
Western Technical College, Diana Drive	6	651	621	465	74.9	465	†	74	†	†	†
Western Technical College, Plaza Circle	6	815	815	646	79.3	646	†	117	†	†	†

See notes at end of table.

Table 312.40. Enrollment and degrees conferred in degree-granting postsecondary institutions that serve large proportions of Hispanic undergraduate students, by institution level and control, percentage Hispanic, degree level, and other selected characteristics: Fall 2013 and 2012–13—Continued

State and institution	Level and control[1]	Total, all enrollment[2,3]	Enrollment, fall 2013 — U.S. citizens and permanent residents only — Total[3]	Hispanic[3]	Percent Hispanic[4]	Hispanic undergraduate	Hispanic postbacca- laureate	Degrees awarded to Hispanics, 2012–13 — Associate's	Bachelor's	Master's	Doctor's[5]
1	2	3	4	5	6	7	8	9	10	11	12
Western Texas College	2	2,044	1,992	587	29.5	587	†	65	†	†	†
Wharton County Junior College	2	7,386	7,381	2,579	34.9	2,579	†	209	†	†	†
Utah											
Art Institute of Salt Lake City	5	466	460	175	38.0	175	†	16	8	†	†
Everest College, Salt Lake City	5	404	404	108	26.7	108	†	11	1	†	†
Vista College, Online	6	207	207	57	27.5	57	†	10	†	†	†
Virginia											
Art Institute of Washington	5	1,499	1,471	571	38.8	571	†	24	26	†	†
Art Institute of Washington, Dulles	5	244	243	67	27.6	67	†	1	2	†	†
Bethel College	3	54	52	11	21.2	11	†	0	0	†	†
Columbia College	6	310	179	56	31.3	56	†	0	†	†	†
Everest College, McLean	6	237	237	73	30.8	73	†	12	†	†	†
ITT Technical Institute, Chantilly	5	573	573	154	26.9	154	†	55	12	†	†
Medtech Institute	6	1,373	1,372	600	43.7	600	†	1	†	†	†
Washington											
Art Institute of Seattle	5	1,573	1,548	475	30.7	475	†	15	30	†	†
Big Bend Community College	2	1,991	1,985	652	32.8	652	†	99	†	†	†
Columbia Basin College	1	6,480	6,473	1,925	29.7	1,925	†	223	9	†	†
Heritage University	3	1,128	1,123	591	52.6	517	74	7	66	35	†
Wenatchee Valley College	2	3,619	3,611	1,126	31.2	1,126	†	133	†	†	†
Yakima Valley Community College	2	4,105	4,100	1,891	46.1	1,891	†	266	†	†	†
Puerto Rico											
American University of Puerto Rico, Bayamon	3	968	968	968	100.0	858	110	24	159	36	†
American University of Puerto Rico, Manati	3	1,082	1,082	1,082	100.0	1,008	74	29	117	22	†
Atenas College	3	1,269	1,269	1,269	100.0	1,269	†	170	54	†	†
Atlantic University College	3	1,429	1,429	1,429	100.0	1,365	64	17	179	36	†
Bayamon Central University	3	2,065	2,065	2,055	99.5	1,647	408	12	175	127	†
Caribbean University, Bayamon	3	1,876	1,876	1,876	100.0	1,578	298	27	153	65	†
Caribbean University, Carolina	3	827	827	827	100.0	704	123	41	46	40	†
Caribbean University, Ponce	3	1,529	1,529	1,529	100.0	1,161	368	21	120	106	†
Caribbean University, Vega Baja	3	604	604	604	100.0	489	115	36	44	43	†
Carlos Albizu University, San Juan	3	919	919	917	99.8	141	776	†	47	155	83
Centro de Estudios Multidisciplinarios, Bayamon	3	631	631	631	100.0	631	†	178	25	†	†
Centro de Estudios Multidisciplinarios, Humacao	3	743	724	724	100.0	724	†	216	43	†	†
Centro de Estudios Multidisciplinarios, San Juan	3	987	987	987	100.0	987	†	365	120	†	†
Colegio de Cinematografía, Artes y Television	6	867	867	867	100.0	867	†	76	†	†	†
Colegio Universitario de San Juan	1	1,387	1,387	1,387	100.0	1,387	†	154	151	†	†
Columbia Centro Universitario, Caguas	5	1,823	1,823	1,823	100.0	1,680	143	254	190	77	†
Columbia Centro Universitario, Yauco	5	402	402	402	100.0	402	†	71	44	†	†
Dewey University, Hato Rey	3	2,565	2,565	2,565	100.0	2,470	95	266	203	†	†
EDIC College	6	752	752	752	100.0	752	†	132	†	†	†
EDP University of Puerto Rico Inc., San Juan	3	1,348	1,348	1,348	100.0	1,275	73	114	73	15	†
EDP University of Puerto Rico Inc., San Sebastian	3	1,195	1,195	1,195	100.0	1,195	†	182	62	†	†
Escuela de Artes Plasticas de Puerto Rico	1	529	528	527	99.8	527	†	†	77	†	†
Huertas College	6	1,255	1,255	1,255	100.0	1,255	†	351	†	†	†
Humacao Community College	3	705	705	705	100.0	705	†	112	21	†	†
ICPR Junior College, Arecibo	6	542	542	542	100.0	542	†	18	†	†	†
ICPR Junior College, General Institutional	6	789	789	789	100.0	789	†	16	†	†	†
ICPR Junior College, Manatí	6	613	613	613	100.0	613	†	†	†	†	†
ICPR Junior College, Mayaguez	6	596	596	596	100.0	596	†	56	†	†	†
Instituto de Banca y Comercio Inc.	6	16,339	16,339	16,339	100.0	16,339	†	50	†	†	†
Instituto Tecnologico de Puerto Rico, Recinto de Guayama	2	861	861	861	100.0	861	†	188	†	†	†
Instituto Tecnologico de Puerto Rico, Recinto de Manati	2	755	755	755	100.0	755	†	211	†	†	†
Instituto Tecnologico de Puerto Rico, Recinto de Ponce	2	644	644	644	100.0	644	†	131	†	†	†
Instituto Tecnologico de Puerto Rico, Recinto de San Juan	2	650	650	650	100.0	650	†	141	†	†	†
Inter American University of Puerto Rico, Aguadilla	3	4,595	4,595	4,588	99.8	4,275	313	115	351	67	†
Inter American University of Puerto Rico, Arecibo	3	4,799	4,799	4,791	99.8	4,305	486	128	441	101	†
Inter American University of Puerto Rico, Barranquitas	3	2,073	2,073	2,068	99.8	2,011	57	115	218	26	†
Inter American University of Puerto Rico, Bayamon	3	4,857	4,857	4,830	99.4	4,688	142	33	477	25	†
Inter American University of Puerto Rico, Fajardo	3	2,259	2,259	2,256	99.9	2,176	80	18	193	6	†
Inter American University of Puerto Rico, Guayama	3	2,169	2,169	2,163	99.7	2,087	76	80	195	10	†
Inter American University of Puerto Rico, Metro	3	9,853	9,853	9,743	98.9	7,037	2,706	84	1,056	524	43
Inter American University of Puerto Rico, Ponce	3	5,821	5,821	5,809	99.8	5,405	404	166	505	51	†
Inter American University of Puerto Rico, San German	3	5,177	5,177	5,153	99.5	4,375	778	53	462	116	19
Mech-Tech College	6	3,262	3,262	3,262	100.0	3,262	†	257	†	†	†
National University College, Arecibo	5	1,650	1,650	1,650	100.0	1,650	†	224	153	†	†
National University College, Bayamon	5	5,213	5,213	5,213	100.0	4,998	215	289	227	5	†
National University College, Caguas	5	920	920	920	100.0	920	†	0	0	†	†
National University College, Ponce	5	1,118	1,118	1,118	100.0	1,118	†	82	151	†	†

See notes at end of table.

Table 312.40. Enrollment and degrees conferred in degree-granting postsecondary institutions that serve large proportions of Hispanic undergraduate students, by institution level and control, percentage Hispanic, degree level, and other selected characteristics: Fall 2013 and 2012–13—Continued

State and institution	Level and control[1]	Total, all enrollment[2,3]	Enrollment, fall 2013					Degrees awarded to Hispanics, 2012–13			
			U.S. citizens and permanent residents only								
			Total[3]	Hispanic[3]	Percent Hispanic[4]	Hispanic under-graduate	Hispanic postbacca-laureate	Associate's	Bachelor's	Master's	Doctor's[5]
1	2	3	4	5	6	7	8	9	10	11	12
National University College, Rio Grande	5	1,869	1,869	1,869	100.0	1,869	†	101	148	†	†
Ponce Paramedical College Inc.	6	2,882	2,882	2,882	100.0	2,882	†	334	†	†	†
Pontifical Catholic University of Puerto Rico, Arecibo	3	986	986	980	99.4	652	328	8	59	55	†
Pontifical Catholic University of Puerto Rico, Mayaguez	3	1,501	1,500	1,499	99.9	1,385	114	7	128	16	†
Pontifical Catholic University of Puerto Rico, Ponce	3	8,341	8,296	8,292	100.0	5,993	2,299	20	608	172	296
Puerto Rico Conservatory of Music	1	492	476	470	98.7	425	45	†	53	11	†
San Juan Bautista School of Medicine	3	295	295	139	47.1	27	112	†	1	1	38
Universal Technology College of Puerto Rico	3	1,260	1,260	1,260	100.0	1,260	†	138	†	†	†
Universidad Adventista de las Antillas	3	1,403	1,360	1,336	98.2	1,226	110	8	154	15	†
Universidad Central Del Caribe	3	467	467	451	96.6	144	307	15	15	5	63
Universidad Del Este	3	13,420	13,420	13,420	100.0	12,287	1,133	376	1,197	228	†
Universidad del Sagrado Corazon	3	5,892	5,892	5,892	100.0	5,159	733	56	783	141	†
Universidad Del Turabo	3	17,287	17,287	17,287	100.0	14,556	2,731	238	1,375	796	42
Universidad Metropolitana	3	13,631	13,631	13,631	100.0	11,503	2,128	203	1,233	674	10
Universidad Pentecostal Mizpa	3	412	412	412	100.0	375	37	13	23	0	†
Universidad Politecnica de Puerto Rico, Hato Rey	3	4,646	4,646	4,638	99.8	3,855	783	†	493	222	†
Universidad Teologica del Caribe	3	202	202	202	100.0	202	†	†	20	†	†
University of Phoenix, Puerto Rico	5	928	918	897	97.7	437	460	†	127	160	†
University of Puerto Rico, Aguadilla	1	2,973	2,973	2,941	98.9	2,941	†	5	336	†	†
University of Puerto Rico, Arecibo	1	3,759	3,759	3,759	100.0	3,759	†	39	519	†	†
University of Puerto Rico, Bayamon	1	5,075	5,075	5,075	100.0	5,075	†	28	529	†	†
University of Puerto Rico, Carolina	1	3,994	3,994	3,876	97.0	3,876	†	64	477	†	†
University of Puerto Rico, Cayey	1	3,816	3,816	3,816	100.0	3,816	†	†	547	†	†
University of Puerto Rico, Humacao	1	3,495	3,493	3,419	97.9	3,419	†	73	511	†	†
University of Puerto Rico, Mayaguez	1	11,838	11,838	11,838	100.0	10,944	894	†	1,696	128	13
University of Puerto Rico, Medical Sciences	1	2,253	2,253	2,220	98.5	489	1,731	43	158	249	176
University of Puerto Rico, Ponce	1	3,120	3,120	3,120	100.0	3,120	†	67	353	†	†
University of Puerto Rico, Rio Piedras	1	15,487	15,477	15,199	98.2	11,954	3,245	†	1,331	201	170
University of Puerto Rico, Utuado	1	1,559	1,559	661	42.4	661	†	79	59	†	†

†Not applicable.

[1]1 = 4-year public; 2 = 2-year public; 3 = 4-year private nonprofit; 4 = 2-year private nonprofit; 5 = 4-year private for-profit; and 6 = 2-year private for-profit.

[2]Includes nonresident alien students as well as U.S. citizens and permanent residents.

[3]Includes graduate as well as undergraduate students.

[4]Hispanic headcount enrollment (U.S. citizens and permanent residents only) as a percentage of total headcount enrollment of U.S. citizens and permanent residents.

[5]Includes Ph.D., Ed.D., and comparable degrees at the doctoral level, as well as such degrees as M.D., D.D.S., and law degrees that were formerly classified as first-professional degrees.

NOTE: Degree-granting institutions grant associate's or higher degrees and participate in Title IV federal financial aid programs. This table includes institutions that serve large proportions of Hispanic undergraduate students, defined as institutions with a full-time-equivalent undergraduate enrollment of Hispanic students at 25 percent or more of full-time-equivalent undergraduate enrollment of U.S. citizens. Data for Hispanics include only persons who were U.S. citizens or permanent residents.

SOURCE: U.S. Department of Education, National Center for Education Statistics, Integrated Postsecondary Education Data System (IPEDS), Spring 2014, Enrollment component; and Fall 2013, Completions component. (This table was prepared May 2015.)

Table 312.50. Fall enrollment and degrees conferred in degree-granting tribally controlled postsecondary institutions, by state and institution: Selected years, fall 2000 through fall 2014, and 2012–13 and 2013–14

State and institution	Level and control[1]	Total fall enrollment							2014				Degrees awarded to American Indians/ Alaska Natives			
									Total	Total American Indian/ Alaska Native	Percent American Indian/ Alaska Native	Under-graduate American Indian/ Alaska Native	Associate's		Bachelor's	
		2000	2005	2008	2010	2011	2012	2013	Total				2012–13	2013–14	2012–13	2013–14
1	2	3	4	5	6	7	8	9	10	11	12	13	14	15	16	17
Tribally controlled institutions[2]	†	13,680	17,167	17,014	21,179	19,126	18,881	18,274	17,879	14,154	79.2	14,020	1,240	1,266	284	295
Alaska																
Ilisagvik College	2	322	278	251	288	226	231	257	243	135	55.6	135	10	5	†	†
Arizona																
Diné College	1	1,712	1,825	1,527	2,033	2,021	1,970	1,466	1,488	1,468	98.7	1,468	115	152	8	7
Tohono O'odham Community College	2	—	270	163	207	295	214	243	225	195	86.7	195	3	6	†	†
Kansas																
Haskell Indian Nations University	1	918	918	997	958	826	846	742	808	808	100.0	808	96	85	102	70
Michigan																
Bay Mills Community College	2	360	406	501	607	575	536	531	555	320	57.7	320	25	25	†	†
Keweenaw Bay Ojibwa Community College	2	—	—	—	—	80	86	106	89	79	88.8	79	6	4	†	†
Saginaw Chippewa Tribal College	2	—	123	133	153	133	127	117	141	119	84.4	119	12	9	†	†
Minnesota																
Fond du Lac Tribal and Community College	2	999	1,981	2,206	2,339	2,319	2,307	2,272	2,215	175	7.9	175	23	33	†	†
Leech Lake Tribal College	2	240	189	228	235	206	338	348	297	287	96.6	287	24	32	†	†
White Earth Tribal and Community College	4	—	61	106	117	88	87	60	69	58	84.1	58	8	10	†	†
Montana																
Aaniiih Nakoda College	2	295	175	168	214	169	221	139	291	256	88.0	256	18	22	†	†
Blackfeet Community College	4	299	485	492	473	464	407	450	495	470	94.9	470	55	76	†	†
Chief Dull Knife College	2	461	554	443	433	374	361	201	192	179	93.2	179	19	27	†	†
Fort Peck Community College	2	400	408	436	452	513	438	405	346	298	86.1	298	15	21	†	†
Little Big Horn College	2	320	259	337	380	366	325	329	263	257	97.7	257	50	47	†	†
Salish Kootenai College	3	1,042	1,142	993	1,158	1,112	906	840	859	655	76.3	655	53	64	35	38
Stone Child College	2	38	344	236	332	410	501	404	458	416	90.8	416	29	21	†	†
Nebraska																
Little Priest Tribal College	4	141	109	116	148	172	144	144	127	114	89.8	114	15	23	†	†
Nebraska Indian Community College	2	170	107	92	177	163	150	199	120	115	95.8	115	9	7	†	†
New Mexico																
Institute of American Indian and Alaska Native Culture[2]	1	139	113	249	313	374	392	422	486	373	76.7	341	8	2	31	31
Navajo Technical College	1	841	333	571	1,019	1,173	1,777	1,956	2,075	2,055	99.0	2,050	56	77	1	5
Southwestern Indian Polytechnic Institute	2	304	614	470	531	480	488	530	481	481	100.0	481	62	71	†	†
North Dakota																
Candkeska Cikana Community College	2	9	198	201	220	219	247	254	185	143	77.3	143	27	27	†	†
Fort Berthold Community College	1	50	241	162	215	199	205	203	158	145	91.8	145	24	15	8	4
Sitting Bull College[2]	1	22	287	296	314	313	277	279	289	255	88.2	253	30	23	14	16
Turtle Mountain Community College	3	686	615	951	969	588	532	602	520	493	94.8	493	90	82	8	6
United Tribes Technical College	3	204	885	375	600	651	505	505	434	377	86.9	377	54	28	3	14
Oklahoma																
College of the Muscogee Nation	2	—	—	—	—	—	—	191	188	187	99.5	187	16	17	†	†
South Dakota																
Oglala Lakota College[2]	1	1,174	1,302	1,531	1,830	1,685	1,583	1,551	1,427	1,366	95.7	1,323	83	68	28	65
Sinte Gleska University[2]	3	900	1,123	1,012	2,473	835	728	689	641	575	89.7	523	41	50	35	23
Sisseton Wahpeton College	2	250	290	227	261	264	175	194	165	150	90.9	150	21	15	†	†
Washington																
Northwest Indian College	1	524	495	554	626	701	699	681	637	553	86.8	553	77	68	9	13
Wisconsin																
College of the Menominee Nation	3	371	532	512	615	699	721	661	560	339	60.5	339	32	31	2	3
Lac Courte Oreilles Ojibwa Community College	2	489	505	478	489	433	357	303	352	258	73.3	258	34	23	†	†

—Not available.
†Not applicable.
[1] 1 = 4-year public; 2 = 2-year public; 3 = 4-year private nonprofit; and 4 = 2-year private nonprofit.
[2] "Total American Indian/Alaska Native" enrollment (column 11) includes graduate students and therefore does not equal "Undergraduate American Indian/Alaska Native" enrollment (column 13).
NOTE: This table only includes institutions that were in operation during the 2014–15 academic year. They are all members of the American Indian Higher Education Consortium and, with few

exceptions, are tribally controlled and located on reservations. Degree-granting institutions grant associate's or higher degrees and participate in Title IV federal financial aid programs. Totals include persons of other racial/ethnic groups not separately identified.
SOURCE: U.S. Department of Education, National Center for Education Statistics, Integrated Postsecondary Education Data System (IPEDS), Spring 2001 through Spring 2015, Fall Enrollment component; and Fall 2013 and Fall 2014, Completions component. (This table was prepared March 2016.)

Table 313.10. Fall enrollment, degrees conferred, and expenditures in degree-granting historically Black colleges and universities, by institution: 2013, 2014, and 2013–14

Institution	State	Level and control[1]	Total enroll-ment, fall 2013	Enrollment, fall 2014		Full-time-equivalent enrollment, fall 2014	Degrees conferred, 2013–14				Total expenditures, 2013–14 (in thousands of current dollars)[3]
				Total	Black enrollment		Associate's	Bachelor's	Master's	Doctor's[2]	
1	2	3	4	5	6	7	8	9	10	11	12
Total..	†	†	303,167	294,316	231,888	254,589	4,224	33,700	7,845	2,423	$7,619,613
Alabama A&M University[4]............................	AL	1	5,020	5,333	4,913	4,925	†	472	223	7	135,120
Alabama State University	AL	1	6,075	5,519	5,024	5,003	†	529	141	55	157,118
Bishop State Community College............................	AL	2	3,896	3,320	2,123	2,362	286	†	†	†	36,282
Concordia College, Alabama............................	AL	3	600	546	503	525	29	34	†	†	13,032
Gadsden State Community College	AL	2	5,797	5,289	1,070	3,603	571	†	†	†	54,148
H. Councill Trenholm State Technical College	AL	2	1,351	1,338	786	902	200	†	†	†	18,502
J. F. Drake State Community and Technical College	AL	2	1,383	1,062	608	719	98	†	†	†	13,819
Lawson State Community College, Birmingham Campus.....	AL	2	3,028	3,090	2,489	2,215	226	†	†	†	35,315
Miles College............................	AL	3	1,666	1,782	1,736	1,740	†	198	†	†	27,892
Oakwood University	AL	3	1,903	1,939	1,690	1,851	1	321	14	†	51,671
Selma University............................	AL	3	611	558	551	483	0	23	10	†	2,953
Shelton State Community College............................	AL	2	5,068	4,978	1,807	3,204	365	†	†	†	45,383
Stillman College............................	AL	3	863	1,056	955	988	†	114	†	†	20,939
Talladega College	AL	3	932	879	758	802	†	81	†	†	16,379
Tuskegee University[4]............................	AL	3	3,118	3,103	2,953	3,017	†	327	50	49	152,573
Arkansas Baptist College	AR	3	1,027	899	847	836	82	45	†	†	17,017
Philander Smith College	AR	3	556	567	512	539	†	108	†	†	15,637
Shorter College	AR	4	330	403	395	349	11	†	†	†	2,380
University of Arkansas at Pine Bluff[4]	AR	1	2,615	2,513	2,301	2,337	0	429	26	0	73,048
Delaware State University[4]	DE	1	4,336	4,397	2,974	4,022	†	550	130	6	124,981
Howard University............................	DC	3	10,297	10,265	8,812	9,589	†	1,033	339	501	848,736
University of the District of Columbia[4]	DC	1	5,011	4,803	3,514	3,195	263	410	86	†	134,230
Bethune-Cookman University	FL	3	3,787	4,044	3,662	3,893	†	480	29	†	76,078
Edward Waters College	FL	3	862	929	838	906	†	106	†	†	22,368
Florida A&M University[4]............................	FL	1	10,743	10,241	8,956	9,332	113	1,560	277	335	294,167
Florida Memorial University	FL	3	1,560	1,528	1,233	1,470	†	207	19	†	36,310
Albany State University............................	GA	1	4,260	3,910	3,543	3,344	†	492	108	†	68,270
Clark Atlanta University	GA	3	3,458	3,485	3,306	3,239	†	459	183	42	85,291
Fort Valley State University[4]	GA	1	3,180	2,594	2,375	2,290	†	431	86	†	70,767
Interdenominational Theological Center............................	GA	3	562	306	295	211	†	†	99	5	8,808
Morehouse College............................	GA	3	2,170	2,109	2,022	2,045	†	339	†	†	87,058
Morehouse School of Medicine	GA	3	372	398	287	395	†	†	26	44	138,225
Paine College	GA	3	924	848	787	809	†	108	†	†	24,429
Savannah State University............................	GA	1	4,772	4,915	4,336	4,549	5	442	74	†	95,218
Spelman College............................	GA	3	2,129	2,135	2,026	2,097	†	464	†	†	86,366
Kentucky State University[4]............................	KY	1	2,533	1,895	1,137	1,626	49	272	49	†	73,682
Dillard University............................	LA	3	1,183	1,200	1,155	1,162	†	186	†	†	43,865
Grambling State University	LA	1	5,071	4,504	4,120	3,970	13	697	251	4	97,172
Southern University and A&M College[4]............................	LA	1	6,777	6,330	5,895	5,499	†	757	272	13	142,446
Southern University at New Orleans	LA	1	2,292	2,103	2,021	1,702	14	303	183	†	43,819
Southern University at Shreveport............................	LA	2	3,018	2,952	2,617	2,350	273	†	†	†	33,699
Xavier University of Louisiana	LA	3	3,121	2,976	2,116	2,869	†	322	58	159	101,151
Bowie State University............................	MD	1	5,561	5,695	4,844	4,766	†	741	278	7	98,430
Coppin State College............................	MD	1	3,383	3,133	2,626	2,562	†	477	83	0	76,693
Morgan State University............................	MD	1	7,546	7,698	6,320	6,769	†	922	227	52	203,169
University of Maryland, Eastern Shore[4]............................	MD	1	4,220	4,279	2,891	3,884	†	585	68	101	109,359
Alcorn State University[4]............................	MS	1	3,848	3,639	3,386	3,083	54	404	128	†	85,187
Coahoma Community College............................	MS	2	2,073	2,045	1,955	1,877	259	†	†	†	34,533
Hinds Community College, Utica Campus............................	MS	2	717	711	674	673	75	†	†	†	—
Jackson State University............................	MS	1	9,134	9,508	8,491	7,843	†	1,093	424	71	193,983
Mississippi Valley State University............................	MS	1	2,203	2,222	2,111	1,957	†	386	70	†	55,674
Rust College	MS	3	922	963	924	930	5	103	†	†	16,662
Tougaloo College	MS	3	878	900	887	883	5	153	†	†	23,576

See notes at end of table.

Table 313.10. Fall enrollment, degrees conferred, and expenditures in degree-granting historically Black colleges and universities, by institution: 2013, 2014, and 2013–14—Continued

Institution	State	Level and control[1]	Total enroll-ment, fall 2013	Enrollment, fall 2014 Total	Black enrollment	Full-time-equivalent enrollment, fall 2014	Degrees conferred, 2013–14 Associate's	Bachelor's	Master's	Doctor's[2]	Total expenditures, 2013–14 (in thousands of current dollars)[3]
1	2	3	4	5	6	7	8	9	10	11	12
Harris-Stowe State University	MO	1	1,298	1,280	1,111	1,095	†	132	†	†	26,168
Lincoln University[4]	MO	1	3,043	3,117	1,298	2,500	80	328	52	†	51,129
Bennett College	NC	3	680	633	595	580	†	105	†	†	18,798
Elizabeth City State University	NC	1	2,421	1,867	1,494	1,727	†	488	55	†	74,329
Fayetteville State University	NC	1	6,179	5,899	3,992	4,912	†	965	193	7	109,956
Johnson C. Smith University	NC	3	1,387	1,402	1,212	1,367	†	248	†	†	44,258
Livingstone College	NC	3	1,175	1,301	1,274	1,296	0	154	†	†	28,663
North Carolina A&T State University[4]	NC	1	10,561	10,725	8,893	9,862	†	1,394	470	43	256,028
North Carolina Central University	NC	1	8,093	7,687	6,073	6,790	†	1,054	427	141	190,426
Saint Augustine's College	NC	3	1,299	1,016	973	1,007	†	226	†	†	34,541
Shaw University	NC	3	2,062	1,802	1,716	1,678	1	286	18	†	47,110
Winston-Salem State University	NC	1	5,399	5,220	3,741	4,707	†	1,371	134	25	142,168
Central State University	OH	1	2,068	1,751	1,686	1,646	†	293	6	†	57,632
Wilberforce University	OH	3	479	387	373	376	†	103	5	†	14,813
Langston University[4]	OK	1	2,533	2,482	2,049	2,185	12	294	110	22	63,156
Cheyney University of Pennsylvania	PA	1	1,212	1,022	924	974	†	150	10	†	46,512
Lincoln University	PA	1	1,963	1,819	1,649	1,668	†	279	160	†	52,246
Allen University	SC	3	651	660	652	649	†	81	†	†	13,369
Benedict College	SC	3	2,512	2,444	2,420	2,420	†	309	†	†	56,967
Claflin College	SC	3	1,884	1,866	1,693	1,825	†	371	25	†	43,663
Clinton College	SC	3	185	194	185	189	26	5	†	†	3,190
Denmark Technical College	SC	2	1,838	1,678	1,615	1,508	82	†	†	†	18,963
Morris College	SC	3	824	780	762	774	†	152	†	†	20,107
South Carolina State University[4]	SC	1	3,463	3,331	3,154	3,002	†	567	112	19	105,507
Voorhees College	SC	3	536	468	461	458	†	117	†	†	16,743
Fisk University	TN	3	646	772	722	749	†	80	6	†	25,817
Lane College	TN	3	1,554	1,262	1,262	1,254	†	239	†	†	24,730
Le Moyne-Owen College	TN	3	1,023	1,006	987	937	†	127	†	†	17,349
Meharry Medical College	TN	3	801	802	645	802	†	†	69	150	132,469
Tennessee State University[4]	TN	1	8,883	9,027	5,798	7,490	104	807	476	85	184,472
Huston-Tillotson University	TX	3	973	1,031	731	967	†	125	†	†	18,737
Jarvis Christian College	TX	3	609	763	623	725	†	65	†	†	15,591
Paul Quinn College	TX	3	243	273	227	265	†	21	†	†	8,124
Prairie View A&M University[4]	TX	1	8,283	8,429	7,236	7,475	†	993	447	22	191,075
Saint Philip's College	TX	2	10,238	10,514	1,119	4,607	511	†	†	†	72,559
Southwestern Christian College	TX	3	172	164	128	157	30	0	†	†	6,307
Texas College	TX	3	971	813	696	792	21	80	†	†	11,543
Texas Southern University	TX	1	8,703	9,233	7,258	8,131	†	867	388	329	199,075
Wiley College	TX	3	1,392	1,351	1,146	1,295	5	176	†	†	23,862
Hampton University	VA	3	4,622	4,393	3,921	4,106	0	710	139	99	151,266
Norfolk State University	VA	1	6,728	6,027	5,163	5,327	95	857	184	9	149,913
Virginia State University[4]	VA	1	5,763	5,025	4,699	4,717	3	793	151	8	138,238
Virginia Union University	VA	3	1,749	1,715	1,669	1,680	†	229	119	9	32,780
Virginia University of Lynchburg	VA	3	582	324	319	249	82	24	11	4	5,377
Bluefield State College	WV	1	1,747	1,563	156	1,377	117	240	†	†	23,364
West Virginia State University[4]	WV	1	2,677	2,884	461	2,343	†	418	17	†	48,268
University of the Virgin Islands[4]	VI	1	2,321	2,280	1,770	1,758	58	214	50	†	78,643

—Not available.
†Not applicable.
[1]1 = 4-year public; 2 = 2-year public; 3 = 4-year private nonprofit; and 4 = 2-year private non-profit.
[2]Includes Ph.D., Ed.D., and comparable degrees at the doctoral level, as well as such degrees as M.D., D.D.S., and law degrees that were formerly classified as first-professional degrees.
[3]Includes private and some public institutions reporting total expenses and deductions under Financial Accounting Standards Board (FASB) reporting standards and public institutions reporting total expenses and deductions under Governmental Accounting Standards Board (GASB) 34/35 reporting standards.
[4]Land-grant institution.

NOTE: Degree-granting institutions grant associate's or higher degrees and participate in Title IV federal financial aid programs. Excludes historically Black colleges and universities that are not participating in Title IV programs. Historically Black colleges and universities are degree-granting institutions established prior to 1964 with the principal mission of educating Black Americans. Federal regulations, 20 U.S. Code, Section 1061 (2), allow for certain exceptions to the founding date. Totals include persons of other racial/ethnic groups not separately identified. Detail may not sum to totals because of rounding.
SOURCE: U.S. Department of Education, National Center for Education Statistics, Integrated Postsecondary Education Data System (IPEDS), Fall 2014, Completions component; Spring 2014 and Spring 2015, Fall Enrollment component; and Spring 2015, Finance component. (This table was prepared March 2016.)

Table 313.20. Fall enrollment in degree-granting historically Black colleges and universities, by sex of student and level and control of institution: Selected years, 1976 through 2014

Year	Total enrollment	Males	Females	4-year	2-year	Public Total	Public 4-year	Public 2-year	Private Total	Private 4-year	Private 2-year
1	2	3	4	5	6	7	8	9	10	11	12
All students											
1976	222,613	104,669	117,944	206,676	15,937	156,836	143,528	13,308	65,777	63,148	2,629
1980	233,557	106,387	127,170	218,009	15,548	168,217	155,085	13,132	65,340	62,924	2,416
1982	228,371	104,897	123,474	212,017	16,354	165,871	151,472	14,399	62,500	60,545	1,955
1984	227,519	102,823	124,696	212,844	14,675	164,116	151,289	12,827	63,403	61,555	1,848
1986	223,275	97,523	125,752	207,231	16,044	162,048	147,631	14,417	61,227	59,600	1,627
1988	239,755	100,561	139,194	223,250	16,505	173,672	158,606	15,066	66,083	64,644	1,439
1990	257,152	105,157	151,995	240,497	16,655	187,046	171,969	15,077	70,106	68,528	1,578
1991	269,335	110,442	158,893	252,093	17,242	197,847	182,204	15,643	71,488	69,889	1,599
1992	279,541	114,622	164,919	261,089	18,452	204,966	188,143	16,823	74,575	72,946	1,629
1993	282,856	116,397	166,459	262,430	20,426	208,197	189,032	19,165	74,659	73,398	1,261
1994	280,071	114,006	166,065	259,997	20,074	206,520	187,735	18,785	73,551	72,262	1,289
1995	278,725	112,637	166,088	259,409	19,316	204,726	186,278	18,448	73,999	73,131	868
1996	273,018	109,498	163,520	253,654	19,364	200,569	182,063	18,506	72,449	71,591	858
1997	269,167	106,865	162,302	248,860	20,307	194,674	175,297	19,377	74,493	73,563	930
1998	273,472	108,752	164,720	248,931	24,541	198,603	174,776	23,827	74,869	74,155	714
1999	274,321	108,301	166,020	249,156	25,165	199,826	175,364	24,462	74,495	73,792	703
2000	275,680	108,164	167,516	250,710	24,970	199,725	175,404	24,321	75,955	75,306	649
2001	289,985	112,874	177,111	260,547	29,438	210,083	181,346	28,737	79,902	79,201	701
2002	299,041	115,466	183,575	269,020	30,021	218,433	189,183	29,250	80,608	79,837	771
2003	306,727	117,795	188,932	274,326	32,401	228,096	196,077	32,019	78,631	78,249	382
2004	308,939	118,129	190,810	276,136	32,803	231,179	198,810	32,369	77,760	77,326	434
2005	311,768	120,023	191,745	272,666	39,102	235,875	197,200	38,675	75,893	75,466	427
2006	308,774	118,865	189,909	272,770	36,004	234,505	198,676	35,829	74,269	74,094	175
2007	306,515	118,640	187,875	270,915	35,600	233,807	198,300	35,507	72,708	72,615	93
2008	313,491	121,873	191,618	274,568	38,923	235,824	197,025	38,799	77,667	77,543	124
2009	322,860	125,728	197,132	280,133	42,727	246,595	204,016	42,579	76,265	76,117	148
2010	326,614	127,437	199,177	283,099	43,515	249,146	205,774	43,372	77,468	77,325	143
2011	323,648	126,160	197,488	281,150	42,498	246,685	204,363	42,322	76,963	76,787	176
2012	312,438	121,719	190,719	273,033	39,405	237,782	198,568	39,214	74,656	74,465	191
2013	303,167	119,291	183,876	264,430	38,737	230,325	191,918	38,407	72,842	72,512	330
2014	294,316	115,837	178,479	256,936	37,380	222,876	185,899	36,977	71,440	71,037	403
Black students											
1976	190,305	84,492	105,813	179,848	10,457	129,770	121,851	7,919	60,535	57,997	2,538
1980	190,989	81,818	109,171	181,237	9,752	131,661	124,236	7,425	59,328	57,001	2,327
1982	182,639	78,874	103,765	171,942	10,697	126,368	117,562	8,806	56,271	54,380	1,891
1984	180,803	76,819	103,984	171,401	9,402	124,445	116,845	7,600	56,358	54,556	1,802
1986	178,628	74,276	104,352	167,971	10,657	123,555	114,502	9,053	55,073	53,469	1,604
1988	194,151	78,268	115,883	183,402	10,749	133,786	124,438	9,348	60,365	58,964	1,401
1990	208,682	82,897	125,785	198,237	10,445	144,204	134,924	9,280	64,478	63,313	1,165
1991	218,366	87,380	130,986	207,449	10,917	152,864	143,411	9,453	65,502	64,038	1,464
1992	228,963	91,949	137,014	217,614	11,349	159,585	149,754	9,831	69,378	67,860	1,518
1993	231,198	93,110	138,088	219,431	11,767	161,444	150,867	10,577	69,754	68,564	1,190
1994	230,162	91,908	138,254	218,565	11,597	161,098	150,682	10,416	69,064	67,883	1,181
1995	229,418	91,132	138,286	218,379	11,039	159,925	149,661	10,264	69,493	68,718	775
1996	224,201	88,306	135,895	213,309	10,892	156,851	146,753	10,098	67,350	66,556	794
1997	222,331	86,641	135,690	210,741	11,590	153,039	142,326	10,713	69,292	68,415	877
1998	223,745	87,163	136,582	211,822	11,923	154,244	142,985	11,259	69,501	68,837	664
1999	226,592	87,987	138,605	213,779	12,813	156,292	144,166	12,126	70,300	69,613	687
2000	227,239	87,319	139,920	215,172	12,067	156,706	145,277	11,429	70,533	69,895	638
2001	238,638	90,718	147,920	224,417	14,221	164,354	150,831	13,523	74,284	73,586	698
2002	247,292	93,538	153,754	231,834	15,458	172,203	157,507	14,696	75,089	74,327	762
2003	253,257	95,703	157,554	236,753	16,504	180,104	163,977	16,127	73,153	72,776	377
2004	257,545	96,750	160,795	241,030	16,515	184,708	168,619	16,089	72,837	72,411	426
2005	256,584	96,891	159,693	238,030	18,554	186,047	167,916	18,131	70,537	70,114	423
2006	255,150	96,508	158,642	238,446	16,704	185,894	169,365	16,529	69,256	69,081	175
2007	253,415	96,313	157,102	236,885	16,530	185,344	168,906	16,438	68,071	67,979	92
2008	258,403	98,634	159,769	240,133	18,270	186,446	168,299	18,147	71,957	71,834	123
2009	264,092	100,590	163,502	243,956	20,136	194,088	174,099	19,989	70,004	69,857	147
2010	265,908	101,605	164,303	245,158	20,750	193,840	173,233	20,607	72,068	71,925	143
2011	263,435	100,526	162,909	242,881	20,554	192,042	171,664	20,378	71,393	71,217	176
2012	251,527	96,079	155,448	232,897	18,630	183,018	164,578	18,440	68,509	68,319	190
2013	241,476	92,454	149,022	223,481	17,995	175,287	157,619	17,668	66,189	65,862	327
2014	231,888	88,469	143,419	214,630	17,258	167,246	150,383	16,863	64,642	64,247	395

NOTE: Historically Black colleges and universities are degree-granting institutions established prior to 1964 with the principal mission of educating Black Americans. Federal regulations, 20 U.S. Code, Section 1061 (2), allow for certain exceptions to the founding date. Data through 1995 are for institutions of higher education, while later data are for degree-granting institutions. Degree-granting institutions grant associate's or higher degrees and participate in Title IV federal financial aid programs. The degree-granting classification is very similar to the earlier higher education classification, but it includes more 2-year colleges and excludes a few higher education institutions that did not grant degrees. Some data have been revised from previously published figures.
SOURCE: U.S. Department of Education, National Center for Education Statistics, Higher Education General Information Survey (HEGIS), "Fall Enrollment in Colleges and Universities," 1976 through 1985 surveys; Integrated Postsecondary Education Data System (IPEDS), "Fall Enrollment Survey" (IPEDS-EF:86–99); and IPEDS Spring 2001 through Spring 2015, Fall Enrollment component. (This table was prepared March 2016.)

Table 313.30. Selected statistics on degree-granting historically Black colleges and universities, by control and level of institution: Selected years, 1990 through 2014

Selected statistics	Total	Public			Private		
		Total	4-year	2-year	Total	4-year	2-year
1	2	3	4	5	6	7	8
Number of institutions, fall 2014	**100**	**51**	**40**	**11**	**49**	**48**	**1**
Fall enrollment							
Total enrollment, fall 1990	257,152	187,046	171,969	15,077	70,106	68,528	1,578
Males	105,157	76,541	70,220	6,321	28,616	28,054	562
Males, Black	82,897	57,255	54,041	3,214	25,642	25,198	444
Females	151,995	110,505	101,749	8,756	41,490	40,474	1,016
Females, Black	125,785	86,949	80,883	6,066	38,836	38,115	721
Total enrollment, fall 2000	275,680	199,725	175,404	24,321	75,955	75,306	649
Males	108,164	78,186	68,322	9,864	29,978	29,771	207
Males, Black	87,319	60,029	56,017	4,012	27,290	27,085	205
Females	167,516	121,539	107,082	14,457	45,977	45,535	442
Females, Black	139,920	96,677	89,260	7,417	43,243	42,810	433
Total enrollment, fall 2010	326,614	249,146	205,774	43,372	77,468	77,325	143
Males	127,437	95,883	78,528	17,355	31,554	31,482	72
Males, Black	101,605	72,629	65,512	7,117	28,976	28,904	72
Females	199,177	153,263	127,246	26,017	45,914	45,843	71
Females, Black	164,303	121,211	107,721	13,490	43,092	43,021	71
Total enrollment, fall 2014	294,316	222,876	185,899	36,977	71,440	71,037	403
Males	115,837	86,571	71,147	15,424	29,266	29,142	124
Males, Black	88,469	62,428	56,178	6,250	26,041	25,919	122
Females	178,479	136,305	114,752	21,553	42,174	41,895	279
Females, Black	143,419	104,818	94,205	10,613	38,601	38,328	273
Full-time enrollment, fall 2014	231,002	164,824	147,352	17,472	66,178	65,865	313
Males	93,326	66,151	58,425	7,726	27,175	27,073	102
Females	137,676	98,673	88,927	9,746	39,003	38,792	211
Part-time enrollment, fall 2014	63,314	58,052	38,547	19,505	5,262	5,172	90
Males	22,511	20,420	12,722	7,698	2,091	2,069	22
Females	40,803	37,632	25,825	11,807	3,171	3,103	68
Earned degrees conferred, 2013–14							
Associate's	4,224	3,926	980	2,946	298	287	11
Males	1,438	1,285	224	1,061	153	149	4
Males, Black	651	511	107	404	140	136	4
Females	2,786	2,641	756	1,885	145	138	7
Females, Black	1,475	1,340	371	969	135	128	7
Bachelor's	33,700	24,456	24,456	†	9,244	9,244	†
Males	12,092	8,810	8,810	†	3,282	3,282	†
Males, Black	9,927	6,929	6,929	†	2,998	2,998	†
Females	21,608	15,646	15,646	†	5,962	5,962	†
Females, Black	17,955	12,484	12,484	†	5,471	5,471	†
Master's	7,845	6,626	6,626	†	1,219	1,219	†
Males	2,331	1,901	1,901	†	430	430	†
Males, Black	1,647	1,291	1,291	†	356	356	†
Females	5,514	4,725	4,725	†	789	789	†
Females, Black	4,019	3,349	3,349	†	670	670	†
Doctor's[1]	2,423	1,361	1,361	†	1,062	1,062	†
Males	999	580	580	†	419	419	†
Males, Black	563	273	273	†	290	290	†
Females	1,424	781	781	†	643	643	†
Females, Black	918	459	459	†	459	459	†
Financial statistics, 2013–14[2]	In thousands of current dollars						
Total revenue	$8,079,150	$5,075,176	$4,693,591	$381,585	$3,003,974	$3,001,508	$2,466
Student tuition and fees	1,825,772	959,451	914,934	44,517	866,321	864,494	1,827
Federal government[3]	2,033,532	1,258,853	1,092,307	166,546	774,679	774,586	93
State governments	1,900,539	1,832,727	1,708,812	123,915	67,812	67,812	0
Local governments	104,177	94,235	63,181	31,054	9,942	9,942	0
Private gifts and grants[4]	265,232	26,610	26,038	572	238,622	238,149	472
Investment return (gain or loss) ...	470,482	80,163	79,771	392	390,319	390,319	0
Auxiliary (essentially self-supporting) enterprises ...	868,553	529,742	523,507	6,235	338,811	338,738	74
Hospitals and other sources	610,864	293,395	285,040	8,355	317,469	317,469	0
Total expenditures	7,619,613	4,884,042	4,520,840	363,203	2,735,570	2,733,190	2,380
Instruction	1,914,052	1,330,125	1,210,706	119,419	583,927	583,560	367
Research	403,596	260,769	260,374	395	142,827	142,827	0
Academic support	522,481	373,829	350,680	23,149	148,653	148,496	157
Institutional support	1,093,096	618,368	564,598	53,771	474,728	474,091	636
Auxiliary (essentially self-supporting) enterprises ...	715,292	532,572	523,458	9,114	182,720	182,589	131
Other expenditures	2,971,095	1,768,379	1,611,024	157,356	1,202,716	1,201,627	1,089

†Not applicable.
[1]Includes Ph.D., Ed.D., and comparable degrees at the doctoral level, as well as such degrees as M.D., D.D.S., and law degrees that were formerly classified as first-professional degrees.
[2]Totals (column 2) of public and private institutions together are approximate because public and private nonprofit institutions fill out different survey forms with different accounting concepts.
[3]Includes independent operations.
[4]Includes contributions from affiliated entities.
NOTE: Degree-granting institutions grant associate's or higher degrees and participate in Title IV federal financial aid programs. Historically Black colleges and universities are degree-granting institutions established prior to 1964 with the principal mission of educating Black Americans. Federal regulations, 20 U.S. Code, Section 1061 (2), allow for certain exceptions to the founding date. Federal, state, and local governments revenue includes appropriations, grants, and contracts. Totals include persons of other racial/ethnic groups not separately identified. Detail may not sum to totals because of rounding.
SOURCE: U.S. Department of Education, National Center for Education Statistics, Integrated Postsecondary Education Data System (IPEDS), "Fall Enrollment Survey" (IPEDS-EF:90); IPEDS Spring 2001, Spring 2011, and Spring 2015, Fall Enrollment component; IPEDS Spring 2015, Finance component; and IPEDS Fall 2014, Completions component. (This table was prepared March 2016.)

Table 314.10. Total and full-time-equivalent (FTE) staff and FTE student/FTE staff ratios in postsecondary institutions participating in Title IV programs, by degree-granting status, control of institution, and primary occupation: Fall 1993, fall 2003, and fall 2013

Degree-granting status, control of institution, and primary occupation	Fall 1993				Fall 2003				Fall 2013			
	Total		Full-time-equivalent (FTE)		Total		Full-time-equivalent (FTE)		Total		Full-time-equivalent (FTE)	
	Number	Percent	Total	FTE students per FTE staff	Number	Percent	Total	FTE students per FTE staff	Number	Percent	Total	FTE students per FTE staff
1	2	3	4	5	6	7	8	9	10	11	12	13
All postsecondary institutions	**2,727,504**	**100.0**	**2,152,184**	**5.2**	**3,237,089**	**100.0**	**2,491,009**	**5.2**	**3,969,226**	**100.0**	**3,003,987**	**5.3**
Faculty (instruction/research/public service)	973,289	35.7	707,820	15.7	1,198,420	37.0	828,883	15.8	1,582,360	39.9	1,068,489	14.8
Graduate assistants	203,049	7.4	67,683	164.6	292,094	9.0	97,365	134.1	363,416	9.2	121,139	130.6
Other staff	1,551,166	56.9	1,376,681	8.1	1,746,575	54.0	1,564,761	8.3	2,023,450	51.0	1,814,360	8.7
Degree-granting institutions[1]												
Total	**2,602,612**	**100.0**	**2,056,544**	**5.0**	**3,187,907**	**100.0**	**2,451,397**	**5.2**	**3,896,053**	**100.0**	**2,946,974**	**5.2**
Faculty (instruction/research/public service)	915,474	35.2	668,962	15.5	1,173,593	36.8	811,259	15.6	1,545,381	39.7	1,042,712	14.8
Graduate assistants	202,819	7.8	67,606	153.1	292,061	9.2	97,354	130.3	363,416	9.3	121,139	127.2
Other staff	1,484,319	57.0	1,319,976	7.8	1,722,253	54.0	1,542,784	8.2	1,987,256	51.0	1,783,123	8.6
Public	1,812,513	100.0	1,408,451	5.5	2,163,336	100.0	1,633,890	5.7	2,527,284	100.0	1,888,157	5.7
Faculty (instruction/research/public service)	650,434	35.9	471,977	16.6	791,766	36.6	547,294	16.9	968,734	38.3	664,555	16.1
Graduate assistants	173,678	9.6	57,893	134.9	239,923	11.1	79,974	115.5	287,852	11.4	95,951	111.5
Other staff	988,401	54.5	878,582	8.9	1,131,647	52.3	1,006,622	9.2	1,270,698	50.3	1,127,651	9.5
Private, nonprofit	766,723	100.0	630,876	3.7	934,992	100.0	755,743	3.7	1,156,998	100.0	920,444	3.7
Faculty (instruction/research/public service)	254,130	33.1	190,083	12.4	330,097	35.3	237,397	11.9	449,072	38.8	318,441	10.6
Graduate assistants	28,065	3.7	9,355	251.5	52,026	5.6	17,342	162.2	75,113	6.5	25,038	134.6
Other staff	484,528	63.2	431,438	5.5	552,869	59.1	501,004	5.6	632,813	54.7	576,965	5.8
Private, for-profit	23,376	100.0	17,217	10.8	89,579	100.0	61,764	10.3	211,771	100.0	138,373	9.7
Faculty (instruction/research/public service)	10,910	46.7	6,903	26.9	51,730	57.7	26,568	23.8	127,575	60.2	59,716	22.5
Graduate assistants	1,076	4.6	359	518.3	112	0.1	37	16,960.9	451	0.2	150	8,948.8
Other staff	11,390	48.7	9,956	18.7	37,737	42.1	35,159	18.0	83,745	39.5	78,507	17.1
Non-degree-granting institutions[2]												
Total	**124,892**	**100.0**	**95,640**	**8.3**	**49,182**	**100.0**	**39,612**	**9.3**	**73,173**	**100.0**	**57,014**	**7.1**
Faculty (instruction/research/public service)	57,815	46.3	38,858	20.3	24,827	50.5	17,624	20.9	36,979	50.5	25,776	15.8
Graduate assistants	230	0.2	77	10,293.8	33	0.1	11	33,429.2	0	0.0	0	†
Other staff	66,847	53.5	56,705	13.9	24,322	49.5	21,977	16.7	36,194	49.5	31,237	13.0
Public	31,554	100.0	24,231	9.5	25,276	100.0	19,665	4.1	22,452	100.0	16,133	4.8
Faculty (instruction/research/public service)	18,142	57.5	12,878	17.9	12,749	50.4	8,358	9.5	11,606	51.7	7,257	10.7
Graduate assistants	22	0.1	7	31,442.6	0	0.0	0	†	0	0.0	0	†
Other staff	13,390	42.4	11,346	20.3	12,527	49.6	11,307	7.1	10,846	48.3	8,876	8.7
Private, nonprofit	34,348	100.0	25,897	5.0	4,091	100.0	3,274	8.8	4,394	100.0	3,401	5.3
Faculty (instruction/research/public service)	12,485	36.3	7,810	16.5	2,021	49.4	1,500	19.3	2,015	45.9	1,440	12.6
Graduate assistants	189	0.6	63	2,049.5	0	0.0	0	†	0	0.0	0	†
Other staff	21,674	63.1	18,023	7.2	2,070	50.6	1,774	16.3	2,379	54.1	1,961	9.2
Private, for-profit	58,990	100.0	45,512	9.4	19,815	100.0	16,672	15.5	46,327	100.0	37,480	8.3
Faculty (instruction/research/public service)	27,188	46.1	18,170	23.6	10,057	50.8	7,766	33.4	23,358	50.4	17,079	18.2
Graduate assistants	19	#	6	67,814.4	33	0.2	11	23,546.0	0	0.0	0	†
Other staff	31,783	53.9	27,336	15.7	9,725	49.1	8,896	29.1	22,969	49.6	20,400	15.2

†Not applicable.
#Rounds to zero.
[1]Data for 1993 are for institutions of higher education, while later data are for degree-granting institutions. Degree-granting institutions grant associate's or higher degrees and participate in Title IV federal financial aid programs. The degree-granting classification is very similar to the earlier higher education classification, but it includes more 2-year colleges and excludes a few higher education institutions that did not grant degrees.
[2]Data are for institutions that did not offer accredited 4-year or 2-year degree programs, but were participating in Title IV federal financial aid programs. Includes some institutions transitioning to higher level program offerings, though still classified at a lower level.

NOTE: Full-time-equivalent staff is the full-time staff, plus the full-time equivalent of the part-time staff. Data for 2013 include institutions with fewer than 15 full-time employees; these institutions did not report staff data prior to 2007. By definition, all graduate assistants are part time. Detail may not sum to totals because of rounding. Some data have been revised from previously published figures.
SOURCE: U.S. Department of Education, National Center for Education Statistics, Integrated Postsecondary Education Data System (IPEDS), "Fall Enrollment Survey" (IPEDS-EF:93) and "Fall Staff Survey" (IPEDS-S:93); IPEDS Spring 2003 and 2013, Enrollment component; and IPEDS Winter 2003–04 and Spring 2014, Human Resources component, Fall Staff section. (This table was prepared March 2016.)

Table 314.20. Employees in degree-granting postsecondary institutions, by sex, employment status, control and level of institution, and primary occupation: Selected years, fall 1991 through fall 2013

Sex, employment status, control and level of institution, and primary occupation	1991	1993	1995	1997	1999	2001	2003	2005	2007	2009	2011	2013	Percent change, 2003 to 2013
1	2	3	4	5	6	7	8	9	10	11	12	13	14
All institutions	2,545,235	2,602,612	2,662,075	2,752,504	2,883,175	3,083,353	3,187,907	3,379,087	3,561,428	3,723,419	3,840,980	3,896,053	22.2
Executive/administrative/managerial	144,755	143,675	147,445	151,363	159,888	152,038	184,913	196,324	217,518	230,579	238,718	(¹)	†
Faculty (instruction/research/public service)	826,252	915,474	931,706	989,813	1,027,830	1,113,183	1,173,593	1,290,426	1,371,390	1,439,144	1,523,615	1,545,381	31.7
Graduate assistants	197,751	202,819	215,909	222,724	239,738	261,136	292,061	317,141	328,979	342,393	355,916	363,416	24.4
Other	1,376,477	1,340,644	1,367,015	1,388,604	1,455,719	1,556,996	1,537,340	1,575,196	1,643,541	1,711,303	1,722,731	1,987,256	†
Males	1,227,591	1,256,037	1,274,676	1,315,311	1,365,812	1,451,773	1,496,867	1,581,498	1,650,350	1,709,636	1,754,713	1,772,803	18.4
Executive/administrative/managerial	85,423	82,748	82,127	81,931	83,883	79,348	91,604	95,223	102,258	106,892	109,374	(¹)	†
Faculty (instruction/research/public service)	525,599	561,123	562,893	587,420	602,469	644,514	663,723	714,453	743,812	761,035	789,197	791,971	19.3
Graduate assistants	119,125	120,384	123,962	125,873	132,607	142,120	156,881	167,529	173,121	180,941	188,468	191,501	22.1
Other	497,444	491,782	505,694	520,087	546,853	585,791	584,659	604,293	631,159	660,768	667,674	789,331	†
Females	1,317,644	1,346,575	1,387,399	1,437,193	1,517,363	1,631,580	1,691,040	1,797,589	1,911,078	2,013,783	2,086,267	2,123,250	25.6
Executive/administrative/managerial	59,332	60,927	65,318	69,432	76,005	72,690	93,309	101,101	115,260	123,687	129,344	(¹)	†
Faculty (instruction/research/public service)	300,653	354,351	368,813	402,393	425,361	468,669	509,870	575,973	627,578	678,109	734,418	753,410	47.8
Graduate assistants	78,626	82,435	91,947	96,851	107,131	119,016	135,180	149,612	155,858	161,452	167,448	171,915	27.2
Other	879,033	848,862	861,321	868,517	908,866	971,205	952,681	970,903	1,012,382	1,050,535	1,055,057	1,197,925	25.7
Full-time	1,812,912	1,783,510	1,801,371	1,828,507	1,918,676	2,043,208	2,083,142	2,179,864	2,281,223	2,381,702	2,435,533	2,472,434	18.7
Executive/administrative/managerial	139,116	137,834	140,990	144,529	153,722	146,523	178,691	190,078	210,257	222,282	231,602	(¹)	†
Faculty (instruction/research/public service)	535,623	545,706	550,822	568,719	590,937	617,868	630,092	675,624	703,463	728,977	761,619	791,378	25.6
Other	1,138,173	1,099,970	1,109,559	1,115,259	1,174,017	1,278,817	1,274,359	1,314,162	1,367,503	1,430,443	1,442,312	1,681,056	†
Part-time	732,323	819,102	860,704	923,997	964,499	1,040,145	1,104,765	1,199,223	1,280,205	1,341,717	1,405,447	1,423,619	28.9
Executive/administrative/managerial	5,639	5,841	6,455	6,834	6,166	5,515	6,222	6,246	7,261	8,297	7,116	(¹)	†
Faculty (instruction/research/public service)	290,629	369,768	380,884	421,094	436,893	495,315	543,501	614,802	667,927	710,167	761,996	754,003	38.7
Graduate assistants	197,751	202,819	215,909	222,724	239,738	261,136	292,061	317,141	328,979	342,393	355,916	363,416	24.4
Other	238,304	240,674	257,456	273,345	281,702	278,179	262,981	261,034	276,038	280,860	280,419	306,200	†
Public 4-year	1,341,914	1,333,533	1,383,476	1,418,661	1,470,842	1,558,576	1,569,870	1,656,709	1,741,699	1,803,724	1,843,204	1,884,854	20.1
Executive/administrative/managerial	63,674	59,678	60,590	61,984	64,336	60,245	70,397	74,241	81,364	84,355	84,911	(¹)	†
Faculty (instruction/research/public service)	358,376	374,021	384,399	404,109	417,086	438,459	450,123	486,691	518,221	539,901	575,534	601,126	33.5
Graduate assistants	144,344	170,916	178,342	182,481	196,393	218,260	239,600	257,578	266,429	275,872	285,905	287,839	20.1
Other	775,520	728,918	760,145	770,087	793,027	841,612	809,750	838,199	875,685	903,596	896,854	995,889	†
Private 4-year	734,509	762,034	770,004	786,634	857,820	912,924	988,895	1,073,764	1,157,226	1,229,784	1,297,486	1,318,760	33.4
Executive/administrative/managerial	57,148	59,230	62,314	62,580	69,626	65,739	84,306	90,415	103,183	111,616	118,268	(¹)	†
Faculty (instruction/research/public service)	232,893	251,948	262,660	278,541	296,737	325,713	364,166	430,305	472,628	498,582	540,093	550,512	51.2
Graduate assistants	23,989	28,880	33,853	36,064	38,597	41,611	52,101	59,147	62,550	66,521	70,011	75,537	45.0
Other	420,479	421,976	411,177	409,449	452,860	479,861	488,322	493,897	518,865	553,065	569,114	692,711	†
Public 2-year	441,414	478,980	482,454	512,086	517,967	578,394	593,466	610,978	620,784	638,352	641,616	642,430	8.3
Executive/administrative/managerial	20,772	21,531	21,806	22,822	21,459	22,566	25,872	26,770	27,363	27,827	27,562	(¹)	†
Faculty (instruction/research/public service)	222,532	276,413	272,434	290,451	296,239	332,665	341,643	354,497	358,925	373,778	377,696	367,608	7.6
Graduate assistants	29,216	2,762	3,401	3,561	4,170	1,215	323	374	0	0	0	13	-96.0
Other	168,894	178,274	184,813	195,252	196,099	221,948	225,628	229,337	234,496	236,747	236,358	274,809	†
Private 2-year	27,398	28,065	26,141	35,123	36,546	33,459	35,676	37,636	41,719	51,559	58,674	50,009	40.2
Executive/administrative/managerial	3,161	3,236	2,735	3,977	4,467	3,488	4,338	4,898	5,608	6,781	7,977	(¹)	†
Faculty (instruction/research/public service)	12,451	13,092	12,213	16,712	17,768	16,346	17,661	18,933	21,616	26,883	30,292	26,135	48.0
Graduate assistants	202	261	313	618	578	50	37	42	0	0	0	27	-27.0
Other	11,584	11,476	10,880	13,816	13,733	13,575	13,640	13,763	14,495	17,895	20,405	23,847	†

†Not applicable.
¹Included in other. Primary occupations were reclassified as of fall 2013; only the faculty and graduate assistant categories are comparable with data from earlier years.
NOTE: Data through 1995 are for institutions of higher education, while later data are for degree-granting institutions. Degree-granting institutions grant associate's or higher degrees and participate in Title IV federal financial aid programs. The degree-granting classification is very similar to the earlier higher education classification, but it includes more 2-year colleges and excludes a few higher education institutions that did not grant degrees. Beginning in 2007, includes institutions with fewer than 15 full-time employees; these institutions did not report staff data prior to 2007. By definition, all graduate assistants are part time. Some data have been revised from previously published figures.
SOURCE: U.S. Department of Education, National Center for Education Statistics, Integrated Postsecondary Education Data System (IPEDS), "Fall Staff Survey" (IPEDS-S:91–99); IPEDS Winter 2001–02 through Winter 2011–12, Human Resources component, Fall Staff section; and IPEDS Spring 2014, Human Resources component, Fall Staff section. (This table was prepared March 2016.)

Table 314.30. Employees in degree-granting postsecondary institutions, by employment status, sex, control and level of institution, and primary occupation: Fall 2013

Control and level of institution and primary occupation	Full-time and part-time Total Number	Percentage distribution	Males	Females Number	Females Percent of all employees	Full-time Total Number	Full-time Total Percent of all employees	Males	Females	Part-time Total	Males	Females
1	2	3	4	5	6	7	8	9	10	11	12	13
All institutions	**3,896,053**	**100.0**	**1,772,803**	**2,123,250**	**54.5**	**2,472,434**	**63.5**	**1,111,721**	**1,360,713**	**1,423,619**	**661,082**	**762,537**
Faculty (instruction/research/public service)	1,545,381	39.7	791,971	753,410	48.8	791,378	51.2	436,470	354,908	754,003	355,501	398,502
Instruction	1,437,789	36.9	731,068	706,721	49.2	705,821	49.1	386,480	319,341	731,968	344,588	387,380
Research	81,670	2.1	48,421	33,249	40.7	67,963	83.2	41,091	26,872	13,707	7,330	6,377
Public service	25,922	0.7	12,482	13,440	51.8	17,594	67.9	8,899	8,695	8,328	3,583	4,745
Graduate assistants	363,416	9.3	191,501	171,915	47.3	†	†	†	†	363,416	191,501	171,915
Librarians, curators, and archivists	44,677	1.1	13,019	31,658	70.9	37,666	84.3	11,336	26,330	7,011	1,683	5,328
Student and academic affairs and other education services	158,653	4.1	52,255	106,398	67.1	100,110	63.1	30,340	69,770	58,543	21,915	36,628
Management	252,615	6.5	113,829	138,786	54.9	244,848	96.9	110,829	134,019	7,767	3,000	4,767
Business and financial operations	193,065	5.0	52,029	141,036	73.1	178,561	92.5	48,120	130,441	14,504	3,909	10,595
Computer, engineering, and science	231,714	5.9	140,140	91,574	39.5	210,155	90.7	130,379	79,776	21,559	9,761	11,798
Community, social service, legal, arts, design, entertainment, sports, and media	167,466	4.3	74,705	92,761	55.4	135,174	80.7	59,460	75,714	32,292	15,245	17,047
Healthcare practitioners and technicians	117,576	3.0	33,215	84,361	71.8	94,854	80.7	27,696	67,158	22,722	5,519	17,203
Service occupations	241,064	6.2	140,612	100,452	41.7	200,353	83.1	118,375	81,978	40,711	22,237	18,474
Sales and related occupations	15,400	0.4	5,374	10,026	65.1	12,503	81.2	4,614	7,889	2,897	760	2,137
Office and administrative support	470,167	12.1	78,893	391,274	83.2	379,996	80.8	54,756	325,240	90,171	24,137	66,034
Natural resources, construction, and maintenance	75,401	1.9	69,198	6,203	8.2	70,692	93.8	65,766	4,926	4,709	3,432	1,277
Production, transportation, and material moving	19,458	0.5	16,062	3,396	17.5	16,144	83.0	13,580	2,564	3,314	2,482	832
Public 4-year	**1,884,854**	**100.0**	**881,207**	**1,003,647**	**53.2**	**1,269,084**	**67.3**	**588,309**	**680,775**	**615,770**	**292,898**	**322,872**
Faculty (instruction/research/public service)	601,126	31.9	325,337	275,789	45.9	401,086	66.7	229,846	171,240	200,040	95,491	104,549
Instruction	535,393	28.4	288,615	246,778	46.1	347,903	65.0	199,382	148,521	187,490	89,233	98,257
Research	51,398	2.7	29,939	21,459	41.8	42,126	82.0	25,102	17,024	9,272	4,837	4,435
Public service	14,335	0.8	6,783	7,552	52.7	11,057	77.1	5,362	5,695	3,278	1,421	1,857
Graduate assistants	287,839	15.3	151,386	136,453	47.4	†	†	†	†	287,839	151,386	136,453
Librarians, curators, and archivists	19,022	1.0	5,735	13,287	69.9	17,302	91.0	5,319	11,983	1,720	416	1,304
Student and academic affairs and other education services	58,198	3.1	19,347	38,851	66.8	40,731	70.0	12,630	28,101	17,467	6,717	10,750
Management	107,423	5.7	50,249	57,174	53.2	103,754	96.6	48,775	54,979	3,669	1,474	2,195
Business and financial operations	109,279	5.8	28,912	80,367	73.5	100,805	92.2	26,723	74,082	8,474	2,189	6,285
Computer, engineering, and science	141,991	7.5	85,695	56,296	39.6	128,585	90.6	79,926	48,659	13,406	5,769	7,637
Community, social service, legal, arts, design, entertainment, sports, and media	77,614	4.1	33,001	44,613	57.5	67,062	86.4	28,792	38,270	10,552	4,209	6,343
Healthcare practitioners and technicians	75,038	4.0	22,157	52,881	70.5	62,240	82.9	19,244	42,996	12,798	2,913	9,885
Service occupations	125,303	6.6	68,297	57,006	45.5	108,009	86.2	59,632	48,377	17,294	8,665	8,629
Sales and related occupations	2,879	0.2	909	1,970	68.4	2,230	77.5	745	1,485	649	164	485
Office and administrative support	217,885	11.6	34,710	183,175	84.1	180,069	82.6	24,160	155,909	37,816	10,550	27,266
Natural resources, construction, and maintenance	48,287	2.6	44,682	3,605	7.5	45,896	95.0	42,924	2,972	2,391	1,758	633
Production, transportation, and material moving	12,970	0.7	10,790	2,180	16.8	11,315	87.2	9,593	1,722	1,655	1,197	458
Public 2-year	**642,430**	**100.0**	**271,794**	**370,636**	**57.7**	**299,509**	**46.6**	**120,709**	**178,800**	**342,921**	**151,085**	**191,836**
Faculty (instruction/research/public service)	367,608	57.2	167,363	200,245	54.5	111,380	30.3	50,073	61,307	256,228	117,290	138,938
Instruction	364,348	56.7	166,121	198,227	54.4	111,033	30.5	49,946	61,087	253,315	116,175	137,140
Research	80	#	38	42	52.5	64	80.0	31	33	16	7	9
Public service	3,180	0.5	1,204	1,976	62.1	283	8.9	96	187	2,897	1,108	1,789
Graduate assistants	13	#	6	7	53.8	†	†	†	†	13	6	7
Librarians, curators, and archivists	5,737	0.9	1,259	4,478	78.1	3,913	68.2	894	3,019	1,824	365	1,459
Student and academic affairs and other education services	47,574	7.4	16,460	31,114	65.4	20,284	42.6	6,119	14,165	27,290	10,341	16,949
Management	32,322	5.0	13,579	18,743	58.0	31,140	96.3	13,099	18,041	1,182	480	702
Business and financial operations	17,932	2.8	4,951	12,981	72.4	15,206	84.8	4,017	11,189	2,726	934	1,792
Computer, engineering, and science	16,579	2.6	11,109	5,470	33.0	13,806	83.3	9,457	4,349	2,773	1,652	1,121
Community, social service, legal, arts, design, entertainment, sports, and media	23,528	3.7	8,845	14,683	62.4	15,944	67.8	5,611	10,333	7,584	3,234	4,350
Healthcare practitioners and technicians	1,755	0.3	557	1,198	68.3	769	43.8	290	479	986	267	719
Service occupations	35,117	5.5	24,563	10,554	30.1	24,843	70.7	18,004	6,839	10,274	6,559	3,715
Sales and related occupations	2,115	0.3	566	1,549	73.2	1,104	52.2	311	793	1,011	255	756
Office and administrative support	83,740	13.0	15,184	68,556	81.9	54,255	64.8	6,643	47,612	29,485	8,541	20,944
Natural resources, construction, and maintenance	7,183	1.1	6,373	810	11.3	6,047	84.2	5,532	515	1,136	841	295
Production, transportation, and material moving	1,227	0.2	979	248	20.2	818	66.7	659	159	409	320	89

See notes at end of table.

Table 314.30. Employees in degree-granting postsecondary institutions, by employment status, sex, control and level of institution, and primary occupation: Fall 2013—Continued

Control and level of institution and primary occupation	Full-time and part-time					Full-time				Part-time		
	Total		Males	Females		Total		Males	Females	Total	Males	Females
	Number	Percentage distribution		Number	Percent of all employees	Number	Percent of all employees					
1	2	3	4	5	6	7	8	9	10	11	12	13
Private nonprofit 4-year	1,151,167	100.0	529,295	621,872	54.0	798,665	69.4	361,384	437,281	352,502	167,911	184,591
Faculty (instruction/research/public service)	446,076	38.7	240,749	205,327	46.0	251,839	56.5	144,202	107,637	194,237	96,547	97,690
Instruction	407,692	35.4	217,893	189,799	46.6	219,913	53.9	124,847	95,066	187,779	93,046	94,733
Research	30,071	2.6	18,394	11,677	38.8	25,697	85.5	15,924	9,773	4,374	2,470	1,904
Public service	8,313	0.7	4,462	3,851	46.3	6,229	74.9	3,431	2,798	2,084	1,031	1,053
Graduate assistants	75,106	6.5	39,938	35,168	46.8	†	†	†	†	75,106	39,938	35,168
Librarians, curators, and archivists	18,204	1.6	5,595	12,609	69.3	15,242	83.7	4,822	10,420	2,962	773	2,189
Student and academic affairs and other education services	39,428	3.4	12,325	27,103	68.7	27,958	70.9	8,144	19,814	11,470	4,181	7,289
Management	95,860	8.3	42,557	53,303	55.6	93,146	97.2	41,589	51,557	2,714	968	1,746
Business and financial operations	58,434	5.1	15,972	42,462	72.7	55,472	94.9	15,268	40,204	2,962	704	2,258
Computer, engineering, and science	70,302	6.1	41,078	29,224	41.6	65,050	92.5	38,828	26,222	5,252	2,250	3,002
Community, social service, legal, arts, design, entertainment, sports, and media	58,198	5.1	29,586	28,612	49.2	44,729	76.9	22,118	22,611	13,469	7,468	6,001
Healthcare practitioners and technicians	40,507	3.5	10,418	30,089	74.3	31,748	78.4	8,133	23,615	8,759	2,285	6,474
Service occupations	78,058	6.8	46,000	32,058	41.1	65,746	84.2	39,493	26,253	12,312	6,507	5,805
Sales and related occupations	4,428	0.4	1,546	2,882	65.1	3,451	77.9	1,268	2,183	977	278	699
Office and administrative support	142,257	12.4	21,827	120,430	84.7	122,166	85.9	17,434	104,732	20,091	4,393	15,698
Natural resources, construction, and maintenance	19,322	1.7	17,629	1,693	8.8	18,280	94.6	16,893	1,387	1,042	736	306
Production, transportation, and material moving	4,987	0.4	4,075	912	18.3	3,838	77.0	3,192	646	1,149	883	266
Private nonprofit 2-year	5,831	100.0	2,268	3,563	61.1	3,502	60.1	1,358	2,144	2,329	910	1,419
Faculty (instruction/research/public service)	2,996	51.4	1,170	1,826	60.9	1,287	43.0	497	790	1,709	673	1,036
Instruction	2,983	51.2	1,162	1,821	61.0	1,281	42.9	493	788	1,702	669	1,033
Research	9	0.2	6	3	33.3	4	44.4	3	1	5	3	2
Public service	4	0.1	2	2	50.0	2	50.0	1	1	2	1	1
Graduate assistants	7	0.1	5	2	28.6	†	†	†	†	7	5	2
Librarians, curators, and archivists	114	2.0	21	93	81.6	69	60.5	13	56	45	8	37
Student and academic affairs and other education services	365	6.3	129	236	64.7	281	77.0	105	176	84	24	60
Management	561	9.6	250	311	55.4	539	96.1	244	295	22	6	16
Business and financial operations	203	3.5	54	149	73.4	169	83.3	48	121	34	6	28
Computer, engineering, and science	114	2.0	92	22	19.3	98	86.0	79	19	16	13	3
Community, social service, legal, arts, design, entertainment, sports, and media	224	3.8	124	100	44.6	155	69.2	72	83	69	52	17
Healthcare practitioners and technicians	23	0.4	3	20	87.0	17	73.9	3	14	6	0	6
Service occupations	300	5.1	201	99	33.0	167	55.7	124	43	133	77	56
Sales and related occupations	112	1.9	39	73	65.2	100	89.3	36	64	12	3	9
Office and administrative support	719	12.3	106	613	85.3	546	75.9	78	468	173	28	145
Natural resources, construction, and maintenance	82	1.4	65	17	20.7	69	84.1	55	14	13	10	3
Production, transportation, and material moving	11	0.2	9	2	18.2	5	45.5	4	1	6	5	1
Private for-profit 4-year	167,593	100.0	72,123	95,470	57.0	73,669	44.0	30,014	43,655	93,924	42,109	51,815
Faculty (instruction/research/public service)	104,436	62.3	48,079	56,357	54.0	16,184	15.5	7,871	8,313	88,252	40,208	48,044
Instruction	104,317	62.2	48,033	56,284	54.0	16,152	15.5	7,856	8,296	88,165	40,177	47,988
Research	55	#	23	32	58.2	27	49.1	13	14	28	10	18
Public service	64	#	23	41	64.1	5	7.8	2	3	59	21	38
Graduate assistants	431	0.3	159	272	63.1	†	†	†	†	431	159	272
Librarians, curators, and archivists	1,151	0.7	297	854	74.2	850	73.8	224	626	301	73	228
Student and academic affairs and other education services	10,376	6.2	3,211	7,165	69.1	8,490	81.8	2,697	5,793	1,886	514	1,372
Management	11,725	7.0	5,265	6,460	55.1	11,607	99.0	5,223	6,384	118	42	76
Business and financial operations	4,772	2.8	1,518	3,254	68.2	4,591	96.2	1,478	3,113	181	40	141
Computer, engineering, and science	2,345	1.4	1,841	504	21.5	2,265	96.6	1,786	479	80	55	25
Community, social service, legal, arts, design, entertainment, sports, and media	7,270	4.3	2,948	4,322	59.4	6,731	92.6	2,689	4,042	539	259	280
Healthcare practitioners and technicians	137	0.1	44	93	67.9	68	49.6	24	44	69	20	49
Service occupations	1,575	0.9	1,089	486	30.9	1,125	71.4	801	324	450	288	162
Sales and related occupations	3,335	2.0	1,415	1,920	57.6	3,264	97.9	1,400	1,864	71	15	56
Office and administrative support	19,526	11.7	5,830	13,696	70.1	18,107	92.7	5,492	12,615	1,419	338	1,081
Natural resources, construction, and maintenance	270	0.2	235	35	13.0	227	84.1	204	23	43	31	12
Production, transportation, and material moving	244	0.1	192	52	21.3	160	65.6	125	35	84	67	17

See notes at end of table.

Table 314.30. Employees in degree-granting postsecondary institutions, by employment status, sex, control and level of institution, and primary occupation: Fall 2013—Continued

Control and level of institution and primary occupation	Full-time and part-time					Full-time				Part-time		
	Total		Males	Females		Total		Males	Females	Total	Males	Females
	Number	Percentage distribution		Number	Percent of all employees	Number	Percent of all employees					
1	2	3	4	5	6	7	8	9	10	11	12	13
Private for-profit 2-year	**44,178**	**100.0**	**16,116**	**28,062**	**63.5**	**28,005**	**63.4**	**9,947**	**18,058**	**16,173**	**6,169**	**10,004**
Faculty (instruction/research/public service)	23,139	52.4	9,273	13,866	59.9	9,602	41.5	3,981	5,621	13,537	5,292	8,245
Instruction	23,056	52.2	9,244	13,812	59.9	9,539	41.4	3,956	5,583	13,517	5,288	8,229
Research	57	0.1	21	36	63.2	45	78.9	18	27	12	3	9
Public service	26	0.1	8	18	69.2	18	69.2	7	11	8	1	7
Graduate assistants	20	#	7	13	65.0	†	†	†	†	20	7	13
Librarians, curators, and archivists	449	1.0	112	337	75.1	290	64.6	64	226	159	48	111
Student and academic affairs and other education services	2,712	6.1	783	1,929	71.1	2,366	87.2	645	1,721	346	138	208
Management	4,724	10.7	1,929	2,795	59.2	4,662	98.7	1,899	2,763	62	30	32
Business and financial operations	2,445	5.5	622	1,823	74.6	2,318	94.8	586	1,732	127	36	91
Computer, engineering, and science	383	0.9	325	58	15.1	351	91.6	303	48	32	22	10
Community, social service, legal, arts, design, entertainment, sports, and media	632	1.4	201	431	68.2	553	87.5	178	375	79	23	56
Healthcare practitioners and technicians	116	0.3	36	80	69.0	12	10.3	2	10	104	34	70
Service occupations	711	1.6	462	249	35.0	463	65.1	321	142	248	141	107
Sales and related occupations	2,531	5.7	899	1,632	64.5	2,354	93.0	854	1,500	177	45	132
Office and administrative support	6,040	13.7	1,236	4,804	79.5	4,853	80.3	949	3,904	1,187	287	900
Natural resources, construction, and maintenance	257	0.6	214	43	16.7	173	67.3	158	15	84	56	28
Production, transportation, and material moving	19	#	17	2	10.5	8	42.1	7	1	11	10	1

†Not applicable.
#Rounds to zero.
NOTE: Degree-granting institutions grant associate's or higher degrees and participate in Title IV federal financial aid programs. Includes institutions with fewer than 15 full-time employees; these institutions did not report staff data prior to 2007. By definition, all graduate assistants are part time. Detail may not sum to totals because of rounding. Some data have been revised from previously published figures.
SOURCE: U.S. Department of Education, National Center for Education Statistics, Integrated Postsecondary Education Data System (IPEDS), Spring 2014, Human Resources component, Fall Staff section. (This table was prepared March 2016.)

Table 314.40. Employees in degree-granting postsecondary institutions, by race/ethnicity, sex, employment status, control and level of institution, and primary occupation: Fall 2013

Sex, employment status, control and level of institution, and primary occupation	Total	White	Minority								Race/ ethnicity unknown	Nonresident alien[2]
			Total	Percent[1]	Black	Hispanic	Asian	Pacific Islander	American Indian/ Alaska Native	Two or more races		
1	2	3	4	5	6	7	8	9	10	11	12	13
All institutions	**3,896,053**	**2,649,651**	**919,977**	**25.8**	**376,778**	**251,119**	**225,285**	**8,852**	**20,967**	**36,976**	**150,847**	**175,578**
Faculty (instruction/research/public service)	1,545,381	1,125,563	296,799	20.9	104,917	67,752	101,974	3,793	7,438	10,925	73,384	49,635
Instruction	1,437,789	1,066,564	274,426	20.5	101,217	63,982	88,265	3,668	7,044	10,250	68,981	27,818
Research	81,670	40,056	16,553	29.2	1,741	2,482	11,516	96	210	508	3,679	21,382
Public service	25,922	18,943	5,820	23.5	1,959	1,288	2,193	29	184	167	724	435
Graduate assistants	363,416	180,062	62,187	25.7	14,415	16,435	24,681	902	1,039	4,715	21,358	99,809
Librarians, curators, and archivists	44,677	35,043	8,305	19.2	3,289	2,139	2,051	76	259	491	1,019	310
Student and academic affairs and other education services	158,653	108,451	41,820	27.8	19,965	12,285	5,862	449	1,314	1,945	6,655	1,727
Management	252,615	196,132	50,021	20.3	24,671	13,067	8,840	321	1,297	1,825	5,302	1,160
Business and financial operations	193,065	135,354	51,617	27.6	21,493	14,884	11,874	402	1,077	1,887	4,867	1,227
Computer, engineering, and science	231,714	156,406	57,358	26.8	14,534	13,761	25,483	384	1,053	2,143	6,286	11,664
Community, social service, legal, arts, design, entertainment, sports, and media	167,466	121,347	39,194	24.4	18,787	11,745	5,257	487	982	1,936	5,862	1,063
Healthcare practitioners and technicians	117,576	76,574	32,488	29.8	12,249	7,085	11,881	163	420	690	4,588	3,926
Service occupations	241,064	131,160	100,668	43.4	55,886	32,713	7,922	580	1,860	1,707	7,224	2,012
Sales and related occupations	15,400	9,677	5,098	34.5	2,726	1,504	444	55	77	292	591	34
Office and administrative support	470,167	305,239	150,984	33.1	72,603	49,351	17,065	1,042	3,220	7,703	11,315	2,629
Natural resources, construction, and maintenance	75,401	55,596	17,698	24.1	8,243	6,520	1,425	170	757	583	1,840	267
Production, transportation, and material moving	19,458	13,047	5,740	30.6	3,000	1,878	526	28	174	134	556	115
Males	**1,772,803**	**1,211,469**	**383,259**	**24.0**	**140,094**	**106,408**	**109,121**	**3,604**	**8,996**	**15,036**	**72,250**	**105,825**
Faculty (instruction/research/public service)	791,971	580,907	143,551	19.8	41,772	33,863	57,673	1,722	3,514	5,007	36,518	30,995
Instruction	731,068	548,657	131,800	19.4	40,349	32,030	49,715	1,668	3,349	4,689	34,156	16,455
Research	48,421	22,993	9,113	28.4	726	1,228	6,790	37	92	240	2,029	14,286
Public service	12,482	9,257	2,638	22.2	697	605	1,168	17	73	78	333	254
Graduate assistants	191,501	90,466	28,897	24.2	5,724	7,622	12,734	159	486	2,172	11,116	61,022
Librarians, curators, and archivists	13,019	10,361	2,207	17.6	727	738	517	18	59	148	341	110
Student and academic affairs and other education services	52,255	35,621	13,321	27.2	5,951	4,082	2,088	134	445	621	2,525	788
Management	113,829	90,748	19,857	18.0	9,097	5,423	3,924	146	557	710	2,605	619
Business and financial operations	52,029	37,424	12,541	25.1	4,760	3,957	2,929	122	274	499	1,625	439
Computer, engineering, and science	140,140	98,125	31,254	24.2	7,718	8,149	13,148	264	637	1,338	3,750	7,011
Community, social service, legal, arts, design, entertainment, sports, and media	74,705	55,261	16,005	22.5	8,420	4,456	1,777	205	394	753	2,933	506
Healthcare practitioners and technicians	33,215	20,269	9,282	31.4	2,798	2,075	4,037	53	120	199	1,545	2,119
Service occupations	140,612	80,371	54,943	40.6	30,374	17,819	4,297	340	1,110	1,003	4,308	990
Sales and related occupations	5,374	3,355	1,784	34.7	975	508	162	26	25	88	226	9
Office and administrative support	78,893	46,096	29,265	38.8	12,379	10,121	4,108	235	559	1,863	2,615	917
Natural resources, construction, and maintenance	69,198	51,606	15,690	23.3	7,068	5,987	1,266	157	677	535	1,687	215
Production, transportation, and material moving	16,062	10,859	4,662	30.0	2,331	1,608	461	23	139	100	456	85
Females	**2,123,250**	**1,438,182**	**536,718**	**27.2**	**236,684**	**144,711**	**116,164**	**5,248**	**11,971**	**21,940**	**78,597**	**69,753**
Faculty (instruction/research/public service)	753,410	544,656	153,248	22.0	63,145	33,889	44,301	2,071	3,924	5,918	36,866	18,640
Instruction	706,721	517,907	142,626	21.6	60,868	31,952	38,550	2,000	3,695	5,561	34,825	11,363
Research	33,249	17,063	7,440	30.4	1,015	1,254	4,726	59	118	268	1,650	7,096
Public service	13,440	9,686	3,182	24.7	1,262	683	1,025	12	111	89	391	181
Graduate assistants	171,915	89,596	33,290	27.1	8,691	8,813	11,947	743	553	2,543	10,242	38,787
Librarians, curators, and archivists	31,658	24,682	6,098	19.8	2,562	1,401	1,534	58	200	343	678	200
Student and academic affairs and other education services	106,398	72,830	28,499	28.1	14,014	8,203	3,774	315	869	1,324	4,130	939
Management	138,786	105,384	30,164	22.3	15,574	7,644	4,916	175	740	1,115	2,697	541
Business and financial operations	141,036	97,930	39,076	28.5	16,733	10,927	8,945	280	803	1,388	3,242	788
Computer, engineering, and science	91,574	58,281	26,104	30.9	6,816	5,612	12,335	120	416	805	2,536	4,653
Community, social service, legal, arts, design, entertainment, sports, and media	92,761	66,086	23,189	26.0	10,367	7,289	3,480	282	588	1,183	2,929	557
Healthcare practitioners and technicians	84,361	56,305	23,206	29.2	9,451	5,010	7,844	110	300	491	3,043	1,807
Service occupations	100,452	50,789	45,725	47.4	25,512	14,894	3,625	240	750	704	2,916	1,022
Sales and related occupations	10,026	6,322	3,314	34.4	1,751	996	282	29	52	204	365	25
Office and administrative support	391,274	259,143	121,719	32.0	60,224	39,230	12,957	807	2,661	5,840	8,700	1,712
Natural resources, construction, and maintenance	6,203	3,990	2,008	33.5	1,175	533	159	13	80	48	153	52
Production, transportation, and material moving	3,396	2,188	1,078	33.0	669	270	65	5	35	34	100	30
Full-time	**2,472,434**	**1,715,774**	**634,998**	**27.0**	**263,365**	**173,874**	**155,473**	**4,730**	**14,239**	**23,317**	**62,097**	**59,565**
Faculty (instruction/research/public service)	791,378	575,507	157,476	21.5	43,148	33,207	71,057	1,209	3,567	5,288	19,988	38,407
Instruction	705,821	529,797	139,296	20.8	40,523	30,295	59,274	1,111	3,319	4,774	16,816	19,912
Research	67,963	32,729	14,187	30.2	1,479	2,032	10,049	78	155	394	2,915	18,132
Public service	17,594	12,981	3,993	23.5	1,146	880	1,734	20	93	120	257	363
Graduate assistants	†	†	†	†	†	†	†	†	†	†	†	†
Librarians, curators, and archivists	37,666	29,665	7,001	19.1	2,746	1,803	1,769	58	219	406	734	266
Student and academic affairs and other education services	100,110	69,073	27,025	28.1	13,275	7,557	3,692	349	958	1,194	2,999	1,013
Management	244,848	189,928	48,763	20.4	24,099	12,764	8,536	317	1,270	1,777	5,083	1,074
Business and financial operations	178,561	124,561	48,598	28.1	20,386	13,953	11,117	365	1,011	1,766	4,305	1,097
Computer, engineering, and science	210,155	142,309	51,838	26.7	13,161	12,204	23,279	356	922	1,916	5,501	10,507
Community, social service, legal, arts, design, entertainment, sports, and media	135,174	97,421	32,888	25.2	15,765	9,824	4,442	408	829	1,620	4,020	845
Healthcare practitioners and technicians	94,854	60,566	27,418	31.2	10,474	6,143	9,756	134	338	573	3,821	3,049
Service occupations	200,353	107,046	86,455	44.7	48,036	28,169	6,883	483	1,512	1,372	5,214	1,638
Sales and related occupations	12,503	7,605	4,432	36.8	2,409	1,296	374	52	59	242	449	17
Office and administrative support	379,996	249,005	121,571	32.8	59,655	39,050	12,794	818	2,713	6,541	8,062	1,358
Natural resources, construction, and maintenance	70,692	52,356	16,591	24.1	7,699	6,206	1,313	155	697	521	1,543	202
Production, transportation, and material moving	16,144	10,732	4,942	31.5	2,512	1,698	461	26	144	101	378	92

See notes at end of table.

Table 314.40. Employees in degree-granting postsecondary institutions, by race/ethnicity, sex, employment status, control and level of institution, and primary occupation: Fall 2013—Continued

Sex, employment status, control and level of institution, and primary occupation	Total	White	Minority								Race/ethnicity unknown	Nonresident alien[2]
			Total	Percent[1]	Black	Hispanic	Asian	Pacific Islander	American Indian/Alaska Native	Two or more races		
1	2	3	4	5	6	7	8	9	10	11	12	13
Part-time	1,423,619	933,877	284,979	23.4	113,413	77,245	69,812	4,122	6,728	13,659	88,750	116,013
Faculty (instruction/research/public service)	754,003	550,056	139,323	20.2	61,769	34,545	30,917	2,584	3,871	5,637	53,396	11,228
Instruction	731,968	536,767	135,130	20.1	60,694	33,687	28,991	2,557	3,725	5,476	52,165	7,906
Research	13,707	7,327	2,366	24.4	262	450	1,467	18	55	114	764	3,250
Public service	8,328	5,962	1,827	23.5	813	408	459	9	91	47	467	72
Graduate assistants	363,416	180,062	62,187	25.7	14,415	16,435	24,681	902	1,039	4,715	21,358	99,809
Librarians, curators, and archivists	7,011	5,378	1,304	19.5	543	336	282	18	40	85	285	44
Student and academic affairs and other education services	58,543	39,378	14,795	27.3	6,690	4,728	2,170	100	356	751	3,656	714
Management	7,767	6,204	1,258	16.9	572	303	304	4	27	48	219	86
Business and financial operations	14,504	10,793	3,019	21.9	1,107	931	757	37	66	121	562	130
Computer, engineering, and science	21,559	14,097	5,520	28.1	1,373	1,557	2,204	28	131	227	785	1,157
Community, social service, legal, arts, design, entertainment, sports, and media	32,292	23,926	6,306	20.9	3,022	1,921	815	79	153	316	1,842	218
Healthcare practitioners and technicians	22,722	16,008	5,070	24.1	1,775	942	2,125	29	82	117	767	877
Service occupations	40,711	24,114	14,213	37.1	7,850	4,544	1,039	97	348	335	2,010	374
Sales and related occupations	2,897	2,072	666	24.3	317	208	70	3	18	50	142	17
Office and administrative support	90,171	56,234	29,413	34.3	12,948	10,301	4,271	224	507	1,162	3,253	1,271
Natural resources, construction, and maintenance	4,709	3,240	1,107	25.5	544	314	112	15	60	62	297	65
Production, transportation, and material moving	3,314	2,315	798	25.6	488	180	65	2	30	33	178	23
Public 4-year	1,884,854	1,247,748	448,701	26.4	170,823	122,114	125,664	3,585	10,579	15,936	64,941	123,464
Faculty (instruction/research/public service)	601,126	430,376	117,634	21.5	31,409	26,115	52,208	1,045	3,062	3,795	23,403	29,713
Instruction	535,393	392,794	104,910	21.1	29,517	23,928	44,321	954	2,754	3,436	20,709	16,980
Research	51,398	26,369	10,243	28.0	1,032	1,602	7,080	74	164	291	2,338	12,448
Public service	14,335	11,213	2,481	18.1	860	585	807	17	144	68	356	285
Graduate assistants	287,839	145,392	48,957	25.2	11,543	13,354	18,722	812	889	3,637	15,142	78,348
Librarians, curators, and archivists	19,022	14,735	3,736	20.2	1,478	1,016	858	19	138	227	425	126
Student and academic affairs and other education services	58,198	39,953	15,101	27.4	7,213	4,410	2,157	166	560	595	2,239	905
Management	107,423	82,980	21,894	20.9	10,927	5,515	4,076	98	568	710	1,966	583
Business and financial operations	109,279	76,449	29,678	28.0	11,726	8,665	7,484	203	660	940	2,436	716
Computer, engineering, and science	141,991	97,562	33,386	25.5	7,889	7,897	15,515	181	663	1,241	3,381	7,662
Community, social service, legal, arts, design, entertainment, sports, and media	77,614	54,883	19,624	26.3	9,033	6,188	2,858	238	474	833	2,520	587
Healthcare practitioners and technicians	75,038	48,628	20,906	30.1	7,519	4,376	8,206	96	299	410	3,167	2,337
Service occupations	125,303	66,040	54,354	45.1	30,739	16,715	4,760	258	1,053	829	3,873	1,036
Sales and related occupations	2,879	1,997	802	28.7	407	217	92	4	16	66	66	14
Office and administrative support	217,885	143,836	68,156	32.2	34,202	22,426	7,433	329	1,575	2,191	4,679	1,214
Natural resources, construction, and maintenance	48,287	36,158	10,715	22.9	4,929	3,854	928	126	492	386	1,268	146
Production, transportation, and material moving	12,970	8,759	3,758	30.0	1,809	1,366	367	10	130	76	376	77
Public 2-year	642,430	463,474	152,392	24.7	68,850	48,584	22,418	2,341	5,059	5,140	22,462	4,102
Faculty (instruction/research/public service)	367,608	280,928	68,167	19.5	29,415	19,550	12,855	1,521	2,379	2,447	16,033	2,480
Instruction	364,348	278,754	67,274	19.4	28,810	19,383	12,795	1,520	2,340	2,426	15,863	2,457
Research	80	50	28	35.9	6	8	4	0	9	1	2	0
Public service	3,180	2,124	865	28.9	599	159	56	1	30	20	168	23
Graduate assistants	13	10	2	16.7	2	0	0	0	0	0	0	1
Librarians, curators, and archivists	5,737	4,368	1,215	21.8	532	348	214	12	55	54	130	24
Student and academic affairs and other education services	47,574	31,733	13,847	30.4	6,461	4,652	1,678	131	440	485	1,803	191
Management	32,322	24,532	7,177	22.6	3,904	1,976	759	46	289	203	524	89
Business and financial operations	17,932	12,088	5,437	31.0	2,544	1,697	762	65	181	188	313	94
Computer, engineering, and science	16,579	11,716	4,458	27.6	1,496	1,505	1,067	59	152	179	282	123
Community, social service, legal, arts, design, entertainment, sports, and media	23,528	15,923	6,927	30.3	3,593	2,112	632	94	243	253	618	60
Healthcare practitioners and technicians	1,755	1,336	305	18.6	158	65	43	1	20	18	107	7
Service occupations	35,117	20,017	13,852	40.9	7,184	4,990	964	114	345	255	926	322
Sales and related occupations	2,115	1,570	486	23.6	196	183	55	5	21	26	54	5
Office and administrative support	83,740	53,300	28,211	34.6	12,289	10,694	3,220	273	786	949	1,563	666
Natural resources, construction, and maintenance	7,183	5,105	1,945	27.6	898	677	144	15	137	74	93	40
Production, transportation, and material moving	1,227	848	363	30.0	178	135	25	5	11	9	16	0
Private nonprofit 4-year	1,151,167	802,307	253,402	24.0	102,983	63,462	68,279	2,137	3,907	12,634	48,188	47,270
Faculty (instruction/research/public service)	446,076	330,360	75,165	18.5	23,487	14,895	31,539	855	1,247	3,142	23,615	16,936
Instruction	407,692	311,241	66,499	17.6	22,325	13,493	25,802	822	1,207	2,850	22,077	7,875
Research	30,071	13,559	6,240	31.5	689	864	4,420	22	32	213	1,338	8,934
Public service	8,313	5,560	2,426	30.4	473	538	1,317	11	8	79	200	127
Graduate assistants	75,106	34,313	13,130	27.7	2,821	3,062	5,948	82	148	1,069	6,208	21,455
Librarians, curators, and archivists	18,204	14,694	2,956	16.7	1,132	641	909	38	58	178	397	157
Student and academic affairs and other education services	39,428	28,629	8,676	23.3	4,143	2,067	1,530	97	252	587	1,514	609
Management	95,860	76,750	16,685	17.9	7,857	4,278	3,409	130	310	701	1,968	457
Business and financial operations	58,434	42,328	14,088	25.0	6,275	3,710	3,210	101	206	586	1,611	407
Computer, engineering, and science	70,302	45,305	18,681	29.2	4,916	4,092	8,652	131	207	683	2,451	3,865
Community, social service, legal, arts, design, entertainment, sports, and media	58,198	45,771	9,983	17.9	5,038	2,587	1,496	100	201	561	2,051	393
Healthcare practitioners and technicians	40,507	26,399	11,221	29.8	4,547	2,632	3,617	65	100	260	1,307	1,580
Service occupations	78,058	43,838	31,261	41.6	17,460	10,452	2,115	203	444	587	2,310	649
Sales and related occupations	4,428	3,150	1,115	26.1	503	392	121	19	18	62	153	10
Office and administrative support	142,257	93,507	44,132	32.1	21,488	12,461	5,286	277	564	4,056	3,984	634
Natural resources, construction, and maintenance	19,322	13,995	4,784	25.5	2,329	1,853	335	29	120	118	462	81
Production, transportation, and material moving	4,987	3,268	1,525	31.8	987	340	112	10	32	44	157	37

See notes at end of table.

Table 314.40. Employees in degree-granting postsecondary institutions, by race/ethnicity, sex, employment status, control and level of institution, and primary occupation: Fall 2013—Continued

Sex, employment status, control and level of institution, and primary occupation	Total	White	Minority Total	Percent[1]	Black	Hispanic	Asian	Pacific Islander	American Indian/ Alaska Native	Two or more races	Race/ ethnicity unknown	Nonresident alien[2]
1	2	3	4	5	6	7	8	9	10	11	12	13
Private nonprofit 2-year	5,831	4,112	1,456	26.1	750	286	163	15	169	73	253	10
Faculty (instruction/research/public service)	2,996	2,113	668	24.0	372	97	80	12	52	55	212	3
Instruction	2,983	2,108	660	23.8	371	97	80	12	45	55	212	3
Research	9	3	6	66.7	1	0	0	0	5	0	0	0
Public service	4	2	2	50.0	0	0	0	0	2	0	0	0
Graduate assistants	7	6	0	0.0	0	0	0	0	0	0	0	1
Librarians, curators, and archivists	114	92	20	17.9	5	5	5	0	4	1	0	2
Student and academic affairs and other education services	365	239	120	33.4	62	32	14	1	8	3	5	1
Management	561	437	115	20.8	53	25	9	0	26	2	8	1
Business and financial operations	203	156	46	22.8	19	10	6	0	11	0	1	0
Computer, engineering, and science	114	86	27	23.9	11	6	5	0	5	0	1	0
Community, social service, legal, arts, design, entertainment, sports, and media	224	154	59	27.7	26	12	3	0	16	2	10	1
Healthcare practitioners and technicians	23	20	3	13.0	2	0	1	0	0	0	0	0
Service occupations	300	197	102	34.1	55	29	5	1	12	0	1	0
Sales and related occupations	112	65	47	42.0	19	16	9	0	1	2	0	0
Office and administrative support	719	492	213	30.2	107	46	25	1	27	7	14	0
Natural resources, construction, and maintenance	82	47	35	42.7	19	7	1	0	7	1	0	0
Production, transportation, and material moving	11	8	1	11.1	0	1	0	0	0	0	1	1
Private for-profit 4-year	167,593	106,334	48,460	31.3	25,679	11,749	7,043	503	1,069	2,417	12,195	604
Faculty (instruction/research/public service)	104,436	67,596	27,790	29.1	16,154	5,301	4,359	224	600	1,152	8,630	420
Instruction	104,317	67,525	27,743	29.1	16,131	5,297	4,342	224	600	1,149	8,629	420
Research	55	45	9	16.7	1	1	4	0	0	3	1	0
Public service	64	26	38	59.4	22	3	13	0	0	0	0	0
Graduate assistants	431	333	86	20.5	44	14	11	7	2	8	8	4
Librarians, curators, and archivists	1,151	833	259	23.7	86	88	51	5	3	26	58	1
Student and academic affairs and other education services	10,376	6,407	3,019	32.0	1,645	691	380	35	36	232	940	10
Management	11,725	8,370	2,806	25.1	1,278	835	430	25	85	153	522	27
Business and financial operations	4,772	3,072	1,355	30.6	477	421	332	21	13	91	342	3
Computer, engineering, and science	2,345	1,502	672	30.9	192	201	214	9	24	32	161	10
Community, social service, legal, arts, design, entertainment, sports, and media	7,270	4,383	2,333	34.7	986	735	244	51	47	270	532	22
Healthcare practitioners and technicians	137	102	26	20.3	7	4	11	1	1	2	7	2
Service occupations	1,575	670	822	55.1	338	392	56	3	4	29	83	0
Sales and related occupations	3,335	1,628	1,546	48.7	927	396	106	18	15	84	160	1
Office and administrative support	19,526	11,144	7,535	40.3	3,486	2,557	822	101	237	332	743	104
Natural resources, construction, and maintenance	270	141	126	47.2	37	79	7	0	1	2	3	0
Production, transportation, and material moving	244	153	85	35.7	22	35	20	3	1	4	6	0
Private for-profit 2-year	44,178	25,676	15,566	37.7	7,693	4,924	1,718	271	184	776	2,808	128
Faculty (instruction/research/public service)	23,139	14,190	7,375	34.2	4,080	1,794	933	136	98	334	1,491	83
Instruction	23,056	14,142	7,340	34.2	4,063	1,784	925	136	98	334	1,491	83
Research	57	30	27	47.4	12	7	8	0	0	0	0	0
Public service	26	18	8	30.8	5	3	0	0	0	0	0	0
Graduate assistants	20	8	12	60.0	5	5	0	1	0	1	0	0
Librarians, curators, and archivists	449	321	119	27.0	56	41	14	2	1	5	9	0
Student and academic affairs and other education services	2,712	1,490	1,057	41.5	441	433	103	19	18	43	154	11
Management	4,724	3,063	1,344	30.5	652	438	157	22	19	56	314	3
Business and financial operations	2,445	1,261	1,013	44.5	452	381	80	12	6	82	164	7
Computer, engineering, and science	383	235	134	36.3	30	60	30	4	2	8	10	4
Community, social service, legal, arts, design, entertainment, sports, and media	632	233	268	53.5	111	111	24	4	1	17	131	0
Healthcare practitioners and technicians	116	89	27	23.3	16	8	3	0	0	0	0	0
Service occupations	711	398	277	41.0	110	135	22	1	2	7	31	5
Sales and related occupations	2,531	1,267	1,102	46.5	674	300	61	9	6	52	158	4
Office and administrative support	6,040	2,960	2,737	48.0	1,031	1,167	279	61	31	168	332	11
Natural resources, construction, and maintenance	257	150	93	38.3	31	50	10	0	0	2	14	0
Production, transportation, and material moving	19	11	8	42.1	4	1	2	0	0	1	0	0

†Not applicable.
[1]Combined total of staff who were Black, Hispanic, Asian, Pacific Islander, American Indian/ Alaska Native, and of Two or more races as a percentage of total staff, excluding race/ethnicity unknown and nonresident alien.
[2]Race/ethnicity not collected.
NOTE: Degree-granting institutions grant associate's or higher degrees and participate in Title IV federal financial aid programs. Includes institutions with fewer than 15 full-time employees;

these institutions did not report staff data prior to 2007. By definition, all graduate assistants are part time. Race categories exclude persons of Hispanic ethnicity. Some data have been revised from previously published figures.
SOURCE: U.S. Department of Education, National Center for Education Statistics, Integrated Postsecondary Education Data System (IPEDS), Spring 2014, Human Resources component, Fall Staff section. (This table was prepared March 2016.)

Table 314.50. Ratios of full-time-equivalent (FTE) students to FTE staff and FTE faculty in public degree-granting postsecondary institutions, by level of institution and state or jurisdiction: Fall 2013

State or jurisdiction	Full-time-equivalent (FTE) staff			FTE faculty			FTE faculty as a percent of FTE staff		FTE students per FTE staff			FTE students per FTE faculty		
	Total	4-year	2-year	Total	4-year	2-year	4-year	2-year	Total	4-year	2-year	Total	4-year	2-year
1	2	3	4	5	6	7	8	9	10	11	12	13	14	15
United States	1,888,157	1,474,341	413,816	664,555	467,766	196,789	31.7	47.6	5.7	4.6	9.4	16.1	14.5	19.8
Alabama	38,441	32,156	6,285	12,146	9,284	2,862	28.9	45.5	5.1	4.3	9.1	16.0	14.8	19.9
Alaska	5,524	5,268	256	2,992	2,894	98	54.9	38.4	3.7	3.7	3.8	6.9	6.8	9.8
Arizona	36,675	25,409	11,266	12,371	7,185	5,186	28.3	46.0	6.6	5.1	9.9	19.4	18.0	21.5
Arkansas..........................	22,322	17,506	4,815	7,024	4,987	2,037	28.5	42.3	5.2	4.6	7.5	16.6	16.1	17.8
California	184,468	127,969	56,499	71,822	40,984	30,837	32.0	54.6	7.7	4.9	14.1	19.9	15.4	25.9
Colorado..........................	38,368	33,103	5,265	15,920	13,386	2,534	40.4	48.1	5.1	4.3	9.7	12.2	10.7	20.1
Connecticut......................	16,946	13,722	3,225	6,122	4,303	1,820	31.4	56.4	5.2	4.2	9.9	14.5	13.2	17.5
Delaware..........................	6,808	5,489	1,319	2,070	1,411	659	25.7	50.0	4.9	4.5	6.7	16.2	17.5	13.5
District of Columbia	922	922	0	456	456	0	49.5	†	3.9	3.9	†	7.8	7.8	†
Florida.............................	78,778	75,417	3,361	26,395	25,025	1,370	33.2	40.8	7.1	7.0	9.8	21.3	21.2	24.0
Georgia............................	58,807	48,005	10,802	18,102	13,167	4,936	27.4	45.7	5.4	4.9	7.7	17.5	17.7	16.8
Hawaii..............................	8,346	6,541	1,805	3,149	2,269	879	34.7	48.7	5.0	3.7	9.4	13.1	10.8	19.2
Idaho...............................	9,271	7,180	2,090	3,333	2,428	905	33.8	43.3	6.0	5.6	7.1	16.6	16.7	16.4
Illinois.............................	70,449	48,874	21,575	20,898	11,728	9,170	24.0	42.5	5.3	3.5	9.5	17.9	14.5	22.3
Indiana............................	45,934	40,441	5,493	15,637	12,824	2,813	31.7	51.2	5.4	4.8	10.2	15.9	15.0	19.9
Iowa................................	25,466	18,185	7,281	8,938	5,482	3,456	30.1	47.5	5.0	3.7	8.1	14.2	12.4	17.0
Kansas.............................	26,231	19,210	7,021	9,488	6,499	2,989	33.8	42.6	5.2	4.4	7.2	14.3	13.0	16.9
Kentucky..........................	33,510	27,154	6,356	10,692	7,631	3,061	28.1	48.2	4.9	3.9	8.8	15.2	14.0	18.2
Louisiana.........................	26,101	22,128	3,973	9,429	7,336	2,092	33.2	52.7	6.4	5.4	12.3	17.8	16.3	23.4
Maine...............................	6,717	5,395	1,321	2,472	1,631	841	30.2	63.7	5.3	4.5	8.7	14.5	15.0	13.6
Maryland...........................	43,483	31,043	12,440	17,173	11,529	5,645	37.1	45.4	4.7	4.1	6.3	12.0	11.0	13.9
Massachusetts..................	30,567	22,410	8,157	11,338	7,812	3,526	34.9	43.2	5.4	4.5	7.6	14.4	13.0	17.7
Michigan...........................	71,768	59,269	12,499	27,347	21,237	6,110	35.8	48.9	5.4	4.4	10.0	14.1	12.3	20.4
Minnesota.........................	32,878	25,603	7,275	12,240	8,561	3,679	33.4	50.6	5.8	4.4	11.0	15.7	13.1	21.8
Mississippi.......................	29,140	22,168	6,972	7,968	4,815	3,153	21.7	45.2	4.6	3.2	8.9	16.6	14.7	19.6
Missouri...........................	37,852	29,642	8,209	11,209	7,690	3,519	25.9	42.9	5.1	4.2	8.3	17.2	16.2	19.4
Montana...........................	7,482	6,453	1,029	2,662	2,242	419	34.8	40.7	5.2	5.1	5.8	14.7	14.8	14.3
Nebraska..........................	17,466	13,948	3,518	5,929	4,163	1,766	29.8	50.2	4.4	3.6	7.4	12.9	12.2	14.6
Nevada............................	9,674	9,090	584	3,544	3,260	284	35.9	48.7	7.2	7.0	9.8	19.6	19.5	20.0
New Hampshire	6,181	4,701	1,480	2,384	1,512	872	32.2	59.0	5.4	5.4	5.6	14.1	16.7	9.6
New Jersey.......................	45,107	34,019	11,087	16,301	11,058	5,243	32.5	47.3	5.9	4.4	10.2	16.2	13.6	21.7
New Mexico.......................	20,014	14,463	5,551	6,775	4,458	2,317	30.8	41.7	4.9	3.6	8.2	14.4	11.7	19.6
New York..........................	78,198	54,615	23,583	31,656	21,010	10,646	38.5	45.1	7.2	6.0	9.9	17.8	15.7	22.0
North Carolina	71,499	48,573	22,926	25,579	14,235	11,344	29.3	49.5	4.8	4.0	6.4	13.3	13.6	13.0
North Dakota.....................	8,019	7,186	833	2,688	2,359	329	32.8	39.5	4.9	4.8	5.3	14.6	14.7	13.5
Ohio................................	78,422	66,060	12,362	23,412	17,583	5,830	26.6	47.2	4.9	4.3	8.5	16.5	16.0	18.1
Oklahoma.........................	29,088	24,477	4,611	9,084	7,258	1,826	29.7	39.6	4.8	4.2	8.2	15.4	14.1	20.7
Oregon.............................	28,997	21,256	7,740	10,664	7,204	3,460	33.9	44.7	5.3	4.1	8.4	14.3	12.2	18.8
Pennsylvania.....................	64,436	54,705	9,731	25,320	20,264	5,056	37.0	52.0	5.2	4.6	8.2	13.2	12.5	15.8
Rhode Island	4,703	3,742	960	1,868	1,345	523	35.9	54.5	6.6	5.8	10.0	16.7	16.1	18.3
South Carolina..................	28,938	22,116	6,822	10,671	7,367	3,304	33.3	48.4	5.6	4.4	9.2	15.1	13.3	19.1
South Dakota.....................	5,975	5,247	728	2,338	1,921	417	36.6	57.3	5.8	5.6	7.5	14.8	15.2	13.0
Tennessee	32,006	26,103	5,903	10,766	7,914	2,851	30.3	48.3	5.5	4.6	9.5	16.5	15.3	19.7
Texas...............................	174,432	131,147	43,285	53,976	34,654	19,322	26.4	44.6	5.2	4.1	8.8	16.9	15.4	19.7
Utah................................	22,594	20,786	1,808	8,646	7,925	722	38.1	39.9	5.3	4.9	9.1	13.8	12.9	22.9
Vermont............................	5,309	4,925	385	2,061	1,844	217	37.4	56.3	3.8	3.6	7.1	9.8	9.5	12.6
Virginia.............................	55,557	45,093	10,463	20,406	15,237	5,169	33.8	49.4	5.4	4.2	10.3	14.7	12.6	20.9
Washington.......................	43,958	34,403	9,555	16,419	12,308	4,111	35.8	43.0	5.6	4.4	9.6	14.9	12.4	22.4
West Virginia.....................	13,232	11,827	1,405	5,330	4,501	830	38.1	59.0	5.7	5.3	9.7	14.2	13.8	16.4
Wisconsin.........................	41,801	32,392	9,409	16,060	11,457	4,602	35.4	48.9	5.2	4.9	6.5	13.6	13.7	13.3
Wyoming...........................	5,689	3,194	2,495	2,213	1,063	1,151	33.3	46.1	4.3	3.4	5.5	11.1	10.3	11.9
U.S. Service Academies	3,609	3,609	0	1,071	1,071	0	29.7	†	4.2	4.2	†	14.0	14.0	†
Other jurisdictions	15,667	14,396	1,270	5,624	5,133	492	35.7	38.7	4.5	4.4	5.8	12.5	12.2	15.1
American Samoa......................	304	304	0	81	81	0	26.6	†	3.4	3.4	†	12.8	12.8	†
Federated States of Micronesia.	384	0	384	105	0	105	†	27.3	5.0	†	5.0	18.1	†	18.1
Guam....................................	898	655	243	279	213	66	32.5	27.2	5.3	4.9	6.4	17.1	15.1	23.5
Marshall Islands.......................	148	0	148	48	0	48	†	32.4	5.3	†	5.3	16.3	†	16.3
Northern Marianas	185	185	0	60	60	0	32.4	†	5.4	5.4	†	16.6	16.6	†
Palau....................................	192	0	192	53	0	53	†	27.4	2.6	†	2.6	9.4	†	9.4
Puerto Rico.............................	12,976	12,673	303	4,780	4,560	220	36.0	72.6	4.5	4.4	8.8	12.2	12.2	12.1
U.S. Virgin Islands...................	580	580	0	219	219	0	37.7	†	3.0	3.0	†	8.1	8.1	†

†Not applicable.
NOTE: Full-time-equivalent staff is the full-time staff, plus the full-time equivalent of the part-time staff. Degree-granting institutions grant associate's or higher degrees and participate in Title IV federal financial aid programs. Data are for all degree-granting institutions, including those with fewer than 15 employees. Detail may not sum to totals because of rounding. Some data have been revised from previously published figures.

SOURCE: U.S. Department of Education, National Center for Education Statistics, Integrated Postsecondary Education Data System (IPEDS), Spring 2014, Human Resources component, Fall Staff section; and Spring 2014, Fall Enrollment component. (This table was prepared March 2016.)

Table 314.60. Ratios of full-time-equivalent (FTE) students to FTE staff and FTE faculty in private degree-granting postsecondary institutions, by level of institution and state or jurisdiction: Fall 2013

State or jurisdiction	Full-time-equivalent (FTE) staff				FTE faculty				FTE faculty as a percent of FTE staff		FTE students per FTE staff		FTE students per FTE faculty	
	All private	Nonprofit 4-year	Nonprofit 2-year	For-profit	All private	Nonprofit 4-year	Nonprofit 2-year	For-profit	Nonprofit 4-year	For-profit	Nonprofit 4-year	For-profit	Nonprofit 4-year	For-profit
1	2	3	4	5	6	7	8	9	10	11	12	13	14	15
United States	1,058,817	916,166	4,278	138,373	378,157	316,585	1,857	59,716	34.6	43.2	3.6	9.7	10.6	22.5
Alabama	6,497	4,563	56	1,879	2,519	1,715	24	781	37.6	41.6	4.9	13.4	13.1	32.3
Alaska	547	161	26	360	205	64	5	136	39.8	37.7	3.0	7.0	7.6	18.6
Arizona	21,690	1,699	0	19,991	9,164	597	0	8,567	35.1	42.9	4.9	14.7	13.9	34.4
Arkansas	3,255	3,012	66	177	1,140	1,016	17	107	33.7	60.4	4.8	8.3	14.3	13.8
California	90,669	72,779	230	17,659	32,806	25,220	83	7,503	34.7	42.5	3.6	9.0	10.4	21.3
Colorado	9,856	5,605	4	4,247	3,907	2,082	1	1,825	37.1	43.0	4.8	9.8	12.9	22.8
Connecticut	24,997	24,146	0	851	8,600	8,283	0	317	34.3	37.3	2.5	7.0	7.2	18.6
Delaware	1,452	1,397	33	22	714	691	13	10	49.5	44.8	8.2	8.1	16.6	18.0
District of Columbia	21,076	20,456	0	621	7,205	6,775	0	429	33.1	69.2	3.3	4.4	9.9	6.4
Florida	46,629	32,914	204	13,511	16,305	10,467	98	5,739	31.8	42.5	4.5	9.5	14.1	22.4
Georgia	25,380	21,428	84	3,868	9,881	8,087	31	1,763	37.7	45.6	3.0	9.8	8.0	21.6
Hawaii	1,995	1,641	0	354	890	712	0	179	43.4	50.4	6.7	10.8	15.4	21.3
Idaho	2,411	2,207	0	204	1,158	1,052	0	107	47.7	52.3	10.6	7.6	22.2	14.5
Illinois	63,612	56,432	82	7,099	22,287	19,551	34	2,703	34.6	38.1	3.4	6.5	9.7	17.2
Indiana	20,809	18,196	71	2,541	7,119	6,223	25	872	34.2	34.3	4.3	6.5	12.7	19.0
Iowa	17,057	10,372	0	6,685	6,814	3,992	0	2,822	38.5	42.2	4.8	13.5	12.4	31.9
Kansas	4,812	4,080	116	617	1,916	1,631	42	243	40.0	39.4	5.0	7.0	12.5	17.7
Kentucky	8,176	6,301	0	1,875	3,348	2,480	0	868	39.4	46.3	5.3	6.5	13.4	14.0
Louisiana	8,464	7,476	122	865	3,112	2,623	56	433	35.1	50.1	3.2	8.4	9.1	16.9
Maine	4,747	4,588	43	116	1,562	1,499	26	37	32.7	31.5	3.8	9.4	11.6	29.8
Maryland	23,947	23,328	0	620	6,952	6,712	0	240	28.8	38.7	1.8	9.7	6.4	25.2
Massachusetts	82,154	81,515	86	553	28,707	28,399	58	251	34.8	45.3	3.0	8.2	8.6	18.0
Michigan	13,949	12,986	0	963	5,817	5,372	0	444	41.4	46.1	6.2	6.8	14.9	14.8
Minnesota	18,191	12,466	28	5,697	7,751	5,107	9	2,635	41.0	46.3	4.8	11.5	11.8	24.8
Mississippi	2,655	2,300	0	355	1,067	896	0	171	39.0	48.1	5.6	6.1	14.4	12.7
Missouri	33,363	30,826	126	2,411	11,875	10,921	69	885	35.4	36.7	3.7	11.3	10.3	30.7
Montana	970	865	105	0	357	333	24	0	38.5	†	4.7	†	12.2	†
Nebraska	5,324	4,981	49	294	1,996	1,856	19	121	37.3	41.0	5.8	7.3	15.5	17.9
Nevada	1,542	652	0	889	748	315	0	433	48.3	48.7	5.0	11.1	10.3	22.9
New Hampshire	8,499	8,089	38	372	2,556	2,378	26	152	29.4	40.9	4.4	6.7	15.0	16.4
New Jersey	16,153	14,839	0	1,314	5,237	4,610	0	627	31.1	47.7	4.2	6.6	13.5	13.9
New Mexico	1,045	276	0	769	494	88	0	406	31.8	52.9	4.0	9.0	12.5	17.1
New York	146,029	139,585	545	5,899	51,622	48,704	292	2,626	34.9	44.5	3.2	7.5	9.2	16.9
North Carolina	37,442	35,566	128	1,748	11,998	11,233	37	728	31.6	41.7	2.4	7.9	7.7	19.1
North Dakota	1,305	1,236	0	69	434	410	0	25	33.1	35.8	3.6	10.1	10.8	28.3
Ohio	31,230	27,099	137	3,993	12,118	10,187	42	1,889	37.6	47.3	4.5	7.2	11.9	15.2
Oklahoma	5,766	4,676	0	1,090	2,153	1,651	0	502	35.3	46.1	4.8	7.6	13.5	16.5
Oregon	7,233	6,396	0	837	3,012	2,625	0	387	41.0	46.3	4.9	7.7	12.0	16.6
Pennsylvania	77,664	71,282	1,274	5,108	27,119	24,184	552	2,384	33.9	46.7	3.5	7.7	10.2	16.5
Rhode Island	9,985	9,985	0	0	3,127	3,127	0	0	31.3	†	3.8	†	12.2	†
South Carolina	8,343	5,965	123	2,256	2,989	2,187	36	766	36.7	34.0	5.1	5.8	13.9	17.0
South Dakota	1,914	1,278	30	607	717	516	14	187	40.4	30.8	4.4	3.1	10.8	10.2
Tennessee	38,349	35,905	72	2,372	9,714	8,577	32	1,105	23.9	46.6	2.1	9.1	8.7	19.6
Texas	36,531	30,527	246	5,757	13,264	10,755	120	2,388	35.2	41.5	3.8	8.6	10.7	20.8
Utah	8,898	7,916	66	916	3,723	3,256	16	451	41.1	49.2	10.5	7.7	25.6	15.7
Vermont	4,043	3,933	0	110	1,387	1,364	0	23	34.7	21.1	4.0	3.6	11.6	16.8
Virginia	22,521	17,624	80	4,817	8,782	6,542	51	2,189	37.1	45.4	5.6	7.8	15.1	17.2
Washington	9,052	8,002	9	1,041	3,779	3,353	5	421	41.9	40.4	4.7	8.5	11.3	21.1
West Virginia	4,135	1,759	0	2,375	1,712	583	0	1,129	33.1	47.5	4.5	11.3	13.6	23.9
Wisconsin	16,261	14,842	0	1,418	6,223	5,578	0	644	37.6	45.4	3.6	6.6	9.5	14.5
Wyoming	194	14	0	180	73	5	0	68	37.2	37.7	5.2	8.1	14.1	21.6
Other jurisdictions	14,737	11,721	0	3,016	6,099	4,848	0	1,251	41.4	41.5	9.9	12.6	23.9	30.4
American Samoa	0	0	0	0	0	0	0	0	†	†	†	†	†	†
Federated States of Micronesia	0	0	0	0	0	0	0	0	†	†	†	†	†	†
Guam	10	10	0	0	6	6	0	0	56.7	†	6.6	†	11.6	†
Marshall Islands	0	0	0	0	0	0	0	0	†	†	†	†	†	†
Northern Marianas	0	0	0	0	0	0	0	0	†	†	†	†	†	†
Palau	0	0	0	0	0	0	0	0	†	†	†	†	†	†
Puerto Rico	14,727	11,711	0	3,016	6,093	4,842	0	1,251	41.3	41.5	9.9	12.6	23.9	30.4
U.S. Virgin Islands	0	0	0	0	0	0	0	0	†	†	†	†	†	†

†Not applicable.
NOTE: Full-time-equivalent staff is the full-time staff, plus the full-time equivalent of the part-time staff. Degree-granting institutions grant associate's or higher degrees and participate in Title IV federal financial aid programs. Data are for all degree-granting institutions, including those with fewer than 15 employees. Detail may not sum to totals because of rounding. Some data have been revised from previously published figures.

SOURCE: U.S. Department of Education, National Center for Education Statistics, Integrated Postsecondary Education Data System (IPEDS), Spring 2014, Human Resources component, Fall Staff section; and Spring 2014, Fall Enrollment component. (This table was prepared March 2016.)

Table 315.10. Number of faculty in degree-granting postsecondary institutions, by employment status, sex, control, and level of institution: Selected years, fall 1970 through fall 2013

Year	Total	Employment status			Sex			Control				Level	
		Full-time	Part-time	Percent full-time	Males	Females	Percent female	Public	Private			4-year	2-year
									Total	Nonprofit	For-profit		
1	2	3	4	5	6	7	8	9	10	11	12	13	14
1970	474,000	369,000	104,000	77.8	—	—	—	314,000	160,000	—	—	382,000	92,000
1971[1]	492,000	379,000	113,000	77.0	—	—	—	333,000	159,000	—	—	387,000	105,000
1972	500,000	380,000	120,000	76.0	—	—	—	343,000	157,000	—	—	384,000	116,000
1973[1]	527,000	389,000	138,000	73.8	—	—	—	365,000	162,000	—	—	401,000	126,000
1974[1]	567,000	406,000	161,000	71.6	—	—	—	397,000	170,000	—	—	427,000	140,000
1975[1]	628,000	440,000	188,000	70.1	—	—	—	443,000	185,000	—	—	467,000	161,000
1976	633,000	434,000	199,000	68.6	—	—	—	449,000	184,000	—	—	467,000	166,000
1977	678,000	448,000	230,000	66.1	—	—	—	492,000	186,000	—	—	485,000	193,000
1979[1]	675,000	445,000	230,000	65.9	—	—	—	488,000	187,000	—	—	494,000	182,000
1980[1]	686,000	450,000	236,000	65.6	—	—	—	495,000	191,000	—	—	494,000	192,000
1981	705,000	461,000	244,000	65.4	—	—	—	509,000	196,000	—	—	493,000	212,000
1982[1]	710,000	462,000	248,000	65.1	—	—	—	506,000	204,000	—	—	493,000	217,000
1983	724,000	471,000	254,000	65.1	—	—	—	512,000	212,000	—	—	504,000	220,000
1984[1]	717,000	462,000	255,000	64.4	—	—	—	505,000	212,000	—	—	504,000	213,000
1985[1]	715,000	459,000	256,000	64.2	—	—	—	503,000	212,000	—	—	504,000	211,000
1986[1]	722,000	459,000	263,000	63.6	—	—	—	510,000	212,000	—	—	506,000	216,000
1987[2]	793,070	523,420	269,650	66.0	529,413	263,657	33.2	552,749	240,321	—	—	547,505	245,565
1989[2]	824,220	524,426	299,794	63.6	534,254	289,966	35.2	577,298	246,922	—	—	583,700	240,520
1991[2]	826,252	535,623	290,629	64.8	525,599	300,653	36.4	580,908	245,344	236,066	9,278	591,269	234,983
1993[2]	915,474	545,706	369,768	59.6	561,123	354,351	38.7	650,434	265,040	254,130	10,910	625,969	289,505
1995[2]	931,706	550,822	380,884	59.1	562,893	368,813	39.6	656,833	274,873	260,900	13,973	647,059	284,647
1997[2]	989,813	568,719	421,094	57.5	587,420	402,393	40.7	694,560	295,253	271,257	23,996	682,650	307,163
1999[2]	1,027,830	590,937	436,893	57.5	602,469	425,361	41.4	713,325	314,505	284,652	29,853	713,823	314,007
2001[2]	1,113,183	617,868	495,315	55.5	644,514	468,669	42.1	771,124	342,059	306,487	35,572	764,172	349,011
2003[2]	1,173,593	630,092	543,501	53.7	663,723	509,870	43.4	791,766	381,827	330,097	51,730	814,289	359,304
2005[2]	1,290,426	675,624	614,802	52.4	714,453	575,973	44.6	841,188	449,238	361,523	87,715	916,996	373,430
2007[2]	1,371,390	703,463	667,927	51.3	743,812	627,578	45.8	877,146	494,244	385,875	108,369	990,849	380,541
2009[2]	1,439,074	729,152	709,922	50.7	761,002	678,072	47.1	913,788	525,286	408,382	116,904	1,038,349	400,725
2011[2]	1,524,469	762,114	762,355	50.0	789,567	734,902	48.2	954,159	570,310	432,630	137,680	1,115,642	408,827
2013[2]	1,545,381	791,378	754,003	51.2	791,971	753,410	48.8	968,734	576,647	449,072	127,575	1,151,638	393,743

—Not available.

[1]Estimated on the basis of enrollment. For methodological details on estimates, see National Center for Education Statistics, *Projections of Education Statistics to 2000.*

[2]Because of revised survey methods, data are not directly comparable with figures for years prior to 1987.

NOTE: Includes faculty members with the title of professor, associate professor, assistant professor, instructor, lecturer, assisting professor, adjunct professor, or interim professor (or the equivalent). Excluded are graduate students with titles such as graduate or teaching fellow who assist senior faculty. Data through 1995 are for institutions of higher education, while later data are for degree-granting institutions. Degree-granting institutions grant associate's or higher degrees and participate in Title IV federal financial aid programs. The degree-granting classification is very similar to the earlier higher education classification, but it includes more 2-year colleges and excludes a few higher education institutions that did not grant degrees. Beginning in 2007, includes institutions with fewer than 15 full-time employees; these institutions did not report staff data prior to 2007. Detail may not sum to totals because of rounding. Some data have been revised from previously published figures.

SOURCE: U.S. Department of Education, National Center for Education Statistics, Higher Education General Information Survey (HEGIS), *Employees in Institutions of Higher Education*, 1970 and 1972, and "Staff Survey" 1976; *Projections of Education Statistics to 2000*; Integrated Postsecondary Education Data System (IPEDS), "Fall Staff Survey" (IPEDS-S:87–99); IPEDS Winter 2001–02 through Winter 2011–12, Human Resources component, Fall Staff section; IPEDS Spring 2014, Human Resources component, Fall Staff section; and U.S. Equal Employment Opportunity Commission, Higher Education Staff Information Survey (EEO-6), 1977, 1981, and 1983. (This table was prepared March 2016.)

Table 315.20. Full-time faculty in degree-granting postsecondary institutions, by race/ethnicity, sex, and academic rank: Fall 2009, fall 2011, and fall 2013

Year, sex, and academic rank	Total	White	Black, Hispanic, Asian, Pacific Islander, American Indian/Alaska Native, and Two or more races									Race/ethnicity unknown	Non-resident-alien[2]
			Total	Percent[1]	Black	Hispanic	Asian/Pacific Islander			American Indian/Alaska Native	Two or more races		
							Total	Asian	Pacific Islander				
1	2	3	4	5	6	7	8	9	10	11	12	13	14
2009													
Total	729,152	551,230	130,903	19.2	39,706	28,022	59,480	—	—	3,458	—	16,059	31,197
Professors	177,566	149,553	24,633	14.1	6,086	4,683	13,281	—	—	580	—	1,923	1,460
Associate professors	148,959	117,241	26,779	18.6	8,162	5,382	12,626	—	—	601	—	2,387	2,560
Assistant professors	171,622	117,794	37,199	24.0	10,974	6,783	18,634	—	—	717	—	4,616	12,104
Instructors	104,554	78,346	20,951	21.1	7,807	6,575	5,546	—	—	1,002	—	3,399	1,879
Lecturers	33,372	24,925	5,851	19.0	1,813	1,583	2,319	—	—	139	—	882	1,711
Other faculty	93,079	63,371	15,490	19.7	4,864	3,016	7,074	—	—	419	—	2,852	11,483
2011													
Total	762,114	564,218	147,495	20.7	41,662	31,335	66,842	65,469	1,373	3,534	4,122	16,999	33,402
Professors	181,509	150,364	27,559	15.5	6,517	5,180	14,617	14,425	192	589	656	2,202	1,384
Associate professors	155,201	119,415	30,605	20.4	8,695	6,144	14,364	14,129	235	597	805	2,477	2,704
Assistant professors	174,052	118,022	39,986	25.3	10,994	7,428	19,820	19,445	375	701	1,043	4,926	11,118
Instructors	109,042	80,690	23,162	22.3	8,602	6,907	5,807	5,448	359	981	865	3,262	1,928
Lecturers	34,473	25,821	6,261	19.5	1,688	1,773	2,455	2,420	35	135	210	848	1,543
Other faculty	107,837	69,906	19,922	22.2	5,166	3,903	9,779	9,602	177	531	543	3,284	14,725
Males	427,214	316,133	79,707	20.1	18,636	16,341	40,989	40,368	621	1,752	1,989	9,600	21,774
Professors	128,649	106,069	19,812	15.7	3,984	3,499	11,550	11,420	130	362	417	1,643	1,125
Associate professors	89,742	68,493	17,820	20.6	4,373	3,437	9,260	9,142	118	313	437	1,574	1,855
Assistant professors	88,173	58,538	19,877	25.3	4,458	3,692	10,970	10,820	150	303	454	2,694	7,064
Instructors	48,124	35,864	9,750	21.4	3,138	3,133	2,668	2,525	143	463	348	1,486	1,024
Lecturers	15,690	11,721	2,740	18.9	751	753	1,110	1,090	20	47	79	410	819
Other faculty	56,836	35,448	9,708	21.5	1,932	1,827	5,431	5,371	60	264	254	1,793	9,887
Females	334,900	248,085	67,788	21.5	23,026	14,994	25,853	25,101	752	1,782	2,133	7,399	11,628
Professors	52,860	44,295	7,747	14.9	2,533	1,681	3,067	3,005	62	227	239	559	259
Associate professors	65,459	50,922	12,785	20.1	4,322	2,707	5,104	4,987	117	284	368	903	849
Assistant professors	85,879	59,484	20,109	25.3	6,536	3,736	8,850	8,625	225	398	589	2,232	4,054
Instructors	60,918	44,826	13,412	23.0	5,464	3,774	3,139	2,923	216	518	517	1,776	904
Lecturers	18,783	14,100	3,521	20.0	937	1,020	1,345	1,330	15	88	131	438	724
Other faculty	51,001	34,458	10,214	22.9	3,234	2,076	4,348	4,231	117	267	289	1,491	4,838
2013[3]													
Total	791,391	575,491	157,480	21.5	43,188	33,217	72,246	71,038	1,208	3,538	5,291	20,013	38,407
Professors	181,530	148,577	29,111	16.4	6,665	5,604	15,417	15,247	170	573	852	2,323	1,519
Associate professors	155,095	116,817	32,580	21.8	8,812	6,381	15,809	15,626	183	591	987	2,859	2,839
Assistant professors	166,045	112,262	38,011	25.3	10,542	7,130	18,402	18,070	332	683	1,254	5,695	10,077
Instructors	99,304	73,859	20,684	21.9	7,448	6,340	5,236	4,950	286	879	781	3,180	1,581
Lecturers	36,728	27,453	6,591	19.4	1,728	2,015	2,436	2,403	33	117	295	1,151	1,533
Other faculty	152,689	96,523	30,503	24.0	7,993	5,747	14,946	14,742	204	695	1,122	4,805	20,858
Males	436,456	316,912	83,905	20.9	18,905	17,198	43,519	42,928	591	1,736	2,547	10,813	24,826
Professors	125,836	102,520	20,450	16.6	4,018	3,669	11,882	11,772	110	350	531	1,664	1,202
Associate professors	87,420	65,320	18,552	22.1	4,321	3,533	9,897	9,810	87	287	514	1,727	1,821
Assistant professors	82,331	54,700	18,387	25.2	4,169	3,506	9,887	9,725	162	304	521	2,957	6,287
Instructors	42,877	32,014	8,665	21.3	2,714	2,888	2,304	2,179	125	430	329	1,349	849
Lecturers	16,588	12,464	2,756	18.1	760	834	992	983	9	39	131	580	788
Other faculty	81,404	49,894	15,095	23.2	2,923	2,768	8,557	8,459	98	326	521	2,536	13,879
Females	354,935	258,579	73,575	22.2	24,283	16,019	28,727	28,110	617	1,802	2,744	9,200	13,581
Professors	55,694	46,057	8,661	15.8	2,647	1,935	3,535	3,475	60	223	321	659	317
Associate professors	67,675	51,497	14,028	21.4	4,491	2,848	5,912	5,816	96	304	473	1,132	1,018
Assistant professors	83,714	57,562	19,624	25.4	6,373	3,624	8,515	8,345	170	379	733	2,738	3,790
Instructors	56,427	41,845	12,019	22.3	4,734	3,452	2,932	2,771	161	449	452	1,831	732
Lecturers	20,140	14,989	3,835	20.4	968	1,181	1,444	1,420	24	78	164	571	745
Other faculty	71,285	46,629	15,408	24.8	5,070	2,979	6,389	6,283	106	369	601	2,269	6,979

—Not available.

[1]Combined total of faculty who were Black, Hispanic, Asian, Pacific Islander, American Indian/Alaska Native, and of Two or more races as a percentage of total faculty, excluding race/ethnicity unknown and nonresident alien.

[2]Race/ethnicity not collected.

[3]Only instructional faculty were classified by academic rank. Primarily research and primarily public service faculty, as well as faculty without ranks, appear under "other faculty."

NOTE: Degree-granting institutions grant associate's or higher degrees and participate in Title IV federal financial aid programs. Includes institutions with fewer than 15 full-time employees; these institutions did not report staff data prior to 2007. Race categories exclude persons of Hispanic ethnicity. Some data have been revised from previously published figures.

SOURCE: U.S. Department of Education, National Center for Education Statistics, Integrated Postsecondary Education Data System (IPEDS), Winter 2009–10 and Winter 2011–12, Human Resources component, Fall Staff section; and IPEDS Spring 2014, Human Resources component, Fall Staff section. (This table was prepared March 2015.)

Table 315.30. Percentage distribution of full-time faculty and instructional staff in degree-granting postsecondary institutions, by level and control of institution, selected instruction activities, and number of classes taught for credit: Fall 2003

[Standard errors appear in parentheses]

Instruction activity and number of classes	All institutions	Research		Doctoral		Comprehensive		Private liberal arts	Public 2-year	Other
		Public	Private	Public	Private	Public	Private			
1	2	3	4	5	6	7	8	9	10	11
Number of full-time faculty and instructional staff										
(in thousands)	681.8 (0.05)	162.1 (0.85)	63.5 (1.58)	51.3 (0.76)	21.7 (0.79)	107.3 (2.98)	41.4 (1.59)	49.6 (1.80)	114.6 (1.09)	70.2 (3.36)
Percentage distribution	100.0 (†)	23.8 (0.12)	9.3 (0.23)	7.5 (0.11)	3.2 (0.12)	15.7 (0.44)	6.1 (0.23)	7.3 (0.26)	16.8 (0.16)	10.3 (0.49)
Average hours worked per week	53.3 (0.13)	55.6 (0.21)	55.8 (0.42)	54.0 (0.38)	52.4 (0.59)	53.2 (0.31)	51.8 (0.53)	54.0 (0.39)	49.2 (0.34)	53.1 (0.49)
Paid activities within institution	45.4 (0.12)	48.8 (0.19)	47.8 (0.36)	45.9 (0.31)	44.7 (0.47)	44.4 (0.27)	42.9 (0.55)	45.6 (0.39)	40.9 (0.27)	45.1 (0.59)
Unpaid activities within institution	3.8 (0.04)	3.1 (0.08)	3.3 (0.15)	3.9 (0.14)	3.8 (0.20)	4.4 (0.13)	4.4 (0.15)	4.4 (0.11)	4.2 (0.12)	3.6 (0.22)
Paid activities outside institution	2.2 (0.05)	1.8 (0.08)	2.7 (0.21)	2.1 (0.13)	2.3 (0.25)	2.3 (0.12)	2.2 (0.17)	2.0 (0.13)	2.3 (0.12)	2.8 (0.24)
Unpaid activities outside institution	1.9 (0.03)	1.9 (0.05)	2.0 (0.09)	2.1 (0.11)	1.7 (0.11)	2.1 (0.09)	2.3 (0.12)	2.0 (0.14)	1.7 (0.08)	1.6 (0.10)
Work time distribution (percent)	100.0 (†)	100.0 (†)	100.0 (†)	100.0 (†)	100.0 (†)	100.0 (†)	100.0 (†)	100.0 (†)	100.0 (†)	100.0 (†)
Teaching	58.2 (0.27)	43.5 (0.43)	43.1 (0.76)	55.5 (0.72)	55.0 (1.15)	64.7 (0.70)	67.5 (0.78)	65.9 (0.80)	78.4 (0.65)	55.0 (1.61)
Research/scholarship	20.0 (0.44)	33.2 (0.42)	34.0 (0.84)	22.3 (0.72)	24.6 (0.84)	15.0 (0.49)	11.2 (0.57)	12.7 (0.67)	3.7 (0.26)	18.7 (0.97)
Other activities (administration, professional growth, etc.)	21.7 (0.17)	23.2 (0.45)	22.8 (0.67)	22.2 (0.64)	20.4 (1.21)	20.4 (0.66)	21.3 (0.75)	21.3 (0.73)	17.9 (0.54)	26.3 (1.27)
Faculty/staff distribution by instruction activity (percent)										
Distribution by hours taught per week	100.0 (†)	100.0 (†)	100.0 (†)	100.0 (†)	100.0 (†)	100.0 (†)	100.0 (†)	100.0 (†)	100.0 (†)	100.0 (†)
Less than 4.0	30.3 (0.44)	48.9 (0.83)	52.2 (1.31)	30.0 (1.70)	26.5 (1.74)	16.3 (1.08)	14.9 (1.06)	15.5 (1.15)	14.5 (0.86)	36.0 (2.35)
4.0 to 5.9	5.8 (0.21)	8.4 (0.50)	8.8 (0.77)	6.0 (0.58)	8.4 (1.37)	4.1 (0.53)	4.1 (0.57)	4.1 (0.57)	2.5 (0.33)	6.7 (0.99)
6.0 to 7.9	13.8 (0.37)	20.0 (0.80)	15.2 (1.20)	22.2 (1.14)	22.0 (1.77)	12.0 (0.78)	11.0 (1.43)	13.3 (1.48)	4.4 (0.60)	9.0 (0.88)
8.0 to 9.9	12.5 (0.30)	9.0 (0.49)	9.3 (0.87)	16.9 (1.20)	19.3 (1.76)	21.5 (0.93)	18.7 (1.78)	19.5 (1.83)	5.7 (0.61)	7.2 (0.98)
10.0 to 14.9	18.2 (0.39)	7.9 (0.55)	8.8 (0.88)	15.1 (1.13)	15.0 (1.53)	31.5 (1.24)	32.7 (2.15)	33.5 (1.93)	14.7 (0.90)	19.6 (1.95)
15.0 or more	19.4 (0.40)	5.8 (0.43)	5.7 (0.67)	9.7 (0.92)	8.7 (1.34)	18.5 (0.93)	18.5 (1.92)	14.1 (1.39)	58.2 (1.47)	21.5 (1.73)
Distribution by number of students taught	100.0 (†)	100.0 (†)	100.0 (†)	100.0 (†)	100.0 (†)	100.0 (†)	100.0 (†)	100.0 (†)	100.0 (†)	100.0 (†)
Less than 25	30.6 (0.46)	46.0 (0.84)	51.5 (1.56)	29.7 (1.53)	31.9 (1.88)	16.8 (1.25)	16.5 (1.23)	20.8 (1.44)	15.9 (0.94)	36.8 (1.96)
25 to 49	17.0 (0.34)	17.0 (0.83)	16.9 (1.06)	17.1 (0.99)	18.8 (1.74)	17.9 (0.96)	22.7 (1.57)	25.4 (1.62)	12.0 (0.77)	13.4 (1.41)
50 to 74	16.2 (0.33)	11.9 (0.69)	10.0 (0.99)	16.3 (1.29)	20.9 (1.64)	18.7 (0.77)	26.5 (1.32)	24.4 (1.40)	16.2 (0.86)	14.4 (1.07)
75 to 99	13.0 (0.30)	7.6 (0.51)	6.2 (0.57)	13.9 (0.91)	11.2 (0.95)	17.5 (0.86)	17.6 (1.15)	15.8 (1.09)	18.1 (0.78)	11.5 (1.03)
100 to 149	14.2 (0.39)	7.6 (0.54)	7.0 (0.78)	13.2 (0.87)	9.9 (1.21)	19.4 (1.22)	13.1 (1.61)	10.6 (0.96)	25.7 (0.98)	14.9 (1.58)
150 or more	9.0 (0.27)	9.8 (0.59)	8.4 (0.73)	9.8 (0.87)	7.4 (1.04)	9.7 (0.85)	3.6 (0.72)	3.0 (0.62)	12.1 (0.86)	8.9 (0.63)
Distribution by student classroom contact hours per week[1]	100.0 (†)	100.0 (†)	100.0 (†)	100.0 (†)	100.0 (†)	100.0 (†)	100.0 (†)	100.0 (†)	100.0 (†)	100.0 (†)
Less than 50	24.2 (0.40)	38.3 (0.83)	42.7 (1.33)	23.2 (1.52)	22.0 (1.53)	11.9 (1.04)	12.6 (1.02)	12.2 (1.05)	11.9 (0.77)	30.8 (1.87)
50 to 99	5.3 (0.23)	7.7 (0.56)	7.0 (0.82)	6.4 (0.68)	7.0 (1.20)	4.3 (0.52)	2.7 (0.55)	4.9 (0.48)	2.5 (0.39)	5.2 (0.88)
100 to 199	7.1 (0.20)	9.4 (0.54)	10.7 (0.87)	8.0 (0.88)	8.6 (1.38)	6.2 (0.62)	4.5 (0.66)	7.2 (1.02)	3.4 (0.43)	6.1 (0.99)
200 to 349	9.0 (0.28)	10.9 (0.52)	10.4 (0.83)	10.4 (0.88)	12.8 (1.74)	8.6 (0.71)	10.9 (1.38)	11.9 (1.27)	3.6 (0.54)	6.8 (0.79)
350 to 499	7.7 (0.24)	8.0 (0.44)	8.1 (0.83)	10.6 (1.03)	11.5 (1.03)	7.9 (0.91)	10.2 (0.79)	12.4 (0.93)	3.5 (0.40)	4.6 (0.70)
500 or more	46.8 (0.44)	25.6 (0.74)	21.2 (1.21)	41.4 (1.36)	38.0 (1.81)	61.1 (1.46)	59.1 (1.75)	51.4 (2.13)	75.0 (1.16)	46.6 (2.30)
Distribution by total classroom credit hours	100.0 (†)	100.0 (†)	100.0 (†)	100.0 (†)	100.0 (†)	100.0 (†)	100.0 (†)	100.0 (†)	100.0 (†)	100.0 (†)
Less than 4.0	31.8 (0.54)	48.9 (0.82)	52.1 (1.55)	30.1 (1.46)	29.0 (1.75)	18.0 (1.03)	17.5 (1.44)	23.7 (2.18)	15.4 (0.84)	38.1 (2.23)
4.0 to 5.9	6.6 (0.22)	9.4 (0.54)	10.2 (0.63)	6.8 (0.67)	10.5 (1.53)	3.5 (0.35)	4.5 (0.61)	5.6 (0.67)	3.7 (0.44)	7.0 (0.83)
6.0 to 7.9	15.0 (0.37)	21.6 (0.66)	14.0 (1.04)	25.1 (1.29)	21.3 (1.71)	14.2 (0.94)	12.2 (1.04)	11.4 (1.15)	6.6 (0.72)	10.1 (1.07)
8.0 to 9.9	14.8 (0.33)	10.4 (0.60)	10.7 (0.84)	19.9 (1.28)	20.8 (1.47)	25.3 (1.15)	23.4 (1.73)	19.1 (1.16)	8.1 (0.60)	10.0 (1.19)
10.0 to 14.9	20.2 (0.38)	7.7 (0.51)	9.7 (0.99)	14.8 (1.17)	13.2 (1.40)	32.0 (1.20)	35.4 (1.94)	32.5 (2.20)	24.3 (1.28)	22.3 (1.38)
15.0 or more	11.6 (0.31)	1.9 (0.24)	3.2 (0.52)	3.3 (0.64)	5.2 (0.99)	7.0 (0.88)	6.9 (0.71)	7.7 (1.28)	41.8 (1.50)	12.5 (1.17)

See notes at end of table.

Table 315.30. Percentage distribution of full-time faculty and instructional staff in degree-granting postsecondary institutions, by level and control of institution, selected instruction activities, and number of classes taught for credit: Fall 2003—Continued

[Standard errors appear in parentheses]

Instruction activity and number of classes	All institutions	Research		Doctoral		Comprehensive		Private liberal arts	Public 2-year	Other
		Public	Private	Public	Private	Public	Private			
1	2	3	4	5	6	7	8	9	10	11
Faculty/staff distribution by number of classes taught for credit (percent)										
Faculty/staff with undergraduate classes only, by total for-credit courses....	100.0 (†)	100.0 (†)	100.0 (†)	100.0 (†)	100.0 (†)	100.0 (†)	100.0 (†)	100.0 (†)	100.0 (†)	100.0 (†)
1	11.0 (0.43)	24.2 (2.40)	20.2 (2.97)	14.1 (2.91)	10.0 (2.52)	10.5 (1.31)	9.3 (1.13)	9.9 (0.98)	8.7 (0.75)	11.2 (2.17)
2	17.4 (0.62)	38.0 (2.80)	31.2 (3.96)	24.2 (3.05)	38.6 (5.05)	14.6 (1.51)	18.5 (2.14)	22.7 (2.32)	10.7 (0.77)	13.7 (2.29)
3	23.7 (0.65)	22.6 (2.21)	30.8 (3.42)	31.1 (2.98)	37.3 (3.60)	28.6 (1.89)	30.3 (2.48)	34.3 (2.57)	16.0 (0.96)	17.3 (2.77)
4	21.9 (0.73)	10.8 (1.43)	11.7 (2.99)	20.4 (1.92)	10.9 (2.75)	33.3 (1.87)	30.7 (2.77)	21.1 (2.22)	16.9 (1.00)	28.4 (2.48)
5 or more	26.1 (0.70)	4.4 (0.86)	6.1 (1.74)	10.1 (1.97)	3.2 ! (1.15)	13.0 (1.56)	11.2 (1.53)	12.0 (1.44)	47.6 (1.49)	29.4 (2.14)
Faculty/staff with graduate classes only, by total for-credit courses....	100.0 (†)	100.0 (†)	100.0 (†)	100.0 (†)	100.0 (†)	100.0 (†)	100.0 (†)	100.0 (†)	‡	100.0 (†)
1	40.1 (1.21)	50.4 (2.17)	48.0 (3.69)	34.3 (3.04)	25.9 (4.02)	23.6 (3.86)	13.0 (3.72)	15.8 ! (6.35)	‡	37.8 (3.15)
2	31.0 (1.07)	26.3 (1.81)	27.9 (2.93)	39.1 (3.32)	50.7 (4.02)	33.6 (5.32)	28.7 (4.00)	31.6 ! (12.42)	‡	32.9 (2.93)
3	16.7 (0.88)	14.3 (1.38)	13.3 (2.60)	16.3 (2.76)	14.1 (3.52)	29.6 (4.35)	36.3 (4.99)	22.7 ! (9.79)	‡	13.4 (2.48)
4	7.1 (0.80)	4.5 (1.24)	7.4 (2.07)	7.4 (2.04)	3.7 ! (1.44)	10.1 ! (3.39)	16.5 (3.92)	16.7 ! (8.04)	‡	7.2 ! (2.21)
5 or more	5.1 (0.52)	4.4 (0.69)	3.4 ! (1.33)	‡ (†)	5.7 ! (2.80)	3.1 ! (1.52)	5.5 ! (2.85)	‡ (†)	‡	8.7 (1.94)
Faculty/staff with both undergraduate and graduate classes, by total for-credit courses....	100.0 (†)	100.0 (†)	100.0 (†)	100.0 (†)	100.0 (†)	100.0 (†)	100.0 (†)	100.0 (†)	100.0 (†)	100.0 (†)
1	23.3 (0.68)	32.5 (1.37)	38.4 (1.89)	21.1 (2.17)	20.2 (2.37)	9.0 (1.04)	10.3 (2.14)	9.4 (2.00)	‡	24.8 (3.18)
2	33.4 (0.83)	44.3 (1.36)	42.8 (2.33)	37.1 (2.15)	37.8 (2.58)	19.6 (1.30)	19.0 (2.78)	18.3 (2.62)	‡	18.7 (3.00)
3	24.3 (0.70)	15.5 (0.99)	12.4 (1.37)	26.5 (1.75)	32.0 (3.01)	38.1 (1.91)	34.8 (2.85)	29.5 (3.77)	‡	21.2 (3.06)
4	12.2 (0.54)	4.5 (0.64)	3.7 (1.06)	10.1 (1.37)	6.6 ! (2.02)	23.4 (1.69)	24.4 (3.39)	27.5 (3.74)	‡	16.6 (3.55)
5 or more	6.7 (0.43)	3.1 (0.45)	2.8 (0.78)	5.2 (0.75)	‡ (†)	9.9 (1.01)	11.4 (2.07)	15.2 (3.65)	‡	18.6 (2.88)

†Not applicable.
!Interpret data with caution. The coefficient of variation (CV) for this estimate is between 30 and 50 percent.
‡Reporting standards not met. Either there are too few cases for a reliable estimate or the coefficient of variation (CV) is 50 percent or greater.
[1]Distribution by student classroom contact hours per week is based on the number of contact hours that faculty and instructional staff spend each week with students during classroom instruction multiplied by the number of students taught.

NOTE: Degree-granting institutions grant associate's or higher degrees and participate in Title IV federal financial aid programs. Totals may differ from figures reported in other tables because of varying survey methodologies. Detail may not sum to totals because of rounding.
SOURCE: U.S. Department of Education, National Center for Education Statistics, 2004 National Study of Postsecondary Faculty (NSOPF:04). (This table was prepared December 2008.)

Table 315.40. Percentage distribution of part-time faculty and instructional staff in degree-granting postsecondary institutions, by level and control of institution, selected instruction activities, and number of classes taught for credit: Fall 2003

[Standard errors appear in parentheses]

Instruction activity and number of classes	All institutions	Research		Doctoral		Comprehensive		Private liberal arts	Public 2-year	Other
		Public	Private	Public	Private	Public	Private			
1	2	3	4	5	6	7	8	9	10	11
Number of part-time faculty and instructional staff (in thousands)	530.0 (0.02)	39.7 (0.78)	23.2 (0.96)	20.8 (0.82)	15.4 (0.83)	60.3 (2.49)	53.5 (2.17)	28.4 (2.19)	230.1 (2.00)	58.7 (3.38)
Percentage distribution	100.0 (†)	7.5 (0.15)	4.4 (0.18)	3.9 (0.15)	2.9 (0.16)	11.4 (0.47)	10.1 (0.41)	5.4 (0.41)	43.4 (0.38)	11.1 (0.64)
Average hours worked per week	39.9 (0.30)	41.1 (0.85)	42.6 (1.24)	43.5 (1.37)	42.1 (1.29)	38.8 (1.01)	42.7 (1.14)	39.6 (1.23)	38.0 (0.45)	41.8 (1.18)
Paid activities within institution	13.7 (0.13)	19.0 (0.61)	14.0 (0.65)	16.4 (0.76)	13.5 (0.97)	14.9 (0.48)	12.1 (0.56)	13.5 (0.73)	12.5 (0.19)	14.2 (0.46)
Unpaid activities within institution	1.7 (0.06)	1.8 (0.25)	2.5 (0.25)	2.3 (0.28)	2.8 (0.37)	2.3 (0.19)	2.7 (0.12)	2.6 (0.17)	2.1 (0.08)	2.5 (0.17)
Paid activities outside institution	22.1 (0.28)	18.3 (0.98)	23.9 (1.34)	23.3 (1.55)	24.1 (1.40)	19.9 (1.00)	26.6 (1.38)	21.9 (0.98)	21.6 (0.41)	23.3 (1.06)
Unpaid activities outside institution	2.3 (0.06)	2.0 (0.25)	2.2 (0.25)	1.6 (0.28)	1.7 (0.37)	1.8 (0.19)	1.3 (0.12)	1.6 (0.17)	1.7 (0.08)	1.8 (0.17)
Work time distribution (percent)	100.0 (†)	100.0 (†)	100.0 (†)	100.0 (†)	100.0 (†)	100.0 (†)	100.0 (†)	100.0 (†)	100.0 (†)	100.0 (†)
Teaching	88.3 (0.32)	74.1 (1.79)	80.6 (1.89)	84.9 (1.71)	87.2 (1.87)	90.8 (0.83)	90.4 (0.70)	90.2 (1.20)	91.3 (0.43)	85.4 (1.19)
Research/scholarship	3.9 (0.80)	13.3 (1.62)	7.0 (0.97)	7.4 (1.35)	5.2 (1.42)	3.2 (0.46)	2.4 (0.49)	2.6 (0.54)	2.1 (0.21)	4.4 (0.61)
Other activities (administration, professional growth, etc.)	7.8 (0.20)	12.6 (1.04)	12.4 (1.75)	7.6 (1.03)	7.6 (1.22)	6.0 (0.63)	7.2 (0.81)	7.2 (0.92)	6.6 (0.40)	10.3 (0.93)
Faculty/staff distribution by instruction activity (percent)										
Distribution by hours taught per week [1]	100.0 (†)	100.0 (†)	100.0 (†)	100.0 (†)	100.0 (†)	100.0 (†)	100.0 (†)	100.0 (†)	100.0 (†)	100.0 (†)
Less than 4.0	45.3 (0.80)	58.1 (2.25)	62.4 (3.87)	53.3 (2.71)	48.0 (2.67)	45.5 (1.68)	39.8 (2.34)	44.8 (2.96)	41.3 (1.30)	46.5 (2.46)
4.0 to 5.9	12.2 (0.48)	9.3 (1.25)	12.9 (2.46)	12.5 (1.49)	15.0 (1.57)	9.7 (1.25)	17.7 (2.07)	13.2 (1.73)	11.7 (0.71)	12.6 (1.62)
6.0 to 7.9	14.3 (0.57)	12.5 (1.50)	10.1 (1.69)	14.5 (1.76)	14.3 (2.01)	19.4 (1.68)	12.9 (2.14)	13.8 (1.98)	14.5 (1.04)	13.0 (1.72)
8.0 to 9.9	10.4 (0.47)	8.9 (1.22)	5.6 (1.46)	8.3 (1.82)	7.8 (1.58)	10.8 (1.11)	11.7 (1.93)	10.7 (1.54)	11.3 (0.73)	9.5 (1.45)
10.0 to 14.9	9.4 (0.47)	7.5 (1.27)	3.0 ! (1.16)	5.5 (1.29)	7.3 (2.03)	8.0 (1.27)	7.7 (1.29)	8.3 (1.55)	11.7 (0.99)	9.8 (1.27)
15.0 or more	8.3 (0.43)	3.6 (0.90)	6.0 ! (1.94)	5.9 (1.50)	7.6 (1.26)	6.5 (1.05)	10.3 (1.61)	9.1 (2.38)	9.5 (0.67)	8.5 (1.19)
Distribution by number of students taught	100.0 (†)	100.0 (†)	100.0 (†)	100.0 (†)	100.0 (†)	100.0 (†)	100.0 (†)	100.0 (†)	100.0 (†)	100.0 (†)
Less than 25	52.0 (0.82)	55.6 (2.16)	68.9 (3.98)	44.6 (2.68)	56.9 (3.29)	41.6 (2.07)	57.9 (2.45)	60.5 (2.34)	49.7 (1.37)	54.0 (3.15)
25 to 49	24.9 (0.58)	17.4 (1.54)	16.9 (2.13)	27.4 (2.51)	20.7 (2.48)	24.5 (2.10)	29.4 (1.90)	24.1 (1.76)	26.7 (0.97)	22.6 (2.74)
50 to 74	12.1 (0.54)	11.6 (1.23)	3.7 ! (1.15)	12.5 (1.71)	9.8 (2.48)	17.5 (1.52)	8.5 (0.77)	10.0 (1.65)	12.9 (0.95)	11.7 (1.55)
75 to 99	5.8 (0.30)	5.4 (0.89)	4.1 ! (1.57)	7.6 (1.52)	6.8 (1.62)	6.7 (1.22)	2.0 (0.44)	3.7 (0.97)	6.2 (0.48)	7.5 (1.18)
100 to 149	3.4 (0.23)	4.8 (1.07)	2.0 ! (0.72)	4.2 ! (1.46)	2.9 ! (0.89)	7.2 (1.14)	1.8 ! (0.55)	‡ (†)	3.2 (0.41)	2.4 ! (0.76)
150 or more	1.9 (0.19)	5.2 (0.96)	4.5 (1.35)	3.7 (0.94)	2.8 ! (1.12)	2.6 (0.59)	‡ (†)	‡ (†)	1.2 (0.35)	1.7 (0.44)
Distribution by student classroom contact hours per week [1]	100.0 (†)	100.0 (†)	100.0 (†)	100.0 (†)	100.0 (†)	100.0 (†)	100.0 (†)	100.0 (†)	100.0 (†)	100.0 (†)
Less than 50	33.9 (0.80)	41.6 (2.52)	53.4 (3.89)	27.7 (2.98)	40.2 (2.67)	25.4 (1.88)	36.0 (2.52)	38.2 (2.66)	31.3 (1.34)	36.7 (3.40)
50 to 99	17.0 (0.54)	13.1 (1.46)	17.5 (2.13)	23.0 (3.38)	17.0 (2.30)	18.9 (1.40)	19.5 (1.53)	17.4 (1.97)	16.6 (0.96)	14.5 (1.65)
100 to 199	13.2 (0.49)	13.3 (1.51)	8.5 (1.44)	14.2 (2.34)	7.5 (1.56)	14.8 (1.72)	13.3 (1.65)	14.1 (2.01)	13.4 (0.82)	13.5 (2.19)
200 to 349	11.2 (0.46)	10.8 (1.29)	5.6 (1.42)	10.9 (1.97)	12.3 (1.88)	10.3 (1.80)	13.5 (0.93)	10.1 (1.26)	11.4 (0.66)	12.1 (1.62)
350 to 499	7.2 (0.34)	6.1 (0.98)	3.0 ! (0.96)	7.7 (1.74)	8.5 (1.74)	10.2 (1.0)	4.5 (0.64)	5.5 (0.95)	8.0 (0.69)	6.0 (0.93)
500 or more	17.5 (0.58)	15.1 (1.89)	12.1 (2.50)	16.5 (2.29)	14.5 (2.58)	20.3 (1.97)	13.3 (1.53)	14.6 (2.85)	19.3 (0.98)	17.2 (1.87)
Distribution by total classroom credit hours	100.0 (†)	100.0 (†)	100.0 (†)	100.0 (†)	100.0 (†)	100.0 (†)	100.0 (†)	100.0 (†)	100.0 (†)	100.0 (†)
Less than 4.0	53.3 (0.89)	59.8 (2.39)	67.5 (3.65)	62.2 (2.96)	55.4 (2.34)	52.0 (2.05)	51.3 (2.05)	58.9 (2.14)	50.2 (1.43)	52.2 (3.00)
4.0 to 5.9	11.7 (0.52)	12.2 (1.52)	11.8 (2.12)	10.8 (1.63)	10.6 (1.81)	9.3 (1.09)	14.1 (1.77)	10.3 (1.68)	12.2 (0.75)	11.5 (1.68)
6.0 to 7.9	16.9 (0.55)	12.8 (1.61)	10.2 (2.20)	14.9 (1.96)	18.7 (2.12)	23.1 (2.10)	18.1 (1.22)	15.4 (1.81)	16.5 (0.98)	17.5 (1.62)
8.0 to 9.9	9.4 (0.42)	8.2 (0.92)	6.2 (1.22)	8.5 (1.64)	8.3 (2.03)	9.5 (0.99)	9.0 (1.08)	8.3 (1.34)	10.8 (0.81)	7.4 (1.33)
10.0 to 14.9	6.6 (0.35)	5.6 (1.48)	1.8 ! (0.75)	3.6 (0.97)	4.8 (1.22)	3.8 (0.81)	5.2 (0.82)	5.1 ! (1.57)	8.1 (0.62)	9.2 (1.54)
15.0 or more	2.1 (0.21)	1.4 ! (0.58)	2.5 ! (0.91)	‡ (†)	2.2 ! (0.78)	2.2 (0.57)	2.3 (0.64)	2.0 ! (0.80)	2.2 (0.31)	2.2 (0.63)

See notes at end of table.

Table 315.40. Percentage distribution of part-time faculty and instructional staff in degree-granting postsecondary institutions, by level and control of institution, selected instruction activities, and number of classes taught for credit: Fall 2003—Continued

[Standard errors appear in parentheses]

Instruction activity and number of classes	All institutions	Research Public	Research Private	Doctoral Public	Doctoral Private	Comprehensive Public	Comprehensive Private	Private liberal arts	Public 2-year	Other
1	2	3	4	5	6	7	8	9	10	11
Faculty/staff distribution by number of classes taught for credit (percent)										
Faculty/staff with undergraduate classes only, by total for-credit courses	100.0 (†)	100.0 (†)	100.0 (†)	100.0 (†)	100.0 (†)	100.0 (†)	100.0 (†)	100.0 (†)	100.0 (†)	100.0 (†)
1	49.2 (0.90)	53.1 (3.85)	62.3 (5.20)	58.8 (4.27)	45.4 (4.58)	48.4 (2.43)	54.1 (2.78)	53.7 (3.42)	47.9 (1.20)	43.2 (3.57)
2	29.7 (0.86)	31.2 (3.04)	28.5 (5.51)	26.9 (3.12)	39.8 (4.33)	33.1 (2.35)	29.2 (2.27)	25.0 (2.20)	29.3 (1.24)	29.7 (2.70)
3	12.5 (0.47)	9.4 (1.83)	6.9 ! (2.33)	11.5 (2.36)	13.1 (3.15)	10.8 (1.26)	9.4 (1.35)	10.2 (1.62)	13.9 (0.84)	13.7 (1.71)
4	5.3 (0.41)	4.6 ! (1.41)	‡ (†)	‡ (†)	‡ (†)	4.0 (1.06)	5.4 (1.08)	5.6 ! (1.95)	5.9 (0.65)	6.9 (1.73)
5 or more	3.3 (0.32)	‡ (†)	‡ (†)	2.6 ! (1.27)	‡ (†)	3.7 (0.95)	1.8 ! (0.77)	5.5 ! (1.69)	3.1 (0.44)	6.5 (1.87)
Faculty/staff with graduate classes only, by total for-credit courses	100.0 (†)	100.0 (†)	100.0 (†)	100.0 (†)	100.0 (†)	100.0 (†)	100.0 (†)	100.0 (†)	100.0 (†)	100.0 (†)
1	72.6 (1.73)	71.7 (5.24)	81.7 (4.89)	81.8 (4.93)	72.2 (5.28)	74.8 (5.62)	62.2 (3.67)	69.9 (6.67)	‡ (†)	75.6 (5.21)
2	16.6 (1.30)	20.6 (4.61)	7.4 ! (3.23)	10.8 ! (4.07)	16.2 (4.50)	12.9 ! (4.45)	23.3 (2.37)	18.8 ! (5.77)	‡ (†)	16.4 (3.91)
3	5.3 (0.93)	‡ (†)	5.7 ! (2.74)	‡ (†)	‡ (†)	‡ (†)	7.6 ! (2.41)	‡ (†)	‡ (†)	‡ (†)
4	3.1 (0.81)	‡ (†)	‡ (†)	‡ (†)	4.0 ! (1.41)	‡ (†)	3.9 ! (1.32)	‡ (†)	‡ (†)	‡ (†)
5 or more	2.4 (0.53)	‡ (†)	‡ (†)	‡ (†)	‡ (†)	‡ (†)	2.9 ! (1.38)	‡ (†)	‡ (†)	3.0 ! (1.45)
Faculty/staff with both undergraduate and graduate classes, by total for-credit courses	100.0 (†)	100.0 (†)	100.0 (†)	100.0 (†)	100.0 (†)	100.0 (†)	100.0 (†)	100.0 (†)	100.0 (†)	100.0 (†)
1	46.5 (2.05)	51.3 (5.19)	46.4 (10.59)	59.3 (5.24)	63.7 (8.93)	38.0 (6.03)	38.9 (4.23)	44.1 (8.69)	‡ (†)	47.4 (6.18)
2	28.7 (1.96)	29.6 (4.47)	36.3 (8.39)	18.5 ! (6.24)	18.1 ! (5.75)	30.7 (3.91)	32.7 (5.11)	35.1 (9.57)	‡ (†)	23.9 (5.54)
3	13.5 (1.79)	11.3 (3.25)	‡ (†)	16.9 ! (6.27)	‡ (†)	17.8 (4.04)	16.6 (3.72)	12.3 ! (4.69)	‡ (†)	‡ (†)
4	5.9 (1.19)	3.3 ! (1.63)	‡ (†)	‡ (†)	‡ (†)	7.9 ! (3.54)	‡ (†)	5.8 ! (2.25)	‡ (†)	10.0 ! (4.03)
5 or more	5.4 (1.18)	4.4 ! (2.08)	‡ (†)	‡ (†)	‡ (†)	5.7 ! (2.75)	6.4 ! (2.36)	‡ (†)	‡ (†)	9.2 ! (4.56)

†Not applicable.
!Interpret data with caution. The coefficient of variation (CV) for this estimate is between 30 and 50 percent.
‡Reporting standards not met. Either there are too few cases for a reliable estimate or the coefficient of variation (CV) is 50 percent or greater.
[1] Distribution by student classroom contact hours per week is based on the number of contact hours that faculty and instructional staff spend each week with students during classroom instruction multiplied by the number of students taught.

NOTE: Degree-granting institutions grant associate's or higher degrees and participate in Title IV federal financial aid programs. Totals may differ from figures reported in other tables because of varying survey methodologies. Detail may not sum to totals because of rounding.
SOURCE: U.S. Department of Education, National Center for Education Statistics, 2004 National Study of Postsecondary Faculty (NSOPF:04). (This table was prepared December 2008.)

Table 315.50. Full-time and part-time faculty and instructional staff in degree-granting postsecondary institutions, by level and control of institution and selected characteristics: Fall 1992, fall 1998, and fall 2003

[Standard errors appear in parentheses]

Selected characteristic	Number (in thousands) 1992	1998	2003	Fall 2003 Total	Research Public	Research Private	Doctoral Public	Doctoral Private	Comprehensive Public	Comprehensive Private	Private liberal arts	Public 2-year	Other
	2	3	4	5	6	7	8	9	10	11	12	13	14
Full-time faculty and instructional staff													
Number (in thousands)	528.3	560.4	681.8 (†)	681.8	162.1 (0.85)	63.5 (1.58)	51.3 (0.76)	21.7 (0.79)	107.3 (2.98)	41.4 (1.59)	49.6 (1.80)	114.6 (1.09)	70.2 (3.36)
Percentage distribution	†	†	†	100.0 (†)	23.8 (0.12)	9.3 (0.23)	7.5 (0.11)	3.2 (0.12)	15.7 (0.44)	6.1 (0.23)	7.3 (0.26)	16.8 (0.16)	10.3 (0.49)
Total	528.3	560.4	681.8	100.0 (†)	100.0 (†)	100.0 (†)	100.0 (†)	100.0 (†)	100.0 (†)	100.0 (†)	100.0 (†)	100.0 (†)	100.0 (†)
Sex													
Male	352.7	356.9	420.4	61.7 (0.35)	69.9 (0.62)	68.8 (0.90)	62.8 (1.29)	66.7 (2.04)	58.8 (0.84)	57.6 (2.03)	59.7 (1.14)	50.5 (1.08)	60.3 (1.41)
Female	175.5	203.5	261.4	38.3 (0.35)	30.1 (0.62)	31.2 (0.90)	37.2 (1.29)	33.3 (2.04)	41.2 (0.84)	42.4 (2.03)	40.3 (1.14)	49.5 (1.08)	39.7 (1.41)
Race/ethnicity													
White	456.7	477.0	547.7	80.3 (0.27)	79.0 (0.50)	77.6 (0.73)	81.3 (1.33)	82.7 (1.55)	78.0 (1.12)	85.6 (1.02)	86.0 (0.81)	80.9 (0.84)	79.8 (1.14)
Black	27.4	28.4	38.1	5.6 (0.17)	3.7 (0.26)	4.9 (0.49)	4.1 (0.50)	5.1 (0.79)	8.7 (0.73)	4.8 (0.65)	6.3 (0.69)	6.9 (0.43)	4.7 (0.81)
Hispanic	13.9	18.5	23.8	3.5 (0.10)	2.9 (0.18)	3.5 (0.36)	2.9 (0.37)	2.2 (0.59)	3.6 (0.23)	2.4 (0.36)	2.3 (0.26)	5.8 (0.44)	3.1 (0.44)
Asian/Pacific Islander	27.7	32.5	62.3	9.1 (0.16)	13.2 (0.45)	12.8 (0.63)	10.1 (1.17)	9.3 (1.40)	7.9 (0.34)	5.9 (0.74)	3.8 (0.33)	4.2 (0.44)	11.3 (0.94)
American Indian/Alaska Native	2.6	4.0	10.0	1.5 (0.11)	1.1 (0.17)	1.2 ! (0.40)	1.6 (0.35)	0.7 ! (0.36)	1.8 (0.50)	1.2 ! (0.38)	1.6 (0.31)	2.2 (0.36)	1.0 ! (0.32)
Age													
Under 30	7.6	8.8	11.9	1.7 (0.13)	1.7 (0.24)	1.5 (0.28)	1.8 (0.37)	1.3 ! (0.44)	1.7 (0.29)	2.3 (0.56)	2.1 (0.41)	1.8 (0.36)	1.7 ! (0.68)
30 to 34	35.4	32.2	47.2	6.9 (0.21)	7.5 (0.44)	8.6 (0.89)	7.2 (0.82)	5.9 (0.73)	6.5 (0.74)	7.0 (0.92)	8.9 (0.73)	5.1 (0.52)	6.4 (0.75)
35 to 39	66.8	60.1	77.1	11.3 (0.29)	12.8 (0.58)	14.3 (1.35)	11.8 (0.95)	8.9 (1.45)	10.1 (0.86)	9.6 (0.88)	12.8 (1.22)	9.0 (0.70)	11.1 (1.05)
40 to 44	90.2	81.9	92.6	13.6 (0.31)	15.3 (0.57)	15.0 (0.75)	11.9 (0.83)	11.8 (1.36)	12.1 (0.78)	14.4 (1.15)	12.3 (0.75)	12.7 (0.88)	14.4 (1.38)
45 to 49	97.7	96.8	105.3	15.4 (0.32)	15.9 (0.53)	14.6 (1.24)	16.5 (1.38)	16.0 (1.89)	15.2 (0.75)	13.0 (1.18)	14.3 (1.10)	14.7 (0.70)	18.0 (1.36)
50 to 54	94.9	104.7	114.4	16.8 (0.34)	16.3 (0.66)	14.6 (0.87)	16.0 (1.09)	14.9 (1.34)	16.6 (0.90)	17.1 (1.26)	16.5 (1.0)	19.3 (0.84)	17.1 (1.35)
55 to 59	67.3	90.2	111.6	16.4 (0.37)	13.9 (0.58)	12.0 (0.61)	15.1 (1.01)	16.5 (1.60)	17.3 (0.89)	16.8 (1.24)	15.6 (0.87)	21.9 (1.05)	16.8 (1.46)
60 to 64	44.6	55.0	78.3	11.5 (0.31)	10.7 (0.58)	10.9 (0.74)	13.8 (0.90)	12.8 (1.54)	13.4 (0.72)	12.9 (1.42)	11.8 (1.10)	10.5 (0.68)	9.4 (0.83)
65 or older	23.8	30.6	43.3	6.3 (0.23)	6.0 (0.40)	8.6 (0.64)	5.9 (0.83)	11.8 (1.53)	7.1 (0.67)	6.8 (0.78)	5.7 (0.80)	4.9 (0.67)	5.2 (0.59)
Highest degree													
Less than bachelor's	6.3	6.7	10.0	1.5 (0.12)	1.5 (0.24)	‡ (†)	0.2 ! (0.09)	‡ (†)	0.1 ! (0.07)	‡ (†)	0.8 ! (0.26)	6.1 (0.58)	2.4 (0.64)
Bachelor's	20.9	22.5	29.4	4.3 (0.24)	2.0 (0.27)	2.0 (0.41)	2.9 (0.51)	1.6 (0.46)	3.1 (0.63)	2.8 (0.58)	2.1 (0.53)	11.1 (0.97)	6.9 (0.82)
Master's	155.8	156.0	179.8	26.4 (0.39)	12.3 (0.49)	9.9 (0.93)	20.3 (1.19)	12.9 (1.17)	22.7 (1.08)	28.7 (2.10)	27.2 (1.71)	63.3 (1.22)	25.5 (1.68)
First-professional	58.3	51.7	56.1	8.2 (0.30)	11.8 (0.53)	18.4 (1.19)	4.7 (0.49)	9.7 (1.47)	2.0 (0.30)	3.5 (0.89)	0.9 (0.18)	1.6 (0.30)	21.3 (1.99)
Doctoral	283.8	323.5	406.6	59.6 (0.48)	73.7 (0.61)	69.4 (1.45)	71.9 (1.30)	75.4 (2.03)	72.1 (1.34)	65.0 (2.47)	69.1 (1.92)	17.9 (1.13)	43.8 (2.47)
Academic rank													
Professor	160.6	172.0	194.4 (3.67)	28.5 (0.54)	33.8 (0.95)	34.0 (1.15)	27.3 (1.34)	30.3 (2.37)	29.8 (1.23)	24.8 (1.61)	28.5 (1.79)	21.7 (1.89)	22.9 (1.39)
Associate professor	123.7	132.0	149.6 (2.56)	21.9 (0.37)	23.3 (0.63)	22.0 (1.12)	25.9 (1.54)	31.6 (1.73)	23.2 (1.30)	27.0 (1.41)	24.6 (1.27)	12.1 (1.22)	22.3 (1.47)
Assistant professor	124.3	125.0	158.1 (2.81)	22.5 (0.41)	22.5 (0.68)	26.6 (1.38)	23.5 (1.36)	21.6 (1.63)	28.3 (1.08)	31.8 (2.0)	30.3 (1.14)	10.5 (1.12)	25.2 (1.37)
Instructor	73.9	74.9	82.7 (2.85)	12.1 (0.42)	4.3 (0.27)	5.0 (0.79)	9.0 (0.94)	4.5 (0.89)	7.6 (0.81)	6.8 (1.02)	6.6 (0.91)	37.5 (2.13)	13.9 (1.30)
Lecturer	11.9	14.1	21.9 (1.48)	3.2 (0.22)	4.6 (0.34)	4.9 (0.59)	5.4 (0.80)	2.5 (0.40)	5.4 (0.99)	1.9 ! (0.67)	1.0 (0.23)	0.3 (0.09)	0.9 (0.27)
Other	17.1	26.3	56.5 (2.15)	8.3 (0.32)	10.6 (0.64)	7.1 (0.54)	8.5 (0.59)	8.9 (1.23)	5.7 (0.94)	7.3 (1.12)	8.8 (1.11)	8.3 (0.80)	7.9 (0.90)
No rank	16.9	15.8	18.6 (1.28)	2.7 (0.19)	0.8 (0.14)	‡ (†)	‡ (†)	‡ (†)	0.1 ! (0.05)	0.5 (0.10)	‡ (†)	9.8 (0.88)	7.0 (1.14)
Base salary													
Under $10,000	13.8	9.7	4.4 (0.49)	0.7 (0.07)	0.8 (0.19)	0.7 ! (0.31)	0.8 ! (0.26)	‡ (†)	0.5 ! (0.20)	‡ (†)	0.6 ! (0.18)	0.6 (0.15)	0.9 ! (0.35)
$10,000 to $24,999	29.4	19.3	19.0 (1.03)	2.8 (0.15)	2.5 (0.28)	3.0 (0.44)	3.8 (0.55)	1.7 ! (0.74)	3.1 (0.36)	2.9 (0.45)	2.6 (0.58)	2.9 (0.42)	2.4 (0.59)
$25,000 to $39,999	181.8	123.7	79.7 (2.90)	11.7 (0.40)	8.0 (0.49)	5.6 (0.66)	13.0 (0.65)	6.6 (1.03)	12.2 (1.12)	12.8 (1.85)	15.2 (1.38)	18.0 (1.44)	12.0 (1.28)
$40,000 to $54,999	163.8	171.1	192.4 (3.09)	28.2 (0.45)	19.2 (0.78)	15.5 (1.13)	27.4 (1.10)	21.3 (2.12)	34.0 (1.40)	38.8 (1.63)	39.6 (1.64)	37.1 (1.48)	25.7 (1.55)
$55,000 to $69,999	76.7	106.2	147.7 (3.54)	21.7 (0.52)	18.9 (0.58)	16.0 (0.99)	22.3 (1.05)	26.4 (2.02)	24.1 (1.26)	24.9 (1.78)	23.1 (1.34)	24.3 (1.58)	20.9 (1.43)
$70,000 to $84,999	32.1	57.9	94.8 (2.19)	13.9 (0.32)	15.3 (0.64)	15.4 (1.01)	14.7 (1.03)	15.6 (1.52)	14.7 (1.21)	10.5 (1.18)	11.2 (1.46)	12.9 (1.10)	12.0 (1.38)
$85,000 to $99,999	11.1	28.1	50.7 (1.98)	7.4 (0.29)	11.1 (0.54)	9.8 (0.80)	7.8 (0.79)	10.1 (1.32)	8.1 (0.78)	4.0 (1.15)	3.7 (0.56)	3.6 (0.59)	5.7 (0.58)
$100,000 or more	19.6	44.4	93.1 (2.29)	13.7 (0.34)	24.1 (0.76)	34.0 (1.20)	10.2 (0.82)	18.2 (1.63)	3.3 (0.46)	5.8 (0.90)	4.0 (0.57)	0.8 (0.21)	20.4 (2.00)

Percentage distribution of full-time faculty and instructional staff

See notes at end of table.

Table 315.50. Full-time and part-time faculty and instructional staff in degree-granting postsecondary institutions, by level and control of institution and selected characteristics: Fall 1992, fall 1998, and fall 2003—Continued

[Standard errors appear in parentheses]

Selected characteristic	Number (in thousands)			Total	Fall 2003								
	1992	1998	2003		Research Public	Research Private	Doctoral Public	Doctoral Private	Comprehensive Public	Comprehensive Private	Private liberal arts	Public 2-year	Other
1	2	3	4	5	6	7	8	9	10	11	12	13	14
Part-time faculty and instructional staff													
Number (in thousands)	376.7	416.0	530.0	530.0 (0.02)	39.7 (0.78)	23.2 (0.96)	20.8 (0.82)	15.4 (0.83)	60.3 (2.49)	53.5 (2.17)	28.4 (2.19)	230.1 (2.00)	58.7 (3.38)
Percentage distribution	†	†	†	100.0 (†)	7.5 (0.15)	4.4 (0.18)	3.9 (0.15)	2.9 (0.16)	11.4 (0.47)	10.1 (0.41)	5.4 (0.41)	43.4 (0.38)	11.1 (0.64)
Percentage distribution of part-time faculty and instructional staff													
Total	376.7	416.0	530.0	100.0 (†)	100.0 (†)	100.0 (†)	100.0 (†)	100.0 (†)	100.0 (†)	100.0 (†)	100.0 (†)	100.0 (†)	100.0 (†)
Sex													
Male	208.7	217.0	275.9	52.1 (0.45)	50.4 (1.97)	60.2 (1.92)	50.2 (2.26)	58.4 (3.34)	50.0 (1.59)	53.9 (1.53)	50.3 (1.95)	50.7 (0.57)	55.4 (1.66)
Female	168.0	199.1	254.1	47.9 (0.45)	49.6 (1.97)	39.8 (1.92)	49.8 (2.26)	41.6 (3.34)	50.0 (1.59)	46.1 (1.53)	49.7 (1.95)	49.3 (0.57)	44.6 (1.66)
Race/ethnicity													
White	332.8	364.4	451.6	85.2 (0.38)	82.4 (1.63)	85.1 (1.78)	87.9 (2.19)	88.9 (1.99)	87.2 (1.89)	91.0 (0.85)	86.2 (1.59)	83.7 (0.54)	83.0 (1.84)
Black	18.3	18.9	29.7	5.6 (0.20)	2.7 (0.72)	4.1 (1.14)	2.4 (1.01)	2.8 ! (0.99)	4.7 (1.20)	2.8 (0.40)	8.1 (1.27)	6.9 (0.25)	7.2 (1.02)
Hispanic	11.2	15.5	18.7	3.5 (0.13)	3.2 (0.56)	2.5 ! (0.78)	4.1 (0.81)	2.8 ! (0.66)	3.1 (0.39)	2.4 (0.30)	2.1 (0.48)	4.4 (0.21)	3.0 (0.57)
Asian/Pacific Islander	12.2	13.2	20.3	3.8 (0.22)	9.9 (1.39)	6.4 (1.05)	4.5 (1.14)	4.9 ! (1.79)	3.3 (0.59)	1.9 ! (0.61)	2.7 (0.63)	2.9 (0.23)	4.7 (1.02)
American Indian/Alaska Native	2.3	4.0	9.7	1.8 (0.22)	1.8 ! (0.68)	‡ (†)	‡ (†)	‡ (†)	1.7 ! (0.61)	1.9 (0.42)	0.9 ! (0.35)	2.1 (0.38)	2.1 ! (0.70)
Age													
Under 30	20.5	15.1	22.8	4.3 (0.30)	5.6 (0.94)	3.1 ! (1.11)	8.9 (1.75)	4.8 ! (1.58)	5.7 (1.04)	1.8 (0.51)	3.8 (0.72)	4.4 (0.46)	3.1 (0.72)
30 to 34	35.9	37.1	43.4	8.2 (0.38)	10.0 (1.32)	8.8 (1.79)	6.8 (1.20)	6.5 (1.81)	8.1 (1.16)	7.9 (1.16)	8.9 (1.33)	8.2 (0.68)	7.6 (1.11)
35 to 39	58.9	47.2	54.6	10.3 (0.48)	8.7 (1.36)	9.4 (1.48)	8.3 (1.74)	12.5 (2.38)	11.1 (1.55)	9.7 (0.88)	10.8 (1.78)	10.4 (0.74)	10.8 (1.35)
40 to 44	70.0	60.4	61.0	11.5 (0.44)	12.9 (1.78)	11.4 (1.81)	11.2 (2.26)	11.2 (1.74)	11.9 (1.34)	10.1 (1.18)	12.2 (1.37)	11.3 (0.78)	11.3 (1.40)
45 to 49	68.0	72.1	76.5	14.4 (0.48)	15.6 (1.51)	16.0 (1.54)	7.9 (2.42)	7.9 (1.93)	11.3 (1.17)	14.3 (1.27)	14.0 (1.95)	14.6 (0.75)	17.1 (1.84)
50 to 54	45.1	69.8	82.8	15.6 (0.42)	14.5 (1.39)	12.2 (1.49)	16.3 (2.27)	16.5 (2.76)	13.6 (1.50)	18.5 (1.24)	15.0 (1.66)	15.9 (0.72)	15.8 (1.57)
55 to 59	28.8	47.1	77.0	14.5 (0.48)	12.1 (1.53)	14.4 (2.14)	16.3 (1.99)	14.2 (2.99)	14.8 (1.35)	14.2 (1.32)	13.7 (1.69)	15.3 (0.71)	14.1 (1.59)
60 to 64	22.9	28.8	51.6	9.7 (0.50)	8.4 (1.38)	9.6 (1.78)	8.0 (1.86)	12.5 (2.58)	11.2 (1.30)	10.5 (1.38)	9.5 (1.41)	9.7 (0.85)	8.5 (1.25)
65 or older	26.6	38.4	60.3	11.4 (0.46)	12.3 (1.49)	15.1 (1.95)	8.7 (1.61)	13.8 (2.90)	12.2 (1.19)	13.1 (1.85)	12.1 (1.93)	10.1 (0.77)	11.7 (2.06)
Highest degree													
Less than bachelor's	17.2	20.3	41.1	7.8 (0.59)	2.2 (0.59)	‡ (1.94)	‡ (2.09)	2.1 (†)	2.1 (0.61)	0.7 ! (0.28)	0.9 ! (0.38)	14.3 (1.21)	7.6 (1.51)
Bachelor's	62.7	58.8	83.8	15.8 (0.55)	9.9 (1.32)	10.9 (3.36)	13.9 (3.16)	7.6 ! (2.48)	13.1 (1.84)	7.5 (1.08)	8.6 (1.52)	21.5 (1.17)	15.9 (1.67)
Master's	190.2	225.1	273.1	51.5 (0.80)	36.5 (2.39)	36.6 (2.68)	53.8 (1.52)	41.7 (3.47)	57.8 (2.32)	64.4 (2.33)	61.0 (2.21)	52.1 (1.63)	44.7 (3.32)
First-professional	39.6	36.0	38.5	7.3 (0.39)	16.7 (1.98)	21.3 (3.88)	7.7 (3.30)	13.6 (2.41)	4.2 (0.79)	4.8 (0.90)	7.2 (1.50)	3.3 (0.49)	14.4 (1.83)
Doctor's	58.9	75.8	93.5	17.6 (0.60)	35.6 (2.56)	28.7	24.1	35.0 (2.65)	22.7 (1.83)	22.6 (1.88)	22.2 (2.09)	8.7 (0.66)	17.4 (2.28)
Academic rank													
Professor	32.3	30.2	23.3 (1.58)	4.4 (0.30)	8.1 (1.54)	5.6 (1.18)	4.6 ! (1.43)	5.7 (1.40)	5.7 (1.01)	2.4 (0.55)	4.4 (0.85)	3.2 (0.52)	6.0 (1.03)
Associate professor	22.5	19.4	14.6 (1.18)	2.8 (0.22)	4.3 (0.94)	6.0 (1.45)	2.6 ! (1.14)	2.9 ! (1.03)	2.1 ! (0.69)	3.1 (0.79)	4.7 (1.11)	1.5 (0.27)	4.8 (1.07)
Assistant professor	24.2	23.1	19.8 (1.53)	3.7 (0.29)	11.0 (1.49)	11.9 (3.02)	3.3 (0.80)	7.0 (1.73)	2.0 (0.49)	3.0 (0.86)	5.1 ! (1.81)	0.8 (0.20)	8.3 (1.24)
Instructor	215.4	205.4	187.7 (4.42)	35.4 (0.83)	20.8 (1.72)	18.2 (1.92)	28.7 (2.27)	20.1 (3.25)	25.4 (2.41)	21.9 (1.64)	24.5 (2.13)	48.5 (1.54)	35.2 (2.66)
Lecturer	45.3	46.3	40.9 (2.15)	7.7 (0.41)	21.5 (1.67)	18.6 (2.30)	13.2 (2.07)	9.6 (1.72)	15.8 (2.18)	8.6 (2.32)	6.7 (1.72)	2.7 (0.42)	2.7 (0.80)
Other	27.6	75.2	230.9 (4.51)	43.6 (0.85)	33.3 (2.17)	38.2 (2.49)	45.4 (2.50)	53.4 (3.25)	47.7 (3.01)	59.7 (3.84)	52.2 (3.03)	40.5 (1.38)	38.3 (3.23)
No rank	9.3	16.5	12.8 (1.07)	2.4 (0.20)	1.0 ! (0.30)	‡ (†)	2.3 ! (0.80)	‡ (†)	1.2 ! (0.39)	1.2 (0.32)	2.3 ! (0.70)	2.8 (0.39)	4.6 (1.10)
Base salary													
Under $10,000	280.5	256.2	340.5 (3.17)	64.2 (0.60)	43.7 (2.35)	54.7 (2.80)	65.1 (2.94)	59.3 (3.10)	66.0 (2.44)	71.8 (2.97)	67.5 (2.75)	66.6 (1.02)	63.5 (1.97)
$10,000 to 24,999	68.1	112.4	140.8 (3.17)	26.6 (0.60)	29.3 (2.32)	27.5 (2.55)	24.7 (2.63)	30.3 (3.38)	26.3 (2.05)	21.4 (2.40)	23.4 (2.00)	28.1 (0.97)	24.6 (1.74)
$25,000 to 39,999	15.8	26.3	27.5 (1.72)	5.2 (0.32)	12.2 (1.38)	5.7 (1.76)	5.7 (1.48)	4.8 ! (1.72)	4.9 (1.09)	4.4 (1.15)	5.3 (1.24)	4.1 (0.46)	4.7 (0.92)
$40,000 to 54,999	5.3	11.8	9.6 (0.74)	1.8 (0.14)	5.8 (1.05)	5.0 (1.18)	1.9 ! (0.70)	3.0 ! (1.00)	1.6 (0.44)	0.9 ! (0.31)	1.1 ! (0.55)	0.5 ! (0.15)	4.0 (0.83)
$55,000 to 69,999	2.2	4.2	4.7 (0.78)	0.9 (0.15)	3.0 (0.65)	2.0 ! (1.00)	‡ (†)	‡ (†)	‡ (†)	0.8 ! (0.31)	1.6 ! (0.65)	0.4 ! (0.14)	‡ (†)
$70,000 to 84,999	1.1	2.4	1.9 (0.35)	0.4 (0.07)	2.2 (0.57)	‡ (†)	‡ (†)	‡ (†)	‡ (†)	‡ (†)	‡ (†)	‡ (†)	0.9 ! (0.30)
$85,000 to 99,999	0.9	#	1.5 (0.39)	0.3 (0.07)	1.0 ! (0.46)	‡ (†)	‡ (†)	‡ (†)	‡ (†)	‡ (†)	‡ (†)	‡ (†)	‡ (†)
$100,000 or more	2.7	#	3.5 (0.53)	0.7 (0.10)	2.9 (0.63)	‡ (†)	‡ (†)	‡ (†)	‡ (†)	‡ (†)	‡ (†)	0.1 ! (0.07)	1.8 ! (0.56)

—Not available.
†Not applicable.
#Rounds to zero.
!Interpret data with caution. The coefficient of variation (CV) for this estimate is between 30 and 50 percent.
‡Reporting standards not met. Either there are too few cases for a reliable estimate or the coefficient of variation (CV) is 50 percent or greater.

NOTE: Degree-granting institutions grant associate's or higher degrees and participate in Title IV federal financial aid programs. Totals may differ from figures reported in other tables because of varying survey methodologies. Race categories exclude persons of Hispanic ethnicity. Detail may not sum to totals because of rounding.
SOURCE: U.S. Department of Education, National Center for Education Statistics, 1993, 1999, and 2004 National Study of Postsecondary Faculty (NSOPF:93;99;04). (This table was prepared January 2009.)

Table 315.60. Full-time and part-time faculty and instructional staff in degree-granting postsecondary institutions, by race/ethnicity, sex, and selected characteristics: Fall 2003

[Standard errors appear in parentheses]

Selected characteristic	Number (in thousands)	Percent	White Male	White Female	Black Male	Black Female	Hispanic Male	Hispanic Female	Asian/Pacific Islander Male	Asian/Pacific Islander Female	American Indian/Alaska Native Male	American Indian/Alaska Native Female
1	2	3	4	5	6	7	8	9	10	11	12	13
Full-time faculty and instructional staff												
Number (in thousands)	681.8 (0.05)	†	338.4 (2.63)	209.3 (2.45)	19.5 (1.03)	18.5 (0.87)	13.4 (0.60)	10.4 (0.56)	43.2 (1.00)	19.0 (1.03)	5.8 (0.57)	4.2 (0.50)
Percentage distribution	† (†)	100.0	49.6 (0.39)	30.7 (0.36)	2.9 (0.15)	2.7 (0.13)	2.0 (0.09)	1.5 (0.08)	6.3 (0.15)	2.8 (0.15)	0.8 (0.08)	0.6 (0.07)
Type and control												
Public research	162.1 (0.85)	100.0	55.4 (0.67)	23.6 (0.59)	2.1 (0.27)	1.7 (0.19)	1.8 (0.16)	1.1 (0.15)	10.0 (0.47)	3.2 (0.35)	0.6 (0.14)	0.6 (0.11)
Private research	63.5 (1.58)	100.0	54.7 (1.00)	22.9 (0.80)	2.2 (0.30)	2.7 (0.37)	2.1 (0.30)	1.4 (0.31)	8.9 (0.66)	3.9 (0.48)	0.8! (0.39)	‡ (†)
Public doctoral	51.3 (0.76)	100.0	50.2 (1.48)	31.1 (1.22)	2.1 (0.44)	2.0 (0.30)	1.6 (0.20)	1.3 (0.27)	7.9 (1.27)	2.2 (0.56)	1.0! (0.32)	0.6! (0.22)
Private doctoral	21.7 (0.79)	100.0	56.0 (2.39)	26.7 (1.94)	3.0 (0.70)	2.1 (0.42)	1.4! (0.49)	0.8! (0.38)	5.8 (1.06)	3.5 (0.93)	‡ (†)	‡ (†)
Public comprehensive	107.3 (2.98)	100.0	45.9 (1.03)	32.1 (0.98)	4.7 (0.64)	4.0 (0.42)	2.1 (0.20)	1.6 (0.19)	5.3 (0.40)	2.6 (0.28)	0.8 (0.23)	1.0! (0.33)
Private comprehensive	41.4 (1.59)	100.0	48.9 (2.00)	36.7 (1.93)	2.3 (0.53)	2.4 (0.44)	1.6 (0.31)	0.8 (0.22)	4.1 (0.65)	1.9 (0.53)	0.6! (0.26)	‡ (†)
Private liberal arts	49.6 (1.80)	100.0	51.9 (1.20)	34.1 (0.99)	3.5 (0.56)	2.8 (0.36)	1.0 (0.20)	1.3 (0.27)	2.2 (0.28)	1.5 (0.29)	1.0 (0.24)	0.6! (0.18)
Public 2-year	114.6 (1.09)	100.0	40.8 (1.19)	40.1 (0.90)	3.1 (0.29)	3.8 (0.34)	3.0 (0.38)	2.7 (0.34)	2.2 (0.27)	2.1 (0.39)	1.3 (0.30)	0.8 (0.19)
Other	70.2 (3.36)	100.0	48.3 (1.65)	31.5 (1.20)	2.4 (0.59)	2.3 (0.59)	1.7 (0.36)	1.5 (0.29)	7.2 (0.87)	4.1 (0.78)	0.7! (0.34)	0.3! (0.14)
Academic rank												
Professor	194.4 (3.67)	100.0	65.5 (0.74)	20.3 (0.61)	2.6 (0.27)	1.1 (0.21)	1.8 (0.13)	0.8 (0.13)	5.7 (0.42)	1.1 (0.21)	0.8 (0.14)	0.4 (0.12)
Associate professor	149.6 (2.56)	100.0	51.6 (0.98)	28.4 (0.78)	3.1 (0.42)	2.4 (0.26)	1.7 (0.19)	1.3 (0.15)	7.0 (0.52)	2.9 (0.36)	1.0 (0.21)	0.5 (0.11)
Assistant professor	158.1 (2.81)	100.0	41.0 (0.83)	33.6 (0.81)	3.1 (0.37)	3.8 (0.38)	2.3 (0.22)	1.9 (0.15)	8.7 (0.49)	4.3 (0.35)	0.7 (0.16)	0.6 (0.15)
Instructor	82.7 (2.85)	100.0	38.2 (1.23)	41.2 (1.09)	3.2 (0.56)	4.4 (0.57)	2.5 (0.37)	2.3 (0.31)	3.1 (0.44)	3.1 (0.48)	0.9 (0.26)	1.1 (0.31)
Lecturer	21.9 (1.48)	100.0	36.7 (2.59)	43.9 (2.21)	2.9! (0.91)	3.0! (0.91)	1.3! (0.38)	3.8 (0.77)	2.4! (0.89)	4.0 (0.99)	1.3! (0.52)	0.7! (0.30)
Other	56.5 (2.15)	100.0	38.8 (1.51)	39.8 (1.37)	2.5 (0.54)	3.9 (0.56)	1.7 (0.22)	2.2 (0.35)	7.0 (0.98)	2.8 (0.56)	0.8! (0.39)	0.6! (0.18)
No rank	18.6 (1.28)	100.0	40.2 (2.37)	43.0 (2.45)	1.5! (0.52)	2.0! (0.83)	2.3! (0.75)	0.7! (0.24)	4.5 (1.17)	3.8! (1.39)	‡ (†)	‡ (†)
Age												
Under 35	59.1 (1.77)	100.0	39.4 (1.31)	33.4 (1.36)	2.9 (0.53)	4.7 (0.62)	2.5 (0.40)	2.8 (0.41)	8.9 (0.85)	4.2 (0.70)	0.6! (0.25)	0.5! (0.17)
35 to 44	169.8 (2.78)	100.0	43.7 (0.96)	30.2 (0.82)	2.7 (0.31)	3.4 (0.36)	2.8 (0.25)	1.8 (0.18)	9.3 (0.45)	5.0 (0.44)	0.8 (0.17)	0.5 (0.16)
45 to 54	219.7 (3.28)	100.0	47.0 (0.86)	34.4 (0.79)	3.1 (0.28)	2.6 (0.22)	1.8 (0.17)	1.6 (0.18)	5.7 (0.32)	2.2 (0.25)	1.0 (0.16)	0.6 (0.12)
55 to 64	190.0 (3.10)	100.0	57.1 (0.74)	28.7 (0.59)	2.8 (0.26)	1.9 (0.17)	1.4 (0.12)	1.1 (0.13)	4.1 (0.36)	1.4 (0.24)	0.9 (0.17)	0.7 (0.12)
65 to 69	31.8 (1.43)	100.0	67.6 (2.05)	20.2 (1.82)	1.7 (0.50)	2.0! (0.61)	1.6 (0.44)	0.4! (0.19)	4.5 (0.94)	1.1! (0.42)	‡ (†)	‡ (†)
70 or older	11.5 (0.67)	100.0	69.0 (3.16)	15.7 (2.71)	5.4 (1.54)	‡ (†)	‡ (†)	‡ (†)	3.8! (1.40)	‡ (†)	‡ (†)	‡ (†)
Base salary												
Under $10,000	4.4 (0.49)	100.0	39.7 (5.71)	34.2 (5.09)	5.8 (0.92)	‡ (†)	‡ (†)	4.4! (1.96)	7.8! (3.27)	‡ (†)	‡ (†)	‡ (†)
$10,000 to 24,999	19.0 (1.03)	100.0	43.2 (2.61)	34.8 (2.40)	1.3 (0.37)	3.2 (0.89)	2.1 (0.61)	2.4 (0.60)	6.5 (1.23)	4.6 (0.93)	1.1! (0.48)	1.1! (0.48)
$25,000 to 39,999	79.7 (2.90)	100.0	36.0 (1.21)	44.5 (1.25)	2.9 (0.55)	3.7 (0.46)	1.8 (0.29)	2.1 (0.28)	3.8 (0.68)	3.6 (0.48)	0.7! (0.26)	0.8 (0.23)
$40,000 to 54,999	192.4 (3.09)	100.0	42.2 (0.95)	38.2 (0.79)	2.7 (0.27)	3.7 (0.37)	1.9 (0.18)	1.8 (0.14)	5.0 (0.43)	2.6 (0.27)	1.0 (0.15)	0.9 (0.14)
$55,000 to 69,999	147.7 (3.54)	100.0	48.7 (0.88)	31.9 (0.80)	3.1 (0.35)	2.5 (0.28)	2.0 (0.25)	1.6 (0.21)	6.0 (0.43)	2.6 (0.31)	1.0 (0.23)	0.6 (0.15)
$70,000 to 84,999	94.8 (2.19)	100.0	55.8 (1.29)	24.2 (1.14)	2.9 (0.39)	1.7 (0.40)	2.4 (0.34)	1.0 (0.20)	8.1 (0.67)	2.6 (0.41)	0.9 (0.23)	0.5! (0.19)
$85,000 to 99,999	50.7 (1.98)	100.0	61.9 (1.58)	18.5 (1.03)	3.8 (0.69)	1.5 (0.38)	1.5 (0.41)	1.0 (0.28)	8.3 (1.06)	2.5 (0.57)	0.8! (0.24)	‡ (†)
$100,000 or more	93.1 (2.29)	100.0	66.9 (0.99)	13.7 (0.74)	2.4 (0.38)	1.6 (0.33)	2.1 (0.29)	0.8 (0.17)	9.0 (0.80)	2.8 (0.50)	0.6 (0.20)	‡ (†)
Total household income												
Under $10,000	† (†)	100.0	‡ (†)	‡ (†)	‡ (†)	‡ (†)	‡ (†)	‡ (†)	‡ (†)	‡ (†)	‡ (†)	‡ (†)
$10,000 to 24,999	3.0 (0.33)	100.0	42.0 (6.54)	29.3 (6.12)	1.4! (1.13)	‡ (†)	‡ (†)	‡ (†)	9.8! (3.74)	8.7! (3.59)	‡ (†)	‡ (†)
$25,000 to 39,999	20.1 (1.13)	100.0	36.5 (2.68)	39.0 (2.28)	3.3! (1.56)	4.5 (0.97)	2.5 (0.43)	1.5 (0.62)	7.3 (1.56)	3.8 (0.95)	0.4! (0.18)	0.9! (0.29)
$40,000 to 54,999	55.0 (1.76)	100.0	39.8 (1.66)	38.4 (1.42)	2.9 (0.59)	4.2 (0.59)	1.9 (0.35)	2.5 (0.29)	6.2 (0.80)	2.5 (0.51)	1.1 (0.26)	1.2 (0.31)
$55,000 to 69,999	86.2 (1.56)	100.0	43.1 (1.23)	34.2 (1.21)	4.1 (0.50)	4.4 (0.42)	2.1 (0.29)	1.9 (0.29)	5.6 (0.56)	2.5 (0.37)	1.0 (0.29)	1.0 (0.29)
$70,000 to 84,999	75.2 (2.19)	100.0	50.6 (1.20)	31.2 (1.11)	2.4 (0.40)	2.8 (0.45)	1.9 (0.26)	1.3 (0.17)	6.3 (0.59)	2.1 (0.40)	0.9! (0.30)	0.5! (0.17)
$85,000 to 99,999	95.0 (2.16)	100.0	46.7 (1.15)	32.5 (0.83)	2.8 (0.39)	3.0 (0.58)	2.7 (0.32)	1.6 (0.24)	7.0 (0.81)	2.5 (0.50)	0.6! (0.18)	0.5 (0.14)
$100,000 or more	347.3 (3.57)	100.0	50.9 (0.52)	27.5 (0.52)	2.6 (0.18)	1.9 (0.16)	1.7 (0.14)	1.3 (0.11)	6.3 (0.29)	3.0 (0.24)	0.9 (0.11)	0.4 (0.07)

See notes at end of table.

Table 315.60. Full-time and part-time faculty and instructional staff in degree-granting postsecondary institutions, by race/ethnicity, sex, and selected characteristics: Fall 2003—Continued

[Standard errors appear in parentheses]

Selected characteristic	Number (in thousands)	Percent	White Male	White Female	Black Male	Black Female	Hispanic Male	Hispanic Female	Asian/Pacific Islander Male	Asian/Pacific Islander Female	American Indian/Alaska Native Male	American Indian/Alaska Native Female
1	2	3	4	5	6	7	8	9	10	11	12	13
Part-time faculty and instructional staff												
Number (in thousands)	530.0 (0.02)	†	235.5 (2.44)	216.1 (2.87)	13.8 (0.91)	15.9 (2.87)	10.2 (0.61)	8.5 (0.56)	10.9 (0.82)	9.4 (0.97)	5.5 (0.78)	4.2 (0.77)
Percentage distribution	‡ (†)	100.0	44.4 (0.46)	40.8 (0.54)	2.6 (0.17)	3.0 (0.54)	1.9 (0.12)	1.6 (0.10)	2.1 (0.15)	1.8 (0.18)	1.0 (0.15)	0.8 (0.15)
Type and control												
Public research	39.7 (0.78)	100.0	41.7 (1.93)	40.7 (2.12)	1.1 ! (0.37)	1.6 ! (0.60)	1.5 (0.40)	1.7 (0.43)	4.5 (1.03)	5.4 (0.90)	1.6 ! (0.67)	‡ (†)
Private research	23.2 (0.96)	100.0	51.1 (2.51)	34.7 (2.29)	2.7 ! (1.00)	1.4 ! (0.57)	1.5 ! (0.62)	‡ (†)	3.6 (1.07)	2.8 (0.77)	‡ (†)	‡ (†)
Public doctoral	20.8 (0.82)	100.0	44.3 (2.27)	43.6 (2.39)	‡ (†)	1.0 ! (0.47)	1.9 ! (0.68)	2.2 (0.61)	2.6 ! (0.86)	1.9 ! (0.83)	‡ (†)	‡ (†)
Private doctoral	15.4 (0.83)	100.0	51.7 (3.99)	37.3 (3.60)	1.7 ! (0.77)	1.1 ! (0.55)	1.6 ! (0.64)	1.2 ! (0.36)	3.4 ! (1.06)	‡ (†)	‡ (†)	‡ (†)
Public comprehensive	60.3 (2.49)	100.0	43.1 (1.34)	44.1 (2.18)	2.3 ! (0.74)	2.4 ! (0.79)	1.6 (0.31)	1.5 (0.32)	2.0 (0.38)	1.3 ! (0.43)	1.0 ! (0.43)	‡ (†)
Private comprehensive	53.5 (2.17)	100.0	49.1 (1.43)	41.9 (1.56)	1.7 (0.34)	1.1 (0.21)	1.0 (0.19)	1.4 (0.26)	1.1 ! (0.54)	0.8 ! (0.35)	1.0 ! (0.30)	0.9 ! (0.32)
Private liberal arts	28.4 (2.19)	100.0	44.2 (1.98)	42.0 (2.14)	2.5 ! (0.85)	5.6 (1.24)	1.1 ! (0.42)	1.0 ! (0.35)	1.7 ! (0.61)	1.1 ! (0.49)	0.9 ! (0.35)	‡ (†)
Public 2-year	230.1 (2.00)	100.0	42.8 (0.70)	41.0 (0.67)	2.9 (0.22)	4.0 (0.18)	2.4 (0.20)	2.0 (0.19)	1.5 (0.18)	1.4 (0.19)	1.1 (0.23)	1.0 (0.25)
Other	58.7 (3.38)	100.0	45.7 (1.83)	37.3 (2.14)	4.2 (0.79)	3.0 (0.74)	2.2 (0.53)	0.8 (0.22)	2.4 ! (0.75)	2.4 ! (0.92)	1.0 ! (0.40)	1.1 ! (0.50)
Academic rank												
Professor	23.3 (1.58)	100.0	59.3 (2.83)	25.0 (2.60)	4.0 (1.17)	2.6 ! (0.84)	‡ (†)	1.0 ! (0.41)	3.6 (0.96)	3.6 (0.93)	‡ (†)	‡ (†)
Associate professor	14.6 (1.18)	100.0	43.7 (4.03)	39.5 (3.88)	2.8 ! (0.84)	‡ (†)	‡ (†)	1.4 ! (0.49)	6.3 ! (2.27)	2.9 (0.45)	‡ (†)	1.2 (0.30)
Assistant professor	19.8 (1.53)	100.0	38.8 (3.39)	42.7 (3.37)	2.8 ! (1.19)	‡ (†)	‡ (†)	1.0 ! (0.42)	4.8 ! (1.65)	1.3 (0.26)	0.9 (0.24)	0.8 ! (0.27)
Instructor	187.7 (4.42)	100.0	41.5 (1.09)	43.9 (1.11)	2.5 (0.30)	3.4 (0.25)	2.2 (0.24)	1.7 (0.22)	1.6 (0.25)	1.6 (0.28)	1.1 (0.26)	0.6 (0.18)
Lecturer	40.9 (2.15)	100.0	41.4 (2.05)	40.1 (1.96)	2.7 (0.63)	2.1 ! (0.77)	2.1 (0.45)	1.7 (0.42)	3.7 (0.80)	4.2 (0.93)	1.6 ! (0.56)	‡ (†)
Other	230.9 (4.51)	100.0	46.5 (1.01)	39.9 (1.04)	2.5 (0.29)	3.1 (0.28)	1.8 (0.23)	1.5 (0.17)	1.5 (0.22)	1.3 (0.31)	0.9 (0.22)	1.0 (0.22)
No rank	12.8 (1.07)	100.0	43.8 (3.52)	39.8 (4.63)	‡ (†)	0.9 ! (0.43)	2.8 ! (1.31)	3.5 ! (1.34)	2.0 ! (0.94)	‡ (†)	‡ (†)	‡ (†)
Age												
Under 35	66.2 (2.30)	100.0	35.3 (1.73)	43.1 (2.04)	3.2 (0.63)	4.3 (0.53)	3.0 (0.49)	3.0 (0.35)	2.4 (0.52)	3.6 (0.93)	1.6 ! (0.68)	‡ (†)
35 to 44	115.6 (3.03)	100.0	40.7 (1.42)	41.5 (1.41)	2.6 (0.39)	3.0 (0.33)	2.5 (0.30)	2.4 (0.32)	2.6 (0.37)	2.9 (0.45)	0.7 ! (0.24)	1.2 (0.30)
45 to 54	159.3 (3.22)	100.0	41.7 (1.13)	44.0 (1.17)	2.9 (0.34)	3.2 (0.33)	1.6 (0.24)	1.5 (0.19)	1.6 (0.35)	1.3 (0.26)	0.9 (0.24)	0.8 ! (0.27)
55 to 64	128.6 (3.31)	100.0	48.2 (1.09)	40.4 (1.06)	2.1 (0.35)	2.8 (0.35)	1.3 (0.30)	0.6 (0.10)	1.6 (0.32)	0.9 (0.23)	1.1 ! (0.34)	1.0 (0.26)
65 to 69	33.5 (1.81)	100.0	62.8 (3.10)	27.6 (2.83)	2.3 ! (0.81)	0.9 ! (0.32)	1.6 ! (0.54)	1.3 ! (0.55)	1.3 ! (0.52)	‡ (†)	1.5 ! (0.63)	‡ (†)
70 or older	26.8 (1.83)	100.0	58.3 (2.99)	30.7 (3.32)	2.4 ! (0.79)	1.6 ! (0.70)	2.5 ! (0.87)	‡ (†)	2.1 ! (0.65)	‡ (†)	‡ (†)	‡ (†)
Base salary												
Under $10,000	340.5 (3.17)	100.0	45.4 (0.68)	39.9 (0.77)	2.6 (0.23)	3.5 (0.23)	1.9 (0.17)	1.6 (0.12)	1.6 (0.17)	1.4 (0.26)	1.1 (0.20)	1.0 (0.20)
$10,000 to 24,999	140.8 (3.17)	100.0	41.3 (1.36)	43.6 (1.50)	2.8 (0.38)	2.3 (0.25)	2.1 (0.26)	1.8 (0.24)	2.3 (0.40)	2.4 (0.40)	0.9 (0.25)	0.5 ! (0.18)
$25,000 to 39,999	27.5 (1.72)	100.0	47.3 (3.06)	38.8 (2.72)	3.3 (0.83)	‡ (†)	1.2 ! (0.58)	1.6 ! (0.55)	3.2 ! (1.02)	1.9 ! (0.61)	‡ (†)	‡ (†)
$40,000 to 54,999	9.6 (0.74)	100.0	48.2 (4.55)	34.0 (4.33)	‡ (†)	1.4 ! (0.68)	3.2 ! (1.19)	‡ (†)	6.2 ! (2.60)	3.8 ! (1.70)	‡ (†)	‡ (†)
$55,000 to 69,999	4.7 (0.78)	100.0	45.5 (6.46)	40.4 (6.35)	‡ (†)	‡ (†)	‡ (†)	2.2 ! (1.08)	‡ (†)	‡ (†)	0.8 ! (0.27)	‡ (†)
$70,000 to 84,999	1.9 (0.35)	100.0	39.0 (11.51)	43.0 (10.25)	‡ (†)	‡ (†)	‡ (†)	‡ (†)	‡ (†)	‡ (†)	1.1 ! (0.41)	1.0 ! (0.37)
$85,000 to 99,999	1.5 (0.39)	100.0	33.4 ! (13.01)	51.7 (13.73)	‡ (†)	‡ (†)	‡ (†)	‡ (†)	‡ (†)	‡ (†)	0.6 ! (0.29)	0.7 ! (0.25)
$100,000 or more	3.5 (0.53)	100.0	47.4 (7.01)	37.1 (5.35)	‡ (†)	‡ (†)	‡ (†)	‡ (†)	10.8 ! (5.15)	‡ (†)	0.8 (0.22)	0.4 ! (0.17)
Total household income												
Under $10,000	1.3 (0.37)	100.0	‡ (†)	46.4 ! (14.12)	‡ (†)	‡ (†)	‡ (†)	‡ (†)	‡ (†)	‡ (†)	‡ (†)	‡ (†)
$10,000 to 24,999	28.5 (1.93)	100.0	36.5 (3.33)	42.5 (3.42)	2.0 ! (0.71)	4.0 (0.80)	1.7 ! (0.53)	2.4 (0.55)	1.6 ! (0.76)	3.5 ! (1.71)	3.7 ! (1.34)	2.2 ! (1.01)
$25,000 to 39,999	47.7 (1.92)	100.0	35.5 (2.27)	46.5 (2.32)	3.4 (0.58)	3.9 (0.66)	2.2 (0.44)	1.8 (0.47)	1.7 ! (0.55)	2.9 ! (0.92)	1.1 ! (0.46)	1.0 ! (0.43)
$40,000 to 54,999	55.7 (2.52)	100.0	38.1 (2.05)	46.2 (2.35)	3.2 (0.71)	3.4 (0.52)	3.1 (0.67)	2.5 (0.60)	1.1 ! (0.40)	1.1 ! (0.35)	‡ (†)	0.5 ! (0.21)
$55,000 to 69,999	87.2 (2.95)	100.0	41.1 (1.50)	43.0 (1.48)	1.9 (0.38)	4.1 (0.38)	1.7 (0.37)	2.5 (0.35)	2.1 (0.42)	1.6 (0.45)	0.8 ! (0.27)	1.0 ! (0.37)
$70,000 to 84,999	58.1 (2.66)	100.0	44.7 (2.15)	41.2 (2.38)	2.3 (0.44)	2.3 (0.57)	2.3 (0.41)	1.3 (0.34)	1.4 (0.41)	2.0 (0.58)	1.1 ! (0.41)	1.1 ! (0.37)
$85,000 to 99,999	66.4 (2.39)	100.0	48.6 (1.85)	38.4 (1.81)	2.4 (0.59)	3.1 (0.52)	1.8 (0.37)	1.2 (0.34)	1.9 (0.49)	1.3 ! (0.41)	0.6 ! (0.29)	0.7 ! (0.25)
$100,000 or more	185.1 (3.59)	100.0	34.9 (0.68)	37.0 (0.91)	2.1 (0.32)	2.1 (0.26)	1.5 (0.21)	1.0 (0.17)	2.8 (0.34)	1.6 (0.25)	0.8 (0.22)	0.4 (0.17)

†Not applicable.

!Interpret data with caution. The coefficient of variation (CV) for this estimate is between 30 and 50 percent.

‡Reporting standards not met. Either there are too few cases for a reliable estimate or the coefficient of variation (CV) is 50 percent or greater.

NOTE: Degree-granting institutions grant associate's or higher degrees and participate in Title IV federal financial aid programs. Totals may differ from figures reported in other tables because of varying survey methodologies. Race categories exclude persons of Hispanic ethnicity. Detail may not sum to totals because of rounding.

SOURCE: U.S. Department of Education, National Center for Education Statistics, 2003 National Study of Postsecondary Faculty (NSOPF:04). (This table was prepared January 2009.)

Table 315.70. Full-time and part-time faculty and instructional staff in degree-granting postsecondary institutions, by field and faculty characteristics: Fall 1992, fall 1998, and fall 2003

[Standard errors appear in parentheses]

Selected faculty and instructional staff characteristic	Number (in thousands) Fall 1992	Fall 1998	Fall 2003	All fields	Agriculture and home economics	Business	Education	Engineering	Fine arts	Health	Humanities[1]	Natural sciences[2]	Social sciences[3]	Other[4]
1	2	3	4	5	6	7	8	9	10	11	12	13	14	15
Full-time faculty and instructional staff														
Number (in thousands)...	528	560	682 (#)	681.8 (0.05)	16.9 (0.80)	43.2 (1.40)	50.9 (1.89)	33.4 (1.32)	43.3 (1.68)	93.9 (2.67)	58.8 (1.82)	127.2 (2.19)	88.7 (2.07)	125.5 (2.36)
Percentage distribution...	†	†	† (†)	100.0 (†)	2.5 (0.12)	6.3 (0.21)	7.5 (0.28)	4.9 (0.19)	6.3 (0.25)	13.8 (0.39)	8.6 (0.27)	18.7 (0.32)	13.0 (0.30)	18.4 (0.35)
Total...	528	560	682 (#)	100.0 (†)	100.0 (†)	100.0 (†)	100.0 (†)	100.0 (†)	100.0 (†)	100.0 (†)	100.0 (†)	100.0 (†)	100.0 (†)	100.0 (†)
				Percentage distribution of full-time faculty and instructional staff										
Sex														
Male...	353	357	420 (—)	61.7 (0.35)	64.6 (2.88)	68.5 (1.61)	39.3 (1.57)	91.5 (1.06)	61.9 (1.38)	46.7 (1.32)	45.3 (1.47)	74.5 (0.88)	64.3 (1.13)	64.0 (0.94)
Female...	176	203	261 (—)	38.3 (0.35)	35.4 (2.88)	31.5 (1.61)	60.7 (1.57)	8.5 (1.06)	38.1 (1.38)	53.3 (1.32)	54.7 (1.47)	25.5 (0.88)	35.7 (1.13)	36.0 (0.94)
Race/ethnicity														
White...	457	477	548 (—)	80.3 (0.27)	87.8 (1.61)	79.5 (1.51)	80.5 (1.26)	70.9 (1.85)	86.4 (1.24)	79.7 (0.84)	80.7 (1.31)	77.8 (0.75)	81.4 (1.09)	82.0 (0.69)
Black...	27	28	38 (—)	5.6 (0.17)	2.3 ! (0.76)	4.5 (0.79)	7.8 (1.01)	5.4 (0.99)	6.0 (0.88)	5.0 (0.50)	5.6 (0.58)	4.1 (0.48)	7.3 (0.72)	6.1 (0.44)
Hispanic...	14	19	24 (—)	3.5 (0.10)	2.5 ! (0.76)	2.3 (0.51)	4.7 (0.63)	2.6 (0.47)	3.3 (0.75)	3.0 (0.32)	6.7 (0.53)	2.9 (0.30)	4.0 (0.47)	2.9 (0.33)
Asian/Pacific Islander...	28	33	62 (—)	9.1 (0.16)	6.4 (1.34)	12.2 (1.22)	4.8 (0.70)	20.1 (1.64)	2.9 (0.74)	10.7 (0.79)	5.2 (0.94)	14.3 (0.69)	5.9 (0.71)	7.1 (0.49)
American Indian/Alaska Native...	3	4	10 (—)	1.5 (0.11)	1.0 ! (0.49)	1.6 (0.37)	2.2 (0.40)	‡ (†)	1.4 (0.38)	1.6 (0.33)	1.8 (0.35)	0.8 (0.17)	1.4 (0.22)	1.8 (0.32)
Age														
Under 30...	8	9	12 (—)	1.7 (0.13)	2.0 ! (0.67)	0.7 ! (0.31)	2.6 (0.78)	1.6 ! (0.48)	1.6 (0.45)	1.1 (0.26)	1.8 (0.33)	1.3 (0.21)	1.8 (0.35)	2.7 (0.41)
30 to 34...	35	32	47 (—)	6.9 (0.21)	5.6 (1.27)	4.0 (0.71)	6.8 (0.83)	7.0 (0.99)	6.2 (0.84)	6.3 (0.60)	8.2 (0.74)	6.8 (0.41)	7.6 (0.47)	7.9 (0.52)
35 to 39...	67	60	77 (—)	11.3 (0.29)	7.5 (1.19)	11.0 (1.15)	7.6 (0.95)	11.3 (1.18)	10.5 (1.20)	13.1 (0.88)	10.9 (0.88)	12.0 (0.65)	12.7 (0.92)	10.9 (0.74)
40 to 44...	90	82	93 (—)	13.6 (0.31)	13.3 (1.63)	11.8 (1.43)	9.9 (1.03)	15.0 (1.21)	12.3 (1.75)	15.0 (0.91)	13.6 (1.15)	15.4 (0.79)	13.7 (0.79)	12.8 (0.69)
45 to 49...	98	97	105 (—)	15.4 (0.32)	15.4 (1.84)	17.9 (1.51)	12.7 (1.04)	17.1 (1.70)	18.0 (1.42)	17.3 (0.95)	14.8 (1.24)	15.5 (0.86)	12.9 (0.79)	15.0 (0.66)
50 to 54...	95	105	114 (—)	16.8 (0.34)	25.3 (2.31)	19.0 (1.30)	17.6 (1.27)	15.2 (1.61)	18.5 (1.38)	19.9 (1.03)	14.1 (1.04)	14.8 (0.64)	14.2 (0.89)	17.1 (0.93)
55 to 59...	67	90	112 (—)	16.4 (0.37)	16.8 (1.83)	18.8 (1.32)	21.9 (1.43)	15.1 (2.32)	16.8 (1.58)	15.4 (0.80)	16.6 (1.07)	13.3 (0.75)	16.2 (0.85)	17.3 (0.73)
60 to 64...	45	55	78 (—)	11.5 (0.31)	10.4 (1.61)	10.9 (1.11)	13.7 (1.27)	10.3 (1.33)	11.4 (1.12)	7.8 (0.62)	12.9 (1.07)	12.5 (0.64)	14.0 (0.76)	10.6 (0.61)
65 or older...	24	31	43 (—)	6.3 (0.23)	3.7 ! (1.20)	5.9 (0.74)	7.2 (0.74)	7.5 (1.09)	4.7 (0.82)	4.1 (0.51)	7.0 (0.81)	8.5 (0.54)	6.8 (0.59)	5.6 (0.53)
Highest degree														
Less than bachelor's...	6	7	10 (—)	1.5 (0.12)	‡ (†)	‡ (†)	1.7 ! (0.74)	2.6 (0.77)	1.4 ! (0.46)	1.7 (0.31)	‡ (†)	‡ (†)	‡ (†)	4.4 (0.54)
Bachelor's...	21	23	29 (—)	4.3 (0.24)	6.4 (1.71)	4.0 (0.80)	4.0 (0.64)	6.5 (1.22)	9.1 (1.10)	5.5 (0.69)	1.1 (0.31)	1.4 (0.23)	1.0 (0.26)	7.9 (0.67)
Master's...	156	156	180 (—)	26.4 (0.39)	29.2 (2.18)	31.8 (1.69)	35.5 (1.37)	13.2 (1.64)	53.9 (1.82)	22.9 (1.16)	35.1 (1.42)	14.9 (0.72)	12.5 (0.72)	34.4 (1.24)
First-professional...	58	52	56 (—)	8.2 (0.30)	‡ (2.74)	2.1 (0.45)	1.1 ! (0.35)	‡ (†)	1.1 ! (0.41)	41.1 (1.32)	0.4 ! (0.18)	3.0 (0.35)	0.5 ! (0.19)	8.7 (0.76)
Doctor's...	284	324	407 (—)	59.6 (0.48)	63.0 (2.74)	61.9 (1.73)	57.7 (1.53)	77.1 (2.08)	34.6 (1.96)	28.9 (1.06)	63.2 (1.43)	80.6 (0.67)	86.0 (0.74)	44.6 (1.23)
Academic rank														
Professor...	161	172	194 (3.67)	28.5 (0.54)	33.0 (2.71)	29.1 (1.66)	21.9 (1.41)	37.6 (1.69)	28.4 (1.85)	20.1 (0.93)	26.2 (1.46)	35.5 (0.87)	35.4 (1.20)	23.5 (1.09)
Associate professor...	124	132	150 (2.56)	21.9 (0.37)	21.0 (2.55)	22.6 (1.32)	17.6 (1.07)	25.3 (1.77)	23.7 (1.64)	23.5 (0.96)	20.0 (1.27)	23.4 (0.93)	22.8 (0.97)	19.9 (1.08)
Assistant professor...	124	125	158 (2.81)	23.2 (0.41)	19.2 (1.79)	23.4 (1.51)	23.8 (1.56)	19.6 (1.67)	23.2 (1.75)	32.2 (1.12)	21.7 (1.30)	21.1 (0.82)	24.8 (1.22)	19.2 (0.73)
Instructor...	74	75	83 (2.85)	12.1 (0.42)	9.9 (1.60)	13.4 (1.37)	12.6 (1.18)	9.1 (1.39)	9.7 (1.01)	15.3 (0.90)	14.9 (1.17)	7.7 (0.56)	5.7 (0.53)	18.7 (1.02)
Lecturer...	12	14	22 (1.48)	3.2 (0.22)	3.4 ! (1.50)	3.6 (0.68)	3.0 (0.60)	2.0 (0.52)	4.3 (0.64)	1.9 (0.37)	7.9 (0.78)	2.1 (0.25)	2.3 (0.42)	3.6 (0.57)
Other...	17	26	57 (2.15)	8.3 (0.32)	11.8 (2.16)	4.9 ! (0.64)	18.2 (1.57)	5.4 (0.82)	7.1 (1.03)	5.5 (0.50)	5.7 (0.69)	6.7 (0.48)	6.4 (0.67)	12.4 (0.76)
No rank...	17	16	19 (1.28)	2.7 (0.19)	‡ (†)	3.0 (0.68)	2.9 ! (1.05)	0.9 ! (0.38)	3.6 ! (1.24)	1.5 (0.27)	3.6 (0.67)	3.5 (0.48)	2.6 (0.47)	2.7 (0.36)

See notes at end of table.

Table 315.70. Full-time and part-time faculty and instructional staff in degree-granting postsecondary institutions, by field and faculty characteristics: Fall 1992, fall 1998, and fall 2003—Continued

[Standard errors appear in parentheses]

Selected faculty and instructional staff characteristic	Number (in thousands)			Fall 2003										
	Fall 1992	Fall 1998	Fall 2003	All fields	Agriculture and home economics	Business	Education	Engineering	Fine arts	Health	Humanities[1]	Natural sciences[2]	Social sciences[3]	Other[4]
1	2	3	4	5	6	7	8	9	10	11	12	13	14	15
Part-time faculty and instructional staff														
Number (in thousands)...	377	416	530 (#)	530.0 (0.02)	7.3 (0.97)	44.9 (2.98)	63.5 (2.57)	14.0 (1.49)	47.8 (3.65)	57.8 (3.06)	58.9 (2.05)	63.7 (2.46)	53.0 (2.39)	119.2 (3.48)
Percentage distribution...	†	†	† (†)	100.0 (†)	1.4 (0.18)	8.5 (0.56)	12.0 (0.48)	2.7 (0.28)	9.0 (0.69)	10.9 (0.58)	11.1 (0.39)	12.0 (0.46)	10.0 (0.45)	22.5 (0.66)
											Percentage distribution of part-time faculty and instructional staff			
Total ...	377	416	530	100.0 (†)	100.0 (†)	100.0 (†)	100.0 (†)	100.0 (†)	100.0 (†)	100.0 (†)	100.0 (†)	100.0 (†)	100.0 (†)	100.0 (†)
Sex														
Male...	209	217	276	52.1 (0.45)	32.0 (6.05)	69.6 (1.89)	29.1 (1.71)	90.8 (2.68)	51.4 (2.26)	34.5 (1.60)	31.6 (1.86)	58.2 (2.22)	60.5 (1.90)	66.2 (1.41)
Female...	168	199	254	47.9 (0.45)	68.0 (6.05)	30.4 (1.89)	70.9 (1.71)	9.2 (2.68)	48.6 (2.26)	65.5 (1.60)	68.4 (1.86)	41.8 (2.22)	39.5 (1.90)	33.8 (1.41)
Race/ethnicity														
White...	333	364	452	85.2 (0.38)	91.4 (3.66)	86.8 (1.54)	85.1 (1.34)	85.4 (2.89)	88.7 (1.22)	85.0 (1.14)	83.0 (1.14)	83.4 (1.35)	84.2 (1.62)	85.5 (0.80)
Black...	18	19	30	5.6 (0.20)	‡ (†)	6.7 (0.96)	6.6 (0.98)	‡ (†)	3.0 (0.70)	5.2 (0.68)	5.0 (0.71)	6.0 (0.66)	5.8 (0.75)	6.5 (0.57)
Hispanic...	11	16	19	3.5 (0.13)	‡ (†)	2.2 ! (0.79)	5.1 (0.71)	2.6 (0.64)	2.7 (0.52)	2.2 (0.47)	6.5 (0.81)	2.2 (0.40)	3.7 ! (0.61)	3.6 (0.39)
Asian/Pacific Islander...	12	13	20	3.8 (0.22)	‡ (†)	3.0 (0.80)	1.6 (0.43)	8.4 (2.11)	2.9 (0.70)	6.5 (1.17)	4.2 (0.71)	7.1 (0.89)	2.7 ! (1.04)	2.5 (0.34)
American Indian/Alaska Native...	2	4	10	1.8 (0.22)	‡ (†)	1.4 ! (0.54)	1.5 (0.37)	‡ (†)	2.8 ! (0.84)	1.0 ! (0.35)	1.3 (0.38)	1.4 ! (0.60)	3.6 (0.91)	1.9 (0.36)
Age														
Under 30...	20	15	23	4.3 (0.30)	6.4 ! (2.51)	2.3 ! (0.70)	2.7 (0.64)	‡ (†)	4.4 (0.79)	3.7 (0.72)	5.7 (0.95)	7.2 (1.15)	3.5 (0.66)	4.3 (0.60)
30 to 34...	36	37	43	8.2 (0.38)	7.7 ! (2.78)	6.7 (1.28)	7.0 (1.03)	‡ (†)	9.4 (1.24)	8.9 (1.01)	10.0 (1.01)	7.6 (1.16)	10.6 (1.17)	7.7 (0.62)
35 to 39...	59	47	55	10.3 (0.48)	5.5 ! (1.97)	9.6 (1.49)	8.7 (1.21)	10.7 ! (3.34)	11.7 (1.38)	9.5 (1.34)	8.7 (1.07)	10.2 (1.16)	9.9 (1.27)	12.6 (1.20)
40 to 44...	70	60	61	11.5 (0.44)	6.3 ! (2.79)	10.5 (1.35)	7.9 (0.88)	15.6 (3.25)	12.0 (1.13)	14.9 (1.54)	9.2 (0.91)	10.1 (1.19)	11.2 (1.26)	13.8 (0.96)
45 to 49...	68	72	76	14.4 (0.48)	17.4 ! (5.26)	13.1 (1.45)	11.7 (1.12)	11.4 ! (3.50)	16.4 (1.68)	19.7 (1.56)	14.3 (1.65)	9.5 (1.05)	13.1 (1.24)	16.5 (1.13)
50 to 54...	45	70	83	15.6 (0.42)	16.4 (4.15)	16.3 (1.42)	17.4 (1.41)	22.3 (3.60)	18.4 (1.76)	15.9 (1.55)	14.1 (1.35)	11.9 (1.34)	11.1 (1.29)	17.1 (1.15)
55 to 59...	29	47	77	14.5 (0.48)	17.6 (4.45)	17.9 (2.01)	15.5 (1.58)	11.7 (2.89)	14.6 (1.78)	11.5 (1.27)	13.8 (1.46)	15.6 (1.56)	17.5 (1.88)	12.8 (0.82)
60 to 64...	23	29	52	9.7 (0.50)	18.0 (5.10)	11.5 (1.25)	13.1 (1.26)	6.5 ! (1.96)	5.7 (1.05)	6.7 (1.13)	12.7 (1.42)	12.8 (1.67)	10.9 (1.29)	6.6 (0.76)
65 or older...	27	38	60	11.4 (0.46)	4.7 ! (2.09)	12.2 (1.65)	15.8 (1.26)	17.2 (3.46)	7.4 (1.33)	9.3 (1.22)	11.6 (1.50)	15.0 (1.99)	12.2 (1.48)	8.6 (0.79)
Highest degree														
Less than bachelor's...	17	20	41	7.8 (0.59)	5.5 ! (2.53)	1.8 ! (0.79)	3.7 (0.96)	17.1 (4.44)	9.1 (1.42)	17.3 (1.86)	‡ (†)	‡ (†)	0.5 ! (0.25)	16.2 (1.31)
Bachelor's...	63	59	84	15.8 (0.55)	26.7 (5.80)	13.9 (1.84)	12.0 (1.25)	17.9 (3.50)	28.2 (2.09)	16.2 (1.61)	12.9 (1.65)	16.1 (1.46)	3.2 (0.82)	19.4 (1.11)
Master's...	190	225	273	51.5 (0.80)	50.3 (6.09)	66.5 (2.34)	63.0 (1.84)	32.3 (4.61)	54.7 (2.95)	30.2 (1.86)	70.2 (2.33)	49.0 (1.94)	55.5 (1.83)	41.6 (1.56)
First-professional...	40	36	39	7.3 (0.39)	‡ (†)	6.3 (1.10)	1.9 (0.45)	0.9 ! (†)	0.9 ! (0.39)	25.2 (2.12)	2.3 (0.55)	4.3 (0.85)	3.1 (0.62)	11.2 (1.00)
Doctor's...	59	76	94	17.6 (0.60)	15.5 (4.57)	11.5 (1.48)	19.4 (1.61)	31.2 (4.13)	7.1 (1.39)	11.1 (1.28)	13.4 (1.80)	29.7 (1.72)	37.7 (1.90)	11.7 (0.94)
Academic rank														
Professor...	32	30	23	4.4 (0.30)	8.9 ! (4.03)	4.6 (1.06)	3.4 (0.55)	5.9 ! (2.27)	3.9 (1.05)	5.4 (0.84)	3.5 (0.75)	4.8 (0.82)	4.7 (1.01)	4.1 (0.63)
Associate professor...	23	19	15	2.8 (0.22)	‡ (†)	2.3 ! (0.74)	1.9 (0.47)	5.7 ! (2.24)	3.7 (0.92)	5.4 (0.89)	1.6 (0.35)	3.3 (0.63)	2.9 (0.60)	1.6 (0.30)
Assistant professor...	24	23	20	3.7 (0.29)	‡ (†)	1.5 ! (0.55)	2.0 (0.50)	‡ (†)	3.6 (0.86)	15.1 (1.64)	1.7 ! (0.64)	2.8 (0.66)	3.7 (0.89)	1.7 (0.34)
Instructor...	215	205	188	35.4 (0.83)	39.9 (5.70)	29.2 (2.00)	37.0 (2.11)	25.3 (4.10)	33.6 (2.12)	36.5 (2.40)	42.9 (2.29)	32.4 (2.05)	30.4 (1.85)	38.2 (1.54)
Lecturer...	45	46	41	7.7 (0.41)	14.8 (4.39)	7.6 (1.52)	6.8 (0.97)	9.3 (2.49)	9.7 (1.16)	4.7 (0.93)	11.2 (1.10)	7.8 (1.02)	9.5 (1.20)	5.8 (0.67)
Other...	28	75	231	43.6 (0.85)	30.8 (5.98)	51.8 (2.46)	46.6 (1.78)	49.4 (5.02)	42.4 (3.00)	30.5 (1.88)	37.4 (2.23)	45.8 (2.02)	46.0 (2.22)	46.6 (1.47)
No rank...	9	16	13	2.4 (0.20)	‡ (†)	3.0 (0.75)	2.1 (0.59)	‡ (†)	3.2 ! (1.10)	2.4 (0.68)	1.7 (0.49)	3.1 (0.79)	2.8 (0.71)	2.1 (0.40)

—Not available.
†Not applicable.
#Rounds to zero.
!Interpret data with caution. The coefficient of variation (CV) for this estimate is between 30 and 50 percent.
‡Reporting standards not met. Either there are too few cases for a reliable estimate or the coefficient of variation (CV) is 50 percent or greater.
[1]Excludes history and philosophy.
[2]Excludes computer sciences.
[3]Includes history.
[4]Includes philosophy, law, occupationally specific programs, computer sciences, and other.
NOTE: Degree-granting institutions grant associate's or higher degrees and participate in Title IV federal financial aid programs. Totals may differ from figures reported in other tables because of varying survey methodologies. Race categories exclude persons of Hispanic ethnicity. Detail may not sum to totals because of survey item nonresponse and rounding.
SOURCE: U.S. Department of Education, National Center for Education Statistics, 1993, 1999, and 2004 National Study of Postsecondary Faculty (NSOPF:93;99;04). (This table was prepared January 2009.)

Table 315.80. Full-time and part-time faculty and instructional staff in degree-granting postsecondary institutions, by race/ethnicity, sex, and program area: Fall 1998 and fall 2003
[Standard errors appear in parentheses]

Program area	Number (in thousands)		Percentage distribution, fall 2003										
	Fall 1998	Fall 2003	Total	White Male	White Female	Black Male	Black Female	Hispanic Male	Hispanic Female	Asian/Pacific Islander Male	Asian/Pacific Islander Female	American Indian/Alaska Native Male	American Indian/Alaska Native Female
1	2	3	4	5	6	7	8	9	10	11	12	13	14
Full-time faculty and instructional staff	560 (4.8)	682 (#)	100.0	49.6 (0.39)	30.7 (0.36)	2.9 (0.15)	2.7 (0.13)	2.0 (0.09)	1.5 (0.08)	6.3 (0.15)	2.8 (0.15)	0.8 (0.08)	0.6 (0.07)
Agriculture and home economics	10 (0.4)	17 (0.8)	100.0	58.9 (3.03)	28.9 (2.72)	‡ (†)	1.8! (0.73)	1.2! (0.46)	1.3! (0.52)	3.6! (1.13)	2.8! (0.86)	‡ (†)	‡ (†)
Business	39 (1.1)	43 (1.4)	100.0	53.2 (1.49)	26.2 (1.71)	2.5 (0.73)	2.0 (0.44)	1.8 (0.48)	0.5! (0.16)	9.7 (1.06)	2.5 (0.46)	1.3 (0.35)	0.4! (0.17)
Communications	10 (1.0)	16 (1.4)	100.0	48.1 (3.39)	38.7 (3.30)	2.0! (0.73)	3.3 (0.94)	1.9! (0.58)	1.5! (0.59)	1.9! (0.87)	‡ (†)	‡ (†)	‡ (†)
Education	40 (1.4)	51 (1.9)	100.0	32.5 (1.49)	48.0 (1.64)	3.0 (0.60)	4.9 (0.64)	1.5 (0.34)	3.2 (0.52)	1.3! (0.43)	3.5 (0.59)	0.9 (0.25)	1.3 (0.34)
Teacher education	14 (0.6)	18 (1.0)	100.0	31.1 (2.31)	54.4 (2.54)	2.1! (0.86)	5.2 (1.10)	‡ (†)	3.1 (0.89)	‡ (†)	2.1! (0.87)	‡ (†)	‡ (†)
Other education	26 (1.3)	33 (1.5)	100.0	33.3 (2.09)	44.4 (2.46)	3.4 (0.84)	4.7 (0.75)	2.2 (0.51)	3.2 (0.57)	1.9! (0.64)	4.2 (0.81)	1.1! (0.40)	1.5! (0.45)
Engineering	25 (0.9)	33 (1.3)	100.0	65.6 (1.93)	5.3 (0.90)	4.9 (0.84)	‡ (†)	2.2 (0.42)	0.4! (0.17)	17.9 (1.61)	2.2 (0.63)	‡ (†)	‡ (†)
Fine arts	33 (1.4)	43 (1.7)	100.0	52.8 (1.68)	33.6 (1.36)	4.4 (0.83)	1.6 (0.34)	2.0 (0.59)	1.3! (0.44)	1.5 (0.42)	1.4! (0.59)	1.2! (0.36)	‡ (†)
Health sciences	84 (2.0)	94 (2.7)	100.0	36.2 (1.23)	43.5 (1.15)	1.6 (0.26)	3.4 (0.44)	1.6 (0.25)	1.4 (0.19)	6.6 (0.60)	4.1 (0.57)	0.7! (0.22)	1.0 (0.28)
First-professional	40 (1.6)	45 (1.7)	100.0	53.9 (1.58)	20.1 (1.42)	2.2 (0.49)	2.5 (0.58)	2.2 (0.40)	1.3 (0.30)	10.6 (1.08)	5.3 (0.89)	1.1! (0.37)	‡ (†)
Nursing	20 (0.6)	20 (1.2)	100.0	3.5 (0.86)	84.6 (2.21)	‡ (†)	5.3 (1.29)	‡ (†)	0.7! (0.27)	‡ (†)	3.4! (1.10)	‡ (†)	1.8! (0.85)
Other health sciences	24 (1.0)	29 (1.4)	100.0	31.0 (1.98)	52.0 (2.05)	1.5! (0.50)	3.6 (0.84)	1.6 (0.44)	1.9 (0.48)	4.8 (1.02)	2.6 (0.71)	‡ (†)	0.7! (0.31)
Humanities	81 (1.8)	90 (2.4)	100.0	47.3 (1.40)	35.0 (1.33)	2.4 (0.43)	2.6 (0.39)	2.2 (0.24)	2.9 (0.31)	2.9 (0.48)	2.9 (0.54)	0.9 (0.23)	0.9 (0.25)
English and literature	40 (1.2)	39 (1.5)	100.0	38.8 (1.90)	46.0 (2.10)	2.1 (0.45)	4.5 (0.70)	1.3 (0.27)	1.9 (0.50)	0.8! (0.34)	2.7! (0.87)	0.5! (0.18)	1.4 (0.39)
Foreign languages	15 (0.8)	20 (1.0)	100.0	36.2 (1.86)	36.7 (2.07)	2.7! (0.89)	0.9! (0.46)	5.1 (0.75)	8.3 (1.07)	4.0 (1.11)	4.5 (1.01)	‡ (†)	‡ (†)
History	14 (0.6)	18 (1.0)	100.0	59.4 (2.90)	23.0 (2.12)	2.7 (0.80)	2.4! (0.94)	1.9! (0.71)	1.2! (0.52)	5.0 (1.49)	3.2 (0.91)	1.0! (0.45)	‡ (†)
Philosophy	12 (0.8)	13 (1.0)	100.0	72.3 (3.55)	16.6 (2.33)	2.3! (1.11)	‡ (†)	1.0! (0.35)	‡ (†)	4.0! (1.49)	‡ (†)	‡ (†)	‡ (†)
Law	8 (0.6)	10 (1.0)	100.0	54.5 (3.56)	29.9 (3.63)	3.3! (1.10)	‡ (†)	‡ (†)	2.4! (1.15)	2.8! (1.36)	‡ (†)	‡ (†)	‡ (†)
Natural sciences	111 (2.1)	151 (2.5)	100.0	57.3 (1.12)	20.3 (0.80)	2.5 (0.31)	1.5 (0.22)	2.0 (0.20)	0.9 (0.15)	11.2 (0.65)	3.3 (0.35)	0.6 (0.16)	0.3! (0.09)
Biological sciences	40 (1.3)	59 (1.7)	100.0	55.4 (1.69)	21.6 (1.30)	2.2 (0.48)	1.2 (0.28)	1.9 (0.39)	1.2 (0.31)	11.1 (1.13)	4.8 (0.67)	‡ (†)	0.3! (0.12)
Physical sciences	27 (0.8)	36 (1.3)	100.0	68.9 (2.03)	12.8 (1.50)	2.6 (0.59)	0.7! (0.31)	1.4 (0.29)	0.6! (0.19)	9.4 (1.05)	3.0 (0.64)	‡ (†)	‡ (†)
Mathematics	26 (1.0)	32 (1.3)	100.0	52.2 (2.15)	22.7 (1.84)	3.8 (0.67)	2.6 (0.67)	2.8 (0.67)	0.7! (0.28)	11.7 (1.41)	1.8! (0.67)	1.2! (0.56)	‡ (†)
Computer sciences	17 (0.9)	24 (1.2)	100.0	51.0 (2.74)	25.1 (2.15)	1.5! (0.59)	2.0 (0.58)	2.3 (0.52)	0.9! (0.31)	13.5 (1.69)	2.0! (0.66)	1.1! (0.48)	‡ (†)
Social sciences	58 (1.3)	70 (1.8)	100.0	52.2 (1.46)	29.0 (1.23)	3.7 (0.45)	4.1 (0.81)	2.6 (0.36)	1.7 (0.35)	3.4 (0.58)	1.9 (0.48)	0.9 (0.25)	0.6 (0.15)
Economics	9 (0.6)	12 (0.7)	100.0	62.3 (3.46)	18.0 (3.09)	3.5 (0.92)	‡ (†)	3.1! (1.13)	‡ (†)	8.9 (2.18)	‡ (†)	‡ (†)	‡ (†)
Political science	8 (0.5)	10 (0.7)	100.0	67.1 (3.74)	16.8 (2.59)	2.8! (1.19)	‡ (†)	5.1! (1.57)	‡ (†)	2.9! (1.31)	‡ (†)	‡ (†)	‡ (†)
Psychology	20 (0.7)	25 (1.1)	100.0	46.3 (2.33)	37.8 (2.16)	3.4 (1.01)	5.0! (1.69)	1.6 (0.42)	2.7 (0.70)	1.1! (0.49)	1.2! (0.39)	‡ (†)	‡ (†)
Sociology	9 (0.4)	9 (0.6)	100.0	49.9 (3.72)	30.1 (3.42)	3.9! (1.69)	8.0! (2.43)	3.0! (0.97)	‡ (†)	‡ (†)	‡ (†)	‡ (†)	‡ (†)
Other social sciences	13 (0.6)	14 (0.9)	100.0	45.2 (3.59)	30.5 (3.09)	4.8 (1.33)	3.9! (1.28)	1.9! (0.80)	2.4 (0.71)	4.7! (1.50)	3.7! (1.22)	1.9! (0.75)	1.1! (0.54)
Occupationally specific programs	16 (0.8)	27 (1.1)	100.0	60.7 (2.47)	24.2 (2.16)	4.2 (1.16)	1.9 (0.55)	2.5 (0.63)	0.8! (0.26)	2.0! (0.92)	1.4! (0.46)	1.9! (0.62)	‡ (†)
All other programs	44 (1.2)	29 (1.4)	100.0	42.0 (2.03)	37.4 (2.00)	4.7 (1.01)	6.0 (1.01)	1.7 (0.44)	1.7! (0.53)	3.2! (0.99)	2.0! (0.64)	0.7! (0.31)	0.6! (0.28)

See notes at end of table.

Table 315.80. Full-time and part-time faculty and instructional staff in degree-granting postsecondary institutions, by race/ethnicity, sex, and program area: Fall 1998 and fall 2003—Continued
[Standard errors appear in parentheses]

	Number (in thousands)		Percentage distribution, fall 2003										
	Fall 1998	Fall 2003	Total	White		Black		Hispanic		Asian/Pacific Islander		American Indian/Alaska Native	
Program area				Male	Female	Male	Female	Male	Female	Male	Female	Male	Female
1	2	3	4	5	6	7	8	9	10	11	12	13	14
Part-time faculty and instructional staff	416 (5.9)	530 (#)	100.0	44.4 (0.46)	40.8 (0.54)	2.6 (0.17)	3.0 (0.14)	1.9 (0.12)	1.6 (0.10)	2.1 (0.15)	1.8 (0.18)	1.0 (0.15)	0.8 (0.15)
Agriculture and home economics	3 (0.2)	7 (1.0)	100.0	30.8 (6.24)	60.6 (6.30)	‡ (†)	‡ (†)	‡ (†)	‡ (†)	‡ (†)	‡ (†)	‡ (†)	‡ (†)
Business	32 (1.8)	45 (3.0)	100.0	60.6 (1.96)	26.2 (1.73)	4.3 (0.70)	2.3 (0.54)	1.7! (0.77)	‡ (†)	2.0! (0.69)	‡ (†)	‡ (†)	‡ (†)
Communications	10 (1.0)	14 (1.2)	100.0	47.7 (3.71)	39.3 (3.89)	2.1! (0.97)	2.8! (0.95)	‡ (†)	‡ (†)	‡ (†)	‡ (†)	‡ (†)	‡ (†)
Education	34 (1.6)	64 (2.6)	100.0	25.3 (1.65)	59.8 (2.11)	1.4 (0.41)	5.2 (0.90)	1.7 (0.37)	3.4 (0.49)	0.4! (0.19)	1.3! (0.38)	0.3! (0.15)	1.2! (0.36)
Teacher education	13 (1.0)	29 (1.8)	100.0	22.2 (2.41)	63.9 (2.84)	0.9! (0.35)	6.4 (1.17)	1.3! (0.41)	2.2 (0.52)	‡ (†)	1.6! (0.60)	‡ (†)	1.6! (0.69)
Other education	20 (1.2)	34 (1.8)	100.0	27.9 (2.53)	56.4 (2.98)	1.9! (0.66)	4.1 (1.17)	2.0 (0.57)	4.5 (0.77)	‡ (†)	‡ (†)	‡ (†)	0.8! (0.37)
Engineering	9 (0.8)	14 (1.5)	100.0	78.6 (3.70)	6.8! (2.77)	‡ (†)	‡ (†)	1.7 (0.46)	‡ (†)	8.0 (2.13)	‡ (†)	‡ (†)	‡ (†)
Fine arts	38 (1.5)	48 (3.6)	100.0	44.8 (2.06)	43.9 (2.44)	1.7! (0.54)	1.3 (0.34)	1.8 (0.49)	0.9 (0.25)	1.0! (0.36)	1.9! (0.58)	2.1! (0.84)	0.7! (0.30)
Health sciences	49 (2.2)	58 (3.1)	100.0	27.9 (1.65)	57.1 (1.74)	1.2! (0.41)	4.0 (0.52)	0.8! (0.26)	1.4 (0.38)	4.0 (0.87)	2.4 (0.72)	‡ (†)	0.5! (0.23)
First-professional	15 (1.3)	17 (1.2)	100.0	47.2 (3.33)	34.7 (3.64)	2.1! (0.92)	2.1! (0.92)	‡ (†)	1.4! (0.56)	6.4! (2.10)	5.1! (2.41)	‡ (†)	‡ (†)
Nursing	12 (0.8)	13 (1.3)	100.0	‡ (†)	86.3 (2.04)	‡ (†)	8.0 (1.30)	‡ (†)	1.4! (0.56)	‡ (†)	‡ (†)	‡ (†)	‡ (†)
Other health sciences	21 (1.7)	28 (2.0)	100.0	29.4 (2.86)	56.4 (3.07)	‡ (†)	3.2 (0.76)	0.8! (0.32)	1.7! (0.70)	4.3 (1.23)	1.4! (0.56)	‡ (†)	‡ (†)
Humanities	74 (2.1)	80 (2.5)	100.0	35.9 (1.52)	49.2 (1.61)	1.6 (0.35)	2.9 (0.45)	2.3 (0.35)	2.9 (0.44)	0.9! (0.30)	2.7 (0.55)	1.0! (0.33)	0.6! (0.22)
English and literature	43 (1.4)	44 (1.9)	100.0	29.5 (2.31)	58.5 (2.47)	1.2 (0.33)	4.3 (0.78)	1.0! (0.35)	1.3 (0.37)	1.0! (0.41)	1.6 (0.46)	0.8! (0.34)	0.8! (0.29)
Foreign languages	12 (1.2)	15 (1.2)	100.0	16.6 (3.57)	52.0 (3.38)	‡ (†)	2.0! (0.80)	7.2 (1.50)	11.4 (1.97)	‡ (†)	7.9 (2.18)	‡ (†)	‡ (†)
History	11 (0.7)	11 (1.0)	100.0	61.1 (4.58)	28.9 (4.15)	‡ (†)	‡ (†)	2.5! (1.05)	‡ (†)	‡ (†)	‡ (†)	‡ (†)	‡ (†)
Philosophy	9 (0.6)	10 (1.2)	100.0	65.7 (4.20)	26.0 (4.60)	‡ (†)	3.5! (1.71)	‡ (†)	‡ (†)	‡ (†)	‡ (†)	‡ (†)	‡ (†)
Law	11 (0.8)	11 (1.2)	100.0	52.6 (4.43)	32.8 (4.18)	4.4! (1.41)	2.0! (0.82)	2.2! (1.05)	‡ (†)	‡ (†)	‡ (†)	‡ (†)	‡ (†)
Natural sciences	65 (2.2)	90 (2.9)	100.0	50.5 (1.72)	32.4 (1.73)	3.8 (0.44)	2.7 (0.36)	1.9 (0.41)	0.7 (0.16)	4.2 (0.61)	2.3 (0.46)	1.0! (0.34)	0.5! (0.26)
Biological sciences	11 (0.9)	16 (1.0)	100.0	41.7 (3.76)	40.1 (3.78)	2.2! (0.67)	2.1! (0.90)	1.0! (0.39)	1.0! (0.40)	5.6! (2.32)	5.3! (1.63)	‡ (†)	‡ (†)
Physical sciences	11 (0.8)	16 (1.1)	100.0	57.8 (3.30)	28.7 (3.42)	3.9! (1.37)	‡ (†)	‡ (†)	0.9! (0.41)	3.1! (1.06)	2.6! (0.99)	‡ (†)	‡ (†)
Mathematics	24 (1.4)	32 (2.3)	100.0	46.6 (3.20)	36.0 (3.04)	4.4 (0.78)	3.1 (0.83)	1.4! (0.48)	0.5! (0.24)	3.9 (0.85)	1.8! (0.64)	‡ (†)	‡ (†)
Computer sciences	19 (1.2)	26 (1.7)	100.0	56.4 (2.98)	25.3 (2.64)	4.1 (1.03)	3.7 (0.60)	3.0! (0.93)	‡ (†)	4.2 (1.10)	4.2 (0.64)	1.4! (0.63)	‡ (†)
Social sciences	41 (2.4)	42 (2.0)	100.0	49.8 (1.85)	32.9 (2.09)	3.7 (0.68)	3.0 (0.66)	2.5 (0.65)	1.5 (0.31)	‡ (†)	‡ (†)	1.5! (0.65)	2.0! (0.62)
Economics	4 (0.5)	5 (0.8)	100.0	68.6 (7.36)	9.3! (4.08)	7.2! (3.52)	‡ (†)	‡ (†)	‡ (†)	‡ (†)	‡ (†)	‡ (†)	‡ (†)
Political science	4 (0.4)	5 (0.8)	100.0	71.1 (5.32)	11.9! (3.93)	5.7! (2.79)	‡ (†)	‡ (†)	‡ (†)	‡ (†)	‡ (†)	‡ (†)	‡ (†)
Psychology	18 (2.1)	18 (1.2)	100.0	42.2 (3.36)	44.4 (3.12)	3.0! (0.76)	3.0! (0.91)	1.4! (0.64)	1.7! (0.58)	‡ (†)	‡ (†)	2.2! (0.93)	2.2! (0.93)
Sociology	6 (0.5)	7 (0.9)	100.0	44.6 (6.09)	30.7 (6.03)	4.0! (1.61)	4.1! (1.54)	‡ (†)	1.6! (0.76)	‡ (†)	‡ (†)	‡ (†)	‡ (†)
Other social sciences	10 (0.9)	8 (0.8)	100.0	46.2 (4.24)	36.4 (4.19)	‡ (†)	4.5! (1.85)	‡ (†)	1.9! (0.83)	‡ (†)	2.8! (1.29)	‡ (†)	‡ (†)
Occupationally specific programs	17 (1.1)	37 (2.4)	100.0	68.2 (2.51)	18.6 (2.19)	1.8! (1.03)	1.8! (0.63)	4.0 (0.92)	0.6! (0.23)	‡ (†)	‡ (†)	1.1! (0.50)	‡ (†)
All other programs	35 (1.6)	19 (1.2)	100.0	41.8 (3.30)	42.6 (2.95)	2.5! (0.81)	5.5 (1.46)	1.9! (0.58)	2.6! (0.90)	‡ (†)	1.2! (0.63)	‡ (†)	‡ (†)

†Not applicable.
#Rounds to zero.
!Interpret data with caution. The coefficient of variation (CV) for this estimate is between 30 and 50 percent.
‡Reporting standards not met. Either there are too few cases for a reliable estimate or the coefficient of variation (CV) is 50 percent or greater.

NOTE: Degree-granting institutions grant associate's or higher degrees and participate in Title IV federal financial aid programs. Totals may differ from figures reported in other tables because of varying survey methodologies. Race categories exclude persons of Hispanic ethnicity. Detail may not sum to totals because of rounding and nonresponse to program area question.
SOURCE: U.S. Department of Education, National Center for Education Statistics, 1999 and 2004 National Study of Postsecondary Faculty (NSOPF:99;04). (This table was prepared December 2008.)

Table 316.10. Average salary of full-time instructional faculty on 9-month contracts in degree-granting postsecondary institutions, by academic rank, control and level of institution, and sex: Selected years, 1970–71 through 2014–15

Sex and academic year	All faculty	Academic rank						Public institutions			Private institutions		
		Professor	Associate professor	Assistant professor	Instructor	Lecturer	No rank	Total	4-year	2-year	Total	4-year	2-year
1	2	3	4	5	6	7	8	9	10	11	12	13	14
							Current dollars						
Total													
1970–71	$12,710	$17,958	$13,563	$11,176	$9,360	$11,196	$12,333	$12,953	$13,121	$12,644	$11,619	$11,824	$8,664
1975–76	16,659	22,649	17,065	13,986	13,672	12,906	15,196	16,942	17,400	15,820	15,921	16,116	10,901
1980–81	23,302	30,753	23,214	18,901	15,178	17,301	22,334	23,745	24,373	22,177	22,093	22,325	15,065
1982–83	27,196	35,540	26,921	22,056	17,601	20,072	25,557	27,488	28,293	25,567	26,393	26,691	16,595
1984–85	30,447	39,743	29,945	24,668	20,230	22,334	27,683	30,646	31,764	27,864	29,910	30,247	18,510
1985–86	32,392	42,268	31,787	26,277	20,918	23,770	29,088	32,750	34,033	29,590	31,402	31,732	19,436
1987–88	35,897	47,040	35,231	29,110	22,728	25,977	31,532	36,231	37,840	32,229	35,049	35,346	21,867
1989–90	40,133	52,810	39,392	32,689	25,030	28,990	34,559	40,416	42,365	35,516	39,464	39,817	24,601
1990–91	42,165	55,540	41,414	34,434	26,332	30,097	36,395	42,317	44,510	37,055	41,788	42,224	24,088
1991–92	43,851	57,433	42,929	35,745	30,916	30,456	37,783	43,641	45,638	38,959	44,376	44,793	25,673
1992–93	44,714	58,788	43,945	36,625	28,499	30,543	37,771	44,197	46,515	38,935	45,985	46,427	26,105
1993–94	46,364	60,649	45,278	37,630	28,828	32,729	40,584	45,920	48,019	41,040	47,465	47,880	28,435
1994–95	47,811	62,709	46,713	38,756	29,665	33,198	41,227	47,432	49,738	42,101	48,741	49,379	25,613
1995–96	49,309	64,540	47,966	39,696	30,344	34,136	42,996	48,837	51,172	43,295	50,466	50,819	31,915
1996–97	50,829	66,659	49,307	40,687	31,193	34,962	44,200	50,303	52,718	44,584	52,112	52,443	32,628
1997–98	52,335	68,731	50,828	41,830	32,449	35,484	45,268	51,638	54,114	45,919	54,039	54,379	33,592
1998–99	54,097	71,322	52,576	43,348	33,819	36,819	46,250	53,319	55,948	47,285	55,981	56,284	34,821
1999–2000	55,888	74,410	54,524	44,978	34,918	38,194	47,389	55,011	57,950	48,240	58,013	58,323	35,925
2001–02	59,742	80,792	58,724	48,796	46,959	41,798	46,569	58,524	62,013	50,837	62,818	63,088	33,139
2002–03	61,330	83,466	60,471	50,552	48,304	42,622	46,338	60,014	63,486	52,330	64,533	64,814	34,826
2003–04	62,579	85,333	61,746	51,798	49,065	43,648	47,725	60,874	64,340	53,076	66,666	66,932	36,322
2004–05	64,234	88,158	63,558	53,308	49,730	44,514	48,942	62,346	66,053	53,932	68,755	68,995	37,329
2005–06	66,172	91,208	65,714	55,106	50,883	45,896	50,425	64,158	67,951	55,405	71,016	71,263	38,549
2006–07	68,585	94,870	68,153	57,143	53,278	47,478	52,161	66,566	70,460	57,466	73,419	73,636	41,138
2007–08	71,085	98,548	70,826	59,294	55,325	49,392	54,405	68,981	72,857	59,646	76,133	76,341	43,402
2008–09	73,570	102,346	73,439	61,550	56,918	51,188	56,370	71,237	75,245	61,433	79,147	79,410	43,542
2009–10	74,620	103,682	74,125	62,245	57,791	52,185	56,803	72,178	76,147	62,264	80,379	80,597	44,748
2010–11	75,481	104,961	75,107	63,136	58,003	52,584	56,549	72,715	76,857	62,359	81,897	82,098	45,146
2011–12	76,567	107,090	76,177	64,011	58,350	53,359	56,898	73,496	77,843	62,553	83,540	83,701	47,805
2012–13	77,278	108,074	77,029	64,673	57,674	53,072	58,752	73,877	78,012	62,907	84,932	85,096	44,978
2013–14	78,625	109,905	78,593	66,025	58,080	54,238	58,902	75,241	79,711	63,198	86,265	86,467	44,566
2014–15	80,203	112,697	80,438	67,677	59,211	55,610	58,201	76,963	81,527	64,304	87,617	88,228	38,168
Males													
1975–76	17,414	22,902	17,209	14,174	14,430	13,579	15,761	17,661	18,121	16,339	16,784	16,946	11,378
1980–81	24,499	31,082	23,451	19,227	15,545	18,281	23,170	24,873	25,509	22,965	23,493	23,669	16,075
1982–83	28,664	35,956	27,262	22,586	18,160	21,225	26,541	28,851	29,661	26,524	28,159	28,380	17,346
1984–85	32,182	40,269	30,392	25,330	21,159	23,557	28,670	32,240	33,344	28,891	32,028	32,278	19,460
1985–86	34,294	42,833	32,273	27,094	21,693	25,238	30,267	34,528	35,786	30,758	33,656	33,900	20,412
1987–88	38,112	47,735	35,823	30,086	23,645	27,652	32,747	38,314	39,898	33,477	37,603	37,817	22,641
1989–90	42,763	53,650	40,131	33,781	25,933	31,162	35,980	42,959	44,834	37,081	42,312	42,595	25,218
1990–91	45,065	56,549	42,239	35,636	27,388	32,398	38,036	45,084	47,168	38,787	45,019	45,319	25,937
1991–92	46,848	58,494	43,814	36,969	33,359	32,843	39,422	46,483	48,401	40,811	47,733	48,042	26,825
1992–93	47,866	59,972	44,855	37,842	29,583	32,512	39,365	47,175	49,392	40,725	49,518	49,837	27,402
1993–94	49,579	61,857	46,229	38,794	29,815	34,796	42,251	48,956	50,989	42,938	51,076	51,397	30,783
1994–95	51,228	64,046	47,705	39,923	30,528	35,082	43,103	50,629	52,874	44,020	52,653	53,036	29,639
1995–96	52,814	65,949	49,037	40,858	30,940	36,135	44,624	52,163	54,448	45,209	54,364	54,649	33,301
1996–97	54,465	68,214	50,457	41,864	31,738	36,932	45,688	53,737	56,162	46,393	56,185	56,453	34,736
1997–98	56,115	70,468	52,041	43,017	33,070	37,481	46,822	55,191	57,744	47,690	58,293	58,576	36,157
1998–99	58,048	73,260	53,830	44,650	34,741	38,976	47,610	57,038	59,805	48,961	60,392	60,641	38,040
1999–2000	60,084	76,478	55,939	46,414	35,854	40,202	48,788	58,984	62,030	50,033	62,631	62,905	38,636
2001–02	64,320	83,356	60,300	50,518	48,844	44,519	48,049	62,835	66,577	52,360	67,871	68,100	33,395
2002–03	66,126	86,191	62,226	52,441	50,272	45,469	47,412	64,564	68,322	53,962	69,726	69,976	34,291
2003–04	67,485	88,262	63,466	53,649	50,985	46,214	48,973	65,476	69,248	54,623	72,021	72,250	35,604
2004–05	69,337	91,290	65,394	55,215	51,380	46,929	50,102	67,130	71,145	55,398	74,318	74,540	34,970
2005–06	71,569	94,733	67,654	57,099	52,519	48,256	51,811	69,191	73,353	56,858	76,941	77,143	38,215
2006–07	74,167	98,563	70,168	59,150	55,061	49,641	53,665	71,797	76,072	58,971	79,491	79,663	41,196
2007–08	76,935	102,555	72,940	61,368	57,116	51,804	56,196	74,389	78,673	61,166	82,681	82,850	42,995
2008–09	79,706	106,759	75,634	63,726	58,819	53,777	58,341	76,897	81,394	62,870	86,008	86,205	43,871
2009–10	80,881	108,225	76,400	64,451	59,793	54,947	58,647	77,948	82,423	63,697	87,382	87,546	44,500
2010–11	81,873	109,656	77,429	65,391	59,851	55,457	58,392	78,609	83,279	63,745	89,000	89,160	44,542
2011–12	83,150	112,066	78,560	66,303	60,066	56,367	58,807	79,544	84,444	63,918	90,840	90,976	45,250
2012–13	83,979	113,311	79,423	67,085	59,350	55,759	61,086	80,016	84,700	64,282	92,385	92,530	42,906
2013–14	85,528	115,455	81,156	68,534	59,614	56,920	61,279	81,560	86,562	64,564	94,016	94,177	44,234
2014–15	87,178	118,412	83,001	70,227	60,730	58,633	60,211	83,363	88,459	65,693	95,467	96,058	37,389

See notes at end of table.

Table 316.10. Average salary of full-time instructional faculty on 9-month contracts in degree-granting postsecondary institutions, by academic rank, control and level of institution, and sex: Selected years, 1970–71 through 2014–15—Continued

Sex and academic year	All faculty	Academic rank						Public institutions			Private institutions		
		Professor	Associate professor	Assistant professor	Instructor	Lecturer	No rank	Total	4-year	2-year	Total	4-year	2-year
1	2	3	4	5	6	7	8	9	10	11	12	13	14
Females													
1975–76	14,308	20,308	16,364	13,522	12,572	11,901	14,094	14,762	14,758	14,769	13,030	13,231	10,201
1980–81	19,996	27,959	22,295	18,302	14,854	16,168	20,843	20,673	20,608	20,778	18,073	18,326	13,892
1982–83	23,261	32,221	25,738	21,130	17,102	18,830	23,855	23,892	23,876	23,917	21,451	21,785	15,845
1984–85	25,941	35,824	28,517	23,575	19,362	21,004	26,050	26,566	26,813	26,172	24,186	24,560	17,575
1985–86	27,576	38,252	30,300	24,966	20,237	22,273	27,171	28,299	28,680	27,693	25,523	25,889	18,504
1987–88	30,499	42,371	33,528	27,600	21,962	24,370	29,605	31,215	31,820	30,228	28,621	28,946	21,215
1989–90	34,183	47,663	37,469	31,090	24,320	26,995	32,528	34,796	35,704	33,307	32,650	33,010	24,002
1990–91	35,881	49,728	39,329	32,724	25,534	28,111	34,179	36,459	37,573	34,720	34,359	34,898	22,585
1991–92	37,534	51,621	40,766	34,063	28,873	28,550	35,622	37,800	38,634	36,517	36,828	37,309	24,683
1992–93	38,385	52,755	41,861	35,032	27,700	28,922	35,792	38,356	39,470	36,710	38,460	38,987	25,068
1993–94	40,058	54,746	43,178	36,169	28,136	31,048	38,474	40,118	41,031	38,707	39,902	40,378	26,142
1994–95	41,369	56,555	44,626	37,352	29,072	31,677	38,967	41,548	42,663	39,812	40,908	41,815	22,851
1995–96	42,871	58,318	45,803	38,345	29,940	32,584	41,085	42,871	43,986	41,086	42,871	43,236	30,671
1996–97	44,325	60,160	47,101	39,350	30,819	33,415	42,474	44,306	45,402	42,531	44,374	44,726	30,661
1997–98	45,775	61,965	48,597	40,504	32,011	33,918	43,491	45,648	46,709	43,943	46,106	46,466	30,995
1998–99	47,421	64,236	50,347	41,894	33,152	35,115	44,723	47,247	48,355	45,457	47,874	48,204	31,524
1999–2000	48,997	67,079	52,091	43,367	34,228	36,607	45,865	48,714	50,168	46,340	49,737	50,052	32,951
2001–02	52,662	72,542	56,186	46,824	45,262	39,538	45,003	52,123	53,895	49,290	54,149	54,434	32,921
2002–03	54,105	75,028	57,716	48,380	46,573	40,265	45,251	53,435	55,121	50,717	55,881	56,158	35,296
2003–04	55,378	76,652	59,095	49,689	47,404	41,536	46,519	54,408	56,117	51,591	57,921	58,192	36,896
2004–05	56,926	79,160	60,809	51,154	48,351	42,455	47,860	55,780	57,714	52,566	59,919	60,143	39,291
2005–06	58,665	81,514	62,860	52,901	49,533	43,934	49,172	57,462	59,437	54,082	61,830	62,092	38,786
2006–07	61,016	85,090	65,237	54,974	51,832	45,693	50,812	59,781	61,875	56,127	64,246	64,481	41,099
2007–08	63,347	88,301	67,816	57,111	53,889	47,407	52,837	62,129	64,226	58,318	66,528	66,745	43,670
2008–09	65,638	91,522	70,375	59,286	55,424	49,078	54,649	64,231	66,393	60,195	69,300	69,593	43,344
2009–10	66,647	92,830	71,017	59,997	56,239	49,957	55,206	65,139	67,276	61,047	70,507	70,746	44,892
2010–11	67,473	94,041	72,003	60,888	56,566	50,270	54,985	65,632	67,935	61,193	72,091	72,306	45,518
2011–12	68,468	95,845	73,057	61,763	57,013	50,994	55,299	66,368	68,897	61,417	73,629	73,788	49,382
2012–13	69,124	96,563	73,966	62,321	56,361	50,963	56,777	66,703	69,083	61,774	74,987	75,149	46,407
2013–14	70,355	98,064	75,388	63,599	56,884	52,156	56,916	67,944	70,713	62,079	76,173	76,390	44,769
2014–15	71,943	100,790	77,297	65,225	58,013	53,233	56,508	69,645	72,583	63,164	77,544	78,132	38,841
					Constant 2014–15 dollars[1]								
Total													
1970–71	75,722	106,989	80,809	66,585	55,764	66,705	73,480	77,175	78,176	75,332	69,222	70,448	51,619
1975–76	71,093	96,659	72,829	59,688	58,349	55,078	64,852	72,303	74,258	67,513	67,945	68,780	46,521
1980–81	63,666	84,023	63,425	51,641	41,469	47,270	61,021	64,876	66,592	60,592	60,363	60,996	41,161
1982–83	65,580	85,700	64,917	53,185	42,443	48,401	61,628	66,284	68,225	61,652	63,644	64,362	40,017
1984–85	68,132	88,934	67,009	55,200	45,269	49,977	61,947	68,577	71,079	62,352	66,930	67,684	41,420
1985–86	70,453	91,933	69,137	57,152	45,497	51,700	63,266	71,231	74,022	64,358	68,299	69,017	42,273
1987–88	73,341	96,108	71,981	59,475	46,435	53,073	64,424	74,024	77,311	65,806	71,609	72,215	44,677
1989–90	74,807	98,435	73,426	60,931	46,655	54,037	64,416	75,334	78,966	66,201	73,559	74,218	45,855
1990–91	74,521	98,158	73,192	60,857	46,537	53,192	64,323	74,789	78,664	65,489	73,853	74,625	42,572
1991–92	75,094	98,352	73,514	61,213	52,942	52,154	64,703	74,734	78,153	66,717	75,992	76,706	43,964
1992–93	74,252	97,623	72,974	60,819	47,326	50,719	62,722	73,393	77,243	64,655	76,362	77,097	43,350
1993–94	75,049	98,171	73,289	60,911	46,663	52,977	65,692	74,330	77,727	66,430	76,830	77,502	46,027
1994–95	75,234	98,676	73,506	60,985	46,679	52,239	64,873	74,637	78,266	66,249	76,696	77,701	40,303
1995–96	75,537	98,869	73,479	60,811	46,484	52,292	65,865	74,813	78,390	66,323	77,308	77,849	48,890
1996–97	75,705	99,282	73,438	60,599	46,459	52,072	65,832	74,921	78,517	66,403	77,616	78,109	48,597
1997–98	76,582	100,575	74,377	61,210	47,482	51,924	66,240	75,562	79,186	67,194	79,076	79,573	49,155
1998–99	77,813	102,590	75,625	62,352	48,645	52,960	66,527	76,694	80,475	68,014	80,524	80,959	50,086
1999–2000	78,134	104,029	76,226	62,882	48,817	53,397	66,252	76,908	81,016	67,442	81,104	81,538	50,224
2001–02	79,350	107,309	77,998	64,811	62,372	55,517	61,853	77,732	82,366	67,522	83,435	83,795	44,015
2002–03	79,707	108,477	78,591	65,701	62,778	55,394	60,224	77,997	82,510	68,011	83,871	84,236	45,261
2003–04	79,590	108,529	78,530	65,878	62,402	55,513	60,698	77,421	81,830	67,504	84,787	85,126	46,195
2004–05	79,308	108,847	78,473	65,818	61,400	54,960	60,427	76,976	81,554	66,588	84,890	85,187	46,089
2005–06	78,704	108,481	78,159	65,541	60,519	54,588	59,974	76,309	80,819	65,898	84,465	84,759	45,849
2006–07	79,517	109,992	79,016	66,251	61,770	55,046	60,476	77,176	81,691	66,626	85,122	85,373	47,696
2007–08	79,471	110,174	79,181	66,289	61,852	55,219	60,823	77,119	81,452	66,683	85,114	85,347	48,523
2008–09	81,117	112,844	80,972	67,864	62,756	56,439	62,152	78,545	82,963	67,735	87,265	87,555	48,008
2009–10	81,486	113,222	80,945	67,972	63,108	56,987	62,030	78,820	83,153	67,993	87,775	88,012	48,865
2010–11	80,804	112,363	80,403	67,588	62,093	56,292	60,537	77,843	82,276	66,756	87,672	87,887	48,329
2011–12	79,633	111,378	79,227	66,574	60,686	55,496	59,177	76,439	80,960	65,058	86,885	87,052	49,719
2012–13	79,057	110,561	78,802	66,161	59,001	54,294	60,104	75,577	79,807	64,355	86,887	87,055	46,013
2013–14	79,198	110,705	79,166	66,506	58,502	54,633	59,331	75,789	80,292	63,658	86,894	87,096	44,891
2014–15	80,203	112,697	80,438	67,677	59,211	55,610	58,201	76,963	81,527	64,304	87,617	88,228	38,168

See notes at end of table.

Table 316.10. Average salary of full-time instructional faculty on 9-month contracts in degree-granting postsecondary institutions, by academic rank, control and level of institution, and sex: Selected years, 1970–71 through 2014–15—Continued

Sex and academic year	All faculty	Academic rank						Public institutions			Private institutions		
		Professor	Associate professor	Assistant professor	Instructor	Lecturer	No rank	Total	4-year	2-year	Total	4-year	2-year
1	2	3	4	5	6	7	8	9	10	11	12	13	14
Males													
1975–76	74,316	97,738	73,441	60,491	61,582	57,950	67,262	75,372	77,333	69,731	71,630	72,319	48,556
1980–81	66,936	84,922	64,073	52,532	42,472	49,947	63,305	67,958	69,696	62,745	64,188	64,668	43,920
1982–83	69,120	86,704	65,739	54,463	43,791	51,182	64,000	69,571	71,524	63,959	67,902	68,435	41,828
1984–85	72,014	90,111	68,009	56,681	47,348	52,714	64,155	72,144	74,615	64,650	71,670	72,229	43,546
1985–86	74,589	93,162	70,194	58,929	47,182	54,893	65,831	75,098	77,835	66,899	73,202	73,733	44,396
1987–88	77,866	97,527	73,190	61,470	48,309	56,496	66,905	78,279	81,516	68,397	76,827	77,264	46,258
1989–90	79,710	100,001	74,802	62,966	48,338	58,084	67,065	80,073	83,569	69,119	78,869	79,395	47,006
1990–91	79,646	99,942	74,650	62,980	48,405	57,258	67,222	79,679	83,361	68,550	79,564	80,095	45,839
1991–92	80,226	100,169	75,030	63,307	57,126	56,243	67,509	79,601	82,885	69,888	81,741	82,270	45,936
1992–93	79,485	99,589	74,487	62,840	49,126	53,990	65,370	78,338	82,021	67,627	82,230	82,760	45,503
1993–94	80,252	100,126	74,829	62,794	48,261	56,323	68,390	79,243	82,534	69,502	82,676	83,195	49,828
1994–95	80,611	100,781	75,067	62,821	48,038	55,204	67,826	79,668	83,200	69,269	82,853	83,456	46,640
1995–96	80,906	101,027	75,120	62,590	47,397	55,355	68,360	79,908	83,409	69,255	83,279	83,717	51,014
1996–97	81,120	101,598	75,150	62,352	47,271	55,006	68,048	80,036	83,647	69,097	83,682	84,080	51,735
1997–98	82,114	103,116	76,152	62,946	48,392	54,846	68,514	80,761	84,497	69,785	85,301	85,715	52,909
1998–99	83,496	105,378	77,428	64,224	49,972	56,062	68,483	82,044	86,024	70,426	86,868	87,226	54,717
1999–2000	83,999	106,919	78,205	64,888	50,126	56,204	68,207	82,462	86,720	69,949	87,561	87,943	54,015
2001–02	85,431	110,714	80,091	67,098	64,875	59,131	63,820	83,458	88,429	69,546	90,147	90,451	44,355
2002–03	85,941	112,018	80,872	68,155	65,336	59,093	61,619	83,910	88,795	70,132	90,619	90,944	44,566
2003–04	85,829	112,254	80,718	68,232	64,844	58,776	62,285	83,274	88,071	69,471	91,599	91,889	45,283
2004–05	85,609	112,713	80,740	68,173	63,437	57,942	61,859	82,884	87,841	68,399	91,759	92,033	43,176
2005–06	85,123	112,674	80,466	67,912	62,465	57,395	61,623	82,294	87,245	67,626	91,512	91,752	45,453
2006–07	85,989	114,273	81,352	68,579	63,838	57,553	62,219	83,241	88,197	68,371	92,162	92,361	47,763
2007–08	86,012	114,654	81,545	68,608	63,854	57,915	62,825	83,165	87,955	68,382	92,436	92,624	48,068
2008–09	87,882	117,710	83,393	70,263	64,852	59,293	64,325	84,785	89,743	69,319	94,830	95,048	48,371
2009–10	88,323	118,183	83,430	70,381	65,294	60,003	64,043	85,120	90,006	69,558	95,422	95,601	48,595
2010–11	87,646	117,389	82,889	70,002	64,072	59,368	62,509	84,152	89,152	68,240	95,276	95,447	47,683
2011–12	86,480	116,553	81,705	68,958	62,471	58,624	61,161	82,729	87,825	66,478	94,477	94,618	47,062
2012–13	85,912	115,919	81,251	68,629	60,716	57,043	62,492	81,858	86,649	65,762	94,511	94,659	43,894
2013–14	86,151	116,296	81,747	69,033	60,048	57,334	61,726	82,154	87,192	65,035	94,701	94,863	44,556
2014–15	87,178	118,412	83,001	70,227	60,730	58,633	60,211	83,363	88,459	65,693	95,467	96,058	37,389
Females													
1975–76	61,060	86,668	69,836	57,707	53,652	50,788	60,148	63,001	62,984	63,028	55,610	56,464	43,533
1980–81	54,633	76,390	60,914	50,005	40,584	44,174	56,947	56,483	56,305	56,770	49,379	50,070	37,956
1982–83	56,091	77,697	62,064	50,952	41,239	45,406	57,523	57,613	57,574	57,673	51,727	52,532	38,208
1984–85	58,049	80,164	63,813	52,754	43,327	47,001	58,293	59,447	60,000	58,566	54,122	54,958	39,328
1985–86	59,978	83,198	65,903	54,301	44,015	48,444	59,097	61,550	62,379	60,232	55,513	56,309	40,246
1987–88	62,313	86,568	68,501	56,390	44,870	49,790	60,486	63,775	65,011	61,759	58,476	59,140	43,344
1989–90	63,716	88,842	69,840	57,950	45,331	50,318	60,632	64,859	66,552	62,083	60,858	61,530	44,739
1990–91	63,413	87,887	69,509	57,835	45,127	49,682	60,405	64,436	66,405	61,362	60,724	61,676	39,916
1991–92	64,275	88,399	69,810	58,332	49,444	48,890	61,002	64,731	66,160	62,535	63,066	63,890	42,269
1992–93	63,741	87,606	69,514	58,175	45,999	48,028	59,436	63,693	65,544	60,961	63,866	64,741	41,628
1993–94	64,841	88,616	69,890	58,545	45,543	50,257	62,276	64,937	66,415	62,654	64,589	65,358	42,315
1994–95	65,097	88,993	70,222	58,776	45,747	49,845	61,317	65,378	67,133	62,646	64,371	65,798	35,958
1995–96	65,674	89,336	70,165	58,741	45,865	49,915	62,938	65,673	67,381	62,940	65,674	66,233	46,985
1996–97	66,017	89,602	70,152	58,608	45,902	49,769	63,261	65,989	67,622	63,345	66,090	66,615	45,667
1997–98	66,982	90,673	71,113	59,269	46,842	49,632	63,640	66,797	68,349	64,302	67,467	67,994	45,355
1998–99	68,210	92,397	72,420	60,260	47,686	50,510	64,329	67,960	69,553	65,385	68,863	69,337	45,344
1999–2000	68,500	93,779	72,825	60,629	47,852	51,178	64,121	68,104	70,137	64,785	69,534	69,975	46,067
2001–02	69,946	96,351	74,627	62,192	60,117	52,514	59,773	69,230	71,585	65,467	71,922	72,300	43,726
2002–03	70,317	97,510	75,011	62,877	60,529	52,330	58,811	69,447	71,638	65,915	72,626	72,986	45,873
2003–04	70,431	97,488	75,159	63,196	60,290	52,827	59,164	69,198	71,372	65,615	73,666	74,010	46,926
2004–05	70,285	97,737	75,079	63,159	59,697	52,418	59,091	68,870	71,258	64,902	73,980	74,257	48,511
2005–06	69,775	96,951	74,764	62,920	58,914	52,254	58,485	68,344	70,693	64,325	73,540	73,851	46,132
2006–07	70,741	98,653	75,636	63,737	60,094	52,977	58,911	69,310	71,738	65,073	74,487	74,759	47,651
2007–08	70,820	98,719	75,816	63,849	60,246	53,000	59,071	69,458	71,803	65,198	74,376	74,619	48,822
2008–09	72,371	100,910	77,594	65,368	61,109	54,112	60,255	70,819	73,203	66,370	76,409	76,732	47,790
2009–10	72,779	101,372	77,551	65,517	61,414	54,554	60,285	71,133	73,466	66,664	76,994	77,255	49,022
2010–11	72,231	100,673	77,081	65,181	60,554	53,815	58,862	70,260	72,726	65,508	77,174	77,404	48,728
2011–12	71,210	99,683	75,982	64,236	59,296	53,036	57,513	69,025	71,656	63,877	76,577	76,743	51,359
2012–13	70,715	98,785	75,668	63,756	57,658	52,136	58,084	68,239	70,673	63,196	76,713	76,879	47,475
2013–14	70,868	98,778	75,937	64,062	57,298	52,535	57,330	68,439	71,228	62,531	76,727	76,946	45,095
2014–15	71,943	100,790	77,297	65,225	58,013	53,233	56,508	69,645	72,583	63,164	77,544	78,132	38,841

[1]Constant dollars based on the Consumer Price Index, prepared by the Bureau of Labor Statistics, U.S. Department of Labor, adjusted to an academic-year basis.
NOTE: Data through 1995–96 are for institutions of higher education, while later data are for degree-granting institutions. Degree-granting institutions grant associate's or higher degrees and participate in Title IV federal financial aid programs. Data for 1987–88 and later years include imputations for nonrespondent institutions.

SOURCE: U.S. Department of Education, National Center for Education Statistics, Higher Education General Information Survey (HEGIS), "Faculty Salaries, Tenure, and Fringe Benefits" surveys, 1970–71 through 1985–86; Integrated Postsecondary Education Data System (IPEDS), "Salaries, Tenure, and Fringe Benefits of Full-Time Instructional Faculty Survey" (IPEDS-SA:87–99); and IPEDS, Winter 2001–02 through Winter 2011–12 and Spring 2013 through Spring 2015, Human Resources component, Salaries section. (This table was prepared November 2015.)

Table 316.20. Average salary of full-time instructional faculty on 9-month contracts in degree-granting postsecondary institutions, by academic rank, sex, and control and level of institution: Selected years, 1999–2000 through 2014–15

Academic year, control and level of institution	Constant 2014–15 dollars[1] All faculty, total	Current dollars — All faculty			Current dollars — Academic rank									
		Total	Males	Females	Professor Total	Professor Males	Professor Females	Associate professor Total	Associate professor Males	Associate professor Females	Assistant professor	Instructor	Lecturer	No academic rank
1	2	3	4	5	6	7	8	9	10	11	12	13	14	15
1999–2000														
All institutions	$78,134	$55,888	$60,084	$48,997	$74,410	$76,478	$67,079	$54,524	$55,939	$52,091	$44,978	$34,918	$38,194	$47,389
Public	76,908	55,011	58,984	48,714	72,475	74,501	65,568	54,641	55,992	52,305	45,285	35,007	37,403	47,990
4-year	81,016	57,950	62,030	50,168	75,204	76,530	69,619	55,681	56,776	53,599	45,822	33,528	37,261	40,579
Doctoral[2]	87,032	62,253	66,882	52,287	81,182	82,445	74,653	57,744	58,999	55,156	48,190	33,345	38,883	39,350
Master's[3]	73,779	52,773	55,565	48,235	66,588	67,128	64,863	53,048	53,686	51,977	43,396	33,214	34,448	43,052
Other 4-year	66,920	47,867	49,829	44,577	60,360	60,748	59,052	49,567	50,133	48,548	42,306	35,754	36,088	38,330
2-year	67,442	48,240	50,033	46,340	57,806	59,441	55,501	48,056	49,425	46,711	41,984	37,634	40,061	48,233
Nonprofit	81,326	58,172	62,788	49,881	78,512	80,557	70,609	54,300	55,836	51,687	44,423	34,670	40,761	41,415
4-year	81,680	58,425	63,028	50,117	78,604	80,622	70,774	54,388	55,898	51,809	44,502	34,813	40,783	41,761
Doctoral[2]	100,481	71,873	77,214	59,586	95,182	96,768	87,342	62,503	63,951	59,536	52,134	39,721	42,693	45,887
Master's[3]	69,722	49,871	52,642	45,718	62,539	63,603	59,353	50,176	51,470	48,165	41,447	33,991	37,923	44,153
Other 4-year	65,395	46,776	48,847	43,544	60,200	60,757	58,364	46,822	47,135	46,365	38,775	31,574	33,058	35,120
2-year	52,543	37,583	39,933	34,733	39,454	38,431	40,571	36,349	37,342	35,608	31,818	27,696	25,965	40,373
For-profit	41,303	29,543	30,023	28,942	45,505	44,248	49,693	48,469	53,548	43,389	33,043	29,894	—	27,958
2009–10														
All institutions	81,486	74,620	80,881	66,647	103,682	108,225	92,830	74,125	76,400	71,017	62,245	57,791	52,185	56,803
Public	78,820	72,178	77,948	65,139	99,208	103,746	88,815	73,379	75,687	70,256	62,160	59,310	50,228	55,864
4-year	83,153	76,147	82,423	67,276	103,948	107,191	95,048	75,251	77,282	72,298	63,442	46,028	50,104	54,005
Doctoral[2]	89,381	81,850	89,186	70,307	113,063	115,829	103,793	78,539	80,830	74,963	66,902	44,406	50,313	53,135
Master's[3]	74,522	68,243	71,574	64,239	87,917	88,929	85,883	70,332	71,340	69,036	59,396	44,422	49,746	55,765
Other 4-year	66,834	61,202	63,678	58,349	76,448	79,143	72,073	65,003	66,297	63,338	55,055	54,050	49,432	54,487
2-year	67,993	62,264	63,697	61,047	72,377	74,423	70,429	60,632	61,565	59,852	54,161	65,503	53,548	56,239
Nonprofit	88,002	80,587	87,600	70,676	112,146	116,401	101,119	75,565	77,764	72,502	62,395	47,842	57,508	62,242
4-year	88,167	80,738	87,720	70,834	112,252	116,472	101,290	75,664	77,827	72,642	62,465	47,885	57,520	62,542
Doctoral[2]	104,265	95,480	104,514	80,888	134,776	138,354	123,283	85,864	88,699	81,499	71,973	53,825	58,932	66,634
Master's[3]	71,828	65,776	68,776	62,128	82,516	84,062	79,452	66,524	67,508	65,309	55,469	45,305	53,637	60,591
Other 4-year	70,560	64,614	67,178	61,326	84,869	85,528	83,480	64,747	64,949	64,478	53,130	42,145	52,422	52,775
2-year	49,939	45,731	44,417	46,529	53,063	55,046	51,310	45,768	45,863	45,717	42,706	46,010	32,393	43,562
For-profit	59,888	54,842	56,689	52,925	79,574	81,765	75,817	71,376	72,429	70,199	66,027	41,742	‡	53,705
2013–14														
All institutions	79,198	78,625	85,528	70,355	109,905	115,455	98,064	78,593	81,156	75,388	66,025	58,080	54,238	58,902
Public	75,789	75,241	81,560	67,944	103,587	109,118	92,281	77,106	79,760	73,783	65,659	59,742	51,923	57,233
4-year	80,292	79,711	86,562	70,713	109,541	113,579	99,646	79,151	81,495	76,009	67,387	48,816	52,055	56,528
Doctoral[2]	86,476	85,851	93,677	74,675	118,814	122,452	108,523	83,032	85,507	79,550	71,429	47,822	53,262	56,347
Master's[3]	69,238	68,737	72,067	64,971	87,794	88,863	85,847	71,355	72,678	69,750	61,117	46,288	48,785	55,818
Other 4-year	61,590	61,145	63,227	58,992	74,333	76,927	70,634	66,053	67,918	63,892	56,116	56,123	47,437	57,110
2-year	63,658	63,198	64,564	62,079	72,737	74,264	71,377	62,258	63,168	61,557	55,423	65,524	48,222	57,498
Nonprofit	87,409	86,777	94,498	76,659	121,995	127,064	110,208	81,478	83,869	78,493	66,690	48,088	60,506	70,174
4-year	87,490	86,858	94,572	76,733	122,042	127,097	110,278	81,494	83,882	78,510	66,719	48,005	60,506	70,411
Doctoral[2]	102,425	101,684	111,792	86,884	146,366	151,239	132,794	92,201	95,342	88,010	75,760	51,412	61,601	74,456
Master's[3]	70,145	69,638	72,555	66,299	86,082	87,087	84,255	70,658	71,961	69,164	59,093	48,322	56,837	69,934
Other 4-year	69,796	69,292	71,765	66,384	90,780	91,178	90,028	69,880	70,079	69,641	57,103	41,388	58,445	56,004
2-year	51,160	50,790	47,259	53,092	51,307	49,960	52,415	59,231	47,530	63,689	41,799	52,227	—	49,582
For-profit	51,093	50,723	52,553	49,176	65,002	65,902	63,875	66,921	68,784	65,184	63,354	42,292	62,743	37,673
2014–15														
All institutions	80,203	80,203	87,178	71,943	112,697	118,412	100,790	80,438	83,001	77,297	67,677	59,211	55,610	58,201
Public	76,963	76,963	83,363	69,645	106,474	112,178	95,084	79,068	81,723	75,814	67,510	60,958	53,171	56,882
4-year	81,527	81,527	88,459	72,583	112,384	116,600	102,397	81,188	83,555	78,094	69,399	49,781	53,235	55,955
Doctoral[2]	87,174	87,174	95,158	76,073	121,703	125,480	111,345	84,740	87,352	81,175	73,284	48,553	53,948	55,379
Master's[3]	71,467	71,467	74,791	67,721	91,025	92,314	88,774	73,921	74,984	72,638	63,226	47,174	51,130	51,478
Other 4-year	63,020	63,020	65,252	60,733	77,827	80,664	73,730	68,333	70,131	66,386	58,116	56,695	51,964	57,848
2-year	64,304	64,304	65,693	63,164	74,831	76,675	73,204	63,896	64,692	63,282	56,667	66,791	51,696	57,230
Nonprofit	88,246	88,246	96,100	78,110	124,537	129,826	112,576	83,161	85,544	80,233	68,026	48,602	62,544	67,947
4-year	88,661	88,661	96,513	78,505	124,598	129,878	112,647	83,171	85,549	80,247	68,059	50,423	63,928	68,209
Doctoral[2]	103,587	103,587	113,743	88,984	149,557	154,775	135,574	93,935	96,951	89,982	77,580	54,408	65,543	70,911
Master's[3]	70,912	70,912	73,847	67,544	87,310	88,150	85,774	71,700	72,897	70,323	59,946	49,300	57,570	69,797
Other 4-year	70,023	70,023	72,649	67,061	92,167	92,881	90,893	70,581	70,963	70,147	57,437	43,853	59,224	57,552
2-year	24,824	24,824	21,204	28,094	53,597	51,613	56,021	47,930	41,621	50,033	45,975	23,163	10,199	47,971
For-profit	49,948	49,948	50,770	49,195	67,647	65,843	70,788	66,768	66,233	67,262	60,978	43,524	70,788	45,996

—Not available.

‡Reporting standards not met (too few cases).

[1]Constant dollars based on the Consumer Price Index, prepared by the Bureau of Labor Statistics, U.S. Department of Labor, adjusted to an academic-year basis.

[2]Institutions that awarded 20 or more doctor's degrees during the previous academic year.

[3]Institutions that awarded 20 or more master's degrees, but less than 20 doctor's degrees, during the previous academic year.

NOTE: Degree-granting institutions grant associate's or higher degrees and participate in Title IV federal financial aid programs.

SOURCE: U.S. Department of Education, National Center for Education Statistics, Integrated Postsecondary Education Data System (IPEDS), "Salaries, Tenure, and Fringe Benefits of Full-Time Instructional Faculty Survey" (IPEDS-SA:99); and IPEDS, Winter 2009–10 and Spring 2013 through Spring 2015, Human Resources component, Salaries section. (This table was prepared November 2015.)

Table 316.30. Average salary of full-time instructional faculty on 9-month contracts in degree-granting postsecondary institutions, by control and level of institution and state or jurisdiction: 2014–15

[In current dollars]

State or jurisdiction	All institutions	Public institutions						Nonprofit institutions						For-profit institutions
		Total	4-year institutions				2-year	Total	4-year institutions				2-year	
			Total	Doctoral[1]	Master's[2]	Other			Total	Doctoral[1]	Master's[2]	Other		
1	2	3	4	5	6	7	8	9	10	11	12	13	14	15
United States	$80,203	$76,963	$81,527	$87,174	$71,467	$63,020	$64,304	$88,246	$88,661	$103,587	$70,912	$70,023	$24,824	$49,948
Alabama	68,645	69,968	76,223	83,107	62,522	68,764	53,185	61,408	61,408	75,302	49,298	49,145	†	‡
Alaska	77,679	78,727	78,905	82,390	76,662	†	65,616	51,007	50,774	†	52,329	‡	‡	†
Arizona	81,138	82,568	85,269	86,600	74,523	51,909	75,872	64,203	64,203	†	45,348	76,909	†	49,935
Arkansas	58,886	59,092	64,240	68,787	53,784	59,516	45,035	57,945	58,217	65,248	59,985	53,757	28,193	17,894
California	94,099	90,833	97,637	109,686	76,502	74,420	82,453	106,818	106,818	116,505	83,693	92,586	†	54,712
Colorado	76,469	75,171	79,544	84,995	61,192	71,223	51,598	86,354	86,354	89,116	83,643	69,109	†	30,609
Connecticut	99,655	92,615	98,488	109,408	87,202	†	74,805	107,143	107,143	114,011	94,278	84,580	†	49,737
Delaware	94,034	95,171	102,378	109,361	63,896	†	64,342	80,725	82,122	128,368	62,853	†	53,000	†
District of Columbia	92,005	80,551	80,551	123,188	76,597	†	†	92,727	103,862	104,751	51,645	‡	9,000	‡
Florida	75,397	74,363	75,053	85,139	76,996	59,322	51,986	79,499	79,499	92,234	69,812	61,861	†	56,733
Georgia	72,174	71,069	72,501	79,669	60,266	54,631	45,891	75,956	75,998	92,989	65,981	60,617	30,863	39,010
Hawaii	82,085	83,443	90,127	92,369	†	71,801	69,005	77,853	77,853	†	76,529	88,571	†	49,377
Idaho	61,190	61,651	64,716	66,090	†	50,302	49,331	56,110	56,110	†	52,445	59,458	†	†
Illinois	84,644	79,199	83,276	86,735	69,733	†	72,196	92,302	92,364	108,860	67,652	62,160	36,028	46,041
Indiana	77,163	76,090	81,412	87,618	64,221	53,980	44,347	79,330	79,330	95,068	61,653	70,125	†	†
Iowa	73,926	79,571	90,103	90,103	†	†	57,538	64,383	64,383	72,855	57,111	64,819	†	47,087
Kansas	65,541	67,908	74,892	79,536	60,086	56,169	51,418	50,635	50,802	†	54,753	43,759	46,291	†
Kentucky	64,467	65,720	71,297	72,730	60,627	†	50,656	59,322	59,322	64,680	52,918	61,166	†	68,328
Louisiana	65,488	61,820	66,665	75,204	55,128	47,303	43,592	81,613	81,613	88,661	57,219	58,552	†	36,642
Maine	76,590	72,552	78,621	85,336	†	62,107	54,915	82,337	82,862	67,610	55,207	93,557	56,734	†
Maryland	80,705	80,640	86,123	90,336	72,436	†	68,829	81,098	81,098	90,007	69,746	71,413	†	21,113
Massachusetts	101,455	83,509	90,595	99,032	77,208	†	63,881	110,387	110,392	126,523	84,792	87,530	‡	67,961
Michigan	84,815	87,787	89,732	91,803	75,245	62,673	78,100	66,150	66,150	78,789	64,200	64,873	†	23,494
Minnesota	75,158	75,527	81,908	99,372	71,079	60,454	64,939	74,326	74,326	75,957	67,698	76,284	†	‡
Mississippi	60,032	60,531	66,364	68,713	55,524	†	51,515	56,000	56,000	61,883	57,166	43,687	†	†
Missouri	72,164	67,911	72,000	79,725	61,380	49,419	54,513	79,628	79,704	97,441	61,226	54,053	66,019	51,351
Montana	62,092	66,078	68,488	72,750	59,817	54,772	48,706	42,229	53,232	†	52,803	53,505	13,986	†
Nebraska	71,189	73,056	77,212	82,632	63,375	†	58,941	65,214	65,359	81,555	56,845	55,590	47,847	†
Nevada	82,388	83,269	84,227	90,469	†	69,061	71,469	57,688	57,688	†	57,688	†	†	39,949
New Hampshire	90,149	85,546	92,225	102,219	77,492	88,434	62,811	96,854	96,854	130,855	67,569	70,786	†	†
New Jersey	99,818	96,904	105,652	108,600	98,428	†	73,046	107,288	107,288	124,832	81,703	69,498	†	29,459
New Mexico	65,704	65,449	71,606	77,205	60,744	47,903	51,364	83,973	83,973	†	83,973	†	†	64,025
New York	92,094	81,856	86,878	101,185	83,619	72,171	71,256	101,991	102,052	112,123	78,125	84,421	64,992	39,984
North Carolina	73,083	68,012	78,000	81,657	68,236	69,732	49,357	86,299	86,538	109,027	61,176	59,648	39,340	97,857
North Dakota	66,832	69,110	70,881	77,883	59,302	54,309	54,743	43,241	43,241	25,628	†	44,778	†	†
Ohio	75,089	76,531	80,326	82,726	57,948	64,634	61,880	72,067	72,067	79,140	65,822	72,160	†	42,872
Oklahoma	67,003	66,808	70,743	76,111	62,460	50,531	49,835	68,166	68,166	80,129	57,938	38,478	†	16,245
Oregon	74,060	73,916	76,698	80,253	59,525	65,674	68,435	75,072	75,072	77,993	65,679	79,946	†	50,525
Pennsylvania	86,531	83,650	87,326	94,343	83,884	70,986	63,666	89,859	90,319	102,248	73,434	79,000	47,351	45,270
Rhode Island	94,306	74,350	78,725	84,445	67,705	†	60,577	108,217	108,217	131,442	92,433	†	†	†
South Carolina	66,617	69,181	77,968	90,361	68,235	57,172	51,045	58,274	58,402	68,716	60,021	54,022	51,029	47,241
South Dakota	61,922	63,487	66,755	67,382	68,684	47,724	49,144	54,435	54,435	†	53,410	55,311	†	†
Tennessee	70,602	67,134	72,563	74,176	60,819	†	49,359	77,794	77,794	99,662	57,246	55,084	†	23,459
Texas	74,985	72,842	80,009	83,949	65,285	55,368	57,115	85,616	85,753	98,340	67,396	56,791	33,887	32,028
Utah	69,170	69,021	70,969	79,663	64,904	66,216	51,404	78,643	79,107	92,464	74,849	†	54,193	27,761
Vermont	77,274	78,025	78,025	88,044	56,627	56,242	†	76,579	76,579	†	80,045	54,741	†	†
Virginia	73,443	79,044	84,100	87,458	67,473	70,147	60,785	60,414	60,405	59,903	57,700	63,592	62,640	32,714
Washington	73,684	73,456	78,385	90,704	75,618	56,149	57,082	74,654	74,684	81,483	62,626	69,977	‡	65,144
West Virginia	63,622	65,457	68,347	75,849	58,845	55,994	47,660	51,143	51,143	55,234	50,650	48,420	†	13,521
Wisconsin	71,756	72,881	74,883	85,416	61,487	92,876	68,325	67,481	67,481	76,060	62,526	60,178	†	‡
Wyoming	70,883	71,387	82,753	82,753	†	†	58,577	†	†	†	†	†	†	57,967
U.S. Service Academies	107,888	107,888	107,888	†	†	107,888	†	†	†	†	†	†	†	†
Other jurisdictions	46,595	52,762	56,908	51,332	65,017	54,439	34,538	29,473	28,986	27,182	34,711	25,905	48,587	18,102
American Samoa	32,891	32,891	32,891	†	†	32,891	†	†	†	†	†	†	†	†
Federated States of Micronesia	26,907	26,907	†	†	†	†	26,907	†	†	†	†	†	†	†
Guam	62,781	62,781	66,547	†	66,547	†	54,355	†	†	†	†	†	†	†
Marshall Islands	†	†	†	†	†	†	†	†	†	†	†	†	†	†
Northern Marianas	42,447	42,447	42,447	†	†	42,447	†	†	†	†	†	†	†	†
Palau	†	†	†	†	†	†	†	†	†	†	†	†	†	†
Puerto Rico	44,418	54,267	56,853	51,332	59,826	58,731	24,964	29,473	28,986	27,182	34,711	25,905	48,587	18,102
U.S. Virgin Islands	63,436	63,436	63,436	†	63,436	†	†	†	†	†	†	†	†	†

†Not applicable.
‡Reporting standards not met (too few cases).
[1]Institutions that awarded 20 or more doctor's degrees during the previous academic year.
[2]Institutions that awarded 20 or more master's degrees, but less than 20 doctor's degrees, during the previous academic year.

NOTE: Degree-granting institutions grant associate's or higher degrees and participate in Title IV federal financial aid programs. Data include imputations for nonrespondent institutions. SOURCE: U.S. Department of Education, National Center for Education Statistics, Integrated Postsecondary Education Data System (IPEDS), Spring 2015, Human Resources component, Salaries section. (This table was prepared November 2015.)

Table 316.40. Average salary of full-time instructional faculty on 9-month contracts in degree-granting postsecondary institutions, by control and level of institution and state or jurisdiction: 2013–14

[In current dollars]

State or jurisdiction	All institutions	Public institutions						Nonprofit institutions						For-profit institutions
		Total	4-year institutions				2-year	Total	4-year institutions				2-year	
			Total	Doctoral[1]	Master's[2]	Other			Total	Doctoral[1]	Master's[2]	Other		
1	2	3	4	5	6	7	8	9	10	11	12	13	14	15
United States	$78,625	$75,241	$79,711	$85,851	$68,737	$61,145	$63,198	$86,777	$86,858	$101,684	$69,638	$69,292	$50,790	$50,723
Alabama	68,313	69,940	75,867	82,746	61,849	69,235	53,485	59,521	59,521	67,352	49,570	52,501	†	46,671
Alaska	75,825	77,107	77,241	79,790	75,604	†	63,167	47,232	46,832	†	46,832	†	53,100	†
Arizona	79,704	80,700	84,601	86,015	72,859	52,000	70,427	60,815	60,815	†	44,027	74,123	†	55,089
Arkansas	58,545	58,690	63,998	67,494	56,122	59,024	44,534	57,893	58,059	64,367	58,590	53,222	39,794	26,072
California	92,595	89,323	95,543	104,868	76,652	74,236	81,984	104,090	104,090	113,411	80,409	91,977	†	48,720
Colorado	75,433	73,887	78,927	83,950	58,625	66,621	49,460	86,028	86,028	88,732	84,169	65,605	†	37,519
Connecticut	96,841	89,490	95,260	106,016	84,040	†	71,797	105,659	105,659	115,867	87,779	82,464	†	60,632
Delaware	93,436	94,561	101,103	107,228	66,484	†	67,071	81,007	81,007	124,890	63,749	†	†	‡
District of Columbia	101,098	82,058	82,058	130,900	77,748	†	†	102,838	102,838	104,016	57,683	†	†	66,982
Florida	73,391	72,214	73,105	82,035	73,464	59,019	51,845	77,691	77,691	90,193	68,091	60,171	†	52,434
Georgia	69,731	68,128	70,315	80,532	59,901	54,144	45,774	74,551	74,566	91,619	63,930	60,166	‡	52,611
Hawaii	80,704	81,530	87,697	89,490	†	71,297	67,597	77,288	77,288	†	75,547	92,747	†	26,173
Idaho	60,003	60,565	63,358	65,636	63,009	50,099	49,944	54,130	54,130	†	52,475	55,648	†	21,256
Illinois	83,057	77,299	80,547	83,623	68,636	†	71,408	91,623	91,623	108,452	69,077	62,098	†	42,079
Indiana	75,527	74,623	79,608	86,037	62,620	54,756	44,771	77,448	77,448	92,602	57,370	67,935	†	26,696
Iowa	71,252	77,111	86,432	86,432	†	†	55,595	62,482	62,482	71,038	55,253	62,382	†	52,587
Kansas	64,913	67,074	73,773	78,241	58,703	65,036	51,277	50,366	50,544	51,820	54,895	44,352	45,549	54,350
Kentucky	63,504	65,155	70,668	80,213	60,996	†	50,638	57,284	57,284	60,391	51,384	61,255	†	63,212
Louisiana	64,609	60,795	65,632	71,748	55,351	46,680	43,171	80,574	80,574	87,988	55,946	52,558	†	22,588
Maine	73,444	68,244	72,598	78,421	†	58,292	54,175	81,018	81,555	66,502	54,460	92,003	53,872	†
Maryland	78,110	75,111	78,952	82,851	67,271	†	67,659	88,252	88,252	101,246	72,987	68,875	†	53,901
Massachusetts	99,515	83,192	90,012	98,953	76,139	†	62,587	107,415	107,415	121,536	84,011	86,814	†	62,966
Michigan	83,540	86,485	88,240	90,192	73,606	62,652	77,156	65,983	65,983	79,801	60,614	66,742	†	22,231
Minnesota	74,191	73,933	80,996	98,117	70,805	58,729	62,292	74,966	74,966	78,369	65,343	78,628	†	39,273
Mississippi	58,187	58,405	64,236	66,473	54,108	†	50,716	56,141	56,141	63,890	59,498	41,952	†	48,391
Missouri	70,919	66,367	70,124	77,228	60,228	48,114	53,223	79,194	79,194	97,590	60,493	52,078	†	48,961
Montana	67,559	70,426	73,540	80,743	58,159	47,290	47,137	49,711	50,889	†	52,612	50,318	36,377	†
Nebraska	71,781	73,790	79,367	85,275	62,930	†	54,285	65,147	65,325	83,515	56,184	54,862	48,600	‡
Nevada	78,430	78,942	80,302	87,844	†	62,300	63,526	60,778	60,778	†	60,778	†	†	29,060
New Hampshire	87,923	82,736	90,191	99,633	76,648	87,700	60,256	95,523	95,523	127,250	67,712	68,627	†	†
New Jersey	98,143	96,043	104,976	112,869	95,775	†	72,488	104,231	104,231	123,769	79,384	73,436	†	50,244
New Mexico	63,318	63,732	70,792	77,237	58,076	45,795	47,613	†	†	†	†	†	†	41,546
New York	91,351	77,324	80,861	98,441	70,523	63,620	70,245	99,455	99,529	110,395	78,344	83,461	71,247	44,359
North Carolina	71,647	67,344	77,902	83,071	68,288	66,680	48,668	83,536	83,790	105,279	54,895	60,458	40,288	82,317
North Dakota	64,948	67,026	68,787	75,004	59,797	52,753	53,401	51,845	51,845	55,421	†	49,453	†	†
Ohio	72,993	74,880	78,742	81,222	57,129	62,560	60,622	69,266	69,266	78,140	63,377	66,700	†	52,855
Oklahoma	64,838	64,799	68,585	75,042	58,802	50,232	49,418	65,258	65,258	78,413	55,338	36,484	†	19,154
Oregon	71,791	71,201	73,660	77,837	58,233	60,922	66,793	73,870	73,870	76,948	64,037	78,730	†	20,455
Pennsylvania	84,832	81,610	84,946	91,998	81,477	68,810	63,764	88,820	89,147	102,294	71,102	80,143	46,434	39,154
Rhode Island	91,302	72,670	76,642	81,049	68,424	†	†	104,135	104,135	126,375	88,606	†	†	†
South Carolina	64,711	66,536	75,472	85,691	67,408	54,527	47,828	58,327	58,450	†	60,949	55,034	51,714	51,829
South Dakota	60,294	61,813	64,768	65,421	66,442	47,352	47,557	53,403	53,403	†	53,478	53,365	†	44,871
Tennessee	69,840	66,808	72,217	74,187	64,007	†	49,373	76,513	76,513	96,160	56,356	54,749	†	41,899
Texas	74,014	72,052	79,175	83,577	65,113	55,910	56,722	83,539	83,658	94,400	66,882	56,440	37,333	38,458
Utah	68,825	69,696	71,728	82,142	62,892	55,327	50,470	61,433	61,522	92,503	53,277	†	56,752	24,780
Vermont	76,077	76,792	76,792	86,208	57,010	56,621	†	75,414	75,414	†	78,937	54,114	†	†
Virginia	72,630	77,966	83,246	87,570	67,820	66,036	60,252	60,530	60,518	60,776	55,606	62,049	63,231	44,359
Washington	71,189	70,358	76,536	85,265	72,073	55,679	56,579	74,194	74,194	80,125	62,286	72,560	†	65,634
West Virginia	62,353	64,027	66,891	74,075	58,823	54,548	47,114	50,069	50,069	53,246	50,177	47,589	†	‡
Wisconsin	71,855	73,431	72,945	83,115	59,835	92,630	74,607	66,136	66,136	74,741	60,782	59,323	†	36,560
Wyoming	70,158	70,181	80,027	80,027	†	†	58,862	‡	‡	†	†	†	‡	†
U.S. Service Academies	101,488	101,488	101,488	†	†	101,488	†	†	†	†	†	†	†	†
Other jurisdictions	44,440	51,872	56,515	51,248	65,393	53,041	32,910	25,996	25,996	33,728	33,767	20,267	†	21,281
American Samoa	25,503	25,503	25,503	†	†	25,503	†	†	†	†	†	†	†	†
Federated States of Micronesia	24,590	24,590	†	†	†	†	24,590	†	†	†	†	†	†	†
Guam	61,982	61,982	65,773	†	65,773	†	53,091	†	†	†	†	†	†	†
Marshall Islands	†	†	†	†	†	†	†	†	†	†	†	†	†	†
Northern Marianas	42,028	42,028	42,028	†	†	42,028	†	†	†	†	†	†	†	†
Palau	†	†	†	†	†	†	†	†	†	†	†	†	†	†
Puerto Rico	41,968	55,047	57,680	51,248	†	59,367	25,059	25,996	25,996	33,728	33,767	20,267	†	21,281
U.S. Virgin Islands	64,918	64,918	64,918	†	64,918	†	†	†	†	†	†	†	†	†

†Not applicable.
‡Reporting standards not met (too few cases).
[1]Institutions that awarded 20 or more doctor's degrees during the previous academic year.
[2]Institutions that awarded 20 or more master's degrees, but less than 20 doctor's degrees, during the previous academic year.

NOTE: Degree-granting institutions grant associate's or higher degrees and participate in Title IV federal financial aid programs. Data include imputations for nonrespondent institutions.
SOURCE: U.S. Department of Education, National Center for Education Statistics, Integrated Postsecondary Education Data System (IPEDS), Spring 2014, Human Resources component, Salaries section. (This table was prepared February 2015.)

Table 316.50. Average salary of full-time instructional faculty on 9-month contracts in 4-year degree-granting postsecondary institutions, by control and classification of institution, academic rank of faculty, and state or jurisdiction: 2014–15

[In current dollars]

State or jurisdiction	Public doctoral[1]			Public master's[2]			Nonprofit doctoral[1]			Nonprofit master's[2]		
	Professor	Associate professor	Assistant professor	Professor	Associate professor	Assistant professor	Professor	Associate professor	Assistant professor	Professor	Associate professor	Assistant professor
1	2	3	4	5	6	7	8	9	10	11	12	13
United States	$121,703	$84,740	$73,284	$91,025	$73,921	$63,226	$149,557	$93,935	$77,580	$87,310	$71,700	$59,946
Alabama	120,615	83,192	68,986	79,783	66,346	57,854	81,319	71,201	65,152	60,732	51,763	45,368
Alaska	106,721	84,932	68,928	105,035	81,494	67,505	†	†	†	58,050	56,843	44,961
Arizona	126,064	86,334	74,984	115,551	87,543	78,780	†	†	†	51,791	47,664	48,874
Arkansas	97,262	73,399	65,578	71,002	59,232	51,626	79,132	66,915	60,312	66,723	62,828	54,063
California	142,154	92,562	83,933	91,297	75,276	69,731	157,411	100,512	87,633	103,633	80,556	68,652
Colorado	117,632	87,687	76,391	78,027	64,025	56,725	128,979	90,316	79,512	112,079	80,535	64,560
Connecticut	148,152	99,675	80,479	102,625	83,564	67,297	165,781	89,769	80,293	130,117	92,286	76,681
Delaware	143,824	100,736	85,424	80,845	68,477	54,520	155,301	122,560	‡	74,623	66,564	54,545
District of Columbia	139,420	118,450	94,673	102,609	75,252	61,765	150,218	98,130	82,458	36,103	72,747	60,420
Florida	117,432	82,969	73,912	124,213	85,380	64,999	128,360	87,161	73,392	90,741	74,565	61,071
Georgia	112,413	80,098	68,660	77,113	63,917	56,475	132,761	86,126	70,273	74,930	61,264	52,162
Hawaii	119,253	88,987	77,610	†	†	†	†	†	†	87,800	84,756	69,679
Idaho	87,371	69,222	60,053	†	†	†	†	†	†	60,802	53,785	47,362
Illinois	124,118	85,525	78,561	95,041	74,793	64,737	163,584	95,456	84,638	80,989	69,352	58,509
Indiana	122,173	86,048	74,633	87,760	68,879	60,379	140,001	89,521	73,492	75,705	62,929	53,522
Iowa	121,109	86,190	76,458	†	†	†	92,784	71,310	60,714	68,220	58,029	53,156
Kansas	112,453	78,007	67,283	75,776	61,185	59,308	†	†	†	63,695	55,788	50,433
Kentucky	102,581	73,032	64,063	79,776	64,925	55,947	78,398	62,766	57,100	62,049	54,261	47,098
Louisiana	101,360	74,834	68,614	72,796	60,623	50,318	126,654	84,581	72,855	62,121	57,053	54,270
Maine	106,550	82,239	63,696	†	†	†	87,972	75,778	68,184	70,834	56,707	49,421
Maryland	124,781	91,513	91,100	92,029	74,697	67,197	135,363	87,039	77,875	86,981	70,706	60,693
Massachusetts	133,659	98,527	82,800	91,564	73,805	64,881	174,766	109,314	93,231	100,709	86,905	69,213
Michigan	124,805	87,566	73,733	92,142	79,195	64,653	100,525	78,665	64,547	74,399	62,698	57,392
Minnesota	131,933	92,060	80,948	84,943	71,137	61,134	98,170	76,181	61,338	78,412	66,723	58,819
Mississippi	96,772	74,846	67,232	68,398	57,782	53,741	74,703	68,787	55,750	73,171	58,734	55,353
Missouri	105,730	76,051	65,098	77,630	62,921	53,511	140,395	88,772	76,671	76,471	63,630	52,065
Montana	90,218	71,308	66,387	75,976	68,391	56,534	†	†	†	60,999	51,484	48,140
Nebraska	109,128	82,087	73,136	79,565	63,360	52,888	103,301	81,448	67,633	65,378	57,006	51,870
Nevada	121,793	88,460	71,075	†	†	†	†	†	†	73,157	66,686	51,840
New Hampshire	123,880	95,734	78,792	90,844	75,680	62,512	164,481	106,458	74,330	82,556	69,743	59,140
New Jersey	147,764	101,896	80,693	122,407	97,032	79,822	178,675	97,242	87,567	100,705	85,612	67,347
New Mexico	102,364	75,590	68,533	74,373	62,966	54,569	†	†	†	†	†	†
New York	135,330	94,964	79,050	106,808	82,102	70,356	158,765	101,492	83,859	96,081	76,983	66,643
North Carolina	117,789	80,958	71,797	88,449	69,808	63,170	158,316	95,485	78,073	75,100	63,116	57,228
North Dakota	106,104	81,431	67,075	79,176	64,920	54,363	†	‡	21,301	†	†	†
Ohio	113,660	81,341	70,251	73,059	63,424	53,601	110,879	76,411	65,410	78,643	67,367	56,313
Oklahoma	107,969	75,966	67,373	79,561	66,917	56,726	101,123	73,340	71,717	68,340	59,655	52,044
Oregon	113,524	85,167	75,019	75,338	60,433	49,559	100,720	76,942	63,248	76,544	70,346	58,967
Pennsylvania	136,477	93,478	72,799	108,525	87,534	70,462	148,347	94,417	81,269	93,412	74,065	62,525
Rhode Island	108,353	80,039	73,127	77,387	66,023	57,152	166,274	110,863	91,739	119,124	92,546	74,579
South Carolina	126,492	88,590	79,129	86,671	69,649	60,965	72,514	66,605	64,249	74,406	59,739	53,205
South Dakota	90,489	71,132	65,096	85,549	72,718	62,415	†	†	†	59,895	56,298	51,026
Tennessee	100,290	75,048	63,851	74,904	62,550	54,409	138,351	89,852	74,172	71,204	56,747	49,844
Texas	122,683	84,319	72,045	88,089	72,689	62,599	134,060	91,986	80,810	84,754	69,161	58,326
Utah	105,748	77,010	66,084	80,725	66,964	59,726	117,391	85,497	70,580	90,182	75,885	60,473
Vermont	118,736	88,571	72,597	70,723	52,775	44,060	†	†	†	101,829	75,967	67,687
Virginia	123,255	84,990	71,802	86,755	70,775	61,183	113,154	81,654	44,778	71,505	58,095	50,246
Washington	120,986	88,680	82,968	94,250	79,908	73,376	110,196	82,424	66,804	79,341	65,816	58,715
West Virginia	99,242	76,987	65,455	70,123	62,826	53,397	67,180	58,505	52,903	65,009	54,346	45,668
Wisconsin	110,888	79,077	72,873	74,227	62,742	60,252	103,884	77,330	67,402	76,069	64,534	55,592
Wyoming	112,269	79,174	72,412	†	†	†	†	†	†	†	†	†
U.S. Service Academies	†	†	†	†	†	†	†	†	†	†	†	†
Other jurisdictions	‡	‡	53,510	84,892	68,061	52,247	†	†	‡	†	†	38,771
American Samoa	†	†	†	†	†	†	†	†	†	†	†	†
Federated States of Micronesia	†	†	†	†	†	†	†	†	†	†	†	†
Guam	†	†	†	89,059	70,570	54,299	†	†	†	†	†	†
Marshall Islands	†	†	†	†	†	†	†	†	†	†	†	†
Northern Marianas	†	†	†	†	†	†	†	†	†	†	†	†
Palau	†	†	†	†	†	†	†	†	†	†	†	†
Puerto Rico	‡	‡	53,510	71,880	†	47,771	†	†	‡	†	†	38,771
U.S. Virgin Islands	†	†	†	81,906	64,446	50,873	†	†	†	†	†	†

†Not applicable.
‡Reporting standards not met (too few cases).
[1]Institutions that awarded 20 or more doctor's degrees during the previous academic year.
[2]Institutions that awarded 20 or more master's degrees, but less than 20 doctor's degrees, during the previous academic year.

NOTE: Degree-granting institutions grant associate's or higher degrees and participate in Title IV federal financial aid programs. Data include imputations for nonrespondent institutions.
SOURCE: U.S. Department of Education, National Center for Education Statistics, Integrated Postsecondary Education Data System (IPEDS), Spring 2015, Human Resources component, Salaries section. (This table was prepared November 2015.)

Table 316.60. Average salary of full-time instructional faculty on 9-month contracts in 4-year degree-granting postsecondary institutions, by control and classification of institution, academic rank of faculty, and state or jurisdiction: 2013–14

[In current dollars]

State or jurisdiction	Public doctoral[1]			Public master's[2]			Nonprofit doctoral[1]			Nonprofit master's[2]		
	Professor	Associate professor	Assistant professor	Professor	Associate professor	Assistant professor	Professor	Associate professor	Assistant professor	Professor	Associate professor	Assistant professor
1	2	3	4	5	6	7	8	9	10	11	12	13
United States	**$118,814**	**$83,032**	**$71,429**	**$87,794**	**$71,355**	**$61,117**	**$146,366**	**$92,201**	**$75,760**	**$86,082**	**$70,658**	**$59,093**
Alabama	120,171	82,219	67,589	79,379	65,427	56,602	78,054	70,300	64,203	61,765	52,132	45,072
Alaska	109,585	81,809	67,816	103,962	79,374	67,277	†	†	†	56,199	50,257	40,222
Arizona	122,633	84,611	72,855	108,007	87,134	76,232	†	†	†	47,223	46,653	‡
Arkansas	95,715	71,017	64,091	69,597	63,398	52,041	77,736	64,875	58,985	65,071	60,709	51,911
California	134,141	88,510	80,199	91,680	74,486	68,541	151,728	99,315	85,001	96,894	78,738	67,968
Colorado	115,045	86,038	73,725	74,413	60,769	52,950	128,374	88,148	77,542	114,541	77,390	62,009
Connecticut	143,133	96,782	77,513	99,139	79,766	64,916	168,263	90,295	79,538	110,606	88,178	72,678
Delaware	142,243	98,352	83,489	76,891	66,542	62,998	151,213	121,916	‡	74,786	64,894	52,705
District of Columbia	149,350	118,450	‡	101,722	76,412	60,670	147,825	96,840	80,391	54,468	66,144	55,257
Florida	112,847	79,427	71,590	120,486	80,434	63,063	124,248	85,140	72,159	88,398	72,506	59,356
Georgia	110,723	78,950	68,914	78,092	63,902	55,815	130,293	82,692	69,005	71,679	60,826	51,587
Hawaii	114,168	86,568	76,287	†	†	†	†	†	†	94,327	80,634	71,059
Idaho	86,027	68,827	58,098	80,115	66,870	59,134	†	†	†	62,147	52,516	47,246
Illinois	119,266	82,356	71,901	93,463	73,687	64,301	163,620	94,672	83,680	85,792	69,406	58,658
Indiana	120,474	84,291	72,214	86,706	67,833	59,260	133,263	84,648	72,962	68,867	57,919	50,724
Iowa	114,915	83,226	72,263	†	†	†	88,775	68,268	61,216	66,686	57,284	50,868
Kansas	108,316	76,570	65,552	73,860	59,352	57,101	63,306	50,976	44,808	63,249	55,811	51,586
Kentucky	110,940	78,327	68,521	80,596	64,493	56,049	72,804	58,263	52,667	61,525	53,673	44,658
Louisiana	99,791	73,612	64,623	72,201	59,938	52,102	126,491	85,308	71,930	65,293	55,272	53,617
Maine	96,483	75,485	60,954	†	†	†	89,097	75,414	65,492	71,541	55,422	49,110
Maryland	116,268	84,878	74,052	85,468	68,340	62,645	147,555	92,859	81,292	82,680	71,958	68,483
Massachusetts	131,921	97,748	81,821	90,261	72,469	64,116	167,977	103,996	88,668	103,175	85,515	67,167
Michigan	121,637	85,385	72,714	96,096	80,159	64,515	102,047	79,122	64,460	71,147	59,950	55,548
Minnesota	128,943	89,749	78,605	85,401	70,263	60,444	102,463	77,175	63,681	76,875	65,516	55,807
Mississippi	93,702	72,302	64,776	67,144	57,048	52,893	77,906	66,454	56,874	73,530	57,744	55,009
Missouri	102,420	74,228	63,463	75,860	61,505	52,729	141,528	90,323	73,784	75,234	61,703	52,970
Montana	102,559	82,388	68,651	71,408	63,081	53,881	†	†	†	63,134	50,447	44,698
Nebraska	110,123	84,065	75,892	78,652	62,714	53,189	110,286	80,712	67,238	65,001	55,529	52,261
Nevada	117,993	85,485	68,344	†	†	†	†	†	†	71,158	62,136	60,570
New Hampshire	120,488	93,349	75,853	90,873	75,074	61,673	162,307	105,049	75,172	84,701	68,074	57,618
New Jersey	154,555	104,441	85,777	117,025	95,561	79,083	176,455	92,763	83,468	96,747	83,654	66,044
New Mexico	93,376	70,694	60,364	73,321	59,836	52,768	†	†	†	†	†	†
New York	132,813	92,985	76,800	90,917	72,348	61,133	155,954	99,995	81,978	98,919	78,220	66,393
North Carolina	119,400	80,828	73,142	89,708	70,623	62,833	152,906	91,454	75,331	63,271	57,929	52,673
North Dakota	101,274	79,189	66,498	79,501	64,853	54,606	65,271	61,393	51,991	†	†	†
Ohio	111,451	79,939	67,862	72,485	61,546	52,597	110,149	75,491	64,442	76,056	64,893	54,574
Oklahoma	104,634	74,846	65,094	77,639	65,452	55,032	99,854	76,793	66,174	63,432	57,183	51,875
Oregon	108,848	82,268	72,348	74,991	60,356	48,121	100,388	75,228	61,765	77,369	67,970	55,494
Pennsylvania	132,876	91,452	70,953	105,841	85,203	68,453	146,382	93,849	82,008	90,918	72,695	60,779
Rhode Island	103,635	76,302	68,143	77,945	66,653	57,817	164,255	107,299	88,505	115,882	86,336	72,131
South Carolina	120,902	84,999	74,153	86,491	68,839	59,579	†	†	†	77,336	60,096	53,706
South Dakota	86,627	70,225	61,855	85,201	69,448	60,349	†	†	†	63,686	56,612	48,615
Tennessee	101,120	74,866	63,219	81,320	66,080	55,829	137,481	88,220	67,304	67,117	55,140	49,115
Texas	120,822	82,758	72,045	85,125	70,105	61,116	129,752	89,240	78,516	86,936	69,042	55,264
Utah	110,791	78,224	69,806	78,088	64,607	57,553	113,141	81,862	69,538	89,014	54,146	63,610
Vermont	117,128	86,451	71,884	68,028	52,977	42,659	†	†	†	103,611	75,119	64,461
Virginia	123,748	84,864	71,463	85,668	70,030	61,332	112,662	82,173	45,656	68,835	57,620	49,686
Washington	112,652	83,321	76,489	89,320	75,582	70,378	107,583	81,067	65,460	78,222	64,170	58,348
West Virginia	97,562	76,450	63,340	70,361	62,827	53,263	65,843	55,725	51,563	61,847	52,113	46,627
Wisconsin	107,566	77,241	70,892	72,542	61,517	57,957	102,103	76,332	65,774	75,169	63,325	53,957
Wyoming	108,737	75,564	68,879	†	†	†	†	†	†	†	†	†
U.S. Service Academies	†	†	†	†	†	†	†	†	†	†	†	†
Other jurisdictions	**‡**	**58,503**	**56,735**	**85,344**	**68,704**	**54,465**	**†**	**†**	**40,738**	**†**	**†**	**40,589**
American Samoa	†	†	†	†	†	†	†	†	†	†	†	†
Federated States of Micronesia	†	†	†	†	†	†	†	†	†	†	†	†
Guam	†	†	†	88,584	70,126	52,965	†	†	†	†	†	†
Marshall Islands	†	†	†	†	†	†	†	†	†	†	†	†
Northern Marianas	†	†	†	†	†	†	†	†	†	†	†	†
Palau	†	†	†	†	†	†	†	†	†	†	†	†
Puerto Rico	‡	58,503	56,735	†	†	†	†	†	40,738	†	†	40,589
U.S. Virgin Islands	†	†	†	81,981	66,743	55,928	†	†	†	†	†	†

†Not applicable.
‡Reporting standards not met (too few cases).
[1]Institutions that awarded 20 or more doctor's degrees during the previous academic year.
[2]Institutions that awarded 20 or more master's degrees, but less than 20 doctor's degrees, during the previous academic year.

NOTE: Degree-granting institutions grant associate's or higher degrees and participate in Title IV federal financial aid programs. Data include imputations for nonrespondent institutions.
SOURCE: U.S. Department of Education, National Center for Education Statistics, Integrated Postsecondary Education Data System (IPEDS), Spring 2014, Human Resources component, Salaries section. (This table was prepared February 2015.)

Table 316.70. Average benefit expenditure for full-time instructional faculty on 9-month contracts in degree-granting postsecondary institutions, by type of benefit and control of institution: Selected years, 1977–78 through 2010–11

Control of institution and year	Average total benefit per full-time faculty member	Retirement plans			Medical/ dental plans	Guaran-teed disability income protection	Tuition plan for depen-dents	Housing plan	Social Security taxes	Unemploy-ment compen-sation taxes	Group life insurance	Worker's compen-sation taxes	Other insurance	Other benefits
		Total	Vested within 5 years	Vested after 5 years										
1	2	3	4	5	6	7	8	9	10	11	12	13	14	15
						Current dollars								
Total														
1977–78	$3,203	$1,725	$1,739	$1,691	$521	$96	$1,410	$886	$899	$109	$105	$80	—	$288
1982–83	5,799	2,731	2,741	2,703	1,111	151	1,993	1,639	1,712	146	138	114	—	915
1987–88	7,227	3,677	3,494	4,028	1,682	132	1,585	2,004	2,379	134	178	190	—	716
1989–90	8,241	4,048	3,974	4,192	2,339	147	2,070	2,643	2,764	121	182	49	—	637
1992–93	10,473	4,397	4,391	4,410	3,266	179	2,196	2,574	3,168	143	237	344	—	874
1997–98	12,263	5,289	5,195	5,498	3,535	218	2,765	4,100	3,562	158	195	340	$1,501	1,043
1998–99	12,580	5,256	5,268	5,228	3,726	213	3,012	3,698	3,668	152	190	347	1,267	845
1999–2000	13,227	5,292	5,365	5,125	3,989	237	3,362	4,187	3,793	146	190	343	1,512	1,303
2001–02	14,408	5,541	5,738	5,126	4,792	250	3,487	4,931	4,079	164	231	402	668	1,267
2002–03	15,552	5,781	6,039	5,208	5,396	264	3,308	4,329	4,158	170	211	411	797	1,263
2003–04	16,437	5,895	6,161	5,281	5,919	261	3,506	6,101	4,260	191	215	435	951	1,452
2004–05	17,269	6,211	6,429	5,682	6,314	272	4,072	4,176	4,354	225	199	481	853	1,637
2005–06	18,082	6,402	6,571	6,010	6,863	280	4,511	5,599	4,451	228	210	473	1,095	1,457
2006–07	18,783	6,710	6,851	6,361	7,217	280	5,029	6,914	4,627	176	217	484	1,226	1,564
2007–08	19,756	7,033	7,142	6,767	7,635	282	5,607	7,436	4,773	168	215	509	1,172	1,706
2008–09	20,332	7,222	7,396	6,797	7,900	291	5,596	9,001	4,918	169	213	498	1,156	1,540
2009–10	20,978	7,292	7,472	6,846	8,389	276	6,016	8,729	4,993	180	211	499	1,155	1,561
2010–11	21,744	7,436	7,672	6,883	8,843	281	6,396	9,071	5,042	219	210	502	1,191	1,546
Public														
1977–78	3,252	1,791	1,833	1,724	560	99	430	846	911	99	105	88	—	94
1982–83	5,920	2,846	2,880	2,776	1,189	153	576	1,027	1,741	139	140	115	—	980
1987–88	7,146	3,815	3,602	4,086	1,757	140	404	1,172	2,399	109	180	192	—	611
1989–90	8,361	4,186	4,128	4,259	2,425	154	605	1,767	2,771	97	182	60	—	602
1992–93	10,280	4,467	4,469	4,464	3,352	188	693	1,135	3,122	117	250	318	—	827
1997–98	12,114	5,432	5,302	5,617	3,646	219	830	2,614	3,482	133	187	340	1,643	1,175
1998–99	12,192	5,249	5,230	5,276	3,830	202	828	1,826	3,553	127	183	348	1,252	709
1999–2000	12,756	5,258	5,297	5,200	4,131	237	962	2,283	3,660	121	176	347	1,603	1,272
2001–02	13,919	5,437	5,641	5,158	4,936	254	994	686	3,930	137	233	402	694	1,162
2002–03	15,097	5,703	5,968	5,323	5,565	274	978	2,415	4,005	142	198	402	872	1,274
2003–04	15,916	5,757	6,044	5,330	6,127	262	1,022	4,589	4,073	173	206	425	901	1,334
2004–05	16,769	6,104	6,321	5,760	6,498	274	1,280	3,655	4,161	202	189	479	866	1,725
2005–06	17,594	6,308	6,458	6,078	7,126	279	1,483	4,418	4,237	210	202	446	1,209	1,299
2006–07	18,299	6,620	6,743	6,419	7,446	281	1,609	393	4,409	149	202	494	1,303	1,523
2007–08	19,245	6,994	7,071	6,872	7,858	289	1,815	3,382	4,542	136	197	520	1,209	1,516
2008–09	19,778	7,156	7,292	6,941	8,079	291	1,876	4,635	4,657	138	194	511	1,245	1,475
2009–10	20,435	7,237	7,387	6,998	8,613	276	1,972	4,276	4,717	148	189	509	1,269	1,543
2010–11	21,234	7,360	7,616	6,977	9,053	269	2,317	4,802	4,750	196	192	514	1,253	1,322
Private														
1977–78	3,071	1,509	1,542	905	404	89	2,025	890	873	131	103	60	—	838
1982–83	5,462	2,340	2,404	1,295	886	146	3,403	1,798	1,648	170	134	113	—	212
1987–88	7,438	3,280	3,306	2,906	1,488	120	3,666	2,303	2,337	197	175	184	—	977
1989–90	7,954	3,657	3,718	2,478	2,112	134	4,259	3,032	2,750	188	182	25	—	712
1992–93	10,958	4,206	4,259	2,877	3,039	163	4,523	2,956	3,267	212	207	402	—	957
1997–98	12,629	4,915	5,023	2,531	3,255	216	5,513	4,228	3,735	222	209	339	1,207	897
1998–99	13,519	5,274	5,327	3,879	3,468	231	6,722	3,936	3,915	219	205	345	1,313	1,020
1999–2000	14,366	5,380	5,471	3,354	3,638	237	6,951	4,349	4,074	213	215	335	1,331	1,342
2001–02	15,644	5,818	5,897	4,518	4,416	245	7,159	5,083	4,414	242	225	403	628	1,450
2002–03	16,660	5,981	6,153	2,983	4,964	249	6,943	4,348	4,490	247	236	429	629	1,248
2003–04	17,687	6,245	6,346	4,225	5,395	259	7,481	6,104	4,667	239	231	457	1,057	1,584
2004–05	18,465	6,483	6,603	4,092	5,849	269	7,600	4,455	4,775	284	217	484	821	1,527
2005–06	19,258	6,637	6,756	5,037	6,195	281	8,594	6,001	4,914	275	223	528	860	1,658
2006–07	19,942	6,935	7,027	5,382	6,632	278	9,610	7,750	5,097	248	246	465	1,049	1,619
2007–08	20,984	7,131	7,257	4,843	7,062	272	10,368	7,474	5,275	253	248	487	1,098	1,944
2008–09	21,656	7,385	7,564	4,195	7,442	292	9,941	9,017	5,489	251	251	472	985	1,628
2009–10	22,258	7,426	7,608	3,951	7,824	275	10,805	8,750	5,590	265	250	479	919	1,580
2010–11	22,927	7,626	7,761	4,797	8,323	299	11,330	9,091	5,664	281	244	479	1,059	1,819

See notes at end of table.

Table 316.70. Average benefit expenditure for full-time instructional faculty on 9-month contracts in degree-granting postsecondary institutions, by type of benefit and control of institution: Selected years, 1977–78 through 2010–11—Continued

Control of institution and year	Average total benefit per full-time faculty member	Average benefit expenditure per full-time faculty member receiving benefit												
		Retirement plans			Medical/ dental plans	Guaranteed disability income protection	Tuition plan for dependents	Housing plan	Social Security taxes	Unemployment compensation taxes	Group life insurance	Worker's compensation taxes	Other insurance	Other benefits
		Total	Vested within 5 years	Vested after 5 years										
1	2	3	4	5	6	7	8	9	10	11	12	13	14	15
Constant 2013–14 dollars[1]														
Total														
1977–78	12,017	6,470	6,525	6,345	1,954	360	5,289	3,326	3,374	407	392	299	—	1,079
1982–83	13,882	6,538	6,562	6,471	2,661	360	4,771	3,923	4,098	350	331	274	—	2,190
1987–88	14,658	7,458	7,087	8,170	3,412	269	3,215	4,065	4,825	272	362	385	—	1,451
1989–90	15,250	7,491	7,354	7,758	4,328	271	3,831	4,892	5,115	225	337	91	—	1,179
1992–93	17,265	7,249	7,240	7,271	5,385	294	3,621	4,243	5,223	236	391	567	—	1,442
1997–98	17,815	7,683	7,547	7,987	5,136	317	4,017	5,956	5,175	229	283	494	2,181	1,515
1998–99	17,964	7,505	7,523	7,465	5,320	304	4,301	5,280	5,237	217	272	496	1,809	1,207
1999–2000	18,358	7,345	7,446	7,113	5,536	329	4,666	5,811	5,265	203	263	477	2,098	1,808
2001–02	18,998	7,306	7,567	6,760	6,318	330	4,598	6,503	5,379	217	304	531	880	1,670
2002–03	20,066	7,459	7,792	6,720	6,963	341	4,268	5,585	5,365	219	272	530	1,028	1,629
2003–04	20,754	7,443	7,778	6,667	7,474	330	4,427	7,704	5,379	241	271	550	1,201	1,833
2004–05	21,167	7,614	7,880	6,965	7,739	334	4,991	5,119	5,337	276	244	589	1,045	2,007
2005–06	21,351	7,559	7,759	7,097	8,104	330	5,326	6,611	5,255	270	247	559	1,293	1,720
2006–07	21,620	7,723	7,885	7,322	8,307	322	5,789	7,958	5,325	203	250	558	1,411	1,800
2007–08	21,927	7,806	7,927	7,511	8,475	313	6,223	8,253	5,298	187	238	565	1,301	1,894
2008–09	22,255	7,905	8,095	7,440	8,647	319	6,126	9,853	5,384	185	234	546	1,266	1,685
2009–10	22,743	7,905	8,100	7,422	9,095	299	6,522	9,463	5,413	195	228	541	1,252	1,692
2010–11	23,109	7,903	8,154	7,315	9,398	299	6,797	9,641	5,359	233	223	534	1,266	1,643
Public														
1977–78	12,199	6,718	6,876	6,467	2,102	373	1,613	3,175	3,418	371	394	331	—	351
1982–83	14,173	6,814	6,895	6,646	2,845	366	1,379	2,459	4,168	332	335	275	—	2,347
1987–88	14,495	7,738	7,307	8,288	3,564	285	820	2,377	4,865	222	365	390	—	1,240
1989–90	15,472	7,746	7,638	7,881	4,488	286	1,120	3,269	5,127	179	337	110	—	1,113
1992–93	16,948	7,365	7,368	7,359	5,526	309	1,142	1,871	5,147	192	413	525	—	1,364
1997–98	17,598	7,891	7,702	8,161	5,296	319	1,205	3,797	5,059	194	272	494	2,386	1,708
1998–99	17,411	7,495	7,469	7,534	5,469	288	1,183	2,607	5,073	181	261	497	1,788	1,013
1999–2000	17,705	7,297	7,352	7,217	5,734	329	1,335	3,168	5,080	168	245	482	2,224	1,766
2001–02	18,353	7,169	7,438	6,801	6,509	335	1,311	905	5,182	181	308	530	915	1,532
2002–03	19,479	7,358	7,701	6,868	7,180	354	1,262	3,116	5,168	183	256	518	1,126	1,643
2003–04	20,096	7,269	7,632	6,729	7,736	331	1,290	5,794	5,143	218	260	537	1,138	1,685
2004–05	20,554	7,481	7,748	7,061	7,965	336	1,569	4,480	5,100	248	232	587	1,061	2,115
2005–06	20,774	7,448	7,625	7,177	8,415	329	1,751	5,216	5,003	248	239	527	1,427	1,534
2006–07	21,063	7,619	7,762	7,388	8,571	324	1,852	453	5,074	172	232	569	1,500	1,753
2007–08	21,359	7,762	7,848	7,627	8,722	321	2,014	3,754	5,041	151	219	577	1,342	1,682
2008–09	21,649	7,833	7,982	7,598	8,843	318	2,054	5,073	5,097	151	212	559	1,363	1,615
2009–10	22,154	7,846	8,008	7,586	9,338	300	2,137	4,636	5,113	161	205	552	1,376	1,673
2010–11	22,567	7,822	8,094	7,415	9,621	286	2,462	5,103	5,049	208	204	546	1,331	1,405
Private														
1977–78	11,523	5,660	5,784	3,396	1,517	334	7,598	3,337	3,273	490	388	225	—	3,143
1982–83	13,076	5,602	5,755	3,101	2,122	349	8,146	4,304	3,945	407	322	270	—	508
1987–88	15,086	6,654	6,707	5,895	3,018	243	7,436	4,672	4,741	400	355	373	—	1,982
1989–90	14,720	6,768	6,880	4,585	3,908	248	7,881	5,611	5,090	349	337	46	—	1,318
1992–93	18,065	6,934	7,021	4,744	5,010	269	7,456	4,873	5,386	349	341	662	—	1,577
1997–98	18,346	7,141	7,298	3,676	4,728	314	8,008	6,143	5,427	323	304	493	1,753	1,303
1998–99	19,305	7,532	7,608	5,539	4,952	329	9,598	5,620	5,590	313	293	492	1,874	1,457
1999–2000	19,939	7,467	7,593	4,655	5,049	329	9,647	6,036	5,655	296	299	465	1,848	1,862
2001–02	20,628	7,671	7,776	5,958	5,823	322	9,440	6,703	5,821	319	297	531	828	1,913
2002–03	21,496	7,717	7,938	3,849	6,405	321	8,959	5,611	5,793	318	305	554	812	1,610
2003–04	22,332	7,885	8,012	5,335	6,811	327	9,446	7,708	5,893	301	292	577	1,335	2,000
2004–05	22,633	7,947	8,094	5,016	7,170	330	9,316	5,461	5,854	348	266	593	1,007	1,871
2005–06	22,740	7,837	7,977	5,947	7,314	332	10,148	7,086	5,803	325	263	623	1,016	1,958
2006–07	22,954	7,982	8,088	6,195	7,634	319	11,062	8,920	5,867	286	283	535	1,207	1,863
2007–08	23,290	7,914	8,055	5,375	7,838	302	11,508	8,296	5,855	281	275	541	1,218	2,158
2008–09	23,704	8,083	8,279	4,591	8,146	320	10,882	9,870	6,009	275	274	517	1,079	1,782
2009–10	24,130	8,051	8,248	4,284	8,482	298	11,714	9,487	6,060	287	271	519	996	1,713
2010–11	24,366	8,105	8,248	5,099	8,845	317	12,042	9,662	6,020	299	259	509	1,126	1,933

—Not available.
[1]Constant dollars based on the Consumer Price Index, prepared by the Bureau of Labor Statistics, U.S. Department of Labor, adjusted to an academic-year basis.
NOTE: Data through 1992–93 are for institutions of higher education, while later data are for degree-granting institutions. Degree-granting institutions grant associate's or higher degrees and participate in Title IV federal financial aid programs.

SOURCE: U.S. Department of Education, National Center for Education Statistics, Higher Education General Information Survey (HEGIS), "Faculty Salaries, Tenure, and Fringe Benefits" surveys, 1977–78 and 1982–83; Integrated Postsecondary Education Data System (IPEDS), "Salaries, Tenure, and Fringe Benefits of Full-Time Instructional Faculty Survey" (IPEDS-SA:87–99); and IPEDS Winter 2001–02 through Winter 2010–11, Human Resources component, Salaries section. (This table was prepared March 2014.)

Table 316.80. Percentage of degree-granting postsecondary institutions with a tenure system and of full-time faculty with tenure at these institutions, by control and level of institution and selected characteristics of faculty: Selected years, 1993–94 through 2013–14

Selected characteristic and academic year	All institutions	Public institutions						Nonprofit institutions						For-profit institutions
		Total	4-year institutions				2-year	Total	4-year institutions				2-year	
			Total	Doctoral[1]	Master's[2]	Other			Total	Doctoral[1]	Master's[2]	Other		
1	2	3	4	5	6	7	8	9	10	11	12	13	14	15
Percent of institutions with a tenure system														
1993–94	62.6	73.6	92.6	100.0	98.3	76.4	62.1	62.0	66.3	90.5	76.5	58.3	26.1	7.8
1999–2000	55.0	72.8	94.6	100.0	95.5	86.3	60.3	59.0	63.4	81.2	72.6	54.9	14.0	4.0
2003–04	52.7	71.3	90.9	100.0	98.0	70.9	59.4	57.9	61.2	86.6	71.6	49.5	14.4	3.6
2005–06	50.9	71.5	90.9	99.5	98.0	71.6	59.4	56.5	59.8	85.1	67.1	49.2	11.5	2.0
2007–08	49.5	70.7	91.0	100.0	98.6	71.6	57.4	57.5	60.2	87.8	66.0	49.0	13.0	1.4
2009–10	47.8	71.2	90.9	99.6	98.5	71.3	57.7	57.1	59.5	80.6	64.4	44.6	12.9	1.5
2011–12	45.3	71.6	90.8	99.6	98.5	70.5	57.8	55.6	58.6	79.5	64.0	42.7	8.0	1.3
2013–14	49.3	74.6	95.8	99.6	98.1	86.6	58.9	59.7	61.8	79.6	63.2	49.0	12.5	1.2
Percent of faculty with tenure at institutions with a tenure system														
All full-time faculty (instruction, research, and public service)														
1993–94	56.2	58.9	56.3	54.5	60.5	51.1	69.9	49.5	49.5	47.6	51.8	50.4	47.9	33.8
1999–2000	53.7	55.9	53.2	50.4	59.1	54.7	67.7	48.2	48.1	43.4	52.3	53.5	59.7	77.4
2003–04	50.4	53.0	50.2	48.9	52.9	51.2	65.2	44.6	44.6	40.1	48.7	51.9	47.7	69.2
2005–06	49.6	51.5	48.7	47.2	52.3	49.1	64.1	45.1	45.1	40.7	49.1	52.5	45.2	69.3
2007–08	48.8	50.5	47.8	46.1	51.9	49.1	63.6	44.7	44.7	40.1	49.8	52.7	41.3	51.3
2009–10	48.7	50.6	47.8	45.7	53.6	51.3	64.1	44.3	44.3	40.4	50.5	54.1	38.5	51.0
2011–12	48.5	50.7	48.0	45.8	54.3	53.4	64.7	43.7	43.7	39.7	50.7	54.3	31.4	31.0
2013–14	48.3	50.4	47.3	44.9	55.4	52.2	67.2	43.8	43.8	39.5	51.7	55.9	31.5	19.8
Full-time instructional faculty in 2013–14														
Total	50.7	52.8	50.0	48.1	55.6	53.5	67.2	46.3	46.4	42.9	51.7	55.9	30.5	19.8
Male	56.6	58.5	56.8	55.5	61.9	56.2	69.6	52.7	52.8	49.9	57.2	61.9	36.7	21.7
Female	43.2	45.7	40.8	37.4	48.5	50.6	65.1	37.7	37.7	32.7	45.4	48.7	26.4	18.3
Professor	90.7	91.9	91.7	90.2	97.8	91.8	93.5	88.4	88.4	86.1	92.1	95.4	79.2	61.3
Male	91.1	92.3	92.1	90.8	97.9	92.6	94.4	88.8	88.8	87.0	91.8	95.4	91.7	64.4
Female	89.9	91.1	90.8	88.3	97.6	90.6	92.7	87.4	87.4	83.6	92.6	95.3	66.7	55.9
Associate professor	77.1	80.6	80.7	77.5	90.2	85.8	79.3	70.4	70.4	63.8	78.6	86.2	42.2	22.9
Male	77.2	80.9	81.0	78.2	90.1	86.1	80.4	70.1	70.1	64.1	78.8	84.7	44.4	20.0
Female	76.8	80.1	80.3	76.6	90.3	85.4	78.4	70.7	70.8	63.4	78.5	87.9	41.7	25.0
Assistant professor	6.8	8.7	5.2	2.0	11.6	23.9	45.2	3.4	3.4	2.1	6.7	4.5	11.1	‡
Male	6.5	8.2	5.0	2.0	11.6	23.5	48.1	3.4	3.4	2.2	6.9	4.7	11.5	‡
Female	7.1	9.3	5.4	2.1	11.6	24.3	43.0	3.3	3.3	1.9	6.6	4.3	10.8	†
Instructor	28.4	34.4	2.1	0.9	1.8	11.6	61.7	0.5	0.5	0.4	0.4	1.6	9.1	66.7
Lecturer	1.6	2.0	1.3	0.7	2.9	4.6	20.9	0.3	0.3	0.1	1.0	1.4	†	†
No academic rank	32.3	41.1	20.4	1.0	7.5	64.0	69.1	9.6	9.5	1.2	19.7	42.3	37.1	11.7

†Not applicable.
‡Reporting standards not met (too few cases).
[1]Institutions that awarded 20 or more doctor's degrees during the previous academic year.
[2]Institutions that awarded 20 or more master's degrees, but less than 20 doctor's degrees, during the previous academic year.

NOTE: Degree-granting institutions grant associate's or higher degrees and participate in Title IV federal financial aid programs. Data include imputations for nonrespondent institutions. Some data have been revised from previously published figures.
SOURCE: U.S. Department of Education, National Center for Education Statistics, Integrated Postsecondary Education Data System (IPEDS), "Fall Staff Survey" (IPEDS-S:93–99); and IPEDS Winter 2003–04 through Winter 2011–12 and Spring 2014, Human Resources component, Fall Staff section. (This table was prepared April 2016.)

Table 317.10. Degree-granting postsecondary institutions, by control and level of institution: Selected years, 1949–50 through 2014–15

Year	All institutions			Public			Private								
								4-year, total	2-year, total	Nonprofit			For-profit		
	Total	4-year	2-year	Total	4-year	2-year	Total			Total	4-year	2-year	Total	4-year	2-year
1	2	3	4	5	6	7	8	9	10	11	12	13	14	15	16
Excluding branch campuses															
1949–50	1,851	1,327	524	641	344	297	1,210	983	227	—	—	—	—	—	—
1959–60	2,004	1,422	582	695	367	328	1,309	1,055	254	—	—	—	—	—	—
1969–70	2,525	1,639	886	1,060	426	634	1,465	1,213	252	—	—	—	—	—	—
1970–71	2,556	1,665	891	1,089	435	654	1,467	1,230	237	—	—	—	—	—	—
1971–72	2,606	1,675	931	1,137	440	697	1,469	1,235	234	—	—	—	—	—	—
1972–73	2,665	1,701	964	1,182	449	733	1,483	1,252	231	—	—	—	—	—	—
1973–74	2,720	1,717	1,003	1,200	440	760	1,520	1,277	243	—	—	—	—	—	—
1974–75	2,747	1,744	1,003	1,214	447	767	1,533	1,297	236	—	—	—	—	—	—
1975–76	2,765	1,767	998	1,219	447	772	1,546	1,320	226	—	—	—	—	—	—
1976–77	2,785	1,783	1,002	1,231	452	779	1,554	1,331	223	—	—	—	—	—	—
1977–78	2,826	1,808	1,018	1,241	454	787	1,585	1,354	231	—	—	—	—	—	—
1978–79	2,954	1,843	1,111	1,308	463	845	1,646	1,380	266	—	—	—	—	—	—
1979–80	2,975	1,863	1,112	1,310	464	846	1,665	1,399	266	—	—	—	—	—	—
1980–81	3,056	1,861	1,195	1,334	465	869	1,722	1,396	326 [1]	—	—	—	—	—	—
1981–82	3,083	1,883	1,200	1,340	471	869	1,743	1,412	331 [1]	—	—	—	—	—	—
1982–83	3,111	1,887	1,224	1,336	472	864	1,775	1,415	360 [1]	—	—	—	—	—	—
1983–84	3,117	1,914	1,203	1,325	474	851	1,792	1,440	352	—	—	—	—	—	—
1984–85	3,146	1,911	1,235	1,329	461	868	1,817	1,450	367	—	—	—	—	—	—
1985–86	3,155	1,915	1,240	1,326	461	865	1,829	1,454	375	—	—	—	—	—	—
Including branch campuses															
1974–75	3,004	1,866	1,138	1,433	537	896	1,571	1,329	242	—	—	—	—	—	—
1975–76	3,026	1,898	1,128	1,442	545	897	1,584	1,353	231	—	—	—	—	—	—
1976–77	3,046	1,913	1,133	1,455	550	905	1,591	1,363	228	1,536	1,348	188	55	15	40
1977–78	3,095	1,938	1,157	1,473	552	921	1,622	1,386	236	—	—	—	—	—	—
1978–79	3,134	1,941	1,193	1,474	550	924	1,660	1,391	269	1,564	1,376	188	96	15	81
1979–80	3,152	1,957	1,195	1,475	549	926	1,677	1,408	269	—	—	—	—	—	—
1980–81	3,231	1,957	1,274	1,497	552	945	1,734	1,405	329 [1]	1,569	1,387	182	165	18	147
1981–82	3,253	1,979	1,274	1,498	558	940	1,755	1,421	334 [1]	—	—	—	—	—	—
1982–83	3,280	1,984	1,296	1,493	560	933	1,787	1,424	363 [1]	—	—	—	—	—	—
1983–84	3,284	2,013	1,271	1,481	565	916	1,803	1,448	355	—	—	—	—	—	—
1984–85	3,331	2,025	1,306	1,501	566	935	1,830	1,459	371	1,616	1,430	186	214	29	185
1985–86	3,340	2,029	1,311	1,498	566	932	1,842	1,463	379	—	—	—	—	—	—
1986–87	3,406	2,070	1,336	1,533	573	960	1,873	1,497	376	1,635	1,462	173	238	35	203
1987–88	3,587	2,135	1,452	1,591	599	992	1,996	1,536	460	1,673	1,487	186	323	49	274
1988–89	3,565	2,129	1,436	1,582	598	984	1,983	1,531	452	1,658	1,478	180	325	53	272
1989–90	3,535	2,127	1,408	1,563	595	968	1,972	1,532	440	1,656	1,479	177	316	53	263
1990–91	3,559	2,141	1,418	1,567	595	972	1,992	1,546	446	1,649	1,482	167	343	64	279
1991–92	3,601	2,157	1,444	1,598	599	999	2,003	1,558	445	1,662	1,486	176	341	72	269
1992–93	3,638	2,169	1,469	1,624	600	1,024	2,014	1,569	445	1,672	1,493	179	342	76	266
1993–94	3,632	2,190	1,442	1,625	604	1,021	2,007	1,586	421	1,687	1,506	181	320	80	240
1994–95	3,688	2,215	1,473	1,641	605	1,036	2,047	1,610	437	1,702	1,510	192	345	100	245
1995–96	3,706	2,244	1,462	1,655	608	1,047	2,051	1,636	415	1,706	1,519	187	345	117	228
1996–97	4,009	2,267	1,742	1,702	614	1,088	2,307	1,653	654	1,693	1,509	184	614	144	470
1997–98	4,064	2,309	1,755	1,707	615	1,092	2,357	1,694	663	1,707	1,528	179	650	166	484
1998–99	4,048	2,335	1,713	1,681	612	1,069	2,367	1,723	644	1,695	1,531	164	672	192	480
1999–2000	4,084	2,363	1,721	1,682	614	1,068	2,402	1,749	653	1,681	1,531	150	721	218	503
2000–01	4,182	2,450	1,732	1,698	622	1,076	2,484	1,828	656	1,695	1,551	144	789	277	512
2001–02	4,197	2,487	1,710	1,713	628	1,085	2,484	1,859	625	1,676	1,541	135	808	318	490
2002–03	4,168	2,466	1,702	1,712	631	1,081	2,456	1,835	621	1,665	1,538	127	791	297	494
2003–04	4,236	2,530	1,706	1,720	634	1,086	2,516	1,896	620	1,664	1,546	118	852	350	502
2004–05	4,216	2,533	1,683	1,700	639	1,061	2,516	1,894	622	1,637	1,525	112	879	369	510
2005–06	4,276	2,582	1,694	1,693	640	1,053	2,583	1,942	641	1,647	1,534	113	936	408	528
2006–07	4,314	2,629	1,685	1,688	643	1,045	2,626	1,986	640	1,640	1,533	107	986	453	533
2007–08	4,352	2,675	1,677	1,685	653	1,032	2,667	2,022	645	1,624	1,532	92	1,043	490	553
2008–09	4,409	2,719	1,690	1,676	652	1,024	2,733	2,067	666	1,629	1,537	92	1,104	530	574
2009–10	4,495	2,774	1,721	1,672	672	1,000	2,823	2,102	721	1,624	1,539	85	1,199	563	636
2010–11	4,599	2,870	1,729	1,656	678	978	2,943	2,192	751	1,630	1,543	87	1,313	649	664
2011–12	4,706	2,968	1,738	1,649	682	967	3,057	2,286	771	1,653	1,553	100	1,404	733	671
2012–13	4,706	2,968	1,738	1,649	682	967	3,057	2,286	771	1,653	1,553	100	1,404	733	671
2013–14	4,724	3,039	1,685	1,625	691	934	3,099	2,348	751	1,675	1,587	88	1,424	761	663
2014–15	4,627	3,011	1,616	1,621	701	920	3,006	2,310	696	1,672	1,584	88	1,334	726	608

—Not available.
[1]Large increases are due to the addition of schools accredited by the Accrediting Commission of Career Schools and Colleges of Technology.
NOTE: Data through 1995–96 are for institutions of higher education, while later data are for degree-granting institutions. Degree-granting institutions grant associate's or higher degrees and participate in Title IV federal financial aid programs. Changes in counts of institutions over time are partly affected by increasing or decreasing numbers of institutions submitting separate data for branch campuses.

SOURCE: U.S. Department of Education, National Center for Education Statistics, *Education Directory, Colleges and Universities*, 1949–50 through 1965–66; Higher Education General Information Survey (HEGIS), "Institutional Characteristics of Colleges and Universities" surveys, 1966–67 through 1985–86; Integrated Postsecondary Education Data System (IPEDS), "Institutional Characteristics Survey" (IPEDS-IC:86–99); and IPEDS Fall 2000 through Fall 2014, Institutional Characteristics component. (This table was prepared October 2015.)

Table 317.20. Degree-granting postsecondary institutions, by control and level of institution and state or jurisdiction: 2014–15

State or jurisdiction	Total institutions	All public institutions	Public 4-year institutions							Public 2-year institutions	All nonprofit institutions	Nonprofit 4-year institutions							Nonprofit 2-year	For-profit institutions		
			Total	Research university, very high[1]	Research university, high[2]	Doctoral/research university[3]	Masters[4]	Baccalaureate[5]	Special focus[6]			Total	Research university, very high[1]	Research university, high[2]	Doctoral/research university[3]	Masters[4]	Baccalaureate[5]	Special focus[6]		Total	4-year	2-year
1	2	3	4	5	6	7	8	9	10	11	12	13	14	15	16	17	18	19	20	21	22	23
United States	4,627	1,621	701	73	73	29	274	206	46	920	1,672	1,584	34	24	48	363	520	595	88	1,334	726	608
Alabama	78	39	14	2	3	0	8	1	0	25	21	20	0	0	0	2	12	6	1	18	11	7
Alaska	10	5	3	0	1	0	2	0	0	2	3	2	0	0	0	1	0	1	1	2	1	1
Arizona	86	28	8	1	1	0	4	0	1	20	14	14	0	0	0	2	4	8	0	44	30	14
Arkansas	52	33	11	1	0	1	6	2	1	22	15	12	0	0	0	1	9	2	3	4	3	1
California	458	149	34	8	1	0	21	2	2	115	144	138	3	1	10	25	24	75	6	165	87	78
Colorado	89	28	14	2	2	1	4	5	0	14	14	14	1	0	0	3	5	5	0	47	26	21
Connecticut	44	21	9	1	0	0	4	4	0	12	19	19	1	0	0	9	5	4	0	4	4	0
Delaware	11	5	2	1	0	0	1	1	0	3	5	4	0	0	1	0	1	2	1	1	1	0
District of Columbia	21	2	2	0	0	0	1	0	1	0	14	13	2	2	1	2	0	6	1	5	4	1
Florida	234	42	38	4	2	2	4	25	1	4	66	62	1	1	3	13	22	22	4	126	65	61
Georgia	131	55	29	3	0	2	9	14	1	26	35	33	1	0	1	4	19	8	2	41	22	19
Hawaii	21	10	4	1	1	0	0	3	0	6	6	6	0	0	0	2	2	2	0	5	3	2
Idaho	19	8	4	0	2	0	1	1	0	4	6	6	0	0	0	1	2	3	0	5	4	1
Illinois	181	60	12	2	2	1	7	0	0	48	83	80	2	2	4	17	19	36	3	38	25	13
Indiana	84	16	15	2	2	1	6	3	1	1	40	39	1	0	0	9	19	10	1	28	18	10
Iowa	65	19	3	2	0	0	1	0	0	16	34	34	0	0	0	6	18	10	0	12	10	2
Kansas	75	33	8	1	2	0	4	0	1	25	26	25	0	0	1	6	12	7	1	16	10	6
Kentucky	76	24	8	1	2	0	5	1	0	16	26	26	1	1	1	6	12	7	0	26	18	8
Louisiana	66	33	17	2	3	0	9	0	3	16	13	11	0	0	0	2	4	4	2	20	5	15
Maine	32	15	8	0	1	0	1	6	0	7	14	12	0	0	0	3	6	3	2	3	2	1
Maryland	60	29	13	1	1	2	7	1	1	16	20	20	0	0	0	6	6	7	0	11	6	5
Massachusetts	124	30	14	1	2	2	7	2	0	16	84	82	5	3	1	16	24	33	2	10	6	4
Michigan	111	46	18	3	2	2	7	4	0	28	50	50	0	0	1	11	22	16	0	15	12	3
Minnesota	115	43	12	1	0	0	8	3	0	31	35	34	0	0	3	6	12	13	1	37	34	3
Mississippi	41	23	8	1	3	0	4	0	0	15	9	9	0	0	0	3	4	2	0	9	2	7
Missouri	129	27	13	1	3	0	6	3	0	14	54	51	1	1	1	11	12	25	3	48	26	22
Montana	22	17	6	1	1	0	1	3	0	11	5	4	0	0	0	0	3	1	1	0	0	0
Nebraska	42	15	7	1	0	1	3	1	1	8	18	16	0	0	0	5	7	4	2	9	5	4
Nevada	24	7	6	0	2	0	0	4	0	1	3	3	0	0	0	1	0	2	0	14	6	8
New Hampshire	27	13	6	0	1	0	2	2	1	7	12	11	1	1	0	5	4	1	1	2	2	0
New Jersey	71	32	13	1	2	0	10	0	0	19	28	28	1	1	1	10	2	13	0	11	6	5
New Mexico	43	28	9	1	1	0	4	1	2	19	3	3	0	0	1	0	0	0	0	12	10	2
New York	302	79	43	4	1	1	21	12	4	36	177	165	6	4	7	39	27	82	12	46	22	24
North Carolina	150	75	16	2	1	3	7	2	1	59	50	49	1	1	0	7	27	13	1	25	17	8
North Dakota	21	14	9	1	1	0	1	4	2	5	6	6	0	0	0	1	1	4	0	1	1	0
Ohio	210	60	35	2	8	0	1	23	1	25	73	68	1	1	2	20	19	25	5	77	29	48
Oklahoma	66	30	17	1	0	0	8	5	2	13	14	14	0	0	1	4	6	3	0	22	11	11
Oregon	64	26	9	2	2	1	3	2	0	17	24	24	0	0	0	5	7	12	0	14	8	6
Pennsylvania	257	62	45	2	1	1	18	21	2	17	118	104	2	2	2	30	35	32	14	77	10	67
Rhode Island	13	3	2	0	1	0	1	0	0	1	10	10	1	0	0	5	1	3	0	0	0	0
South Carolina	78	33	13	2	1	0	5	4	1	20	23	22	0	0	0	5	14	3	1	22	14	8
South Dakota	25	12	7	0	2	1	2	1	1	5	8	7	0	1	0	0	5	1	1	5	5	0
Tennessee	107	22	9	1	1	0	3	0	0	13	50	47	1	1	2	11	16	17	3	35	18	17
Texas	267	107	44	3	6	7	17	4	7	63	68	59	1	2	2	17	14	23	9	92	42	50
Utah	40	8	7	1	1	0	2	3	0	1	11	10	0	1	0	2	3	4	1	21	18	3

See notes at end of table.

Table 317.20. Degree-granting postsecondary institutions, by control and level of institution and state or jurisdiction: 2014–15—Continued

State or jurisdiction	Total institutions	All public institutions	Public 4-year: Total	Public 4-year: Research university, very high[1]	Public 4-year: Research university, high[2]	Public 4-year: Doctoral/research university[3]	Public 4-year: Master's[4]	Public 4-year: Baccalaureate[5]	Public 4-year: Special focus[6]	Public 2-year	All nonprofit institutions	Nonprofit 4-year: Total	Nonprofit 4-year: Research university, very high[1]	Nonprofit 4-year: Research university, high[2]	Nonprofit 4-year: Doctoral/research university[3]	Nonprofit 4-year: Master's[4]	Nonprofit 4-year: Baccalaureate[5]	Nonprofit 4-year: Special focus[6]	Nonprofit 2-year	For-profit: Total	For-profit: 4-year	For-profit: 2-year
1	2	3	4	5	6	7	8	9	10	11	12	13	14	15	16	17	18	19	20	21	22	23
Vermont	24	6	5	0	1	0	1	3	0	1	17	17	0	0	0	4	11	2	0	1	1	0
Virginia	130	40	16	3	3	0	7	2	1	24	40	38	0	0	1	7	18	12	2	50	29	21
Washington	87	43	23	2	0	0	6	13	2	20	24	23	0	0	0	10	5	8	1	20	11	9
West Virginia	43	22	13	0	1	0	3	8	1	9	9	9	0	0	0	0	7	2	0	12	3	9
Wisconsin	86	31	14	1	1	0	10	2	0	17	30	30	0	0	3	8	10	9	0	25	23	2
Wyoming	10	8	1	0	1	0	0	0	0	7	1	1	0	0	0	0	0	1	0	1	0	1
U.S. Service Academies	5	5	5	0	0	0	0	5	0	0	†	†	†	†	†	†	†	†	†	†	†	†
Other jurisdictions	**98**	**26**	**18**	**0**	**1**	**1**	**1**	**12**	**3**	**8**	**50**	**46**	**0**	**0**	**3**	**12**	**16**	**15**	**4**	**22**	**12**	**10**
American Samoa	1	1	1	0	0	0	0	1	0	0	0	0	0	0	0	0	0	0	0	0	0	0
Federated States of Micronesia	1	1	0	0	0	0	0	0	0	1	0	0	0	0	0	0	0	0	0	0	0	0
Guam	3	2	1	0	0	0	1	0	0	1	1	1	0	0	0	0	0	1	0	0	0	0
Marshall Islands	1	1	0	0	0	0	0	0	0	1	0	0	0	0	0	0	0	0	0	0	0	0
Northern Marianas	1	1	1	0	0	0	0	1	0	0	0	0	0	0	0	0	0	0	0	0	0	0
Palau	1	1	0	0	0	0	0	0	0	1	0	0	0	0	0	0	0	0	0	0	0	0
Puerto Rico	89	18	14	0	1	1	0	9	3	4	49	45	0	0	3	12	16	14	4	22	12	10
U.S. Virgin Islands	1	1	1	0	0	0	0	1	0	0	0	0	0	0	0	0	0	0	0	0	0	0

†Not applicable.

[1]Research universities with a very high level of research activity.

[2]Research universities with a high level of research activity.

[3]Institutions that award at least 20 doctor's degrees per year, but did not have a high level of research activity.

[4]Institutions that award at least 50 master's degrees per year.

[5]Institutions that primarily emphasize undergraduate education. Also includes institutions classified as 4-year under the IPEDS system, which had been classified as 2-year in the Carnegie classification system because they primarily award associate's degrees.

[6]Four-year institutions that award degrees primarily in single fields of study, such as medicine, business, fine arts, theology, and engineering.

NOTE: Branch campuses are counted as separate institutions. Relative levels of research activity for research universities were determined by an analysis of research and development expenditures, science and engineering research staffing, and doctoral degrees conferred, by field. Further information on the research index ranking may be obtained from http://carnegieclassifications.iu.edu/. Degree-granting institutions grant associate's or higher degrees and participate in Title IV federal financial aid programs.

SOURCE: U.S. Department of Education, National Center for Education Statistics, Integrated Postsecondary Education Data System (IPEDS), Fall 2014, Institutional Characteristics component. (This table was prepared October 2015.)

Table 317.30. Number of non-degree-granting Title IV institutions offering postsecondary education, by control of institution and state or jurisdiction: Selected years, 2000–01 through 2014–15

State or jurisdiction	2000–01, total	2005–06, total	2010–11, total	2012–13 Total	2012–13 Public	2012–13 Private Total	2012–13 Private Non-profit	2012–13 Private For-profit	2013–14 Total	2013–14 Public	2013–14 Private Total	2013–14 Private Non-profit	2013–14 Private For-profit	2014–15 Total	2014–15 Public	2014–15 Private Total	2014–15 Private Non-profit	2014–15 Private For-profit
1	2	3	4	5	6	7	8	9	10	11	12	13	14	15	16	17	18	19
United States	2,297	2,187	2,422	2,528	358	2,169	168	2,001	2,512	355	2,157	159	1,998	2,524	343	2,181	155	2,026
Alabama	10	9	9	12	0	13	1	12	14	0	14	1	13	14	0	14	1	13
Alaska	3	2	3	2	1	1	1	0	0	0	0	0	0	0	0	0	0	0
Arizona	33	34	42	48	2	48	1	47	47	2	45	0	45	48	2	46	0	46
Arkansas	36	32	32	36	2	32	2	30	33	2	31	2	29	31	2	29	1	28
California	230	235	248	262	12	253	24	229	258	14	244	22	222	252	12	240	22	218
Colorado	21	26	33	39	3	37	3	34	39	3	36	3	33	39	3	36	3	33
Connecticut	37	36	59	56	11	39	3	36	48	11	37	3	34	48	10	38	3	35
Delaware	4	6	8	8	0	8	1	7	8	0	8	1	7	8	0	8	1	7
District of Columbia	5	6	5	4	0	4	1	3	4	0	4	1	3	4	0	4	1	3
Florida	124	126	150	153	42	110	4	106	155	43	112	3	109	168	45	123	3	120
Georgia	38	44	46	46	1	44	1	43	46	1	45	2	43	47	1	46	3	43
Hawaii	6	5	5	7	0	6	0	6	5	0	5	0	5	5	0	5	0	5
Idaho	11	13	17	19	1	22	0	22	23	1	22	0	22	23	1	22	0	22
Illinois	88	94	108	117	3	113	10	103	119	2	117	8	109	117	2	115	7	108
Indiana	34	28	42	48	4	45	1	44	48	2	46	1	45	48	1	47	1	46
Iowa	27	26	26	28	0	28	2	26	27	0	27	2	25	27	0	27	2	25
Kansas	23	25	22	22	1	24	0	24	22	1	21	0	21	19	1	18	0	18
Kentucky	52	32	30	32	0	32	2	30	33	0	33	2	31	33	0	33	2	31
Louisiana	57	57	47	51	0	52	2	50	51	0	51	3	48	57	0	57	2	55
Maine	11	9	7	8	0	8	0	8	9	0	9	0	9	8	0	8	0	8
Maryland	34	27	32	33	0	31	0	31	35	0	35	0	35	38	0	38	0	38
Massachusetts	60	61	75	73	11	57	3	54	68	12	56	3	53	67	12	55	3	52
Michigan	72	65	89	86	1	82	2	80	82	1	81	3	78	84	1	83	3	80
Minnesota	20	21	26	26	0	27	2	25	27	0	27	2	25	27	0	27	2	25
Mississippi	16	20	20	20	0	20	0	20	20	0	20	0	20	20	0	20	0	20
Missouri	69	61	74	80	30	47	3	44	77	29	48	2	46	72	23	49	3	46
Montana	10	8	8	9	0	9	0	9	8	0	8	0	8	8	0	8	0	8
Nebraska	12	10	7	7	0	7	1	6	7	0	7	1	6	7	0	7	1	6
Nevada	10	9	18	20	0	23	1	22	23	0	23	1	22	21	0	21	1	20
New Hampshire	11	14	14	15	0	15	1	14	15	0	15	1	14	15	0	15	1	14
New Jersey	89	91	87	90	5	89	8	81	95	5	90	7	83	90	5	85	7	78
New Mexico	6	7	7	8	0	8	0	8	8	0	8	0	8	8	0	8	0	8
New York	152	133	151	156	33	122	30	92	152	33	119	26	93	156	33	123	24	99
North Carolina	36	29	42	43	1	43	2	41	45	1	44	3	41	46	1	45	3	42
North Dakota	5	5	8	8	0	8	0	8	9	0	9	0	9	9	0	9	0	9
Ohio	130	119	138	139	53	87	6	81	138	51	87	6	81	144	50	94	7	87
Oklahoma	84	78	83	82	47	31	0	31	79	49	30	0	30	79	48	31	0	31
Oregon	28	27	26	30	0	29	3	26	30	0	30	3	27	31	0	31	3	28
Pennsylvania	167	131	126	127	34	91	21	70	126	34	92	20	72	126	33	93	21	72
Rhode Island	12	10	11	11	0	11	2	9	11	0	11	2	9	11	0	11	2	9
South Carolina	14	21	27	33	1	32	1	31	33	1	32	1	31	30	1	29	1	28
South Dakota	5	6	6	6	0	6	3	3	6	0	6	3	3	6	0	6	3	3
Tennessee	54	58	66	72	26	46	1	45	72	26	46	1	45	76	26	50	1	49
Texas	161	169	170	174	0	175	4	171	174	0	174	4	170	179	0	179	3	176
Utah	26	24	34	38	7	33	0	33	40	7	33	0	33	40	7	33	0	33
Vermont	3	4	4	4	0	3	0	3	3	0	3	0	3	2	0	2	0	2
Virginia	56	42	33	36	8	32	4	28	40	6	34	3	31	41	6	35	3	32
Washington	42	37	37	37	1	37	3	34	35	1	34	4	30	35	1	34	5	29
West Virginia	36	31	33	32	17	16	5	11	34	17	17	5	12	30	16	14	3	11
Wisconsin	24	22	30	34	0	32	3	29	30	0	30	4	26	29	0	29	3	26
Wyoming	3	2	1	1	0	1	0	1	1	0	1	0	1	1	0	1	0	1
Other jurisdictions	74	74	68	70	2	70	13	57	71	2	69	12	57	61	1	60	6	54
American Samoa	0	0	0	0	0	0	0	0	0	0	0	0	0	0	0	0	0	0
Guam	0	0	0	0	0	0	0	0	0	0	0	0	0	0	0	0	0	0
Northern Marianas	0	0	0	0	0	0	0	0	0	0	0	0	0	0	0	0	0	0
Palau	0	0	0	0	0	0	0	0	0	0	0	0	0	0	0	0	0	0
Puerto Rico	74	74	68	70	2	70	13	57	71	2	69	12	57	61	1	60	6	54
U.S. Virgin Islands	0	0	0	0	0	0	0	0	0	0	0	0	0	0	0	0	0	0

NOTE: Includes all institutions that participated in Title IV federal financial aid programs but did not grant degrees at the associate's or higher level.

SOURCE: U.S. Department of Education, National Center for Education Statistics, Integrated Postsecondary Education Data System (IPEDS), Fall 2000 through Fall 2014, Institutional Characteristics component. (This table was prepared December 2015.)

Table 317.40. Number of degree-granting postsecondary institutions and enrollment in these institutions, by enrollment size, control, and level of institution: Fall 2014

Control and level of institution	Number of institutions, by enrollment size of institution[1]									
	Total	Under 200	200 to 499	500 to 999	1,000 to 2,499	2,500 to 4,999	5,000 to 9,999	10,000 to 19,999	20,000 to 29,999	30,000 or more
1	2	3	4	5	6	7	8	9	10	11
Total	**4,614**	**612**	**791**	**609**	**892**	**643**	**495**	**341**	**142**	**89**
Research university, very high[2]	107	0	0	0	1	0	9	22	32	43
Research university, high[3]	97	0	0	0	1	2	14	42	27	11
Doctoral/research university[4]	88	1	1	4	9	15	21	26	9	2
Master's[5]	675	3	10	21	136	207	178	86	20	14
Baccalaureate[6]	853	28	95	175	356	136	33	18	4	8
Special-focus institutions[7]	1,183	367	375	217	146	55	13	6	3	1
2-year	1,611	213	310	192	243	228	227	141	47	10
Public	1,621	10	34	66	287	361	384	281	125	73
Research university, very high[2]	73	0	0	0	0	0	2	6	25	40
Research university, high[3]	73	0	0	0	0	0	7	32	24	10
Doctoral/research university[4]	29	0	0	0	1	1	4	16	7	0
Master's[5]	274	0	1	0	11	54	112	71	19	6
Baccalaureate[6]	207	0	1	19	59	71	31	16	3	7
Special-focus institutions[7]	45	2	7	10	11	13	2	0	0	0
Art, music, or design	2	0	0	1	1	0	0	0	0	0
Business and management	2	0	0	1	0	0	1	0	0	0
Engineering or technology	2	0	0	0	0	2	0	0	0	0
Law	6	1	3	1	1	0	0	0	0	0
Medical or other health	25	0	2	5	6	11	1	0	0	0
Tribal	8	1	2	2	3	0	0	0	0	0
2-year	920	8	25	37	205	222	226	140	47	10
Private nonprofit	1,666	288	256	233	472	247	99	50	12	9
Research university, very high[2]	34	0	0	0	1	0	7	16	7	3
Research university, high[3]	24	0	0	0	1	2	7	10	3	1
Doctoral/research university[4]	48	1	1	0	5	14	16	9	2	0
Master's[5]	363	2	7	13	112	148	65	12	0	4
Baccalaureate[6]	520	15	51	110	279	63	0	1	0	1
Special-focus institutions[7]	591	240	156	98	71	20	4	2	0	0
Art, music, or design	57	12	13	17	11	3	0	1	0	0
Business and management	40	9	11	11	4	3	2	0	0	0
Engineering or technology	13	6	2	2	2	0	0	1	0	0
Law	21	3	5	7	6	0	0	0	0	0
Medical or other health	141	22	43	29	36	10	1	0	0	0
Theological	298	180	78	26	10	3	1	0	0	0
Tribal	5	0	1	4	0	0	0	0	0	0
Other special focus	16	8	3	2	2	1	0	0	0	0
2-year	86	30	41	12	3	0	0	0	0	0
Private for-profit	1,327	314	501	310	133	35	12	10	5	7
Doctoral/research university[4]	11	0	0	4	3	0	1	1	0	2
Master's[5]	38	1	2	8	13	5	1	3	1	4
Baccalaureate[6]	126	13	43	46	18	2	2	1	1	0
Special-focus institutions[7]	547	125	212	109	64	22	7	4	3	1
Art, music, or design	89	16	25	18	24	4	1	1	0	0
Business and management	220	52	75	40	27	15	5	2	3	1
Engineering or technology	153	30	87	33	0	2	1	0	0	0
Law	9	1	2	3	3	0	0	0	0	0
Medical or other health	71	25	21	15	9	0	0	1	0	0
Other special focus	5	1	2	0	1	1	0	0	0	0
2-year	605	175	244	143	35	6	1	1	0	0

See notes at end of table.

Table 317.40. Number of degree-granting postsecondary institutions and enrollment in these institutions, by enrollment size, control, and level of institution: Fall 2014—Continued

Control and level of institution	Total	Under 200	200 to 499	500 to 999	1,000 to 2,499	2,500 to 4,999	5,000 to 9,999	10,000 to 19,999	20,000 to 29,999	30,000 or more
1	12	13	14	15	16	17	18	19	20	21
Total	20,207,369	69,031	266,824	434,332	1,480,334	2,304,192	3,542,720	4,717,412	3,476,118	3,916,406
Research university, very high[2]	2,963,505	0	0	0	2,209	0	63,677	321,086	824,619	1,751,914
Research university, high[3]	1,807,492	0	0	0	2,160	7,296	107,788	623,645	673,394	393,209
Doctoral/research university[4]	854,781	88	291	3,124	15,054	53,583	152,701	332,439	210,252	87,249
Master's[5]	4,607,954	463	3,329	15,045	247,460	756,900	1,272,104	1,168,696	464,352	679,605
Baccalaureate[6]	2,103,907	3,051	34,715	128,412	573,830	463,848	220,912	260,757	98,240	320,142
Special-focus institutions[7]	1,155,245	40,937	122,818	151,297	220,604	186,888	87,181	81,625	68,836	195,059
2-year	6,714,485	24,492	105,671	136,454	419,017	835,677	1,638,357	1,929,164	1,136,425	489,228
Public	14,655,015	1,506	12,716	52,348	507,752	1,328,046	2,774,495	3,906,638	3,075,542	2,995,972
Research university, very high[2]	2,398,724	0	0	0	0	0	14,361	103,073	653,215	1,628,075
Research university, high[3]	1,502,013	0	0	0	0	0	57,500	480,393	601,395	362,725
Doctoral/research university[4]	420,049	0	0	0	2,200	3,331	31,653	216,857	166,008	0
Master's[5]	2,682,609	0	469	0	21,821	208,793	817,351	958,955	442,794	232,426
Baccalaureate[6]	1,166,559	0	488	14,848	98,899	256,158	206,228	230,715	75,705	283,518
Special-focus institutions[7]	87,296	311	2,349	8,022	18,205	44,145	14,264	0	0	0
Art, music, or design	3,053	0	0	958	2,095	0	0	0	0	0
Business and management	8,879	0	0	891	0	0	7,988	0	0	0
Engineering or technology	6,458	0	0	0	0	6,458	0	0	0	0
Law	2,708	153	908	644	1,003	0	0	0	0	0
Medical or other health	58,830	0	666	4,084	10,117	37,687	6,276	0	0	0
Tribal	7,368	158	775	1,445	4,990	0	0	0	0	0
2-year	6,397,765	1,195	9,410	29,478	366,627	815,619	1,633,138	1,916,645	1,136,425	489,228
Private nonprofit	3,996,089	31,336	85,559	170,750	780,783	859,901	688,786	676,299	287,647	415,028
Research university, very high[2]	564,781	0	0	0	2,209	0	49,316	218,013	171,404	123,839
Research university, high[3]	305,479	0	0	0	2,160	7,296	50,288	143,252	71,999	30,484
Doctoral/research university[4]	322,680	88	291	0	8,532	50,252	114,851	104,422	44,244	0
Master's[5]	1,586,703	359	2,337	9,666	205,265	531,265	447,751	165,979	0	224,081
Baccalaureate[6]	812,195	1,693	18,847	83,961	450,186	201,774	0	19,110	0	36,624
Special-focus institutions[7]	373,886	26,036	50,256	68,830	107,347	69,314	26,580	25,523	0	0
Art, music, or design	60,883	1,268	4,560	11,545	18,966	13,197	0	11,347	0	0
Business and management	40,475	1,236	3,668	7,843	5,871	8,933	12,924	0	0	0
Engineering or technology	20,274	618	722	1,300	3,458	0	0	14,176	0	0
Law	15,406	528	1,852	5,447	7,579	0	0	0	0	0
Medical or other health	132,164	2,581	14,635	20,921	51,951	35,141	6,935	0	0	0
Theological	92,618	18,978	23,551	17,489	16,614	9,265	6,721	0	0	0
Tribal	3,014	0	434	2,580	0	0	0	0	0	0
Other special focus	9,052	827	834	1,705	2,908	2,778	0	0	0	0
2-year	30,365	3,160	13,828	8,293	5,084	0	0	0	0	0
Private for-profit	1,556,265	36,189	168,549	211,234	191,799	116,245	79,439	134,475	112,929	505,406
Doctoral/research university[4]	112,052	0	0	3,124	4,322	0	6,197	11,160	0	87,249
Master's[5]	338,642	104	523	5,379	20,374	16,842	7,002	43,762	21,558	223,098
Baccalaureate[6]	125,153	1,358	15,380	29,603	24,745	5,916	14,684	10,932	22,535	0
Special-focus institutions[7]	694,063	14,590	70,213	74,445	95,052	73,429	46,337	56,102	68,836	195,059
Art, music, or design	96,215	1,771	8,821	13,430	34,590	13,008	9,383	15,212	0	0
Business and management	466,297	6,262	23,978	27,740	41,722	49,748	30,727	22,225	68,836	195,059
Engineering or technology	67,799	3,644	29,202	21,161	0	7,565	6,227	0	0	0
Law	6,492	118	802	2,074	3,498	0	0	0	0	0
Medical or other health	51,590	2,618	6,592	10,040	13,675	0	0	18,665	0	0
Other special focus	5,670	177	818	0	1,567	3,108	0	0	0	0
2-year	286,355	20,137	82,433	98,683	47,306	20,058	5,219	12,519	0	0

[1]Excludes 13 institutions that had no enrollment.
[2]Research universities with a very high level of research activity.
[3]Research universities with a high level of research activity.
[4]Institutions that award at least 20 doctor's degrees per year, but did not have a high level of research activity.
[5]Institutions that award at least 50 master's degrees per year.
[6]Institutions that primarily emphasize undergraduate education. Also includes institutions classified as 4-year under the IPEDS system, which had been classified as 2-year in the Carnegie system because they primarily award associate's degrees.

[7]Four-year institutions that award degrees primarily in single fields of study, such as medicine, business, fine arts, theology, and engineering.
NOTE: Degree-granting institutions grant associate's or higher degrees and participate in Title IV federal financial aid programs. Relative levels of research activity for research universities were determined by an analysis of research and development expenditures, science and engineering research staffing, and doctoral degrees conferred, by field. Further information on the research index ranking may be obtained from http://carnegieclassifications.iu.edu/.
SOURCE: U.S. Department of Education, National Center for Education Statistics, Integrated Postsecondary Education Data System (IPEDS), Spring 2015, Fall Enrollment component. (This table was prepared October 2015.)

Table 317.50. Degree-granting postsecondary institutions that have closed their doors, by control and level of institution: 1969–70 through 2014–15

Year	All institutions			Public			Private								
							Total			Nonprofit			For-profit		
	Total	4-year	2-year	Total	4-year	2-year	Total	4-year	2-year	Total	4-year	2-year	Total	4-year	2-year
1	2	3	4	5	6	7	8	9	10	11	12	13	14	15	16
1969–70	24	10	14	5	1	4	19	9	10	—	—	—	—	—	—
1970–71	35	10	25	11	0	11	24	10	14	—	—	—	—	—	—
1971–72	14	5	9	3	0	3	11	5	6	—	—	—	—	—	—
1972–73	21	12	9	4	0	4	17	12	5	—	—	—	—	—	—
1973–74	20	12	8	1	0	1	19	12	7	—	—	—	—	—	—
1974–75	18	13	5	4	0	4	14	13	1	—	—	—	—	—	—
1975–76	9	7	2	2	1	1	7	6	1	—	—	—	—	—	—
1976–77	9	6	3	0	0	0	9	6	3	—	—	—	—	—	—
1977–78	12	9	3	0	0	0	12	9	3	—	—	—	—	—	—
1978–79	9	4	5	0	0	0	9	4	5	—	—	—	—	—	—
1979–80	6	5	1	0	0	0	6	5	1	—	—	—	—	—	—
1980–81	4	3	1	0	0	0	4	3	1	—	—	—	—	—	—
1981–82	7	6	1	0	0	0	7	6	1	—	—	—	—	—	—
1982–83	7	4	3	0	0	0	7	4	3	—	—	—	—	—	—
1983–84	5	5	0	1	1	0	4	4	0	—	—	—	—	—	—
1984–85	4	4	0	0	0	0	4	4	0	—	—	—	—	—	—
1985–86	12	8	4	1	1	0	11	7	4	—	—	—	—	—	—
1986–87 and 1987–88	26	19	7	1	0	1	25	19	6	—	—	—	—	—	—
1988–89	14	6	8	0	0	0	14	6	8	—	—	—	—	—	—
1989–90	19	8	11	0	0	0	19	8	11	—	—	—	—	—	—
1990–91	18	6	12	0	0	0	18	6	12	7	5	2	11	1	10
1991–92	26	8	18	1	0	1	25	8	17	8	7	1	17	1	16
1992–93	23	6	17	0	0	0	23	6	17	6	5	1	17	1	16
1993–94	38	11	27	1	0	1	37	11	26	13	10	3	24	1	23
1994–95	15	8	7	2	0	2	13	8	5	8	7	1	5	1	4
1995–96	21	8	13	1	1	0	20	7	13	9	7	2	11	0	11
1996–97	36	13	23	2	0	2	34	13	21	14	10	4	20	3	17
1997–98	5	0	5	0	0	0	5	0	5	1	0	1	4	0	4
1998–99	7	1	6	1	0	1	6	1	5	2	0	2	4	1	3
1999–2000	16	3	13	3	0	3	13	3	10	8	3	5	5	0	5
2000–01	14	9	5	0	0	0	14	9	5	8	8	0	6	1	5
2001–02	14	2	12	0	0	0	14	2	12	1	1	0	13	1	12
2002–03	13	7	6	0	0	0	13	7	6	6	6	0	7	1	6
2003–04	12	5	7	0	0	0	12	5	7	8	5	3	4	0	4
2004–05	3	1	2	0	0	0	3	1	2	1	1	0	2	0	2
2005–06	11	6	5	1	1	0	10	5	5	5	4	1	5	1	4
2006–07	13	4	9	0	0	0	13	4	9	6	4	2	7	0	7
2007–08	26	10	16	0	0	0	26	10	16	9	6	3	17	4	13
2008–09	16	6	10	0	0	0	16	6	10	6	5	1	10	1	9
2009–10	17	11	6	0	0	0	17	11	6	9	9	0	8	2	6
2010–11	20	9	11	0	0	0	20	9	11	7	6	1	13	3	10
2011–12	10	5	5	4	0	4	6	5	1	2	2	0	4	3	1
2012–13	21	3	18	1	1	0	20	2	18	4	2	2	16	0	16
2013–14	20	8	12	1	1	0	19	7	12	4	3	1	15	4	11
2014–15	54	7	47	0	0	0	54	7	47	5	3	2	49	4	45

—Not available.
NOTE: This table indicates the year by which the institution no longer operated (generally it closed at the end of or during the prior year). Data through 1995–96 are for institutions of higher education, while later data are for degree-granting institutions. Degree-granting institutions grant associate's or higher degrees and participate in Title IV federal financial aid programs. The degree-granting classification is very similar to the earlier higher education classification, but it includes more 2-year colleges and excludes a few higher education institutions that did not grant degrees.

SOURCE: U.S. Department of Education, National Center for Education Statistics, *Education Directory, Higher Education*, 1969–70 through 1974–75; *Education Directory, Colleges and Universities*, 1975–76 through 1985–86; *1982–83 Supplement to the Education Directory, Colleges and Universities*; Integrated Postsecondary Education Data System (IPEDS), "Institutional Characteristics Survey" (IPEDS-IC:86–99); and IPEDS Fall 2000 through Fall 2014, Institutional Characteristics component. (This table was prepared July 2016.)

Table 318.10. Degrees conferred by postsecondary institutions, by level of degree and sex of student: Selected years, 1869–70 through 2025–26

Year	Associate's degrees				Bachelor's degrees				Master's degrees				Doctor's degrees[1]			
	Total	Males	Females	Percent female	Total	Males	Females	Percent female	Total	Males	Females	Percent female	Total	Males	Females	Percent female
1	2	3	4	5	6	7	8	9	10	11	12	13	14	15	16	17
1869–70	—	—	—	—	9,371 [2]	7,993 [2]	1,378 [2]	14.7	0	0	0	—	1	1	0	0.0
1879–80	—	—	—	—	12,896 [2]	10,411 [2]	2,485 [2]	19.3	879	868	11	1.3	54	51	3	5.6
1889–90	—	—	—	—	15,539 [2]	12,857 [2]	2,682 [2]	17.3	1,015	821	194	19.1	149	147	2	1.3
1899–1900	—	—	—	—	27,410 [2]	22,173 [2]	5,237 [2]	19.1	1,583	1,280	303	19.1	382	359	23	6.0
1909–10	—	—	—	—	37,199 [2]	28,762 [2]	8,437 [2]	22.7	2,113	1,555	558	26.4	443	399	44	9.9
1919–20	—	—	—	—	48,622 [2]	31,980 [2]	16,642 [2]	34.2	4,279	2,985	1,294	30.2	615	522	93	15.1
1929–30	—	—	—	—	122,484 [2]	73,615 [2]	48,869 [2]	39.9	14,969	8,925	6,044	40.4	2,299	1,946	353	15.4
1939–40	—	—	—	—	186,500 [2]	109,546 [2]	76,954 [2]	41.3	26,731	16,508	10,223	38.2	3,290	2,861	429	13.0
1949–50	—	—	—	—	432,058 [2]	328,841 [2]	103,217 [2]	23.9	58,183	41,220	16,963	29.2	6,420	5,804	616	9.6
1959–60	—	—	—	—	392,440 [2]	254,063 [2]	138,377 [2]	35.3	74,435	50,898	23,537	31.6	9,829	8,801	1,028	10.5
1969–70	206,023	117,432	88,591	43.0	792,316	451,097	341,219	43.1	213,589	130,799	82,790	38.8	59,486	53,792	5,694	9.6
1970–71	252,311	144,144	108,167	42.9	839,730	475,594	364,136	43.4	235,564	143,083	92,481	39.3	64,998	58,137	6,861	10.6
1971–72	292,014	166,227	125,787	43.1	887,273	500,590	386,683	43.6	257,201	155,010	102,191	39.7	71,206	63,353	7,853	11.0
1972–73	316,174	175,413	140,761	44.5	922,362	518,191	404,171	43.8	268,654	159,569	109,085	40.6	79,512	69,959	9,553	12.0
1973–74	343,924	188,591	155,333	45.2	945,776	527,313	418,463	44.2	282,074	162,606	119,468	42.4	82,591	71,131	11,460	13.9
1974–75	360,171	191,017	169,154	47.0	922,933	504,841	418,092	45.3	297,545	166,318	131,227	44.1	84,904	71,025	13,879	16.3
1975–76	391,454	209,996	181,458	46.4	925,746	504,925	420,821	45.5	317,477	172,519	144,958	45.7	91,007	73,888	17,119	18.8
1976–77	406,377	210,842	195,535	48.1	919,549	495,545	424,004	46.1	323,025	173,090	149,935	46.4	91,730	72,209	19,521	21.3
1977–78	412,246	204,718	207,528	50.3	921,204	487,347	433,857	47.1	317,987	166,857	151,130	47.5	92,345	70,283	22,062	23.9
1978–79	402,702	192,091	210,611	52.3	921,390	477,344	444,046	48.2	307,686	159,111	148,575	48.3	94,971	70,452	24,519	25.8
1979–80	400,910	183,737	217,173	54.2	929,417	473,611	455,806	49.0	305,196	156,882	148,314	48.6	95,631	69,526	26,105	27.3
1980–81	416,377	188,638	227,739	54.7	935,140	469,883	465,257	49.8	302,637	152,979	149,658	49.5	98,016	69,567	28,449	29.0
1981–82	434,526	196,944	237,582	54.7	952,998	473,364	479,634	50.3	302,447	151,349	151,098	50.0	97,838	68,630	29,208	29.9
1982–83	449,620	203,991	245,629	54.6	969,510	479,140	490,370	50.6	296,415	150,092	146,323	49.4	99,335	67,757	31,578	31.8
1983–84	452,240	202,704	249,536	55.2	974,309	482,319	491,990	50.5	291,141	149,268	141,873	48.7	100,799	67,769	33,030	32.8
1984–85	454,712	202,932	251,780	55.4	979,477	482,528	496,949	50.7	293,472	149,276	144,196	49.1	100,785	66,269	34,516	34.2
1985–86	446,047	196,166	249,881	56.0	987,823	485,923	501,900	50.8	295,850	149,373	146,477	49.5	100,280	65,215	35,065	35.0
1986–87	436,304	190,839	245,465	56.3	991,264	480,782	510,482	51.5	296,530	147,063	149,467	50.4	98,477	62,790	35,687	36.2
1987–88	435,085	190,047	245,038	56.3	994,829	477,203	517,626	52.0	305,783	150,243	155,540	50.9	99,139	63,019	36,120	36.4
1988–89	436,764	186,316	250,448	57.3	1,018,755	483,346	535,409	52.6	316,626	153,993	162,633	51.4	100,571	63,055	37,516	37.3
1989–90	455,102	191,195	263,907	58.0	1,051,344	491,696	559,648	53.2	330,152	158,052	172,100	52.1	103,508	63,963	39,545	38.2
1990–91	481,720	198,634	283,086	58.8	1,094,538	504,045	590,493	53.9	342,863	160,842	182,021	53.1	105,547	64,242	41,305	39.1
1991–92	504,231	207,481	296,750	58.9	1,136,553	520,811	615,742	54.2	358,089	165,867	192,222	53.7	109,554	66,603	42,951	39.2
1992–93	514,756	211,964	302,792	58.8	1,165,178	532,881	632,297	54.3	375,032	173,354	201,678	53.8	112,072	67,130	44,942	40.1
1993–94	530,632	215,261	315,371	59.4	1,169,275	532,422	636,853	54.5	393,037	180,571	212,466	54.1	112,636	66,773	45,863	40.7
1994–95	539,691	218,352	321,339	59.5	1,160,134	526,131	634,003	54.6	403,609	183,043	220,566	54.6	114,266	67,324	46,942	41.1
1995–96	555,216	219,514	335,702	60.5	1,164,792	522,454	642,338	55.1	412,180	183,481	228,699	55.5	115,507	67,189	48,318	41.8
1996–97	571,226	223,948	347,278	60.8	1,172,879	520,515	652,364	55.6	425,260	185,270	239,990	56.4	118,747	68,387	50,360	42.4
1997–98	558,555	217,613	340,942	61.0	1,184,406	519,956	664,450	56.1	436,037	188,718	247,319	56.7	118,735	67,232	51,503	43.4
1998–99	564,984	220,508	344,476	61.0	1,202,239	519,961	682,278	56.8	446,038	190,230	255,808	57.4	116,700	65,340	51,360	44.0
1999–2000	564,933	224,721	340,212	60.2	1,237,875	530,367	707,508	57.2	463,185	196,129	267,056	57.7	118,736	64,930	53,806	45.3
2000–01	578,865	231,645	347,220	60.0	1,244,171	531,840	712,331	57.3	473,502	197,770	275,732	58.2	119,585	64,171	55,414	46.3
2001–02	595,133	238,109	357,024	60.0	1,291,900	549,816	742,084	57.4	487,313	202,604	284,709	58.4	119,663	62,731	56,932	47.6
2002–03	634,016	253,451	380,565	60.0	1,348,811	573,258	775,553	57.5	518,699	215,172	303,527	58.5	121,579	62,730	58,849	48.4
2003–04	665,301	260,033	405,268	60.9	1,399,542	595,425	804,117	57.5	564,272	233,056	331,216	58.7	126,087	63,981	62,106	49.3
2004–05	696,660	267,536	429,124	61.6	1,439,264	613,000	826,264	57.4	580,151	237,155	342,996	59.1	134,387	67,257	67,130	50.0
2005–06	713,066	270,095	442,971	62.1	1,485,242	630,600	854,642	57.5	599,731	241,656	358,075	59.7	138,056	68,912	69,144	50.1
2006–07	728,114	275,187	452,927	62.2	1,524,092	649,570	874,522	57.4	610,597	242,189	368,408	60.3	144,690	71,308	73,382	50.7
2007–08	750,164	282,521	467,643	62.3	1,563,069	667,928	895,141	57.3	630,666	250,169	380,497	60.3	149,378	73,453	75,925	50.8
2008–09	787,243	298,066	489,177	62.1	1,601,399	685,422	915,977	57.2	662,082	263,515	398,567	60.2	154,564	75,674	78,890	51.0
2009–10	848,856	322,747	526,109	62.0	1,649,919	706,660	943,259	57.2	693,313	275,317	417,996	60.3	158,590	76,610	81,980	51.7
2010–11	943,506	361,408	582,098	61.7	1,716,053	734,159	981,894	57.2	730,922	291,680	439,242	60.1	163,827	79,672	84,155	51.4
2011–12	1,021,718	393,479	628,239	61.5	1,792,163	765,772	1,026,391	57.3	755,967	302,484	453,483	60.0	170,217	82,670	87,547	51.4
2012–13	1,007,427	389,195	618,232	61.4	1,840,381	787,408	1,052,973	57.2	751,718	301,552	450,166	59.9	175,026	85,080	89,946	51.4
2013–14	1,003,364	390,805	612,559	61.1	1,869,814	801,692	1,068,122	57.1	754,475	302,807	451,668	59.9	177,580	85,587	91,993	51.8
2014–15[3]	979,000	379,000	600,000	61.3	1,868,000	802,000	1,066,000	57.1	763,000	308,000	454,000	59.6	178,000	85,000	92,000	51.9
2015–16[3]	999,000	389,000	610,000	61.0	1,853,000	794,000	1,058,000	57.1	773,000	319,000	454,000	58.7	179,000	86,000	93,000	52.1
2016–17[3]	1,018,000	385,000	633,000	62.1	1,863,000	796,000	1,067,000	57.3	798,000	333,000	465,000	58.3	181,000	86,000	94,000	52.2
2017–18[3]	1,074,000	401,000	673,000	62.7	1,830,000	780,000	1,050,000	57.4	823,000	342,000	481,000	58.5	183,000	89,000	95,000	51.7
2018–19[3]	1,104,000	407,000	697,000	63.1	1,854,000	785,000	1,069,000	57.6	846,000	352,000	494,000	58.4	188,000	91,000	97,000	51.7
2019–20[3]	1,135,000	414,000	721,000	63.5	1,888,000	795,000	1,093,000	57.9	867,000	362,000	505,000	58.3	192,000	92,000	100,000	52.0
2020–21[3]	1,162,000	420,000	742,000	63.8	1,920,000	807,000	1,113,000	58.0	887,000	370,000	517,000	58.3	195,000	94,000	102,000	52.0
2021–22[3]	1,188,000	427,000	761,000	64.1	1,947,000	817,000	1,130,000	58.0	908,000	378,000	529,000	58.3	199,000	95,000	103,000	52.1
2022–23[3]	1,213,000	432,000	780,000	64.3	1,968,000	825,000	1,144,000	58.1	929,000	387,000	542,000	58.3	201,000	96,000	105,000	52.2
2023–24[3]	1,240,000	439,000	801,000	64.6	1,993,000	834,000	1,159,000	58.2	950,000	396,000	554,000	58.3	204,000	97,000	107,000	52.3
2024–25[3]	1,266,000	445,000	821,000	64.9	2,015,000	843,000	1,173,000	58.2	968,000	403,000	565,000	58.4	207,000	99,000	108,000	52.4
2025–26[3]	1,290,000	451,000	840,000	65.1	2,037,000	851,000	1,187,000	58.2	982,000	408,000	573,000	58.4	209,000	100,000	110,000	52.4

—Not available.
[1]Includes Ph.D., Ed.D., and comparable degrees at the doctoral level. Includes most degrees formerly classified as first-professional, such as M.D., D.D.S., and law degrees.
[2]Includes some degrees classified as master's or doctor's degrees in later years.
[3]Projected.
NOTE: Data through 1994–95 are for institutions of higher education, while later data are for degree-granting institutions. Degree-granting institutions grant associate's or higher degrees and participate in Title IV federal financial aid programs. Some data have been revised from previously published figures. Detail may not sum to totals because of rounding.
SOURCE: U.S. Department of Education, National Center for Education Statistics, *Earned Degrees Conferred*, 1869–70 through 1964–65; Higher Education General Information Survey (HEGIS), "Degrees and Other Formal Awards Conferred" surveys, 1965–66 through 1985–86; Integrated Postsecondary Education Data System (IPEDS), "Completions Survey" (IPEDS-C:87–99); IPEDS Fall 2000 through Fall 2014, Completions component; and Degrees Conferred Projection Model, 1980–81 through 2025–26. (This table was prepared March 2016.)

Table 318.20. Bachelor's, master's, and doctor's degrees conferred by postsecondary institutions, by field of study: Selected years, 1970–71 through 2013–14

Degree and year	Number of degrees conferred								Percentage distribution of degrees conferred							
	Total degrees	Humanities[1]	Social and behavioral sciences[2]	Natural sciences and mathematics[3]	Computer sciences and engineering[4]	Education	Business	Other fields[5]	Total degrees	Humanities[1]	Social and behavioral sciences[2]	Natural sciences and mathematics[3]	Computer sciences and engineering[4]	Education	Business	Other fields[5]
1	2	3	4	5	6	7	8	9	10	11	12	13	14	15	16	17
Bachelor's degrees																
1970–71	839,730	143,549	193,511	81,916	52,570	176,307	115,396	76,481	100.0	17.1	23.0	9.8	6.3	21.0	13.7	9.1
1975–76	925,746	150,736	176,674	91,596	52,328	154,437	143,171	156,804	100.0	16.3	19.1	9.9	5.7	16.7	15.5	16.9
1980–81	935,140	134,139	141,581	78,092	90,476	108,074	200,521	182,257	100.0	14.3	15.1	8.4	9.7	11.6	21.4	19.5
1985–86	987,823	132,891	134,468	76,228	139,459	87,147	236,700	180,930	100.0	13.5	13.6	7.7	14.1	8.8	24.0	18.3
1990–91	1,094,538	172,485	183,762	70,209	104,910	110,807	249,165	203,200	100.0	15.8	16.8	6.4	9.6	10.1	22.8	18.6
1995–96	1,164,792	193,404	199,895	93,443	102,503	105,384	226,623	243,540	100.0	16.6	17.2	8.0	8.8	9.0	19.5	20.9
2000–01	1,244,171	214,107	201,681	89,772	117,011	105,458	263,515	252,627	100.0	17.2	16.2	7.2	9.4	8.5	21.2	20.3
2005–06	1,485,242	261,696	249,619	105,899	128,886	107,238	318,042	313,862	100.0	17.6	16.8	7.1	8.7	7.2	21.4	21.1
2009–10	1,649,919	281,056	269,997	125,801	128,328	101,287	358,119	385,331	100.0	17.0	16.4	7.6	7.8	6.1	21.7	23.4
2010–11	1,716,053	288,446	278,075	131,871	136,163	104,008	365,133	412,357	100.0	16.8	16.2	7.7	7.9	6.1	21.3	24.0
2011–12	1,792,163	295,182	287,633	141,355	146,060	105,656	367,235	449,042	100.0	16.5	16.0	7.9	8.1	5.9	20.5	25.1
2012–13	1,840,381	297,322	292,213	148,899	153,958	104,698	360,887	482,404	100.0	16.2	15.9	8.1	8.4	5.7	19.6	26.2
2013–14	1,869,814	291,507	290,394	154,917	164,336	98,854	358,079	511,727	100.0	15.6	15.5	8.3	8.8	5.3	19.2	27.4
Master's degrees																
1970–71	235,564	34,510	22,256	17,152	18,535	87,666	26,490	28,955	100.0	14.6	9.4	7.3	7.9	37.2	11.2	12.3
1975–76	317,477	37,079	26,120	15,742	19,403	126,061	42,592	50,480	100.0	11.7	8.2	5.0	6.1	39.7	13.4	15.9
1980–81	302,637	35,130	22,168	13,579	21,434	96,713	57,888	55,725	100.0	11.6	7.3	4.5	7.1	32.0	19.1	18.4
1985–86	295,850	34,834	20,409	14,055	30,216	74,816	66,676	54,844	100.0	11.8	6.9	4.8	10.2	25.3	22.5	18.5
1990–91	342,863	35,984	23,582	13,664	34,774	87,352	78,255	69,252	100.0	10.5	6.9	4.0	10.1	25.5	22.8	20.2
1995–96	412,180	40,795	30,164	16,154	39,422	104,936	93,554	87,155	100.0	9.9	7.3	3.9	9.6	25.5	22.7	21.1
2000–01	473,502	40,625	30,330	15,360	44,098	127,829	115,602	99,658	100.0	8.6	6.4	3.2	9.3	27.0	24.4	21.0
2005–06	599,731	49,584	37,139	19,574	50,444	174,620	146,406	121,964	100.0	8.3	6.2	3.3	8.4	29.1	24.4	20.3
2009–10	693,313	54,957	43,997	22,435	57,346	182,165	177,748	154,665	100.0	7.9	6.3	3.2	8.3	26.3	25.6	22.3
2010–11	730,922	57,160	46,147	23,576	62,695	185,127	187,178	169,039	100.0	7.8	6.3	3.2	8.6	25.3	25.6	23.1
2011–12	755,967	59,901	48,943	25,576	66,041	179,047	191,606	184,853	100.0	7.9	6.5	3.4	8.7	23.7	25.3	24.5
2012–13	751,718	60,655	49,378	27,271	68,110	164,652	188,617	193,035	100.0	8.1	6.6	3.6	9.1	21.9	25.1	25.7
2013–14	754,475	59,761	49,441	28,217	71,858	154,636	189,328	201,234	100.0	7.9	6.6	3.7	9.5	20.5	25.1	26.7
Doctor's degrees[6]																
1970–71	64,998	4,402	5,804	9,126	3,816	6,041	774	35,035	100.0	6.8	8.9	14.0	5.9	9.3	1.2	53.9
1975–76	91,007	5,461	7,314	7,591	3,118	7,202	906	59,415	100.0	6.0	8.0	8.3	3.4	7.9	1.0	65.3
1980–81	98,016	4,827	6,698	7,473	2,860	7,279	808	68,071	100.0	4.9	6.8	7.6	2.9	7.4	0.8	69.4
1985–86	100,280	4,648	6,548	7,668	3,800	6,610	923	70,083	100.0	4.6	6.5	7.6	3.8	6.6	0.9	69.9
1990–91	105,547	4,858	6,944	9,378	6,006	6,189	1,185	70,987	100.0	4.6	6.6	8.9	5.7	5.9	1.1	67.3
1995–96	115,507	6,356	7,901	10,997	7,223	6,246	1,366	75,418	100.0	5.5	6.8	9.5	6.3	5.4	1.2	65.3
2000–01	119,585	6,466	9,021	10,190	6,315	6,284	1,180	80,129	100.0	5.4	7.5	8.5	5.3	5.3	1.0	67.0
2005–06	138,056	6,628	8,835	12,097	8,734	7,584	1,711	92,467	100.0	4.8	6.4	8.8	6.3	5.5	1.2	67.0
2009–10	158,590	7,742	9,778	14,333	9,372	9,237	2,249	105,879	100.0	4.9	6.2	9.0	5.9	5.8	1.4	66.8
2010–11	163,827	8,359	10,241	14,574	10,013	9,642	2,286	108,712	100.0	5.1	6.3	8.9	6.1	5.9	1.4	66.4
2011–12	170,217	8,732	10,533	14,974	10,554	10,118	2,538	112,768	100.0	5.1	6.2	8.8	6.2	5.9	1.5	66.2
2012–13	175,026	8,582	10,936	15,276	11,301	10,572	2,828	115,531	100.0	4.9	6.2	8.7	6.5	6.0	1.6	66.0
2013–14	177,580	8,398	11,358	15,971	12,099	10,920	3,039	115,795	100.0	4.7	6.4	9.0	6.8	6.1	1.7	65.2

[1] Includes degrees in Area, ethnic, cultural, gender, and group studies; English language and literature/letters; Foreign languages, literatures, and linguistics; Liberal arts and sciences, general studies, and humanities; Multi/interdisciplinary studies; Philosophy and religious studies; Theology and religious vocations; and Visual and performing arts.
[2] Includes Psychology; Social sciences; and History.
[3] Includes Biological and biomedical sciences; Mathematics and statistics; and Physical sciences and science technologies.
[4] Includes Computer and information sciences; Engineering; and Engineering technologies.
[5] Includes Agriculture and natural resources; Architecture and related services; Communication, journalism, and related programs; Communications technologies; Family and consumer sciences/human sciences; Health professions and related programs; Homeland security, law enforcement, and firefighting; Legal professions and studies; Library science; Military technologies and applied sciences; Parks, recreation, leisure, and fitness studies; Precision production; Public administration and social services; Transportation and materials moving; and Not classified by field of study.
[6] Includes Ph.D., Ed.D., and comparable degrees at the doctoral level. Includes most degrees formerly classified as first-professional, such as M.D., D.D.S., and law degrees.

NOTE: Data are for postsecondary institutions participating in Title IV federal financial aid programs. The new Classification of Instructional Programs was initiated in 2009–10. The figures for earlier years have been reclassified when necessary to make them conform to the new taxonomy. To facilitate trend comparisons, certain aggregations have been made of the degree fields as reported in the Integrated Postsecondary Education Data System (IPEDS): "Agriculture and natural resources" includes Agriculture, agriculture operations, and related sciences and Natural resources and conservation; "Business" includes Business, management, marketing, and related support services and Personal and culinary services; and "Engineering technologies" includes Engineering technologies and engineering-related fields, Construction trades, and Mechanic and repair technologies/technicians. Detail may not sum to totals because of rounding. Some data have been revised from previously published figures.
SOURCE: U.S. Department of Education, National Center for Education Statistics, Higher Education General Information Survey (HEGIS), "Degrees and Other Formal Awards Conferred" surveys, 1970–71 through 1985–86; Integrated Postsecondary Education Data System (IPEDS), "Completions Survey" (IPEDS-C:91–96); and IPEDS Fall 2001 through Fall 2014, Completions component. (This table was prepared October 2015.)

Table 318.30. Bachelor's, master's, and doctor's degrees conferred by postsecondary institutions, by sex of student and discipline division: 2013–14

Discipline division	Bachelor's degrees			Master's degrees			Doctor's degrees[1]		
	Total	Males	Females	Total	Males	Females	Total	Males	Females
1	2	3	4	5	6	7	8	9	10
All fields, total	1,869,814	801,692	1,068,122	754,475	302,807	451,668	177,580	85,587	91,993
Agriculture and natural resources	35,116	17,249	17,867	6,544	2,966	3,578	1,407	739	668
Agriculture, agriculture operations, and related sciences	18,036	8,437	9,599	2,704	1,201	1,503	823	426	397
Agriculture, general	1,854	975	879	282	105	177	16	8	8
Agricultural business and management, general	1,171	762	409	73	47	26	0	0	0
Agribusiness/agricultural business operations	1,533	999	534	18	7	11	0	0	0
Agricultural economics	1,555	1,113	442	420	234	186	153	89	64
Farm/farm and ranch management	130	89	41	12	8	4	0	0	0
Agricultural/farm supplies retailing and wholesaling	71	31	40	0	0	0	0	0	0
Agricultural business technology	17	10	7	0	0	0	0	0	0
Agricultural business and management, other	31	12	19	3	1	2	0	0	0
Agricultural mechanization, general	339	313	26	1	1	0	0	0	0
Agricultural mechanics and equipment/machine technology	5	5	0	0	0	0	0	0	0
Agricultural production operations, general	108	62	46	11	5	6	0	0	0
Animal/livestock husbandry and production	205	70	135	0	0	0	0	0	0
Aquaculture	53	38	15	32	17	15	12	8	4
Crop production	45	37	8	2	2	0	3	3	0
Dairy husbandry and production	6	1	5	0	0	0	0	0	0
Horse husbandry/equine science and management	123	5	118	5	0	5	0	0	0
Agroecology and sustainable agriculture	97	58	39	55	24	31	13	7	6
Viticulture and enology	98	52	46	10	4	6	0	0	0
Agricultural and food products processing	92	48	44	0	0	0	0	0	0
Equestrian/equine studies	334	11	323	0	0	0	0	0	0
Agricultural and domestic animal services, other	0	0	0	0	0	0	0	0	0
Applied horticulture/horticultural operations, general	174	104	70	33	13	20	4	0	4
Ornamental horticulture	49	35	14	8	5	3	2	2	0
Landscaping and groundskeeping	142	101	41	8	3	5	0	0	0
Plant nursery operations and management	1	1	0	0	0	0	0	0	0
Turf and turfgrass management	108	105	3	10	9	1	0	0	0
Floriculture/floristry operations and management	3	2	1	0	0	0	0	0	0
Applied horticulture/horticultural business services, other	19	16	3	0	0	0	0	0	0
International agriculture	35	15	20	50	18	32	0	0	0
Agricultural and extension education services	58	21	37	75	22	53	5	1	4
Agricultural communication/journalism	332	81	251	23	5	18	0	0	0
Agricultural public services, other	89	44	45	3	0	3	0	0	0
Animal sciences, general	5,108	1,034	4,074	382	139	243	152	68	84
Agricultural animal breeding	0	0	0	5	0	5	5	1	4
Animal health	2	2	0	2	1	1	0	0	0
Animal nutrition	0	0	0	0	0	0	2	1	1
Dairy science	142	63	79	10	3	7	2	1	1
Livestock management	15	7	8	1	0	1	2	1	1
Poultry science	79	39	40	15	8	7	9	4	5
Animal sciences, other	72	10	62	4	2	2	0	0	0
Food science	1,414	471	943	447	144	303	125	48	77
Food technology and processing	6	4	2	16	5	11	3	2	1
Food science and technology, other	2	0	2	12	4	8	2	0	2
Plant sciences, general	432	290	142	105	56	49	45	23	22
Agronomy and crop science	570	449	121	212	144	68	93	64	29
Horticultural science	600	363	237	90	36	54	39	21	18
Agricultural and horticultural plant breeding	2	1	1	11	5	6	12	10	2
Plant protection and integrated pest management	42	28	14	18	10	8	2	2	0
Range science and management	149	93	56	33	14	19	9	3	6
Plant sciences, other	37	25	12	54	27	27	31	14	17
Soil science and agronomy, general	211	144	67	107	56	51	65	37	28
Soil chemistry and physics	22	19	3	0	0	0	0	0	0
Soil sciences, other	28	16	12	13	7	6	6	4	2
Agriculture, agriculture operations, and related sciences, other	226	163	63	33	10	23	11	4	7
Natural resources and conservation	17,080	8,812	8,268	3,840	1,765	2,075	584	313	271
Natural resources/conservation, general	1,385	739	646	602	253	349	73	46	27
Environmental studies	5,925	2,679	3,246	893	410	483	79	37	42
Environmental science	5,542	2,697	2,845	1,017	438	579	169	88	81
Natural resources conservation and research, other	25	12	13	77	39	38	21	10	11
Natural resources management and policy	616	390	226	428	191	237	36	20	16
Natural resource economics	60	35	25	9	5	4	14	7	7
Water, wetlands, and marine resources management	90	60	30	146	50	96	2	1	1
Land use planning and management/development	56	41	15	51	21	30	10	2	8
Natural resource recreation and tourism	67	46	21	27	14	13	3	1	2
Natural resources law enforcement and protective services	33	29	4	0	0	0	0	0	0
Natural resources management and policy, other	189	96	93	11	4	7	1	0	1
Fishing and fisheries sciences and management	347	206	141	36	19	17	17	10	7
Forestry, general	600	466	134	140	83	57	28	18	10
Forest sciences and biology	218	175	43	126	81	45	58	31	27
Forest management/forest resources management	177	147	30	50	26	24	13	7	6
Urban forestry	9	3	6	8	4	4	0	0	0
Wood science and wood products/pulp and paper technology	46	40	6	13	11	2	6	6	0
Forest resources production and management	5	5	0	17	9	8	7	6	1
Forest technology/technician	5	5	0	0	0	0	0	0	0
Forestry, other	43	34	9	13	5	8	8	3	5
Wildlife, fish, and wildlands science and management	1,374	757	617	150	90	60	34	17	17
Natural resources and conservation, other	268	150	118	26	12	14	5	3	2
Architecture and related services	9,144	5,173	3,971	8,048	4,122	3,926	247	134	113
Architecture	5,952	3,444	2,508	4,285	2,436	1,849	119	63	56
City/urban, community and regional planning	827	502	325	2,222	1,030	1,192	90	44	46
Environmental design/architecture	595	339	256	125	54	71	21	12	9
Interior architecture	416	50	366	205	33	172	0	0	0
Landscape architecture	871	540	331	738	290	448	5	5	0
Architectural history and criticism, general	71	30	41	43	12	31	3	3	0
Architectural technology/technician	214	145	69	0	0	0	0	0	0
Architectural and building sciences/technology	62	50	12	85	53	32	5	4	1
Real estate development	0	0	0	232	174	58	0	0	0
Architecture and related services, other	136	73	63	113	40	73	4	3	1

See notes at end of table.

Table 318.30. Bachelor's, master's, and doctor's degrees conferred by postsecondary institutions, by sex of student and discipline division: 2013–14—Continued

Discipline division	Bachelor's degrees			Master's degrees			Doctor's degrees[1]		
	Total	Males	Females	Total	Males	Females	Total	Males	Females
1	2	3	4	5	6	7	8	9	10
Area, ethnic, cultural, gender, and group studies	8,275	2,466	5,809	1,824	623	1,201	336	130	206
African studies	87	26	61	36	12	24	8	2	6
American/United States studies/civilization	1,303	501	802	247	89	158	103	39	64
Asian studies/civilization	755	317	438	111	37	74	3	1	2
East Asian studies	428	180	248	172	58	114	18	10	8
Russian, Central European, East European and Eurasian studies	20	9	11	33	11	22	0	0	0
European studies/civilization	100	26	74	30	13	17	0	0	0
Latin American studies	384	140	244	218	78	140	5	1	4
Near and Middle Eastern studies	196	65	131	168	87	81	40	20	20
Pacific Area/Pacific Rim studies	18	10	8	7	3	4	0	0	0
Russian studies	81	39	42	48	23	25	0	0	0
Scandinavian studies	13	4	9	3	2	1	4	3	1
South Asian studies	26	8	18	17	10	7	5	2	3
Southeast Asian studies	2	1	1	20	7	13	0	0	0
Western European studies	5	1	4	35	11	24	0	0	0
Canadian studies	2	1	1	0	0	0	0	0	1
Slavic studies	4	0	4	1	1	0	1	0	1
Ural-Altaic and Central Asian studies	0	0	0	9	6	3	3	2	1
Regional studies (U.S., Canadian, foreign)	32	5	27	24	8	16	4	3	1
Chinese studies	47	19	28	14	7	7	0	0	0
French studies	54	10	44	18	8	10	15	8	7
German studies	81	30	51	12	3	9	6	3	3
Italian studies	34	12	22	12	6	6	1	0	1
Japanese studies	51	22	29	5	5	0	0	0	0
Korean studies	0	0	0	4	2	2	0	0	0
Spanish and Iberian studies	28	8	20	0	0	0	0	0	0
Irish studies	0	0	0	2	0	2	0	0	0
Latin American and Caribbean studies	46	14	32	21	6	15	0	0	0
Area studies, other	784	244	540	59	26	33	4	1	3
Ethnic studies	140	39	101	16	5	11	6	3	3
African-American/Black studies	639	205	434	75	23	52	25	10	15
American Indian/Native American studies	228	79	149	32	6	26	8	1	7
Hispanic-American, Puerto Rican, and Mexican-American/Chicano studies	456	125	331	30	17	13	15	8	7
Asian-American studies	120	49	71	11	2	9	0	0	0
Women's studies	1,357	94	1,263	184	13	171	22	1	21
Gay/lesbian studies	19	0	19	0	0	0	0	0	0
Folklore studies	17	6	11	26	9	17	13	6	7
Disability studies	5	1	4	41	12	29	2	1	1
Ethnic, cultural minority, gender, and group studies, other	713	176	537	83	17	66	25	5	20
Biological and biomedical sciences	104,633	43,427	61,206	13,960	6,072	7,888	8,302	3,884	4,418
Biology/biological sciences, general	69,402	27,668	41,734	3,465	1,453	2,012	1,053	488	565
Biomedical sciences, general	2,922	1,145	1,777	1,503	760	743	504	226	278
Biochemistry	7,312	3,785	3,527	280	136	144	530	257	273
Biophysics	142	101	41	28	18	10	139	88	51
Molecular biology	717	343	374	212	96	116	268	128	140
Molecular biochemistry	439	239	200	82	19	63	62	33	29
Molecular biophysics	0	0	0	3	2	1	17	11	6
Structural biology	0	0	0	2	2	0	6	4	2
Radiation biology/radiobiology	11	1	10	8	7	1	11	5	6
Biochemistry and molecular biology	800	449	351	97	54	43	182	103	79
Biochemistry, biophysics and molecular biology, other	198	99	99	5	5	0	23	17	6
Botany/plant biology	212	113	99	87	35	52	120	50	70
Plant pathology/phytopathology	13	4	9	74	31	43	85	39	46
Plant physiology	0	0	0	3	3	0	7	6	1
Plant molecular biology	0	0	0	0	0	0	13	10	3
Botany/plant biology, other	17	7	10	9	2	7	0	0	0
Cell/cellular biology and histology	415	205	210	46	20	26	149	56	93
Anatomy	365	145	220	142	73	69	43	28	15
Developmental biology and embryology	42	19	23	29	8	21	48	20	28
Cell/cellular and molecular biology	2,330	1,088	1,242	193	91	102	474	221	253
Cell biology and anatomy	5	1	4	10	5	5	46	22	24
Cell/cellular biology and anatomical sciences, other	127	56	71	105	43	62	137	50	87
Microbiology, general	1,752	850	902	183	77	106	207	90	117
Medical microbiology and bacteriology	603	284	319	155	60	95	127	50	77
Virology	0	0	0	0	0	0	20	13	7
Parasitology	0	0	0	1	0	1	0	0	0
Immunology	0	0	0	38	16	22	183	80	103
Microbiology and immunology	92	34	58	33	9	24	74	24	50
Microbiological sciences and immunology, other	125	46	79	55	16	39	63	28	35
Zoology/animal biology	1,633	527	1,106	179	56	123	79	34	45
Entomology	118	54	64	170	79	91	99	55	44
Animal physiology	72	33	39	59	21	38	25	11	14
Animal behavior and ethology	49	10	39	6	2	4	1	1	0
Wildlife biology	361	178	183	16	7	9	9	8	1
Zoology/animal biology, other	36	12	24	34	13	21	4	2	2
Genetics, general	247	89	158	57	18	39	153	67	86
Molecular genetics	162	62	100	20	10	10	72	31	41
Animal genetics	22	5	17	25	11	14	51	16	35
Plant genetics	5	4	1	7	3	4	23	10	13
Human/medical genetics	0	0	0	115	14	101	84	32	52
Genome sciences/genomics	0	0	0	1	1	0	7	3	4
Genetics, other	0	0	0	3	0	3	12	7	5
Physiology, general	1,505	645	860	554	313	241	159	83	76
Molecular physiology	0	0	0	5	3	2	21	14	7
Cell physiology	0	0	0	23	12	11	25	9	16
Endocrinology	0	0	0	2	2	0	9	3	6
Reproductive biology	0	0	0	9	5	4	2	1	1
Cardiovascular science	0	0	0	7	2	5	11	9	2
Exercise physiology	2,252	1,113	1,139	241	98	143	56	32	24
Vision science/physiological optics	21	13	8	26	10	16	10	5	5
Pathology/experimental pathology	27	9	18	91	33	58	207	94	113
Oncology and cancer biology	0	0	0	35	20	15	111	48	63
Physiology, pathology, and related sciences, other	0	0	0	1	1	0	6	5	1

See notes at end of table.

Table 318.30. Bachelor's, master's, and doctor's degrees conferred by postsecondary institutions, by sex of student and discipline division: 2013–14—Continued

Discipline division	Bachelor's degrees			Master's degrees			Doctor's degrees[1]		
	Total	Males	Females	Total	Males	Females	Total	Males	Females
1	2	3	4	5	6	7	8	9	10
Pharmacology	55	34	21	166	80	86	243	106	137
Molecular pharmacology	0	0	0	5	0	5	39	18	21
Neuropharmacology	0	0	0	14	9	5	0	0	0
Toxicology	122	30	92	44	17	27	95	47	48
Molecular toxicology	0	0	0	0	0	0	4	2	2
Environmental toxicology	30	13	17	33	7	26	42	17	25
Pharmacology and toxicology	62	28	34	72	26	46	54	29	25
Biometry/biometrics	20	7	13	29	20	9	20	14	6
Biostatistics	25	10	15	458	187	271	181	82	99
Bioinformatics	141	88	53	262	148	114	129	85	44
Computational biology	41	23	18	8	6	2	31	20	11
Biomathematics, bioinformatics, and computational biology, other	31	16	15	37	27	10	19	11	8
Biotechnology	656	319	337	1,213	546	667	8	2	6
Ecology	759	331	428	125	43	82	172	74	98
Marine biology and biological oceanography	1,200	421	779	254	86	168	55	29	26
Evolutionary biology	125	51	74	15	7	8	32	18	14
Aquatic biology/limnology	79	41	38	13	6	7	0	0	0
Environmental biology	285	119	166	48	18	30	11	9	2
Population biology	0	0	0	3	1	2	1	1	0
Conservation biology	141	45	96	118	36	82	17	7	10
Systematic biology/biological systematics	0	0	0	1	0	1	9	4	5
Epidemiology	24	6	18	1,073	315	758	273	100	173
Ecology and evolutionary biology	360	157	203	40	14	26	89	37	52
Ecology, evolution, systematics and population biology, other	136	50	86	22	7	15	38	6	32
Molecular medicine	0	0	0	16	8	8	58	23	35
Neuroscience	4,006	1,529	2,477	150	69	81	548	278	270
Neuroanatomy	0	0	0	0	0	0	0	0	0
Neurobiology and anatomy	606	272	334	11	5	6	106	59	47
Neurobiology and behavior	82	29	53	26	12	14	11	1	10
Neurobiology and neurosciences, other	4	1	3	0	0	0	5	1	4
Biological and biomedical sciences, other	1,092	371	721	1,170	597	573	185	77	108
Business, management, marketing, and personal and culinary services	358,079	188,418	169,661	189,328	101,043	88,285	3,039	1,722	1,317
Business, management, marketing, and related support services	356,747	187,818	168,929	189,284	101,036	88,248	3,039	1,722	1,317
Business/commerce, general	23,248	12,502	10,746	10,562	6,336	4,226	349	181	168
Business administration and management, general	134,243	70,929	63,314	109,368	60,891	48,477	1,589	962	627
Purchasing, procurement/acquisitions and contracts management	627	360	267	568	307	261	4	2	2
Logistics, materials, and supply chain management	3,314	2,313	1,001	782	518	264	3	1	2
Office management and supervision	261	102	159	0	0	0	0	0	0
Operations management and supervision	3,030	1,948	1,082	759	472	287	11	8	3
Nonprofit/public/organizational management	486	173	313	1,809	574	1,235	11	4	7
Customer service management	93	28	65	1	0	1	0	0	0
E-commerce/electronic commerce	181	105	76	189	96	93	1	1	0
Transportation/mobility management	295	236	59	121	85	36	1	0	1
Research and development management	8	7	1	47	7	40	0	0	0
Project management	1,064	819	245	1,242	754	488	16	11	5
Retail management	231	31	200	10	1	9	0	0	0
Organizational leadership	2,305	1,060	1,245	2,878	1,321	1,557	222	103	119
Business administration, management and operations, other	10,329	4,962	5,367	5,949	3,016	2,933	41	25	16
Accounting	49,421	24,046	25,375	18,354	8,537	9,817	47	30	17
Accounting technology/technician and bookkeeping	99	54	45	0	0	0	0	0	0
Auditing	34	10	24	66	30	36	0	0	0
Accounting and finance	527	306	221	1,299	475	824	0	0	0
Accounting and business/management	2,188	627	1,561	289	154	135	0	0	0
Accounting and related services, other	203	116	87	266	149	117	2	2	0
Administrative assistant and secretarial science, general	56	23	33	0	0	0	0	0	0
Business/office automation/technology/data entry	55	24	31	0	0	0	0	0	0
General office occupations and clerical services	13	3	10	0	0	0	0	0	0
Parts, warehousing, and inventory management operations	0	0	0	0	0	0	0	0	0
Business operations support and secretarial services, other				49	21	28	0	0	0
Business/corporate communications	655	250	405	158	38	120	0	0	0
Business/managerial economics	4,858	3,330	1,528	294	140	154	70	43	27
Entrepreneurship/entrepreneurial studies	2,234	1,516	718	715	472	243	14	10	4
Small business administration/management	61	38	23	20	14	6	0	0	0
Entrepreneurial and small business operations, other	41	23	18	13	7	6	2	1	1
Finance, general	31,365	21,875	9,490	6,705	4,118	2,587	48	31	17
Banking and financial support services	499	302	197	49	35	14	0	0	0
Financial planning and services	251	176	75	339	192	147	7	6	1
International finance	6	3	3	35	21	14	0	0	0
Investments and securities	81	64	17	224	136	88	0	0	0
Public finance	24	19	5	0	0	0	0	0	0
Finance and financial management services, other	154	111	43	283	193	90	1	0	1
Hospitality administration/management, general	7,930	2,437	5,493	475	141	334	22	12	10
Tourism and travel services management	564	144	420	130	34	96	0	0	0
Hotel/motel administration/management	1,867	656	1,211	180	59	121	4	3	1
Restaurant/food services management	799	361	438	0	0	0	0	0	0
Resort management	214	92	122	0	0	0	0	0	0
Meeting and event planning	429	38	391	0	0	0	0	0	0
Casino management	6	3	3	0	0	0	0	0	0
Hotel, motel, and restaurant management	154	54	100	0	0	0	0	0	0
Hospitality administration/management, other	476	186	290	69	25	44	2	0	2
Human resources management/personnel administration, general	7,120	1,993	5,127	4,457	1,129	3,328	38	12	26
Labor and industrial relations	766	380	386	794	249	545	20	7	13
Organizational behavior studies	2,878	1,255	1,623	2,010	749	1,261	267	123	144
Labor studies	43	15	28	25	11	14	1	1	0
Human resources development	539	149	390	1,191	336	855	19	9	10
Human resources management and services, other	222	53	169	1,179	436	743	0	0	0
International business/trade/commerce	5,334	2,651	2,683	2,424	1,444	980	33	23	10
Management information systems, general	7,477	5,581	1,896	2,950	2,051	899	41	27	14
Information resources management	224	172	52	630	441	189	27	20	7
Knowledge management	12	8	4	53	42	11	0	0	0
Management information systems and services, other	188	128	60	19	13	6	0	0	0
Management science, general	2,762	1,683	1,079	1,346	781	565	28	20	8
Business statistics	84	55	29	106	54	52	0	0	0

See notes at end of table.

Table 318.30. Bachelor's, master's, and doctor's degrees conferred by postsecondary institutions, by sex of student and discipline division: 2013–14—Continued

Discipline division	Bachelor's degrees			Master's degrees			Doctor's degrees[1]		
	Total	Males	Females	Total	Males	Females	Total	Males	Females
1	2	3	4	5	6	7	8	9	10
Actuarial science	1,099	650	449	378	216	162	0	0	0
Management sciences and quantitative methods, other	289	183	106	559	354	205	10	7	3
Marketing/marketing management, general	29,769	14,238	15,531	1,997	771	1,226	23	11	12
Marketing research	60	26	34	117	51	66	0	0	0
International marketing	156	33	123	103	27	76	5	2	3
Marketing, other	932	451	481	221	98	123	3	1	2
Real estate	536	391	145	755	554	201	1	1	0
Taxation	0	0	0	1,787	893	894	0	0	0
Insurance	773	514	259	94	49	45	2	1	1
Sales, distribution, and marketing operations, general	1,231	682	549	314	106	208	2	0	2
Merchandising and buying operations	13	0	13	23	0	23	0	0	0
Retailing and retail operations	247	55	192	3	0	3	0	0	0
Selling skills and sales operations	339	225	114	0	0	0	0	0	0
General merchandising/sales/related marketing operations, other	107	52	55	7	6	1	0	0	0
Fashion merchandising	2,511	128	2,383	17	2	15	0	0	0
Apparel and accessories marketing operations	755	72	683	7	3	4	0	0	0
Tourism and travel services marketing operations	35	19	16	0	0	0	0	0	0
Tourism promotion operations	67	7	60	0	0	0	0	0	0
Vehicle and vehicle parts and accessories marketing operations	66	61	5	0	0	0	0	0	0
Special products marketing operations	204	81	123	15	5	10	0	0	0
Hospitality and recreation marketing operations	81	67	14	0	0	0	0	0	0
Specialized merchandising/sales/related marketing operations, other	83	32	51	57	17	40	0	0	0
Construction management	1,862	1,695	167	277	212	65	0	0	0
Telecommunications management	1	1	0	3	2	1	0	0	0
Business/management/marketing/related support services, other	2,903	1,570	1,333	1,069	565	504	52	21	31
Personal and culinary services	1,332	600	732	44	7	37	0	0	0
Funeral service and mortuary science, general	113	35	78	0	0	0	0	0	0
Funeral direction/service	24	7	17	0	0	0	0	0	0
Cosmetology/cosmetologist, general	0	0	0	0	0	0	0	0	0
Cooking and related culinary arts, general	0	0	0	0	0	0	0	0	0
Baking and pastry arts/baker/pastry chef	76	10	66	0	0	0	0	0	0
Culinary arts/chef training	332	154	178	0	0	0	0	0	0
Restaurant, culinary, and catering management/manager	716	364	352	0	0	0	0	0	0
Food service, waiter/waitress, and dining room management	0	0	0	0	0	0	0	0	0
Culinary science/culinology	26	15	11	0	0	0	0	0	0
Culinary arts and related services, other	43	15	28	44	7	37	0	0	0
Personal and culinary services, other	2	0	2	0	0	0	0	0	0
Communication and communications technologies	92,591	34,370	58,221	9,928	3,129	6,799	614	267	347
Communication, journalism, and related programs	87,604	30,955	56,649	9,347	2,807	6,540	611	266	345
Communication, general	8,037	2,582	5,455	504	141	363	60	20	40
Speech communication and rhetoric	31,812	11,163	20,649	2,076	646	1,430	244	100	144
Mass communication/media studies	9,522	3,438	6,084	944	277	667	141	64	77
Communication and media studies, other	1,806	600	1,206	777	224	553	59	24	35
Journalism	12,009	3,947	8,062	1,751	536	1,215	34	20	14
Broadcast journalism	1,014	443	571	58	22	36	0	0	0
Photojournalism	147	48	99	23	11	12	0	0	0
Journalism, other	796	257	539	193	57	136	0	0	0
Radio and television	5,161	2,779	2,382	184	79	105	8	2	6
Digital communication and media/multimedia	2,154	1,133	1,021	380	185	195	27	23	4
Radio, television, and digital communication, other	846	475	371	17	11	6	0	0	0
Public relations, advertising, and applied communication	1,213	328	885	42	13	29	0	0	0
Organizational communication, general	1,167	380	787	121	28	93	2	1	1
Public relations/image management	4,634	974	3,660	600	161	439	0	0	0
Advertising	4,625	1,486	3,139	327	112	215	4	0	4
Political communication	74	21	53	22	7	15	0	0	0
Health communication	53	6	47	146	12	134	6	1	5
Sports communication	100	71	29	14	8	6	0	0	0
International and intercultural communication	31	12	19	84	14	70	0	0	0
Technical and scientific communication	42	10	32	12	4	8	7	3	4
Public relations, advertising and applied communication, other	1,029	266	763	180	52	128	0	0	0
Publishing	4	1	3	173	24	149	0	0	0
Communication, journalism, and related programs, other	1,328	535	793	719	183	536	19	8	11
Communications technologies/technicians and support services	4,987	3,415	1,572	581	322	259	3	1	2
Communications technology/technician	91	62	29	42	17	25	3	1	2
Photographic and film/video technology/technician and assistant	77	56	21	0	0	0	0	0	0
Radio and television broadcasting technology/technician	472	298	174	122	43	79	0	0	0
Recording arts technology/technician	1,248	1,101	147	33	22	11	0	0	0
Audiovisual communications technologies/technicians, other	153	123	30	0	0	0	0	0	0
Graphic communications, general	293	101	192	0	0	0	0	0	0
Printing management	88	41	47	2	2	0	0	0	0
Prepress/desktop publishing and digital imaging design	65	24	41	0	0	0	0	0	0
Animation/interactive technology/video graphics/special effects	2,228	1,483	745	355	225	130	0	0	0
Graphic and printing equipment operator, general production	35	17	18	0	0	0	0	0	0
Printing press operator	12	6	6	0	0	0	0	0	0
Graphic communications, other	42	13	29	13	5	8	0	0	0
Communications technologies/technicians and support services, other	183	90	93	14	8	6	0	0	0
Computer and information sciences and support services	55,367	45,393	9,974	24,532	17,484	7,048	1,982	1,566	416
Computer and information sciences, general	12,523	10,546	1,977	5,188	3,917	1,271	667	537	130
Artificial intelligence	0	0	0	112	85	27	39	32	7
Information technology	6,833	5,484	1,349	3,203	2,172	1,031	63	44	19
Informatics	649	505	144	319	114	205	13	9	4
Computer and information sciences, other	329	265	64	99	74	25	27	14	13
Computer programming/programmer, general	1,229	1,047	182	78	56	22	2	1	1
Computer programming, specific applications	242	228	14	37	32	5	0	0	0
Computer programming, other	0	0	0	0	0	0	0	0	0
Data processing and data processing technology/technician	75	69	6	0	0	0	0	0	0
Information science/studies	6,097	4,730	1,367	4,487	2,774	1,713	163	107	56
Computer systems analysis/analyst	1,542	1,204	338	358	248	110	0	0	0
Computer science	13,220	11,306	1,914	6,689	5,114	1,575	954	783	171
Web page, digital/multimedia and information resources design	1,667	1,025	642	252	120	132	0	0	0
Data modeling/warehousing and database administration	186	123	63	93	60	33	0	0	0
Computer graphics	1,626	1,056	570	177	111	66	0	0	0
Modeling, virtual environments and simulation	217	192	25	50	47	3	1	1	0

See notes at end of table.

Table 318.30. Bachelor's, master's, and doctor's degrees conferred by postsecondary institutions, by sex of student and discipline division: 2013–14—Continued

Discipline division	Bachelor's degrees			Master's degrees			Doctor's degrees[1]		
	Total	Males	Females	Total	Males	Females	Total	Males	Females
1	2	3	4	5	6	7	8	9	10
Computer software and media applications, other	250	228	22	38	23	15	0	0	0
Computer systems networking and telecommunications	1,779	1,602	177	666	530	136	3	3	0
Network and system administration/administrator	668	595	73	45	30	15	0	0	0
System, networking, and LAN/WAN management/manager	244	205	39	22	14	8	0	0	0
Computer and information systems security/information assurance	4,432	3,832	600	1,804	1,424	380	16	13	3
Web/multimedia management and webmaster	417	257	160	13	8	5	0	0	0
Information technology project management	371	306	65	190	119	71	6	5	1
Computer support specialist	34	28	6	0	0	0	0	0	0
Computer/information tech. services admin. and management, other	420	313	107	212	141	71	0	0	0
Computer and information sciences and support services, other	317	247	70	400	271	129	28	17	11
Education	98,854	20,353	78,501	154,636	35,984	118,652	10,920	3,464	7,456
Education, general	3,761	645	3,116	22,071	5,190	16,881	2,048	585	1,463
Bilingual and multilingual education	227	19	208	328	52	276	12	2	10
Multicultural education	0	0	0	172	38	134	37	16	21
Indian/Native American education	4	1	3	0	0	0	0	0	0
Bilingual, multilingual, and multicultural education, other	0	0	0	3	0	3	0	0	0
Curriculum and instruction	215	45	170	15,442	2,751	12,691	1,325	305	1,020
Educational leadership and administration, general	2	2	0	18,226	6,427	11,799	3,972	1,460	2,512
Administration of special education	0	0	0	69	8	61	17	2	15
Adult and continuing education administration	7	4	3	876	242	634	55	19	36
Educational, instructional, and curriculum supervision	43	9	34	976	265	711	65	12	53
Higher education/higher education administration	7	4	3	2,712	793	1,919	523	206	317
Community college education	0	0	0	46	15	31	40	14	26
Elementary and middle school administration/principalship	69	5	64	649	294	355	27	8	19
Secondary school administration/principalship	0	0	0	448	182	266	0	0	0
Urban education and leadership	113	44	69	485	127	358	53	17	36
Superintendency and educational system administration	0	0	0	520	183	337	58	30	28
Educational administration and supervision, other	1	0	1	1,270	435	835	317	124	193
Educational/instructional technology	53	32	21	4,388	1,299	3,089	147	46	101
Educational evaluation and research	0	0	0	49	10	39	69	25	44
Educational statistics and research methods	0	0	0	48	18	30	39	15	24
Educational assessment, testing, and measurement	0	0	0	70	6	64	9	4	5
Learning sciences	50	6	44	23	6	17	2	0	2
Educational assessment, evaluation, and research, other	14	3	11	103	28	75	32	10	22
International and comparative education	35	6	29	267	47	220	16	3	13
Social and philosophical foundations of education	30	6	24	512	139	373	113	39	74
Special education and teaching, general	7,697	884	6,813	11,869	1,955	9,914	226	30	196
Education/teaching of individuals with hearing impairments/deafness	102	7	95	140	12	128	8	3	5
Education/teaching of the gifted and talented	0	0	0	318	29	289	2	1	1
Education/teaching of individuals with emotional disturbances	81	17	64	83	21	62	11	1	10
Education/teaching of individuals with mental retardation	141	15	126	97	15	82	3	0	3
Education/teaching of individuals with multiple disabilities	131	10	121	294	45	249	0	0	0
Educ./teach. of individuals with orthopedic/physical health impair.	0	0	0	17	2	15	0	0	0
Education/teaching of individuals with vision impairments/blindness	27	5	22	127	24	103	0	0	0
Educ./teach. of individuals with specific learning disabilities	193	21	172	356	45	311	1	0	1
Education/teaching of individuals with speech/language impairments	192	9	183	221	12	209	0	0	0
Education/teaching of individuals with autism	0	0	0	351	31	320	0	0	0
Education/teaching of individuals who are developmentally delayed	15	0	15	156	25	131	0	0	0
Educ./teach. of individuals in early childhood spec. educ. programs	444	16	428	1,143	110	1,033	0	0	0
Education/teaching of individuals in elementary special educ. programs	219	15	204	1,426	132	1,294	0	0	0
Educ./teach. of individuals in jr. high/middle school special educ. prog.	16	5	11	241	76	165	0	0	0
Education/teaching of individuals in secondary special educ. prog.	45	14	31	376	111	265	0	0	0
Special education and teaching, other	335	44	291	576	80	496	6	2	4
Counselor education/school counseling and guidance services	6	0	6	11,614	2,027	9,587	295	74	221
College student counseling and personnel services	0	0	0	1,059	289	770	25	7	18
Student counseling and personnel services, other	2	0	2	300	48	252	6	0	6
Adult and continuing education and teaching	32	7	25	1,117	312	805	152	40	112
Elementary education and teaching	31,772	2,915	28,857	9,810	1,166	8,644	74	12	62
Junior high/intermediate/middle school education and teaching	3,165	852	2,313	876	219	657	2	1	1
Secondary education and teaching	3,849	1,594	2,255	6,498	2,525	3,973	26	8	18
Teacher education, multiple levels	1,626	297	1,329	3,474	871	2,603	19	4	15
Montessori teacher education	6	0	6	213	13	200	0	0	0
Waldorf/Steiner teacher education	0	0	0	0	0	0	0	0	0
Kindergarten/preschool education and teaching	1,384	67	1,317	267	11	256	12	5	7
Early childhood education and teaching	13,855	542	13,313	3,047	96	2,951	21	0	21
Teacher educ. and prof. dev., specific levels and methods, other	166	26	140	3,532	832	2,700	69	21	48
Agricultural teacher education	577	229	348	251	86	165	29	9	20
Art teacher education	1,178	181	997	893	151	742	25	5	20
Business teacher education	230	89	141	113	51	62	0	0	0
Driver and safety teacher education	0	0	0	5	3	2	0	0	0
English/language arts teacher education	2,445	503	1,942	790	204	586	10	3	7
Foreign language teacher education	108	15	93	183	29	154	12	3	9
Health teacher education	1,609	460	1,149	644	149	495	35	13	22
Family and consumer sciences/home economics teacher education	257	10	247	62	4	58	3	1	2
Technology teacher education/industrial arts teacher education	330	281	49	331	137	194	1	1	0
Sales and marketing operations/marketing and dist. teacher educ.	11	4	7	9	4	5	0	0	0
Mathematics teacher education	2,056	703	1,353	1,609	527	1,082	60	22	38
Music teacher education	3,835	1,577	2,258	1,145	460	685	92	43	49
Physical education teaching and coaching	8,175	4,806	3,369	1,957	1,172	785	36	19	17
Reading teacher education	85	12	73	6,018	352	5,666	78	8	70
Science teacher education/general science teacher education	617	264	353	891	303	588	55	14	41
Social science teacher education	500	289	211	111	56	55	0	0	0
Social studies teacher education	1,618	940	678	479	254	225	3	1	2
Technical teacher education	219	121	98	231	92	139	58	28	30
Trade and industrial teacher education	686	407	279	222	96	126	4	2	2
Computer teacher education	59	10	49	233	66	167	10	4	6
Biology teacher education	430	139	291	292	93	199	1	0	1
Chemistry teacher education	85	30	55	67	27	40	2	1	1
Drama and dance teacher education	131	12	119	72	16	56	0	0	0
French language teacher education	43	6	37	30	7	23	0	0	0
German language teacher education	12	5	7	0	0	0	0	0	0
Health occupations teacher education	10	0	10	74	9	65	67	1	66
History teacher education	598	347	251	93	43	50	0	0	0

See notes at end of table.

Table 318.30. Bachelor's, master's, and doctor's degrees conferred by postsecondary institutions, by sex of student and discipline division: 2013–14—Continued

Discipline division	Bachelor's degrees			Master's degrees			Doctor's degrees[1]		
	Total	Males	Females	Total	Males	Females	Total	Males	Females
1	2	3	4	5	6	7	8	9	10
Physics teacher education	60	38	22	62	42	20	0	0	0
Spanish language teacher education	398	75	323	149	44	105	0	0	0
Speech teacher education	20	5	15	46	8	38	11	3	8
Geography teacher education	2	0	2	2	0	2	0	0	0
Latin teacher education	4	0	4	14	7	7	0	0	0
School librarian/library media specialist	1	1	0	145	14	131	0	0	0
Psychology teacher education	12	3	9	0	0	0	0	0	0
Earth science teacher education	55	18	37	66	30	36	0	0	0
Environmental education	3	2	1	4	1	3	0	0	0
Teacher educ. and prof. dev., specific subject areas, other	300	111	189	1,852	381	1,471	35	14	21
Teaching English as a second/foreign language/ESL language instructor	325	59	266	3,301	653	2,648	27	11	16
Teaching French as a second or foreign language	0	0	0	0	0	0	0	0	0
Teaching English or French as a second or foreign lang., other	35	13	22	0	0	0	0	0	0
Teacher assistant/aide	1	1	0	17	5	12	0	0	0
Adult literacy tutor/instructor	0	0	0	10	1	9	1	0	1
Education, other	1,602	394	1,208	2,812	718	2,094	331	107	224
Engineering and engineering technologies	108,969	88,938	20,031	47,326	35,777	11,549	10,117	7,820	2,297
Engineering	92,162	73,903	18,259	42,372	32,158	10,214	10,010	7,739	2,271
Engineering, general	2,171	1,671	500	2,083	1,596	487	417	330	87
Pre-engineering	17	10	7	0	0	0	0	0	0
Aerospace, aeronautical and astronautical engineering	3,565	3,077	488	1,311	1,104	207	336	283	53
Agricultural engineering	971	639	332	305	162	143	145	99	46
Architectural engineering	675	493	182	129	95	34	14	10	4
Bioengineering and biomedical engineering	5,430	3,255	2,175	1,925	1,165	760	955	590	365
Ceramic sciences and engineering	81	64	17	9	6	3	7	4	3
Chemical engineering	7,969	5,320	2,649	1,473	989	484	980	694	286
Chemical and biomolecular engineering	134	73	61	37	27	10	12	10	2
Chemical engineering, other	0	0	0	8	5	3	0	0	0
Civil engineering, general	12,794	9,976	2,818	5,107	3,738	1,369	936	704	232
Geotechnical and geoenvironmental engineering	0	0	0	1	1	0	0	0	0
Structural engineering	173	142	31	217	163	54	9	9	0
Transportation and highway engineering	0	0	0	95	59	36	9	6	3
Water resources engineering	9	2	7	65	32	33	12	6	6
Civil engineering, other	17	7	10	16	13	3	6	6	0
Computer engineering, general	5,061	4,540	521	1,964	1,508	456	332	289	43
Computer hardware engineering	0	0	0	71	65	6	0	0	0
Computer software engineering	660	612	48	1,197	827	370	6	4	2
Computer engineering, other	1	1	0	9	8	1	4	4	0
Electrical and electronics engineering	13,757	12,052	1,705	9,537	7,595	1,942	2,267	1,906	361
Laser and optical engineering	15	12	3	36	30	6	16	11	5
Telecommunications engineering	3	3	0	205	161	44	0	0	0
Electrical, electronics and communications engineering, other	77	68	9	51	39	12	18	16	2
Engineering mechanics	94	75	19	89	66	23	67	54	13
Engineering physics/applied physics	499	427	72	103	83	20	64	48	16
Engineering science	474	362	112	298	219	79	131	95	36
Environmental/environmental health engineering	1,261	720	541	905	484	421	166	98	68
Materials engineering	1,185	868	317	925	657	268	589	437	152
Mechanical engineering	24,301	21,265	3,036	6,182	5,248	934	1,387	1,183	204
Metallurgical engineering	104	72	32	43	35	8	16	11	5
Mining and mineral engineering	277	241	36	52	47	5	15	14	1
Naval architecture and marine engineering	440	393	47	48	40	8	12	11	1
Nuclear engineering	572	482	90	299	243	56	162	138	24
Ocean engineering	175	146	29	121	94	27	15	13	2
Petroleum engineering	1,406	1,206	200	458	367	91	110	92	18
Systems engineering	808	619	189	2,088	1,632	456	118	92	26
Textile sciences and engineering	252	71	181	43	19	24	32	13	19
Polymer/plastics engineering	98	81	17	113	86	27	61	42	19
Construction engineering	387	349	38	97	72	25	0	0	0
Forest engineering	24	22	2	2	2	0	1	0	1
Industrial engineering	4,101	2,892	1,209	2,286	1,615	671	342	236	106
Manufacturing engineering	339	303	36	257	220	37	4	1	3
Operations research	436	281	155	667	437	230	65	47	18
Surveying engineering	28	27	1	15	12	3	0	0	0
Geological/geophysical engineering	197	138	59	159	127	32	18	14	4
Paper science and engineering	9	5	4	6	2	4	2	1	1
Electromechanical engineering	59	53	6	0	0	0	0	0	0
Mechatronics, robotics, and automation engineering	32	29	3	86	72	14	17	16	1
Biochemical engineering	60	33	27	2	1	1	0	0	0
Engineering chemistry	3	2	1	0	0	0	0	0	0
Biological/biosystems engineering	210	134	76	21	9	12	15	11	4
Engineering, other	751	590	161	1,156	881	275	120	91	29
Engineering technologies/construction trades/mechanics and repairers	16,807	15,035	1,772	4,954	3,619	1,335	107	81	26
Engineering technologies and engineering-related fields	16,221	14,495	1,726	4,954	3,619	1,335	107	81	26
Engineering technology, general	1,309	1,156	153	270	219	51	7	5	2
Architectural engineering technology/technician	386	332	54	15	12	3	0	0	0
Civil engineering technology/technician	532	460	72	0	0	0	0	0	0
Electrical/electronic/communications eng. technology/technician	1,736	1,615	121	39	32	7	0	0	0
Laser and optical technology/technician	0	0	0	0	0	0	0	0	0
Telecommunications technology/technician	73	58	15	94	76	18	0	0	0
Electrical/electronic eng. technologies/technicians, other	793	731	62	2	2	0	0	0	0
Biomedical technology/technician	117	90	27	5	4	1	3	0	3
Electromechanical technology/electromechanical eng. technology	84	80	4	5	3	2	0	0	0
Instrumentation technology/technician	47	41	6	0	0	0	0	0	0
Robotics technology/technician	4	4	0	0	0	0	0	0	0
Automation engineer technology/technician	49	47	2	0	0	0	0	0	0
Electromechanical/instrumentation and maintenance technol./tech.	12	9	3	0	0	0	0	0	0
Heating, ventilation, air conditioning and refrig. eng. technol./tech.	2	2	0	0	0	0	0	0	0
Energy management and systems technology/technician	102	95	7	77	55	22	0	0	0
Solar energy technology/technician	63	61	2	12	11	1	0	0	0
Water quality/wastewater treatment manage./recycling technol./tech.	15	6	9	0	0	0	0	0	0
Environmental engineering technology/environmental technology	112	86	26	77	39	38	3	3	0
Hazardous materials management and waste technology/technician	0	0	0	0	0	0	0	0	0
Environmental control technologies/technicians, other	8	6	2	57	35	22	0	0	0

See notes at end of table.

Table 318.30. Bachelor's, master's, and doctor's degrees conferred by postsecondary institutions, by sex of student and discipline division: 2013–14—Continued

Discipline division	Bachelor's degrees			Master's degrees			Doctor's degrees[1]		
	Total	Males	Females	Total	Males	Females	Total	Males	Females
1	2	3	4	5	6	7	8	9	10
Plastics and polymer engineering technology/technician	83	75	8	7	4	3	0	0	0
Industrial technology/technician	1,649	1,491	158	240	170	70	14	13	1
Manufacturing engineering technology/technician	535	510	25	47	41	6	0	0	0
Welding engineering technology/technician	8	7	1	0	0	0	0	0	0
Industrial production technologies/technicians, other	257	222	35	2	2	0	0	0	0
Occupational safety and health technology/technician	1,268	1,048	220	487	352	135	0	0	0
Quality control technology/technician	21	13	8	113	57	56	0	0	0
Industrial safety technology/technician	113	95	18	25	23	2	0	0	0
Quality control and safety technologies/technicians, other	43	40	3	0	0	0	0	0	0
Aeronautical/aerospace engineering technology/technician	98	88	10	46	37	9	0	0	0
Automotive engineering technology/technician	249	241	8	28	21	7	1	1	0
Mechanical engineering/mechanical technology/technician	1,574	1,486	88	29	20	9	0	0	0
Mechanical engineering related technologies/technicians, other	183	165	18	0	0	0	0	0	0
Mining technology/technician	4	3	1	0	0	0	0	0	0
Petroleum technology/technician	18	17	1	0	0	0	0	0	0
Mining and petroleum technologies/technicians, other	0	0	0	0	0	0	0	0	0
Construction engineering technology/technician	1,680	1,538	142	148	115	33	3	2	1
Surveying technology/surveying	159	145	14	2	1	1	8	6	2
Hydraulics and fluid power technology/technician	6	6	0	0	0	0	0	0	0
Engineering-related technologies, other	0	0	0	0	0	0	0	0	0
Computer engineering technology/technician	488	439	49	0	0	0	0	0	0
Computer technology/computer systems technology	287	249	38	6	4	2	1	1	0
Computer hardware technology/technician	0	0	0	0	0	0	0	0	0
Computer software technology/technician	39	36	3	0	0	0	1	1	0
Computer engineering technologies/technicians, other	13	13	0	0	0	0	0	0	0
Drafting and design technologies/technicians, general	69	54	15	0	0	0	0	0	0
CAD/CADD drafting and/or design technology/technician	86	72	14	1	1	0	0	0	0
Architectural drafting and architectural CAD/CADD	2	2	0	0	0	0	0	0	0
Civil drafting and civil engineering CAD/CADD	3	3	0	0	0	0	0	0	0
Mechanical drafting and mechanical drafting CAD/CADD	33	24	9	0	0	0	0	0	0
Drafting/design engineering technologies/technicians, other	7	1	6	0	0	0	0	0	0
Nuclear engineering technology/technician	169	153	16	0	0	0	0	0	0
Engineering/industrial management	705	580	125	2,886	2,152	734	52	40	12
Engineering design	0	0	0	40	23	17	3	2	1
Packaging science	285	214	71	38	23	15	4	4	0
Engineering-related fields, other	12	10	2	4	1	3	7	3	4
Nanotechnology	4	4	0	26	18	8	0	0	0
Engineering tech. and engineering-related fields, other	627	572	55	126	66	60	0	0	0
Construction trades	268	243	25	0	0	0	0	0	0
Construction trades, general	0	0	0	0	0	0	0	0	0
Mason/masonry	0	0	0	0	0	0	0	0	0
Electrician	0	0	0	0	0	0	0	0	0
Building/property maintenance	0	0	0	0	0	0	0	0	0
Building/construction site management/manager	156	139	17	0	0	0	0	0	0
Building construction technology	63	59	4	0	0	0	0	0	0
Building/construction finishing, mgmt., and inspection, other	49	45	4	0	0	0	0	0	0
Construction trades, other	0	0	0	0	0	0	0	0	0
Mechanic and repair technologies/technicians	318	297	21	0	0	0	0	0	0
Communications systems installation and repair technology	0	0	0	0	0	0	0	0	0
Industrial electronics technology/technician	1	1	0	0	0	0	0	0	0
Heating, air conditioning, ventilation and refrig. main. tech.	1	1	0	0	0	0	0	0	0
Heavy equipment maintenance technology/technician	10	10	0	0	0	0	0	0	0
Autobody/collision and repair technology/technician	0	0	0	0	0	0	0	0	0
Automobile/automotive mechanics technology/technician	49	48	1	0	0	0	0	0	0
Diesel mechanics technology/technician	29	28	1	0	0	0	0	0	0
Airframe mechanics and aircraft maintenance technology/technician	55	51	4	0	0	0	0	0	0
Aircraft powerplant technology/technician	66	61	5	0	0	0	0	0	0
Avionics maintenance technology/technician	104	94	10	0	0	0	0	0	0
Vehicle maintenance and repair technologies, other	3	3	0	0	0	0	0	0	0
English language and literature/letters	50,404	15,809	34,595	9,292	3,113	6,179	1,393	557	836
English language and literature, general	39,996	12,168	27,828	5,044	1,604	3,440	1,196	481	715
Writing, general	602	230	372	125	41	84	0	0	0
Creative writing	2,937	1,010	1,927	3,215	1,212	2,003	9	6	3
Professional, technical, business, and scientific writing	682	218	464	314	94	220	24	10	14
Rhetoric and composition	4,946	1,832	3,114	264	82	182	116	46	70
Rhetoric and composition/writing studies, other	31	6	25	7	2	5	0	0	0
General literature	225	60	165	34	9	25	8	3	5
American literature (United States)	32	3	29	7	0	7	0	0	0
English literature (British and Commonwealth)	244	67	177	117	25	92	10	2	8
Children's and adolescent literature	9	0	9	0	0	0	0	0	0
Literature, other	10	2	8	0	0	0	0	0	0
English language and literature/letters, other	690	213	477	165	44	121	30	9	21
Family and consumer sciences/human sciences	24,722	3,014	21,708	3,121	422	2,699	335	62	273
Work and family studies	1	0	1	0	0	0	0	0	0
Family and consumer sciences/human sciences, general	3,650	343	3,307	528	94	434	69	14	55
Business family and consumer sciences/human sciences	169	55	114	4	2	2	0	0	0
Family and consumer sciences/human sciences communication	17	0	17	0	0	0	0	0	0
Consumer merchandising/retailing management	170	24	146	6	3	3	2	0	2
Family and consumer sciences/human sciences business services, other	7	0	7	0	0	0	0	0	0
Family resource management studies, general	748	217	531	58	14	44	6	1	5
Consumer economics	194	73	121	0	0	0	0	0	0
Consumer services and advocacy	19	2	17	0	0	0	0	0	0
Family and consumer economics and related services, other	359	45	314	4	0	4	8	1	7
Foods, nutrition, and wellness studies, general	2,645	535	2,110	581	85	496	34	8	26
Human nutrition	790	152	638	357	63	294	23	6	17
Food service systems administration/management	1,010	398	612	8	0	8	0	0	0
Foods, nutrition, and related services, other	14	1	13	34	3	31	0	0	0
Housing and human environments, general	226	39	187	24	5	19	5	0	5
Facilities planning and management	59	56	3	11	8	3	0	0	0
Housing and human environments, other	13	3	10	0	0	0	0	0	0
Human development and family studies, general	8,191	650	7,541	602	61	541	112	23	89
Adult development and aging	18	1	17	171	18	153	1	0	1
Family systems	506	47	459	24	1	23	7	0	7

See notes at end of table.

Table 318.30. Bachelor's, master's, and doctor's degrees conferred by postsecondary institutions, by sex of student and discipline division: 2013–14—Continued

Discipline division	Bachelor's degrees			Master's degrees			Doctor's degrees[1]		
	Total	Males	Females	Total	Males	Females	Total	Males	Females
1	2	3	4	5	6	7	8	9	10
Child development	1,808	63	1,745	235	14	221	16	1	15
Family and community services	1,121	151	970	212	21	191	31	4	27
Child care and support services management	223	8	215	39	1	38	0	0	0
Child care provider/assistant	13	0	13	5	0	5	0	0	0
Human development, family studies, and related services, other	470	40	430	58	8	50	8	1	7
Apparel and textiles, general	1,868	88	1,780	72	11	61	9	3	6
Apparel and textile manufacture	49	4	45	0	0	0	0	0	0
Textile science	1	0	1	0	0	0	0	0	0
Apparel and textile marketing management	321	16	305	46	4	42	4	0	4
Fashion and fabric consultant	2	0	2	0	0	0	0	0	0
Apparel and textiles, other	15	0	15	1	0	1	0	0	0
Family and consumer sciences/human sciences, other	25	3	22	41	6	35	0	0	0
Foreign languages, literatures, and linguistics	20,335	6,266	14,069	3,482	1,222	2,260	1,231	498	733
Foreign languages and literatures, general	1,586	469	1,117	256	61	195	22	6	16
Linguistics	2,068	670	1,398	665	268	397	231	94	137
Language interpretation and translation	39	16	23	152	41	111	7	3	4
Comparative literature	788	235	553	136	49	87	156	71	85
Applied linguistics	18	5	13	16	6	10	4	0	4
Linguistic/comparative/related language studies and serv., other	139	33	106	33	8	25	5	0	5
African languages, literatures, and linguistics	6	1	5	3	2	1	4	2	2
East Asian languages, literatures, and linguistics, general	157	60	97	77	36	41	32	15	17
Chinese language and literature	497	255	242	46	5	41	3	0	3
Japanese language and literature	625	290	335	25	11	14	4	2	2
Korean language and literature	32	12	20	10	3	7	8	0	8
East Asian languages, literatures, and linguistics, other	102	35	67	19	11	8	22	8	14
Slavic languages, literatures, and linguistics, general	66	28	38	46	13	33	34	14	20
Russian language and literature	371	191	180	14	8	6	1	0	1
Polish language and literature	4	3	1	0	0	0	0	0	0
Slavic/Baltic/Albanian languages, lit., and linguistics, other	0	0	0	1	0	1	0	0	0
Germanic languages, literatures, and linguistics, general	68	26	42	23	9	14	32	17	15
German language and literature	878	408	470	123	44	79	44	21	23
Scandinavian languages, literatures, and linguistics	7	3	4	3	0	3	4	0	4
Danish language and literature	2	0	2	0	0	0	0	0	0
Dutch/Flemish language and literature	1	0	1	0	0	0	0	0	0
Norwegian language and literature	9	5	4	0	0	0	0	0	0
Swedish language and literature	1	0	1	0	0	0	0	0	0
Germanic languages, literatures, and linguistics, other	1	1	0	0	0	0	0	0	0
Modern Greek language and literature	2	2	0	0	0	0	1	1	0
South Asian languages, literatures, and linguistics, general	2	2	0	2	2	0	4	1	3
Iranian languages, literatures, and linguistics	13	9	4	2	1	1	0	0	0
Romance languages, literatures, and linguistics, general	152	34	118	74	23	51	53	22	31
French language and literature	2,044	492	1,552	308	91	217	107	31	76
Italian language and literature	271	85	186	58	14	44	29	10	19
Portuguese language and literature	50	23	27	19	7	12	6	3	3
Spanish language and literature	8,034	2,029	6,005	832	250	582	193	66	127
Hispanic and Latin American languages, lit., and linguistics, general	85	23	62	21	8	13	14	6	8
Romance languages, literatures, and linguistics, other	68	17	51	40	11	29	47	16	31
American Indian/Native American languages, literatures, and linguistics	0	0	0	9	2	7	0	0	0
Middle/Near Eastern and Semitic languages, lit., and linguistics, general	20	11	9	27	15	12	16	8	8
Arabic language and literature	165	87	78	6	4	2	0	0	0
Hebrew language and literature	60	26	34	30	20	10	9	3	6
Ancient Near Eastern and biblical languages, lit., and linguistics	39	26	13	26	21	5	4	3	1
Middle/Near Eastern and Semitic languages, lit., and ling., other	80	29	51	38	18	20	29	17	12
Classics and classical languages, lit., and linguistics, general	994	456	538	194	106	88	87	50	37
Ancient/classical Greek language and literature	17	7	10	1	0	1	0	0	0
Latin language and literature	55	22	33	20	11	9	0	0	0
Classics and classical languages, lit., and linguistics, other	19	9	10	23	16	7	1	1	0
Celtic languages, literatures, and linguistics	2	1	1	0	0	0	2	0	2
Filipino/Tagalog language and literature	6	2	4	0	0	0	0	0	0
Turkish language and literature	0	0	0	0	0	0	0	0	0
Uralic languages, literatures, and linguistics	0	0	0	0	0	0	0	0	0
American sign language (ASL)	124	9	115	31	12	19	0	0	0
Sign language interpretation and translation	313	36	277	29	5	24	0	0	0
American sign language, other	2	1	1	0	0	0	0	0	0
Foreign languages, literatures, and linguistics, other	253	82	171	44	10	34	16	7	9
Health professions and related programs	198,770	30,931	167,839	97,403	17,749	79,654	67,448	28,084	39,364
Health and wellness, general	9,944	2,394	7,550	672	258	414	177	51	126
Chiropractic	0	0	0	0	0	0	2,420	1,464	956
Communication sciences and disorders, general	4,852	258	4,594	1,898	87	1,811	32	6	26
Audiology/audiologist	253	19	234	119	9	110	605	100	505
Speech-language pathology/pathologist	1,383	49	1,334	2,881	118	2,763	25	2	23
Audiology/audiologist and speech-language pathology/pathologist	4,539	228	4,311	2,649	120	2,529	212	30	182
Communication disorders sciences and services, other	80	2	78	110	3	107	14	4	10
Dentistry	0	0	0	0	0	0	5,407	2,839	2,568
Dental clinical sciences, general	0	0	0	347	199	148	7	3	4
Advanced general dentistry	0	0	0	8	6	2	0	0	0
Oral biology and oral maxillofacial pathology	0	0	0	92	50	42	16	8	8
Dental public health and education	0	0	0	8	1	7	1	0	1
Dental materials	0	0	0	0	0	0	0	0	0
Endodontics/endodontology	0	0	0	30	20	10	2	1	1
Oral/maxillofacial surgery	0	0	0	0	0	0	0	0	0
Orthodontics/orthodontology	0	0	0	84	40	44	5	3	2
Pediatric dentistry/pedodontics	0	0	0	26	9	17	0	0	0
Periodontics/periodontology	0	0	0	36	20	16	1	1	0
Prosthodontics/prosthodontology	0	0	0	25	17	8	5	3	2
Advanced/graduate dentistry and oral sciences, other	0	0	0	57	27	30	4	3	1
Dental assisting/assistant	1	0	1	0	0	0	0	0	0
Dental hygiene/hygienist	2,059	72	1,987	82	4	78	0	0	0
Dental laboratory technology/technician	0	0	0	13	8	5	0	0	0
Dental services and allied professions, other	13	0	13	4	2	2	0	0	0
Health/health care administration/management	9,249	1,826	7,423	7,836	2,359	5,477	189	58	131
Hospital and health care facilities administration/management	4,400	572	3,828	938	308	630	1	1	0
Health unit manager/ward supervisor	0	0	0	4	1	3	0	0	0

See notes at end of table.

Table 318.30. Bachelor's, master's, and doctor's degrees conferred by postsecondary institutions, by sex of student and discipline division: 2013–14—Continued

Discipline division	Bachelor's degrees			Master's degrees			Doctor's degrees[1]		
	Total	Males	Females	Total	Males	Females	Total	Males	Females
1	2	3	4	5	6	7	8	9	10
Medical office management/administration	10	1	9	0	0	0	0	0	0
Health information/medical records administration/administrator	1,577	258	1,319	295	108	187	0	0	0
Health information/medical records technology/technician	42	15	27	29	4	25	0	0	0
Medical office assistant/specialist	5	2	3	0	0	0	0	0	0
Medical/health management and clinical assistant/specialist	111	24	87	6	1	5	0	0	0
Medical staff services technology/technician	0	0	0	0	0	0	0	0	0
Long term care administration/management	472	43	429	11	2	9	0	0	0
Clinical research coordinator	9	0	9	62	12	50	0	0	0
Health and medical administrative services, other	571	128	443	294	70	224	14	5	9
Medical/clinical assistant	4	1	3	13	5	8	0	0	0
Occupational therapist assistant	0	0	0	0	0	0	0	0	0
Pharmacy technician/assistant	0	0	0	0	0	0	0	0	0
Physical therapy technician/assistant	8	6	2	0	0	0	0	0	0
Veterinary/animal health technology/technician and vet. assistant	384	33	351	0	0	0	0	0	0
Anesthesiologist assistant	0	0	0	124	59	65	0	0	0
Pathology/pathologist assistant	11	3	8	67	13	54	0	0	0
Respiratory therapy technician/assistant	15	8	7	0	0	0	0	0	0
Radiologist assistant	0	0	0	10	3	7	0	0	0
Allied health and medical assisting services, other	356	99	257	156	50	106	0	0	0
Cardiovascular technology/technologist	83	22	61	0	0	0	0	0	0
Emergency medical technology/technician (EMT paramedic)	242	172	70	17	13	4	0	0	0
Nuclear medical technology/technologist	300	99	201	0	0	0	0	0	0
Perfusion technology/perfusionist	6	5	1	62	36	26	0	0	0
Medical radiologic technology/science radiation therapist	1,186	307	879	63	32	31	0	0	0
Respiratory care therapy/therapist	1,100	346	754	25	6	19	0	0	0
Surgical technology/technologist	3	0	3	15	3	12	0	0	0
Diagnostic medical sonography/sonographer and ultrasound technician	647	115	532	9	2	7	0	0	0
Radiologic technology/science radiographer	1,246	326	920	49	23	26	3	2	1
Physician assistant	485	126	359	6,542	1,638	4,904	10	9	1
Athletic training/trainer	3,630	1,495	2,135	548	219	329	1	1	0
Gene/genetic therapy	11	4	7	0	0	0	1	0	1
Cardiopulmonary technology/technologist	6	1	5	0	0	0	0	0	0
Radiation protection/health physics technician	13	2	11	8	7	1	0	0	0
Magnetic resonance imaging (MRI) technology/technician	31	13	18	0	0	0	0	0	0
Allied health diagnostic/intervention/treatment professions, other	325	85	240	13	7	6	143	33	110
Blood bank technology specialist	0	0	0	0	0	0	0	0	0
Cytotechnology/cytotechnologist	45	17	28	8	2	6	0	0	0
Hematology technology/technician	0	0	0	9	5	4	0	0	0
Clinical/medical laboratory technician	125	35	90	0	0	0	0	0	0
Clinical laboratory science/medical technology/technologist	2,700	783	1,917	170	60	110	0	0	0
Histologic technology/histotechnologist	13	1	12	4	0	4	0	0	0
Cytogenetics/genetics/clinical genetics technology/technologist	51	14	37	0	0	0	0	0	0
Clinical/medical laboratory science and allied professions, other	269	80	189	91	31	60	6	4	2
Pre-dentistry studies	13	8	5	0	0	0	0	0	0
Pre-medicine/pre-medical studies	859	367	492	30	13	17	0	0	0
Pre-pharmacy studies	21	8	13	0	0	0	0	0	0
Pre-veterinary studies	302	45	257	0	0	0	0	0	0
Pre-nursing studies	16	2	14	0	0	0	0	0	0
Pre-occupational therapy studies	138	9	129	0	0	0	0	0	0
Pre-optometry studies	1	0	1	0	0	0	0	0	0
Pre-physical therapy studies	215	86	129	0	0	0	0	0	0
Health/medical preparatory programs, other	1,382	394	988	95	38	57	0	0	0
Medicine	0	0	0	0	0	0	17,606	9,234	8,372
Medical scientist	0	0	0	483	245	238	15	8	7
Substance abuse/addiction counseling	457	114	343	421	115	306	0	0	0
Psychiatric/mental health services technician	245	48	197	31	1	30	0	0	0
Clinical/medical social work	212	31	181	586	73	513	5	0	5
Community health services/liaison/counseling	1,104	225	879	245	48	197	9	1	8
Marriage and family therapy/counseling	0	0	0	3,006	463	2,543	113	24	89
Clinical pastoral counseling/patient counseling	38	5	33	95	32	63	34	9	25
Psychoanalysis and psychotherapy	0	0	0	6	3	3	8	2	6
Mental health counseling/counselor	9	1	8	4,891	743	4,148	15	3	12
Genetic counseling/counselor	0	0	0	138	6	132	0	0	0
Mental and social health services and allied professions, other	585	77	508	129	29	100	16	1	15
Optometry	0	0	0	0	0	0	1,523	535	988
Ophthalmic technician/technologist	5	1	4	0	0	0	0	0	0
Orthoptics/orthoptist	2	0	2	0	0	0	0	0	0
Ophthalmic/optometric support services/allied professions, other	10	7	3	20	9	11	3	2	1
Osteopathic medicine/osteopathy	0	0	0	0	0	0	4,990	2,662	2,328
Pharmacy	954	368	586	2	2	0	13,919	5,427	8,492
Pharmacy admin. and pharmacy policy and regulatory affairs	0	0	0	361	139	222	23	9	14
Pharmaceutics and drug design	151	72	79	122	59	63	150	74	76
Medicinal and pharmaceutical chemistry	25	14	11	63	32	31	104	60	44
Natural products chemistry and pharmacognosy	0	0	0	2	1	1	4	3	1
Clinical and industrial drug development	24	6	18	136	36	100	0	0	0
Pharmacoeconomics/pharmaceutical economics	0	0	0	5	2	3	94	41	53
Clinical, hospital, and managed care pharmacy	0	0	0	3	2	1	0	0	0
Industrial and physical pharmacy and cosmetic sciences	2	0	2	14	1	13	0	0	0
Pharmaceutical sciences	613	248	365	210	97	113	157	81	76
Pharmaceutical marketing and management	53	21	32	22	10	12	0	0	0
Pharmacy, pharmaceutical sciences, and administration, other	456	181	275	327	111	216	38	24	14
Podiatric medicine/podiatry	0	0	0	0	0	0	567	338	229
Public health, general	3,050	669	2,381	8,115	2,110	6,005	363	105	258
Environmental health	348	161	187	532	187	345	92	34	58
Health/medical physics	42	23	19	122	87	35	45	29	16
Occupational health and industrial hygiene	152	113	39	114	72	42	15	8	7
Public health education and promotion	2,493	459	2,034	815	104	711	79	14	65
Community health and preventive medicine	1,145	225	920	189	37	152	29	7	22
Maternal and child health	17	0	17	153	4	149	23	2	21
International public health/international health	62	15	47	493	114	379	15	8	7
Health services administration	817	143	674	628	217	411	12	4	8
Behavioral aspects of health	137	43	94	119	13	106	24	4	20
Public health, other	1,045	288	757	553	136	417	78	22	56

See notes at end of table.

Table 318.30. Bachelor's, master's, and doctor's degrees conferred by postsecondary institutions, by sex of student and discipline division: 2013–14—Continued

Discipline division	Bachelor's degrees			Master's degrees			Doctor's degrees[1]		
	Total	Males	Females	Total	Males	Females	Total	Males	Females
1	2	3	4	5	6	7	8	9	10
Art therapy/therapist	194	7	187	452	18	434	4	0	4
Dance therapy/therapist	0	0	0	68	0	68	0	0	0
Music therapy/therapist	293	44	249	115	20	95	1	0	1
Occupational therapy/therapist	890	96	794	5,498	618	4,880	302	25	277
Orthotist/prosthetist	16	10	6	115	44	71	0	0	0
Physical therapy/therapist	304	114	190	179	57	122	10,207	3,416	6,791
Therapeutic recreation/recreational therapy	597	84	513	48	6	42	0	0	0
Vocational rehabilitation counseling/counselor	323	58	265	1,023	220	803	21	3	18
Kinesiotherapy/kinesiotherapist	51	17	34	20	2	18	0	0	0
Assistive/augmentative technology and rehabilitation engineering	0	0	0	10	6	4	0	0	0
Animal-assisted therapy	8	0	8	6	0	6	0	0	0
Rehabilitation science	575	143	432	114	47	67	49	17	32
Rehabilitation and therapeutic professions, other	720	139	581	351	72	279	23	7	16
Veterinary medicine	0	0	0	0	0	0	2,686	565	2,121
Veterinary sciences/veterinary clinical sciences, general	42	4	38	179	55	124	176	63	113
Veterinary physiology	0	0	0	0	0	0	7	4	3
Veterinary microbiology and immunobiology	29	10	19	4	1	3	5	2	3
Veterinary pathology and pathobiology	0	0	0	7	2	5	16	3	13
Large animal/food animal/equine surgery and medicine	0	0	0	1	0	1	1	0	1
Small/companion animal surgery and medicine	0	0	0	4	1	3	0	0	0
Comparative and laboratory animal medicine	0	0	0	36	8	28	0	0	0
Veterinary preventive medicine epidemiology/public health	0	0	0	10	6	4	0	0	0
Veterinary infectious diseases	0	0	0	0	0	0	6	4	2
Medical illustration/medical illustrator	50	4	46	33	5	28	0	0	0
Medical informatics	119	40	79	457	215	242	62	40	22
Dietetics/dietitian	3,096	335	2,761	491	35	456	1	0	1
Clinical nutrition/nutritionist	159	19	140	286	52	234	8	1	7
Dietetic technician	0	0	0	0	0	0	0	0	0
Dietetics and clinical nutrition services, other	313	54	259	89	10	79	0	0	0
Bioethics/medical ethics	13	4	9	246	75	171	21	4	17
Alternative and complementary medicine and medical systems, general	0	0	0	22	7	15	8	2	6
Acupuncture and oriental medicine	91	29	62	1,425	418	1,007	83	37	46
Traditional Chinese medicine and Chinese herbology	0	0	0	251	63	188	16	5	11
Naturopathic medicine/naturopathy	0	0	0	0	0	0	294	73	221
Holistic health	157	33	124	30	7	23	0	0	0
Alternative and complementary medicine and medical systems, other	176	30	146	18	1	17	0	0	0
Direct entry midwifery	20	0	20	14	0	14	0	0	0
Massage therapy/therapeutic massage	0	0	0	0	0	0	0	0	0
Asian bodywork therapy	0	0	0	0	0	0	0	0	0
Movement therapy and movement education	54	30	24	22	0	22	6	2	4
Herbalism/herbalist	12	4	8	16	0	16	0	0	0
Energy and biologically based therapies, other	0	0	0	0	0	0	0	0	0
Registered nursing/registered nurse	110,817	13,454	97,363	14,201	1,442	12,759	643	59	584
Nursing administration	979	80	899	4,552	480	4,072	294	34	260
Adult health nurse/nursing	73	6	67	1,089	97	992	15	0	15
Nurse anesthetist	0	0	0	1,650	648	1,002	80	32	48
Family practice nurse/nursing	298	44	254	5,480	605	4,875	211	17	194
Maternal/child health and neonatal nurse/nursing	0	0	0	235	12	223	1	0	1
Nurse midwife/nursing midwifery	0	0	0	328	0	328	11	0	11
Nursing science	1,145	127	1,018	2,181	233	1,948	643	40	603
Pediatric nurse/nursing	0	0	0	295	12	283	12	0	12
Psychiatric/mental health nurse/nursing	0	0	0	314	52	262	14	1	13
Public health/community nurse/nursing	17	1	16	159	8	151	0	0	0
Perioperative/operating room and surgical nurse/nursing	0	0	0	74	5	69	0	0	0
Clinical nurse specialist	62	6	56	330	43	287	45	4	41
Critical care nursing	0	0	0	233	30	203	13	1	12
Occupational and environmental health nursing	0	0	0	18	3	15	2	0	2
Emergency room/trauma nursing	0	0	0	26	9	17	0	0	0
Nursing education	28	0	28	1,800	112	1,688	21	2	19
Nursing practice	804	98	706	236	17	219	1,768	185	1,583
Palliative care nursing	4	0	4	9	2	7	0	0	0
Clinical nurse leader	11	0	11	336	43	293	0	0	0
Geriatric nurse/nursing	0	0	0	242	37	205	2	0	2
Women's health nurse/nursing	0	0	0	146	0	146	0	0	0
Reg. nursing, nursing admin., nursing research and clinical nursing, other	1,617	187	1,430	1,175	99	1,076	161	15	146
Licensed practical/vocational nurse training	30	5	25	0	0	0	0	0	0
Practical nursing, vocational nursing and nursing assistants, other	73	6	67	23	0	23	0	0	0
Health professions and related clinical sciences, other	4,445	1,043	3,402	736	221	515	40	15	25
Homeland security, law enforcement, firefighting and related prot. services	62,409	33,383	29,026	9,310	4,665	4,645	152	66	86
Corrections	481	209	272	18	5	13	0	0	0
Criminal justice/law enforcement administration	19,363	10,035	9,328	3,039	1,370	1,669	28	11	17
Criminal justice/safety studies	31,415	16,452	14,963	2,869	1,247	1,622	101	41	60
Forensic science and technology	1,184	317	867	612	163	449	0	0	0
Criminal justice/police science	2,854	1,682	1,172	60	17	43	3	2	1
Security and loss prevention services	23	16	7	17	13	4	0	0	0
Juvenile corrections	30	6	24	6	2	4	5	3	2
Criminalistics and criminal science	200	63	137	51	14	37	0	0	0
Securities services administration/management	967	555	412	286	224	62	0	0	0
Corrections administration	90	48	42	11	3	8	0	0	0
Law enforcement investigation and interviewing	10	4	6	0	0	0	0	0	0
Cyber/computer forensics and counterterrorism	201	163	38	110	77	33	0	0	0
Financial forensics and fraud investigation	39	12	27	111	43	68	0	0	0
Law enforcement intelligence analysis	22	17	5	11	5	6	0	0	0
Critical incident response/special police operations	0	0	0	0	0	0	0	0	0
Protective services operations	0	0	0	0	0	0	0	0	0
Corrections and criminal justice, other	1,662	737	925	173	68	105	0	0	0
Fire prevention and safety technology/technician	147	135	12	12	8	4	0	0	0
Fire services administration	533	495	38	122	91	31	2	0	2
Fire science/firefighting	661	619	42	0	0	0	0	0	0
Fire/arson investigation and prevention	15	12	3	0	0	0	0	0	0
Fire protection, other	34	30	4	1	1	0	0	0	0
Homeland security	691	549	142	483	377	106	0	0	0
Crisis/emergency/disaster management	676	470	206	448	308	140	11	7	4

See notes at end of table.

Table 318.30. Bachelor's, master's, and doctor's degrees conferred by postsecondary institutions, by sex of student and discipline division: 2013–14—Continued

Discipline division	Bachelor's degrees			Master's degrees			Doctor's degrees[1]		
	Total	Males	Females	Total	Males	Females	Total	Males	Females
1	2	3	4	5	6	7	8	9	10
Critical infrastructure protection	55	34	21	86	62	24	0	0	0
Terrorism and counterterrorism operations	0	0	0	12	9	3	0	0	0
Homeland security, other	79	56	23	138	102	36	0	0	0
Homeland sec., law enforcement, firefighting and related prot. serv., other	977	667	310	634	456	178	2	2	0
Legal professions and studies	4,513	1,456	3,057	7,655	3,567	4,088	44,169	23,495	20,674
Pre-law studies	300	156	144	0	0	0	0	0	0
Legal studies, general	1,846	667	1,179	407	127	280	11	2	9
Law	0	0	0	0	0	0	43,772	23,278	20,494
Advanced legal research/studies, general	118	64	54	1,713	766	947	81	51	30
Programs for foreign lawyers	0	0	0	1,064	552	512	0	0	0
American/U.S. law/legal studies/jurisprudence	30	12	18	306	120	186	35	14	21
Banking, corporate, finance, and securities law	0	0	0	280	140	140	1	1	0
Comparative law	0	0	0	51	33	18	0	0	0
Energy, environment, and natural resources law	2	1	1	91	52	39	4	4	0
Health law	0	0	0	215	46	169	4	3	1
International law and legal studies	2	1	1	583	247	336	20	9	11
International business, trade, and tax law	0	0	0	237	129	108	0	0	0
Tax law/taxation	0	0	0	741	477	264	25	12	13
Intellectual property law	0	0	0	137	58	79	24	12	12
Legal research and advanced professional studies, other	0	0	0	801	381	420	104	64	40
Legal administrative assistant/secretary	21	6	15	0	0	0	0	0	0
Legal assistant/paralegal	1,826	421	1,405	103	15	88	0	0	0
Court reporting/court reporter	10	0	10	0	0	0	0	0	0
Legal support services, other	0	0	0	11	4	7	0	0	0
Legal professions and studies, other	358	128	230	915	420	495	88	45	43
Liberal arts and sciences, general studies and humanities	45,260	16,485	28,775	3,002	1,209	1,793	90	29	61
Liberal arts and sciences/liberal studies	24,689	8,175	16,514	1,950	802	1,148	24	8	16
General studies	15,105	6,224	8,881	143	55	88	1	0	1
Humanities/humanistic studies	2,499	806	1,693	574	214	360	60	19	41
Liberal arts and sciences, general studies and humanities, other	2,967	1,280	1,687	335	138	197	5	2	3
Library science	127	14	113	5,839	1,060	4,779	52	14	38
Library and information science	127	14	113	5,703	1,043	4,660	52	14	38
Library science, other	0	0	0	136	17	119	0	0	0
Mathematics and statistics	20,980	11,967	9,013	7,273	4,256	3,017	1,863	1,325	538
Mathematics, general	16,914	9,494	7,420	2,900	1,746	1,154	1,131	846	285
Analysis and functional analysis	1	1	0	0	0	0	0	0	0
Topology and foundations	0	0	0	0	0	0	3	1	2
Mathematics, other	322	192	130	37	14	23	9	4	5
Applied mathematics, general	1,607	1,009	598	802	532	270	250	178	72
Computational mathematics	113	90	23	26	18	8	22	17	5
Computational and applied mathematics	82	50	32	63	42	21	30	25	5
Financial mathematics	107	61	46	773	473	300	1	0	1
Mathematical biology	19	9	10	0	0	0	0	0	0
Applied mathematics, other	111	81	30	119	78	41	9	6	3
Statistics, general	1,205	695	510	2,317	1,207	1,110	374	228	146
Mathematical statistics and probability	178	95	83	112	71	41	14	10	4
Mathematics and statistics	58	24	34	50	30	20	0	0	0
Statistics, other	56	35	21	36	25	11	4	2	2
Mathematics and statistics, other	207	131	76	38	20	18	16	8	8
Military technologies and applied sciences	185	161	24	29	21	8	0	0	0
Intelligence, general	75	72	3	0	0	0	0	0	0
Strategic intelligence	0	0	0	25	18	7	0	0	0
Intelligence, command control and information operations, other	0	0	0	4	3	1	0	0	0
Military applied sciences, other	54	49	5	0	0	0	0	0	0
Military technologies and applied sciences, other	56	40	16	0	0	0	0	0	0
Multi/interdisciplinary studies	48,348	16,119	32,229	8,075	3,061	5,014	769	322	447
Multi/interdisciplinary studies, general	3,356	1,251	2,105	80	30	50	21	13	8
Biological and physical sciences	2,291	971	1,320	428	174	254	49	26	23
Peace studies and conflict resolution	464	162	302	554	180	374	16	9	7
Systems science and theory	258	159	99	221	111	110	24	16	8
Mathematics and computer science	260	200	60	26	16	10	20	14	6
Biopsychology	186	49	137	8	4	4	4	0	4
Gerontology	306	28	278	457	58	399	28	6	22
Historic preservation and conservation	100	25	75	225	51	174	3	2	1
Cultural resource management and policy analysis	0	0	0	26	8	18	0	0	0
Historic preservation and conservation, other	0	0	0	6	0	6	0	0	0
Medieval and renaissance studies	37	12	25	25	11	14	8	6	2
Museology/museum studies	19	1	18	542	64	478	2	2	0
Science, technology and society	666	362	304	124	48	76	29	15	14
Accounting and computer science	2	1	1	4	3	1	0	0	0
Behavioral sciences	5,727	1,097	4,630	46	13	33	22	5	17
Natural sciences	625	234	391	96	40	56	13	8	5
Nutrition sciences	1,932	336	1,596	685	110	575	118	25	93
International/global studies	5,513	2,174	3,339	1,208	715	493	1	0	1
Holocaust and related studies	7	2	5	15	6	9	0	0	0
Ancient studies/civilization	99	35	64	6	1	5	4	1	3
Classical, ancient Mediterranean/Near Eastern studies/archaeology	100	34	66	4	0	4	3	1	2
Intercultural/multicultural and diversity studies	186	49	137	137	37	100	2	0	2
Cognitive science	902	347	555	72	35	37	32	21	11
Cultural studies/critical theory and analysis	137	59	78	37	19	18	2	1	1
Human biology	741	215	526	0	0	0	0	0	0
Dispute resolution	0	0	0	288	112	176	40	20	20
Maritime studies	13	6	7	0	0	0	0	0	0
Computational science	15	11	4	56	43	13	12	11	1
Human computer interaction	37	28	9	130	69	61	3	3	0
Marine sciences	62	25	37	51	15	36	17	12	5
Sustainability studies	312	155	157	327	146	181	1	0	1
Multi/interdisciplinary studies, other	23,995	8,091	15,904	2,191	942	1,249	297	107	190
Parks, recreation, leisure, and fitness studies	46,042	24,713	21,329	7,609	4,338	3,271	317	158	159
Parks, recreation and leisure studies	3,186	1,589	1,597	236	116	120	26	15	11
Parks, recreation and leisure facilities management	3,045	1,517	1,528	412	208	204	23	9	14
Golf course operation and grounds management	12	12	0	0	0	0	0	0	0
Parks, recreation and leisure facilities management, other	3	2	1	0	0	0	0	0	0

See notes at end of table.

Table 318.30. Bachelor's, master's, and doctor's degrees conferred by postsecondary institutions, by sex of student and discipline division: 2013–14—Continued

Discipline division	Bachelor's degrees			Master's degrees			Doctor's degrees[1]		
	Total	Males	Females	Total	Males	Females	Total	Males	Females
1	2	3	4	5	6	7	8	9	10
Health and physical education/fitness, general	9,087	4,592	4,495	1,079	596	483	23	13	10
Sport and fitness administration/management	8,435	6,141	2,294	3,482	2,209	1,273	8	7	1
Kinesiology and exercise science	20,670	9,949	10,721	2,182	1,100	1,082	208	106	102
Physical fitness technician	55	30	25	0	0	0	0	0	0
Sports studies	217	162	55	105	51	54	0	0	0
Health and physical education/fitness, other	1,062	549	513	47	22	25	23	7	16
Outdoor education	99	67	32	52	26	26	0	0	0
Parks, recreation, leisure, and fitness studies, other	171	103	68	14	10	4	6	1	5
Philosophy and religious studies	11,997	7,582	4,415	2,095	1,312	783	698	461	237
Philosophy and religious studies, general	91	54	37	7	2	5	16	7	9
Philosophy	6,774	4,762	2,012	865	656	209	411	294	117
Logic	1	0	1	10	7	3	1	1	0
Ethics	77	21	56	59	29	30	0	0	0
Applied and professional ethics	12	4	8	16	7	9	0	0	0
Philosophy, other	208	113	95	5	4	1	13	9	4
Religion/religious studies	3,904	2,102	1,802	516	287	229	209	133	76
Buddhist studies	0	0	0	2	0	2	1	0	1
Christian studies	365	238	127	364	195	169	0	0	0
Islamic studies	12	4	8	13	8	5	3	1	2
Jewish/Judaic studies	211	76	135	85	31	54	14	6	8
Religion/religious studies, other	87	45	42	45	20	25	11	4	7
Philosophy and religious studies, other	255	162	93	108	66	42	19	6	13
Physical sciences and science technologies	29,304	17,802	11,502	6,984	4,312	2,672	5,806	3,873	1,933
Physical sciences	28,808	17,533	11,275	6,950	4,294	2,656	5,805	3,873	1,932
Physical sciences	396	205	191	58	33	25	49	33	16
Astronomy	220	136	84	103	57	46	100	64	36
Astrophysics	167	103	64	33	21	12	36	27	9
Planetary astronomy and science	9	6	3	12	7	5	24	11	13
Astronomy and astrophysics, other	33	14	19	12	9	3	19	15	4
Atmospheric sciences and meteorology, general	518	332	186	233	131	102	99	68	31
Atmospheric physics and dynamics	0	0	0	0	0	0	1	1	0
Meteorology	206	140	66	29	20	9	19	12	7
Atmospheric sciences and meteorology, other	27	21	6	1	1	0	7	4	3
Chemistry, general	13,730	7,174	6,556	2,234	1,204	1,030	2,673	1,614	1,059
Analytical chemistry	10	1	9	23	10	13	6	3	3
Inorganic chemistry	0	0	0	0	0	0	8	5	3
Organic chemistry	0	0	0	2	2	0	8	5	3
Physical chemistry	1	1	0	1	0	1	3	2	1
Polymer chemistry	1	1	0	51	37	14	40	30	10
Chemical physics	30	23	7	1	1	0	17	14	3
Environmental chemistry	5	2	3	1	0	1	4	3	1
Forensic chemistry	59	14	45	0	0	0	0	0	0
Theoretical chemistry	4	3	1	0	0	0	0	0	0
Chemistry, other	602	288	314	44	20	24	45	28	17
Geology/earth science, general	4,984	3,107	1,877	1,429	852	577	434	234	200
Geochemistry	14	7	7	6	1	5	4	1	3
Geophysics and seismology	126	81	45	134	90	44	88	58	30
Paleontology	1	1	0	4	2	2	0	0	0
Hydrology and water resources science	53	30	23	64	45	19	15	9	6
Geochemistry and petrology	0	0	0	0	0	0	0	0	0
Oceanography, chemical and physical	255	133	122	152	66	86	129	57	72
Geological and earth sciences/geosciences, other	526	274	252	144	73	71	65	43	22
Physics, general	6,002	4,878	1,124	1,666	1,281	385	1,622	1,329	293
Atomic/molecular physics	0	0	0	3	3	0	3	3	0
Elementary particle physics	0	0	0	0	0	0	0	0	0
Nuclear physics	1	1	0	1	1	0	3	2	1
Optics/optical sciences	39	32	7	76	59	17	51	37	14
Condensed matter and materials physics	0	0	0	2	1	1	5	3	2
Acoustics	9	9	0	11	9	2	7	7	0
Theoretical and mathematical physics	11	10	1	0	0	0	1	1	0
Physics, other	199	152	47	107	78	29	76	55	21
Materials science	143	97	46	193	124	69	122	85	37
Materials chemistry	6	6	0	12	10	2	5	4	1
Materials sciences, other	0	0	0	0	0	0	1	1	0
Physical sciences, other	421	251	170	108	46	62	24	10	14
Science technologies/technicians	496	269	227	34	18	16	1	0	1
Science technologies/technicians, general	23	19	4	0	0	0	0	0	0
Biology technician/biotechnology laboratory technician	33	11	22	0	0	0	1	0	1
Nuclear/nuclear power technology/technician	9	8	1	0	0	0	0	0	0
Nuclear and industrial radiologic technologies/technicians, other	0	0	0	0	0	0	0	0	0
Chemical technology/technician	0	0	0	5	2	3	0	0	0
Physical science technologies/technicians, other	0	0	0	0	0	0	0	0	0
Science technologies/technicians, other	431	231	200	29	16	13	0	0	0
Precision production	37	21	16	15	10	5	0	0	0
Tool and die technology/technician	0	0	0	0	0	0	0	0	0
Welding technology/welder	7	7	0	0	0	0	0	0	0
Furniture design and manufacturing	30	14	16	15	10	5	0	0	0
Psychology	117,298	27,304	89,994	27,966	5,731	22,235	6,634	1,680	4,954
Psychology, general	109,165	25,492	83,673	6,368	1,593	4,775	1,895	572	1,323
Cognitive psychology and psycholinguistics	81	22	59	5	2	3	7	6	1
Comparative psychology	0	0	0	5	4	1	0	0	0
Developmental and child psychology	706	65	641	356	29	327	58	8	50
Experimental psychology	860	226	634	180	53	127	123	46	77
Personality psychology	15	3	12	7	1	6	10	1	9
Physiological psychology/psychobiology	1,158	367	791	28	3	25	12	5	7
Social psychology	1,033	224	809	49	19	30	49	15	34
Psychometrics and quantitative psychology	0	0	0	13	3	10	7	4	3
Psychopharmacology	0	0	0	36	15	21	0	0	0
Research and experimental psychology, other	971	271	700	18	6	12	63	24	39
Clinical psychology	101	30	71	2,798	590	2,208	2,564	579	1,985
Community psychology	461	70	391	225	43	182	25	7	18
Counseling psychology	676	106	570	9,193	1,696	7,497	500	113	387
Industrial and organizational psychology	272	90	182	1,044	342	702	140	48	92

See notes at end of table.

Table 318.30. Bachelor's, master's, and doctor's degrees conferred by postsecondary institutions, by sex of student and discipline division: 2013–14—Continued

Discipline division	Bachelor's degrees			Master's degrees			Doctor's degrees[1]		
	Total	Males	Females	Total	Males	Females	Total	Males	Females
1	2	3	4	5	6	7	8	9	10
School psychology	0	0	0	1,675	236	1,439	315	49	266
Educational psychology	117	13	104	1,279	234	1,045	421	115	306
Clinical child psychology	0	0	0	17	1	16	34	3	31
Environmental psychology	31	16	15	71	32	39	13	2	11
Geropsychology	0	0	0	1	1	0	0	0	0
Health/medical psychology	39	7	32	32	8	24	18	1	17
Family psychology	17	3	14	44	10	34	2	2	0
Forensic psychology	538	100	438	831	119	712	100	22	78
Applied psychology	577	108	469	548	88	460	5	1	4
Applied behavior analysis	133	32	101	294	32	262	48	4	44
Clinical, counseling and applied psychology, other	25	6	19	457	92	365	90	12	78
Psychology, other	322	53	269	2,392	479	1,913	135	41	94
Public administration and social service professions	33,483	5,917	27,566	44,490	10,833	33,657	1,047	346	701
Human services, general	7,272	971	6,301	2,499	485	2,014	55	9	46
Community organization and advocacy	1,754	423	1,331	568	180	388	7	3	4
Public administration	3,247	1,608	1,639	13,252	5,489	7,763	282	144	138
Public policy analysis, general	1,319	578	741	2,715	1,200	1,515	205	85	120
Education policy analysis	1	0	1	40	6	34	24	7	17
Health policy analysis	78	14	64	105	52	53	9	3	6
International policy analysis	14	1	13	43	32	11	0	0	0
Public policy analysis, other	1	1	0	57	15	42	9	4	5
Social work	19,400	2,228	17,172	24,460	3,192	21,268	363	74	289
Youth services/administration	90	10	80	60	8	52	0	0	0
Social work, other	29	5	24	167	28	139	0	0	0
Public administration and social service professions, other	278	78	200	524	146	378	93	17	76
Social sciences and history	173,096	88,233	84,863	21,475	10,750	10,725	4,724	2,494	2,230
Social sciences	141,990	69,480	72,510	17,520	8,548	8,972	3,684	1,901	1,783
Social sciences, general	8,166	3,047	5,119	572	188	384	21	6	15
Research methodology and quantitative methods	4	1	3	11	4	7	0	0	0
Anthropology	10,909	3,090	7,819	1,193	380	813	567	218	349
Physical and biological anthropology	26	7	19	18	1	17	1	0	1
Medical anthropology	4	1	3	0	0	0	0	0	0
Cultural anthropology	53	9	44	19	3	16	4	3	1
Anthropology, other	60	21	39	26	9	17	16	4	12
Archeology	215	78	137	60	23	37	18	3	15
Criminology	7,113	3,617	3,496	749	290	459	46	17	29
Demography and population studies	0	0	0	34	12	22	18	8	10
Economics, general	28,382	19,737	8,645	2,883	1,812	1,071	993	676	317
Applied economics	244	164	80	392	246	146	26	13	13
Econometrics and quantitative economics	546	363	183	81	44	37	6	2	4
Development economics and international development	232	65	167	389	160	229	7	3	4
International economics	228	120	108	215	114	101	15	8	7
Economics, other	363	240	123	155	75	80	12	6	6
Geography	4,476	2,855	1,621	792	476	316	289	136	153
Geographic information science and cartography	259	202	57	298	194	104	10	5	5
Geography, other	156	86	70	20	13	7	7	4	3
International relations and affairs	9,331	3,731	5,600	4,398	2,131	2,267	80	39	41
National security policy studies	33	24	9	195	131	64	0	0	0
International relations and national security studies, other	130	76	54	118	65	53	0	0	0
Political science and government, general	36,258	20,401	15,857	2,018	1,160	858	785	452	333
American government and politics (United States)	191	112	79	174	117	57	0	0	0
Political economy	179	99	80	0	0	0	1	1	0
Political science and government, other	733	388	345	102	46	56	6	3	3
Sociology	30,059	9,418	20,641	1,611	519	1,092	674	249	425
Urban studies/affairs	1,044	492	552	444	194	250	53	28	25
Sociology and anthropology	507	145	362	9	4	5	0	0	0
Rural sociology	33	11	22	0	0	0	0	0	0
Social sciences, other	2,056	880	1,176	544	137	407	29	17	12
History	31,106	18,753	12,353	3,955	2,202	1,753	1,040	593	447
History, general	30,361	18,316	12,045	3,327	1,818	1,509	966	550	416
American history (United States)	47	38	9	76	24	52	9	7	2
European history	20	12	8	0	0	0	0	0	0
History and philosophy of science and technology	133	52	81	28	9	19	41	23	18
Public/applied history	32	12	20	141	34	107	0	0	0
Asian history	1	1	0	0	0	0	2	1	1
Military history	64	53	11	207	184	23	0	0	0
History, other	448	269	179	176	133	43	22	12	10
Theology and religious vocations	9,642	6,594	3,048	14,128	9,245	4,883	2,103	1,522	581
Bible/biblical studies	2,728	1,773	955	511	381	130	55	50	5
Missions/missionary studies and missiology	444	158	286	250	129	121	111	98	13
Religious education	965	532	433	503	234	269	61	36	25
Religious/sacred music	320	189	131	114	64	50	0	0	0
Theology/theological studies	999	689	310	4,077	2,772	1,305	603	477	126
Divinity/ministry	248	160	88	5,704	3,834	1,870	514	311	203
Pre-theology/pre-ministerial studies	155	118	37	2	2	0	0	0	0
Rabbinical studies	0	0	0	109	72	37	12	12	0
Talmudic studies	1,777	1,777	0	466	466	0	18	18	0
Theological and ministerial studies, other	350	227	123	678	451	227	313	240	73
Pastoral studies/counseling	500	310	190	788	331	457	127	87	40
Youth ministry	584	370	214	45	25	20	0	0	0
Urban ministry	23	11	12	23	7	16	15	11	4
Women's ministry	2	0	2	0	0	0	0	0	0
Lay ministry	101	55	46	79	26	53	0	0	0
Pastoral counseling and specialized ministries, other	112	36	76	185	88	97	39	26	13
Theology and religious vocations, other	334	189	145	594	363	231	235	156	79
Transportation and materials moving	4,588	4,053	535	1,243	1,020	223	7	6	1
Aeronautics/aviation/aerospace science and technology, general	2,268	2,025	243	937	788	149	5	4	1
Airline/commercial/professional pilot and flight crew	897	813	84	0	0	0	0	0	0
Aviation/airway management and operations	806	681	125	242	187	55	2	2	0
Air traffic controller	240	196	44	0	0	0	0	0	0
Flight instructor	7	7	0	0	0	0	0	0	0

See notes at end of table.

Table 318.30. Bachelor's, master's, and doctor's degrees conferred by postsecondary institutions, by sex of student and discipline division: 2013–14—Continued

Discipline division	Bachelor's degrees			Master's degrees			Doctor's degrees[1]		
	Total	Males	Females	Total	Males	Females	Total	Males	Females
1	2	3	4	5	6	7	8	9	10
Air transportation, other	20	18	2	58	40	18	0	0	0
Marine science/merchant marine officer	348	311	37	0	0	0	0	0	0
Transportation and materials moving, other	2	2	0	6	5	1	0	0	0
Visual and performing arts	97,246	38,081	59,165	17,863	7,711	10,152	1,778	869	909
Visual and performing arts, general	1,746	647	1,099	166	64	102	16	10	6
Digital arts	573	347	226	137	92	45	0	0	0
Crafts/craft design, folk art and artisanry	130	35	95	7	2	5	0	0	0
Dance, general	2,168	239	1,929	215	36	179	6	0	6
Ballet	42	4	38	0	0	0	0	0	0
Dance, other	24	1	23	2	0	2	4	0	4
Design and visual communications, general	3,177	1,067	2,110	508	182	326	3	1	2
Commercial and advertising art	1,326	482	844	88	35	53	0	0	0
Industrial and product design	1,608	976	632	189	111	78	0	0	0
Commercial photography	509	164	345	20	9	11	0	0	0
Fashion/apparel design	2,308	216	2,092	246	18	228	0	0	0
Interior design	3,290	357	2,933	409	66	343	0	0	0
Graphic design	6,186	2,335	3,851	301	103	198	0	0	0
Illustration	1,844	640	1,204	159	68	91	0	0	0
Game and interactive media design	1,331	1,080	251	167	119	48	0	0	0
Design and applied arts, other	667	250	417	272	81	191	7	2	5
Drama and dramatics/theatre arts, general	9,229	3,426	5,803	975	387	588	101	42	59
Technical theatre/theatre design and technology	566	290	276	160	65	95	0	0	0
Playwriting and screenwriting	239	120	119	220	126	94	0	0	0
Theatre literature, history and criticism	35	18	17	8	1	7	3	2	1
Acting	779	310	469	251	129	122	0	0	0
Directing and theatrical production	72	25	47	84	32	52	0	0	0
Musical theatre	429	174	255	0	0	0	0	0	0
Costume design	16	3	13	6	2	4	0	0	0
Dramatic/theatre arts and stagecraft, other	308	108	200	56	25	31	4	1	3
Film/cinema/video studies	3,261	1,912	1,349	322	163	159	42	21	21
Cinematography and film/video production	4,742	3,179	1,563	859	493	366	5	2	3
Photography	1,858	566	1,292	282	153	129	0	0	0
Documentary production	32	10	22	24	11	13	0	0	0
Film/video and photographic arts, other	917	539	378	178	106	72	0	0	0
Art/art studies, general	12,320	3,622	8,698	757	297	460	7	1	6
Fine/studio arts, general	10,247	3,226	7,021	1,521	632	889	0	0	0
Art history, criticism and conservation	3,167	448	2,719	941	119	822	255	57	198
Drawing	302	98	204	21	12	9	0	0	0
Intermedia/multimedia	454	203	251	59	32	27	0	0	0
Painting	693	215	478	190	96	94	0	0	0
Sculpture	279	99	180	62	35	27	0	0	0
Printmaking	172	57	115	44	11	33	0	0	0
Ceramic arts and ceramics	227	61	166	41	15	26	0	0	0
Fiber, textile and weaving arts	218	21	197	30	2	28	2	1	1
Metal and jewelry arts	119	13	106	35	5	30	0	0	0
Fine arts and art studies, other	1,018	302	716	338	118	220	1	1	0
Music, general	7,897	4,234	3,663	2,029	1,057	972	526	313	213
Music history, literature, and theory	97	51	46	44	17	27	18	6	12
Music performance, general	4,226	2,262	1,964	2,345	1,184	1,161	464	227	237
Music theory and composition	816	654	162	291	194	97	67	49	18
Musicology and ethnomusicology	25	16	9	85	41	44	48	23	25
Conducting	9	3	6	107	74	33	47	41	6
Keyboard instruments	140	55	85	189	85	104	47	11	36
Voice and opera	352	89	263	231	87	144	28	18	10
Jazz/jazz studies	340	292	48	137	109	28	7	6	1
Stringed instruments	181	97	84	183	83	100	10	4	6
Music pedagogy	73	19	54	40	11	29	9	2	7
Music technology	277	235	42	64	52	12	5	3	2
Brass instruments	44	34	10	32	23	9	0	0	0
Woodwind instruments	40	16	24	52	29	23	3	2	1
Percussion instruments	24	23	1	17	12	5	1	1	0
Music, other	785	511	274	200	124	76	22	15	7
Arts, entertainment, and media management, general	496	271	225	591	254	337	0	0	0
Fine and studio arts management	800	214	586	455	89	366	5	2	3
Music management	1,450	885	565	30	18	12	0	0	0
Theatre/theatre arts management	119	36	83	55	15	40	0	0	0
Arts, entertainment, and media management, other	25	15	10	1	1	0	0	0	0
Visual and performing arts, other	402	184	218	335	99	236	15	5	10
Not classified by field of study	0	0	0	0	0	0	0	0	0

[1]Includes Ph.D., Ed.D., and comparable degrees at the doctoral level. Includes most degrees formerly classified as first-professional, such as M.D., D.D.S., and law degrees.
NOTE: Data are for postsecondary institutions participating in Title IV federal financial aid programs. Aggregations by field of study derived from the Classification of Instructional Programs developed by the National Center for Education Statistics.

SOURCE: U.S. Department of Education, National Center for Education Statistics, Integrated Postsecondary Education Data System (IPEDS), Fall 2014, Completions component. (This table was prepared September 2015.)

Table 318.40. Degrees/certificates conferred by postsecondary institutions, by control of institution and level of degree: 1970–71 through 2013–14

Year	Public institutions					Private institutions — Total					Private institutions — Nonprofit					Private institutions — For-profit				
	Certificates below the associate's	Associate's degrees	Bachelor's degrees	Master's degrees	Doctor's degrees[1]	Certificates below the associate's	Associate's degrees	Bachelor's degrees	Master's degrees	Doctor's degrees[1]	Certificates below the associate's	Associate's degrees	Bachelor's degrees	Master's degrees	Doctor's degrees[1]	Certificates below the associate's	Associate's degrees	Bachelor's degrees	Master's degrees	Doctor's degrees[1]
1	2	3	4	5	6	7	8	9	10	11	12	13	14	15	16	17	18	19	20	21
1970–71	—	215,645	557,996	151,603	36,927	—	36,666	281,734	83,961	28,071	—	—	—	—	—	—	—	—	—	—
1971–72	—	255,218	599,615	167,075	40,297	—	36,796	287,658	90,126	30,909	—	—	—	—	—	—	—	—	—	—
1972–73	—	278,132	630,899	174,405	44,229	—	38,042	291,463	94,249	35,283	—	—	—	—	—	—	—	—	—	—
1973–74	—	303,188	651,544	184,632	45,018	—	40,736	294,232	97,442	37,573	—	—	—	—	—	—	—	—	—	—
1974–75	—	318,474	634,785	193,804	45,788	—	41,697	288,148	103,741	39,116	—	—	—	—	—	—	—	—	—	—
1975–76	—	345,006	635,161	206,298	47,517	—	46,448	290,585	111,179	43,490	—	—	—	—	—	—	—	—	—	—
1976–77	—	355,550	630,463	208,901	47,573	—	50,727	289,086	114,124	44,157	—	—	—	—	—	—	—	—	—	—
1977–78	—	358,874	627,903	202,099	47,553	—	53,372	293,301	115,888	44,792	—	—	—	—	—	—	—	—	—	—
1978–79	—	346,808	621,666	192,016	48,602	—	55,894	299,724	115,670	46,369	—	—	—	—	—	—	—	—	—	—
1979–80	—	344,536	624,084	187,499	48,550	—	56,374	305,333	117,697	47,081	—	—	—	—	—	—	—	—	—	—
1980–81	—	352,391	626,452	184,384	50,023	—	63,986 [2]	308,688	118,253	47,993	—	—	—	—	—	—	—	—	—	—
1981–82	—	366,732	636,475	182,295	50,500	—	67,794 [2]	316,523	120,152	47,338	—	—	—	—	—	—	—	—	—	—
1982–83	—	377,817	646,317	176,246	50,943	—	71,803 [2]	323,193	120,169	48,392	—	—	—	—	—	—	—	—	—	—
1983–84	—	379,249	646,013	170,693	50,727	—	72,991	328,296	120,448	50,072	—	—	—	—	—	—	—	—	—	—
1984–85	—	377,625	652,246	170,000	51,489	—	77,087	327,231	123,472	49,296	—	—	—	—	—	—	—	—	—	—
1985–86	—	369,052	658,586	169,903	51,001	—	76,995	329,237	125,947	49,279	—	—	—	—	—	—	—	—	—	—
1986–87	—	358,811	659,260	167,797	51,216	—	77,493	332,004	128,733	47,261	—	—	—	—	—	—	—	—	—	—
1987–88	—	354,180	658,491	173,778	51,641	—	80,905	336,338	132,005	47,498	—	—	—	—	—	—	—	—	—	—
1988–89	—	357,001	675,675	179,109	51,963	—	79,763	343,080	137,517	48,608	—	—	—	—	—	—	—	—	—	—
1989–90	—	375,635	700,015	186,104	53,451	—	79,467	351,329	144,048	50,057	—	42,497	344,569	142,681	49,655	—	36,970	6,760	1,367	402
1990–91	—	398,055	724,062	193,057	55,235	—	83,665	370,476	149,806	50,312	—	45,821	360,634	146,161	49,841	—	37,844	9,842	3,645	471
1991–92	—	420,265	759,475	203,398	56,186	—	83,966	377,078	154,691	53,368	—	45,700	370,718	153,291	52,830	—	38,266	6,360	1,400	538
1992–93	—	430,321	785,112	213,843	57,020	—	84,435	380,066	161,189	55,052	—	47,713	373,346	159,562	54,399	—	36,722	6,720	1,627	653
1993–94	—	444,373	789,148	221,428	58,366	—	86,259	380,127	171,609	54,270	—	48,493	371,561	168,718	53,502	—	37,766	8,566	2,891	768
1994–95	—	451,539	776,670	224,152	58,788	—	88,152	383,464	179,457	55,478	—	48,643	373,454	176,485	54,675	—	39,509	10,010	2,972	803
1995–96	307,358	454,291	774,070	227,179	59,398	313,311	100,925	390,722	185,001	56,109	34,259	50,678	379,916	181,142	55,506	279,052	50,247	10,806	3,859	603
1996–97	326,687	465,494	776,677	233,237	61,081	272,237	105,732	396,202	192,023	57,666	35,560	49,168	384,086	186,963	56,864	236,677	56,564	12,116	5,060	802
1997–98	305,910	455,084	784,296	235,922	60,948	246,571	103,471	400,110	200,115	57,787	32,166	47,625	386,455	194,048	57,089	214,405	55,846	13,655	6,067	698
1998–99	304,294	452,616	792,392	238,954	60,028	251,589	112,368	409,847	207,084	56,672	29,402	47,757	394,749	198,481	55,663	222,187	64,611	15,098	8,603	1,009
1999–2000	294,912	448,446	810,855	243,157	60,655	263,217	116,487	427,020	220,028	58,081	28,580	46,337	406,958	209,720	56,972	234,637	70,150	20,062	10,308	1,109
2000–01	309,624	456,487	812,438	246,054	60,820	242,879	122,378	431,733	227,448	58,765	29,336	45,761	408,701	215,815	57,722	213,543	76,667	23,032	11,633	1,043
2001–02	319,291	471,660	841,180	249,820	61,661	264,957	123,473	450,720	237,493	58,602	32,904	45,761	424,322	223,259	57,707	232,053	77,712	26,398	14,264	895
2002–03	355,727	498,279	875,596	265,643	61,611	290,698	135,737	473,215	253,056	59,968	36,926	46,183	442,060	238,069	58,894	253,772	89,554	31,155	14,987	1,074
2003–04	364,053	524,875	905,718	285,138	64,205	323,734	140,426	496,821	279,134	61,882	35,316	45,759	451,518	250,894	60,447	288,418	94,667	42,306	28,240	1,435
2004–05	370,683	547,511	932,443	291,505	67,511	340,190	149,141	506,821	288,646	66,876	35,968	45,344	451,963	253,564	65,278	304,222	103,797	48,858	35,082	1,598
2005–06	371,211	557,134	955,369	293,517	70,036	344,190	155,932	529,873	306,214	68,020	35,888	46,442	467,836	261,090	66,066	308,302	109,490	62,037	45,124	1,954
2006–07	389,640	566,535	975,513	291,971	73,085	339,397	161,579	548,579	318,626	71,605	34,195	43,829	477,805	267,690	69,239	305,202	117,750	70,774	50,936	2,366
2007–08	399,081	578,520	996,435	299,983	75,533	350,802	171,644	566,634	330,683	73,845	34,084	44,788	490,685	275,829	70,679	316,718	126,856	75,949	54,854	3,166
2008–09	428,849	596,391	1,020,521	308,215	77,270	375,771	190,852	580,878	353,867	77,294	31,939	46,930	496,353	290,401	73,583	343,832	143,922	84,525	63,466	3,711
2009–10	472,428	640,265	1,049,179	322,389	78,805	463,291	208,591	600,740	370,924	79,785	35,652	46,673	503,264	300,053	75,172	427,639	161,918	97,476	70,871	4,613
2010–11	519,711	696,884	1,088,722	339,420	82,013	510,766	246,622	627,331	391,502	81,814	36,534	51,967	512,821	313,317	76,595	474,232	194,655	114,510	78,185	5,219
2011–12	525,264	756,484	1,131,885	349,349	84,730	463,797	265,234	660,278	406,618	85,487	32,856	54,347	526,022	325,175	79,498	430,941	210,887	134,256	81,443	5,989
2012–13	545,446	772,978	1,163,616	346,751	86,411	421,768	234,449	676,765	404,967	88,615	30,913	55,651	535,958	327,013	81,543	390,855	178,798	140,807	77,954	7,072
2013–14	576,258	793,180	1,186,397	346,101	88,904	393,095	210,184	683,417	408,374	88,676	30,730	53,127	544,213	333,580	80,894	362,365	157,057	139,204	74,794	7,782

—Not available.
[1] Includes Ph.D., Ed.D., and comparable degrees at the doctoral level. Includes most degrees formerly classified as first-professional, such as M.D., D.D.S., and law degrees.
[2] Part of the increase is due to the addition of schools accredited by the Accrediting Commission of Career Schools and Colleges of Technology.

NOTE: Data through 1990–91 are for institutions of higher education, while later data are for postsecondary institutions that participate in Title IV federal financial aid programs. Data for associate's degrees and higher awards are for degree-granting institutions. Some data have been revised from previously published figures.
SOURCE: U.S. Department of Education, National Center for Education Statistics, Higher Education General Information Survey (HEGIS), "Degrees and Other Formal Awards Conferred" surveys, 1970–71 through 1985–86; Integrated Postsecondary Education Data System (IPEDS), "Completions Survey" (IPEDS-C:87–99); and IPEDS Fall 2000 through Fall 2014, Completions component. (This table was prepared September 2015.)

Table 318.50. Degrees conferred by postsecondary institutions, by control of institution, level of degree, and field of study: 2013–14

Field of study	All institutions				Public institutions				Private nonprofit institutions				Private for-profit institutions			
	Associate's degrees	Bachelor's degrees	Master's degrees	Doctor's degrees[1]	Associate's degrees	Bachelor's degrees	Master's degrees	Doctor's degrees[1]	Associate's degrees	Bachelor's degrees	Master's degrees	Doctor's degrees[1]	Associate's degrees	Bachelor's degrees	Master's degrees	Doctor's degrees[1]
1	2	3	4	5	6	7	8	9	10	11	12	13	14	15	16	17
All fields, total	1,003,364	1,869,814	754,475	177,580	793,180	1,186,397	346,101	88,904	53,127	544,213	333,580	80,894	157,057	139,204	74,794	7,782
Agriculture and natural resources	7,051	35,116	6,544	1,407	6,741	29,125	5,121	1,342	310	5,263	1,296	65	0	728	127	0
Architecture and related services	414	9,144	8,048	247	404	6,407	4,744	181	10	2,650	3,215	66	0	87	89	0
Area, ethnic, cultural, gender, and group studies	362	8,275	1,824	336	346	5,407	1,045	201	16	2,868	779	135	0	0	0	0
Biological and biomedical sciences	4,479	104,633	13,960	8,302	4,376	71,453	8,219	5,486	102	33,052	5,741	2,816	1	128	0	0
Business	129,661	358,079	189,328	3,039	87,011	201,897	67,635	1,036	11,035	108,169	89,991	831	31,615	48,013	31,702	1,172
Communication, journalism, and related programs	4,935	87,604	9,347	611	4,631	61,552	3,871	495	119	24,713	5,147	116	185	1,339	329	0
Communications technologies	4,703	4,987	581	3	3,187	1,467	51	0	138	1,460	312	3	1,378	2,060	218	0
Computer and information sciences	37,601	55,367	24,532	1,982	21,430	29,282	12,274	1,362	1,577	12,957	9,945	522	14,594	13,128	2,313	98
Construction trades	4,831	268	0	0	3,915	267	0	0	174	0	0	0	742	1	0	0
Education	17,504	98,854	154,636	10,920	14,675	67,929	74,723	5,694	695	26,821	67,533	3,540	2,134	4,104	12,380	1,686
Engineering	4,269	92,162	42,372	10,010	4,155	71,914	27,805	7,388	22	19,985	14,400	2,622	92	263	167	0
Engineering technologies and engineering-related fields[2]	31,768	16,221	4,954	107	22,824	12,138	2,709	72	1,150	1,711	1,875	35	7,794	2,372	370	0
English language and literature/letters	2,075	50,404	9,292	1,393	1,761	34,767	5,945	1,043	16	14,826	3,211	350	298	811	136	0
Family and consumer sciences	8,657	24,722	3,121	335	8,053	19,846	1,979	274	396	4,379	857	42	208	497	285	19
Foreign languages, literatures, and linguistics	2,276	20,335	3,482	1,231	1,957	14,683	2,445	795	319	5,628	1,037	436	0	24	0	0
Health professions and related programs	208,660	198,770	97,403	67,448	130,449	110,329	41,937	33,967	18,182	62,446	41,985	32,057	60,029	25,995	13,481	1,424
Homeland security, law enforcement, and firefighting	45,650	62,409	9,310	152	30,665	35,200	3,842	98	1,469	13,168	3,048	10	13,516	14,041	2,420	44
Legal professions and studies	10,496	4,513	7,655	44,169	6,223	2,291	2,039	15,274	602	1,393	5,398	26,969	3,671	829	218	1,926
Liberal arts and sciences, general studies, and humanities	353,438	45,260	3,002	90	340,430	31,514	1,317	40	9,850	13,418	1,632	34	3,158	328	53	16
Library science	192	127	5,839	52	192	96	4,856	47	0	0	983	5	0	31	0	0
Mathematics and statistics	2,140	20,980	7,273	1,863	2,128	14,367	4,918	1,345	9	6,607	2,355	518	3	6	0	0
Mechanic and repair technologies/technicians	20,052	318	0	0	13,143	203	0	0	2,106	115	0	0	4,803	0	0	0
Military technologies and applied sciences	1,084	185	29	0	1,047	60	25	0	1	73	4	0	36	52	0	0
Multi/interdisciplinary studies	28,164	48,348	8,075	769	25,097	31,986	4,074	568	440	10,883	3,313	201	2,627	5,479	688	0
Parks, recreation, leisure and fitness studies	4,348	46,042	7,609	317	2,760	34,333	5,316	303	356	11,118	2,076	14	1,232	591	217	0
Philosophy and religious studies	435	11,997	2,095	698	176	5,349	698	283	259	6,580	1,227	414	0	68	170	1
Physical sciences and science technologies	6,935	29,304	6,984	5,806	6,856	20,808	5,329	4,168	74	8,491	1,655	1,638	5	5	0	0
Precision production	3,903	37	15	0	3,434	6	0	0	138	31	15	0	331	0	0	0
Psychology	7,530	117,298	27,966	6,634	7,050	78,797	8,851	2,561	322	35,263	14,521	2,925	158	3,238	4,594	1,148
Public administration and social service professions	8,900	33,483	44,490	1,047	6,293	20,791	25,414	515	522	9,128	17,140	291	2,085	3,564	1,936	241
Social sciences and history	16,528	173,096	21,475	4,724	16,399	118,653	11,340	3,098	91	52,678	9,200	1,625	38	1,765	935	1
Social sciences	15,454	141,990	17,520	3,684	15,356	97,493	8,798	2,417	83	43,102	8,261	1,266	15	1,395	461	1
History	1,074	31,106	3,955	1,040	1,043	21,160	2,542	681	8	9,576	939	359	23	370	474	0
Theology and religious vocations	944	9,642	14,128	2,103	1	5	0	0	934	9,416	14,074	2,098	9	221	54	5
Transportation and materials moving	2,099	4,588	1,243	7	1,499	2,252	129	0	527	2,308	1,106	7	73	28	8	0
Visual and performing arts	21,280	97,246	17,863	1,778	13,872	51,223	7,450	1,268	1,166	36,615	8,509	509	6,242	9,408	1,904	1

[1] Includes Ph.D., Ed.D., and comparable degrees at the doctoral level, as well as such degrees as M.D., D.D.S., and law degrees that were formerly classified as first-professional degrees.
[2] Excludes "Construction trades" and "Mechanic and repair technologies/technicians," which are listed separately.
NOTE: Data are for degree-granting postsecondary institutions, which are institutions that grant associate's or higher degrees and participate in Title IV federal financial aid programs. To facilitate trend comparisons, certain aggregations have been made of the degree fields as reported in the Integrated Postsecondary Education Data System (IPEDS): "Agriculture and natural resources" includes Agriculture, agriculture operations, and related sciences and Natural resources and conservation; and "Business" includes Business management, marketing, and related support services and Personal and culinary services. SOURCE: U.S. Department of Education, National Center for Education Statistics, Integrated Postsecondary Education Data System (IPEDS), Fall 2014, Completions component. (This table was prepared April 2016.)

Table 318.60. Number of postsecondary institutions conferring degrees, by control of institution, level of degree, and field of study: 2013–14

Field of study	All institutions				Public institutions				Private nonprofit institutions				Private for-profit institutions			
	Associate's degrees	Bachelor's degrees	Master's degrees	Doctor's degrees[1]	Associate's degrees	Bachelor's degrees	Master's degrees	Doctor's degrees[1]	Associate's degrees	Bachelor's degrees	Master's degrees	Doctor's degrees[1]	Associate's degrees	Bachelor's degrees	Master's degrees	Doctor's degrees[1]
1	2	3	4	5	6	7	8	9	10	11	12	13	14	15	16	17
All fields, total	3,006	2,588	1,902	939	1,241	659	530	326	627	1,327	1,126	555	1,138	602	246	58
Agriculture and natural resources	501	722	238	98	472	322	178	90	29	390	57	8	0	10	3	0
Architecture and related services	75	195	153	38	71	121	102	28	4	71	49	10	0	3	2	0
Area, ethnic, cultural, gender, and group studies	73	487	143	55	67	238	92	36	6	249	51	19	0	0	0	0
Biological and biomedical sciences	282	1,353	494	258	266	526	344	180	15	820	150	78	1	7	0	0
Business	1,981	2,027	1,231	207	1,088	593	432	102	270	948	611	73	623	486	188	32
Communication, journalism, and related programs	305	1,189	347	78	264	461	217	60	29	675	126	18	12	53	4	0
Communications technologies	321	202	20	1	274	54	6	0	12	72	10	1	35	76	4	0
Computer and information sciences	1,546	1,538	512	168	906	521	289	115	98	658	157	50	542	359	66	3
Construction trades	350	10	0	0	312	9	0	0	12	0	0	0	26	1	0	0
Education	732	1,249	1,185	406	625	465	471	226	73	757	641	152	34	27	73	28
Engineering	345	519	318	215	329	286	211	154	9	216	101	61	7	17	6	0
Engineering technologies and engineering-related fields[2]	1,160	404	176	18	845	228	118	12	48	65	55	6	267	111	3	0
English language and literature/letters	190	1,341	492	151	177	514	323	101	11	816	167	50	2	11	2	0
Family and consumer sciences/human sciences	531	340	155	49	499	195	109	38	23	137	42	10	9	8	4	1
Foreign languages, literatures, and linguistics	196	926	222	95	187	413	163	65	9	511	59	30	0	2	0	0
Health professions and related programs	2,005	1,467	1,025	500	1,061	527	398	228	236	706	508	250	708	234	119	22
Homeland security, law enforcement, and firefighting	1,408	1,056	321	27	857	350	173	23	98	393	110	3	453	313	38	1
Legal professions and studies	768	258	147	212	412	74	56	85	47	116	87	119	309	68	4	8
Liberal arts and sciences, general studies, and humanities	1,397	930	185	16	1,084	387	94	7	289	518	89	8	24	25	2	1
Library science	36	9	64	13	36	8	52	11	0	0	12	2	0	2	0	0
Mathematics and statistics	207	1,196	349	173	200	498	271	124	6	697	78	49	1	1	0	0
Mechanic and repair technologies/technicians	702	20	0	0	623	12	0	0	24	8	0	0	55	0	0	0
Military technologies and applied sciences	12	8	2	0	9	3	1	0	1	3	1	0	2	2	0	0
Multi/interdisciplinary studies	397	926	368	111	370	367	207	78	23	525	159	33	4	34	2	0
Parks, recreation, leisure and fitness studies	318	837	279	48	259	341	196	43	20	483	76	5	39	13	7	0
Philosophy and religious studies	65	920	229	117	48	319	96	56	17	600	132	60	0	1	1	1
Physical sciences and science technologies	362	1,100	328	216	347	481	243	150	12	618	85	66	3	1	0	0
Precision production	370	6	2	0	348	1	0	0	11	5	2	0	11	0	0	0
Psychology	236	1,447	693	329	206	525	323	162	25	872	325	141	5	50	45	26
Public administration and social services	354	805	509	122	304	347	298	80	31	414	169	40	19	44	42	2
Social sciences and history	272	1,368	463	192	246	533	317	134	21	817	143	57	5	18	3	1
Social sciences	261	1,281	384	177	238	516	263	124	19	748	119	52	4	17	2	1
History	126	1,238	362	138	121	492	277	95	4	741	83	43	1	5	2	0
Theology and religious vocations	102	414	363	154	1	1	0	0	100	411	362	153	0	2	1	1
Transportation and materials moving	115	84	18	2	98	50	7	0	11	30	9	2	6	4	2	0
Visual and performing arts	887	1,465	461	114	594	498	253	77	63	838	191	36	230	129	17	1

[1]Includes Ph.D., Ed.D., and comparable degrees at the doctoral level, as well as such degrees as M.D., D.D.S., and law degrees that were formerly classified as first-professional degrees.
[2]Excludes "Construction trades" and "Mechanic and repair technologies/technicians," which are listed separately.
NOTE: Data are for degree-granting postsecondary institutions, which are institutions that grant associate's or higher degrees and participate in Title IV federal financial aid programs. To facilitate trend comparisons, certain aggregations have been made of the degree fields as reported in the Integrated Postsecondary Education Data System (IPEDS): "Agriculture and natural resources" includes Agriculture, agriculture operations, and related sciences and Natural resources and conservation; and "Business" includes Business management, marketing, and related support services and Personal and culinary services. SOURCE: U.S. Department of Education, National Center for Education Statistics, Integrated Postsecondary Education Data System (IPEDS), Fall 2014, Completions component. (This table was prepared April 2016.)

Table 319.10. Degrees conferred by postsecondary institutions, by control of institution, level of degree, and state or jurisdiction: 2013–14

State or jurisdiction	Public				Private nonprofit				Private for-profit			
	Associate's degrees	Bachelor's degrees	Master's degrees	Doctor's degrees[1]	Associate's degrees	Bachelor's degrees	Master's degrees	Doctor's degrees[1]	Associate's degrees	Bachelor's degrees	Master's degrees	Doctor's degrees[1]
1	2	3	4	5	6	7	8	9	10	11	12	13
United States	793,180	1,186,397	346,101	88,904	53,127	544,213	333,580	80,894	157,057	139,204	74,794	7,782
Alabama	9,644	22,617	8,797	1,835	129	3,424	679	445	3,530	3,475	1,870	6
Alaska	1,409	1,855	644	52	12	79	63	8	384	99	0	0
Arizona	18,107	25,718	7,631	1,781	226	806	1,182	730	23,513	34,756	20,016	1,393
Arkansas	8,586	12,671	4,305	895	136	2,633	527	90	128	184	64	0
California	105,374	133,269	28,555	7,080	1,578	38,160	35,415	10,289	23,010	27,829	10,551	950
Colorado	8,651	24,400	7,221	1,783	574	3,967	4,122	643	4,952	5,045	3,592	491
Connecticut	5,882	11,282	3,044	787	929	9,589	6,244	1,262	325	839	233	0
Delaware	1,918	4,299	892	245	158	2,017	1,935	309	4	22	15	0
District of Columbia	263	410	90	103	267	8,386	10,866	3,415	236	455	521	0
Florida	72,474	65,981	17,931	4,686	6,907	22,583	13,230	3,730	16,951	8,440	2,916	697
Georgia	14,269	35,579	10,454	2,504	1,033	10,227	4,602	1,695	3,471	3,025	1,919	447
Hawaii	4,440	4,408	1,179	467	476	2,152	719	0	532	355	177	39
Idaho	3,309	6,482	1,622	400	1,774	4,066	251	12	332	155	15	0
Illinois	34,869	33,688	12,467	3,075	1,285	30,604	24,861	5,191	4,362	10,666	4,349	180
Indiana	12,267	31,065	9,545	2,652	1,504	14,900	4,680	885	3,959	1,021	132	0
Iowa	12,391	12,494	2,732	1,514	645	10,313	2,035	1,318	4,036	5,318	2,914	118
Kansas	9,542	15,256	5,170	1,326	793	4,050	1,699	134	1,464	968	518	0
Kentucky	10,417	17,095	5,735	1,656	439	4,556	3,330	280	2,765	617	442	90
Louisiana	5,827	18,800	5,085	1,563	336	3,331	2,134	932	1,077	408	129	0
Maine	2,638	4,156	898	174	139	3,234	1,135	354	416	86	2	0
Maryland	15,126	25,107	10,553	2,178	16	6,459	7,520	730	616	597	317	0
Massachusetts	11,965	19,748	6,138	773	1,454	38,496	29,774	7,548	704	468	123	0
Michigan	27,533	45,278	16,799	4,426	3,935	12,950	4,346	1,669	861	680	147	0
Minnesota	17,454	21,251	5,227	1,825	609	11,212	4,987	1,192	3,150	3,988	11,868	2,274
Mississippi	12,086	12,012	3,381	995	58	2,247	1,429	264	496	7	12	0
Missouri	12,826	21,472	6,880	1,517	2,989	18,397	13,447	3,234	2,752	941	234	0
Montana	2,231	5,239	1,086	420	186	725	75	0	0	0	0	0
Nebraska	4,983	8,917	2,562	793	268	5,417	2,286	710	501	151	26	0
Nevada	4,600	6,963	1,540	513	0	259	361	409	1,132	858	247	0
New Hampshire	2,069	5,173	1,236	231	556	4,707	3,252	311	345	257	89	0
New Jersey	21,377	30,228	8,620	2,214	138	9,965	6,551	946	995	834	116	0
New Mexico	7,983	8,099	2,923	644	0	114	204	0	665	933	209	0
New York	51,179	61,669	18,712	3,155	7,946	69,241	51,754	11,863	9,467	3,916	1,107	1
North Carolina	26,361	36,981	11,675	2,495	1,103	14,740	6,226	2,102	1,770	881	475	408
North Dakota	1,989	5,425	1,382	437	130	684	443	32	286	59	0	0
Ohio	24,192	45,868	14,776	4,527	3,007	21,380	7,677	1,622	6,274	1,040	327	0
Oklahoma	11,225	16,587	5,129	1,330	189	3,780	1,410	327	1,192	287	77	0
Oregon	12,397	17,179	4,051	1,035	58	5,086	4,351	961	916	474	85	0
Pennsylvania	17,076	48,189	11,849	3,449	3,280	42,679	24,707	6,543	8,061	1,840	335	0
Rhode Island	1,708	4,118	855	241	2,072	7,337	1,763	512	0	0	0	0
South Carolina	9,855	17,647	4,414	1,437	407	5,514	1,047	151	1,623	1,190	417	278
South Dakota	2,243	4,324	1,033	393	214	1,082	278	2	239	270	25	0
Tennessee	9,858	20,870	5,933	1,783	774	12,205	5,691	1,689	2,375	1,059	501	21
Texas	64,939	95,688	35,737	8,408	1,260	20,208	9,487	2,382	4,930	2,889	1,064	20
Utah	11,242	15,291	3,339	826	1,163	13,869	5,867	225	1,204	688	359	220
Vermont	962	3,353	425	220	182	2,806	1,870	138	78	62	0	0
Virginia	18,456	35,779	11,778	3,371	1,315	15,553	10,117	1,849	5,420	4,462	1,949	129
Washington	28,292	24,323	5,744	1,803	79	7,387	3,308	735	693	796	240	20
West Virginia	3,229	9,384	2,591	884	82	1,168	333	125	2,603	4,973	3,882	0
Wisconsin	12,596	27,041	5,257	1,781	304	9,464	3,310	901	2,001	841	188	0
Wyoming	2,871	2,007	476	222	13	5	0	0	261	0	0	0
U.S. Service Academies	0	3,662	3	0	†	†	†	†	†	†	†	†
Other jurisdictions	2,355	7,937	927	550	3,650	11,762	4,114	912	3,189	1,428	280	0
American Samoa	228	3	0	0	0	0	0	0	0	0	0	0
Federated States of Micronesia	267	0	0	0	0	0	0	0	0	0	0	0
Guam	155	414	106	0	0	10	0	0	0	0	0	0
Marshall Islands	106	0	0	0	0	0	0	0	0	0	0	0
Northern Marianas	123	35	0	0	0	0	0	0	0	0	0	0
Palau	88	0	0	0	0	0	0	0	0	0	0	0
Puerto Rico	1,330	7,271	771	550	3,650	11,752	4,114	912	3,189	1,428	280	0
U.S. Virgin Islands	58	214	50	0	0	0	0	0	0	0	0	0

†Not applicable.
[1]Includes Ph.D., Ed.D., and comparable degrees at the doctoral level. Includes most degrees formerly classified as first-professional, such as M.D., D.D.S., and law degrees.
NOTE: Data are for postsecondary institutions participating in Title IV federal financial aid programs.

SOURCE: U.S. Department of Education, National Center for Education Statistics, Integrated Postsecondary Education Data System (IPEDS), Fall 2014, Completions component. (This table was prepared April 2016.)

Table 319.20. Degrees conferred by postsecondary institutions, by level of degree and state or jurisdiction: 2011–12 through 2013–14

State or jurisdiction	2011–12				2012–13				2013–14			
	Associate's degrees	Bachelor's degrees	Master's degrees	Doctor's degrees[1]	Associate's degrees	Bachelor's degrees	Master's degrees	Doctor's degrees[1]	Associate's degrees	Bachelor's degrees	Master's degrees	Doctor's degrees[1]
1	2	3	4	5	6	7	8	9	10	11	12	13
United States	1,021,718	1,792,163	755,967	170,217	1,007,427	1,840,381	751,718	175,026	1,003,364	1,869,814	754,475	177,580
Alabama	14,197	28,277	11,539	2,256	13,758	29,876	11,670	2,297	13,303	29,516	11,346	2,286
Alaska	1,706	1,750	703	50	1,758	1,895	724	54	1,805	2,033	707	60
Arizona	62,994	64,707	36,178	3,533	48,911	66,304	30,579	3,771	41,846	61,280	28,829	3,904
Arkansas	8,645	14,190	5,320	913	8,499	14,317	5,225	980	8,850	15,488	4,896	985
California	114,613	172,419	68,502	17,448	120,550	180,529	69,257	18,761	129,962	199,258	74,521	18,319
Colorado	16,939	31,136	15,406	2,352	15,550	32,446	15,009	2,747	14,177	33,412	14,935	2,917
Connecticut	6,511	20,710	9,457	1,954	6,826	21,470	9,570	1,964	7,136	21,710	9,521	2,049
Delaware	1,947	5,885	2,680	585	2,072	6,230	2,753	558	2,080	6,338	2,842	554
District of Columbia	463	9,212	10,211	3,567	686	9,299	10,995	3,621	766	9,251	11,477	3,518
Florida	103,158	91,225	33,859	9,485	100,877	94,505	32,945	9,029	96,332	97,004	34,077	9,113
Georgia	18,728	45,936	17,674	4,267	18,889	47,655	17,888	4,410	18,773	48,831	16,975	4,646
Hawaii	4,199	6,016	2,115	533	4,402	6,363	1,978	556	5,448	6,915	2,075	506
Idaho	4,952	9,781	2,041	331	5,762	10,336	2,049	398	5,415	10,703	1,888	412
Illinois	41,925	72,541	43,664	8,132	40,584	75,992	43,254	8,598	40,516	74,958	41,677	8,446
Indiana	19,430	45,534	14,230	3,465	18,838	46,551	14,663	3,475	17,730	46,986	14,357	3,537
Iowa	20,515	40,676	12,100	2,957	18,751	41,462	12,127	3,031	17,072	28,125	7,681	2,950
Kansas	10,218	18,999	7,021	1,452	10,647	19,622	6,625	1,474	11,799	20,274	7,387	1,460
Kentucky	14,680	21,531	9,411	1,935	13,853	21,872	9,860	1,951	13,621	22,268	9,507	2,026
Louisiana	7,706	22,015	7,275	2,585	7,150	22,334	7,552	2,532	7,240	22,539	7,348	2,495
Maine	3,321	7,596	1,902	383	3,167	7,335	1,935	489	3,193	7,476	2,035	528
Maryland	15,156	30,863	17,845	2,822	15,387	31,729	18,444	3,043	15,758	32,163	18,390	2,908
Massachusetts	13,645	55,593	35,748	8,146	13,742	57,134	35,438	8,289	14,123	58,712	36,035	8,321
Michigan	33,322	57,815	21,392	5,884	34,187	58,540	21,047	6,053	32,329	58,908	21,292	6,095
Minnesota	21,868	35,428	22,424	4,420	21,664	36,326	22,202	4,813	21,213	36,451	22,082	5,291
Mississippi	12,996	13,516	4,809	1,217	12,140	14,076	4,804	1,261	12,640	14,266	4,822	1,259
Missouri	19,895	43,688	20,979	4,669	19,821	40,963	20,577	4,682	18,567	40,810	20,561	4,751
Montana	2,364	5,384	1,286	372	2,296	5,644	1,280	395	2,417	5,964	1,161	420
Nebraska	5,761	14,248	5,178	1,392	5,944	14,119	5,008	1,495	5,752	14,485	4,874	1,503
Nevada	5,350	7,639	2,604	950	5,375	7,949	2,194	936	5,732	8,080	2,148	922
New Hampshire	3,119	9,270	3,825	480	2,824	9,769	3,878	501	2,970	10,137	4,577	542
New Jersey	21,631	39,804	15,490	3,122	21,647	40,295	14,267	2,335	22,510	41,027	15,287	3,160
New Mexico	7,709	8,259	3,259	614	8,941	8,586	3,239	629	8,648	9,146	3,336	644
New York	69,654	129,429	71,406	14,809	68,104	132,614	70,407	15,332	68,592	134,826	71,573	15,019
North Carolina	27,673	50,737	16,948	4,420	28,551	51,782	17,301	4,824	29,234	52,602	18,376	5,005
North Dakota	2,523	5,742	1,725	480	2,386	5,983	1,676	465	2,405	6,168	1,825	469
Ohio	35,871	66,736	24,148	5,992	33,570	66,193	22,994	6,117	33,473	68,288	22,780	6,149
Oklahoma	11,513	19,846	6,481	1,728	12,405	20,047	6,497	1,658	12,606	20,654	6,616	1,657
Oregon	12,637	21,114	7,541	1,910	14,272	22,085	7,504	1,959	13,371	22,739	8,487	1,996
Pennsylvania	29,875	90,688	36,832	9,384	28,794	91,392	37,151	9,788	28,417	92,708	36,891	9,992
Rhode Island	3,537	11,013	2,566	745	3,727	11,079	2,654	742	3,780	11,455	2,618	753
South Carolina	10,790	22,973	5,972	1,604	11,628	24,004	6,120	1,741	11,885	24,351	5,878	1,866
South Dakota	2,699	5,392	1,467	353	2,610	5,641	1,512	335	2,696	5,676	1,336	395
Tennessee	13,548	32,309	11,929	3,152	13,230	33,766	11,946	3,298	13,007	34,134	12,125	3,493
Texas	67,768	111,312	45,325	10,108	68,898	115,114	46,464	10,426	71,129	118,785	46,288	10,810
Utah	13,280	26,554	7,669	1,184	13,021	28,597	8,412	1,247	13,609	29,848	9,565	1,271
Vermont	1,196	6,283	2,474	415	1,280	6,206	3,191	434	1,222	6,221	2,295	358
Virginia	26,199	52,998	21,516	5,328	25,789	54,749	22,782	5,193	25,191	55,794	23,844	5,349
Washington	28,977	32,376	9,595	2,561	29,281	32,689	9,519	2,601	29,064	32,506	9,292	2,558
West Virginia	4,897	13,284	5,892	986	5,411	14,357	6,409	1,032	5,914	15,525	6,806	1,009
Wisconsin	16,494	36,005	9,856	2,590	15,807	36,927	9,653	2,507	14,901	37,346	8,755	2,682
Wyoming	2,924	2,064	489	197	3,125	2,057	486	199	3,145	2,012	476	222
U.S. Service Academies	0	3,665	9	0	0	3,576	4	0	0	3,662	3	0
Other jurisdictions	9,135	20,358	5,309	1,405	8,293	20,870	5,224	1,471	9,194	21,127	5,321	1,462
American Samoa	269	2	0	0	235	5	0	0	228	3	0	0
Federated States of Micronesia	262	0	0	0	293	0	0	0	267	0	0	0
Guam	278	408	132	0	137	395	113	0	155	424	106	0
Marshall Islands	71	0	0	0	79	0	0	0	106	0	0	0
Northern Marianas	103	14	0	0	133	29	0	0	123	35	0	0
Palau	85	0	0	0	99	0	0	0	88	0	0	0
Puerto Rico	7,994	19,697	5,124	1,405	7,252	20,230	5,055	1,471	8,169	20,451	5,165	1,462
U.S. Virgin Islands	73	237	53	0	65	211	56	0	58	214	50	0

[1] Includes Ph.D., Ed.D., and comparable degrees at the doctoral level. Includes most degrees formerly classified as first-professional, such as M.D., D.D.S., and law degrees.
NOTE: Data are for postsecondary institutions participating in Title IV federal financial aid programs. Some data have been revised from previously published figures.

SOURCE: U.S. Department of Education, National Center for Education Statistics, Integrated Postsecondary Education Data System (IPEDS), Fall 2012 through Fall 2014, Completions component. (This table was prepared April 2016.)

Table 319.30. Bachelor's degrees conferred by postsecondary institutions, by field of study and state or jurisdiction: 2013–14

State or jurisdiction	Total	Humanities[1]	Psychology	Social sciences and history	Natural sciences[2]	Computer sciences	Engineering[3]	Education	Business/ management[4]	Health professions and related programs	Other fields[5]
1	2	3	4	5	6	7	8	9	10	11	12
United States	1,869,814	291,507	117,298	173,096	154,917	55,367	108,969	98,854	358,079	198,770	312,957
Alabama	29,516	2,513	1,466	1,584	2,166	636	2,496	2,380	7,141	3,324	5,810
Alaska	2,033	336	132	153	192	31	192	100	379	217	301
Arizona	61,280	8,558	2,293	2,763	2,864	3,089	1,769	3,332	14,963	11,009	10,640
Arkansas	15,488	2,347	794	1,057	1,253	282	672	1,504	2,825	1,981	2,773
California	199,258	36,267	15,177	25,816	18,315	5,184	11,534	4,668	36,723	14,812	30,762
Colorado	33,412	4,901	2,054	3,387	3,076	1,254	2,251	273	6,905	3,425	5,886
Connecticut	21,710	4,056	1,730	2,885	1,876	271	941	671	3,495	2,355	3,430
Delaware	6,338	742	353	554	329	160	420	516	1,426	758	1,080
District of Columbia	9,251	1,261	565	2,801	554	192	288	64	1,682	671	1,173
Florida	97,004	12,082	6,429	8,310	6,653	2,943	4,687	5,146	22,070	11,085	17,599
Georgia	48,831	6,931	3,132	4,182	4,382	1,864	2,843	3,824	9,800	4,281	7,592
Hawaii	6,915	1,016	432	701	490	221	183	426	1,568	741	1,137
Idaho	10,703	1,714	512	763	871	294	607	965	1,691	1,391	1,895
Illinois	74,958	11,752	4,291	5,805	5,767	2,500	4,001	4,202	13,919	10,480	12,241
Indiana	46,986	6,424	2,140	3,272	3,259	1,454	3,824	2,936	9,461	6,513	7,703
Iowa	28,125	3,164	1,783	1,771	1,919	789	1,653	1,995	5,822	3,157	6,072
Kansas	20,274	2,831	788	1,269	1,184	405	1,383	1,656	4,805	2,413	3,540
Kentucky	22,268	3,040	1,224	1,501	1,649	415	1,162	2,144	3,497	2,439	5,197
Louisiana	22,539	3,660	1,292	1,621	1,975	362	1,576	1,684	4,398	2,727	3,244
Maine	7,476	1,196	474	889	836	97	440	462	844	1,057	1,181
Maryland	32,163	4,046	2,174	3,861	2,962	2,525	1,550	1,589	5,649	2,675	5,132
Massachusetts	58,712	9,726	4,302	7,391	5,684	1,695	3,775	1,584	10,548	5,546	8,461
Michigan	58,908	7,321	3,523	4,346	5,059	1,713	4,670	3,307	11,380	6,786	10,803
Minnesota	36,451	5,215	2,528	2,960	3,865	1,202	1,430	2,440	7,142	3,879	5,790
Mississippi	14,266	1,763	836	878	1,263	153	800	1,804	2,594	1,701	2,474
Missouri	40,810	5,247	2,615	2,368	3,032	985	2,115	3,174	9,159	5,139	6,976
Montana	5,964	813	303	523	631	105	631	517	798	484	1,159
Nebraska	14,485	1,361	723	854	1,010	508	508	1,462	3,746	1,724	2,589
Nevada	8,080	994	495	626	663	209	442	407	2,179	834	1,231
New Hampshire	10,137	1,724	897	1,113	736	320	541	501	1,969	792	1,544
New Jersey	41,027	7,431	3,605	4,418	3,714	990	2,330	1,819	7,155	3,371	6,194
New Mexico	9,146	1,816	567	615	740	181	715	786	1,589	777	1,360
New York	134,826	26,531	10,578	15,215	11,071	3,723	6,601	6,132	23,876	12,034	19,065
North Carolina	52,602	6,267	3,663	5,250	5,115	1,339	2,850	3,592	8,825	4,725	10,976
North Dakota	6,168	585	255	192	406	116	492	609	1,176	850	1,487
Ohio	68,288	8,939	3,507	5,108	5,076	1,310	4,755	5,430	12,510	10,353	11,300
Oklahoma	20,654	3,550	973	957	1,373	426	1,509	1,607	4,256	2,071	3,932
Oregon	22,739	4,385	1,463	3,008	2,000	466	1,249	615	3,485	2,016	4,052
Pennsylvania	92,708	13,807	5,602	8,494	8,677	3,120	6,161	5,042	16,809	10,725	14,271
Rhode Island	11,455	1,511	612	1,039	870	311	432	441	2,828	813	2,598
South Carolina	24,351	3,281	1,594	2,273	2,710	513	1,211	1,762	5,375	2,001	3,631
South Dakota	5,676	487	228	369	412	189	451	563	733	1,139	1,105
Tennessee	34,134	6,363	1,916	2,589	2,360	654	1,694	2,449	5,880	3,630	6,599
Texas	118,785	23,113	6,242	8,632	9,883	2,513	7,753	2,053	23,209	12,946	22,441
Utah	29,848	3,409	1,221	2,277	1,914	1,937	1,268	3,237	5,522	4,906	4,157
Vermont	6,221	1,283	422	831	572	169	245	300	762	418	1,219
Virginia	55,794	10,757	4,604	6,334	4,547	2,571	3,269	1,425	10,086	4,504	7,697
Washington	32,506	6,204	2,008	4,013	3,595	1,219	2,017	1,404	5,087	2,294	4,665
West Virginia	15,525	3,179	753	1,252	851	572	742	843	2,577	1,045	3,711
Wisconsin	37,346	5,095	1,883	3,263	3,824	1,020	2,252	2,787	7,274	3,494	6,454
Wyoming	2,012	153	117	142	253	18	210	225	235	262	397
U.S. Service Academies	3,662	360	28	821	439	152	1,379	0	252	0	231
Other jurisdictions	21,127	1,036	1,224	761	2,051	763	1,268	1,608	4,953	4,373	3,090
American Samoa	3	0	0	0	0	0	0	3	0	0	0
Guam	424	43	7	25	29	13	0	74	83	24	126
Northern Marianas	35	0	0	0	0	0	0	35	0	0	0
Puerto Rico	20,451	986	1,196	734	1,981	745	1,268	1,475	4,779	4,338	2,949
U.S. Virgin Islands	214	7	21	2	41	5	0	21	91	11	15

[1]Includes degrees in area, ethnic, cultural, gender, and group studies; English language and literature/letters; foreign languages, literatures, and linguistics; liberal arts and sciences, general studies and humanities; multi/interdisciplinary studies; philosophy and religious studies; theology and religious vocations; and visual and performing arts.
[2]Includes biological and biomedical sciences; physical sciences; science technologies/technicians; and mathematics and statistics.
[3]Includes engineering; engineering technologies/technicians; mechanic and repair technologies/technicians; and construction trades.
[4]Includes business management, marketing, and related support services; and personal and culinary services.
[5]Includes agriculture, agricultural operations, and related sciences; natural resources and conservation; architecture and related services; communication, journalism, and related

programs; communications technologies/technicians and support services; family and consumer services/human sciences; legal professions and studies; library science; military technologies and applied sciences; parks, recreation, leisure, and fitness studies; homeland security, law enforcement, and firefighting; public administration and social service professions; transportation and materials moving; and precision production.
NOTE: Data are for postsecondary institutions participating in Title IV federal financial aid programs. This table includes only those jurisdictions with 4-year institutions.
SOURCE: U.S. Department of Education, National Center for Education Statistics, Integrated Postsecondary Education Data System (IPEDS), Fall 2014, Completions component. (This table was prepared April 2016.)

Table 319.40. Master's degrees conferred by postsecondary institutions, by field of study and state or jurisdiction: 2013–14

State or jurisdiction	Total	Humanities[1]	Psychology	Social sciences and history	Natural sciences[2]	Computer sciences	Engineering[3]	Education	Business/ management[4]	Health professions and related programs	Other fields[5]
1	2	3	4	5	6	7	8	9	10	11	12
United States	754,475	59,761	27,966	21,475	28,217	24,532	47,326	154,636	189,328	97,403	103,831
Alabama	11,346	350	337	213	295	147	982	2,342	2,975	2,041	1,664
Alaska	707	32	32	15	62	2	52	258	107	35	112
Arizona	28,829	808	2,292	249	353	672	957	7,292	9,616	4,252	2,338
Arkansas	4,896	202	39	81	168	81	310	2,051	606	688	670
California	74,521	7,572	4,473	1,992	2,665	2,107	6,305	13,517	16,919	8,201	10,770
Colorado	14,935	907	881	524	524	839	1,041	2,173	5,023	1,239	1,784
Connecticut	9,521	886	329	226	588	272	666	2,086	1,985	1,221	1,262
Delaware	2,842	92	17	61	109	101	86	614	954	387	421
District of Columbia	11,477	1,188	182	1,451	771	405	626	748	2,444	1,020	2,642
Florida	34,077	1,925	1,126	624	1,256	560	2,591	4,697	10,887	4,852	5,559
Georgia	16,975	1,625	345	365	713	601	1,168	3,086	4,625	2,490	1,957
Hawaii	2,075	181	132	51	66	39	61	455	502	209	379
Idaho	1,888	126	12	40	93	19	163	531	295	272	337
Illinois	41,677	2,951	1,364	927	1,526	1,928	2,087	7,773	12,489	4,871	5,761
Indiana	14,357	1,353	290	308	512	375	1,077	2,595	4,468	1,688	1,691
Iowa	7,681	475	397	78	230	407	296	1,497	2,157	1,163	981
Kansas	7,387	670	189	147	193	100	427	1,985	1,721	804	1,151
Kentucky	9,507	703	473	182	255	189	351	2,937	1,364	1,539	1,514
Louisiana	7,348	632	159	171	417	118	305	1,338	1,634	1,311	1,263
Maine	2,035	145	38	10	59	11	34	610	289	459	380
Maryland	18,390	1,198	286	1,002	1,034	1,879	1,257	2,661	5,294	2,245	1,534
Massachusetts	36,035	2,827	951	1,337	1,280	1,122	2,463	7,206	9,392	3,983	5,474
Michigan	21,292	1,324	537	513	926	562	2,127	3,875	5,441	2,670	3,317
Minnesota	22,082	967	1,704	375	425	522	456	5,642	3,972	5,608	2,411
Mississippi	4,822	185	95	93	493	80	135	1,465	958	635	683
Missouri	20,561	1,166	687	567	521	421	909	4,003	7,296	2,660	2,331
Montana	1,161	97	38	44	83	14	55	332	114	191	193
Nebraska	4,874	304	98	317	197	188	100	1,298	1,098	754	520
Nevada	2,148	86	39	70	80	39	100	680	508	298	248
New Hampshire	4,577	212	25	71	72	131	221	907	1,913	610	415
New Jersey	15,287	1,499	466	330	853	662	1,653	3,016	3,270	1,536	2,002
New Mexico	3,336	328	59	123	163	52	277	879	668	455	332
New York	71,573	7,459	1,968	2,622	2,805	2,492	3,990	16,193	14,213	8,071	11,760
North Carolina	18,376	1,646	209	546	875	670	1,240	4,017	4,356	2,473	2,344
North Dakota	1,825	47	70	37	62	29	87	392	396	402	303
Ohio	22,780	1,829	731	566	1,219	388	1,781	4,573	5,184	3,595	2,914
Oklahoma	6,616	765	285	118	220	187	448	1,227	1,778	750	838
Oregon	8,487	773	254	134	308	78	360	3,706	1,239	884	751
Pennsylvania	36,891	2,713	1,357	856	1,361	1,773	2,824	7,319	8,171	5,596	4,921
Rhode Island	2,618	219	101	106	111	64	121	435	832	178	451
South Carolina	5,878	433	138	114	235	86	390	1,446	1,411	728	897
South Dakota	1,336	71	80	27	66	65	101	348	215	163	200
Tennessee	12,125	955	383	204	379	154	478	2,949	2,899	2,389	1,335
Texas	46,288	3,571	1,962	1,323	1,952	1,852	3,260	9,111	12,997	4,969	5,291
Utah	9,565	273	161	110	238	532	350	2,163	3,360	1,612	766
Vermont	2,295	580	83	390	41	37	82	328	267	110	377
Virginia	23,844	3,295	1,228	550	507	811	1,108	5,164	5,320	1,911	3,950
Washington	9,292	707	406	142	438	398	509	1,745	1,865	1,227	1,855
West Virginia	6,806	830	117	782	105	92	168	1,180	1,383	628	1,521
Wisconsin	8,755	514	337	270	247	173	637	1,703	2,397	1,299	1,178
Wyoming	476	65	4	21	66	6	51	88	61	31	83
U.S. Service Academies	3	0	0	0	0	0	3	0	0	0	0
Other jurisdictions	5,321	267	356	44	145	103	294	1,202	1,458	801	651
American Samoa	0	0	0	0	0	0	0	0	0	0	0
Guam	106	2	5	0	3	0	0	58	6	0	32
Northern Marianas	0	0	0	0	0	0	0	0	0	0	0
Puerto Rico	5,165	265	351	44	142	103	294	1,128	1,430	801	607
U.S. Virgin Islands	50	0	0	0	0	0	0	16	22	0	12

[1]Includes degrees in area, ethnic, cultural, gender, and group studies; English language and literature/letters; foreign languages, literatures, and linguistics; liberal arts and sciences, general studies and humanities; multi/interdisciplinary studies; philosophy and religious studies; theology and religious vocations; and visual and performing arts.
[2]Includes biological and biomedical sciences; physical sciences; science technologies/technicians; and mathematics and statistics.
[3]Includes engineering; engineering technologies/technicians; mechanic and repair technologies/technicians; and construction trades.
[4]Includes business management, marketing, and related support services; and personal and culinary services.
[5]Includes agriculture, agricultural operations, and related sciences; natural resources and conservation; architecture and related services; communication, journalism, and related programs; communications technologies/technicians and support services; family and consumer sciences/human sciences; legal professions and studies; library science; military technologies and applied sciences; parks, recreation, leisure, and fitness studies; homeland security, law enforcement, and firefighting; public administration and social service professions; transportation and materials moving; and precision production.
NOTE: Data are for postsecondary institutions participating in Title IV federal financial aid programs. This table includes only those jurisdictions with 4-year institutions.
SOURCE: U.S. Department of Education, National Center for Education Statistics, Integrated Postsecondary Education Data System (IPEDS), Fall 2014, Completions component. (This table was prepared April 2016.)

Table 320.10. Certificates below the associate's degree level conferred by postsecondary institutions, by length of curriculum, sex of student, institution level and control, and discipline division: 2013–14

Discipline division	Less-than-1-year certificates								1- to less-than-4-year certificates							
	Sex			Institution level		Institution control			Sex			Institution level		Institution control		
	Total	Males	Females	Non-degree-granting (less-than-2-year)	Degree-granting (2-year and 4-year)	Public	Nonprofit	For-profit	Total	Males	Females	Non-degree-granting (less-than-2-year)	Degree-granting (2-year and 4-year)	Public	Nonprofit	For-profit
1	2	3	4	5	6	7	8	9	10	11	12	13	14	15	16	17
Total	479,574	213,414	266,160	118,214	361,360	343,129	13,390	123,055	489,779	177,380	312,399	186,021	303,758	233,129	17,340	239,310
Agriculture and natural resources	3,322	2,095	1,227	90	3,232	3,143	17	162	2,330	1,463	867	178	2,152	2,111	121	98
Agriculture, agriculture operations, and related sciences	2,711	1,701	1,010	90	2,621	2,576	0	135	2,207	1,370	837	176	2,031	1,990	119	98
Natural resources and conservation	611	394	217	0	611	567	17	27	123	93	30	2	121	121	2	0
Architecture and related services	243	148	95	0	243	193	49	1	109	71	38	0	109	72	37	0
Area, ethnic, cultural, gender, and group studies	442	116	326	0	442	422	20	0	151	32	119	0	151	147	4	0
Biological and biomedical sciences	732	202	530	25	707	711	5	16	194	67	127	83	111	117	54	23
Business, management, marketing, and support services	50,889	17,407	33,482	3,401	47,488	45,929	983	3,977	24,198	6,680	17,518	3,154	21,044	20,293	1,198	2,707
Accounting and related services	9,905	2,995	6,910	601	9,304	8,844	75	986	5,597	1,315	4,282	616	4,981	4,837	436	324
Business/commerce, general	2,133	906	1,227	0	2,133	2,086	39	8	1,639	838	801	0	1,639	1,477	7	155
Business administration, management, and operations	10,969	4,295	6,674	17	10,952	10,473	116	380	4,127	1,491	2,636	45	4,082	3,690	47	390
Management information systems and services	949	558	391	274	675	490	62	397	250	132	118	79	171	234	0	16
Business operations support and assistant services	11,499	2,948	8,551	1,691	9,808	10,004	103	1,392	7,771	1,208	6,563	1,908	5,863	6,076	364	1,331
Business and management, other	15,434	5,705	9,729	818	14,616	14,032	588	814	4,814	1,696	3,118	506	4,308	3,979	344	491
Communication, journalism, and related programs	1,993	963	1,030	237	1,756	1,731	106	156	1,860	1,109	751	1,292	568	460	139	1,261
Communications technologies	2,353	1,433	920	465	1,888	1,897	28	428	3,201	2,514	687	1,793	1,408	1,381	15	1,805
Computer and information sciences and support services	23,485	16,647	6,838	2,514	20,971	20,337	240	2,908	10,250	7,719	2,531	2,206	8,044	7,426	236	2,588
Construction trades	12,568	11,916	652	3,355	9,213	10,951	629	988	12,968	12,457	511	3,857	9,111	8,323	530	4,115
Education	5,929	803	5,126	71	5,858	4,754	751	424	3,652	423	3,229	377	3,275	2,480	857	315
Engineering	595	497	98	235	360	486	0	109	329	268	61	39	290	269	50	10
Engineering technologies and engineering-related fields[1]	18,129	15,776	2,353	2,460	15,669	15,710	221	2,198	14,207	12,916	1,291	2,469	11,738	9,012	322	4,873
English language and literature/letters	1,006	324	682	187	819	622	370	14	1,115	390	725	775	340	134	92	889
Family and consumer sciences/human sciences	14,143	1,240	12,903	1,073	13,070	13,986	51	106	3,734	271	3,463	310	3,424	3,664	47	23
Foreign languages, literatures, and linguistics	1,197	256	941	0	1,197	1,041	149	7	598	97	501	1	597	543	55	0
Health professions and related programs	177,063	34,359	142,704	55,211	121,852	102,894	5,330	68,839	183,142	25,921	157,221	60,856	122,286	70,464	8,342	104,336
Dental assisting	8,101	772	7,329	3,232	4,869	1,519	251	6,331	14,113	1,307	12,806	4,222	9,891	4,517	59	9,537
Emergency medical technician (EMT paramedic)	16,457	10,914	5,543	1,122	15,335	15,891	92	474	5,198	3,927	1,271	481	4,717	4,640	265	293
Clinical/medical lab science	9,471	1,392	8,079	2,372	7,099	6,549	182	2,740	2,326	611	1,715	596	1,730	692	666	968
Medical assisting	21,387	2,102	19,285	11,072	10,315	2,682	1,523	17,182	51,708	4,714	46,994	19,774	31,934	6,347	1,625	43,736
Pharmacy assisting	6,473	1,567	4,906	2,967	3,506	2,157	654	3,662	7,788	1,740	6,048	1,676	6,112	1,970	89	5,729
Other allied health assisting	7,470	2,349	5,121	1,841	5,629	4,741	55	2,674	3,297	418	2,879	1,442	1,855	947	221	2,129
Nursing and patient care assistant	46,534	5,911	40,623	11,261	35,273	38,335	754	7,445	982	102	880	317	665	418	0	564
Practical nursing	6,257	682	5,575	852	5,405	5,542	79	636	49,825	5,643	44,182	16,353	33,472	33,836	1,355	14,634
Nursing, registered nurse and other	1,599	198	1,401	0	1,599	1,476	123	0	3,402	473	2,929	2,167	1,235	1,038	2,037	327
Health sciences, other	53,314	8,472	44,842	20,492	32,822	24,002	1,617	27,695	44,503	6,986	37,517	13,828	30,675	16,059	2,025	26,419
Homeland security, law enforcement, and firefighting	27,237	20,160	7,077	3,001	24,236	26,360	429	448	7,159	4,661	2,498	162	6,997	6,514	167	478
Criminal justice and corrections	20,464	14,115	6,349	1,441	19,023	19,911	366	187	5,778	3,470	2,308	152	5,626	5,250	54	474
Fire control and safety	6,096	5,612	484	1,438	4,658	6,073	7	16	1,213	1,112	101	10	1,203	1,213	0	0
Homeland security and related protective services, other	677	433	244	122	555	376	56	245	168	79	89	89	168	51	113	4
Legal professions and studies	2,006	350	1,656	165	1,841	1,228	234	544	3,444	598	2,846	561	2,883	2,642	286	516
Liberal arts and sciences, general studies, and humanities	3,224	1,239	1,985	0	3,224	3,214	10	0	36,266	14,316	21,950	0	36,266	36,193	73	0
Library science	224	31	193	0	224	224	0	0	60	10	50	0	60	60	0	0

See notes at end of table.

Table 320.10. Certificates below the associate's degree level conferred by postsecondary institutions, by length of curriculum, sex of student, institution level and control, and discipline division: 2013–14—Continued

Discipline division	Less-than-1-year certificates								1- to less-than-4-year certificates							
	Sex			Institution level		Institution control			Total	Sex		Institution level		Institution control		
	Total	Males	Females	Non-degree-granting (less-than-2-year)	Degree-granting (2-year and 4-year)	Public	Nonprofit	For-profit		Males	Females	Non-degree-granting (less-than-2-year)	Degree-granting (2-year and 4-year)	Public	Nonprofit	For-profit
1	2	3	4	5	6	7	8	9	10	11	12	13	14	15	16	17
Mathematics and statistics	166	124	42	0	166	146	20	0	17	14	3	0	17	12	5	0
Mechanic and repair technologies/technicians	32,423	30,565	1,858	3,788	28,635	30,143	559	1,721	50,338	48,443	1,895	22,413	27,925	22,360	973	27,005
Military technologies and applied sciences	25	20	5	0	25	9	0	16	36	25	11	0	36	36	0	0
Multi/interdisciplinary studies	1,525	647	878	5	1,520	1,152	55	318	1,203	627	576	0	1,203	1,168	34	1
Parks, recreation, leisure, and fitness studies	2,400	1,121	1,279	687	1,713	1,572	34	794	650	357	293	97	553	431	5	214
Personal and culinary services	38,157	5,545	32,612	27,158	10,999	10,065	276	27,816	98,125	14,332	83,793	78,804	19,321	13,967	1,168	82,990
Philosophy and religious studies	59	27	32	0	59	43	16	0	11	2	9	0	11	5	6	0
Physical sciences and science technologies	886	618	268	73	813	881	5	0	998	671	327	0	998	998	0	0
Physical sciences	197	126	71	0	197	192	5	0	17	13	4	0	17	17	0	0
Science technologies/technicians	689	492	197	73	616	689	0	0	981	658	323	0	981	981	0	0
Precision production	21,616	20,501	1,115	3,421	18,195	19,280	700	1,636	15,900	15,096	804	4,703	11,197	11,740	867	3,293
Psychology	209	35	174	0	209	69	140	0	64	9	55	0	64	59	5	0
Public administration and social services	1,176	279	897	14	1,162	1,034	97	45	1,179	206	973	0	1,179	1,111	63	5
Social sciences and history	1,089	612	477	8	1,081	968	121	0	368	201	167	0	368	353	15	0
Social sciences	1,064	604	460	8	1,056	944	120	0	361	196	165	0	361	346	15	0
History	25	8	17	0	25	24	1	0	7	5	2	0	7	7	0	0
Theology and religious vocations	297	129	168	0	297	2	295	0	819	349	470	437	382	1	818	0
Transportation and materials moving	27,803	25,166	2,637	9,644	18,159	18,298	777	8,728	979	914	65	316	663	631	18	330
Visual and performing arts	4,963	2,063	2,900	926	4,037	3,634	673	656	10,125	4,151	5,974	1,138	8,987	7,952	738	1,435
Fine and studio arts	787	293	494	658	129	116	529	142	5,411	1,999	3,412	5	5,406	5,339	71	1
Music and dance	280	170	110	0	280	197	4	79	431	288	143	93	338	126	148	157
Visual and performing arts, other[2]	3,896	1,600	2,296	268	3,628	3,321	140	435	4,283	1,864	2,419	1,040	3,243	2,487	519	1,277

[1]Excludes "Construction trades" and "Mechanic and repair technologies/technicians," which are listed separately.
[2]Includes design and applied arts, drama and theatre arts, film and photographic arts, and all other arts not included under "Fine and studio arts" or "Music and dance."

NOTE: Data are for postsecondary institutions participating in Title IV federal financial aid programs. Degree-granting institutions grant degrees at the associate's or higher level, while non-degree-granting institutions grant only awards below that level.
SOURCE: U.S. Department of Education, National Center for Education Statistics, Integrated Postsecondary Education Data System (IPEDS), Fall 2014, Completions component. (This table was prepared April 2016.)

Table 320.20. Certificates below the associate's degree level conferred by postsecondary institutions, by race/ethnicity and sex of student: 1998–99 through 2013–14

Year and sex	Number of certificates conferred to U.S. citizens and nonresident aliens								Percentage distribution of certificates conferred to U.S. citizens						
	Total	White	Black	Hispanic	Asian/ Pacific Islander	American Indian/ Alaska Native	Two or more races	Non-resident alien	Total	White	Black	Hispanic	Asian/ Pacific Islander	American Indian/ Alaska Native	Two or more races
1	2	3	4	5	6	7	8	9	10	11	12	13	14	15	16
Total															
1998–99	555,883	345,359	92,800	76,833	27,920	7,510	—	5,461	100.0	62.7	16.9	14.0	5.1	1.4	—
1999–2000	558,129	337,546	97,329	81,132	29,361	6,966	—	5,795	100.0	61.1	17.6	14.7	5.3	1.3	—
2000–01	552,503	333,478	99,397	78,528	28,123	6,598	—	6,379	100.0	61.1	18.2	14.4	5.1	1.2	—
2001–02	584,248	352,559	106,647	83,950	27,490	7,430	—	6,172	100.0	61.0	18.4	14.5	4.8	1.3	—
2002–03	646,425	382,289	120,582	95,499	32,981	8,117	—	6,957	100.0	59.8	18.9	14.9	5.2	1.3	—
2003–04	687,787	402,989	129,891	107,216	32,819	8,375	—	6,497	100.0	59.2	19.1	15.7	4.8	1.2	—
2004–05	710,873	415,670	133,601	114,089	32,783	8,150	—	6,580	100.0	59.0	19.0	16.2	4.7	1.2	—
2005–06	715,401	412,077	135,460	118,853	34,110	8,400	—	6,501	100.0	58.1	19.1	16.8	4.8	1.2	—
2006–07	729,037	420,585	139,995	119,501	32,962	8,793	—	7,201	100.0	58.3	19.4	16.6	4.6	1.2	—
2007–08	749,883	430,187	145,181	122,676	35,985	8,596	—	7,258	100.0	57.9	19.5	16.5	4.8	1.2	—
2008–09	804,620	450,562	161,487	138,301	37,941	9,485	—	6,844	100.0	56.5	20.2	17.3	4.8	1.2	—
2009–10	935,719	511,186	191,657	172,015	41,407	12,003	—	7,451	100.0	55.1	20.6	18.5	4.5	1.3	—
2010–11	1,030,477	557,595	207,693	187,433	44,294	11,204	14,999	7,259	100.0	54.5	20.3	18.3	4.3	1.1	1.5
2011–12	989,061	535,621	190,253	187,014	43,048	10,638	14,140	8,347	100.0	54.6	19.4	19.1	4.4	1.1	1.4
2012–13	967,214	524,000	177,006	186,248	44,196	10,824	17,642	7,298	100.0	54.6	18.4	19.4	4.6	1.1	1.8
2013–14	969,353	523,184	177,881	185,588	43,810	10,817	19,931	8,142	100.0	54.4	18.5	19.3	4.6	1.1	2.1
Males															
1998–99	219,872	144,735	29,875	27,719	11,742	3,061	—	2,740	100.0	66.7	13.8	12.8	5.4	1.4	—
1999–2000	226,110	143,634	33,792	30,337	13,082	2,862	—	2,403	100.0	64.2	15.1	13.6	5.8	1.3	—
2000–01	223,951	143,144	34,381	28,685	12,072	2,719	—	2,950	100.0	64.8	15.6	13.0	5.5	1.2	—
2001–02	235,275	152,226	36,482	29,749	10,938	3,226	—	2,654	100.0	65.4	15.7	12.8	4.7	1.4	—
2002–03	254,238	161,001	40,080	33,925	12,930	3,506	—	2,796	100.0	64.0	15.9	13.5	5.1	1.4	—
2003–04	257,138	161,684	40,809	36,157	12,713	3,135	—	2,640	100.0	63.5	16.0	14.2	5.0	1.2	—
2004–05	259,261	161,126	41,644	38,297	12,448	3,068	—	2,678	100.0	62.8	16.2	14.9	4.9	1.2	—
2005–06	259,737	158,747	41,863	40,752	12,790	3,219	—	2,366	100.0	61.7	16.3	15.8	5.0	1.3	—
2006–07	269,589	164,939	44,870	40,958	12,622	3,527	—	2,673	100.0	61.8	16.8	15.3	4.7	1.3	—
2007–08	283,266	172,398	48,024	43,085	13,527	3,452	—	2,780	100.0	61.5	17.1	15.4	4.8	1.2	—
2008–09	302,449	179,813	53,879	47,860	14,427	3,856	—	2,614	100.0	60.0	18.0	16.0	4.8	1.3	—
2009–10	355,381	205,404	65,487	60,771	15,940	5,067	—	2,712	100.0	58.2	18.6	17.2	4.5	1.4	—
2010–11	391,676	223,755	71,867	66,514	16,944	4,760	4,884	2,952	100.0	57.6	18.5	17.1	4.4	1.2	1.3
2011–12	374,086	213,833	65,224	65,838	16,180	4,507	4,952	3,552	100.0	57.7	17.6	17.8	4.4	1.2	1.3
2012–13	375,928	215,432	61,668	67,377	17,352	4,446	6,511	3,142	100.0	57.8	16.5	18.1	4.7	1.2	1.7
2013–14	390,794	223,229	65,632	68,758	17,283	4,732	7,752	3,408	100.0	57.6	16.9	17.7	4.5	1.2	2.0
Females															
1998–99	336,011	200,624	62,925	49,114	16,178	4,449	—	2,721	100.0	60.2	18.9	14.7	4.9	1.3	—
1999–2000	332,019	193,912	63,537	50,795	16,279	4,104	—	3,392	100.0	59.0	19.3	15.5	5.0	1.2	—
2000–01	328,552	190,334	65,016	49,843	16,051	3,879	—	3,429	100.0	58.5	20.0	15.3	4.9	1.2	—
2001–02	348,973	200,333	70,165	54,201	16,552	4,204	—	3,518	100.0	58.0	20.3	15.7	4.8	1.2	—
2002–03	392,187	221,288	80,502	61,574	20,051	4,611	—	4,161	100.0	57.0	20.7	15.9	5.2	1.2	—
2003–04	430,649	241,305	89,082	71,059	20,106	5,240	—	3,857	100.0	56.5	20.9	16.6	4.7	1.2	—
2004–05	451,612	254,544	91,957	75,792	20,335	5,082	—	3,902	100.0	56.9	20.5	16.9	4.5	1.1	—
2005–06	455,664	253,330	93,597	78,101	21,320	5,181	—	4,135	100.0	56.1	20.7	17.3	4.7	1.1	—
2006–07	459,448	255,646	95,125	78,543	20,340	5,266	—	4,528	100.0	56.2	20.9	17.3	4.5	1.2	—
2007–08	466,617	257,789	97,157	79,591	22,458	5,144	—	4,478	100.0	55.8	21.0	17.2	4.9	1.1	—
2008–09	502,171	270,749	107,608	90,441	23,514	5,629	—	4,230	100.0	54.4	21.6	18.2	4.7	1.1	—
2009–10	580,338	305,782	126,170	111,244	25,467	6,936	—	4,739	100.0	53.1	21.9	19.3	4.4	1.2	—
2010–11	638,801	333,840	135,826	120,919	27,350	6,444	10,115	4,307	100.0	52.6	21.4	19.1	4.3	1.0	1.6
2011–12	614,975	321,788	125,029	121,176	26,868	6,131	9,188	4,795	100.0	52.7	20.5	19.9	4.4	1.0	1.5
2012–13	591,286	308,568	115,338	118,871	26,844	6,378	11,131	4,156	100.0	52.6	19.6	20.2	4.6	1.1	1.9
2013–14	578,559	299,955	112,249	116,830	26,527	6,085	12,179	4,734	100.0	52.3	19.6	20.4	4.6	1.1	2.1

—Not available.
NOTE: Includes less-than-1-year awards and 1- to less-than-4-year awards (excluding associate's degrees) conferred by postsecondary institutions participating in Title IV federal financial aid programs. Race categories exclude persons of Hispanic ethnicity. Reported racial/ethnic distributions of students by level of degree, field of degree, and sex were used to estimate race/ethnicity for students whose race/ethnicity was not reported.

Some data have been revised from previously published figures. Detail may not sum to totals because of rounding.
SOURCE: U.S. Department of Education, National Center for Education Statistics, Integrated Postsecondary Education Data System (IPEDS), "Completions Survey" (IPEDS-C:99); and IPEDS Fall 2000 through Fall 2014, Completions component. (This table was prepared September 2015.)

Table 321.10. Associate's degrees conferred by postsecondary institutions, by sex of student and discipline division: 2003–04 through 2013–14

Discipline division	2003–04	2004–05	2005–06	2006–07	2007–08	2008–09	2009–10	2010–11	2011–12	2012–13	2013–14 Total	2013–14 Males	2013–14 Females
1	2	3	4	5	6	7	8	9	10	11	12	13	14
Total..	665,301	696,660	713,066	728,114	750,164	787,243	848,856	943,506	1,021,718	1,007,427	1,003,364	390,805	612,559
Agriculture and natural resources.................	6,283	6,404	6,168	5,838	5,738	5,724	5,852	6,430	7,068	6,826	7,051	4,410	2,641
Agriculture, agriculture operations, and related sciences....	4,959	5,137	4,958	4,638	4,554	4,525	4,615	4,925	5,400	5,227	5,417	3,223	2,194
Natural resources and conservation	1,324	1,267	1,210	1,200	1,184	1,199	1,237	1,505	1,668	1,599	1,634	1,187	447
Architecture and related services	492	583	656	517	568	605	553	569	593	468	414	279	135
Area, ethnic, cultural, gender, and group studies....	105	115	124	164	169	174	199	209	194	271	362	130	232
Biological and biomedical sciences..................	1,456	1,709	1,827	2,060	2,200	2,337	2,664	3,276	3,834	4,185	4,479	1,465	3,014
Business, management, marketing, and support services	92,065	96,067	96,933	99,998	104,566	111,524	116,798	121,735	123,014	114,842	112,804	41,610	71,194
Accounting and related services	14,506	13,988	13,620	14,232	15,965	16,707	17,925	20,180	20,270	18,061	17,386	4,789	12,597
Business/commerce, general	13,387	12,050	13,297	12,725	12,473	13,100	14,553	15,083	17,301	17,211	17,290	7,412	9,878
Business administration, management, and operations	31,522	37,258	39,152	43,667	47,911	52,938	46,086	46,253	45,879	49,816	50,010	21,476	28,534
Management information systems and services..............	4,214	2,812	2,179	2,007	1,237	1,103	1,221	1,244	1,164	1,085	1,176	804	372
Business operations support and assistant services	11,400	11,196	10,044	8,864	7,841	7,550	7,399	8,259	7,986	7,320	754	6,566
Business and management, other	17,036	18,763	18,641	18,503	19,139	20,126	29,614	30,716	29,423	20,683	19,622	6,375	13,247
Communication, journalism, and related programs........	2,444	2,545	2,629	2,609	2,620	2,722	2,841	3,051	3,495	4,299	4,935	2,197	2,738
Communications technologies	3,401	3,516	3,380	3,095	4,237	4,805	4,418	4,209	5,004	5,028	4,703	3,278	1,425
Computer and information sciences and support services....	41,845	36,173	31,246	27,712	28,296	29,912	32,351	37,689	41,250	38,954	37,601	29,913	7,688
Construction trades....................................	3,560	3,512	3,850	3,895	4,309	4,252	4,684	5,402	5,750	5,038	4,831	4,580	251
Education...	12,465	13,329	14,475	13,021	13,108	14,123	17,346	20,460	20,762	18,744	17,504	2,112	15,392
Engineering..	2,726	2,430	2,154	2,128	2,279	2,170	2,508	2,825	3,382	3,732	4,269	3,704	565
Engineering technologies and engineering-related fields[1].....	36,915	33,548	30,461	29,199	29,334	30,441	31,883	35,519	36,642	33,752	31,768	27,882	3,886
English language and literature/letters	828	995	1,105	1,249	1,402	1,534	1,658	2,019	2,137	2,089	2,075	678	1,397
Family and consumer sciences/human sciences	9,478	9,707	9,488	9,124	8,613	9,035	9,515	8,532	9,506	8,996	8,657	362	8,295
Foreign languages, literatures, and linguistics	1,047	1,234	1,161	1,207	1,258	1,630	1,683	1,888	1,980	2,131	2,276	478	1,798
Health professions and related programs	106,208	122,520	134,931	145,436	155,816	165,015	177,321	202,920	219,491	214,040	208,660	33,607	175,053
Dental assisting.....................................	5,652	5,813	6,085	6,313	6,642	6,574	7,063	7,498	7,790	7,823	7,986	382	7,604
Emergency medical technician (EMT paramedic)...............	1,617	1,825	1,980	2,008	2,140	2,270	2,413	2,895	3,352	3,520	3,516	2,459	1,057
Clinical/medical lab science	1,786	2,055	2,163	2,306	2,316	2,538	2,621	2,811	3,240	3,387	3,510	892	2,618
Medical and other health assisting...................	15,543	19,005	22,267	23,491	24,276	25,858	29,776	39,277	46,950	41,921	39,121	5,359	33,762
Nursing and patient care assistant..................	4	38	101	158	329	385	1	33	36	35	38	7	31
Practical nursing....................................	1,049	1,388	1,481	1,509	1,417	1,299	1,973	2,069	2,366	2,361	2,230	212	2,018
Nursing, registered nurse and other.................	51,552	58,007	62,095	66,516	73,277	77,922	81,281	83,023	84,569	86,380	86,280	12,557	73,723
Health sciences, other..............................	29,005	34,389	38,759	43,135	45,419	48,169	52,193	65,314	71,188	68,613	65,979	11,739	54,240
Homeland security, law enforcement, and firefighting	20,573	23,749	26,425	28,208	29,590	33,012	37,154	44,922	51,318	48,460	45,650	25,328	20,322
Criminal justice and corrections.....................	17,040	19,942	22,351	23,917	25,588	28,998	32,648	40,022	45,971	42,785	40,181	20,424	19,757
Fire control and safety..............................	3,012	3,366	3,554	3,811	3,937	3,947	4,307	4,603	4,779	4,910	4,644	4,331	313
Homeland security and related protective services, other.	521	441	520	480	65	67	199	297	568	765	825	573	252
Legal professions and studies	9,466	9,885	10,509	10,391	9,465	9,062	9,999	11,619	12,315	11,862	10,496	1,660	8,836
Liberal arts and sciences, general studies, and humanities...	227,650	240,131	244,689	250,030	254,012	263,947	284,954	306,674	336,938	344,171	353,438	136,296	217,142
Library science	114	108	136	84	117	116	112	160	159	181	192	28	164
Mathematics and statistics............................	801	807	753	827	855	933	1,051	1,644	1,529	1,801	2,140	1,492	648
Mechanic and repair technologies/technicians.........	12,553	13,619	14,454	15,432	15,297	16,059	16,326	19,969	20,715	20,487	20,052	19,011	1,041
Military technologies and applied sciences............	293	355	610	781	851	721	668	856	986	1,002	1,084	898	186
Multi/interdisciplinary studies	14,794	13,888	14,473	15,838	16,255	15,472	17,279	23,729	27,263	27,407	28,164	11,396	16,768
Parks, recreation, leisure, and fitness studies........	923	966	1,128	1,251	1,344	1,587	2,006	2,366	3,123	3,455	4,348	2,827	1,521
Personal and culinary services.......................	14,239	16,311	17,162	16,103	16,592	16,358	16,467	18,259	20,376	19,272	16,857	6,697	10,160
Philosophy and religious studies	404	422	367	375	458	193	256	283	308	326	435	283	152
Physical sciences and science technologies	2,687	2,825	2,910	3,412	3,395	3,650	4,141	5,078	5,827	6,376	6,935	4,089	2,846
Physical sciences...................................	1,599	1,637	1,741	2,023	1,980	2,196	2,378	3,148	3,652	4,083	4,518	2,653	1,865
Science technologies/technicians...................	1,088	1,188	1,169	1,389	1,415	1,454	1,763	1,930	2,175	2,293	2,417	1,436	981
Precision production..................................	1,968	2,039	1,977	1,973	1,968	2,127	2,794	3,254	3,320	3,345	3,903	3,686	217
Psychology..	1,887	1,942	1,944	2,213	2,412	3,957	6,582	3,866	4,717	6,122	7,530	1,795	5,735
Public administration and social services.............	3,728	4,027	4,415	4,338	4,192	4,177	4,522	7,472	9,222	8,788	8,900	1,275	7,625
Social sciences and history	6,245	6,533	6,730	7,080	7,812	9,157	10,649	12,772	14,132	15,668	16,528	6,190	10,338
Social sciences.....................................	5,875	6,233	6,308	6,673	7,358	8,670	10,108	12,072	13,321	14,749	15,454	5,531	9,923
History..	370	300	422	407	454	487	541	700	811	919	1,074	659	415
Theology and religious vocations	492	581	570	608	582	676	613	758	839	881	944	456	488
Transportation and materials moving	1,217	1,435	1,472	1,674	1,550	1,430	1,444	1,698	2,098	2,119	2,099	1,766	333
Visual and performing arts............................	23,949	22,650	21,754	20,244	18,890	18,606	19,565	21,394	22,431	22,309	21,280	8,947	12,333
Fine and studio arts	1,450	1,614	1,638	1,753	1,705	2,019	2,277	2,414	2,339	2,541	2,683	873	1,810
Music and dance...................................	2,584	2,333	2,389	2,290	1,317	1,152	1,335	1,356	1,683	1,743	1,712	1,123	589
Visual and performing arts, other[2]................	19,915	18,703	17,727	16,201	15,868	15,435	15,953	17,624	18,409	18,025	16,885	6,951	9,934
Not classified by field of study......................	0	0	0	0	14	0	0	0	0	0	0	0	0

[1]Excludes "Construction trades" and "Mechanic and repair technologies/technicians," which are listed separately.
[2]Includes design and applied arts, drama and theatre arts, film and photographic arts, and all other arts not included under "Fine and studio arts" or "Music and dance."
NOTE: Data are for degree-granting postsecondary institutions, which are institutions that grant associate's or higher degrees and participate in Title IV federal financial aid programs. Some data have been revised from previously published figures.

SOURCE: U.S. Department of Education, National Center for Education Statistics, Integrated Postsecondary Education Data System (IPEDS), "Completions Survey" (IPEDS-C:98–99); and IPEDS Fall 2003 through Fall 2004 through Fall 2014, Completions component. (This table was prepared September 2015.)

Table 321.20. Associate's degrees conferred by postsecondary institutions, by race/ethnicity and sex of student: Selected years, 1976–77 through 2013–14

Year and sex	Number of degrees conferred to U.S. citizens and nonresident aliens								Percentage distribution of degrees conferred to U.S. citizens						
	Total	White	Black	Hispanic	Asian/ Pacific Islander	American Indian/ Alaska Native	Two or more races	Non-resident alien	Total	White	Black	Hispanic	Asian/ Pacific Islander	American Indian/ Alaska Native	Two or more races
1	2	3	4	5	6	7	8	9	10	11	12	13	14	15	16
Total															
1976–77[1]	404,956	342,290	33,159	16,636	7,044	2,498	—	3,329	100.0	85.2	8.3	4.1	1.8	0.6	—
1980–81[2]	410,174	339,167	35,330	17,800	8,650	2,584	—	6,643	100.0	84.0	8.8	4.4	2.1	0.6	—
1990–91	481,720	391,264	38,835	25,540	15,257	3,871	—	6,953	100.0	82.4	8.2	5.4	3.2	0.8	—
1997–98	558,555	413,561	55,314	45,876	25,196	6,246	—	12,362	100.0	75.7	10.1	8.4	4.6	1.1	—
1998–99	564,984	412,985	58,417	48,845	27,628	6,395	—	10,714	100.0	74.5	10.5	8.8	5.0	1.2	—
1999–2000	564,933	408,822	60,208	51,563	27,778	6,474	—	10,088	100.0	73.7	10.9	9.3	5.0	1.2	—
2000–01	578,865	411,075	63,855	57,288	28,463	6,623	—	11,561	100.0	72.5	11.3	10.1	5.0	1.2	—
2001–02	595,133	417,733	67,343	60,003	30,945	6,832	—	12,277	100.0	71.7	11.6	10.3	5.3	1.2	—
2002–03	634,016	438,261	75,609	66,673	32,629	7,461	—	13,383	100.0	70.6	12.2	10.7	5.3	1.2	—
2003–04	665,301	456,047	81,183	72,270	33,149	8,119	—	14,533	100.0	70.1	12.5	11.1	5.1	1.2	—
2004–05	696,660	475,513	86,402	78,557	33,669	8,435	—	14,084	100.0	69.7	12.7	11.5	4.9	1.2	—
2005–06	713,066	485,297	89,784	80,854	35,201	8,552	—	13,378	100.0	69.4	12.8	11.6	5.0	1.2	—
2006–07	728,114	491,572	91,529	85,410	37,266	8,583	—	13,754	100.0	68.8	12.8	12.0	5.2	1.2	—
2007–08	750,164	501,079	95,702	91,274	38,843	8,849	—	14,417	100.0	68.1	13.0	12.4	5.3	1.2	—
2008–09	787,243	521,834	101,631	98,408	41,364	8,823	—	15,183	100.0	67.6	13.2	12.7	5.4	1.1	—
2009–10	848,856	552,376	113,867	112,403	44,026	10,101	—	16,083	100.0	66.3	13.7	13.5	5.3	1.2	—
2010–11	943,506	604,745	129,044	126,297	45,489	10,180	11,126	16,625	100.0	65.2	13.9	13.6	4.9	1.1	1.2
2011–12	1,021,718	635,755	142,512	151,807	48,861	10,738	14,858	17,187	100.0	63.3	14.2	15.1	4.9	1.1	1.5
2012–13	1,007,427	617,308	135,892	157,989	49,474	10,546	19,383	16,835	100.0	62.3	13.7	15.9	5.0	1.1	2.0
2013–14	1,003,364	601,383	134,483	167,120	50,333	10,334	22,634	17,077	100.0	61.0	13.6	16.9	5.1	1.0	2.3
Males															
1976–77[1]	209,672	178,236	15,330	9,105	3,630	1,216	—	2,155	100.0	85.9	7.4	4.4	1.7	0.6	—
1980–81[2]	183,819	151,242	14,290	8,327	4,557	1,108	—	4,295	100.0	84.2	8.0	4.6	2.5	0.6	—
1990–91	198,634	161,858	14,143	10,738	7,164	1,439	—	3,292	100.0	82.9	7.2	5.5	3.7	0.7	—
1997–98	217,613	161,212	18,686	19,108	10,953	2,252	—	5,402	100.0	76.0	8.8	9.0	5.2	1.1	—
1998–99	220,508	162,339	19,844	19,484	11,688	2,234	—	4,919	100.0	75.3	9.2	9.0	5.4	1.0	—
1999–2000	224,721	164,317	20,968	20,947	12,009	2,222	—	4,258	100.0	74.5	9.5	9.5	5.4	1.0	—
2000–01	231,645	166,322	22,147	23,350	12,339	2,294	—	5,193	100.0	73.4	9.8	10.3	5.4	1.0	—
2001–02	238,109	170,622	22,806	23,963	13,256	2,308	—	5,154	100.0	73.2	9.8	10.3	5.7	1.0	—
2002–03	253,451	179,163	25,591	26,461	14,057	2,618	—	5,561	100.0	72.3	10.3	10.7	5.7	1.1	—
2003–04	260,033	183,819	25,961	27,828	13,907	2,740	—	5,778	100.0	72.3	10.2	10.9	5.5	1.1	—
2004–05	267,536	188,569	27,151	29,658	13,802	2,774	—	5,582	100.0	72.0	10.4	11.3	5.3	1.1	—
2005–06	270,095	190,139	27,619	30,040	14,224	2,774	—	5,299	100.0	71.8	10.4	11.3	5.4	1.0	—
2006–07	275,187	191,565	28,273	31,646	15,510	2,873	—	5,320	100.0	71.0	10.5	11.7	5.7	1.1	—
2007–08	282,521	194,099	30,016	33,817	15,936	3,003	—	5,650	100.0	70.1	10.8	12.2	5.8	1.1	—
2008–09	298,066	202,670	32,004	36,919	17,305	3,075	—	6,093	100.0	69.4	11.0	12.6	5.9	1.1	—
2009–10	322,747	215,977	36,148	42,210	18,268	3,555	—	6,589	100.0	68.3	11.4	13.4	5.8	1.1	—
2010–11	361,408	238,012	41,649	47,911	19,085	3,727	4,197	6,827	100.0	67.1	11.7	13.5	5.4	1.1	1.2
2011–12	393,479	251,964	46,377	57,926	20,537	3,924	5,569	7,182	100.0	65.2	12.0	15.0	5.3	1.0	1.4
2012–13	389,195	243,868	45,458	60,536	21,223	3,638	7,434	7,038	100.0	63.8	11.9	15.8	5.6	1.0	1.9
2013–14	390,805	239,076	45,806	64,293	21,811	3,680	8,953	7,186	100.0	62.3	11.9	16.8	5.7	1.0	2.3
Females															
1976–77[1]	195,284	164,054	17,829	7,531	3,414	1,282	—	1,174	100.0	84.5	9.2	3.9	1.8	0.7	—
1980–81[2]	226,355	187,925	21,040	9,473	4,093	1,476	—	2,348	100.0	83.9	9.4	4.2	1.8	0.7	—
1990–91	283,086	229,406	24,692	14,802	8,093	2,432	—	3,661	100.0	82.1	8.8	5.3	2.9	0.9	—
1997–98	340,942	252,349	36,628	26,768	14,243	3,994	—	6,960	100.0	75.6	11.0	8.0	4.3	1.2	—
1998–99	344,476	250,646	38,573	29,361	15,940	4,161	—	5,795	100.0	74.0	11.4	8.7	4.7	1.2	—
1999–2000	340,212	244,505	39,240	30,616	15,769	4,252	—	5,830	100.0	73.1	11.7	9.2	4.7	1.3	—
2000–01	347,220	244,753	41,708	33,938	16,124	4,329	—	6,368	100.0	71.8	12.2	10.0	4.7	1.3	—
2001–02	357,024	247,111	44,537	36,040	17,689	4,524	—	7,123	100.0	70.6	12.7	10.3	5.1	1.3	—
2002–03	380,565	259,098	50,018	40,212	18,572	4,843	—	7,822	100.0	69.5	13.4	10.8	5.0	1.3	—
2003–04	405,268	272,228	55,222	44,442	19,242	5,379	—	8,755	100.0	68.7	13.9	11.2	4.9	1.4	—
2004–05	429,124	286,944	59,251	48,899	19,867	5,661	—	8,502	100.0	68.2	14.1	11.6	4.7	1.3	—
2005–06	442,971	295,158	62,165	50,814	20,977	5,778	—	8,079	100.0	67.9	14.3	11.7	4.8	1.3	—
2006–07	452,927	300,007	63,256	53,764	21,756	5,710	—	8,434	100.0	67.5	14.2	12.1	4.9	1.3	—
2007–08	467,643	306,980	65,686	57,457	22,907	5,846	—	8,767	100.0	66.9	14.3	12.5	5.0	1.3	—
2008–09	489,177	319,164	69,627	61,489	24,059	5,748	—	9,090	100.0	66.5	14.5	12.8	5.0	1.2	—
2009–10	526,109	336,399	77,719	70,193	25,758	6,546	—	9,494	100.0	65.1	15.0	13.6	5.0	1.3	—
2010–11	582,098	366,733	87,395	78,386	26,404	6,453	6,929	9,798	100.0	64.1	15.3	13.7	4.6	1.1	1.2
2011–12	628,239	383,791	96,135	93,881	28,324	6,814	9,289	10,005	100.0	62.1	15.5	15.2	4.6	1.1	1.5
2012–13	618,232	373,440	90,434	97,453	28,251	6,908	11,949	9,797	100.0	61.4	14.9	16.0	4.6	1.1	2.0
2013–14	612,559	362,307	88,677	102,827	28,522	6,654	13,681	9,891	100.0	60.1	14.7	17.1	4.7	1.1	2.3

—Not available.
[1]Excludes 1,170 males and 251 females whose racial/ethnic group was not available.
[2]Excludes 4,819 males and 1,384 females whose racial/ethnic group was not available.
NOTE: Data through 1990–91 are for institutions of higher education, while later data are for degree-granting postsecondary institutions, which are institutions that grant associate's or higher degrees and participate in Title IV federal financial aid programs. Race categories exclude persons of Hispanic ethnicity. For 1989–90 and later years, reported racial/ethnic distributions of students by level of degree, field of degree, and sex were used to estimate race/eth-

nicity for students whose race/ethnicity was not reported. Detail may not sum to totals because of rounding. Some data have been revised from previously published figures.
SOURCE: U.S. Department of Education, National Center for Education Statistics, Higher Education General Information Survey (HEGIS), "Degrees and Other Formal Awards Conferred" surveys, 1976–77 and 1980–81; Integrated Postsecondary Education Data System (IPEDS), "Completions Survey" (IPEDS-C:90–99); and IPEDS Fall 2000 through Fall 2014, Completions component. (This table was prepared September 2015.)

Table 321.30. Associate's degrees conferred by postsecondary institutions, by race/ethnicity and field of study: 2012–13 and 2013–14

Field of study	2012–13 Total	White	Black	Hispanic	Asian/Pacific Islander Total	Asian	Pacific Islander	American Indian/ Alaska Native	Two or more races	Nonresident alien	2013–14 Total	White	Black	Hispanic	Asian/Pacific Islander Total	Asian	Pacific Islander	American Indian/ Alaska Native	Two or more races	Nonresident alien
1	2	3	4	5	6	7	8	9	10	11	12	13	14	15	16	17	18	19	20	21
All fields, total	1,007,427	617,308	135,892	157,989	49,474	45,620	3,854	10,546	19,383	16,835	1,003,364	601,383	134,483	167,120	50,333	46,601	3,732	10,334	22,634	17,077
Agriculture and natural resources	6,826	6,175	92	301	55	46	9	109	67	27	7,051	6,344	92	309	58	50	8	124	91	33
Architecture and related services	468	187	21	192	40	40	0	2	4	22	414	171	25	171	28	28	0	0	5	14
Area, ethnic, cultural, gender, and group studies	271	58	29	66	23	12	11	74	15	6	362	74	40	94	32	15	17	86	26	10
Biological and biomedical sciences	4,185	1,907	358	1,090	544	522	22	82	94	110	4,479	2,047	377	1,210	568	548	20	71	97	109
Business	134,114	77,830	21,570	18,901	7,891	7,318	573	1,520	2,413	3,989	129,661	72,630	21,100	19,438	8,108	7,569	539	1,464	2,719	4,202
Communication, journalism, and related programs	4,299	2,483	396	905	229	212	17	26	129	131	4,935	2,527	500	1,288	285	271	14	25	162	148
Communications technologies	5,028	3,114	673	691	192	166	26	43	221	94	4,703	2,765	628	738	180	167	13	33	270	89
Computer and information sciences	38,954	24,529	6,103	4,646	2,083	1,918	165	390	676	527	37,601	23,024	6,090	4,696	2,058	1,918	140	383	798	552
Construction trades	5,038	3,813	544	435	76	62	14	100	55	15	4,831	3,564	510	399	146	126	20	85	115	12
Education	18,744	11,446	3,045	3,027	324	290	34	471	236	195	17,504	10,505	2,773	2,982	317	278	39	463	275	189
Engineering	3,732	2,313	256	557	326	305	21	44	61	175	4,269	2,523	316	708	394	372	22	37	94	197
Engineering technologies and engineering-related fields[1]	33,752	23,200	4,180	4,038	1,148	1,047	101	409	516	261	31,768	21,799	3,889	3,773	1,122	1,050	72	373	548	264
English language and literature/letters	2,089	1,060	201	563	151	140	11	13	67	34	2,075	1,056	184	587	117	111	6	13	83	35
Family and consumer sciences/human sciences	8,996	4,569	1,741	1,911	441	409	32	106	114	114	8,657	4,167	1,727	2,026	394	372	22	104	131	108
Foreign languages, literatures, and linguistics	2,131	1,276	92	569	79	74	5	17	39	59	2,276	1,252	112	664	91	84	7	19	59	79
Health professions and related programs	214,040	143,141	29,632	24,618	9,682	8,960	722	2,056	3,452	1,459	208,660	138,255	28,371	25,427	9,762	9,012	750	1,987	3,543	1,315
Homeland security, law enforcement, and firefighting	48,460	27,317	8,230	10,312	1,149	959	190	441	822	189	45,650	24,924	7,758	10,314	1,113	951	162	438	922	181
Legal professions and studies	11,862	7,356	1,891	1,910	287	263	24	160	199	59	10,496	6,578	1,596	1,672	250	226	24	104	233	63
Liberal arts and sciences, general studies, and humanities	344,171	206,750	44,298	59,929	16,130	14,850	1,280	3,137	7,309	6,618	353,438	208,376	45,471	63,875	16,720	15,396	1,324	3,150	8,966	6,880
Library science	181	132	6	27	12	12	0	1	3	0	192	145	12	22	8	8	0	1	3	1
Mathematics and statistics	1,801	809	73	491	294	291	3	14	51	69	2,140	877	63	704	325	322	3	22	54	95
Mechanic and repair technologies/technicians	20,487	14,303	1,845	2,784	660	550	110	315	426	154	20,052	13,732	1,791	2,903	739	631	108	286	464	137
Military technologies and applied sciences	1,002	687	116	129	41	38	3	8	21	0	1,084	679	155	151	34	27	7	5	60	0
Multi/interdisciplinary studies	27,407	14,745	2,228	5,876	3,196	3,084	112	194	618	550	28,164	14,864	2,257	6,616	2,983	2,869	114	194	759	491
Parks, recreation, leisure, and fitness studies	3,455	1,982	424	686	149	137	12	43	87	84	4,348	2,440	507	933	212	191	21	44	143	69
Philosophy and religious studies	326	160	69	67	14	12	2	1	13	2	435	206	107	89	20	17	3	2	9	2
Physical sciences and science technologies	6,376	3,389	700	1,045	674	650	24	74	188	306	6,935	3,566	714	1,242	766	740	26	71	225	351
Precision production	3,345	2,707	166	275	87	76	11	45	54	11	3,903	3,185	178	305	106	93	13	48	77	4
Psychology	6,122	2,839	487	2,046	419	388	31	90	179	62	7,530	3,234	609	2,745	521	497	24	106	235	80
Public administration and social services	8,788	4,671	2,417	1,229	147	119	28	136	134	54	8,900	4,533	2,552	1,359	106	90	16	125	168	57
Social sciences and history	15,668	6,937	1,440	4,672	1,632	1,480	152	209	495	283	16,528	6,910	1,478	5,519	1,507	1,397	110	229	614	271
Social sciences	14,749	6,390	1,406	4,428	1,591	1,440	151	197	456	281	15,454	6,312	1,435	5,188	1,470	1,367	103	217	565	267
History	919	547	34	244	41	40	1	12	39	2	1,074	598	43	331	37	30	7	12	49	4
Theology and religious vocations	881	566	215	70	15	10	5	11	6	6	944	627	207	78	3	3	0	11	7	11
Transportation and materials moving	2,119	1,345	184	319	104	94	10	11	52	104	2,099	1,357	172	314	88	79	9	19	69	80
Visual and performing arts	22,309	13,512	2,170	3,612	1,180	1,086	94	202	567	1,066	21,280	12,447	2,122	3,769	1,172	1,093	79	212	610	948
Other and not classified	0	0	0	0	0	0	0	0	0	0	0	0	0	0	0	0	0	0	0	0

[1] Excludes "Construction trades" and "Mechanic and repair technologies/technicians," which are listed separately.

NOTE: Data are for degree-granting postsecondary institutions, which are institutions that grant associate's or higher degrees and participate in Title IV federal financial aid programs. Race categories exclude persons of Hispanic ethnicity. Reported racial/ethnic distributions of students by level of degree, field of degree, and sex were used to estimate race/ethnicity for students whose race/ethnicity was not reported. To facilitate trend comparisons, certain aggregations have been made of the degree fields as reported in the integrated Postsecondary Education Data System (IPEDS): "Agriculture and natural resources" includes Agriculture, agriculture operations, and related sciences and Natural resources and conservation; and "Business" includes Business management, marketing, and related support services and Personal and culinary services. Some data have been revised from previously published figures.
SOURCE: U.S. Department of Education, National Center for Education Statistics, Integrated Postsecondary Education Data System (IPEDS), Fall 2013 and Fall 2014, Completions component. (This table was prepared September 2015.)

Table 321.40. Associate's degrees conferred to males by postsecondary institutions, by race/ethnicity and field of study: 2012–13 and 2013–14

Field of study	2012–13 Total	White	Black	Hispanic	Asian/Pacific Islander Total	Asian	Pacific Islander	American Indian/Alaska Native	Two or more races	Nonresident alien	2013–14 Total	White	Black	Hispanic	Asian/Pacific Islander Total	Asian	Pacific Islander	American Indian/Alaska Native	Two or more races	Nonresident alien
1	2	3	4	5	6	7	8	9	10	11	12	13	14	15	16	17	18	19	20	21
All fields, total	**389,195**	**243,868**	**45,458**	**60,536**	**21,223**	**19,514**	**1,709**	**3,638**	**7,434**	**7,038**	**390,805**	**239,076**	**45,806**	**64,293**	**21,811**	**20,152**	**1,659**	**3,680**	**8,953**	**7,186**
Agriculture and natural resources	4,306	3,924	69	175	31	27	4	60	36	11	4,410	3,970	65	199	40	35	5	70	50	16
Architecture and related services	305	127	15	129	22	22	0	1	2	9	279	124	20	110	16	16	0	0	3	6
Area, ethnic, cultural, gender, and group studies	101	21	11	30	11	6	5	23	5	0	130	25	22	34	7	4	3	34	7	1
Biological and biomedical sciences	1,337	613	103	337	191	182	9	27	30	36	1,465	695	119	358	198	188	10	18	35	42
Business	49,629	29,096	7,111	7,200	3,236	3,005	231	464	881	1,641	48,307	27,070	7,123	7,576	3,414	3,201	213	457	963	1,704
Communication, journalism, and related programs	1,969	1,207	180	383	108	102	6	18	43	30	2,197	1,189	212	548	116	111	5	16	73	43
Communications technologies	3,491	2,106	507	519	119	100	19	23	160	57	3,278	1,861	470	547	114	103	11	16	213	57
Computer and information sciences	30,721	19,705	4,427	3,747	1,659	1,537	122	262	531	390	29,913	18,691	4,497	3,797	1,648	1,529	119	278	598	404
Construction trades	4,802	3,657	502	416	71	59	12	93	49	14	4,580	3,425	483	377	125	107	18	73	87	10
Education	2,193	1,417	326	288	36	35	1	75	28	23	2,112	1,272	335	311	45	38	7	85	39	25
Engineering	3,218	2,046	222	449	264	246	18	32	56	149	3,704	2,240	276	597	325	305	20	28	74	164
Engineering technologies and engineering-related fields[1]	29,633	20,588	3,556	3,534	987	902	85	329	424	215	27,882	19,329	3,348	3,295	930	869	61	305	457	218
English language and literature/letters	681	353	57	182	54	52	2	2	27	6	678	329	49	224	42	40	2	2	22	10
Family and consumer sciences/human sciences	376	174	72	81	25	24	1	3	7	14	362	157	72	91	27	23	4	4	5	6
Foreign languages, literatures, and linguistics	435	219	13	141	28	28	0	4	10	20	478	238	19	149	32	29	3	3	16	21
Health professions and related programs	33,595	21,322	3,982	4,546	2,604	2,380	224	274	558	309	33,607	20,770	4,088	4,834	2,666	2,445	221	312	612	325
Homeland security, law enforcement, and firefighting	26,515	16,700	3,062	5,242	809	694	115	199	393	110	25,328	15,592	2,934	5,254	771	667	104	216	465	96
Legal professions and studies	1,690	975	286	314	61	59	2	20	24	10	1,660	918	302	312	58	55	3	16	37	17
Liberal arts and sciences, general studies, and humanities	132,614	81,914	15,221	22,071	6,797	6,255	542	1,068	2,718	2,825	136,296	82,955	15,420	23,393	7,112	6,569	543	1,057	3,458	2,901
Library science	29	22	0	6	1	1	0	0	0	0	28	20	3	4	0	0	0	0	1	0
Mathematics and statistics	1,242	571	45	336	197	194	3	9	37	47	1,492	625	49	505	217	214	3	13	31	52
Mechanic and repair technologies/technicians	19,446	13,616	1,735	2,637	627	521	106	287	399	145	19,011	13,096	1,660	2,745	691	589	102	256	435	128
Military technologies and applied sciences	773	550	73	97	32	29	3	7	14	10	898	573	121	127	24	18	6	5	48	0
Multi/interdisciplinary studies	10,864	6,038	781	2,158	1,353	1,304	49	55	240	239	11,396	6,324	832	2,455	1,249	1,204	45	69	272	195
Parks, recreation, leisure, and fitness studies	2,158	1,253	286	406	83	77	6	23	49	58	2,827	1,616	349	563	136	120	16	26	89	48
Philosophy and religious studies	212	110	32	49	12	10	2	0	8	1	283	150	49	66	9	9	0	2	6	1
Physical sciences and science technologies	3,793	2,119	313	657	367	354	13	42	121	174	4,089	2,166	337	752	431	416	15	40	149	214
Precision production	3,116	2,534	152	252	82	73	9	37	49	10	3,686	3,020	160	291	104	91	13	40	67	4
Psychology	1,498	678	128	488	134	129	5	18	38	14	1,795	759	130	653	183	174	9	12	46	12
Public administration and social services	1,237	650	358	163	24	21	3	22	15	5	1,275	603	404	180	20	19	1	28	31	9
Social sciences and history	5,770	2,676	457	1,581	675	607	68	68	198	115	6,190	2,774	535	1,912	572	521	51	66	236	95
Social sciences	5,202	2,326	443	1,436	648	580	68	61	174	114	5,531	2,406	507	1,704	549	503	46	59	213	93
History	568	350	14	145	27	27	0	7	24	1	659	368	28	208	23	18	5	7	23	2
Theology and religious vocations	425	275	103	31	8	4	4	1	3	4	456	310	92	41	2	2	0	1	2	6
Transportation and materials moving	1,743	1,156	153	252	77	73	4	8	37	60	1,766	1,188	141	245	70	63	7	15	53	54
Visual and performing arts	9,278	5,456	1,120	1,639	438	402	36	84	244	297	8,947	5,002	1,090	1,748	417	378	39	115	273	302
Other and not classified	0	0	0	0	0	0	0	0	0	0	0	0	0	0	0	0	0	0	0	0

[1] Excludes "Construction trades" and "Mechanic and repair technologies/technicians," which are listed separately.

NOTE: Data are for degree-granting postsecondary institutions, which are institutions that grant associate's or higher degrees and participate in Title IV federal financial aid programs. Race categories exclude persons of Hispanic ethnicity. Reported racial/ethnic distributions of students by level of degree, field of degree, and sex were used to estimate race/ethnicity for students whose race/ethnicity was not reported. To facilitate trend comparisons, certain aggregations have been made of the degree fields as reported in the Integrated Postsecondary Education Data System (IPEDS): "Agriculture and natural resources" includes Agriculture, agriculture operations, and related sciences and Natural resources and conservation; and "Business" includes Business management, marketing, and related support services and Personal and culinary services. Some data have been revised from previously published figures.

SOURCE: U.S. Department of Education, National Center for Education Statistics, Integrated Postsecondary Education Data System (IPEDS), Fall 2013 and Fall 2014, Completions component. (This table was prepared September 2015.)

Table 321.50. Associate's degrees conferred to females by postsecondary institutions, by race/ethnicity and field of study: 2012–13 and 2013–14

Field of study	2012–13										2013–14									
	Total	White	Black	Hispanic	Asian/Pacific Islander			American Indian/Alaska Native	Two or more races	Non-resident alien	Total	White	Black	Hispanic	Asian/Pacific Islander			American Indian/Alaska Native	Two or more races	Non-resident alien
					Total	Asian	Pacific Islander								Total	Asian	Pacific Islander			
1	2	3	4	5	6	7	8	9	10	11	12	13	14	15	16	17	18	19	20	21
All fields, total	**618,232**	**373,440**	**90,434**	**97,453**	**28,251**	**26,106**	**2,145**	**6,908**	**11,949**	**9,797**	**612,559**	**362,307**	**88,677**	**102,827**	**28,522**	**26,449**	**2,073**	**6,654**	**13,681**	**9,891**
Agriculture and natural resources	2,520	2,251	23	126	24	19	5	49	31	16	2,641	2,374	27	110	18	15	3	54	41	17
Architecture and related services	163	60	6	63	18	18	0	1	2	13	135	47	5	61	12	12	0	0	2	8
Area, ethnic, cultural, gender, and group studies	170	37	18	36	12	6	6	51	10	6	232	49	18	60	25	11	14	52	19	9
Biological and biomedical sciences	2,848	1,294	255	753	353	340	13	55	64	74	3,014	1,352	258	852	370	360	10	53	62	67
Business	84,485	48,734	14,459	11,701	4,655	4,313	342	1,056	1,532	2,348	81,354	45,560	13,977	11,862	4,694	4,368	326	1,007	1,756	2,498
Communication, journalism, and related programs	2,330	1,276	216	522	121	110	11	8	86	101	2,738	1,338	288	740	169	160	9	9	89	105
Communications technologies	1,537	1,008	166	172	73	66	7	20	61	37	1,425	904	158	191	66	64	2	17	57	32
Computer and information sciences	8,233	4,824	1,676	899	424	381	43	128	145	137	7,688	4,333	1,593	899	410	389	21	105	200	148
Construction trades	236	156	42	19	5	3	2	7	6	1	251	139	27	22	21	19	2	12	28	2
Education	16,551	10,029	2,719	2,739	288	255	33	396	208	172	15,392	9,233	2,438	2,671	272	240	32	378	236	164
Engineering	514	267	34	108	62	59	3	12	5	26	565	283	40	111	69	67	2	9	20	33
Engineering technologies and engineering-related fields[1]	4,119	2,612	624	504	161	145	16	80	92	46	3,886	2,470	541	478	192	181	11	68	91	46
English language and literature/letters	1,408	707	144	381	97	88	9	11	40	28	1,397	727	135	363	75	71	4	11	61	25
Family and consumer sciences/human sciences	8,620	4,395	1,669	1,830	416	385	31	103	107	100	8,295	4,010	1,655	1,935	367	349	18	100	126	102
Foreign languages, literatures, and linguistics	1,696	1,057	79	428	51	46	5	13	29	39	1,798	1,014	93	515	59	55	4	16	43	58
Health professions and related programs	180,445	121,819	25,650	20,072	7,078	6,580	498	1,782	2,894	1,150	175,053	117,485	24,283	20,593	7,096	6,567	529	1,675	2,931	990
Homeland security, law enforcement, and firefighting	21,945	10,617	5,168	5,070	340	265	75	242	429	79	20,322	9,332	4,824	5,060	342	284	58	222	457	85
Legal professions and studies	10,172	6,381	1,605	1,596	226	204	22	140	175	49	8,836	5,660	1,294	1,360	192	171	21	88	196	46
Liberal arts and sciences, general studies, and humanities	211,557	124,836	29,077	37,858	9,333	8,595	738	2,069	4,591	3,793	217,142	125,421	30,051	40,482	9,608	8,827	781	2,093	5,508	3,979
Library science	152	110	6	21	11	11	0	1	3	0	164	125	9	18	8	8	0	1	2	1
Mathematics and statistics	559	238	28	155	97	97	0	5	14	22	648	252	14	199	108	108	0	9	23	43
Mechanic and repair technologies/technicians	1,041	687	110	147	33	29	4	28	27	9	1,041	636	131	158	48	42	6	30	29	9
Military technologies and applied sciences	229	137	43	32	5	9	0	1	7	0	186	106	34	24	10	9	1	0	12	0
Multi/interdisciplinary studies	16,543	8,707	1,447	3,718	1,843	1,780	63	139	378	311	16,768	8,540	1,425	4,161	1,734	1,665	69	125	487	296
Parks, recreation, leisure, and fitness studies	1,297	729	138	280	66	60	6	20	38	26	1,521	824	158	370	76	71	5	18	54	21
Philosophy and religious studies	114	50	37	18	2	2	0	1	5	1	152	56	58	23	11	8	3	0	3	1
Physical sciences and science technologies	2,583	1,270	387	388	307	296	11	32	67	132	2,846	1,400	377	490	335	324	11	31	76	137
Precision production	229	173	14	23	5	3	2	8	5	48	217	165	18	14	2	2	0	8	10	0
Psychology	4,624	2,161	359	1,558	285	259	26	72	141	49	5,735	2,475	479	2,092	338	323	15	94	189	68
Public administration and social services	7,551	4,021	2,059	1,066	123	98	25	114	119	168	7,625	3,930	2,148	1,179	86	71	15	97	137	48
Social sciences and history	9,898	4,261	983	3,091	957	873	84	141	297	167	10,338	4,136	943	3,607	935	876	59	163	378	176
Social sciences	9,547	4,064	963	2,992	943	860	83	136	282	1	9,923	3,906	928	3,484	921	864	57	158	352	174
History	351	197	20	99	14	13	1	5	15	2	415	230	15	123	14	12	2	5	26	2
Theology and religious vocations	456	291	112	39	7	6	1	2	3	44	488	317	115	37	1	1	0	8	5	5
Transportation and materials moving	376	189	31	67	27	21	6	3	15	769	333	169	31	69	18	16	2	4	16	26
Visual and performing arts	13,031	8,056	1,050	1,973	742	684	58	118	323	0	12,333	7,445	1,032	2,021	755	715	40	97	337	646
Other and not classified	0	0	0	0	0	0	0	0	0	0	0	0	0	0	0	0	0	0	0	0

[1]Excludes "Construction trades" and "Mechanic and repair technologies/technicians," which are listed separately.
NOTE: Data are for degree-granting postsecondary institutions, which are institutions that grant associate's or higher degrees and participate in Title IV federal financial aid programs. Race categories exclude persons of Hispanic ethnicity. Reported racial/ethnic distributions of students by level of degree, field of degree, and sex were used to estimate race/ethnicity for students whose race/ethnicity was not reported. To facilitate trend comparisons, certain aggregations have been made of the degree fields as reported in the Inte-grated Postsecondary Education Data System (IPEDS): "Agriculture and natural resources" includes Agriculture, agriculture operations, and related sciences and Natural resources and conservation; and "Business" includes Business management, marketing, and related support services and Personal and culinary services. Some data have been revised from previously published figures.
SOURCE: U.S. Department of Education, National Center for Education Statistics, Integrated Postsecondary Education Data System (IPEDS), Fall 2013 and Fall 2014, Completions component. (This table was prepared September 2015.)

Table 322.10. Bachelor's degrees conferred by postsecondary institutions, by field of study: Selected years, 1970–71 through 2013–14

Field of study	1970–71	1975–76	1980–81	1985–86	1990–91	1995–96	2000–01	2003–04	2004–05	2005–06	2006–07	2007–08	2008–09	2009–10	2010–11	2011–12	2012–13	2013–14
1	2	3	4	5	6	7	8	9	10	11	12	13	14	15	16	17	18	19
Total	839,730	925,746	935,140	987,823	1,094,538	1,164,792	1,244,171	1,399,542	1,439,264	1,485,242	1,524,092	1,563,069	1,601,399	1,649,919	1,716,053	1,792,163	1,840,381	1,869,814
Agriculture and natural resources	12,672	19,402	21,886	16,823	13,124	21,425	23,370	22,835	23,002	23,053	23,133	24,113	24,982	26,343	28,630	30,972	33,592	35,116
Architecture and related services	5,570	9,146	9,455	9,119	9,781	8,352	8,480	8,838	9,237	9,515	9,717	9,805	10,119	10,051	9,831	9,727	9,757	9,144
Area, ethnic, cultural, gender, and group studies	2,579	3,577	2,887	3,021	4,776	5,633	6,160	7,181	7,569	7,879	8,194	8,454	8,772	8,620	8,955	9,228	8,850	8,275
Biological and biomedical sciences	35,705	54,154	43,078	38,395	39,482	61,014	60,576	62,624	65,915	70,607	76,832	79,829	82,828	86,391	89,984	95,850	100,397	104,633
Business	115,396	143,171	200,521	236,700	249,165	226,623	263,515	307,149	311,574	318,042	327,531	335,254	348,056	358,119	365,133	367,235	360,887	358,079
Communication, journalism, and related programs	10,324	20,045	29,428	41,666	51,650	47,320	58,013	70,968	72,715	73,955	74,783	76,382	77,984	81,280	83,231	83,771	84,818	87,604
Communications technologies	478	1,237	1,854	1,479	1,397	853	1,178	2,034	2,523	2,981	3,637	4,666	5,100	4,782	4,858	4,983	4,987	4,987
Computer and information sciences	2,388	5,652	15,121	42,337	25,159	24,506	44,142	59,488	54,111	47,480	42,170	38,476	37,992	39,593	43,066	47,406	50,961	55,367
Education	176,307	154,437	108,074	87,147	110,807	105,384	105,458	106,278	105,451	107,238	105,641	102,582	101,716	101,287	104,008	105,656	104,698	98,854
Engineering	45,034	38,733	63,642	77,391	62,448	62,168	58,209	63,410	64,707	66,841	66,874	68,431	68,911	72,657	76,356	81,371	85,987	92,162
Engineering technologies	5,148	7,943	11,713	19,731	17,303	15,829	14,660	14,669	14,837	14,565	14,980	15,177	15,493	16,078	16,741	17,283	17,010	16,807
English language and literature/letters	63,914	41,452	31,922	34,083	51,064	49,928	50,569	53,984	54,379	55,096	55,122	55,038	55,465	53,229	52,754	53,765	52,401	50,404
Family and consumer sciences/human sciences	11,167	17,409	18,370	13,847	13,920	14,353	16,421	19,172	20,074	20,775	21,400	21,870	21,906	21,832	22,438	23,441	23,930	24,722
Foreign languages, literatures, and linguistics	20,988	17,068	11,638	11,550	13,937	14,832	16,128	17,754	18,386	19,410	20,275	20,977	21,169	21,507	21,705	21,756	21,647	20,335
Health professions and related programs	25,223	53,885	63,665	65,309	59,875	86,087	75,933	73,934	80,685	91,973	101,810	111,478	120,420	129,623	143,463	163,675	181,149	198,770
Homeland security, law enforcement, and firefighting	2,045	12,507	13,707	12,704	16,806	24,810	25,211	28,175	30,723	35,319	39,206	40,235	41,788	43,613	47,600	54,091	60,264	62,409
Legal professions and studies	545	531	776	1,223	1,827	2,123	1,991	2,841	3,161	3,302	3,596	3,771	3,822	3,886	4,429	4,595	4,425	4,513
Liberal arts and sciences, general studies, and humanities	7,481	18,855	21,643	21,336	30,526	33,997	37,962	42,106	43,751	44,898	44,255	46,940	47,095	46,963	46,717	46,961	46,790	45,260
Library science	1,013	843	375	155	90	58	52	72	76	76	82	68	78	85	96	95	102	127
Mathematics and statistics	24,801	15,984	11,078	16,122	14,393	12,713	11,171	13,327	14,351	14,770	14,954	15,192	15,507	16,029	17,182	18,841	20,449	20,980
Military technologies and applied sciences	357	952	42	255	183	7	21	10	40	33	168	39	55	56	64	86	105	185
Multi/interdisciplinary studies	6,324	13,709	12,986	13,754	17,774	26,885	26,478	28,047	28,939	30,583	32,111	34,174	35,376	37,717	42,473	45,717	47,658	48,348
Parks, recreation, leisure and fitness studies	1,621	5,182	5,729	4,623	4,315	12,974	17,948	22,164	22,888	25,490	27,430	29,931	31,683	33,332	35,934	38,998	42,628	46,042
Philosophy and religious studies	8,149	8,447	6,776	6,396	7,423	7,541	8,717	11,152	11,584	11,985	11,969	12,257	12,448	12,503	12,830	12,645	12,792	11,997
Physical sciences and science technologies	21,410	21,458	23,936	21,711	16,334	19,716	18,025	18,131	19,104	20,522	21,291	22,179	22,691	23,381	24,705	26,664	28,053	29,304
Precision production	0	0	0	2	2	12	31	61	64	55	23	33	29	29	43	37	36	37
Psychology	38,187	50,278	41,068	40,628	58,655	73,416	73,645	82,098	85,614	88,134	90,039	92,587	94,273	97,215	100,906	109,099	114,446	117,298
Public administration and social services	5,466	15,440	16,707	11,887	14,350	19,849	19,447	20,552	21,769	21,986	23,147	23,493	23,852	25,421	26,799	29,695	31,950	33,483
Social sciences and history	155,324	126,396	100,513	93,840	125,107	126,479	128,036	150,357	156,892	161,485	164,183	167,363	168,517	172,782	177,169	178,534	177,767	173,096
Theology and religious vocations	3,720	5,490	5,808	5,510	4,799	5,292	6,945	8,126	9,284	8,548	8,696	8,992	8,940	8,719	9,073	9,304	9,385	9,642
Transportation and materials moving	0	225	263	1,838	2,622	3,561	3,748	4,824	4,904	5,349	5,657	5,203	5,189	4,998	4,941	4,876	4,661	4,588
Visual and performing arts	30,394	42,138	40,479	37,241	42,186	49,296	61,148	77,181	80,955	83,297	85,186	87,703	89,143	91,798	93,939	95,806	97,799	97,246
Not classified by field of study	0				13,258	1,756	783	0	0	0	0	377	0	0	0	0	0	0

NOTE: Data through 1990–91 are for institutions of higher education, while later data are for postsecondary institutions that participate in Title IV federal financial aid programs. The new Classification of Instructional Programs was initiated in 2009–10. The figures for earlier years have been reclassified when necessary to make them conform to the new taxonomy. To facilitate trend comparisons, certain aggregations have been made of the degree fields as reported in the Integrated Postsecondary Education Data System (IPEDS): "Agriculture and natural resources" includes Agriculture, agriculture operations, and related sciences and Natural resources and conservation; "Business" includes Business, management, marketing, and related support services and Personal and culinary services; and "Engineering technologies" includes Engineering technologies and engineering-related fields, Construction trades, and Mechanic and repair technologies/technicians. Some data have been revised from previously published figures.
SOURCE: U.S. Department of Education, National Center for Education Statistics, Higher Education General Information Survey (HEGIS), "Degrees and Other Formal Awards Conferred" surveys, 1970–71 through 1985–86; Integrated Postsecondary Education Data System (IPEDS), "Completions Survey" (IPEDS-C:91–99); and IPEDS Fall 2000 through Fall 2014, Completions component. (This table was prepared September 2015.)

Table 322.20. Bachelor's degrees conferred by postsecondary institutions, by race/ethnicity and sex of student: Selected years, 1976–77 through 2013–14

Year and sex	Number of degrees conferred to U.S. citizens and nonresident aliens								Percentage distribution of degrees conferred to U.S. citizens						
	Total	White	Black	Hispanic	Asian/Pacific Islander	American Indian/Alaska Native	Two or more races	Non-resident alien	Total	White	Black	Hispanic	Asian/Pacific Islander	American Indian/Alaska Native	Two or more races
1	2	3	4	5	6	7	8	9	10	11	12	13	14	15	16
Total															
1976–77[1]	917,900	807,688	58,636	18,743	13,793	3,326	—	15,714	100.0	89.5	6.5	2.1	1.5	0.4	—
1980–81[2]	934,800	807,319	60,673	21,832	18,794	3,593	—	22,589	100.0	88.5	6.7	2.4	2.1	0.4	—
1990–91	1,094,538	914,093	66,375	37,342	42,529	4,583	—	29,616	100.0	85.8	6.2	3.5	4.0	0.4	—
1997–98	1,184,406	901,344	98,251	66,005	71,678	7,903	—	39,225	100.0	78.7	8.6	5.8	6.3	0.7	—
1998–99	1,202,239	909,562	101,910	69,735	74,126	8,658	—	38,248	100.0	78.1	8.8	6.0	6.4	0.7	—
1999–2000	1,237,875	929,102	108,018	75,063	77,909	8,717	—	39,066	100.0	77.5	9.0	6.3	6.5	0.7	—
2000–01	1,244,171	927,357	111,307	77,745	78,902	9,049	—	39,811	100.0	77.0	9.2	6.5	6.6	0.8	—
2001–02	1,291,900	958,597	116,623	82,966	83,093	9,165	—	41,456	100.0	76.7	9.3	6.6	6.6	0.7	—
2002–03	1,348,811	994,616	124,253	89,029	87,964	9,875	—	43,074	100.0	76.2	9.5	6.8	6.7	0.8	—
2003–04	1,399,542	1,026,114	131,241	94,644	92,073	10,638	—	44,832	100.0	75.7	9.7	7.0	6.8	0.8	—
2004–05	1,439,264	1,049,141	136,122	101,124	97,209	10,307	—	45,361	100.0	75.3	9.8	7.3	7.0	0.7	—
2005–06	1,485,242	1,075,561	142,420	107,588	102,376	10,940	—	46,357	100.0	74.7	9.9	7.5	7.1	0.8	—
2006–07	1,524,092	1,099,850	146,653	114,936	105,297	11,455	—	45,901	100.0	74.4	9.9	7.8	7.1	0.8	—
2007–08	1,563,069	1,122,675	152,457	123,048	109,058	11,509	—	44,322	100.0	73.9	10.0	8.1	7.2	0.8	—
2008–09	1,601,399	1,144,628	156,603	129,473	112,581	12,221	—	45,893	100.0	73.6	10.1	8.3	7.2	0.8	—
2009–10	1,649,919	1,167,322	164,789	140,426	117,391	12,405	—	47,586	100.0	72.9	10.3	8.8	7.3	0.8	—
2010–11	1,716,053	1,182,690	172,731	154,450	121,118	11,935	20,589	52,540	100.0	71.1	10.4	9.3	7.3	0.7	1.2
2011–12	1,792,163	1,212,417	185,916	169,736	126,177	11,498	27,234	59,185	100.0	70.0	10.7	9.8	7.3	0.7	1.6
2012–13	1,840,381	1,221,908	191,233	186,677	130,129	11,432	34,128	64,874	100.0	68.8	10.8	10.5	7.3	0.6	1.9
2013–14	1,869,814	1,218,792	191,298	202,412	131,680	10,786	45,423	69,423	100.0	67.7	10.6	11.2	7.3	0.6	2.5
Males															
1976–77[1]	494,424	438,161	25,147	10,318	7,638	1,804	—	11,356	100.0	90.7	5.2	2.1	1.6	0.4	—
1980–81[2]	469,625	406,173	24,511	10,810	10,107	1,700	—	16,324	100.0	89.6	5.4	2.4	2.2	0.4	—
1990–91	504,045	421,290	24,800	16,598	21,203	1,938	—	18,216	100.0	86.7	5.1	3.4	4.4	0.4	—
1997–98	519,956	399,553	34,510	27,677	33,445	3,151	—	21,620	100.0	80.2	6.9	5.6	6.7	0.6	—
1998–99	519,961	398,310	34,856	28,477	34,179	3,407	—	20,732	100.0	79.8	7.0	5.7	6.8	0.7	—
1999–2000	530,367	402,954	37,029	30,304	35,853	3,463	—	20,764	100.0	79.1	7.3	5.9	7.0	0.7	—
2000–01	531,840	401,780	38,103	31,368	35,865	3,700	—	21,024	100.0	78.7	7.5	6.1	7.0	0.7	—
2001–02	549,816	414,892	39,196	32,951	37,660	3,624	—	21,493	100.0	78.5	7.4	6.2	7.1	0.7	—
2002–03	573,258	430,248	41,494	35,101	40,230	3,870	—	22,315	100.0	78.1	7.5	6.4	7.3	0.7	—
2003–04	595,425	445,483	43,851	37,288	41,360	4,244	—	23,199	100.0	77.9	7.7	6.5	7.2	0.7	—
2004–05	613,000	456,592	45,810	39,490	43,711	4,143	—	23,254	100.0	77.4	7.8	6.7	7.4	0.7	—
2005–06	630,600	467,467	48,079	41,814	45,809	4,203	—	23,228	100.0	77.0	7.9	6.9	7.5	0.7	—
2006–07	649,570	480,558	49,685	44,750	47,582	4,505	—	22,490	100.0	76.6	7.9	7.1	7.6	0.7	—
2007–08	667,928	492,137	52,247	47,884	49,485	4,523	—	21,652	100.0	76.1	8.1	7.4	7.7	0.7	—
2008–09	685,422	503,396	53,465	50,596	50,773	4,849	—	22,343	100.0	75.9	8.1	7.6	7.7	0.7	—
2009–10	706,660	513,711	56,136	55,139	53,365	4,879	—	23,430	100.0	75.2	8.2	8.1	7.8	0.7	—
2010–11	734,159	519,992	59,015	60,869	55,321	4,798	8,028	26,136	100.0	73.4	8.3	8.6	7.8	0.7	1.1
2011–12	765,772	532,463	63,736	67,083	57,521	4,476	10,945	29,548	100.0	72.3	8.7	9.1	7.8	0.6	1.5
2012–13	787,408	535,358	67,351	74,067	59,806	4,611	13,834	32,381	100.0	70.9	8.9	9.8	7.9	0.6	1.8
2013–14	801,692	535,839	68,259	80,297	59,848	4,171	18,138	35,140	100.0	69.9	8.9	10.5	7.8	0.5	2.4
Females															
1976–77[1]	423,476	369,527	33,489	8,425	6,155	1,522	—	4,358	100.0	88.2	8.0	2.0	1.5	0.4	—
1980–81[2]	465,175	401,146	36,162	11,022	8,687	1,893	—	6,265	100.0	87.4	7.9	2.4	1.9	0.4	—
1990–91	590,493	492,803	41,575	20,744	21,326	2,645	—	11,400	100.0	85.1	7.2	3.6	3.7	0.5	—
1997–98	664,450	501,791	63,741	38,328	38,233	4,752	—	17,605	100.0	77.6	9.9	5.9	5.9	0.7	—
1998–99	682,278	511,252	67,054	41,258	39,947	5,251	—	17,516	100.0	76.9	10.1	6.2	6.0	0.8	—
1999–2000	707,508	526,148	70,989	44,759	42,056	5,254	—	18,302	100.0	76.3	10.3	6.5	6.1	0.8	—
2000–01	712,331	525,577	73,204	46,377	43,037	5,349	—	18,787	100.0	75.8	10.6	6.7	6.2	0.8	—
2001–02	742,084	543,705	77,427	50,015	45,433	5,541	—	19,963	100.0	75.3	10.7	6.9	6.3	0.8	—
2002–03	775,553	564,368	82,759	53,928	47,734	6,005	—	20,759	100.0	74.8	11.0	7.1	6.3	0.8	—
2003–04	804,117	580,631	87,390	57,356	50,713	6,394	—	21,633	100.0	74.2	11.2	7.3	6.5	0.8	—
2004–05	826,264	592,549	90,312	61,634	53,498	6,164	—	22,107	100.0	73.7	11.2	7.7	6.7	0.8	—
2005–06	854,642	608,094	94,341	65,774	56,567	6,737	—	23,129	100.0	73.1	11.3	7.9	6.8	0.8	—
2006–07	874,522	619,292	96,968	70,186	57,715	6,950	—	23,411	100.0	72.8	11.4	8.2	6.8	0.8	—
2007–08	895,141	630,538	100,210	75,164	59,573	6,986	—	22,670	100.0	72.3	11.5	8.6	6.8	0.8	—
2008–09	915,977	641,232	103,138	78,877	61,808	7,372	—	23,550	100.0	71.9	11.6	8.8	6.9	0.8	—
2009–10	943,259	653,611	108,653	85,287	64,026	7,526	—	24,156	100.0	71.1	11.8	9.3	7.0	0.8	—
2010–11	981,894	662,698	113,716	93,581	65,797	7,137	12,561	26,404	100.0	69.4	11.9	9.8	6.9	0.7	1.3
2011–12	1,026,391	679,954	122,180	102,653	68,656	7,022	16,289	29,637	100.0	68.2	12.3	10.3	6.9	0.7	1.6
2012–13	1,052,973	686,550	123,882	112,610	70,323	6,821	20,294	32,493	100.0	67.3	12.1	11.0	6.9	0.7	2.0
2013–14	1,068,122	682,953	123,039	122,115	71,832	6,615	27,285	34,283	100.0	66.1	11.9	11.8	6.9	0.6	2.6

—Not available.

[1]Excludes 1,121 males and 528 females whose racial/ethnic group was not available.
[2]Excludes 258 males and 82 females whose racial/ethnic group was not available.
NOTE: Data through 1990–91 are for institutions of higher education, while later data are for postsecondary institutions participating in Title IV federal financial aid programs. Race categories exclude persons of Hispanic ethnicity. For 1989–90 and later years, reported racial/ethnic distributions of students by level of degree, field of degree, and sex were used to esti-

mate race/ethnicity for students whose race/ethnicity was not reported. Detail may not sum to totals because of rounding. Some data have been revised from previously published figures.
SOURCE: U.S. Department of Education, National Center for Education Statistics, Higher Education General Information Survey (HEGIS), "Degrees and Other Formal Awards Conferred" surveys, 1976–77 and 1980–81; Integrated Postsecondary Education Data System (IPEDS), "Completions Survey" (IPEDS-C:90–99); and IPEDS Fall 2000 through Fall 2014, Completions component. (This table was prepared September 2015.)

Table 322.30. Bachelor's degrees conferred by postsecondary institutions, by race/ethnicity and field of study: 2012–13 and 2013–14

	2012–13											2013–14									
					Asian/Pacific Islander			American Indian/ Alaska Native	Two or more races	Non-resident alien					Asian/Pacific Islander			American Indian/ Alaska Native	Two or more races	Non-resident alien
Field of study	Total	White	Black	Hispanic	Total	Asian	Pacific Islander				Total	White	Black	Hispanic	Total	Asian	Pacific Islander			
1	2	3	4	5	6	7	8	9	10	11	12	13	14	15	16	17	18	19	20	21
All fields, total	1,840,381	1,221,908	191,233	186,677	130,129	125,074	5,055	11,432	34,128	64,874	1,869,814	1,218,792	191,298	202,412	131,680	126,487	5,193	10,786	45,423	69,423
Agriculture and natural resources	33,592	27,648	960	2,049	1,358	1,283	75	285	649	643	35,116	28,670	1,052	2,262	1,354	1,271	83	229	851	698
Architecture and related services	9,757	6,252	505	1,257	891	870	21	35	163	654	9,144	5,747	512	1,282	737	723	14	32	167	667
Area, ethnic, cultural, gender, and group studies	8,850	4,303	1,148	1,588	1,008	957	51	225	360	218	8,275	3,829	1,171	1,569	844	803	41	191	406	265
Biological and biomedical sciences	100,397	61,781	7,649	8,892	16,509	16,256	253	539	2,094	2,933	104,633	63,810	7,712	10,008	16,724	16,450	274	495	3,075	2,809
Business	360,887	225,466	42,466	35,437	27,081	25,902	1,179	2,078	5,287	23,072	358,079	221,420	39,841	37,404	26,479	25,348	1,131	1,995	6,858	24,082
Communication, journalism, and related programs	84,818	59,425	9,113	8,223	3,651	3,449	202	425	1,690	2,291	87,604	59,925	9,676	9,213	3,616	3,442	174	380	2,353	2,441
Communications technologies	4,987	3,166	622	609	242	237	5	22	120	206	4,987	3,124	633	613	254	235	19	29	171	163
Computer and information sciences	50,961	31,723	6,016	4,500	5,103	4,934	169	292	946	2,381	55,367	33,845	5,937	5,122	6,001	5,809	192	301	1,343	2,818
Construction trades	244	186	6	36	6	3	2	1	9	1	268	198	9	41	13	11	2	1	5	1
Education	104,698	84,202	8,299	7,170	2,127	1,931	196	726	1,249	925	98,854	78,692	7,666	7,164	2,168	1,942	226	724	1,552	888
Engineering	85,987	56,129	3,621	7,041	10,591	10,395	196	359	1,469	6,777	92,162	59,537	3,686	8,131	10,717	10,530	187	322	2,192	7,577
Engineering technologies and engineering-related fields[1]	16,493	11,762	1,684	1,369	728	693	35	167	186	597	16,221	11,298	1,699	1,430	719	684	35	146	269	660
English language and literature/letters	52,401	38,524	4,102	5,308	2,429	2,335	94	280	1,205	553	50,404	36,182	4,070	5,510	2,212	2,123	89	260	1,598	572
Family and consumer sciences/human sciences	23,930	16,409	3,033	2,267	1,335	1,274	61	141	408	337	24,722	16,397	3,089	2,735	1,365	1,291	74	181	564	391
Foreign languages, literatures, and linguistics	21,647	14,134	964	4,135	1,274	1,244	30	118	549	473	20,335	12,937	909	4,207	1,128	1,090	38	75	639	440
Health professions and related programs	181,149	124,575	22,061	14,437	13,616	12,967	649	1,101	3,016	2,343	198,770	134,427	23,751	17,629	15,479	14,708	771	1,084	4,019	2,381
Homeland security, law enforcement, and firefighting	60,264	34,526	12,296	9,836	1,757	1,552	205	482	1,003	364	62,409	35,362	12,460	10,569	1,798	1,556	242	441	1,337	442
Legal professions and studies	4,425	2,713	759	590	202	194	8	30	87	44	4,513	2,606	771	650	217	209	8	52	111	106
Liberal arts and sciences, general studies, and humanities	46,790	30,709	6,624	5,301	1,686	1,547	139	511	1,023	936	45,260	29,099	6,672	5,430	1,562	1,439	123	440	1,215	842
Library science	102	90	6	4	0	0	0	0	2	0	127	108	11	5	0	0	0	1	2	0
Mathematics and statistics	20,449	13,274	1,022	1,526	2,117	2,078	39	78	351	2,081	20,990	13,001	1,009	1,758	2,195	2,166	29	62	517	2,438
Mechanic and repair technologies/technicians	273	204	10	14	12	11	1	6	4	23	318	238	16	20	10	10	0	3	9	22
Military technologies and applied sciences	105	61	29	12	1	1	0	1	0	1	185	119	38	16	4	2	2	1	5	3
Multi/interdisciplinary studies	47,658	30,522	5,575	6,475	2,754	2,603	151	359	1,006	967	48,348	30,363	5,764	6,580	2,914	2,762	152	319	1,294	1,114
Parks, recreation, leisure, and fitness studies	42,628	31,463	4,136	3,728	1,671	1,555	116	260	774	596	46,042	33,005	4,613	4,437	1,970	1,826	144	288	1,038	691
Philosophy and religious studies	12,792	9,227	1,027	1,175	749	721	28	76	315	223	11,997	8,517	920	1,180	664	630	34	64	386	266
Physical sciences and science technologies	28,053	19,664	1,519	1,982	2,883	2,821	62	156	537	1,312	29,304	20,103	1,562	2,236	3,016	2,966	50	165	820	1,402
Precision production	36	25	0	2	6	6	0	0	1	2	37	26	0	4	3	3	0	1	1	2
Psychology	114,446	72,081	14,123	15,172	7,594	7,312	282	704	2,545	2,227	117,298	71,648	14,235	17,115	7,692	7,410	282	688	3,465	2,455
Public administration and social services	31,950	17,849	7,527	4,230	1,118	1,015	103	300	589	337	33,483	18,855	7,450	4,715	1,048	937	111	305	764	346
Social sciences and history	177,767	114,131	16,958	21,338	12,879	12,466	413	1,007	4,111	7,343	173,096	107,818	16,622	22,020	12,294	11,895	399	894	5,258	8,190
Social sciences	143,579	87,069	15,299	18,205	11,712	11,350	362	825	3,384	7,085	141,990	83,672	14,995	18,944	11,319	10,970	349	721	4,413	7,926
History	34,188	27,062	1,659	3,133	1,167	1,116	51	182	727	258	31,106	24,146	1,627	3,076	975	925	50	173	845	264
Theology and religious vocations	9,385	7,673	689	444	244	218	26	41	101	193	9,642	7,733	763	499	242	225	17	49	131	225
Transportation and materials moving	4,661	3,442	360	364	235	203	32	22	107	131	4,588	3,376	322	358	202	175	27	34	122	174
Visual and performing arts	97,799	68,569	6,324	10,166	6,273	6,041	232	605	2,172	3,690	97,246	66,777	6,657	10,500	6,039	5,816	223	535	2,886	3,852
Other and not classified	0	0	0	0	0	0	0	0	0	0	0	0	0	0	0	0	0	0	0	0

[1]Excludes "Construction trades" and "Mechanic and repair technologies/technicians," which are listed separately.
NOTE: Data are for postsecondary institutions participating in Title IV federal financial aid programs. Race categories exclude persons of Hispanic ethnicity. Reported racial/ethnic distributions of students by level of degree, field of degree, and sex were used to estimate race/ethnicity for students whose race/ethnicity was not reported. To facilitate trend comparisons, certain aggregations have been made of the degree fields as reported in the Integrated Postsecondary Education Data System (IPEDS): "Agriculture and natu-

ral resources" includes Agriculture, agriculture operations, and related sciences and Natural resources and conservation; and "Business" includes Business management, marketing, and related support services and Personal and culinary services. Some data have been revised from previously published figures.
SOURCE: U.S. Department of Education, National Center for Education Statistics, Integrated Postsecondary Education Data System (IPEDS), Fall 2013 and Fall 2014, Completions component. (This table was prepared September 2015.)

Table 322.40. Bachelor's degrees conferred to males by postsecondary institutions, by race/ethnicity and field of study: 2012–13 and 2013–14

Field of study	2012–13										2013–14									
	Total	White	Black	Hispanic	Asian/Pacific Islander Total	Asian	Pacific Islander	American Indian/Alaska Native	Two or more races	Non-resident alien	Total	White	Black	Hispanic	Asian/Pacific Islander Total	Asian	Pacific Islander	American Indian/Alaska Native	Two or more races	Non-resident alien
1	2	3	4	5	6	7	8	9	10	11	12	13	14	15	16	17	18	19	20	21
All fields, total	787,408	535,358	67,351	74,067	59,806	57,560	2,246	4,611	13,834	32,381	801,692	535,839	68,259	80,297	59,848	57,610	2,238	4,171	18,138	35,140
Agriculture and natural resources	16,618	14,127	418	864	496	463	33	139	300	274	17,249	14,587	446	968	534	505	29	108	314	292
Architecture and related services	5,581	3,685	284	756	446	432	14	22	82	306	5,173	3,391	275	751	352	344	8	19	80	305
Area, ethnic, cultural, gender, and group studies	2,623	1,292	320	419	329	309	20	84	104	75	2,466	1,147	368	425	264	243	21	58	123	81
Biological and biomedical sciences	41,556	26,198	2,363	3,578	7,183	7,074	109	221	857	1,156	43,427	27,310	2,371	4,043	7,223	7,120	103	192	1,171	1,117
Business	187,843	124,498	17,299	16,842	13,879	13,310	569	979	2,672	11,674	188,418	123,490	16,935	18,042	13,354	12,833	521	883	3,412	12,302
Communication, journalism, and related programs	30,148	21,603	3,317	2,698	1,165	1,091	74	144	535	686	30,955	21,709	3,468	3,012	1,179	1,107	72	130	721	736
Communications technologies	3,522	2,213	446	468	152	150	2	20	86	137	3,415	2,158	428	468	129	116	13	22	109	101
Computer and information sciences	41,874	26,960	4,359	3,619	4,075	3,933	142	218	744	1,899	45,393	28,681	4,339	4,205	4,690	4,537	153	239	1,057	2,182
Construction trades	225	173	6	30	5	3	2	1	9	1	243	187	8	32	11	9	2	1	4	0
Education	21,824	17,473	1,892	1,296	463	417	46	170	296	234	20,353	16,222	1,767	1,221	448	392	56	127	341	227
Engineering	69,430	46,200	2,738	5,565	8,214	8,056	158	277	1,130	5,306	73,903	48,727	2,724	6,415	8,207	8,056	151	240	1,662	5,928
Engineering technologies and engineering-related fields[1]	14,742	10,668	1,414	1,194	624	594	30	149	166	527	14,495	10,226	1,433	1,254	639	608	31	125	237	581
English language and literature/letters	16,508	12,295	1,090	1,757	768	732	36	99	340	159	15,809	11,512	1,103	1,777	700	663	37	93	476	148
Family and consumer sciences/human sciences	2,872	1,809	429	283	199	187	12	17	59	76	3,014	1,852	462	317	225	213	12	16	65	77
Foreign languages, literatures, and linguistics	6,842	4,608	295	1,162	426	412	14	43	176	132	6,266	4,159	249	1,179	329	314	15	31	188	131
Health professions and related programs	28,208	18,305	3,104	2,502	3,050	2,900	150	189	503	555	30,931	19,686	3,448	2,962	3,454	3,284	170	165	663	553
Homeland security, law enforcement, and firefighting	31,795	20,474	4,784	4,555	1,123	1,013	110	205	467	187	33,383	21,222	4,969	4,954	1,140	1,003	137	224	646	228
Legal professions and studies	1,308	844	197	148	67	66	1	10	31	11	1,456	898	210	198	70	67	3	14	27	39
Liberal arts and sciences, general studies, and humanities	16,991	11,615	2,397	1,550	554	502	52	168	356	351	16,485	11,003	2,428	1,598	535	491	44	170	381	370
Library science	12	11	0	1	0	0	0	0	0	0	14	12	1	1	0	0	0	0	0	0
Mathematics and statistics	11,599	7,558	503	840	1,295	1,271	24	49	194	1,160	11,967	7,446	490	971	1,331	1,317	14	35	299	1,395
Mechanic and repair technologies/technicians	248	185	10	11	12	11	1	6	3	21	297	225	16	16	8	8	0	2	9	21
Military technologies and applied sciences	80	54	15	10	0	0	0	0	1	0	161	111	30	12	2	1	1	0	3	1
Multi/interdisciplinary studies	15,332	10,321	1,629	1,608	938	886	52	138	324	374	16,119	10,479	1,789	1,859	1,012	943	69	89	443	448
Parks, recreation, leisure, and fitness studies	23,170	16,810	2,485	2,065	914	850	64	137	414	345	24,713	17,480	2,661	2,445	1,081	1,001	80	128	523	395
Philosophy and religious studies	8,149	5,972	582	756	461	442	19	50	187	141	7,582	5,536	517	749	365	344	21	31	232	152
Physical sciences and science technologies	17,142	12,515	670	1,201	1,610	1,576	34	71	308	767	17,802	12,785	694	1,363	1,610	1,584	26	83	459	808
Precision production	23	18	0	0	0	3	0	0	0	2	21	15	1	3	1	1	0	0	1	0
Psychology	26,814	16,994	2,903	3,381	2,171	2,090	81	182	611	572	27,304	16,905	2,864	3,780	2,169	2,099	70	174	790	622
Public administration and social services	5,664	3,228	1,161	740	295	277	18	54	110	76	5,917	3,432	1,215	778	238	213	25	54	131	69
Social sciences and history	90,143	61,907	6,681	9,256	6,269	6,042	227	474	1,842	3,714	88,233	58,895	6,761	9,494	6,041	5,830	211	429	2,374	4,239
Social sciences	69,682	45,350	5,849	7,481	5,622	5,431	191	366	1,442	3,572	69,480	44,037	5,896	7,747	5,474	5,287	187	332	1,904	4,090
History	20,461	16,557	832	1,775	647	611	36	108	400	142	18,753	14,858	865	1,747	567	543	24	97	470	149
Theology and religious vocations	6,351	5,349	363	271	143	122	21	33	50	142	6,594	5,438	429	298	159	146	13	30	78	162
Transportation and materials moving	4,108	3,065	307	310	207	177	30	17	94	108	4,053	3,029	270	297	168	147	21	28	109	152
Visual and performing arts	38,063	26,331	2,890	4,330	2,270	2,169	101	245	784	1,213	38,081	25,884	3,091	4,410	2,180	2,071	109	231	1,010	1,275
Other and not classified	0	0	0	0	0	0	0	0	0	0	0	0	0	0	0	0	0	0	0	0

[1]Excludes "Construction trades" and "Mechanic and repair technologies/technicians," which are listed separately.
NOTE: Data are for postsecondary institutions participating in Title IV federal financial aid programs. Race categories exclude persons of Hispanic ethnicity. Reported racial/ethnic distributions of students by level of degree, field of degree, and sex were used to estimate race/ethnicity for students whose race/ethnicity was not reported. To facilitate trend comparisons, certain aggregations have been made of the degree fields as reported in the Integrated Postsecondary Education Data System (IPEDS): "Agriculture and natural resources" includes Agriculture, agriculture operations, and related sciences and Natural resources and conservation; and "Business" includes Business management, marketing, and related support services and Personal and culinary services. Some data have been revised from previously published figures.
SOURCE: U.S. Department of Education, National Center for Education Statistics, Integrated Postsecondary Education Data System (IPEDS), Fall 2013 and Fall 2014, Completions component. (This table was prepared September 2015.)

Table 322.50. Bachelor's degrees conferred to females by postsecondary institutions, by race/ethnicity and field of study: 2012–13 and 2013–14

Field of study	2012–13				Asian/Pacific Islander			American Indian/Alaska Native	Two or more races	Non-resident alien	2013–14				Asian/Pacific Islander			American Indian/Alaska Native	Two or more races	Non-resident alien
	Total	White	Black	Hispanic	Total	Asian	Pacific Islander				Total	White	Black	Hispanic	Total	Asian	Pacific Islander			
1	2	3	4	5	6	7	8	9	10	11	12	13	14	15	16	17	18	19	20	21
All fields, total	**1,052,973**	**686,550**	**123,882**	**112,610**	**70,323**	**67,514**	**2,809**	**6,821**	**20,294**	**32,493**	**1,068,122**	**682,953**	**123,039**	**122,115**	**71,832**	**68,877**	**2,955**	**6,615**	**27,285**	**34,283**
Agriculture and natural resources	16,974	13,521	542	1,185	862	820	42	146	349	369	17,867	14,083	606	1,294	820	766	54	121	537	406
Architecture and related services	4,176	2,567	221	501	445	438	7	13	81	348	3,971	2,356	237	531	385	379	6	13	87	362
Area, ethnic, cultural, gender, and group studies	6,227	3,011	828	1,169	679	648	31	141	256	143	5,809	2,682	803	1,144	580	560	20	133	283	184
Biological and biomedical sciences	58,841	35,583	5,286	5,314	9,326	9,182	144	318	1,237	1,777	61,206	36,500	5,341	5,965	9,501	9,330	171	303	1,904	1,692
Business	173,044	100,968	25,167	18,595	13,202	12,592	610	1,099	2,615	11,398	169,661	97,930	22,906	19,362	13,125	12,515	610	1,112	3,446	11,780
Communication, journalism, and related programs	54,670	37,822	5,796	5,525	2,486	2,358	128	281	1,155	1,605	56,649	38,216	6,208	6,201	2,437	2,335	102	250	1,632	1,705
Communications technologies	1,465	953	176	141	90	87	3	2	34	69	1,572	966	205	145	125	119	6	7	62	62
Computer and information sciences	9,087	4,763	1,657	881	1,028	1,001	27	74	202	482	9,974	5,164	1,598	917	1,311	1,272	39	62	286	636
Construction trades	19	13	0	6	0	0	0	0	0	0	25	11	1	9	2	2	0	0	1	1
Education	82,874	66,729	6,407	5,874	1,664	1,514	150	556	953	691	78,501	62,470	5,899	5,943	1,720	1,550	170	597	1,211	661
Engineering	16,557	9,929	883	1,476	2,377	2,339	38	82	339	1,471	18,259	10,810	962	1,716	2,510	2,474	36	82	530	1,649
Engineering technologies and engineering-related fields[1]	1,751	1,094	270	175	104	99	5	18	20	70	1,726	1,072	266	176	80	76	4	21	32	79
English language and literature/letters	35,893	26,229	3,012	3,551	1,661	1,603	58	181	865	394	34,595	24,670	2,967	3,733	1,512	1,460	52	167	1,122	424
Family and consumer sciences/human sciences	21,058	14,600	2,604	1,984	1,136	1,087	49	124	349	261	21,708	14,545	2,627	2,418	1,140	1,078	62	165	499	314
Foreign languages, literatures, and linguistics	14,805	9,526	669	2,973	848	832	16	75	373	341	14,069	8,778	660	3,028	799	776	23	44	451	309
Health professions and related programs	152,941	106,270	18,957	11,935	10,566	10,067	499	912	2,513	1,788	167,839	114,741	20,303	14,667	12,025	11,424	601	919	3,356	1,828
Homeland security, law enforcement, and firefighting	28,469	14,052	7,512	5,281	634	539	95	277	536	177	29,026	14,140	7,491	5,615	658	553	105	217	691	214
Legal professions and studies	3,117	1,869	562	442	135	128	7	20	56	33	3,057	1,708	561	452	147	142	5	38	84	67
Liberal arts and sciences, general studies, and humanities	29,799	19,094	4,227	3,751	1,132	1,045	87	343	667	585	28,775	18,096	4,244	3,832	1,027	948	79	270	834	472
Library science	90	79	6	3	0	0	0	0	2	0	113	96	10	4	0	0	0	1	2	0
Mathematics and statistics	8,850	5,716	519	686	822	807	15	29	157	921	9,013	5,555	519	787	864	849	15	27	218	1,043
Mechanic and repair technologies/technicians	25	19	0	3	0	0	0	1	1	2	21	13	0	4	2	2	0	0	0	1
Military technologies and applied sciences	25	7	14	2	1	1	0	0	1	0	24	8	8	4	2	2	1	1	0	0
Multi/interdisciplinary studies	32,326	20,201	3,946	4,867	1,816	1,717	99	221	682	593	32,229	19,884	3,975	4,721	1,902	1,819	83	230	851	666
Parks, recreation, leisure, and fitness studies	19,458	14,653	1,651	1,663	757	705	52	123	360	251	21,329	15,525	1,952	1,992	889	825	64	160	515	296
Philosophy and religious studies	4,643	3,255	445	419	288	279	9	26	128	82	4,415	2,981	403	431	299	286	13	33	154	114
Physical sciences and science technologies	10,911	7,149	849	781	1,273	1,245	28	85	229	545	11,502	7,318	868	873	1,406	1,382	24	82	361	594
Precision production	13	7	0	1	3	3	0	0	1	1	16	11	0	1	2	2	0	0	0	1
Psychology	87,632	55,087	11,220	11,791	5,423	5,222	201	522	1,934	1,655	89,994	54,743	11,371	13,335	5,523	5,311	212	514	2,675	1,833
Public administration and social services	26,286	14,621	6,366	3,490	823	738	85	246	479	261	27,566	15,423	6,235	3,937	810	724	86	251	633	277
Social sciences and history	87,624	52,224	10,277	12,082	6,610	6,424	186	533	2,269	3,629	84,863	48,923	9,861	12,526	6,253	6,065	188	465	2,884	3,951
Social sciences	73,897	41,719	9,450	10,724	6,090	5,919	171	459	1,942	3,513	72,510	39,635	9,099	11,197	5,845	5,683	162	389	2,509	3,836
History	13,727	10,505	827	1,358	520	505	15	74	327	116	12,353	9,288	762	1,329	408	382	26	76	375	115
Theology and religious vocations	3,034	2,324	326	173	101	96	5	8	51	51	3,048	2,295	334	201	83	79	4	19	53	63
Transportation and materials moving	553	377	53	54	28	26	2	5	13	23	535	347	52	61	34	28	6	6	22	22
Visual and performing arts	59,736	42,238	3,434	5,836	4,003	3,872	131	360	1,388	2,477	59,165	40,893	3,566	6,090	3,859	3,745	114	304	1,876	2,577
Other and not classified	0	0	0	0	0	0	0	0	0	0	0	0	0	0	0	0	0	0	0	0

[1]Excludes "Construction trades" and "Mechanic and repair technologies/technicians," which are listed separately.

NOTE: Data are for postsecondary institutions participating in Title IV federal financial aid programs. Race categories exclude persons of Hispanic ethnicity. Reported racial/ethnic distributions of students by level of degree, field of degree, and sex were used to estimate race/ethnicity for students whose race/ethnicity was not reported. To facilitate trend comparisons, certain aggregations have been made of the degree fields as reported in the Integrated Postsecondary Education Data System (IPEDS): "Agriculture and natu-

ral resources" includes Agriculture, agriculture operations, and related sciences and Natural resources and conservation; and "Business" includes Business management, marketing, and related support services and Personal and culinary services. Some data have been revised from previously published figures.

SOURCE: U.S. Department of Education, National Center for Education Statistics, Integrated Postsecondary Education Data System (IPEDS), Fall 2013 and Fall 2014, Completions component. (This table was prepared September 2014.)

Table 323.10. Master's degrees conferred by postsecondary institutions, by field of study: Selected years, 1970–71 through 2013–14

Field of study	1970–71	1975–76	1980–81	1985–86	1990–91	1995–96	2000–01	2003–04	2004–05	2005–06	2006–07	2007–08	2008–09	2009–10	2010–11	2011–12	2012–13	2013–14
1	2	3	4	5	6	7	8	9	10	11	12	13	14	15	16	17	18	19
Total	235,564	317,477	302,637	295,850	342,863	412,180	473,502	564,272	580,151	599,731	610,597	630,666	662,082	693,313	730,922	755,967	751,718	754,475
Agriculture and natural resources	2,457	3,340	4,003	3,801	3,295	4,551	4,272	4,783	4,746	4,640	4,623	4,684	4,878	5,215	5,766	6,390	6,336	6,544
Architecture and related services	1,705	3,215	3,153	3,260	3,490	3,993	4,302	5,424	5,674	5,743	5,951	6,065	6,587	7,280	7,788	8,448	8,095	8,048
Area, ethnic, cultural, gender, and group studies	1,032	993	802	915	1,233	1,652	1,555	1,683	1,755	2,080	1,699	1,778	1,779	1,775	1,913	1,947	1,897	1,824
Biological and biomedical sciences	5,625	6,457	5,766	5,064	4,834	6,593	7,017	7,732	8,284	8,781	8,898	9,689	10,018	10,730	11,324	12,419	13,300	13,960
Business	26,490	42,592	57,888	66,676	78,255	93,554	115,602	139,347	142,617	146,406	150,211	155,637	168,404	177,748	187,178	191,606	188,617	189,328
Communication, journalism, and related programs	1,770	2,961	2,896	3,500	4,123	5,080	5,218	6,535	6,762	7,244	6,773	6,915	7,042	7,630	8,302	9,005	8,760	9,347
Communications technologies	86	165	209	308	204	481	427	365	433	501	499	631	475	463	502	497	577	581
Computer and information sciences	1,588	2,603	4,218	8,070	9,324	10,579	16,911	20,143	18,416	17,055	16,232	17,087	17,907	17,955	19,516	20,925	22,782	24,532
Education	87,666	126,061	96,713	74,816	87,352	104,936	127,829	162,345	167,490	174,620	176,572	175,880	178,538	182,165	185,127	179,047	164,652	154,636
Engineering	16,813	16,472	16,893	21,529	24,454	26,789	25,174	32,554	32,488	30,848	29,299	31,557	34,546	35,133	38,664	40,323	40,420	42,372
Engineering technologies	134	328	323	617	996	2,054	2,013	2,499	2,500	2,541	2,690	2,873	3,462	4,258	4,515	4,793	4,908	4,954
English language and literature/letters	10,441	8,599	5,742	5,335	6,784	7,657	6,763	7,956	8,468	8,845	8,742	9,161	9,262	9,202	9,475	9,938	9,755	9,292
Family and consumer sciences/human sciences	1,452	2,179	2,570	2,011	1,541	1,712	1,838	1,794	1,827	1,983	2,080	2,199	2,453	2,592	2,918	3,155	3,255	3,121
Foreign languages, literatures, and linguistics	5,480	4,432	2,934	2,690	3,049	3,443	3,035	3,124	3,407	3,539	3,443	3,565	3,592	3,756	3,727	3,827	3,708	3,482
Health professions and related programs	5,330	12,164	16,176	18,603	21,354	33,920	43,623	44,939	46,703	51,380	54,531	58,120	62,642	69,112	75,571	84,355	90,933	97,403
Homeland security, law enforcement, and firefighting	194	1,197	1,538	1,074	1,108	1,812	2,514	3,717	3,991	4,277	4,906	5,760	6,125	6,717	7,433	8,420	8,868	9,310
Legal professions and studies	955	1,442	1,832	1,924	2,057	2,751	3,829	4,243	4,170	4,453	4,486	4,815	5,150	5,767	6,475	6,614	7,013	7,655
Liberal arts and sciences, general studies, and humanities	885	2,633	2,375	1,586	2,213	2,778	3,193	3,697	3,680	3,702	3,634	3,797	3,729	3,822	3,997	3,792	3,264	3,002
Library science	7,001	8,037	4,859	3,564	4,763	5,099	4,727	6,015	6,213	6,448	6,767	7,162	7,091	7,448	7,729	7,443	6,983	5,839
Mathematics and statistics	5,191	3,857	2,567	3,131	3,549	3,651	3,209	4,191	4,477	4,730	4,884	4,980	5,211	5,639	5,866	6,246	6,957	7,273
Military technologies and applied sciences	2	0	43	83	0	136	0	0	0	0	202	0	3	0	0	29	32	29
Multi/interdisciplinary studies	924	1,283	2,356	2,869	2,079	2,713	3,413	3,972	4,167	4,391	4,611	5,165	5,225	5,947	6,762	7,746	7,953	8,075
Parks, recreation, leisure, and fitness studies	218	571	643	570	483	1,684	2,354	3,199	3,740	3,992	4,110	4,440	4,825	5,617	6,546	7,047	7,139	7,609
Philosophy and religious studies	1,326	1,358	1,231	1,193	1,471	1,363	1,386	1,578	1,647	1,739	1,716	1,879	1,859	2,045	1,839	2,003	1,934	2,095
Physical sciences and science technologies	6,336	5,428	5,246	5,860	5,281	5,910	5,134	5,714	5,823	6,063	6,012	6,061	5,862	6,066	6,386	6,911	7,014	6,984
Precision production	0	0	0	0	0	8	2	13	6	9	5	3	10	10	5	11	9	15
Psychology	5,717	10,167	10,223	9,845	11,349	15,152	16,539	17,898	18,830	19,770	21,037	21,431	23,415	23,763	25,062	27,052	27,787	27,966
Public administration and social services	7,785	15,209	17,803	15,692	17,905	24,229	25,268	28,250	29,552	30,510	31,131	33,029	33,934	35,740	38,614	41,737	43,591	44,490
Social sciences and history	16,539	15,953	11,945	10,564	12,233	15,012	13,791	16,110	16,952	17,369	17,665	18,495	19,241	20,234	21,085	21,891	21,591	21,475
Theology and religious vocations	7,747	8,964	11,061	11,826	10,498	10,909	9,876	10,818	11,348	11,758	12,436	12,578	12,851	12,848	13,170	13,341	14,275	14,128
Transportation and materials moving	0	0	0	454	406	919	756	728	802	784	985	982	1,048	1,074	1,390	1,702	1,444	1,243
Visual and performing arts	6,675	8,817	8,629	8,420	8,657	10,280	11,404	12,906	13,183	13,530	13,767	14,164	14,918	15,562	16,277	17,307	17,869	17,863
Not classified by field of study	0	0	0	0	8,523	780	528	0	0	0	0	84	0	0	0	0	0	0

NOTE: Data through 1990–91 are for institutions of higher education, while later data are for postsecondary institutions that participate in Title IV federal financial aid programs. The new Classification of Instructional Programs was initiated in 2009–10. The figures for earlier years have been reclassified when necessary to make them conform to the new taxonomy. To facilitate trend comparisons, certain aggregations have been made of the degree fields as reported in the Integrated Postsecondary Education Data System (IPEDS). "Agriculture and natural resources" includes Agriculture, agriculture operations, and related sciences and Natural resources and conservation; "Business" includes Business, management, marketing, and related support services and Personal and culinary services; and "Engineering technologies" includes Engineering technolo-gies and engineering-related fields, Construction trades, and Mechanic and repair technologies/technicians. Some data have been revised from previously published figures.
SOURCE: U.S. Department of Education, National Center for Education Statistics, Higher Education General Information Survey (HEGIS), "Degrees and Other Formal Awards Conferred" surveys, 1970–71 through 1985–86; Integrated Postsecondary Education Data System (IPEDS), "Completions Survey" (IPEDS-C:91–99); and IPEDS Fall 2000 through Fall 2014, Completions component. (This table was prepared September 2015.)

Table 323.20. Master's degrees conferred by postsecondary institutions, by race/ethnicity and sex of student: Selected years, 1976–77 through 2013–14

Year and sex	Number of degrees conferred to U.S. citizens and nonresident aliens								Percentage distribution of degrees conferred to U.S. citizens						
	Total	White	Black	Hispanic	Asian/ Pacific Islander	American Indian/ Alaska Native	Two or more races	Non-resident alien	Total	White	Black	Hispanic	Asian/ Pacific Islander	American Indian/ Alaska Native	Two or more races
1	2	3	4	5	6	7	8	9	10	11	12	13	14	15	16
Total															
1976–77[1]	322,463	271,402	21,252	6,136	5,127	1,018	—	17,528	100.0	89.0	7.0	2.0	1.7	0.3	—
1980–81[2]	301,081	247,475	17,436	6,534	6,348	1,044	—	22,244	100.0	88.8	6.3	2.3	2.3	0.4	—
1990–91	342,863	265,927	17,023	8,981	11,869	1,189	—	37,874	100.0	87.2	5.6	2.9	3.9	0.4	—
1997–98	436,037	312,752	30,703	16,370	21,415	2,068	—	52,729	100.0	81.6	8.0	4.3	5.6	0.5	—
1998–99	446,038	318,555	33,010	17,781	22,262	2,075	—	52,355	100.0	80.9	8.4	4.5	5.7	0.5	—
1999–2000	463,185	324,990	36,606	19,379	23,523	2,263	—	56,424	100.0	79.9	9.0	4.8	5.8	0.6	—
2000–01	473,502	324,211	38,853	21,661	24,544	2,496	—	61,737	100.0	78.7	9.4	5.3	6.0	0.6	—
2001–02	487,313	331,427	41,006	22,517	25,681	2,632	—	64,050	100.0	78.3	9.7	5.3	6.1	0.6	—
2002–03	518,699	346,003	45,150	25,200	27,492	2,886	—	71,968	100.0	77.5	10.1	5.6	6.2	0.6	—
2003–04	564,272	373,448	51,402	29,806	31,202	3,206	—	75,208	100.0	76.4	10.5	6.1	6.4	0.7	—
2004–05	580,151	383,246	55,330	31,639	33,042	3,310	—	73,584	100.0	75.7	10.9	6.2	6.5	0.7	—
2005–06	599,731	397,439	59,806	32,567	34,289	3,519	—	72,111	100.0	75.3	11.3	6.2	6.5	0.7	—
2006–07	610,597	403,562	63,412	34,967	36,491	3,589	—	68,576	100.0	74.5	11.7	6.5	6.7	0.7	—
2007–08	630,666	413,179	65,914	36,972	37,722	3,777	—	73,102	100.0	74.1	11.8	6.6	6.8	0.7	—
2008–09	662,082	427,713	70,772	39,567	40,510	3,777	—	79,743	100.0	73.4	12.2	6.8	7.0	0.6	—
2009–10	693,313	445,158	76,472	43,603	42,520	3,965	—	81,595	100.0	72.8	12.5	7.1	7.0	0.6	—
2010–11	730,922	462,922	80,742	46,823	43,482	3,946	6,597	86,410	100.0	71.8	12.5	7.3	6.7	0.6	1.0
2011–12	755,967	470,822	86,007	50,994	45,379	3,681	9,823	89,261	100.0	70.6	12.9	7.6	6.8	0.6	1.5
2012–13	751,718	455,896	87,989	52,991	44,906	3,693	11,794	94,449	100.0	69.4	13.4	8.1	6.8	0.6	1.8
2013–14	754,475	444,700	88,515	55,965	44,613	3,494	13,411	103,777	100.0	68.3	13.6	8.6	6.9	0.5	2.1
Males															
1976–77[1]	172,703	144,042	7,970	3,328	3,128	565	—	13,670	100.0	90.6	5.0	2.1	2.0	0.4	—
1980–81[2]	151,602	120,927	6,418	3,155	3,830	507	—	16,765	100.0	89.7	4.8	2.3	2.8	0.4	—
1990–91	160,842	117,993	6,201	4,017	6,765	495	—	25,371	100.0	87.1	4.6	3.0	5.0	0.4	—
1997–98	188,718	128,987	9,978	6,612	10,500	792	—	31,849	100.0	82.2	6.4	4.2	6.7	0.5	—
1998–99	190,230	129,912	10,346	7,044	10,638	794	—	31,496	100.0	81.8	6.5	4.4	6.7	0.5	—
1999–2000	196,129	131,221	11,642	7,738	11,299	845	—	33,384	100.0	80.6	7.2	4.8	6.9	0.5	—
2000–01	197,770	128,516	11,878	8,371	11,561	925	—	36,519	100.0	79.7	7.4	5.2	7.2	0.6	—
2001–02	202,604	131,316	12,119	8,539	11,956	995	—	37,679	100.0	79.6	7.3	5.2	7.2	0.6	—
2002–03	215,172	135,938	13,224	9,389	12,704	1,043	—	42,874	100.0	78.9	7.7	5.4	7.4	0.6	—
2003–04	233,056	146,369	15,027	10,929	14,551	1,137	—	45,043	100.0	77.9	8.0	5.8	7.7	0.6	—
2004–05	237,155	150,076	16,136	11,501	15,238	1,167	—	43,037	100.0	77.3	8.3	5.9	7.8	0.6	—
2005–06	241,656	153,666	17,384	11,739	16,031	1,252	—	41,584	100.0	76.8	8.7	5.9	8.0	0.6	—
2006–07	242,189	154,241	18,333	12,473	16,728	1,275	—	39,139	100.0	76.0	9.0	6.1	8.2	0.6	—
2007–08	250,169	157,596	18,761	13,189	17,476	1,293	—	41,854	100.0	75.7	9.0	6.3	8.4	0.6	—
2008–09	263,515	162,863	20,146	14,314	18,865	1,349	—	45,978	100.0	74.9	9.3	6.6	8.7	0.6	—
2009–10	275,317	170,243	22,121	15,554	19,423	1,419	—	46,557	100.0	74.4	9.7	6.8	8.5	0.6	—
2010–11	291,680	177,786	23,746	17,183	19,918	1,409	2,540	49,098	100.0	73.3	9.8	7.1	8.2	0.6	1.0
2011–12	302,484	183,222	25,284	18,633	20,751	1,298	3,518	49,778	100.0	72.5	10.0	7.4	8.2	0.5	1.4
2012–13	301,552	177,208	26,417	19,441	20,456	1,280	4,472	52,278	100.0	71.1	10.6	7.8	8.2	0.5	1.8
2013–14	302,807	173,278	26,575	20,569	19,981	1,211	4,888	56,305	100.0	70.3	10.8	8.3	8.1	0.5	2.0
Females															
1976–77[1]	149,760	127,360	13,282	2,808	1,999	453	—	3,858	100.0	87.3	9.1	1.9	1.4	0.3	—
1980–81[2]	149,479	126,548	11,018	3,379	2,518	537	—	5,479	100.0	87.9	7.7	2.3	1.7	0.4	—
1990–91	182,021	147,934	10,822	4,964	5,104	694	—	12,503	100.0	87.3	6.4	2.9	3.0	0.4	—
1997–98	247,319	183,765	20,725	9,758	10,915	1,276	—	20,880	100.0	81.2	9.2	4.3	4.8	0.6	—
1998–99	255,808	188,643	22,664	10,737	11,624	1,281	—	20,859	100.0	80.3	9.6	4.6	4.9	0.5	—
1999–2000	267,056	193,769	24,964	11,641	12,224	1,418	—	23,040	100.0	79.4	10.2	4.8	5.0	0.6	—
2000–01	275,732	195,695	26,975	13,290	12,983	1,571	—	25,218	100.0	78.1	10.8	5.3	5.2	0.6	—
2001–02	284,709	200,111	28,887	13,978	13,725	1,637	—	26,371	100.0	77.5	11.2	5.4	5.3	0.6	—
2002–03	303,527	210,065	31,926	15,811	14,788	1,843	—	29,094	100.0	76.5	11.6	5.8	5.4	0.7	—
2003–04	331,216	227,079	36,375	18,877	16,651	2,069	—	30,165	100.0	75.4	12.1	6.3	5.5	0.7	—
2004–05	342,996	233,170	39,194	20,138	17,804	2,143	—	30,547	100.0	74.6	12.5	6.4	5.7	0.7	—
2005–06	358,075	243,773	42,422	20,828	18,258	2,267	—	30,527	100.0	74.4	13.0	6.4	5.6	0.7	—
2006–07	368,408	249,321	45,079	22,494	19,763	2,314	—	29,437	100.0	73.6	13.3	6.6	5.8	0.7	—
2007–08	380,497	255,583	47,153	23,783	20,246	2,484	—	31,248	100.0	73.2	13.5	6.8	5.8	0.7	—
2008–09	398,567	264,850	50,626	25,253	21,645	2,428	—	33,765	100.0	72.6	13.9	6.9	5.9	0.7	—
2009–10	417,996	274,915	54,351	28,049	23,097	2,546	—	35,038	100.0	71.8	14.2	7.3	6.0	0.7	—
2010–11	439,242	285,136	56,996	29,640	23,564	2,537	4,057	37,312	100.0	70.9	14.2	7.4	5.9	0.6	1.0
2011–12	453,483	287,600	60,723	32,361	24,628	2,383	6,305	39,483	100.0	69.5	14.7	7.8	5.9	0.6	1.5
2012–13	450,166	278,688	61,572	33,550	24,450	2,413	7,322	42,171	100.0	68.3	15.1	8.2	6.0	0.6	1.8
2013–14	451,668	271,422	61,940	35,396	24,632	2,283	8,523	47,472	100.0	67.2	15.3	8.8	6.1	0.6	2.1

—Not available.
[1]Excludes 387 males and 175 females whose racial/ethnic group was not available.
[2]Excludes 1,377 males and 179 females whose racial/ethnic group was not available.
NOTE: Data through 1990–91 are for institutions of higher education, while later data are for postsecondary institutions participating in Title IV federal financial aid programs. Race categories exclude persons of Hispanic ethnicity. For 1989–90 and later years, reported racial/ethnic distributions of students by level of degree, field of degree, and sex were used to estimate race/ethnicity for students whose race/ethnicity was not reported. Detail may not sum to totals because of rounding. Some data have been revised from previously published figures.
SOURCE: U.S. Department of Education, National Center for Education Statistics, Higher Education General Information Survey (HEGIS), "Degrees and Other Formal Awards Conferred" surveys, 1976–77 and 1980–81; Integrated Postsecondary Education Data System (IPEDS), "Completions Survey" (IPEDS-C:90–99); and IPEDS Fall 2000 through Fall 2014, Completions component. (This table was prepared September 2015.)

Table 323.30. Master's degrees conferred by postsecondary institutions, by race/ethnicity and field of study: 2012–13 and 2013–14

Field of study	2012–13 Total	White	Black	Hispanic	Asian/Pacific Islander Total	Asian	Pacific Islander	American Indian/ Alaska Native	Two or more races	Non-resident alien	2013–14 Total	White	Black	Hispanic	Asian/Pacific Islander Total	Asian	Pacific Islander	American Indian/ Alaska Native	Two or more races	Non-resident alien
1	2	3	4	5	6	7	8	9	10	11	12	13	14	15	16	17	18	19	20	21
All fields, total	751,718	455,896	87,989	52,991	44,906	43,100	1,806	3,693	11,794	94,449	754,475	444,700	88,515	55,965	44,613	42,752	1,861	3,494	13,411	103,777
Agriculture and natural resources	6,336	4,540	233	256	221	206	15	41	112	933	6,544	4,673	228	294	218	212	6	25	125	981
Architecture and related services	8,095	4,955	338	623	521	513	8	21	169	1,468	8,048	4,426	335	718	527	517	10	22	168	1,852
Area, ethnic, cultural, gender, and group studies	1,897	981	168	228	125	117	8	30	69	296	1,824	873	169	262	114	104	10	26	69	311
Biological and biomedical sciences	13,300	7,371	866	741	1,812	1,790	22	41	309	2,160	13,960	7,677	900	877	1,871	1,851	20	55	302	2,278
Business	188,617	100,909	28,356	12,824	14,916	14,341	575	875	2,580	28,157	189,328	99,150	27,494	13,501	14,444	13,856	588	817	2,859	31,063
Communication, journalism, and related programs	8,760	5,109	957	665	375	362	13	20	205	1,429	9,347	5,127	1,119	763	358	349	9	32	258	1,690
Communications technologies	577	230	49	36	44	43	1	0	4	214	581	234	51	32	35	35	0	1	4	224
Computer and information sciences	22,782	7,442	2,031	875	2,012	1,984	28	51	262	10,109	24,532	7,738	2,054	936	2,185	2,145	40	64	330	11,225
Construction trades	6	6	0	0	0	0	0	0	0	0	6	6	0	0	0	0	0	0	0	0
Education	164,652	120,690	18,670	13,155	4,872	4,463	409	947	2,252	4,066	154,636	110,800	17,984	13,226	4,778	4,382	396	830	2,415	4,603
Engineering	40,420	15,510	1,192	1,864	3,969	3,935	34	80	496	17,309	42,372	15,633	1,162	1,991	3,751	3,718	33	50	574	19,211
Engineering technologies and engineering-related fields[1]	4,902	2,342	400	224	401	399	2	23	65	1,447	4,954	2,343	386	240	287	281	6	24	84	1,590
English language and literature/letters	9,755	7,599	530	596	322	309	13	54	257	397	9,292	7,158	511	679	312	293	19	35	258	339
Family and consumer sciences/human sciences	3,255	2,133	500	207	126	122	4	15	63	211	3,121	2,040	449	201	116	107	9	14	70	231
Foreign languages, literatures, and linguistics	3,708	1,988	78	636	146	141	5	14	57	789	3,482	1,862	98	549	138	124	14	13	77	745
Health professions and related programs	90,933	61,409	11,375	5,804	6,856	6,533	323	517	1,292	3,680	97,403	64,661	12,462	6,660	7,556	7,239	317	497	1,793	3,774
Homeland security, law enforcement, and firefighting	8,868	5,409	1,948	869	245	212	33	73	158	166	9,310	5,515	2,126	905	268	233	35	75	212	209
Legal professions and studies	7,013	2,041	464	317	235	227	8	23	78	3,855	7,655	2,111	535	383	284	280	4	31	67	4,244
Liberal arts and sciences, general studies, and humanities	3,264	2,264	408	265	94	91	3	27	81	125	3,002	2,034	404	232	75	71	4	26	55	176
Library science	6,983	5,739	284	436	246	238	8	36	148	94	5,839	4,726	267	355	239	218	21	35	122	95
Mathematics and statistics	6,957	2,806	220	290	572	571	1	6	86	2,977	7,273	2,822	195	267	546	543	3	5	69	3,369
Mechanic and repair technologies/technicians	0	0	0	0	0	0	0	0	0	0	0	0	0	0	0	0	0	0	0	0
Military technologies and applied sciences	32	23	0	3	2	1	1	0	3	1	29	25	0	1	0	0	0	0	2	2
Multi/interdisciplinary studies	7,953	5,070	679	650	415	403	12	60	170	909	8,075	5,008	742	588	391	366	25	37	242	1,067
Parks, recreation, leisure, and fitness studies	7,139	5,214	835	363	164	157	7	26	130	407	7,609	5,445	912	478	168	153	15	54	168	384
Philosophy and religious studies	1,934	1,435	149	125	69	66	3	12	31	113	2,095	1,445	221	129	91	84	7	8	47	154
Physical sciences and science technologies	7,014	4,019	202	274	406	396	10	34	135	1,944	6,984	4,020	185	311	358	353	5	17	120	1,973
Precision production	9	9	0	0	0	0	0	0	0	0	15	6	0	1	1	1	0	0	1	6
Psychology	27,787	18,340	3,718	2,750	1,191	1,124	67	167	575	1,046	27,966	18,449	3,823	2,794	1,166	1,086	80	175	616	943
Public administration and social services	43,591	24,973	8,681	4,561	1,791	1,687	104	276	955	2,354	44,490	24,945	8,773	5,058	1,733	1,639	94	312	1,138	2,531
Social sciences and history	21,591	13,050	1,599	1,555	1,002	981	21	96	456	3,833	21,475	12,537	1,609	1,613	936	909	27	93	539	4,148
Social sciences	17,508	9,689	1,467	1,300	930	912	18	68	367	3,687	17,520	9,366	1,471	1,313	855	833	22	62	442	4,011
History	4,083	3,361	132	255	72	69	3	28	89	146	3,955	3,171	138	300	81	76	5	31	97	137
Theology and religious vocations	14,275	9,750	2,071	604	706	671	35	46	162	936	14,128	9,435	2,200	642	708	679	29	51	163	929
Transportation and materials moving	1,444	1,042	125	113	50	43	7	17	20	77	1,243	893	103	108	38	33	5	9	27	65
Visual and performing arts	17,869	11,503	863	1,082	999	974	25	65	414	2,943	17,863	10,889	1,018	1,171	921	891	30	61	438	3,365
Other and not classified	0	0	0	0	0	0	0	0	0	0	0	0	0	0	0	0	0	0	0	0

[1]Excludes "Construction trades" and "Mechanic and repair technologies/technicians," which are listed separately.

NOTE: Data are for postsecondary institutions participating in Title IV federal financial aid programs. Race categories exclude persons of Hispanic ethnicity. Reported racial/ethnic distributions of students by level of degree, field of degree, and sex were used to estimate race/ethnicity for students whose race/ethnicity was not reported. To facilitate trend comparisons, certain aggregations have been made of the degree fields as reported in the Integrated Postsecondary Education Data System (IPEDS): "Agriculture and natural resources" includes Agriculture, agriculture operations, and related sciences and Natural resources and conservation; and "Business" includes Business management, marketing, and related support services and Personal and culinary services. Some data have been revised from previously published figures.

SOURCE: U.S. Department of Education, National Center for Education Statistics, Integrated Postsecondary Education Data System (IPEDS), Fall 2013 and Fall 2014, Completions component. (This table was prepared September 2015.)

Table 323.40. Master's degrees conferred to males by postsecondary institutions, by race/ethnicity and field of study: 2012–13 and 2013–14

Field of study	2012–13				Asian/Pacific Islander			American Indian/ Alaska Native	Two or more races	Non-resident alien	2013–14				Asian/Pacific Islander			American Indian/ Alaska Native	Two or more races	Non-resident alien
	Total	White	Black	Hispanic	Total	Asian	Pacific Islander				Total	White	Black	Hispanic	Total	Asian	Pacific Islander			
1	2	3	4	5	6	7	8	9	10	11	12	13	14	15	16	17	18	19	20	21
All fields, total	**301,552**	**177,208**	**26,417**	**19,441**	**20,456**	**19,737**	**719**	**1,280**	**4,472**	**52,278**	**302,807**	**173,278**	**26,575**	**20,569**	**19,981**	**19,256**	**725**	**1,211**	**4,888**	**56,305**
Agriculture and natural resources	2,912	2,143	95	105	76	70	6	12	48	433	2,966	2,151	98	112	92	89	3	13	62	438
Architecture and related services	4,261	2,760	189	326	229	223	6	12	89	656	4,122	2,451	162	378	209	204	5	8	79	835
Area, ethnic, cultural, gender, and group studies	667	379	44	83	38	34	4	8	26	89	623	342	40	93	31	27	4	5	24	88
Biological and biomedical sciences	5,783	3,351	257	316	797	785	12	19	125	918	6,072	3,478	304	384	821	812	9	24	118	943
Business	101,599	58,679	10,652	6,582	8,481	8,178	303	450	1,352	15,403	101,043	57,498	10,311	6,989	8,116	7,817	299	384	1,423	16,322
Communication, journalism, and related programs	2,684	1,702	240	188	95	91	4	3	66	390	2,807	1,706	285	214	87	82	5	11	69	435
Communications technologies	337	156	14	20	29	29	0	0	0	118	322	143	28	24	22	22	0	0	0	105
Computer and information sciences	16,539	5,856	1,234	678	1,412	1,389	23	35	176	7,148	17,484	5,948	1,291	709	1,457	1,430	27	39	235	7,805
Construction trades	4	2	0	0	0	0	0	0	0	2	0	0	0	0	0	0	0	0	0	0
Education	37,816	27,953	3,999	2,991	1,073	960	113	207	553	1,040	35,984	26,081	3,865	2,965	1,061	962	99	202	579	1,231
Engineering	30,856	12,423	872	1,406	2,887	2,862	25	58	380	12,830	32,158	12,520	857	1,498	2,701	2,675	26	42	429	14,111
Engineering technologies and engineering-related fields[1]	3,636	1,827	267	158	272	270	2	15	47	1,050	3,619	1,816	252	176	206	201	5	17	60	1,092
English language and literature/letters	3,213	2,554	149	207	91	84	7	15	76	121	3,113	2,427	138	245	102	94	8	12	78	111
Family and consumer sciences/human sciences	434	275	62	30	14	14	0	3	8	42	422	282	56	18	20	19	1	0	7	39
Foreign languages, literatures, and linguistics	1,235	709	32	190	31	29	2	4	24	245	1,222	676	41	177	45	40	5	4	26	253
Health professions and related programs	16,747	10,483	1,741	1,214	1,694	1,615	79	105	245	1,265	17,749	10,854	2,003	1,330	1,862	1,786	76	103	317	1,280
Homeland security, law enforcement, and firefighting	4,351	2,904	741	368	125	109	16	39	78	96	4,665	3,099	770	410	133	112	21	39	99	115
Legal professions and studies	3,329	1,032	134	138	107	106	1	7	24	1,887	3,567	1,069	160	161	134	133	1	8	22	2,013
Liberal arts and sciences, general studies, and humanities	1,302	953	125	103	35	33	2	10	28	48	1,209	849	147	96	26	26	0	12	20	59
Library science	1,295	1,064	42	83	51	49	2	4	29	22	1,060	861	51	63	43	34	9	5	15	22
Mathematics and statistics	4,178	1,767	149	190	342	342	0	4	57	1,669	4,256	1,749	118	179	312	310	2	4	43	1,851
Mechanic and repair technologies/technicians	0	0	0	0	0	0	0	0	0	0	0	0	0	0	0	0	0	0	0	0
Military technologies and applied sciences	17	14	0	0	2	1	1	0	0	0	21	19	0	1	0	0	0	0	1	0
Multi/interdisciplinary studies	2,999	1,916	238	257	141	135	6	21	61	365	3,061	1,913	257	236	147	135	12	16	84	408
Parks, recreation, leisure, and fitness studies	4,038	2,957	490	211	92	90	2	22	65	201	4,338	3,129	516	273	87	77	10	37	87	209
Philosophy and religious studies	1,262	969	76	77	44	42	2	9	19	68	1,312	950	102	82	52	47	5	3	31	92
Physical sciences and science technologies	4,377	2,521	110	186	234	227	7	18	84	1,224	4,312	2,528	88	199	206	202	4	14	63	1,214
Precision production	4	4	0	0	0	0	0	0	0	0	10	5	1	1	1	1	0	0	0	3
Psychology	5,715	3,901	603	548	258	245	13	25	123	257	5,731	3,942	628	539	257	238	19	39	117	209
Public administration and social services	10,864	6,391	1,701	1,046	469	439	30	61	204	992	10,833	6,129	1,747	1,166	469	446	23	68	251	1,003
Social sciences and history	10,811	6,917	610	741	452	444	8	46	200	1,845	10,750	6,565	612	766	434	421	13	44	238	2,091
Social sciences	8,532	5,018	544	603	419	412	7	33	151	1,764	8,548	4,767	565	592	390	380	10	28	191	2,015
History	2,279	1,899	66	138	33	32	1	13	49	81	2,202	1,798	47	174	44	41	3	16	47	76
Theology and religious vocations	9,484	6,723	1,033	401	495	469	26	30	94	708	9,245	6,396	1,105	427	494	477	17	30	94	704
Transportation and materials moving	1,193	875	104	84	38	35	3	10	15	67	1,020	748	78	87	32	27	5	10	17	53
Visual and performing arts	7,610	5,048	414	514	352	338	14	28	176	1,078	7,711	4,954	465	571	322	310	12	22	206	1,171
Other and not classified	0	0	0	0	0	0	0	0	0	0	0	0	0	0	0	0	0	0	0	0

[1]Excludes "Construction trades" and "Mechanic and repair technologies/technicians," which are listed separately.
NOTE: Data are for postsecondary institutions participating in Title IV federal financial aid programs. Race categories exclude persons of Hispanic ethnicity. Reported racial/ethnic distributions of students by level of degree, field of degree, and sex were used to estimate race/ethnicity for students whose race/ethnicity was not reported. To facilitate trend comparisons, certain aggregations have been made of the degree fields as reported in the Integrated Postsecondary Education Data System (IPEDS): "Agriculture and natural resources" includes Agriculture, agriculture operations, and related sciences and Natural resources and conservation; and "Business" includes Business management, marketing, and related support services and Personal and culinary services. Some data have been revised from previously published figures.
SOURCE: U.S. Department of Education, National Center for Education Statistics, Integrated Postsecondary Education Data System (IPEDS), Fall 2013 and Fall 2014, Completions component. (This table was prepared September 2015.)

Table 323.50. Master's degrees conferred to females by postsecondary institutions, by race/ethnicity and field of study: 2012–13 and 2013–14

Field of study	2012–13				Asian/Pacific Islander			American Indian/ Alaska Native	Two or more races	Non-resident alien	2013–14				Asian/Pacific Islander			American Indian/ Alaska Native	Two or more races	Non-resident alien
	Total	White	Black	Hispanic	Total	Asian	Pacific Islander				Total	White	Black	Hispanic	Total	Asian	Pacific Islander			
1	2	3	4	5	6	7	8	9	10	11	12	13	14	15	16	17	18	19	20	21
All fields, total	450,166	278,688	61,572	33,550	24,450	23,363	1,087	2,413	7,322	42,171	451,668	271,422	61,940	35,396	24,632	23,496	1,136	2,283	8,523	47,472
Agriculture and natural resources	3,424	2,397	138	151	145	136	9	29	64	500	3,578	2,522	130	182	126	123	3	12	63	543
Architecture and related services	3,834	2,195	149	297	292	290	2	9	80	812	3,926	1,975	173	340	318	313	5	14	89	1,017
Area, ethnic, cultural, gender, and group studies	1,230	602	124	145	87	83	4	22	43	207	1,201	531	129	169	83	77	6	21	45	223
Biological and biomedical sciences	7,517	4,020	609	425	1,015	1,005	10	22	184	1,242	7,888	4,199	596	493	1,050	1,039	11	31	184	1,335
Business	87,018	42,230	17,704	6,242	6,435	6,163	272	425	1,228	12,754	88,285	41,652	17,183	6,512	6,328	6,039	289	433	1,436	14,741
Communication, journalism, and related programs	6,076	3,407	717	477	280	271	9	17	139	1,039	6,540	3,421	834	549	271	267	4	21	189	1,255
Communications technologies	240	74	35	16	15	14	1	0	4	96	259	91	23	8	13	13	0	1	4	119
Computer and information sciences	6,243	1,586	797	197	600	595	5	16	86	2,961	7,048	1,790	763	227	728	715	13	25	95	3,420
Construction trades	2	2			0	0	0	0	0	1	0	0	0	0	0	0	0	0	0	0
Education	126,836	92,737	14,671	10,164	3,799	3,503	296	740	1,699	3,026	118,652	84,719	14,119	10,261	3,717	3,420	297	628	1,836	3,372
Engineering	9,564	3,087	320	458	1,082	1,073	9	22	116	4,479	10,214	3,113	305	493	1,050	1,043	7	8	145	5,100
Engineering technologies and engineering-related fields[1]	1,266	515	133	66	129	129	0	8	18	397	1,335	527	134	64	81	80	1	7	24	498
English language and literature/letters	6,542	5,045	381	389	231	225	6	39	181	276	6,179	4,731	373	434	210	199	11	23	180	228
Family and consumer sciences/human sciences	2,821	1,858	438	177	112	108	4	12	55	169	2,699	1,758	393	183	96	88	8	14	63	192
Foreign languages, literatures, and linguistics	2,473	1,279	46	446	115	112	3	10	33	544	2,260	1,186	57	372	93	84	9	9	51	492
Health professions and related programs	74,186	50,926	9,634	4,590	5,162	4,918	244	412	1,047	2,415	79,654	53,807	10,459	5,330	5,694	5,453	241	394	1,476	2,494
Homeland security, law enforcement, and firefighting	4,517	2,505	1,207	501	120	103	17	34	80	70	4,645	2,416	1,356	495	135	121	14	36	113	94
Legal professions and studies	3,684	1,009	330	179	128	121	7	16	54	1,968	4,088	1,042	375	222	150	147	3	23	45	2,231
Liberal arts and sciences, general studies, and humanities	1,962	1,311	283	162	59	58	1	17	53	77	1,793	1,185	257	136	49	45	4	14	35	117
Library science	5,688	4,675	242	353	195	189	6	32	119	72	4,779	3,865	216	292	196	184	12	30	107	73
Mathematics and statistics	2,779	1,039	71	100	230	229	1	2	29	1,308	3,017	1,073	77	88	234	233	1	1	26	1,518
Mechanic and repair technologies/technicians	0	0	0	0	0	0	0	0	0	0	0	0	0	0	0	0	0	0	0	0
Military technologies and applied sciences	15	9	0	3	0	0	0	0	3	0	8	6	0	0	0	0	0	0	0	2
Multi/interdisciplinary studies	4,954	3,154	441	393	274	268	6	39	109	544	5,014	3,095	485	352	244	231	13	21	158	659
Parks, recreation, leisure, and fitness studies	3,101	2,257	345	152	72	67	5	4	65	206	3,271	2,316	396	205	81	76	5	17	81	175
Philosophy and religious studies	672	466	73	48	25	24	1	3	12	45	783	495	119	47	39	37	2	5	16	62
Physical sciences and science technologies	2,637	1,498	92	88	172	169	3	16	51	720	2,672	1,492	97	112	152	151	1	3	57	759
Precision production	5	3			1	1	0	0	0	0	5	1						0	1	3
Psychology	22,072	14,439	3,115	2,202	933	879	54	142	452	789	22,235	14,507	3,195	2,255	909	848	61	136	499	734
Public administration and social services	32,727	18,582	6,980	3,515	1,322	1,248	74	215	751	1,362	33,657	18,816	7,026	3,892	1,264	1,193	71	244	887	1,528
Social sciences and history	10,780	6,133	989	814	550	537	13	50	256	1,988	10,725	5,972	997	847	502	488	14	49	301	2,057
Social sciences	8,976	4,671	923	697	511	500	11	35	216	1,923	8,972	4,599	906	721	465	453	12	34	251	1,996
History	1,804	1,462	66	117	39	37	2	15	40	65	1,753	1,373	91	126	37	35	2	15	50	61
Theology and religious vocations	4,791	3,027	1,038	203	211	202	9	16	68	228	4,883	3,039	1,095	215	214	202	12	20	75	225
Transportation and materials moving	251	167	21	29	12	8	4	7	5	10	223	145	25	21	6	6	0	4	10	12
Visual and performing arts	10,259	6,455	449	568	647	636	11	37	238	1,865	10,152	5,935	553	600	599	581	18	39	232	2,194
Other and not classified	0	0	0	0	0	0	0	0	0	0	0	0	0	0	0	0	0	0	0	0

[1] Excludes "Construction trades" and "Mechanic and repair technologies/technicians," which are listed separately.
NOTE: Data are for postsecondary institutions participating in Title IV federal financial aid programs. Race categories exclude persons of Hispanic ethnicity. Reported racial/ethnic distributions of students by level of degree, field of degree, and sex were used to estimate race/ethnicity for students whose race/ethnicity was not reported. To facilitate trend comparisons, certain aggregations have been made of the degree fields as reported in the Integrated Postsecondary Education Data System (IPEDS). "Agriculture and natural resources" includes Agriculture, agriculture operations, and related sciences and Natural resources and conservation; and "Business" includes Business management, marketing, and related support services and Personal and culinary services. Some data have been revised from previously published figures.
SOURCE: U.S. Department of Education, National Center for Education Statistics, Integrated Postsecondary Education Data System (IPEDS), Fall 2013 and Fall 2014, Completions component. (This table was prepared September 2015.)

Table 324.10. Doctor's degrees conferred by postsecondary institutions, by field of study: Selected years, 1970–71 through 2013–14

Field of study	1970–71	1975–76	1980–81	1985–86	1990–91	1995–96	2000–01	2003–04	2004–05	2005–06	2006–07	2007–08	2008–09	2009–10	2010–11	2011–12	2012–13	2013–14
1	2	3	4	5	6	7	8	9	10	11	12	13	14	15	16	17	18	19
Total	64,998	91,007	98,016	100,280	105,547	115,507	119,585	126,087	134,387	138,056	144,690	149,378	154,564	158,590	163,827	170,217	175,026	177,580
Agriculture and natural resources	1,086	928	1,067	1,158	1,185	1,259	1,127	1,185	1,173	1,194	1,272	1,257	1,328	1,149	1,246	1,333	1,411	1,407
Architecture and related services	36	82	93	156	135	141	153	173	179	201	178	199	212	210	205	255	247	247
Area, ethnic, cultural, gender, and group studies	143	186	161	156	159	183	216	209	189	226	233	270	239	253	278	302	291	336
Biological and biomedical sciences	3,603	3,347	3,640	3,405	4,152	5,250	5,225	5,538	5,935	6,162	6,764	7,400	7,499	7,672	7,693	7,935	7,939	8,302
Business	774	906	808	923	1,185	1,366	1,180	1,481	1,498	1,711	2,029	2,084	2,123	2,249	2,286	2,538	2,828	3,039
Communication, journalism, and related programs	145	196	171	212	259	338	368	418	465	461	479	489	533	570	577	563	612	611
Communications technologies	0	8	11	6	13	7	2	8	3	3	1	7	2	3	1	4	0	3
Computer and information sciences	128	244	252	344	676	869	768	909	1,119	1,416	1,595	1,698	1,580	1,599	1,588	1,698	1,834	1,982
Education	6,041	7,202	7,279	6,610	6,189	6,246	6,284	7,088	7,681	7,584	8,261	8,491	9,028	9,237	9,642	10,118	10,572	10,920
Engineering	3,687	2,872	2,598	3,444	5,316	6,304	5,485	5,801	6,413	7,243	7,867	7,922	7,744	7,706	8,369	8,722	9,356	10,010
Engineering technologies	1	2	10	12	14	50	62	58	54	75	61	55	59	67	56	134	111	107
English language and literature/letters	1,554	1,514	1,040	895	1,056	1,395	1,330	1,207	1,212	1,254	1,178	1,262	1,271	1,334	1,344	1,427	1,377	1,393
Family and consumer sciences/human sciences	123	178	247	307	229	375	354	329	331	340	337	323	333	296	320	325	351	335
Foreign languages, literatures, and linguistics	1,084	1,245	931	768	889	1,020	1,078	1,031	1,027	1,074	1,059	1,078	1,111	1,091	1,158	1,231	1,304	1,231
Health professions and related programs	15,988	25,267	29,595	31,922	29,842	32,678	39,019	41,861	44,201	45,677	48,943	51,675	54,846	57,750	60,221	62,097	64,192	67,448
Homeland security, law enforcement, and firefighting	1	9	21	21	28	38	44	54	94	80	85	88	97	106	131	117	147	152
Legal professions and studies	17,441	32,369	36,391	35,898	38,035	39,919	38,190	40,328	43,521	43,569	43,629	43,880	44,304	44,627	44,853	46,836	47,246	44,169
Liberal arts and sciences, general studies, and humanities	32	162	121	90	70	75	102	95	109	84	77	76	67	96	95	93	98	90
Library science	39	71	71	62	56	53	58	47	42	44	52	64	35	64	50	60	50	52
Mathematics and statistics	1,199	856	728	742	978	1,158	997	1,060	1,176	1,293	1,351	1,360	1,535	1,596	1,586	1,669	1,823	1,863
Multi/interdisciplinary studies	101	156	236	352	306	549	512	580	626	600	683	660	731	631	660	727	730	769
Parks, recreation, leisure, and fitness studies	2	15	42	39	28	104	177	222	207	194	218	228	285	266	257	288	295	317
Philosophy and religious studies	555	556	411	480	464	550	600	595	586	578	637	635	686	667	804	778	794	698
Physical sciences and science technologies	4,324	3,388	3,105	3,521	4,248	4,589	3,968	3,937	4,248	4,642	5,041	4,994	5,237	5,065	5,295	5,370	5,514	5,806
Psychology	2,144	3,157	3,576	3,593	3,932	4,141	5,091	4,827	5,106	4,921	5,153	5,296	5,477	5,540	5,851	5,936	6,326	6,634
Public administration and social services	174	292	362	382	430	499	574	649	673	704	726	760	812	838	851	890	979	1,047
Social sciences and history	3,660	4,157	3,122	2,955	3,012	3,760	3,930	3,811	3,819	3,914	3,844	4,059	4,234	4,238	4,390	4,597	4,610	4,724
Theology and religious vocations	312	1,022	1,273	1,185	1,076	1,517	1,461	1,304	1,422	1,429	1,573	1,615	1,587	2,071	2,374	2,446	2,174	2,103
Transportation and materials moving	0	0	0	0	0	0	0	0	0	0	0	0	0	0	0	0	0	7
Visual and performing arts	621	620	654	722	838	1,067	1,167	1,282	1,278	1,383	1,364	1,453	1,569	1,599	1,646	1,728	1,814	1,778
Not classified by field of study	0	0	0	0	747	7	63	0	0	0	0	0	0	0	0	0	0	0

NOTE: Data through 1990–91 are for institutions of higher education, while later data are for postsecondary institutions that participate in Title IV federal financial aid programs. The new Classification of Instructional Programs was initiated in 2009–10. Includes Ph.D., Ed.D., and comparable degrees at the doctoral level, as well as such degrees as M.D., D.D.S., and law degrees that were formerly classified as first-professional degrees. The figures for earlier years have been reclassified when necessary to make them conform to the new taxonomy. To facilitate trend comparisons, certain aggregations have been made of the degree fields as reported in the Integrated Postsecondary Education Data System (IPEDS). "Agriculture and natural resources" includes Agriculture, agriculture operations, and related sciences and Natural resources and conservation;

"Business" includes Business, management, marketing, and related support services and Personal and culinary services; and "Engineering technologies" includes Engineering technologies and engineering-related fields, Construction trades, and Mechanic and repair technologies/technicians. Some data have been revised from previously published figures. SOURCE: U.S. Department of Education, National Center for Education Statistics, Higher Education General Information Survey (HEGIS), "Degrees and Other Formal Awards Conferred" surveys, 1970–71 through 1985–86; Integrated Postsecondary Education Data System (IPEDS), "Completions Survey" (IPEDS-C:91–99); and IPEDS Fall 2000 through Fall 2014, Completions component. (This table was prepared September 2015.)

Table 324.20. Doctor's degrees conferred by postsecondary institutions, by race/ethnicity and sex of student: Selected years, 1976–77 through 2013–14

Year and sex	Number of degrees conferred[1] to U.S. citizens and nonresident aliens								Percentage distribution of degrees conferred[1] to U.S. citizens						
	Total	White	Black	Hispanic	Asian/ Pacific Islander	American Indian/ Alaska Native	Two or more races	Non-resident alien	Total	White	Black	Hispanic	Asian/ Pacific Islander	American Indian/ Alaska Native	Two or more races
1	2	3	4	5	6	7	8	9	10	11	12	13	14	15	16
Total															
1976–77[2]	91,218	79,932	3,575	1,533	1,674	240	—	4,264	100.0	91.9	4.1	1.8	1.9	0.3	—
1980–81[3]	97,281	84,200	3,893	1,924	2,267	312	—	4,685	100.0	90.9	4.2	2.1	2.4	0.3	—
1990–91	105,547	81,791	4,429	3,210	5,120	356	—	10,641	100.0	86.2	4.7	3.4	5.4	0.4	—
1997–98	118,735	83,690	7,018	4,705	9,814	732	—	12,776	100.0	79.0	6.6	4.4	9.3	0.7	—
1998–99	116,700	82,066	7,004	4,959	10,025	774	—	11,872	100.0	78.3	6.7	4.7	9.6	0.7	—
1999–2000	118,736	82,984	7,078	5,042	10,682	708	—	12,242	100.0	77.9	6.6	4.7	10.0	0.7	—
2000–01	119,585	82,321	7,035	5,204	11,587	705	—	12,733	100.0	77.0	6.6	4.9	10.8	0.7	—
2001–02	119,663	81,995	7,570	5,267	11,633	753	—	12,445	100.0	76.5	7.1	4.9	10.8	0.7	—
2002–03	121,579	82,549	7,537	5,503	12,008	759	—	13,223	100.0	76.2	7.0	5.1	11.1	0.7	—
2003–04	126,087	84,695	8,089	5,795	12,371	771	—	14,366	100.0	75.8	7.2	5.2	11.1	0.7	—
2004–05	134,387	89,763	8,527	6,115	13,176	788	—	16,018	100.0	75.8	7.2	5.2	11.1	0.7	—
2005–06	138,056	91,050	8,523	6,202	13,686	929	—	17,666	100.0	75.6	7.1	5.2	11.4	0.8	—
2006–07	144,690	94,248	9,377	6,593	14,924	918	—	18,630	100.0	74.8	7.4	5.2	11.8	0.7	—
2007–08	149,378	97,839	9,463	6,949	15,203	932	—	18,992	100.0	75.0	7.3	5.3	11.7	0.7	—
2008–09	154,564	101,400	10,188	7,497	15,840	978	—	18,661	100.0	74.6	7.5	5.5	11.7	0.7	—
2009–10	158,590	104,419	10,413	8,085	16,560	952	—	18,161	100.0	74.4	7.4	5.8	11.8	0.7	—
2010–11	163,827	105,990	10,934	8,662	17,078	947	1,251	18,965	100.0	73.2	7.5	6.0	11.8	0.7	0.9
2011–12	170,217	109,365	11,794	9,223	17,896	915	1,571	19,453	100.0	72.5	7.8	6.1	11.9	0.6	1.0
2012–13	175,026	110,759	12,085	10,108	18,406	900	2,440	20,328	100.0	71.6	7.8	6.5	11.9	0.6	1.6
2013–14	177,580	110,156	12,615	10,665	19,118	861	2,966	21,199	100.0	70.4	8.1	6.8	12.2	0.6	1.9
Males															
1976–77[2]	71,709	62,977	2,338	1,216	1,311	182	—	3,685	100.0	92.6	3.4	1.8	1.9	0.3	—
1980–81[3]	68,853	59,574	2,206	1,338	1,589	223	—	3,923	100.0	91.8	3.4	2.1	2.4	0.3	—
1990–91	64,242	48,812	1,991	1,835	3,038	196	—	8,370	100.0	87.4	3.6	3.3	5.4	0.4	—
1997–98	67,232	47,189	2,808	2,525	5,171	364	—	9,175	100.0	81.3	4.8	4.3	8.9	0.6	—
1998–99	65,340	45,802	2,793	2,533	5,382	402	—	8,428	100.0	80.5	4.9	4.5	9.5	0.7	—
1999–2000	64,930	45,308	2,762	2,602	5,467	333	—	8,458	100.0	80.2	4.9	4.6	9.7	0.6	—
2000–01	64,171	44,131	2,655	2,564	5,759	346	—	8,716	100.0	79.6	4.8	4.6	10.4	0.6	—
2001–02	62,731	43,014	2,821	2,586	5,645	357	—	8,308	100.0	79.0	5.2	4.8	10.4	0.7	—
2002–03	62,730	42,569	2,735	2,671	5,683	358	—	8,714	100.0	78.8	5.1	4.9	10.5	0.7	—
2003–04	63,981	43,014	2,888	2,731	5,620	357	—	9,371	100.0	78.8	5.3	5.0	10.3	0.7	—
2004–05	67,257	44,749	2,904	2,863	5,913	370	—	10,458	100.0	78.8	5.1	5.0	10.4	0.7	—
2005–06	68,912	45,476	2,949	2,850	5,977	429	—	11,231	100.0	78.8	5.1	4.9	10.4	0.7	—
2006–07	71,308	46,228	3,225	3,049	6,597	421	—	11,788	100.0	77.7	5.4	5.1	11.1	0.7	—
2007–08	73,453	48,203	3,296	3,146	6,535	447	—	11,826	100.0	78.2	5.3	5.1	10.6	0.7	—
2008–09	75,674	49,880	3,531	3,388	6,914	460	—	11,501	100.0	77.7	5.5	5.3	10.8	0.7	—
2009–10	76,610	50,707	3,609	3,642	7,184	430	—	11,038	100.0	77.3	5.5	5.6	11.0	0.7	—
2010–11	79,672	51,688	3,838	3,990	7,545	454	557	11,600	100.0	75.9	5.6	5.9	11.1	0.7	0.8
2011–12	82,670	53,488	4,121	4,218	7,792	418	701	11,932	100.0	75.6	5.8	6.0	11.0	0.6	1.0
2012–13	85,080	54,196	4,310	4,473	8,190	400	1,085	12,426	100.0	74.6	5.9	6.2	11.3	0.6	1.5
2013–14	85,587	53,377	4,509	4,788	8,270	365	1,297	12,981	100.0	73.5	6.2	6.6	11.4	0.5	1.8
Females															
1976–77[2]	19,509	16,955	1,237	317	363	58	—	579	100.0	89.6	6.5	1.7	1.9	0.3	—
1980–81[3]	28,428	24,626	1,687	586	678	89	—	762	100.0	89.0	6.1	2.1	2.5	0.3	—
1990–91	41,305	32,979	2,438	1,375	2,082	160	—	2,271	100.0	84.5	6.2	3.5	5.3	0.4	—
1997–98	51,503	36,501	4,210	2,180	4,643	368	—	3,601	100.0	76.2	8.8	4.6	9.7	0.8	—
1998–99	51,360	36,264	4,211	2,426	4,643	372	—	3,444	100.0	75.7	8.8	5.1	9.7	0.8	—
1999–2000	53,806	37,676	4,316	2,440	5,215	375	—	3,784	100.0	75.3	8.6	4.9	10.4	0.7	—
2000–01	55,414	38,190	4,380	2,640	5,828	359	—	4,017	100.0	74.3	8.5	5.1	11.3	0.7	—
2001–02	56,932	38,981	4,749	2,681	5,988	396	—	4,137	100.0	73.8	9.0	5.1	11.3	0.8	—
2002–03	58,849	39,980	4,802	2,832	6,325	401	—	4,509	100.0	73.6	8.8	5.2	11.6	0.7	—
2003–04	62,106	41,681	5,201	3,064	6,751	414	—	4,995	100.0	73.0	9.1	5.4	11.8	0.7	—
2004–05	67,130	45,014	5,623	3,252	7,263	418	—	5,560	100.0	73.1	9.1	5.3	11.8	0.7	—
2005–06	69,144	45,574	5,574	3,352	7,709	500	—	6,435	100.0	72.7	8.9	5.3	12.3	0.8	—
2006–07	73,382	48,020	6,152	3,544	8,327	497	—	6,842	100.0	72.2	9.2	5.3	12.5	0.7	—
2007–08	75,925	49,636	6,167	3,803	8,668	485	—	7,166	100.0	72.2	9.0	5.5	12.6	0.7	—
2008–09	78,890	51,520	6,657	4,109	8,926	518	—	7,160	100.0	71.8	9.3	5.7	12.4	0.7	—
2009–10	81,980	53,712	6,804	4,443	9,376	522	—	7,123	100.0	71.8	9.1	5.9	12.5	0.7	—
2010–11	84,155	54,302	7,096	4,672	9,533	493	694	7,365	100.0	70.7	9.2	6.1	12.4	0.6	0.9
2011–12	87,547	55,877	7,673	5,005	10,104	497	870	7,521	100.0	69.8	9.6	6.3	12.6	0.6	1.1
2012–13	89,946	56,563	7,775	5,635	10,216	500	1,355	7,902	100.0	68.9	9.5	6.9	12.5	0.6	1.7
2013–14	91,993	56,779	8,106	5,877	10,848	496	1,669	8,218	100.0	67.8	9.7	7.0	12.9	0.6	2.0

—Not available.
[1]Includes Ph.D., Ed.D., and comparable degrees at the doctoral level, as well as such degrees as M.D., D.D.S., and law degrees that were formerly classified as first-professional degrees.
[2]Excludes 500 males and 12 females whose racial/ethnic group was not available.
[3]Excludes 714 males and 21 females whose racial/ethnic group was not available.
NOTE: Data through 1990–91 are for institutions of higher education, while later data are for postsecondary institutions participating in Title IV federal financial aid programs. Race categories exclude persons of Hispanic ethnicity. For 1989–90 and later years, reported racial/ethnic

distributions of students by level of degree, field of degree, and sex were used to estimate race/ethnicity for students whose race/ethnicity was not reported. Detail may not sum to totals because of rounding. Some data have been revised from previously published figures.
SOURCE: U.S. Department of Education, National Center for Education Statistics, Higher Education General Information Survey (HEGIS), "Degrees and Other Formal Awards Conferred" surveys, 1976–77 and 1980–81; Integrated Postsecondary Education Data System (IPEDS), "Completions Survey" (IPEDS-C:90–99); and IPEDS Fall 2000 through Fall 2014, Completions component. (This table was prepared September 2015.)

Table 324.25. Doctor's degrees conferred by postsecondary institutions, by race/ethnicity and field of study: 2012–13 and 2013–14

Field of study	2012–13										2013–14									
					Asian/Pacific Islander			American Indian/Alaska Native	Two or more races	Non-resident alien					Asian/Pacific Islander			American Indian/Alaska Native	Two or more races	Non-resident alien
	Total	White	Black	Hispanic	Total	Asian	Pacific Islander				Total	White	Black	Hispanic	Total	Asian	Pacific Islander			
1	2	3	4	5	6	7	8	9	10	11	12	13	14	15	16	17	18	19	20	21
All fields, total	**175,026**	**110,759**	**12,085**	**10,108**	**18,406**	**18,020**	**386**	**900**	**2,440**	**20,328**	**177,580**	**110,156**	**12,615**	**10,665**	**19,118**	**18,790**	**328**	**861**	**2,966**	**21,199**
Agriculture and natural resources	1,411	707	45	53	39	38	1	4	7	556	1,407	691	41	55	47	46	1	5	6	562
Architecture and related services	247	97	13	10	30	29	1	0	7	90	247	76	20	13	21	20	1	5	5	112
Area, ethnic, cultural, gender, and group studies	291	148	43	30	21	21	0	11	2	36	336	151	53	28	31	30	1	7	12	54
Biological and biomedical sciences	7,939	4,248	323	409	735	728	7	27	69	2,128	8,302	4,493	299	376	721	707	14	18	119	2,276
Business	2,828	1,332	488	126	200	196	4	15	20	647	3,039	1,440	592	127	188	187	1	10	17	665
Communication, journalism, and related programs	612	372	45	22	25	25	0	4	7	137	611	381	32	35	16	16	0	3	5	139
Communications technologies	0	0	0	0	0	0	0	0	0	0	3	1	1	0	1	1	0	0	0	0
Computer and information sciences	1,834	617	63	46	147	147	0	0	3	958	1,982	670	69	37	129	129	0	9	8	1,060
Construction trades	0	0	0	0	0	0	0	0	0	0	0	0	0	0	0	0	0	0	0	0
Education	10,572	6,651	1,982	703	429	396	33	82	101	624	10,920	6,828	2,091	815	406	383	23	73	112	595
Engineering	9,356	2,911	191	213	644	636	8	7	63	5,327	10,010	3,132	180	265	705	696	9	14	81	5,633
Engineering technologies and engineering-related fields[1]	111	41	4	4	7	7	0	1	7	54	107	47	1	0	3	3	0	1	1	54
English language and literature/letters	1,377	1,070	61	61	51	51	0	7	17	110	1,393	1,092	48	56	49	48	1	9	17	122
Family and consumer sciences/human sciences	351	182	49	10	20	20	0	2	3	85	335	199	35	8	19	19	0	2	2	72
Foreign languages, literatures, and linguistics	1,304	674	16	136	46	45	1	8	12	412	1,231	679	19	118	62	62	0	4	8	341
Health professions and related programs	64,192	42,846	3,736	3,355	11,015	10,868	147	292	863	2,085	67,448	44,236	4,031	3,571	12,019	11,869	150	297	1,167	2,127
Homeland security, law enforcement, and firefighting	147	100	19	2	4	4	0	0	0	22	152	98	31	10	3	3	0	3	1	9
Legal professions and studies	47,246	33,921	3,494	3,824	3,670	3,509	161	327	1,013	997	44,169	30,985	3,303	3,910	3,360	3,256	104	313	1,105	1,193
Liberal arts and sciences, general studies, and humanities	98	75	7	5	0	0	0	1	0	10	90	72	5	1	4	4	0	1	2	5
Library science	50	28	5	0	1	1	0	0	0	16	52	30	4	3	0	0	0	0	0	15
Mathematics and statistics	1,823	716	30	38	112	112	0	3	12	912	1,863	776	30	39	87	86	1	1	14	916
Mechanics and repair technologies/technicians	0	0	0	0	0	0	0	0	0	0	0	0	0	0	0	0	0	0	0	0
Military technologies and applied sciences	0	0	0	0	0	0	0	0	0	0	0	0	0	0	0	0	0	0	0	0
Multi/interdisciplinary studies	730	433	55	29	41	40	1	5	6	161	769	439	83	26	44	44	0	2	11	164
Parks, recreation, leisure, and fitness studies	295	198	24	5	8	7	1	4	0	56	317	220	16	12	8	6	2	0	4	57
Philosophy and religious studies	794	546	28	29	35	34	1	0	17	139	698	489	43	28	24	24	0	6	8	100
Physical sciences and science technologies	5,514	2,716	120	154	265	265	0	13	48	2,198	5,806	2,730	137	174	280	277	3	19	57	2,409
Precision production	0	0	0	0	0	0	0	0	0	0	0	0	0	0	0	0	0	0	0	0
Psychology	6,326	4,566	497	436	350	342	8	44	83	350	6,634	4,675	561	520	380	366	14	30	115	353
Public administration and social services	979	538	168	36	53	51	2	1	8	175	1,047	569	229	48	40	39	1	9	10	142
Social sciences and history	4,610	2,665	204	234	213	208	5	25	44	1,225	4,724	2,674	217	250	229	228	1	22	41	1,291
Social sciences	3,607	1,933	159	170	181	177	4	14	39	1,111	3,684	1,938	164	181	192	192	0	19	33	1,157
History	1,003	732	45	64	32	31	1	11	5	114	1,040	736	53	69	37	36	1	3	8	134
Theology and religious vocations	2,174	1,261	335	56	122	118	4	15	13	372	2,103	1,162	402	65	132	131	1	5	18	319
Transportation and materials moving	1	1	0	0	0	0	0	0	0	0	7	5	0	1	0	0	0	0	1	0
Visual and performing arts	1,814	1,099	40	82	123	122	1	2	22	446	1,778	1,116	42	74	110	110	0	2	20	414
Other and not classified	0	0	0	0	0	0	0	0	0	0	0	0	0	0	0	0	0	0	0	0

[1]Excludes "Construction trades" and "Mechanic and repair technologies/technicians," which are listed separately.
NOTE: Data are for postsecondary institutions participating in Title IV federal financial aid programs. Race categories exclude persons of Hispanic ethnicity. Reported racial/ethnic distributions of students by level of degree, field of degree, and sex were used to estimate race/ethnicity for students whose race/ethnicity was not reported. To facilitate trend comparisons, certain aggregations have been made of the degree fields as reported in the Integrated Postsecondary Education Data System (IPEDS). "Agricul-

ture and natural resources" includes Agriculture, agriculture operations, and related sciences and Natural resources and conservation; and "Business" includes Business management, marketing, and related support services and Personal and culinary services. Some data have been revised from previously published figures.
SOURCE: U.S. Department of Education, National Center for Education Statistics, Integrated Postsecondary Education Data System (IPEDS), Fall 2013 and Fall 2014, Completions component. (This table was prepared September 2015.)

Table 324.30. Doctor's degrees conferred to males by postsecondary institutions, by race/ethnicity and field of study: 2012–13 and 2013–14

Field of study	2012–13 Total	White	Black	Hispanic	Asian/Pacific Islander Total	Asian	Pacific Islander	American Indian/Alaska Native	Two or more races	Nonresident alien	2013–14 Total	White	Black	Hispanic	Asian/Pacific Islander Total	Asian	Pacific Islander	American Indian/Alaska Native	Two or more races	Nonresident alien
1	2	3	4	5	6	7	8	9	10	11	12	13	14	15	16	17	18	19	20	21
All fields, total	85,080	54,196	4,310	4,473	8,190	8,009	181	400	1,085	12,426	85,587	53,377	4,509	4,788	8,270	8,117	153	365	1,297	12,981
Agriculture and natural resources	767	385	18	23	24	23	1	1	4	312	739	368	20	33	18	17	1	3	2	295
Architecture and related services	134	52	9	8	11	10	1	0	1	53	134	41	8	7	10	10	0	0	2	66
Area, ethnic, cultural, gender, and group studies	125	66	22	11	6	6	0	4	0	16	130	63	14	13	14	13	1	1	5	20
Biological and biomedical sciences	3,689	2,029	117	177	302	300	2	10	26	1,028	3,884	2,151	104	177	301	297	4	4	59	1,088
Business	1,605	783	217	70	114	112	2	9	9	403	1,722	857	276	74	110	110	0	5	8	392
Communication, journalism, and related programs	246	164	14	5	5	5	0	3	3	52	266	186	11	9	3	3	0	2	2	53
Communications technologies	0	0	0	0	0	0	0	0	0	0	1	1	0	0	0	0	0	0	0	0
Computer and information sciences	1,480	502	39	37	111	111	0	0	2	789	1,566	550	48	24	87	87	0	7	7	843
Construction trades	0	0	0	0	0	0	0	0	0	0	0	0	0	0	0	0	0	0	0	0
Education	3,418	2,239	536	223	120	110	10	31	38	231	3,464	2,265	563	246	118	105	13	27	25	220
Engineering	7,231	2,282	126	144	435	428	7	7	48	4,189	7,739	2,452	110	193	470	463	7	12	62	4,440
Engineering technologies and engineering-related fields[1]	74	29	2	3	4	4	0	1	0	35	81	32	1	0	3	3	0	0	1	44
English language and literature/letters	554	435	18	21	21	21	0	4	6	49	557	436	11	28	14	13	1	6	8	54
Family and consumer sciences/human sciences	79	46	8	2	3	3	0	0	0	20	62	45	2	1	1	1	0	0	0	13
Foreign languages, literatures, and linguistics	531	299	7	45	11	10	1	2	7	160	498	299	7	41	14	14	0	2	2	133
Health professions and related programs	26,852	18,198	1,199	1,363	4,737	4,667	70	122	345	888	28,084	18,607	1,322	1,544	5,107	5,035	72	121	460	923
Homeland security, law enforcement, and firefighting	72	52	6	1	1	1	0	1	0	13	66	35	15	7	2	2	0	0	0	7
Legal professions and studies	25,321	19,212	1,416	1,855	1,720	1,642	78	150	477	491	23,495	17,614	1,290	1,869	1,467	1,421	46	139	541	575
Liberal arts and sciences, general studies, and humanities	42	35	1	2	1	0	0	1	0	3	29	24	2	0	1	1	0	0	0	2
Library science	23	10	2	0	1	1	0	0	0	10	14	8	1	0	0	0	0	0	0	5
Mathematics and statistics	1,292	529	23	31	75	75	0	2	9	623	1,325	580	20	31	53	52	1	0	10	631
Mechanic and repair technologies/technicians	0	0	0	0	0	0	0	0	0	0	0	0	0	0	0	0	0	0	0	0
Military technologies and applied sciences	0	0	0	0	0	0	0	0	0	0	0	0	0	0	0	0	0	0	0	0
Multi/interdisciplinary studies	307	178	17	12	14	14	0	2	1	83	322	176	37	9	15	15	0	1	5	79
Parks, recreation, leisure, and fitness studies	159	96	11	4	5	4	1	2	0	41	158	107	4	4	5	3	2	0	2	36
Philosophy and religious studies	550	385	16	21	20	19	1	0	11	97	461	323	32	21	14	14	0	2	4	65
Physical sciences and science technologies	3,646	1,814	59	93	148	148	0	11	31	1,490	3,873	1,829	75	121	158	157	1	11	35	1,644
Precision production	0	0	0	0	0	0	0	0	0	0	0	0	0	0	0	0	0	0	0	0
Psychology	1,628	1,223	91	104	76	75	1	12	21	101	1,680	1,255	104	112	67	65	2	8	24	110
Public administration and social services	351	195	45	13	17	16	1	0	2	79	346	181	76	16	7	7	0	2	4	60
Social sciences and history	2,461	1,454	88	107	81	79	2	14	22	695	2,494	1,417	100	115	93	92	1	9	10	750
Social sciences	1,908	1,037	67	78	62	61	1	7	18	639	1,901	991	75	74	76	76	0	7	8	670
History	553	417	21	29	19	18	1	7	4	56	593	426	25	41	17	16	1	2	2	80
Theology and religious vocations	1,592	915	183	48	95	93	2	7	11	329	1,522	853	232	48	96	95	1	2	11	280
Transportation and materials moving	1	1	0	0	0	0	0	0	0	0	6	5	0	0	0	0	0	1	0	0
Visual and performing arts	850	588	20	51	33	32	1	1	11	146	869	617	24	45	22	22	0	0	8	153
Other and not classified	0	0	0	0	0	0	0	0	0	0	0	0	0	0	0	0	0	0	0	0

[1]Excludes "Construction trades" and "Mechanic and repair technologies/technicians," which are listed separately.

NOTE: Data are for postsecondary institutions participating in Title IV federal financial aid programs. Race categories exclude persons of Hispanic ethnicity. Reported racial/ethnic distributions of students by level of degree, field of degree, and sex were used to estimate race/ethnicity for students whose race/ethnicity was not reported. To facilitate trend comparisons, certain aggregations have been made of the degree fields as reported in the Integrated Postsecondary Education Data System

(IPEDS). "Agriculture and natural resources" includes Agriculture, agriculture operations, and related sciences and Natural resources and conservation; and "Business" includes Business management, marketing, and related support services and Personal and culinary services. Some data have been revised from previously published figures.
SOURCE: U.S. Department of Education, National Center for Education Statistics, Integrated Postsecondary Education Data System (IPEDS), Fall 2013 and Fall 2014, Completions component. (This table was prepared September 2015.)

Table 324.35. Doctor's degrees conferred to females by postsecondary institutions, by race/ethnicity and field of study: 2012–13 and 2013–14

Field of study	2012–13										2013–14									
					Asian/Pacific Islander			American Indian/ Alaska Native	Two or more races	Non-resident alien					Asian/Pacific Islander			American Indian/ Alaska Native	Two or more races	Non-resident alien
	Total	White	Black	Hispanic	Total	Asian	Pacific Islander				Total	White	Black	Hispanic	Total	Asian	Pacific Islander			
1	2	3	4	5	6	7	8	9	10	11	12	13	14	15	16	17	18	19	20	21
All fields, total	**89,946**	**56,563**	**7,775**	**5,635**	**10,216**	**10,011**	**205**	**500**	**1,355**	**7,902**	**91,993**	**56,779**	**8,106**	**5,877**	**10,848**	**10,673**	**175**	**496**	**1,669**	**8,218**
Agriculture and natural resources	644	322	27	30	15	15	0	3	3	244	668	323	21	22	29	29	0	2	4	267
Architecture and related services	113	45	4	2	19	19	0	0	6	37	113	35	12	6	11	10	1	0	3	46
Area, ethnic, cultural, gender, and group studies	166	82	21	19	15	15	0	7	2	20	206	88	39	15	17	17	0	6	7	34
Biological and biomedical sciences	4,250	2,219	206	232	433	428	5	17	43	1,100	4,418	2,342	195	199	420	410	10	14	60	1,188
Business	1,223	549	271	56	86	84	2	6	11	244	1,317	583	316	53	78	77	1	5	9	273
Communication, journalism, and related programs	366	208	31	17	20	20	0	1	4	85	345	195	21	26	13	13	0	1	3	86
Communications technologies	0	0	0	0	0	0	0	0	0	0	2	0	1	0	1	1	0	0	0	0
Computer and information sciences	354	115	24	9	36	36	0	0	1	169	416	120	21	13	42	42	0	2	1	217
Construction trades	0	0	0	0	0	0	0	0	0	0	0	0	0	0	0	0	0	0	0	0
Education	7,154	4,412	1,446	480	309	286	23	51	63	393	7,456	4,563	1,528	569	288	278	10	46	87	375
Engineering	2,125	629	65	69	209	208	1	0	15	1,138	2,271	680	70	72	235	233	2	2	19	1,193
Engineering technologies and engineering-related fields[1]	37	12	2	1	3	3	0	0	0	19	26	15	0	0	0	0	0	1	0	10
English language and literature/letters	823	635	43	40	30	30	0	3	11	61	836	656	37	28	35	35	0	3	9	68
Family and consumer sciences/human sciences	272	136	41	8	17	17	0	2	3	65	273	154	33	7	18	18	0	2	2	59
Foreign languages, literatures, and linguistics	773	375	9	91	35	35	0	6	5	252	733	380	12	77	48	48	0	6	6	208
Health professions and related programs	37,340	24,648	2,537	1,992	6,278	6,201	77	170	518	1,197	39,364	25,629	2,709	2,027	6,912	6,834	78	176	707	1,204
Homeland security, law enforcement, and firefighting	75	48	13	2	3	3	0	0	0	9	86	63	16	3	1	1	0	0	1	2
Legal professions and studies	21,925	14,709	2,078	1,969	1,950	1,867	83	177	536	506	20,674	13,371	2,013	2,041	1,893	1,835	58	174	564	618
Liberal arts and sciences, general studies, and humanities	56	40	6	3	0	0	0	0	0	7	61	48	3	1	3	3	0	1	2	3
Library science	27	18	3	0	0	0	0	0	0	6	38	22	3	3	0	0	0	0	0	10
Mathematics and statistics	531	187	7	7	37	37	0	1	3	289	538	196	10	8	34	34	0	1	4	285
Mechanic and repair technologies/technicians	0	0	0	0	0	0	0	0	0	0	0	0	0	0	0	0	0	0	0	0
Military technologies and applied sciences	0	0	0	0	0	0	0	0	0	0	0	0	0	0	0	0	0	0	0	0
Multi/interdisciplinary studies	423	255	38	17	27	26	1	3	5	78	447	263	46	17	29	29	0	1	6	85
Parks, recreation, leisure, and fitness studies	136	102	13	1	3	3	0	2	0	15	159	113	12	8	3	3	0	0	2	21
Philosophy and religious studies	244	161	12	8	15	15	0	0	6	42	237	166	11	7	10	10	0	4	4	35
Physical sciences and science technologies	1,868	902	61	61	117	117	0	2	17	708	1,933	901	62	53	122	120	2	8	22	765
Precision production	0	0	0	0	0	0	0	0	0	0	0	0	0	0	0	0	0	0	0	0
Psychology	4,698	3,343	406	332	274	267	7	32	62	249	4,954	3,420	457	408	313	301	12	22	91	243
Public administration and social services	628	343	123	23	36	35	1	1	6	96	701	388	153	32	33	32	1	7	6	82
Social sciences and history	2,149	1,211	116	127	132	129	3	11	22	530	2,230	1,257	117	135	136	136	0	13	31	541
Social sciences	1,699	896	92	92	119	116	3	7	21	472	1,783	947	89	107	116	116	0	12	25	487
History	450	315	24	35	13	13	0	4	1	58	447	310	28	28	20	20	0	1	6	54
Theology and religious vocations	582	346	152	8	27	25	2	4	0	43	581	309	170	17	36	36	0	3	7	39
Transportation and materials moving	0	0	0	0	0	0	0	0	0	0	1	0	0	1	0	0	0	0	0	0
Visual and performing arts	964	511	20	31	90	90	0	1	11	300	909	499	18	29	88	88	0	2	12	261
Other and not classified	0	0	0	0	0	0	0	0	0	0	0	0	0	0	0	0	0	0	0	0

[1]Excludes "Construction trades" and "Mechanic and repair technologies/technicians," which are listed separately.

NOTE: Data are for postsecondary institutions participating in Title IV federal financial aid programs. Race categories exclude persons of Hispanic ethnicity. Reported racial/ethnic distributions of students by level of degree, field of degree, and sex were used to estimate race/ethnicity for students whose race/ethnicity was not reported. To facilitate trend comparisons, certain aggregations have been made of the degree fields as reported in the Integrated Postsecondary Education Data System

(IPEDS); "Agriculture and natural resources" includes Agriculture, agriculture operations, and related sciences and Natural resources and conservation; and "Business" includes Business management, marketing, and related support services and Personal and culinary services. Some data have been revised from previously published figures.

SOURCE: U.S. Department of Education, National Center for Education Statistics, Integrated Postsecondary Education Data System (IPEDS), Fall 2013 and Fall 2014, Completions component. (This table was prepared September 2015.)

Table 324.40. Number of postsecondary institutions conferring doctor's degrees in dentistry, medicine, and law, and number of such degrees conferred, by sex of student: Selected years, 1949–50 through 2013–14

Year	Dentistry (D.D.S. or D.M.D.)				Medicine (M.D.)				Law (LL.B. or J.D.)			
	Number of institutions conferring degrees	Number of degrees conferred			Number of institutions conferring degrees	Number of degrees conferred			Number of institutions conferring degrees	Number of degrees conferred		
		Total	Males	Females		Total	Males	Females		Total	Males	Females
1	2	3	4	5	6	7	8	9	10	11	12	13
1949–50	40	2,579	2,561	18	72	5,612	5,028	584	—	—	—	—
1951–52	41	2,918	2,895	23	72	6,201	5,871	330	—	—	—	—
1953–54	42	3,102	3,063	39	73	6,712	6,377	335	—	—	—	—
1955–56	42	3,009	2,975	34	73	6,810	6,464	346	131	8,262	7,974	288
1957–58	43	3,065	3,031	34	75	6,816	6,469	347	131	9,394	9,122	272
1959–60	45	3,247	3,221	26	79	7,032	6,645	387	134	9,240	9,010	230
1961–62	46	3,183	3,166	17	81	7,138	6,749	389	134	9,364	9,091	273
1963–64	46	3,180	3,168	12	82	7,303	6,878	425	133	10,679	10,372	307
1964–65	46	3,108	3,086	22	81	7,304	6,832	472	137	11,583	11,216	367
1965–66	47	3,178	3,146	32	84	7,673	7,170	503	136	13,246	12,776	470
1967–68	48	3,422	3,375	47	85	7,944	7,318	626	138	16,454	15,805	649
1968–69	—	3,408	3,376	32	—	8,025	7,415	610	—	17,053	16,373	680
1969–70	48	3,718	3,684	34	86	8,314	7,615	699	145	14,916	14,115	801
1970–71	48	3,745	3,703	42	89	8,919	8,110	809	147	17,421	16,181	1,240
1971–72	48	3,862	3,819	43	92	9,253	8,423	830	147	21,764	20,266	1,498
1972–73	51	4,047	3,992	55	97	10,307	9,388	919	152	27,205	25,037	2,168
1973–74	52	4,440	4,355	85	99	11,356	10,093	1,263	151	29,326	25,986	3,340
1974–75	52	4,773	4,627	146	104	12,447	10,818	1,629	154	29,296	24,881	4,415
1975–76	56	5,425	5,187	238	107	13,426	11,252	2,174	166	32,293	26,085	6,208
1976–77	57	5,138	4,764	374	109	13,461	10,891	2,570	169	34,104	26,447	7,657
1977–78	57	5,189	4,623	566	109	14,279	11,210	3,069	169	34,402	25,457	8,945
1978–79	58	5,434	4,794	640	109	14,786	11,381	3,405	175	35,206	25,180	10,026
1979–80	58	5,258	4,558	700	112	14,902	11,416	3,486	179	35,647	24,893	10,754
1980–81	58	5,460	4,672	788	116	15,505	11,672	3,833	176	36,331	24,563	11,768
1981–82	59	5,282	4,467	815	119	15,814	11,867	3,947	180	35,991	23,965	12,026
1982–83	59	5,585	4,631	954	118	15,484	11,350	4,134	177	36,853	23,550	13,303
1983–84	60	5,353	4,302	1,051	119	15,813	11,359	4,454	179	37,012	23,382	13,630
1984–85	59	5,339	4,233	1,106	120	16,041	11,167	4,874	181	37,491	23,070	14,421
1985–86	59	5,046	3,907	1,139	120	15,938	11,022	4,916	181	35,844	21,874	13,970
1986–87	58	4,741	3,603	1,138	121	15,428	10,431	4,997	179	36,056	21,561	14,495
1987–88	57	4,477	3,300	1,177	122	15,358	10,278	5,080	180	35,397	21,067	14,330
1988–89	58	4,265	3,124	1,141	124	15,460	10,310	5,150	182	35,634	21,069	14,565
1989–90	57	4,100	2,834	1,266	124	15,075	9,923	5,152	182	36,485	21,079	15,406
1990–91	55	3,699	2,510	1,189	121	15,043	9,629	5,414	179	37,945	21,643	16,302
1991–92	52	3,593	2,431	1,162	120	15,243	9,796	5,447	177	38,848	22,260	16,588
1992–93	55	3,605	2,383	1,222	122	15,531	9,679	5,852	184	40,302	23,182	17,120
1993–94	53	3,787	2,330	1,457	121	15,368	9,544	5,824	185	40,044	22,826	17,218
1994–95	53	3,897	2,480	1,417	119	15,537	9,507	6,030	183	39,349	22,592	16,757
1995–96	53	3,697	2,374	1,323	119	15,341	9,061	6,280	183	39,828	22,508	17,320
1996–97	52	3,784	2,387	1,397	118	15,571	9,121	6,450	184	40,079	22,548	17,531
1997–98	53	4,032	2,490	1,542	117	15,424	9,006	6,418	185	39,331	21,876	17,455
1998–99	53	4,143	2,673	1,470	118	15,566	8,972	6,594	185	38,297	21,102	17,195
1999–2000	54	4,250	2,547	1,703	118	15,286	8,761	6,525	190	38,152	20,638	17,514
2000–01	54	4,391	2,696	1,695	118	15,403	8,728	6,675	192	37,904	19,981	17,923
2001–02	53	4,239	2,608	1,631	118	15,237	8,469	6,768	192	38,981	20,254	18,727
2002–03	53	4,345	2,654	1,691	118	15,034	8,221	6,813	194	39,067	19,916	19,151
2003–04	53	4,335	2,532	1,803	118	15,442	8,273	7,169	195	40,209	20,332	19,877
2004–05	53	4,454	2,505	1,949	120	15,461	8,151	7,310	198	43,423	22,297	21,126
2005–06	54	4,389	2,435	1,954	119	15,455	7,900	7,555	197	43,440	22,597	20,843
2006–07	55	4,596	2,548	2,048	120	15,730	7,987	7,743	200	43,486	22,777	20,709
2007–08	55	4,795	2,661	2,134	120	15,646	7,935	7,711	201	43,769	23,197	20,572
2008–09	55	4,918	2,637	2,281	120	15,987	8,164	7,823	203	44,045	23,860	20,185
2009–10	55	5,062	2,745	2,317	120	16,356	8,468	7,888	205	44,346	23,384	20,962
2010–11	55	5,071	2,764	2,307	120	16,863	8,701	8,162	206	44,421	23,481	20,940
2011–12	55	5,109	2,748	2,361	120	16,927	8,809	8,118	207	46,445	24,576	21,869
2012–13	56	5,219	2,707	2,512	122	17,264	8,976	8,288	209	46,811	25,087	21,724
2013–14	57	5,407	2,839	2,568	124	17,606	9,234	8,372	210	43,772	23,278	20,494

—Not available.

NOTE: Data are for postsecondary institutions participating in Title IV federal financial aid programs. Some data have been revised from previously published figures.
SOURCE: U.S. Department of Education, National Center for Education Statistics, *Earned Degrees Conferred*, 1949–50 through 1964–65; Higher Education General Information Survey (HEGIS), "Degrees and Other Formal Awards Conferred" surveys, 1965–66 through 1985–86; Integrated Postsecondary Education Data System (IPEDS), "Completions Survey" (IPEDS-C:87–99); and IPEDS Fall 2000 through Fall 2014, Completions component. (This table was prepared April 2016.)

Table 324.50. Degrees conferred by postsecondary institutions in selected professional fields, by sex of student, control of institution, and field of study: Selected years, 1985–86 through 2013–14

Control of institution and field of study	1985-86	1990-91	1995-96	2000-01	2003-04	2004-05	2005-06	2006-07	2007-08	2008-09	2009-10	2010-11	2011-12			2012-13			2013-14		
													Total	Males	Females	Total	Males	Females	Total	Males	Females
1	2	3	4	5	6	7	8	9	10	11	12	13	14	15	16	17	18	19	20	21	22
Total, all institutions	73,910	71,948	76,734	79,707	83,041	87,289	87,655	90,064	91,394	92,173	94,453	95,980	98,998	50,391	48,607	100,729	51,579	49,150	99,404	50,562	48,842
Dentistry (D.D.S. or D.M.D.)	5,046	3,699	3,697	4,391	4,335	4,454	4,389	4,596	4,795	4,918	5,062	5,071	5,109	2,748	2,361	5,219	2,707	2,512	5,407	2,839	2,568
Medicine (M.D.)	15,938	15,043	15,341	15,403	15,442	15,461	15,455	15,730	15,646	15,987	16,356	16,863	16,927	8,809	8,118	17,264	8,976	8,288	17,606	9,234	8,372
Optometry (O.D.)	1,029	1,115	1,231	1,289	1,275	1,252	1,198	1,311	1,304	1,338	1,335	1,322	1,361	476	885	1,521	557	964	1,523	535	988
Osteopathic medicine (D.O.)	1,547	1,459	1,895	2,450	2,722	2,762	2,718	2,992	3,232	3,665	3,890	4,141	4,336	2,283	2,053	4,691	2,489	2,202	4,990	2,662	2,328
Pharmacy (Pharm.D.)	903	1,244	2,555	6,324	8,221	8,885	9,292	10,439	10,932	11,291	11,873	12,271	12,943	4,971	7,972	13,374	5,141	8,233	13,921	5,429	8,492
Podiatry (Pod.D. or D.P.) or podiatric medicine (D.P.M.)	612	589	650	528	382	343	347	331	555	431	491	543	535	342	193	471	296	175	567	338	229
Veterinary medicine (D.V.M.)	2,270	2,032	2,109	2,248	2,228	2,354	2,370	2,443	2,504	2,377	2,478	2,564	2,616	588	2,028	2,610	593	2,017	2,686	565	2,121
Chiropractic (D.C. or D.C.M.)	3,395	2,640	3,379	3,796	2,730	2,560	2,564	2,525	2,639	2,512	2,601	2,694	2,496	1,538	958	2,219	1,363	856	2,420	1,464	956
Law (LL.B. or J.D.)	35,844	37,945	39,828	37,904	40,209	43,423	43,440	43,486	43,769	44,045	44,346	44,421	46,445	24,576	21,869	46,811	25,087	21,724	43,772	23,278	20,494
Theology (M. Div, M.H.L., B.D., or Ord. and M.H.L./Rav., B.D., or Ord.)	7,283	5,695	5,879	5,026	5,332	5,533	5,666	5,990	5,751	5,367	5,696	5,832	5,931	3,998	1,933	6,276	4,322	1,954	6,218	4,145	2,073
Other[1]	43	487	170	348	165	262	216	221	267	242	325	258	299	62	237	273	48	225	294	73	221
Total, public institutions	29,568	29,554	29,882	32,633	34,499	35,768	36,269	36,855	37,278	37,357	38,132	39,071	39,776	19,589	20,187	39,774	19,598	20,176	40,376	19,963	20,413
Dentistry (D.D.S. or D.M.D.)	2,827	2,308	2,198	2,477	2,498	2,577	2,669	2,769	2,760	2,870	2,984	3,008	3,053	1,708	1,345	2,972	1,582	1,390	3,187	1,688	1,499
Medicine (M.D.)	9,991	9,364	9,370	9,408	9,418	9,536	9,650	9,733	9,646	9,795	10,043	10,577	10,626	5,591	5,035	10,654	5,593	5,061	11,077	5,906	5,171
Optometry (O.D.)	441	477	499	497	476	477	462	518	492	517	507	515	508	178	330	520	189	331	514	194	320
Osteopathic medicine (D.O.)	486	493	528	562	586	568	585	637	634	679	817	856	841	442	399	854	441	413	1,024	507	517
Pharmacy (Pharm.D.)	473	808	1,557	3,876	4,930	5,352	5,523	5,903	6,218	6,395	6,587	6,888	6,919	2,679	4,240	6,897	2,596	4,301	6,933	2,720	4,213
Podiatry (Pod.D. or D.P.) or podiatric medicine (D.P.M.)	0	0	0	84	64	64	65	66	73	68	85	87	204	128	76	105	72	33	202	125	77
Veterinary medicine (D.V.M.)	1,931	1,814	1,889	2,017	1,912	2,033	2,048	2,116	2,123	1,968	2,048	2,134	2,168	493	1,675	2,184	495	1,689	2,251	481	1,770
Chiropractic (D.C. or D.C.M.)	0	0	0	0	0	0	0	0	0	0	0	0	0	0	0	0	0	0	0	0	0
Law (LL.B. or J.D.)	13,419	14,290	13,841	13,712	14,615	15,161	15,267	15,113	15,332	15,065	15,061	15,006	15,457	8,370	7,087	15,588	8,630	6,958	15,188	8,342	6,846
Theology (M. Div, M.H.L., B.D., or Ord. and M.H.L./Rav., B.D., or Ord.)	0	0	0	0	0	0	0	0	0	0	0	0	0	0	0	0	0	0	0	0	0
Other[1]	0	0	0	0	0	0	0	0	0	0	0	0	0	0	0	0	0	0	0	0	0
Total, private institutions	44,342	42,394	46,852	47,074	48,542	51,521	51,386	53,209	54,116	54,816	56,321	56,909	59,222	30,802	28,420	60,955	31,981	28,974	59,028	30,599	28,429
Dentistry (D.D.S. or D.M.D.)	2,219	1,391	1,499	1,914	1,837	1,877	1,720	1,827	2,035	2,048	2,078	2,063	2,056	1,040	1,016	2,247	1,125	1,122	2,220	1,151	1,069
Medicine (M.D.)	5,947	5,679	5,971	5,995	6,024	5,925	5,805	5,997	6,000	6,192	6,313	6,286	6,301	3,218	3,083	6,610	3,383	3,227	6,529	3,328	3,201
Optometry (O.D.)	588	638	732	792	799	775	736	793	812	821	828	807	853	298	555	1,001	368	633	1,009	341	668
Osteopathic medicine (D.O.)	1,061	966	1,367	1,888	2,136	2,194	2,133	2,355	2,598	2,986	3,073	3,285	3,495	1,841	1,654	3,837	2,048	1,789	3,966	2,155	1,811
Pharmacy (Pharm.D.)	430	436	998	2,448	3,291	3,533	3,769	4,536	4,714	4,896	5,286	5,383	6,024	2,292	3,732	6,477	2,545	3,932	6,988	2,709	4,279
Podiatry (Pod.D. or D.P.) or podiatric medicine (D.P.M.)	612	589	650	444	318	279	282	265	482	363	406	456	331	214	117	366	224	142	365	213	152
Veterinary medicine (D.V.M.)	339	218	220	231	316	321	322	327	381	409	430	430	448	95	353	426	98	328	435	84	351
Chiropractic (D.C. or D.C.M.)	3,395	2,640	3,379	3,796	2,730	2,560	2,564	2,525	2,639	2,512	2,601	2,694	2,496	1,538	958	2,219	1,363	856	2,420	1,464	956
Law (LL.B. or J.D.)	22,425	23,655	25,987	24,192	25,594	28,262	28,173	28,373	28,437	28,980	29,285	29,415	30,988	16,206	14,782	31,223	16,457	14,766	28,584	14,936	13,648
Theology (M. Div, M.H.L., B.D., or Ord. and M.H.L./Rav., B.D., or Ord.)	7,283	5,695	5,879	5,026	5,332	5,533	5,666	5,990	5,751	5,367	5,696	5,832	5,931	3,998	1,933	6,276	4,322	1,954	6,218	4,145	2,073
Other[1]	43	487	170	348	165	262	216	221	267	242	325	258	299	62	237	273	48	225	294	73	221

[1] Includes naturopathic medicine and degrees that were not classified by field by the reporting institution.

NOTE: Data are for postsecondary institutions participating in Title IV federal financial aid programs. Includes degrees that require at least 6 years of college work for completion (including at least 2 years of preprofessional training). Some data have been revised from previously published figures.

SOURCE: U.S. Department of Education, National Center for Education Statistics, Higher Education General Information Survey (HEGIS), "Degrees and Other Formal Awards Conferred," 1985–86; Integrated Postsecondary Education Data System (IPEDS), "Completions Survey" (IPEDS-C:91–99); and IPEDS Fall 2000 through Fall 2014, Completions component. (This table was prepared May 2016.)

Table 324.55. Degrees conferred by postsecondary institutions in selected professional fields, by race/ethnicity and field of study: 2012–13 and 2013–14

Field of study	2012–13				Asian/Pacific Islander			American Indian/Alaska Native	Two or more races	Non-resident alien	2013–14				Asian/Pacific Islander			American Indian/Alaska Native	Two or more races	Non-resident alien
	Total	White	Black	Hispanic	Total	Asian	Pacific Islander				Total	White	Black	Hispanic	Total	Asian	Pacific Islander			
1	2	3	4	5	6	7	8	9	10	11	12	13	14	15	16	17	18	19	20	21
All fields, total	100,729	68,417	7,219	6,606	13,747	13,463	284	540	1,737	2,463	99,404	65,909	7,256	6,820	14,267	14,069	198	528	2,014	2,610
Dentistry (D.D.S. or D.M.D.)	5,219	3,066	227	313	1,114	1,103	11	25	41	433	5,407	3,129	259	365	1,168	1,152	16	16	71	399
Medicine (M.D.)	17,264	10,887	1,096	1,067	3,632	3,606	26	71	275	236	17,606	10,761	1,161	1,127	3,888	3,859	29	73	340	256
Optometry (O.D.)	1,521	872	35	61	437	434	3	5	18	93	1,523	822	36	59	448	448	0	7	34	117
Osteopathic medicine (D.O.)	4,691	3,387	116	148	887	876	11	20	105	28	4,990	3,534	125	153	1,030	1,022	8	22	109	17
Pharmacy (Pharm.D.)	13,374	7,921	1,014	576	3,296	3,250	46	44	148	375	13,921	8,121	1,016	611	3,561	3,537	24	50	204	358
Podiatry (Pod.D. or D.P.) or podiatric medicine (D.P.M.)	471	289	15	26	106	104	2	13	10	12	567	348	19	41	118	117	1	9	18	14
Veterinary medicine (D.V.M.)	2,610	2,134	67	273	74	74	0	11	40	11	2,686	2,258	51	170	135	132	3	9	50	13
Chiropractic (D.C. or D.C.M.)	2,219	1,755	75	115	174	163	11	16	26	58	2,420	1,923	97	136	166	158	8	12	25	61
Law (LL.B. or J.D.)	46,811	33,816	3,449	3,783	3,611	3,457	154	308	990	854	43,772	30,965	3,219	3,887	3,332	3,236	96	299	1,081	989
Theology (M.Div, M.H.L./Rav, B.D., or Ord.)	6,276	4,093	1,109	237	387	367	20	26	72	352	6,218	3,844	1,252	260	398	385	13	29	65	370
Other[1]	273	197	16	7	29	29	0	1	12	11	294	204	21	11	23	23	0	2	17	16

[1]Includes naturopathic medicine and degrees that were not classified by field by the reporting institution.
NOTE: Data are for postsecondary institutions participating in Title IV federal financial aid programs. Includes degrees that require at least 6 years of college work for completion (including at least 2 years of preprofessional training). Race categories exclude persons of Hispanic ethnicity. Reported racial/ethnic distributions of students by level of degree, field of degree, and sex were used to estimate race/ethnicity for students whose race/ethnicity was not reported. Some data have been revised from previously published figures.
SOURCE: U.S. Department of Education, National Center for Education Statistics, Integrated Postsecondary Education Data System (IPEDS), Fall 2013 and Fall 2014, Completions component. (This table was prepared May 2016.)

Table 324.60. Degrees conferred to males by postsecondary institutions in selected professional fields, by race/ethnicity and field of study: 2012–13 and 2013–14

Field of study	2012–13				Asian/Pacific Islander			American Indian/Alaska Native	Two or more races	Non-resident alien	2013–14				Asian/Pacific Islander			American Indian/Alaska Native	Two or more races	Non-resident alien
	Total	White	Black	Hispanic	Total	Asian	Pacific Islander				Total	White	Black	Hispanic	Total	Asian	Pacific Islander			
1	2	3	4	5	6	7	8	9	10	11	12	13	14	15	16	17	18	19	20	21
All fields, total	51,579	36,971	2,910	3,108	6,284	6,137	147	259	788	1,259	50,562	35,485	2,940	3,297	6,343	6,246	97	232	926	1,339
Dentistry (D.D.S. or D.M.D.)	2,707	1,783	97	129	472	468	4	11	18	197	2,839	1,859	98	171	492	483	9	10	27	182
Medicine (M.D.)	8,976	6,003	383	510	1,809	1,795	14	36	120	115	9,234	5,949	427	572	1,953	1,936	17	32	167	134
Optometry (O.D.)	557	362	11	17	127	126	2	2	5	33	535	352	12	17	103	103	0	4	11	36
Osteopathic medicine (D.O.)	2,489	1,837	44	78	454	449	5	10	49	17	2,662	1,965	46	78	509	506	3	12	43	9
Pharmacy (Pharm.D.)	5,141	3,094	371	223	1,210	1,186	24	19	63	161	5,429	3,215	410	256	1,313	1,302	11	16	75	144
Podiatry (Pod.D. or D.P.) or podiatric medicine (D.P.M.)	296	197	5	11	65	63	2	7	3	8	338	224	6	25	62	61	1	2	9	10
Veterinary medicine (D.V.M.)	593	487	17	60	18	18	0	2	6	3	565	476	8	40	27	26	1	3	9	2
Chiropractic (D.C. or D.C.M.)	1,363	1,100	26	64	118	113	5	11	13	31	1,464	1,176	43	77	107	103	4	6	16	39
Law (LL.B. or J.D.)	25,087	19,160	1,380	1,840	1,689	1,614	75	141	465	412	23,278	17,589	1,253	1,863	1,460	1,417	43	131	526	456
Theology (M.Div, M.H.L./Rav, B.D., or Ord.)	4,322	2,911	574	175	318	301	17	20	43	281	4,145	2,626	633	194	312	304	8	16	38	326
Other[1]	48	37	2	1	4	4	0	0	3	1	73	54	4	1	5	5	0	0	5	1

[1]Includes naturopathic medicine and degrees that were not classified by field by the reporting institution.
NOTE: Data are for postsecondary institutions participating in Title IV federal financial aid programs. Includes degrees that require at least 6 years of college work for completion (including at least 2 years of preprofessional training). Race categories exclude persons of Hispanic ethnicity. Reported racial/ethnic distributions of students by level of degree, field of degree, and sex were used to estimate race/ethnicity for students whose race/ethnicity was not reported. Some data have been revised from previously published figures.
SOURCE: U.S. Department of Education, National Center for Education Statistics, Integrated Postsecondary Education Data System (IPEDS), Fall 2013 and Fall 2014, Completions component. (This table was prepared May 2016.)

Table 324.70. Degrees conferred to females by postsecondary institutions in selected professional fields, by race/ethnicity and field of study: 2012–13 and 2013–14

Field of study	2012–13										2013–14									
					Asian/Pacific Islander			American Indian/ Alaska Native	Two or more races	Non-resident alien					Asian/Pacific Islander			American Indian/ Alaska Native	Two or more races	Non-resident alien
	Total	White	Black	Hispanic	Total	Asian	Pacific Islander				Total	White	Black	Hispanic	Total	Asian	Pacific Islander			
1	2	3	4	5	6	7	8	9	10	11	12	13	14	15	16	17	18	19	20	21
All fields, total	**49,150**	**31,446**	**4,309**	**3,498**	**7,463**	**7,326**	**137**	**281**	**949**	**1,204**	**48,842**	**30,424**	**4,316**	**3,523**	**7,924**	**7,823**	**101**	**296**	**1,088**	**1,271**
Dentistry (D.D.S. or D.M.D.)	2,512	1,283	130	184	642	635	7	14	23	236	2,568	1,270	161	194	676	669	7	6	44	217
Medicine (M.D.)	8,288	4,884	713	557	1,823	1,811	12	35	155	121	8,372	4,812	734	555	1,935	1,923	12	41	173	122
Optometry (O.D.)	964	510	24	44	310	308	2	3	13	60	988	470	24	42	345	345	0	3	23	81
Osteopathic medicine (D.O.)	2,202	1,550	72	70	433	427	6	10	56	11	2,328	1,569	79	75	521	516	5	10	66	8
Pharmacy (Pharm.D.)	8,233	4,827	643	353	2,086	2,064	22	25	85	214	8,492	4,906	606	355	2,248	2,235	13	34	129	214
Podiatry (Pod.D. or D.P) or podiatric medicine (D.P.M.)	175	92	10	15	41	41	0	6	7	4	229	124	13	16	56	56	0	7	9	4
Veterinary medicine (D.V.M.)	2,017	1,647	50	213	56	56	0	9	34	8	2,121	1,782	43	130	108	106	2	6	41	11
Chiropractic (D.C. or D.C.M.)	856	655	49	51	56	50	6	5	13	27	956	747	54	59	59	55	4	6	9	22
Law (LL.B. or J.D.)	21,724	14,656	2,069	1,943	1,922	1,843	79	167	525	442	20,494	13,376	1,966	2,024	1,872	1,819	53	168	555	533
Theology (M.Div, M.H.L./Rav., B.D., or Ord.)	1,954	1,182	535	62	69	66	3	6	29	71	2,073	1,218	619	66	86	81	5	13	27	44
Other[1]	225	160	14	6	25	25	0	1	9	10	221	150	17	7	18	18	0	2	12	15

[1]Includes naturopathic medicine and degrees that were not classified by field by the reporting institution.
NOTE: Data are for postsecondary institutions participating in Title IV federal financial aid programs. Includes degrees that require at least 6 years of college work for completion (including at least 2 years of preprofessional training). Race categories exclude persons of Hispanic ethnicity. Reported racial/ethnic distributions of students by level of degree, field of degree, and sex were used to estimate race/ethnicity for students whose race/ethnicity was not reported. Some data have been revised from previously published figures.
SOURCE: U.S. Department of Education, National Center for Education Statistics, Integrated Postsecondary Education Data System (IPEDS), Fall 2013 and Fall 2014, Completions component. (This table was prepared May 2016.)

Table 324.80. Statistical profile of persons receiving doctor's degrees, by field of study and selected characteristics: 2012–13 and 2013–14

Selected characteristic	Field of study, 2012–13								
	All fields	Education	Engineering	Humanities	Life sciences	Physical sciences, mathematics, and computer science[1] Total	Mathematics	Social sciences and psychology	Other fields
1	2	3	4	5	6	7	8	9	10
Number of doctor's degrees conferred	52,760	4,944	8,963	5,662	12,305	9,290	1,817	8,401	3,195
Sex (percent)[2]									
Male	53.7	31.9	77.1	48.7	44.7	70.9	71.0	40.7	50.2
Female	46.2	68.1	22.9	51.2	55.3	29.0	29.0	59.3	49.7
Race/ethnicity (percent)[3]									
White	72.9	69.8	68.9	78.4	71.6	77.1	74.9	72.5	70.7
Black	6.4	12.5	4.6	3.7	6.2	2.9	3.0	7.3	9.3
Hispanic	6.3	6.5	5.1	7.4	6.6	4.6	3.9	7.0	5.8
Asian	8.5	5.4	15.1	4.3	10.5	9.6	12.4	6.1	8.8
American Indian/Alaska Native	0.4	0.6	0.1	0.5	0.4	0.1	0.0	0.4	0.2
Two or more races	2.5	2.0	2.3	2.5	2.5	2.5	2.3	3.0	2.2
Other and unknown[4]	3.1	3.3	3.9	3.1	2.2	3.1	3.6	3.6	2.9
Citizenship (percent)									
U.S. citizen/permanent resident	64.3	83.3	41.7	79.8	68.6	52.4	47.9	75.0	61.3
Temporary visa holder	29.7	10.4	52.8	13.3	25.8	42.1	46.4	19.3	30.5
Unknown	6.0	6.3	5.5	6.9	5.7	5.5	5.7	5.7	8.2
Median age at doctorate (years)	31.8	38.8	30.1	34.2	31.1	29.9	29.5	32.4	34.9
Percent with bachelor's degree in same field as doctorate	54.9	25.1	76.5	51.4	50.1	67.4	71.8	52.2	36.0
Median time lapse to doctorate (years)									
Since bachelor's degree completion	9.0	15.0	7.3	11.0	8.4	7.3	7.0	9.4	11.6
Since starting graduate school	7.5	11.7	6.6	9.2	6.9	6.5	6.2	7.7	9.3
Postdoctoral plans (percent)[5]									
Definite postdoctoral study[6]	23.9	5.0	20.4	8.1	36.6	34.7	31.9	24.4	5.3
Fellowship	12.4	2.3	6.4	6.6	20.7	14.5	17.0	16.8	3.0
Research associateship	10.8	2.4	13.6	1.3	14.7	19.6	14.5	6.2	2.0
Other[7]	0.7	0.3	0.4	0.3	1.1	0.6	0.3	1.4	0.2
Definite postdoctoral employment[8]	36.8	58.5	37.3	43.5	20.4	30.1	35.8	43.0	62.5
Postsecondary educational institution[9]	19.1	34.8	6.3	36.0	9.6	9.7	18.9	26.7	50.4
Government	2.9	2.0	3.6	1.2	2.6	1.9	1.6	5.3	2.9
Industry, business	10.6	2.6	26.1	2.0	5.7	17.4	14.0	5.9	5.0
Nonprofit organization	2.0	3.0	1.0	2.2	1.9	0.7	0.9	3.6	3.1
Other and unknown[10]	2.2	16.0	0.3	2.2	0.6	0.5	0.5	1.5	1.1
Seeking employment or study	34.9	32.8	38.0	44.7	36.0	32.2	28.9	29.8	29.0
Other/unknown	4.3	3.7	4.3	3.6	7.0	3.0	3.5	2.7	3.2
Primary work activity after doctorate (percent)[11]									
Research and development	41.7	12.4	74.8	9.4	43.5	65.4	48.5	37.9	35.8
Teaching	35.7	43.5	7.6	76.8	28.4	22.3	41.2	38.0	48.4
Management or administration	11.3	33.0	6.0	7.4	12.6	3.4	1.6	7.9	9.8
Professional services	9.6	10.5	8.7	4.6	13.0	6.8	7.6	15.2	5.3
Other	1.7	0.7	3.0	1.7	2.5	2.1	1.1	1.0	0.7
Location after doctorate (percent)[12]									
New England	8.3	4.1	8.0	9.3	9.3	9.3	8.3	8.9	5.8
Middle Atlantic	12.6	9.8	10.8	17.2	12.5	12.7	14.6	13.5	12.6
East North Central	12.3	15.3	11.4	13.4	11.2	11.4	15.0	12.5	14.9
West North Central	5.4	9.1	3.7	5.8	6.7	3.2	4.2	5.3	5.6
South Atlantic	16.3	21.1	13.0	15.4	18.4	12.7	13.2	18.3	17.3
East South Central	3.8	8.6	2.8	4.7	3.7	2.3	2.6	3.4	4.2
West South Central	7.6	9.9	8.7	7.5	7.0	6.3	5.6	7.0	9.2
Mountain	5.5	8.2	6.0	5.3	4.7	5.8	4.1	4.3	5.6
Pacific and insular	17.0	8.9	23.7	11.3	17.2	23.5	15.2	13.4	9.2
Foreign	10.8	4.7	11.6	9.9	8.8	12.5	16.8	13.0	15.0
Region unknown	0.1	0.2	0.1	0.1	0.1	0.1	0.1	0.1	0.2

See notes at end of table.

Table 324.80. Statistical profile of persons receiving doctor's degrees, by field of study and selected characteristics: 2012–13 and 2013–14—Continued

Selected characteristic	All fields	Education	Engineering	Humanities	Life sciences	Physical sciences, mathematics, and computer science[1] Total	Mathematics	Social sciences and psychology	Other fields
1	11	12	13	14	15	16	17	18	19
Number of doctor's degrees conferred	54,070	4,793	9,568	5,486	12,504	9,859	1,879	8,657	3,203
Sex (percent)[2]									
Male	53.7	30.6	76.8	49.2	43.7	71.0	71.1	40.2	49.5
Female	46.0	69.2	22.8	50.8	56.0	28.6	28.5	59.5	50.1
Race/ethnicity (percent)[3]									
White	73.0	69.0	69.5	79.1	72.2	75.5	77.6	73.9	68.8
Black	6.4	13.3	4.1	3.8	5.9	3.5	4.0	6.7	11.2
Hispanic	6.5	6.5	6.0	7.2	6.3	5.4	4.1	7.2	6.2
Asian	8.5	5.0	14.3	4.3	10.3	9.8	9.3	6.3	8.2
American Indian/Alaska Native	0.3	0.5	0.1	0.4	0.2	0.3	0.2	0.4	0.1
Two or more races[4]	2.6	2.3	2.6	2.7	2.7	2.5	1.8	2.7	2.0
Other and unknown[4]	2.8	3.4	3.4	2.5	2.2	3.0	3.0	2.8	3.5
Citizenship (percent)									
U.S. citizen/permanent resident	62.9	82.0	42.1	79.5	67.5	51.3	49.7	72.4	59.9
Temporary visa holder	29.3	10.0	51.6	12.9	25.2	41.5	43.6	17.9	29.0
Unknown	7.8	8.0	6.3	7.7	7.3	7.1	6.7	9.7	11.1
Median age at doctorate (years)	31.6	38.3	30.0	34.2	31.0	29.9	29.5	32.5	35.1
Percent with bachelor's degree in same field as									
doctorate	54.7	24.6	76.3	52.4	50.6	64.3	70.9	50.9	36.4
Median time lapse to doctorate (years)									
Since bachelor's degree completion	8.8	14.7	7.3	11.0	8.3	7.3	7.0	9.4	11.5
Since starting graduate school	7.3	11.7	6.5	9.2	6.7	6.5	6.3	7.8	9.2
Postdoctoral plans (percent)[5]									
Definite postdoctoral study[6]	23.4	5.1	18.6	9.6	36.5	31.6	32.0	24.3	4.9
Fellowship	12.5	2.6	6.2	8.0	21.0	13.1	17.0	17.7	2.9
Research associateship	10.3	2.2	12.2	1.5	14.6	18.0	14.5	5.5	1.8
Other[7]	0.6	0.3	0.3	0.1	0.9	0.6	0.5	1.1	0.2
Definite postdoctoral employment[8]	35.9	56.8	36.5	41.9	19.7	30.9	33.9	42.4	60.4
Postsecondary educational institution[9]	18.2	34.1	6.6	34.9	9.4	9.4	17.4	26.0	47.8
Government	2.8	2.9	3.8	0.9	2.2	1.9	1.7	4.8	2.9
Industry, business	11.1	2.1	25.1	1.8	5.8	18.5	13.3	6.7	6.2
Nonprofit organization	1.9	2.6	0.8	2.3	1.8	0.7	0.7	3.5	2.7
Other and unknown[10]	1.9	15.0	0.2	1.9	0.4	0.5	0.7	1.4	0.8
Seeking employment or study	35.9	34.3	40.1	44.1	36.6	33.6	30.6	29.9	30.4
Other/unknown	4.8	3.8	4.8	4.4	7.2	3.8	3.6	3.4	4.3
Primary work activity after doctorate (percent)[11]									
Research and development	42.4	11.3	72.6	9.9	45.3	66.3	52.6	36.9	35.0
Teaching	34.7	44.3	8.8	75.5	29.2	20.1	38.5	37.5	47.1
Management or administration	10.8	32.2	5.1	8.4	10.6	3.3	‡	9.2	10.5
Professional services	10.0	10.9	10.1	5.0	12.5	7.4	5.3	15.2	6.0
Other	2.1	1.3	3.5	1.3	2.4	2.8	‡	1.2	1.3
Location after doctorate (percent)[12]									
New England	8.3	4.7	8.0	8.7	9.9	8.7	8.9	8.6	5.4
Middle Atlantic	12.5	10.4	9.5	17.2	12.1	11.9	15.0	14.8	13.0
East North Central	11.8	15.0	12.3	13.0	11.0	10.4	13.8	10.6	14.7
West North Central	5.3	7.4	3.7	6.0	6.5	4.1	7.0	5.3	5.4
South Atlantic	16.3	20.0	13.5	14.2	18.1	12.6	13.0	19.3	18.1
East South Central	3.8	8.2	3.3	4.3	3.7	2.0	2.1	3.4	5.1
West South Central	8.0	11.0	8.7	7.7	7.3	7.0	6.8	7.1	9.8
Mountain	5.2	7.5	5.7	4.5	4.5	5.4	4.9	4.3	5.5
Pacific and insular	18.0	10.1	24.5	12.5	18.1	24.8	13.0	13.2	11.1
Foreign	10.6	5.4	10.4	11.6	8.4	12.5	15.2	13.0	11.6
Region unknown	0.2	0.2	0.2	0.2	0.2	0.2	0.3	0.1	0.2

‡Reporting standards not met (too few cases).
[1]Includes mathematics, computer science, physics and astronomy, chemistry, and earth, atmospheric, and marine sciences.
[2]Distribution based on respondents reporting sex data.
[3]Distribution based on U.S. citizens and permanent residents.
[4]Includes Native Hawaiians and other Pacific Islanders.
[5]Percentages are based on only those doctorate recipients who responded to questions about postgraduation plans.
[6]Percentages are based on only those doctorate recipients who indicated definite postgraduation plans for study and who indicated the type of study.
[7]Includes respondents who indicated definite postgraduation study plans for traineeship, internship/clinical residency, or other study.
[8]Percentages are based on only those doctorate recipients who indicated definite postgraduation plans for employment and who indicated the sector of employment.
[9]Includes 2-year, 4-year, and foreign colleges and universities, and medical schools.
[10]Other is mainly composed of elementary and secondary schools.
[11]Percentages are based on only those doctorate recipients who indicated definite postgraduation plans for employment and who indicated their primary work activity.

[12]Percentages are based on only those doctorate recipients who indicated definite postgraduation plans and type of plans.
NOTE: The above classification of degrees by field differs somewhat from that in most publications of the National Center for Education Statistics (NCES). One major difference is that history is included under humanities rather than social sciences. Includes Ph.D., Ed.D., and comparable degrees at the doctoral level. Includes only graduates of research programs, which typically require the preparation and defense of a dissertation based on original research, or the planning and execution of an original project demonstrating substantial artistic or scholarly achievement. Excludes nonresearch professional practice doctor's degrees (e.g., M.D., D.D.S., and J.D.) that are conferred upon completion of a program providing the knowledge and skills for the recognition, credential, or license required for professional practice in such fields as health and theology. The number of doctor's degrees in this table differs from that reported in the NCES Integrated Postsecondary Education Data System (IPEDS), which includes both the research and nonresearch degrees. Race categories exclude persons of Hispanic ethnicity. Detail may not sum to totals because of rounding.
SOURCE: *Doctorate Recipients From U.S. Universities: 2013 and 2014*, Survey of Earned Doctorates, National Science Foundation, National Institutes of Health, U.S. Department of Education, National Endowment for the Humanities, U.S. Department of Agriculture, and the National Aeronautics and Space Administration. (This table was prepared March 2016.)

Table 324.90. Doctor's degrees conferred by the 60 institutions conferring the most doctor's degrees, by rank order: 2004–05 through 2013–14

Institution	Rank order[1]	Total, 2004–05 to 2013–14	2004–05	2005–06	2006–07	2007–08	2008–09	2009–10	2010–11	2011–12	2012–13	2013–14
1	2	3	4	5	6	7	8	9	10	11	12	13
United States, all institutions	†	1,566,315	134,387	138,056	144,690	149,378	154,564	158,590	163,827	170,217	175,026	177,580
Total, 60 institutions conferring most doctorates	†	603,218	53,704	55,360	58,243	59,476	60,506	61,109	62,616	63,424	64,632	64,148
University of Florida	1	19,655	1,665	1,732	1,957	2,107	2,028	2,127	2,127	1,954	1,964	1,994
Nova Southeastern University	2	17,340	1,629	1,521	1,913	1,772	1,732	1,806	1,699	1,800	1,729	1,739
University of Minnesota, Twin Cities	3	16,426	1,455	1,536	1,667	1,563	1,594	1,618	1,692	1,680	1,826	1,795
Ohio State University, Main Campus	4	15,857	1,432	1,549	1,501	1,611	1,617	1,596	1,658	1,628	1,661	1,604
University of Michigan, Ann Arbor	5	15,408	1,406	1,514	1,496	1,483	1,576	1,534	1,550	1,566	1,647	1,636
University of Southern California	6	14,631	1,361	1,312	1,378	1,523	1,571	1,459	1,474	1,518	1,554	1,481
Harvard University	7	14,367	1,288	1,393	1,476	1,468	1,418	1,401	1,450	1,474	1,464	1,535
New York University	8	14,208	1,385	1,321	1,331	1,413	1,419	1,444	1,413	1,481	1,494	1,507
University of Wisconsin, Madison	9	14,060	1,314	1,261	1,425	1,407	1,430	1,355	1,417	1,514	1,440	1,497
University of Texas at Austin	10	13,815	1,404	1,443	1,358	1,439	1,379	1,382	1,309	1,372	1,351	1,378
University of California, Los Angeles	11	13,385	1,225	1,271	1,307	1,361	1,382	1,358	1,330	1,326	1,393	1,432
Rutgers University, New Brunswick[2]	12	13,277	1,131	1,182	1,226	1,341	1,382	1,401	1,424	1,430	1,495	1,265
Columbia University in the City of New York	13	12,927	1,231	1,300	1,203	1,218	1,281	1,295	1,291	1,329	1,382	1,397
University of California, Berkeley	14	12,368	1,151	1,110	1,280	1,218	1,216	1,245	1,292	1,264	1,304	1,288
University of Washington, Seattle Campus	15	11,963	1,003	1,124	1,130	1,125	1,176	1,224	1,251	1,273	1,329	1,328
University of Pennsylvania	16	11,827	1,170	1,162	1,136	1,105	1,190	1,212	1,212	1,189	1,207	1,244
Temple University	17	11,788	1,119	1,205	1,194	1,220	1,169	1,144	1,246	1,154	1,191	1,146
University of North Carolina at Chapel Hill	18	11,523	1,069	1,098	1,113	1,204	1,101	1,155	1,172	1,179	1,203	1,229
Boston University	19	11,205	926	1,062	1,210	1,161	1,179	1,097	1,111	1,177	1,175	1,107
Texas A&M University, College Station[3]	20	11,811	971	987	1,094	1,079	1,107	1,206	1,256	1,324	1,344	1,443
University of Illinois at Urbana-Champaign	21	10,794	971	998	1,018	1,067	1,081	1,066	1,106	1,210	1,159	1,118
University of Pittsburgh, Pittsburgh Campus	22	10,243	936	926	996	1,026	1,022	944	1,113	1,059	1,086	1,135
George Washington University	23	9,923	879	937	949	956	1,011	1,005	974	1,050	1,071	1,091
Stanford University	24	9,796	904	954	969	944	920	978	1,053	1,019	1,052	1,003
University of Tennessee, Knoxville	25	9,758	790	873	895	912	994	1,024	1,002	1,110	1,104	1,054
University of Iowa	26	9,462	924	887	926	926	937	920	949	948	1,045	1,000
University at Buffalo	27	9,439	933	905	970	938	964	919	948	913	992	957
Georgetown University	28	9,298	890	844	923	926	967	950	936	934	973	955
Michigan State University	29	9,042	774	768	855	770	876	921	951	962	993	1,172
University of California, Davis	30	9,003	791	812	876	900	894	891	927	1,002	1,009	901
Northwestern University	31	8,972	798	837	878	876	872	891	927	898	1,009	986
University of Illinois at Chicago	32	8,916	789	807	862	873	851	965	914	912	974	969
University of Virginia, Main Campus	33	8,875	826	840	852	925	907	861	933	904	908	919
Western Michigan University--Thomas M. Cooley Law School	34	8,808	524	614	756	845	981	955	1,039	1,080	1,143	871
University of Georgia	35	8,728	818	828	858	832	897	854	889	903	901	948
Purdue University, Main Campus	36	8,647	763	785	837	840	882	845	924	880	926	965
University of Maryland, Baltimore	37	8,254	750	813	767	775	775	835	875	900	889	875
Duke University	38	8,222	615	570	680	682	718	820	887	1,010	1,100	1,140
University of Arizona	39	8,021	696	698	814	778	824	824	813	850	854	870
University of Houston	40	7,906	824	772	778	809	786	757	831	798	796	755
University of Miami	41	7,789	685	673	707	703	758	860	803	911	874	815
University of Kansas	42	7,696	562	585	789	781	766	819	856	821	870	847
Cornell University[4]	43	7,671	740	754	752	752	785	779	782	775	771	781
Wayne State University	44	7,567	682	703	688	758	772	717	856	807	777	807
University of Kentucky	45	7,532	670	634	653	717	719	734	783	888	864	870
Capella University	46	7,500	272	499	667	814	700	841	819	810	889	1,189
Washington University in St. Louis	47	7,438	641	678	727	730	760	737	805	783	806	771
Indiana University-Purdue University, Indianapolis	48	7,254	655	669	719	720	687	751	755	771	755	772
Florida State University	49	7,119	577	601	631	730	680	683	818	850	736	813
Indiana University, Bloomington	50	7,116	683	667	651	695	729	718	693	748	771	761
University of the Pacific	51	7,075	733	684	691	708	681	713	749	732	760	624
Pennsylvania State University, Main Campus	52	6,997	571	646	664	643	703	718	736	755	800	761
Case Western Reserve University	53	6,968	636	681	654	718	750	781	730	658	705	655
University of Chicago	54	6,901	638	695	653	704	682	682	711	715	710	711
Yale University	55	6,894	625	622	640	671	685	752	686	712	758	743
A.T. Still University of Health Sciences	56	6,879	477	551	644	694	730	815	810	755	732	671
University of Connecticut	57	6,776	554	629	609	576	687	746	720	773	720	762
University of South Carolina, Columbia	58	6,748	636	642	641	639	703	643	703	674	748	719
Yeshiva University	59	6,704	659	627	635	649	657	680	690	684	726	697
Arizona State University, Tempe	60	6,646	478	569	574	656	766	656	746	828	723	650

†Not applicable.

[1] Institutions are ranked by the total number of doctor's degrees conferred during the 10-year period from July 1, 2004, to June 30, 2014.

[2] Includes degrees conferred by the University of Medicine and Dentistry of New Jersey, which merged with Rutgers University in 2013–14.

[3] Includes law degrees conferred by Texas Wesleyan University, which was acquired by Texas A&M in 2013, as well as degrees in all fields from Texas A&M Health Sciences Center.

[4] Includes degrees conferred by the Endowed and Statutory Colleges.

NOTE: Includes Ph.D., Ed.D., and comparable degrees at the doctoral level, as well as such degrees as M.D., D.D.S., and law degrees that were formerly classified as first-professional degrees. Some data have been revised from previously published figures.

SOURCE: U.S. Department of Education, National Center for Education Statistics, Integrated Postsecondary Education Data System (IPEDS), Fall 2005 through Fall 2014, Completions component. (This table was prepared April 2016.)

Table 325.10. Degrees in agriculture and natural resources conferred by postsecondary institutions, by level of degree and sex of student: 1970–71 through 2013–14

	Bachelor's degrees					Master's degrees			Doctor's degrees		
	Total				Females as a percent of total						
Year	Number	Annual percent change	Males	Females		Total	Males	Females	Total	Males	Females
1	2	3	4	5	6	7	8	9	10	11	12
1970–71	12,672	†	12,136	536	4.2	2,457	2,313	144	1,086	1,055	31
1971–72	13,516	6.7	12,779	737	5.5	2,680	2,490	190	971	945	26
1972–73	14,756	9.2	13,661	1,095	7.4	2,807	2,588	219	1,059	1,031	28
1973–74	16,253	10.1	14,684	1,569	9.7	2,928	2,640	288	930	897	33
1974–75	17,528	7.8	15,061	2,467	14.1	3,067	2,703	364	991	958	33
1975–76	19,402	10.7	15,845	3,557	18.3	3,340	2,862	478	928	867	61
1976–77	21,467	10.6	16,690	4,777	22.3	3,724	3,177	547	893	831	62
1977–78	22,650	5.5	17,069	5,581	24.6	4,023	3,268	755	971	909	62
1978–79	23,134	2.1	16,854	6,280	27.1	3,994	3,187	807	950	877	73
1979–80	22,802	-1.4	16,045	6,757	29.6	3,976	3,082	894	991	879	112
1980–81	21,886	-4.0	15,154	6,732	30.8	4,003	3,061	942	1,067	940	127
1981–82	21,029	-3.9	14,443	6,586	31.3	4,163	3,114	1,049	1,079	925	154
1982–83	20,909	-0.6	14,085	6,824	32.6	4,254	3,129	1,125	1,149	1,004	145
1983–84	19,317	-7.6	13,206	6,111	31.6	4,178	2,989	1,189	1,172	1,001	171
1984–85	18,107	-6.3	12,477	5,630	31.1	3,928	2,846	1,082	1,213	1,036	177
1985–86	16,823	-7.1	11,544	5,279	31.4	3,801	2,701	1,100	1,158	966	192
1986–87	14,991	-10.9	10,314	4,677	31.2	3,522	2,460	1,062	1,049	871	178
1987–88	14,222	-5.1	9,744	4,478	31.5	3,479	2,427	1,052	1,142	926	216
1988–89	13,492	-5.1	9,298	4,194	31.1	3,245	2,231	1,014	1,183	950	233
1989–90	12,900	-4.4	8,822	4,078	31.6	3,382	2,239	1,143	1,295	1,038	257
1990–91	13,124	1.7	8,832	4,292	32.7	3,295	2,160	1,135	1,185	953	232
1991–92	15,113	15.2	9,867	5,246	34.7	3,730	2,409	1,321	1,205	955	250
1992–93	16,769	11.0	11,079	5,690	33.9	3,959	2,474	1,485	1,159	869	290
1993–94	18,056	7.7	11,746	6,310	34.9	4,110	2,512	1,598	1,262	969	293
1994–95	19,832	9.8	12,686	7,146	36.0	4,234	2,541	1,693	1,256	955	301
1995–96	21,425	8.0	13,531	7,894	36.8	4,551	2,642	1,909	1,259	926	333
1996–97	22,597	5.5	13,791	8,806	39.0	4,505	2,601	1,904	1,202	875	327
1997–98	23,276	3.0	13,806	9,470	40.7	4,464	2,545	1,919	1,290	924	366
1998–99	24,179	3.9	14,045	10,134	41.9	4,376	2,360	2,016	1,249	869	380
1999–2000	24,238	0.2	13,843	10,395	42.9	4,360	2,356	2,004	1,168	803	365
2000–01	23,370	-3.6	12,840	10,530	45.1	4,272	2,251	2,021	1,127	741	386
2001–02	23,331	-0.2	12,630	10,701	45.9	4,503	2,340	2,163	1,148	760	388
2002–03	23,348	0.1	12,343	11,005	47.1	4,492	2,232	2,260	1,229	790	439
2003–04	22,835	-2.2	11,889	10,946	47.9	4,783	2,306	2,477	1,185	758	427
2004–05	23,002	0.7	11,987	11,015	47.9	4,746	2,288	2,458	1,173	763	410
2005–06	23,053	0.2	12,063	10,990	47.7	4,640	2,280	2,360	1,194	710	484
2006–07	23,133	0.3	12,309	10,824	46.8	4,623	2,174	2,449	1,272	768	504
2007–08	24,113	4.2	12,634	11,479	47.6	4,684	2,180	2,504	1,257	742	515
2008–09	24,982	3.6	13,096	11,886	47.6	4,878	2,328	2,550	1,328	741	587
2009–10	26,343	5.4	13,524	12,819	48.7	5,215	2,512	2,703	1,149	626	523
2010–11	28,630	8.7	14,678	13,952	48.7	5,766	2,746	3,020	1,246	675	571
2011–12	30,972	8.2	15,485	15,487	50.0	6,390	3,026	3,364	1,333	721	612
2012–13	33,592	8.5	16,618	16,974	50.5	6,336	2,912	3,424	1,411	767	644
2013–14	35,116	4.5	17,249	17,867	50.9	6,544	2,966	3,578	1,407	739	668
Percent change											
2003–04 to 2008–09	9.4	†	10.2	8.6	†	2.0	1.0	2.9	12.1	-2.2	37.5
2008–09 to 2013–14	40.6	†	31.7	50.3	†	34.2	27.4	40.3	5.9	-0.3	13.8

†Not applicable.
NOTE: Data are for postsecondary institutions participating in Title IV federal financial aid programs. Includes degrees in agriculture, agriculture operations, and related sciences and in natural resources and conservation. Some data have been revised from previously published figures.

SOURCE: U.S. Department of Education, National Center for Education Statistics, Higher Education General Information Survey (HEGIS), "Degrees and Other Formal Awards Conferred" surveys, 1970–71 through 1985–86; Integrated Postsecondary Education Data System (IPEDS), "Completions Survey" (IPEDS-C:87–99); and IPEDS Fall 2000 through Fall 2014, Completions component. (This table was prepared September 2015.)

Table 325.15. Degrees in architecture and related services conferred by postsecondary institutions, by level of degree and sex of student: Selected years, 1949–50 through 2013–14

Year	Bachelor's degrees					Master's degrees			Doctor's degrees		
	Total				Females as a percent of total						
	Number	Annual percent change	Males	Females		Total	Males	Females	Total	Males	Females
1	2	3	4	5	6	7	8	9	10	11	12
1949–50	2,563	†	2,441	122	4.8	166	159	7	1	1	0
1959–60	1,801	†	1,744	57	3.2	319	305	14	17	17	0
1967–68	3,057	†	2,931	126	4.1	1,021	953	68	15	15	0
1969–70	4,105	†	3,888	217	5.3	1,427	1,260	167	35	33	2
1970–71	5,570	35.7	4,906	664	11.9	1,705	1,469	236	36	33	3
1971–72	6,440	15.6	5,667	773	12.0	1,899	1,626	273	50	43	7
1972–73	6,962	8.1	6,042	920	13.2	2,307	1,943	364	58	54	4
1973–74	7,822	12.4	6,665	1,157	14.8	2,702	2,208	494	69	65	4
1974–75	8,226	5.2	6,791	1,435	17.4	2,938	2,343	595	69	58	11
1975–76	9,146	11.2	7,396	1,750	19.1	3,215	2,545	670	82	69	13
1976–77	9,222	0.8	7,249	1,973	21.4	3,213	2,489	724	73	62	11
1977–78	9,250	0.3	7,054	2,196	23.7	3,115	2,304	811	73	57	16
1978–79	9,273	0.2	6,876	2,397	25.8	3,113	2,226	887	96	74	22
1979–80	9,132	-1.5	6,596	2,536	27.8	3,139	2,245	894	79	66	13
1980–81	9,455	3.5	6,800	2,655	28.1	3,153	2,234	919	93	73	20
1981–82	9,728	2.9	6,825	2,903	29.8	3,327	2,242	1,085	80	58	22
1982–83	9,823	1.0	6,403	3,420	34.8	3,357	2,224	1,133	97	74	23
1983–84	9,186	-6.5	5,895	3,291	35.8	3,223	2,197	1,026	84	62	22
1984–85	9,325	1.5	6,019	3,306	35.5	3,275	2,148	1,127	89	66	23
1985–86	9,119	-2.2	5,824	3,295	36.1	3,260	2,129	1,131	73	56	17
1986–87	8,950	-1.9	5,617	3,333	37.2	3,163	2,086	1,077	92	66	26
1987–88	8,603	-3.9	5,271	3,332	38.7	3,159	2,042	1,117	98	66	32
1988–89	9,150	6.4	5,545	3,605	39.4	3,383	2,192	1,191	86	63	23
1989–90	9,364	2.3	5,703	3,661	39.1	3,499	2,228	1,271	103	73	30
1990–91	9,781	4.5	5,788	3,993	40.8	3,490	2,244	1,246	135	101	34
1991–92	8,753	-10.5	5,805	2,948	33.7	3,640	2,271	1,369	132	93	39
1992–93	9,167	4.7	5,940	3,227	35.2	3,808	2,376	1,432	148	105	43
1993–94	8,975	-2.1	5,764	3,211	35.8	3,943	2,428	1,515	161	111	50
1994–95	8,756	-2.4	5,741	3,015	34.4	3,923	2,310	1,613	141	95	46
1995–96	8,352	-4.6	5,340	3,012	36.1	3,993	2,361	1,632	141	96	45
1996–97	7,944	-4.9	5,090	2,854	35.9	4,034	2,336	1,698	135	93	42
1997–98	7,652	-3.7	4,966	2,686	35.1	4,347	2,537	1,810	131	80	51
1998–99	8,245	7.7	5,145	3,100	37.6	4,235	2,435	1,800	119	76	43
1999–2000	8,462	2.6	5,193	3,269	38.6	4,268	2,508	1,760	129	85	44
2000–01	8,480	0.2	5,086	3,394	40.0	4,302	2,515	1,787	153	83	70
2001–02	8,808	3.9	5,224	3,584	40.7	4,566	2,606	1,960	183	117	66
2002–03	9,056	2.8	5,331	3,725	41.1	4,925	2,832	2,093	152	83	69
2003–04	8,838	-2.4	5,059	3,779	42.8	5,424	3,049	2,375	173	94	79
2004–05	9,237	4.5	5,222	4,015	43.5	5,674	3,180	2,494	179	110	69
2005–06	9,515	3.0	5,414	4,101	43.1	5,743	3,165	2,578	201	108	93
2006–07	9,717	2.1	5,393	4,324	44.5	5,951	3,304	2,647	178	104	74
2007–08	9,805	0.9	5,579	4,226	43.1	6,065	3,252	2,813	199	103	96
2008–09	10,119	3.2	5,797	4,322	42.7	6,587	3,657	2,930	212	113	99
2009–10	10,051	-0.7	5,694	4,357	43.3	7,280	4,012	3,268	210	116	94
2010–11	9,831	-2.2	5,698	4,133	42.0	7,788	4,265	3,523	205	110	95
2011–12	9,727	-1.1	5,566	4,161	42.8	8,448	4,504	3,944	255	147	108
2012–13	9,757	0.3	5,581	4,176	42.8	8,095	4,261	3,834	247	134	113
2013–14	9,144	-6.3	5,173	3,971	43.4	8,048	4,122	3,926	247	134	113
Percent change											
2003–04 to 2008–09	14.5	†	14.6	14.4	†	21.4	19.9	23.4	22.5	20.2	25.3
2008–09 to 2013–14	-9.6	†	-10.8	-8.1	†	22.2	12.7	34.0	16.5	18.6	14.1

†Not applicable.
NOTE: Data are for postsecondary institutions participating in Title IV federal financial aid programs. Some data have been revised from previously published figures.
SOURCE: U.S. Department of Education, National Center for Education Statistics, *Earned Degrees Conferred*, 1949–50 and 1959–60; Higher Education General Information Survey (HEGIS), "Degrees and Other Formal Awards Conferred" surveys, 1967–68 through 1985–86; Integrated Postsecondary Education Data System (IPEDS), "Completions Survey" (IPEDS-C:87–99); and IPEDS Fall 2000 through Fall 2014, Completions component. (This table was prepared September 2015.)

Table 325.20. Degrees in the biological and biomedical sciences conferred by postsecondary institutions, by level of degree and sex of student: Selected years, 1951–52 through 2013–14

	Bachelor's degrees					Master's degrees			Doctor's degrees		
	Total				Females as a percent of total						
Year	Number	Annual percent change	Males	Females		Total	Males	Females	Total	Males	Females
1	2	3	4	5	6	7	8	9	10	11	12
1951–52	11,094	†	8,212	2,882	26.0	2,307	1,908	399	764	680	84
1953–54	9,279	†	6,710	2,569	27.7	1,610	1,287	323	1,077	977	100
1955–56	12,423	†	9,515	2,908	23.4	1,759	1,379	380	1,025	908	117
1957–58	14,308	†	11,159	3,149	22.0	1,852	1,448	404	1,125	987	138
1959–60	15,576	†	11,654	3,922	25.2	2,154	1,668	486	1,205	1,086	119
1961–62	16,915	†	12,136	4,779	28.3	2,642	1,982	660	1,338	1,179	159
1963–64	22,723	†	16,321	6,402	28.2	3,296	2,348	948	1,625	1,432	193
1965–66	26,916	†	19,368	7,548	28.0	4,232	3,085	1,147	2,097	1,792	305
1967–68	31,826	†	22,986	8,840	27.8	5,506	3,959	1,547	2,784	2,345	439
1969–70	34,034	†	23,919	10,115	29.7	5,800	3,975	1,825	3,289	2,820	469
1970–71	35,705	4.9	25,319	10,386	29.1	5,625	3,782	1,843	3,603	3,018	585
1971–72	37,269	4.4	26,314	10,955	29.4	5,989	4,056	1,933	3,587	2,981	606
1972–73	42,207	13.2	29,625	12,582	29.8	6,156	4,317	1,839	3,583	2,892	691
1973–74	48,244	14.3	33,217	15,027	31.1	6,408	4,512	1,896	3,358	2,684	674
1974–75	51,609	7.0	34,580	17,029	33.0	6,429	4,554	1,875	3,334	2,612	722
1975–76	54,154	4.9	35,498	18,656	34.4	6,457	4,466	1,991	3,347	2,631	716
1976–77	53,464	-1.3	34,178	19,286	36.1	6,953	4,670	2,283	3,335	2,627	708
1977–78	51,360	-3.9	31,673	19,687	38.3	6,651	4,353	2,298	3,255	2,481	774
1978–79	48,713	-5.2	29,173	19,540	40.1	6,638	4,198	2,440	3,459	2,593	866
1979–80	46,254	-5.0	26,797	19,457	42.1	6,339	4,042	2,297	3,568	2,651	917
1980–81	43,078	-6.9	24,124	18,954	44.0	5,766	3,602	2,164	3,640	2,620	1,020
1981–82	41,501	-3.7	22,722	18,779	45.2	5,679	3,384	2,295	3,662	2,611	1,051
1982–83	39,924	-3.8	21,572	18,352	46.0	5,711	3,298	2,413	3,386	2,306	1,080
1983–84	38,593	-3.3	20,565	18,028	46.7	5,489	3,123	2,366	3,496	2,416	1,080
1984–85	38,354	-0.6	20,071	18,283	47.7	5,109	2,775	2,334	3,465	2,335	1,130
1985–86	38,395	0.1	20,000	18,395	47.9	5,064	2,733	2,331	3,405	2,273	1,132
1986–87	38,074	-0.8	19,684	18,390	48.3	4,995	2,646	2,349	3,469	2,268	1,201
1987–88	36,688	-3.6	18,267	18,421	50.2	4,871	2,530	2,341	3,688	2,389	1,299
1988–89	36,068	-1.7	17,998	18,070	50.1	5,034	2,598	2,436	3,617	2,299	1,318
1989–90	37,304	3.4	18,363	18,941	50.8	4,941	2,509	2,432	3,922	2,478	1,444
1990–91	39,482	5.8	19,418	20,064	50.8	4,834	2,417	2,417	4,152	2,618	1,534
1991–92	42,892	8.6	20,816	22,076	51.5	4,862	2,437	2,425	4,442	2,749	1,693
1992–93	47,009	9.6	22,870	24,139	51.3	5,026	2,540	2,486	4,749	2,866	1,883
1993–94	51,296	9.1	25,071	26,225	51.1	5,462	2,681	2,781	4,891	2,910	1,981
1994–95	55,983	9.1	26,734	29,249	52.2	5,873	2,920	2,953	5,069	3,012	2,057
1995–96	61,014	9.0	28,921	32,093	52.6	6,593	3,212	3,381	5,250	3,062	2,188
1996–97	63,973	4.8	29,562	34,411	53.8	6,986	3,419	3,567	5,313	3,014	2,299
1997–98	65,917	3.0	29,663	36,254	55.0	6,848	3,336	3,512	5,474	3,123	2,351
1998–99	65,310	-0.9	28,507	36,803	56.4	6,966	3,279	3,687	5,250	3,010	2,240
1999–2000	63,630	-2.6	26,579	37,051	58.2	6,850	3,171	3,679	5,463	3,068	2,395
2000–01	60,576	-4.8	24,600	35,976	59.4	7,017	3,075	3,942	5,225	2,923	2,302
2001–02	60,309	-0.4	23,694	36,615	60.7	7,011	3,033	3,978	5,104	2,836	2,268
2002–03	61,294	1.6	23,356	37,938	61.9	7,050	3,015	4,035	5,268	2,866	2,402
2003–04	62,624	2.2	23,691	38,933	62.2	7,732	3,271	4,461	5,538	2,975	2,563
2004–05	65,915	5.3	25,104	40,811	61.9	8,284	3,361	4,923	5,935	3,025	2,910
2005–06	70,607	7.1	27,183	43,424	61.5	8,781	3,709	5,072	6,162	3,138	3,024
2006–07	76,832	8.8	30,600	46,232	60.2	8,898	3,639	5,259	6,764	3,440	3,324
2007–08	79,829	3.9	32,401	47,428	59.4	9,689	4,094	5,595	7,400	3,645	3,755
2008–09	82,828	3.8	33,707	49,121	59.3	10,018	4,250	5,768	7,499	3,549	3,950
2009–10	86,391	4.3	35,866	50,525	58.5	10,730	4,612	6,118	7,672	3,603	4,069
2010–11	89,984	4.2	36,888	53,096	59.0	11,324	4,869	6,455	7,693	3,648	4,045
2011–12	95,850	6.5	39,542	56,308	58.7	12,419	5,378	7,041	7,935	3,708	4,227
2012–13	100,397	4.7	41,556	58,841	58.6	13,300	5,783	7,517	7,939	3,689	4,250
2013–14	104,633	4.2	43,427	61,206	58.5	13,960	6,072	7,888	8,302	3,884	4,418
Percent change											
2003–04 to 2008–09	32.3	†	42.3	26.2	†	29.6	29.9	29.3	35.4	19.3	54.1
2008–09 to 2013–14	26.3	†	28.8	24.6	†	39.3	42.9	36.8	10.7	9.4	11.8

†Not applicable.
NOTE: Data are for postsecondary institutions participating in Title IV federal financial aid programs. Some data have been revised from previously published figures.
SOURCE: U.S. Department of Education, National Center for Education Statistics, *Earned Degrees Conferred*, 1951–52 through 1963–64; Higher Education General Information Survey (HEGIS), "Degrees and Other Formal Awards Conferred" surveys, 1965–66 through 1985–86; Integrated Postsecondary Education Data System (IPEDS), "Completions Survey" (IPEDS-C:87–99); and IPEDS Fall 2000 through Fall 2014, Completions component. (This table was prepared September 2015.)

Table 325.22. Degrees in biology, microbiology, and zoology conferred by postsecondary institutions, by level of degree: 1970–71 through 2013–14

Year	Biology, general[1]			Microbiology[2]			Zoology[3]		
	Bachelor's	Master's	Doctor's	Bachelor's	Master's	Doctor's	Bachelor's	Master's	Doctor's
1	2	3	4	5	6	7	8	9	10
1970–71	26,294	2,665	536	1,475	456	365	5,721	1,027	878
1971–72	27,473	2,943	580	1,548	470	351	5,518	1,040	836
1972–73	31,185	2,959	627	1,940	517	344	5,763	1,042	803
1973–74	36,188	3,186	657	2,311	505	384	6,128	1,091	677
1974–75	38,748	3,109	637	2,767	552	345	6,110	1,039	697
1975–76	40,163	3,177	624	2,927	585	364	6,077	976	645
1976–77	39,530	3,322	608	2,884	659	325	5,574	985	696
1977–78	37,598	3,094	664	2,695	615	353	5,096	958	624
1978–79	35,962	3,093	663	2,670	597	395	4,738	946	669
1979–80	33,523	2,911	718	2,631	596	376	4,301	922	639
1980–81	31,323	2,598	734	2,414	482	370	3,873	881	613
1981–82	29,651	2,579	678	2,377	470	350	3,615	868	625
1982–83	28,022	2,354	521	2,324	499	358	3,407	738	533
1983–84	27,379	2,313	617	2,349	505	388	3,231	700	521
1984–85	27,593	2,130	658	2,207	471	319	3,069	664	508
1985–86	27,618	2,173	574	2,257	392	362	2,894	618	548
1986–87	27,465	2,022	537	2,159	451	380	2,791	623	464
1987–88	26,838	1,981	576	2,061	404	442	2,537	629	492
1988–89	26,229	2,097	527	1,833	449	423	2,549	634	466
1989–90	27,213	1,998	551	1,973	403	441	2,473	548	545
1990–91	29,285	1,956	632	1,788	343	443	2,641	551	516
1991–92	31,909	1,995	657	1,750	372	532	2,811	530	494
1992–93	34,932	2,000	671	1,798	367	621	3,036	559	465
1993–94	38,103	2,178	665	1,872	359	591	3,162	658	503
1994–95	41,658	2,350	729	1,992	326	572	3,149	586	487
1995–96	44,818	2,606	768	2,220	364	606	3,463	677	501
1996–97	46,632	2,742	693	2,530	363	612	3,438	720	474
1997–98	47,054	2,617	809	2,926	401	585	3,653	685	465
1998–99	46,172	2,616	718	2,885	406	544	3,508	606	462
1999–2000	44,982	2,599	727	3,049	383	551	3,226	616	481
2000–01	42,310	2,582	780	2,779	334	553	3,045	560	380
2001–02	42,281	2,424	689	2,622	325	538	2,979	578	413
2002–03	42,699	2,340	680	2,455	297	507	2,488	379	355
2003–04	43,465	2,529	681	2,365	350	599	2,454	367	245
2004–05	45,540	2,564	712	2,318	390	610	2,159	384	268
2005–06	48,855	2,719	776	2,243	372	612	2,140	384	254
2006–07	52,527	2,679	788	2,347	369	667	2,223	416	263
2007–08	54,384	2,935	866	2,458	353	734	2,235	381	281
2008–09	55,859	2,987	896	2,480	291	716	2,140	347	297
2009–10	58,700	3,087	919	2,449	303	767	2,147	360	243
2010–11	61,236	3,283	935	2,466	337	739	2,062	338	230
2011–12	64,616	3,494	964	2,532	395	687	2,174	346	258
2012–13	66,692	3,479	1,003	2,582	402	704	2,246	416	231
2013–14	69,402	3,465	1,053	2,572	465	674	2,269	464	217
Percent change									
2003–04 to 2008–09	28.5	18.1	31.6	4.9	-16.9	19.5	-12.8	-5.4	21.2
2008–09 to 2013–14	24.2	16.0	17.5	3.7	59.8	-5.9	6.0	33.7	-26.9

[1]Includes biology/biological sciences, general.
[2]Includes microbiology, general; medical microbiology and bacteriology; virology; parasitology; immunology; and microbiological sciences and immunology, other.
[3]Includes zoology/animal biology; entomology; animal physiology; animal behavior and ethology; wildlife biology; and zoology/animal biology, other.
NOTE: Data are for postsecondary institutions participating in Title IV federal financial aid programs. Some data have been revised from previously published figures.

SOURCE: U.S. Department of Education, National Center for Education Statistics, Higher Education General Information Survey (HEGIS), "Degrees and Other Formal Awards Conferred" surveys, 1970–71 through 1985–86; Integrated Postsecondary Education Data System (IPEDS), "Completions Survey" (IPEDS-C:87–99); and IPEDS Fall 2000 through Fall 2014, Completions component. (This table was prepared September 2015.)

Table 325.25. Degrees in business conferred by postsecondary institutions, by level of degree and sex of student: Selected years, 1955–56 through 2013–14

Year	Bachelor's degrees					Master's degrees			Doctor's degrees		
	Total				Females as a percent of total						
	Number	Annual percent change	Males	Females		Total	Males	Females	Total	Males	Females
1	2	3	4	5	6	7	8	9	10	11	12
1955–56	42,813	†	38,706	4,107	9.6	3,280	3,118	162	129	127	2
1957–58	51,991	†	48,063	3,928	7.6	4,223	4,072	151	110	105	5
1959–60	51,076	†	47,262	3,814	7.5	4,643	4,476	167	135	133	2
1961–62	49,017	†	45,184	3,833	7.8	7,691	7,484	207	226	221	5
1963–64	55,474	†	51,056	4,418	8.0	9,251	9,008	243	275	268	7
1965–66	62,721	†	57,516	5,205	8.3	12,959	12,628	331	387	370	17
1967–68	79,074	†	72,126	6,948	8.8	17,795	17,186	609	441	427	14
1969–70	105,580	†	96,346	9,234	8.7	21,561	20,792	769	620	610	10
1970–71	115,396	9.3	104,936	10,460	9.1	26,490	25,458	1,032	774	753	21
1971–72	121,917	5.7	110,331	11,586	9.5	30,509	29,317	1,192	876	857	19
1972–73	126,717	3.9	113,337	13,380	10.6	31,208	29,689	1,519	917	864	53
1973–74	132,304	4.4	115,363	16,941	12.8	32,691	30,557	2,134	922	873	49
1974–75	133,639	1.0	111,983	21,656	16.2	36,315	33,274	3,041	939	900	39
1975–76	143,171	7.1	114,986	28,185	19.7	42,592	37,654	4,938	906	856	50
1976–77	152,010	6.2	116,394	35,616	23.4	46,505	39,852	6,653	839	785	54
1977–78	160,775	5.8	117,103	43,672	27.2	48,347	40,224	8,123	834	760	74
1978–79	172,392	7.2	119,765	52,627	30.5	50,397	40,766	9,631	852	752	100
1979–80	186,264	8.0	123,639	62,625	33.6	55,008	42,744	12,264	767	650	117
1980–81	200,521	7.7	126,798	73,723	36.8	57,888	43,411	14,477	808	686	122
1981–82	215,190	7.3	130,693	84,497	39.3	61,251	44,230	17,021	826	676	150
1982–83	226,442	5.2	131,451	94,991	41.9	64,741	45,987	18,754	770	638	132
1983–84	229,013	1.1	129,296	99,717	43.5	66,129	46,167	19,962	926	727	199
1984–85	232,282	1.4	127,467	104,815	45.1	66,981	46,199	20,782	827	685	142
1985–86	236,700	1.9	128,415	108,285	45.7	66,676	45,927	20,749	923	720	203
1986–87	240,346	1.5	128,506	111,840	46.5	67,093	44,913	22,180	1,062	808	254
1987–88	242,859	1.0	129,467	113,392	46.7	69,230	45,980	23,250	1,063	810	253
1988–89	246,262	1.4	131,098	115,164	46.8	73,065	48,540	24,525	1,100	800	300
1989–90	248,568	0.9	132,284	116,284	46.8	76,676	50,585	26,091	1,093	818	275
1990–91	249,165	0.2	131,557	117,608	47.2	78,255	50,883	27,372	1,185	876	309
1991–92	256,298	2.9	135,263	121,035	47.2	84,517	54,609	29,908	1,242	953	289
1992–93	256,473	0.1	135,368	121,105	47.2	89,425	57,504	31,921	1,346	969	377
1993–94	246,265	-4.0	128,946	117,319	47.6	93,285	59,223	34,062	1,364	980	384
1994–95	233,895	-5.0	121,663	112,232	48.0	93,540	58,931	34,609	1,391	1,011	380
1995–96	226,623	-3.1	116,545	110,078	48.6	93,554	58,400	35,154	1,366	972	394
1996–97	225,934	-0.3	116,023	109,911	48.6	97,204	59,333	37,871	1,336	947	389
1997–98	232,079	2.7	119,379	112,700	48.6	101,652	62,357	39,295	1,290	885	405
1998–99	239,924	3.4	121,741	118,183	49.3	106,830	64,271	42,559	1,216	848	368
1999–2000	256,070	6.7	128,521	127,549	49.8	111,532	67,078	44,454	1,194	812	382
2000–01	263,515	2.9	132,275	131,240	49.8	115,602	68,471	47,131	1,180	783	397
2001–02	278,217	5.6	138,343	139,874	50.3	119,725	70,463	49,262	1,156	746	410
2002–03	293,391	5.5	145,075	148,316	50.6	127,685	75,239	52,446	1,252	820	432
2003–04	307,149	4.7	152,513	154,636	50.3	139,347	80,858	58,489	1,481	960	521
2004–05	311,574	1.4	155,940	155,634	50.0	142,617	82,151	60,466	1,498	901	597
2005–06	318,042	2.1	159,683	158,359	49.8	146,406	83,550	62,856	1,711	1,049	662
2006–07	327,531	3.0	166,350	161,181	49.2	150,211	84,115	66,096	2,029	1,188	841
2007–08	335,254	2.4	170,978	164,276	49.0	155,637	86,258	69,379	2,084	1,250	834
2008–09	348,056	3.8	177,924	170,132	48.9	168,404	91,991	76,413	2,123	1,302	821
2009–10	358,119	2.9	183,272	174,847	48.8	177,748	96,742	81,006	2,249	1,338	911
2010–11	365,133	2.0	187,116	178,017	48.8	187,178	101,440	85,738	2,286	1,357	929
2011–12	367,235	0.6	190,180	177,055	48.2	191,606	103,250	88,356	2,538	1,461	1,077
2012–13	360,887	-1.7	187,843	173,044	47.9	188,617	101,599	87,018	2,828	1,605	1,223
2013–14	358,079	-0.8	188,418	169,661	47.4	189,328	101,043	88,285	3,039	1,722	1,317
Percent change											
2003–04 to 2008–09	13.3	†	16.7	10.0	†	20.9	13.8	30.6	43.3	35.6	57.6
2008–09 to 2013–14	2.9	†	5.9	-0.3	†	12.4	9.8	15.5	43.1	32.3	60.4

†Not applicable.
NOTE: Data are for postsecondary institutions participating in Title IV federal financial aid programs. Includes degrees in business, management, marketing, and related support services and in personal and culinary services. Some data have been revised from previously published figures.
SOURCE: U.S. Department of Education, National Center for Education Statistics, *Earned Degrees Conferred*, 1955–56 through 1963–64; Higher Education General Information Survey (HEGIS), "Degrees and Other Formal Awards Conferred" surveys, 1965–66 through 1985–86; Integrated Postsecondary Education Data System (IPEDS), "Completions Survey" (IPEDS-C:87–99); and IPEDS Fall 2000 through Fall 2014, Completions component. (This table was prepared September 2015.)

Table 325.30. Degrees in communication, journalism, and related programs and in communications technologies conferred by postsecondary institutions, by level of degree and sex of student: 1970–71 through 2013–14

Year	Bachelor's degrees Total Number	Bachelor's degrees Total Annual percent change	Bachelor's degrees Males	Bachelor's degrees Females	Females as a percent of total	Master's degrees Total	Master's degrees Males	Master's degrees Females	Doctor's degrees Total	Doctor's degrees Males	Doctor's degrees Females
1	2	3	4	5	6	7	8	9	10	11	12
1970–71	10,802	†	6,989	3,813	35.3	1,856	1,214	642	145	126	19
1971–72	12,340	14.2	7,964	4,376	35.5	2,200	1,443	757	111	96	15
1972–73	14,317	16.0	9,074	5,243	36.6	2,406	1,546	860	139	114	25
1973–74	17,096	19.4	10,536	6,560	38.4	2,640	1,668	972	175	146	29
1974–75	19,248	12.6	11,455	7,793	40.5	2,794	1,618	1,176	165	119	46
1975–76	21,282	10.6	12,458	8,824	41.5	3,126	1,818	1,308	204	154	50
1976–77	23,214	9.1	12,932	10,282	44.3	3,091	1,719	1,372	171	130	41
1977–78	25,400	9.4	13,480	11,920	46.9	3,296	1,673	1,623	191	138	53
1978–79	26,457	4.2	13,266	13,191	49.9	2,882	1,483	1,399	192	138	54
1979–80	28,616	8.2	13,656	14,960	52.3	3,082	1,527	1,555	193	121	72
1980–81	31,282	9.3	14,179	17,103	54.7	3,105	1,448	1,657	182	107	75
1981–82	34,222	9.4	14,917	19,305	56.4	3,327	1,578	1,749	200	136	64
1982–83	38,647	12.9	16,213	22,434	58.0	3,600	1,660	1,940	208	123	85
1983–84	40,203	4.0	16,662	23,541	58.6	3,620	1,578	2,042	216	129	87
1984–85	42,102	4.7	17,233	24,869	59.1	3,657	1,574	2,083	232	141	91
1985–86	43,145	2.5	17,681	25,464	59.0	3,808	1,603	2,205	218	116	102
1986–87	45,521	5.5	18,201	27,320	60.0	3,881	1,584	2,297	275	158	117
1987–88	46,916	3.1	18,672	28,244	60.2	3,916	1,568	2,348	233	133	100
1988–89	48,889	4.2	19,357	29,532	60.4	4,249	1,734	2,515	248	137	111
1989–90	51,572	5.5	20,374	31,198	60.5	4,353	1,705	2,648	272	145	127
1990–91	53,047	2.9	20,806	32,241	60.8	4,327	1,711	2,616	272	150	122
1991–92	55,144	4.0	21,601	33,543	60.8	4,463	1,692	2,771	255	132	123
1992–93	54,907	-0.4	22,154	32,753	59.7	5,179	1,969	3,210	301	146	155
1993–94	52,033	-5.2	21,484	30,549	58.7	5,388	2,088	3,300	345	174	171
1994–95	48,969	-5.9	20,501	28,468	58.1	5,559	2,086	3,473	321	162	159
1995–96	48,173	-1.6	19,868	28,305	58.8	5,561	2,153	3,408	345	190	155
1996–97	47,894	-0.6	19,771	28,123	58.7	5,552	1,989	3,563	300	155	145
1997–98	50,263	4.9	20,103	30,160	60.0	6,097	2,369	3,728	359	171	188
1998–99	52,397	4.2	20,943	31,454	60.0	5,582	2,001	3,581	348	182	166
1999–2000	57,058	8.9	22,152	34,906	61.2	5,525	2,030	3,495	357	168	189
2000–01	59,191	3.7	22,542	36,649	61.9	5,645	1,964	3,681	370	190	180
2001–02	64,036	8.2	23,692	40,344	63.0	5,980	2,169	3,811	383	168	215
2002–03	69,828	9.0	25,338	44,490	63.7	6,495	2,301	4,194	398	179	219
2003–04	73,002	4.5	25,813	47,189	64.6	6,900	2,329	4,571	426	186	240
2004–05	75,238	3.1	26,926	48,312	64.2	7,195	2,535	4,660	468	195	273
2005–06	76,936	2.3	28,142	48,794	63.4	7,745	2,611	5,134	464	207	257
2006–07	78,420	1.9	29,009	49,411	63.0	7,272	2,485	4,787	480	188	292
2007–08	81,048	3.4	30,384	50,664	62.5	7,546	2,580	4,966	496	209	287
2008–09	83,084	2.5	31,207	51,877	62.4	7,517	2,446	5,071	535	225	310
2009–10	86,062	3.6	32,048	54,014	62.8	8,093	2,656	5,437	573	225	348
2010–11	88,089	2.4	33,018	55,071	62.5	8,804	2,819	5,985	578	207	371
2011–12	88,754	0.8	33,525	55,229	62.2	9,502	3,068	6,434	567	242	325
2012–13	89,805	1.2	33,670	56,135	62.5	9,337	3,021	6,316	612	246	366
2013–14	92,591	3.1	34,370	58,221	62.9	9,928	3,129	6,799	614	267	347
Percent change											
2003–04 to 2008–09	13.8	†	20.9	9.9	†	8.9	5.0	10.9	25.6	21.0	29.2
2008–09 to 2013–14	11.4	†	10.1	12.2	†	32.1	27.9	34.1	14.8	18.7	11.9

†Not applicable.
NOTE: Data are for postsecondary institutions participating in Title IV federal financial aid programs. Some data have been revised from previously published figures.
SOURCE: U.S. Department of Education, National Center for Education Statistics, Higher Education General Information Survey (HEGIS), "Degrees and Other Formal Awards Conferred" surveys, 1970–71 through 1985–86; Integrated Postsecondary Education Data System (IPEDS), "Completions Survey" (IPEDS-C:87–99); and IPEDS Fall 2000 through Fall 2014, Completions component. (This table was prepared September 2015.)

Table 325.35. Degrees in computer and information sciences conferred by postsecondary institutions, by level of degree and sex of student: 1970–71 through 2013–14

	Bachelor's degrees					Master's degrees			Doctor's degrees		
	Total				Females as a percent of total						
Year	Number	Annual percent change	Males	Females		Total	Males	Females	Total	Males	Females
1	2	3	4	5	6	7	8	9	10	11	12
1970–71	2,388	†	2,064	324	13.6	1,588	1,424	164	128	125	3
1971–72	3,402	42.5	2,941	461	13.6	1,977	1,752	225	167	155	12
1972–73	4,304	26.5	3,664	640	14.9	2,113	1,888	225	196	181	15
1973–74	4,756	10.5	3,976	780	16.4	2,276	1,983	293	198	189	9
1974–75	5,033	5.8	4,080	953	18.9	2,299	1,961	338	213	199	14
1975–76	5,652	12.3	4,534	1,118	19.8	2,603	2,226	377	244	221	23
1976–77	6,407	13.4	4,876	1,531	23.9	2,798	2,332	466	216	197	19
1977–78	7,201	12.4	5,349	1,852	25.7	3,038	2,471	567	196	181	15
1978–79	8,719	21.1	6,272	2,447	28.1	3,055	2,480	575	236	206	30
1979–80	11,154	27.9	7,782	3,372	30.2	3,647	2,883	764	240	213	27
1980–81	15,121	35.6	10,202	4,919	32.5	4,218	3,247	971	252	227	25
1981–82	20,267	34.0	13,218	7,049	34.8	4,935	3,625	1,310	251	230	21
1982–83	24,565	21.2	15,641	8,924	36.3	5,321	3,813	1,508	262	228	34
1983–84	32,439	32.1	20,416	12,023	37.1	6,190	4,379	1,811	251	225	26
1984–85	39,121	20.6	24,737	14,384	36.8	7,101	5,064	2,037	248	223	25
1985–86	42,337	8.2	27,208	15,129	35.7	8,070	5,658	2,412	344	299	45
1986–87	39,767	-6.1	25,962	13,805	34.7	8,481	5,985	2,496	374	322	52
1987–88	34,651	-12.9	23,414	11,237	32.4	9,197	6,726	2,471	428	380	48
1988–89	30,560	-11.8	21,143	9,417	30.8	9,414	6,775	2,639	551	466	85
1989–90	27,347	-10.5	19,159	8,188	29.9	9,677	6,960	2,717	627	534	93
1990–91	25,159	-8.0	17,771	7,388	29.4	9,324	6,563	2,761	676	584	92
1991–92	24,821	-1.3	17,685	7,136	28.7	9,655	6,980	2,675	772	669	103
1992–93	24,519	-1.2	17,606	6,913	28.2	10,353	7,557	2,796	805	689	116
1993–94	24,527	#	17,528	6,999	28.5	10,568	7,836	2,732	810	685	125
1994–95	24,737	0.9	17,684	7,053	28.5	10,595	7,805	2,790	887	726	161
1995–96	24,506	-0.9	17,757	6,749	27.5	10,579	7,729	2,850	869	743	126
1996–97	25,422	3.7	18,527	6,895	27.1	10,513	7,526	2,987	857	721	136
1997–98	27,829	9.5	20,372	7,457	26.8	11,765	8,343	3,422	858	718	140
1998–99	30,552	9.8	22,289	8,263	27.0	12,843	8,866	3,977	806	656	150
1999–2000	37,788	23.7	27,185	10,603	28.1	14,990	9,978	5,012	779	648	131
2000–01	44,142	16.8	31,923	12,219	27.7	16,911	11,195	5,716	768	632	136
2001–02	50,365	14.1	36,462	13,903	27.6	17,173	11,447	5,726	752	581	171
2002–03	57,433	14.0	41,950	15,483	27.0	19,509	13,267	6,242	816	648	168
2003–04	59,488	3.6	44,585	14,903	25.1	20,143	13,868	6,275	909	709	200
2004–05	54,111	-9.0	42,125	11,986	22.2	18,416	13,136	5,280	1,119	905	214
2005–06	47,480	-12.3	37,705	9,775	20.6	17,055	12,470	4,585	1,416	1,109	307
2006–07	42,170	-11.2	34,342	7,828	18.6	16,232	11,985	4,247	1,595	1,267	328
2007–08	38,476	-8.8	31,694	6,782	17.6	17,087	12,513	4,574	1,698	1,323	375
2008–09	37,992	-1.3	31,213	6,779	17.8	17,907	13,063	4,844	1,580	1,226	354
2009–10	39,593	4.2	32,414	7,179	18.1	17,955	13,019	4,936	1,599	1,250	349
2010–11	43,066	8.8	35,477	7,589	17.6	19,516	14,010	5,506	1,588	1,267	321
2011–12	47,406	10.1	38,796	8,610	18.2	20,925	15,132	5,793	1,698	1,332	366
2012–13	50,961	7.5	41,874	9,087	17.8	22,782	16,539	6,243	1,834	1,480	354
2013–14	55,367	8.6	45,393	9,974	18.0	24,532	17,484	7,048	1,982	1,566	416
Percent change											
2003–04 to 2008–09	-36.1	†	-30.0	-54.5	†	-11.1	-5.8	-22.8	73.8	72.9	77.0
2008–09 to 2013–14	45.7	†	45.4	47.1	†	37.0	33.8	45.5	25.4	27.7	17.5

†Not applicable.
#Rounds to zero.
NOTE: Data are for postsecondary institutions participating in Title IV federal financial aid programs. Some data have been revised from previously published figures.
SOURCE: U.S. Department of Education, National Center for Education Statistics, Higher Education General Information Survey (HEGIS), "Degrees and Other Formal Awards Conferred" surveys, 1970–71 through 1985–86; Integrated Postsecondary Education Data System (IPEDS), "Completions Survey" (IPEDS-C:87–99); and IPEDS Fall 2000 through Fall 2014, Completions component. (This table was prepared September 2015.)

Table 325.40. Degrees in education conferred by postsecondary institutions, by level of degree and sex of student: Selected years, 1949–50 through 2013–14

Year	Bachelor's degrees					Master's degrees			Doctor's degrees		
	Total				Females as a percent of total	Total	Males	Females	Total	Males	Females
	Number	Annual percent change	Males	Females							
1	2	3	4	5	6	7	8	9	10	11	12
1949–50	61,472	†	31,398	30,074	48.9	20,069	12,025	8,044	953	797	156
1959–60	89,002	†	25,556	63,446	71.3	33,433	18,057	15,376	1,591	1,279	312
1967–68	133,965	†	31,926	102,039	76.2	63,399	30,672	32,727	4,078	3,250	828
1969–70	163,964	†	40,420	123,544	75.3	78,020	34,832	43,188	5,588	4,479	1,109
1970–71	176,307	7.5	44,896	131,411	74.5	87,666	38,365	49,301	6,041	4,771	1,270
1971–72	190,880	8.3	49,344	141,536	74.1	96,668	41,141	55,527	6,648	5,104	1,544
1972–73	193,984	1.6	51,300	142,684	73.6	103,777	43,298	60,479	6,857	5,191	1,666
1973–74	184,907	-4.7	48,997	135,910	73.5	110,402	44,112	66,290	6,757	4,974	1,783
1974–75	166,758	-9.8	44,463	122,295	73.3	117,841	44,430	73,411	6,975	4,856	2,119
1975–76	154,437	-7.4	42,004	112,433	72.8	126,061	44,831	81,230	7,202	4,826	2,376
1976–77	143,234	-7.3	39,867	103,367	72.2	124,267	42,308	81,959	7,338	4,832	2,506
1977–78	135,821	-5.2	37,410	98,411	72.5	116,916	37,662	79,254	7,018	4,281	2,737
1978–79	125,873	-7.3	33,743	92,130	73.2	109,866	34,410	75,456	7,170	4,174	2,996
1979–80	118,038	-6.2	30,901	87,137	73.8	101,819	30,300	71,519	7,314	4,100	3,214
1980–81	108,074	-8.4	27,039	81,035	75.0	96,713	27,548	69,165	7,279	3,843	3,436
1981–82	100,932	-6.6	24,380	76,552	75.8	91,601	25,339	66,262	6,999	3,612	3,387
1982–83	97,908	-3.0	23,651	74,257	75.8	83,254	22,824	60,430	7,063	3,550	3,513
1983–84	92,310	-5.7	22,200	70,110	76.0	75,700	21,164	54,536	6,914	3,448	3,466
1984–85	88,078	-4.6	21,254	66,824	75.9	74,667	20,539	54,128	6,614	3,174	3,440
1985–86	87,147	-1.1	20,982	66,165	75.9	74,816	20,302	54,514	6,610	3,088	3,522
1986–87	86,788	-0.4	20,705	66,083	76.1	72,619	18,955	53,664	5,905	2,745	3,160
1987–88	90,928	4.8	20,947	69,981	77.0	75,270	18,777	56,493	5,568	2,530	3,038
1988–89	96,740	6.4	21,643	75,097	77.6	79,793	19,616	60,177	5,884	2,522	3,362
1989–90	105,112	8.7	23,007	82,105	78.1	84,890	20,469	64,421	6,503	2,776	3,727
1990–91	110,807	5.4	23,417	87,390	78.9	87,352	20,448	66,904	6,189	2,614	3,575
1991–92	107,836	-2.7	22,655	85,181	79.0	91,225	20,897	70,328	6,423	2,652	3,771
1992–93	107,578	-0.2	23,199	84,379	78.4	94,497	21,857	72,640	6,581	2,712	3,869
1993–94	107,440	-0.1	24,424	83,016	77.3	97,427	22,656	74,771	6,450	2,555	3,895
1994–95	105,929	-1.4	25,619	80,310	75.8	99,835	23,511	76,324	6,475	2,490	3,985
1995–96	105,384	-0.5	26,214	79,170	75.1	104,936	24,955	79,981	6,246	2,404	3,842
1996–97	105,116	-0.3	26,242	78,874	75.0	108,720	25,518	83,202	6,297	2,367	3,930
1997–98	105,833	0.7	26,285	79,548	75.2	113,374	26,814	86,560	6,261	2,334	3,927
1998–99	107,372	1.5	26,321	81,051	75.5	118,226	28,077	90,149	6,471	2,297	4,174
1999–2000	108,034	0.6	26,103	81,931	75.8	123,045	29,081	93,964	6,409	2,295	4,114
2000–01	105,458	-2.4	24,580	80,878	76.7	127,829	29,997	97,832	6,284	2,237	4,047
2001–02	106,295	0.8	24,049	82,246	77.4	135,189	31,907	103,282	6,549	2,211	4,338
2002–03	105,845	-0.4	22,604	83,241	78.6	147,883	34,033	113,850	6,832	2,314	4,518
2003–04	106,278	0.4	22,802	83,476	78.5	162,345	37,843	124,502	7,088	2,403	4,685
2004–05	105,451	-0.8	22,513	82,938	78.7	167,490	38,863	128,627	7,681	2,557	5,124
2005–06	107,238	1.7	22,448	84,790	79.1	174,620	40,700	133,920	7,584	2,664	4,920
2006–07	105,641	-1.5	22,516	83,125	78.7	176,572	40,164	136,408	8,261	2,681	5,580
2007–08	102,582	-2.9	21,828	80,754	78.7	175,880	40,055	135,825	8,491	2,773	5,718
2008–09	101,716	-0.8	21,163	80,553	79.2	178,538	40,312	138,226	9,028	2,956	6,072
2009–10	101,287	-0.4	20,739	80,548	79.5	182,165	41,284	140,881	9,237	3,023	6,214
2010–11	104,008	2.7	21,206	82,802	79.6	185,127	42,043	143,084	9,642	3,070	6,572
2011–12	105,656	1.6	21,714	83,942	79.4	179,047	41,364	137,683	10,118	3,262	6,856
2012–13	104,698	-0.9	21,824	82,874	79.2	164,652	37,816	126,836	10,572	3,418	7,154
2013–14	98,854	-5.6	20,353	78,501	79.4	154,636	35,984	118,652	10,920	3,464	7,456
Percent change											
2003–04 to 2008–09	-4.3	†	-7.2	-3.5	†	10.0	6.5	11.0	27.4	23.0	29.6
2008–09 to 2013–14	-2.8	†	-3.8	-2.5	†	-13.4	-10.7	-14.2	21.0	17.2	22.8

†Not applicable.
NOTE: Data are for postsecondary institutions participating in Title IV federal financial aid programs. Some data have been revised from previously published figures.
SOURCE: U.S. Department of Education, National Center for Education Statistics, *Earned Degrees Conferred*, 1949–50 and 1959–60; Higher Education General Information Survey (HEGIS), "Degrees and Other Formal Awards Conferred" surveys, 1967–68 through 1985–86; Integrated Postsecondary Education Data System (IPEDS), "Completions Survey" (IPEDS-C:87–99); and Fall 2000 through Fall 2014, Completions component. (This table was prepared September 2015.)

Table 325.45. Degrees in engineering and engineering technologies conferred by postsecondary institutions, by level of degree and sex of student: Selected years, 1949–50 through 2013–14

	Bachelor's degrees					Master's degrees			Doctor's degrees		
	Total										
Year	Number	Annual percent change	Males	Females	Females as a percent of total	Total	Males	Females	Total	Males	Females
1	2	3	4	5	6	7	8	9	10	11	12
1949–50	52,246	†	52,071	175	0.3	4,496	4,481	15	417	416	1
1959–60	37,679	†	37,537	142	0.4	7,159	7,133	26	786	783	3
1969–70	44,479	†	44,149	330	0.7	15,593	15,421	172	3,681	3,657	24
1970–71	50,182	12.8	49,775	407	0.8	16,947	16,734	213	3,688	3,663	25
1971–72	51,258	2.1	50,726	532	1.0	17,299	17,009	290	3,708	3,685	23
1972–73	51,384	0.2	50,766	618	1.2	16,988	16,694	294	3,513	3,459	54
1973–74	50,412	-1.9	49,611	801	1.6	15,851	15,470	381	3,374	3,318	56
1974–75	47,131	-6.5	46,105	1,026	2.2	15,837	15,426	411	3,181	3,113	68
1975–76	46,676	-1.0	45,184	1,492	3.2	16,800	16,174	626	2,874	2,805	69
1976–77	49,482	6.0	47,238	2,244	4.5	16,659	15,891	768	2,622	2,547	75
1977–78	56,150	13.5	52,353	3,797	6.8	16,887	15,940	947	2,483	2,424	59
1978–79	62,898	12.0	57,603	5,295	8.4	16,012	14,971	1,041	2,545	2,459	86
1979–80	69,387	10.3	62,877	6,510	9.4	16,765	15,535	1,230	2,546	2,447	99
1980–81	75,355	8.6	67,573	7,782	10.3	17,216	15,761	1,455	2,608	2,499	109
1981–82	80,632	7.0	71,305	9,327	11.6	18,475	16,747	1,728	2,676	2,532	144
1982–83	89,811	11.4	78,673	11,138	12.4	19,949	18,038	1,911	2,871	2,742	129
1983–84	95,295	6.1	82,841	12,454	13.1	21,197	18,916	2,281	3,032	2,864	168
1984–85	97,099	1.9	83,991	13,108	13.5	22,124	19,688	2,436	3,269	3,055	214
1985–86	97,122	#	84,050	13,072	13.5	22,146	19,545	2,601	3,456	3,220	236
1986–87	93,560	-3.7	80,543	13,017	13.9	23,101	20,137	2,964	3,854	3,585	269
1987–88	89,406	-4.4	76,886	12,520	14.0	23,839	20,815	3,024	4,237	3,941	296
1988–89	85,982	-3.8	74,020	11,962	13.9	25,066	21,731	3,335	4,572	4,160	412
1989–90	82,480	-4.1	70,859	11,621	14.1	25,294	21,753	3,541	5,030	4,576	454
1990–91	79,751	-3.3	68,482	11,269	14.1	25,450	21,780	3,670	5,330	4,834	496
1991–92	78,036	-2.2	67,086	10,950	14.0	26,373	22,397	3,976	5,499	4,967	532
1992–93	78,619	0.7	67,214	11,405	14.5	29,103	24,721	4,382	5,870	5,300	570
1993–94	78,580	#	66,867	11,713	14.9	30,102	25,394	4,708	5,954	5,288	666
1994–95	78,483	-0.1	66,157	12,326	15.7	29,949	25,028	4,921	6,108	5,378	730
1995–96	77,997	-0.6	65,362	12,635	16.2	28,843	23,840	5,003	6,354	5,559	795
1996–97	75,659	-3.0	62,994	12,665	16.7	27,016	22,047	4,969	6,166	5,408	758
1997–98	74,557	-1.5	61,880	12,677	17.0	27,244	21,800	5,444	5,966	5,230	736
1998–99	72,796	-2.4	59,859	12,937	17.8	26,689	21,348	5,341	5,413	4,643	770
1999–2000	73,323	0.7	59,668	13,655	18.6	26,648	21,047	5,601	5,367	4,539	828
2000–01	72,869	-0.6	59,489	13,380	18.4	27,187	21,341	5,846	5,547	4,630	917
2001–02	74,588	2.4	60,417	14,171	19.0	26,987	21,212	5,775	5,181	4,285	896
2002–03	77,231	3.5	62,821	14,410	18.7	30,583	24,097	6,486	5,252	4,353	899
2003–04	78,079	1.1	63,401	14,678	18.8	35,053	27,561	7,492	5,859	4,821	1,038
2004–05	79,544	1.9	65,033	14,511	18.2	34,988	27,049	7,939	6,467	5,263	1,204
2005–06	81,406	2.3	66,866	14,540	17.9	33,389	25,568	7,821	7,318	5,848	1,470
2006–07	81,854	0.6	68,081	13,773	16.8	31,989	24,746	7,243	7,928	6,285	1,643
2007–08	83,608	2.1	69,540	14,068	16.8	34,430	26,461	7,969	7,977	6,263	1,714
2008–09	84,404	1.0	70,504	13,900	16.5	38,008	29,458	8,550	7,803	6,123	1,680
2009–10	88,735	5.1	73,838	14,897	16.8	39,391	30,554	8,837	7,773	5,986	1,787
2010–11	93,097	4.9	77,080	16,017	17.2	43,179	33,372	9,807	8,425	6,548	1,877
2011–12	98,654	6.0	81,364	17,290	17.5	45,116	34,712	10,404	8,856	6,838	2,018
2012–13	102,997	4.4	84,645	18,352	17.8	45,328	34,496	10,832	9,467	7,305	2,162
2013–14	108,969	5.8	88,938	20,031	18.4	47,326	35,777	11,549	10,117	7,820	2,297
Percent change											
2003–04 to 2008–09	8.1	†	11.2	-5.3	†	8.4	6.9	14.1	33.2	27.0	61.8
2008–09 to 2013–14	29.1	†	26.1	44.1	†	24.5	21.5	35.1	29.7	27.7	36.7

†Not applicable.
#Rounds to zero.
NOTE: Data are for postsecondary institutions participating in Title IV federal financial aid programs. Includes degrees in engineering, engineering-related technologies, mechanic and repair technologies, and construction trades for 1969–70 and later years. Degrees in engineering include degrees in all areas of engineering—for example, chemical, civil, electrical, and mechanical engineering—as well as degrees in general engineering. Some data have been revised from previously published figures.

SOURCE: U.S. Department of Education, National Center for Education Statistics, *Earned Degrees Conferred*, 1949–50 and 1959–60; Higher Education General Information Survey (HEGIS), "Degrees and Other Formal Awards Conferred" surveys, 1969–70 through 1985–86; Integrated Postsecondary Education Data System (IPEDS), "Completions Survey" (IPEDS-C:87–99); and IPEDS Fall 2000 through Fall 2014, Completions component. (This table was prepared September 2015.)

Table 325.47. Degrees in chemical, civil, electrical, and mechanical engineering conferred by postsecondary institutions, by level of degree: 1970–71 through 2013–14

Year	Chemical engineering			Civil engineering			Electrical, electronics, and communications engineering			Mechanical engineering		
	Bachelor's	Master's	Doctor's	Bachelor's	Master's	Doctor's	Bachelor's	Master's	Doctor's	Bachelor's	Master's	Doctor's
1	2	3	4	5	6	7	8	9	10	11	12	13
1970–71	3,579	1,100	406	6,526	2,425	446	12,198	4,282	879	8,858	2,237	438
1971–72	3,625	1,154	394	6,803	2,487	415	12,101	4,206	824	8,530	2,282	411
1972–73	3,578	1,051	397	7,390	2,627	397	12,313	3,895	791	8,523	2,141	370
1973–74	3,399	1,044	400	8,017	2,652	368	11,316	3,499	705	7,677	1,843	385
1974–75	3,070	990	346	7,651	2,769	356	10,161	3,469	701	6,890	1,858	340
1975–76	3,140	1,031	308	7,923	2,999	370	9,791	3,774	649	6,800	1,907	305
1976–77	3,524	1,086	291	8,228	2,964	309	9,936	3,788	566	7,703	1,952	283
1977–78	4,569	1,235	259	9,135	2,685	277	11,133	3,740	503	8,875	1,942	279
1978–79	5,568	1,149	304	9,809	2,646	253	12,338	3,591	586	10,107	1,877	271
1979–80	6,320	1,270	284	10,326	2,683	270	13,821	3,836	525	11,808	2,060	281
1980–81	6,527	1,267	300	10,678	2,891	325	14,938	3,901	535	13,329	2,291	276
1981–82	6,740	1,285	311	10,524	2,995	329	16,455	4,462	526	13,922	2,399	333
1982–83	7,185	1,368	319	9,989	3,074	340	18,049	4,531	550	15,675	2,511	299
1983–84	7,475	1,514	330	9,693	3,146	369	19,943	5,078	585	16,629	2,797	319
1984–85	7,146	1,544	418	9,162	3,172	377	21,691	5,153	660	16,794	3,053	409
1985–86	5,877	1,361	446	8,679	2,926	395	23,742	5,534	722	16,194	3,075	426
1986–87	4,991	1,184	497	8,147	2,901	451	24,547	6,183	724	15,450	3,198	528
1987–88	3,917	1,088	579	7,488	2,836	481	23,597	6,688	860	14,900	3,329	596
1988–89	3,663	1,093	602	7,312	2,903	505	21,908	7,028	998	14,843	3,498	633
1989–90	3,430	1,035	562	7,252	2,812	516	20,711	7,225	1,162	14,336	3,424	742
1990–91	3,444	903	611	7,314	2,927	536	19,320	7,095	1,220	13,977	3,516	757
1991–92	3,754	956	590	8,034	3,113	540	17,958	7,360	1,282	14,067	3,653	851
1992–93	4,459	990	595	8,868	3,610	577	17,281	7,870	1,413	14,464	3,982	871
1993–94	5,163	1,032	604	9,479	3,873	651	15,823	7,791	1,470	15,030	4,099	887
1994–95	5,901	1,085	571	9,927	4,077	625	14,929	7,693	1,543	14,794	4,213	890
1995–96	6,319	1,176	670	10,607	3,905	616	13,900	7,103	1,591	14,177	3,881	940
1996–97	6,564	1,131	650	10,437	3,833	640	13,336	6,393	1,512	13,493	3,608	913
1997–98	6,319	1,128	652	9,926	3,795	610	12,995	6,737	1,458	13,071	3,441	933
1998–99	6,038	1,130	575	9,178	3,656	534	12,606	6,708	1,309	12,753	3,268	788
1999–2000	5,807	1,078	590	8,136	3,433	543	12,930	6,926	1,392	12,807	3,273	776
2000–01	5,611	1,083	610	7,588	3,310	571	13,091	6,815	1,417	12,817	3,371	849
2001–02	5,462	973	605	7,665	3,295	574	13,056	6,587	1,235	13,058	3,391	772
2002–03	5,109	1,065	542	7,836	3,596	599	13,627	7,621	1,256	13,693	3,695	747
2003–04	4,742	1,165	623	7,827	3,790	636	14,123	9,511	1,440	14,050	4,420	787
2004–05	4,397	1,183	773	8,186	3,834	713	14,171	9,054	1,566	14,609	4,637	915
2005–06	4,326	1,116	819	9,090	3,768	750	13,966	8,123	1,860	15,850	4,443	1,096
2006–07	4,492	957	835	9,671	3,482	805	13,089	7,777	2,042	16,601	4,294	1,106
2007–08	4,795	933	853	10,455	3,595	752	12,375	8,631	1,996	17,367	4,497	1,109
2008–09	5,036	994	789	10,785	3,794	763	11,620	9,178	1,812	17,352	4,620	1,142
2009–10	5,740	1,043	830	11,335	4,079	717	11,450	9,052	1,869	18,498	4,818	996
2010–11	6,311	1,283	831	12,557	4,860	751	11,575	9,691	2,037	19,171	5,802	1,106
2011–12	7,027	1,389	823	12,808	5,359	787	12,110	9,696	2,119	20,541	5,840	1,213
2012–13	7,529	1,450	835	13,262	5,353	868	12,835	9,485	2,118	21,990	5,872	1,321
2013–14	8,103	1,518	992	12,993	5,501	972	13,852	9,829	2,301	24,301	6,182	1,387
Percent change												
2003–04 to 2008–09	6.2	-14.7	26.6	37.8	0.1	20.0	-17.7	-3.5	25.8	23.5	4.5	45.1
2008–09 to 2013–14	60.9	52.7	25.7	20.5	45.0	27.4	19.2	7.1	27.0	40.0	33.8	21.5

NOTE: Data are for postsecondary institutions participating in Title IV federal financial aid programs. From 1970–71 through 1981–82, civil engineering includes construction and transportation engineering. From 1991–92, civil engineering includes geotechnical, structural, transportation, and water resources engineering. Degrees in engineering technologies are not included in this table. Some data have been revised from previously published figures.

SOURCE: U.S. Department of Education, National Center for Education Statistics, Higher Education General Information Survey (HEGIS), "Degrees and Other Formal Awards Conferred" surveys, 1970–71 through 1985–86; Integrated Postsecondary Education Data System (IPEDS), "Completions Survey" (IPEDS-C:87–99); and IPEDS Fall 2000 through Fall 2014, Completions component. (This table was prepared September 2015.)

Table 325.50. Degrees in English language and literature/letters conferred by postsecondary institutions, by level of degree and sex of student: Selected years, 1949–50 through 2013–14

Year	Bachelor's degrees					Master's degrees			Doctor's degrees		
	Total				Females as a percent of total						
	Number	Annual percent change	Males	Females		Total	Males	Females	Total	Males	Females
1	2	3	4	5	6	7	8	9	10	11	12
1949–50	17,240	†	8,221	9,019	52.3	2,259	1,320	939	230	181	49
1959–60	20,128	†	7,580	12,548	62.3	2,931	1,458	1,473	397	314	83
1967–68	47,977	†	15,700	32,277	67.3	7,916	3,434	4,482	977	717	260
1969–70	56,410	†	18,650	37,760	66.9	8,517	3,326	5,191	1,213	837	376
1970–71	63,914	13.3	22,005	41,909	65.6	10,441	4,126	6,315	1,554	1,107	447
1971–72	63,707	-0.3	22,580	41,127	64.6	10,412	4,066	6,346	1,734	1,173	561
1972–73	60,607	-4.9	22,022	38,585	63.7	10,035	3,988	6,047	1,817	1,189	628
1973–74	54,190	-10.6	20,082	34,108	62.9	9,573	3,824	5,749	1,755	1,142	613
1974–75	47,062	-13.2	17,689	29,373	62.4	9,178	3,463	5,715	1,595	974	621
1975–76	41,452	-11.9	15,898	25,554	61.6	8,599	3,290	5,309	1,514	895	619
1976–77	37,343	-9.9	14,135	23,208	62.1	7,824	2,907	4,917	1,373	768	605
1977–78	34,799	-6.8	12,972	21,827	62.7	7,444	2,623	4,821	1,272	698	574
1978–79	33,218	-4.5	12,085	21,133	63.6	6,503	2,307	4,196	1,186	639	547
1979–80	32,187	-3.1	11,237	20,950	65.1	6,026	2,181	3,845	1,196	635	561
1980–81	31,922	-0.8	11,082	20,840	65.3	5,742	2,026	3,716	1,040	497	543
1981–82	33,078	3.6	11,300	21,778	65.8	5,593	1,916	3,677	986	467	519
1982–83	31,327	-5.3	10,699	20,628	65.8	4,866	1,653	3,213	877	419	458
1983–84	32,296	3.1	11,007	21,289	65.9	4,814	1,681	3,133	899	413	486
1984–85	32,686	1.2	11,195	21,491	65.7	4,987	1,723	3,264	915	414	501
1985–86	34,083	4.3	11,657	22,426	65.8	5,335	1,811	3,524	895	390	505
1986–87	35,667	4.6	12,133	23,534	66.0	5,298	1,819	3,479	853	367	486
1987–88	38,106	6.8	12,687	25,419	66.7	5,366	1,796	3,570	858	380	478
1988–89	41,786	9.7	13,729	28,057	67.1	5,716	1,930	3,786	929	405	524
1989–90	46,803	12.0	15,437	31,366	67.0	6,317	2,125	4,192	986	444	542
1990–91	51,064	9.1	16,891	34,173	66.9	6,784	2,203	4,581	1,056	469	587
1991–92	54,250	6.2	18,314	35,936	66.2	7,215	2,441	4,774	1,142	484	658
1992–93	55,289	1.9	19,007	36,282	65.6	7,537	2,570	4,967	1,201	495	706
1993–94	53,150	-3.9	18,214	34,936	65.7	7,611	2,620	4,991	1,205	512	693
1994–95	51,170	-3.7	17,581	33,589	65.6	7,612	2,672	4,940	1,393	589	804
1995–96	49,928	-2.4	17,007	32,921	65.9	7,657	2,727	4,930	1,395	535	860
1996–97	48,641	-2.6	16,325	32,316	66.4	7,487	2,650	4,837	1,431	610	821
1997–98	49,016	0.8	16,280	32,736	66.8	7,587	2,568	5,019	1,489	611	878
1998–99	49,877	1.8	16,332	33,545	67.3	7,326	2,452	4,874	1,412	554	858
1999–2000	50,106	0.5	16,124	33,982	67.8	7,022	2,315	4,707	1,470	611	859
2000–01	50,569	0.9	15,997	34,572	68.4	6,763	2,160	4,603	1,330	533	797
2001–02	52,375	3.6	16,457	35,918	68.6	7,097	2,270	4,827	1,291	532	759
2002–03	53,699	2.5	16,738	36,961	68.8	7,428	2,433	4,995	1,246	492	754
2003–04	53,984	0.5	16,792	37,192	68.9	7,956	2,459	5,497	1,207	479	728
2004–05	54,379	0.7	17,154	37,225	68.5	8,468	2,615	5,853	1,212	494	718
2005–06	55,096	1.3	17,316	37,780	68.6	8,845	2,860	5,985	1,254	510	744
2006–07	55,122	#	17,475	37,647	68.3	8,742	2,867	5,875	1,178	478	700
2007–08	55,038	#	17,681	37,357	67.9	9,161	3,027	6,134	1,262	453	809
2008–09	55,465	0.8	17,973	37,492	67.6	9,262	3,000	6,262	1,271	464	807
2009–10	53,229	-4.0	17,050	36,179	68.0	9,202	3,006	6,196	1,334	523	811
2010–11	52,754	-0.9	16,917	35,837	67.9	9,475	3,137	6,338	1,344	529	815
2011–12	53,765	1.9	16,976	36,789	68.4	9,938	3,403	6,535	1,427	548	879
2012–13	52,401	-2.5	16,508	35,893	68.5	9,755	3,213	6,542	1,377	554	823
2013–14	50,404	-3.8	15,809	34,595	68.6	9,292	3,113	6,179	1,393	557	836
Percent change											
2003–04 to 2008–09	2.7	†	7.0	0.8	†	16.4	22.0	13.9	5.3	-3.1	10.9
2008–09 to 2013–14	-9.1	†	-12.0	-7.7	†	0.3	3.8	-1.3	9.6	20.0	3.6

†Not applicable.
#Rounds to zero.
NOTE: Data are for postsecondary institutions participating in Title IV federal financial aid programs. Some data have been revised from previously published figures.
SOURCE: U.S. Department of Education, National Center for Education Statistics, *Earned* *Degrees Conferred*, 1949–50 and 1959–60; Higher Education General Information Survey (HEGIS), "Degrees and Other Formal Awards Conferred" surveys, 1967–68 through 1985–86; Integrated Postsecondary Education Data System (IPEDS), "Completions Survey" (IPEDS-C:87–99); and IPEDS Fall 2000 through Fall 2014, Completions component. (This table was prepared September 2015.)

Table 325.55. Degrees in foreign languages and literatures conferred by postsecondary institutions, by level of degree and sex of student: Selected years, 1959–60 through 2013–14

	Bachelor's degrees					Master's degrees			Doctor's degrees		
	Total										
Year	Number	Annual percent change	Males	Females	Females as a percent of total	Total	Males	Females	Total	Males	Females
1	2	3	4	5	6	7	8	9	10	11	12
1959–60	5,462	†	2,090	3,372	61.7	1,125	590	535	229	166	63
1967–68	19,254	†	5,253	14,001	72.7	4,849	2,068	2,781	707	503	204
1969–70	21,109	†	5,613	15,496	73.4	5,137	1,917	3,220	869	579	290
1970–71	20,988	-0.6	5,508	15,480	73.8	5,480	1,961	3,519	1,084	714	370
1971–72	19,890	-5.2	5,196	14,694	73.9	5,283	1,919	3,364	1,134	742	392
1972–73	20,170	1.4	5,119	15,051	74.6	5,068	1,909	3,159	1,347	829	518
1973–74	20,197	0.1	5,063	15,134	74.9	4,851	1,788	3,063	1,248	703	545
1974–75	19,103	-5.4	4,723	14,380	75.3	4,721	1,672	3,049	1,220	665	555
1975–76	17,068	-10.7	4,270	12,798	75.0	4,432	1,581	2,851	1,245	643	602
1976–77	15,496	-9.2	3,965	11,531	74.4	4,056	1,365	2,691	1,103	574	529
1977–78	14,334	-7.5	3,684	10,650	74.3	3,624	1,194	2,430	1,002	490	512
1978–79	13,211	-7.8	3,391	9,820	74.3	3,248	1,092	2,156	960	471	489
1979–80	12,480	-5.5	3,226	9,254	74.2	3,067	1,026	2,041	857	412	445
1980–81	11,638	-6.7	3,013	8,625	74.1	2,934	1,039	1,895	931	460	471
1981–82	11,175	-4.0	2,919	8,256	73.9	2,892	997	1,895	869	407	462
1982–83	11,170	#	3,048	8,122	72.7	2,706	1,001	1,705	790	362	428
1983–84	10,985	-1.7	3,098	7,887	71.8	2,814	984	1,830	779	353	426
1984–85	11,436	4.1	3,186	8,250	72.1	2,708	932	1,776	761	342	419
1985–86	11,550	1.0	3,374	8,176	70.8	2,690	878	1,812	768	338	430
1986–87	11,706	1.4	3,374	8,332	71.2	2,574	847	1,727	769	332	437
1987–88	11,515	-1.6	3,223	8,292	72.0	2,680	931	1,749	725	330	395
1988–89	12,403	7.7	3,432	8,971	72.3	2,837	955	1,882	727	317	410
1989–90	13,133	5.9	3,625	9,508	72.4	3,018	987	2,031	816	348	468
1990–91	13,937	6.1	4,008	9,929	71.2	3,049	1,018	2,031	889	396	493
1991–92	14,634	5.0	4,225	10,409	71.1	3,229	1,074	2,155	984	434	550
1992–93	15,305	4.6	4,435	10,870	71.0	3,513	1,182	2,331	977	417	560
1993–94	15,242	-0.4	4,573	10,669	70.0	3,612	1,199	2,413	1,033	418	615
1994–95	14,558	-4.5	4,496	10,062	69.1	3,439	1,124	2,315	1,081	479	602
1995–96	14,832	1.9	4,514	10,318	69.6	3,443	1,141	2,302	1,020	446	574
1996–97	14,487	-2.3	4,388	10,099	69.7	3,361	1,104	2,257	1,064	450	614
1997–98	15,279	5.5	4,585	10,694	70.0	3,181	1,033	2,148	1,118	473	645
1998–99	15,835	3.6	4,738	11,097	70.1	3,109	976	2,133	1,049	443	606
1999–2000	15,886	0.3	4,616	11,270	70.9	3,037	944	2,093	1,086	446	640
2000–01	16,128	1.5	4,695	11,433	70.9	3,035	969	2,066	1,078	420	658
2001–02	16,258	0.8	4,685	11,573	71.2	3,075	958	2,117	1,003	418	585
2002–03	16,912	4.0	4,996	11,916	70.5	3,049	874	2,175	1,042	424	618
2003–04	17,754	5.0	5,215	12,539	70.6	3,124	957	2,167	1,031	410	621
2004–05	18,386	3.6	5,370	13,016	70.8	3,407	1,056	2,351	1,027	410	617
2005–06	19,410	5.6	5,842	13,568	69.9	3,539	1,049	2,490	1,074	436	638
2006–07	20,275	4.5	6,173	14,102	69.6	3,443	1,058	2,385	1,059	437	622
2007–08	20,977	3.5	6,254	14,723	70.2	3,565	1,128	2,437	1,078	431	647
2008–09	21,169	0.9	6,305	14,864	70.2	3,592	1,211	2,381	1,111	426	685
2009–10	21,507	1.6	6,607	14,900	69.3	3,756	1,254	2,502	1,091	446	645
2010–11	21,705	0.9	6,719	14,986	69.0	3,727	1,256	2,471	1,158	477	681
2011–12	21,756	0.2	6,629	15,127	69.5	3,827	1,280	2,547	1,231	497	734
2012–13	21,647	-0.5	6,842	14,805	68.4	3,708	1,235	2,473	1,304	531	773
2013–14	20,335	-6.1	6,266	14,069	69.2	3,482	1,222	2,260	1,231	498	733
Percent change											
2003–04 to 2008–09	19.2	†	20.9	18.5	†	15.0	26.5	9.9	7.8	3.9	10.3
2008–09 to 2013–14	-3.9	†	-0.6	-5.3	†	-3.1	0.9	-5.1	10.8	16.9	7.0

†Not applicable.
#Rounds to zero.
NOTE: Data are for postsecondary institutions participating in Title IV federal financial aid programs. Some data have been revised from previously published figures.
SOURCE: U.S. Department of Education, National Center for Education Statistics, *Earned Degrees Conferred*, 1949–50 and 1959–60; Higher Education General Information Survey (HEGIS), "Degrees and Other Formal Awards Conferred" surveys, 1967–68 through 1985–86; Integrated Postsecondary Education Data System (IPEDS), "Completions Survey" (IPEDS-C:87–99); and IPEDS Fall 2000 through Fall 2014, Completions component. (This table was prepared September 2015.)

Table 325.57. Degrees in French, German, Italian, and Spanish language and literature conferred by postsecondary institutions, by level of degree: Selected years, 1949–50 through 2013–14

Year	French			German			Italian			Spanish		
	Bachelor's	Master's	Doctor's	Bachelor's	Master's	Doctor's	Bachelor's	Master's	Doctor's	Bachelor's	Master's	Doctor's
1	2	3	4	5	6	7	8	9	10	11	12	13
1949–50	1,471	299	53	540	121	40	—	—	—	2,122	373	34
1959–60	1,927	316	58	659	126	21	—	—	—	1,610	261	31
1967–68	7,068	1,301	152	2,368	771	117	—	—	—	6,381	1,188	123
1969–70	7,624	1,409	181	2,652	669	118	242	71	14	7,226	1,372	139
1970–71	7,306	1,437	192	2,601	690	144	201	87	10	7,068	1,456	168
1971–72	6,822	1,421	193	2,477	608	167	287	104	19	6,847	1,421	152
1972–73	6,705	1,277	203	2,520	598	176	313	78	27	7,209	1,298	206
1973–74	6,263	1,195	213	2,425	550	149	292	81	19	7,250	1,217	203
1974–75	5,745	1,077	200	2,289	480	147	329	100	13	6,719	1,228	202
1975–76	4,783	914	190	1,983	471	164	342	85	19	5,984	1,080	176
1976–77	4,228	875	177	1,820	394	126	325	89	16	5,359	930	153
1977–78	3,708	692	155	1,647	357	101	301	58	19	4,832	822	113
1978–79	3,558	576	143	1,524	344	106	236	60	14	4,563	720	118
1979–80	3,285	513	128	1,466	309	94	272	49	9	4,331	685	103
1980–81	3,178	460	115	1,286	294	79	205	65	13	3,870	592	131
1981–82	3,054	485	92	1,327	324	76	208	55	14	3,633	568	140
1982–83	2,871	360	106	1,367	281	68	224	45	18	3,349	506	129
1983–84	2,876	418	86	1,292	241	63	206	41	13	3,254	537	102
1984–85	2,991	385	74	1,411	240	58	190	44	9	3,415	505	115
1985–86	3,015	409	86	1,396	249	73	240	42	10	3,385	521	95
1986–87	3,062	421	85	1,366	234	70	219	53	17	3,450	504	104
1987–88	3,082	437	89	1,350	244	71	224	45	7	3,416	553	93
1988–89	3,297	444	83	1,428	263	59	239	45	17	3,748	552	101
1989–90	3,259	478	115	1,437	253	67	247	38	19	4,176	573	108
1990–91	3,355	480	98	1,543	242	58	253	36	21	4,480	609	125
1991–92	3,371	465	112	1,616	273	85	238	55	18	4,768	647	143
1992–93	3,280	513	98	1,572	317	86	274	50	13	5,233	667	145
1993–94	3,094	479	104	1,580	298	61	264	47	24	5,505	691	160
1994–95	2,764	470	118	1,352	278	83	271	69	31	5,602	709	161
1995–96	2,655	446	113	1,290	305	75	232	44	22	5,995	769	151
1996–97	2,468	414	119	1,214	281	80	234	49	18	6,161	677	175
1997–98	2,530	389	104	1,181	209	94	252	60	25	6,595	781	160
1998–99	2,565	365	115	1,237	242	78	257	41	12	6,992	697	153
1999–2000	2,514	343	129	1,125	184	76	237	48	13	7,031	718	175
2000–01	2,371	376	115	1,143	242	73	286	42	11	7,164	716	185
2001–02	2,396	356	89	1,092	208	64	263	46	15	7,243	792	193
2002–03	2,294	348	75	1,097	188	77	307	54	20	7,619	791	190
2003–04	2,362	361	85	1,031	153	30	279	49	31	7,991	833	199
2004–05	2,394	356	80	1,103	180	56	277	70	12	8,304	919	190
2005–06	2,410	395	84	1,106	172	48	321	94	17	8,690	981	192
2006–07	2,462	364	95	1,055	158	56	280	97	20	9,013	982	195
2007–08	2,432	359	102	1,085	173	51	359	88	25	9,278	990	193
2008–09	2,450	386	86	1,058	163	47	341	76	34	9,333	878	218
2009–10	2,488	391	87	1,028	143	46	336	73	23	9,138	962	199
2010–11	2,490	366	81	1,019	156	43	313	83	28	8,920	955	179
2011–12	2,358	341	96	1,001	130	67	332	72	35	8,714	991	189
2012–13	2,278	332	115	931	102	52	284	73	27	8,419	928	205
2013–14	2,044	308	107	878	123	44	271	58	29	8,034	832	193
Percent change												
2003–04 to 2008–09	3.7	6.9	1.2	2.6	6.5	56.7	22.2	55.1	9.7	16.8	5.4	9.5
2008–09 to 2013–14	-16.6	-20.2	24.4	-17.0	-24.5	-6.4	-20.5	-23.7	-14.7	-13.9	-5.2	-11.5

—Not available.
NOTE: Data are for postsecondary institutions participating in Title IV federal financial aid programs. Some data have been revised from previously published figures.
SOURCE: U.S. Department of Education, National Center for Education Statistics, *Earned Degrees Conferred*, 1949–50 and 1959–60; Higher Education General Information Survey (HEGIS), "Degrees and Other Formal Awards Conferred" surveys, 1967–68 through 1985–86; Integrated Postsecondary Education Data System (IPEDS), "Completions Survey" (IPEDS-C:87–99); and IPEDS Fall 2000 through Fall 2014, Completions component. (This table was prepared September 2015.)

Table 325.59. Degrees in Arabic, Chinese, Korean, and Russian language and literature conferred by postsecondary institutions, by level of degree: 1969–70 through 2013–14

Year	Arabic			Chinese			Korean			Russian		
	Bachelor's	Master's	Doctor's	Bachelor's	Master's	Doctor's	Bachelor's	Master's	Doctor's	Bachelor's	Master's	Doctor's
1	2	3	4	5	6	7	8	9	10	11	12	13
1969–70	—	—	—	81	34	0	—	—	—	768	172	24
1970–71	15	6	4	89	22	8	—	—	—	715	110	14
1971–72	10	4	0	103	20	11	—	—	—	658	150	15
1972–73	12	3	1	98	29	13	—	—	—	622	120	27
1973–74	20	5	1	121	37	5	—	—	—	624	100	27
1974–75	13	11	2	141	26	12	—	—	—	598	106	20
1975–76	10	7	2	150	23	6	—	—	—	531	81	13
1976–77	7	15	1	112	32	6	—	—	—	528	66	19
1977–78	8	3	1	116	23	4	—	—	—	442	50	12
1978–79	4	4	5	91	22	12	—	—	—	465	51	9
1979–80	13	2	5	79	33	7	—	—	—	402	60	6
1980–81	6	7	0	73	20	6	—	—	—	409	68	8
1981–82	15	4	4	68	14	10	—	—	—	324	49	7
1982–83	12	4	1	92	15	7	—	—	—	342	33	5
1983–84	6	2	0	115	14	10	—	—	—	340	39	3
1984–85	9	4	0	97	21	3	—	—	—	432	47	6
1985–86	5	4	0	87	23	11	—	—	—	493	33	3
1986–87	8	1	1	110	16	10	—	—	—	502	54	8
1987–88	9	4	0	103	31	9	—	—	—	472	54	8
1988–89	6	2	1	138	27	8	—	—	—	469	55	6
1989–90	4	0	1	144	33	8	—	—	—	549	52	5
1990–91	9	0	1	150	24	9	—	—	—	593	70	6
1991–92	13	0	0	183	36	14	—	—	—	629	68	7
1992–93	8	3	2	129	54	8	—	—	—	612	68	4
1993–94	8	2	0	112	48	18	—	—	—	611	71	3
1994–95	10	1	1	107	63	16	—	—	—	572	66	3
1995–96	8	3	2	136	42	19	—	—	—	494	58	7
1996–97	9	3	0	152	31	15	—	—	—	455	46	9
1997–98	16	2	1	161	21	13	—	—	—	383	49	9
1998–99	13	3	1	178	20	14	—	—	—	398	29	4
1999–2000	6	4	5	183	18	15	—	—	—	340	33	10
2000–01	7	2	3	183	13	7	—	—	—	335	24	7
2001–02	13	2	2	189	16	12	—	—	—	277	34	5
2002–03	13	3	0	190	12	9	5	0	0	271	16	6
2003–04	13	3	1	186	15	5	9	2	1	301	21	3
2004–05	21	5	0	208	21	8	8	0	0	298	18	0
2005–06	26	4	2	241	20	10	17	4	3	279	28	7
2006–07	68	2	0	261	30	2	13	0	0	311	18	4
2007–08	57	8	1	289	35	5	15	4	1	294	20	1
2008–09	85	14	1	384	45	11	24	2	1	325	21	1
2009–10	121	10	6	456	51	12	27	19	1	356	19	1
2010–11	141	5	1	449	51	8	28	10	3	340	11	3
2011–12	143	8	7	496	46	9	38	8	3	392	17	2
2012–13	167	12	1	510	61	12	43	14	0	392	11	5
2013–14	165	6	0	497	46	3	32	10	8	371	14	1
Percent change												
2003–04 to 2008–09	553.8	366.7	0	106.5	200.0	120.0	166.7	0	0	8.0	0	-66.7
2008–09 to 2013–14	94.1	-57.1	-100.0	29.4	2.2	-72.7	33.3	400.0	700.0	14.2	-33.3	0

—Not available.
NOTE: Data are for postsecondary institutions participating in Title IV federal financial aid programs. Some data have been revised from previously published figures.
SOURCE: U.S. Department of Education, National Center for Education Statistics, Higher Education General Information Survey (HEGIS), "Degrees and Other Formal Awards Con-ferred" surveys, 1969–70 through 1985–86; Integrated Postsecondary Education Data System (IPEDS), "Completions Survey" (IPEDS-C:87–99); and IPEDS Fall 2000 through Fall 2014, Completions component. (This table was prepared September 2015.)

Table 325.60. Degrees in the health professions and related programs conferred by postsecondary institutions, by level of degree and sex of student: 1970–71 through 2013–14

Year	Bachelor's degrees					Master's degrees			Doctor's degrees		
	Total										
	Number	Annual percent change	Males	Females	Females as a percent of total	Total	Males	Females	Total	Males	Females
1	2	3	4	5	6	7	8	9	10	11	12
1970–71	25,223	†	5,785	19,438	77.1	5,330	2,165	3,165	15,988	14,863	1,125
1971–72	28,611	13.4	7,005	21,606	75.5	6,811	2,749	4,062	16,538	15,373	1,165
1972–73	33,562	17.3	7,752	25,810	76.9	7,978	3,189	4,789	18,215	16,870	1,345
1973–74	41,421	23.4	9,347	32,074	77.4	9,232	3,444	5,788	20,094	18,287	1,807
1974–75	49,002	18.3	10,844	38,158	77.9	10,277	3,686	6,591	22,191	19,808	2,383
1975–76	53,885	10.0	11,386	42,499	78.9	12,164	3,837	8,327	25,267	21,980	3,287
1976–77	57,222	6.2	11,896	45,326	79.2	12,627	3,865	8,762	24,972	21,022	3,950
1977–78	59,445	3.9	11,600	47,845	80.5	14,027	3,972	10,055	26,516	21,622	4,894
1978–79	62,095	4.5	11,214	50,881	81.9	15,110	4,155	10,955	27,766	22,194	5,572
1979–80	63,848	2.8	11,330	52,518	82.3	15,374	4,060	11,314	28,190	22,157	6,033
1980–81	63,665	-0.3	10,531	53,134	83.5	16,176	4,024	12,152	29,595	22,792	6,803
1981–82	63,660	#	10,110	53,550	84.1	16,212	3,743	12,469	30,096	22,968	7,128
1982–83	65,642	3.1	10,247	55,395	84.4	16,941	4,138	12,803	30,800	22,920	7,880
1983–84	65,305	-0.5	10,068	55,237	84.6	17,351	4,124	13,227	31,655	22,851	8,804
1984–85	65,331	#	9,741	55,590	85.1	17,442	4,046	13,396	31,493	22,045	9,448
1985–86	65,309	#	9,629	55,680	85.3	18,603	4,355	14,248	31,922	22,069	9,853
1986–87	63,963	-2.1	9,137	54,826	85.7	18,442	3,818	14,624	29,500	19,686	9,814
1987–88	61,614	-3.7	8,955	52,659	85.5	18,774	4,004	14,770	30,060	19,853	10,207
1988–89	59,850	-2.9	8,878	50,972	85.2	19,493	4,197	15,296	30,546	19,893	10,653
1989–90	58,983	-1.4	9,075	49,908	84.6	20,406	4,486	15,920	30,101	19,118	10,983
1990–91	59,875	1.5	9,619	50,256	83.9	21,354	4,423	16,931	29,842	18,492	11,350
1991–92	62,779	4.9	10,330	52,449	83.5	23,671	4,794	18,877	31,479	19,362	12,117
1992–93	68,434	9.0	11,605	56,829	83.0	26,190	5,249	20,941	31,089	18,446	12,643
1993–94	75,890	10.9	13,377	62,513	82.4	28,442	5,813	22,629	30,959	17,988	12,971
1994–95	81,596	7.5	14,812	66,784	81.8	31,770	6,718	25,052	32,124	18,463	13,661
1995–96	86,087	5.5	15,942	70,145	81.5	33,920	7,017	26,903	32,678	18,495	14,183
1996–97	87,997	2.2	16,440	71,557	81.3	36,162	7,536	28,626	34,971	19,619	15,352
1997–98	86,843	-1.3	15,700	71,143	81.9	39,567	8,644	30,923	35,369	19,370	15,999
1998–99	84,989	-2.1	15,191	69,798	82.1	40,628	9,152	31,476	35,939	19,673	16,266
1999–2000	80,863	-4.9	13,342	67,521	83.5	42,593	9,500	33,093	37,829	19,984	17,845
2000–01	75,933	-6.1	12,514	63,419	83.5	43,623	9,711	33,912	39,019	20,260	18,759
2001–02	72,887	-4.0	10,869	62,018	85.1	43,560	9,588	33,972	39,435	19,760	19,675
2002–03	71,261	-2.2	10,096	61,165	85.8	42,748	9,280	33,468	39,799	19,493	20,306
2003–04	73,934	3.8	10,017	63,917	86.5	44,939	9,670	35,269	41,861	19,587	22,274
2004–05	80,685	9.1	10,858	69,827	86.5	46,703	9,816	36,887	44,201	19,697	24,504
2005–06	91,973	14.0	12,914	79,059	86.0	51,380	10,630	40,750	45,677	19,640	26,037
2006–07	101,810	10.7	14,325	87,485	85.9	54,531	10,636	43,895	48,943	20,522	28,421
2007–08	111,478	9.5	16,286	95,192	85.4	58,120	11,010	47,110	51,675	21,616	30,059
2008–09	120,420	8.0	17,776	102,644	85.2	62,642	11,848	50,794	54,846	22,678	32,168
2009–10	129,623	7.6	19,309	110,314	85.1	69,112	12,874	56,238	57,750	23,946	33,804
2010–11	143,463	10.7	21,540	121,923	85.0	75,571	14,034	61,537	60,221	25,386	34,835
2011–12	163,675	14.1	24,905	138,770	84.8	84,355	15,675	68,680	62,097	26,074	36,023
2012–13	181,149	10.7	28,208	152,941	84.4	90,933	16,747	74,186	64,192	26,852	37,340
2013–14	198,770	9.7	30,931	167,839	84.4	97,403	17,749	79,654	67,448	28,084	39,364
Percent change											
2003–04 to 2008–09	62.9	†	77.5	60.6	†	39.4	22.5	44.0	31.0	15.8	44.4
2008–09 to 2013–14	65.1	†	74.0	63.5	†	55.5	49.8	56.8	23.0	23.8	22.4

†Not applicable.
#Rounds to zero.
NOTE: Data are for postsecondary institutions participating in Title IV federal financial aid programs. Doctor's degrees include medicine (M.D.), dentistry (D.D.S. and D.M.D), and other medical specialty degrees that were formerly classified as first-professional. Some data have been revised from previously published figures.

SOURCE: U.S. Department of Education, National Center for Education Statistics, Higher Education General Information Survey (HEGIS), "Degrees and Other Formal Awards Conferred" surveys, 1970–71 through 1985–86; Integrated Postsecondary Education Data System (IPEDS), "Completions Survey" (IPEDS-C:87–99); and IPEDS Fall 2000 through Fall 2014, Completions component. (This table was prepared September 2015.)

Table 325.65. Degrees in mathematics and statistics conferred by degree-granting institutions, by level of degree and sex of student: Selected years, 1949–50 through 2013–14

	Bachelor's degrees					Master's degrees			Doctor's degrees		
	Total										
Year	Number	Annual percent change	Males	Females	Females as a percent of total	Total	Males	Females	Total	Males	Females
1	2	3	4	5	6	7	8	9	10	11	12
1949–50	6,382	†	4,942	1,440	22.6	974	784	190	160	151	9
1959–60	11,399	†	8,293	3,106	27.2	1,757	1,422	335	303	285	18
1967–68	23,513	†	14,782	8,731	37.1	5,527	4,199	1,328	947	895	52
1969–70	27,442	†	17,177	10,265	37.4	5,636	3,966	1,670	1,236	1,140	96
1970–71	24,801	-9.6	15,369	9,432	38.0	5,191	3,673	1,518	1,199	1,106	93
1971–72	23,713	-4.4	14,454	9,259	39.0	5,198	3,655	1,543	1,128	1,039	89
1972–73	23,067	-2.7	13,796	9,271	40.2	5,028	3,525	1,503	1,068	966	102
1973–74	21,635	-6.2	12,791	8,844	40.9	4,834	3,337	1,497	1,031	931	100
1974–75	18,181	-16.0	10,586	7,595	41.8	4,327	2,905	1,422	975	865	110
1975–76	15,984	-12.1	9,475	6,509	40.7	3,857	2,547	1,310	856	762	94
1976–77	14,196	-11.2	8,303	5,893	41.5	3,695	2,396	1,299	823	714	109
1977–78	12,569	-11.5	7,398	5,171	41.1	3,373	2,228	1,145	805	681	124
1978–79	11,806	-6.1	6,899	4,907	41.6	3,036	1,985	1,051	730	608	122
1979–80	11,378	-3.6	6,562	4,816	42.3	2,860	1,828	1,032	724	624	100
1980–81	11,078	-2.6	6,342	4,736	42.8	2,567	1,692	875	728	614	114
1981–82	11,599	4.7	6,593	5,006	43.2	2,727	1,821	906	681	587	94
1982–83	12,294	6.0	6,888	5,406	44.0	2,810	1,838	972	697	581	116
1983–84	13,087	6.5	7,290	5,797	44.3	2,723	1,773	950	695	569	126
1984–85	15,009	14.7	8,080	6,929	46.2	2,859	1,858	1,001	699	590	109
1985–86	16,122	7.4	8,623	7,499	46.5	3,131	2,028	1,103	742	618	124
1986–87	16,257	0.8	8,673	7,584	46.7	3,283	1,995	1,288	723	598	125
1987–88	15,712	-3.4	8,408	7,304	46.5	3,413	2,052	1,361	750	625	125
1988–89	15,017	-4.4	8,081	6,936	46.2	3,405	2,061	1,344	866	700	166
1989–90	14,276	-4.9	7,674	6,602	46.2	3,624	2,172	1,452	917	754	163
1990–91	14,393	0.8	7,580	6,813	47.3	3,549	2,096	1,453	978	790	188
1991–92	14,468	0.5	7,668	6,800	47.0	3,558	2,151	1,407	1,048	825	223
1992–93	14,384	-0.6	7,566	6,818	47.4	3,644	2,151	1,493	1,138	867	271
1993–94	14,171	-1.5	7,594	6,577	46.4	3,682	2,237	1,445	1,125	880	245
1994–95	13,494	-4.8	7,154	6,340	47.0	3,820	2,289	1,531	1,181	919	262
1995–96	12,713	-5.8	6,847	5,866	46.1	3,651	2,178	1,473	1,158	919	239
1996–97	12,401	-2.5	6,649	5,752	46.4	3,504	2,055	1,449	1,134	861	273
1997–98	11,795	-4.9	6,247	5,548	47.0	3,409	1,985	1,424	1,215	903	312
1998–99	12,011	1.8	6,206	5,805	48.3	3,304	1,912	1,392	1,107	812	295
1999–2000	11,418	-4.9	5,955	5,463	47.8	3,208	1,749	1,459	1,075	803	272
2000–01	11,171	-2.2	5,791	5,380	48.2	3,209	1,857	1,352	997	715	282
2001–02	11,950	7.0	6,333	5,617	47.0	3,350	1,913	1,437	923	658	265
2002–03	12,505	4.6	6,784	5,721	45.7	3,620	1,996	1,624	1,007	734	273
2003–04	13,327	6.6	7,203	6,124	46.0	4,191	2,302	1,889	1,060	762	298
2004–05	14,351	7.7	7,937	6,414	44.7	4,477	2,525	1,952	1,176	841	335
2005–06	14,770	2.9	8,115	6,655	45.1	4,730	2,712	2,018	1,293	911	382
2006–07	14,954	1.2	8,360	6,594	44.1	4,884	2,859	2,025	1,351	949	402
2007–08	15,192	1.6	8,490	6,702	44.1	4,980	2,860	2,120	1,360	938	422
2008–09	15,507	2.1	8,801	6,706	43.2	5,211	3,064	2,147	1,535	1,059	476
2009–10	16,029	3.4	9,087	6,942	43.3	5,639	3,378	2,261	1,596	1,118	478
2010–11	17,182	7.2	9,782	7,400	43.1	5,866	3,459	2,407	1,586	1,132	454
2011–12	18,841	9.7	10,722	8,119	43.1	6,246	3,695	2,551	1,669	1,198	471
2012–13	20,449	8.5	11,599	8,850	43.3	6,957	4,178	2,779	1,823	1,292	531
2013–14	20,980	2.6	11,967	9,013	43.0	7,273	4,256	3,017	1,863	1,325	538
Percent change											
2003–04 to 2008–09	16.4	†	22.2	9.5	†	24.3	33.1	13.7	44.8	39.0	59.7
2008–09 to 2013–14	35.3	†	36.0	34.4	†	39.6	38.9	40.5	21.4	25.1	13.0

†Not applicable.
NOTE: Data are for postsecondary institutions participating in Title IV federal financial aid programs. Some data have been revised from previously published figures.
SOURCE: U.S. Department of Education, National Center for Education Statistics, *Earned Degrees Conferred*, 1949–50 and 1959–60; Higher Education General Information Survey (HEGIS), "Degrees and Other Formal Awards Conferred" surveys, 1967–68 through 1985–86; Integrated Postsecondary Education Data System (IPEDS), "Completions Survey" (IPEDS-C:87–99); and IPEDS Fall 2000 through Fall 2014, Completions component. (This table was prepared September 2015.)

Table 325.70. Degrees in the physical sciences and science technologies conferred by postsecondary institutions, by level of degree and sex of student: Selected years, 1959–60 through 2013–14

| Year | Bachelor's degrees | | | | | Master's degrees | | | Doctor's degrees | | |
| | Total | | | | | | | | | | |
	Number	Annual percent change	Males	Females	Females as a percent of total	Total	Males	Females	Total	Males	Females
1	2	3	4	5	6	7	8	9	10	11	12
1959–60	16,007	†	14,013	1,994	12.5	3,376	3,049	327	1,838	1,776	62
1967–68	19,380	†	16,739	2,641	13.6	5,499	4,869	630	3,593	3,405	188
1969–70	21,439	†	18,522	2,917	13.6	5,908	5,069	839	4,271	4,038	233
1970–71	21,410	-0.1	18,457	2,953	13.8	6,336	5,495	841	4,324	4,082	242
1971–72	20,743	-3.1	17,661	3,082	14.9	6,268	5,390	878	4,075	3,805	270
1972–73	20,692	-0.2	17,622	3,070	14.8	6,230	5,388	842	3,961	3,698	263
1973–74	21,170	2.3	17,669	3,501	16.5	6,019	5,157	862	3,558	3,312	246
1974–75	20,770	-1.9	16,986	3,784	18.2	5,782	4,949	833	3,577	3,284	293
1975–76	21,458	3.3	17,349	4,109	19.1	5,428	4,622	806	3,388	3,097	291
1976–77	22,482	4.8	17,985	4,497	20.0	5,281	4,411	870	3,295	2,981	314
1977–78	22,975	2.2	18,083	4,892	21.3	5,507	4,583	924	3,073	2,763	310
1978–79	23,197	1.0	17,976	5,221	22.5	5,418	4,438	980	3,061	2,717	344
1979–80	23,407	0.9	17,861	5,546	23.7	5,167	4,210	957	3,044	2,669	375
1980–81	23,936	2.3	18,052	5,884	24.6	5,246	4,172	1,074	3,105	2,733	372
1981–82	24,045	0.5	17,861	6,184	25.7	5,446	4,274	1,172	3,246	2,804	442
1982–83	23,374	-2.8	16,988	6,386	27.3	5,250	4,131	1,119	3,214	2,767	447
1983–84	23,645	1.2	17,112	6,533	27.6	5,541	4,249	1,292	3,269	2,789	480
1984–85	23,694	0.2	17,065	6,629	28.0	5,752	4,425	1,327	3,349	2,808	541
1985–86	21,711	-8.4	15,750	5,961	27.5	5,860	4,443	1,417	3,521	2,946	575
1986–87	20,060	-7.6	14,365	5,695	28.4	5,586	4,193	1,393	3,629	3,004	625
1987–88	17,797	-11.3	12,385	5,412	30.4	5,696	4,300	1,396	3,758	3,085	673
1988–89	17,179	-3.5	12,071	5,108	29.7	5,691	4,180	1,511	3,795	3,046	749
1989–90	16,056	-6.5	11,026	5,030	31.3	5,410	3,996	1,414	4,116	3,328	788
1990–91	16,334	1.7	11,170	5,164	31.6	5,281	3,823	1,458	4,248	3,417	831
1991–92	16,970	3.9	11,443	5,527	32.6	5,397	3,935	1,462	4,378	3,433	945
1992–93	17,577	3.6	11,853	5,724	32.6	5,392	3,840	1,552	4,372	3,426	946
1993–94	18,474	5.1	12,271	6,203	33.6	5,718	4,069	1,649	4,652	3,657	995
1994–95	19,247	4.2	12,556	6,691	34.8	5,798	4,058	1,740	4,486	3,443	1,043
1995–96	19,716	2.4	12,634	7,082	35.9	5,910	4,031	1,879	4,589	3,543	1,046
1996–97	19,594	-0.6	12,285	7,309	37.3	5,616	3,799	1,817	4,501	3,479	1,022
1997–98	19,454	-0.7	11,999	7,455	38.3	5,411	3,484	1,927	4,592	3,451	1,141
1998–99	18,448	-5.2	11,119	7,329	39.7	5,241	3,454	1,787	4,229	3,206	1,023
1999–2000	18,427	-0.1	11,019	7,408	40.2	4,888	3,167	1,721	4,017	3,002	1,015
2000–01	18,025	-2.2	10,628	7,397	41.0	5,134	3,276	1,858	3,968	2,914	1,054
2001–02	17,890	-0.7	10,349	7,541	42.2	5,082	3,186	1,896	3,824	2,766	1,058
2002–03	18,038	0.8	10,625	7,413	41.1	5,196	3,284	1,912	3,939	2,854	1,085
2003–04	18,131	0.5	10,577	7,554	41.7	5,714	3,470	2,244	3,937	2,855	1,082
2004–05	19,104	5.4	11,065	8,039	42.1	5,823	3,569	2,254	4,248	3,071	1,177
2005–06	20,522	7.4	11,978	8,544	41.6	6,063	3,666	2,397	4,642	3,258	1,384
2006–07	21,291	3.7	12,604	8,687	40.8	6,012	3,675	2,337	5,041	3,454	1,587
2007–08	22,179	4.2	13,143	9,036	40.7	6,061	3,762	2,299	4,994	3,513	1,481
2008–09	22,691	2.3	13,465	9,226	40.7	5,862	3,576	2,286	5,237	3,554	1,683
2009–10	23,381	3.0	13,866	9,515	40.7	6,066	3,654	2,412	5,065	3,406	1,659
2010–11	24,705	5.7	14,778	9,927	40.2	6,386	3,907	2,479	5,295	3,608	1,687
2011–12	26,664	7.9	15,972	10,692	40.1	6,911	4,299	2,612	5,370	3,609	1,761
2012–13	28,053	5.2	17,142	10,911	38.9	7,014	4,377	2,637	5,514	3,646	1,868
2013–14	29,304	4.5	17,802	11,502	39.3	6,984	4,312	2,672	5,806	3,873	1,933
Percent change											
2003–04 to 2008–09	25.2	†	27.3	22.1	†	2.6	3.1	1.9	33.0	24.5	55.5
2008–09 to 2013–14	29.1	†	32.2	24.7	†	19.1	20.6	16.9	10.9	9.0	14.9

†Not applicable.
NOTE: Data are for postsecondary institutions participating in Title IV federal financial aid programs. Some data have been revised from previously published figures.
SOURCE: U.S. Department of Education, National Center for Education Statistics, *Earned Degrees Conferred*, 1959–60; Higher Education General Information Survey (HEGIS), "Degrees and Other Formal Awards Conferred" surveys, 1967–68 through 1985–86; Integrated Postsecondary Education Data System (IPEDS), "Completions Survey" (IPEDS-C:87–99); and IPEDS Fall 2000 through Fall 2014, Completions component. (This table was prepared September 2015.)

Table 325.72. Degrees in chemistry, geology and earth science, and physics conferred by postsecondary institutions, by level of degree: 1970–71 through 2013–14

Year	Chemistry			Geology and earth science[1]			Physics[2]		
	Bachelor's	Master's	Doctor's	Bachelor's	Master's	Doctor's	Bachelor's	Master's	Doctor's
1	2	3	4	5	6	7	8	9	10
1970–71	11,061	2,244	2,093	3,312	1,074	408	5,071	2,188	1,482
1971–72	10,588	2,229	1,943	3,766	1,233	433	4,634	2,033	1,344
1972–73	10,124	2,198	1,827	4,117	1,296	430	4,259	1,747	1,338
1973–74	10,430	2,082	1,755	4,526	1,479	416	3,952	1,655	1,115
1974–75	10,541	1,961	1,773	4,566	1,320	433	3,706	1,574	1,080
1975–76	11,015	1,745	1,578	4,677	1,384	445	3,544	1,451	997
1976–77	11,200	1,717	1,522	5,280	1,446	480	3,420	1,319	945
1977–78	11,304	1,832	1,461	5,648	1,633	419	3,330	1,294	873
1978–79	11,499	1,724	1,475	5,753	1,596	414	3,337	1,319	918
1979–80	11,229	1,671	1,500	5,785	1,623	440	3,396	1,192	830
1980–81	11,331	1,616	1,586	6,332	1,702	404	3,441	1,294	866
1981–82	11,058	1,683	1,682	6,650	1,848	452	3,472	1,284	873
1982–83	10,789	1,582	1,691	6,981	1,784	406	3,793	1,369	873
1983–84	10,698	1,632	1,707	7,524	1,747	408	3,907	1,532	953
1984–85	10,472	1,675	1,735	7,194	1,927	401	4,097	1,523	951
1985–86	10,110	1,712	1,878	5,760	2,036	395	4,180	1,501	1,010
1986–87	9,660	1,695	1,932	3,943	1,835	399	4,318	1,543	1,074
1987–88	9,043	1,671	1,944	3,204	1,722	462	4,100	1,675	1,093
1988–89	8,618	1,742	1,974	2,847	1,609	492	4,352	1,736	1,112
1989–90	8,122	1,643	2,135	2,372	1,399	562	4,155	1,831	1,192
1990–91	8,311	1,637	2,196	2,367	1,336	600	4,236	1,725	1,209
1991–92	8,629	1,746	2,233	2,784	1,245	549	4,098	1,834	1,337
1992–93	8,903	1,822	2,216	3,123	1,195	626	4,063	1,777	1,277
1993–94	9,417	1,968	2,298	3,456	1,221	577	4,001	1,945	1,465
1994–95	9,706	2,062	2,211	4,032	1,280	539	3,823	1,817	1,424
1995–96	10,395	2,214	2,228	4,019	1,288	555	3,679	1,678	1,462
1996–97	10,609	2,203	2,202	4,023	1,258	564	3,376	1,496	1,410
1997–98	10,528	2,108	2,291	3,866	1,227	588	3,441	1,371	1,393
1998–99	10,109	2,019	2,175	3,570	1,196	533	3,200	1,326	1,257
1999–2000	9,989	1,857	2,028	3,516	1,186	492	3,342	1,232	1,208
2000–01	9,466	1,952	2,056	3,495	1,220	472	3,418	1,365	1,169
2001–02	9,084	1,823	1,984	3,449	1,263	494	3,627	1,344	1,096
2002–03	9,013	1,777	2,092	3,381	1,323	466	3,900	1,438	1,089
2003–04	9,016	2,009	2,033	3,312	1,389	463	4,118	1,625	1,119
2004–05	9,664	1,879	2,148	3,276	1,420	476	4,182	1,785	1,254
2005–06	10,606	2,044	2,403	3,322	1,476	505	4,541	1,846	1,341
2006–07	10,994	2,097	2,514	3,319	1,437	640	4,843	1,777	1,442
2007–08	11,568	2,194	2,410	3,561	1,350	577	4,862	1,791	1,507
2008–09	11,852	2,085	2,556	3,809	1,352	614	4,824	1,653	1,580
2009–10	12,107	2,123	2,470	4,093	1,447	613	4,984	1,793	1,571
2010–11	12,656	2,272	2,599	4,611	1,568	567	5,199	1,769	1,670
2011–12	13,473	2,435	2,537	5,111	1,807	612	5,531	1,873	1,752
2012–13	13,814	2,396	2,617	5,539	1,845	657	6,082	1,975	1,740
2013–14	14,442	2,357	2,796	5,959	1,933	735	6,261	1,866	1,768
Percent change									
2003–04 to 2008–09	31.5	3.8	25.7	15.0	-2.7	32.6	17.1	1.7	41.2
2008–09 to 2013–14	21.9	13.0	9.4	56.4	43.0	19.7	29.8	12.9	11.9

[1]Includes geology/earth science, general; geochemistry; geophysics; paleontology; hydrology; oceanography; and geological and earth sciences, other.
[2]Includes physics, general; atomic/molecular physics; elementary particle physics; nuclear physics; optics; acoustics; theoretical physics; and physics, other.
NOTE: Data are for postsecondary institutions participating in Title IV federal financial aid programs. Some data have been revised from previously published figures.

SOURCE: U.S. Department of Education, National Center for Education Statistics, Higher Education General Information Survey (HEGIS), "Degrees and Other Formal Awards Conferred" surveys, 1970–71 through 1985–86; Integrated Postsecondary Education Data System (IPEDS), "Completions Survey" (IPEDS-C:87–99); and IPEDS Fall 2000 through Fall 2014, Completions component. (This table was prepared September 2015.)

Table 325.80. Degrees in psychology conferred by postsecondary institutions, by level of degree and sex of student: Selected years, 1949–50 through 2013–14

	Bachelor's degrees					Master's degrees			Doctor's degrees		
	Total										
Year	Number	Annual percent change	Males	Females	Females as a percent of total	Total	Males	Females	Total	Males	Females
1	2	3	4	5	6	7	8	9	10	11	12
1949–50	9,569	†	6,055	3,514	36.7	1,316	948	368	283	241	42
1959–60	8,061	†	4,773	3,288	40.8	1,406	981	425	641	544	97
1967–68	23,819	†	13,792	10,027	42.1	3,479	2,321	1,158	1,268	982	286
1969–70	33,679	†	19,077	14,602	43.4	5,158	2,975	2,183	1,962	1,505	457
1970–71	38,187	13.4	21,227	16,960	44.4	5,717	3,395	2,322	2,144	1,629	515
1971–72	43,433	13.7	23,352	20,081	46.2	6,764	3,934	2,830	2,277	1,694	583
1972–73	47,940	10.4	25,117	22,823	47.6	7,619	4,325	3,294	2,550	1,797	753
1973–74	52,139	8.8	25,868	26,271	50.4	8,796	4,983	3,813	2,872	1,987	885
1974–75	51,245	-1.7	24,284	26,961	52.6	9,394	5,035	4,359	2,913	1,979	934
1975–76	50,278	-1.9	22,898	27,380	54.5	10,167	5,136	5,031	3,157	2,115	1,042
1976–77	47,861	-4.8	20,627	27,234	56.9	10,859	5,293	5,566	3,386	2,127	1,259
1977–78	44,879	-6.2	18,422	26,457	59.0	10,282	4,670	5,612	3,164	1,974	1,190
1978–79	42,697	-4.9	16,540	26,157	61.3	10,132	4,405	5,727	3,228	1,895	1,333
1979–80	42,093	-1.4	15,440	26,653	63.3	9,938	4,096	5,842	3,395	1,921	1,474
1980–81	41,068	-2.4	14,332	26,736	65.1	10,223	4,066	6,157	3,576	2,002	1,574
1981–82	41,212	0.4	13,645	27,567	66.9	9,947	3,823	6,124	3,461	1,856	1,605
1982–83	40,460	-1.8	13,131	27,329	67.5	9,981	3,647	6,334	3,602	1,838	1,764
1983–84	39,955	-1.2	12,812	27,143	67.9	9,525	3,400	6,125	3,535	1,774	1,761
1984–85	39,900	-0.1	12,706	27,194	68.2	9,891	3,452	6,439	3,447	1,739	1,708
1985–86	40,628	1.8	12,605	28,023	69.0	9,845	3,347	6,498	3,593	1,724	1,869
1986–87	43,152	6.2	13,395	29,757	69.0	11,000	3,516	7,484	4,062	1,801	2,261
1987–88	45,371	5.1	13,579	31,792	70.1	10,488	3,256	7,232	3,973	1,783	2,190
1988–89	49,083	8.2	14,265	34,818	70.9	11,329	3,465	7,864	4,143	1,773	2,370
1989–90	53,952	9.9	15,336	38,616	71.6	10,730	3,377	7,353	3,811	1,566	2,245
1990–91	58,655	8.7	16,067	42,588	72.6	11,349	3,329	8,020	3,932	1,520	2,412
1991–92	63,683	8.6	17,062	46,621	73.2	11,659	3,335	8,324	3,814	1,490	2,324
1992–93	66,931	5.1	17,942	48,989	73.2	12,518	3,380	9,138	4,100	1,570	2,530
1993–94	69,419	3.7	18,668	50,751	73.1	13,723	3,763	9,960	4,021	1,497	2,524
1994–95	72,233	4.1	19,570	52,663	72.9	15,378	4,210	11,168	4,252	1,562	2,690
1995–96	73,416	1.6	19,836	53,580	73.0	15,152	4,090	11,062	4,141	1,380	2,761
1996–97	74,308	1.2	19,408	54,900	73.9	15,769	4,155	11,614	4,507	1,495	3,012
1997–98	74,107	-0.3	18,976	55,131	74.4	15,142	3,978	11,164	4,541	1,470	3,071
1998–99	73,747	-0.5	18,376	55,371	75.1	15,560	3,959	11,601	4,678	1,528	3,150
1999–2000	74,194	0.6	17,451	56,743	76.5	15,740	3,821	11,919	4,731	1,529	3,202
2000–01	73,645	-0.7	16,585	57,060	77.5	16,539	3,892	12,647	5,091	1,598	3,493
2001–02	76,775	4.3	17,284	59,491	77.5	16,357	3,814	12,543	4,759	1,503	3,256
2002–03	78,650	2.4	17,514	61,136	77.7	17,161	3,839	13,322	4,835	1,483	3,352
2003–04	82,098	4.4	18,193	63,905	77.8	17,898	3,789	14,109	4,827	1,496	3,331
2004–05	85,614	4.3	19,000	66,614	77.8	18,830	3,900	14,930	5,106	1,466	3,640
2005–06	88,134	2.9	19,865	68,269	77.5	19,770	4,079	15,691	4,921	1,347	3,574
2006–07	90,039	2.2	20,343	69,696	77.4	21,037	4,265	16,772	5,153	1,382	3,771
2007–08	92,587	2.8	21,202	71,385	77.1	21,431	4,356	17,075	5,296	1,440	3,856
2008–09	94,273	1.8	21,490	72,783	77.2	23,415	4,789	18,626	5,477	1,478	3,999
2009–10	97,215	3.1	22,262	74,953	77.1	23,763	4,799	18,964	5,540	1,478	4,062
2010–11	100,906	3.8	23,230	77,676	77.0	25,062	5,127	19,935	5,851	1,481	4,370
2011–12	109,099	8.1	25,420	83,679	76.7	27,052	5,482	21,570	5,936	1,525	4,411
2012–13	114,446	4.9	26,814	87,632	76.6	27,787	5,715	22,072	6,326	1,628	4,698
2013–14	117,298	2.5	27,304	89,994	76.7	27,966	5,731	22,235	6,634	1,680	4,954
Percent change											
2003–04 to 2008–09	14.8	†	18.1	13.9	†	30.8	26.4	32.0	13.5	-1.2	20.1
2008–09 to 2013–14	24.4	†	27.1	23.6	†	19.4	19.7	19.4	21.1	13.7	23.9

†Not applicable.
NOTE: Data are for postsecondary institutions participating in Title IV federal financial aid programs. Some data have been revised from previously published figures.
SOURCE: U.S. Department of Education, National Center for Education Statistics, *Earned Degrees Conferred*, 1949–50 and 1959–60; Higher Education General Information Survey (HEGIS), "Degrees and Other Formal Awards Conferred" surveys, 1967–68 through 1985–86; Integrated Postsecondary Education Data System (IPEDS), "Completions Survey" (IPEDS-C:87–99); and IPEDS Fall 2000 through Fall 2014, Completions component. (This table was prepared September 2015.)

Table 325.85. Degrees in public administration and social services conferred by postsecondary institutions, by level of degree and sex of student: 1970–71 through 2013–14

	Bachelor's degrees					Master's degrees			Doctor's degrees		
	Total										
Year	Number	Annual percent change	Males	Females	Females as a percent of total	Total	Males	Females	Total	Males	Females
1	2	3	4	5	6	7	8	9	10	11	12
1970–71	5,466	†	1,726	3,740	68.4	7,785	3,893	3,892	174	132	42
1971–72	7,508	37.4	2,588	4,920	65.5	8,756	4,537	4,219	193	150	43
1972–73	10,690	42.4	3,998	6,692	62.6	10,068	5,271	4,797	198	160	38
1973–74	11,966	11.9	4,266	7,700	64.3	11,415	6,028	5,387	201	154	47
1974–75	13,661	14.2	4,630	9,031	66.1	13,617	7,200	6,417	257	192	65
1975–76	15,440	13.0	5,706	9,734	63.0	15,209	7,969	7,240	292	192	100
1976–77	16,136	4.5	5,544	10,592	65.6	17,026	8,810	8,216	292	197	95
1977–78	16,607	2.9	5,096	11,511	69.3	17,337	8,513	8,824	357	237	120
1978–79	17,328	4.3	4,938	12,390	71.5	17,306	8,051	9,255	315	215	100
1979–80	16,644	-3.9	4,451	12,193	73.3	17,560	7,866	9,694	342	216	126
1980–81	16,707	0.4	4,248	12,459	74.6	17,803	7,460	10,343	362	212	150
1981–82	16,495	-1.3	4,176	12,319	74.7	17,416	6,975	10,441	372	205	167
1982–83	14,414	-12.6	3,343	11,071	76.8	16,046	5,961	10,085	347	184	163
1983–84	12,570	-12.8	2,998	9,572	76.1	15,060	5,634	9,426	420	230	190
1984–85	11,754	-6.5	2,829	8,925	75.9	15,575	5,573	10,002	431	213	218
1985–86	11,887	1.1	2,966	8,921	75.0	15,692	5,594	10,098	382	171	211
1986–87	12,328	3.7	2,993	9,335	75.7	16,432	5,673	10,759	398	216	182
1987–88	12,385	0.5	2,923	9,462	76.4	16,424	5,631	10,793	470	238	232
1988–89	13,162	6.3	3,214	9,948	75.6	17,020	5,615	11,405	428	210	218
1989–90	13,908	5.7	3,334	10,574	76.0	17,399	5,634	11,765	508	235	273
1990–91	14,350	3.2	3,215	11,135	77.6	17,905	5,679	12,226	430	190	240
1991–92	15,987	11.4	3,479	12,508	78.2	19,243	5,769	13,474	432	204	228
1992–93	16,775	4.9	3,801	12,974	77.3	20,634	6,105	14,529	459	215	244
1993–94	17,815	6.2	3,919	13,896	78.0	21,833	6,406	15,427	519	238	281
1994–95	18,586	4.3	3,935	14,651	78.8	23,501	6,870	16,631	556	274	282
1995–96	19,849	6.8	4,205	15,644	78.8	24,229	6,927	17,302	499	220	279
1996–97	20,649	4.0	4,177	16,472	79.8	24,781	6,957	17,824	518	243	275
1997–98	20,408	-1.2	3,881	16,527	81.0	25,144	7,025	18,119	499	223	276
1998–99	20,323	-0.4	3,799	16,524	81.3	25,038	6,621	18,417	534	240	294
1999–2000	20,185	-0.7	3,816	16,369	81.1	25,594	6,808	18,786	537	227	310
2000–01	19,447	-3.7	3,670	15,777	81.1	25,268	6,544	18,724	574	263	311
2001–02	19,392	-0.3	3,706	15,686	80.9	25,448	6,505	18,943	571	250	321
2002–03	19,900	2.6	3,726	16,174	81.3	25,903	6,391	19,512	599	265	334
2003–04	20,552	3.3	3,793	16,759	81.5	28,250	7,001	21,249	649	275	374
2004–05	21,769	5.9	4,209	17,560	80.7	29,552	7,370	22,182	673	272	401
2005–06	21,986	1.0	4,126	17,860	81.2	30,510	7,572	22,938	704	285	419
2006–07	23,147	5.3	4,354	18,793	81.2	31,131	7,758	23,373	726	253	473
2007–08	23,493	1.5	4,202	19,291	82.1	33,029	8,140	24,889	760	269	491
2008–09	23,852	1.5	4,373	19,479	81.7	33,934	8,346	25,588	812	306	506
2009–10	25,421	6.6	4,578	20,843	82.0	35,740	8,868	26,872	838	323	515
2010–11	26,799	5.4	4,913	21,886	81.7	38,614	9,791	28,823	851	327	524
2011–12	29,695	10.8	5,386	24,309	81.9	41,737	10,494	31,243	890	343	547
2012–13	31,950	7.6	5,664	26,286	82.3	43,591	10,864	32,727	979	351	628
2013–14	33,483	4.8	5,917	27,566	82.3	44,490	10,833	33,657	1,047	346	701
Percent change											
2003–04 to 2008–09	16.1	†	15.3	16.2	†	20.1	19.2	20.4	25.1	11.3	35.3
2008–09 to 2013–14	40.4	†	35.3	41.5	†	31.1	29.8	31.5	28.9	13.1	38.5

†Not applicable.
NOTE: Data are for postsecondary institutions participating in Title IV federal financial aid programs. Some data have been revised from previously published figures.
SOURCE: U.S. Department of Education, National Center for Education Statistics, Higher Education General Information Survey (HEGIS), "Degrees and Other Formal Awards Conferred" surveys, 1970–71 through 1985–86; Integrated Postsecondary Education Data System (IPEDS), "Completions Survey" (IPEDS-C:87–99); and IPEDS Fall 2000 through Fall 2014, Completions component. (This table was prepared September 2015.)

Table 325.90. Degrees in the social sciences and history conferred by postsecondary institutions, by level of degree and sex of student: 1970–71 through 2013–14

	Bachelor's degrees					Master's degrees			Doctor's degrees		
	Total				Females as a percent of total						
Year	Number	Annual percent change	Males	Females		Total	Males	Females	Total	Males	Females
1	2	3	4	5	6	7	8	9	10	11	12
1970–71	155,324	†	98,173	57,151	36.8	16,539	11,833	4,706	3,660	3,153	507
1971–72	158,060	1.8	100,895	57,165	36.2	17,445	12,540	4,905	4,081	3,483	598
1972–73	155,970	-1.3	99,735	56,235	36.1	17,477	12,605	4,872	4,234	3,573	661
1973–74	150,320	-3.6	95,650	54,670	36.4	17,293	12,321	4,972	4,124	3,383	741
1974–75	135,190	-10.1	84,826	50,364	37.3	16,977	11,875	5,102	4,212	3,334	878
1975–76	126,396	-6.5	78,691	47,705	37.7	15,953	10,918	5,035	4,157	3,262	895
1976–77	117,040	-7.4	71,128	45,912	39.2	15,533	10,413	5,120	3,802	2,957	845
1977–78	112,952	-3.5	67,217	45,735	40.5	14,718	9,845	4,873	3,594	2,722	872
1978–79	108,059	-4.3	62,852	45,207	41.8	12,963	8,395	4,568	3,371	2,501	870
1979–80	103,662	-4.1	58,511	45,151	43.6	12,176	7,794	4,382	3,230	2,357	873
1980–81	100,513	-3.0	56,131	44,382	44.2	11,945	7,457	4,488	3,122	2,274	848
1981–82	99,705	-0.8	55,196	44,509	44.6	12,002	7,468	4,534	3,061	2,237	824
1982–83	95,228	-4.5	52,771	42,457	44.6	11,205	6,974	4,231	2,931	2,042	889
1983–84	93,323	-2.0	52,154	41,169	44.1	10,577	6,551	4,026	2,911	2,030	881
1984–85	91,570	-1.9	51,226	40,344	44.1	10,503	6,475	4,028	2,851	1,933	918
1985–86	93,840	2.5	52,724	41,116	43.8	10,564	6,419	4,145	2,955	1,970	985
1986–87	96,342	2.7	53,949	42,393	44.0	10,506	6,373	4,133	2,916	2,026	890
1987–88	100,460	4.3	56,377	44,083	43.9	10,412	6,310	4,102	2,781	1,849	932
1988–89	108,151	7.7	60,121	48,030	44.4	11,023	6,599	4,424	2,885	1,949	936
1989–90	118,083	9.2	65,887	52,196	44.2	11,634	6,898	4,736	3,010	2,019	991
1990–91	125,107	5.9	68,701	56,406	45.1	12,233	7,016	5,217	3,012	1,956	1,056
1991–92	133,974	7.1	73,001	60,973	45.5	12,702	7,237	5,465	3,218	2,126	1,092
1992–93	135,703	1.3	73,589	62,114	45.8	13,471	7,671	5,800	3,460	2,203	1,257
1993–94	133,680	-1.5	72,006	61,674	46.1	14,561	8,152	6,409	3,627	2,317	1,310
1994–95	128,154	-4.1	68,139	60,015	46.8	14,845	8,207	6,638	3,725	2,319	1,406
1995–96	126,479	-1.3	65,872	60,607	47.9	15,012	8,093	6,919	3,760	2,339	1,421
1996–97	124,891	-1.3	64,115	60,776	48.7	14,787	7,830	6,957	3,989	2,479	1,510
1997–98	125,040	0.1	63,537	61,503	49.2	14,938	7,960	6,978	4,127	2,445	1,682
1998–99	124,815	-0.2	61,843	62,972	50.5	14,396	7,440	6,956	3,873	2,290	1,583
1999–2000	127,101	1.8	62,062	65,039	51.2	14,066	7,024	7,042	4,095	2,407	1,688
2000–01	128,036	0.7	61,749	66,287	51.8	13,791	6,816	6,975	3,930	2,302	1,628
2001–02	132,874	3.8	64,170	68,704	51.7	14,112	6,941	7,171	3,902	2,219	1,683
2002–03	143,256	7.8	69,517	73,739	51.5	14,630	7,202	7,428	3,850	2,196	1,654
2003–04	150,357	5.0	73,834	76,523	50.9	16,110	7,810	8,300	3,811	2,188	1,623
2004–05	156,892	4.3	77,702	79,190	50.5	16,952	8,256	8,696	3,819	2,184	1,635
2005–06	161,485	2.9	80,799	80,686	50.0	17,369	8,415	8,954	3,914	2,218	1,696
2006–07	164,183	1.7	82,417	81,766	49.8	17,665	8,577	9,088	3,844	2,110	1,734
2007–08	167,363	1.9	84,868	82,495	49.3	18,495	9,349	9,146	4,059	2,194	1,865
2008–09	168,517	0.7	85,202	83,315	49.4	19,241	9,605	9,636	4,234	2,353	1,881
2009–10	172,782	2.5	87,404	85,378	49.4	20,234	9,967	10,267	4,238	2,292	1,946
2010–11	177,169	2.5	89,809	87,360	49.3	21,085	10,578	10,507	4,390	2,331	2,059
2011–12	178,534	0.8	90,628	87,906	49.2	21,891	10,987	10,904	4,597	2,464	2,133
2012–13	177,767	-0.4	90,143	87,624	49.3	21,591	10,811	10,780	4,610	2,461	2,149
2013–14	173,096	-2.6	88,233	84,863	49.0	21,475	10,750	10,725	4,724	2,494	2,230
Percent change											
2003–04 to 2008–09	12.1	†	15.4	8.9	†	19.4	23.0	16.1	11.1	7.5	15.9
2008–09 to 2013–14	2.7	†	3.6	1.9	†	11.6	11.9	11.3	11.6	6.0	18.6

†Not applicable.
NOTE: Data are for postsecondary institutions participating in Title IV federal financial aid programs. Some data have been revised from previously published figures.
SOURCE: U.S. Department of Education, National Center for Education Statistics, Higher Education General Information Survey (HEGIS), "Degrees and Other Formal Awards Conferred" surveys, 1970–71 through 1985–86; Integrated Postsecondary Education Data System (IPEDS), "Completions Survey" (IPEDS-C:87–99); and IPEDS Fall 2000 through Fall 2014, Completions component. (This table was prepared September 2015.)

Table 325.92. Degrees in economics, history, political science and government, and sociology conferred by postsecondary institutions, by level of degree: Selected years, 1949–50 through 2013–14

Year	Economics			History			Political science and government			Sociology		
	Bachelor's	Master's	Doctor's	Bachelor's	Master's	Doctor's	Bachelor's	Master's	Doctor's	Bachelor's	Master's	Doctor's
1	2	3	4	5	6	7	8	9	10	11	12	13
1949–50	14,568	921	200	13,542	1,801	275	6,336	710	127	7,870	552	98
1951–52	8,593	695	239	10,187	1,445	317	4,911	525	147	6,648	517	141
1953–54	6,719	609	245	9,363	1,220	355	5,314	534	153	5,692	440	184
1955–56	6,555	581	232	10,510	1,114	259	5,633	509	203	5,878	402	170
1957–58	7,457	669	239	12,840	1,397	297	6,116	665	170	6,568	397	150
1959–60	7,453	708	237	14,737	1,794	342	6,596	722	201	7,147	440	161
1961–62	8,366	853	268	17,340	2,163	343	8,326	839	214	8,120	578	173
1963–64	10,583	1,104	385	23,668	2,705	507	12,126	1,163	263	10,943	646	198
1965–66	11,555	1,522	458	28,612	3,883	599	15,242	1,429	336	15,038	981	244
1967–68	15,193	1,916	600	35,291	4,845	688	20,387	1,937	457	21,710	1,193	367
1969–70	17,197	1,988	794	43,386	5,049	1,038	25,713	2,105	525	30,436	1,813	534
1970–71	15,758	1,995	721	44,663	5,157	991	27,482	2,318	700	33,263	1,808	574
1971–72	15,231	2,224	794	43,695	5,217	1,133	28,135	2,451	758	35,216	1,944	636
1972–73	14,770	2,225	845	40,943	5,030	1,140	30,100	2,398	747	35,436	1,923	583
1973–74	14,285	2,141	788	37,049	4,533	1,114	30,744	2,448	766	35,491	2,196	632
1974–75	14,046	2,127	815	31,470	4,226	1,117	29,126	2,333	680	31,488	2,112	693
1975–76	14,741	2,087	763	28,400	3,658	1,014	28,302	2,191	723	27,634	2,009	729
1976–77	15,296	2,158	758	25,433	3,393	921	26,411	2,222	641	24,713	1,830	714
1977–78	15,661	1,995	706	23,004	3,033	813	26,069	2,069	636	22,750	1,611	599
1978–79	16,409	1,955	712	21,019	2,536	756	25,628	2,037	563	20,285	1,415	612
1979–80	17,863	1,821	677	19,301	2,367	712	25,457	1,938	535	18,881	1,341	583
1980–81	18,753	1,911	727	18,301	2,237	643	24,977	1,875	484	17,272	1,240	610
1981–82	19,876	1,964	677	17,146	2,210	636	25,658	1,954	513	16,042	1,145	558
1982–83	20,517	1,972	734	16,467	2,041	575	25,791	1,829	435	14,105	1,112	522
1983–84	20,719	1,891	729	16,643	1,940	561	25,719	1,769	457	13,145	1,008	520
1984–85	20,711	1,992	749	16,049	1,921	468	25,834	1,500	441	11,968	1,022	480
1985–86	21,602	1,937	789	16,415	1,961	497	26,439	1,704	439	12,271	965	504
1986–87	22,378	1,855	750	16,997	2,021	534	26,817	1,618	435	12,239	950	451
1987–88	22,911	1,847	770	18,207	2,093	517	27,207	1,579	391	13,024	984	452
1988–89	23,454	1,886	827	20,159	2,121	487	30,450	1,598	452	14,435	1,135	451
1989–90	23,923	1,950	806	22,476	2,369	570	33,560	1,580	480	16,035	1,198	432
1990–91	23,488	1,951	802	24,541	2,591	606	35,737	1,772	468	17,550	1,260	465
1991–92	23,423	2,106	866	26,966	2,754	644	37,805	1,908	535	19,568	1,347	501
1992–93	21,321	2,292	879	27,774	2,952	690	37,931	1,943	529	20,896	1,521	536
1993–94	19,496	2,521	869	27,503	3,009	752	36,097	2,147	616	22,368	1,639	530
1994–95	17,673	2,400	910	26,598	3,091	816	33,013	2,019	637	22,886	1,748	546
1995–96	16,674	2,533	916	26,005	2,898	805	30,775	2,024	634	24,071	1,772	527
1996–97	16,539	2,433	968	25,214	2,901	873	28,969	1,909	686	24,672	1,731	591
1997–98	17,074	2,435	928	25,726	2,895	937	28,044	1,957	705	24,806	1,737	596
1998–99	17,577	2,332	819	24,742	2,618	931	27,476	1,667	694	24,979	1,940	521
1999–2000	18,441	2,168	851	25,247	2,573	984	27,635	1,627	693	25,598	1,996	595
2000–01	19,437	2,139	851	25,090	2,365	931	27,792	1,596	688	25,268	1,845	546
2001–02	20,927	2,330	826	26,001	2,420	924	29,354	1,641	625	25,202	1,928	534
2002–03	23,007	2,582	836	27,757	2,521	861	33,205	1,664	671	26,095	1,897	591
2003–04	24,069	2,824	849	29,808	2,522	855	35,581	1,869	618	26,939	2,009	558
2004–05	24,217	3,092	973	31,398	2,893	819	38,107	1,983	636	28,473	1,499	527
2005–06	23,807	2,941	930	33,153	2,992	852	39,409	2,054	649	28,467	1,547	562
2006–07	23,916	2,962	941	34,446	3,144	807	39,899	2,102	614	28,960	1,545	569
2007–08	25,278	3,187	1,025	34,441	3,403	860	40,259	2,156	639	28,815	1,560	585
2008–09	26,301	3,233	1,015	34,713	3,543	918	39,202	2,171	709	28,735	1,580	628
2009–10	27,623	3,358	983	35,191	3,858	888	39,462	2,252	745	28,650	1,428	603
2010–11	28,517	3,731	1,018	35,008	4,003	908	40,133	2,488	722	29,281	1,559	656
2011–12	27,994	3,890	1,130	35,122	4,155	969	39,792	2,510	746	30,136	1,696	626
2012–13	28,449	3,872	1,076	34,188	4,083	1,003	38,466	2,332	821	30,531	1,603	615
2013–14	29,995	4,115	1,059	31,106	3,955	1,040	37,361	2,294	792	30,059	1,611	674
Percent change												
2003–04 to 2008–09	9.3	14.5	19.6	16.5	40.5	7.4	10.2	16.2	14.7	6.7	-21.4	12.5
2008–09 to 2013–14	14.0	27.3	4.3	-10.4	11.6	13.3	-4.7	5.7	11.7	4.6	2.0	7.3

NOTE: Data are for postsecondary institutions participating in Title IV federal financial aid programs. Some data have been revised from previously published figures.
SOURCE: U.S. Department of Education, National Center for Education Statistics, *Earned Degrees Conferred*, 1949–50 through 1963–64; Higher Education General Information Survey (HEGIS), "Degrees and Other Formal Awards Conferred" surveys, 1965–66 through 1985–86; Integrated Postsecondary Education Data System (IPEDS), "Completions Survey" (IPEDS-C:87–99); and IPEDS Fall 2000 through Fall 2014, Completions component. (This table was prepared September 2015.)

Table 325.95. Degrees in visual and performing arts conferred by postsecondary institutions, by level of degree and sex of student: 1970–71 through 2013–14

Year	Bachelor's degrees					Master's degrees			Doctor's degrees		
	Total										
	Number	Annual percent change	Males	Females	Females as a percent of total	Total	Males	Females	Total	Males	Females
1	2	3	4	5	6	7	8	9	10	11	12
1970–71	30,394	†	12,256	18,138	59.7	6,675	3,510	3,165	621	483	138
1971–72	33,831	11.3	13,580	20,251	59.9	7,537	4,049	3,488	572	428	144
1972–73	36,017	6.5	14,267	21,750	60.4	7,254	4,005	3,249	616	449	167
1973–74	39,730	10.3	15,821	23,909	60.2	8,001	4,325	3,676	585	440	145
1974–75	40,782	2.6	15,532	25,250	61.9	8,362	4,448	3,914	649	446	203
1975–76	42,138	3.3	16,491	25,647	60.9	8,817	4,507	4,310	620	447	173
1976–77	41,793	-0.8	16,166	25,627	61.3	8,636	4,211	4,425	662	447	215
1977–78	40,951	2.0	15,572	25,379	62.0	9,036	4,327	4,709	708	448	260
1978–79	40,969	#	15,380	25,589	62.5	8,524	3,933	4,591	700	454	246
1979–80	40,892	-0.2	15,065	25,827	63.2	8,708	4,067	4,641	655	413	242
1980–81	40,479	-1.0	14,798	25,681	63.4	8,629	4,056	4,573	654	396	258
1981–82	40,422	-0.1	14,819	25,603	63.3	8,746	3,866	4,880	670	380	290
1982–83	39,804	-1.5	14,695	25,109	63.1	8,763	4,013	4,750	692	404	288
1983–84	40,131	0.8	15,089	25,042	62.4	8,526	3,897	4,629	730	406	324
1984–85	38,285	-4.6	14,518	23,767	62.1	8,720	3,896	4,824	696	407	289
1985–86	37,241	-2.7	14,236	23,005	61.8	8,420	3,775	4,645	722	396	326
1986–87	36,873	-1.0	13,980	22,893	62.1	8,508	3,756	4,752	793	447	346
1987–88	37,150	0.8	14,225	22,925	61.7	7,939	3,442	4,497	727	424	303
1988–89	38,420	3.4	14,698	23,722	61.7	8,267	3,611	4,656	753	446	307
1989–90	39,934	3.9	15,189	24,745	62.0	8,481	3,706	4,775	849	472	377
1990–91	42,186	5.6	15,761	26,425	62.6	8,657	3,830	4,827	838	466	372
1991–92	46,522	10.3	17,616	28,906	62.1	9,353	4,078	5,275	906	504	402
1992–93	47,761	2.7	18,610	29,151	61.0	9,440	4,099	5,341	882	478	404
1993–94	49,053	2.7	19,538	29,515	60.2	9,925	4,229	5,696	1,054	585	469
1994–95	48,690	-0.7	19,781	28,909	59.4	10,277	4,374	5,903	1,080	545	535
1995–96	49,296	1.2	20,126	29,170	59.2	10,280	4,361	5,919	1,067	524	543
1996–97	50,083	1.6	20,729	29,354	58.6	10,627	4,470	6,157	1,060	525	535
1997–98	52,077	4.0	21,483	30,594	58.7	11,145	4,596	6,549	1,163	566	597
1998–99	54,446	4.5	22,270	32,176	59.1	10,762	4,544	6,218	1,117	567	550
1999–2000	58,791	8.0	24,003	34,788	59.2	10,918	4,672	6,246	1,127	537	590
2000–01	61,148	4.0	24,967	36,181	59.2	11,404	4,788	6,616	1,167	568	599
2001–02	66,773	9.2	27,130	39,643	59.4	11,595	4,912	6,683	1,114	490	624
2002–03	71,482	7.1	27,922	43,560	60.9	11,982	4,975	7,007	1,293	613	680
2003–04	77,181	8.0	30,037	47,144	61.1	12,906	5,531	7,375	1,282	572	710
2004–05	80,955	4.9	31,355	49,600	61.3	13,183	5,646	7,537	1,278	594	684
2005–06	83,297	2.9	32,117	51,180	61.4	13,530	5,801	7,729	1,383	639	744
2006–07	85,186	2.3	32,729	52,457	61.6	13,767	5,910	7,857	1,364	625	739
2007–08	87,703	3.0	33,862	53,841	61.4	14,164	5,998	8,166	1,453	675	778
2008–09	89,143	1.6	35,055	54,088	60.7	14,918	6,325	8,593	1,569	726	843
2009–10	91,798	3.0	35,768	56,030	61.0	15,562	6,531	9,031	1,599	700	899
2010–11	93,939	2.3	36,342	57,597	61.3	16,277	6,881	9,396	1,646	770	876
2011–12	95,806	2.0	37,164	58,642	61.2	17,307	7,320	9,987	1,728	790	938
2012–13	97,799	2.1	38,063	59,736	61.1	17,869	7,610	10,259	1,814	850	964
2013–14	97,246	-0.6	38,081	59,165	60.8	17,863	7,711	10,152	1,778	869	909
Percent change											
2003–04 to 2008–09	15.5	†	16.7	14.7	†	15.6	14.4	16.5	22.4	26.9	18.7
2008–09 to 2013–14	9.1	†	8.6	9.4	†	19.7	21.9	18.1	13.3	19.7	7.8

†Not applicable.
#Rounds to zero.
NOTE: Data are for postsecondary institutions participating in Title IV federal financial aid programs. Some data have been revised from previously published figures.

SOURCE: U.S. Department of Education, National Center for Education Statistics, Higher Education General Information Survey (HEGIS), "Degrees and Other Formal Awards Conferred" surveys, 1970–71 through 1985–86; Integrated Postsecondary Education Data System (IPEDS), "Completions Survey" (IPEDS-C:87–99); and IPEDS Fall 2000 through Fall 2014, Completions component. (This table was prepared September 2015.)

Table 326.10. Graduation rate from first institution attended for first-time, full-time bachelor's degree-seeking students at 4-year postsecondary institutions, by race/ethnicity, time to completion, sex, control of institution, and acceptance rate: Selected cohort entry years, 1996 through 2008

Time to completion, sex, control of institution, cohort entry year, and acceptance rate	Total	White	Black	Hispanic	Asian/Pacific Islander Total	Asian	Pacific Islander	American Indian/ Alaska Native	Two or more races	Nonresident alien
1	2	3	4	5	6	7	8	9	10	11
Graduating within 4 years after start, males and females										
All 4-year institutions										
1996 starting cohort	33.7	36.3	19.5	22.8	37.5	—	—	18.8	—	41.7
2000 starting cohort	36.1	38.9	21.3	25.9	41.0	—	—	21.0	—	41.9
2002 starting cohort	36.4	39.3	20.4	26.4	42.8	—	—	20.5	—	38.7
2003 starting cohort	37.0	40.2	20.2	26.7	43.9	—	—	20.6	—	39.4
2004 starting cohort	38.0	41.3	20.5	27.9	45.0	—	—	21.8	—	43.7
2005 starting cohort	38.3	41.8	20.2	28.2	45.1	45.5	22.2	21.8	44.1	44.0
2006 starting cohort	39.1	42.7	20.6	29.3	46.0	46.4	24.2	21.9	46.6	44.1
2007 starting cohort	39.4	43.3	20.8	29.8	46.2	46.7	25.8	23.0	49.1	44.6
2008 starting cohort	39.8	43.7	21.4	30.4	47.1	47.7	26.7	23.0	46.5	46.4
Public institutions										
1996 starting cohort	26.0	28.3	15.0	15.8	28.5	—	—	14.5	—	30.9
2000 starting cohort	29.0	31.4	17.9	18.9	33.7	—	—	16.4	—	32.7
2002 starting cohort	29.9	32.3	16.9	20.1	35.8	—	—	16.0	—	33.4
2003 starting cohort	30.7	33.5	16.5	20.7	37.5	—	—	17.0	—	33.8
2004 starting cohort	31.4	34.2	16.4	21.5	38.0	—	—	17.2	—	34.4
2005 starting cohort	32.0	35.1	16.8	22.4	38.7	39.1	16.9	17.9	28.7	33.5
2006 starting cohort	32.9	36.1	17.2	23.1	40.0	40.4	18.6	17.9	30.5	33.9
2007 starting cohort	33.5	36.9	17.4	24.0	39.8	40.2	20.9	19.5	35.9	34.4
2008 starting cohort	34.4	37.9	18.6	24.8	41.1	41.6	22.1	19.1	35.2	38.0
Nonprofit institutions										
1996 starting cohort	48.6	51.3	29.3	39.9	57.9	—	—	33.7	—	50.4
2000 starting cohort	50.3	53.5	28.2	42.9	58.8	—	—	36.0	—	50.3
2002 starting cohort	51.0	54.0	29.4	44.1	61.0	—	—	36.6	—	54.8
2003 starting cohort	51.6	54.7	29.8	44.0	61.5	—	—	34.4	—	55.3
2004 starting cohort	52.6	55.5	30.6	46.2	62.8	—	—	39.0	—	57.4
2005 starting cohort	52.2	55.4	29.2	45.1	62.3	62.8	34.9	35.2	59.9	57.4
2006 starting cohort	52.9	56.2	29.7	47.4	62.8	63.5	37.2	38.3	62.1	56.8
2007 starting cohort	52.8	56.4	29.7	46.7	63.6	64.2	40.1	37.0	62.6	56.9
2008 starting cohort	52.7	56.3	29.7	47.2	63.4	63.9	44.8	37.0	59.3	57.1
For-profit institutions										
1996 starting cohort	21.8	26.3	14.8	20.1	24.6	—	—	16.5	—	33.8
2000 starting cohort	25.7	30.3	22.5	27.4	42.7	—	—	28.0	—	36.5
2002 starting cohort	14.2	17.5	10.0	19.1	29.4	—	—	11.2	—	3.4
2003 starting cohort	14.8	18.2	10.4	19.5	25.5	—	—	8.4	—	4.7
2004 starting cohort	20.6	27.3	13.3	20.7	31.4	—	—	9.4	—	10.6
2005 starting cohort	20.0	27.9	11.0	19.6	31.7	33.8	15.4	15.2	24.7	15.4
2006 starting cohort	22.8	32.5	12.7	23.0	30.1	32.4	9.4	13.0	27.6	22.4
2007 starting cohort	22.5	32.7	11.6	22.7	32.2	36.4	8.2	12.6	27.2	24.4
2008 starting cohort	17.5	26.4	9.6	20.9	30.7	34.8	8.7	12.8	30.1	19.7
Graduating within 4 years after start, males										
All 4-year institutions										
1996 starting cohort	28.5	30.6	13.9	19.0	32.2	—	—	15.1	—	38.6
2000 starting cohort	31.1	33.4	15.5	21.8	35.7	—	—	17.1	—	39.3
2002 starting cohort	31.3	33.8	14.7	21.8	37.4	—	—	17.2	—	36.6
2003 starting cohort	32.2	34.8	14.7	22.5	39.0	—	—	17.7	—	37.7
2004 starting cohort	33.0	35.7	15.1	23.3	39.9	—	—	18.9	—	39.7
2005 starting cohort	33.5	36.4	15.0	24.2	39.9	40.2	19.6	18.8	40.2	40.1
2006 starting cohort	34.3	37.2	15.7	24.9	41.2	41.6	21.6	17.6	43.2	39.6
2007 starting cohort	34.5	37.7	15.7	25.4	41.1	41.5	24.0	18.6	44.7	39.3
2008 starting cohort	34.8	38.1	16.2	25.7	42.1	42.5	25.0	18.9	40.7	41.0
Public institutions										
1996 starting cohort	20.8	22.6	9.9	12.5	23.4	—	—	10.9	—	28.6
2000 starting cohort	23.6	25.5	11.7	14.5	27.8	—	—	11.9	—	30.2
2002 starting cohort	24.5	26.6	11.0	15.8	30.4	—	—	12.7	—	30.3
2003 starting cohort	25.7	27.9	10.9	16.4	32.5	—	—	14.1	—	30.8
2004 starting cohort	26.2	28.5	11.2	16.9	32.9	—	—	14.5	—	30.1
2005 starting cohort	27.1	29.6	11.7	18.3	33.5	33.8	14.1	15.0	26.4	29.8
2006 starting cohort	27.9	30.4	12.1	18.8	34.9	35.2	15.4	13.8	29.2	29.7
2007 starting cohort	28.3	31.1	12.1	19.5	34.8	35.0	18.8	14.7	33.8	29.4
2008 starting cohort	29.3	32.1	13.3	20.0	36.1	36.5	18.7	15.3	30.7	33.1
Nonprofit institutions										
1996 starting cohort	43.6	46.2	22.1	35.0	53.5	—	—	28.9	—	47.0
2000 starting cohort	46.0	48.9	22.3	38.2	56.1	—	—	33.2	—	48.0
2002 starting cohort	46.3	49.1	22.9	38.8	57.6	—	—	32.1	—	50.6
2003 starting cohort	47.0	49.8	23.1	39.9	58.6	—	—	30.7	—	51.3
2004 starting cohort	47.8	50.6	23.2	41.2	59.0	—	—	35.4	—	53.2
2005 starting cohort	47.5	50.5	22.6	40.7	58.8	59.3	29.4	30.8	55.7	52.7
2006 starting cohort	48.2	51.2	23.4	42.4	60.2	60.8	34.5	34.2	58.4	52.2
2007 starting cohort	47.8	51.4	23.0	42.3	60.0	60.5	37.3	32.2	57.8	51.4
2008 starting cohort	47.7	51.3	23.0	42.4	59.5	59.9	43.5	31.5	53.9	51.6

See notes at end of table.

Table 326.10. Graduation rate from first institution attended for first-time, full-time bachelor's degree-seeking students at 4-year postsecondary institutions, by race/ethnicity, time to completion, sex, control of institution, and acceptance rate: Selected cohort entry years, 1996 through 2008—Continued

Time to completion, sex, control of institution, cohort entry year, and acceptance rate	Total	White	Black	Hispanic	Asian/Pacific Islander			American Indian/ Alaska Native	Two or more races	Nonresident alien
					Total	Asian	Pacific Islander			
1	2	3	4	5	6	7	8	9	10	11
For-profit institutions										
1996 starting cohort	22.3	25.5	16.1	23.0	27.7	—	—	25.6	—	33.1
2000 starting cohort	30.1	34.3	23.7	30.9	44.5	—	—	28.7	—	36.7
2002 starting cohort	17.0	20.9	11.8	20.1	33.3	—	—	17.6	—	4.0
2003 starting cohort	17.4	20.9	11.8	20.8	28.1	—	—	11.1	—	6.4
2004 starting cohort	23.5	30.5	15.0	21.6	36.6	—	—	12.1	—	10.7
2005 starting cohort	23.6	31.4	12.0	22.2	32.2	33.2	24.0	20.8	25.2	16.7
2006 starting cohort	27.8	37.2	16.6	26.0	33.7	35.2	17.2	14.7	30.1	23.7
2007 starting cohort	28.4	39.3	15.3	25.7	35.8	38.3	14.1	19.0	25.8	26.9
2008 starting cohort	20.7	30.5	11.1	22.0	34.0	35.9	16.2	12.4	27.8	14.9
Graduating within 4 years after start, females										
All 4-year institutions										
1996 starting cohort	38.0	41.1	23.2	25.8	42.2	—	—	21.7	—	45.8
2000 starting cohort	40.2	43.5	25.2	29.0	45.7	—	—	24.0	—	45.3
2002 starting cohort	40.5	43.9	24.3	29.9	47.4	—	—	23.0	—	41.0
2003 starting cohort	41.0	44.8	23.9	29.8	48.1	—	—	22.8	—	41.1
2004 starting cohort	42.2	45.9	24.2	31.4	49.4	—	—	24.0	—	48.1
2005 starting cohort	42.2	46.4	23.7	31.3	49.6	50.1	24.2	24.1	47.3	48.4
2006 starting cohort	43.1	47.4	23.9	32.5	50.2	50.8	26.2	25.2	49.1	49.3
2007 starting cohort	43.5	48.0	24.3	33.1	50.7	51.3	27.0	26.3	52.3	50.8
2008 starting cohort	43.9	48.6	24.9	33.9	51.6	52.4	27.8	26.0	50.6	52.5
Public institutions										
1996 starting cohort	30.3	33.3	18.3	18.4	33.2	—	—	17.3	—	34.1
2000 starting cohort	33.5	36.3	22.0	22.2	39.1	—	—	19.9	—	36.2
2002 starting cohort	34.3	37.2	20.9	23.4	40.8	—	—	18.5	—	37.0
2003 starting cohort	35.0	38.3	20.2	23.9	42.0	—	—	19.2	—	37.2
2004 starting cohort	35.7	39.2	19.9	24.9	42.6	—	—	19.3	—	39.6
2005 starting cohort	36.2	39.9	20.2	25.5	43.5	43.9	19.0	20.1	30.7	37.7
2006 starting cohort	37.2	41.1	20.6	26.4	44.7	45.1	21.3	21.1	31.5	39.1
2007 starting cohort	37.8	42.0	21.0	27.5	44.6	45.1	22.5	23.1	37.5	40.8
2008 starting cohort	38.8	43.1	22.2	28.5	45.8	46.4	24.5	21.9	38.7	44.0
Nonprofit institutions										
1996 starting cohort	52.6	55.5	34.2	43.5	61.6	—	—	37.5	—	54.4
2000 starting cohort	53.7	57.3	32.3	46.2	60.9	—	—	38.1	—	53.2
2002 starting cohort	54.7	57.8	34.0	47.8	63.6	—	—	39.9	—	59.2
2003 starting cohort	55.3	58.6	34.4	46.7	63.7	—	—	37.0	—	59.7
2004 starting cohort	56.4	59.4	35.9	49.6	65.6	—	—	41.5	—	61.9
2005 starting cohort	55.9	59.2	34.1	48.1	64.9	65.5	38.6	38.5	63.1	62.7
2006 starting cohort	56.7	60.1	34.4	50.8	64.9	65.7	39.2	40.9	64.4	61.8
2007 starting cohort	56.7	60.4	34.7	49.8	66.4	67.2	41.8	40.6	65.6	62.8
2008 starting cohort	56.7	60.4	34.8	50.5	66.5	67.1	45.8	41.0	62.5	62.8
For-profit institutions										
1996 starting cohort	21.1	27.5	13.7	16.1	20.3	—	—	9.6	—	34.6
2000 starting cohort	20.7	24.5	21.4	23.1	39.3	—	—	27.2	—	36.3
2002 starting cohort	11.6	14.0	8.7	18.1	23.9	—	—	6.0	—	3.1
2003 starting cohort	12.8	15.9	9.5	18.3	22.8	—	—	6.7	—	3.7
2004 starting cohort	17.8	23.8	12.2	19.9	25.0	—	—	7.4	—	10.5
2005 starting cohort	16.9	24.1	10.4	17.3	30.9	34.6	5.9	11.4	24.0	14.4
2006 starting cohort	18.1	26.7	10.1	20.3	26.2	29.3	3.7	11.8	24.1	21.3
2007 starting cohort	17.0	24.5	9.2	19.9	28.8	34.4	5.1	8.1	29.4	22.3
2008 starting cohort	14.7	22.2	8.6	19.9	27.5	33.7	5.6	13.1	33.3	23.7
Graduating within 5 years after start, males and females										
All 4-year institutions										
1996 starting cohort	50.2	53.3	33.3	38.9	56.4	—	—	33.3	—	54.3
2000 starting cohort	52.6	55.7	36.0	42.4	60.1	—	—	35.1	—	55.2
2002 starting cohort	52.3	55.7	34.3	42.5	61.0	—	—	33.8	—	50.6
2003 starting cohort	53.2	56.9	34.2	43.0	62.1	—	—	33.7	—	52.1
2004 starting cohort	54.1	57.7	34.5	44.0	62.9	—	—	34.7	—	57.2
2005 starting cohort	54.2	58.0	34.2	44.6	63.2	63.6	40.6	34.7	58.6	58.1
2006 starting cohort	54.9	58.7	34.9	45.8	64.4	64.9	41.7	35.6	61.8	59.0
2007 starting cohort	55.1	59.1	35.5	46.4	64.2	64.7	42.6	36.3	63.9	58.9
2008 starting cohort	55.3	59.5	35.7	47.1	65.1	65.7	43.8	36.3	60.5	60.8
Public institutions										
1996 starting cohort	45.9	49.0	30.5	34.1	51.3	—	—	30.0	—	46.5
2000 starting cohort	49.1	51.9	34.6	38.0	56.8	—	—	31.9	—	49.8
2002 starting cohort	49.2	52.2	32.9	38.8	57.7	—	—	30.8	—	50.4
2003 starting cohort	50.3	53.6	32.4	39.5	59.0	—	—	31.6	—	51.4
2004 starting cohort	50.7	54.1	32.2	40.2	59.3	—	—	31.6	—	51.9
2005 starting cohort	51.1	54.7	32.6	41.4	59.9	60.2	39.1	32.5	47.6	51.3
2006 starting cohort	51.9	55.5	33.5	42.2	61.6	62.0	41.3	32.9	50.1	51.9
2007 starting cohort	52.3	56.0	34.1	43.3	61.0	61.4	41.1	34.4	54.9	51.9
2008 starting cohort	53.1	56.7	35.0	44.4	62.1	62.6	41.8	34.1	52.1	55.1

See notes at end of table.

Table 326.10. Graduation rate from first institution attended for first-time, full-time bachelor's degree-seeking students at 4-year postsecondary institutions, by race/ethnicity, time to completion, sex, control of institution, and acceptance rate: Selected cohort entry years, 1996 through 2008—Continued

Time to completion, sex, control of institution, cohort entry year, and acceptance rate	Total	White	Black	Hispanic	Asian/Pacific Islander			American Indian/ Alaska Native	Two or more races	Nonresident alien
					Total	Asian	Pacific Islander			
1	2	3	4	5	6	7	8	9	10	11
Nonprofit institutions										
1996 starting cohort	59.2	61.8	40.2	51.4	68.7	—	—	45.2	—	60.4
2000 starting cohort	60.8	63.8	39.9	55.1	70.0	—	—	46.9	—	60.4
2002 starting cohort	61.3	64.2	40.2	55.7	71.1	—	—	46.7	—	64.7
2003 starting cohort	62.3	65.2	41.2	56.1	72.0	—	—	44.4	—	65.6
2004 starting cohort	63.0	65.8	41.8	57.8	73.1	—	—	47.9	—	67.9
2005 starting cohort	62.6	65.6	40.5	56.6	73.1	73.6	49.4	44.0	71.5	67.9
2006 starting cohort	63.2	66.1	41.2	59.0	73.5	74.2	47.4	48.8	74.5	68.6
2007 starting cohort	63.1	66.3	41.5	58.5	74.2	74.8	53.9	45.9	74.1	68.2
2008 starting cohort	63.2	66.4	41.4	58.6	74.3	74.7	57.7	46.6	70.7	68.6
For-profit institutions										
1996 starting cohort	25.4	30.1	17.8	23.1	27.3	—	—	19.8	—	51.6
2000 starting cohort	30.0	34.8	28.0	31.3	45.1	—	—	29.4	—	44.0
2002 starting cohort	17.2	20.7	12.5	22.7	32.0	—	—	12.6	—	6.0
2003 starting cohort	20.2	23.6	15.6	24.4	30.4	—	—	11.4	—	10.0
2004 starting cohort	25.9	32.9	19.1	25.8	36.5	—	—	15.5	—	17.7
2005 starting cohort	25.5	33.3	15.8	26.0	38.2	40.2	23.1	18.9	27.3	24.1
2006 starting cohort	28.0	37.2	17.8	29.8	38.0	40.2	18.7	16.8	30.5	30.3
2007 starting cohort	27.8	37.6	16.7	29.1	38.9	43.1	14.4	16.2	31.0	34.6
2008 starting cohort	22.9	31.7	14.8	27.7	37.4	40.7	19.6	16.7	34.7	33.3
Graduating within 5 years after start, males										
All 4-year institutions										
1996 starting cohort	46.2	49.2	27.0	34.4	51.8	—	—	31.2	—	51.5
2000 starting cohort	49.0	52.0	29.9	37.8	56.5	—	—	31.6	—	53.0
2002 starting cohort	48.7	52.1	28.2	37.5	57.4	—	—	30.9	—	49.3
2003 starting cohort	49.9	53.5	28.5	38.6	58.6	—	—	31.1	—	50.9
2004 starting cohort	50.6	54.2	28.8	39.3	59.3	—	—	31.9	—	53.5
2005 starting cohort	50.9	54.7	28.8	40.7	59.4	59.7	39.0	33.1	55.6	54.2
2006 starting cohort	51.6	55.2	29.8	41.4	61.1	61.5	39.7	31.8	59.3	54.5
2007 starting cohort	51.6	55.5	29.9	42.2	60.3	60.7	42.1	32.6	60.4	53.9
2008 starting cohort	51.6	55.6	30.1	42.3	61.4	61.8	42.8	32.9	56.1	55.5
Public institutions										
1996 starting cohort	41.6	44.6	24.0	29.4	46.4	—	—	27.7	—	44.1
2000 starting cohort	44.8	47.6	27.4	32.6	52.1	—	—	27.7	—	47.2
2002 starting cohort	45.3	48.3	26.0	33.7	53.7	—	—	27.5	—	47.0
2003 starting cohort	46.7	50.0	26.3	34.7	55.1	—	—	28.7	—	48.2
2004 starting cohort	47.0	50.4	26.3	35.2	55.4	—	—	28.6	—	47.2
2005 starting cohort	47.8	51.3	26.9	37.2	56.0	56.3	37.1	31.2	44.9	46.9
2006 starting cohort	48.4	51.8	27.8	37.4	57.7	58.0	38.8	29.0	48.5	47.0
2007 starting cohort	48.6	52.2	28.1	38.6	56.9	57.2	40.7	30.2	53.5	46.8
2008 starting cohort	49.1	52.7	29.1	39.0	58.1	58.5	39.1	31.2	47.4	50.3
Nonprofit institutions										
1996 starting cohort	55.8	58.5	34.0	47.4	65.9	—	—	42.9	—	57.7
2000 starting cohort	58.5	61.3	35.1	51.7	69.9	—	—	45.9	—	58.9
2002 starting cohort	58.5	61.5	34.7	51.4	70.0	—	—	44.0	—	61.9
2003 starting cohort	59.3	62.3	35.0	53.2	70.7	—	—	41.5	—	62.2
2004 starting cohort	60.1	62.9	35.6	54.0	71.2	—	—	46.0	—	64.4
2005 starting cohort	59.5	62.5	34.7	53.3	70.6	71.0	45.2	40.4	69.3	63.9
2006 starting cohort	60.2	63.2	35.6	55.4	72.1	72.9	44.6	45.7	72.8	64.4
2007 starting cohort	59.7	63.2	35.0	55.1	71.5	72.0	50.8	42.5	70.9	63.1
2008 starting cohort	59.6	63.1	35.0	54.8	72.1	72.5	56.9	41.7	68.6	63.0
For-profit institutions										
1996 starting cohort	25.6	29.2	18.1	25.4	29.9	—	—	30.8	—	51.0
2000 starting cohort	33.6	38.1	27.6	34.4	46.4	—	—	28.7	—	43.1
2002 starting cohort	19.9	24.1	14.3	23.6	35.4	—	—	18.5	—	6.3
2003 starting cohort	22.6	26.3	16.0	24.9	32.0	—	—	16.0	—	10.2
2004 starting cohort	27.8	35.1	19.1	25.9	41.6	—	—	15.0	—	16.8
2005 starting cohort	28.7	36.4	16.4	27.4	38.1	38.7	33.3	23.8	28.5	24.9
2006 starting cohort	32.5	41.5	20.9	32.0	40.8	42.1	25.9	18.2	34.0	32.4
2007 starting cohort	32.7	43.3	19.5	30.7	41.8	44.2	21.1	23.1	27.7	34.8
2008 starting cohort	25.0	34.9	14.7	27.4	40.3	42.0	25.0	14.2	31.1	26.7
Graduating within 5 years after start, females										
All 4-year institutions										
1996 starting cohort	53.6	56.8	37.5	42.4	60.5	—	—	34.9	—	57.9
2000 starting cohort	55.6	58.8	40.2	45.9	63.4	—	—	37.8	—	58.0
2002 starting cohort	55.2	58.6	38.4	46.2	64.1	—	—	36.0	—	52.0
2003 starting cohort	55.9	59.7	38.0	46.2	65.1	—	—	35.8	—	53.5
2004 starting cohort	56.9	60.7	38.3	47.6	66.0	—	—	36.8	—	61.4
2005 starting cohort	56.8	60.8	37.8	47.5	66.5	66.9	41.9	35.9	61.2	62.4
2006 starting cohort	57.6	61.7	38.4	49.0	67.4	68.0	43.2	38.5	63.7	64.2
2007 starting cohort	58.1	62.2	39.3	49.7	67.7	68.4	42.9	39.0	66.3	64.9
2008 starting cohort	58.5	62.8	39.6	50.8	68.4	69.1	44.5	38.8	63.6	66.8

See notes at end of table.

Table 326.10. Graduation rate from first institution attended for first-time, full-time bachelor's degree-seeking students at 4-year postsecondary institutions, by race/ethnicity, time to completion, sex, control of institution, and acceptance rate: Selected cohort entry years, 1996 through 2008—Continued

Time to completion, sex, control of institution, cohort entry year, and acceptance rate	Total	White	Black	Hispanic	Asian/Pacific Islander			American Indian/ Alaska Native	Two or more races	Nonresident alien
					Total	Asian	Pacific Islander			
1	2	3	4	5	6	7	8	9	10	11
Public institutions										
1996 starting cohort	49.5	52.7	34.8	37.8	56.0	—	—	31.8	—	50.0
2000 starting cohort	52.7	55.5	39.3	42.1	61.0	—	—	35.1	—	53.5
2002 starting cohort	52.5	55.4	37.6	42.6	61.5	—	—	33.2	—	54.4
2003 starting cohort	53.3	56.8	36.5	43.1	62.6	—	—	33.9	—	55.0
2004 starting cohort	53.8	57.4	36.2	44.0	62.9	—	—	34.0	—	57.6
2005 starting cohort	53.9	57.7	36.3	44.5	63.4	63.7	40.5	33.5	50.0	56.5
2006 starting cohort	54.9	58.7	37.2	45.7	65.2	65.6	43.3	36.0	51.3	58.0
2007 starting cohort	55.5	59.4	38.1	46.8	64.8	65.3	41.4	37.6	56.0	58.4
2008 starting cohort	56.5	60.3	39.1	48.4	65.9	66.6	43.7	36.2	55.7	61.0
Nonprofit institutions										
1996 starting cohort	61.8	64.5	44.5	54.3	71.0	—	—	47.0	—	63.7
2000 starting cohort	62.7	65.8	43.2	57.4	70.0	—	—	47.7	—	62.3
2002 starting cohort	63.5	66.4	44.0	58.7	71.9	—	—	48.6	—	67.7
2003 starting cohort	64.6	67.5	45.5	58.0	73.0	—	—	46.5	—	69.3
2004 starting cohort	65.4	68.0	46.3	60.4	74.6	—	—	49.3	—	71.6
2005 starting cohort	65.1	68.0	44.8	58.8	75.0	75.5	52.3	46.7	73.1	72.4
2006 starting cohort	65.7	68.5	45.4	61.5	74.5	75.2	49.5	50.8	75.5	73.3
2007 starting cohort	65.9	68.9	46.4	60.7	76.3	76.9	55.8	48.5	76.2	73.7
2008 starting cohort	66.0	69.0	46.1	61.3	76.0	76.5	58.2	50.1	71.9	74.5
For-profit institutions										
1996 starting cohort	25.1	31.4	17.6	20.0	23.7	—	—	11.5	—	52.2
2000 starting cohort	25.9	30.0	28.4	27.5	42.6	—	—	30.4	—	45.1
2002 starting cohort	14.7	17.3	11.2	21.7	27.1	—	—	8.0	—	5.8
2003 starting cohort	18.3	21.4	15.3	23.9	28.8	—	—	8.5	—	9.9
2004 starting cohort	24.2	30.5	19.1	25.6	30.3	—	—	15.8	—	18.3
2005 starting cohort	22.6	29.9	15.5	24.7	38.3	42.3	11.8	15.5	26.0	23.5
2006 starting cohort	23.8	31.8	15.8	27.8	35.1	38.1	13.6	15.8	25.9	28.5
2007 starting cohort	23.2	30.5	14.8	27.6	36.1	42.0	10.9	11.4	35.8	34.4
2008 starting cohort	21.2	28.5	14.8	27.9	34.5	39.4	17.3	18.7	39.8	38.9
Graduating within 6 years after start, males and females										
All 4-year institutions										
1996 starting cohort	55.4	58.1	38.9	45.7	63.4	—	—	38.0	—	58.0
2000 starting cohort	57.5	60.2	42.1	49.1	66.7	—	—	40.2	—	59.6
2002 starting cohort	57.2	60.2	40.1	48.9	67.1	—	—	38.3	—	55.3
2003 starting cohort	57.8	61.1	39.5	49.1	68.1	—	—	38.7	—	56.1
2004 starting cohort	58.4	61.6	39.6	50.2	68.7	—	—	39.4	—	61.6
2005 starting cohort	58.6	62.0	39.5	51.0	69.2	69.6	48.3	39.3	64.2	62.6
2006 starting cohort	59.2	62.5	40.2	51.9	70.1	70.6	48.5	40.2	66.6	63.6
2007 starting cohort	59.4	62.9	40.8	52.5	70.0	70.5	49.6	40.6	67.8	63.9
2008 starting cohort[1]	59.6	63.2	40.9	53.5	70.6	71.2	50.0	41.0	65.2	65.6
Open admissions	36.3	43.3	23.9	32.0	45.0	46.4	32.6	18.1	37.0	44.8
90 percent or more accepted	43.8	47.7	27.9	36.2	43.3	42.9	51.5	27.5	41.0	52.5
75.0 to 89.9 percent accepted	56.0	58.4	38.0	51.8	62.1	62.5	47.8	41.2	54.7	56.3
50.0 to 74.9 percent accepted	61.7	65.2	44.4	53.6	68.0	68.6	50.4	42.7	64.0	64.4
25.0 to 49.9 percent accepted	68.9	74.6	47.1	62.7	77.7	77.8	65.9	58.8	79.5	72.8
Less than 25.0 percent accepted	88.6	88.7	79.2	86.3	94.9	94.9	89.2	73.7	92.7	89.9
Public institutions										
1996 starting cohort	51.7	54.3	36.8	42.1	59.5	—	—	35.3	—	51.3
2000 starting cohort	54.8	57.1	40.8	46.0	64.1	—	—	37.5	—	54.6
2002 starting cohort	54.9	57.4	39.4	46.3	64.7	—	—	35.7	—	55.5
2003 starting cohort	55.8	58.7	38.6	47.0	65.9	—	—	37.2	—	56.4
2004 starting cohort	56.1	59.0	38.5	47.9	66.3	—	—	37.0	—	57.2
2005 starting cohort	56.6	59.6	38.8	48.9	67.0	67.2	49.7	37.8	55.7	57.3
2006 starting cohort	57.2	60.3	39.7	49.5	68.2	68.5	49.1	38.2	57.0	57.7
2007 starting cohort	57.7	60.7	40.3	50.7	68.0	68.3	49.6	39.5	60.4	58.2
2008 starting cohort[1]	58.5	61.4	41.2	52.3	68.9	69.4	49.2	39.7	58.9	61.0
Open admissions	34.5	39.9	23.6	26.7	39.4	41.2	18.2	13.3	32.3	42.5
90 percent or more accepted	42.7	46.4	26.5	35.2	40.8	40.7	46.7	25.8	36.7	51.4
75.0 to 89.9 percent accepted	55.0	56.9	38.5	51.8	62.7	63.1	47.0	40.5	51.4	55.5
50.0 to 74.9 percent accepted	61.4	64.8	45.1	52.6	67.9	68.5	47.2	42.0	60.2	63.0
25.0 to 49.9 percent accepted	66.1	71.9	45.2	61.2	74.6	74.6	69.0	60.6	79.8	64.0
Less than 25.0 percent accepted	85.0	83.1	71.8	81.9	93.9	93.9	87.8	59.5	87.2	87.0
Nonprofit institutions										
1996 starting cohort	63.1	65.7	44.6	55.7	73.5	—	—	48.1	—	63.4
2000 starting cohort	64.5	67.0	45.9	59.0	75.2	—	—	50.9	—	64.5
2002 starting cohort	64.6	67.2	44.9	59.5	75.3	—	—	49.8	—	68.3
2003 starting cohort	65.1	67.8	45.0	59.4	76.0	—	—	47.6	—	69.3
2004 starting cohort	65.5	67.9	45.0	60.6	76.2	—	—	50.8	—	71.3
2005 starting cohort	65.2	67.8	43.9	60.4	76.5	77.0	52.6	46.5	75.2	71.0
2006 starting cohort	65.5	68.1	44.5	62.0	76.8	77.5	52.6	51.3	77.5	71.9
2007 starting cohort	65.3	68.3	44.7	60.9	77.0	77.5	58.2	47.9	76.8	71.5

See notes at end of table.

Table 326.10. Graduation rate from first institution attended for first-time, full-time bachelor's degree-seeking students at 4-year postsecondary institutions, by race/ethnicity, time to completion, sex, control of institution, and acceptance rate: Selected cohort entry years, 1996 through 2008—Continued

| Time to completion, sex, control of institution, cohort entry year, and acceptance rate | Total | White | Black | Hispanic | Asian/Pacific Islander | | | American Indian/ Alaska Native | Two or more races | Nonresident alien |
					Total	Asian	Pacific Islander			
1	2	3	4	5	6	7	8	9	10	11
2008 starting cohort[1]	65.4	68.3	44.6	61.5	76.9	77.3	60.6	48.7	73.2	72.1
Open admissions	41.4	49.7	25.1	42.4	56.2	56.1	57.5	26.0	51.4	49.6
90 percent or more accepted	50.0	53.0	33.7	45.7	53.4	53.4	53.6	42.5	48.6	54.8
75.0 to 89.9 percent accepted	59.7	63.0	38.5	52.9	60.4	60.9	48.8	45.3	59.8	57.6
50.0 to 74.9 percent accepted	62.8	66.4	43.2	57.2	68.8	68.9	63.4	46.1	69.2	66.7
25.0 to 49.9 percent accepted	74.7	78.9	51.7	70.8	84.5	84.8	62.8	57.3	80.9	78.0
Less than 25.0 percent accepted	90.2	91.0	81.5	89.0	95.6	95.7	90.9	79.6	93.8	90.5
For-profit institutions										
1996 starting cohort	28.0	33.2	19.2	24.6	28.9	—	—	23.1	—	54.0
2000 starting cohort	32.6	38.1	29.7	33.8	47.3	—	—	30.4	—	47.5
2002 starting cohort	22.0	25.5	16.3	27.5	35.5	—	—	17.1	—	12.5
2003 starting cohort	23.5	27.3	18.3	26.8	33.3	—	—	13.9	—	11.8
2004 starting cohort	28.6	35.5	21.4	29.0	38.8	—	—	19.0	—	21.8
2005 starting cohort	29.1	36.2	19.8	30.2	42.3	44.3	27.3	22.3	27.8	28.4
2006 starting cohort	31.5	40.3	21.1	33.7	42.5	44.4	25.2	18.8	32.4	35.5
2007 starting cohort	31.9	39.9	22.4	35.0	43.1	46.9	21.2	19.6	32.5	41.1
2008 starting cohort	26.5	34.5	18.8	31.7	41.2	44.1	26.1	19.8	35.5	41.3
Graduating within 6 years after start, males										
All 4-year institutions										
1996 starting cohort	52.0	54.8	32.8	41.3	59.5	—	—	36.2	—	55.4
2000 starting cohort	54.3	57.1	35.6	44.6	62.9	—	—	37.1	—	56.8
2002 starting cohort	54.1	57.3	34.0	44.1	64.0	—	—	35.1	—	53.9
2003 starting cohort	55.1	58.4	34.1	44.9	65.1	—	—	36.7	—	55.0
2004 starting cohort	55.6	58.9	34.3	45.7	65.7	—	—	37.5	—	58.5
2005 starting cohort	56.0	59.4	34.2	47.2	66.3	66.6	48.6	37.9	61.3	59.2
2006 starting cohort	56.5	59.8	35.2	47.8	67.4	67.8	46.4	37.2	64.5	60.1
2007 starting cohort	56.5	60.0	35.3	48.6	66.7	67.1	50.0	37.3	64.8	59.8
2008 starting cohort[1]	56.5	60.1	35.3	48.9	67.6	68.0	49.9	38.6	61.7	61.6
Open admissions	34.7	41.7	20.5	29.1	43.3	43.9	33.9	18.5	33.0	40.1
90 percent or more accepted	39.8	43.9	23.9	32.1	39.3	38.4	60.0	21.9	35.2	49.2
75.0 to 89.9 percent accepted	52.8	55.1	33.4	47.3	59.7	60.2	42.4	39.9	52.4	51.9
50.0 to 74.9 percent accepted	58.3	61.9	39.2	48.6	64.9	65.2	50.2	40.5	59.9	60.2
25.0 to 49.9 percent accepted	65.6	71.7	39.0	57.7	74.4	74.5	62.0	51.9	75.8	69.6
Less than 25.0 percent accepted	87.2	88.0	72.7	84.6	93.8	93.9	86.4	72.4	90.1	87.7
Public institutions										
1996 starting cohort	48.1	50.8	30.3	37.5	55.2	—	—	33.1	—	48.8
2000 starting cohort	51.3	53.8	34.1	41.1	60.0	—	—	33.6	—	52.1
2002 starting cohort	51.7	54.4	32.9	41.4	61.3	—	—	32.2	—	52.5
2003 starting cohort	52.9	55.9	32.9	42.4	62.7	—	—	35.0	—	53.5
2004 starting cohort	53.2	56.2	32.9	43.1	63.0	—	—	34.9	—	53.1
2005 starting cohort	53.9	57.0	33.3	44.9	64.0	64.2	50.9	36.8	52.7	53.3
2006 starting cohort	54.4	57.4	34.2	45.0	65.1	65.4	47.2	35.3	56.1	53.7
2007 starting cohort	54.6	57.7	34.7	46.3	64.4	64.7	49.5	35.8	59.1	54.1
2008 starting cohort[1]	55.2	58.2	35.4	47.3	65.6	65.9	47.7	37.9	54.9	57.4
Open admissions	31.9	37.1	19.8	22.5	38.0	39.2	20.8	14.0	27.2	39.4
90 percent or more accepted	39.1	42.9	23.3	30.9	36.8	36.6	50.0	18.9	30.7	47.7
75.0 to 89.9 percent accepted	52.1	54.0	33.6	47.3	60.3	60.8	40.0	40.2	50.0	51.5
50.0 to 74.9 percent accepted	58.2	61.6	40.0	47.6	64.7	65.1	46.8	40.4	54.5	59.4
25.0 to 49.9 percent accepted	61.9	67.8	36.9	55.6	70.8	70.8	68.0	53.5	74.3	61.6
Less than 25.0 percent accepted	83.1	82.5	64.4	80.0	92.3	92.4	84.6	69.0	85.4	83.9
Nonprofit institutions										
1996 starting cohort	60.4	63.0	38.9	52.1	71.5	—	—	46.7	—	60.9
2000 starting cohort	61.7	64.4	39.3	55.3	73.1	—	—	50.1	—	61.7
2002 starting cohort	61.9	64.8	38.6	55.4	73.8	—	—	46.6	—	65.4
2003 starting cohort	62.5	65.3	38.9	56.7	74.2	—	—	45.4	—	65.8
2004 starting cohort	63.0	65.7	39.3	57.1	74.5	—	—	49.5	—	68.3
2005 starting cohort	62.5	65.3	38.2	57.2	74.6	75.1	49.2	42.8	73.5	67.4
2006 starting cohort	62.9	65.6	39.2	58.7	75.6	76.3	49.1	48.6	76.2	68.8
2007 starting cohort	62.3	65.5	38.3	58.1	74.9	75.3	58.1	44.5	74.3	67.3
2008 starting cohort[1]	62.3	65.6	38.3	57.8	75.0	75.3	60.7	44.3	72.2	67.9
Open admissions	38.8	48.4	20.4	35.3	51.4	51.1	57.1	25.4	59.1	45.7
90 percent or more accepted	44.7	48.1	26.2	40.8	48.1	44.9	64.5	45.9	44.8	52.7
75.0 to 89.9 percent accepted	55.2	58.8	34.2	48.1	57.3	57.8	48.1	39.1	56.9	52.3
50.0 to 74.9 percent accepted	59.0	62.9	38.1	52.5	65.7	65.8	62.9	42.1	68.2	62.0
25.0 to 49.9 percent accepted	73.1	77.6	44.3	68.1	82.7	83.0	55.3	50.6	79.8	74.2
Less than 25.0 percent accepted	89.2	90.7	75.4	87.2	94.9	94.9	88.9	74.1	91.8	88.5
For-profit institutions										
1996 starting cohort	28.0	32.3	19.4	26.7	31.7	—	—	30.8	—	53.0
2000 starting cohort	35.5	40.2	29.8	36.2	48.4	—	—	30.3	—	46.3
2002 starting cohort	23.6	27.8	16.6	26.7	38.4	—	—	23.5	—	11.7
2003 starting cohort	25.7	29.3	18.5	26.9	35.0	—	—	18.8	—	12.1
2004 starting cohort	30.3	37.2	21.5	29.0	43.6	—	—	18.6	—	23.7
2005 starting cohort	31.6	38.8	19.5	30.4	42.5	43.3	36.0	27.7	28.5	29.4
2006 starting cohort	35.4	43.9	23.5	35.4	44.0	45.5	27.6	19.6	34.6	37.4
2007 starting cohort	35.7	45.0	23.4	36.0	43.7	45.9	23.9	27.2	28.9	41.4
2008 starting cohort	27.8	37.1	17.9	30.7	43.0	44.5	29.4	18.9	31.8	33.4

See notes at end of table.

Table 326.10. Graduation rate from first institution attended for first-time, full-time bachelor's degree-seeking students at 4-year postsecondary institutions, by race/ethnicity, time to completion, sex, control of institution, and acceptance rate: Selected cohort entry years, 1996 through 2008—Continued

Time to completion, sex, control of institution, cohort entry year, and acceptance rate	Total	White	Black	Hispanic	Asian/Pacific Islander			American Indian/ Alaska Native	Two or more races	Nonresident alien
					Total	Asian	Pacific Islander			
1	2	3	4	5	6	7	8	9	10	11
Graduating within 6 years after start, females										
All 4-year institutions										
1996 starting cohort............................	58.2	60.9	43.0	49.1	66.8	—	—	39.5	—	61.5
2000 starting cohort............................	60.2	62.8	46.4	52.4	70.1	—	—	42.7	—	63.1
2002 starting cohort............................	59.7	62.5	44.2	52.5	69.8	—	—	40.7	—	56.7
2003 starting cohort............................	60.0	63.3	43.2	52.2	70.7	—	—	40.2	—	57.3
2004 starting cohort............................	60.7	63.9	43.3	53.5	71.3	—	—	40.9	—	65.0
2005 starting cohort............................	60.8	64.2	43.0	53.8	71.8	72.2	48.1	40.3	66.7	66.6
2006 starting cohort............................	61.4	64.9	43.6	54.9	72.6	73.1	50.2	42.5	68.1	67.6
2007 starting cohort............................	61.9	65.4	44.6	55.5	73.0	73.6	49.3	43.1	69.9	68.7
2008 starting cohort[1]	62.3	65.9	44.8	57.0	73.4	74.1	50.1	42.8	67.6	70.2
Open admissions.....................	37.9	45.0	26.9	34.6	46.7	49.1	32.0	17.9	40.4	50.6
90 percent or more accepted.........	47.4	51.2	31.2	39.9	47.5	47.7	44.4	32.5	44.8	57.3
75.0 to 89.9 percent accepted.......	58.8	61.2	41.2	55.3	64.3	64.7	52.2	42.3	56.6	61.8
50.0 to 74.9 percent accepted.......	64.4	68.0	47.9	57.3	70.9	71.5	50.5	44.4	66.6	69.2
25.0 to 49.9 percent accepted.......	71.5	77.1	52.2	66.4	80.5	80.7	67.9	63.7	81.8	76.1
Less than 25.0 percent accepted....	90.0	89.4	84.5	87.8	95.8	95.8	93.3	74.8	95.0	92.3
Public institutions										
1996 starting cohort......................	54.7	57.4	41.0	45.7	63.5	—	—	37.0	—	54.9
2000 starting cohort......................	57.7	59.9	45.2	49.7	67.8	—	—	40.5	—	58.1
2002 starting cohort......................	57.5	59.9	43.7	50.0	67.7	—	—	38.3	—	59.0
2003 starting cohort......................	58.2	61.0	42.4	50.4	68.8	—	—	38.9	—	59.7
2004 starting cohort......................	58.6	61.5	42.3	51.5	69.2	—	—	38.5	—	62.3
2005 starting cohort......................	58.8	61.8	42.4	51.9	69.7	70.0	48.7	38.5	58.4	62.0
2006 starting cohort......................	59.6	62.7	43.3	52.9	71.1	71.5	50.7	40.5	57.8	62.6
2007 starting cohort......................	60.3	63.3	44.1	54.1	71.3	71.8	49.7	42.3	61.4	63.4
2008 starting cohort[1]...................	61.2	64.3	45.1	56.1	72.0	72.6	50.3	41.1	62.0	65.3
Open admissions......................	36.8	42.6	26.6	30.1	40.9	43.3	16.1	12.8	36.0	46.5
90 percent or more accepted......	45.9	49.6	29.1	39.0	45.0	45.0	43.8	31.8	41.0	57.0
75.0 to 89.9 percent accepted.....	57.5	59.5	41.8	55.4	65.0	65.4	52.9	40.8	52.5	60.5
50.0 to 74.9 percent accepted.....	64.0	67.6	48.3	56.2	70.9	71.7	47.5	43.2	64.2	67.5
25.0 to 49.9 percent accepted.....	69.5	75.5	50.7	65.2	78.0	78.2	69.4	65.7	84.0	66.3
Less than 25.0 percent accepted.	87.1	84.0	79.0	83.6	95.2	95.2	93.3	48.6	91.2	91.1
Nonprofit institutions										
1996 starting cohort......................	65.4	67.9	48.4	58.3	75.0	—	—	49.2	—	66.4
2000 starting cohort......................	66.7	69.1	50.4	61.7	76.7	—	—	51.5	—	67.9
2002 starting cohort......................	66.7	69.1	49.4	62.2	76.3	—	—	52.1	—	71.5
2003 starting cohort......................	67.2	69.8	49.2	61.3	77.3	—	—	49.3	—	73.2
2004 starting cohort......................	67.4	69.7	49.2	63.0	77.6	—	—	51.7	—	74.5
2005 starting cohort......................	67.3	69.8	48.1	62.6	77.9	78.4	54.9	49.2	76.5	75.1
2006 starting cohort......................	67.6	70.1	48.5	64.2	77.7	78.4	55.1	53.0	78.3	75.4
2007 starting cohort......................	67.7	70.4	49.4	62.9	78.7	79.3	58.2	50.5	78.4	76.0
2008 starting cohort[1]...................	67.8	70.5	49.4	64.1	78.4	78.9	60.6	51.8	73.8	76.5
Open admissions......................	43.9	51.0	29.5	48.6	61.2	61.5	57.7	26.4	48.0	54.5
90 percent or more accepted......	54.7	57.4	40.4	49.8	58.1	60.9	44.7	38.9	50.6	57.5
75.0 to 89.9 percent accepted.....	63.0	66.0	42.3	56.2	62.5	63.1	49.3	50.2	61.7	64.2
50.0 to 74.9 percent accepted.....	65.7	69.1	47.2	60.3	71.0	71.3	63.8	48.9	69.8	71.4
25.0 to 49.9 percent accepted.....	76.1	80.0	56.2	72.8	85.8	86.2	66.7	61.9	81.5	81.7
Less than 25.0 percent accepted.	91.2	91.3	86.4	90.6	96.3	96.3	93.3	83.8	95.4	92.5
For-profit institutions										
1996 starting cohort......................	27.9	34.5	19.0	21.9	24.9	—	—	17.3	—	55.1
2000 starting cohort......................	29.1	35.1	29.7	30.9	45.2	—	—	30.4	—	48.9
2002 starting cohort......................	20.5	23.1	16.1	28.3	31.3	—	—	12.0	—	13.0
2003 starting cohort......................	21.8	25.6	18.2	26.7	31.6	—	—	10.8	—	11.6
2004 starting cohort......................	26.9	33.6	21.3	28.9	33.1	—	—	19.3	—	20.4
2005 starting cohort......................	26.9	33.3	20.0	30.0	42.1	45.8	17.6	18.7	26.9	27.7
2006 starting cohort......................	28.0	35.8	19.5	32.1	40.8	43.3	23.5	18.2	29.3	33.9
2007 starting cohort......................	28.3	33.7	21.7	34.1	42.6	48.0	19.7	14.3	37.6	40.8
2008 starting cohort......................	25.4	31.9	19.4	32.7	39.5	43.7	24.7	20.6	40.7	48.0

—Not available.
[1]Includes data for institutions not reporting admissions data, which are not separately shown.
NOTE: Data are for 4-year degree-granting postsecondary institutions participating in Title IV federal financial aid programs. Graduation rates refer to students receiving bachelor's degrees from their initial institutions of attendance only. Totals include data for persons whose race/ethnicity was not reported. Race categories exclude persons of Hispanic ethnicity. Some data have been revised from previously published figures.
SOURCE: U.S. Department of Education, National Center for Education Statistics, Integrated Postsecondary Education Data System (IPEDS), Spring 2002 through Spring 2013, Winter 2013–14, and Winter 2014–15, Graduation Rates component; and IPEDS Fall 2008, Institutional Characteristics component. (This table was prepared December 2015.)

Table 326.20. Graduation rate from first institution attended within 150 percent of normal time for first-time, full-time degree/certificate-seeking students at 2-year postsecondary institutions, by race/ethnicity, sex, and control of institution: Selected cohort entry years, 2000 through 2011

Sex, control of institution, and cohort entry year	Percent graduating with a certificate or associate's degree within 150 percent of normal time									
	Total	White	Black	Hispanic	Asian/Pacific Islander			American Indian/ Alaska Native	Two or more races	Nonresident alien
					Total	Asian	Pacific Islander			
1	2	3	4	5	6	7	8	9	10	11
Males and females										
All 2-year institutions										
2000 starting cohort	30.5	31.5	26.1	30.1	33.3	—	—	29.3	—	25.5
2002 starting cohort	29.3	30.4	24.2	30.7	31.4	—	—	26.3	—	26.7
2003 starting cohort	29.1	29.9	24.2	30.2	31.7	—	—	25.9	—	27.2
2004 starting cohort	27.8	29.0	22.9	26.3	30.2	—	—	26.7	—	32.9
2005 starting cohort	27.5	28.5	22.6	25.7	31.5	—	—	24.9	—	32.2
2006 starting cohort	29.2	29.3	24.4	30.7	33.9	—	—	24.4	—	30.1
2007 starting cohort	29.8	29.4	25.4	33.3	33.1	—	—	25.5	—	30.9
2008 starting cohort	31.2	30.1	27.6	35.1	34.3	35.2	24.1	25.7	33.3	33.7
2009 starting cohort	30.9	30.1	26.4	36.3	35.1	36.0	25.0	25.7	30.5	34.6
2010 starting cohort	29.4	29.4	23.7	33.8	35.4	35.2	37.9	24.0	26.0	36.2
2011 starting cohort	27.9	29.1	20.2	29.9	33.6	33.7	32.1	22.5	24.5	34.3
Public institutions										
2000 starting cohort	23.6	25.7	17.8	16.8	25.5	—	—	19.6	—	23.2
2002 starting cohort	21.9	24.5	13.2	16.7	23.8	—	—	18.8	—	25.5
2003 starting cohort	21.5	24.1	12.7	16.3	24.8	—	—	17.9	—	25.8
2004 starting cohort	20.3	22.9	11.5	15.0	24.2	—	—	17.8	—	30.5
2005 starting cohort	20.6	22.9	12.1	15.6	25.8	—	—	18.2	—	29.9
2006 starting cohort	20.4	23.1	12.0	15.5	25.4	—	—	16.9	—	25.0
2007 starting cohort	20.3	22.9	11.8	15.9	25.3	—	—	17.4	—	25.5
2008 starting cohort	20.2	22.8	11.8	15.8	26.2	27.2	15.2	15.4	17.0	30.5
2009 starting cohort	19.8	22.5	11.3	15.9	26.1	27.3	11.9	15.9	18.5	32.6
2010 starting cohort	19.5	22.4	10.8	16.2	26.7	27.5	15.6	15.0	17.4	32.6
2011 starting cohort	20.0	23.4	9.8	17.5	27.2	28.1	14.0	14.4	17.6	31.0
Nonprofit institutions										
2000 starting cohort	50.1	49.6	37.5	56.3	61.4	—	—	62.1	—	43.1
2002 starting cohort	49.1	55.1	36.5	46.1	49.5	—	—	20.3	—	45.3
2003 starting cohort	49.0	56.0	35.8	39.4	50.1	—	—	17.9	—	64.2
2004 starting cohort	44.4	48.9	37.3	35.6	36.6	—	—	19.5	—	54.7
2005 starting cohort	48.2	52.3	41.6	47.3	41.6	—	—	14.8	—	51.7
2006 starting cohort	52.8	55.0	46.5	47.5	51.2	—	—	22.6	—	69.3
2007 starting cohort	51.0	56.1	43.6	46.1	51.0	—	—	15.3	—	63.9
2008 starting cohort	56.6	59.7	53.4	62.4	52.9	53.9	‡	25.0	55.8	59.5
2009 starting cohort	62.3	66.0	59.7	68.3	57.9	57.7	‡	30.4	66.5	50.0
2010 starting cohort	53.6	55.9	51.0	62.1	51.7	52.2	‡	18.2	39.5	52.5
2011 starting cohort	51.2	56.3	46.5	57.5	47.0	48.0	35.7	21.6	45.6	51.5
For-profit institutions										
2000 starting cohort	59.1	63.1	47.6	60.3	64.4	—	—	60.3	—	55.4
2002 starting cohort	57.1	61.0	49.3	59.7	61.7	—	—	58.1	—	58.9
2003 starting cohort	57.2	61.8	48.4	60.0	55.8	—	—	59.1	—	36.5
2004 starting cohort	58.2	64.3	48.4	59.6	65.4	—	—	59.0	—	71.1
2005 starting cohort	57.7	62.9	47.8	61.4	65.8	—	—	55.8	—	57.7
2006 starting cohort	58.3	62.8	46.9	62.7	72.1	—	—	57.5	—	65.6
2007 starting cohort	60.6	65.0	49.7	65.1	68.8	—	—	59.0	—	67.6
2008 starting cohort	61.7	64.1	52.6	67.9	69.9	70.2	66.2	60.3	57.4	62.0
2009 starting cohort	62.7	65.1	52.9	68.4	70.8	71.6	64.0	60.7	59.9	61.7
2010 starting cohort	62.8	65.8	53.3	68.3	72.4	73.4	68.9	61.4	59.0	69.7
2011 starting cohort	58.4	62.6	48.5	62.3	65.8	66.3	63.6	55.5	56.7	63.6
Males										
All 2-year institutions										
2000 starting cohort	28.7	30.0	23.1	27.9	30.1	—	—	28.3	—	22.9
2002 starting cohort	27.2	28.6	21.3	27.0	28.7	—	—	23.7	—	22.5
2003 starting cohort	27.2	28.5	20.6	26.8	29.4	—	—	22.4	—	22.6
2004 starting cohort	25.7	27.3	19.1	22.6	27.9	—	—	23.6	—	30.1
2005 starting cohort	25.3	27.0	18.6	21.8	28.4	—	—	23.4	—	29.4
2006 starting cohort	26.3	27.2	20.3	25.4	30.5	—	—	22.6	—	27.4
2007 starting cohort	26.2	27.0	20.3	26.6	29.3	—	—	23.7	—	27.1
2008 starting cohort	27.4	27.7	22.7	29.1	30.3	30.9	23.8	23.0	28.8	30.5
2009 starting cohort	27.2	27.8	22.1	30.0	30.9	31.7	21.6	23.6	24.6	31.5
2010 starting cohort	26.2	27.6	19.4	27.7	31.5	31.5	31.8	21.4	22.3	33.2
2011 starting cohort	25.3	27.5	16.9	25.7	29.8	29.9	28.7	20.6	21.7	31.5
Public institutions										
2000 starting cohort	22.2	24.2	16.5	15.4	22.6	—	—	19.3	—	20.4
2002 starting cohort	20.9	23.2	13.1	15.2	21.8	—	—	16.9	—	21.4
2003 starting cohort	20.8	23.0	12.5	15.2	22.7	—	—	16.4	—	21.3
2004 starting cohort	19.6	21.8	11.5	13.8	22.6	—	—	17.5	—	27.8
2005 starting cohort	19.9	22.1	12.0	14.6	23.5	—	—	18.7	—	27.4
2006 starting cohort	19.8	22.2	12.2	14.7	23.7	—	—	16.3	—	22.5
2007 starting cohort	19.8	22.2	11.9	15.1	23.6	—	—	18.6	—	22.1
2008 starting cohort	19.6	22.1	12.0	14.9	24.3	25.1	15.2	15.2	16.7	28.1
2009 starting cohort	19.3	22.0	11.4	14.8	24.4	25.4	12.4	16.0	16.8	29.9
2010 starting cohort	19.0	21.9	10.7	15.1	24.6	25.4	14.6	14.1	16.2	30.2
2011 starting cohort	19.5	23.0	9.8	16.4	24.6	25.4	13.0	14.2	16.3	28.2

See notes at end of table.

Table 326.20. Graduation rate from first institution attended within 150 percent of normal time for first-time, full-time degree/certificate-seeking students at 2-year postsecondary institutions, by race/ethnicity, sex, and control of institution: Selected cohort entry years, 2000 through 2011—Continued

Sex, control of institution, and cohort entry year	Percent graduating with a certificate or associate's degree within 150 percent of normal time									
					Asian/Pacific Islander			American Indian/ Alaska Native	Two or more races	Nonresident alien
	Total	White	Black	Hispanic	Total	Asian	Pacific Islander			
1	2	3	4	5	6	7	8	9	10	11
Nonprofit institutions										
2000 starting cohort............	49.5	49.3	31.7	54.3	62.5	—	—	64.5	—	42.6
2002 starting cohort............	51.1	58.8	33.0	42.9	56.0	—	—	21.7	—	35.3
2003 starting cohort............	49.6	57.0	31.4	42.4	48.1	—	—	16.8	—	51.6
2004 starting cohort............	43.2	46.4	38.3	36.4	40.3	—	—	17.5	—	52.0
2005 starting cohort............	44.5	49.1	38.7	42.9	43.7	—	—	10.4	—	47.7
2006 starting cohort............	51.3	52.6	45.1	45.6	54.0	—	—	21.8	—	68.2
2007 starting cohort............	50.1	56.4	45.5	41.1	49.3	—	—	10.3	—	58.1
2008 starting cohort............	49.8	53.8	47.3	49.4	45.4	46.3	‡	14.6	46.7	52.1
2009 starting cohort............	53.6	57.5	51.0	58.2	47.4	47.7	‡	22.4	56.1	45.1
2010 starting cohort............	46.2	49.4	42.5	52.1	47.6	48.8	‡	19.8	27.0	44.0
2011 starting cohort............	45.7	52.0	38.0	48.9	41.1	42.8	‡	19.2	42.0	50.3
For-profit institutions										
2000 starting cohort............	59.3	63.7	45.6	58.2	63.1	—	—	55.9	—	55.0
2002 starting cohort............	56.6	62.0	45.9	56.1	59.7	—	—	58.4	—	61.9
2003 starting cohort............	58.0	63.7	45.7	56.9	62.0	—	—	59.5	—	36.7
2004 starting cohort............	58.1	65.4	44.6	55.4	64.3	—	—	59.6	—	69.4
2005 starting cohort............	57.7	64.8	43.1	57.5	65.7	—	—	56.3	—	56.3
2006 starting cohort............	56.5	62.2	42.3	57.6	69.7	—	—	57.5	—	63.8
2007 starting cohort............	58.4	65.1	45.0	59.5	66.8	—	—	56.7	—	67.9
2008 starting cohort............	58.9	63.9	48.2	63.1	67.7	68.1	65.1	54.6	58.2	54.6
2009 starting cohort............	59.6	63.7	49.3	63.8	67.7	68.7	59.2	59.4	55.2	59.9
2010 starting cohort............	60.8	65.9	49.4	63.4	71.2	72.8	65.5	59.4	57.4	66.4
2011 starting cohort............	57.7	63.3	45.7	60.0	65.8	65.5	67.1	53.6	56.2	62.6
Females										
All 2-year institutions										
2000 starting cohort............	32.1	33.0	28.1	31.8	36.3	—	—	30.0	—	28.3
2002 starting cohort............	30.9	32.0	26.1	33.4	33.9	—	—	28.2	—	30.4
2003 starting cohort............	30.7	31.2	26.3	32.7	33.9	—	—	28.4	—	31.5
2004 starting cohort............	29.6	30.5	25.2	29.0	32.6	—	—	28.8	—	35.3
2005 starting cohort............	29.3	29.9	25.2	28.6	34.6	—	—	25.9	—	34.8
2006 starting cohort............	31.5	31.2	26.9	34.5	37.4	—	—	25.7	—	32.5
2007 starting cohort............	32.7	31.5	28.5	37.9	37.0	—	—	26.8	—	34.4
2008 starting cohort............	34.4	32.3	30.9	39.4	38.3	39.6	24.3	27.9	36.2	36.7
2009 starting cohort............	34.1	32.3	29.4	40.9	39.3	40.3	28.0	27.3	35.0	37.6
2010 starting cohort............	32.2	31.1	26.7	38.2	39.4	38.9	43.2	26.0	28.8	39.0
2011 starting cohort............	30.1	30.5	22.6	33.2	37.6	37.9	35.2	24.0	26.8	37.1
Public institutions										
2000 starting cohort............	24.8	27.1	18.8	17.9	28.4	—	—	19.9	—	26.2
2002 starting cohort............	22.8	25.8	13.2	17.8	25.9	—	—	20.2	—	29.2
2003 starting cohort............	22.2	25.1	12.8	17.3	27.1	—	—	19.0	—	30.0
2004 starting cohort............	21.0	24.0	11.5	16.0	26.1	—	—	17.9	—	32.8
2005 starting cohort............	21.2	23.8	12.1	16.4	28.2	—	—	17.8	—	32.2
2006 starting cohort............	20.9	23.9	11.8	16.2	27.3	—	—	17.5	—	27.3
2007 starting cohort............	20.7	23.6	11.7	16.7	27.1	—	—	16.4	—	28.7
2008 starting cohort............	20.7	23.5	11.7	16.5	28.3	29.6	15.2	15.6	17.3	32.9
2009 starting cohort............	20.2	23.0	11.2	16.8	28.0	29.5	11.4	15.8	20.0	35.4
2010 starting cohort............	20.0	23.0	10.8	17.2	29.0	30.0	16.7	15.7	18.6	35.0
2011 starting cohort............	20.4	23.8	9.7	18.5	30.3	31.3	15.2	14.6	18.8	33.9
Nonprofit institutions										
2000 starting cohort............	50.7	50.0	43.1	58.3	60.1	—	—	60.2	—	43.8
2002 starting cohort............	47.3	51.4	39.2	48.9	44.3	—	—	19.3	—	55.0
2003 starting cohort............	48.5	55.0	38.8	37.5	51.4	—	—	18.7	—	75.4
2004 starting cohort............	45.4	51.1	36.3	35.1	34.3	—	—	21.0	—	57.4
2005 starting cohort............	51.3	54.9	44.9	49.6	40.1	—	—	18.0	—	55.2
2006 starting cohort............	54.0	56.7	47.7	48.5	48.8	—	—	23.2	—	70.4
2007 starting cohort............	51.8	55.8	41.6	49.5	52.2	—	—	18.9	—	69.9
2008 starting cohort............	59.9	63.2	55.8	67.7	56.8	57.7	‡	31.5	58.3	66.8
2009 starting cohort............	66.6	70.8	63.4	72.5	63.2	62.7	‡	34.5	70.3	54.5
2010 starting cohort............	57.7	60.0	55.0	66.8	54.5	54.5	‡	17.3	45.5	58.7
2011 starting cohort............	54.1	59.2	50.2	60.8	50.0	50.6	‡	23.6	47.7	52.7
For-profit institutions										
2000 starting cohort............	58.9	62.6	48.6	61.8	65.3	—	—	63.8	—	55.7
2002 starting cohort............	57.4	60.3	50.8	61.7	63.3	—	—	58.0	—	56.7
2003 starting cohort............	56.8	60.4	49.4	61.9	52.1	—	—	59.0	—	36.4
2004 starting cohort............	58.3	63.4	49.9	61.9	66.2	—	—	58.7	—	72.3
2005 starting cohort............	57.7	61.6	49.4	63.3	65.8	—	—	55.7	—	58.6
2006 starting cohort............	59.3	63.2	48.8	65.1	73.7	—	—	57.4	—	67.0
2007 starting cohort............	61.6	64.9	51.4	67.4	70.0	—	—	60.0	—	67.5
2008 starting cohort............	63.2	64.2	54.7	70.3	71.2	71.4	67.3	64.0	57.1	67.6
2009 starting cohort............	64.4	66.0	54.7	70.7	72.7	73.4	66.9	61.5	61.9	62.8
2010 starting cohort............	63.8	65.8	55.0	70.7	73.1	73.8	71.0	62.6	59.8	72.7
2011 starting cohort............	58.9	62.2	49.8	63.4	65.8	66.9	61.4	56.6	57.0	64.5

—Not available.
‡Reporting standards not met (too few cases).
NOTE: Data are for 2-year degree-granting postsecondary institutions participating in Title IV federal financial aid programs. Graduation rates refer to students receiving associate's degrees or certificates from their initial institutions of attendance only. Totals include data for persons whose race/ethnicity was not reported. Race categories exclude persons of Hispanic ethnicity. Some data have been revised from previously published figures.

SOURCE: U.S. Department of Education, National Center for Education Statistics, Integrated Postsecondary Education Data System (IPEDS), Spring 2002 through Spring 2013, Winter 2013–14, and Winter 2014–15, Graduation Rates component. (This table was prepared December 2015.)

Table 326.30. Retention of first-time degree-seeking undergraduates at degree-granting postsecondary institutions, by attendance status, level and control of institution, and percentage of applications accepted: Selected years, 2006 to 2014

Attendance status, level, control, and percent of applications accepted	First-time degree-seekers (adjusted entry cohort),[1] by entry year							Students from adjusted cohort returning in the following year							Percent of first-time undergraduates retained						
	2006	2008	2009	2010	2011	2012	2013	2007	2009	2010	2011	2012	2013	2014	2006 to 2007	2008 to 2009	2009 to 2010	2010 to 2011	2011 to 2012	2012 to 2013	2013 to 2014
1	2	3	4	5	6	7	8	9	10	11	12	13	14	15	16	17	18	19	20	21	22
Full-time students																					
All institutions	2,171,714	2,294,973	2,371,220	2,340,415	2,271,908	2,223,481	2,221,384	1,542,175	1,646,507	1,705,242	1,678,241	1,631,396	1,621,301	1,642,199	71.0	71.7	71.9	71.7	71.8	72.9	73.9
Public institutions	1,524,044	1,654,851	1,732,822	1,698,150	1,666,828	1,637,612	1,646,239	1,072,644	1,167,982	1,222,688	1,192,140	1,170,856	1,168,799	1,192,882	70.4	70.6	70.7	70.2	70.2	71.4	72.5
Nonprofit institutions	466,139	476,059	478,755	487,746	484,388	483,953	483,621	369,084	378,339	381,364	389,124	386,563	388,539	392,197	79.2	79.5	79.7	79.8	79.8	80.3	81.1
For-profit institutions	181,531	164,063	159,643	154,519	120,692	101,916	91,524	100,447	100,186	101,190	96,977	73,977	63,963	57,120	55.3	61.1	63.4	62.8	61.3	62.8	62.4
4-year institutions	1,458,731	1,511,258	1,452,575	1,460,795	1,472,189	1,466,842	1,482,853	1,115,529	1,176,183	1,146,534	1,151,786	1,159,681	1,167,016	1,193,644	76.5	77.8	78.9	78.8	78.8	79.6	80.5
Public institutions	912,401	936,840	973,212	940,660	957,744	957,853	977,381	711,490	745,703	746,121	745,747	758,616	765,747	789,743	78.0	78.6	79.6	79.3	79.2	79.9	80.8
Open admissions	62,724	76,596	45,458	43,031	41,111	35,041	34,566	38,839	49,281	28,675	26,485	24,978	21,189	21,413	61.9	64.3	63.1	61.5	60.8	60.5	61.9
90 percent or more accepted	68,835	63,404	45,453	74,553	50,200	47,775	55,149	49,274	45,743	46,280	53,975	35,197	33,969	40,118	71.6	72.1	72.9	72.4	71.1	71.1	72.7
75.0 to 89.9 percent accepted	244,177	213,394	212,573	205,403	230,328	226,673	261,407	185,457	163,639	163,677	176,676	185,677	174,316	203,267	76.0	76.1	77.0	77.3	76.9	76.7	77.8
50.0 to 74.9 percent accepted	417,093	464,239	462,554	469,026	451,184	469,245	461,424	336,199	375,310	376,021	379,353	363,305	381,576	381,505	80.6	80.8	81.3	80.9	80.5	81.3	82.7
25.0 to 49.9 percent accepted	103,118	133,409	131,241	131,782	169,908	164,067	147,849	88,908	113,365	112,209	112,006	145,215	141,671	127,595	86.2	85.0	85.5	85.0	85.5	86.3	86.3
Less than 25.0 percent accepted	7,716	14,540	14,540	13,996	9,468	8,843	15,315	7,048	13,780	13,649	13,302	13,649	9,013	14,651	91.3	94.8	95.3	95.0	95.2	94.5	95.7
Information not available	8,738	7,630	7,235	2,869	5,545	6,209	1,671	5,765	5,402	5,230	2,323	4,232	4,669	1,194	66.0	70.8	72.3	81.0	76.3	75.2	71.5
Nonprofit institutions	457,556	468,126	470,795	476,794	473,690	476,215	476,441	363,760	373,610	376,668	382,427	380,126	383,994	387,721	79.5	79.8	80.0	80.2	80.2	80.6	81.4
Open admissions	26,679	23,712	22,613	22,853	21,972	22,493	12,549	16,116	16,124	14,349	14,304	13,835	14,351	7,653	60.4	68.0	63.5	62.6	63.0	63.8	61.0
90 percent or more accepted	13,684	15,241	15,135	14,102	13,537	12,348	22,841	9,549	10,835	10,953	9,859	9,292	8,516	16,881	69.8	71.1	72.4	69.9	68.6	69.0	73.9
75.0 to 89.9 percent accepted	102,218	82,985	80,301	83,326	80,566	79,817	86,040	78,495	63,646	62,196	64,730	62,725	62,184	68,481	76.8	76.7	77.5	77.7	77.9	77.9	79.6
50.0 to 74.9 percent accepted	190,079	214,266	218,072	222,880	218,224	220,080	207,435	148,781	166,608	170,232	175,151	170,519	173,261	162,951	78.3	77.8	78.1	78.6	78.1	78.7	78.6
25.0 to 49.9 percent accepted	93,560	95,727	98,312	92,723	93,743	95,784	98,202	81,880	82,558	84,941	79,654	80,260	81,876	85,506	87.5	86.2	86.4	85.9	85.6	85.5	87.1
Less than 25.0 percent accepted	26,696	32,644	32,980	38,511	44,290	44,735	45,222	25,639	31,409	31,790	37,056	42,698	43,215	43,522	96.0	96.2	96.4	96.2	96.4	96.6	96.2
Information not available	4,650	3,551	3,382	2,399	1,358	958	4,152	3,300	2,430	2,207	1,673	797	581	2,727	71.0	68.4	65.3	69.7	58.7	60.6	65.7
For-profit institutions	88,764	69,920	44,940	43,341	40,755	32,774	29,031	40,279	37,238	24,163	23,238	20,939	17,285	16,180	45.4	53.3	53.8	53.6	51.4	52.7	55.7
Open admissions	45,273	21,906	16,826	16,783	20,710	16,811	19,206	18,735	12,545	9,260	9,034	10,769	8,331	10,053	41.4	57.3	55.0	53.8	52.0	49.6	52.3
90 percent or more accepted	6,285	15,104	3,722	2,475	5,360	3,337	700	3,454	6,916	1,311	1,460	2,511	1,650	504	55.0	45.8	35.2	59.0	46.7	49.4	72.0
75.0 to 89.9 percent accepted	3,703	2,544	3,224	2,536	2,857	1,880	2,990	2,081	1,408	1,549	1,369	1,352	1,224	1,865	56.2	55.3	48.0	54.0	47.3	65.1	63.9
50.0 to 74.9 percent accepted	12,845	18,996	12,061	10,122	4,849	6,245	3,690	6,536	9,685	6,839	5,443	2,691	3,608	2,472	50.9	51.0	56.7	53.8	55.5	57.8	67.0
25.0 to 49.9 percent accepted	18,142	8,662	6,098	7,214	6,687	2,908	419	8,036	5,229	3,423	3,942	3,451	1,554	293	44.3	60.4	56.1	54.6	51.6	53.4	69.9
Less than 25.0 percent accepted	—	15	3	—	0	0	0	—	7	0	2	0	—	—	†	46.7	66.7	†	†	†	†
Information not available	2,516	2,693	3,006	4,211	272	1,593	2,096	1,437	1,448	1,779	1,990	165	918	993	57.1	53.8	59.2	47.3	60.7	57.6	47.4
2-year institutions	712,983	783,715	918,645	879,620	799,719	756,639	738,531	426,646	470,324	558,708	526,455	471,715	454,285	448,555	59.8	60.0	60.8	59.9	59.0	60.0	60.7
Public institutions	611,643	681,639	795,982	757,490	709,084	679,759	668,858	361,154	402,647	466,985	446,019	412,240	403,052	403,139	59.0	59.1	59.9	58.9	58.1	59.3	60.3
Nonprofit institutions	8,573	7,933	7,960	10,952	10,698	7,738	7,180	5,324	4,729	4,696	6,697	6,437	4,555	4,476	62.1	59.6	59.0	61.1	60.2	58.9	62.3
For-profit institutions	92,767	94,143	114,703	111,178	79,937	69,142	62,493	60,168	62,948	77,027	73,739	53,038	46,678	40,940	64.9	66.9	67.2	66.3	66.3	67.5	65.5
Part-time students																					
All institutions	463,234	518,634	545,635	548,178	532,017	516,025	490,020	191,586	210,937	229,566	228,329	224,401	222,420	213,497	41.4	40.7	42.1	41.7	42.2	43.1	43.6
Public institutions	419,006	476,900	497,453	500,615	494,294	483,211	461,845	171,746	192,636	209,164	210,466	209,013	209,110	202,505	41.0	40.4	42.0	42.0	42.3	43.3	43.8
Nonprofit institutions	14,585	11,199	10,359	9,805	9,788	9,935	9,341	7,018	5,472	4,892	4,325	4,395	3,996	3,884	48.1	48.9	47.2	44.1	44.9	40.2	41.6
For-profit institutions	29,643	30,635	37,823	37,758	27,935	22,879	18,836	12,822	12,829	15,510	13,538	10,993	9,314	7,108	43.3	41.9	41.0	35.9	39.4	40.7	37.7
4-year institutions	82,367	96,353	72,046	69,397	57,810	53,825	49,367	38,257	45,400	32,344	29,023	25,142	23,701	22,328	46.4	47.1	44.9	41.8	43.5	44.0	45.2
Public institutions	48,353	63,669	33,327	29,934	28,281	27,517	26,540	23,631	31,962	16,944	15,354	14,044	13,803	13,921	48.9	50.0	50.8	51.3	49.7	50.2	52.5
Open admissions	20,223	38,361	8,356	6,303	5,971	5,553	5,243	8,298	18,048	3,586	2,616	2,249	1,991	2,093	41.0	47.0	42.9	41.5	37.7	35.9	39.9
90 percent or more accepted	3,745	4,199	4,004	4,974	2,294	2,223	2,098	1,909	2,023	1,959	2,796	1,008	1,005	1,061	51.0	48.2	48.9	56.2	43.9	45.2	50.6
75.0 to 89.9 percent accepted	8,969	7,192	6,493	5,650	6,003	5,226	7,386	4,196	3,572	3,268	2,856	3,109	2,595	3,946	46.8	49.7	50.3	50.5	51.8	49.7	53.4
50.0 to 74.9 percent accepted	11,599	10,805	11,254	10,650	10,785	10,671	7,154	6,766	6,189	6,053	5,690	5,798	5,840	5,149	58.3	57.3	53.8	53.4	53.8	54.7	56.2
25.0 to 49.9 percent accepted	3,373	3,062	3,046	2,262	2,947	2,854	2,553	2,223	1,989	1,982	1,330	1,739	1,774	1,617	65.9	65.0	65.1	58.8	59.0	62.2	64.7
Less than 25.0 percent accepted	65	57	44	43	41	49	51	50	43	35	31	27	38	33	76.9	75.4	79.5	81.4	65.9	77.6	40.0
Information not available	379	193	130	52	240	941	55	189	98	61		114	560	22	49.9	50.8	46.9	59.6	47.5	59.5	

See notes at end of table.

Table 326.30. Retention of first-time degree-seeking undergraduates at degree-granting postsecondary institutions, by attendance status, level and control of institution, and percentage of applications accepted: Selected years, 2006 to 2014—Continued

Attendance status, level, control, and percent of applications accepted	First-time degree-seekers (adjusted entry cohort),[1] by entry year							Students from adjusted cohort returning in the following year							Percent of first-time undergraduates retained						
	2006	2008	2009	2010	2011	2012	2013	2007	2009	2010	2011	2012	2013	2014	2006 to 2007	2008 to 2009	2009 to 2010	2010 to 2011	2011 to 2012	2012 to 2013	2013 to 2014
1	2	3	4	5	6	7	8	9	10	11	12	13	14	15	16	17	18	19	20	21	22
Nonprofit institutions	12,828	9,869	9,599	9,046	8,833	9,195	8,502	6,045	4,767	4,491	3,951	3,881	3,628	3,449	47.1	48.3	46.8	43.7	43.9	39.5	40.6
Open admissions	5,446	3,566	3,821	3,896	4,226	4,433	2,434	2,579	1,639	1,693	1,575	1,634	1,400	848	47.4	46.0	44.3	40.4	38.7	31.6	34.8
90 percent or more accepted	523	321	393	474	843	915	1,159	237	122	199	175	358	377	468	45.3	38.0	50.6	36.9	42.5	41.2	40.4
75.0 to 89.9 percent accepted	2,459	1,873	1,164	975	1,278	1,177	1,332	1,047	1,033	550	462	683	521	622	42.6	55.2	47.3	47.4	53.4	44.3	46.7
50.0 to 74.9 percent accepted	3,131	3,123	3,256	2,924	1,869	1,829	1,516	1,406	1,423	1,531	1,330	844	865	702	44.9	45.6	47.0	45.5	45.2	47.3	46.3
25.0 to 49.9 percent accepted	853	766	715	647	466	584	606	452	398	366	319	240	278	305	53.0	52.0	51.2	49.3	51.5	47.6	50.3
Less than 25.0 percent accepted	112	77	93	84	116	126	115	86	70	78	67	104	106	101	76.8	90.9	83.9	79.8	89.7	84.1	87.8
Information not available	304	143	157	46	35	131	1,340	238	82	74	23	18	81	403	78.3	57.3	47.1	50.0	51.4	61.8	30.1
For-profit institutions	21,186	22,615	29,120	30,417	20,696	17,113	14,325	8,581	8,671	10,909	9,718	7,217	6,270	4,958	40.5	38.3	37.5	31.9	34.9	36.6	34.6
Open admissions	10,515	11,179	10,926	13,567	10,634	9,561	10,395	4,105	4,164	4,299	4,875	4,253	3,909	3,751	39.0	37.2	39.3	35.9	40.0	40.9	36.1
90 percent or more accepted	2,212	1,623	1,372	2,159	2,234	360	121	639	548	375	504	637	137	59	28.9	33.8	27.3	23.3	28.5	38.1	48.8
75.0 to 89.9 percent accepted	2,838	3,026	3,151	2,407	4,145	854	1,232	1,342	1,218	1,093	527	1,106	250	353	47.3	40.3	34.7	21.9	26.7	29.3	28.7
50.0 to 74.9 percent accepted	2,774	4,886	4,591	6,237	524	1,819	2,471	1,134	2,049	2,249	1,996	220	594	755	40.9	41.9	49.0	32.0	42.0	32.7	30.6
25.0 to 49.9 percent accepted	2,033	1,675	1,099	1,826	2,932	2,537	73	627	629	342	583	936	727	25	30.8	37.6	31.1	31.9	31.9	28.7	34.2
Less than 25.0 percent accepted	0	0	0	0	0	0	0	0	0	0	0	0	0	0	†	†	†	†	†	†	†
Information not available	814	226	7,981	4,221	227	1,982	33	734	63	2,551	1,233	65	653	15	90.2	27.9	32.0	29.2	28.6	32.9	45.5
2-year institutions	380,867	422,281	473,589	478,781	474,207	462,200	440,655	153,329	165,537	197,222	199,306	199,259	198,719	191,169	40.3	39.2	41.6	41.6	42.0	43.0	43.4
Public institutions	370,653	412,931	464,126	470,681	466,013	455,694	435,305	148,115	160,674	192,220	195,112	194,969	195,307	188,584	40.0	38.9	41.4	41.5	41.8	42.9	43.3
Nonprofit institutions	1,757	1,330	760	759	955	740	839	973	705	401	374	514	368	435	55.4	53.0	52.8	53.8	49.7	49.7	51.8
For-profit institutions	8,457	8,020	8,703	7,341	7,239	5,766	4,511	4,241	4,158	4,601	3,820	3,776	3,044	2,150	50.1	51.8	52.9	52.2	52.8	52.8	47.7

†Not applicable.

[1]Adjusted student counts exclude students who died or were totally and permanently disabled, served in the armed forces (including those called to active duty), served with a foreign aid service of the federal government (e.g., Peace Corps), or served on official church missions.

NOTE: Returning students data for 2-year institutions include returning students, plus students who completed their program.
SOURCE: U.S. Department of Education, National Center for Education Statistics, Integrated Postsecondary Education Data System (IPEDS), Spring 2008 through Spring 2015, Fall Enrollment component; and IPEDS Fall 2006 through Fall 2013, Institutional Characteristics component. (This table was prepared December 2015.)

Table 326.40. Percentage distribution of first-time postsecondary students starting at 2- and 4-year institutions during the 2003–04 academic year, by highest degree attained, enrollment status, and selected characteristics: Spring 2009

[Standard errors appear in parentheses]

Selected characteristic	Students starting at 2-year institutions							Students starting at 4-year institutions					
	Highest degree attained				No degree, still enrolled	No degree, not enrolled		Highest degree attained				No degree, still enrolled	No degree, not enrolled
	Total, any degree[1]	Certificate	Associate's	Bachelor's[2]				Total, any degree[1]	Certificate	Associate's	Bachelor's[2]		
1	2	3	4	5	6	7		8	9	10	11	12	13
Total	35.1 (0.86)	9.5 (0.68)	15.0 (0.63)	10.6 (0.63)	18.5 (0.98)	46.4 (1.01)		64.2 (1.18)	1.7 (0.24)	4.6 (0.49)	58.0 (1.34)	12.2 (0.60)	23.6 (0.97)
Sex													
Male	33.3 (1.54)	9.4 (1.19)	13.7 (1.00)	10.3 (0.79)	19.1 (1.64)	47.6 (1.54)		61.4 (1.40)	1.2 (0.29)	5.1 (0.72)	55.1 (1.54)	13.9 (0.86)	24.8 (1.18)
Female	36.5 (1.18)	9.6 (0.90)	16.0 (0.92)	10.9 (0.83)	18.1 (0.93)	45.4 (1.37)		66.5 (1.45)	2.1 (0.34)	4.2 (0.51)	60.2 (1.58)	10.9 (0.71)	22.6 (1.24)
Age when first enrolled													
18 years old or younger	39.4 (1.63)	6.1 (0.78)	15.5 (1.24)	17.9 (1.36)	20.6 (1.70)	40.0 (1.58)		69.1 (1.27)	1.6 (0.29)	3.7 (0.45)	63.8 (1.41)	11.2 (0.76)	19.8 (1.07)
19 years old	37.7 (2.04)	8.9 (2.01)	16.2 (1.46)	12.6 (1.21)	17.7 (1.57)	44.6 (1.75)		65.1 (1.43)	1.0 (0.24)	4.2 (0.63)	59.9 (1.51)	12.3 (0.92)	22.6 (1.16)
20 to 23 years old	29.1 (1.94)	10.3 (1.38)	14.6 (1.68)	4.1 (0.69)	21.9 (1.92)	49.0 (2.10)		41.9 (3.78)	4.1! (1.62)	8.4 (1.74)	29.4 (3.71)	17.8 (2.91)	40.3 (3.49)
24 to 29 years old	28.8 (4.04)	15.6 (3.98)	10.8 (1.98)	2.5 (0.74)	17.2 (2.62)	53.9 (4.05)		32.7 (5.77)	‡ (†)	9.4! (4.28)	20.4 (5.06)	18.8 (4.87)	48.6 (5.81)
30 years old or over	31.7 (2.43)	14.4 (2.08)	15.0 (1.89)	‡ (†)	10.4 (1.97)	57.9 (2.65)		33.7 (7.09)	3.9! (1.84)	13.4! (5.05)	16.4! (6.14)	14.8 (3.97)	51.4 (7.32)
Race/ethnicity													
White	38.9 (1.16)	9.8 (1.00)	16.6 (0.82)	12.5 (0.85)	16.2 (1.21)	44.9 (1.31)		68.9 (1.04)	1.5 (0.31)	4.8 (0.54)	62.6 (1.31)	9.8 (0.58)	21.4 (0.94)
Black	28.1 (2.60)	11.3 (1.66)	11.4 (2.12)	5.3 (1.10)	22.0 (2.04)	50.0 (2.79)		46.9 (3.16)	2.2 (0.91)	4.2! (1.48)	40.5 (3.03)	19.6 (2.21)	33.6 (3.08)
Hispanic	28.3 (2.18)	8.2 (1.67)	12.7 (1.51)	7.4 (1.10)	18.8 (2.03)	52.9 (2.58)		48.8 (3.24)	2.2! (0.83)	5.1 (1.39)	41.5 (2.96)	18.6 (2.36)	32.5 (3.34)
Asian/Pacific Islander	38.3 (4.50)	6.5! (2.29)	14.6 (2.91)	17.2 (3.50)	29.0 (4.58)	32.7 (3.51)		72.8 (3.21)	1.4! (0.67)	2.1! (0.94)	69.3 (3.22)	11.9 (2.23)	15.2 (2.59)
American Indian/Alaska Native	32.1 (9.62)	‡ (†)	‡ (†)	‡ (†)	28.4! (10.89)	39.6 (10.68)		51.5 (9.53)	‡ (†)	‡ (†)	39.3 (9.11)	19.3! (8.63)	29.3! (10.85)
Two or more races	33.9 (5.51)	9.0! (3.65)	14.6! (4.39)	10.3 (2.87)	21.4 (4.98)	44.7 (5.50)		57.1 (5.42)	‡ (†)	4.0! (1.83)	50.4 (5.57)	19.2 (4.71)	23.6 (4.32)
Highest education level of parents													
High school diploma or less	32.0 (1.42)	11.0 (1.30)	14.3 (1.05)	6.7 (0.72)	17.1 (1.18)	50.9 (1.51)		49.9 (2.12)	2.9 (0.83)	6.6 (0.97)	40.4 (2.01)	15.4 (1.33)	34.7 (1.98)
Some college/vocational	38.3 (2.24)	9.6 (1.48)	17.6 (1.17)	11.1 (1.07)	18.0 (1.70)	43.8 (2.06)		59.1 (1.90)	2.3! (0.76)	7.0 (1.08)	49.8 (2.11)	13.4 (1.24)	27.5 (1.84)
Bachelor's degree	39.4 (1.91)	8.2 (1.60)	14.1 (1.87)	17.2 (1.74)	20.6 (2.09)	40.0 (2.53)		70.1 (1.60)	1.2 (0.28)	3.4 (0.58)	65.6 (1.62)	11.0 (0.87)	18.9 (1.41)
Advanced (higher than bachelor's degree)	37.2 (3.03)	6.2 (1.70)	13.7 (1.81)	17.2 (2.09)	22.4 (2.56)	40.4 (3.74)		75.8 (1.44)	0.6! (0.24)	2.1 (0.39)	73.1 (1.51)	9.2 (0.78)	15.0 (1.35)
Dependency status when first enrolled													
Dependent	39.4 (1.26)	7.5 (0.76)	16.7 (0.85)	15.2 (0.88)	19.6 (1.19)	41.0 (1.15)		68.3 (1.06)	1.4 (0.22)	4.2 (0.45)	62.7 (1.22)	11.6 (0.63)	20.1 (0.90)
Independent	28.3 (1.44)	12.8 (1.26)	12.3 (1.13)	3.3 (0.60)	16.8 (1.42)	54.9 (1.75)		31.4 (3.08)	3.7 (1.10)	7.5 (1.92)	20.2 (2.84)	17.3 (2.61)	51.3 (3.25)
Dependent student family income in 2002													
Less than $25,000	34.6 (2.35)	8.4 (1.48)	14.5 (1.54)	11.7 (1.73)	18.0 (1.91)	47.4 (2.43)		52.7 (2.28)	2.8! (1.09)	5.0 (1.00)	44.9 (2.40)	15.9 (1.63)	31.4 (2.38)
$25,000 to $44,999	36.0 (2.12)	7.3 (1.36)	16.4 (1.75)	12.3 (1.60)	19.0 (2.24)	45.0 (2.67)		62.7 (2.31)	1.9 (0.53)	5.4 (1.03)	55.3 (2.50)	13.1 (1.69)	24.2 (1.97)
$45,000 to $69,999	41.3 (2.13)	7.1 (1.29)	17.6 (1.59)	16.6 (1.58)	22.0 (1.92)	36.7 (1.86)		67.1 (1.94)	1.5 (0.34)	5.1 (0.77)	60.6 (2.00)	12.8 (1.27)	20.1 (1.86)
$70,000 to $99,999	43.1 (3.50)	7.6! (3.67)	16.3 (2.58)	19.1 (2.14)	18.4 (2.75)	38.5 (2.76)		71.9 (1.64)	0.9! (0.30)	4.4 (0.88)	66.7 (1.85)	9.4 (0.83)	18.7 (1.37)
$100,000 or more	45.0 (3.56)	6.6 (1.77)	19.6 (3.74)	18.8 (2.40)	20.5 (3.25)	34.4 (3.61)		80.0 (1.30)	0.7! (0.29)	1.9 (0.37)	77.5 (1.38)	8.5 (0.94)	11.4 (0.99)
Timing of postsecondary enrollment													
Delayed entry	29.1 (1.25)	11.0 (1.11)	13.2 (1.02)	4.9 (0.63)	17.2 (1.26)	53.7 (1.44)		36.6 (2.80)	3.8 (1.01)	7.9 (1.54)	24.9 (2.53)	17.8 (2.06)	45.6 (2.75)
Did not delay entry[3]	41.0 (1.36)	7.8 (0.86)	17.0 (0.99)	16.2 (1.00)	20.1 (1.44)	38.8 (1.16)		69.2 (1.05)	1.3 (0.21)	4.0 (0.40)	64.0 (1.17)	11.1 (0.61)	19.6 (0.91)
Intensity of enrollment through 2009													
Always full-time	44.9 (1.66)	11.4 (1.50)	18.0 (1.42)	15.5 (1.11)	10.1 (0.87)	44.9 (1.65)		73.7 (1.15)	1.2 (0.26)	3.8 (0.55)	68.7 (1.41)	6.7 (0.46)	19.6 (1.03)
Always part-time	13.9 (2.80)	8.4! (2.79)	5.5 (1.12)	‡ (†)	13.3 (1.79)	72.8 (2.68)		12.5! (4.93)	‡ (†)	‡ (†)	‡ (†)	13.8! (4.23)	73.6 (6.59)
Mixed	36.6 (1.32)	8.7 (0.83)	16.6 (1.10)	11.4 (0.99)	26.1 (1.34)	37.2 (1.69)		48.3 (1.59)	2.7 (0.47)	6.1 (0.72)	39.5 (1.60)	23.3 (1.39)	28.4 (1.42)
Remedial course taken in 2003–04													
No	35.4 (0.95)	10.0 (0.84)	14.5 (0.81)	10.9 (0.78)	17.6 (0.99)	47.0 (1.21)		65.2 (1.23)	1.8 (0.28)	4.4 (0.53)	59.0 (1.43)	11.5 (0.62)	23.4 (1.05)
Yes	34.3 (2.10)	8.3 (1.62)	16.2 (1.37)	9.8 (0.98)	21.0 (1.70)	44.7 (1.92)		59.6 (1.98)	1.2 (0.32)	5.4 (0.92)	53.0 (2.13)	15.7 (1.44)	24.6 (1.81)

See notes at end of table.

Table 326.40. Percentage distribution of first-time postsecondary students starting at 2- and 4-year institutions during the 2003–04 academic year, by highest degree attained, enrollment status, and selected characteristics: Spring 2009—Continued

[Standard errors appear in parentheses]

Selected characteristic	Students starting at 2-year institutions						Students starting at 4-year institutions					
	Highest degree attained				No degree, still enrolled	No degree, not enrolled	Highest degree attained				No degree, still enrolled	No degree, not enrolled
	Total, any degree[1]	Certificate	Associate's	Bachelor's[2]			Total, any degree[1]	Certificate	Associate's	Bachelor's[2]		
1	2	3	4	5	6	7	8	9	10	11	12	13
Highest degree expected in 2003–04												
No degree or certificate	‡ (†)	(†)	‡ (†)	# (†)	‡ (†)	87.3 (4.75)	‡ (†)	‡ (†)	‡ (†)	‡ (†)	‡ (†)	‡ (†)
Certificate	44.8 (5.47)	42.8 (5.28)	‡ (†)	‡ (†)	6.9 (2.02)	48.3 (5.60)	41.2! (18.43)	‡ (†)	‡ (†)	‡ (†)	‡ (†)	‡ (†)
Associate's degree	34.6 (2.38)	13.9 (2.05)	19.3 (1.86)	1.4! (0.49)	12.3 (1.69)	53.1 (2.80)	43.7 (8.43)	16.2! (5.50)	21.3! (7.06)	6.1! (2.93)	12.8! (5.09)	43.5 (7.70)
Bachelor's degree[4]	32.7 (1.81)	8.0 (1.49)	15.4 (1.02)	9.3 (1.03)	18.1 (1.50)	49.3 (1.60)	55.2 (2.02)	2.2 (0.52)	6.8 (1.02)	46.2 (2.07)	15.1 (1.37)	29.7 (1.59)
Master's degree[4]	38.2 (1.72)	7.0 (1.32)	14.8 (1.21)	16.4 (1.19)	22.7 (1.63)	39.1 (1.66)	66.7 (1.42)	1.0 (0.25)	4.1 (0.62)	61.7 (1.42)	11.2 (0.77)	22.1 (1.32)
Doctoral/first-professional degree[4]	34.7 (2.30)	4.8 (0.93)	13.8 (2.02)	16.0 (1.65)	22.4 (2.54)	42.9 (3.25)	70.6 (1.57)	1.3 (0.36)	1.9 (0.36)	67.4 (1.69)	11.0 (0.95)	18.3 (1.35)
Work intensity (including work-study) in 2003–04												
Did not work	34.7 (1.79)	11.2 (1.57)	15.8 (1.20)	7.7 (0.85)	19.9 (1.80)	45.3 (2.16)	69.9 (1.35)	0.8 (0.18)	3.4 (0.55)	65.8 (1.47)	10.9 (0.92)	19.1 (1.08)
Worked part time	39.9 (2.08)	7.9 (1.20)	17.4 (1.00)	14.6 (1.04)	17.2 (1.28)	42.8 (1.70)	66.2 (1.42)	1.7 (0.31)	5.2 (0.69)	59.3 (1.44)	12.1 (0.85)	21.7 (1.21)
Worked full time	28.6 (1.96)	10.6 (1.63)	10.9 (1.08)	7.2 (0.94)	19.3 (1.53)	52.1 (2.10)	40.1 (2.93)	4.1 (1.22)	5.9 (1.20)	30.1 (2.60)	16.5 (1.77)	43.4 (2.86)
Control of first institution												
Public	34.4 (0.95)	8.5 (0.68)	14.4 (0.61)	11.6 (0.68)	19.6 (1.03)	46.0 (1.00)	64.8 (1.22)	1.6 (0.23)	3.8 (0.45)	59.5 (1.32)	12.9 (0.73)	22.2 (0.98)
Private, nonprofit	46.2 (8.52)	13.3! (6.56)	21.5! (6.76)	11.3! (4.99)	10.4! (3.32)	43.4 (8.28)	69.9 (1.45)	1.5 (0.37)	3.8 (0.95)	64.6 (1.89)	11.1 (1.02)	19.0 (1.18)
Private, for profit	39.5 (3.70)	19.6 (4.78)	19.5 (3.51)	‡ (†)	9.6 (2.61)	50.9 (4.64)	33.9 (4.37)	‡ (†)	14.6 (3.45)	15.7 (3.78)	11.3 (2.44)	54.8 (3.82)
Income quartile in 2003–04[5]												
Lowest quartile	30.6 (1.45)	9.4 (1.27)	13.0 (1.14)	8.3 (0.84)	18.4 (1.46)	51.0 (1.78)	49.5 (1.91)	2.7 (0.73)	4.6 (0.74)	42.2 (2.15)	16.2 (1.37)	34.3 (1.75)
Second quartile	37.1 (1.58)	10.5 (1.56)	15.8 (1.26)	10.8 (0.97)	19.7 (1.58)	43.2 (1.86)	60.5 (2.04)	2.4 (0.51)	6.5 (1.10)	51.6 (2.20)	13.5 (1.16)	26.0 (1.82)
Third quartile	36.3 (2.51)	9.6 (1.71)	15.0 (1.35)	11.6 (1.53)	18.7 (1.64)	45.0 (2.18)	67.2 (1.58)	1.3 (0.31)	4.9 (0.80)	61.0 (1.85)	11.2 (0.88)	21.6 (1.55)
Highest quartile	38.6 (2.51)	8.1 (1.49)	17.3 (1.96)	13.2 (1.65)	16.5 (2.30)	45.0 (3.20)	76.8 (1.37)	0.6! (0.25)	2.4 (0.46)	73.8 (1.42)	8.7 (0.80)	14.4 (1.18)

†Not applicable.
#Rounds to zero.
!Interpret data with caution. The coefficient of variation (CV) for this estimate is between 30 and 50 percent.
‡Reporting standards not met. Either there are too few cases for a reliable estimate or the coefficient of variation (CV) is 50 percent or greater.
[1]Includes a small percentage of students who had attained a degree and were still enrolled. Includes recipients of degrees not shown separately.
[2]Includes a small percentage of students who had attained an advanced degree.

[3]Includes students with a standard high school diploma who enrolled in postsecondary education in the same year as their graduation.
[4]Students starting at 2-year institutions include students whose goal was to transfer to a 4-year institution.
[5]Indicates the income quartile of the student, based on the student's total income in 2002 for independent students or the parents' total income in 2002 for dependent students. Income quartiles were determined separately for dependent and independent students based on percentile rankings and then combined into one variable.
NOTE: Race categories exclude persons of Hispanic ethnicity. Detail may not sum to totals because of rounding.
SOURCE: U.S. Department of Education, National Center for Education Statistics, 2004/09 Beginning Postsecondary Students Longitudinal Study (BPS:04/09). (This table was prepared November 2011.)

Table 327.10. Average scores and standard deviations on Graduate Record Examination (GRE) general and subject tests: 1965 through 2014

[Standard deviations appear in square brackets]

Columns 4–7 are General test sections; columns 8–17 are Subject tests[2]. General test section scores are on the Former scale (200–800)[4].

Academic year ending	Number of GRE takers	GRE takers as a percent of bachelor's degrees[1]	Verbal	Quantitative	Analytical reasoning[3]	Analytical writing[3]	Biochemistry, cell and molecular biology	Biology	Chemistry	Computer science	Education	Engineering	Literature	Mathematics	Physics	Psychology
1	2	3	4	5	6	7	8	9	10	11	12	13	14	15	16	17
1965	93,792	18.7	530 [124]	533 [137]	†	†	†	617 [117]	628 [114]	†	481 [86]	618 [108]	591 [95]	— [†]	— [†]	556 [91]
1966	123,960	23.8	520 [124]	528 [133]	†	†	†	610 [115]	618 [110]	†	474 [87]	609 [106]	588 [94]	— [†]	— [†]	552 [91]
1967	151,134	27.0	519 [125]	528 [134]	†	†	†	613 [114]	615 [104]	†	476 [90]	603 [104]	582 [91]	— [†]	— [†]	553 [93]
1968	182,432	28.8	520 [124]	527 [135]	†	†	†	614 [114]	617 [104]	†	478 [87]	601 [105]	572 [91]	— [†]	— [†]	547 [93]
1969	206,113	28.3	515 [124]	524 [132]	†	†	†	613 [112]	613 [104]	†	477 [88]	591 [103]	569 [89]	— [†]	— [†]	543 [89]
1970	265,359	33.5	503 [123]	516 [132]	†	†	†	603 [111]	613 [113]	†	462 [92]	586 [110]	556 [90]	— [†]	— [†]	532 [91]
1971	293,600	35.0	497 [125]	512 [134]	†	†	†	603 [114]	618 [117]	†	457 [95]	587 [115]	546 [91]	— [†]	— [†]	530 [92]
1972	293,506	33.1	494 [126]	508 [136]	†	†	†	606 [114]	624 [124]	†	446 [93]	594 [119]	544 [96]	— [†]	— [†]	528 [92]
1973	290,104	31.5	497 [125]	512 [135]	†	†	†	619 [110]	630 [114]	†	459 [96]	593 [114]	545 [96]	— [†]	— [†]	529 [92]
1974	301,070	31.8	492 [126]	509 [137]	†	†	†	624 [110]	634 [115]	†	452 [93]	591 [121]	547 [99]	— [†]	— [†]	530 [95]
1975	298,335	32.3	493 [125]	508 [137]	†	†	†	— [†]	— [†]	†	— [†]	— [†]	— [†]	— [†]	— [†]	— [†]
1976	299,292	32.3	492 [127]	510 [138]	†	†	†	627 [112]	627 [107]	—	454 [93]	594 [119]	539 [101]	— [†]	— [†]	531 [93]
1977	287,715	31.3	490 [129]	514 [139]	†	†	†	625 [113]	630 [109]	—	453 [93]	592 [115]	532 [101]	— [†]	— [†]	532 [95]
1978	286,383	31.1	484 [128]	518 [135]	†	†	†	622 [113]	624 [108]	—	452 [91]	594 [114]	530 [102]	— [†]	— [†]	529 [97]
1979	282,482	30.7	476 [130]	517 [135]	†	†	†	621 [117]	623 [104]	—	451 [89]	592 [114]	525 [102]	— [†]	— [†]	530 [97]
1980	272,281	29.3	474 [131]	522 [136]	†	†	†	619 [115]	618 [105]	—	449 [90]	590 [116]	521 [105]	— [†]	— [†]	534 [98]
1981	262,855	28.1	475 [128]	523 [136]	†	†	†	617 [115]	615 [103]	—	453 [90]	590 [116]	520 [99]	— [†]	— [†]	532 [97]
1982	256,381	26.9	477 [130]	533 [137]	498 [126]	†	†	616 [114]	616 [105]	—	456 [89]	593 [115]	521 [100]	— [†]	— [†]	532 [97]
1983	263,674	27.2	483 [123]	541 [138]	504 [128]	†	†	623 [115]	620 [105]	—	459 [90]	599 [114]	527 [98]	— [†]	— [†]	542 [95]
1984	265,221	27.2	484 [125]	541 [139]	512 [129]	†	†	622 [115]	619 [102]	—	461 [90]	604 [114]	530 [97]	— [†]	— [†]	543 [96]
1985	271,972	27.8	486 [123]	545 [140]	516 [129]	†	†	619 [114]	621 [101]	—	459 [89]	615 [120]	531 [95]	— [†]	— [†]	541 [95]
1986	279,428	28.3	485 [122]	552 [140]	520 [129]	†	†	612 [114]	628 [106]	—	464 [87]	616 [119]	527 [96]	— [†]	— [†]	542 [97]
1987	293,560	29.6	483 [120]	550 [140]	521 [128]	†	†	616 [116]	629 [104]	—	465 [86]	619 [119]	526 [95]	— [†]	— [†]	536 [95]
1988	303,703	30.5	481 [117]	557 [140]	528 [128]	†	—	615 [114]	631 [108]	—	467 [85]	622 [120]	525 [94]	— [†]	— [†]	537 [94]
1989	326,096	32.0	479 [116]	560 [142]	530 [129]	†	—	612 [114]	642 [117]	—	465 [87]	626 [116]	528 [91]	— [†]	— [†]	538 [95]
1990	344,572	32.8	477 [115]	562 [143]	534 [128]	†	—	612 [114]	662 [123]	—	461 [84]	617 [111]	523 [92]	— [†]	— [†]	537 [95]
1991	379,882	34.7	473 [114]	562 [141]	536 [129]	†	—	609 [113]	660 [123]	—	457 [85]	611 [111]	523 [93]	— [†]	— [†]	535 [95]
1992	411,528	36.2	472 [113]	561 [140]	537 [129]	†	—	605 [113]	654 [128]	—	462 [82]	610 [117]	525 [92]	— [†]	— [†]	536 [95]
1993	400,246	34.4	471 [113]	557 [140]	541 [129]	†	—	606 [114]	662 [133]	—	462 [80]	602 [115]	516 [94]	— [†]	— [†]	536 [97]
1994	399,395[5]	34.2	468 [114]	553 [139]	545 [129]	†	—	620 [116]	627 [113]	—	493[6] [104]	601 [115]	517 [95]	— [†]	— [†]	538 [96]
1995	389,539[5]	33.6	466 [115]	553 [140]	544 [131]	†	—	622 [116]	675 [138]	—	488[6] [102]	596 [113]	513 [96]	— [†]	— [†]	544 [98]
1996	376,013[5]	32.3	467 [114]	558 [139]	549 [131]	†	—	614 [114]	678 [135]	—	489[6] [104]	604 [119]	512 [97]	— [†]	— [†]	547 [99]
1997	376,062[5]	32.1	466 [113]	562 [139]	548 [129]	†	—	620 [115]	684 [143]	—	487[6] [103]	602 [114]	525 [100]	— [†]	— [†]	554 [99]
1998	364,554[5]	30.8	469 [113]	569 [141]	543 [133]	†	—	628 [113]	686 [137]	—	477[6] [100]	609 [118]	530 [100]	— [†]	— [†]	563 [100]
1999[7]	396,330	33.0	468 [114]	565 [143]	542 [133]	†	—	626 [114]	684 [137]	—	†	604 [115]	527 [100]	— [†]	— [†]	559 [99]

See notes at end of table.

Table 327.10. Average scores and standard deviations on Graduate Record Examination (GRE) general and subject tests: 1965 through 2014—Continued

[Standard deviations appear in square brackets]

Academic year ending	Number of GRE takers	GRE takers as a percent of bachelor's degrees[1]	General test sections				Subject tests[2]									
			Verbal	Quantitative	Analytical reasoning[3]	Analytical writing[3]	Biochemistry, cell and molecular biology	Biology	Chemistry	Computer science	Education	Engineering	Literature	Mathematics	Physics	Psychology
1	2	3	4	5	6	7	8	9	10	11	12	13	14	15	16	17
2000[7]	387,422	31.3	465 [116]	578 [147]	562 [141]	† [†]	— [†]	629 [114]	686 [133]	— [†]	†	— [†]	530 [99]	— [†]	— [†]	563 [98]
2001	433,109	34.8	— [†]	— [†]	— [†]	† [†]	— [†]	— [†]	— [†]	— [†]	†	— [†]	— [†]	— [†]	— [†]	— [†]
2002	536,523	41.5	473 [123]	597 [151]	571 [139]	† [†]	— [†]	— [†]	— [†]	— [†]	†	†	— [†]	— [†]	— [†]	— [†]
2003[8,9]	440,982	32.7	470 [121]	598 [148]	†	4.2 [1.0]	517 [100]	635 [114]	682 [125]	712 [97]	†	†	538 [98]	620 [131]	669 [151]	580 [101]
2004[8,9,10]	446,661	31.9	469 [120]	597 [148]	†	4.2 [1.0]	517 [101]	643 [115]	675 [120]	715 [93]	†	†	537 [97]	621 [130]	665 [148]	586 [101]
2005[9,10]	474,594	33.0	467 [118]	591 [148]	†	4.2 [0.9]	518 [100]	647 [117]	675 [117]	715 [91]	†	†	540 [97]	623 [130]	672 [151]	592 [101]
2006[8,10,11]	508,445	34.2	465 [117]	584 [149]	†	4.1 [0.9]	519 [99]	650 [118]	677 [116]	717 [92]	†	†	541 [97]	627 [129]	678 [153]	598 [101]
2007[8,10,11]	561,014	36.8	462 [119]	584 [151]	†	4.0 [0.9]	521 [97]	650 [120]	689 [115]	715 [91]	†	†	542 [98]	636 [130]	686 [155]	600 [101]
2008[8,10,11]	545,311	34.9	457 [121]	586 [152]	†	3.9 [0.9]	525 [97]	651 [120]	694 [116]	712 [92]	†	†	541 [98]	640 [131]	692 [156]	603 [101]
2009[8,10,11]	600,702	37.5	456 [120]	590 [150]	†	3.8 [0.9]	523 [97]	650 [120]	699 [115]	708 [91]	†	†	541 [97]	648 [134]	692 [156]	605 [103]
2010[8]	630,028	38.2	— [†]	— [†]	†	— [†]	525 [97]	651 [121]	700 [115]	702 [96]	†	†	542 [98]	650 [134]	692 [157]	609 [103]
			Revised scale (130–170)[4]													
2011[8,12]	700,755	40.8	151[12] [8.5]	151[12] [8.7]	†	3.7[12] [0.9]	525 [97]	651 [122]	703 [114]	698 [99]	†	†	547 [98]	655 [135]	689 [156]	612 [103]
2012[8,12]	586,370	32.7	151[12] [8.4]	151[12] [8.8]	†	3.6[12] [0.9]	526 [95]	658 [123]	703 [115]	693 [100]	†	†	549 [99]	657 [136]	696 [158]	616 [102]
2013[8,12]	663,439	36.0	151[12] [8.4]	151[12] [8.8]	†	3.6[12] [0.9]	526 [95]	658 [123]	703 [115]	693 [100]	†	†	549 [99]	657 [136]	696 [158]	616 [102]
2014[8,12]	684,345	36.6	150 [8.0]	152 [9.0]	†	3.6 [0.9]	522 [92]	671 [121]	699 [113]	— (†)	†	†	546 [99]	659 [137]	705 [156]	615 [102]

—Not available.
†Not applicable.

[1]GRE takers include examinees from inside and outside of the United States, while the bachelor's degrees include only those conferred by U.S. institutions.
[2]Subject test scores are reported on a 200 to 990 scale, in 10-point increments, although the score range for any particular subject test is usually smaller. The education subject test was administered for the final time in April 1998. The engineering subject test was administered for the final time in April 2001.
[3]The analytical reasoning section of the GRE, a multiple-choice test, was discontinued in September 2002 and replaced by the analytical writing section, an essay-based test. Scores for the analytical writing section range from 0 to 6, in half-point increments.
[4]Prior to 2011, GRE scores for the verbal and quantitative sections ranged from 200 to 800, in 10-point increments, as did scores for the analytical reasoning section until it was replaced by the analytical writing section in 2002. On August 1, 2011, the GRE revised general test was introduced. Scores for the revised verbal reasoning and quantitative reasoning sections range from 130 to 170, in 1-point increments. In the revised general test, the score scale for the analytical writing section continues to range from 0 to 6, in half-point increments.
[5]Total includes examinees who received no score on one or more general test measures.
[6]Data reported for 1994 through 1998 are from the revised education test.
[7]Subject test score data reflect the 3-year average for all examinees who tested between October 1 three years prior to the reported test year and September 30 of the reported test year. These data are not directly comparable with data for most other years.
[8]Subject test score data reflect the 3-year average for all examinees who tested between July 1 three years prior to the reported test year and June 30 of the reported test year. These data are not directly comparable with previous years, except for 1999 and 2000.

[9]Analytical writing test score data reflect the average for all examinees who tested between October 1, 2002, and June 30 of the reported test year.
[10]Verbal and quantitative test score data reflect the 3-year average for all examinees who tested between July 1 three years prior to the reported test year and June 30 of the reported test year. These data are not directly comparable with previous years.
[11]Analytical writing test score data reflect the 3-year average for all examinees who tested between July 1 three years prior to the reported test year and June 30 of the reported test year.
[12]For all three sections of the revised general test (verbal, quantitative, and analytical writing), scores for 2011, 2012, and 2013 reflect the average for all examinees who tested between August 1, 2011, and April 30 of the reported test year. Scores for 2014 reflect the average for all examinees who tested between August 1, 2011, and June 30, 2014. General test scores for 2011 through 2014 are not comparable with scores from previous years.
NOTE: GRE data include test takers from both within and outside of the United States.
SOURCE: Graduate Record Examination Board, Examinee and Score Trends for the GRE General Test, 1964–65 through 1985–86; A Summary of Data Collected From Graduate Record Examinations Test-Takers During 1986–87; Guide to the Use of Scores, 1987–88 through 2015–16; GRE Volumes by Country, 2000–2015; and Interpreting Your GRE Scores, 2005–06 through 2011–12. U.S. Department of Education, National Center for Education Statistics, Higher Education General Information Survey (HEGIS), "Degrees and Other Formal Awards Conferred" surveys, 1964–65 through 1985–86; Integrated Postsecondary Education Data System (IPEDS), "Completions Survey" (IPEDS-C:87–99); and IPEDS Fall 2000 through Fall 2014, Completions component. (This table was prepared May 2016.)

Table 329.10.   On-campus crimes, arrests, and referrals for disciplinary action at degree-granting postsecondary institutions, by location of incident, control and level of institution, and type of incident: 2001 through 2013

Control and level of institution and type of incident	Number of incidents														
	Total, in residence halls and at other locations												2013		
	2001	2002	2003	2004	2005	2006	2007	2008	2009	2010	2011	2012	Total	In residence halls	At other locations
1	2	3	4	5	6	7	8	9	10	11	12	13	14	15	16
All institutions															
Selected crimes against persons and property	41,596	42,521	43,064	43,555	42,710	44,492	41,829	40,296	34,054	32,097	30,407	29,832	27,567	13,215	14,352
Murder[1]	17	20	9	15	11	8	44	12	16	15	16	12	23	3	20
Negligent manslaughter[2]	2	0	1	0	2	0	3	3	0	1	1	1	0	0	0
Sex offenses—forcible[3]	2,201	2,327	2,595	2,667	2,674	2,670	2,694	2,639	2,544	2,927	3,375	4,017	4,964	3,627	1,337
Sex offenses—nonforcible[4]	461	261	60	27	42	43	40	35	65	33	46	46	45	20	25
Robbery[5]	1,663	1,802	1,625	1,550	1,551	1,547	1,561	1,576	1,409	1,392	1,285	1,374	1,330	196	1,134
Aggravated assault[6]	2,947	2,804	2,832	2,721	2,656	2,817	2,604	2,495	2,327	2,221	2,239	2,424	2,085	719	1,366
Burglary[7]	26,904	28,038	28,639	29,480	29,256	31,260	29,488	28,737	23,083	21,335	19,472	18,228	15,500	8,285	7,215
Motor vehicle theft[8]	6,221	6,181	6,285	6,062	5,531	5,231	4,619	4,104	3,977	3,441	3,334	3,026	2,993	14	2,979
Arson[9]	1,180	1,088	1,018	1,033	987	916	776	695	633	732	639	704	627	351	276
Weapons-, drug-, and liquor-related arrests and referrals															
Arrests[10]	40,348	43,407	44,581	47,939	49,024	50,187	50,558	50,639	50,066	51,519	54,285	52,819	47,764	24,966	22,798
Illegal weapons possession	1,073	1,142	1,094	1,263	1,316	1,316	1,318	1,190	1,077	1,112	1,023	1,027	1,044	279	765
Drug law violations	11,854	12,041	12,467	12,775	13,707	13,952	14,135	15,146	15,871	18,589	20,729	21,389	20,148	10,744	9,404
Liquor law violations	27,421	30,224	31,020	33,901	34,001	34,919	35,105	34,303	33,118	31,818	32,533	30,403	26,572	13,943	12,629
Referrals for disciplinary action[10]	155,201	167,319	184,915	196,775	202,816	218,040	216,600	217,526	220,987	230,269	249,694	251,724	246,438	222,654	23,784
Illegal weapons possession	1,277	1,287	1,566	1,799	1,882	1,871	1,658	1,455	1,275	1,314	1,282	1,411	1,434	975	459
Drug law violations	23,900	26,038	25,753	25,762	25,356	27,251	28,476	32,469	36,344	42,022	51,562	54,131	54,135	46,222	7,913
Liquor law violations	130,024	139,994	157,596	169,214	175,578	188,918	186,466	183,602	183,368	186,933	196,850	196,182	190,869	175,457	15,412
Public 4-year															
Selected crimes against persons and property	18,710	19,563	19,789	19,984	19,582	20,648	19,579	18,695	15,975	15,503	14,675	14,520	13,240	6,300	6,940
Murder[1]	9	9	5	8	4	5	42	9	8	9	10	7	10	2	8
Negligent manslaughter[2]	2	0	1	0	1	0	2	1	1	0	1	1	0	0	0
Sex offenses—forcible[3]	1,245	1,278	1,358	1,482	1,398	1,400	1,425	1,317	1,214	1,461	1,638	1,972	2,257	1,646	611
Sex offenses—nonforcible[4]	207	113	28	16	25	15	23	12	40	15	17	17	17	9	8
Robbery[5]	584	659	669	612	696	680	722	750	647	662	612	660	641	120	521
Aggravated assault[6]	1,434	1,320	1,381	1,269	1,280	1,338	1,258	1,182	1,134	1,076	1,076	1,192	1,019	355	664
Burglary[7]	11,520	12,523	12,634	13,026	12,935	14,027	13,371	12,970	10,708	10,219	9,373	8,839	7,379	3,919	3,460
Motor vehicle theft[8]	3,072	3,092	3,116	2,964	2,667	2,662	2,266	2,027	1,824	1,604	1,592	1,405	1,513	8	1,505
Arson[9]	637	569	597	607	576	521	470	427	400	457	356	427	404	241	163
Weapons-, drug-, and liquor-related arrests and referrals															
Arrests[10]	31,077	33,831	34,657	36,746	38,051	39,900	39,570	40,607	40,780	41,992	44,891	43,587	38,701	20,060	18,641
Illegal weapons possession	692	745	697	811	878	859	825	759	659	669	629	624	657	209	448
Drug law violations	9,125	9,238	9,389	9,620	10,606	10,850	10,693	11,714	12,186	14,362	16,323	16,931	15,810	8,516	7,294
Liquor law violations	21,260	23,848	24,571	26,315	26,567	28,191	28,052	28,134	27,935	26,961	27,939	26,032	22,234	11,335	10,899
Referrals for disciplinary action[10]	79,152	84,636	94,365	100,588	100,211	107,289	106,148	104,585	108,756	116,029	129,667	132,552	127,851	116,424	11,427
Illegal weapons possession	678	675	847	1,001	1,097	972	867	792	669	664	610	649	623	442	181
Drug law violations	13,179	13,943	13,811	13,658	13,020	13,798	14,458	16,656	18,260	21,451	27,339	29,021	28,732	24,486	4,246
Liquor law violations	65,295	70,018	79,707	85,929	86,094	92,519	90,823	87,137	89,827	93,914	101,718	102,882	98,496	91,496	7,000
Nonprofit 4-year															
Selected crimes against persons and property	14,844	14,859	15,179	15,523	15,574	16,864	15,452	14,892	11,964	11,202	10,740	10,803	10,420	6,116	4,304
Murder[1]	5	9	2	4	5	3	2	1	6	5	3	2	5	0	5
Negligent manslaughter[2]	0	0	0	0	1	0	1	0	0	0	0	0	0	0	0
Sex offenses—forcible[3]	820	914	1,048	1,026	1,088	1,080	1,065	1,083	1,102	1,225	1,431	1,741	2,368	1,876	492
Sex offenses—nonforcible[4]	113	81	14	5	6	10	8	16	11	8	13	10	12	4	8
Robbery[5]	649	735	538	577	500	502	460	437	366	319	320	387	377	53	324
Aggravated assault[6]	882	900	773	838	744	834	768	754	661	641	631	668	690	267	423
Burglary[7]	10,471	10,561	11,066	11,426	11,657	13,051	11,941	11,551	8,810	8,138	7,421	7,058	6,098	3,803	2,295
Motor vehicle theft[8]	1,471	1,273	1,385	1,316	1,248	1,077	984	859	834	641	704	710	694	6	688
Arson[9]	433	386	353	331	325	307	223	191	174	225	217	227	176	107	69
Weapons-, drug-, and liquor-related arrests and referrals															
Arrests[10]	6,329	6,548	6,856	7,722	7,406	6,134	6,732	6,112	5,777	5,459	5,444	5,515	5,729	3,438	2,291
Illegal weapons possession	167	162	166	184	150	146	178	158	148	137	129	127	133	45	88
Drug law violations	1,628	1,723	1,869	1,751	1,691	1,650	1,804	1,883	2,080	2,248	2,425	2,436	2,541	1,658	883
Liquor law violations	4,534	4,663	4,821	5,787	5,565	4,338	4,750	4,071	3,549	3,074	2,890	2,952	3,055	1,735	1,320
Referrals for disciplinary action[10]	71,293	77,641	85,184	90,749	96,646	103,484	103,254	105,289	103,457	104,939	110,607	110,396	110,019	99,314	10,705
Illegal weapons possession	443	424	537	608	590	622	545	457	358	393	417	498	540	430	110
Drug law violations	9,688	11,100	10,885	10,903	11,208	12,114	12,685	14,157	15,845	17,841	21,240	22,197	22,337	19,606	2,731
Liquor law violations	61,162	66,117	73,762	79,238	84,848	90,748	90,024	90,675	87,254	86,705	88,950	87,701	87,142	79,278	7,864
For-profit 4-year															
Selected crimes against persons and property	505	592	720	718	829	641	612	574	525	561	446	384	542	180	362
Murder[1]	0	0	0	0	0	0	0	0	0	0	1	0	1	1	0
Negligent manslaughter[2]	0	0	0	0	0	0	0	0	0	0	0	0	0	0	0
Sex offenses—forcible[3]	4	4	8	5	4	12	12	9	9	22	26	19	20	14	6
Sex offenses—nonforcible[4]	13	1	2	0	1	0	2	0	1	1	0	3	2	0	2
Robbery[5]	64	71	43	46	43	25	31	38	86	70	74	53	90	13	77
Aggravated assault[6]	23	45	41	38	59	31	31	63	43	51	36	47	68	38	30
Burglary[7]	347	376	542	524	607	489	446	385	299	350	249	200	282	113	169
Motor vehicle theft[8]	52	94	80	100	110	78	89	79	85	65	58	61	77	0	77
Arson[9]	2	1	4	5	5	6	1	0	2	2	2	1	2	1	1
Weapons-, drug-, and liquor-related arrests and referrals															
Arrests[10]	11	17	11	41	28	52	28	40	54	165	152	128	86	31	55
Illegal weapons possession	2	3	2	5	2	5	3	8	6	13	11	11	12	2	10
Drug law violations	4	9	4	12	16	14	16	14	22	66	41	50	56	25	31
Liquor law violations	5	5	5	24	10	33	9	18	26	86	100	67	18	4	14
Referrals for disciplinary action[10]	316	399	465	298	529	513	519	566	882	760	718	668	1,166	1,051	115
Illegal weapons possession	11	25	24	11	42	13	11	13	23	9	16	23	18	12	6
Drug law violations	92	133	130	99	128	138	132	159	231	221	233	254	540	476	64
Liquor law violations	213	241	311	188	359	362	376	394	628	530	469	391	608	563	45

See notes at end of table.

Table 329.10. On-campus crimes, arrests, and referrals for disciplinary action at degree-granting postsecondary institutions, by location of incident, control and level of institution, and type of incident: 2001 through 2013—Continued

Control and level of institution and type of incident	Number of incidents															
	Total, in residence halls and at other locations													2013		
	2001	2002	2003	2004	2005	2006	2007	2008	2009	2010	2011	2012	Total	In residence halls	At other locations
1	2	3	4	5	6	7	8	9	10	11	12	13	14	15	16
Public 2-year															
Selected crimes against persons and property.	6,817	6,860	6,637	6,637	5,981	5,669	5,381	5,464	4,984	4,396	4,141	3,760	3,117	566	2,551
Murder[1]	2	1	2	3	2	0	0	2	2	1	2	3	7	0	7
Negligent manslaughter[2]	0	0	0	0	0	0	0	0	0	1	0	0	0	0	0
Sex offenses—forcible[3]	118	118	160	142	175	167	181	210	205	210	262	265	304	84	220
Sex offenses—nonforcible[4]	119	61	14	6	10	16	7	7	12	8	16	13	12	5	7
Robbery[5]	245	234	230	213	248	284	279	285	251	298	262	244	194	6	188
Aggravated assault[6]	545	503	589	497	501	546	462	401	431	409	406	437	286	52	234
Burglary[7]	4,132	4,158	3,973	4,068	3,541	3,261	3,202	3,430	2,920	2,398	2,235	1,972	1,615	417	1,198
Motor vehicle theft[8]	1,552	1,661	1,607	1,620	1,428	1,319	1,174	1,059	1,109	1,028	899	777	655	0	655
Arson[9]	104	124	62	88	76	76	76	70	54	43	59	49	44	2	42
Weapons-, drug-, and liquor-related arrests and referrals															
Arrests[10]	2,660	2,844	2,950	3,270	3,416	3,993	4,124	3,764	3,335	3,811	3,723	3,486	3,121	1,365	1,756
Illegal weapons possession	198	221	220	255	278	300	304	258	256	282	248	253	234	21	213
Drug law violations	989	996	1,141	1,312	1,326	1,378	1,563	1,490	1,507	1,866	1,892	1,901	1,652	499	1,153
Liquor law violations	1,473	1,627	1,589	1,703	1,812	2,315	2,257	2,016	1,572	1,663	1,583	1,332	1,235	845	390
Referrals for disciplinary action[10]	3,529	3,744	4,036	4,371	4,688	5,897	5,987	6,425	7,241	8,017	8,174	7,589	6,876	5,369	1,507
Illegal weapons possession	127	146	145	167	133	238	218	183	210	242	228	225	242	85	157
Drug law violations	761	692	679	858	819	908	1,006	1,302	1,745	2,336	2,573	2,469	2,304	1,454	850
Liquor law violations	2,641	2,906	3,212	3,346	3,736	4,751	4,763	4,940	5,286	5,439	5,373	4,895	4,330	3,830	500
Nonprofit 2-year															
Selected crimes against persons and property.	248	230	189	166	314	250	258	272	147	120	148	107	61	34	27
Murder[1]	1	0	0	0	0	0	0	0	0	0	0	0	0	0	0
Negligent manslaughter[2]	0	0	0	0	0	0	0	1	0	0	0	0	0	0	0
Sex offenses—forcible[3]	2	7	6	3	8	3	9	16	8	7	11	8	4	1	3
Sex offenses—nonforcible[4]	2	2	0	0	0	3	1	0	0	0	0	0	2	2	0
Robbery[5]	54	56	64	22	9	7	2	13	9	5	1	2	5	2	3
Aggravated assault[6]	23	17	12	17	22	35	52	66	5	9	53	46	9	1	8
Burglary[7]	142	123	83	111	266	187	178	160	120	95	74	47	38	28	10
Motor vehicle theft[8]	23	21	23	13	7	14	14	9	4	2	7	4	3	0	3
Arson[9]	1	4	1	0	2	3	3	7	1	2	2	0	0	0	0
Weapons-, drug-, and liquor-related arrests and referrals															
Arrests[10]	108	39	23	48	76	67	59	93	58	49	52	52	66	34	32
Illegal weapons possession	1	2	3	2	5	3	4	3	4	6	5	5	5	1	4
Drug law violations	21	10	16	16	32	34	27	33	35	18	34	31	49	22	27
Liquor law violations	86	27	4	30	39	30	28	57	19	25	13	16	12	11	1
Referrals for disciplinary action[10]	624	569	552	447	514	537	519	413	348	377	360	300	320	306	14
Illegal weapons possession	2	3	6	5	12	19	10	6	7	4	1	6	7	4	3
Drug law violations	91	65	52	58	47	74	73	85	100	105	109	103	129	121	8
Liquor law violations	531	501	494	384	455	444	436	322	241	268	250	191	184	181	3
For-profit 2-year															
Selected crimes against persons and property.	472	417	550	527	430	420	547	399	459	315	257	258	187	19	168
Murder[1]	0	1	0	0	0	0	0	0	1	0	0	0	0	0	0
Negligent manslaughter[2]	0	0	0	0	0	0	0	1	0	0	0	0	0	0	0
Sex offenses—forcible[3]	12	6	15	9	1	8	2	4	6	2	7	12	11	6	5
Sex offenses—nonforcible[4]	7	3	2	0	0	1	0	0	1	1	0	3	0	0	0
Robbery[5]	67	47	81	80	55	49	67	53	50	38	16	28	23	2	21
Aggravated assault[6]	40	19	36	62	50	33	33	29	53	35	37	34	13	6	7
Burglary[7]	292	297	341	325	250	245	350	241	226	135	120	112	88	5	83
Motor vehicle theft[8]	51	40	74	49	71	81	92	71	121	101	74	69	51	0	51
Arson[9]	3	4	1	2	3	3	3	0	2	3	3	0	1	0	1
Weapons-, drug-, and liquor-related arrests and referrals															
Arrests[10]	163	128	84	112	47	41	45	23	62	43	23	51	61	38	23
Illegal weapons possession	13	9	6	6	3	3	4	4	4	5	1	7	3	1	2
Drug law violations	87	65	48	64	36	26	32	12	41	29	14	40	40	24	16
Liquor law violations	63	54	30	42	8	12	9	7	17	9	8	4	18	13	5
Referrals for disciplinary action[10]	287	330	313	322	228	320	173	248	303	147	168	219	206	190	16
Illegal weapons possession	16	14	7	7	8	7	7	4	8	2	10	10	4	2	2
Drug law violations	89	105	196	186	134	219	122	110	163	68	68	87	93	79	14
Liquor law violations	182	211	110	129	86	94	44	134	132	77	90	122	109	109	0

[1]Excludes suicides, fetal deaths, traffic fatalities, accidental deaths, and justifiable homicide (such as the killing of a felon by a law enforcement officer in the line of duty).
[2]Killing of another person through gross negligence (excludes traffic fatalities).
[3]Any sexual act directed against another person forcibly and/or against that person's will.
[4]Includes only statutory rape or incest.
[5]Taking or attempting to take anything of value using actual or threatened force or violence.
[6]Attack upon a person for the purpose of inflicting severe or aggravated bodily injury.
[7]Unlawful entry of a structure to commit a felony or theft.
[8]Theft or attempted theft of a motor vehicle.
[9]Willful or malicious burning or attempt to burn a dwelling house, public building, motor vehicle, or personal property of another.
[10]If an individual is both arrested and referred to college officials for disciplinary action for a single offense, only the arrest is counted.

NOTE: Data are for degree-granting institutions, which are institutions that grant associate's or higher degrees and participate in Title IV federal financial aid programs. Some institutions that report Clery data—specifically, non-degree-granting institutions and institutions outside of the 50 states and the District of Columbia—are excluded from this table. Crimes, arrests, and referrals include incidents involving students, staff, and on-campus guests. Excludes off-campus crimes and arrests even if they involve college students or staff. Some data have been revised from previously published figures.
SOURCE: U.S. Department of Education, Office of Postsecondary Education, Campus Safety and Security Reporting System, 2001 through 2013; and National Center for Education Statistics, Integrated Postsecondary Education Data System (IPEDS), Fall 2002 through Fall 2014, Institutional Characteristics component. (This table was prepared August 2015.)

Table 329.20. On-campus crimes, arrests, and referrals for disciplinary action per 10,000 full-time-equivalent (FTE) students at degree-granting postsecondary institutions, by whether institution has residence halls, control and level of institution, and type of incident: 2001 through 2013

Control and level of institution and type of incident	Number of incidents per 10,000 full-time-equivalent (FTE) students[1]														
	Total, institutions with and without residence halls												2013		
	2001	2002	2003	2004	2005	2006	2007	2008	2009	2010	2011	2012	Total	Institutions with residence halls	Institutions without residence halls
1	2	3	4	5	6	7	8	9	10	11	12	13	14	15	16
All institutions															
Selected crimes against persons and property	35.619	34.649	34.040	33.580	32.864	33.347	30.568	28.987	22.955	20.869	20.027	19.793	18.378	24.209	6.181
Murder[2]	0.015	0.016	0.007	0.012	0.008	0.006	0.032	0.009	0.011	0.010	0.011	0.008	0.015	0.014	0.019
Negligent manslaughter[3]	0.002	0.000	0.001	0.000	0.002	0.000	0.002	0.002	0.000	0.001	0.001	0.001	0.000	0.000	0.000
Sex offenses—forcible[4]	1.885	1.896	2.051	2.056	2.058	2.001	1.969	1.898	1.715	1.903	2.223	2.665	3.309	4.646	0.513
Sex offenses—nonforcible[5]	0.395	0.213	0.047	0.021	0.032	0.032	0.029	0.025	0.044	0.021	0.030	0.031	0.030	0.035	0.019
Robbery[6]	1.424	1.468	1.284	1.195	1.193	1.159	1.141	1.134	0.950	0.905	0.846	0.912	0.887	1.048	0.548
Aggravated assault[7]	2.524	2.285	2.239	2.098	2.044	2.111	1.903	1.795	1.569	1.444	1.475	1.608	1.390	1.792	0.548
Burglary[8]	23.038	22.847	22.638	22.728	22.511	23.429	21.549	20.672	15.559	13.872	12.825	12.094	10.333	13.908	2.857
Motor vehicle theft[9]	5.327	5.037	4.968	4.674	4.256	3.921	3.375	2.952	2.681	2.237	2.196	2.008	1.995	2.191	1.587
Arson[10]	1.010	0.887	0.805	0.796	0.759	0.687	0.567	0.500	0.427	0.476	0.421	0.467	0.418	0.574	0.091
Weapons-, drug-, and liquor-related arrests and referrals															
Arrests[11]	34.550	35.371	35.239	36.960	37.722	37.615	36.947	36.428	33.748	33.497	35.755	35.045	31.842	45.542	3.188
Illegal weapons possession	0.919	0.931	0.865	0.974	1.013	0.986	0.963	0.856	0.726	0.723	0.674	0.681	0.696	0.829	0.418
Drug law violations	10.151	9.812	9.854	9.849	10.547	10.457	10.330	10.895	10.698	12.086	13.653	14.191	13.432	18.809	2.185
Liquor law violations	23.481	24.629	24.520	26.137	26.163	26.172	25.654	24.676	22.324	20.687	21.428	20.172	17.714	25.904	0.585
Referrals for disciplinary action[11]	132.899	136.344	146.165	151.708	156.060	163.421	158.288	156.479	148.959	149.716	164.460	167.017	164.290	241.127	3.576
Illegal weapons possession	1.093	1.049	1.238	1.387	1.448	1.402	1.212	1.047	0.859	0.854	0.844	0.936	0.956	1.284	0.270
Drug law violations	20.466	21.218	20.356	19.862	19.511	20.425	20.810	23.357	24.498	27.322	33.961	35.916	36.090	52.605	1.546
Liquor law violations	111.340	114.077	124.571	130.459	135.101	141.594	136.267	132.076	123.602	121.540	129.654	130.165	127.244	187.238	1.760
Public 4-year															
Selected crimes against persons and property	36.191	36.334	35.725	35.522	34.295	35.532	32.837	30.531	24.898	23.448	21.958	21.652	19.633	20.933	6.306
Murder[2]	0.017	0.017	0.009	0.014	0.007	0.009	0.070	0.015	0.012	0.014	0.015	0.010	0.015	0.015	0.017
Negligent manslaughter[3]	0.004	0.000	0.002	0.000	0.002	0.000	0.003	0.002	0.000	0.000	0.001	0.001	0.000	0.000	0.000
Sex offenses—forcible[4]	2.408	2.374	2.452	2.634	2.448	2.409	2.390	2.151	1.892	2.210	2.451	2.941	3.347	3.624	0.500
Sex offenses—nonforcible[5]	0.400	0.210	0.051	0.028	0.044	0.026	0.039	0.020	0.062	0.023	0.025	0.025	0.025	0.026	0.017
Robbery[6]	1.130	1.224	1.208	1.088	1.219	1.170	1.211	1.225	1.008	1.001	0.916	0.984	0.950	0.990	0.551
Aggravated assault[7]	2.774	2.452	2.493	2.256	2.242	2.302	2.110	1.930	1.767	1.627	1.610	1.778	1.511	1.608	0.517
Burglary[8]	22.283	23.259	22.808	23.154	22.654	24.138	22.425	21.181	16.689	15.456	14.025	13.181	10.942	11.707	3.103
Motor vehicle theft[9]	5.942	5.743	5.625	5.269	4.671	4.581	3.800	3.310	2.843	2.426	2.382	2.095	2.244	2.313	1.535
Arson[10]	1.232	1.057	1.078	1.079	1.009	0.897	0.788	0.697	0.623	0.691	0.533	0.637	0.599	0.651	0.067
Weapons-, drug-, and liquor-related arrests and referrals															
Arrests[11]	60.113	62.833	62.566	65.318	66.641	68.662	66.366	66.315	63.558	63.512	67.169	64.997	57.387	62.562	4.337
Illegal weapons possession	1.339	1.384	1.258	1.442	1.538	1.478	1.384	1.240	1.027	1.012	0.941	0.931	0.974	1.027	0.434
Drug law violations	17.651	17.158	16.950	17.100	18.575	18.671	17.934	19.130	18.993	21.722	24.424	25.248	23.444	25.434	3.036
Liquor law violations	41.123	44.292	44.358	46.776	46.529	48.513	47.048	45.945	43.539	40.778	41.804	38.819	32.969	36.101	0.867
Referrals for disciplinary action[11]	153.104	157.192	170.355	178.800	175.506	184.628	178.029	170.797	169.503	175.490	194.017	197.663	189.581	207.918	1.618
Illegal weapons possession	1.311	1.254	1.529	1.779	1.921	1.673	1.454	1.293	1.043	1.004	0.913	0.968	0.924	1.007	0.067
Drug law violations	25.492	25.896	24.933	24.278	22.803	23.744	24.249	27.201	28.459	32.444	40.907	43.276	42.605	46.663	1.001
Liquor law violations	126.301	130.043	143.893	152.743	150.782	159.211	152.326	142.303	140.001	142.042	152.198	153.419	146.053	160.248	0.551
Nonprofit 4-year															
Selected crimes against persons and property	57.358	55.445	54.891	54.728	54.165	57.681	52.039	49.315	38.613	35.193	33.154	32.730	31.341	33.383	9.371
Murder[2]	0.019	0.034	0.007	0.014	0.017	0.010	0.007	0.003	0.019	0.016	0.009	0.006	0.015	0.013	0.035
Negligent manslaughter[3]	0.000	0.000	0.000	0.000	0.003	0.000	0.003	0.000	0.000	0.000	0.000	0.000	0.000	0.000	0.000
Sex offenses—forcible[4]	3.169	3.410	3.790	3.617	3.784	3.694	3.587	3.586	3.557	3.848	4.417	5.275	7.122	7.686	1.061
Sex offenses—nonforcible[5]	0.437	0.302	0.051	0.018	0.021	0.034	0.027	0.053	0.036	0.025	0.040	0.030	0.036	0.036	0.035
Robbery[6]	2.508	2.743	1.946	2.034	1.739	1.717	1.549	1.447	1.181	1.002	0.988	1.173	1.134	1.154	0.919
Aggravated assault[7]	3.408	3.358	2.795	2.954	2.588	2.853	2.586	2.497	2.133	2.014	1.948	2.024	2.075	2.199	0.743
Burglary[8]	40.460	39.407	40.017	40.284	40.542	44.639	40.214	38.251	28.434	25.567	22.908	21.384	18.341	19.547	5.375
Motor vehicle theft[9]	5.684	4.750	5.008	4.640	4.340	3.684	3.314	2.845	2.692	2.014	2.173	2.151	2.087	2.170	1.202
Arson[10]	1.673	1.440	1.277	1.167	1.130	1.050	0.751	0.632	0.562	0.707	0.670	0.688	0.529	0.579	0.000
Weapons-, drug-, and liquor-related arrests and referrals															
Arrests[11]	24.456	24.433	24.793	27.225	25.758	20.981	22.672	20.240	18.645	17.150	16.805	16.709	17.231	18.656	1.909
Illegal weapons possession	0.645	0.604	0.600	0.649	0.522	0.499	0.599	0.523	0.478	0.430	0.398	0.385	0.400	0.434	0.035
Drug law violations	6.291	6.429	6.759	6.173	5.881	5.644	6.075	6.236	6.713	7.062	7.486	7.380	7.643	8.241	1.202
Liquor law violations	17.520	17.399	17.434	20.403	19.355	14.838	15.997	13.481	11.454	9.657	8.921	8.944	9.189	9.980	0.672
Referrals for disciplinary action[11]	275.480	289.709	308.044	319.945	336.127	353.954	347.734	348.663	333.904	329.679	341.437	334.473	330.910	359.218	26.414
Illegal weapons possession	1.712	1.582	1.942	2.144	2.052	2.127	1.835	1.513	1.155	1.235	1.287	1.509	1.624	1.759	0.177
Drug law violations	37.435	41.418	39.363	38.440	38.981	41.434	42.720	46.881	51.139	56.050	65.567	67.251	67.184	73.026	4.349
Liquor law violations	236.333	246.708	266.740	279.362	295.095	310.392	303.179	300.269	281.609	272.395	274.583	265.713	262.101	284.433	21.888
For-profit 4-year															
Selected crimes against persons and property	19.109	17.840	17.605	13.650	17.049	9.552	8.095	10.320	7.513	6.499	6.003	5.234	7.493	20.129	3.717
Murder[2]	0.000	0.000	0.000	0.000	0.000	0.000	0.000	0.000	0.000	0.000	0.013	0.000	0.014	0.060	0.000
Negligent manslaughter[3]	0.000	0.000	0.000	0.000	0.000	0.000	0.000	0.000	0.000	0.000	0.000	0.000	0.000	0.000	0.000
Sex offenses—forcible[4]	0.151	0.121	0.196	0.095	0.082	0.179	0.159	0.162	0.129	0.255	0.350	0.259	0.277	0.961	0.072
Sex offenses—nonforcible[5]	0.492	0.030	0.049	0.000	0.021	0.000	0.026	0.000	0.014	0.012	0.000	0.041	0.028	0.000	0.036
Robbery[6]	2.422	2.140	1.051	0.875	0.884	0.373	0.410	0.683	1.231	0.811	0.996	0.722	1.244	3.545	0.557
Aggravated assault[7]	0.870	1.356	1.003	0.722	1.213	0.462	0.410	1.133	0.615	0.591	0.485	0.641	0.940	3.004	0.323
Burglary[8]	13.130	11.331	13.253	9.962	12.484	7.287	5.899	6.922	4.279	4.055	3.351	2.726	3.899	10.876	1.814
Motor vehicle theft[9]	1.968	2.833	1.956	1.901	2.262	1.162	1.177	1.420	1.216	0.753	0.781	0.831	1.065	1.622	0.898
Arson[10]	0.076	0.030	0.098	0.095	0.103	0.089	0.013	0.000	0.029	0.023	0.027	0.014	0.028	0.060	0.018
Weapons-, drug-, and liquor-related arrests and referrals															
Arrests[11]	0.416	0.512	0.269	0.779	0.576	0.775	0.370	0.719	0.773	1.911	2.046	1.745	1.189	3.365	0.539
Illegal weapons possession	0.076	0.090	0.049	0.095	0.041	0.075	0.040	0.144	0.086	0.151	0.148	0.150	0.166	0.421	0.090
Drug law violations	0.151	0.271	0.098	0.228	0.329	0.209	0.212	0.252	0.315	0.765	0.552	0.681	0.774	2.343	0.305
Liquor law violations	0.189	0.151	0.122	0.456	0.206	0.492	0.119	0.324	0.372	0.996	1.346	0.913	0.249	0.601	0.144
Referrals for disciplinary action[11]	11.957	12.024	11.370	5.665	10.880	7.645	6.865	10.177	12.623	8.804	9.663	9.104	16.120	68.438	0.485
Illegal weapons possession	0.416	0.753	0.587	0.209	0.864	0.194	0.145	0.234	0.329	0.104	0.215	0.313	0.249	0.901	0.054
Drug law violations	3.481	4.008	3.179	1.882	2.632	2.057	1.746	2.859	3.306	2.560	3.136	3.462	7.466	31.545	0.269
Liquor law violations	8.060	7.263	7.605	3.574	7.383	5.395	4.973	7.084	8.988	6.140	6.312	5.329	8.406	35.991	0.162

See notes at end of table.

Table 329.20. On-campus crimes, arrests, and referrals for disciplinary action per 10,000 full-time-equivalent (FTE) students at degree-granting postsecondary institutions, by whether institution has residence halls, control and level of institution, and type of incident: 2001 through 2013—Continued

Control and level of institution and type of incident	Number of incidents per 10,000 full-time-equivalent (FTE) students[1]															
	Total, institutions with and without residence halls													2013		
	2001	2002	2003	2004	2005	2006	2007	2008	2009	2010	2011	2012	Total	Institutions with residence halls	Institutions without residence halls
1	2	3	4	5	6	7	8	9	10	11	12	13	14	15	16
Public 2-year															
Selected crimes against persons and property	19.867	18.834	18.044	17.903	16.389	15.423	14.388	13.991	11.745	10.195	9.998	9.387	7.994	14.793	6.309
Murder[2]	0.006	0.003	0.005	0.008	0.005	0.000	0.000	0.005	0.005	0.002	0.005	0.007	0.018	0.000	0.022
Negligent manslaughter[3]	0.000	0.000	0.000	0.000	0.000	0.000	0.000	0.000	0.000	0.002	0.000	0.000	0.000	0.000	0.000
Sex offenses—forcible[4]	0.344	0.324	0.435	0.383	0.480	0.454	0.484	0.538	0.483	0.487	0.633	0.662	0.780	1.626	0.570
Sex offenses—nonforcible[5]	0.347	0.167	0.038	0.016	0.027	0.044	0.019	0.018	0.028	0.019	0.039	0.032	0.031	0.090	0.016
Robbery[6]	0.714	0.642	0.625	0.575	0.680	0.773	0.746	0.730	0.591	0.691	0.633	0.609	0.498	0.529	0.490
Aggravated assault[7]	1.588	1.381	1.601	1.341	1.373	1.485	1.235	1.027	1.016	0.949	0.980	1.091	0.734	1.304	0.592
Burglary[8]	12.042	11.416	10.801	10.974	9.703	8.872	8.561	8.783	6.881	5.561	5.396	4.923	4.142	9.746	2.753
Motor vehicle theft[9]	4.523	4.560	4.369	4.370	3.913	3.588	3.139	2.712	2.613	2.384	2.171	1.940	1.680	1.420	1.744
Arson[10]	0.303	0.340	0.169	0.237	0.208	0.207	0.203	0.179	0.127	0.100	0.142	0.122	0.113	0.077	0.122
Weapons-, drug-, and liquor-related arrests and referrals															
Arrests[11]	7.752	7.808	8.020	8.821	9.360	10.863	11.027	9.638	7.859	8.838	8.989	8.703	8.005	25.159	3.751
Illegal weapons possession	0.577	0.607	0.598	0.688	0.762	0.816	0.813	0.661	0.603	0.654	0.599	0.632	0.600	0.839	0.541
Drug law violations	2.882	2.735	3.102	3.539	3.633	3.749	4.179	3.815	3.551	4.328	4.568	4.746	4.237	10.959	2.570
Liquor law violations	4.293	4.467	4.320	4.594	4.965	6.298	6.035	5.162	3.704	3.857	3.822	3.325	3.167	13.360	0.640
Referrals for disciplinary action[11]	10.284	10.279	10.973	11.791	12.846	16.043	16.008	16.451	17.063	18.592	19.735	18.946	17.635	77.865	2.701
Illegal weapons possession	0.370	0.401	0.394	0.450	0.364	0.648	0.583	0.469	0.495	0.561	0.550	0.562	0.621	1.639	0.368
Drug law violations	2.218	1.900	1.846	2.314	2.244	2.470	2.690	3.334	4.112	5.417	6.212	6.164	5.909	22.809	1.719
Liquor law violations	7.697	7.978	8.732	9.026	10.237	12.926	12.735	12.649	12.456	12.614	12.972	12.220	11.105	53.416	0.615
Nonprofit 2-year															
Selected crimes against persons and property	63.955	58.903	51.594	48.535	91.263	81.948	103.819	99.299	55.883	48.448	45.531	34.764	23.425	53.231	10.021
Murder[2]	0.258	0.000	0.000	0.000	0.000	0.000	0.000	0.000	0.000	0.000	0.000	0.000	0.000	0.000	0.000
Negligent manslaughter[3]	0.000	0.000	0.000	0.000	0.000	0.000	0.000	0.365	0.000	0.000	0.000	0.000	0.000	0.000	0.000
Sex offenses—forcible[4]	0.516	1.793	1.638	0.877	2.325	0.983	3.622	5.841	3.041	2.826	3.384	2.599	1.536	2.476	1.113
Sex offenses—nonforcible[5]	0.516	0.512	0.000	0.000	0.000	0.328	0.000	0.000	0.000	0.000	0.000	0.000	0.768	2.476	0.000
Robbery[6]	13.926	14.342	17.471	6.432	2.616	2.295	0.805	4.746	3.421	2.019	0.308	0.650	1.920	3.714	1.113
Aggravated assault[7]	5.931	4.354	3.276	4.970	6.394	11.473	20.925	24.095	1.901	3.634	16.305	14.945	3.456	6.190	2.227
Burglary[8]	36.620	31.500	22.658	32.454	77.312	61.297	71.627	58.411	45.619	38.354	22.766	15.270	14.592	37.138	4.454
Motor vehicle theft[9]	5.931	5.378	6.279	3.801	2.035	4.589	5.634	3.286	1.521	0.807	2.154	1.300	1.152	1.238	1.113
Arson[10]	0.258	1.024	0.273	0.000	0.581	0.983	1.207	2.555	0.380	0.807	0.615	0.000	0.000	0.000	0.000
Weapons-, drug-, and liquor-related arrests and referrals															
Arrests[11]	27.852	9.988	6.279	14.034	22.089	21.962	23.741	33.952	22.049	19.783	15.998	16.895	25.345	66.848	6.680
Illegal weapons possession	0.258	0.512	0.819	0.585	1.453	0.983	1.610	1.095	1.521	2.422	1.538	1.624	1.920	6.190	0.000
Drug law violations	5.416	2.561	4.368	4.678	9.301	11.145	10.865	12.047	13.305	7.267	10.460	10.072	18.816	45.803	6.680
Liquor law violations	22.178	6.915	1.092	8.771	11.335	9.834	11.267	20.809	7.223	10.093	3.999	5.198	4.608	14.855	0.000
Referrals for disciplinary action[11]	160.920	145.722	150.688	130.694	149.393	176.025	208.845	150.774	132.294	152.206	110.752	97.469	122.883	389.948	2.783
Illegal weapons possession	0.516	0.768	1.638	1.462	3.488	6.228	4.024	2.190	2.661	1.615	0.308	1.949	2.688	6.190	1.113
Drug law violations	23.468	16.647	14.195	16.958	13.660	24.257	29.375	31.031	38.016	42.392	33.533	33.464	49.537	157.217	1.113
Liquor law violations	136.937	128.307	134.855	112.274	132.244	145.540	175.446	117.553	91.618	108.200	76.911	62.055	70.658	226.541	0.557
For-profit 2-year															
Selected crimes against persons and property	25.385	21.447	24.700	21.845	17.851	18.237	23.658	14.826	13.033	8.167	7.503	8.744	6.602	21.150	5.916
Murder[2]	0.000	0.051	0.000	0.000	0.000	0.000	0.000	0.000	0.000	0.000	0.000	0.000	0.000	0.000	0.000
Negligent manslaughter[3]	0.000	0.000	0.000	0.000	0.000	0.000	0.000	0.037	0.000	0.000	0.000	0.000	0.000	0.000	0.000
Sex offenses—forcible[4]	0.645	0.309	0.674	0.373	0.042	0.347	0.087	0.149	0.170	0.052	0.204	0.407	0.388	4.700	0.185
Sex offenses—nonforcible[5]	0.376	0.154	0.090	0.000	0.000	0.043	0.000	0.000	0.028	0.026	0.000	0.102	0.000	0.000	0.000
Robbery[6]	3.603	2.417	3.638	3.316	2.283	2.128	2.898	1.969	1.420	0.985	0.467	0.949	0.812	1.567	0.776
Aggravated assault[7]	2.151	0.977	1.617	2.570	2.076	1.433	1.427	1.078	1.505	0.907	1.080	1.152	0.459	4.700	0.259
Burglary[8]	15.704	15.275	15.314	13.472	10.378	10.638	15.138	8.955	6.417	3.500	3.503	3.796	3.107	7.050	2.921
Motor vehicle theft[9]	2.743	2.057	3.323	2.031	2.947	3.517	3.979	2.638	3.436	2.619	2.160	2.338	1.801	3.133	1.738
Arson[10]	0.161	0.206	0.045	0.083	0.125	0.130	0.130	0.000	0.057	0.078	0.088	0.000	0.035	0.000	0.037
Weapons-, drug-, and liquor-related arrests and referrals															
Arrests[11]	8.766	6.583	3.772	4.643	1.951	1.780	1.946	0.855	1.760	1.115	0.671	1.728	2.154	32.900	0.702
Illegal weapons possession	0.699	0.463	0.269	0.249	0.125	0.130	0.173	0.149	0.114	0.130	0.029	0.237	0.106	0.783	0.074
Drug law violations	4.679	3.343	2.156	2.653	1.495	1.129	1.384	0.446	1.164	0.752	0.409	1.356	1.412	21.933	0.444
Liquor law violations	3.388	2.777	1.347	1.741	0.332	0.521	0.389	0.260	0.483	0.233	0.234	0.136	0.636	10.183	0.185
Referrals for disciplinary action[11]	15.435	16.972	14.057	13.348	9.465	13.895	7.482	9.215	8.603	3.811	4.905	7.422	7.273	149.616	0.555
Illegal weapons possession	0.861	0.720	0.314	0.290	0.332	0.304	0.303	0.149	0.227	0.052	0.292	0.339	0.141	1.567	0.074
Drug law violations	4.787	5.400	8.802	7.710	5.563	9.509	5.277	4.087	4.628	1.763	1.985	2.949	3.284	62.666	0.481
Liquor law violations	9.788	10.852	4.940	5.347	3.570	4.082	1.903	4.979	3.748	1.996	2.627	4.135	3.848	85.383	0.000

[1]Although crimes, arrests, and referrals include incidents involving students, staff, and campus guests, they are expressed as a ratio to FTE students because comprehensive FTE counts of all these groups are not available.
[2]Excludes suicides, fetal deaths, traffic fatalities, accidental deaths, and justifiable homicide (such as the killing of a felon by a law enforcement officer in the line of duty).
[3]Killing of another person through gross negligence (excludes traffic fatalities).
[4]Any sexual act directed against another person forcibly and/or against that person's will.
[5]Includes only statutory rape or incest.
[6]Taking or attempting to take anything of value using actual or threatened force or violence.
[7]Attack upon a person for the purpose of inflicting severe or aggravated bodily injury.
[8]Unlawful entry of a structure to commit a felony or theft.
[9]Theft or attempted theft of a motor vehicle.
[10]Willful or malicious burning or attempt to burn a dwelling house, public building, motor vehicle, or personal property of another.

[11]If an individual is both arrested and referred to college officials for disciplinary action for a single offense, only the arrest is counted.
NOTE: Data are for degree-granting institutions, which are institutions that grant associate's or higher degrees and participate in Title IV federal financial aid programs. Some institutions that report Clery data—specifically, non-degree-granting institutions and institutions outside of the 50 states and the District of Columbia—are excluded from this table. Crimes, arrests, and referrals include incidents involving students, staff, and on-campus guests. Excludes off-campus crimes and arrests even if they involve college students or staff. Detail may not sum to totals because of rounding. Some data have been revised from previously published figures.
SOURCE: U.S. Department of Education, Office of Postsecondary Education, Campus Safety and Security Reporting System, 2001 through 2013; and National Center for Education Statistics, Integrated Postsecondary Education Data System (IPEDS), Spring 2002 through Spring 2014, Fall Enrollment component. (This table was prepared August 2015.)

Table 329.30. On-campus hate crimes at degree-granting postsecondary institutions, by level and control of institution, type of crime, and category of bias motivating the crime: 2009 through 2013

Type of crime and category of bias motivating the crime[1]	Total, 2009	Total, 2010	Total, 2011	2012 Total	2012 4-year Public	2012 4-year Non-profit	2012 4-year For-profit	2012 2-year Public	2012 2-year Non-profit	2012 2-year For-profit	2013 Total	2013 4-year Public	2013 4-year Non-profit	2013 4-year For-profit	2013 2-year Public	2013 2-year Non-profit	2013 2-year For-profit
1	2	3	4	5	6	7	8	9	10	11	12	13	14	15	16	17	18
All on-campus hate crimes	672	928	761	787	328	303	12	138	2	4	781	295	349	25	106	1	5
Murder[2]	0	0	0	0	0	0	0	0	0	0	0	0	0	0	0	0	0
Negligent manslaughter[3]	0	0	0	0	0	0	0	0	0	0	0	0	0	0	0	0	0
Sex offenses–forcible[4]	11	7	9	4	1	1	0	2	0	0	7	1	6	0	0	0	0
Race	0	0	0	1	0	0	0	1	0	0	2	0	2	0	0	0	0
Ethnicity	0	0	2	0	0	0	0	0	0	0	0	0	0	0	0	0	0
Religion	0	0	1	2	1	0	0	1	0	0	1	0	1	0	0	0	0
Sexual orientation	0	4	6	1	0	1	0	0	0	0	4	1	3	0	0	0	0
Gender	3	3	0	0	0	0	0	0	0	0	0	0	0	0	0	0	0
Disability	8	0	0	0	0	0	0	0	0	0	0	0	0	0	0	0	0
Sex offenses–nonforcible[5]	0	0	0	0	0	0	0	0	0	0	0	0	0	0	0	0	0
Robbery[6]	5	2	2	5	2	0	0	3	0	0	1	0	1	0	0	0	0
Race	3	1	1	4	2	0	0	2	0	0	0	0	0	0	0	0	0
Ethnicity	0	1	0	0	0	0	0	0	0	0	1	0	1	0	0	0	0
Religion	0	0	0	0	0	0	0	0	0	0	0	0	0	0	0	0	0
Sexual orientation	2	0	1	0	0	0	0	0	0	0	0	0	0	0	0	0	0
Gender	0	0	0	0	0	0	0	0	0	0	0	0	0	0	0	0	0
Disability	0	0	0	1	0	0	0	1	0	0	0	0	0	0	0	0	0
Aggravated assault[7]	9	17	13	14	6	4	1	3	0	0	6	3	1	0	2	0	0
Race	3	6	5	6	3	1	0	2	0	0	4	2	0	0	2	0	0
Ethnicity	1	1	0	0	0	0	0	0	0	0	1	1	0	0	0	0	0
Religion	0	1	2	1	1	0	0	0	0	0	0	0	0	0	0	0	0
Sexual orientation	4	9	6	5	2	2	1	0	0	0	1	0	1	0	0	0	0
Gender	1	0	0	1	0	0	0	1	0	0	0	0	0	0	0	0	0
Disability	0	0	0	1	0	1	0	0	0	0	0	0	0	0	0	0	0
Burglary[8]	8	11	8	5	0	0	0	4	0	1	4	1	2	0	1	0	0
Race	4	7	4	0	0	0	0	0	0	0	1	0	1	0	0	0	0
Ethnicity	2	0	0	0	0	0	0	0	0	0	0	0	0	0	0	0	0
Religion	0	0	2	0	0	0	0	0	0	1	1	0	1	0	0	0	0
Sexual orientation	1	2	1	0	0	0	0	0	0	0	0	0	0	0	0	0	0
Gender	1	1	1	4	0	0	0	4	0	0	2	1	0	0	1	0	0
Disability	0	1	0	0	0	0	0	0	0	0	0	0	0	0	0	0	0
Motor vehicle theft[9]	0	0	0	0	0	0	0	0	0	0	0	0	0	0	0	0	0
Arson[10]	0	0	1	0	0	0	0	0	0	0	0	0	0	0	0	0	0
Race	0	0	0	0	0	0	0	0	0	0	0	0	0	0	0	0	0
Ethnicity	0	0	0	0	0	0	0	0	0	0	0	0	0	0	0	0	0
Religion	0	0	1	0	0	0	0	0	0	0	0	0	0	0	0	0	0
Sexual orientation	0	0	0	0	0	0	0	0	0	0	0	0	0	0	0	0	0
Gender	0	0	0	0	0	0	0	0	0	0	0	0	0	0	0	0	0
Disability	0	0	0	0	0	0	0	0	0	0	0	0	0	0	0	0	0
Simple assault[11]	58	67	67	79	43	19	2	12	1	2	89	39	39	5	6	0	0
Race	23	25	22	36	20	11	1	2	0	2	34	15	14	2	3	0	0
Ethnicity	5	5	10	5	2	1	0	2	0	0	7	5	2	0	0	0	0
Religion	1	4	8	9	6	2	0	1	0	0	5	2	3	0	0	0	0
Sexual orientation	18	23	16	21	13	4	1	3	0	0	26	11	11	1	3	0	0
Gender	7	9	8	5	2	1	0	1	1	0	17	6	9	2	0	0	0
Disability	4	1	3	3	0	0	0	3	0	0	0	0	0	0	0	0	0
Larceny[12]	10	9	15	9	1	4	0	2	1	1	15	1	6	1	3	1	3
Race	0	1	2	2	0	1	0	1	0	0	5	1	2	1	2	0	0
Ethnicity	3	3	3	2	2	1	0	0	1	0	2	0	2	0	0	0	0
Religion	1	1	2	2	1	0	0	0	0	1	3	0	2	0	0	0	3
Sexual orientation	2	1	3	3	3	0	2	0	1	0	3	1	2	0	1	1	0
Gender	4	3	3	0	0	0	0	0	0	0	2	0	0	0	1	1	0
Disability	0	0	2	0	0	0	0	0	0	0	0	0	0	0	0	0	0
Intimidation[13]	175	260	282	268	94	120	7	47	0	0	295	100	139	14	42	0	0
Race	58	79	111	120	47	45	2	26	0	0	110	43	48	4	15	0	0
Ethnicity	23	17	22	23	6	14	1	2	0	0	49	14	29	1	5	0	0
Religion	20	38	24	29	12	14	1	2	0	0	24	7	16	1	0	0	0
Sexual orientation	57	87	91	70	25	31	0	14	0	0	69	26	31	3	9	0	0
Gender	13	37	31	22	1	15	3	3	0	0	37	7	14	5	11	0	0
Disability	4	2	3	4	3	1	0	0	0	0	6	3	1	0	2	0	0
Destruction, damage, and vandalism[14]	396	555	364	403	181	155	2	65	0	0	364	150	155	5	52	0	2
Race	174	257	166	186	91	56	0	39	0	0	151	58	61	5	27	0	0
Ethnicity	28	43	30	34	21	8	1	4	0	0	37	11	19	0	5	0	2
Religion	72	103	57	70	18	43	1	8	0	0	48	21	24	0	3	0	0
Sexual orientation	109	135	104	104	47	46	0	11	0	0	112	57	44	0	11	0	0
Gender	13	17	7	9	4	2	0	3	0	0	14	3	6	0	5	0	0
Disability	0	0	0	0	0	0	0	0	0	0	2	0	1	0	1	0	0

[1]Bias categories correspond to characteristics against which the bias is directed (i.e., race, ethnicity, religion, sexual orientation, gender, or disability).

[2]Excludes suicides, fetal deaths, traffic fatalities, accidental deaths, and justifiable homicide (such as the killing of a felon by a law enforcement officer in the line of duty).

[3]Killing of another person through gross negligence (excludes traffic fatalities).

[4]Any sexual act directed against another person forcibly and/or against that person's will.

[5]Includes only statutory rape or incest.

[6]Taking or attempting to take anything of value using actual or threatened force or violence.

[7]Attack upon a person for the purpose of inflicting severe or aggravated bodily injury.

[8]Unlawful entry of a structure to commit a felony or theft.

[9]Theft or attempted theft of a motor vehicle.

[10]Willful or malicious burning or attempt to burn a dwelling house, public building, motor vehicle, or personal property of another.

[11]A physical attack by one person upon another where neither the offender displays a weapon, nor the victim suffers obvious severe or aggravated bodily injury involving apparent broken bones, loss of teeth, possible internal injury, severe laceration, or loss of consciousness.

[12]The unlawful taking, carrying, leading, or riding away of property from the possession of another.

[13]Placing another person in reasonable fear of bodily harm through the use of threatening words and/or other conduct, but without displaying a weapon or subjecting the victim to actual physical attack.

[14]Willfully or maliciously destroying, damaging, defacing, or otherwise injuring real or personal property without the consent of the owner or the person having custody or control of it.

NOTE: Data are for degree-granting institutions, which are institutions that grant associate's or higher degrees and participate in Title IV federal financial aid programs. Some institutions that report Clery data–specifically, non-degree-granting institutions and institutions outside of the 50 states and the District of Columbia–are excluded from this table. A hate crime is a criminal offense that is motivated, in whole or in part, by the perpetrator's bias against a group of people based on their race, ethnicity, religion, sexual orientation, gender, or disability. Includes on-campus incidents involving students, staff, and on-campus guests. Excludes off-campus crimes and arrests even if they involve college students or staff.

SOURCE: U.S. Department of Education, Office of Postsecondary Education, Campus Safety and Security Reporting System, 2009 through 2013. (This table was prepared August 2015.)

Table 330.10. Average undergraduate tuition and fees and room and board rates charged for full-time students in degree-granting postsecondary institutions, by level and control of institution: 1963–64 through 2014–15

Year and control of institution	Constant 2014–15 dollars[1]												Current dollars											
	Total tuition, fees, room and board			Tuition and required fees[2]			Dormitory rooms			Board[3]			Total tuition, fees, room, and board			Tuition and required fees[2]			Dormitory rooms			Board[3]		
	All institutions	4-year	2-year	All institutions	4-year	2-year	All institutions	4-year	2-year	All institutions	4-year	2-year	All institutions	4-year	2-year	All institutions	4-year	2-year	All institutions	4-year	2-year	All institutions	4-year	2-year
1	2	3	4	5	6	7	8	9	10	11	12	13	14	15	16	17	18	19	20	21	22	23	24	25
All institutions																								
1963–64	$9,576	$9,869	$5,951	$3,900	$4,240	$1,314	$2,167	$2,138	$1,605	$3,510	$3,491	$3,032	$1,248	$1,286	$775	$508	$553	$171	$282	$279	$209	$457	$455	$395
1964–65	9,722	10,044	6,374	4,016	4,396	1,419	2,240	2,207	1,800	3,465	3,441	3,155	1,283	1,325	841	530	580	187	296	291	238	457	454	416
1965–66	9,819	10,200	6,560	4,069	4,499	1,505	2,300	2,281	1,917	3,447	3,420	3,138	1,324	1,375	884	549	607	203	311	308	258	465	461	423
1966–67	9,908	10,348	6,656	4,127	4,604	1,541	2,362	2,352	2,013	3,419	3,393	3,102	1,378	1,439	926	574	640	214	328	327	280	476	472	431
1967–68	9,849	10,348	6,847	4,089	4,612	1,615	2,380	2,374	2,097	3,380	3,365	3,134	1,415	1,487	984	588	663	232	342	341	301	486	483	450
1968–69	9,679	10,254	6,987	3,957	4,534	1,662	2,391	2,390	2,169	3,331	3,330	3,156	1,459	1,545	1,053	596	683	250	360	360	327	502	502	476
1969–70	9,774	10,491	6,825	4,042	4,730	1,550	2,439	2,455	2,174	3,294	3,306	3,102	1,560	1,674	1,089	645	755	247	389	392	347	526	528	495
1970–71	9,846	10,631	6,675	4,099	4,848	1,486	2,495	2,514	2,201	3,252	3,269	2,988	1,653	1,784	1,120	688	814	249	419	422	369	546	549	501
1971–72	9,953	10,799	6,739	4,163	4,977	1,443	2,559	2,579	2,248	3,231	3,243	3,048	1,730	1,878	1,172	724	865	251	445	448	391	562	564	530
1972–73	10,142	11,227	7,054	4,199	5,254	1,586	2,697	2,723	2,293	3,246	3,251	3,175	1,834	2,031	1,276	759	950	287	488	492	415	587	588	574
1973–74	9,660	10,660	6,895	4,039	4,998	1,667	2,515	2,537	2,181	3,107	3,111	3,047	1,903	2,097	1,358	796	985	328	495	500	430	612	613	600
1974–75	9,062	9,992	6,542	3,699	4,607	1,497	2,413	2,434	2,103	2,951	2,951	2,942	1,983	2,187	1,432	809	1,008	328	528	533	460	646	646	644
1975–76	8,976	10,049	6,288	3,538	4,580	1,268	2,428	2,459	2,023	3,010	3,011	2,997	2,103	2,355	1,473	829	1,073	297	569	576	474	705	706	702
1976–77	9,175	10,391	6,443	3,726	4,913	1,393	2,433	2,463	2,027	3,015	3,015	3,023	2,275	2,577	1,598	924	1,218	346	603	611	503	748	748	750
1977–78	9,110	10,297	6,437	3,720	4,880	1,429	2,438	2,471	1,983	2,951	2,946	3,025	2,411	2,725	1,703	984	1,291	378	645	654	525	781	780	801
1978–79	8,937	10,080	6,316	3,706	4,826	1,420	2,377	2,403	1,987	2,854	2,851	2,910	2,587	2,917	1,828	1,073	1,397	411	688	696	575	826	825	842
1979–80	8,563	9,655	6,035	3,545	4,612	1,375	2,285	2,315	1,914	2,729	2,728	2,745	2,809	3,167	1,979	1,163	1,513	451	751	759	628	895	895	900
1980–81	8,473	9,561	6,093	3,521	4,586	1,437	2,285	2,311	1,925	2,668	2,664	2,731	3,101	3,499	2,230	1,289	1,679	526	836	846	705	976	975	1,000
1981–82	8,776	9,936	6,226	3,663	4,797	1,483	2,389	2,418	1,993	2,723	2,722	2,750	3,489	3,951	2,476	1,457	1,907	590	950	961	793	1,083	1,082	1,094
1982–83	9,348	10,624	6,543	3,920	5,159	1,627	2,565	2,599	2,106	2,863	2,866	2,810	3,877	4,406	2,713	1,626	2,139	675	1,064	1,078	873	1,187	1,189	1,165
1983–84	9,690	11,039	6,638	4,145	5,450	1,698	2,663	2,702	2,130	2,882	2,887	2,809	4,167	4,747	2,854	1,783	2,344	730	1,145	1,162	916	1,239	1,242	1,208
1984–85	10,210	11,548	7,115	4,443	5,745	1,838	2,835	2,869	2,367	2,932	2,933	2,910	4,563	5,160	3,179	1,985	2,567	821	1,267	1,282	1,058	1,310	1,311	1,301
1985–86[4]	10,624	11,972	7,323	4,744	6,056	1,932	2,911	2,947	2,408	2,970	2,969	2,983	4,885	5,504	3,295	2,181	2,784	888	1,338	1,355	1,107	1,365	1,365	1,372
1986–87	11,077	12,690	7,012	4,919	6,473	1,909	2,989	3,035	2,200	3,168	3,182	2,902	5,206	5,964	3,263	2,312	3,042	897	1,405	1,427	1,034	1,489	1,495	1,364
1987–88	11,226	12,815	6,987	5,022	6,540	1,653	3,039	3,098	2,059	3,184	3,200	2,935	5,494	6,272	3,263	2,458	3,201	809	1,488	1,516	1,017	1,549	1,555	1,437
1988–89	11,461	13,134	7,201	5,190	6,781	1,913	3,075	3,142	2,118	3,196	3,212	2,947	5,869	6,725	3,573	2,658	3,472	979	1,575	1,609	1,085	1,636	1,644	1,509
1989–90	11,570	13,442	6,906	5,292	7,083	1,823	3,053	3,122	2,059	3,225	3,237	3,024	6,207	7,212	3,705	2,839	3,800	978	1,638	1,675	1,105	1,730	1,737	1,622
1990–91	11,597	13,435	6,946	5,331	7,085	1,922	3,081	3,149	2,090	3,185	3,200	2,935	6,562	7,602	3,930	3,016	4,009	1,087	1,743	1,782	1,182	1,802	1,811	1,660
1991–92	12,119	14,107	7,007	5,626	7,510	2,036	3,209	3,290	2,073	3,284	3,307	2,898	7,077	8,238	4,092	3,286	4,385	1,189	1,874	1,921	1,210	1,918	1,931	1,692
1992–93	12,376	14,543	6,987	5,841	7,891	2,118	3,220	3,306	2,059	3,315	3,346	2,809	7,452	8,758	4,207	3,517	4,752	1,276	1,939	1,991	1,240	1,996	2,015	1,692
1993–94	12,838	15,048	7,201	6,195	8,286	2,264	3,330	3,416	2,156	3,313	3,345	2,781	7,931	9,296	4,449	3,827	5,119	1,399	2,057	2,111	1,332	2,047	2,067	1,718
1994–95	13,069	15,308	7,291	6,364	8,483	2,341	3,376	3,461	2,197	3,329	3,364	2,753	8,306	9,728	4,633	4,044	5,391	1,488	2,145	2,200	1,396	2,116	2,138	1,750
1995–96	13,481	15,824	7,238	6,645	8,863	2,332	3,468	3,551	2,256	3,368	3,410	2,650	8,800	10,330	4,725	4,338	5,786	1,522	2,264	2,318	1,473	2,199	2,226	1,730
1996–97	13,711	16,146	7,291	6,798	9,113	2,298	3,523	3,607	2,268	3,390	3,427	2,725	9,206	10,841	4,895	4,564	6,118	1,543	2,365	2,422	1,522	2,276	2,301	1,830
1997–98	14,029	16,502	7,597	6,958	9,293	2,480	3,576	3,669	2,338	3,495	3,540	2,780	9,588	11,277	5,192	4,755	6,351	1,695	2,444	2,507	1,598	2,389	2,419	1,900
1998–99	14,493	17,100	7,610	7,211	9,670	2,482	3,678	3,777	2,324	3,604	3,654	2,804	10,076	11,888	5,291	5,013	6,723	1,725	2,557	2,626	1,616	2,506	2,540	1,950
1999–2000	14,582	17,265	7,577	7,300	9,843	2,416	3,755	3,845	2,477	3,527	3,576	2,685	10,430	12,349	5,420	5,222	7,040	1,728	2,686	2,751	1,771	2,523	2,558	1,920
2000–01	14,625	17,468	7,389	7,468	9,964	2,295	3,814	3,910	2,407	3,543	3,593	2,686	10,820	12,922	5,466	5,377	7,377	1,698	2,820	2,893	1,781	2,621	2,658	1,987
2001–02	15,115	18,116	7,595	7,500	10,342	2,390	3,960	4,064	2,455	3,656	3,710	2,750	11,380	13,639	5,718	5,646	7,786	1,800	2,981	3,060	1,848	2,753	2,793	2,070
2002–03	15,613	18,766	8,126	7,801	10,798	2,474	4,132	4,241	2,699	3,681	3,727	2,953	12,014	14,439	6,252	6,002	8,309	1,903	3,179	3,263	2,077	2,832	2,867	2,272
2003–04	16,475	19,720	8,528	8,404	11,483	2,766	4,272	4,385	2,808	3,798	3,852	2,954	12,953	15,505	6,705	6,608	9,029	2,174	3,359	3,448	2,208	2,986	3,028	2,322
2004–05	17,030	20,384	8,760	8,793	11,984	2,886	4,410	4,521	2,906	3,827	3,879	2,968	13,793	16,510	7,095	7,122	9,706	2,338	3,572	3,662	2,354	3,100	3,142	2,404
2005–06	17,405	20,756	8,606	9,041	12,225	2,875	4,532	4,644	2,867	3,832	3,887	2,864	14,634	17,451	7,236	7,601	10,279	2,417	3,810	3,905	2,411	3,222	3,268	2,408
2006–07	17,951	21,415	8,656	9,382	12,673	2,894	4,659	4,772	2,930	3,910	3,970	2,832	15,483	18,471	7,466	8,092	10,931	2,496	4,019	4,116	2,527	3,372	3,424	2,443
2007–08	18,146	21,647	8,538	9,484	12,805	2,817	4,711	4,826	2,946	3,950	4,016	2,776	16,231	19,363	7,637	8,483	11,454	2,519	4,214	4,317	2,635	3,534	3,592	2,483
2008–09	18,845	22,502	9,083	9,805	13,281	2,887	4,902	5,024	3,065	4,139	4,197	3,131	17,092	20,409	8,238	8,893	12,045	2,618	4,446	4,557	2,780	3,754	3,807	2,839
2009–10	19,274	23,070	9,327	9,975	13,545	3,192	5,087	5,225	3,269	4,212	4,299	2,885	17,650	21,126	8,541	9,135	12,404	2,923	4,658	4,785	2,994	3,857	3,937	2,624
2010–11	19,778	23,630	9,493	10,250	13,858	3,275	5,222	5,374	3,291	4,306	4,398	2,927	18,475	22,074	8,868	9,575	12,945	3,060	4,878	5,020	3,074	4,023	4,108	2,734
2011–12	20,178	23,932	9,721	10,586	14,115	3,374	5,289	5,433	3,329	4,303	4,383	3,017	19,401	23,011	9,347	10,179	13,572	3,244	5,085	5,224	3,201	4,138	4,215	2,901
2012–13	20,699	23,871	9,794	10,927	14,424	3,398	5,418	5,558	3,417	4,354	4,438	2,978	20,233	23,871	9,573	10,681	14,099	3,322	5,296	5,433	3,340	4,256	4,338	2,911
2013–14	21,148	24,878	9,959	11,154	14,667	3,394	5,560	5,695	3,566	4,434	4,517	3,000	20,995	24,699	9,887	11,074	14,561	3,370	5,520	5,654	3,540	4,402	4,484	2,978
2014–15	21,728	25,409	10,153	11,487	14,957	3,389	5,719	5,851	3,655	4,523	4,602	3,109	21,728	25,409	10,153	11,487	14,957	3,389	5,719	5,851	3,655	4,523	4,602	3,109

See notes at end of table.

Table 330.10. Average undergraduate tuition and fees and room and board rates charged for full-time students in degree-granting postsecondary institutions, by level and control of institution: 1963–64 through 2014–15—Continued

Columns 2–13 are in **Constant 2014–15 dollars[1]**; columns 14–25 are in **Current dollars**.

Year and control of institution	Total tuition, fees, room, and board			Tuition and required fees[2]			Dormitory rooms			Board[3]			Total tuition, fees, room, and board			Tuition and required fees[2]			Dormitory rooms			Board[3]		
	All institutions	4-year	2-year	All institutions	4-year	2-year	All institutions	4-year	2-year	All institutions	4-year	2-year	All institutions	4-year	2-year	All institutions	4-year	2-year	All institutions	4-year	2-year	All institutions	4-year	2-year
1	2	3	4	5	6	7	8	9	10	11	12	13	14	15	16	17	18	19	20	21	22	23	24	25
Public institutions																								
1963–64	7,002	7,126	4,835	1,796	1,867	744	1,917	1,945	1,320	3,290	3,314	2,770	912	929	630	234	243	97	250	253	172	429	432	361
1964–65	7,060	7,208	4,835	1,841	1,938	750	1,979	2,007	1,349	3,240	3,263	2,736	932	951	638	243	256	99	261	265	178	428	431	361
1965–66	7,179	7,385	4,970	1,906	2,061	809	2,037	2,064	1,439	3,236	3,259	2,722	968	996	670	257	278	109	275	278	194	436	439	367
1966–67	7,295	7,542	5,105	1,977	2,174	870	2,094	2,120	1,531	3,224	3,248	2,703	1,015	1,049	710	275	302	121	291	295	213	448	452	376
1967–68	7,346	7,576	5,491	1,970	2,158	1,002	2,159	2,181	1,691	3,217	3,237	2,798	1,055	1,089	789	283	310	144	310	313	243	462	465	402
1968–69	7,376	7,584	5,859	1,958	2,130	1,128	2,217	2,236	1,845	3,201	3,218	2,887	1,112	1,143	883	295	321	170	334	337	278	482	485	435
1969–70	7,497	7,756	5,958	2,024	2,245	1,115	2,293	2,314	1,930	3,181	3,197	2,913	1,197	1,238	951	323	358	178	366	369	308	508	510	465
1970–71	7,603	7,900	5,946	2,091	2,346	1,114	2,367	2,390	2,014	3,144	3,164	2,818	1,276	1,326	998	351	394	187	397	401	338	528	531	473
1971–72	7,747	8,080	6,171	2,163	2,460	1,104	2,449	2,472	2,105	3,136	3,148	2,962	1,347	1,405	1,073	376	428	192	426	430	366	545	547	515
1972–73	8,030	8,589	6,618	2,250	2,779	1,288	2,606	2,633	2,200	3,174	3,177	3,129	1,452	1,553	1,197	407	503	233	471	476	398	574	575	566
1973–74	7,690	8,102	6,467	2,223	2,607	1,391	2,429	2,454	2,076	3,038	3,040	3,000	1,515	1,596	1,274	438	514	274	479	483	409	598	599	591
1974–75	7,134	7,525	6,119	1,974	2,342	1,266	2,309	2,336	1,938	2,852	2,847	2,916	1,561	1,647	1,339	432	512	277	505	511	424	624	623	638
1975–76	7,097	7,594	5,915	1,848	2,314	1,046	2,319	2,355	1,886	2,930	2,926	2,983	1,663	1,780	1,386	433	542	245	543	552	442	687	686	699
1976–77	7,214	7,803	6,011	1,930	2,486	1,143	2,349	2,387	1,874	2,935	2,930	2,993	1,789	1,935	1,491	479	617	283	582	592	465	728	727	742
1977–78	7,133	7,700	6,007	1,933	2,474	1,158	2,346	2,385	1,836	2,853	2,841	3,013	1,888	2,038	1,590	512	655	306	621	631	486	755	752	797
1978–79	6,888	7,410	5,842	1,875	2,376	1,131	2,263	2,294	1,820	2,750	2,740	2,891	1,994	2,145	1,691	543	688	327	655	664	527	796	793	837
1979–80	6,600	7,095	5,553	1,779	2,249	1,082	2,180	2,211	1,749	2,642	2,636	2,722	2,165	2,327	1,822	583	738	355	715	725	574	867	865	893
1980–81	6,484	6,968	5,538	1,795	2,196	1,069	2,182	2,216	1,754	2,568	2,556	2,716	2,373	2,550	2,027	635	804	391	799	811	642	940	936	994
1981–82	6,697	7,220	5,593	1,795	2,287	1,093	2,287	2,328	1,769	2,614	2,605	2,732	2,663	2,871	2,224	714	909	434	909	925	703	1,039	1,036	1,086
1982–83	7,101	7,707	5,762	1,925	2,487	1,141	2,436	2,485	1,821	2,740	2,735	2,801	2,945	3,196	2,390	798	1,031	473	1,010	1,030	755	1,136	1,134	1,162
1983–84	7,339	7,983	5,892	2,073	2,669	1,228	2,528	2,581	1,862	2,738	2,733	2,802	3,156	3,433	2,534	891	1,148	528	1,087	1,110	801	1,178	1,175	1,205
1984–85	7,626	8,238	6,281	2,172	2,748	1,307	2,676	2,723	2,060	2,778	2,768	2,914	3,408	3,682	2,807	971	1,228	584	1,196	1,217	921	1,241	1,237	1,302
1985–86*	7,768	8,392	6,484	2,272	2,866	1,394	2,701	2,747	2,083	2,795	2,779	3,002	3,571	3,859	2,981	1,045	1,318	641	1,242	1,263	960	1,285	1,278	1,380
1986–87	8,096	8,804	6,359	2,354	3,008	1,405	2,768	2,814	2,083	2,974	2,982	2,871	3,805	4,138	2,989	1,106	1,414	660	1,301	1,323	979	1,398	1,401	1,349
1987–88	8,274	8,996	6,263	2,489	3,141	1,442	2,815	2,880	1,926	2,970	2,975	2,895	4,050	4,403	3,066	1,218	1,537	706	1,378	1,410	943	1,454	1,456	1,417
1988–89	8,347	9,136	6,216	2,509	3,215	1,426	2,845	2,921	1,884	2,993	3,000	2,906	4,274	4,678	3,183	1,285	1,646	730	1,457	1,496	965	1,533	1,536	1,488
1989–90	8,395	9,274	6,150	2,528	3,317	1,409	2,821	2,903	1,793	3,047	3,054	2,947	4,504	4,975	3,299	1,356	1,780	756	1,513	1,557	962	1,635	1,638	1,581
1990–91	8,407	9,265	6,128	2,570	3,337	1,456	2,849	2,928	1,855	2,988	3,001	2,817	4,757	5,243	3,467	1,454	1,888	824	1,612	1,657	1,050	1,691	1,698	1,594
1991–92	8,799	9,750	6,204	2,788	3,625	1,603	2,964	3,056	1,840	3,048	3,068	2,761	5,138	5,693	3,623	1,628	2,117	936	1,731	1,785	1,074	1,780	1,792	1,612
1992–93	8,932	9,997	6,308	2,958	3,901	1,702	2,916	3,016	1,837	3,057	3,079	2,769	5,379	6,020	3,799	1,782	2,349	1,025	1,756	1,816	1,106	1,841	1,854	1,668
1993–94	9,217	10,303	6,468	3,144	4,106	1,820	3,031	3,130	1,926	3,043	3,067	2,722	5,694	6,365	3,996	1,942	2,537	1,125	1,873	1,934	1,190	1,880	1,895	1,681
1994–95	9,386	10,496	6,509	3,237	4,218	1,876	3,083	3,183	1,938	3,067	3,095	2,694	5,965	6,670	4,137	2,057	2,681	1,192	1,959	2,023	1,232	1,949	1,967	1,712
1995–96	9,583	10,744	6,460	3,338	4,362	1,899	3,152	3,249	1,986	3,094	3,133	2,575	6,256	7,014	4,217	2,179	2,848	1,239	2,057	2,121	1,297	2,020	2,045	1,681
1996–97	9,725	10,924	6,559	3,383	4,449	1,900	3,199	3,297	1,994	3,144	3,177	2,664	6,530	7,334	4,404	2,271	2,987	1,276	2,148	2,214	1,339	2,111	2,133	1,789
1997–98	9,970	11,228	6,599	3,454	4,550	1,923	3,256	3,367	2,050	3,260	3,312	2,626	6,813	7,673	4,509	2,360	3,110	1,314	2,225	2,301	1,401	2,228	2,263	1,795
1998–99	10,222	11,546	6,623	3,496	4,644	1,908	3,351	3,465	2,086	3,376	3,436	2,629	7,107	8,027	4,604	2,430	3,229	1,327	2,330	2,409	1,450	2,347	2,389	1,828
1999–2000	10,217	11,568	6,613	3,500	4,682	1,884	3,411	3,522	2,165	3,305	3,364	2,563	7,308	8,274	4,730	2,504	3,349	1,348	2,440	2,519	1,549	2,364	2,406	1,834
2000–01	10,254	11,697	6,541	3,463	4,732	1,801	3,472	3,588	2,163	3,319	3,378	2,576	7,586	8,653	4,839	2,562	3,501	1,333	2,569	2,654	1,600	2,455	2,495	1,906
2001–02	10,654	12,215	6,824	3,586	4,961	1,833	3,617	3,741	2,287	3,451	3,512	2,704	8,022	9,196	5,137	2,700	3,735	1,380	2,723	2,816	1,722	2,598	2,645	2,036
2002–03	11,049	12,570	7,280	3,772	5,259	1,927	3,808	3,936	2,539	3,469	3,505	2,813	8,502	9,787	5,601	2,903	4,046	1,483	2,930	3,029	1,954	2,669	2,712	2,164
2003–04	11,760	13,576	7,646	4,221	5,833	2,165	3,950	4,085	2,657	3,589	3,657	2,825	9,247	10,674	6,012	3,319	4,587	1,702	3,106	3,212	2,089	2,822	2,876	2,221
2004–05	12,179	14,107	7,871	4,481	6,206	2,283	4,080	4,221	2,684	3,619	3,680	2,905	9,864	11,426	6,375	3,629	5,027	1,849	3,304	3,418	2,174	2,931	2,981	2,353
2005–06	12,434	14,401	7,721	4,607	6,364	2,302	4,217	4,358	2,677	3,610	3,679	2,742	10,454	12,108	6,492	3,874	5,351	1,935	3,545	3,664	2,251	3,035	3,093	2,306
2006–07	12,810	14,837	7,901	4,756	6,569	2,339	4,356	4,497	2,791	3,699	3,771	2,791	11,049	12,797	6,815	4,102	5,666	2,018	3,757	3,878	2,407	3,191	3,253	2,390
2007–08	12,938	15,013	7,798	4,797	6,644	2,304	4,418	4,563	2,801	3,724	3,805	2,693	11,573	13,429	6,975	4,291	5,943	2,061	3,952	4,082	2,506	3,331	3,404	2,409
2008–09	13,513	15,725	8,344	4,975	6,959	2,355	4,619	4,775	2,937	3,919	3,990	3,053	12,256	14,262	7,568	4,512	6,312	2,136	4,190	4,331	2,664	3,554	3,619	2,769
2009–10	13,999	16,419	8,417	5,201	7,335	2,493	4,806	4,984	3,116	3,992	4,101	2,808	12,819	15,036	7,708	4,763	6,717	2,283	4,401	4,564	2,854	3,655	3,755	2,571
2010–11	14,522	17,042	8,648	5,453	7,635	2,613	4,974	5,172	3,164	4,116	4,235	2,872	13,566	15,919	8,079	5,075	7,132	2,441	4,646	4,832	2,955	3,845	3,956	2,683
2011–12	14,934	17,459	8,962	5,786	8,022	2,757	5,044	5,232	3,224	4,104	4,204	2,980	14,359	16,787	8,617	5,563	7,713	2,651	4,849	5,031	3,100	3,946	4,042	2,866
2012–13	15,367	17,877	9,133	6,034	8,256	2,886	5,178	5,362	3,322	4,154	4,259	2,955	15,021	17,475	8,927	5,889	8,070	2,792	5,062	5,241	3,247	4,061	4,163	2,888
2013–14	15,743	18,231	9,349	6,166	8,372	2,903	5,342	5,519	3,472	4,235	4,340	2,974	15,630	18,100	9,281	6,122	8,312	2,882	5,304	5,479	3,447	4,205	4,308	2,953
2014–15	16,188	18,632	9,586	6,371	8,543	2,955	5,504	5,677	3,559	4,313	4,412	3,072	16,188	18,632	9,586	6,371	8,543	2,955	5,504	5,677	3,559	4,313	4,412	3,072

See notes at end of table.

Table 330.10. Average undergraduate tuition and fees and room and board rates charged for full-time students in degree-granting postsecondary institutions, by level and control of institution: 1963–64 through 2014–15—Continued

Year and control of institution	Constant 2014–15 dollars[1]												Current dollars											
	Total tuition, fees, room, and board			Tuition and required fees[2]			Dormitory rooms			Board[3]			Total tuition, fees, room, and board			Tuition and required fees[2]			Dormitory rooms			Board[3]		
	All institu-tions	4-year	2-year	All institu-tions	4-year	2-year	All institu-tions	4-year	2-year	All institu-tions	4-year	2-year	All institu-tions	4-year	2-year	All institu-tions	4-year	2-year	All institu-tions	4-year	2-year	All institu-tions	4-year	2-year
1	2	3	4	5	6	7	8	9	10	11	12	13	14	15	16	17	18	19	20	21	22	23	24	25
Private nonprofit and for-profit institutions																								
1963–64........	13,928	13,887	10,076	7,766	7,757	4,927	2,425	2,400	1,872	3,737	3,731	3,277	1,815	1,810	1,313	1,012	1,011	642	316	313	244	487	486	427
1964–65........	14,451	14,520	11,026	8,245	8,312	5,320	2,508	2,504	2,190	3,698	3,704	3,516	1,907	1,916	1,455	1,088	1,097	702	331	330	289	488	489	464
1965–66........	14,872	14,924	11,549	8,560	8,622	5,697	2,641	2,626	2,344	3,672	3,676	3,508	2,005	2,012	1,557	1,154	1,162	768	356	354	316	495	496	473
1966–67........	15,272	15,310	12,072	8,865	8,995	6,076	2,768	2,743	2,495	3,638	3,637	3,502	2,124	2,129	1,679	1,233	1,241	845	385	382	347	506	506	487
1967–68........	15,346	15,474	12,263	9,026	9,166	6,208	2,728	2,717	2,547	3,591	3,591	3,508	2,205	2,223	1,762	1,297	1,317	892	392	390	366	516	516	504
1968–69........	15,402	15,635	12,449	9,177	9,404	6,344	2,681	2,684	2,595	3,543	3,547	3,510	2,321	2,356	1,876	1,383	1,417	956	404	405	391	534	534	529
1969–70........	15,836	16,032	12,487	9,605	9,786	6,478	2,720	2,729	2,586	3,511	3,517	3,421	2,527	2,559	1,993	1,533	1,562	1,034	434	436	413	560	561	546
1970–71........	16,259	16,411	12,529	10,033	10,166	6,607	2,755	2,765	2,586	3,471	3,480	3,336	2,729	2,754	2,103	1,684	1,706	1,109	462	464	434	583	584	560
1971–72........	16,693	16,787	12,573	10,468	10,538	6,741	2,792	2,805	2,582	3,432	3,444	3,250	2,902	2,919	2,186	1,820	1,832	1,172	486	488	449	597	599	565
1972–73........	16,786	17,091	12,567	10,494	10,772	6,751	2,891	2,912	2,527	3,401	3,408	3,290	3,036	3,091	2,273	1,898	1,948	1,221	523	527	457	615	616	595
1973–74........	16,052	16,354	12,234	10,097	10,378	6,614	2,701	2,715	2,452	3,255	3,261	3,168	3,182	3,222	2,410	1,989	2,045	1,303	532	535	483	641	642	624
1974–75........	15,483	15,556	11,840	9,674	9,735	6,247	2,641	2,645	2,577	3,167	3,176	3,016	3,388	3,404	2,591	2,117	2,130	1,367	578	579	564	693	695	660
1975–76........	15,552	15,657	11,570	9,696	9,778	6,090	2,669	2,683	2,441	3,187	3,196	3,039	3,644	3,669	2,711	2,272	2,291	1,427	625	629	572	747	749	712
1976–77........	15,751	16,037	11,980	9,947	10,219	6,420	2,617	2,627	2,449	3,188	3,192	3,111	3,906	3,977	2,971	2,467	2,534	1,592	649	651	607	790	791	772
1977–78........	15,713	16,010	11,895	9,914	10,204	6,445	2,638	2,653	2,386	3,161	3,166	3,064	4,158	4,240	3,148	2,624	2,700	1,706	698	702	631	836	838	811
1978–79........	15,597	15,926	11,711	9,908	10,220	6,326	2,618	2,630	2,419	3,072	3,077	2,966	4,514	4,609	3,389	2,867	2,958	1,831	758	761	700	889	890	858
1979–80........	14,976	15,282	11,436	9,543	9,832	6,285	2,522	2,533	2,336	2,912	2,917	2,815	4,912	5,013	3,751	3,130	3,225	2,062	827	831	766	955	957	923
1980–81........	14,945	15,283	11,756	9,557	9,882	6,593	2,507	2,515	2,381	2,881	2,886	2,783	5,470	5,594	4,303	3,498	3,617	2,413	918	921	871	1,054	1,056	1,019
1981–82........	15,506	15,919	11,937	9,941	10,345	6,551	2,609	2,612	2,571	2,956	2,963	2,815	6,166	6,330	4,746	3,953	4,113	2,605	1,038	1,039	1,022	1,175	1,178	1,119
1982–83........	16,687	17,183	12,935	10,704	11,186	7,253	2,848	2,849	2,839	3,135	3,148	2,843	6,920	7,126	5,364	4,439	4,639	3,008	1,181	1,181	1,177	1,300	1,306	1,179
1983–84........	17,459	18,043	12,954	11,279	11,843	7,206	2,971	2,974	2,913	3,209	3,226	2,835	7,608	7,759	5,571	4,851	5,093	3,099	1,278	1,279	1,253	1,380	1,387	1,219
1984–85........	18,354	18,910	13,881	11,892	12,432	7,798	3,191	3,191	3,187	3,271	3,287	2,896	8,202	8,451	6,203	5,315	5,556	3,485	1,426	1,426	1,424	1,462	1,469	1,294
1985–86[4]....	19,324	20,071	14,164	12,591	13,312	7,987	3,379	3,386	3,263	3,354	3,373	2,915	8,885	9,228	6,512	5,789	6,121	3,672	1,553	1,557	1,500	1,542	1,551	1,340
1986–87........	20,589	21,361	13,583	13,438	14,168	7,838	3,529	3,561	2,694	3,621	3,633	3,051	9,676	10,039	6,384	6,316	6,658	3,684	1,658	1,673	1,266	1,702	1,708	1,434
1987–88........	21,476	21,778	14,461	14,274	14,539	8,501	3,571	3,596	2,820	3,627	3,643	3,140	10,512	10,659	7,078	6,988	7,116	4,161	1,748	1,760	1,380	1,775	1,783	1,537
1988–89........	21,852	22,408	15,559	14,571	15,080	9,408	3,611	3,639	3,008	3,671	3,689	3,143	11,189	11,474	7,967	7,461	7,722	4,817	1,849	1,863	1,540	1,880	1,889	1,609
1989–90........	22,402	22,897	16,161	15,186	15,650	9,686	3,585	3,607	3,100	3,631	3,640	3,375	12,018	12,284	8,670	8,147	8,396	5,196	1,923	1,935	1,663	1,948	1,953	1,811
1990–91........	22,816	23,395	16,440	15,504	16,050	9,844	3,647	3,672	3,082	3,666	3,671	3,514	12,910	13,237	9,302	8,772	9,083	5,570	2,063	2,077	1,744	2,074	2,077	1,989
1991–92........	23,790	24,416	16,495	16,130	16,713	9,854	3,804	3,837	3,063	3,856	3,865	3,579	13,892	14,258	9,632	9,419	9,759	5,754	2,221	2,241	1,788	2,252	2,257	2,090
1992–93........	24,301	24,925	16,446	16,495	17,093	10,061	3,899	3,922	3,271	3,892	3,909	3,113	14,634	15,009	9,903	9,942	10,294	6,059	2,348	2,362	1,970	2,344	2,354	1,875
1993–94........	25,082	25,743	16,844	17,112	17,728	10,311	4,030	4,057	3,345	3,940	3,958	3,189	15,496	15,904	10,406	10,572	10,952	6,370	2,490	2,506	2,067	2,434	2,445	1,970
1994–95........	25,502	26,124	17,577	17,484	18,066	10,880	4,072	4,093	3,515	3,947	3,965	3,183	16,207	16,602	11,170	11,111	11,481	6,914	2,587	2,601	2,233	2,509	2,520	2,023
1995–96........	26,361	26,979	17,714	18,175	18,755	10,868	4,194	4,214	3,632	3,992	4,009	3,214	17,208	17,612	11,563	11,864	12,243	7,094	2,738	2,751	2,371	2,606	2,617	2,098
1996–97........	26,867	27,468	17,805	18,614	19,185	10,773	4,286	4,303	3,779	3,967	3,980	3,248	18,039	18,442	11,954	12,498	12,881	7,236	2,878	2,889	2,537	2,663	2,672	2,181
1997–98........	27,095	27,905	18,908	18,731	19,527	10,923	4,322	4,337	3,910	4,042	4,041	4,075	18,516	19,070	12,921	12,801	13,344	7,464	2,954	2,964	2,672	2,762	2,761	2,785
1998–99........	27,859	28,666	19,158	19,315	20,099	11,296	4,422	4,446	3,713	4,122	4,121	4,149	19,368	19,929	13,319	13,428	13,973	7,854	3,075	3,091	2,581	2,865	2,865	2,884
1999–2000...	28,259	28,991	19,635	19,713	20,434	11,499	4,524	4,532	4,288	4,022	4,025	3,848	20,213	20,737	14,045	14,100	14,616	8,225	3,236	3,242	3,067	2,877	2,879	2,753
2000–01........	28,891	29,543	20,151	20,276	20,912	12,256	4,572	4,585	4,064	4,043	4,046	3,831	21,373	21,856	14,907	15,000	15,470	9,067	3,382	3,392	3,006	2,991	2,993	2,834
2001–02........	29,770	30,411	21,019	20,909	21,532	13,383	4,738	4,750	4,139	4,123	4,129	3,497	22,413	22,896	15,825	15,742	16,211	10,076	3,567	3,576	3,116	3,104	3,109	2,633
2002–03........	30,334	30,915	23,073	21,292	21,868	13,842	4,876	4,892	4,201	4,166	4,155	5,030	23,340	23,787	17,753	16,383	16,826	10,651	3,752	3,764	3,232	3,206	3,197	3,870
2003–04........	31,317	31,884	24,875	22,021	22,592	14,684	5,018	5,027	4,554	4,278	4,266	5,637	24,624	25,070	19,558	17,315	17,763	11,545	3,945	3,952	3,581	3,364	3,354	4,432
2004–05........	31,875	32,422	25,061	22,414	22,970	14,967	5,158	5,152	5,526	4,303	4,301	4,568	25,817	26,260	20,297	18,154	18,604	12,122	4,178	4,173	4,475	3,485	3,483	3,700
2005–06........	32,004	32,509	25,457	22,435	22,945	14,803	5,233	5,238	4,964	4,336	4,326	5,686	26,908	27,333	21,404	18,862	19,292	12,450	4,400	4,404	4,173	3,645	3,637	4,781
2006–07........	32,972	33,528	23,517	23,243	23,788	14,733	5,341	5,348	4,808	4,389	4,392	3,976	28,439	28,919	20,284	20,048	20,517	12,708	4,606	4,613	4,147	3,785	3,788	3,429
2007–08........	33,279	33,792	24,243	23,446	23,955	14,675	5,370	5,375	5,013	4,463	4,462	4,555	29,767	30,226	21,685	20,972	21,427	13,126	4,804	4,808	4,484	3,992	3,991	4,074
2008–09........	33,964	34,481	25,057	23,783	24,297	14,954	5,541	5,548	5,002	4,640	4,637	5,101	30,804	31,273	22,726	21,570	22,036	13,562	5,025	5,032	4,537	4,209	4,206	4,627
2009–10........	34,225	34,777	26,714	23,766	24,318	16,230	5,731	5,731	5,691	4,728	4,727	4,794	31,341	31,847	24,463	21,764	22,269	14,862	5,248	5,248	5,211	4,329	4,329	4,390
2010–11........	34,123	34,810	24,730	23,596	24,276	14,653	5,784	5,791	5,287	4,743	4,742	4,791	31,875	32,517	23,101	22,042	22,677	13,687	5,403	5,410	4,939	4,430	4,430	4,475
2011–12........	34,382	35,026	24,550	23,765	24,403	14,475	5,847	5,853	5,376	4,769	4,770	4,654	33,058	33,677	23,605	22,850	23,464	13,961	5,622	5,627	5,169	4,586	4,586	4,475
2012–13........	35,277	35,879	23,892	24,495	25,087	14,475	5,965	5,971	5,348	4,817	4,820	4,069	34,483	35,071	23,355	23,943	24,523	14,149	5,831	5,837	5,228	4,709	4,712	3,977
2013–14........	36,247	36,854	24,033	25,283	25,883	14,271	6,065	6,070	5,533	4,898	4,901	4,229	35,985	36,587	23,859	25,101	25,696	14,168	6,021	6,026	5,493	4,863	4,865	4,198
2014–15........	37,424	37,990	24,317	26,184	26,740	14,254	6,221	6,229	5,504	5,019	5,021	4,560	37,424	37,990	24,317	26,184	26,740	14,254	6,221	6,229	5,504	5,019	5,021	4,560

See notes at end of table.

Table 330.10. Average undergraduate tuition and fees and room and board rates charged for full-time students in degree-granting postsecondary institutions, by level and control of institution: 1963–64 through 2014–15—Continued

Columns 2–13 are in **Constant 2014–15 dollars[1]**; columns 14–25 are in **Current dollars**. Within each, the groups are Total tuition, fees, room, and board; Tuition and required fees[2]; Dormitory rooms; and Board[3].

Year and control of institution	Total all inst.	Total 4-year	Total 2-year	Tuition all inst.	Tuition 4-year	Tuition 2-year	Dorm all inst.	Dorm 4-year	Dorm 2-year	Board all inst.	Board 4-year	Board 2-year	Total all inst.	Total 4-year	Total 2-year	Tuition all inst.	Tuition 4-year	Tuition 2-year	Dorm all inst.	Dorm 4-year	Dorm 2-year	Board all inst.	Board 4-year	Board 2-year
1	2	3	4	5	6	7	8	9	10	11	12	13	14	15	16	17	18	19	20	21	22	23	24	25
Nonprofit																								
1999–2000	29,344	29,682	16,340	20,846	21,154	9,636	4,479	4,502	2,957	4,019	4,025	3,747	20,989	21,231	11,688	14,911	15,131	6,893	3,204	3,221	2,115	2,875	2,879	2,680
2000–01	29,649	29,968	15,838	21,082	21,373	9,419	4,524	4,549	2,714	4,043	4,046	3,704	21,934	22,170	11,717	15,596	15,811	6,968	3,347	3,365	2,008	2,991	2,993	2,740
2001–02	30,655	30,890	17,227	21,886	22,053	10,794	4,696	4,708	3,060	4,123	4,129	3,373	23,080	23,257	12,970	16,440	16,604	8,126	3,536	3,544	2,304	3,104	3,109	2,540
2002–03	31,551	31,771	18,769	22,561	22,767	11,576	4,838	4,849	3,439	4,152	4,155	3,755	24,277	24,446	14,442	17,359	17,517	8,907	3,723	3,731	2,646	3,195	3,197	2,889
2003–04	32,667	32,881	19,801	23,438	23,636	12,193	4,969	4,979	3,629	4,260	4,266	3,980	25,685	25,853	15,569	18,429	18,584	9,587	3,907	3,915	2,853	3,349	3,354	3,129
2004–05	33,439	33,651	19,639	24,074	24,264	12,235	5,078	5,086	3,617	4,287	4,301	3,787	27,083	27,255	15,906	19,498	19,652	9,910	4,113	4,119	2,929	3,472	3,483	3,067
2005–06	33,921	34,126	19,421	24,463	24,658	12,272	5,132	5,142	3,588	4,326	4,326	3,561	28,520	28,692	16,329	20,568	20,732	10,318	4,315	4,323	3,017	3,637	3,637	2,994
2006–07	34,973	35,153	20,499	25,323	25,500	12,679	5,255	5,261	4,146	4,395	4,392	3,674	30,165	30,320	17,681	21,841	21,994	10,936	4,532	4,537	3,576	3,791	3,788	3,169
2007–08	35,687	35,831	21,082	25,938	26,081	13,180	5,283	5,288	4,244	4,465	4,462	3,658	31,921	32,050	18,857	23,201	23,328	11,789	4,725	4,730	3,796	3,994	3,991	3,272
2008–09	37,134	37,272	22,350	27,015	27,164	13,896	5,465	5,471	4,288	4,654	4,637	4,167	33,679	33,804	20,271	24,502	24,636	12,603	4,957	4,962	3,889	4,221	4,206	3,779
2009–10	38,133	38,267	22,665	27,732	27,885	13,798	5,649	5,655	4,495	4,751	4,727	4,372	34,920	35,042	20,756	25,396	25,535	12,636	5,173	5,178	4,116	4,351	4,329	4,004
2010–11	38,863	38,984	21,508	28,305	28,456	13,562	5,779	5,786	4,260	4,779	4,742	3,686	36,304	36,416	20,092	26,441	26,581	12,668	5,398	5,404	3,980	4,464	4,430	3,444
2011–12	39,215	39,350	23,844	28,542	28,722	14,642	5,853	5,859	4,452	4,820	4,770	4,750	37,705	37,835	22,926	27,443	27,616	13,785	5,628	5,633	4,281	4,634	4,586	4,567
2012–13	40,072	40,204	22,657	29,224	29,405	14,102	5,973	5,978	4,506	4,876	4,820	4,049	39,171	39,299	22,148	28,566	28,743	14,002	5,838	5,844	4,405	4,766	4,712	3,958
2013–14	40,908	41,003	23,169	29,864	30,016	14,104	6,081	6,086	4,843	4,963	4,901	4,222	40,612	40,706	23,001	29,648	29,799	14,002	6,037	6,042	4,808	4,927	4,865	4,191
2014–15	41,970	42,065	23,576	30,643	30,790	14,287	6,249	6,254	5,038	5,078	5,021	4,252	41,970	42,065	23,576	30,643	30,790	14,287	6,249	6,254	5,038	5,078	5,021	4,252
For-profit																								
1999–2000	22,542	23,134	21,996	12,173	12,108	12,255	5,937	6,475	5,469	4,433	4,551	4,273	16,124	16,547	15,734	8,707	8,661	8,766	4,247	4,631	3,912	3,171	3,255	3,056
2000–01	22,909	24,629	23,062	13,777	14,073	13,444	6,092	6,705	5,346	4,101	3,851	4,273	16,948	18,220	17,061	10,192	10,411	9,945	4,507	4,960	3,955	2,988	2,849	3,161
2001–02	24,673	26,262	22,522	14,424	14,702	14,118	6,149	7,168	4,754	4,101	4,392	3,650	18,576	19,772	16,956	10,860	11,069	10,629	4,629	5,396	3,579	3,087	3,307	2,748
2002–03	25,595	26,044	25,219	14,699	14,825	14,464	5,950	6,997	4,588	4,946	4,222	6,168	19,694	20,039	19,404	11,310	11,407	11,129	4,578	5,384	3,530	3,806	3,249	4,746
2003–04	27,753	27,831	28,452	15,616	15,768	15,292	6,476	7,318	5,077	5,661	4,744	8,083	21,822	21,883	22,371	12,278	12,398	12,024	5,092	5,754	3,992	4,451	3,730	6,355
2004–05	28,519	28,910	27,598	16,095	16,295	15,566	6,983	7,239	6,358	5,441	5,377	5,675	23,098	23,415	22,353	13,036	13,197	12,607	5,655	5,863	5,149	4,407	4,355	4,596
2005–06	28,019	27,624	30,532	15,744	15,836	15,413	7,238	7,713	5,681	5,037	4,075	9,438	23,557	23,225	25,670	13,237	13,315	12,959	6,085	6,485	4,776	4,235	3,426	7,935
2006–07	27,832	28,648	24,638	16,553	16,919	15,170	7,194	7,696	5,178	4,085	4,034	4,290	24,005	24,710	21,250	14,277	14,593	13,085	6,205	6,638	4,466	3,523	3,479	3,700
2007–08	27,665	28,042	26,296	16,108	16,372	14,999	7,206	7,581	5,479	4,351	4,090	5,878	24,745	25,083	23,522	14,409	14,644	13,363	6,445	6,781	4,901	3,892	3,658	5,258
2008–09	26,817	26,985	27,199	15,777	15,902	15,133	6,849	7,102	5,402	4,192	3,950	6,664	24,322	24,447	24,669	14,309	14,423	13,725	6,212	6,441	4,899	3,802	3,583	6,044
2009–10	26,338	26,083	28,362	15,320	15,036	16,524	6,816	6,915	6,206	4,201	4,131	5,633	24,118	23,885	25,973	14,029	13,769	15,132	6,242	6,332	5,683	3,847	3,783	5,158
2010–11	24,602	24,488	27,605	14,708	14,695	14,765	5,845	5,865	5,702	4,050	3,928	7,138	22,982	22,875	25,787	13,739	13,727	13,792	5,460	5,479	5,327	3,783	3,669	6,668
2011–12	23,892	23,841	24,426	14,301	14,261	14,502	5,780	5,773	5,852	3,810	3,807	4,072	22,972	22,923	23,486	13,751	13,712	13,944	5,558	5,551	5,627	3,663	3,660	3,915
2012–13	23,699	23,620	24,569	14,087	14,006	14,539	5,872	5,879	5,800	3,739	3,735	4,230	23,166	23,088	24,016	13,770	13,691	14,212	5,740	5,747	5,669	3,655	3,651	4,135
2013–14	23,303	23,213	24,521	13,888	13,812	14,296	5,846	5,837	5,934	3,570	3,564	4,291	23,135	23,045	24,344	13,787	13,712	14,193	5,803	5,795	5,891	3,544	3,538	4,260
2014–15	23,372	23,278	25,615	13,971	13,926	14,248	5,795	5,798	5,773	3,605	3,554	5,594	23,372	23,278	25,615	13,971	13,926	14,248	5,795	5,798	5,773	3,605	3,554	5,594

[1]Constant dollars based on the Consumer Price Index, prepared by the Bureau of Labor Statistics, U.S. Department of Labor, adjusted to a school-year basis.

[2]For public institutions, in-state tuition and required fees are used.

[3]Data for 1986–87 and later years reflect a basis of 20 meals per week, while data for earlier years are for meals served 7 days a week (the number of meals per day was not specified). Because of this revision in data collection and tabulation procedures, data are not entirely comparable with figures for previous years. In particular, data on board rates are somewhat higher than in earlier years because they reflect the basis of 20 meals per week rather than meals served 7 days a week. Since many institutions serve fewer than 3 meals each day, the 1986–87 and later data reflect a more accurate accounting of total board costs.

[4]Room and board data are estimated.

NOTE: Data are for the entire academic year and are average charges for full-time students. Tuition and fees were weighted by the number of full-time-equivalent undergraduates, but were not adjusted to reflect student residency. Room and board are based on full-time students. Data through 1995–96 are for institutions of higher education, while later data are for degree-granting institutions.

Degree-granting institutions grant associate's or higher degrees and participate in Title IV federal financial aid programs. The degree-granting classification is very similar to the earlier higher education classification, but it includes more 2-year colleges and excludes a few higher education institutions that did not grant degrees. Because of their low response rate, data for private 2-year colleges must be interpreted with caution. Some data have been revised from previously published figures. Detail may not sum to totals because of rounding.

SOURCE: U.S. Department of Education, National Center for Education Statistics, *Projections of Education Statistics to 1986–87*; Higher Education General Information Survey (HEGIS), "Institutional Characteristics of Colleges and Universities" surveys, 1969–70 through 1985–86; "Fall Enrollment in Institutions of Higher Education" surveys, 1963 through 1985; Integrated Postsecondary Education Data System (IPEDS), "Fall Enrollment Survey" (IPEDS-EF:86–99) and "Institutional Characteristics Survey" (IPEDS-IC:86–99); IPEDS Spring 2001 through Spring 2015, Fall Enrollment component; and IPEDS Fall 2000 through Fall 2014, Institutional Characteristics component. (This table was prepared December 2015.)

Table 330.20. Average undergraduate tuition and fees and room and board rates charged for full-time students in degree-granting postsecondary institutions, by control and level of institution and state or jurisdiction: 2013–14 and 2014–15

[In current dollars]

State or jurisdiction	Public 4-year							Private 4-year						Public 2-year, tuition and required fees		
	In-state, 2013–14		In-state, 2014–15				Out-of-state tuition and required fees, 2014–15	2013–14		2014–15				In-state, 2013–14	In-state, 2014–15	Out-of-state, 2014–15
	Total	Tuition and required fees	Total	Tuition and required fees	Room	Board		Total	Tuition and required fees	Total	Tuition and required fees	Room	Board			
1	2	3	4	5	6	7	8	9	10	11	12	13	14	15	16	17
United States	$18,100	$8,312	$18,632	$8,543	$5,677	$4,412	$23,523	$36,587	$25,696	$37,990	$26,740	$6,229	$5,021	$2,882	$2,955	$7,122
Alabama	17,245	8,503	17,859	8,871	5,012	3,976	22,499	22,973	14,201	23,883	14,759	4,651	4,473	4,108	4,120	8,096
Alaska..........................	15,693	6,141	16,814	6,356	6,298	4,160	19,185	30,261	20,943	25,961	19,136	3,881	2,944	4,652	3,340	3,340
Arizona	19,781	9,906	19,839	9,775	6,422	3,641	23,180	20,195	11,462	20,928	12,201	4,549	4,178	1,949	2,025	8,086
Arkansas......................	14,651	6,894	15,320	7,261	4,534	3,526	17,219	26,475	19,104	27,486	19,974	3,918	3,594	2,812	2,973	4,781
California	21,280	8,903	21,749	9,008	7,110	5,630	30,175	41,889	29,678	38,468	27,388	6,179	4,902	1,233	1,244	6,731
Colorado	18,977	8,228	19,710	8,722	5,554	5,434	27,059	31,470	20,359	32,916	21,603	6,254	5,060	3,160	3,347	8,769
Connecticut..................	21,638	10,128	22,435	10,535	6,416	5,483	31,004	48,715	35,407	49,824	36,304	7,548	5,971	3,824	3,869	11,561
Delaware	22,682	11,278	23,161	11,492	7,008	4,661	28,279	24,221	13,444	24,904	13,720	5,563	5,621	3,380	3,530	8,282
District of Columbia	7,255	7,255	†	5,251	†	†	11,233	49,892	36,723	51,857	37,949	8,869	5,038	†	†	†
Florida	14,369	4,423	14,677	4,456	5,905	4,316	17,771	31,286	20,971	32,418	21,578	6,059	4,781	2,513	2,383	8,862
Georgia	16,060	6,614	16,522	6,753	5,910	3,860	21,739	34,658	23,521	36,107	24,493	6,364	5,250	2,926	3,177	7,769
Hawaii	18,023	8,216	19,131	8,831	5,208	5,092	26,150	27,265	15,073	27,483	15,233	5,344	6,906	2,608	2,800	7,646
Idaho............................	13,817	6,315	13,644	6,834	3,189	3,621	19,633	14,162	6,736	13,009	6,456	2,449	4,104	2,963	3,023	7,336
Illinois	23,093	12,520	23,792	13,084	6,146	4,561	27,672	38,627	27,504	39,778	28,481	6,596	4,702	3,306	3,499	9,871
Indiana.........................	18,249	8,443	18,393	8,633	5,157	4,603	28,035	37,961	28,035	39,129	29,050	5,211	4,868	3,605	4,055	7,932
Iowa	16,533	7,839	16,708	7,858	4,297	4,554	23,778	24,517	17,492	32,610	24,076	4,075	4,459	4,253	4,355	5,548
Kansas.........................	14,633	7,387	15,584	7,726	3,903	3,956	20,155	27,962	20,122	24,655	16,635	3,865	4,155	2,890	3,015	4,197
Kentucky	17,280	8,715	17,530	9,189	4,404	3,936	21,409	29,526	21,271	31,594	23,039	4,359	4,196	3,487	3,650	12,478
Louisiana	15,238	6,585	16,045	7,296	5,227	3,523	21,409	41,042	30,257	42,620	31,175	6,344	5,100	3,178	3,502	6,659
Maine	19,121	9,368	18,914	9,166	4,687	5,062	25,273	44,057	32,534	44,991	33,205	5,945	5,841	3,545	3,663	6,455
Maryland.......................	18,879	8,320	19,375	8,482	6,151	4,741	21,031	47,022	34,316	49,648	36,402	7,515	5,731	3,550	3,668	8,841
Massachusetts..............	21,814	10,702	22,214	10,900	6,888	4,426	26,213	51,481	38,009	53,172	39,298	7,953	5,920	4,216	4,333	9,742
Michigan	20,412	11,295	20,843	11,507	4,617	4,720	33,666	27,835	19,372	29,423	20,718	4,270	4,435	2,922	3,062	6,323
Minnesota	18,387	10,355	18,726	10,400	4,575	3,752	17,376	36,246	27,104	37,684	28,123	4,956	4,605	5,387	5,327	5,960
Mississippi	14,411	6,612	15,710	6,880	4,975	3,855	17,262	21,699	15,042	22,844	15,643	3,763	3,438	2,409	2,518	4,676
Missouri	16,785	7,998	17,143	8,065	5,324	3,754	19,410	28,414	19,523	30,402	21,465	4,931	4,007	2,850	2,890	5,514
Montana........................	14,081	6,323	14,448	6,378	3,713	4,357	21,481	28,731	20,868	29,635	21,630	3,826	4,180	3,202	3,215	8,923
Nebraska	15,635	7,081	16,199	7,223	4,784	4,193	18,180	27,882	19,832	28,930	20,501	4,355	4,074	2,670	2,743	3,743
Nevada	16,034	5,029	15,138	5,016	5,301	4,822	20,064	30,745	16,169	30,812	17,325	7,290	6,198	2,700	2,700	9,345
New Hampshire	25,245	14,469	25,821	14,538	6,435	4,848	26,131	43,487	31,029	44,995	31,868	8,115	5,013	7,230	6,979	15,202
New Jersey	24,243	12,266	24,825	12,541	7,542	4,741	26,556	44,235	32,010	45,434	32,986	7,161	5,288	3,929	3,982	6,926
New Mexico	14,103	5,973	14,778	6,003	4,557	4,217	15,285	27,468	17,657	28,464	18,779	5,441	4,244	1,443	1,475	4,636
New York	19,754	6,892	20,549	7,272	8,582	4,695	18,825	47,053	33,825	48,845	35,095	8,146	5,604	4,507	4,711	8,344
North Carolina	15,195	6,578	15,771	6,658	5,136	3,977	22,676	37,541	27,284	38,918	28,177	5,504	5,236	2,304	2,355	8,269
North Dakota	13,711	6,824	14,217	7,050	2,846	4,320	17,316	18,122	12,408	19,502	13,255	2,761	3,486	3,978	4,283	8,441
Ohio.............................	19,997	9,443	20,537	9,631	5,932	4,974	22,756	36,853	26,917	37,976	27,761	5,273	4,942	3,544	3,610	7,512
Oklahoma	13,493	6,043	14,147	6,345	4,352	3,451	17,633	29,988	21,411	31,093	22,309	4,396	4,388	3,062	3,244	7,940
Oregon.........................	19,152	8,616	19,654	8,891	6,296	4,467	27,341	42,383	31,599	44,215	33,108	5,753	5,354	3,935	4,023	7,552
Pennsylvania.................	22,575	12,607	23,519	13,171	6,120	4,228	24,741	46,237	34,313	47,894	35,622	6,725	5,547	4,352	4,589	11,732
Rhode Island	21,761	10,809	22,030	10,868	6,953	4,209	27,110	46,704	35,036	48,870	36,205	6,993	5,671	3,944	3,950	10,582
South Carolina...............	19,502	11,066	20,354	11,448	5,448	3,459	27,814	30,169	21,769	30,957	22,241	4,395	4,321	3,928	4,061	8,537
South Dakota	14,429	7,735	14,983	7,744	3,522	3,718	10,923	27,521	20,114	28,531	21,018	3,659	3,855	4,800	5,014	4,886
Tennessee	16,263	7,958	17,147	8,495	4,700	3,951	23,949	31,707	22,561	33,183	23,893	5,226	4,064	3,637	3,820	14,859
Texas	16,209	7,476	16,872	7,870	4,733	4,269	21,135	36,290	26,382	37,743	27,552	5,690	4,502	1,898	1,948	5,398
Utah	12,800	5,656	12,970	5,942	3,032	3,996	17,899	15,362	7,765	15,435	7,747	3,883	3,805	3,342	3,469	11,011
Vermont	24,071	13,952	24,986	14,495	6,623	3,869	35,241	47,908	36,449	49,211	37,391	6,518	5,301	5,668	5,886	11,622
Virginia.........................	19,845	10,531	20,941	11,057	5,530	4,354	30,416	31,825	22,280	32,501	22,835	4,810	4,856	4,095	4,318	9,019
Washington...................	19,282	8,766	18,863	8,299	5,515	5,049	28,539	41,863	31,599	43,285	32,964	5,588	4,733	4,026	3,992	6,887
West Virginia.................	14,834	5,998	15,644	6,420	4,938	4,285	17,882	19,696	11,050	19,681	11,055	4,178	4,447	3,403	3,628	8,215
Wisconsin	15,720	8,406	15,938	8,441	4,422	3,075	20,020	35,653	26,637	37,416	28,094	5,204	4,118	4,233	4,323	7,220
Wyoming.......................	12,949	3,756	13,457	3,968	4,160	5,329	12,152	16,620	16,620	†	16,968	†	†	2,579	2,694	6,658

†Not applicable.

NOTE: Data are for the entire academic year and are average charges for full-time students. In-state tuition and fees were weighted by the number of full-time-equivalent undergraduates, but were not adjusted to reflect the number of students who were state residents. Out-of-state tuition and fees were weighted by the number of first-time freshmen attending the institution in fall 2014 from out of state. Institutional room and board rates are weighted by the number of full-time students. Degree-granting institutions grant associate's or higher degrees and par-

ticipate in Title IV federal financial aid programs. Some data have been revised from previously published figures. Detail may not sum to totals because of rounding.
SOURCE: U.S. Department of Education, National Center for Education Statistics, Integrated Postsecondary Education Data System (IPEDS), Fall 2013 and Fall 2014, Institutional Characteristics component; and Spring 2014 and Spring 2015, Fall Enrollment component. (This table was prepared December 2015.)

Table 330.30. Average undergraduate tuition, fees, room, and board rates for full-time students in degree-granting postsecondary institutions, by percentile of charges and control and level of institution: Selected years, 2000–01 through 2014–15

Control and level of institution, and year	Current dollars										Constant 2014–15 dollars				
	Tuition, fees, room, and board					Tuition and required fees					Tuition and required fees				
	10th percentile	25th percentile	Median (50th percentile)	75th percentile	90th percentile	10th percentile	25th percentile	Median (50th percentile)	75th percentile	90th percentile	10th percentile	25th percentile	Median (50th percentile)	75th percentile	90th percentile
1	2	3	4	5	6	7	8	9	10	11	12	13	14	15	16
Public institutions[1]															
2000–01	$5,741	$6,880	$8,279	$9,617	$11,384	$612	$1,480	$2,403	$3,444	$4,583	$827	$2,001	$3,248	$4,655	$6,195
2005–06	7,700	9,623	11,348	13,543	16,264	990	2,070	3,329	5,322	6,972	1,177	2,462	3,959	6,330	8,292
2010–11	9,889	12,856	15,234	17,860	21,593	1,230	2,626	4,632	7,115	9,420	1,317	2,811	4,959	7,617	10,084
2012–13	11,283	14,426	17,013	19,481	23,298	1,536	3,048	5,576	8,132	10,514	1,571	3,118	5,704	8,319	10,756
2013–14	11,817	14,954	17,665	20,167	23,943	1,560	3,217	5,963	8,506	10,918	1,571	3,240	6,006	8,568	10,998
2014–15	12,596	15,601	18,012	20,667	24,525	1,630	3,348	6,313	8,878	11,471	1,630	3,348	6,313	8,878	11,471
Public 4-year[1]															
2000–01	6,503	7,347	8,468	9,816	11,611	2,118	2,520	3,314	4,094	5,085	2,863	3,406	4,480	5,534	6,874
2005–06	8,863	10,219	11,596	13,830	16,443	3,094	3,822	5,084	6,458	8,097	3,680	4,546	6,047	7,681	9,630
2010–11	12,048	13,604	15,823	18,419	22,191	4,336	5,091	6,779	8,689	11,029	4,642	5,450	7,257	9,302	11,807
2012–13	13,324	15,102	17,561	19,713	23,686	4,982	6,180	7,554	9,769	12,692	5,097	6,322	7,728	9,994	12,984
2013–14	13,782	15,653	18,239	20,411	24,228	5,086	6,343	7,816	10,037	12,864	5,123	6,389	7,873	10,110	12,958
2014–15	14,289	16,181	18,576	21,080	24,922	5,250	6,497	7,994	10,382	13,160	5,250	6,497	7,994	10,382	13,160
Public 2-year[1]															
2000–01	3,321	3,804	4,627	5,750	6,871	310	724	1,387	1,799	2,460	419	979	1,875	2,432	3,325
2005–06	4,380	4,822	6,234	7,567	8,993	691	1,109	1,920	2,589	3,100	822	1,319	2,284	3,079	3,687
2010–11	5,347	6,327	7,339	9,370	11,312	700	1,412	2,537	3,315	3,840	749	1,512	2,716	3,549	4,111
2012–13	5,812	6,536	8,291	10,282	12,464	1,183	1,627	2,804	3,717	4,352	1,210	1,664	2,869	3,803	4,452
2013–14	6,144	6,952	8,763	10,729	13,369	1,178	1,560	2,954	3,826	4,550	1,187	1,571	2,976	3,854	4,583
2014–15	6,287	7,202	8,815	11,438	14,462	1,183	1,551	3,000	3,963	4,754	1,183	1,551	3,000	3,963	4,754
Private nonprofit institutions															
2000–01	13,514	17,552	22,493	27,430	32,659	7,800	11,730	15,540	19,600	24,532	10,543	15,856	21,006	26,494	33,161
2005–06	18,243	23,258	29,497	35,918	41,707	9,981	15,375	21,070	26,265	31,690	11,871	18,287	25,060	31,239	37,691
2010–11	23,143	29,884	38,063	47,061	52,235	11,930	19,625	26,920	34,536	40,082	12,771	21,009	28,818	36,971	42,908
2012–13	24,955	32,582	41,412	51,744	56,419	11,940	21,140	29,312	37,830	43,204	12,215	21,627	29,987	38,701	44,198
2013–14	26,280	34,020	43,047	53,659	58,612	12,550	22,080	30,390	39,120	44,848	12,641	22,241	30,611	39,405	45,175
2014–15	27,640	35,274	44,582	55,440	60,770	12,525	22,760	31,370	40,660	46,467	12,525	22,760	31,370	40,660	46,467
Nonprofit 4-year															
2000–01	13,972	17,714	22,554	27,476	32,659	8,450	11,920	15,746	19,730	24,532	11,422	16,113	21,284	26,670	33,161
2005–06	18,350	23,322	29,598	36,028	41,774	10,300	15,560	21,190	26,500	31,690	12,251	18,507	25,203	31,519	37,691
2010–11	23,548	30,042	38,129	47,061	52,235	12,220	19,854	27,100	34,580	40,082	13,082	21,254	29,011	37,018	42,908
2012–13	25,183	32,668	41,476	51,750	56,419	12,464	21,496	29,460	38,000	43,204	12,751	21,991	30,138	38,875	44,198
2013–14	26,663	34,095	43,233	53,667	58,612	12,700	22,252	30,579	39,330	44,848	12,792	22,414	30,802	39,616	45,175
2014–15	27,778	35,425	44,775	55,440	60,770	12,920	22,950	31,480	40,670	46,467	12,920	22,950	31,480	40,670	46,467
Nonprofit 2-year															
2000–01	6,850	6,850	9,995	14,209	20,240	2,430	4,825	7,250	8,266	11,100	3,285	6,522	9,800	11,173	15,004
2005–06	8,030	15,680	16,830	20,829	28,643	4,218	8,640	9,940	12,270	14,472	5,017	10,276	11,822	14,594	17,213
2010–11	10,393	19,718	21,186	27,386	30,758	3,840	9,730	12,000	14,640	18,965	4,111	10,416	12,846	15,672	20,302
2012–13	20,135	22,399	24,480	28,882	30,114	7,124	11,640	14,944	16,162	20,050	7,288	11,908	15,288	16,534	20,511
2013–14	21,146	23,815	25,400	29,677	31,200	3,060	10,500	15,533	16,345	20,660	3,082	10,576	15,646	16,464	20,810
2014–15	22,044	23,200	25,705	30,400	32,120	4,200	11,330	15,579	16,678	21,260	4,200	11,330	15,579	16,678	21,260
Private for-profit institutions															
2000–01	13,396	15,778	19,403	21,400	21,845	6,900	8,202	9,644	12,090	14,600	9,327	11,087	13,036	16,342	19,735
2005–06	17,278	19,098	25,589	26,499	31,903	7,632	10,011	12,450	14,335	17,740	9,077	11,907	14,808	17,050	21,100
2010–11	16,097	16,097	17,484	26,175	31,639	10,194	10,194	13,520	15,750	18,048	10,913	10,913	14,473	16,861	19,321
2012–13	16,115	16,115	16,115	22,612	32,239	9,936	11,202	12,685	16,156	18,650	10,165	11,460	12,977	16,528	19,079
2013–14	16,466	16,466	16,745	28,348	34,316	10,312	10,878	13,049	16,156	18,313	10,387	10,957	13,144	16,274	18,446
2014–15	16,942	16,942	23,107	25,619	34,114	10,480	10,702	13,500	17,132	18,748	10,480	10,702	13,500	17,132	18,748
For-profit 4-year															
2000–01	13,396	15,818	20,417	21,400	21,400	7,206	8,305	9,675	12,800	15,090	9,741	11,226	13,078	17,302	20,398
2005–06	17,383	19,098	25,589	26,499	31,903	7,632	10,418	12,900	14,450	17,735	9,077	12,391	15,343	17,187	21,094
2010–11	16,097	16,097	17,484	26,175	31,639	10,194	10,194	13,560	16,500	18,048	10,913	10,913	14,516	17,664	19,321
2012–13	16,115	16,115	16,115	22,612	32,239	9,936	11,202	12,110	16,156	18,650	10,165	11,460	12,389	16,528	19,079
2013–14	16,466	16,466	16,745	28,348	34,316	10,312	10,878	12,435	16,360	18,748	10,387	10,957	12,526	16,479	18,885
2014–15	16,942	16,942	23,107	25,619	34,114	10,480	10,702	12,975	17,173	18,885	10,480	10,702	12,975	17,173	18,885
For-profit 2-year															
2000–01	15,778	15,778	19,403	21,845	21,845	6,025	7,365	9,644	12,000	14,255	8,144	9,955	13,036	16,221	19,269
2005–06	13,010	18,281	43,425	43,425	43,425	7,870	9,285	11,550	14,196	19,425	9,360	11,043	13,737	16,884	23,104
2010–11	23,687	23,687	25,161	25,161	25,161	10,075	12,049	13,418	15,263	17,918	10,785	12,899	14,364	16,339	19,181
2012–13	23,600	23,600	23,600	25,866	25,866	10,425	12,400	13,240	15,552	18,048	10,665	12,685	13,545	15,910	18,463
2013–14	24,019	24,019	26,295	26,295	26,295	10,360	12,307	13,620	15,356	18,000	10,435	12,397	13,719	15,468	18,131
2014–15	25,028	25,028	25,028	25,028	25,028	10,437	12,450	13,620	15,119	17,339	10,437	12,450	13,620	15,119	17,339

[1]Average undergraduate tuition and fees are based on in-state students only.
NOTE: Data are for the entire academic year and are average charges for full-time students. Student charges were weighted by the number of full-time-equivalent undergraduates, but were not adjusted to reflect student residency. Degree-granting institutions grant associate's or higher degrees and participate in Title IV federal financial aid programs. Some data have been revised from previously published figures.

SOURCE: U.S. Department of Education, National Center for Education Statistics, Integrated Postsecondary Education Data System (IPEDS), Fall 2000 through Fall 2014, Institutional Characteristics component; and Spring 2001 through Spring 2015, Fall Enrollment component. (This table was prepared December 2015.)

Table 330.40. Average total cost of attendance for first-time, full-time undergraduate students in degree-granting postsecondary institutions, by control and level of institution, living arrangement, and component of student costs: Selected years, 2009–10 through 2014–15

Level of institution, living arrangement, and component of student costs	2009–10				2011–12				2012–13				2013–14				2014–15			
	All institutions	Public, in-state	Private Nonprofit	Private For-profit	All institutions	Public, in-state	Private Nonprofit	Private For-profit	All institutions	Public, in-state	Private Nonprofit	Private For-profit	All institutions	Public, in-state	Private Nonprofit	Private For-profit	All institutions	Public, in-state	Private Nonprofit	Private For-profit
1	2	3	4	5	6	7	8	9	10	11	12	13	14	15	16	17	18	19	20	21
Current dollars																				
4-year institutions																				
Average total cost, by living arrangement																				
On campus	$26,283	$19,219	$38,254	$28,916	$28,457	$20,997	$41,375	$29,887	$29,531	$21,677	$42,887	$31,099	$30,177	$22,148	$44,353	$29,816	$31,058	$22,752	$45,763	$30,406
Off campus, living with family	19,091	11,950	30,500	19,318	20,705	13,344	32,982	21,526	21,346	13,595	34,107	23,194	21,522	13,562	35,210	21,975	22,145	13,920	36,319	22,407
Off campus, not living with family	28,829	20,724	38,824	28,836	29,322	22,261	41,413	28,840	30,372	22,655	42,546	31,542	30,116	22,827	43,727	28,393	31,007	23,373	45,249	29,118
Component of student costs																				
Tuition and required fees	13,734	6,773	25,676	12,873	15,077	7,703	27,931	14,609	15,763	7,997	29,029	16,299	16,104	8,199	30,108	15,241	16,628	8,445	31,177	15,463
Books and supplies	1,192	1,165	1,182	1,389	1,237	1,230	1,230	1,373	1,246	1,241	1,239	1,361	1,248	1,250	1,251	1,190	1,266	1,275	1,248	1,283
Room, board, and other expenses																				
On campus																				
Room and board	8,583	8,155	9,114	10,082	9,255	8,839	9,824	9,660	9,598	9,187	10,179	9,228	9,910	9,495	10,506	9,499	10,198	9,760	10,827	9,859
Other	2,774	3,126	2,282	4,573	2,889	3,225	2,389	4,245	2,925	3,253	2,441	4,212	2,916	3,203	2,488	3,886	2,965	3,272	2,511	3,802
Off campus, living with family																				
Other	4,165	4,012	3,642	5,057	4,391	4,411	3,821	5,544	4,337	4,358	3,839	5,534	4,171	4,113	3,850	5,545	4,250	4,200	3,893	5,661
Off campus, not living with family																				
Room and board	8,862	8,722	8,164	8,997	8,572	9,206	8,327	7,898	8,971	9,282	8,410	8,697	8,633	9,435	8,481	7,393	8,873	9,663	8,516	7,760
Other	5,041	4,065	3,801	5,578	4,437	4,122	3,925	4,960	4,393	4,136	3,868	5,184	4,132	3,943	3,886	4,569	4,239	3,990	4,308	4,612
2-year institutions																				
Average total cost, by living arrangement																				
On campus	$14,351	$11,886	$23,352	$27,721	$14,049	$12,796	$26,246	$27,873	$14,436	$13,265	$27,692	$28,035	$14,646	$13,503	$29,373	$28,382	$14,984	$13,847	$29,695	$28,710
Off campus, living with family	9,731	7,581	16,639	18,982	9,115	8,129	19,066	19,810	9,171	8,314	19,990	20,037	9,268	8,469	21,291	19,817	9,408	8,603	21,270	20,072
Off campus, not living with family	17,063	14,758	24,969	26,556	16,562	15,567	27,528	27,015	16,807	15,879	29,752	27,857	16,989	16,157	29,448	27,617	17,241	16,371	29,749	28,297
Component of student costs																				
Tuition and required fees	4,705	2,619	12,326	13,511	3,912	2,940	14,007	14,298	3,925	3,081	14,338	14,510	3,949	3,161	15,354	14,304	4,061	3,270	15,634	14,428
Books and supplies	1,259	1,241	1,205	1,371	1,315	1,311	1,332	1,368	1,341	1,347	1,315	1,254	1,371	1,378	1,264	1,257	1,417	1,422	1,237	1,351
Room, board, and other expenses																				
On campus																				
Room and board	5,481	5,171	7,096	8,729	5,913	5,630	8,011	9,417	6,072	5,765	8,529	9,362	6,317	6,005	9,095	9,767	6,461	6,133	9,459	9,898
Other	2,906	2,856	2,726	4,111	2,910	2,915	2,896	2,789	3,099	3,072	3,510	2,909	3,010	2,959	3,661	3,054	3,046	3,022	3,366	3,032
Off campus, living with family																				
Other	3,767	3,721	3,108	4,101	3,888	3,878	3,726	4,143	3,905	3,886	4,338	4,273	3,948	3,931	4,673	4,256	3,930	3,911	4,399	4,293
Off campus, not living with family																				
Room and board	7,334	7,240	8,095	7,588	7,514	7,524	7,680	7,390	7,656	7,630	9,027	7,723	7,802	7,810	8,258	7,657	7,931	7,918	8,369	8,015
Other	3,765	3,659	3,343	4,087	3,822	3,792	4,508	3,959	3,886	3,821	5,073	4,370	3,867	3,809	4,573	4,399	3,832	3,761	4,509	4,504
Constant 2014–15 dollars[1]																				
4-year institutions																				
Average total cost, by living arrangement																				
On campus	$28,701	$20,988	$41,774	$31,577	$29,597	$21,838	$43,031	$31,084	$30,211	$22,176	$43,874	$31,815	$30,397	$22,309	$44,676	$30,033	$31,058	$22,752	$45,763	$30,406
Off campus, living with family	20,847	13,049	33,306	21,096	21,534	13,878	34,303	22,388	21,837	13,908	34,892	23,728	21,679	13,661	35,466	22,135	22,145	13,920	36,319	22,407
Off campus, not living with family	31,482	22,631	42,396	31,490	30,497	23,152	43,071	29,995	31,071	23,177	43,525	32,268	30,336	22,994	44,046	28,599	31,007	23,373	45,249	29,118
Tuition and required fees	14,998	7,396	28,038	14,057	15,680	8,012	29,050	15,194	16,126	8,181	29,697	16,674	16,221	8,258	30,327	15,352	16,628	8,445	31,177	15,463
2-year institutions																				
Average total cost, by living arrangement																				
On campus	15,671	12,980	25,501	30,272	14,612	13,309	27,297	28,989	14,768	13,570	28,329	28,680	14,752	13,601	29,587	28,589	14,984	13,847	29,695	28,710
Off campus, living with family	10,626	8,278	18,170	20,729	9,480	8,454	19,829	20,603	9,382	8,505	20,450	20,498	9,336	8,531	21,446	19,961	9,408	8,603	21,270	20,072
Off campus, not living with family	18,633	16,116	27,266	28,999	17,225	16,190	28,630	28,097	17,194	16,245	30,437	28,498	17,112	16,275	29,663	27,818	17,241	16,371	29,749	28,297
Tuition and required fees	5,138	2,860	13,460	14,754	4,068	3,058	14,568	14,871	4,015	3,152	14,668	14,844	3,978	3,184	15,466	14,408	4,061	3,270	15,634	14,428

[1]Constant dollars based on the Consumer Price Index, prepared by the Bureau of Labor Statistics, U.S. Department of Labor, adjusted to a school-year basis.
NOTE: Excludes students who previously attended another postsecondary institution or who began their studies on a part-time basis. Tuition and fees at public institutions are the lower of either in-district or in-state tuition and fees. Data illustrating the average total cost of attendance for all students are weighted by the number of students at the institution receiving Title IV aid. Detail may not sum to totals because of rounding. Some data have been revised from previously published figures.
SOURCE: U.S. Department of Education, National Center for Education Statistics, Integrated Postsecondary Education Data System (IPEDS), Spring 2010 through Spring 2011 and Winter 2011–12 through Winter 2014–15, Student Financial Aid component; and Fall 2009 through Fall 2014, Institutional Characteristics component. (This table was prepared December 2015.)

Table 330.50. Average graduate tuition and required fees in degree-granting postsecondary institutions, by control of institution and percentile of charges: 1989–90 through 2014–15

Year	Total	Public institutions[1]	Private institutions			Public institutions,[1] by percentile			Nonprofit institutions, by percentile		
			Total	Nonprofit	For-profit	25th percentile	Median (50th percentile)	75th percentile	25th percentile	Median (50th percentile)	75th percentile
1	2	3	4	5	6	7	8	9	10	11	12
					Current dollars						
1989–90	$4,135	$1,999	$7,881	—	—	—	—	—	—	—	—
1990–91	4,488	2,206	8,507	—	—	—	—	—	—	—	—
1991–92	5,116	2,524	9,592	—	—	—	—	—	—	—	—
1992–93	5,475	2,791	10,008	—	—	—	—	—	—	—	—
1993–94	5,973	3,050	10,790	—	—	—	—	—	—	—	—
1994–95	6,247	3,250	11,338	—	—	—	—	—	—	—	—
1995–96	6,741	3,449	12,083	—	—	—	—	—	—	—	—
1996–97	7,111	3,607	12,537	—	—	—	—	—	—	—	—
1997–98	7,246	3,744	12,774	—	—	—	—	—	—	—	—
1998–99	7,685	3,897	13,299	—	—	—	—	—	—	—	—
1999–2000	8,069	4,042	13,821	$14,123	$9,611	$2,640	$3,637	$5,163	$7,998	$12,870	$20,487
2000–01	8,429	4,243	14,420	14,457	13,229	2,931	3,822	5,347	8,276	13,200	21,369
2001–02	8,857	4,496	15,165	15,232	13,414	3,226	4,119	5,596	8,583	14,157	22,054
2002–03	9,226	4,842	14,983	15,676	9,644	3,395	4,452	5,927	8,690	14,140	22,700
2003–04	10,312	5,544	16,209	16,807	12,542	3,795	5,103	7,063	9,072	15,030	25,600
2004–05	11,004	6,080	16,751	17,551	13,133	4,236	5,663	7,616	9,300	16,060	26,140
2005–06	11,621	6,493	17,244	18,171	13,432	4,608	6,209	7,977	9,745	16,222	26,958
2006–07	12,312	6,894	18,108	19,033	14,421	4,909	6,594	8,341	10,346	17,057	29,118
2007–08	13,002	7,415	18,878	19,896	14,713	5,176	6,990	9,288	10,705	17,647	30,247
2008–09	13,647	7,999	19,230	20,485	14,418	5,612	7,376	9,912	11,290	18,270	30,514
2009–10	14,542	8,763	20,078	21,317	14,512	6,074	7,983	10,658	12,290	19,460	31,730
2010–11	15,017	9,238	20,397	21,993	13,811	6,550	8,788	10,937	12,510	19,586	33,215
2011–12	15,845	9,978	21,230	22,899	14,285	7,506	9,440	11,954	12,936	20,625	34,680
2012–13	16,407	10,408	21,907	23,642	14,418	7,706	9,900	12,590	12,960	21,352	36,820
2013–14	16,946	10,725	22,607	24,467	14,210	7,791	10,242	12,779	13,567	22,018	36,660
2014–15	17,385	10,979	23,266	25,171	14,265	7,914	10,428	12,829	13,872	22,170	38,948
					Constant 2014–15 dollars						
1989–90	$7,707	$3,726	$14,690	—	—	—	—	—	—	—	—
1990–91	7,932	3,899	15,035	—	—	—	—	—	—	—	—
1991–92	8,761	4,322	16,426	—	—	—	—	—	—	—	—
1992–93	9,092	4,635	16,619	—	—	—	—	—	—	—	—
1993–94	9,668	4,937	17,465	—	—	—	—	—	—	—	—
1994–95	9,830	5,115	17,842	—	—	—	—	—	—	—	—
1995–96	10,326	5,283	18,509	—	—	—	—	—	—	—	—
1996–97	10,591	5,372	18,673	—	—	—	—	—	—	—	—
1997–98	10,603	5,479	18,692	—	—	—	—	—	—	—	—
1998–99	11,054	5,605	19,129	—	—	—	—	—	—	—	—
1999–2000	11,281	5,651	19,322	$19,745	$13,437	$3,691	$5,085	$7,218	$11,182	$17,993	$28,642
2000–01	11,394	5,736	19,492	19,541	17,882	3,962	5,166	7,228	11,187	17,843	28,885
2001–02	11,764	5,971	20,143	20,232	17,816	4,285	5,471	7,433	11,400	18,804	29,292
2002–03	11,990	6,292	19,472	20,373	12,534	4,412	5,786	7,703	11,294	18,377	29,502
2003–04	13,115	7,051	20,615	21,376	15,952	4,827	6,490	8,983	11,538	19,116	32,559
2004–05	13,587	7,507	20,683	21,670	16,215	5,230	6,992	9,403	11,482	19,829	32,274
2005–06	13,822	7,723	20,510	21,612	15,976	5,481	7,385	9,488	11,591	19,294	32,063
2006–07	14,274	7,993	20,994	22,067	16,720	5,691	7,645	9,671	11,995	19,776	33,759
2007–08	14,536	8,290	21,105	22,244	16,449	5,787	7,815	10,384	11,968	19,729	33,815
2008–09	15,047	8,819	21,202	22,587	15,897	6,188	8,133	10,929	12,448	20,144	33,644
2009–10	15,880	9,570	21,926	23,279	15,848	6,633	8,718	11,639	13,421	21,251	34,650
2010–11	16,076	9,889	21,835	23,544	14,785	7,012	9,408	11,708	13,392	20,967	35,557
2011–12	16,479	10,378	22,080	23,816	14,857	7,807	9,818	12,433	13,454	21,451	36,069
2012–13	16,785	10,648	22,411	24,186	14,750	7,883	10,128	12,880	13,258	21,843	37,667
2013–14	17,069	10,803	22,771	24,645	14,313	7,848	10,317	12,872	13,666	22,178	36,927
2014–15	17,385	10,979	23,266	25,171	14,265	7,914	10,428	12,829	13,872	22,170	38,948

—Not available.

[1]Data are based on in-state tuition only.

NOTE: Average graduate student tuition weighted by fall full-time-equivalent graduate enrollment. Excludes doctoral students in professional practice programs. Data through 1995–96 are for institutions of higher education, while later data are for degree-granting institutions. Degree-granting institutions grant associate's or higher degrees and participate in Title IV federal financial aid programs. The degree-granting classification is very similar to the earlier higher education classification, but it includes more 2-year colleges and excludes a few higher education institutions that did not grant degrees. Some data have been revised from previously published figures.

SOURCE: U.S. Department of Education, National Center for Education Statistics, Integrated Postsecondary Education Data System (IPEDS), "Fall Enrollment Survey" (IPEDS-EF:89–99); "Completions Survey" (IPEDS-C:90–99); "Institutional Characteristics Survey" (IPEDS-IC:89–99); IPEDS Fall 2000 through Fall 2014, Institutional Characteristics component; and IPEDS Spring 2001 through Spring 2015, Fall Enrollment component. (This table was prepared December 2015.)

Table 331.10. Percentage of undergraduates receiving financial aid, by type and source of aid and selected student characteristics: 2011–12
[Standard errors appear in parentheses]

Selected student characteristic	Number of undergraduates[1] (in thousands)	Any aid			Grants			Loans			Work study
		Total[2]	Federal[3]	Nonfederal	Total	Federal	Nonfederal	Total[4]	Federal[4]	Nonfederal	Total[5]
1	2	3	4	5	6	7	8	9	10	11	12
All undergraduates	23,055	70.7 (0.56)	59.4 (0.51)	40.4 (0.44)	59.1 (0.45)	41.5 (0.36)	36.3 (0.42)	41.9 (0.14)	40.3 (0.10)	6.5 (0.14)	5.9 (0.14)
Sex											
Male	9,921	68.4 (0.72)	56.7 (0.73)	39.8 (0.55)	55.1 (0.57)	36.7 (0.55)	35.6 (0.53)	39.0 (0.35)	37.3 (0.35)	6.4 (0.18)	6.0 (0.22)
Female	13,135	72.5 (0.53)	61.5 (0.46)	40.9 (0.47)	62.1 (0.46)	45.1 (0.36)	36.7 (0.45)	44.1 (0.22)	42.6 (0.22)	6.5 (0.17)	5.9 (0.15)
Race/ethnicity											
White	13,345	68.1 (0.59)	55.3 (0.53)	40.0 (0.49)	54.5 (0.47)	33.7 (0.38)	35.9 (0.48)	41.9 (0.34)	40.2 (0.32)	6.8 (0.19)	6.0 (0.17)
Black	3,709	81.0 (0.81)	75.2 (0.87)	36.8 (0.78)	71.4 (0.72)	62.1 (0.80)	32.2 (0.72)	52.3 (0.84)	51.0 (0.82)	6.5 (0.34)	5.1 (0.27)
Hispanic	3,696	72.3 (0.85)	61.9 (0.91)	43.0 (0.89)	64.0 (0.81)	50.1 (0.81)	38.9 (0.90)	35.6 (0.83)	34.2 (0.84)	5.6 (0.27)	5.3 (0.30)
Asian	1,292	60.8 (1.64)	46.3 (1.45)	44.2 (1.46)	53.0 (1.49)	33.4 (1.22)	41.2 (1.36)	28.4 (1.12)	27.0 (1.06)	5.0 (0.49)	9.0 (0.66)
Pacific Islander	119	68.3 (3.58)	56.7 (3.66)	37.4 (3.15)	55.1 (3.32)	39.3 (3.23)	34.9 (3.14)	37.9 (3.28)	37.3 (3.22)	4.6 (1.02)	4.5 ! (1.46)
American Indian/Alaska Native	209	76.3 (3.13)	69.0 (3.23)	40.9 (3.05)	67.6 (3.18)	55.3 (3.10)	37.6 (3.02)	43.0 (3.17)	41.9 (3.12)	5.1 (0.91)	4.7 (1.15)
Two or more races	686	74.8 (1.48)	63.6 (1.43)	46.7 (1.76)	63.9 (1.59)	45.7 (1.45)	41.9 (1.75)	46.1 (1.46)	44.1 (1.40)	8.4 (0.84)	7.2 (0.68)
Age											
15 to 23 years old	12,956	72.1 (0.49)	59.2 (0.41)	48.2 (0.47)	60.9 (0.42)	38.0 (0.29)	44.4 (0.47)	42.8 (0.28)	41.1 (0.25)	7.4 (0.15)	9.0 (0.21)
24 to 29 years old	4,253	70.4 (1.05)	61.9 (1.09)	31.8 (0.76)	59.0 (0.89)	49.1 (0.83)	27.1 (0.70)	41.6 (0.68)	39.9 (0.64)	5.8 (0.30)	2.4 (0.18)
30 years old or over	5,846	67.9 (0.89)	58.2 (0.92)	29.5 (0.64)	55.1 (0.76)	43.7 (0.77)	25.0 (0.60)	40.4 (0.52)	39.1 (0.51)	4.9 (0.25)	1.6 (0.13)
Marital status											
Not married[6]	18,507	71.9 (0.50)	60.6 (0.41)	43.0 (0.46)	60.9 (0.43)	42.2 (0.30)	38.8 (0.44)	43.5 (0.17)	41.9 (0.15)	7.0 (0.14)	7.0 (0.17)
Married	4,087	63.9 (1.21)	52.2 (1.28)	30.0 (0.71)	49.4 (0.92)	35.5 (1.00)	26.0 (0.68)	33.8 (0.75)	32.4 (0.70)	4.3 (0.32)	1.4 (0.14)
Separated	461	82.0 (1.72)	76.6 (1.91)	30.8 (1.62)	74.2 (1.92)	67.1 (2.07)	26.3 (1.72)	50.8 (2.09)	50.0 (2.07)	5.3 (0.88)	1.6 (0.47)
Attendance status[7]											
Full-time, full-year	8,864	84.4 (0.36)	72.8 (0.51)	56.9 (0.46)	72.4 (0.41)	47.4 (0.50)	52.6 (0.45)	56.7 (0.53)	55.5 (0.54)	9.2 (0.22)	11.9 (0.25)
Part-time or part-year	14,192	62.1 (1.05)	51.1 (1.10)	30.1 (0.60)	50.8 (0.87)	37.8 (0.85)	26.1 (0.56)	32.7 (0.48)	30.9 (0.45)	4.8 (0.17)	2.2 (0.12)
Dependency status and family income											
Dependent	11,231	71.6 (0.49)	58.2 (0.40)	49.9 (0.50)	59.6 (0.44)	34.9 (0.30)	46.1 (0.50)	43.4 (0.31)	41.7 (0.29)	7.8 (0.17)	9.8 (0.22)
Less than $20,000	1,775	88.3 (0.68)	83.5 (0.79)	53.2 (1.01)	87.0 (0.67)	82.1 (0.78)	50.8 (1.00)	45.5 (0.84)	44.3 (0.84)	4.9 (0.35)	10.7 (0.56)
$20,000–$39,999	2,011	81.5 (0.88)	74.1 (0.92)	54.7 (0.99)	79.1 (0.92)	70.9 (0.92)	52.0 (1.03)	42.8 (0.80)	41.6 (0.82)	5.6 (0.35)	11.6 (0.54)
$40,000–$59,999	1,389	79.7 (0.89)	70.0 (0.96)	57.5 (1.06)	72.1 (0.97)	54.7 (0.91)	54.3 (1.07)	51.0 (0.96)	49.9 (0.99)	8.5 (0.50)	11.2 (0.53)
$60,000–$79,999	1,535	65.7 (1.06)	49.6 (1.07)	49.0 (0.97)	48.3 (1.00)	14.2 (0.62)	44.3 (1.01)	46.0 (1.02)	43.9 (0.97)	9.8 (0.62)	9.9 (0.59)
$80,000–$99,999	1,339	61.6 (1.29)	45.0 (0.95)	44.5 (1.22)	40.4 (1.17)	2.7 (0.28)	39.6 (1.17)	43.9 (0.91)	41.4 (0.89)	10.2 (0.62)	9.3 (0.65)
$100,000 or more	3,183	59.5 (0.79)	38.7 (0.64)	44.5 (0.74)	40.2 (0.74)	0.7 (0.09)	39.9 (0.74)	38.0 (0.63)	35.9 (0.59)	8.5 (0.34)	7.6 (0.37)
Independent	11,825	69.9 (0.81)	60.6 (0.85)	31.4 (0.55)	58.6 (0.67)	47.7 (0.68)	26.9 (0.52)	40.5 (0.33)	39.0 (0.30)	5.2 (0.20)	2.3 (0.10)
Less than $10,000	3,561	78.6 (0.72)	71.6 (0.74)	35.2 (0.75)	73.5 (0.76)	66.5 (0.76)	30.3 (0.76)	46.7 (0.72)	45.1 (0.73)	5.8 (0.30)	4.4 (0.25)
$10,000–$19,999	2,349	77.0 (1.09)	71.1 (1.05)	32.1 (0.93)	71.2 (1.14)	65.5 (1.12)	27.0 (0.83)	46.9 (0.86)	45.6 (0.87)	5.7 (0.35)	2.3 (0.23)
$20,000–$29,999	1,702	71.4 (1.14)	62.9 (1.41)	30.4 (1.06)	56.6 (1.14)	45.7 (1.20)	25.7 (1.04)	42.3 (0.90)	40.6 (0.91)	5.7 (0.41)	1.8 (0.24)
$30,000–$49,999	1,895	65.5 (1.23)	53.6 (1.36)	30.2 (1.11)	48.7 (1.17)	34.0 (0.98)	25.8 (1.13)	36.8 (0.91)	35.1 (0.92)	5.1 (0.34)	0.8 (0.13)
$50,000 or more	2,318	51.8 (1.73)	37.1 (1.54)	26.6 (0.94)	32.3 (1.08)	13.7 (0.75)	23.2 (0.88)	26.2 (1.25)	25.2 (1.14)	3.7 (0.37)	0.6 (0.12)
Housing status[8]											
School-owned	2,800	85.3 (0.52)	69.6 (0.59)	71.8 (0.63)	74.5 (0.59)	35.5 (0.60)	68.1 (0.64)	63.0 (0.64)	61.4 (0.62)	11.6 (0.39)	23.0 (0.63)
Off-campus, not with parents	10,619	68.1 (0.88)	57.4 (0.87)	34.4 (0.59)	56.1 (0.69)	42.1 (0.67)	30.0 (0.54)	39.1 (0.41)	37.5 (0.39)	5.8 (0.19)	3.1 (0.15)
With parents	7,734	68.3 (0.74)	57.8 (0.69)	36.9 (0.69)	57.7 (0.69)	43.2 (0.65)	33.1 (0.67)	36.5 (0.53)	35.0 (0.53)	5.2 (0.24)	3.6 (0.19)

! Interpret data with caution. The coefficient of variation (CV) for this estimate is between 30 and 50 percent.
[1] Numbers of undergraduates may not equal figures reported in other tables, since these data are based on a sample survey of students who enrolled at any time during the school year. Includes all postsecondary institutions.
[2] Includes students who reported they were awarded aid, but did not specify the source or type of aid.
[3] Includes Department of Veterans Affairs and Department of Defense benefits.
[4] Includes Parent Loans for Undergraduate Students (PLUS).
[5] Details on federal and nonfederal work-study participants are not available.
[6] Includes students who were single, divorced, or widowed.

[7] Full-time, full-year includes students enrolled full time for 9 or more months. Part-time or part-year includes students enrolled part time for 9 or more months and students enrolled less than 9 months either part time or full time.
[8] Excludes students attending more than one institution.
NOTE: Detail may not sum to totals because of rounding and because some students receive multiple types of aid and aid from different sources. Data include undergraduates in degree-granting and non-degree-granting institutions. Data exclude Puerto Rico. Race categories exclude persons of Hispanic ethnicity. In 2012, no students were reported in the "Other" race category.
SOURCE: U.S. Department of Education, National Center for Education Statistics, 2011–12 National Postsecondary Student Aid Study (NPSAS:12). (This table was prepared January 2014.)

Table 331.20. Full-time, first-time degree/certificate-seeking undergraduate students enrolled in degree-granting postsecondary institutions, by participation and average amount awarded in financial aid programs, and control and level of institution: 2000–01 through 2013–14

Control and level of institution, and year	Number enrolled	Number receiving financial aid	Percent receiving aid	Percent of enrolled students in student aid programs				Average award for students in aid programs[1]							
								Current dollars				Constant 2014–15 dollars			
				Federal grants	State/local grants	Institutional grants	Student loans[2]	Federal grants	State/local grants	Institutional grants	Student loans[2]	Federal grants	State/local grants	Institutional grants	Student loans[2]
1	2	3	4	5	6	7	8	9	10	11	12	13	14	15	16
All institutions															
2000–01	1,976,600	1,390,527	70.3	31.6	31.2	31.1	40.1	$2,486	$2,039	$4,740	$3,764	$3,361	$2,756	$6,407	$5,088
2001–02	2,050,016	1,481,592	72.3	33.3	32.5	31.5	40.7	2,739	2,057	4,918	3,970	3,638	2,732	6,532	5,273
2002–03	2,135,613	1,553,024	72.7	34.1	30.9	31.5	41.4	2,947	2,189	5,267	4,331	3,830	2,845	6,845	5,628
2003–04	2,178,517	1,610,967	73.9	34.6	31.2	31.9	43.1	2,934	2,226	5,648	4,193	3,731	2,831	7,183	5,333
2004–05	2,260,590	1,689,910	74.8	35.2	31.3	31.7	44.0	2,939	2,343	5,958	4,463	3,629	2,893	7,356	5,510
2005–06	2,309,543	1,731,315	75.0	33.7	30.8	32.7	44.6	2,959	2,441	6,213	4,831	3,520	2,903	7,390	5,746
2006–07	2,427,043	1,766,257	72.8	32.1	30.0	32.2	43.5	3,125	2,526	6,593	5,014	3,624	2,928	7,643	5,814
2007–08	2,532,955	1,914,567	75.6	35.4	30.6	33.6	45.6	3,376	2,580	6,791	6,009	3,775	2,884	7,592	6,718
2008–09	2,542,748	1,974,063	77.6	36.4	31.7	34.6	46.6	3,927	2,706	7,518	6,723	4,330	2,984	8,290	7,413
2009–10	2,855,241	2,323,706	81.4	46.2	28.6	33.3	51.2	4,693	2,771	7,693	7,019	5,125	3,026	8,401	7,665
2010–11	2,648,101	2,179,582	82.3	47.8	31.0	35.8	50.1	4,758	2,843	8,393	6,624	5,094	3,043	8,985	7,091
2011–12	2,571,120	2,140,556	83.3	47.6	30.8	37.9	51.2	4,424	2,912	8,767	6,641	4,601	3,029	9,118	6,907
2012–13	2,511,146	2,077,316	82.7	45.5	31.2	39.8	49.4	4,452	3,052	9,220	6,899	4,555	3,123	9,432	7,058
2013–14	2,504,847	2,076,901	82.9	45.3	32.2	41.3	47.4	4,531	3,102	9,606	7,012	4,564	3,125	9,676	7,063
Public															
2000–01	1,333,236	872,109	65.4	30.0	33.5	22.7	30.7	2,408	1,707	2,275	3,050	3,255	2,307	3,075	4,123
2005–06	1,510,268	1,066,041	70.6	31.1	34.8	25.1	34.2	2,926	2,226	3,162	3,866	3,480	2,648	3,761	4,599
2007–08	1,648,583	1,173,222	71.2	32.6	35.8	25.9	34.7	3,368	2,351	3,530	4,803	3,765	2,628	3,947	5,369
2008–09	1,701,017	1,245,890	73.2	33.6	36.6	26.5	36.2	3,886	2,485	3,780	5,590	4,284	2,740	4,167	6,163
2009–10	1,804,745	1,383,660	76.7	41.1	36.6	26.3	38.6	3,698	2,555	3,903	5,682	5,130	2,790	4,262	6,205
2010–11	1,802,335	1,421,369	78.9	46.0	35.9	27.2	40.2	4,765	2,676	4,160	5,780	5,101	2,865	4,454	6,188
2011–12	1,766,428	1,418,651	80.3	46.8	35.7	29.6	42.5	4,400	2,772	4,439	5,909	4,576	2,883	4,617	6,145
2012–13	1,736,952	1,390,827	80.1	45.0	36.2	31.1	41.4	4,427	2,916	4,693	6,127	4,529	2,984	4,801	6,268
2013–14	1,751,924	1,409,393	80.4	44.9	37.3	32.4	39.9	4,517	2,962	4,951	6,206	4,550	2,983	4,987	6,251
4-year															
2000–01	804,793	573,430	71.3	26.6	36.5	29.6	40.7	2,569	2,068	2,616	3,212	3,473	2,795	3,536	4,341
2005–06	906,948	695,017	76.6	26.6	36.8	34.2	44.4	3,071	2,752	3,573	4,166	3,652	3,273	4,250	4,955
2007–08	976,830	753,643	77.2	28.0	37.4	36.2	45.2	3,675	2,963	3,956	5,190	4,109	3,313	4,423	5,803
2008–09	1,007,672	791,177	78.5	28.1	37.6	37.2	46.6	4,191	3,158	4,215	6,038	4,621	3,482	4,647	6,657
2009–10	1,021,273	833,194	81.6	34.4	37.4	38.9	50.1	4,966	3,302	4,345	6,065	5,423	3,606	4,744	6,623
2010–11	1,039,126	858,424	82.6	38.9	38.2	39.6	51.5	4,983	3,469	4,634	6,127	5,335	3,713	4,961	6,559
2011–12	1,059,837	878,933	82.9	39.1	37.1	42.1	52.6	4,472	3,531	4,895	6,326	4,651	3,673	5,091	6,579
2012–13	1,056,185	872,769	82.6	37.8	37.3	43.8	50.9	4,508	3,670	5,165	6,579	4,612	3,754	5,283	6,731
2013–14	1,076,346	892,158	82.9	38.0	37.4	45.3	49.6	4,596	3,725	5,437	6,652	4,629	3,752	5,476	6,701
2-year															
2000–01	528,443	298,679	56.5	35.2	28.8	12.1	15.3	2,222	1,009	1,004	2,396	3,004	1,364	1,357	3,238
2005–06	603,320	371,024	61.5	38.0	31.9	11.3	19.0	2,774	1,314	1,297	2,812	3,299	1,563	1,542	3,345
2007–08	671,753	419,579	62.5	39.1	33.4	10.8	19.4	3,048	1,354	1,458	3,488	3,408	1,514	1,630	3,900
2008–09	693,345	454,713	65.6	41.5	35.5	11.0	21.1	3,584	1,448	1,637	4,150	3,952	1,597	1,805	4,576
2009–10	783,472	550,466	70.3	49.7	33.3	9.9	23.7	4,455	1,461	1,647	4,629	4,865	1,595	1,798	5,055
2010–11	763,209	562,945	73.8	55.7	32.8	10.3	24.9	4,557	1,418	1,677	4,802	4,879	1,518	1,795	5,141
2011–12	706,591	539,718	76.4	58.2	33.4	10.9	27.5	4,327	1,508	1,789	4,711	4,500	1,568	1,861	4,899
2012–13	680,767	518,058	76.1	56.3	34.4	11.4	26.8	4,342	1,648	1,891	4,797	4,442	1,686	1,935	4,908
2013–14	675,578	517,235	76.6	56.0	37.2	11.8	24.4	4,431	1,736	1,977	4,763	4,464	1,749	1,991	4,798
Private nonprofit															
2000–01	439,369	363,044	82.6	28.4	31.8	68.1	57.7	2,879	2,998	7,368	4,019	3,891	4,052	9,959	5,433
2005–06	471,069	401,908	85.3	26.5	31.3	73.8	59.8	3,426	3,117	9,932	5,270	4,075	3,707	11,813	6,268
2007–08	494,088	424,943	86.0	27.3	30.0	74.4	60.2	3,928	3,386	11,465	6,415	4,392	3,785	12,818	7,172
2008–09	496,594	433,231	87.2	27.5	30.2	76.7	60.5	4,446	3,527	12,691	7,618	4,902	3,889	13,993	8,400
2009–10	501,227	445,500	88.9	33.1	27.8	78.4	63.0	5,059	3,642	13,642	7,445	5,525	3,978	14,897	8,130
2010–11	517,831	462,840	89.4	36.4	27.7	78.4	64.3	5,076	3,556	14,324	7,296	5,434	3,806	15,334	7,810
2011–12	512,754	457,227	89.2	34.9	27.0	79.4	63.3	4,656	3,573	15,067	7,480	4,842	3,679	15,670	7,780
2012–13	515,423	459,216	89.1	33.8	26.1	79.9	62.0	4,668	3,671	15,948	7,886	4,775	3,756	16,315	8,068
2013–14	513,574	458,513	89.3	33.7	26.1	81.1	61.1	4,733	3,762	16,830	8,064	4,768	3,789	16,952	8,123

See notes at end of table.

Table 331.20. Full-time, first-time degree/certificate-seeking undergraduate students enrolled in degree-granting postsecondary institutions, by participation and average amount awarded in financial aid programs, and control and level of institution: 2000–01 through 2013–14—Continued

Control and level of institution, and year	Number enrolled	Number receiving financial aid	Percent receiving aid	Percent of enrolled students in student aid programs				Average award for students in aid programs[1] Current dollars				Constant 2014–15 dollars			
				Federal grants	State/local grants	Institutional grants	Student loans[2]	Federal grants	State/local grants	Institutional grants	Student loans[2]	Federal grants	State/local grants	Institutional grants	Student loans[2]
1	2	3	4	5	6	7	8	9	10	11	12	13	14	15	16
4-year															
2000–01	419,499	347,638	82.9	27.4	32.2	70.1	58.1	2,930	3,001	7,458	4,000	3,961	4,057	10,081	5,407
2005–06	460,832	393,429	85.4	26.0	31.2	74.6	59.8	3,437	3,121	10,002	5,264	4,088	3,712	11,897	6,261
2007–08	484,021	416,405	86.0	26.7	30.0	75.1	60.3	3,960	3,391	11,539	6,435	4,427	3,791	12,900	7,194
2008–09	487,034	424,917	87.2	26.9	30.1	77.4	60.6	4,484	3,526	12,772	7,647	4,944	3,888	14,082	8,432
2009–10	491,140	436,485	88.9	32.4	27.8	79.2	63.1	5,092	3,656	13,737	7,471	5,560	3,993	15,001	8,158
2010–11	504,715	451,012	89.4	35.4	27.7	79.6	64.3	5,105	3,574	14,414	7,305	5,464	3,826	15,431	7,820
2011–12	499,901	445,144	89.0	33.9	27.0	80.6	63.2	4,683	3,554	15,178	7,493	4,871	3,696	15,786	7,793
2012–13	505,099	449,905	89.1	33.1	26.0	80.8	62.0	4,698	3,678	16,058	7,905	4,806	3,763	16,428	8,087
2013–14	504,584	450,215	89.2	33.1	26.1	81.6	61.0	4,753	3,764	16,964	8,069	4,788	3,792	17,088	8,128
2-year															
2000–01	19,870	15,406	77.5	49.2	23.9	25.7	49.5	2,269	2,892	2,168	4,509	3,068	3,909	2,930	6,095
2005–06	10,237	8,479	82.8	51.6	36.1	38.5	55.9	3,176	2,974	3,799	5,531	3,778	3,537	4,519	6,578
2007–08	10,067	8,538	84.8	53.3	31.6	37.5	54.1	3,161	3,138	4,364	5,323	3,534	3,509	4,879	5,951
2008–09	9,560	8,314	87.0	59.3	32.1	37.5	58.1	3,564	3,554	4,194	6,081	3,930	3,918	4,625	6,705
2009–10	10,087	9,015	89.4	66.9	29.1	41.5	58.6	4,294	3,000	4,798	6,078	4,689	3,276	5,239	6,637
2010–11	13,116	11,828	90.2	73.3	26.8	29.8	64.3	4,553	2,835	5,059	6,944	4,874	3,035	5,416	7,434
2011–12	12,853	12,083	94.0	76.3	24.3	31.8	65.5	4,180	2,830	4,075	7,014	4,348	2,944	4,238	7,295
2012–13	10,324	9,311	90.2	67.1	30.3	37.6	60.6	3,939	3,374	4,347	6,971	4,030	3,452	4,448	7,132
2013–14	8,990	8,298	92.3	70.6	27.3	49.5	65.5	4,216	3,618	4,346	7,818	4,246	3,644	4,378	7,875
Private for-profit															
4-year															
2000–01	203,995	155,374	76.2	49.3	15.2	6.2	63.5	2,312	2,494	1,540	5,517	3,125	3,371	2,081	7,458
2005–06	328,206	263,366	80.1	55.6	11.4	8.8	70.4	2,725	2,796	1,423	6,454	3,241	3,325	1,693	7,676
2007–08	390,284	316,402	81.1	57.8	9.5	14.0	72.9	3,066	2,996	1,154	8,010	3,428	3,350	1,290	8,955
2008–09	345,137	294,942	85.5	63.4	9.1	14.0	77.7	3,710	3,194	1,677	8,323	4,091	3,522	1,849	9,177
2009–10	549,269	494,546	90.0	74.8	6.3	15.2	81.5	4,538	3,275	1,218	8,800	4,956	3,576	1,330	9,610
2010–11	327,935	295,373	90.1	75.7	9.0	15.5	82.0	4,494	3,028	1,884	8,064	4,811	3,242	2,017	8,633
2011–12	291,938	264,678	90.7	75.3	8.4	15.3	82.3	4,327	2,992	2,102	7,797	4,500	3,112	2,186	8,110
2012–13	258,771	227,273	87.8	71.9	7.8	18.2	77.4	4,357	3,158	2,350	8,098	4,458	3,231	2,404	8,284
2013–14	239,349	208,995	87.3	72.8	8.1	21.5	73.2	4,395	3,277	2,499	8,336	4,427	3,301	2,517	8,397
2-year															
2000–01	81,075	51,739	63.8	36.1	11.9	8.3	57.7	2,295	2,889	1,616	5,749	3,103	3,905	2,184	7,771
2005–06	157,705	116,237	73.7	46.8	8.9	10.9	67.2	2,490	2,945	1,641	7,046	2,962	3,503	1,952	8,381
2007–08	210,468	159,991	76.0	51.5	7.2	20.4	68.7	3,030	2,922	1,235	8,799	3,387	3,266	1,381	9,837
2008–09	125,211	107,014	85.5	57.8	11.7	21.5	77.9	3,554	3,172	2,324	9,356	3,919	3,497	2,562	10,316
2009–10	241,369	222,795	92.3	75.9	6.6	23.7	86.6	4,578	2,899	1,379	9,667	5,000	3,166	1,506	10,557
2010–11	112,706	102,000	90.5	73.6	11.3	23.6	82.9	4,733	2,950	2,805	8,561	5,067	3,158	3,002	9,165
2011–12	112,969	102,357	90.6	75.5	10.7	22.4	82.7	4,692	2,994	2,860	8,231	4,880	3,114	2,975	8,561
2012–13	100,541	89,411	88.9	73.5	9.7	26.9	79.1	4,664	2,941	3,040	8,300	4,771	3,008	3,110	8,491
2013–14	90,408	80,758	89.3	72.4	10.5	34.4	78.0	4,628	3,023	3,082	8,585	4,661	3,045	3,104	8,648
2-year															
2000–01	122,920	103,635	84.3	58.0	17.3	4.8	67.3	2,319	2,314	1,453	5,387	3,135	3,128	1,963	7,281
2005–06	170,501	147,129	86.3	63.6	13.7	6.8	73.4	2,885	2,706	1,098	5,951	3,431	3,218	1,307	7,079
2007–08	179,816	156,411	87.0	65.0	12.3	8.4	77.9	3,100	3,047	924	7,195	3,466	3,407	1,033	8,044
2008–09	219,926	187,928	85.5	66.6	7.6	9.8	77.5	3,787	3,215	865	7,733	4,176	3,544	953	8,526
2009–10	307,900	271,751	88.3	74.0	6.1	8.5	77.5	4,506	3,596	865	8,040	4,921	3,926	945	8,780
2010–11	215,229	193,373	89.8	76.8	7.8	11.3	81.5	4,374	3,088	875	7,799	4,682	3,306	936	8,349
2011–12	178,969	162,321	90.7	75.2	6.9	10.8	82.0	4,095	2,990	1,108	7,521	4,259	3,110	1,153	7,822
2012–13	158,230	137,862	87.1	70.9	6.6	12.7	76.2	4,155	3,359	1,421	7,964	4,251	3,437	1,454	8,147
2013–14	148,941	128,237	86.1	73.0	6.7	13.6	70.3	4,254	3,517	1,602	8,168	4,285	3,543	1,614	8,228

[1]Average amounts for students participating in indicated programs.
[2]Includes only loans made directly to students. Does not include Parent Loans for Undergraduate Students (PLUS) and other loans made directly to parents.
NOTE: Degree-granting institutions grant associate's or higher degrees and participate in Title IV federal financial aid programs.

SOURCE: U.S. Department of Education, National Center for Education Statistics, Integrated Postsecondary Education Data System (IPEDS), Spring 2001 through Spring 2011 and Winter 2011–12 through Winter 2013–14, Student Financial Aid component. (This table was prepared December 2015.)

Table 331.30. Average amount of grant and scholarship aid and average net price for first-time, full-time students receiving Title IV aid, by control and level of institution and income level: Selected years, 2009–10 through 2013–14

Level of institution and income level	2009–10				2011–12				2012–13				2013–14			
	All institutions	Public	Private		All institutions	Public	Private		All institutions	Public	Private		All institutions	Public	Private	
			Nonprofit	For-profit			Nonprofit	For-profit			Nonprofit	For-profit			Nonprofit	For-profit
1	2	3	4	5	6	7	8	9	10	11	12	13	14	15	16	17
	Current dollars															
4-year institutions																
Grant and scholarship aid[1]																
All income levels	$9,050	$5,980	$15,560	$4,420	$9,680	$6,240	$16,920	$4,890	$10,280	$6,520	$17,930	$5,150	$10,820	$6,790	$18,980	$5,310
$0 to $30,000	10,290	9,080	17,460	5,110	10,670	9,180	18,130	5,350	11,380	9,600	19,200	5,520	11,900	9,780	19,980	5,760
$30,001 to $48,000	11,170	8,330	18,710	4,530	11,820	8,540	20,190	5,010	12,420	8,880	21,290	5,490	13,010	9,300	22,510	5,740
$48,001 to $75,000	9,140	4,910	16,810	2,430	9,840	5,210	18,540	3,300	10,600	5,650	19,730	3,630	11,310	6,150	21,050	3,990
$75,001 to $110,000	7,150	2,270	14,650	1,220	7,910	2,440	16,380	1,700	8,480	2,690	17,460	2,180	9,100	2,950	18,680	2,190
$110,001 or more	6,300	1,590	11,560	1,020	7,180	1,610	13,160	1,480	7,590	1,720	14,040	2,190	8,170	1,860	15,240	2,070
Net price[2]																
All income levels	15,900	11,070	21,780	22,590	16,820	12,290	23,450	21,460	17,190	12,640	24,070	21,500	17,230	12,660	24,510	20,850
$0 to $30,000	12,570	7,720	15,970	21,770	13,260	9,130	17,650	20,930	13,420	9,340	18,180	21,020	13,080	9,230	18,610	20,000
$30,001 to $48,000	13,110	9,260	17,200	23,590	14,010	10,770	18,620	22,410	14,060	10,970	18,980	21,910	13,920	10,760	19,180	21,770
$48,001 to $75,000	16,610	13,290	20,270	26,710	17,500	14,600	21,560	25,260	17,660	14,760	21,940	24,790	17,460	14,530	21,910	24,470
$75,001 to $110,000	19,860	16,410	23,900	29,830	21,000	17,890	25,170	28,050	21,230	18,160	25,480	27,540	21,330	18,240	25,630	27,450
$110,001 or more	24,080	17,880	30,210	32,910	25,580	19,530	31,730	30,780	26,030	20,020	32,360	29,980	26,190	20,290	32,520	30,060
2-year institutions																
Grant and scholarship aid[1]																
All income levels	4,460	4,540	5,180	4,090	4,480	4,520	5,740	4,140	4,600	4,610	6,080	4,380	4,800	4,790	7,060	4,620
$0 to $30,000	5,250	5,450	5,540	4,590	5,290	5,400	5,970	4,700	5,430	5,520	6,160	4,870	5,650	5,740	6,960	5,080
$30,001 to $48,000	4,380	4,520	5,080	3,670	4,440	4,580	5,950	3,540	4,700	4,760	6,120	3,980	5,020	5,060	8,040	4,290
$48,001 to $75,000	2,240	2,250	4,150	1,960	2,430	2,430	5,120	1,990	2,620	2,600	6,280	2,280	2,940	2,910	7,420	2,710
$75,001 to $110,000	800	750	3,240	830	770	720	4,620	570	840	780	4,960	860	970	880	6,160	1,100
$110,001 or more	610	600	2,940	470	480	420	3,620	490	640	550	5,600	680	640	550	5,440	790
Net price[2]																
All income levels	8,930	6,290	16,270	18,360	9,070	6,990	18,130	19,330	9,030	7,080	18,610	20,080	8,920	7,050	18,910	20,020
$0 to $30,000	8,560	5,380	16,500	18,240	8,600	6,180	17,690	19,210	8,600	6,230	18,130	19,760	8,410	6,110	18,100	19,590
$30,001 to $48,000	8,720	6,330	16,620	19,070	9,250	6,990	19,150	19,990	8,670	6,990	19,670	21,120	8,360	6,820	19,440	20,590
$48,001 to $75,000	10,690	8,810	18,650	21,290	10,710	9,230	20,440	22,560	10,560	9,270	20,380	22,870	10,220	9,090	20,770	22,200
$75,001 to $110,000	12,230	10,630	20,760	23,020	12,460	11,150	21,400	24,150	12,470	11,270	22,410	24,450	12,470	11,340	22,370	24,380
$110,001 or more	12,760	10,820	20,930	24,620	12,860	11,400	22,440	25,230	12,780	11,520	22,990	24,570	12,770	11,740	23,080	24,950
	Constant 2014–15 dollars[3]															
4-year institutions																
Grant and scholarship aid[1]																
All income levels	$9,880	$6,530	$16,990	$4,820	$10,070	$6,490	$17,600	$5,080	$10,520	$6,670	$18,340	$5,260	$10,900	$6,840	$19,120	$5,350
$0 to $30,000	11,240	9,910	19,060	5,580	11,100	9,550	18,860	5,560	11,650	9,820	19,640	5,650	11,990	9,960	20,130	5,810
$30,001 to $48,000	12,190	9,100	20,440	4,950	12,290	8,880	21,000	5,210	12,700	9,090	21,780	5,620	13,100	9,370	22,680	5,780
$48,001 to $75,000	9,980	5,370	18,360	2,650	10,240	5,410	19,280	3,430	10,840	5,780	20,180	3,710	11,400	6,190	21,210	4,020
$75,001 to $110,000	7,810	2,480	16,000	1,330	8,230	2,540	17,040	1,760	8,680	2,750	17,860	2,230	9,170	2,970	18,820	2,200
$110,001 or more	6,880	1,730	12,630	1,110	7,470	1,670	13,690	1,540	7,770	1,760	14,360	2,240	8,230	1,880	15,350	2,090
Net price[2]																
All income levels	17,360	12,090	23,790	24,670	17,500	12,790	24,390	22,320	17,590	12,930	24,620	22,000	17,350	12,750	24,690	21,000
$0 to $30,000	13,730	8,430	17,440	23,780	13,790	9,490	18,350	21,770	13,730	9,560	18,600	21,510	13,180	9,300	18,740	20,140
$30,001 to $48,000	14,320	10,110	18,790	25,760	14,580	11,200	19,360	23,310	14,380	11,220	19,420	22,420	14,020	10,840	19,320	21,930
$48,001 to $75,000	18,140	14,510	22,130	29,160	18,200	15,190	22,430	26,270	18,060	15,100	22,450	25,360	17,590	14,640	22,070	24,650
$75,001 to $110,000	21,680	17,920	26,100	32,570	21,840	18,600	26,180	29,170	21,710	18,570	26,070	28,180	21,480	18,380	25,810	27,650
$110,001 or more	26,300	19,530	32,990	35,940	26,600	20,310	33,000	32,010	26,630	20,480	33,100	30,670	26,380	20,430	32,760	30,280

See notes at end of table.

Table 331.30. Average amount of grant and scholarship aid and average net price for first-time, full-time students receiving Title IV aid, by control and level of institution and income level: Selected years, 2009–10 through 2013–14—Continued

Level of institution and income level	2009–10				2011–12				2012–13				2013–14			
	All institutions	Public	Private Nonprofit	For-profit	All institutions	Public	Private Nonprofit	For-profit	All institutions	Public	Private Nonprofit	For-profit	All institutions	Public	Private Nonprofit	For-profit
1	2	3	4	5	6	7	8	9	10	11	12	13	14	15	16	17
2-year institutions																
Grant and scholarship aid[1]																
All income levels......	4,870	4,960	5,660	4,470	4,660	4,700	5,970	4,310	4,710	4,710	6,230	4,480	4,830	4,830	7,110	4,650
$0 to $30,000......	5,730	5,950	6,050	5,010	5,500	5,620	6,210	4,890	5,550	5,650	6,300	4,980	5,690	5,780	7,010	5,110
$30,001 to $48,000......	4,780	4,940	5,540	4,000	4,620	4,760	6,190	3,680	4,810	4,870	6,260	4,070	5,060	5,100	8,100	4,320
$48,001 to $75,000......	2,450	2,460	4,540	2,140	2,530	2,530	5,320	2,070	2,680	2,660	6,430	2,330	2,970	2,930	7,470	2,730
$75,001 to $110,000......	870	820	3,540	910	800	740	4,810	590	860	790	5,070	880	980	890	6,200	1,110
$110,001 or more......	670	650	3,210	520	500	430	3,770	510	650	570	5,730	700	650	560	5,480	800
Net price[2]																
All income levels......	9,750	6,870	17,770	20,050	9,430	7,270	18,860	20,100	9,240	7,240	19,040	20,540	8,980	7,100	19,040	20,170
$0 to $30,000......	9,350	5,870	18,010	19,910	8,940	6,430	18,400	19,970	8,800	6,370	18,550	20,210	8,470	6,150	18,230	19,730
$30,001 to $48,000......	9,520	6,910	18,150	20,820	9,620	7,270	19,920	20,790	8,870	7,160	20,130	21,610	8,420	6,870	19,590	20,740
$48,001 to $75,000......	11,670	9,630	20,370	23,250	11,140	9,600	21,250	23,460	10,800	9,490	20,850	23,400	10,300	9,150	20,920	22,360
$75,001 to $110,000......	13,350	11,610	22,670	25,140	12,960	11,600	22,260	25,120	12,760	11,530	22,930	25,020	12,560	11,420	22,530	24,550
$110,001 or more......	13,940	11,810	22,860	26,890	13,370	11,860	23,340	26,240	13,070	11,790	23,520	25,140	12,860	11,820	23,240	25,140

[1]Grant and scholarship aid consists of federal Title IV grants, as well as other grant or scholarship aid from the federal government, state or local governments, or institutional sources. Title IV grants include Federal Pell Grants, Federal Supplemental Educational Opportunity Grants (FSEOGs), Academic Competitiveness Grants (ACGs), National Science and Mathematics Access to Retain Talent Grants (National SMART Grants), and Teacher Education Assistance for College and Higher Education (TEACH) Grants. The average amount of grant and scholarship aid by income level was calculated based on all students who received any type of Title IV aid, even those students who received zero Title IV aid in the form of grants and received Title IV aid only in the form of work-study aid or loan aid.
[2]Net price is the total cost of attendance minus grant and scholarship aid from the federal government, state or local governments, or institutional sources. However, average net price by income level was calculated based on all students who received any type of Title IV aid, even those who received zero Title IV aid in the form of grants and received Title IV aid only in the form of work-study aid or loan aid.

[3]Constant dollars based on the Consumer Price Index, prepared by the Bureau of Labor Statistics, U.S. Department of Labor, adjusted to a school-year basis.
NOTE: Excludes students who previously attended another postsecondary institution or who began their studies on a part-time basis. Includes only first-time, full-time students who paid the in-state or in-district tuition rate (if they attended public institutions) and who received Title IV aid. Totals include students for whom income data were not available. Some data have been revised from previously published figures.
SOURCE: U.S. Department of Education, National Center for Education Statistics, Integrated Postsecondary Education Data System (IPEDS), Spring 2010 and Winter 2011–12 through Winter 2013–14, Student Financial Aid component. (This table was prepared December 2015.)

Table 331.35. Percentage of full-time, full-year undergraduates receiving financial aid, and average annual amount received, by source of aid and selected student characteristics: Selected years, 1999–2000 through 2011–12

[Standard errors appear in parentheses. Amounts in constant 2014–15 dollars]

Year and selected student characteristic	Number enrolled (in thousands)	Any aid — Percent receiving — Total[2]	Federal[3]	Nonfederal	Any aid — Average amount — Total[2]	Federal[3]	Nonfederal	Grants — Percent receiving — Total	Pell	Grants — Average amount — Total	Pell	Loans[1] — Percent receiving	Average amount
1	2	3	4	5	6	7	8	9	10	11	12	13	14
1999–2000													
Total	6,145 (—)	71.9 (0.59)	56.7 (0.44)	52.3 (0.67)	$11,840 (139)	$8,340 (81)	$7,220 (133)	58.5 (0.60)	28.3 (0.43)	$7,130 (113)	$3,200 (21)	45.6 (0.44)	$8,430 (82)
Sex													
Male	2,687 (—)	69.1 (0.74)	53.9 (0.65)	49.7 (0.79)	11,810 (215)	8,450 (118)	7,250 (207)	53.9 (0.83)	24.5 (0.59)	7,100 (173)	3,130 (29)	43.8 (0.67)	8,610 (144)
Female	3,458 (—)	74.0 (0.73)	59.0 (0.62)	54.3 (0.86)	11,860 (159)	8,260 (94)	7,200 (134)	62.1 (0.75)	31.3 (0.61)	7,150 (118)	3,240 (28)	46.9 (0.64)	8,300 (102)
Race/ethnicity													
White	4,335 (—)	69.9 (0.73)	53.1 (0.59)	52.2 (0.73)	11,960 (187)	8,390 (104)	7,480 (171)	55.2 (0.70)	21.5 (0.53)	7,170 (144)	3,020 (30)	45.3 (0.61)	8,640 (112)
Black	675 (—)	88.0 (1.16)	78.6 (1.49)	54.7 (2.09)	11,610 (403)	8,680 (240)	6,200 (351)	76.2 (1.24)	55.7 (1.38)	6,690 (210)	3,430 (47)	59.2 (2.36)	7,690 (266)
Hispanic	500 (—)	77.1 (1.41)	65.6 (1.84)	53.1 (2.20)	10,820 (422)	7,840 (294)	6,020 (330)	66.7 (1.78)	45.4 (2.10)	6,470 (261)	3,340 (54)	42.7 (1.99)	8,260 (270)
Asian	372 (—)	60.3 (1.65)	47.8 (1.79)	47.9 (1.55)	12,430 (787)	8,180 (306)	7,490 (721)	53.0 (1.67)	31.7 (1.62)	8,250 (650)	3,490 (86)	33.0 (2.03)	7,920 (235)
Pacific Islander	41 (—)	62.3 (6.39)	56.0 (5.70)	48.8 (5.63)	12,210 (1,137)	7,340 (627)	7,160 (1,067)	53.1 (6.29)	31.9 (5.85)	7,330 (843)	3,140 (262)	40.7 (5.58)	8,610 (1,198)
American Indian/Alaska Native	42 (—)	81.5 (4.72)	75.0 (5.05)	61.7 (6.64)	12,200 (1,041)	7,650 (767)	6,810 (959)	78.7 (4.73)	50.8 (7.04)	7,470 (676)	3,540 (175)	44.6 (7.94)	7,790 (766)
Two or more races	93 (—)	75.6 (3.00)	60.6 (3.36)	57.1 (3.44)	12,460 (664)	8,000 (405)	8,000 (556)	62.0 (3.22)	34.2 (3.30)	8,440 (600)	3,340 (181)	43.8 (2.76)	8,210 (369)
Other	86 (—)	61.9 (3.54)	45.2 (3.64)	46.9 (4.04)	11,260 (1,021)	7,470 (474)	7,670 (1,013)	51.4 (4.32)	26.0 (3.70)	7,770 (820)	3,030 (227)	29.8 (4.02)	8,260 (867)
Dependency status and family income													
Dependent	4,612 (—)	70.2 (0.65)	53.4 (0.52)	53.7 (0.75)	12,250 (165)	8,020 (93)	8,040 (166)	56.2 (0.70)	21.1 (0.52)	7,790 (137)	2,970 (26)	45.6 (0.50)	8,340 (104)
Low-income[4]	990 (—)	85.4 (0.90)	78.1 (1.03)	65.2 (1.43)	12,540 (223)	8,050 (124)	6,800 (195)	82.3 (0.94)	70.4 (1.12)	8,010 (152)	3,390 (28)	50.5 (1.27)	7,030 (143)
Middle-income[4]	2,383 (—)	70.6 (0.85)	53.4 (0.85)	54.5 (1.01)	12,500 (250)	7,660 (112)	8,500 (246)	54.3 (1.00)	11.6 (0.47)	7,730 (181)	1,900 (48)	49.8 (0.80)	8,220 (120)
High-income[4]	1,238 (—)	57.3 (1.10)	33.7 (0.77)	42.6 (1.07)	11,590 (226)	9,090 (259)	8,420 (183)	38.8 (1.08)	‡ (†)	7,560 (181)	‡ (†)	33.5 (0.72)	10,250 (267)
Independent	1,533 (—)	76.9 (0.88)	66.8 (0.80)	48.1 (1.11)	10,700 (194)	9,110 (128)	4,450 (141)	65.5 (0.84)	50.0 (0.72)	5,430 (111)	3,480 (33)	45.6 (1.17)	8,700 (104)
2003–04													
Total	7,562 (—)	75.3 (0.62)	60.3 (0.49)	54.9 (0.63)	$12,420 (118)	$8,910 (76)	$7,230 (150)	62.2 (0.58)	31.4 (0.31)	$7,210 (128)	$3,870 (23)	48.6 (0.42)	$8,900 (91)
Sex													
Male	3,340 (—)	72.8 (0.89)	57.2 (0.83)	53.8 (0.78)	12,560 (156)	9,070 (104)	7,340 (165)	58.6 (0.82)	28.0 (0.62)	7,180 (145)	3,790 (34)	46.8 (0.77)	9,210 (129)
Female	4,222 (—)	77.3 (0.56)	62.7 (0.51)	55.8 (0.70)	12,310 (137)	8,800 (81)	7,150 (171)	65.0 (0.61)	34.2 (0.46)	7,240 (141)	3,930 (26)	50.0 (0.45)	8,670 (94)
Race/ethnicity													
White	5,137 (—)	73.3 (0.86)	56.3 (0.79)	55.2 (0.81)	12,370 (150)	8,890 (88)	7,360 (163)	59.0 (0.79)	23.9 (0.54)	7,050 (150)	3,680 (29)	48.4 (0.68)	9,070 (97)
Black	895 (—)	88.7 (0.90)	81.3 (1.08)	55.5 (1.68)	12,930 (279)	9,470 (189)	6,600 (252)	79.0 (1.27)	61.5 (1.64)	7,380 (232)	4,120 (36)	59.2 (1.90)	8,440 (227)
Hispanic	718 (—)	78.8 (1.09)	67.8 (1.21)	55.0 (1.32)	12,020 (262)	8,560 (163)	6,680 (260)	68.1 (1.15)	46.7 (1.17)	7,340 (187)	4,050 (57)	46.3 (1.19)	8,580 (228)
Asian	459 (—)	65.1 (1.55)	51.4 (1.46)	50.6 (1.70)	12,660 (311)	8,190 (227)	7,970 (267)	54.5 (1.74)	30.6 (1.40)	8,730 (260)	4,100 (73)	35.7 (1.28)	8,340 (296)
Pacific Islander	34 (—)	71.1 (5.10)	61.5 (4.79)	46.2 (4.95)	12,090 (1,184)	8,630 (882)	7,120 (1,154)	53.0 (5.12)	28.1 (4.85)	7,410 (779)	3,710 (290)	45.0 (5.02)	9,350 (1,074)
American Indian/Alaska Native	59 (—)	81.1 (5.18)	66.2 (6.31)	64.5 (4.42)	11,490 (794)	8,740 (461)	5,470 (951)	73.8 (5.79)	43.4 (4.64)	6,910 (747)	3,870 (197)	46.5 (5.70)	8,090 (534)
Two or more races	156 (—)	77.1 (2.12)	61.6 (2.12)	55.9 (2.11)	12,640 (516)	9,250 (362)	7,240 (444)	63.8 (2.18)	31.5 (2.39)	7,110 (377)	3,870 (112)	49.3 (2.34)	9,420 (490)
Other	104 (—)	72.2 (2.56)	56.6 (2.71)	53.2 (2.58)	11,530 (627)	8,670 (418)	6,420 (572)	61.7 (2.89)	35.5 (2.94)	6,630 (401)	3,950 (138)	42.9 (2.65)	8,770 (553)
Dependency status and family income													
Dependent	5,574 (—)	73.3 (0.79)	56.3 (0.68)	57.2 (0.74)	12,840 (148)	8,550 (81)	8,040 (165)	59.6 (0.74)	23.6 (0.39)	7,790 (159)	3,640 (26)	47.5 (0.62)	9,040 (103)
Low-income[4]	1,250 (—)	87.9 (0.70)	77.8 (0.80)	66.6 (1.00)	13,660 (259)	9,150 (153)	7,330 (247)	84.8 (0.80)	70.8 (0.92)	8,960 (210)	4,300 (25)	51.0 (0.91)	7,380 (166)
Middle-income[4]	2,886 (—)	72.7 (1.01)	55.4 (0.89)	58.0 (0.97)	12,570 (175)	8,000 (106)	8,120 (183)	57.2 (0.88)	14.8 (0.42)	7,190 (180)	2,280 (35)	50.4 (0.80)	9,050 (125)
High-income[4]	1,438 (—)	61.6 (0.98)	39.3 (0.82)	47.4 (0.91)	12,470 (217)	9,050 (153)	8,700 (216)	42.5 (1.02)	‡ (†)	7,410 (214)	‡ (†)	38.8 (0.83)	10,910 (191)
Independent	1,988 (—)	80.9 (0.77)	71.5 (0.79)	48.5 (0.91)	11,330 (134)	9,720 (114)	4,570 (126)	69.4 (0.79)	53.5 (0.82)	5,820 (86)	4,160 (31)	51.6 (0.85)	8,540 (114)
2007–08													
Total	7,527 (—)	80.1 (0.28)	63.9 (0.31)	63.7 (0.36)	$14,520 (110)	$9,140 (57)	$9,090 (99)	64.6 (0.37)	32.7 (0.29)	$8,110 (79)	$3,630 (16)	54.8 (0.32)	$10,640 (86)
Sex													
Male	3,277 (—)	77.1 (0.44)	60.0 (0.47)	61.8 (0.49)	14,630 (158)	9,280 (103)	9,240 (123)	60.8 (0.54)	27.7 (0.42)	8,160 (106)	3,590 (25)	52.1 (0.56)	10,850 (131)
Female	4,249 (—)	82.4 (0.36)	66.9 (0.42)	65.2 (0.47)	14,440 (129)	9,040 (63)	8,990 (125)	67.6 (0.47)	36.6 (0.41)	8,070 (95)	3,660 (23)	56.9 (0.43)	10,490 (96)
Race/ethnicity													
White	4,983 (—)	78.1 (0.39)	59.6 (0.44)	63.2 (0.46)	14,520 (141)	9,030 (79)	9,420 (128)	61.1 (0.51)	24.1 (0.37)	8,000 (101)	3,460 (24)	54.0 (0.45)	10,930 (109)
Black	889 (—)	92.1 (0.58)	83.9 (0.86)	67.8 (0.85)	15,160 (186)	10,030 (124)	8,180 (181)	79.6 (0.92)	61.5 (1.06)	7,940 (157)	3,870 (42)	70.3 (0.84)	9,950 (167)
Hispanic	844 (—)	84.3 (0.71)	71.8 (0.88)	65.8 (0.91)	13,790 (217)	8,750 (121)	8,120 (201)	72.0 (0.85)	50.5 (1.02)	7,850 (137)	3,740 (37)	52.0 (0.92)	10,420 (231)
Asian	489 (—)	69.5 (1.35)	53.7 (1.33)	57.6 (1.47)	14,240 (318)	8,360 (201)	9,410 (281)	57.0 (1.21)	32.2 (1.21)	9,890 (269)	3,850 (49)	38.6 (1.29)	9,750 (277)
Pacific Islander	45 (—)	81.4 (3.79)	67.3 (3.81)	64.1 (4.44)	15,160 (1,003)	10,040 (797)	8,710 (820)	69.0 (4.14)	36.1 (4.59)	7,040 (582)	3,530 (235)	53.8 (4.44)	12,480 (1,074)
American Indian/Alaska Native	50 (—)	85.9 (3.32)	71.3 (3.81)	61.8 (4.53)	12,270 (879)	8,600 (582)	7,130 (721)	76.3 (3.20)	48.3 (4.15)	7,490 (668)	3,670 (188)	48.7 (4.70)	9,060 (669)
Two or more races	199 (—)	83.4 (1.31)	68.1 (1.72)	67.1 (2.01)	15,490 (440)	9,630 (259)	9,480 (392)	67.9 (1.66)	37.6 (1.87)	9,240 (375)	3,730 (97)	59.1 (1.92)	10,010 (382)
Other	17 (—)	79.8 (5.18)	72.9 (5.30)	50.9 (6.42)	14,000 (1,387)	8,820 (665)	9,340 (1,302)	67.3 (5.59)	51.9 (5.87)	8,450 (1,243)	3,520 (266)	54.7 (5.64)	8,200 (829)

See notes at end of table.

Table 331.35. Percentage of full-time, full-year undergraduates receiving financial aid, and average annual amount received, by source of aid and selected student characteristics: Selected years, 1999–2000 through 2011–12—Continued

[Standard errors appear in parentheses. Amounts in constant 2014–15 dollars]

Year and selected student characteristic	Number enrolled (in thousands)	Any aid — Percent receiving: Total[2]	Federal[3]	Nonfederal	Any aid — Average amount: Total[2]	Federal[3]	Nonfederal	Grants — Percent receiving: Total	Pell	Grants — Average amount: Total	Pell	Loans[1] — Percent receiving	Average amount
1	2	3	4	5	6	7	8	9	10	11	12	13	14
Dependency status and family income													
Dependent	5,675	78.0 (0.34)	59.5 (0.37)	65.1 (0.40)	14,980 (134)	8,830 (72)	9,900 (115)	62.7 (0.44)	25.2 (0.27)	8,880 (98)	3,560 (19)	51.9 (0.39)	10,870 (109)
Low-income[4]	1,203	92.3 (0.49)	85.9 (0.59)	74.9 (0.62)	15,440 (177)	9,280 (88)	8,390 (146)	89.2 (0.57)	80.9 (0.66)	9,960 (124)	4,170 (18)	56.7 (0.75)	8,410 (159)
Middle-income[4]	2,825	79.3 (0.41)	59.4 (0.50)	67.1 (0.48)	14,900 (164)	8,290 (95)	10,280 (149)	61.6 (0.50)	16.1 (0.33)	8,440 (130)	2,250 (31)	56.0 (0.50)	10,870 (123)
High-income[4]	1,647	65.5 (0.66)	40.3 (0.65)	54.4 (0.76)	14,680 (233)	9,510 (212)	10,620 (181)	45.2 (0.84)	‡ (†)	8,340 (167)	‡ (†)	41.4 (0.68)	13,310 (225)
Independent	1,851	86.4 (0.47)	77.4 (0.59)	59.6 (0.74)	13,240 (134)	9,860 (86)	6,390 (114)	70.5 (0.64)	55.8 (0.64)	6,000 (78)	3,740 (29)	63.6 (0.74)	10,070 (110)
2011–12													
Total	8,864	84.4 (0.36)	72.8 (0.51)	56.9 (0.46)	$16,130 (111)	$11,250 (78)	$9,530 (115)	72.4 (0.41)	47.1 (0.50)	$9,600 (96)	$4,600 (17)	56.7 (0.53)	$10,500 (78)
Sex													
Male	3,868	82.3 (0.50)	70.1 (0.65)	56.2 (0.61)	16,340 (175)	11,440 (113)	9,670 (181)	68.9 (0.58)	42.9 (0.60)	9,790 (155)	4,580 (25)	53.9 (0.70)	10,590 (117)
Female	4,996	86.0 (0.42)	74.9 (0.60)	57.5 (0.53)	15,980 (139)	11,120 (91)	9,420 (146)	75.1 (0.46)	50.4 (0.62)	9,470 (114)	4,620 (22)	58.8 (0.58)	10,430 (98)
Race/ethnicity[5]													
White	5,369	82.6 (0.45)	68.5 (0.63)	57.0 (0.50)	15,990 (152)	11,190 (105)	9,740 (144)	68.8 (0.50)	37.8 (0.57)	9,430 (120)	4,410 (26)	56.4 (0.67)	10,700 (103)
Black	1,209	94.0 (0.54)	90.7 (0.70)	52.8 (1.24)	16,770 (267)	12,360 (163)	8,600 (312)	84.6 (0.72)	73.5 (1.07)	8,940 (199)	4,820 (27)	71.9 (1.12)	10,390 (173)
Hispanic	1,274	88.3 (0.74)	79.1 (0.91)	60.4 (1.12)	15,320 (322)	10,580 (163)	8,530 (331)	79.9 (0.84)	62.7 (0.94)	9,650 (278)	4,770 (36)	51.2 (1.09)	9,830 (187)
Asian	603	71.4 (1.77)	58.5 (1.82)	56.4 (1.60)	16,860 (557)	9,900 (257)	11,120 (533)	63.3 (1.71)	40.8 (1.60)	12,210 (462)	4,740 (66)	38.4 (1.59)	9,860 (416)
Pacific Islander	42	82.1 (3.87)	71.5 (5.20)	55.0 (4.22)	18,530 (1,725)	12,390 (906)	11,550 (1,945)	67.3 (4.42)	44.6 (4.76)	12,440 (1,772)	5,010 (153)	50.7 (5.38)	11,180 (1,218)
American Indian/Alaska Native	67	93.0 (2.55)	86.4 (2.44)	57.1 (3.82)	15,350 (1,031)	10,380 (534)	9,290 (1,174)	85.4 (3.24)	69.5 (3.37)	9,720 (816)	4,630 (174)	62.3 (3.60)	8,320 (632)
Two or more races	301	85.8 (1.46)	76.3 (1.76)	59.6 (2.14)	17,750 (566)	11,950 (307)	10,230 (596)	73.1 (1.71)	49.4 (1.94)	10,470 (432)	4,720 (87)	59.3 (2.06)	11,330 (367)
Age													
15 to 23	6,650	82.7 (0.39)	68.6 (0.54)	62.4 (0.46)	16,840 (131)	10,880 (94)	10,360 (129)	70.9 (0.43)	39.7 (0.44)	10,750 (116)	4,570 (19)	54.0 (0.53)	10,720 (103)
24 to 29	1,048	87.5 (0.76)	83.1 (0.91)	43.4 (1.01)	14,680 (250)	12,240 (171)	6,190 (369)	76.7 (0.95)	68.6 (1.11)	6,820 (210)	4,670 (38)	61.9 (1.20)	10,090 (128)
30 or over	1,165	91.1 (0.72)	87.2 (0.80)	37.8 (1.14)	13,690 (218)	12,090 (151)	5,110 (244)	77.0 (0.90)	70.3 (1.01)	6,040 (130)	4,640 (38)	67.3 (1.08)	9,840 (127)
Marital status[6]													
Not married	7,920	84.0 (0.37)	71.6 (0.53)	59.1 (0.47)	16,520 (115)	11,240 (82)	9,840 (120)	72.5 (0.41)	45.3 (0.50)	10,000 (101)	4,610 (18)	56.4 (0.54)	10,610 (84)
Married	828	86.9 (0.90)	80.6 (1.06)	38.4 (1.18)	12,880 (264)	11,220 (185)	5,590 (348)	69.5 (1.15)	59.5 (1.28)	6,200 (194)	4,470 (49)	57.3 (1.16)	9,640 (175)
Separated	117	97.2 (1.02)	95.9 (1.25)	37.5 (2.73)	13,660 (538)	11,820 (372)	5,170 (849)	88.6 (2.00)	85.0 (2.35)	6,250 (315)	4,830 (76)	71.4 (2.68)	9,310 (327)
Dependency status and family income													
Dependent	6,141	82.3 (0.39)	67.7 (0.56)	63.3 (0.46)	17,110 (137)	10,920 (99)	10,560 (130)	69.9 (0.43)	37.0 (0.43)	11,000 (122)	4,510 (21)	54.3 (0.55)	10,860 (109)
Low-income[4]	1,361	94.2 (0.58)	90.6 (0.73)	67.9 (0.64)	17,300 (233)	10,950 (121)	9,390 (279)	93.6 (0.61)	89.2 (0.76)	11,820 (213)	5,420 (16)	56.1 (0.89)	8,370 (137)
Middle-income[4]	3,045	83.2 (0.50)	69.0 (0.68)	66.8 (0.64)	17,160 (190)	10,510 (116)	10,670 (178)	70.1 (0.59)	34.6 (0.55)	10,680 (168)	3,470 (32)	58.2 (0.70)	10,770 (133)
High-income[4]	1,735	71.3 (0.73)	47.4 (0.89)	55.4 (0.81)	16,840 (312)	11,940 (263)	11,460 (290)	50.9 (0.83)	0.4 (0.07)	10,590 (281)	3,440 (439)	46.1 (0.92)	13,430 (251)
Independent	2,723	89.2 (0.54)	84.3 (0.64)	42.5 (0.80)	14,080 (172)	11,850 (108)	6,060 (231)	78.1 (0.67)	70.0 (0.79)	6,780 (123)	4,710 (26)	62.0 (0.86)	9,780 (93)
Housing status													
School-owned	2,219	88.2 (0.50)	72.9 (0.66)	76.3 (0.59)	23,100 (261)	12,630 (167)	14,430 (259)	78.1 (0.59)	35.9 (0.67)	14,970 (267)	4,550 (38)	65.9 (0.75)	11,860 (146)
Off-campus, not with parents	3,222	84.4 (0.63)	74.6 (0.73)	48.9 (0.73)	14,020 (176)	11,220 (117)	7,090 (179)	71.6 (0.63)	53.0 (0.77)	7,470 (128)	4,620 (28)	56.1 (0.74)	10,230 (129)
With parents	2,502	82.7 (0.69)	72.0 (0.85)	52.0 (0.86)	12,880 (174)	9,940 (102)	6,710 (201)	71.2 (0.73)	52.1 (0.87)	7,630 (146)	4,640 (32)	49.4 (0.88)	9,540 (137)
Attended more than one institution	921	79.9 (0.74)	68.2 (0.94)	51.5 (0.87)	14,520 (233)	11,100 (149)	7,830 (246)	64.9 (0.90)	40.0 (0.86)	8,130 (190)	4,470 (41)	56.3 (1.00)	9,880 (152)

—Not available.
†Not applicable.
‡Reporting standards not met. Either there are too few cases for a reliable estimate or the coefficient of variation (CV) is 50 percent or greater.
[1]Includes Parent Loans for Undergraduate Students (PLUS).
[2]Includes students who reported they were awarded aid but did not specify the source of aid.
[3]Includes Department of Veterans Affairs and Department of Defense benefits.
[4]Low-income students have family incomes below the 25th percentile, middle-income students have family incomes from the 25th to the 75th percentile, and high-income students have family incomes above the 75th percentile.
[5]The 2012 questionnaire did not offer students the option of choosing an "Other" race category.

[6]Includes students who were single, divorced, or widowed.
NOTE: Full-time, full-year undergraduates are those who were enrolled full time for 9 or more months at one or more institutions. Data include undergraduates in degree-granting and non-degree-granting institutions. Constant dollars based on the Consumer Price Index, prepared by the Bureau of Labor Statistics. U.S. Department of Labor, adjusted to an academic-year basis. Detail may not sum to totals because some students receive multiple types of aid and aid from different sources. Data exclude Puerto Rico. Race categories exclude persons of Hispanic ethnicity.
SOURCE: U.S. Department of Education, National Center for Education Statistics, 1999–2000, 2003–04, 2007–08, and 2011–12 National Postsecondary Student Aid Study (NPSAS:2000, NPSAS:04, NPSAS:08, and NPSAS:12). (This table was prepared April 2016.)

Table 331.37. Percentage of part-time or part-year undergraduates receiving financial aid, and average annual amount received, by source of aid and selected student characteristics: Selected years, 1999–2000 through 2011–12

[Standard errors appear in parentheses. Amounts in constant 2014–15 dollars]

Year and selected student characteristic	Number enrolled (in thousands)	Any aid — Percent receiving Total[2]	Federal[3]	Nonfederal	Any aid — Average amount Total[2]	Federal[3]	Nonfederal	Grants — Percent receiving Total	Pell	Grants — Average amount Total	Pell	Loans[1] Percent receiving	Loans[1] Average amount
1	2	3	4	5	6	7	8	9	10	11	12	13	14
1999–2000 Total	10,186 (—)	44.2 (0.66)	29.3 (0.34)	27.5 (0.72)	$5,260 (92)	$5,440 (67)	$2,660 (80)	35.3 (0.62)	17.9 (0.25)	$2,740 (47)	$2,090 (22)	18.6 (0.28)	$6,400 (88)
Sex													
Male	4,467 (—)	41.5 (0.91)	26.7 (0.60)	26.1 (0.80)	5,410 (177)	5,700 (151)	2,770 (119)	31.6 (0.79)	14.3 (0.48)	2,740 (67)	2,050 (42)	17.5 (0.66)	6,550 (171)
Female	5,719 (—)	46.4 (0.80)	31.4 (0.62)	28.7 (0.80)	5,150 (93)	5,260 (65)	2,580 (92)	38.2 (0.72)	20.8 (0.44)	2,750 (59)	2,120 (24)	19.4 (0.49)	6,300 (92)
Race/ethnicity													
White	6,682	41.9 (0.56)	26.7 (0.37)	26.9 (0.52)	5,300 (85)	5,510 (74)	2,790 (83)	32.6 (0.49)	14.4 (0.33)	2,740 (58)	1,980 (28)	18.1 (0.32)	6,420 (107)
Black	1,349	59.9 (2.01)	43.2 (1.52)	33.2 (2.84)	5,020 (263)	5,230 (181)	2,260 (196)	49.8 (2.26)	32.0 (1.30)	2,620 (109)	2,170 (47)	23.8 (1.46)	6,350 (197)
Hispanic	1,189	46.2 (1.92)	32.3 (1.52)	28.1 (1.66)	5,130 (226)	5,420 (238)	2,210 (149)	38.4 (1.55)	22.9 (1.16)	2,640 (100)	2,250 (67)	18.7 (1.35)	6,230 (304)
Asian	494	31.8 (2.19)	21.3 (1.69)	21.6 (1.69)	6,090 (683)	5,960 (522)	3,110 (342)	26.4 (1.90)	15.3 (1.25)	3,660 (308)	2,590 (149)	13.2 (1.61)	6,460 (536)
Pacific Islander	86	33.9 (5.65)	28.4 (5.17)	19.4 (3.47)	5,390 (500)	5,110 (803)	1,940 (608)	26.4 (4.13)	18.6 (3.88)	2,670 (381)	1,950 (266)	13.3 (3.33)	7,160 (1,051)
American Indian/Alaska Native	114	49.0 (4.71)	33.3 (4.13)	27.8 (3.76)	4,340 (428)	4,410 (411)	2,360 (411)	40.4 (4.34)	23.5 (3.88)	2,820 (333)	2,020 (111)	16.1 (2.69)	4,810 (428)
Two or more races	170	42.1 (3.26)	28.6 (2.70)	25.8 (2.43)	5,400 (492)	4,970 (424)	3,290 (458)	33.7 (3.17)	17.9 (2.46)	3,040 (378)	2,030 (201)	15.7 (1.61)	7,080 (554)
Other	103	35.9 (3.91)	23.7 (3.57)	24.5 (3.03)	6,860 (898)	5,790 (632)	4,460 (986)	28.7 (3.38)	15.4 (2.94)	3,200 (406)	2,140 (216)	17.2 (2.74)	8,170 (1,187)
Dependency status and family income													
Dependent	3,472	43.5 (0.82)	31.6 (0.65)	27.1 (0.67)	6,410 (157)	5,450 (86)	3,940 (179)	32.6 (0.69)	15.3 (0.50)	3,700 (134)	2,130 (48)	23.2 (0.55)	6,250 (109)
Low-income[4]	895	61.1 (1.17)	52.2 (1.38)	35.5 (1.30)	6,070 (220)	5,000 (149)	3,100 (175)	57.3 (1.13)	46.1 (1.37)	3,610 (151)	2,360 (52)	27.3 (1.08)	5,410 (193)
Middle-income[4]	1,798	40.4 (1.12)	27.1 (0.93)	25.9 (0.75)	6,340 (231)	5,510 (143)	4,120 (241)	26.8 (0.90)	6.6 (0.54)	3,580 (200)	1,330 (51)	23.5 (0.77)	6,250 (157)
High-income[4]	779	30.6 (1.56)	18.1 (1.12)	20.1 (1.16)	7,380 (369)	6,750 (308)	5,130 (456)	17.7 (1.15)	‡ (†)	4,410 (366)	‡ (†)	17.8 (1.16)	7,720 (334)
Independent	6,714	44.6 (0.82)	28.2 (0.39)	27.8 (0.93)	4,680 (107)	5,430 (81)	2,010 (69)	36.7 (0.79)	19.3 (0.30)	2,310 (37)	2,080 (23)	16.2 (0.38)	6,520 (117)
2003–04 Total	11,306 (—)	54.0 (0.82)	38.1 (0.81)	31.6 (0.59)	$5,810 (80)	$5,560 (81)	$3,220 (78)	43.1 (0.76)	23.5 (0.65)	$3,090 (44)	$2,390 (29)	24.5 (0.24)	$6,440 (94)
Sex													
Male	4,661	50.6 (1.05)	34.1 (0.91)	30.5 (0.73)	6,060 (128)	5,870 (107)	3,470 (117)	37.9 (0.92)	17.4 (0.63)	3,150 (64)	2,380 (36)	22.5 (0.48)	6,870 (164)
Female	6,646	56.3 (0.78)	40.9 (0.85)	32.3 (0.63)	5,660 (77)	5,380 (88)	3,060 (83)	46.8 (0.76)	27.8 (0.76)	3,050 (50)	2,400 (31)	25.9 (0.35)	6,180 (80)
Race/ethnicity													
White	6,841	51.5 (1.09)	33.8 (1.11)	31.7 (0.67)	5,740 (107)	5,640 (89)	3,300 (97)	40.0 (0.95)	18.3 (0.81)	2,990 (55)	2,270 (29)	23.6 (0.57)	6,590 (118)
Black	1,778	68.9 (0.94)	55.8 (1.09)	34.2 (1.06)	5,890 (197)	5,570 (193)	2,800 (112)	57.8 (0.91)	41.0 (0.93)	3,120 (77)	2,470 (50)	33.2 (1.60)	5,920 (134)
Hispanic	1,559	53.0 (1.24)	40.8 (1.10)	29.6 (1.15)	5,700 (152)	5,200 (120)	3,050 (141)	44.0 (1.17)	28.7 (0.97)	3,150 (82)	2,510 (37)	22.6 (0.94)	6,300 (201)
Asian	570	39.4 (2.05)	25.7 (1.65)	26.8 (1.67)	6,390 (286)	5,710 (227)	3,910 (277)	31.2 (1.86)	15.2 (1.13)	3,910 (223)	2,810 (120)	14.8 (1.23)	7,230 (419)
Pacific Islander	66	59.2 (3.54)	26.9 (4.62)	26.1 (4.75)	5,870 (862)	5,000 (571)	3,710 (803)	30.6 (4.95)	16.4 (3.80)	3,140 (530)	2,360 (293)	14.5 (3.44)	7,940 (1,313)
American Indian/Alaska Native	116	59.2 (3.54)	40.5 (3.38)	34.8 (3.02)	4,720 (414)	4,670 (354)	2,580 (320)	51.1 (3.38)	26.0 (3.39)	2,890 (286)	2,420 (136)	21.8 (3.00)	5,350 (681)
Two or more races	233	51.7 (1.97)	38.9 (2.03)	29.8 (1.98)	7,030 (437)	5,860 (295)	4,540 (481)	41.7 (2.15)	25.8 (2.09)	3,570 (273)	2,280 (128)	24.7 (1.96)	7,550 (464)
Other	143	61.6 (3.04)	48.2 (3.00)	35.7 (2.44)	6,440 (350)	5,850 (333)	3,210 (309)	48.3 (3.04)	30.2 (2.79)	3,280 (179)	2,710 (132)	28.8 (2.65)	6,800 (431)
Dependency status and family income													
Dependent	3,943	50.2 (1.05)	37.3 (0.89)	31.0 (0.78)	6,880 (165)	5,490 (107)	4,540 (156)	37.9 (0.94)	19.3 (0.67)	3,960 (95)	2,460 (33)	26.6 (0.58)	6,660 (174)
Low-income[4]	1,069	67.0 (1.17)	56.6 (1.09)	37.7 (1.09)	6,520 (166)	5,160 (106)	3,850 (160)	62.5 (1.17)	50.4 (1.02)	4,140 (103)	2,770 (37)	27.9 (0.82)	5,600 (176)
Middle-income[4]	2,018	48.4 (1.02)	34.6 (0.88)	30.9 (0.88)	6,790 (202)	5,440 (146)	4,550 (193)	32.4 (0.89)	11.1 (0.57)	3,620 (117)	1,710 (44)	29.4 (0.80)	6,610 (203)
High-income[4]	855	33.2 (1.72)	19.7 (1.13)	22.6 (1.30)	8,110 (357)	6,830 (293)	5,950 (351)	20.0 (1.22)	‡ (†)	4,530 (297)	‡ (†)	18.5 (1.08)	8,860 (357)
Independent	7,364	56.0 (0.86)	38.6 (0.90)	31.9 (0.62)	5,300 (65)	5,600 (96)	2,540 (57)	45.9 (0.80)	25.8 (0.74)	2,700 (34)	2,370 (32)	23.4 (0.34)	6,310 (80)
2007–08 Total	12,984 (—)	56.6 (0.47)	38.9 (0.31)	37.8 (0.47)	$6,580 (83)	$5,880 (59)	$3,810 (77)	43.0 (0.48)	23.8 (0.30)	$2,990 (44)	$2,150 (17)	30.1 (0.22)	$7,280 (87)
Sex													
Male	5,539	51.3 (0.66)	32.7 (0.57)	35.0 (0.64)	6,580 (130)	6,080 (137)	3,960 (99)	37.1 (0.64)	17.3 (0.41)	3,060 (64)	2,130 (31)	25.4 (0.55)	7,510 (159)
Female	7,445	60.6 (0.56)	43.4 (0.47)	39.9 (0.55)	6,580 (92)	5,770 (60)	3,710 (86)	47.4 (0.56)	28.7 (0.45)	2,960 (49)	2,160 (20)	33.7 (0.42)	7,150 (97)
Race/ethnicity													
White	7,723	54.0 (0.60)	35.3 (0.45)	37.0 (0.54)	6,590 (111)	5,920 (87)	3,990 (104)	39.3 (0.64)	18.9 (0.38)	3,000 (54)	2,080 (25)	29.3 (0.44)	7,310 (124)
Black	2,093	69.0 (1.00)	54.1 (1.10)	42.1 (0.89)	6,830 (136)	5,890 (92)	3,630 (120)	55.6 (0.97)	39.3 (0.92)	2,850 (60)	2,210 (36)	40.6 (1.13)	7,120 (142)
Hispanic	1,874	59.1 (1.07)	41.0 (0.91)	39.5 (1.15)	6,150 (188)	5,740 (159)	3,230 (137)	47.5 (1.11)	29.0 (0.83)	2,850 (85)	2,200 (38)	27.2 (0.91)	7,470 (204)
Asian	731	41.2 (1.54)	25.2 (1.25)	29.9 (1.37)	6,740 (372)	5,930 (335)	4,290 (343)	29.0 (1.32)	16.3 (1.00)	3,950 (311)	2,390 (88)	17.3 (1.16)	7,370 (367)
Pacific Islander	104	54.8 (4.74)	33.5 (4.88)	35.2 (4.17)	5,680 (515)	5,720 (561)	3,400 (463)	43.8 (4.67)	25.0 (4.76)	2,650 (342)	2,090 (167)	24.8 (4.56)	7,010 (745)
American Indian/Alaska Native	122	64.0 (3.87)	47.5 (3.74)	42.4 (3.91)	5,570 (612)	5,060 (624)	2,740 (287)	53.8 (3.82)	30.9 (3.84)	3,160 (371)	2,270 (124)	30.6 (3.99)	5,370 (620)
Two or more races	293	57.3 (2.28)	43.8 (2.08)	37.2 (2.08)	7,540 (319)	6,360 (263)	4,110 (334)	53.1 (2.12)	26.5 (1.72)	3,440 (219)	2,170 (78)	29.9 (1.98)	7,600 (335)
Other	43	57.8 (5.95)	37.0 (4.66)	38.1 (5.90)	6,220 (897)	5,510 (650)	4,090 (1,184)	42.0 (5.75)	23.4 (3.36)	2,360 (235)	2,220 (164)	29.5 (4.75)	8,550 (1,191)

See notes at end of table.

Table 331.37. Percentage of part-time or part-year undergraduates receiving financial aid, and average annual amount received, by source of aid and selected student characteristics: Selected years, 1999–2000 through 2011–12—Continued

[Standard errors appear in parentheses. Amounts in constant 2014–15 dollars]

Year and selected student characteristic	Number enrolled (in thousands)	Any aid — Percent receiving — Total[2]	Federal[3]	Nonfederal	Any aid — Average amount — Total[2]	Federal[3]	Nonfederal	Grants — Percent receiving — Total	Pell	Grants — Average amount — Total	Pell	Loans[1] — Percent receiving	Loans[1] — Average amount
1	2	3	4	5	6	7	8	9	10	11	12	13	14
Dependency status and family income													
Dependent	4,852 (—)	52.6 (0.66)	35.9 (0.52)	36.8 (0.59)	7,400 (167)	5,820 (116)	4,880 (149)	37.0 (0.61)	18.0 (0.39)	3,840 (103)	2,270 (28)	29.2 (0.51)	7,770 (168)
Low-income[4]	1,265 (—)	67.5 (1.16)	55.7 (1.16)	42.6 (1.03)	6,560 (162)	5,300 (137)	3,460 (110)	60.4 (1.09)	49.2 (1.07)	3,700 (82)	2,550 (28)	30.8 (1.12)	6,410 (187)
Middle-income[4]	2,575 (—)	49.8 (0.84)	31.7 (0.67)	36.5 (0.77)	7,580 (207)	5,880 (167)	5,250 (180)	31.3 (0.76)	9.7 (0.41)	3,730 (140)	1,550 (42)	30.6 (0.64)	7,870 (220)
High-income[4]	1,012 (—)	40.9 (1.11)	22.0 (0.94)	30.5 (0.95)	8,540 (332)	7,230 (341)	6,260 (315)	22.4 (0.89)	‡ (†)	4,680 (288)	‡ (†)	23.8 (0.91)	9,650 (332)
Independent	8,132 (—)	59.0 (0.59)	40.6 (0.41)	38.4 (0.58)	6,150 (68)	5,920 (56)	3,200 (67)	46.6 (0.58)	27.3 (0.38)	2,590 (32)	2,110 (20)	30.7 (0.29)	7,000 (85)
2011–12 Total	14,192 (—)	62.1 (1.05)	51.1 (1.10)	30.1 (0.60)	7,030 (73)	6,590 (66)	3,320 (90)	50.8 (0.87)	37.6 (0.85)	3,570 (47)	2,740 (22)	32.7 (0.48)	6,820 (58)
Sex													
Male	6,053	59.4 (1.28)	48.1 (1.40)	29.3 (0.72)	7,030 (109)	6,650 (89)	3,320 (108)	46.3 (1.02)	32.4 (1.07)	3,490 (67)	2,670 (29)	29.6 (0.72)	6,810 (89)
Female	8,139	64.2 (0.97)	53.3 (0.96)	30.7 (0.65)	7,030 (87)	6,550 (76)	3,320 (111)	54.1 (0.86)	41.4 (0.79)	3,610 (59)	2,780 (27)	35.1 (0.45)	6,830 (69)
Race/ethnicity[5]													
White	7,977	58.3 (1.10)	46.5 (1.15)	28.7 (0.62)	7,160 (99)	6,750 (80)	3,610 (115)	45.0 (0.88)	30.6 (0.84)	3,600 (67)	2,690 (25)	32.2 (0.64)	6,850 (79)
Black	2,500	74.8 (1.18)	67.7 (1.29)	29.1 (0.94)	7,320 (126)	6,690 (131)	3,250 (170)	65.0 (1.05)	56.3 (1.19)	3,540 (84)	2,750 (39)	42.8 (0.91)	6,720 (110)
Hispanic	2,422	63.9 (1.35)	52.8 (1.44)	33.9 (1.14)	6,280 (146)	6,020 (135)	2,470 (118)	55.7 (1.29)	43.3 (1.27)	3,320 (74)	2,790 (38)	27.4 (1.04)	6,770 (128)
Asian	688	51.5 (2.42)	35.7 (2.11)	33.5 (1.97)	7,020 (366)	6,510 (336)	3,870 (372)	44.0 (2.24)	26.7 (1.83)	4,370 (285)	3,000 (111)	19.5 (1.53)	7,500 (534)
Pacific Islander	77	60.8 (5.54)	48.7 (5.57)	27.8 (3.98)	6,600 (549)	6,730 (487)	2,660 (464)	48.4 (4.83)	36.4 (4.84)	3,270 (322)	2,810 (187)	30.9 (4.47)	7,420 (648)
American Indian/Alaska Native	142	68.4 (4.29)	60.8 (4.35)	33.3 (3.82)	6,870 (559)	6,360 (434)	2,510 (399)	59.1 (4.21)	46.7 (3.92)	3,500 (318)	2,760 (147)	33.9 (3.63)	6,480 (414)
Two or more races	386	66.3 (2.20)	53.7 (2.10)	36.7 (2.38)	7,300 (287)	6,680 (247)	3,420 (308)	56.7 (2.35)	42.0 (2.03)	3,720 (177)	2,680 (87)	35.8 (1.86)	6,660 (288)
Age													
15 to 23	6,306	60.8 (1.09)	49.2 (1.08)	33.2 (0.72)	7,200 (121)	6,190 (86)	4,020 (141)	50.3 (0.92)	35.7 (0.82)	4,180 (87)	2,820 (27)	30.9 (0.53)	6,680 (111)
24 to 29	3,205	64.8 (1.47)	55.0 (1.57)	28.0 (0.94)	6,810 (114)	6,690 (102)	2,600 (117)	53.3 (1.27)	42.4 (1.24)	3,050 (61)	2,640 (33)	34.9 (0.93)	6,710 (86)
30 or over	4,681	62.1 (1.16)	51.0 (1.23)	27.4 (0.71)	6,980 (89)	7,050 (102)	2,690 (106)	49.7 (0.98)	36.8 (1.02)	3,100 (63)	2,710 (31)	33.7 (0.71)	7,090 (79)
Marital status													
Not married[6]	10,588	62.9 (1.00)	52.4 (1.01)	30.8 (0.66)	7,130 (88)	6,490 (69)	3,520 (105)	52.1 (0.89)	39.4 (0.80)	3,720 (54)	2,760 (22)	33.9 (0.45)	6,780 (69)
Married	3,260	58.1 (1.51)	45.0 (1.60)	27.9 (0.81)	6,640 (134)	6,920 (138)	2,660 (134)	44.3 (1.16)	29.1 (1.24)	3,030 (83)	2,600 (45)	27.8 (0.95)	7,000 (101)
Separated	344	76.9 (2.18)	70.1 (2.43)	28.5 (1.92)	7,290 (258)	6,900 (258)	2,720 (276)	69.3 (2.29)	60.9 (2.42)	3,280 (114)	2,860 (90)	43.8 (2.44)	6,750 (219)
Dependency status and family income													
Dependent	5,090	58.7 (1.10)	46.8 (1.03)	33.8 (0.81)	7,340 (140)	6,140 (102)	4,230 (155)	47.2 (0.94)	31.8 (0.78)	4,410 (99)	2,830 (30)	30.3 (0.58)	6,870 (132)
Low-income[4]	1,342	77.9 (1.22)	71.1 (1.35)	38.4 (1.35)	6,640 (144)	5,510 (114)	3,240 (160)	75.5 (1.19)	69.1 (1.33)	4,330 (92)	3,130 (37)	31.8 (1.01)	5,510 (126)
Middle-income[4]	2,676	56.5 (1.16)	43.6 (1.11)	34.7 (0.97)	7,460 (149)	6,180 (117)	4,370 (191)	43.2 (1.06)	25.7 (0.79)	4,250 (139)	2,410 (42)	32.0 (0.70)	6,980 (158)
High-income[4]	1,071	40.1 (1.78)	24.4 (1.15)	25.8 (1.43)	8,610 (404)	8,220 (387)	5,600 (455)	21.8 (1.30)	0.5 ! (0.20)	5,510 (507)	‡ (†)	24.1 (1.16)	8,720 (378)
Independent	9,102	64.1 (1.16)	53.5 (1.26)	28.1 (0.66)	6,880 (71)	6,820 (83)	2,710 (88)	52.7 (0.99)	40.8 (1.04)	3,150 (44)	2,700 (25)	34.1 (0.58)	6,800 (53)
Housing status													
School-owned	582	74.4 (1.83)	56.8 (1.95)	54.4 (1.86)	13,120 (486)	9,300 (399)	8,230 (413)	60.7 (1.88)	31.6 (1.50)	7,840 (398)	2,860 (86)	51.9 (2.07)	8,910 (383)
Off-campus, not with parents	7,397	60.9 (1.33)	50.0 (1.38)	28.1 (0.68)	6,720 (79)	6,570 (82)	2,900 (94)	49.3 (1.07)	37.1 (1.07)	3,270 (50)	2,720 (26)	31.7 (0.66)	6,710 (70)
With parents	5,232	61.5 (1.20)	51.0 (1.19)	29.6 (0.94)	6,420 (124)	6,090 (98)	2,840 (161)	51.2 (1.12)	38.7 (1.11)	3,350 (83)	2,720 (36)	30.3 (0.75)	6,450 (97)
Attended more than one institution	982	67.6 (1.07)	57.0 (1.18)	33.3 (1.10)	8,140 (174)	7,580 (167)	3,530 (158)	53.0 (1.19)	38.8 (1.18)	3,890 (112)	2,970 (55)	42.0 (1.26)	7,400 (139)

—Not available.
†Not applicable.
!Interpret data with caution. The coefficient of variation (CV) for this estimate is between 30 and 50 percent.
‡Reporting standards not met. Either there are too few cases for a reliable estimate or the coefficient of variation (CV) is 50 percent or greater.
[1]Includes Parent Loans for Undergraduate Students (PLUS).
[2]Includes students who reported they were awarded aid but did not specify the source of aid.
[3]Includes Department of Veterans Affairs and Department of Defense benefits.
[4]Low-income students have family incomes below the 25th percentile, middle-income students have family incomes between the 25th to the 75th percentile, and high-income students have family incomes above the 75th percentile.
[5]The 2012 questionnaire did not offer students the option of choosing an "Other" race category.

[6]Includes students who were single, divorced, or widowed.
NOTE: Part-time or part-year undergraduates include those who were enrolled part time for 9 or more months and those who were enrolled less than 9 months either part time or full time. Data include undergraduates in degree-granting and non-degree-granting institutions. Constant dollars based on the Consumer Price Index, prepared by the Bureau of Labor Statistics, U.S. Department of Labor, adjusted to an academic-year basis. Detail may not sum to totals because of rounding and because some students receive multiple types of aid and aid from different sources. Data exclude Puerto Rico. Race categories exclude persons of Hispanic ethnicity.
SOURCE: U.S. Department of Education, National Center for Education Statistics, 1999–2000, 2003–04, 2007–08, and 2011–12 National Postsecondary Student Aid Study (NPSAS:2000, NPSAS:04, NPSAS:08, and NPSAS:12). (This table was prepared April 2016.)

Table 331.40. Average amount of financial aid awarded to full-time, full-year undergraduates, by type and source of aid and selected student characteristics: 2011–12

[In current dollars. Standard errors appear in parentheses]

Selected student characteristic	Any aid Total[1]	Any aid Federal[2]	Any aid Nonfederal	Grants Total	Grants Federal	Grants Nonfederal	Loans Total[3]	Loans Federal[3]	Loans Nonfederal	Work study Total[4]
1	2	3	4	5	6	7	8	9	10	11
All full-time, full-year undergraduates	$15,510 (106)	$10,820 (75)	$9,160 (110)	$9,230 (92)	$4,580 (20)	$8,590 (115)	$10,090 (75)	$9,160 (69)	$6,980 (187)	$2,250 (48)
Sex										
Male	15,710 (168)	11,000 (109)	9,300 (174)	9,420 (149)	4,550 (27)	8,750 (178)	10,180 (112)	9,240 (98)	6,910 (255)	2,300 (59)
Female	15,360 (134)	10,690 (88)	9,060 (141)	9,100 (109)	4,590 (26)	8,480 (140)	10,030 (94)	9,100 (91)	7,040 (275)	2,200 (57)
Race/ethnicity										
White	15,380 (146)	10,760 (101)	9,370 (138)	9,060 (115)	4,370 (27)	8,670 (144)	10,280 (99)	9,250 (97)	7,230 (181)	2,200 (67)
Black	16,120 (257)	11,890 (157)	8,270 (300)	8,600 (191)	4,780 (30)	7,850 (313)	9,990 (167)	9,320 (157)	6,360 (406)	2,320 (86)
Hispanic	14,730 (310)	10,190 (157)	8,200 (319)	9,280 (267)	4,750 (40)	7,920 (340)	9,450 (180)	8,670 (163)	6,330 (338)	2,350 (87)
Asian	16,230 (536)	9,520 (248)	10,690 (512)	11,740 (444)	4,780 (82)	10,310 (498)	9,480 (400)	8,500 (303)	7,500 (1,734)	2,350 (119)
Pacific Islander	17,820 (1,659)	11,910 (872)	11,100 (1,870)	11,960 (1,704)	4,990 (164)	11,100 (1,983)	10,750 (1,171)	10,240 (1,057)	‡ (†)	‡ (†)
American Indian/Alaska Native	14,760 (992)	9,980 (514)	8,930 (1,129)	9,350 (785)	4,970 (260)	8,490 (1,048)	8,000 (607)	7,300 (487)	6,620 ! (2,584)	‡ (†)
Two or more races	17,060 (544)	11,490 (295)	9,840 (573)	10,070 (416)	4,750 (94)	9,110 (536)	10,890 (353)	9,750 (300)	6,710 (955)	2,120 (153)
Age										
15 to 23 years old	16,190 (126)	10,460 (90)	9,960 (124)	10,340 (112)	4,570 (22)	9,380 (124)	10,300 (99)	9,320 (94)	6,900 (215)	2,220 (50)
24 to 29 years old	14,120 (240)	11,770 (165)	5,950 (355)	6,550 (202)	4,600 (39)	5,000 (389)	9,700 (123)	8,770 (82)	7,790 (482)	2,530 (159)
30 years old or over	13,160 (210)	11,620 (145)	4,910 (234)	5,800 (125)	4,570 (39)	4,000 (266)	9,460 (122)	8,760 (86)	6,750 (367)	2,550 (157)
Marital status										
Not married[5]	15,890 (111)	10,810 (79)	9,460 (115)	9,620 (97)	4,600 (20)	8,880 (117)	10,200 (81)	9,230 (75)	6,980 (197)	2,240 (47)
Married	12,390 (254)	10,790 (178)	5,380 (335)	5,990 (187)	4,400 (50)	4,680 (380)	9,270 (168)	8,610 (114)	6,800 (619)	2,630 (339)
Separated	13,130 (517)	11,360 (358)	4,970 (817)	6,010 (303)	4,750 (80)	4,070 (857)	8,950 (314)	8,260 (222)	8,150 (1,369)	‡ (†)
Dependency status and family income										
Dependent	16,460 (132)	10,500 (95)	10,150 (125)	10,580 (117)	4,520 (24)	9,570 (128)	10,440 (105)	9,450 (101)	6,840 (219)	2,210 (52)
Less than $20,000	16,380 (272)	10,530 (137)	8,800 (328)	11,150 (255)	5,460 (28)	8,560 (330)	8,010 (149)	7,590 (143)	5,180 (426)	2,140 (78)
$20,000–$39,999	17,000 (284)	10,440 (134)	9,450 (278)	11,530 (239)	5,010 (31)	9,250 (284)	8,350 (148)	7,880 (145)	4,610 (347)	2,250 (99)
$40,000–$59,999	16,700 (313)	9,770 (161)	9,930 (293)	10,030 (265)	2,980 (50)	9,380 (278)	9,700 (215)	8,930 (185)	5,330 (397)	2,250 (112)
$60,000–$79,999	16,080 (387)	9,870 (221)	10,330 (353)	9,690 (356)	2,090 (70)	9,680 (378)	10,660 (245)	9,460 (216)	6,680 (373)	2,160 (95)
$80,000–$99,999	16,180 (398)	10,460 (277)	10,690 (388)	9,880 (382)	2,350 (184)	9,880 (387)	11,620 (267)	10,360 (268)	6,950 (425)	2,110 (87)
$100,000 or more	16,310 (276)	11,380 (241)	11,160 (253)	10,300 (243)	2,900 (327)	10,300 (244)	12,810 (240)	11,360 (229)	8,530 (517)	2,280 (84)
Independent	13,540 (166)	11,390 (104)	5,820 (222)	6,520 (118)	4,640 (28)	5,010 (239)	9,410 (89)	8,600 (60)	7,350 (299)	2,480 (99)
Less than $10,000	14,400 (255)	11,600 (148)	6,210 (333)	7,510 (185)	5,070 (31)	5,490 (340)	9,180 (134)	8,360 (96)	7,560 (552)	2,330 (106)
$10,000–$19,999	13,700 (282)	11,590 (195)	5,580 (369)	6,160 (188)	4,440 (53)	4,760 (404)	9,440 (137)	8,650 (104)	7,170 (388)	2,700 (279)
$20,000–$29,999	12,670 (295)	11,120 (210)	4,840 (380)	5,550 (189)	4,450 (69)	3,920 (412)	9,080 (207)	8,440 (159)	6,550 (489)	3,230 (384)
$30,000–$49,999	12,920 (409)	11,390 (262)	5,820 (743)	5,750 (374)	4,320 (65)	4,940 (798)	9,650 (217)	8,810 (134)	7,440 (837)	1,920 (257)
$50,000 or more	11,770 (359)	10,420 (240)	5,940 (534)	4,690 (363)	2,750 (97)	4,820 (573)	10,410 (292)	9,330 (166)	7,890 (1,159)	‡ (†)
Housing status										
School-owned	22,220 (251)	12,340 (160)	13,880 (249)	14,390 (257)	4,690 (44)	13,060 (259)	11,410 (140)	10,190 (145)	7,690 (269)	2,140 (67)
Off-campus, not with parents	13,480 (169)	10,780 (113)	6,820 (172)	7,190 (123)	4,550 (28)	6,230 (191)	9,830 (124)	8,990 (110)	6,580 (268)	2,410 (69)
With parents	12,380 (167)	9,550 (98)	6,460 (193)	7,340 (141)	4,580 (36)	5,900 (197)	9,170 (132)	8,360 (100)	6,900 (439)	2,490 (92)
Attended more than one institution	13,960 (224)	10,670 (143)	7,530 (237)	7,810 (182)	4,430 (45)	7,010 (237)	9,500 (146)	8,750 (122)	6,170 (339)	2,050 (90)

†Not applicable.
!Interpret data with caution. The coefficient of variation (CV) for this estimate is between 30 and 50 percent.
‡Reporting standards not met (too few cases for a reliable estimate).
[1]Includes students who reported they were awarded aid, but did not specify the source or type of aid.
[2]Includes Department of Veterans Affairs and Department of Defense benefits.
[3]Includes Parent Loans for Undergraduate Students (PLUS).
[4]Details on federal and nonfederal work-study participants are not available.

[5]Includes students who were single, divorced, or widowed.
NOTE: Aid averages are for those students who received the specified type of aid. Detail may not sum to totals because of rounding and because some students receive multiple types of aid and aid from different sources. Full-time, full-year undergraduates were enrolled full time for 9 or more months in degree-granting and non-degree-granting institutions. Data include undergraduates at one or more institutions. Data include Puerto Rico. Race categories exclude persons of Hispanic ethnicity.
SOURCE: U.S. Department of Education, National Center for Education Statistics, 2011–12 National Postsecondary Student Aid Study (NPSAS:12). (This table was prepared January 2014.)

Table 331.45. Average amount of financial aid awarded to part-time or part-year undergraduates, by type and source of aid and selected student characteristics: 2011–12

[In current dollars. Standard errors appear in parentheses]

Selected student characteristic	Any aid — Total[1]	Any aid — Federal[2]	Any aid — Nonfederal	Grants — Total	Grants — Federal	Grants — Nonfederal	Loans — Total[3]	Loans — Federal[3]	Loans — Nonfederal	Work study — Total[4]
1	2	3	4	5	6	7	8	9	10	11
All part-time or part-year undergraduates	$6,760 (70)	$6,340 (63)	$3,190 (86)	$3,430 (45)	$2,680 (22)	$2,790 (86)	$6,560 (55)	$6,270 (47)	$4,420 (131)	$2,350 (82)
Sex										
Male	6,760 (105)	6,400 (86)	3,200 (104)	3,360 (64)	2,620 (28)	2,770 (107)	6,550 (86)	6,240 (76)	4,480 (191)	2,600 (157)
Female	6,760 (84)	6,300 (73)	3,190 (107)	3,470 (57)	2,710 (27)	2,810 (111)	6,570 (66)	6,280 (56)	4,370 (163)	2,160 (107)
Race/ethnicity										
White	6,880 (95)	6,490 (77)	3,470 (111)	3,460 (64)	2,630 (25)	3,030 (113)	6,590 (76)	6,280 (65)	4,740 (190)	2,310 (112)
Black	7,040 (121)	6,440 (126)	3,130 (164)	3,400 (81)	2,690 (38)	2,810 (189)	6,470 (106)	6,210 (103)	3,850 (202)	2,210 (254)
Hispanic	6,040 (140)	5,790 (130)	2,370 (114)	3,200 (71)	2,740 (39)	1,970 (104)	6,510 (123)	6,200 (107)	4,150 (238)	2,910 (246)
Asian	6,750 (352)	6,260 (323)	3,720 (358)	4,200 (274)	2,920 (107)	3,480 (356)	7,210 (514)	7,000 (514)	3,980 (516)	2,040 (205)
Pacific Islander	6,350 (528)	6,470 (469)	2,560 (447)	3,140 (309)	2,740 (185)	2,060 (457)	7,140 (514)	6,840 (586)	‡ (†)	‡ (†)
American Indian/Alaska Native	6,610 (537)	6,110 (417)	2,410 (384)	3,370 (305)	2,720 (154)	2,240 (359)	6,230 (399)	6,030 (375)	‡ (†)	‡ (†)
Two or more races	7,020 (276)	6,430 (237)	3,290 (296)	3,570 (170)	2,610 (83)	2,880 (285)	6,410 (277)	6,140 (238)	4,400 (758)	1,870 (309)
Age										
15 to 23 years old	6,920 (116)	5,950 (83)	3,860 (136)	4,020 (84)	2,760 (27)	3,540 (135)	6,420 (107)	6,110 (101)	4,370 (173)	2,290 (101)
24 to 29 years old	6,540 (110)	6,430 (98)	2,500 (113)	2,930 (58)	2,580 (32)	1,950 (98)	6,450 (82)	6,110 (73)	4,670 (223)	2,640 (239)
30 years old or over	6,710 (85)	6,780 (98)	2,590 (102)	2,990 (60)	2,650 (31)	2,140 (112)	6,820 (76)	6,570 (67)	4,310 (270)	2,300 (198)
Marital status[5]										
Not married[5]	6,860 (85)	6,240 (66)	3,390 (101)	3,580 (52)	2,700 (21)	2,970 (100)	6,520 (66)	6,200 (57)	4,520 (150)	2,300 (80)
Married	6,380 (129)	6,660 (133)	2,550 (129)	2,910 (79)	2,550 (44)	2,240 (132)	6,730 (97)	6,560 (87)	3,930 (248)	2,820 (404)
Separated	7,010 (248)	6,630 (248)	2,610 (265)	3,150 (110)	2,800 (87)	1,950 (251)	6,490 (211)	6,110 (200)	4,570 (585)	‡ (†)
Dependency status and family income										
Dependent	7,050 (135)	5,900 (98)	4,070 (149)	4,240 (96)	2,770 (30)	3,730 (146)	6,600 (127)	6,270 (118)	4,430 (198)	2,230 (105)
Less than $20,000	6,530 (171)	5,420 (131)	3,140 (180)	4,190 (106)	3,080 (45)	2,930 (190)	5,270 (136)	5,080 (136)	3,640 (255)	2,050 (343)
$20,000–$39,999	6,690 (215)	5,360 (124)	3,640 (334)	4,340 (188)	2,930 (45)	3,380 (340)	5,660 (166)	5,410 (158)	3,880 (418)	1,910 (177)
$40,000–$59,999	6,990 (260)	5,740 (194)	3,530 (220)	3,560 (156)	2,020 (53)	3,230 (211)	6,790 (252)	6,440 (254)	3,650 (388)	2,160 (261)
$60,000–$79,999	7,070 (344)	6,210 (258)	4,270 (299)	3,910 (262)	1,620 (118)	3,930 (289)	6,760 (288)	6,480 (257)	4,110 (405)	2,290 (280)
$80,000–$99,999	7,260 (352)	6,280 (272)	4,960 (328)	4,310 (324)	1,760 (244)	4,310 (343)	7,060 (298)	6,420 (271)	5,770 (554)	2,170 (248)
$100,000 or more	8,280 (374)	7,810 (344)	5,440 (392)	5,220 (425)	4,390 (605)	5,160 (433)	8,380 (345)	8,070 (351)	5,310 (551)	2,830 (268)
Independent	6,610 (69)	6,560 (80)	2,600 (85)	3,030 (42)	2,640 (25)	2,140 (88)	6,540 (51)	6,260 (42)	4,410 (169)	2,530 (145)
Less than $10,000	6,800 (110)	6,430 (101)	2,710 (135)	3,330 (59)	2,860 (31)	2,200 (139)	6,010 (75)	5,690 (66)	4,620 (235)	2,280 (177)
$10,000–$19,999	6,990 (131)	6,590 (137)	2,580 (137)	3,090 (68)	2,580 (40)	2,050 (152)	6,490 (95)	6,190 (91)	4,480 (218)	2,710 (319)
$20,000–$29,999	6,610 (143)	6,520 (160)	2,500 (161)	2,910 (80)	2,560 (51)	1,970 (147)	6,580 (131)	6,300 (111)	4,250 (372)	2,490 (613)
$30,000–$49,999	6,370 (152)	6,610 (135)	2,470 (150)	2,820 (97)	2,610 (51)	1,970 (140)	6,950 (128)	6,720 (118)	4,540 (548)	3,600 (530)
$50,000 or more	6,000 (172)	6,770 (192)	2,650 (137)	2,420 (108)	1,700 (63)	2,400 (138)	7,350 (135)	7,180 (132)	3,940 (318)	2,750 (709)
Housing status										
School-owned	12,620 (468)	8,940 (383)	7,910 (397)	7,540 (382)	2,870 (81)	7,420 (428)	8,560 (368)	7,880 (353)	6,350 (709)	1,700 (143)
Off-campus, not with parents	6,460 (120)	6,320 (79)	2,790 (91)	3,140 (48)	2,650 (26)	2,340 (98)	6,450 (67)	6,180 (59)	4,430 (188)	2,550 (165)
With parents	6,170 (167)	5,850 (94)	2,730 (155)	3,220 (80)	2,660 (36)	2,380 (149)	6,200 (93)	5,960 (76)	4,010 (200)	2,610 (156)
Attended more than one institution	7,830 (167)	7,290 (161)	3,390 (152)	3,740 (108)	2,900 (53)	2,960 (163)	7,110 (133)	6,760 (129)	4,220 (255)	2,180 (223)

†Not applicable.
‡Reporting standards not met (too few cases for a reliable estimate).
[1]Includes students who reported they were awarded aid, but did not specify the source or type of aid.
[2]Includes Department of Veterans Affairs and Department of Defense benefits.
[3]Includes Parent Loans for Undergraduate Students (PLUS).
[4]Details on federal and nonfederal work-study participants are not available.
[5]Includes students who were single, divorced, or widowed.

NOTE: Aid averages are for those students who received the specified type of aid. Detail may not sum to totals because of rounding and because some students receive multiple types of aid and aid from different sources. Part-time or part-year undergraduates include students enrolled part time for 9 or more months and students enrolled less than 9 months either part time or full time. Data include undergraduates in degree-granting and non-degree-granting institutions. Data exclude Puerto Rico. Race categories exclude persons of Hispanic ethnicity.
SOURCE: U.S. Department of Education, National Center for Education Statistics, 2011–12 National Postsecondary Student Aid Study (NPSAS:12). (This table was prepared January 2014.)

Table 331.50. Amount borrowed, aid status, and sources of aid for full-time and part-time undergraduates, by control and level of institution: 2007–08 and 2011–12

[Standard errors appear in parentheses]

Control and level of institution	Number of undergraduates[1] (in thousands)	Cumulative amount borrowed for undergraduate education[2] — In current dollars		In constant 2014–15 dollars[3]		Aid status (percent of students) — Nonaided		Source of aid — Any aid[4,5]		Federal[5]		State		Institutional		Other[4]	
1	2	3		4		5		6		7		8		9		10	
2007–08																	
Full-time, full-year students																	
All institutions	7,527	(—)	$15,270	(128)	$17,070	(143)	19.9	(0.28)	80.1	(0.28)	63.9	(0.31)	28.3	(0.39)	34.5	(0.47)	32.9	(0.32)
Public	5,159	(—)	13,170	(117)	14,730	(131)	24.6	(0.33)	75.4	(0.33)	58.7	(0.36)	29.8	(0.42)	27.1	(0.39)	26.5	(0.32)
4-year doctoral	2,522	(—)	14,720	(169)	16,450	(189)	22.2	(0.40)	77.8	(0.40)	59.6	(0.48)	30.6	(0.61)	33.6	(0.59)	30.8	(0.43)
Other 4-year	1,031	(—)	13,510	(203)	15,100	(226)	17.5	(0.59)	82.5	(0.59)	67.6	(0.68)	34.6	(0.96)	25.5	(0.91)	29.6	(0.68)
2-year	1,584	(—)	8,710	(176)	9,740	(197)	33.1	(0.69)	66.9	(0.69)	51.4	(0.73)	25.8	(0.76)	18.1	(0.71)	17.6	(0.56)
Less-than-2-year	22	(—)	10,000	(996)	11,180	(1,114)	30.9	(3.87)	69.1	(3.87)	58.6	(3.84)	17.1	(4.00)	‡	(†)	21.6	(3.23)
Private, nonprofit	1,672	(—)	19,610	(335)	21,920	(374)	10.5	(0.57)	89.5	(0.57)	71.2	(0.62)	32.0	(1.05)	68.5	(1.58)	43.7	(0.70)
4-year doctoral	844	(—)	20,980	(479)	23,460	(535)	14.5	(0.93)	85.5	(0.93)	67.1	(1.12)	27.5	(0.94)	66.2	(1.84)	42.0	(1.01)
Other 4-year	814	(—)	18,430	(456)	20,600	(510)	6.4	(0.74)	93.6	(0.74)	75.1	(1.12)	36.5	(1.99)	71.7	(2.48)	45.6	(1.07)
Less-than-4-year	14	(—)	13,970	(1,706)	15,620	(1,907)	8.0 !	(2.79)	92.0	(2.79)	84.4	(3.65)	35.4 !	(11.44)	23.3 !	(8.37)	31.2	(6.68)
Private, for-profit	695	(—)	16,170	(390)	18,070	(435)	7.4	(0.70)	92.6	(0.70)	84.6	(1.24)	8.0	(1.06)	7.9	(1.61)	54.8	(1.29)
2-year and above	599	(—)	17,160	(456)	19,180	(510)	7.6	(0.79)	92.4	(0.79)	84.2	(1.41)	8.4	(1.21)	7.9	(1.86)	57.2	(1.44)
Less-than-2-year	96	(—)	9,910	(220)	11,080	(245)	6.4	(0.82)	93.6	(0.82)	87.4	(1.74)	5.5 !	(1.82)	8.0	(1.69)	40.0	(1.49)
Part-time or part-year students																	
All institutions	12,984	(—)	$12,820	(117)	$14,340	(131)	43.4	(0.47)	56.6	(0.47)	38.9	(0.31)	10.5	(0.23)	12.0	(0.36)	24.0	(0.35)
Public	10,386	(—)	11,810	(114)	13,200	(128)	50.8	(0.54)	49.2	(0.54)	30.3	(0.36)	10.6	(0.25)	10.6	(0.33)	19.0	(0.31)
4-year doctoral	1,683	(—)	16,390	(250)	18,320	(279)	35.8	(0.73)	64.2	(0.73)	44.0	(0.74)	15.9	(0.57)	16.6	(0.59)	26.7	(0.77)
Other 4-year	1,150	(—)	13,710	(287)	15,330	(321)	40.0	(1.02)	60.0	(1.02)	42.9	(0.95)	11.2	(0.56)	7.4	(0.42)	25.3	(0.96)
2-year	7,477	(—)	9,360	(152)	10,460	(170)	55.8	(0.68)	44.3	(0.68)	25.2	(0.42)	9.4	(0.32)	9.8	(0.44)	16.4	(0.36)
Less-than-2-year	76	(—)	8,140	(574)	9,100	(642)	53.3	(2.17)	46.7	(2.17)	31.4	(1.91)	9.9 !	(3.86)	4.0 !	(1.25)	15.5	(1.43)
Private, nonprofit	1,109	(—)	18,880	(365)	21,100	(408)	23.5	(0.92)	76.5	(0.92)	53.7	(0.86)	15.1	(0.83)	29.1	(1.22)	41.9	(0.97)
4-year doctoral	455	(—)	20,610	(584)	23,050	(653)	24.8	(1.38)	75.2	(1.38)	48.9	(1.82)	12.2	(0.88)	31.3	(2.06)	43.6	(1.46)
Other 4-year	599	(—)	18,130	(501)	20,270	(560)	22.2	(1.32)	77.8	(1.32)	56.4	(1.50)	17.2	(1.26)	29.1	(1.54)	41.8	(1.49)
Less-than-4-year	54	(—)	13,220	(1,901)	14,780	(2,125)	27.7	(4.93)	72.4	(4.93)	63.0	(3.97)	16.6 !	(6.35)	9.9 !	(4.11)	27.9	(2.67)
Private, for-profit	1,489	(—)	12,580	(336)	14,070	(375)	6.6	(0.56)	93.4	(0.56)	87.8	(0.72)	6.3	(0.68)	9.0	(1.80)	45.2	(1.66)
2-year and above	1,169	(—)	13,500	(410)	15,090	(459)	5.2	(0.70)	94.8	(0.70)	89.9	(0.88)	6.9	(0.81)	9.3	(2.21)	47.6	(2.03)
Less-than-2-year	319	(—)	8,980	(203)	10,040	(227)	11.8	(0.84)	88.2	(0.84)	80.0	(1.21)	4.1	(0.93)	7.8	(2.05)	36.5	(1.46)
2011–12																	
Full-time, full-year students																	
All institutions	8,864	(—)	$18,960	(146)	$19,720	(152)	15.6	(0.36)	84.4	(0.36)	72.8	(0.51)	24.0	(0.43)	33.9	(0.48)	28.1	(0.36)
Public	5,997	(—)	16,550	(165)	17,210	(171)	19.6	(0.47)	80.4	(0.47)	68.4	(0.61)	26.5	(0.58)	26.2	(0.59)	24.3	(0.36)
4-year doctoral	2,893	(—)	18,080	(196)	18,810	(204)	16.1	(0.46)	83.9	(0.46)	70.9	(0.47)	30.6	(0.68)	33.2	(0.90)	28.1	(0.49)
Other 4-year	969	(—)	16,980	(347)	17,660	(361)	16.5	(0.93)	83.5	(0.93)	72.7	(1.34)	30.2	(1.36)	22.9	(1.33)	27.5	(0.90)
2-year	2,104	(—)	12,740	(416)	13,250	(433)	25.5	(1.03)	74.5	(1.03)	63.0	(1.24)	19.3	(0.98)	18.5	(0.97)	17.8	(0.57)
Less-than-2-year	31	(—)	12,740	(3,005)	13,250	(3,125)	28.4	(4.50)	71.6	(4.50)	67.8	(4.72)	18.2 !	(6.85)	‡	(†)	18.9	(4.08)
Private, nonprofit	1,875	(—)	21,780	(425)	22,650	(442)	8.4	(0.55)	91.6	(0.55)	76.1	(0.75)	25.3	(0.87)	73.7	(0.97)	39.6	(0.96)
4-year doctoral	990	(—)	22,190	(756)	23,080	(786)	9.6	(0.84)	90.4	(0.84)	74.3	(0.94)	23.3	(1.29)	74.5	(1.29)	38.9	(1.50)
Other 4-year	849	(—)	21,500	(466)	22,360	(484)	6.9	(0.68)	93.1	(0.68)	78.0	(1.20)	28.0	(1.24)	74.3	(1.38)	40.5	(1.08)
Less-than-4-year	36	(—)	17,230	(1,989)	17,920	(2,064)	9.8	(4.12)	90.2	(4.12)	78.1	(5.04)	19.5 !	(7.60)	34.5 !	(11.90)	38.4	(4.24)
Private, for-profit	992	(—)	23,830	(303)	24,780	(315)	5.2	(0.46)	94.8	(0.46)	93.1	(0.51)	6.9	(0.70)	4.8	(0.72)	29.2	(0.89)
2-year and above	859	(—)	25,440	(351)	26,460	(366)	5.4	(0.53)	94.6	(0.53)	92.8	(0.59)	7.5	(0.78)	5.4	(0.83)	30.7	(0.96)
Less-than-2-year	133	(—)	13,080	(356)	13,600	(370)	4.1	(0.75)	95.9	(0.75)	95.2	(0.79)	‡	(†)	‡	(†)	19.3	(2.30)
Part-time or part-year students																	
All institutions	14,192	(—)	$16,350	(186)	$17,010	(194)	37.9	(1.05)	62.1	(1.05)	51.1	(1.10)	10.1	(0.36)	12.1	(0.52)	16.4	(0.34)
Public	10,929	(—)	14,870	(202)	15,460	(210)	44.0	(1.18)	56.0	(1.18)	44.5	(1.22)	10.8	(0.41)	11.8	(0.64)	13.4	(0.36)
4-year doctoral	1,875	(—)	20,940	(368)	21,780	(383)	33.9	(1.04)	66.1	(1.04)	53.4	(0.81)	14.8	(0.60)	13.9	(0.88)	20.7	(0.73)
Other 4-year	1,477	(—)	15,890	(452)	16,520	(470)	40.5	(1.46)	59.5	(1.46)	49.7	(1.66)	11.7	(0.75)	7.0	(0.80)	16.9	(0.94)
2-year	7,521	(—)	12,080	(248)	12,560	(258)	47.3	(1.36)	52.7	(1.36)	41.2	(1.39)	9.6	(0.53)	12.3	(0.88)	10.9	(0.39)
Less-than-2-year	56	(—)	11,420	(2,303)	11,880	(2,395)	29.8	(4.21)	70.2	(4.21)	60.3	(4.47)	19.7	(5.84)	3.1 !	(1.37)	9.2	(2.44)
Private, nonprofit	1,135	(—)	23,120	(850)	24,040	(884)	22.6	(1.47)	77.4	(1.47)	61.0	(1.61)	13.5	(1.28)	30.2	(1.95)	28.7	(1.58)
4-year doctoral	557	(—)	24,890	(1,518)	25,890	(1,579)	24.0	(1.87)	76.0	(1.87)	57.9	(2.12)	9.5	(1.49)	30.1	(2.15)	28.1	(2.61)
Other 4-year	527	(—)	22,300	(946)	23,190	(984)	20.8	(2.42)	79.2	(2.42)	64.0	(2.54)	18.6	(2.12)	32.3	(3.36)	30.2	(2.14)
Less-than-4-year	51	(—)	12,630	(1,266)	13,140	(1,317)	25.7	(4.47)	74.3	(4.47)	64.3	(3.22)	‡	(†)	‡	(†)	18.2	(4.18)
Private, for-profit	2,128	(—)	17,450	(245)	18,150	(255)	14.6	(1.02)	85.4	(1.02)	79.7	(0.83)	4.2	(0.52)	3.7	(0.71)	25.3	(1.09)
2-year and above	1,790	(—)	18,680	(281)	19,420	(292)	14.7	(1.20)	85.3	(1.20)	78.8	(0.97)	4.2	(0.49)	3.6	(0.68)	27.0	(1.22)
Less-than-2-year	337	(—)	11,170	(344)	11,610	(358)	14.1	(1.39)	85.9	(1.39)	84.6	(1.40)	‡	(†)	‡	(†)	16.3	(1.71)

—Not available.
†Not applicable.
!Interpret data with caution. The coefficient of variation (CV) for this estimate is between 30 and 50 percent.
‡Reporting standards not met. The coefficient of variation (CV) for this estimate is 50 percent or greater.
[1]Numbers of undergraduates may not equal figures reported in other tables, since these data are based on a sample survey of students who enrolled at any time during the academic year.
[2]Includes only those students who borrowed to finance their undergraduate education. Excludes loans from family sources.

[3]Constant dollars based on the Consumer Price Index, prepared by the Bureau of Labor Statistics, U.S. Department of Labor, adjusted to a school-year basis.
[4]Includes students who reported that they were awarded aid, but did not specify the source of the aid.
[5]Includes Department of Veterans Affairs and Department of Defense benefits.
NOTE: Excludes students whose attendance status was not reported. Detail may not sum to totals because of rounding and because some students receive multiple types of aid and aid from different sources. Data exclude Puerto Rico. Some data have been revised from previously published figures.
SOURCE: U.S. Department of Education, National Center for Education Statistics, 2007–08 and 2011–12 National Postsecondary Student Aid Study (NPSAS:08 and NPSAS:12). (This table was prepared September 2015.)

Table 331.60. Percentage of full-time, full-year undergraduates receiving financial aid, by type and source of aid and control and level of institution: Selected years, 1992–93 through 2011–12

[Standard errors appear in parentheses]

Control and level of institution	Any aid			Grants			Loans			Work study[1]	
	Total[2]	Federal[3]	Nonfederal	Total	Federal	Nonfederal	Total[4]	Federal[4]	Nonfederal	Total	Federal
1	2	3	4	5	6	7	8	9	10	11	12
1992–93, all institutions	58.2 (0.50)	45.0 (0.50)	37.9 (0.58)	48.3 (0.51)	28.6 (0.47)	34.9 (0.51)	34.0 (0.61)	33.1 (0.61)	2.7 (0.22)	10.3 (0.38)	6.8 (0.30)
Public	52.4 (0.67)	39.8 (0.60)	32.7 (0.69)	42.8 (0.58)	27.4 (0.50)	29.6 (0.64)	27.1 (0.57)	26.3 (0.54)	2.0 (0.27)	6.8 (0.36)	4.2 (0.23)
4-year doctoral	54.0 (0.94)	39.1 (0.80)	34.7 (0.82)	42.2 (0.80)	23.6 (0.65)	31.2 (0.79)	33.1 (0.86)	32.3 (0.86)	2.4 (0.29)	7.1 (0.50)	4.3 (0.34)
Other 4-year	56.5 (1.07)	45.4 (1.19)	36.7 (1.27)	45.4 (1.29)	31.1 (1.24)	32.4 (1.32)	34.4 (0.98)	33.4 (0.93)	2.8 (0.69)	9.7 (0.77)	5.6 (0.57)
2-year	47.2 (1.93)	36.0 (1.70)	27.0 (1.62)	41.9 (1.68)	29.9 (1.43)	25.7 (1.65)	12.7 (1.23)	12.3 (1.17)	0.7! (0.28)	4.1 (0.77)	3.0 (0.54)
Less-than-2-year	35.4 (3.60)	31.6 (4.08)	15.7 (4.47)	30.3 (2.53)	26.6 (2.91)	13.3! (4.75)	3.0! (1.30)	3.0! (1.30)	‡ (†)	‡ (†)	‡ (†)
Private, nonprofit	69.5 (1.38)	52.3 (1.42)	58.9 (1.49)	62.0 (1.36)	25.8 (1.59)	55.9 (1.47)	47.6 (1.33)	45.9 (1.40)	5.1 (0.47)	22.5 (1.10)	16.1 (1.00)
4-year doctoral	63.5 (1.65)	44.3 (1.37)	54.7 (1.76)	56.0 (1.61)	17.0 (0.97)	52.7 (1.68)	41.7 (1.27)	39.8 (1.27)	6.1 (0.74)	18.9 (1.33)	13.2 (1.40)
Other 4-year	75.4 (1.91)	59.4 (2.08)	64.3 (2.46)	68.4 (2.11)	33.0 (2.79)	60.6 (2.81)	53.8 (1.88)	52.4 (1.99)	4.3 (0.80)	27.7 (1.75)	20.1 (1.58)
Less-than-4-year	70.7 (3.80)	59.5 (4.15)	44.4 (6.26)	56.6 (4.50)	40.9 (3.70)	39.2 (6.82)	43.5 (5.33)	41.7 (5.08)	2.8! (1.17)	4.1! (1.90)	2.3! (1.00)
Private, for-profit	77.0 (2.18)	72.0 (2.17)	16.8 (2.32)	56.2 (1.75)	49.9 (1.71)	13.6 (2.41)	55.4 (4.82)	55.1 (4.79)	2.2! (0.91)	1.9! (0.78)	0.7! (0.25)
2-year and above	82.2 (4.50)	76.5 (4.35)	24.1 (4.65)	50.3 (4.06)	40.5 (2.52)	21.0 (5.02)	48.5 (5.41)	68.5 (5.41)	‡ (†)	3.6! (1.62)	1.4! (0.54)
Less-than-2-year	73.2 (2.46)	68.8 (2.64)	11.5 (2.49)	60.4 (2.46)	56.7 (2.31)	8.3! (2.53)	46.0 (5.63)	45.4 (5.56)	1.5! (0.53)	† (†)	0.2! (0.09)
1999–2000, all institutions	71.9 (0.59)	56.7 (0.44)	52.3 (0.67)	58.5 (0.60)	29.0 (0.44)	49.0 (0.69)	45.6 (0.44)	44.5 (0.41)	6.8 (0.31)	11.6 (0.46)	8.9 (0.36)
Public	66.9 (0.73)	51.6 (0.51)	46.4 (0.86)	52.8 (0.69)	29.3 (0.43)	43.0 (0.81)	37.9 (0.50)	36.9 (0.46)	4.4 (0.30)	7.5 (0.47)	5.6 (0.38)
4-year doctoral	71.1 (0.79)	54.4 (0.68)	49.7 (0.77)	53.3 (0.87)	25.1 (0.74)	45.6 (0.68)	49.0 (0.73)	47.9 (0.69)	5.6 (0.41)	8.7 (0.51)	6.1 (0.42)
Other 4-year	75.7 (1.29)	63.0 (1.43)	50.6 (2.13)	57.5 (1.38)	33.7 (1.53)	46.6 (2.10)	51.5 (1.66)	50.7 (1.66)	4.7 (0.45)	11.0 (1.33)	8.1 (1.12)
2-year	55.7 (1.47)	40.5 (1.08)	39.5 (1.51)	49.2 (1.34)	31.9 (0.97)	37.3 (1.49)	14.9 (0.75)	13.9 (0.62)	2.5 (0.40)	3.8 (0.69)	3.5 (0.68)
Less-than-2-year	58.4 (6.03)	45.0 (6.96)	35.0 (5.14)	48.4 (7.50)	39.7 (7.40)	26.4 (6.54)	4.7! (2.14)	4.7! (2.13)	‡ (†)	# (†)	# (†)
Private, nonprofit	84.0 (0.77)	67.3 (0.75)	73.5 (1.37)	74.9 (1.13)	24.2 (1.24)	71.1 (1.42)	62.6 (0.83)	61.2 (0.89)	14.2 (0.89)	25.8 (1.27)	19.8 (0.88)
4-year doctoral	79.0 (1.03)	62.7 (1.22)	71.0 (1.27)	70.4 (1.19)	20.6 (1.80)	68.2 (1.33)	60.0 (1.16)	58.4 (1.19)	16.0 (1.08)	25.7 (1.16)	21.7 (1.05)
Other 4-year	88.7 (1.08)	72.2 (1.31)	76.3 (2.29)	78.9 (1.63)	26.3 (1.80)	74.1 (2.28)	67.4 (1.41)	66.0 (1.45)	13.4 (1.20)	26.7 (2.24)	19.0 (1.55)
Less-than-4-year	77.2 (4.01)	53.3 (2.88)	64.0 (5.11)	72.7 (4.37)	37.0 (3.48)	62.5 (5.62)	27.4 (2.59)	27.3 (2.60)	3.1 (0.62)	13.7 (2.56)	10.0 (2.71)
Private, for-profit	89.9 (1.11)	87.0 (1.39)	33.4 (3.08)	63.5 (2.14)	52.9 (2.59)	26.6 (2.83)	82.7 (2.19)	82.0 (1.50)	7.8 (1.62)	2.2 (0.87)	1.9! (0.86)
2-year and above	88.6 (1.50)	85.7 (1.77)	37.5 (4.17)	60.8 (2.81)	47.3 (3.29)	32.6 (3.88)	82.9 (2.19)	82.2 (2.19)	6.9 (2.04)	2.9! (1.17)	2.5! (1.15)
Less-than-2-year	93.7 (1.32)	91.1 (1.88)	20.8 (2.75)	71.9 (2.96)	69.8 (2.97)	8.6 (2.27)	81.9 (3.65)	81.5 (3.64)	10.4 (1.93)	‡ (†)	‡ (0.18)
2007–08, all institutions	80.1 (0.28)	63.9 (0.31)	63.7 (0.36)	64.6 (0.37)	33.1 (0.29)	53.6 (0.41)	54.8 (0.32)	51.0 (0.32)	20.5 (0.31)	13.8 (0.29)	10.6 (0.23)
Public	75.4 (0.33)	58.7 (0.36)	58.0 (0.39)	59.2 (0.38)	32.3 (0.29)	49.6 (0.40)	46.2 (0.34)	42.7 (0.33)	14.2 (0.25)	9.5 (0.25)	7.1 (0.22)
4-year doctoral	77.8 (0.40)	59.6 (0.48)	62.8 (0.49)	59.9 (0.55)	27.8 (0.38)	53.8 (0.53)	54.7 (0.50)	50.8 (0.50)	17.4 (0.38)	10.2 (0.35)	7.6 (0.32)
Other 4-year	82.5 (0.59)	67.6 (0.68)	62.7 (0.80)	63.2 (0.81)	35.2 (0.66)	52.7 (0.85)	57.5 (0.72)	54.4 (0.72)	16.4 (0.61)	11.5 (0.60)	8.7 (0.45)
2-year	66.9 (0.69)	51.4 (0.73)	55.5 (0.79)	55.5 (0.63)	37.3 (0.65)	41.3 (0.76)	25.5 (0.59)	22.3 (0.57)	7.8 (0.37)	7.1 (0.36)	5.5 (0.29)
Less-than-2-year	69.1 (3.87)	58.6 (3.84)	33.0 (4.74)	56.6 (3.58)	50.0 (3.97)	16.1 (2.88)	26.5 (4.79)	23.6 (4.33)	10.7 (2.75)	# (†)	# (†)
Private, nonprofit	89.5 (0.57)	71.2 (0.62)	83.2 (0.79)	80.9 (0.85)	27.4 (0.67)	77.5 (1.02)	68.1 (0.66)	64.3 (0.61)	30.4 (0.74)	32.2 (1.08)	25.0 (0.86)
4-year doctoral	85.5 (0.93)	67.1 (1.12)	79.4 (1.11)	76.5 (1.18)	23.6 (0.82)	73.6 (1.38)	64.2 (1.21)	60.0 (1.22)	29.7 (1.02)	30.3 (1.10)	24.5 (1.04)
Other 4-year	93.6 (0.74)	75.1 (1.12)	87.5 (1.06)	85.8 (1.11)	31.0 (1.18)	82.1 (1.40)	72.3 (1.18)	68.8 (1.21)	31.2 (1.06)	34.7 (1.88)	26.0 (1.45)
Less-than-4-year	92.0 (2.79)	84.4 (3.65)	61.8 (10.16)	61.3 (4.96)	45.3 (5.77)	48.2 (9.77)	60.2 (7.26)	56.8 (7.31)	26.0 (7.94)	5.8 (1.50)	4.7! (1.63)
Private, for-profit	92.6 (0.70)	84.6 (1.24)	59.8 (1.60)	65.5 (1.48)	53.0 (1.50)	25.8 (1.66)	86.5 (1.19)	81.2 (1.29)	43.1 (1.67)	1.8 (0.29)	1.6 (0.28)
2-year and above	92.4 (0.79)	84.2 (1.41)	61.7 (1.82)	64.7 (1.69)	50.7 (1.70)	27.8 (1.90)	86.4 (1.36)	81.3 (1.46)	44.1 (1.92)	2.0 (0.34)	1.8 (0.33)
Less-than-2-year	93.6 (0.82)	87.4 (1.74)	47.6 (2.52)	70.8 (2.12)	67.6 (2.14)	13.5 (2.33)	87.2 (1.70)	80.7 (2.44)	36.9 (1.61)	0.7! (0.27)	‡ (†)
2011–12, all institutions	84.4 (0.36)	72.8 (0.51)	56.9 (0.46)	72.4 (0.41)	47.4 (0.50)	52.6 (0.45)	56.7 (0.53)	55.5 (0.54)	9.2 (0.22)	11.9 (0.25)	10.5 (0.24)
Public	80.4 (0.47)	68.4 (0.61)	53.3 (0.58)	67.3 (0.49)	46.1 (0.59)	49.7 (0.56)	48.5 (0.57)	47.4 (0.57)	6.3 (0.19)	6.9 (0.24)	6.2 (0.23)
4-year doctoral	83.9 (0.46)	70.9 (0.47)	61.2 (0.63)	67.8 (0.51)	41.1 (0.40)	56.8 (0.61)	61.6 (0.44)	60.4 (0.43)	8.6 (0.31)	8.3 (0.37)	7.4 (0.37)
Other 4-year	83.5 (0.93)	72.7 (1.34)	54.1 (1.23)	69.2 (0.99)	48.3 (1.10)	50.1 (1.32)	55.5 (1.49)	54.3 (1.51)	7.4 (0.60)	9.3 (0.70)	8.6 (0.61)
2-year	74.5 (1.03)	63.0 (1.24)	42.5 (1.14)	65.7 (1.09)	51.6 (1.30)	40.2 (1.15)	27.5 (0.99)	26.6 (1.00)	2.7 (0.24)	3.9 (0.28)	3.4 (0.28)
Less-than-2-year	71.6 (4.50)	67.8 (4.72)	33.5 (5.54)	68.6 (4.05)	63.7 (4.54)	27.2 (3.90)	20.5 (5.20)	20.2 (5.20)	‡ (†)	1.0! (0.46)	# (†)
Private, nonprofit	91.6 (0.55)	76.1 (0.75)	83.1 (0.77)	85.4 (0.77)	37.6 (0.65)	80.3 (0.85)	68.4 (0.90)	66.7 (0.88)	15.3 (0.65)	33.1 (0.85)	29.2 (0.81)
4-year doctoral	90.4 (0.84)	74.3 (0.94)	82.9 (1.13)	84.2 (1.17)	34.9 (0.80)	80.4 (1.21)	66.7 (1.08)	65.3 (1.05)	15.0 (0.92)	33.2 (1.27)	30.0 (1.26)
Other 4-year	93.1 (0.68)	78.0 (1.20)	84.2 (0.98)	87.2 (0.92)	40.3 (1.10)	81.3 (1.15)	70.7 (1.41)	68.7 (1.44)	15.8 (0.91)	33.9 (1.22)	29.1 (1.14)
Less-than-4-year	90.2 (4.12)	78.1 (5.04)	60.2 (7.07)	77.8 (6.09)	48.5 (6.54)	51.1 (8.78)	61.2 (5.71)	59.0 (7.42)	12.2 (2.62)	‡ (†)	‡ (†)
Private, for-profit	94.6 (0.46)	93.1 (0.51)	29.3 (1.05)	77.4 (0.76)	73.9 (0.82)	17.4 (0.94)	84.1 (0.85)	83.4 (0.89)	14.8 (0.75)	1.9 (0.21)	1.8 (0.20)
2-year and above	94.6 (0.53)	92.8 (0.59)	30.7 (1.16)	77.4 (0.86)	72.2 (0.92)	18.9 (1.05)	84.2 (0.85)	83.4 (0.89)	15.0 (0.82)	2.2 (0.24)	2.1 (0.23)
Less-than-2-year	95.9 (0.75)	95.2 (0.79)	20.3 (2.64)	86.2 (1.54)	85.4 (1.63)	7.5 (1.82)	83.8 (3.56)	83.0 (3.52)	13.5 (1.58)	‡ (†)	‡ (†)

†Not applicable.

#Rounds to zero.

!Interpret data with caution. The coefficient of variation (CV) for this estimate is between 30 and 50 percent.

‡Reporting standards not met. The coefficient of variation (CV) for this estimate is 50 percent or greater.

[1]Details on nonfederal work-study participants are not available.

[2]Includes students who reported they were awarded aid, but did not specify the source of aid.

[3]Includes Department of Veterans Affairs and Department of Defense benefits.

[4]Includes Parent Loans for Undergraduate Students (PLUS).

NOTE: Excludes students whose attendance status was not reported. Detail may not sum to totals because of rounding and because some students receive multiple types of aid and aid from different sources. Data exclude Puerto Rico. Some data have been revised from previously published figures.

SOURCE: U.S. Department of Education, National Center for Education Statistics, 1992–93, 1999–2000, 2007–08, and 2011–12 National Postsecondary Student Aid Study (NPSAS:93, NPSAS:2000, NPSAS:08, and NPSAS:12). (This table was prepared August 2014.)

Table 331.70. Average amount of financial aid awarded to full-time, full-year undergraduates, by type and source of aid and control and level of institution: Selected years, 1992–93 through 2011–12

[Standard errors appear in parentheses]

Control and level of institution	Any aid			Grants			Loans			Work study[1]	
	Total[2]	Federal[3]	Nonfederal	Total[4]	Federal	Nonfederal	Total[5]	Federal[5]	Nonfederal	Total	Federal
1	2	3	4	5	6	7	8	9	10	11	12
					Current dollars						
1992–93, all institutions	$5,600 (80)	$4,320 (54)	$3,390 (85)	$3,520 (63)	$2,000 (17)	$3,250 (85)	$3,860 (59)	$3,750 (54)	$2,640 (133)	$1,360 (34)	$1,280 (38)
Public	4,030 (39)	3,740 (40)	1,860 (34)	2,420 (28)	1,900 (18)	1,740 (34)	3,350 (42)	3,290 (40)	2,020 (133)	1,380 (48)	1,350 (52)
4-year doctoral	4,720 (60)	4,390 (49)	2,330 (55)	2,750 (45)	1,970 (26)	2,230 (55)	3,660 (46)	3,590 (43)	2,150 (142)	1,440 (57)	1,360 (55)
Other 4-year	4,240 (92)	3,850 (68)	1,710 (68)	2,430 (48)	1,960 (26)	1,530 (52)	3,200 (65)	3,120 (71)	2,150 (198)	1,240 (59)	1,260 (69)
2-year	2,720 (88)	2,640 (87)	1,170 ! (84)	1,940 (59)	1,760 (42)	1,120 (88)	2,500 (125)	2,530 (112)	‡ (†)	1,500 (179)	1,490 (155)
Less-than-2-year	2,250 (198)	1,950 (192)	1,100 ! (476)	1,930 (154)	1,760 (60)	880 (154)	3,310 (472)	3,120 (621)	‡ (†)	‡ (†)	‡ (†)
Private, nonprofit	9,040 (184)	5,280 (94)	5,880 (206)	6,010 (183)	2,320 (39)	5,600 (171)	4,360 (86)	4,140 (67)	3,350 (274)	1,320 (44)	1,230 (48)
4-year doctoral	10,160 (250)	5,650 (147)	7,060 (225)	6,940 (201)	2,420 (74)	6,590 (200)	4,910 (140)	4,560 (106)	3,750 (411)	1,520 (64)	1,360 (79)
Other 4-year	8,460 (253)	5,120 (130)	5,100 (276)	5,500 (275)	2,290 (56)	4,970 (233)	4,000 (115)	3,880 (103)	2,750 (272)	1,190 (48)	1,140 (51)
Less-than-4-year	4,910 (507)	3,980 (258)	2,490 (434)	2,890 (431)	2,140 (149)	1,940 (427)	3,520 (260)	3,410 (257)	‡ (†)	‡ (†)	‡ (†)
Private, for-profit	5,460 (321)	5,130 (301)	2,590 (377)	2,290 (116)	1,950 (47)	2,320 (452)	4,910 (276)	4,840 (254)	2,410 (373)	† (†)	† (†)
2-year and above	6,670 (296)	6,130 (251)	2,820 (528)	2,780 (265)	2,060 (93)	2,670 (582)	5,590 (291)	5,480 (260)	‡ (†)	† (†)	† (†)
Less-than-2-year	4,480 (425)	4,330 (416)	2,240 (533)	2,010 (95)	1,890 (68)	1,680 (532)	4,180 (383)	4,150 (372)	‡ (†)	† (†)	† (†)
1995–96, all institutions	$6,880 (159)	$5,250 (61)	$4,000 (163)	$3,990 (138)	$2,000 (23)	$3,710 (162)	$4,830 (61)	$4,770 (59)	$2,790 (232)	$1,410 (40)	$1,350 (37)
Public	5,160 (105)	4,670 (77)	2,410 (74)	2,740 (68)	1,920 (23)	2,110 (74)	4,390 (87)	4,370 (81)	2,440 (476)	1,390 (63)	1,350 (63)
4-year doctoral	6,230 (124)	5,490 (122)	3,050 (82)	3,250 (107)	1,920 (35)	2,790 (105)	4,910 (149)	4,850 (140)	2,750 (500)	1,330 (100)	1,290 (89)
Other 4-year	5,440 (235)	4,790 (166)	2,170 (81)	2,720 (48)	1,970 (25)	1,870 (60)	4,100 (139)	4,090 (137)	‡ (†)	1,450 (56)	1,380 (58)
2-year	3,130 (162)	3,110 (101)	1,530 ! (213)	2,020 (106)	1,900 (53)	1,100 (140)	3,140 (120)	3,210 (137)	‡ (†)	1,430 (254)	1,410 (234)
Less-than-2-year	2,440 ! (887)	2,040 (267)	2,120 ! (897)	2,190 (485)	1,650 (127)	2,360 ! (882)	2,870 (441)	2,870 (441)	‡ (†)	‡ (†)	‡ (†)
Private, nonprofit	10,870 (388)	6,470 (137)	6,740 (331)	6,640 (312)	2,280 (75)	6,230 (305)	5,600 (128)	5,470 (126)	3,210 (328)	1,430 (52)	1,350 (45)
4-year doctoral	13,130 (727)	7,160 (176)	8,720 (735)	8,370 (674)	2,350 (63)	8,000 (641)	6,260 (188)	6,120 (160)	3,610 (933)	1,660 (84)	1,550 (63)
Other 4-year	10,220 (453)	6,310 (179)	6,040 (357)	6,090 (349)	2,280 (106)	5,590 (345)	5,340 (162)	5,220 (160)	3,300 (417)	1,320 (40)	1,250 (39)
Less-than-4-year	5,310 (229)	4,150 (229)	3,050 (201)	3,230 (364)	2,060 (159)	2,780 (340)	4,520 (189)	4,480 (181)	‡ (†)	1,260 (81)	1,210 (241)
Private, for-profit	6,150 (137)	5,540 (162)	3,010 (188)	2,470 (123)	1,940 (30)	2,350 (211)	4,940 (237)	4,920 (212)	2,300 (210)	† (†)	† (†)
2-year and above	6,850 (235)	6,110 (310)	3,340 (157)	2,880 (264)	2,010 (40)	2,860 (148)	5,330 (164)	5,250 (200)	‡ (†)	† (†)	† (†)
Less-than-2-year	5,520 (337)	5,020 (318)	2,700 (284)	2,120 (67)	1,880 (43)	1,520 (264)	4,550 (525)	4,570 (443)	2,080 (160)	† (†)	† (†)
1999–2000, all institutions	$8,470 (100)	$5,970 (58)	$5,160 (95)	$5,100 (81)	$2,520 (19)	$4,590 (92)	$6,030 (59)	$5,430 (51)	$4,870 (155)	$1,680 (37)	$1,570 (39)
Public	6,140 (84)	5,260 (65)	2,990 (85)	3,520 (77)	2,490 (22)	2,630 (53)	5,180 (72)	4,870 (55)	3,820 (194)	1,720 (56)	1,630 (69)
4-year doctoral	7,410 (175)	6,180 (136)	3,840 (105)	4,170 (91)	2,530 (33)	3,480 (80)	5,620 (81)	5,300 (68)	3,850 (209)	1,780 (45)	1,680 (42)
Other 4-year	6,190 (135)	5,280 (96)	2,690 (96)	3,270 (91)	2,430 (28)	2,290 (83)	4,770 (179)	4,520 (147)	3,540 (426)	1,650 (148)	1,580 (194)
2-year	3,990 (383)	3,670 (387)	1,860 (296)	2,800 (234)	2,490 (45)	1,560 (80)	4,190 (198)	3,750 (122)	4,090 (841)	1,650 (118)	1,580 (105)
Less-than-2-year	3,490	3,050	1,900	2,930	2,410 (167)	1,750 (357)	5,090 (950)	5,040 (975)	‡ (†)	‡ (†)	‡ (†)
Private, nonprofit	14,050 (307)	7,280 (104)	9,390 (238)	8,710 (235)	2,660 (52)	8,280 (218)	7,460 (117)	6,300 (93)	5,750 (211)	1,620 (41)	1,500 (33)
4-year doctoral	16,060 (359)	7,890 (149)	10,910 (326)	10,140 (302)	2,860 (81)	9,600 (283)	8,240 (156)	6,700 (131)	6,430 (237)	1,810 (51)	1,700 (51)
Other 4-year	12,930 (424)	6,930 (162)	8,480 (318)	7,880 (317)	2,530 (70)	7,490 (291)	6,910 (166)	6,020 (149)	5,070 (312)	1,490 (69)	1,330 (47)
Less-than-4-year	7,700 (780)	5,540 (645)	4,680 (485)	5,070 (459)	2,640 (196)	4,340 (550)	6,010 (186)	5,380 (176)	5,590 (1,440)	950 (96)	850 (63)
Private, for-profit	8,730 (285)	7,440 (240)	4,120 (296)	3,380 (144)	2,490 (77)	3,110 (285)	6,590 (285)	6,070 (266)	5,970 (474)	† (†)	† (†)
2-year and above	9,430 (381)	7,920 (315)	4,190 (375)	3,730 (197)	2,550 (109)	3,240 (321)	7,030 (367)	6,530 (345)	6,620 (663)	† (†)	† (†)
Less-than-2-year	6,730 (354)	6,080 (330)	3,700 (556)	2,490 (64)	2,370 (63)	1,570 (385)	5,240 (355)	4,670 (319)	4,660 (800)	† (†)	† (†)
2003–04, all institutions	$9,760 (93)	$7,010 (60)	$5,690 (118)	$5,670 (101)	$3,230 (22)	$4,930 (125)	$6,060 (72)	$6,060 (57)	$6,100 (138)	$1,940 (36)	$1,790 (37)
Public	7,400 (95)	6,260 (90)	3,620 (45)	4,230 (45)	3,190 (31)	3,110 (45)	5,520 (72)	5,100 (64)	6,060 (114)	2,020 (45)	1,860 (51)
4-year doctoral	8,970 (109)	7,360 (99)	4,500 (70)	4,890 (64)	3,220 (39)	3,930 (63)	6,150 (100)	5,510 (81)	5,510 (160)	2,070 (64)	1,900 (66)
Other 4-year	7,870 (183)	6,440 (146)	3,560 (84)	4,230 (118)	3,150 (64)	2,900 (91)	5,280 (127)	5,260 (112)	5,260 (227)	1,930 (86)	1,820 (100)
2-year	4,690 (130)	4,420 (143)	2,140 (84)	3,330 (64)	3,180 (45)	1,810 (86)	3,850 (146)	3,850 (147)	3,700 (207)	2,010 (100)	1,830 (109)
Less-than-2-year	4,770 (389)	4,490 (368)	2,920 (250)	3,180 (206)	2,800 (157)	2,500 (243)	5,090 (621)	4,740 (402)	4,230 (802)	2,460 ! (1,180)	‡ (†)
Private, nonprofit	16,250 (258)	8,480 (127)	10,270 (234)	9,620 (261)	3,390 (49)	8,860 (250)	7,040 (178)	7,430 (135)	8,800 (273)	1,810 (52)	1,670 (51)
4-year doctoral	17,650 (367)	9,000 (204)	11,590 (383)	10,660 (465)	3,460 (101)	9,950 (466)	7,600 (272)	8,220 (190)	9,790 (333)	2,120 (78)	1,980 (75)
Other 4-year	15,650 (352)	8,260 (161)	9,580 (303)	9,130 (295)	3,340 (57)	8,280 (283)	6,910 (219)	6,740 (161)	8,270 (391)	1,620 (56)	1,470 (52)
Less-than-4-year	8,910 (647)	6,240 (375)	5,160 (534)	5,720 (547)	3,560 (333)	4,600 (607)	6,200 (584)	5,630 (470)	6,920 (774)	1,570 ! (549)	1,580 ! (557)
Private, for-profit	10,480 (328)	8,550 (222)	5,070 (285)	4,300 (167)	3,230 (72)	3,880 (317)	6,580 (267)	6,950 (190)	5,730 (525)	2,660 (275)	2,730 (328)
2-year and above	11,380 (433)	9,100 (297)	5,330 (349)	4,660 (222)	3,370 (101)	4,030 (369)	8,140 (351)	6,950 (253)	6,050 (657)	2,890 (308)	2,890 (361)
Less-than-2-year	7,810 (139)	6,890 (93)	3,980 (157)	3,210 (102)	2,850 (58)	3,010 (185)	6,050 (140)	5,350 (112)	4,560 (205)	1,570 (129)	1,570 (108)

See notes at end of table.

Table 331.70. Average amount of financial aid awarded to full-time, full-year undergraduates, by type and source of aid and control and level of institution: Selected years, 1992–93 through 2011–12—Continued

[Standard errors appear in parentheses]

Control and level of institution	Any aid Total[2]	Any aid Federal[3]	Any aid Nonfederal	Grants Total[4]	Grants Federal	Grants Nonfederal	Loans Total[5]	Loans Federal[5]	Loans Nonfederal	Work study[1] Total	Work study[1] Federal
	2	3	4	5	6	7	8	9	10	11	12
2007–08, all institutions	$12,990 (98)	$8,170 (51)	$8,130 (89)	$7,250 (71)	$3,680 (19)	$6,470 (79)	$9,520 (77)	$7,080 (56)	$7,800 (112)	$2,270 (26)	$2,160 (30)
Public	9,680 (62)	7,250 (51)	5,240 (50)	5,420 (40)	3,670 (18)	4,080 (43)	7,990 (60)	6,470 (58)	6,520 (108)	2,430 (37)	2,360 (44)
4-year doctoral	11,670 (96)	8,320 (82)	6,550 (83)	6,410 (71)	3,780 (33)	5,170 (67)	8,870 (90)	7,100 (83)	7,130 (156)	2,440 (42)	2,290 (46)
Other 4-year	10,040 (136)	7,430 (110)	5,200 (95)	5,420 (88)	3,690 (32)	4,040 (99)	7,690 (123)	6,240 (95)	6,300 (204)	2,280 (69)	2,110 (81)
2-year	5,750 (68)	5,160 (63)	2,510 (45)	3,750 (44)	3,530 (29)	1,860 (35)	5,450 (91)	4,600 (73)	4,670 (150)	2,560 (107)	2,760 (122)
Less-than-2-year	6,210 (528)	5,200 (441)	3,750 (477)	3,610 (212)	3,320 (153)	2,390 (351)	6,910 (500)	5,550 (387)	4,920 (284)	‡ (†)	‡ (†)
Private, nonprofit	21,640 (307)	10,020 (158)	14,700 (221)	12,470 (186)	4,090 (51)	11,570 (176)	12,320 (207)	8,350 (164)	9,930 (224)	2,090 (35)	1,930 (35)
4-year doctoral	22,880 (388)	10,380 (192)	15,850 (289)	13,170 (250)	4,280 (82)	12,320 (231)	13,420 (253)	8,840 (213)	11,140 (351)	2,230 (52)	2,080 (55)
Other 4-year	20,620 (447)	9,720 (224)	13,710 (341)	11,880 (268)	3,920 (60)	10,940 (263)	11,330 (313)	7,920 (223)	8,750 (263)	1,970 (40)	1,780 (43)
Less-than-4-year	12,530 (1,097)	8,340 (1,134)	7,270 (1,107)	6,970 (1,588)	4,710 (935)	4,440 (1,230)	11,310 (613)	8,000 (1,208)	8,740 (1,011)	‡ (†)	‡ (†)
Private, for-profit	12,890 (294)	9,160 (176)	6,990 (269)	4,050 (96)	3,200 (60)	3,720 (201)	10,260 (233)	7,040 (133)	7,340 (307)	3,650 (392)	3,840 (385)
2-year and above	13,270 (340)	9,270 (203)	7,220 (303)	4,130 (113)	3,180 (73)	3,810 (216)	10,600 (269)	7,140 (153)	7,610 (350)	3,760 (402)	3,940 (386)
Less-than-2-year	10,540 (234)	8,510 (186)	5,100 (250)	3,590 (86)	3,270 (52)	2,470 (381)	8,150 (215)	6,380 (166)	5,320 (212)	‡ (†)	‡ (†)
2011–12, all institutions	$15,510 (106)	$10,820 (75)	$9,160 (110)	$9,230 (92)	$4,580 (20)	$8,590 (115)	$10,090 (75)	$9,160 (69)	$6,980 (187)	$2,250 (48)	$2,180 (37)
Public	11,420 (93)	9,400 (71)	5,170 (75)	6,610 (62)	4,560 (22)	4,730 (75)	8,860 (87)	8,300 (81)	5,790 (237)	2,330 (60)	2,290 (60)
4-year doctoral	14,130 (125)	11,000 (106)	6,610 (108)	7,880 (101)	4,610 (27)	6,070 (112)	9,750 (112)	9,040 (109)	6,400 (289)	2,410 (80)	2,320 (79)
Other 4-year	11,730 (229)	9,800 (150)	4,920 (170)	6,440 (133)	4,650 (49)	4,410 (155)	8,790 (186)	8,210 (152)	5,630 (483)	2,020 (106)	2,050 (112)
2-year	7,120 (117)	6,740 (91)	2,480 (76)	4,910 (76)	4,460 (41)	2,320 (74)	6,200 (78)	6,060 (79)	3,380 (208)	2,460 (130)	2,460 (146)
Less-than-2-year	7,300 (989)	6,360 (1,018)	2,740 (813)	5,050 (458)	4,510 (464)	2,170 ! (676)	7,260 (950)	7,060 (939)	‡ (†)	‡ (†)	‡ (†)
Private, nonprofit	27,250 (300)	13,300 (217)	17,870 (265)	17,780 (264)	4,710 (46)	16,720 (266)	12,550 (200)	10,930 (190)	8,460 (437)	2,150 (67)	2,050 (44)
4-year doctoral	29,080 (456)	13,700 (355)	19,410 (383)	19,380 (410)	4,690 (81)	18,260 (396)	13,120 (356)	11,420 (330)	8,700 (728)	2,280 (65)	2,220 (60)
Other 4-year	25,630 (384)	12,870 (216)	16,400 (355)	16,370 (336)	4,720 (46)	15,210 (348)	11,960 (167)	10,430 (172)	8,200 (385)	1,980 (130)	1,830 (69)
Less-than-4-year	16,190 (2,359)	12,830 (1,038)	7,610 ! (2,474)	7,410 (1,336)	4,870 (140)	6,670 ! (2,156)	11,600 (1,621)	10,330 (1,239)	8,170 ! (3,055)	2,750 (478)	2,790 (508)
Private, for-profit	15,070 (214)	13,300 (173)	6,480 (205)	5,270 (85)	4,520 (49)	4,600 (257)	10,610 (139)	9,440 (107)	7,170 (211)	3,690 (272)	3,760 (291)
2-year and above	15,520 (219)	13,660 (181)	6,530 (218)	5,310 (85)	4,500 (40)	4,580 (267)	10,960 (151)	9,740 (117)	7,350 (222)	3,750 (281)	3,830 (299)
Less-than-2-year	12,170 (633)	10,990 (483)	5,960 (551)	5,050 (268)	4,670 (230)	4,880 (532)	8,370 (313)	7,510 (211)	5,810 (675)	‡ (†)	‡ (†)
Constant 2014–15 dollars[6]											
All institutions											
1992–93	$9,310 (133)	$7,180 (90)	$5,630 (140)	$5,850 (104)	$3,310 (28)	$5,390 (141)	$6,420 (97)	$6,230 (90)	$4,380 (221)	$2,260 (57)	$2,120 (64)
1995–96	10,530 (244)	8,040 (94)	6,130 (249)	6,110 (212)	3,070 (35)	5,680 (249)	7,400 (93)	7,310 (89)	4,280 (356)	2,160 (61)	2,060 (56)
1999–2000	11,840 (139)	8,340 (81)	7,220 (133)	7,130 (113)	3,530 (26)	6,420 (129)	8,430 (82)	7,590 (71)	6,810 (216)	2,350 (50)	2,190 (55)
2003–04	12,420 (118)	8,910 (76)	7,230 (150)	7,210 (128)	4,110 (29)	6,280 (159)	8,900 (91)	7,710 (72)	7,760 (176)	2,460 (45)	2,270 (47)
2007–08	14,520 (110)	9,140 (57)	9,090 (99)	8,110 (79)	4,110 (21)	7,230 (88)	10,640 (86)	7,920 (62)	8,720 (125)	2,540 (29)	2,410 (33)
2011–12	16,130 (111)	11,250 (78)	9,530 (115)	9,600 (96)	4,760 (21)	8,940 (120)	10,500 (78)	9,530 (72)	7,260 (194)	2,340 (49)	2,260 (38)

†Not applicable.
!Interpret data with caution. The coefficient of variation (CV) for this estimate is between 30 and 50 percent.
‡Reporting standards not met. Either there are too few cases for a reliable estimate or the coefficient of variation (CV) is 50 percent or greater.
[1]Details on nonfederal work-study participants are not available.
[2]Includes students who reported that they were awarded aid, but did not specify the source or type of aid.
[3]Includes Department of Veterans Affairs and Department of Defense benefits.
[4]Indicates all grants, scholarships, or tuition waivers received from federal, state, institutional, or private sources, including employers.
[5]Includes Parent Loans for Undergraduate Students (PLUS)

[6]Constant dollars based on the Consumer Price Index, prepared by the Bureau of Labor Statistics, U.S. Department of Labor, adjusted to a school-year basis.
NOTE: Aid averages are for those students who received the specified type of aid. Full-time, full-year students were enrolled full time for 9 or more months from July 1 through June 30. Data exclude Puerto Rico. Some data have been revised from previously published figures.
SOURCE: U.S. Department of Education, National Center for Education Statistics, 1992–93, 1995–96, 1999–2000, 2003–04, 2007–08, and 2011–12 National Postsecondary Student Aid Study (NPSAS:93, NPSAS:96, NPSAS:2000, NPSAS:04, NPSAS:08, and NPSAS:12). (This table was prepared September 2015.)

Table 331.80. Percentage of part-time or part-year undergraduates receiving financial aid, by type and source of aid and control and level of institution: Selected years, 1992–93 through 2011–12

[Standard errors appear in parentheses]

Control and level of institution	Any aid			Grants			Loans			Work study[1]	
	Total[2]	Federal[3]	Nonfederal	Total	Federal	Nonfederal	Total[4]	Federal[4]	Nonfederal	Total	Federal
1	2	3	4	5	6	7	8	9	10	11	12
1992–93, all institutions	**37.3** (0.49)	**24.7** (0.34)	**16.5** (0.45)	**32.0** (0.40)	**18.3** (0.26)	**19.3** (0.43)	**13.9** (0.36)	**13.5** (0.37)	**0.8** (0.10)	**2.1** (0.10)	**1.2** (0.07)
Public	31.7 (0.49)	19.9 (0.29)	14.5 (0.48)	27.6 (0.44)	15.3 (0.24)	17.2 (0.50)	9.6 (0.26)	9.2 (0.27)	0.6 (0.11)	1.7 (0.10)	0.9 (0.08)
4-year doctoral	40.5 (0.72)	27.8 (0.74)	19.5 (0.67)	31.2 (0.81)	17.0 (0.69)	20.7 (0.73)	21.8 (0.76)	21.4 (0.75)	1.1 (0.19)	3.6 (0.27)	2.1 (0.22)
Other 4-year	39.5 (0.65)	28.5 (1.13)	19.1 (1.05)	33.8 (0.78)	22.0 (0.92)	20.1 (0.87)	16.8 (0.85)	16.3 (0.81)	1.3! (0.40)	3.1 (0.40)	1.5 (0.26)
2-year	28.6 (0.65)	16.6 (0.44)	12.7 (0.64)	25.9 (0.56)	13.7 (0.32)	16.2 (0.66)	5.8 (0.34)	5.5 (0.33)	0.4 (0.10)	1.1 (0.12)	0.6 (0.10)
Less-than-2-year	21.2 (1.69)	15.1 (1.09)	6.9 (1.48)	19.4 (1.62)	13.8 (1.06)	8.0 (1.85)	0.7! (0.31)	0.7! (0.31)	# (†)	‡ (†)	‡ (†)
Private, nonprofit	54.6 (1.33)	32.5 (1.43)	34.5 (1.20)	48.2 (1.19)	19.9 (1.06)	38.8 (1.16)	25.0 (1.31)	24.4 (1.33)	1.9 (0.19)	6.0 (0.69)	3.9 (0.51)
4-year doctoral	51.4 (1.87)	28.5 (1.31)	33.0 (1.98)	44.3 (1.97)	12.6 (0.88)	43.0 (1.85)	23.8 (1.33)	23.8 (1.33)	2.7 (0.52)	5.4 (0.98)	3.1 (0.69)
Other 4-year	56.8 (1.88)	34.1 (2.31)	36.9 (1.79)	50.8 (1.73)	21.7 (2.10)	43.0 (1.95)	25.8 (1.95)	25.8 (1.95)	1.6 (0.29)	7.7 (1.18)	5.0 (0.81)
2-year	52.7 (4.06)	34.5 (2.94)	28.4 (3.54)	46.0 (3.73)	26.5 (2.29)	31.3 (3.79)	20.7 (2.96)	20.7 (3.00)	1.2! (0.41)	1.6 (0.20)	‡ (†)
Less-than-4-year	70.9 (2.20)	64.3 (2.02)	11.9 (1.31)	55.0 (1.31)	48.4 (0.95)	11.3 (1.41)	42.8 (3.57)	42.8 (3.52)	1.5! (0.57)	1.2! (0.37)	‡ (†)
Private, for-profit	63.7 (4.57)	54.1 (3.69)	14.7 (3.04)	44.9 (2.97)	33.3 (1.26)	17.8 (3.61)	47.7 (4.16)	47.5 (4.10)	1.2! (0.57)	0.8 (0.20)	0.3! (0.08)
2-year and above	63.7 (4.57)	54.1 (3.69)	14.7 (3.04)	44.9 (2.97)	33.3 (1.26)	17.8 (3.61)	47.7 (4.16)	47.5 (4.10)	1.5! (0.57)	1.2! (0.37)	0.5! (0.24)
Less-than-2-year	75.5 (1.80)	70.9 (1.73)	10.2 (1.75)	61.5 (1.37)	58.1 (1.11)	7.1 (1.45)	40.3 (4.97)	39.7 (4.93)	1.8! (0.63)	0.5! (0.23)	0.2! (0.08)
1999–2000, all institutions	**44.2** (0.66)	**29.3** (0.34)	**27.5** (0.72)	**35.3** (0.62)	**18.2** (0.25)	**25.2** (0.68)	**18.6** (0.28)	**17.9** (0.27)	**2.1** (0.13)	**1.9** (0.09)	**1.4** (0.08)
Public	38.9 (0.77)	23.9 (0.36)	25.4 (0.80)	31.4 (0.70)	15.5 (0.26)	23.4 (0.76)	12.6 (0.24)	12.0 (0.22)	1.3 (0.12)	1.5 (0.11)	1.1 (0.09)
4-year doctoral	51.8 (0.73)	37.8 (0.77)	30.6 (0.84)	36.1 (0.70)	18.1 (0.71)	27.3 (0.73)	33.0 (0.81)	31.8 (0.72)	3.4 (0.47)	3.3 (0.30)	2.1 (0.27)
Other 4-year	53.0 (1.18)	39.2 (1.27)	30.4 (1.23)	40.0 (1.20)	22.2 (1.10)	28.2 (1.22)	30.4 (1.06)	29.5 (1.08)	2.6 (0.35)	3.3 (0.52)	2.7 (0.45)
2-year	33.4 (1.07)	18.0 (0.43)	23.4 (1.10)	28.9 (1.01)	13.8 (0.37)	21.8 (1.05)	4.8 (0.14)	4.4 (0.11)	0.6 (0.09)	0.8 (0.10)	0.6 (0.08)
Less-than-2-year	36.9 (2.46)	19.7 (3.00)	22.6 (1.47)	28.4 (2.64)	16.7 (2.68)	14.6 (2.36)	‡ (†)	‡ (†)	‡ (†)	1.6 (0.50)	0.9! (0.37)
Private, nonprofit	65.5 (0.86)	44.9 (1.29)	49.2 (1.35)	54.3 (1.02)	20.5 (1.30)	46.9 (1.48)	37.6 (1.17)	36.4 (1.13)	6.5 (0.57)	6.4 (0.36)	4.3 (0.29)
4-year doctoral	61.2 (1.65)	42.4 (1.75)	49.1 (1.92)	50.9 (1.68)	16.5 (1.49)	46.7 (1.81)	37.4 (2.00)	36.5 (2.04)	8.2 (1.48)	7.2 (0.87)	5.3 (0.73)
Other 4-year	67.8 (1.19)	45.9 (2.08)	50.3 (2.19)	55.7 (1.56)	20.6 (1.73)	48.1 (2.49)	39.4 (1.93)	37.9 (1.81)	6.2 (0.65)	6.3 (0.51)	4.0 (0.42)
2-year	64.0 (4.98)	46.2 (5.18)	39.8 (6.19)	56.8 (4.67)	36.0 (4.62)	37.0 (6.29)	22.9 (2.57)	22.3 (2.48)	2.0! (0.72)	4.1 (1.40)	3.1! (1.09)
Less-than-4-year	87.3 (1.08)	83.0 (1.08)	21.9 (1.98)	60.3 (1.59)	54.7 (1.70)	14.6 (1.64)	75.3 (1.61)	74.3 (1.55)	6.5 (0.83)	‡ (†)	‡ (†)
Private, for-profit	86.0 (1.60)	83.0 (1.08)	25.5 (3.00)	56.5 (2.60)	48.0 (2.56)	19.3 (2.38)	77.9 (2.46)	77.1 (2.38)	6.6 (1.29)	‡ (†)	‡ (†)
2-year and above	89.1 (1.77)	85.2 (1.66)	17.2 (2.78)	65.3 (2.27)	63.3 (2.20)	8.5 (2.21)	72.0 (3.97)	70.7 (3.96)	6.4 (1.14)	‡ (†)	‡ (†)
Less-than-2-year	85.2 (1.77)	85.2 (1.66)	17.2 (2.78)	65.3 (2.27)	63.3 (2.20)	8.5 (2.21)	72.0 (3.97)	70.7 (3.96)	6.4 (1.14)	‡ (†)	‡ (†)
2007–08, all institutions	**56.6** (0.47)	**38.9** (0.31)	**37.8** (0.47)	**43.0** (0.48)	**23.9** (0.30)	**28.4** (0.46)	**30.1** (0.22)	**26.2** (0.18)	**11.6** (0.26)	**3.4** (0.16)	**2.6** (0.11)
Public	49.2 (0.54)	30.3 (0.36)	33.3 (0.46)	38.0 (0.54)	19.1 (0.31)	27.7 (0.46)	19.6 (0.21)	15.9 (0.17)	6.6 (0.17)	2.9 (0.17)	2.2 (0.10)
4-year doctoral	64.2 (1.02)	44.0 (0.74)	45.0 (0.71)	43.1 (0.61)	19.7 (0.57)	34.3 (0.61)	42.6 (0.81)	36.8 (0.76)	14.0 (0.56)	4.5 (0.30)	3.4 (0.26)
Other 4-year	60.0 (1.02)	42.9 (0.95)	36.0 (1.08)	42.2 (0.77)	25.0 (0.75)	26.8 (0.84)	35.1 (0.95)	29.8 (0.83)	10.8 (0.64)	3.2 (0.29)	2.4 (0.27)
2-year	44.3 (0.68)	25.2 (0.42)	30.4 (0.58)	36.2 (0.69)	18.0 (0.38)	26.4 (0.60)	12.1 (0.20)	9.1 (0.13)	4.3 (0.18)	2.5 (0.22)	2.0 (0.13)
Less-than-2-year	46.7 (2.17)	31.4 (1.91)	26.5 (4.22)	38.5 (1.87)	27.6 (1.43)	15.8 (2.14)	14.6 (1.79)	11.3 (1.91)	5.7 (1.24)	# (†)	# (†)
Private, nonprofit	76.5 (0.92)	53.7 (0.86)	60.6 (1.05)	59.1 (1.08)	22.3 (0.87)	51.5 (1.14)	51.5 (0.83)	46.9 (0.87)	20.2 (0.77)	9.5 (0.75)	7.1 (0.66)
4-year doctoral	75.2 (1.32)	48.9 (1.50)	62.3 (1.39)	58.3 (1.67)	18.8 (1.02)	51.6 (1.90)	49.9 (1.60)	43.5 (1.92)	21.4 (1.24)	10.9 (1.45)	8.1 (1.22)
Other 4-year	77.8 (1.32)	56.4 (1.50)	60.8 (1.39)	60.5 (1.41)	23.6 (1.28)	51.7 (1.46)	51.7 (1.47)	49.3 (1.50)	19.2 (1.19)	9.1 (0.85)	6.8 (0.77)
2-year	72.4 (4.93)	63.0 (3.97)	44.5 (5.84)	49.8 (4.95)	37.7 (6.05)	25.4 (4.39)	51.7 (4.57)	48.3 (5.29)	20.9 (3.05)	2.0! (0.74)	1.5! (0.51)
Less-than-4-year	93.4 (0.56)	87.8 (0.72)	51.9 (1.75)	66.0 (1.01)	58.8 (1.16)	17.6 (1.80)	87.9 (0.75)	82.6 (0.84)	40.1 (1.69)	2.0 (0.35)	1.7 (0.35)
Private, for-profit	94.8 (0.70)	89.9 (0.88)	53.9 (2.16)	66.5 (1.25)	58.2 (1.44)	18.9 (2.23)	90.3 (0.82)	86.0 (0.97)	41.7 (2.06)	2.5 (0.44)	2.1 (0.44)
2-year and above	94.8 (0.70)	89.9 (0.88)	53.9 (2.16)	66.5 (1.25)	58.2 (1.44)	18.9 (2.23)	90.3 (0.82)	86.0 (0.97)	41.7 (2.06)	2.5 (0.44)	2.1 (0.44)
Less-than-2-year	88.2 (0.84)	80.0 (1.21)	44.2 (2.01)	64.3 (1.33)	60.8 (1.21)	13.1 (2.20)	79.1 (1.69)	69.9 (1.87)	34.2 (1.65)	† (†)	† (†)
2011–12, all institutions	**62.1** (1.05)	**51.1** (1.10)	**30.1** (0.60)	**50.8** (0.87)	**37.8** (0.85)	**26.1** (0.56)	**32.7** (0.48)	**30.9** (0.45)	**4.8** (0.17)	**2.2** (0.12)	**2.0** (0.12)
Public	56.0 (1.18)	44.5 (1.22)	28.9 (0.67)	46.5 (0.93)	33.6 (0.90)	26.3 (0.64)	23.6 (0.45)	22.2 (0.43)	2.9 (0.13)	1.7 (0.11)	1.6 (0.11)
4-year doctoral	66.1 (1.04)	53.4 (0.81)	36.8 (1.02)	47.7 (1.05)	30.9 (0.65)	31.2 (1.02)	47.3 (0.60)	44.3 (0.61)	7.0 (0.41)	2.7 (0.26)	2.5 (0.26)
Other 4-year	59.5 (1.46)	49.7 (1.66)	27.0 (1.13)	46.2 (1.23)	35.7 (1.21)	23.1 (0.98)	30.8 (1.17)	28.5 (1.16)	4.5 (0.53)	2.5 (0.36)	2.4 (0.33)
2-year	52.7 (1.36)	41.2 (1.39)	27.4 (0.86)	46.1 (1.08)	35.7 (1.09)	25.8 (0.83)	16.4 (0.47)	15.4 (0.42)	1.6 (0.13)	1.3 (0.14)	1.3 (0.14)
Less-than-2-year	70.2 (4.21)	60.3 (4.47)	28.4 (5.72)	63.7 (4.42)	54.0 (4.12)	19.4 (4.26)	20.8 (3.99)	20.8 (4.28)	# (†)	# (†)	# (†)
Private, nonprofit	77.4 (1.47)	61.0 (1.61)	51.5 (2.10)	60.8 (1.91)	34.9 (1.51)	45.6 (2.13)	53.6 (1.60)	49.8 (1.59)	10.5 (1.01)	8.9 (0.86)	7.1 (0.76)
4-year doctoral	76.0 (1.87)	57.9 (2.12)	49.0 (2.65)	57.4 (2.68)	29.3 (1.78)	43.2 (2.63)	52.6 (2.12)	48.5 (1.99)	10.2 (1.62)	9.7 (1.21)	6.9 (0.96)
Other 4-year	79.2 (2.42)	64.0 (2.54)	56.6 (3.34)	63.9 (2.81)	38.7 (2.60)	50.8 (3.36)	55.6 (2.61)	52.0 (2.45)	11.0 (1.52)	8.9 (1.26)	7.8 (1.15)
2-year	74.3 (4.47)	64.3 (3.22)	26.6 (6.12)	63.9 (4.68)	57.9 (2.94)	18.3! (6.47)	45.0 (4.55)	40.8 (3.99)	8.5! (2.85)	2.0 (0.74)	‡ (†)
Less-than-4-year	85.4 (1.02)	79.7 (0.83)	24.7 (1.17)	67.2 (1.33)	60.8 (1.08)	14.5 (1.26)	68.2 (0.78)	65.7 (0.51)	11.3 (0.64)	1.0 (0.13)	0.9 (0.14)
Private, for-profit	85.3 (1.20)	78.8 (0.97)	25.5 (1.30)	65.9 (1.56)	58.6 (1.24)	15.6 (1.47)	67.3 (0.56)	64.5 (0.64)	11.3 (0.68)	1.2 (0.15)	1.1 (0.16)
2-year and above	85.3 (1.20)	78.8 (0.97)	25.5 (1.30)	65.9 (1.56)	58.6 (1.24)	15.6 (1.47)	67.3 (0.56)	64.5 (0.64)	11.3 (0.68)	1.2 (0.15)	1.1 (0.16)
Less-than-2-year	85.9 (1.39)	84.6 (1.40)	20.7 (3.40)	74.2 (1.66)	72.3 (1.58)	8.6 (2.47)	73.3 (1.35)	71.6 (1.71)	12.5 (1.71)	0.2! (0.08)	0.2! (0.07)

†Not applicable.
#Rounds to zero.
!Interpret data with caution. The coefficient of variation (CV) for this estimate is between 30 and 50 percent.
‡Reporting standards not met. Either there are too few cases for a reliable estimate or the coefficient of variation (CV) is 50 percent or greater.
[1]Details on nonfederal work-study participants are not available.
[2]Includes students who reported they were awarded aid, but did not specify the source of aid.
[3]Includes Department of Veterans Affairs and Department of Defense benefits.
[4]Includes Parent Loans for Undergraduate Students (PLUS).
NOTE: Excludes students whose attendance status was not reported. Detail may not sum to totals because of rounding and because some students receive multiple types of aid and aid from different sources. Data exclude Puerto Rico. Some data have been revised from previously published figures.
SOURCE: U.S. Department of Education, National Center for Education Statistics, 1992–93, 1999–2000, 2007–08, and 2011–12 National Postsecondary Student Aid Study (NPSAS:93, NPSAS:2000, NPSAS:08, and NPSAS:12). (This table was prepared August 2014.)

Table 331.90. Percentage of full-time and part-time undergraduates receiving federal aid, by aid program and control and level of institution: 2007–08 and 2011–12

[Standard errors appear in parentheses]

Control and level of institution	Number of undergraduates[1] (in thousands)		Any federal aid		Any Title IV aid		Pell		SEOG[3]		CWS[4]		Perkins[5]		Stafford[6]		PLUS[7]	
1	2		3		4		5		6		7		8		9		10	
2007–08																		
Full-time, full-year students																		
All institutions	7,527	(—)	63.9	(0.31)	62.9	(0.31)	32.7	(0.29)	8.9	(0.20)	10.6	(0.23)	6.0	(0.17)	50.2	(0.32)	7.5	(0.20)
Public	5,159	(—)	58.7	(0.36)	57.6	(0.36)	32.0	(0.29)	6.8	(0.18)	7.1	(0.22)	4.1	(0.15)	41.9	(0.33)	6.1	(0.21)
4-year doctoral	2,522	(—)	59.6	(0.48)	58.7	(0.48)	27.3	(0.37)	6.5	(0.23)	7.6	(0.32)	6.1	(0.27)	49.7	(0.49)	9.3	(0.39)
Other 4-year	1,031	(—)	67.6	(0.68)	66.6	(0.70)	34.9	(0.66)	7.9	(0.37)	8.7	(0.45)	5.0	(0.42)	53.8	(0.72)	6.4	(0.40)
2-year	1,584	(—)	51.4	(0.73)	49.9	(0.75)	37.2	(0.65)	6.6	(0.36)	5.5	(0.29)	0.4	(0.08)	22.1	(0.58)	1.1	(0.12)
Less-than-2-year	22	(—)	58.6	(3.84)	57.1	(4.15)	49.7	(4.14)	‡	(†)	#	(†)	#	(†)	23.6	(4.33)	‡	(†)
Private, nonprofit	1,672	(—)	71.2	(0.62)	70.4	(0.62)	26.6	(0.65)	13.1	(0.51)	25.0	(0.86)	13.8	(0.63)	62.9	(0.65)	12.2	(0.59)
4-year doctoral	844	(—)	67.1	(1.12)	66.1	(1.14)	22.2	(0.79)	11.7	(0.60)	24.5	(1.04)	16.3	(1.02)	58.4	(1.28)	12.3	(0.69)
Other 4-year	814	(—)	75.1	(1.12)	74.7	(1.12)	30.8	(1.19)	14.5	(0.80)	26.0	(1.45)	11.5	(0.80)	67.7	(1.23)	12.2	(0.93)
Less-than-4-year	14	(—)	84.4	(3.65)	82.8	(4.17)	43.3	(6.07)	12.6 !	(5.08)	4.7 !	(1.63)	‡	(†)	56.2	(7.28)	‡	(†)
Private, for-profit	695	(—)	84.6	(1.24)	83.9	(1.36)	52.9	(1.48)	13.6	(1.27)	1.6	(0.28)	1.0	(0.19)	81.0	(1.30)	5.8	(0.63)
2-year and above	599	(—)	84.2	(1.41)	83.4	(1.55)	50.5	(1.69)	12.2	(1.45)	1.8	(0.33)	1.1	(0.22)	81.2	(1.46)	4.9	(0.69)
Less-than-2-year	96	(—)	87.4	(1.74)	87.1	(1.84)	67.5	(2.15)	22.3	(2.49)	‡	(†)	‡	(†)	79.8	(2.50)	11.3	(1.16)
Part-time or part-year students																		
All institutions	12,984	(—)	38.9	(0.31)	37.3	(0.30)	23.8	(0.30)	4.3	(0.23)	2.6	(0.11)	0.9	(0.05)	26.0	(0.18)	1.6	(0.10)
Public	10,386	(—)	30.3	(0.36)	28.6	(0.34)	19.0	(0.31)	2.1	(0.11)	2.2	(0.10)	0.6	(0.04)	15.7	(0.16)	0.9	(0.06)
Private, nonprofit	1,109	(—)	53.7	(0.86)	51.4	(0.86)	22.1	(0.85)	5.9	(0.51)	7.1	(0.66)	3.6	(0.49)	46.3	(0.86)	3.6	(0.44)
Private, for-profit	1,489	(—)	87.8	(0.72)	87.3	(0.72)	58.6	(1.15)	18.6	(1.68)	1.7	(0.35)	0.9	(0.13)	82.4	(0.84)	5.3	(0.59)
2011–12																		
Full-time, full-year students																		
All institutions	8,864	(—)	72.8	(0.51)	71.4	(0.54)	47.1	(0.50)	9.0	(0.24)	10.5	(0.24)	4.2	(0.18)	55.1	(0.54)	9.1	(0.23)
Public	5,997	(—)	68.4	(0.61)	67.1	(0.64)	45.8	(0.59)	6.6	(0.26)	6.2	(0.23)	2.7	(0.15)	47.1	(0.57)	7.1	(0.28)
4-year doctoral	2,893	(—)	70.9	(0.47)	70.1	(0.48)	40.8	(0.39)	7.1	(0.39)	7.4	(0.37)	4.3	(0.30)	60.0	(0.43)	11.4	(0.45)
Other 4-year	969	(—)	72.7	(1.34)	71.4	(1.43)	48.1	(1.07)	6.5	(0.52)	8.6	(0.61)	2.8	(0.35)	54.0	(1.53)	8.1	(0.67)
2-year	2,104	(—)	63.0	(1.24)	61.0	(1.29)	51.4	(1.30)	5.9	(0.40)	3.4	(0.28)	0.3	(0.06)	26.5	(0.99)	1.0	(0.11)
Less-than-2-year	31	(—)	67.8	(4.72)	66.4	(5.20)	62.4	(5.04)	‡	(†)	‡	(†)	#	(†)	19.7	(4.83)	‡	(†)
Private, nonprofit	1,875	(—)	76.1	(0.75)	74.9	(0.75)	37.2	(0.64)	12.2	(0.60)	29.2	(0.81)	10.6	(0.61)	66.0	(0.90)	16.5	(0.67)
4-year doctoral	990	(—)	74.3	(0.94)	73.4	(0.96)	34.5	(0.77)	11.0	(0.89)	30.0	(1.26)	13.3	(0.97)	64.4	(1.08)	16.7	(1.10)
Other 4-year	849	(—)	78.0	(1.20)	76.7	(1.17)	39.8	(1.11)	13.6	(0.74)	29.1	(1.14)	8.0	(0.69)	68.2	(1.48)	16.2	(0.76)
Less-than-4-year	36	(—)	78.1	(5.04)	74.6	(5.35)	48.5	(6.54)	13.1 !	(5.38)	‡	(†)	‡	(†)	59.0	(7.42)	13.9	(3.36)
Private, for-profit	992	(—)	93.1	(0.51)	90.4	(0.52)	73.8	(0.81)	17.8	(0.87)	1.8	(0.20)	1.4	(0.23)	83.2	(0.90)	7.1	(0.44)
2-year and above	859	(—)	92.8	(0.59)	89.7	(0.59)	72.1	(0.91)	15.7	(0.81)	2.1	(0.23)	1.6	(0.27)	83.3	(0.91)	7.3	(0.48)
Less-than-2-year	133	(—)	95.2	(0.79)	95.1	(0.80)	85.0	(1.46)	31.4	(4.40)	‡	(†)	‡	(†)	82.9	(3.51)	5.9	(0.77)
Part-time or part-year students																		
All institutions	14,192	(—)	51.1	(1.10)	48.4	(1.09)	37.6	(0.85)	4.4	(0.19)	2.0	(0.12)	0.9	(0.08)	30.7	(0.44)	1.6	(0.10)
Public	10,929	(—)	44.5	(1.22)	42.4	(1.13)	33.4	(0.89)	2.6	(0.14)	1.6	(0.11)	0.5	(0.05)	22.1	(0.43)	1.0	(0.08)
4-year doctoral	1,875	(—)	53.4	(0.81)	51.2	(0.75)	30.6	(0.65)	2.9	(0.32)	2.5	(0.26)	2.1	(0.26)	44.0	(0.63)	4.1	(0.32)
Other 4-year	1,477	(—)	49.7	(1.66)	47.2	(1.51)	35.4	(1.18)	2.6	(0.36)	2.4	(0.33)	0.9	(0.26)	28.3	(1.16)	1.7	(0.40)
2-year	7,521	(—)	41.2	(1.39)	39.1	(1.31)	33.6	(1.08)	2.5	(0.17)	1.3	(0.14)	0.1	(0.02)	15.4	(0.41)	0.1	(0.02)
Less-than-2-year	56	(—)	60.3	(4.47)	59.6	(4.47)	53.9	(4.11)	‡	(†)	#	(†)	#	(†)	20.7	(4.33)	‡	(†)
Private, nonprofit	1,135	(—)	61.0	(1.61)	56.5	(1.99)	34.8	(1.51)	6.8	(0.66)	7.1	(0.76)	1.9	(0.30)	49.5	(1.57)	4.3	(0.51)
4-year doctoral	557	(—)	57.9	(2.12)	53.3	(2.19)	29.1	(1.77)	4.2	(0.73)	6.9	(0.96)	2.4	(0.47)	48.3	(2.00)	3.9	(0.65)
Other 4-year	527	(—)	64.0	(2.54)	59.1	(2.91)	38.6	(2.59)	8.2	(1.21)	7.8	(1.15)	1.6	(0.41)	51.6	(2.42)	4.9	(0.96)
Less-than-4-year	51	(—)	64.3	(3.22)	64.2	(3.18)	57.9	(2.94)	21.0	(5.35)	‡	(†)	‡	(†)	40.6	(3.92)	2.0 !	(0.81)
Private, for-profit	2,128	(—)	79.7	(0.83)	75.2	(1.16)	60.5	(1.09)	12.8	(0.83)	0.9	(0.14)	2.0	(0.47)	65.3	(0.47)	3.4	(0.32)
2-year and above	1,790	(—)	78.8	(0.97)	73.6	(1.35)	58.4	(1.25)	11.8	(0.84)	1.1	(0.16)	2.4	(0.56)	64.1	(0.51)	3.2	(0.33)
Less-than-2-year	337	(—)	84.6	(1.40)	83.6	(1.33)	71.9	(1.60)	18.1	(2.38)	0.2 !	(0.07)	‡	(†)	71.5	(1.36)	4.2	(0.84)

—Not available.
†Not applicable.
#Rounds to zero.
!Interpret data with caution. The coefficient of variation (CV) for this estimate is between 30 and 50 percent.
‡Reporting standards not met. The coefficient of variation (CV) for this estimate is 50 percent or greater.
[1]Numbers of undergraduates may not equal figures reported in other tables, since these data are based on a sample survey of students who enrolled at any point during the year.
[2]Title IV of the Higher Education Act.
[3]Supplemental Educational Opportunity Grants.

[4]College Work Study. Prior to October 17, 1986, private for-profit institutions were prohibited by law from spending CWS funds for on-campus work. Includes persons who participated in the program but had no earnings.
[5]Formerly National Direct Student Loans (NDSL).
[6]Formerly Guaranteed Student Loans (GSL).
[7]Parent Loans for Undergraduate Students.
NOTE: Excludes students whose attendance status was not reported. Detail may not sum to totals because of rounding and because some students receive multiple types of aid and aid from different sources. Data exclude Puerto Rico. Some data have been revised from previously published figures.
SOURCE: U.S. Department of Education, National Center for Education Statistics, 2007–08 and 2011–12 National Postsecondary Student Aid Study (NPSAS:08 and NPSAS:12). (This table was prepared July 2014.)

Table 331.95. Percentage of undergraduate students ages 18 to 24 in their 4th (senior) year or above who ever received federal loans, nonfederal loans, or Parent Loans for Undergraduates (PLUS), and average cumulative amount borrowed, by selected student characteristics and control and level of institution: 1989–90, 1999–2000, and 2011–12

[Standard errors appear in parentheses]

Percent of students with loans

Selected student characteristic or control and level of institution (1)	1989–90 Total[1] (2)	1989–90 Stafford Loans[3] (3)	1989–90 Perkins Loans (4)	1989–90 Parent PLUS Loans[4] (5)	1999–2000 Total[1] (6)	1999–2000 Federal loans to students[2] (7)	1999–2000 Parent PLUS Loans[4] (8)	2011–12 Total[1] (9)	2011–12 Federal loans to students (10)	2011–12 Nonfederal loans (11)	2011–12 Parent PLUS Loans[4] (12)
Total	50.5 (0.81)	38.0 (0.77)	13.0 (0.65)	4.1 (0.22)	60.2 (0.66)	58.1 (0.69)	12.4 (0.51)	67.7 (0.74)	64.3 (0.71)	29.0 (0.73)	19.9 (0.70)
Sex											
Male	51.8 (1.24)	37.9 (1.18)	12.6 (0.76)	3.8 (0.29)	58.2 (0.98)	55.8 (0.99)	12.4 (0.56)	67.2 (1.14)	63.4 (1.10)	29.2 (1.09)	19.9 (1.07)
Female	49.3 (0.90)	37.9 (0.88)	13.1 (0.72)	4.4 (0.30)	61.8 (0.87)	59.9 (0.88)	12.3 (0.70)	68.0 (1.01)	65.1 (1.05)	28.9 (0.96)	19.9 (0.91)
Race/ethnicity											
White	49.5 (0.97)	36.8 (0.92)	11.9 (0.64)	4.2 (0.27)	58.9 (0.79)	56.9 (0.82)	12.4 (0.57)	65.5 (0.87)	62.1 (0.81)	29.6 (0.92)	19.9 (0.88)
Black	68.9 (2.24)	57.1 (2.16)	23.2 (2.42)	7.0 (1.06)	76.8 (2.53)	74.5 (2.49)	15.5 (1.47)	90.3 (1.34)	88.1 (1.74)	31.3 (3.03)	30.4 (2.25)
Hispanic	57.3 (3.71)	42.3 (4.17)	15.9 (1.65)	4.3 (0.99)	67.4 (2.28)	64.3 (1.88)	14.0 (1.79)	72.3 (1.93)	70.2 (1.98)	28.4 (2.19)	19.3 (2.06)
Asian[5]	40.5 (1.78)	27.5 (2.30)	13.4 (2.68)	‡ (†)	50.6 (2.16)	49.5 (2.22)	7.5 (1.29)	50.8 (2.88)	45.2 (2.72)	21.4 (2.76)	9.9 (1.58)
Pacific Islander[5]	‡ (†)	‡ (†)	‡ (†)	‡ (†)	55.3 (9.93)	55.3 (9.93)	14.2 ! (5.01)	‡ (†)	‡ (†)	‡ (†)	‡ (†)
American Indian/Alaska Native	‡ (†)	‡ (†)	‡ (†)	‡ (†)	46.9 (9.93)	38.7 (9.01)	‡ (†)	‡ (†)	‡ (†)	‡ (†)	‡ (†)
Two or more races	— (†)	— (†)	— (†)	— (†)	50.1 (4.67)	48.5 (4.93)	9.4 ! (2.91)	77.9 (3.68)	76.4 (3.84)	36.1 (4.68)	20.2 (4.44)
Dependency status											
Dependent	47.5 (0.96)	35.6 (0.93)	11.7 (0.56)	4.4 (0.25)	59.6 (0.74)	57.4 (0.75)	13.7 (0.60)	66.5 (0.79)	63.4 (0.78)	29.2 (0.79)	21.0 (0.80)
Independent	59.6 (1.51)	45.0 (1.30)	16.7 (1.28)	3.4 (0.36)	62.4 (1.33)	60.7 (1.30)	7.4 (0.59)	73.1 (1.82)	69.0 (1.85)	28.3 (1.99)	14.7 (1.50)
Public institutions											
4-year doctoral	49.5 (1.41)	36.4 (1.32)	11.8 (1.07)	3.5 (0.30)	57.4 (1.13)	55.2 (1.15)	11.2 (0.62)	64.6 (0.89)	61.9 (0.88)	25.0 (0.87)	16.5 (0.83)
Other 4-year	49.6 (2.01)	34.5 (1.92)	11.5 (0.76)	3.5 (0.52)	58.6 (1.81)	57.1 (1.81)	9.0 (1.33)	64.9 (2.05)	60.1 (1.96)	27.1 (1.94)	16.5 (1.55)
2-year	‡ (†)	‡ (†)	‡ (†)	‡ (†)	46.2 (4.35)	42.6 (4.16)	5.4 (1.41)	‡ (†)	‡ (†)	‡ (†)	‡ (†)
Private nonprofit institutions											
4-year doctoral	50.5 (1.76)	42.7 (1.98)	20.7 (1.35)	5.2 (0.48)	63.1 (1.71)	61.2 (1.69)	17.5 (1.26)	74.1 (2.82)	69.2 (2.69)	36.9 (2.87)	29.0 (3.14)
Other 4-year	61.8 (1.81)	51.7 (1.59)	14.9 (1.72)	7.4 (0.76)	72.3 (1.86)	70.2 (1.94)	17.7 (1.80)	74.2 (2.69)	71.8 (2.73)	38.2 (2.28)	25.9 (2.16)
Private for-profit institutions											
2-year and above	‡ (†)	‡ (†)	‡ (†)	‡ (†)	86.2 (3.62)	84.9 (3.76)	28.4 (5.58)	85.4 (3.16)	84.3 (3.43)	38.0 (3.73)	38.6 (4.07)

Average cumulative loan amount for students with loans (constant 2014–15 dollars)[6]

Selected student characteristic or control and level of institution (1)	1989–90 Total[1] (2)	1989–90 Stafford Loans[3] (3)	1989–90 Perkins Loans (4)	1989–90 Parent PLUS Loans[4] (5)	1999–2000 Total[1] (6)	1999–2000 Federal loans to students[2] (7)	1999–2000 Parent PLUS Loans[4] (8)	2011–12 Total[1] (9)	2011–12 Federal loans to students (10)	2011–12 Nonfederal loans (11)	2011–12 Parent PLUS Loans[4] (12)
Total	$15,300 (320)	$11,900 (210)	$4,500 (150)	$9,100 (260)	$22,300 (200)	$19,500 (150)	$19,500 (770)	$26,400 (410)	$21,000 (230)	$15,000 (740)	$28,400 (1,260)
Sex											
Male	15,800 (350)	12,200 (260)	4,300 (220)	9,700 (410)	22,200 (300)	19,600 (190)	20,200 (990)	26,800 (660)	20,800 (320)	16,600 (1,270)	29,700 (2,140)
Female	14,800 (410)	11,600 (230)	4,600 (170)	8,700 (440)	22,300 (300)	19,400 (230)	18,900 (1,020)	26,200 (490)	21,300 (300)	13,700 (810)	27,200 (1,460)
Race/ethnicity											
White	16,000 (330)	12,100 (260)	4,400 (130)	9,500 (250)	22,100 (270)	19,200 (170)	20,200 (920)	26,400 (490)	20,400 (280)	15,500 (780)	28,700 (1,620)
Black	12,100 (720)	12,200 (500)	5,600 (620)	‡ (†)	25,600 (780)	23,100 (680)	15,200 (1,390)	31,100 (1,180)	26,500 (680)	15,000 (2,230)	26,400 (3,330)
Hispanic	10,400 (1,000)	10,200 (580)	4,000 (300)	‡ (†)	21,400 (890)	18,700 (590)	18,200 (1,800)	25,300 (1,100)	20,400 (710)	14,100 (2,260)	24,900 (3,480)
Asian[5]	13,400 (850)	9,600 (550)	4,400 (730)	‡ (†)	19,700 (580)	18,100 (550)	15,600 (3,430)	20,700 (1,200)	18,400 (770)	10,300 (1,990)	29,300 (3,670)
Pacific Islander[5]	‡ (†)	‡ (†)	‡ (†)	‡ (†)	18,800 (2,710)	16,600 (1,810)	‡ (†)	‡ (†)	‡ (†)	‡ (†)	‡ (†)
American Indian/Alaska Native	‡ (†)	‡ (†)	‡ (†)	‡ (†)	22,800 (3,820)	22,300 (2,980)	‡ (†)	‡ (†)	‡ (†)	‡ (†)	‡ (†)
Two or more races	— (†)	— (†)	— (†)	— (†)	24,100 (1,660)	21,200 (1,400)	‡ (†)	26,500 (2,990)	19,500 (1,210)	15,900 ! (5,300)	‡ (†)
Dependency status											
Dependent	15,600 (330)	11,700 (200)	4,600 (170)	9,300 (300)	22,100 (220)	19,100 (150)	20,100 (840)	26,200 (450)	20,500 (240)	15,200 (800)	28,300 (1,120)
Independent	14,500 (560)	12,500 (350)	4,300 (180)	8,200 (520)	22,900 (530)	21,000 (470)	14,900 (1,240)	27,600 (940)	23,500 (730)	14,000 (1,720)	28,700 (6,320)
Public institutions											
4-year doctoral	13,700 (530)	11,200 (290)	4,000 (240)	9,200 (420)	21,200 (300)	19,200 (250)	16,500 (790)	24,200 (450)	20,200 (320)	12,300 (680)	23,100 (1,110)
Other 4-year	10,200 (400)	9,500 (610)	3,600 (250)	7,700 (590)	19,900 (540)	18,000 (470)	12,800 (710)	21,800 (850)	18,700 (610)	10,700 (1,220)	20,200 (1,790)
2-year	‡ (†)	‡ (†)	‡ (†)	‡ (†)	12,500 (1,290)	11,900 (1,170)	‡ (†)	‡ (†)	‡ (†)	‡ (†)	‡ (†)

See notes at end of table.

Table 331.95. Percentage of undergraduate students ages 18 to 24 in their 4th (senior) year or above who ever received federal loans, nonfederal loans, or Parent Loans for Undergraduates (PLUS), and average cumulative amount borrowed, by selected student characteristics and control and level of institution: 1989–90, 1999–2000, and 2011–12—Continued

[Standard errors appear in parentheses]

Selected student characteristic or control and level of institution	1989–90				1999–2000			2011–12			
	Federal loans to students[2]										
	Total[1]	Stafford Loans[3]	Perkins Loans	Parent PLUS Loans[4]	Total[1]	Federal loans to students[2]	Parent PLUS Loans[4]	Total[1]	Federal loans to students	Nonfederal loans	Parent PLUS Loans[4]
1	2	3	4	5	6	7	8	9	10	11	12
Private nonprofit institutions											
4-year doctoral............	23,800 (420)	14,400 (330)	5,700 (310)	9,800 (550)	27,800 (680)	22,500 (490)	28,100 (1,720)	31,500 (1,900)	23,200 (720)	19,900 (3,200)	42,700 (4,980)
Other 4-year................	19,900 (990)	14,000 (450)	5,900 (490)	9,300 (700)	26,100 (690)	21,600 (390)	24,200 (2,140)	32,700 (1,330)	22,800 (600)	20,600 (2,380)	30,900 (2,160)
Private for-profit institutions											
2-year and above........	‡ (†)	‡ (†)	‡ (†)	‡ (†)	24,200 (1,790)	20,000 (1,960)	19,100 (4,860)	40,500 (2,060)	32,500 (1,280)	19,000 (3,520)	34,300 (4,170)

—Not available.
†Not applicable.
‡Reporting standards not met. Either there are too few cases for a reliable estimate or the coefficient of variation (CV) is 50 percent or greater.

Interpret data with caution. The coefficient of variation (CV) for this estimate is between 30 and 50 percent.
[1]For 1989–90 data, total borrowed includes loans from family and friends. For 1999–2000 and 2011–12 data, total borrowed excludes loans from family and friends.
[2]Includes Stafford Loans and Perkins Loans only.
[3]Cumulative Stafford Loan amounts shown in the table include federal subsidized and unsubsidized Stafford Loans as well as any Supplemental Loans for Students (SLS) received in prior years. The SLS program was an unsubsidized student loan program limited to independent students and some dependent students with special circumstances. Beginning in 1993–94, the SLS program was replaced by unsubsidized Stafford Loans, which are available to both independent and dependent students regardless of need. Subsidized Stafford Loans are available only to students with demonstrated financial need. Stafford Loans were

available through both the William D. Ford Federal Direct Loan Program and the Federal Family Education Loan Program (FFELP) until FFELP was discontinued in 2010. Since then, Stafford Loans have been referred to as Direct Loans.
[4]Parent PLUS Loans are taken out by parents of dependent students and are used toward the students' undergraduate education. Parent PLUS Loans were available through both the William D. Ford Federal Direct Loan Program and the Federal Family Education Loan Program (FFELP) until FFELP was discontinued in 2010. Since then, Parent PLUS Loans have been referred to as Direct PLUS Loans.
[5]Includes Pacific Islanders in 1989–90.
[6]Average loan amounts were calculated only for students who took out a loan (or whose parents took out a PLUS loan on their behalf). Constant dollars based on the Consumer Price Index, prepared by the Bureau of Labor Statistics, U.S. Department of Labor, adjusted to a school-year basis.
NOTE: Data exclude Puerto Rico. Some data have been revised from previously published figures.
SOURCE: U.S. Department of Education, National Center for Education Statistics, 1989–90, 1999–2000, and 2011–12 National Postsecondary Student Aid Study (NPSAS:90, NPSAS:2000, and NPSAS:12). (This table was prepared August 2015.)

Table 332.10. Amount borrowed, aid status, and sources of aid for full-time, full-year postbaccalaureate students, by level of study and control and level of institution: Selected years, 1992–93 through 2011–12

[Standard errors appear in parentheses]

Level of study, control and level of institution	Cumulative borrowing for undergraduate and graduate education[1]						Aid status (percent of students)										
	Percent who borrowed		Average amount for those who borrowed						Source of aid								
			Current dollars		Constant 2014–15 dollars[4]		Nonaided		Any aid[2]		Federal[3]		State		Institutional		Employer	
1	2		3		4		5		6		7		8		9		10	
1992–93, all institutions	—	(†)	—	(†)	—	(†)	30.7	(1.43)	69.3	(1.43)	44.3	(1.42)	6.9	(0.64)	40.6	(2.02)	5.3	(0.59)
Master's degree	—	(†)	—	(†)	—	(†)	35.5	(2.54)	64.5	(2.54)	33.8	(1.91)	5.8	(0.79)	42.4	(2.97)	8.3	(1.01)
Public	—	(†)	—	(†)	—	(†)	32.7	(2.40)	67.3	(2.40)	33.9	(2.04)	7.8	(1.10)	44.1	(2.68)	7.6	(1.24)
4-year doctoral	—	(†)	—	(†)	—	(†)	32.4	(2.59)	67.6	(2.59)	32.4	(2.23)	6.7	(0.96)	46.4	(3.19)	7.7	(1.28)
Other 4-year	—	(†)	—	(†)	—	(†)	34.6	(4.38)	65.4	(4.38)	42.5	(5.30)	14.4	(4.13)	30.5	(3.67)	6.8	(2.66)
Private	—	(†)	—	(†)	—	(†)	39.2	(4.74)	60.8	(4.74)	33.7	(3.62)	3.2	(0.89)	40.2	(6.34)	9.4	(1.88)
4-year doctoral	—	(†)	—	(†)	—	(†)	37.4	(4.70)	62.6	(4.70)	34.2	(4.09)	2.9	(1.00)	42.9	(6.75)	8.9	(1.88)
Other 4-year	—	(†)	—	(†)	—	(†)	50.5	(10.60)	49.5	(10.60)	30.5	(7.06)	5.1	(2.98)	22.8	(9.39)	12.1	(6.81)
Doctor's degree	—	(†)	—	(†)	—	(†)	30.1	(2.32)	69.9	(2.32)	28.3	(2.14)	4.4	(0.71)	51.6	(2.70)	3.0	(0.79)
Public	—	(†)	—	(†)	—	(†)	29.9	(2.99)	70.1	(2.99)	22.3	(2.26)	6.5	(1.14)	55.5	(3.01)	3.9	(1.00)
Private	—	(†)	—	(†)	—	(†)	30.4	(3.27)	69.6	(3.27)	37.8	(3.54)	1.1	(0.73)	45.5	(3.52)	1.7	(1.19)
First-professional	—	(†)	—	(†)	—	(†)	22.6	(0.96)	77.4	(0.96)	68.2	(1.54)	9.9	(1.34)	37.0	(1.81)	2.3	(0.52)
Public	—	(†)	—	(†)	—	(†)	20.4	(1.02)	79.6	(1.02)	72.5	(1.29)	13.4	(1.75)	37.7	(1.67)	2.3	(0.59)
Private	—	(†)	—	(†)	—	(†)	24.6	(1.66)	75.4	(1.66)	64.2	(2.42)	6.8	(1.19)	36.4	(3.29)	2.3	(0.70)
Other graduate	—	(†)	—	(†)	—	(†)	38.3	(6.82)	61.7	(6.82)	42.1	(4.26)	6.6	(1.81)	23.0	(4.05)	6.0	(2.98)
1999–2000, all institutions	69.4	(0.74)	$41,920	(863)	$58,610	(1,207)	18.3	(0.66)	81.7	(0.66)	52.5	(0.76)	6.0	(0.60)	49.7	(1.03)	6.0	(0.57)
Master's degree	68.3	(1.12)	31,930	(1,097)	44,640	(1,534)	20.6	(1.15)	79.4	(1.15)	50.6	(1.23)	5.1	(0.66)	45.4	(1.61)	9.2	(1.03)
Public	63.2	(1.60)	28,070	(1,079)	39,240	(1,508)	22.3	(1.52)	77.7	(1.52)	44.8	(1.82)	7.3	(1.14)	49.8	(2.16)	7.0	(1.04)
4-year doctoral	62.5	(1.56)	27,510	(1,234)	38,460	(1,725)	20.2	(1.46)	79.8	(1.46)	43.3	(1.71)	7.0	(1.31)	54.3	(2.02)	7.3	(1.20)
Other 4-year	70.9	(6.04)	31,920	(2,822)	44,630	(3,946)	29.9	(5.08)	70.1	(5.08)	54.7	(6.88)	10.2 !	(3.32)	27.4	(6.85)	5.1 !	(1.79)
Private	74.4	(1.55)	35,890	(1,855)	50,180	(2,593)	18.6	(1.59)	81.4	(1.59)	57.8	(1.88)	2.5	(0.63)	40.2	(2.63)	11.8	(1.89)
4-year doctoral	73.3	(1.76)	38,420	(2,521)	53,710	(3,525)	17.1	(1.93)	82.9	(1.93)	58.3	(2.36)	2.9 !	(0.90)	50.5	(3.22)	8.3	(1.31)
Other[5]	76.9	(3.74)	30,770	(1,850)	43,020	(2,586)	21.8	(2.75)	78.2	(2.75)	56.6	(4.41)	‡	(†)	18.1	(3.91)	19.1	(5.24)
Doctor's degree	56.8	(1.95)	38,990	(3,421)	54,510	(4,782)	12.0	(1.38)	88.0	(1.38)	29.6	(2.80)	2.6	(0.54)	77.4	(1.65)	5.4	(0.64)
Public	54.5	(1.92)	33,600	(1,564)	46,970	(2,187)	11.4	(1.38)	88.6	(1.38)	26.1	(1.86)	3.2	(0.75)	80.0	(1.59)	7.3	(0.88)
Private	60.5	(3.62)	46,680	(7,288)	65,260	(10,190)	13.0	(2.80)	87.0	(2.80)	35.2	(6.26)	‡	(†)	73.2	(3.22)	2.3	(0.55)
First-professional	85.1	(1.14)	60,860	(1,713)	85,080	(2,395)	13.4	(1.18)	86.6	(1.18)	77.1	(1.29)	9.9	(1.65)	41.4	(2.40)	1.7 !	(0.53)
Public	86.8	(1.70)	52,790	(1,954)	73,800	(2,732)	13.8	(1.82)	86.2	(1.82)	78.3	(2.13)	12.7	(2.57)	38.9	(2.84)	1.8 !	(0.87)
Private	83.6	(1.63)	67,820	(3,213)	94,820	(4,492)	13.1	(1.49)	86.9	(1.49)	76.1	(1.84)	7.5	(2.11)	43.4	(3.65)	1.7 !	(0.66)
Other graduate	57.5	(3.81)	27,840	(2,036)	38,920	(2,847)	39.3	(3.68)	60.7	(3.68)	44.9	(3.72)	8.1	(2.37)	25.3	(3.22)	2.8 !	(1.20)
2007–08, all institutions	71.3	(1.04)	$55,110	(993)	$61,610	(1,110)	13.1	(0.80)	86.9	(0.80)	56.6	(1.18)	3.8	(0.28)	43.9	(1.17)	11.6	(0.93)
Master's degree	71.8	(1.77)	43,250	(1,374)	48,350	(1,536)	15.6	(1.34)	84.4	(1.34)	55.5	(1.93)	2.9	(0.40)	35.5	(1.48)	16.3	(1.76)
Public	66.5	(1.79)	37,770	(1,473)	42,230	(1,647)	13.3	(1.27)	86.7	(1.27)	50.7	(1.91)	4.1	(0.83)	52.2	(2.40)	13.4	(1.49)
4-year doctoral	65.1	(1.95)	38,450	(1,644)	42,990	(1,838)	12.1	(1.34)	87.9	(1.34)	50.1	(2.07)	4.2	(0.93)	56.0	(2.62)	14.5	(1.68)
Other 4-year	77.1	(4.81)	33,440	(2,285)	37,380	(2,555)	22.7	(3.92)	77.3	(3.92)	55.6	(5.96)	‡	(†)	23.5	(4.89)	5.1 !	(1.92)
Private	75.5	(2.58)	46,590	(1,974)	52,090	(2,206)	17.2	(1.96)	82.8	(1.96)	58.8	(2.81)	2.0	(0.35)	24.0	(1.59)	18.3	(2.79)
4-year doctoral	71.4	(1.85)	46,510	(1,654)	52,000	(1,849)	19.1	(1.45)	80.9	(1.45)	55.1	(1.51)	2.4	(0.50)	36.0	(2.46)	14.4	(1.17)
Other[5]	80.8	(5.13)	46,670	(3,671)	52,180	(4,104)	14.8	(3.91)	85.2	(3.91)	63.6	(5.96)	1.6	(0.43)	8.4	(1.44)	23.4	(6.23)
Doctor's degree	59.8	(1.73)	55,200	(2,108)	61,710	(2,357)	7.1	(0.88)	92.9	(0.88)	38.4	(2.18)	2.9	(0.41)	70.7	(3.03)	7.9	(0.79)
Public	52.3	(2.17)	44,190	(1,604)	49,400	(1,793)	7.9	(1.48)	92.1	(1.48)	29.7	(1.80)	3.6	(0.65)	81.1	(1.89)	7.7	(0.93)
Private	67.8	(2.41)	64,120	(3,123)	71,680	(3,492)	6.2	(1.08)	93.8	(1.08)	47.6	(3.43)	2.2 !	(0.65)	59.8	(5.02)	8.0	(1.36)
First-professional	84.9	(1.29)	81,400	(1,782)	91,000	(1,992)	11.5	(1.12)	88.5	(1.12)	81.7	(1.35)	7.5	(0.83)	35.7	(1.89)	4.6	(0.75)
Public	84.4	(1.96)	73,230	(2,717)	81,870	(3,038)	11.5	(1.65)	88.5	(1.65)	81.8	(2.12)	10.6	(1.46)	34.0	(2.67)	4.9	(1.44)
Private	85.4	(1.57)	87,800	(2,183)	98,160	(2,441)	11.5	(1.46)	88.5	(1.46)	81.5	(1.67)	5.1	(0.85)	37.0	(2.56)	4.4	(0.72)
Other graduate	62.4	(6.48)	43,740	(3,904)	48,900	(4,365)	30.8	(6.54)	69.2	(6.54)	51.0	(6.62)	‡	(†)	25.5	(5.78)	6.2 !	(2.33)

See notes at end of table.

Table 332.10. Amount borrowed, aid status, and sources of aid for full-time, full-year postbaccalaureate students, by level of study and control and level of institution: Selected years, 1992–93 through 2011–12—Continued

[Standard errors appear in parentheses]

Level of study, control and level of institution	Percent who borrowed		Current dollars		Constant 2014–15 dollars[4]		Nonaided		Any aid[2]		Federal[3]		State		Institutional		Employer	
			Average amount for those who borrowed						Source of aid									
1	2		3		4		5		6		7		8		9		10	
2011–12, all institutions.........	73.3	(0.90)	$74,710	(996)	$77,700	(1,036)	13.9	(0.77)	86.1	(0.77)	62.3	(0.93)	2.4	(0.34)	42.2	(1.19)	10.2	(0.48)
Master's degree	73.5	(1.45)	58,590	(1,142)	60,940	(1,188)	17.4	(1.28)	82.6	(1.28)	63.0	(1.44)	1.8	(0.35)	35.1	(1.53)	8.8	(0.70)
Public	71.8	(2.24)	50,200	(1,816)	52,210	(1,889)	16.2	(1.84)	83.8	(1.84)	58.2	(2.41)	3.7	(0.80)	45.6	(2.35)	10.3	(1.17)
4-year doctoral	70.7	(2.41)	50,620	(2,015)	52,650	(2,095)	16.3	(2.03)	83.7	(2.03)	57.0	(2.60)	4.0	(0.89)	47.1	(2.56)	10.8	(1.28)
Other 4-year	82.2	(3.71)	46,900	(2,538)	48,780	(2,640)	15.4	(4.13)	84.6	(4.13)	69.5	(5.18)	‡	(†)	31.2	(3.46)	5.9	(1.68)
Private...	74.8	(1.95)	64,510	(1,456)	67,090	(1,514)	18.2	(1.80)	81.8	(1.80)	66.5	(2.13)	0.4 !	(0.19)	27.5	(2.09)	7.8	(0.88)
4-year doctoral	70.1	(2.41)	67,130	(2,165)	69,820	(2,252)	19.6	(2.06)	80.4	(2.06)	59.5	(2.45)	‡	(†)	35.2	(2.96)	7.8	(1.23)
Other[5]...................................	81.8	(3.20)	61,140	(1,816)	63,590	(1,889)	16.1	(3.09)	83.9	(3.09)	77.0	(3.66)	‡	(†)	15.9	(2.70)	7.6	(1.04)
Doctor's degree—research/ scholarship	50.5	(1.42)	65,090	(2,343)	67,700	(2,437)	6.6	(0.73)	93.4	(0.73)	27.8	(1.19)	1.5 !	(0.49)	79.8	(1.27)	24.0	(1.25)
Public	47.9	(2.23)	55,500	(2,291)	57,720	(2,383)	5.9	(1.04)	94.1	(1.04)	24.2	(1.41)	2.1 !	(0.78)	87.2	(1.59)	27.0	(1.93)
Private...	54.0	(1.86)	76,180	(4,351)	79,230	(4,525)	7.5	(1.07)	92.5	(1.07)	32.3	(2.30)	‡	(†)	70.1	(2.28)	20.1	(1.06)
Doctor's degree—professional practice and other[6].....................	88.3	(0.90)	110,570	(1,848)	115,000	(1,922)	9.3	(0.88)	90.7	(0.88)	84.4	(1.03)	4.5	(0.96)	35.1	(1.66)	4.4	(0.51)
Public	88.3	(1.00)	102,220	(2,726)	106,310	(2,835)	8.9	(1.09)	91.1	(1.09)	84.4	(1.31)	8.1	(2.27)	40.6	(2.51)	5.4	(0.82)
Private...	88.3	(1.28)	116,000	(2,490)	120,640	(2,589)	9.6	(1.22)	90.4	(1.22)	84.4	(1.50)	2.2	(0.53)	31.5	(2.19)	3.7	(0.62)
Other graduate..............................	74.9	(6.28)	57,540	(5,456)	59,840	(5,674)	29.1	(6.46)	70.9	(6.46)	61.4	(7.24)	‡	(†)	16.9	(4.78)	5.5 !	(2.47)

—Not available.
†Not applicable.
!Interpret data with caution. The coefficient of variation (CV) for this estimate is between 30 and 50 percent.
‡Reporting standards not met. Either there are too few cases for a reliable estimate or the coefficient of variation (CV) is 50 percent or greater.
[1]Includes all loans ever taken out for both graduate and undergraduate education. Does not include Parent Loans for Undergraduate Students (PLUS) or loans from families and friends.
[2]Includes students who reported they were awarded aid, but did not specify the source of aid.
[3]Includes Department of Veterans Affairs and Department of Defense benefits.
[4]Constant dollars based on the Consumer Price Index, prepared by the Bureau of Labor Statistics, U.S. Department of Labor, adjusted to a school-year basis.

[5]Includes nonprofit 4-year nondoctoral institutions and for-profit 2-year-and-above institutions.
[6]Professional practice doctor's degrees include most degrees formerly classified as first-professional (such as M.D., D.D.S., and J.D.). "Other" doctor's degrees are those that are neither research/scholarship degrees nor professional practice degrees.
NOTE: Excludes students whose attendance status was not reported. Total includes some students whose level of study or control of institution was unknown. Detail may not sum to totals because of rounding and because some students receive multiple types of aid and aid from different sources. Data exclude Puerto Rico. Some data have been revised from previously published figures.
SOURCE: U.S. Department of Education, National Center for Education Statistics, 1992–93, 1999–2000, 2007–08, and 2011–12 National Postsecondary Student Aid Study (NPSAS:93, NPSAS:2000, NPSAS:08, and NPSAS:12). (This table was prepared September 2015.)

Table 332.20. Amount borrowed, aid status, and sources of aid for part-time or part-year postbaccalaureate students, by level of study and control and level of institution: Selected years, 1992–93 through 2011–12

[Standard errors appear in parentheses]

Level of study, control and level of institution	Cumulative borrowing for undergraduate and graduate education[1]						Aid status (percent of students)									
	Percent who borrowed		Average amount for those who borrowed						Source of aid							
			Current dollars		Constant 2014–15 dollars[4]		Nonaided		Any aid[2]		Federal[3]		State		Institutional		Employer	
1	2		3		4		5		6		7		8		9		10	
1992–93, all institutions	—	(†)	—	(†)	—	(†)	63.2	(0.81)	36.8	(0.81)	10.8	(0.53)	1.9	(0.14)	12.7	(0.53)	16.7	(0.71)
Master's degree	—	(†)	—	(†)	—	(†)	62.5	(0.85)	37.5	(0.85)	10.5	(0.61)	1.6	(0.18)	11.1	(0.70)	18.7	(0.91)
Public	—	(†)	—	(†)	—	(†)	66.4	(1.00)	33.6	(1.00)	10.1	(0.57)	2.5	(0.30)	11.7	(0.77)	14.6	(0.83)
4-year doctoral	—	(†)	—	(†)	—	(†)	62.2	(1.25)	37.8	(1.25)	11.9	(0.81)	2.5	(0.48)	15.3	(1.11)	14.6	(1.06)
Other 4-year	—	(†)	—	(†)	—	(†)	73.7	(1.39)	26.3	(1.39)	6.9	(0.76)	2.4	(0.55)	5.5	(1.11)	14.4	(1.09)
Private	—	(†)	—	(†)	—	(†)	57.0	(1.56)	43.0	(1.56)	11.1	(1.06)	0.4	(0.12)	10.3	(1.04)	24.5	(1.46)
4-year doctoral	—	(†)	—	(†)	—	(†)	55.2	(1.91)	44.8	(1.91)	12.1	(1.15)	0.3	(0.16)	12.1	(1.57)	25.1	(1.72)
Other 4-year	—	(†)	—	(†)	—	(†)	60.4	(2.84)	39.6	(2.84)	9.1	(1.73)	0.6	(0.28)	6.9	(1.33)	23.3	(2.36)
Doctor's degree	—	(†)	—	(†)	—	(†)	51.7	(2.56)	48.3	(2.56)	8.7	(1.18)	3.5	(0.79)	32.9	(2.46)	12.0	(1.49)
Public	—	(†)	—	(†)	—	(†)	51.6	(3.09)	48.4	(3.09)	8.5	(1.38)	4.4	(1.25)	33.0	(3.05)	12.9	(1.89)
Private	—	(†)	—	(†)	—	(†)	51.8	(5.53)	48.2	(5.53)	8.9	(2.49)	1.6	(0.68)	32.6	(4.51)	10.2	(2.47)
First-professional	—	(†)	—	(†)	—	(†)	41.4	(3.04)	58.6	(3.04)	44.9	(3.13)	3.3	(0.71)	25.7	(2.07)	6.1	(1.34)
Public	—	(†)	—	(†)	—	(†)	48.3	(4.43)	51.7	(4.43)	42.8	(3.96)	3.6	(1.11)	22.2	(3.35)	5.0	(1.61)
Private	—	(†)	—	(†)	—	(†)	37.4	(3.43)	62.6	(3.43)	46.1	(3.92)	3.2	(0.91)	27.8	(2.44)	6.7	(1.81)
Other graduate	—	(†)	—	(†)	—	(†)	73.0	(1.42)	27.0	(1.42)	7.6	(0.76)	1.7	(0.42)	8.4	(0.85)	13.4	(1.00)
1999–2000, all institutions	55.7	(0.78)	$22,060	(408)	$30,840	(571)	51.3	(0.72)	48.7	(0.72)	19.2	(0.50)	1.7	(0.21)	16.0	(0.51)	20.2	(0.66)
Master's degree	56.9	(0.90)	20,800	(400)	29,080	(559)	48.8	(0.83)	51.2	(0.83)	20.6	(0.66)	1.4	(0.26)	14.1	(0.59)	23.2	(0.81)
Public	55.9	(1.22)	18,030	(499)	25,210	(698)	53.0	(1.19)	47.0	(1.19)	16.9	(0.82)	2.0	(0.38)	15.3	(0.95)	20.7	(1.32)
4-year doctoral	56.3	(1.53)	18,640	(686)	26,060	(959)	49.6	(1.56)	50.4	(1.56)	18.2	(1.21)	2.1	(0.51)	18.1	(1.22)	21.4	(1.62)
Other 4-year	54.5	(2.19)	16,320	(649)	22,820	(907)	60.8	(1.96)	39.2	(1.96)	14.2	(1.45)	2.0	(0.50)	9.5	(1.52)	18.5	(2.28)
Private	58.2	(1.24)	24,180	(666)	33,800	(931)	43.5	(1.26)	56.5	(1.26)	25.2	(1.05)	0.6 !	(0.23)	12.6	(0.94)	26.5	(1.15)
4-year doctoral	57.6	(1.62)	25,620	(918)	35,820	(1,283)	42.3	(1.43)	57.7	(1.43)	25.2	(1.38)	0.9 !	(0.34)	14.8	(1.12)	25.5	(1.23)
Other[5]	59.4	(2.15)	21,610	(1,068)	30,210	(1,494)	45.9	(2.26)	54.1	(2.26)	25.3	(1.96)	‡	(†)	8.4	(1.63)	28.3	(2.23)
Doctor's degree	53.1	(1.73)	28,140	(1,966)	39,340	(2,749)	45.5	(1.81)	54.5	(1.81)	15.0	(1.41)	0.9	(0.17)	37.3	(1.66)	14.0	(1.35)
Public	48.6	(1.86)	25,050	(1,478)	35,020	(2,066)	46.7	(2.34)	53.3	(2.34)	13.1	(1.17)	1.4	(0.25)	40.5	(2.04)	12.1	(1.46)
Private	62.5	(3.81)	33,250	(4,031)	46,480	(5,635)	42.9	(2.95)	57.1	(2.95)	19.3	(3.46)	#	(†)	30.6	(2.65)	18.1	(3.16)
First-professional	77.2	(4.07)	47,480	(3,827)	66,380	(5,350)	24.4	(3.17)	75.6	(3.17)	55.4	(4.94)	5.0 !	(1.80)	28.0	(2.97)	11.0	(2.09)
Public	78.6	(6.98)	40,590	(3,682)	56,750	(5,147)	27.3	(6.84)	72.7	(6.84)	54.4	(8.28)	4.8 !	(2.30)	21.7	(6.36)	8.0 !	(3.85)
Private	76.7	(4.80)	50,550	(5,236)	70,670	(7,321)	23.2	(3.14)	76.8	(3.14)	55.9	(6.37)	5.0 !	(2.46)	30.7	(2.91)	12.3	(2.85)
Other graduate	48.7	(2.02)	15,810	(711)	22,100	(994)	67.0	(1.77)	33.0	(1.77)	9.8	(1.25)	2.2	(0.47)	10.2	(1.07)	15.3	(1.31)
2007–08, all institutions	66.9	(0.76)	$36,280	(840)	$40,560	(939)	33.2	(0.85)	66.8	(0.85)	32.0	(0.71)	1.9	(0.50)	18.7	(0.65)	27.2	(0.93)
Master's degree	67.3	(1.08)	34,110	(906)	38,130	(1012)	31.0	(1.10)	69.0	(1.10)	34.4	(0.98)	2.0 !	(0.68)	15.9	(0.71)	29.8	(1.22)
Public	65.2	(1.30)	30,880	(702)	34,520	(785)	34.3	(1.39)	65.7	(1.39)	29.7	(0.94)	1.7	(0.37)	18.0	(0.92)	27.8	(1.43)
4-year doctoral	65.4	(1.38)	31,440	(816)	35,150	(912)	32.3	(1.60)	67.7	(1.60)	29.7	(1.17)	1.8	(0.47)	20.3	(1.15)	29.4	(1.71)
Other 4-year	64.7	(3.08)	29,080	(1,639)	32,510	(1,832)	40.6	(2.99)	59.4	(2.99)	29.7	(2.67)	1.2 !	(0.48)	10.4	(1.40)	22.7	(2.56)
Private	69.5	(1.57)	37,180	(1,517)	41,570	(1,697)	27.7	(1.59)	72.3	(1.59)	39.1	(1.49)	‡	(†)	13.8	(1.12)	31.7	(1.85)
4-year doctoral	66.6	(1.37)	37,230	(909)	41,620	(1,017)	29.0	(1.52)	71.0	(1.52)	34.1	(1.53)	1.5	(0.40)	15.9	(1.27)	32.9	(1.20)
Other[5]	74.1	(3.29)	37,090	(3,292)	41,470	(3,680)	25.6	(3.25)	74.4	(3.25)	47.2	(2.91)	‡	(†)	10.4	(1.68)	29.9	(4.50)
Doctor's degree	64.8	(3.47)	52,080	(5,396)	58,220	(6,033)	20.1	(1.92)	79.9	(1.92)	32.0	(4.96)	1.5	(0.33)	48.4	(3.16)	19.2	(1.73)
Public	54.8	(1.94)	36,790	(1,355)	41,130	(1,515)	23.2	(1.57)	76.8	(1.57)	18.0	(1.21)	2.2	(0.42)	60.2	(1.77)	19.6	(1.43)
Private	77.9	(5.58)	66,360	(9,120)	74,190	(10,196)	16.0	(3.95)	84.0	(3.95)	50.5	(9.18)	‡	(†)	32.7	(5.18)	18.6	(4.11)
First-professional	82.7	(2.34)	64,520	(3,850)	72,130	(4,304)	14.4	(2.54)	85.6	(2.54)	64.0	(4.52)	3.0 !	(1.36)	31.7	(3.39)	16.5	(2.21)
Public	78.2	(4.97)	63,520	(5,656)	71,010	(6,323)	11.7	(4.96)	88.3	(4.96)	65.4	(7.23)	6.3 !	(2.74)	32.9	(5.87)	16.3	(3.79)
Private	85.1	(2.51)	65,010	(5,405)	72,680	(6,043)	15.9	(3.09)	84.1	(3.09)	63.3	(6.18)	‡	(†)	31.1	(4.56)	16.7	(2.86)
Other graduate	64.0	(2.69)	28,950	(1,970)	32,370	(2,203)	56.1	(3.07)	43.9	(3.07)	16.1	(1.59)	1.2	(0.32)	7.5	(1.09)	23.4	(2.79)

See notes at end of table.

Table 332.20. Amount borrowed, aid status, and sources of aid for part-time or part-year postbaccalaureate students, by level of study and control and level of institution: Selected years, 1992–93 through 2011–12—Continued

[Standard errors appear in parentheses]

Level of study, control and level of institution	Cumulative borrowing for undergraduate and graduate education[1]						Aid status (percent of students)										
	Percent who borrowed		Average amount for those who borrowed						Source of aid								
			Current dollars		Constant 2014–15 dollars[4]		Nonaided		Any aid[2]		Federal[3]		State		Institutional		Employer	
1	2		3		4		5		6		7		8		9		10	
2011–12, all institutions	**63.6**	**(0.90)**	**$49,410**	**(968)**	**$51,390**	**(1,007)**	**39.1**	**(0.99)**	**60.9**	**(0.99)**	**35.8**	**(0.66)**	**1.0**	**(0.14)**	**18.0**	**(0.76)**	**17.0**	**(0.88)**
Master's degree	65.1	(1.13)	45,860	(1,055)	47,700	(1,097)	37.5	(1.29)	62.5	(1.29)	39.4	(0.88)	0.9	(0.18)	16.1	(0.89)	17.3	(1.13)
Public	61.5	(1.63)	40,340	(1,364)	41,960	(1,419)	42.9	(1.51)	57.1	(1.51)	34.3	(1.28)	1.6	(0.33)	17.0	(1.17)	14.7	(1.02)
4-year doctoral	60.2	(1.87)	40,870	(1,584)	42,510	(1,648)	41.5	(1.74)	58.5	(1.74)	34.1	(1.47)	1.8	(0.39)	18.6	(1.38)	15.6	(1.15)
Other 4-year	68.2	(2.74)	38,070	(2,079)	39,590	(2,162)	49.8	(2.32)	50.2	(2.32)	35.4	(2.04)	‡	(†)	9.0	(1.31)	10.3	(1.66)
Private	68.3	(1.73)	50,210	(1,536)	52,220	(1,597)	32.7	(1.94)	67.3	(1.94)	43.9	(1.31)	‡	(†)	15.3	(1.31)	19.5	(1.91)
4-year doctoral	63.6	(2.49)	49,510	(1,979)	51,490	(2,058)	34.3	(2.07)	65.7	(2.07)	37.9	(1.65)	‡	(†)	15.9	(1.77)	21.2	(2.02)
Other 4-year	74.4	(1.75)	51,000	(2,306)	53,040	(2,399)	30.6	(3.63)	69.4	(3.63)	51.7	(2.22)	‡	(†)	14.4	(2.05)	17.3	(3.39)
Doctor's degree—research/ scholarship	57.7	(1.52)	66,220	(2,390)	68,870	(2,486)	29.1	(1.67)	70.9	(1.67)	25.6	(1.54)	1.2	(0.21)	43.4	(2.01)	20.9	(1.35)
Public	50.2	(1.96)	51,810	(2,294)	53,880	(2,386)	30.1	(2.12)	69.9	(2.12)	16.6	(1.62)	1.3	(0.25)	51.6	(2.40)	23.6	(1.77)
Private	72.8	(1.72)	86,290	(3,951)	89,750	(4,109)	26.9	(2.56)	73.1	(2.56)	43.7	(2.76)	0.8 !	(0.38)	26.9	(2.44)	15.5	(1.78)
Doctor's degree—professional practice and other[6]	69.4	(3.45)	100,780	(4,860)	104,820	(5,055)	31.5	(3.09)	68.5	(3.09)	48.7	(3.68)	2.0	(0.59)	19.3	(2.20)	12.1	(1.83)
Public	61.6	(4.88)	79,230	(5,498)	82,400	(5,718)	41.7	(4.51)	58.3	(4.51)	38.1	(4.14)	3.6 !	(1.32)	23.3	(3.59)	12.6	(2.94)
Private	74.7	(4.23)	112,960	(6,242)	117,480	(6,492)	24.5	(3.48)	75.5	(3.48)	56.0	(5.04)	‡	(†)	16.6	(2.60)	11.8	(2.64)
Other graduate	56.0	(2.72)	39,690	(2,498)	41,280	(2,598)	59.4	(2.66)	40.6	(2.66)	16.5	(1.63)	1.1 !	(0.33)	11.5	(2.13)	14.6	(1.91)

—Not available.
†Not applicable.
#Rounds to zero.
!Interpret data with caution. The coefficient of variation (CV) for this estimate is between 30 and 50 percent.
‡Reporting standards not met. The coefficient of variation (CV) for this estimate is 50 percent or greater.
[1]Includes all loans ever taken out for both graduate and undergraduate education. Does not include Parent Loans for Undergraduate Students (PLUS) or loans from families or friends.
[2]Includes students who reported they were awarded aid, but did not specify the source of aid.
[3]Includes Department of Veterans Affairs and Department of Defense benefits.
[4]Constant dollars based on the Consumer Price Index, prepared by the Bureau of Labor Statistics, U.S. Department of Labor, adjusted to a school-year basis.

[5]Includes nonprofit 4-year nondoctoral institutions and for-profit 2-year-and-above institutions.
[6]Professional practice doctor's degrees include most degrees formerly classified as first-professional (such as M.D., D.D.S., and J.D.) "Other" doctor's degrees are those that are neither research/scholarship degrees nor professional practice degrees.
NOTE: Excludes students whose attendance status was not reported. Total includes some students whose level of study or control of institution was unknown. Detail may not sum to totals because of rounding and because some students receive multiple types of aid and aid from different sources. Data exclude Puerto Rico. Some data have been revised from previously published figures.
SOURCE: U.S. Department of Education, National Center for Education Statistics, 1992–93, 1999–2000, 2007–08, and 2011–12 National Postsecondary Student Aid Study (NPSAS:93, NPSAS:2000, NPSAS:08, and NPSAS:12). (This table was prepared September 2015.)

Table 332.30. Percentage of full-time, full-year postbaccalaureate students receiving financial aid, by type of aid, level of study, and control and level of institution: Selected years, 1992–93 through 2011–12

[Standard errors appear in parentheses]

Level of study, control and level of institution	Number of students (in thousands)	Any aid[2]	Fellowship grants	Tuition waivers	Assistantships[3]	Employer (includes college staff)	Any loans	Stafford[4]	Perkins[5]
1	2	3	4	5	6	7	8	9	10
1992–93, all institutions	672 (—)	69.3 (1.43)	[6] (†)	12.4 (1.00)	14.3 (1.32)	5.3 (0.59)	43.3 (1.36)	41.1 (1.40)	9.0 (0.89)
Master's degree	281 (—)	64.5 (2.54)	[6] (†)	15.7 (1.53)	18.1 (2.01)	8.3 (1.01)	32.3 (1.80)	30.5 (1.84)	5.0 (0.89)
Public	162 (—)	67.3 (2.40)	[6] (†)	20.6 (2.40)	22.4 (1.83)	7.6 (1.24)	32.1 (1.96)	30.9 (1.99)	4.0 (0.87)
4-year doctoral	139 (—)	67.6 (2.59)	[6] (†)	23.4 (2.76)	23.6 (2.25)	7.7 (1.28)	30.6 (2.15)	29.6 (2.16)	3.3 (0.85)
Other 4-year	24 (—)	65.4 (4.38)	[6] (†)	4.4 ! (2.12)	15.8 (3.11)	6.8 ! (2.66)	40.4 (5.65)	38.4 (5.72)	8.3 ! (3.50)
Private	118 (—)	60.8 (4.74)	[6] (†)	8.9 (1.74)	12.2 ! (4.44)	9.4 (1.88)	32.7 (3.39)	29.9 (3.42)	6.4 (1.50)
4-year doctoral	103 (—)	62.6 (4.70)	[6] (†)	9.5 (1.92)	13.6 ! (4.86)	8.9 (1.88)	33.3 (3.97)	30.8 (4.04)	6.7 (1.66)
Other 4-year	16 (—)	49.5 (10.60)	[6] (†)	‡ (†)	‡ (†)	‡ (†)	28.7 (5.35)	24.6 (5.32)	‡ (†)
Doctor's degree	120 (—)	69.9 (2.32)	[6] (†)	19.4 (1.91)	27.0 (2.36)	3.0 (0.79)	25.8 (2.33)	23.9 (2.16)	3.5 (0.71)
Public	74 (—)	70.1 (2.99)	[6] (†)	23.1 (2.78)	31.6 (2.31)	3.9 (1.00)	20.6 (2.04)	18.9 (2.07)	2.9 (0.85)
Private	46 (—)	69.6 (3.27)	[6] (†)	13.6 (2.50)	19.9 (3.74)	‡ (†)	34.1 (4.20)	31.9 (3.67)	4.3 (1.16)
First-professional	210 (—)	77.4 (0.96)	[6] (†)	5.6 (0.99)	4.3 (0.69)	2.3 (0.52)	67.8 (1.49)	65.6 (1.47)	19.3 (1.65)
Public	101 (—)	79.6 (1.02)	[6] (†)	5.4 (1.11)	4.2 (0.53)	2.3 (0.59)	71.9 (1.30)	70.0 (1.19)	23.3 (2.25)
Private	110 (—)	75.4 (1.66)	[6] (†)	5.8 (1.40)	4.4 (1.24)	2.3 ! (0.70)	64.0 (2.33)	61.5 (2.35)	15.7 (1.92)
Other graduate	61 (—)	61.7 (6.82)	[6] (†)	7.6 (1.65)	6.2 (1.62)	6.0 ! (2.98)	43.3 (4.26)	39.3 (4.04)	2.6 ! (0.87)
1999–2000, all institutions	873 (—)	81.7 (0.66)	20.5 (0.97)	11.9 (0.49)	24.0 (0.92)	6.0 (0.57)	52.4 (0.77)	50.6 (0.80)	8.3 (0.64)
Master's degree	406 (—)	79.4 (1.15)	16.8 (1.12)	11.5 (0.87)	21.9 (1.37)	9.2 (1.03)	50.5 (1.26)	48.9 (1.35)	5.8 (0.54)
Public	222 (—)	77.7 (1.52)	15.5 (1.45)	18.3 (1.46)	30.5 (1.89)	7.0 (1.04)	43.5 (1.82)	42.3 (1.91)	2.8 (0.57)
4-year doctoral	179 (—)	79.8 (1.46)	16.4 (1.64)	19.6 (1.59)	34.0 (2.06)	7.3 (1.20)	41.8 (1.68)	41.2 (1.66)	3.0 (0.67)
Other 4-year	37 (—)	70.1 (5.08)	11.2 (3.31)	14.6 ! (4.91)	14.1 ! (4.31)	5.1 ! (1.79)	54.4 (6.55)	53.1 (6.84)	‡ (†)
Private	184 (—)	81.4 (1.59)	18.3 (1.76)	3.2 (0.75)	11.6 (1.64)	11.8 (1.89)	59.1 (1.81)	56.8 (2.08)	9.5 (1.18)
4-year doctoral	125 (—)	82.9 (1.93)	23.9 (2.29)	4.1 (1.05)	13.9 (1.70)	8.3 (1.31)	60.7 (2.14)	57.4 (2.61)	11.9 (1.64)
Other[7]	58 (—)	78.2 (2.75)	6.3 ! (2.12)	1.4 ! (0.53)	‡ (†)	19.1 (5.24)	55.5 (4.49)	55.5 (4.49)	4.3 ! (1.52)
Doctor's degree	184 (—)	88.0 (1.38)	37.7 (1.43)	23.3 (1.40)	54.8 (3.13)	5.4 (0.64)	28.9 (2.89)	27.3 (2.84)	‡ (†)
Public	113 (—)	88.6 (1.38)	30.0 (1.28)	34.9 (1.66)	62.8 (1.80)	7.3 (0.88)	25.8 (1.96)	24.0 (1.89)	1.1 ! (0.37)
Private	71 (—)	87.0 (2.80)	49.8 (3.31)	5.1 (1.10)	42.1 (6.85)	2.3 (0.55)	33.7 (6.36)	32.4 (6.32)	‡ (†)
First-professional	222 (—)	86.6 (1.18)	17.3 (2.25)	4.3 (0.80)	6.9 (0.99)	1.7 ! (0.53)	77.9 (1.35)	75.5 (1.38)	17.5 (1.85)
Public	101 (—)	86.2 (1.82)	12.3 (1.72)	7.6 (1.52)	7.0 (1.51)	1.8 ! (0.87)	78.5 (2.17)	77.1 (2.16)	18.7 (2.22)
Private	121 (—)	86.9 (1.49)	21.4 (3.78)	1.6 ! (0.60)	6.8 (1.51)	1.7 ! (0.66)	77.3 (1.85)	74.2 (1.97)	16.5 (2.88)
Other graduate	61 (—)	60.7 (3.68)	5.5 (1.57)	8.5 (1.93)	7.1 (1.96)	2.8 ! (1.20)	42.7 (3.71)	42.5 (3.69)	3.4 ! (1.45)
2007–08, all institutions	1,139 (—)	86.9 (0.80)	23.6 (0.87)	12.2 (0.62)	25.1 (0.87)	11.6 (0.93)	58.4 (1.21)	55.2 (1.18)	6.1 (0.38)
Master's degree	592 (—)	84.4 (1.34)	17.8 (1.04)	10.7 (0.90)	19.3 (1.01)	16.3 (1.76)	59.5 (2.03)	54.9 (1.93)	4.4 (0.50)
Public	242 (—)	86.7 (1.27)	20.0 (1.83)	21.1 (1.99)	35.3 (1.78)	13.4 (1.49)	53.4 (1.87)	50.2 (1.88)	4.7 (0.96)
4-year doctoral	213 (—)	87.9 (1.34)	21.9 (2.03)	23.1 (2.18)	37.4 (1.98)	14.5 (1.68)	52.4 (2.02)	49.5 (2.05)	4.5 (1.01)
Other 4-year	28 (—)	77.3 (3.92)	5.2 ! (2.19)	6.0 ! (2.38)	19.8 (4.57)	5.1 ! (1.92)	61.1 (5.94)	55.6 (5.96)	6.2 ! (2.87)
Private	350 (—)	82.8 (1.96)	16.2 (1.33)	3.5 (0.61)	8.2 (0.74)	18.3 (2.79)	63.7 (2.89)	58.1 (2.79)	4.2 (0.54)
4-year doctoral	197 (—)	80.9 (1.45)	25.6 (2.19)	3.8 (0.63)	13.0 (1.18)	14.4 (1.17)	58.0 (1.52)	54.0 (1.51)	7.1 (0.95)
Other 4-year	153 (—)	85.2 (3.91)	4.1 (0.85)	3.2 ! (1.14)	2.0 (0.51)	23.4 (6.23)	71.0 (6.08)	63.5 (5.96)	‡ (†)
Doctor's degree	280 (—)	92.9 (0.88)	35.2 (1.91)	25.4 (1.70)	53.1 (2.55)	7.9 (0.79)	37.3 (2.32)	35.4 (2.23)	2.6 (0.46)
Public	143 (—)	92.1 (1.48)	30.8 (2.40)	39.2 (2.33)	66.4 (2.70)	7.7 (0.93)	29.1 (1.71)	27.8 (1.71)	2.5 (0.60)
Private	136 (—)	93.8 (1.08)	39.8 (3.42)	10.9 (1.91)	39.1 (3.41)	8.0 (1.36)	46.0 (3.85)	43.4 (3.74)	2.8 (0.69)
First-professional	235 (—)	88.5 (1.12)	26.2 (1.78)	1.7 (0.42)	7.9 (0.78)	4.6 (0.75)	81.8 (1.38)	80.4 (1.41)	14.6 (1.26)
Public	104 (—)	88.5 (1.65)	22.1 (2.16)	3.2 (0.90)	9.4 (1.39)	4.9 (1.44)	81.7 (2.25)	80.6 (2.26)	14.7 (2.04)
Private	131 (—)	88.5 (1.46)	29.4 (2.57)	0.5 ! (0.18)	6.7 (0.93)	4.4 (0.72)	81.9 (1.62)	80.2 (1.70)	14.6 (1.66)
Other graduate	33 (—)	69.2 (6.54)	10.4 ! (3.71)	3.2 ! (1.27)	16.0 ! (5.08)	6.2 ! (2.33)	49.3 (6.72)	47.4 (6.58)	4.7 ! (2.12)
2011–12, all institutions	1,391 (—)	86.1 (0.77)	26.3 (1.06)	10.0 (0.60)	20.7 (0.79)	10.2 (0.48)	61.6 (0.90)	60.0 (0.91)	3.9 (0.39)
Master's degree	777 (—)	82.6 (1.28)	21.5 (1.36)	7.4 (0.73)	15.9 (1.13)	8.8 (0.70)	62.6 (1.43)	60.8 (1.40)	3.1 (0.47)
Public	329 (—)	83.8 (1.84)	24.0 (2.28)	12.1 (1.40)	24.6 (1.98)	10.3 (1.17)	57.5 (2.27)	56.2 (2.31)	3.8 (0.83)
4-year doctoral	297 (—)	83.7 (2.03)	25.5 (2.49)	12.5 (1.57)	25.0 (2.17)	10.8 (1.28)	56.2 (2.43)	54.8 (2.48)	4.0 (0.91)
Other 4-year	32 (—)	84.6 (4.13)	10.1 (2.79)	7.5 (2.05)	21.1 (2.80)	5.9 (1.68)	69.5 (5.14)	69.0 (5.14)	1.5 ! (0.65)
Private	448 (—)	81.8 (1.80)	19.6 (1.76)	4.0 (0.71)	9.6 (1.33)	7.8 (0.88)	66.4 (1.99)	64.3 (2.00)	2.7 (0.47)
4-year doctoral	269 (—)	80.4 (2.06)	25.3 (2.64)	5.2 (1.04)	13.1 (1.69)	7.8 (1.23)	61.0 (2.15)	57.9 (2.35)	4.3 (0.76)
Other 4-year	180 (—)	83.9 (3.09)	11.0 (2.25)	2.1 ! (0.76)	4.3 ! (1.88)	7.6 (1.04)	74.5 (3.59)	73.8 (3.45)	‡ (†)
Doctor's degree—research/ scholarship	235 (—)	93.4 (0.73)	42.6 (1.58)	28.1 (1.56)	62.2 (1.29)	24.0 (1.25)	25.4 (1.20)	23.9 (1.13)	1.2 ! (0.38)
Public	133 (—)	94.1 (1.04)	39.8 (2.10)	33.3 (2.32)	72.7 (1.65)	27.0 (1.93)	22.2 (1.49)	20.9 (1.46)	1.1 ! (0.46)
Private	102 (—)	92.5 (1.07)	46.3 (2.46)	21.3 (2.16)	48.5 (1.96)	20.1 (1.06)	29.5 (2.23)	27.8 (2.06)	1.3 ! (0.58)
Doctor's degree—professional practice and other[8]	342 (—)	90.7 (0.88)	28.5 (1.55)	4.7 (0.70)	4.0 (0.48)	4.4 (0.51)	84.2 (1.05)	82.9 (1.00)	7.6 (1.10)
Public	135 (—)	91.1 (1.09)	32.3 (2.24)	7.5 (1.38)	5.5 (0.92)	5.4 (0.82)	83.9 (1.23)	83.3 (1.25)	7.5 (1.17)
Private	207 (—)	90.4 (1.22)	25.9 (2.11)	2.8 (0.73)	3.0 (0.53)	3.7 (0.62)	84.4 (1.51)	82.7 (1.45)	7.7 (1.64)
Other graduate	37 (—)	70.9 (6.46)	6.6 ! (2.45)	‡ (†)	10.7 ! (3.85)	5.5 ! (2.47)	61.7 (7.20)	58.9 (7.45)	2.3 ! (1.10)

—Not available.
†Not applicable.
!Interpret data with caution. The coefficient of variation (CV) for this estimate is between 30 and 50 percent.
‡Reporting standards not met. Either there are too few cases for a reliable estimate or the coefficient of variation (CV) is 50 percent or greater.
[1]Numbers of full-time, full-year postbaccalaureate students may not equal figures reported in other tables, since these data are based on a sample survey of all postbaccalaureate students who enrolled at any time during the school year.
[2]Includes students who reported they were awarded aid, but did not specify the source of aid.
[3]Includes students who received teaching or research assistantships and/or participated in work-study programs.
[4]Formerly Guaranteed Student Loans (GSL).
[5]Formerly National Direct Student Loans (NDSL). Includes subsidized amounts only.

[6]Fellowship estimates for 1992–93 were based primarily on information provided by institutions and are not comparable to data for 1999–2000 and later years, which were based on information provided by both students and institutions.
[7]Includes nonprofit 4-year nondoctoral institutions and for-profit 2-year-and-above institutions.
[8]Professional practice doctor's degrees include most degrees formerly classified as first-professional (such as M.D., D.D.S., and J.D). "Other" doctor's degrees are those that are neither research/scholarship degrees nor professional practice degrees.
NOTE: Excludes students whose attendance status was not reported. Total includes some students whose level of study or control of institution was unknown. Detail may not sum to totals because of rounding and because some students receive aid from multiple sources. Data exclude Puerto Rico. Some data have been revised from previously published figures.
SOURCE: U.S. Department of Education, National Center for Education Statistics, 1992–93, 1999–2000, 2007–08, and 2011–12 National Postsecondary Student Aid Study (NPSAS:93, NPSAS:2000, NPSAS:08, and NPSAS:12). (This table was prepared August 2014.)

Table 332.40. Percentage of part-time or part-year postbaccalaureate students receiving financial aid, by type of aid, level of study, and control and level of institution: Selected years, 1992–93 through 2011–12

[Standard errors appear in parentheses]

Level of study, control and level of institution	Number of students[1] (in thousands)		Percent receiving aid													
			Any aid[2]		Fellowship grants		Tuition waivers		Assistantships[3]		Employer (includes college staff)		Loans					
													Any loans		Stafford[4]		Perkins[5]	
1	2		3		4		5		6		7		8		9		10	
1992–93, all institutions	1,975	(—)	36.8	(0.81)	[6]	(†)	5.1	(0.38)	4.2	(0.27)	16.7	(0.71)	10.5	(0.52)	9.4	(0.48)	1.0	(0.13)
Master's degree	1,319	(—)	37.5	(0.85)	[6]	(†)	4.6	(0.48)	3.8	(0.37)	18.7	(0.91)	10.3	(0.62)	9.2	(0.54)	0.9	(0.15)
Public	772	(—)	33.6	(1.00)	[6]	(†)	4.9	(0.49)	5.2	(0.46)	14.6	(0.83)	9.8	(0.65)	8.9	(0.55)	1.2	(0.23)
4-year doctoral	488	(—)	37.8	(1.25)	[6]	(†)	6.5	(0.66)	6.7	(0.70)	14.6	(1.06)	11.8	(0.90)	10.7	(0.74)	1.5	(0.33)
Other 4-year	284	(—)	26.3	(1.39)	[6]	(†)	2.2	(0.59)	2.6	(0.62)	14.4	(1.09)	6.5	(0.76)	6.0	(0.76)	0.6 !	(0.21)
Private	547	(—)	43.0	(1.56)	[6]	(†)	4.2	(0.69)	1.8 !	(0.60)	24.5	(1.46)	10.9	(1.03)	9.6	(0.89)	0.5 !	(0.18)
4-year doctoral	357	(—)	44.8	(1.91)	[6]	(†)	4.4	(0.89)	2.5 !	(0.82)	25.1	(1.72)	11.9	(1.16)	10.5	(0.99)	0.6 !	(0.26)
Other 4-year	191	(—)	39.6	(2.84)	[6]	(†)	3.8	(1.11)	0.7 !	(0.31)	23.3	(2.36)	9.1	(1.60)	7.9	(1.33)	‡	(†)
Doctor's degree	148	(—)	48.3	(2.56)	[6]	(†)	12.7	(2.19)	16.8	(1.75)	12.0	(1.49)	7.3	(1.16)	6.9	(1.20)	0.8 !	(0.35)
Public	97	(—)	48.4	(3.09)	[6]	(†)	15.0	(2.91)	16.6	(2.11)	12.9	(1.89)	7.1	(1.20)	6.5	(1.20)	‡	(†)
Private	51	(—)	48.2	(5.53)	[6]	(†)	8.3	(2.05)	17.0	(4.31)	10.2	(2.47)	7.6 !	(2.76)	7.5 !	(2.79)	‡	(†)
First-professional	64	(—)	58.6	(3.04)	[6]	(†)	5.9	(1.41)	3.1	(0.92)	6.1	(1.34)	45.6	(3.35)	42.0	(3.20)	6.2	(0.84)
Public	24	(—)	51.7	(4.43)	[6]	(†)	6.8	(1.65)	6.1 !	(2.23)	5.0 !	(1.61)	42.4	(3.99)	41.4	(3.86)	8.5	(1.77)
Private	40	(—)	62.6	(3.43)	[6]	(†)	5.4 !	(1.77)	1.4 !	(0.50)	6.7	(1.81)	47.5	(4.28)	42.3	(3.94)	4.9	(0.96)
Other graduate	414	(—)	27.0	(1.42)	[6]	(†)	3.4	(0.55)	1.6	(0.32)	13.4	(1.00)	7.1	(0.68)	5.9	(0.59)	‡	(†)
1999–2000, all institutions	1,724	(—)	48.7	(0.72)	4.9	(0.27)	5.8	(0.33)	5.4	(0.34)	20.2	(0.66)	19.1	(0.51)	18.1	(0.47)	0.9	(0.13)
Master's degree	1,131	(—)	51.2	(0.83)	4.5	(0.37)	5.0	(0.32)	4.7	(0.36)	23.2	(0.81)	20.4	(0.68)	19.3	(0.63)	0.7	(0.14)
Public	633	(—)	47.0	(1.19)	3.8	(0.52)	6.4	(0.55)	6.2	(0.56)	20.7	(1.32)	16.9	(0.86)	15.8	(0.79)	0.7	(0.16)
4-year doctoral	436	(—)	50.4	(1.54)	4.2	(0.48)	7.4	(0.71)	8.0	(0.79)	21.4	(1.62)	17.8	(1.24)	16.7	(1.18)	0.5 !	(0.17)
Other 4-year	188	(—)	39.2	(1.96)	3.2 !	(1.41)	4.2	(0.93)	2.3	(0.46)	18.5	(2.28)	14.4	(1.47)	13.6	(1.49)	1.2 !	(0.41)
Private	498	(—)	56.5	(1.26)	5.3	(0.55)	3.2	(0.41)	2.8	(0.50)	26.5	(1.15)	24.9	(1.05)	23.8	(1.04)	0.8 !	(0.29)
4-year doctoral	322	(—)	57.7	(1.43)	6.5	(0.68)	3.5	(0.55)	3.3	(0.52)	25.5	(1.23)	24.7	(1.25)	23.5	(1.26)	0.8 !	(0.33)
Other[7]	176	(—)	54.1	(2.26)	3.1	(0.93)	2.6	(0.62)	1.9 !	(0.92)	28.3	(2.23)	25.3	(2.00)	24.2	(2.03)	‡	(†)
Doctor's degree	159	(—)	54.5	(1.81)	10.8	(0.95)	15.0	(1.24)	20.9	(1.60)	14.0	(1.35)	14.7	(1.34)	14.1	(1.37)	‡	(†)
Public	108	(—)	53.3	(2.34)	8.8	(0.85)	19.5	(1.34)	25.7	(1.98)	12.1	(1.46)	12.6	(1.13)	12.0	(1.12)	‡	(†)
Private	51	(—)	57.1	(2.95)	15.1	(2.49)	5.5	(1.60)	10.8	(1.83)	18.1	(3.16)	19.2	(3.16)	18.5	(3.29)	‡	(†)
First-professional	72	(—)	75.6	(3.17)	10.2	(2.70)	5.3 !	(1.62)	‡	(†)	11.0	(2.09)	57.7	(4.43)	54.8	(5.09)	6.8 !	(2.70)
Public	22	(—)	72.7	(6.84)	8.5 !	(3.72)	‡	(†)	‡	(†)	8.0 !	(3.85)	57.4	(8.37)	54.4	(8.28)	4.7 !	(1.93)
Private	50	(—)	76.8	(3.14)	11.0 !	(3.67)	6.0 !	(2.17)	2.7 !	(1.34)	12.3	(2.85)	57.8	(5.44)	54.9	(6.63)	7.8 !	(3.72)
Other graduate	363	(—)	33.0	(1.77)	2.6	(0.44)	4.4	(0.80)	1.3	(0.33)	15.3	(1.31)	9.5	(1.09)	8.9	(1.09)	0.4 !	(0.18)
2007–08, all institutions	2,337	(—)	66.8	(0.85)	6.6	(0.50)	6.8	(0.34)	9.7	(0.38)	27.2	(0.93)	34.6	(0.70)	30.5	(0.65)	0.9	(0.09)
Master's degree	1,646	(—)	69.0	(1.10)	5.5	(0.45)	5.6	(0.40)	7.5	(0.40)	29.8	(1.22)	36.8	(0.97)	32.7	(0.93)	0.9	(0.12)
Public	829	(—)	65.7	(1.39)	4.4	(0.53)	7.2	(0.69)	10.6	(0.72)	27.8	(1.43)	32.8	(1.16)	27.8	(0.90)	1.0	(0.16)
4-year doctoral	631	(—)	67.7	(1.60)	4.9	(0.64)	8.4	(0.81)	12.0	(0.94)	29.4	(1.71)	32.3	(1.36)	28.0	(1.16)	1.0	(0.18)
Other 4-year	198	(—)	59.4	(2.99)	3.0 !	(0.97)	3.6 !	(1.18)	6.0	(1.17)	22.7	(2.56)	34.5	(2.98)	27.2	(2.63)	1.2 !	(0.37)
Private	818	(—)	72.3	(1.59)	6.5	(0.74)	4.0	(0.51)	4.3	(0.43)	31.7	(1.85)	40.9	(1.42)	37.6	(1.41)	0.8	(0.19)
4-year doctoral	509	(—)	71.0	(1.52)	8.0	(0.95)	3.8	(0.52)	5.5	(0.57)	32.9	(1.20)	36.5	(1.33)	32.8	(1.24)	1.1	(0.29)
Other[7]	309	(—)	74.4	(3.25)	4.0	(0.79)	4.4	(1.00)	2.4	(0.57)	29.9	(4.50)	48.3	(2.89)	45.5	(2.86)	0.2 !	(0.12)
Doctor's degree	270	(—)	79.9	(1.92)	17.1	(2.09)	16.4	(1.78)	34.0	(3.40)	19.2	(1.73)	33.3	(4.81)	30.4	(5.07)	0.5 !	(0.25)
Public	154	(—)	76.8	(1.57)	16.8	(1.67)	24.2	(1.52)	47.2	(2.02)	19.6	(1.43)	18.9	(1.26)	15.9	(1.15)	‡	(†)
Private	116	(—)	84.0	(3.95)	17.5	(4.59)	6.0 !	(2.03)	16.4	(4.27)	18.6	(4.11)	52.4	(8.69)	49.6	(9.37)	‡	(†)
First-professional	58	(—)	85.6	(2.54)	20.5	(3.99)	6.5 !	(2.52)	10.3	(2.01)	16.5	(2.21)	68.5	(3.89)	62.9	(4.62)	4.1 !	(1.48)
Public	20	(—)	88.3	(4.96)	13.8	(3.97)	11.0 !	(4.26)	18.5	(4.72)	16.3	(3.79)	68.4	(5.79)	62.7	(7.17)	7.9 !	(3.25)
Private	38	(—)	84.1	(3.09)	24.0	(5.43)	‡	(†)	6.0	(1.69)	16.7	(2.86)	68.6	(5.46)	63.0	(6.20)	‡	(†)
Other graduate	363	(—)	43.9	(3.07)	1.5	(0.37)	4.9	(0.97)	1.5	(0.41)	23.4	(2.79)	20.0	(2.10)	15.5	(1.58)	0.5 !	(0.25)
2011–12, all institutions	2,291	(—)	60.9	(0.99)	8.6	(0.55)	6.7	(0.56)	6.4	(0.43)	17.0	(0.88)	35.0	(0.61)	32.7	(0.60)	0.8	(0.17)
Master's degree	1,715	(—)	62.5	(1.29)	7.6	(0.61)	5.6	(0.62)	4.8	(0.47)	17.3	(1.13)	38.1	(0.83)	36.0	(0.83)	0.7	(0.17)
Public	800	(—)	57.1	(1.51)	7.2	(0.83)	5.8	(0.72)	7.5	(0.85)	14.7	(1.02)	33.7	(1.19)	31.2	(1.12)	1.2 !	(0.37)
4-year doctoral	664	(—)	58.5	(1.74)	8.1	(1.00)	6.2	(0.84)	7.9	(1.02)	15.6	(1.15)	33.4	(1.36)	31.1	(1.29)	1.2 !	(0.43)
Other 4-year	136	(—)	50.2	(2.32)	2.7	(0.76)	3.8	(1.07)	5.3	(1.06)	10.3	(1.66)	35.0	(2.15)	31.7	(2.10)	‡	(†)
Private	914	(—)	67.3	(1.94)	8.0	(0.92)	5.5	(0.91)	2.5	(0.55)	19.5	(1.91)	41.9	(1.32)	40.1	(1.30)	0.2 !	(0.08)
4-year doctoral	515	(—)	65.7	(2.07)	10.1	(1.49)	3.7	(0.91)	2.7	(0.72)	21.2	(2.02)	37.9	(1.67)	35.4	(1.72)	‡	(†)
Other 4-year	399	(—)	69.4	(3.63)	5.2	(0.93)	7.8	(1.71)	2.1 !	(0.95)	17.3	(3.39)	47.2	(2.03)	46.1	(1.92)	‡	(†)
Doctor's degree—research/ scholarship	198	(—)	70.9	(1.67)	18.1	(1.31)	20.0	(1.27)	30.4	(1.98)	20.9	(1.35)	24.4	(1.46)	22.4	(1.44)	0.3 !	(0.10)
Public	133	(—)	69.9	(2.12)	20.0	(1.76)	25.2	(1.78)	39.4	(2.56)	23.6	(1.77)	14.7	(1.34)	13.5	(1.28)	0.4 !	(0.15)
Private	66	(—)	73.1	(2.56)	14.2	(1.34)	9.6	(1.24)	12.2	(1.77)	15.5	(1.78)	44.0	(2.68)	40.5	(2.75)	‡	(†)
Doctor's degree—professional practice and other[8]	100	(—)	68.5	(3.09)	13.8	(1.88)	4.6	(0.98)	2.3 !	(0.79)	12.1	(1.83)	51.5	(3.52)	47.3	(3.67)	4.7 !	(2.12)
Public	41	(—)	58.3	(4.51)	16.0	(2.83)	7.3	(1.96)	3.8 !	(1.75)	12.6	(2.94)	40.3	(4.01)	37.4	(4.10)	3.0 !	(1.32)
Private	59	(—)	75.5	(3.48)	12.3	(2.41)	2.7 !	(1.02)	1.3 !	(0.50)	11.8	(2.64)	59.1	(4.83)	54.1	(5.03)	‡	(†)
Other graduate	278	(—)	40.6	(2.66)	6.5	(1.57)	4.6 !	(1.47)	0.7 !	(0.34)	14.6	(1.91)	17.9	(1.76)	14.9	(1.64)	‡	(†)

—Not available.
†Not applicable.
!Interpret data with caution. The coefficient of variation (CV) for this estimate is between 30 and 50 percent.
‡Reporting standards not met. The coefficient of variation (CV) for this estimate is 50 percent or greater.
[1]Numbers of part-time or part-year postbaccalaureate students may not equal figures reported in other tables, since these data are based on a sample survey of all postbaccalaureate students enrolled at any time during the school year.
[2]Includes students who reported they were awarded aid, but did not specify the source of aid.
[3]Includes students who received teaching or research assistantships and/or participated in work-study programs.
[4]Formerly Guaranteed Student Loans (GSL).
[5]Formerly National Direct Student Loans (NDSL). Includes subsidized amounts only.

[6]Fellowship estimates for 1992–93 were based primarily on information provided by institutions and are not comparable to data for 1999–2000 and later years, which were based on information provided by both students and institutions.
[7]Includes nonprofit 4-year nondoctoral institutions and for-profit 2-year-and-above institutions.
[8]Professional practice doctor's degrees include most degrees formerly classified as first-professional (such as M.D., D.D.S., and J.D). "Other" doctor's degrees are those that are neither research/scholarship degrees nor professional practice degrees.
NOTE: Excludes students whose attendance status was not reported. Total includes some students whose level of study or control of institution was unknown. Detail may not sum to totals because of rounding and because some students receive aid from multiple sources. Data exclude Puerto Rico. Some data have been revised from previously published figures.
SOURCE: U.S. Department of Education, National Center for Education Statistics, 1992–93, 1999–2000, 2007–08, and 2011–12 National Postsecondary Student Aid Study (NPSAS:93, NPSAS:2000, NPSAS:08, and NPSAS:12). (This table was prepared August 2014.)

Table 332.50. Number of postsecondary students who entered the student loan repayment phase, number of students who defaulted, and student loan cohort default rates, by 2-year or 3-year default period and level and control of institution: Fiscal years 2010 through 2012

Fiscal year and level and control of institution	For student loan cohorts over a 2-year period			For student loan cohorts over a 3-year period		
	Number entering repayment phase in given fiscal year[1]	Number defaulting by end of next fiscal year[2]	2-year default rate[3,4]	Number entering repayment phase in given fiscal year[1]	Number defaulting by end of second following fiscal year[2]	3-year default rate[4,5]
1	2	3	4	5	6	7
Fiscal year 2010						
All institutions[6]	4,100,778	374,940	9.1	4,082,570	600,545	14.7
Public	1,928,054	161,815	8.3	1,922,773	250,661	13.0
Private nonprofit	882,005	46,481	5.2	879,269	72,347	8.2
Private for-profit	1,281,215	166,364	12.9	1,270,965	277,088	21.8
Less-than-2-year institutions	179,650	21,274	11.8	178,904	37,223	20.8
Public	8,261	831	10.0	7,963	1,315	16.5
Private nonprofit	4,953	676	13.6	5,020	1,097	21.8
Private for-profit	166,436	19,767	11.8	165,921	34,811	20.9
2-year institutions	966,842	124,136	12.8	950,143	199,922	21.0
Public	604,872	81,120	13.4	599,467	125,764	20.9
Private nonprofit	18,384	1,573	8.5	16,217	2,305	14.2
Private for-profit	343,586	41,443	12.0	334,459	71,853	21.4
4-year institutions	2,944,782	229,250	7.8	2,943,960	362,951	12.3
Public	1,314,921	79,864	6.0	1,315,343	123,582	9.3
Private nonprofit	858,668	44,232	5.1	858,032	68,945	8.0
Private for-profit	771,193	105,154	13.6	770,585	170,424	22.1
Fiscal year 2011						
All institutions[6]	4,739,481	475,538	10.0	4,732,793	650,727	13.7
Public	2,253,463	218,418	9.6	2,252,334	292,012	12.9
Private nonprofit	967,956	51,153	5.2	969,156	70,186	7.2
Private for-profit	1,507,562	205,681	13.6	1,500,812	288,126	19.1
Less-than-2-year institutions	211,988	29,576	14.0	202,526	41,526	20.5
Public	8,779	824	9.3	8,750	1,196	13.6
Private nonprofit	5,219	734	14.0	6,567	1,644	25.0
Private for-profit	197,990	28,018	14.1	187,209	38,686	20.6
2-year institutions	1,179,508	172,265	14.6	1,174,583	237,571	20.2
Public	774,772	116,966	15.0	767,073	158,104	20.6
Private nonprofit	17,458	1,445	8.2	16,861	2,026	12.0
Private for-profit	387,278	53,854	13.9	390,649	77,441	19.8
4-year institutions	3,337,485	273,411	8.2	3,345,193	371,227	11.1
Public	1,469,912	100,628	6.8	1,476,511	132,712	8.9
Private nonprofit	945,279	48,974	5.1	945,728	66,516	7.0
Private for-profit	922,294	123,809	13.4	922,954	171,999	18.6
Fiscal year 2012						
All institutions[6]	—	—	—	5,143,918	610,956	11.8
Public	—	—	—	2,563,157	301,453	11.7
Private nonprofit	—	—	—	1,083,328	73,747	6.8
Private for-profit	—	—	—	1,486,162	235,384	15.8
Less-than-2-year institutions	—	—	—	209,036	36,952	17.7
Public	—	—	—	10,151	1,241	12.2
Private nonprofit	—	—	—	10,336	2,318	22.4
Private for-profit	—	—	—	188,549	33,393	17.7
2-year institutions	—	—	—	1,301,109	242,471	18.6
Public	—	—	—	905,058	173,628	19.1
Private nonprofit	—	—	—	42,274	6,193	14.6
Private for-profit	—	—	—	353,777	62,650	17.7
4-year institutions	—	—	—	3,622,502	331,161	9.1
Public	—	—	—	1,647,948	126,584	7.6
Private nonprofit	—	—	—	1,030,718	65,236	6.3
Private for-profit	—	—	—	943,836	139,341	14.7

—Not available.

[1]The repayment phase is the period when student loans must be repaid; it generally begins 6 months after a student leaves an institution. Students who enter the repayment phase during a particular federal fiscal year (October 1 through September 30) make up the cohort for that fiscal year. For example, members of the fiscal year (FY) 2012 cohort entered the repayment phase any time from October 1, 2011, through September 30, 2012.

[2]Borrowers are considered to be in default if they make no payments for 360 days after missing a regularly scheduled payment.

[3]The 2-year cohort default rate is the percentage of borrowers entering repayment during one fiscal year and defaulting by the end of the next fiscal year. For example, the 2-year cohort default rate for FY 2010 is the percentage of borrowers who entered repayment during FY 2010 (any time from October 1, 2009, through September 30, 2010) and who defaulted by the end of FY 2011 (September 30, 2011).

[4]For purposes of computing default rates, if an individual or entity affiliated with the institution makes a payment to prevent a borrower's default on a loan, the borrower is still considered in default.

[5]The 3-year cohort default rate is the percentage of borrowers entering repayment during the specified fiscal year and defaulting by the end of the second fiscal year that follows. For exam-

ple, the 3-year cohort default rate for FY 2010 is the percentage of borrowers who entered repayment during FY 2010 (any time from October 1, 2009, through September 30, 2010) and who defaulted by the end of FY 2012 (September 30, 2012).

[6]Includes borrowers from foreign and unclassified schools, which account for less than 1 percent of borrowers and are not included elsewhere.

NOTE: Data are for certain loans under the Federal Family Education Loan (FFEL) Program and the William D. Ford Federal Direct Loan Program (commonly referred to as the Direct Loan Program). Includes Federal Stafford Loans. Does not include PLUS loans, Federal Insured Student Loans (FISLs), or Federal Perkins Loans. For more details, see http://ifap.ed.gov/Default Management/guide/attachments/CDRGuideCh2Pt1CDRCalculation.pdf. The Office of Federal Student Aid currently publishes only 3-year default rates. The 2-year default rates shown in this table are no longer available online; therefore, no source for the 2-year rates can be provided.

SOURCE: U.S. Department of Education, Office of Federal Student Aid, Direct Loan and Federal Family Education Loan Programs, Cohort Default Rate Database; retrieved October 13, 2015, from http://www2.ed.gov/offices/OSFAP/defaultmanagement/schooltyperates.pdf. (This table was prepared October 2015.)

Table 333.10. Revenues of public degree-granting postsecondary institutions, by source of revenue and level of institution: 2007–08 through 2013–14

Level of institution and year	Total revenues	Operating revenue							
		Tuition and fees[1]	Grants and contracts			Sales and services of auxiliary enterprises[1]	Sales and services of hospitals	Independent operations	Other operating revenues[2]
			Federal	State	Local and private				
1	2	3	4	5	6	7	8	9	10
					In thousands of current dollars				
All levels									
2007–08............	$273,109,306	$48,070,012	$25,522,915	$7,831,530	$8,699,329	$20,488,319	$25,183,379	$1,174,836	$14,108,986
2008–09............	267,421,029	51,846,428	26,077,431	7,403,668	9,557,483	21,360,263	27,390,973	1,036,660	14,068,011
2009–10............	303,341,758	55,955,342	28,380,803	6,901,666	9,620,236	22,173,993	29,236,931	1,343,230	14,817,094
2010–11............	324,473,342	60,268,927	29,821,416	7,019,420	10,110,953	23,605,640	30,998,993	1,330,334	15,758,118
2011–12............	317,289,436	65,396,118	29,133,188	6,830,670	10,161,247	24,276,751	33,508,840	1,356,861	16,296,364
2012–13............	327,932,633	68,095,088	28,430,717	6,687,856	10,779,776	24,666,058	34,940,780	1,359,043	17,336,700
2013–14............	353,095,490	70,498,077	27,533,487	7,093,767	11,186,060	25,476,347	37,596,888	1,432,772	18,204,327
4-year									
2007–08............	223,566,529	40,083,063	23,518,933	5,715,188	8,106,887	18,507,934	25,183,379	1,174,836	13,135,633
2008–09............	216,470,957	43,478,018	24,172,034	5,527,110	8,988,911	19,391,219	27,390,973	1,036,660	13,193,521
2009–10............	248,093,564	46,964,829	26,257,423	5,301,243	9,062,160	20,099,430	29,236,931	1,343,230	13,896,518
2010–11............	266,688,058	51,046,786	27,656,656	5,480,573	9,543,780	21,506,767	30,998,993	1,330,334	14,830,150
2011–12............	261,158,738	55,978,667	27,235,518	5,352,808	9,590,518	22,240,828	33,508,840	1,356,861	15,343,535
2012–13............	272,356,474	58,627,864	26,601,896	5,196,508	10,251,194	22,714,712	34,940,780	1,359,043	16,456,904
2013–14............	297,230,653	61,155,700	25,756,710	5,521,827	10,656,459	23,643,409	37,596,888	1,432,772	17,327,733
2-year									
2007–08............	49,542,777	7,986,949	2,003,982	2,116,343	592,442	1,980,385	0	0	973,353
2008–09............	50,950,072	8,368,411	1,905,397	1,876,558	568,572	1,969,043	0	0	874,490
2009–10............	55,248,194	8,990,512	2,123,380	1,600,423	558,076	2,074,563	0	0	920,576
2010–11............	57,785,284	9,222,142	2,164,760	1,538,848	567,174	2,098,872	0	0	927,968
2011–12............	56,130,698	9,417,451	1,897,670	1,477,862	570,729	2,035,923	0	0	952,830
2012–13............	55,576,159	9,467,224	1,828,820	1,491,347	528,582	1,951,346	0	0	879,795
2013–14............	55,864,837	9,342,377	1,776,776	1,571,939	529,602	1,832,937	0	0	876,594
					Percentage distribution				
All levels									
2007–08............	100.00	17.60	9.35	2.87	3.19	7.50	9.22	0.43	5.17
2008–09............	100.00	19.39	9.75	2.77	3.57	7.99	10.24	0.39	5.26
2009–10............	100.00	18.45	9.36	2.28	3.17	7.31	9.64	0.44	4.88
2010–11............	100.00	18.57	9.19	2.16	3.12	7.28	9.55	0.41	4.86
2011–12............	100.00	20.61	9.18	2.15	3.20	7.65	10.56	0.43	5.14
2012–13............	100.00	20.76	8.67	2.04	3.29	7.52	10.65	0.41	5.29
2013–14............	100.00	19.97	7.80	2.01	3.17	7.22	10.65	0.41	5.16
4-year									
2007–08............	100.00	17.93	10.52	2.56	3.63	8.28	11.26	0.53	5.88
2008–09............	100.00	20.08	11.17	2.55	4.15	8.96	12.65	0.48	6.09
2009–10............	100.00	18.93	10.58	2.14	3.65	8.10	11.78	0.54	5.60
2010–11............	100.00	19.14	10.37	2.06	3.58	8.06	11.62	0.50	5.56
2011–12............	100.00	21.43	10.43	2.05	3.67	8.52	12.83	0.52	5.88
2012–13............	100.00	21.53	9.77	1.91	3.76	8.34	12.83	0.50	6.04
2013–14............	100.00	20.58	8.67	1.86	3.59	7.95	12.65	0.48	5.83
2-year									
2007–08............	100.00	16.12	4.04	4.27	1.20	4.00	0.00	0.00	1.96
2008–09............	100.00	16.42	3.74	3.68	1.12	3.86	0.00	0.00	1.72
2009–10............	100.00	16.27	3.84	2.90	1.01	3.75	0.00	0.00	1.67
2010–11............	100.00	15.96	3.75	2.66	0.98	3.63	0.00	0.00	1.61
2011–12............	100.00	16.78	3.38	2.63	1.02	3.63	0.00	0.00	1.70
2012–13............	100.00	17.03	3.29	2.68	0.95	3.51	0.00	0.00	1.58
2013–14............	100.00	16.72	3.18	2.81	0.95	3.28	0.00	0.00	1.57
					Revenue per full-time-equivalent student in constant 2014–15 dollars[3]				
All levels									
2007–08............	$31,349	$5,518	$2,930	$899	$999	$2,352	$2,891	$135	$1,619
2008–09............	29,304	5,681	2,858	811	1,047	2,341	3,002	114	1,542
2009–10............	30,824	5,686	2,884	701	978	2,253	2,971	136	1,506
2010–11............	31,524	5,855	2,897	682	982	2,293	3,012	129	1,531
2011–12............	30,123	6,209	2,766	649	965	2,305	3,181	129	1,547
2012–13............	31,115	6,461	2,698	635	1,023	2,340	3,315	129	1,645
2013–14............	33,253	6,639	2,593	668	1,053	2,399	3,541	135	1,714
4-year									
2007–08............	41,697	7,476	4,386	1,066	1,512	3,452	4,697	219	2,450
2008–09............	38,875	7,808	4,341	993	1,614	3,482	4,919	186	2,369
2009–10............	41,988	7,948	4,444	897	1,534	3,402	4,948	227	2,352
2010–11............	43,023	8,235	4,462	884	1,540	3,470	5,001	215	2,392
2011–12............	40,334	8,646	4,206	827	1,481	3,435	5,175	210	2,370
2012–13............	41,191	8,867	4,023	786	1,550	3,435	5,284	206	2,489
2013–14............	44,088	9,071	3,820	819	1,581	3,507	5,577	213	2,570
2-year									
2007–08............	14,788	2,384	598	632	177	591	0	0	291
2008–09............	14,322	2,352	536	528	160	554	0	0	246
2009–10............	14,049	2,286	540	407	142	528	0	0	234
2010–11............	14,114	2,252	529	376	139	513	0	0	227
2011–12............	13,832	2,321	468	364	141	502	0	0	235
2012–13............	14,152	2,411	466	380	135	497	0	0	224
2013–14............	14,411	2,410	458	405	137	473	0	0	226

See notes at end of table.

Table 333.10. Revenues of public degree-granting postsecondary institutions, by source of revenue and level of institution: 2007–08 through 2013–14—Continued

Level of institution and year	Nonoperating revenue									Other revenues and additions			
	Appropriations			Nonoperating grants			Gifts	Investment income	Other nonoperating revenues	Capital appropriations	Capital grants and gifts	Additions to permanent endowments	Other
	Federal	State	Local	Federal	State	Local							
1	11	12	13	14	15	16	17	18	19	20	21	22	23
In thousands of current dollars													
All levels													
2007–08	$1,849,775	$68,375,062	$9,319,219	$10,022,315	$1,909,570	$177,555	$6,070,499	$5,278,643	$2,251,324	$7,578,049	$3,090,589	$1,133,783	$4,973,618
2008–09	2,010,843	65,475,631	9,787,019	12,760,291	2,720,848	265,789	5,893,938	-9,401,624	3,010,295	7,049,628	2,938,605	851,289	5,317,562
2009–10	2,152,228	62,438,851	9,954,504	20,728,610	3,123,358	231,104	5,872,441	10,043,969	5,243,618	6,042,653	3,780,010	873,870	4,427,245
2010–11	1,946,965	63,063,322	10,023,157	24,231,846	3,404,970	228,055	6,287,358	14,215,863	6,888,955	5,645,126	3,745,699	965,007	4,913,217
2011–12	1,835,767	58,789,575	10,214,576	23,204,292	3,559,591	232,167	6,522,320	6,170,822	4,193,110	5,544,504	3,724,162	825,587	5,512,923
2012–13	1,747,391	58,634,067	10,725,798	22,393,312	3,830,396	279,760	7,117,638	11,298,624	4,990,501	5,195,685	3,614,091	928,928	4,880,426
2013–14	1,843,674	62,700,662	11,112,188	21,925,929	4,035,063	300,706	8,114,163	20,024,438	6,543,828	5,313,456	3,835,939	1,123,705	7,200,016
4-year													
2007–08	1,776,452	53,268,648	453,280	5,177,569	1,201,394	103,824	5,798,732	4,430,479	1,770,108	5,637,968	2,762,277	1,120,806	4,639,141
2008–09	1,934,958	50,851,970	484,689	6,425,434	1,729,985	131,427	5,635,304	-9,871,846	2,601,303	5,001,830	2,554,107	838,025	4,975,326
2009–10	2,006,623	48,701,730	431,615	10,308,365	2,088,155	134,608	5,642,265	9,663,671	4,606,436	4,005,260	3,312,752	857,605	4,172,713
2010–11	1,853,109	49,025,814	507,010	11,812,776	2,320,005	130,451	6,061,629	13,781,509	6,061,802	3,884,591	3,249,844	943,748	4,661,730
2011–12	1,715,489	45,755,610	517,219	11,263,074	2,398,688	130,598	6,255,956	5,994,582	3,492,667	3,884,832	3,356,930	815,973	4,969,547
2012–13	1,634,057	45,842,103	551,917	11,126,358	2,516,165	153,773	6,864,121	11,126,073	4,356,413	3,619,996	3,260,502	899,534	4,256,561
2013–14	1,732,216	49,198,717	562,506	11,187,296	2,659,043	179,126	7,867,481	19,709,539	5,873,842	3,867,745	3,563,297	1,106,470	6,631,877
2-year													
2007–08	73,324	15,106,414	8,865,938	4,844,746	708,176	73,731	271,766	848,164	481,216	1,940,082	328,312	12,978	334,477
2008–09	75,885	14,623,660	9,302,330	6,334,857	990,863	134,362	258,634	470,222	408,992	2,047,798	384,498	13,263	342,236
2009–10	145,606	13,737,120	9,522,890	10,420,246	1,035,203	96,496	230,175	380,298	637,182	2,037,393	467,258	16,265	254,532
2010–11	93,856	14,037,508	9,516,147	12,419,069	1,084,965	97,604	225,730	434,353	827,153	1,760,535	495,855	21,258	251,487
2011–12	120,279	13,033,965	9,697,357	11,941,218	1,160,903	101,569	266,364	176,240	700,443	1,659,672	367,232	9,614	543,376
2012–13	113,334	12,791,964	10,173,882	11,266,954	1,314,232	125,987	253,517	172,551	634,088	1,575,688	353,588	29,394	623,866
2013–14	111,459	13,501,945	10,549,682	10,738,632	1,376,020	121,580	246,683	314,899	669,985	1,445,711	272,641	17,236	568,140
Percentage distribution													
All levels													
2007–08	0.68	25.04	3.41	3.67	0.70	0.07	2.22	1.93	0.82	2.77	1.13	0.42	1.82
2008–09	0.75	24.48	3.66	4.77	1.02	0.10	2.20	-3.52	1.13	2.64	1.10	0.32	1.99
2009–10	0.71	20.58	3.28	6.83	1.03	0.08	1.94	3.31	1.73	1.99	1.25	0.29	1.46
2010–11	0.60	19.44	3.09	7.47	1.05	0.07	1.94	4.38	2.12	1.74	1.15	0.30	1.51
2011–12	0.58	18.53	3.22	7.31	1.12	0.07	2.06	1.94	1.32	1.75	1.17	0.26	1.74
2012–13	0.53	17.88	3.27	6.83	1.17	0.09	2.17	3.45	1.52	1.58	1.10	0.28	1.49
2013–14	0.52	17.76	3.15	6.21	1.14	0.09	2.30	5.67	1.85	1.50	1.09	0.32	2.04
4-year													
2007–08	0.79	23.83	0.20	2.32	0.54	0.05	2.59	1.98	0.79	2.52	1.24	0.50	2.08
2008–09	0.89	23.49	0.22	2.97	0.80	0.06	2.60	-4.56	1.20	2.31	1.18	0.39	2.30
2009–10	0.81	19.63	0.17	4.16	0.84	0.05	2.27	3.90	1.86	1.61	1.34	0.35	1.68
2010–11	0.69	18.38	0.19	4.43	0.87	0.05	2.27	5.17	2.27	1.46	1.22	0.35	1.75
2011–12	0.66	17.52	0.20	4.31	0.92	0.05	2.40	2.30	1.34	1.49	1.29	0.31	1.90
2012–13	0.60	16.83	0.20	4.09	0.92	0.06	2.52	4.09	1.60	1.33	1.20	0.33	1.56
2013–14	0.58	16.55	0.19	3.76	0.89	0.06	2.65	6.63	1.98	1.30	1.20	0.37	2.23
2-year													
2007–08	0.15	30.49	17.90	9.78	1.43	0.15	0.55	1.71	0.97	3.92	0.66	0.03	0.68
2008–09	0.15	28.70	18.26	12.43	1.94	0.26	0.51	0.92	0.80	4.02	0.75	0.03	0.67
2009–10	0.26	24.86	17.24	18.86	1.87	0.17	0.42	0.69	1.15	3.69	0.85	0.03	0.46
2010–11	0.16	24.29	16.47	21.49	1.88	0.17	0.39	0.75	1.43	3.05	0.86	0.04	0.44
2011–12	0.21	23.22	17.28	21.27	2.07	0.18	0.47	0.31	1.25	2.96	0.65	0.02	0.97
2012–13	0.20	23.02	18.31	20.27	2.36	0.23	0.46	0.31	1.14	2.84	0.64	0.05	1.12
2013–14	0.20	24.17	18.88	19.22	2.46	0.22	0.44	0.56	1.20	2.59	0.49	0.03	1.02
Revenue per full-time-equivalent student in constant 2014–15 dollars[3]													
All levels													
2007–08	$212	$7,848	$1,070	$1,150	$219	$20	$697	$606	$258	$870	$355	$130	$571
2008–09	220	7,175	1,072	1,398	298	29	646	-1,030	330	773	322	93	583
2009–10	219	6,345	1,012	2,106	317	23	597	1,021	533	614	384	89	450
2010–11	189	6,127	974	2,354	331	22	611	1,381	669	548	364	94	477
2011–12	174	5,581	970	2,203	338	22	619	586	398	526	354	78	523
2012–13	166	5,563	1,018	2,125	363	27	675	1,072	474	493	343	88	463
2013–14	174	5,905	1,046	2,065	380	28	764	1,886	616	500	361	106	678
4-year													
2007–08	331	9,935	85	966	224	19	1,082	826	330	1,052	515	209	865
2008–09	347	9,132	87	1,154	311	24	1,012	-1,773	467	898	459	150	894
2009–10	340	8,242	73	1,745	353	23	955	1,635	780	678	561	145	706
2010–11	299	7,909	82	1,906	374	21	978	2,223	978	627	524	152	752
2011–12	265	7,067	80	1,740	370	20	966	926	539	600	518	126	768
2012–13	247	6,933	83	1,683	381	23	1,038	1,683	659	547	493	136	644
2013–14	257	7,298	83	1,659	394	27	1,167	2,923	871	574	529	164	984
2-year													
2007–08	22	4,509	2,646	1,446	211	22	81	253	144	579	98	4	100
2008–09	21	4,111	2,615	1,781	279	38	73	132	115	576	108	4	96
2009–10	37	3,493	2,422	2,650	263	25	59	97	162	518	119	4	65
2010–11	23	3,429	2,324	3,033	265	24	55	106	202	430	121	5	61
2011–12	30	3,212	2,390	2,943	286	25	66	43	173	409	90	2	134
2012–13	29	3,257	2,591	2,869	335	32	65	44	161	401	90	7	159
2013–14	29	3,483	2,721	2,770	355	31	64	81	173	373	70	4	147

[1]After deducting discounts and allowances.
[2]Includes sales and services of educational activities.
[3]Constant dollars based on the Consumer Price Index, prepared by the Bureau of Labor Statistics, U.S. Department of Labor, adjusted to a school-year basis.
NOTE: Degree-granting institutions grant associate's or higher degrees and participate in Title IV federal financial aid programs. Includes data for public institutions reporting data according to either the Governmental Accounting Standards Board (GASB) or the Financial Accounting Standards Board (FASB) questionnaire. Some data have been revised from previously published figures. Detail may not sum to totals because of rounding.
SOURCE: U.S. Department of Education, National Center for Education Statistics, Integrated Postsecondary Education Data System (IPEDS), Spring 2008 through Spring 2014, Fall Enrollment component; and Spring 2009 through Spring 2015, Finance component. (This table was prepared October 2015.)

Table 333.20. Revenues of public degree-granting postsecondary institutions, by source of revenue and state or jurisdiction: 2013–14

[In thousands of current dollars]

State or jurisdiction	Total revenues	Operating revenue							Nonoperating revenue[1]			Other revenues and additions
		Total	Tuition and fees[2]	Federal grants and contracts	State, local, and private grants and contracts	Sales and services of auxiliary enterprises[2]	Sales and services of hospitals	Independent operations and other[3]	Total	State appro-priations	Local appro-priations	
1	2	3	4	5	6	7	8	9	10	11	12	13
United States......	$353,095,490	$199,021,724	$70,498,077	$27,533,487	$18,279,827	$25,476,347	$37,596,888	$19,637,099	$136,600,650	$62,700,662	$11,112,188	$17,473,116
Alabama	7,144,384	4,930,337	1,610,285	656,950	252,855	417,042	1,647,047	346,158	2,099,129	1,317,764	1,895	114,917
Alaska........................	1,049,003	388,273	126,748	123,150	77,688	40,032	0	20,655	481,384	392,451	10,789	179,345
Arizona......................	5,841,870	3,053,345	1,793,304	545,626	155,844	398,734	0	159,836	2,679,158	789,580	798,085	109,367
Arkansas....................	3,801,308	2,361,940	509,171	214,968	204,130	255,140	919,366	259,165	1,356,994	783,427	32,279	82,373
California...................	49,191,306	27,231,786	6,576,492	3,513,089	2,468,950	1,996,833	8,055,683	4,620,740	19,105,353	8,171,790	3,005,606	2,854,166
Colorado....................	6,055,720	4,993,088	1,904,190	906,457	579,022	530,689	648,766	423,964	922,089	32,718	83,364	140,543
Connecticut...............	3,545,779	1,803,353	626,586	176,299	92,853	290,926	308,708	307,982	1,313,433	1,080,009	0	428,993
Delaware....................	1,391,945	825,566	450,974	138,177	50,194	142,732	0	43,489	558,378	234,102	0	8,000
District of Columbia......	159,720	55,507	30,457	12,816	7,639	455	0	4,139	81,314	66,691	0	22,898
Florida.......................	11,473,089	5,427,688	2,352,048	1,039,779	1,070,893	789,818	2,012	173,138	5,586,872	3,356,433	0	458,529
Georgia.....................	7,798,148	4,520,863	1,918,056	782,502	542,361	865,082	189,029	223,833	3,077,695	2,003,786	400	199,591
Hawaii.......................	1,633,045	810,176	249,334	353,524	78,577	97,978	0	30,763	640,799	391,266	0	182,070
Idaho.........................	1,267,010	653,189	324,395	105,750	57,435	115,366	0	50,244	575,706	346,115	27,176	38,115
Illinois.......................	12,306,204	5,906,496	2,353,565	794,628	405,595	898,100	672,662	781,947	6,286,481	1,844,938	1,048,852	113,227
Indiana......................	7,070,983	4,284,578	2,233,388	544,891	309,494	787,029	0	409,776	2,636,593	1,452,440	7,760	149,812
Iowa..........................	5,506,899	3,888,908	918,065	504,378	159,894	501,764	1,461,969	342,838	1,449,205	818,015	125,607	168,786
Kansas......................	3,509,730	1,985,657	836,557	317,999	225,276	336,683	0	269,141	1,372,354	731,298	265,604	151,719
Kentucky....................	5,493,107	3,672,664	1,024,907	396,107	202,452	323,459	1,329,520	396,220	1,711,104	923,182	20,377	109,339
Louisiana...................	3,947,179	2,467,508	959,277	298,919	515,532	375,069	147,649	171,062	1,338,102	807,568	0	141,569
Maine........................	905,086	481,252	221,258	64,020	50,888	90,283	0	54,803	397,824	258,412	0	26,011
Maryland....................	6,505,436	3,790,369	1,556,478	705,175	419,780	699,294	0	409,642	2,338,783	1,480,786	329,689	376,284
Massachusetts...........	5,010,522	3,124,545	1,296,731	372,668	264,443	497,998	0	692,705	1,671,000	1,168,001	0	214,977
Michigan....................	16,299,324	10,339,057	3,878,068	1,412,797	467,212	1,072,906	3,001,292	506,784	5,451,403	1,600,635	531,528	508,864
Minnesota..................	5,466,024	2,918,995	1,281,936	485,747	355,521	620,718	0	175,073	2,303,669	1,183,311	0	243,360
Mississippi	4,271,987	2,456,234	606,824	291,042	193,776	294,110	910,959	159,524	1,612,660	946,620	64,212	203,093
Missouri	5,177,981	3,208,473	1,126,698	238,586	178,200	771,827	733,291	159,870	1,894,030	852,967	147,973	75,478
Montana.....................	1,022,967	652,931	292,172	152,535	36,131	92,129	0	79,964	342,763	211,658	9,156	27,274
Nebraska...................	2,585,957	1,305,307	432,489	208,582	201,133	322,429	26,081	114,593	1,146,049	666,757	138,933	134,601
Nevada......................	1,608,047	794,384	372,396	147,181	74,708	92,056	0	108,043	788,386	478,282	0	25,277
New Hampshire...........	1,093,629	752,685	393,596	74,927	49,586	203,117	0	31,459	214,586	109,724	0	126,359
New Jersey.................	7,409,557	4,377,767	2,155,396	446,579	403,031	606,433	487,578	278,750	2,772,975	1,569,437	199,631	258,815
New Mexico................	3,462,441	1,891,089	288,149	392,974	169,181	114,121	671,214	255,450	1,488,384	749,949	134,655	82,967
New York....................	15,884,730	7,944,546	2,604,024	740,897	1,199,900	672,664	2,499,595	227,466	7,282,983	4,593,055	803,784	657,202
North Carolina............	10,846,550	4,713,325	1,707,181	879,754	330,203	1,579,331	0	216,856	5,689,573	3,474,851	217,480	443,652
North Dakota..............	1,208,427	714,017	294,322	142,747	68,657	105,321	0	102,970	421,827	334,094	3,082	72,583
Ohio..........................	13,521,773	9,102,680	3,579,698	702,520	548,494	1,127,627	2,808,465	335,877	4,119,231	1,917,249	164,764	299,861
Oklahoma..................	4,286,400	2,609,029	867,911	274,985	328,923	502,153	77,174	557,883	1,532,249	915,806	56,899	145,121
Oregon......................	6,427,174	4,445,266	1,228,548	658,589	180,234	489,593	1,624,606	263,696	1,755,374	634,748	230,607	226,534
Pennsylvania	14,288,542	10,362,602	4,042,860	1,239,071	430,688	1,017,593	2,968,771	663,620	3,831,440	1,211,416	111,246	94,499
Rhode Island.............	775,576	511,979	274,261	74,853	24,538	109,714	0	28,613	219,312	148,310	0	44,284
South Carolina...........	4,335,333	2,950,170	1,406,699	410,690	397,235	435,158	0	300,387	1,250,492	538,507	64,358	134,672
South Dakota..............	830,944	505,057	235,110	96,262	49,281	72,473	0	51,931	273,946	180,855	0	51,940
Tennessee.................	4,540,388	2,248,216	1,083,863	288,249	291,405	306,780	0	277,918	2,040,738	1,117,533	5,707	251,434
Texas........................	40,011,641	14,917,459	4,968,851	2,013,315	2,288,264	1,362,680	2,215,483	2,068,865	19,907,784	5,394,667	1,623,483	5,186,399
Utah..........................	5,379,665	3,925,547	736,349	395,350	151,950	219,354	1,579,004	843,541	1,293,216	737,380	0	160,902
Vermont	871,552	679,764	358,086	127,324	58,943	104,931	0	30,480	186,815	70,618	0	4,973
Virginia.....................	10,458,605	6,491,774	2,529,739	864,907	211,398	1,292,544	1,262,465	330,723	3,454,418	1,674,472	3,886	512,413
Washington................	8,897,290	6,090,617	1,847,536	1,233,600	719,278	632,632	1,206,918	450,653	2,537,607	1,195,297	0	269,067
West Virginia..............	1,845,096	1,181,613	568,567	128,751	197,567	231,604	0	55,124	594,336	401,966	653	69,147
Wisconsin..................	6,403,153	3,654,136	1,379,834	672,274	412,368	458,248	0	731,412	2,562,796	1,012,034	795,338	186,221
Wyoming....................	838,597	301,238	83,823	55,288	65,581	59,212	0	37,334	488,382	327,692	47,331	48,977
U.S. Service Academies.............	2,438,669	318,678	826	115,239	4,649	56,383	141,582	0	1,463,475	0	0	656,516
Other jurisdictions.	1,746,762	421,758	92,185	169,400	43,441	12,548	67,698	36,488	1,315,294	995,154	46,378	9,710
American Samoa	19,401	10,656	3,926	6,316	0	202	0	212	8,745	3,000	0	0
Federated States of Micronesia	28,418	17,425	836	4,802	2,772	1,762	0	7,253	10,993	0	0	0
Guam........................	140,406	62,096	15,493	33,777	2,942	2,383	0	7,501	78,310	32,131	17,423	0
Marshall Islands	15,630	4,751	492	3,084	0	976	0	200	10,879	2,875	0	0
Northern Marianas.......	18,834	11,683	1,436	8,997	0	1,248	0	2	7,151	4,114	0	0
Palau........................	10,361	4,927	2,662	1,707	0	125	0	433	5,434	2,461	0	0
Puerto Rico.................	1,434,948	273,719	53,015	94,382	35,373	2,812	67,698	20,440	1,155,512	950,573	2,431	5,718
U.S. Virgin Islands........	78,762	36,500	14,324	16,335	2,354	3,041	0	447	38,270	0	26,525	3,992

[1]Includes other categories not separately shown.
[2]After deducting discounts and allowances.
[3]Includes sales and services of educational activities.
NOTE: Degree-granting institutions grant associate's or higher degrees and participate in Title IV federal financial aid programs. Includes data for public institutions reporting data according to either the Governmental Accounting Standards Board (GASB) or the Financial Accounting Standards Board (FASB) questionnaire. Detail may not sum to totals because of rounding.
SOURCE: U.S. Department of Education, National Center for Education Statistics, Integrated Postsecondary Education Data System (IPEDS), Spring 2015, Finance component. (This table was prepared October 2015.)

Table 333.25. Revenues of public degree-granting postsecondary institutions, by source of revenue and state or jurisdiction: 2011–12

[In thousands of current dollars]

State or jurisdiction	Total revenues	Operating revenue							Nonoperating revenue[1]			Other revenues and additions
		Total	Tuition and fees[2]	Federal grants and contracts	State, local, and private grants and contracts	Sales and services of auxiliary enterprises[2]	Sales and services of hospitals	Independent operations and other[3]	Total	State appropriations	Local appropriations	
1	2	3	4	5	6	7	8	9	10	11	12	13
United States......	$317,289,436	$186,960,039	$65,396,118	$29,133,188	$16,991,917	$24,276,751	$33,508,840	$17,653,225	$114,722,221	$58,789,575	$10,214,576	$15,607,176
Alabama.............	6,898,551	4,470,826	1,445,641	638,664	234,802	377,327	1,430,697	343,695	2,266,648	1,332,025	1,277	161,078
Alaska................	984,645	323,106	124,504	63,452	75,364	40,611	0	19,175	494,218	358,441	10,031	167,322
Arizona..............	5,417,482	2,794,932	1,548,148	577,593	174,917	338,428	0	155,846	2,524,426	783,210	749,180	98,124
Arkansas............	3,746,046	2,299,638	441,167	298,138	187,638	246,418	876,544	249,734	1,338,735	755,308	31,131	107,673
California............	43,262,371	24,997,632	6,064,944	3,788,696	2,422,968	1,892,987	6,817,495	4,010,541	15,543,874	7,397,375	2,561,870	2,720,866
Colorado............	5,477,203	4,538,936	1,708,810	946,582	558,641	490,313	478,461	356,129	748,878	30,648	78,374	189,389
Connecticut........	3,112,449	1,705,133	590,081	173,699	98,321	270,590	289,388	283,054	1,117,577	892,046	0	289,739
Delaware............	1,133,613	784,390	423,082	145,096	40,460	128,887	0	46,863	320,566	222,253	0	28,658
District of Columbia......	167,230	56,749	27,050	13,854	12,207	377	0	3,260	84,445	67,362	0	26,036
Florida...............	10,622,365	5,055,543	2,097,380	1,084,379	940,208	771,409	0	162,165	5,205,271	3,037,050	0	361,551
Georgia..............	7,664,812	4,299,845	1,780,346	776,296	529,480	802,114	196,911	214,698	2,979,565	1,847,510	44	385,401
Hawaii................	1,584,602	780,940	238,172	346,662	60,956	87,631	0	47,518	616,659	375,754	0	187,003
Idaho.................	1,282,864	660,724	322,712	120,035	51,578	121,301	0	45,097	581,949	308,986	20,559	40,191
Illinois...............	11,780,728	5,996,283	2,393,531	888,551	394,977	910,618	655,563	753,043	5,582,666	1,815,619	1,015,855	201,779
Indiana...............	6,611,275	4,149,360	2,141,648	609,029	262,448	724,944	0	411,292	2,376,556	1,415,835	9,012	85,359
Iowa..................	5,035,497	3,699,260	843,756	577,340	143,341	470,520	1,319,642	344,661	1,250,437	709,408	114,880	85,799
Kansas...............	3,320,431	1,898,469	758,564	367,193	188,492	307,221	0	276,999	1,323,151	719,033	233,851	98,812
Kentucky............	5,148,333	3,425,174	954,277	438,238	245,000	300,764	1,084,839	402,057	1,623,158	969,989	17,501	100,000
Louisiana...........	4,000,467	2,386,961	791,720	333,795	442,797	340,265	287,764	190,621	1,463,053	944,649	0	150,453
Maine................	919,695	493,225	216,316	67,108	68,063	92,353	0	49,385	374,279	255,518	0	52,191
Maryland............	6,381,736	3,731,747	1,548,101	784,837	413,076	649,640	0	336,091	2,242,606	1,411,746	310,463	407,383
Massachusetts.....	4,648,600	2,903,740	1,193,215	401,434	241,733	428,542	0	638,816	1,454,496	1,046,090	0	290,364
Michigan............	13,321,669	9,633,297	3,564,224	1,469,930	435,807	1,071,907	2,601,803	489,625	3,382,901	1,490,701	523,771	305,471
Minnesota..........	5,053,633	2,918,488	1,265,215	513,955	348,166	597,554	0	193,597	1,937,790	1,095,626	0	197,354
Mississippi.........	3,993,870	2,223,603	548,043	370,314	174,346	267,205	704,269	159,426	1,612,497	939,075	59,716	157,771
Missouri.............	4,736,828	3,021,550	1,023,031	265,314	187,060	734,490	656,903	154,752	1,623,104	836,519	146,266	92,174
Montana.............	1,018,201	660,995	278,828	174,268	34,242	86,022	15,484	72,150	325,630	192,319	8,404	31,576
Nebraska............	2,351,516	1,248,587	404,450	245,921	175,016	286,557	25,752	110,892	1,008,319	616,412	127,737	94,609
Nevada..............	1,362,281	694,960	335,187	141,148	65,159	91,760	0	61,706	643,010	466,961	0	24,312
New Hampshire....	939,405	724,302	371,385	65,790	64,294	198,475	0	24,358	174,129	80,192	0	40,975
New Jersey.........	7,319,202	4,630,767	2,025,059	497,186	410,975	585,610	920,868	191,069	2,531,469	1,495,920	194,452	156,965
New Mexico........	3,203,410	1,822,786	273,385	385,027	157,246	120,755	624,117	262,256	1,301,481	675,069	126,890	79,143
New York............	15,687,238	7,840,647	2,410,166	795,823	1,048,339	927,283	2,459,479	199,557	7,120,420	4,248,791	797,232	726,171
North Carolina.....	10,263,991	4,289,664	1,539,459	823,784	309,500	1,427,382	974	188,566	5,330,955	3,387,420	200,980	643,372
North Dakota.......	1,115,052	691,468	275,366	164,278	58,833	113,007	0	79,984	365,624	276,228	2,686	57,960
Ohio..................	12,202,046	8,689,965	3,427,072	791,674	502,995	1,116,246	2,550,550	301,429	3,278,851	1,861,830	158,190	233,230
Oklahoma...........	4,042,219	2,363,087	771,736	269,595	292,237	456,635	67,631	505,254	1,533,106	898,544	50,986	146,025
Oregon..............	5,722,757	4,105,013	1,122,000	675,695	172,101	459,727	1,442,402	233,088	1,493,524	583,336	210,454	124,220
Pennsylvania.......	12,076,791	9,495,751	3,841,626	1,300,138	330,584	984,355	2,412,708	626,339	2,480,199	1,189,943	111,524	100,840
Rhode Island.......	780,754	522,339	264,236	87,381	38,536	102,825	0	29,361	209,791	141,208	0	48,624
South Carolina.....	4,063,314	2,755,593	1,304,733	416,150	360,754	398,300	0	275,654	1,155,894	465,402	62,126	151,828
South Dakota.......	800,354	512,259	214,192	125,186	43,018	66,209	0	63,654	247,252	159,652	0	40,843
Tennessee..........	4,297,676	2,151,942	992,372	332,362	257,387	299,677	0	270,145	1,903,832	1,002,136	5,655	241,901
Texas................	30,181,917	13,574,916	4,658,797	2,082,244	2,023,194	1,258,911	1,922,484	1,629,287	12,954,728	5,022,641	1,452,266	3,652,272
Utah..................	5,016,569	3,455,190	674,688	433,497	141,904	195,995	1,267,170	741,935	1,107,769	677,217	0	453,610
Vermont.............	760,959	645,422	348,332	127,751	43,807	102,133	0	23,398	105,702	67,894	0	9,835
Virginia..............	9,215,536	6,003,793	2,302,342	850,969	199,854	1,171,606	1,173,193	305,829	2,562,990	1,441,710	5,141	648,753
Washington.........	7,679,810	5,557,645	1,615,340	1,289,869	623,460	522,263	1,097,525	409,189	1,881,257	1,074,462	0	240,907
West Virginia.......	1,922,218	1,128,696	517,199	146,773	185,225	221,689	0	57,811	625,209	429,716	874	168,313
Wisconsin...........	6,404,192	3,558,863	1,294,046	712,773	452,724	482,556	0	616,764	2,393,871	943,010	769,923	451,458
Wyoming............	804,486	281,495	78,962	45,014	62,851	59,262	0	35,405	494,402	333,566	45,274	28,589
U.S. Service Academies............	1,750,547	304,344	1,480	92,709	4,838	77,093	128,223	0	1,423,303	0	0	22,900
Other jurisdictions.	1,833,942	585,852	122,708	239,924	76,116	14,326	86,819	45,959	1,240,687	891,770	40,258	7,403
American Samoa........	25,002	14,919	4,208	10,036	0	669	0	6	10,083	1,948	0	0
Federated States of Micronesia........	23,179	6,283	612	2,180	1,206	1,874	0	412	16,896	0	0	0
Guam..................	147,097	68,274	15,693	34,233	3,322	2,559	0	12,467	77,719	34,197	14,569	1,104
Marshall Islands...........	18,067	2,157	534	0	250	1,012	0	362	15,909	2,875	0	0
Northern Marianas......	19,824	13,279	2,527	9,473	0	1,265	0	16	6,545	3,749	0	0
Palau................	11,548	4,767	3,092	1,320	0	139	0	216	6,781	2,654	0	0
Puerto Rico.........	1,508,112	434,319	81,275	162,460	68,421	3,216	86,819	32,128	1,071,487	846,348	2	2,307
U.S. Virgin Islands.......	81,113	41,854	14,768	20,223	2,917	3,593	0	354	35,267	0	25,687	3,992

[1]Includes other categories not separately shown.
[2]After deducting discounts and allowances.
[3]Includes sales and services of educational activities.
NOTE: Degree-granting institutions grant associate's or higher degrees and participate in Title IV federal financial aid programs. Includes data for public institutions reporting data according to either the Governmental Accounting Standards Board (GASB) or the Financial Accounting Standards Board (FASB) questionnaire. Some data have been revised from previously published figures. Detail may not sum to totals because of rounding.
SOURCE: U.S. Department of Education, National Center for Education Statistics, Integrated Postsecondary Education Data System (IPEDS), Spring 2013, Finance component. (This table was prepared October 2015.)

Table 333.30. Appropriations from state and local governments for public degree-granting postsecondary institutions, by state or jurisdiction: Selected years, 1990–91 through 2013–14

[In thousands of current dollars]

State or jurisdiction	State appropriations						Local appropriations					
	1990–91	2000–01	2010–11	2011–12	2012–13	2013–14	1990–91	2000–01	2010–11	2011–12	2012–13	2013–14
1	2	3	4	5	6	7	8	9	10	11	12	13
United States	$35,898,653	$56,268,990	$63,063,322	$58,789,575	$58,634,067	$62,700,662	$3,159,789	$5,582,287	$10,023,157	$10,214,576	$10,725,798	$11,112,188
Alabama	708,191	991,302	1,281,923	1,332,025	1,289,898	1,317,764	6,796	4,829	1,204	1,277	1,337	1,895
Alaska	168,395	190,650	346,644	358,441	377,504	392,451	260	10,340	9,681	10,031	10,031	10,789
Arizona	591,656	903,196	1,006,196	783,210	772,257	789,580	149,337	310,762	746,962	749,180	763,521	798,085
Arkansas..................	315,372	583,794	753,573	755,308	759,693	783,427	216	9,496	30,375	31,131	30,714	32,279
California	5,313,052	7,891,669	9,367,909	7,397,375	7,353,389	8,171,790	771,160	1,764,717	2,490,057	2,561,870	2,870,210	3,005,606
Colorado	423,710	655,037	33,667	30,648	30,479	32,718	22,400	36,840	82,141	78,374	84,923	83,364
Connecticut..............	363,427	664,356	1,018,015	892,046	926,224	1,080,009	0	0	0	0	0	0
Delaware..................	115,729	193,695	214,445	222,253	236,730	234,102	0	0	0	0	0	0
District of Columbia ...	0	3,019	66,420	67,362	75,405	66,691	73,495	46,933	0	0	0	0
Florida.....................	1,638,218	2,656,376	3,243,232	3,037,050	2,765,668	3,356,433	1,850	2	0	0	0	0
Georgia	915,303	1,826,961	1,938,523	1,847,730	1,887,336	2,003,786	25,705	21,615	23	44	69	400
Hawaii	304,131	395,884	359,077	375,754	372,872	391,266	0	0	0	0	0	0
Idaho.......................	177,918	290,746	312,809	308,986	334,283	346,115	6,161	11,148	13,398	20,559	26,483	27,176
Illinois.....................	1,296,895	1,760,300	1,789,707	1,815,619	1,830,155	1,844,938	284,635	520,136	1,001,566	1,015,855	1,028,222	1,048,852
Indiana....................	886,124	1,257,919	1,431,488	1,415,835	1,393,030	1,452,440	1,507	6,190	7,951	9,012	8,241	7,760
Iowa........................	544,945	813,805	731,485	709,408	752,635	818,015	21,624	36,129	107,022	114,880	117,353	125,607
Kansas.....................	437,413	664,201	741,285	719,033	743,076	731,298	87,026	160,873	228,630	233,851	255,347	265,604
Kentucky	617,915	939,047	971,263	969,989	920,031	923,182	4,682	14,930	18,261	17,501	19,349	20,377
Louisiana	566,798	834,643	1,018,696	944,649	874,193	807,568	1,462	517	0	0	0	0
Maine	174,737	212,144	252,786	255,518	251,703	258,412	0	0	0	0	0	0
Maryland..................	724,223	999,723	1,392,864	1,411,746	1,426,571	1,480,786	117,913	185,034	319,337	310,463	318,138	329,689
Massachusetts..........	471,368	1,038,998	1,034,211	1,046,090	1,042,983	1,168,001	0	0	0	0	0	0
Michigan	1,326,884	1,991,098	1,713,747	1,490,701	1,551,995	1,600,635	159,202	288,112	551,945	523,771	511,749	531,528
Minnesota	744,381	1,174,797	1,206,301	1,095,626	1,099,848	1,183,311	2,040	0	0	0	0	0
Mississippi	365,574	758,242	868,311	939,075	905,656	946,620	25,670	38,167	58,179	59,716	63,053	64,212
Missouri	563,430	945,746	904,594	836,519	841,745	852,967	38,097	101,562	148,970	146,266	148,724	147,973
Montana...................	110,199	137,341	173,250	192,319	193,116	211,658	3,310	4,069	8,151	8,404	8,622	9,156
Nebraska	318,482	514,235	621,957	616,412	631,041	666,757	36,569	19,892	120,979	127,737	134,270	138,933
Nevada	161,581	333,117	539,712	466,961	464,295	478,282	0	0	0	0	0	0
New Hampshire	71,226	96,157	131,878	80,192	94,372	109,724	6	0	7	0	0	0
New Jersey	854,989	1,246,554	1,495,505	1,495,920	1,127,237	1,569,437	145,010	172,667	211,638	194,452	194,041	199,631
New Mexico	307,083	538,822	724,046	675,069	711,375	749,949	34,364	60,183	120,930	126,890	128,028	134,655
New York..................	2,313,128	4,461,671	4,247,113	4,248,791	4,311,984	4,593,055	372,650	431,415	762,484	797,232	802,810	803,784
North Carolina	1,351,111	2,221,600	3,434,423	3,387,420	3,549,146	3,474,851	62,785	113,448	196,168	200,980	206,763	217,480
North Dakota	129,986	188,047	268,488	276,228	312,859	334,094	9	21	2,459	2,686	3,025	3,082
Ohio........................	1,360,141	1,922,571	1,888,347	1,861,830	1,875,678	1,917,249	63,899	101,647	163,891	158,190	151,995	164,764
Oklahoma	473,898	754,540	924,623	898,544	899,841	915,806	12,822	28,367	49,857	50,986	56,133	56,899
Oregon	377,476	640,347	537,918	583,336	471,202	634,748	118,499	106,436	206,762	210,454	219,987	230,607
Pennsylvania.............	962,121	1,331,544	1,401,316	1,189,943	1,216,803	1,211,416	62,794	94,338	117,967	111,524	113,607	111,246
Rhode Island	113,614	157,137	137,071	141,208	141,512	148,310	0	0	0	0	0	0
South Carolina..........	578,794	853,139	480,329	465,402	506,615	538,507	18,670	36,060	62,799	62,126	62,217	64,358
South Dakota............	81,859	129,680	157,444	159,652	168,873	180,855	0	0	0	0	0	0
Tennessee	663,536	969,316	1,250,509	1,002,136	1,032,518	1,117,533	1,779	3,824	5,327	5,655	5,684	5,707
Texas......................	2,627,916	4,236,852	5,179,075	5,022,641	4,891,792	5,394,667	210,934	439,342	1,377,390	1,452,266	1,539,448	1,623,483
Utah........................	304,738	531,975	661,823	677,217	697,252	737,380	0	0	0	0	0	0
Vermont	40,997	53,605	72,466	67,894	67,725	70,618	4	0	0	0	0	0
Virginia....................	886,208	1,395,308	1,534,717	1,441,710	1,608,217	1,674,472	973	1,570	3,737	5,141	3,698	3,886
Washington..............	828,700	1,200,392	1,329,108	1,074,462	1,060,355	1,195,297	2,470	0	0	0	0	0
West Virginia............	263,269	382,269	395,050	429,716	439,393	401,966	574	503	316	874	719	653
Wisconsin	841,192	1,186,415	1,151,462	943,010	986,520	1,012,034	197,712	379,648	757,773	769,923	789,097	795,338
Wyoming..................	120,623	149,009	326,523	333,566	358,988	327,692	12,721	20,525	38,818	45,274	48,190	47,331
U.S. Service Academies...........	0	0	0	0	0	0	0	0	0	0	0	0
Other jurisdictions.	337,393	709,473	883,692	891,770	954,953	995,154	12,724	20,612	46,944	40,258	43,362	46,378
American Samoa......	0	0	0	1,948	1,830	3,000	0	0	0	0	0	0
Federated States of Micronesia	0	40	0	0	0	0	0	3,327	0	0	0	0
Guam.......................	28,283	29,122	31,936	34,197	32,661	32,131	10,028	12,826	15,700	14,569	16,156	17,423
Marshall Islands........	0	1,924	2,000	2,875	2,901	2,875	0	0	0	0	0	0
Northern Marianas	0	9,055	4,385	3,749	4,474	4,114	0	0	0	0	0	0
Palau.......................	644	2,345	2,039	2,654	2,411	2,461	0	0	0	0	0	0
Puerto Rico..............	277,295	647,623	843,332	846,348	910,675	950,573	2,375	4,459	1,824	2	2,319	2,431
U.S. Virgin Islands	31,170	19,365	0	0	0	0	320	0	29,420	25,687	24,887	26,525

NOTE: Data for 1990–91 are for institutions of higher education, while later data are for degree-granting institutions. Degree-granting institutions grant associate's or higher degrees and participate in Title IV federal financial aid programs. The degree-granting classification is very similar to the earlier higher education classification, but it includes more 2-year colleges and excludes a few higher education institutions that did not grant degrees. Includes data for public institutions reporting data according to either the Governmental Accounting Standards Board (GASB) or the Financial Accounting Standards Board (FASB) questionnaire. Some data have been revised from previously published figures. Detail may not sum to totals because of rounding.
SOURCE: U.S. Department of Education, National Center for Education Statistics, Integrated Postsecondary Education Data System (IPEDS), "Finance Survey" (IPEDS-F:FY91); and selected years, Spring 2002 through Spring 2015, Finance component. (This table was prepared October 2015.)

Table 333.40. Total revenue of private nonprofit degree-granting postsecondary institutions, by source of funds and level of institution: 1999–2000 through 2013–14

Level of institution and year	Total	Student tuition and fees (net of allowances)	Federal appropriations, grants, and contracts[1]	State and local appropriations, grants, and contracts	Private gifts, grants, and contracts			Investment return (gain or loss)	Educational activities	Auxiliary enterprises (net of allowances)	Hospitals	Other
					Total	Private grants and contracts	Private gifts and contributions from affiliated entities					
1	2	3	4	5	6	7	8	9	10	11	12	13

In thousands of current dollars

All levels												
1999–2000	$120,625,806	$29,651,812	$12,191,827	$1,697,979	$16,488,984	—	—	$37,763,518	$2,865,606	$8,317,607	$7,208,600	$4,439,874
2000–01	82,174,492	31,318,106	13,378,019	1,684,425	15,859,313	—	—	-3,602,326	3,468,680	8,742,610	7,126,343	4,199,323
2001–02	84,346,652	33,499,121	14,790,235	1,796,930	15,394,353	—	—	-6,545,330	3,220,868	9,317,922	8,083,935	4,788,618
2002–03	105,672,753	36,019,267	16,625,072	1,988,977	14,380,351	—	—	9,340,400	3,056,259	9,833,972	8,942,047	5,486,409
2003–04	134,230,762	38,505,631	18,335,784	1,941,273	15,847,571	—	—	30,896,917	3,290,420	10,325,606	9,657,753	5,429,805
2004–05	140,150,716	41,394,424	19,699,204	1,957,921	16,738,916	—	—	30,431,521	3,595,559	10,823,963	10,377,808	5,131,401
2005–06	152,744,665	44,263,227	19,683,291	2,075,850	18,346,525	—	—	35,634,520	3,716,409	11,610,762	11,536,658	5,877,423
2006–07	182,381,275	47,481,431	20,193,637	2,165,371	20,193,231	—	—	55,907,662	4,105,289	12,291,973	12,636,904	7,405,779
2007–08	139,250,857	50,736,003	20,204,523	2,385,888	20,991,936	—	—	6,446,982	4,849,728	12,928,521	13,299,928	7,407,348
2008–09	69,064,340	53,698,893	21,026,721	2,391,238	17,670,642	—	—	-64,204,943	4,787,360	13,579,506	14,790,231	5,324,691
2009–10	168,688,480	56,386,895	22,913,755	2,193,062	18,019,300	$4,189,574	$13,829,726	28,427,192	4,821,683	14,080,329	16,541,461	5,304,802
2010–11	207,132,349	60,069,691	24,319,663	2,165,584	22,096,853	4,379,206	17,717,647	53,574,169	4,979,595	14,797,601	17,521,091	7,608,102
2011–12	161,843,203	63,010,873	24,147,131	1,964,921	21,619,470	4,446,517	17,172,953	4,538,153	5,082,873	15,500,185	18,658,649	7,320,948
2012–13	202,084,062	65,595,255	23,714,629	1,938,964	22,336,587	4,834,524	17,502,063	38,537,742	5,534,688	15,957,898	19,011,711	9,456,589
2013–14	228,806,703	67,682,150	23,655,533	1,976,193	25,821,258	5,134,270	20,686,988	57,147,116	6,280,766	16,405,110	20,667,484	9,171,093
4–year												
1999–2000	119,708,625	29,257,523	12,133,829	1,673,707	16,346,616	—	—	37,698,219	2,837,784	8,261,507	7,208,600	4,290,841
2000–01	81,568,928	30,996,381	13,318,572	1,659,505	15,788,869	—	—	-3,623,323	3,452,731	8,703,316	7,125,648	4,147,227
2001–02	83,764,907	33,165,965	14,708,582	1,771,383	15,328,974	—	—	-6,547,915	3,206,440	9,263,171	8,083,935	4,784,371
2002–03	105,064,157	35,676,736	16,515,854	1,957,729	14,319,622	—	—	9,338,684	3,041,307	9,779,275	8,942,047	5,492,904
2003–04	133,594,668	38,181,648	18,236,313	1,903,374	15,789,672	—	—	30,854,091	3,277,767	10,287,215	9,657,753	5,406,836
2004–05	139,528,763	41,045,608	19,622,002	1,931,021	16,671,017	—	—	30,408,545	3,581,869	10,784,161	10,377,808	5,106,733
2005–06	152,150,193	43,944,766	19,607,858	2,045,814	18,288,085	—	—	35,603,805	3,699,630	11,573,115	11,536,658	5,850,463
2006–07	181,853,949	47,211,041	20,137,112	2,144,350	20,143,850	—	—	55,857,220	4,097,001	12,253,297	12,636,904	7,373,173
2007–08	138,749,560	50,431,352	20,143,833	2,361,511	20,938,774	—	—	6,459,197	4,838,649	12,890,431	13,299,928	7,385,886
2008–09	68,617,705	53,399,912	20,967,794	2,370,169	17,624,319	—	—	-64,172,755	4,781,845	13,542,690	14,790,231	5,313,500
2009–10	168,169,216	56,087,965	22,843,520	2,179,050	17,968,453	4,185,607	13,782,846	28,406,397	4,814,283	14,044,652	16,541,461	5,283,434
2010–11	206,473,105	59,603,541	24,260,568	2,150,124	22,057,300	4,376,381	17,680,919	53,557,782	4,975,158	14,762,888	17,521,091	7,584,652
2011–12	161,246,877	62,571,879	24,098,863	1,953,307	21,580,612	4,444,004	17,136,608	4,532,992	5,079,866	15,471,860	18,658,649	7,298,849
2012–13	201,568,379	65,246,827	23,668,765	1,925,440	22,294,772	4,832,217	17,462,555	38,524,192	5,531,823	15,928,400	19,011,711	9,436,448
2013–14	228,233,132	67,326,758	23,594,264	1,963,783	25,770,492	5,131,305	20,639,187	57,104,740	6,278,456	16,374,118	20,667,484	9,153,035
2–year												
1999–2000	917,181	394,289	57,998	24,272	142,368	—	—	65,299	27,822	56,100	0	149,033
2000–01	605,564	321,724	59,446	24,920	70,444	—	—	20,996	15,949	39,294	694	52,096
2001–02	581,745	333,156	81,653	25,547	65,379	—	—	2,585	14,429	54,750	0	4,246
2002–03	608,596	342,531	109,217	31,247	60,729	—	—	1,716	14,953	54,697	0	-6,495
2003–04	636,094	323,983	99,471	37,900	57,900	—	—	42,826	12,653	38,391	0	22,969
2004–05	621,953	348,815	77,202	26,900	67,899	—	—	22,976	13,690	39,802	0	24,668
2005–06	594,473	318,460	75,433	30,036	58,441	—	—	30,716	16,778	37,648	0	26,960
2006–07	527,327	270,389	56,525	21,021	49,381	—	—	50,442	8,288	38,675	0	32,606
2007–08	501,297	304,651	60,689	24,377	53,162	—	—	-12,214	11,080	38,091	0	21,462
2008–09	446,635	298,981	58,927	21,069	46,323	—	—	-32,187	5,515	36,816	0	11,191
2009–10	519,264	298,930	70,235	14,012	50,847	3,967	46,880	20,795	7,400	35,677	0	21,368
2010–11	659,244	466,149	59,095	15,460	39,553	2,825	36,727	16,388	4,437	34,712	0	23,450
2011–12	596,326	438,994	48,269	11,614	38,858	2,513	36,345	5,161	3,007	28,325	0	22,099
2012–13	515,683	348,427	45,863	13,524	41,815	2,307	39,508	13,550	2,865	29,498	0	20,140
2013–14	573,571	355,392	61,269	12,409	50,766	2,965	47,800	42,376	2,311	30,991	0	18,058

Percentage distribution

All levels												
1999–2000	100.00	24.58	10.11	1.41	13.67	—	—	31.31	2.38	6.90	5.98	3.68
2000–01	100.00	38.11	16.28	2.05	19.30	—	—	-4.38	4.22	10.64	8.67	5.11
2001–02	100.00	39.72	17.54	2.13	18.25	—	—	-7.76	3.82	11.05	9.58	5.68
2002–03	100.00	34.09	15.73	1.88	13.61	—	—	8.84	2.89	9.31	8.46	5.19
2003–04	100.00	28.69	13.66	1.45	11.81	—	—	23.02	2.45	7.69	7.19	4.05
2004–05	100.00	29.54	14.06	1.40	11.94	—	—	21.71	2.57	7.72	7.40	3.66
2005–06	100.00	28.98	12.89	1.36	12.01	—	—	23.33	2.43	7.60	7.55	3.85
2006–07	100.00	26.03	11.07	1.19	11.07	—	—	30.65	2.25	6.74	6.93	4.06
2007–08	100.00	36.43	14.51	1.71	15.07	—	—	4.63	3.48	9.28	9.55	5.32
2008–09	100.00	77.75	30.45	3.46	25.59	—	—	-92.96	6.93	19.66	21.42	7.71
2009–10	100.00	33.43	13.58	1.30	10.68	2.48	8.20	16.85	2.86	8.35	9.81	3.14
2010–11	100.00	29.00	11.74	1.05	10.67	2.11	8.55	25.86	2.40	7.14	8.46	3.67
2011–12	100.00	38.93	14.92	1.21	13.36	2.75	10.61	2.80	3.14	9.58	11.53	4.52
2012–13	100.00	32.46	11.74	0.96	11.05	2.39	8.66	19.07	2.74	7.90	9.41	4.68
2013–14	100.00	29.58	10.34	0.86	11.29	2.24	9.04	24.98	2.75	7.17	9.03	4.01
4–year												
1999–2000	100.00	24.44	10.14	1.40	13.66	—	—	31.49	2.37	6.90	6.02	3.58
2000–01	100.00	38.00	16.33	2.03	19.36	—	—	-4.44	4.23	10.67	8.74	5.08
2001–02	100.00	39.59	17.56	2.11	18.30	—	—	-7.82	3.83	11.06	9.65	5.71
2002–03	100.00	33.96	15.72	1.86	13.63	—	—	8.89	2.89	9.31	8.51	5.23
2003–04	100.00	28.58	13.65	1.42	11.82	—	—	23.10	2.45	7.70	7.23	4.05
2004–05	100.00	29.42	14.06	1.38	11.95	—	—	21.79	2.57	7.73	7.44	3.66
2005–06	100.00	28.88	12.89	1.34	12.02	—	—	23.40	2.43	7.61	7.58	3.85
2006–07	100.00	25.96	11.07	1.18	11.08	—	—	30.72	2.25	6.74	6.95	4.05
2007–08	100.00	36.35	14.52	1.70	15.09	—	—	4.66	3.49	9.29	9.59	5.32
2008–09	100.00	77.82	30.56	3.45	25.68	—	—	-93.52	6.97	19.74	21.55	7.74

See notes at end of table.

Table 333.40. Total revenue of private nonprofit degree-granting postsecondary institutions, by source of funds and level of institution: 1999–2000 through 2013–14—Continued

Level of institution and year	Total	Student tuition and fees (net of allowances)	Federal appropriations, grants, and contracts[1]	State and local appropriations, grants, and contracts	Private gifts, grants, and contracts			Investment return (gain or loss)	Educational activities	Auxiliary enterprises (net of allowances)	Hospitals	Other
					Total	Private grants and contracts	Private gifts and contributions from affiliated entities					
1	2	3	4	5	6	7	8	9	10	11	12	13
2009–10	100.00	33.35	13.58	1.30	10.68	2.49	8.20	16.89	2.86	8.35	9.84	3.14
2010–11	100.00	28.87	11.75	1.04	10.68	2.12	8.56	25.94	2.41	7.15	8.49	3.67
2011–12	100.00	38.81	14.95	1.21	13.38	2.76	10.63	2.81	3.15	9.60	11.57	4.53
2012–13	100.00	32.37	11.74	0.96	11.06	2.40	8.66	19.11	2.74	7.90	9.43	4.68
2013–14	100.00	29.50	10.34	0.86	11.29	2.25	9.04	25.02	2.75	7.17	9.06	4.01
2-year												
1999–2000	100.00	42.99	6.32	2.65	15.52	—	—	7.12	3.03	6.12	0.00	16.25
2000–01	100.00	53.13	9.82	4.12	11.63	—	—	3.47	2.63	6.49	0.11	8.60
2001–02	100.00	57.27	14.04	4.39	11.24	—	—	0.44	2.48	9.41	0.00	0.73
2002–03	100.00	56.28	17.95	5.13	9.98	—	—	0.28	2.46	8.99	0.00	-1.07
2003–04	100.00	50.93	15.64	5.96	9.10	—	—	6.73	1.99	6.04	0.00	3.61
2004–05	100.00	56.08	12.41	4.33	10.92	—	—	3.69	2.20	6.40	0.00	3.97
2005–06	100.00	53.57	12.69	5.05	9.83	—	—	5.17	2.82	6.33	0.00	4.54
2006–07	100.00	51.28	10.72	3.99	9.36	—	—	9.57	1.57	7.33	0.00	6.18
2007–08	100.00	60.77	12.11	4.86	10.60	—	—	-2.44	2.21	7.60	0.00	4.28
2008–09	100.00	66.94	13.19	4.72	10.37	—	—	-7.21	1.23	8.24	0.00	2.51
2009–10	100.00	57.57	13.53	2.70	9.79	0.76	9.03	4.00	1.43	6.87	0.00	4.12
2010–11	100.00	70.71	8.96	2.35	6.00	0.43	5.57	2.49	0.67	5.27	0.00	3.56
2011–12	100.00	73.62	8.09	1.95	6.52	0.42	6.09	0.87	0.50	4.75	0.00	3.71
2012–13	100.00	67.57	8.89	2.62	8.11	0.45	7.66	2.63	0.56	5.72	0.00	3.91
2013–14	100.00	61.96	10.68	2.16	8.85	0.52	8.33	7.39	0.40	5.40	0.00	3.15
Revenue per full-time-equivalent student in constant 2014–15 dollars[2]												
All levels												
1999–2000	$66,422	$16,328	$6,713	$935	$9,080	—	—	$20,794	$1,578	$4,580	$3,969	$2,445
2000–01	42,899	16,350	6,984	879	8,279	—	—	-1,881	1,811	4,564	3,720	2,192
2001–02	42,338	16,815	7,424	902	7,727	—	—	-3,285	1,617	4,677	4,058	2,404
2002–03	50,225	17,120	7,902	945	6,835	—	—	4,439	1,453	4,674	4,250	2,608
2003–04	60,942	17,482	8,325	881	7,195	—	—	14,028	1,494	4,688	4,385	2,465
2004–05	60,304	17,811	8,476	842	7,202	—	—	13,094	1,547	4,657	4,465	2,208
2005–06	62,449	18,097	8,047	849	7,501	—	—	14,569	1,519	4,747	4,717	2,403
2006–07	71,402	18,589	7,906	848	7,906	—	—	21,888	1,607	4,812	4,947	2,899
2007–08	51,282	18,685	7,441	879	7,731	—	—	2,374	1,786	4,761	4,898	2,728
2008–09	24,702	19,206	7,521	855	6,320	—	—	-22,964	1,712	4,857	5,290	1,904
2009–10	58,201	19,455	7,906	757	6,217	$1,445	$4,772	9,808	1,664	4,858	5,707	1,830
2010–11	67,503	19,576	7,926	706	7,201	1,427	5,774	17,459	1,623	4,822	5,710	2,479
2011–12	50,799	19,778	7,579	617	6,786	1,396	5,390	1,424	1,595	4,865	5,857	2,298
2012–13	61,648	20,010	7,234	592	6,814	1,475	5,339	11,756	1,688	4,868	5,800	2,885
2013–14	68,604	20,293	7,093	593	7,742	1,539	6,203	17,135	1,883	4,919	6,197	2,750
4-year												
1999–2000	67,329	16,456	6,825	941	9,194	—	—	21,203	1,596	4,647	4,054	2,413
2000–01	43,248	16,434	7,062	880	8,371	—	—	-1,921	1,831	4,615	3,778	2,199
2001–02	42,674	16,897	7,493	902	7,809	—	—	-3,336	1,634	4,719	4,118	2,437
2002–03	50,607	17,185	7,955	943	6,897	—	—	4,498	1,465	4,710	4,307	2,646
2003–04	61,428	17,556	8,385	875	7,260	—	—	14,187	1,507	4,730	4,441	2,486
2004–05	60,765	17,876	8,545	841	7,260	—	—	13,243	1,560	4,697	4,520	2,224
2005–06	62,882	18,162	8,104	846	7,558	—	—	14,715	1,529	4,783	4,768	2,418
2006–07	71,813	18,643	7,952	847	7,955	—	—	22,058	1,618	4,839	4,990	2,912
2007–08	51,556	18,739	7,485	877	7,780	—	—	2,400	1,798	4,790	4,942	2,744
2008–09	24,751	19,262	7,563	855	6,357	—	—	-23,147	1,725	4,885	5,335	1,917
2009–10	58,499	19,511	7,946	758	6,250	1,456	4,794	9,881	1,675	4,886	5,754	1,838
2010–11	68,010	19,633	7,991	708	7,265	1,442	5,824	17,641	1,639	4,863	5,771	2,498
2011–12	51,114	19,835	7,639	619	6,841	1,409	5,432	1,437	1,610	4,904	5,915	2,314
2012–13	62,007	20,072	7,281	592	6,858	1,487	5,372	11,851	1,702	4,900	5,848	2,903
2013–14	68,984	20,350	7,131	594	7,789	1,551	6,238	17,260	1,898	4,949	6,247	2,767
2-year												
1999–2000	24,074	10,349	1,522	637	3,737	—	—	1,714	730	1,473	0	3,912
2000–01	20,565	10,926	2,019	846	2,392	—	—	713	542	1,334	24	1,769
2001–02	19,838	11,361	2,784	871	2,229	—	—	88	492	1,867	0	145
2002–03	21,813	12,277	3,915	1,120	2,177	—	—	62	536	1,960	0	-233
2003–04	22,909	11,668	3,582	1,365	2,085	—	—	1,542	456	1,383	0	827
2004–05	22,301	12,507	2,768	965	2,435	—	—	824	491	1,427	0	885
2005–06	22,603	12,109	2,868	1,142	2,222	—	—	1,168	638	1,431	0	1,025
2006–07	24,022	12,317	2,575	958	2,250	—	—	2,298	378	1,762	0	1,485
2007–08	20,765	12,620	2,514	1,010	2,202	—	—	-506	459	1,578	0	889
2008–09	18,968	12,697	2,503	895	1,967	—	—	-1,367	234	1,564	0	475
2009–10	21,989	12,659	2,974	593	2,153	168	1,985	881	313	1,511	0	905
2010–11	20,233	14,307	1,814	474	1,214	87	1,127	503	136	1,065	0	720
2011–12	19,055	14,028	1,542	371	1,242	80	1,161	165	96	905	0	706
2012–13	18,871	12,751	1,678	495	1,530	84	1,446	496	105	1,079	0	737
2013–14	21,484	13,312	2,295	465	1,902	111	1,790	1,587	87	1,161	0	676

—Not available.
[1]Includes independent operations.
[2]Constant dollars based on the Consumer Price Index, prepared by the Bureau of Labor Statistics, U.S. Department of Labor, adjusted to a school-year basis.
NOTE: Degree-granting institutions grant associate's or higher degrees and participate in Title IV federal financial aid programs. Some data have been revised from previously published figures. Detail may not sum to totals because of rounding.

SOURCE: U.S. Department of Education, National Center for Education Statistics, Integrated Postsecondary Education Data System (IPEDS), "Fall Enrollment Survey" (IPEDS-EF:99); and Spring 2001 through Spring 2007, Enrollment component; Spring 2008 through Spring 2014, Fall Enrollment component; and Spring 2001 through Spring 2015, Finance component. (This table was prepared November 2015.)

Table 333.50. Total revenue of private nonprofit degree-granting postsecondary institutions, by source of funds and classification of institution: 2013–14

Classification of institution	Total	Student tuition and fees (net of allowances)	Federal appropriations, grants, and contracts[1]	State and local appropriations, grants, and contracts	Private grants and contracts	Private gifts and contributions from affiliated entities	Investment return (gain or loss)	Educational activities	Auxiliary enterprises (net of allowances)	Hospitals	Other
1	2	3	4	5	6	7	8	9	10	11	12
In thousands of current dollars											
Total	$228,806,703	$67,682,150	$23,655,533	$1,976,193	$5,134,270	$20,686,988	$57,147,116	$6,280,766	$16,405,110	$20,667,484	$9,171,093
4-year	228,233,132	67,326,758	23,594,264	1,963,783	5,131,305	20,639,187	57,104,740	6,278,456	16,374,118	20,667,484	9,153,035
Research university, very high[2]	116,156,076	14,961,425	18,183,002	883,457	3,577,126	10,173,916	37,247,144	4,757,896	4,317,283	16,196,364	5,858,463
Research university, high[3]	14,928,569	6,349,616	1,156,599	142,768	198,034	1,574,928	2,312,746	633,093	1,572,421	434,199	554,165
Doctoral/research[4]	9,785,706	5,995,835	207,198	75,805	110,719	558,175	1,295,240	65,284	996,374	0	481,077
Master's[5]	33,809,636	21,105,526	985,377	336,513	154,165	2,313,975	3,620,728	164,277	4,266,940	67,503	794,631
Baccalaureate[6]	32,120,799	11,924,551	732,338	179,899	206,514	3,827,690	10,085,520	145,056	4,387,750	342	631,137
Special-focus institutions[7]	21,432,346	6,989,805	2,329,750	345,341	884,748	2,190,504	2,543,363	512,850	833,350	3,969,076	833,561
Art, music, or design	2,707,646	1,586,102	54,046	12,699	23,298	282,302	402,954	17,804	247,440	0	81,001
Business and management	844,297	575,397	24,859	8,346	966	41,587	95,429	6,864	80,854	0	9,994
Engineering or technology	364,804	205,910	3,496	892	204	25,471	90,359	2,167	27,645	0	8,660
Law	611,727	458,984	8,624	2,328	4,564	24,796	89,682	915	14,984	0	6,851
Medical or other health	13,984,306	3,323,005	2,102,246	312,107	805,219	1,089,870	1,127,580	456,313	248,702	3,969,076	550,187
Theological	2,488,360	634,396	44,311	2,640	44,198	690,264	708,395	16,415	188,063	0	159,677
Tribal[8]	107,516	10,379	79,461	2,233	1,634	671	860	611	1,398	0	10,269
Other special focus	323,689	195,632	12,706	4,097	4,664	35,543	28,103	11,760	24,263	0	6,921
2-year	573,571	355,392	61,269	12,409	2,965	47,800	42,376	2,311	30,991	0	18,058
Associate's of arts	553,672	354,704	49,179	11,623	2,772	47,104	42,185	2,311	30,856	0	12,937
Tribal[8]	19,899	688	12,089	786	193	696	191	0	135	0	5,121
Percentage distribution											
Total	100.00	29.58	10.34	0.86	2.24	9.04	24.98	2.75	7.17	9.03	4.01
4-year	100.00	29.50	10.34	0.86	2.25	9.04	25.02	2.75	7.17	9.06	4.01
Research university, very high[2]	100.00	12.88	15.65	0.76	3.08	8.76	32.07	4.10	3.72	13.94	5.04
Research university, high[3]	100.00	42.53	7.75	0.96	1.33	10.55	15.49	4.24	10.53	2.91	3.71
Doctoral/research[4]	100.00	61.27	2.12	0.77	1.13	5.70	13.24	0.67	10.18	0.00	4.92
Master's[5]	100.00	62.42	2.91	1.00	0.46	6.84	10.71	0.49	12.62	0.20	2.35
Baccalaureate[6]	100.00	37.12	2.28	0.56	0.64	11.92	31.40	0.45	13.66	#	1.96
Special-focus institutions[7]	100.00	32.61	10.87	1.61	4.13	10.22	11.87	2.39	3.89	18.52	3.89
Art, music, or design	100.00	58.58	2.00	0.47	0.86	10.43	14.88	0.66	9.14	0.00	2.99
Business and management	100.00	68.15	2.94	0.99	0.11	4.93	11.30	0.81	9.58	0.00	1.18
Engineering or technology	100.00	56.44	0.96	0.24	0.06	6.98	24.77	0.59	7.58	0.00	2.37
Law	100.00	75.03	1.41	0.38	0.75	4.05	14.66	0.15	2.45	0.00	1.12
Medical or other health	100.00	23.76	15.03	2.23	5.76	7.79	8.06	3.26	1.78	28.38	3.93
Theological	100.00	25.49	1.78	0.11	1.78	27.74	28.47	0.66	7.56	0.00	6.42
Tribal[8]	100.00	9.65	73.91	2.08	1.52	0.62	0.80	0.57	1.30	0.00	9.55
Other special focus	100.00	60.44	3.93	1.27	1.44	10.98	8.68	3.63	7.50	0.00	2.14
2-year	100.00	61.96	10.68	2.16	0.52	8.33	7.39	0.40	5.40	0.00	3.15
Associate's of arts	100.00	64.06	8.88	2.10	0.50	8.51	7.62	0.42	5.57	0.00	2.34
Tribal[8]	100.00	3.46	60.75	3.95	0.97	3.50	0.96	0.00	0.68	0.00	25.73
Revenue per full-time-equivalent student in current dollars											
Total	$68,108	$20,147	$7,041	$588	$1,528	$6,158	$17,011	$1,870	$4,883	$6,152	$2,730
4-year	68,486	20,203	7,080	589	1,540	6,193	17,135	1,884	4,913	6,202	2,747
Research university, very high[2]	229,320	29,538	35,898	1,744	7,062	20,086	73,535	9,393	8,523	31,976	11,566
Research university, high[3]	55,561	23,632	4,305	531	737	5,862	8,607	2,356	5,852	1,616	2,062
Doctoral/research[4]	36,712	22,494	777	284	415	2,094	4,859	245	3,738	0	1,805
Master's[5]	26,981	16,843	786	269	123	1,847	2,889	131	3,405	54	634
Baccalaureate[6]	44,050	16,353	1,004	247	283	5,249	13,831	199	6,017	#	866
Special-focus institutions[7]	69,470	22,657	7,552	1,119	2,868	7,100	8,244	1,662	2,701	12,865	2,702
Art, music, or design	47,436	27,787	947	222	408	4,946	7,059	312	4,335	0	1,419
Business and management	27,825	18,963	819	275	32	1,371	3,145	226	2,665	0	329
Engineering or technology	24,516	13,838	235	60	14	1,712	6,073	146	1,858	0	582
Law	44,035	33,039	621	168	329	1,785	6,456	66	1,079	0	493
Medical or other health	128,407	30,513	19,303	2,866	7,394	10,007	10,354	4,190	2,284	36,445	5,052
Theological	33,743	8,603	601	36	599	9,360	9,606	223	2,550	0	2,165
Tribal[8]	41,803	4,035	30,895	868	635	261	334	238	544	0	3,993
Other special focus	45,629	27,577	1,791	577	657	5,010	3,962	1,658	3,420	0	976
2-year	21,329	13,216	2,278	461	110	1,777	1,576	86	1,152	0	672
Associate's of arts	21,023	13,468	1,867	441	105	1,789	1,602	88	1,172	0	491
Tribal[8]	35,790	1,237	21,743	1,414	348	1,252	343	0	243	0	9,210

#Rounds to zero.
[1]Includes independent operations.
[2]Research universities with a very high level of research activity.
[3]Research universities with a high level of research activity.
[4]Institutions that award at least 20 doctor's degrees per year, but did not have high levels of research activity.
[5]Institutions that award at least 50 master's degrees per year.
[6]Institutions that primarily emphasize undergraduate education. Also includes institutions classified as 4-year under the IPEDS system, which had been classified as 2-year in the Carnegie classification system because they primarily award associate's degrees.
[7]Four-year institutions that award degrees primarily in single fields of study, such as medicine, business, fine arts, theology, and engineering.

[8]Tribally controlled colleges, which are located on reservations and are members of the American Indian Higher Education Consortium.
NOTE: Relative levels of research activity for research universities were determined by an analysis of research and development expenditures, science and engineering research staffing, and doctoral degrees conferred, by field. Further information on the Carnegie 2005 classification system used in this table may be obtained from http://carnegieclassifications.iu.edu/. Degree-granting institutions grant associate's or higher degrees and participate in Title IV federal financial aid programs. Detail may not sum to totals because of rounding.
SOURCE: U.S. Department of Education, National Center for Education Statistics, Integrated Postsecondary Education Data System (IPEDS), Spring 2014, Fall Enrollment component; and Spring 2015, Finance component. (This table was prepared November 2015.)

Table 333.55. Total revenue of private for-profit degree-granting postsecondary institutions, by source of funds and level of institution: Selected years, 1999–2000 through 2013–14

Level of institution and year	Total	Student tuition and fees (net of allowances)	Federal appropriations, grants, and contracts	State and local appropriations, grants, and contracts	Private gifts, grants, and contracts	Investment income and gains (losses)	Educational activities	Auxiliary enterprises (net of allowances)	Other
1	2	3	4	5	6	7	8	9	10
					In thousands of current dollars				
All levels									
1999–2000	$4,321,985	$3,721,032	$198,923	$71,904	$2,151	$18,537	$70,672	$156,613	$82,153
2008–09	19,401,359	16,767,748	1,407,615	130,378	80,345	38,680	368,034	395,589	212,970
2009–10	24,689,264	22,402,076	1,706,901	95,277	37,570	40,115	424,471	485,443	-502,589
2010–11	28,285,216	25,157,459	1,583,370	157,290	31,272	32,551	402,206	542,622	378,447
2011–12	26,922,849	24,344,390	1,220,844	101,443	9,386	36,726	351,917	511,364	346,778
2012–13	24,780,997	22,483,997	1,092,117	96,650	14,700	58,267	312,065	484,747	238,453
2013–14	22,659,062	20,476,030	941,370	77,986	12,206	43,032	256,219	482,560	369,658
4-year									
1999–2000	2,381,042	2,050,136	103,865	39,460	1,109	10,340	33,764	102,103	40,266
2008–09	14,793,302	12,982,049	897,503	80,021	71,601	35,434	327,474	297,626	101,595
2009–10	18,985,251	17,342,058	1,356,142	65,148	35,630	35,949	366,044	372,513	-588,234
2010–11	21,690,069	19,483,895	1,113,186	118,054	29,118	28,671	346,786	405,604	164,755
2011–12	21,204,786	19,251,785	836,741	69,747	7,298	30,546	308,359	404,301	296,009
2012–13	19,574,783	17,783,754	809,567	64,261	12,233	49,224	265,836	395,722	194,187
2013–14	17,845,848	16,187,061	709,416	51,830	10,232	36,012	222,739	395,510	233,049
2-year									
1999–2000	1,940,943	1,670,896	95,058	32,444	1,042	8,197	36,908	54,510	41,888
2008–09	4,608,057	3,785,699	510,112	50,358	8,745	3,246	40,560	97,964	111,374
2009–10	5,704,013	5,060,018	350,759	30,129	1,940	4,166	58,427	112,930	85,644
2010–11	6,595,147	5,673,564	470,183	39,236	2,154	3,880	55,420	137,018	213,692
2011–12	5,718,063	5,092,606	384,103	31,696	2,087	6,180	43,558	107,063	50,770
2012–13	5,206,214	4,700,243	282,550	32,390	2,467	9,043	46,230	89,025	44,266
2013–14	4,813,214	4,288,969	231,954	26,157	1,975	7,021	33,480	87,050	136,609
					Percentage distribution				
All levels									
1999–2000	100.00	86.10	4.60	1.66	0.05	0.43	1.64	3.62	1.90
2008–09	100.00	86.43	7.26	0.67	0.41	0.20	1.90	2.04	1.10
2009–10	100.00	90.74	6.91	0.39	0.15	0.16	1.72	1.97	-2.04
2010–11	100.00	88.94	5.60	0.56	0.11	0.12	1.42	1.92	1.34
2011–12	100.00	90.42	4.53	0.38	0.03	0.14	1.31	1.90	1.29
2012–13	100.00	90.73	4.41	0.39	0.06	0.24	1.26	1.96	0.96
2013–14	100.00	90.37	4.15	0.34	0.05	0.19	1.13	2.13	1.63
4-year									
1999–2000	100.00	86.10	4.36	1.66	0.05	0.43	1.42	4.29	1.69
2008–09	100.00	87.76	6.07	0.54	0.48	0.24	2.21	2.01	0.69
2009–10	100.00	91.34	7.14	0.34	0.19	0.19	1.93	1.96	-3.10
2010–11	100.00	89.83	5.13	0.54	0.13	0.13	1.60	1.87	0.76
2011–12	100.00	90.79	3.95	0.33	0.03	0.14	1.45	1.91	1.40
2012–13	100.00	90.85	4.14	0.33	0.06	0.25	1.36	2.02	0.99
2013–14	100.00	90.70	3.98	0.29	0.06	0.20	1.25	2.22	1.31
2-year									
1999–2000	100.00	86.09	4.90	1.67	0.05	0.42	1.90	2.81	2.16
2008–09	100.00	82.15	11.07	1.09	0.19	0.07	0.88	2.13	2.42
2009–10	100.00	88.71	6.15	0.53	0.03	0.07	1.02	1.98	1.50
2010–11	100.00	86.03	7.13	0.59	0.03	0.06	0.84	2.08	3.24
2011–12	100.00	89.06	6.72	0.55	0.04	0.11	0.76	1.87	0.89
2012–13	100.00	90.28	5.43	0.62	0.05	0.17	0.89	1.71	0.85
2013–14	100.00	89.11	4.82	0.54	0.04	0.15	0.70	1.81	2.84
					Revenue per full-time-equivalent student in constant 2014–15 dollars[1]				
All levels									
1999–2000	$15,710	$13,526	$723	$261	$8	$67	$257	$569	$299
2008–09	16,795	14,515	1,219	113	70	33	319	342	184
2009–10	18,096	16,420	1,251	70	28	29	311	356	-368
2010–11	18,312	16,287	1,025	102	20	21	260	351	245
2011–12	17,370	15,706	788	65	6	24	227	330	224
2012–13	17,913	16,252	789	70	11	42	226	350	172
2013–14	21,557	19,480	896	74	12	41	244	459	352
4-year									
1999–2000	15,945	13,729	696	264	7	69	226	684	270
2008–09	16,645	14,607	1,010	90	81	40	368	335	114
2009–10	18,549	16,944	1,325	64	35	35	358	364	-575
2010–11	18,461	16,583	947	100	25	24	295	345	140
2011–12	17,602	15,980	695	58	6	25	256	336	246
2012–13	18,086	16,431	748	59	11	45	246	366	179
2013–14	23,092	20,946	918	67	13	47	288	512	302
2-year									
1999–2000	15,431	13,284	756	258	8	65	293	433	333
2008–09	17,295	14,209	1,915	189	33	12	152	368	418
2009–10	16,737	14,848	1,029	88	6	12	171	331	251
2010–11	17,837	15,344	1,272	106	6	10	150	371	578
2011–12	16,561	14,750	1,112	92	6	18	126	310	147
2012–13	17,289	15,609	938	108	8	30	154	296	147
2013–14	17,294	15,410	833	94	7	25	120	313	491

[1]Constant dollars based on the Consumer Price Index, prepared by the Bureau of Labor Statistics, U.S. Department of Labor, adjusted to a school-year basis.
NOTE: Degree-granting institutions grant associate's or higher degrees and participate in Title IV federal financial aid programs. Some data have been revised from previously published figures. Detail may not sum to totals because of rounding.

SOURCE: U.S. Department of Education, National Center for Education Statistics, Integrated Postsecondary Education Data System (IPEDS), "Fall Enrollment Survey" (IPEDS-EF:99); Spring 2009 through Spring 2014, Fall Enrollment component; and selected years, Spring 2001 through Spring 2015, Finance component. (This table was prepared November 2015.)

Table 333.60. Total revenue of private for-profit degree-granting postsecondary institutions, by source of funds and classification of institution: 2013–14

Classification of institution	Total	Student tuition and fees (net of allowances)	Federal appropriations, grants, and contracts	State and local appropriations, grants, and contracts	Private gifts, grants, and contracts	Investment income and gains (losses)	Educational activities	Auxiliary enterprises (net of allowances)	Other
1	2	3	4	5	6	7	8	9	10
In thousands of current dollars									
Total	$22,659,062	$20,476,030	$941,370	$77,986	$12,206	$43,032	$256,219	$482,560	$369,658
4-year	17,845,848	16,187,061	709,416	51,830	10,232	36,012	222,739	395,510	233,049
Doctoral/research[1]	1,238,552	1,178,680	6,132	225	0	13,048	566	1,984	37,917
Master's[2]	4,018,182	3,857,058	24,271	1,081	0	3,277	11,002	95,303	26,191
Baccalaureate[3]	2,132,025	1,927,516	110,337	6,164	6,737	2,266	15,653	39,359	23,992
Special-focus institutions[4]	10,457,089	9,223,807	568,676	44,360	3,494	17,421	195,518	258,863	144,949
Art, music, or design	2,346,574	1,781,444	336,452	32,919	1,703	1,366	120	151,889	40,680
Business and management	5,605,852	5,132,441	194,664	7,140	1,373	4,441	179,412	64,611	21,770
Engineering or technology	1,263,322	1,199,092	24,037	3,945	101	5,170	3,980	17,404	9,594
Law	203,856	203,102	0	0	63	26	306	45	315
Medical or other health	882,290	837,707	13,523	356	255	4,735	8,255	8,108	9,350
Theological	110,629	31,751	0	0	0	1,479	0	14,943	62,455
Other special focus	44,567	38,270	0	0	0	204	3,445	1,864	785
2-year	4,813,214	4,288,969	231,954	26,157	1,975	7,021	33,480	87,050	136,609
Percentage distribution									
Total	100.00	90.37	4.15	0.34	0.05	0.19	1.13	2.13	1.63
4-year	100.00	90.70	3.98	0.29	0.06	0.20	1.25	2.22	1.31
Doctoral/research[1]	100.00	95.17	0.50	0.02	0.00	1.05	0.05	0.16	3.06
Master's[2]	100.00	95.99	0.60	0.03	0.00	0.08	0.27	2.37	0.65
Baccalaureate[3]	100.00	90.41	5.18	0.29	0.32	0.11	0.73	1.85	1.13
Special-focus institutions[4]	100.00	88.21	5.44	0.42	0.03	0.17	1.87	2.48	1.39
Art, music, or design	100.00	75.92	14.34	1.40	0.07	0.06	0.01	6.47	1.73
Business and management	100.00	91.56	3.47	0.13	0.02	0.08	3.20	1.15	0.39
Engineering or technology	100.00	94.92	1.90	0.31	0.01	0.41	0.32	1.38	0.76
Law	100.00	99.63	0.00	0.00	0.03	0.01	0.15	0.02	0.15
Medical or other health	100.00	94.95	1.53	0.04	0.03	0.54	0.94	0.92	1.06
Theological	100.00	28.70	0.00	0.00	0.00	1.34	0.00	13.51	56.45
Other special focus	100.00	85.87	0.00	0.00	0.00	0.46	7.73	4.18	1.76
2-year	100.00	89.11	4.82	0.54	0.04	0.15	0.70	1.81	2.84
Revenue per full-time-equivalent student in current dollars									
Total	$21,401	$19,339	$889	$74	$12	$41	$242	$456	$349
4-year	22,925	20,794	911	67	13	46	286	508	299
Doctoral/research[1]	17,459	16,615	86	3	0	184	8	28	535
Master's[2]	17,071	16,386	103	5	0	14	47	405	111
Baccalaureate[3]	19,851	17,947	1,027	57	63	21	146	366	223
Special-focus institutions[4]	28,672	25,291	1,559	122	10	48	536	710	397
Art, music, or design	27,134	20,599	3,890	381	20	16	1	1,756	470
Business and management	32,380	29,645	1,124	41	8	26	1,036	373	126
Engineering or technology	21,292	20,210	405	66	2	87	67	293	162
Law	32,317	32,198	0	0	10	4	49	7	50
Medical or other health	26,040	24,724	399	11	8	140	244	239	276
Theological	36,439	10,458	0	0	0	487	0	4,922	20,571
Other special focus	17,505	15,031	0	0	0	80	1,353	732	308
2-year	17,169	15,299	827	93	7	25	119	311	487
Revenue per full-time-equivalent student in constant 2014–15 dollars[5]									
Total	$21,557	$19,480	$896	$74	$12	$41	$244	$459	$352
4-year	23,092	20,946	918	67	13	47	288	512	302
Doctoral/research[1]	17,587	16,736	87	3	0	185	8	28	538
Master's[2]	17,195	16,506	104	5	0	14	47	408	112
Baccalaureate[3]	19,996	18,078	1,035	58	63	21	147	369	225
Special-focus institutions[4]	28,881	25,475	1,571	123	10	48	540	715	400
Art, music, or design	27,332	20,749	3,919	383	20	16	1	1,769	474
Business and management	32,616	29,861	1,133	42	8	26	1,044	376	127
Engineering or technology	21,447	20,357	408	67	2	88	68	295	163
Law	32,552	32,432	0	0	10	4	49	7	50
Medical or other health	26,230	24,904	402	11	8	141	245	241	278
Theological	36,704	10,534	0	0	0	491	0	4,958	20,721
Other special focus	17,632	15,141	0	0	0	81	1,363	737	311
2-year	17,294	15,410	833	94	7	25	120	313	491

[1]Institutions that award at least 20 doctor's degrees per year, but did not have high levels of research activity.

[2]Institutions that award at least 50 master's degrees per year.

[3]Institutions that primarily emphasize undergraduate education. Also includes institutions classified as 4-year under the IPEDS system, which had been classified as 2-year in the Carnegie classification system because they primarily award associate's degrees.

[4]Four-year institutions that award degrees primarily in single fields of study, such as medicine, business, fine arts, theology, and engineering.

[5]Constant dollars based on the Consumer Price Index, prepared by the Bureau of Labor Statistics, U.S. Department of Labor, adjusted to a school-year basis.

NOTE: Degree-granting institutions grant associate's or higher degrees and participate in Title IV federal financial aid. Further information on the Carnegie 2005 classification system used in this table may be obtained from http://carnegieclassifications.iu.edu/. Detail may not sum to totals because of rounding.

SOURCE: U.S. Department of Education, National Center for Education Statistics, Integrated Postsecondary Education Data System (IPEDS), Spring 2014, Fall Enrollment component; and Spring 2015, Finance component. (This table was prepared November 2015.)

Table 333.70. Revenue received from the federal government by the 120 degree-granting postsecondary institutions receiving the largest amounts, by control and rank order: 2013–14

Institution	Control[1]	Rank order	Revenue from the federal govern-ment[2] (in thousands)	Institution	Control[1]	Rank order	Revenue from the federal govern-ment[2] (in thousands)
1	2	3	4	1	2	3	4
United States (all institutions)	†	†	$77,332,765				
120 institutions receiving the largest amounts	†	†	45,778,300				
Johns Hopkins University (MD)	2	1	2,373,018	Icahn School of Medicine at Mount Sinai (NY)	2	61	285,380
California Institute of Technology	2	2	1,865,247	Oregon Health & Science University	1	62	284,219
University of Chicago (IL)	2	3	1,486,511	Princeton University (NJ)	2	63	271,319
Massachusetts Institute of Technology	2	4	1,273,847	Purdue University, Main Campus (IN)	1	64	266,069
New York University	2	5	1,139,890	University of Rochester (NY)	2	65	261,997
University of Washington, Seattle Campus	1	6	1,067,422	Virginia Polytechnic Institute and State University	1	66	254,660
Stanford University (CA)	2	7	1,031,747	University of Kentucky	1	67	245,970
Weill Cornell Medical College (NY)	2	8	962,303	University of Miami (FL)	2	68	242,029
University of Michigan, Ann Arbor	1	9	855,601	Boston University (MA)	2	69	240,247
University of Utah	1	10	777,384	University of South Florida, Main Campus	1	70	235,610
University of Pennsylvania	2	11	765,192	University of New Mexico, Main Campus	1	71	228,861
Columbia University in the City of New York	2	12	756,604	University of Virginia, Main Campus	1	72	224,687
University of North Carolina at Chapel Hill	1	13	715,272	University of Texas Health Science Center at Houston	1	73	221,941
University of California, San Diego	1	14	687,433	University of Maryland, Baltimore	1	74	215,629
University of Southern California	2	15	656,344	Colorado State University, Fort Collins	1	75	211,536
University of California, San Francisco	1	16	648,682	Iowa State University	1	76	210,849
United States Air Force Academy (CO)	1	17	634,201	Indiana University-Purdue University, Indianapolis	1	77	206,777
University of Pittsburgh, Pittsburgh Campus (PA)	1	18	610,717	University of Massachusetts Medical School, Worcester	1	78	204,290
Harvard University (MA)	2	19	610,580	Ivy Tech Community College (IN)	1	79	202,168
University of California, Los Angeles	1	20	606,857	Oregon State University	1	80	200,258
University of Wisconsin, Madison	1	21	539,992	Yeshiva University (NY)	2	81	193,269
Duke University (NC)	2	22	532,977	University of Kansas	1	82	193,057
University of Minnesota, Twin Cities	1	23	525,232	Miami-Dade College (FL)	1	83	191,729
Yale University (CT)	2	24	512,637	North Carolina State University at Raleigh	1	84	190,000
Georgia Institute of Technology, Main Campus	1	25	505,556	Florida State University	1	85	189,140
Pennsylvania State University, Main Campus	1	26	498,597	University of Texas Southwestern Medical Center	1	86	188,868
Vanderbilt University (TN)	2	27	478,563	Utah State University	1	87	179,405
University of Oklahoma Health Sciences Center	1	28	452,230	Virginia Commonwealth University	1	88	176,979
University of Illinois at Urbana, Champaign	1	29	451,371	Washington State University	1	89	169,985
Washington University in St. Louis (MO)	2	30	438,726	University of Central Florida	1	90	166,334
University of California, Davis	1	31	436,095	Stony Brook University (NY)	1	91	166,049
United States Naval Academy (MD)	1	32	430,165	Wake Forest University (NC)	2	92	164,873
University of Texas at Austin	1	33	425,604	Florida International University	1	93	163,561
University of Florida	1	34	415,467	University of California, Santa Barbara	1	94	158,649
Emory University (GA)	2	35	414,915	University of Missouri, Columbia	1	95	154,141
University of California, Berkeley	1	36	412,589	University of Georgia	1	96	154,068
Northwestern University (IL)	2	37	401,885	Indiana University, Bloomington	1	97	149,530
Ohio State University, Main Campus	1	38	400,176	Louisiana State University and Ag. & Mech. College	1	98	148,791
University of Arizona	1	39	387,578	University of Cincinnati, Main Campus (OH)	1	99	147,540
Texas A & M University, College Station	1	40	379,176	University of South Carolina, Columbia	1	100	147,390
University of Connecticut	1	41	364,865	University of Nebraska, Lincoln	1	101	146,552
University of Maryland, College Park	1	42	362,768	Tulane University of Louisiana	2	102	146,393
Rutgers University, New Brunswick (NJ)	1	43	356,318	University at Buffalo (NY)	1	103	142,510
Arizona State University, Tempe	1	44	353,375	Wayne State University (MI)	1	104	142,370
Michigan State University	1	45	346,128	Mississippi State University	1	105	141,556
University of Colorado, Boulder	1	46	343,974	Medical University of South Carolina	1	106	132,107
University of Alabama at Birmingham	1	47	342,701	New Mexico State University, Main Campus	1	107	131,215
Cornell University (NY)	2	48	339,697	University of Massachusetts, Amherst	1	108	130,515
Carnegie Mellon University (PA)	2	49	337,465	University of California, Santa Cruz	1	109	129,696
United States Military Academy (NY)	1	50	331,820	Brown University (RI)	2	110	129,439
Case Western Reserve University (OH)	2	51	314,010	Dartmouth College (NH)	2	111	129,198
Howard University (DC)	2	52	313,601	University of Texas Medical Branch	1	112	127,509
University of Tennessee, Knoxville	1	53	307,586	Tufts University (MA)	2	113	126,452
University of Colorado, Denver	1	54	303,220	Temple University (PA)	1	114	123,713
George Washington University (DC)	2	55	301,120	University of Vermont	1	115	123,604
University of California, Irvine	1	56	298,563	Georgetown University (DC)	2	116	123,494
Baylor College of Medicine (TX)	2	57	298,468	State University of New York at Albany	1	117	120,854
University of Illinois at Chicago	1	58	296,729	University of Oregon	1	118	119,359
University of Iowa	1	59	296,334	Medical College of Wisconsin	2	119	118,474
University of Hawaii at Manoa	1	60	294,655	University of Houston (TX)	1	120	117,655

†Not applicable.

[1]Publicly controlled institutions are identified by a "1"; private nonprofit, by a "2"; and private for-profit, by a "3."

[2]Includes federal appropriations; operating, nonoperating, unrestricted, and restricted federal contracts and grants; and revenue for independent operations. Independent operations generally include only the revenues associated with major federally funded research and development centers. Pell grants are included for public institutions and may also be included for private nonprofit institutions that do not treat Pell grants as pass-through trans-actions. Data for public, private nonprofit, and private for-profit institutions are only roughly comparable because they were collected using different survey instruments.

NOTE: Degree-granting institutions grant associate's or higher degrees and participate in Title IV federal financial aid programs.

SOURCE: U.S. Department of Education, National Center for Education Statistics, Integrated Postsecondary Education Data System (IPEDS), Spring 2015, Finance component. (This table was prepared February 2016.)

Table 333.80. Voluntary support for degree-granting postsecondary institutions, by source and purpose of support: Selected years, 1949–50 through 2013–14

Year	Total voluntary support, in millions of constant 2014–15 dollars[1]	In millions of current dollars										Voluntary support as a percent of total expenditures[2]
		Total voluntary support	Sources							Purpose		
			Alumni	Nonalumni individuals	Corporations	Foundations	Religious organizations	Other organizations	Current operations	Capital purposes	
1	2	3	4	5	6	7	8	9	10	11	12
1949–50	$2,398	$240	$60	$60	$28	$60	$16	$16	$101	$139	10.7
1959–60	6,565	815	191	194	130	163	80	57	385	430	14.6
1965–66	10,681	1,440	310	350	230	357	108	85	675	765	11.5
1970–71	11,082	1,860	458	495	259	418	104	126	1,050	810	8.0
1975–76	10,285	2,410	588	569	379	549	130	195	1,480	930	6.2
1980–81	11,557	4,230	1,049	1,007	778	922	140	334	2,590	1,640	6.6
1985–86	16,095	7,400	1,825	1,781	1,702	1,363	211	518	4,022	3,378	7.6
1989–90	18,267	9,800	2,540	2,230	2,170	1,920	240	700	5,440	4,360	7.3
1990–91	18,027	10,200	2,680	2,310	2,230	2,030	240	710	5,830	4,370	7.0
1993–94	19,991	12,350	3,410	2,800	2,510	2,540	240	850	6,710	5,640	7.1
1994–95	20,063	12,750	3,600	2,940	2,560	2,460	250	940	7,230	5,520	7.0
1995–96	21,829	14,250	4,040	3,400	2,800	2,815	255	940	7,850	6,400	7.5
1996–97	23,830	16,000	4,650	3,850	3,050	3,200	250	1,000	8,500	7,500	8.0
1997–98	26,925	18,400	5,500	4,500	3,250	3,800	300	1,050	9,000	9,400	8.8
1998–99	29,343	20,400	5,930	4,810	3,610	4,530	330	1,190	9,900	10,500	9.3
1999–2000	32,434	23,200	6,800	5,420	4,150	5,080	370	1,380	11,270	11,930	9.8
2000–01	32,712	24,200	6,830	5,200	4,350	6,000	370	1,450	12,200	12,000	9.3
2001–02	31,744	23,900	5,900	5,400	4,370	6,300	360	1,570	12,400	11,500	8.5
2002–03	30,672	23,600	6,570	4,280	4,250	6,600	360	1,540	12,900	10,700	7.8
2003–04	31,033	24,400	6,700	5,200	4,400	6,200	350	1,550	13,600	10,800	7.7
2004–05	31,608	25,600	7,100	5,000	4,400	7,000	370	1,730	14,200	11,400	7.6
2005–06	33,303	28,000	8,400	5,700	4,600	7,100	375	1,825	15,000	13,000	7.9
2006–07	34,492	29,750	8,270	5,650	4,800	8,500	380	2,150	16,100	13,650	7.9
2007–08	35,328	31,600	8,700	6,120	4,900	9,100	380	2,400	17,070	14,530	7.7
2008–09	30,707	27,850	7,130	4,995	4,620	8,235	325	2,545	16,955	10,895	6.5
2009–10	30,576	28,000	7,100	4,920	4,730	8,400	305	2,545	17,000	11,000	6.3
2010–11	32,437	30,300	7,800	5,650	5,020	8,675	305	2,850	17,800	12,500	6.4
2011–12	32,241	31,000	7,700	5,825	5,250	9,150	275	2,800	18,900	12,100	6.4
2012–13	34,578	33,800	9,000	6,200	5,100	10,000	300	3,200	20,200	13,600	6.8
2013–14	37,723	37,450	9,850	6,500	5,750	11,200	(3)	4,150	21,800	15,650	7.2

[1]Constant dollars based on the Consumer Price Index, prepared by the Bureau of Labor statistics, U.S. Department of Labor, adjusted to a school-year basis.
[2]Total expenditures include current-fund expenditures and additions to plant value through 1995–96.
[3]For 2013–14, voluntary support from religious organizations is included with that from other organizations.
NOTE: Data rounding is consistent with the original source material. Voluntary support data are from the Council for Aid to Education, while the percentage of total expendi-

tures is based on total expenditures reported through the Integrated Postsecondary Education Data System.
SOURCE: Council for Aid to Education, *Voluntary Support of Education*, selected years, 1949–50 through 2013–14. U.S. Department of Education, National Center for Education Statistics, Higher Education General Information Survey (HEGIS), selected years, 1965–66 through 1985–86; *Financial Statistics of Institutions of Higher Education*, 1949–50 and 1959–60; Integrated Postsecondary Education Data System (IPEDS), "Finance Survey" (IPEDS-F:FY87–99); and IPEDS Spring 2001 through Spring 2015, Finance component. (This table was prepared March 2016.)

Table 333.90. Endowment funds of the 120 degree-granting postsecondary institutions with the largest endowments, by rank order: Fiscal year 2014

Institution	Rank order, end of FY[1]	Market value of endowment Beginning of FY (in thousands)	End of FY (in thousands)	Percent change[2]	Institution	Rank order, end of FY[1]	Market value of endowment Beginning of FY (in thousands)	End of FY (in thousands)	Percent change[2]
1	2	3	4	5	1	2	3	4	5
United States (all institutions)...........	†	$465,793,112	$535,186,040	14.9					
120 institutions with the largest amounts......	†	344,599,413	398,543,954	15.7					
Harvard University (MA)...........	1	32,689,489	36,429,256	11.4	Texas Christian University............	61	1,256,030	1,393,241	10.9
University of Texas System Office	2	19,740,283	25,445,315	28.9	University of Delaware............	62	1,171,166	1,310,133	11.9
Yale University (CT)............	3	20,708,793	23,858,561	15.2	University of Illinois at Urbana-Champaign..........	63	1,050,492	1,289,584	22.8
Stanford University (CA)............	4	18,688,868	21,466,006	14.9	University of Iowa............	64	1,094,803	1,251,356	14.3
Princeton University (NJ)............	5	18,786,132	20,576,361	9.5	Soka University of America (CA)............	65	1,117,424	1,249,761	11.8
Massachusetts Institute of Technology............	6	10,857,976	12,425,131	14.4	Weill Cornell Medical College (NY)............	66	1,138,386	1,243,815	9.3
Texas A & M University, College Station............	7	8,238,774	10,521,034	27.7	Carnegie Mellon University (PA)............	67	1,066,149	1,235,968	15.9
University of Michigan, Ann Arbor	8	8,272,366	9,603,919	16.1	Bowdoin College (ME)............	68	1,038,640	1,216,030	17.1
University of Pennsylvania............	9	8,174,165	9,582,335	17.2	Lehigh University (PA)............	69	1,103,449	1,215,926	10.2
Columbia University in the City of New York (NY)............	10	8,197,880	9,223,047	12.5	University of Kentucky............	70	1,054,448	1,215,226	15.2
University of Notre Dame (IN)............	11	6,959,051	8,189,096	17.7	Trinity University (TX)............	71	1,013,929	1,187,929	17.2
Northwestern University (IL)............	12	6,283,130	7,501,116	19.4	Syracuse University (NY)............	72	1,053,214	1,183,244	12.3
University of California System Admin. Central Office..	13	6,402,600	7,413,709	15.8	University of Cincinnati, Main Campus (OH)............	73	1,044,198	1,182,040	13.2
Duke University (NC)............	14	6,040,973	7,036,776	16.5	Tulane University of Louisiana............	74	1,031,661	1,169,060	13.3
Emory University (GA)............	15	6,115,582	6,981,308	14.2	Baylor University (TX)............	75	1,061,157	1,151,200	8.5
Washington University in St. Louis (MO)............	16	5,749,297	6,719,449	16.9	Wake Forest University (NC)............	76	1,061,638	1,148,026	8.1
University of Chicago (IL)............	17	5,886,968	6,539,290	11.1	Berea College (KY)............	77	1,012,401	1,137,222	12.3
University of Virginia, Main Campus............	18	5,106,876	5,876,310	15.1	Middlebury College (VT)............	78	972,992	1,081,894	11.2
Rice University (TX)............	19	4,895,299	5,553,717	13.5	Saint Louis University (MO)............	79	956,014	1,076,959	12.7
Cornell University (NY)............	20	4,133,842	4,646,134	12.4	Princeton Theological Seminary (NJ)............	80	941,110	1,042,191	10.7
University of Southern California............	21	3,868,355	4,593,014	18.7	University of Tulsa (OK)............	81	893,055	1,023,412	14.6
Dartmouth College (NH)............	22	3,733,596	4,468,220	19.7	Juilliard School (NY)............	82	882,012	999,769	13.4
Vanderbilt University (TN)............	23	3,635,343	4,046,250	11.3	University of Texas Southwestern Medical Center......	83	878,855	988,251	12.4
Ohio State University, Main Campus............	24	3,130,942	3,595,323	14.8	Baylor College of Medicine (TX)............	84	844,261	988,247	17.1
University of Pittsburgh, Pittsburgh Campus (PA)........	25	2,956,739	3,470,665	17.4	Vassar College (NY)............	85	868,741	974,180	12.1
New York University............	26	2,980,027	3,435,034	15.3	University of Oklahoma, Norman Campus............	86	845,635	965,937	14.2
Johns Hopkins University (MD)............	27	2,918,546	3,392,529	16.2	Indiana University, Bloomington............	87	835,123	961,054	15.1
University of Texas at Austin............	28	3,012,895	3,376,824	12.1	University of Arkansas............	88	819,814	929,693	13.4
University of Wisconsin, Madison............	29	2,295,273	3,133,197	36.5	Hamilton College (NY)............	89	773,828	927,520	19.9
Brown University (RI)............	30	2,669,948	2,999,749	12.4	Berry College (GA)............	90	861,107	925,698	7.5
University of Minnesota, Twin Cities............	31	2,610,544	2,992,707	14.6	University of California, San Francisco............	91	766,144	912,957	19.2
University of Washington, Seattle Campus............	32	2,432,421	2,915,058	19.8	North Carolina State University at Raleigh............	92	769,404	885,055	15.0
University of North Carolina at Chapel Hill............	33	2,344,280	2,659,759	13.5	University of Louisville (KY)............	93	757,336	876,825	15.8
Michigan State University............	34	2,007,498	2,549,137	27.0	Washington State University............	94	777,644	868,091	11.6
Purdue University, Main Campus (IN)............	35	2,189,202	2,445,542	11.7	Oberlin College (OH)............	95	765,804	866,830	13.2
University of Richmond (VA)............	36	2,025,996	2,313,305	14.2	Colgate University (NY)............	96	760,825	865,882	13.8
Pennsylvania State University, Main Campus............	37	1,924,143	2,264,414	17.7	University of Miami (FL)............	97	777,947	865,435	11.2
Amherst College (MA)............	38	1,823,748	2,149,203	17.8	Brandeis University (MA)............	98	766,205	861,152	12.4
Williams College (MA)............	39	1,902,112	2,143,153	12.7	Bryn Mawr College (PA)............	99	710,168	839,226	18.2
California Institute of Technology............	40	1,960,435	2,118,100	8.0	Clemson University (SC)............	100	518,606	836,152	61.2
Boston College (MA)............	41	1,868,699	2,105,654	12.7	Indiana University, Purdue University, Indianapolis......	101	709,877	834,834	17.6
Pomona College (CA)............	42	1,823,441	2,101,461	15.2	Lafayette College (PA)............	102	749,031	832,811	11.2
University of Rochester (NY)............	43	1,730,829	2,015,283	16.4	University of Missouri, Columbia............	103	692,853	806,717	16.4
Georgia Institute of Technology, Main Campus............	44	1,714,876	1,889,014	10.2	Denison University (OH)............	104	691,740	799,108	15.5
Swarthmore College (PA)............	45	1,634,685	1,876,669	14.8	College of William and Mary (VA)............	105	697,724	797,592	14.3
Wellesley College (MA)............	46	1,576,337	1,834,137	16.4	Wesleyan University (CT)............	106	688,643	793,334	15.2
Grinnell College (IA)............	47	1,553,629	1,829,521	17.8	Carleton College (MN)............	107	700,540	792,737	13.2
Case Western Reserve University (OH)............	48	1,595,300	1,758,570	10.2	Pepperdine University (CA)............	108	715,660	790,483	10.5
Smith College (MA)............	49	1,557,427	1,755,755	12.7	Virginia Polytechnic Institute and State U............	109	653,700	788,800	20.7
University of California, Berkeley............	50	1,411,707	1,671,939	18.4	University of Tennessee, Knoxville............	110	662,942	782,734	18.1
University of California, Los Angeles............	51	1,411,797	1,616,045	14.5	Rutgers University, New Brunswick (NJ)............	111	655,125	763,561	16.6
Boston University (MA)............	52	1,403,061	1,616,004	15.2	University of Arizona............	112	611,746	760,679	24.3
Tufts University (MA)............	53	1,440,527	1,590,045	10.4	Rochester Institute of Technology (NY)............	113	669,132	753,951	12.7
George Washington University (DC)............	54	1,375,202	1,576,508	14.6	Bucknell University (PA)............	114	666,563	750,913	12.7
University of Florida............	55	1,360,073	1,519,964	11.8	Macalester College (MN)............	115	694,311	749,550	8.0
University of Kansas............	56	1,310,655	1,494,881	14.1	Medical College of Wisconsin............	116	597,865	748,637	25.2
Washington and Lee University (VA)............	57	1,345,356	1,477,923	9.9	Colby College (ME)............	117	649,992	740,631	13.9
Brigham Young University, Provo (UT)............	58	1,053,241	1,470,770	39.6	Northeastern University (MA)............	118	631,395	729,034	15.5
Georgetown University (DC)............	59	1,286,322	1,461,276	13.6	College of the Holy Cross (MA)............	119	634,912	726,232	14.4
Southern Methodist University (TX)............	60	1,268,079	1,425,146	12.4	University of Utah............	120	642,219	723,827	12.7

†Not applicable.
[1]Institutions ranked by size of endowment at end of 2014 fiscal year.
[2]Change in market value of endowment. Includes growth from gifts and returns on investments, as well as reductions from expenditures and withdrawals.

NOTE: Degree-granting institutions grant associate's or higher degrees and participate in Title IV federal financial aid programs.
SOURCE: U.S. Department of Education, National Center for Education Statistics, Integrated Postsecondary Education Data System (IPEDS), Spring 2015, Finance component. (This table was prepared January 2016.)

Table 334.10. Expenditures of public degree-granting postsecondary institutions, by purpose of expenditure and level of institution: 2007–08 through 2013–14

Level of institution and year	Total expenditures	Instruction Total[1]	Instruction Salaries and wages	Research	Public service	Academic support	Student services	Institutional support	Operation and maintenance of plant	Depreciation	Scholarships and fellowships[2]	Auxiliary enterprises	Hospitals	Independent operations	Interest	Other
1	2	3	4	5	6	7	8	9	10	11	12	13	14	15	16	17
								In thousands of current dollars								
All levels																
2007–08	$261,045,829	$71,807,253	$48,691,508	$25,331,167	$10,800,588	$17,871,280	$12,205,110	$22,145,030	$17,032,966	$12,814,049	$9,664,173	$19,533,181	$23,974,721	$931,838	$4,301,708	$12,632,765
2008–09	273,018,676	75,087,547	51,151,497	26,643,578	11,243,089	18,803,731	12,939,241	23,072,985	17,839,425	13,719,433	11,107,945	20,587,662	25,944,900	1,177,848	2,972,642	11,878,652
2009–10	281,390,445	76,331,795	51,808,563	28,102,054	11,511,735	18,890,370	13,124,073	22,679,459	18,037,657	14,307,677	15,494,246	20,482,149	26,595,704	1,236,092	5,062,000	9,535,082
2010–11	296,862,854	79,412,245	53,586,472	29,401,389	12,012,207	19,351,676	13,577,155	23,815,431	18,898,138	15,441,148	17,487,275	21,727,625	27,980,574	1,153,975	5,476,865	11,127,150
2011–12	305,537,590	80,881,773	54,341,187	29,665,476	11,930,514	20,380,843	14,184,601	24,099,951	19,286,569	16,467,330	16,611,881	22,172,526	30,833,717	1,204,016	6,138,489	11,679,905
2012–13	311,424,709	82,946,384	55,555,811	29,860,945	11,905,234	21,259,036	14,688,802	25,269,318	19,717,247	17,436,827	16,221,476	22,490,098	31,838,319	1,224,309	6,364,472	10,202,242
2013–14	323,888,217	85,688,549	57,583,231	29,474,988	12,197,163	22,169,321	15,529,411	26,543,793	20,704,034	18,369,899	15,962,246	23,172,857	34,427,527	1,417,050	6,552,127	11,679,253
4-year																
2007–08	215,474,080	54,371,328	36,618,879	25,312,279	10,055,606	14,471,795	8,051,799	15,812,151	13,047,228	10,959,500	6,467,362	17,296,774	23,974,721	931,838	3,523,683	11,198,015
2008–09	225,343,545	57,273,583	38,666,427	26,621,961	10,497,618	15,298,522	8,612,602	16,500,601	13,802,983	11,719,701	7,146,645	18,292,903	25,944,900	1,177,848	2,354,694	10,098,986
2009–10	230,212,346	58,307,342	39,032,863	28,081,694	10,758,002	15,366,887	8,763,305	16,342,588	13,661,203	12,312,930	9,103,655	18,145,849	26,595,704	1,236,092	4,091,226	7,445,889
2010–11	242,591,219	60,644,416	40,420,752	29,380,202	11,225,195	15,732,164	9,122,182	17,255,818	14,305,617	13,213,721	10,088,873	19,334,526	27,980,574	1,153,975	4,379,246	8,774,710
2011–12	251,518,494	62,225,401	41,334,687	29,645,195	11,174,292	16,732,590	9,659,034	17,376,744	14,805,020	14,102,984	9,737,295	19,801,700	30,833,717	1,204,016	4,779,600	9,440,966
2012–13	257,543,514	64,142,742	42,541,275	29,842,594	11,178,539	17,528,570	10,103,438	18,349,595	15,212,898	14,870,558	9,819,766	20,191,850	31,838,319	1,224,309	5,071,595	8,168,742
2013–14	269,892,768	66,829,678	44,567,421	29,453,355	11,492,915	18,322,501	10,865,041	19,522,528	16,088,167	15,667,606	9,899,892	20,985,004	34,427,527	1,417,050	5,200,722	9,720,781
2-year																
2007–08	45,571,749	17,435,926	12,072,630	18,887	744,982	3,399,485	4,153,311	6,332,879	3,985,738	1,854,549	3,196,811	2,236,407	0	0	778,025	1,434,749
2008–09	47,675,131	17,813,964	12,485,070	21,617	745,470	3,505,209	4,326,639	6,572,385	4,036,442	1,999,732	3,961,299	2,294,759	0	0	617,948	1,779,666
2009–10	51,178,098	18,024,453	12,775,700	20,711	753,733	3,523,483	4,360,768	6,336,871	4,376,455	1,994,747	6,390,591	2,336,300	0	0	970,774	2,089,213
2010–11	54,271,635	18,767,830	13,165,721	21,187	787,012	3,619,512	4,454,973	6,559,613	4,592,521	2,227,427	6,398,402	2,393,099	0	0	1,097,619	2,352,441
2011–12	54,019,096	18,656,373	13,006,500	20,281	756,282	3,648,252	4,525,567	6,723,207	4,481,549	2,364,346	6,874,585	2,370,826	0	0	1,358,889	2,238,939
2012–13	53,881,195	18,803,642	13,014,536	18,351	726,695	3,730,467	4,585,363	6,919,723	4,504,349	2,566,269	6,401,710	2,298,249	0	0	1,292,877	2,033,500
2013–14	53,995,449	18,858,870	13,015,810	21,633	704,248	3,846,819	4,664,370	7,021,265	4,615,867	2,702,294	6,062,353	2,187,853	0	0	1,351,405	1,958,472
								Percentage distribution								
All levels																
2007–08	100.00	27.51	18.65	9.70	4.14	6.85	4.68	8.48	6.52	4.91	3.70	7.48	9.18	0.36	1.65	4.84
2008–09	100.00	27.50	18.74	9.76	4.12	6.89	4.74	8.45	6.53	5.03	4.07	7.54	9.50	0.43	1.09	4.35
2009–10	100.00	27.13	18.41	9.99	4.09	6.71	4.66	8.06	6.41	5.08	5.51	7.28	9.45	0.44	1.80	3.39
2010–11	100.00	26.75	18.05	9.90	4.05	6.52	4.57	8.02	6.37	5.20	5.89	7.32	9.43	0.39	1.84	3.75
2011–12	100.00	26.47	17.79	9.71	3.90	6.67	4.64	7.89	6.31	5.39	5.44	7.26	10.09	0.39	2.01	3.82
2012–13	100.00	26.63	17.84	9.59	3.82	6.83	4.72	8.11	6.33	5.60	5.21	7.22	10.22	0.39	2.04	3.28
2013–14	100.00	26.46	17.78	9.10	3.77	6.84	4.79	8.20	6.39	5.67	4.93	7.15	10.63	0.44	2.02	3.61
4-year																
2007–08	100.00	25.23	16.99	11.75	4.67	6.72	3.74	7.34	6.06	5.09	3.00	8.03	11.13	0.43	1.64	5.20
2008–09	100.00	25.42	17.16	11.81	4.66	6.79	3.82	7.32	6.13	5.20	3.17	8.12	11.51	0.52	1.04	4.48
2009–10	100.00	25.33	16.96	12.20	4.67	6.68	3.81	7.10	5.93	5.35	3.95	7.88	11.55	0.54	1.78	3.23
2010–11	100.00	25.00	16.66	12.11	4.63	6.49	3.76	7.11	5.90	5.45	4.16	7.97	11.53	0.48	1.81	3.62
2011–12	100.00	24.74	16.43	11.79	4.44	6.65	3.84	6.91	5.89	5.61	3.87	7.87	12.26	0.48	1.90	3.75
2012–13	100.00	24.91	16.52	11.59	4.34	6.81	3.92	7.12	5.91	5.77	3.81	7.84	12.36	0.48	1.97	3.17
2013–14	100.00	24.76	16.51	10.91	4.26	6.79	4.03	7.23	5.96	5.81	3.67	7.78	12.76	0.53	1.93	3.60
2-year																
2007–08	100.00	38.26	26.49	0.04	1.63	7.46	9.11	13.90	8.75	4.07	7.01	4.91	0.00	0.00	1.71	3.15
2008–09	100.00	37.37	26.19	0.05	1.56	7.35	9.08	13.79	8.47	4.19	8.31	4.81	0.00	0.00	1.30	3.73
2009–10	100.00	35.22	24.96	0.04	1.47	6.88	8.52	12.38	8.55	3.90	12.49	4.57	0.00	0.00	1.90	4.08
2010–11	100.00	34.58	24.26	0.04	1.45	6.67	8.21	12.09	8.46	4.10	13.63	4.41	0.00	0.00	2.02	4.33
2011–12	100.00	34.54	24.08	0.04	1.40	6.75	8.38	12.45	8.30	4.38	13.73	4.39	0.00	0.00	2.52	4.14
2012–13	100.00	34.90	24.15	0.03	1.35	6.92	8.51	12.84	8.36	4.76	11.88	4.27	0.00	0.00	2.40	3.77
2013–14	100.00	34.93	24.11	0.04	1.30	7.12	8.64	13.00	8.55	5.00	11.23	4.05	0.00	0.00	2.50	3.63

See notes at end of table.

Table 334.10. Expenditures of public degree-granting postsecondary institutions, by purpose of expenditure and level of institution: 2007–08 through 2013–14—Continued

Level of institution and year	Total expenditures	Instruction Total[1]	Instruction Salaries and wages	Research	Public service	Academic support	Student services	Institutional support	Operation and maintenance of plant	Depreciation	Scholarships and fellowships[2]	Auxiliary enterprises	Hospitals	Independent operations	Interest	Other
1	2	3	4	5	6	7	8	9	10	11	12	13	14	15	16	17

Expenditures per full-time-equivalent student in current dollars

Level of institution and year	2	3	4	5	6	7	8	9	10	11	12	13	14	15	16	17
All levels																
2007–08	$26,802	$7,373	$4,999	$2,601	$1,109	$1,835	$1,253	$2,274	$1,749	$1,316	$992	$2,006	$2,462	$96	$442	$1,297
2008–09	27,134	7,463	5,084	2,648	1,117	1,869	1,286	2,293	1,773	1,364	1,104	2,046	2,579	117	295	1,181
2009–10	26,184	7,103	4,821	2,615	1,071	1,758	1,221	2,110	1,678	1,331	1,442	1,906	2,475	115	471	887
2010–11	26,942	7,207	4,863	2,668	1,090	1,756	1,232	2,161	1,715	1,401	1,587	1,972	2,539	105	497	1,010
2011–12	27,891	7,383	4,961	2,708	1,089	1,860	1,295	2,200	1,761	1,503	1,516	2,024	2,815	110	560	1,066
2012–13	28,884	7,693	5,153	2,770	1,104	1,972	1,362	2,344	1,829	1,617	1,505	2,086	2,953	114	590	946
2013–14	30,282	8,011	5,384	2,756	1,140	2,073	1,452	2,482	1,936	1,717	1,492	2,167	3,219	132	613	1,092
4-year																
2007–08	35,947	9,071	6,109	4,223	1,678	2,414	1,343	2,638	2,177	1,828	1,079	2,886	4,000	155	588	1,868
2008–09	36,704	9,329	6,298	4,336	1,710	2,492	1,403	2,688	2,248	1,909	1,164	2,980	4,226	192	384	1,645
2009–10	35,678	9,037	6,049	4,352	1,667	2,382	1,358	2,533	2,117	1,908	1,411	2,812	4,122	192	634	1,154
2010–11	36,558	9,139	6,091	4,428	1,692	2,371	1,375	2,600	2,156	1,991	1,520	2,914	4,217	174	660	1,322
2011–12	37,350	9,240	6,138	4,402	1,659	2,485	1,434	2,580	2,199	2,094	1,446	2,941	4,579	179	710	1,402
2012–13	38,075	9,483	6,289	4,412	1,653	2,591	1,494	2,713	2,249	2,198	1,452	2,985	4,707	181	750	1,208
2013–14	39,743	9,841	6,563	4,337	1,692	2,698	1,600	2,875	2,369	2,307	1,458	3,090	5,070	209	766	1,431
2-year																
2007–08	12,167	4,655	3,223	5	199	908	1,109	1,691	1,064	495	854	597	0	0	208	383
2008–09	12,155	4,542	3,183	6	190	894	1,103	1,676	1,029	510	1,010	585	0	0	158	454
2009–10	11,918	4,197	2,975	5	176	821	1,015	1,476	1,019	465	1,488	544	0	0	226	487
2010–11	12,382	4,282	3,004	5	180	826	1,016	1,497	1,048	508	1,688	546	0	0	250	537
2011–12	12,799	4,420	3,082	5	179	864	1,072	1,593	1,062	560	1,629	562	0	0	322	530
2012–13	13,411	4,680	3,239	5	181	929	1,141	1,722	1,121	639	1,593	572	0	0	322	506
2013–14	13,828	4,830	3,333	6	180	985	1,194	1,798	1,182	692	1,553	560	0	0	346	502

Expenditures per full-time-equivalent student in constant 2014–15 dollars[3]

Level of institution and year	2	3	4	5	6	7	8	9	10	11	12	13	14	15	16	17
All levels																
2007–08	$29,964	$8,242	$5,589	$2,908	$1,240	$2,051	$1,401	$2,542	$1,955	$1,471	$1,109	$2,242	$2,752	$107	$494	$1,450
2008–09	29,917	8,228	5,605	2,920	1,232	2,061	1,418	2,528	1,955	1,503	1,217	2,256	2,843	129	326	1,302
2009–10	28,593	7,756	5,264	2,856	1,170	1,920	1,334	2,305	1,833	1,454	1,574	2,081	2,703	126	514	969
2010–11	28,841	7,715	5,206	2,816	1,167	1,880	1,319	2,314	1,836	1,500	1,699	2,111	2,718	112	532	1,081
2011–12	29,008	7,679	5,159	2,833	1,133	1,935	1,347	2,288	1,831	1,563	1,577	2,105	2,927	114	583	1,109
2012–13	29,549	7,870	5,271	2,833	1,130	2,017	1,394	2,398	1,871	1,654	1,539	2,134	3,021	116	604	968
2013–14	30,502	8,070	5,423	2,776	1,149	2,088	1,462	2,500	1,950	1,730	1,503	2,182	3,242	133	617	1,100
4-year																
2007–08	40,188	10,141	6,830	4,721	1,875	2,699	1,502	2,949	2,433	2,044	1,206	3,226	4,471	174	657	2,089
2008–09	40,469	10,286	6,944	4,781	1,885	2,747	1,547	2,963	2,479	2,105	1,283	3,285	4,659	212	423	1,814
2009–10	38,961	9,868	6,606	4,753	1,821	2,601	1,483	2,766	2,312	2,084	1,541	3,071	4,501	209	692	1,260
2010–11	39,136	9,783	6,521	4,740	1,811	2,538	1,472	2,784	2,308	2,132	1,628	3,119	4,514	186	706	1,416
2011–12	38,845	9,610	6,384	4,579	1,726	2,584	1,492	2,684	2,287	2,178	1,504	3,058	4,762	186	738	1,458
2012–13	38,951	9,701	6,434	4,513	1,691	2,651	1,528	2,775	2,301	2,249	1,485	3,054	4,815	185	767	1,235
2013–14	40,033	9,913	6,611	4,369	1,705	2,718	1,612	2,896	2,386	2,324	1,468	3,113	5,107	210	771	1,442
2-year																
2007–08	13,603	5,204	3,604	6	222	1,015	1,240	1,890	1,190	554	954	668	0	0	232	428
2008–09	13,402	5,008	3,510	6	210	985	1,216	1,848	1,135	562	1,114	645	0	0	174	500
2009–10	13,014	4,584	3,249	5	192	896	1,109	1,611	1,113	507	1,625	594	0	0	247	531
2010–11	13,256	4,584	3,216	5	192	884	1,088	1,602	1,122	544	1,807	585	0	0	268	575
2011–12	13,311	4,597	3,205	5	186	899	1,115	1,657	1,104	583	1,694	584	0	0	335	552
2012–13	13,720	4,788	3,314	5	185	950	1,168	1,762	1,147	653	1,630	585	0	0	329	518
2013–14	13,928	4,865	3,357	6	182	992	1,203	1,811	1,191	697	1,564	564	0	0	349	505

[1]Includes other categories not separately shown.
[2]Excludes discounts and allowances.
[3]Constant dollars based on the Consumer Price Index, prepared by the Bureau of Labor Statistics, U.S. Department of Labor, adjusted to a school-year basis.
NOTE: Degree-granting institutions grant associate's or higher degrees and participate in Title IV federal financial aid programs. Includes data for public institutions reporting data according to either the Governmental Accounting Standards Board (GASB) or the Financial Accounting Standards Board (FASB) questionnaire. All expenditures reported by institutions for operation and mainte- nance of plant have been aggregated in the operation and maintenance of plant category, even in cases where they originally were

reported by purpose. Similarly, all expenditures reported by institutions for depreciation have been aggregated in the depreciation category, even in cases where they originally were reported by purpose. In addition, all expenditures reported by institutions for interest have been aggregated in the interest category, even in cases where they originally were reported by purpose. Some data have been revised from previously published figures. Detail may not sum to totals because of rounding.
SOURCE: U.S. Department of Education, National Center for Education Statistics, Integrated Postsecondary Education Data Sys- tem (IPEDS), Spring 2008 through Spring 2014, Fall Enrollment component; and Spring 2009 through Spring 2015, Finance com- ponent. (This table was prepared November 2015.)

Table 334.20. Expenditures of public degree-granting postsecondary institutions, by level of institution, purpose of expenditure, and state or jurisdiction: 2010–11 through 2013–14

[In thousands of current dollars]

State or jurisdiction	Total expenditures, 2010–11	Total expenditures, 2011–12	Total expenditures, 2012–13			2013–14					
			All institutions	4-year institutions	2-year institutions	All institutions		4-year institutions		2-year institutions	
						Total[1]	Instruction[2]	Total[1]	Instruction[2]	Total[1]	Instruction[2]
1	2	3	4	5	6	7	8	9	10	11	12
United States	$296,862,854	$305,537,590	$311,424,709	$257,543,514	$53,881,195	$323,888,217	$85,688,549	$269,892,768	$66,829,678	$53,995,449	$18,858,870
Alabama	6,649,467	6,249,206	6,499,646	5,761,237	738,409	6,762,386	1,525,817	6,030,666	1,252,625	731,720	273,192
Alaska	800,218	829,978	845,578	809,679	35,899	852,991	226,417	823,759	217,287	29,231	9,130
Arizona	4,968,606	5,126,746	5,372,323	3,908,951	1,463,372	5,600,337	1,671,395	4,139,515	1,205,371	1,460,823	466,024
Arkansas	3,454,422	3,592,033	3,614,017	3,115,538	498,479	3,704,972	772,425	3,207,504	608,748	497,468	163,677
California	43,624,464	45,485,482	45,915,560	34,830,021	11,085,538	47,558,693	10,974,319	36,032,725	7,591,689	11,525,968	3,382,630
Colorado	4,837,724	5,145,208	5,342,995	4,756,073	586,922	5,698,854	1,649,462	5,109,318	1,417,891	589,536	231,570
Connecticut	2,974,554	2,931,898	3,030,961	2,565,900	465,062	3,295,856	946,450	2,798,124	749,362	497,732	197,088
Delaware	1,032,228	1,128,190	1,121,660	965,973	155,687	1,153,297	435,992	989,869	363,890	163,428	72,102
District of Columbia	152,640	147,034	141,338	141,338	0	134,230	40,618	134,230	40,618	0	0
Florida	10,413,803	10,559,827	10,659,595	10,272,223	387,372	11,087,586	3,273,040	10,762,561	3,183,978	325,025	89,062
Georgia	7,032,754	7,298,882	7,409,996	6,310,205	1,099,791	7,564,411	1,975,429	6,573,904	1,618,310	990,506	357,119
Hawaii	1,523,301	1,609,315	1,647,129	1,395,933	251,196	1,680,041	488,730	1,426,337	371,762	253,705	116,968
Idaho	1,116,296	1,216,909	1,182,070	974,156	207,914	1,188,089	356,948	981,948	287,096	206,141	69,852
Illinois	10,302,240	10,888,678	11,603,379	8,567,709	3,035,670	11,777,464	3,394,502	8,704,462	2,388,822	3,073,002	1,005,680
Indiana	5,959,191	6,105,284	6,227,063	5,587,045	640,018	6,395,776	2,213,282	5,780,882	2,007,494	614,894	205,789
Iowa	4,332,274	4,726,859	4,846,304	3,957,757	888,547	5,047,472	1,010,442	4,155,763	677,225	891,709	333,217
Kansas	3,053,391	3,214,748	3,306,016	2,562,868	743,148	3,364,787	1,054,428	2,622,331	798,777	742,456	255,651
Kentucky	4,889,725	5,136,705	5,180,174	4,454,346	725,828	5,235,067	1,176,627	4,592,917	952,428	642,150	224,199
Louisiana	4,163,519	4,204,018	4,151,993	3,656,295	495,698	4,010,882	1,154,288	3,509,182	963,131	501,700	191,157
Maine	837,119	844,272	847,717	725,066	122,652	859,812	242,296	732,026	189,034	127,787	53,263
Maryland	5,627,221	5,829,195	5,979,533	4,623,170	1,356,363	6,228,564	1,695,862	4,825,353	1,199,583	1,403,211	496,280
Massachusetts	4,224,820	4,297,014	4,442,564	3,610,605	831,958	4,703,032	1,304,970	3,826,904	972,337	876,128	332,633
Michigan	12,796,769	13,384,740	13,788,962	11,940,315	1,848,647	14,155,072	3,524,124	12,421,602	2,893,847	1,733,470	630,277
Minnesota	4,841,837	4,810,022	5,019,669	3,976,182	1,043,487	5,271,821	1,483,381	4,229,591	1,056,753	1,042,230	426,627
Mississippi	3,717,313	3,800,955	3,855,187	2,976,363	878,824	4,017,008	897,484	3,138,675	599,261	878,333	298,224
Missouri	4,370,406	4,563,353	4,619,674	3,823,178	796,496	4,772,178	1,316,991	3,991,095	1,028,336	781,083	288,655
Montana	961,380	981,509	992,536	866,457	126,079	1,012,355	264,210	885,121	230,207	127,234	34,004
Nebraska	2,119,516	2,176,505	2,226,961	1,838,167	388,794	2,312,160	678,915	1,913,185	529,519	398,975	149,396
Nevada	1,452,203	1,374,536	1,442,757	1,375,441	67,316	1,508,447	520,231	1,439,569	492,907	68,878	27,324
New Hampshire	916,009	894,369	901,393	769,683	131,710	937,896	279,538	803,389	233,204	134,507	46,334
New Jersey	6,814,524	7,080,502	5,474,962	4,147,457	1,327,505	7,090,602	2,105,237	5,771,315	1,654,899	1,319,287	450,338
New Mexico	3,195,659	3,150,710	3,252,357	2,643,255	609,102	3,316,771	652,622	2,689,810	441,810	626,962	210,812
New York	15,481,165	16,037,336	15,844,606	12,689,386	3,155,220	16,292,947	4,802,726	13,020,834	3,484,970	3,272,112	1,317,757
North Carolina	9,639,567	9,563,597	9,964,777	7,766,190	2,198,588	10,156,317	3,138,226	7,973,839	2,255,953	2,182,478	882,273
North Dakota	993,822	1,041,219	1,068,159	977,140	91,019	1,108,117	382,282	1,007,083	347,147	101,034	35,135
Ohio	11,618,184	11,808,427	12,192,587	10,636,363	1,556,224	12,303,835	3,236,387	10,809,969	2,698,065	1,493,866	538,322
Oklahoma	3,721,375	3,859,701	3,924,755	3,432,762	491,994	4,083,901	1,136,627	3,577,738	950,594	506,163	186,033
Oregon	5,209,651	5,531,213	5,744,633	4,529,658	1,214,975	6,000,874	1,275,419	4,812,288	886,843	1,188,585	388,576
Pennsylvania	11,287,473	11,823,354	12,176,869	10,975,980	1,200,889	12,566,618	3,001,192	11,358,294	2,565,821	1,208,324	435,370
Rhode Island	683,831	717,329	719,733	603,025	116,707	746,067	206,859	625,392	154,628	120,675	52,232
South Carolina	3,715,311	3,827,663	4,030,358	3,202,729	827,629	4,168,222	1,318,877	3,332,306	1,031,911	835,916	286,967
South Dakota	707,073	739,971	744,419	669,445	74,974	777,182	239,126	695,739	206,139	81,443	32,987
Tennessee	3,980,862	4,156,217	4,193,989	3,522,799	671,191	4,317,495	1,519,514	3,659,273	1,264,015	658,222	255,499
Texas	26,326,215	26,426,890	27,655,846	22,880,541	4,775,306	29,539,462	7,335,228	24,677,131	5,693,243	4,862,331	1,641,985
Utah	4,232,743	4,461,853	4,744,745	4,539,033	205,712	4,995,994	806,841	4,789,432	724,002	206,562	82,840
Vermont	793,941	799,662	843,550	806,021	37,529	853,311	223,049	817,070	213,154	36,241	9,895
Virginia	7,930,362	8,367,116	8,757,065	7,615,345	1,141,720	9,099,520	2,393,790	7,941,651	1,935,864	1,157,869	457,925
Washington	7,312,805	7,403,283	7,740,652	6,429,794	1,310,858	8,207,793	2,241,170	7,157,286	1,846,327	1,050,507	394,843
West Virginia	1,738,447	1,813,682	1,761,432	1,600,198	161,234	1,762,607	527,757	1,606,576	481,677	156,031	46,080
Wisconsin	5,974,368	5,942,717	6,044,715	4,704,511	1,340,203	6,346,355	1,887,933	5,000,620	1,251,567	1,345,735	636,366
Wyoming	706,777	752,127	744,748	469,004	275,744	761,062	231,331	484,984	141,818	276,078	89,513
U.S. Service Academies	1,653,288	1,679,549	1,585,003	1,585,003	0	1,501,631	477,739	1,501,631	477,739	0	0
Other jurisdictions	1,698,347	1,728,527	1,684,136	1,591,208	92,928	1,699,654	495,286	1,599,556	462,634	100,099	32,653
American Samoa	15,942	15,097	14,449	14,449	0	14,060	4,537	14,060	4,537	0	0
Federated States of Micronesia	21,048	23,134	22,472	0	22,472	27,695	6,635	0	0	27,695	6,635
Guam	125,565	136,515	129,808	96,962	32,846	136,246	30,303	99,906	18,231	36,340	12,072
Marshall Islands	17,259	18,381	13,552	0	13,552	15,117	3,544	0	0	15,117	3,544
Northern Marianas	20,214	18,085	18,031	18,031	0	17,849	7,647	17,849	7,647	0	0
Palau	4,856	10,488	10,384	0	10,384	9,834	4,097	0	0	9,834	4,097
Puerto Rico	1,406,063	1,418,143	1,393,668	1,379,994	13,674	1,400,211	424,617	1,389,098	418,312	11,113	6,304
U.S. Virgin Islands	87,400	88,683	81,772	81,772	0	78,643	13,906	78,643	13,906	0	0

[1]Includes other categories not separately shown.
[2]Excludes expenditures for operations and maintenance, interest, and depreciation, which are included in the total.
NOTE: Degree-granting institutions grant associate's or higher degrees and participate in Title IV federal financial aid programs. Includes data for public institutions reporting data according to either the Governmental Accounting Standards Board (GASB) or the Financial Accounting Standards Board (FASB) questionnaire. Some data have been revised from previously published figures. Detail may not sum to totals because of rounding.
SOURCE: U.S. Department of Education, National Center for Education Statistics, Integrated Postsecondary Education Data System (IPEDS), Spring 2012 through Spring 2015, Finance component. (This table was prepared November 2015.)

Table 334.30. Total expenditures of private nonprofit degree-granting postsecondary institutions, by purpose and level of institution: 1999–2000 through 2013–14

Level of institution and year	Total	Instruction	Research	Public service	Academic support	Student services	Institutional support	Auxiliary enterprises[1]	Net grant aid to students[2]	Hospitals	Independent operations	Other
1	2	3	4	5	6	7	8	9	10	11	12	13
						In thousands of current dollars						
All levels												
1999–2000	$80,613,037	$26,012,599	$8,381,926	$1,446,958	$6,510,951	$5,688,499	$10,585,850	$8,300,021	$1,180,882	$7,355,110	$2,753,679	$2,396,563
2000–01	85,625,016	27,607,324	9,025,739	1,473,292	7,368,263	6,117,195	11,434,074	9,010,853	1,176,160	7,255,376	3,134,609	2,022,132
2001–02	92,192,297	29,689,041	10,035,480	1,665,884	7,802,637	6,573,185	12,068,120	9,515,829	1,188,690	7,633,043	3,397,979	2,622,409
2002–03	99,748,076	32,062,218	11,079,532	1,878,380	8,156,688	7,096,223	13,157,744	9,936,478	1,173,845	7,586,208	3,879,736	3,741,024
2003–04	104,317,870	33,909,179	12,039,531	1,972,351	8,759,743	7,544,021	13,951,408	10,508,719	1,101,738	8,374,128	4,222,980	1,934,070
2004–05	110,394,127	36,258,473	12,812,857	2,000,437	9,342,064	8,191,737	14,690,328	10,944,342	1,069,591	9,180,775	4,223,779	1,679,741
2005–06	116,817,913	38,465,058	13,242,343	1,941,519	10,217,274	8,965,704	15,667,101	11,741,258	708,158	9,645,428	4,203,523	2,020,548
2006–07	124,557,725	41,223,483	13,704,450	2,036,588	10,882,028	9,591,334	16,831,353	12,451,087	728,139	10,400,055	4,680,393	2,028,816
2007–08	133,503,539	44,226,329	14,474,367	2,182,676	11,884,345	10,363,476	18,364,513	13,319,602	721,487	10,754,966	4,887,609	2,324,170
2008–09	141,363,564	46,456,178	15,264,804	2,298,520	12,585,948	11,016,097	19,403,346	13,713,701	754,752	11,930,840	5,158,480	2,780,898
2009–10	145,115,244	47,566,210	16,221,823	2,090,243	12,953,023	11,422,737	19,438,608	13,890,396	826,379	13,174,405	5,154,851	2,376,569
2010–11	152,501,429	49,759,574	17,362,082	2,255,075	13,601,137	12,198,263	20,214,683	14,460,084	759,683	14,239,347	5,376,016	2,275,486
2011–12	159,831,378	52,163,647	17,483,157	2,333,298	14,215,689	12,881,102	21,175,119	14,948,315	845,525	15,474,737	5,450,038	2,860,752
2012–13	165,573,669	54,257,906	17,514,795	2,318,128	14,922,229	13,685,488	21,857,624	15,330,575	851,647	16,701,193	5,436,746	2,697,338
2013–14	172,547,895	56,706,803	17,734,816	2,459,838	15,449,364	14,550,938	22,621,924	15,975,048	867,482	17,377,766	5,693,990	3,109,927
4-year												
1999–2000	79,699,659	25,744,199	8,376,568	1,438,544	6,476,338	5,590,978	10,398,914	8,228,409	1,162,570	7,355,110	2,752,019	2,176,011
2000–01	85,048,123	27,413,897	9,019,966	1,467,325	7,333,851	6,036,478	11,292,310	8,957,973	1,160,660	7,253,479	3,133,099	1,979,086
2001–02	91,612,337	29,492,583	10,035,394	1,658,782	7,768,870	6,497,127	11,914,149	9,470,557	1,173,725	7,632,942	3,396,831	2,571,376
2002–03	99,137,236	31,866,310	11,079,332	1,871,274	8,122,181	7,014,149	12,996,836	9,876,937	1,161,441	7,586,208	3,854,471	3,708,098
2003–04	103,733,257	33,712,542	12,039,080	1,964,898	8,726,505	7,466,472	13,774,084	10,464,984	1,084,880	8,374,128	4,221,611	1,904,075
2004–05	109,789,731	36,051,084	12,812,326	1,993,767	9,307,600	8,101,214	14,516,197	10,899,456	1,051,216	9,180,775	4,223,779	1,652,317
2005–06	116,247,359	38,249,125	13,241,769	1,931,804	10,177,381	8,894,330	15,524,004	11,696,510	699,462	9,645,428	4,203,523	1,984,024
2006–07	124,061,478	41,056,590	13,703,502	2,028,364	10,850,270	9,522,535	16,693,987	12,414,609	714,398	10,400,055	4,680,393	1,996,775
2007–08	132,967,352	44,041,162	14,473,394	2,176,695	11,847,922	10,286,780	18,216,170	13,281,694	711,903	10,754,966	4,887,609	2,289,058
2008–09	140,866,945	46,289,898	15,264,459	2,294,909	12,544,436	10,947,638	19,261,017	13,676,329	747,586	11,930,840	5,158,480	2,751,352
2009–10	144,624,598	47,400,673	16,221,238	2,085,201	12,910,113	11,353,608	19,303,251	13,855,994	819,196	13,174,405	5,154,851	2,346,068
2010–11	151,878,613	49,550,398	17,361,796	2,252,726	13,547,801	12,111,973	20,048,321	14,430,101	758,318	14,239,347	5,376,016	2,201,817
2011–12	159,245,924	51,959,761	17,482,484	2,331,249	14,164,326	12,795,619	21,024,665	14,924,702	843,453	15,474,737	5,450,038	2,794,891
2012–13	165,073,451	54,076,793	17,514,466	2,316,357	14,883,058	13,617,897	21,719,080	15,304,071	846,965	16,701,193	5,436,746	2,656,826
2013–14	171,992,210	56,508,677	17,734,396	2,458,106	15,400,899	14,460,267	22,499,119	15,944,610	863,119	17,377,766	5,693,990	3,051,263
2-year												
1999–2000	913,378	268,400	5,358	8,415	34,612	97,521	186,936	71,612	18,311	0	1,660	220,553
2000–01	576,893	193,428	5,772	5,967	34,412	80,717	141,764	52,880	15,500	1,896	1,510	43,046
2001–02	579,960	196,459	86	7,102	33,767	76,058	153,971	45,271	14,965	100	1,147	51,033
2002–03	610,840	195,909	200	7,106	34,506	82,074	160,908	59,541	12,404	0	25,265	32,926
2003–04	584,612	196,637	451	7,453	33,238	77,549	177,324	43,735	16,859	0	1,369	29,995
2004–05	604,395	207,389	532	6,670	34,464	90,523	174,131	44,886	18,375	0	0	27,425
2005–06	570,554	215,934	574	9,715	39,893	71,374	143,096	44,748	8,696	0	0	36,524
2006–07	496,247	166,893	947	8,224	31,758	68,799	137,366	36,478	13,741	0	0	32,041
2007–08	536,187	185,167	973	5,982	36,423	76,696	148,343	37,908	9,584	0	0	35,112
2008–09	496,620	166,280	345	3,612	41,511	68,459	142,330	37,372	7,165	0	0	29,546
2009–10	490,645	165,538	585	5,041	42,909	69,129	135,357	34,402	7,183	0	0	30,502
2010–11	622,815	209,176	285	2,349	53,336	86,290	166,362	29,983	1,365	0	0	73,669
2011–12	585,454	203,885	673	2,049	51,363	85,483	150,455	23,613	2,072	0	0	65,861
2012–13	500,218	181,113	329	1,771	39,171	67,591	138,543	26,505	4,682	0	0	40,512
2013–14	555,685	198,126	420	1,732	48,465	90,671	122,804	30,438	4,364	0	0	58,664
						Percentage distribution						
All levels												
1999–2000	100.00	32.27	10.40	1.79	8.08	7.06	13.13	10.30	1.46	9.12	3.42	2.97
2000–01	100.00	32.24	10.54	1.72	8.61	7.14	13.35	10.52	1.37	8.47	3.66	2.36
2001–02	100.00	32.20	10.89	1.81	8.46	7.13	13.09	10.32	1.29	8.28	3.69	2.84
2002–03	100.00	32.14	11.11	1.88	8.18	7.11	13.19	9.96	1.18	7.61	3.89	3.75
2003–04	100.00	32.51	11.54	1.89	8.40	7.23	13.37	10.07	1.06	8.03	4.05	1.85
2004–05	100.00	32.84	11.61	1.81	8.46	7.42	13.31	9.91	0.97	8.32	3.83	1.52
2005–06	100.00	32.93	11.34	1.66	8.75	7.67	13.41	10.05	0.61	8.26	3.60	1.73
2006–07	100.00	33.10	11.00	1.64	8.74	7.70	13.51	10.00	0.58	8.35	3.76	1.63
2007–08	100.00	33.13	10.84	1.63	8.90	7.76	13.76	9.98	0.54	8.06	3.66	1.74
2008–09	100.00	32.86	10.80	1.63	8.90	7.79	13.73	9.70	0.53	8.44	3.65	1.97
2009–10	100.00	32.78	11.18	1.44	8.93	7.87	13.40	9.57	0.57	9.08	3.55	1.64
2010–11	100.00	32.63	11.38	1.48	8.92	8.00	13.26	9.48	0.50	9.34	3.53	1.49
2011–12	100.00	32.64	10.94	1.46	8.89	8.06	13.25	9.35	0.53	9.68	3.41	1.79
2012–13	100.00	32.77	10.58	1.40	9.01	8.27	13.20	9.26	0.51	10.09	3.28	1.63
2013–14	100.00	32.86	10.28	1.43	8.95	8.43	13.11	9.26	0.50	10.07	3.30	1.80
4-year												
1999–2000	100.00	32.30	10.51	1.80	8.13	7.02	13.05	10.32	1.46	9.23	3.45	2.73
2000–01	100.00	32.23	10.61	1.73	8.62	7.10	13.28	10.53	1.36	8.53	3.68	2.33
2001–02	100.00	32.19	10.95	1.81	8.48	7.09	13.00	10.34	1.28	8.33	3.71	2.81
2002–03	100.00	32.14	11.18	1.89	8.19	7.08	13.11	9.96	1.17	7.65	3.89	3.74
2003–04	100.00	32.50	11.61	1.89	8.41	7.20	13.28	10.09	1.05	8.07	4.07	1.84
2004–05	100.00	32.84	11.67	1.82	8.48	7.38	13.22	9.93	0.96	8.36	3.85	1.50
2005–06	100.00	32.90	11.39	1.66	8.75	7.65	13.35	10.06	0.60	8.30	3.62	1.71
2006–07	100.00	33.09	11.05	1.63	8.75	7.68	13.46	10.01	0.58	8.38	3.77	1.61
2007–08	100.00	33.12	10.88	1.64	8.91	7.74	13.70	9.99	0.54	8.09	3.68	1.72
2008–09	100.00	32.86	10.84	1.63	8.91	7.77	13.67	9.71	0.53	8.47	3.66	1.95
2009–10	100.00	32.77	11.22	1.44	8.93	7.85	13.35	9.58	0.57	9.11	3.56	1.62
2010–11	100.00	32.63	11.43	1.48	8.92	7.97	13.20	9.50	0.50	9.38	3.54	1.45
2011–12	100.00	32.63	10.98	1.46	8.89	8.04	13.20	9.37	0.53	9.72	3.42	1.76
2012–13	100.00	32.76	10.61	1.40	9.02	8.25	13.16	9.27	0.51	10.12	3.29	1.61
2013–14	100.00	32.86	10.31	1.43	8.95	8.41	13.08	9.27	0.50	10.10	3.31	1.77

See notes at end of table.

Table 334.30. Total expenditures of private nonprofit degree-granting postsecondary institutions, by purpose and level of institution: 1999–2000 through 2013–14—Continued

Level of institution and year	Total	Instruction	Research	Public service	Academic support	Student services	Institutional support	Auxiliary enterprises[1]	Net grant aid to students[2]	Hospitals	Independent operations	Other
1	2	3	4	5	6	7	8	9	10	11	12	13
2-year												
1999–2000	100.00	29.39	0.59	0.92	3.79	10.68	20.47	7.84	2.00	0.00	0.18	24.15
2000–01	100.00	33.53	1.00	1.03	5.96	13.99	24.57	9.17	2.69	0.33	0.26	7.46
2001–02	100.00	33.87	0.01	1.22	5.82	13.11	26.55	7.81	2.58	0.02	0.20	8.80
2002–03	100.00	32.07	0.03	1.16	5.65	13.44	26.34	9.75	2.03	0.00	4.14	5.39
2003–04	100.00	33.64	0.08	1.27	5.69	13.27	30.33	7.48	2.88	0.00	0.23	5.13
2004–05	100.00	34.31	0.09	1.10	5.70	14.98	28.81	7.43	3.04	0.00	0.00	4.54
2005–06	100.00	37.85	0.10	1.70	6.99	12.51	25.08	7.84	1.52	0.00	0.00	6.40
2006–07	100.00	33.63	0.19	1.66	6.40	13.86	27.68	7.35	2.77	0.00	0.00	6.46
2007–08	100.00	34.53	0.18	1.12	6.79	14.30	27.67	7.07	1.79	0.00	0.00	6.55
2008–09	100.00	33.48	0.07	0.73	8.36	13.78	28.66	7.53	1.44	0.00	0.00	5.95
2009–10	100.00	33.74	0.12	1.03	8.75	14.09	27.59	7.01	1.46	0.00	0.00	6.22
2010–11	100.00	33.59	0.05	0.38	8.56	13.85	26.71	4.81	0.22	0.00	0.00	11.83
2011–12	100.00	34.83	0.11	0.35	8.77	14.60	25.70	4.03	0.35	0.00	0.00	11.25
2012–13	100.00	36.21	0.07	0.35	7.83	13.51	27.70	5.30	0.94	0.00	0.00	8.10
2013–14	100.00	35.65	0.08	0.31	8.72	16.32	22.10	5.48	0.79	0.00	0.00	10.56
	Expenditure per full-time-equivalent student in constant 2014–15 dollars[3]											
All levels												
1999–2000	$44,389	$14,324	$4,615	$797	$3,585	$3,132	$5,829	$4,570	$650	$4,050	$1,516	$1,320
2000–01	44,701	14,412	4,712	769	3,847	3,194	5,969	4,704	614	3,788	1,636	1,056
2001–02	46,276	14,903	5,037	836	3,917	3,299	6,058	4,777	597	3,831	1,706	1,316
2002–03	47,410	15,239	5,266	893	3,877	3,373	6,254	4,723	558	3,606	1,844	1,778
2003–04	47,363	15,396	5,466	895	3,977	3,425	6,334	4,771	500	3,802	1,917	878
2004–05	47,500	15,601	5,513	861	4,020	3,525	6,321	4,709	460	3,950	1,817	723
2005–06	47,761	15,726	5,414	794	4,177	3,666	6,405	4,800	290	3,944	1,719	826
2006–07	48,764	16,139	5,365	797	4,260	3,755	6,589	4,875	285	4,072	1,832	794
2007–08	49,166	16,287	5,331	804	4,377	3,817	6,763	4,905	266	3,961	1,800	856
2008–09	50,561	16,616	5,460	822	4,502	3,940	6,940	4,905	270	4,267	1,845	995
2009–10	50,068	16,411	5,597	721	4,469	3,941	6,707	4,792	285	4,545	1,779	820
2010–11	49,699	16,216	5,658	735	4,433	3,975	6,588	4,712	248	4,641	1,752	742
2011–12	50,168	16,373	5,488	732	4,462	4,043	6,646	4,692	265	4,857	1,711	898
2012–13	50,510	16,552	5,343	707	4,552	4,175	6,668	4,677	260	5,095	1,659	823
2013–14	51,736	17,003	5,318	738	4,632	4,363	6,783	4,790	260	5,210	1,707	932
4-year												
1999–2000	44,827	14,480	4,711	809	3,643	3,145	5,849	4,628	654	4,137	1,548	1,224
2000–01	45,093	14,535	4,782	778	3,888	3,201	5,987	4,750	615	3,846	1,661	1,049
2001–02	46,672	15,025	5,113	845	3,958	3,310	6,070	4,825	598	3,889	1,731	1,310
2002–03	47,752	15,349	5,337	901	3,912	3,379	6,260	4,758	559	3,654	1,857	1,786
2003–04	47,698	15,502	5,536	903	4,013	3,433	6,334	4,812	499	3,851	1,941	876
2004–05	47,814	15,700	5,580	868	4,054	3,528	6,322	4,747	458	3,998	1,839	720
2005–06	48,044	15,808	5,473	798	4,206	3,676	6,416	4,834	289	3,986	1,737	820
2006–07	48,991	16,213	5,411	801	4,285	3,760	6,592	4,902	282	4,107	1,848	789
2007–08	49,408	16,365	5,378	809	4,402	3,822	6,769	4,935	265	3,996	1,816	851
2008–09	50,811	16,697	5,506	828	4,525	3,949	6,948	4,933	270	4,304	1,861	992
2009–10	50,309	16,489	5,643	725	4,491	3,949	6,715	4,820	285	4,583	1,793	816
2010–11	50,028	16,321	5,719	742	4,463	3,990	6,604	4,753	250	4,690	1,771	725
2011–12	50,480	16,471	5,542	739	4,490	4,056	6,665	4,731	267	4,905	1,728	886
2012–13	50,781	16,635	5,388	713	4,578	4,189	6,681	4,708	261	5,138	1,672	817
2013–14	51,985	17,080	5,360	743	4,655	4,371	6,800	4,819	261	5,252	1,721	922
2-year												
1999–2000	23,974	7,045	141	221	909	2,560	4,907	1,880	481	0	44	5,789
2000–01	19,592	6,569	196	203	1,169	2,741	4,814	1,796	526	64	51	1,462
2001–02	19,777	6,699	3	242	1,151	2,594	5,250	1,544	510	3	39	1,740
2002–03	21,893	7,022	7	255	1,237	2,942	5,767	2,134	445	0	906	1,180
2003–04	21,062	7,084	16	269	1,198	2,794	6,389	1,576	607	0	49	1,081
2004–05	21,671	7,436	19	239	1,236	3,246	6,244	1,609	659	0	0	983
2005–06	21,694	8,210	22	369	1,517	2,714	5,441	1,701	331	0	0	1,389
2006–07	22,606	7,603	43	375	1,447	3,134	6,258	1,662	626	0	0	1,460
2007–08	22,211	7,670	40	248	1,509	3,177	6,145	1,570	397	0	0	1,454
2008–09	21,091	7,062	15	153	1,763	2,907	6,045	1,587	304	0	0	1,255
2009–10	20,778	7,010	25	213	1,817	2,927	5,732	1,457	304	0	0	1,292
2010–11	19,115	6,420	9	72	1,637	2,648	5,106	920	42	0	0	2,261
2011–12	18,708	6,515	22	65	1,641	2,732	4,808	755	66	0	0	2,105
2012–13	18,306	6,628	12	65	1,433	2,474	5,070	970	171	0	0	1,483
2013–14	20,814	7,421	16	65	1,815	3,396	4,600	1,140	163	0	0	2,197

[1]Essentially self-supporting operations of institutions that furnish a service to students, faculty, or staff, such as residence halls and food services.
[2]Excludes tuition, fee, and auxiliary enterprise allowances and agency transactions, such as student awards made from contributed funds or grant funds. These exclusions account for the majority of total student grants.
[3]Constant dollars based on the Consumer Price Index, prepared by the Bureau of Labor Statistics, U.S. Department of Labor, adjusted to a school-year basis.

NOTE: Degree-granting institutions grant associate's or higher degrees and participate in Title IV federal financial aid programs. Some data have been revised from previously published figures. Detail may not sum to totals because of rounding.
SOURCE: U.S. Department of Education, National Center for Education Statistics, Integrated Postsecondary Education Data System (IPEDS), "Fall Enrollment Survey" (IPEDS-EF:99); Spring 2001 through Spring 2007, Enrollment component; Spring 2008 through Spring 2014, Fall Enrollment component; and Spring 2001 through Spring 2015, Finance component. (This table was prepared November 2015.)

Table 334.40. Total expenditures of private nonprofit degree-granting postsecondary institutions, by purpose and classification of institution: 2013–14

Classification of institution	Total	Instruction	Research	Public service	Academic support	Student services	Institutional support	Auxiliary enterprises[1]	Net grant aid to students[2]	Hospitals	Independent operations	Other
1	2	3	4	5	6	7	8	9	10	11	12	13
	In thousands of current dollars											
Total	$172,547,895	$56,706,803	$17,734,816	$2,459,838	$15,449,364	$14,550,938	$22,621,924	$15,975,048	$867,482	$17,377,766	$5,693,990	$3,109,927
4-year	171,992,210	56,508,677	17,734,396	2,458,106	15,400,899	14,460,267	22,499,119	15,944,610	863,119	17,377,766	5,693,990	3,051,263
Research university, very high[3]	81,674,629	25,076,817	14,209,367	841,371	5,876,903	3,163,824	6,998,927	5,206,552	566,931	13,423,613	4,512,389	1,797,933
Research university, high[4]	12,449,099	4,523,567	1,020,637	179,572	1,835,801	958,259	1,658,653	1,524,309	22,379	495,685	55,457	174,779
Doctoral/research[5]	8,064,790	3,251,029	232,506	121,960	921,489	1,005,620	1,423,866	1,027,763	6,756	0	17,933	55,870
Master's[6]	28,648,501	11,016,240	281,531	296,349	2,914,859	4,616,036	5,329,868	3,708,088	87,939	31,986	128,585	237,021
Baccalaureate[7]	22,964,541	8,163,501	247,539	211,106	1,996,206	3,713,390	4,405,133	3,724,056	125,877	6,621	64,161	306,950
Special-focus institutions[8]	18,190,650	4,477,522	1,742,817	807,748	1,855,640	1,003,137	2,682,673	753,842	53,236	3,419,861	915,464	478,710
Art, music, or design	2,189,912	892,914	858	24,312	254,527	222,468	483,109	222,536	7,385	0	26,690	55,113
Business and management	714,741	237,701	7,296	740	93,625	109,924	171,783	70,215	619	0	2,409	20,427
Engineering or technology	295,415	133,085	2,935	0	20,879	47,834	65,883	18,734	2,942	0	49	3,073
Law	586,418	259,813	5,514	15,278	85,803	71,732	127,858	16,684	1,220	0	454	2,061
Medical or other health	12,155,664	2,221,126	1,714,569	681,191	1,176,313	336,052	1,245,936	198,779	10,177	3,419,861	875,117	276,544
Theological	1,854,769	588,040	7,972	58,154	188,833	173,112	492,656	203,407	29,565	0	10,744	102,285
Tribal[9]	106,488	28,695	1,087	11,048	6,193	15,956	23,677	2,088	1,154	0	0	16,590
Other special focus	287,244	116,149	2,586	17,024	29,467	26,059	71,771	21,399	173	0	0	2,617
2-year	555,685	198,126	420	1,732	48,465	90,671	122,804	30,438	4,364	0	0	58,664
Associate's of arts	536,040	193,764	107	1,571	44,044	88,847	118,432	30,144	1,223	0	0	57,908
Tribal[9]	19,646	4,362	313	161	4,421	1,825	4,373	295	3,140	0	0	756
	Percentage distribution											
Total	100.00	32.86	10.28	1.43	8.95	8.43	13.11	9.26	0.50	10.07	3.30	1.80
4-year	100.00	32.86	10.31	1.43	8.95	8.41	13.08	9.27	0.50	10.10	3.31	1.77
Research university, very high[3]	100.00	30.70	17.40	1.03	7.20	3.87	8.57	6.37	0.69	16.44	5.52	2.20
Research university, high[4]	100.00	36.34	8.20	1.44	14.75	7.70	13.32	12.24	0.18	3.98	0.45	1.40
Doctoral/research[5]	100.00	40.31	2.88	1.51	11.43	12.47	17.66	12.74	0.08	0.00	0.22	0.69
Master's[6]	100.00	38.45	0.98	1.03	10.17	16.11	18.60	12.94	0.31	0.11	0.45	0.83
Baccalaureate[7]	100.00	35.55	1.08	0.92	8.69	16.17	19.18	16.22	0.55	0.03	0.28	1.34
Special-focus institutions[8]	100.00	24.61	9.58	4.44	10.20	5.51	14.75	4.14	0.29	18.80	5.03	2.63
Art, music, or design	100.00	40.77	0.04	1.11	11.62	10.16	22.06	10.16	0.34	0.00	1.22	2.52
Business and management	100.00	33.26	1.02	0.10	13.10	15.38	24.03	9.82	0.09	0.00	0.34	2.86
Engineering or technology	100.00	45.05	0.99	0.00	7.07	16.19	22.30	6.34	1.00	0.00	0.02	1.04
Law	100.00	44.31	0.94	2.61	14.63	12.23	21.80	2.85	0.21	0.00	0.08	0.35
Medical or other health	100.00	18.27	14.11	5.60	9.68	2.76	10.25	1.64	0.08	28.13	7.20	2.28
Theological	100.00	31.70	0.43	3.14	10.18	9.33	26.56	10.97	1.59	0.00	0.58	5.51
Tribal[9]	100.00	26.95	1.02	10.37	5.82	14.98	22.23	1.96	1.08	0.00	0.00	15.58
Other special focus	100.00	40.44	0.90	5.93	10.26	9.07	24.99	7.45	0.06	0.00	0.00	0.91
2-year	100.00	35.65	0.08	0.31	8.72	16.32	22.10	5.48	0.79	0.00	0.00	10.56
Associate's of arts	100.00	36.15	0.02	0.29	8.22	16.57	22.09	5.62	0.23	0.00	0.00	10.80
Tribal[9]	100.00	22.21	1.59	0.82	22.50	9.29	22.26	1.50	15.98	0.00	0.00	3.85
	Expenditure per full-time-equivalent student in current dollars											
Total	$51,362	$16,880	$5,279	$732	$4,599	$4,331	$6,734	$4,755	$258	$5,173	$1,695	$926
4-year	51,610	16,956	5,322	738	4,621	4,339	6,751	4,784	259	5,215	1,709	916
Research university, very high[3]	161,246	49,508	28,053	1,661	11,602	6,246	13,818	10,279	1,119	26,501	8,909	3,550
Research university, high[4]	46,333	16,836	3,799	668	6,832	3,566	6,173	5,673	83	1,845	206	650
Doctoral/research[5]	30,256	12,196	872	458	3,457	3,773	5,342	3,856	25	0	67	210
Master's[6]	22,862	8,791	225	236	2,326	3,684	4,253	2,959	70	26	103	189
Baccalaureate[7]	31,494	11,195	339	290	2,738	5,093	6,041	5,107	173	9	88	421
Special-focus institutions[8]	58,963	14,513	5,649	2,618	6,015	3,252	8,696	2,443	173	11,085	2,967	1,552
Art, music, or design	38,366	15,643	15	426	4,459	3,897	8,464	3,899	129	0	468	966
Business and management	23,555	7,834	240	24	3,086	3,623	5,661	2,314	20	0	79	673
Engineering or technology	19,853	8,944	197	0	1,403	3,215	4,428	1,259	198	0	3	207
Law	42,213	18,702	397	1,100	6,176	5,164	9,204	1,201	88	0	33	148
Medical or other health	111,616	20,395	15,744	6,255	10,801	3,086	11,440	1,825	93	31,402	8,036	2,539
Theological	25,151	7,974	108	789	2,561	2,347	6,681	2,758	401	0	146	1,387
Tribal[9]	41,403	11,157	423	4,295	2,408	6,204	9,206	812	449	0	0	6,450
Other special focus	40,491	16,373	364	2,400	4,154	3,673	10,117	3,016	24	0	0	369
2-year	20,664	7,367	16	64	1,802	3,372	4,567	1,132	162	0	0	2,181
Associate's of arts	20,354	7,357	4	60	1,672	3,374	4,497	1,145	46	0	0	2,199
Tribal[9]	35,334	7,846	563	290	7,952	3,282	7,864	530	5,648	0	0	1,359

[1]Essentially self-supporting operations of institutions that furnish a service to students, faculty, or staff, such as residence halls and food services.
[2]Excludes tuition, fee, and auxiliary enterprise allowances and agency transactions, such as student awards made from contributed funds or grant funds. These exclusions account for the majority of total student grants.
[3]Research universities with a very high level of research activity.
[4]Research universities with a high level of research activity.
[5]Institutions that award at least 20 doctor's degrees per year, but did not have high levels of research activity.
[6]Institutions that award at least 50 master's degrees per year.
[7]Institutions that primarily emphasize undergraduate education. Also includes institutions classified as 4-year under the IPEDS system, which had been classified as 2-year in the Carnegie classification system because they primarily award associate's degrees.

[8]Four-year institutions that award degrees primarily in single fields of study, such as medicine, business, fine arts, theology, and engineering.
[9]Tribally controlled colleges, which are located on reservations and are members of the American Indian Higher Education Consortium.
NOTE: Relative levels of research activity for research universities were determined by an analysis of research and development expenditures, science and engineering research staffing, and doctoral degrees conferred, by field. Further information on the Carnegie 2005 classification system used in this table may be obtained from http://carnegieclassifications.iu.edu/. Degree-granting institutions grant associate's or higher degrees and participate in Title IV federal financial aid programs. Detail may not sum to totals because of rounding.
SOURCE: U.S. Department of Education, National Center for Education Statistics, Integrated Postsecondary Education Data System (IPEDS), Spring 2014, Fall Enrollment component; and Spring 2015, Finance component. (This table was prepared November 2015.)

Table 334.50. Total expenditures of private for-profit degree-granting postsecondary institutions, by purpose and level of institution: 1999–2000 through 2013–14

Year and level of institution	Total	Instruction	Research and public service	Student services, academic and institutional support	Auxiliary enterprises[1]	Net grant aid to students[2]	Other
1	2	3	4	5	6	7	8
	In thousands of current dollars						
All levels							
1999–2000	$3,846,246	$1,171,732	$24,738	$2,041,594	$144,305	$26,278	$437,599
2000–01	4,235,781	1,310,054	22,896	2,337,151	181,243	43,788	340,649
2001–02	5,087,292	1,517,389	16,632	2,977,225	213,195	23,283	339,567
2002–03	6,110,378	1,747,725	17,987	3,670,218	240,380	36,031	398,037
2003–04	7,364,012	1,883,733	8,606	4,592,730	249,472	56,467	573,004
2004–05	8,830,792	2,313,895	7,583	5,693,200	269,883	54,819	491,411
2005–06	10,208,845	2,586,870	8,445	6,569,329	276,587	66,569	701,044
2006–07	12,152,366	2,884,481	6,087	7,760,044	332,887	68,300	1,100,568
2007–08	13,940,442	3,238,406	9,547	9,322,781	421,714	82,072	865,922
2008–09	16,375,034	3,876,258	9,939	11,069,416	396,715	44,440	978,267
2009–10	19,973,034	4,759,300	13,257	13,230,271	466,040	120,032	1,384,134
2010–11	22,632,244	5,656,167	19,327	14,853,799	486,433	87,151	1,529,368
2011–12	22,713,683	5,538,070	42,657	15,111,978	489,409	54,579	1,476,991
2012–13	21,940,185	5,424,430	27,729	14,357,843	464,188	53,555	1,612,440
2013–14	20,658,825	5,535,512	16,450	13,097,041	472,200	36,569	1,501,053
4–year							
1999–2000	2,022,622	595,976	4,393	1,104,001	92,071	11,805	214,377
2000–01	2,414,655	726,328	4,878	1,385,095	113,371	18,519	166,465
2001–02	3,046,929	883,899	3,192	1,842,373	134,740	8,229	174,495
2002–03	3,754,727	1,030,470	5,339	2,337,388	153,528	14,813	213,190
2003–04	4,821,864	1,143,050	3,705	3,108,697	168,069	32,603	365,740
2004–05	5,989,792	1,430,196	3,513	4,110,514	180,036	38,639	226,894
2005–06	7,218,830	1,680,603	4,065	4,985,531	179,064	54,291	315,276
2006–07	8,837,598	1,857,765	4,303	5,909,914	228,624	56,930	780,063
2007–08	10,424,536	2,149,651	7,534	7,335,592	312,834	71,324	547,602
2008–09	12,409,748	2,585,133	7,629	8,893,714	276,211	33,417	613,644
2009–10	15,286,893	3,268,070	10,726	10,732,002	337,499	72,082	866,514
2010–11	17,141,926	3,925,347	15,582	12,031,073	343,319	74,921	751,684
2011–12	17,407,585	3,928,903	37,912	12,153,860	349,405	51,818	885,687
2012–13	16,779,710	3,897,632	24,432	11,443,167	356,202	46,446	1,011,832
2013–14	16,031,478	4,077,757	15,193	10,540,173	371,014	32,306	995,035
2–year							
1999–2000	1,823,624	575,756	20,345	937,593	52,234	14,473	223,223
2000–01	1,821,126	583,727	18,019	952,056	67,872	25,269	174,184
2001–02	2,040,363	633,490	13,440	1,134,853	78,455	15,054	165,071
2002–03	2,355,650	717,255	12,648	1,332,830	86,853	21,218	184,846
2003–04	2,542,148	740,683	4,901	1,484,033	81,403	23,864	207,264
2004–05	2,840,999	883,699	4,070	1,582,687	89,846	16,181	264,517
2005–06	2,990,015	906,267	4,381	1,583,798	97,523	12,278	385,768
2006–07	3,314,768	1,026,716	1,784	1,850,129	104,264	11,370	320,505
2007–08	3,515,906	1,088,755	2,014	1,987,189	108,880	10,747	318,320
2008–09	3,965,287	1,291,124	2,310	2,175,703	120,504	11,023	364,623
2009–10	4,686,142	1,491,230	2,531	2,498,269	128,542	47,950	517,619
2010–11	5,490,318	1,730,820	3,744	2,822,726	143,113	12,230	777,685
2011–12	5,306,098	1,609,167	4,745	2,958,118	140,004	2,761	591,304
2012–13	5,160,475	1,526,798	3,297	2,914,676	107,986	7,109	600,609
2013–14	4,627,347	1,457,755	1,257	2,556,868	101,186	4,263	506,018
	Percentage distribution						
All levels							
1999–2000	100.00	30.46	0.64	53.08	3.75	0.68	11.38
2000–01	100.00	30.93	0.54	55.18	4.28	1.03	8.04
2001–02	100.00	29.83	0.33	58.52	4.19	0.46	6.67
2002–03	100.00	28.60	0.29	60.07	3.93	0.59	6.51
2003–04	100.00	25.58	0.12	62.37	3.39	0.77	7.78
2004–05	100.00	26.20	0.09	64.47	3.06	0.62	5.56
2005–06	100.00	25.34	0.08	64.35	2.71	0.65	6.87
2006–07	100.00	23.74	0.05	63.86	2.74	0.56	9.06
2007–08	100.00	23.23	0.07	66.88	3.03	0.59	6.21
2008–09	100.00	23.67	0.06	67.60	2.42	0.27	5.97
2009–10	100.00	23.83	0.07	66.24	2.33	0.60	6.93
2010–11	100.00	24.99	0.09	65.63	2.15	0.39	6.76
2011–12	100.00	24.38	0.19	66.53	2.15	0.24	6.50
2012–13	100.00	24.72	0.13	65.44	2.12	0.24	7.35
2013–14	100.00	26.79	0.08	63.40	2.29	0.18	7.27
4–year							
1999–2000	100.00	29.47	0.22	54.58	4.55	0.58	10.60
2000–01	100.00	30.08	0.20	57.36	4.70	0.77	6.89
2001–02	100.00	29.01	0.10	60.47	4.42	0.27	5.73
2002–03	100.00	27.44	0.14	62.25	4.09	0.39	5.68
2003–04	100.00	23.71	0.08	64.47	3.49	0.68	7.59
2004–05	100.00	23.88	0.06	68.63	3.01	0.65	3.79
2005–06	100.00	23.28	0.06	69.06	2.48	0.75	4.37
2006–07	100.00	21.02	0.05	66.87	2.59	0.64	8.83
2007–08	100.00	20.62	0.07	70.37	3.00	0.68	5.25
2008–09	100.00	20.83	0.06	71.67	2.23	0.27	4.94
2009–10	100.00	21.38	0.07	70.20	2.21	0.47	5.67
2010–11	100.00	22.90	0.09	70.19	2.00	0.44	4.39
2011–12	100.00	22.57	0.22	69.82	2.01	0.30	5.09
2012–13	100.00	23.23	0.15	68.20	2.12	0.28	6.03
2013–14	100.00	25.44	0.09	65.75	2.31	0.20	6.21

See notes at end of table.

Table 334.50. Total expenditures of private for-profit degree-granting postsecondary institutions, by purpose and level of institution: 1999–2000 through 2013–14—Continued

Year and level of institution	Total	Instruction	Research and public service	Student services, academic and institutional support	Auxiliary enterprises[1]	Net grant aid to students[2]	Other
1	2	3	4	5	6	7	8
2-year							
1999–2000	100.00	31.57	1.12	51.41	2.86	0.79	12.24
2000–01	100.00	32.05	0.99	52.28	3.73	1.39	9.56
2001–02	100.00	31.05	0.66	55.62	3.85	0.74	8.09
2002–03	100.00	30.45	0.54	56.58	3.69	0.90	7.85
2003–04	100.00	29.14	0.19	58.38	3.20	0.94	8.15
2004–05	100.00	31.11	0.14	55.71	3.16	0.57	9.31
2005–06	100.00	30.31	0.15	52.97	3.26	0.41	12.90
2006–07	100.00	30.97	0.05	55.81	3.15	0.34	9.67
2007–08	100.00	30.97	0.06	56.52	3.10	0.31	9.05
2008–09	100.00	32.56	0.06	54.87	3.04	0.28	9.20
2009–10	100.00	31.82	0.05	53.31	2.74	1.02	11.05
2010–11	100.00	31.52	0.07	51.41	2.61	0.22	14.16
2011–12	100.00	30.33	0.09	55.75	2.64	0.05	11.14
2012–13	100.00	29.59	0.06	56.48	2.09	0.14	11.64
2013–14	100.00	31.50	0.03	55.26	2.19	0.09	10.94

Total expenditures per full-time-equivalent student in constant 2014–15 dollars[3]

Year and level of institution	Total	Instruction	Research and public service	Student services, academic and institutional support	Auxiliary enterprises[1]	Net grant aid to students[2]	Other
All levels							
1999–2000	$13,981	$4,259	$90	$7,421	$525	$96	$1,591
2000–01	14,573	4,507	79	8,041	624	151	1,172
2001–02	14,801	4,415	48	8,662	620	68	988
2002–03	14,688	4,201	43	8,822	578	87	957
2003–04	14,475	3,703	17	9,028	490	111	1,126
2004–05	13,835	3,625	12	8,919	423	86	770
2005–06	13,483	3,417	11	8,676	365	88	926
2006–07	14,933	3,545	7	9,536	409	84	1,352
2007–08	15,123	3,513	10	10,113	457	89	939
2008–09	14,175	3,356	9	9,583	343	38	847
2009–10	14,640	3,488	10	9,697	342	88	1,015
2010–11	14,652	3,662	13	9,616	315	56	990
2011–12	14,654	3,573	28	9,750	316	35	953
2012–13	15,859	3,921	20	10,378	336	39	1,166
2013–14	19,654	5,266	16	12,460	449	35	1,428
4-year							
1999–2000	13,545	3,991	29	7,393	617	79	1,436
2000–01	14,313	4,305	29	8,210	672	110	987
2001–02	14,638	4,246	15	8,851	647	40	838
2002–03	14,116	3,874	20	8,788	577	56	802
2003–04	14,360	3,404	11	9,258	501	97	1,089
2004–05	13,357	3,189	8	9,166	401	86	506
2005–06	12,961	3,017	7	8,951	322	97	566
2006–07	14,552	3,059	7	9,731	376	94	1,284
2007–08	14,771	3,046	11	10,394	443	101	776
2008–09	13,963	2,909	9	10,007	311	38	690
2009–10	14,936	3,193	10	10,485	330	70	847
2010–11	14,590	3,341	13	10,240	292	64	640
2011–12	14,450	3,261	31	10,089	290	43	735
2012–13	15,504	3,601	23	10,573	329	43	935
2013–14	20,745	5,277	20	13,639	480	42	1,288
2-year							
1999–2000	14,498	4,577	162	7,454	415	115	1,775
2000–01	14,934	4,787	148	7,807	557	207	1,428
2001–02	15,052	4,673	99	8,372	579	111	1,218
2002–03	15,701	4,781	84	8,884	579	141	1,232
2003–04	14,698	4,283	28	8,580	471	138	1,198
2004–05	14,964	4,655	21	8,337	473	85	1,393
2005–06	14,937	4,527	22	7,912	487	61	1,927
2006–07	16,055	4,973	9	8,961	505	55	1,552
2007–08	16,272	5,039	9	9,197	504	50	1,473
2008–09	14,883	4,846	9	8,166	452	41	1,369
2009–10	13,751	4,376	7	7,331	377	141	1,519
2010–11	14,849	4,681	10	7,634	387	33	2,103
2011–12	15,368	4,661	14	8,568	405	8	1,713
2012–13	17,137	5,070	11	9,679	359	24	1,995
2013–14	16,626	5,238	5	9,187	364	15	1,818

[1]Essentially self-supporting operations of institutions that furnish a service to students, faculty, or staff, such as residence halls and food services.
[2]Excludes tuition, fee, and auxiliary enterprise allowances and agency transactions, such as student awards made from contributed funds or grant funds.
[3]Constant dollars based on the Consumer Price Index, prepared by the Bureau of Labor Statistics, U.S. Department of Labor, adjusted to a school-year basis.

NOTE: Degree-granting institutions grant associate's or higher degrees and participate in Title IV federal financial aid programs. Some data have been revised from previously published figures. Detail may not sum to totals because of rounding.
SOURCE: U.S. Department of Education, National Center for Education Statistics, Integrated Postsecondary Education Data System (IPEDS), "Fall Enrollment Survey" (IPEDS-EF:99); Spring 2001 through Spring 2007, Enrollment component; Spring 2008 through Spring 2014, Fall Enrollment component; and Spring 2001 through Spring 2015, Finance component. (This table was prepared November 2015.)

Table 334.60. Total expenditures of private for-profit degree-granting postsecondary institutions, by purpose and classification of institution: 2013–14

Classification of institution	Total	Instruction	Research	Public service	Academic support	Student services	Institutional support	Auxiliary enterprises[1]	Net grant aid to students[2]	Hospitals	Other
1	2	3	4	5	6	7	8	9	10	11	12
					In thousands of current dollars						
Total	$20,658,825	$5,535,512	$5,204	$11,246	$1,830,679	$4,130,801	$7,135,561	$472,200	$36,569	$27	$1,501,026
4-year	16,031,478	4,077,757	5,136	10,057	1,462,951	3,433,300	5,643,922	371,014	32,306	27	995,008
Doctoral/research[3]	1,105,001	278,123	374	818	114,294	113,231	461,429	3,360	61	0	133,311
Master's[4]	3,461,345	774,344	2,112	1,173	243,412	968,872	1,159,454	49,288	0	0	262,691
Baccalaureate[5]	1,933,735	647,141	872	313	151,332	371,258	631,711	42,279	826	0	88,002
Special-focus institutions[6]	9,531,397	2,378,149	1,778	7,752	953,913	1,979,939	3,391,328	276,087	31,419	27	511,004
Art, music, or design	2,270,306	666,137	124	21	104,004	462,048	725,726	176,987	947	0	134,313
Business and management	4,880,142	1,107,427	83	6,660	630,000	1,232,849	1,607,462	60,770	19,515	0	215,376
Engineering or technology	1,285,688	252,817	0	20	84,426	120,991	766,814	14,837	713	0	45,069
Law	185,506	53,255	82	0	32,421	20,979	66,201	621	10,119	0	1,827
Medical or other health	755,363	260,823	419	1,051	94,424	131,954	202,381	8,716	126	27	55,442
Theological	109,776	20,852	1,071	0	5,748	8,222	8,270	12,635	0	0	52,979
Other special focus	44,616	16,838	0	0	2,889	2,895	14,472	1,523	0	0	5,999
2-year	4,627,347	1,457,755	67	1,189	367,728	697,501	1,491,639	101,186	4,263	0	506,018
					Percentage distribution						
Total	100.00	26.79	0.03	0.05	8.86	20.00	34.54	2.29	0.18	#	7.27
4-year	100.00	25.44	0.03	0.06	9.13	21.42	35.21	2.31	0.20	#	6.21
Doctoral/research[3]	100.00	25.17	0.03	0.07	10.34	10.25	41.76	0.30	0.01	0.00	12.06
Master's[4]	100.00	22.37	0.06	0.03	7.03	27.99	33.50	1.42	0.00	0.00	7.59
Baccalaureate[5]	100.00	33.47	0.05	0.02	7.83	19.20	32.67	2.19	0.04	0.00	4.55
Special-focus institutions[6]	100.00	24.95	0.02	0.08	10.01	20.77	35.58	2.90	0.33	#	5.36
Art, music, or design	100.00	29.34	0.01	#	4.58	20.35	31.97	7.80	0.04	0.00	5.92
Business and management	100.00	22.69	0.00	0.14	12.91	25.26	32.94	1.25	0.40	0.00	4.41
Engineering or technology	100.00	19.66	#	#	6.57	9.41	59.64	1.15	0.06	0.00	3.51
Law	100.00	28.71	0.04	0.00	17.48	11.31	35.69	0.33	5.45	0.00	0.99
Medical or other health	100.00	34.53	0.06	0.14	12.50	17.47	26.79	1.15	0.02	#	7.34
Theological	100.00	18.99	0.98	0.00	5.24	7.49	7.53	11.51	0.00	0.00	48.26
Other special focus	100.00	37.74	0.00	0.00	6.47	6.49	32.44	3.41	0.00	0.00	13.44
2-year	100.00	31.50	#	0.03	7.95	15.07	32.24	2.19	0.09	0.00	10.94
				Expenditure per full-time-equivalent student in current dollars							
Total	$19,512	$5,228	$5	$11	$1,729	$3,901	$6,739	$446	$35	$#	$1,418
4-year	20,595	5,238	7	13	1,879	4,411	7,250	477	42	#	1,278
Doctoral/research[3]	15,577	3,921	5	12	1,611	1,596	6,505	47	1	0	1,879
Master's[4]	14,705	3,290	9	5	1,034	4,116	4,926	209	0	0	1,116
Baccalaureate[5]	18,005	6,026	8	3	1,409	3,457	5,882	394	8	0	819
Special-focus institutions[6]	26,134	6,521	5	21	2,616	5,429	9,299	757	86	#	1,401
Art, music, or design	26,252	7,703	1	#	1,203	5,343	8,392	2,047	11	0	1,553
Business and management	28,188	6,397	0	38	3,639	7,121	9,285	351	113	0	1,244
Engineering or technology	21,669	4,261	#	#	1,423	2,039	12,924	250	12	0	760
Law	29,408	8,442	13	0	5,140	3,326	10,495	98	1,604	0	290
Medical or other health	22,294	7,698	12	31	2,787	3,895	5,973	257	4	1	1,636
Theological	36,158	6,868	353	0	1,893	2,708	2,724	4,162	0	0	17,450
Other special focus	17,524	6,614	0	0	1,135	1,137	5,684	598	0	0	2,356
2-year	16,506	5,200	#	4	1,312	2,488	5,321	361	15	0	1,805
				Expenditure per full-time-equivalent student in constant 2014–15 dollars[7]							
Total	$19,654	$5,266	$5	$11	$1,742	$3,930	$6,788	$449	$35	$#	$1,428
4-year	20,745	5,277	7	13	1,893	4,443	7,303	480	42	#	1,288
Doctoral/research[3]	15,690	3,949	5	12	1,623	1,608	6,552	48	1	0	1,893
Master's[4]	14,812	3,314	9	5	1,042	4,146	4,962	211	0	0	1,124
Baccalaureate[5]	18,136	6,069	8	3	1,419	3,482	5,925	397	8	0	825
Special-focus institutions[6]	26,324	6,568	5	21	2,635	5,468	9,366	763	87	#	1,411
Art, music, or design	26,443	7,759	1	#	1,211	5,382	8,453	2,061	11	0	1,564
Business and management	28,393	6,443	0	39	3,665	7,173	9,352	354	114	0	1,253
Engineering or technology	21,827	4,292	#	#	1,433	2,054	13,018	252	12	0	765
Law	29,622	8,504	13	0	5,177	3,350	10,571	99	1,616	0	292
Medical or other health	22,456	7,754	12	31	2,807	3,923	6,017	259	4	1	1,648
Theological	36,421	6,918	355	0	1,907	2,728	2,744	4,192	0	0	17,577
Other special focus	17,651	6,662	0	0	1,143	1,145	5,726	603	0	0	2,373
2-year	16,626	5,238	#	4	1,321	2,506	5,359	364	15	0	1,818

#Rounds to zero.
[1]Essentially self-supporting operations of institutions that furnish a service to students, faculty, or staff, such as residence halls and food services.
[2]Excludes tuition, fee, and auxiliary enterprise allowances and agency transactions, such as student awards made from contributed funds or grant funds.
[3]Institutions that award at least 20 doctor's degrees per year, but did not have high levels of research activity.
[4]Institutions that award at least 50 master's degrees per year.
[5]Institutions that primarily emphasize undergraduate education. Also includes institutions classified as 4-year under the IPEDS system, which had been classified as 2-year in the Carnegie classification system because they primarily award associate's degrees.

[6]Four-year institutions that award degrees primarily in single fields of study, such as medicine, business, fine arts, theology, and engineering.
[7]Constant dollars based on the Consumer Price Index, prepared by the Bureau of Labor Statistics, U.S. Department of Labor, adjusted to a school-year basis.
NOTE: Degree-granting institutions grant associate's or higher degrees and participate in Title IV federal financial aid programs. Further information on the Carnegie 2005 classification system used in this table may be obtained from http://carnegieclassifications.iu.edu/. Detail may not sum to totals because of rounding.
SOURCE: U.S. Department of Education, National Center for Education Statistics, Integrated Postsecondary Education Data System (IPEDS), Spring 2014, Fall Enrollment component; and Spring 2015, Finance component. (This table was prepared November 2015.)

Table 334.70. Total expenditures of private nonprofit and for-profit degree-granting postsecondary institutions, by state or jurisdiction: Selected years, 1999–2000 through 2013–14

[In thousands of current dollars]

State or jurisdiction	Nonprofit institutions						For-profit institutions					
	1999–2000	2004–05	2009–10	2011–12	2012–13	2013–14	1999–2000	2004–05	2009–10	2011–12	2012–13	2013–14
1	2	3	4	5	6	7	8	9	10	11	12	13
United States ...	$80,613,037	$110,394,127	$145,115,244	$159,831,378	$165,573,669	$172,547,895	$3,846,246	$8,830,792	$19,973,034	$22,713,683	$21,940,185	$20,658,825
Alabama	393,465	459,250	561,968	604,992	629,327	657,549	88,190	60,629	139,366	218,257	235,259	230,833
Alaska	19,042	21,076	16,249	17,245	20,965	20,503	3,559	3,986	19,302	53,164	59,584	56,715
Arizona	143,698	147,825	176,443	237,638	251,981	313,229	278,286	1,095,783	3,412,261	3,173,032	3,003,342	2,652,208
Arkansas	230,860	239,357	289,868	341,827	353,657	365,289	5,828	11,574	31,263	27,918	23,245	18,418
California	7,871,651	10,728,872	13,925,287	15,355,141	15,815,988	16,959,940	666,020	1,243,346	2,551,481	2,990,108	3,016,715	3,506,661
Colorado	376,887	524,349	626,838	692,467	776,700	751,330	154,801	320,550	661,384	737,110	719,598	717,552
Connecticut	2,094,981	2,882,963	3,950,481	4,337,333	4,557,470	4,724,751	18,110	41,931	59,726	95,460	118,571	109,443
Delaware	52,533	87,617	132,851	150,054	148,481	141,488	†	†	4,042	5,171	4,480	3,219
District of Columbia ..	2,267,409	2,824,081	3,687,042	3,929,951	3,976,868	4,117,223	59,375	127,859	66,677	68,595	70,981	57,139
Florida	2,031,623	3,067,443	4,592,898	5,354,744	5,570,552	5,623,110	315,721	781,280	1,825,704	2,033,099	2,083,657	2,000,148
Georgia	2,635,438	3,442,374	4,497,299	5,346,024	5,530,320	5,698,108	106,794	261,219	678,839	807,701	707,447	628,350
Hawaii	209,135	195,152	210,680	251,071	262,526	255,366	9,422	24,996	34,299	44,990	51,477	49,490
Idaho	118,150	164,694	228,589	261,954	300,184	315,995	5,932	13,073	32,602	50,310	36,771	30,718
Illinois	5,668,566	7,113,842	9,512,165	10,531,366	11,212,425	11,578,652	166,956	620,678	1,100,032	1,541,661	1,274,607	1,201,548
Indiana	1,343,315	1,796,767	2,251,554	2,502,296	2,557,015	2,672,361	89,932	211,310	591,600	729,623	613,850	557,521
Iowa	740,760	921,320	1,156,393	1,248,348	1,261,785	1,298,494	34,311	146,688	1,000,405	1,189,516	1,165,192	549,337
Kansas	208,729	265,476	364,286	414,219	444,498	456,307	9,156	11,213	47,645	58,077	84,242	138,197
Kentucky	400,513	470,392	597,495	683,702	728,838	712,235	55,010	114,564	242,672	287,956	269,760	249,044
Louisiana	746,629	940,075	1,089,736	1,192,748	1,202,971	1,216,894	31,675	70,241	111,844	108,489	106,710	99,281
Maine	316,114	422,938	552,463	619,223	640,969	670,634	7,137	5,648	12,409	13,111	13,023	16,405
Maryland	2,205,880	3,497,182	4,792,089	5,278,869	5,535,099	5,748,151	5,354	41,717	115,071	107,285	100,249	98,850
Massachusetts	7,591,344	10,799,206	13,862,598	15,252,538	15,940,319	16,388,566	34,893	64,126	118,526	126,833	120,182	109,120
Michigan	995,384	1,327,051	1,638,367	1,751,050	1,731,507	1,740,691	25,340	55,391	120,070	149,564	163,271	127,760
Minnesota	1,004,427	1,297,457	1,622,869	1,729,682	1,757,253	1,795,111	123,571	325,758	928,396	1,178,779	1,168,273	1,163,083
Mississippi	150,123	178,142	225,484	248,970	257,215	252,514	†	8,369	21,061	29,852	32,917	31,127
Missouri	2,144,299	3,128,635	3,958,548	4,356,136	4,479,649	4,674,575	100,307	196,447	331,391	430,642	342,705	264,185
Montana	69,426	91,446	116,161	107,390	111,276	111,050	†	†	†	†	†	†
Nebraska	387,569	557,724	709,182	744,788	733,066	707,006	12,051	25,524	41,559	43,219	39,015	36,602
Nevada	7,006	9,637	73,701	98,835	130,845	111,867	29,278	104,949	143,358	150,189	149,537	133,061
New Hampshire	589,823	883,914	1,085,570	1,159,703	1,289,111	1,382,865	21,831	41,599	36,737	44,532	42,598	48,589
New Jersey	1,362,090	1,873,156	2,591,234	2,747,352	2,803,276	2,971,977	61,109	85,429	126,833	125,496	141,366	165,994
New Mexico	54,280	54,076	30,447	32,930	34,809	34,667	25,806	35,073	83,708	108,572	110,443	100,078
New York	12,519,671	17,680,799	23,511,385	25,903,697	26,742,737	28,137,325	326,329	624,764	762,214	871,255	899,389	884,033
North Carolina	3,530,337	4,808,306	6,451,308	7,001,839	7,263,282	7,705,625	4,041	38,078	186,514	260,476	286,151	297,354
North Dakota	56,000	88,860	87,938	114,109	118,499	131,991	1,145	7,885	20,198	15,292	12,964	11,857
Ohio	2,211,035	3,017,764	3,582,655	3,803,772	3,900,304	3,919,070	122,531	232,685	564,498	657,252	564,238	506,201
Oklahoma	338,276	392,427	523,630	583,898	601,224	607,899	32,527	72,537	110,336	144,428	139,022	140,970
Oregon	456,683	550,322	734,883	832,852	879,799	937,306	23,175	86,156	120,490	133,403	134,361	112,339
Pennsylvania	7,590,629	9,960,675	13,154,197	14,464,172	14,638,232	15,436,516	306,135	530,515	842,052	860,312	863,594	746,170
Rhode Island	828,715	1,237,106	1,564,624	1,702,209	1,727,591	1,812,414	4,519	10,073	†	†	†	†
South Carolina	408,127	563,952	680,369	739,911	744,752	758,663	6,627	18,374	226,848	288,920	289,924	288,939
South Dakota	69,555	99,575	119,974	125,509	132,514	134,738	18,061	23,477	41,594	51,505	50,760	36,047
Tennessee	1,971,564	3,140,336	4,500,016	4,918,450	5,120,422	5,247,334	50,921	142,256	331,287	337,188	342,166	290,090
Texas	2,490,597	3,379,710	4,376,280	4,804,428	5,043,913	5,318,949	172,327	343,221	803,401	842,359	823,269	769,819
Utah	648,035	867,956	1,012,997	1,177,439	1,370,858	1,457,704	36,348	62,880	144,226	210,120	116,470	117,056
Vermont	347,293	510,623	717,199	782,385	792,944	839,679	24,841	24,914	17,126	16,288	13,159	11,298
Virginia	944,905	1,311,743	1,841,075	1,923,966	2,015,158	2,120,835	65,804	258,642	614,287	661,698	670,139	647,248
Washington	600,315	778,678	988,571	1,073,689	1,104,511	1,129,947	51,134	104,107	161,645	162,644	159,308	163,075
West Virginia	170,653	181,181	211,877	179,112	186,523	195,658	17,926	28,634	165,043	259,876	315,675	300,580
Wisconsin	999,502	1,410,625	1,929,430	2,119,356	2,141,821	2,186,164	16,333	36,044	131,140	172,180	156,315	152,576
Wyoming	†	†	†	†	1,643	1,579	19,766	34,596	39,869	40,176	34,218	32,498
Other jurisdictions..	431,216	615,990	742,820	855,651	845,821	848,925	56,116	70,535	222,515	257,832	263,553	299,949
Guam	†	1,535	2,551	1,756	1,639	1,158	†	†	†	†	†	†
Puerto Rico	431,216	614,455	740,269	853,895	844,183	847,767	56,116	70,535	222,515	257,832	263,553	299,949

†Not applicable.
NOTE: Degree-granting institutions grant associate's or higher degrees and participate in Title IV federal financial aid programs. Some data have been revised from previously published figures. Detail may not sum to totals because of rounding.

SOURCE: U.S. Department of Education, National Center for Education Statistics, Integrated Postsecondary Education Data System (IPEDS), selected years, Spring 2001 through Spring 2015, Finance component. (This table was prepared November 2015.)

CHAPTER 4
Federal Funds for Education and Related Activities

This chapter provides information on federal support for education. The tables include detailed data on funding by specific federal agencies, funding for different levels of education and types of education-related activities, and funding for specific programs. Preceding the tables is a brief chronology of federal education legislation enacted since 1787, which provides historical context for the education funding data.

The data in this chapter primarily reflect outlays and appropriations of federal agencies. The data are compiled from budget information prepared by federal agencies. In contrast, most of the federal revenue data reported in other chapters are compiled by educational institutions or state education agencies and reported to the federal government through standardized survey forms. Tabulations based on institution- or state-reported revenue data differ substantially from federal budget reports because of numerous variations in methodology and definitions. Federal dollars are not necessarily spent by recipient institutions in the same year in which they are appropriated. In some cases, institutions cannot identify the source of federal revenues because they flow through state agencies. Some types of revenues, such as tuition and fees, are reported as revenues from students even though they may be supported by federal student aid programs. Some institutions that receive federal education funds (e.g., Department of Defense overseas and domestic schools, state education agencies, Head Start programs, and federal libraries) are not included in regular surveys, censuses, and administrative data collections conducted by the National Center for Education Statistics (NCES). Thus, the federal programs data tabulated in this chapter are not comparable with figures reported in other chapters. Readers should also be careful about comparing the data on obligations shown in table 402.10 with the data on outlays and appropriations appearing in other tables in this chapter.

Federal Education Funding

Federal on-budget funding (federal appropriations) for education increased an estimated 413 percent from fiscal year (FY) 1965 to FY 2014, after adjustment for inflation (table D, table 401.10, and figure 20). From FY 1965 to FY 1975, federal on-budget funding for education increased by 152 percent. From FY 1975 to FY 1985, there was a decrease of 16 percent. Thereafter, federal on-budget funding for education generally increased. From FY 1990 to FY 2000, after adjustment for inflation, federal on-budget funding for education increased by 30 percent. From FY 2000 to FY 2014, it increased by 63 percent.

Table D. Federal on-budget funding for education, by category: Selected fiscal years, 1965 through 2014

[In billions of constant fiscal year (FY) 2015 dollars]

Year	Total	Elementary/ secondary	Post- secondary	Other education	Research at educational institutions
1965	$37.7	$13.7	$8.5	$2.6	$12.8
1975	94.8	43.2	31.1	6.5	13.9
1980	95.7	44.5	30.8	4.3	16.1
1985	79.7	34.5	22.8	4.3	18.1
1990	90.8	38.7	24.0	5.9	22.2
1995	107.6	50.5	26.5	7.1	23.5
2000	118.3	60.3	20.7	7.5	29.8
2005	178.6	83.3	46.6	8.3	40.4
2010	198.6	94.0	54.4	10.1	40.1
2014	193.0	80.5	70.4	9.6	32.6

NOTE: Detail may not sum to totals because of rounding.
SOURCE: U.S. Department of Education, Budget Service and National Center for Education Statistics, unpublished tabulations. U.S. Office of Management and Budget, *Budget of the U.S. Government, Appendix,* various FYs. National Science Foundation, *Federal Funds for Research and Development,* various FYs.

Between FY 1990 and FY 2000, after adjustment for inflation, federal on-budget funding increased for three of the four major categories reported: elementary and secondary education (by 56 percent), other education (by 27 percent), and research at educational institutions (by 34 percent) (table D, table 401.10, and figure 20). During the same period, funding for postsecondary education decreased by 14 percent. From FY 2000 to FY 2014, after adjustment for inflation, federal on-budget funding showed a net increase of 34 percent for elementary and secondary education, 241 percent for postsecondary education, 27 percent for other education, and 9 percent for research at educational institutions. In FY 2009, federal on-budget funding for elementary and secondary education was at a record-high level ($189.4 billion in FY 2015 dollars) due to funds from the American Recovery and Reinvestment Act of 2009 (ARRA) (table 401.10).[1] For FY 2015, federal program funds totaled $77.6 billion for elementary and secondary education, $77.0 billion for postsecondary education, $9.5 billion for other education programs, and an estimated $32.5 billion for research at educational institutions (tables 401.10 and 401.30).

[1] Throughout this chapter, all education funds from ARRA are included in FY 2009. Most of these funds had a 2-year availability, meaning that they were available for the U.S. Department of Education to obligate during FY 2009 and FY 2010.

After adjustment for inflation, off-budget support (federal support for education not tied to appropriations) and nonfederal funds generated by federal legislation (e.g., private loans, grants, and aid) showed an increase of 134 percent between FY 1990 ($19.6 billion in FY 2015 dollars) and FY 2000 ($46.0 billion in FY 2015 dollars) (table 401.10). In FY 2014, these same funds totaled $101.9 billion in FY 2015 dollars, an increase of 122 percent over FY 2000. In FY 2015, these funds totaled $101.5 billion.

In FY 2014, federal on-budget funds for education totaled $190.5 billion in current dollars (figure 21 and table 401.20). The U.S. Department of Education provided 50 percent ($95.7 billion) of this total. Funds exceeding $3 billion also came from the U.S. Department of Health and Human Services ($28.9 billion), the U.S. Department of Agriculture ($23.1 billion), the U.S. Department of Veterans Affairs ($13.1 billion), the U.S. Department of Defense ($7.3 billion), the National Science Foundation ($5.5 billion), the U.S. Department of Labor ($5.5 billion), and the U.S. Department of Energy ($3.3 billion).

Chronology of Federal Education Legislation

A capsule view of the history of federal education activities is provided in the following list of selected legislation:

1787 *Northwest Ordinance* authorized land grants for the establishment of educational institutions.

1802 *An Act Fixing the Military Peace Establishment of the United States* established the U.S. Military Academy. (The U.S. Naval Academy was established in 1845 by the Secretary of the Navy.)

1862 *First Morrill Act* authorized public land grants to the states for the establishment and maintenance of agricultural and mechanical colleges.

1867 *Department of Education Act* authorized the establishment of the U.S. Department of Education.[2]

1876 *Appropriation Act*, U.S. Department of the Treasury, established the U.S. Coast Guard Academy.

1890 *Second Morrill Act* provided for monetary grants for support of instruction in the agricultural and mechanical colleges.

1911 *State Marine School Act* authorized federal funds to be used for the benefit of any nautical school in any of 11 specified seaport cities.

1917 *Smith-Hughes Act* provided for grants to states for support of vocational education.

---

[2] The U.S. Department of Education as established in 1867 was later known as the Office of Education. In 1980, under Public Law 96-88, it became a cabinet-level department. Therefore, for purposes of consistency, it is referred to as the "U.S. Department of Education" even in those tables covering years when it was officially the Office of Education.

1918 *Vocational Rehabilitation Act* provided for grants for rehabilitation through training of World War I veterans.

1920 *Smith-Bankhead Act* authorized grants to states for vocational rehabilitation programs.

1935 *Bankhead-Jones Act* (Public Law 74-182) authorized grants to states for agricultural experiment stations.

Agricultural Adjustment Act (Public Law 74-320) authorized 30 percent of the annual customs receipts to be used to encourage the exportation and domestic consumption of agricultural commodities. Commodities purchased under this authorization began to be used in school lunch programs in 1936. The National School Lunch Act of 1946 continued and expanded this assistance.

1936 *An Act to Further the Development and Maintenance of an Adequate and Well-Balanced American Merchant Marine* (Public Law 74-415) established the U.S. Merchant Marine Academy.

1937 *National Cancer Institute Act* (Public Law 75-244) established the Public Health Service fellowship program.

1941 *Amendment to Lanham Act of 1940* authorized federal aid for construction, maintenance, and operation of schools in federally impacted areas. Such assistance was continued under Public Law 815 and Public Law 874, 81st Congress, in 1950.

1943 *Vocational Rehabilitation Act* (Public Law 78-16) provided assistance to veterans with disabilities.

School Lunch Indemnity Plan (Public Law 78-129) provided funds for local lunch food purchases.

1944 *Servicemen's Readjustment Act* (Public Law 78-346), known as the GI Bill, provided assistance for the education of veterans.

Surplus Property Act (Public Law 78-457) authorized transfer of surplus property to educational institutions.

1946 *National School Lunch Act* (Public Law 79-396) authorized assistance through grants-in-aid and other means to states to assist in providing adequate foods and facilities for the establishment, maintenance, operation, and expansion of nonprofit school lunch programs.

George-Barden Act (Public Law 80-402) expanded federal support of vocational education.

1948 *United States Information and Educational Exchange Act* (Public Law 80-402) provided for the interchange of people, knowledge, and skills between the United States and other countries.

1949 *Federal Property and Administrative Services Act* (Public Law 81-152) provided for donation of surplus property to educational institutions and for other public purposes.

1950 *Financial Assistance for Local Educational Agencies Affected by Federal Activities* (Public Law 81-815 and Public Law 81-874) provided assistance for construction (Public Law 815) and operation (Public Law 874) of schools in federally affected areas.

Housing Act (Public Law 81-475) authorized loans for construction of college housing facilities.

1954 *An Act for the Establishment of the United States Air Force Academy and Other Purposes* (Public Law 83-325) established the U.S. Air Force Academy.

Educational Research Act (Public Law 83-531) authorized cooperative arrangements with universities, colleges, and state educational agencies for educational research.

School Milk Program Act (Public Law 83-597) provided funds for purchase of milk for school lunch programs.

1956 *Library Services Act* (Public Law 84-597) provided grants to states for extension and improvement of rural public library services.

1957 *Practical Nurse Training Act* (Public Law 84-911) provided grants to states for practical nurse training.

1958 *National Defense Education Act* (Public Law 85-864) provided assistance to state and local school systems for instruction in science, mathematics, modern foreign languages, and other critical subjects; state statistical services; guidance, counseling, and testing services and training institutes; higher education student loans and fellowships as well as foreign language study and training; experimentation and dissemination of information on more effective use of television, motion pictures, and related media for educational purposes; and vocational education for technical occupations necessary to the national defense.

Education of Mentally Retarded Children Act (Public Law 85-926) authorized federal assistance for training teachers of the disabled.

Captioned Films for the Deaf Act (Public Law 85-905) authorized a loan service of captioned films for the deaf.

1961 *Area Redevelopment Act* (Public Law 87-27) included provisions for training or retraining of people in redevelopment areas.

1962 *Manpower Development and Training Act* (Public Law 87-415) provided training in new and improved skills for the unemployed and underemployed.

Migration and Refugee Assistance Act of 1962 (Public Law 87-510) authorized loans, advances, and grants for education and training of refugees.

1963 *Health Professions Educational Assistance Act of 1963* (Public Law 88-129) provided funds to expand teaching facilities and for loans to students in the health professions.

Vocational Education Act of 1963 (Public Law 88-210, Part A) increased federal support of vocational education schools; vocational work-study programs; and research, training, and demonstrations in vocational education.

Higher Education Facilities Act of 1963 (Public Law 88-204) authorized grants and loans for classrooms, libraries, and laboratories in public community colleges and technical institutes, as well as undergraduate and graduate facilities in other higher education institutions.

1964 *Civil Rights Act of 1964* (Public Law 88-352) authorized the Commissioner of Education to arrange for support for higher education institutions and school districts to provide inservice programs for assisting instructional staff in dealing with problems caused by desegregation.

Economic Opportunity Act of 1964 (Public Law 88-452) authorized grants for college work-study programs for students from low-income families; established a Job Corps program and authorized support for work-training programs to provide education and vocational training and work experience opportunities in welfare programs; authorized support of education and training activities and of community action programs, including Head Start, Follow Through, and Upward Bound; and authorized the establishment of Volunteers in Service to America (VISTA).

1965 *Elementary and Secondary Education Act of 1965* (Public Law 89-10) authorized grants for elementary and secondary school programs for children of low-income families; school library resources, textbooks, and other instructional materials for school children; supplementary educational centers and services; strengthening state education agencies; and educational research and research training.

Health Professions Educational Assistance Amendments of 1965 (Public Law 89-290) authorized scholarships to aid needy students in the health professions.

Higher Education Act of 1965 (Public Law 89-329) provided grants for university community service programs, college library assistance, library training and research, strengthening developing institutions, teacher training programs, and undergraduate instructional equipment. Authorized insured student loans, established a National Teacher Corps, and provided for graduate teacher training fellowships.

National Foundation on the Arts and the Humanities Act (Public Law 89-209) authorized grants and loans for projects in the creative and performing arts and for research, training, and scholarly publications in the humanities.

National Technical Institute for the Deaf Act (Public Law 89-36) provided for the establishment, construction, equipping, and operation of a residential school for postsecondary education and technical training of the deaf.

School Assistance in Disaster Areas Act (Public Law 89-313) provided for assistance to local education agencies to help meet exceptional costs resulting from a major disaster.

1966 *International Education Act* (Public Law 89-698) provided grants to higher education institutions for the establishment, strengthening, and operation of centers for research and training in international studies and the international aspects of other fields of study.

National Sea Grant College and Program Act (Public Law 89-688) authorized the establishment and operation of Sea Grant Colleges and programs by initiating and supporting programs of education and research in the various fields relating to the development of marine resources.

Adult Education Act (Public Law 89-750) authorized grants to states for the encouragement and expansion of educational programs for adults, including training of teachers of adults and demonstrations in adult education (previously part of Economic Opportunity Act of 1964).

Model Secondary School for the Deaf Act (Public Law 89-694) authorized the establishment and operation, by Gallaudet College, of a model secondary school for the deaf.

1967 *Education Professions Development Act* (Public Law 90-35) amended the Higher Education Act of 1965 for the purpose of improving the quality of teaching and to help meet critical shortages of adequately trained educational personnel.

Public Broadcasting Act of 1967 (Public Law 90-129) established a Corporation for Public Broadcasting to assume major responsibility in channeling federal funds to noncommercial radio and television stations, program production groups, and educational television networks; conduct research, demonstration, or training in matters related to noncommercial broadcasting; and award grants for construction of educational radio and television facilities.

1968 *Elementary and Secondary Education Amendments of 1968* (Public Law 90-247) modified existing programs and authorized support of regional centers for education of children with disabilities, model centers and services for deaf-blind children, recruitment of personnel and dissemination of information on education of children with disabilities; technical assistance in education to rural areas; support of dropout prevention projects; and support of bilingual education programs.

Handicapped Children's Early Education Assistance Act (Public Law 90-538) authorized preschool and early education programs for children with disabilities.

Vocational Education Amendments of 1968 (Public Law 90-576) modified existing programs and provided for a National Advisory Council on Vocational Education and collection and dissemination of information for programs administered by the Commissioner of Education.

1970 *Elementary and Secondary Education Assistance Programs, Extension* (Public Law 91-230) authorized comprehensive planning and evaluation grants to state and local education agencies; provided for the establishment of a National Commission on School Finance.

National Commission on Libraries and Information Science Act (Public Law 91-345) established a National Commission on Libraries and Information Science to effectively utilize the nation's educational resources.

Office of Education Appropriation Act (Public Law 91-380) provided emergency school assistance to desegregating local education agencies.

Environmental Education Act (Public Law 91-516) established an Office of Environmental Education to develop curriculum and initiate and maintain environmental education programs at the elementary/secondary levels; disseminate information; provide training programs for teachers and other educational, public, community, labor, and industrial leaders and employees; provide community education programs; and distribute material dealing with the environment and ecology.

Drug Abuse Education Act of 1970 (Public Law 91-527) provided for development, demonstration, and evaluation of curricula on the problems of drug abuse.

1971 *Comprehensive Health Manpower Training Act of 1971* (Public Law 92-257) amended Title VII of the Public Health Service Act, increasing and expanding provisions for health manpower training and training facilities.

1972 *Drug Abuse Office and Treatment Act of 1972* (Public Law 92-255) established a Special Action Office for Drug Abuse Prevention to provide overall planning and policy for all federal drug-abuse prevention functions; a National Advisory Council for Drug Abuse Prevention; community assistance grants for community mental health centers for treatment and rehabilitation of people with drug-abuse problems; and, in December 1974, a National Institute on Drug Abuse.

Education Amendments of 1972 (Public Law 92-318) established the Education Division in the U.S. Department of Health, Education, and Welfare and the National Institute of Education; general aid for higher education institutions; federal matching grants for state Student Incentive Grants; a National Commission on Financing Postsecondary Education; State Advisory Councils on Community Colleges; a Bureau of Occupational and Adult Education and State Grants for the design, establishment, and conduct of postsecondary occupational education; and a bureau-level Office of Indian Education. Amended current U.S. Department of Education programs to increase their effectiveness and better meet special needs. Prohibited sex bias in admission to vocational, professional, and graduate schools, and public institutions of undergraduate higher education.

1973 *Older Americans Comprehensive Services Amendment of 1973* (Public Law 93-29) made available to older citizens comprehensive programs of health, education, and social services.

Comprehensive Employment and Training Act of 1973 (Public Law 93-203) provided for employment and training opportunities for unemployed and underemployed people. Extended and expanded provisions in the Manpower Development and Training Act of 1962, Title I of the Economic Opportunity Act of 1962, Title I of the Economic Opportunity Act of 1964, and the Emergency Employment Act of 1971 as in effect prior to June 30, 1973.

1974 *Education Amendments of 1974* (Public Law 93-380) provided for the consolidation of certain programs and established a National Center for Education Statistics.

Juvenile Justice and Delinquency Prevention Act of 1974 (Public Law 93-415) provided for technical assistance, staff training, centralized research, and resources to develop and implement programs to keep students in elementary and secondary schools; and established, in the U.S. Department of Justice, a National Institute for Juvenile Justice and Delinquency Prevention.

1975 *Indian Self-Determination and Education Assistance Act* (Public Law 93-638) provided for increased participation of American Indians/Alaska Natives in the establishment and conduct of their education programs and services.

Harry S Truman Memorial Scholarship Act (Public Law 93-642) established the Harry S Truman Scholarship Foundation and created a perpetual education scholarship fund for young Americans to prepare for and pursue careers in public service.

Education for All Handicapped Children Act (Public Law 94-142) provided that all children with disabilities have available to them a free appropriate education designed to meet their unique needs.

1976 *Educational Broadcasting Facilities and Telecommunications Demonstration Act of 1976* (Public Law 94-309) established a telecommunications demonstration program to promote the development of nonbroadcast telecommunications facilities and services for the transmission, distribution, and delivery of health, education, and public or social service information.

1977 *Youth Employment and Demonstration Projects Act of 1977* (Public Law 95-93) established a youth employment training program including, among other activities, promotion of education-to-work transition, literacy training and bilingual training, and attainment of certificates of high school equivalency.

Career Education Incentive Act (Public Law 95-207) authorized the establishment of a career education program for elementary and secondary schools.

1978 *Tribally Controlled Community College Assistance Act of 1978* (Public Law 95-471) provided federal funds for the operation and improvement of tribally controlled community colleges for American Indian/Alaska Native students.

Middle Income Student Assistance Act (Public Law 95-566) modified the provisions for student financial assistance programs to allow middle-income as well as low-income students attending college or other postsecondary institutions to qualify for federal education assistance.

1979 *Department of Education Organization Act* (Public Law 96-88) established a U.S. Department of Education containing functions from the Education Division of the U.S. Department of Health, Education, and Welfare (HEW) along with other selected education programs from HEW, the U.S. Department of Justice, U.S. Department of Labor, and the National Science Foundation.

1980 *Asbestos School Hazard Detection and Control Act of 1980* (Public Law 96-270) established a program for inspection of schools for detection of hazardous asbestos materials and provided loans to assist educational agencies to contain or remove and replace such materials.

1981 *Education Consolidation and Improvement Act of 1981* (Part of Public Law 97-35) consolidated 42 programs into 7 programs to be funded under the elementary and secondary block grant authority.

1983 *Student Loan Consolidation and Technical Amendments Act of 1983* (Public Law 98-79) established an 8 percent interest rate for Guaranteed Student Loans and an extended Family Contribution Schedule.

Challenge Grant Amendments of 1983 (Public Law 98-95) amended Title III of the Higher Education Act of 1965, and added authorization of the Challenge Grant program. The Challenge Grant program provides funds to eligible institutions on a matching basis as an incentive to seek alternative sources of funding.

Education of the Handicapped Act Amendments of 1983 (Public Law 98-199) added the Architectural Barrier amendment (providing funds for altering existing buildings and equipment to make them accessible to those with physical disabilities) and clarified participation of children with disabilities in private schools.

1984 *Education for Economic Security Act* (Public Law 98-377) added new science and mathematics programs for elementary, secondary, and postsecondary education. The new programs included magnet schools, excellence in education, and equal access.

Carl D. Perkins Vocational Education Act (Public Law 98-524) continued federal assistance for vocational education through FY 1989. The act replaced the Vocational Education Act of 1963. It provided aid to the states to make vocational education programs accessible to all people, including disabled and disadvantaged, single parents and homemakers, and the incarcerated.

Human Services Reauthorization Act (Public Law 98-558) created a Carl D. Perkins scholarship program, a National Talented Teachers Fellowship program, a Federal Merit Scholarships program, and a Leadership in Educational Administration program.

1985 *Montgomery GI Bill—Active Duty* (Public Law 98-525), brought about a new GI Bill for individuals who initially entered active military duty on or after July 1, 1985.

Montgomery GI Bill—Selected Reserve (Public Law 98-525), established an education program for members of the Selected Reserve (which includes the National Guard) who enlist, reenlist, or extend an enlistment after June 30, 1985, for a 6-year period.

1986 *Handicapped Children's Protection Act of 1986* (Public Law 99-372) allowed parents of children with disabilities to collect attorneys' fees in cases brought under the Education of the Handicapped Act and provided that the Education of the Handicapped Act does not preempt other laws, such as Section 504 of the Rehabilitation Act.

Drug-Free Schools and Communities Act of 1986 (Part of Public Law 99-570) established programs for drug abuse education and prevention, coordinated with related community efforts and resources, through the use of federal financial assistance.

1988 *Augustus F. Hawkins-Robert T. Stafford Elementary and Secondary School Improvement Amendments of 1988* (Public Law 100-297) reauthorized through 1993 major elementary and secondary education programs, including Chapter 1, Chapter 2, Bilingual Education, Math-Science Education, Magnet Schools, Impact Aid, Indian Education, Adult Education, and other smaller education programs.

Stewart B. McKinney Homeless Assistance Amendments Act of 1988 (Public Law 100-628) extended for 2 additional years programs providing assistance to the homeless, including literacy training for homeless adults and education for homeless youths.

Tax Reform Technical Amendments (Public Law 100-647) authorized an Education Savings Bond for the purpose of postsecondary educational expenses. The bill grants tax exclusion for interest earned on regular series EE savings bonds.

1989 *Childhood Education and Development Act of 1989* (Part of Public Law 101-239) authorized the appropriations to expand Head Start programs and programs carried out under the Elementary and Secondary Education Act of 1965 to include child care services.

1990 *Excellence in Mathematics, Science and Engineering Education Act of 1990* (Public Law 101-589) created a national mathematics and science clearinghouse and created several other mathematics, science, and engineering education programs.

Student Right-To-Know and Campus Security Act (Public Law 101-542) required higher education institutions receiving federal financial assistance to provide certain information about graduation rates of student-athletes and about campus crime statistics and security policies. (The 1990 campus crime and security legislation, along with later acts that amended it, is generally referred to as "the Clery Act.")

Americans with Disabilities Act of 1990 (Public Law 101-336) prohibited discrimination against people with disabilities.

National and Community Service Act of 1990 (Public Law 101-610) increased school and college-based community service opportunities and authorized the President's Points of Light Foundation.

1991 *National Literacy Act of 1991* (Public Law 102-73) established the National Institute for Literacy, the National Institute Board, and the Interagency Task Force on Literacy. Amended various federal laws to establish and extend various literacy programs.

High-Performance Computing Act of 1991 (Public Law 102-194) directed the President to implement a National High-Performance Computing Program. Provided for (1) establishment of a National Research and Education Network; (2) standards and guidelines for high-performance networks; and (3) the responsibility of certain federal departments and agencies with regard to the Network.

Veterans' Educational Assistance Amendments of 1991 (Public Law 102-127) restored certain educational benefits available to reserve and active-duty personnel under the Montgomery GI Bill to students whose courses of studies were interrupted by the Persian Gulf War.

Civil Rights Act of 1991 (Public Law 102-166) amended the Civil Rights Act of 1964, the Age Discrimination in Employment Act of 1967, and the Americans with Disabilities Act of 1990, with regard to employment discrimination. Established the Technical Assistance Training Institute.

1992 *Ready-To-Learn Act* (Public Law 102-545) amended the General Education Provisions Act to establish Ready-To-Learn Television programs to support educational programming and related materials for preschool and elementary school children and their parents, child care providers, and educators.

1993 *Student Loan Reform Act* (Public Law 103-66) reformed the student aid process by phasing in a system of direct lending designed to provide savings for taxpayers and students. Allows students to choose among a variety of repayment options, including income contingency.

National Service Trust Act (Public Law 103-82) amended the National and Community Service Act of 1990 to establish a Corporation for National Service. In addition, provided education grants up to $4,725 per year for 2 years to people age 17 or older who perform community service before, during, or after postsecondary education.

1994 *Goals 2000: Educate America Act* (Public Law 103-227) established a new federal partnership through a system of grants to states and local communities to reform the nation's education system. The Act formalized the national education goals and established the National Education Goals Panel.

School-to-Work Opportunities Act of 1994 (Public Law 103-239) established a national framework within which states and communities can develop School-to-Work Opportunities systems to prepare young people for first jobs and continuing education. The Act also provided money to states and communities to develop a system of programs that include work-based learning, school-based learning, and connecting activities components.

Safe Schools Act of 1994 (Part of Public Law 103-227) authorized the award of competitive grants to local educational agencies with serious crime to implement violence prevention activities such as conflict resolution and peer mediation.

1996 *Contract With America: Unfunded Mandates* (Public Law 104-4) ended the imposition, in the absence of full consideration by Congress, of federal mandates on state, local, and tribal governments without adequate funding, in a manner that may displace other essential governmental priorities; and ensured that the federal government pays the costs incurred by those governments in complying with certain requirements under federal statutes and regulations.

1997 *The Taxpayer Relief Act of 1997* (Public Law 105-34) enacted the Hope Scholarship and Life-Long Learning Tax Credit provisions into law.

Emergency Student Loan Consolidation Act of 1997 (Public Law 105-78) amended the Higher Education Act of 1965 to provide for improved student loan consolidation services.

1998 *Workforce Investment Act of 1998* (Public Law 105-220) enacted the Adult Education and Family Literacy Act, and substantially revised and extended, through FY 2003, the Rehabilitation Act of 1973.

Jeanne Clery Disclosure of Campus Security Policy and Campus Crime Statistics Act (Public Law 105-244) expanded crime categories that must be reported by postsecondary institutions.

Omnibus Consolidated and Emergency Supplemental Appropriations Act, 1999 (Public Law 105-277) enacted the Reading Excellence Act, to promote the ability of children to read independently by the third grade; and earmarked funds to help states and school districts reduce class sizes in the early grades.

Charter School Expansion Act (Public Law 105-278) amended the charter school program, enacted in 1994 as Title X, Part C of the Elementary and Secondary Education Act of 1965.

Carl D. Perkins Vocational and Applied Technology Education Amendments of 1998 (Public Law 105-332) revised, in its entirety, the Carl D. Perkins Vocational and Applied Technology Education Act, and reauthorized the Act through FY 2003.

Assistive Technology Act of 1998 (Public Law 105-394) replaced the Technology-Related Assistance for Individuals with Disabilities Act of 1988 with a new Act, authorized through FY 2004, to address the assistive-technology needs of individuals with disabilities.

1999 *Education Flexibility Partnership Act of 1999* (Public Law 106-25) authorized the Secretary of Education to allow all states to participate in the Education Flexibility Partnership program.

District of Columbia College Access Act of 1999 (Public Law 106-98) established a program to afford high school graduates from the District of Columbia the benefits of in-state tuition at state colleges and universities outside the District of Columbia.

2000 *The National Defense Authorization Act for Fiscal Year 2001* (Public Law 106-398) included, as Title XVIII, the Impact Aid Reauthorization Act of 2000, which extended the Impact Aid programs through FY 2003.

College Scholarship Fraud Prevention Act of 2000 (Public Law 106-420) enhanced federal penalties for offenses involving scholarship fraud; required an annual scholarship fraud report by the Attorney General, the Secretary of Education, and the Federal Trade Commission (FTC); and required the Secretary of Education, in conjunction with the FTC, to maintain a scholarship fraud awareness website.

Consolidated Appropriations Act 2001 (Public Law 106-554) created a new program of assistance for school repair and renovation, and amended the Elementary and Secondary Education Act of 1965 to authorize credit enhancement initiatives to help charter schools obtain, construct, or repair facilities; reauthorized the Even Start program; and enacted the Children's Internet Protection Act.

2001 *50th Anniversary of Brown v. the Board of Education* (Public Law 107-41) established a commission for the purpose of encouraging and providing for the commemoration of the 50th anniversary of the 1954 Supreme Court decision *Brown* v. *Board of Education.*

2002 *No Child Left Behind Act of 2001* (Public Law 107-110) provided for the comprehensive reauthorization of the Elementary and Secondary Education Act of 1965, incorporating specific proposals in such areas as testing, accountability, parental choice, and early reading.

Education Sciences Reform Act (Public Law 107-279) established the Institute of Education Sciences within the U.S. Department of Education to carry out a coordinated, focused agenda of high-quality research, statistics, and evaluation that is relevant to the educational challenges of the nation.

The Higher Education Relief Opportunities for Students Act of 2001 (Public Law 107-122) provided the Secretary of Education with waiver authority over student financial aid programs under Title IV of the Higher Education Act of 1965, to deal with student and family situations resulting from the September 11, 2001, terrorist attacks.

Public Law 107-139 amended Title IV of the Higher Education Act to establish fixed interest rates for student and parent borrowers.

2003 *The Higher Education Relief Opportunities for Students Act of 2003* (Public Law 108-76) provided the Secretary of Education with waiver authority over student financial aid programs under Title IV of the Higher Education Act of 1965, to deal with student and family situations resulting from wars or national emergencies.

2004 *Assistive Technology Act of 2004* (Public Law 108-364) reauthorized the Assistive Technology program, administered by the Department of Education.

Taxpayer-Teacher Protection Act of 2004 (Public Law 108-409) temporarily stopped excessive special allowance payments to certain lenders under the Federal Family Education Loan (FFEL) Program and increased the amount of loans that can be forgiven for certain borrowers who are highly qualified mathematics, science, and special education teachers who serve in high-poverty schools for 5 years.

Individuals with Disabilities Education Improvement Act of 2004 (Public Law 108-446) provided a comprehensive reauthorization of the Individuals with Disabilities Education Act.

2005 *Student Grant Hurricane and Disaster Relief Act* (Public Law 109-67) authorized the Secretary of Education to waive certain repayment requirements for students receiving campus-based federal grant assistance if they were residing in, employed in, or attending an institution of higher education located in a major disaster area, or their attendance was interrupted because of the disaster.

Natural Disaster Student Aid Fairness Act (Public Law 109-86) authorized the Secretary of Education during FY 2006 to reallocate campus-based student aid funds to institutions of higher learning in Louisiana, Mississippi, Alabama, and Texas, or institutions that had accepted students displaced by Hurricane Katrina or Rita. The law also waived requirements for matching funds that are normally imposed on institutions and students.

Hurricane Education Recovery Act (Public Law 109-148, provision in the Defense Department Appropriations Act for FY 2006) provided funds for states affected by Hurricane Katrina to restart school operations, provide temporary emergency aid for displaced students, and assist homeless youth. The law also permitted the Secretary of Education to extend deadlines under the Individuals with Disabilities Education Act for those affected by Katrina or Rita.

2006 *Higher Education Reconciliation Act of 2005* (Public Law 109-171) made various amendments to programs of student financial assistance under Title IV of the Higher Education Act of 1965.

Public Law 109-211 reauthorized the "ED-FLEX" program (under the Education Flexibility Partnership Act of 1999), under which the Secretary of Education permits states to waive certain requirements of federal statutes and regulations if they meet certain conditions.

Carl D. Perkins Career and Technical Education Improvement Act of 2006 (Public Law 109-270) reauthorized the vocational and technical education programs under the Perkins Act through 2012.

2007 *America COMPETES Act* (or "*America Creating Opportunities to Meaningfully Promote Excellence in Technology, Education, and Science Act*") (Public Law 110-69) created new STEM (science, technology, engineering, and mathematics) education programs in various agencies, including the Department of Education.

College Cost Reduction and Access Act of 2007 (Public Law 110-84) reduced interest rates on student loans and made other amendments to the Higher Education Act of 1965 to make college more accessible and affordable.

Public Law 110-93 made permanent the waiver authority of the Secretary of Education with respect to student financial assistance during a war or other military operation or national emergency.

2008 *Ensuring Continued Access to Student Loans Act of 2008* (Public Law 110-227) provided various authorities to the Department of Education, among other provisions, to help ensure that college students and their parents continue to have access to loans in the tight credit market.

Higher Education Opportunity Act (Public Law 110-315) provided a comprehensive reauthorization of the Higher Education Act of 1965.

2009 *American Recovery and Reinvestment Act of 2009* (Public Law 111-5) provided about $100 billion to state education systems and supplemental appropriations for several Department of Education programs.

Public Law 111-39 made miscellaneous and technical amendments to the Higher Education Act of 1965.

2010 *Health Care and Education Reconciliation Act of 2010* (Public Law 111-152) included, as Title II, the "SAFRA Act" (also known as the "Student Aid and Fiscal Responsibility Act"). The SAFRA Act ended the federal government's role in subsidizing financial institutions that make student loans through the Federal Family Education Loan (FFEL) Program under Part B of Title IV of the Higher Education Act of 1965 (HEA), and correspondingly expanded the Federal Direct Student Loan Program administered by the Department of Education under Part D of Title IV of the HEA.

Public Law 111-226 provided an additional $10 billion to states and school districts, through an "Education Jobs Fund" modeled closely on the State Fiscal Stabilization Fund created by the 2009 Recovery Act, to hire (or avoid laying off) teachers and other educators.

2013 *The Bipartisan Student Loan Certainty Act of 2013* (Public Law 113-28) amended the Higher Education Act of 1965 (HEA) to govern the interest rates on the various categories of student loans under Title IV of the HEA.

Violence Against Women Reauthorization Act of 2013 (Public Law 113-4) amended the Clery Act, increasing the responsibility of postsecondary institutions to prevent, address, and report crimes on campus.

2014 *Workforce Innovation and Opportunity Act* (Public Law 113-128) amended the Workforce Investment Act of 1998 to strengthen the U.S. workforce development system through innovation in, and alignment and improvement of, employment, training, and education programs in the United States, and to promote individual and national economic growth, and for other purposes.

Public Law 113-174 extended the National Advisory Committee on Institutional Quality and Integrity and the Advisory Committee on Student Financial Assistance for 1 year.

2015 *Need-Based Educational Aid Act of 2015* (Public Law 114-44) amended the Improving America's Schools Act of 1994 to extend through FY 2022 the antitrust exemption that allows higher education institutions that admit all students on a need-blind basis to enter or attempt to enter into agreements among themselves regarding the administration of need-based financial aid.

STEM Education Act of 2015 (Public Law 114-59) defined STEM education to include computer science, and provided for continued support for existing STEM education programs at the National Science Foundation.

Every Student Succeeds Act (Public Law 114-95) reauthorized and amended the Elementary and Secondary Education Act of 1965, incorporating provisions to expand state responsibility over schools, provide grants to charter schools, and reduce the federal test-based accountability system of the No Child Left Behind Act.

Federal Perkins Loan Program Extension Act of 2015 (Public Law 114-105) temporarily extended the Federal Perkins Loan program, allowing continued disbursement of loans to current undergraduate borrowers through September 30, 2017.

Figure 20. Federal on-budget funds for education, by level or other educational purpose: Selected years, 1965 through 2015

Billions of constant fiscal year 2015 dollars

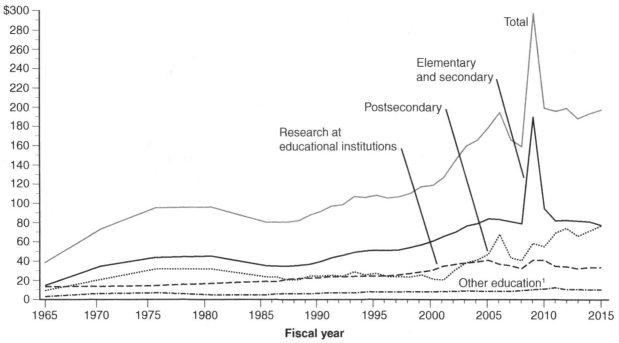

[1]Other education includes libraries, museums, cultural activities, and miscellaneous research.

NOTE: The increase in postsecondary expenditures in 2006 resulted primarily from an accounting adjustment. Amounts for 2009 include funds from the American Recovery and Reinvestment Act of 2009 (ARRA). Data for research at educational institutions are estimated for 2015.

SOURCE: U.S. Department of Education, Budget Service, unpublished tabulations. U.S. Department of Education, National Center for Education Statistics, unpublished tabulations. U.S. Office of Management and Budget, *Budget of the U.S. Government, Appendix,* fiscal years 1967 through 2016. National Science Foundation, *Federal Funds for Research and Development,* fiscal years 1967 through 2015.

Figure 21. Percentage distribution of federal on-budget funds for education, by agency: Fiscal year 2014

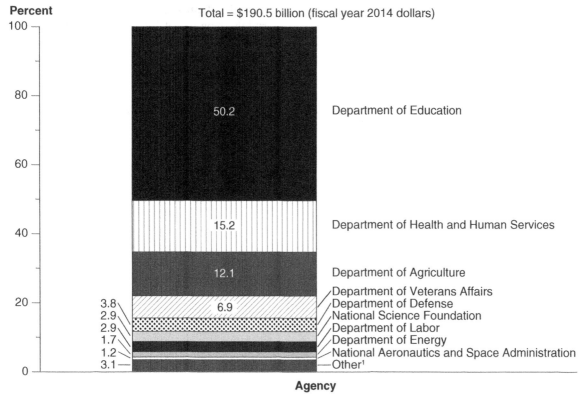

[1]In addition to the nine agencies shown in this figure, other agencies provide smaller amounts of funding for education.

NOTE: On-budget funds are tied to federal appropriations for education programs. Detail may not sum to totals because of rounding.

SOURCE: U.S. Department of Education, National Center for Education Statistics, unpublished tabulations. U.S. Office of Management and Budget, *Budget of the U.S. Government, Appendix,* fiscal year 2015. National Science Foundation, *Federal Funds for Research and Development,* fiscal year 2014.

Table 401.10. Federal support and estimated federal tax expenditures for education, by category: Selected fiscal years, 1965 through 2015.
[In thousands of dollars]

Fiscal year	Total on-budget support, off-budget support, and nonfederal funds generated by federal legislation	On-budget support[1] Total	Elementary and secondary	Post-secondary	Other education[3]	Research at educational institutions	Off-budget support and nonfederal funds generated by federal legislation — Off-budget support Total	Direct Loan Program[4]	Federal Family Education Loan Program[5]	Nonfederal funds — Perkins Loans[6]	Income Contingent Loans[7]	Leveraging Educational Assistance Partnerships[8]	Supplemental Educational Opportunity Grants[9]	Work-Study Aid[10]	Estimated federal tax expenditures for education[2]
1	2	3	4	5	6	7	8	9	10	11	12	13	14	15	16
Current dollars															
1965	$5,324,767	$5,331,016	$1,942,577	$1,197,511	$374,652	$1,816,276	-$6,249	†	†	$16,111	†	†	†	-$22,360	—
1970	13,365,315	12,526,499	5,830,442	3,447,697	964,719	2,283,641	838,816	†	$770,000	20,976	†	†	†	47,840	—
1975	24,451,787	23,288,120	10,617,195	7,644,037	1,608,478	3,418,410	1,163,667	†	1,233,000	35,667	†	$20,000	†	-125,000	$8,605,000
1980	39,310,241	34,493,502	16,027,686	11,115,882	1,548,730	5,801,204	4,816,739	†	4,598,000	31,778	†	76,800	†	110,161	13,320,000
1985	47,655,763	39,027,876	16,901,334	11,174,379	2,107,588	8,844,575	8,627,887	†	8,467,000	21,387	†	76,000	†	63,500	19,105,000
1986	48,260,015	39,962,901	17,049,940	11,283,589	2,620,021	9,009,351	8,297,114	†	8,142,000	20,203	†	72,700	†	62,211	20,425,000
1987	50,606,736	41,194,718	17,535,707	10,299,998	2,820,407	10,538,606	9,412,018	†	9,272,000	20,889	$556	76,000	†	42,573	20,830,000
1988	53,965,521	43,454,424	18,564,859	10,657,530	2,981,571	11,250,464	10,511,097	†	10,380,000	20,637	479	72,800	$65,140	37,181	17,025,000
1989	59,418,905	48,269,575	19,809,528	13,269,888	3,180,334	12,009,825	11,149,330	†	10,938,000	20,390	549	71,900		53,351	17,755,000
1990	62,778,792	51,624,342	21,984,361	13,650,915	3,383,031	12,606,035	11,154,450	†	10,826,000	15,014	500	59,181	127,719	126,036	19,040,000
1991	70,349,116	57,599,477	25,418,031	14,707,407	3,698,617	13,775,422	12,749,639	†	12,372,000	17,349	500	63,530	131,115	165,145	18,995,000
1992	74,481,656	60,483,092	27,926,887	14,387,387	3,991,955	14,176,863	13,998,564	†	13,568,000	17,333	542	72,000	175,656	165,033	19,950,000
1993	84,692,869	67,740,617	30,834,326	17,844,015	4,107,193	14,955,083	16,952,252	†	16,524,000	29,255	†	72,429	172,023	154,545	21,010,000
1994	92,718,577	68,254,205	32,304,356	16,177,051	4,483,704	15,289,094	24,464,372	$813,000	23,214,000	52,667	†	72,429	172,000	140,276	22,630,000
1995	95,763,287	71,639,520	33,623,809	17,618,137	4,719,655	15,677,919	24,123,767	5,161,000	18,519,000	52,667	500	63,400	181,000	146,700	24,600,000
1996	96,795,962	72,362,362	34,391,501	15,775,508	4,828,038	16,332,315	25,468,600	8,357,000	16,711,000	31,100	500	31,400	179,000	159,100	26,340,000
1997	103,140,145	73,731,845	35,478,905	15,959,425	5,021,163	17,272,352	29,408,300	9,838,000	19,163,000	52,700	542	50,000	228,200	76,400	28,125,000
1998	107,706,075	76,909,233	37,486,166	15,799,570	5,148,492	18,475,005	30,796,842	10,400,100	20,002,500	45,000	†	25,000	240,950	83,292	29,540,000
1999	113,285,097	82,863,597	39,937,911	17,651,199	5,318,020	19,956,467	30,421,500	9,953,000	20,107,000	33,300	†	25,000	255,900	47,300	37,360,000
2000	119,367,271	85,944,203	43,790,783	15,008,715	5,484,571	21,660,134	33,423,068	10,347,000	22,711,000	33,300	†	50,000	276,743	5,025	39,475,000
2001	130,618,224	94,846,476	48,530,061	14,938,278	5,880,007	25,498,130	35,771,748	10,635,000	24,694,000	25,000	†	80,000	316,655	21,093	41,460,000
2002	150,030,786	109,211,419	52,754,118	22,964,176	6,297,697	27,195,488	40,819,307	11,689,000	28,606,000	25,000	†	104,000	308,811	86,496	—
2003	170,677,327	124,374,489	59,274,219	29,499,694	6,532,502	29,068,074	46,302,838	11,969,000	33,791,000	33,000	†	103,000	304,671	102,167	—
2004	185,040,371	132,420,703	62,653,231	32,432,974	6,576,821	30,757,677	52,619,668	12,840,000	39,266,000	33,000	†	102,000	295,143	83,525	—
2005	204,558,951	147,878,146	68,957,711	38,587,287	6,913,451	33,419,698	56,680,805	12,930,000	43,284,000	0	†	101,000	305,644	60,161	—
2006[11]	226,951,151	166,495,661	70,948,229	57,757,738	7,074,484	30,715,210	60,455,490	12,677,000	47,307,000	0	†	100,000	309,608	61,882	—
2007	210,509,705	145,697,988	70,735,875	37,465,287	7,214,906	30,281,920	64,811,717	13,022,000	51,320,000	0	†	100,000	287,126	82,591	—
2008	220,360,440	144,338,889	71,272,580	36,386,271	7,882,220	28,797,817	76,021,551	18,213,000	57,296,000	0	†	98,000	281,812	132,739	—
2009[12]	368,486,844	271,297,568	172,660,784	53,085,401	8,853,694	36,697,689	97,189,276	29,738,000	66,778,000	0	†	98,000	309,058	266,218	—
2010	288,081,805	183,189,989	86,681,783	50,188,459	9,326,441	36,993,306	104,891,816	84,703,000	19,618,000	0	†	98,000	255,108	217,708	—
2011	293,297,670	183,942,414	76,406,315	64,422,753	11,096,234	32,017,112	109,355,256	108,926,300	0	0	†	0	231,480	197,476	—
2012	295,441,149	190,400,108	78,529,067	70,304,347	9,390,511	32,176,184	105,441,041	105,041,041	0	0	†	0	243,871	184,162	—
2013	284,367,652	182,297,588	78,965,899	63,353,225	9,638,631	30,339,833	104,613,008	104,156,082	0	0	†	0	192,116	146,869	—
2014	291,094,418	190,498,209	79,411,320	69,439,861	9,443,392	32,203,636	102,070,064	101,731,079	0	0	†	0	244,918 [13]	195,209 [13]	—
2015	297,974,582	196,456,123	77,565,989	76,955,169	9,467,086	32,467,878 [13]	101,518,459	101,088,453	0	0	†	0	243,383 [13]	186,622 [13]	—
Constant fiscal year 2015 dollars[14]															
1965	$37,612,810	$37,656,951	$13,721,874	$8,458,915	$2,646,447	$12,829,715	-$44,141	†	†	$113,804	†	†	†	-$157,945	—
1970	77,207,744	72,362,135	33,680,858	19,916,396	5,572,916	13,191,965	4,845,609	†	$4,448,078	121,173	†	†	†	276,359	—
1975	99,494,104	94,759,153	43,201,272	31,103,519	6,544,883	13,909,480	4,734,951	†	5,017,066	145,129	†	$81,380	†	-508,624	$35,013,668
1980	109,090,145	95,723,177	44,478,552	30,847,768	4,297,892	16,098,965	13,366,969	†	12,759,944	88,187	†	213,128	†	305,709	36,964,432
1985	97,298,291	79,682,821	34,507,283	22,814,617	4,303,041	18,057,880	17,615,470	†	17,286,989	43,666	†	155,168	†	129,647	39,006,486
1986	96,484,849	79,896,669	34,087,451	22,558,952	5,238,132	18,012,134	16,588,179	†	16,278,065	40,391	$1,081	145,347	†	124,377	40,835,110
1987	98,362,136	80,068,401	34,083,399	22,019,663	5,481,904	20,483,435	18,293,734	†	18,021,588	40,601	†	147,718	†	82,747	40,486,375
1988	101,457,029	81,695,807	34,902,571	20,036,522	5,605,456	21,151,258	19,761,222	†	19,514,756	38,798	900	136,866	$117,938	69,902	32,007,584
1989	107,579,697	87,393,504	35,865,741	24,025,528	5,758,089	21,744,146	20,186,194	†	19,803,575	36,917	994	130,177		96,594	32,145,956

See notes at end of table.

Table 401.10. Federal support and estimated federal tax expenditures for education, by category: Selected fiscal years, 1965 through 2015—Continued
[In thousands of dollars]

Fiscal year	Total on-budget support, off-budget support, and nonfederal funds generated by federal legislation	On-budget support[1] Total	Elementary and secondary	Post-secondary	Other education[3]	Research at educational institutions	Off-budget support and nonfederal funds generated by federal legislation Total	Off-budget support Direct Loan Program[4]	Nonfederal funds Federal Family Education Loan Program[5]	Perkins Loans[6]	Income Contingent Loans[7]	Leveraging Educational Assistance Partnerships[8]	Supplemental Educational Opportunity Grants[9]	Work-Study Aid[10]	Estimated federal tax expenditures for education[2]
1	2	3	4	5	6	7	8	9	10	11	12	13	14	15	16
1990	110,401,306	90,785,353	38,661,180	24,006,178	5,949,319	22,168,676	19,615,953	†	19,038,349	26,403	879	104,074	224,604	221,644	33,483,296
1991	118,236,526	96,808,068	42,720,362	24,718,899	6,216,306	23,152,502	21,428,457	†	20,793,755	29,159	840	106,776	220,366	277,561	31,925,103
1992	120,653,244	97,976,893	45,238,918	23,306,207	6,466,590	22,965,178	22,676,351	†	21,978,878	28,078	878	116,633	284,546	267,338	32,317,115
1993	133,239,749	106,570,281	48,508,900	28,072,400	6,461,481	23,527,500	26,669,469	†	25,995,738	46,024	†	113,946	270,628	243,132	33,053,162
1994	143,256,731	105,457,553	49,912,505	24,994,683	6,927,638	23,622,727	37,799,178	$1,256,142	35,867,265	81,374	†	111,908	265,752	216,736	34,964,944
1995	143,769,435	107,552,420	50,479,429	26,450,111	7,085,619	23,537,262	36,217,014	7,748,210	27,802,577	79,069	†	95,182	271,735	220,241	36,931,983
1996	142,339,370	104,887,555	50,573,025	23,198,033	7,099,675	24,016,822	37,451,815	12,289,047	24,573,682	45,733	†	46,174	263,221	233,958	38,733,217
1997	148,639,962	106,258,321	51,130,266	22,999,854	7,236,227	24,891,973	42,381,641	14,177,990	27,616,672	75,948	†	72,057	328,869	110,104	40,532,219
1998	153,825,757	109,841,725	53,537,722	22,564,937	7,353,073	26,385,992	43,984,033	14,853,417	28,567,560	64,269	†	35,705	344,125	118,958	42,189,012
1999	159,775,972	116,869,864	56,327,961	24,895,044	7,500,473	28,146,367	42,906,127	14,037,594	28,358,677	46,966	†	35,260	360,918	66,711	52,692,106
2000	164,277,878	118,279,752	60,266,578	20,655,577	7,548,080	29,809,518	45,998,125	14,239,944	31,255,761	45,829	†	68,812	380,864	6,916	54,327,029
2001	175,083,323	127,134,145	65,050,680	20,023,572	7,881,681	34,178,212	47,949,178	14,265,370	33,100,340	33,511	†	107,234	424,451	28,273	55,573,827
2002	197,817,034	143,996,385	69,556,812	30,278,487	8,303,574	35,857,512	53,820,649	15,412,059	37,717,286	32,963	†	137,125	407,170	114,046	—
2003	218,858,010	159,484,295	76,006,801	37,827,194	8,376,569	37,273,731	59,373,715	15,347,742	43,329,897	42,316	†	132,076	390,677	131,008	—
2004	231,221,423	165,469,314	78,289,776	40,527,364	8,218,217	38,433,958	65,752,108	16,044,515	49,065,727	41,236	†	127,456	368,803	104,371	—
2005	247,056,225	178,599,941	83,283,726	46,603,824	8,349,725	40,362,665	68,456,284	15,616,217	52,276,283	0	†	121,983	369,142	72,659	—
2006[11]	264,969,575	194,386,697	82,833,341	67,433,204	8,259,588	35,860,563	70,582,878	14,800,627	55,231,778	0	†	116,752	361,473	72,248	—
2007	239,453,698	165,730,706	80,461,691	42,616,570	8,206,918	34,445,527	73,722,992	14,812,457	58,376,234	0	†	113,749	326,604	93,947	—
2008	242,195,574	158,641,179	78,334,857	39,991,724	8,663,256	31,651,343	83,554,395	20,017,695	62,973,361	0	†	107,711	309,736	145,892	—
2009[12]	404,230,067	297,613,432	189,408,880	58,234,685	9,712,502	40,257,365	106,616,636	32,622,586	73,255,466	0	†	107,506	339,037	292,041	—
2010	312,309,260	198,596,124	93,971,653	54,409,269	10,110,788	40,104,414	113,713,136	91,826,456	21,267,858	0	†	106,242	276,562	236,017	—
2011	311,831,308	195,565,835	81,234,471	68,493,662	11,797,411	34,040,291	116,265,474	115,809,412	0	0	†	0	246,107	209,955	—
2012	308,313,300	198,695,699	81,950,520	73,367,455	9,799,648	33,578,077	109,617,601	109,170,919	0	0	†	0	254,496	192,186	—
2013	292,664,710	187,616,525	81,269,904	65,201,696	9,919,859	31,225,065	105,048,185	104,699,309	0	0	†	0	197,721	151,154	—
2014	294,993,604	193,049,917	80,475,028	70,370,002	9,569,885	32,635,001	101,943,687	101,497,665	0	0	†	0	248,199[13]	197,823[13]	—
2015	297,974,582	196,456,123	77,565,989	76,955,169	9,467,086	32,467,878[13]	101,518,459	101,088,453	0	0	†	0	243,383[13]	186,622[13]	—

—Not available.
†Not applicable.
[1]On-budget support includes federal funds for education programs tied to appropriations. Excludes federal support for medical education benefits under Medicare in the U.S. Department of Health and Human Services. Benefits excluded because data before fiscal year (FY) 1990 are not available. This program existed since Medicare began, but was not available as a separate budget item until FY 1990. Excluded amounts range from an estimated $4,440,000,000 in FY 1990 to an estimated $11,800,000,000 in FY 2015.
[2]Losses of tax revenue attributable to provisions of the federal income tax laws that allow a special exclusion, exemption, or deduction from gross income or provide a special credit, preferential rate of tax, or a deferral of tax liability affecting individual or corporate income tax liabilities.
[3]Other education includes libraries, museums, cultural activities, and miscellaneous research.
[4]The William D. Ford Federal Direct Loan Program (commonly referred to as the Direct Loan Program) provides students with the same benefits they were eligible to receive under the Federal Family Education Loan (FFEL) Program, but provides loans to students through federal capital rather than through private lenders.
[5]The Federal Family Education Loan (FFEL) Program, formerly known as the Guaranteed Student Loan Program, provided student loans guaranteed by the federal government and disbursed to borrowers. After June 30, 2010, no new FFEL loans have been originated; all new loans are originated through the Direct Loan Program.
[6]Student loans created from institutional matching funds (since 1993 one-third of federal capital contributions). Excludes repayments of outstanding loans.
[7]Student loans created from institutional matching funds (one-ninth of federal contributions). This was a demonstration project that involved only 10 institutions and had unsubsidized interest rates. Program repealed in fiscal 1992.

[8]Formerly the State Student Incentive Grant Program. Starting in fiscal year 2000, amounts under $30.0 million have required dollar-for-dollar state matching contributions, while amounts over $30.0 million have required two-to-one state matching contributions.
[9]Institutions award grants to undergraduate students, and the federal share of such grants may not exceed 75 percent of the total grant.
[10]Employer contributions to student earnings are generally one-third of federal allocation.
[11]The increase in postsecondary expenditures in 2006 resulted primarily from an accounting adjustment.
[12]All education funds from the American Recovery and Reinvestment Act of 2009 (ARRA) are included in the FY 2009 row of this table. Most of these funds had a 2-year availability, meaning that they were available for the Department of Education to obligate during FY 2009 and FY 2010.
[13]Estimated.
Data adjusted by the federal budget composite deflator, as reported in the U.S. Office of Management and Budget's *Budget of the U.S. Government, Historical Tables, Fiscal Year 2016.*
NOTE: To the extent possible, federal education funds data do not represent obligations, but instead represent appropriations or (especially for earlier years) outlays. Negative amounts occur when program receipts exceed outlays. Some data have been revised from previously published figures. Detail may not sum to totals because of rounding.
SOURCE: U.S. Department of Education, Budget Service, unpublished tabulations. U.S. Department of Education, National Center for Education Statistics, unpublished tabulations. U.S. Office of Management and Budget, *Budget of the U.S. Government, Appendix,* fiscal years 1967 through 2016. National Science Foundation, *Federal Funds for Research and Development,* fiscal years 1967 through 2015. (This table was prepared May 2016.)

Table 401.20. Federal on-budget funds for education, by agency: Selected fiscal years, 1970 through 2014
[In thousands of dollars]

Agency	1970	1980	1990[1]	2000[1]	2005[1]	2010[1]	2011[1]	2012[1]	2013[1]	2014[1]
1	2	3	4	5	6	7	8	9	10	11
					Current dollars					
Total	$12,526,499	$34,493,502	$51,624,342	$85,944,203	$147,878,146	$183,189,989	$183,942,414	$190,400,108	$182,297,588	$190,498,209
Department of Education[2]	4,625,224	13,137,785	23,198,575	34,106,697	72,893,301	91,893,199	93,777,295	99,129,939	91,129,538	95,665,940
Department of Agriculture	960,910	4,562,467	6,260,843	11,080,031	13,817,553	19,260,881	20,241,295	22,120,982	23,135,596	23,145,081
Department of Commerce	13,990	135,561	53,835	114,575	243,948	303,000	242,778	205,085	235,936	275,521
Department of Defense	821,388	1,560,301	3,605,509	4,525,080	7,986,654	7,686,288	7,617,359	7,400,880	7,036,469	7,297,021
Department of Energy	551,527	1,605,558	2,561,950	3,577,004	4,339,879	3,402,600	2,994,903	2,983,055	2,941,159	3,288,681
Department of Health and Human Services	1,796,854	5,613,930	7,956,011	17,670,867	26,112,807	31,961,852	28,359,740	28,578,464	27,074,506	28,904,559
Department of Homeland Security	†	†	†	†	624,860	540,229	2,006,390	333,630	358,580	372,386
Department of Housing and Urban Development	114,709	5,314	118	1,400	1,100	400	1,600	300	4,500	100
Department of the Interior	190,975	440,547	630,537	959,802	1,254,533	1,042,901	1,041,115	971,805	904,600	975,564
Department of Justice	15,728	60,721	99,775	278,927	608,148	205,692	203,988	217,850	229,791	237,025
Department of Labor	424,494	1,862,738	2,511,380	4,696,100	5,764,500	6,826,000	6,121,000	5,802,000	5,188,004	5,463,123
Department of State	59,742	25,188	51,225	388,349	533,309	778,180	741,670	725,222	797,102	819,041
Department of Transportation	27,534	54,712	76,186	117,054	126,900	160,243	160,741	173,888	178,502	168,000
Department of the Treasury	18	1,247,463	41,715	83,000	†	†	†	†	†	†
Department of Veterans Affairs	1,032,918	2,351,233	757,476	1,577,374	4,293,624	8,795,010	10,581,209	10,895,478	12,616,642	13,104,028
Other agencies and programs										
ACTION	88,034	2,833	8,472	†	†	†	†	†	†	†
Agency for International Development	37,838	176,770	249,786	332,500	602,100	557,900	621,900	629,900	603,900	594,039
Appalachian Regional Commission	†	19,032	93	7,243	8,542	5,070	11,902	11,124	13,070	13,073
Barry Goldwater Scholarship and Excellence in Education Foundation	†	†	1,033	3,000	3,000	4,000	3,000	4,000	4,000	3,000
Corporation for National and Community Service	†	†	†	386,000	472,000	965,000	983,000	750,252	711,009	756,849
Environmental Protection Agency	19,446	41,083	87,481	98,900	83,400	54,700	79,200	87,200	73,700	86,100
Estimated education share of federal aid to the District of Columbia	33,019	81,847	104,940	127,127	154,962	159,670	155,643	151,381	217,160	210,732
Federal Emergency Management Agency[3]	290	1,946	215	14,894	†	†	†	†	†	†
General Services Administration	14,775	34,800	†	†	†	†	†	†	†	†
Harry S Truman Scholarship fund	†	-1,895	2,883	3,000	3,000	2,000	1,000	1,200	1,500	1,000
Institute of American Indian and Alaska Native Culture and Arts Development	†	†	4,305	2,000	6,000	8,000	8,284	8,500	9,550	11,369
Institute of Museum and Library Services	†	†	†	166,000	250,000	265,000	274,000	242,605	231,954	225,813
James Madison Memorial Fellowship Commission	†	†	†	7,000	2,000	2,000	2,000	2,000	2,000	2,000
Japanese-United States Friendship Commission	†	2,294	191	3,000	3,000	2,000	3,700	3,700	3,700	3,000
Library of Congress	29,478	151,871	2,299	299,000	430,000	516,000	521,000	521,000	470,202	485,757
National Aeronautics and Space Administration	258,366	255,511	189,827	2,077,830	2,763,120	1,585,500	1,430,761	2,289,837	2,200,143	2,287,755
National Archives and Records Administration	†	†	77,397	121,879	276,000	339,000	349,000	339,000	373,000	370,706
National Commission on Libraries and Information Science	†	†	3,281	2,000	1,000	†	†	†	†	†
National Endowment for the Arts	340	2,090	5,577	10,048	10,976	14,413	13,495	16,595	13,910	15,426
National Endowment for the Humanities	8,459	142,586	141,048	100,014	117,825	142,654	131,135	136,100	114,171	117,533
National Science Foundation	295,628	808,392	1,588,891	2,955,244	3,993,216	5,560,700	5,127,990	5,534,426	5,302,011	5,478,258
Nuclear Regulatory Commission	†	32,590	42,328	12,200	15,100	14,500	14,000	8,600	5,400	9,400
Office of Economic Opportunity	1,092,410	†	†	†	†	†	†	†	†	†
Smithsonian Institution	2,461	5,153	5,779	25,764	45,890	63,107	67,322	65,109	65,483	68,529
U.S. Arms Control and Disarmament Agency	100	661	25	†	†	†	†	†	†	†
United States Information Agency	8,423	66,210	201,547	13,000	†	†	†	†	†	†
United States Institute of Peace	†	†	7,621	†	28,000	58,000	47,000	44,000	47,000	37,000
Other agencies	1,421	990	885	300	7,900	14,300	6,000	5,000	3,800	4,800

See notes at end of table.

Table 401.20. Federal on-budget funds for education, by agency: Selected fiscal years, 1970 through 2014—Continued

[In thousands of dollars]

Agency	1970	1980	1990[1]	2000[1]	2005[1]	2010[1]	2011[1]	2012[1]	2013[1]	2014[1]
					Constant fiscal year 2015 dollars[4]					
1	2	3	4	5	6	7	8	9	10	11
Total	**$72,362,135**	**$95,723,177**	**$90,785,353**	**$118,279,752**	**$178,599,941**	**$198,596,124**	**$195,565,835**	**$198,695,699**	**$187,616,525**	**$193,049,917**
Department of Education[2]	26,718,645	36,458,766	40,796,468	46,938,962	88,036,938	99,621,345	99,703,133	103,448,957	93,788,445	96,947,378
Department of Agriculture	5,550,912	12,661,336	11,010,171	15,248,769	16,688,159	20,880,706	21,520,353	23,084,777	23,810,628	23,455,107
Department of Commerce	80,816	376,196	94,673	157,683	294,628	328,482	258,119	214,020	242,820	279,212
Department of Defense	4,744,932	4,330,003	6,340,563	6,227,591	9,645,887	8,332,699	8,098,704	7,723,331	7,241,774	7,394,764
Department of Energy	3,186,020	4,455,596	4,505,585	4,922,812	5,241,492	3,688,756	3,184,152	3,113,024	3,026,974	3,332,732
Department of Health and Human Services	10,379,931	15,579,259	13,991,253	24,319,334	31,537,762	34,649,819	30,151,807	29,823,606	27,864,465	29,291,733
Department of Homeland Security	†	†	†	†	754,675	585,662	2,133,175	348,166	369,043	377,374
Department of Housing and Urban Development	662,642	14,747	208	1,927	1,329	434	1,701	313	101	4,631
Department of the Interior	1,103,210	1,222,565	1,108,848	1,320,917	1,515,163	1,130,608	1,106,904	1,014,146	930,993	988,631
Department of Justice	90,856	168,507	175,462	383,870	734,491	222,991	216,878	227,342	236,495	240,200
Department of Labor	2,452,185	5,169,298	4,416,454	6,462,955	6,962,955	7,400,061	6,507,789	6,054,789	5,339,376	5,536,301
Department of State	345,113	69,899	90,083	534,461	644,104	843,624	788,537	756,819	820,359	830,012
Department of Transportation	159,056	151,832	133,979	161,094	153,264	173,719	170,898	181,464	183,710	170,250
Department of the Treasury	104	3,461,844	73,359	114,228	†	†	†	†	†	†
Department of Veterans Affairs	5,966,883	6,524,924	1,332,079	2,170,843	5,185,628	9,534,663	11,249,841	11,380,622	12,984,761	13,279,555
Other agencies and programs										
ACTION	508,548	490,556	14,899	†	†	†	†	†	†	†
Agency for International Development	218,580	52,816	439,268	457,599	727,187	604,819	661,198	657,344	621,520	601,996
Appalachian Regional Commission	†	†	164	9,968	10,317	5,496	12,654	11,609	13,451	13,248
Barry Goldwater Scholarship and Excellence in Education Foundation	†	†	1,817	4,129	3,623	4,336	3,190	4,174	4,117	3,040
Corporation for National and Community Service	†	†	†	531,228	570,058	1,046,156	1,045,116	782,940	731,754	766,987
Environmental Protection Agency	112,334	114,010	153,842	136,110	100,726	59,300	84,205	90,999	75,850	87,253
Estimated education share of federal aid to the District of Columbia[3]	190,742	227,134	184,545	174,957	187,155	173,098	165,478	157,977	223,496	213,555
Federal Emergency Management Agency[3]	1,675	5,400	378	20,498	†	†	†	†	†	†
General Services Administration	85,351	96,574	†	†	†	†	†	†	†	†
Harry S Truman Scholarship fund	†	-5,259	5,070	4,129	3,623	2,168	1,063	1,252	1,544	1,013
Institute of American Indian and Alaska Native Culture and Arts Development	†	†	7,571	2,752	7,247	8,673	8,807	8,870	9,829	11,521
Institute of Museum and Library Services	†	†	†	228,456	301,938	287,286	291,314	253,175	238,722	228,837
James Madison Memorial Fellowship Foundation	†	†	336	9,634	2,416	2,168	2,126	2,087	2,058	2,027
Japanese-United States Friendship Commission	†	6,366	4,043	4,129	3,623	2,168	3,934	3,861	3,808	3,040
Library of Congress	170,286	421,458	333,825	411,495	519,333	559,395	553,922	543,700	483,921	492,264
National Aeronautics and Space Administration	1,492,509	709,070	1,922,657	2,859,590	3,337,160	1,718,839	1,521,171	2,389,604	2,264,337	2,318,399
National Archives and Records Administration	†	†	136,109	167,735	333,339	367,510	371,053	353,770	383,883	375,672
National Commission on Libraries and Information Science	†	5,800	5,770	2,752	1,208	†	†	†	†	†
National Endowment for the Arts	1,964	14,486	9,808	13,828	13,256	15,625	14,348	17,318	14,316	15,633
National Endowment for the Humanities	48,865	395,691	248,044	137,644	142,303	154,651	139,421	142,030	117,502	119,107
National Science Foundation	1,707,762	2,243,375	2,794,186	4,067,122	4,822,810	6,028,351	5,452,030	5,775,557	5,456,709	5,551,639
Nuclear Regulatory Commission	†	90,441	74,437	16,790	18,237	15,719	14,885	8,975	5,558	9,526
Office of Economic Opportunity	6,310,552	†	†	†	†	†	†	†	†	†
Smithsonian Institution	14,217	14,300	10,163	35,457	55,424	68,414	71,576	67,946	67,394	69,447
U.S. Arms Control and Disarmament Agency	578	1,834	44	†	†	†	†	†	†	†
United States Information Agency	48,657	183,740	354,436	†	†	†	†	†	†	†
United States Institute of Peace	†	†	13,402	17,891	33,817	62,878	49,970	45,917	48,371	37,496
Other agencies	8,209	2,747	1,556	413	9,541	15,503	6,379	5,218	3,911	4,864

†Not applicable.

[1]Excludes federal support for medical education benefits under Medicare in the U.S. Department of Health and Human Services. Benefits excluded from total because data before fiscal year (FY) 1990 are not available. This program existed since Medicare began, but was not available as a separate budget item until FY 1990. Excluded amounts are estimated as follows: $4,440,000,000 in FY 1990, $8,020,000,000 in FY 2000, $8,290,000,000 in FY 2005, $9,080,000,000 in FY 2010, $9,200,000,000 in FY 2011, $9,800,000,000 in FY 2012, $10,000,000,000 in FY 2013, and $11,330,000,000 in FY 2014.

[2]The U.S. Department of Education was created in May 1980. It formerly was the Office of Education in the U.S. Department of Health, Education, and Welfare. All education funds from the American Recovery and Reinvestment Act of 2009 (ARRA) are included in the Department of Education amount for FY 2009. Most of these funds had a 2-year availability, meaning that they were available for the Department of Education to obligate during FY 2009 and FY 2010.

[3]The Federal Emergency Management Agency (FEMA) was created in 1979, representing a combination of five existing agencies. The FY 1970 funds shown for FEMA were in other agencies. FEMA was transferred to the U.S. Department of Homeland Security in March of 2003.

[4]Data adjusted by the federal budget composite deflator, as reported in the U.S. Office of Management and Budget's Budget of the U.S. Government, Historical Tables, Fiscal Year 2016.

NOTE: To the extent possible, amounts reported do not represent obligations, but instead represent appropriations or (especially for earlier years) outlays. Negative amounts occur when program receipts exceed outlays. Some data have been revised from previously published figures. Detail may not sum to totals because of rounding.

SOURCE: U.S. Department of Education, National Center for Education Statistics, unpublished tabulations. U.S. Office of Management and Budget, Budget of the U.S. Government, Appendix, fiscal years 1972 through 2015. National Science Foundation, Federal Funds for Research and Development, fiscal years 1970 to 2014. (This table was prepared May 2016.)

Table 401.30. Federal on-budget funds for education, by level/educational purpose, agency, and program: Selected fiscal years, 1970 through 2015

[In thousands of current dollars]

Level/educational purpose, agency, and program	1970	1980	1990	1995	2000[1]	2005[1]	2010[1]	2011[1]	2012[1]	2013[1]	2014[1]	2015[1,2]
1	2	3	4	5	6	7	8	9	10	11	12	13
Total	$12,526,499	$34,493,502	$51,624,342	$71,639,520	$85,944,203	$147,878,146	$183,189,989	$183,942,414	$190,400,108	$182,297,588	$190,498,209	$196,456,123
Elementary/secondary education	5,830,442	16,027,686	21,984,361	33,623,809	43,790,783	68,957,711	86,681,783	76,406,315	78,529,067	78,965,899	79,411,320	77,565,989
Department of Education[3]	2,719,204	6,629,095	9,681,313	14,029,000	20,039,563	37,477,594	49,621,475	38,652,240	38,600,066	38,705,852	37,771,972	37,394,190
Education for the disadvantaged	1,339,014	3,204,664	4,494,111	6,808,000	8,529,111	14,635,566	15,864,666	15,515,444	15,741,703	15,590,733	15,552,693	15,536,107
Impact aid program[4]	656,372	690,170	816,366	808,000	877,101	1,262,174	1,276,183	1,273,631	1,291,186	1,299,088	1,288,603	1,288,603
School improvement programs[5]	288,304	788,918	1,189,158	1,397,000	2,549,971	7,918,091	16,999,862	6,738,485	6,327,886	6,543,628	5,883,351	5,478,097
Indian education	†	93,365	69,451	71,000	65,285	121,911	127,282	127,027	130,779	131,579	123,939	123,939
English Language Acquisition	21,250	169,540	188,919	225,000	362,662	667,485	750,000	733,530	732,144	736,624	723,400	737,400
Special education	79,090	821,777	1,616,623	3,177,000	4,948,977	10,940,312	12,587,035	12,526,672	12,640,709	12,661,256	12,497,300	12,522,358
Vocational and adult education	335,174	860,661	1,306,685	1,482,000	1,462,977	1,967,086	2,016,447	1,737,451	1,735,659	1,742,944	1,702,686	1,707,686
Education Reform—Goals 2000[6]	†	†	†	61,000	1,243,479	-35,031	†	†	†	†	†	†
Hurricane Education Recovery	†	†	†	†	†	†	†	†	†	†	†	†
Department of Agriculture	760,477	4,064,497	5,528,950	8,201,294	10,051,278	12,577,265	17,875,561	18,843,607	20,849,143	21,931,420	21,818,519	20,617,097
Child nutrition programs[7]	299,131	3,377,056	4,977,075	7,644,789	9,554,028	11,901,943	16,383,421	17,290,601	19,504,343	20,487,229	20,487,299	19,287,957
McGovern-Dole International Food for Education and Child Nutrition Program[8]	†	†	†	†	†	86,000	343,500	196,400	196,400	197,126	260,000	192,000
Agricultural Marketing Service—commodities[9]	341,597	388,000	350,441	400,000	400,000	399,322	1,100,000	1,006,000	952,000	1,053,000	888,000	1,029,000
Special Milk Program	83,800	159,293	18,707	(7)	(7)	(7)	(7)	(7)	(7)	(7)	(7)	(7)
Estimated education share of Forest Service permanent appropriations	35,949	140,148	182,727	156,505	97,250	190,000	182,140	203,506	196,400	194,065	183,220	108,140
Department of Commerce	†	54,816	†	†	†	†	†	†	†	†	†	†
Local public works program—school facilities[10]	†	54,816	†	†	†	†	†	†	†	†	†	†
Department of Defense	143,100	370,846	1,097,876	1,295,547	1,485,611	1,786,253	1,981,321	2,047,825	2,132,046	2,220,611	2,193,877	2,134,713
Junior Reserve Officers Training Corps (JROTC)	12,100	32,000	39,300	155,600	210,432	315,122	359,689	377,526	391,682	407,335	450,229	381,306
Overseas dependents schools	131,000	338,846	864,958	855,772	904,829	1,060,920	1,186,560	1,193,636	1,235,707	1,262,545	1,187,691	1,170,596
Domestic schools	†	†	193,618	284,175	370,350	410,211	435,072	476,663	504,657	550,731	555,957	582,811
Department of Energy	200	77,633	15,563	12,646	†	†	†	†	†	†	†	†
Energy conservation for school buildings[11]	†	77,240	15,213	10,746	†	†	†	†	†	†	†	†
Pre-engineering program	200	393	350	1,900	†	†	†	†	†	†	†	†
Department of Health and Human Services	167,333	1,077,000	2,396,793	5,116,559	6,011,036	8,003,348	8,547,000	8,871,364	9,298,710	8,894,300	9,963,200	9,981,200
Head Start[12]	†	735,000	1,447,758	3,534,000	5,267,000	6,842,348	7,234,000	7,559,164	7,969,210	7,573,000	8,598,000	8,598,000
Payments to states for Aid to Families with Dependent Children (AFDC) work programs[13]	†	†	459,221	953,000	15,000	—	—	—	—	—	—	—
Social Security student benefits[14]	167,333	342,000	489,814	629,559	729,036	1,161,000	1,313,000	1,312,200	1,329,500	1,321,300	1,365,200	1,383,200
Department of Homeland Security	†	†	†	†	†	500	505	504	454	364	341	346
Tuition assistance for educational accreditation—Coast Guard personnel[15]	†	†	†	†	†	500	505	504	454	364	341	346
Department of the Interior	140,705	318,170	445,267	493,124	725,423	938,506	781,075	815,877	782,335	742,546	782,405	807,193
Mineral Leasing Act and other funds												
Payments to states—estimated education share	12,294	62,636	123,811	18,750	24,610	60,290	23,000	24,380	26,450	24,770	28,100	24,100
Payments to counties—estimated education share	16,359	48,953	102,522	37,490	53,500	79,686	50,000	53,000	58,000	53,970	61,300	52,500
Indian Education												
Bureau of Indian Education schools	95,850	178,112	192,841	411,524	466,905	517,647	580,492	583,572	631,477	597,412	622,382	641,353
Johnson-O'Malley assistance[16]	16,080	28,081	25,556	24,359	17,387	16,510	13,589	13,415	13,304	12,615	14,338	14,739
Education construction	†	388	538	1,000	161,021	263,373	112,994	140,509	52,104	52,779	55,285	74,501
Education expenses for children of employees, Yellowstone National Park	122	†	†	†	2,000	1,000	1,000	1,000	1,000	1,000	1,000	†
Department of Justice	8,237	23,890	65,997	128,850	224,800	554,500	137,529	140,525	149,587	160,684	151,630	—
Advanced occupational education	†	†	†	†	†	0	137,529	140,525	149,587	160,684	151,630	—
Vocational training expenses for prisoners in federal prisons	2,720	4,966	2,066	3,000	1,000	554,500	†	†	†	†	†	—
Inmate programs[17]	5,517	18,924	63,931	125,850	223,800	†	†	†	†	†	†	†

See notes at end of table.

Table 401.30. Federal on-budget funds for education, by level/educational purpose, agency, and program: Selected fiscal years, 1970 through 2015—Continued

[In thousands of current dollars]

Level/educational purpose, agency, and program	1970	1980	1990	1995[1]	2000[1]	2005[1]	2010[1]	2011[1]	2012[1]	2013[1]	2014[1]	2015[1,2]
1	2	3	4	5	6	7	8	9	10	11	12	13
Department of Labor	420,927	1,849,800	2,505,487	3,957,800	4,683,200	5,654,000	6,826,000	6,121,000	5,802,000	5,188,004	5,463,123	5,314,155
Job Corps	†	469,800	739,376	1,029,000	1,256,000	1,521,000	1,850,000	1,660,000	1,789,000	1,650,004	1,691,123	1,688,155
Training programs—estimated funds for education programs[18]	420,927	1,380,000	1,766,111	2,928,800	3,427,200	4,133,000	4,976,000	4,461,000	4,013,000	3,538,000	3,772,000	3,626,000
Department of Transportation	45	60	46	62	188	†	†	†	†	†	†	†
Tuition assistance for educational accreditation—Coast Guard personnel[15]	45	60	46	62	188	†	†	†	†	†	†	†
Department of the Treasury	†	935,903	†	†	†	†	†	†	†	†	†	†
Estimated education share of general revenue sharing[19]												
State[20]	†	525,019	†	†	†	†	†	†	†	†	†	†
Local	†	410,884	†	†	†	†	†	†	†	†	†	†
Department of Veterans Affairs	338,910	545,786	155,351	311,768	445,052	1,815,000	760,476	759,457	790,688	930,750	1,079,667	1,201,493
Noncollegiate and job training programs[21]	281,640	439,993	12,848	298,132	438,635	1,815,000	760,476	759,457	790,688	930,750	1,079,667	1,201,493
Vocational rehabilitation for disabled veterans[22]	41,700	87,980	136,780	5,961	6,417	†	†	†	†	†	†	†
Veteran Dependents' education[23]	15,570	17,813	5,723	7,675	†	†	†	†	†	†	—	†
Service members occupational conversion training act of 1992	†	†	†	†	†	†	†	†	†	†	†	†
Other agencies												
Appalachian Regional Commission	33,161	9,157	93	2,173	2,588	2,962	986	2,290	962	1,689	3,163	1,574
National Endowment for the Arts[24]	†	4,989	4,641	7,117	6,002	8,470	11,530	12,125	10,450	10,427	10,924	9,777
Arts in education	†	4,989	4,641	7,117	6,002	8,470	11,530	12,125	10,450	10,427	10,924	9,777
National Endowment for the Humanities	20	330	404	997	812	603	125	75	100	333	181	243
Office of Economic Opportunity	1,072,375	†	†	†	†	†	†	†	†	†	†	†
Head Start[25]	325,700	†	†	†	†	†	†	†	†	†	†	†
Other elementary and secondary programs[26]	42,809	†	†	†	†	†	†	†	†	†	†	†
Job Corps[27]	144,000	†	†	†	†	†	†	†	†	†	†	†
Youth Corps and other training programs[27]	553,368	†	†	†	†	†	†	†	†	†	†	†
Volunteers in Service to America (VISTA)[28]	6,498	†	†	†	†	†	†	†	†	†	†	†
Other programs												
Estimated education share of federal aid to the District of Columbia	25,748	65,714	86,579	66,871	115,230	138,710	138,200	139,426	112,526	178,919	172,318	104,008
Postsecondary education	**$3,447,697**	**$11,115,882**	**$13,650,915**	**$17,618,137**	**$15,008,715**	**$38,587,287**	**$50,188,459**	**$64,422,753**	**$70,304,347**	**$63,353,225**	**$69,439,861**	**$76,955,169**
Department of Education[3]	1,187,962	5,682,242	11,175,978	14,234,000	10,727,315	31,420,023	36,539,655	49,260,330	54,470,178	46,130,198	51,896,533	57,908,189
Student financial assistance	†	3,682,789	5,920,328	7,047,000	9,060,317	15,209,515	25,959,478	43,753,247	43,324,872	37,319,312	30,589,493	30,278,081
Direct Loan Program[29]	†	†	†	840,000	-2,862,240	3,020,992	3,481,859	2,781,709	6,917,373	3,273,880	16,254,117	23,660,742
Federal Family Education Loan Program[30]	2,323	1,407,977	4,372,446	5,190,000	2,707,473	10,777,470	3,932,994	-91,796	1,498,353	2,787,755	2,269,320	1,362,692
Higher education	1,029,131	399,787	659,492	871,000	1,530,779	2,053,288	2,740,665	2,388,946	2,297,656	2,302,753	2,322,592	2,161,224
Facilities—loans and insurance[31]	114,199	-19,031	19,219	-6,000	-2,174	-1,464	-8,360	-4,607	-8,513	-156	-109	-156
College housing loans[31]	774	14,082	-57,167	-46,000	-41,886	-33,521	-16,725	-13,265	-16,725	-1,176	-1,176	-1,176
Educational activities overseas	†	†	82	†	150	169	†	†	†	†	†	†
Historically Black Colleges and Universities Capital Financing, Program Account	†	†	†	†	†	†	23,330	23,289	32,160	20,227	55,184	37,670
Gallaudet College and Howard University	38,559	176,829	230,327	292,000	291,060	339,823	357,977	357,261	359,580	361,781	340,821	342,096
National Technical Institute for the Deaf	2,976	16,248	31,251	46,000	43,836	53,751	68,437	65,546	65,422	65,822	66,291	67,016
Department of Agriculture	†	10,453	31,273	33,373	30,676	61,957	80,697	81,658	81,658	75,387	82,986	82,986
Agriculture Extension Service, Second Morrill Act payments to agricultural and mechanical colleges and Tuskegee Institute	†	10,453	31,273	33,373	30,676	61,957	80,697	81,658	81,658	75,387	82,986	82,986
Department of Commerce	8,277	29,971	3,312	3,487	3,800	—	—	—	—	—	—	—
Sea Grant Program[32]	6,160	3,123	3,312	3,487	3,800	—	—	—	—	—	—	—
Merchant Marine Academy[33]	†	14,809	†	†	†	†	†	†	†	†	†	†
State marine schools[33]	2,117	12,039	†	†	†	†	†	†	†	†	†	†

See notes at end of table.

Table 401.30. Federal on-budget funds for education, by level/educational purpose, agency, and program: Selected fiscal years, 1970 through 2015—Continued

[In thousands of current dollars]

Level/educational purpose, agency, and program	1970	1980	1990[1]	1995[1]	2000[1]	2005[1]	2010[1]	2011[1]	2012[1]	2013[1]	2014[1]	2015[1,2]
1	2	3	4	5	6	7	8	9	10	11	12	13
Department of Defense	322,100	545,000	635,769	729,500	1,147,759	1,858,301	2,550,667	2,297,234	2,407,629	2,420,958	2,314,444	2,204,083
Tuition assistance for military personnel	57,500	—	95,300	127,000	263,303	608,109	669,892	567,412	590,626	564,604	580,848	520,817
Service academies	78,700	106,100	120,613	163,300	212,678	300,760	402,640	348,836	375,250	372,726	225,163	227,413
Senior Reserve Officers Training Corps (SROTC)	108,100	—	193,056	219,400	363,461	537,525	885,500	851,910	844,498	843,018	856,900	840,384
Professional development education[34]	77,800	—	226,800	219,800	308,317	411,907	592,635	529,076	597,255	640,610	651,533	615,469
Department of Energy												
University laboratory cooperative program	3,000	57,701	25,502	28,027	†	†	†	†	†	†	†	†
Teacher development projects	3,000	2,800	9,402	8,552	†	†	†	†	†	†	†	†
Energy conservation for buildings—higher education[11]	†	1,400	†	†	†	†	†	†	†	†	†	†
Minority honors vocational training	†	53,501	7,459	7,381	†	†	†	†	†	†	†	†
Honors research program	†	†	6,472	2,221	†	†	†	†	†	†	†	†
Students and teachers	†	†	2,169	9,873	†	†	†	†	†	†	†	†
Department of Health and Human Services	981,483	2,412,058	578,542	796,035	954,190	1,433,516	1,278,936	1,368,129	1,311,009	1,254,548	1,308,245	1,302,908
Health professions training programs[35]	353,029	460,736	230,600	298,302	340,361	581,661	406,000	498,000	459,000	438,039	469,236	438,721
Indian health manpower	†	7,187	9,508	27,000	16,000	27,000	46,000	41,000	41,000	32,000	32,000	48,000
National Health Service Corps scholarships	†	70,667	4,759	78,206	33,300	45,000	41,000	46,400	38,300	39,800	43,300	38,500
National Institutes of Health training grants[36]	†	176,388	241,356	380,502	550,220	756,014	775,186	772,000	762,000	734,000	753,000	767,000
National Institute of Occupational Safety and Health training grants[37]	8,088	12,899	10,461	11,660	14,198	23,841	10,750	10,729	10,709	10,709	10,709	10,687
Alcohol, drug abuse, and mental health training programs[38]	118,366	122,103	81,353	†	†	†	†	†	†	†	†	†
Health teaching facilities[39]	†	3,078	505	†	†	†	†	†	†	†	†	†
Social Security postsecondary students' benefits[40]	502,000	1,559,000	†	365	110	†	†	†	†	†	†	†
Department of Homeland Security	†	†	†	†	†	36,400	45,824	49,604	48,592	43,468	36,142	35,905
Coast Guard Academy[15]	†	†	†	†	†	16,400	26,326	27,581	26,803	24,359	25,407	23,905
Postgraduate training for Coast Guard officers[41]	†	†	†	†	†	8,700	4,645	4,883	5,891	6,198	5,417	5,345
Tuition assistance to Coast Guard military personnel[15]	†	†	†	†	†	11,300	14,853	17,140	15,898	12,911	5,318	6,655
Department of Housing and Urban Development[31]	114,199	†	†	†	†	†	†	†	†	†	†	†
College housing loans[31]	114,199	†	†	†	†	†	†	†	†	†	†	†
Department of the Interior	31,749	80,202	135,480	159,054	187,179	249,227	177,626	116,465	124,065	110,702	116,337	115,172
Shared revenues, Mineral Leasing Act and other receipts—estimated education share	6,949	35,403	69,980	82,810	98,740	146,235	16,250	20,430	29,900	20,310	23,100	19,800
Indian programs												
Continuing education	9,380	16,909	34,911	43,907	57,576	76,271	126,791	61,603	61,435	58,832	61,887	64,182
Higher education scholarships	15,420	27,890	30,589	32,337	30,863	26,721	34,585	34,432	32,730	31,560	31,350	31,190
Department of State	30,850	†	2,167	3,000	319,000	424,000	657,660	620,050	601,770	577,864	567,811	589,900
Educational exchange[42]	30,850	†	†	†	319,000	424,000	657,660	620,050	601,770	577,864	567,811	589,900
Mutual educational and cultural exchange activities	30,454	†	†	†	303,000	402,000	635,000	599,550	583,200	559,180	567,811	589,900
International educational exchange activities[43]	396	†	†	†	16,000	22,000	22,660	20,500	18,570	18,684	†	†
Russian, Eurasian, and East European Research and Training	†	†	2,167	3,000	†	†	†	†	†	†	†	†
Department of Transportation	11,197	12,530	46,025	59,257	60,300	73,000	89,997	95,806	102,268	97,993	96,800	97,650
Merchant Marine Academy[33]	†	†	20,926	30,850	34,000	61,000	74,057	79,897	85,168	81,787	79,500	79,150
State marine schools[33]	†	†	8,269	8,980	7,000	12,000	15,940	15,909	17,100	16,206	17,300	18,500
Coast Guard Academy[15]	9,342	10,000	12,074	13,500	15,500	†	†	†	†	†	†	†
Postgraduate training for Coast Guard officers[41]	1,655	2,230	4,173	5,513	2,500	†	†	†	†	†	†	†
Tuition assistance to Coast Guard military personnel[15]	200	300	582	414	1,300	†	†	†	†	†	†	†
Department of the Treasury	†	296,750	†	†	†	†	†	†	†	†	†	†
General revenue sharing—estimated state share to higher education[19,20]	†	296,750	†	†	†	†	†	†	†	†	†	†
Department of Veterans Affairs	693,490	1,803,847	599,825	1,010,114	1,132,322	2,478,624	8,034,534	9,821,752	10,114,790	11,685,892	12,024,361	13,605,271
Vietnam-era veterans	638,260	1,579,974	46,998	†	†	†	†	†	†	†	†	†
College student support	†	1,560,081	39,458	†	†	†	†	†	†	†	†	†
Work-study	†	19,893	7,540	†	†	†	†	†	†	†	†	†

See notes at end of table.

Table 401.30. Federal on-budget funds for education, by level/educational purpose, agency, and program: Selected fiscal years, 1970 through 2015—Continued

[In thousands of current dollars]

Level/educational purpose, agency, and program	1970	1980	1990[1]	1995[1]	2000[1]	2005[1]	2010[1]	2011[1]	2012[1]	2013[1]	2014[1]	2015[1,2]
1	2	3	4	5	6	7	8	9	10	11	12	13
Service persons college support	18,900	46,617	8,911	†	†	1,136	†	†	†	†	†	†
Post-Vietnam veterans	†	922	161,475	33,596	3,958	†	1,496	1,343	932	615	425	398
All-volunteer-force educational assistance	†	†	269,947	868,394	984,068	2,070,996	1,854,917	1,587,376	1,086,585	928,847	680,312	605,763
Veterans	†	†	183,765	760,390	876,434	1,887,239	1,659,694	1,385,943	931,756	775,382	530,508	478,735
Reservists	†	†	86,182	108,004	107,634	183,757	195,223	201,433	154,829	153,465	149,804	127,028
Post 9-11 GI Bill[44]	†	†	†	†	†	†	5,542,843	7,656,490	8,476,227	10,184,499	10,754,649	12,407,886
Veteran dependents' education	36,330	176,334	100,494	95,124	131,296	388,719	507,294	462,877	455,318	483,281	513,633	540,801
Payments to state education agencies	†	†	12,000	13,000	13,000	13,000	18,958	18,342	18,985	18,980	18,985	19,000
Reserve Education Assistance Program (REAP)[45]	†	†	†	†	†	17,773	109,026	95,324	76,990	69,670	56,357	31,423
Other agencies												
Appalachian Regional Commission	4,105	1,751	—	2,741	2,286	4,407	2,464	6,098	6,653	4,443	7,471	17,062
National Endowment for the Humanities	3,349	56,451	50,938	56,481	28,395	29,253	47,949	40,168	45,000	39,399	39,824	42,900
National Science Foundation	42,000	64,583	161,884	211,800	389,000	490,000	646,000	636,060	937,160	858,130	894,000	893,350
Science and engineering education programs	37,000	64,583	161,884	211,800	389,000	490,000	646,000	636,060	937,160	858,130	894,000	893,350
Sea Grant Program[39]	5,000	†	†	†	†	†	†	†	†	†	†	†
United States Information Agency[46]	8,423	51,095	181,172	260,800	†	†	†	†	†	†	†	†
Educational and cultural affairs[42]	†	49,546	35,862	13,600	†	†	†	†	†	†	†	†
Educational and cultural exchange programs[47]	†	†	145,307	247,200	†	†	†	†	†	†	†	†
Educational exchange activities, international	†	1,549	3	†	†	†	†	†	†	†	†	†
Information center and library activities	8,423	†	†	†	†	†	†	†	†	†	†	†
Other programs												
Barry Goldwater Scholarship and Excellence in Education Foundation	†	†	1,033	3,000	3,000	3,000	4,000	3,000	4,000	4,000	3,000	3,000
Estimated education share of federal aid to the District of Columbia[48]	5,513	13,143	14,637	9,468	11,493	14,578	20,450	15,115	37,875	37,193	37,538	42,324
Harry S Truman Scholarship fund	†	-1,895	2,883	3,000	3,000	3,000	2,000	1,000	1,200	1,500	1,000	1,000
Institute of American Indian and Alaska Native Culture and Arts Development	†	†	4,305	13,000	2,000	6,000	8,000	8,284	8,500	9,550	11,369	11,469
James Madison Memorial Fellowship Foundation	†	†	191	2,000	7,000	2,000	2,000	2,000	2,000	2,000	2,000	2,000
Other education	**$964,719**	**$1,548,730**	**$3,383,031**	**$4,719,655**	**$5,484,571**	**$6,913,451**	**$9,326,441**	**$11,096,234**	**$9,390,511**	**$9,638,631**	**$9,443,392**	**$9,467,086**
Department of Education[3]	630,235	747,706	2,251,801	2,861,000	3,223,355	3,538,862	5,073,063	5,255,939	5,466,031	5,696,191	5,420,500	5,457,928
Administration	47,456	187,317	328,293	404,000	458,054	548,842	1,531,232	1,755,384	1,928,821	2,048,098	1,971,955	1,965,715
Libraries[49]	108,284	129,127	137,264	117,000	†	†	†	†	†	†	†	†
Rehabilitative services and disability research	473,091	426,886	1,780,360	2,333,000	2,755,468	2,973,346	3,506,861	3,474,718	3,511,281	3,622,925	3,422,749	3,466,393
American Printing House for the Blind	1,404	4,349	5,736	7,000	9,368	16,538	24,600	24,551	24,505	24,655	24,456	24,931
Trust funds and contributions	0	27	148	0	465	136	10,370	1,286	1,424	513	1,340	889
Department of Agriculture	135,637	271,112	352,511	422,878	444,477	468,631	567,423	552,030	547,081	549,989	545,676	548,176
Extension Service	131,734	263,584	337,907	405,371	424,174	445,631	543,423	530,030	526,081	528,989	521,676	524,176
National Agricultural Library	3,903	7,528	14,604	17,507	20,303	23,000	24,000	22,000	21,000	21,000	24,000	24,000
Department of Commerce	1,226	2,479	†	†	†	†	†	†	†	†	†	†
Maritime Administration	†	†	†	†	†	†	†	†	†	†	†	†
Training for private sector employees[33]	1,226	2,479	†	†	†	†	†	†	†	†	†	†
Department of Health and Human Services	24,273	37,819	77,962	138,000	214,000	317,947	339,716	339,716	338,278	337,639	327,723	336,939
National Library of Medicine	24,273	37,819	77,962	138,000	214,000	317,947	339,716	339,716	338,278	337,639	327,723	336,939
Department of Homeland Security	†	†	†	†	†	278,243	341,100	1,851,832	215,884	243,111	258,730	259,595
Federal Law Enforcement Training Center[50]	†	†	†	†	†	159,000	323,000	270,832	271,413	243,111	258,730	259,595
Estimated disaster relief[51]	†	†	†	†	†	119,243	18,100	1,581,000	-55,529	—	—	—
Department of Justice	5,546	27,642	26,920	36,296	34,727	26,148	33,563	33,563	33,563	30,207	30,095	30,814
Federal Bureau of Investigation National Academy	2,066	7,234	6,028	12,831	22,479	15,619	19,443	19,443	19,443	21,268	21,291	21,409
Federal Bureau of Investigation Field Police Academy	2,500	7,715	10,548	11,140	11,962	10,456	14,120	14,120	14,120	8,939	8,804	9,405
Narcotics and dangerous drug training	980	2,416	850	325	286	73	†	†	†	†	†	†
National Institute of Corrections	†	10,277	9,494	12,000	†	†	†	†	†	†	†	†

See notes at end of table.

Table 401.30. Federal on-budget funds for education, by level/educational purpose, agency, and program: Selected fiscal years, 1970 through 2015—Continued

[In thousands of current dollars]

Level/educational purpose, agency, and program	1970	1980	1990[1]	1995[1]	2000[1]	2005[1]	2010[1]	2011[1]	2012[1]	2013[1]	2014[1]	2015[1,2]
1	2	3	4	5	6	7	8	9	10	11	12	13
Department of State	20,672	25,000	47,539	51,648	69,349	109,309	120,520	121,620	123,452	219,238	251,230	234,337
Foreign Service Institute	15,857	25,000	47,539	51,648	69,349	109,309	120,520	121,620	123,452	219,238	251,230	234,337
Center for Cultural and Technical Interchange[42]	4,815	†	†	—	†	†	†	†	†	†	†	†
Department of Transportation	3,964	10,212	1,507	650	700	1,100	146	135	120	—	—	—
Highways training and education grants	2,418	3,412	—	—								
Maritime Administration												
Training for private sector employees[31]	†	†	†	†								
Urban mass transportation—managerial training grants	1,546	500	1,507	650	700	1,100	146	135	120	—	—	—
Federal Aviation Administration												
Air traffic controllers second career program	—	6,300	—	—								
Department of the Treasury	18	14,584	41,488	48,000	83,000	†	†	†	†	†	†	†
Federal Law Enforcement Training Center[60]	18	14,584	41,488	48,000	83,000	†	†	†	†	†	†	†
Other agencies												
ACTION[62]	†	2,833	8,472	†	†	†	†	†	†	†	†	†
Estimated education funds	†	2,833	8,472	†	†	†	†	†	†	†	†	†
Agency for International Development	88,034	99,707	170,371	260,408	299,000	574,000	542,700	599,500	598,800	574,000	576,439	589,900
Education and human resources	61,570	80,518	142,801	248,408	299,000	574,000	542,700	599,500	598,800	574,000	576,439	589,900
American schools and hospitals abroad	26,464	19,189	27,570	12,000	†	†	†	†	†	†	†	†
Appalachian Regional Commission	572	8,124	†	5,709	2,369	1,173	1,620	3,514	3,510	6,938	2,439	5,045
Corporation for National and Community Service[52]	†	†	†	214,600	386,000	472,000	965,000	983,000	750,252	711,009	756,849	758,349
Federal Emergency Management Agency[63]	290	281	215	170,400	14,894	†	†	†	†	†	†	†
Estimated architect/engineer student development program	40	31	200	—	—							
Estimated other training programs[54]	250	250	15	—	—							
Estimated disaster relief[61]	†	—	—	170,400	14,894	†	†	†	†	†	†	†
General Services Administration	14,775	34,800	†	†	†	†	†	†	†	†	†	†
Libraries and other archival activities[55]	14,775	34,800	†	†	†	†	†	†	†	†	†	†
Institute of Museum and Library Services[49]	†	†	†	†	166,000	250,000	265,000	274,000	242,605	231,954	225,813	226,448
Japanese-United States Friendship Commission	†	2,294	2,299	2,000	3,000	3,000	2,000	3,700	3,700	3,700	3,000	3,000
Library of Congress	29,478	151,871	189,827	241,000	299,000	430,000	516,000	521,000	521,000	470,202	485,757	469,605
Salaries and expenses	20,700	102,364	148,985	198,000	247,000	383,000	439,000	446,000	442,625	422,625	433,830	419,357
Books for the blind and the physically handicapped	6,195	31,436	37,473	39,000	46,000	47,000	77,000	75,000	79,000	47,577	51,927	50,248
Special foreign currency program	2,273	3,492	10	†	†	†	†	†	†	†	†	†
Furniture and furnishings	310	14,579	3,359	4,000	6,000	†	†	†	†	†	†	†
National Aeronautics and Space Administration	350	882	3,300	5,923	6,800	†	†	†	†	†	†	†
Aerospace education services project	350	882	3,300	5,923	6,800	†	†	†	†	†	†	†
National Archives and Records Administration	†	†	77,397	105,172	121,879	276,000	339,000	349,000	339,000	373,000	370,706	360,000
Libraries and other archival activities[55]	†	†	77,397	105,172	121,879	276,000	339,000	349,000	339,000	373,000	370,706	360,000
National Commission on Libraries and Information Science[56]	†	2,090	3,281	1,000	2,000	1,000	†	†	†	†	†	†
National Endowment for the Arts[24]	340	231	936	2,304	4,046	2,506	2,883	1,370	6,145	3,483	4,502	3,732
National Endowment for the Humanities	5,090	85,805	89,706	94,249	70,807	87,969	94,580	90,891	91,000	74,439	77,528	77,073
Smithsonian Institution	2,461	5,153	5,779	9,961	25,764	45,890	63,107	67,322	65,109	65,483	68,529	70,053
Museum programs and related research	2,261	3,254	690	3,190	18,000	32,000	52,000	56,000	54,000	54,313	57,915	59,553
National Gallery of Art extension service	200	426	474	771	764	890	107	119	122	115	114	—
Woodrow Wilson International Center for Scholars	†	1,473	4,615	6,000	7,000	13,000	11,000	11,203	10,987	11,055	10,500	10,500

See notes at end of table.

Table 401.30. Federal on-budget funds for education, by level/educational purpose, agency, and program: Selected fiscal years, 1970 through 2015—Continued

[In thousands of current dollars]

Level/educational purpose, agency, and program	1970	1980	1990	1995[1]	2000[1]	2005[1]	2010[1]	2011[1]	2012[1]	2013[1]	2014[1]	2015[1,2]
1	2	3	4	5	6	7	8	9	10	11	12	13
United States Information Agency—Center for Cultural and Technical Interchange[42]	†	15,115	20,375	34,000	†	†	†	†	†	†	†	†
United States Institute of Peace	†	†	7,621	12,000	13,000	28,000	58,000	47,000	44,000	47,000	37,000	35,000
Other programs												
Estimated education share of federal aid for the District of Columbia	1,758	2,990	3,724	2,457	404	1,674	1,020	1,102	980	1,048	876	1,092
Research programs at universities and related institutions[57]	$2,283,641	$5,801,204	$12,606,035	$15,677,919	$21,560,134	$33,419,698	$36,993,306	$32,017,112	$32,176,184	$30,339,833	$32,203,636	$32,467,878
Department of Education[58]	87,823	78,742	89,483	279,000	116,464	456,822	659,006	608,786	593,664	597,297	576,935	$573,935
Department of Agriculture	64,796	216,405	348,109	434,544	553,600	709,700	737,200	764,000	643,100	578,800	697,900	794,100
Department of Commerce	4,487	48,295	50,523	85,442	110,775	243,948	303,000	242,778	205,085	235,936	275,521	294,768
Department of Defense	356,188	644,455	1,871,864	1,853,955	1,891,710	4,342,100	3,154,300	3,272,300	2,861,205	2,394,900	2,788,700	2,940,200
Department of Energy	548,327	1,470,224	2,520,885	2,651,641	3,577,004	4,339,879	3,402,600	2,994,903	2,983,055	2,941,159	3,288,681	3,099,413
Department of Health and Human Services	623,765	2,087,053	4,902,714	6,418,969	10,491,641	16,357,996	21,796,200	17,780,531	17,630,467	16,588,019	17,305,391	17,416,327
Department of Homeland Security	†	†	†	†	†	309,717	152,800	104,450	68,700	71,637	77,173	78,176
Department of Housing and Urban Development	510	†	118	1,613	1,400	1,100	400	1,600	300	4,500	100	1,500
Department of the Interior	18,521	5,314	49,790	50,618	47,200	66,800	84,200	108,774	65,405	51,352	76,822	52,400
Department of Justice	1,945	9,189	6,858	7,204	19,400	27,500	34,600	29,900	34,700	38,900	55,300	54,800
Department of Labor	3,567	12,938	5,893	10,114	12,900	110,500	†	†	†	†	†	†
Department of State	8,220	188	1,519	23	†	†	†	†	†	†	†	†
Department of Transportation	12,328	31,910	28,608	75,847	55,866	52,800	70,100	64,800	71,500	80,509	71,200	6,800
Department of the Treasury	†	226	227	1,496	†	†	†	†	†	†	†	†
Department of Veterans Affairs	518	1,600	2,300	2,500	†	†	†	†	†	†	†	†
Agency for International Development	19,446	77,063	79,415	30,172	33,500	28,100	15,200	22,400	31,100	29,900	17,600	17,900
Environmental Protection Agency	†	41,083	87,481	125,721	98,900	83,400	54,700	79,200	87,200	73,700	86,100	68,000
Federal Emergency Management Agency	†	1,665	†	†	†	†	†	†	†	†	†	†
National Aeronautics and Space Administration	258,016	254,629	1,090,003	1,751,977	2,071,030	2,763,120	1,585,500	1,430,761	2,289,837	2,200,143	2,287,755	2,333,069
National Science Foundation	253,628	743,809	1,427,007	1,874,395	2,566,244	3,503,216	4,914,700	4,491,930	4,597,266	4,443,881	4,584,258	4,723,391
Nuclear Regulatory Commission	†	32,590	42,328	22,188	12,200	15,100	14,500	14,000	8,600	5,400	9,400	6,200
Office of Economic Opportunity	20,035	†	†	†	†	†	†	†	†	†	†	†
U.S. Arms Control and Disarmament Agency	100	661	25	†	†	†	†	†	†	†	†	†
Other agencies	1,421	990	885	500	300	7,900	14,300	6,000	5,000	3,800	4,800	6,900

See notes at end of table.

Table 401.30. Federal on-budget funds for education, by level/educational purpose, agency, and program: Selected fiscal years, 1970 through 2014—Continued

—Not available.

†Not applicable.

[1]Excludes federal support for medical education benefits under Medicare in the U.S. Department of Health and Human Services. Benefits excluded from total because data before fiscal year (FY) 1990 are not available. This program existed since Medicare began, but was not available as a separate budget item until FY 1990. Excluded amounts are estimated as follows: $4,440,000,000 in FY 1990, $7,510,000,000 in FY 1995, $8,020,000,000 in FY 2000, $8,290,000,000 in FY 2005, $9,080,000,000 in FY 2010, $9,200,000,000 in FY 2011, $9,800,000,000 in FY 2012, $10,000,000,000 in FY 2013, $11,330,000,000 in FY 2014, and $11,800,000,000 in FY 2015.

[2]Data for research programs at universities and related institutions are estimated.

[3]The U.S. Department of Education was created in May 1980. It formerly was the Office of Education in the U.S. Department of Health, Education, and Welfare.

[4]Arranges for the education of children who reside on federal property when no suitable local school district can or will provide for the education of these children.

[5]Includes many programs, such as No Child Left Behind, 21st Century Community Learning Centers, Class Size Reduction, and Charter Schools, Safe and Drug-Free Schools, and Innovative programs.

[6]Included the School-To-Work Opportunities program, which initiated a national system to be administered jointly by the U.S. Departments of Education and Labor. Programs in the Education Reform program were transferred to the school improvement programs or discontinued in FY 2002. Amounts after FY 2002 reflect balances that are spending out from prior-year appropriations.

[7]Starting in FY 1994, the Special Milk Program has been included in the child nutrition programs.

[8]The Farm Security and Rural Investment Act of 2002 (Public Law 107-171) carries out preschool and school feeding programs in foreign countries to help reduce the incidence of hunger and malnutrition, and improve literacy and primary education.

[9]These commodities are purchased under Section 32 of the Agricultural Adjustment Act of 1935 (Public Law 74-320), for use in the child nutrition programs.

[10]Assisted in the construction of public facilities, such as vocational schools, through grants or loans. No funds have been appropriated for this program since FY 1977, and it was completely phased out in FY 1984.

[11]Established in 1979, with funds first appropriated in FY 1980.

[12]Formerly in the Office of Economic Opportunity. In FY 1972, funds were transferred to the U.S. Department of Health, Education, and Welfare, Office of Child Development.

[13]Created by the Family Support Act of 1988 (Public Law 100-485) to provide funds for the Job Opportunities and Basic Skills Training program. Later incorporated into Temporary Assistance for Needy Families program.

[14]After age 18, benefits terminate at the end of the school term or in 3 months, whichever comes first.

[15]Transferred from the U.S. Department of Transportation to the U.S. Department of Homeland Security in March 2003.

[16]Provides funding for supplemental programs for eligible American Indian students in public schools.

[17]Finances the cost of academic, social, and occupational education courses for inmates in federal prisons.

[18]Some of the work and training programs were in the Office of Economic Opportunity and were transferred to the U.S. Department of Labor in FYs 1971 and 1972. From FY 1994 through FY 2001, included the School-to-Work Opportunities program, which was administered jointly by the U.S. Departments of Education and Labor.

[19]Established in FY 1972 and closed in FY 1986.

[20]The states' share of revenue-sharing funds could not be spent on education in FYs 1981 through 1986.

[21]Provided educational assistance allowances in order to restore lost educational opportunities to those individuals whose careers were interrupted or impeded by reason of active military service between January 31, 1955, and January 1, 1977.

[22]This program is in Readjustment Benefits program, Chapter 31, and covers the costs of subsistence, tuition, books, supplies, and equipment for disabled veterans requiring vocational rehabilitation.

[23]This program is in Readjustment Benefits program, Chapter 35, and provides benefits to children and spouses of veterans.

[24]"Elementary/secondary" obligations for FYs 2014 and 2015 include those items that impact elementary and secondary (K–12) students, and that are standards based. "Other education" obligations include all other arts education items not meeting the terms of "elementary/secondary."

[25]Head Start program funds were transferred to the U.S. Department of Health, Education, and Welfare, Office of Child Development, in FY 1972.

[26]Most of these programs were transferred to the U.S. Department of Health, Education, and Welfare, Office of Education, in FY 1972.

[27]Transferred to the U.S. Department of Labor in FYs 1971 and 1972.

[28]Transferred to the ACTION Agency in FY 1972.

[29]Under the William D. Ford Federal Direct Loan Program (commonly referred to as the Direct Loan Program), the federal government uses Treasury funds to provide loan capital directly to schools, which then disburse loan funds to students.

[30]The Federal Family Education Loan (FFEL) Program eliminated the authorization to originate new FFEL loans after June 30, 2010; all new loans are originated under the Direct Loan Program. The FFEL Program made loan capital available to students and their families through private lenders. State and private nonprofit guaranty agencies administer the federal guar-

antee protecting FFEL lenders against losses related to borrower default. These agencies also collect on defaulted loans and provide other services to lenders.

[31]Transferred from the U.S. Department of Housing and Urban Development to the U.S. Department of Health, Education, and Welfare, Office of Education, in FY 1979.

[32]Transferred from the National Science Foundation to the U.S. Department of Commerce in October 1970.

[33]Transferred from the U.S. Department of Commerce to the U.S. Department of Transportation in FY 1981.

[34]Includes special education programs (military and civilian); legal education program; flight training; advanced degree program; college degree program (officers); and Armed Forces Health Professions Scholarship program.

[35]Does not include Health Education Assistance Loans (HEAL).

[36]Alcohol, drug abuse, and mental health training programs are included starting in FY 1992.

[37]From 2008 onward, funding came from Harwood Training Grants.

[38]Beginning in FY 1992, data were included in the National Institutes of Health training grants program.

[39]This program closed in FY 2004.

[40]Postsecondary student benefits were ended by the Omnibus Budget Reconciliation Act of 1981 (Public Law 97-35) and were completely phased out by August 1985.

[41]Includes flight training. Transferred to the U.S. Department of Homeland Security in March 2003.

[42]Transferred from the U.S. Department of State to the United States Information Agency in 1977, then transferred back to the U.S. Department of State in FY 1998.

[43]In FY 2014, the Regional Graduate Fellowship program was consolidated with the Fulbright Program.

[44]Chapter 33 was enacted in the Post 9-11 Veterans Educational Assistance Act of 2008 (Public Law 110-252).

[45]Part of the Ronald W. Reagan National Defense Authorization Act for FY 2005 (Public Law 108-375), enacted October 28, 2004. The Reserve Education Assistance Program (REAP) provides educational assistance to members of the National Guard and Reserves who serve on active duty in support of a contingency operation under federal authority on or after September 11, 2001.

[46]Abolished in FY 1998, with functions transferred to the U.S. Department of State and the newly created Broadcasting Board of Governors.

[47]Included in the Educational and Cultural Affairs program in FYs 1980 through 1983, and became an independent program in FY 1984.

[48]Includes funding for D.C. College Tuition Assistance Grant (DC TAG), D.C. Adoption Scholarship Program, Robert C. Byrd Honors Scholarship Program, United States Senate Youth Program (USSYP), Advanced Placement Test Fee Program, the Early College Grant, and the College Access Challenge Grant.

[49]Transferred from U.S. Department of Education to the Institute of Museum and Library Services in FY 1997.

[50]Transferred to the U.S. Department of Homeland Security in FY 2003.

[51]The disaster relief program repairs and replaces damaged and destroyed school buildings. This program was transferred from the Federal Emergency Management Agency to the U.S. Department of Homeland Security in FY 2003.

[52]The National Service Trust Act of 1993 (Public Law 103-82) established the Corporation for National and Community Service. In 1993, ACTION became part of this agency.

[53]The Federal Emergency Management Agency was created in 1979, representing a combination of five existing agencies. The funds for the Federal Emergency Management Agency in FY 1970 were in other agencies. This agency was transferred to the U.S. Department of Homeland Security in March 2003.

[54]These programs include the Fall-Out Shelter Analysis, Blast Protection Design through FY 1992. Starting in FY 1993, earthquake training and safety for teachers and administrators for grades 1 through 12 are included.

[55]Transferred from the General Services Administration in April 1985.

[56]The Consolidated Appropriations Act of 2008 (Public Law 110-161) transferred the National Commission on Libraries and Information Science to the Institute of Museum and Library Services starting in FY 2008.

[57]Includes federal obligations for research and development (research, and R & D plant administered by colleges and universities. FY 2015 data are estimated, except the U.S. Department of Education data, which are actual numbers.

[58]FY 1970 includes outlays for the Research and Training program. FY 1980 includes outlays for the National Institute of Education program. FY 1990 through FY 2000 amounts are outlays for the Office of Educational Research and Improvement. Amounts for FY 2005 and later years are for the Institute of Education Sciences; these amounts are outlays for years prior to FY 2010 and appropriations for later years.

NOTE: To the extent possible, amounts reported do not represent obligations, but instead represent appropriations or (especially for earlier years) outlays. Negative amounts occur when program receipts exceed outlays. Some data have been revised from previously published figures. Detail may not sum to totals because of rounding.

SOURCE: U.S. Department of Education, Budget Service, unpublished tabulations. U.S. Office of Management and Budget, *Budget of the U.S. Government, Appendix*, fiscal years 1972 through 2016. National Science Foundation, Federal Funds for Research and Development, fiscal years 1970 through 2015. (This table was prepared May 2016.)

Table 401.60. U.S. Department of Education appropriations for major programs, by state or jurisdiction: Fiscal year 2014

[In thousands of current dollars]

State or jurisdiction	Total	Grants for the disadvantaged[1]	Block grants to states for school improvement[2]	School assistance in federally affected areas[3]	Career/ technical and adult education[4]	Special education[5]	Language assistance[6]	American Indian education	Student financial assistance[7]	Rehabilitation services[8]
1	2	3	4	5	6	7	8	9	10	11
Total, 50 states and D.C.[9]	$69,873,570	$14,676,651	$4,024,201	$1,040,434	$1,622,315	$11,984,134	$664,423	$100,381	$32,759,496	$3,001,536
Total, 50 states, D.C., other activities, and other jurisdictions	72,342,512	15,312,923	4,260,867	1,216,955	1,681,553	12,264,584	723,400	100,381	33,627,028	3,154,820
Alabama	1,161,215	231,586	67,627	2,452	28,375	190,766	3,971	1,530	574,052	60,855
Alaska	313,248	47,029	21,209	127,825	5,244	39,443	1,189	12,383	47,768	11,159
Arizona	2,437,713	343,891	76,305	147,376	36,272	201,977	15,178	10,437	1,540,434	65,843
Arkansas	711,121	169,775	45,574	385	16,807	119,386	3,218	260	306,858	48,859
California	8,559,688	1,879,925	443,404	55,870	209,783	1,294,029	150,817	5,691	4,212,432	307,737
Colorado	1,016,228	165,139	48,310	26,283	22,508	166,020	8,610	651	536,532	42,177
Connecticut	669,449	120,173	38,574	4,684	14,674	139,786	6,309	30	318,441	26,777
Delaware	197,628	46,342	21,024	42	6,341	37,787	1,465	0	70,218	14,409
District of Columbia	277,732	44,795	20,702	295	5,475	19,698	881	0	167,499	18,387
Florida	4,176,246	828,823	191,393	6,632	98,948	673,866	43,667	107	2,156,419	176,390
Georgia	2,273,371	534,528	122,548	18,064	56,142	351,312	15,158	0	1,112,356	63,264
Hawaii	274,353	56,161	21,318	41,186	7,616	42,300	3,813	0	87,910	14,050
Idaho	362,890	64,187	24,004	4,893	8,587	59,750	1,911	424	181,063	18,071
Illinois	3,004,056	671,808	172,075	13,320	60,609	532,649	27,322	192	1,413,737	112,345
Indiana	1,584,207	274,577	72,532	95	34,343	272,346	8,481	0	860,467	61,366
Iowa	767,564	89,710	35,338	102	15,439	128,308	3,785	286	465,285	29,312
Kansas	628,563	121,743	36,755	34,010	13,834	113,564	4,269	1,022	282,234	21,131
Kentucky	1,006,424	237,294	67,783	664	26,299	171,261	3,613	0	450,755	48,754
Louisiana	1,093,089	305,731	87,403	8,903	30,016	198,564	3,035	918	421,834	36,684
Maine	297,411	55,033	24,081	1,445	7,163	58,537	726	158	131,860	18,410
Maryland	1,021,494	205,957	58,240	5,618	24,347	211,224	9,835	80	457,474	48,718
Massachusetts	1,267,565	224,262	69,702	494	27,597	297,178	13,702	86	580,576	53,967
Michigan	2,326,922	547,272	152,205	3,418	50,529	417,505	11,225	2,418	1,049,031	93,318
Minnesota	1,152,830	152,368	55,384	18,393	22,305	201,289	8,532	3,589	637,694	53,274
Mississippi	800,922	194,644	60,428	1,184	19,356	126,255	1,589	459	351,547	45,459
Missouri	1,348,099	248,958	75,727	23,352	30,120	237,637	5,288	76	663,001	63,941
Montana	260,828	47,344	26,340	39,978	6,380	40,115	556	3,532	82,288	14,296
Nebraska	392,765	78,682	25,920	10,215	9,114	78,595	2,965	875	165,714	20,686
Nevada	429,325	119,908	27,232	2,735	15,142	76,587	7,155	731	161,638	18,196
New Hampshire	278,924	45,065	23,433	5	7,128	50,466	1,054	0	139,612	12,161
New Jersey	1,586,588	320,298	89,114	10,487	37,291	378,446	20,953	33	669,182	60,784
New Mexico	602,877	115,332	34,657	77,601	12,091	95,903	4,306	7,855	232,662	22,471
New York	4,721,724	1,136,338	304,225	37,531	92,151	805,320	59,771	1,797	2,137,598	146,994
North Carolina	1,993,777	433,807	104,617	14,181	52,451	350,292	14,187	3,560	913,061	107,621
North Dakota	184,294	34,715	21,758	22,527	5,177	30,865	646	1,878	55,819	10,909
Ohio	2,440,942	589,882	155,217	1,194	57,985	456,491	10,101	0	1,057,605	112,466
Oklahoma	851,266	162,123	56,234	31,961	21,063	155,168	5,020	23,995	350,469	45,233
Oregon	855,630	163,730	45,017	2,060	18,775	135,369	7,008	1,867	430,905	50,898
Pennsylvania	2,450,301	578,464	156,003	840	58,209	448,310	15,157	0	1,068,228	125,090
Rhode Island	274,035	50,589	21,180	1,288	7,683	46,898	2,460	0	129,562	14,375
South Carolina	1,005,723	224,026	57,202	1,033	26,658	187,372	3,550	18	448,248	57,615
South Dakota	285,822	44,520	22,017	46,119	5,397	36,863	995	3,729	115,273	10,909
Tennessee	1,335,678	286,904	76,995	2,731	34,279	249,249	5,273	0	607,178	73,068
Texas	5,775,497	1,424,950	352,539	88,180	146,182	1,043,902	103,674	510	2,371,373	244,188
Utah	736,374	94,422	29,848	8,414	15,390	118,330	4,113	1,357	424,518	39,983
Vermont	167,601	35,519	20,762	7	5,100	29,914	500	217	58,474	17,109
Virginia	1,539,662	243,292	72,344	31,030	36,311	299,534	12,284	11	771,305	73,550
Washington	1,190,650	239,359	68,203	38,295	29,985	234,506	16,666	4,104	504,135	55,395
West Virginia	515,150	92,212	34,799	11	11,980	80,406	680	0	257,127	37,935
Wisconsin	1,108,889	217,398	68,041	12,074	26,647	221,362	7,260	2,612	488,596	64,898
Wyoming	159,220	36,059	20,861	12,952	5,018	31,432	500	904	41,445	10,050
Other activities/jurisdictions										
Indian Tribe Set-Aside	273,856	95,732	22,661	0	13,970	99,219	5,000	0	0	37,275
Other nonstate allocations	416,742	45,462	80,957	176,521	11,875	15,000	47,021	0	0	39,905
American Samoa	31,875	11,226	4,785	0	579	6,956	1,104	0	6,089	1,136
Freely Associated States[10]	24,586	0	0	0	171	6,579	0	0	17,835	0
Guam	62,578	16,777	7,435	0	1,059	15,560	1,350	0	17,556	2,841
Northern Marianas	23,639	7,174	3,361	0	689	5,290	1,068	0	4,940	1,117
Puerto Rico	1,599,444	447,492	112,610	0	29,818	122,107	3,339	0	815,270	68,808
U.S. Virgin Islands	36,221	12,409	4,858	0	1,076	9,740	95	0	5,842	2,201

[1]Title I grants. Includes Grants to Local Education Agencies (Basic, Concentration, Targeted, and Education Finance Incentive Grants); School Turnaround Grants; Migrant Education Grants; and Neglected and Delinquent Children Grants.
[2]Title VI grants. Includes Improving Teacher Quality State Grants; Mathematics and Science Partnerships; 21st Century Community Learning Centers; Assessing Achievement, including No Child Left Behind; Rural and Low-Income Schools Program; Small, Rural School Achievement Program; and Homeless Children and Youth Education.
[3]Includes Impact Aid—Basic Support Payments; Impact Aid—Payments for Children with Disabilities; and Impact Aid—Construction.
[4]Includes Career and Technical Education State Grants; Adult Basic and Literacy Education State Grants; and English Literacy and Civics Education State Grants.
[5]Includes Special Education—Grants to States; Special Education—Preschool Grants; and Grants for Infants and Families.

[6]Includes English Language Acquisition.
[7]Includes Pell Grants; Federal Supplemental Educational Opportunity Grants; Federal Work-Study; College Access Challenge Grant; and Student Loan Program interest subsidies.
[8]Includes Vocational Rehabilitation State Grants; Client Assistance State Grants; Protection and Advocacy of Individual Rights; Supported Employment State Grants; and Services for Older Blind Individuals.
[9]Total excludes other activities and other jurisdictions.
[10]Includes the Marshall Islands, the Federated States of Micronesia, and Palau.
NOTE: Data reflect revisions to figures in the Budget of the United States Government, Fiscal Year 2016. Detail may not sum to totals because of rounding.
SOURCE: U.S. Department of Education, Budget Service, retrieved November 25, 2015, from http://www2.ed.gov/about/overview/budget/statetables/index.html; and unpublished tabulations. (This table was prepared November 2015.)

Table 401.70. Appropriations for Title I and selected other programs under the No Child Left Behind Act of 2001, by program and state or jurisdiction: Fiscal years 2014 and 2015

[In thousands of current dollars]

State or jurisdiction	Title I total, 2014	Title I, 2015					Assessing Achievement, 2015	Improving Teacher Quality State Grants, 2015
		Total	Grants to local education agencies[1]	State agency programs		Turn-around Grants		
				Neglected and Delinquent	Migrant			
1	2	3	4	5	6	7	8	9
Total, 50 states and D.C.[2]	$14,676,651	$14,717,694	$13,843,293	$45,928	$364,751	$463,722	$360,104	$2,190,206
Total, 50 states, D.C., other activities, and other jurisdictions	15,312,923	15,337,923	14,409,802	47,614	374,751	505,756	378,000	2,349,830
Alabama	231,586	231,649	221,675	669	2,038	7,267	6,135	36,285
Alaska	47,029	45,994	37,335	325	6,895	1,440	3,508	10,833
Arizona	343,891	341,799	322,822	1,835	6,506	10,636	7,592	35,496
Arkansas	169,775	165,232	154,451	481	5,218	5,082	4,987	22,040
California	1,879,925	1,874,266	1,684,977	1,215	128,658	59,416	28,595	254,340
Colorado	165,139	162,514	150,086	405	6,965	5,057	6,515	25,437
Connecticut	120,173	120,861	115,996	1,064	0	3,801	5,260	21,574
Delaware	46,342	46,376	44,349	288	289	1,450	3,570	10,833
District of Columbia	44,795	44,391	42,820	177	0	1,394	3,279	10,833
Florida	828,823	825,820	775,326	1,567	22,495	26,432	14,450	102,926
Georgia	534,528	525,067	499,248	1,580	7,809	16,430	10,059	59,838
Hawaii	56,161	49,798	47,045	409	794	1,550	3,837	10,833
Idaho	64,187	63,373	57,304	537	3,532	2,000	4,223	10,853
Illinois	671,808	688,240	663,791	640	1,887	21,922	11,475	93,723
Indiana	274,577	272,993	258,436	558	5,437	8,562	7,483	38,852
Iowa	89,710	96,206	91,259	314	1,591	3,043	5,046	17,873
Kansas	121,743	119,543	104,127	237	11,413	3,766	5,013	18,241
Kentucky	237,294	227,306	211,876	1,091	7,310	7,029	5,840	35,840
Louisiana	305,731	298,550	284,811	2,010	2,443	9,287	6,104	52,095
Maine	55,033	53,123	50,087	230	1,156	1,649	3,749	10,833
Maryland	205,957	204,400	195,845	1,524	500	6,531	6,782	33,206
Massachusetts	224,262	243,232	231,735	2,160	1,591	7,745	6,950	41,946
Michigan	547,272	523,850	498,742	1,029	8,459	15,620	9,376	91,173
Minnesota	152,368	156,404	148,649	753	2,046	4,956	6,599	31,236
Mississippi	194,644	198,203	190,654	397	1,024	6,128	5,071	34,059
Missouri	248,958	251,840	240,817	1,621	1,499	7,902	6,927	39,456
Montana	47,344	48,148	45,473	187	995	1,494	3,632	10,833
Nebraska	78,682	76,709	68,871	376	5,032	2,431	4,297	11,110
Nevada	119,908	121,131	116,689	358	234	3,851	4,877	11,417
New Hampshire	45,065	41,851	39,727	682	144	1,297	3,781	10,833
New Jersey	320,298	344,633	330,260	1,438	1,938	10,996	8,705	52,363
New Mexico	115,332	121,289	116,205	350	910	3,823	4,407	18,096
New York	1,136,338	1,153,476	1,104,146	2,776	9,764	36,789	14,739	188,307
North Carolina	433,807	437,051	416,987	609	5,567	13,888	9,479	49,793
North Dakota	34,715	34,938	33,486	123	231	1,098	3,453	10,833
Ohio	589,882	580,183	558,414	1,054	2,621	18,094	10,511	85,802
Oklahoma	162,123	163,261	156,253	356	1,515	5,137	5,650	26,237
Oregon	163,730	157,216	140,708	1,515	10,121	4,872	5,424	22,084
Pennsylvania	578,464	571,697	544,019	836	8,946	17,895	10,658	93,503
Rhode Island	50,589	51,444	49,334	476	0	1,634	3,609	10,833
South Carolina	224,026	235,440	225,816	1,554	554	7,515	6,063	28,553
South Dakota	44,520	45,878	43,470	140	827	1,441	3,578	10,833
Tennessee	286,904	293,915	283,633	359	568	9,355	7,219	38,844
Texas	1,424,950	1,425,719	1,320,435	2,199	58,218	44,867	22,896	186,990
Utah	94,422	93,035	87,185	1,046	1,823	2,982	5,514	14,923
Vermont	35,519	35,073	33,196	148	626	1,102	3,352	10,833
Virginia	243,292	254,065	243,634	1,563	784	8,084	8,222	40,760
Washington	239,359	254,977	230,297	1,706	14,921	8,054	7,458	37,521
West Virginia	92,212	92,927	89,209	793	0	2,925	4,071	19,680
Wisconsin	217,398	217,429	208,522	1,380	627	6,900	6,697	37,733
Wyoming	36,059	35,178	33,060	788	230	1,100	3,386	10,833
Other activities/jurisdictions								
Indian Tribe Set-Aside	95,732	98,993	95,806	0	0	3,187	1,845	11,690
Other nonstate allocations	45,462	45,462	8,984	1,190	10,000	25,288	8,949	65,795
American Samoa	11,226	10,662	10,321	0	0	342	359	2,673
Guam	16,777	15,925	15,424	0	0	502	809	4,496
Northern Marianas	7,174	6,808	6,595	0	0	213	262	1,644
Puerto Rico	447,492	431,198	418,467	496	0	12,235	5,257	70,448
U.S. Virgin Islands	12,409	11,180	10,913	0	0	267	415	2,878

[1]Includes Basic, Concentration, Targeted, and Education Finance Incentive Grants.
[2]Total excludes other activities and other jurisdictions.
NOTE: Detail may not sum to totals because of rounding. Data for fiscal year 2014 are revised from previously published figures. Estimates for fiscal year 2015 are preliminary.

SOURCE: U.S. Department of Education, Budget Service, Elementary, Secondary, and Vocational Education Analysis Division, retrieved September 15, 2015, from http://www2.ed.gov/about/overview/budget/statetables/16stbyprogram.pdf. (This table was prepared September 2015.)

Table 402.10. Federal obligations for research, development, and R&D plant, by category of obligation, performers, and fields of science: Fiscal years 2007 through 2015

[In millions]

Category of obligation, performers, and fields of science	Actual							Estimated		Percent change, 2014 to 2015
	2007	2008	2009	2010	2011	2012	2013	2014	2015	
1	2	3	4	5	6	7	8	9	10	11
	Current dollars									
Total obligations for research, development, and R&D plant.....	$129,431.1	$129,049.4	$144,760.5	$146,967.8	$139,661.5	$140,635.8	$127,291.1	$132,496.3	$132,751.8	0.2
Research and development obligations....	127,262.7	127,105.6	141,092.5	140,354.5	135,490.8	138,485.1	125,386.0	130,278.7	129,435.0	-0.6
Performers										
Federal intramural[1]	29,932.5	29,637.9	31,546.4	30,911.8	35,144.7	34,367.8	32,963.1	34,736.1	33,373.7	-3.9
Industrial firms...............................	55,342.3	56,337.6	59,749.3	59,867.8	53,550.2	58,910.1	49,538.1	50,236.5	50,580.4	0.7
Federally funded research and development centers (FFRDCs) administered by industrial firms	2,691.6	4,119.9	4,067.1	3,946.2	4,424.5	3,611.7	3,796.1	4,207.5	4,558.1	8.3
Universities and colleges	25,547.8	26,026.5	31,557.7	31,192.3	27,680.3	27,509.5	25,772.0	27,429.3	27,736.6	1.1
FFRDCs administered by universities and colleges	4,171.2	1,988.6	3,402.7	3,370.5	3,437.8	3,694.2	3,711.7	3,800.8	3,661.8	-3.7
Other nonprofit institutions	5,984.4	5,965.0	7,049.7	7,245.3	6,636.6	6,347.0	5,915.0	6,134.9	6,037.3	-1.6
FFRDCs administered by nonprofit institutions........................	2,520.3	2,083.0	2,730.7	2,784.1	2,923.7	2,752.2	2,571.9	2,557.1	2,366.2	-7.5
State and local governments.................	362.0	389.0	392.0	426.7	716.2	453.2	385.6	446.4	476.1	6.7
Foreign	710.6	558.1	596.9	609.9	976.8	839.5	732.4	730.1	644.6	-11.7
Research obligations........................	54,093.5	53,893.6	63,694.3	63,728.0	58,023.7	61,946.9	59,198.2	62,908.8	63,419.9	0.8
Performers										
Federal intramural[1]	11,816.4	11,921.7	13,321.2	13,280.9	12,663.4	14,295.0	13,416.8	14,305.6	14,747.5	3.1
Industrial firms...............................	6,074.2	5,782.4	6,280.2	6,625.5	6,037.4	7,794.0	7,365.5	8,057.5	7,935.2	-1.5
FFRDCs administered by industrial firms	1,863.0	2,929.7	3,070.5	2,960.1	2,984.4	2,678.7	2,713.8	3,217.5	3,445.1	7.1
Universities and colleges...................	23,966.9	24,323.2	30,168.8	29,607.8	26,253.2	26,289.9	24,771.7	26,110.1	26,382.9	1.0
FFRDCs administered by universities and colleges................	2,942.4	1,623.1	2,148.1	2,151.6	2,224.4	2,856.9	3,089.7	3,090.9	2,885.8	-6.6
Other nonprofit institutions..................	5,416.7	5,397.5	6,500.7	6,687.0	5,760.8	5,812.9	5,445.5	5,648.4	5,652.6	0.1
FFRDCs administered by nonprofit institutions........................	1,283.0	1,205.7	1,462.0	1,633.6	1,447.7	1,457.0	1,686.8	1,725.7	1,599.9	-7.3
State and local governments..............	297.6	338.8	343.6	352.8	282.2	352.2	313.5	394.7	427.5	8.3
Foreign	433.3	371.5	399.3	428.6	370.2	410.3	394.8	358.5	343.5	-4.2
Fields of science										
Engineering	8,989.7	8,975.5	10,285.0	11,081.2	10,057.2	11,403.4	10,948.2	11,887.5	11,768.6	-1.0
Environmental sciences	3,170.5	2,984.6	3,751.1	3,338.9	3,207.2	3,884.3	4,041.0	4,365.8	4,384.6	0.4
Life sciences.................................	29,463.6	28,918.8	33,267.1	33,909.1	29,408.6	30,966.7	29,328.4	30,668.2	30,972.7	1.0
Mathematics and computer sciences ..	2,945.7	3,047.3	3,611.6	3,411.8	3,374.3	3,527.5	3,427.0	3,883.2	4,179.8	7.6
Physical sciences...........................	5,136.1	5,072.6	5,821.1	5,870.8	5,426.6	6,407.5	6,281.9	6,483.1	6,486.9	0.1
Psychology...................................	1,837.9	1,740.8	2,086.3	2,155.6	1,886.8	2,086.6	1,935.2	1,968.0	2,016.4	2.5
Social sciences..............................	1,147.1	977.0	1,159.2	1,197.3	1,262.4	1,124.5	1,237.3	1,435.1	1,284.0	-10.5
Other sciences	1,403.1	2,177.1	3,712.7	2,763.2	3,400.5	2,546.3	1,999.3	2,217.9	2,326.8	4.9
Development obligations	73,169.2	73,211.9	77,398.2	76,626.5	77,467.1	76,538.3	66,187.8	67,369.9	66,015.1	-2.0
Performers										
Federal intramural[1]	18,116.1	17,716.1	18,225.2	17,630.9	22,481.3	20,072.8	19,546.3	20,430.5	18,626.2	-8.8
Industrial firms...............................	49,268.1	50,555.2	53,467.0	53,242.3	47,512.8	51,116.1	42,172.6	42,179.1	42,645.2	1.1
FFRDCs administered by industrial firms	828.6	1,190.2	996.6	986.1	1,440.1	933.0	1,082.3	990.0	1,113.0	12.4
Universities and colleges...................	1,580.9	1,703.3	1,389.0	1,584.5	1,427.1	1,219.6	1,000.2	1,319.2	1,353.8	2.6
FFRDCs administered by universities and colleges	1,228.8	365.5	1,254.6	1,218.9	1,213.3	837.3	622.1	709.9	776.0	9.3
Other nonprofit institutions	567.7	567.5	549.0	558.3	875.8	534.1	469.5	486.5	384.7	-20.9
FFRDCs administered by nonprofit institutions........................	1,237.3	877.3	1,268.7	1,150.4	1,476.0	1,295.2	885.1	831.5	766.3	-7.8
State and local governments..............	64.4	50.2	48.4	73.9	434.0	101.0	72.1	51.6	48.7	-5.7
Foreign	277.3	186.6	197.6	181.3	606.6	429.2	337.6	371.6	301.1	-19.0
R&D plant obligations	2,168.4	1,943.8	3,668.0	6,613.3	4,170.7	2,150.7	1,905.1	2,217.6	3,316.8	49.6
Performers										
Federal intramural[1]	593.4	494.0	804.7	1,953.3	846.5	486.2	673.3	642.5	697.4	8.5
Industrial firms...............................	401.4	449.0	396.3	1,751.2	2,030.0	460.5	231.5	323.3	1,331.6	311.9
FFRDCs administered by industrial firms..............................	27.6	175.6	127.7	167.7	118.3	51.8	79.5	91.2	98.7	8.3
Universities and colleges	265.6	210.2	607.0	1,532.6	286.0	372.5	236.6	325.8	377.3	15.8
FFRDCs administered by universities and colleges	498.4	334.4	706.5	491.4	242.9	248.1	246.2	308.5	356.2	15.5
Other nonprofit institutions	79.7	23.7	154.4	245.9	141.3	200.8	184.1	212.8	384.2	80.6
FFRDCs administered by nonprofit institutions........................	296.2	253.8	868.2	465.3	491.0	323.1	249.8	309.8	69.7	-77.5
State and local governments.................	#	#	1.2	2.0	0.2	#	0.2	0.3	#	-86.8
Foreign	6.1	3.1	2.0	4.0	14.6	7.6	3.9	3.4	1.7	-50.0

See notes at end of table.

Table 402.10. Federal obligations for research, development, and R&D plant, by category of obligation, performers, and fields of science: Fiscal years 2007 through 2015—Continued

[In millions]

Category of obligation, performers, and fields of science	Actual							Estimated		Percent change, 2014 to 2015
	2007	2008	2009	2010	2011	2012	2013	2014	2015	
1	2	3	4	5	6	7	8	9	10	11
	Constant fiscal year 2015 dollars[2]									
Total obligations for research, development, and R&D plant.....	$147,227.2	$141,836.7	$158,802.3	$159,327.7	$148,486.8	$146,763.2	$131,005.1	$134,271.1	$132,751.8	-1.1
Research and development obligations	144,760.7	139,700.3	154,778.5	152,158.2	144,052.5	144,518.8	129,044.4	132,023.8	129,435.0	-2.0
Performers										
Federal intramural[1]	34,048.1	32,574.7	34,606.4	33,511.5	37,365.5	35,865.2	33,924.9	35,201.4	33,373.7	-5.2
Industrial firms.................................	62,951.6	61,920.0	65,545.0	64,902.6	56,934.1	61,476.8	50,983.5	50,909.4	50,580.4	-0.6
Federally funded research and development centers (FFRDCs) administered by industrial firms	3,061.7	4,528.1	4,461.6	4,278.1	4,704.1	3,769.1	3,906.9	4,263.9	4,558.1	6.9
Universities and colleges	29,060.5	28,605.4	34,618.8	33,815.5	29,429.4	28,708.1	26,524.0	27,796.7	27,736.6	-0.2
FFRDCs administered by universities and colleges..................	4,744.7	2,185.6	3,732.8	3,654.0	3,655.0	3,855.2	3,820.0	3,851.7	3,661.8	-4.9
Other nonprofit institutions	6,807.2	6,556.1	7,733.5	7,854.6	7,056.0	6,623.5	6,087.6	6,217.1	6,037.3	-2.9
FFRDCs administered by nonprofit institutions...........................	2,866.8	2,289.4	2,995.6	3,018.2	3,108.5	2,872.1	2,646.9	2,591.4	2,366.2	-8.7
State and local governments................	411.8	427.5	430.0	462.6	761.5	472.9	396.9	452.4	476.1	5.2
Foreign	808.3	613.4	654.8	661.2	1,038.5	876.1	753.8	739.9	644.6	-12.9
Research obligations............................	61,531.1	59,233.8	69,872.6	69,087.5	61,690.2	64,645.9	60,925.4	63,751.5	63,419.9	-0.5
Performers										
Federal intramural[1]	13,441.1	13,103.0	14,613.4	14,397.8	13,463.6	14,917.8	13,808.3	14,497.2	14,747.5	1.7
Industrial firms.................................	6,909.4	6,355.4	6,889.4	7,182.7	6,418.9	8,133.6	7,580.4	8,165.4	7,935.2	-2.8
FFRDCs administered by industrial firms	2,119.2	3,220.0	3,368.3	3,209.0	3,173.0	2,795.4	2,793.0	3,260.6	3,445.1	5.7
Universities and colleges.....................	27,262.2	26,733.3	33,095.2	32,097.8	27,912.2	27,435.3	25,494.5	26,459.8	26,382.9	-0.3
FFRDCs administered by universities and colleges	3,347.0	1,783.9	2,356.5	2,332.5	2,365.0	2,981.4	3,179.8	3,132.3	2,885.8	-7.9
Other nonprofit institutions	6,161.5	5,932.3	7,131.3	7,249.4	6,124.8	6,066.2	5,604.4	5,724.1	5,652.6	-1.2
FFRDCs administered by nonprofit institutions........................	1,459.4	1,325.2	1,603.8	1,771.0	1,539.2	1,520.5	1,736.0	1,748.8	1,599.9	-8.5
State and local governments..............	338.5	372.4	376.9	382.5	300.0	367.5	322.6	400.0	427.5	6.9
Foreign	492.9	408.3	438.0	464.6	393.6	428.2	406.3	363.3	343.5	-5.5
Fields of science										
Engineering	10,225.7	9,864.9	11,282.6	12,013.1	10,692.7	11,900.2	11,267.6	12,046.7	11,768.6	-2.3
Environmental sciences	3,606.4	3,280.3	4,115.0	3,619.7	3,409.9	4,053.5	4,158.9	4,424.3	4,384.6	-0.9
Life sciences	33,514.7	31,784.3	36,494.0	36,760.8	31,266.9	32,315.9	30,184.1	31,079.0	30,972.7	-0.3
Mathematics and computer sciences ..	3,350.7	3,349.3	3,962.1	3,698.7	3,587.5	3,681.2	3,527.0	3,935.2	4,179.8	6.2
Physical sciences...............................	5,842.3	5,575.2	6,385.7	6,364.5	5,769.5	6,686.7	6,465.2	6,569.9	6,486.9	-1.3
Psychology...	2,090.6	1,913.3	2,288.7	2,336.9	2,006.0	2,177.5	1,991.7	1,994.4	2,016.4	1.1
Social sciences..................................	1,304.8	1,073.8	1,271.6	1,298.0	1,342.2	1,173.5	1,273.4	1,454.3	1,284.0	-11.7
Other sciences	1,596.0	2,392.8	4,072.8	2,995.6	3,615.4	2,657.2	2,057.6	2,247.6	2,326.8	3.5
Development obligations	83,229.6	80,466.3	84,905.8	83,070.7	82,362.3	79,873.0	68,119.0	68,272.3	66,015.1	-3.3
Performers										
Federal intramural[1]	20,607.0	19,471.6	19,993.0	19,113.6	23,901.9	20,947.4	20,116.6	20,704.2	18,626.2	-10.0
Industrial firms.................................	56,042.2	55,564.6	58,653.3	57,719.9	50,515.2	53,343.2	43,403.1	42,744.1	42,645.2	-0.2
FFRDCs administered by industrial firms	942.5	1,308.1	1,093.3	1,069.0	1,531.1	973.7	1,113.9	1,003.3	1,113.0	10.9
Universities and colleges.....................	1,798.3	1,872.1	1,523.7	1,717.8	1,517.3	1,272.7	1,029.4	1,336.9	1,353.8	1.3
FFRDCs administered by universities and colleges	1,397.8	401.7	1,376.3	1,321.4	1,290.0	873.8	640.3	719.4	776.0	7.9
Other nonprofit institutions	645.8	623.7	602.3	605.3	931.1	557.4	483.2	493.0	384.7	-22.0
FFRDCs administered by nonprofit institutions........................	1,407.4	964.2	1,391.8	1,247.1	1,569.3	1,351.6	910.9	842.6	766.3	-9.1
State and local governments..............	73.3	55.2	53.1	80.1	461.4	105.4	74.2	52.3	48.7	-6.9
Foreign	315.4	205.1	216.8	196.5	644.9	447.9	347.5	376.6	301.1	-20.0
R&D plant obligations	2,466.5	2,136.4	4,023.8	7,169.5	4,434.2	2,244.4	1,960.7	2,247.3	3,316.8	47.6
Performers										
Federal intramural[1]	675.0	542.9	882.8	2,117.6	900.0	507.4	692.9	651.1	697.4	7.1
Industrial firms.................................	456.6	493.5	434.7	1,898.5	2,158.3	480.6	238.3	327.6	1,331.6	306.4
FFRDCs administered by industrial firms	31.4	193.0	140.1	181.8	125.8	54.1	81.8	92.4	98.7	6.8
Universities and colleges	302.1	231.0	665.9	1,661.5	304.1	388.7	243.5	330.2	377.3	14.3
FFRDCs administered by universities and colleges	566.9	367.5	775.0	532.7	258.2	258.9	253.4	312.6	356.2	13.9
Other nonprofit institutions	90.7	26.0	169.4	266.6	150.2	209.5	189.5	215.7	384.2	78.2
FFRDCs administered by nonprofit institutions........................	336.9	278.9	952.4	504.4	522.0	337.2	257.1	313.9	69.7	-77.8
State and local governments................	#	#	1.3	2.2	0.2	#	0.2	0.3	#	-86.8
Foreign	6.9	3.4	2.2	4.3	15.5	7.9	4.0	3.4	1.7	-50.7

#Rounds to zero.
[1]Includes costs associated with the administration of intramural and extramural programs by federal personnel as well as actual intramural performance.
[2]Data adjusted by the federal budget composite deflator reported in U.S. Office of Management and Budget, *Budget of the U.S. Government, Historical Tables, Fiscal Year 2016.*

NOTE: Some data have been revised from previously published figures. Detail may not sum to totals because of rounding. Totals do not include the U.S. Department of Homeland Security.
SOURCE: National Science Foundation, National Center for Science and Engineering Statistics, Survey of Federal Funds for Research and Development, 2006 through 2015, retrieved May 16, 2016, from https://ncsesdata.nsf.gov/fedfunds/2014/. (This table was prepared May 2016.)

CHAPTER 5
Outcomes of Education

This chapter contains tables comparing educational attainment and workforce characteristics. The data show labor force status, income levels, and occupations of high school dropouts and high school and college graduates. Most of these tables are based on data from the U.S. Census Bureau and the U.S. Bureau of Labor Statistics. Population characteristics are provided for many of the measures to allow for comparisons among various demographic groups. While most of the tables in this chapter focus on labor market outcomes, the chapter ends with a few tables on adults' attitudes, skills, and participation in continuing education.

Statistics related to outcomes of education appear in other sections of the *Digest*. For example, statistics on educational attainment of the entire population are in chapter 1. More detailed data on the numbers of high school and college graduates can be found in chapters 2 and 3. Chapter 3 contains trend data on the percentage of high school completers going to college. Chapter 6 includes international comparisons of employment rates by educational attainment. Additional data on earnings by educational attainment may be obtained from the U.S. Census Bureau's Current Population Reports, Series P-60. The U.S. Bureau of Labor Statistics has a series of publications regarding the educational characteristics of the labor force. Further information on survey methodologies can be found in Appendix A: Guide to Sources and in the publications cited in the table source notes.

Labor Force

The labor force participation rate—that is, the percentage of people either employed or actively seeking employment—was generally higher for adults with higher levels of educational attainment than for those with less education. Among 25- to 64-year-old adults, 86 percent of those with a bachelor's or higher degree participated in the labor force in 2014, compared with 72 percent of those who had completed only high school and 60 percent of those who had not completed high school (table 501.10). Within each education level, the labor force participation rate also varied by race/ethnicity. For 25- to 64-year-olds who had completed only high school, the 2014 labor force participation rate was highest for Hispanics (76 percent), followed by Asians (74 percent), then Whites (72 percent),

then Blacks (68 percent), and then American Indians/Alaska Natives (61 percent). For 25- to 64-year-olds with a bachelor's or higher degree in 2014, the labor force participation rate was highest for Blacks (88 percent), followed by Hispanics and Whites (86 percent), and then Asians (83 percent). The labor force participation rate for American Indians/Alaska Natives with a bachelor's or higher degree (82 percent) was lower than the rates for Blacks, Hispanics, and Whites, but not measurably different from the rate for Asians.

The unemployment rate—that is, the percentage of people in the labor force who are not employed and who have made specific efforts to find employment sometime during the prior 4 weeks—was generally higher for people with lower levels of educational attainment than for those with more education. In 2015, the unemployment rate for 25- to 64-year-old adults who had not completed high school was 9 percent, compared with 6 percent for those who had completed only high school and 2 percent for those with a bachelor's or higher degree (table 501.80). Within each education level, the unemployment rates for 16- to 19-year-olds and 20- to 24-year-olds tended to be higher than the unemployment rate for 25- to 64-year-olds. For example, among 20- to 24-year-olds who had not completed high school and were not enrolled in school, the 2015 unemployment rate was 20 percent, compared with 9 percent for 25- to 64-year-olds with the same level of educational attainment. Among adults in the 25- to 34-year-old age group, the 2015 unemployment rate was 12 percent for those who had not completed high school, 9 percent for high school completers, and 2 percent for those with a bachelor's or higher degree (table 501.80 and figure 22).

The employment to population ratio—that is, the percentage of the population that is employed—was generally higher for people with higher levels of educational attainment than for those with less education. Among 25- to 34-year-olds, for example, 85 percent of those with a bachelor's or higher degree were employed in 2015, compared with 70 percent of those who had completed only high school and 57 percent of those who had not completed high school (table 501.50 and figure 23).

The relative difficulties that high school dropouts encounter in entering the job market are highlighted by comparing the labor force participation and employment rates of recent high school dropouts with those of recent high school completers. In October 2014, about 41 percent of 2013–14 dropouts participated in the labor force (i.e., were either employed or looking for work), with 29 percent employed and 12 percent looking for work (table 504.20 and figure 24). In contrast, the labor force participation rate was 73 percent for 2013–14 high school completers who were not enrolled in college, with 52 percent employed and 21 percent looking for work (table 504.10 and figure 24).

Earnings

Median annual earnings were generally higher for adults with higher levels of educational attainment than for those with lower levels of educational attainment. Among full-time year-round workers age 25 and over, both males and females who had more education generally earned more than people of the same sex who had less education. In 2014, for example, males whose highest level of educational attainment was a bachelor's degree earned 67 percent more than males whose highest level of attainment was high school completion, and females who had attained a bachelor's degree earned 68 percent more than females who had only completed high school (table E, table 502.20, and figure 25).

Among full-time year-round workers age 25 and over, the earnings of females were lower than the earnings of males overall, as well as by education level. For example, median 2014 earnings for full-time year-round workers with a bachelor's degree were 33 percent higher for males than for females. Among those who had only completed high school, median 2014 earnings were 34 percent higher for males than for females.

From 1995 to 2014, net percentage changes in earnings (after adjustment for inflation) varied by highest level of educational attainment and sex. In constant 2014 dollars, the median annual earnings of male full-time year-round workers age 25 and over who had started but not completed high school decreased 9 percent from 1995 ($34,050) to 2014 ($30,840), and the median earnings of those who had completed high school decreased 10 percent from 1995 ($45,290) to 2014 ($40,930). For males with a bachelor's degree, median annual earnings in constant 2014 dollars were not significantly different in 1995 ($69,480) than in 2014 ($68,160). In constant 2014 dollars, the median annual earnings of female full-time year-round workers who had started but not completed high school decreased 9 percent from 1995 ($24,290) to 2014 ($21,990), and the median earnings of those who had completed high school decreased 2 percent from 1995 ($31,410) to 2014 ($30,650). For females with a bachelor's degree, median annual earnings in constant 2014 dollars were not significantly different in 1995 ($49,190) than in 2014 ($51,350).

Table E. Median annual earnings of full-time year-round workers 25 years old and over, by selected levels of educational attainment and sex: Selected years, 1995 through 2014
[In constant 2014 dollars]

Sex and year	Some high school, no completion	High school completion	Bachelor's degree
Males			
1995	$34,050	$45,290	$69,480
2000	34,090	46,600	76,520
2005	32,560	43,480	71,890
2014	30,840	40,930	68,160
Females			
1995	24,290	31,410	49,190
2000	24,340	33,920	54,900
2005	24,100	31,490	50,510
2014	21,990	30,650	51,350

SOURCE: U.S. Department of Commerce, Census Bureau, Current Population Reports, Series P-60, *Money Income in the United States*, 1995 and 2000; and Current Population Survey (CPS), 2005 and 2014 Annual Social and Economic Supplement.

In 2009, the median annual salary of bachelor's degree recipients employed full time 1 year after graduation was $39,700 in constant 2014 dollars (table 505.50 and figure 26). Full-time median annual salaries varied by degree field, however. In 2009, graduates employed full time 1 year after receiving bachelor's degrees in engineering had the highest median annual salary ($59,600 in constant 2014 dollars), followed by those with degrees in the health professions ($50,700) and mathematics/computer science ($49,600), and then those with degrees in business/management ($44,100). Among the lowest full-time median annual salaries were those earned by graduates with degrees in the humanities ($32,000) and psychology ($32,400).

Overall, the inflation-adjusted median annual salary of graduates employed full time 1 year after receiving their bachelor's degree was 7 percent lower in 2009 than in 2001. However, the change in median annual salary from 2001 to 2009 varied by degree field, ranging from an increase of 7 percent for graduates with degrees in the health professions to a decrease of 19 percent for those with degrees in mathematics/computer science and a decrease of 16 percent for those with degrees in the humanities. Although the overall median annual salary of graduates employed full time 1 year after graduation decreased from 2001 to 2009, it had previously increased 13 percent from 1991 to 2001. From 1991 to 2009, there was a net increase of 5 percent in the overall median salary.

In 2014, 25- to 29-year-olds with a bachelor's or higher degree had median annual earnings of $45,340 (table 505.10). Median annual earnings varied by bachelor's degree field. For example, 25- to 29-year-olds with a bachelor's degree in computer engineering had median annual earnings of $70,120, while those with a bachelor's degree in theology and religious vocations had median annual earnings of $34,910.

Figure 22. Unemployment rates of persons 25 to 34 years old, by highest level of educational attainment: Selected years, 1990 through 2015

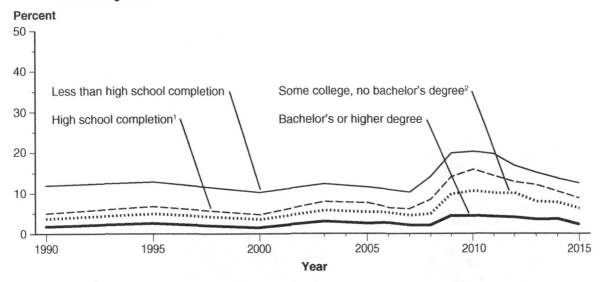

[1] Includes equivalency credentials, such as the GED credential.
[2] Includes persons with no college degree as well as those with an associate's degree.
NOTE: The unemployment rate is the percentage of persons in the civilian labor force who are not working and who made specific efforts to find employment sometime during the prior 4 weeks. The civilian labor force consists of all civilians who are employed or seeking employment.
SOURCE: U.S. Department of Commerce, Census Bureau, Current Population Survey (CPS), Annual Social and Economic Supplement, selected years, 1990 through 2015.

Figure 23. Employment to population ratios of persons 25 to 34 years old, by highest level of educational attainment: Selected years, 1990 through 2015

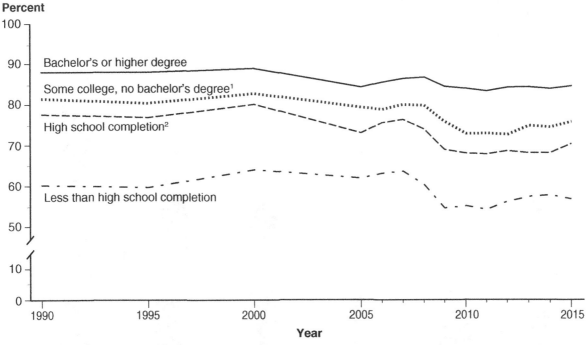

[1] Includes persons with no college degree as well as those with an associate's degree.
[2] Includes equivalency credentials, such as the GED credential.
NOTE: The employment to population ratio is the number of persons employed as a percentage of the civilian population.
SOURCE: U.S. Department of Commerce, Census Bureau, Current Population Survey (CPS), Annual Social and Economic Supplement, selected years, 1990 through 2015.

Figure 24. Percentage distribution of 2013–14 high school dropouts and high school completers not enrolled in college, by labor force status: October 2014

NOTE: Data are for 16- to 24-year-olds who were enrolled in school in October 2013 but were no longer enrolled in October 2014. Dropouts are those who left school without completing a high school credential, while completers are those who received a high school credential, including recipients of equivalency credentials as well as diploma recipients. Detail may not sum to totals because of rounding.
SOURCE: U.S. Department of Commerce, Census Bureau, Current Population Survey (CPS), October 2014.

Figure 25. Median annual earnings of full-time year-round workers 25 years old and over, by highest level of educational attainment and sex: 2014

[In current dollars]

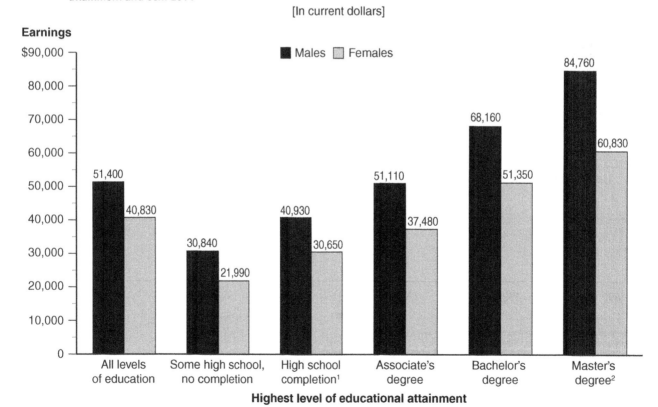

[1]Includes equivalency credentials, such as the GED credential.
[2]Includes only persons whose highest level of education is a master's degree. Doctor's and professional degree recipients are not included.
SOURCE: U.S. Department of Commerce, Census Bureau, Current Population Survey (CPS), Annual Social and Economic Supplement, 2015. Retrieved January 28, 2016, from http://www.census.gov/hhes/www/cpstables/032015/perinc/pinc03_000.htm.

Figure 26. Median annual salaries of bachelor's degree recipients employed full time 1 year after graduation, by field of study: 1991, 2001, and 2009

[In constant 2014 dollars]

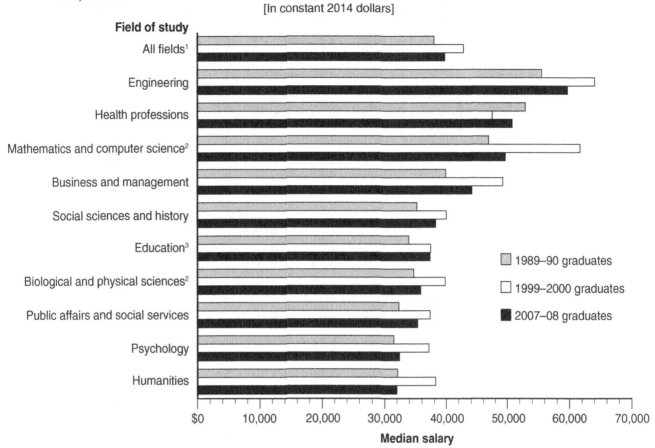

[1]Includes graduates in other fields not separately shown.
[2]For 1989–90 graduates, physical sciences are included with mathematics and computer science instead of with biological sciences.
[3]Most educators work 9- to 10-month contracts.
SOURCE: U.S. Department of Education, National Center for Education Statistics, "Recent College Graduates" survey, 1991; and 2000/01 and 2008/09 Baccalaureate and Beyond Longitudinal Study (B&B:2000/01 and B&B:08/09).

Table 501.10. Labor force participation, employment, and unemployment of persons 25 to 64 years old, by sex, race/ethnicity, age group, and educational attainment: 2012, 2013, and 2014

[Standard errors appear in parentheses]

Sex, race/ethnicity, age group, and educational attainment	Labor force participation rate[1] 2012	2013	2014	Number of participants (in thousands) 2014	Employment to population ratio[2] 2012	2013	2014	Number employed (in thousands) 2014	Unemployment rate[3] 2012	2013	2014	Number unemployed (in thousands) 2014
1	2	3	4	5	6	7	8	9	10	11	12	13
All persons 25 to 64 years old, all education levels	**77.5 (0.04)**	**77.2 (0.04)**	**77.1 (0.04)**	**128,728 (86.0)**	**71.5 (0.04)**	**71.9 (0.04)**	**72.5 (0.05)**	**121,021 (91.3)**	**7.8 (0.03)**	**7.0 (0.03)**	**6.0 (0.03)**	**7,706 (39.6)**
Less than high school completion[4]	60.7 (0.14)	60.7 (0.14)	60.2 (0.15)	11,804 (52.3)	52.1 (0.14)	53.0 (0.16)	53.6 (0.15)	10,511 (50.1)	14.1 (0.14)	12.7 (0.14)	11.0 (0.13)	1,293 (15.6)
High school completion[4]	73.2 (0.09)	72.8 (0.09)	72.3 (0.09)	31,787 (77.6)	65.9 (0.09)	66.2 (0.09)	66.7 (0.09)	29,320 (72.0)	10.0 (0.07)	9.1 (0.06)	7.8 (0.07)	2,467 (24.4)
Some college, no degree	78.0 (0.09)	77.5 (0.09)	77.5 (0.09)	27,877 (64.6)	71.2 (0.10)	71.5 (0.09)	72.4 (0.10)	26,054 (59.8)	8.7 (0.07)	7.7 (0.07)	6.5 (0.06)	1,824 (18.0)
Associate's degree	82.2 (0.13)	82.0 (0.13)	81.6 (0.13)	12,122 (46.3)	76.7 (0.15)	77.2 (0.15)	77.5 (0.15)	11,508 (46.0)	6.6 (0.09)	5.8 (0.09)	5.1 (0.08)	614 (9.2)
Bachelor's or higher degree	86.1 (0.06)	86.0 (0.05)	85.8 (0.06)	45,138 (110.6)	82.5 (0.07)	82.7 (0.06)	83.0 (0.07)	43,629 (106.6)	4.2 (0.04)	3.8 (0.03)	3.3 (0.04)	1,509 (17.4)
Sex												
Male, all education levels	**82.9 (0.05)**	**82.7 (0.05)**	**82.6 (0.05)**	**67,901 (51.1)**	**76.4 (0.05)**	**76.8 (0.06)**	**77.6 (0.06)**	**63,846 (60.3)**	**7.9 (0.04)**	**7.0 (0.04)**	**6.0 (0.04)**	**4,055 (27.1)**
Less than high school completion[4]	69.7 (0.19)	69.8 (0.18)	69.9 (0.18)	7,466 (38.9)	60.7 (0.20)	61.7 (0.21)	63.0 (0.19)	6,730 (37.5)	13.0 (0.14)	11.5 (0.16)	9.9 (0.16)	736 (12.4)
High school completion[4]	79.2 (0.11)	78.7 (0.10)	78.3 (0.12)	18,407 (53.7)	71.0 (0.12)	71.4 (0.12)	72.2 (0.13)	16,980 (53.3)	10.4 (0.10)	9.2 (0.09)	7.8 (0.09)	1,428 (12.1)
Some college, no degree	83.0 (0.10)	82.6 (0.13)	82.7 (0.12)	14,335 (47.8)	76.1 (0.13)	76.5 (0.14)	77.5 (0.12)	13,442 (46.0)	8.3 (0.09)	7.4 (0.11)	6.2 (0.08)	893 (12.1)
Associate's degree	86.6 (0.16)	86.4 (0.16)	86.4 (0.16)	5,444 (29.2)	81.0 (0.18)	81.5 (0.18)	82.0 (0.21)	5,170 (29.2)	6.5 (0.11)	5.8 (0.13)	5.0 (0.11)	274 (6.1)
Bachelor's or higher degree	91.5 (0.06)	91.4 (0.06)	91.1 (0.07)	22,248 (60.5)	87.8 (0.08)	87.9 (0.07)	88.2 (0.08)	21,524 (58.4)	4.0 (0.05)	3.8 (0.05)	3.3 (0.05)	725 (11.5)
Female, all education levels	**72.2 (0.06)**	**72.0 (0.06)**	**71.8 (0.05)**	**60,827 (54.9)**	**66.7 (0.07)**	**67.0 (0.06)**	**67.5 (0.06)**	**57,175 (59.9)**	**7.7 (0.04)**	**6.9 (0.04)**	**6.0 (0.04)**	**3,651 (27.2)**
Less than high school completion[4]	49.8 (0.23)	49.8 (0.21)	48.7 (0.19)	4,338 (25.1)	41.8 (0.23)	42.5 (0.22)	42.4 (0.19)	3,781 (24.5)	15.9 (0.26)	14.7 (0.25)	12.9 (0.20)	558 (8.9)
High school completion[4]	66.5 (0.14)	66.1 (0.13)	65.3 (0.13)	13,379 (45.8)	60.1 (0.15)	60.2 (0.14)	60.2 (0.12)	12,340 (43.5)	9.6 (0.10)	8.9 (0.11)	7.8 (0.10)	1,040 (13.9)
Some college, no degree	73.4 (0.14)	72.7 (0.13)	72.7 (0.12)	13,542 (43.8)	66.7 (0.15)	66.9 (0.13)	67.7 (0.13)	12,612 (40.6)	9.1 (0.10)	7.9 (0.09)	6.9 (0.10)	931 (14.4)
Associate's degree	78.9 (0.16)	78.7 (0.17)	78.1 (0.17)	6,677 (31.4)	73.6 (0.18)	74.0 (0.18)	74.2 (0.17)	6,338 (30.7)	6.7 (0.13)	5.9 (0.11)	5.1 (0.10)	339 (6.9)
Bachelor's or higher degree	81.3 (0.09)	81.2 (0.08)	81.3 (0.09)	22,889 (67.0)	77.8 (0.10)	78.1 (0.10)	78.5 (0.09)	22,105 (64.7)	4.3 (0.05)	3.8 (0.05)	3.4 (0.05)	784 (12.8)
Race/ethnicity												
White, all education levels	**78.5 (0.05)**	**78.2 (0.05)**	**78.1 (0.05)**	**82,330 (52.9)**	**73.4 (0.06)**	**73.7 (0.05)**	**74.2 (0.05)**	**78,284 (58.0)**	**6.5 (0.04)**	**5.8 (0.03)**	**4.9 (0.03)**	**4,046 (25.6)**
Less than high school completion[4]	54.3 (0.23)	54.3 (0.23)	53.3 (0.26)	3,546 (27.9)	45.7 (0.21)	46.6 (0.21)	46.5 (0.26)	3,092 (25.4)	15.8 (0.20)	14.2 (0.24)	12.8 (0.23)	455 (8.9)
High school completion[4]	73.5 (0.11)	72.9 (0.11)	72.2 (0.11)	19,845 (54.5)	67.1 (0.12)	67.2 (0.11)	67.5 (0.11)	18,551 (51.1)	8.7 (0.08)	7.9 (0.07)	6.5 (0.07)	1,293 (15.6)
Some college, no degree	78.0 (0.10)	77.4 (0.10)	77.4 (0.10)	17,951 (48.2)	72.3 (0.13)	72.4 (0.10)	73.1 (0.10)	16,958 (45.1)	7.3 (0.09)	6.5 (0.07)	5.5 (0.06)	993 (12.0)
Associate's degree	82.5 (0.16)	82.0 (0.15)	81.8 (0.15)	8,446 (36.1)	77.8 (0.19)	77.8 (0.17)	78.3 (0.19)	8,082 (36.6)	5.8 (0.12)	5.1 (0.10)	4.3 (0.10)	364 (8.1)
Bachelor's or higher degree	86.1 (0.07)	86.1 (0.06)	86.0 (0.06)	32,542 (75.0)	83.0 (0.08)	83.2 (0.06)	83.5 (0.07)	31,601 (72.5)	3.7 (0.04)	3.3 (0.04)	2.9 (0.03)	941 (11.6)
Black, all education levels	**72.9 (0.13)**	**72.9 (0.12)**	**72.9 (0.14)**	**14,977 (33.4)**	**62.9 (0.15)**	**63.9 (0.12)**	**65.0 (0.14)**	**13,357 (33.4)**	**13.6 (0.11)**	**12.3 (0.11)**	**10.8 (0.10)**	**1,620 (15.0)**
Less than high school completion[4]	47.3 (0.43)	47.8 (0.40)	47.1 (0.40)	1,236 (15.2)	34.9 (0.39)	35.8 (0.39)	36.8 (0.40)	964 (13.5)	26.2 (0.48)	25.1 (0.52)	22.0 (0.51)	272 (7.1)
High school completion[4]	68.3 (0.26)	68.1 (0.20)	68.1 (0.20)	4,428 (32.1)	57.1 (0.24)	58.0 (0.23)	58.9 (0.27)	3,831 (29.3)	16.4 (0.22)	14.9 (0.24)	13.5 (0.23)	597 (11.0)
Some college, no degree	76.8 (0.24)	76.4 (0.22)	76.5 (0.26)	4,141 (25.2)	66.2 (0.30)	67.4 (0.26)	68.5 (0.26)	3,705 (22.7)	13.7 (0.26)	11.8 (0.21)	10.5 (0.21)	435 (9.5)
Associate's degree	81.9 (0.40)	82.6 (0.41)	81.0 (0.33)	1,429 (17.5)	73.3 (0.46)	75.0 (0.48)	74.6 (0.41)	1,314 (16.8)	10.5 (0.32)	9.2 (0.32)	8.0 (0.30)	114 (4.5)
Bachelor's or higher degree	88.5 (0.20)	88.1 (0.18)	88.2 (0.19)	3,744 (26.2)	82.7 (0.27)	82.4 (0.22)	83.4 (0.22)	3,542 (26.6)	6.5 (0.19)	6.4 (0.16)	5.4 (0.17)	202 (6.3)
Hispanic, all education levels	**77.3 (0.09)**	**76.9 (0.11)**	**76.9 (0.11)**	**20,834 (33.3)**	**70.3 (0.11)**	**70.7 (0.13)**	**71.7 (0.11)**	**19,424 (33.1)**	**9.1 (0.09)**	**8.0 (0.09)**	**6.8 (0.08)**	**1,410 (17.2)**
Less than high school completion[4]	70.1 (0.19)	69.8 (0.21)	69.6 (0.21)	6,130 (38.6)	62.6 (0.22)	63.3 (0.25)	64.1 (0.23)	5,650 (38.8)	10.7 (0.19)	9.3 (0.17)	7.8 (0.16)	480 (9.8)
High school completion[4]	77.3 (0.20)	76.8 (0.23)	76.5 (0.22)	5,740 (32.3)	69.6 (0.21)	70.1 (0.25)	70.9 (0.21)	5,320 (31.1)	10.0 (0.16)	8.8 (0.15)	7.3 (0.16)	420 (9.7)
Some college, no degree	80.8 (0.23)	80.1 (0.25)	80.4 (0.25)	4,040 (24.8)	73.4 (0.28)	73.5 (0.28)	75.2 (0.24)	3,778 (22.5)	9.1 (0.19)	8.2 (0.20)	6.5 (0.15)	261 (6.6)
Associate's degree	83.7 (0.38)	83.4 (0.41)	83.2 (0.41)	1,418 (16.7)	78.2 (0.38)	78.2 (0.44)	78.1 (0.48)	1,331 (16.7)	7.4 (0.27)	6.3 (0.28)	6.1 (0.30)	87 (4.3)
Bachelor's or higher degree	87.1 (0.23)	86.8 (0.22)	86.4 (0.18)	3,507 (27.8)	82.4 (0.26)	82.5 (0.26)	82.4 (0.23)	3,345 (26.6)	5.4 (0.16)	5.0 (0.17)	4.6 (0.17)	162 (6.2)
Asian, all education levels	**78.4 (0.16)**	**78.6 (0.15)**	**78.1 (0.13)**	**7,528 (19.8)**	**73.5 (0.18)**	**74.3 (0.17)**	**74.4 (0.15)**	**7,176 (20.8)**	**6.2 (0.12)**	**5.5 (0.10)**	**4.7 (0.10)**	**352 (7.4)**
Less than high school completion[4]	64.5 (0.52)	63.8 (0.50)	63.1 (0.55)	663 (9.8)	58.5 (0.54)	57.8 (0.49)	58.5 (0.55)	615 (8.8)	9.3 (0.43)	9.3 (0.45)	7.3 (0.38)	48 (2.8)
High school completion[4]	74.3 (0.49)	73.8 (0.43)	73.6 (0.48)	1,019 (12.5)	67.9 (0.50)	68.8 (0.48)	68.6 (0.53)	951 (11.9)	8.6 (0.39)	6.8 (0.31)	6.7 (0.38)	69 (4.1)
Some college, no degree	78.0 (0.48)	78.2 (0.49)	76.5 (0.51)	952 (13.4)	71.3 (0.49)	72.6 (0.51)	72.1 (0.53)	898 (13.2)	8.6 (0.39)	7.2 (0.32)	5.7 (0.30)	54 (2.9)
Associate's degree	76.4 (0.68)	79.1 (0.56)	78.7 (0.69)	529 (8.7)	71.3 (0.70)	74.3 (0.61)	75.0 (0.67)	504 (8.4)	6.6 (0.41)	6.1 (0.43)	4.8 (0.33)	25 (1.8)
Bachelor's or higher degree	82.7 (0.21)	82.8 (0.22)	82.5 (0.20)	4,365 (22.7)	79.0 (0.21)	79.4 (0.24)	79.6 (0.22)	4,209 (22.2)	4.5 (0.13)	4.2 (0.11)	3.6 (0.11)	156 (4.8)
American Indian/Alaska Native, all education levels	**66.2 (0.56)**	**65.1 (0.58)**	**64.4 (0.51)**	**696 (8.8)**	**57.2 (0.60)**	**56.7 (0.60)**	**57.2 (0.54)**	**618 (8.6)**	**13.7 (0.44)**	**12.9 (0.45)**	**11.2 (0.42)**	**78 (3.0)**
Less than high school completion[4]	44.0 (1.21)	45.8 (1.50)	43.0 (1.43)	72 (3.2)	33.0 (1.13)	35.3 (1.47)	33.3 (1.31)	56 (2.7)	24.9 (1.88)	22.9 (1.59)	22.5 (1.26)	16 (1.1)
High school completion[4]	64.7 (0.96)	62.5 (0.84)	60.9 (0.83)	224 (5.2)	54.4 (1.03)	52.4 (0.97)	53.0 (0.94)	196 (5.4)	16.0 (0.94)	16.1 (0.96)	12.9 (0.90)	29 (2.0)
Some college, no degree	68.5 (1.14)	67.2 (0.98)	67.5 (0.99)	196 (4.9)	59.0 (1.13)	59.1 (1.05)	60.6 (1.10)	176 (4.8)	13.8 (0.85)	12.0 (0.77)	10.2 (0.73)	20 (1.5)
Associate's degree	75.0 (1.75)	74.8 (1.55)	75.5 (1.68)	73 (3.0)	67.4 (1.69)	68.3 (1.64)	67.9 (1.72)	66 (2.8)	10.0 (1.04)	8.6 (1.18)	10.0 (1.10)	7 (0.9)
Bachelor's or higher degree	84.4 (1.13)	82.1 (1.25)	82.3 (1.16)	131 (4.9)	79.9 (1.16)	78.0 (1.35)	78.9 (1.24)	125 (4.9)	5.2 (0.65)	5.0 (0.71)	4.2 (0.67)	6 (0.9)

See notes at end of table.

Table 501.10. Labor force participation, employment, and unemployment of persons 25 to 64 years old, by sex, race/ethnicity, age group, and educational attainment: 2012, 2013, and 2014—Continued

[Standard errors appear in parentheses]

Sex, race/ethnicity, age group, and educational attainment	Labor force participation				Employment				Unemployment			
	Labor force participation rate[1]			Number of participants (in thousands)	Employment to population ratio[2]			Number employed (in thousands)	Unemployment rate[3]			Number unemployed (in thousands)
	2012	2013	2014	2014	2012	2013	2014	2014	2012	2013	2014	2014
1	2	3	4	5	6	7	8	9	10	11	12	13
Age group												
25 to 34, all education levels	**82.0** (0.06)	**81.8** (0.08)	**81.8** (0.07)	**35,094** (39.1)	**74.1** (0.07)	**74.6** (0.09)	**75.6** (0.09)	**32,436** (46.4)	**9.7** (0.06)	**8.7** (0.06)	**7.6** (0.07)	**2,658** (22.4)
Less than high school completion[4]	65.5 (0.29)	65.3 (0.30)	64.6 (0.32)	3,011 (23.6)	53.7 (0.32)	54.4 (0.30)	55.0 (0.33)	2,566 (22.5)	18.0 (0.31)	16.7 (0.26)	14.8 (0.30)	445 (9.4)
High school completion[4]	78.0 (0.17)	77.1 (0.18)	76.9 (0.16)	7,919 (38.6)	67.2 (0.17)	67.5 (0.21)	68.5 (0.19)	7,045 (36.8)	13.9 (0.15)	12.5 (0.15)	11.0 (0.16)	874 (12.9)
Some college, no degree	82.0 (0.17)	81.8 (0.19)	82.0 (0.15)	8,050 (36.1)	72.9 (0.20)	73.8 (0.20)	75.0 (0.19)	7,358 (33.3)	11.2 (0.15)	9.8 (0.14)	8.6 (0.15)	692 (13.0)
Associate's degree	86.7 (0.22)	86.6 (0.21)	86.5 (0.22)	3,279 (21.8)	80.1 (0.26)	80.8 (0.23)	81.2 (0.30)	3,078 (21.4)	7.7 (0.22)	6.7 (0.15)	6.1 (0.20)	200 (6.7)
Bachelor's or higher degree	89.7 (0.10)	89.6 (0.11)	89.4 (0.11)	12,835 (51.8)	85.8 (0.11)	85.9 (0.11)	86.3 (0.11)	12,388 (50.0)	4.3 (0.08)	4.1 (0.06)	3.5 (0.07)	447 (9.6)
35 to 44, all education levels	**82.5** (0.08)	**82.1** (0.08)	**82.1** (0.10)	**33,412** (45.3)	**76.3** (0.09)	**76.6** (0.09)	**77.3** (0.09)	**31,460** (41.9)	**7.5** (0.06)	**6.7** (0.06)	**5.8** (0.06)	**1,952** (19.5)
Less than high school completion[4]	68.4 (0.24)	68.0 (0.28)	67.3 (0.28)	3,349 (23.2)	59.3 (0.26)	59.8 (0.31)	60.1 (0.30)	2,989 (23.3)	13.4 (0.22)	12.0 (0.27)	10.8 (0.25)	361 (8.4)
High school completion[4]	79.0 (0.18)	78.4 (0.18)	78.0 (0.18)	7,701 (33.8)	70.9 (0.18)	71.1 (0.20)	71.6 (0.20)	7,075 (33.3)	10.3 (0.16)	9.3 (0.15)	8.1 (0.13)	626 (10.6)
Some college, no degree	83.1 (0.18)	82.3 (0.17)	82.4 (0.18)	6,990 (36.1)	76.1 (0.23)	76.0 (0.20)	77.1 (0.20)	6,638 (34.5)	8.5 (0.15)	7.7 (0.14)	6.5 (0.12)	452 (8.5)
Associate's degree	86.5 (0.24)	86.1 (0.23)	86.2 (0.24)	3,168 (22.5)	80.8 (0.27)	81.2 (0.30)	82.0 (0.28)	3,012 (23.0)	6.6 (0.22)	5.7 (0.14)	4.9 (0.18)	155 (5.7)
Bachelor's or higher degree	89.1 (0.11)	89.1 (0.10)	89.1 (0.11)	12,204 (43.3)	85.8 (0.12)	86.2 (0.11)	86.5 (0.11)	11,847 (41.8)	3.7 (0.08)	3.2 (0.06)	2.9 (0.06)	357 (8.0)
45 to 54, all education levels	**80.3** (0.07)	**80.0** (0.07)	**79.8** (0.08)	**34,557** (44.9)	**74.6** (0.08)	**75.0** (0.08)	**75.6** (0.08)	**32,731** (47.7)	**7.0** (0.05)	**6.3** (0.05)	**5.3** (0.05)	**1,826** (17.4)
Less than high school completion[4]	61.9 (0.26)	62.1 (0.29)	62.2 (0.27)	3,299 (23.6)	53.8 (0.27)	55.0 (0.30)	56.2 (0.27)	2,980 (22.8)	13.0 (0.22)	11.5 (0.23)	9.7 (0.21)	319 (7.2)
High school completion[4]	76.9 (0.16)	76.4 (0.14)	75.8 (0.15)	9,266 (35.8)	70.5 (0.17)	70.5 (0.15)	70.9 (0.16)	8,665 (34.0)	8.6 (0.10)	7.7 (0.09)	6.5 (0.10)	601 (10.0)
Some college, no degree	81.3 (0.13)	80.9 (0.18)	80.6 (0.17)	7,273 (30.4)	75.3 (0.16)	75.7 (0.19)	76.3 (0.18)	6,885 (30.3)	7.3 (0.11)	6.5 (0.11)	5.3 (0.11)	388 (7.9)
Associate's degree	84.6 (0.21)	84.7 (0.22)	84.4 (0.24)	3,298 (23.2)	79.5 (0.27)	80.3 (0.22)	80.6 (0.24)	3,150 (21.7)	6.0 (0.17)	5.2 (0.13)	4.5 (0.12)	148 (4.3)
Bachelor's or higher degree	89.4 (0.12)	89.0 (0.11)	89.0 (0.11)	11,422 (37.7)	85.9 (0.14)	85.7 (0.13)	86.1 (0.12)	11,051 (35.9)	4.0 (0.07)	3.8 (0.08)	3.2 (0.05)	371 (6.1)
55 to 64, all education levels	**64.1** (0.08)	**64.3** (0.08)	**64.1** (0.08)	**25,665** (32.3)	**59.9** (0.08)	**60.5** (0.09)	**60.9** (0.08)	**24,394** (34.5)	**6.6** (0.06)	**5.9** (0.06)	**4.9** (0.06)	**1,270** (14.3)
Less than high school completion[4]	45.5 (0.26)	46.0 (0.26)	46.1 (0.26)	2,145 (18.7)	40.5 (0.26)	41.5 (0.27)	42.5 (0.26)	1,975 (18.1)	10.8 (0.24)	9.9 (0.25)	7.9 (0.22)	169 (4.8)
High school completion[4]	59.3 (0.15)	59.8 (0.17)	59.5 (0.16)	6,900 (28.6)	54.9 (0.15)	55.8 (0.17)	56.3 (0.16)	6,534 (27.3)	7.4 (0.11)	6.6 (0.12)	5.3 (0.11)	366 (8.2)
Some college, no degree	64.4 (0.19)	64.1 (0.19)	64.4 (0.18)	5,565 (26.1)	59.8 (0.20)	60.1 (0.19)	61.0 (0.19)	5,273 (25.1)	7.2 (0.12)	6.2 (0.13)	5.2 (0.10)	291 (6.0)
Associate's degree	69.2 (0.31)	69.1 (0.28)	68.4 (0.32)	2,378 (17.7)	65.2 (0.34)	65.2 (0.30)	65.2 (0.32)	2,268 (17.0)	6.2 (0.19)	5.7 (0.18)	4.6 (0.17)	110 (4.1)
Bachelor's or higher degree	74.5 (0.15)	74.6 (0.14)	74.2 (0.13)	8,677 (30.1)	71.0 (0.16)	71.5 (0.14)	71.4 (0.15)	8,344 (30.8)	4.8 (0.08)	4.2 (0.07)	3.8 (0.08)	334 (6.7)

[1]Percentage of the civilian population who are employed or seeking employment.
[2]Number of persons employed as a percentage of the civilian population.
[3]The percentage of persons in the civilian labor force who are not working and who made specific efforts to find employment sometime during the prior 4 weeks.
[4]Includes equivalency credentials, such as the GED credential.

NOTE: Race categories exclude persons of Hispanic ethnicity. Totals include racial/ethnic groups not separately shown. Standard errors were computed using replicate weights.
SOURCE: U.S. Department of Commerce, Census Bureau, American Community Survey (ACS), 2012, 2013, and 2014, unpublished tabulations. (This table was prepared February 2016.)

Table 501.20. Labor force participation, employment, and unemployment of persons 16 to 24 years old who are not enrolled in school, by age group, sex, race/ethnicity, and educational attainment: 2012, 2013, and 2014

[Standard errors appear in parentheses]

Age group, sex, race/ethnicity, and educational attainment	Labor force participation rate[1] 2012	2013	2014	Number of participants (in thousands) 2014	Employment to population ratio[2] 2012	2013	2014	Number employed (in thousands) 2014	Unemployment rate[3] 2012	2013	2014	Number unemployed (in thousands) 2014
1	2	3	4	5	6	7	8	9	10	11	12	13
16 to 19 years old												
All persons, all education levels	64.1 (0.39)	64.3 (0.40)	65.0 (0.39)	1,573 (15.1)	43.5 (0.41)	45.5 (0.39)	48.2 (0.43)	1,166 (13.6)	32.1 (0.50)	29.2 (0.48)	25.8 (0.46)	406 (8.1)
Less than high school completion	47.9 (0.72)	47.1 (0.81)	49.3 (0.86)	338 (9.1)	27.6 (0.63)	28.4 (0.76)	32.0 (0.73)	220 (6.8)	42.5 (1.06)	39.7 (1.19)	35.0 (1.06)	119 (4.9)
High school completion[4]	70.3 (0.53)	70.2 (0.52)	70.6 (0.53)	1,020 (12.8)	48.6 (0.54)	50.3 (0.53)	53.4 (0.58)	770 (11.4)	30.8 (0.61)	28.4 (0.57)	24.5 (0.54)	249 (6.1)
At least some college	77.1 (1.03)	76.4 (1.09)	74.3 (1.00)	215 (5.8)	61.1 (1.22)	62.7 (1.09)	61.0 (1.11)	176 (5.3)	20.8 (1.12)	18.0 (0.92)	17.8 (1.15)	38 (2.7)
Male, all education levels	66.0 (0.52)	66.9 (0.61)	66.9 (0.48)	903 (11.7)	44.9 (0.49)	46.6 (0.55)	49.4 (0.52)	667 (10.3)	32.0 (0.59)	30.4 (0.56)	26.1 (0.56)	236 (5.8)
Less than high school completion	51.2 (1.09)	50.1 (1.13)	51.5 (1.11)	209 (7.1)	30.1 (0.90)	30.1 (0.96)	34.0 (0.90)	138 (5.5)	41.2 (1.30)	40.0 (1.37)	33.9 (1.24)	71 (3.4)
High school completion[4]	72.5 (0.63)	73.9 (0.71)	73.9 (0.64)	588 (9.8)	50.7 (0.65)	52.1 (0.66)	55.1 (0.71)	443 (8.9)	30.1 (0.75)	29.5 (0.72)	24.6 (0.68)	145 (4.3)
At least some college	77.2 (1.43)	76.6 (1.68)	75.4 (1.51)	106 (4.1)	62.6 (1.58)	62.6 (1.74)	61.2 (1.70)	86 (3.7)	22.1 (1.75)	18.2 (1.42)	18.8 (1.61)	20 (1.9)
Female, all education levels	61.5 (0.66)	60.9 (0.56)	62.7 (0.62)	670 (9.7)	41.6 (0.65)	44.1 (0.65)	46.7 (0.69)	499 (9.0)	32.3 (0.82)	27.5 (0.75)	25.5 (0.78)	171 (5.8)
Less than high school completion	43.0 (1.05)	42.7 (1.16)	46.0 (1.31)	129 (5.1)	23.8 (0.89)	26.0 (1.04)	29.0 (1.11)	82 (3.5)	44.7 (1.70)	39.1 (1.76)	36.8 (1.86)	48 (2.8)
High school completion[4]	67.2 (0.78)	65.5 (0.87)	67.6 (0.85)	432 (7.8)	45.8 (0.92)	48.0 (0.87)	51.2 (0.95)	327 (7.5)	31.8 (1.03)	26.8 (0.88)	24.3 (0.93)	105 (4.2)
At least some college	77.0 (1.34)	76.3 (1.33)	73.2 (1.36)	109 (4.1)	62.0 (1.56)	62.7 (1.68)	60.8 (1.39)	91 (3.8)	19.5 (1.57)	17.8 (1.48)	16.9 (1.56)	18 (1.8)
White, all education levels	68.8 (0.51)	68.5 (0.57)	69.2 (0.56)	818 (11.3)	50.4 (0.58)	51.4 (0.53)	53.8 (0.56)	636 (9.4)	26.7 (0.57)	24.9 (0.58)	22.2 (0.48)	182 (4.7)
Less than high school completion	49.6 (1.07)	49.5 (1.19)	50.9 (1.14)	155 (5.9)	29.1 (1.01)	29.1 (1.00)	31.2 (1.00)	105 (4.4)	41.3 (1.47)	36.9 (1.64)	32.1 (1.47)	50 (3.1)
High school completion[4]	74.8 (0.64)	74.1 (0.66)	75.3 (0.68)	545 (9.4)	56.1 (0.71)	56.3 (0.66)	59.3 (0.80)	429 (8.6)	24.8 (0.70)	24.3 (0.62)	21.2 (0.68)	115 (4.0)
At least some college	81.8 (1.20)	79.5 (1.30)	76.6 (1.46)	119 (4.4)	68.5 (1.36)	69.2 (1.22)	65.7 (1.50)	102 (4.0)	16.2 (1.36)	13.0 (1.18)	14.3 (1.16)	17 (1.5)
Black, all education levels	55.6 (1.12)	55.7 (0.82)	57.5 (1.15)	233 (7.1)	27.6 (1.02)	30.4 (0.97)	34.9 (0.96)	141 (5.0)	50.3 (1.39)	45.5 (1.55)	39.4 (1.43)	92 (4.6)
Less than high school completion	35.4 (1.75)	36.0 (1.65)	35.9 (2.13)	40 (3.0)	12.6 (1.25)	14.1 (1.41)	17.6 (1.81)	20 (2.0)	64.4 (2.97)	61.0 (3.33)	50.9 (3.68)	21 (2.0)
High school completion[4]	63.2 (1.36)	64.0 (1.34)	66.1 (1.36)	161 (5.6)	31.8 (1.47)	35.9 (1.38)	40.4 (1.35)	100 (4.3)	49.6 (1.85)	43.9 (1.90)	37.9 (1.77)	61 (3.7)
At least some college	75.8 (2.88)	68.6 (2.20)	69.8 (2.87)	31 (2.5)	46.7 (2.69)	46.7 (2.78)	47.6 (3.87)	21 (2.2)	33.9 (2.90)	31.9 (3.60)	31.8 (4.54)	10 (1.6)
Hispanic, all education levels	61.9 (0.72)	63.3 (0.88)	62.8 (0.82)	418 (9.8)	42.1 (0.67)	46.0 (0.83)	47.6 (0.87)	316 (8.4)	32.0 (0.96)	27.4 (0.96)	24.3 (0.86)	101 (4.2)
Less than high school completion	52.8 (1.48)	51.9 (1.66)	53.4 (1.57)	119 (5.2)	34.7 (1.27)	34.1 (1.60)	36.4 (1.52)	81 (4.2)	34.3 (1.79)	34.3 (1.97)	31.8 (1.90)	38 (2.8)
High school completion[4]	66.6 (1.05)	67.6 (1.19)	66.9 (1.10)	253 (7.2)	44.8 (1.11)	50.0 (1.13)	51.9 (1.14)	196 (6.2)	32.7 (1.33)	26.0 (1.18)	22.4 (0.99)	57 (2.9)
At least some college	71.2 (2.70)	75.9 (2.13)	71.8 (2.49)	46 (3.0)	56.1 (2.83)	61.4 (2.61)	60.9 (2.58)	39 (2.8)	21.2 (2.42)	19.1 (2.27)	15.2 (1.89)	7 (0.9)
Asian, all education levels	57.5 (3.08)	49.6 (3.11)	54.3 (3.21)	25 (2.3)	48.3 (3.36)	34.5 (2.34)	40.7 (3.11)	19 (1.9)	16.0 (2.76)	30.5 (3.48)	25.1 (3.45)	6 (1.0)
Less than high school completion	34.6 (5.69)	29.3 (3.44)	34.4 (4.91)	4 (0.8)	27.5 (5.25)	20.3 (3.55)	24.1 (4.95)	‡ (†)	20.5 (5.60)	30.8 (7.86)	29.7 (8.25)	‡ (†)
High school completion[4]	65.3 (4.12)	57.4 (4.60)	60.2 (4.60)	15 (1.7)	56.0 (4.27)	35.2 (3.77)	45.3 (4.41)	11 (1.4)	14.3 (3.29)	38.7 (5.59)	24.8 (4.55)	4 (0.8)
At least some college	61.8 (7.32)	67.4 (5.89)	64.2 (6.71)	6 (1.1)	49.6 (8.50)	56.7 (5.60)	49.6 (7.32)	5 (1.0)	19.8 ! (8.49)	15.9 ! (5.22)	22.7 ! (7.26)	‡ (†)
American Indian/Alaska Native, all education levels	56.1 (3.26)	53.2 (3.11)	54.3 (3.43)	14 (1.4)	28.3 (3.43)	34.1 (3.22)	37.4 (3.56)	10 (1.3)	49.6 (5.04)	35.8 (4.24)	31.2 (4.61)	4 (0.7)
Less than high school completion	45.7 (5.02)	42.0 (4.72)	41.9 (4.97)	4 (0.6)	17.3 (3.98)	26.3 (4.69)	25.3 (5.26)	‡ (†)	62.1 (8.22)	37.5 (7.65)	39.5 (9.25)	‡ (†)
High school completion[4]	63.6 (4.40)	61.8 (4.20)	55.1 (4.80)	7 (1.0)	36.4 (4.67)	40.1 (5.21)	37.5 (6.20)	5 (0.9)	42.7 (5.70)	35.1 (†)	31.9 (6.20)	2 (0.5)
At least some college	66.7 (7.65)	58.2 (8.60)	79.1 (6.33)	3 (0.7)	38.0 (8.74)	63.3 (8.31)	63.3 (8.90)	‡ (†)	42.6 (11.01)	‡ (†)	20.0 ! (9.31)	‡ (†)
20 to 24 years old												
All persons, all education levels	80.5 (0.13)	80.7 (0.15)	80.7 (0.15)	10,595 (38.5)	66.6 (0.18)	67.9 (0.19)	69.5 (0.19)	9,122 (39.1)	17.3 (0.18)	15.9 (0.18)	13.9 (0.17)	1,473 (18.1)
Less than high school completion	64.2 (0.47)	63.5 (0.51)	63.5 (0.48)	1,148 (12.0)	45.3 (0.44)	46.7 (0.53)	48.4 (0.51)	874 (11.1)	29.5 (0.58)	26.2 (0.50)	23.9 (0.55)	274 (6.9)
High school completion[4]	78.4 (0.24)	78.5 (0.27)	77.9 (0.19)	4,209 (24.9)	62.4 (0.30)	63.6 (0.34)	64.7 (0.25)	3,494 (23.4)	20.4 (0.30)	18.9 (0.28)	17.0 (0.27)	716 (12.3)
Some college, no degree	85.3 (0.27)	85.8 (0.31)	85.4 (0.26)	2,842 (21.8)	72.7 (0.36)	74.0 (0.34)	75.6 (0.35)	2,515 (21.1)	14.7 (0.33)	13.7 (0.27)	11.5 (0.29)	327 (8.4)
Associate's degree	89.4 (0.60)	90.8 (0.43)	90.6 (0.46)	611 (11.4)	81.2 (0.72)	82.9 (0.54)	84.5 (0.60)	569 (10.8)	9.2 (0.53)	8.7 (0.53)	6.9 (0.39)	42 (2.5)
Bachelor's or higher degree	93.8 (0.25)	93.4 (0.21)	93.3 (0.27)	1,785 (18.6)	87.0 (0.35)	87.1 (0.27)	87.3 (0.34)	1,670 (18.1)	7.2 (0.27)	6.7 (0.25)	6.4 (0.25)	115 (4.5)

See notes at end of table.

Table 501.20. Labor force participation, employment, and unemployment of persons 16 to 24 years old who are not enrolled in school, by age group, sex, race/ethnicity, and educational attainment: 2012, 2013, and 2014—Continued

[Standard errors appear in parentheses]

Age group, sex, race/ethnicity, and educational attainment	Labor force participation rate[1]			Number of participants (in thousands)	Employment to population ratio[2]			Number employed (in thousands)	Unemployment rate[3]			Number unemployed (in thousands)
	2012	2013	2014	2014	2012	2013	2014	2014	2012	2013	2014	2014
1	2	3	4	5	6	7	8	9	10	11	12	13
Male, all education levels	82.9 (0.17)	83.0 (0.18)	83.0 (0.22)	5,839 (27.8)	67.8 (0.24)	69.1 (0.24)	71.0 (0.26)	4,997 (26.7)	18.2 (0.23)	16.6 (0.23)	14.4 (0.21)	842 (12.8)
Less than high school completion	68.4 (0.57)	68.4 (0.62)	68.4 (0.59)	734 (10.8)	50.7 (0.65)	52.0 (0.68)	53.7 (0.65)	576 (9.6)	27.1 (0.74)	24.0 (0.61)	21.5 (0.68)	158 (5.6)
High school completion[4]	81.8 (0.27)	81.3 (0.30)	81.3 (0.29)	2,567 (19.7)	65.1 (0.39)	66.3 (0.40)	67.5 (0.33)	2,129 (17.4)	20.5 (0.38)	19.0 (0.36)	17.1 (0.32)	438 (9.1)
Some college, no degree	88.4 (0.31)	88.1 (0.37)	88.1 (0.36)	1,495 (17.8)	74.7 (0.45)	75.6 (0.49)	78.0 (0.48)	1,323 (16.5)	15.2 (0.41)	14.5 (0.40)	11.5 (0.37)	172 (5.9)
Associate's degree	93.2 (0.70)	92.1 (0.59)	92.1 (0.74)	280 (7.4)	82.8 (1.02)	85.3 (0.88)	85.9 (0.95)	261 (7.1)	10.2 (0.85)	8.5 (0.77)	6.8 (0.56)	19 (1.6)
Bachelor's or higher degree	94.9 (0.30)	94.9 (0.34)	94.9 (0.31)	763 (11.2)	87.0 (0.87)	87.3 (0.49)	88.0 (0.42)	707 (10.7)	8.4 (0.39)	7.2 (0.42)	7.2 (0.38)	55 (3.1)
Female, all education levels	78.2 (0.21)	78.1 (0.22)	78.1 (0.20)	4,756 (23.8)	65.1 (0.27)	66.5 (0.26)	67.8 (0.27)	4,125 (24.8)	16.2 (0.24)	15.0 (0.22)	13.3 (0.26)	632 (12.3)
Less than high school completion	55.5 (0.81)	56.4 (0.76)	56.4 (0.72)	415 (7.7)	37.0 (0.74)	38.6 (0.73)	40.6 (0.70)	298 (6.4)	33.9 (1.07)	30.4 (0.90)	28.1 (0.95)	117 (4.7)
High school completion[4]	73.9 (0.39)	73.1 (0.45)	73.1 (0.37)	1,642 (16.3)	58.6 (0.48)	59.9 (0.51)	60.7 (0.48)	1,365 (16.5)	20.6 (0.46)	18.8 (0.42)	16.9 (0.48)	277 (7.9)
Some college, no degree	83.1 (0.42)	82.7 (0.46)	82.7 (0.39)	1,347 (14.0)	70.7 (0.54)	72.3 (0.51)	73.2 (0.51)	1,192 (13.8)	14.0 (0.47)	13.0 (0.40)	11.5 (0.43)	155 (6.0)
Associate's degree	88.6 (0.89)	89.7 (0.72)	89.7 (0.66)	331 (8.0)	79.7 (1.01)	80.7 (0.84)	83.4 (0.80)	308 (7.7)	8.3 (0.65)	8.9 (0.74)	7.0 (0.54)	23 (1.9)
Bachelor's or higher degree	93.0 (0.32)	93.0 (0.31)	93.0 (0.41)	1,022 (13.7)	87.0 (0.41)	87.1 (0.42)	86.8 (0.49)	962 (13.3)	6.4 (0.33)	6.3 (0.32)	5.9 (0.32)	60 (3.4)
White, all education levels	84.0 (0.17)	83.8 (0.19)	83.8 (0.18)	5,903 (28.5)	72.4 (0.20)	73.0 (0.25)	74.4 (0.22)	5,238 (28.3)	14.0 (0.20)	13.2 (0.21)	11.3 (0.20)	665 (12.0)
Less than high school completion	64.1 (0.80)	63.9 (0.70)	63.9 (0.78)	424 (7.9)	45.0 (0.70)	46.6 (0.78)	49.3 (0.85)	328 (7.1)	30.2 (1.00)	27.4 (0.81)	22.8 (0.86)	97 (4.0)
High school completion[4]	81.0 (0.34)	80.1 (0.34)	80.1 (0.27)	2,215 (20.8)	66.6 (0.39)	67.4 (0.44)	68.3 (0.34)	1,889 (19.7)	17.8 (0.35)	16.7 (0.37)	14.7 (0.33)	325 (7.7)
Some college, no degree	87.1 (0.35)	86.5 (0.38)	86.5 (0.35)	1,578 (15.9)	76.7 (0.45)	77.1 (0.50)	78.2 (0.39)	1,427 (15.6)	11.6 (0.38)	11.4 (0.38)	9.6 (0.32)	151 (5.2)
Associate's degree	92.2 (0.61)	91.8 (0.55)	91.8 (0.59)	408 (8.5)	84.5 (0.78)	85.8 (0.69)	86.6 (0.71)	385 (8.3)	7.7 (0.59)	6.9 (0.55)	5.7 (0.46)	23 (1.9)
Bachelor's or higher degree	95.6 (0.24)	94.9 (0.25)	95.1 (0.24)	1,278 (14.3)	89.9 (0.31)	89.6 (0.32)	90.0 (0.35)	1,209 (13.4)	6.0 (0.27)	5.6 (0.28)	5.4 (0.28)	68 (3.8)
Black, all education levels	73.0 (0.45)	74.0 (0.48)	74.5 (0.44)	1,583 (17.2)	50.4 (0.61)	53.8 (0.52)	56.0 (0.50)	1,190 (15.7)	30.9 (0.61)	27.4 (0.55)	24.8 (0.51)	393 (9.0)
Less than high school completion	53.3 (1.09)	52.9 (1.09)	52.9 (1.05)	183 (5.7)	25.6 (0.95)	27.4 (1.04)	29.1 (0.91)	101 (4.0)	52.1 (1.60)	46.6 (1.43)	45.0 (1.47)	82 (3.8)
High school completion[4]	73.2 (0.72)	72.6 (0.69)	72.6 (0.69)	704 (13.4)	47.7 (0.76)	51.3 (0.71)	52.0 (0.80)	505 (11.3)	32.9 (0.81)	29.9 (0.72)	28.3 (0.78)	199 (6.5)
Some college, no degree	84.0 (0.72)	84.2 (0.69)	84.2 (0.78)	493 (11.0)	63.0 (1.08)	66.1 (0.90)	69.4 (0.93)	406 (10.4)	25.0 (1.01)	22.0 (0.91)	17.7 (0.77)	87 (4.0)
Associate's degree	86.3 (1.98)	89.7 (1.66)	88.4 (1.83)	63 (4.0)	73.0 (2.75)	77.1 (2.23)	76.8 (2.44)	55 (3.6)	15.4 (2.47)	14.1 (2.21)	13.2 (2.27)	8 (1.6)
Bachelor's or higher degree	92.9 (1.03)	92.9 (1.08)	92.1 (1.08)	141 (5.3)	81.1 (1.46)	83.0 (1.51)	81.3 (1.40)	124 (5.1)	12.7 (1.37)	10.7 (1.24)	11.7 (1.10)	16 (1.6)
Hispanic, all education levels	78.3 (0.32)	78.3 (0.34)	79.1 (0.33)	2,390 (17.8)	64.5 (0.38)	66.6 (0.44)	68.8 (0.42)	2,080 (18.7)	17.1 (0.38)	15.0 (0.38)	13.0 (0.36)	310 (8.6)
Less than high school completion	69.4 (0.72)	69.5 (0.79)	69.5 (0.77)	477 (9.2)	55.0 (0.83)	57.1 (0.88)	58.2 (0.85)	400 (8.6)	20.7 (0.81)	17.5 (0.74)	16.2 (0.83)	77 (4.3)
High school completion[4]	78.0 (0.51)	78.4 (0.48)	78.4 (0.41)	1,057 (13.8)	64.3 (0.60)	65.3 (0.64)	67.3 (0.52)	908 (12.9)	17.9 (0.57)	16.2 (0.51)	14.1 (0.50)	149 (5.6)
Some college, no degree	84.7 (0.54)	84.9 (0.69)	84.9 (0.72)	585 (11.1)	71.2 (0.73)	74.1 (0.81)	75.8 (0.91)	522 (10.9)	14.6 (0.67)	12.5 (0.69)	10.7 (0.64)	63 (3.8)
Associate's degree	84.0 (1.80)	87.6 (1.34)	88.9 (1.22)	102 (4.4)	74.5 (1.90)	76.7 (1.81)	82.1 (1.34)	94 (3.9)	11.4 (1.46)	12.5 (1.66)	7.6 (1.25)	8 (1.4)
Bachelor's or higher degree	91.2 (0.85)	91.7 (0.89)	92.3 (0.85)	170 (6.1)	81.7 (1.31)	83.3 (1.13)	84.9 (1.16)	156 (5.9)	10.4 (1.30)	9.1 (0.94)	8.0 (0.80)	14 (1.4)
Asian, all education levels	77.3 (0.73)	78.6 (0.77)	78.9 (0.86)	324 (7.0)	68.3 (0.97)	68.4 (0.94)	70.6 (1.00)	291 (6.8)	13.4 (0.83)	15.0 (0.79)	10.2 (0.74)	33 (2.5)
Less than high school completion	60.2 (3.18)	61.9 (3.95)	61.9 (3.49)	24 (2.0)	49.3 (3.69)	50.7 (3.99)	49.6 (3.14)	19 (1.6)	19.5 (3.45)	19.9 (3.50)	19.9 (3.10)	5 (0.9)
High school completion[4]	71.8 (1.75)	71.7 (1.68)	71.7 (1.96)	69 (3.9)	65.6 (2.13)	61.4 (2.19)	64.0 (2.22)	62 (3.8)	14.8 (1.93)	14.4 (1.85)	10.7 (1.48)	7 (1.0)
Some college, no degree	80.0 (2.00)	82.9 (2.27)	82.9 (1.77)	68 (3.2)	68.2 (2.29)	67.3 (2.31)	71.4 (2.23)	60 (3.0)	16.9 (1.70)	14.8 (1.40)	12.3 (1.68)	8 (1.2)
Associate's degree	81.2 (3.87)	87.3 (4.04)	87.3 (2.87)	18 (1.5)	71.8 (4.44)	70.7 (5.08)	82.2 (3.39)	17 (1.4)	11.5 (3.42)	12.3 (3.61)	5.9 ! (2.06)	‡ (†)
Bachelor's or higher degree	82.7 (1.23)	83.2 (1.03)	83.2 (1.06)	145 (4.0)	74.5 (1.42)	75.5 (1.20)	76.7 (1.14)	133 (3.8)	10.0 (1.07)	9.9 (1.01)	7.8 (0.80)	11 (1.2)
American Indian/Alaska Native, all education levels	71.8 (1.39)	67.9 (1.75)	67.1 (1.53)	85 (3.4)	50.6 (1.72)	48.0 (1.72)	51.2 (1.75)	65 (3.3)	29.5 (1.82)	29.3 (1.94)	23.6 (1.76)	20 (1.5)
Less than high school completion	55.9 (3.41)	52.5 (3.50)	56.2 (2.98)	14 (1.5)	32.1 (3.53)	30.6 (3.58)	34.3 (2.93)	9 (1.1)	42.5 (4.49)	41.8 (5.16)	38.9 (4.09)	6 (0.8)
High school completion[4]	73.0 (1.68)	65.0 (2.44)	65.0 (2.15)	41 (2.2)	50.3 (2.25)	45.2 (2.58)	50.2 (2.22)	31 (2.1)	31.0 (2.44)	30.8 (3.13)	22.8 (2.31)	9 (1.0)
Some college, no degree	79.0 (2.84)	75.4 (2.32)	75.4 (3.02)	23 (2.2)	61.2 (3.13)	60.7 (3.32)	60.2 (3.41)	18 (2.0)	22.5 (2.76)	23.9 (3.62)	20.2 (3.27)	5 (0.9)
Associate's degree	86.3 (5.12)	89.8 (5.17)	85.7 (6.60)	‡ (†)	76.3 (7.99)	75.2 (6.10)	83.0 (8.81)	‡ (†)	‡ (†)	‡ (†)	‡ (†)	‡ (†)
Bachelor's or higher degree	89.7 (4.84)	87.7 (4.03)	87.6 (6.14)	4 (0.9)	66.7 (10.74)	72.4 (7.86)	66.7 (6.73)	‡ (†)	23.9 ! (9.08)	‡ (†)	‡ (†)	‡ (†)

†Not applicable.
!Interpret data with caution. The coefficient of variation (CV) for this estimate is between 30 and 50 percent.
‡Reporting standards not met. Either there are too few cases for a reliable estimate or the coefficient of variation (CV) is 50 percent or greater.
[1]Percentage of the civilian population who are employed or seeking employment.
[2]Number of persons employed as a percentage of the civilian population.
[3]The percentage of persons in the civilian labor force who are not working and who made specific efforts to find employment sometime during the prior 4 weeks.
[4]Includes equivalency credentials, such as the GED credential.
NOTE: Table excludes persons enrolled in school. Race categories exclude persons of Hispanic ethnicity. Totals include racial/ethnic groups not separately shown. Standard errors were computed using replicate weights.
SOURCE: U.S. Department of Commerce, Census Bureau, American Community Survey (ACS), 2012, 2013, and 2014, unpublished tabulations. (This table was prepared February 2016.)

Table 501.30. Number and percentage of persons 18 to 24 years old who were neither enrolled in school nor working, by educational attainment, age group, sex, family poverty status, and race/ethnicity: 2015

[Standard errors appear in parentheses]

Age group, sex, family poverty status, and race/ethnicity	Total (in thousands)		Neither enrolled in school nor working												
			Number (in thousands)		Percentage distribution		Percent, by educational attainment									
							Total		Less than high school completion		High school completion[1]		Some college, no bachelor's degree[2]		Bachelor's or higher degree	
1	2		3		4		5		6		7		8		9	
Total, 18 and 19 years old	**7,900**	**(82.2)**	**1,018**	**(44.4)**	**100.0**	**(†)**	**12.9**	**(0.54)**	**10.4**	**(0.81)**	**24.6**	**(1.28)**	**4.8**	**(0.56)**	**‡**	**(†)**
Male	3,962	(59.1)	534	(31.9)	52.5	(2.16)	13.5	(0.77)	10.5	(0.92)	24.2	(1.72)	5.9	(1.00)	‡	(†)
Female	3,938	(61.3)	484	(30.5)	47.5	(2.16)	12.3	(0.74)	10.3	(1.24)	25.1	(1.90)	4.0	(0.71)	‡	(†)
White	4,293	(61.3)	476	(31.4)	46.7	(2.21)	11.1	(0.69)	7.9	(0.89)	23.8	(1.85)	3.6	(0.68)	‡	(†)
Black	1,094	(35.6)	196	(19.2)	19.2	(1.68)	17.9	(1.63)	15.2	(2.40)	30.3	(3.89)	7.7 !	(2.57)	‡	(†)
Hispanic	1,771	(39.3)	285	(21.8)	28.0	(1.78)	16.1	(1.19)	14.4	(1.63)	25.0	(2.59)	7.6	(1.65)	‡	(†)
Asian	379	(21.2)	‡	(†)	1.8 !	(0.55)	4.8	(1.42)	‡	(†)	8.3 !	(3.56)	3.9 !	(1.82)	‡	(†)
Pacific Islander	36	(8.6)	‡	(†)	‡	(†)	‡	(†)	‡	(†)	‡	(†)	‡	(†)	‡	(†)
American Indian/Alaska Native	76	(11.0)	‡	(†)	1.3 !	(0.44)	18.0	(5.00)	8.5 !	(3.94)	‡	(†)	‡	(†)	‡	(†)
Two or more races	251	(17.9)	‡	(†)	2.6	(0.71)	10.6	(2.80)	‡	(†)	22.0	(6.20)	‡	(†)	‡	(†)
Poor[3]	1,503	(57.8)	386	(28.1)	37.9	(2.11)	25.7	(1.61)	21.6	(2.57)	43.8	(3.44)	9.3	(2.28)	‡	(†)
Nonpoor[3]	6,398	(91.0)	632	(33.9)	62.1	(2.11)	9.9	(0.50)	7.3	(0.71)	19.8	(1.38)	4.1	(0.56)	‡	(†)
Total, 20 to 24 years old	**22,215**	**(21.7)**	**3,852**	**(96.9)**	**100.0**	**(†)**	**17.3**	**(0.44)**	**41.2**	**(1.91)**	**28.4**	**(0.89)**	**8.7**	**(0.42)**	**7.8**	**(0.76)**
Male	11,201	(21.1)	1,741	(72.7)	45.2	(1.27)	15.5	(0.65)	32.9	(2.46)	24.8	(1.24)	7.5	(0.66)	6.5	(1.21)
Female	11,014	(3.9)	2,112	(63.6)	54.8	(1.27)	19.2	(0.58)	50.4	(2.99)	32.9	(1.24)	9.8	(0.63)	8.8	(1.06)
White	12,219	(33.8)	1,793	(74.1)	46.5	(1.26)	14.7	(0.60)	43.3	(3.66)	25.8	(1.34)	8.0	(0.66)	6.3	(0.93)
Black	3,249	(23.7)	755	(38.9)	19.6	(0.94)	23.2	(1.20)	48.0	(4.29)	35.8	(2.39)	10.9	(1.34)	10.8	(3.15)
Hispanic	4,717	(7.4)	1,014	(42.9)	26.3	(1.02)	21.5	(0.91)	36.9	(2.54)	28.9	(1.63)	10.0	(0.95)	11.6	(2.29)
Asian	1,268	(29.6)	115	(15.6)	3.0	(0.39)	9.1	(1.21)	‡	(†)	12.4 !	(3.75)	5.8	(1.30)	11.1	(2.43)
Pacific Islander	81	(14.2)	‡	(†)	0.5 !	(0.14)	22.1	(6.00)	‡	(†)	24.0 !	(8.88)	‡	(†)	‡	(†)
American Indian/Alaska Native	204	(23.9)	78	(13.2)	2.0	(0.34)	38.4	(5.05)	61.6	(11.93)	57.8	(7.42)	15.7 !	(6.97)	‡	(†)
Two or more races	476	(26.6)	79	(13.5)	2.1	(0.35)	16.6	(2.57)	‡	(†)	29.0	(5.37)	7.2 !	(2.78)	14.9 !	(5.24)
Family poverty status																
Poor[3]	4,451	(111.1)	1,368	(57.5)	100.0	(†)	30.7	(1.17)	53.7	(2.52)	44.8	(2.05)	13.4	(1.40)	12.2	(2.60)
White	2,098	(83.7)	592	(42.7)	43.2	(2.28)	28.2	(1.88)	57.5	(5.71)	46.9	(3.38)	13.0	(2.07)	10.2 !	(3.06)
Black	915	(42.4)	332	(28.6)	24.3	(1.75)	36.3	(2.63)	53.4	(6.21)	48.8	(4.34)	17.1	(3.51)	‡	(†)
Hispanic	1,017	(47.5)	352	(26.1)	25.7	(1.84)	34.6	(2.12)	49.3	(3.60)	38.2	(3.79)	14.0	(2.72)	35.3 !	(12.11)
Asian	265	(31.0)	‡	(†)	1.8	(0.53)	9.4	(2.62)	‡	(†)	‡	(†)	6.8 !	(2.79)	‡	(†)
Pacific Islander	‡	(†)	‡	(†)	0.7 !	(0.31)	49.2	(13.84)	‡	(†)	‡	(†)	‡	(†)	‡	(†)
American Indian/Alaska Native	45	(9.5)	‡	(†)	1.9 !	(0.59)	59.6	(10.63)	‡	(†)	‡	(†)	‡	(†)	‡	(†)
Two or more races	91	(16.1)	‡	(†)	2.2	(0.64)	33.9	(7.98)	‡	(†)	‡	(†)	‡	(†)	‡	(†)
Nonpoor[3]	17,764	(114.3)	2,484	(80.7)	100.0	(†)	14.0	(0.44)	32.7	(2.28)	23.8	(0.95)	7.7	(0.44)	7.2	(0.79)
White	10,122	(85.3)	1,201	(60.7)	48.4	(1.62)	11.9	(0.59)	33.6	(4.12)	21.3	(1.31)	7.0	(0.69)	5.7	(0.97)
Black	2,334	(46.6)	423	(33.2)	17.0	(1.29)	18.1	(1.35)	43.4	(6.07)	29.3	(2.68)	9.0	(1.31)	9.3 !	(3.26)
Hispanic	3,700	(48.3)	662	(37.1)	26.7	(1.30)	17.9	(0.94)	28.9	(3.21)	26.3	(1.81)	9.3	(1.00)	8.5	(2.11)
Asian	1,003	(38.0)	90	(14.3)	3.6	(0.55)	9.0	(1.35)	‡	(†)	13.3	(3.99)	5.5	(1.39)	12.6	(2.92)
Pacific Islander	60	(13.1)	‡	(†)	0.3 !	(0.15)	12.8 !	(5.74)	‡	(†)	‡	(†)	‡	(†)	‡	(†)
American Indian/Alaska Native	160	(21.4)	52	(10.9)	2.1	(0.44)	32.5	(5.72)	‡	(†)	55.4	(8.33)	14.8 !	(7.40)	‡	(†)
Two or more races	386	(25.2)	49	(10.1)	2.0	(0.41)	12.6	(2.40)	‡	(†)	21.1	(5.38)	7.1 !	(2.99)	14.7 !	(5.32)

†Not applicable.
!Interpret data with caution. The coefficient of variation (CV) for this estimate is between 30 and 50 percent.
‡Reporting standards not met. Either there are too few cases for a reliable estimate or the coefficient of variation (CV) is 50 percent or greater.
[1]Includes equivalency credentials, such as the GED credential.
[2]Includes persons with no college degree as well as those with an associate's degree.

[3]Poor is defined to include families with incomes below the poverty threshold. Nonpoor is defined to include families with incomes at or above the poverty threshold. For information about how the Census Bureau determines who is in poverty, see http://www.census.gov/hhes/www/poverty/about/overview/measure.html.
NOTE: Race categories exclude persons of Hispanic ethnicity. Standard errors were computed using replicate weights. Detail may not sum to totals because of rounding.
SOURCE: U.S. Department of Commerce, Census Bureau, Current Population Survey (CPS), Annual Social and Economic Supplement, 2015. (This table was prepared October 2015.)

Table 501.40. Percentage distribution of 25- to 34-year-olds with various levels of educational attainment, by labor force status, sex, race/ethnicity, and U.S. nativity and citizenship status: 2014

[Standard errors appear in parentheses]

Sex, race/ethnicity, and U.S. nativity and citizenship status	All 25- to 34-year-olds: In labor force — Employed	Unemployed (seeking employment)	Not in labor force	Less than high school completion: In labor force — Employed	Unemployed (seeking employment)	Not in labor force	High school completion[1]: In labor force — Employed	Unemployed (seeking employment)	Not in labor force	Some college, no bachelor's degree[2]: In labor force — Employed	Unemployed (seeking employment)	Not in labor force	Bachelor's or higher degree: In labor force — Employed	Unemployed (seeking employment)	Not in labor force
	2	3	4	5	6	7	8	9	10	11	12	13	14	15	16
Total	75.6 (0.09)	6.2 (0.05)	18.2 (0.07)	55.0 (0.33)	9.5 (0.20)	35.4 (0.32)	68.5 (0.19)	8.5 (0.12)	23.1 (0.16)	76.7 (0.15)	6.6 (0.10)	16.7 (0.13)	86.3 (0.11)	3.1 (0.07)	10.6 (0.11)
Sex															
Male	80.2 (0.11)	6.6 (0.07)	13.3 (0.09)	65.2 (0.40)	9.5 (0.24)	25.4 (0.39)	74.4 (0.21)	8.6 (0.16)	16.9 (0.16)	81.7 (0.22)	6.6 (0.14)	11.7 (0.16)	90.3 (0.16)	3.4 (0.10)	6.3 (0.14)
Female	71.0 (0.13)	5.8 (0.07)	23.2 (0.11)	41.2 (0.48)	9.6 (0.30)	49.2 (0.48)	60.3 (0.34)	8.3 (0.18)	31.4 (0.30)	72.1 (0.21)	6.5 (0.13)	21.4 (0.21)	83.1 (0.19)	2.9 (0.08)	14.0 (0.17)
Race/ethnicity															
White	78.7 (0.12)	5.2 (0.07)	16.1 (0.10)	49.1 (0.59)	11.5 (0.35)	39.4 (0.53)	70.1 (0.26)	7.6 (0.16)	22.3 (0.24)	78.1 (0.19)	5.6 (0.10)	16.3 (0.18)	88.2 (0.13)	2.6 (0.07)	9.2 (0.12)
Black	67.5 (0.28)	11.3 (0.11)	21.2 (0.21)	35.6 (0.81)	16.9 (0.66)	47.6 (0.85)	59.2 (0.48)	14.0 (0.39)	26.8 (0.42)	73.8 (0.46)	10.6 (0.20)	15.6 (0.33)	86.8 (0.53)	5.3 (0.32)	7.9 (0.41)
Hispanic	73.2 (0.21)	6.2 (0.11)	20.6 (0.20)	64.3 (0.44)	6.5 (0.27)	29.2 (0.42)	71.8 (0.41)	6.8 (0.26)	21.4 (0.41)	77.0 (0.82)	6.2 (0.31)	16.7 (0.76)	84.4 (0.42)	4.3 (0.24)	11.3 (0.35)
Asian	74.5 (0.32)	4.0 (0.16)	21.5 (0.29)	61.2 (1.72)	6.3 (0.76)	32.6 (1.79)	69.6 (1.10)	5.8 (0.67)	24.6 (1.07)	71.2 (1.11)	5.0 (0.35)	23.8 (1.00)	77.5 (0.41)	3.1 (0.16)	19.4 (0.40)
Pacific Islander	72.3 (1.96)	6.8 (1.18)	20.9 (1.96)	56.9 (5.39)	3.7 ! (1.81)	39.3 (5.45)	72.0 (3.40)	7.9 (2.12)	20.0 (2.88)	73.4 (3.51)	7.0 (1.35)	19.7 (3.00)	85.0 (3.75)	5.9 (2.37)	9.1 ! (2.92)
American Indian/Alaska Native[3]	56.6 (0.91)	10.7 (0.63)	32.7 (0.92)	32.2 (2.26)	14.6 (1.67)	53.3 (2.46)	49.6 (1.68)	13.6 (1.15)	36.8 (1.79)	64.6 (1.79)	8.3 (1.03)	27.2 (1.76)	82.1 (2.42)	5.0 (1.61)	12.9 (1.92)
American Indian	56.7 (1.02)	10.2 (0.71)	33.1 (1.04)	30.0 (2.49)	15.2 (1.87)	54.7 (2.49)	48.8 (1.81)	12.4 (1.22)	38.8 (1.79)	64.9 (1.91)	8.0 (1.12)	27.2 (1.88)	84.5 (2.23)	5.3 ! (1.77)	10.2 (1.61)
Alaska Native	54.6 (3.84)	15.6 (3.60)	29.8 (3.56)	24.0 ! (8.39)	27.3 ! (8.61)	48.7 (10.99)	57.3 (5.61)	16.2 (3.32)	26.6 (5.07)	61.7 (7.33)	13.1 ! (4.03)	25.2 (5.83)	‡ (†)	‡ (†)	‡ (†)
Two or more races	73.2 (0.62)	7.5 (0.38)	19.3 (0.49)	46.3 (2.51)	9.1 (1.55)	44.6 (2.41)	65.3 (1.45)	9.8 (0.91)	24.9 (1.18)	72.6 (0.99)	8.3 (0.71)	19.1 (0.77)	83.8 (0.80)	4.9 (0.52)	11.3 (0.66)
Race/ethnicity by sex															
Male															
White	83.1 (0.15)	5.8 (0.29)	11.1 (0.11)	57.9 (0.79)	12.4 (0.45)	29.7 (0.70)	76.3 (0.30)	8.1 (0.22)	15.6 (0.24)	84.2 (0.24)	5.6 (0.15)	10.2 (0.19)	91.7 (0.16)	3.0 (0.10)	5.2 (0.14)
Black	64.4 (0.41)	12.0 (0.29)	23.7 (0.34)	30.4 (1.04)	17.3 (0.88)	52.3 (1.14)	58.3 (0.69)	13.8 (0.54)	27.9 (0.57)	73.6 (0.76)	11.0 (0.51)	15.4 (0.55)	86.9 (0.80)	5.4 (0.49)	7.7 (0.58)
Hispanic	82.1 (0.24)	5.9 (0.17)	12.0 (0.20)	79.5 (0.45)	5.5 (0.29)	15.0 (0.41)	81.4 (0.43)	6.4 (0.34)	12.2 (0.34)	82.9 (0.47)	6.2 (0.30)	10.9 (0.40)	88.7 (0.53)	4.5 (0.39)	6.8 (0.46)
Asian	82.1 (0.44)	4.4 (0.23)	13.5 (0.40)	71.0 (2.24)	8.5 (1.29)	20.5 (2.05)	78.9 (1.31)	6.3 (1.01)	14.8 (0.92)	74.5 (1.11)	6.4 (0.53)	19.1 (1.00)	86.4 (0.52)	3.0 (0.25)	10.6 (0.48)
Pacific Islander	80.5 (2.83)	6.6 (1.79)	12.9 (2.53)	‡ (†)	‡ (†)	14.6 ! (5.11)	76.1 (4.29)	8.9 ! (3.12)	13.0 (3.53)	80.1 (5.51)	‡ (†)	15.5 ! (4.90)	90.0 (4.86)	7.5 ! (3.46)	‡ (†)
American Indian/Alaska Native[3]	57.5 (1.48)	12.6 (1.11)	29.9 (1.21)	36.4 (3.04)	14.7 (2.08)	48.9 (3.16)	52.2 (2.49)	16.1 (1.89)	31.6 (2.00)	66.2 (2.88)	9.2 (1.86)	24.6 (2.43)	80.7 (4.09)	8.0 (3.90)	11.7 (2.72)
American Indian	58.0 (1.54)	12.0 (1.16)	30.0 (1.39)	32.7 (3.45)	15.4 (2.37)	51.9 (3.58)	53.7 (2.67)	14.3 (1.86)	32.0 (2.47)	66.3 (3.13)	9.3 (2.04)	24.4 (2.59)	83.0 (4.07)	‡ (†)	9.0 (2.30)
Alaska Native	51.5 (5.48)	17.3 (3.24)	31.2 (4.59)	‡ (†)	‡ (†)	‡ (†)	54.5 (8.17)	17.2 (3.93)	28.3 (7.00)	‡ (†)	‡ (†)	‡ (†)	‡ (†)	‡ (†)	‡ (†)
Two or more races	76.2 (0.95)	8.0 (0.63)	15.9 (0.66)	53.7 (3.25)	8.8 (1.99)	37.5 (3.04)	70.3 (1.85)	10.1 (1.33)	19.6 (1.41)	75.9 (1.60)	8.4 (1.10)	15.8 (1.24)	86.4 (1.19)	5.7 (0.85)	7.9 (0.96)
Female															
White	74.3 (0.16)	4.6 (0.09)	21.1 (0.15)	36.8 (0.85)	10.2 (0.55)	53.0 (0.84)	61.1 (0.47)	6.8 (0.25)	32.1 (0.42)	72.2 (0.27)	5.5 (0.15)	22.2 (0.28)	85.3 (0.22)	2.3 (0.08)	12.4 (0.20)
Black	70.4 (0.38)	10.7 (0.29)	18.9 (0.30)	42.4 (1.31)	16.3 (0.83)	41.3 (1.33)	60.2 (0.86)	14.2 (0.58)	25.5 (0.80)	73.9 (0.49)	10.3 (0.36)	15.7 (0.55)	86.7 (0.63)	5.3 (0.38)	8.1 (0.53)
Hispanic	63.5 (0.36)	6.5 (0.16)	30.0 (0.33)	43.0 (0.66)	7.8 (0.42)	49.2 (0.73)	59.6 (0.68)	7.2 (0.37)	34.2 (0.62)	71.8 (0.57)	6.3 (0.26)	21.9 (0.55)	81.2 (0.63)	4.2 (0.28)	14.5 (0.54)
Asian	67.6 (0.51)	3.6 (0.19)	28.8 (0.49)	51.5 (2.55)	4.1 (0.86)	44.4 (2.58)	60.6 (1.67)	5.2 (0.71)	34.2 (1.83)	68.1 (1.20)	3.7 (0.43)	28.2 (1.31)	69.9 (0.60)	3.2 (0.19)	26.8 (0.58)
Pacific Islander	64.7 (3.17)	7.0 (1.54)	28.4 (3.09)	35.5 (8.33)	‡ (†)	60.5 (8.72)	64.8 (5.56)	6.8 ! (2.05)	28.5 (5.14)	68.0 (4.40)	9.0 ! (2.87)	23.0 (3.79)	81.6 (5.99)	3.2 (0.96)	13.2 ! (4.73)
American Indian/Alaska Native[3]	55.8 (1.32)	8.8 (0.73)	35.4 (1.29)	27.4 (3.13)	14.5 (2.84)	58.1 (3.38)	46.5 (2.45)	10.5 (1.41)	42.9 (2.51)	63.2 (2.46)	7.4 (1.12)	29.4 (2.43)	83.0 (2.87)	3.4 ! (1.09)	13.7 (2.80)
American Indian	55.4 (1.44)	8.5 (0.76)	36.0 (1.43)	27.2 (3.35)	15.1 (3.08)	57.8 (3.63)	43.1 (2.62)	10.3 (1.54)	46.5 (2.79)	63.6 (2.54)	6.8 (1.12)	29.6 (2.54)	85.6 (2.46)	‡ (†)	11.0 (2.27)
Alaska Native	57.7 (5.36)	14.0 (3.60)	28.4 (5.39)	‡ (†)	‡ (†)	‡ (†)	60.6 (7.51)	15.0 ! (5.20)	24.5 (6.94)	59.9 (9.42)	14.9 ! (6.12)	25.2 (7.49)	‡ (†)	‡ (†)	‡ (†)
Two or more races	70.5 (0.86)	7.0 (0.50)	22.5 (0.80)	37.3 (3.57)	9.4 (2.53)	53.3 (3.97)	58.2 (2.00)	9.4 (1.36)	32.4 (1.99)	69.9 (1.27)	8.3 (0.92)	21.9 (1.12)	81.7 (1.15)	4.3 (0.62)	14.0 (1.01)
Nativity															
Hispanic															
Born within United States[4]	73.5 (0.25)	7.1 (0.17)	19.4 (0.21)	53.3 (0.82)	10.6 (0.59)	36.1 (0.81)	70.1 (0.54)	8.3 (0.39)	21.6 (0.44)	77.2 (0.45)	6.3 (0.24)	16.5 (0.40)	86.4 (0.48)	4.3 (0.29)	9.3 (0.40)
Born outside United States[4]	72.8 (0.33)	5.1 (0.15)	22.2 (0.33)	68.9 (0.49)	4.7 (0.24)	26.4 (0.46)	73.8 (0.53)	5.1 (0.28)	21.1 (0.53)	76.6 (0.71)	6.0 (0.44)	17.4 (0.68)	79.3 (0.98)	4.5 (0.44)	16.2 (0.84)
Asian															
Born within United States[4]	81.3 (0.55)	4.6 (0.27)	14.1 (0.48)	49.2 (3.70)	10.2 (2.58)	40.6 (3.51)	70.5 (1.88)	8.1 (1.28)	21.4 (1.63)	75.7 (1.29)	5.8 (0.58)	18.6 (1.18)	86.9 (0.61)	3.3 (0.30)	9.7 (0.52)
Born outside United States[4]	71.4 (0.37)	3.7 (0.18)	24.9 (0.36)	63.5 (1.88)	5.5 (0.77)	31.0 (1.98)	69.2 (1.39)	4.8 (0.77)	26.0 (1.32)	68.5 (1.01)	4.6 (0.36)	27.0 (1.00)	73.5 (0.48)	3.0 (0.21)	23.5 (0.48)
Citizenship status															
U.S.-born citizen	76.3 (0.10)	6.5 (0.06)	17.3 (0.08)	46.2 (0.40)	12.7 (0.28)	41.2 (0.43)	67.7 (0.21)	9.1 (0.14)	23.0 (0.19)	77.1 (0.16)	6.7 (0.16)	16.2 (0.21)	88.5 (0.11)	3.0 (0.07)	8.5 (0.10)
Naturalized citizen	78.9 (0.35)	4.8 (0.19)	16.3 (0.35)	66.2 (1.47)	5.2 (0.67)	28.6 (1.46)	74.6 (0.77)	5.3 (0.45)	20.0 (0.75)	77.8 (0.62)	5.5 (0.40)	16.7 (0.61)	84.7 (0.51)	3.9 (0.26)	11.4 (0.52)
Noncitizen	69.7 (0.26)	4.9 (0.12)	25.4 (0.26)	68.0 (0.47)	5.0 (0.22)	27.0 (0.43)	71.5 (0.54)	5.5 (0.29)	23.1 (0.49)	70.2 (0.62)	5.9 (0.40)	23.9 (0.59)	69.9 (0.42)	3.6 (0.20)	26.5 (0.45)

†Not applicable.
!Interpret data with caution. The coefficient of variation (CV) for this estimate is between 30 and 50 percent.
‡Reporting standards not met. Either there are too few cases for a reliable estimate or the coefficient of variation (CV) is 50 percent or greater.
[1]Data are for all persons with high school completion as their highest level of education, including those with equivalency credentials, such as the GED credential.
[2]Includes persons with no college degree as well as those with an associate's degree.
[3]Includes persons reporting American Indian alone, persons reporting Alaska Native alone, and persons from American Indian and/or Alaska Native tribes specified or not specified.

[4]United States refers to the 50 states, the District of Columbia, Puerto Rico, American Samoa, Guam, the U.S. Virgin Islands, and the Northern Marianas. Children born abroad to U.S. citizen parents are also counted as born within the United States.
NOTE: Estimates are for the entire population in the indicated age range, including persons living in households and persons living in group quarters (such as college residence halls, residential treatment centers, military barracks, and correctional facilities). The labor force consists of all employed persons plus those seeking employment. Standard errors were computed using replicate weights. Detail may not sum to totals because of rounding. Race categories exclude persons of Hispanic ethnicity.
SOURCE: U.S. Department of Commerce, Census Bureau, American Community Survey (ACS), 2014. (This table was prepared May 2016.)

Table 501.50. Employment to population ratios of persons 16 to 64 years old, by age group and highest level of educational attainment: Selected years, 1975 through 2015

[Standard errors appear in parentheses]

Age group and highest level of educational attainment	1975	1980	1985	1990	1995	2000	2005	2008	2009	2010	2011	2012	2013	2014	2015
1	2	3	4	5	6	7	8	9	10	11	12	13	14	15	16
16 to 19 years old, all education levels[1]	—	—	(†)	60.8 (2.03)	58.0 (2.13)	62.6 (2.09)	53.7 (1.40)	53.5 (1.41)	46.6 (1.36)	43.2 (1.30)	44.8 (1.40)	45.8 (1.43)	46.3 (1.40)	51.0 (1.67)	49.2 (1.36)
Less than high school completion	—	—	(†)	44.2 (3.08)	44.0 (3.13)	52.2 (3.19)	39.4 (2.01)	37.5 (1.90)	31.1 (1.89)	29.4 (1.83)	31.1 (2.21)	28.5 (2.05)	32.6 (2.03)	39.7 (2.63)	35.3 (2.03)
High school completion[2]	—	—	(†)	74.2 (2.54)	70.1 (2.99)	70.1 (2.92)	65.0 (2.04)	64.3 (1.96)	53.6 (1.72)	51.1 (1.84)	50.3 (2.01)	53.6 (1.90)	52.7 (2.15)	58.5 (2.22)	56.1 (1.83)
At least some college	—	—	(†)	76.8 (9.32)	71.6 (6.38)	78.2 (6.22)	66.6 (4.54)	65.3 (3.89)	65.4 (3.70)	57.5 (3.99)	61.5 (3.63)	64.3 (4.07)	63.5 (3.96)	60.5 (5.27)	65.7 (3.40)
20 to 24 years old, all education levels[1]	—	—	(†)	75.6 (0.90)	73.7 (0.93)	77.4 (0.93)	73.2 (0.66)	73.4 (0.60)	68.3 (0.66)	65.5 (0.72)	67.0 (0.59)	68.7 (0.67)	68.5 (0.72)	69.4 (0.74)	71.4 (0.66)
Less than high school completion	—	—	(†)	54.4 (2.29)	52.7 (2.41)	60.8 (2.43)	55.7 (1.27)	55.1 (1.73)	50.6 (1.60)	44.4 (1.58)	46.8 (1.71)	47.7 (1.95)	46.8 (1.88)	46.6 (2.62)	51.4 (2.17)
High school completion[2]	—	—	(†)	76.6 (1.26)	72.2 (1.46)	76.5 (1.46)	72.3 (0.91)	69.8 (0.97)	63.9 (1.03)	61.5 (1.01)	62.9 (1.07)	64.2 (0.99)	63.5 (1.16)	63.7 (1.31)	66.9 (1.01)
Some college, no bachelor's degree[3]	—	—	(†)	85.6 (1.69)	83.6 (1.52)	86.6 (1.49)	80.3 (1.19)	81.8 (1.09)	80.3 (1.32)	72.9 (1.27)	73.2 (1.01)	75.3 (1.19)	75.3 (1.15)	75.0 (1.29)	76.4 (1.03)
Bachelor's or higher degree	—	—	(†)	93.3 (1.57)	90.9 (1.76)	87.8 (2.07)	89.3 (1.16)	89.6 (1.21)	87.2 (1.26)	86.5 (1.37)	85.2 (1.41)	87.3 (1.16)	86.6 (1.46)	88.1 (1.47)	88.9 (1.05)
25 to 64 years old, all education levels	65.8 (0.33)	70.2 (0.30)	71.6 (0.30)	75.0 (0.29)	75.5 (0.28)	77.7 (0.27)	75.0 (0.19)	75.5 (0.16)	72.2 (0.19)	71.5 (0.19)	71.2 (0.19)	71.7 (0.18)	72.1 (0.19)	72.3 (0.26)	73.1 (0.19)
Less than high school completion	55.3 (0.62)	55.5 (0.66)	53.1 (0.74)	54.9 (0.80)	53.8 (0.85)	57.8 (0.91)	57.2 (0.51)	56.2 (0.51)	52.5 (0.57)	52.1 (0.60)	51.1 (0.56)	52.9 (0.60)	53.2 (0.60)	54.9 (0.78)	54.7 (0.58)
High school completion[2]	65.5 (0.53)	70.4 (0.48)	70.7 (0.48)	74.4 (0.46)	73.3 (0.49)	75.5 (0.49)	71.5 (0.34)	71.6 (0.28)	67.0 (0.33)	67.0 (0.36)	66.2 (0.39)	66.5 (0.35)	66.7 (0.38)	67.0 (0.44)	67.3 (0.37)
Some college, no bachelor's degree[3]	71.7 (0.86)	76.1 (0.70)	77.8 (0.66)	80.2 (0.60)	79.5 (0.51)	80.7 (0.50)	77.7 (0.33)	77.5 (0.31)	73.9 (0.33)	72.7 (0.30)	72.2 (0.30)	72.2 (0.30)	73.1 (0.31)	72.6 (0.44)	74.1 (0.32)
Bachelor's or higher degree	82.5 (0.68)	84.5 (0.55)	85.6 (0.51)	86.7 (0.47)	86.5 (0.44)	86.4 (0.42)	83.7 (0.26)	84.4 (0.27)	82.2 (0.25)	81.6 (0.24)	81.5 (0.26)	82.1 (0.24)	81.9 (0.26)	82.0 (0.34)	82.8 (0.26)
25 to 34 years old, all education levels	67.7 (0.59)	74.5 (0.49)	76.2 (0.48)	78.6 (0.47)	78.5 (0.48)	81.6 (0.49)	76.8 (0.31)	78.1 (0.31)	74.2 (0.36)	73.2 (0.34)	73.0 (0.35)	73.8 (0.31)	74.6 (0.33)	74.5 (0.43)	76.0 (0.35)
Less than high school completion	52.9 (1.43)	58.3 (1.46)	57.0 (1.54)	60.3 (1.50)	59.8 (1.59)	64.1 (1.76)	60.4 (0.95)	60.4 (0.93)	54.6 (1.07)	55.1 (0.95)	54.2 (1.17)	58.2 (1.14)	57.4 (1.03)	57.8 (1.37)	56.5 (1.11)
High school completion[2]	65.5 (0.92)	72.0 (0.81)	74.3 (0.78)	77.0 (0.74)	77.0 (0.84)	80.2 (0.91)	73.1 (0.60)	74.0 (0.60)	69.0 (0.66)	68.1 (0.72)	67.9 (0.67)	68.7 (0.75)	68.2 (0.68)	68.2 (0.73)	70.4 (0.72)
Some college, no bachelor's degree[3]	71.7 (1.33)	77.8 (1.01)	80.1 (0.97)	81.6 (0.96)	80.5 (0.87)	82.8 (0.90)	79.4 (0.54)	79.9 (0.52)	75.9 (0.60)	72.9 (0.57)	73.0 (0.62)	72.7 (0.68)	74.9 (0.65)	74.5 (0.74)	76.4 (0.60)
Bachelor's or higher degree	82.0 (1.04)	85.4 (0.82)	86.6 (0.79)	88.1 (0.76)	88.1 (0.75)	89.0 (0.73)	84.4 (0.52)	86.8 (0.46)	84.5 (0.49)	84.0 (0.49)	83.4 (0.45)	84.3 (0.45)	84.4 (0.45)	84.0 (0.59)	84.8 (0.48)
35 to 44 years old, all education levels	70.3 (0.66)	76.5 (0.58)	78.1 (0.54)	81.6 (0.48)	80.2 (0.46)	81.8 (0.45)	79.9 (0.26)	80.1 (0.30)	76.7 (0.29)	76.0 (0.30)	76.0 (0.35)	76.9 (0.35)	77.0 (0.35)	77.1 (0.40)	78.3 (0.31)
Less than high school completion	61.4 (1.31)	63.4 (1.39)	60.0 (1.58)	62.5 (1.66)	58.6 (1.66)	64.8 (1.64)	64.3 (0.93)	64.3 (1.05)	60.2 (1.01)	58.2 (1.13)	57.5 (1.04)	59.6 (1.13)	61.6 (1.03)	61.3 (1.25)	62.3 (0.84)
High school completion[2]	69.6 (1.02)	76.6 (0.90)	76.6 (0.88)	80.0 (0.80)	78.6 (0.82)	81.0 (0.79)	78.0 (0.52)	76.9 (0.57)	72.6 (0.63)	72.4 (0.64)	71.8 (0.64)	72.1 (0.68)	72.6 (0.66)	72.6 (0.80)	72.5 (0.63)
Some college, no bachelor's degree[3]	74.5 (1.74)	80.9 (1.33)	81.6 (1.15)	85.0 (0.93)	83.3 (0.81)	84.4 (0.80)	82.0 (0.48)	82.4 (0.58)	78.5 (0.53)	76.9 (0.53)	76.9 (0.62)	78.2 (0.61)	77.0 (0.64)	77.3 (0.68)	79.6 (0.53)
Bachelor's or higher degree	84.5 (1.31)	87.1 (1.00)	88.8 (0.80)	89.5 (0.72)	88.5 (0.71)	87.6 (0.74)	84.4 (0.41)	86.4 (0.40)	84.8 (0.42)	84.7 (0.39)	84.8 (0.43)	85.0 (0.41)	84.4 (0.43)	85.0 (0.57)	86.7 (0.39)
45 to 54 years old, all education levels	68.4 (0.65)	71.7 (0.65)	73.5 (0.67)	77.6 (0.62)	78.8 (0.55)	81.2 (0.50)	78.4 (0.32)	78.4 (0.33)	75.2 (0.34)	74.7 (0.35)	74.3 (0.32)	74.6 (0.30)	74.9 (0.30)	76.2 (0.43)	75.9 (0.33)
Less than high school completion	59.8 (1.14)	61.8 (1.24)	58.7 (1.52)	60.7 (1.63)	58.4 (1.79)	60.3 (1.89)	59.0 (1.04)	56.0 (1.02)	54.0 (1.13)	52.5 (1.05)	51.7 (0.84)	54.7 (1.06)	53.3 (1.04)	59.4 (1.50)	56.8 (1.16)
High school completion[2]	68.8 (1.03)	72.0 (1.02)	74.0 (1.03)	77.5 (0.97)	75.9 (1.01)	78.2 (0.95)	75.1 (0.64)	75.4 (0.57)	71.6 (0.53)	71.0 (0.65)	70.1 (0.58)	70.4 (0.62)	70.1 (0.60)	70.7 (0.84)	70.9 (0.63)
Some college, no bachelor's degree[3]	74.7 (1.81)	76.5 (1.72)	79.2 (1.63)	81.9 (1.38)	81.7 (1.03)	83.4 (0.91)	80.4 (0.57)	80.2 (0.51)	77.3 (0.58)	77.3 (0.54)	76.6 (0.53)	76.2 (0.53)	77.4 (0.53)	77.4 (0.76)	77.1 (0.60)
Bachelor's or higher degree	87.1 (1.36)	87.3 (1.21)	87.9 (1.16)	89.4 (0.97)	89.5 (0.78)	89.7 (0.71)	87.5 (0.45)	88.1 (0.45)	85.2 (0.45)	84.4 (0.45)	84.9 (0.45)	84.7 (0.48)	84.7 (0.47)	85.9 (0.54)	85.7 (0.43)
55 to 64 years old, all education levels	54.6 (0.77)	54.1 (0.73)	52.1 (0.77)	53.4 (0.81)	55.0 (0.82)	58.1 (0.79)	60.8 (0.48)	62.8 (0.41)	60.8 (0.42)	60.6 (0.41)	60.2 (0.43)	60.6 (0.41)	61.3 (0.43)	60.9 (0.52)	61.9 (0.37)
Less than high school completion	48.5 (1.11)	43.2 (1.16)	41.8 (1.29)	39.5 (1.46)	38.1 (1.67)	40.4 (1.84)	39.4 (1.13)	41.0 (1.24)	38.2 (1.19)	40.0 (1.19)	39.4 (1.15)	39.1 (1.08)	38.5 (1.32)	39.6 (1.34)	42.4 (1.12)
High school completion[2]	56.5 (1.32)	57.5 (1.19)	52.1 (1.22)	54.0 (1.29)	53.7 (1.34)	55.4 (1.34)	55.3 (0.79)	57.8 (0.69)	55.8 (0.73)	55.1 (0.71)	54.4 (0.81)	54.6 (0.75)	56.3 (0.74)	57.6 (0.90)	56.9 (0.74)
Some college, no bachelor's degree[3]	62.6 (2.48)	62.5 (2.08)	58.9 (2.21)	60.4 (2.12)	62.0 (1.74)	62.4 (1.64)	64.8 (0.90)	64.3 (0.80)	61.6 (0.74)	61.8 (0.76)	61.2 (0.78)	61.2 (0.70)	62.3 (0.72)	60.5 (0.99)	63.2 (0.68)
Bachelor's or higher degree	72.6 (2.34)	71.9 (1.96)	71.3 (1.83)	70.5 (1.79)	70.0 (1.72)	71.9 (1.49)	73.5 (0.74)	74.0 (0.68)	72.7 (0.63)	72.0 (0.65)	71.8 (0.71)	73.1 (0.66)	72.4 (0.67)	71.7 (0.90)	72.3 (0.62)

—Not available.
†Not applicable.
[1]Data for 16- to 19-year-olds and 20- to 24-year-olds exclude persons enrolled in school.
[2]Includes equivalency credentials, such as the GED credential.
[3]Includes persons with no college degree as well as those with an associate's degree.

NOTE: For each age group, the employment to population ratio is the number of persons in that age group who are employed as a percentage of the civilian population in that age group.
SOURCE: U.S. Department of Commerce, Census Bureau, Current Population Survey (CPS), Annual Social and Economic Supplement, selected years, 1975 through 2015. (This table was prepared October 2015.)

Table 501.60. Employment to population ratios of males 16 to 64 years old, by age group and highest level of educational attainment: Selected years, 1975 through 2015

[Standard errors appear in parentheses]

Age group and highest level of educational attainment	1975	1980	1985	1990	1995	2000	2005	2008	2009	2010	2011	2012	2013	2014	2015
1	2	3	4	5	6	7	8	9	10	11	12	13	14	15	16
16 to 19 years old, all education levels[1]	— (†)	— (†)	— (†)	65.3 (2.82)	63.6 (2.87)	69.2 (2.70)	56.2 (2.10)	58.7 (1.72)	45.8 (1.77)	44.0 (1.72)	47.0 (1.94)	48.1 (2.00)	48.1 (1.92)	51.9 (2.37)	51.2 (1.92)
Less than high school completion	— (†)	— (†)	— (†)	51.5 (4.20)	50.6 (4.26)	63.1 (4.09)	47.0 (3.07)	45.8 (2.44)	34.0 (2.70)	31.5 (2.64)	37.4 (3.03)	34.7 (3.25)	33.9 (2.63)	43.6 (3.64)	37.2 (2.72)
High school completion[2]	— (†)	— (†)	— (†)	78.7 (3.51)	76.1 (3.87)	74.4 (3.77)	63.1 (2.88)	67.1 (2.47)	51.1 (2.35)	51.0 (2.37)	51.2 (2.84)	52.5 (2.51)	55.8 (2.86)	58.1 (3.28)	58.7 (2.49)
At least some college	— (†)	— (†)	— (†)	83.1 (13.41)	75.9 (8.99)	77.0 (9.81)	70.4 (5.98)	74.3 (4.67)	62.9 (5.37)	61.4 (6.00)	60.2 (5.67)	64.2 (5.72)	65.9 (5.64)	57.6 (8.04)	63.9 (4.71)
20 to 24 years old, all education levels[1]	— (†)	— (†)	— (†)	83.5 (1.10)	81.2 (1.16)	83.3 (1.16)	78.9 (0.86)	79.1 (0.68)	70.6 (0.86)	68.4 (0.97)	69.5 (0.84)	72.1 (0.96)	71.4 (0.95)	72.4 (1.04)	74.9 (0.98)
Less than high school completion	— (†)	— (†)	— (†)	70.0 (2.84)	69.3 (2.99)	72.1 (2.93)	69.5 (1.80)	68.2 (2.11)	59.2 (2.28)	52.9 (2.06)	57.3 (2.43)	56.6 (2.42)	57.0 (2.54)	58.3 (3.16)	60.3 (2.76)
High school completion[2]	— (†)	— (†)	— (†)	84.6 (1.50)	81.1 (1.73)	82.7 (1.78)	78.0 (1.21)	76.9 (1.05)	78.0 (1.38)	66.0 (1.31)	66.2 (1.31)	68.0 (1.43)	68.0 (1.47)	66.6 (1.77)	71.1 (1.39)
Some college, no bachelor's degree[3]	— (†)	— (†)	— (†)	91.8 (1.98)	87.5 (1.97)	92.6 (1.65)	84.6 (1.43)	85.2 (1.38)	77.7 (1.69)	74.8 (1.71)	75.2 (1.66)	80.5 (1.59)	77.9 (1.51)	78.6 (1.82)	79.9 (1.57)
Bachelor's or higher degree	— (†)	— (†)	— (†)	94.9 (2.07)	91.1 (2.70)	89.1 (3.07)	90.6 (1.82)	92.4 (1.51)	86.4 (1.94)	86.3 (2.04)	84.7 (2.16)	88.7 (1.77)	86.1 (2.11)	90.6 (1.93)	90.6 (1.71)
25 to 64 years old, all education levels	84.6 (0.36)	85.0 (0.34)	83.1 (0.36)	84.5 (0.34)	83.0 (0.34)	84.6 (0.33)	81.9 (0.25)	81.6 (0.22)	77.0 (0.25)	76.3 (0.27)	76.3 (0.27)	77.4 (0.25)	78.2 (0.27)	78.2 (0.35)	79.4 (0.26)
Less than high school completion	74.3 (0.77)	72.4 (0.84)	67.6 (0.98)	67.9 (1.04)	64.2 (1.13)	69.6 (1.17)	69.7 (0.70)	66.6 (0.78)	61.6 (0.80)	61.2 (0.93)	61.0 (0.81)	63.0 (0.77)	64.0 (0.75)	66.3 (1.04)	67.2 (0.75)
High school completion[2]	87.2 (0.56)	87.0 (0.54)	83.5 (0.58)	85.1 (0.55)	81.9 (0.61)	82.9 (0.61)	78.6 (0.44)	78.3 (0.42)	72.1 (0.49)	71.7 (0.50)	71.8 (0.50)	72.6 (0.45)	73.1 (0.51)	73.6 (0.59)	74.7 (0.48)
Some college, no bachelor's degree[3]	88.8 (0.83)	88.3 (0.73)	87.1 (0.75)	87.9 (0.70)	86.1 (0.63)	86.1 (0.63)	83.7 (0.44)	82.9 (0.42)	78.1 (0.41)	76.6 (0.42)	75.9 (0.45)	77.3 (0.43)	78.3 (0.46)	77.5 (0.59)	79.6 (0.48)
Bachelor's or higher degree	93.8 (0.55)	93.6 (0.48)	92.4 (0.50)	92.5 (0.48)	91.4 (0.48)	91.8 (0.47)	89.4 (0.35)	90.0 (0.31)	87.6 (0.34)	86.9 (0.33)	86.9 (0.35)	87.5 (0.33)	88.0 (0.33)	87.7 (0.42)	88.0 (0.32)
25 to 34 years old, all education levels	87.4 (0.59)	88.1 (0.52)	86.9 (0.54)	87.9 (0.52)	87.1 (0.55)	89.4 (0.55)	84.6 (0.40)	84.6 (0.41)	79.1 (0.46)	78.4 (0.48)	78.5 (0.51)	80.1 (0.48)	81.3 (0.46)	80.9 (0.56)	83.2 (0.44)
Less than high school completion	76.2 (1.78)	76.3 (1.80)	75.1 (1.87)	75.6 (1.77)	73.7 (1.91)	78.4 (2.04)	73.5 (1.23)	73.5 (1.40)	66.2 (1.45)	66.6 (1.42)	66.3 (1.47)	70.1 (1.51)	70.2 (1.32)	73.1 (1.88)	73.1 (1.59)
High school completion[2]	88.4 (0.93)	88.4 (0.86)	86.1 (0.88)	88.6 (0.80)	86.6 (0.94)	89.1 (0.98)	81.7 (0.77)	81.7 (0.83)	73.4 (0.87)	73.0 (0.85)	74.3 (0.91)	76.5 (0.90)	77.3 (0.82)	77.2 (0.93)	79.6 (0.87)
Some college, no bachelor's degree[3]	87.7 (1.31)	88.5 (1.06)	89.7 (1.04)	89.7 (1.08)	89.6 (0.98)	90.7 (1.02)	86.4 (0.82)	86.3 (0.73)	81.4 (0.82)	78.7 (0.83)	77.5 (0.90)	78.2 (0.97)	80.7 (0.95)	79.1 (1.25)	83.0 (0.86)
Bachelor's or higher degree	93.5 (0.87)	93.4 (0.76)	92.2 (0.85)	93.1 (0.83)	93.1 (0.83)	93.6 (0.82)	89.6 (0.69)	91.7 (0.62)	89.5 (0.68)	89.2 (0.74)	89.0 (0.70)	89.3 (0.67)	89.8 (0.57)	88.8 (0.78)	89.6 (0.59)
35 to 44 years old, all education levels	90.1 (0.61)	91.1 (0.55)	89.1 (0.57)	90.2 (0.52)	88.6 (0.55)	88.8 (0.52)	87.2 (0.37)	87.1 (0.41)	82.7 (0.41)	82.3 (0.42)	82.4 (0.43)	83.3 (0.43)	84.7 (0.47)	83.8 (0.56)	85.6 (0.42)
Less than high school completion	81.6 (1.48)	80.1 (1.65)	74.6 (1.99)	73.9 (2.13)	66.7 (2.15)	76.5 (2.00)	75.9 (1.26)	73.3 (1.51)	69.4 (1.47)	69.5 (1.61)	70.9 (1.59)	70.6 (1.47)	74.8 (1.38)	73.9 (1.75)	76.9 (1.24)
High school completion[2]	91.3 (0.95)	92.3 (0.85)	88.6 (1.00)	89.1 (0.91)	85.9 (0.98)	87.1 (0.93)	83.7 (0.71)	83.3 (0.76)	77.6 (0.80)	77.6 (0.92)	76.8 (0.83)	78.2 (0.97)	79.4 (0.88)	78.2 (1.17)	80.4 (0.82)
Some college, no bachelor's degree[3]	93.8 (1.34)	93.8 (1.13)	90.2 (1.25)	92.6 (0.97)	88.8 (0.99)	90.2 (0.95)	89.4 (0.60)	89.0 (0.71)	83.9 (0.74)	82.7 (0.73)	83.1 (0.86)	83.9 (0.76)	84.6 (0.78)	83.9 (1.04)	85.4 (0.85)
Bachelor's or higher degree	97.0 (0.77)	97.1 (0.65)	96.3 (0.62)	96.3 (0.59)	95.1 (0.66)	95.1 (0.67)	94.6 (0.45)	94.9 (0.41)	92.3 (0.56)	92.3 (0.56)	91.4 (0.51)	92.2 (0.51)	92.9 (0.48)	92.4 (0.75)	93.6 (0.53)
45 to 54 years old, all education levels	86.6 (0.68)	87.4 (0.67)	85.8 (0.76)	87.1 (0.70)	84.9 (0.68)	86.5 (0.62)	83.9 (0.45)	83.7 (0.43)	78.8 (0.44)	78.3 (0.50)	78.9 (0.45)	79.9 (0.44)	79.7 (0.38)	81.8 (0.61)	81.3 (0.46)
Less than high school completion	78.2 (1.34)	79.6 (1.42)	73.2 (1.90)	74.3 (2.05)	66.4 (2.41)	66.5 (2.52)	69.9 (1.55)	65.5 (1.49)	61.4 (1.50)	58.8 (1.48)	58.6 (1.25)	62.5 (1.45)	61.1 (1.33)	67.3 (1.96)	65.0 (1.56)
High school completion[2]	90.3 (1.01)	89.3 (1.08)	87.3 (1.18)	87.5 (1.15)	82.1 (1.35)	84.6 (1.21)	80.7 (0.86)	80.4 (0.81)	74.2 (0.80)	74.6 (0.91)	75.2 (0.78)	75.2 (0.88)	74.2 (0.78)	76.4 (1.12)	76.7 (0.86)
Some college, no bachelor's degree[3]	91.0 (1.66)	89.4 (1.78)	89.3 (1.76)	88.9 (1.58)	87.2 (1.29)	86.4 (1.18)	84.5 (0.84)	85.6 (0.64)	80.1 (0.84)	79.4 (0.80)	79.2 (0.81)	81.9 (0.69)	82.1 (0.69)	83.5 (0.95)	82.4 (0.87)
Bachelor's or higher degree	95.6 (1.02)	96.0 (0.88)	94.8 (1.00)	95.2 (0.88)	93.8 (0.80)	94.6 (0.72)	92.2 (0.53)	93.5 (0.46)	90.2 (0.58)	89.4 (0.58)	90.5 (0.53)	90.2 (0.60)	90.7 (0.51)	91.4 (0.65)	91.2 (0.50)
55 to 64 years old, all education levels	71.3 (1.00)	69.7 (0.98)	64.6 (1.05)	64.0 (1.12)	63.2 (1.13)	64.9 (1.09)	67.3 (0.66)	68.0 (0.54)	65.2 (0.59)	64.4 (0.61)	64.1 (0.61)	65.1 (0.58)	66.0 (0.54)	65.7 (0.76)	67.1 (0.53)
Less than high school completion	64.5 (1.51)	58.3 (1.65)	53.4 (1.85)	49.6 (2.13)	46.9 (2.46)	51.2 (2.71)	48.8 (1.70)	48.3 (1.60)	44.3 (1.75)	45.0 (1.81)	45.2 (1.68)	44.6 (1.48)	45.5 (1.73)	48.4 (1.96)	52.6 (1.61)
High school completion[2]	74.9 (1.73)	66.1 (1.61)	66.1 (1.80)	66.0 (1.89)	62.7 (1.99)	61.0 (1.97)	61.8 (1.15)	62.9 (1.10)	59.3 (1.19)	58.5 (1.12)	58.2 (1.12)	59.1 (1.05)	61.1 (1.04)	62.6 (1.34)	62.2 (1.03)
Some college, no bachelor's degree[3]	80.8 (2.87)	77.2 (2.53)	67.5 (3.01)	67.7 (2.93)	67.8 (2.41)	66.6 (2.31)	69.6 (1.31)	67.9 (1.10)	64.5 (1.06)	63.0 (1.10)	63.0 (1.08)	64.3 (1.11)	63.3 (1.29)	63.3 (1.29)	67.6 (1.00)
Bachelor's or higher degree	84.1 (2.52)	83.8 (2.04)	80.7 (1.98)	77.9 (2.03)	74.9 (2.04)	77.0 (1.82)	78.6 (0.89)	78.6 (0.81)	77.4 (0.83)	76.2 (0.82)	76.3 (0.84)	77.7 (0.85)	77.8 (0.91)	77.2 (1.18)	76.8 (0.87)

—Not available.
†Not applicable.
[1]Data for 16- to 19-year-olds and 20- to 24-year-olds exclude persons enrolled in school.
[2]Includes equivalency credentials, such as the GED credential.
[3]Includes persons with no college degree as well as those with an associate's degree.

NOTE: For each age group, the employment to population ratio of males is the number of males in that age group who are employed as a percentage of the male civilian population in that age group.
SOURCE: U.S. Department of Commerce, Census Bureau, Current Population Survey (CPS), Annual Social and Economic Supplement, selected years, 1975 through 2015. (This table was prepared October 2015.)

Table 501.70. Employment to population ratios of females 16 to 64 years old, by age group and highest level of educational attainment: Selected years, 1975 through 2015

[Standard errors appear in parentheses]

Age group and highest level of educational attainment	1975	1980	1985	1990	1995	2000	2005	2008	2009	2010	2011	2012	2013	2014	2015
1	2	3	4	5	6	7	8	9	10	11	12	13	14	15	16
16 to 19 years old, all education levels[1]	(†)	(†)	(†)	56.6 (2.72)	52.2 (2.93)	55.1 (2.98)	51.0 (1.88)	47.3 (2.14)	47.7 (1.81)	42.3 (1.88)	42.3 (2.14)	43.1 (2.03)	44.3 (1.90)	50.0 (2.39)	46.9 (1.88)
Less than high school completion	—	—	—	36.0 (4.13)	36.5 (4.23)	38.9 (4.42)	30.3 (2.72)	25.9 (2.84)	27.3 (2.57)	26.8 (2.75)	23.5 (2.92)	22.6 (2.88)	31.0 (3.10)	34.5 (3.67)	33.3 (2.82)
High school completion[2]	—	—	—	70.5 (3.38)	64.1 (4.22)	65.2 (4.22)	67.0 (2.60)	61.2 (2.94)	56.7 (2.54)	51.2 (2.99)	49.1 (2.91)	55.2 (2.97)	48.9 (2.96)	59.0 (3.35)	52.8 (2.83)
At least some college	(†)	(†)	(†)	73.1 (11.73)	68.3 (8.37)	79.1 (7.56)	63.6 (6.23)	55.9 (5.75)	67.6 (4.82)	54.4 (5.29)	62.5 (5.31)	64.3 (5.68)	61.7 (4.61)	63.0 (7.14)	67.7 (5.08)
20 to 24 years old, all education levels[1]	(†)	(†)	(†)	68.2 (1.29)	66.3 (1.34)	71.5 (1.35)	67.0 (1.01)	67.2 (0.97)	65.8 (0.94)	62.4 (1.01)	64.1 (0.92)	65.0 (0.94)	65.2 (1.01)	66.3 (1.06)	67.7 (0.88)
Less than high school completion	(†)	(†)	(†)	36.7 (3.08)	33.6 (3.18)	46.2 (3.57)	38.5 (2.20)	37.5 (2.47)	38.6 (2.32)	33.3 (2.50)	33.2 (2.31)	36.2 (2.84)	33.4 (2.55)	30.5 (3.57)	42.0 (3.18)
High school completion[2]	(†)	(†)	(†)	68.8 (1.84)	62.2 (2.19)	70.0 (2.15)	65.0 (1.47)	60.8 (1.55)	59.9 (1.53)	55.6 (1.43)	58.5 (1.77)	59.2 (1.55)	58.4 (1.78)	60.2 (1.86)	61.6 (1.41)
Some college, no bachelor's degree[3]	(†)	(†)	(†)	80.9 (2.39)	80.3 (2.12)	81.4 (2.23)	76.6 (1.72)	78.7 (1.56)	72.4 (1.67)	72.4 (1.65)	71.2 (1.65)	70.6 (1.64)	71.6 (1.64)	71.6 (1.89)	72.9 (1.54)
Bachelor's or higher degree	(†)	(†)	(†)	92.0 (2.12)	90.8 (2.19)	86.9 (2.61)	88.4 (1.53)	87.8 (1.55)	87.7 (1.60)	86.7 (1.67)	85.5 (1.81)	86.4 (1.53)	87.0 (1.64)	86.3 (1.96)	87.6 (1.42)
25 to 64 years old, all education levels	48.5 (0.46)	56.5 (0.44)	60.8 (0.43)	66.0 (0.42)	68.3 (0.40)	71.2 (0.39)	68.4 (0.23)	69.6 (0.23)	67.6 (0.24)	66.9 (0.23)	66.2 (0.24)	66.3 (0.25)	66.4 (0.23)	66.6 (0.32)	67.1 (0.24)
Less than high school completion	37.7 (0.80)	39.8 (0.86)	39.1 (0.97)	41.8 (1.06)	43.2 (1.15)	45.8 (1.24)	43.4 (0.72)	43.8 (0.74)	41.9 (0.67)	41.6 (0.81)	39.7 (0.71)	41.6 (0.89)	40.6 (0.82)	41.5 (0.89)	40.5 (0.81)
High school completion[2]	50.1 (0.70)	58.2 (0.65)	60.8 (0.65)	65.6 (0.64)	65.7 (0.69)	68.6 (0.70)	64.2 (0.44)	64.7 (0.43)	63.2 (0.42)	61.9 (0.44)	60.1 (0.51)	60.0 (0.49)	59.8 (0.47)	59.7 (0.58)	59.1 (0.48)
Some college, no bachelor's degree[3]	53.8 (1.30)	63.7 (1.07)	69.0 (0.98)	73.2 (0.88)	73.8 (0.71)	76.0 (0.70)	72.8 (0.42)	73.0 (0.43)	70.4 (0.44)	69.4 (0.45)	69.1 (0.37)	67.9 (0.43)	68.6 (0.46)	68.3 (0.58)	69.3 (0.45)
Bachelor's or higher degree	65.6 (1.29)	71.8 (1.01)	76.7 (0.88)	79.8 (0.78)	80.8 (0.71)	80.8 (0.66)	78.1 (0.40)	79.1 (0.40)	77.3 (0.38)	76.9 (0.36)	76.6 (0.39)	77.2 (0.38)	76.6 (0.40)	77.1 (0.47)	78.2 (0.35)
25 to 34 years old, all education levels	49.3 (0.83)	61.6 (0.73)	65.9 (0.72)	69.6 (0.70)	70.2 (0.71)	74.1 (0.74)	69.0 (0.48)	71.7 (0.47)	69.3 (0.51)	68.0 (0.44)	67.5 (0.42)	67.7 (0.44)	68.0 (0.45)	68.2 (0.55)	69.0 (0.51)
Less than high school completion	33.7 (1.74)	42.3 (1.91)	38.7 (2.05)	42.5 (2.12)	43.5 (2.25)	47.6 (2.56)	42.7 (1.44)	42.4 (1.37)	39.5 (1.50)	40.2 (1.35)	37.5 (1.55)	38.9 (1.69)	40.7 (1.49)	40.2 (1.86)	36.5 (1.73)
High school completion[2]	48.1 (1.72)	59.4 (1.12)	63.9 (1.11)	67.5 (1.11)	67.2 (1.27)	70.7 (1.43)	62.5 (0.99)	64.3 (0.92)	63.2 (0.98)	61.4 (1.14)	59.5 (0.94)	59.1 (1.05)	57.1 (1.07)	56.3 (1.19)	58.6 (1.08)
Some college, no bachelor's degree[3]	53.6 (2.06)	66.3 (1.58)	71.0 (1.46)	74.5 (1.40)	73.0 (1.26)	76.3 (1.31)	73.0 (0.81)	74.4 (0.81)	70.8 (0.86)	67.7 (0.80)	69.1 (0.79)	67.7 (0.90)	69.7 (0.84)	70.3 (0.91)	70.6 (0.83)
Bachelor's or higher degree	66.3 (1.88)	75.5 (1.42)	80.6 (1.26)	83.2 (1.18)	83.4 (1.16)	84.7 (1.11)	80.1 (0.72)	82.8 (0.66)	80.7 (0.73)	79.9 (0.63)	78.8 (0.60)	80.3 (0.63)	80.1 (0.67)	80.2 (0.77)	80.9 (0.67)
35 to 44 years old, all education levels	51.9 (0.95)	62.8 (0.87)	67.7 (0.80)	73.3 (0.72)	73.8 (0.68)	75.1 (0.67)	72.8 (0.38)	73.3 (0.40)	70.9 (0.42)	69.9 (0.42)	69.8 (0.48)	70.7 (0.48)	69.6 (0.47)	70.7 (0.57)	71.3 (0.42)
Less than high school completion	42.8 (1.76)	46.4 (1.90)	46.4 (2.13)	51.0 (2.35)	49.7 (2.33)	52.5 (2.35)	51.5 (1.33)	53.1 (1.57)	48.9 (1.47)	44.8 (1.54)	42.5 (1.41)	47.0 (1.49)	45.8 (1.52)	45.6 (1.61)	45.5 (1.44)
High school completion[2]	53.9 (1.38)	64.7 (1.28)	67.8 (1.22)	72.7 (1.13)	71.7 (1.19)	74.7 (1.18)	71.6 (0.74)	69.6 (0.78)	66.9 (0.94)	66.3 (0.87)	65.8 (0.87)	64.9 (1.02)	64.8 (0.92)	65.8 (1.07)	62.8 (0.99)
Some college, no bachelor's degree[3]	55.1 (2.67)	67.8 (2.14)	73.6 (1.73)	77.9 (1.44)	78.5 (1.16)	76.1 (1.16)	76.1 (0.67)	76.9 (0.81)	74.0 (0.79)	72.2 (0.74)	71.8 (0.87)	73.4 (0.90)	70.3 (0.90)	71.7 (1.06)	74.5 (0.70)
Bachelor's or higher degree	63.2 (2.73)	73.0 (1.97)	78.5 (1.53)	81.6 (1.18)	81.5 (1.19)	80.2 (1.20)	78.1 (0.66)	78.9 (0.63)	78.1 (0.61)	78.3 (0.63)	78.9 (0.68)	78.8 (0.64)	80.1 (0.71)	79.0 (0.80)	81.0 (0.57)
45 to 54 years old, all education levels	51.5 (0.93)	57.1 (0.94)	62.1 (0.98)	68.6 (0.92)	72.9 (0.80)	76.0 (0.73)	73.2 (0.46)	73.2 (0.46)	71.8 (0.46)	71.3 (0.44)	70.0 (0.44)	69.6 (0.42)	70.3 (0.41)	70.8 (0.58)	70.8 (0.46)
Less than high school completion	41.5 (1.55)	43.9 (1.71)	44.3 (2.06)	47.6 (2.22)	50.6 (2.43)	52.3 (2.57)	47.8 (1.40)	44.6 (1.30)	45.5 (1.47)	45.2 (1.61)	44.1 (1.25)	45.8 (1.53)	43.8 (1.52)	49.6 (2.11)	47.3 (1.50)
High school completion[2]	53.8 (1.37)	60.2 (1.37)	64.2 (1.41)	69.9 (1.35)	71.1 (1.36)	72.9 (1.33)	69.5 (0.83)	70.1 (0.80)	68.8 (0.85)	68.0 (0.72)	64.4 (0.89)	65.5 (0.82)	65.7 (0.84)	64.8 (1.17)	64.5 (0.93)
Some college, no bachelor's degree[3]	58.1 (2.78)	64.7 (2.56)	69.7 (2.45)	75.2 (2.08)	76.9 (1.46)	80.6 (1.28)	76.9 (0.72)	75.9 (0.74)	75.0 (0.73)	75.5 (0.74)	74.4 (0.71)	71.4 (0.77)	73.6 (0.78)	72.6 (1.03)	72.8 (0.80)
Bachelor's or higher degree	72.2 (2.87)	72.3 (2.55)	77.3 (2.24)	81.8 (1.76)	83.8 (1.36)	84.5 (1.17)	82.8 (0.72)	83.0 (0.73)	80.5 (0.69)	79.6 (0.72)	79.6 (0.68)	79.6 (0.71)	79.2 (0.71)	80.6 (0.83)	80.8 (0.63)
55 to 64 years old, all education levels	39.7 (0.99)	40.5 (0.94)	41.1 (0.99)	44.0 (1.05)	47.5 (1.08)	51.9 (1.06)	54.8 (0.61)	58.1 (0.55)	56.7 (0.55)	57.1 (0.53)	56.4 (0.51)	56.5 (0.57)	57.1 (0.57)	56.4 (0.63)	57.0 (0.49)
Less than high school completion	33.5 (1.39)	29.4 (1.41)	31.2 (1.60)	30.5 (1.80)	30.3 (2.07)	30.9 (2.26)	30.5 (1.33)	34.1 (1.70)	32.1 (1.47)	35.1 (1.54)	33.6 (1.46)	34.0 (1.57)	32.1 (1.57)	30.4 (1.69)	32.1 (1.42)
High school completion[2]	42.6 (1.65)	45.8 (1.48)	42.8 (1.48)	45.7 (1.60)	47.5 (1.66)	51.3 (1.69)	50.5 (0.95)	53.8 (0.90)	52.9 (0.97)	52.2 (0.92)	51.1 (0.95)	50.6 (0.97)	52.0 (0.93)	52.9 (1.09)	51.8 (0.99)
Some college, no bachelor's degree[3]	45.9 (3.37)	48.2 (2.87)	51.1 (2.95)	54.1 (2.81)	57.0 (2.32)	58.8 (2.17)	60.9 (1.06)	62.0 (1.04)	59.1 (1.02)	59.9 (1.08)	59.6 (1.08)	58.7 (1.01)	60.2 (1.03)	58.2 (1.19)	59.4 (0.92)
Bachelor's or higher degree	57.8 (3.72)	54.0 (3.27)	55.1 (3.18)	58.6 (2.98)	61.9 (2.81)	65.1 (2.28)	67.5 (1.22)	68.7 (1.04)	67.5 (0.96)	67.5 (0.98)	67.0 (1.04)	68.3 (1.03)	67.2 (0.93)	66.6 (1.25)	68.1 (0.86)

—Not available.
†Not applicable.
[1]Data for 16- to 19-year-olds and 20- to 24-year-olds exclude persons enrolled in school.
[2]Includes equivalency credentials, such as the GED credential.
[3]Includes persons with no college degree as well as those with an associate's degree.

NOTE: For each age group, the employment to population ratio of females in that age group is the number of females who are employed as a percentage of the female civilian population in that age group.
SOURCE: U.S. Department of Commerce, Census Bureau, Current Population Survey (CPS), Annual Social and Economic Supplement, selected years, 1975 through 2015. (This table was prepared October 2015.)

Table 501.80. Unemployment rates of persons 16 to 64 years old, by age group and highest level of educational attainment: Selected years, 1975 through 2015

[Standard errors appear in parentheses]

Age group and highest level of educational attainment	1975	1980	1985	1990	1995	2000	2005	2008	2009	2010	2011	2012	2013	2014	2015
1	2	3	4	5	6	7	8	9	10	11	12	13	14	15	16
16 to 19 years old, all education levels[1]	(†)	(†)	(†)	17.0 (1.83)	21.0 (2.06)	17.2 (1.89)	22.8 (1.39)	20.9 (1.36)	30.3 (1.58)	31.9 (1.59)	28.8 (1.62)	30.6 (1.57)	29.4 (1.57)	22.9 (1.83)	22.5 (1.35)
Less than high school completion	—	—	—	26.2 (3.54)	30.3 (3.67)	21.4 (3.23)	30.3 (2.34)	30.8 (2.40)	38.9 (3.05)	41.7 (3.14)	35.1 (3.42)	41.1 (3.01)	36.3 (2.70)	22.9 (3.38)	25.6 (2.67)
High school completion[2]	—	—	—	11.7 (2.05)	15.1 (2.59)	15.3 (2.54)	19.1 (2.02)	17.2 (1.62)	29.1 (1.80)	29.6 (2.08)	28.9 (2.18)	28.7 (2.00)	29.2 (2.12)	25.0 (2.32)	23.3 (1.90)
At least some college	—	—	—	‡ (†)	12.4! (5.19)	‡! (†)	15.8 (3.54)	11.3 (2.99)	18.1 (3.68)	18.1 (3.65)	16.2 (3.55)	19.6 (3.83)	16.2 (3.32)	15.1 (4.16)	13.2 (2.96)
20 to 24 years old, all education levels[1]	(†)	(†)	(†)	8.2 (0.63)	10.7 (0.72)	9.2 (0.70)	10.9 (0.48)	10.7 (0.43)	17.0 (0.62)	18.8 (0.66)	18.1 (0.60)	15.5 (0.55)	15.2 (0.62)	14.9 (0.70)	12.3 (0.53)
Less than high school completion	—	—	—	17.4 (2.15)	19.5 (2.37)	16.6 (2.18)	18.9 (1.24)	19.2 (1.66)	29.0 (1.69)	32.3 (1.80)	30.1 (1.95)	27.6 (2.12)	29.2 (2.27)	25.3 (2.75)	19.9 (1.99)
High school completion[2]	—	—	—	7.8 (0.88)	12.0 (1.18)	10.0 (1.12)	12.0 (0.73)	13.0 (0.70)	20.3 (1.05)	22.3 (0.95)	21.6 (1.02)	18.3 (0.96)	17.5 (0.91)	18.9 (1.18)	15.8 (0.92)
Some college, no bachelor's degree[3]	—	—	—	4.8 (1.09)	7.3 (1.13)	5.2 (1.02)	7.3 (0.76)	6.8 (0.67)	12.1 (0.94)	14.2 (1.07)	14.0 (0.98)	12.7 (0.89)	12.2 (1.02)	12.2 (1.16)	9.6 (0.89)
Bachelor's or higher degree	—	—	—	3.1! (1.12)	4.1! (1.26)	5.0 (1.43)	5.4 (0.91)	4.5 (0.78)	7.9 (1.02)	7.9 (1.15)	8.7 (1.05)	6.0 (0.95)	7.0 (1.09)	6.7 (1.09)	5.1 (0.72)
25 to 64 years old, all education levels	6.8 (0.21)	5.0 (0.17)	6.1 (0.18)	3.6 (0.14)	4.8 (0.15)	3.3 (0.13)	4.4 (0.09)	4.4 (0.09)	8.1 (0.12)	9.1 (0.13)	8.3 (0.13)	7.4 (0.11)	6.6 (0.12)	5.8 (0.14)	4.7 (0.10)
Less than high school completion	10.5 (0.49)	8.4 (0.48)	11.4 (0.61)	7.7 (0.55)	10.0 (0.66)	7.9 (0.63)	9.0 (0.36)	10.1 (0.44)	15.8 (0.54)	16.8 (0.54)	16.2 (0.55)	14.3 (0.49)	12.7 (0.46)	10.6 (0.63)	9.2 (0.44)
High school completion[2]	6.8 (0.34)	5.1 (0.27)	6.9 (0.31)	3.8 (0.23)	5.2 (0.28)	3.8 (0.25)	5.5 (0.17)	5.8 (0.18)	10.4 (0.21)	12.1 (0.26)	10.9 (0.27)	9.2 (0.25)	8.7 (0.27)	7.4 (0.29)	6.2 (0.21)
Some college, no bachelor's degree[3]	5.5 (0.50)	4.3 (0.38)	4.7 (0.37)	3.1 (0.29)	4.5 (0.29)	3.0 (0.24)	4.2 (0.17)	4.2 (0.17)	8.0 (0.22)	8.8 (0.23)	8.1 (0.20)	7.9 (0.24)	6.5 (0.21)	6.1 (0.27)	4.9 (0.16)
Bachelor's or higher degree	2.4 (0.30)	1.9 (0.23)	2.4 (0.24)	1.7 (0.19)	2.5 (0.21)	1.5 (0.16)	2.3 (0.13)	2.1 (0.11)	4.3 (0.15)	4.7 (0.15)	4.4 (0.15)	4.1 (0.14)	3.8 (0.13)	3.4 (0.16)	2.4 (0.11)
25 to 34 years old, all education levels	8.6 (0.41)	6.8 (0.32)	7.3 (0.33)	4.8 (0.27)	5.8 (0.30)	4.0 (0.27)	5.8 (0.18)	5.9 (0.21)	10.1 (0.27)	10.8 (0.28)	10.0 (0.28)	9.2 (0.26)	8.0 (0.23)	7.4 (0.30)	5.9 (0.20)
Less than high school completion	17.2 (1.36)	13.7 (1.24)	15.5 (1.38)	12.0 (1.21)	12.9 (1.32)	10.3 (1.33)	11.6 (0.69)	14.2 (0.93)	19.9 (1.05)	20.3 (1.02)	19.7 (1.09)	16.8 (1.09)	15.1 (0.97)	13.7 (1.24)	12.5 (1.01)
High school completion[2]	9.4 (0.67)	7.9 (0.55)	9.1 (0.57)	5.1 (0.44)	6.8 (0.56)	4.8 (0.54)	7.7 (0.41)	8.5 (0.49)	14.1 (0.57)	15.9 (0.62)	14.3 (0.55)	12.8 (0.57)	12.1 (0.57)	10.5 (0.68)	8.9 (0.50)
Some college, no bachelor's degree[3]	6.7 (0.85)	6.0 (0.64)	5.4 (0.60)	3.8 (0.51)	5.0 (0.52)	3.6 (0.49)	5.4 (0.36)	5.0 (0.33)	9.8 (0.46)	10.6 (0.44)	10.1 (0.46)	10.1 (0.51)	8.0 (0.42)	7.8 (0.52)	6.5 (0.39)
Bachelor's or higher degree	2.9 (0.50)	2.5 (0.39)	2.8 (0.41)	1.9 (0.34)	2.7 (0.40)	1.6 (0.31)	2.6 (0.26)	2.2 (0.21)	4.5 (0.29)	4.5 (0.28)	4.3 (0.31)	4.1 (0.28)	3.6 (0.25)	3.7 (0.30)	2.4 (0.20)
35 to 44 years old, all education levels	6.4 (0.41)	4.3 (0.31)	5.6 (0.33)	3.3 (0.24)	4.6 (0.27)	3.5 (0.23)	4.2 (0.14)	4.3 (0.17)	7.9 (0.18)	9.2 (0.24)	8.2 (0.23)	7.1 (0.22)	6.4 (0.19)	5.7 (0.24)	4.4 (0.17)
Less than high school completion	11.2 (1.02)	9.0 (1.00)	12.4 (1.29)	8.3 (1.17)	10.5 (1.28)	8.4 (1.14)	8.7 (0.63)	9.1 (0.79)	15.3 (0.87)	17.8 (1.07)	15.9 (1.04)	14.1 (0.88)	11.5 (0.80)	11.5 (1.08)	8.4 (0.74)
High school completion[2]	5.7 (0.60)	4.2 (0.48)	6.1 (0.55)	3.7 (0.41)	5.1 (0.48)	3.9 (0.43)	5.2 (0.31)	6.0 (0.35)	10.6 (0.44)	11.9 (0.51)	11.3 (0.44)	9.1 (0.44)	8.5 (0.50)	7.4 (0.48)	6.3 (0.41)
Some college, no bachelor's degree[3]	4.6 (0.95)	3.1 (0.64)	4.8 (0.39)	2.8 (0.47)	4.7 (0.49)	3.1 (0.41)	3.9 (0.25)	3.8 (0.27)	7.2 (0.36)	9.2 (0.42)	7.5 (0.39)	7.6 (0.40)	6.7 (0.40)	6.1 (0.49)	4.5 (0.31)
Bachelor's or higher degree	2.3 (0.59)	1.6 (0.41)	2.2 (0.39)	1.6 (0.31)	2.2 (0.34)	1.8 (0.31)	2.0 (0.19)	1.9 (0.17)	4.2 (0.26)	4.6 (0.26)	4.6 (0.29)	3.6 (0.23)	3.6 (0.23)	3.2 (0.30)	2.1 (0.20)
45 to 54 years old, all education levels	5.9 (0.39)	3.9 (0.32)	5.4 (0.39)	2.5 (0.26)	3.9 (0.29)	2.4 (0.22)	3.9 (0.16)	3.9 (0.16)	7.4 (0.21)	8.4 (0.22)	7.5 (0.20)	6.8 (0.18)	6.0 (0.18)	4.9 (0.24)	4.1 (0.15)
Less than high school completion	8.5 (0.81)	6.6 (0.78)	10.2 (1.16)	4.7 (0.89)	7.9 (1.24)	6.1 (1.16)	7.0 (0.66)	8.9 (0.74)	13.6 (0.95)	15.6 (0.98)	16.3 (0.92)	13.5 (0.92)	12.3 (0.94)	8.0 (0.95)	8.6 (0.80)
High school completion[2]	5.6 (0.60)	3.4 (0.48)	5.4 (0.60)	2.3 (0.39)	4.0 (0.53)	2.7 (0.42)	4.6 (0.33)	4.7 (0.34)	8.8 (0.42)	11.0 (0.43)	9.3 (0.42)	7.8 (0.36)	7.8 (0.40)	6.1 (0.50)	5.2 (0.34)
Some college, no bachelor's degree[3]	4.7 (1.00)	3.0 (0.78)	3.2 (0.79)	2.6 (0.62)	3.9 (0.56)	2.4 (0.40)	3.7 (0.40)	4.0 (0.32)	7.5 (0.39)	7.6 (0.40)	7.1 (0.35)	6.9 (0.36)	5.2 (0.35)	4.8 (0.44)	4.1 (0.18)
Bachelor's or higher degree	2.0! (0.61)	1.3! (0.44)	2.1 (0.54)	1.4 (0.38)	2.4 (0.41)	1.3 (0.28)	2.5 (0.26)	1.9 (0.18)	4.3 (0.29)	4.8 (0.30)	4.0 (0.27)	3.9 (0.27)	3.8 (0.26)	3.2 (0.29)	2.2 (0.18)
55 to 64 years old, all education levels	5.5 (0.46)	3.2 (0.35)	4.6 (0.44)	2.8 (0.36)	3.9 (0.42)	2.8 (0.35)	3.7 (0.20)	3.3 (0.18)	6.7 (0.25)	7.3 (0.25)	6.9 (0.25)	6.6 (0.23)	5.7 (0.23)	5.2 (0.28)	4.2 (0.20)
Less than high school completion	7.1 (0.79)	5.2 (0.77)	7.1 (1.01)	3.9 (0.90)	6.7 (1.35)	5.2 (1.28)	7.5 (0.90)	5.6 (0.77)	12.7 (1.25)	10.1 (0.99)	10.0 (1.02)	11.5 (1.05)	11.2 (1.19)	8.2 (1.21)	6.9 (0.84)
High school completion[2]	5.1 (0.76)	2.7 (0.51)	4.5 (0.69)	3.0 (0.59)	3.4 (0.65)	3.1 (0.62)	4.3 (0.39)	3.4 (0.35)	7.8 (0.50)	7.8 (0.56)	8.4 (0.58)	7.1 (0.50)	6.4 (0.47)	5.6 (0.53)	4.4 (0.38)
Some college, no bachelor's degree[3]	4.1! (1.26)	2.0! (0.77)	3.0! (1.00)	2.2! (0.82)	3.2 (0.80)	2.8 (0.70)	3.5 (0.39)	3.7 (0.37)	7.0 (0.50)	7.7 (0.52)	7.3 (0.45)	5.8 (0.40)	5.8 (0.54)	5.5 (0.54)	4.3 (0.40)
Bachelor's or higher degree	1.5! (0.75)	‡! (†)	2.2! (0.70)	1.8! (0.62)	3.3 (0.79)	1.4! (0.46)	2.3 (0.30)	2.4 (0.26)	4.3 (0.33)	5.0 (0.34)	4.9 (0.35)	4.8 (0.38)	4.2 (0.29)	4.0 (0.39)	3.3 (0.30)

—Not available.
†Not applicable.
!Interpret data with caution. The coefficient of variation (CV) for this estimate is between 30 and 50 percent.
‡Reporting standards not met. The coefficient of variation (CV) for this estimate is 50 percent or greater.
[1]Data for 16- to 19-year-olds and 20- to 24-year-olds exclude persons enrolled in school.
[2]Includes equivalency credentials, such as the GED credential.
[3]Includes persons with no college degree as well as those with an associate's degree.

NOTE: The unemployment rate is the percentage of persons in the civilian labor force who are not working and who made specific efforts to find employment sometime during the prior 4 weeks. The civilian labor force consists of all civilians who are employed or seeking employment.
SOURCE: U.S. Department of Commerce, Census Bureau, Current Population Survey (CPS), Annual Social and Economic Supplement, selected years, 1975 through 2015. (This table was prepared October 2015.)

Table 501.85. Unemployment rates of males 16 to 64 years old, by age group and highest level of educational attainment: Selected years, 1975 through 2015

[Standard errors appear in parentheses]

Age group and highest level of educational attainment	1975	1980	1985	1990	1995	2000	2005	2008	2009	2010	2011	2012	2013	2014	2015
1	2	3	4	5	6	7	8	9	10	11	12	13	14	15	16
16 to 19 years old, all education levels[1]	— (†)	— (†)	(†)	18.9 (2.58)	21.3 (2.71)	16.0 (2.36)	25.2 (1.83)	22.3 (1.79)	35.1 (2.08)	35.6 (2.07)	31.2 (2.10)	31.4 (2.05)	29.7 (2.00)	24.4 (2.40)	22.5 (1.79)
Less than high school completion	— (†)	— (†)	(†)	27.9 (4.45)	30.6 (4.60)	17.6 (3.69)	29.9 (2.88)	30.7 (2.87)	41.2 (3.89)	44.7 (4.07)	32.0 (4.05)	37.1 (3.82)	36.1 (3.57)	23.1 (4.25)	26.6 (3.61)
High school completion[2]	— (†)	— (†)	(†)	12.1 (2.96)	14.4 (3.38)	15.0 (3.30)	23.4 (2.77)	18.9 (2.43)	34.4 (2.46)	33.0 (2.59)	32.7 (2.96)	31.8 (2.68)	28.8 (2.70)	26.7! (3.29)	23.0 (2.47)
At least some college	— (†)	— (†)	(†)	(†)	‡ (†)	‡ (†)	12.7 (4.34)	9.1! (3.09)	22.4 (5.43)	19.0 (5.64)	21.4! (5.91)	20.2! (5.03)	17.5 (4.79)	17.7! (7.00)	11.5 (3.68)
20 to 24 years old, all education levels[1]	— (†)	— (†)	(†)	8.4 (0.86)	11.1 (0.97)	9.4 (0.94)	11.4 (0.61)	11.5 (0.58)	19.8 (0.85)	21.4 (0.88)	19.7 (0.81)	16.6 (0.83)	16.5 (0.80)	17.0 (0.92)	13.6 (0.75)
Less than high school completion	— (†)	— (†)	(†)	16.9 (2.53)	17.4 (2.68)	16.5 (2.61)	16.1 (1.37)	18.2 (1.89)	29.2 (2.06)	32.4 (2.20)	27.0 (2.23)	27.8 (2.48)	26.4 (2.72)	23.6 (3.04)	19.0 (2.52)
High school completion[2]	— (†)	— (†)	(†)	7.4 (1.15)	11.6 (1.48)	9.6 (1.45)	12.4 (0.97)	13.3 (0.85)	22.7 (1.31)	23.7 (1.25)	22.9 (1.31)	19.0 (1.28)	19.0 (1.24)	21.1 (1.60)	16.6 (1.16)
Some college, no bachelor's degree[3]	— (†)	— (†)	(†)	4.6! (1.54)	8.0 (1.65)	4.8 (1.36)	7.8 (1.04)	7.1 (0.97)	13.7 (1.39)	16.4 (1.58)	15.2 (1.46)	12.0 (1.23)	12.8 (1.36)	13.8 (1.56)	11.5 (1.46)
Bachelor's or higher degree	— (†)	— (†)	(†)	‡ (†)	5.6! (2.22)	5.5! (2.32)	6.8 (1.54)	4.7 (1.19)	10.1 (1.71)	9.8 (1.82)	10.8 (1.82)	6.6 (1.54)	8.5 (1.89)	7.3 (1.71)	5.1 (1.18)
25 to 64 years old, all education levels	6.5 (0.26)	4.9 (0.22)	6.1 (0.24)	3.6 (0.19)	5.1 (0.21)	3.3 (0.18)	4.7 (0.14)	4.9 (0.13)	9.5 (0.18)	10.5 (0.19)	9.2 (0.18)	8.0 (0.16)	6.9 (0.16)	5.9 (0.19)	5.0 (0.14)
Less than high school completion	10.3 (0.59)	8.2 (0.58)	11.2 (0.76)	7.3 (0.68)	10.9 (0.86)	7.1 (0.75)	7.9 (0.44)	10.9 (0.60)	16.5 (0.72)	17.8 (0.79)	16.7 (0.70)	13.6 (0.59)	11.9 (0.58)	9.4 (0.70)	8.4 (0.54)
High school completion[2]	6.6 (0.43)	5.3 (0.37)	7.2 (0.43)	3.8 (0.32)	5.7 (0.40)	3.9 (0.34)	6.0 (0.25)	6.3 (0.24)	12.4 (0.32)	13.8 (0.39)	12.2 (0.38)	10.1 (0.33)	9.2 (0.37)	7.8 (0.37)	6.7 (0.27)
Some college, no bachelor's degree[3]	5.0 (0.59)	4.4 (0.49)	4.5 (0.49)	3.0 (0.38)	4.4 (0.39)	3.1 (0.34)	4.3 (0.27)	4.2 (0.25)	9.3 (0.31)	10.2 (0.35)	8.7 (0.33)	8.2 (0.34)	6.5 (0.30)	5.9 (0.37)	4.9 (0.23)
Bachelor's or higher degree	2.1 (0.34)	1.7 (0.26)	2.4 (0.30)	1.8 (0.25)	2.6 (0.28)	1.6 (0.22)	2.5 (0.19)	2.0 (0.15)	4.7 (0.23)	5.1 (0.22)	4.6 (0.20)	4.3 (0.20)	3.7 (0.18)	3.4 (0.25)	2.8 (0.16)
25 to 34 years old, all education levels	8.3 (0.50)	6.8 (0.41)	7.3 (0.43)	4.5 (0.35)	5.9 (0.40)	4.2 (0.37)	6.0 (0.27)	6.5 (0.28)	11.9 (0.40)	12.6 (0.40)	11.3 (0.38)	10.0 (0.38)	8.4 (0.31)	7.5 (0.41)	6.2 (0.27)
Less than high school completion	17.3 (1.65)	13.4 (1.53)	13.9 (1.60)	10.3 (1.36)	12.5 (1.57)	8.8 (1.51)	9.7 (0.84)	14.8 (1.18)	19.2 (1.27)	20.7 (1.36)	19.2 (1.30)	14.3 (1.17)	13.2 (1.19)	10.8 (1.37)	10.2 (1.15)
High school completion[2]	9.0 (0.85)	8.2 (0.75)	9.5 (0.77)	4.6 (0.55)	6.6 (0.72)	4.9 (0.70)	7.8 (0.52)	8.5 (0.64)	16.1 (0.77)	17.8 (0.77)	15.2 (0.74)	13.5 (0.70)	11.8 (0.69)	10.1 (0.81)	9.1 (0.63)
Some college, no bachelor's degree[3]	6.6 (1.03)	6.0 (0.81)	4.9 (0.76)	3.6 (0.68)	4.6 (0.70)	3.8 (0.69)	5.6 (0.57)	5.0 (0.48)	11.3 (0.68)	11.8 (0.69)	11.2 (0.71)	11.1 (0.75)	8.5 (0.63)	7.8 (0.76)	6.1 (0.51)
Bachelor's or higher degree	2.6 (0.57)	2.4 (0.48)	2.8 (0.54)	1.9 (0.46)	2.8 (0.55)	1.8 (0.46)	2.7 (0.36)	2.1 (0.30)	5.1 (0.52)	4.8 (0.45)	4.5 (0.47)	4.2 (0.45)	3.9 (0.40)	3.8 (0.51)	2.8 (0.34)
35 to 44 years old, all education levels	6.0 (0.50)	4.1 (0.39)	5.7 (0.44)	3.2 (0.32)	4.9 (0.37)	3.4 (0.31)	4.4 (0.20)	4.7 (0.24)	9.2 (0.30)	10.1 (0.33)	8.9 (0.32)	7.6 (0.31)	6.3 (0.29)	5.7 (0.33)	4.6 (0.26)
Less than high school completion	10.8 (1.24)	8.4 (1.22)	12.3 (1.63)	7.9 (1.46)	11.8 (1.69)	6.3 (1.27)	7.8 (0.76)	9.9 (1.05)	16.5 (1.23)	18.4 (1.42)	15.8 (1.34)	13.5 (1.13)	10.3 (0.97)	9.8 (1.22)	7.5 (0.90)
High school completion[2]	5.8 (0.80)	4.2 (0.65)	6.5 (0.79)	3.4 (0.56)	5.6 (0.68)	4.2 (0.58)	5.7 (0.46)	6.4 (0.45)	12.2 (0.62)	12.9 (0.71)	12.4 (0.66)	9.7 (0.66)	8.8 (0.63)	8.2 (0.68)	6.3 (0.54)
Some college, no bachelor's degree[3]	3.3! (1.01)	2.9 (0.81)	5.3 (0.96)	2.8 (0.63)	4.8 (0.69)	2.9 (0.56)	4.1 (0.38)	4.1 (0.43)	8.3 (0.61)	9.9 (0.63)	7.4 (0.60)	7.4 (0.64)	6.1 (0.58)	5.5 (0.69)	4.9 (0.46)
Bachelor's or higher degree	1.9! (0.61)	1.3! (0.44)	2.2 (0.49)	1.7 (0.41)	2.0 (0.55)	1.7 (0.42)	2.1 (0.27)	1.7 (0.24)	4.6 (0.40)	4.6 (0.38)	4.7 (0.39)	4.1 (0.40)	3.1 (0.33)	2.6 (0.43)	2.2 (0.28)
45 to 54 years old, all education levels	5.5 (0.48)	3.7 (0.40)	5.4 (0.51)	2.7 (0.36)	4.6 (0.42)	2.5 (0.30)	4.1 (0.25)	4.3 (0.23)	8.6 (0.31)	9.9 (0.33)	8.2 (0.30)	7.0 (0.22)	6.5 (0.22)	4.9 (0.33)	4.5 (0.23)
Less than high school completion	8.3 (0.97)	6.1 (0.92)	10.9 (1.48)	4.7 (1.12)	9.4 (1.74)	6.9 (1.60)	6.3 (0.81)	9.7 (0.97)	14.1 (1.24)	16.8 (1.29)	16.6 (1.15)	13.7 (1.12)	12.3 (1.23)	8.7 (1.17)	8.8 (1.05)
High school completion[2]	4.9 (0.76)	3.3 (0.64)	5.5 (0.84)	2.8 (0.61)	5.5 (0.87)	2.4 (0.55)	5.1 (0.51)	5.4 (0.47)	10.7 (0.59)	12.6 (0.67)	10.3 (0.56)	8.7 (0.51)	8.9 (0.58)	6.2 (0.65)	5.7 (0.49)
Some college, no bachelor's degree[3]	4.4 (1.21)	3.5! (1.11)	2.6! (0.94)	2.5! (0.82)	4.0 (0.79)	2.6 (0.58)	3.8 (0.47)	3.9 (0.45)	8.6 (0.64)	9.5 (0.63)	8.1 (0.56)	6.3 (0.49)	5.0 (0.47)	4.3 (0.48)	4.1 (0.48)
Bachelor's or higher degree	1.8! (0.67)	1.1! (0.47)	2.0! (0.63)	1.4! (0.49)	2.7 (0.55)	1.3 (0.38)	2.7 (0.38)	1.9 (0.28)	5.3 (0.43)	5.3 (0.42)	3.9 (0.37)	3.8 (0.34)	3.7 (0.33)	3.1 (0.39)	2.4 (0.25)
55 to 64 years old, all education levels	5.5 (0.58)	3.6 (0.46)	4.7 (0.57)	3.3 (0.51)	4.3 (0.59)	3.2 (0.49)	3.9 (0.30)	3.4 (0.25)	7.6 (0.36)	8.6 (0.37)	7.9 (0.34)	7.1 (0.33)	6.1 (0.32)	5.6 (0.37)	4.6 (0.28)
Less than high school completion	6.9 (0.96)	5.9 (1.01)	7.4 (1.28)	4.6 (1.24)	7.7 (1.84)	5.5! (1.67)	6.7 (1.01)	5.7 (1.06)	14.8 (1.75)	11.6 (1.48)	13.4 (1.53)	12.1 (1.27)	11.7 (1.56)	7.2 (1.50)	6.9 (1.05)
High school completion[2]	5.5 (1.02)	2.8 (0.70)	4.6 (0.96)	3.7 (0.91)	3.6 (0.95)	3.5 (0.93)	5.2 (0.63)	4.0 (0.48)	9.4 (0.78)	11.1 (0.88)	10.2 (0.88)	7.7 (0.68)	6.7 (0.64)	6.5 (0.76)	5.1 (0.56)
Some college, no bachelor's degree[3]	3.1! (1.39)	2.5! (1.06)	3.6! (1.43)	‡ (†)	3.7! (1.16)	3.4! (1.06)	3.3 (0.52)	3.5 (0.51)	8.5 (0.80)	9.2 (0.77)	7.5 (0.65)	8.0 (0.70)	6.2 (0.62)	5.9 (0.80)	4.1 (0.48)
Bachelor's or higher degree	‡ (†)	(†)	2.2! (0.80)	2.1! (0.78)	3.6 (1.00)	1.7! (0.63)	2.6 (0.41)	2.4 (0.34)	3.9 (0.47)	5.8 (0.48)	5.3 (0.47)	5.2 (0.55)	4.4 (0.42)	4.3 (0.53)	3.9 (0.50)

—Not available.
†Not applicable.
!Interpret data with caution. The coefficient of variation (CV) for this estimate is between 30 and 50 percent.
‡Reporting standards not met. The coefficient of variation (CV) for this estimate is 50 percent or greater.
[1]Data for 16- to 19-year-olds and 20- to 24-year-olds exclude persons enrolled in school.
[2]Includes equivalency credentials, such as the GED credential.

[3]Includes persons with no college degree as well as those with an associate's degree.
NOTE: The unemployment rate is the percentage of persons in the civilian labor force who are not working and who made specific efforts to find employment sometime during the prior 4 weeks. The civilian labor force consists of all civilians who are employed or seeking employment.
SOURCE: U.S. Department of Commerce, Census Bureau, Current Population Survey (CPS), Annual Social and Economic Supplement, selected years, 1975 through 2015. (This table was prepared October 2015.)

Table 501.90. Unemployment rates of females 16 to 64 years old, by age group and highest level of educational attainment: Selected years, 1975 through 2015

[Standard errors appear in parentheses]

Age group and highest level of educational attainment	1975	1980	1985	1990	1995	2000	2005	2008	2009	2010	2011	2012	2013	2014	2015
	2	3	4	5	6	7	8	9	10	11	12	13	14	15	16
16 to 19 years old, all education levels[1]	— (†)	— (†)	(†)	14.7 (2.39)	20.6 (2.93)	18.9 (2.85)	19.7 (1.86)	18.8 (2.01)	23.8 (2.10)	26.9 (2.14)	25.5 (2.45)	29.6 (2.48)	28.9 (2.31)	20.9 (2.54)	22.4 (2.07)
Less than high school completion	—	—	(†)	23.4 (5.31)	29.7 (5.57)	27.9 (5.53)	31.0 (3.88)	30.9 (4.44)	34.9 (4.60)	36.4 (4.75)	40.4 (5.78)	46.2 (5.08)	36.5 (4.27)	22.5 (4.49)	24.4 (4.00)
High school completion[2]	—	—	(†)	11.3 (2.64)	16.0 (3.69)	15.7 (3.66)	14.2 (2.34)	15.0 (2.09)	22.2 (2.59)	24.9 (3.03)	23.8 (2.91)	24.5 (3.01)	29.6 (3.16)	22.9 (3.54)	23.7 (2.88)
At least some college	—	—	(†)	(‡)	(‡)	(‡)	18.3 (5.47)	14.2 ! (5.49)	14.0 (4.16)	17.3 (4.41)	11.8 ! (4.28)	18.7 ! (5.62)	15.2 (3.92)	12.9 ! (4.87)	14.8 (4.26)
20 to 24 years old, all education levels[1]	— (†)	— (†)	(†)	7.8 (0.86)	10.2 (1.00)	8.9 (0.96)	10.3 (0.73)	9.7 (0.63)	13.5 (0.78)	15.6 (0.86)	16.0 (0.75)	14.1 (0.78)	13.4 (0.85)	12.4 (0.89)	10.7 (0.69)
Less than high school completion	—	—	(†)	18.6 (3.70)	24.3 (4.34)	17.0 (3.60)	24.5 (2.79)	21.6 (3.02)	28.4 (2.94)	32.2 (3.38)	36.3 (3.46)	27.3 (3.57)	34.9 (3.85)	29.3 (5.22)	21.2 (3.60)
High school completion[2]	—	—	(†)	8.1 (1.26)	12.7 (1.78)	10.6 (1.63)	11.5 (1.14)	12.5 (1.17)	16.6 (1.37)	19.9 (1.46)	19.5 (1.43)	17.1 (1.31)	15.1 (1.44)	15.8 (1.72)	14.6 (1.38)
Some college, no bachelor's degree[3]	—	—	(†)	4.9 (1.43)	6.7 (1.43)	5.7 (1.42)	6.8 (1.01)	6.5 (0.94)	10.5 (1.18)	12.1 (1.33)	12.8 (1.27)	13.4 (1.28)	11.5 (1.36)	10.6 (1.41)	7.5 (0.97)
Bachelor's or higher degree	— (†)	— (†)	(†)	3.5 ! (1.47)	3.1 ! (1.35)	4.6 ! (1.70)	4.4 (1.05)	4.4 (1.01)	6.1 (1.13)	6.3 (1.29)	7.2 (1.27)	5.6 (1.14)	5.6 (1.01)	6.3 (1.38)	5.2 (1.01)
25 to 64 years old, all education levels	7.3 (0.33)	5.0 (0.25)	6.0 (0.26)	3.7 (0.20)	4.4 (0.21)	3.2 (0.18)	4.2 (0.12)	4.0 (0.12)	6.6 (0.12)	7.5 (0.15)	7.2 (0.17)	6.8 (0.15)	6.3 (0.15)	5.7 (0.19)	4.3 (0.13)
Less than high school completion	10.8 (0.79)	8.9 (0.76)	11.7 (0.96)	8.3 (0.88)	8.6 (0.95)	9.1 (1.00)	10.9 (0.65)	8.5 (0.62)	14.5 (0.72)	15.0 (0.71)	15.2 (0.74)	15.4 (0.83)	14.1 (0.84)	12.7 (0.98)	10.6 (0.68)
High school completion[2]	7.1 (0.49)	5.0 (0.37)	6.5 (0.41)	3.9 (0.32)	4.6 (0.36)	3.6 (0.33)	4.8 (0.23)	5.1 (0.27)	7.9 (0.26)	9.8 (0.30)	9.1 (0.36)	8.1 (0.31)	8.1 (0.35)	6.8 (0.42)	5.6 (0.31)
Some college, no bachelor's degree[3]	6.3 (0.84)	4.1 (0.54)	4.8 (0.53)	3.2 (0.40)	4.5 (0.38)	2.9 (0.31)	4.0 (0.22)	4.2 (0.21)	6.7 (0.27)	7.5 (0.27)	7.5 (0.27)	7.7 (0.30)	6.4 (0.26)	6.3 (0.36)	5.0 (0.23)
Bachelor's or higher degree	3.1 (0.57)	2.2 (0.39)	2.5 (0.36)	1.6 (0.27)	2.4 (0.30)	1.4 (0.22)	2.2 (0.17)	2.1 (0.15)	4.0 (0.19)	4.3 (0.19)	4.3 (0.21)	3.8 (0.19)	3.8 (0.19)	3.4 (0.22)	2.1 (0.13)
25 to 34 years old, all education levels	9.1 (0.65)	6.8 (0.47)	7.3 (0.47)	5.1 (0.39)	5.7 (0.42)	3.9 (0.37)	5.6 (0.27)	5.3 (0.29)	8.0 (0.28)	8.7 (0.33)	8.6 (0.33)	8.2 (0.32)	7.5 (0.32)	7.3 (0.36)	5.6 (0.29)
Less than high school completion	17.0 (2.18)	14.2 (1.93)	18.5 (2.37)	15.1 (2.17)	13.7 (2.20)	12.9 (2.33)	15.7 (1.36)	12.8 (1.53)	21.5 (1.79)	19.5 (1.52)	20.8 (1.84)	22.0 (1.99)	19.3 (1.65)	19.1 (2.42)	17.5 (1.85)
High school completion[2]	10.0 (1.01)	7.6 (0.76)	8.6 (0.78)	5.7 (0.65)	6.9 (0.81)	4.8 (0.78)	7.6 (0.62)	8.7 (0.67)	10.8 (0.67)	12.6 (0.86)	12.9 (0.78)	11.6 (0.82)	12.5 (0.88)	11.1 (1.04)	8.7 (0.74)
Some college, no bachelor's degree[3]	6.9 (1.38)	5.9 (0.94)	6.0 (0.88)	4.0 (0.72)	5.4 (0.73)	3.5 (0.63)	5.1 (0.46)	5.1 (0.45)	8.2 (0.56)	9.3 (0.57)	9.0 (0.61)	9.1 (0.59)	7.4 (0.57)	7.7 (0.68)	6.9 (0.58)
Bachelor's or higher degree	3.5 (0.88)	2.6 (0.60)	2.7 (0.57)	2.0 (0.47)	2.6 (0.53)	1.4 (0.39)	2.5 (0.31)	2.3 (0.29)	4.1 (0.37)	4.3 (0.35)	4.1 (0.35)	3.9 (0.38)	3.3 (0.33)	3.6 (0.38)	1.9 (0.26)
35 to 44 years old, all education levels	7.1 (0.66)	4.7 (0.47)	5.4 (0.46)	3.5 (0.34)	4.3 (0.36)	3.7 (0.33)	3.9 (0.20)	3.8 (0.22)	6.4 (0.25)	8.2 (0.29)	7.4 (0.30)	6.5 (0.29)	6.6 (0.27)	5.6 (0.34)	4.1 (0.20)
Less than high school completion	11.9 (1.65)	10.0 (1.56)	12.7 (1.95)	8.9 (1.79)	8.4 (1.75)	11.3 (1.94)	10.1 (1.22)	7.7 (1.03)	13.0 (1.33)	16.7 (1.32)	16.1 (1.51)	15.2 (1.29)	13.6 (1.57)	14.9 (1.99)	10.2 (1.26)
High school completion[2]	5.7 (0.85)	4.1 (0.65)	5.7 (0.72)	4.0 (0.57)	4.5 (0.63)	3.6 (0.58)	4.5 (0.40)	5.3 (0.50)	8.4 (0.63)	10.5 (0.67)	9.6 (0.66)	8.3 (0.71)	8.1 (0.70)	6.2 (0.68)	6.3 (0.61)
Some college, no bachelor's degree[3]	6.8 (1.76)	3.3 (0.97)	4.3 (0.91)	2.8 (0.64)	4.7 (0.66)	3.3 (0.57)	3.7 (0.36)	3.6 (0.35)	6.2 (0.46)	8.5 (0.51)	7.6 (0.56)	7.4 (0.54)	7.3 (0.53)	6.7 (0.70)	4.2 (0.39)
Bachelor's or higher degree	3.5 ! (1.29)	2.3 ! (0.76)	2.2 (0.61)	1.4 ! (0.42)	2.4 (0.52)	1.8 (0.44)	1.9 (0.26)	2.1 (0.24)	3.7 (0.37)	4.5 (0.35)	4.5 (0.41)	3.1 (0.31)	4.0 (0.35)	3.0 (0.40)	2.1 (0.25)
45 to 54 years old, all education levels	6.5 (0.62)	4.1 (0.49)	5.3 (0.56)	2.3 (0.35)	3.1 (0.36)	2.4 (0.30)	3.6 (0.20)	3.5 (0.20)	6.1 (0.23)	6.8 (0.27)	6.7 (0.28)	6.5 (0.28)	5.6 (0.25)	4.9 (0.32)	3.7 (0.19)
Less than high school completion	9.0 (1.33)	7.6 (1.32)	9.2 (1.71)	4.7 (1.33)	5.8 (1.55)	5.1 ! (1.52)	8.2 (1.08)	7.3 (1.08)	12.7 (1.38)	13.6 (1.41)	15.8 (1.50)	13.1 (1.49)	12.1 (1.43)	6.7 (1.32)	8.3 (1.09)
High school completion[2]	6.3 (0.88)	3.6 (0.66)	5.4 (0.80)	1.8 (0.46)	2.7 (0.57)	3.0 (0.59)	4.0 (0.39)	3.7 (0.41)	6.6 (0.50)	9.0 (0.56)	8.0 (0.62)	6.7 (0.48)	6.4 (0.45)	6.1 (0.69)	4.4 (0.51)
Some college, no bachelor's degree[3]	5.3 ! (1.61)	2.3 ! (0.99)	4.0 ! (1.23)	2.7 ! (0.89)	3.7 (0.73)	2.2 (0.52)	3.6 (0.41)	4.2 (0.40)	6.5 (0.47)	5.9 (0.43)	6.2 (0.43)	5.4 (0.57)	5.4 (0.44)	5.3 (0.64)	4.1 (0.39)
Bachelor's or higher degree	2.6 ! (1.18)	1.9 ! (0.90)	2.4 ! (0.92)	1.3 ! (0.56)	2.1 (0.57)	1.3 ! (0.39)	2.2 (0.24)	1.9 (0.24)	3.8 (0.34)	4.3 (0.36)	4.1 (0.38)	3.9 (0.38)	3.9 (0.38)	3.3 (0.40)	2.0 (0.25)
55 to 64 years old, all education levels	5.4 (0.71)	2.5 (0.47)	4.5 (0.63)	2.2 (0.47)	3.3 (0.55)	2.4 (0.45)	3.4 (0.29)	3.2 (0.24)	5.6 (0.33)	6.0 (0.32)	5.9 (0.34)	6.0 (0.31)	5.4 (0.33)	4.7 (0.38)	3.7 (0.26)
Less than high school completion	7.3 (1.28)	3.7 (1.06)	6.7 (1.49)	2.9 ! (1.17)	5.3 ! (1.78)	4.8 ! (1.84)	8.6 (1.51)	5.6 (1.10)	9.7 (1.45)	8.0 (1.36)	4.8 (1.05)	10.8 (1.78)	10.5 (1.69)	9.8 (2.00)	7.0 (1.51)
High school completion[2]	4.6 (1.05)	2.6 (0.69)	4.5 (0.93)	2.2 ! (0.68)	3.2 (0.84)	2.8 (0.77)	3.3 (0.46)	2.9 (0.45)	6.3 (0.64)	7.5 (0.68)	6.7 (0.65)	6.5 (0.69)	6.0 (0.64)	4.6 (0.65)	3.5 (0.54)
Some college, no bachelor's degree[3]	5.6 ! (2.23)	(†)	(†)	2.4 ! (1.15)	2.8 ! (1.00)	2.2 ! (0.84)	3.7 (0.54)	3.9 (0.51)	5.5 (0.63)	6.3 (0.65)	7.1 (0.66)	6.3 (0.58)	5.5 (0.50)	5.1 (0.68)	4.5 (0.55)
Bachelor's or higher degree	(†)	(†)	(†)	(‡)	2.6 ! (1.16)	(‡)	1.9 (0.39)	2.3 (0.36)	4.3 (0.50)	4.1 (0.49)	4.4 (0.52)	4.4 (0.51)	4.0 (0.44)	3.6 (0.58)	2.7 (0.36)

—Not available.
†Not applicable.
!Interpret data with caution. The coefficient of variation (CV) for this estimate is between 30 and 50 percent.
‡Reporting standards not met. The coefficient of variation (CV) for this estimate is 50 percent or greater.
[1]Data for 16- to 19-year-olds and 20- to 24-year-olds exclude persons enrolled in school.
[2]Includes equivalency credentials, such as the GED credential.

[3]Includes persons with no college degree as well as those with an associate's degree.
NOTE: The unemployment rate is the percentage of persons in the civilian labor force who are not working and who made specific efforts to find employment sometime during the prior 4 weeks. The civilian labor force consists of all civilians who are employed or seeking employment.
SOURCE: U.S. Department of Commerce, Census Bureau, Current Population Survey (CPS), Annual Social and Economic Supplement, selected years, 1975 through 2015. (This table was prepared October 2015.)

Table 502.10. Occupation of employed persons 25 years old and over, by highest level of educational attainment and sex: 2014 and 2015

[Standard errors appear in parentheses]

Sex and occupation	Total employed (in thousands)	Total	Less than high school completion	High school completion (includes equivalency)	Some college, no degree	Associate's degree	Bachelor's degree	Master's or higher degree
1	2	3	4	5	6	7	8	9
2014								
All persons	127,863 (227.9)	100.0	7.7 (0.09)	26.5 (0.14)	16.5 (0.12)	11.1 (0.10)	24.1 (0.14)	14.1 (0.11)
Management, professional, and related	52,674 (224.1)	100.0	1.2 (0.05)	10.5 (0.15)	11.1 (0.16)	10.4 (0.15)	36.9 (0.24)	29.9 (0.23)
Management, business, and financial operations	22,144 (161.3)	100.0	2.0 (0.11)	15.6 (0.28)	14.2 (0.27)	8.9 (0.22)	39.0 (0.38)	20.3 (0.31)
Professional and related	30,531 (184.4)	100.0	0.6 (0.05)	6.8 (0.17)	8.8 (0.19)	11.5 (0.21)	35.4 (0.32)	36.9 (0.32)
Education, training, and library	7,972 (100.9)	100.0	0.5 (0.09)	6.0 (0.31)	6.4 (0.32)	5.6 (0.30)	34.7 (0.62)	46.9 (0.65)
Preschool and kindergarten teachers	591 (28.1)	100.0	‡ (†)	12.7 (1.58)	13.2 (1.61)	14.4 (1.67)	40.3 (2.33)	18.8 (1.86)
Elementary and middle school teachers	2,955 (62.3)	100.0	0.2 ! (0.10)	2.1 (0.30)	2.6 (0.34)	2.5 (0.33)	42.8 (1.05)	49.7 (1.06)
Secondary school teachers	1,044 (37.2)	100.0	‡ (†)	1.1 ! (0.37)	1.5 (0.44)	1.1 ! (0.38)	41.3 (1.76)	54.7 (1.78)
Special education teachers	320 (20.7)	100.0	‡ (†)	3.4 ! (1.18)	2.5 ! (1.01)	5.3 (1.45)	34.4 (3.07)	54.7 (3.22)
Postsecondary teachers	1,170 (39.4)	100.0	‡ (†)	0.9 ! (0.33)	2.0 (0.47)	3.2 (0.60)	13.4 (1.15)	80.3 (1.35)
Other education, training, and library workers	1,892 (50.0)	100.0	1.2 (0.29)	16.2 (0.98)	16.3 (0.98)	11.4 (0.85)	30.0 (1.22)	24.9 (1.15)
Service occupations	20,013 (154.4)	100.0	15.9 (0.30)	36.7 (0.39)	20.2 (0.33)	11.8 (0.26)	12.7 (0.27)	2.7 (0.13)
Sales and office occupations	27,778 (177.5)	100.0	4.1 (0.14)	31.3 (0.32)	23.2 (0.29)	12.4 (0.23)	24.0 (0.30)	5.0 (0.15)
Natural resources, construction, and maintenance	12,097 (122.9)	100.0	20.1 (0.42)	42.3 (0.52)	17.2 (0.40)	12.2 (0.34)	7.0 (0.27)	1.2 (0.12)
Production, transportation, and material moving	15,301 (136.9)	100.0	16.3 (0.35)	46.7 (0.47)	18.0 (0.36)	9.0 (0.27)	8.5 (0.26)	1.5 (0.12)
Males	68,284 (152.2)	100.0	9.4 (0.13)	28.4 (0.20)	16.3 (0.16)	9.6 (0.13)	23.0 (0.18)	13.3 (0.15)
Management, professional, and related	25,606 (154.8)	100.0	1.5 (0.09)	11.2 (0.22)	11.4 (0.23)	8.1 (0.19)	37.1 (0.34)	30.7 (0.33)
Management, business, and financial operations	12,569 (118.6)	100.0	2.4 (0.16)	16.5 (0.38)	14.0 (0.35)	7.9 (0.27)	38.3 (0.49)	20.9 (0.41)
Professional and related	13,037 (120.4)	100.0	0.7 (0.08)	6.0 (0.24)	8.9 (0.28)	8.3 (0.27)	36.0 (0.48)	40.1 (0.49)
Education, training, and library	2,052 (51.0)	100.0	0.3 ! (0.15)	3.0 (0.43)	4.7 (0.53)	2.9 (0.42)	32.9 (1.18)	56.2 (1.25)
Service occupations	8,642 (100.7)	100.0	16.2 (0.45)	34.8 (0.58)	20.4 (0.49)	10.4 (0.37)	15.2 (0.44)	3.0 (0.21)
Sales and office occupations	10,535 (109.9)	100.0	4.5 (0.23)	28.1 (0.50)	21.7 (0.46)	10.0 (0.33)	29.3 (0.50)	6.4 (0.27)
Natural resources, construction, and maintenance	11,562 (114.4)	100.0	19.9 (0.42)	42.7 (0.52)	17.2 (0.40)	12.3 (0.35)	6.8 (0.27)	1.1 (0.11)
Production, transportation, and material moving	11,939 (116.0)	100.0	15.3 (0.38)	47.3 (0.52)	18.4 (0.40)	9.1 (0.30)	8.5 (0.29)	1.5 (0.12)
Females	59,579 (158.8)	100.0	5.8 (0.11)	24.3 (0.19)	16.8 (0.17)	12.8 (0.15)	25.3 (0.20)	15.1 (0.16)
Management, professional, and related	27,069 (152.0)	100.0	0.8 (0.06)	10.0 (0.20)	10.8 (0.21)	12.6 (0.22)	36.7 (0.32)	29.1 (0.30)
Management, business, and financial operations	9,575 (101.9)	100.0	1.5 (0.14)	14.5 (0.40)	14.5 (0.40)	10.1 (0.34)	39.9 (0.55)	19.4 (0.45)
Professional and related	17,494 (131.0)	100.0	0.5 (0.06)	7.4 (0.22)	8.8 (0.24)	13.9 (0.29)	34.9 (0.40)	34.4 (0.40)
Education, training, and library	5,919 (81.9)	100.0	0.5 (0.10)	7.0 (0.37)	7.0 (0.37)	6.5 (0.35)	35.3 (0.68)	43.6 (0.71)
Service occupations	11,371 (109.9)	100.0	15.6 (0.37)	38.2 (0.50)	20.0 (0.41)	13.0 (0.35)	10.8 (0.32)	2.5 (0.16)
Sales and office occupations	17,243 (130.2)	100.0	3.8 (0.16)	33.3 (0.40)	24.1 (0.36)	13.9 (0.29)	20.7 (0.34)	4.2 (0.17)
Natural resources, construction, and maintenance	534 (25.4)	100.0	24.5 (2.05)	33.5 (2.25)	16.5 (1.77)	9.9 (1.42)	12.4 (1.57)	3.4 (0.86)
Production, transportation, and material moving	3,362 (62.7)	100.0	19.7 (0.75)	44.8 (0.94)	16.5 (0.70)	8.5 (0.53)	8.7 (0.53)	1.8 (0.25)
2015								
All persons	130,077 (225.3)	100.0	7.8 (0.09)	25.7 (0.14)	16.6 (0.12)	10.9 (0.10)	24.4 (0.14)	14.6 (0.11)
Management, professional, and related	54,504 (226.3)	100.0	1.3 (0.06)	10.2 (0.15)	11.1 (0.16)	10.2 (0.15)	37.0 (0.24)	30.3 (0.23)
Management, business, and financial operations	23,093 (164.3)	100.0	2.2 (0.11)	15.1 (0.27)	14.3 (0.27)	8.8 (0.22)	39.1 (0.37)	20.5 (0.31)
Professional and related	31,410 (186.5)	100.0	0.6 (0.05)	6.6 (0.16)	8.8 (0.18)	11.1 (0.21)	35.5 (0.31)	37.4 (0.32)
Education, training, and library	8,124 (101.9)	100.0	0.5 (0.09)	6.1 (0.31)	6.5 (0.32)	4.9 (0.28)	34.8 (0.61)	47.2 (0.64)
Preschool and kindergarten teachers	605 (28.4)	100.0	1.0 ! (0.47)	12.9 (1.57)	13.1 (1.58)	13.4 (1.60)	38.2 (2.28)	21.5 (1.93)
Elementary and middle school teachers	2,994 (62.7)	100.0	0.3 ! (0.11)	1.9 (0.29)	2.2 (0.31)	2.1 (0.31)	43.7 (1.05)	49.9 (1.06)
Secondary school teachers	1,079 (37.9)	100.0	‡ (†)	0.9 ! (0.34)	2.2 (0.52)	1.2 ! (0.38)	37.5 (1.70)	57.9 (1.74)
Special education teachers	321 (20.7)	100.0	‡ (†)	4.0 ! (1.27)	3.4 ! (1.17)	3.4 ! (1.17)	34.9 (3.08)	53.9 (3.22)
Postsecondary teachers	1,233 (40.5)	100.0	‡ (†)	0.9 ! (0.31)	1.7 (0.43)	2.6 (0.52)	15.4 (1.19)	79.2 (1.34)
Other education, training, and library workers	1,892 (50.0)	100.0	1.3 (0.30)	17.1 (1.00)	17.1 (1.00)	10.6 (0.82)	30.9 (1.23)	22.9 (1.12)
Service occupations	20,042 (154.5)	100.0	16.2 (0.30)	36.2 (0.39)	19.9 (0.33)	12.0 (0.27)	12.8 (0.27)	2.9 (0.14)
Sales and office occupations	27,800 (177.6)	100.0	4.0 (0.14)	30.3 (0.32)	23.6 (0.29)	12.5 (0.23)	24.3 (0.30)	5.3 (0.16)
Natural resources, construction, and maintenance	12,271 (123.7)	100.0	20.5 (0.42)	41.2 (0.51)	17.1 (0.39)	11.9 (0.34)	7.7 (0.28)	1.5 (0.13)
Production, transportation, and material moving	15,461 (137.6)	100.0	16.4 (0.34)	45.9 (0.46)	18.6 (0.36)	8.7 (0.26)	8.6 (0.26)	1.8 (0.13)
Males	69,604 (149.4)	100.0	9.4 (0.13)	27.7 (0.19)	16.2 (0.16)	9.6 (0.13)	23.5 (0.18)	13.6 (0.15)
Management, professional, and related	26,577 (156.6)	100.0	1.6 (0.09)	10.8 (0.22)	11.4 (0.22)	8.1 (0.19)	37.6 (0.34)	30.4 (0.32)
Management, business, and financial operations	13,085 (120.6)	100.0	2.7 (0.16)	16.0 (0.36)	14.0 (0.34)	8.0 (0.27)	39.0 (0.49)	20.3 (0.40)
Professional and related	13,492 (122.1)	100.0	0.6 (0.07)	5.8 (0.23)	8.9 (0.28)	8.1 (0.27)	36.3 (0.47)	40.3 (0.48)
Education, training, and library	2,141 (52.0)	100.0	‡ (†)	3.2 (0.43)	4.8 (0.52)	2.8 (0.41)	32.6 (1.15)	56.4 (1.22)
Service occupations	8,623 (100.6)	100.0	16.7 (0.46)	34.6 (0.58)	19.5 (0.49)	10.9 (0.38)	15.2 (0.44)	3.1 (0.21)
Sales and office occupations	10,612 (110.3)	100.0	4.2 (0.22)	27.6 (0.49)	21.7 (0.45)	10.5 (0.34)	29.4 (0.50)	6.6 (0.27)
Natural resources, construction, and maintenance	11,717 (115.1)	100.0	20.3 (0.42)	41.7 (0.52)	17.1 (0.40)	11.9 (0.34)	7.5 (0.28)	1.5 (0.13)
Production, transportation, and material moving	12,074 (116.6)	100.0	15.5 (0.37)	46.6 (0.52)	18.9 (0.41)	8.8 (0.29)	8.4 (0.29)	1.9 (0.14)
Females	60,474 (157.7)	100.0	5.8 (0.10)	23.3 (0.19)	17.0 (0.17)	12.5 (0.15)	25.5 (0.20)	15.8 (0.16)
Management, professional, and related	27,926 (153.4)	100.0	0.9 (0.06)	9.6 (0.19)	10.9 (0.20)	12.1 (0.22)	36.4 (0.32)	30.1 (0.30)
Management, business, and financial operations	10,008 (103.9)	100.0	1.5 (0.14)	13.9 (0.38)	14.8 (0.39)	9.9 (0.33)	39.1 (0.54)	20.8 (0.45)
Professional and related	17,918 (132.2)	100.0	0.6 (0.06)	7.2 (0.21)	8.7 (0.23)	13.4 (0.28)	34.8 (0.39)	35.3 (0.39)
Education, training, and library	5,983 (82.3)	100.0	0.7 (0.11)	7.1 (0.36)	7.1 (0.37)	5.7 (0.33)	35.6 (0.68)	43.9 (0.71)
Service occupations	11,419 (110.1)	100.0	15.8 (0.38)	37.4 (0.50)	20.3 (0.41)	12.9 (0.34)	11.0 (0.32)	2.7 (0.17)
Sales and office occupations	17,188 (130.1)	100.0	3.9 (0.16)	32.0 (0.39)	24.7 (0.36)	13.7 (0.29)	21.2 (0.34)	4.5 (0.17)
Natural resources, construction, and maintenance	554 (25.8)	100.0	24.9 (2.02)	31.0 (2.16)	15.9 (1.71)	11.2 (1.47)	14.1 (1.63)	2.5 (0.73)
Production, transportation, and material moving	3,387 (62.9)	100.0	19.5 (0.75)	43.6 (0.94)	17.5 (0.72)	8.3 (0.52)	9.4 (0.55)	1.7 (0.25)

†Not applicable.
!Interpret data with caution. The coefficient of variation (CV) for this estimate is between 30 and 50 percent.
‡Reporting standards not met. Either there are too few cases for a reliable estimate or the coefficient of variation (CV) is 50 percent or greater.

NOTE: Detail may not sum to totals because of rounding.
SOURCE: U.S. Department of Labor, Bureau of Labor Statistics, Office of Employment and Unemployment Statistics, unpublished 2014 and 2015 annual average data from the Current Population Survey (CPS). (This table was prepared May 2016.)

Table 502.20. Median annual earnings, number, and percentage of full-time year-round workers 25 years old and over, by highest level of educational attainment and sex: 1990 through 2014

[Standard errors appear in parentheses]

		Elementary/secondary			College							
							Bachelor's or higher degree[4]				
Sex and year	Total	Less than 9th grade	Some high school, no completion[1]	High school completion (includes equivalency)[2]	Some college, no degree[3]	Associate's degree	Total	Bachelor's degree[5]	Master's degree	Professional degree[4]	Doctor's degree
1	2	3	4	5	6	7	8	9	10	11	12
					Current dollars						
Males											
1990	$30,730 (—)	$17,390 (—)	$20,900 (—)	$26,650 (—)	$31,730 (—)	$33,820[6] (†)	$42,670 (—)	$39,240 (—)	$49,730[6] (†)	$74,000[6] (†)	$57,190[6] (†)
1991	31,610 (—)	17,390 (—)	21,400 (—)	26,780 (—)	31,660 (—)	33,430 (—)	45,140 (—)	40,910 (—)	49,970 (—)	76,220 (—)	57,420 (—)
1992	32,060 (120)	17,290 (—)	21,270 (—)	27,280 (175)	32,100 (—)	33,690 (—)	45,800 (—)	41,360 (304)	51,870 (—)	76,550 (—)	63,150 (—)
1993	32,360 (124)	16,860 (—)	21,750 (204)	27,370 (204)	32,080 (—)	33,690 (—)	47,740 (—)	42,760 (536)	51,870 (—)	80,550 (—)	80,150 (—)
1994	33,440 (246)	17,530 (453)	22,050 (319)	28,040 (322)	32,280 (300)	35,790 (430)	49,230 (707)	43,660 (633)	53,500 (854)	75,010 (3,040)	61,920 (1,619)
1995	34,550 (275)	18,350 (545)	22,190 (342)	29,510 (358)	33,880 (517)	35,200 (535)	50,480 (312)	45,270 (510)	55,220 (973)	79,670 (2,582)	65,340 (2,188)
1996	35,620 (150)	17,960 (594)	22,720 (414)	30,710 (184)	34,850 (456)	37,130 (435)	51,440 (303)	45,850 (458)	60,510 (945)	85,960 (3,317)	71,230 (3,362)
1997	36,680 (149)	19,290 (629)	24,730 (466)	31,220 (171)	35,550 (293)	38,020 (774)	53,450 (755)	48,620 (851)	61,690 (771)	85,010 (4,253)	76,230 (3,611)
1998	37,910 (291)	19,380 (600)	23,960 (547)	31,480 (169)	36,930 (291)	40,270 (539)	56,520 (421)	51,410 (349)	62,240 (847)	94,740 (12,105)	75,080 (2,507)
1999	40,330 (144)	20,430 (444)	25,040 (535)	33,180 (388)	39,220 (581)	41,640 (459)	60,200 (439)	52,990 (722)	66,240 (690)	100,000 ! (37,836)	81,690 (3,953)
2000	41,060 (156)	20,790 (376)	25,100 (436)	34,300 (457)	40,340 (312)	41,950 (460)	61,870 (303)	56,330 (573)	68,320 (1,506)	99,410 (20,832)	80,250 (2,446)
2001	41,620 (104)	21,360 (235)	26,210 (251)	34,720 (299)	41,050 (214)	42,780 (561)	62,220 (279)	55,930 (335)	70,900 (687)	100,000 (—)	86,970 (3,013)
2002	41,150 (100)	20,920 (213)	25,900 (207)	33,210 (311)	40,850 (195)	42,860 (673)	61,700 (201)	56,080 (385)	67,280 (1,294)	100,000 (—)	83,310 (2,076)
2003	41,940 (90)	21,220 (227)	26,470 (280)	33,410 (168)	41,350 (182)	42,870 (719)	62,080 (187)	56,500 (365)	70,640 (562)	100,000 (—)	87,130 (2,528)
2004	42,090 (89)	21,660 (191)	26,280 (234)	35,730 (148)	41,900 (175)	44,400 (931)	62,800 (798)	57,220 (393)	71,530 (490)	100,000 (—)	82,400 (2,423)
2005	43,320 (367)	22,330 (220)	27,190 (237)	36,300 (141)	42,420 (323)	47,180 (367)	66,170 (356)	60,020 (653)	75,030 (1,229)	100,000 (—)	85,860 (3,061)
2006	45,780 (134)	22,710 (398)	27,650 (573)	37,030 (164)	43,830 (812)	47,070 (390)	66,930 (346)	60,910 (235)	75,430 (859)	100,000 (—)	100,000 (1,894)
2007	47,000 (130)	23,380 (544)	29,320 (590)	37,860 (406)	44,900 (585)	49,040 (801)	70,400 (241)	62,090 (236)	76,280 (416)	100,000 (—)	92,090 (—)
2008	49,000 (339)	24,260 (631)	29,680 (458)	39,010 (399)	45,820 (276)	50,150 (344)	72,220 (236)	65,800 (388)	80,960 (468)	100,000 (—)	100,000 (519)
2009	49,990 (201)	23,950 (394)	28,020 (542)	39,480 (379)	47,100 (347)	50,300 (238)	71,470 (239)	62,440 (707)	79,340 (1,568)	123,240 (2,539)	100,740 (—)
2010	50,360 (93)	24,450 (597)	29,440 (684)	40,060 (237)	46,430 (348)	50,280 (245)	71,780 (267)	63,740 (1,115)	80,960 (453)	115,300 (4,891)	101,220 (653)
2011	50,660 (25)	25,220 (23)	30,420 (300)	40,450 (87)	47,070 (78)	50,930 (212)	73,850 (490)	66,200 (25)	83,030 (755)	119,470 (1,917)	106,770 (192)
2012	50,950 (144)	25,160 (440)	30,530 (430)	40,350 (194)	47,190 (407)	50,960 (329)	75,320 (565)	66,150 (570)	85,120 (1,412)	116,350 (5,632)	106,470 (4,656)
2013	51,120 (149)	26,160 (531)	30,570 (551)	40,290 (227)	47,650 (739)	51,000 (493)	76,110 (485)	67,240 (992)	86,310 (1,429)	126,730 (8,647)	105,280 (4,631)
2014	51,400 (133)	26,580 (382)	30,840 (382)	40,930 (197)	46,900 (429)	51,110 (345)	75,910 (391)	68,160 (1,282)	84,760 (1,988)	121,750 (5,986)	100,710 (852)
Females											
1990	21,370 (—)	12,250 (—)	14,430 (—)	18,320 (—)	22,230 (—)	25,000[6] (†)	30,380 (—)	28,020 (—)	34,950[6] (†)	46,740[6] (†)	43,300[6] (†)
1991	22,040 (159)	12,070 (—)	14,460 (—)	18,840 (—)	22,140 (—)	25,620 (—)	31,310 (—)	29,080 (294)	36,040 (—)	46,260 (—)	45,790 (—)
1992	23,140 (166)	12,960 (—)	14,560 (—)	19,430 (176)	23,060 (—)	25,880 (—)	32,300 (—)	30,330 (310)	38,610 (—)	50,210 (—)	47,250 (—)
1993	23,630 (165)	12,420 (—)	15,390 (173)	19,960 (173)	23,160 (—)	25,940 (—)	34,310 (—)	31,200 (314)	39,460 (606)	50,620 (—)	51,120 (—)
1994	24,400 (165)	12,430 (427)	15,130 (328)	20,370 (158)	23,510 (327)	25,940 (295)	35,380 (290)	31,740 (314)	39,460 (606)	50,620 (2,154)	51,120 (2,888)
1995	24,880 (160)	13,580 (490)	15,830 (293)	20,460 (162)	24,000 (274)	27,310 (428)	35,260 (313)	32,050 (273)	40,260 (556)	50,000 (2,532)	48,140 (2,373)
1996	25,810 (131)	14,410 (559)	16,950 (333)	21,180 (143)	25,180 (267)	28,080 (526)	36,460 (296)	33,530 (437)	41,900 (564)	57,620 (3,635)	56,270 (3,300)
1997	26,970 (134)	14,160 (492)	16,700 (335)	22,070 (148)	26,340 (291)	28,810 (660)	38,040 (481)	35,380 (295)	44,950 (837)	61,050 (4,737)	53,040 (3,626)
1998	27,960 (199)	14,470 (429)	16,480 (322)	22,780 (254)	27,420 (271)	29,920 (513)	39,790 (408)	36,560 (305)	45,280 (760)	57,570 (1,705)	57,800 (1,881)
1999	28,840 (216)	15,100 (492)	17,020 (298)	23,060 (279)	27,760 (369)	30,920 (318)	41,750 (275)	37,990 (614)	48,100 (862)	59,900 (4,479)	60,080 (3,130)
2000	30,330 (138)	15,800 (327)	17,920 (434)	24,970 (236)	28,700 (364)	31,070 (307)	42,710 (439)	40,420 (284)	50,140 (735)	58,960 (3,552)	57,080 (2,999)
2001	31,360 (91)	16,690 (255)	19,160 (359)	25,300 (132)	30,420 (186)	32,150 (211)	44,780 (367)	40,990 (231)	50,670 (328)	61,750 (3,976)	62,120 (2,228)
2002	31,010 (83)	16,910 (297)	19,310 (360)	25,180 (121)	29,400 (299)	31,630 (241)	43,250 (568)	40,850 (173)	48,890 (595)	65,020 (2,421)	65,720 (2,268)
2003	31,570 (85)	16,910 (256)	18,940 (327)	26,070 (118)	30,140 (176)	32,250 (241)	45,120 (291)	41,330 (204)	50,160 (454)	66,490 (3,469)	67,210 (2,462)
2004	31,990 (80)	17,020 (241)	19,160 (298)	26,030 (116)	30,820 (135)	33,480 (489)	45,910 (229)	41,680 (172)	51,320 (263)	75,040 (2,436)	68,880 (2,450)
2005	33,080 (242)	16,140 (250)	20,130 (274)	26,290 (134)	31,400 (165)	33,940 (497)	46,950 (232)	42,170 (179)	51,410 (283)	80,460 (2,774)	66,850 (2,490)
2006	35,100 (113)	18,130 (408)	20,130 (270)	26,740 (136)	31,950 (165)	35,160 (376)	49,570 (441)	45,410 (259)	52,440 (561)	76,240 (2,488)	70,520 (1,779)
2007	35,090 (105)	18,260 (461)	20,400 (292)	27,240 (133)	32,840 (415)	36,330 (283)	50,400 (158)	45,770 (237)	55,430 (412)	71,100 (910)	68,990 (2,155)
2008	36,700 (109)	18,630 (494)	20,410 (295)	28,380 (283)	32,630 (355)	36,760 (243)	51,410 (145)	47,030 (237)	57,510 (745)	71,300 (2,859)	74,030 (2,144)
2009	37,260 (107)	18,480 (451)	21,230 (301)	29,150 (273)	34,090 (483)	37,270 (310)	51,880 (169)	46,830 (260)	61,070 (304)	83,910 (3,210)	76,580 (912)
2010	38,290 (272)	18,240 (592)	20,880 (334)	29,860 (260)	33,400 (410)	37,770 (588)	51,940 (159)	47,440 (336)	59,100 (1,021)	76,740 (2,723)	77,390 (2,174)
2011	38,910 (216)	20,060 (250)	21,110 (131)	30,010 (145)	34,590 (512)	39,290 (40)	52,140 (88)	49,110 (103)	60,300 (533)	80,720 (135)	77,460 (21)
2012	39,980 (294)	20,060 (514)	21,390 (285)	30,410 (165)	35,060 (452)	37,320 (455)	53,690 (888)	50,170 (290)	60,930 (464)	94,470 (6,655)	77,900 (3,616)
2013	40,610 (134)	19,840 (502)	22,250 (544)	30,800 (173)	35,240 (312)	37,700 (751)	55,720 (416)	50,750 (341)	61,280 (561)	85,400 (6,196)	75,090 (3,515)
2014	40,830 (151)	20,990 (279)	21,990 (322)	30,650 (151)	34,380 (891)	37,480 (591)	55,940 (333)	51,350 (230)	60,830 (442)	91,810 (8,587)	80,540 (2,875)

See notes at end of table.

Table 502.20. Median annual earnings, number, and percentage of full-time year-round workers 25 years old and over, by highest level of educational attainment and sex: 1990 through 2014—Continued

[Standard errors appear in parentheses]

Constant 2014 dollars[7]

Sex and year	Elementary/secondary					College						
	Total	Less than 9th grade	Some high school, no completion[1]	High school completion (includes equivalency)[2]	Some college, no degree[3]	Associate's degree	Bachelor's or higher degree[4]					
							Total	Bachelor's degree[5]	Master's degree	Professional degree	Doctor's degree
1	2	3	4	5	6	7	8	9	10	11	12
Males											
1990	$55,000	$31,130	$37,410	$47,700	$56,790	$58,080	$76,370	$70,220	$85,420	$127,080	$98,220
1991	54,290	30,270	36,760	45,990	54,380	55,740	77,520	70,250	83,320	127,080	95,730
1992	53,450	28,830	35,470	45,480	53,520	54,540	76,360	68,950	83,960	130,390	102,230
1993	52,380	27,300	35,210	44,310	51,930	—	77,280	69,210	—	—	—
1994	52,780	27,670	34,800	44,250	50,950	56,500	77,700	68,920	84,440	118,390	97,730
1995	53,030	28,170	34,050	45,290	52,010	54,030	77,480	69,480	84,750	122,280	100,280
1996	53,110	26,780	33,870	45,780	51,950	55,360	76,680	68,350	90,210	128,160	106,190
1997	53,460	28,120	36,040	45,490	52,390	55,410	77,900	70,850	89,910	123,900	111,100
1998	54,400	27,810	34,380	45,170	53,000	57,800	81,120	73,770	89,320	135,950	107,740
1999	56,630	28,680	35,150	46,590	55,070	58,460	84,530	74,390	93,010	140,410 !	114,690
2000	55,770	28,240	34,090	46,600	54,790	56,990	84,040	76,520	92,810	135,040	109,010
2001	54,970	28,210	34,620	45,860	54,210	56,500	82,180	73,870	93,640	132,080	114,860
2002	53,510	27,200	33,680	43,180	53,120	55,720	80,230	72,910	87,480	130,030	108,320
2003	53,320	26,970	33,650	45,020	52,560	54,500	78,910	71,830	89,800	127,130	110,770
2004	52,110	26,820	32,540	44,240	51,880	54,990	77,760	70,860	88,580	123,830	102,040
2005	51,880	26,750	32,560	43,480	50,810	56,510	79,250	71,890	89,860	119,770	102,840
2006	53,090	26,350	32,090	42,970	50,860	54,620	77,660	70,670	87,520	116,030	116,030
2007	53,030	26,370	33,070	42,710	50,650	55,330	79,420	70,040	86,060	112,820	103,890
2008	53,240	26,350	32,240	42,380	49,780	54,480	78,460	71,490	87,960	108,650	108,650
2009	54,510	26,110	30,550	43,040	51,350	54,850	77,920	68,080	86,510	134,380	109,840
2010	54,020	26,230	31,580	42,970	49,810	53,940	77,000	68,370	86,850	123,680	108,580
2011	52,680	26,230	31,640	42,060	48,950	52,960	76,800	68,840	86,340	124,240	104,790
2012	51,910	25,600	30,900	41,110	48,070	51,920	76,740	67,400	86,720	118,540	108,470
2013	51,920	26,570	31,050	40,930	48,400	51,800	77,310	68,300	87,670	118,730	106,940
2014	51,400	26,580	30,840	40,930	46,900	51,110	75,910	68,160	84,760	121,750	100,710
Females											
1990	$38,250	$21,930	$25,820	$32,790	$39,780	$42,940	$54,370	$50,140	$60,020	$80,280	$74,370
1991	37,860	20,720	24,830	32,350	38,030	42,720	53,770	49,940	60,080	77,120	76,340
1992	38,580	21,600	24,270	32,390	38,610	41,900	53,360	50,560	62,500	81,280	76,480
1993	38,250	20,100	24,910	32,320	37,320	—	55,540	50,500	—	—	—
1994	38,510	19,620	23,890	32,160	37,110	40,940	55,840	50,100	62,280	79,890	80,690
1995	38,180	20,840	24,290	31,410	36,830	41,920	54,120	49,190	61,800	76,740	73,890
1996	38,480	21,490	25,270	31,570	37,520	41,870	54,360	49,980	62,470	85,910	83,890
1997	39,310	20,640	24,330	32,160	38,380	41,990	55,440	51,560	65,510	88,980	77,300
1998	40,120	20,760	23,650	32,690	39,350	42,940	57,100	52,460	64,980	82,610	82,940
1999	40,500	21,200	23,890	32,380	38,970	43,410	58,620	53,340	67,530	84,110	84,350
2000	41,200	21,460	24,340	33,920	38,010	42,210	58,010	54,900	68,110	80,090	77,540
2001	41,420	22,050	25,300	33,420	40,180	42,470	59,140	54,150	66,920	81,560	82,050
2002	40,320	21,470	24,080	32,740	38,230	41,120	56,230	53,120	63,570	74,140	85,450
2003	40,130	21,490	24,080	33,150	38,320	41,000	57,360	52,540	63,770	84,530	85,450
2004	39,610	21,080	23,730	32,230	38,160	41,460	56,850	51,610	63,540	92,920	85,290
2005	39,610	19,330	24,100	31,490	37,610	40,650	56,230	50,510	61,580	96,370	80,070
2006	40,720	21,040	23,360	31,020	37,080	40,790	57,520	52,690	60,840	88,460	81,820
2007	40,710	20,600	23,010	30,730	37,050	40,990	56,860	51,640	62,530	80,210	77,830
2008	39,870	20,240	22,170	30,840	35,450	39,940	55,850	51,090	62,480	77,460	80,420
2009	40,630	20,150	23,140	31,780	37,170	40,630	56,560	51,060	66,580	91,480	83,500
2010	41,080	19,570	22,400	32,030	35,830	40,520	55,720	50,890	63,400	82,320	83,020
2011	40,460	20,900	21,960	31,210	35,970	40,850	54,220	51,070	62,710	83,940	80,550
2012	40,730	20,440	21,790	30,980	35,720	40,040	54,700	51,120	62,070	96,250	79,370
2013	41,250	20,150	22,600	31,290	35,800	38,300	56,600	51,550	62,250	86,740	76,280
2014	40,830	20,990	21,990	30,650	34,380	37,480	55,940	51,350	60,830	91,810	80,540

See notes at end of table.

Table 502.20. Median annual earnings, number, and percentage of full-time year-round workers 25 years old and over, by highest level of educational attainment and sex: 1990 through 2014—Continued

[Standard errors appear in parentheses]

Number of persons with earnings who worked full time, year round (in thousands)

Sex and year	Total	Elementary/secondary			College			Bachelor's or higher degree[4]			
		Less than 9th grade	Some high school, no completion[1]	High school completion (includes equivalency)[2]	Some college, no degree[3]	Associate's degree	Total	Bachelor's degree[5]	Master's degree	Professional degree[4]	Doctor's degree
1	2	3	4	5	6	7	8	9	10	11	12

Sex and year	2	3	4	5	6	7	8	9	10	11	12
Males											
1990	44,406 (268.6)	2,250 (73.9)	3,315 (89.3)	16,394 (188.0)	9,113 (144.6)	[6] (†)	13,334 (171.8)	7,569 (132.6)	[6] (†)	[6] (†)	[6] (†)
1991	44,199 (268.3)	1,807 (66.3)	3,083 (86.2)	15,025 (181.1)	8,034 (136.4)	2,899 (83.6)	13,350 (171.9)	8,456 (139.7)	3,073 (86.1)	1,147 (53.0)	674 (40.7)
1992	44,752 (269.1)	1,815 (66.5)	3,009 (85.2)	14,604 (179.5)	8,067 (136.6)	3,203 (87.8)	13,937 (175.2)	8,719 (141.7)	3,178 (87.5)	1,295 (56.3)	745 (42.8)
1993	45,873 (270.6)	1,790 (66.0)	3,083 (86.2)	14,604 (178.9)	8,493 (140.0)	3,557 (92.4)	14,346 (177.5)	9,178 (145.1)	3,131 (86.8)	1,231 (54.9)	808 (44.5)
1994	47,566 (303.0)	1,895 (69.2)	3,057 (87.6)	15,109 (188.5)	8,783 (146.2)	3,735 (96.6)	14,987 (187.8)	9,636 (152.8)	3,225 (89.9)	1,258 (56.4)	868 (46.9)
1995	48,500 (306.1)	1,946 (72.8)	3,335 (94.9)	15,331 (195.6)	8,908 (152.3)	3,926 (102.8)	15,054 (194.0)	9,597 (157.8)	3,395 (95.7)	1,208 (57.5)	853 (48.4)
1996	49,764 (301.1)	2,041 (69.2)	3,441 (89.6)	15,840 (186.5)	9,173 (144.2)	3,931 (95.6)	15,339 (183.7)	9,898 (149.6)	3,272 (87.4)	1,277 (54.8)	893 (45.9)
1997	50,807 (299.0)	1,914 (67.0)	3,548 (90.9)	16,225 (187.8)	9,170 (143.9)	4,086 (97.4)	15,864 (185.9)	10,349 (152.4)	3,228 (86.7)	1,321 (55.8)	966 (47.7)
1998	52,381 (306.4)	1,870 (66.3)	3,613 (91.7)	16,442 (189.7)	9,375 (145.7)	4,347 (100.4)	16,733 (191.2)	11,058 (157.6)	3,414 (89.2)	1,264 (54.6)	998 (48.5)
1999	53,062 (307.8)	1,993 (68.4)	3,295 (87.7)	16,589 (190.5)	9,684 (148.0)	4,359 (100.6)	17,142 (193.3)	11,142 (158.2)	3,725 (93.1)	1,267 (54.6)	1,008 (48.8)
2000	54,065 (309.7)	1,968 (68.0)	3,354 (88.4)	16,834 (191.7)	9,792 (148.8)	4,729 (104.7)	17,387 (194.6)	11,395 (159.9)	3,680 (92.6)	1,274 (54.8)	1,038 (49.5)
2001	54,013 (224.8)	2,207 (51.4)	3,503 (64.5)	16,314 (135.4)	9,494 (104.9)	4,714 (74.7)	17,780 (140.9)	11,479 (114.8)	3,961 (68.5)	1,298 (39.5)	1,041 (35.4)
2002	54,108 (225.0)	2,154 (50.7)	3,680 (66.1)	16,005 (134.2)	9,603 (105.5)	4,399 (72.2)	18,267 (142.7)	11,829 (116.5)	4,065 (69.4)	1,308 (39.6)	1,065 (35.8)
2003	54,253 (225.2)	2,209 (51.4)	3,369 (63.3)	16,285 (135.0)	9,340 (104.1)	4,696 (74.5)	18,354 (143.0)	11,846 (116.6)	4,124 (69.9)	1,348 (40.2)	1,037 (35.5)
2004	55,469 (227.0)	2,427 (53.8)	3,468 (64.2)	17,067 (138.3)	9,257 (103.6)	4,913 (76.2)	18,338 (142.9)	11,701 (115.9)	4,243 (70.9)	1,305 (39.6)	1,088 (36.1)
2005	56,717 (228.7)	2,425 (53.8)	3,652 (65.9)	17,266 (139.0)	9,532 (105.1)	5,022 (77.0)	18,820 (144.7)	12,032 (117.4)	4,275 (71.2)	1,369 (40.5)	1,144 (37.1)
2006	58,109 (230.6)	2,361 (53.1)	3,872 (67.8)	17,369 (139.4)	9,493 (104.9)	5,110 (77.7)	19,903 (148.4)	12,764 (120.7)	4,542 (73.3)	1,425 (41.3)	1,172 (37.5)
2007	58,147 (230.7)	2,142 (50.6)	3,451 (64.0)	17,224 (138.9)	9,867 (106.8)	5,244 (78.7)	20,218 (149.5)	12,962 (121.6)	4,800 (75.3)	1,332 (40.0)	1,125 (36.7)
2008	55,655 (227.2)	1,982 (48.7)	3,118 (60.9)	16,195 (135.0)	9,515 (105.0)	5,020 (77.0)	19,825 (148.1)	12,609 (120.0)	4,709 (74.6)	1,388 (40.8)	1,119 (36.7)
2009	52,445 (222.5)	1,561 (43.2)	2,795 (57.7)	15,258 (131.3)	8,609 (100.1)	4,828 (75.5)	19,395 (146.7)	12,290 (118.6)	4,575 (73.6)	1,319 (39.8)	1,212 (38.1)
2010	52,890 (223.2)	1,600 (43.8)	2,615 (55.9)	15,104 (130.7)	8,541 (99.7)	5,042 (77.2)	19,990 (148.7)	12,836 (121.1)	4,670 (74.3)	1,237 (38.5)	1,246 (38.7)
2011	54,279 (225.2)	1,848 (47.0)	2,715 (56.9)	15,335 (131.6)	8,752 (100.9)	5,206 (78.4)	20,423 (150.1)	13,013 (121.8)	4,839 (75.6)	1,300 (39.5)	1,271 (39.0)
2012	55,208 (226.6)	1,793 (46.3)	2,671 (56.4)	15,295 (131.4)	8,974 (102.1)	5,423 (80.0)	21,052 (152.2)	13,315 (123.2)	5,003 (76.9)	1,301 (39.5)	1,433 (41.4)
2013	56,703 (289.3)	1,944 (61.0)	2,910 (74.5)	16,034 (170.0)	8,960 (129.0)	5,605 (102.8)	21,249 (193.4)	13,378 (156.2)	5,146 (98.6)	1,249 (49.0)	1,476 (53.2)
2014	58,435 (256.1)	1,994 (54.0)	3,012 (66.2)	16,429 (150.3)	9,281 (114.7)	5,622 (90.0)	22,098 (172.1)	13,969 (139.3)	5,401 (88.2)	1,359 (44.6)	1,369 (44.8)
Females											
1990	28,636 (234.7)	847 (45.6)	1,861 (67.3)	11,810 (162.8)	6,462 (123.1)	[6] (†)	7,655 (133.3)	4,704 (105.8)	[6] (†)	[6] (†)	[6] (†)
1991	29,474 (237.1)	733 (42.4)	1,819 (66.5)	10,959 (157.8)	5,633 (115.3)	2,523 (78.1)	7,807 (134.6)	5,263 (111.6)	2,025 (70.1)	312 (27.7)	206 (22.5)
1992	30,346 (239.6)	734 (42.4)	1,659 (63.6)	11,039 (157.9)	5,904 (117.9)	2,655 (80.1)	8,355 (138.9)	5,604 (115.0)	2,192 (72.9)	334 (28.7)	225 (23.5)
1993	30,683 (240.5)	765 (43.3)	1,576 (62.0)	10,513 (154.4)	6,279 (121.4)	3,067 (86.0)	8,483 (139.9)	5,735 (116.3)	2,166 (72.5)	323 (28.2)	260 (25.3)
1994	31,379 (259.2)	696 (42.0)	1,675 (65.1)	10,785 (161.2)	6,256 (124.2)	3,210 (89.7)	8,756 (146.0)	5,901 (120.8)	2,174 (74.0)	398 (31.8)	283 (26.8)
1995	32,673 (268.2)	774 (46.1)	1,763 (69.3)	11,064 (168.6)	6,329 (129.5)	3,336 (94.9)	9,406 (156.3)	6,434 (130.5)	2,268 (78.5)	421 (34.0)	283 (27.9)
1996	33,549 (259.0)	750 (42.1)	1,751 (64.1)	11,363 (159.7)	6,582 (122.9)	3,468 (89.9)	9,636 (147.7)	6,689 (123.9)	2,213 (72.0)	413 (31.2)	322 (27.6)
1997	34,624 (260.1)	791 (43.2)	1,765 (64.4)	11,475 (160.0)	6,628 (123.2)	3,538 (90.7)	10,427 (153.0)	7,173 (128.0)	2,448 (75.7)	488 (34.0)	318 (27.4)
1998	35,528 (265.4)	814 (43.8)	1,878 (66.4)	11,613 (161.3)	7,070 (127.3)	3,527 (90.7)	10,725 (155.4)	7,288 (129.2)	2,639 (78.6)	468 (33.3)	329 (27.9)
1999	37,091 (269.7)	886 (45.7)	1,883 (66.5)	11,824 (162.7)	7,453 (130.6)	3,804 (94.1)	11,242 (158.9)	7,607 (131.9)	2,818 (81.2)	470 (33.3)	346 (28.6)
2000	37,762 (271.6)	930 (46.8)	1,950 (67.7)	11,789 (162.5)	7,391 (130.0)	4,118 (97.8)	11,584 (161.2)	7,899 (134.3)	2,823 (81.2)	509 (34.7)	353 (28.9)
2001	38,228 (197.6)	927 (33.4)	1,869 (47.3)	11,690 (115.8)	7,283 (92.3)	4,190 (70.5)	12,269 (118.5)	8,257 (98.1)	3,089 (60.6)	531 (25.3)	392 (21.7)
2002	38,510 (197.6)	858 (32.1)	1,841 (46.9)	11,687 (115.8)	7,354 (92.7)	4,285 (71.2)	12,484 (119.5)	8,229 (97.9)	3,281 (62.5)	572 (26.1)	402 (22.0)
2003	38,681 (197.9)	882 (32.6)	1,739 (45.6)	11,587 (115.3)	7,341 (92.6)	4,397 (72.2)	12,735 (120.6)	8,330 (98.5)	3,376 (63.4)	567 (26.1)	462 (23.6)
2004	39,072 (198.7)	917 (33.2)	1,797 (46.4)	11,392 (114.4)	7,330 (92.6)	4,505 (73.0)	13,131 (122.4)	8,664 (100.4)	3,451 (64.0)	564 (26.0)	452 (23.3)
2005	40,021 (200.6)	902 (32.9)	1,740 (45.6)	11,419 (114.5)	7,452 (93.3)	4,751 (74.9)	13,758 (125.1)	9,074 (102.6)	3,591 (65.3)	657 (28.1)	437 (22.9)
2006	41,311 (203.2)	934 (33.5)	1,802 (46.4)	11,652 (115.6)	7,613 (94.3)	4,760 (75.0)	14,549 (128.4)	9,645 (105.7)	3,746 (66.7)	662 (28.2)	497 (24.5)
2007	42,196 (204.9)	823 (31.5)	1,649 (44.4)	11,447 (114.7)	7,916 (96.1)	4,891 (76.0)	15,469 (132.1)	9,931 (107.2)	4,389 (72.1)	666 (28.3)	484 (24.1)
2008	40,979 (202.5)	814 (31.3)	1,568 (43.3)	10,851 (111.8)	7,456 (93.3)	4,955 (76.5)	15,335 (131.6)	9,856 (106.8)	4,176 (70.3)	753 (30.1)	550 (25.7)
2009	40,376 (201.4)	776 (30.5)	1,519 (42.7)	10,467 (109.9)	7,164 (91.6)	4,924 (76.3)	15,526 (132.4)	10,066 (107.9)	4,261 (71.0)	606 (27.0)	592 (26.7)
2010	40,196 (201.0)	732 (29.7)	1,371 (40.5)	10,117 (108.1)	7,150 (91.5)	4,999 (76.8)	15,826 (133.5)	9,903 (107.0)	4,576 (73.6)	622 (27.4)	725 (29.5)
2011	40,885 (202.4)	779 (30.6)	1,380 (40.7)	10,040 (107.7)	6,989 (90.5)	5,131 (77.8)	16,566 (136.4)	10,537 (110.2)	4,700 (74.6)	635 (27.6)	694 (28.9)
2012	41,319 (203.2)	690 (28.8)	1,351 (40.3)	9,870 (106.8)	6,899 (89.9)	5,246 (78.7)	17,263 (139.0)	10,961 (112.3)	4,887 (76.0)	670 (28.4)	745 (29.9)
2013	42,021 (258.8)	788 (38.9)	1,309 (50.1)	9,990 (135.9)	7,070 (115.1)	5,253 (99.6)	17,611 (177.5)	11,124 (143.1)	4,963 (96.9)	793 (39.1)	732 (37.5)
2014	42,957 (228.5)	796 (34.2)	1,356 (44.6)	9,802 (117.7)	7,241 (101.7)	5,426 (88.4)	18,336 (158.1)	11,420 (126.6)	5,310 (87.5)	776 (33.8)	830 (34.9)

See notes at end of table.

Table 502.20. Median annual earnings, number, and percentage of full-time year-round workers 25 years old and over, by highest level of educational attainment and sex: 1990 through 2014—Continued

[Standard errors appear in parentheses]

Percent of persons with earnings who worked full time, year round[8]

| | | Elementary/secondary | | | | College | | Bachelor's or higher degree[4] | | | | |
Sex and year	Total	Less than 9th grade	Some high school, no completion[1]	High school completion (includes equivalency)[2]	Some college, no degree[3]	Associate's degree	Total	Bachelor's degree[5]	Master's degree	Professional degree	Doctor's degree
1	2	3	4	5	6	7	8	9	10	11	12
Males											
1996	78.2 (0.25)	64.5 (1.31)	66.9 (1.01)	77.2 (0.45)	78.8 (0.58)	83.8 (0.83)	82.9 (0.43)	83.2 (0.53)	80.6 (0.95)	85.4 (1.40)	85.1 (1.69)
1997	81.6 (0.24)	63.9 (1.35)	69.5 (0.99)	78.7 (0.44)	79.5 (0.58)	83.7 (0.84)	83.3 (0.42)	83.9 (0.51)	80.8 (0.96)	85.4 (1.38)	83.4 (1.68)
1998	81.0 (0.24)	66.8 (1.37)	73.5 (0.97)	80.3 (0.43)	81.0 (0.56)	85.3 (0.76)	84.6 (0.39)	85.9 (0.47)	81.6 (0.92)	86.0 (1.39)	80.0 (1.74)
1999	81.1 (0.24)	70.3 (1.32)	71.5 (1.02)	80.3 (0.43)	81.3 (0.55)	84.2 (0.78)	84.7 (0.39)	85.3 (0.48)	83.5 (0.86)	85.6 (1.40)	81.8 (1.69)
2000	81.7 (0.23)	69.2 (1.33)	71.8 (1.01)	80.9 (0.42)	82.2 (0.54)	86.6 (0.71)	84.8 (0.39)	85.6 (0.47)	82.8 (0.87)	85.8 (1.39)	82.5 (1.65)
2001	80.1 (0.17)	69.7 (0.90)	70.9 (0.71)	79.4 (0.31)	80.2 (0.40)	84.1 (0.54)	83.3 (0.28)	83.6 (0.35)	82.4 (0.60)	84.6 (1.01)	82.2 (1.18)
2002	79.4 (0.17)	70.1 (0.91)	71.3 (0.69)	77.8 (0.32)	78.8 (0.41)	81.4 (0.58)	83.9 (0.27)	84.4 (0.34)	82.2 (0.60)	85.7 (0.99)	82.8 (1.16)
2003	79.5 (0.17)	71.5 (0.89)	70.1 (0.73)	78.7 (0.31)	78.8 (0.41)	82.1 (0.56)	83.1 (0.28)	84.0 (0.34)	83.1 (0.60)	84.4 (1.00)	80.3 (1.22)
2004	80.0 (0.17)	74.7 (0.84)	71.2 (0.71)	79.1 (0.30)	79.3 (0.41)	83.6 (0.53)	83.0 (0.28)	83.1 (0.35)	83.1 (0.58)	83.3 (1.03)	81.7 (1.16)
2005	80.3 (0.16)	74.0 (0.84)	73.8 (0.69)	79.5 (0.30)	80.0 (0.40)	82.5 (0.54)	82.9 (0.27)	83.0 (0.34)	82.7 (0.58)	83.7 (1.00)	82.4 (1.12)
2006	81.1 (0.16)	73.6 (0.85)	72.9 (0.67)	79.6 (0.30)	80.1 (0.40)	85.3 (0.50)	84.7 (0.26)	85.2 (0.32)	83.5 (0.55)	85.9 (0.94)	83.4 (1.09)
2007	80.5 (0.16)	71.1 (0.91)	70.8 (0.72)	79.4 (0.30)	79.5 (0.40)	83.3 (0.52)	84.5 (0.26)	85.1 (0.32)	83.5 (0.54)	83.1 (1.03)	83.5 (1.11)
2008	77.0 (0.17)	66.3 (0.95)	64.6 (0.76)	74.6 (0.32)	76.5 (0.42)	79.4 (0.56)	82.6 (0.27)	83.2 (0.33)	80.9 (0.57)	82.4 (1.02)	83.1 (1.12)
2009	73.9 (0.18)	56.2 (1.03)	61.8 (0.79)	70.1 (0.34)	73.4 (0.45)	77.9 (0.58)	80.8 (0.28)	79.9 (0.35)	82.0 (0.56)	85.1 (0.99)	81.2 (1.11)
2010	74.8 (0.18)	58.8 (1.04)	61.6 (0.82)	71.9 (0.34)	72.9 (0.45)	78.2 (0.56)	81.4 (0.27)	81.8 (0.34)	80.0 (0.58)	81.6 (1.10)	82.2 (1.08)
2011	76.6 (0.17)	67.2 (0.98)	64.2 (0.81)	74.2 (0.33)	75.2 (0.44)	78.0 (0.56)	82.0 (0.27)	82.1 (0.33)	82.3 (0.55)	81.6 (1.07)	81.0 (1.09)
2012	76.5 (0.17)	65.4 (1.00)	64.4 (0.82)	74.5 (0.33)	73.7 (0.44)	78.8 (0.54)	82.1 (0.26)	82.5 (0.33)	80.8 (0.55)	84.4 (1.01)	81.4 (1.12)
2013	78.1 (0.21)	69.3 (1.21)	68.9 (0.99)	76.5 (0.41)	76.2 (0.55)	79.6 (0.67)	82.4 (0.33)	82.6 (0.41)	82.5 (0.67)	83.2 (1.34)	79.7 (1.30)
2014	79.2 (0.18)	72.2 (1.03)	69.4 (0.85)	78.3 (0.35)	76.7 (0.47)	79.9 (0.58)	83.3 (0.28)	83.7 (0.35)	82.7 (0.57)	83.5 (1.12)	81.2 (1.15)
Females											
1996	60.7 (0.32)	47.9 (1.94)	49.4 (1.29)	60.0 (0.55)	62.0 (0.73)	63.7 (1.00)	63.5 (0.60)	63.4 (0.72)	62.4 (1.25)	68.4 (2.91)	70.0 (3.29)
1997	61.7 (0.32)	48.7 (1.91)	49.3 (1.29)	61.0 (0.55)	61.9 (0.72)	64.3 (0.99)	65.4 (0.58)	64.6 (0.70)	65.7 (1.20)	73.6 (2.63)	72.1 (3.29)
1998	62.5 (0.31)	51.8 (1.94)	53.1 (1.29)	61.9 (0.55)	63.3 (0.70)	64.9 (1.00)	65.0 (0.57)	64.0 (0.69)	66.2 (1.15)	71.9 (2.71)	68.5 (3.26)
1999	63.7 (0.31)	53.0 (1.88)	54.0 (1.30)	63.0 (0.54)	64.8 (0.69)	65.1 (0.96)	66.2 (0.56)	65.9 (0.68)	66.5 (1.12)	68.4 (2.73)	68.2 (3.18)
2000	64.6 (0.30)	53.5 (1.84)	56.5 (1.30)	64.1 (0.54)	65.3 (0.69)	66.6 (0.92)	66.5 (0.55)	66.7 (0.67)	64.9 (1.11)	70.6 (2.61)	71.5 (3.13)
2001	64.3 (0.22)	54.0 (1.32)	55.3 (0.94)	63.5 (0.39)	65.1 (0.49)	65.8 (0.65)	66.6 (0.38)	66.6 (0.47)	65.6 (0.76)	70.3 (1.83)	70.9 (2.12)
2002	64.1 (0.21)	52.6 (1.36)	55.5 (0.95)	63.2 (0.39)	65.0 (0.49)	65.6 (0.65)	66.5 (0.38)	65.9 (0.47)	66.1 (0.74)	74.3 (1.73)	73.8 (2.07)
2003	64.4 (0.21)	56.5 (1.38)	53.8 (0.96)	64.4 (0.39)	64.2 (0.49)	65.6 (0.64)	66.4 (0.37)	65.8 (0.46)	66.3 (0.73)	72.3 (1.75)	71.9 (1.95)
2004	64.5 (0.21)	56.3 (1.35)	56.1 (0.96)	64.5 (0.40)	64.2 (0.49)	64.6 (0.63)	66.7 (0.37)	66.3 (0.45)	66.3 (0.72)	71.5 (1.77)	71.2 (1.97)
2005	65.3 (0.21)	56.5 (1.36)	54.5 (0.97)	65.1 (0.40)	63.5 (0.49)	67.2 (0.61)	68.2 (0.36)	68.0 (0.44)	68.3 (0.70)	71.2 (1.64)	67.3 (2.02)
2006	66.2 (0.21)	58.5 (1.35)	56.0 (0.96)	65.6 (0.39)	65.9 (0.48)	67.3 (0.61)	68.6 (0.35)	68.4 (0.43)	67.5 (0.69)	73.6 (1.61)	74.0 (1.86)
2007	66.7 (0.21)	56.8 (1.43)	55.3 (1.00)	65.7 (0.39)	66.7 (0.48)	67.3 (0.60)	69.3 (0.34)	68.4 (0.42)	70.6 (0.63)	74.1 (1.60)	71.2 (1.91)
2008	64.4 (0.21)	51.6 (1.38)	52.8 (1.01)	62.4 (0.40)	64.7 (0.49)	65.5 (0.60)	67.9 (0.34)	67.8 (0.43)	66.9 (0.65)	74.0 (1.51)	70.0 (1.80)
2009	64.3 (0.21)	52.0 (1.42)	54.5 (1.04)	62.4 (0.41)	63.9 (0.50)	64.5 (0.60)	68.0 (0.34)	68.3 (0.42)	67.5 (0.65)	66.4 (1.72)	68.3 (1.74)
2010	64.4 (0.21)	51.7 (1.46)	52.4 (1.07)	62.6 (0.42)	63.3 (0.50)	64.3 (0.60)	68.5 (0.34)	67.7 (0.42)	68.5 (0.62)	73.9 (1.66)	76.3 (1.51)
2011	65.0 (0.21)	52.2 (1.42)	49.1 (1.04)	63.0 (0.42)	62.9 (0.50)	66.3 (0.59)	69.6 (0.33)	69.4 (0.41)	69.0 (0.62)	72.8 (1.65)	73.6 (1.58)
2012	64.8 (0.21)	50.0 (1.48)	51.1 (1.07)	62.3 (0.42)	61.7 (0.50)	64.7 (0.58)	70.0 (0.32)	70.6 (0.40)	68.0 (0.60)	73.2 (1.61)	73.9 (1.52)
2013	65.6 (0.26)	56.0 (1.84)	52.3 (1.07)	63.8 (0.46)	63.4 (0.62)	65.1 (0.79)	69.6 (0.40)	70.4 (0.50)	67.4 (0.82)	73.9 (1.86)	69.4 (1.97)
2014	66.1 (0.23)	53.5 (1.57)	54.1 (1.21)	63.6 (0.47)	64.3 (0.55)	66.5 (0.63)	70.0 (0.34)	70.3 (0.44)	69.2 (0.64)	73.8 (1.65)	68.1 (1.62)

—Not available.
†Not applicable.
‡Interpret data with caution. The coefficient of variation (CV) for this estimate is between 30 and 50 percent.
[1]Includes 1 to 3 years of high school for 1990.
[2]Includes 4 years of high school for 1990.
[3]Includes 1 to 3 years of college and associate's degrees for 1990.
[4]Includes 4 or more years of college for 1990.
[5]Includes 4 years of college for 1990.
[6]Not reported separately for 1990.

[7]Constant dollars based on the Consumer Price Index, prepared by the Bureau of Labor Statistics, U.S. Department of Labor.
[8]Data not available for 1990 through 1995.
NOTE: Detail may not sum to totals because of rounding.
SOURCE: U.S. Department of Commerce, Census Bureau, Current Population Reports, Series P-60, *Money Income of Households, Families, and Persons in the United States and Income, Poverty, and Valuation of Noncash Benefits, 1990 through 1994*; Series P-60, *Money Income in the United States, 1995 through 2002*; and Current Population Survey (CPS), Annual Social and Economic Supplement, 2004 through 2015. Retrieved January 28, 2016, from http://www.census.gov/hhes/www/cpstables/032015/perinc/pinc03_000.htm. (This table was prepared January 2015.)

Table 502.30. Median annual earnings of full-time year-round workers 25 to 34 years old and full-time year-round workers as a percentage of the labor force, by sex, race/ethnicity, and educational attainment: Selected years, 1995 through 2014

[Amounts in constant 2014 dollars. Standard errors appear in parentheses]

Sex, race/ethnicity, and educational attainment	1995	2000	2004	2005	2007	2009	2010	2011	2012	2013	2014
1	2	3	4	5	6	7	8	9	10	11	12
Total, all full-time year-round workers 25 to 34 years old											
Median annual earnings, all education levels.....	$38,840 (215)	$41,240 (131)	$40,700 (939)	$39,980 (1,092)	$39,960 (#)	$41,890 (1,090)	$40,580 (840)	$39,940 (99)	$39,180 (901)	$40,650 (#)	$40,000 (80)
Less than high school completion.....	24,620 (391)	24,880 (540)	25,030 (23)	24,900 (776)	25,030 (707)	22,990 (797)	22,790 (853)	24,060 (869)	23,630 (840)	24,330 (726)	24,960 (1,440)
High school completion[1].....	32,290 (308)	34,360 (241)	33,740 (457)	33,810 (1,136)	33,070 (716)	33,020 (17)	32,470 (33)	31,520 (25)	30,890 (16)	30,480 (2)	30,000 (2)
Some college, no degree.....	36,110 (673)	39,660 (516)	39,060 (1,017)	38,030 (777)	37,530 (880)	36,600 (1,264)	35,720 (937)	33,670 (526)	33,870 (740)	34,630 (1,185)	31,810 (827)
Associate's degree.....	38,550 (632)	41,240 (390)	41,180 (1,313)	41,170 (1,044)	39,730 (157)	39,610 (1,062)	40,150 (1,118)	38,980 (1,525)	36,830 (1,495)	38,150 (2,157)	34,970 (455)
Bachelor's or higher degree.....	51,230 (874)	54,980 (284)	53,860 (1,381)	53,180 (1,077)	54,640 (1,467)	54,990 (35)	52,910 (1,090)	52,620 (359)	51,510 (17)	50,810 (1,298)	51,980 (783)
Bachelor's degree.....	48,100 (391)	54,870 (406)	51,210 (1,111)	49,460 (1,336)	51,180 (905)	49,640 (299)	48,850 (675)	47,330 (661)	48,360 (920)	49,320 (1,737)	49,880 (150)
Master's or higher degree.....	61,590 (1,132)	65,870 (2,034)	62,190 (288)	60,540 (54)	63,560 (2,243)	65,340 (2,231)	59,340 (1,076)	62,340 (1,581)	61,480 (1,168)	60,540 (454)	59,080 (1,258)
Percent,[2] all education levels.....	63.6 (0.44)	68.4 (0.32)	66.2 (0.38)	66.6 (0.37)	67.8 (0.36)	61.0 (0.41)	61.9 (0.42)	63.3 (0.41)	64.2 (0.44)	65.1 (0.49)	67.1 (0.40)
Less than high school completion.....	49.6 (1.37)	59.4 (1.02)	60.1 (1.26)	60.0 (1.32)	56.5 (1.26)	47.0 (1.25)	44.9 (1.52)	48.1 (1.43)	48.6 (1.38)	53.3 (1.72)	55.1 (1.51)
High school completion[1].....	62.8 (0.79)	67.2 (0.59)	65.6 (0.71)	66.9 (0.75)	67.0 (0.71)	55.3 (0.74)	57.0 (0.80)	59.1 (0.78)	60.3 (0.80)	61.7 (1.07)	65.3 (0.87)
Some college, no degree.....	61.5 (0.99)	67.8 (0.71)	63.1 (0.93)	63.5 (0.83)	64.8 (0.92)	58.7 (0.91)	58.1 (0.92)	59.0 (0.99)	59.2 (1.00)	59.0 (1.10)	61.6 (0.84)
Associate's degree.....	67.4 (1.41)	70.9 (1.01)	65.8 (1.16)	67.8 (1.16)	67.8 (1.23)	65.1 (1.18)	63.6 (1.29)	65.4 (1.17)	64.8 (1.18)	67.5 (1.51)	65.8 (1.17)
Bachelor's or higher degree.....	70.4 (0.79)	72.3 (0.55)	70.7 (0.70)	70.2 (0.67)	73.5 (0.59)	69.4 (0.63)	71.4 (0.59)	71.4 (0.62)	72.8 (0.62)	72.1 (0.71)	73.5 (0.63)
Bachelor's degree.....	70.5 (0.90)	73.1 (0.62)	70.9 (0.74)	70.9 (0.76)	73.2 (0.70)	69.1 (0.77)	71.2 (0.71)	71.1 (0.72)	72.9 (0.75)	71.9 (0.84)	73.4 (0.72)
Master's or higher degree.....	69.8 (1.65)	69.6 (1.18)	70.1 (1.42)	68.2 (1.27)	74.4 (1.21)	70.0 (1.10)	71.7 (1.23)	72.2 (1.25)	72.5 (1.20)	72.6 (1.32)	73.5 (1.14)
Male											
Median annual earnings, all education levels.....	41,840 (286)	43,990 (210)	43,870 (#)	42,430 (#)	43,320 (100)	44,140 (#)	43,290 (31)	42,010 (34)	41,240 (1)	40,650 (355)	40,950 (1,006)
Less than high school completion.....	27,590 (728)	27,390 (342)	26,040 (129)	26,560 (1,055)	26,250 (572)	25,000 (1,245)	26,050 (842)	26,270 (1,115)	25,360 (1,008)	24,780 (393)	25,000 (829)
High school completion[1].....	37,190 (611)	39,610 (650)	37,560 (150)	36,220 (49)	35,200 (1,067)	36,290 (982)	35,610 (909)	34,150 (870)	33,850 (742)	32,220 (485)	32,970 (1,154)
Some college, no degree.....	40,310 (555)	43,720 (369)	43,660 (501)	42,320 (319)	41,880 (1,567)	46,000 (1,697)...	41,120 (999)	38,610 (1,257)	38,840 (868)	38,960 (1,438)	35,790 (822)
Associate's degree.....	40,070 (1,029)	48,080 (751)	46,310 (1,115)	47,130 (1,880)	45,360 (379)	46,000 (1,697)	43,330 (466)	44,040 (1,822)	45,000 (2,828)	42,420 (2,467)	40,060 (1,548)
Bachelor's or higher degree.....	57,750 (895)	63,120 (570)	62,580 (720)	60,580 (1,934)	58,880 (1,119)	60,060 (606)	57,280 (1,931)	57,220 (1,089)	56,540 (529)	57,870 (2,179)	57,890 (1,704)
Bachelor's degree.....	54,330 (719)	61,550 (824)	57,600 (1,616)	54,510 (1,303)	56,950 (52)	55,700 (1,416)	54,050 (165)	52,370 (128)	51,530 (602)	52,790 (1,277)	54,710 (559)
Master's or higher degree.....	68,760 (2,204)	75,460 (2,043)	65,070 (3,830)	66,660 (4,044)	70,440 (3,434)	76,410 (3,202)	69,660 (1,521)	71,560 (2,473)	67,020 (2,435)	67,850 (2,567)	64,630 (1,440)
Percent,[2] all education levels.....	69.7 (0.57)	75.1 (0.40)	72.3 (0.52)	72.5 (0.48)	72.2 (0.51)	62.8 (0.58)	64.5 (0.56)	67.4 (0.57)	68.4 (0.53)	69.5 (0.62)	72.4 (0.55)
Less than high school completion.....	54.3 (1.71)	67.8 (1.22)	67.0 (1.43)	66.7 (1.54)	61.1 (1.51)	49.2 (1.71)	47.4 (1.81)	55.5 (1.74)	54.1 (1.88)	59.9 (2.06)	63.0 (1.85)
High school completion[1].....	69.3 (1.00)	73.6 (0.73)	71.0 (0.95)	73.5 (0.91)	71.9 (0.94)	57.4 (1.01)	60.6 (1.01)	63.8 (1.00)	65.5 (1.00)	67.0 (1.27)	71.4 (1.00)
Some college, no degree.....	68.5 (1.31)	76.1 (0.91)	69.7 (1.22)	70.7 (1.13)	71.1 (1.31)	62.7 (1.31)	62.0 (1.17)	64.2 (1.33)	64.3 (1.41)	63.9 (1.56)	67.8 (1.19)
Associate's degree.....	78.6 (1.81)	80.9 (1.31)	74.9 (1.63)	75.1 (1.67)	73.4 (1.70)	70.1 (1.65)	68.6 (1.77)	71.6 (1.61)	71.8 (1.70)	76.3 (2.03)	71.0 (1.79)
Bachelor's or higher degree.....	75.9 (1.04)	78.0 (0.72)	77.1 (0.82)	74.6 (0.93)	77.7 (0.94)	71.8 (0.94)	75.3 (0.80)	75.3 (0.84)	77.1 (0.87)	75.7 (1.01)	78.7 (0.87)
Bachelor's degree.....	76.4 (1.19)	78.8 (0.81)	77.2 (0.93)	74.5 (1.01)	78.0 (1.07)	70.6 (1.15)	75.4 (0.91)	74.7 (0.98)	77.3 (0.94)	74.8 (1.34)	78.5 (1.02)
Master's or higher degree.....	74.6 (2.11)	75.3 (1.58)	76.7 (1.72)	75.1 (2.00)	76.8 (1.93)	75.6 (1.61)	74.0 (1.88)	77.3 (1.63)	76.4 (1.82)	78.0 (1.83)	79.2 (1.61)
Female											
Median annual earnings, all education levels.....	33,880 (279)	38,100 (327)	37,550 (17)	36,320 (35)	37,610 (442)	38,530 (230)	37,880 (37)	36,790 (21)	36,090 (810)	37,530 (800)	35,960 (695)
Less than high school completion.....	20,100 (784)	20,590 (576)	22,060 (951)	20,360 (774)	20,340 (922)	20,930 (639)	19,300 (716)	19,930 (494)	18,460 (797)	20,230 (587)	19,950 (324)
High school completion[1].....	27,360 (461)	30,120 (329)	29,900 (815)	28,970 (197)	27,440 (1,103)	27,530 (28)	27,110 (68)	27,270 (772)	25,760 (9)	25,390 (14)	30,000 (353)
Some college, no degree.....	31,050 (449)	34,330 (336)	34,950 (1,561)	33,840 (481)	34,150 (820)	32,220 (1,080)	32,040 (1,102)	30,460 (1,152)	30,260 (647)	30,230 (139)	28,040 (1,016)
Associate's degree.....	37,200 (1,386)	36,620 (492)	37,310 (314)	35,550 (433)	35,390 (1,186)	34,090 (1,331)	37,630 (927)	33,760 (1,405)	32,590 (999)	32,950 (1,040)	29,740 (271)
Bachelor's or higher degree.....	46,250 (654)	49,490 (343)	50,050 (135)	48,200 (127)	48,990 (1,093)	49,600 (26)	47,760 (1,276)	47,250 (60)	48,300 (715)	47,560 (1,554)	44,990 (957)
Bachelor's degree.....	43,340 (939)	47,970 (383)	47,210 (802)	45,460 (1,109)	45,490 (106)	44,240 (1,283)	43,410 (1,226)	43,100 (1,403)	44,280 (1,274)	45,340 (490)	44,490 (144)
Master's or higher degree.....	53,660 (1,482)	57,160 (1,151)	56,150 (1,419)	56,910 (2,229)	57,300 (1,725)	59,580 (2,331)	54,100 (96)	54,160 (1,635)	55,190 (1,504)	54,790 (1,480)	54,590 (644)
Percent,[2] all education levels.....	56.6 (0.67)	60.7 (0.49)	58.9 (0.56)	59.6 (0.57)	62.7 (0.57)	58.9 (0.53)	58.7 (0.53)	58.6 (0.52)	59.3 (0.63)	59.9 (0.76)	60.8 (0.56)
Less than high school completion.....	41.3 (2.24)	45.3 (1.68)	47.0 (1.95)	45.9 (1.83)	45.9 (2.22)	42.7 (2.03)	39.4 (2.22)	34.1 (2.03)	37.8 (1.96)	41.1 (2.70)	38.5 (1.98)
High school completion[1].....	54.4 (1.23)	58.5 (0.96)	57.4 (1.23)	57.0 (1.11)	59.4 (1.13)	51.8 (1.12)	51.1 (1.19)	51.6 (1.19)	51.9 (1.24)	52.4 (1.64)	54.9 (1.29)
Some college, no degree.....	53.9 (1.46)	59.2 (1.08)	55.8 (1.35)	55.7 (1.19)	57.9 (1.22)	54.1 (1.28)	53.6 (1.29)	53.3 (1.33)	53.3 (1.22)	53.4 (1.69)	54.6 (1.28)
Associate's degree.....	57.6 (2.05)	62.7 (1.45)	56.9 (1.54)	60.8 (1.57)	62.7 (1.75)	60.8 (1.65)	59.1 (1.67)	59.5 (1.75)	58.8 (1.69)	59.6 (2.13)	61.1 (1.51)
Bachelor's or higher degree.....	64.7 (1.17)	66.8 (0.82)	64.9 (1.03)	66.0 (0.99)	69.9 (0.76)	67.2 (0.82)	68.0 (0.77)	68.0 (0.84)	68.9 (0.90)	68.9 (0.98)	68.7 (0.83)
Bachelor's degree.....	64.9 (1.32)	67.6 (0.93)	65.0 (1.10)	67.4 (1.18)	68.7 (0.92)	67.9 (1.04)	67.2 (0.94)	67.8 (1.06)	68.5 (1.13)	69.1 (1.16)	68.6 (0.94)
Master's or higher degree.....	63.9 (2.57)	64.2 (1.71)	64.4 (2.05)	62.6 (1.76)	72.6 (1.52)	65.7 (1.58)	70.0 (1.63)	68.6 (1.76)	69.7 (1.71)	68.5 (1.79)	68.9 (1.58)

See notes at end of table.

Table 502.30. Median annual earnings of full-time year-round workers 25 to 34 years old and full-time year-round workers as a percentage of the labor force, by sex, race/ethnicity, and educational attainment: Selected years, 1995 through 2014—Continued

[Amounts in constant 2014 dollars. Standard errors appear in parentheses]

Sex, race/ethnicity, and educational attainment	1995	2000	2004	2005	2007	2009	2010	2011	2012	2013	2014
1	2	3	4	5	6	7	8	9	10	11	12
White											
Median annual earnings, all education levels	**40,380** (244)	**44,990** (386)	**44,950** (290)	**42,430** (94)	**45,640** (1,357)	**44,140** (#)	**43,380** (24)	**42,090** (152)	**42,230** (1,268)	**42,640** (333)	**42,940** (745)
Less than high school completion	27,300 (1,089)	28,580 (567)	30,640 (498)	27,820 (1,587)	27,350 (1,642)	27,210 (1,082)	27,130 (430)	29,170 (1,244)	25,400 (1,112)	30,490 (2,007)	28,540 (1,945)
High school completion[1]	34,140 (384)	37,960 (508)	37,570 (14)	36,270 (44)	34,230 (20)	35,240 (785)	34,690 (928)	33,620 (651)	33,340 (712)	32,190 (635)	32,940 (1,216)
Some college, no degree	37,280 (703)	41,110 (353)	40,590 (903)	38,650 (411)	39,960 (858)	38,610 (213)	37,810 (823)	36,530 (1,159)	36,010 (1,148)	35,540 (806)	34,940 (162)
Associate's degree	40,270 (784)	43,570 (425)	43,350 (427)	42,000 (453)	41,980 (1,509)	43,970 (1,620)	43,070 (815)	41,610 (1,403)	39,840 (1,926)	40,630 (15)	36,490 (1,346)
Bachelor's or higher degree	52,750 (927)	54,990 (314)	55,150 (1,304)	54,100 (914)	54,740 (1,084)	55,000 (39)	53,780 (862)	52,250 (94)	51,500 (19)	50,810 (1,503)	52,840 (1,111)
Bachelor's degree	49,700 (482)	54,890 (362)	52,520 (273)	49,670 (1,086)	51,210 (68)	49,650 (873)	49,850 (1,228)	49,400 (1,223)	48,910 (1,093)	50,520 (2,046)	49,920 (50)
Master's or higher degree	61,750 (1,076)	65,770 (2,260)	62,130 (905)	60,540 (61)	62,400 (952)	63,540 (1,873)	58,980 (931)	61,820 (1,692)	58,720 (2,551)	59,740 (835)	57,850 (1,475)
Percent,[2] all education levels	**64.5** (0.52)	**68.2** (0.39)	**66.1** (0.52)	**66.9** (0.49)	**68.3** (0.47)	**62.5** (0.52)	**63.3** (0.52)	**65.6** (0.54)	**66.0** (0.54)	**66.3** (0.68)	**68.7** (0.49)
Less than high school completion	48.6 (2.03)	55.2 (1.76)	55.6 (2.31)	58.7 (2.29)	51.8 (2.28)	41.0 (2.43)	39.5 (2.78)	41.2 (2.70)	45.0 (2.44)	47.3 (3.27)	47.1 (2.69)
High school completion[1]	62.7 (0.94)	66.2 (0.75)	64.2 (0.94)	66.6 (0.92)	66.9 (0.89)	55.9 (1.04)	57.1 (1.08)	60.8 (1.15)	61.7 (1.10)	62.4 (1.41)	66.6 (1.17)
Some college, no degree	62.3 (1.18)	67.6 (0.88)	62.7 (1.19)	64.2 (1.02)	63.7 (1.18)	59.0 (1.14)	57.0 (1.20)	60.7 (1.25)	59.2 (1.39)	60.5 (1.53)	62.1 (1.23)
Associate's degree	66.7 (1.44)	68.2 (1.23)	63.4 (1.36)	66.9 (1.41)	69.6 (1.51)	65.4 (1.54)	63.9 (1.60)	65.7 (1.29)	66.2 (1.45)	66.9 (1.85)	67.1 (1.44)
Bachelor's or higher degree	70.5 (0.87)	72.2 (0.63)	71.4 (0.77)	72.8 (0.79)	72.7 (0.65)	69.5 (0.77)	71.7 (0.69)	72.4 (0.76)	72.8 (0.74)	71.9 (0.91)	74.2 (0.74)
Bachelor's degree	70.6 (0.99)	72.2 (0.72)	71.6 (0.81)	72.0 (0.92)	72.7 (0.77)	69.4 (0.90)	71.5 (0.79)	72.2 (0.84)	73.2 (0.88)	72.0 (1.03)	73.9 (0.87)
Master's or higher degree	70.3 (1.84)	69.9 (1.36)	71.0 (1.66)	68.8 (1.56)	73.3 (1.48)	69.5 (1.43)	72.3 (1.47)	72.8 (1.44)	71.9 (1.38)	71.7 (1.76)	74.9 (1.35)
Black											
Median annual earnings, all education levels	**32,550** (559)	**34,360** (362)	**34,420** (1,135)	**34,630** (1,227)	**34,170** (44)	**33,090** (134)	**34,300** (778)	**33,560** (765)	**32,780** (482)	**33,830** (1,713)	**30,810** (1,015)
Less than high school completion	21,460 (1,689)	22,780 (1,066)	24,340 (934)	24,710 (1,436)	21,440 (2,087)	24,500 (3,868)	22,010 (2,005)	20,470 (772)	21,740 (1,748)	20,810 (1,299)	20,480 (2,189)
High school completion[1]	27,890 (896)	30,050 (497)	29,800 (724)	27,820 (1,223)	29,490 (1,496)	27,540 (957)	27,140 (794)	26,620 (1,103)	27,260 (1,371)	25,420 (1,370)	24,970 (681)
Some college, no degree	34,130 (1,321)	35,660 (714)	37,370 (1,848)	35,190 (1,697)	34,100 (172)	32,020 (1,703)	31,780 (421)	30,860 (609)	30,930 (1,331)	32,190 (1,535)	27,270 (1,258)
Associate's degree	34,050 (1,406)	34,220 (980)	35,950 (1,731)	33,740 (1,528)	33,630 (830)	30,600 (2,106)	34,110 (2,347)	35,420 (2,478)	32,580 (2,611)	34,730 (4,480)	30,980 (1,631)
Bachelor's or higher degree	42,540 (1,453)	47,520 (1,285)	48,690 (1,781)	46,960 (1,758)	45,430 (1,252)	49,180 (944)	44,540 (1,553)	43,700 (1,889)	45,450 (2,008)	45,320 (766)	46,800 (2,441)
Bachelor's degree	40,340 (1,322)	45,020 (1,968)	44,730 (1,682)	42,760 (2,606)	44,530 (1,304)	44,140 (1,715)	42,870 (534)	41,200 (1,036)	40,690 (846)	40,580 (3,074)	44,840 (1,712)
Master's or higher degree	51,440 (1,938)	51,510 (2,553)	59,030 (4,952)	52,200 (3,680)	51,320 (2,668)	58,590 (2,959)	53,310 (6,466)	52,020 (1,090)	56,360 (2,279)	55,400 (5,867)	49,170 (1,237)
Percent,[2] all education levels	**62.4** (1.30)	**69.7** (1.28)	**66.3** (1.12)	**64.5** (1.19)	**65.0** (1.21)	**57.4** (1.13)	**57.7** (1.26)	**55.7** (1.33)	**58.5** (1.23)	**59.6** (1.51)	**61.7** (1.12)
Less than high school completion	42.4 (4.02)	48.8 (4.46)	48.6 (4.06)	40.3 (3.98)	43.9 (4.11)	38.1 (4.26)	30.5 (3.73)	30.3 (3.80)	27.5 (4.20)	40.9 (5.90)	39.0 (5.19)
High school completion[1]	60.7 (2.11)	68.3 (2.16)	64.5 (1.92)	64.0 (2.01)	60.4 (2.11)	48.9 (1.93)	53.6 (2.03)	50.8 (2.16)	51.4 (2.22)	51.2 (2.64)	58.5 (1.78)
Some college, no degree	62.2 (2.51)	69.8 (2.57)	61.5 (2.28)	59.3 (2.65)	65.5 (2.78)	57.7 (2.21)	56.2 (2.42)	50.8 (2.40)	58.0 (2.18)	54.6 (2.94)	58.9 (2.36)
Associate's degree	69.2 (4.29)	78.0 (3.79)	68.6 (4.20)	72.2 (3.57)	57.9 (3.78)	63.2 (3.58)	61.5 (3.25)	69.0 (3.32)	58.9 (3.34)	64.2 (4.19)	59.3 (3.23)
Bachelor's or higher degree	77.3 (2.85)	78.6 (2.58)	72.0 (2.16)	79.0 (1.94)	82.0 (1.95)	73.5 (2.05)	72.4 (2.11)	69.1 (2.13)	76.2 (2.12)	78.2 (2.27)	74.2 (2.07)
Bachelor's degree	76.1 (3.15)	79.4 (2.80)	71.7 (2.66)	79.9 (2.14)	82.5 (2.44)	73.1 (2.46)	71.1 (2.70)	68.5 (2.41)	75.1 (2.47)	74.3 (2.99)	73.4 (2.52)
Master's or higher degree	84.0 (6.41)	74.9 (6.52)	72.8 (4.96)	76.5 (3.95)	80.5 (3.78)	74.7 (3.60)	76.5 (3.65)	70.6 (4.32)	79.3 (3.96)	88.6 (3.30)	76.4 (3.53)
Hispanic											
Median annual earnings, all education levels	**29,110** (679)	**30,790** (460)	**30,080** (1,090)	**30,290** (10)	**30,810** (769)	**31,810** (1,399)	**32,530** (642)	**31,520** (22)	**30,830** (45)	**30,120** (123)	**30,000** (103)
Less than high school completion	23,100 (626)	23,370 (482)	24,520 (1,675)	24,100 (75)	23,500 (819)	21,950 (83)	21,630 (282)	22,800 (989)	23,130 (1,205)	23,180 (1,800)	23,820 (909)
High school completion[1]	29,250 (1,214)	31,570 (820)	29,900 (650)	29,020 (1,055)	29,460 (947)	28,390 (877)	30,220 (980)	29,410 (1,353)	28,430 (788)	28,730 (1,138)	29,990 (822)
Some college, no degree	30,320 (1,384)	36,360 (968)	37,580 (1,445)	37,990 (1,727)	35,290 (1,096)	35,610 (1,013)	31,550 (1,493)	31,550 (821)	32,760 (1,398)	30,370 (1,077)	31,060 (1,338)
Associate's degree	36,910 (2,218)	40,710 (1,746)	37,250 (1,757)	41,110 (1,969)	34,230 (1,484)	33,910 (1,609)	36,790 (1,422)	36,510 (1,523)	34,370 (1,791)	33,130 (2,304)	29,920 (1,540)
Bachelor's or higher degree	46,280 (1,802)	49,960 (1,770)	49,510 (1,896)	49,370 (2,270)	49,440 (1,804)	50,290 (1,657)	47,880 (2,144)	43,350 (1,846)	46,040 (592)	46,560 (1,500)	47,390 (2,413)
Bachelor's degree	43,590 (2,076)	48,130 (1,319)	46,430 (2,750)	47,830 (841)	45,670 (2,380)	48,930 (1,074)	45,290 (3,273)	41,690 (313)	44,040 (2,105)	45,690 (1,485)	45,690 (1,400)
Master's or higher degree	64,830 (8,743)	52,470 (3,216)	61,580 (2,300)	60,970 (4,268)	66,100 (3,068)	58,400 (4,377)	53,010 (3,882)	53,550 (2,628)	51,560 (4,168)	50,350 (5,655)	57,130 (2,404)
Percent,[2] all education levels	**60.5** (1.32)	**68.7** (1.14)	**68.0** (0.84)	**68.1** (0.82)	**67.9** (0.86)	**58.2** (0.96)	**59.4** (0.85)	**61.4** (0.89)	**61.8** (0.87)	**64.7** (1.04)	**65.9** (0.94)
Less than high school completion	53.5 (2.27)	64.4 (2.00)	64.8 (1.52)	64.9 (1.67)	61.1 (1.72)	51.8 (1.67)	50.4 (1.77)	54.9 (1.69)	54.4 (1.81)	58.9 (2.15)	62.0 (1.96)
High school completion[1]	66.0 (2.31)	70.5 (2.00)	70.8 (1.57)	71.3 (1.40)	72.1 (1.31)	58.2 (1.57)	59.0 (1.64)	61.5 (1.49)	63.3 (1.53)	66.9 (1.78)	67.8 (1.70)
Some college, no degree	58.4 (3.18)	69.5 (2.89)	67.3 (2.16)	66.6 (1.93)	67.9 (2.06)	61.1 (2.28)	64.5 (1.85)	63.0 (2.09)	61.7 (2.13)	58.2 (2.44)	63.3 (1.79)
Associate's degree	67.0 (5.34)	79.0 (3.95)	73.1 (2.69)	70.0 (2.63)	65.6 (3.15)	66.2 (3.03)	65.1 (2.70)	65.3 (3.06)	65.2 (2.90)	73.5 (2.81)	64.4 (2.84)
Bachelor's or higher degree	66.9 (3.73)	70.1 (3.27)	68.9 (2.11)	69.5 (2.11)	73.5 (1.92)	64.4 (2.12)	68.1 (2.10)	65.3 (1.84)	68.4 (1.84)	71.1 (2.00)	70.8 (1.84)
Bachelor's degree	66.3 (4.12)	71.1 (3.57)	68.8 (2.52)	69.3 (2.40)	71.6 (2.15)	64.2 (2.23)	68.1 (2.29)	68.6 (2.13)	67.6 (2.21)	72.2 (2.27)	70.6 (2.10)
Master's or higher degree	69.8 (8.84)	65.5 (8.05)	69.3 (4.88)	70.4 (4.19)	80.2 (3.55)	65.3 (4.32)	68.2 (3.89)	67.1 (3.97)	71.3 (4.09)	67.5 (4.31)	71.5 (4.16)

See notes at end of table.

Table 502.30. Median annual earnings of full-time year-round workers 25 to 34 years old and full-time year-round workers as a percentage of the labor force, by sex, race/ethnicity, and educational attainment: Selected years, 1995 through 2014—Continued

[Amounts in constant 2014 dollars. Standard errors appear in parentheses]

Sex, race/ethnicity, and educational attainment	1995	2000	2004	2005	2007	2009	2010	2011	2012	2013	2014
1	2	3	4	5	6	7	8	9	10	11	12
Asian[3]											
Median annual earnings, all education levels	39,290 (1,094)	49,290 (836)	49,350 (1,238)	48,310 (1,966)	51,080 (2,088)	54,290 (814)	49,640 (2,781)	51,800 (2,763)	55,510 (2,577)	51,260 (2,011)	49,520 (681)
Less than high school completion	‡ (†)	25,290 (2,268)	24,120 (3,963)	‡ (†)	‡ (†)	‡ (†)	‡ (†)	‡ (†)	‡ (†)	‡ (†)	‡ (†)
High school completion[1]	30,840 (2,256)	34,360 (1,244)	31,440 (1,391)	32,610 (1,712)	31,830 (2,915)	28,550 (2,232)	31,700 (1,870)	26,250 (1,354)	30,440 (841)	28,390 (2,562)	29,810 (1,870)
Some college, no degree	28,770 (2,706)	39,550 (2,047)	37,110 (3,288)	35,960 (2,524)	39,750 (2,748)	41,910 (3,622)	37,720 (1,549)	32,510 (1,892)	34,240 (2,716)	35,240 (4,790)	29,410 (2,938)
Associate's degree	31,070 (1,905)	40,560 (2,026)	36,100 (5,890)	41,250 (5,116)	40,100 (5,198)	40,040 (4,221)	38,960 (2,914)	36,400 (6,856)	44,440 (3,260)	32,110 (3,058)	33,840 (3,942)
Bachelor's or higher degree	51,110 (2,202)	67,800 (1,402)	61,960 (1,169)	60,600 (1,103)	62,740 (5,200)	65,410 (1,548)	64,980 (1,173)	64,310 (2,488)	66,220 (1,726)	60,880 (2,420)	61,190 (3,195)
Bachelor's degree	46,840 (988)	61,650 (2,483)	59,530 (2,581)	60,590 (3,939)	56,280 (1,955)	54,960 (1,240)	58,640 (4,306)	53,980 (3,488)	61,130 (1,985)	59,080 (2,765)	55,960 (2,275)
Master's or higher degree	58,950 (5,643)	78,640 (6,034)	64,130 (2,676)	65,970 (4,839)	73,940 (2,483)	77,240 (3,319)	74,140 (5,325)	77,060 (4,698)	71,890 (2,024)	75,860 (5,396)	73,080 (4,500)
Percent,[2] all education levels	63.4 (2.98)	68.5 (1.78)	67.1 (1.79)	64.8 (1.57)	71.2 (1.63)	66.7 (1.51)	65.1 (1.46)	65.1 (1.73)	67.9 (1.57)	66.0 (1.79)	68.2 (1.46)
Less than high school completion	46.6 (9.98)	61.6 (8.31)	61.8 (6.81)	49.4 (7.62)	58.3 (8.93)	52.4 (11.87)	46.6 (11.24)	56.2 (6.80)	50.9 (7.17)	53.3 (9.35)	50.8 (7.91)
High school completion[1]	66.9 (7.05)	68.9 (4.59)	73.6 (4.04)	62.5 (4.82)	68.5 (4.09)	59.3 (4.15)	55.9 (3.97)	53.7 (4.47)	64.6 (3.36)	62.4 (5.45)	66.8 (4.47)
Some college, no degree	51.8 (8.46)	63.4 (4.59)	62.4 (5.22)	66.5 (4.65)	73.4 (4.48)	57.4 (5.03)	58.2 (4.93)	58.3 (4.37)	51.7 (4.31)	57.2 (5.79)	58.6 (5.25)
Associate's degree	77.1 (8.01)	72.2 (5.92)	65.1 (6.35)	66.3 (5.93)	70.6 (5.49)	70.3 (4.25)	56.5 (5.57)	55.1 (5.88)	60.6 (5.79)	69.3 (5.81)	72.8 (5.10)
Bachelor's or higher degree	65.6 (4.18)	69.9 (2.35)	67.1 (2.55)	66.0 (2.07)	72.4 (2.04)	70.5 (1.84)	71.1 (1.89)	70.4 (2.08)	72.9 (1.80)	68.5 (2.24)	70.5 (1.65)
Bachelor's degree	68.0 (5.27)	70.8 (2.87)	67.6 (2.65)	68.7 (2.69)	71.6 (2.40)	69.7 (2.46)	72.2 (2.22)	69.6 (2.59)	73.7 (2.31)	67.6 (3.04)	72.9 (2.14)
Master's or higher degree	62.0 (6.80)	67.9 (4.11)	66.1 (3.98)	61.3 (3.08)	73.6 (3.25)	71.6 (3.17)	69.4 (3.15)	71.8 (3.20)	71.7 (2.85)	70.0 (3.51)	66.9 (2.83)
Median annual earnings for other race groups, all education levels											
Pacific Islander[4]	[3]	(†)	38,260 (8,298)	36,630 (3,907)	39,250 (3,695)	32,050 (5,746)	37,180 (1,428)	36,040 (2,705)	33,090 (5,056)	39,630 (4,420)	34,110 (3,654)
American Indian/Alaska Native[4]	30,800 (3,084)	34,350 (1,506)	32,280 (2,607)	35,760 (2,065)	35,040 (1,992)	33,110 (4,351)	34,190 (3,434)	30,830 (1,763)	33,910 (2,799)	32,750 (6,664)	29,830 (1,358)
Two or more races[4]	—	(†)	38,920 (2,300)	41,210 (1,729)	37,020 (3,516)	37,080 (2,970)	37,780 (1,511)	38,620 (1,733)	36,680 (1,563)	37,170 (3,416)	34,360 (1,974)
Percent[2] for other race groups, all education levels											
Pacific Islander[4]	[3]	[3]	64.3 (6.81)	53.7 (6.81)	70.2 (5.06)	46.9 (7.15)	62.2 (6.71)	56.9 (5.50)	69.4 (6.03)	77.2 (6.48)	63.9 (5.09)
American Indian/Alaska Native[4]	46.9 (8.10)	57.6 (4.94)	54.3 (4.25)	60.2 (4.01)	64.3 (4.58)	59.8 (4.30)	52.9 (4.14)	52.2 (4.58)	55.8 (5.05)	59.4 (5.26)	61.0 (3.84)
Two or more races[4]	—	—	60.7 (2.46)	61.9 (3.46)	59.5 (3.21)	50.2 (2.95)	60.2 (2.87)	58.1 (2.93)	59.0 (2.94)	61.0 (3.73)	61.6 (3.23)

—Not available.
†Not applicable.
#Rounds to zero.
‡Reporting standards not met (too few cases for a reliable estimate).
[1]Includes equivalency credentials, such as the GED credential.
[2]Full-time year-round workers as a percentage of the population ages 25 through 34 who reported working or looking for work in the given year.
[3]For 1995 and 2000, data for Asians and Pacific Islanders were not reported separately; therefore, Pacific Islanders are included with Asians for 1995 and 2000.

[4]For Pacific Islanders, American Indians/Alaska Natives, and persons of Two or more races, data by educational attainment are omitted because these data did not meet reporting standards. All data shown for these three race categories are for persons of all education levels.
NOTE: Beginning in 2004, standard errors were computed using replicate weights, which produced more precise values than the generalized variance function methodology used in prior years. Race categories exclude persons of Hispanic ethnicity. Constant dollars based on the Consumer Price Index, prepared by the Bureau of Labor Statistics, U.S. Department of Labor.
SOURCE: U.S. Department of Commerce, Census Bureau, Current Population Survey (CPS), Annual Social and Economic Supplement, 1996 through 2015. (This table was prepared November 2015.)

Table 502.40. Annual earnings of persons 25 years old and over, by highest level of educational attainment and sex: 2014

[Standard errors appear in parentheses]

Sex and earnings	Total	Elementary/secondary				College		Bachelor's or higher degree				
		Less than 9th grade	Some high school, no completion	High school completion (includes equivalency)	Some college, no degree	Associate's degree	Total	Bachelor's degree	Master's degree	Professional degree	Doctor's degree
1	2	3	4	5	6	7	8	9	10	11	12
Number of persons											
(in thousands)	212,132 (231.8)	9,896 (120.5)	14,686 (145.3)	62,575 (268.3)	35,164 (215.0)	20,867 (171.0)	68,945 (276.9)	43,500 (234.6)	18,471 (161.7)	3,365 (71.2)	3,609 (73.7)
With earnings	138,766 (310.2)	4,249 (79.8)	6,846 (100.8)	36,388 (218.1)	23,370 (180.0)	15,202 (147.7)	52,712 (252.5)	32,928 (209.1)	14,201 (143.0)	2,680 (63.6)	2,903 (66.2)
For persons with earnings											
Percentage distribution, by total annual earnings[1]	100.0 (†)	100.0 (†)	100.0 (†)	100.0 (†)	100.0 (†)	100.0 (†)	100.0 (†)	100.0 (†)	100.0 (†)	100.0 (†)	100.0 (†)
$1 to $4,999 or loss[2]	4.7 (0.07)	6.7 (0.47)	8.2 (0.41)	5.1 (0.14)	5.6 (0.19)	5.1 (0.22)	3.3 (0.10)	3.5 (0.13)	3.0 (0.18)	2.5 (0.38)	2.5 (0.36)
$5,000 to $9,999	4.5 (0.07)	7.9 (0.51)	9.0 (0.43)	5.5 (0.15)	5.5 (0.18)	4.1 (0.20)	2.8 (0.09)	2.9 (0.11)	2.6 (0.17)	2.2 (0.35)	2.5 (0.36)
$10,000 to $14,999	6.2 (0.08)	14.4 (0.66)	12.9 (0.50)	7.9 (0.17)	7.0 (0.21)	5.8 (0.23)	3.3 (0.10)	3.7 (0.13)	3.0 (0.18)	1.6 (0.30)	2.0 (0.32)
$15,000 to $19,999	6.5 (0.08)	16.5 (0.70)	12.9 (0.52)	8.5 (0.18)	7.3 (0.24)	6.0 (0.24)	3.1 (0.09)	3.6 (0.13)	2.4 (0.20)	2.2 (0.35)	2.3 (0.34)
$20,000 to $24,999	8.1 (0.09)	16.3 (0.70)	14.0 (0.52)	10.8 (0.20)	9.7 (0.24)	8.4 (0.28)	4.1 (0.11)	4.7 (0.14)	3.7 (0.20)	2.0 (0.34)	2.3 (0.34)
$25,000 to $29,999	7.0 (0.08)	9.4 (0.55)	9.5 (0.44)	9.8 (0.19)	8.5 (0.23)	7.5 (0.26)	3.8 (0.10)	4.6 (0.14)	2.9 (0.17)	1.9 (0.32)	1.6 (0.29)
$30,000 to $34,999	7.7 (0.09)	9.8 (0.56)	8.1 (0.41)	10.4 (0.20)	8.9 (0.23)	8.4 (0.26)	4.8 (0.11)	5.6 (0.16)	3.8 (0.20)	1.6 (0.30)	2.9 (0.38)
$35,000 to $39,999	6.3 (0.08)	4.4 (0.39)	4.6 (0.31)	7.7 (0.17)	7.2 (0.21)	7.4 (0.26)	5.1 (0.12)	6.1 (0.16)	3.9 (0.20)	2.0 (0.33)	2.3 (0.34)
$40,000 to $49,999	11.4 (0.11)	5.3 (0.43)	8.4 (0.42)	11.2 (0.20)	12.0 (0.26)	14.0 (0.35)	11.5 (0.17)	12.3 (0.22)	11.1 (0.33)	6.9 (0.61)	8.3 (0.63)
$50,000 to $74,999	18.4 (0.13)	6.0 (0.45)	8.1 (0.41)	14.8 (0.23)	16.5 (0.30)	19.9 (0.40)	23.7 (0.23)	23.7 (0.29)	25.7 (0.45)	16.1 (0.88)	20.3 (0.92)
$75,000 to $99,999	8.3 (0.09)	1.4 (0.23)	2.3 (0.22)	5.0 (0.14)	6.2 (0.20)	7.5 (0.26)	13.2 (0.18)	12.3 (0.22)	15.4 (0.37)	10.9 (0.74)	14.5 (0.81)
$100,000 or more	10.7 (0.10)	1.9 (0.26)	2.0 (0.21)	3.3 (0.12)	5.7 (0.19)	5.8 (0.23)	21.3 (0.22)	17.0 (0.26)	22.5 (0.43)	50.2 (1.19)	38.4 (1.12)
Median annual earnings[1]	$38,430 (343)	$20,940 (207)	$21,860 (223)	$30,730 (138)	$32,330 (162)	$37,320 (322)	$56,470 (283)	$51,310 (185)	$61,390 (352)	$100,070 (5,533)	$77,750 (2,772)
Number of males											
(in thousands)	101,887 (143.3)	4,911 (84.7)	7,278 (102.1)	30,997 (186.6)	16,772 (148.1)	9,006 (112.6)	32,923 (190.1)	20,696 (161.3)	8,157 (107.6)	1,965 (54.3)	2,105 (56.2)
With earnings	73,743 (204.5)	2,761 (64.1)	4,338 (79.8)	20,972 (162.1)	12,106 (128.7)	7,040 (100.5)	26,526 (177.0)	16,681 (147.8)	6,533 (97.0)	1,628 (49.5)	1,685 (50.3)
For males with earnings											
Percentage distribution, by total annual earnings[1]	100.0 (†)	100.0 (†)	100.0 (†)	100.0 (†)	100.0 (†)	100.0 (†)	100.0 (†)	100.0 (†)	100.0 (†)	100.0 (†)	100.0 (†)
$1 to $4,999 or loss[2]	3.3 (0.08)	4.0 (0.46)	6.0 (0.45)	3.7 (0.16)	3.6 (0.21)	3.4 (0.27)	2.3 (0.11)	2.4 (0.15)	1.9 (0.21)	2.1 (0.44)	2.6 (0.47)
$5,000 to $9,999	3.2 (0.08)	5.4 (0.53)	6.3 (0.46)	3.6 (0.16)	4.0 (0.22)	2.8 (0.24)	1.8 (0.10)	1.9 (0.13)	1.5 (0.19)	1.8 (0.41)	2.0 (0.42)
$10,000 to $14,999	4.7 (0.10)	10.5 (0.72)	9.8 (0.56)	5.6 (0.20)	5.3 (0.25)	4.2 (0.30)	2.4 (0.12)	2.5 (0.15)	2.5 (0.24)	0.9! (0.29)	1.5 (0.37)
$15,000 to $19,999	5.4 (0.10)	15.9 (0.86)	11.0 (0.59)	6.6 (0.21)	6.0 (0.27)	3.8 (0.28)	2.6 (0.12)	2.9 (0.16)	1.8 (0.20)	2.2 (0.45)	2.7 (0.49)
$20,000 to $24,999	6.7 (0.11)	16.2 (0.87)	13.8 (0.65)	8.4 (0.24)	7.3 (0.29)	6.0 (0.35)	3.1 (0.13)	3.5 (0.18)	3.0 (0.26)	1.9 (0.42)	1.8 (0.40)
$25,000 to $29,999	6.3 (0.11)	10.6 (0.73)	10.3 (0.57)	9.0 (0.24)	6.7 (0.28)	5.4 (0.33)	3.1 (0.13)	3.8 (0.18)	2.0 (0.21)	1.3 (0.35)	1.5 (0.36)
$30,000 to $34,999	7.1 (0.12)	12.5 (0.78)	9.5 (0.55)	10.0 (0.26)	7.9 (0.30)	6.8 (0.37)	3.7 (0.14)	4.4 (0.20)	2.8 (0.25)	1.5 (0.38)	1.7 (0.38)
$35,000 to $39,999	6.3 (0.11)	5.2 (0.52)	5.8 (0.44)	8.2 (0.23)	7.5 (0.30)	7.5 (0.39)	4.1 (0.15)	5.0 (0.21)	3.0 (0.26)	1.0 (0.31)	1.7 (0.38)
$40,000 to $49,999	11.3 (0.14)	7.0 (0.60)	10.9 (0.58)	13.2 (0.29)	12.8 (0.37)	14.3 (0.52)	8.8 (0.22)	10.1 (0.29)	7.1 (0.39)	4.7 (0.65)	7.1 (0.77)
$50,000 to $74,999	20.5 (0.18)	8.6 (0.66)	10.7 (0.58)	19.8 (0.34)	21.0 (0.46)	25.2 (0.64)	22.5 (0.32)	23.9 (0.41)	22.1 (0.63)	14.9 (1.09)	17.8 (1.15)
$75,000 to $99,999	10.2 (0.14)	1.9 (0.32)	3.3 (0.33)	7.2 (0.22)	9.1 (0.32)	10.8 (0.46)	15.0 (0.27)	14.5 (0.34)	17.3 (0.58)	11.1 (0.96)	13.6 (1.03)
$100,000 or more	15.0 (0.16)	2.4 (0.36)	2.5 (0.29)	4.7 (0.18)	8.8 (0.32)	9.7 (0.44)	30.7 (0.35)	25.0 (0.41)	35.0 (0.73)	56.5 (1.52)	46.1 (1.50)
Median annual earnings[1]	$45,390 (205)	$23,880 (786)	$25,970 (385)	$36,290 (228)	$40,730 (274)	$46,410 (449)	$69,400 (1,051)	$61,730 (269)	$76,690 (702)	$106,450 (5,279)	$90,910 (2,388)

See notes at end of table.

Table 502.40. Annual earnings of persons 25 years old and over, by highest level of educational attainment and sex: 2014—Continued

[Standard errors appear in parentheses]

Sex and earnings	Total	Elementary/secondary — Less than 9th grade	Some high school, no completion	High school completion (includes equivalency)	Some college, no degree	Associate's degree	College — Total	Bachelor's degree	Master's degree	Professional degree	Doctor's degree
1	2	3	4	5	6	7	8	9	10	11	12
Number of females (in thousands)	**110,245** (149.6)	**4,985** (85.5)	**7,408** (103.2)	**31,578** (190.3)	**18,391** (154.9)	**11,861** (128.1)	**36,021** (198.5)	**22,804** (169.0)	**10,314** (120.3)	**1,400** (46.0)	**1,504** (47.6)
With earnings	65,023 (220.2)	1,488 (47.4)	2,508 (61.3)	15,415 (143.8)	11,263 (125.2)	8,163 (108.0)	26,186 (178.1)	16,248 (147.1)	7,668 (104.9)	1,052 (39.9)	1,218 (42.9)
For females with earnings											
Percentage distribution, by total annual earnings[1]	100.0 (†)	100.0 (†)	100.0 (†)	100.0 (†)	100.0 (†)	100.0 (†)	100.0 (†)	100.0 (†)	100.0 (†)	100.0 (†)	100.0 (†)
$1 to $4,999 or loss[2]	6.3 (0.12)	11.8 (1.03)	11.8 (0.80)	7.0 (0.25)	7.7 (0.31)	6.6 (0.34)	4.3 (0.16)	4.7 (0.20)	4.0 (0.28)	3.2 (0.67)	2.5 (0.55)
$5,000 to $9,999	6.1 (0.12)	12.5 (1.06)	13.6 (0.84)	8.0 (0.27)	7.0 (0.30)	5.2 (0.30)	3.7 (0.14)	3.9 (0.19)	3.6 (0.26)	2.9 (0.63)	3.2 (0.62)
$10,000 to $14,999	8.0 (0.13)	21.6 (1.32)	18.4 (0.96)	11.0 (0.31)	8.9 (0.33)	7.2 (0.35)	4.3 (0.16)	5.0 (0.21)	3.5 (0.26)	2.8 (0.62)	2.6 (0.57)
$15,000 to $19,999	7.7 (0.13)	17.5 (1.22)	16.1 (0.91)	11.2 (0.31)	8.7 (0.33)	7.9 (0.37)	3.7 (0.14)	4.3 (0.20)	2.8 (0.23)	2.1 (0.54)	1.8 (0.47)
$20,000 to $24,999	9.8 (0.14)	16.6 (1.19)	14.3 (0.86)	14.0 (0.35)	12.3 (0.38)	10.4 (0.42)	5.1 (0.17)	5.9 (0.23)	4.3 (0.29)	2.2 (0.56)	3.0 (0.61)
$25,000 to $29,999	7.8 (0.13)	7.0 (0.82)	8.1 (0.67)	10.8 (0.31)	10.4 (0.35)	9.3 (0.40)	4.6 (0.16)	5.3 (0.22)	3.7 (0.26)	2.8 (0.62)	1.8 (0.47)
$30,000 to $34,999	8.2 (0.13)	4.8 (0.69)	5.7 (0.57)	10.9 (0.31)	10.0 (0.35)	9.8 (0.41)	5.9 (0.18)	6.9 (0.25)	4.6 (0.30)	1.7 (0.49)	4.5 (0.73)
$35,000 to $39,999	6.4 (0.12)	3.0 (0.54)	2.7 (0.40)	7.1 (0.26)	7.0 (0.30)	7.3 (0.36)	6.0 (0.18)	7.1 (0.25)	4.6 (0.30)	3.4 (0.69)	3.2 (0.62)
$40,000 to $49,999	11.6 (0.16)	2.4 (0.49)	4.2 (0.50)	8.5 (0.28)	11.1 (0.37)	13.7 (0.47)	14.2 (0.27)	14.6 (0.34)	14.5 (0.50)	10.3 (1.16)	9.9 (1.06)
$50,000 to $74,999	16.0 (0.18)	1.2 (0.35)	3.5 (0.45)	8.1 (0.27)	11.6 (0.37)	15.3 (0.49)	24.8 (0.33)	23.5 (0.41)	28.7 (0.64)	17.9 (1.46)	23.8 (1.51)
$75,000 to $99,999	6.2 (0.12)	0.5 ! (0.23)	0.6 ! (0.18)	1.9 (0.14)	3.1 (0.20)	4.7 (0.29)	11.4 (0.24)	10.0 (0.29)	13.8 (0.49)	10.6 (1.17)	15.7 (1.29)
$100,000 or more	5.9 (0.11)	0.9 ! (0.31)	1.0 (0.25)	1.4 (0.12)	2.4 (0.18)	2.5 (0.21)	11.8 (0.25)	8.7 (0.27)	11.8 (0.46)	40.3 (1.87)	27.9 (1.59)
Median annual earnings[1]	$31,680 (124)	$15,960 (377)	$16,630 (341)	$24,300 (350)	$27,090 (273)	$31,020 (231)	$47,690 (527)	$42,440 (458)	$51,920 (372)	$75,960 (5,396)	$66,650 (2,560)

†Not applicable.
!Interpret data with caution. The coefficient of variation (CV) for this estimate is between 30 and 50 percent.
[1]Excludes persons without earnings.
[2]A negative amount (a net loss) may be reported by self-employed persons.

NOTE: Detail may not sum to totals because of rounding.
SOURCE: U.S. Department of Commerce, Census Bureau, Current Population Survey (CPS), Annual Social and Economic Supplement, 2015; retrieved April 15, 2016, from http://www.census.gov/hhes/www/cpstables/032015/perinc/pinc03_000.htm. (This table was prepared April 2016.)

Table 503.10. Percentage of high school students age 16 and over who were employed, by age group, sex, race/ethnicity, family income, nativity, and hours worked per week: Selected years, 1970 through 2014

[Standard errors appear in parentheses]

Year	Total	Age group		Sex		Race/ethnicity			Family income[1]			Nativity	
		16 and 17 years old	18 years old and over	Male	Female	White	Black	Hispanic	Low income	Middle income	High income	U.S.-born	Foreign-born
1	2	3	4	5	6	7	8	9	10	11	12	13	14

Percent employed[2]

Year	Total	16–17	18+	Male	Female	White	Black	Hispanic	Low income	Middle income	High income	U.S.-born	Foreign-born
1970	31.9 (0.88)	30.8 (0.93)	39.7 (2.55)	35.2 (1.24)	28.3 (1.22)	— (†)	— (†)	— (†)	22.0 (2.51)	31.5 (1.12)	35.9 (1.64)	— (†)	— (†)
1975	33.2 (0.85)	32.9 (0.91)	34.9 (2.40)	35.0 (1.19)	31.2 (1.22)	38.0 (1.00)	13.9 (1.63)	21.8 (3.59)	18.4 (2.22)	31.8 (1.10)	40.4 (1.59)	— (†)	— (†)
1980	35.6 (0.87)	34.9 (0.94)	39.6 (2.28)	36.9 (1.22)	34.2 (1.24)	41.2 (1.03)	15.0 (1.64)	24.1 (3.65)	19.4 (2.10)	35.2 (1.15)	42.3 (1.59)	— (†)	— (†)
1985	31.6 (0.93)	30.8 (1.00)	36.1 (2.47)	32.1 (1.29)	31.0 (1.33)	37.9 (1.15)	15.0 (1.85)	17.6 (2.63)	14.7 (1.85)	31.0 (1.23)	41.1 (1.81)	— (†)	— (†)
1990	32.3 (0.98)	31.2 (1.08)	37.1 (2.33)	33.1 (1.37)	31.3 (1.39)	37.8 (1.24)	17.3 (2.05)	26.4 (2.86)	21.4 (2.16)	33.1 (1.29)	36.8 (1.97)	— (†)	— (†)
1995	33.6 (0.92)	32.7 (1.02)	37.5 (2.19)	33.1 (1.26)	34.2 (1.35)	40.8 (1.18)	18.0 (1.91)	22.2 (2.41)	17.4 (1.82)	34.4 (1.23)	42.1 (1.88)	34.9 (0.97)	20.1 (2.65)
2000	34.1 (0.93)	33.3 (1.03)	37.7 (2.15)	33.2 (1.28)	35.1 (1.36)	41.3 (1.20)	21.3 (2.14)	20.9 (2.18)	22.0 (2.11)	34.1 (1.22)	40.7 (1.85)	35.1 (0.99)	24.4 (2.74)
2001	32.4 (0.86)	31.1 (0.95)	37.8 (1.99)	30.6 (1.17)	34.5 (1.27)	38.9 (1.11)	18.7 (1.85)	23.6 (2.23)	21.4 (2.04)	33.3 (1.12)	36.1 (1.70)	33.3 (0.90)	23.0 (2.64)
2002	30.6 (0.84)	29.2 (0.93)	35.9 (1.92)	28.0 (1.13)	33.4 (1.24)	37.5 (1.11)	16.9 (1.81)	21.1 (1.94)	18.4 (1.83)	31.4 (1.11)	35.3 (1.64)	31.6 (0.89)	21.3 (2.34)
2003	27.0 (0.79)	25.3 (0.86)	34.6 (1.97)	26.7 (1.09)	27.3 (1.15)	33.3 (1.07)	15.2 (1.68)	18.8 (1.82)	14.3 (1.64)	27.8 (1.05)	31.8 (1.57)	28.0 (0.84)	17.7 (2.17)
2004	27.2 (0.80)	25.6 (0.87)	34.7 (2.03)	26.2 (1.09)	28.3 (1.17)	32.9 (1.08)	15.1 (1.71)	21.2 (1.92)	12.0 (1.55)	27.5 (1.05)	34.4 (1.64)	27.8 (0.85)	20.8 (2.43)
2005	26.4 (0.77)	25.2 (0.84)	32.2 (1.95)	25.3 (1.05)	27.6 (1.14)	31.8 (1.05)	13.7 (1.63)	19.4 (1.78)	14.8 (1.61)	26.9 (1.03)	31.7 (1.55)	26.8 (0.81)	21.7 (2.49)
2006	27.6 (0.79)	26.0 (0.86)	34.1 (1.87)	26.5 (1.08)	28.8 (1.16)	33.6 (1.08)	20.1 (1.85)	17.5 (1.72)	17.8 (1.72)	27.5 (1.04)	33.5 (1.59)	27.9 (0.82)	23.9 (2.64)
2007	26.2 (0.78)	24.8 (0.85)	32.2 (1.87)	25.0 (1.06)	27.6 (1.14)	31.3 (1.06)	15.1 (1.68)	21.1 (1.83)	17.3 (1.74)	25.9 (1.01)	32.1 (1.62)	26.0 (0.81)	28.5 (2.64)
2008	22.6 (0.74)	21.0 (0.80)	29.5 (1.83)	20.0 (0.99)	25.4 (1.10)	27.7 (1.04)	15.5 (1.69)	15.1 (1.54)	13.5 (1.54)	22.6 (0.96)	28.4 (1.59)	23.1 (0.78)	18.0 (2.35)
2009	17.0 (0.67)	15.2 (0.72)	23.8 (1.65)	16.0 (0.91)	18.1 (0.98)	21.5 (0.96)	10.5 (1.43)	11.9 (1.39)	9.7 (1.33)	16.3 (0.85)	23.5 (1.51)	17.0 (0.70)	16.9 (2.32)
2010[3]	16.2 (0.55)	15.0 (0.59)	20.8 (1.52)	14.0 (0.78)	18.5 (0.86)	20.9 (0.86)	9.6 (1.28)	10.4 (1.18)	8.5 (1.01)	16.5 (0.80)	20.9 (1.31)	16.4 (0.60)	13.4 (2.20)
2011[3]	16.9 (0.67)	16.4 (0.77)	18.7 (1.28)	14.7 (0.76)	19.4 (1.09)	22.2 (1.07)	10.2 (1.43)	11.3 (1.11)	10.2 (1.29)	17.5 (0.83)	19.6 (1.39)	17.3 (0.74)	12.4 (1.91)
2012[3]	18.0 (0.71)	16.0 (0.75)	24.5 (1.88)	16.6 (0.83)	19.4 (1.13)	23.2 (0.99)	12.7 (2.17)	11.4 (1.23)	13.0 (1.42)	16.4 (0.88)	24.9 (1.55)	18.6 (0.76)	12.0 (2.01)
2013[3]	17.9 (0.65)	15.8 (0.69)	24.7 (1.73)	17.6 (0.89)	18.3 (0.94)	23.3 (0.99)	11.8 (1.42)	14.0 (1.19)	9.7 (1.26)	16.9 (0.90)	25.4 (1.69)	17.8 (0.66)	19.0 (2.67)
2014[3]	19.2 (0.70)	17.3 (0.71)	25.5 (1.63)	18.1 (0.90)	20.3 (1.03)	23.2 (1.00)	14.0 (1.65)	14.7 (1.47)	12.6 (1.52)	19.3 (0.88)	23.2 (1.54)	19.2 (0.75)	18.8 (2.20)

Percent working less than 15 hours per week[4]

Year	Total	16–17	18+	Male	Female	White	Black	Hispanic	Low income	Middle income	High income	U.S.-born	Foreign-born
1970	13.6 (0.64)	14.5 (0.71)	7.5 (1.37)	12.3 (0.85)	14.9 (0.97)	— (†)	— (†)	— (†)	9.9 (1.81)	12.6 (0.80)	16.8 (1.28)	— (†)	— (†)
1975	13.4 (0.62)	14.9 (0.67)	8.8 (1.43)	12.5 (0.82)	14.3 (0.92)	15.5 (0.75)	5.3 (1.05)	6.6 ! (2.15)	6.8 (1.44)	12.3 (0.78)	17.4 (1.23)	— (†)	— (†)
1980	14.0 (0.63)	14.9 (0.70)	8.9 (1.33)	13.7 (0.87)	14.2 (0.91)	16.4 (0.77)	4.6 (0.96)	9.4 (2.49)	7.7 (1.41)	13.2 (0.82)	17.7 (1.23)	— (†)	— (†)
1985	12.3 (0.65)	12.8 (0.72)	9.5 (1.51)	11.7 (0.89)	12.9 (0.96)	15.2 (0.85)	6.2 (1.25)	3.0 ! (1.18)	3.6 (0.97)	11.8 (0.86)	17.5 (1.40)	— (†)	— (†)
1990	11.7 (0.67)	12.3 (0.78)	6.8 (1.21)	11.3 (0.92)	12.2 (0.98)	14.7 (0.90)	6.0 (1.28)	4.8 (1.39)	5.9 (1.24)	11.5 (0.88)	15.6 (1.48)	— (†)	— (†)
1995	11.9 (0.63)	13.1 (0.73)	6.8 (1.14)	11.1 (0.84)	12.9 (0.96)	14.8 (0.85)	6.5 (1.22)	6.5 (1.42)	4.4 (0.98)	11.3 (0.82)	18.1 (1.47)	12.6 (0.68)	5.1 (1.46)
2000	11.9 (0.64)	12.9 (0.73)	7.8 (1.19)	11.2 (0.86)	12.6 (0.94)	15.4 (0.88)	6.3 (1.27)	3.7 (1.01)	5.4 (1.15)	11.3 (0.82)	16.5 (1.40)	12.6 (0.68)	5.2 (1.42)
2001	11.6 (0.59)	12.6 (0.68)	7.7 (1.10)	9.8 (0.75)	13.7 (0.91)	15.0 (0.82)	4.3 (0.96)	6.1 (1.26)	5.7 (1.15)	10.8 (0.74)	16.4 (1.31)	12.2 (0.63)	5.5 (1.43)
2002	11.1 (0.57)	12.1 (0.66)	7.2 (1.04)	9.7 (0.74)	12.7 (0.87)	15.0 (0.82)	4.5 (1.00)	3.6 (0.89)	6.0 (1.12)	10.0 (0.72)	16.1 (1.26)	11.9 (0.62)	4.1 (1.13)
2003	9.6 (0.52)	10.0 (0.59)	7.8 (1.11)	9.0 (0.70)	10.2 (0.82)	12.4 (0.77)	4.5 (0.96)	5.5 (1.06)	4.8 (1.00)	9.1 (0.67)	13.1 (1.14)	10.2 (0.59)	3.7 (1.07)
2004	10.4 (0.55)	10.9 (0.62)	8.4 (1.18)	9.9 (0.74)	11.0 (0.82)	14.0 (0.80)	4.9 (1.03)	4.4 (0.96)	3.5 (0.87)	8.5 (0.66)	18.1 (1.33)	11.0 (0.59)	5.2 (1.33)
2005	10.1 (0.53)	10.7 (0.60)	7.2 (1.08)	8.9 (0.69)	11.4 (0.81)	13.4 (0.77)	3.7 (0.89)	5.0 (0.99)	3.7 (0.85)	9.9 (0.69)	13.9 (1.16)	10.6 (0.56)	4.6 (1.26)
2006	9.9 (0.53)	10.7 (0.61)	6.4 (0.97)	8.8 (0.69)	11.0 (0.80)	12.8 (0.76)	5.2 (1.03)	4.2 (0.91)	3.7 (0.85)	9.2 (0.67)	14.7 (1.20)	10.5 (0.58)	3.0 ! (1.06)
2007	10.6 (0.54)	11.4 (0.63)	7.0 (1.02)	9.5 (0.72)	11.7 (0.82)	14.2 (0.80)	3.0 (0.80)	6.0 (1.06)	6.1 (1.10)	9.6 (0.68)	15.3 (1.25)	11.1 (0.58)	5.7 (1.36)
2008	9.2 (0.51)	9.9 (0.59)	6.1 (0.96)	8.1 (0.68)	10.3 (0.77)	12.4 (0.77)	3.2 (0.82)	4.1 (0.85)	3.1 (0.78)	9.1 (0.66)	13.0 (1.18)	9.6 (0.54)	4.6 (1.28)
2009	7.6 (0.47)	8.0 (0.54)	6.2 (0.94)	6.8 (0.62)	8.4 (0.71)	10.1 (0.71)	3.6 (0.86)	4.7 (0.91)	3.6 (0.83)	6.9 (0.58)	11.8 (1.15)	7.8 (0.50)	5.2 (1.38)
2010[3]	7.3 (0.42)	7.5 (0.49)	6.8 (0.94)	6.3 (0.50)	8.4 (0.69)	9.5 (0.65)	4.1 (0.82)	4.5 (0.79)	3.0 (0.63)	7.1 (0.54)	10.9 (1.01)	7.7 (0.45)	3.4 ! (1.21)
2011[3]	7.3 (0.40)	8.1 (0.50)	4.4 (0.71)	5.8 (0.51)	9.0 (0.66)	11.0 (0.66)	2.2 (0.60)	2.7 (0.54)	3.7 (0.81)	7.0 (0.55)	10.2 (0.94)	7.7 (0.44)	2.8 ! (0.98)
2012[3]	8.2 (0.46)	8.5 (0.53)	7.3 (0.95)	7.1 (0.57)	9.4 (0.73)	12.2 (0.73)	3.7 (0.92)	2.4 (0.58)	4.2 (0.89)	7.2 (0.53)	13.3 (1.27)	8.8 (0.50)	2.4 ! (0.75)
2013[3]	7.9 (0.50)	8.2 (0.54)	6.8 (0.99)	6.9 (0.61)	8.9 (0.77)	12.2 (0.81)	2.6 (0.71)	3.4 (0.62)	2.9 (0.78)	7.0 (0.54)	13.1 (1.38)	8.1 (0.50)	5.5 ! (1.75)
2014[3]	7.8 (0.43)	8.4 (0.49)	5.7 (0.85)	6.5 (0.54)	9.1 (0.67)	10.7 (0.67)	3.5 (0.91)	3.5 (0.65)	3.8 (0.90)	7.6 (0.57)	10.9 (1.04)	8.2 (0.46)	3.7 ! (1.14)

Percent working 15 or more hours per week[4]

Year	Total	16–17	18+	Male	Female	White	Black	Hispanic	Low income	Middle income	High income	U.S.-born	Foreign-born
1970	17.5 (0.71)	15.6 (0.73)	30.8 (2.41)	22.1 (1.08)	12.6 (0.90)	— (†)	— (†)	— (†)	10.6 (1.87)	18.4 (0.93)	18.1 (1.32)	— (†)	— (†)
1975	19.2 (0.71)	18.2 (0.75)	25.7 (2.20)	21.7 (1.03)	16.4 (0.97)	21.8 (0.85)	8.3 (1.30)	14.7 (3.08)	11.3 (1.81)	19.0 (0.93)	22.1 (1.34)	— (†)	— (†)
1980	20.5 (0.73)	19.0 (0.77)	29.4 (2.12)	22.1 (1.05)	18.9 (1.02)	23.5 (0.89)	10.1 (1.39)	14.3 (2.99)	11.4 (1.69)	21.3 (0.98)	23.1 (1.36)	— (†)	— (†)
1985	18.4 (0.77)	17.2 (0.81)	25.5 (2.24)	19.5 (1.09)	17.3 (1.09)	21.7 (0.97)	8.4 (1.44)	13.7 (2.37)	10.0 (1.57)	18.4 (1.03)	22.6 (1.54)	— (†)	— (†)
1990	19.7 (0.83)	17.5 (0.88)	29.1 (2.19)	21.0 (1.19)	18.3 (1.16)	22.1 (1.06)	10.6 (1.67)	21.5 (2.66)	15.0 (1.88)	20.8 (1.11)	20.2 (1.64)	— (†)	— (†)
1995	20.5 (0.79)	18.4 (0.84)	29.7 (2.07)	20.8 (1.09)	20.2 (1.14)	24.5 (1.03)	10.9 (1.55)	15.1 (2.07)	12.7 (1.60)	21.9 (1.07)	22.5 (1.59)	21.1 (0.83)	14.9 (2.35)

See notes at end of table.

Table 503.10. Percentage of high school students age 16 and over who were employed, by age group, sex, race/ethnicity, family income, nativity, and hours worked per week: Selected years, 1970 through 2014—Continued

[Standard errors appear in parentheses]

Year	Total	Age group		Sex		Race/ethnicity			Family income[1]			Nativity	
		16 and 17 years old	18 years old and over	Male	Female	White	Black	Hispanic	Low income	Middle income	High income	U.S.-born	Foreign-born
1	2	3	4	5	6	7	8	9	10	11	12	13	14
2000	21.1 (0.80)	19.2 (0.86)	28.8 (2.01)	21.1 (1.11)	21.0 (1.16)	24.6 (1.05)	13.8 (1.80)	16.3 (1.98)	15.6 (1.85)	21.5 (1.06)	23.1 (1.59)	21.3 (0.84)	19.0 (2.50)
2001	19.4 (0.73)	17.1 (0.77)	28.3 (1.85)	19.6 (1.01)	19.1 (1.05)	22.2 (0.95)	13.4 (1.62)	17.0 (1.97)	14.6 (1.76)	20.9 (0.97)	18.4 (1.37)	19.6 (0.76)	16.9 (2.35)
2002	18.5 (0.71)	16.1 (0.75)	27.9 (1.80)	17.5 (0.95)	19.7 (1.04)	21.4 (0.94)	11.9 (1.57)	16.8 (1.78)	12.3 (1.55)	20.7 (0.97)	17.4 (1.30)	18.7 (0.75)	16.5 (2.12)
2003	16.4 (0.66)	14.3 (0.69)	25.9 (1.82)	16.8 (0.92)	16.0 (0.94)	19.5 (0.90)	10.4 (1.42)	13.1 (1.57)	9.1 (1.35)	17.6 (0.89)	17.7 (1.29)	16.7 (0.70)	13.6 (1.95)
2004	16.0 (0.66)	13.8 (0.68)	26.2 (1.88)	15.5 (0.90)	16.6 (0.97)	17.8 (0.88)	10.2 (1.45)	16.6 (1.75)	8.1 (1.30)	18.3 (0.91)	15.2 (1.24)	16.1 (0.69)	15.2 (2.15)
2005	15.2 (0.63)	13.4 (0.66)	23.5 (1.77)	15.5 (0.88)	14.8 (0.90)	17.0 (0.84)	9.6 (1.40)	13.6 (1.55)	10.8 (1.40)	15.9 (0.85)	16.1 (1.23)	15.1 (0.66)	16.5 (2.24)
2006	17.0 (0.66)	14.4 (0.69)	27.0 (1.75)	16.8 (0.91)	17.1 (0.96)	19.5 (0.90)	14.5 (1.63)	13.3 (1.54)	13.8 (1.55)	17.7 (0.89)	17.3 (1.27)	16.6 (0.68)	20.8 (2.51)
2007	15.0 (0.63)	12.8 (0.66)	24.2 (1.72)	14.8 (0.87)	15.2 (0.92)	16.2 (0.85)	11.4 (1.49)	14.9 (1.59)	10.9 (1.44)	15.6 (0.83)	15.8 (1.27)	14.3 (0.65)	22.2 (2.43)
2008	12.8 (0.59)	10.3 (0.60)	22.7 (1.68)	11.4 (0.79)	14.1 (0.88)	14.3 (0.82)	11.9 (1.51)	10.6 (1.32)	9.9 (1.34)	12.8 (0.77)	14.4 (1.23)	12.7 (0.62)	13.0 (2.06)
2009	8.7 (0.50)	6.4 (0.49)	17.3 (1.47)	8.4 (0.69)	9.1 (0.73)	10.4 (0.71)	6.5 (1.15)	7.2 (1.11)	5.9 (1.06)	8.9 (0.66)	9.9 (1.07)	8.4 (0.52)	11.7 (1.99)
2010[3]	8.3 (0.45)	6.9 (0.47)	13.4 (1.24)	7.2 (0.62)	9.4 (0.70)	10.5 (0.67)	5.3 (1.01)	5.6 (0.84)	5.3 (0.88)	9.0 (0.58)	8.7 (1.16)	8.1 (0.46)	9.6 (1.83)
2011[3]	9.0 (0.52)	7.7 (0.56)	13.6 (1.10)	8.4 (0.63)	9.8 (0.78)	10.5 (0.77)	7.4 (1.30)	8.4 (1.06)	6.3 (1.10)	10.0 (0.69)	8.5 (0.94)	9.0 (0.55)	9.6 (1.84)
2012[3]	8.9 (0.55)	6.7 (0.51)	16.5 (1.62)	8.4 (0.62)	9.5 (0.84)	10.0 (0.69)	8.2 (1.97)	8.4 (1.04)	8.3 (1.22)	8.7 (0.68)	9.9 (1.30)	8.9 (0.59)	9.6 (1.76)
2013[3]	9.7 (0.56)	7.3 (0.53)	17.4 (1.57)	10.3 (0.85)	9.1 (0.67)	10.6 (0.81)	9.1 (1.37)	10.6 (1.10)	6.7 (1.19)	9.7 (0.82)	11.7 (1.12)	9.4 (0.60)	13.4 (2.15)
2014[3]	10.7 (0.55)	8.2 (0.48)	19.3 (1.49)	10.8 (0.72)	10.6 (0.81)	11.6 (0.75)	9.4 (1.52)	11.0 (1.30)	8.6 (1.34)	11.1 (0.73)	11.1 (1.25)	10.2 (0.56)	15.1 (2.12)

—Not available.
†Not applicable.
‡Interpret data with caution. The coefficient of variation (CV) for this estimate is between 30 and 50 percent.
[1]Low income refers to the bottom 20 percent of all family incomes; high income refers to the top 20 percent of all family incomes; and middle income refers to the 60 percent in between.
[2]Percent employed includes those who were employed but not at work during the survey week.
[3]Beginning in 2010, standard errors were computed using replicate weights, which produced more precise values than the generalized variance function methodology used in prior years.

[4]Hours worked per week refers to the number of hours the respondent worked at all jobs during the survey week. The estimates of the percentage of high school students age 16 and over who worked less than 15 hours per week or 15 or more hours per week exclude those who were employed but not at work during the survey week. Therefore, detail may not sum to total percentage employed.
NOTE: Race categories exclude persons of Hispanic ethnicity. Totals include racial/ethnic groups not shown separately.
SOURCE: U.S. Department of Commerce, Census Bureau, Current Population Survey (CPS), October, 1970 through 2014. (This table was prepared November 2015.)

Table 503.20. Percentage of college students 16 to 24 years old who were employed, by attendance status, hours worked per week, and control and level of institution: Selected years, October 1970 through 2014

[Standard errors appear in parentheses]

Control and level of institution and year	Full-time students				Part-time students			
	Percent employed[1]	Hours worked per week[2]			Percent employed[1]	Hours worked per week[2]		
		Less than 20 hours	20 to 34 hours	35 or more hours		Less than 20 hours	20 to 34 hours	35 or more hours
1	2	3	4	5	6	7	8	9
Total, all institutions								
1970	33.8 (0.88)	19.0 (0.73)	10.4 (0.57)	3.7 (0.35)	82.1 (1.81)	5.0 (1.03)	15.9 (1.72)	60.1 (2.31)
1975	35.3 (0.83)	18.0 (0.67)	12.0 (0.56)	4.6 (0.36)	80.8 (1.55)	6.0 (0.94)	19.4 (1.56)	52.6 (1.97)
1980	40.0 (0.84)	21.3 (0.70)	14.0 (0.59)	3.9 (0.33)	84.7 (1.38)	7.9 (1.04)	22.5 (1.60)	52.7 (1.91)
1985	44.2 (0.88)	21.7 (0.73)	17.3 (0.67)	4.3 (0.36)	85.9 (1.41)	5.7 (0.94)	26.9 (1.80)	52.2 (2.03)
1990	45.7 (0.89)	20.6 (0.73)	19.3 (0.71)	4.8 (0.38)	83.7 (1.50)	4.0 (0.80)	26.0 (1.78)	52.7 (2.03)
1991	47.2 (0.88)	20.9 (0.72)	19.8 (0.70)	5.6 (0.41)	85.9 (1.45)	8.2 (1.15)	25.4 (1.82)	51.0 (2.09)
1992	47.2 (0.87)	20.3 (0.70)	20.3 (0.70)	5.5 (0.40)	83.4 (1.50)	7.5 (1.06)	27.2 (1.79)	47.8 (2.01)
1993	46.3 (0.89)	20.8 (0.72)	19.5 (0.71)	5.1 (0.39)	84.6 (1.43)	8.5 (1.10)	31.4 (1.84)	43.7 (1.96)
1994	48.6 (0.87)	20.1 (0.70)	21.7 (0.72)	5.8 (0.41)	86.3 (1.28)	9.8 (1.10)	31.1 (1.72)	43.8 (1.84)
1995	47.2 (0.87)	19.1 (0.69)	20.3 (0.70)	6.5 (0.43)	82.9 (1.45)	8.6 (1.08)	30.4 (1.77)	42.3 (1.90)
1996	49.2 (0.88)	18.2 (0.68)	22.3 (0.74)	7.0 (0.45)	84.8 (1.47)	8.3 (1.13)	27.5 (1.83)	48.0 (2.05)
1997	47.8 (0.86)	18.3 (0.67)	21.4 (0.71)	7.4 (0.45)	84.4 (1.46)	9.4 (1.17)	26.2 (1.77)	47.7 (2.01)
1998	50.2 (0.86)	20.2 (0.69)	20.6 (0.70)	8.0 (0.47)	84.1 (1.45)	7.0 (1.01)	26.8 (1.76)	49.3 (1.98)
1999	50.4 (0.86)	19.0 (0.68)	22.3 (0.72)	7.8 (0.46)	82.3 (1.55)	6.2 (0.98)	28.8 (1.85)	45.9 (2.03)
2000	52.0 (0.86)	20.1 (0.69)	21.7 (0.71)	8.9 (0.49)	84.9 (1.38)	8.6 (1.08)	27.8 (1.73)	47.5 (1.93)
2001	47.1 (0.80)	17.4 (0.61)	20.6 (0.65)	7.9 (0.43)	84.4 (1.29)	8.0 (0.97)	25.8 (1.56)	48.9 (1.78)
2002	47.8 (0.78)	17.3 (0.59)	20.9 (0.64)	8.5 (0.44)	78.9 (1.51)	8.7 (1.04)	25.3 (1.61)	43.4 (1.84)
2003	47.7 (0.78)	17.1 (0.59)	20.7 (0.63)	8.8 (0.44)	79.0 (1.44)	7.8 (0.95)	27.2 (1.58)	42.8 (1.75)
2004	49.0 (0.76)	17.7 (0.58)	21.6 (0.62)	8.6 (0.43)	81.5 (1.44)	8.5 (1.04)	27.4 (1.66)	44.1 (1.84)
2005	49.1 (0.75)	17.8 (0.58)	21.1 (0.61)	9.0 (0.43)	85.0 (1.30)	10.2 (1.10)	27.1 (1.62)	47.1 (1.82)
2006	46.5 (0.76)	15.1 (0.55)	22.0 (0.63)	8.1 (0.42)	81.0 (1.41)	7.3 (0.94)	27.6 (1.61)	45.5 (1.80)
2007	45.5 (0.74)	15.4 (0.54)	20.7 (0.60)	8.7 (0.42)	81.2 (1.39)	6.8 (0.90)	27.2 (1.59)	45.9 (1.78)
2008	45.3 (0.72)	15.6 (0.53)	20.1 (0.58)	8.7 (0.41)	79.4 (1.51)	9.3 (1.09)	24.7 (1.61)	44.4 (1.86)
2009	40.6 (0.69)	15.6 (0.51)	17.6 (0.54)	6.2 (0.34)	76.2 (1.57)	10.1 (1.11)	27.5 (1.65)	36.9 (1.78)
2010[3]	39.8 (1.01)	14.9 (0.57)	17.2 (0.77)	6.6 (0.46)	73.4 (2.03)	10.7 (1.24)	28.3 (1.92)	32.8 (2.19)
2011[3]	41.3 (0.94)	15.8 (0.67)	17.4 (0.66)	7.0 (0.44)	75.5 (1.93)	9.7 (1.21)	28.4 (1.99)	35.5 (2.16)
2012[3]	41.0 (0.83)	15.1 (0.72)	17.8 (0.71)	7.2 (0.44)	71.7 (2.07)	9.0 (1.27)	29.5 (2.09)	32.1 (2.07)
2012[3]	39.5 (1.00)	14.0 (0.67)	18.5 (0.77)	6.6 (0.50)	75.7 (2.06)	10.5 (1.44)	28.7 (1.76)	35.4 (2.11)
2014[3]	41.3 (0.97)	15.6 (0.69)	17.9 (0.80)	6.6 (0.48)	80.3 (1.81)	13.8 (1.58)	26.9 (2.33)	38.5 (2.36)
Public 4-year institutions								
1990	43.0 (1.18)	19.8 (0.95)	18.6 (0.93)	3.7 (0.45)	87.4 (2.25)	4.2 ! (1.37)	27.9 (3.05)	54.7 (3.39)
1995	48.8 (1.16)	19.4 (0.92)	22.6 (0.97)	5.6 (0.53)	86.7 (2.08)	9.6 (1.80)	30.8 (2.83)	45.0 (3.05)
2000	50.5 (1.15)	19.1 (0.90)	21.5 (0.94)	9.0 (0.66)	87.3 (1.91)	8.5 (1.60)	26.4 (2.53)	50.9 (2.87)
2005	49.6 (0.99)	17.8 (0.76)	22.7 (0.83)	8.0 (0.54)	86.3 (1.90)	9.0 (1.58)	26.8 (2.45)	49.7 (2.76)
2008	44.1 (0.96)	15.1 (0.70)	19.2 (0.76)	8.8 (0.55)	83.9 (2.25)	9.3 (1.78)	24.7 (2.64)	49.5 (3.06)
2009	40.6 (0.91)	14.7 (0.66)	18.7 (0.73)	5.8 (0.44)	78.7 (2.45)	11.1 (1.88)	25.7 (2.61)	39.8 (2.92)
2010[3]	40.8 (1.27)	15.2 (0.88)	18.0 (0.93)	6.6 (0.64)	70.4 (3.58)	10.5 (2.04)	26.9 (2.82)	32.1 (3.59)
2011[3]	41.0 (1.20)	15.0 (0.91)	17.6 (0.85)	7.4 (0.63)	77.5 (3.27)	7.8 (1.65)	28.4 (3.18)	39.7 (3.29)
2012[3]	41.0 (1.13)	14.9 (0.95)	18.6 (0.99)	6.7 (0.57)	77.6 (3.20)	9.9 (2.41)	28.0 (3.44)	38.8 (3.36)
2013[3]	40.1 (1.31)	13.9 (0.88)	19.2 (0.98)	6.6 (0.63)	78.8 (2.88)	9.8 (1.94)	26.6 (2.80)	41.1 (3.84)
2014[3]	41.1 (1.31)	14.6 (0.91)	18.4 (0.99)	6.9 (0.69)	83.4 (2.86)	12.2 (2.61)	28.4 (3.69)	42.3 (3.81)
Private 4-year institutions								
1990	38.1 (1.89)	24.0 (1.66)	9.9 (1.17)	3.5 (0.72)	89.9 (4.27)	‡ (†)	31.9 (6.62)	53.1 (7.09)
1995	38.6 (1.78)	21.6 (1.51)	10.7 (1.13)	4.6 (0.77)	80.1 (4.85)	14.9 (4.32)	26.8 (5.38)	36.5 (5.84)
2000	45.8 (1.88)	23.6 (1.60)	14.9 (1.34)	5.4 (0.85)	78.0 (5.36)	‡ (†)	18.5 (5.02)	52.6 (6.46)
2005	42.3 (1.64)	20.1 (1.33)	13.8 (1.15)	7.0 (0.85)	88.5 (3.32)	10.6 ! (3.20)	34.5 (4.94)	43.2 (5.15)
2008	38.0 (1.68)	18.5 (1.35)	12.4 (1.14)	5.6 (0.80)	84.4 (4.44)	‡ (†)	21.4 (5.01)	55.3 (6.08)
2009	35.2 (1.64)	18.6 (1.33)	10.7 (1.06)	5.1 (0.76)	93.9 (2.89)	7.5 ! (3.17)	22.1 (5.00)	62.4 (5.84)
2010[3]	35.6 (2.37)	15.7 (1.63)	12.2 (1.52)	6.0 (1.08)	78.6 (7.00)	‡ (†)	23.4 ! (7.49)	45.6 (9.01)
2011[3]	36.3 (2.07)	20.0 (1.61)	10.1 (1.34)	4.5 (0.82)	79.4 (6.01)	‡ (†)	34.2 (7.03)	38.2 (7.67)
2012[3]	40.4 (2.39)	19.9 (1.80)	12.2 (1.40)	6.7 (1.13)	84.4 (5.35)	9.5 ! (4.53)	33.9 (6.58)	36.9 (7.38)
2013[3]	34.0 (2.27)	14.9 (1.55)	12.8 (1.33)	5.6 (1.13)	86.9 (4.71)	21.9 (6.40)	29.8 (7.01)	35.2 (6.56)
2014[3]	37.8 (2.29)	18.7 (1.72)	12.0 (1.62)	5.3 (1.00)	77.1 (6.82)	12.9 ! (4.92)	13.5 ! (5.59)	50.8 (8.76)
Public 2-year institutions								
1990	61.2 (1.94)	19.1 (1.57)	31.2 (1.85)	9.2 (1.15)	81.5 (2.17)	4.1 (1.12)	24.9 (2.42)	51.1 (2.80)
1995	52.9 (1.97)	15.6 (1.43)	25.3 (1.72)	10.9 (1.23)	81.1 (2.21)	6.1 (1.35)	32.5 (2.64)	40.5 (2.77)
2000	63.9 (1.79)	20.6 (1.51)	29.9 (1.71)	11.9 (1.21)	85.5 (2.09)	9.9 (1.77)	30.0 (2.72)	44.9 (2.95)
2005	54.2 (1.69)	15.6 (1.23)	24.2 (1.46)	13.4 (1.16)	82.0 (2.20)	10.8 (1.77)	25.8 (2.50)	44.8 (2.84)
2008	52.9 (1.43)	14.6 (1.01)	26.9 (1.27)	10.7 (0.89)	74.8 (2.29)	9.7 (1.56)	25.9 (2.31)	37.8 (2.56)
2009	45.4 (1.45)	16.0 (1.07)	20.5 (1.18)	7.8 (0.78)	71.8 (2.36)	10.3 (1.60)	30.6 (2.42)	29.4 (2.39)
2010[3]	40.6 (1.90)	14.0 (1.20)	19.1 (1.50)	6.8 (0.78)	74.7 (2.51)	11.6 (1.93)	30.1 (2.86)	31.0 (3.08)
2011[3]	45.6 (2.00)	14.7 (1.45)	22.1 (1.47)	8.1 (1.01)	73.6 (2.58)	11.3 (1.73)	27.5 (3.12)	32.4 (3.21)
2012[3]	41.2 (1.76)	12.0 (1.17)	19.8 (1.44)	8.4 (0.95)	66.1 (2.98)	8.3 (1.60)	30.0 (2.70)	26.9 (2.79)
2013[3]	41.8 (1.89)	13.8 (1.37)	20.5 (1.55)	7.1 (1.05)	71.1 (3.02)	8.8 (1.92)	29.8 (2.85)	31.2 (3.09)
2014[3]	45.0 (2.28)	15.9 (1.57)	21.3 (1.82)	6.9 (0.91)	77.5 (2.64)	15.2 (2.35)	28.3 (3.35)	32.4 (3.58)

†Not applicable.
!Interpret data with caution. The coefficient of variation (CV) for this estimate is between 30 and 50 percent.
‡Reporting standards not met. Either there are too few cases for a reliable estimate or the coefficient of variation (CV) is 50 percent or greater.
[1]Includes those who were employed but not at work during the survey week.
[2]Excludes those who were employed but not at work during the survey week; therefore, detail may not sum to total percentage employed. "Hours worked per week" refers to the number of hours worked at all jobs during the survey week.

[3]Beginning in 2010, standard errors were computed using replicate weights, which produced more precise values than the generalized variance function methodology used in prior years.
NOTE: Students were classified as full time if they were taking at least 12 hours of classes (or at least 9 hours of graduate classes) during an average school week and as part time if they were taking fewer hours.
SOURCE: U.S. Department of Commerce, Census Bureau, Current Population Survey (CPS), October, selected years, 1970 through 2014. (This table was prepared September 2015.)

Table 503.30. Percentage of college students 16 to 24 years old who were employed, by attendance status, hours worked per week, and selected characteristics: October 2012 through 2014

[Standard errors appear in parentheses]

Year and selected characteristic	Full-time students				Part-time students			
	Percent employed[1]	Hours worked per week[2]			Percent employed[1]	Hours worked per week[2]		
		Less than 20 hours	20 to 34 hours	35 or more hours		Less than 20 hours	20 to 34 hours	35 or more hours
1	2	3	4	5	6	7	8	9
2012								
Total	41.0 (0.83)	15.1 (0.72)	17.8 (0.71)	7.2 (0.44)	71.7 (2.07)	9.0 (1.27)	29.5 (2.09)	32.1 (2.07)
Sex								
Male..................................	39.1 (1.27)	13.0 (0.93)	17.0 (1.08)	7.9 (0.69)	74.0 (2.68)	7.9 (2.04)	30.9 (3.08)	35.1 (3.26)
Female	42.7 (1.19)	17.0 (0.98)	18.4 (0.98)	6.5 (0.57)	69.9 (2.61)	9.9 (1.72)	28.3 (2.60)	29.5 (2.46)
2013								
Total	39.5 (1.00)	14.0 (0.67)	18.5 (0.77)	6.6 (0.50)	75.7 (2.06)	10.5 (1.44)	28.7 (1.76)	35.4 (2.11)
Sex								
Male..................................	35.9 (1.36)	12.2 (0.94)	16.6 (1.05)	6.6 (0.78)	70.9 (3.16)	7.4 (1.95)	28.8 (2.84)	33.9 (2.98)
Female	42.7 (1.31)	15.6 (0.99)	20.2 (0.97)	6.6 (0.67)	79.4 (2.50)	12.9 (1.93)	28.6 (2.49)	36.5 (2.93)
Level and control of institution								
2-year...............................	42.0 (1.84)	13.6 (1.32)	20.7 (1.52)	7.3 (1.01)	71.3 (2.90)	9.0 (1.92)	30.0 (2.75)	31.0 (2.99)
Public...........................	41.8 (1.89)	13.8 (1.37)	20.5 (1.55)	7.1 (1.05)	71.1 (3.02)	8.8 (1.92)	29.8 (2.85)	31.2 (3.09)
Private..........................	45.1 (8.22)	10.1 ! (4.13)	24.5 (6.99)	10.5 ! (5.01)	‡ (†)	‡ (†)	‡ (†)	‡ (†)
4-year...............................	38.7 (1.15)	14.1 (0.76)	17.8 (0.87)	6.3 (0.53)	80.4 (2.59)	12.2 (2.03)	27.2 (2.45)	39.9 (3.29)
Public...........................	40.1 (1.31)	13.9 (0.88)	19.2 (0.98)	6.6 (0.63)	78.8 (2.88)	9.8 (1.94)	26.6 (2.80)	41.1 (3.84)
Private..........................	34.0 (2.27)	14.9 (1.55)	12.8 (1.33)	5.6 (1.13)	86.9 (4.71)	21.9 (6.40)	29.8 (7.01)	35.2 (6.56)
2014								
Total	41.3 (0.97)	15.6 (0.69)	17.9 (0.80)	6.6 (0.48)	80.3 (1.81)	13.8 (1.58)	26.9 (2.33)	38.5 (2.36)
Sex								
Male..................................	37.3 (1.40)	12.9 (0.98)	17.2 (1.13)	6.1 (0.63)	82.8 (2.83)	13.6 (2.35)	25.0 (3.20)	42.5 (3.15)
Female	44.9 (1.36)	18.0 (0.99)	18.6 (1.02)	7.1 (0.63)	78.4 (2.48)	14.0 (2.10)	28.4 (3.23)	35.5 (3.12)
Race/ethnicity								
White................................	46.1 (1.26)	18.2 (0.93)	19.4 (1.02)	7.2 (0.62)	85.9 (2.40)	15.3 (2.24)	28.9 (3.07)	40.6 (3.18)
Black.................................	32.2 (2.64)	8.4 (1.60)	14.9 (2.00)	6.7 (1.45)	69.2 (6.11)	11.5 ! (5.03)	26.1 (6.89)	31.6 (7.22)
Hispanic............................	41.5 (2.36)	14.5 (1.71)	19.4 (1.87)	6.9 (1.17)	76.6 (3.67)	9.1 (2.55)	27.0 (4.05)	38.9 (4.48)
Asian.................................	23.6 (2.71)	11.4 (2.00)	9.2 (2.06)	3.0 ! (1.09)	80.6 (6.88)	25.5 ! (7.87)	20.7 ! (7.52)	34.4 (8.68)
Pacific Islander.................	‡ (†)	‡ (†)	‡ (†)	‡ (†)	‡ (†)	‡ (†)	‡ (†)	‡ (†)
American Indian/Alaska Native..........	15.0 ! (6.42)	‡ (†)	‡ (†)	‡ (†)	‡ (†)	‡ (†)	‡ (†)	‡ (†)
Two or more races	40.1 (5.79)	14.1 ! (4.45)	21.5 (5.10)	‡ (†)	‡ (†)	‡ (†)	‡ (†)	‡ (†)
Level and control of institution								
2-year...............................	44.5 (2.15)	15.7 (1.42)	21.0 (1.72)	7.0 (0.89)	78.5 (2.57)	15.2 (2.33)	27.8 (3.24)	33.9 (3.49)
Public...........................	45.0 (2.28)	15.9 (1.57)	21.3 (1.82)	6.9 (0.91)	77.5 (2.64)	15.2 (2.35)	28.3 (3.35)	32.4 (3.58)
Private..........................	39.4 (6.92)	13.6 ! (5.65)	17.5 ! (5.75)	8.3 ! (3.25)	‡ (†)	‡ (†)	‡ (†)	‡ (†)
4-year...............................	40.3 (1.15)	15.5 (0.81)	17.0 (0.86)	6.5 (0.59)	82.4 (2.57)	12.3 (2.23)	25.9 (3.25)	43.7 (3.32)
Public...........................	41.1 (1.31)	14.6 (0.91)	18.4 (0.99)	6.9 (0.69)	83.4 (2.86)	12.2 (2.61)	28.4 (3.69)	42.3 (3.81)
Private..........................	37.8 (2.29)	18.7 (1.72)	12.0 (1.62)	5.3 (1.00)	77.1 (6.82)	12.9 ! (4.92)	13.5 ! (5.59)	50.8 (8.76)
Student enrollment level								
Undergraduate	40.9 (1.00)	15.8 (0.74)	17.9 (0.85)	6.0 (0.47)	80.1 (2.00)	14.4 (1.72)	29.0 (2.47)	35.6 (2.45)
Sex								
Male..............................	36.8 (1.42)	13.2 (1.04)	17.2 (1.20)	5.4 (0.62)	83.3 (2.96)	14.8 (2.58)	26.1 (3.37)	40.4 (3.32)
Female	44.6 (1.41)	18.1 (1.05)	18.5 (1.10)	6.5 (0.64)	77.6 (2.78)	14.0 (2.22)	31.3 (3.60)	31.8 (3.14)
Race/ethnicity								
White...........................	45.4 (1.30)	18.2 (0.97)	19.4 (1.08)	6.4 (0.61)	84.7 (2.71)	15.7 (2.55)	31.7 (3.38)	35.9 (3.31)
Black............................	31.7 (2.78)	9.1 (1.76)	14.3 (2.05)	6.0 (1.46)	71.6 (6.58)	12.4 ! (5.45)	28.2 (7.41)	31.0 (7.71)
Hispanic.......................	40.8 (2.40)	14.8 (1.74)	19.0 (1.87)	6.3 (1.15)	76.2 (3.80)	9.0 (2.66)	28.2 (4.26)	37.3 (4.64)
Asian...........................	23.6 (2.83)	12.0 (2.23)	9.0 (2.28)	2.6 ! (1.08)	87.3 (5.94)	31.6 (9.04)	22.2 ! (7.86)	33.5 (9.36)
Pacific Islander	‡ (†)	‡ (†)	‡ (†)	‡ (†)	‡ (†)	‡ (†)	‡ (†)	‡ (†)
American Indian/Alaska Native ...	18.0 ! (7.69)	‡ (†)	‡ (†)	‡ (†)	‡ (†)	‡ (†)	‡ (†)	‡ (†)
Two or more races.........	41.3 (6.03)	14.3 ! (4.70)	22.4 (5.23)	‡ (†)	‡ (†)	‡ (†)	‡ (†)	‡ (†)
Level and control of institution								
2-year	43.6 (2.20)	15.4 (1.45)	20.8 (1.76)	6.7 (0.87)	79.8 (2.57)	16.2 (2.50)	29.8 (3.38)	32.1 (3.62)
Public........................	44.0 (2.33)	15.5 (1.59)	21.0 (1.85)	6.7 (0.89)	78.9 (2.65)	16.3 (2.51)	30.3 (3.50)	30.7 (3.68)
Private.......................	38.7 (7.16)	14.1 ! (5.95)	17.9 ! (5.90)	6.7 ! (2.83)	‡ (†)	‡ (†)	‡ (†)	‡ (†)
4-year	40.0 (1.20)	15.9 (0.88)	17.0 (0.94)	5.8 (0.56)	80.6 (3.01)	12.0 (2.58)	27.9 (3.66)	40.2 (3.75)
Public........................	40.5 (1.39)	14.9 (0.98)	18.2 (1.07)	6.2 (0.67)	81.2 (3.29)	13.0 (2.97)	29.4 (4.09)	38.2 (4.12)
Private.......................	38.0 (2.32)	19.7 (1.96)	12.3 (1.78)	4.1 (0.87)	76.3 (8.81)	‡ (†)	18.3 ! (7.54)	52.2 (10.87)
Graduate...........................	46.1 (3.29)	13.2 (2.09)	18.3 (2.37)	14.2 (2.56)	81.6 (5.25)	9.9 ! (4.15)	12.2 ! (4.54)	59.6 (5.76)

†Not applicable.

!Interpret data with caution. The coefficient of variation (CV) for this estimate is between 30 and 50 percent.

‡Reporting standards not met. Either there are too few cases for a reliable estimate or the coefficient of variation (CV) is 50 percent or greater.

[1]Includes those who were employed but not at work during the survey week.

[2]Excludes those who were employed but not at work during the survey week; therefore, detail may not sum to total percentage employed. "Hours worked per week" refers to the number of hours worked at all jobs during the survey week.

NOTE: Students were classified as full time if they were taking at least 12 hours of classes (or at least 9 hours of graduate classes) during an average school week and as part time if they were taking fewer hours. Race categories exclude persons of Hispanic ethnicity.

SOURCE: U.S. Department of Commerce, Census Bureau, Current Population Survey (CPS), October, 2011 through 2012 through 2014. (This table was prepared September 2015.)

Table 504.10. Labor force status of 2012, 2013, and 2014 high school completers, by college enrollment status, sex, and race/ethnicity: October 2012, 2013, and 2014

[Standard errors appear in parentheses]

College enrollment status, sex, and race/ethnicity	Total number of high school completers (in thousands)	Separately for those enrolled in college vs. those not enrolled	For all high school completers	Employed	Unemployed (seeking employment)	Not in labor force	Labor force participation rate of all high school completers[1]	Total, all completers in labor force	Employed	Unemployed (seeking employment)	Unemployment rate	High school completers not in labor force (in thousands)
1	2	3	4	5	6	7	8	9	10	11	12	13
2012 high school completers[3]												
Total	3,203 (96.2)	† (†)	100.0 (†)	36.3 (1.53)	12.6 (1.15)	51.2 (1.61)	48.8 (1.61)	1,563 (67.9)	1,161 (57.7)	402 (38.9)	25.7 (2.13)	1,639 (73.1)
Male	1,622 (70.1)	† (†)	50.6 (1.25)	33.7 (2.21)	14.5 (1.75)	51.8 (2.29)	48.2 (2.29)	783 (49.3)	547 (42.8)	235 (29.5)	30.0 (3.29)	840 (52.7)
Female	1,581 (54.0)	† (†)	49.4 (1.25)	38.8 (1.92)	10.6 (1.29)	50.6 (2.16)	49.4 (2.16)	781 (42.2)	614 (36.0)	167 (21.1)	21.4 (2.31)	800 (44.7)
White	1,820 (62.8)	† (†)	56.8 (1.52)	42.5 (2.07)	10.9 (1.31)	46.6 (2.02)	53.4 (2.02)	971 (49.9)	774 (46.1)	198 (24.8)	20.3 (2.35)	849 (46.7)
Black	413 (33.9)	† (†)	12.9 (0.98)	26.4 (4.59)	23.2 (4.11)	50.4 (4.88)	49.6 (4.88)	205 (26.1)	109 (19.8)	96 (19.3)	46.8 (7.23)	208 (26.4)
Hispanic	697 (54.9)	† (†)	21.8 (1.41)	32.1 (3.10)	10.2 (2.13)	57.6 (3.29)	42.4 (3.29)	296 (28.7)	224 (25.2)	‡ (†)	24.2 (4.60)	402 (42.7)
Enrolled in college, 2012	2,121 (76.4)	100.0 (†)	66.2 (1.59)	31.5 (1.66)	6.8 (0.92)	61.8 (1.84)	38.2 (1.84)	811 (46.7)	667 (41.0)	143 (20.0)	17.7 (2.18)	1,310 (63.9)
Male	994 (53.3)	46.9 (1.66)	31.0 (1.31)	27.4 (2.39)	7.0 (1.37)	65.6 (2.58)	34.4 (2.58)	342 (29.7)	272 (27.0)	‡ (†)	20.4 (3.65)	652 (45.6)
Female	1,127 (49.9)	53.1 (1.66)	35.2 (1.41)	35.1 (2.19)	6.5 (1.20)	58.4 (2.43)	41.6 (2.43)	469 (32.6)	395 (29.0)	‡ (†)	15.7 (2.60)	658 (42.0)
2-year	921 (57.7)	43.4 (2.07)	28.8 (1.57)	39.9 (3.10)	8.0 (1.57)	52.1 (3.22)	47.9 (3.22)	441 (35.2)	367 (32.0)	‡ (†)	16.7 (3.09)	480 (47.1)
4-year	1,200 (58.3)	56.6 (2.07)	37.5 (1.60)	25.0 (1.92)	5.8 (1.14)	69.2 (2.17)	30.8 (2.17)	370 (31.8)	300 (27.6)	‡ (†)	18.8 (3.32)	830 (47.5)
Full-time students	1,863 (71.3)	87.8 (1.31)	58.2 (1.61)	28.1 (1.74)	5.8 (0.87)	66.1 (1.89)	33.9 (1.89)	632 (41.6)	523 (36.6)	109 (16.8)	17.2 (2.34)	1,231 (60.3)
Part-time students	258 (29.7)	12.2 (1.31)	8.1 (0.90)	55.9 (5.63)	13.4 (3.98)	30.8 (5.73)	69.2 (5.73)	179 (25.8)	144 (22.3)	‡ (†)	19.3 (5.36)	‡ (†)
White	1,196 (52.7)	56.4 (1.88)	37.3 (1.50)	35.0 (2.32)	6.6 (1.16)	58.3 (2.46)	41.7 (2.46)	498 (35.5)	419 (32.1)	79 (14.3)	15.9 (2.61)	698 (44.0)
Black	233 (30.4)	11.0 (1.38)	7.3 (0.93)	24.4 (5.79)	10.8 ! (4.25)	64.7 (6.27)	35.3 (6.27)	‡ (†)	‡ (†)	‡ (†)	‡ (†)	151 (24.1)
Hispanic	490 (43.3)	23.1 (1.71)	15.3 (1.16)	31.7 (3.98)	4.7 ! (1.83)	63.6 (4.00)	36.4 (4.00)	178 (22.7)	155 (22.0)	‡ (†)	12.9 ! (4.91)	312 (36.1)
Not enrolled in college, 2012	1,082 (63.3)	100.0 (†)	33.8 (1.59)	45.7 (2.52)	23.9 (2.62)	30.4 (2.69)	69.6 (2.69)	753 (53.4)	494 (40.9)	259 (31.4)	34.4 (3.24)	329 (34.5)
Male	628 (45.9)	58.1 (2.47)	19.6 (1.22)	43.8 (3.64)	26.3 (3.63)	29.8 (3.64)	70.2 (3.64)	441 (39.1)	275 (31.1)	166 (25.0)	37.5 (4.55)	187 (27.0)
Female	454 (37.3)	41.9 (2.47)	14.2 (1.09)	48.2 (3.92)	20.5 (3.35)	31.3 (3.78)	68.7 (3.78)	312 (29.8)	219 (25.1)	93 (16.5)	29.9 (4.50)	142 (21.3)
White	624 (42.3)	57.7 (2.63)	19.5 (1.21)	56.9 (3.29)	18.9 (2.69)	24.2 (3.11)	75.8 (3.11)	473 (39.3)	355 (34.3)	118 (17.9)	25.0 (3.32)	151 (20.9)
Black	180 (22.0)	16.6 (1.84)	5.6 (0.66)	28.8 (6.82)	39.2 (7.43)	31.9 (7.23)	68.1 (7.23)	122 (19.9)	‡ (†)	‡ (†)	57.6 (9.06)	‡ (†)
Hispanic	207 (28.4)	19.1 (2.25)	6.5 (0.85)	33.2 (6.32)	23.4 (5.69)	43.4 (5.64)	56.6 (5.64)	117 (18.0)	‡ (†)	‡ (†)	41.4 (9.35)	90 (18.2)
2013 high school completers[3]												
Total	2,977 (84.4)	† (†)	100.0 (†)	35.4 (1.58)	12.3 (1.25)	52.2 (1.64)	47.8 (1.64)	1,422 (69.5)	1,054 (60.7)	367 (39.0)	25.8 (2.38)	1,556 (58.3)
Male	1,524 (62.9)	† (†)	51.2 (1.43)	35.5 (2.24)	14.5 (1.80)	50.0 (2.46)	50.0 (2.46)	763 (49.7)	542 (40.6)	221 (29.4)	29.0 (3.16)	762 (48.0)
Female	1,453 (57.0)	† (†)	48.8 (1.43)	35.3 (2.41)	10.1 (1.49)	54.6 (2.43)	45.4 (2.43)	659 (46.4)	513 (42.7)	146 (22.3)	22.2 (3.13)	794 (43.8)
White	1,737 (63.0)	† (†)	58.3 (1.61)	39.0 (2.08)	11.2 (1.63)	49.8 (2.15)	50.2 (2.15)	872 (51.7)	677 (44.7)	195 (29.8)	22.4 (2.97)	865 (45.7)
Black	378 (36.2)	† (†)	12.7 (1.13)	33.6 (5.31)	14.8 (3.39)	51.7 (5.48)	48.3 (5.48)	183 (27.2)	127 (23.5)	‡ (†)	30.6 (6.64)	195 (27.7)
Hispanic	571 (42.6)	† (†)	19.2 (1.32)	31.1 (3.71)	14.3 (2.81)	54.6 (4.00)	45.4 (4.00)	260 (30.4)	178 (25.3)	‡ (†)	31.5 (5.53)	312 (32.4)
Enrolled in college, 2013	1,962 (74.1)	100.0 (†)	65.9 (1.58)	27.2 (1.86)	6.9 (1.11)	65.9 (1.86)	34.1 (1.86)	669 (47.1)	534 (43.0)	135 (22.8)	20.2 (3.11)	1,293 (56.7)
Male	968 (53.9)	49.4 (1.90)	32.5 (1.48)	24.4 (2.71)	9.3 (1.90)	66.3 (3.01)	33.7 (3.01)	326 (34.7)	236 (28.7)	90 (19.5)	27.5 (4.99)	642 (45.6)
Female	994 (51.0)	50.6 (1.90)	33.4 (1.48)	29.9 (2.62)	4.6 (1.23)	65.5 (2.61)	34.5 (2.61)	343 (31.9)	297 (30.3)	‡ (†)	13.2 (3.47)	651 (41.3)
2-year	709 (48.8)	36.1 (2.07)	23.8 (1.44)	33.8 (3.35)	11.4 (2.40)	54.8 (3.62)	45.2 (3.62)	320 (36.3)	240 (30.5)	‡ (†)	25.2 (4.79)	389 (33.9)
4-year	1,253 (62.3)	63.9 (2.07)	42.1 (1.76)	23.5 (2.17)	4.3 (1.07)	72.2 (2.24)	27.8 (2.24)	348 (33.8)	294 (31.3)	‡ (†)	15.6 (3.66)	904 (51.5)
Full-time students	1,820 (70.6)	92.8 (1.11)	61.1 (1.60)	25.1 (1.82)	5.9 (1.12)	69.0 (1.94)	31.0 (1.94)	564 (44.7)	458 (38.9)	107 (21.4)	18.9 (3.32)	1,256 (54.6)
Part-time students	141 (22.8)	7.2 (1.11)	4.8 (0.75)	53.7 (7.40)	20.1 (5.38)	26.2 (6.13)	73.8 (6.13)	104 (19.8)	76 (16.5)	‡ (†)	27.2 (7.29)	‡ (†)

See notes at end of table.

Table 504.10. Labor force status of 2012, 2013, and 2014 high school completers, by college enrollment status, sex, and race/ethnicity: October 2012, 2013, and 2014—Continued

[Standard errors appear in parentheses]

College enrollment status, sex, and race/ethnicity	Total number of high school completers (in thousands)	Percent: Separately for those enrolled in college vs. those not enrolled	Percent: For all high school completers	Percentage distribution: Employed	Percentage distribution: Unemployed (seeking employment)	Percentage distribution: Not in labor force	Labor force participation rate of all high school completers[1]	Number (in thousands): Total, all completers in labor force[2]	Number: Employed	Number: Unemployed (seeking employment)	Unemployment rate	High school completers not in labor force (in thousands)
1	2	3	4	5	6	7	8	9	10	11	12	13
White	1,196 (52.8)	60.9 (2.02)	40.2 (1.52)	30.9 (2.36)	5.6 (1.47)	63.5 (2.38)	36.5 (2.38)	436 (33.8)	369 (32.0)	‡ (†)	15.4 (3.84)	759 (44.5)
Black	215 (29.5)	10.9 (1.38)	7.2 (0.95)	24.5 (7.01)	7.8! (3.43)	67.6 (7.27)	32.4 (7.27)	‡ (†)	‡ (†)	‡ (†)	‡ (†)	145 (24.9)
Hispanic	342 (35.3)	17.4 (1.61)	11.5 (1.12)	22.3 (3.85)	11.1 (3.17)	66.7 (4.52)	33.3 (4.52)	114 (19.6)	‡ (†)	‡ (†)	33.2 (7.94)	228 (28.0)
Not enrolled in college, 2013	1,016 (54.1)	100.0 (†)	34.1 (1.58)	51.3 (3.14)	22.9 (2.84)	25.8 (2.90)	74.2 (2.90)	753 (51.3)	521 (43.2)	232 (31.5)	30.9 (3.53)	262 (31.6)
Male	556 (39.2)	54.8 (2.55)	18.7 (1.22)	54.9 (3.73)	23.6 (3.60)	21.5 (3.43)	78.5 (3.43)	437 (34.6)	305 (27.9)	132 (22.3)	30.1 (4.18)	119 (21.3)
Female	459 (35.8)	45.2 (2.55)	15.4 (1.13)	46.9 (4.79)	22.0 (3.77)	31.2 (4.56)	68.8 (4.56)	316 (33.1)	215 (28.7)	101 (18.7)	31.9 (5.18)	143 (23.3)
White	542 (39.1)	53.3 (2.80)	18.2 (1.24)	56.9 (3.88)	23.7 (3.62)	19.4 (3.27)	80.6 (3.27)	436 (39.1)	308 (32.3)	128 (22.2)	29.4 (4.21)	105 (17.8)
Black	164 (26.1)	16.1 (2.32)	5.5 (0.86)	45.4 (8.24)	23.9 (6.59)	30.7 (7.76)	69.3 (7.76)	114 (22.4)	‡ (†)	‡ (†)	34.5 (9.08)	‡ (†)
Hispanic	229 (24.8)	22.6 (2.22)	7.7 (0.82)	44.3 (6.65)	19.2 (5.20)	36.5 (6.68)	63.5 (6.68)	146 (21.4)	102 (18.6)	‡ (†)	30.2 (7.57)	‡ (†)
2014 high school completers[3]												
Total	2,868 (78.5)	† (†)	100.0 (†)	38.5 (1.84)	10.4 (0.99)	51.1 (1.87)	48.9 (1.87)	1,403 (62.2)	1,105 (57.7)	298 (29.5)	21.2 (1.95)	1,465 (70.6)
Male	1,423 (58.1)	† (†)	49.6 (1.48)	39.9 (2.56)	10.7 (1.47)	49.5 (2.48)	50.5 (2.48)	719 (44.7)	568 (42.8)	152 (21.4)	21.1 (2.85)	704 (46.6)
Female	1,445 (57.5)	† (†)	50.4 (1.48)	37.2 (2.37)	10.1 (1.28)	52.7 (2.61)	47.3 (2.61)	684 (44.0)	538 (38.7)	146 (19.1)	21.4 (2.45)	761 (50.9)
White	1,685 (64.8)	† (†)	58.8 (1.73)	40.3 (2.29)	9.9 (1.25)	49.8 (2.30)	50.2 (2.30)	845 (48.3)	679 (45.1)	166 (21.7)	19.7 (2.40)	840 (52.7)
Black	340 (32.9)	† (†)	11.9 (1.08)	30.9 (4.97)	10.7 (3.20)	58.3 (5.41)	41.7 (5.41)	142 (20.7)	105 (18.8)	‡ (†)	25.8 (6.85)	198 (28.8)
Hispanic	566 (46.9)	† (†)	19.8 (1.49)	40.8 (4.60)	13.2 (2.62)	46.0 (4.65)	54.0 (4.65)	306 (32.3)	231 (28.8)	‡ (†)	24.5 (4.68)	260 (37.5)
Enrolled in college, 2014	1,961 (71.4)	100.0 (†)	68.4 (1.67)	32.4 (2.14)	5.5 (0.89)	62.1 (2.19)	37.9 (2.19)	744 (46.6)	636 (45.0)	108 (17.6)	14.5 (2.28)	1,217 (66.8)
Male	911 (48.0)	46.5 (1.81)	31.8 (1.41)	32.9 (3.01)	3.2! (1.09)	63.9 (3.02)	36.1 (3.02)	329 (31.0)	300 (30.9)	‡ (†)	8.9! (2.96)	582 (43.2)
Female	1,050 (53.0)	53.5 (1.81)	36.6 (1.59)	32.0 (2.70)	7.5 (1.41)	60.5 (3.03)	39.5 (3.03)	415 (35.3)	336 (30.9)	‡ (†)	18.9 (3.16)	635 (48.4)
2-year	706 (50.8)	36.0 (2.12)	24.6 (1.56)	41.2 (3.63)	7.9 (1.75)	50.9 (3.88)	49.1 (3.88)	347 (34.2)	291 (31.7)	‡ (†)	16.1 (3.31)	359 (40.4)
4-year	1,254 (58.8)	64.0 (2.12)	43.7 (1.81)	27.5 (2.42)	4.1 (1.09)	68.4 (2.47)	31.6 (2.47)	397 (33.6)	345 (32.9)	‡ (†)	13.0 (3.35)	858 (54.8)
Full-time students	1,810 (69.2)	92.3 (1.21)	63.1 (1.70)	29.7 (2.15)	5.1 (0.94)	65.2 (2.22)	34.8 (2.22)	630 (42.7)	537 (41.4)	‡ (†)	14.8 (2.59)	1,180 (65.9)
Part-time students	151 (24.6)	7.7 (1.21)	5.3 (0.85)	65.6 (6.92)	9.6! (3.95)	24.8 (6.28)	75.2 (6.28)	113 (20.3)	99 (18.3)	‡ (†)	12.8! (5.22)	‡ (†)
White	1,141 (57.9)	58.2 (2.15)	39.8 (1.79)	34.2 (2.69)	3.7 (1.00)	62.1 (2.70)	37.9 (2.70)	432 (34.8)	390 (34.3)	‡ (†)	9.8 (2.58)	708 (51.0)
Black	239 (29.6)	12.2 (1.43)	8.3 (0.99)	19.3 (5.12)	10.9! (3.71)	69.8 (6.11)	30.2 (6.11)	‡ (†)	‡ (†)	‡ (†)	‡ (†)	167 (26.3)
Hispanic	369 (41.3)	18.8 (1.93)	12.9 (1.37)	41.3 (5.65)	7.8! (2.43)	50.8 (5.46)	49.2 (5.46)	181 (25.6)	153 (25.0)	‡ (†)	15.9! (5.04)	188 (31.8)
Not enrolled in college, 2014	907 (54.3)	100.0 (†)	31.6 (1.67)	51.7 (2.97)	21.0 (2.41)	27.3 (2.78)	72.7 (2.78)	659 (46.8)	469 (39.6)	190 (24.0)	28.8 (3.10)	248 (29.2)
Male	512 (40.2)	56.4 (3.34)	17.8 (1.31)	52.3 (3.88)	23.9 (3.34)	23.8 (3.44)	76.2 (3.44)	390 (33.8)	268 (28.8)	122 (18.7)	31.4 (4.11)	122 (20.8)
Female	395 (40.4)	43.6 (3.34)	13.8 (1.35)	50.9 (4.76)	17.1 (3.47)	32.0 (4.33)	68.0 (4.33)	269 (32.3)	201 (30.1)	‡ (†)	25.1 (4.91)	126 (21.3)
White	544 (43.2)	60.0 (2.76)	19.0 (1.41)	53.1 (3.81)	22.8 (3.03)	24.1 (3.31)	75.9 (3.31)	413 (37.7)	289 (31.5)	124 (18.8)	30.0 (3.84)	131 (20.4)
Black	101 (16.6)	11.2 (1.80)	3.5 (0.58)	58.3 (9.62)	‡ (†)	31.4 (9.15)	68.6 (9.15)	‡ (†)	‡ (†)	‡ (†)	‡ (†)	‡ (†)
Hispanic	197 (25.8)	21.8 (2.61)	6.9 (0.87)	39.8 (6.98)	23.3 (5.83)	36.9 (6.72)	63.1 (6.72)	124 (20.0)	‡ (†)	‡ (†)	36.9 (8.55)	‡ (†)

†Not applicable.
!Interpret data with caution. The coefficient of variation (CV) for this estimate is between 30 and 50 percent.
‡Reporting standards not met (too few cases for a reliable estimate).
[1]The labor force participation rate is the percentage of persons who are either employed or seeking employment.
[2]The labor force includes all employed persons plus those seeking employment. The unemployment rate is the percentage of persons in the labor force who are not working and who made specific efforts to find employment sometime during the prior 4 weeks.
[3]Includes 16- to 24-year-olds who completed high school between October of the previous year and October of the given year. Includes recipients of equivalency credentials as well as diploma recipients.

NOTE: Data are for October of given year. Data are based on sample surveys of the civilian noninstitutional population. Percentages are only shown when the base is 75,000 or greater. Standard errors were computed using replicate weights. Totals include race categories not separately shown. Race categories exclude persons of Hispanic ethnicity. Detail may not sum to totals because of rounding.
SOURCE: U.S. Department of Commerce, Census Bureau, Current Population Survey (CPS), October 2012, 2013, and 2014. (This table was prepared January 2016.)

Table 504.20. Labor force status of high school dropouts, by sex and race/ethnicity: Selected years, October 1980 through 2014
[Standard errors appear in parentheses]

Year, sex, and race/ethnicity	Number of dropouts (in thousands)	Percent of all dropouts	Percentage distribution of dropouts — Employed	Unemployed (seeking employment)	Not in labor force	Labor force participation rate of dropouts[1]	Dropouts in civilian labor force[2] — Number (in thousands) — Total	Unemployed (seeking employment)	Unemployment rate	Dropouts not in labor force (in thousands)
1	2	3	4	5	6	7	8	9	10	11
				Estimates for individual years						
All dropouts										
1980..................	738 (44.0)	100.0 (†)	43.8 (2.97)	20.0 (2.37)	36.2 (2.87)	63.8 (2.87)	471 (35.2)	148 (19.5)	31.4 (3.44)	267 (26.5)
1990..................	412 (36.0)	100.0 (†)	46.3 (4.37)	21.6 (3.57)	32.2 (4.09)	67.8 (4.09)	279 (29.7)	89 (16.6)	31.8 (4.90)	132 (20.4)
2000..................	515 (28.5)	100.0 (†)	48.7 (2.77)	19.2 (3.01)	32.0 (2.59)	68.0 (2.59)	350 (23.5)	99 (17.2)	28.1 (4.16)	165 (16.2)
2005..................	407 (35.3)	100.0 (†)	38.3 (4.22)	18.9 (3.42)	42.8 (3.32)	57.2 (4.30)	233 (26.7)	77 (15.4)	32.9 (5.42)	174 (17.9)
2010[3]..................	340 (29.0)	100.0 (†)	30.9 (4.24)	23.0 (4.29)	46.1 (4.78)	53.9 (4.78)	183 (21.5)	78 (16.0)	42.7 (6.67)	157 (21.9)
2013[3]..................	529 (45.1)	100.0 (†)	31.0 (3.87)	12.0 (2.33)	57.1 (4.13)	42.9 (4.13)	227 (29.7)	‡ (†)	27.9 (5.06)	302 (33.2)
2014[3]..................	575 (41.4)	100.0 (†)	28.7 (3.40)	12.5 (2.29)	58.8 (3.34)	41.2 (3.34)	237 (25.2)	‡ (†)	30.3 (5.37)	338 (31.7)
				3-year moving averages[4]						
All dropouts										
1980..................	748 (44.3)	100.0 (†)	44.4 (1.70)	19.9 (1.38)	35.7 (1.27)	64.3 (1.64)	481 (35.6)	149 (19.9)	30.9 (1.99)	267 (20.5)
1990..................	413 (36.1)	100.0 (†)	43.5 (2.50)	21.5 (2.08)	35.0 (1.86)	65.0 (2.41)	268 (29.1)	89 (16.8)	33.1 (2.96)	144 (16.5)
2000..................	515 (41.8)	100.0 (†)	44.1 (2.33)	19.0 (1.85)	36.9 (1.75)	63.1 (2.27)	325 (33.2)	98 (18.3)	30.1 (2.72)	190 (19.7)
2005..................	449 (37.1)	100.0 (†)	36.8 (2.30)	17.7 (1.83)	45.5 (1.84)	54.5 (2.38)	245 (27.4)	79 (15.7)	32.5 (3.04)	205 (19.4)
2010..................	365 (33.4)	100.0 (†)	28.7 (2.39)	23.7 (2.26)	47.6 (2.04)	52.4 (2.64)	191 (24.2)	87 (16.4)	45.2 (3.65)	174 (17.8)
2013..................	491 (38.8)	100.0 (†)	28.3 (2.06)	15.0 (1.64)	56.7 (1.75)	43.3 (2.26)	213 (25.5)	74 (15.1)	34.7 (3.32)	278 (22.6)
2014..................	552 (36.9)	100.0 (†)	29.8 (2.17)	12.2 (1.78)	58.0 (2.32)	42.0 (2.34)	232 (24.0)	67 (14.8)	29.1 (3.80)	320 (27.9)
Sex										
Male										
1980..............	393 (31.6)	52.6 (1.69)	55.5 (2.31)	19.5 (1.84)	25.0 (2.01)	75.0 (2.01)	295 (27.4)	77 (14.0)	25.9 (2.35)	98 (15.8)
1990..............	216 (25.7)	52.3 (2.48)	50.9 (3.44)	25.2 (2.98)	23.9 (2.93)	76.1 (2.93)	164 (22.4)	55 (12.9)	33.1 (3.71)	52 (12.6)
2000..............	279 (30.3)	54.1 (2.30)	49.8 (3.14)	19.6 (2.49)	30.7 (2.90)	69.3 (2.90)	193 (25.2)	55 (13.4)	28.2 (3.39)	85 (16.8)
2005..............	254 (27.4)	56.5 (2.33)	40.0 (3.06)	19.0 (2.45)	41.0 (3.07)	59.0 (3.07)	150 (21.1)	48 (12.0)	32.2 (3.80)	104 (17.6)
2010..............	196 (24.1)	53.6 (2.60)	32.1 (3.32)	22.4 (2.97)	45.5 (3.54)	54.5 (3.54)	107 (17.8)	44 (11.4)	41.2 (4.74)	89 (16.3)
2013..............	262 (27.9)	53.3 (2.24)	29.7 (2.81)	15.2 (2.21)	55.1 (3.06)	44.9 (3.06)	118 (18.7)	40 (10.9)	34.0 (4.35)	144 (20.7)
2014..............	297 (29.5)	53.8 (2.58)	29.2 (3.20)	11.5 (2.25)	59.3 (3.46)	40.7 (3.46)	121 (18.9)	‡ (†)	28.3 (4.97)	176 (22.8)
Female										
1980..............	354 (29.1)	47.4 (1.63)	32.1 (2.21)	20.4 (1.91)	47.5 (2.37)	52.5 (2.37)	186 (21.1)	72 (13.1)	38.9 (3.19)	168 (20.0)
1990..............	197 (23.7)	47.7 (2.40)	35.4 (3.33)	17.4 (2.64)	47.2 (3.48)	52.8 (3.48)	104 (17.2)	34 (9.9)	33.0 (4.51)	93 (16.3)
2000..............	236 (27.0)	45.9 (2.23)	37.4 (3.19)	18.3 (2.55)	44.3 (3.28)	55.7 (3.28)	132 (20.1)	43 (11.6)	32.9 (4.15)	105 (18.0)
2005..............	196 (23.3)	43.5 (2.25)	32.6 (3.23)	16.0 (2.52)	51.4 (3.44)	48.6 (3.44)	95 (16.2)	31 (9.3)	32.9 (4.64)	101 (16.7)
2010..............	169 (21.7)	46.4 (2.51)	24.9 (3.20)	25.1 (3.21)	50.0 (3.70)	50.0 (3.70)	85 (15.3)	43 (10.9)	50.2 (5.23)	85 (15.3)
2013..............	229 (25.2)	46.7 (2.17)	26.7 (2.81)	14.8 (2.26)	58.5 (3.13)	41.5 (3.13)	95 (16.3)	34 (9.7)	35.6 (4.73)	134 (19.3)
2014..............	255 (26.6)	46.2 (2.51)	30.5 (3.40)	13.1 (2.49)	56.4 (3.67)	43.6 (3.67)	111 (17.6)	‡ (†)	30.0 (5.13)	144 (20.0)
Race/ethnicity										
White										
1980..............	494 (36.0)	66.0 (1.62)	50.9 (2.11)	17.6 (1.61)	31.5 (1.52)	68.5 (1.96)	338 (29.8)	87 (15.2)	25.7 (2.24)	156 (15.7)
1990..............	240 (27.5)	58.0 (2.49)	51.4 (3.31)	19.3 (2.63)	29.3 (2.33)	70.7 (3.02)	170 (23.1)	46 (12.1)	27.3 (3.53)	70 (11.5)
2000..............	279 (30.8)	54.1 (2.34)	48.3 (3.19)	18.7 (2.50)	33.0 (2.32)	67.0 (3.00)	187 (25.2)	52 (13.4)	27.8 (3.51)	92 (13.7)
2005..............	215 (25.7)	48.0 (2.38)	41.6 (3.40)	14.2 (2.42)	44.2 (2.64)	55.8 (3.42)	120 (19.2)	31 ! (9.7)	25.5 (4.04)	95 (13.2)
2010..............	164 (22.4)	45.0 (2.63)	32.7 (3.70)	20.8 (3.22)	46.4 (3.04)	53.6 (3.93)	88 (16.4)	34 ! (10.3)	38.9 (5.28)	76 (11.8)
2013..............	214 (25.6)	43.7 (2.26)	30.7 (3.18)	9.8 (2.06)	59.5 (2.62)	40.5 (3.39)	87 (16.3)	21 ! (8.1)	24.2 (4.67)	128 (15.3)
2014..............	279 (26.3)	50.5 (2.37)	31.6 (3.10)	9.5 (2.24)	58.9 (3.25)	41.1 (3.28)	115 (16.9)	‡ (†)	23.2 (5.02)	164 (20.0)
Black										
1980..............	154 (21.3)	20.6 (1.47)	21.0 (3.27)	28.3 (3.62)	50.6 (4.01)	49.4 (4.01)	76 (15.0)	44 (11.4)	57.4 (5.65)	78 (15.2)
1990..............	96 (18.5)	23.3 (2.27)	27.1 (4.93)	29.0 (5.04)	43.9 (5.51)	56.1 (5.51)	54 (13.8)	28 ! (10.0)	51.7 (7.41)	42 (12.3)
2000..............	102 (19.7)	19.8 (1.98)	28.0 (5.03)	22.2 (4.65)	49.8 (5.60)	50.2 (5.60)	51 (14.0)	‡ (†)	44.2 (7.85)	51 (13.9)
2005..............	88 (17.4)	19.5 (2.01)	21.5 (4.71)	27.7 (5.13)	50.9 (5.73)	49.1 (5.73)	43 (12.2)	‡ (†)	56.3 (8.11)	45 (12.4)
2010..............	70 (15.6)	19.3 (2.22)	22.4 (5.33)	30.4 (5.88)	47.2 (6.38)	52.8 (6.38)	37 ! (11.3)	‡ (†)	57.5 (8.69)	33 ! (10.7)
2013..............	94 (18.0)	19.2 (1.91)	13.1 (3.72)	24.5 (4.75)	62.4 (5.35)	37.6 (5.35)	35 ! (11.1)	‡ (†)	65.3 (8.58)	59 (14.3)
2014..............	85 (17.4)	15.4 (2.06)	17.1 ! (5.48)	17.1 ! (5.49)	65.8 (6.91)	34.2 (6.91)	‡ (†)	‡ (†)	‡ (†)	56 (14.2)
Hispanic										
1980..............	84 (18.7)	11.3 (1.36)	48.2 (6.40)	19.5 (5.07)	32.3 (5.99)	67.7 (5.99)	57 (15.4)	‡ (†)	28.8 (7.05)	27 ! (10.6)
1990..............	66 (15.3)	15.9 (1.96)	39.3 (6.56)	19.9 (5.36)	40.8 (6.60)	59.2 (6.60)	39 ! (11.8)	‡ (†)	33.5 (8.24)	27 ! (9.8)
2000..............	113 (20.8)	21.9 (2.06)	50.4 (5.32)	17.7 (4.06)	31.9 (4.96)	68.1 (4.96)	77 (17.1)	‡ (†)	26.0 (5.66)	36 ! (11.7)
2005..............	125 (20.8)	27.9 (2.27)	39.2 (4.68)	16.1 (3.52)	44.7 (4.77)	55.3 (4.77)	69 (15.4)	‡ (†)	29.1 (5.86)	56 (13.9)
2010..............	102 (18.8)	28.0 (2.52)	25.8 (4.64)	24.3 (4.55)	49.9 (5.30)	50.1 (5.30)	51 (13.3)	25 ! (9.3)	48.4 (7.49)	51 (13.3)
2013..............	150 (22.7)	30.6 (2.23)	33.2 (4.12)	15.1 (3.13)	51.7 (4.37)	48.3 (4.37)	73 (15.8)	‡ (†)	31.3 (5.84)	78 (16.4)
2014..............	158 (22.8)	28.7 (2.48)	32.8 (4.80)	12.6 (3.39)	54.6 (5.09)	45.4 (5.09)	72 (15.4)	‡ (†)	27.7 (6.79)	86 (16.9)

†Not applicable.
!Interpret data with caution. The coefficient of variation (CV) for this estimate is between 30 and 50 percent.
‡Reporting standards not met. Either there are too few cases for a reliable estimate or the coefficient of variation (CV) is 50 percent or greater.
[1]The labor force participation rate is the percentage of persons who are either employed or seeking employment.
[2]The labor force includes all employed persons plus those seeking employment. The unemployment rate is the percentage of persons in the labor force who are not working and who made specific efforts to find employment sometime during the prior 4 weeks.
[3]Beginning in 2010, standard errors for the individual year estimates were computed using replicate weights in order to produce more precise values. This methodology can only be used for these estimates. For all other estimates in the table, standard errors were computed using generalized variance function methodology.

[4]A 3-year moving average is the arithmetic average of the year indicated, the year immediately preceding, and the year immediately following. For example, the estimates shown for 2000 reflect an average of 1999, 2000, and 2001. Use of a moving average increases the sample size, thereby reducing the size of sampling errors and producing more stable estimates. For the final year of available data, a 2-year moving average is used; thus, the estimates for 2014 reflect the average of 2013 and 2014.
NOTE: Data are based on sample surveys of the civilian noninstitutional population. Data are for October of a given year. Dropouts are considered persons 16 to 24 years old who dropped out of school in the 12-month period ending in October of years shown. Includes dropouts from any grade, including a small number from elementary and middle schools. Percentages are only shown when the base is 75,000 or greater. Totals include race categories not separately shown. Race categories exclude persons of Hispanic ethnicity. Detail may not sum to totals because of rounding.
SOURCE: U.S. Department of Commerce, Census Bureau, Current Population Survey (CPS), selected years, October 1979 through 2014. (This table was prepared May 2016.)

Table 504.30. Among special education students out of high school up to 8 years, percentage attending and completing postsecondary education, living independently, and working competitively, by type of disability: 2007 and 2009

[Standard errors appear in parentheses]

Year, postsecondary status and institution type, and living and employment status	All disabilities[1]	Specific learning disabilities	Speech or language impairments	Intellectual disability	Emotional disturbance	Hearing impairments	Orthopedic impairments	Other health impairments[2]	Visual impairments	Multiple disabilities	Deaf-blindness	Autism	Traumatic brain injury
1	2	3	4	5	6	7	8	9	10	11	12	13	14
2007 (out of high school up to 6 years)													
Ever attended institution													
Any postsecondary	55.0 (2.62)	60.9 (3.88)	63.0 (3.77)	28.2 (3.65)	44.6 (4.36)	70.9 (4.61)	59.8 (4.59)	56.6 (4.14)	70.8 (5.23)	31.3 (5.28)	48.8 (6.63)	46.6 (5.25)	56.2 (7.49)
4-year	14.7 (1.87)	15.6 (2.89)	29.8 (3.57)	6.2! (1.96)	7.7! (2.34)	31.4 (4.71)	22.5 (3.91)	19.5 (3.31)	42.8 (5.70)	8.0! (3.08)	18.2 (5.28)	15.7! (3.82)	15.7! (5.49)
2-year	37.3 (2.55)	40.8 (3.91)	41.0 (3.84)	21.2 (3.32)	30.0 (4.02)	44.9 (5.05)	45.5 (4.66)	44.6 (4.16)	47.0 (5.74)	17.2 (4.29)	29.1 (6.21)	32.6 (4.93)	33.5 ! (7.12)
Vocational/technical	28.3 (2.37)	31.4 (3.69)	20.3 (3.14)	16.0 (2.97)	27.5 (3.92)	37.8 (4.92)	21.5 (3.84)	28.1 (3.76)	21.2 (4.71)	14.8 (4.04)	18.9 (5.35)	21.8 (4.35)	33.2 (7.11)
Graduation rate, by type of institution[3]													
Any postsecondary	38.4 (4.41)	37.5 (6.13)	48.4 (6.64)	40.0 (10.17)	41.1 (7.55)	38.9 (8.80)	35.7 (7.55)	33.8 (6.09)	49.7 (9.35)	32.1 ! (10.55)	‡ (†)	35.3 (10.36)	50.4 (12.59)
4-year	29.4 (8.30)	‡ (†)	39.8 ! (12.46)	‡ (†)	‡ (†)	37.2 ! (13.80)	35.7 ! (16.18)	‡ (†)	58.7 (13.84)	‡ (†)	‡ (†)	‡ (†)	‡ (†)
2-year	29.7 (4.83)	29.4 (6.81)	40.2 (7.79)	28.1 ! (11.70)	26.7 ! (8.47)	30.6 ! (10.78)	23.1 ! (8.41)	32.6 (6.63)	42.9 (11.33)	‡ (†)	‡ (†)	33.0 ! (13.39)	24.8 ! (12.11)
Vocational/technical	54.6 (7.22)	55.1 (9.66)	69.8 (10.43)	50.3 ! (15.09)	56.5 (11.38)	33.0 ! (14.56)	44.4 (11.95)	47.1 (11.65)	50.9 ! (19.67)	‡ (†)	‡ (†)	49.2 ! (15.05)	‡ (†)
Living independently[4]	35.7 (2.53)	40.6 (3.91)	30.4 (3.60)	21.2 (3.32)	34.4 (4.17)	28.5 (4.60)	14.0 (3.26)	30.8 (3.86)	31.3 (5.35)	10.6! (3.51)	13.7 ! (4.69)	11.8 (3.39)	24.8 (6.52)
Competitively employed[5]													
Currently	61.1 (2.86)	70.4 (4.12)	61.4 (4.17)	31.6 (4.22)	53.2 (4.94)	49.4 (5.85)	26.2 (4.36)	60.3 (4.51)	34.4 (5.98)	31.6 (6.13)	15.0 ! (5.46)	32.7 (5.63)	32.6 (7.47)
In the past 2 years	78.6 (2.27)	85.9 (2.92)	78.8 (3.30)	49.8 (4.32)	78.9 (3.77)	70.3 (4.93)	42.8 (4.62)	78.8 (3.54)	54.6 (5.97)	41.0 (5.99)	26.4 (6.17)	44.1 (5.40)	63.6 (7.50)
2009 (out of high school up to 8 years)													
Ever attended institution													
Any postsecondary	59.2 (2.64)	65.3 (3.93)	67.0 (3.62)	29.5 (3.62)	53.0 (4.53)	74.8 (4.24)	62.0 (4.42)	65.2 (4.05)	70.7 (5.01)	33.2 (5.09)	56.8 (7.09)	44.2 (4.66)	60.4 (7.40)
4-year	18.4 (2.08)	20.9 (3.36)	30.9 (3.56)	6.2! (1.92)	11.0 (2.84)	34.7 (4.66)	23.5 (3.87)	19.1 (3.34)	41.5 (5.43)	7.3 ! (2.82)	23.7 (6.09)	17.4 (3.56)	18.5 ! (5.87)
2-year	44.4 (2.67)	49.7 (4.13)	46.5 (3.86)	19.7 (3.16)	38.0 (4.40)	53.4 (4.88)	50.9 (4.57)	53.2 (4.25)	51.2 (5.51)	21.7 (4.45)	36.9 (6.91)	32.2 (4.39)	42.1 (7.47)
Vocational/technical	31.3 (2.49)	34.1 (3.92)	28.5 (3.48)	17.2 (2.99)	33.0 (4.27)	40.3 (4.79)	26.5 (4.03)	33.1 (4.00)	25.6 (4.81)	17.6 (4.11)	21.6 (5.89)	22.1 (3.90)	34.5 (7.20)
Currently attending institution													
Any postsecondary	15.1 (1.93)	17.3 (3.13)	20.1 (3.09)	‡ (†)	12.9 (3.04)	25.0 (4.23)	23.3 (3.87)	16.1 (3.13)	25.0 (4.79)	8.2 ! (2.99)	24.5 (6.19)	14.0 (3.26)	14.6 ! (5.34)
4-year	5.2 (1.20)	5.9 ! (1.95)	10.6 (2.38)	‡ (†)	3.9 ! (1.76)	15.0 (3.51)	8.0 ! (2.47)	3.1 ! (1.48)	15.1 (3.94)	‡ (†)	9.1 ! (4.11)	5.3 ! (2.12)	‡ (†)
2-year	9.0 (1.54)	10.3 (2.52)	8.3 (2.14)	‡ (†)	8.6 (2.56)	11.6 (3.15)	13.2 (3.10)	10.9 (2.67)	8.9 ! (3.16)	‡ (†)	16.7 ! (5.34)	8.2 ! (2.59)	9.2 ! (4.38)
Vocational/technical	2.2 ! (0.79)	‡ (†)	2.7 ! (1.24)	‡ (†)	‡ (†)	‡ (†)	5.5 ! (2.09)	2.9 ! (1.43)	‡ (†)	‡ (†)	‡ (†)	‡ (†)	‡ (†)
Graduation rate, by type of institution[3]													
Any postsecondary	47.6 (3.92)	47.8 (5.49)	53.5 (5.35)	39.8 (8.45)	45.9 (6.45)	58.7 (6.67)	45.3 (6.40)	44.8 (5.64)	58.4 (7.24)	58.9 (9.71)	‡ (†)	50.7 (8.15)	61.8 (10.33)
4-year	45.3 (7.28)	47.7 (10.07)	60.1 (8.80)	‡ (†)	‡ (†)	49.5 (9.93)	48.8 (11.86)	30.6 ! (9.72)	63.1 (10.01)	‡ (†)	‡ (†)	59.0 (12.15)	‡ (†)
2-year	37.2 (4.46)	38.2 (6.16)	39.2 (6.35)	28.2 ! (9.90)	33.3 (7.61)	42.5 (8.53)	32.9 (7.24)	35.1 (6.12)	45.9 (9.06)	44.3 (12.86)	‡ (†)	43.3 (10.61)	35.7 ! (11.88)
Vocational/technical	54.6 (5.96)	52.7 (8.29)	64.3 (8.39)	51.2 (12.94)	62.5 (8.67)	63.8 (10.75)	50.7 (10.12)	58.7 (8.28)	47.3 (12.97)	46.5 (12.73)	‡ (†)	53.2 (12.43)	73.9 (14.00)
Living independently[4]	44.7 (2.68)	51.0 (4.15)	38.7 (3.75)	25.7 (3.48)	44.3 (4.52)	40.3 (4.79)	24.9 (3.95)	39.2 (4.17)	41.4 (5.43)	11.2! (3.41)	20.5 (5.79)	7.1 ! (2.42)	24.0 (6.48)
Competitively employed[5]													
Currently	53.1 (2.82)	62.4 (4.27)	58.5 (3.93)	25.7 (3.60)	40.9 (4.65)	47.4 (5.14)	26.4 (4.03)	53.8 (4.48)	34.1 (5.36)	21.5 (4.63)	23.1 (6.19)	24.2 (4.07)	41.7 (7.52)
In the past 2 years	70.1 (2.52)	78.1 (3.51)	77.2 (3.28)	38.7 (3.98)	68.6 (4.31)	65.0 (4.81)	40.2 (4.53)	72.2 (3.92)	47.2 (5.61)	32.1 (5.15)	34.9 (6.96)	33.9 (4.54)	53.3 (7.64)

†Not applicable.
!Interpret data with caution. The coefficient of variation (CV) for this estimate is between 30 and 50 percent.
‡Reporting standards not met. The coefficient of variation (CV) for this estimate is 50 percent or greater.
[1]Includes disability categories not shown separately.
[2]Other health impairments include having limited strength, vitality, or alertness that is due to chronic or acute health problems (such as a heart condition, rheumatic fever, asthma, hemophilia, and leukemia) and that adversely affects educational performance.
[3]Among students who had ever attended the type of institution specified, the percentage who received a diploma, certificate, or license.
[4]Living independently includes living alone, with a spouse or roommate, in a college dormitory, in Job Corps housing, or in military housing as a service member.

[5]Competitively employed refers to those receiving more than minimum wage and working in an environment where the majority of workers are not disabled.
NOTE: Data based on students who had been out of high school up to 6 years in 2007 and up to 8 years in 2009 and had attended special or regular schools in the 1999–2000 or 2000–01 school year. Apparent discrepancies in attendance and graduation percentages between 2007 and 2009 may be due to inconsistent reporting by respondents and smaller numbers of respondents for the 2009 survey wave. Some data have been revised from previously published figures.
SOURCE: U.S. Department of Education, Institute of Education Sciences, National Center for Special Education Research, National Longitudinal Transition Study-2 (NLTS2), Waves 4 and 5, 2007 and 2009, unpublished tabulations. (This table was prepared July 2010.)

Table 505.10. Number, percentage distribution, unemployment rates, and median earnings of 25- to 29-year-old bachelor's degree holders and percentage of degree holders among all 25- to 29-year-olds, by field of study: 2010 and 2014

[Standard errors appear in parentheses]

Field of study	2010 — 25- to 29-year-old bachelor's degree holders					2014 — 25- to 29-year-old bachelor's degree holders				
	Number, in thousands	Percentage distribution	Unemployment rate	Median annual earnings (in current dollars)	Percent of all 25- to 29-year-olds with degree in specific field	Number, in thousands	Percentage distribution	Unemployment rate	Median annual earnings (in current dollars)	Percent of all 25- to 29-year-olds with degree in specific field
	2	3	4	5	6	7	8	9	10	11
Total, all bachelor's degrees	6,366 (30.5)	100.0 (†)	5.6 (0.13)	$44,330 (564)	30.5 (0.14)	7,078 (33.6)	100.0 (†)	3.9 (0.10)	$45,340 (1,667)	32.4 (0.15)
Agriculture	59 (2.8)	0.9 (0.04)	3.8 (0.99)	40,180 (508)	0.3 (0.01)	66 (3.5)	0.9 (0.05)	2.2 ! (0.96)	44,540 (1,667)	0.3 (0.02)
Architecture	47 (2.5)	0.7 (0.04)	13.8 (2.49)	44,250 (2,733)	0.2 (0.01)	62 (3.4)	0.9 (0.05)	4.6 (1.10)	45,110 (1,051)	0.3 (0.02)
Area, ethnic, and civilization studies	28 (1.9)	0.4 (0.03)	5.2 ! (1.61)	43,360 (3,152)	0.1 (0.01)	33 (2.4)	0.5 (0.03)	5.0 (1.48)	40,160 (1,410)	0.2 (0.01)
Arts, fine and commercial										
Fine arts	245 (5.4)	3.8 (0.08)	6.1 (0.69)	37,770 (943)	1.2 (0.03)	292 (7.7)	4.1 (0.11)	5.8 (0.53)	37,120 (1,267)	1.3 (0.03)
Commercial art and graphic design	89 (3.9)	1.4 (0.06)	8.6 (1.09)	40,220 (726)	0.4 (0.02)	111 (4.2)	1.6 (0.06)	3.9 (0.85)	42,060 (1,746)	0.5 (0.02)
Business										
Business, general	222 (5.5)	3.5 (0.09)	5.7 (0.66)	46,290 (1,329)	1.1 (0.03)	260 (6.9)	3.7 (0.10)	3.9 (0.49)	47,850 (1,491)	1.2 (0.03)
Accounting	194 (5.7)	3.0 (0.09)	5.8 (0.68)	50,200 (196)	0.9 (0.03)	210 (5.8)	3.0 (0.08)	2.5 (0.50)	53,140 (956)	1.0 (0.03)
Business management and administration	339 (7.2)	5.3 (0.11)	6.5 (0.57)	44,220 (1,291)	1.6 (0.03)	352 (8.4)	5.0 (0.11)	4.0 (0.44)	45,320 (1,009)	1.6 (0.04)
Marketing and marketing research	187 (5.5)	2.9 (0.08)	4.6 (0.57)	45,050 (906)	0.9 (0.03)	189 (6.0)	2.7 (0.08)	3.5 (0.56)	46,820 (1,973)	0.8 (0.03)
Finance	170 (5.5)	2.7 (0.09)	4.9 (0.61)	53,050 (2,086)	0.8 (0.03)	174 (5.6)	2.5 (0.08)	2.9 (0.50)	57,080 (1,591)	0.8 (0.03)
Management information systems and statistics	23 (1.6)	0.4 (0.03)	3.4 ! (1.12)	55,110 (1,915)	0.1 (0.01)	23 (1.9)	0.3 (0.03)	5.6 (1.67)	54,990 (3,125)	0.1 (0.01)
Business, other and medical administration	118 (3.7)	1.9 (0.06)	4.5 (0.57)	44,750 (515)	0.6 (0.02)	148 (4.8)	2.1 (0.07)	3.9 (0.69)	49,400 (1,428)	0.7 (0.02)
Communications and communications technologies	373 (8.2)	5.9 (0.12)	6.4 (0.45)	40,290 (286)	1.8 (0.04)	410 (8.2)	5.8 (0.11)	4.2 (0.39)	43,110 (955)	1.9 (0.04)
Computer and information systems	249 (6.2)	3.9 (0.10)	5.6 (0.55)	57,780 (1,764)	1.2 (0.03)	245 (7.4)	3.5 (0.10)	3.7 (0.55)	59,790 (288)	1.1 (0.03)
Construction/electrical/transportation technologies	35 (2.6)	0.5 (0.04)	4.8 ! (1.64)	49,770 (1,616)	0.2 (0.01)	41 (2.8)	0.6 (0.04)	‡ (†)	55,000 (1,774)	0.2 (0.01)
Criminal justice and fire protection	140 (4.7)	2.2 (0.07)	6.2 (0.74)	40,230 (504)	0.7 (0.02)	168 (5.1)	2.4 (0.07)	4.1 (0.63)	39,550 (1,103)	0.8 (0.02)
Education										
General education	151 (5.3)	2.4 (0.09)	4.7 (0.80)	39,290 (1,040)	0.7 (0.03)	162 (5.6)	2.3 (0.08)	3.1 (0.66)	39,620 (853)	0.7 (0.03)
Early childhood education	32 (2.0)	0.5 (0.03)	1.2 ! (0.58)	36,900 (1,641)	0.2 (0.01)	36 (2.2)	0.5 (0.03)	2.7 ! (1.09)	34,230 (1,117)	0.2 (0.01)
Elementary education	181 (5.0)	2.8 (0.08)	3.2 (0.53)	38,200 (706)	0.9 (0.02)	151 (5.1)	2.1 (0.07)	2.7 (0.55)	37,130 (924)	0.7 (0.02)
Secondary teacher education	19 (1.4)	0.3 (0.02)	2.5 ! (1.08)	36,070 (984)	0.1 (0.01)	18 (1.8)	0.3 (0.03)	‡ (†)	38,580 (1,787)	0.1 (0.01)
Education, other	190 (4.8)	3.0 (0.07)	2.9 (0.45)	39,210 (856)	0.9 (0.02)	183 (5.5)	2.6 (0.08)	2.0 (0.40)	38,420 (1,135)	0.8 (0.03)
Engineering and engineering-related fields										
General engineering	63 (3.0)	1.0 (0.05)	4.3 ! (1.44)	60,210 (613)	0.3 (0.01)	63 (3.6)	0.9 (0.05)	2.9 ! (1.12)	60,330 (2,431)	0.3 (0.02)
Chemical engineering	28 (2.2)	0.4 (0.03)	4.4 ! (1.42)	68,100 (2,580)	0.1 (0.01)	35 (2.2)	0.5 (0.03)	4.3 ! (1.76)	67,540 (1,848)	0.2 (0.01)
Civil engineering	46 (2.9)	0.7 (0.05)	6.6 (1.69)	59,520 (1,152)	0.2 (0.01)	56 (2.7)	0.8 (0.04)	2.6 ! (0.90)	59,360 (2,167)	0.3 (0.01)
Computer engineering	45 (2.8)	0.7 (0.04)	7.1 (1.50)	65,670 (1,115)	0.2 (0.01)	54 (2.9)	0.8 (0.04)	1.8 ! (0.81)	70,120 (3,269)	0.2 (0.01)
Electrical engineering	86 (4.3)	1.3 (0.07)	5.1 (1.13)	65,150 (1,069)	0.4 (0.02)	92 (4.5)	1.3 (0.06)	3.4 (0.84)	68,220 (1,005)	0.4 (0.02)
Mechanical engineering	86 (3.9)	1.3 (0.06)	3.7 (0.77)	61,780 (1,316)	0.4 (0.02)	103 (4.0)	1.5 (0.06)	2.4 (0.59)	67,470 (2,107)	0.5 (0.02)
Engineering, other	78 (3.6)	1.2 (0.06)	4.9 (1.01)	59,970 (556)	0.4 (0.02)	96 (3.7)	1.4 (0.05)	3.4 (0.76)	65,130 (1,079)	0.4 (0.02)
Engineering technologies	42 (2.5)	0.7 (0.04)	4.7 (1.17)	56,470 (2,265)	0.2 (0.01)	45 (2.9)	0.6 (0.04)	2.7 ! (1.05)	56,220 (4,690)	0.2 (0.01)
English language and literature	194 (5.2)	3.0 (0.08)	7.6 (0.73)	38,220 (712)	0.9 (0.02)	219 (5.6)	3.1 (0.08)	5.9 (0.77)	40,260 (47)	1.0 (0.03)
Family and consumer sciences	55 (3.1)	0.9 (0.05)	3.9 (0.97)	36,580 (1,577)	0.3 (0.01)	59 (3.0)	0.8 (0.04)	2.9 (0.87)	35,290 (2,116)	0.3 (0.01)
Health professions										
General medical and health services	200 (6.5)	3.1 (0.10)	3.6 (0.54)	46,620 (1,564)	1.0 (0.03)	253 (6.2)	3.6 (0.09)	3.2 (0.50)	49,600 (2,005)	1.2 (0.03)
Nursing	179 (5.5)	2.8 (0.08)	3.0 (0.57)	54,410 (1,666)	0.9 (0.03)	237 (5.9)	3.4 (0.08)	1.7 (0.34)	54,020 (1,529)	1.1 (0.03)
History	138 (4.5)	2.2 (0.07)	8.4 (0.77)	41,990 (1,385)	0.7 (0.02)	145 (5.2)	2.0 (0.07)	4.1 (0.73)	40,670 (928)	0.7 (0.02)
Liberal arts and humanities	76 (3.4)	1.2 (0.05)	7.2 (1.19)	40,190 (60)	0.4 (0.02)	79 (4.7)	1.1 (0.07)	5.2 (1.08)	39,530 (764)	0.4 (0.02)
Linguistics and comparative language and literature	68 (3.5)	1.1 (0.05)	8.6 (1.73)	39,140 (1,694)	0.3 (0.02)	75 (3.1)	1.1 (0.04)	7.0 (1.25)	41,150 (1,101)	0.3 (0.01)
Mathematics	78 (3.8)	1.2 (0.06)	4.6 (1.04)	50,190 (854)	0.4 (0.02)	75 (3.3)	1.1 (0.05)	4.7 (1.29)	50,360 (1,665)	0.3 (0.01)
Multi/interdisciplinary studies	55 (2.6)	0.9 (0.04)	5.4 (0.96)	41,190 (1,863)	0.3 (0.01)	74 (4.0)	1.0 (0.06)	5.2 (1.23)	41,250 (1,519)	0.3 (0.02)
Natural sciences										
Biology	364 (8.1)	5.7 (0.13)	4.9 (0.50)	43,300 (883)	1.7 (0.04)	429 (8.3)	6.1 (0.11)	3.3 (0.37)	45,190 (351)	2.0 (0.04)
Environmental science	42 (2.8)	0.7 (0.04)	9.7 (1.98)	40,100 (792)	0.2 (0.01)	49 (2.9)	0.7 (0.04)	5.0 (1.37)	39,330 (1,706)	0.2 (0.01)
Physical sciences	180 (4.8)	2.8 (0.08)	4.7 (0.76)	42,230 (1,627)	0.9 (0.02)	197 (6.8)	2.8 (0.10)	2.9 (0.45)	43,820 (2,476)	0.9 (0.03)

See notes at end of table.

Table 505.10. Number, percentage distribution, unemployment rates, and median earnings of 25- to 29-year-old bachelor's degree holders and percentage of degree holders among all 25- to 29-year-olds, by field of study: 2010 and 2014—Continued

[Standard errors appear in parentheses]

Field of study	2010					2014				
	25- to 29-year-old bachelor's degree holders				Percent of all 25- to 29-year-olds with degree in specific field	25- to 29-year-old bachelor's degree holders				Percent of all 25- to 29-year-olds with degree in specific field
	Number, in thousands	Percentage distribution	Unemployment rate	Median annual earnings (in current dollars)		Number, in thousands	Percentage distribution	Unemployment rate	Median annual earnings (in current dollars)	
1	2	3	4	5	6	7	8	9	10	11
Physical fitness, parks, recreation and leisure	101 (3.6)	1.6 (0.06)	3.5 (0.68)	40,270 (270)	0.5 (0.02)	136 (4.5)	1.9 (0.06)	4.1 (0.79)	39,880 (1,957)	0.6 (0.02)
Philosophy and religious studies	53 (2.3)	0.8 (0.04)	7.8 (1.56)	41,290 (2,496)	0.3 (0.01)	54 (3.2)	0.8 (0.04)	3.7 (0.99)	44,410 (4,247)	0.2 (0.01)
Psychology	378 (7.9)	5.9 (0.12)	5.9 (0.48)	38,230 (640)	1.8 (0.04)	409 (7.9)	5.8 (0.11)	4.7 (0.49)	37,650 (672)	1.9 (0.04)
Public administration and public policy	12 (1.6)	0.2 (0.02)	‡ (†)	52,350 (5,582)	0.1 (0.01)	13 (1.3)	0.2 (0.02)	14.1 ! (4.97)	40,840 (1,583)	0.1 (0.01)
Social sciences										
Anthropology and archeology	33 (2.0)	0.5 (0.03)	4.5 (1.14)	39,210 (2,106)	0.2 (0.01)	40 (2.6)	0.6 (0.04)	8.0 (2.15)	39,470 (2,179)	0.2 (0.01)
Economics	126 (4.4)	2.0 (0.07)	8.2 (1.00)	54,200 (1,552)	0.6 (0.02)	147 (5.5)	2.1 (0.08)	4.7 (0.80)	58,710 (2,521)	0.7 (0.03)
Geography	15 (1.7)	0.2 (0.03)	9.2 ! (3.53)	44,030 (2,749)	0.1 (0.01)	14 (1.4)	0.2 (0.02)	6.6 ! (2.48)	44,350 (3,398)	0.1 (0.01)
International relations	23 (2.0)	0.4 (0.03)	7.1 ! (2.75)	49,100 (1,918)	0.1 (0.01)	35 (3.0)	0.5 (0.04)	6.6 (1.75)	57,630 (3,939)	0.2 (0.01)
Political science and government	173 (4.8)	2.7 (0.08)	5.9 (0.70)	45,310 (1,071)	0.8 (0.02)	182 (4.9)	2.6 (0.07)	6.7 (0.78)	47,850 (1,803)	0.8 (0.02)
Sociology	116 (4.3)	1.8 (0.07)	7.6 (1.15)	39,750 (1,438)	0.6 (0.02)	107 (4.4)	1.5 (0.06)	4.6 (1.14)	39,800 (315)	0.5 (0.02)
Miscellaneous social sciences	32 (2.0)	0.5 (0.03)	5.3 (1.38)	40,280 (1,627)	0.2 (0.01)	37 (2.8)	0.5 (0.04)	4.8 (1.41)	39,940 (736)	0.2 (0.01)
Social work and human services	59 (2.8)	0.9 (0.04)	5.6 (1.38)	34,950 (152)	0.3 (0.01)	75 (4.1)	1.1 (0.06)	5.7 (1.41)	35,480 (658)	0.3 (0.02)
Theology and religious vocations	28 (2.0)	0.4 (0.03)	3.9 ! (1.88)	33,590 (1,456)	0.1 (0.01)	36 (2.4)	0.5 (0.03)	5.0 ! (1.94)	34,910 (2,229)	0.2 (0.01)
Other fields	26 (2.0)	0.4 (0.03)	9.0 (2.31)	37,770 (4,192)	0.1 (0.01)	25 (2.2)	0.4 (0.03)	4.8 ! (1.72)	37,210 (5,291)	0.1 (0.01)

†Not applicable.
!Interpret data with caution. The coefficient of variation (CV) for this estimate is between 30 and 50 percent.
‡Reporting standards not met. Either there are too few cases for a reliable estimate or the coefficient of variation (CV) is 50 percent or greater.

NOTE: The first bachelor's degree major reported by respondents was used to classify their field of study, even though they were able to report a second bachelor's degree major and may possess advanced degrees in other fields. Detail may not sum to totals because of rounding.
SOURCE: U.S. Department of Commerce, Census Bureau, 2010 and 2014 American Community Survey (ACS) Public Use Microdata Sample (PUMS) data. (This table was prepared February 2016.)

Table 505.15. Number, percentage distribution, and median annual earnings of 25- to 34-year-olds with a bachelor's or higher degree, by sex, race/ethnicity, and selected employment and occupational characteristics: 2014

[Standard errors appear in parentheses]

Selected employment or occupational characteristic	Total	Sex Male	Sex Female	Race/ethnicity White	Race/ethnicity Black	Race/ethnicity Hispanic	Race/ethnicity Asian	Race/ethnicity Pacific Islander	Race/ethnicity American Indian/Alaska Native	Race/ethnicity Two or more races
1	2	3	4	5	6	7	8	9	10	11
All 25- to 34-year-olds with a bachelor's or higher degree *(Number in thousands)*	14,360 (56.6)	6,324 (30.3)	8,036 (36.4)	9,703 (38.6)	1,158 (14.1)	1,316 (17.3)	1,770 (13.6)	11 (1.3)	37 (2.4)	327 (8.5)
All 25- to 34-year-olds with a bachelor's or higher degree *(Percentage distribution)*	100.0 (†)	100.0 (†)	100.0 (†)	100.0 (†)	100.0 (†)	100.0 (†)	100.0 (†)	100.0 (†)	100.0 (†)	100.0 (†)
Employment status										
Employed	86.3 (0.11)	90.3 (0.16)	83.1 (0.19)	88.2 (0.13)	86.8 (0.53)	84.4 (0.42)	77.5 (0.41)	85.0 (3.75)	82.1 (2.42)	83.8 (0.80)
Full-time	75.7 (0.14)	82.3 (0.19)	70.4 (0.22)	77.4 (0.17)	76.5 (0.60)	73.1 (0.46)	68.3 (0.40)	75.8 (4.81)	74.8 (2.64)	71.6 (0.92)
Part-time	10.6 (0.11)	8.0 (0.13)	12.7 (0.15)	10.8 (0.12)	10.2 (0.42)	11.3 (0.34)	9.2 (0.27)	9.2! (3.69)	7.3 (1.64)	12.3 (0.67)
Less than 20 hours per week	2.5 (0.04)	1.6 (0.06)	3.2 (0.06)	2.5 (0.05)	2.3 (0.19)	2.6 (0.18)	2.4 (0.14)	‡ (†)	1.5! (0.68)	3.1 (0.38)
20 to 29 hours per week	4.5 (0.07)	3.5 (0.09)	5.4 (0.10)	4.5 (0.07)	4.4 (0.26)	5.1 (0.23)	4.5 (0.19)	‡ (†)	4.3! (1.31)	5.1 (0.50)
30 to 34 hours per week	3.6 (0.07)	2.9 (0.07)	4.1 (0.09)	3.8 (0.09)	3.5 (0.24)	3.6 (0.24)	2.3 (0.14)	‡ (†)	1.5! (0.60)	4.1 (0.40)
Unemployed	3.1 (0.07)	3.4 (0.10)	2.9 (0.08)	2.6 (0.07)	5.3 (0.32)	4.3 (0.24)	3.1 (0.16)	5.9! (2.37)	5.0! (1.61)	4.9 (0.52)
Not in labor force	10.6 (0.11)	6.3 (0.14)	14.0 (0.17)	9.2 (0.12)	7.9 (0.41)	11.3 (0.35)	19.4 (0.40)	9.1! (2.92)	12.9 (1.92)	11.3 (0.66)
Enrolled in graduate school	2.9 (0.05)	3.1 (0.09)	2.8 (0.08)	2.4 (0.05)	2.5 (0.21)	2.8 (0.18)	6.0 (0.24)	‡ (†)	2.4! (0.92)	3.9 (0.48)
Not enrolled in graduate school	7.7 (0.10)	3.2 (0.10)	11.2 (0.16)	6.8 (0.11)	5.4 (0.35)	8.5 (0.29)	13.3 (0.30)	8.7! (2.86)	10.5 (1.64)	7.3 (0.52)
Major occupation group[1]	100.0 (†)	100.0 (†)	100.0 (†)	100.0 (†)	100.0 (†)	100.0 (†)	100.0 (†)	100.0 (†)	100.0 (†)	100.0 (†)
Management	12.4 (0.12)	14.2 (0.20)	10.8 (0.15)	12.9 (0.13)	10.8 (0.44)	12.0 (0.43)	10.7 (0.35)	12.2! (4.48)	10.6 (1.97)	11.1 (0.69)
Business and financial operations	10.5 (0.11)	10.4 (0.17)	10.6 (0.14)	10.4 (0.14)	10.7 (0.40)	9.9 (0.37)	11.6 (0.34)	17.0! (5.36)	4.4 (1.16)	9.7 (0.70)
Computer and mathematical	6.8 (0.10)	11.2 (0.18)	3.1 (0.08)	5.3 (0.09)	4.6 (0.29)	3.8 (0.24)	20.1 (0.43)	‡ (†)	3.0! (0.93)	7.4 (0.69)
Architecture and engineering	3.9 (0.09)	6.7 (0.16)	1.6 (0.06)	3.8 (0.10)	1.9 (0.20)	3.9 (0.27)	6.0 (0.30)	‡ (†)	‡ (†)	4.0 (0.46)
Life, physical, and social sciences	2.5 (0.06)	2.6 (0.08)	2.4 (0.07)	2.4 (0.06)	1.5 (0.17)	1.9 (0.19)	4.1 (0.22)	‡ (†)	1.6! (0.69)	3.3 (0.42)
Community and social services	3.8 (0.07)	2.4 (0.08)	5.0 (0.10)	3.5 (0.08)	7.6 (0.36)	5.0 (0.24)	1.2 (0.14)	‡ (†)	5.2 (1.27)	4.7 (0.53)
Legal	2.5 (0.06)	2.6 (0.09)	2.4 (0.08)	2.6 (0.08)	2.0 (0.18)	2.3 (0.20)	1.9 (0.15)	‡ (†)	‡ (†)	2.5 (0.39)
Education, training, and library	13.8 (0.12)	8.9 (0.16)	18.1 (0.19)	15.1 (0.14)	12.4 (0.51)	13.3 (0.40)	8.1 (0.30)	9.4! (3.37)	14.1 (2.12)	12.3 (0.72)
Arts, design, entertainment, sports, and media	4.3 (0.08)	4.5 (0.14)	4.1 (0.09)	4.6 (0.11)	2.4 (0.19)	4.2 (0.26)	3.1 (0.22)	‡ (†)	2.9! (1.01)	5.4 (0.51)
Healthcare practitioners and technicians	10.2 (0.11)	5.3 (0.13)	14.4 (0.16)	10.3 (0.12)	9.6 (0.47)	7.7 (0.34)	12.2 (0.41)	15.9! (5.07)	10.6 (2.54)	9.6 (0.82)
Healthcare support	1.0 (0.04)	0.5 (0.04)	1.4 (0.06)	0.8 (0.04)	1.8 (0.18)	1.4 (0.14)	1.0 (0.13)	‡ (†)	‡ (†)	1.3 (0.23)
Protective service	1.8 (0.04)	3.0 (0.08)	0.8 (0.04)	1.8 (0.05)	2.7 (0.23)	2.4 (0.20)	0.6 (0.09)	‡ (†)	1.8 (0.78)	1.8 (0.35)
Food preparation and serving	2.3 (0.06)	2.1 (0.08)	2.3 (0.08)	2.4 (0.07)	1.5 (0.17)	2.9 (0.21)	1.6 (0.15)	‡ (†)	2.4! (0.78)	2.6 (0.36)
Building and grounds cleaning and maintenance	0.5 (0.03)	0.8 (0.04)	0.3 (0.03)	0.5 (0.03)	0.5 (0.11)	1.1 (0.15)	0.2 (0.05)	‡ (†)	‡ (†)	0.3! (0.12)
Personal care and service	1.9 (0.05)	1.1 (0.06)	2.6 (0.09)	1.8 (0.06)	3.1 (0.33)	2.2 (0.19)	1.5 (0.12)	‡ (†)	5.6! (1.75)	1.9 (0.33)
Sales and related	8.4 (0.12)	9.9 (0.19)	7.1 (0.14)	8.8 (0.13)	8.1 (0.42)	8.8 (0.36)	5.9 (0.27)	‡ (†)	8.1 (1.90)	8.6 (0.74)
Office and administrative support	9.3 (0.09)	6.7 (0.13)	11.5 (0.14)	8.7 (0.11)	14.1 (0.54)	11.3 (0.45)	7.5 (0.28)	10.1! (3.23)	13.7 (2.68)	9.2 (0.64)
Farming, fishing, and forestry	0.2 (0.01)	0.2 (0.02)	0.1 (0.01)	0.2 (0.02)	0.1! (0.03)	0.2 (0.05)	0.1! (0.03)	‡ (†)	‡ (†)	‡ (†)
Construction and extraction	0.8 (0.03)	1.5 (0.07)	0.1 (0.02)	0.8 (0.04)	0.5 (0.10)	1.5 (0.18)	0.2! (0.05)	‡ (†)	‡ (†)	0.3! (0.15)
Installation, maintenance, and repair	0.7 (0.03)	1.3 (0.06)	0.2 (0.02)	0.6 (0.03)	0.8 (0.13)	0.9 (0.10)	0.5 (0.07)	‡ (†)	‡ (†)	1.3! (0.49)
Production	1.4 (0.05)	2.1 (0.09)	0.9 (0.04)	1.4 (0.06)	1.7 (0.22)	1.7 (0.14)	1.3 (0.13)	‡ (†)	6.3! (2.49)	1.2 (0.27)
Transportation and material moving	1.2 (0.04)	2.2 (0.08)	0.4 (0.03)	1.2 (0.05)	1.6 (0.18)	1.6 (0.18)	0.7 (0.09)	‡ (†)	2.9! (1.22)	1.4 (0.26)
Military-specific	‡ (†)	‡ (†)	‡ (†)	‡ (†)	‡ (†)	‡ (†)	‡ (†)	‡ (†)	‡ (†)	‡ (†)
Class of worker[1]	100.0 (†)	100.0 (†)	100.0 (†)	100.0 (†)	100.0 (†)	100.0 (†)	100.0 (†)	100.0 (†)	100.0 (†)	100.0 (†)
Private for-profit wage and salary	65.7 (0.20)	72.1 (0.23)	60.3 (0.29)	64.7 (0.21)	61.6 (0.78)	65.1 (0.62)	75.9 (0.41)	63.2 (6.97)	55.6 (3.87)	63.8 (1.22)
Employee of private company	64.0 (0.21)	69.8 (0.23)	59.0 (0.30)	62.8 (0.22)	60.5 (0.78)	63.6 (0.61)	74.5 (0.43)	61.0 (7.08)	54.1 (3.95)	62.3 (1.23)
Self-employed in own incorporated business	1.7 (0.04)	2.3 (0.07)	1.2 (0.05)	1.9 (0.06)	1.1 (0.17)	1.4 (0.14)	1.4 (0.12)	‡ (†)	1.5! (0.70)	1.5 (0.25)
Private nonprofit wage and salary	12.8 (0.12)	9.2 (0.15)	15.9 (0.19)	13.3 (0.14)	12.6 (0.54)	11.2 (0.39)	10.4 (0.33)	20.1 (5.79)	12.0 (2.27)	14.8 (0.75)
Government	18.6 (0.14)	15.7 (0.17)	21.2 (0.21)	18.8 (0.15)	24.3 (0.64)	20.8 (0.54)	11.6 (0.34)	14.7! (4.53)	28.8 (3.20)	18.0 (0.86)
Local	8.6 (0.10)	6.6 (0.11)	10.4 (0.15)	8.9 (0.13)	10.2 (0.42)	11.1 (0.37)	4.0 (0.21)	‡ (†)	14.4 (2.65)	7.2 (0.70)
State	7.1 (0.10)	5.8 (0.11)	8.2 (0.15)	7.2 (0.11)	8.6 (0.42)	6.6 (0.32)	5.4 (0.22)	8.9! (3.78)	8.4 (1.67)	7.4 (0.52)
Federal	2.9 (0.07)	3.3 (0.09)	2.6 (0.09)	2.6 (0.07)	5.6 (0.38)	3.2 (0.24)	2.3 (0.17)	‡ (†)	6.0 (1.74)	3.4 (0.40)
Self-employed in own nonincorporated business	2.8 (0.07)	3.0 (0.09)	2.7 (0.08)	3.1 (0.1)	1.5 (0.18)	2.9 (0.24)	1.9 (0.14)	‡ (†)	3.6! (1.44)	3.3 (0.48)
Unpaid family	0.1 (0.01)	0.1 (0.01)	0.1 (0.01)	# (0.01)	‡ (†)	# (0.02)	0.2 (0.04)	‡ (†)	‡ (†)	‡ (†)

See notes at end of table.

Table 505.15. Number, percentage distribution, and median annual earnings of 25- to 34-year-olds with a bachelor's or higher degree, by sex, race/ethnicity, and selected employment and occupational characteristics: 2014—Continued

[Standard errors appear in parentheses]

Median annual earnings (in current dollars)

Selected employment or occupational characteristic	Total	Sex — Male	Sex — Female	Race/ethnicity — White	Black	Hispanic	Asian	Pacific Islander	American Indian/ Alaska Native	Two or more races
1	2	3	4	5	6	7	8	9	10	11
All 25- to 34-year-old bachelor's degree holders who were full-time year-round workers²	$50,370 (4)	$55,460 (1)	$46,290 (561)	$50,380 (4)	$42,210 (113)	$45,360 (262)	$62,590 (972)	$46,990 (3,049)	$37,280 (2,157)	$48,350 (1,038)
Major occupation group¹										
Management	60,370 (36)	65,280 (163)	54,850 (260)	60,440 (42)	50,100 (1,120)	54,900 (550)	70,390 (2,173)	47,350 (8,191)	51,760 (14,328)	58,880 (3,836)
Business and financial operations	55,460 (909)	60,280 (75)	51,770 (491)	56,400 (553)	49,950 (1,644)	50,130 (989)	64,650 (1,114)	44,850 (8,072)	49,050 (3,166)	51,540 (3,569)
Computer and mathematical	70,050 (182)	70,560 (1,238)	64,910 (685)	67,490 (1,174)	55,340 (4,100)	62,730 (3,711)	78,930 (1,926)	53,680 (6,953)	35,690 (5,854)	60,430 (5,399)
Architecture and engineering	70,330 (73)	70,460 (89)	65,230 (1,124)	70,020 (1,026)	59,210 (3,376)	65,510 (2,354)	77,170 (1,952)	‡ (†)	49,940 (6,652)	64,700 (5,817)
Life, physical, and social sciences	48,090 (749)	48,370 (1,264)	47,280 (1,018)	48,020 (1,016)	46,040 (3,049)	49,610 (1,626)	47,450 (3,358)	‡ (†)	35,830 (1,277)	48,580 (2,744)
Community and social services	38,820 (666)	39,930 (221)	38,250 (347)	38,770 (640)	38,000 (1,294)	38,320 (2,052)	44,480 (2,729)	‡ (†)	‡ (†)	39,510 (4,220)
Legal	70,310 (878)	80,020 (2,152)	61,960 (2,885)	75,030 (2,031)	60,370 (3,963)	53,760 (3,781)	74,790 (9,674)	‡ (†)	31,360 (1,391)	73,000 (11,354)
Education, training, and library	40,330 (115)	41,310 (767)	40,320 (9)	41,090 (881)	38,910 (801)	43,200 (574)	36,000 (2,027)	‡ (†)	51,880 (6,890)	42,730 (1,115)
Arts, design, entertainment, sports, and media	46,350 (937)	48,040 (1,229)	45,370 (617)	46,310 (1,047)	42,220 (2,216)	45,280 (3,986)	50,230 (1,808)	50,150 (2,535)	41,200 (4,732)	45,260 (1,692)
Healthcare practitioners and technicians	58,190 (1,038)	60,160 (119)	57,250 (727)	58,020 (748)	53,550 (1,523)	54,030 (2,008)	64,270 (2,016)	‡ (†)	29,660 (7,801)	55,910 (3,074)
Healthcare support	30,020 (168)	29,630 (422)	30,070 (561)	30,070 (534)	29,510 (1,110)	32,290 (2,727)	27,990 (5,159)	22,180! (8,750)	26,740 (3,857)	28,640 (881)
Protective service	50,070 (222)	50,360 (1,468)	46,380 (1,536)	50,360 (1,152)	41,750 (3,468)	49,840 (2,772)	56,420 (5,610)	‡ (†)	28,780 (4,214)	44,490 (5,747)
Food preparation and serving	27,180 (1,168)	29,200 (1,391)	26,080 (1,131)	28,160 (1,253)	22,000 (3,069)	24,660 (3,288)	29,120 (2,699)	‡ (†)	‡ (†)	30,670 (5,334)
Building and grounds cleaning and maintenance	30,350 (2,323)	32,520 (2,633)	34,330 (2,831)	34,330 (2,116)	30,560 (4,553)	24,600 (2,064)	28,070 (4,667)	‡ (†)	33,890 (6,186)	24,940 (3,170)
Personal care and service	29,960 (1,561)	32,020 (1,199)	27,140 (1,289)	30,060 (324)	26,930 (1,979)	31,010 (2,214)	24,130 (2,761)	36,540 (1,591)	35,380 (6,541)	36,840 (1,225)
Sales and related	50,350 (22)	54,600 (488)	45,340 (33)	50,420 (1,316)	40,260 (678)	44,440 (1,864)	48,300 (1,349)	25,200 (3,076)	36,760 (6,421)	44,370 (3,939)
Office and administrative support	37,260 (250)	40,270 (17)	36,120 (844)	38,640 (810)	33,180 (1,407)	35,200 (1,263)	39,400 (803)	‡ (†)	‡ (†)	35,280 (1,388)
Farming, fishing, and forestry	32,200 (2,263)	32,130 (2,052)	32,270 (6,874)	31,820 (2,480)	41,190 (6,424)	31,740 (4,921)	‡ (†)	‡ (†)	27,400 (4,966)	‡ (†)
Construction and extraction	41,580 (1,803)	42,260 (1,796)	33,750 (4,130)	41,310 (1,637)	39,850 (7,558)	33,730 (6,926)	76,870! (29,172)	‡ (†)	‡ (†)	42,700 (9,619)
Installation, maintenance, and repair	43,200 (1,818)	44,200 (1,835)	38,000 (5,378)	44,870 (1,695)	40,310 (4,879)	39,990 (3,006)	39,950 (10,027)	‡ (†)	‡ (†)	69,680! (26,350)
Production	43,150 (2,086)	45,180 (902)	38,000 (1,747)	44,620 (601)	35,940 (2,616)	35,940 (5,193)	49,430 (4,261)	‡ (†)	‡ (†)	42,260 (11,445)
Transportation and material moving	39,510 (1,236)	40,060 (251)	32,300 (3,241)	40,330 (2,279)	34,400 (3,603)	‡ (†)	28,230 (3,456)	‡ (†)	44,350 (7,667)	29,440 (2,974)
Military-specific	‡ (†)	‡ (†)	‡ (†)	‡ (†)	‡ (†)	‡ (†)	‡ (†)	‡ (†)	‡ (†)	‡ (†)
Class of worker¹										
Private for-profit wage and salary	53,350 (66)	60,290 (21)	49,320 (933)	54,350 (216)	42,250 (611)	47,210 (1,184)	67,200 (1,076)	42,580 (5,214)	40,380 (3,276)	50,280 (640)
Employee of private company	53,340 (65)	59,920 (59)	49,340 (819)	54,340 (217)	42,260 (684)	46,380 (1,293)	67,200 (1,047)	44,440 (5,162)	40,390 (3,179)	50,280 (634)
Self-employed in own incorporated business	55,400 (1,475)	60,420 (462)	45,290 (2,969)	55,410 (2,105)	41,200 (6,805)	56,070 (5,789)	65,680 (7,206)	‡ (†)	27,620 (1,545)	47,500 (10,244)
Private nonprofit wage and salary	45,330 (15)	47,900 (892)	44,580 (864)	45,340 (18)	40,270 (707)	40,370 (929)	50,560 (954)	49,970 (1,473)	35,390 (1,868)	42,710 (2,048)
Government	45,680 (735)	50,180 (42)	44,350 (487)	45,720 (747)	42,320 (844)	46,310 (981)	51,140 (1,308)	44,260 (4,597)	35,010 (3,214)	47,900 (1,259)
Local	45,340 (17)	48,350 (442)	44,340 (772)	45,330 (18)	41,240 (1,279)	46,120 (856)	52,990 (1,995)	‡ (†)	33,720 (2,126)	47,470 (2,179)
State	42,310 (33)	45,190 (754)	41,290 (569)	42,330 (394)	38,240 (1,385)	42,210 (1,076)	47,210 (1,410)	‡ (†)	39,700 (7,787)	45,560 (1,261)
Federal	64,330 (809)	68,400 (2,059)	59,960 (339)	68,260 (1,702)	55,230 (1,887)	59,910 (2,042)	64,150 (3,416)	39,230 (11,633)	‡ (†)	55,120 (5,963)
Self-employed in own nonincorporated business	40,090 (474)	42,270 (2,961)	35,100 (1,880)	40,130 (243)	35,890 (5,442)	39,560 (4,925)	38,200 (1,584)	‡ (†)	‡ (†)	32,800 (5,583)
Unpaid family	25,520 (6,458)	30,720 (7,754)	21,690 (5,279)	33,470! (12,707)	‡ (†)	17,790 (4,843)	28,000 (7,607)	‡ (†)	‡ (†)	‡ (†)

†Not applicable.
#Rounds to zero.
!Interpret data with caution. The coefficient of variation (CV) for this estimate is between 30 and 50 percent.
‡Reporting standards not met. Either there are too few cases for a reliable estimate or the coefficient of variation (CV) is 50 percent or greater.
¹Estimates by major occupation group and class of worker are restricted to individuals currently employed.
²Estimates of median annual earnings are restricted to individuals working full time and year round.

NOTE: Estimates are for the entire population of civilian 25- to 34-year-old bachelor's degree holders, including persons living in households and persons living in group quarters (such as college residence halls, residential treatment centers, and correctional facilities). Standard errors were computed using replicate weights. Detail may not sum to totals because of rounding. Totals include other racial/ethnic groups not separately shown. Race categories exclude persons of Hispanic ethnicity.
SOURCE: U.S. Department of Commerce, Census Bureau, American Community Survey (ACS), 2014. (This table was prepared January 2016.)

Table 505.20. Unemployment rate of 25- to 34-year-olds with a bachelor's or higher degree, by undergraduate field of study, sex, race/ethnicity, and U.S. nativity and citizenship status: 2014

[Standard errors appear in parentheses]

Sex, race/ethnicity, and U.S. nativity and citizenship status	Total, all fields	Bachelor's degree in a science, technology, engineering, or mathematics (STEM) field									Bachelor's degree in a non-STEM field			
		STEM total	Agriculture/ natural resources	Architecture	Computer and information sciences	Engineering/ engineering technologies	Biology/ biomedical sciences	Mathematics/ statistics	Physical/ social sciences	Health studies	Non-STEM total	Business	Education	All other fields of study
1	2	3	4	5	6	7	8	9	10	11	12	13	14	15
Total[1]	3.5 (0.07)	3.1 (0.10)	2.9 (0.48)	3.9 (0.66)	3.2 (0.33)	2.7 (0.18)	2.9 (0.26)	3.4 (0.67)	3.9 (0.22)	2.2 (0.23)	3.7 (0.10)	3.3 (0.14)	2.4 (0.20)	4.2 (0.15)
Sex														
Male	3.6 (0.10)	3.2 (0.15)	3.4 (0.76)	4.3 (0.90)	2.9 (0.34)	2.4 (0.19)	3.1 (0.38)	4.4 (0.95)	4.4 (0.42)	1.9 (0.48)	3.9 (0.14)	3.3 (0.19)	2.9 (0.45)	4.4 (0.20)
Female	3.4 (0.09)	3.1 (0.14)	2.3 (0.44)	3.2! (1.00)	4.8 (0.84)	3.7 (0.47)	2.8 (0.30)	2.0! (0.64)	3.6 (0.25)	2.3 (0.25)	3.5 (0.12)	3.3 (0.17)	2.2 (0.22)	4.1 (0.17)
Race/ethnicity														
White	2.9 (0.07)	2.7 (0.12)	2.7 (0.54)	3.3 (0.76)	2.7 (0.39)	2.2 (0.23)	2.3 (0.24)	3.0 (0.77)	3.5 (0.23)	1.9 (0.26)	3.0 (0.10)	2.5 (0.13)	2.0 (0.19)	3.5 (0.14)
Black	5.7 (0.34)	5.1 (0.44)	†	‡ (†)	4.6 (1.17)	8.3! (1.39)	5.3 (1.41)	†	5.1 (0.78)	3.4 (0.90)	6.1 (0.46)	5.9 (0.71)	3.0! (0.94)	6.8 (0.63)
Hispanic	4.8 (0.27)	4.4 (0.37)	†	8.3! (3.15)	7.1! (2.21)	4.5 (0.93)	3.8 (0.88)	†	4.7 (0.65)	1.9! (0.74)	5.1 (0.36)	4.2 (0.51)	4.4 (1.03)	5.9 (0.52)
Asian	3.9 (0.20)	2.9 (0.21)	†	†	2.7 (0.45)	2.0 (0.29)	3.4 (0.60)	4.4! (1.72)	4.2 (0.61)	2.9 (0.58)	5.4 (0.41)	4.7 (0.50)	5.0! (1.82)	6.2 (0.67)
Pacific Islander	6.4! (2.55)	†	†	†	†	†	†	†	†	†	7.2! (2.71)	†	†	6.5! (2.99)
American Indian/Alaska Native[2]	5.7! (1.83)	3.0! (1.14)	†	†	†	†	†	†	†	†	7.3! (2.92)	†	†	6.3! (3.08)
American Indian	5.8! (1.95)	3.4! (1.25)	†	†	†	†	†	†	†	†	†	†	†	†
Alaska Native	†	†	†	†	†	†	†	†	†	†	†	†	†	†
Two or more races	5.5 (0.58)	5.9 (0.92)	13.4! (6.51)	†	7.3! (3.16)	7.0 (1.73)	3.7! (1.25)	†	6.7 (1.66)	†	5.2 (0.67)	5.4 (1.34)	†	5.2 (0.91)
Race/ethnicity by sex														
Male														
White	3.2 (0.11)	2.9 (0.19)	2.8 (0.79)	4.4 (1.11)	2.5 (0.43)	2.3 (0.27)	2.6 (0.42)	4.2 (1.03)	4.0 (0.44)	1.6 (0.44)	3.3 (0.14)	2.7 (0.20)	2.6 (0.46)	3.8 (0.20)
Black	5.8 (0.53)	4.8 (0.71)	†	†	4.9! (1.57)	7.9! (1.67)	5.7! (2.36)	†	3.4! (1.17)	†	6.3 (0.70)	6.3 (1.17)	†	6.7 (0.96)
Hispanic	4.7 (0.41)	4.4 (0.55)	†	†	5.3! (2.15)	4.0 (0.99)	4.7! (1.46)	†	4.6 (0.98)	†	5.0 (0.60)	3.9 (0.66)	2.3! (0.90)	6.1 (0.95)
Asian	3.3 (0.28)	2.5 (0.23)	†	†	2.2 (0.50)	1.0! (0.21)	3.3 (0.82)	4.2! (1.90)	5.7 (1.06)	†	5.2 (0.68)	4.5 (0.79)	†	6.0 (1.14)
Pacific Islander	8.5! (3.87)	†	†	†	†	†	†	†	†	†	12.1! (5.32)	†	†	†
American Indian/Alaska Native[2]	8.8! (4.24)	4.1! (1.74)	†	†	†	†	†	†	†	†	12.1! (5.75)	†	†	†
American Indian	†	4.5! (1.84)	†	†	†	†	†	†	†	†	†	†	†	†
Alaska Native	†	†	†	†	†	†	†	†	†	†	†	†	†	†
Two or more races	6.1 (0.90)	7.1 (1.50)	†	†	†	7.0 (2.08)	†	†	9.2! (3.80)	†	5.2 (1.02)	4.1! (1.38)	†	5.7 (1.55)
Female														
White	2.6 (0.09)	2.4 (0.16)	2.5 (0.51)	†	4.0 (1.14)	1.4! (0.40)	2.1 (0.26)	†	3.1 (0.28)	1.9 (0.29)	2.7 (0.12)	2.3 (0.17)	1.9 (0.22)	3.2 (0.17)
Black	5.7 (0.41)	5.3 (0.59)	†	†	17.2! (8.20)	9.5! (3.10)	5.2! (1.59)	†	5.9 (1.01)	3.7 (1.05)	5.9 (0.50)	5.7 (0.74)	2.6 (0.69)	6.9 (0.78)
Hispanic	4.9 (0.33)	4.4 (0.56)	†	13.8! (6.19)	4.1 (1.07)	6.3! (2.59)	3.0! (1.12)	†	4.8 (0.86)	1.9! (0.76)	5.2 (0.47)	4.5 (0.77)	5.1 (1.35)	5.7 (0.64)
Asian	4.4 (0.26)	3.5 (0.34)	†	†	†	4.8 (0.91)	3.6 (0.85)	†	2.8 (0.62)	3.0 (0.56)	5.5 (0.49)	4.9 (0.62)	4.5! (1.47)	6.3 (0.77)
Pacific Islander	†	†	†	†	†	†	†	†	†	†	†	†	†	†
American Indian/Alaska Native[2]	3.7! (1.09)	†	†	†	†	†	†	†	†	†	3.4! (1.53)	†	†	5.3! (2.63)
American Indian	3.8! (1.21)	†	†	†	†	†	†	†	†	†	†	†	†	†
Alaska Native	†	†	†	†	†	†	†	†	†	†	†	†	†	†
Two or more races	4.9 (0.71)	4.6 (0.99)	†	†	†	†	4.0! (1.65)	†	5.1! (1.60)	†	5.2 (0.92)	6.9! (2.28)	†	4.9 (1.11)
Nativity														
Hispanic														
U.S.-born[3]	4.6 (0.31)	3.8 (0.41)	†	†	†	4.7 (1.24)	3.5! (1.10)	†	4.6 (0.74)	1.7! (0.77)	5.1 (0.40)	4.6 (0.59)	3.2! (1.03)	5.8 (0.58)
Foreign-born	5.4 (0.54)	5.8 (0.84)	†	16.7! (7.06)	14.6! (4.98)	4.2! (1.54)	4.6! (1.94)	†	5.3 (1.24)	†	5.1 (0.63)	3.5 (0.79)	8.2! (2.66)	6.0 (1.18)
Asian														
U.S.-born[3]	3.7 (0.33)	3.3 (0.46)	†	†	2.0! (0.95)	3.0 (0.87)	2.2! (0.67)	†	4.2 (0.83)	3.7! (1.30)	4.0 (0.55)	2.9 (0.76)	†	5.2 (0.81)
Foreign-born	4.0 (0.27)	2.8 (0.25)	†	†	2.8 (0.51)	1.8 (0.32)	4.4 (0.91)	3.4! (1.35)	4.1 (0.75)	2.4 (0.55)	6.4 (0.57)	5.8 (0.70)	6.3! (2.70)	7.1 (1.01)
Citizenship status														
U.S.-born citizen	3.2 (0.08)	3.0 (0.11)	2.8 (0.49)	2.9 (0.63)	3.1 (0.36)	2.6 (0.19)	2.5 (0.24)	3.4 (0.84)	3.9 (0.23)	2.0 (0.22)	3.4 (0.10)	3.0 (0.14)	2.1 (0.18)	4.0 (0.14)
Naturalized citizen	4.4 (0.29)	3.9 (0.39)	†	†	5.3 (1.33)	3.0 (0.69)	3.7 (0.79)	4.3! (2.00)	4.9 (0.87)	2.6! (0.77)	4.9 (0.45)	4.4 (0.60)	3.2! (1.19)	5.7 (0.72)
Noncitizen	4.9 (0.26)	3.5 (0.23)	5.3! (2.32)	11.7! (3.59)	2.8 (0.57)	2.9 (0.37)	5.2 (1.11)	3.2! (1.32)	3.6 (0.68)	4.6 (0.92)	7.2 (0.57)	6.2 (0.74)	11.0 (2.56)	7.6 (0.80)

†Not applicable.
!Interpret data with caution. The coefficient of variation (CV) for this estimate is between 30 and 50 percent.
‡Reporting standards not met. Either there are too few cases for a reliable estimate or the coefficient of variation (CV) is 50 percent or greater.
[1]Total includes other racial/ethnic groups not shown separately.
[2]Includes persons reporting American Indian alone, persons reporting Alaska Native alone, and persons from American Indian and/or Alaska Native tribes specified or not specified.
[3]Includes those born in the 50 states, the District of Columbia, Puerto Rico, American Samoa, Guam, the U.S. Virgin Islands, and the Northern Marianas, as well as those born abroad to U.S.-citizen parents.
NOTE: The unemployment rate is the percentage of labor force participants who are not employed but are actively seeking work. The labor force consists of persons who are employed as well as persons who are not employed but are looking for work. (It does not include those who are neither employed nor looking for work.) Estimates are for the entire population of bachelor's degree holders in the indicated age range, including persons living in households and persons living in group quarters (such as college residence halls, residential treatment centers, military barracks, and correctional facilities). The first bachelor's degree major reported by respondents was used to classify their field of study, even though they were able to report a second bachelor's degree major and may possess advanced degrees in other fields. STEM fields, as defined here, consist of the fields specified in columns 4 through 11. Data were assembled based on major field aggregations, except that management of STEM activities was counted as a STEM field instead of a business field. Race categories exclude persons of Hispanic ethnicity.
SOURCE: U.S. Department of Commerce, Census Bureau, American Community Survey (ACS), 2014. (This table was prepared December 2015.)

Table 505.30. Among employed 25- to 34-year-olds with a bachelor's degree in a science, technology, engineering, or mathematics (STEM) field, percentage with STEM and non-STEM occupations, by sex, race/ethnicity, and U.S. nativity and citizenship status: 2014

[Standard errors appear in parentheses]

Sex, race/ethnicity, and U.S. nativity and citizenship status	Total, all occupation types	Science, technology, engineering, or mathematics (STEM) occupation					Non-STEM occupation								
		STEM total	Computer scientists and mathematicians	Engineers and architects	Life, physical, and social scientists	Medical professionals	Non-STEM total	Healthcare support workers	Agriculture and forestry workers	Business workers/managers	Educators	Legal professionals	Human/protective services workers	Military personnel	Other
1	2	3	4	5	6	7	8	9	10	11	12	13	14	15	16
Total[1]	100.0 (†)	46.7 (0.30)	12.2 (0.19)	8.7 (0.22)	5.0 (0.11)	20.8 (0.25)	53.3 (0.30)	1.3 (0.08)	0.2 (0.03)	20.1 (0.24)	8.6 (0.15)	1.5 (0.07)	5.0 (0.12)	0.3 (0.04)	16.2 (0.19)
Sex															
Male	100.0 (†)	47.7 (0.43)	19.2 (0.33)	13.8 (0.35)	4.8 (0.17)	9.9 (0.25)	52.3 (0.43)	0.7 (0.06)	0.3 (0.04)	22.3 (0.32)	7.0 (0.22)	1.5 (0.09)	3.6 (0.15)	0.6 (0.06)	16.4 (0.31)
Female	100.0 (†)	45.6 (0.39)	5.2 (0.18)	3.6 (0.16)	5.1 (0.15)	31.7 (0.37)	54.4 (0.39)	2.0 (0.13)	0.2 (0.03)	18.0 (0.30)	10.2 (0.22)	1.5 (0.08)	6.5 (0.19)	0.1 (0.03)	16.0 (0.28)
Race/ethnicity															
White	100.0 (†)	45.7 (0.38)	9.2 (0.19)	9.1 (0.26)	5.1 (0.13)	22.3 (0.28)	54.3 (0.38)	1.0 (0.08)	0.3 (0.04)	20.9 (0.29)	8.9 (0.20)	1.7 (0.09)	5.1 (0.14)	0.4 (0.05)	16.1 (0.25)
Black	100.0 (†)	36.2 (1.16)	8.0 (0.61)	4.4 (0.51)	2.8 (0.39)	21.0 (1.06)	63.8 (1.16)	2.8 (0.33)	0.2! (0.08)	20.0 (0.95)	8.8 (0.65)	1.2 (0.21)	10.4 (0.74)	0.2! (0.10)	20.2 (0.90)
Hispanic	100.0 (†)	36.4 (0.90)	6.5 (0.47)	8.9 (0.66)	3.7 (0.38)	17.3 (0.76)	63.6 (0.90)	2.6 (0.33)	0.4 (0.11)	20.2 (0.78)	8.4 (0.57)	1.2 (0.19)	7.1 (0.49)	0.4! (0.14)	23.3 (0.88)
Asian	100.0 (†)	60.4 (0.72)	28.3 (0.65)	9.3 (0.46)	5.8 (0.33)	16.9 (0.61)	39.6 (0.72)	1.2 (0.18)	‡ (†)	17.1 (0.55)	7.4 (0.34)	1.1 (0.13)	1.4 (0.16)	0.1! (0.05)	11.2 (0.42)
Pacific Islander	100.0 (†)	43.3 (7.91)	6.5! (2.36)	‡ (†)	4.3! (1.77)	28.4 (8.52)	56.7 (7.91)	‡ (†)	‡ (†)	25.9 (7.27)	7.1! (2.45)	‡ (†)	4.2! (1.61)	‡ (†)	16.4 (5.33)
American Indian/Alaska Native[2]	100.0 (†)	37.9 (6.37)	4.5! (1.92)	‡ (†)	4.5! (1.88)	24.1 (5.30)	62.1 (6.37)	‡ (†)	‡ (†)	15.9 (3.80)	7.9! (2.68)	‡ (†)	4.7! (1.83)	‡ (†)	30.2 (5.34)
American Indian	100.0 (†)	37.7 (6.72)	‡ (†)	‡ (†)	‡ (†)	25.5 (5.89)	62.3 (6.72)	‡ (†)	‡ (†)	13.4 (3.69)	‡ (†)	‡ (†)	‡ (†)	‡ (†)	31.1 (5.76)
Alaska Native	100.0 (†)	‡ (†)	‡ (†)	‡ (†)	‡ (†)	‡ (†)	‡ (†)	‡ (†)	‡ (†)	‡ (†)	‡ (†)	‡ (†)	‡ (†)	‡ (†)	‡ (†)
Two or more races	100.0 (†)	44.6 (2.00)	12.4 (1.31)	7.6 (1.02)	6.2 (0.81)	18.4 (1.50)	55.4 (2.00)	1.4 (0.38)	‡ (†)	19.4 (1.49)	10.1 (1.11)	0.9! (0.34)	5.8 (1.00)	‡ (†)	17.4 (1.39)
Race/ethnicity by sex															
Male															
White	100.0 (†)	45.3 (0.49)	15.2 (0.33)	14.9 (0.39)	4.9 (0.20)	10.2 (0.27)	54.7 (0.49)	0.5 (0.07)	0.4 (0.06)	24.1 (0.38)	6.9 (0.25)	1.7 (0.12)	3.8 (0.20)	0.7 (0.09)	16.6 (0.37)
Black	100.0 (†)	34.9 (1.73)	14.7 (1.22)	8.5 (1.09)	2.7 (0.64)	9.0 (1.11)	65.1 (1.73)	1.8! (0.55)	0.7! (0.21)	23.8 (1.65)	7.1 (1.05)	1.4! (0.44)	7.7 (0.95)	0.2! (0.11)	22.8 (1.39)
Hispanic	100.0 (†)	37.5 (1.60)	14.3 (0.91)	14.3 (1.15)	3.2 (0.47)	8.8 (0.87)	62.5 (1.60)	1.4 (0.39)	0.7! (0.21)	21.3 (1.11)	6.5 (0.66)	0.7! (0.18)	4.9 (0.57)	0.8! (0.26)	26.3 (1.23)
Asian	100.0 (†)	63.9 (0.96)	37.0 (0.92)	12.1 (0.68)	5.6 (0.40)	9.2 (0.57)	36.1 (0.96)	0.6 (0.14)	‡ (†)	16.4 (0.73)	7.4 (0.54)	1.1 (0.18)	0.9 (0.16)	0.1! (0.06)	9.5 (0.52)
Pacific Islander	100.0 (†)	31.9 (8.81)	11.7! (5.29)	‡ (†)	‡ (†)	8.3! (3.92)	68.1 (8.81)	‡ (†)	‡ (†)	14.8! (5.28)	‡ (†)	‡ (†)	‡ (†)	‡ (†)	40.1 (8.03)
American Indian/Alaska Native[2]	100.0 (†)	31.2 (8.94)	‡ (†)	‡ (†)	‡ (†)	‡ (†)	68.8 (8.94)	‡ (†)	‡ (†)	12.4! (5.78)	‡ (†)	‡ (†)	‡ (†)	‡ (†)	40.9 (9.04)
American Indian	100.0 (†)	‡ (†)	‡ (†)	‡ (†)	‡ (†)	‡ (†)	‡ (†)	‡ (†)	‡ (†)	‡ (†)	‡ (†)	‡ (†)	‡ (†)	‡ (†)	‡ (†)
Alaska Native	100.0 (†)	‡ (†)	‡ (†)	‡ (†)	‡ (†)	‡ (†)	‡ (†)	‡ (†)	‡ (†)	‡ (†)	‡ (†)	‡ (†)	‡ (†)	‡ (†)	‡ (†)
Two or more races	100.0 (†)	47.5 (2.78)	20.5 (2.11)	10.0 (1.81)	6.1 (1.33)	10.9 (1.71)	52.5 (2.78)	‡ (†)	‡ (†)	21.5 (2.21)	7.7 (1.63)	‡ (†)	4.3 (1.12)	‡ (†)	17.5 (1.79)
Female															
White	100.0 (†)	46.1 (0.52)	3.2 (0.17)	3.3 (0.18)	5.3 (0.20)	34.3 (0.44)	53.9 (0.52)	1.6 (0.14)	0.2 (0.04)	17.8 (0.32)	10.9 (0.29)	1.6 (0.12)	6.3 (0.21)	0.1! (0.03)	15.5 (0.35)
Black	100.0 (†)	37.0 (1.55)	3.9 (0.53)	1.9 (0.46)	2.9 (0.43)	28.3 (1.55)	63.0 (1.55)	3.4 (0.49)	‡ (†)	17.7 (1.06)	9.9 (0.85)	1.1 (0.35)	12.1 (0.95)	‡ (†)	18.6 (1.17)
Hispanic	100.0 (†)	35.4 (1.31)	2.0 (0.29)	3.7 (0.63)	4.2 (0.55)	25.4 (1.37)	64.6 (1.31)	3.8 (0.58)	‡ (†)	19.2 (1.13)	10.1 (0.86)	1.1 (0.18)	9.1 (0.82)	0.8! (0.35)	20.4 (1.17)
Asian	100.0 (†)	55.7 (1.12)	16.7 (0.85)	5.6 (0.49)	6.1 (0.47)	27.3 (1.03)	44.3 (1.12)	1.9 (0.35)	‡ (†)	18.2 (0.89)	7.5 (0.50)	1.1 (0.18)	1.9 (0.30)	‡ (†)	13.5 (0.71)
Pacific Islander	100.0 (†)	41.4 (7.61)	‡ (†)	‡ (†)	‡ (†)	33.5 (7.38)	58.6 (7.61)	‡ (†)	‡ (†)	16.5! (5.00)	9.3! (3.57)	‡ (†)	4.3! (2.15)	‡ (†)	24.4 (7.07)
American Indian/Alaska Native[2]	100.0 (†)	41.3 (8.22)	‡ (†)	‡ (†)	‡ (†)	35.0 (8.09)	58.7 (8.22)	‡ (†)	‡ (†)	13.9! (4.86)	10.0! (3.75)	‡ (†)	‡ (†)	‡ (†)	25.6 (7.60)
American Indian	100.0 (†)	‡ (†)	‡ (†)	‡ (†)	‡ (†)	‡ (†)	‡ (†)	‡ (†)	‡ (†)	‡ (†)	‡ (†)	‡ (†)	‡ (†)	‡ (†)	‡ (†)
Alaska Native	100.0 (†)	‡ (†)	‡ (†)	‡ (†)	‡ (†)	‡ (†)	‡ (†)	‡ (†)	‡ (†)	‡ (†)	‡ (†)	‡ (†)	‡ (†)	‡ (†)	‡ (†)
Two or more races	100.0 (†)	41.8 (2.39)	4.8 (1.06)	5.3 (1.20)	6.3 (1.13)	25.4 (2.07)	58.2 (2.39)	2.2 (0.65)	‡ (†)	17.4 (1.97)	12.3 (1.65)	1.2! (0.56)	7.2 (1.45)	‡ (†)	17.2 (1.92)
Nativity															
Hispanic															
U.S.-born[3]	100.0 (†)	36.5 (1.06)	5.8 (0.54)	7.6 (0.71)	3.8 (0.42)	19.3 (0.85)	63.5 (1.06)	2.5 (0.41)	0.6 (0.16)	20.6 (0.89)	8.8 (0.67)	1.4 (0.23)	8.7 (0.62)	0.5! (0.17)	20.5 (1.00)
Foreign-born	100.0 (†)	36.1 (1.91)	8.0 (1.04)	11.9 (1.33)	3.6 (0.75)	12.6 (1.36)	63.9 (1.91)	2.8 (0.79)	‡ (†)	19.2 (1.71)	7.4 (0.99)	0.7! (0.29)	3.2 (0.65)	‡ (†)	30.1 (2.11)
Asian															
U.S.-born[3]	100.0 (†)	53.0 (1.33)	12.7 (0.71)	8.3 (0.80)	5.4 (0.63)	26.6 (1.25)	47.0 (1.33)	1.6 (0.36)	‡ (†)	21.1 (1.07)	5.6 (0.60)	2.1 (0.31)	2.8 (0.51)	‡ (†)	13.7 (0.78)
Foreign-born	100.0 (†)	63.2 (0.82)	34.3 (0.83)	9.7 (0.54)	6.0 (0.37)	13.2 (0.64)	36.8 (0.82)	1.0 (0.18)	‡ (†)	15.6 (0.54)	8.1 (0.41)	0.7 (0.12)	0.8 (0.12)	0.1! (0.05)	10.3 (0.48)
Citizenship status															
U.S.-born citizen	100.0 (†)	44.4 (0.35)	8.7 (0.18)	8.5 (0.22)	4.7 (0.12)	22.5 (0.28)	55.6 (0.35)	1.3 (0.08)	0.3 (0.03)	20.9 (0.25)	8.5 (0.17)	1.6 (0.08)	5.9 (0.15)	0.4 (0.04)	16.7 (0.22)
Naturalized citizen	100.0 (†)	50.1 (1.08)	12.5 (0.70)	8.8 (0.59)	3.6 (0.36)	25.2 (0.96)	49.9 (1.08)	1.9 (0.33)	‡ (†)	20.7 (0.84)	6.3 (0.49)	1.6 (0.13)	3.6 (0.36)	0.3! (0.13)	15.5 (0.76)
Noncitizen	100.0 (†)	57.9 (0.87)	32.3 (0.83)	10.1 (0.52)	7.2 (0.34)	8.3 (0.46)	42.1 (0.87)	1.0 (0.18)	0.1! (0.04)	15.0 (0.59)	10.5 (0.46)	0.5 (0.09)	3.8 (0.14)	‡ (†)	14.1 (0.61)

†Not applicable.
!Interpret data with caution. The coefficient of variation (CV) for this estimate is between 30 and 50 percent.
‡Reporting standards not met. Either there are too few cases for a reliable estimate or the coefficient of variation (CV) is 50 percent or greater.
[1]Total includes other racial/ethnic groups not shown separately.
[2]Includes persons reporting American Indian alone, and persons from American Indian and/or Alaska Native tribes specified or not specified.
[3]Includes those born in the 50 states, the District of Columbia, Puerto Rico, American Samoa, Guam, the U.S. Virgin Islands, and the Northern Marianas, as well as those born abroad to U.S.-citizen parents.

NOTE: Estimates include persons in the indicated age range who in households as well as those who live in group quarters (such as college residence halls, military barracks, and correctional facilities). This table includes only employed persons who have a bachelor's degree in a STEM field of study. The first bachelor's degree major reported by respondents was used to classify their field of study, even though they were able to report a second bachelor's degree major and may possess advanced degrees in other fields. Aggregated occupation classifications were used to assemble the data, except that managers of STEM activities were counted as practitioners of STEM occupations instead of "Business workers/managers." Detail may not sum to totals because of rounding. Race categories exclude persons of Hispanic ethnicity. SOURCE: U.S. Department of Commerce, Census Bureau, American Community Survey (ACS), 2014. (This table was prepared December 2015.)

Table 505.40. Percentage distribution of recipients of bachelor's degrees in various fields of study 1 year after graduation, by time to completion, enrollment and employment status, and occupation: 2001 and 2009

[Standard errors appear in parentheses]

Time to completion, enrollment and employment status, and occupation	1999–2000 graduates in 2001, total		2007–08 graduates in 2009 Total[1]		Engineering		Biological and physical sciences		Mathematics and computer science		Social sciences		History		Humanities		Health professions		Business and management		Education[2]		Psychology		Public affairs and social services	
1	2	(t)	3	(t)	4	(t)	5	(t)	6	(t)	7	(t)	8	(t)	9	(t)	10	(t)	11	(t)	12	(t)	13	(t)	14	(t)
Total graduates	100.0	(t)	100.0	(t)	100.0	(t)	100.0	(t)	100.0	(t)	100.0	(t)	100.0	(t)	100.0	(t)	100.0	(t)	100.0	(t)	100.0	(t)	100.0	(t)	100.0	(t)
Time between high school graduation and degree completion																										
4 years or less	32.7	(0.83)	40.3	(0.64)	35.5	(2.68)	56.2	(2.24)	36.3	(3.27)	53.4	(2.08)	44.1	(3.78)	50.4	(2.02)	28.9	(2.01)	37.5	(1.53)	32.5	(1.65)	48.9	(2.17)	29.1	(3.42)
More than 4, up to 5 years	22.9	(0.58)	20.7	(0.51)	31.0	(2.58)	17.8	(1.74)	16.9	(2.62)	19.2	(1.62)	20.4	(2.81)	20.7	(1.57)	18.1	(1.41)	17.4	(1.09)	25.5	(1.59)	19.5	(1.73)	16.0	(2.85)
More than 5, up to 6 years	10.8	(0.48)	9.5	(0.35)	11.2	(1.69)	9.8	(1.59)	8.4	(1.79)	7.6	(1.09)	12.2	(2.87)	7.9	(1.01)	8.9	(1.14)	8.0	(0.79)	13.2	(1.34)	7.7	(1.10)	10.4	(2.12)
More than 6, up to 10 years	14.8	(0.59)	13.4	(0.42)	11.1	(1.64)	8.9	(1.21)	13.8	(2.25)	11.9	(1.21)	12.4	(2.87)	12.6	(1.40)	16.3	(1.64)	14.1	(1.01)	13.8	(1.32)	11.8	(1.54)	19.0	(3.09)
More than 10 years	18.8	(0.59)	16.0	(0.52)	11.2	(1.89)	7.3	(1.24)	24.6	(2.58)	7.8	(1.05)	10.9	(2.55)	8.3	(1.02)	27.8	(2.13)	23.1	(1.25)	15.0	(1.41)	12.1	(1.61)	25.5	(2.74)
Enrollment status																										
Enrolled	20.8	(0.51)	21.7	(0.47)	22.8	(1.98)	40.9	(2.33)	19.9	(2.58)	23.5	(1.65)	38.1	(3.99)	23.6	(1.48)	23.5	(1.93)	13.9	(1.01)	19.9	(1.36)	36.6	(2.15)	24.3	(3.28)
Not enrolled	79.2	(0.51)	78.3	(0.47)	77.2	(1.98)	59.1	(2.33)	80.1	(2.58)	76.5	(1.65)	61.9	(3.99)	76.4	(1.48)	76.5	(1.93)	86.1	(1.01)	80.1	(1.36)	63.4	(2.15)	75.7	(3.28)
Employment status																										
Employed	87.4	(0.46)	83.8	(0.49)	88.4	(1.54)	69.6	(1.92)	88.9	(1.88)	78.9	(1.72)	74.9	(3.93)	79.4	(1.58)	86.6	(1.64)	88.1	(0.95)	90.2	(1.12)	79.7	(1.91)	81.2	(2.92)
Full time	76.5	(0.52)	65.0	(0.62)	76.1	(2.12)	49.0	(2.38)	75.1	(2.67)	61.2	(1.94)	46.1	(4.35)	47.6	(2.12)	68.5	(1.86)	76.7	(1.18)	70.7	(1.74)	46.6	(2.40)	69.8	(3.44)
Part time	10.9	(0.40)	18.8	(0.48)	12.3	(1.88)	20.7	(1.84)	13.8	(2.11)	17.6	(1.72)	28.8	(3.66)	31.9	(1.72)	18.0	(1.59)	11.4	(0.92)	19.4	(1.54)	33.1	(2.33)	11.4	(2.15)
Unemployed[3]	6.1	(0.33)	9.2	(0.38)	6.7	(1.15)	7.2	(1.06)	5.8	(1.28)	11.3	(1.32)	14.5	(3.24)	11.8	(1.32)	6.4	(1.07)	8.5	(0.83)	5.1	(0.76)	10.2	(1.42)	13.5	(2.63)
Not in labor force[4]	6.4	(0.35)	7.0	(0.31)	4.9	(1.08)	23.1	(1.99)	5.3	(1.51)	9.9	(1.32)	10.6	(2.99)	8.8	(1.03)	7.0	(1.27)	3.4	(0.51)	4.7	(0.91)	10.0	(1.44)	5.2	(1.52)
Unemployment rate (labor force participants only)[5]	6.5	(—)	9.9	(—)	7.0	(—)	9.4	(—)	6.1	(—)	12.5	(—)	16.2	(—)	12.9	(—)	6.9	(—)	8.8	(—)	5.4	(—)	11.3	(—)	14.3	(—)
Total employed	100.0	(—)	100.0	(—)	100.0	(—)	100.0	(—)	100.0	(—)	100.0	(—)	100.0	(—)	100.0	(—)	100.0	(—)	100.0	(—)	100.0	(—)	100.0	(—)	100.0	(—)
Occupation																										
Administrative/clerical	4.5	(0.28)	2.6	(0.21)	‡	(t)	1.9 !	(0.61)	‡	(t)	4.1	(0.88)	4.6 !	(2.17)	4.9	(1.01)	‡	(t)	2.6	(0.51)	‡	(t)	2.9	(0.65)	5.8 !	(2.10)
Arts/communications	4.2	(0.30)	4.5	(0.32)	2.3 !	(1.09)	‡	(t)	1.6 !	(0.65)	3.0 !	(0.92)	‡	(t)	14.4	(1.54)	‡	(t)	1.3	(0.37)	1.0 !	(0.35)	‡	(t)	#	(t)
Business																										
Management	12.5	(0.47)	8.4	(0.41)	10.8	(2.08)	3.2 !	(0.96)	3.4 !	(1.24)	9.5	(1.45)	5.0 !	(1.83)	4.8	(0.99)	5.1	(1.10)	14.5	(1.08)	1.6	(0.45)	6.9	(1.43)	11.1	(2.98)
Nonmanagement	15.1	(0.58)	21.1	(0.61)	7.0	(1.54)	10.5	(1.63)	17.0	(2.82)	26.3	(2.05)	19.5	(3.67)	15.8	(1.93)	6.4	(1.14)	43.5	(1.76)	4.0	(0.76)	16.8	(1.98)	11.6	(2.91)
Computer information systems/mathematics[6]	6.8	(0.34)	4.6	(0.27)	7.0	(1.19)	‡	(t)	50.6	(3.28)	3.0	(0.89)	‡	(t)	1.0 !	(0.39)	‡	(t)	4.6	(0.69)	0.6 !	(0.27)	1.8 !	(0.77)	#	(t)
Construction/trade/transportation	3.1	(0.26)	3.3	(0.23)	5.0	(1.22)	2.5	(0.72)	2.0 !	(0.70)	2.2	(0.61)	5.1 !	(2.51)	4.2	(1.01)	‡	(t)	4.2	(0.59)	0.9 !	(0.31)	1.7	(0.50)	‡	(t)
Education	18.1	(0.52)	15.6	(0.43)	5.2	(1.26)	16.3	(2.12)	12.5	(2.01)	11.4	(1.45)	27.9	(3.49)	19.1	(1.74)	3.5	(0.72)	3.1	(0.55)	78.7	(1.61)	12.7	(1.41)	13.1	(2.69)
Engineering/engineering technician/science professions	8.4	(0.33)	6.2	(0.30)	55.6	(3.02)	28.8	(2.39)	2.2 !	(0.93)	1.0 !	(0.38)	‡	(t)	0.8 !	(0.32)	‡	(t)	1.3	(0.35)	0.2 !	(0.09)	1.7 !	(0.74)	#	(t)
Health professions	7.8	(0.26)	8.6	(0.30)	1.1 !	(0.53)	13.5	(1.62)	‡	(t)	3.3	(0.84)	3.7 !	(1.68)	2.4 !	(0.78)	74.4	(2.00)	1.2	(0.32)	1.2	(0.48)	7.0	(1.38)	2.3 !	(1.06)
Military/protective service	2.4	(0.20)	2.9	(0.24)	1.6 !	(0.72)	2.9 !	(0.89)	2.3 !	(1.12)	6.3	(1.08)	6.5 !	(2.23)	0.9 !	(0.39)	‡	(t)	2.4	(0.46)	0.8 !	(0.35)	1.8 !	(0.69)	7.0 !	(2.79)
Sales	6.8	(0.31)	7.9	(0.40)	2.1	(0.61)	7.4	(1.78)	1.6 !	(0.70)	7.4	(1.29)	8.9 !	(3.28)	9.8	(1.34)	1.9 !	(0.68)	12.9	(1.12)	1.7	(0.44)	7.4	(1.37)	5.5 !	(2.21)
Other occupations	10.2	(0.42)	14.3	(0.43)	2.0 !	(0.65)	10.9	(1.65)	4.3 !	(1.40)	22.4	(2.16)	13.0	(2.53)	21.8	(1.77)	4.6	(0.87)	8.8	(1.08)	9.2	(1.22)	38.5	(2.19)	42.4	(4.03)

—Not available.
†Not applicable.
#Rounds to zero.
!Interpret data with caution. The coefficient of variation (CV) for this estimate is between 30 and 50 percent.
‡Reporting standards not met. The coefficient of variation (CV) for this estimate is 50 percent or greater.
[1]Includes graduates in other fields not separately shown.
[2]Includes graduates who have not finished all requirements for teaching certification or were previously qualified to teach.
[3]Percentage of all graduates who are not employed, but are looking for work.
[4]Percentage of all graduates who are neither employed nor looking for work.

[5]The labor force is made up of persons who are employed and persons who are not employed but are looking for work. (It does not include those who are neither employed nor looking for work.) The unemployment rate is the percentage of labor force participants who are not employed but are actively seeking work.
[6]For 2001, does not include mathematics professions.
NOTE: Data exclude bachelor's degree recipients from U.S. Service Academies, deceased graduates, and graduates living at foreign addresses at the time of the survey. Detail may not sum to totals because of rounding.
SOURCE: U.S. Department of Education, National Center for Education Statistics, 2000/01 and 2008/09 Baccalaureate and Beyond Longitudinal Study (B&B:2000/01 and B&B:08/09). (This table was prepared August 2011.)

Table 505.50. Percentage, selected employment characteristics, and annual salaries of bachelor's degree recipients employed full time 1 year after graduation, by field of study: 1991, 2001, and 2009

[Standard errors appear in parentheses]

Selected employment characteristic and annual salary	All fields of study[1]	Engineering	Biological and physical sciences[2]	Mathematics and computer science[2]	Social sciences and history	Humanities	Health professions	Business and management	Education[3]	Psychology	Public affairs and social services
1	2	3	4	5	6	7	8	9	10	11	12
Employment characteristics											
Percent of recipients employed full time											
1989–90 recipients in June 1991	73.8 (0.36)	85.2 (0.95)	50.6 (1.72)	71.2 (1.30)	66.2 (0.94)	59.2 (1.32)	80.9 (1.35)	83.2 (0.57)	77.0 (0.74)	59.8 (1.64)	77.0 (2.06)
1999–2000 recipients in July 2001	76.5 (0.52)	86.0 (1.77)	58.6 (2.04)	83.7 (2.06)	68.3 (1.88)	67.5 (1.65)	74.8 (1.50)	85.5 (1.27)	84.0 (1.29)	64.0 (2.64)	85.1 (2.25)
2007–08 recipients in June 2009	65.0 (0.62)	76.1 (2.12)	49.0 (2.38)	75.1 (2.67)	58.0 (1.81)	50.4 (1.82)	68.5 (1.86)	77.2 (1.20)	70.6 (1.75)	46.6 (2.40)	69.8 (3.44)
Percent of full-time employees looking for a different job[4]											
1989–90 recipients in June 1991	21.5 (0.35)	12.9 (1.05)	21.0 (1.95)	16.6 (1.08)	24.5 (1.20)	25.8 (1.44)	9.2 (1.10)	20.7 (0.78)	25.5 (0.92)	21.8 (1.57)	26.8 (2.36)
1999–2000 recipients in July 2001	24.6 (0.66)	19.2 (2.30)	22.9 (2.64)	18.3 (2.36)	27.1 (2.06)	28.3 (2.13)	20.9 (1.93)	24.4 (1.51)	17.4 (1.45)	23.9 (2.54)	25.8 (2.80)
2007–08 recipients in June 2009	31.2 (0.74)	20.2 (2.53)	28.5 (3.47)	27.7 (3.37)	35.3 (2.47)	39.2 (2.56)	21.8 (2.40)	32.0 (1.61)	23.6 (1.78)	37.3 (2.99)	30.4 (4.86)
Percent of full-time employees in job closely related to field of study											
1989–90 recipients in June 1991	52.5 (0.55)	57.5 (1.24)	49.4 (2.31)	66.4 (1.34)	20.2 (1.12)	32.2 (2.07)	88.2 (2.10)	49.8 (0.79)	79.2 (0.89)	40.3 (2.13)	57.6 (2.56)
1999–2000 recipients in July 2001	56.1 (0.65)	70.0 (3.35)	48.6 (3.00)	72.7 (2.58)	28.7 (2.03)	41.5 (2.16)	77.5 (2.45)	58.7 (1.67)	84.3 (1.68)	40.1 (3.65)	61.2 (3.11)
2007–08 recipients in June 2009	49.7 (0.78)	61.3 (2.86)	49.0 (3.36)	61.9 (3.57)	21.6 (2.07)	27.6 (2.56)	81.7 (2.10)	49.3 (1.76)	82.0 (1.68)	26.6 (3.04)	57.2 (4.93)
Annual salaries of full-time employees[5]											
Average salary, in current dollars											
1989–90 recipients in June 1991	$23,600 (180)	$30,900 (390)	$21,100 (410)	$27,200 (400)	$22,100 (330)	$19,100 (350)	$31,500 (860)	$24,700 (330)	$19,100 (140)	$19,200 (310)	$20,900 (470)
1999–2000 recipients in July 2001	35,400 (300)	47,900 (840)	31,000 (710)	47,400 (1,080)	33,000 (700)	30,000 (690)	39,400 (1,110)	41,000 (860)	27,600 (370)	28,800 (990)	30,400 (1,030)
2007–08 recipients in June 2009	40,100 (340)	53,900 (1,080)	34,600 (1,220)	48,800 (1,570)	36,600 (980)	31,100 (780)	49,100 (1,290)	44,200 (890)	33,000 (490)	30,600 (910)	35,000 (1,700)
Average salary, in constant 2014 dollars											
1989–90 recipients in June 1991	$41,100 (310)	$53,800 (680)	$36,600 (720)	$47,200 (690)	$38,400 (580)	$33,200 (620)	$54,700 (1,490)	$43,000 (570)	$33,200 (240)	$33,300 (550)	$36,300 (810)
1999–2000 recipients in July 2001	47,300 (400)	64,100 (1,120)	41,400 (950)	63,400 (1,440)	44,100 (940)	40,200 (930)	52,700 (1,480)	54,800 (1,150)	36,900 (490)	38,600 (1,320)	40,600 (1,380)
2007–08 recipients in June 2009	44,200 (370)	59,500 (1,200)	38,200 (1,340)	53,900 (1,740)	40,400 (1,080)	34,300 (860)	54,200 (1,420)	48,700 (980)	36,400 (540)	33,800 (1,010)	38,600 (1,880)
Percent change in average salary, in constant 2014 dollars											
1991 to 2009	7.6	10.6	4.4	14.1	5.1	3.5	-0.8	13.2	9.5	1.5	6.6
1991 to 2001	15.2	19.2	13.2	34.3	14.7	21.4	-3.6	27.4	11.2	15.8	12.1
2001 to 2009	-6.6	-7.2	-7.7	-15.0	-8.4	-14.7	2.8	-11.1	-1.5	-12.4	-4.9
Median salary, in current dollars											
1989–90 recipients in June 1991	$21,800 (210)	$31,900 (470)	$20,000 (430)	$27,000 (510)	$20,300 (250)	$18,500 (360)	$30,400 (760)	$23,000 (300)	$19,500 (220)	$18,100 (320)	$18,600 (410)
1999–2000 recipients in July 2001	32,000 (90)	47,800 (880)	29,800 (470)	46,100 (1,990)	29,900 (360)	28,600 (700)	35,500 (770)	36,800 (700)	27,900 (410)	27,700 (1,180)	27,900 (710)
2007–08 recipients in June 2009	36,000 (220)	54,000 (900)	32,500 (1,570)	45,000 (1,830)	34,600 (920)	29,000 (1,060)	45,900 (920)	40,000 (300)	33,800 (570)	29,300 (1,040)	32,000 (1,430)
Median salary, in constant 2014 dollars											
1989–90 recipients in June 1991	$37,900 (360)	$55,400 (820)	$34,700 (740)	$46,800 (890)	$35,200 (430)	$32,100 (620)	$52,800 (1,320)	$39,900 (520)	$33,900 (380)	$31,500 (560)	$32,300 (710)
1999–2000 recipients in July 2001	42,200 (120)	63,900 (1,180)	39,900 (630)	61,600 (2,660)	40,000 (470)	38,200 (930)	47,400 (1,030)	49,200 (940)	37,400 (550)	37,100 (1,570)	37,300 (950)
2007–08 recipients in June 2009	39,700 (240)	59,600 (990)	35,800 (1,740)	49,600 (2,020)	38,200 (1,010)	32,000 (1,170)	50,700 (1,020)	44,100 (330)	37,300 (630)	32,400 (1,150)	35,300 (1,580)
Percent change in median salary, in constant 2014 dollars											
1991 to 2009	4.9	7.5	3.2	6.0	8.5	-0.3	-4.1	10.5	10.0	2.8	9.2
1991 to 2001	12.8	15.4	14.9	31.5	13.5	19.1	-10.2	23.2	10.1	17.9	15.4
2001 to 2009	-7.0	-6.8	-10.1	-19.4	-4.5	-16.3	6.9	-10.3	-0.1	-12.7	-5.4

—Not available.
[1]Includes graduates in other fields not separately shown.
[2]For 1991, physical sciences not included in column 4 with biological sciences; instead, they are included in column 5 with mathematics and computer science.
[3]Most educators work 9- to 10-month contracts.
[4]In 1991, respondents were asked whether they were "looking for a different principal job." In 2001 and 2009, they were asked whether they were "looking for a different job" (instead of "a different principal job").

[5]In all years, reported salaries of full-time workers under $1,000 were excluded from the tabulations. In addition, salaries reported as above $500,000 were set to $500,000 in 2001, and salaries reported as above $250,000 were set to $250,000 in 2009. In all years, only a tiny fraction of reported full-time salaries were either below $1,000 or above $250,000.
NOTE: Data exclude bachelor's degree recipients from U.S. Service Academies, deceased graduates, and graduates living at foreign addresses at the time of the survey. Constant dollars based on the Consumer Price Index, prepared by the Bureau of Labor Statistics, U.S. Department of Labor. Some data have been revised from previously published figures.
SOURCE: U.S. Department of Education, National Center for Education Statistics, "Recent College Graduates" survey, 1991; and 2000/01 and 2008/09 Baccalaureate and Beyond Longitudinal Study (B&B:2000/01 and B&B:08/09). (This table was prepared August 2015.)

Table 506.10. Percentage of 1972 high school seniors, 1992 high school seniors, and 2004 high school seniors who felt that certain life values were "very important," by sex: Selected years, 1972 through 2004

[Standard errors appear in parentheses]

Year and sex	Being successful in work	Finding steady work	Having lots of money	Being a leader in the community	Helping others in the community	Correcting inequalities	Having children	Having a happy family life	Giving my children better opportunities	Living close to parents or relatives	Moving from area	Having strong friendships	Having leisure time
1	2	3	4	5	6	7	8	9	10	11	12	13	14
1972 seniors													
In 1972													
Total	84.5 (0.35)	78.2 (0.39)	17.9 (0.36)	11.4 (0.29)	—	27.1 (0.41)	(†)	82.1 (0.36)	67.7 (0.44)	8.0 (0.25)	14.3 (0.33)	79.1 (0.37)	(†)
Male	86.4 (0.47)	82.3 (0.52)	25.8 (0.58)	14.9 (0.47)	—	23.0 (0.55)	(†)	79.0 (0.55)	67.4 (0.62)	7.4 (0.34)	14.0 (0.46)	80.5 (0.52)	(†)
Female	82.6 (0.51)	74.1 (0.58)	10.1 (0.38)	7.9 (0.34)	—	31.2 (0.60)	(†)	85.2 (0.47)	67.9 (0.61)	8.7 (0.37)	14.7 (0.47)	77.6 (0.53)	(†)
In 1974													
Total	77.2 (0.40)	66.9 (0.44)	13.1 (0.31)	6.1 (0.21)	—	16.6 (0.34)	(†)	84.8 (0.34)	59.4 (0.45)	9.9 (0.28)	7.6 (0.25)	75.4 (0.40)	57.9 (0.46)
Male	80.3 (0.54)	74.4 (0.59)	17.6 (0.51)	8.2 (0.35)	—	15.8 (0.47)	(†)	82.7 (0.51)	58.8 (0.65)	8.0 (0.36)	7.9 (0.36)	76.2 (0.57)	60.6 (0.65)
Female	74.2 (0.58)	59.7 (0.64)	8.6 (0.36)	4.1 (0.25)	—	17.3 (0.48)	(†)	86.9 (0.44)	60.0 (0.63)	11.8 (0.42)	7.3 (0.34)	74.7 (0.56)	55.4 (0.65)
In 1976													
Total	74.5 (0.41)	70.4 (0.43)	13.0 (0.31)	6.2 (0.22)	—	16.1 (0.34)	(†)	85.1 (0.34)	57.9 (0.46)	9.3 (0.27)	6.4 (0.23)	74.3 (0.41)	62.6 (0.45)
Male	79.8 (0.55)	79.3 (0.55)	17.1 (0.50)	8.7 (0.36)	—	15.6 (0.48)	(†)	84.2 (0.50)	58.8 (0.65)	7.2 (0.34)	6.6 (0.33)	76.4 (0.57)	65.1 (0.64)
Female	69.3 (0.61)	61.6 (0.64)	9.0 (0.37)	3.8 (0.24)	—	16.5 (0.48)	(†)	85.9 (0.46)	57.1 (0.64)	11.4 (0.42)	6.3 (0.32)	72.3 (0.58)	60.0 (0.64)
1992 seniors													
In 1992													
Total	88.8 (0.44)	88.5 (0.41)	37.1 (0.63)	(†)	33.8 (0.63)	20.2 (0.55)	44.6 (0.65)	79.0 (0.57)	76.0 (0.56)	16.6 (0.46)	20.6 (0.55)	80.0 (0.52)	64.0 (0.64)
Male	88.3 (0.69)	87.8 (0.59)	45.6 (0.98)	(†)	27.9 (0.93)	17.1 (0.72)	39.5 (0.96)	75.8 (0.89)	74.6 (0.83)	14.9 (0.60)	20.9 (0.83)	79.8 (0.70)	66.3 (0.95)
Female	89.3 (0.53)	89.2 (0.56)	28.6 (0.79)	(†)	39.7 (0.86)	23.3 (0.83)	49.7 (0.87)	82.1 (0.72)	77.3 (0.75)	18.2 (0.68)	20.3 (0.71)	80.3 (0.77)	61.7 (0.84)
In 1994													
Total	89.7 (0.38)	89.7 (0.40)	36.9 (0.63)	(†)	(†)	(†)	(†)	—	91.3 (0.34)	—	—	86.2 (0.44)	(†)
Male	89.6 (0.55)	89.1 (0.61)	41.3 (0.94)	(†)	(†)	(†)	(†)	—	91.1 (0.52)	—	—	87.2 (0.58)	(†)
Female	89.7 (0.52)	90.3 (0.52)	32.5 (0.86)	(†)	(†)	(†)	(†)	—	91.5 (0.43)	—	—	85.1 (0.65)	(†)
2004 seniors													
In 2004													
Total	91.3 (0.33)	87.3 (0.40)	35.1 (0.58)	(†)	41.7 (0.57)	19.7 (0.46)	49.3 (0.55)	81.0 (0.46)	82.5 (0.45)	24.5 (0.50)	18.3 (0.45)	85.5 (0.41)	69.0 (0.55)
Male	89.7 (0.49)	85.6 (0.55)	42.7 (0.80)	(†)	35.2 (0.77)	18.1 (0.60)	45.4 (0.75)	80.1 (0.63)	82.1 (0.64)	22.3 (0.65)	18.6 (0.63)	84.9 (0.56)	70.2 (0.69)
Female	92.9 (0.40)	89.0 (0.49)	27.6 (0.69)	(†)	48.1 (0.74)	21.2 (0.67)	53.2 (0.78)	81.9 (0.64)	82.9 (0.58)	26.6 (0.74)	17.9 (0.59)	86.1 (0.57)	67.8 (0.74)

—Not available.
†Not applicable.
SOURCE: U.S. Department of Education, National Center for Education Statistics, National Longitudinal Study of the High School Class of 1972 "Base Year" (NLS:72), "Second Follow-up" (NLS:72/74), and "Third Follow-up" (NLS:72/76); National Education Longitudinal Study of 1988, "Second Follow-up, Student Survey, 1992" (NELS:88/92) and "Third Follow-up, 1994" (NELS:88/94); and Education Longitudinal Study of 2002, "First Follow-up" (ELS:02/04). (This table was prepared October 2011.)

Table 507.10. Literacy skills of adults, by type of literacy, proficiency levels, and selected characteristics: 1992 and 2003

[Standard errors appear in parentheses]

Selected characteristic	Prose literacy[1] Average score 1992	2003	Below Basic	Basic	Intermediate	Proficient	Document literacy[2] Average score 1992	2003	Below Basic	Basic	Intermediate	Proficient	Quantitative literacy[3] Average score 1992	2003	Below Basic	Basic	Intermediate	Proficient
1	2	3	4	5	6	7	8	9	10	11	12	13	14	15	16	17	18	19
Total	276 (1.1)	275 (1.3)	14 (0.6)	29 (0.6)	44 (0.7)	13 (0.6)	271 (1.1)	271 (1.2)	12 (0.5)	22 (0.5)	53 (0.7)	13 (0.6)	275 (1.1)	283 (1.2)	22 (0.6)	33 (0.5)	33 (0.5)	13 (0.5)
Sex																		
Male	276 (1.2)	272 (1.5)	15 (0.6)	29 (0.7)	43 (0.7)	13 (0.6)	274 (1.2)	269 (1.5)	14 (0.6)	23 (0.5)	51 (0.8)	13 (0.6)	283 (1.4)	286 (1.3)	21 (0.6)	31 (0.5)	33 (0.5)	16 (0.6)
Female	277 (1.3)	277 (1.4)	12 (0.6)	29 (0.6)	46 (0.8)	14 (0.6)	268 (1.2)	272 (1.2)	11 (0.6)	22 (0.6)	54 (0.8)	13 (0.6)	269 (1.2)	279 (1.3)	22 (0.8)	35 (0.7)	32 (0.7)	11 (0.6)
Age																		
16 to 18 years old	270 (2.3)	267 (2.3)	11 (1.7)	37 (2.5)	48 (2.7)	5 (1.4)	270 (2.2)	268 (2.9)	11 (1.4)	24 (1.8)	56 (2.4)	9 (1.7)	264 (2.5)	267 (3.1)	28 (2.3)	38 (2.1)	28 (2.1)	6 (1.3)
19 to 24 years old	280 (2.0)	276 (2.4)	11 (1.1)	29 (1.3)	48 (1.5)	12 (1.1)	282 (2.2)	282 (2.5)	9 (1.1)	20 (1.2)	58 (1.7)	13 (1.5)	277 (2.0)	279 (2.3)	21 (1.4)	36 (1.3)	33 (1.4)	10 (1.1)
25 to 39 years old	288 (1.3)	283 (1.7)	12 (0.6)	25 (0.7)	45 (0.7)	18 (0.8)	286 (1.3)	286 (1.8)	8 (0.7)	19 (0.7)	56 (1.1)	17 (1.1)	286 (1.3)	292 (1.8)	17 (0.8)	31 (0.8)	35 (0.8)	17 (0.9)
40 to 54 years old	293 (2.0)	282 (1.9)	11 (0.9)	27 (1.1)	47 (1.2)	15 (0.8)	284 (1.9)	277 (1.8)	10 (0.7)	20 (0.8)	54 (1.2)	15 (1.1)	292 (1.8)	289 (1.9)	19 (0.9)	32 (0.8)	34 (0.8)	16 (0.9)
55 to 64 years old	269 (1.4)	278 (1.9)	13 (0.8)	27 (0.9)	44 (1.1)	15 (1.1)	258 (1.4)	270 (2.1)	12 (0.9)	23 (0.9)	54 (1.2)	12 (1.1)	272 (1.8)	289 (1.9)	19 (1.0)	30 (0.8)	34 (0.9)	17 (0.8)
65 years old and older	235 (1.7)	248 (2.0)	23 (1.3)	38 (1.2)	34 (1.4)	4 (0.6)	221 (2.2)	235 (2.0)	27 (1.5)	33 (1.0)	38 (1.4)	3 (0.4)	235 (2.7)	257 (2.2)	34 (1.6)	37 (1.2)	24 (1.2)	5 (0.6)
Race/ethnicity																		
White	287 (1.2)	288 (1.5)	7 (0.5)	25 (0.8)	51 (0.9)	17 (0.9)	281 (1.2)	282 (1.5)	8 (0.5)	19 (0.7)	58 (1.0)	15 (1.0)	288 (1.1)	297 (1.3)	13 (0.7)	32 (0.7)	39 (0.8)	17 (0.8)
Black	237 (1.4)	243 (1.8)	24 (1.4)	43 (1.2)	31 (1.4)	2 (0.4)	230 (1.4)	238 (2.1)	24 (1.7)	35 (1.4)	40 (1.9)	2 (0.5)	222 (1.6)	238 (2.1)	47 (1.8)	36 (1.3)	15 (1.1)	2 (0.4)
Hispanic	234 (2.3)	216 (3.5)	44 (1.8)	30 (1.0)	23 (1.1)	4 (0.4)	238 (2.3)	224 (3.6)	36 (1.6)	36 (0.8)	33 (1.2)	5 (0.5)	233 (1.6)	233 (3.2)	50 (1.7)	34 (0.9)	17 (0.9)	4 (0.5)
Asian/Pacific Islander	255 (6.1)	271 (4.0)	14 (2.0)	32 (2.2)	42 (2.5)	12 (2.5)	259 (6.1)	272 (5.0)	11 (2.2)	22 (2.1)	54 (3.0)	13 (2.3)	268 (7.8)	285 (5.1)	19 (3.0)	34 (2.9)	35 (2.8)	12 (2.5)
Highest level of education																		
Still in high school	268 (2.5)	262 (3.7)	14 (2.5)	37 (2.8)	45 (3.1)	4 ! (1.5)	270 (2.4)	265 (4.3)	13 (2.3)	24 (2.2)	54 (3.0)	9 (1.9)	263 (3.2)	261 (4.2)	31 (2.9)	38 (2.5)	25 (2.3)	5 (1.4)
Less than high school completion	216 (1.4)	207 (2.4)	50 (1.4)	33 (1.0)	16 (0.9)	1 (0.2)	211 (1.5)	208 (2.6)	45 (1.4)	29 (0.7)	25 (1.0)	2 (0.3)	209 (2.1)	211 (2.2)	64 (1.3)	25 (0.8)	10 (0.7)	1 (0.2)
GED/high school equivalency	265 (2.2)	260 (2.1)	10 (1.8)	45 (2.9)	43 (3.0)	3 ! (1.1)	259 (2.3)	257 (2.5)	13 (1.9)	30 (2.3)	53 (2.8)	4 ! (1.2)	265 (2.3)	265 (3.1)	26 (3.1)	43 (3.1)	28 (2.9)	3 ! (1.2)
High school graduate	268 (1.0)	262 (1.3)	13 (1.0)	39 (1.2)	44 (1.3)	4 (0.6)	261 (1.4)	258 (1.6)	13 (1.0)	29 (1.1)	54 (1.4)	5 (0.7)	267 (1.2)	269 (1.6)	24 (1.4)	42 (1.3)	29 (1.3)	5 (0.7)
Vocational/trade/business	278 (2.1)	268 (2.7)	7 (1.8)	36 (2.6)	49 (2.7)	9 (2.1)	273 (1.6)	267 (2.5)	5 (1.5)	26 (2.3)	59 (2.7)	7 (1.5)	280 (1.7)	279 (2.2)	18 (2.1)	41 (2.3)	35 (1.8)	6 (1.4)
Some college	292 (1.4)	287 (1.8)	5 (0.7)	20 (1.4)	56 (1.4)	19 (1.7)	288 (1.6)	280 (1.7)	5 (0.8)	19 (1.5)	65 (1.5)	11 (1.5)	294 (1.7)	294 (1.7)	16 (1.2)	36 (1.8)	43 (1.8)	11 (1.5)
Associate's degree	306 (1.9)	298 (2.4)	4 (0.7)	20 (1.5)	56 (2.0)	19 (2.0)	301 (1.9)	291 (2.0)	5 (0.7)	15 (1.5)	66 (2.3)	10 (2.2)	305 (2.0)	305 (2.1)	7 (1.1)	30 (1.9)	45 (2.1)	18 (2.1)
Bachelor's degree	325 (1.9)	314 (2.1)	3 (0.5)	14 (1.0)	53 (1.7)	31 (1.8)	317 (1.9)	303 (2.2)	2 ! (0.6)	11 (1.2)	62 (2.5)	25 (2.7)	324 (1.8)	323 (1.8)	4 (0.6)	22 (1.2)	43 (1.5)	31 (1.9)
Graduate studies/degree	340 (2.0)	327 (2.8)	1 ! (0.4)	10 (1.2)	48 (2.3)	41 (2.6)	328 (1.9)	311 (2.2)	1 ! (0.4)	9 (1.1)	59 (2.6)	31 (2.8)	336 (2.1)	332 (2.1)	3 (0.6)	18 (1.5)	43 (2.1)	36 (2.6)
Employment																		
Full-time	290 (1.2)	285 (1.5)	— (†)	— (†)	— (†)	— (†)	286 (1.2)	281 (1.2)	— (†)	— (†)	— (†)	— (†)	292 (1.3)	296 (1.1)	— (†)	— (†)	— (†)	— (†)
Part-time	285 (1.7)	281 (2.2)	— (†)	— (†)	— (†)	— (†)	279 (1.8)	277 (1.8)	— (†)	— (†)	— (†)	— (†)	281 (1.7)	287 (2.2)	— (†)	— (†)	— (†)	— (†)
Unemployed	263 (2.3)	269 (2.8)	— (†)	— (†)	— (†)	— (†)	261 (2.2)	265 (0.3)	— (†)	— (†)	— (†)	— (†)	261 (3.2)	270 (3.6)	— (†)	— (†)	— (†)	— (†)
Not in labor force	252 (1.4)	255 (1.7)	— (†)	— (†)	— (†)	— (†)	244 (1.5)	250 (1.9)	— (†)	— (†)	— (†)	— (†)	247 (1.9)	261 (1.8)	— (†)	— (†)	— (†)	— (†)
Language spoken before starting school																		
English only	282 (1.2)	283 (1.4)	9 (0.5)	27 (0.7)	49 (0.8)	15 (0.7)	275 (1.2)	276 (1.3)	9 (0.6)	21 (0.6)	56 (0.8)	13 (0.7)	280 (1.2)	289 (1.2)	18 (0.6)	33 (0.6)	35 (0.6)	15 (0.6)
English and Spanish	255 (2.9)	262 (3.1)	14 (2.1)	38 (2.2)	42 (2.4)	6 (1.3)	253 (3.6)	259 (3.8)	12 (2.5)	29 (3.0)	54 (3.8)	5 ! (1.3)	247 (4.6)	261 (3.8)	31 (3.3)	39 (2.6)	26 (2.8)	4 ! (1.3)
English and other language	273 (4.0)	278 (3.1)	7 (1.5)	33 (2.8)	51 (3.1)	9 (2.1)	260 (4.5)	268 (3.2)	10 (2.0)	25 (2.3)	57 (2.9)	8 (2.0)	271 (5.6)	289 (4.1)	15 (2.7)	38 (2.7)	34 (3.0)	14 (2.6)
Spanish	205 (2.9)	188 (3.8)	61 (1.8)	25 (1.1)	13 (0.9)	1 ! (0.3)	216 (2.8)	199 (4.6)	49 (2.0)	25 (1.0)	23 (1.3)	3 (0.4)	212 (3.3)	211 (4.6)	62 (2.2)	25 (1.2)	11 (1.1)	2 (0.5)
Other language	239 (3.4)	249 (4.6)	26 (2.2)	33 (2.0)	34 (2.3)	7 (1.3)	241 (3.7)	257 (4.2)	24 (1.9)	24 (1.3)	46 (2.3)	10 (1.2)	246 (4.3)	270 (4.3)	28 (2.3)	33 (1.7)	29 (1.9)	10 (1.5)

—Not available.
†Not applicable.
!Interpret data with caution. The coefficient of variation (CV) for this estimate is between 30 and 50 percent.
[1]Prose literacy refers to the knowledge and skills needed to search, comprehend, and use information from continuous texts. Adults at the *Below Basic* level, rated 0 to 209, range from being nonliterate in English to being able to locate easily identifiable information in short, commonplace prose texts. At the *Basic* level, rated 210 to 264, adults are able to read and understand information in short, commonplace prose texts. At the *Intermediate* level, rated 265 to 339, adults are able to read and understand moderately dense, less commonplace prose texts as well as summarize, make simple inferences, determine cause and effect, and recognize the author's purpose. At the *Proficient* level, rated 340 to 500, adults are able to read lengthy, complex, abstract prose texts as well as synthesize information and make complex inferences.
[2]Document literacy refers to the knowledge and skills needed to search, comprehend, and use information from noncontinuous texts in various formats. Adults at the *Below Basic* level, rated 0 to 204, range from being nonliterate in English to being able to locate easily identifiable information and follow instructions in simple documents (e.g., charts or forms). At the *Basic* level, rated 205 to 249, adults are able to read and understand information in simple documents. At the *Intermediate* level, rated 250 to 334, adults are able to locate information in dense, complex documents and make simple inferences about the information. At the *Proficient* level, rated 335 to 500, adults are able to integrate, synthesize, and analyze multiple pieces of information located in complex documents.

[3]Quantitative literacy refers to the knowledge and skills required to identify and perform computations, either alone or sequentially, using numbers embedded in printed materials. Adults at the *Below Basic* level, rated 0 to 234, range from being nonliterate in English to being able to locate numbers and use them to perform simple quantitative operations (primarily addition) when the mathematical information is very concrete and familiar. At the *Basic* level, rated 235 to 289, adults are able to locate easily identifiable quantitative information and use it to solve simple, one-step problems when the arithmetic operation is specified or easily inferred. At the *Intermediate* level, rated 290 to 349, adults are able to locate less familiar quantitative information and use it to solve problems when the arithmetic operation is not specified or easily inferred. At the *Proficient* level, rated 350 to 500, adults are able to locate more abstract quantitative information and use it to solve multistep problems when the arithmetic operations are not easily inferred and the problems are more complex.
NOTE: Adults are defined as people age 16 and older living in households or prisons. Adults who could not be interviewed due to language spoken or cognitive or mental disabilities (3 percent in 2003 and 4 percent in 1992) are excluded from this table. Race categories exclude persons of Hispanic ethnicity. Totals include racial/ethnic groups not separately shown. Detail may not sum to totals because of rounding.
SOURCE: U.S. Department of Education, National Center for Education Statistics, 1992 National Adult Literacy Survey (NALS) and 2003 National Assessment of Adult Literacy (NAAL), *A First Look at the Literacy of America's Adults in the 21st Century,* and supplemental data retrieved July 6, 2006, from http://nces.ed.gov/naal/Excel/2006470_DataTable.xls. (This table was prepared July 2006.)

Table 507.20. Participants in state-administered adult basic education, secondary education, and English as a second language programs, by type of program and state or jurisdiction: Selected fiscal years, 2000 through 2014

State or jurisdiction	2000, total	2005, total	2010, total	2013				2014			
				Total	Adult basic education	Adult secondary education	English as a second language	Total	Adult basic education	Adult secondary education	English as a second language
1	2	3	4	5	6	7	8	9	10	11	12
United States	2,629,643	2,543,953	1,990,118	1,584,037	735,601	181,182	667,254	1,518,550	679,313	171,722	667,515
Alabama.................	23,666	19,827	24,339	22,016	16,212	3,632	2,172	19,721	13,775	3,791	2,155
Alaska...................	5,312	3,791	3,176	2,423	1,454	180	789	1,975	981	180	814
Arizona	31,136	26,881	18,552	16,059	8,742	1,161	6,156	13,500	7,322	917	5,261
Arkansas................	38,867	37,102	27,603	20,274	12,529	3,700	4,045	16,946	9,882	3,400	3,664
California	473,050	591,893	392,918	305,182	84,049	39,731	181,402	304,831	79,741	43,164	181,926
Colorado	13,818	15,011	12,873	10,457	3,808	903	5,746	9,249	3,310	841	5,098
Connecticut............	30,844	31,958	25,924	22,565	6,194	5,047	11,324	20,212	5,193	4,525	10,494
Delaware...............	4,342	6,329	4,961	4,678	2,806	608	1,264	4,124	2,433	387	1,304
District of Columbia	3,667	3,646	3,808	3,286	1,441	163	1,682	2,914	1,388	201	1,325
Florida...................	404,912	348,119	239,653	151,384	68,227	14,939	68,218	171,116	69,982	15,031	86,103
Georgia	108,004	95,434	64,668	47,197	34,508	3,560	9,129	44,225	31,111	3,206	9,908
Hawaii	10,525	7,461	9,058	6,289	2,739	1,484	2,066	6,066	2,900	1,332	1,834
Idaho....................	10,506	7,744	6,675	5,086	2,948	392	1,746	5,053	2,752	480	1,821
Illinois..................	122,043	118,296	96,620	78,741	26,245	8,445	44,051	74,313	25,859	6,446	42,008
Indiana	42,135	43,498	28,571	29,738	21,019	4,430	4,289	28,107	18,872	4,182	5,053
Iowa	20,161	11,989	11,167	9,991	4,739	1,272	3,980	12,203	5,859	1,445	4,899
Kansas..................	11,248	9,475	8,100	8,609	4,423	1,094	3,092	7,183	3,373	844	2,966
Kentucky................	31,050	30,931	38,654	32,831	20,838	7,825	4,168	28,676	17,363	7,158	4,155
Louisiana	30,929	29,367	27,270	22,266	17,530	2,640	2,096	22,405	17,223	2,276	2,906
Maine...................	12,430	8,151	6,776	6,340	3,395	1,252	1,693	5,730	3,031	1,078	1,621
Maryland................	22,702	27,055	32,833	30,054	12,834	2,602	14,618	27,997	11,318	2,764	13,915
Massachusetts..........	24,053	21,448	20,314	19,244	4,659	3,241	11,344	19,235	4,521	3,094	11,620
Michigan	56,096	34,768	25,745	28,625	17,898	2,425	8,302	27,443	16,644	2,235	8,564
Minnesota	42,039	47,174	46,009	39,135	16,074	4,942	18,119	38,612	14,804	6,185	17,623
Mississippi	37,947	25,675	16,854	13,269	11,294	1,734	241	10,785	9,464	1,088	233
Missouri.................	41,089	37,052	31,397	22,243	15,528	1,879	4,836	19,565	12,994	1,548	5,023
Montana.................	4,892	3,291	3,494	2,437	1,783	495	159	2,023	1,490	378	155
Nebraska...............	7,917	10,226	8,485	7,007	3,368	629	3,010	6,344	2,903	514	2,927
Nevada	22,992	9,981	8,673	9,297	1,966	526	6,805	8,838	2,063	177	6,598
New Hampshire	5,962	5,804	5,740	4,664	1,307	1,139	2,218	4,258	1,119	1,013	2,126
New Jersey	44,317	40,889	30,976	33,488	12,038	1,311	20,139	21,694	8,507	1,126	12,061
New Mexico	23,243	24,132	21,466	16,796	9,136	1,215	6,445	15,353	8,422	1,089	5,842
New York	176,239	157,486	122,833	106,616	42,065	5,487	59,064	102,784	38,893	4,736	59,155
North Carolina	107,504	109,047	115,312	91,061	52,156	14,880	24,025	77,092	43,169	12,006	21,917
North Dakota	2,124	2,063	1,581	1,553	813	379	361	1,597	765	303	529
Ohio	65,579	50,869	41,692	32,650	22,588	3,571	6,491	29,751	19,658	3,194	6,899
Oklahoma	20,101	20,447	18,329	15,493	10,167	1,408	3,918	14,557	9,083	1,193	4,281
Oregon	25,228	21,668	20,851	16,204	7,833	1,811	6,560	13,807	6,000	2,040	5,767
Pennsylvania............	49,369	54,274	30,577	22,468	13,249	2,541	6,678	21,884	12,618	2,316	6,950
Rhode Island	5,592	6,697	6,012	5,587	2,434	337	2,816	4,927	1,794	272	2,861
South Carolina............	94,452	65,901	49,484	39,350	26,454	7,316	5,580	31,641	20,403	6,335	4,903
South Dakota	5,637	3,517	2,423	2,060	1,178	306	576	2,062	1,086	304	672
Tennessee	40,615	48,924	28,170	24,203	17,678	2,504	4,021	22,711	15,845	2,207	4,659
Texas	111,585	119,867	99,333	71,676	26,385	2,290	43,001	83,534	40,674	2,612	40,248
Utah.....................	30,714	29,320	24,686	20,390	12,309	2,224	5,857	19,374	11,386	2,164	5,824
Vermont	1,146	2,015	1,590	2,650	1,493	804	353	2,073	911	809	353
Virginia..................	35,261	29,222	28,220	22,902	9,085	2,274	11,543	20,598	7,563	1,503	11,532
Washington..............	53,460	50,386	61,392	49,811	20,658	3,350	25,803	45,562	18,706	3,183	23,673
West Virginia............	13,072	9,444	9,785	8,620	6,505	1,840	275	7,789	5,735	1,797	257
Wisconsin	27,304	26,029	21,523	16,614	9,483	2,751	4,380	14,211	7,473	2,277	4,461
Wyoming	2,767	2,379	2,973	2,458	1,337	513	608	1,900	952	376	572
Other jurisdictions ...	44,785	37,328	22,045	14,719	3,225	10,422	1,072	16,090	3,226	9,992	3,369
American Samoa............	662	838	225	188	0	48	140	199	0	55	144
Federated States of Micronesia	0	0	0	0	0	0	0	0	0	0	0
Guam....................	1,092	1,062	539	524	392	73	59	503	419	25	59
Marshall Islands..........	335	0	0	0	0	0	0	0	0	0	0
Northern Marianas	680	740	607	262	47	188	27	241	150	71	20
Palau....................	132	206	56	55	0	55	0	41	0	41	0
Puerto Rico..............	41,043	33,463	20,464	13,135	2,252	10,044	839	15,106	2,160	9,800	3,146
U.S. Virgin Islands	841	1,019	154	555	534	14	7	‡	497	‡	0

‡Reporting standards not met (too few cases).
NOTE: Adult basic education provides instruction in basic skills for adults 16 and over functioning at literacy levels below the secondary level. Adult secondary education provides instruction at the high school level for adults who are seeking to pass the GED or obtain an adult high school creden-tial. English as a second language instruction is for adults who lack proficiency in English and who seek to improve their literacy and competence in English.
SOURCE: U.S. Department of Education, Office of Vocational and Adult Education (OVAE), OVAE National Reporting System, retrieved February 25, 2016, from http://wdcrobcolp01.ed.gov/CFAPPS/OVAE/NRS/reports/index.cfm. (This table was prepared February 2016.)

Table 507.30. Participation of employed persons, 17 years old and over, in career-related adult education during the previous 12 months, by selected characteristics of participants: 1995, 1999, and 2005

[Standard errors appear in parentheses]

Characteristic of employed person	1995 Percent of adults participating in career- or job-related courses	1995 Number of career- or job-related courses taken, per employed adult	1999 Percent of adults participating in career- or job-related courses	1999 Number of career- or job-related courses taken, per employed adult	2005 Employed persons, in thousands	2005 In career- or job-related courses[1]	2005 In apprenticeship programs	2005 In personal interest courses	2005 In informal learning activities for personal interest	2005 Number of career- or job-related courses taken In thousands	2005 Number of career- or job-related courses taken Per employed adult
1	2	3	4	5	6	7	8	9	10	11	12
Total	31.1 (0.54)	0.8 (0.02)	30.5 (1.14)	0.7 (0.03)	133,386 (1,508.1)	38.8 (0.83)	1.4 (0.24)	21.8 (0.94)	73.5 (1.01)	108,443	0.8 (0.03)
Sex											
Male	29.0 (0.72)	0.7 (0.02)	28.3 (1.15)	0.6 (0.03)	71,754 (934.7)	31.7 (1.22)	2.0 (0.37)	18.5 (1.30)	73.4 (1.52)	44,512	0.6 (0.03)
Female	33.4 (0.83)	0.9 (0.03)	32.9 (1.14)	0.8 (0.03)	61,632 (1,219.3)	47.1 (1.43)	0.8 (0.23)	25.8 (1.23)	73.6 (1.37)	63,931	1.0 (0.05)
Age											
17 through 24 years old	18.6 (1.01)	0.4 (0.02)	19.1 (1.91)	0.4 (0.06)	15,027 (1,030.4)	26.4 (3.01)	3.0 ! (1.03)	25.2 (3.37)	71.4 (3.15)	8,024	0.5 (0.09)
25 through 29 years old	31.2 (1.46)	0.8 (0.05)	34.3 (2.44)	0.8 (0.08)	14,555 (918.4)	36.1 (2.94)	3.1 ! (1.12)	24.5 (3.66)	70.9 (4.49)	9,493	0.7 (0.06)
30 through 34 years old	31.6 (1.30)	0.8 (0.04)	34.4 (2.50)	0.7 (0.08)	15,250 (977.2)	41.0 (3.06)	2.7 ! (1.10)	23.7 (2.63)	74.0 (2.54)	12,681	0.8 (0.07)
35 through 39 years old	35.1 (1.02)	0.9 (0.03)	29.2 (2.15)	0.7 (0.07)	15,286 (922.4)	41.7 (4.16)	1.0 ! (0.46)	21.6 (3.15)	77.7 (3.00)	13,807	0.9 (0.14)
40 through 44 years old	36.6 (1.29)	0.9 (0.04)	36.4 (2.44)	0.8 (0.07)	18,141 (946.5)	39.8 (2.73)	‡ (†)	23.3 (2.60)	71.2 (3.15)	15,586	0.9 (0.07)
45 through 49 years old	39.6 (1.94)	1.0 (0.06)	30.4 (2.42)	0.7 (0.06)	18,149 (842.5)	45.0 (2.15)	0.7 ! (0.29)	19.0 (2.09)	73.5 (2.68)	16,809	0.9 (0.06)
50 through 54 years old	34.4 (1.69)	0.9 (0.04)	34.7 (2.57)	0.8 (0.07)	14,624 (732.1)	42.6 (2.49)	0.7 ! (0.32)	19.5 (1.92)	76.3 (2.27)	14,881	1.0 (0.10)
55 through 59 years old	26.7 (1.86)	0.7 (0.06)	30.3 (2.83)	0.6 (0.08)	10,522 (676.0)	44.7 (2.98)	‡ (†)	18.3 (1.93)	73.0 (2.95)	9,901	0.9 (0.09)
60 through 64 years old	21.1 (2.41)	0.5 (0.06)	27.2 (3.80)	0.7 (0.15)	6,021 (498.8)	38.9 (3.97)	‡ (†)	23.4 (3.52)	73.0 (4.22)	4,919	0.8 (0.10)
65 years old and over	13.7 (1.86)	0.4 (0.06)	20.3 (4.21)	0.4 (0.08)	5,812 (493.3)	21.6 (3.48)	# (†)	17.4 (3.13)	74.2 (3.75)	2,343	0.4 (0.07)
65 through 69	13.1 (2.28)	0.4 (0.08)	— (†)	— (†)	3,385 (415.5)	19.1 (4.05)	# (†)	20.9 (4.88)	75.4 (5.18)	1,102	0.3 (0.08)
70 and over	14.6 (2.85)	0.4 (0.09)	— (†)	— (†)	2,427 (282.3)	25.1 (5.81)	# (†)	12.6 (2.93)	72.6 (6.11)	1,241	0.5 (0.14)
Race/ethnicity											
White	33.2 (0.61)	0.8 (0.02)	32.8 (0.98)	0.6 (0.03)	94,881 (1,538.6)	41.3 (0.93)	1.2 (0.25)	22.2 (1.11)	75.3 (1.17)	82,511	0.9 (0.03)
Black	26.2 (1.46)	0.7 (0.04)	28.1 (2.34)	1.0 (0.07)	13,773 (533.2)	39.2 (3.82)	1.7 ! (0.83)	23.5 (3.04)	66.9 (3.02)	10,311	0.7 (0.11)
Hispanic	18.1 (1.00)	0.4 (0.02)	16.4 (1.83)	0.5 (0.05)	15,741 (681.1)	25.0 (2.66)	2.9 (0.85)	16.2 (2.31)	65.8 (3.39)	8,786	0.6 (0.11)
Asian	— (†)	—	— (†)	—	3,770 (520.7)	36.9 (7.00)	‡ (†)	32.3 (7.26)	81.1 (5.88)	2,207	0.6 (0.12)
Pacific Islander	— (†)	—	— (†)	—	‡ (†)	‡ (†)	‡ (†)	‡ (†)	‡ (†)	‡	‡ (†)
Asian/Pacific Islander	25.5 (2.69)	0.6 (0.07)	32.8 (4.84)	0.4 ! (0.15)	— (†)	— (†)	— (†)	— (†)	— (†)	—	— (†)
American Indian/Alaska Native	34.0 (6.32)	0.9 (0.20)	29.5 ! (11.52)	‡	‡ (†)	‡ (†)	‡ (†)	‡ (†)	‡ (†)	‡	‡ (†)
Two or more races	— (†)	—	— (†)	—	3,786 (562.7)	39.1 (6.85)	‡ (†)	22.6 (6.34)	77.6 (8.40)	3,083	0.8 (0.15)
Other races	25.3 (2.99)	0.7 (0.09)	— (†)	—	‡ (†)	‡ (†)	‡ (†)	‡ (†)	‡ (†)	‡	‡ (†)
Highest level of education completed											
Less than high school completion	8.8 (1.05)	0.1 (0.02)	7.9 (2.29)	0.4 (0.05)	16,627 (838.2)	10.4 (2.11)	2.4 ! (0.90)	8.8 (1.54)	57.0 (3.76)	2,592	0.2 (0.03)
8th grade or less	6.1 ! (2.00)	0.1 ! (0.04)	— (†)	—	5,016 (599.7)	2.7 (1.12)	‡ (†)	3.8 ! (1.71)	46.7 (7.11)	197	# (†)
9th through 12th grade, no completion	10.0 (1.27)	0.2 (0.02)	— (†)	— (†)	11,610 (792.8)	13.7 (2.99)	‡ (†)	11.0 (2.06)	61.5 (4.05)	2,396	0.2 (0.04)
High school completion	20.9 (0.79)	0.4 (0.02)	21.4 (1.45)	0.8 (0.03)	34,121 (1,147.2)	24.7 (1.76)	1.3 ! (0.46)	17.1 (1.89)	63.4 (2.55)	16,640	0.5 (0.05)
Some vocational/technical	32.3 (2.50)	0.8 (0.07)	28.7 (5.76)	0.9 (0.17)	3,744 (393.1)	48.2 (5.92)	‡ (†)	25.5 (4.61)	74.0 (5.54)	3,802	1.0 (0.17)
Some college	29.9 (0.91)	0.7 (0.03)	29.0 (1.78)	0.7 (0.06)	24,479 (1,067.7)	39.9 (2.36)	1.9 ! (0.69)	25.2 (2.50)	79.8 (2.04)	18,437	0.8 (0.05)
Associate's degree	39.2 (1.58)	1.0 (0.05)	39.7 (3.07)	0.9 (0.09)	9,943 (730.7)	50.4 (3.71)	2.3 ! (0.84)	19.1 (2.86)	78.4 (3.88)	14,224	1.4 (0.21)
Bachelor's degree	44.6 (1.33)	1.2 (0.04)	43.8 (2.01)	1.0 (0.06)	26,475 (902.7)	53.1 (1.88)	‡ (†)	29.0 (1.77)	78.7 (1.94)	28,099	1.1 (0.06)
Some graduate work (or study)	50.2 (1.63)	1.4 (0.05)	46.8 (4.17)	1.2 (0.14)	17,998 (735.4)	61.1 (2.16)	‡ (†)	28.6 (2.01)	88.8 (1.16)	24,649	1.4 (0.07)
No degree	44.3 (3.18)	1.2 (0.10)	54.2 (4.94)	1.2 (0.14)	2,125 (227.9)	53.8 (5.79)	‡ (†)	39.3 (6.05)	75.0 (5.64)	2,412	1.1 (0.16)
Master's	50.5 (1.99)	1.4 (0.06)	45.3 (2.97)	1.1 (0.11)	11,330 (614.7)	62.7 (2.98)	‡ (†)	28.2 (2.27)	90.5 (1.40)	15,394	1.4 (0.09)
Doctor's	40.4 (6.42)	1.0 (0.16)	34.4 (4.79)	0.7 (0.12)	1,600 (227.2)	49.0 (5.80)	‡ (†)	28.8 (4.76)	87.8 (4.35)	2,204	1.4 (0.36)
Professional	67.6 (3.89)	2.0 (0.15)	67.6 (6.98)	1.9 (0.31)	2,943 (382.7)	66.5 (6.39)	‡ (†)	22.1 (5.05)	92.9 (2.21)	4,639	1.6 (0.21)

See notes at end of table.

Table 507.30. Participation of employed persons, 17 years old and over, in career-related adult education during the previous 12 months, by selected characteristics of participants: 1995, 1999, and 2005—Continued

[Standard errors appear in parentheses]

Characteristic of employed person	1995		1999		2005					Number of career- or job-related courses taken[1]	
	Percent of adults participating in career- or job-related courses	Number of career- or job-related courses taken, per employed adult	Percent of adults participating in career- or job-related courses	Number of career- or job-related courses taken, per employed adult	Employed persons, in thousands	Percent of adults participating				In thousands	Per employed adult
						In career- or job-related courses[1]	In apprenticeship programs[1]	In personal interest courses	In informal learning activities for personal interest		
1	2	3	4	5	6	7	8	9	10	11	12
Locale[2]											
City	—(†)	—(†)	—(†)	—(†)	39,283 (1,391.3)	39.6 (1.67)	2.2 (0.60)	23.1 (1.43)	74.0 (1.77)	34,327	0.9 (0.05)
Suburban	—(†)	—(†)	—(†)	—(†)	48,452 (1,555.0)	41.1 (1.87)	1.2 (0.32)	23.3 (1.38)	74.2 (1.49)	39,802	0.8 (0.04)
Town	—(†)	—(†)	—(†)	—(†)	17,616 (1,060.7)	36.0 (2.64)	‡ (†)	19.6 (2.83)	71.7 (3.02)	12,947	0.7 (0.07)
Rural	—(†)	—(†)	—(†)	—(†)	27,847 (885.2)	35.4 (2.14)	1.4 ! (0.58)	19.0 (2.19)	72.7 (2.22)	21,135	0.8 (0.06)
Occupation											
Executive, administrative, or managerial occupations	42.9 (1.49)	1.2 (0.05)	40.6 (2.06)	1.0 (0.07)	14,596 (707.6)	53.6 (2.79)	‡ (†)	29.5 (2.89)	77.7 (2.87)	16,567	1.1 (0.09)
Engineers, surveyors, and architects	44.2 (4.46)	1.1 (0.12)	52.1 (6.96)	1.0 (0.16)	1,987 (244.9)	56.3 (5.68)	‡ (†)	30.5 (6.36)	81.0 (4.73)	2,323	1.2 (0.16)
Natural scientists and mathematicians	59.7 (3.97)	1.7 (0.15)	46.0 (6.61)	0.8 (0.14)	4,130 (445.4)	51.5 (5.64)	‡ (†)	31.2 (4.83)	85.3 (5.44)	3,693	0.9 (0.11)
Social scientists and workers, religious workers, and lawyers	59.5 (2.61)	1.8 (0.11)	56.9 (5.66)	1.7 (0.24)	4,697 (480.9)	66.8 (4.48)	‡ (†)	28.3 (3.81)	88.6 (2.95)	7,822	1.7 (0.29)
Teachers, elementary/secondary	53.9 (2.23)	1.5 (0.08)	52.1 (3.53)	1.2 (0.11)	7,085 (568.5)	67.7 (4.16)	‡ (†)	31.5 (3.93)	83.0 (2.79)	12,233	1.7 (0.13)
Teachers, postsecondary and counselors, librarians, and archivists	41.6 (4.57)	1.0 (0.15)	35.6 (5.85)	0.7 (0.14)	2,393 (420.9)	53.1 (8.63)	‡ (†)	17.7 (4.91)	90.9 (3.97)	2,122	0.9 (0.09)
Health diagnosing and treating practitioners	68.6 (5.85)	2.0 (0.23)	65.2 (11.99)	1.5 ! (0.50)	978 (208.8)	78.9 (7.10)	‡ (†)	27.4 ! (9.60)	86.6 (5.37)	1,951	2.0 (0.25)
Registered nurses, pharmacists, dieticians, therapists, and physician's assistants	72.8 (3.02)	2.2 (0.14)	72.2 (5.04)	1.8 (0.21)	2,794 (238.8)	79.7 (4.60)	‡ (†)	29.4 (4.17)	84.3 (3.70)	4,984	1.8 (0.15)
Writers, artists, entertainers, and athletes	23.4 (2.89)	0.5 (0.07)	30.6 (6.21)	0.6 (0.18)	2,969 (405.2)	29.9 (5.69)	‡ (†)	31.8 (6.15)	88.9 (4.39)	1,865	0.6 (0.15)
Health technologists and technicians	50.0 (4.08)	1.4 (0.12)	41.8 (6.00)	1.0 (0.19)	3,060 (436.7)	70.6 (7.31)	‡ (†)	27.8 (6.48)	77.5 (6.40)	4,473	1.5 (0.18)
Technologists and technicians, except health	43.8 (2.67)	1.1 (0.10)	37.6 (4.87)	1.0 (0.15)	1,774 (336.5)	29.4 (8.10)	‡ (†)	5.3 ! (2.02)	75.2 (8.98)	1,015	0.6 (0.17)
Marketing and sales occupations	25.2 (1.26)	0.6 (0.03)	21.1 (2.27)	0.4 (0.06)	14,845 (971.9)	32.3 (3.17)	‡ (†)	20.8 (2.64)	70.5 (3.53)	7,724	0.5 (0.05)
Administrative support occupations, including clerical	30.8 (1.15)	0.7 (0.03)	27.4 (2.02)	0.6 (0.05)	21,167 (1,179.4)	36.1 (2.95)	0.8 ! (0.40)	28.2 (2.28)	72.9 (2.37)	15,443	0.7 (0.10)
Service occupations	22.6 (1.25)	0.6 (0.04)	21.0 (2.15)	0.5 (0.07)	17,180 (1,033.7)	33.7 (3.13)	1.1 ! (0.36)	16.2 (2.31)	69.0 (2.74)	13,029	0.8 (0.10)
Agriculture, forestry, and fishing occupations	12.4 (2.47)	0.3 (0.07)	12.2 ! (4.09)	0.2 ! (0.07)	2,522 (423.8)	22.4 ! (7.61)	‡ (†)	23.0 ! (11.03)	62.9 (11.04)	960	0.4 ! (0.12)
Mechanics and repairers	29.1 (2.62)	0.7 (0.08)	15.0 (3.40)	0.3 (0.09)	5,241 (521.6)	28.3 (4.47)	4.0 ! (1.44)	12.6 (3.24)	69.3 (4.36)	2,669	0.5 (0.09)
Construction and extractive occupations	18.6 (2.33)	0.3 (0.04)	13.2 (3.16)	0.2 (0.06)	6,827 (647.1)	12.4 (3.04)	5.3 ! (2.26)	7.8 (1.88)	69.0 (5.25)	2,323	0.3 ! (0.13)
Precision production[3]	25.6 (4.04)	0.6 (0.12)	18.3 ! (6.52)	0.4 ! (0.12)	10,483 (839.3)	23.5 (3.79)	‡ (†)	14.0 (3.34)	64.9 (3.74)	4,904	0.5 (0.07)
Production workers	14.8 (1.13)	0.3 (0.02)	23.0 (3.17)	0.5 (0.08)	—(†)	—(†)	—(†)	—(†)	—(†)	—	—(†)

See notes at end of table.

Table 507.30. Participation of employed persons, 17 years old and over, in career-related adult education during the previous 12 months, by selected characteristics of participants: 1995, 1999, and 2005—Continued

[Standard errors appear in parentheses]

Characteristic of employed person	1995		1999			2005 Percent of adults participating				2005 Number of career- or job-related courses taken[1]	
	Percent of adults participating in career- or job-related courses	Number of career- or job-related courses taken, per employed adult	Percent of adults participating in career- or job-related courses	Number of career- or job-related courses taken, per employed adult	Employed persons, in thousands	In career- or job-related courses[1]	In apprenticeship programs	In personal interest courses	In informal learning activities for personal interest	In thousands	Per employed adult
1	2	3	4	5	6	7	8	9	10	11	12
Transportation and material moving...	15.8 (1.83)	0.3 (0.04)	18.4 (3.62)	0.3 (0.06)	7,858 (742.5)	15.2 (2.81)	‡ (†)	10.5 (3.10)	62.5 (5.32)	1,935	0.2 (0.05)
Handlers, equipment cleaners, helpers, and laborers...	11.7 (2.77)	0.2 (0.06)	‡ (†)	‡ !	— (†)	— (†)	‡ (†)	— (†)	— (†)	—	— (†)
Miscellaneous occupations...	38.8 (3.50)	1.0 (0.11)	14.2 ! (4.62)	0.3 ! (0.08)	801 (189.4)	17.2 ! (6.87)	‡ (†)	8.7 ! (4.31)	48.3 (13.96)	409	‡ (†)
Annual household income											
$10,000 or less...	12.6 (1.31)	0.2 (0.03)	9.5 ! (3.09)	0.2 ! (0.05)	4,425 (444.8)	16.7 (4.35)	‡ (†)	26.2 ! (7.96)	69.7 (5.72)	1,556	0.4 ! (0.12)
$5,000 or less...	8.7 (1.91)	0.1 (0.03)	— (†)	— (†)	1,635 (252.7)	19.1 (6.52)	‡ (†)	22.9 ! (7.91)	60.9 (8.84)	850	‡ (†)
$5,001 to $10,000...	15.1 (1.62)	0.3 (0.04)	— (†)	— (†)	2,791 (454.1)	15.3 (5.68)	‡ (†)	28.1 ! (12.27)	74.8 (6.88)	706	0.3 ! (0.10)
$10,001 to $15,000...	15.1 (1.71)	0.4 (0.04)	8.3 (1.88)	0.1 (0.03)	4,814 (633.4)	22.2 (5.77)	‡ (†)	17.3 ! (5.25)	64.5 (7.57)	2,189	0.5 (0.12)
$15,001 to $20,000...	20.1 (1.36)	0.4 (0.03)	16.3 (2.75)	0.3 (0.05)	4,515 (398.8)	18.2 (3.09)	5.7 ! (2.71)	11.5 (1.96)	60.4 (5.11)	1,322	0.3 (0.05)
$20,001 to $25,000...	20.4 (1.52)	0.5 (0.05)	18.8 (2.79)	0.4 (0.08)	5,593 (490.2)	23.8 (4.02)	1.1 ! (0.51)	13.3 (3.21)	71.5 (4.11)	2,817	0.5 (0.10)
$25,001 to $30,000...	24.7 (1.34)	0.5 (0.03)	22.2 (2.73)	0.5 (0.07)	7,444 (680.4)	31.4 (4.88)	‡ (†)	16.7 (3.77)	73.5 (3.91)	4,322	0.6 (0.11)
$30,001 to $40,000...	30.2 (1.13)	0.8 (0.03)	26.6 (2.82)	0.6 (0.07)	13,123 (928.5)	35.1 (3.45)	1.5 ! (0.65)	21.7 (3.71)	69.1 (3.55)	8,224	0.6 (0.06)
$40,001 to $50,000...	34.7 (1.30)	0.8 (0.04)	32.3 (2.34)	0.7 (0.07)	13,647 (1,058.4)	31.5 (3.01)	1.8 ! (0.72)	20.1 (3.32)	73.5 (2.78)	10,072	0.7 (0.10)
$50,001 to $75,000...	40.0 (1.18)	1.0 (0.04)	36.6 (1.86)	0.9 (0.06)	33,665 (1,430.4)	42.7 (1.80)	1.2 ! (0.51)	20.9 (2.10)	71.3 (2.55)	28,991	0.9 (0.06)
More than $75,000...	45.2 (1.40)	1.3 (0.04)	42.5 (1.79)	1.0 (0.06)	46,160 (1,263.3)	48.1 (1.57)	1.3 ! (0.39)	26.0 (1.37)	79.2 (1.55)	48,951	1.1 (0.05)

—Not available.
†Not applicable.
#Rounds to zero.
!Interpret data with caution. The coefficient of variation (CV) for this estimate is between 30 and 50 percent.
‡Reporting standards not met. The coefficient of variation (CV) for this estimate is 50 percent or greater.
[1]The 2005 estimates on participation in career- or job-related courses were based on responses to multiple questions. Specifically, respondents were first asked what courses they had taken, and then whether each course was career- or job-related. In contrast, 1995 and 1999 respondents were asked a single, general question about whether they had participated in any career- or job-related courses. Therefore, 2005 results may not be comparable to results from the earlier years.

[2]Detail may not sum to totals due to missing locale information.
[3]For 2005, figures include "Production workers" occupations data.
NOTE: Data do not include persons enrolled in high school or below. Race categories exclude persons of Hispanic ethnicity. Detail may not sum to totals because of rounding.
SOURCE: U.S. Department of Education, National Center for Education Statistics, Adult Education Survey (AE-NHES:1995, AE-NHES:1999, and AE-NHES:2005) of the National Household Education Surveys Program. (This table was prepared October 2010.)

Table 507.40. Participation rate of persons, 17 years old and over, in adult education during the previous 12 months, by selected characteristics of participants: Selected years, 1991 through 2005

[Standard errors appear in parentheses]

Characteristic of participant	Percent taking any program, class, or course					Percent taking specific programs, classes, or courses, 2005						Percent doing informal learning activities for personal interest, 2005
	1991	1995	1999	2001	2005	Basic skills/General Educational Development (GED) classes	English as a second language (ESL) classes	Part-time postsecondary education[1]	Career- or job-related courses	Apprenticeship programs	Personal-interest courses	
1	2	3	4	5	6	7	8	9	10	11	12	13
Total	33.0 (0.68)	40.2 (0.48)	44.5 (0.77)	46.4 (0.55)	44.4 (0.74)	1.3 (0.22)	0.9 (0.17)	5.0 (0.29)	27.0 (0.63)	1.2 (0.18)	21.4 (0.71)	70.5 (0.79)
Sex												
Male	32.6 (1.09)	38.2 (0.65)	41.7 (1.15)	43.1 (0.83)	41.0 (1.20)	1.4 (0.41)	0.9! (0.29)	5.0 (0.44)	24.5 (0.99)	1.7 (0.31)	18.3 (1.08)	70.8 (1.10)
Female	33.2 (0.97)	42.1 (0.59)	47.1 (1.02)	49.5 (0.78)	47.5 (1.01)	1.2 (0.19)	0.9 (0.15)	5.1 (0.37)	29.2 (0.95)	0.7 (0.15)	24.2 (0.88)	70.2 (1.03)
Age												
17 to 24 years old	37.8 (1.46)	47.0 (1.12)	49.9 (2.34)	52.8 (2.04)	52.8 (2.79)	6.0 (1.48)	1.7! (0.61)	11.5 (1.34)	21.3 (2.22)	2.7 (0.76)	26.3 (2.60)	69.2 (2.54)
25 to 29 years old	40.0 (2.33)	49.6 (1.31)	56.5 (2.53)	52.9 (2.60)	51.6 (3.82)	1.8 (0.48)	3.3! (1.48)	9.1 (1.50)	29.5 (2.48)	3.2! (1.06)	20.9 (2.78)	66.8 (3.75)
30 to 34 years old	37.6 (2.88)	47.3 (1.41)	56.2 (2.57)	53.7 (2.18)	52.7 (2.52)	1.9! (0.66)	1.6! (0.64)	8.4 (1.28)	33.8 (2.71)	2.5! (0.89)	23.2 (2.23)	73.8 (2.22)
35 to 39 years old	42.1 (2.71)	47.7 (1.15)	50.1 (2.43)	54.0 (1.71)	48.6 (3.21)	0.4! (0.16)	0.7! (0.26)	6.1 (0.90)	32.6 (3.29)	0.9! (0.36)	20.7 (2.67)	75.5 (2.69)
40 to 44 years old	49.2 (3.28)	50.9 (1.15)	53.5 (2.43)	53.5 (1.88)	48.9 (2.62)	0.8! (0.31)	0.6! (0.23)	4.7 (0.77)	34.8 (2.30)	0.9! (0.42)	23.4 (2.29)	71.5 (2.62)
45 to 49 years old	40.0 (2.43)	48.7 (1.66)	49.8 (2.69)	55.4 (2.02)	49.0 (2.09)	† (†)	0.6! (0.25)	3.2 (0.48)	37.7 (1.83)	0.5! (0.23)	19.3 (1.88)	71.6 (2.52)
50 to 54 years old	26.8 (3.31)	42.5 (1.38)	47.2 (2.51)	51.1 (2.22)	46.6 (2.36)	† (†)	0.3! (0.15)	4.5 (0.75)	35.2 (2.25)	0.6! (0.28)	20.3 (1.64)	75.6 (1.89)
55 to 59 years old	29.0 (3.74)	32.2 (1.66)	38.0 (2.60)	44.1 (1.98)	42.2 (2.78)	† (†)	† (†)	1.9 (0.43)	31.9 (2.39)	† (†)	18.0 (1.63)	69.5 (2.56)
60 to 64 years old	17.4 (1.90)	23.7 (1.89)	31.4 (2.83)	30.8 (2.18)	37.9 (3.00)	† (†)	† (†)	0.9! (0.36)	20.9 (2.07)	† (†)	24.1 (2.40)	71.4 (3.04)
65 to 69 years old	14.2 (2.97)	18.1 (1.46)	25.4 (2.54)	20.5 (1.74)	26.2 (2.67)	† (†)	† (†)	0.5! (0.22)	8.1 (1.36)	† (†)	20.9 (2.41)	67.6 (2.52)
70 years old and over	8.6 (1.25)	13.8 (1.09)	15.0 (1.38)	21.7 (1.37)	21.5 (1.44)	5.1! (2.17)	† (†)	† (†)	4.0 (0.78)	† (†)	17.9 (1.33)	62.9 (1.82)
Racial/ethnic group												
White	34.1 (0.82)	41.5 (0.54)	44.4 (0.89)	47.4 (0.59)	45.6 (0.84)	0.9 (0.23)	0.2! (0.08)	4.9 (0.35)	29.1 (0.70)	0.9 (0.17)	22.1 (0.87)	73.0 (0.92)
Black	25.9 (2.23)	37.0 (1.45)	46.3 (2.30)	43.3 (1.50)	46.4 (2.81)	1.9 (0.49)	† (†)	5.4 (0.97)	27.0 (2.53)	1.5! (0.73)	23.7 (2.11)	65.3 (2.02)
Hispanic	31.4 (2.63)	33.7 (1.18)	41.3 (2.51)	41.7 (2.28)	37.8 (2.43)	2.6 (0.72)	5.6 (1.22)	5.7 (1.55)	16.9 (1.72)	2.2 (0.63)	15.4 (1.75)	57.5 (2.86)
Asian	—	† (†)	—	—	48.3 (5.39)	‡ (†)	2.6! (1.03)	7.6! (2.62)	27.2 (4.70)	‡ (†)	26.5 (5.06)	81.1 (4.10)
Pacific Islander	—	—	—	—	—	—	—	—	—	—	—	—
Asian/Pacific Islander	35.9 (5.55)	39.7 (2.92)	51.1 (4.63)	49.5 (3.81)	36.3 (10.17)	‡ (†)	‡ (†)	4.4! (1.82)	23.0! (8.51)	‡ (†)	13.0! (6.16)	70.6 (9.18)
American Indian/Alaska Native	29.3! (11.55)	38.8 (4.85)	36.3 (9.16)	50.2 (8.28)	39.4 (4.94)	5.1! (2.17)	‡ (†)	3.2! (1.07)	23.8 (4.06)	1.3! (0.59)	21.0 (4.13)	77.6 (5.28)
Two or more races	—	—	† (†)	—	—	—	—	—	—	—	—	—
Highest level of education completed												
8th grade or less	7.7 (1.44)	10.0 (1.38)	14.7 (2.92)	19.7 (2.84)	15.5 (2.47)	1.9 (0.57)	4.3! (1.70)	‡ (†)	1.7! (0.55)	‡ (†)	7.3 (1.24)	38.1 (3.27)
9th through 12th grade, no completion	15.8 (2.25)	20.7 (1.38)	25.6 (2.55)	25.5 (1.53)	27.2 (2.40)	7.9 (1.69)	1.1! (0.41)	2.1 (0.57)	7.6 (1.44)	1.5! (0.61)	12.5 (1.53)	55.7 (2.52)
High school completion	24.1 (1.10)	30.7 (0.84)	34.8 (1.37)	33.9 (1.07)	33.0 (1.62)	0.5! (0.24)	0.7! (0.24)	2.5 (0.36)	17.2 (1.18)	1.1 (0.35)	16.8 (1.27)	63.6 (1.93)
Some vocational/technical	34.2 (3.80)	41.9 (2.16)	41.1 (3.97)	50.7 (3.51)	43.3 (4.30)	‡ (†)	‡ (†)	4.5! (1.42)	28.3 (3.71)	1.4! (0.47)	23.2 (3.09)	77.6 (3.98)
Some college	41.4 (1.67)	49.3 (0.92)	51.1 (1.76)	57.4 (1.29)	51.1 (1.79)	‡ (†)	1.1! (0.51)	8.6 (1.06)	28.8 (1.54)	1.9! (0.66)	26.8 (1.80)	79.8 (1.52)
Associate's degree	49.2 (5.82)	56.1 (1.85)	56.6 (2.93)	62.5 (2.15)	56.5 (1.56)	† (†)	0.4! (0.17)	6.6 (1.42)	40.8 (3.27)	0.4! (0.17)	20.1 (2.48)	75.9 (3.70)
Bachelor's degree	51.1 (2.46)	56.9 (1.20)	60.3 (1.84)	64.5 (1.39)	59.8 (1.99)	† (†)	‡ (†)	6.3 (0.82)	44.1 (1.61)	‡ (†)	28.6 (1.55)	79.3 (1.72)
Some graduate work (or study)	55.1 (2.90)	59.9 (1.55)	63.6 (1.96)	68.9 (1.64)	66.3 (1.99)	† (†)	‡ (†)	8.7 (0.86)	49.3 (2.15)	‡ (†)	30.7 (1.77)	88.0 (1.06)
No degree	—	62.2 (2.67)	64.7 (4.39)	64.2 (3.54)	65.3 (4.84)	† (†)	‡ (†)	14.5 (2.55)	40.5 (4.68)	‡ (†)	38.7 (4.81)	78.2 (4.34)
Master's	—	59.1 (1.88)	65.7 (2.64)	70.7 (2.10)	67.5 (2.59)	† (†)	‡ (†)	8.9 (1.31)	51.4 (2.81)	‡ (†)	30.6 (2.04)	88.8 (1.33)
Doctor's	—	54.0 (6.99)	53.1 (4.73)	63.7 (3.98)	58.0 (4.94)	† (†)	‡ (†)	10.1! (3.14)	34.0 (4.53)	‡ (†)	31.4 (3.95)	90.3 (3.26)
Professional	—	65.9 (3.91)	72.5 (5.75)	72.8 (3.79)	68.2 (5.77)	† (†)	‡ (†)	‡ (†)	59.0 (6.35)	‡ (†)	23.9 (4.35)	91.6 (2.15)
Urbanicity												
City	—	—	—	—	45.8 (1.46)	1.4 (0.31)	1.6 (0.38)	5.7 (0.59)	26.3 (1.24)	1.8 (0.43)	22.5 (1.10)	69.2 (1.39)
Suburban	—	—	—	—	46.9 (1.33)	0.9 (0.23)	0.9! (0.36)	5.8 (0.55)	29.7 (1.26)	0.9 (0.22)	23.4 (1.16)	73.4 (1.28)
Town	—	—	—	—	41.8 (2.33)	2.7! (1.16)	0.4! (0.14)	4.2 (0.87)	25.6 (1.74)	0.5! (0.21)	18.5 (1.96)	70.5 (2.43)
Rural	—	—	—	—	39.5 (2.04)	0.8 (0.22)	‡ (†)	3.3 (0.59)	24.2 (1.38)	1.2! (0.40)	18.3 (1.76)	67.6 (1.76)
Labor force status												
In labor force	40.7 (0.96)	49.8 (0.69)	52.1 (0.94)	† (†)	52.3 (0.93)	1.4 (0.32)	0.8 (0.19)	6.4 (0.39)	37.1 (0.83)	1.5 (0.24)	21.9 (0.91)	73.0 (0.94)
Employed	42.0 (1.00)	50.7 (0.53)	52.5 (0.96)	† (†)	53.4 (0.94)	1.1 (0.31)	0.7 (0.20)	6.5 (0.39)	38.8 (0.83)	1.4 (0.24)	21.8 (0.94)	73.5 (1.01)
Unemployed	26.0 (3.24)	36.6 (1.91)	44.9 (4.60)	† (†)	37.8 (4.26)	5.8 (1.60)	1.9! (0.79)	5.2 (1.37)	13.5 (2.16)	‡ (†)	22.1 (3.99)	66.7 (3.80)
Not in labor force	15.7 (0.91)	21.3 (0.69)	24.9 (1.17)	† (†)	27.6 (1.18)	1.1 (0.24)	1.3 (0.36)	2.3 (0.45)	5.7 (0.55)	0.6! (0.22)	20.5 (0.97)	65.2 (1.27)

See notes at end of table.

Table 507.40. Participation rate of persons, 17 years old and over, in adult education during the previous 12 months, by selected characteristics of participants: Selected years, 1991 through 2005—Continued

[Standard errors appear in parentheses]

Characteristic of participant	Percent taking any program, class, or course					Percent taking specific programs, classes, or courses, 2005						Percent doing informal learning activities for personal interest, 2005
	1991	1995	1999	2001	2005	Basic skills/General Educational Development (GED) classes	English as a second language (ESL) classes	Part-time postsecondary education[1]	Career- or job-related courses	Apprenticeship programs	Personal-interest courses	
1	2	3	4	5	6	7	8	9	10	11	12	13
Occupation												
Executive, administrative, or managerial occupations	49.3 (3.45)	55.8 (1.92)	57.0 (2.11)	66.2 (1.61)	64.1 (2.73)	‡ (†)	‡ (†)	6.0 (1.10)	51.8 (2.82)	‡ (†)	28.8 (2.89)	78.6 (2.71)
Engineers, surveyors, and architects	62.6 (7.85)	65.5 (4.18)	79.8 (6.01)	68.1 (4.46)	71.2 (5.68)	‡ (†)	‡ (†)	9.3 ! (3.21)	55.6 (5.60)	‡ (†)	31.4 (6.19)	81.1 (4.63)
Natural scientists and mathematicians	48.2 (9.86)	72.3 (3.52)	60.5 (6.74)	74.0 (4.46)	69.1 (4.63)	‡ (†)	‡ (†)	9.2 (2.49)	49.6 (5.27)	‡ (†)	30.2 (4.53)	85.5 (5.16)
Social scientists and workers, religious workers, and lawyers	55.6 (6.01)	76.6 (2.61)	79.3 (4.35)	83.5 (3.05)	77.7 (4.11)	‡ (†)	‡ (†)	12.8 (3.16)	64.3 (4.42)	‡ (†)	29.2 (3.52)	89.4 (2.78)
Teachers, elementary/secondary	56.0 (4.20)	54.8 (4.64)	66.5 (5.61)	79.9 (2.95)	79.7 (2.59)	‡ (†)	‡ (†)	8.3 ! (3.16)	65.0 (3.99)	‡ (†)	31.7 (3.78)	83.8 (2.62)
Teachers: college, university, postsecondary institutions	45.5 (8.31)	76.7 (1.98)	78.4 (3.11)	69.4 (4.60)	61.3 (6.96)	‡ (†)	‡ (†)	‡ (†)	49.0 (8.50)	‡ (†)	19.5 (4.98)	91.7 (3.58)
Health diagnosing and treating practitioners	67.1 (13.73)	71.1 (5.78)	79.8 (9.02)	78.5 (6.38)	88.8 (5.59)	‡ (†)	‡ (†)	15.4 (2.47)	79.5 (6.59)	‡ (†)	31.9 (9.15)	84.5 (5.63)
Registered nurses, pharmacists, dieticians, therapists, and physician's assistants	59.6 (6.69)	86.7 (2.47)	85.4 (4.10)	82.7 (3.83)	85.4 (4.05)	‡ (†)	‡ (†)	7.9 (2.17)	78.2 (4.89)	‡ (†)	27.4 (3.73)	83.1 (3.92)
Writers, artists, entertainers, and athletes	42.9 (6.63)	49.9 (4.37)	50.0 (6.93)	46.8 (6.03)	52.5 (6.59)	‡ (†)	‡ (†)	5.4 ! (2.16)	27.8 (5.02)	‡ (†)	35.3 (6.42)	88.2 (3.89)
Health technologists and technicians	68.6 (10.03)	74.8 (3.64)	66.9 (6.16)	85.6 (3.25)	72.1 (8.37)	‡ (†)	‡ (†)	6.0 ! (2.11)	63.2 (8.67)	‡ (†)	24.6 (5.91)	75.6 (7.26)
Technologists and technicians, except health and engineering	53.0 (6.49)	64.3 (2.84)	59.6 (5.07)	70.2 (3.32)	33.8 (8.53)	‡ (†)	‡ (†)	7.1 ! (3.19)	29.1 (7.68)	‡ (†)	6.2 ! (2.14)	76.0 (8.80)
Marketing and sales occupations	34.4 (2.38)	44.2 (1.34)	44.4 (2.73)	51.1 (2.10)	45.7 (3.00)	1.7 ! (0.59)	‡ (†)	4.5 (0.88)	30.2 (2.77)	‡ (†)	21.5 (2.43)	68.9 (3.37)
Administrative support occupations, including clerical	29.9 (1.74)	51.7 (1.25)	50.1 (2.29)	58.7 (1.72)	54.6 (2.70)	1.1 ! (0.53)	‡ (†)	6.6 (0.98)	33.5 (2.70)	‡ (†)	27.7 (2.18)	73.8 (2.33)
Service occupations	25.2 (1.82)	46.5 (1.38)	50.9 (2.74)	49.3 (2.24)	44.7 (2.47)	1.6 (0.39)	1.9 ! (0.88)	6.8 (1.42)	28.5 (2.64)	1.4 ! (0.57)	17.5 (2.10)	65.4 (2.71)
Agriculture, forestry, and fishing occupations	14.3 ! (5.19)	26.4 (3.55)	34.3 (7.16)	46.4 (6.80)	44.4 (9.02)	‡ (†)	‡ (†)	‡ (†)	20.3 ! (6.92)	‡ (†)	21.6 ! (10.05)	64.0 (10.03)
Mechanics and repairers	32.1 (4.72)	47.6 (2.70)	42.2 (5.44)	35.1 (3.40)	40.1 (5.10)	‡ (†)	‡ (†)	6.0 ! (1.89)	27.4 (4.26)	3.8 ! (1.38)	12.7 (3.18)	69.3 (4.27)
Construction and extractive occupations	21.9 (3.38)	38.0 (2.45)	34.5 (4.78)	32.3 (3.19)	27.6 (3.73)	‡ (†)	1.1 ! (0.49)	3.2 ! (1.08)	12.3 (2.54)	5.2 ! (1.89)	11.4 (2.72)	72.3 (4.48)
Precision production[2]	31.2 (6.09)	43.0 (4.32)	38.3 (8.48)	35.1 (6.19)	33.0 (3.98)	‡ (†)	0.4 ! (0.16)	4.2 ! (1.42)	22.2 (3.41)	‡ (†)	13.3 (2.99)	63.9 (3.46)
Transportation, material moving	21.1 (2.31)	30.7 (1.29)	38.0 (3.47)	39.4 (2.82)	— (†)	— (†)	— (†)	— (†)	— (†)	— (†)	— (†)	— (†)
Production workers	20.7 (4.69)	28.4 (2.32)	33.3 (4.25)	30.4 (3.29)	34.6 (5.27)	‡ (†)	‡ (†)	‡ (†)	14.7 (2.63)	3.2 ! (1.57)	11.2 (2.85)	60.8 (4.98)
Handler, equipment, cleaners, helpers, and laborers	— (†)	25.1 (2.70)	19.6 (4.56)	18.2 (3.20)	— (†)	— (†)	— (†)	— (†)	— (†)	— (†)	— (†)	— (†)
Miscellaneous occupations	20.8 (3.49)	56.6 (3.61)	43.0 (7.98)	64.9 (7.07)	39.2 (11.25)	‡ (†)	‡ (†)	‡ (†)	15.7 ! (5.81)	‡ (†)	7.8 ! (3.63)	52.2 (12.32)
Annual household income												
$5,000 or less	13.6 (1.70)	21.3 (1.59)	21.0 (3.22)	25.1 (2.92)	35.9 (4.83)	2.4 ! (0.92)	1.5 ! (0.71)	3.6 ! (1.52)	13.7 (4.00)	‡ (†)	17.2 (3.59)	52.9 (4.97)
$5,001 to $10,000	17.5 (2.14)	23.9 (1.37)	24.5 (3.39)	28.0 (2.74)	29.6 (4.49)	2.4 (0.69)	0.8 ! (0.33)	1.7 ! (0.81)	8.4 (2.11)	‡ (†)	21.8 (4.75)	61.0 (3.75)
$10,001 to $15,000	22.8 (2.60)	26.7 (1.61)	22.8 (2.45)	28.6 (2.30)	25.0 (3.41)	1.0 ! (0.38)	‡ (†)	3.3 ! (1.17)	11.3 (2.52)	‡ (†)	15.5 (3.14)	58.6 (4.43)
$15,001 to $20,000	21.9 (2.35)	31.8 (1.55)	31.4 (2.75)	30.2 (2.48)	24.3 (2.54)	1.7 ! (0.78)	1.9 ! (0.62)	3.3 ! (1.19)	10.1 (1.37)	2.6 ! (1.20)	12.9 (2.00)	61.1 (3.17)
$20,001 to $25,000	26.7 (3.20)	31.4 (1.27)	35.8 (2.81)	35.2 (2.27)	28.2 (2.51)	‡ (†)	1.3 ! (0.61)	4.4 (1.26)	12.8 (2.04)	1.1 ! (0.50)	13.6 (1.88)	63.2 (3.11)
$25,001 to $30,000	32.1 (2.51)	37.9 (1.47)	36.7 (2.61)	38.3 (2.43)	38.6 (3.63)	‡ (†)	1.0 ! (0.49)	6.8 ! (2.09)	20.2 (3.37)	‡ (†)	18.4 (2.52)	71.0 (3.38)
$30,001 to $40,000	35.6 (1.84)	42.7 (0.86)	45.2 (2.05)	44.6 (1.54)	42.7 (2.65)	1.9 ! (0.65)	1.0 ! (0.49)	3.7 (0.68)	22.8 (2.27)	1.1 ! (0.39)	23.0 (2.49)	68.7 (2.36)
$40,001 to $50,000	44.8 (1.84)	46.8 (1.39)	47.9 (2.31)	49.1 (1.93)	41.4 (2.92)	1.6 (0.53)	‡ (†)	2.9 (0.55)	22.4 (2.00)	1.5 ! (0.56)	23.0 (2.47)	71.9 (2.62)
$50,001 to $75,000	46.6 (2.03)	52.0 (0.94)	55.1 (1.80)	55.7 (1.48)	47.7 (1.74)	0.4 ! (0.19)	‡ (†)	5.8 (0.69)	33.0 (1.37)	0.9 ! (0.36)	20.5 (1.67)	70.6 (2.15)
More than $75,000	48.7 (3.15)	58.0 (1.27)	56.9 (1.66)	— (†)	— (†)	— (†)	— (†)	— (†)	— (†)	— (†)	— (†)	— (†)
$75,001 to $100,000	— (†)	— (†)	—	59.7 (1.91)	56.4 (2.28)	‡ (†)	‡ (†)	7.5 (0.89)	38.6 (2.26)	1.8 ! (0.64)	25.3 (1.51)	75.0 (1.97)
More than $100,000	— (†)	— (†)	—	59.3 (1.82)	58.4 (2.11)	‡ (†)	‡ (†)	6.1 (0.70)	39.4 (1.80)	‡ (†)	28.2 (1.62)	81.2 (1.68)

—Not available.

†Not applicable.

!Interpret data with caution. The coefficient of variation (CV) for this estimate is between 30 and 50 percent.

‡Reporting standards not met. Either there are too few cases for a reliable estimate or the coefficient of variation (CV) is 50 percent or greater.

[1]Includes college and university degree programs, post-degree certificate programs, and vocational certificate programs.

[2]For 2005, figures include "Production workers" occupations data.

NOTE: Adult education is defined as all education activities, except full-time enrollment in higher education credential programs. Data do not include persons enrolled in high school or below. Race categories exclude persons of Hispanic ethnicity.

SOURCE: U.S. Department of Education, National Center for Education Statistics, Adult Education Survey (AE-NHES:1991, AE-NHES:1995, AE-NHES:1999, and AE-NHES:2005) and Adult Education and Lifelong Learning Survey (AELL-NHES:2001) of the National Household Education Surveys Program. (This table was prepared November 2010.)

CHAPTER 6
International Comparisons of Education

This chapter offers a broad perspective on education across the nations of the world. It also provides an international context for examining the condition of education in the United States. Insights into the educational practices and outcomes of the United States are obtained by comparing them with those of other education systems. Most of the education systems represent countries; however, some of the tables in this chapter also include data for subnational entities with separate education systems, such as Hong Kong. The National Center for Education Statistics (NCES) carries out a variety of activities in order to provide statistical data for international comparisons of education.

This chapter presents data drawn from materials prepared by the United Nations Educational, Scientific, and Cultural Organization (UNESCO); the Organization for Economic Cooperation and Development (OECD); and the International Association for the Evaluation of Educational Achievement (IEA). Basic summary data on enrollments and enrollment ratios, teachers, educational attainment, and finances were synthesized from data published by the OECD in the Online Education Database and the annual *Education at a Glance* report, as well as from data collected by UNESCO. Even though these tabulations are carefully prepared, international data users should be cautioned about the many problems of definition and reporting involved in the collection of data about the education systems of the world, which vary greatly in structure from country to country (see the UNESCO entry at the end of Appendix A: Guide to Sources).

Also presented in this chapter are data from two international assessments of student achievement that are carried out under the aegis of IEA and supported by NCES. The Trends in International Mathematics and Science Study (TIMSS), formerly known as the Third International Mathematics and Science Study, assesses the mathematics and science knowledge and skills of fourth- and eighth-graders every 4 years. The Progress in International Reading Literacy Study (PIRLS) measures the reading knowledge and skills of fourth-graders every 5 years.

This chapter includes additional information from two OECD assessments supported by NCES. The Program for International Student Assessment (PISA) provides performance scores of 15-year-olds in the areas of reading, mathematics, and science literacy; it also measures general, or cross-curricular, competencies such as learning strategies. The Program for the International Assessment of Adult Competencies (PIAAC) assesses the cognitive skills of adults in the areas of literacy, numeracy, and problem solving in technology-rich environments. PIAAC measures relationships between adults' skills in these areas and their educational background, workplace experiences, occupational attainment, and use of information and communication technology. While PISA and PIAAC focus on OECD countries, data from some non-OECD education systems are also provided.

Further information on survey methodologies is in Appendix A: Guide to Sources and in the publications cited in the table source notes.

Population

Among the reporting OECD countries, Mexico had the largest percentage of its population made up of young people ages 5 to 14 (20 percent) in 2012, followed by Israel (18 percent) and Turkey (17 percent) (table 601.30). OECD countries with small percentages of people in this age group included the Czech Republic, Germany, Greece, Italy, Japan, and Slovenia (all at 9 percent), and Austria, Estonia, Hungary, the Republic of Korea, Poland, Portugal, the Slovak Republic, Spain, and Switzerland (all at 10 percent). In the United States, the proportion of 5- to 14-year-olds was 13 percent, which was higher than in most of the other OECD countries.

Enrollments

In 2013, about 1.5 billion students were enrolled in schools around the world (table 601.10). Of these students, 714 million were in elementary-level programs, 569 million were in secondary programs, and 199 million were in postsecondary programs.

From 2000 to 2013, enrollment changes varied from region to region. Changes in elementary enrollment ranged from increases of 59 percent in Africa, 36 percent in Oceania, and less than 1 percent in Asia to decreases of 10 percent in Europe, 7 percent in Central and South America (including Latin America and the Caribbean), and 3 percent in Northern America (including Bermuda, Canada, Greenland, St. Pierre and Miquelon, and the United States) (table F, table 601.10, and figure 27). Over the same period, secondary enrollment increased by 83 percent in Africa, 34 percent in Asia, 17 percent in Central and South America, 7 percent in Northern America, and 4 percent in Oceania but decreased by 17 percent in Europe. At the postsecondary level, enrollments increased in all major areas of the world from 2000 to 2013. Postsecondary enrollment rose by 164 percent in Asia, 105 percent in Central and South America, 99 percent in Africa, 61 percent in Oceania, 48 percent in Northern America, and 23 percent in Europe.

Table F. Population and enrollment at different levels in major areas of the world: 2000 and 2013

[In millions]

Area of the world	Population	Enrollment		
		Elementary	Secondary	Postsecondary
World total				
2000...................	6,088.6	655.6	450.1	99.6
2013...................	7,101.0	713.6	568.5	198.6
Africa				
2000...................	802.7	109.5	38.6	6.1
2013...................	1,102.6	173.6	70.8	12.2
Asia				
2000...................	3,693.8	404.8	257.5	41.0
2013...................	4,262.1	406.0	344.8	108.2
Europe				
2000...................	730.5	41.7	70.5	25.5
2013...................	744.0	37.7	58.4	31.5
Central and South America				
2000...................	517.8	70.0	55.0	11.5
2013...................	604.9	65.4	64.2	23.7
Northern America				
2000...................	313.4	27.4	25.1	14.4
2013...................	351.2	26.6	26.8	21.3
Oceania				
2000...................	30.4	3.1	3.4	1.0
2013...................	36.3	4.3	3.5	1.7

SOURCE: United Nations Educational, Scientific, and Cultural Organization, unpublished tabulations, and U.S. Department of Commerce, Census Bureau, International Data Base.

Across OECD countries in 2013, an average enrollment rate of 98 percent was reported for the 5- to 14-year-old population, and the enrollment rate was at least 94 percent in all 31 of the OECD countries that reported data for this age group (table 601.35). For 15-year-olds in 2013, the OECD average enrollment rate was 97 percent, with only 2 out of 33 reporting countries having a rate of less than 90 percent (Mexico, at 71 percent, and Turkey, at 88 percent) (table 601.40). The OECD average enrollment rate for youth decreased with each additional year of age, from 94 percent for 16-year-olds to 51 percent for 20-year-olds. Although the U.S. enrollment rates for 15-year-olds (99 percent) and 19-year-olds (60 percent) were higher than the OECD average, the U.S. enrollment rates at ages 16 through 18 were lower than the OECD average.

In all reporting OECD countries, the majority of enrollment was still at the secondary level for 17-year-olds. For older students, however, patterns of enrollment at the secondary and postsecondary levels varied across OECD countries. For example, of the 32 countries that reported separate secondary and postsecondary enrollment rates, 14 countries had a higher percentage of their 19-year-olds enrolled at the secondary level, while 18 countries had a higher percentage enrolled at the postsecondary level. The percentage of 19-year-olds enrolled at the secondary level was at least 5 times higher than the percentage enrolled at the postsecondary level in 3 countries: Iceland (70 percent of 19-year-olds enrolled at the secondary level vs. 4 percent enrolled at the postsecondary level), Italy (22 percent vs. 2 percent), and Denmark (58 percent vs. 8 percent). At the other end of the spectrum, 5 countries reported a percentage of 19-year-olds enrolled at the postsecondary level that was at least 5 times higher than the percentage enrolled at the secondary level: the Republic of Korea (74 percent of 19-year-olds enrolled at the postsecondary level vs. less than 1 percent enrolled at the secondary level), Ireland (57 percent vs. 4 percent), the United States (52 percent vs. 6 percent), Israel (13 percent vs. 2 percent), and Turkey (40 percent vs. 7 percent).

Achievement

Mathematics and Science at Grades 4 and 8

The 2011 Trends in International Mathematics and Science Study (TIMSS) assessed students' mathematics and science performance at grade 4 in 45 countries and at grade 8 in 38 countries. A number of subnational entities also participated in TIMSS as separate education systems. Examples of subnational participants include the cities of Hong Kong and Taipei, several U.S. states and Canadian provinces, Northern Ireland and England within the United Kingdom, and the Flemish community in Belgium. Results for individual U.S. states are based on public school students only, while U.S. national results are based on both public and private school students. TIMSS assessments are curriculum based and measure what students have actually learned against the subject matter that is expected to be taught by the end of grades 4 and 8, as described in the TIMSS mathematics and science frameworks, which guide assessment development. At both grades, TIMSS scores are reported on a scale of 0 to 1,000, with the scale average set at 500.

In 2011, the average mathematics scores of U.S. fourth-graders (541) and eighth-graders (509) were higher than the TIMSS scale average of 500 (tables 602.20 and 602.30). The average U.S. fourth-grade mathematics score was higher than the average score in 37 of the 44 other countries participating at grade 4, lower than the average score in 3 countries, and not measurably different from the average score in the remaining 4 countries (table 602.20). The 3 countries that outperformed the United States in fourth-grade mathematics were Singapore, the Republic of Korea, and Japan. At grade 8, the average U.S. mathematics score was higher than the average score in 27 of the 37 other participating countries, lower than the average score in 4 countries, and not measurably different from the average score in the remaining 6 countries (table 602.30). The 4 countries that outperformed the United States in eighth-grade mathematics were the Republic of Korea, Singapore, Japan, and the Russian Federation.

Of the two U.S. states that participated in the 2011 TIMSS as separate education systems at grade 4, one state—North Carolina—had an average score for public schools that was higher than both the TIMSS scale average and the U.S. national average in mathematics (table 602.20). Public schools in the other state, Florida, had an average fourth-grade mathematics score that was higher than the TIMSS scale average but not measurably different from the U.S. national average. Of the nine U.S. states that participated separately at grade 8, four states—Massachusetts, Minnesota,

North Carolina, and Indiana—had public school average scores that were higher than both the TIMSS scale average and the U.S. national average in mathematics (table 602.30). The public schools in three states—Colorado, Connecticut, and Florida—had average eighth-grade mathematics scores that were higher than the TIMSS scale average but not measurably different from the U.S. national average. The average eighth-grade score for public schools in California was not measurably different from the TIMSS scale average but was lower than the U.S. national average, while Alabama's public school average was lower than both the TIMSS scale average and the U.S. national average in mathematics.

The average science scores of both U.S. fourth-graders (544) and U.S. eighth-graders (525) were higher than the TIMSS scale average of 500 in 2011 (tables 602.20 and 602.30). The average U.S. fourth-grade science score was higher than the average score in 39 of the 44 other countries participating at grade 4 and lower than the average score in 5 countries (table 602.20). The 5 countries that outperformed the United States in fourth-grade science were the Republic of Korea, Singapore, Finland, Japan, and the Russian Federation. At grade 8, the average U.S. science score was higher than the average score in 28 of the 37 other participating countries in 2011, lower than the average score in 6 countries, and not measurably different from the average score in the remaining 3 countries (table 602.30). The 6 countries that outperformed the United States in eighth-grade science were Singapore, the Republic of Korea, Japan, Finland, Slovenia, and the Russian Federation.

Public schools in both Florida and North Carolina, which were the two U.S. states participating in the 2011 TIMSS at grade 4, had average fourth-grade science scores that were higher than the TIMSS scale average but not measurably different from the U.S. national average (table 602.20). Of the nine U.S. states that participated at grade 8, three states—Massachusetts, Minnesota, and Colorado—had public school average scores that were higher than both the TIMSS scale average and the U.S. national average in science (table 602.30). Public schools in four states—Indiana, Connecticut, North Carolina, and Florida—had average eighth-grade science scores that were higher than the TIMSS scale average but not measurably different from the U.S. national average. The average eighth-grade score for public schools in California was not measurably different from the TIMSS scale average but was lower than the U.S. national average, while Alabama's public school average was lower than both the TIMSS scale average and the U.S. national average in science.

Reading Literacy at Grade 4

The Progress in International Reading Literacy Study (PIRLS) has conducted international assessments of fourth-grade reading literacy in 2001, 2006, and 2011. In 2011, PIRLS participants consisted of 40 countries as well as a number of subnational education systems. Examples of subnational participants include the cities of Hong Kong and Taipei, the public school system of the U.S. state of Florida,

several Canadian provinces, Northern Ireland and England within the United Kingdom, and the Flemish community in Belgium. PIRLS scores are reported on a scale from 0 to 1,000, with the scale average set at 500.

On the 2011 PIRLS, U.S. fourth-graders had an average reading literacy score of 556 (table 602.10). The U.S. average score in 2011 was 14 points higher than in 2001 and 16 points higher than in 2006. In all 3 assessment years, the U.S. average score was higher than the PIRLS scale average.

In 2011, the average reading literacy score of fourth-graders in the United States was higher than the average score in 33 of the 39 other participating countries, lower than the average score in 3 countries, and not measurably different from the average in the remaining 3 countries. The 3 countries that outperformed the United States on the 2011 PIRLS were the Russian Federation, Finland, and Singapore. Public school students in Florida scored higher than both the PIRLS scale average and the U.S. national average.

In the United States, the 2011 average reading literacy score for females (562) was higher than the average score for males (551). In 34 of the 39 other participating countries, the average score for females was also higher than the average score for males, while there was no measurable difference between females' and males' average scores in the remaining 5 countries.

Reading, Mathematics, and Science Literacy at Age 15

The Program for International Student Assessment (PISA) assesses 15-year-old students' application of reading, mathematics, and science literacy to problems within a real-life context. In 2012, PISA assessed students in the 34 OECD countries as well as in a number of other education systems. Some subnational entities participated as separate education systems, including the U.S. states of Connecticut, Florida, and Massachusetts. Results for individual U.S. states are based on public school students only, while U.S. national results are based on both public and private school students. PISA scores are reported on a scale of 0 to 1,000.

On the 2012 PISA assessment, U.S. 15-year-olds' average score in reading literacy was 498, which was not measurably different from the OECD average of 496 (table 602.50). The average reading literacy score in the United States was lower than the average score in 13 of the 33 other OECD countries, higher than the average score in 10 of the other OECD countries, and not measurably different from the average score in 10 of the OECD countries. The average reading literacy scores of public school students in Massachusetts (527) and Connecticut (521) were higher than both the U.S. average and the OECD average, while the average score in Florida (492) was not measurably different from either the U.S. average or the OECD average. In all participating education systems, females outperformed males in reading (table 602.40). The U.S. gender gap in reading (31 points) was smaller than the OECD average gap (38 points) and smaller than the gaps in 14 of the OECD countries.

In mathematics literacy, U.S. 15-year-olds' average score of 481 on the 2012 PISA assessment was lower than the OECD average score of 494 (table 602.60). The average mathematics literacy score in the United States was lower than the average in 21 of the 33 other OECD countries, higher than the average in 5 OECD countries, and not measurably different from the average in 7 OECD countries. The average mathematics literacy score of public school students in Massachusetts (514) was higher than both the U.S. average and the OECD average, while the average score in Connecticut (506) was higher than the U.S. average but not measurably different from the OECD average. The average score in Florida (467) was lower than both the U.S. average and the OECD average. In 25 of the OECD countries, males outperformed females in mathematics literacy (table 602.40). In the United States, however, the average score of males (484) was not measurably different from that of females (479).

In science literacy, U.S. 15-year-olds' average score of 497 was not measurably different from the OECD average score of 501 (table 602.70). The average science literacy score in the United States was lower than the average in 15 OECD countries, higher than the average in 8 OECD countries, and not measurably different from the average in 10 OECD countries. The average science literacy scores of public school students in Massachusetts (527) and Connecticut (521) were higher than both the U.S. average and the OECD average. The average score in Florida (485) was not measurably different from the U.S. average but was lower than the OECD average.

Educational Attainment

In 2014, the percentage of 25- to 64-year-olds who had completed high school varied among reporting OECD countries (table 603.10). The OECD country reporting the highest percentage of 25- to 64-year-olds who had completed high school was the Czech Republic (93 percent), followed by Estonia, the Slovak Republic, and Poland (all at 91 percent). High school completers made up 90 percent of 25- to 64-year-olds in 2 OECD countries (Canada and the United States), and 12 OECD countries reported percentages between 80 and 88 percent. The OECD country reporting the lowest percentage of high school completers among 25- to 64-year-olds was Mexico (34 percent), followed by Turkey (36 percent) and then Portugal (43 percent).

In 2014, the OECD country reporting the highest percentage of 25- to 64-year-olds with a postsecondary degree (i.e., any degree at the associate's level or above) was Canada (54 percent), followed by Israel (49 percent), Luxembourg (46 percent), the Republic of Korea (45 percent), and the United States (44 percent) (table 603.20). An additional 6 OECD countries reported that at least 40 percent of their 25- to 64-year-olds had a postsecondary degree. The OECD countries reporting the lowest percentages of 25- to 64-year-olds with a postsecondary degree were Italy and Turkey (both at 17 percent), followed by Mexico (19 percent).

Among younger adults (those 25 to 34 years old) in OECD countries, the percentage with a postsecondary degree also varied in 2014 (table 603.20 and figure 28). The OECD country reporting the highest percentage of younger adults with a postsecondary degree was the Republic of Korea (68 percent), followed by Canada (58 percent) and then Luxembourg (53 percent). At least 40 percent of younger adults had a postsecondary degree in 18 additional countries, including the United States (46 percent). The OECD country reporting the lowest percentage of younger adults with a degree in 2014 was Italy (24 percent), followed by Mexico and Turkey (both at 25 percent).

Degrees

In 27 of the 30 reporting OECD countries, more than half of all postsecondary degrees (i.e., all degrees at the associate's level or above) were awarded to women in 2013 (table 603.60). However, the proportion of degrees awarded to women varied by field. For example, 29 of the 30 countries reported that at least 70 percent of education degrees were awarded to women. In contrast, 18 of the countries reported that less than 25 percent of degrees in the combined field of engineering, manufacturing, and construction were awarded to women.

The percentages of bachelor's degrees that were awarded in mathematics and science fields—including natural sciences, mathematics and computer science, and engineering—varied across the 32 OECD countries that reported these data in 2013 (table 603.70). Three of the reporting OECD countries awarded 30 percent or more of their bachelor's degrees in mathematics and science fields: Germany (36 percent), the Republic of Korea (33 percent), and Greece (30 percent). Two countries awarded less than 15 percent of their bachelor's degrees in mathematics and science fields: Norway (13 percent) and the Netherlands (14 percent). In 2013, the United States awarded 17 percent of its bachelor's degrees in mathematics and science fields, a lower percentage than most other reporting countries.

The percentages of graduate degrees awarded in mathematics and science fields—including natural sciences, mathematics and computer science, and engineering—varied widely across OECD countries in 2013 (table 603.80). In most of the countries, a higher percentage of degrees were awarded in mathematics and science fields at the doctoral level than at the master's level. In 2013, data at the master's level were reported by 32 OECD countries. Five of the reporting OECD countries awarded 30 percent or more of their master's degrees in mathematics and science fields: Japan (42 percent), Greece and Sweden (both at 32 percent), Germany (31 percent), and Estonia (30 percent). Six OECD countries awarded less than 15 percent of their master's degrees in mathematics and science fields: Chile (6 percent), Mexico (11 percent), Israel and the United States (both at 12 percent), and Ireland and the Netherlands (both at 14 percent). Data at the doctoral level were reported by 31 OECD countries in 2013. Six of the reporting OECD countries awarded more than half of their doctor's degrees in mathematics and science fields: France (62 percent), Chile (59 percent), Canada (56 percent), Israel (52 percent), and Estonia and Sweden (both at 51 percent). Only 2 OECD countries reported awarding less than 30 percent of their doctor's degrees in mathematics and science fields: Turkey (20 percent) and Mexico (28 percent). The United States awarded 41 percent of its doctor's degrees in mathematics and science fields.

Skills of Adults

The Program for the International Assessment of Adult Competencies (PIAAC) assesses the cognitive skills of adults in three areas—literacy, numeracy, and problem solving in technology-rich environments—that are seen as key to facilitating the social and economic participation of adults in advanced economies. The discussion below focuses on the areas of literacy and numeracy. PIAAC 2012 results are available for adults in 24 participating countries and regions, including 22 that belong to the OECD. Participating countries and regions are referred to collectively as "education systems" in the *Digest*. The education systems that participated in the 2012 assessment were primarily countries, but also included three subnational education systems: Northern Ireland and England within the United Kingdom, and the Flemish community in Belgium. PIAAC literacy and numeracy scores are reported on a scale of 0 to 500.

In 2012, average scores on the PIAAC literacy scale for adults ages 25 to 65 ranged from 249 in Italy and 250 in Spain to 296 in Japan (table 604.10). U.S. 25- to 65-year-olds had an average PIAAC literacy score of 269, which was not measurably different from the OECD average score of 271. Across education systems, adults' average literacy scores generally increased with higher levels of educational attainment. In the United States, for example, 25- to 65-year-olds whose highest level of attainment was high school completion had an average literacy score of 259, compared with an average score of 302 for those who had a bachelor's or higher degree. The literacy score for U.S. high school completers in the 25- to 65-year-old age group was lower than the OECD average of 268 for high school completers in this age group, while the literacy score for U.S. 25- to 65-year-olds with a bachelor's or higher degree was not measurably different from the OECD average of 302 for those with a bachelor's or higher degree.

On the PIAAC numeracy scale, 2012 average scores for adults ages 25 to 65 ranged from 245 in Spain and 246 in

Italy to 289 in Japan. U.S. 25- to 65-year-olds had an average PIAAC numeracy score of 254, which was lower than the OECD average score of 268. Across education systems, adults' average numeracy scores generally increased with higher levels of educational attainment. In the United States, for example, 25- to 65-year-olds whose highest level of attainment was high school completion had an average numeracy score of 241, compared with an average score of 293 for those who had a bachelor's or higher degree. The numeracy score for U.S. 25- to 65-year-olds who had completed only high school was lower than the OECD average of 265 for those with the same level of educational attainment. Likewise, the average numeracy score of U.S. 25- to 65-year-olds with a bachelor's or higher degree was lower than the OECD average of 303 for those with a bachelor's or higher degree.

Finances

In 2012, expenditures per full-time-equivalent (FTE) student at the combined elementary and secondary level of education were at least $11,000 (in current U.S. dollars) in 6 of the 32 OECD countries that reported finance data for this level of education (table 605.10). Specifically, Luxembourg spent $20,200 per elementary/secondary student; Switzerland spent $15,500; Norway spent $13,600; Austria spent $12,200; the United States spent $11,700; and Belgium spent $11,000. At the higher education level, 9 of 31 reporting countries had expenditures of over $17,000 per FTE student in 2012: Luxembourg ($32,900), the United States ($26,600), Switzerland ($25,300), the United Kingdom ($24,300), Sweden ($22,500), Norway ($20,000), the Netherlands ($19,300), Finland ($17,900), and Germany ($17,200). These expenditures were adjusted to U.S. dollars using the purchasing-power-parity (PPP) index. This index is considered more stable and comparable than indexes using currency exchange rates; for more information, see appendix B.

A comparison of public direct expenditures on all education levels as a percentage of gross domestic product (GDP) in reporting OECD countries shows that public investment in education in 2012 ranged from 3.5 percent in Japan and the Slovak Republic to 6.5 percent in Norway (table 605.20 and figure 29). Among reporting OECD countries, the average public direct expenditure on education in 2012 was 4.7 percent of GDP. In the United States, the public direct expenditure on education as a percentage of GDP was 4.7 percent.

Figure 27. Percentage change in enrollment, by major areas of the world and level of education: 2000 to 2013

Percent change

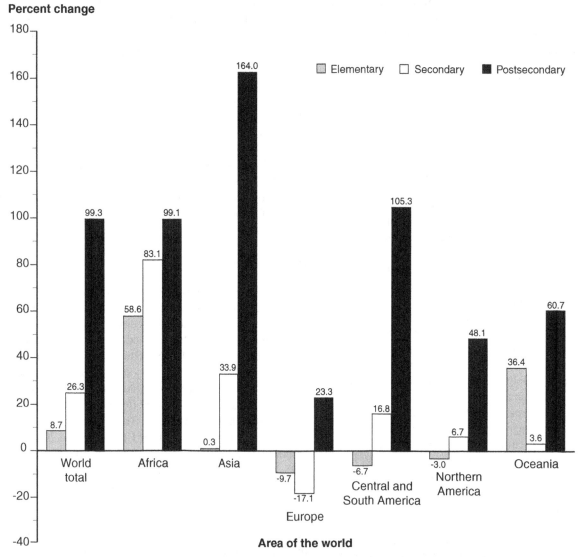

NOTE: Europe includes all countries of the former Union of Soviet Socialist Republics (U.S.S.R.) except Armenia, Azerbaijan, Georgia, Kazakhstan, Kyrgyzstan, Tajikistan, Turkmenistan, and Uzbekistan, which are included in Asia. Asia also includes Turkey, the Arab states (except those located in Africa), and Israel. Central and South America includes Latin America and the Caribbean. Northern America includes Bermuda, Canada, Greenland, St. Pierre and Miquelon, and the United States. Data include imputed values for nonrespondent countries.
SOURCE: United Nations Educational, Scientific, and Cultural Organization (UNESCO), unpublished tabulations. U.S. Department of Commerce, Census Bureau, International Data Base (March 2016).

Figure 28. Percentage of the population 25 to 34 years old with an associate's or higher degree, by OECD country: 2014

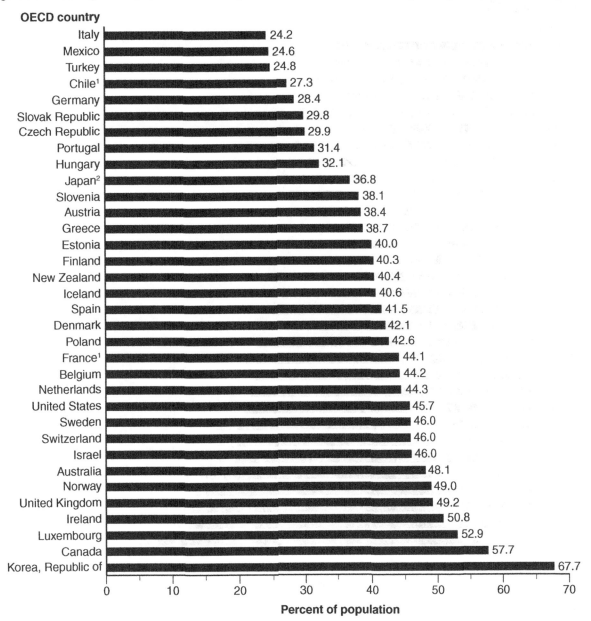

OECD country

Country	Percent
Italy	24.2
Mexico	24.6
Turkey	24.8
Chile[1]	27.3
Germany	28.4
Slovak Republic	29.8
Czech Republic	29.9
Portugal	31.4
Hungary	32.1
Japan[2]	36.8
Slovenia	38.1
Austria	38.4
Greece	38.7
Estonia	40.0
Finland	40.3
New Zealand	40.4
Iceland	40.6
Spain	41.5
Denmark	42.1
Poland	42.6
France[1]	44.1
Belgium	44.2
Netherlands	44.3
United States	45.7
Sweden	46.0
Switzerland	46.0
Israel	46.0
Australia	48.1
Norway	49.0
United Kingdom	49.2
Ireland	50.8
Luxembourg	52.9
Canada	57.7
Korea, Republic of	67.7

Percent of population

[1]Data from 2013 are reported for 2014.
[2]Excludes short-cycle tertiary education, which corresponds to the associate's degree in the United States.
NOTE: All data in this figure were calculated using International Standard Classification of Education (ISCED) 2011. The data refer to total tertiary degrees, which correspond to all degrees at the associate's level and above in the United States and include the following ISCED 2011 levels: level 5 (corresponding to the associate's degree in the United States), level 6 (bachelor's or equivalent degree), level 7 (master's or equivalent degree), and level 8 (doctoral or equivalent degree).
SOURCE: Organization for Economic Cooperation and Development (OECD), *Education at a Glance, 2015.*

Figure 29. Public direct expenditures on education institutions as a percentage of gross domestic product (GDP), by selected OECD country: 2012

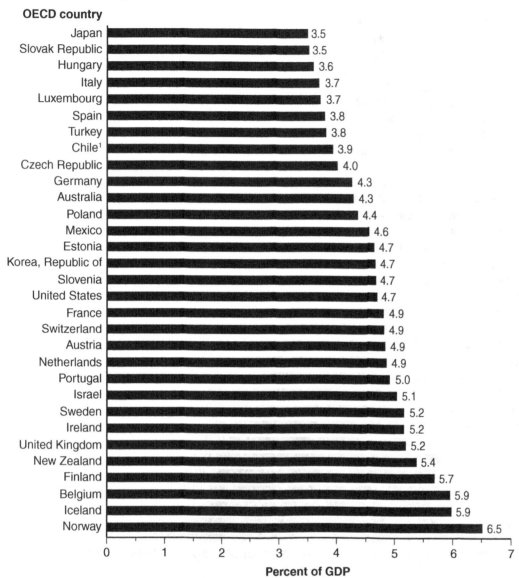

OECD country

Country	Percent of GDP
Japan	3.5
Slovak Republic	3.5
Hungary	3.6
Italy	3.7
Luxembourg	3.7
Spain	3.8
Turkey	3.8
Chile[1]	3.9
Czech Republic	4.0
Germany	4.3
Australia	4.3
Poland	4.4
Mexico	4.6
Estonia	4.7
Korea, Republic of	4.7
Slovenia	4.7
United States	4.7
France	4.9
Switzerland	4.9
Austria	4.9
Netherlands	4.9
Portugal	5.0
Israel	5.1
Sweden	5.2
Ireland	5.2
United Kingdom	5.2
New Zealand	5.4
Finland	5.7
Belgium	5.9
Iceland	5.9
Norway	6.5

Percent of GDP

[1]Data are for 2013 instead of 2012. Data for 2012 were not available.
NOTE: Includes public direct expenditures on all levels of education institutions. Public direct expenditures on education institutions include public subsidies to households for payments to education institutions; direct expenditures on education institutions from international sources; amounts spent directly by governments to hire education personnel and to procure other resources; and amounts provided by governments to public or private institutions.
SOURCE: Organization for Economic Cooperation and Development (OECD), *Education at a Glance, 2015.*

Table 601.10. Population, school enrollment, and number of teachers, by major areas of the world and level of education: Selected years, 1980 through 2013

[In thousands]

Year and selected characteristic	World total[1]	Major areas of the world					
		Africa	Asia[1,2]	Europe[2]	Central and South America[3]	Northern America[3]	Oceania
1	2	3	4	5	6	7	8
1980							
Population, all ages[4]	4,451,363	478,543	2,644,522	695,225	358,609	251,929	22,534
Enrollment, all levels	869,566	78,324	493,917	134,429	97,146	60,542	5,207
Primary (elementary)[5]	525,601	61,541	334,056	47,661	56,801	22,893	2,649
Secondary[6]	294,322	15,080	146,867	69,983	35,550	24,695	2,147
Postsecondary[7]	49,644	1,703	12,995	16,785	4,796	12,955	411
Teachers, all levels	39,584	2,325	19,270	—	4,407	—	276
Primary (elementary)[5]	18,475	1,646	10,711	2,499	1,872	—	134
Secondary[6]	17,202	586	7,418	—	2,153	1,309	112
Postsecondary[7]	3,906	92	1,141	—	383	815	31
1990							
Population, all ages[4]	5,288,956	630,010	3,191,764	722,628	440,609	277,533	26,412
Enrollment, all levels	985,773	107,320	561,993	132,628	116,498	61,543	5,790
Primary (elementary)[5]	577,034	78,099	361,455	45,195	65,049	24,629	2,607
Secondary[6]	341,284	26,386	177,769	68,827	44,201	21,534	2,566
Postsecondary[7]	67,455	2,836	22,768	18,607	7,248	15,380	617
Teachers, all levels	47,877	3,630	24,523	—	5,538	3,938	314
Primary (elementary)[5]	22,103	2,288	13,063	2,610	2,396	1,608	139
Secondary[6]	20,751	1,201	9,744	5,791	2,541	1,340	134
Postsecondary[7]	5,024	141	1,717	—	601	991	41
2000							
Population, all ages[4]	6,088,571	802,705	3,693,777	730,523	517,756	313,388	30,421
Enrollment, all levels	1,206,331	154,222	703,297	137,693	136,593	66,968	7,559
Primary (elementary)[5]	656,568	109,452	404,809	41,699	70,043	27,435	3,131
Secondary[6]	450,115	38,643	257,507	70,453	55,011	25,117	3,384
Postsecondary[7]	99,649	6,127	40,981	25,541	11,539	14,416	1,044
Teachers, all levels	56,535	4,917	29,336	10,705	6,527	4,648	—
Primary (elementary)[5]	24,862	2,843	14,569	2,739	2,751	1,806	155
Secondary[6]	24,987	1,790	12,323	6,096	2,900	1,682	—
Postsecondary[7]	6,686	285	2,444	1,870	876	1,161	50
2005							
Population, all ages[4]	6,473,045	907,737	3,918,933	733,244	552,438	328,033	32,659
Enrollment, all levels	1,326,269	194,285	772,684	135,543	143,471	72,389	7,898
Primary (elementary)[5]	679,003	136,505	405,256	38,472	68,848	26,780	3,142
Secondary[6]	507,988	49,168	304,929	64,895	58,496	27,039	3,462
Postsecondary[7]	139,278	8,612	62,499	32,176	16,127	18,570	1,295
Teachers, all levels	64,255	5,937	34,432	10,826	7,628	5,007	—
Primary (elementary)[5]	26,796	3,449	15,735	2,674	2,917	1,865	—
Secondary[6]	28,302	2,139	14,831	5,864	3,484	1,774	—
Postsecondary[7]	9,157	349	3,866	2,288	1,227	1,368	59
2010							
Population, all ages[4]	6,866,332	1,025,744	4,136,475	740,296	585,639	343,239	34,940
Enrollment, all levels	1,423,325	233,885	827,834	128,692	149,189	75,166	8,558
Primary (elementary)[5]	696,711	159,515	403,576	36,751	66,682	26,565	3,622
Secondary[6]	544,881	62,957	332,852	58,234	60,667	26,809	3,362
Postsecondary[7]	181,734	11,413	91,407	33,708	21,840	21,792	1,574
Teachers, all levels	71,591	7,284	39,761	10,520	8,143	5,454	—
Primary (elementary)[5]	28,547	4,006	16,850	2,676	2,922	1,920	—
Secondary[6]	31,993	2,821	18,077	5,420	3,586	1,898	—
Postsecondary[7]	11,052	457	4,833	2,424	1,634	1,637	67
2013							
Population, all ages[4]	7,101,028	1,102,597	4,262,082	743,962	604,918	351,199	36,271
Enrollment, all levels	1,480,690	256,560	859,031	127,582	153,299	74,766	9,453
Primary (elementary)[5]	713,581	173,601	406,046	37,663	65,378	26,624	4,269
Secondary[6]	568,543	70,762	344,813	58,434	64,234	26,795	3,505
Postsecondary[7]	198,567	12,197	108,172	31,485	23,687	21,347	1,679
Teachers, all levels	74,026	8,314	—	10,332	8,423	5,234	—
Primary (elementary)[5]	29,486	4,519	17,304	2,676	2,977	1,820	—
Secondary[6]	32,740	3,276	18,328	5,353	3,792	1,787	—
Postsecondary[7]	11,800	519	—	2,303	1,654	1,627	68

—Not available.
[1]Enrollment and teacher data for the world total and Asia exclude Taiwan.
[2]Europe includes all countries of the former Union of Soviet Socialist Republics (U.S.S.R.) except Armenia, Azerbaijan, Georgia, Kazakhstan, Kyrgyzstan, Tajikistan, Turkmenistan, and Uzbekistan, which are included in Asia. Asia also includes Turkey, the Arab states (with the exception of those located in Africa), and Israel.
[3]Central and South America includes Latin America and the Caribbean. Northern America includes Bermuda, Canada, Greenland, St. Pierre and Miquelon, and the United States.
[4]Estimate of midyear population.
[5]This level generally corresponds to grades 1–6 in the United States.
[6]Includes general education, teacher training (at the secondary level), and technical and vocational education. This level generally corresponds to grades 7–12 in the United States.

[7]Includes college and university enrollment, and technical and vocational education beyond the secondary level.
NOTE: Detail may not sum to totals because of rounding. Data include imputed values for nonrespondent countries. Enrollment and teacher data exclude several island countries or territories with small populations (less than 150,000). Some data have been revised from previously published figures.
SOURCE: United Nations Educational, Scientific, and Cultural Organization (UNESCO), unpublished tabulations. U.S. Department of Commerce, Census Bureau, International Data Base, retrieved March 31, 2016, from http://www.census.gov/population/international/data/idb/informationGateway.php. (This table was prepared March 2016.)

Table 601.20. Selected population and enrollment statistics for countries with populations of at least 10 million in 2013, by continent and country: Selected years, 1990 through 2013

	Midyear population (in millions)			Persons per square kilometer, 2013	Primary (elementary)[2]					Secondary[3]					Postsecondary[4]				
					Enrollment (in thousands)		Gross enrollment ratio[5]			Enrollment (in thousands)		Gross enrollment ratio[5]			Enrollment (in thousands)		Gross enrollment ratio[5]		
Continent and country[1]	1991	2000	2013	2013	1999–2000	2012–13	1990–91	1999–2000	2012–13	1999–2000	2012–13	1990–91	1999–2000	2012–13	1999–2000	2012–13	1990–91	1999–2000	2012–13
1	2	3	4	5	6	7	8	9	10	11	12	13	14	15	16	17	18	19	20
World total[6]	5,372	6,089	7,101	54	655,727	712,994[7]	99	98	108[7]	449,304	567,831[7]	52	59	75[7]	99,301	198,020	14	19	33
Africa																			
Algeria[8]	26	31	38	16	4,843	3,609	94	105	120	2,994	—	58	65	—	—	1,253	11	—	34
Angola	10	13	19	15	—	—	72	—	85	355	—	11	14	—	—	219	1	—	10
Burkina Faso	9	12	18	65	852	2,466	34	45	85	190	762	7	10	28	6	74	1	1	5
Burundi	6	7	10	392	705	2,010	69	57	130	—	491	6	—	32	66	45	1	5	4
Cameroon	12	16	23	48	2,237[9]	—	95	83[9]	—	700	1,813	27	27	52	6	—	3	1	—
Chad	6	8	11	9	914	2,331	51	64	101	137	—	—	11	—	—	—	—	—	—
Congo, Democratic Republic of the	41	52	76	33	1,943	12,601	79	74	103	—	3,996	—	—	41	—	443	3	—	7
Cote d'Ivoire	13	17	22	70	—	3,021	69	—	87	—	—	—	—	—	—	169	—	—	9
Egypt[8]	56	65	85	86	7,947[7]	11,103	93	93[7]	106	8,028[7]	8,152	75	81[7]	86	—	2,477	13	—	30
Ethiopia	49	64	94	94	5,847	—	32	55	108	1,195	2,357	14	14	—	68	—	1	—	—
Ghana[8]	16	19	25	111	2,561	4,106	80	86	—	1,057	—	—	41	61	—	355	1	3	14
Guinea	7	8	11	46	790	1,666	37	57	90	—	—	12	—	—	—	109	—	2	10
Kenya[8]	24	31	44	77	5,035	—	98	96	—	1,909	—	—	39	—	89	—	—	—	—
Madagascar	12	16	23	39	2,208	4,483	100	100	145	487	853	17	30	38	32	97	3	3	4
Malawi	10	11	17	179	2,695	3,952	76	136	146	258[7]	882	7	17	41	4	—	1	#	—
Mali	9	11	16	13	1,017	—	28	57	76	—	—	7	—	—	20	—	1	2	—
Morocco[8]	24	28	33	73	3,670	4,021	64	92	117	1,541	—	36	38	—	296	708	10	10	22
Mozambique[8]	13	18	24	31	2,544	5,526	61	74	104	124	758	7	6	25	12	128	1	1	5
Niger	8	11	17	13	579	2,166	28	33	70	106[7]	468	7	7[7]	18	—	—	1	1	—
Nigeria[8]	99	124	173	190	19,151	—	85	98	—	4,104	—	16	24	—	—	—	—	10	—
Rwanda[8]	7	8	12	487	1,432	2,402	75	106	138	130	582	16	11	40	9	77	1	—	8
Senegal	8	9	13	69	1,108	—	55	68	—	250	—	16	16	—	—	—	—	—	—
Somalia	6	8	10	16	—	—	—	—	—	—	—	—	—	—	—	—	—	—	—
South Africa	39	45	52	43	7,445	7,064	109	104	99	4,142	5,201	70	87	98	182	1,036	12	—	20
South Sudan[8]	5	6	11	17	—	—	—	—	—	—	—	—	—	—	—	—	—	—	—
Sudan[8]	22	27	35	19	—	—	70	—	—	—	—	—	—	—	—	640	—	—	17
Tanzania	26	33	48	55	4,382	8,232	70	68	87	—	2,052	5	—	32	21	158	#	1	4
Tunisia	8	10	11	70	1,414	1,063	115	115	111	1,104[7]	1,072	45	75[7]	90	180	337	9	19	34
Uganda	17	23	35	176	6,559	8,459	71	132	110	547	1,421	11	17	28	56	—	—	3	—
Zambia	8	10	14	19	1,590	—	92	77	—	—	—	11	—	—	—	—	5	—	—
Zimbabwe	10	12	13	34	2,461	3,075	102	100	104	844	—	47	43	—	—	94	—	—	6
Asia																			
Afghanistan[8]	14	22	31	48	749	5,986	29	22	110	—	2,538	16	—	57	—	—	—	—	—
Bangladesh	114	132	164	1,257	—	—	—	—	123	10,329	13,314	—	48	58	727	—	—	5	—
Cambodia	10	12	15	86	2,248	2,225	101	106	109	351	—	28	17	—	22	—	1	2	—
China	1,168	1,268	1,355	145	113,613	98,871	126	95	111	81,488	94,324	40	61	96	7,364	34,091	3	8	30
India	854	1,006	1,221	411	—	141,155	92	—	106	71,031	119,401	45	45	69	9,404	28,175	6	10	24
Indonesia	185	214	251	139	28,509	30,109	113	100	118	14,720	22,322	55	—	82	3,126	6,423	9	15	31
Iran	60	69	80	52	—	7,858	109	100	102	9,955	5,869	55	79	87	1,405	4,368	—	—	58
Iraq	17	23	35	79	3,639	—	108	97	111	1,224	—	55	37	—	289	—	—	—	—
Japan	124	127	127	349	7,529	6,802	101	101	105	8,782	7,281	98	102	102	3,982	3,863	30[10]	49	62
Kazakhstan	17	16	18	7	1,208	1,057	118	96	106	1,994	1,659	98	93	102	418	781	39	32	50
Korea, Democratic People's Republic of	21	23	25	205	—	—	106	101	—	—	—	—	—	—	—	—	—	—	—
Korea, Republic of	43	47	49	505	4,030	2,959	94	98	—	3,959	3,783	92	98	99	3,003	3,357	38	78	97
Malaysia	18	23	30	90	3,026	3,246	99	98	—	2,205	2,751	55	66	71	549	1,117	8	26	39
Myanmar	41	47	55	84	4,858	4,577	—	120[9]	—	2,268	3,111[7]	21	36	66[7]	94	477	—	—	17
Nepal[8]	19	25	30	212	3,780[9]	—	113	74[10]	139	1,348	—	25	36	40	—	—	6	4	—
Pakistan[8]	122	152	193	251	13,987[10]	18,150	—	—	90	—	10,794	—	—	—	—	1,915	—	—	10
Philippines	63	76	98	328	12,708	14,460	109	109	117	—	7,220	72	—	88	—	3,317	27	—	34

See notes at end of table.

Table 601.20. Selected population and enrollment statistics for countries with populations of at least 10 million in 2013, by continent and country: Selected years, 1990 through 2013—Continued

Continent and country[1]	Midyear population (in millions)			Persons per square kilometer, 2013	Primary (elementary)[2]					Secondary[3]					Postsecondary[4]				
					Enrollment (in thousands)		Gross enrollment ratio[5]			Enrollment (in thousands)		Gross enrollment ratio[5]			Enrollment (in thousands)		Gross enrollment ratio[5]		
	1991	2000	2013	2013	1999–2000	2012–13	1990–91	1999–2000	2012–13	1999–2000	2012–13	1990–91	1999–2000	2012–13	1999–2000	2012–13	1990–91	1999–2000	2012–13
	2	3	4	5	6	7	8	9	10	11	12	13	14	15	16	17	18	19	20
Saudi Arabia	16	21	27	13	—	3,636	—	—	107	—	3,400[7]	—	—	108[7]	404	1,357	10	22	55
Sri Lanka[8]	17	19	22	335	—	1,767	110	—	101	—	2,606	72	—	100	—	298	—	—	19
Syria	13	17	20	110	2,775	1,547	107	108	80	1,069	1,857	48	44	50	—	660	18	—	35
Taiwan	20	22	23	722	—	—	—	—	98	—	—	—	—	86	—	—	—	—	—
Thailand	57	63	67	132	6,101	4,955	100	98	98	5,658	4,655	30	73	115	1,900	2,405	14	35	51
Turkey	58	66	77	101	6,562	5,594	104	103	107	3,566	10,563	52	86	—	—	4,976	17	13	79
Uzbekistan	21	25	29	67	2,602	—	111	101	—	—	—	99	—	—	305	—	2	9	—
Vietnam	69	79	92	298	10,063	7,203	106	109	108	—	—	—	—	49	732	2,250	—	—	25
Yemen	13	17	25	48	—	3,875	—	—	97	—	1,768	—	—	—	—	—	—	—	—
Europe																			
Belgium	10	10	11	368	774	764	100	105	105	1,058	1,207	103	145	163	356	488	40	58	72
Czech Republic	10	10	11	137	645	492	97	103	99	958	801	90	88	104	254	427	16	28	65
France	59	61	66	103	3,885	4,171	109	105	106	5,929	5,914	101	109	111	2,015	2,338	39	54	62
Germany[11]	80	82	81	233	3,656	2,890	102	107	103	8,307	7,289	99	100	102	—	2,780	34	—	61
Greece	10	11	11	83	645	634	99	97	99	739	695	95	90	108	422	659	36	52	110
Italy[8]	57	58	61	209	2,836	2,861	99	103	102	4,404	4,594	81	92	102	1,770	1,873	32	49	63
Netherlands[8]	15	16	17	496	1,279	1,255[7]	103	109	106[7]	1,379	1,555[7]	120	124	131[7]	488	618	40	53	71
Poland[8]	38	39	39	127	3,319	2,161	98	98	101	3,988	2,778	88	99	109	1,580	1,903	22	50	66
Portugal	10	10	11	118	811	693	120	123	110	831	799	68	105	120	374	371	23	48	52
Romania[8]	23	22	22	95	1,189	—	85	97	100	2,226	1,669	89	79	98	453	—	10	24	78
Russian Federation	148	147	143	9	6,138	5,652	110	103	106	—	9,092	96	—	99	6,331	7,528	52	56	87
Spain[8]	39	41	47	95	2,540	2,935	105	104	108	3,246	3,296	103	110	131	1,829	1,969	37	58	80
Ukraine[8]	52	49	45	78	2,079	1,638	119	115	108	5,204	2,803	92	104	98	1,812	2,206	47	49	80
United Kingdom[8]	58	59	63	262	4,632	4,622	105	100	109	5,315	6,497	88	102	124	2,024	2,386	29	59	57
North America																			
Canada	28	31	35	4	2,456	—	104	100	—	2,519	—	101	102	—	1,212	—	95	59	—
Cuba	11	11	11	101	1,046	772	98	101	98	790	787	90	83	93	159	373	21	22	49
Dominican Republic	7	8	10	212	1,364	1,291	100	114	103	654	920	23	59	78	—	—	—	—	—
Guatemala	9	11	14	134	1,909	2,499	77	102	108	504	1,160	52	36	64	—	294	14	19	18
Mexico	86	100	119	61	14,766	14,837	110	106	104	9,094	12,467	52	70	87	1,963	3,300	14	19	29
United States	253	282	316	35	24,973	24,418	104	103	99	22,594	24,095	91	93	96	13,203	19,973	73	68	89
South America																			
Argentina	34	37	43	16	4,728	4,792	109	113	111	3,428	4,406	72	86	106	1,767[7]	2,768	38	53[7]	80
Bolivia	7	8	10	10	1,492	1,349	102	120	—	877[7]	1,113	—	78[7]	85	279	—	—	34	—
Brazil	152	174	201	24	20,212	16,761	—	—	100	—	24,881	—	—	—	2,781	7,323	—	—	84
Chile	13	15	17	23	1,799	1,472	107	109	—	1,391	1,571	96	87	100	452	1,174	21	37	84
Colombia	34	39	46	44	5,221	4,708	102	121	116	3,569	4,910	52	70	102	934	2,109	15	23	50
Ecuador	10	12	15	56	1,925	2,103	122	111	103	917	1,835	57	58	102	—	586	20	—	40
Peru	22	26	30	23	4,338	3,545	117	121	102	2,374	2,732	66	85	98	900	—	32	35	—
Venezuela	20	23	28	32	3,328	3,520	109	99	—	1,543	2,575	56	59	92	668	—	28	29	—
Oceania																			
Australia[8]	17	19	22	3	1,906	2,128	106	100	107	2,589	2,384	—	163	138	845	1,390	38	67	87

—Not available.
#Rounds to zero.
[1] Selection based on total population for midyear 2013.
[2] This level generally corresponds to grades 1–6 in the United States.
[3] Includes general education, teacher training (at the secondary level), and technical and vocational education. This level generally corresponds to grades 7–12 in the United States.
[4] Includes college and university enrollment, and technical and vocational education beyond the secondary level.
[5] Data represent the total enrollment of all ages in the school level divided by the population of the specific age groups that correspond to the school level. Adjustments have been made for the varying lengths of primary and secondary programs. Ratios may exceed 100 because some countries have many students from outside the normal age range.
[6] Enrollment totals and ratios exclude the Democratic People's Republic of Korea (North Korea).

[7] Estimated by the United Nations Educational, Scientific, and Cultural Organization (UNESCO) Institute for Statistics.
[8] Classification or data coverage of levels has been revised. Data by level may not be comparable over time.
[9] Policy change in 1999–2000: introduction of free universal primary education.
[10] National estimation.
[11] Data include both former East and West Germany.

NOTE: Data do not include adult education or special education provided outside regular schools. Some data have been revised from previously published figures.
SOURCE: United Nations Educational, Scientific, and Cultural Organization (UNESCO), *Statistical Yearbook, 1999*, unpublished tabulations; and tabulations from the UNESCO Institute for Statistics Online Data Center, retrieved May 16, 2016, from http://data.uis.unesco.org/; U.S. Department of Commerce, Census Bureau, International Data Base, retrieved May 16, 2016, from http://www.census.gov/population/international/data/idb/informationGateway.php. (This table was prepared May 2016.)

Table 601.30. School-age populations as a percentage of total population, by age group and country: Selected years, 1985 through 2012

Country	5- to 14-year-olds as a percent of total population											15- to 19-year-olds as a percent of total population										
	1985[1]	1990[1]	1995[1]	2005	2006	2007	2008	2009	2010	2011	2012	1985[2]	1990[2]	1995[2]	2005	2006	2007	2008	2009	2010	2011	2012
1	2	3	4	5	6	7	8	9	10	11	12	13	14	15	16	17	18	19	20	21	22	23
OECD average[3]	—	—	—	**12.7**	**12.5**	**12.3**	**12.0**	**11.9**	**11.8**	**11.7**	**11.6**	—	—	—	**6.7**	**6.7**	**6.6**	**6.6**	**6.5**	**6.4**	**6.3**	**6.2**
Australia	14.5	13.1	12.9	13.4	13.2	13.0	12.8	12.6	12.4	12.3	12.3	—	6.4	5.6	6.8	6.8	6.9	6.9	6.8	6.7	6.6	6.4
Austria	—	—	—	11.3	11.1	10.8	10.6	10.4	10.2	10.0	9.8	—	—	—	5.9	5.9	6.0	6.0	6.0	6.0	5.9	5.8
Belgium	11.4	10.9	10.7	11.7	11.6	11.4	11.2	11.1	11.1	11.7	11.1	5.8	5.1	4.9	5.9	6.0	6.1	6.1	6.1	6.0	6.2	5.8
Canada	12.8	12.4	12.2	12.6	12.4	12.1	11.7	11.4	11.5	11.1	10.8	6.1	5.5	5.4	6.7	6.6	6.7	6.8	6.8	6.8	6.6	6.3
Chile	—	—	—	17.9	16.8	15.9	15.5	15.5	15.0	14.8	14.6	—	—	—	8.8	8.9	8.8	8.8	8.8	8.7	8.4	8.2
Czech Republic	(⁴)	(⁴)	11.6	10.4	10.0	9.6	9.3	8.9	8.8	8.9	9.0	(⁴)	(⁴)	6.5	6.4	6.4	6.3	6.2	6.1	5.9	5.5	5.2
Denmark	12.0	10.1	9.7	12.8	12.7	12.7	12.5	12.4	12.2	12.0	12.0	5.8	5.7	4.7	5.6	5.8	5.9	6.1	6.2	6.3	6.4	6.4
Estonia	(⁴)	(⁴)	11.4	10.6	10.1	9.9	9.6	9.4	9.4	9.5	9.6	(⁴)	4.9	5.1	8.0	7.9	7.7	7.4	6.9	6.3	5.7	5.3
Finland	11.5	11.8	11.4	12.0	11.8	11.6	11.4	11.2	11.0	10.9	10.8	5.6	5.8	5.1	6.1	6.1	6.2	6.3	6.3	6.3	6.2	6.1
France	12.8	12.1	12.0	12.3	12.3	12.2	12.2	12.3	12.3	12.3	12.4	6.2	5.8	5.3	6.5	6.5	6.4	6.3	6.3	6.2	6.1	6.1
Germany	9.1[5]	8.7	10.0	10.0	9.8	9.6	9.5	9.4	9.3	9.2	9.1	6.1[5]	4.1	4.3	5.8	5.9	5.8	5.6	5.5	5.3	5.1	5.0
Greece	—	—	10.7	9.7	9.6	9.5	9.4	9.4	9.3	9.3	9.3	—	5.5	5.8	5.5	5.4	5.3	5.2	5.1	5.1	5.0	4.9
Hungary	15.7	15.0	14.3	10.9	10.7	10.4	10.2	10.0	9.9	9.8	9.8	6.7	6.8	6.4	6.3	6.2	6.2	6.2	6.1	6.0	5.9	5.7
Iceland	15.7	15.0	14.3	15.2	14.8	14.3	13.9	13.7	13.6	13.5	13.4	6.7	6.8	6.4	7.3	7.4	7.5	7.5	7.5	7.5	7.3	7.3
Ireland	17.9	17.5	15.2	13.5	13.3	13.3	13.2	13.3	13.5	13.5	13.7	7.7	8.0	7.8	7.2	7.0	6.8	6.5	6.3	6.1	6.2	6.0
Israel	12.7	10.3	9.1	18.1	18.1	18.2	18.2	18.2	17.9	18.0	17.9	6.5	6.0	4.8	8.3	8.2	8.1	8.1	8.0	7.9	7.8	7.8
Italy	14.0	11.8	10.2	9.4	9.4	9.4	9.3	9.3	9.3	9.3	9.4	6.2	6.5	5.4	4.9	5.0	5.0	5.0	5.0	4.9	4.8	4.8
Japan	—	—	10.8	9.4	9.3	9.3	9.3	9.2	9.1	9.0	8.9	—	—	5.7	5.3	5.1	5.0	4.9	4.8	4.8	4.8	4.8
Korea, Republic of	—	—	14.5	13.9	13.7	13.3	12.8	12.2	11.7	10.9	10.5	—	—	7.1	6.5	6.5	6.6	6.7	6.9	7.0	7.0	6.8
Luxembourg	10.2	10.1	10.5	12.6	12.5	12.5	12.4	12.2	12.0	11.9	11.5	5.5	4.4	4.4	5.8	5.8	5.9	5.9	5.9	5.9	5.9	6.0
Mexico	—	—	—	21.4	21.3	21.0	20.7	20.3	19.8	19.4	19.6	6.8	5.4	4.8	10.1	10.0	10.0	9.9	9.8	9.7	9.6	9.6
Netherlands	12.0	10.7	10.8	12.3	12.2	12.2	12.1	12.1	12.0	11.9	11.8	7.5	6.7	5.7	6.0	6.1	6.1	6.1	6.1	6.1	6.0	6.0
New Zealand	15.3	13.5	13.5	14.6	14.3	14.1	13.8	13.6	13.3	13.2	13.1	6.4	5.8	4.9	7.5	7.5	7.6	7.6	7.5	7.4	7.2	7.0
Norway	12.5	11.0	11.2	13.5	13.3	13.2	13.0	12.8	12.6	12.5	12.3	—	—	—	6.3	6.4	6.6	6.7	6.7	6.6	6.6	6.5
Poland	—	—	—	12.0	11.6	11.1	10.7	10.3	10.0	9.8	9.7	—	—	—	7.8	7.5	7.3	7.1	6.9	6.6	6.3	6.0
Portugal	—	—	—	10.4	10.3	10.3	10.3	10.3	10.3	10.3	10.3	—	—	—	5.7	5.6	5.5	5.5	5.4	5.3	5.2	5.3
Slovak Republic	(⁴)	(⁴)	—	12.2	11.8	11.3	10.8	10.4	10.2	10.0	10.0	(⁴)	(⁴)	—	7.8	7.6	7.4	7.2	7.0	6.8	6.4	6.1
Slovenia	(⁴)	(⁴)	—	9.9	9.7	9.5	9.3	9.1	9.0	9.0	9.0	(⁴)	(⁴)	—	6.3	6.1	5.9	5.7	5.4	5.2	5.0	4.9
Spain	15.0	12.9	10.2	9.5	9.4	9.4	9.4	9.5	9.6	9.7	9.8	6.8	6.8	6.2	6.3	6.1	5.9	5.7	5.4	5.2	4.8	4.7
Sweden	11.3	10.2	10.8	12.2	11.8	11.4	11.1	10.9	10.7	10.7	10.7	5.4	5.2	4.6	6.4	6.6	6.8	6.9	6.9	6.8	6.6	6.2
Switzerland	10.6	10.1	10.4	11.3	11.1	10.9	10.6	10.4	10.3	10.2	10.0	5.8	4.8	4.5	5.8	5.9	6.0	6.0	5.9	5.8	5.7	5.6
Turkey	20.6	20.6	19.7	19.3	19.2	19.2	18.2	17.9	17.5	17.2	17.0	8.7	8.9	8.8	8.8	8.7	8.7	8.7	8.6	8.6	8.5	8.5
United Kingdom	11.4	11.1	11.6	12.4	12.1	11.8	11.6	11.4	11.3	11.2	11.2	6.3	5.2	4.8	6.6	6.6	6.6	6.5	6.5	6.3	6.2	6.1
United States	12.6	12.8	13.0	13.8	13.6	13.4	13.2	13.3	13.2	13.2	13.2	6.2	5.4	5.5	7.1	7.1	7.1	7.1	7.1	7.0	7.1	6.9
Other reporting countries																						
Argentina	—	—	—	—	—	—	—	—	—	—	—	—	—	—	—	—	—	—	—	8.5	8.5	8.3
Brazil	—	—	—	19.1	19.1	18.2	17.8	17.2	—	—	—	—	—	—	—	9.6	9.1	8.9	8.8	8.9	8.7	8.7
China	—	—	—	—	—	—	—	—	13.4	12.7	11.5	—	—	—	—	9.6	—	—	—	7.9	7.4	7.0
Colombia	—	—	—	24.6	—	—	—	—	—	—	18.8	—	—	—	—	—	—	—	—	—	—	—
India	—	—	—	—	—	—	—	—	20.1	19.7	19.9	—	—	—	9.7	—	—	—	—	9.8	9.6	9.6
Indonesia	—	—	—	—	—	—	—	—	17.1	17.8	19.3	—	—	—	—	—	—	—	—	9.3	8.7	8.7
Latvia	—	—	14.3	10.5	10.0	—	—	9.4	—	—	9.2	—	—	—	—	—	—	7.2	6.5	—	5.9	5.4
Russian Federation	(⁴)	—	—	—	—	—	—	—	21.2	20.4	19.5	(⁴)	—	—	—	8.3	7.8	7.2	6.5	6.0	5.9	5.3
Saudi Arabia	—	—	—	—	—	—	—	—	—	—	—	—	—	—	8.5	—	—	—	—	—	—	—
South Africa	—	—	—	—	—	—	—	—	20.1	19.9	19.0	—	—	—	—	—	—	—	—	10.0	9.7	9.2

—Not available.

[1] Data are for the 5- to 13-year-old population.
[2] Data are for the 14- to 17-year-old population.
[3] Refers to the mean of the data values for all reporting Organization for Economic Cooperation and Development (OECD) countries, to which each country reporting data contributes equally. The average includes all current OECD countries for which a given year's data are available, even if they were not members of OECD in that year. However, if data were reported for less than 75 percent of the countries, the average for that year is omitted.
[4] Country did not exist in its current form in the given year.
[5] Data for 1985 are for the former West Germany.

SOURCE: Organization for Economic Cooperation and Development (OECD), *Education at a Glance*, selected years, 1987 through 2001; and Online Education Database, retrieved February 8, 2016, from http://stats.oecd.org/Index.aspx. (This table was prepared February 2016.)

Table 601.35. Percentage of 3- and 4-year-olds and 5- to 14-year-olds enrolled in school, by country: 2000 through 2013

Country	Percent of 3- and 4-year-olds enrolled		Percent of 5- to 14-year-olds enrolled													
	2012	2013	2000	2001	2002	2003	2004	2005	2006	2007	2008	2009	2010	2011	2012	2013
1	2	3	4	5	6	7	8	9	10	11	12	13	14	15	16	17
OECD average[1]	76.2	80.5	97.8	98.1	98.3	98.0	98.0	98.2	98.3	98.5	98.7	98.5	98.8	98.6	98.4	98.3
Australia	46.6	72.1	100.0	100.1	99.3	98.2	98.5	99.1	99.6	99.3	99.3	99.3	99.2	99.4	101.1	100.6
Austria	77.8	81.4	98.2	98.7	98.9	98.5	98.5	98.4	98.1	98.3	98.5	98.4	98.4	98.2	98.2	98.4
Belgium	98.6	97.9	99.1	100.2	100.1	100.3	100.4 [2]	99.6 [2]	99.4	99.3	99.1	98.9	98.6	98.5	98.5	97.9
Canada	—	—	97.1	97.2	—	—	—	—	—	—	—	98.7	98.8	98.9	99.9	—
Chile	62.1	67.3	93.6	—	92.1	90.8	89.5	88.3	91.2	96.1	96.1	93.2	95.1	94.3	93.9	97.3
Czech Republic	70.3	70.9	99.8	99.8	99.3	99.8	99.7	99.8	99.9	99.8	98.7	98.7	98.1	97.7	98.6	98.1
Denmark	97.5	96.9	99.2	97.2	99.1	99.1	98.0	97.1	97.4	98.0	97.6	97.6	99.1	99.4	99.3	99.4
Estonia	88.9	89.2	—	—	—	—	—	104.6	102.2	100.4	100.4	100.0	96.4	95.7	95.2	96.4
Finland	55.1	71.4	91.6	93.5	94.4	94.6	95.1	95.1	95.1	95.3	95.5	95.5	95.5	95.7	95.7	96.8
France	99.1	100.1	99.8	101.0	101.1	101.4	101.6	101.3	101.0	100.9	100.7	99.8	99.6	99.4	99.1	99.1
Germany	93.3	94.0	99.4	100.1	97.5	97.6	97.9	98.3	98.8	99.2	99.3	99.4	99.4	98.5	99.4	98.7
Greece	25.6	—	99.8	98.1	96.3	96.7	97.2	97.5	98.1	97.7	98.9	100.1	100.7	100.0	99.2	—
Hungary	83.6	84.3	99.9	99.4	100.3	100.4	100.5	100.3	100.3	99.8	99.6	98.9	98.5	98.1	97.6	97.1
Iceland	96.1	96.4	98.5	98.9	98.5	98.8	98.8	98.9	98.8	98.3	98.5	98.2	98.5	98.6	98.8	98.5
Ireland	69.1	69.9	100.5	100.6	101.4	100.4	100.9	101.1	101.2	102.6	101.5	101.7	102.1	101.1	100.9	100.0
Israel	89.1	100.0	96.6	96.9	96.1	96.8	96.6	96.0	95.8	96.1	95.7	96.2	97.8	96.8	97.8	98.2
Italy	94.2	96.5	99.7	99.4	101.7	101.9	101.6	101.2	100.7	100.3	100.3	99.8	99.5	99.0	98.6	100.0
Japan	85.9	88.2	101.2	101.0	100.8	100.7	100.7	100.7	100.7	100.5	100.7	101.0	101.5	101.1	101.3	100.0
Korea, Republic of	86.3	—	92.3	92.6	92.7	93.2	93.5	94.1	94.9	95.7	95.1	95.7	99.7	99.1	98.8	—
Luxembourg	85.4	85.1	95.3	92.2	93.4	96.7	96.4	96.7	96.2	95.9	95.8	95.6	95.8	96.0	97.9	97.1
Mexico	63.3	66.1	94.8	95.0	95.7	96.9	97.7	99.9	100.9	102.1	103.4	104.6	106.1	107.7	100.2	100.0
Netherlands	91.4	91.5	99.4	99.3	99.3	99.7	99.6	99.0	99.6	99.5	99.6	99.5	99.5	99.8	99.8	99.5
New Zealand	90.7	98.2	99.0	99.3	99.5	100.1	100.5	100.9	101.0	99.7	100.2	100.6	100.9	101.0	100.7	100.0
Norway	96.1	96.2	97.4	97.6	97.9	98.1	98.3	98.4	98.8	99.2	99.5	99.5	99.5	99.6	99.5	99.5
Poland	58.0	60.0	93.6	94.3	94.4	94.2	94.5	94.6	94.5	94.5	94.0	94.1	94.9	95.3	95.5	95.9
Portugal	84.9	84.2	105.2	107.0	106.0	105.3	104.1	103.9	103.8	104.2	104.1	103.1	102.4	102.1	102.1	100.0
Slovak Republic	67.5	68.1	—	97.9	98.1	97.3	97.3	97.1	96.8	96.8	96.6	96.1	95.8	95.5	94.5	94.2
Slovenia	87.1	86.7	—	—	—	—	—	96.5	96.4	96.2	96.8	97.1	97.1	97.1	97.4	97.1
Spain	96.1	96.2	104.4	103.6	103.8	102.5	101.8	101.4	101.0	100.7	100.4	100.1	99.5	99.0	97.8	97.5
Sweden	93.4	93.7	97.8	98.1	98.2	98.6	99.1	99.5	98.8	100.3	99.3	98.7	98.5	97.4	99.0	98.5
Switzerland	21.6	22.2	98.8	98.7	98.6	99.3	99.6	99.6	100.3	100.4	100.2	100.0	100.1	99.5	99.3	99.6
Turkey	12.0	21.7	80.2	83.5	—	82.0	81.2	81.8	82.9	84.3	91.9	91.3	94.1	94.9	95.2	96.3
United Kingdom	95.5	96.3	98.9	98.7	98.9	100.5	100.4	101.0	100.7	99.3	101.5	101.4	103.1	100.7	98.0	98.2
United States	53.5	53.7	99.3	102.1	96.9	97.1	97.3	97.7	98.0	98.3	98.6	97.1	96.8	96.2	97.3	96.9
Other reporting countries																
Argentina	—	—	105.6	104.1	104.3	—	—	—	—	—	—	107.3	107.6	106.7	—	—
Brazil	49.3	65.3	89.8	91.3	91.8	—	93.0	93.1	—	91.7	95.6	96.5	96.2	94.9	94.8	94.9
China	—	—	79.6	81.7	80.7	85.9	—	—	—	—	—	—	—	—	26.9	—
Colombia	21.9	61.5	—	—	—	—	—	—	—	—	—	—	—	—	91.2	93.2
India	2.5	—	—	65.0	—	65.7	—	—	—	—	—	—	77.7	—	79.6	—
Indonesia	14.9	26.6	—	86.4	93.4	89.2	—	—	—	—	95.1	—	101.2	92.8	87.5	89.9
Latvia	83.4	86.1	—	—	—	—	—	—	—	—	—	—	—	—	98.2	97.8
Russian Federation	73.4	75.8	—	83.3	84.6	94.2	90.4	81.5	—	—	93.8	93.5	93.1	92.1	92.7	93.2
Saudi Arabia	—	17.3	—	—	—	—	—	—	—	—	—	—	—	—	79.3	88.0
South Africa	—	—	—	—	—	—	—	—	—	—	—	—	—	—	76.8	—

—Not available.

[1]Refers to the mean of the data values for all reporting Organization for Economic Cooperation and Development (OECD) countries, to which each country reporting data contributes equally. The average includes all current OECD countries for which a given year's data are available, even if they were not members of OECD in that year.
[2]Excludes the German-speaking Community of Belgium.
NOTE: For each country, this table shows the number of persons in each age group who are enrolled in that country as a percentage of that country's total population in the specified age group. However, some of a country's population may be enrolled in a different

country, and some persons enrolled in the country may be residents of a different country. Enrollment rates may be underestimated for countries such as Luxembourg that are net exporters of students and may be overestimated for countries that are net importers. If a country enrolls many residents of other countries, the country's total population in the specified age group can be smaller than the total number enrolled, resulting in enrollment estimates exceeding 100 percent.
SOURCE: Organization for Economic Cooperation and Development (OECD), *Education at a Glance*, 2002 through 2015. (This table was prepared November 2015.)

Table 601.40. Percentage of 15- to 29-year-olds enrolled in school, by selected levels of education, age, and country: 2013

Country	All levels of education[1]							Secondary education[2]						Total tertiary education (postsecondary degree programs)[3]			
	15 years old	16 years old	17 years old	18 years old	19 years old	20 years old	20 to 29 years old	15 years old	16 years old	17 years old	18 years old	19 years old	20 years old	17 years old	18 years old	19 years old	20 years old
1	2	3	4	5	6	7	8	9	10	11	12	13	14	15	16	17	18
OECD average[4]	97.3	94.4	90.5	75.1	58.4	51.4	28.3	97.0	94.1	88.4	56.6	25.8	12.6	1.6	17.1	30.9	37.3
Australia	100.9	98.3	89.6	74.2	70.2	66.2	34.0	100.8	97.8	82.9	39.1	23.9	19.4	5.6	31.9	42.7	43.5
Austria	94.7	91.0	88.6	74.0	51.2	41.2	26.6	94.7	90.9	74.6	44.0	19.2	8.5	13.3	28.8	30.3	30.9
Belgium	99.6	99.2	98.4	83.4	79.6	77.1	34.2	99.4	99.0	97.2	50.7	26.5	15.3	1.0	30.3	49.1	53.3
Canada	92.7	91.0	79.8	56.2	49.5	44.9	22.0	92.7	90.9	76.9	26.7	11.0	6.6	2.8	29.5	38.5	38.3
Chile	94.7	93.9	89.2	62.8	55.3	51.3	28.4	93.1	93.1	88.6	33.6	10.4	4.0	0.2	29.0	44.7	47.3
Czech Republic	99.8	97.8	95.6	89.5	72.5	56.6	26.0	99.7	97.8	95.4	88.3	49.3	14.3	0.1	1.2	23.2	42.3
Denmark	99.1	95.1	90.9	86.9	66.0	55.0	44.9	98.9	95.1	90.9	86.4	58.0	32.6	#	0.5	8.0	22.4
Estonia	98.4	97.4	93.6	85.5	65.2	56.4	29.7	98.3	97.4	93.4	79.0	22.7	9.4	0.2	5.6	35.3	39.2
Finland	98.1	94.8	94.8	94.1	50.7	47.6	41.3	98.1	94.8	94.6	93.2	33.8	18.4	0.1	0.9	16.9	29.1
France	98.1	93.7	90.3	77.1	63.9	52.9	21.0	97.4	92.9	87.0	40.0	16.3	6.9	2.6	35.8	46.6	45.4
Germany	98.2	97.4	93.3	85.0	72.9	62.7	33.5	98.1	96.1	89.5	75.1	40.4	22.6	0.3	4.6	15.1	24.2
Greece	—	—	—	—	—	—	—	—	—	—	—	—	—	—	—	—	—
Hungary	97.3	94.2	93.0	84.4	70.3	60.3	27.3	97.1	94.1	92.6	72.3	31.8	13.1	0.3	6.3	23.3	33.7
Iceland	99.1	96.0	90.2	82.5	73.9	54.0	40.4	99.1	96.0	90.1	81.9	69.7	33.2	#	0.5	4.3	20.5
Ireland	101.3	101.3	97.7	106.9	74.1	66.5	22.1	101.2	101.1	89.6	47.1	4.2	1.2	4.4	31.5	56.7	57.1
Israel	96.6	94.7	89.6	25.7	14.8	15.3	22.2	96.2	94.3	89.2	17.4	1.5	0.8	0.4	8.2	12.8	13.9
Italy	99.6	97.1	91.7	78.6	23.9	39.7	25.2	99.6	96.7	91.0	77.4	21.6	8.0	#	#	2.3	30.9
Japan	99.2	96.1	95.6	4.0	1.0	#	—	99.2	96.1	95.6	3.1	1.0	#	—	—	—	—
Korea, Republic of	99.7	96.8	96.3	70.3	74.1	70.3	31.4	99.7	96.8	95.2	7.6	0.4	0.1	1.0	62.7	73.8	70.2
Luxembourg[5]	97.3	86.5	81.9	72.0	50.6	35.0	12.8	97.3	86.5	81.7	69.5	41.7	24.5	0.2	2.3	8.5	9.8
Mexico	71.1	65.9	57.1	41.1	34.1	30.1	14.0	70.4	65.9	54.4	23.4	10.4	5.6	2.7	17.7	23.7	24.5
Netherlands	99.2	98.5	96.0	86.3	77.5	68.2	31.3	99.1	98.3	89.1	62.7	42.0	27.1	6.8	23.5	35.5	41.1
New Zealand	101.9	102.1	91.9	66.9	58.6	53.6	27.5	101.8	101.2	86.9	28.2	10.4	6.4	2.5	31.4	41.3	42.0
Norway	100.3	95.3	92.7	89.6	57.0	52.5	30.3	100.3	95.3	92.7	89.3	39.5	19.9	#	0.4	17.3	32.2
Poland	96.4	96.7	95.7	92.5	71.7	65.9	33.0	95.8	96.5	95.4	92.3	42.2	12.1	0.1	0.1	24.7	45.0
Portugal	101.5	100.5	94.8	80.6	65.4	56.5	24.2	99.0	99.2	93.5	53.6	29.1	15.5	0.5	25.6	34.6	39.5
Slovak Republic	97.8	93.2	90.0	84.2	62.8	45.6	20.8	97.1	92.9	89.7	77.7	33.1	5.6	#	3.0	23.6	36.3
Slovenia	97.8	97.5	96.3	92.1	78.2	66.5	33.6	97.8	97.4	96.3	87.6	25.1	8.7	#	4.5	53.0	57.8
Spain	97.3	95.5	91.8	80.2	71.8	63.9	29.3	96.7	95.5	91.6	45.8	28.5	18.2	#	34.0	43.1	45.5
Sweden	99.3	99.7	98.4	96.3	43.0	40.0	34.9	99.3	99.6	98.0	94.9	24.5	13.3	0.2	1.1	16.7	23.9
Switzerland	97.9	93.2	91.3	84.6	62.8	46.2	26.3	97.8	92.8	90.1	79.7	50.4	24.8	0.4	3.8	11.2	20.1
Turkey	87.8	81.9	73.5	55.2	47.2	51.1	30.9	86.4	80.4	69.9	31.3	7.3	5.8	2.2	23.9	39.9	45.3
United Kingdom	99.1	93.8	90.3	67.2	58.6	53.1	21.0	99.1	93.4	88.0	38.5	19.9	12.9	2.3	28.8	38.7	40.2
United States	98.8	89.4	88.1	69.2	59.9	49.1	26.0	98.8	89.1	86.9	29.6	5.6	#	1.1	38.2	52.0	47.0
Other reporting countries																	
Brazil	92.6	88.5	73.7	50.1	40.3	32.9	19.7	89.9	86.3	66.6	33.9	19.5	11.3	4.8	13.1	18.0	19.2
Colombia	82.7	73.6	53.9	41.7	32.9	29.3	16.9	79.5	68.3	39.0	18.7	8.4	4.8	13.6	22.0	23.8	23.9
Indonesia	92.6	80.9	83.2	54.1	43.0	30.5	12.6	92.6	80.9	83.2	46.7	14.2	4.0	#	7.4	28.9	26.5
Latvia	98.7	98.6	98.3	93.0	82.5	58.8	28.2	97.6	98.0	97.4	90.2	43.0	12.7	0.3	2.5	36.7	43.7
Russian Federation	96.4	91.3	92.3	76.7	65.8	52.9	20.1	87.7	58.1	38.2	3.5	0.1	#	39.9	60.7	59.8	50.5
Saudi Arabia	101.1	94.6	90.4	48.0	20.4	15.9	4.8	97.1	94.3	90.1	47.7	20.1	15.7	—	—	—	—

—Not available.
#Rounds to zero.
[1]In addition to secondary and tertiary education, may include enrollment in the following International Standard Classification of Education (ISCED) 2011 education levels that are not shown separately: level 1 (primary or elementary education) and level 4 (nontertiary education that typically corresponds to postsecondary vocational programs below the associate's degree level in the United States).
[2]Refers to ISCED 2011 level 2 (lower secondary education) and level 3 (upper secondary education). Secondary education generally corresponds to grades 7–12 in the United States.
[3]Total tertiary education corresponds to all postsecondary programs leading to associate's and higher degrees in the United States. Tertiary education includes ISCED 2011 level 5 (corresponding to U.S. programs at the associate's degree level), level 6 (bachelor's or equivalent level), level 7 (master's or equivalent level), and level 8 (doctoral or equivalent level). Enrollment rates may not be directly comparable across countries due to differing definitions of tertiary education and the age at which it begins.

[4]Refers to the mean of the data values for all reporting Organization for Economic Cooperation and Development (OECD) countries, to which each country reporting data contributes equally.
[5]Tertiary students from Luxembourg generally study for no more than 1 year in Luxembourg and must complete their studies in other countries.
NOTE: For each country, this table shows the number of persons at a given age who are enrolled in that country as a percentage of that country's total population at the specified age. If a country enrolls many residents of other countries, the country's total population at the specified age can be smaller than the total number enrolled, resulting in enrollment estimates exceeding 100 percent. Conversely, if a country has many residents who are enrolled outside of the country, the country's enrollment rates may be underestimated. Enrollment estimates can also be affected if population and enrollment data were collected at different times. Includes both full-time and part-time students.
SOURCE: Organization for Economic Cooperation and Development (OECD), Online Education Database, retrieved April 5, 2016, from http://stats.oecd.org/Index.aspx. (This table was prepared April 2016.)

Table 601.50. Pupil/teacher ratios in public and private elementary and secondary schools, by level of education and country: Selected years, 2000 through 2013

Country	Elementary school							Junior high school (lower secondary)							Senior high school (upper secondary)						
	2000	2005	2009	2010	2011	2012	2013	2000	2005	2009	2010	2011	2012	2013	2000	2005	2009	2010	2011	2012	2013
	2	3	4	5	6	7	8	9	10	11	12	13	14	15	16	17	18	19	20	21	22
OECD average[1]	**17.7**	**17.0**	**16.0**	**15.9**	**15.4**	**15.1**	**15.2**	**—**	**14.0**	**13.5**	**13.6**	**13.3**	**13.3**	**13.4**	**13.7**	**13.5**	**13.4**	**13.6**	**13.7**	**13.5**	**13.3**
Australia	17.3	16.2	15.8	15.7	15.6	15.5	15.6	—	10.6	9.6	9.3	9.1	9.0	9.0	—	12.1[2,3]	12.0[2,3]	12.0[2,3]	12.0[2,3]	12.0[2,3]	12.0[2,3]
Austria	15.0[4]	14.1	12.6	12.2	12.1	12.5	11.9	—	9.4	8.1[5]	9.3	9.1	9.0	9.0[5]	—	11.3	10.2	10.1	9.8	9.8	9.9[5]
Belgium	18.1	12.8	12.5[5]	12.4[5]	12.4	12.5	12.7[5]	—	—	8.1[5]	9.5[4,7]	10.3[5]	9.9	9.8	9.7[3,6]	9.9[5]	10.2[5,6]	10.1[5,6]	10.1[5,6]	10.1[5,6]	9.5[5]
Canada	—	—	—	—	—	—	—	—	—	—	—	—	—	—	9.5	9.9[5]	9.4[6,10]	9.4[10]	9.7[6,10]	9.6[6]	9.3[6]
Chile	—	25.9	22.4	24.6	23.1	22.1	22.5	18.1	25.9	22.4	25.1	23.6	22.4	24.3	26.6	24.7	26.1	25.4	24.0	25.1	
Czech Republic	19.7	17.5	18.4	18.7	18.7	18.9	18.8	14.7	13.5[7]	11.5[7]	11.7[7]	11.8[7]	11.9[7]	11.2	11.5	12.8	12.2	12.1	11.7	11.3	11.1
Denmark	10.4	—	—	—	—	—	—	11.4	—	—	—	—	—	—	—	—	—	—	—	—	—
Estonia	16.9	15.9	16.2	16.2	16.0	15.9	13.0	10.7	10.4	15.7[7]	14.9[7]	10.3	9.9	9.8	18.0[6,8]	18.0[6,8]	16.6[6]	17.1[6]	13.7[6]	14.1[6]	11.3[6]
Finland	16.9	19.4[5]	13.6[5]	14.0[5]	13.2[5]	13.6[5]	13.0	14.7	10.0	15.7	14.9	10.3	9.9[5]	9.4	16.8	18.0[6,8]	16.6[6]	17.1[6]	16.3[6]	16.1[6]	13.6[6]
France	19.8	19.4	19.7[5]	18.7[5]	18.4[5]	18.9[5]	19.3	14.7	14.2	14.9[5]	15.0[5]	14.8[5]	15.5[5]	15.4	10.3	10.3	9.6[5]	9.7[5]	10.0[5]	9.9[5]	10.1
Germany	19.8	18.8[1]	17.4	16.7	16.3	16.2	15.6	15.7	15.9	15.1	14.9	14.2	14.0	13.6	13.9	14.0	13.9	13.2	13.8	13.7	13.2
Greece	13.4	10.6	10.7[10]	10.8	10.7	10.7	9.5[9]	10.9	10.4	10.8[7]	10.7[7]	10.6	10.6	10.4[9]	10.5	12.2[6]	12.8[6]	12.5	12.4	12.5	12.1[6]
Hungary	10.9	10.6	10.7	10.8	10.7	10.6	10.4	10.4	10.4	10.8	10.3[7]	10.6	10.6	10.5	9.7[4,6]	12.6[6]	12.6	11.5	11.5	12.0[6]	12.0[6]
Iceland	—	11.3[7]	—	—	—	—	—	12.7	11.3[7]	9.9[7]	10.3[7]	—	—	—	15.9[3,6]	15.5[3,6]	12.6[3,6,10]	14.4[3,6,10]	14.4[3,6]	15.0[3,6]	13.9[3,10]
Ireland	21.5	17.9	15.9	15.9	15.7	16.2	16.4[10]	—	—	—	—	—	—	—	—	—	—	—	—	—	—
Israel	11.0	17.3[10]	17.0[10]	20.6[10]	15.9[10]	15.2[10]	15.3	10.4	13.4	13.7[10]	12.8[10]	13.6[10]	13.6	13.5	10.2	13.4	10.8[10]	11.0[10]	11.3[10]	11.0[10]	11.0[10]
Italy	10.9	10.4	10.7[10]	11.8[10]	11.7[10]	12.1[10]	15.3	16.8	10.1	10.0	12.8[10]	11.5[10]	14.1	11.7	14.0	13.0	12.6[6]	12.5	12.6	12.6	12.6
Japan	20.9	28.0	18.5[10]	18.4	18.1	17.7	17.4	21.5	15.1	14.5[7]	14.4	14.2	14.1	17.5	20.9	13.0[6]	16.7	16.5	12.6	15.4	15.1
Korea, Republic of	32.1	28.0	22.5	20.6[10]	18.6	10.7	11.2	11.5	12.7	19.9[10]	19.7[10]	18.8	10.7	11.2	20.9	9.0[3,10]	9.1[3]	9.1[3]	9.6[3]	7.6	7.1
Luxembourg	15.9[10]	11.7	11.6	10.1	9.9	9.2	8.8	—	—	—	—	—	—	—	—	—	—	—	—	—	—
Mexico	27.2[4]	28.3[4]	28.1[4,10]	28.1[4,10]	28.1	28.0	27.7	34.8	33.7	33.0	32.7	31.9	31.9	32.2	26.5[3]	25.8[3]	25.6[3,6,10]	26.9[3,6,10]	26.8	26.9	27.3[10]
Netherlands	20.6	18.1	15.8[4,10]	15.7[4,10]	15.8	16.4	17.0[4]	19.9	16.8	16.3	16.3	16.3	16.4	16.0	17.1[3]	16.2[3]	16.1[3,6]	14.4	16.9[6]	13.7[6]	19.0[10]
New Zealand	20.4	18.0	16.3[10]	16.2	16.3	16.3	16.4	19.9	16.8	16.9	16.3	16.3	16.4	16.8	13.7	12.9	9.4[6,10]	9.7[6,10]	9.7[6,10]	9.6[6]	10.3[6,8]
Poland	12.4	11.7	10.2	10.0	10.4	10.3	11.1	11.5	12.7	12.9	12.7	11.3	10.9	9.9	16.9	12.9	12.0	12.1	11.1	10.9	11.0
Portugal	12.1	10.8	11.3	10.9	11.2[11]	11.9	13.2	10.4	8.2[1]	7.6	7.9	8.2[11]	9.6	10.4	7.9	8.0	7.7[6]	7.2[6]	7.3[6,11]	7.6[6]	8.4[6]
Slovak Republic	18.3	18.1	15.8[10]	17.1	16.0	16.8	16.0	13.5	14.1	14.0	13.6	13.1	12.8	12.5	12.8	14.3	15.1[6]	14.6[6]	14.3[6]	13.9[6]	13.6[6]
Slovenia	14.9	15.0	16.7	16.2	13.2	13.4	12.7	—	11.1	10.1	10.1	10.3	10.6	11.6	11.9[3]	14.1	14.3[6]	14.1[6]	14.8	14.1[6]	13.5
Spain	12.8	12.2	13.3	13.2	13.2	13.4	12.7	12.8	12.0	11.3	11.4	11.3	11.3	12.0	15.2	14.0	13.2	13.1	13.0	13.2	12.8
Sweden	14.9	11.6	11.7	11.7	11.3	11.8	12.7	12.8	12.0	11.3	11.4	11.3	11.3	12.0	15.2	14.0	13.2	13.1	13.0	13.2	12.8
Switzerland[10]	—	14.6	15.4	14.9	14.6	20.1	15.0	—	11.7	12.0	11.8	†	20.1	12.0	14.0	10.5	10.4[2]	10.3[2]	17.8[3]	16.2[3]	15.6[3]
Turkey	30.5	25.8[10]	22.9	21.7[10]	21.0	20.1	19.8	—	17.0	16.1	17.1	15.2	20.2	18.3	14.0[2]	16.2[2]	16.9[3]	15.6	17.8	17.1	15.6
United Kingdom	15.8	20.7	22.9	19.8	19.9	20.1	20.7	17.6[2]	15.1	14.3	14.0	15.2	20.2	18.5	14.1	16.0	15.1	15.0	15.3	15.3	15.4
United States	15.8	14.9	14.8	14.5	15.3	15.3	15.3	16.3[2]	15.1	14.3	14.0	15.2	15.3	15.4	14.1	16.0	15.1	15.0	15.3	15.3	15.4
Other reporting countries																					
Argentina	22.7[10,12]	22.9	16.0[13]	23.4	22.5	21.7	21.2	13.2[10,12]	18.1	15.3[13]	20.4	19.8	19.1	18.5	9.0[10,12]	17.6	8.8[13]	17.3	16.9	16.8	15.7
Brazil	26.6[12]	—	24.0	17.2	17.1	17.5	16.9	34.2[12]	—	25.6	15.0	14.6	12.8	13.4	38.7[12]	—	18.1	18.4	18.4	16.2	17.0
China	20.2[12]	—	17.6	19.9	20.3	25.2	25.0	17.6[12]	—	15.6	—	18.3	21.6	26.6	13.8[12]	—	18.2	—	20.1	22.8	22.9
Colombia	—	—	—	19.9	20.3	20.1[10]	20.7	22.0[10,12]	—	15.9	17.0	18.3	7.9	18.0	9.2[10,12]	—	16.8	16.1	—	15.3[10]	22.6[10]
India	43.0[10,12]	—	20.8	19.9	20.3	25.2	20.7	22.0[10,12]	—	15.9	17.0	18.3	7.9	18.0	9.2[10,12]	11.2[6,15]	8.8[13]	11.3[3,6,10]	8.7[3,6,10]	15.3[10]	8.9[3]
Indonesia	27.1[14]	—	—	—	11.1	10.1	7.8	19.6[14]	—	—	—	—	8.9[10]	9.7	17.8[14]	—	8.7[3,6,16]	11.0	10.9	10.7	
Latvia	—	—	17.9[10]	19.2[10]	20.0[10]	20.1[10]	20.3	—	15.9	—	8.8	9.7	9.7	9.8	—	—	24.4[3]	—	—	—	—
Russian Federation	17.3[14]	—	—	11.2[10]	11.0[10]	10.9	—	—	—	—	—	—	—	—	—	—	—	—	—	—	—
Saudi Arabia	—	—	—	—	—	—	—	—	—	—	—	—	—	—	—	—	—	—	—	—	—
South Africa	—	—	33.6[4]	—	—	—	—	—	—	—	—	—	—	—	—	—	—	—	—	—	—

—Not available.

†Not applicable. This level of education is not part of the national education structure; students in the age group normally associated with this education level were reported in other levels.

[1] Refers to the mean of the data values for all reporting Organization for Economic Cooperation and Development (OECD) countries, to which each country reporting data contributes equally. The average includes all current OECD countries for which a given year's data are available, even if they were not members of OECD in that year. However, if data were reported for less than 75 percent of the countries, the average for that year is omitted.
[2] Includes only general programs.
[3] Includes junior high school data.
[4] Includes preprimary data.
[5] Excludes independent private institutions.
[6] Includes postsecondary non-higher-education.
[7] Includes elementary school data.
[8] Includes occupation-specific education corresponding to that offered at the vocational associate's degree level in the United States.
[9] Includes data on management personnel.

[10] Public institutions only.
[11] Based on a head count of teachers, rather than full-time equivalents.
[12] Data from 1999 reported for 2000.
[13] Data from 2008 reported for 2009.
[14] Data from 2001 reported for 2000.
[15] Excludes general programs.
[16] Excludes part-time personnel in public institutions.
NOTE: The pupil/teacher ratio is the number of full-time-equivalent students divided by the number of full-time-equivalent teachers, including teachers for students with disabilities and other special teachers. Data for 2012 and earlier years were calculated using the International Standard Classification of Education (ISCED) 1997. Data for 2013 used the ISCED 2011 classification and may not be comparable to data for earlier years. In this table, elementary school corresponds to ISCED 1997 and ISCED 2011 level 1 (U.S. grades 1 through 6), junior high school corresponds to ISCED 1997 and ISCED 2011 level 2 (U.S. grades 7 through 9), and senior high school corresponds to ISCED 1997 and ISCED 2011 level 3 (U.S. grades 10 through 12).
SOURCE: Organization for Economic Cooperation and Development (OECD), Online Education Database; and Education at a Glance, 2002 through 2015. (This table was prepared February 2016.)

Table 601.60. Teachers' statutory teaching and total working time and average class size in public elementary and secondary schools, by level of education and country: 2013

Country	Statutory teaching and total working time												Average class size	
	Number of weeks teaching			Number of days teaching			Net teaching time in hours			Total working time in hours				
	Elementary school	Junior high school (lower secondary)[1]	Senior high school (upper secondary)[1]	Elementary school	Junior high school (lower secondary)[1]	Senior high school (upper secondary)[1]	Elementary school	Junior high school (lower secondary)[1]	Senior high school (upper secondary)[1]	Elementary school	Junior high school (lower secondary)[1]	Senior high school (upper secondary)[1]	Elementary school	Junior high school (lower secondary)
1	2	3	4	5	6	7	8	9	10	11	12	13	14	15
OECD average[2]	38	37	37	183	182	181	772	694	643	1,600	1,618	1,603	21	24
Australia[3]	40	40	40	196	196	194	879	821	812	†	†	†	23	23
Austria[3]	38	38	38	180	180	180	779	607	589	1,776	1,776	†	18	21
Belgium (Flemish)[3]	37	37	37	177	179	179	752	669	625	†	†	†	—	—
Belgium (French)[3]	37	37	37	181	181	181	721	661	601	962	†	†	20	—
Canada[3]	37	37	37	183	183	183	796	743	745	†	†	†	—	—
Chile[4]	38	38	38	181	181	181	1,129	1,129	1,129	1,989	1,989	1,989	29	31
Czech Republic[3]	39	39	39	188	188	188	827	620	592	1,760	1,760	1,760	20	22
Denmark[5]	†	†	†	†	†	†	662	662	369 [6]	1,680	1,680	1,680	21	21
England[5]	38	38	38	190	190	190	722	745	745	1,265	1,265	1,265	—	—
Estonia[4]	35	35	35	172	172	172	619	619	568	1,540	1,540	1,540	17	15
Finland[7]	38	38	38	188	188	188	677	592	550	†	†	†	19	20
France[3]	36	36	36	144	†	†	924	648	648	1,607	1,607	1,607	23	25
Germany[3]	40	40	40	193	193	193	800	752	715	1,768	1,768	1,768	21	24
Greece[3]	35	31	31	171	152	152	569	415	415	1,864	†	†	17	22
Hungary[7]	36	36	36	182	182	181	601	601	597	1,864	1,864	1,864	21	21
Iceland[3]	37	37	35	180	180	170	624	624	544	1,800	1,800	1,800	19	20
Ireland[3]	37	33	33	183	167	167	915	735	735	†	†	†	25	—
Israel[3]	38	36	36	182	175	175	840	644	570	1,225	985	811	28	29
Italy[3]	39	39	39	171	171	171	752	616	616	—	—	—	19	22
Japan[5]	40	40	39	201	202	197	736	608	513	1,899	1,899	1,899	27	32
Korea, Republic of[7]	38	38	38	190	190	190	667	557	549	1,520	1,520	1,520	24	33
Luxembourg[3]	36	36	36	176	176	176	810	739	739	†	†	†	15	19
Mexico[3]	42	42	36	200	200	171	800	1,047	838	†	†	†	20	28
Netherlands[4]	40	—	—	195	—	—	930	750	750	1,659	1,659	1,659	23 [8]	—
New Zealand[3]	38	38	38	192	191	190	922	841	760	†	†	†	—	—
Norway[4]	38	38	38	190	190	190	741	663	523	1,688	1,688	1,688	—	—
Poland[5]	38	37	37	184	182	179	629	555	551	1,504	1,488	1,472	19	23
Portugal[4]	36	36	36	166	166	166	747	609	609	1,282	1,282	1,282	21	22
Scotland[4]	38	38	38	190	190	190	855	855	855	1,365	1,365	1,365	—	—
Slovak Republic[3]	38	38	38	187	187	187	832	645	617	1,568	1,568	1,568	18	19
Slovenia[3]	40	40	40	190	190	190	627	627	570	—	—	—	19	20
Spain[3]	37	37	36	176	176	171	880	713	693	1,425	1,425	1,425	21	25
Sweden[3]	†	†	†	†	†	†	†	†	†	1,767	1,767	1,767	—	—
Switzerland	—	—	—	—	—	—	—	—	—	—	—	—	—	—
Turkey[3]	38	38	38	180	180	180	720	504	504	1,576	1,576	1,576	23	28
United Kingdom	—	—	—	—	—	—	—	—	—	—	—	—	27	20
United States[5]	36	36	36	180	180	180	—	981	—	1,922	1,936	1,960	22	28
Other reporting countries														
Brazil	42	42	42	203	203	203	—	—	—	—	—	—	25	28
China	—	—	—	—	—	—	—	—	—	—	—	—	37	50
Colombia[3]	40	40	40	200	200	200	1,000	1,200	1,200	1,600	1,600	1,600	24	30
Indonesia	—	—	—	—	—	—	—	—	—	—	—	—	26	31
Latvia	35	35	35	165	165	165	825	825	990	1,760	1,760	1,760	16	15
Russian Federation[5]	34	35	35	170	210	210	561	483	483	—	—	—	18	19

—Not available.
†Not applicable according to the Organization for Economic Cooperation and Development (OECD).
[1]General programs only.
[2]Refers to the mean of the data values for all reporting OECD countries, to which each country or country component reporting data contributes equally.
[3]Typical teaching time reported.
[4]Maximum teaching time reported.
[5]Actual teaching time reported.

[6]Data from 2011 reported for 2013.
[7]Minimum teaching time reported.
[8]Data for government-dependent private institutions are included.
NOTE: In this table, elementary school corresponds to International Standard Classification of Education (ISCED) 2011 level 1 (U.S. grades 1 through 6), junior high school corresponds to ISCED 2011 level 2 (U.S. grades 7 through 9), and senior high school corresponds to ISCED 2011 level 3 (U.S. grades 10 through 12).
SOURCE: Organization for Economic Cooperation and Development (OECD), *Education at a Glance,* 2015. (This table was prepared February 2016.)

Table 602.10. Average reading literacy scale scores of fourth-graders and percentage whose schools emphasize reading skills and strategies at or before second grade or at third grade, by sex and country or other education system: 2001, 2006, and 2011

[Standard errors appear in parentheses]

Country or other education system[1]	2001		2006		Average reading literacy scale score[2] 2011 Total		2011 Male		2011 Female		Percent of fourth-graders in 2011, by grade at which reading skills and strategies emphasized[3] At or before second grade		At third grade	
1	2		3		4		5		6		7		8	
PIRLS average[4]	500	(†)	500	(†)	500	(†)	504	(0.5)	520	(0.5)	28	(0.5)	68	(0.5)
Australia	—	(†)	—	(†)	527	(2.2)	519	(2.7)	536	(2.7)	73	(4.0)	27	(4.0)
Austria	—	(†)	538	(2.2)	529	(2.0)	525	(2.3)	533	(2.2)	29	(4.2)	71	(4.2)
Azerbaijan[5]	—	(†)	—	(†)	462 [6]	(3.3)	456 [6]	(3.5)	470 [6]	(3.6)	19	(3.6)	79[5]	(3.8)
Belgium (French)-BEL	—	(†)	500	(2.6)	506 [6,7]	(2.9)	504 [6,7]	(3.1)	509 [6,7]	(3.1)	29	(5.0)	70	(5.1)
Bulgaria	550	(3.8)	547	(4.4)	532	(4.1)	524	(4.3)	539	(4.5)	25	(3.5)	74	(3.6)
Canada	—	(†)	—	(†)	548 [6]	(1.6)	542 [6]	(2.1)	555 [6]	(1.7)	55	(2.7)	44	(2.7)
Chinese Taipei-CHN	—	(†)	535	(2.0)	553	(1.9)	546	(2.1)	561	(2.1)	17	(3.0)	80	(3.0)
Colombia	422	(4.4)	—	(†)	448	(4.1)	448	(4.6)	447	(4.6)	13	(3.3)	81	(3.6)
Croatia	—	(†)	—	(†)	553 [6]	(1.9)	546 [6]	(2.2)	560 [6]	(2.1)	31	(4.1)	68	(4.2)
Czech Republic	537	(2.3)	—	(†)	545	(2.2)	542	(2.5)	549	(2.5)	24	(3.8)	74	(4.0)
Denmark	—	(†)	546	(2.3)	554 [6]	(1.7)	548 [6]	(2.1)	560 [6]	(1.9)	21	(2.4)	79	(2.4)
England-GBR	553 [4,5]	(3.4)	539	(2.6)	552 [7]	(2.6)	540 [7]	(3.1)	563 [7]	(3.0)	84	(3.3)	15	(3.2)
Finland	—	(†)	—	(†)	568	(1.9)	558	(2.2)	578	(2.3)	10	(2.6)	87	(2.8)
France	525	(2.4)	522	(2.1)	520	(2.6)	518	(2.4)	522	(3.4)	18	(3.3)	81	(3.4)
Georgia[5]	—	(†)	471 [6,8]	(3.1)	488 [8]	(3.1)	477 [8]	(4.0)	499 [8]	(2.7)	20	(2.8)	79	(2.9)
Germany	539	(1.9)	548	(2.2)	541	(2.2)	537	(2.7)	545	(2.3)	30	(3.4)	69	(3.3)
Hong Kong-CHN	528	(3.1)	564	(2.4)	571 [9]	(2.3)	563 [9]	(2.5)	579 [9]	(2.3)	16	(3.5)	81	(3.8)
Hungary	543	(2.2)	551	(3.0)	539	(2.9)	532	(3.2)	547	(3.2)	28	(4.1)	71	(4.0)
Indonesia	—	(†)	405	(4.1)	428	(4.2)	419	(4.3)	437	(4.5)	‡	(†)	88	(3.2)
Iran, Islamic Republic of	414	(4.2)	421	(3.1)	457	(2.8)	448	(4.3)	467	(4.3)	7	(1.6)	85	(2.4)
Ireland	—	(†)	—	(†)	552	(2.3)	544	(3.0)	559	(2.9)	40	(4.0)	60	(4.0)
Israel	509 [10]	(2.8)	512 [10]	(3.3)	541 [9]	(2.7)	538 [9]	(3.4)	544 [9]	(3.1)	59	(4.7)	41	(4.7)
Italy	541	(2.4)	551	(2.9)	541	(2.2)	540	(2.7)	543	(2.4)	15	(2.5)	84	(2.5)
Lithuania	543 [8]	(2.6)	537 [8]	(1.6)	528 [6,8]	(2.0)	520 [6,8]	(2.4)	537 [6,8]	(2.4)	23	(3.3)	76	(3.4)
Malta	—	(†)	—	(†)	477	(1.4)	468	(2.0)	486	(1.9)	14	(0.1)	86	(0.1)
Morocco	350 [11]	(9.6)	323	(5.9)	310 [12]	(3.9)	296 [12]	(4.6)	326 [12]	(4.0)	‡ [13]	(†)	48	(4.0)
Netherlands	554 [7]	(1.5)	547 [7]	(1.5)	546 [7]	(1.9)	543 [7]	(2.2)	549 [7]	(2.1)	22 [13]	(4.4)	78 [13]	(4.4)
New Zealand	529	(3.6)	532	(2.0)	531	(1.9)	521	(2.7)	541	(2.2)	73	(3.6)	27	(3.6)
Northern Ireland-GBR	—	(†)	—	(†)	558 [7]	(2.4)	550 [7]	(3.2)	567 [7]	(2.5)	55 [13]	(4.6)	45 [13]	(4.6)
Norway	499	(2.9)	498 [13]	(2.6)	507 [11]	(1.9)	500 [11]	(2.7)	514 [11]	(2.2)	14	(3.4)	83	(3.9)
Oman	—	(†)	—	(†)	391 [14]	(2.8)	371 [14]	(3.4)	411 [14]	(3.0)	4	(0.9)	86	(2.0)
Poland	—	(†)	519	(2.4)	526	(2.1)	519	(2.7)	533	(2.5)	6 !	(2.1)	94	(2.1)
Portugal	—	(†)	—	(†)	541	(2.6)	534	(2.8)	548	(3.0)	25	(4.1)	75	(4.1)
Qatar	—	(†)	353	(1.1)	425 [6]	(3.5)	411 [6]	(4.2)	441 [6]	(4.7)	24	(3.0)	66	(3.4)
Romania	512	(4.6)	489	(5.0)	502	(4.3)	495	(4.3)	510	(4.8)	14	(3.4)	85	(3.5)
Russian Federation	528 [6]	(4.4)	565 [6]	(3.4)	568	(2.7)	559	(3.1)	578	(2.8)	50	(3.7)	50	(3.7)
Saudi Arabia	—	(†)	—	(†)	430	(4.4)	402	(8.2)	456	(3.1)	7	(1.7)	78	(3.5)
Singapore	528	(5.2)	558	(2.9)	567 [6]	(3.3)	559 [6]	(3.6)	576 [6]	(3.5)	46	(#)	54	(#)
Slovak Republic	518	(2.8)	531	(2.8)	535	(2.8)	530	(2.8)	540	(3.1)	24	(3.2)	76	(3.3)
Slovenia	502	(2.0)	522	(2.1)	530	(2.0)	523	(2.7)	539	(2.2)	8	(1.8)	87	(2.4)
Spain	—	(†)	513	(2.5)	513	(2.3)	511	(2.8)	516	(2.5)	29	(3.2)	71	(3.2)
Sweden	561	(2.2)	549	(2.3)	542	(2.1)	535	(2.5)	549	(2.4)	37 [13]	(4.5)	63 [13]	(4.5)
Trinidad and Tobago	—	(†)	436	(4.9)	471	(3.8)	456	(4.3)	487	(4.5)	32	(3.8)	66	(4.0)
United Arab Emirates	—	(†)	—	(†)	439	(2.2)	425	(3.5)	452	(3.0)	15	(1.3)	68	(2.2)
United States	542 [6,7]	(3.8)	540 [7]	(3.5)	556 [6]	(1.5)	551 [6]	(1.7)	562 [6]	(1.9)	75 [13]	(2.7)	24 [13]	(2.7)
Benchmarking education systems														
Abu Dhabi-UAE	—	(†)	—	(†)	424	(4.7)	406	(6.3)	442	(5.5)	11	(2.6)	61	(4.4)
Alberta-CAN	—	(†)	560 [6]	(2.4)	548 [6]	(2.9)	543 [6]	(3.1)	553 [6]	(3.1)	52	(4.5)	48	(4.5)
Andalusia-ESP	—	(†)	—	(†)	515	(2.3)	511	(2.8)	519	(2.4)	26	(3.6)	74	(3.6)
Dubai-UAE	—	(†)	—	(†)	476	(2.0)	470	(3.5)	483	(3.9)	28	(0.3)	66	(0.3)
Florida-USA[15]	—	(†)	—	(†)	569 [8,10]	(2.9)	561 [8,10]	(3.0)	576 [8,10]	(3.4)	82 [13]	(4.7)	18 [13]	(4.7)
Maltese-MLT	—	(†)	—	(†)	457	(1.5)	445	(2.2)	470	(2.0)	14	(0.1)	86	(0.1)
Ontario-CAN	548 [6]	(3.3)	555 [6]	(2.7)	552 [6]	(2.6)	546 [6]	(2.8)	558 [6]	(3.3)	75	(4.0)	25	(4.0)
Quebec-CAN	537	(3.0)	533	(2.8)	538	(2.1)	531	(2.4)	544	(2.6)	23	(3.9)	75	(4.1)

—Not available.
†Not applicable.
#Rounds to zero.
!Interpret data with caution. The coefficient of variation (CV) for this estimate is between 30 and 50 percent.
‡Reporting standards not met. The coefficient of variation (CV) for this estimate is 50 percent or greater.
[1]Most of the education systems represent complete countries, but some represent subnational entities such as U.S. states, Canadian provinces, and England (which is part of the United Kingdom). The name of each subnational entity appears in italics and includes as a suffix the three-letter International Organization for Standardization (ISO) abbreviation for its complete country. Examples include Florida-USA, Ontario-CAN, and England-GBR.
[2]Progress in International Reading Literacy Study (PIRLS) scores are reported on a scale from 0 to 1,000, with the scale average set at 500 and the standard deviation set at 100.
[3]Based on principals' reports of the earliest grade at which each of 11 reading skills and strategies first receive a major emphasis in instruction. A school is counted as emphasizing reading skills and strategies at a certain grade (or before) only if its principal reported that all 11 skills and strategies are emphasized at that grade (or before). A small percentage of fourth-graders (1 percent in the United States) are not shown because their schools first emphasized reading skills and strategies at fourth grade or later.
[4]The PIRLS average includes only education systems that are members of the International Association for the Evaluation of Educational Achievement (IAE), which develops and implements PIRLS

at the international level. "Benchmarking" education systems are not members of the IEA and are therefore not included in the average.
[5]Exclusion rates for Azerbaijan and Georgia are slightly underestimated as some conflict zones were not covered and no official statistics were available for 2011.
[6]National Defined Population covers 90 percent to 95 percent of National Target Population.
[7]Met guidelines for sample participation rates only after replacement schools were included.
[8]National Target Population does not include all of the International Target Population.
[9]National Defined Population covers less than 90 percent of National Target Population.
[10]National Defined Population covers less than 80 percent of National Target Population.
[11]Nearly satisfied guidelines for sample participation rates after replacement schools were included.
[12]The TIMSS & PIRLS International Study Center has reservations about the reliability of the average achievement score because the percentage of students with achievement too low for estimation exceeds 25 percent.
[13]Data are available for at least 70 percent but less than 85 percent of students.
[14]The TIMSS & PIRLS International Study Center has reservations about the reliability of the average achievement score because the percentage of students with achievement too low for estimation exceeds 15 percent, though it is less than 25 percent.
[15]All data for Florida are based on public schools only.
SOURCE: International Association for the Evaluation of Educational Achievement (IEA), Progress in International Reading Literacy Study (PIRLS), 2001, 2006, and 2011. (This table was prepared February 2013).

Table 602.20.   Average fourth-grade scores and annual instructional time in mathematics and science, by country or other education system: 2011

[Standard errors appear in parentheses]

Country or other education system[1]	Total instructional hours per year		Mathematics						Science					
			Average score[2]		Instructional time in mathematics				Average score[2]		Instructional time in science			
					Hours per year		As a percent of total instructional hours				Hours per year		As a percent of total instructional hours	
1	2		3		4		5		6		7		8	
TIMSS average[3]	897	(2.0)	500	(†)	162	(0.5)	18	(0.1)	500	(†)	85	(0.5)	10	(0.1)
Armenia	851 [4]	(17.1)	452	(3.5)	139 [4]	(1.7)	16	(0.2)	416	(3.8)	54 [5]	(0.6)	6	(0.1)
Australia	1,008	(6.9)	516	(2.9)	230 [5]	(5.8)	23	(0.6)	516	(2.8)	65 [5]	(2.3)	6	(0.2)
Austria	808	(6.9)	508	(2.6)	146	(2.1)	18	(0.3)	532	(2.8)	96	(2.3)	12	(0.3)
Azerbaijan[6,7]	804	(27.7)	463	(5.8)	130	(3.3)	18	(0.7)	438	(5.6)	61	(1.4)	8	(0.3)
Bahrain	964	(10.8)	436	(3.3)	131 [4]	(4.4)	14	(0.4)	449	(3.5)	85 [4]	(2.7)	9	(0.3)
Belgium (Flemish)-BEL	1,010 [4]	(16.8)	549	(1.9)	224 [4]	(4.1)	21	(0.3)	509	(2.0)	—	(†)	—	(†)
Chile	1,228 [4]	(22.6)	462	(2.3)	231 [5]	(6.7)	19	(0.6)	480	(2.4)	161 [5]	(6.4)	13	(0.5)
Chinese Taipei-CHN	989 [4]	(13.4)	591	(2.0)	133	(3.9)	12	(0.4)	552	(2.2)	90	(2.3)	9	(0.3)
Croatia[6]	776	(19.4)	490	(1.9)	134	(2.3)	18	(0.4)	516	(2.1)	95	(2.4)	13	(0.4)
Czech Republic	782	(8.2)	511	(2.4)	163	(3.0)	21	(0.4)	536	(2.5)	60	(2.2)	8	(0.3)
Denmark[6]	863 [4]	(9.4)	537	(2.6)	124 [5]	(2.0)	15	(0.3)	528	(2.8)	62 [5]	(1.9)	7	(0.2)
England-GBR	970 [4]	(8.3)	542	(3.5)	188 [5]	(3.3)	19	(0.4)	529	(2.9)	76 [5]	(3.2)	8	(0.3)
Finland	779	(9.8)	545	(2.3)	139	(2.5)	18	(0.4)	570	(2.6)	98	(1.9)	13	(0.4)
Georgia[7,8]	748 [4]	(18.7)	450	(3.7)	148 [4]	(3.9)	21	(0.6)	455	(3.8)	110 [4]	(2.7)	16	(0.4)
Germany	863 [4]	(11.2)	528	(2.2)	163 [4]	(3.1)	19	(0.3)	528	(2.9)	75 [5]	(3.5)	8	(0.4)
Hong Kong-CHN[6]	1,059 [4]	(11.2)	602	(3.4)	158 [4]	(3.0)	15	(0.3)	535	(3.8)	88 [4]	(4.2)	8	(0.4)
Hungary	760	(12.2)	515	(3.4)	148	(3.3)	20	(0.5)	534	(3.7)	72	(2.2)	10	(0.3)
Iran, Islamic Republic of	727	(11.2)	431	(3.5)	146	(3.9)	20	(0.4)	453	(3.7)	106	(3.2)	14	(0.4)
Ireland	854	(#)	527	(2.6)	150	(2.8)	18	(0.3)	516	(3.4)	63	(6.6)	7	(0.8)
Italy	1,085	(12.6)	508	(2.6)	214	(3.9)	20	(0.4)	524	(2.7)	78 [4]	(1.8)	7	(0.2)
Japan	891	(3.7)	585	(1.7)	150	(1.6)	17	(0.1)	559	(1.9)	91	(0.8)	10	(0.1)
Kazakhstan[6]	779	(10.6)	501	(4.5)	140	(2.7)	18	(0.4)	495	(5.1)	57	(1.3)	8	(0.2)
Korea, Republic of	789	(11.4)	605	(1.9)	121	(3.0)	15	(0.4)	587	(2.0)	92	(2.5)	11	(0.4)
Kuwait[8]	928 [4]	(23.1)	342 [9]	(3.4)	120 [4]	(4.9)	13	(0.4)	347 [10]	(4.7)	85 [5]	(5.8)	10	(0.6)
Lithuania[6,8]	649	(9.0)	534	(2.4)	133	(2.6)	21	(0.5)	515	(2.4)	60	(1.5)	9	(0.3)
Malta	891 [4]	(0.2)	496	(1.3)	183 [4]	(0.1)	21	(#)	446	(1.9)	39 [4]	(0.1)	4	(#)
Morocco	1,040 [4]	(23.6)	335 [9]	(4.0)	174 [5]	(3.5)	17	(0.4)	264 [9]	(4.5)	44 [5]	(5.5)	5	(0.6)
Netherlands[11]	1,074 [5]	(9.9)	540	(1.7)	195 [5]	(7.0)	18	(0.5)	531	(2.2)	42 [5]	(2.4)	4	(0.2)
New Zealand	925	(3.9)	486	(2.6)	168	(2.4)	18	(0.3)	497	(2.3)	52 [5]	(3.0)	6	(0.3)
Northern Ireland-GBR[11]	970 [4]	(11.0)	562	(2.9)	232 [5]	(6.1)	24	(0.6)	517	(2.6)	72 [5]	(3.9)	8	(0.4)
Norway[12]	817	(10.7)	495	(2.8)	157	(4.1)	19	(0.6)	494	(2.3)	55	(2.2)	7	(0.3)
Oman	999 [5]	(17.4)	385 [10]	(2.9)	170 [5]	(3.1)	17	(0.3)	377	(4.3)	120 [5]	(2.4)	12	(0.2)
Poland	764 [4]	(13.5)	481	(2.2)	157 [4]	(3.0)	21	(0.5)	505	(2.6)	64 [4]	(3.1)	8	(0.4)
Portugal	940 [4]	(13.1)	532	(3.4)	250 [4]	(4.3)	27	(0.4)	522	(3.9)	162 [4]	(4.1)	17	(0.8)
Qatar[6]	1,068	(9.1)	413	(3.5)	185	(6.3)	17	(0.6)	394	(4.3)	135	(6.8)	13	(0.6)
Romania	796	(17.9)	482	(5.8)	148	(3.9)	19	(0.5)	505	(5.9)	56	(6.2)	7	(0.8)
Russian Federation	660 [4]	(8.0)	542	(3.7)	104	(1.0)	16	(0.2)	552	(3.5)	49	(0.7)	8	(0.2)
Saudi Arabia[6]	977 [4]	(19.4)	410	(5.3)	147 [4]	(6.6)	15	(0.5)	429	(5.4)	82 [4]	(4.2)	8	(0.5)
Serbia[6]	778	(18.5)	516	(3.0)	153	(2.1)	20	(0.5)	516	(3.1)	72	(5.0)	10	(0.9)
Singapore[6]	1,012	(#)	606	(3.2)	208	(3.2)	21	(0.3)	583	(3.4)	96	(2.1)	9	(0.2)
Slovak Republic	780	(8.8)	507	(3.8)	147	(1.4)	19	(0.1)	532	(3.8)	101	(4.3)	13	(0.6)
Slovenia	684	(#)	513	(2.2)	169	(2.6)	25	(0.4)	520	(2.7)	101	(1.2)	15	(0.2)
Spain	884 [4]	(9.7)	482	(2.9)	167 [4]	(2.3)	19	(0.2)	505	(3.0)	145 [4]	(2.6)	16	(0.3)
Sweden	849 [4]	(11.3)	504	(2.0)	138 [5]	(3.8)	17	(0.5)	533	(2.7)	75 [5]	(3.0)	9	(0.4)
Thailand	1,201 [4]	(20.9)	458	(4.8)	167	(5.2)	14	(0.6)	472	(5.6)	109	(4.9)	9	(0.5)
Tunisia	963 [4]	(22.9)	359 [10]	(3.9)	175 [4]	(2.9)	19	(0.3)	346 [10]	(5.3)	93 [4]	(5.4)	10	(0.6)
Turkey	900	(19.3)	469	(4.7)	126	(2.5)	15	(0.4)	463	(4.5)	94	(1.8)	11	(0.3)
United Arab Emirates	1,025 [4]	(8.5)	434	(2.0)	154 [5]	(2.4)	15	(0.2)	428	(2.5)	108 [5]	(3.0)	11	(0.3)
United States[6]	1,078	(7.3)	541	(1.8)	206 [4]	(4.6)	19	(0.5)	544	(2.1)	105 [4]	(3.1)	10	(0.3)
Yemen	831 [4]	(14.1)	248 [9]	(6.0)	135 [4]	(6.4)	16	(0.7)	209 [9]	(7.3)	91 [4]	(5.6)	11	(0.6)
Benchmarking education systems														
Abu Dhabi-UAE	1,033 [4]	(18.1)	417	(4.6)	150 [5]	(4.3)	15	(0.4)	411	(4.9)	110 [5]	(6.8)	11	(0.6)
Alberta-CAN[6]	1,006	(8.8)	507	(2.5)	169 [5]	(3.2)	17	(0.4)	541	(2.4)	130 [5]	(4.1)	13	(0.6)
Dubai-UAE	993 [4]	(0.7)	468	(1.6)	158 [5]	(2.3)	16	(0.2)	461	(2.3)	99 [5]	(1.6)	10	(0.2)
Florida-USA[8,13,14]	1,073 [4]	(19.7)	545	(2.9)	217 [5]	(8.8)	20	(0.9)	545	(3.7)	113 [5]	(9.6)	10	(0.8)
North Carolina-USA[6,8,14]	1,113 [4]	(22.9)	554	(4.2)	221 [4]	(13.5)	20	(1.2)	538	(4.6)	94 [4]	(6.0)	9	(0.4)
Ontario-CAN	969	(7.4)	518	(3.1)	201 [4]	(4.1)	21	(0.5)	528	(3.0)	92 [4]	(3.2)	10	(0.3)
Quebec-CAN	916	(5.1)	533	(2.4)	229	(5.0)	25	(0.6)	516	(2.7)	50	(1.7)	5	(0.2)

—Not available.
†Not applicable.
#Rounds to zero.

[1]Most of the education systems represent complete countries, but some represent subnational entities such as U.S. states, Canadian provinces, and England (which is part of the United Kingdom). The name of each subnational entity appears in italics and includes as a suffix the three-letter International Organization for Standardization (ISO) abbreviation for its complete country. Examples include *Florida-USA*, *Ontario-CAN*, and *England-GBR*.
[2]Trends in International Mathematics and Science Study (TIMSS) scores are reported on a scale from 0 to 1,000, with the scale average set at 500 and the standard deviation set at 100.
[3]The TIMSS average includes only education systems that are members of the International Association for the Evaluation of Educational Achievement (IAE), which develops and implements TIMSS at the international level. "Benchmarking" education systems are not members of the IEA and are therefore not included in the average.
[4]Data are available for at least 70 percent but less than 85 percent of students.
[5]Data are available for at least 50 percent but less than 70 percent of students.
[6]National Defined Population covers 90 to 95 percent of National Target Population.
[7]Exclusion rates for Azerbaijan and Georgia are slightly underestimated as some conflict zones were not covered and no official statistics were available.
[8]National Target Population does not include all of the International Target Population defined by TIMSS.
[9]The TIMSS & PIRLS International Study Center has reservations about the reliability of the average achievement score because the percentage of students with achievement too low for estimation exceeds 25 percent.

[10]The TIMSS & PIRLS International Study Center has reservations about the reliability of the average achievement score because the percentage of students with achievement too low for estimation exceeds 15 percent, though it is less than 25 percent.
[11]Met guidelines for sample participation rates only after replacement schools were included.
[12]Nearly satisfied guidelines for sample participation rates after replacement schools were included.
[13]National Defined Population covers less than 90 percent of National Target Population (but at least 77 percent).
[14]All U.S. state data are based on public school students only.
NOTE: Countries were required to sample students in the grade that corresponded to the end of 4 years of formal schooling, providing that the mean age at the time of testing was at least 9.5 years. Instructional times shown in this table are actual or implemented times (as opposed to intended times prescribed by the curriculum). Principals reported total instructional hours per day and school days per year. Total instructional hours per year were calculated by multiplying the number of school days per year by the number of instructional hours per day. Teachers reported instructional hours per week in mathematics and science. Instructional hours per year in mathematics and science were calculated by dividing weekly instructional hours by the number of school days per week and then multiplying by the number of school days per year.
SOURCE: International Association for the Evaluation of Educational Achievement (IEA), Trends in International Mathematics and Science Study (TIMSS), 2011; *TIMSS 2011 International Results in Mathematics*, by Ina V.S. Mullis et al.; and *TIMSS 2011 International Results in Science*, by Michael O. Martin et al. (This table was prepared December 2012.)

Table 602.30. Average eighth-grade scores and annual instructional time in mathematics and science, by country or other education system: 2011

[Standard errors appear in parentheses]

Country or other education system[1]	Total instructional hours per year		Mathematics						Science					
					Instructional time in mathematics						Instructional time in science[3]			
			Average score[2]		Hours per year		As a percent of total instructional hours		Average score[2]		Hours per year		As a percent of total instructional hours	
1	2		3		4		5		6		7		8	
TIMSS average[4]	1,031	(2.3)	500	(†)	138	(0.5)	14	(0.1)	500	(†)	158	(0.8)	11	(0.1)
Armenia	979[5]	(12.8)	467	(2.7)	143[5]	(3.0)	15	(0.2)	437	(3.1)	240[6]	(4.9)	‡	(†)
Australia	1,039	(7.2)	505	(5.1)	143[6]	(3.5)	14	(0.3)	519	(4.8)	131[6]	(4.5)	12	(0.4)
Bahrain	1,019	(1.1)	409[7]	(2.0)	142[5]	(2.5)	14	(0.3)	452	(2.0)	130[5]	(2.8)	13	(0.3)
Chile	1,245[5]	(23.5)	416	(2.6)	193[5]	(4.5)	15	(0.3)	461	(2.5)	134[5]	(3.8)	11	(0.3)
Chinese Taipei-CHN	1,153	(11.7)	609	(3.2)	166	(2.4)	15	(0.2)	564	(2.3)	157	(2.7)	14	(0.3)
England-GBR[8]	992[5]	(8.4)	507	(5.5)	116[5]	(2.1)	11	(0.3)	533	(4.9)	102[6]	(3.1)	10	(0.4)
Finland	934	(11.7)	514	(2.5)	105	(1.8)	11	(0.2)	552	(2.5)	190[5]	(6.0)	‡	(†)
Georgia[9,10]	833[5]	(10.8)	431	(3.8)	123[5]	(3.3)	15	(0.5)	420	(3.0)	198[5]	(6.8)	‡	(†)
Ghana	1,153[5]	(18.9)	331[11]	(4.3)	165[5]	(6.8)	14	(0.6)	306[7]	(5.2)	148[5]	(6.1)	13	(0.4)
Hong Kong-CHN	1,026[5]	(11.3)	586	(3.8)	138[5]	(2.9)	13	(0.3)	535	(3.4)	103[5]	(4.6)	10	(0.4)
Hungary	836	(12.2)	505	(3.5)	119	(1.9)	15	(0.3)	522	(3.1)	236	(4.8)	28 !	(13.1)
Indonesia	1,494[5]	(40.9)	386[7]	(4.3)	173[5]	(7.9)	12	(0.6)	406	(4.5)	190[5]	(12.2)	10	(0.5)
Iran, Islamic Republic of	994	(15.9)	415[7]	(4.3)	124	(3.3)	13	(0.3)	474	(4.0)	120	(3.6)	12	(0.4)
Israel[12]	1,108[5]	(14.1)	516	(4.1)	165[5]	(3.0)	15	(0.2)	516	(4.0)	132	(3.9)	12	(0.4)
Italy	1,085	(9.4)	498	(2.4)	155	(2.5)	14	(0.2)	501	(2.5)	73	(1.0)	7	(0.1)
Japan	1,016	(6.7)	570	(2.6)	108	(1.4)	11	(0.1)	558	(2.4)	128	(1.7)	12	(0.3)
Jordan	1,041	(11.9)	406[7]	(3.7)	130	(3.8)	13	(0.4)	449	(4.0)	134	(3.1)	13	(0.4)
Kazakhstan	920	(9.9)	487	(4.0)	117	(3.2)	13	(0.4)	490	(4.3)	244	(4.8)	27 !	(11.0)
Korea, Republic of	1,006	(12.1)	613	(2.9)	137	(1.8)	13	(0.2)	560	(2.0)	126	(2.5)	11	(0.2)
Lebanon	1,028[5]	(12.7)	449	(3.7)	178[5]	(3.9)	17	(0.4)	406	(4.9)	‡	(†)	‡	(†)
Lithuania[9]	898	(13.9)	502	(2.5)	132	(2.7)	15	(0.4)	514	(2.6)	251[5]	(5.2)	‡	(†)
Macedonia, Republic of	1,023[5]	(21.4)	426[7]	(5.2)	122[6]	(4.6)	13	(0.6)	407	(5.4)	334[6]	(14.7)	‡	(†)
Malaysia	1,198[5]	(13.7)	440	(5.4)	123[5]	(3.4)	10	(0.3)	426	(6.3)	126	(3.6)	10	(0.3)
Morocco	1,303[5]	(24.9)	371[11]	(2.0)	148[5]	(2.1)	12	(0.2)	376	(2.2)	144[5]	(2.0)	‡	(†)
New Zealand	959	(4.4)	488	(5.5)	141	(1.8)	15	(0.2)	512	(4.6)	130[5]	(2.6)	14	(0.3)
Norway	880	(6.3)	475	(2.4)	125	(3.4)	14	(0.4)	494	(2.6)	101	(3.3)	11	(0.4)
Oman	1,044[5]	(17.7)	366[7]	(2.8)	161[5]	(5.1)	16	(0.4)	420	(3.2)	161[6]	(3.8)	16	(0.3)
Palestinian National Authority	918	(7.3)	404[7]	(3.5)	134	(4.0)	15	(0.4)	420	(3.2)	107	(3.4)	12	(0.4)
Qatar	1,054	(1.3)	410[7]	(3.1)	162	(3.6)	15	(0.4)	419	(3.4)	131	(6.9)	12	(0.5)
Romania	984	(15.5)	458	(4.0)	145	(3.7)	15	(0.3)	465	(3.5)	281	(10.1)	‡	(†)
Russian Federation[13]	882	(8.7)	539	(3.6)	142	(2.0)	16	(0.3)	542	(3.2)	208	(1.6)	24 !	(8.8)
Saudi Arabia	1,050[5]	(20.9)	394[7]	(4.6)	134[5]	(5.4)	13	(0.4)	436	(3.9)	124[5]	(6.8)	12	(0.5)
Singapore[13]	1,106	(#)	611	(3.8)	138	(1.7)	13	(0.2)	590	(4.3)	115	(2.1)	11	(0.2)
Slovenia	798	(#)	505	(2.2)	121	(1.5)	15	(0.2)	543	(2.7)	251	(4.6)	31	(4.6)
Sweden	969[5]	(13.4)	484	(1.9)	97[6]	(2.2)	10	(0.3)	509	(2.5)	94[6]	(3.1)	9	(0.4)
Syrian Arab Republic	811	(14.2)	380[7]	(4.5)	118[5]	(4.7)	15	(0.5)	426	(3.9)	150[5]	(7.5)	‡	(†)
Thailand	1,270[5]	(15.1)	427	(4.3)	129	(4.3)	10	(0.3)	451	(3.9)	119	(2.9)	9	(0.3)
Tunisia	1,299[5]	(25.4)	425	(2.8)	131[5]	(3.0)	10	(0.2)	439	(2.5)	64[5]	(1.9)	5	(0.1)
Turkey	889	(16.7)	452	(3.9)	117	(1.8)	14	(0.3)	483	(3.4)	99	(1.1)	12	(0.2)
Ukraine	901	(10.7)	479	(3.9)	132	(3.5)	15	(0.4)	501	(3.4)	239	(4.0)	27 !	(11.4)
United Arab Emirates	1,046[5]	(8.0)	456	(2.1)	157[5]	(2.9)	15	(0.3)	465	(2.4)	115[6]	(2.7)	11	(0.3)
United States[13]	1,114	(6.6)	509	(2.6)	157[6]	(3.2)	14	(0.3)	525	(2.6)	139[14]	(2.4)	13[14]	(0.2)
Benchmarking education systems														
Abu Dhabi-UAE[13]	1,045[5]	(16.6)	449	(3.7)	158[5]	(5.8)	15	(0.5)	461	(4.0)	111[6]	(4.8)	11	(0.5)
Alabama-USA[9,15]	1,135[5]	(16.0)	466	(5.9)	166[6]	(8.9)	15	(0.9)	485	(6.2)	167[6]	(6.0)	15	(0.5)
Alberta-CAN[13]	1,031	(10.0)	505	(2.6)	156	(4.2)	19	(0.4)	546	(2.4)	145[5]	(4.0)	10	(0.4)
California-USA[9,13,15]	1,040[5]	(15.2)	493	(4.9)	173[6]	(8.0)	17	(0.7)	499	(4.6)	‡	(†)	14	(0.7)
Colorado-USA[9,15]	1,148	(17.0)	518	(4.9)	173[5]	(8.6)	15	(0.8)	542	(4.4)	138[6]	(6.0)	12	(0.5)

See notes at end of table.

Table 602.30. Average eighth-grade scores and annual instructional time in mathematics and science, by country or other education system: 2011—Continued

[Standard errors appear in parentheses]

Country or other education system[1]	Total instructional hours per year	Mathematics			Science		
		Average score[2]	Instructional time in mathematics		Average score[2]	Instructional time in science[3]	
			Hours per year	As a percent of total instructional hours		Hours per year	As a percent of total instructional hours
1	2	3	4	5	6	7	8
Connecticut-USA[9,13,15]	1,071 (19.3)	518 (4.8)	144 [5] (4.4)	14 (0.5)	532 (4.6)	139 [6] (6.2)	13 (0.6)
Dubai-UAE	1,022 [5] (1.5)	478 (2.1)	155 [5] (3.6)	15 (0.3)	485 (2.5)	125 [6] (3.6)	11 (0.3)
Florida-USA[9,13,15]	1,119 [5] (17.0)	513 (6.4)	144 [6] (7.4)	13 (0.7)	530 (7.3)	‡ (†)	13 (0.8)
Indiana-USA[9,13,15]	1,133 [5] (14.9)	522 (5.1)	149 [6] (6.9)	13 (0.7)	533 (4.8)	132 [6] (6.5)	12 (0.6)
Massachusetts-USA[9,13,15]	1,087 (13.6)	561 (5.3)	154 [5] (5.4)	14 (0.6)	567 (5.1)	156 [6] (6.1)	15 (0.6)
Minnesota-USA[9,15]	1,043 (14.8)	545 (4.6)	142 [5] (7.5)	14 (0.7)	553 (4.6)	140 [6] (8.3)	14 (0.9)
North Carolina-USA[9,12,15]	1,159 (16.0)	537 (6.8)	185 [6] (9.7)	16 (0.8)	532 (6.3)	‡ (†)	16 (1.2)
Ontario-CAN[13]	971 [5] (7.5)	512 (2.5)	181 [5] (3.9)	16 (0.5)	521 (2.5)	96 [5] (3.5)	11 (0.3)
Quebec-CAN	913 (3.3)	532 (2.3)	147 (4.1)	15 (0.5)	520 (2.5)	102 [5] (3.0)	14 (0.4)

†Not applicable.
#Rounds to zero.
!Interpret data with caution. The coefficient of variation (CV) for this estimate is between 30 and 50 percent.
‡Reporting standards not met. Either data are available for less than 50 percent of the students or the coefficient of variation (CV) is 50 percent or greater.
[1]Most of the education systems represent complete countries, but some represent subnational entities such as U.S. states, Canadian provinces, and England (which is part of the United Kingdom). The name of each subnational entity appears in italics and includes as a suffix the three-letter International Organization for Standardization (ISO) abbreviation for its complete country. Examples include _Florida-USA_, _Ontario-CAN_, and _England-GBR_.
[2]Trends in International Mathematics and Science Study (TIMSS) scores are reported on a scale from 0 to 1,000, with the scale average set at 500 and the standard deviation set at 100.
[3]General/integrated science instructional time is shown for the 27 participating countries that teach science as a general or integrated subject at the eighth grade. For the 15 participating countries that teach the sciences as separate subjects (biology, chemistry, etc.) at the eighth grade, total instructional time across science subjects is shown.
[4]The TIMSS average includes only education systems that are members of the International Association for the Evaluation of Educational Achievement (IAE), which develops and implements TIMSS at the international level. "Benchmarking" education systems are not members of the IEA and are therefore not included in the average.
[5]Data are available for at least 70 percent but less than 85 percent of students.
[6]Data are available for at least 50 percent but less than 70 percent of students.
[7]The TIMSS & PIRLS International Study Center has reservations about the reliability of the average achievement score because the percentage of students with achievement too low for estimation exceeds 15 percent, though it is less than 25 percent.
[8]Nearly satisfied guidelines for sample participation rate after replacement schools were included.

[9]National Target Population does not include all of the International Target Population defined by TIMSS.
[10]Exclusion rates for Georgia are slightly underestimated as some conflict zones were not covered and no official statistics were available.
[11]The TIMSS & PIRLS International Study Center has reservations about the reliability of the average achievement score because the percentage of students with achievement too low for estimation exceeds 25 percent.
[12]National Defined Population covers less than 90 percent of National Target Population (but at least 77 percent).
[13]National Defined Population covers 90 to 95 percent of National Target Population.
[14]Data are for 2007 and are from _TIMSS 2007 International Results in Science_. Met guidelines for sample participation rates only after replacement schools were included. Data are available for at least 50 percent but less than 70 percent of students.
[15]All U.S. state data are based on public school students only.
NOTE: Countries were required to sample students in the grade that corresponded to the end of 8 years of formal schooling, providing that the mean age at the time of testing was at least 13.5 years. Instructional times shown in this table are actual or implemented times (as opposed to intended times prescribed by the curriculum). Principals reported total instructional hours per day and school days per year. Total instructional hours per year were calculated by multiplying the number of school days per year by the number of instructional hours per day. Teachers reported instructional hours per week in mathematics and science. Instructional hours per year in mathematics and science were calculated by dividing weekly instructional hours by the number of school days per week and then multiplying by the number of school days per year.
SOURCE: International Association for the Evaluation of Educational Achievement (IEA), Trends in International Mathematics and Science Study (TIMSS), 2011; _TIMSS 2011 International Results in Mathematics_, by Ina V.S. Mullis et al.; and _TIMSS 2011 International Results in Science_, by Michael O. Martin et al. (This table was prepared December 2012.)

Table 602.40. Average reading literacy, mathematics literacy, and science literacy scores of 15-year-old students, by sex and country or other education system: 2009 and 2012

[Standard errors appear in parentheses]

Country or other education system	Reading literacy 2009	2012 Total	2012 Male	2012 Female	Mathematics literacy 2009	2012 Total	2012 Male	2012 Female	Science literacy 2009	2012 Total	2012 Male	2012 Female
1	2	3	4	5	6	7	8	9	10	11	12	13
OECD average[1]	493 (0.5)	496 (0.5)	478 (0.6)	515 (0.5)	496 (0.5)	494 (0.5)	499 (0.6)	489 (0.5)	501 (0.5)	501 (0.5)	502 (0.6)	500 (0.5)
Australia	515 (2.3)	512 (1.6)	495 (2.3)	530 (2.0)	514 (2.5)	504 (1.6)	510 (2.4)	498 (2.0)	527 (2.5)	521 (1.8)	524 (2.5)	519 (2.1)
Austria	470 (2.9)	490 (2.8)	471 (4.0)	508 (3.4)	496 (2.7)	506 (2.7)	517 (3.9)	494 (3.3)	494 (3.2)	506 (2.7)	510 (3.9)	501 (3.4)
Belgium	506 (2.3)	509 (2.3)	493 (3.0)	525 (2.7)	515 (2.3)	515 (2.1)	520 (2.9)	509 (2.6)	507 (2.5)	505 (2.2)	507 (3.0)	503 (2.6)
Canada	524 (1.5)	523 (1.9)	506 (2.3)	541 (2.1)	527 (1.6)	518 (1.8)	523 (2.1)	513 (2.1)	529 (1.6)	525 (1.9)	527 (2.4)	524 (2.0)
Chile	449 (3.1)	441 (2.9)	430 (3.8)	452 (3.2)	421 (3.1)	423 (3.1)	436 (3.8)	411 (3.1)	447 (2.9)	445 (2.9)	448 (3.7)	442 (2.9)
Czech Republic	478 (2.9)	493 (2.9)	474 (3.3)	513 (3.4)	493 (2.8)	499 (2.9)	505 (3.7)	493 (3.6)	500 (3.0)	508 (3.0)	509 (3.7)	508 (3.5)
Denmark	495 (2.1)	496 (2.6)	481 (3.3)	512 (2.6)	503 (2.6)	500 (2.3)	507 (2.9)	493 (2.3)	499 (2.5)	498 (2.7)	504 (3.5)	493 (2.5)
Estonia	501 (2.6)	516 (2.0)	494 (2.4)	538 (2.3)	512 (2.6)	521 (2.0)	523 (2.6)	518 (2.2)	528 (2.7)	541 (1.9)	540 (2.5)	543 (2.3)
Finland	536 (2.3)	524 (2.4)	494 (3.1)	556 (2.4)	541 (2.2)	519 (1.9)	517 (2.6)	520 (2.2)	554 (2.3)	545 (2.2)	537 (3.0)	554 (2.3)
France	496 (3.4)	505 (2.8)	483 (3.8)	527 (3.0)	497 (3.1)	495 (2.5)	499 (3.4)	491 (2.5)	498 (3.6)	499 (2.6)	498 (3.8)	500 (2.4)
Germany	497 (2.7)	508 (2.8)	486 (2.9)	530 (3.1)	513 (2.9)	514 (2.9)	520 (3.0)	507 (3.4)	520 (2.8)	524 (3.0)	524 (3.1)	524 (3.5)
Greece	483 (4.3)	477 (3.3)	452 (4.1)	502 (3.1)	466 (3.9)	453 (2.5)	457 (3.3)	449 (2.6)	470 (4.0)	467 (3.1)	460 (3.8)	473 (3.0)
Hungary	494 (3.2)	488 (3.2)	468 (3.9)	508 (3.3)	490 (3.5)	477 (3.2)	482 (3.7)	473 (3.6)	503 (3.1)	494 (2.9)	496 (3.4)	493 (3.3)
Iceland	500 (1.4)	483 (1.8)	457 (2.4)	508 (2.5)	507 (1.4)	493 (1.7)	490 (2.3)	496 (2.3)	496 (1.4)	478 (2.1)	477 (2.7)	480 (2.9)
Ireland	496 (3.0)	523 (2.6)	509 (3.5)	538 (3.0)	487 (2.5)	501 (2.2)	509 (3.3)	494 (2.6)	508 (3.3)	522 (2.5)	524 (3.4)	520 (3.1)
Israel	474 (3.6)	486 (5.0)	463 (8.2)	507 (3.9)	447 (3.3)	466 (4.7)	472 (7.8)	461 (3.5)	455 (3.1)	470 (5.0)	470 (7.9)	470 (4.0)
Italy	486 (1.6)	490 (2.0)	471 (2.5)	510 (2.3)	483 (1.9)	485 (2.0)	494 (2.4)	476 (2.2)	489 (1.8)	494 (1.9)	495 (2.2)	492 (2.4)
Japan	520 (3.5)	538 (3.7)	527 (4.7)	551 (3.6)	529 (3.3)	536 (3.6)	545 (4.6)	527 (3.6)	539 (3.4)	547 (3.6)	552 (4.7)	541 (3.5)
Korea, Republic of	539 (3.5)	536 (3.9)	525 (5.0)	548 (4.5)	546 (4.0)	554 (4.6)	562 (5.6)	544 (5.1)	538 (3.4)	538 (3.7)	539 (4.7)	536 (4.2)
Luxembourg	472 (1.3)	488 (1.5)	473 (1.9)	503 (1.8)	489 (1.2)	490 (1.1)	502 (1.5)	477 (1.4)	484 (1.2)	491 (1.3)	499 (1.7)	483 (1.7)
Mexico	425 (2.0)	424 (1.5)	411 (1.7)	435 (1.6)	419 (1.8)	413 (1.4)	420 (1.6)	406 (1.4)	416 (1.8)	415 (1.3)	418 (1.5)	412 (1.3)
Netherlands	508 (5.1)	511 (3.5)	498 (4.0)	525 (3.5)	526 (4.7)	523 (3.5)	528 (3.6)	518 (3.9)	522 (5.4)	522 (3.5)	524 (3.7)	520 (3.9)
New Zealand	521 (2.4)	512 (2.4)	495 (3.3)	530 (3.5)	519 (2.3)	500 (2.2)	507 (3.2)	492 (2.9)	532 (2.6)	516 (2.1)	518 (3.2)	513 (3.3)
Norway	503 (2.6)	504 (3.2)	481 (3.3)	528 (3.9)	498 (2.4)	489 (2.7)	490 (2.8)	488 (3.4)	500 (2.6)	495 (3.1)	493 (3.2)	496 (3.7)
Poland	500 (2.6)	518 (3.1)	497 (3.7)	539 (3.1)	495 (2.8)	518 (3.6)	520 (4.3)	516 (3.8)	508 (2.4)	526 (3.1)	524 (3.7)	527 (3.2)
Portugal	489 (3.1)	488 (3.8)	468 (4.2)	508 (3.7)	487 (2.9)	487 (3.8)	493 (4.1)	481 (3.9)	493 (2.9)	489 (3.7)	488 (4.1)	490 (3.8)
Slovak Republic	477 (2.5)	463 (4.2)	444 (4.6)	483 (5.1)	497 (3.1)	482 (3.4)	486 (4.1)	477 (4.1)	490 (3.0)	471 (3.6)	475 (4.3)	467 (4.2)
Slovenia	483 (1.0)	481 (1.2)	454 (1.7)	510 (1.8)	501 (1.2)	501 (1.2)	503 (2.0)	499 (2.0)	512 (1.1)	514 (1.3)	510 (1.9)	519 (1.9)
Spain	481 (2.0)	488 (1.9)	474 (2.3)	503 (1.9)	483 (2.1)	484 (1.9)	492 (2.4)	476 (2.0)	488 (2.1)	496 (1.8)	500 (2.3)	493 (1.9)
Sweden	497 (2.9)	483 (3.0)	458 (4.0)	509 (2.8)	494 (2.9)	478 (2.3)	477 (3.0)	480 (2.4)	495 (2.7)	485 (3.0)	481 (3.9)	489 (2.8)
Switzerland	501 (2.4)	509 (2.6)	491 (3.1)	527 (2.5)	534 (3.3)	531 (3.0)	537 (3.5)	524 (3.1)	517 (2.8)	515 (2.7)	518 (3.3)	512 (2.7)
Turkey	464 (3.5)	475 (4.2)	453 (4.6)	499 (4.3)	445 (4.4)	448 (4.8)	452 (5.1)	444 (5.7)	454 (3.6)	463 (3.9)	458 (4.5)	469 (4.3)
United Kingdom	494 (2.3)	499 (3.5)	487 (4.5)	512 (3.8)	492 (2.4)	494 (3.3)	500 (4.2)	488 (3.8)	514 (2.5)	514 (3.4)	521 (4.5)	508 (3.7)
United States	500 (3.7)	498 (3.7)	482 (4.1)	513 (3.8)	487 (3.6)	481 (3.6)	484 (3.8)	479 (3.9)	502 (3.6)	497 (3.8)	497 (4.1)	498 (4.0)
Non-OECD education systems												
Albania	385 (4.0)	394 (3.2)	387 (3.8)	401 (3.7)	377 (4.0)	394 (2.0)	394 (2.6)	395 (2.6)	391 (3.9)	397 (2.4)	394 (3.0)	401 (2.9)
Argentina	398 (4.6)	396 (3.7)	377 (4.5)	414 (3.6)	388 (4.1)	388 (3.5)	396 (4.2)	382 (3.4)	401 (4.6)	406 (3.9)	402 (4.5)	409 (4.0)
Brazil	412 (2.7)	410 (2.1)	394 (2.4)	425 (2.2)	386 (2.4)	391 (2.1)	401 (2.2)	383 (2.3)	405 (2.4)	405 (2.1)	406 (2.3)	404 (2.3)
Bulgaria	429 (6.7)	436 (6.0)	403 (6.3)	472 (5.6)	428 (5.9)	439 (4.0)	438 (4.7)	440 (4.2)	439 (5.9)	446 (4.8)	437 (5.6)	457 (4.6)
Chinese Taipei	— (†)	523 (3.0)	507 (4.3)	539 (4.3)	— (†)	560 (3.3)	563 (5.4)	557 (5.7)	— (†)	523 (2.3)	524 (3.9)	523 (4.0)
Colombia	413 (3.7)	403 (3.4)	394 (3.9)	412 (3.8)	381 (3.2)	376 (2.9)	390 (3.4)	364 (3.2)	402 (3.6)	399 (3.1)	408 (3.4)	390 (3.6)
Connecticut-USA[2]	— (†)	521 (6.5)	510 (7.1)	532 (6.7)	— (†)	506 (6.2)	513 (6.9)	499 (6.3)	— (†)	521 (5.7)	528 (6.2)	514 (6.1)
Costa Rica	— (†)	441 (3.5)	427 (3.9)	452 (3.5)	— (†)	407 (3.0)	420 (3.6)	396 (3.1)	— (†)	429 (2.9)	436 (3.5)	424 (3.2)
Croatia	476 (2.9)	485 (3.3)	461 (4.1)	509 (3.3)	460 (3.1)	471 (3.5)	477 (4.4)	465 (3.7)	486 (2.8)	491 (3.1)	490 (3.9)	493 (3.3)
Cyprus	— (†)	449 (1.2)	418 (1.9)	481 (1.9)	— (†)	440 (1.1)	440 (1.5)	440 (1.6)	— (†)	438 (1.2)	431 (1.8)	444 (1.7)
Florida-USA[2]	— (†)	492 (6.1)	481 (7.0)	503 (5.9)	— (†)	467 (5.8)	474 (6.3)	460 (6.0)	— (†)	485 (6.4)	491 (7.4)	478 (6.2)
Hong Kong-China	533 (2.1)	545 (2.8)	533 (3.8)	558 (3.3)	555 (2.7)	561 (3.2)	568 (4.6)	553 (3.9)	549 (2.8)	555 (2.6)	558 (3.6)	551 (3.1)
Indonesia	402 (3.7)	396 (4.2)	382 (4.8)	410 (4.3)	371 (3.7)	375 (4.0)	377 (4.4)	373 (4.3)	383 (3.8)	382 (3.8)	380 (4.1)	383 (4.1)
Jordan	405 (3.3)	399 (3.6)	361 (5.5)	436 (3.1)	387 (3.7)	386 (3.1)	375 (5.4)	396 (3.1)	415 (3.5)	409 (3.1)	388 (5.4)	430 (2.9)
Kazakhstan	390 (3.1)	393 (2.7)	374 (3.4)	411 (2.6)	405 (3.0)	432 (3.0)	432 (3.4)	432 (3.3)	400 (3.1)	425 (3.0)	420 (3.4)	429 (3.2)
Latvia	484 (3.0)	489 (2.4)	462 (3.3)	516 (2.7)	482 (3.1)	491 (2.8)	489 (3.4)	493 (3.2)	494 (3.1)	502 (2.8)	495 (3.6)	510 (2.8)
Liechtenstein	499 (2.8)	516 (4.1)	504 (6.2)	529 (5.8)	536 (4.1)	535 (4.0)	546 (6.0)	523 (5.8)	520 (3.4)	525 (3.5)	533 (5.8)	516 (5.7)
Lithuania	468 (2.4)	477 (2.5)	450 (2.8)	505 (2.6)	477 (2.6)	479 (2.6)	479 (2.8)	479 (3.0)	491 (2.9)	496 (2.6)	488 (3.0)	503 (2.6)
Macao-China	487 (0.9)	509 (0.9)	492 (1.4)	527 (1.1)	525 (0.9)	538 (1.0)	540 (1.4)	537 (1.3)	511 (1.0)	521 (0.8)	520 (1.3)	521 (1.2)
Malaysia	— (†)	398 (3.3)	377 (3.9)	418 (3.3)	— (†)	421 (3.2)	416 (3.7)	424 (3.7)	— (†)	420 (3.0)	414 (3.8)	425 (3.1)
Montenegro, Republic of	408 (1.7)	422 (1.2)	391 (2.3)	453 (1.5)	403 (2.0)	410 (1.1)	410 (1.6)	410 (1.6)	401 (2.0)	410 (1.1)	402 (1.6)	419 (1.6)
Peru	370 (4.0)	384 (4.3)	373 (4.0)	395 (4.4)	365 (4.0)	368 (3.7)	378 (3.6)	359 (4.8)	369 (3.5)	373 (3.6)	376 (3.5)	370 (4.6)
Massachusetts-USA[2]	— (†)	527 (6.1)	511 (6.2)	542 (6.6)	— (†)	514 (6.2)	518 (6.3)	509 (7.1)	— (†)	527 (6.0)	529 (6.1)	526 (6.8)
Qatar	372 (0.8)	388 (0.8)	354 (1.1)	424 (1.2)	368 (0.7)	376 (0.8)	369 (1.1)	385 (0.9)	379 (0.9)	384 (0.7)	367 (1.2)	402 (1.1)
Romania	424 (4.1)	438 (4.0)	417 (4.5)	457 (4.2)	427 (3.4)	445 (3.8)	447 (4.3)	443 (4.0)	428 (3.4)	439 (3.3)	436 (3.7)	441 (3.5)
Russian Federation	459 (3.3)	475 (3.0)	455 (3.5)	495 (3.2)	468 (3.3)	482 (3.0)	481 (3.7)	483 (3.1)	478 (3.3)	486 (2.9)	484 (3.5)	489 (2.9)
Serbia, Republic of	442 (2.4)	446 (3.4)	423 (3.9)	469 (3.8)	442 (2.9)	449 (3.4)	453 (4.1)	444 (3.7)	443 (2.4)	445 (3.4)	443 (4.0)	447 (3.8)
Shanghai-China	556 (2.4)	570 (2.9)	557 (3.3)	581 (2.8)	600 (2.8)	613 (3.3)	616 (4.0)	610 (3.4)	575 (2.3)	580 (3.0)	583 (3.5)	578 (3.1)
Singapore	526 (1.1)	542 (1.4)	527 (1.9)	559 (1.9)	562 (1.4)	573 (1.3)	572 (1.9)	575 (1.8)	542 (1.4)	551 (1.5)	551 (2.1)	552 (1.9)
Thailand	421 (2.6)	441 (3.1)	410 (3.6)	465 (3.3)	419 (3.2)	427 (3.4)	419 (3.6)	433 (4.1)	425 (3.0)	444 (2.9)	433 (3.3)	452 (3.4)
Tunisia	404 (2.9)	404 (4.5)	388 (5.0)	418 (4.4)	371 (3.0)	388 (3.9)	396 (4.3)	381 (4.0)	401 (2.7)	398 (3.5)	399 (3.9)	398 (3.6)
United Arab Emirates	— (†)	442 (2.5)	413 (3.9)	469 (3.2)	— (†)	434 (2.4)	432 (3.8)	436 (3.0)	— (†)	448 (2.8)	434 (4.1)	462 (3.7)
Uruguay	426 (2.6)	411 (3.2)	392 (3.9)	428 (3.2)	427 (2.6)	409 (2.8)	415 (3.5)	404 (2.9)	427 (2.6)	416 (2.8)	415 (3.4)	416 (3.1)
Vietnam	— (†)	508 (4.4)	492 (5.0)	523 (4.0)	— (†)	511 (4.8)	517 (5.6)	507 (4.7)	— (†)	528 (4.3)	529 (5.0)	528 (4.1)

—Not available.
†Not applicable.
[1]Refers to the mean of the data values for all Organization for Economic Cooperation and Development (OECD) countries, to which each country contributes equally regardless of the absolute size of the student population of each country.

[2]Results are for public school students only.
NOTE: Program for International Student Assessment (PISA) scores are reported on a scale from 0 to 1,000.
SOURCE: Organization for Economic Cooperation and Development (OECD), Program for International Student Assessment (PISA), 2009 and 2012. (This table was prepared July 2014.)

Table 602.50. Average reading literacy scores of 15-year-old students and percentage attaining reading literacy proficiency levels, by country or other education system: 2012

[Standard errors appear in parentheses]

Country or other education system	Average reading literacy score	Percentage attaining reading literacy proficiency levels[1]									
		Below level 2				At level 2	At level 3	At level 4	At or above level 5		
		Total below level 2	Below level 1b	At level 1b	At level 1a				Total at or above level 5	At level 5	At level 6
1	2	3	4	5	6	7	8	9	10	11	12
OECD average[2]	496 (0.5)	18.0 (0.18)	1.3 (0.05)	4.4 (0.08)	12.3 (0.13)	23.5 (0.16)	29.1 (0.17)	21.0 (0.16)	8.4 (0.12)	7.3 (0.10)	1.1 (0.04)
Australia	512 (1.6)	14.2 (0.46)	0.9 (0.11)	3.1 (0.21)	10.2 (0.42)	21.6 (0.47)	29.1 (0.53)	23.3 (0.51)	11.7 (0.54)	9.8 (0.46)	1.9 (0.19)
Austria	490 (2.8)	19.5 (1.07)	0.8 (0.24)	4.8 (0.64)	13.8 (0.84)	24.2 (0.89)	29.6 (0.92)	21.2 (0.94)	5.5 (0.61)	5.2 (0.59)	0.3 (0.10)
Belgium	509 (2.3)	16.2 (0.77)	1.6 (0.31)	4.1 (0.40)	10.4 (0.55)	20.4 (0.62)	27.3 (0.70)	24.4 (0.71)	12.3 (0.55)	10.4 (0.54)	1.4 (0.17)
Canada	523 (1.9)	10.9 (0.45)	0.5 (0.09)	2.4 (0.19)	8.0 (0.36)	19.4 (0.55)	31.0 (0.72)	25.8 (0.59)	12.9 (0.62)	10.8 (0.53)	2.1 (0.22)
Chile	441 (2.9)	33.0 (1.67)	1.0 (0.19)	8.1 (0.79)	23.9 (1.08)	35.1 (1.08)	24.3 (1.06)	6.9 (0.62)	0.6 (0.10)	0.6 (0.11)	‡ (†)
Czech Republic	493 (2.9)	16.9 (1.21)	0.6! (0.27)	3.5 (0.56)	12.7 (0.94)	26.4 (1.30)	31.3 (1.23)	19.4 (1.13)	6.1 (0.55)	5.3 (0.49)	0.8 (0.16)
Denmark	496 (2.6)	14.6 (1.07)	0.8! (0.30)	3.1 (0.39)	10.7 (0.77)	25.8 (0.92)	33.6 (0.85)	20.5 (0.86)	5.4 (0.62)	5.1 (0.58)	0.4! (0.12)
Estonia	516 (2.0)	9.1 (0.65)	‡ (†)	1.3 (0.28)	7.7 (0.61)	22.7 (0.94)	35.0 (1.06)	24.9 (1.08)	8.3 (0.72)	7.5 (0.71)	0.9 (0.18)
Finland	524 (2.4)	11.3 (0.71)	0.7 (0.16)	2.4 (0.38)	8.2 (0.57)	19.1 (0.81)	29.3 (0.70)	26.8 (0.84)	13.5 (0.64)	11.3 (0.60)	2.2 (0.26)
France	505 (2.8)	18.9 (0.98)	2.1 (0.40)	4.9 (0.43)	11.9 (0.70)	18.9 (0.85)	26.3 (0.84)	23.0 (0.67)	12.9 (0.85)	10.6 (0.62)	2.3 (0.41)
Germany	508 (2.8)	14.5 (0.91)	0.5! (0.18)	3.3 (0.40)	10.7 (0.67)	22.1 (0.93)	29.9 (0.86)	24.6 (0.88)	8.9 (0.70)	8.3 (0.64)	0.7! (0.23)
Greece	477 (3.3)	22.6 (1.24)	2.6 (0.40)	5.9 (0.64)	14.2 (0.83)	25.1 (1.06)	30.0 (1.02)	17.2 (1.19)	5.1 (0.61)	4.6 (0.59)	0.5 (0.13)
Hungary	488 (3.2)	19.7 (1.22)	0.7! (0.24)	5.2 (0.64)	13.8 (0.88)	24.3 (1.17)	29.9 (1.00)	20.4 (1.05)	5.6 (0.75)	5.3 (0.68)	0.4! (0.13)
Iceland	483 (1.8)	21.0 (0.72)	2.3 (0.33)	5.4 (0.47)	13.3 (0.92)	24.7 (0.92)	29.9 (1.09)	18.6 (1.12)	5.8 (0.51)	5.2 (0.41)	0.6! (0.21)
Ireland	523 (2.6)	9.6 (0.88)	0.3! (0.13)	1.9 (0.35)	7.5 (0.69)	19.6 (1.19)	33.4 (1.17)	26.0 (0.90)	11.4 (0.65)	10.1 (0.67)	1.3 (0.35)
Israel	486 (5.0)	23.6 (1.64)	3.8 (0.59)	6.9 (0.74)	12.9 (0.96)	20.8 (0.87)	25.3 (0.81)	20.6 (1.03)	9.6 (0.84)	8.1 (0.77)	1.5 (0.30)
Italy	490 (2.0)	19.5 (0.67)	1.6 (0.15)	5.2 (0.29)	12.7 (0.48)	23.7 (0.57)	29.7 (0.53)	20.5 (0.62)	6.7 (0.35)	6.1 (0.33)	0.6 (0.07)
Japan	538 (3.7)	9.8 (0.92)	0.6 (0.16)	2.4 (0.37)	6.7 (0.67)	16.6 (0.89)	26.7 (0.98)	28.4 (1.08)	18.5 (1.27)	14.6 (0.99)	3.9 (0.59)
Korea, Republic of	536 (3.9)	7.6 (0.89)	0.4 (0.13)	1.7 (0.39)	5.5 (0.60)	16.4 (0.94)	30.8 (1.00)	31.0 (1.06)	14.1 (1.24)	12.6 (1.05)	1.6 (0.32)
Luxembourg	488 (1.5)	22.2 (0.74)	2.0 (0.21)	6.3 (0.33)	13.8 (0.81)	23.4 (0.71)	25.8 (0.64)	19.7 (0.64)	8.9 (0.39)	7.5 (0.35)	1.4 (0.20)
Mexico	424 (1.5)	41.1 (0.90)	2.6 (0.22)	11.0 (0.70)	27.5 (0.70)	34.5 (0.62)	19.6 (0.54)	4.5 (0.25)	0.4 (0.09)	0.4 (0.08)	‡ (†)
Netherlands	511 (3.5)	14.0 (1.23)	‡ (†)	2.8 (0.46)	10.3 (0.93)	21.0 (1.27)	29.2 (1.32)	26.1 (1.36)	9.8 (0.82)	9.0 (0.72)	0.8 (0.19)
New Zealand	512 (2.4)	16.3 (0.83)	1.3 (0.28)	4.0 (0.46)	11.0 (0.67)	20.8 (0.76)	26.3 (1.06)	22.7 (1.06)	14.0 (0.77)	10.9 (0.62)	3.0 (0.37)
Norway	504 (3.2)	16.2 (1.03)	1.7 (0.31)	3.7 (0.36)	10.8 (0.69)	21.9 (1.03)	29.4 (1.35)	22.3 (1.21)	10.2 (0.74)	8.5 (0.61)	1.7 (0.31)
Poland	518 (3.1)	10.6 (0.80)	0.3! (0.11)	2.1 (0.35)	8.1 (0.74)	21.4 (0.90)	32.0 (0.89)	26.0 (0.96)	10.0 (0.93)	8.6 (0.76)	1.4 (0.37)
Portugal	488 (3.8)	18.8 (1.42)	1.3 (0.30)	5.1 (0.77)	12.3 (0.98)	25.5 (1.16)	30.2 (1.46)	19.7 (1.07)	5.8 (0.61)	5.3 (0.57)	0.5! (0.15)
Slovak Republic	463 (4.2)	28.2 (1.78)	4.1 (0.77)	7.9 (0.80)	16.2 (1.06)	25.0 (1.08)	26.8 (1.38)	15.7 (0.96)	4.4 (0.68)	4.1 (0.60)	‡ (†)
Slovenia	481 (1.2)	21.1 (0.68)	1.2 (0.14)	4.9 (0.37)	15.0 (0.71)	27.2 (0.77)	28.4 (0.94)	18.2 (0.63)	5.0 (0.43)	4.7 (0.45)	0.3! (0.12)
Spain	488 (1.9)	18.3 (0.76)	1.3 (0.17)	4.4 (0.38)	12.6 (0.47)	25.8 (0.81)	31.2 (0.68)	19.2 (0.62)	5.5 (0.30)	5.0 (0.30)	0.5 (0.10)
Sweden	483 (3.0)	22.7 (1.15)	2.9 (0.39)	6.0 (0.64)	13.9 (0.72)	23.5 (0.88)	27.3 (0.73)	18.6 (0.93)	7.9 (0.64)	6.7 (0.53)	1.2 (0.20)
Switzerland	509 (2.6)	13.7 (0.76)	0.5 (0.14)	2.9 (0.34)	10.3 (0.59)	21.9 (0.86)	31.5 (0.71)	23.8 (0.84)	9.1 (0.68)	8.2 (0.60)	1.0 (0.25)
Turkey	475 (4.2)	21.6 (1.43)	0.6 (0.15)	4.5 (0.57)	16.6 (1.07)	30.8 (1.39)	28.7 (1.34)	14.5 (1.39)	4.3 (0.85)	4.1 (0.79)	0.3! (0.13)
United Kingdom	499 (3.5)	16.6 (1.30)	1.5 (0.27)	4.0 (0.54)	11.2 (0.79)	23.5 (1.01)	29.9 (1.08)	21.3 (1.14)	8.8 (0.74)	7.5 (0.59)	1.3 (0.24)
United States	498 (3.7)	16.6 (1.26)	0.8! (0.24)	3.6 (0.49)	12.3 (0.89)	24.9 (0.99)	30.5 (0.88)	20.1 (1.08)	7.9 (0.67)	6.9 (0.59)	1.0 (0.22)

See notes at end of table.

Table 602.50. Average reading literacy scores of 15-year-old students and percentage attaining reading literacy proficiency levels, by country or other education system: 2012—Continued

[Standard errors appear in parentheses]

Country or other education system	Average reading literacy score	Percentage attaining reading literacy proficiency levels[1]									
		Below level 2				At level 2	At level 3	At level 4	At or above level 5		
		Total below level 2	Below level 1b	At level 1b	At level 1a				Total at or above level 5	At level 5	At level 6
1	2	3	4	5	6	7	8	9	10	11	12
Non-OECD education systems											
Albania	394 (3.2)	52.3 (1.28)	12.0 (0.84)	15.9 (1.00)	24.4 (1.23)	24.7 (1.01)	15.9 (0.73)	5.9 (0.61)	1.2 (0.25)	1.1 (0.24)	‡ (†)
Argentina	396 (3.7)	53.6 (1.73)	8.1 (0.80)	17.7 (1.20)	27.7 (1.34)	27.3 (1.12)	14.6 (0.91)	4.0 (0.57)	0.5 (0.14)	0.5 (0.15)	‡ (†)
Brazil	410 (2.1)	49.2 (1.13)	4.0 (0.36)	14.8 (0.64)	30.4 (0.79)	30.1 (0.77)	15.8 (0.63)	4.4 (0.37)	0.5 (0.12)	0.5 (0.12)	‡ (†)
Bulgaria	436 (6.0)	39.4 (2.21)	8.0 (1.07)	12.8 (1.15)	18.6 (1.10)	22.2 (1.16)	21.4 (1.10)	12.7 (1.03)	4.3 (0.64)	3.8 (0.56)	0.5 ! (0.18)
Chinese Taipei	523 (3.0)	11.5 (0.87)	0.6 (0.15)	2.5 (0.32)	8.4 (0.65)	18.1 (0.83)	29.9 (0.92)	28.7 (1.01)	11.8 (0.84)	10.4 (0.73)	1.4 (0.32)
Colombia	403 (3.4)	51.4 (1.78)	5.0 (0.76)	15.4 (0.98)	31.0 (1.29)	30.5 (1.22)	14.5 (0.91)	3.2 (0.50)	0.3 ! (0.13)	0.3 ! (0.12)	‡ (†)
Connecticut-USA[3]	521 (6.5)	13.2 (1.76)	‡ (†)	3.2 (0.87)	9.7 (1.26)	19.6 (1.49)	28.2 (1.32)	24.4 (1.83)	14.5 (1.68)	11.7 (1.38)	2.9 (0.54)
Costa Rica	441 (3.5)	32.4 (1.81)	0.8 ! (0.24)	7.3 (1.02)	24.3 (1.25)	38.1 (1.40)	22.9 (1.42)	6.0 (0.78)	0.6 ! (0.19)	0.6 ! (0.19)	‡ (†)
Croatia	485 (3.3)	18.7 (1.29)	0.7 ! (0.25)	4.0 (0.59)	13.9 (0.97)	27.8 (1.07)	31.2 (1.24)	17.8 (1.09)	4.4 (0.69)	4.2 (0.66)	0.2 ! (0.11)
Cyprus	449 (1.2)	32.8 (0.67)	6.1 (0.32)	9.7 (0.44)	17.0 (0.61)	25.1 (0.78)	24.9 (0.75)	13.2 (0.64)	4.0 (0.32)	3.5 (0.34)	0.5 (0.12)
Florida-USA[3]	492 (6.1)	17.5 (2.00)	0.7 ! (0.31)	3.6 (0.75)	13.2 (1.46)	25.8 (1.56)	30.9 (1.50)	20.4 (2.06)	5.5 (1.02)	4.9 (1.00)	‡ (†)
Hong Kong-China	545 (2.8)	6.8 (0.72)	0.2 ! (0.09)	1.3 (0.24)	5.3 (0.61)	14.3 (0.79)	29.2 (1.21)	32.9 (1.39)	16.8 (1.16)	14.9 (1.00)	1.9 (0.39)
Indonesia	396 (4.2)	55.2 (2.18)	4.1 (0.81)	16.3 (1.28)	34.8 (1.56)	31.6 (1.54)	11.5 (1.28)	1.5 ! (0.53)	‡ (†)	‡ (†)	‡ (†)
Jordan	399 (3.6)	50.7 (1.57)	7.5 (0.84)	14.9 (0.79)	28.3 (1.01)	30.8 (1.14)	15.5 (0.83)	2.9 (0.63)	‡ (†)	‡ (†)	‡ (†)
Kazakhstan	393 (2.7)	57.1 (1.56)	4.2 (0.47)	17.3 (1.24)	35.6 (1.15)	31.3 (1.12)	10.4 (0.87)	1.2 (0.24)	‡ (†)	‡ (†)	‡ (†)
Latvia	489 (2.4)	17.0 (1.14)	0.7 ! (0.24)	3.7 (0.54)	12.6 (0.96)	26.7 (1.31)	33.1 (1.05)	19.1 (0.88)	4.2 (0.55)	3.9 (0.56)	0.3 ! (0.11)
Liechtenstein	516 (4.1)	12.4 (1.88)	# (†)	‡ (†)	10.5 (1.85)	22.4 (3.44)	28.6 (4.53)	25.7 (2.44)	10.9 (2.89)	10.4 (2.44)	‡ (†)
Lithuania	477 (2.5)	21.2 (1.18)	1.0 (0.19)	4.6 (0.49)	15.6 (1.06)	28.1 (1.13)	31.1 (0.94)	16.3 (0.78)	3.3 (0.37)	3.1 (0.35)	0.2 ! (0.07)
Macao-China	509 (0.9)	11.5 (0.42)	0.3 ! (0.11)	2.1 (0.22)	9.0 (0.42)	23.3 (0.58)	34.3 (0.67)	24.0 (0.60)	7.0 (0.41)	6.4 (0.48)	0.6 ! (0.21)
Malaysia	398 (3.3)	52.7 (1.71)	5.8 (0.59)	16.4 (1.03)	30.5 (0.99)	31.0 (1.09)	13.6 (1.11)	2.5 (0.45)	‡ (†)	‡ (†)	‡ (†)
Massachusetts-USA[3]	527 (6.1)	11.5 (1.37)	‡ (†)	2.3 (0.55)	8.6 (1.19)	18.5 (1.76)	29.8 (1.52)	24.2 (1.82)	16.1 (1.98)	12.9 (1.59)	3.2 (0.86)
Montenegro, Republic of	422 (1.2)	43.3 (0.75)	4.4 (0.53)	13.2 (0.62)	25.7 (0.94)	29.2 (0.77)	19.9 (0.76)	6.6 (0.53)	1.0 (0.19)	0.9 (0.19)	‡ (†)
Peru	384 (4.3)	59.9 (1.95)	9.8 (0.87)	20.6 (1.11)	29.5 (0.98)	24.9 (1.02)	11.4 (0.96)	3.3 (0.61)	0.5 ! (0.21)	0.5 ! (0.21)	‡ (†)
Qatar	388 (0.8)	57.1 (0.42)	13.6 (0.32)	18.9 (0.87)	24.6 (0.44)	21.9 (0.50)	13.5 (0.43)	5.8 (0.21)	1.6 (0.14)	1.4 (0.13)	0.2 (0.05)
Romania	438 (4.0)	37.3 (1.87)	2.5 (0.38)	10.3 (0.82)	24.4 (1.28)	30.6 (1.12)	21.8 (1.17)	8.7 (0.88)	1.6 (0.38)	1.5 (0.35)	‡ (†)
Russian Federation	475 (3.0)	22.3 (1.29)	1.1 (0.18)	5.2 (0.49)	16.0 (1.03)	29.5 (1.08)	28.3 (1.05)	15.3 (0.93)	4.6 (0.58)	4.2 (0.51)	0.5 (0.12)
Serbia, Republic of	446 (3.4)	33.1 (1.66)	2.6 (0.40)	9.3 (0.73)	21.3 (1.09)	30.8 (1.20)	23.3 (1.15)	10.5 (0.81)	2.2 (0.41)	2.0 (0.39)	0.2 ! (0.08)
Shanghai-China	570 (2.9)	2.9 (0.39)	‡ (†)	0.3 ! (0.11)	2.5 (0.34)	11.0 (0.85)	25.3 (0.85)	35.7 (1.07)	25.1 (1.19)	21.3 (0.98)	3.8 (0.65)
Singapore	542 (1.4)	9.9 (0.42)	0.5 (0.12)	1.9 (0.27)	7.5 (0.41)	16.7 (0.65)	25.4 (0.66)	26.8 (0.79)	21.2 (0.60)	16.2 (0.73)	5.0 (0.43)
Thailand	441 (3.1)	33.0 (1.40)	1.2 (0.29)	7.7 (0.77)	24.1 (0.98)	36.0 (1.12)	23.5 (1.13)	6.7 (0.79)	0.8 (0.22)	0.8 (0.21)	‡ (†)
Tunisia	404 (4.5)	49.3 (2.24)	6.2 (0.91)	15.5 (1.20)	27.6 (1.31)	31.4 (1.43)	15.6 (1.15)	3.5 (0.69)	‡ (†)	‡ (†)	‡ (†)
United Arab Emirates	442 (2.5)	35.5 (1.08)	3.3 (0.34)	10.4 (0.65)	21.8 (0.72)	28.6 (0.72)	24.0 (0.77)	9.7 (0.58)	2.2 (0.29)	2.1 (0.28)	0.2 ! (0.06)
Uruguay	411 (3.2)	47.0 (1.42)	6.4 (0.70)	14.7 (0.84)	25.9 (0.88)	28.9 (1.00)	17.4 (0.71)	5.7 (0.62)	0.9 (0.27)	0.9 (0.26)	‡ (†)
Vietnam	508 (4.4)	9.4 (1.43)	‡ (†)	1.5 ! (0.48)	7.8 (1.10)	23.7 (1.40)	39.0 (1.47)	23.4 (1.47)	4.5 (0.81)	4.2 (0.71)	0.4 ! (0.16)

†Not applicable.
#Rounds to zero.
!Interpret data with caution. The coefficient of variation (CV) for this estimate is between 30 and 50 percent.
‡Reporting standards not met. Either there are too few cases for a reliable estimate or the coefficient of variation (CV) is 50 percent or greater.
[1]To reach a particular proficiency level, a student must correctly answer a majority of items at that level. Students were classified into reading literacy levels according to their scores. Exact cut scores are as follows: below level 1b (a score less than or equal to 262.04); level 1b (a score greater than 262.04 and less than or equal to 334.75); level 1a (a score greater than 334.75 and less than or equal to 407.47); level 2 (a score greater than 407.47 and less than or equal to 480.18); level 3 (a score greater than 480.18 and less than

or equal to 552.89); level 4 (a score greater than 552.89 and less than or equal to 625.61); level 5 (a score greater than 625.61 and less than or equal to 698.32); and level 6 (a score greater than 698.32).
[2]Refers to the mean of the data values for all Organization for Economic Cooperation and Development (OECD) countries, to which each country contributes equally, regardless of the absolute size of the student population of each country.
[3]Results are for public school students only.
NOTE: Program for International Student Assessment (PISA) scores are reported on a scale from 0 to 1,000. Detail may not sum to totals because of rounding.
SOURCE: Organization for Economic Cooperation and Development (OECD), Program for International Student Assessment (PISA), 2012. (This table was prepared November 2013.)

Table 602.60. Average mathematics literacy scores of 15-year-old students and percentage attaining mathematics literacy proficiency levels, by country or other education system: 2012

[Standard errors appear in parentheses]

Country or other education system	Average mathematics literacy score	Percentage attaining mathematics literacy proficiency levels[1] Below level 2			At level 2	At level 3	At level 4	At or above level 5 Total at or above level 5		
		Total below level 2	Below level 1	At level 1				Total at or above level 5	At level 5	At level 6
1	2	3	4	5	6	7	8	9	10	11
OECD average[2]	494 (0.5)	23.0 (0.17)	8.0 (0.12)	15.0 (0.13)	22.5 (0.15)	23.7 (0.15)	18.1 (0.14)	12.7 (0.14)	9.3 (0.11)	3.3 (0.08)
Australia	504 (1.6)	19.7 (0.60)	6.1 (0.35)	13.5 (0.57)	21.9 (0.76)	24.6 (0.65)	19.0 (0.50)	14.8 (0.64)	10.5 (0.43)	4.3 (0.36)
Austria	506 (2.7)	18.7 (0.96)	5.7 (0.59)	13.0 (0.74)	21.9 (0.87)	24.2 (0.84)	21.0 (0.90)	14.3 (0.95)	11.0 (0.75)	3.3 (0.41)
Belgium	515 (2.1)	19.0 (0.82)	7.0 (0.58)	12.0 (0.52)	18.4 (0.58)	22.4 (0.70)	20.6 (0.63)	19.5 (0.76)	13.4 (0.73)	6.1 (0.43)
Canada	518 (1.8)	13.8 (0.55)	3.6 (0.29)	10.2 (0.45)	21.0 (0.64)	26.4 (0.63)	22.4 (0.49)	16.4 (0.64)	12.1 (0.47)	4.3 (0.29)
Chile	423 (3.1)	51.5 (1.67)	22.0 (1.35)	29.5 (1.01)	25.3 (1.00)	15.4 (0.78)	6.2 (0.60)	1.6 (0.22)	1.5 (0.21)	0.1 ! (0.04)
Czech Republic	499 (2.9)	21.0 (1.20)	6.8 (0.76)	14.2 (0.97)	21.7 (0.83)	24.8 (1.07)	19.7 (0.90)	12.9 (0.82)	9.6 (0.66)	3.2 (0.31)
Denmark	500 (2.3)	16.8 (0.98)	4.4 (0.49)	12.5 (0.70)	24.4 (0.97)	29.0 (1.03)	19.8 (0.69)	10.0 (0.66)	8.3 (0.57)	1.7 (0.32)
Estonia	521 (2.0)	10.5 (0.63)	2.0 (0.26)	8.6 (0.57)	22.0 (0.84)	29.4 (0.79)	23.4 (0.91)	14.6 (0.76)	11.0 (0.67)	3.6 (0.37)
Finland	519 (1.9)	12.3 (0.67)	3.3 (0.39)	8.9 (0.49)	20.5 (0.66)	28.8 (0.78)	23.2 (0.78)	15.3 (0.74)	11.7 (0.60)	3.5 (0.30)
France	495 (2.5)	22.4 (0.87)	8.7 (0.72)	13.6 (0.76)	22.1 (0.95)	23.8 (0.82)	18.9 (0.79)	12.9 (0.77)	9.8 (0.55)	3.1 (0.40)
Germany	514 (2.9)	17.7 (1.03)	5.5 (0.65)	12.2 (0.81)	19.4 (0.81)	23.7 (0.79)	21.7 (0.73)	17.5 (0.94)	12.8 (0.71)	4.7 (0.49)
Greece	453 (2.5)	35.7 (1.34)	14.5 (0.92)	21.2 (0.85)	27.2 (1.02)	22.1 (0.86)	11.2 (0.79)	3.9 (0.43)	3.3 (0.43)	0.6 (0.15)
Hungary	477 (3.2)	28.1 (1.31)	9.9 (0.77)	18.2 (1.04)	25.3 (1.21)	23.0 (1.02)	14.4 (0.86)	9.3 (1.12)	7.1 (0.73)	2.1 (0.51)
Iceland	493 (1.7)	21.5 (0.74)	7.5 (0.54)	14.0 (0.83)	23.6 (0.89)	25.7 (0.95)	18.1 (0.79)	11.2 (0.69)	8.9 (0.61)	2.3 (0.35)
Ireland	501 (2.2)	16.9 (0.99)	4.8 (0.55)	12.1 (0.70)	23.9 (0.72)	28.2 (0.87)	20.3 (0.76)	10.7 (0.54)	8.5 (0.51)	2.2 (0.23)
Israel	466 (4.7)	33.5 (1.68)	15.9 (1.23)	17.6 (0.93)	21.6 (0.93)	21.0 (0.87)	14.6 (0.88)	9.4 (0.99)	7.2 (0.74)	2.2 (0.39)
Italy	485 (2.0)	24.7 (0.76)	8.5 (0.39)	16.1 (0.51)	24.1 (0.55)	24.6 (0.62)	16.7 (0.48)	9.9 (0.57)	7.8 (0.44)	2.2 (0.25)
Japan	536 (3.6)	11.1 (0.98)	3.2 (0.49)	7.9 (0.69)	16.9 (0.85)	24.7 (1.00)	23.7 (0.89)	23.7 (1.46)	16.0 (0.89)	7.6 (0.84)
Korea, Republic of	554 (4.6)	9.1 (0.95)	2.7 (0.46)	6.4 (0.62)	14.7 (0.85)	21.4 (0.99)	23.9 (1.23)	30.9 (1.83)	18.8 (0.92)	12.1 (1.26)
Luxembourg	490 (1.1)	24.3 (0.54)	8.8 (0.54)	15.5 (0.54)	22.3 (0.72)	23.6 (0.72)	18.5 (0.58)	11.2 (0.42)	8.6 (0.38)	2.6 (0.25)
Mexico	413 (1.4)	54.7 (0.82)	22.8 (0.68)	31.9 (0.58)	27.8 (0.53)	13.1 (0.41)	3.7 (0.23)	0.6 (0.08)	0.6 (0.07)	‡ (†)
Netherlands	523 (3.5)	14.8 (1.28)	3.8 (0.57)	11.0 (0.93)	17.9 (1.08)	24.2 (1.19)	23.8 (1.11)	19.3 (1.21)	14.9 (0.99)	4.4 (0.56)
New Zealand	500 (2.2)	22.6 (0.80)	7.5 (0.58)	15.1 (0.66)	21.6 (0.83)	22.7 (0.76)	18.1 (0.84)	15.0 (0.88)	10.5 (0.75)	4.5 (0.40)
Norway	489 (2.7)	22.3 (1.06)	7.2 (0.78)	15.1 (0.88)	24.3 (0.84)	25.7 (1.01)	18.3 (0.96)	9.4 (0.67)	7.3 (0.56)	2.1 (0.30)
Poland	518 (3.6)	14.4 (0.89)	3.3 (0.38)	11.1 (0.77)	22.1 (0.93)	25.5 (0.94)	21.3 (1.12)	16.7 (1.33)	11.7 (0.78)	5.0 (0.80)
Portugal	487 (3.8)	24.9 (1.52)	8.9 (0.79)	16.0 (0.98)	22.8 (0.88)	24.0 (0.84)	17.7 (0.88)	10.6 (0.79)	8.5 (0.73)	2.1 (0.33)
Slovak Republic	482 (3.4)	27.5 (1.28)	11.1 (1.03)	16.4 (0.94)	23.1 (1.10)	22.1 (1.09)	16.4 (1.08)	11.0 (0.94)	7.8 (0.64)	3.1 (0.55)
Slovenia	501 (1.2)	20.1 (0.65)	5.1 (0.48)	15.0 (0.69)	23.6 (0.95)	23.9 (0.96)	18.7 (0.80)	13.7 (0.55)	10.3 (0.64)	3.4 (0.43)
Spain	484 (1.9)	23.6 (0.85)	7.8 (0.50)	15.8 (0.57)	24.9 (0.65)	26.0 (0.59)	17.6 (0.56)	8.0 (0.43)	6.7 (0.42)	1.3 (0.15)
Sweden	478 (2.3)	27.1 (1.12)	9.5 (0.68)	17.5 (0.76)	24.7 (0.92)	23.9 (0.78)	16.3 (0.69)	8.0 (0.52)	6.5 (0.49)	1.6 (0.25)
Switzerland	531 (3.0)	12.4 (0.70)	3.6 (0.35)	8.9 (0.59)	17.8 (1.06)	24.5 (1.02)	23.9 (0.80)	21.4 (1.19)	14.6 (0.78)	6.8 (0.69)
Turkey	448 (4.8)	42.0 (1.93)	15.5 (1.08)	26.5 (1.28)	25.5 (1.16)	16.5 (1.05)	10.1 (1.09)	5.9 (1.13)	4.7 (0.81)	1.2 ! (0.46)
United Kingdom	494 (3.3)	21.8 (1.30)	7.8 (0.77)	14.0 (0.76)	23.2 (0.81)	24.8 (0.85)	18.4 (0.78)	11.8 (0.81)	9.0 (0.63)	2.9 (0.42)
United States	481 (3.6)	25.8 (1.39)	8.0 (0.73)	17.9 (0.98)	26.3 (0.84)	23.3 (0.93)	15.8 (0.91)	8.8 (0.78)	6.6 (0.61)	2.2 (0.34)

See notes at end of table.

Table 602.60. Average mathematics literacy scores of 15-year-old students and percentage attaining mathematics literacy proficiency levels, by country or other education system: 2012—Continued

[Standard errors appear in parentheses]

Country or other education system	Average mathematics literacy score	Percentage attaining mathematics literacy proficiency levels[1]						At or above level 5		
		Below level 2			At level 2	At level 3	At level 4	Total at or above level 5	At level 5	At level 6
		Total below level 2	Below level 1	At level 1						
1	2	3	4	5	6	7	8	9	10	11
Non-OECD education systems										
Albania	394 (2.0)	60.7 (0.95)	32.5 (1.03)	28.1 (0.97)	22.9 (0.91)	12.0 (0.92)	3.6 (0.35)	0.8 (0.19)	0.8 (0.20)	‡ (†)
Argentina	388 (3.5)	66.5 (2.03)	34.9 (1.95)	31.6 (1.22)	22.2 (1.36)	9.2 (0.88)	1.8 (0.35)	0.3 ! (0.10)	0.3 ! (0.10)	‡ (†)
Brazil	391 (2.1)	67.1 (1.03)	35.2 (0.93)	31.9 (0.70)	20.4 (0.67)	8.9 (0.47)	2.9 (0.35)	0.8 (0.20)	0.7 (0.19)	‡ (†)
Bulgaria	439 (4.0)	43.8 (1.78)	20.0 (1.45)	23.8 (0.95)	24.4 (1.12)	17.9 (0.91)	9.9 (0.83)	4.1 (0.62)	3.4 (0.50)	0.7 (0.19)
Chinese Taipei	560 (3.3)	12.8 (0.84)	4.5 (0.53)	8.3 (0.61)	13.1 (0.61)	17.1 (0.65)	19.7 (0.75)	37.2 (1.24)	19.2 (0.89)	18.0 (1.00)
Colombia	376 (2.9)	73.8 (1.43)	41.6 (1.71)	32.2 (1.05)	17.8 (0.90)	6.4 (0.61)	1.6 (0.28)	0.3 ! (0.11)	0.3 ! (0.10)	‡ (†)
Connecticut-USA[3]	506 (6.2)	20.6 (2.14)	6.8 (1.18)	13.8 (1.33)	20.0 (1.28)	24.3 (1.36)	18.6 (1.79)	16.4 (1.91)	11.5 (1.46)	4.9 (0.83)
Costa Rica	407 (3.0)	59.9 (1.87)	23.6 (1.68)	36.2 (1.22)	26.8 (1.29)	10.1 (0.99)	2.6 (0.46)	0.6 ! (0.19)	0.5 ! (0.16)	‡ (†)
Croatia	471 (3.5)	29.9 (1.36)	9.5 (0.74)	20.4 (1.02)	26.7 (0.95)	22.9 (1.12)	13.5 (0.80)	7.0 (1.15)	5.4 (0.76)	1.6 ! (0.51)
Cyprus	440 (1.1)	42.0 (0.63)	19.0 (0.58)	23.0 (0.65)	25.5 (0.62)	19.2 (0.58)	9.6 (0.44)	3.7 (0.27)	3.1 (0.25)	0.6 ! (0.20)
Florida-USA[3]	467 (5.8)	30.4 (2.65)	9.7 (1.44)	20.6 (1.87)	27.9 (1.42)	23.0 (1.64)	13.0 (1.34)	5.8 (1.18)	4.9 (1.04)	0.9 ! (0.39)
Hong Kong-China	561 (3.2)	8.5 (0.79)	2.6 (0.36)	5.9 (0.61)	12.0 (0.77)	19.7 (0.97)	26.1 (1.09)	33.7 (1.35)	21.4 (0.96)	12.3 (0.95)
Indonesia	375 (4.0)	75.7 (2.05)	42.3 (2.14)	33.4 (1.59)	16.8 (1.12)	5.7 (0.90)	1.5 ! (0.54)	‡ (†)	‡ (†)	‡ (†)
Jordan	386 (3.1)	68.6 (1.50)	36.5 (1.59)	32.1 (0.95)	21.0 (1.04)	8.1 (0.63)	1.8 (0.33)	‡ (†)	‡ (†)	‡ (†)
Kazakhstan	432 (3.0)	45.2 (1.70)	14.5 (0.90)	30.7 (1.40)	31.5 (0.95)	16.9 (1.11)	5.4 (0.79)	0.9 ! (0.29)	0.9 ! (0.27)	‡ (†)
Latvia	491 (2.8)	19.9 (1.13)	4.8 (0.53)	15.1 (0.96)	26.6 (1.29)	27.8 (0.92)	17.6 (0.90)	8.0 (0.78)	6.5 (0.65)	1.5 (0.28)
Liechtenstein	535 (4.0)	14.1 (2.02)	3.5 ! (1.31)	10.6 (1.81)	15.2 (2.52)	22.7 (2.81)	23.2 (3.01)	24.8 (2.55)	17.4 (3.17)	7.4 (1.86)
Lithuania	479 (2.6)	26.0 (1.18)	8.7 (0.68)	17.3 (0.89)	25.9 (0.80)	24.6 (1.01)	15.4 (0.70)	8.1 (0.60)	6.6 (0.49)	1.4 (0.24)
Macao-China	538 (1.0)	10.8 (0.49)	3.2 (0.29)	7.6 (0.53)	16.4 (0.71)	24.0 (0.69)	24.4 (0.87)	24.3 (0.56)	16.8 (0.63)	7.6 (0.35)
Malaysia	421 (3.2)	51.8 (1.68)	23.0 (1.19)	28.8 (1.12)	26.0 (0.95)	14.9 (0.93)	6.0 (0.69)	1.3 (0.30)	1.2 (0.28)	0.1 ! (0.05)
Massachusetts-USA[3]	514 (6.2)	17.8 (1.46)	5.3 (0.83)	12.5 (1.17)	20.4 (1.61)	24.3 (1.49)	18.9 (1.18)	18.5 (2.47)	12.7 (1.61)	5.8 (1.11)
Montenegro, Republic of.	410 (1.1)	56.6 (1.02)	27.5 (0.64)	29.1 (1.14)	24.2 (1.06)	13.1 (0.73)	4.9 (0.48)	1.0 (0.20)	0.9 (0.20)	‡ (†)
Peru	368 (3.7)	74.6 (1.75)	47.0 (1.79)	27.6 (0.88)	16.1 (1.00)	6.7 (0.68)	2.1 (0.38)	0.6 ! (0.21)	0.5 ! (0.20)	‡ (†)
Qatar	376 (0.8)	69.6 (0.46)	47.0 (0.42)	22.6 (0.53)	15.2 (0.39)	8.8 (0.34)	4.5 (0.28)	2.0 (0.21)	1.7 (0.20)	0.3 (0.07)
Romania	445 (3.8)	40.8 (1.93)	14.0 (1.15)	26.8 (1.23)	28.3 (1.09)	19.2 (1.07)	8.4 (0.81)	3.2 (0.61)	2.6 (0.45)	0.6 ! (0.27)
Russian Federation	482 (3.0)	24.0 (1.13)	7.5 (0.70)	16.5 (0.80)	26.6 (0.99)	26.0 (0.97)	15.7 (0.78)	7.8 (0.85)	6.3 (0.64)	1.5 (0.31)
Serbia, Republic of	449 (3.4)	38.9 (1.54)	15.5 (1.16)	23.4 (0.93)	26.5 (1.12)	19.5 (1.03)	10.5 (0.69)	4.6 (0.71)	3.5 (0.52)	1.1 (0.31)
Shanghai-China	613 (3.3)	3.8 (0.55)	0.8 (0.21)	2.9 (0.46)	7.5 (0.64)	13.1 (0.77)	20.2 (0.83)	55.4 (1.37)	24.6 (1.04)	30.8 (1.24)
Singapore	573 (1.3)	8.3 (0.48)	2.2 (0.23)	6.1 (0.40)	12.2 (0.68)	17.5 (0.66)	22.0 (0.62)	40.0 (0.71)	21.0 (0.58)	19.0 (0.51)
Thailand	427 (3.4)	49.7 (1.74)	19.1 (1.07)	30.6 (1.20)	27.3 (1.00)	14.5 (1.15)	5.8 (0.74)	2.6 (0.51)	2.0 (0.38)	0.5 ! (0.19)
Tunisia	388 (3.9)	67.7 (1.83)	36.5 (1.88)	31.3 (1.09)	21.1 (1.17)	8.0 (0.79)	2.3 (0.68)	0.8 ! (0.37)	0.7 ! (0.32)	‡ (†)
United Arab Emirates	434 (2.4)	46.3 (1.22)	20.5 (0.92)	25.8 (0.81)	24.9 (0.69)	16.9 (0.64)	8.5 (0.54)	3.5 (0.29)	2.9 (0.25)	0.5 (0.11)
Uruguay	409 (2.8)	55.8 (1.31)	29.2 (1.20)	26.5 (0.76)	23.0 (0.93)	14.4 (0.87)	5.4 (0.60)	1.4 (0.32)	1.3 (0.28)	‡ (†)
Vietnam	511 (4.8)	14.2 (1.75)	3.6 (0.80)	10.6 (1.26)	22.8 (1.28)	28.4 (1.52)	21.3 (1.22)	13.3 (1.47)	9.8 (0.99)	3.5 (0.75)

†Not applicable.
#Rounds to zero.
!Interpret data with caution. The coefficient of variation (CV) for this estimate is between 30 and 50 percent.
‡Reporting standards not met. Either there are too few cases for a reliable estimate or the coefficient of variation (CV) is 50 percent or greater.
[1]To reach a particular proficiency level, a student must correctly answer a majority of items at that level. Students were classified into mathematics literacy levels according to their scores. Exact cut scores are as follows: below level 1 (a score less than or equal to 357.77); level 1 (a score greater than 357.77 and less than or equal to 420.07); level 2 (a score greater than 420.07 and less than or equal to 482.38 and less than or equal to 544.68 and

less than or equal to 606.99); level 5 (a score greater than 606.99 and less than or equal to 669.30); and level 6 (a score greater than 669.30).
[2]Refers to the mean of the data values for all Organization for Economic Cooperation and Development (OECD) countries, to which each country contributes equally, regardless of the absolute size of the student population of each country.
[3]Results are for public school students only.
NOTE: Program for International Student Assessment (PISA) scores are reported on a scale from 0 to 1,000. Detail may not sum to totals because of rounding.
SOURCE: Organization for Economic Cooperation and Development (OECD), Program for International Student Assessment (PISA), 2012. (This table was prepared November 2013.)

Table 602.70. Average science literacy scores of 15-year-old students and percentage attaining science literacy proficiency levels, by country or other education system: 2012

[Standard errors appear in parentheses]

Country or other education system	Average science literacy score	Percentage attaining science literacy proficiency levels[1]								
		Below level 2			At level 2	At level 3	At level 4	At or above level 5		
		Total below level 2	Below level 1	At level 1				Total at or above level 5	At level 5	At level 6
1	2	3	4	5	6	7	8	9	10	11
OECD average[2]	501 (0.5)	17.8 (0.17)	4.8 (0.09)	13.0 (0.14)	24.5 (0.16)	28.8 (0.17)	20.5 (0.15)	8.4 (0.11)	7.2 (0.10)	1.1 (0.04)
Australia	521 (1.8)	13.6 (0.48)	3.4 (0.25)	10.2 (0.41)	21.5 (0.47)	28.5 (0.68)	22.8 (0.63)	13.6 (0.55)	10.9 (0.47)	2.6 (0.25)
Austria	506 (2.7)	15.8 (1.00)	3.6 (0.54)	12.2 (0.92)	24.3 (1.05)	30.1 (0.85)	21.9 (0.81)	7.9 (0.70)	7.0 (0.62)	0.8 (0.20)
Belgium	505 (2.2)	17.7 (0.86)	5.9 (0.53)	11.8 (0.58)	21.5 (0.63)	28.7 (0.71)	23.0 (0.66)	9.1 (0.43)	8.1 (0.42)	0.9 (0.16)
Canada	525 (1.9)	10.4 (0.47)	2.4 (0.24)	8.0 (0.38)	21.0 (0.65)	32.0 (0.54)	25.3 (0.58)	11.3 (0.55)	9.5 (0.47)	1.8 (0.20)
Chile	445 (2.9)	34.5 (1.58)	8.1 (0.80)	26.3 (1.11)	34.6 (1.06)	22.4 (0.96)	7.5 (0.60)	1.0 (0.15)	1.0 (0.15)	# (†)
Czech Republic	508 (3.0)	13.8 (1.13)	3.3 (0.62)	10.5 (1.03)	24.7 (0.99)	31.7 (1.23)	22.2 (0.96)	7.6 (0.58)	6.7 (0.53)	0.9 (0.18)
Denmark	498 (2.7)	16.7 (0.97)	4.7 (0.55)	12.0 (0.69)	25.7 (0.80)	31.3 (0.90)	19.6 (0.79)	6.8 (0.70)	6.1 (0.67)	0.7 (0.17)
Estonia	541 (1.9)	5.0 (0.45)	0.5 (0.14)	4.5 (0.43)	19.0 (0.87)	34.5 (0.87)	28.7 (0.96)	12.8 (0.73)	11.1 (0.66)	1.7 (0.25)
Finland	545 (2.2)	7.7 (0.58)	1.8 (0.28)	5.9 (0.48)	16.8 (0.69)	29.6 (0.77)	28.8 (0.73)	17.1 (0.66)	13.9 (0.62)	3.2 (0.38)
France	499 (2.6)	18.7 (1.01)	6.1 (0.67)	12.6 (0.71)	22.9 (1.08)	29.2 (1.12)	21.3 (0.87)	7.9 (0.77)	6.9 (0.68)	1.0 (0.21)
Germany	524 (3.0)	12.2 (0.90)	2.9 (0.46)	9.3 (0.73)	20.5 (0.82)	28.9 (0.89)	26.2 (1.05)	12.2 (0.95)	10.6 (0.80)	1.6 (0.28)
Greece	467 (3.1)	25.5 (1.47)	7.4 (0.70)	18.1 (1.14)	31.0 (1.10)	28.8 (1.02)	12.2 (0.81)	2.5 (0.40)	2.3 (0.40)	‡ (†)
Hungary	494 (2.9)	18.0 (1.14)	4.1 (0.61)	14.0 (1.04)	26.4 (1.08)	30.9 (1.16)	18.7 (0.98)	5.9 (0.75)	5.5 (0.73)	0.5 ! (0.18)
Iceland	478 (2.1)	24.0 (0.78)	8.0 (0.56)	16.0 (0.72)	27.5 (0.87)	27.2 (0.86)	16.2 (0.74)	5.2 (0.61)	4.6 (0.60)	0.6 (0.17)
Ireland	522 (2.5)	11.1 (0.88)	2.6 (0.40)	8.5 (0.76)	22.0 (1.15)	31.1 (1.03)	25.0 (0.94)	10.7 (0.58)	9.3 (0.63)	1.5 (0.25)
Israel	470 (5.0)	28.9 (1.67)	11.2 (1.08)	17.7 (0.93)	24.8 (0.93)	24.4 (1.19)	16.1 (1.12)	5.8 (0.65)	5.2 (0.58)	0.6 ! (0.22)
Italy	494 (1.9)	18.7 (0.68)	4.9 (0.35)	13.8 (0.52)	26.0 (0.58)	30.1 (0.66)	19.1 (0.59)	6.1 (0.41)	5.5 (0.37)	0.6 (0.08)
Japan	547 (3.6)	8.5 (0.88)	2.0 (0.39)	6.4 (0.61)	16.3 (0.79)	27.5 (0.92)	29.5 (1.06)	18.2 (1.21)	14.8 (0.93)	3.4 (0.49)
Korea, Republic of	538 (3.7)	6.6 (0.77)	1.2 (0.25)	5.5 (0.60)	18.0 (1.02)	33.6 (1.11)	30.1 (1.24)	11.7 (1.13)	10.6 (0.93)	1.1 ! (0.39)
Luxembourg	491 (1.3)	22.2 (0.63)	7.2 (0.42)	15.1 (0.67)	24.2 (0.63)	26.2 (0.60)	19.2 (0.53)	8.2 (0.54)	7.0 (0.49)	1.2 (0.17)
Mexico	415 (1.3)	47.0 (0.81)	12.6 (0.52)	34.4 (0.58)	37.0 (0.59)	13.8 (0.52)	2.1 (0.16)	0.1 ! (0.04)	0.1 ! (0.04)	† (†)
Netherlands	522 (3.5)	13.1 (1.12)	3.1 (0.53)	10.1 (0.83)	20.1 (1.35)	29.1 (1.28)	25.8 (1.24)	11.8 (1.06)	10.5 (0.98)	1.3 (0.28)
New Zealand	516 (2.1)	16.3 (0.86)	4.7 (0.39)	11.6 (0.76)	21.7 (0.94)	26.4 (0.95)	22.3 (0.85)	13.4 (0.69)	10.7 (0.62)	2.7 (0.25)
Norway	495 (3.1)	19.6 (1.10)	6.0 (0.63)	13.6 (0.71)	24.8 (0.80)	28.9 (0.91)	19.0 (0.79)	7.5 (0.57)	6.4 (0.56)	1.1 (0.24)
Poland	526 (3.1)	9.0 (0.75)	1.3 (0.32)	7.7 (0.70)	22.5 (0.98)	33.1 (0.92)	24.5 (0.96)	10.8 (1.01)	9.1 (0.76)	1.7 (0.35)
Portugal	489 (3.7)	19.0 (1.44)	4.7 (0.66)	14.3 (1.09)	27.3 (0.96)	31.4 (1.25)	17.8 (1.06)	4.5 (0.55)	4.2 (0.55)	0.3 ! (0.11)
Slovak Republic	471 (3.6)	26.9 (1.58)	9.2 (0.95)	17.6 (1.14)	27.0 (1.30)	26.2 (1.62)	15.0 (1.02)	4.9 (0.72)	4.3 (0.58)	0.6 ! (0.25)
Slovenia	514 (1.3)	12.9 (0.56)	2.4 (0.19)	10.4 (0.55)	24.5 (1.00)	30.0 (1.02)	23.0 (0.92)	9.6 (0.72)	8.4 (0.71)	1.2 (0.24)
Spain	496 (1.8)	15.7 (0.71)	3.7 (0.33)	12.0 (0.51)	27.3 (0.64)	32.8 (0.60)	19.4 (0.53)	4.8 (0.29)	4.5 (0.26)	0.3 (0.08)
Sweden	485 (3.0)	22.2 (1.11)	7.3 (0.62)	15.0 (0.80)	26.2 (0.84)	28.0 (0.84)	17.2 (0.77)	6.3 (0.50)	5.6 (0.45)	0.7 (0.14)
Switzerland	515 (2.7)	12.8 (0.72)	3.0 (0.31)	9.8 (0.62)	22.8 (0.82)	31.3 (0.74)	23.7 (0.86)	9.3 (0.77)	8.3 (0.70)	1.0 (0.22)
Turkey	463 (3.9)	26.4 (1.50)	4.4 (0.50)	21.9 (1.27)	35.4 (1.43)	25.1 (1.28)	11.3 (1.28)	1.8 (0.36)	1.8 (0.34)	‡ (†)
United Kingdom	514 (3.4)	15.0 (1.07)	4.3 (0.48)	10.7 (0.86)	22.4 (1.00)	28.4 (0.98)	23.0 (0.91)	11.2 (0.79)	9.3 (0.70)	1.8 (0.34)
United States	497 (3.8)	18.1 (1.33)	4.2 (0.54)	14.0 (1.08)	26.7 (1.08)	28.9 (1.07)	18.8 (1.07)	7.5 (0.74)	6.3 (0.64)	1.1 (0.20)

See notes at end of table.

Table 602.70. Average science literacy scores of 15-year-old students and percentage attaining science literacy proficiency levels, by country or other education system: 2012—Continued

[Standard errors appear in parentheses]

Country or other education system	Average science literacy score	Percentage attaining science literacy proficiency levels[1]						At or above level 5		
		Below level 2			At level 2	At level 3	At level 4	Total at or above level 5	At level 5	At level 6
		Total below level 2	Below level 1	At level 1						
1	2	3	4	5	6	7	8	9	10	11
Non-OECD education systems										
Albania	397 (2.4)	53.1 (1.20)	23.5 (1.04)	29.6 (0.94)	28.5 (1.19)	14.4 (0.78)	3.6 (0.41)	0.4 ! (0.13)	0.4 ! (0.14)	‡ (†)
Argentina	406 (3.9)	50.9 (2.21)	19.8 (1.39)	31.0 (1.46)	31.1 (1.33)	14.8 (1.20)	3.0 (0.43)	0.2 ! (0.10)	0.2 ! (0.10)	‡ (†)
Brazil	405 (2.1)	53.7 (1.14)	18.6 (0.78)	35.1 (0.79)	30.7 (0.78)	12.5 (0.68)	2.8 (0.37)	0.3 ! (0.10)	0.3 ! (0.10)	‡ (†)
Bulgaria	446 (4.8)	36.9 (2.02)	14.4 (1.34)	22.5 (1.15)	26.3 (1.07)	22.5 (1.09)	11.2 (0.84)	3.1 (0.58)	2.8 (0.50)	0.3 ! (0.12)
Chinese Taipei	523 (2.3)	9.8 (0.77)	1.6 (0.25)	8.2 (0.64)	20.8 (0.89)	33.7 (0.97)	27.3 (1.00)	8.3 (0.61)	7.8 (0.56)	0.6 (0.13)
Colombia	399 (3.1)	56.2 (1.61)	19.8 (1.36)	36.3 (1.10)	30.8 (1.08)	11.0 (0.83)	1.9 (0.25)	‡ (†)	‡ (†)	‡ (†)
Connecticut-USA[3]	521 (5.7)	13.5 (1.70)	3.3 (0.82)	10.2 (1.36)	21.4 (1.58)	29.4 (1.69)	22.8 (1.46)	12.9 (1.34)	10.7 (1.13)	2.2 (0.60)
Costa Rica	429 (2.9)	39.3 (1.75)	8.6 (0.79)	30.7 (1.30)	39.2 (1.25)	17.8 (1.12)	3.4 (0.57)	0.2 ! (0.10)	0.2 ! (0.11)	‡ (†)
Croatia	491 (3.1)	17.3 (0.93)	3.2 (0.38)	14.0 (0.74)	29.1 (0.99)	31.4 (1.19)	17.6 (1.16)	4.6 (0.79)	4.3 (0.75)	‡ (†)
Cyprus	438 (1.2)	38.0 (0.67)	14.4 (0.47)	23.7 (0.66)	30.3 (0.89)	21.3 (0.73)	8.4 (0.43)	2.0 (0.29)	1.8 (0.29)	0.2 ! (0.08)
Florida-USA[3]	485 (6.4)	21.3 (2.15)	5.1 (0.96)	16.1 (1.61)	28.4 (1.61)	28.2 (2.00)	16.6 (1.64)	5.5 (1.05)	4.9 (1.01)	‡ (†)
Hong Kong-China	555 (2.6)	5.6 (0.62)	1.2 (0.23)	4.4 (0.52)	13.0 (0.72)	29.8 (1.06)	34.9 (0.99)	16.7 (1.05)	14.9 (0.91)	1.8 (0.36)
Indonesia	382 (3.8)	66.6 (2.20)	24.7 (1.96)	41.9 (1.42)	26.3 (1.54)	6.5 (1.02)	‡ (†)	‡ (†)	‡ (†)	‡ (†)
Jordan	409 (3.1)	49.6 (1.55)	18.2 (1.21)	31.4 (0.96)	32.2 (1.04)	15.0 (0.86)	3.0 (0.57)	0.2 ! (†)	‡ (†)	‡ (†)
Kazakhstan	425 (3.0)	41.9 (1.83)	11.3 (0.99)	30.7 (1.49)	36.8 (1.16)	17.8 (1.19)	3.3 (0.45)	0.2 ! (0.09)	0.2 ! (0.09)	‡ (†)
Latvia	502 (2.8)	12.4 (0.96)	1.8 (0.39)	10.5 (0.90)	28.2 (1.20)	35.1 (1.02)	20.0 (1.05)	4.4 (0.51)	4.0 (0.47)	0.3 ! (0.13)
Liechtenstein	525 (3.5)	10.4 (1.96)	‡ (†)	9.6 (1.94)	22.0 (3.94)	30.8 (3.79)	26.7 (2.58)	10.1 (1.80)	9.1 (1.47)	‡ (†)
Lithuania	496 (2.6)	16.1 (1.08)	3.4 (0.48)	12.7 (0.84)	27.6 (1.00)	32.9 (1.08)	18.3 (0.88)	5.1 (0.49)	4.7 (0.47)	0.4 (0.09)
Macao-China	521 (0.8)	8.8 (0.46)	1.4 (0.20)	7.4 (0.49)	22.2 (0.60)	36.2 (0.81)	26.2 (0.73)	6.7 (0.36)	6.2 (0.35)	0.4 (0.10)
Malaysia	420 (3.0)	45.5 (1.55)	14.5 (1.13)	31.0 (1.21)	33.9 (1.10)	16.5 (1.07)	3.7 (0.54)	0.3 ! (0.12)	0.3 ! (0.13)	‡ (†)
Massachusetts-USA[3]	527 (6.0)	11.5 (1.18)	2.6 (0.65)	8.9 (1.03)	21.2 (1.96)	29.4 (1.50)	23.8 (1.84)	14.2 (1.94)	11.3 (1.48)	2.9 (0.73)
Montenegro, Republic of.	410 (1.1)	50.7 (0.72)	18.7 (0.74)	32.0 (0.98)	29.7 (0.94)	15.4 (0.76)	3.8 (0.47)	0.4 ! (0.14)	0.4 ! (0.14)	‡ (†)
Peru	373 (3.6)	68.5 (1.95)	31.5 (1.61)	37.0 (1.26)	23.5 (1.29)	7.0 (0.85)	1.0 (0.28)	‡ (†)	‡ (†)	‡ (†)
Qatar	384 (0.7)	62.6 (0.53)	34.6 (0.38)	28.0 (0.58)	19.6 (0.71)	11.2 (0.39)	5.1 (0.40)	1.5 (0.12)	1.3 (0.11)	0.1 (0.04)
Romania	439 (3.3)	37.3 (1.64)	8.7 (0.77)	28.7 (1.32)	34.6 (1.23)	21.0 (1.12)	6.2 (0.77)	0.9 ! (0.29)	0.9 (0.26)	‡ (†)
Russian Federation	486 (2.9)	18.8 (1.15)	3.6 (0.39)	15.1 (0.96)	30.1 (1.08)	31.2 (0.89)	15.7 (0.98)	4.3 (0.59)	3.9 (0.51)	0.3 ! (0.16)
Serbia, Republic of.	445 (3.4)	35.0 (1.81)	10.3 (0.99)	24.7 (1.15)	32.4 (1.21)	22.8 (1.06)	8.1 (0.63)	1.7 (0.36)	1.6 (0.35)	‡ (†)
Shanghai-China	580 (3.0)	2.7 (0.41)	0.3 ! (0.11)	2.4 (0.36)	10.0 (0.86)	24.6 (0.87)	35.5 (1.11)	27.2 (1.32)	23.0 (1.09)	4.2 (0.57)
Singapore	551 (1.5)	9.6 (0.51)	2.2 (0.27)	7.4 (0.48)	16.7 (0.73)	24.0 (0.73)	27.0 (0.87)	22.7 (0.81)	16.9 (0.94)	5.8 (0.41)
Thailand	444 (2.9)	33.6 (1.56)	7.0 (0.64)	26.6 (1.33)	37.5 (1.07)	21.6 (1.14)	6.4 (0.74)	0.9 (0.27)	0.9 ! (0.27)	‡ (†)
Tunisia	398 (3.5)	55.3 (1.87)	21.3 (1.45)	34.0 (1.07)	31.1 (1.36)	11.7 (1.00)	1.8 (0.49)	‡ (†)	‡ (†)	‡ (†)
United Arab Emirates	448 (2.8)	35.2 (1.30)	11.3 (0.76)	23.8 (0.99)	29.9 (0.83)	22.3 (0.88)	10.1 (0.60)	2.5 (0.27)	2.3 (0.25)	0.3 (0.07)
Uruguay	416 (2.8)	46.9 (1.25)	19.7 (1.06)	27.2 (0.92)	29.3 (1.00)	17.1 (0.95)	5.6 (0.53)	1.0 (0.25)	1.0 (0.24)	‡ (†)
Vietnam	528 (4.3)	6.7 (1.09)	0.9 ! (0.26)	5.8 (0.90)	20.7 (1.40)	37.5 (1.48)	27.0 (1.50)	8.1 (1.09)	7.1 (0.90)	1.0 ! (0.32)

†Not applicable.
#Rounds to zero.
!Interpret data with caution. The coefficient of variation (CV) for this estimate is between 30 and 50 percent.
‡Reporting standards not met. Either there are too few cases for a reliable estimate or the coefficient of variation (CV) is 50 percent or greater.
[1]To reach a particular proficiency level, a student must correctly answer a majority of items at that level. Students were classified into science literacy levels according to their scores. Exact cut scores are as follows: below level 1 (a score less than or equal to 334.94); level 1 (a score greater than 334.94 and less than or equal to 409.54); level 2 (a score greater than 409.54 and less than or equal to 484.14); level 3 (a score greater than 484.14 and less than or equal to 558.73 and less than or equal to 633.33); level 5 (a score greater than 633.33 and less than or equal to 707.93); and level 6 (a score greater than 707.93).

[2]Refers to the mean of the data values for all Organization for Economic Cooperation and Development (OECD) countries, to which each country contributes equally, regardless of the absolute size of the student population of each country.
[3]Results are for public school students only.
NOTE: Program for International Student Assessment (PISA) scores are reported on a scale from 0 to 1,000. Detail may not sum to totals because of rounding.
SOURCE: Organization for Economic Cooperation and Development (OECD), Program for International Student Assessment (PISA), 2012. (This table was prepared November 2013.)

Table 603.10. Percentage of the population 25 to 64 years old who completed high school, by age group and country: Selected years, 2001 through 2014

[Standard errors appear in parentheses]

Country	2001 Total, 25 to 64 years old	2001 25 to 34 years old	2005 Total, 25 to 64 years old	2005 25 to 34 years old	2012 Total, 25 to 64 years old		2012 25 to 34 years old		2014 Total, 25 to 64 years old		2014 25 to 34 years old		2014 35 to 44 years old		2014 45 to 54 years old		2014 55 to 64 years old	
1	2	3	4	5	6		7		8		9		10		11		12	
OECD average[1]	**64.2**	**74.0**	**72.8**	**82.6**	**75.2**	**(0.03)**	**82.5**	**(0.07)**	**76.3**	**(0.03)**	**83.2**	**(0.07)**	**80.3**	**(0.06)**	**74.2**	**(0.07)**	**66.2**	**(0.08)**
Australia	58.9	70.7	65.0	78.6	76.4	(0.25)	86.6	(0.41)	77.1	(0.25)	86.7	(0.40)	82.3	(0.45)	71.2	(0.53)	65.3	(0.60)
Austria[2,3]	75.7	83.3	80.6	87.5	83.1	(0.24)	88.6	(0.50)	83.9	(0.20)	90.0	(0.34)	86.1	(0.37)	83.4	(0.34)	75.2	(0.48)
Belgium[2]	58.5	75.3	66.1	80.9	71.6	(0.19)	81.9	(0.35)	73.6	(0.21)	82.3	(0.38)	80.4	(0.37)	72.4	(0.39)	58.7	(0.46)
Canada	81.9	89.3	85.2	90.8	89.1	(0.13)	92.2	(0.19)	90.0	(0.12)	92.6	(0.19)	92.8	(0.18)	89.2	(0.20)	85.4	(0.25)
Chile[2,4,5,6]	45.9	57.9	50.0	64.3	57.5	(0.16)	76.6	(0.27)	61.4	(0.15)	80.0	(0.24)	65.9	(0.29)	53.4	(0.29)	41.7	(0.33)
Czech Republic	86.2	92.5	89.9	93.9	92.5	(0.07)	93.7	(0.15)	93.2	(0.07)	94.6	(0.15)	95.9	(0.11)	94.1	(0.14)	87.6	(0.18)
Denmark	80.2	86.3	81.0	87.4	77.9	(0.16)	81.7	(0.36)	79.6	(0.16)	82.2	(0.36)	84.0	(0.30)	80.4	(0.28)	71.6	(0.34)
Estonia	—	—	89.1	87.4	89.8	(0.41)	86.4	(0.95)	91.0	(0.25)	89.0	(0.57)	89.0	(0.52)	94.0	(0.40)	92.0	(0.47)
Finland	73.8	86.8	78.8	89.4	84.8	(0.18)	90.0	(0.32)	86.5	(0.12)	90.2	(0.22)	90.3	(0.21)	89.0	(0.21)	77.2	(0.27)
France[6,7]	63.9	78.4	66.3	81.1	72.5	(0.09)	83.3	(0.16)	74.8	(0.08)	85.3	(0.15)	81.1	(0.15)	72.3	(0.16)	61.0	(0.18)
Germany	82.6	85.5	83.1	84.1	86.3	(0.12)	86.8	(0.32)	86.9	(0.12)	87.3	(0.32)	87.0	(0.32)	87.4	(0.28)	85.8	(0.31)
Greece	51.4	72.6	57.1	73.6	68.5	(0.13)	82.5	(0.23)	68.3	(0.13)	81.7	(0.24)	75.1	(0.24)	64.7	(0.26)	49.8	(0.27)
Hungary	70.2	80.9	76.4	85.0	82.1	(0.10)	87.5	(0.18)	83.1	(0.10)	87.0	(0.20)	85.6	(0.18)	82.6	(0.21)	77.2	(0.21)
Iceland	56.9	61.2	62.9	69.0	71.0	(0.48)	75.0	(0.87)	73.3	(0.48)	73.8	(0.95)	77.7	(0.92)	72.9	(0.95)	68.1	(1.02)
Ireland	57.6	73.4	64.5	81.1	74.6	(0.13)	85.9	(0.19)	78.8	(0.22)	90.1	(0.25)	85.6	(0.26)	74.4	(0.36)	58.9	(0.46)
Israel	—	—	79.2	85.7	84.5	(0.15)	90.3	(0.23)	85.4	(0.14)	90.8	(0.22)	87.0	(0.26)	82.5	(0.31)	78.2	(0.35)
Italy	43.3	57.5	50.1	65.9	57.2	(0.14)	71.8	(0.37)	59.3	(0.15)	73.8	(0.38)	64.7	(0.31)	54.0	(0.28)	46.1	(0.29)
Japan	83.1	93.6	—	—	—	(†)	—	(†)	—	(†)	—	(†)	—	(†)	—	(†)	—	(†)
Korea, Republic of	68.0	94.6	75.5	97.3	82.4	(0.20)	98.2	(0.14)	85.0	(0.13)	98.3	(0.13)	97.4	(0.15)	84.1	(0.35)	54.4	(0.63)
Luxembourg	52.7	59.4	65.9	76.5	78.3	(0.31)	86.1	(0.58)	82.0	(0.44)	86.9	(0.92)	86.4	(0.77)	79.3	(0.86)	73.1	(0.97)
Mexico	21.6	25.4	21.3	24.0	37.3	(0.06)	45.8	(0.12)	33.7	(0.06)	45.6	(0.12)	33.3	(0.12)	28.3	(0.13)	19.9	(0.14)
Netherlands[2,7]	65.0	74.0	71.8	81.3	73.4	(0.09)	83.3	(0.17)	75.9	(0.09)	85.2	(0.17)	80.2	(0.17)	74.1	(0.16)	64.9	(0.18)
New Zealand	75.7	81.8	78.7	85.2	74.1	(0.37)	80.0	(0.72)	74.1	(0.37)	81.1	(0.69)	78.1	(0.68)	71.0	(0.72)	65.6	(0.81)
Norway[2]	85.2	93.4	77.2	83.5	82.1	(0.16)	82.1	(0.36)	81.9	(0.17)	81.4	(0.36)	86.0	(0.29)	79.7	(0.33)	80.4	(0.35)
Poland	45.9	51.7	51.4	62.5	89.6	(0.06)	94.4	(0.10)	90.5	(0.07)	94.2	(0.11)	93.0	(0.12)	90.8	(0.13)	84.2	(0.15)
Portugal	19.9	32.5	26.5	42.8	37.6	(0.17)	57.9	(0.39)	43.3	(0.17)	64.7	(0.38)	52.3	(0.32)	34.2	(0.30)	22.9	(0.27)
Slovak Republic	85.1	93.7	85.7	93.0	91.7	(0.23)	94.1	(0.41)	90.8	(0.12)	92.5	(0.25)	94.0	(0.21)	91.6	(0.24)	84.5	(0.29)
Slovenia	—	—	80.3	91.2	85.0	(0.19)	94.2	(0.27)	85.7	(0.18)	93.9	(0.27)	90.7	(0.33)	84.1	(0.36)	74.6	(0.44)
Spain	40.0	57.1	48.8	63.9	54.6	(0.08)	64.2	(0.17)	56.6	(0.28)	65.6	(0.61)	65.4	(0.51)	53.0	(0.52)	38.6	(0.56)
Sweden	80.6	90.7	83.6	90.6	87.5	(0.08)	90.8	(0.14)	81.6	(0.09)	81.8	(0.20)	86.2	(0.17)	83.8	(0.17)	73.7	(0.21)
Switzerland	87.4	91.8	83.0	87.9	86.3	(0.13)	89.4	(0.28)	88.0	(0.11)	91.0	(0.24)	88.8	(0.21)	87.4	(0.20)	84.3	(0.25)
Turkey	24.3	30.2	27.2	35.7	33.9	(0.09)	45.9	(0.18)	35.6	(0.09)	49.5	(0.19)	35.3	(0.18)	24.6	(0.17)	21.0	(0.18)
United Kingdom[3,7,8]	63.0	68.0	66.7	72.9	78.1	(0.09)	84.8	(0.16)	79.2	(0.09)	86.2	(0.16)	81.6	(0.17)	76.5	(0.18)	71.3	(0.20)
United States	87.7	88.1	87.8	86.7	89.3	(0.16)	89.3	(0.29)	89.6	(0.15)	90.0	(0.29)	89.0	(0.26)	89.4	(0.29)	89.9	(0.29)
Other reporting countries																		
Argentina	41.9	51.5	—	—	—	(†)	—	(†)	—	(†)	—	(†)	—	(†)	—	(†)	—	(†)
Brazil[4,6]	27.2	31.8	29.5	38.0	44.9	(0.11)	58.9	(0.19)	46.4	(0.26)	60.8	(0.33)	47.6	(0.35)	40.0	(0.37)	28.4	(0.40)
China[9]	14.9	15.8	—	—	24.5	(—)	35.7	(—)	—	(†)	—	(†)	—	(†)	—	(†)	—	(†)
Colombia[5]	—	—	—	—	41.8	(—)	—	(†)	52.0	(0.25)	67.4	(0.31)	53.3	(0.37)	41.7	(0.39)	32.9	(0.48)
Costa Rica	—	—	—	—	—	(†)	—	(†)	39.6	(—)	47.2	(—)	37.3	(—)	35.7	(—)	34.7	(—)
Indonesia[5]	21.4	32.8	—	—	31.0	(—)	40.0	(—)	—	(†)	—	(†)	—	(†)	—	(†)	—	(†)
Latvia	—	—	—	—	89.1	(0.27)	85.4	(0.69)	89.5	(0.33)	86.0	(0.72)	87.5	(0.64)	94.7	(0.38)	89.7	(0.53)
Lithuania	—	—	—	—	—	(†)	—	(†)	91.2	(0.15)	88.4	(0.44)	88.3	(0.36)	95.8	(0.19)	91.4	(0.29)
Russian Federation[6,10]	88.0	91.0	—	—	94.3	(0.05)	94.4	(0.10)	94.7	(0.05)	94.8	(0.10)	95.2	(0.10)	96.2	(0.08)	92.3	(0.14)
Saudi Arabia[4,6]	—	—	34.2	—	—	(†)	—	(†)	51.0	(—)	64.8	(—)	49.0	(—)	39.9	(—)	27.7	(—)
South Africa	—	—	—	—	64.9	(—)	77.4	(—)	—	(†)	—	(†)	—	(†)	—	(†)	—	(†)

—Not available.
†Not applicable.
[1]Refers to the mean of the data values for all reporting Organization for Economic Cooperation and Development (OECD) countries, to which each country reporting data contributes equally. The average includes all current OECD countries for which a given year's data are available, even if they were not members of OECD in that year.
[2]Data from 2000 reported for 2001.
[3]Data in 2005 columns include some International Standard Classification of Education (ISCED) 3C short secondary programs.
[4]Data from 2004 reported for 2005.
[5]Data from 2011 reported for 2012.
[6]Data from 2013 reported for 2014.
[7]Data in 2001 columns include some short secondary (ISCED 3C) programs.
[8]Data for 2014 include some persons (18 percent of the total) who have completed a sufficient volume and standard of programs, any one of which individually would be classified as a program that only partially completes the high school (or upper secondary) level of education.

[9]Data from 2010 reported for 2012.
[10]Data from 2002 reported for 2001.
NOTE: The International Standard Classification of Education (ISCED) was revised in 2011. The previous version, ISCED 1997, was used to calculate all data for 2012 and earlier years. For most countries, data for 2014 were calculated using ISCED 2011 and may not be comparable to data for earlier years. (The countries for which 2014 data were calculated using ISCED 1997 are Brazil, the Russian Federation, and Saudi Arabia.) Data in this table refer to degrees classified as ISCED level 3, which corresponds to high school completion in the United States, with the following exceptions: Programs classified under ISCED 1997 as level 3C short programs do not correspond to high school completion; these short programs are excluded from this table except where otherwise noted. Programs classified under ISCED 2011 as only partially completing level 3 are also excluded except where otherwise noted. Standard errors are not available for 2001 and 2005.
SOURCE: Organization for Economic Cooperation and Development (OECD), *Education at a Glance*, selected years, 2002 through 2015. (This table was prepared January 2016.)

Table 603.20. Percentage of the population 25 to 64 years old who attained any postsecondary degree, by age group and country: Selected years, 2001 through 2014

[Standard errors appear in parentheses]

Country	2001 Total 25 to 64	2001 25 to 34	2005 Total 25 to 64	2005 25 to 34	2008 Total 25 to 64	2008 25 to 34	2010 Total 25 to 64	2010 25 to 34	2012 Total 25 to 64	2012 25 to 34	2014 Total 25 to 64	2014 25 to 34	2014 35 to 44	2014 45 to 54	2014 55 to 64
1	2	3	4	5	6	7	8	9	10	11	12	13	14	15	16
OECD average[1]	**22.5**	**27.8**	**26.2**	**32.1**	**28.9**	**35.5**	**30.7** (0.05)	**37.8** (0.10)	**32.2** (0.04)	**39.2** (0.09)	**33.5** (0.04)	**40.7** (0.09)	**37.7** (0.08)	**29.6** (0.07)	**25.0** (0.07)
Australia	29.0	33.5	31.7	38.1	36.1	42.0	37.6 (0.45)	44.4 (0.85)	41.3 (0.27)	47.2 (0.56)	41.9 (0.29)	48.1 (0.59)	45.9 (0.58)	38.0 (0.57)	33.5 (0.59)
Austria	14.1	14.3	17.8	19.7	18.1	19.4	19.3 (0.26)	20.8 (0.54)	20.0 (0.23)	23.0 (0.50)	29.9 (0.26)	38.4 (0.57)	33.2 (0.52)	26.5 (0.44)	21.3 (0.43)
Belgium	27.6	37.5	31.0	40.6	32.3	42.3	35.0 (0.20)	43.8 (0.44)	35.3 (0.20)	43.0 (0.45)	36.9 (0.24)	44.2 (0.50)	42.2 (0.48)	34.5 (0.44)	26.3 (0.42)
Canada	41.9	50.5	46.1	53.8	48.8	55.9	50.6 (0.23)	56.5 (0.43)	52.6 (0.23)	57.7 (0.40)	53.6 (0.25)	57.7 (0.41)	60.6 (0.41)	51.3 (0.34)	45.1 (0.40)
Chile[2,3,4]	—	—	13.2	18.3	24.2	33.7	26.8 (0.18)	38.5 (0.34)	17.8 (0.12)	22.5 (0.26)	21.1 (0.12)	27.3 (0.26)	24.2 (0.26)	16.9 (0.22)	14.5 (0.24)
Czech Republic	11.1	11.3	13.1	14.2	14.5	17.7	16.8 (0.10)	22.6 (0.25)	19.3 (0.11)	27.8 (0.28)	21.5 (0.12)	29.9 (0.30)	21.2 (0.23)	19.6 (0.24)	15.1 (0.20)
Denmark	28.4	29.0	33.5	39.8	34.5	43.1	33.3 (0.19)	37.8 (0.50)	34.8 (0.19)	40.2 (0.46)	35.8 (0.19)	42.1 (0.40)	40.6 (0.40)	32.6 (0.33)	29.1 (0.34)
Estonia	—	—	33.5	32.8	34.5	35.8	35.3 (0.79)	37.8 (1.73)	37.3 (0.69)	39.8 (1.46)	38.0 (0.42)	40.0 (0.89)	39.0 (0.81)	35.0 (0.80)	36.0 (0.82)
Finland	32.3	38.2	34.6	37.5	36.6	38.3	38.1 (0.24)	39.2 (0.52)	39.7 (0.17)	39.7 (0.52)	41.8 (0.17)	40.3 (0.37)	49.9 (0.36)	43.7 (0.33)	34.2 (0.31)
France[2]	23.0	34.2	24.8	39.3	27.4	40.7	29.0 (0.09)	42.9 (0.21)	30.9 (0.09)	42.9 (0.21)	32.1 (0.09)	44.1 (0.22)	39.1 (0.19)	25.6 (0.16)	20.3 (0.15)
Germany	23.2	21.8	24.6	22.5	25.4	23.9	26.6 (0.08)	26.1 (0.19)	28.1 (0.08)	29.0 (0.19)	27.1 (0.08)	28.4 (0.19)	28.5 (0.19)	26.2 (0.16)	25.5 (0.18)
Greece	18.0	24.0	21.3	25.4	23.4	28.2	24.6 (0.33)	30.9 (0.59)	26.7 (0.12)	34.7 (0.29)	28.1 (0.13)	38.7 (0.31)	27.1 (0.25)	25.6 (0.24)	21.1 (0.22)
Hungary	14.0	14.7	17.1	19.6	19.2	24.0	20.1 (0.10)	26.0 (0.24)	22.0 (0.11)	30.4 (0.26)	23.4 (0.12)	32.1 (0.28)	24.5 (0.23)	20.3 (0.23)	16.9 (0.19)
Iceland	24.6	26.5	30.5	35.8	31.3	32.8	32.5 (0.50)	36.2 (0.99)	35.2 (0.50)	38.4 (0.98)	37.1 (0.52)	40.6 (1.06)	42.0 (1.09)	36.1 (1.02)	28.8 (0.99)
Ireland	23.6	47.8	29.1	40.6	33.9	45.1	37.3 (0.13)	48.2 (0.26)	39.7 (0.14)	49.2 (0.28)	41.0 (0.27)	50.8 (0.48)	49.0 (0.40)	34.2 (0.38)	24.3 (0.37)
Israel	10.0	11.8	45.8	50.0	44.0	42.3	45.6 (0.20)	44.2 (0.38)	46.4 (0.20)	44.5 (0.38)	48.5 (0.20)	46.0 (0.38)	52.8 (0.39)	47.5 (0.41)	47.4 (0.43)
Italy	34.1	47.7	12.2	16.1	14.4	19.9	14.8 (0.07)	20.7 (0.19)	15.7 (0.08)	20.7 (0.21)	16.9 (0.08)	24.2 (0.22)	19.4 (0.17)	12.9 (0.14)	12.3 (0.16)
Japan[5]	25.0	39.5	39.9	53.2	42.8	55.1	44.8 (0.20)	56.7 (0.40)	46.6 (0.19)	58.6 (0.40)	27.6 (0.17)	36.8 (0.40)	56.4 (0.34)	25.5 (0.36)	20.8 (0.37)
Korea, Republic of	34.1	39.5	31.6	51.0	32.5	57.9	39.7 (0.25)	65.0 (0.46)	41.7 (0.25)	65.7 (0.46)	44.6 (0.25)	67.7 (0.45)	56.4 (0.46)	33.3 (0.46)	17.3 (0.48)
Luxembourg	18.1	23.4	26.5	37.0	27.7	38.7	35.5 (0.46)	44.2 (1.08)	39.1 (0.36)	49.9 (0.83)	45.9 (0.57)	52.9 (1.35)	55.8 (1.11)	39.7 (1.03)	31.7 (1.01)
Mexico	15.1	17.9	14.9	18.1	16.0	19.7	17.4 (0.00)	21.8 (0.00)	18.1 (0.00)	24.1 (0.00)	18.5 (0.05)	24.6 (0.10)	17.5 (0.09)	15.8 (0.10)	13.2 (0.10)
Netherlands	23.2	26.5	30.1	35.4	32.2	39.8	32.4 (0.10)	40.8 (0.23)	34.4 (0.10)	43.0 (0.23)	34.4 (0.10)	44.3 (0.24)	37.6 (0.21)	30.1 (0.17)	26.9 (0.17)
New Zealand	29.0	28.5	27.1	30.8	36.0	47.6	40.7 (0.41)	46.4 (0.89)	40.6 (0.41)	46.9 (0.89)	35.6 (0.40)	40.4 (0.87)	38.5 (0.81)	32.1 (0.74)	28.9 (0.77)
Norway	30.2	37.9	32.7	40.9	36.0	45.6	37.3 (0.20)	47.3 (0.45)	38.6 (0.21)	45.0 (0.46)	41.8 (0.21)	49.0 (0.46)	48.7 (0.42)	36.2 (0.39)	31.7 (0.41)
Poland	11.9	15.2	16.9	25.5	19.6	32.1	22.9 (0.09)	37.4 (0.21)	24.5 (0.10)	40.8 (0.25)	27.0 (0.10)	42.6 (0.23)	31.9 (0.22)	18.2 (0.18)	13.7 (0.14)
Portugal	9.2	13.7	12.8	19.1	14.3	23.2	15.4 (0.51)	24.8 (1.02)	18.5 (0.13)	28.3 (0.36)	21.7 (0.14)	31.4 (0.37)	26.4 (0.28)	16.6 (0.23)	12.8 (0.22)
Slovak Republic	10.9	11.9	13.7	16.3	14.8	18.4	17.3 (0.16)	24.0 (0.29)	19.0 (0.17)	27.0 (0.77)	20.4 (0.17)	29.8 (0.43)	20.7 (0.35)	15.3 (0.31)	13.9 (0.27)
Slovenia	—	—	20.2	24.7	22.6	30.0	23.7 (0.22)	31.3 (0.51)	26.4 (0.24)	35.4 (0.55)	28.6 (0.24)	38.1 (0.54)	34.7 (0.53)	24.3 (0.43)	17.9 (0.38)
Spain	23.6	35.5	28.2	39.7	29.2	38.8	30.7 (0.08)	39.2 (0.17)	32.3 (0.08)	39.3 (0.18)	34.7 (0.08)	41.5 (0.19)	42.8 (0.16)	30.2 (0.14)	21.2 (0.14)
Sweden	25.6	36.9	29.6	37.3	32.0	41.6	34.2 (0.11)	42.2 (0.23)	35.7 (0.11)	43.5 (0.24)	38.7 (0.12)	46.0 (0.25)	46.1 (0.24)	32.3 (0.22)	29.9 (0.21)
Switzerland	25.4	26.6	28.8	31.0	33.7	38.5	35.2 (0.16)	40.5 (0.39)	36.6 (0.18)	40.6 (0.46)	40.2 (0.17)	46.0 (0.41)	44.8 (0.32)	38.1 (0.30)	31.1 (0.32)
Turkey	8.4	10.2	9.7	11.8	12.0	15.5	13.1 (0.07)	17.4 (0.13)	15.3 (0.07)	21.0 (0.15)	16.7 (0.07)	24.8 (0.16)	15.9 (0.13)	9.9 (0.12)	10.0 (0.13)
United Kingdom	26.1	29.5	29.6	35.0	32.5	38.4	38.2 (0.21)	46.0 (0.46)	41.0 (0.11)	47.9 (0.23)	42.2 (0.11)	49.2 (0.23)	45.8 (0.22)	38.3 (0.20)	34.8 (0.21)
United States	37.3	39.1	39.0	39.2	41.1	41.6	41.7 (0.24)	42.3 (0.38)	43.1 (0.24)	44.0 (0.42)	44.2 (0.28)	45.7 (0.53)	47.2 (0.44)	43.0 (0.48)	41.0 (0.53)
Other reporting countries															
Brazil[2,4,6]	—	—	7.8	7.9	10.8	11.0	10.9 (0.07)	11.6 (0.12)	13.0 (0.07)	14.5 (0.12)	13.7 (0.19)	15.3 (0.26)	14.1 (0.25)	13.6 (0.26)	10.7 (0.27)
China[7]	4.6	6.1	—	—	—	—	9.7	17.9	(†)	(†)	(†)	(†)	(†)	(†)	(†)
Colombia[3]	—	—	—	—	—	—	—	—	19.7	—	22.4 (†)	27.7 (†)	23.0 (†)	18.3 (†)	16.1 (†)
Costa Rica	—	—	—	—	—	—	—	—	18.0	—	18.0 (0.25)	20.0 (0.32)	18.3 (0.35)	16.4 (0.33)	16.2 (0.38)
Indonesia[3,5,8]	—	—	—	—	4.5	—	7.5	—	8.5	10.3 (0.95)	(†)	(†)	(†)	(†)	(†)
Latvia	—	—	—	—	—	—	—	—	29.2 (0.40)	38.7 (0.95)	30.2 (0.67)	39.4 (1.15)	31.4 (1.19)	26.7 (0.98)	23.0 (0.96)
Lithuania	—	—	—	—	—	—	—	—	— (0.26)	38.7 (0.95)?	36.7 (0.26)	52.6 (0.69)	37.6 (0.54)	30.2 (0.42)	27.6 (0.46)
Russian Federation[2,4]	—	35.5	14.9	—	—	—	—	—	53.5	57.0	54.3 (0.11)	58.2 (0.23)	55.3 (0.23)	53.3 (0.21)	49.6 (0.27)
Saudi Arabia[2,4]	—	—	—	—	—	—	—	—	—	—	21.9 (†)	25.7	22.0 (†)	18.3 (†)	14.2 (†)
South Africa[8]	—	—	—	—	4.3	—	—	—	6.6	5.2	(†)	(†)	(†)	(†)	(†)

—Not available.
†Not applicable.

[1] Refers to the mean of the data values for all reporting Organization for Economic Cooperation and Development (OECD) countries, to which each country reporting data contributes equally. The average includes all current OECD countries for which a given year's data are available, even if they were not members of OECD in that year.
[2] Data from 2013 reported for 2014.
[3] Data from 2011 reported for 2012.
[4] Data from 2004 reported for 2005.
[5] Data for 2014 exclude short-cycle tertiary education, which corresponds to the associate's degree in the United States.
[6] Data from 2009 reported for 2010.
[7] Data from 2000 reported for 2001.

[8] Data from 2007 reported for 2008.
NOTE: Data in this table include all tertiary degrees, which correspond to all degrees at the associate's level and above in the United States. The International Standard Classification of Education (ISCED) was revised in 2011. The previous version, ISCED 1997, was used to calculate all data for 2012 and earlier years. For 2014 were calculated using ISCED 2011 and may not be comparable to data for earlier years. (The countries for which 2014 data were calculated using ISCED 1997 are Brazil, the Russian Federation, and Saudi Arabia.) Under ISCED 2011, tertiary degrees are classified at the following levels: level 5 (corresponding to an associate's degree in the United States), level 6 (a bachelor's or equivalent degree), level 7 (a master's or equivalent degree), and level 8 (a doctoral or equivalent degree). Standard errors are not available for years prior to 2010.
SOURCE: Organization for Economic Cooperation and Development (OECD), Education at a Glance, selected years, 2003 through 2015. (This table was prepared January 2016.)

Table 603.30. Percentage of the population 25 to 64 years old who attained a postsecondary degree, by highest degree attained, age group, and country: 2014

[Standard errors appear in parentheses]

Country	Associate's degree (short-cycle tertiary)					Bachelor's or equivalent degree				
	Total, 25 to 64 years old	25 to 34 years old	35 to 44 years old	45 to 54 years old	55 to 64 years old	Total, 25 to 64 years old	25 to 34 years old	35 to 44 years old	45 to 54 years old	55 to 64 years old
1	2	3	4	5	6	7	8	9	10	11
OECD average[1]	7.6 (0.02)	7.4 (0.05)	9.0 (0.05)	7.9 (0.05)	7.8 (0.05)	15.1 (0.03)	20.7 (0.07)	16.6 (0.06)	12.3 (0.05)	10.4 (0.05)
Australia	11.4 (0.19)	9.9 (0.35)	12.9 (0.39)	12.2 (0.39)	10.5 (0.39)	23.8 (0.25)	30.2 (0.54)	25.3 (0.51)	19.9 (0.47)	18.0 (0.48)
Austria	15.5 (0.19)	17.4 (0.44)	16.8 (0.39)	15.1 (0.35)	12.5 (0.32)	2.1 (0.08)	5.3 (0.25)	1.7 (0.16)	0.9 (0.09)	0.5 (0.07)
Belgium	0.4 (0.03)	0.4 (0.06)	0.5 (0.06)	0.3 (0.05)	‡ (†)	20.2 (0.19)	23.1 (0.41)	22.5 (0.39)	19.7 (0.35)	15.4 (0.33)
Canada[2]	25.1 (0.17)	24.5 (0.32)	27.0 (0.32)	26.0 (0.28)	22.9 (0.29)	19.4 (0.19)	24.1 (0.35)	22.6 (0.36)	17.0 (0.27)	14.0 (0.28)
Chile[2,3]	7.2 (0.08)	8.6 (0.17)	8.7 (0.17)	6.8 (0.14)	4.1 (0.13)	12.6 (0.10)	17.6 (0.23)	13.9 (0.21)	9.0 (0.16)	9.2 (0.19)
Czech Republic	0.1 (0.01)	0.2 (0.03)	‡ (†)	‡ (†)	‡ (†)	5.1 (0.06)	10.6 (0.20)	5.1 (0.12)	2.8 (0.10)	1.5 (0.07)
Denmark	4.5 (0.08)	4.1 (0.18)	5.2 (0.18)	4.7 (0.15)	3.9 (0.15)	19.5 (0.16)	22.4 (0.39)	20.2 (0.33)	17.9 (0.27)	18.0 (0.29)
Estonia	7.0 (0.22)	1.0 (0.18)	7.0 (0.43)	9.0 (0.48)	12.0 (0.56)	10.0 (0.26)	23.0 (0.76)	11.0 (0.52)	3.0 (0.29)	1.0 (0.17)
Finland	12.5 (0.11)	0.5 (0.05)	11.5 (0.23)	19.8 (0.26)	17.1 (0.24)	14.7 (0.12)	25.8 (0.33)	18.3 (0.28)	8.6 (0.18)	7.2 (0.17)
France[3]	14.0 (0.07)	17.5 (0.17)	17.4 (0.15)	12.4 (0.12)	8.9 (0.11)	8.9 (0.06)	12.1 (0.14)	11.9 (0.13)	6.2 (0.09)	5.8 (0.09)
Germany	0.7 (0.01)	0.4 (0.02)	0.6 (0.03)	0.8 (0.03)	0.7 (0.03)	14.3 (0.06)	14.3 (0.14)	14.4 (0.14)	14.7 (0.12)	13.8 (0.13)
Greece	1.7 (0.04)	1.2 (0.07)	0.9 (0.05)	2.6 (0.09)	2.2 (0.08)	23.4 (0.12)	33.7 (0.30)	22.0 (0.23)	20.4 (0.22)	17.5 (0.21)
Hungary	1.3 (0.03)	3.0 (0.10)	1.3 (0.06)	0.6 (0.04)	‡ (†)	12.8 (0.09)	15.7 (0.22)	13.4 (0.18)	12.0 (0.18)	10.3 (0.15)
Iceland	3.5 (0.20)	2.6 (0.34)	4.1 (0.44)	3.6 (0.40)	3.9 (0.42)	20.1 (0.43)	25.7 (0.94)	21.5 (0.91)	17.9 (0.82)	14.5 (0.77)
Ireland	11.8 (0.12)	11.8 (0.22)	14.9 (0.24)	11.1 (0.21)	8.4 (0.19)	20.8 (0.19)	28.7 (0.39)	23.7 (0.31)	16.4 (0.27)	11.4 (0.26)
Israel	14.0 (0.14)	11.4 (0.24)	14.1 (0.27)	15.3 (0.29)	16.5 (0.32)	22.0 (0.17)	26.9 (0.34)	24.6 (0.34)	17.6 (0.31)	16.2 (0.32)
Italy	‡ (†)	‡ (†)	‡ (†)	‡ (†)	‡ (†)	3.3 (0.04)	8.8 (0.14)	2.7 (0.07)	1.7 (0.06)	1.0 (0.05)
Japan	— (†)	— (†)	— (†)	— (†)	— (†)	— (†)	— (†)	— (†)	— (†)	— (†)
Korea, Republic of[4]	13.3 (0.17)	23.2 (0.41)	17.8 (0.36)	7.8 (0.26)	3.3 (0.23)	31.3 (0.23)	44.5 (0.48)	38.6 (0.45)	25.5 (0.42)	14.0 (0.44)
Luxembourg	9.3 (0.33)	9.9 (0.81)	10.5 (0.69)	8.3 (0.58)	8.3 (0.60)	15.0 (0.41)	16.6 (1.01)	17.7 (0.86)	13.5 (0.72)	11.3 (0.69)
Mexico[4]	0.6 (0.01)	0.7 (0.02)	0.7 (0.02)	0.5 (0.02)	0.3 (0.02)	17.9 (0.05)	23.8 (0.10)	16.8 (0.09)	15.2 (0.10)	12.9 (0.10)
Netherlands	2.5 (0.03)	1.8 (0.10)	2.6 (0.07)	2.9 (0.06)	2.4 (0.06)	19.7 (0.08)	26.4 (0.21)	21.1 (0.17)	16.5 (0.13)	15.8 (0.14)
New Zealand	5.3 (0.19)	3.7 (0.33)	4.7 (0.35)	5.6 (0.36)	7.4 (0.45)	25.6 (0.36)	32.0 (0.82)	30.2 (0.76)	22.1 (0.66)	17.5 (0.65)
Norway	11.9 (0.14)	14.0 (0.32)	13.5 (0.29)	10.9 (0.25)	8.9 (0.25)	19.1 (0.17)	22.3 (0.38)	21.6 (0.35)	16.2 (0.30)	15.8 (0.32)
Poland	0.1 (0.01)	0.1 (0.01)	0.1 (0.01)	0.1 (0.01)	0.2 (0.02)	5.6 (0.05)	11.3 (0.15)	5.7 (0.11)	2.5 (0.07)	2.4 (0.06)
Portugal	‡ (†)	‡ (†)	‡ (†)	‡ (†)	‡ (†)	4.6 (0.07)	10.1 (0.24)	3.6 (0.12)	2.5 (0.10)	3.0 (0.11)
Slovak Republic	0.3 (0.02)	0.3! (0.05)	‡ (†)	0.4! (0.05)	‡ (†)	3.2 (0.08)	6.0 (0.22)	3.3 (0.15)	1.8 (0.11)	1.3 (0.09)
Slovenia	6.8 (0.13)	6.0 (0.26)	6.5 (0.28)	7.4 (0.26)	7.2 (0.26)	6.4 (0.13)	12.5 (0.37)	7.3 (0.29)	4.0 (0.19)	2.0 (0.14)
Spain	10.7 (0.05)	13.0 (0.13)	13.8 (0.11)	9.5 (0.09)	5.3 (0.08)	9.4 (0.05)	11.2 (0.12)	11.2 (0.10)	7.8 (0.08)	6.9 (0.09)
Sweden	9.8 (0.07)	10.3 (0.15)	8.9 (0.14)	9.4 (0.14)	10.6 (0.14)	15.5 (0.09)	22.2 (0.21)	18.9 (0.19)	11.1 (0.15)	9.4 (0.14)
Switzerland[5]	[5]	[5]	[5]	[5]	[5]	19.8 (0.14)	24.4 (0.35)	20.9 (0.27)	18.3 (0.24)	15.2 (0.24)
Turkey	4.9 (0.04)	7.1 (0.10)	4.2 (0.07)	3.3 (0.07)	3.9 (0.09)	10.1 (0.06)	15.5 (0.13)	9.9 (0.11)	5.6 (0.09)	5.3 (0.10)
United Kingdom	11.2 (0.07)	7.8 (0.12)	14.7 (0.15)	11.7 (0.13)	10.9 (0.14)	21.8 (0.09)	30.5 (0.21)	22.2 (0.18)	17.9 (0.16)	15.9 (0.16)
United States	10.8 (0.16)	10.3 (0.29)	11.3 (0.27)	10.9 (0.27)	10.5 (0.32)	21.6 (0.23)	24.9 (0.46)	22.5 (0.36)	20.8 (0.42)	18.1 (0.39)

See notes at end of table.

Table 603.30. Percentage of the population 25 to 64 years old who attained a postsecondary degree, by highest degree attained, age group, and country: 2014—Continued

[Standard errors appear in parentheses]

Country	Master's or equivalent degree					Doctoral or equivalent degree				
	Total, 25 to 64 years old	25 to 34 years old	35 to 44 years old	45 to 54 years old	55 to 64 years old	Total, 25 to 64 years old	25 to 34 years old	35 to 44 years old	45 to 54 years old	55 to 64 years old
1	12	13	14	15	16	17	18	19	20	21
OECD average[1]	11.4 (0.03)	13.6 (0.07)	13.4 (0.06)	10.1 (0.05)	8.2 (0.05)	1.0 (0.01)	0.7 (0.02)	1.3 (0.02)	1.1 (0.02)	1.0 (0.02)
Australia	5.6 (0.14)	7.2 (0.30)	6.4 (0.28)	4.8 (0.23)	3.6 (0.23)	1.2 (0.06)	0.8 (0.11)	1.4 (0.14)	1.2 (0.13)	1.4 (0.15)
Austria	11.1 (0.18)	14.8 (0.41)	13.2 (0.38)	9.2 (0.27)	7.2 (0.27)	1.3 (0.07)	0.9 (0.11)	1.6 (0.15)	1.3 (0.11)	1.2 (0.12)
Belgium	15.6 (0.18)	20.1 (0.41)	18.5 (0.37)	13.8 (0.31)	10.1 (0.28)	0.6 (0.04)	0.7 (0.08)	0.8 (0.08)	0.6 (0.07)	0.5 (0.06)
Canada[2]	9.1 (0.14)	9.1 (0.24)	11.0 (0.28)	8.2 (0.20)	8.1 (0.22)	[²]	[²]	[²]	[²]	[²]
Chile[2,3]	1.3 (0.03)	1.1 (0.06)	1.6 (0.08)	1.2 (0.07)	1.2 (0.07)	[²]	[²]	[²]	[²]	[²]
Czech Republic	15.8 (0.11)	18.6 (0.25)	15.4 (0.20)	16.3 (0.18)	12.9 (0.18)	0.5 (0.02)	0.4 (0.04)	0.5 (0.04)	0.4 (0.04)	0.6 (0.04)
Denmark	10.9 (0.12)	14.8 (0.33)	13.6 (0.28)	9.0 (0.20)	6.9 (0.19)	0.9 (0.04)	0.8 (0.08)	1.6 (0.10)	0.9 (0.07)	0.4 ! (0.05)
Estonia	20.0 (0.34)	16.0 (0.66)	20.0 (0.67)	22.0 (0.71)	22.0 (0.71)	1.0 (0.09)	‡ (†)	1.0 (0.17)	‡ (†)	‡ (†)
Finland	13.4 (0.12)	13.6 (0.26)	18.4 (0.28)	13.7 (0.23)	8.5 (0.18)	1.2 (0.04)	0.4 (0.04)	1.6 (0.09)	1.6 (0.08)	1.3 (0.07)
France[3]	8.4 (0.05)	13.8 (0.15)	8.9 (0.11)	6.2 (0.09)	4.9 (0.08)	0.8 (0.02)	0.6 (0.03)	0.9 (0.04)	0.8 (0.03)	0.8 (0.03)
Germany	10.8 (0.06)	12.7 (0.13)	11.8 (0.12)	9.3 (0.10)	9.7 (0.11)	1.3 (0.02)	1.0 (0.04)	1.7 (0.05)	1.4 (0.04)	1.3 (0.04)
Greece	2.4 (0.04)	3.4 (0.11)	3.3 (0.10)	1.9 (0.07)	0.9 (0.05)	0.6 (0.02)	0.4 (0.04)	0.9 (0.05)	0.6 (0.04)	0.5 (0.04)
Hungary	8.6 (0.08)	12.7 (0.20)	9.3 (0.15)	7.0 (0.14)	5.7 (0.12)	0.7 (0.02)	0.7 (0.05)	0.6 (0.04)	0.6 (0.04)	0.7 (0.04)
Iceland	12.3 (0.36)	12.2 (0.70)	14.9 (0.79)	13.0 (0.72)	8.7 (0.62)	1.2 (0.12)	‡ (†)	1.5 (0.27)	1.6 (0.27)	1.7 (0.28)
Ireland	7.5 (0.12)	9.5 (0.24)	9.5 (0.21)	5.9 (0.16)	4.1 (0.15)	0.8 (0.03)	0.8 (0.06)	0.9 (0.06)	0.7 (0.05)	0.5 (0.05)
Israel	11.3 (0.13)	7.4 (0.20)	12.9 (0.26)	13.2 (0.28)	13.0 (0.29)	1.2 (0.04)	0.4 (0.05)	1.3 (0.09)	1.5 (0.10)	1.7 (0.11)
Italy	13.2 (0.07)	14.9 (0.18)	16.1 (0.16)	10.7 (0.13)	11.2 (0.15)	0.4 (0.01)	0.4 (0.03)	0.6 (0.04)	0.4 (0.03)	0.1 (0.02)
Japan	— (†)	— (†)	— (†)	— (†)	— (†)	— (†)	— (†)	— (†)	— (†)	— (†)
Korea, Republic of[4]	[⁴] (†)	[⁴]	[⁴]	[⁴]	[⁴]	[⁴] (†)	[⁴]	[⁴]	[⁴]	[⁴]
Luxembourg	20.1 (0.46)	25.5 (1.18)	25.8 (0.98)	16.7 (0.79)	9.8 (0.65)	1.4 (0.14)	0.9 (0.25)	1.8 (0.29)	1.1 (0.22)	2.3 (0.32)
Mexico[4]	[⁴] (†)	[⁴]	[⁴]	[⁴]	[⁴]	[⁴] (†)	[⁴]	[⁴]	[⁴]	[⁴]
Netherlands	11.6 (0.06)	15.6 (0.17)	13.1 (0.14)	10.0 (0.11)	8.2 (0.10)	0.6 (0.02)	0.5 (0.03)	0.8 (0.04)	0.6 (0.03)	0.5 (0.03)
New Zealand	3.9 (0.16)	4.4 (0.36)	4.7 (0.35)	3.3 (0.28)	3.2 (0.30)	0.9 (0.08)	0.3 (0.10)	1.2 (0.18)	1.1 (0.17)	0.8 (0.15)
Norway	9.9 (0.13)	12.3 (0.30)	12.6 (0.28)	7.9 (0.22)	6.1 (0.21)	0.9 (0.04)	0.4 (0.06)	1.0 (0.08)	1.2 (0.09)	0.9 (0.08)
Poland	20.7 (0.09)	30.8 (0.21)	25.3 (0.20)	15.1 (0.16)	10.6 (0.13)	0.5 (0.02)	0.4 (0.03)	0.8 (0.04)	0.5 (0.03)	0.5 (0.03)
Portugal	16.6 (0.12)	21.0 (0.33)	22.2 (0.27)	13.3 (0.21)	9.4 (0.19)	0.6 (0.03)	‡ (†)	0.6 (0.05)	0.9 (0.05)	0.4 (0.04)
Slovak Republic	16.4 (0.16)	22.9 (0.39)	16.5 (0.32)	12.8 (0.28)	11.9 (0.26)	0.6 (0.03)	0.6 (0.07)	0.7 (0.07)	0.4 ! (0.05)	0.5 (0.06)
Slovenia	13.3 (0.18)	17.8 (0.43)	17.7 (0.43)	10.6 (0.31)	7.6 (0.27)	2.1 (0.08)	1.9 (0.15)	3.2 (0.20)	2.2 (0.15)	1.1 (0.10)
Spain	13.9 (0.06)	17.0 (0.14)	16.9 (0.12)	12.1 (0.10)	8.3 (0.09)	0.7 (0.01)	0.3 (0.02)	0.8 (0.03)	0.8 (0.03)	0.7 (0.03)
Sweden	12.0 (0.08)	12.9 (0.17)	16.3 (0.18)	10.0 (0.14)	8.5 (0.13)	1.5 (0.03)	0.7 (0.04)	2.0 (0.07)	1.8 (0.06)	1.4 (0.05)
Switzerland[5]	17.3 (0.13)	19.3 (0.33)	19.8 (0.26)	16.7 (0.23)	12.8 (0.23)	3.2 (0.06)	2.4 (0.13)	4.0 (0.13)	3.1 (0.11)	3.1 (0.12)
Turkey	1.3 (0.02)	2.0 (0.05)	1.4 (0.04)	0.7 (0.03)	0.5 (0.03)	0.3 (0.01)	0.1 (0.01)	0.4 (0.02)	0.3 (0.02)	0.2 (0.02)
United Kingdom	8.0 (0.06)	9.9 (0.14)	7.6 (0.12)	7.5 (0.11)	6.8 (0.11)	1.2 (0.02)	1.0 (0.05)	1.2 (0.05)	1.2 (0.05)	1.2 (0.05)
United States	10.2 (0.16)	9.3 (0.32)	11.5 (0.28)	9.7 (0.28)	10.5 (0.31)	1.6 (0.06)	1.2 (0.11)	1.9 (0.13)	1.6 (0.12)	1.9 (0.14)

—Not available.
†Not applicable.
‡Reporting standards not met (too few cases for a reliable estimate).
!Interpret data with caution. Country indicated that this value fell below a specified reliability threshold, which varies from country to country. (For more information, see http://www.oecd.org/edu/EAG2015-Annex3-ChapterA.pdf.)
[1] Refers to the mean of the data values for all reporting Organization for Economic Cooperation and Development (OECD) countries, to which each country reporting data contributes equally.
[2] Doctoral or equivalent degree data are included in columns for master's or equivalent degree.
[3] Data from 2013 reported for 2014.

[4] Master's or equivalent degree data and doctoral or equivalent degree data are included in columns for bachelor's or equivalent degree.
[5] Associate's degree data are included in columns for bachelor's or equivalent, master's or equivalent, and doctoral or equivalent degrees.
NOTE: All data in this table were calculated using the International Standard Classification of Education (ISCED) 2011 classification of tertiary degrees. Includes degrees at ISCED 2011 level 5 (short-cycle tertiary, which corresponds to the associate's degree in the United States), level 6 (bachelor's or equivalent degree), level 7 (master's or equivalent degree), and level 8 (doctoral or equivalent degree).
SOURCE: Organization for Economic Cooperation and Development (OECD), Education at a Glance, 2015. (This table was prepared January 2016.)

Table 603.40. Percentage of the population 25 to 64 years old who attained a postsecondary vocational degree, by age group and country: Selected years, 1999 through 2012

[Standard errors appear in parentheses]

Country	1999 Total, 25 to 64 years old	1999 25 to 34 years old	2001 Total, 25 to 64 years old	2001 25 to 34 years old	2005 Total, 25 to 64 years old	2005 25 to 34 years old	2008 Total, 25 to 64 years old	2008 25 to 34 years old	2009 Total, 25 to 64 years old	2009 25 to 34 years old	2010 Total, 25 to 64 years old	2010 25 to 34 years old	2012 Total, 25 to 64 years old	2012 25 to 34 years old
	2	3	4	5	6	7	8	9	10	11	12	13	14	15
OECD average[1]	**8.4**	**10.5**	**8.9**	**10.8**	**8.6**	**9.6**	**9.7**	**10.4**	**10.4** (0.03)	**11.0** (0.07)	**10.2** (0.04)	**10.9** (0.07)	**9.8** (0.03)	**10.0** (0.06)
Australia	9.0	8.8	9.7	9.7	9.0	8.9	10.1	9.8	10.1 (0.20)	10.2 (0.39)	10.7 (0.29)	10.2 (0.52)	11.5 (0.17)	10.5 (0.33)
Austria[2]	4.7	5.8	7.3	7.4	8.7	8.1	7.4	5.9	7.6 (0.08)	5.8 (0.16)	7.3 (0.19)	5.4 (0.29)	7.3 (0.14)	5.2 (0.29)
Belgium	13.9	17.9	14.9	19.7	17.3	21.5	15.9	19.5	15.9 (0.15)	18.3 (0.34)	17.8 (0.16)	20.5 (0.36)	16.9 (0.16)	18.2 (0.35)
Canada[3,4,5]	20.2	23.7	21.2	25.4	22.8	25.6	23.6	26.1	24.1 (0.16)	26.0 (0.32)	24.2 (0.17)	25.8 (0.38)	24.9 (0.16)	25.5 (0.32)
Chile[2,3,4,5]	0.9	1.4	1.0	1.6	2.8	4.1	8.5	11.5	8.0 (0.11)	11.0 (0.22)	10.3 (0.13)	13.1 (0.23)	5.8 (0.07)	6.1 (0.15)
Denmark	—	—	5.3	5.8	7.6	9.1	7.0	8.2	7.2 (0.11)	8.5 (0.35)	6.3 (0.10)	6.2 (0.25)	5.6 (0.09)	5.3 (0.21)
Estonia	—	—	—	—	11.1	8.7	12.0	12.3	13.2 (0.33)	14.8 (0.75)	13.3 (0.55)	14.0 (1.24)	12.6 (0.45)	13.1 (0.98)
Finland	17.4	21.8	17.5	20.2	16.6	11.0	15.0	5.4	14.7 (0.11)	3.4 (0.13)	14.7 (0.18)	2.5 (0.17)	13.5 (0.17)	0.9 (0.10)
France	10.5	15.6	11.2	16.7	10.0	17.0	11.1	16.9	11.6 (0.07)	17.5 (0.18)	11.5 (0.06)	16.9 (0.16)	11.9 (0.06)	16.1 (0.16)
Germany	9.9	8.6	9.7	8.2	9.7	7.4	9.0	6.5	9.3 (0.05)	6.8 (0.09)	9.6 (0.05)	7.2 (0.10)	11.1 (0.06)	9.5 (0.11)
Greece	5.5	8.6	5.4	—	6.7	8.4	6.6	9.6	6.7 (0.06)	10.1 (0.16)	7.2 (0.16)	10.9 (0.34)	8.8 (0.08)	13.5 (0.21)
Hungary	—	—	—	—	0.2	0.5	#	1.0	# (t)	1.0 (#)	0.6 (0.02)	1.4 (0.06)	0.7 (0.02)	1.5 (0.07)
Iceland	4.6	5.3	6.0	5.5	4.7	3.3	3.4	2.2	3.9 (0.21)	2.5 (0.31)	3.8 (0.20)	2.2 (0.30)	4.1 (0.21)	2.6 (0.32)
Ireland[2]	10.5	13.4	21.6	28.1	10.6	14.4	11.7	14.5	14.9 (0.10)	18.7 (0.20)	15.6 (0.10)	18.4 (0.20)	14.8 (0.10)	16.0 (0.20)
Israel	—	—	—	—	16.0	15.1	15.1	13.4	15.5 (0.14)	13.4 (0.26)	15.0 (0.14)	12.4 (0.25)	13.9 (0.14)	11.7 (0.25)
Italy	—	—	—	—	0.5	0.6	#	#	# (t)	# (t)	# (t)	# (t)	0.3 (—)	0.2 (—)
Japan	13.4	22.1	14.6	23.4	17.7	25.3	18.5	24.1	19.1 (0.16)	23.9 (0.25)	19.5 (0.16)	23.7 (0.34)	20.2 (0.15)	23.4 (0.35)
Korea, Republic of	5.8	11.9	6.7	14.5	8.9	19.3	10.9	23.3	11.6 (0.16)	25.5 (0.42)	12.2 (0.17)	26.0 (0.43)	13.3 (0.17)	25.8 (0.43)
Luxembourg	6.6	8.1	6.7	8.3	9.6	13.2	7.7	10.8	14.6 (0.34)	20.4 (0.87)	14.7 (0.34)	18.1 (0.84)	13.1 (0.25)	14.1 (0.58)
Mexico	1.3	2.2	1.7	2.7	1.1	1.2	1.1	1.2	1.1 (0.01)	1.2 (0.03)	1.1 (#)	1.3 (#)	1.2 (#)	1.4 (#)
Netherlands	2.5	2.4	2.3	2.4	1.8	1.6	2.4	2.2	2.8 (0.03)	2.5 (0.07)	2.5 (0.03)	2.4 (0.07)	2.8 (0.03)	2.6 (0.07)
New Zealand	13.9	10.4	15.3	11.6	7.4	4.6	14.9	13.9	16.9 (0.36)	15.9 (0.76)	16.4 (0.31)	14.9 (0.64)	15.3 (0.30)	14.1 (0.62)
Norway[2]	2.0	2.2	2.6	2.6	2.4	1.9	2.4	1.8	2.2 (0.06)	1.4 (0.11)	2.1 (0.06)	1.0 (0.09)	2.4 (0.06)	0.8 (0.08)
Portugal	2.7	3.0	2.4	3.1	—	—	—	—	— (t)	— (t)	— (t)	— (t)	— (t)	— (t)
Slovak Republic	—	—	0.6	0.6	0.8	0.9	0.8	0.6	0.8 (0.04)	0.9 (0.08)	0.7 (0.04)	0.6 (0.05)	1.3 (0.09)	1.2 (0.19)
Slovenia	—	—	—	—	9.6	9.5	10.8	11.7	10.8 (0.16)	11.7 (0.35)	10.6 (0.16)	12.2 (0.36)	11.7 (0.18)	13.8 (0.40)
Spain	6.2	11.4	6.7	11.6	8.3	12.8	9.2	13.0	9.5 (0.05)	13.2 (0.11)	9.2 (0.05)	12.2 (0.11)	9.7 (0.05)	12.5 (0.12)
Sweden	15.6	20.7	14.7	17.1	9.1	8.9	8.6	8.4	8.7 (0.07)	8.5 (0.15)	8.8 (0.06)	8.2 (0.13)	9.1 (0.07)	9.4 (0.14)
Switzerland	9.1	9.3	9.6	9.7	9.7	9.1	10.4	9.7	10.3 (0.17)	9.4 (0.36)	10.8 (0.11)	9.9 (0.24)	10.8 (0.12)	9.0 (0.25)
United Kingdom	8.2	8.4	8.0	9.0	8.8	8.1	9.0	7.7	10.0 (0.06)	8.5 (0.12)	10.2 (0.13)	8.1 (0.25)	10.0 (0.06)	7.7 (0.12)
United States	8.3	8.7	9.0	9.2	9.4	9.0	9.6	9.3	9.8 (0.08)	8.9 (0.15)	10.0 (0.12)	9.5 (0.22)	10.4 (0.12)	9.9 (0.20)
Other reporting countries														
Russian Federation[6]	—	—	33.5	34.2	—	—	—	—	— (t)	— (t)	— (t)	— (t)	25.7 (—)	21.5 (—)

—Not available.
†Not applicable.
#Rounds to zero.
[1]Refers to the mean of the data values for all reporting Organization for Economic Cooperation and Development (OECD) countries, to which each country reporting data contributes equally. The average includes all current OECD countries for which a given year's data are available, even if they were not members of OECD in that year.
[2]Data from 1998 reported for 1999.
[3]Data from 2000 reported for 2001.
[4]Data from 2004 reported for 2005.
[5]Data from 2011 reported for 2012.
[6]Data from 2002 reported for 2001.

NOTE: Data in this table refer to degrees classified as International Standard Classification of Education (ISCED) 1997 level 5B. ISCED level 5B corresponds to the associate's degree in the United States. Data for the Czech Republic, Poland, and Turkey are not shown because these countries do not separate tertiary degrees at this level. Standard errors are not available for years prior to 2009.
SOURCE: Organization for Economic Cooperation and Development (OECD), Education at a Glance, 2001 through 2014. (This table was prepared December 2014.)

Table 603.50. Number of bachelor's degree recipients per 100 persons at the typical minimum age of graduation, by sex and country: Selected years, 2005 through 2012

Country	Typical age of graduation[1] 2012	Total							Male							Female						
		2005	2007	2008	2009	2010	2011	2012	2005	2007	2008	2009	2010	2011	2012	2005	2007	2008	2009	2010	2011	2012
1	2	3	4	5	6	7	8	9	10	11	12	13	14	15	16	17	18	19	20	21	22	23
OECD average[2]	—	34.7	37.5	39.1	38.9	39.8	39.7	40.8	27.5	30.0	31.0	31.0	31.5	31.8	32.7	42.3	45.3	47.5	47.1	48.5	48.0	49.3
Australia	23	59.9	60.7	58.9	58.5	58.6	59.0	63.4	47.9	48.6	47.0	46.9	46.5	47.0	50.6	72.5	73.4	71.4	70.8	71.4	71.8	76.7
Austria	22–25	20.4	22.4	25.8	30.3	30.7	33.7	36.4	19.0	20.8	22.7	25.9	26.3	28.5	29.7	21.8	24.0	29.1	34.7	35.2	39.0	43.3
Belgium (Flemish)[3]	21	18.4	35.4	27.0	—	—	—	—	17.0	32.6	24.4	—	—	—	—	19.8	38.2	29.6	—	—	—	—
Canada	22	33.6	35.2	39.5	38.9	38.6	37.6	35.1	25.2	26.5	29.1	29.3	29.1	28.5	26.8	42.2	44.3	50.6	49.0	48.6	47.2	43.9
Chile	23–26	11.5	14.5	14.7	17.6	18.1	18.5	19.0	9.7	11.9	11.7	13.2	14.9	15.5	16.1	13.4	17.3	17.8	22.1	21.5	21.6	21.9
Czech Republic	22–26	26.0	36.4	39.2	39.7	42.3	42.8	45.2	22.6	31.0	32.2	30.4	31.1	30.8	32.9	29.5	42.1	46.6	49.7	54.4	55.5	57.9
Denmark	24–26	52.9	50.9	50.3	48.3	50.7	50.6	49.3	37.2	38.3	38.3	35.3	37.5	38.3	37.1	69.2	63.9	62.6	61.7	64.3	63.3	62.0
Estonia	22–24	28.5	27.3	23.8	22.9	22.3	23.8	22.1	17.6	17.6	14.9	13.7	14.0	15.4	15.1	39.5	37.3	32.8	32.7	31.6	32.6	29.4
Finland[4]	24	53.8	58.8	79.8	42.3	46.4	50.3	52.0	38.8	41.3	55.3	28.7	33.1	36.4	38.4	69.7	77.4	105.6	56.6	60.3	65.0	66.3
France	19–24	—	33.8	33.9	33.0	—	—	—	—	30.2	30.3	29.8	—	—	—	—	37.5	37.6	36.3	—	—	—
Germany	24–27	20.5	23.2	25.5	28.9	30.4	31.0	30.5	20.0	22.0	24.0	27.4	28.7	29.6	29.0	21.1	24.4	27.0	30.5	32.2	32.5	32.0
Greece[3]	23–24	23.9	21.7	26.6	—	25.4	27.3	26.7	16.3	14.7	18.3	—	17.5	18.6	18.7	32.2	29.4	35.5	—	34.0	36.7	35.5
Hungary	21–24	41.5	38.8	37.6	39.0	38.4	32.8	29.9	29.6	26.2	25.2	27.1	28.0	25.0	23.0	54.5	51.8	50.4	51.2	49.1	41.0	37.2
Iceland	23–25	56.3	62.8	55.9	50.7	65.4	—	57.7	33.6	38.0	34.1	30.7	40.1	—	38.8	80.5	88.0	78.9	72.2	91.3	—	77.9
Ireland	21	40.7	44.8	46.0	47.1	52.2	46.8	48.3	33.3	36.4	36.9	38.5	45.3	40.0	40.7	48.0	53.4	55.2	55.4	58.9	53.5	56.1
Israel	26–29	32.9	36.1	36.3	36.4	36.8	38.5	41.1	25.7	29.1	29.6	30.8	30.6	31.8	33.6	40.2	43.1	43.1	42.0	43.1	45.3	48.7
Italy	23–25	44.8	38.7	35.8	34.6	33.6	34.3	33.1	37.3	31.6	29.5	28.5	26.9	27.3	25.9	52.7	46.1	42.3	40.9	40.6	41.6	40.6
Japan	21–23	36.9	38.8	40.6	41.5	41.3	44.8	46.3	41.3	42.9	44.9	46.1	45.4	49.2	50.1	32.2	34.4	36.0	36.7	37.1	40.2	42.3
Korea, Republic of	22–26	35.5	42.9	48.7	50.0	50.7	49.9	49.0	34.8	42.7	49.0	51.0	50.9	49.2	47.3	36.2	43.2	48.5	48.8	50.4	50.7	51.1
Mexico	23	15.2	18.2	17.8	19.0	19.5	20.9	21.3	14.5	16.8	16.2	17.4	17.7	19.3	20.0	15.9	19.7	19.3	20.7	21.2	22.4	22.6
Netherlands	23	47.2	47.8	46.0	45.6	44.7	45.3	49.2	40.2	41.7	39.8	39.4	38.6	38.5	42.2	54.3	54.1	52.3	51.9	51.0	52.2	56.2
New Zealand	21–23	49.0	53.8	50.0	50.7	47.3	51.0	54.8	36.6	41.6	37.6	38.9	36.7	37.6	40.2	62.0	66.0	63.0	63.1	58.6	65.1	70.6
Norway	22–25	42.1	45.0	46.1	44.3	46.1	46.1	44.3	28.8	31.8	33.9	33.4	33.7	33.4	32.5	55.8	58.7	58.8	57.3	58.8	59.3	56.5
Poland	23–25	45.0	46.6	48.2	49.4	56.9	60.6	55.7	32.8	34.4	35.0	35.9	40.5	42.9	40.3	57.6	59.2	61.9	63.3	73.8	79.1	71.6
Portugal	22	33.7	46.0	50.4	44.3	44.6	42.9	44.4	21.7	35.0	40.3	35.9	34.5	34.2	36.0	46.0	57.4	60.9	53.1	55.2	52.1	53.0
Slovak Republic	21–23	30.1	37.9	57.6	61.7	50.9	48.6	46.3	25.6	26.8	38.7	42.8	35.2	33.9	32.7	34.8	49.6	77.3	81.5	67.3	63.6	60.5
Slovenia	23–26	21.6	21.1	22.6	27.9	34.7	38.1	45.6	14.3	13.9	14.4	17.2	21.7	25.2	31.1	29.4	29.0	31.7	39.6	49.2	52.1	61.4
Spain	20–22	35.0	34.7	35.5	37.4	39.5	45.1	43.1	27.1	26.6	27.3	28.8	30.7	35.7	35.7	43.3	43.3	44.2	46.4	48.5	54.9	51.0
Sweden	25	44.0	42.2	40.9	38.1	35.7	38.5	35.1	30.8	29.1	27.9	25.8	23.6	25.0	23.8	57.6	55.8	54.7	51.0	48.6	52.7	47.0
Switzerland	24–26	25.0	28.9	30.6	29.2	28.8	28.0	28.7	26.1	28.7	29.2	27.0	26.7	25.4	26.4	23.9	29.2	32.0	31.5	31.0	30.7	31.2
Turkey	23–24	11.3	17.0	19.5	20.8	23.1	22.7	27.1	11.8	17.9	20.6	22.4	24.9	23.9	27.4	10.7	15.9	18.4	19.2	21.2	21.4	26.8
United Kingdom	20–24	39.8	39.0	40.2	39.9	41.9	43.4	45.5	34.1	32.9	33.5	33.8	35.6	36.6	38.5	45.7	45.4	47.2	46.3	48.6	50.6	52.8
United States	21	34.2	36.5	37.3	37.8	38.2	38.8	38.8	28.1	30.1	31.0	31.4	31.8	32.4	32.4	40.7	43.4	43.9	44.5	45.0	45.4	45.3
Other reporting countries																						
Brazil	22	17.5	22.7	25.6	24.9	23.1	25.9	26.9	13.3	18.4	19.9	17.9	16.9	19.0	19.2	21.6	27.0	31.3	32.0	29.4	32.8	35.1
Russian Federation	22–24	45.9	48.6	52.7	51.8	55.1	58.6	60.3	—	—	—	—	—	—	46.4	—	—	—	—	—	—	74.6

—Not available.

[1]The typical age of graduation is based on full-time attendance and normal progression through the education system (without repeating coursework, taking time off, etc.); this age varies across countries because of differences in their education systems and differences in program duration. In countries where the typical duration of bachelor's degree programs varies, an age span is shown. For example, if a typical program duration can be as little as 3 years or as much as 6 years, then the first age in the span represents those who graduate after 3 years, while the final age represents those who graduate after 6 years. The typical age of graduation is presented for the most recent year of data and may differ from previous years; please see previously published volumes of the Digest of Education Statistics for the typical age in previous years.

[2]Refers to the mean of the data values for all reporting Organization for Economic Cooperation and Development (OECD) countries, to which each country reporting data contributes equally. The average includes all current OECD countries for which a given year's data are available, even if they were not members of OECD in that year.

[3]Reference year for typical age of graduation is 2008.

[4]Structural changes in the Finnish higher education system accounted for much of the increase in Finnish degree recipients in 2008, as well as the decrease in 2009. Students had a strong incentive to complete their degrees in 2008. Students who did not complete their degrees in 2008 may have had to spend extra time or take additional courses in order to meet new requirements that went into effect in 2009.

NOTE: Data in this table refer to degrees classified by OECD as International Standard Classification of Education (ISCED) 1997 level 5A, first award. This level corresponds to the bachelor's degree in the United States. The recipients-per-100-persons ratio relates the number of people of all ages earning bachelor's degrees in a particular year to the number of people in the population at the typical minimum age of graduation. Some countries have two types of awards that correspond to the bachelor's degree (with different typical minimum ages of graduation). The typical minimum age for an award that requires 3 to 5 years for completion would be based on graduation after 3 years, and the typical minimum age for an award that requires 5 to 6 years would be based on graduation after 5 years. The recipients-per-100-persons ratio is the sum of all persons earning the two different award types, divided by the sum of all persons at the minimum graduation age for each of the award types. Data for Luxembourg are not shown because students generally attend no more than 1 year of higher education in Luxembourg and must complete their degrees in other countries.

SOURCE: Organization for Economic Cooperation and Development (OECD), Education at a Glance, 2006 through 2014; and Online Education Database, retrieved November 26, 2014, from http://stats.oecd.org/Index.aspx. (This table was prepared December 2014.)

Table 603.60. Percentage of postsecondary degrees awarded to women, by field of study and country: 2013

Country	All fields[1]	Education	Humanities and arts	Health and welfare	Social sciences, business, and law	Personal, transport, environmental protection, and security services	Engineering, manufacturing, and construction	Sciences, mathematics, and computer science	Agriculture
1	2	3	4	5	6	7	8	9	10
OECD average[2]	**57.2**	**78.4**	**65.3**	**76.9**	**58.5**	**50.9**	**24.1**	**39.1**	**50.9**
Australia	57.6	75.0	62.7	77.3	56.1	56.1	21.8	37.0	51.4
Austria	56.0	83.7	70.5	70.8	58.6	79.3	21.2	33.3	55.9
Belgium	59.1	78.9	61.6	76.7	58.6	51.7	22.4	29.4	54.1
Canada[3]	58.7	75.3	63.2	84.4	58.8	50.6	18.9	45.4	57.8
Chile	56.6	76.1	58.4	77.8	58.0	47.0	17.6	22.9	46.5
Czech Republic	61.8	83.1	71.1	83.3	68.3	48.5	28.2	38.3	59.7
Denmark	57.5	72.5	66.8	80.0	53.5	21.1	35.3	35.4	67.4
Estonia	65.4	95.0	76.2	90.1	71.0	49.9	30.3	45.2	51.7
Finland	60.1	82.3	72.9	85.1	63.5	65.1	21.7	42.5	57.6
France	56.1	76.5	69.3	74.4	60.6	51.1	25.6	37.8	50.1
Germany	50.7	77.7	70.2	69.7	55.6	49.9	19.4	38.6	41.4
Greece	58.8	78.5	76.5	80.9	63.3	54.9	32.8	46.0	41.7
Hungary	63.9	81.9	66.9	78.0	70.8	61.9	23.7	35.4	48.4
Iceland	—	—	—	—	—	—	—	—	—
Ireland	53.6	75.0	60.4	76.5	53.7	54.1	14.1	34.0	24.9
Israel	—	—	—	—	—	—	—	—	—
Italy	59.5	89.4	72.5	67.9	59.0	50.0	34.3	52.7	48.2
Japan	48.8	71.7	69.0	63.5	39.1	77.3	12.5	26.0	39.4
Korea, Republic of	51.0	76.2	68.6	71.9	49.3	48.3	24.3	38.4	43.2
Mexico	53.1	72.3	58.3	66.6	58.8	28.0	28.5	46.1	36.1
Netherlands	56.9	79.6	58.1	74.5	53.8	53.9	21.5	28.4	54.4
New Zealand	59.5	84.2	62.9	79.4	56.7	51.8	26.2	38.3	69.9
Norway	58.7	73.9	62.3	83.6	57.6	36.7	19.6	35.9	58.9
Poland	—	—	—	—	—	—	—	—	—
Portugal	59.8	81.5	60.0	78.9	62.1	48.7	32.5	55.7	59.9
Slovak Republic	63.6	76.9	69.6	81.9	68.5	42.9	30.9	45.6	50.9
Slovenia	61.1	89.2	71.5	80.2	70.1	53.6	24.1	42.2	60.8
Spain	55.8	78.6	59.5	74.5	60.5	46.3	25.2	36.6	43.0
Sweden	61.7	82.0	59.8	81.4	63.4	63.4	29.2	39.0	63.5
Switzerland	48.3	70.2	61.4	74.4	48.4	43.1	14.0	31.8	30.1
Turkey[3]	47.1	60.5	56.4	63.4	48.5	27.4	24.8	48.2	45.0
United Kingdom	57.1	76.4	62.3	77.3	53.2	62.8	22.2	45.7	64.1
United States	58.6	78.1	59.9	81.3	55.9	53.4	18.9	40.3	49.8
Other reporting countries									
Colombia	55.3	67.3	50.4	72.0	62.5	30.6	32.1	41.8	40.9
Latvia	69.0	91.3	80.0	92.3	71.5	58.4	26.8	38.7	48.7
Russian Federation	44.0	56.8	56.0	36.3	56.1	32.6	17.3	25.9	40.4
Saudi Arabia	51.1	53.9	68.7	52.0	42.7	63.7	3.4	57.2	29.6
South Africa[3]	59.8	73.8	60.2	73.7	60.3	79.3	28.5	49.1	48.6

—Not available.
[1]Includes degrees in unknown or unspecified fields of study.
[2]Refers to the mean of the data values for all reporting Organization for Economic Cooperation and Development (OECD) countries, to which each country reporting data contributes equally.
[3]Data are for 2012 instead of 2013.
NOTE: All data in this table were calculated using International Standard Classification of Education (ISCED) 2011. The data refer to total tertiary degrees, which correspond to degrees at

the associate's level and above in the United States. Includes degrees at ISCED 2011 level 5 (corresponding to the associate's degree in the United States), level 6 (bachelor's or equivalent degree), level 7 (master's or equivalent degree), and level 8 (doctoral or equivalent degree). Data for Luxembourg are not included because students generally attend no more than 1 year of higher education in Luxembourg and must complete their degrees in other countries.
SOURCE: Organization for Economic Cooperation and Development (OECD), *Education at a Glance, 2015*. (This table was prepared April 2016.)

Table 603.70. Percentage of bachelor's or equivalent degrees awarded in mathematics, science, and engineering, by field of study and country: 2013

Country	All mathematics, science, and engineering fields[1]	Natural sciences			Mathematics and computer science			Engineering, manufacturing, and construction
		Total	Life science	Physical science	Total	Mathematics and statistics	Computer science	
1	2	3	4	5	6	7	8	9
OECD average[2]	**21.9**	**4.5**	**2.7**	**1.8**	**4.2**	**1.0**	**3.2**	**13.3**
Australia	16.4	5.9	3.9 [3]	2.0 [3]	3.5	0.4 [3]	3.1 [3]	7.0
Austria	25.5	6.1	3.5	2.6	5.6	0.7	4.9	13.8
Belgium	15.3	2.1	0.7	1.4	2.2	0.2	2.0	11.0
Canada	21.4	10.0	7.1	2.9	3.4	1.4	2.0	8.1
Chile	22.4	1.0	0.6	0.4	4.1	3.9	0.2	17.3
Czech Republic	22.0	4.3	2.1	2.2	5.8	0.9	4.9	11.9
Denmark	16.4	2.7	1.5	1.2	3.7	0.4	3.3	9.9
Estonia	21.7	4.1	2.1	2.0	6.1	0.9	5.2	11.5
Finland	27.4	1.8	0.8	1.0	3.4	0.4	3.0	22.0
France	19.8	6.3	3.8	2.5	4.9	1.5	3.4	7.5
Germany	35.8	5.4	2.2	3.2	6.0	1.2	4.8	24.4
Greece	30.1	3.8	1.1	2.7	7.2	2.6	4.6	19.2
Hungary	17.6	2.7	0.9	1.8	2.5	0.5	2.0	12.4
Iceland	—	—	—	—	—	—	—	—
Ireland	22.9	6.1	4.1	2.0	4.4	0.6	3.8	12.3
Israel	20.8	3.8	2.5	1.3	4.5	0.9	3.6	12.6
Italy	22.5	5.4	3.5	1.9	2.2	1.0	1.2	14.8
Japan	20.4	—	—	—	—	—	—	16.9
Korea, Republic of	33.4	4.8	3.0	1.8	5.1	1.3	3.8	23.5
Mexico	27.9	2.4	1.9	0.5	3.2	0.4	2.8	22.3
Netherlands	13.9	1.7	1.0	0.7	4.1	0.2	3.9	8.1
New Zealand	18.1	6.5	4.5	2.0	5.1	1.0	4.1	6.4
Norway	13.1	1.9	0.9	1.0	3.4	0.3	3.1	7.6
Poland	17.3	2.4	1.3	1.1	4.0	0.8	3.2	10.8
Portugal	24.6	4.6	3.2	1.4	1.9	0.4	1.5	18.2
Slovak Republic	20.7	3.7	2.2	1.5	4.0	0.9	3.1	13.0
Slovenia	25.2	4.8	3.1	1.7	5.4	1.4	4.0	15.1
Spain	27.3	2.5	1.8	0.7	4.5	0.3	4.2	20.2
Sweden	15.9	2.1	1.4	0.7	3.6	0.5	3.1	10.1
Switzerland	21.8	3.3	1.8	1.5	3.1	0.4	2.7	15.5
Turkey	17.6	6.0	1.7	4.3	3.2	2.2	1.0	8.4
United Kingdom	28.6	13.9	9.8	4.1	6.0	2.1	3.9	8.7
United States	17.0	6.9	5.4	1.5	3.9	1.1	2.8	6.1
Other reporting countries								
Brazil	13.8	1.8	1.1	0.7	3.7	0.1	3.6	8.2
Colombia	24.2	2.0	1.4	0.6	0.3	0.2	0.1	21.9
Latvia	17.4	1.8	0.6	1.2	3.5	0.5	3.0	12.2
Russian Federation	24.8	3.4	0.9	2.5	6.9	0.5	6.4	14.4
Saudi Arabia	23.0	—	—	—	—	—	—	5.0
South Africa	18.1	—	—	—	—	—	—	7.1

—Not available.

[1]Includes life science; physical science; mathematics/statistics; computer science; and engineering, manufacturing, and construction.
[2]Refers to the mean of the data values for all reporting Organization for Economic Cooperation and Development (OECD) countries, to which each country reporting data contributes equally.
[3]Includes data from another category.
NOTE: Data in this table refer to degrees classified as International Standard Classification of Education (ISCED) 2011 level 6 (bachelor's or equivalent degree). Data for Luxembourg are not included because students generally attend no more than 1 year of higher education in Luxembourg and must complete their degrees in other countries. Detail may not sum to totals because of rounding.
SOURCE: Organization for Economic Cooperation and Development (OECD), Online Education Database, retrieved April 5, 2016, from http://stats.oecd.org/Index.aspx; and unpublished tabulations. (This table was prepared April 2016.)

Table 603.80. Percentage of master's or equivalent degrees and of doctoral or equivalent degrees awarded in mathematics, science, and engineering, by field of study and country: 2013

Country	All mathematics, science, and engineering fields[1]		Natural sciences[2]		Mathematics and computer science[3]		Engineering, manufacturing, and construction	
	Master's	Doctoral	Master's	Doctoral	Master's	Doctoral	Master's	Doctoral
1	2	3	4	5	6	7	8	9
OECD average[4]	**21.9**	**43.6**	**5.0**	**20.7**	**3.9**	**6.0**	**13.0**	**17.0**
Australia	16.1	39.1	1.6	18.7	5.5	5.3	9.0	15.2
Austria	21.2	47.3	5.4	19.8	4.3	7.7	11.5	19.7
Belgium	20.8	46.8	4.3	16.3	2.3	4.9	14.2	25.5
Canada	19.0	55.9	6.6	29.8	3.1	7.0	9.3	19.1
Chile	5.9	58.5	1.6	35.5	1.1	4.4	3.2	18.6
Czech Republic	24.5	48.0	4.7	22.9	5.3	5.7	14.5	19.3
Denmark	22.8	43.2	5.4	#	7.2	17.7	10.3	25.5
Estonia	30.0	50.7	6.1	27.9	6.0	6.9	17.9	15.9
Finland	27.3	41.5	4.9	12.8	4.4	4.8	17.9	23.7
France	26.9	61.9	4.7	39.6	4.9	8.9	16.8	13.4
Germany	31.3	43.8	9.0	27.2	7.5	5.6	14.8	11.0
Greece	32.1	39.1	7.2	12.6	10.0	8.1	14.8	18.4
Hungary	17.9	37.2	3.8	20.5	2.4	7.7	11.6	9.0
Iceland	—	—	—	—	—	—	—	—
Ireland	13.6	44.4	1.6	23.9	7.8	7.0	4.2	13.5
Israel	11.7	52.4	4.7	37.3	2.5	5.7	4.6	9.3
Italy	25.1	45.4	5.1	21.5	2.0	4.1	18.0	19.8
Japan	42.3	38.3	—	—	—	—	32.7	23.0
Korea, Republic of	22.4	38.7	4.0	10.7	1.6	2.3	16.8	25.7
Mexico	11.1	27.9	3.0	13.6	1.2	1.7	6.9	12.6
Netherlands	13.9	33.6	3.4	—	2.9	—	7.6	18.7
New Zealand	28.8	46.2	9.7	26.0	3.7	6.6	15.4	13.6
Norway	23.6	41.7	6.0	8.1	3.8	3.5	13.5	9.9
Poland	18.1	—	3.3	—	3.0	—	11.8	—
Portugal	26.2	43.0	6.2	17.5	2.0	5.0	17.9	20.6
Slovak Republic	19.5	40.9	3.4	12.7	3.4	3.5	12.8	24.7
Slovenia	23.1	40.0	4.4	16.0	3.6	6.5	15.1	17.5
Spain	21.4	45.1	6.8	28.7	3.1	7.6	11.6	8.8
Sweden	31.5	51.2	4.8	17.4	3.0	6.3	23.7	27.4
Switzerland	21.8	42.4	7.0	25.1	3.0	4.4	11.8	12.9
Turkey	19.6	20.4	6.9	10.5	3.4	2.7	9.3	7.2
United Kingdom	20.7	46.6	6.8	26.0	4.0	6.7	9.7	13.8
United States	12.1	41.4	2.4	20.9	3.4	5.6	6.3	14.9
Other reporting countries								
Colombia	8.0	47.4	0.9	22.6	1.5	1.9	5.6	22.9
Latvia	22.6	40.0	3.5	15.5	5.3	6.0	13.9	18.4
Russian Federation	21.8	40.5	1.5	15.5	3.1	9.4	17.2	15.6
Saudi Arabia	8.7	9.4	—	—	—	—	2.5	3.8
South Africa	24.1	37.8	—	—	—	—	11.1	7.8

—Not available.
#Rounds to zero.
[1]Includes life science; physical science; mathematics/statistics; computer science; and engineering, manufacturing, and construction.
[2]Includes life science and physical science.
[3]Includes mathematics/statistics and computer science.
[4]Refers to the mean of the data values for all reporting Organization for Economic Cooperation and Development (OECD) countries, to which each country reporting data contributes equally.

NOTE: Data in this table refer to degrees classified as International Standard Classification of Education (ISCED) 2011 level 7 (master's or equivalent degree) and ISCED 2011 level 8 (doctoral or equivalent degree). Data for Luxembourg are not included because students generally attend no more than 1 year of higher education in Luxembourg and must complete their degrees in other countries. Detail may not sum to totals because of rounding.
SOURCE: Organization for Economic Cooperation and Development (OECD), Online Education Database, retrieved April 5, 2016, from http://stats.oecd.org/Index.aspx; and unpublished tabulations. (This table was prepared April 2016.)

Table 603.90. Employment to population ratios of 25- to 64-year-olds, by sex, highest level of educational attainment, and country: 2014

Country	Total population, 25 to 64 years old				Male				Female			
	All levels of education	Less than high school completion	High school completion	Associate's or higher degree	All levels of education	Less than high school completion	High school completion	Associate's or higher degree	All levels of education	Less than high school completion	High school completion	Associate's or higher degree
1	2	3	4	5	6	7	8	9	10	11	12	13
OECD average[1]	73.3	55.7	73.8	83.3	80.4	65.9	80.8	87.8	66.3	45.9	66.0	79.2
Australia	75.6	59.7	77.3	82.9	83.0	69.2	84.7	88.9	68.5	51.5	67.8	78.0
Austria	75.0	53.0	75.9	85.3	79.6	59.1	79.8	87.2	70.5	49.5	71.6	83.3
Belgium	70.5	47.5	72.8	84.7	75.1	56.1	78.1	87.2	65.9	38.1	66.9	82.6
Canada	76.2	55.8	73.9	81.6	80.2	64.5	79.2	84.9	72.2	44.6	67.3	79.0
Chile[2]	70.2	61.3	71.6	84.0	86.4	84.2	86.3	90.7	56.3	41.8	58.7	78.2
Czech Republic	76.7	43.0	77.6	84.5	85.4	53.5	85.6	92.3	67.8	37.1	68.7	77.2
Denmark	78.3	61.7	79.4	86.3	82.0	69.4	83.0	89.2	74.5	52.8	75.1	84.2
Estonia	76.7	60.3	74.4	84.0	81.1	65.7	80.0	89.5	72.6	51.0	67.5	80.8
Finland	74.8	53.5	73.2	83.5	76.0	58.1	75.0	85.6	73.6	46.5	70.9	81.9
France[2]	72.1	54.3	73.3	84.4	76.4	61.8	76.8	87.3	68.0	47.7	69.5	81.9
Germany	79.1	58.0	79.7	88.1	84.1	67.4	83.5	91.3	74.1	50.9	76.0	84.0
Greece	56.0	46.9	54.5	68.5	65.7	58.6	67.1	72.5	46.6	34.4	42.9	64.8
Hungary	69.6	45.3	71.8	81.8	76.8	54.7	78.2	88.4	62.8	38.1	64.6	77.0
Iceland	85.5	76.8	86.6	90.8	89.2	83.3	89.6	93.5	81.8	70.7	82.1	88.8
Ireland	68.8	46.6	67.9	81.1	75.4	58.1	76.4	85.6	62.4	31.9	59.4	77.4
Israel	75.5	48.6	72.3	86.1	80.3	63.6	76.9	89.5	70.8	32.2	66.7	83.4
Italy	62.9	49.6	69.8	77.8	73.4	64.1	79.1	83.2	52.7	34.1	60.6	73.7
Japan	78.7	—	—	—	89.7	—	—	—	67.6	—	—	—
Korea, Republic of	73.6	66.2	72.1	77.4	86.5	78.9	84.9	89.7	60.4	58.3	59.1	62.6
Luxembourg	75.8	60.9	72.1	84.6	82.6	70.0	79.8	88.9	68.8	53.5	64.2	79.7
Mexico	67.7	63.3	73.1	79.1	87.9	87.6	90.0	87.3	50.0	43.8	54.8	70.8
Netherlands	76.6	58.8	77.9	87.7	82.8	70.9	83.0	90.3	70.5	47.8	72.5	84.9
New Zealand	80.3	70.9	80.3	87.2	87.8	78.1	89.5	92.9	73.5	64.8	70.0	82.8
Norway	81.5	61.9	81.5	89.9	84.1	66.5	85.3	91.4	78.7	56.8	76.7	88.6
Poland	69.0	39.2	66.2	86.2	76.3	49.5	75.3	90.7	61.9	29.0	55.9	83.0
Portugal	70.4	63.0	77.6	82.7	74.5	69.1	81.1	85.5	66.6	56.4	74.4	80.9
Slovak Republic	69.4	32.7	71.1	80.0	76.6	37.0	78.1	87.4	62.2	29.5	63.4	73.9
Slovenia	70.4	48.5	69.5	83.2	74.3	55.7	73.5	86.5	66.3	42.3	64.1	80.7
Spain	62.7	49.4	65.9	77.2	68.2	57.4	71.6	80.8	57.1	40.7	60.1	74.0
Sweden	82.9	65.9	84.7	89.0	85.3	72.7	87.1	90.2	80.3	58.2	81.4	88.1
Switzerland	83.4	69.2	82.3	88.9	88.8	78.3	87.6	92.3	77.9	62.4	77.7	84.4
Turkey	57.1	50.8	61.9	76.1	77.8	74.6	81.1	84.3	33.4	27.0	32.0	64.7
United Kingdom[3]	77.8	60.1	80.0	84.6	83.7	70.4	85.3	88.6	72.0	51.0	74.1	80.9
United States	71.9	54.8	67.9	80.1	77.5	66.2	73.7	85.0	66.5	41.5	61.9	75.9

—Not available.

[1]Refers to the mean of the data values for all reporting Organization for Economic Cooperation and Development (OECD) countries, to which each country reporting data contributes equally.

[2]Data are for 2013 instead of 2014.

[3]High school completion data include some persons (18 percent of the total) who have completed a sufficient volume and standard of programs, any one of which individually would be classified as a program that only partially completes the high school (or upper secondary) level of education.

NOTE: All data in this table were calculated using International Standard Classification of Education (ISCED) 2011. High school completion refers to completion of ISCED 2011 level 3 (upper secondary education); programs classified under ISCED 2011 as only partially completing level 3 are not included in the high school completion data except where otherwise noted. In this table, persons completing ISCED 2011 level 4 are also considered to have high school completion as their highest level of educational attainment. ISCED level 4 typically corresponds to postsecondary vocational programs below the associate's degree level in the United States. Associate's or higher degrees include ISCED 2011 level 5 (corresponding to the associate's degree in the United States), level 6 (bachelor's or equivalent degree), level 7 (master's or equivalent degree), and level 8 (doctoral or equivalent degree). For each country, the employment to population ratio of 25- to 64-year-olds is the number of persons in this age group who are employed as a percentage of the total civilian population in this age group.

SOURCE: Organization for Economic Cooperation and Development (OECD), *Education at a Glance, 2015*. (This table was prepared April 2016.)

Table 604.10. Average literacy and numeracy scale scores of 25- to 65-year-olds, by sex, age group, highest level of educational attainment, and country or other education system: 2012

[Standard errors appear in parentheses]

Country or other education system[1]	Total population of 25- to 65-year-olds		Sex				Age group								Highest level of educational attainment[2]							
			Male		Female		25 to 34		35 to 44		45 to 54		55 to 65		Less than high school completion		High school completion		Associate's degree		Bachelor's or higher degree	
1	2		3		4		5		6		7		8		9		10		11		12	
Literacy scale score[3]																						
OECD average[4]	**271**	**(0.2)**	**273**	**(0.3)**	**270**	**(0.2)**	**284**	**(0.4)**	**279**	**(0.3)**	**268**	**(0.3)**	**255**	**(0.3)**	**235**	**(0.5)**	**268**	**(0.3)**	**286**	**(0.5)**	**302**	**(0.3)**
Austria	268	(0.8)	270	(1.1)	266	(1.0)	280	(1.5)	275	(1.7)	266	(1.4)	250	(1.6)	239	(2.1)	268	(0.9)	282	(2.2)	305	(1.7)
Canada	273	(0.6)	274	(0.9)	271	(0.9)	285	(1.3)	279	(1.4)	268	(1.3)	260	(1.1)	219	(2.1)	265	(1.1)	278	(1.2)	300	(1.0)
Czech Republic	273	(1.0)	274	(1.3)	271	(1.5)	287	(1.8)	275	(2.0)	266	(1.7)	262	(2.0)	242	(3.4)	269	(1.0)	293	(4.6)	303	(2.5)
Denmark	270	(0.7)	270	(1.1)	269	(0.9)	282	(1.7)	281	(1.6)	266	(1.4)	252	(1.1)	234	(2.1)	264	(1.2)	286	(1.3)	298	(1.5)
England (UK)	274	(1.1)	275	(1.4)	273	(1.4)	280	(2.1)	279	(1.6)	271	(1.8)	265	(2.0)	241	(1.6)	273	(1.5)	283	(2.4)	302	(1.9)
Estonia	273	(0.8)	273	(1.2)	274	(0.9)	286	(1.7)	278	(1.2)	269	(1.4)	261	(1.5)	244	(2.0)	267	(1.0)	276	(1.5)	298	(1.4)
Finland	286	(0.8)	284	(1.4)	287	(1.2)	309	(1.7)	299	(2.1)	284	(1.8)	260	(1.4)	245	(2.8)	276	(1.4)	294	(1.5)	318	(1.6)
Flanders (Belgium)	274	(0.9)	277	(1.1)	270	(1.1)	291	(1.8)	282	(1.6)	272	(1.6)	255	(1.6)	232	(2.0)	265	(1.2)	294	(1.6)	313	(1.7)
France	259	(0.6)	260	(0.9)	259	(0.8)	278	(1.4)	267	(1.3)	254	(1.2)	242	(1.3)	224	(1.3)	258	(0.9)	287	(1.4)	297	(1.2)
Germany	268	(1.0)	271	(1.2)	265	(1.3)	281	(1.8)	275	(1.6)	264	(1.7)	254	(1.7)	220	(3.0)	262	(1.1)	280	(2.3)	301	(1.6)
Ireland	266	(1.0)	267	(1.3)	264	(1.2)	276	(1.5)	271	(1.8)	259	(2.1)	251	(1.8)	232	(1.8)	266	(1.5)	279	(1.9)	301	(1.7)
Italy	249	(1.1)	249	(1.6)	248	(1.4)	260	(2.2)	253	(1.9)	249	(1.8)	233	(2.2)	231	(1.6)	263	(1.3)	‡	(†)	282	(1.6)
Japan	296	(0.7)	297	(1.0)	294	(0.9)	309	(1.7)	307	(1.0)	297	(1.5)	273	(1.6)	260	(2.6)	287	(1.0)	304	(1.4)	320	(1.1)
Korea, Republic of	269	(0.6)	273	(0.9)	264	(0.9)	290	(1.2)	278	(1.2)	259	(1.4)	244	(1.4)	230	(1.7)	265	(1.0)	282	(1.4)	297	(1.3)
Netherlands	282	(0.8)	286	(1.2)	278	(1.0)	298	(2.0)	294	(1.8)	277	(1.7)	261	(1.6)	246	(1.7)	283	(1.3)	293	(3.4)	312	(1.3)
Northern Ireland (UK)	268	(2.1)	271	(2.7)	265	(2.0)	278	(2.9)	274	(2.3)	262	(2.6)	255	(3.2)	239	(2.6)	270	(2.6)	280	(3.3)	303	(2.9)
Norway	279	(0.7)	281	(1.1)	277	(1.1)	289	(1.8)	288	(1.6)	277	(1.5)	262	(1.5)	251	(1.8)	271	(1.4)	288	(3.1)	303	(1.1)
Poland	264	(0.7)	260	(1.1)	267	(1.0)	277	(1.5)	268	(1.9)	259	(1.7)	249	(1.7)	227	(2.6)	254	(1.0)	—	(†)	297	(1.3)
Slovak Republic	273	(0.7)	273	(1.0)	274	(0.9)	278	(1.4)	278	(1.4)	270	(1.3)	266	(1.3)	238	(1.9)	275	(0.9)	—	(†)	295	(1.4)
Spain	250	(0.8)	253	(1.1)	248	(1.2)	263	(1.5)	260	(1.3)	248	(1.5)	227	(1.9)	225	(1.3)	258	(1.4)	266	(2.1)	288	(1.3)
Sweden	278	(0.8)	280	(1.2)	276	(1.2)	290	(1.9)	287	(1.8)	276	(1.7)	262	(1.3)	238	(2.2)	277	(1.2)	294	(2.4)	309	(1.4)
United States	269	(1.1)	270	(1.3)	269	(1.4)	275	(2.0)	273	(1.8)	266	(1.7)	263	(1.5)	211	(2.7)	259	(1.4)	282	(2.8)	302	(1.7)
Non-OECD education systems																						
Cyprus[5]	269	(0.9)	269	(1.3)	270	(1.1)	275	(1.7)	270	(1.5)	270	(1.7)	261	(1.6)	248	(1.9)	266	(1.2)	273	(2.0)	290	(1.5)
Russian Federation[6]	275	(3.0)	274	(3.3)	277	(3.1)	273	(4.1)	278	(3.9)	277	(3.7)	275	(3.9)	248	(7.5)	272	(4.2)	276	(2.8)	282	(3.1)
Numeracy scale score[3]																						
OECD average[4]	**268**	**(0.2)**	**275**	**(0.3)**	**262**	**(0.3)**	**279**	**(0.4)**	**275**	**(0.4)**	**266**	**(0.4)**	**253**	**(0.4)**	**227**	**(0.5)**	**265**	**(0.3)**	**283**	**(0.9)**	**303**	**(0.4)**
Austria	274	(0.9)	281	(1.3)	267	(1.1)	282	(1.7)	281	(2.0)	274	(1.7)	257	(1.7)	237	(2.3)	276	(1.1)	292	(2.6)	315	(1.8)
Canada	265	(0.8)	273	(1.0)	257	(1.0)	276	(1.4)	272	(1.5)	260	(1.4)	251	(1.4)	206	(2.5)	255	(1.2)	271	(1.5)	295	(1.0)
Czech Republic	275	(1.0)	280	(1.5)	270	(1.4)	288	(1.8)	277	(1.8)	272	(2.2)	263	(2.0)	235	(3.3)	271	(1.0)	287	(6.1)	313	(2.5)
Denmark	279	(0.8)	285	(1.4)	273	(1.0)	287	(1.9)	290	(1.6)	277	(1.6)	265	(1.2)	241	(2.4)	275	(1.3)	295	(1.4)	309	(1.8)
England (UK)	263	(1.1)	270	(1.4)	256	(1.6)	267	(2.2)	269	(1.9)	259	(1.9)	257	(1.9)	226	(1.9)	262	(1.5)	271	(3.0)	295	(2.2)
Estonia	272	(0.6)	276	(1.0)	269	(0.9)	284	(1.7)	275	(1.1)	269	(1.4)	259	(1.3)	236	(1.8)	265	(0.9)	275	(1.4)	300	(1.3)
Finland	282	(0.8)	286	(1.3)	277	(1.2)	302	(2.1)	292	(2.2)	279	(2.0)	260	(1.3)	244	(2.8)	271	(1.3)	291	(1.6)	314	(1.7)
Flanders (Belgium)	280	(0.9)	289	(1.2)	271	(1.3)	295	(1.9)	289	(1.8)	280	(1.9)	260	(1.6)	235	(1.9)	272	(1.2)	300	(1.5)	323	(1.8)
France	252	(0.7)	258	(1.0)	247	(1.0)	269	(1.5)	262	(1.6)	246	(1.4)	234	(1.3)	208	(1.3)	251	(1.0)	287	(1.7)	299	(1.4)
Germany	271	(1.1)	280	(1.4)	262	(1.4)	282	(1.8)	279	(2.0)	268	(1.9)	256	(1.9)	210	(3.4)	264	(1.2)	287	(2.5)	310	(1.7)
Ireland	255	(1.0)	261	(1.4)	249	(1.3)	266	(1.7)	260	(1.7)	250	(2.1)	238	(2.3)	218	(2.2)	254	(1.6)	274	(2.1)	294	(1.9)
Italy	246	(1.1)	253	(1.6)	240	(1.4)	262	(2.3)	251	(1.9)	244	(2.0)	229	(2.2)	225	(1.5)	265	(1.5)	‡	(†)	280	(2.1)
Japan	289	(0.8)	296	(1.2)	282	(1.1)	297	(1.6)	297	(1.3)	291	(1.7)	273	(1.6)	247	(2.5)	281	(1.3)	291	(1.3)	319	(1.2)
Korea, Republic of	260	(0.7)	266	(1.0)	254	(1.1)	281	(1.4)	271	(1.5)	251	(1.4)	232	(1.7)	215	(1.9)	256	(1.0)	275	(1.6)	293	(1.5)
Netherlands	279	(0.8)	288	(1.3)	270	(1.1)	293	(1.8)	287	(2.1)	277	(1.7)	262	(1.7)	243	(1.9)	281	(1.2)	292	(3.5)	310	(1.3)
Northern Ireland (UK)	258	(1.8)	265	(2.2)	251	(2.0)	268	(2.9)	266	(2.4)	252	(2.1)	245	(3.1)	225	(2.9)	261	(2.1)	273	(3.0)	298	(2.4)
Norway	280	(0.9)	288	(1.3)	272	(1.2)	285	(2.0)	289	(1.9)	280	(1.7)	265	(1.7)	246	(2.2)	273	(1.5)	296	(3.7)	306	(1.3)
Poland	258	(1.0)	259	(1.5)	257	(1.0)	270	(1.5)	262	(2.2)	254	(2.1)	244	(1.9)	216	(3.1)	250	(1.2)	—	(†)	290	(1.5)
Slovak Republic	275	(0.9)	277	(1.2)	274	(1.1)	279	(1.6)	281	(1.7)	275	(1.6)	265	(1.6)	226	(2.4)	278	(1.0)	—	(†)	306	(1.5)
Spain	245	(0.7)	251	(1.1)	238	(1.1)	257	(1.3)	255	(1.3)	242	(1.6)	221	(1.7)	217	(1.3)	254	(1.5)	264	(2.4)	283	(1.3)
Sweden	279	(1.0)	286	(1.5)	272	(1.2)	288	(2.0)	286	(2.0)	276	(2.3)	268	(1.7)	237	(2.6)	277	(1.4)	297	(2.6)	311	(1.5)
United States	254	(1.2)	262	(1.3)	246	(1.5)	260	(2.2)	258	(1.9)	250	(2.1)	247	(1.8)	185	(3.1)	241	(1.5)	266	(3.1)	293	(1.7)
Non-OECD education systems																						
Cyprus[5]	265	(0.9)	270	(1.2)	260	(1.3)	273	(2.0)	269	(1.6)	265	(1.8)	250	(1.8)	230	(2.3)	264	(1.4)	270	(2.1)	292	(1.6)
Russian Federation[6]	269	(2.8)	268	(3.3)	271	(3.0)	269	(4.2)	270	(3.6)	272	(3.2)	267	(3.9)	234	(8.5)	265	(4.0)	268	(2.6)	280	(3.0)

—Not available.
†Not applicable.
‡Reporting standards not met (too few cases).
[1]Most of the education systems represent complete countries, but three of them represent subnational entities: England (which is part of the United Kingdom), Flanders (which is part of Belgium), and Northern Ireland (which is part of the United Kingdom).
[2]High school completion includes International Standard Classification of Education (ISCED) 1997 levels 3 and 4, with the exception of ISCED level 3C short programs. ISCED 3C short programs do not correspond to high school completion in the United States and are included in the "less than high school completion" column in this table. The associate's degree data in this table refer to degrees classified as ISCED 1997 level 5B. The data for bachelor's or higher degree refer to degrees classified as ISCED 1997 level 5A and as level 6.

[3]Scale scores range from 0 to 500.
[4]Refers to the mean of the data values for all reporting Organization for Economic Cooperation and Development (OECD) countries and subnational education systems, to which each country or subnational education system reporting data contributes equally, with the exception of England (UK) and Northern Ireland (UK), which contribute to the mean as a combined entity, England/Northern Ireland (UK).
[5]Cyprus includes only the population under the effective control of the Government of the Republic of Cyprus. For the educational attainment data (columns 9 through 12), the item response rate for Cyprus is below 85 percent; missing data have not been explicitly accounted for.
[6]The Russian Federation does not include the population of the Moscow municipal region.
SOURCE: Organization for Economic Cooperation and Development (OECD), Program for the International Assessment of Adult Competencies (PIAAC), 2012. (This table was prepared May 2016.)

Table 604.20. Percentage distribution of 25- to 65-year-olds, by literacy proficiency level, numeracy proficiency level, selected levels of educational attainment, and country or other education system: 2012

[Standard errors appear in parentheses]

Country or other education system[1]	Total population of 25- to 65-year-olds				Highest level of educational attainment[2]							
					High school completion				Bachelor's or higher degree			
	At or below level 1	At level 2	At level 3	At level 4 or level 5	At or below level 1	At level 2	At level 3	At level 4 or level 5	At or below level 1	At level 2	At level 3	At level 4 or level 5
1	2	3	4	5	6	7	8	9	10	11	12	13
Percentage distribution, by literacy proficiency level												
OECD average[3]	16.6 (0.15)	34.0 (0.21)	37.6 (0.21)	11.8 (0.13)	15.1 (0.23)	39.7 (0.34)	38.0 (0.33)	7.2 (0.18)	4.0 (0.16)	18.7 (0.35)	49.5 (0.45)	27.8 (0.40)
Austria	16.3 (0.70)	39.0 (1.06)	36.7 (1.04)	8.0 (0.47)	14.3 (0.86)	41.9 (1.38)	37.9 (1.40)	5.9 (0.60)	2.5! (0.79)	16.8 (1.99)	52.9 (2.47)	27.8 (2.03)
Canada	17.3 (0.47)	31.9 (0.70)	36.7 (0.74)	14.2 (0.55)	18.2 (0.85)	39.0 (1.05)	35.4 (1.13)	7.5 (0.80)	5.9 (0.49)	21.3 (0.88)	44.1 (1.20)	28.7 (1.20)
Czech Republic	12.5 (0.87)	38.5 (1.87)	40.9 (1.76)	8.1 (0.77)	12.4 (1.11)	43.4 (2.34)	39.5 (1.97)	4.8 (0.73)	1.9! (0.89)	17.1 (3.16)	57.2 (3.80)	23.8 (3.21)
Denmark	16.7 (0.58)	33.9 (0.83)	39.4 (0.81)	10.0 (0.57)	16.6 (1.01)	41.7 (1.48)	36.3 (1.46)	5.4 (0.64)	5.8 (0.69)	17.0 (1.20)	51.9 (1.86)	25.2 (1.87)
England (UK)	16.1 (0.77)	32.8 (0.97)	36.7 (1.01)	14.4 (0.89)	14.4 (1.36)	35.4 (1.81)	39.2 (1.58)	11.0 (1.07)	5.5 (1.06)	18.1 (1.55)	46.2 (2.37)	30.1 (2.26)
Estonia	14.3 (0.62)	35.5 (0.68)	39.3 (0.93)	10.9 (0.67)	16.0 (0.95)	40.4 (1.11)	37.2 (1.07)	6.5 (0.65)	4.4 (0.70)	22.8 (1.42)	48.4 (1.94)	24.5 (1.65)
Finland	11.6 (0.57)	27.5 (0.90)	39.2 (0.92)	21.7 (0.61)	13.3 (0.99)	33.8 (1.65)	39.6 (1.55)	13.2 (1.03)	2.9 (0.66)	11.0 (1.23)	39.7 (2.01)	46.4 (1.74)
Flanders (Belgium)	15.8 (0.66)	32.0 (0.96)	39.4 (1.06)	12.8 (0.65)	16.7 (1.13)	41.7 (1.53)	35.9 (1.76)	5.7 (0.68)	2.1! (0.65)	10.3 (1.62)	51.1 (2.84)	36.5 (2.44)
France	23.6 (0.55)	36.6 (0.77)	32.5 (0.69)	7.3 (0.39)	20.4 (0.95)	45.2 (1.08)	31.1 (0.96)	3.4 (0.44)	5.1 (0.71)	20.2 (1.40)	52.2 (1.56)	22.5 (1.51)
Germany	18.7 (0.86)	35.3 (1.12)	35.9 (1.00)	10.2 (0.64)	19.9 (1.13)	41.6 (1.55)	32.8 (1.33)	5.7 (0.73)	4.2 (0.90)	19.1 (1.66)	50.6 (1.84)	26.2 (1.80)
Ireland	18.5 (0.87)	37.2 (0.91)	35.6 (0.89)	8.8 (0.62)	14.7 (1.18)	42.3 (1.62)	37.6 (1.78)	5.3 (0.90)	3.0 (0.71)	20.7 (1.64)	52.2 (1.96)	24.2 (1.87)
Italy	29.2 (1.18)	42.5 (1.01)	25.1 (1.01)	3.2 (0.34)	16.6 (1.30)	44.6 (1.55)	34.9 (1.77)	3.9 (0.73)	9.2 (1.27)	30.9 (2.28)	48.2 (2.63)	11.7 (1.72)
Japan	5.3 (0.43)	23.4 (0.90)	48.4 (1.06)	22.9 (0.75)	5.8 (0.78)	30.1 (1.42)	51.1 (1.45)	13.0 (1.03)	1.1! (0.35)	8.2 (0.96)	46.2 (2.06)	44.5 (1.93)
Korea, Republic of	14.9 (0.60)	39.6 (0.92)	38.5 (0.96)	6.9 (0.43)	13.0 (0.92)	48.0 (1.67)	35.4 (1.47)	3.6 (0.50)	2.1 (0.56)	22.8 (1.48)	57.6 (1.66)	17.5 (1.30)
Netherlands	13.4 (0.56)	27.5 (0.82)	41.1 (0.84)	18.0 (0.74)	8.9 (0.96)	30.9 (1.47)	46.5 (1.56)	13.8 (1.04)	2.7 (0.59)	12.7 (1.09)	47.5 (1.52)	37.0 (1.56)
Northern Ireland (UK)	18.4 (1.29)	37.0 (1.71)	34.7 (1.76)	9.9 (0.78)	13.8 (1.97)	41.1 (2.91)	37.6 (3.61)	7.5 (1.21)	3.2! (0.99)	17.8 (2.14)	51.6 (2.26)	27.5 (2.55)
Norway	12.5 (0.67)	30.1 (0.90)	42.6 (0.86)	14.9 (0.67)	13.1 (1.26)	37.7 (1.62)	41.5 (1.47)	7.7 (0.95)	4.5 (0.57)	16.3 (1.09)	50.1 (1.44)	29.0 (1.26)
Poland	20.7 (0.73)	37.5 (1.09)	32.7 (1.05)	9.0 (0.60)	24.0 (1.08)	43.6 (1.39)	28.6 (1.15)	3.8 (0.53)	4.4 (0.77)	24.5 (1.53)	48.1 (2.05)	23.0 (1.68)
Slovak Republic	11.9 (0.69)	36.7 (1.18)	44.0 (1.02)	7.4 (0.53)	8.7 (0.68)	39.2 (1.53)	46.1 (1.48)	6.0 (0.60)	2.7! (0.84)	23.3 (2.01)	57.4 (2.04)	16.6 (1.85)
Spain	29.2 (0.84)	39.1 (0.84)	27.0 (0.76)	4.8 (0.43)	21.0 (1.42)	46.1 (1.96)	29.5 (1.81)	3.5 (0.82)	5.8 (0.90)	29.3 (1.76)	50.1 (2.15)	14.8 (1.40)
Sweden	14.1 (0.71)	29.0 (1.13)	40.5 (0.99)	16.4 (0.62)	11.7 (0.96)	32.9 (1.71)	44.9 (1.83)	10.5 (0.90)	4.9 (0.64)	13.2 (1.35)	44.5 (1.78)	37.4 (1.90)
United States	19.2 (0.88)	32.8 (1.15)	35.5 (1.08)	12.5 (0.79)	22.0 (1.32)	41.7 (1.83)	30.8 (1.38)	5.5 (0.79)	3.7 (0.68)	18.9 (1.28)	49.6 (1.79)	27.8 (2.02)
Non-OECD education systems												
Cyprus[4]	14.4 (0.73)	39.7 (1.31)	38.7 (1.18)	7.1 (0.53)	14.5 (1.20)	43.1 (2.24)	37.5 (2.17)	4.8 (0.79)	4.6 (0.94)	29.9 (2.42)	49.3 (2.27)	16.2 (1.45)
Russian Federation[5]	12.9 (1.63)	34.7 (1.92)	41.5 (2.17)	10.9 (1.93)	15.0 (2.46)	35.8 (2.59)	39.9 (3.68)	9.4! (2.87)	9.8 (1.85)	31.2 (3.01)	45.3 (3.29)	13.7 (2.60)
Percentage distribution, by numeracy proficiency level												
OECD average[3]	19.8 (0.16)	33.1 (0.20)	34.3 (0.20)	12.8 (0.14)	18.4 (0.25)	38.8 (0.33)	34.6 (0.33)	8.2 (0.19)	5.0 (0.18)	19.6 (0.35)	45.3 (0.45)	30.1 (0.40)
Austria	15.0 (0.72)	34.2 (0.96)	37.0 (1.05)	13.8 (0.66)	11.7 (0.90)	37.1 (1.27)	39.6 (1.41)	11.5 (0.88)	2.5! (0.94)	12.9 (1.90)	44.6 (2.56)	40.0 (2.33)
Canada	23.3 (0.57)	31.8 (0.65)	32.2 (0.76)	12.7 (0.50)	26.8 (1.21)	38.0 (1.25)	29.2 (1.17)	6.0 (0.58)	8.3 (0.67)	23.5 (1.12)	42.0 (1.58)	26.2 (1.23)
Czech Republic	13.2 (0.87)	35.4 (1.31)	39.9 (1.24)	11.5 (0.81)	12.7 (1.02)	40.1 (1.72)	40.7 (1.76)	6.6 (0.84)	1.1! (0.44)	13.5 (2.52)	50.0 (3.70)	35.4 (3.22)
Denmark	14.3 (0.58)	29.7 (0.78)	38.3 (0.82)	17.7 (0.56)	12.8 (1.07)	35.4 (1.41)	39.8 (1.37)	12.0 (0.95)	5.5 (0.64)	14.0 (1.36)	41.9 (1.70)	38.7 (1.91)
England (UK)	24.1 (1.04)	32.8 (1.15)	30.7 (1.08)	12.3 (0.85)	22.4 (1.43)	37.1 (1.79)	31.8 (2.03)	8.8 (1.35)	8.1 (1.61)	23.2 (1.95)	42.1 (2.07)	26.6 (1.92)
Estonia	15.0 (0.55)	36.6 (0.71)	37.4 (0.63)	11.0 (0.46)	16.5 (0.95)	42.3 (1.15)	34.6 (1.07)	6.5 (0.60)	4.2 (0.64)	21.4 (1.48)	49.0 (2.02)	25.5 (1.55)
Finland	13.5 (0.58)	29.3 (0.70)	37.5 (0.91)	19.7 (0.66)	16.4 (0.98)	35.7 (1.27)	36.0 (1.39)	11.8 (1.04)	3.3 (0.67)	13.5 (1.38)	41.9 (1.94)	41.3 (1.89)
Flanders (Belgium)	14.7 (0.68)	29.2 (0.83)	37.8 (1.03)	18.3 (0.78)	15.0 (1.04)	37.1 (1.55)	38.0 (1.57)	10.0 (1.06)	1.7! (0.63)	8.4 (1.45)	41.4 (2.45)	48.4 (2.52)
France	29.9 (0.69)	33.5 (0.79)	28.3 (0.59)	8.4 (0.37)	26.8 (1.02)	43.0 (1.16)	26.8 (0.99)	3.4 (0.42)	5.9 (0.79)	20.0 (1.13)	48.2 (1.40)	25.9 (1.37)
Germany	19.1 (0.79)	31.5 (0.91)	34.9 (0.90)	14.5 (0.68)	19.7 (1.05)	38.7 (1.30)	33.4 (1.42)	8.1 (0.74)	3.4 (0.88)	15.6 (1.65)	45.5 (1.71)	35.5 (1.86)
Ireland	25.8 (0.94)	37.7 (0.96)	28.7 (0.89)	7.8 (0.66)	23.8 (1.57)	43.6 (1.58)	28.1 (1.37)	4.5 (0.72)	5.2 (0.89)	26.8 (1.74)	46.5 (2.31)	21.5 (2.14)
Italy	32.4 (1.13)	39.0 (1.15)	24.1 (1.03)	4.6 (0.37)	17.4 (1.38)	40.7 (1.92)	35.3 (1.81)	6.6 (0.75)	11.8 (1.65)	31.7 (2.32)	42.3 (2.59)	14.2 (1.80)
Japan	8.2 (0.55)	27.7 (0.92)	44.4 (0.94)	19.7 (0.70)	8.6 (1.01)	34.0 (1.56)	46.3 (1.61)	11.0 (1.10)	1.0! (0.41)	10.4 (0.99)	45.0 (1.86)	43.5 (1.76)
Korea, Republic of	21.3 (0.64)	40.3 (0.98)	32.1 (0.89)	6.3 (0.52)	20.3 (1.14)	49.4 (1.34)	27.5 (1.40)	2.8 (0.56)	3.3 (0.67)	26.4 (1.65)	53.3 (2.00)	17.0 (1.55)
Netherlands	14.5 (0.60)	28.6 (0.85)	39.3 (1.00)	17.6 (0.72)	10.5 (1.13)	32.4 (1.78)	43.3 (1.93)	13.8 (1.10)	2.8 (0.64)	15.6 (1.14)	46.8 (1.78)	34.9 (1.78)
Northern Ireland (UK)	26.0 (1.54)	36.1 (1.36)	29.4 (1.34)	8.5 (0.74)	20.4 (2.01)	42.9 (2.24)	30.9 (2.52)	5.8 (1.19)	4.8 (1.10)	21.5 (2.20)	49.2 (2.74)	24.5 (2.32)
Norway	14.4 (0.62)	28.1 (0.89)	38.3 (0.96)	19.1 (0.73)	15.0 (1.19)	34.8 (1.58)	38.3 (1.46)	11.8 (1.24)	5.4 (0.61)	15.8 (1.07)	44.2 (1.57)	34.5 (1.46)
Poland	24.9 (0.88)	37.5 (1.03)	29.4 (1.10)	8.1 (0.63)	28.2 (1.11)	42.7 (1.52)	25.3 (1.25)	3.9 (0.62)	7.3 (1.00)	28.0 (1.77)	44.7 (2.28)	20.0 (1.63)
Slovak Republic	14.1 (0.65)	32.5 (0.96)	40.8 (1.07)	12.6 (0.72)	9.9 (0.71)	36.0 (1.21)	44.0 (1.32)	10.2 (0.93)	2.0! (0.65)	18.1 (1.58)	51.0 (2.49)	28.9 (2.12)
Spain	32.1 (0.72)	39.6 (0.97)	24.2 (0.78)	4.1 (0.37)	22.8 (1.63)	46.9 (2.07)	26.8 (1.88)	3.6 (0.73)	7.0 (0.88)	33.7 (1.85)	47.4 (2.18)	11.9 (1.35)
Sweden	15.2 (0.79)	27.9 (1.08)	37.5 (1.02)	19.4 (0.76)	13.1 (1.02)	31.5 (1.70)	40.9 (1.90)	14.5 (1.16)	4.9 (0.68)	14.0 (1.69)	40.8 (1.85)	40.2 (2.00)
United States	29.8 (0.93)	32.9 (1.05)	27.7 (0.90)	9.6 (0.66)	36.4 (1.34)	39.3 (1.69)	20.6 (1.58)	3.7 (0.67)	7.5 (0.73)	24.1 (1.56)	45.9 (1.82)	22.6 (1.82)
Non-OECD education systems												
Cyprus[4]	18.9 (0.81)	38.6 (1.17)	33.9 (1.17)	8.7 (0.62)	17.4 (1.30)	42.1 (1.93)	34.1 (1.99)	6.4 (1.08)	5.6 (0.96)	28.5 (2.07)	46.1 (2.26)	19.9 (1.62)
Russian Federation[5]	14.4 (1.66)	39.8 (1.95)	38.1 (1.74)	7.7 (1.44)	17.1 (3.00)	41.5 (3.33)	35.5 (3.59)	5.9 (1.74)	8.5 (1.59)	36.7 (2.84)	42.9 (2.56)	11.9 (2.27)

!Interpret data with caution. The coefficient of variation (CV) for this estimate is between 30 and 50 percent.
[1]Most of the education systems represent complete countries, but three of them represent subnational entities: England (which is part of the United Kingdom), Flanders (which is part of Belgium), and Northern Ireland (which is part of the United Kingdom).
[2]High school completion includes International Standard Classification of Education (ISCED) 1997 levels 3 and 4, with the exception of ISCED level 3C short programs. ISCED 3C short programs do not correspond to high school completion in the United States and are not included in the high school completion columns in this table. The data for bachelor's or higher degree refer to degrees classified as ISCED 1997 level 5A and as level 6.
[3]Refers to the mean of the data values for all reporting Organization for Economic Cooperation and Development (OECD) countries and subnational education systems, to which each country or subnational education system reporting data contributes equally, with the exception of England (UK) and Northern Ireland (UK), which contribute to the mean as a combined entity, England/Northern Ireland (UK).

[4]Cyprus includes only the population under the effective control of the Government of the Republic of Cyprus. For the educational attainment data (columns 6 through 13), the item response rate for Cyprus is below 85 percent; missing data have not been explicitly accounted for.
[5]The Russian Federation does not include the population of the Moscow municipal region.
NOTE: In this table, scores below level 1 and scores at level 1 are combined into the "at or below level 1" reporting category; scores at level 4 and scores at level 5 are combined into the "at level 4 or level 5" reporting category. For both literacy and numeracy, the proficiency-level reporting categories correspond to the score ranges shown in parentheses: at or below level 1 (0–225.9), at level 2 (226.0–275.9), at level 3 (276.0–325.9), at level 4 or level 5 (326.0–500.0).
SOURCE: Organization for Economic Cooperation and Development (OECD), Program for the International Assessment of Adult Competencies (PIAAC), 2012. (This table was prepared May 2016.)

Table 604.30. Employment rates and mean monthly earnings of 25- to 65-year-olds, by literacy proficiency level, numeracy proficiency level, and country or other education system: 2012

[Standard errors appear in parentheses]

Country or other education system[1]	Total population of 25- to 65-year-olds		Proficiency level[2]								
			At or below level 1		At level 2		At level 3		At level 4 or level 5	
	Employment rate of labor force[3]	Mean monthly earnings (in current dollars)	Employment rate of labor force[3]	Mean monthly earnings (in current dollars)[4]	Employment rate of labor force[3]	Mean monthly earnings (in current dollars)[4]	Employment rate of labor force[3]	Mean monthly earnings (in current dollars)[4]	Employment rate of labor force[3]	Mean monthly earnings (in current dollars)[4]
1	2	3	4	5	6	7	8	9	10	11
Literacy										
OECD average[5]	93.7 (0.08)	$2,930 (9)	89.7 (0.36)	$2,170 (24)	93.1 (0.19)	$2,580 (16)	95.1 (0.16)	$3,140 (16)	96.4 (0.30)	$3,740 (36)
Austria	96.2 (0.38)	— (†)	92.9 (1.54)	— (†)	96.0 (0.79)	— (†)	97.2 (0.60)	— (†)	97.8 (1.28)	— (†)
Canada	95.9 (0.22)	— (†)	93.7 (0.92)	— (†)	95.4 (0.55)	— (†)	96.7 (0.46)	— (†)	97.3 (0.61)	— (†)
Czech Republic	94.2 (0.20)	1,620 (22)	91.3 (2.62)	1,320 (66)	92.6 (0.93)	1,470 (43)	95.6 (0.87)	1,720 (43)	97.7 (1.39)	2,030 (96)
Denmark	94.5 (0.38)	4,090 (28)	90.8 (1.45)	3,210 (84)	94.5 (0.75)	3,730 (53)	95.0 (0.62)	4,390 (58)	96.4 (1.44)	4,850 (139)
England (UK)	94.0 (0.08)	3,180 (43)	87.5 (1.65)	2,140 (108)	92.5 (0.91)	2,610 (91)	96.2 (0.55)	3,440 (96)	97.3 (0.79)	4,380 (151)
Estonia	93.4 (0.34)	1,750 (25)	89.5 (1.48)	1,420 (75)	92.1 (0.75)	1,560 (42)	94.5 (0.53)	1,820 (41)	97.4 (0.74)	2,260 (87)
Finland	95.5 (0.39)	3,250 (18)	92.5 (2.04)	2,670 (120)	95.3 (0.84)	2,920 (56)	95.8 (0.59)	3,330 (43)	96.1 (0.63)	3,590 (56)
Flanders (Belgium)	98.0 (0.21)	3,650 (35)	96.5 (0.93)	2,790 (106)	97.4 (0.55)	3,220 (67)	98.6 (0.40)	3,860 (69)	98.9 (0.68)	4,470 (151)
France	92.9 (0.19)	2,490 (17)	89.4 (1.08)	1,910 (39)	92.9 (0.66)	2,340 (33)	94.3 (0.64)	2,760 (33)	95.0 (1.39)	3,270 (84)
Germany	95.2 (0.40)	— (†)	91.1 (1.53)	— (†)	94.9 (0.84)	— (†)	96.3 (0.63)	— (†)	98.3 (0.73)	— (†)
Ireland	89.2 (0.53)	3,410 (52)	83.6 (1.95)	2,370 (106)	86.7 (1.12)	2,950 (68)	92.0 (1.02)	3,820 (90)	95.8 (1.36)	4,610 (206)
Italy	87.7 (0.66)	2,510 (36)	84.1 (1.91)	2,290 (103)	87.2 (1.30)	2,360 (68)	90.8 (1.34)	2,800 (75)	93.5 (3.39)	3,140 (248)
Japan	97.6 (0.22)	3,000 (37)	98.9 (1.01)	2,210 (199)	99.1 (0.63)	2,540 (84)	97.5 (0.45)	3,000 (60)	96.2 (0.83)	3,550 (100)
Korea, Republic of	96.8 (0.27)	3,000 (32)	97.4 (0.86)	2,180 (86)	97.0 (0.53)	2,820 (60)	96.7 (0.59)	3,290 (63)	95.5 (1.71)	3,960 (133)
Netherlands	95.8 (0.41)	3,490 (30)	91.5 (2.00)	2,350 (117)	94.7 (0.93)	2,930 (75)	97.0 (0.59)	3,640 (63)	96.8 (0.88)	4,230 (90)
Northern Ireland (UK)	94.7 (0.49)	2,750 (42)	90.6 (2.03)	1,820 (90)	94.4 (0.96)	2,330 (96)	95.9 (1.01)	3,070 (92)	96.0 (2.10)	3,870 (188)
Norway	97.1 (0.31)	4,090 (30)	93.6 (1.66)	2,910 (110)	96.8 (0.74)	3,630 (66)	97.6 (0.45)	4,340 (56)	98.8 (0.65)	4,850 (99)
Poland	91.9 (0.49)	1,610 (22)	88.0 (1.75)	1,260 (56)	90.8 (1.08)	1,430 (52)	93.9 (0.89)	1,780 (56)	95.5 (1.56)	2,190 (90)
Slovak Republic	90.7 (0.48)	1,570 (25)	79.6 (2.60)	1,060 (63)	90.4 (1.06)	1,380 (39)	92.5 (0.80)	1,700 (46)	93.3 (2.09)	2,110 (150)
Spain	82.7 (0.63)	2,390 (32)	75.1 (1.60)	1,910 (55)	82.5 (1.32)	2,260 (48)	87.4 (1.19)	2,680 (61)	92.1 (2.30)	3,280 (157)
Sweden	94.9 (0.44)	— (†)	85.3 (2.21)	— (†)	94.2 (1.01)	— (†)	96.3 (0.69)	— (†)	98.4 (0.73)	— (†)
United States	92.5 (0.44)	4,260 (80)	89.0 (1.53)	2,730 (150)	90.8 (1.13)	3,480 (110)	93.8 (0.85)	4,740 (148)	97.1 (0.72)	6,310 (323)
Non-OECD education systems										
Cyprus[6]	92.0 (0.64)	2,860 (38)	87.3 (2.50)	2,490 (149)	91.8 (1.22)	2,660 (73)	93.1 (1.03)	3,010 (73)	93.9 (2.04)	3,440 (197)
Russian Federation[7]	94.9 (1.02)	840 (25)	95.0 (2.53)	790 (55)	95.9 (1.48)	770 (31)	95.0 (1.33)	870 (36)	91.7 (2.82)	1,000 (61)
Numeracy										
OECD average[5]	93.7 (0.08)	$2,930 (9)	88.8 (0.36)	$2,110 (21)	93.2 (0.20)	$2,560 (16)	95.5 (0.17)	$3,180 (18)	97.0 (0.27)	$3,940 (38)
Austria	96.2 (0.38)	— (†)	92.7 (1.56)	— (†)	95.9 (0.79)	— (†)	97.0 (0.56)	— (†)	97.6 (0.88)	— (†)
Canada	95.9 (0.22)	— (†)	93.0 (0.83)	— (†)	95.7 (0.57)	— (†)	96.8 (0.54)	— (†)	98.4 (0.58)	— (†)
Czech Republic	94.2 (0.20)	1,620 (22)	87.3 (2.81)	1,280 (56)	92.8 (0.92)	1,460 (38)	95.9 (0.69)	1,690 (43)	97.9 (1.82)	2,060 (86)
Denmark	94.5 (0.38)	4,090 (28)	89.4 (1.72)	3,100 (84)	93.2 (1.02)	3,580 (66)	95.6 (0.60)	4,210 (64)	96.8 (0.77)	4,980 (98)
England (UK)	94.0 (0.08)	3,180 (43)	87.6 (1.25)	2,120 (90)	94.1 (0.83)	2,690 (81)	96.5 (0.74)	3,650 (102)	97.6 (0.87)	4,530 (179)
Estonia	93.4 (0.34)	1,750 (25)	87.6 (1.53)	1,250 (65)	92.2 (0.76)	1,520 (46)	94.9 (0.58)	1,850 (45)	98.0 (0.73)	2,470 (83)
Finland	95.5 (0.39)	3,250 (18)	90.8 (2.06)	2,510 (89)	94.9 (0.94)	2,880 (57)	96.3 (0.58)	3,320 (47)	96.8 (0.62)	3,830 (73)
Flanders (Belgium)	98.0 (0.21)	3,650 (35)	96.8 (0.99)	2,640 (96)	97.4 (0.62)	3,100 (65)	98.5 (0.39)	3,740 (57)	98.5 (0.51)	4,650 (129)
France	92.9 (0.19)	2,490 (17)	89.1 (0.87)	1,850 (31)	92.4 (0.75)	2,300 (32)	95.5 (0.84)	2,860 (37)	95.7 (1.42)	3,440 (87)
Germany	95.2 (0.40)	— (†)	89.8 (1.52)	— (†)	94.5 (0.89)	— (†)	96.4 (0.61)	— (†)	98.8 (0.58)	— (†)
Ireland	89.2 (0.53)	3,410 (52)	84.1 (1.85)	2,340 (96)	88.2 (1.12)	3,030 (85)	92.1 (1.17)	3,970 (113)	94.9 (1.77)	4,990 (281)
Italy	87.7 (0.66)	2,510 (36)	82.5 (1.91)	2,260 (105)	88.0 (1.28)	2,330 (60)	90.8 (1.28)	2,770 (84)	95.0 (2.64)	3,290 (205)
Japan	97.6 (0.22)	3,000 (37)	98.8 (0.95)	1,980 (141)	96.9 (0.83)	2,420 (85)	97.6 (0.54)	2,990 (66)	98.1 (0.64)	4,030 (99)
Korea, Republic of	96.8 (0.27)	3,000 (32)	96.4 (0.85)	2,210 (72)	96.8 (0.52)	2,880 (61)	96.9 (0.61)	3,370 (68)	97.1 (1.17)	4,040 (145)
Netherlands	95.8 (0.41)	3,490 (30)	90.1 (1.95)	2,280 (116)	95.5 (0.92)	2,900 (79)	96.9 (0.57)	3,650 (70)	97.2 (0.96)	4,470 (106)
Northern Ireland (UK)	94.7 (0.49)	2,750 (42)	91.2 (1.54)	1,810 (81)	94.5 (1.19)	2,400 (70)	96.4 (1.06)	3,230 (107)	96.0 (2.39)	3,990 (213)
Norway	97.1 (0.31)	4,090 (30)	92.9 (1.65)	2,880 (119)	96.6 (0.77)	3,480 (69)	97.9 (0.45)	4,250 (61)	98.5 (0.56)	5,110 (101)
Poland	91.9 (0.49)	1,610 (22)	86.5 (1.75)	1,260 (53)	91.8 (1.15)	1,430 (38)	94.0 (0.86)	1,800 (49)	96.4 (1.47)	2,290 (107)
Slovak Republic	90.7 (0.48)	1,570 (25)	75.3 (2.92)	1,030 (62)	89.5 (1.12)	1,320 (52)	93.4 (0.77)	1,660 (43)	94.9 (1.41)	2,090 (94)
Spain	82.7 (0.63)	2,390 (32)	74.2 (1.59)	1,830 (51)	82.7 (1.45)	2,270 (53)	88.9 (1.51)	2,800 (68)	93.3 (2.70)	3,300 (170)
Sweden	94.9 (0.44)	— (†)	86.2 (2.24)	— (†)	93.9 (1.33)	— (†)	96.5 (0.68)	— (†)	98.2 (0.63)	— (†)
United States	92.5 (0.44)	4,260 (80)	88.2 (1.36)	2,760 (94)	91.3 (1.13)	3,690 (120)	95.6 (0.92)	5,110 (157)	98.1 (0.71)	6,780 (370)
Non-OECD education systems										
Cyprus[6]	92.0 (0.64)	2,860 (38)	86.6 (2.24)	2,250 (112)	91.7 (1.26)	2,630 (75)	93.4 (1.04)	3,050 (74)	95.9 (1.57)	3,640 (163)
Russian Federation[7]	94.9 (1.02)	840 (25)	96.3 (2.04)	750 (55)	95.5 (1.41)	780 (35)	94.9 (1.53)	890 (38)	90.5 (3.89)	990 (68)

—Not available.
†Not applicable.
[1]Most of the education systems represent complete countries, but three of them represent subnational entities: England (which is part of the United Kingdom), Flanders (which is part of Belgium), and Northern Ireland (which is part of the United Kingdom).
[2]In this table, scores below level 1 and scores at level 1 are combined into the "at or below level 1" reporting category; scores at level 4 and scores at level 5 are combined into the "at level 4 or level 5" reporting category. For both literacy and numeracy, the proficiency-level reporting categories correspond to the score ranges shown in parentheses: at or below level 1 (0–225.9), at level 2 (226.0–275.9), at level 3 (276.0–325.9), at level 4 or level 5 (326.0–500.0).
[3]The employment rate is the percentage of the labor force that is employed. The labor force consists of those who are employed as well as those who are unemployed but actively looking for work.

[4]Mean monthly earnings for those who are employed. Data adjusted to U.S. dollars using the purchasing power parity (PPP) index.
[5]Refers to the mean of the data values for all reporting Organization for Economic Cooperation and Development (OECD) countries and subnational education systems, to which each country or subnational education system reporting data contributes equally, with the exception of England (UK) and Northern Ireland (UK), which contribute to the mean as a combined entity, England/Northern Ireland (UK).
[6]Cyprus includes only the population under the effective control of the Government of the Republic of Cyprus.
[7]The Russian Federation does not include the population of the Moscow municipal region.
SOURCE: Organization for Economic Cooperation and Development (OECD), Program for the International Assessment of Adult Competencies (PIAAC), 2012. (This table was prepared March 2016.)

Table 605.10. Gross domestic product per capita and public and private education expenditures per full-time-equivalent (FTE) student, by level of education and country: Selected years, 2005 through 2012

Country	Gross domestic product per capita						Elementary and secondary education expenditures per FTE student						Higher education expenditures per FTE student					
	2005	2008	2009	2010	2011	2012	2005	2008	2009	2010	2011	2012	2005	2008	2009	2010	2011	2012
1	2	3	4	5	6	7	8	9	10	11	12	13	14	15	16	17	18	19
										Current dollars								
OECD average[1]	$28,772	$33,886	$33,206	$33,471	$35,491	$36,852	$6,751	$8,180	$8,632	$8,501	$8,832	$8,954	$11,342	$13,391	$13,707	$13,211	$13,881	$14,815
Australia	33,983	39,532	39,971	40,801	43,208	43,158	7,142	7,814	9,139	9,803	9,383	8,790	14,579	15,043	16,074	15,142	16,267	16,859
Austria	34,107	39,849	38,834	40,411	42,978	44,892	9,436	10,994	11,681	11,693	12,509	12,164	14,775	15,043	14,257	15,007	14,895	15,549
Belgium	32,077	36,879	36,698	37,878	40,093	41,684	7,306	9,706	9,783	10,123	10,722	11,007	11,960	15,020	15,443	15,179	15,420	15,503
Canada	—	38,522	40,136	37,480	42,585	—	7,774 2,3	8,997 2,3	9,774 2,3	10,078 2,3	10,226 2,3	—	22,810 4,5	20,903 4	22,475 4	23,226 4	22,006 4	—
Chile	12,635	14,106	14,578	15,107	17,312	21,486	2,099	2,245	2,635	2,935	3,203	4,522	6,873	6,829	6,829	6,863	7,101	8,333
Czech Republic	20,280	25,845	25,614	25,364	27,046	28,679	4,098	5,236	5,615	5,532	6,128	6,419	6,649	8,318	8,237	7,635	9,392	10,319
Denmark	33,626	39,494	38,299	40,600	41,843	43,564	8,997 6	10,429 6	11,094 6	11,404 6	10,290 6	10,780	14,959 6	17,634 6	18,556 6	18,977 6	21,254 6	—
Estonia	16,660	21,802	19,789	20,093	23,088	24,689	3,736	6,054	6,149	5,984	6,055	6,334	3,869	6,022 5	6,373	6,501	7,868	8,206
Finland	30,468	37,795	35,848	36,030	38,611	40,209	6,610	8,068	8,314	8,591	9,180	9,353	12,285	15,402	16,569	16,714	18,002	17,863
France	29,644	34,233	33,724	34,395	36,391	37,347	7,456	8,559 3	8,861 3	9,070 3	9,329 3	9,338 3	10,995	14,079	14,642	15,067	15,375	15,281
Germany	30,496	37,171	36,048	37,661	40,990	42,730	7,039	7,859	8,534	—	9,521	9,843	12,446	15,390	15,711	—	16,723	17,157
Greece	25,472	29,920	29,381	27,539	26,622	25,462	5,493 2	—	—	—	—	—	6,130	—	—	—	—	—
Hungary	17,014	20,700	20,154	20,625	22,413	22,494	4,027 4	4,626 4	4,506 4	4,555 4	4,527 4	4,371	6,244 4	7,327 4	8,518 4	8,745 4	9,210 4	8,876
Iceland	35,571	39,029	36,718	35,509	38,224	40,464	8,815 6	9,745	9,309	8,592	9,326	9,333	9,474 4	10,429	9,939	8,728	8,612	9,377
Ireland	38,061	42,644	39,750	41,000	42,943	45,210	6,411	8,915 4	9,615 4	9,638 4	9,830 4	9,893 4	10,468	16,284 4	16,420 4	16,008 4	16,095 4	14,922 4
Israel	21,474	27,690	27,454	26,552	30,168	31,296	5,041	5,780	5,464	5,692	6,277	6,325	10,919	12,568	11,214	10,730	11,554	12,338
Italy[3]	27,750	33,271	32,397	32,110	33,870	35,334	7,410 4	9,071 4	8,943 4	8,489 4	8,534 4	8,450 4	8,026 4	9,553	9,562	9,580	9,990	10,071
Japan[6]	30,290	33,902	32,324	35,238	34,967	35,695	7,343	8,301	8,502	9,168	9,102	9,408	12,326	14,890	15,951	16,015	16,446	16,872
Korea, Republic of	21,342	26,877	27,171	28,829	29,035	32,022	5,638 2,3,4	6,723	8,122	7,396	7,652	7,934	7,606	9,081	9,513	9,972	9,927	9,866
Luxembourg	69,984	89,732	82,972	84,672	88,668	91,754	15,930 2,3,4	16,909 3	18,018 3	19,050 3	19,600 3	20,153	—	—	—	—	—	32,876 4
Mexico	11,299	15,190	14,397	15,195	17,125	16,767	2,025	2,284	2,339	2,464	2,765	2,801	6,402	7,504	8,020	7,872	7,889	8,115
Netherlands	34,724	42,887	41,089	41,682	43,150	46,062	7,045	9,251	10,030	10,075	10,268	10,464	13,883	17,245	17,849	17,161	17,549	19,276
New Zealand	24,882	29,231	29,204	29,629	31,487	32,165	5,659	6,496	7,556	7,681	8,831	8,445	10,262	10,526	10,619	10,418	10,582	13,740
Norway[7]	47,620	43,659	54,708	44,825	46,696	51,368	9,975	12,070	12,971	13,067	13,219	13,611 8	15,552	18,942	19,269	18,512	18,840	20,016 8
Poland[4]	13,573	18,062	18,910	20,034	21,753	22,869	3,165	4,682	5,167	5,693	6,066	6,764	5,593	7,063	7,776	8,866	9,659	9,799
Portugal[4]	19,967	24,962	24,935	25,519	25,672	27,204	5,646 3	6,276 3	7,288 3	7,419 3	7,282 3	7,444 6	8,787	10,373	10,481	10,578	9,640	9,196 6
Slovak Republic[3]	15,881	23,205	22,620	23,194	25,130	25,725	2,740	4,006	4,781	5,066	5,105	5,231	5,783	6,560	6,758	6,904	8,177	9,022
Slovenia	23,043	29,241	27,150	26,649	28,156	28,455	7,065	8,555	8,670	8,505	8,867	8,457	8,573	9,263	9,311	9,693	10,413	11,002
Spain	27,270	33,173	32,146	31,574	32,157	32,775	6,411	8,522	8,818	8,479	8,476	8,152	10,089	13,366	13,614	13,373	13,173	12,356
Sweden	32,770	39,321	37,192	39,251	41,761	43,869	7,861	9,524	9,709	10,044	10,548	10,652	15,946	20,014	19,961	19,562	20,818	22,534
Switzerland[4]	35,500	45,517	44,773	48,962	51,582	55,623	10,721	13,775	13,411	13,510	14,623	15,512	21,734	21,648	21,577	21,893	22,882	25,264
Turkey	—	14,963	14,442	15,775	17,781	18,002	—	—	—	2,020	2,501	2,784	—	—	—	—	8,193	7,779
United Kingdom	31,580	36,817	34,483	35,299	33,886	37,170	6,888	9,169	9,602	9,980	9,738	10,056	13,506	15,310	16,338	15,862	14,223	24,338
United States[9]	41,674	46,901	45,087	46,548	49,321	49,895	9,771	11,107	11,818	11,826	11,841	11,732	23,435	27,499	27,066	25,576	26,021	26,562

See notes at end of table.

Table 605.10. Gross domestic product per capita and public and private education expenditures per full-time-equivalent (FTE) student, by level of education and country: Selected years, 2005 through 2012—Continued

Country	Gross domestic product per capita						Elementary and secondary education expenditures per FTE student						Higher education expenditures per FTE student					
	2005	2008	2009	2010	2011	2012	2005	2008	2009	2010	2011	2012	2005	2008	2009	2010	2011	2012
1	2	3	4	5	6	7	8	9	10	11	12	13	14	15	16	17	18	19
									Constant 2014 dollars									
OECD average[1]	$34,878	$37,259	$36,642	$36,339	$37,353	$37,998	$8,183	$8,994	$9,525	$9,230	$9,295	$9,232	$13,749	$14,724	$15,126	$14,343	$14,609	$15,276
Australia	41,195	43,467	44,107	44,297	45,474	44,500	8,657	8,592	10,085	10,643	9,875	9,063	17,673	16,540	17,737	16,439	17,120	17,383
Austria	41,345	43,816	42,852	43,873	45,232	46,289	11,439	12,088	12,889	12,695	13,165	12,543	17,911	16,541	15,733	16,293	15,676	16,032
Belgium	38,884	40,551	40,495	41,123	42,195	42,981	8,856	10,672	10,796	10,990	11,285	11,350	14,499	16,516	17,041	16,479	16,229	15,985
Canada	—	42,356	44,289	40,691	—	—	9,424 [2,3]	9,892 [2,3]	10,786 [2,3]	10,941 [2,3]	10,762 [2,3]	—	27,650 [4,5]	22,984 [4]	24,801 [4]	25,216 [4]	23,160 [4]	—
Chile	15,316	15,510	16,086	16,401	18,219	22,155	2,544	2,468	2,908	3,187	3,371	4,663	8,331	7,509	7,536	7,451	7,473	8,592
Czech Republic	24,584	28,418	28,265	27,537	28,464	29,571	4,967	5,758	6,196	6,006	6,450	6,618	8,060	9,146	9,089	8,289	9,884	10,640
Denmark	40,762	43,426	42,262	44,078	44,037	44,920	10,906 [6]	11,467 [6]	12,242 [6]	12,380 [6]	10,766 [6]	11,116	18,133 [6]	19,389 [6]	20,476 [6]	20,603 [6]	22,369 [6]	—
Estonia	20,195	23,973	21,836	21,815	24,299	25,457	4,529	6,656	6,786	6,497	6,373	6,531	4,690	6,622 [5]	7,032	7,058	8,281	8,462
Finland	36,934	41,558	39,557	39,116	40,636	41,460	8,013	8,871	9,174	9,326	9,661	9,643	14,892	16,935	18,283	18,146	18,946	18,419
France	35,935	37,641	37,214	37,341	38,299	38,509	9,039	9,411 [3]	9,778 [3]	9,847 [3]	9,818 [3]	9,628 [3]	13,329	15,480	16,157	16,358	16,181	15,757
Germany	36,967	40,871	39,778	40,887	43,139	44,060	8,532	8,641	9,417	—	10,020	10,149	15,087	16,922	17,337	—	17,600	17,691
Greece	30,878	32,898	32,421	29,898	28,019	26,255	6,659 [2]	—	—	—	—	—	7,432	—	—	—	—	—
Hungary	20,625	22,761	22,240	22,392	23,589	23,194	4,881 [4]	5,087 [4]	4,973 [4]	4,945 [4]	4,765 [4]	4,507	7,569 [4]	8,057 [4]	9,399 [4]	9,494 [4]	9,693 [4]	9,152
Iceland	43,120	42,914	40,517	38,552	40,229	41,722	10,686 [6]	10,715	10,272	9,328	9,815	9,623	11,485 [5]	11,468	10,967	9,476	9,064	9,669
Ireland	46,138	46,889	43,863	44,513	45,195	46,616	7,771	9,802 [4]	10,610 [4]	10,463 [4]	10,345 [4]	10,201 [4]	12,689	17,905 [4]	18,119 [4]	17,379 [4]	16,939 [4]	15,386 [4]
Israel	26,031	30,447	30,295	28,827	31,750	32,270	6,110	6,355	6,029	6,180	6,606	6,522	13,236	13,820	12,375	11,649	12,160	12,721
Italy[3]	33,639	36,583	35,749	34,861	35,646	36,433	8,982 [4]	9,974 [4]	9,868 [4]	9,216 [4]	8,981 [4]	8,713 [4]	9,729 [4]	10,505	10,551	10,400	10,514	10,384
Japan[6]	36,718	37,277	35,669	38,257	36,801	36,805	8,902	9,127	9,381	9,953	9,580	9,701	14,942	16,372	17,608	17,387	17,308	17,397
Korea, Republic of	25,871	29,552	29,983	31,299	30,557	33,018	6,835	7,392	8,963	8,030	8,053	8,181	9,220	9,985	10,498	10,826	10,447	10,173
Luxembourg	84,836	98,665	91,558	91,926	93,318	94,608	19,311 [2,3,4]	18,593 [3]	19,882 [3]	20,682 [3]	20,628 [3]	20,780	—	—	—	—	—	33,899 [4]
Mexico	13,697	16,702	15,887	16,497	18,023	17,288	2,455	2,511	2,581	2,675	2,910	2,888	7,761	8,251	8,850	8,547	8,303	8,368
Netherlands	42,093	47,157	45,341	45,252	45,413	47,495	8,540	10,172	11,068	10,938	10,806	10,789	16,829	18,961	19,696	18,632	18,470	19,876
New Zealand	30,162	32,152	32,226	32,168	33,138	33,166	6,861	7,142	8,338	8,339	9,294	8,707	12,439	11,574	11,718	11,311	11,137	14,168
Norway[7]	57,726	48,005	60,368	48,666	49,145	52,966	12,092	13,272	14,313	14,186	13,912	14,035 [8]	18,853	20,827	21,263	20,098	19,828	20,639 [8]
Poland[4]	16,453	19,860	20,867	21,750	22,894	23,580	3,836	5,148	5,701	6,181	6,384	6,974	6,780	7,766	8,581	9,625	10,165	10,104
Portugal[4]	24,205	27,447	27,516	27,705	27,018	28,050	6,844 [3]	6,901 [3]	8,042 [3]	8,055 [3]	7,664 [3]	7,676 [6]	10,652	11,405	11,565	11,485	10,145	9,482 [6]
Slovak Republic[8]	19,251	25,515	24,960	25,181	26,448	26,525	3,321	4,405	5,275	5,500	5,373	5,394	7,011	7,213	7,457	7,495	8,606	9,303
Slovenia	27,934	32,152	29,959	28,932	29,632	29,341	8,564	9,407	9,568	9,234	9,332	8,720	10,392	10,185	10,275	10,523	10,960	11,344
Spain	33,057	36,476	35,473	34,278	33,843	33,794	7,771	9,370	9,731	9,205	8,920	8,406	12,230	14,697	15,023	14,519	13,864	12,740
Sweden	39,725	43,236	41,040	42,614	43,952	45,234	9,530	10,472	10,714	10,905	11,101	10,983	19,330	22,006	22,026	21,238	21,910	23,235
Switzerland[4]	43,033	50,048	49,406	53,157	54,287	57,353	12,996	15,146	14,798	14,668	15,390	15,994	26,347	23,803	23,810	23,769	24,082	26,050
Turkey	—	16,452	15,936	17,127	18,713	18,562	—	—	—	2,193	2,632	2,871	—	—	—	—	8,623	8,021
United Kingdom	38,282	40,483	38,051	38,323	35,663	38,327	8,350	10,082	10,596	10,835	10,249	10,368	16,373	16,834	18,029	17,221	14,969	25,095
United States[9]	50,518	51,570	49,753	50,536	51,908	51,447	11,844	12,213	13,040	12,839	12,462	12,097	28,408	30,237	29,867	27,767	27,386	27,388

—Not available.

[1] Refers to the mean of the data values for all reporting Organization for Economic Cooperation and Development (OECD) countries, to which each country reporting data contributes equally. The average includes all current OECD countries for which a given year's data are available, even if they were not members of OECD in that year.
[2] Includes preprimary education (for children ages 3 and older).
[3] Education expenditures exclude postsecondary non-higher-education.
[4] Education expenditures include public institutions only.
[5] Excludes occupation-specific education corresponding to that offered at the vocational associate's degree level in the United States.
[6] Postsecondary non-higher-education included in both secondary and higher education.
[7] The GDP mainland market value is used for Norway.
[8] Occupation-specific education corresponding to that offered at the vocational associate's degree level in the United States is included in elementary and secondary education instead of in higher education.

[9] Postsecondary non-higher-education included in higher education.
NOTE: Includes all expenditures by public and private education institutions (such as administration, instruction, ancillary services for students and families, and research and development) unless otherwise noted. Expenditures for International Standard Classification of Education (ISCED) level 4 (postsecondary non-higher-education) are included in elementary and secondary education unless otherwise noted. Data adjusted to U.S. dollars using the purchasing power parity (PPP) index. Constant dollars based on the Consumer Price Index, prepared by the Bureau of Labor Statistics. U.S. Department of Labor. Data for 2011 and earlier years were calculated using the ISCED 1997 classification. Data for 2012 used the ISCED 2011 classification and may not be comparable to data for earlier years.
SOURCE: Organization for Economic Cooperation and Development (OECD). Education at a Glance, 2008 through 2015. (This table was prepared December 2015.)

Table 605.20. Public and private direct expenditures on education institutions as a percentage of gross domestic product, by level of education and country: Selected years, 2000 through 2012

Country	All institutions								Elementary and secondary institutions[1] (excludes preprimary unless otherwise noted)								Higher education institutions							
	Public direct expenditures[1] (includes preprimary education, not separately shown)					Direct expenditures, 2012			Public direct expenditures[1]					Direct expenditures, 2012			Public direct expenditures[1]					Direct expenditures, 2012		
	2000	2005	2009	2010	2011	Public[1]	Private	Total	2000	2005	2009	2010	2011	Public[1]	Private	Total	2000	2005	2009	2010	2011	Public[1]	Private	Total
1	2	3	4	5	6	7	8	9	10	11	12	13	14	15	16	17	18	19	20	21	22	23	24	25
OECD average[2]	4.9	5.0	5.4	5.4	5.2	4.7	0.6	5.3	3.4	3.5	3.7	3.7	3.5	3.5	0.2	3.7	1.0	1.0	1.1	1.1	1.1	1.1	0.4	1.5
Australia	4.6	4.3	4.5	4.6	4.3	4.3	1.3	5.6	3.7	3.4	3.6	3.7	3.5	3.4	0.6	4.0	0.8	0.8	0.7	0.8	0.7	0.9	0.7	1.6
Austria	5.4[3]	5.2	5.5	5.6	5.5	4.9	0.0	4.9	3.7[3]	3.5	3.8	3.5	3.5	3.1	0.0	3.1	1.2[3]	1.2	1.4	1.5	1.4	1.7	0.0	1.7
Belgium	5.1	5.8	6.4	6.4	6.4	5.9	0.0	5.9	3.4[5]	3.9	4.3	4.3[6,7]	4.3[6,7]	4.3	0.0	4.3	1.2[4]	1.2	1.4	1.4	1.3	1.4	0.0	1.4
Canada	5.2	4.8	6.0	5.2	4.7	—	—	—	3.3	3.3[5]	4.3[6,7]	3.6[6,7]	—	—	—	—	1.6[5]	1.5	1.5	1.6	1.5	—	—	—
Chile	4.2	3.3	4.1	4.3	3.9	3.9[8]	2.2[8]	6.1[8]	3.2	2.7	3.3	2.9	2.7	2.8[8]	0.8[8]	3.6[8]	0.6	0.3	0.3	0.8	0.7	1.0[8]	1.5[8]	2.5[8]
Czech Republic	4.2	4.1	4.2	4.1	4.4	4.0	0.4	4.4	2.8[4]	2.7	2.6	2.6	2.6	2.6	0.2	2.8	0.8[4]	0.8	1.0	1.0	1.2	1.2	0.2	1.4
Denmark	6.4[3]	6.7	7.5	7.6	7.5	—	—	—	4.1[3,9]	4.4[9]	4.1[9]	4.7[9]	4.3[9]	4.7	0.0	4.7	1.5[3,9]	1.6[9]	1.8[9]	1.8[9]	1.8[9]	1.8	0.0	1.8
Estonia	—	—	—	—	—	4.7	0.1	4.9	—	3.5	4.1	3.9	3.3[9]	3.2	0.0	3.2	—	1.7	1.3	1.3	1.4	1.4	0.2	1.6
Finland	5.5	5.9	6.3	6.4	6.3	5.7	0.1	5.8	3.5	3.8	4.1	4.1	4.1	3.9	0.0	3.9	1.7	1.7	1.8	1.9	1.9	1.8	0.0	1.8
France	5.7	5.6	6.0	5.8	5.6	4.9	0.4	5.3	4.0	3.8	3.9	3.8[7]	3.7[7]	3.6[7]	0.2	3.8[7]	1.0	1.1	1.3	1.3	1.3	1.3	0.2	1.4
Germany	4.3	4.2	4.5	—	4.4	4.3	0.1	4.4	2.9	2.8	2.9	—	2.8	2.9	0.2	3.1	1.0	0.9	1.1	—	1.1	1.2	0.0	1.2
Greece	3.7[3]	4.0	—	—	—	—	—	—	2.9[3,6]	2.7[3,6]	—	—	—	—	—	—	0.9[3]	1.4	1.0	0.8	1.0	—	—	—
Hungary	4.4	5.1	4.8	4.6	4.4	3.6	0.5	4.1	2.8[3]	3.2	3.0	2.8	2.6	2.6	0.1	2.6	0.9	1.0	1.2	1.3	1.1	0.8	0.4	1.2
Iceland	5.7[3]	7.2	7.3	7.0	6.9	5.9	0.5	6.4	4.6[3]	5.2	5.0	4.7	4.6	4.5	0.2	4.7	0.8[3]	1.1[9]	1.4	1.3	1.1	1.0	0.4	1.3
Ireland	4.1	4.3	6.0	6.0	5.7	5.2	0.4	5.6	2.9[4]	3.3	4.6	4.6	4.4	4.2	0.2	4.4	1.2[4]	1.0	1.0	—	1.2	1.0	0.1	1.3
Israel[7]	6.6	6.2	5.0	5.9	5.6	5.1[10]	1.3[10]	6.5[10]	4.5	4.2	3.4	3.7	3.7	4.4[10]	0.3	4.6[10]	1.1	1.0	0.8	0.8	0.9	0.7[10]	1.0[10]	1.6[10]
Italy[7]	4.5	3.4	4.8	4.3	4.2	3.5	0.2[10]	3.9[10]	3.2	2.6	3.8	3.4	3.3	2.9[10]	0.1[10]	3.0[10]	0.9[3]	0.6	0.5	0.8	0.8	0.7[10]	0.1[10]	0.9[10]
Japan	3.5	4.3	3.6	3.6	3.6	3.5	1.5	5.0	2.7[9]	2.6	2.7[9]	2.8	2.7[9]	2.7[9]	0.2[9]	2.9[9]	0.5[9]	0.5	0.7	0.7	0.5[9]	0.5[9,10]	1.0[9]	1.6[9,10]
Korea, Republic of	4.3	4.3	4.9	4.8	4.9	3.7	1.3	5.0	3.3	3.4	3.6	3.4	3.5	3.3	0.5	3.7	0.6	0.6	0.7	0.9	0.7	0.9	1.0	1.9
Luxembourg	—	—	—	—	—	3.7	0.0	3.7	—	—	—	—	3.7[6,7]	3.3	0.0	3.3	—	—	—	—	—	0.4	0.0	0.4
Mexico	4.7	5.3	5.0	5.1	5.0	4.6	0.8	5.4	3.3	3.7	3.8	3.4	3.3	3.4	0.5	3.9	0.8	0.9	1.0	1.0	0.9	1.0	0.4	1.3
Netherlands	4.3	4.6	5.0	5.4	5.3	4.9	0.6	5.5	3.3	3.3	3.7	3.7	3.6	3.5	0.3	3.8	0.9	0.9	1.1	1.3	1.3	1.4	0.7	1.9
New Zealand	5.8	5.2	6.1	6.0	6.3	5.0	1.5	6.5	4.6	4.0	4.4	4.4	4.8	4.2	0.8	5.0	0.9	0.9	1.1	1.0	1.0	1.0	0.7	1.7
Norway	5.8[3]	5.7	7.0	7.5	7.3	6.5	0.1	6.5	4.6	4.0	4.5	5.1	5.4	4.6[11]	0.0[11]	4.6[11]	1.3	1.2	1.3	1.6	1.6[11]	1.6[11]	0.1	1.6[11]
Poland	5.2[3]	5.4	5.0	5.0	4.8	4.4	0.4	4.8	3.7[3]	3.7	3.2	3.4	3.2	3.2	0.2	3.4	0.8[3]	1.2	1.1	1.0	1.2	1.2	0.1	1.3
Portugal	5.6[3]	5.3	5.0	5.1	5.1	4.9	0.9	5.9	3.9[3,11]	3.8[11]	4.0[7,11]	3.9[11]	3.7[7,11]	3.9	0.5[9]	4.5	1.0[3]	0.9	0.7[9,11]	0.7[11]	0.8[11]	0.9	0.1[11]	1.0[11]
Slovak Republic	4.0[3]	3.7	4.1	4.0	3.8	2.5[11]	0.2[11]	2.7[11]	2.7[3,4,11]	2.5[11]	2.7[11]	2.8[11]	2.5[11]	2.5[11]	0.2[11]	2.7[11]	0.7[3,4,11]	0.7[11]	1.1	0.7[11]	1.1	1.0	0.2	1.2
Slovenia	—	—	—	—	—	3.5	0.3	3.8	3.1[4]	2.7	3.1	3.0	2.9	2.8	0.3	3.0	0.9[4]	1.0	1.1	1.1	1.0	1.0	0.2	1.2
Spain	4.3	4.1	5.3	5.2	4.7	4.0	0.5	4.3	3.1[4]	3.0	3.6	3.6	2.9	2.8	0.3	3.1	1.5[4]	1.0	1.1	1.1	1.6	1.0	0.2	1.2
Sweden	6.3	6.2	6.6	6.3	6.2	5.2	0.2	5.4	4.4	4.2	4.2	4.0	3.9	3.7	0.0	3.7	—	1.5	1.6	1.6	1.6	1.5	0.2	1.7
Switzerland	5.3[3]	5.6	5.5	5.2	5.2	4.9	0.0	4.9	3.8	3.9	3.8	3.6	3.6	3.5	0.4	3.9	1.2[3]	1.4	1.4	1.3	1.3	1.2	0.2	1.4
Turkey	3.4[3]	—	—	—	—	—	—	—	2.4[3]	—	—	—	—	2.6	0.3	3.0	0.7[3]	0.9	0.6	0.7	0.9	1.2	0.6	1.4
United Kingdom[5]	4.5	5.0	5.3	5.9	5.6	5.2	1.0	6.3	3.8	3.8	4.5	4.8	4.4	4.0	0.6	4.5	0.8	0.9	1.1	1.1	0.9	1.2	0.6	1.8
United States[5]	4.6	4.9	5.3	5.1	4.7	4.7	1.7	6.4	3.5	3.6	3.8	3.7	3.4	3.3	0.3	3.6	0.8	1.0	1.6	1.6	1.6	1.4	1.4	2.8
Other reporting countries																								
Argentina	4.5[3]	—	—	—	—	—	—	—	3.2[3]	3.3	4.4	4.2	4.5	—	—	—	0.8[3]	0.8	1.1	1.1	1.2	—	—	—
Brazil	4.1[3]	4.4	5.5	5.6	6.2	5.6	0.0[8]	5.6[8]	2.9[3]	—	4.3	4.3	4.4	4.6[8]	0.0[8]	4.6[8]	0.8[3]	—	0.8	0.9	0.9	0.9[8]	0.0[8]	0.9[8]
Colombia	—	—	—	—	5.9	4.9[8]	1.9[8]	6.8[8]	—	—	—	—	—	3.6[8]	0.9[8]	4.5[8]	—	—	—	—	—	0.8	1.0[8]	1.9[8]
Indonesia	—	—	—	—	—	3.3[8]	0.4[8]	3.7[8]	—	—	—	—	—	2.3[8]	0.2[8]	2.5[8]	0.4[3,4]	—	0.5[9]	0.5	—	0.6[8]	0.2[8]	0.8[8]
Latvia	1.5[3,4]	—	—	3.0	—	3.9[8]	0.3	4.2	1.1[3,4]	—	—	2.0	2.0	2.9	0.0	2.8	—	—	—	0.5	—	0.9	0.5	1.4
Russian Federation	—	—	—	—	—	3.4	0.6	4.0	—	—	—	—	—	2.2	0.1	2.3	—	—	—	—	—	1.2	—	—
South Africa	3.0[3]	3.8	4.7	4.1	3.9	—	—	—	1.7	1.9	2.3	2.0	2.0	—	—	—	0.5	0.8	1.2	1.0	0.9	—	—	—

—Not available.
[1]Unless otherwise noted, includes public subsidies to households for payments to education institutions and direct expenditures on education institutions from international sources.
[2]Refers to the mean of the data values for all reporting Organization for Economic Cooperation and Development (OECD) countries, to which each country reporting data contributes equally. The average includes all current OECD countries for which a given year's data are available, even if they were not members of OECD in that year.
[3]Excludes public subsidies to households.
[4]Direct expenditures on education institutions from international sources exceed 1.5 percent of all public expenditures.
[5]Postsecondary non-higher-education included in higher education.
[6]Includes preprimary education (for children ages 3 and older).
[7]Excludes postsecondary non-higher-education.
[8]Data are for 2013 instead of 2012.
[9]Postsecondary non-higher-education included in both secondary and higher education.

[10]Excludes occupation-specific education corresponding to that offered at the vocational associate's degree level in the United States.
[11]Occupation-specific education corresponding to that offered at the vocational associate's degree level in the United States is included in elementary and secondary education instead of in higher education.
NOTE: Public direct expenditures on education include both amounts spent directly by governments to hire education personnel and to procure other resources, and amounts provided by governments to public or private institutions. Private direct expenditures exclude public subsidies that are used for payments to education institutions. Postsecondary non-higher-education is included in elementary and secondary education unless otherwise noted. Data for "all institutions" include expenditures that could not be reported by level of education. Data for 2011 and earlier years were calculated using the International Standard Classification of Education (ISCED) 1997 classification. Data for 2012 used the ISCED 2011 classification and may not be comparable to data for earlier years. Detail may not sum to totals because of rounding.
SOURCE: Organization for Economic Cooperation and Development (OECD), Online Education Database; and Education at a Glance, selected years, 2003 through 2015. (This table was prepared December 2015.)

CHAPTER 7
Libraries and Internet Use

This chapter presents statistics on elementary and secondary school libraries, college and university libraries (including institution-level information for the 60 largest college libraries in the country), and public libraries. It contains data on library collections, staff, and expenditures, as well as library usage. The chapter ends with a table on internet usage among persons of various racial/ethnic groups, age groups, educational attainment levels, and income levels. Tables on the use of technology and distance education in elementary and secondary schools and in postsecondary institutions can be found in chapters 2 and 3.

Libraries

Among public schools that had a library in 2011–12, the average number of library staff per school was 1.8, including 0.9 certified library/media specialists (table 701.10). On average, public school libraries had larger numbers of books on a per student basis in 2011–12 (2,188 per 100 students) than in 1999–2000 (1,803 per 100 students), 2003–04 (1,891 per 100 students), and 2007–08 (2,015 per 100 students). In 2011–12, public elementary school libraries had larger holdings than public secondary school libraries on a per student basis (2,570 books per 100 students, compared with 1,474 books per 100 students).

At degree-granting postsecondary institutions, library operating expenditures per full-time-equivalent (FTE) student were 1 percent higher in 2001–02 than in 1991–92, after adjustment for inflation (table 701.40). From 2001–02 to 2011–12, library operating expenditures per FTE student dropped by 25 percent in inflation-adjusted dollars. Overall, there was a net decrease of 24 percent in library operating expenditures per FTE student between 1991–92 and 2011–12. In 2011–12, library operating expenditures per FTE student averaged $441 (in current dollars) across all degree-granting institutions. The amount varied widely by institution control, however. Library operating expenditures averaged $372 per FTE student attending a public institution in 2011–12, compared with $844 per FTE student attending a private nonprofit institution and $78 per FTE student attending a private for-profit institution. In 2011–12, the average number of volumes (including books, bound periodicals, and other print materials) per FTE student also differed for public institutions (61 volumes), private nonprofit institutions (128 volumes), and private for-profit institutions (4 volumes). Across all degree-granting institutions, the average number of volumes per FTE student in 2011–12 was 69, which was 4 percent less than in 1991–92. The calculations of library operating expenditures and number of volumes per FTE student include both institutions with libraries and those without libraries. In 2011–12, there were libraries at 81 percent of degree-granting institutions overall, 95 percent of public institutions, 88 percent of private nonprofit institutions, and 55 percent of private for-profit institutions.

In 2013, there were 9,091 public libraries in the United States with a total of 775 million books and serial volumes (table 701.60). The annual number of visits per capita—that is, per resident of the areas served by the libraries—was 4.8, the annual number of reference transactions per capita was 0.9, and the annual number of uses of public-access internet computers per capita was 1.1.

Computer and Internet Use

In 2013, 71 percent of the U.S. population age 3 and over used the Internet (table 702.10). Comparing the White, Black, and Hispanic populations age 3 and over, the percentage of internet users was highest among Whites (75 percent), followed by Blacks (64 percent), and then Hispanics (61 percent). The percentage of internet users in the population age 3 and over was generally higher for those with higher family income levels. For example, 72 percent of people with family incomes from $40,000 to $49,999 used the Internet, compared to 85 percent of people with family incomes of $100,000 or more. Among persons age 25 and over, the percentage of internet users tended to be higher for those with higher levels of educational attainment. For example, 54 percent of persons who had not completed high school used the Internet, compared with 64 percent of those who had completed only a high school diploma or equivalent and 89 percent of those with a bachelor's or higher degree.

Table 701.10. Selected statistics on public school libraries/media centers, by level of school: Selected years, 1999–2000 through 2011–12

[Standard errors appear in parentheses]

Selected statistic	1999–2000	2003–04	2007–08 Total	Elementary	Secondary	Combined elementary/ secondary	2011–12 Total	Elementary	Secondary	Combined elementary/ secondary
1	2	3	4	5	6	7	8	9	10	11
Number of schools with libraries/media centers	77,300 (421)	78,300 (548)	81,900 (634)	59,700 (492)	17,800 (414)	4,400 (239)	81,200 (510)	58,000 (418)	17,100 (357)	6,100 (373)
Average number of staff per library/media center	1.89 (0.018)	1.76 (0.014)	1.72 (0.017)	1.65 (0.019)	2.04 (0.039)	1.42 (0.057)	1.77 (0.017)	1.72 (0.020)	1.93 (0.027)	1.76 (0.056)
Certified library/media specialists	0.81 (0.007)	0.79 (0.009)	0.78 (0.011)	0.73 (0.013)	0.98 (0.013)	0.66 (0.033)	0.90 (0.012)	0.88 (0.014)	0.99 (0.017)	0.88 (0.031)
Full-time	0.65 (0.007)	0.65 (0.009)	0.66 (0.010)	0.61 (0.012)	0.88 (0.018)	0.49 (0.032)	0.71 (0.010)	0.67 (0.012)	0.84 (0.017)	0.69 (0.029)
Part-time	0.16 (0.006)	0.14 (0.007)	0.13 (0.007)	0.13 (0.010)	0.10 (0.009)	0.18 (0.020)	0.20 (0.008)	0.21 (0.010)	0.15 (0.010)	0.19 (0.020)
Other professional staff	0.17 (0.007)	0.19 (0.008)	0.22 (0.010)	0.22 (0.013)	0.21 (0.021)	0.24 (0.027)	0.19 (0.007)	0.18 (0.009)	0.17 (0.014)	0.27 (0.026)
Full-time	0.12 (0.005)	0.13 (0.007)	0.13 (0.008)	0.13 (0.010)	0.14 (0.017)	0.15 (0.022)	0.12 (0.006)	0.11 (0.007)	0.13 (0.013)	0.16 (0.022)
Part-time	0.06 (0.004)	0.05 (0.005)	0.08 (0.007)	0.08 (0.009)	0.07 (0.013)	0.08 (0.017)	0.07 (0.005)	0.07 (0.007)	0.05 (0.005)	0.11 (0.014)
Other paid employees	0.91 (0.014)	0.78 (0.011)	0.72 (0.013)	0.70 (0.016)	0.86 (0.027)	0.51 (0.036)	0.68 (0.011)	0.66 (0.012)	0.76 (0.021)	0.61 (0.040)
Full-time	0.49 (0.008)	0.46 (0.009)	0.43 (0.013)	0.39 (0.016)	0.60 (0.022)	0.27 (0.028)	0.40 (0.008)	0.37 (0.009)	0.52 (0.017)	0.39 (0.031)
Part-time	0.41 (0.014)	0.33 (0.012)	0.29 (0.011)	0.31 (0.014)	0.26 (0.018)	0.24 (0.028)	0.28 (0.009)	0.29 (0.012)	0.24 (0.012)	0.22 (0.027)
Percent of libraries/media centers with certain media equipment										
Automated catalog	72.8 (0.69)	82.7 (0.66)	87.2 (0.71)	87.5 (0.94)	90.6 (1.08)	69.8 (2.88)	88.3 (0.49)	89.1 (0.60)	90.3 (0.78)	74.4 (2.16)
Automated circulation system	74.4 (0.65)	86.9 (0.61)	89.5 (0.68)	89.9 (0.87)	92.6 (0.98)	72.4 (3.15)	90.3 (0.47)	91.7 (0.59)	90.1 (0.75)	77.8 (2.17)
Media retrieval system[1]	— (†)	— (†)	34.9 (1.05)	35.9 (1.33)	35.1 (1.66)	20.6 (2.32)	32.5 (0.76)	33.6 (0.99)	32.3 (0.91)	22.4 (1.92)
Connection to Internet	90.1 (0.57)	95.1 (0.35)	96.7 (0.40)	96.5 (0.51)	98.6 (0.51)	91.6 (1.90)	95.9 (0.34)	96.2 (0.46)	97.3 (0.49)	89.6 (1.82)
Digital video disc (DVD) player/video cassette recorder (VCR)	— (†)	87.8 (0.60)	87.2 (0.77)	86.7 (1.02)	89.6 (1.00)	84.5 (2.20)	83.2 (0.76)	82.8 (0.98)	86.7 (0.76)	77.7 (2.00)
Disability assistance technologies, such as TDD	— (†)	11.9 (0.50)	23.9 (1.05)	23.0 (1.33)	26.4 (1.34)	25.9 (2.76)	31.0 (0.75)	29.9 (0.94)	34.3 (1.02)	31.9 (1.95)
Percent of libraries/media centers with certain services										
Students permitted to check out laptops	— (†)	— (†)	27.5 (1.02)	26.9 (1.27)	29.8 (1.34)	26.1 (2.57)	40.2 (0.69)	39.3 (0.85)	42.4 (1.08)	41.8 (2.67)
Staff permitted to check out laptops	— (†)	— (†)	45.9 (1.07)	45.2 (1.35)	50.1 (1.50)	38.5 (2.85)	54.3 (0.85)	53.9 (0.99)	55.5 (1.23)	54.2 (2.43)
Number of library computer workstations per 100 students	— (†)	2.3 (0.04)	2.6 (0.05)	2.5 (0.07)	2.9 (0.06)	3.0 (0.17)	3.1 (0.05)	2.8 (0.06)	3.6 (0.08)	3.3 (0.23)
Number of holdings per 100 students at the end of the school year[2]										
Books (number of volumes)	1,803 (19.7)	1,891 (45.1)	2,015 (30.5)	2,316 (40.2)	1,432 (36.6)	2,439 (132.3)	2,188 (42.4)	2,570 (58.5)	1,474 (24.7)	2,066 (87.3)
Audio and video materials	59 (0.9)	80 (3.7)	90 (3.8)	93 (5.6)	81 (5.2)	107 (13.3)	81 (2.4)	85 (3.3)	71 (2.9)	97 (8.3)
Number of additions per 100 students during the school year[2]										
Books (number of volumes)	— (†)	99.3 (2.08)	95.3 (2.21)	113.3 (3.26)	62.1 (2.67)	103.4 (7.41)	89.4 (3.47)	104.8 (5.45)	58.9 (2.08)	92.5 (6.54)
Audio and video materials	— (†)	5.1 (0.19)	5.4 (0.49)	5.9 (0.77)	4.5 (0.41)	5.7 (0.84)	4.3 (0.37)	3.8 (0.32)	4.2 (0.70)	8.2 ! (3.28)
Expenditures for library/media materials per pupil[2] in current dollars										
Total[3]	$23.37 (0.438)	$16.24 (0.322)	$16.11 (0.461)	$16.18 (0.591)	$15.90 (0.647)	$17.00 (1.216)	$16.00 (0.691)	$16.48 (1.099)	$14.80 (0.584)	$17.26 (1.215)
Books	9.97 (0.153)	10.99 (0.299)	11.40 (0.291)	11.99 (0.389)	10.26 (0.504)	12.10 (1.094)	10.28 (0.343)	10.73 (0.480)	9.41 (0.526)	10.27 (0.830)
Audio and video materials	1.66 (0.032)	1.14 (0.045)	1.08 (0.055)	1.06 (0.088)	1.11 (0.054)	1.16 (0.152)	0.84 (0.072)	0.80 (0.113)	0.89 (0.062)	0.89 (0.131)
Current serial subscriptions	1.26 (0.016)	1.38 (0.025)	(†)	(†)	(†)	(†)	(†)	(†)	(†)	(†)
Electronic subscriptions	0.81 (0.018)	0.88 (0.033)	(†)	(†)	(†)	(†)	(†)	(†)	(†)	(†)
Expenditures for library/media materials per pupil[2] in constant 2014–15 dollars[4]										
Total[3]	$32.67 (0.612)	$20.65 (0.409)	$18.01 (0.515)	$18.08 (0.660)	$17.78 (0.724)	$19.00 (1.360)	$16.64 (0.719)	$17.14 (1.143)	$15.39 (0.607)	$17.95 (1.263)
Books	13.94 (0.214)	13.98 (0.380)	12.74 (0.326)	13.40 (0.435)	11.48 (0.564)	13.53 (1.207)	10.70 (0.357)	11.16 (0.499)	9.79 (0.547)	10.68 (0.863)
Audio and video materials	2.33 (0.045)	1.45 (0.057)	1.21 (0.062)	1.18 (0.098)	1.24 (0.060)	1.30 (0.166)	0.87 (0.075)	0.83 (0.118)	0.93 (0.065)	0.93 (0.136)
Current serial subscriptions	1.76 (0.022)	1.76 (0.032)	(†)	(†)	(†)	(†)	(†)	(†)	(†)	(†)
Electronic subscriptions	1.13 (0.025)	1.12 (0.042)	(†)	(†)	(†)	(†)	(†)	(†)	(†)	(†)

—Not available.
†Not applicable.
!Interpret data with caution. The coefficient of variation (CV) for this estimate is between 30 percent and 50 percent.
[1]Centralized video distribution equipment with a scheduling and control server that telecasts video to classrooms.
[2]Holdings, additions, and expenditures are from the prior school year, while enrollment counts are from the current school year.
[3]Includes other expenditures not separately shown.
[4]Constant dollars based on the Consumer Price Index, prepared by the Bureau of Labor Statistics, U.S. Department of Labor, adjusted to a school-year basis.
NOTE: Detail may not sum to totals because of rounding.
SOURCE: U.S. Department of Education, National Center for Education Statistics, Schools and Staffing Survey (SASS), "Public School Library Media Center Questionnaire," 1999–2000, 2003–04, 2007–08, and 2011–12; and "Charter School Questionnaire," 1999–2000. (This table was prepared May 2016.)

Table 701.20. Selected statistics on public school libraries/media centers, by level and enrollment size of school: 2011–12

[Standard errors appear in parentheses]

Selected statistic	All public school libraries/media centers — Total	Elementary school enrollment size — Total	Less than 150	150 to 499	500 to 749	750 or more	Secondary school enrollment size — Total	Less than 500	500 to 749	750 to 1,499	1,500 or more
1	2	3	4	5	6	7	8	9	10	11	12
Number of schools with libraries/media centers	81,200 (510)	58,000 (418)	3,000 (308)	29,700 (658)	16,600 (591)	8,600 (426)	17,100 (357)	6,400 (289)	3,100 (170)	4,600 (188)	3,000 (160)
Average number of staff per library/media center	1.77 (0.017)	1.72 (0.020)	1.76 (0.226)	1.66 (0.022)	1.75 (0.032)	1.87 (0.040)	1.93 (0.027)	1.58 (0.041)	1.76 (0.050)	2.07 (0.045)	2.63 (0.062)
Certified library/media specialists	0.90 (0.012)	0.88 (0.014)	0.90 (0.176)	0.86 (0.016)	0.88 (0.019)	0.92 (0.024)	0.99 (0.017)	0.78 (0.029)	0.95 (0.029)	1.10 (0.024)	1.32 (0.039)
Full-time	0.71 (0.010)	0.67 (0.012)	0.47 ! (0.171)	0.61 (0.015)	0.74 (0.016)	0.81 (0.022)	0.84 (0.017)	0.59 (0.029)	0.81 (0.025)	0.99 (0.021)	1.21 (0.037)
Part-time	0.20 (0.008)	0.21 (0.010)	0.44 ! (0.054)	0.26 (0.014)	0.14 (0.014)	0.11 (0.017)	0.15 (0.010)	0.19 (0.018)	0.15 (0.025)	0.11 (0.019)	0.14 (0.018)
Other professional staff	0.19 (0.007)	0.18 (0.009)	0.27 ! (0.081)	0.18 (0.020)	0.18 (0.020)	0.16 (0.019)	0.17 (0.014)	0.21 (0.027)	0.19 (0.030)	0.14 (0.015)	0.14 (0.019)
Full-time	0.12 (0.006)	0.11 (0.007)	0.19 ! (0.076)	0.10 (0.010)	0.09 (0.011)	0.13 (0.020)	0.13 (0.013)	0.14 (0.025)	0.12 (0.030)	0.11 (0.014)	0.13 (0.019)
Part-time	0.07 (0.005)	0.07 (0.007)	0.08 ! (0.034)	0.08 (0.010)	0.09 (0.016)	0.03 ! (0.009)	0.05 (0.005)	0.07 (0.013)	0.07 (0.017)	0.02 (0.006)	0.02 ! (0.005)
Other paid employees	0.68 (0.011)	0.66 (0.012)	0.59 (0.063)	0.61 (0.016)	0.69 (0.026)	0.79 (0.035)	0.76 (0.021)	0.59 (0.032)	0.62 (0.036)	0.84 (0.032)	1.16 (0.049)
Full-time	0.40 (0.008)	0.37 (0.009)	0.29 (0.048)	0.32 (0.013)	0.39 (0.017)	0.51 (0.027)	0.52 (0.017)	0.35 (0.024)	0.39 (0.030)	0.61 (0.028)	0.87 (0.044)
Part-time	0.28 (0.009)	0.29 (0.012)	0.30 (0.061)	0.29 (0.015)	0.30 (0.022)	0.28 (0.029)	0.24 (0.012)	0.24 (0.020)	0.23 (0.026)	0.22 (0.024)	0.29 (0.027)
Percent of libraries/media centers with certain media equipment											
Automated catalog	88.3 (0.49)	89.1 (0.60)	75.2 (4.05)	88.0 (0.97)	90.0 (1.14)	96.2 (0.81)	90.3 (0.78)	80.4 (1.72)	93.3 (1.72)	97.2 (0.73)	97.1 (0.82)
Automated circulation system	90.3 (0.47)	91.7 (0.59)	77.0 (4.30)	91.4 (0.80)	93.0 (1.07)	95.7 (0.97)	90.1 (0.75)	81.2 (1.60)	94.1 (1.62)	96.2 (0.94)	95.3 (1.00)
Media retrieval system[1]	32.5 (0.76)	33.6 (0.99)	15.9 (3.35)	27.3 (1.48)	39.2 (1.77)	51.1 (2.24)	32.3 (0.91)	25.2 (1.89)	36.8 (2.56)	38.7 (1.99)	32.7 (2.19)
Connection to Internet	95.5 (0.34)	96.2 (0.46)	88.6 (3.28)	95.7 (0.66)	97.3 (0.79)	98.5 (0.64)	97.3 (0.49)	93.9 (1.18)	98.4 (0.67)	99.4 (0.33)	100.0 (†)
Digital video disc (DVD) player/video cassette recorder (VCR)[1]	83.2 (0.76)	82.8 (0.98)	66.0 (5.70)	83.1 (1.33)	84.3 (1.49)	84.6 (2.02)	86.7 (0.76)	83.9 (1.50)	89.5 (1.82)	88.4 (1.23)	87.0 (1.88)
Disability assistance technologies, such as TDD	31.0 (0.75)	29.9 (0.94)	20.7 (3.54)	26.8 (1.33)	33.2 (2.00)	37.4 (2.25)	34.3 (1.02)	30.8 (2.29)	34.6 (2.53)	36.8 (2.17)	37.6 (2.67)
Percent of libraries/media centers with certain services											
Students permitted to check out laptops	40.2 (0.69)	39.3 (0.85)	31.7 (4.21)	38.5 (1.52)	39.7 (2.01)	44.1 (2.02)	42.4 (1.08)	42.7 (2.07)	40.3 (2.72)	44.3 (2.12)	40.9 (2.77)
Staff permitted to check out laptops	54.3 (0.85)	53.9 (0.99)	38.9 (4.84)	51.8 (1.65)	57.5 (1.89)	59.6 (2.20)	55.5 (1.23)	52.6 (2.24)	55.6 (2.76)	58.1 (2.31)	57.8 (2.37)
Number of library computer workstations per 100 students	2.8 (0.05)	2.8 (0.06)	12.0 (1.49)	3.7 (0.13)	2.3 (0.09)	2.1 (0.07)	3.6 (0.08)	7.2 (0.35)	4.4 (0.16)	3.5 (0.09)	2.6 (0.12)
Number of holdings per 100 students at the end of the school year[2]											
Books (number of volumes)	2,188 (42.4)	2,570 (58.5)	9,505 (1472.0)	3,273 (115.0)	2,366 (101.2)	1,692 (53.5)	1,474 (24.7)	3,252 (98.6)	1,908 (74.2)	1,338 (21.2)	976 (20.9)
Audio and video materials	81 (2.4)	85 (3.3)	201 (58.1)	100 (6.6)	80 (4.5)	67 (5.9)	71 (2.9)	131 (8.7)	83 (7.3)	73 (5.4)	50 (4.0)
Number of additions per 100 students during the school year[2]											
Books (number of volumes)	89.4 (3.47)	104.8 (5.45)	423.0 (83.50)	126.3 (6.91)	99.5 (12.14)	73.4 (4.29)	58.9 (2.08)	124.0 (9.17)	77.5 (5.52)	50.0 (2.54)	43.0 (3.70)
Audio and video materials	4.3 (0.37)	3.8 (0.32)	10.6 ! (4.33)	4.7 (0.50)	3.2 (0.29)	3.2 (0.79)	4.2 (0.70)	5.8 (0.66)	4.3 (0.55)	3.5 (0.67)	4.5 ! (1.50)
Total expenditures for library/media materials per pupil[2,3]	$16.00 (0.691)	$16.48 (1.099)	$46.34 (7.286)	$20.40 (1.625)	$15.81 (2.409)	$11.31 (0.649)	$14.80 (0.584)	$27.69 (2.135)	$18.59 (2.051)	$13.48 (0.571)	$11.26 (1.169)
Books	10.28 (0.343)	10.73 (0.480)	32.08 (5.256)	12.82 (0.566)	9.83 (1.001)	8.47 (0.505)	9.41 (0.526)	16.28 (1.284)	12.55 (2.077)	8.06 (0.451)	7.70 (1.025)
Audio and video materials	0.84 (0.072)	0.80 (0.113)	1.02 (0.257)	0.80 (0.074)	1.00 (0.294)	0.56 (0.064)	0.89 (0.062)	1.50 (0.238)	0.79 (0.072)	0.88 (0.080)	0.77 (0.113)

†Not applicable.
!Interpret data with caution. The coefficient of variation (CV) for this estimate is between 30 percent and 50 percent.
[1]Centralized video distribution equipment with a scheduling and control server that telecasts video to classrooms.
[2]Holdings, additions, and expenditures are from the prior school year, while enrollment counts are from the current school year.
[3]Includes other expenditures not separately shown.

NOTE: Total includes combined elementary/secondary schools not separately shown. Detail may not sum to totals because of rounding.
SOURCE: U.S. Department of Education, National Center for Education Statistics, Schools and Staffing Survey (SASS), "Public School Library Media Center Questionnaire," 2011–12. (This table was prepared December 2013.)

Table 701.30. Selected statistics on public school libraries/media centers, by state: 2011–12

[Standard errors appear in parentheses]

State	Automated catalog	Automated circulation system	Percent of libraries/media centers offering selected services/equipment — Laptops for student use outside of library/media center	Laptops for staff use outside of library/media center	Media retrieval system[1]	Connection to the Internet	DVD player/VCR	Average number of staff per library/media center[2]	Books (number of volumes) held at end of year per 100 students[3]	Books (number of volumes) acquired during year per 100 students[3]	Total expenditure for materials per student[3]	Number of library computer workstations per 100 students
1	2	3	4	5	6	7	8	9	10	11	12	13
United States	88.3 (0.49)	90.3 (0.47)	40.2 (0.69)	54.3 (0.85)	32.5 (0.76)	95.9 (0.34)	83.2 (0.76)	1.8 (0.02)	2,188 (42.4)	89 (3.5)	$16.00 (0.691)	3.1 (0.05)
Alabama	96.0 (1.59)	98.5 (0.74)	46.7 (4.48)	59.9 (3.98)	29.6 (3.44)	97.2 (1.38)	95.4 (1.47)	1.6 (0.05)	2,114 (117.4)	48 (4.0)	7.31 (0.630)	2.4 (0.13)
Alaska	63.1 (5.91)	58.0 (6.01)	50.6 (5.49)	46.2 (5.49)	10.0 ! (3.22)	79.7 (6.31)	69.9 (6.51)	1.5 (0.11)	5,077 (351.4)	190 (29.7)	25.19 (3.742)	5.9 (0.66)
Arizona	77.5 (5.11)	78.5 (4.74)	33.0 (4.44)	51.4 (3.89)	35.2 (3.94)	88.7 (3.97)	78.8 (4.58)	1.5 (0.09)	1,988 (97.3)	57 (7.8)	9.60 (1.505)	2.7 (0.15)
Arkansas	97.4 (1.15)	97.4 (1.15)	29.5 (3.73)	48.1 (5.16)	30.6 (4.85)	100.0 (†)	94.2 (2.46)	1.8 (0.10)	1,880 (102.6)	96 (9.5)	16.00 (1.328)	2.7 (0.27)
California	78.5 (3.00)	82.5 (2.27)	20.8 (2.96)	40.7 (4.08)	13.1 (2.55)	93.6 (1.77)	58.9 (4.36)	1.5 (0.05)	2,065 (161.6)	75 (13.4)	10.25 (2.611)	2.2 (0.17)
Colorado	93.2 (3.07)	88.9 (3.73)	52.7 (4.25)	64.5 (4.58)	34.7 (4.91)	98.2 (0.90)	91.1 (2.64)	1.8 (0.10)	2,101 (137.0)	89 (8.4)	11.23 (1.648)	4.3 (0.30)
Connecticut	84.5 (4.76)	84.1 (4.79)	41.6 (7.41)	61.1 (6.05)	21.5 (4.98)	86.6 (2.11)	86.6 (3.83)	2.0 (0.08)	2,405 (105.1)	111 (29.0)	17.01 (1.330)	4.8 (0.46)
Delaware	95.1 (1.69)	97.1 (1.57)	48.6 (5.58)	48.6 (5.83)	24.4 (5.13)	98.2 (1.45)	81.4 (4.88)	1.2 (0.07)	2,835 (752.6)	61 (6.0)	9.41 (0.690)	3.0 (0.25)
District of Columbia	93.9 (2.05)	91.4 (2.67)	40.5 (4.01)	70.2 (4.51)	73.9 (3.17)	97.4 (0.94)	89.6 (2.88)	1.6 (0.05)	1,904 (114.0)	68 (5.9)	10.98 (1.115)	2.6 (†)
Florida	96.3 (1.26)	98.2 (0.78)	51.2 (4.92)	78.7 (3.79)	73.1 (4.13)	99.3 (0.37)	97.6 (1.38)	2.0 (0.06)	1,909 (81.2)	85 (7.8)	13.06 (0.806)	2.3 (0.16)
Georgia	75.5 (5.06)	85.6 (3.70)	9.9 (2.35)	22.1 (4.21)	24.5 (4.39)	97.4 (1.81)	81.5 (6.08)	1.6 (0.12)	2,378 (179.4)	64 (6.9)	8.45 (0.954)	3.0 (0.22)
Hawaii	80.3 (3.31)	81.6 (3.25)	39.4 (4.92)	48.1 (4.94)	15.2 (2.39)	94.9 (2.41)	79.9 (4.00)	2.1 (0.21)	2,453 (206.1)	110 (17.5)	20.31 (3.342)	3.6 (0.22)
Idaho	89.7 (3.52)	88.9 (4.46)	33.2 (4.58)	50.2 (5.73)	31.7 (5.41)	96.9 (1.75)	89.6 (3.38)	2.0 (0.09)	2,486 (142.5)	84 (7.5)	14.54 (1.057)	2.9 (0.27)
Illinois												
Indiana												
Iowa	94.5 (2.53)	95.8 (1.94)	59.5 (4.38)	66.3 (4.73)	26.5 (5.18)	98.0 (1.26)	86.4 (3.45)	2.3 (0.09)	2,603 (143.2)	101 (9.8)	14.44 (1.345)	5.8 (0.59)
Kansas	92.2 (4.50)	99.2 (0.40)	58.0 (4.86)	58.2 (5.34)	28.3 (4.63)	93.0 (3.36)	97.7 (1.27)	2.0 (0.09)	3,564 (259.0)	101 (14.2)	22.42 (5.432)	4.2 (0.43)
Kentucky	91.0 (2.31)	93.0 (2.16)	34.2 (4.76)	51.3 (4.59)	56.3 (4.89)	95.0 (2.02)	86.0 (3.27)	1.5 (0.08)	2,026 (91.2)	96 (8.4)	17.68 (1.388)	3.2 (0.14)
Louisiana	83.9 (4.21)	98.3 (0.96)	48.4 (5.33)	66.8 (5.40)	31.5 (5.98)	95.0 (1.48)	85.9 (4.22)	1.4 (0.10)	1,951 (119.4)	66 (7.2)	17.58 (4.543)	3.5 (0.31)
Maine	85.6 (4.05)	88.6 (3.44)	48.1 (4.85)	53.1 (4.18)	11.3 (3.20)	84.7 (3.91)	75.8 (4.94)	1.7 (0.10)	3,393 (283.8)	109 (9.9)	22.60 (1.615)	2.6 (0.22)
Maryland	68.1 ‡ (4.03)	70.9 (4.42)	33.6 (4.95)	42.6 (5.18)	20.0 (4.09)	96.8 (1.82)	84.5 (3.77)	1.3 (†)	1,664 (121.0)	61 (7.5)	13.79 (2.749)	3.4 (0.26)
Massachusetts	83.6 (2.79)	87.1 (2.74)	39.9 (3.62)	51.3 (3.63)	45.9 (3.56)	98.3 (0.77)	80.8 (3.40)	1.7 (0.07)	2,065 (117.9)	58 (5.1)	10.13 (1.086)	4.5 (0.30)
Michigan	91.5 (2.23)	92.1 (2.41)	39.8 (3.67)	57.6 (4.04)	34.4 (3.50)	94.4 (1.86)	86.3 (2.82)	2.2 (0.07)	2,760 (139.9)	105 (24.4)	16.40 (2.140)	5.4 (0.35)
Minnesota	71.9 (5.72)	86.5 (3.53)	22.7 (3.97)	46.3 (5.13)	26.8 (3.50)	97.0 (1.86)	89.5 (3.43)	1.5 (0.08)	1,862 (110.5)	106 (22.0)	13.03 (1.871)	1.9 (0.15)
Mississippi												
Missouri	93.8 (1.87)	97.3 (1.37)	34.8 (3.06)	44.1 (3.32)	19.8 (2.78)	98.2 (1.40)	89.2 (2.91)	1.9 (0.09)	2,624 (93.4)	106 (6.2)	21.23 (0.896)	4.4 (0.20)
Montana	77.6 (6.74)	87.9 (4.59)	34.8 (6.14)	50.6 (7.14)	17.0 (5.97)	96.2 (2.31)	93.3 (2.57)	1.8 (0.10)	3,570 (325.3)	118 (9.4)	21.51 (2.129)	6.1 (0.73)
Nebraska	90.0 (3.18)	93.3 (2.83)	71.8 (4.06)	71.8 (4.32)	33.6 (4.96)	95.0 (2.14)	92.5 (2.55)	2.1 (0.11)	3,629 (430.3)	137 (18.6)	21.64 (1.246)	5.8 (0.44)
Nevada	97.8 (1.08)	98.3 (0.96)	28.6 (4.31)	41.2 (4.77)	34.4 (3.34)	97.4 (1.78)	65.2 (5.29)	1.6 (0.12)	1,674 (55.0)	74 (5.3)	10.23 (0.490)	1.9 (0.13)
New Hampshire	91.3 (4.46)	94.4 (4.05)	58.4 (7.08)	66.7 (6.26)	7.9 ‡ (3.66)	100.0 (†)	96.1 (2.84)	1.8 (0.12)	2,134 (124.6)	81 (5.5)	21.78 (1.383)	3.7 (0.31)
New Jersey	85.7 (3.03)	86.5 (2.85)	46.5 (4.19)	45.4 (4.10)	20.7 (3.29)	96.0 (2.08)	79.9 (3.22)	1.4 (0.06)	2,172 (121.3)	68 (8.2)	15.47 (1.072)	3.1 (0.19)
New Mexico	87.3 (10.18)	86.3 (10.49)	36.4 (3.90)	65.2 (5.93)	37.6 (7.31)	95.8 (2.70)	83.7 (6.05)	1.8 (0.24)	3,057 (631.5)	95 (16.1)	‡ (1.274)	2.5 ! (1.21)
New York	94.2 (2.24)	93.8 (2.49)	38.3 (3.94)	45.8 (4.46)	21.4 (3.23)	98.5 (0.98)	81.3 (2.94)	1.8 (0.06)	1,898 (97.3)	101 (17.8)	19.25 (1.086)	2.5 ! (0.18)
North Carolina	95.9 (2.17)	95.5 (1.67)	57.3 (4.17)	86.1 (2.53)	55.4 (3.83)	98.5 (1.01)	93.6 (2.74)	1.6 (0.06)	1,940 (97.3)	88 (10.1)	15.85 (1.164)	3.5 (0.26)
North Dakota	77.6 (3.93)	80.5 (3.66)	45.1 (5.00)	52.7 (4.42)	20.1 (3.23)	96.6 (1.43)	75.6 (3.99)	2.0 (0.09)	3,728 (230.1)	172 (16.8)	24.28 (1.378)	4.8 (0.61)
Ohio	91.1 (2.25)	94.1 (2.23)	45.5 (3.69)	48.5 (3.52)	42.0 (4.60)	94.4 (1.88)	81.5 (3.43)	1.8 (0.07)	1,889 (75.4)	64 (6.2)	9.06 (0.502)	3.3 (0.20)
Oklahoma	84.1 (4.75)	86.4 (4.26)	42.3 (5.72)	46.2 (5.72)	26.7 (5.71)	94.1 (2.45)	87.7 (3.89)	1.7 (0.10)	2,676 (229.2)	133 (33.8)	15.91 (2.051)	3.0 (0.22)
Oregon	90.0 (3.18)	93.3 (2.83)	35.5 (5.04)	50.4 (5.10)	28.7 (5.09)	97.5 (1.54)	74.4 (5.11)	1.7 (0.08)	2,569 (116.8)	77 (10.6)	11.28 (1.628)	4.0 (0.42)
Pennsylvania	89.4 (3.12)	91.0 (2.86)	39.5 (4.85)	46.3 (4.96)	19.9 (3.71)	92.1 (3.19)	75.7 (4.33)	1.8 (0.11)	2,302 (181.0)	81 (10.1)	16.68 (1.792)	3.3 (0.22)
Rhode Island	72.9 (5.12)	76.7 (4.20)	26.0 (5.81)	22.9 (5.38)	5.1 ‡ (2.06)	94.3 (3.60)	72.4 (7.05)	1.7 (0.11)	1,993 (110.8)	62 (9.1)	9.22 (0.978)	3.3 (0.40)
South Carolina	95.2 (2.02)	97.2 (1.55)	49.1 (4.63)	79.0 (3.80)	81.6 (4.22)	100.0 (†)	96.1 (1.89)	1.8 (0.07)	2,246 (401.6)	79 (5.9)	15.47 (1.105)	3.5 (0.24)
South Dakota	75.1 (4.80)	69.3 (5.65)	48.0 (5.49)	51.9 (6.10)	25.8 (4.22)	98.1 (5.62)	55.3 (5.53)	1.7 (0.07)	3,370 (329.1)	81 (9.3)	22.94 (1.947)	3.5 (0.45)
Tennessee	92.3 (2.75)	98.1 (1.28)	46.3 (5.01)	57.9 (4.83)	28.0 (3.68)	96.1 (1.23)	90.5 (3.57)	1.7 (0.06)	1,756 (60.8)	81 (9.3)	11.96 (1.448)	2.5 (0.21)
Texas	93.2 (1.98)	96.8 (1.28)	42.1 (3.37)	59.2 (3.89)	32.9 (3.57)	98.1 (1.41)	90.2 (2.07)	1.8 (0.06)	2,261 (250.8)	113 (23.0)	23.54 (4.438)	2.3 (0.10)
Utah	86.1 (5.81)	85.8 (6.20)	28.0 (5.07)	34.2 (5.33)	44.5 (5.72)	84.8 (5.15)	84.8 (5.98)	1.7 (0.13)	1,652 (90.6)	85 (12.2)	10.03 (0.862)	2.1 (0.18)
Vermont	84.5 (4.69)	80.6 (4.24)	58.5 (5.72)	64.5 (4.95)	11.2 (2.48)	93.1 (2.97)	80.2 (4.12)	1.8 (0.09)	4,010 (145.6)	155 (9.1)	32.89 (1.796)	4.8 (0.48)
Virginia	95.7 (2.26)	97.3 (1.38)	60.8 (3.91)	74.7 (4.14)	49.5 (4.90)	96.8 (1.33)	90.1 (3.92)	1.9 (0.09)	2,018 (78.9)	122 (24.9)	18.86 (3.017)	3.1 (0.50)
Washington	92.2 (2.67)	93.6 (2.49)	29.0 (4.38)	47.9 (4.47)	28.1 (4.08)	96.3 (3.28)	84.1 (3.53)	1.9 (0.11)	2,325 (107.8)	82 (9.4)	9.46 (0.680)	3.9 (0.27)
West Virginia	69.0 (4.92)	74.9 (5.24)	42.1 (4.40)	47.5 (5.04)	22.0 (2.80)	92.8 (2.48)	68.6 (5.32)	1.0 (0.07)	1,923 (109.7)	110 (32.3)	15.04 (2.674)	4.5 (0.80)
Wisconsin	96.0 (2.31)	97.9 (1.07)	50.4 (4.28)	63.0 (4.58)	27.2 (3.97)	98.6 (1.35)	95.7 (2.36)	2.4 (0.09)	3,125 (149.7)	159 (8.7)	37.93 (2.217)	5.2 (0.41)
Wyoming	95.5 (4.10)	95.5 (4.10)	56.8 (5.80)	51.1 (4.62)	19.3 (5.06)	98.7 (0.80)	81.2 (5.71)	1.8 (0.10)	3,714 (330.4)	211 (33.4)	32.02 (5.222)	4.8 (0.67)

†Not applicable.
!Interpret data with caution. The coefficient of variation (CV) for this estimate is between 30 percent and 50 percent.
‡Reporting standards not met. Either the response rate is under 50 percent or there are too few cases for a reliable estimate.
[1]Centralized video distribution equipment with a scheduling and control server that telecasts video to classrooms.
[2]Includes professional and nonprofessional staff.
[3]Books held, books acquired, and expenditures are from the current school year, while enrollment counts are from the prior school year.

SOURCE: U.S. Department of Education, National Center for Education Statistics, Schools and Staffing Survey (SASS), "Public School Library Media Center Questionnaire," 2011–12. (This table was prepared December 2013.)

Table 701.40. Collections, staff, and operating expenditures of degree-granting postsecondary institution libraries: Selected years, 1981–82 through 2011–12

Collections, staff, and operating expenditures	1981–82	1987–88	1991–92	1997–98	2001–02	2005–06	2007–08	2009–10	2011–12 Total	Public	Private nonprofit	Private for-profit
1	2	3	4	5	6	7	8	9	10	11	12	13
Number of libraries	3,104	3,438	3,274	3,658	3,568	3,617	3,827	3,689	3,793	1,560	1,461	772
Percentage of institutions with libraries	—	—	—	90.0	85.0	84.6	87.9	82.1	80.6	94.6	88.4	55.0
Number of circulation transactions (in thousands)	—	—	—	216,067	189,248	187,236	178,766	176,736	154,409	99,897	51,930	2,582
Number of circulation transactions per full-time equivalent (FTE) student	—	—	—	20	16	14	13	11	10	9	16	2
Enrollment (in thousands)												
Total enrollment[1]	12,372	12,767	14,359	14,502	15,928	17,487	18,248	20,428	20,994	15,110	3,927	1,957
Full-time-equivalent (FTE) enrollment[1]	9,015	9,230	10,361	10,615	11,766	13,201	13,783	15,496	15,886	10,949	3,321	1,616
Collections (in thousands)												
Number of volumes at end of year	567,826	718,504	749,429	878,906	954,030	1,015,658	1,052,531	1,076,027	1,099,951	669,521	424,671	5,760
Number of volumes added during year	19,507	21,907	20,982	24,551	24,574	22,241	23,990	27,164	27,605	17,134	9,984	488
Number of serial subscriptions at end of year[2]	4,890	6,416	6,966	10,908	9,855	16,361	25,342	25,041	—	—	—	—
Microform units at end of year	—	—	—	1,062,082	1,143,678	1,166,295	1,157,365	1,124,941	1,044,521	705,525	337,405	1,591
E-books at end of year	—	—	—	—	10,318	64,366	102,502	158,652	252,599	136,181	102,413	14,006
Number of volumes per FTE student	63	78	72	83	81	77	76	69	69	61	128	4
Full-time-equivalent (FTE) library staff												
Total staff in regular positions[3]	58,476	67,251	67,166	68,337	69,526	69,615	69,328	66,562	65,242	39,776	23,770	1,696
Librarians and professional staff	23,816	25,115	26,341	30,041	32,053	33,265	34,520	34,147	34,423	19,601	13,382	1,440
Other paid staff	34,660	40,733	40,421	38,026	37,473	36,350	34,808	32,415	30,819	20,175	10,388	256
Contributed services	—	1,403	404	270	—	—	—	—	—	—	—	—
Student assistants	—	33,821	29,075	28,373	25,305	23,976	24,110	22,382	20,509	11,288	8,498	724
FTE student enrollment per FTE staff member	154	137	154	155	169	190	199	233	243	275	140	953
Library operating expenditures[4]												
Total operating expenditures (in thousands of current dollars)	$1,943,769	$2,770,075	$3,648,654	$4,592,657	$5,416,716	$6,234,192	$6,785,542	$6,829,108	$7,008,114	$4,077,793	$2,803,864	$126,457
Salaries and wages	914,379 [5]	1,451,551	1,889,368	2,314,380	2,753,404	3,102,561	3,342,082	3,401,649	3,443,831	2,060,066	1,308,607	75,158
Student hourly wages	100,847	(6)	(6)	(5)	(6)	(6)	(6)	(6)	(6)	(6)	(6)	(6)
Fringe benefits	167,515	—	—	—	—	—	—	—	—	—	—	—
Furniture/equipment	—	—	—	57,013	—	—	—	—	—	—	—	—
Computer hardware/software	—	—	—	164,379	155,791	153,002	158,698	142,652	143,660	90,583	51,050	2,028
Bibliographic utilities/networks/consortia	—	—	—	89,618	92,242	106,268	113,427	117,838	123,650	71,925	50,694	1,031
Information resources	591,550	925,425	1,240,419	1,643,914	1,990,989	2,375,485	2,663,082	2,680,298	2,790,039	1,572,279	1,172,378	45,383
Books and serial backfiles—paper	—	—	—	514,048	563,007	572,228	611,192	515,942	503,851	248,460	244,454	10,938
Books and serial backfiles—electronic	—	—	—	28,061	44,792	93,778	133,586	152,359	180,570	100,553	74,724	5,292
Current serials—paper	—	—	—	849,399	926,105	830,137	699,906	536,357	487,265	272,219	207,707	7,339
Current serials—electronic	—	—	—	125,470	297,657	691,585	1,004,393	1,249,726	1,436,671	856,062	562,111	18,498
Audiovisual materials	—	—	23,879	30,623	37,041	39,029	43,849	55,659	37,022	19,486	15,609	1,926
Document delivery/interlibrary loan	—	—	—	19,309	22,913	26,513	30,496	33,679	32,490	20,069	11,768	652
Preservation	30,351	34,144	43,126	42,919	46,499	41,102	41,591	31,212	26,838	14,382	12,392	63
Other collection expenditures	561,199	891,281	1,173,414	34,086	52,976	81,113	98,069	105,364	85,334	41,047	43,612	675
Other library operating expenditures	169,478	393,099	518,867	323,354	424,290	496,877	508,253	486,672	506,934	282,941	221,136	2,857
Operating expenditures per full-time-equivalent (FTE) student												
In current dollars	216	300	352	433	460	472	492	441	441	372	844	78
In constant 2014–15 dollars[7]	542	613	603	633	611	562	550	481	459	387	878	81
Information resource expenditures per FTE student												
In current dollars	66	100	120	155	169	180	193	173	176	144	353	28
In constant 2014–15 dollars[7]	165	205	205	227	225	214	216	189	183	149	367	29
Operating expenditures (percentage distribution)	100.0	100.0	100.0	100.0	100.0	100.0	100.0	100.0	100.0	100.0	100.0	100.0
Salaries and wages	47.0	52.4	51.8	50.4	50.8	49.8	49.3	49.8	49.1	50.5	46.7	59.4
Student hourly wages	5.2	(6)	(6)	(6)	(6)	(6)	(6)	(6)	(6)	(6)	(6)	(6)
Fringe benefits	8.6	—	—	—	—	—	—	—	—	—	—	—
Preservation	1.6	1.2	1.2	0.9	0.9	0.7	0.6	0.5	0.4	0.4	0.4	0.1
Information resources	28.9	32.2	32.8	34.9	35.9	37.4	38.6	38.8	39.4	38.2	41.4	35.8
Other[8]	8.7	14.2	14.2	13.8	12.4	12.1	11.5	10.9	11.0	10.9	11.5	4.7
Library operating expenditures as a percent of total institutional expenditures for educational and general purposes	3.5	3.2	3.0	—	—	—	—	—	—	—	—	—

—Not available.
[1]Fall enrollment for the academic year specified.
[2]For 1997–98 and later years, includes microform and electronic serials.
[3]Excludes student assistants.
[4]Excludes capital outlay.
[5]Includes salary equivalents of contributed services staff.
[6]Included under salaries and wages.
[7]Constant dollars based on the Consumer Price Index, prepared by the Bureau of Labor Statistics, U.S. Department of Labor, adjusted to a school-year basis.
[8]Includes furniture/equipment, computer hardware/software, and bibliographic utilities/networks/consortia as well as expenditures classified as "other library operating expenditures."

NOTE: Data through 1995 are for institutions of higher education, while later data are for degree-granting institutions. Degree-granting institutions grant associate's or higher degrees and participate in Title IV federal financial aid programs. The degree-granting classification is very similar to the earlier higher education classification, but it includes more 2-year colleges and excludes a few higher education institutions that did not grant degrees. Detail may not sum to totals because of rounding.
SOURCE: U.S. Department of Education, National Center for Education Statistics, *Library Statistics of Colleges and Universities*, 1981–82; Integrated Postsecondary Education Data System (IPEDS), "Academic Libraries Survey" (IPEDS-L:88–98), "Fall Enrollment Survey" (IPEDS-EF:87–98), and IPEDS Spring 2002 through Spring 2012, Enrollment component; Academic Libraries Survey (ALS), 2000 through 2012. (This table was prepared May 2016.)

Table 701.50. Collections, staff, operating expenditures, public service hours, and reference services of the 60 largest college and university libraries: Fiscal year 2012

Institution	Rank order, by number of volumes	Number of volumes at end of year (in thousands)	Number of e-books at end of year	Full-time-equivalent staff		Operating expenditures (in thousands of current dollars)		Public service hours per typical week	Gate count per typical week[1]	Annual reference information services to individuals[2]
				Total	Librarians	Total	Salaries and wages			
1	2	3	4	5	6	7	8	9	10	11
Harvard University (MA)	1	17,225	402,473	1,073	400	$134,533	$83,834	168	27,194 [3]	187,903
Yale University (CT)	2	13,504	1,090,187	600	163	81,221	35,235	111	27,194 [3]	31,783
University of Illinois at Urbana-Champaign	3	12,937	645,398	437	77	43,703	20,744	152	93,818	110,973
University of California, Berkeley	4	11,537	1,097,969	434	74	47,325	24,022	77	39,081 [3]	70,986
University of Michigan, Ann Arbor	5	11,458	1,926,938	690	186	63,828	32,553	168	114,557	211,469
University of Chicago (IL)	6	11,397	1,251,085	309	68	36,112	13,450	148	28,732	16,610
Columbia University in the City of New York	7	11,291	1,329,421	526	162	57,422	26,244	107	84,930	58,489
University of Texas at Austin	8	10,185	752,892	489	104	43,968	20,476	120	101,797	119,058
University of California, Los Angeles	9	9,981	1,288,821	527	133	50,171	27,406	96	81,905	113,725
Indiana University, Bloomington	10	9,276	1,363,894	395	90	33,371	15,259	101	64,700	138,542
Stanford University (CA)	11	9,025	841,538	653	153	69,922	31,704	105	20,491 [3]	105,636
University of Wisconsin, Madison	12	7,841	656,536	533	202	38,018	18,778	148	103,845	650
Tarrant County College District (TX)	13	7,828	83,036	73	24	3,878	2,723	84	26,583	—
Cornell University (NY)	14	7,684	903,397	468	110	45,471	21,917	145	73,193	62,429
Princeton University (NJ)	15	7,486	322,690	382	87	50,222	20,476	120	8,508	19,018
University of Washington, Seattle Campus	16	7,375	460,477	385	122	36,649	17,592	135	135,000	56,062
University of Minnesota, Twin Cities	17	6,918	484,151	355	87	39,526	17,992	107	45,000	46,021
Michigan State University	18	6,702	2,715,914	236	70	27,496	10,389	140	37,453	50,633
University of Pittsburgh, Main Campus (PA)	19	6,663	988,230	319	118	31,800	11,881	118	39,081 [3]	80,695
Duke University (NC)	20	6,540	875,488	321	114	41,043	17,127	149	95,437	80,518
University of Colorado at Boulder	21	6,510	675,723	232	62	24,263	10,114	128	66,545	57,345
University of North Carolina at Chapel Hill	22	6,437	996,453	409	130	38,135	18,921	146	90,160	84,345
University of Pennsylvania	23	6,108	1,100,111	416	137	41,535	19,601	116	31,779	6,500
Ohio State University, Main Campus	24	6,050	526,075	449	75	43,185	17,349	168	128,852	27,876
University of Arizona	25	6,030	1,184,441	194	51	23,350	8,410	142	38,585	17,247
University of Florida	26	5,611	815,537	301	90	28,657	13,434	138	53,235	44,945
Rutgers University, New Brunswick (NJ)	27	5,478	595,141	272	56	25,958	14,493	115	60,618	25,656
Pennsylvania State University, Main Campus	28	5,351	316,913	539	143	50,972	25,757	148	139,775	85,211
University of Iowa	29	5,310	772,023	221	66	24,728	9,883	116	34,623	52,416
University of Virginia, Main Campus	30	5,247	460,840	344	97	33,796	16,775	149	76,921	76,853
University of California, Davis	31	5,204	582,966	185	54	18,506	8,783	102	34,482	78,595
New York University	32	5,196	1,101,383	465	68	51,534	21,977	126	65,163	132,850
Northwestern University (IL)	33	5,140	139,418	362	111	32,029	14,629	122	21,560	23,444
University of Oklahoma, Norman Campus	34	5,139	1,168,077	142	34	17,000	4,727	117	26,456	21,693
University of Georgia	35	4,947	555,015	283	76	24,101	10,262	109	61,786	42,991
University of Southern California	36	4,845	877,824	329	84	66,405	17,589	159	53,335	110,159
Brown University (RI)	37	4,724	979,523	172	48	21,368	8,709	112	27,890	11,568
Texas A&M University, College Station	38	4,531	1,073,198	321	78	35,350	12,945	145	63,798	44,988
Arizona State University	39	4,531	403,504	288	73	25,459	9,795	149	39,081 [3]	42,726
University of South Carolina, Columbia	40	4,460	206,886	265	71	21,752	7,785	111	38,470	85,215
Johns Hopkins University (MD)	41	4,396	985,644	271	29	37,396	13,445	120	34,500	28,667
University of Cincinnati, Main Campus (OH)	42	4,336	1,243,527	188	44	21,019	8,588	106	33,229	119,451
Tulane University of Louisiana	43	4,320	927,113	172	55	17,813	6,275	118	20,000	21,633
Auburn University (AL)	44	4,318	821,083	106	29	12,762	4,502	146	28,066	98,072
University of Kansas	45	4,285	404,676	249	59	20,282	9,362	140	42,000	91,236
Miami University-Oxford (OH)	46	4,225	595,932	121	44	9,654	4,533	168	29,976	12,947
University at Buffalo (NY)	47	4,119	726,127	173	52	19,414	9,663	168	48,000	35,367
University of Maryland, College Park	48	4,094	599,198	250	80	29,353	11,724	138	58,461	386,001
University of Utah	49	4,068	334,463	322	79	25,130	12,508	142	55,008	165,837
University of Kentucky	50	4,023	588,428	238	74	21,285	8,741	140	51,632	29,825
University of Alabama	51	3,974	855,794	200	64	19,417	7,290	135	35,307	29,854
Brigham Young University (UT)	52	3,946	526,051	352	61	26,686	11,771	101	72,336	57,917
Washington University in St. Louis (MO)	53	3,890	590,299	245	97	32,570	10,042	120	28,000	52,905
Emory University (GA)	54	3,878	555,313	287	97	37,737	14,269	106	35,117	8,935
Syracuse University (NY)	55	3,815	942,224	207	59	19,271	8,613	136	34,993	21,395
Louisiana State University and Agricultural & Mechanical College	56	3,802	402,264	124	43	15,718	—	99	34,772	28,978
University of Notre Dame (IN)	57	3,796	466,168	249	77	26,934	10,880	147	26,544	20,612
Vanderbilt University (TN)	58	3,720	606,267	196	61	23,624	9,181	147	40,417	18,507
North Carolina State University at Raleigh	59	3,653	514,635	280	103	27,504	12,395	146	44,540	32,916
Temple University (PA)	60	3,573	635,008	196	55	23,382	8,263	145	80,009	73,889

—Not available.
[1]The number of entries into the library in an average week. A single person can be counted more than once.
[2]Includes both in-person and virtual services.
[3]Imputed.

SOURCE: U.S. Department of Education, National Center for Education Statistics, Academic Libraries Survey (ALS), fiscal year 2012. (This table was prepared March 2014.)

Table 701.60. Public libraries, books and serial volumes, and per capita usage of selected library services per year, by state: Fiscal years 2012 and 2013

State	Number of public libraries[1]		Number of books and serial volumes				Per capita[2] usage of selected services per year							
			In thousands		Per capita[2]		Number of library visits[3]		Circulation (number of materials lent)		Reference transactions[4]		Uses of public-access internet computers	
	2012	2013	2012	2013	2012	2013	2012	2013	2012	2013	2012	2013	2012	2013
1	2	3	4	5	6	7	8	9	10	11	12	13	14	15
United States	9,082	9,091	783,882	774,706	2.6	2.5	4.9	4.8	8.0	7.8	0.9	0.9	1.1	1.1
Alabama	219	220	9,671	9,636	2.1	2.1	3.6	3.5	4.5	4.5	0.9	0.9	1.0	1.0
Alaska	77	81	2,354	2,415	3.6	3.7	5.1	5.2	7.1	7.1	0.7	0.6	1.6	1.2
Arizona	91	90	8,399	8,427	1.3	1.3	4.3	4.2	7.8	7.2	0.7	0.9	1.0	1.0
Arkansas	56	57	6,501	6,579	2.5	2.5	4.1	4.0	5.4	5.5	0.8	0.9	0.8	0.8
California	183	183	68,912	67,641	1.8	1.8	4.3	4.4	6.1	6.0	0.6	0.6	0.9	0.9
Colorado	115	114	11,367	10,823	2.2	2.1	6.5	6.4	13.1	12.9	0.9	0.8	1.4	1.4
Connecticut	183	183	14,522	14,464	4.3	4.2	6.9	6.5	9.7	9.2	1.1	1.0	1.5	1.4
Delaware	21	21	1,697	1,642	1.9	1.8	5.1	4.1	7.0	6.7	0.5	0.4	0.9	0.7
District of Columbia	1	1	1,334	1,802	2.1	2.9	4.0	3.9	5.3	5.2	1.5	1.4	1.3	1.4
Florida	79	80	32,481	31,351	1.7	1.6	4.3	4.1	6.6	6.3	1.6	1.4	1.0	1.0
Georgia	61	61	16,637	16,089	1.6	1.5	3.2	2.9	4.2	3.9	0.9	0.9	1.3	1.2
Hawaii	1	1	3,394	3,372	2.5	2.4	3.9	3.7	5.0	4.8	0.5	0.5	0.4	0.5
Idaho	101	102	4,350	4,348	3.1	3.2	6.8	6.6	10.9	11.0	0.9	0.9	1.3	1.5
Illinois	622	623	43,846	43,378	3.7	3.7	6.6	6.5	10.3	10.2	1.2	0.9	1.3	1.2
Indiana	237	237	24,321	24,066	4.0	3.9	6.3	6.1	12.7	12.7	0.9	0.7	1.3	1.3
Iowa	533	534	12,105	11,959	4.1	4.0	6.5	6.2	9.7	9.4	0.6	0.6	1.3	1.2
Kansas	321	319	9,473	9,289	3.8	3.7	6.0	5.7	10.7	10.6	0.8	0.8	1.6	1.6
Kentucky	119	119	8,803	8,878	2.0	2.0	4.5	4.4	6.8	6.9	0.9	0.9	1.1	1.1
Louisiana	68	68	11,934	11,649	2.6	2.5	3.7	3.6	4.5	4.4	0.9	0.9	1.4	1.4
Maine	229	232	5,964	6,121	5.2	5.3	6.2	6.0	8.4	8.2	0.6	0.6	1.2	1.1
Maryland	24	24	13,022	12,927	2.3	2.2	5.1	4.9	10.0	10.0	1.5	1.4	1.2	1.2
Massachusetts	359	368	32,668	32,110	5.0	4.9	6.5	6.5	9.9	9.6	0.8	0.8	1.2	1.2
Michigan	389	388	33,728	33,411	3.4	3.4	5.7	5.4	8.9	8.8	1.0	1.0	1.2	1.2
Minnesota	138	137	15,164	14,779	2.8	2.8	4.9	4.7	10.5	10.1	0.6	0.7	1.2	1.1
Mississippi	51	52	5,734	5,687	1.9	1.9	3.2	3.2	2.8	2.7	0.5	0.5	0.9	0.9
Missouri	147	149	17,220	17,157	3.2	3.1	5.6	5.5	10.0	10.3	0.7	0.7	1.2	1.2
Montana	82	82	2,700	2,630	2.7	2.7	4.7	4.7	7.6	6.3	0.5	0.5	1.6	1.5
Nebraska	265	263	5,949	5,888	4.1	3.9	6.0	5.7	9.4	8.3	0.6	0.5	1.6	1.5
Nevada	22	21	4,441	4,128	1.6	1.5	4.1	3.9	7.4	7.6	0.7	0.6	0.9	0.9
New Hampshire	218	218	5,874	5,864	6.0	6.0	7.7	7.6	11.6	11.0	0.8	0.8	1.2	1.0
New Jersey	297	295	29,075	28,579	3.3	3.3	5.5	5.4	7.1	6.8	0.9	0.9	1.2	1.2
New Mexico	85	83	4,271	4,230	2.6	2.6	4.5	4.4	5.7	5.6	0.6	0.7	1.2	1.3
New York	756	756	70,074	70,955	3.6	3.7	5.9	5.7	8.2	7.9	1.6	1.5	1.2	1.2
North Carolina	77	80	16,519	16,517	1.7	1.7	4.2	3.7	5.7	5.4	1.1	0.9	0.9	0.9
North Dakota	75	75	2,294	2,298	3.7	3.6	3.8	3.5	6.7	6.5	0.6	0.6	1.0	0.9
Ohio	251	251	44,120	43,543	3.8	3.8	7.6	7.5	16.4	16.1	1.8	1.9	1.8	1.9
Oklahoma	118	117	7,441	7,271	2.4	2.3	4.7	4.5	7.1	7.3	1.0	0.9	1.3	1.2
Oregon	128	129	9,926	9,948	2.7	2.7	6.3	6.0	17.2	16.3	0.7	0.7	1.3	1.1
Pennsylvania	456	455	26,694	26,392	2.2	2.1	3.8	3.7	5.6	5.5	0.6	0.6	0.7	0.8
Rhode Island	48	48	4,428	4,364	4.2	4.2	5.8	5.8	7.1	6.8	0.7	0.7	1.4	1.4
South Carolina	42	42	9,343	9,206	2.0	2.0	3.9	4.0	5.6	5.7	0.7	0.7	1.0	1.1
South Dakota	112	111	2,988	2,848	4.0	3.9	5.3	5.4	8.9	9.5	0.6	0.6	1.9	1.8
Tennessee	185	186	11,525	11,640	1.8	1.8	3.4	3.2	4.2	4.1	0.6	0.6	0.8	0.8
Texas	551	544	40,707	39,977	1.7	1.7	3.2	3.1	5.5	5.0	0.6	0.6	0.8	0.8
Utah	72	71	6,964	6,705	2.5	2.4	6.8	6.5	13.5	13.2	1.2	1.2	1.2	1.1
Vermont	163	167	2,881	2,857	4.9	4.8	6.5	6.4	7.8	7.7	0.9	0.9	1.5	1.5
Virginia	91	91	18,332	18,059	2.3	2.3	5.0	4.8	9.7	9.5	0.9	0.9	1.3	1.0
Washington	61	61	14,842	14,271	2.2	2.1	6.4	6.2	12.1	12.4	0.8	0.8	1.6	1.6
West Virginia	97	97	5,140	5,081	2.8	2.7	3.2	3.0	3.6	3.5	0.4	0.3	0.7	0.6
Wisconsin	382	381	19,265	18,997	3.4	3.3	6.3	6.1	11.1	11.0	0.8	0.8	1.2	1.1
Wyoming	23	23	2,488	2,459	4.4	4.3	6.4	6.3	8.8	8.6	0.9	0.9	1.7	1.6

[1]"Number of public libraries" refers to the number of administrative entities that are legally established under local or state law to provide public library service to the population of a local jurisdiction. A public library (administrative entity) may have a single outlet that provides direct service to the public, or it may have multiple service outlets. In 2013, a total of 17,214 service outlets were open to the public: 8,905 central libraries, 7,640 branch libraries, and 669 bookmobiles.
[2]Per capita (or per person) data are based on unduplicated populations of the areas served by public libraries.
[3]Includes only the number of physical visits (entering the library for any purpose). The survey does not collect data on the number of online visits.

[4]A reference transaction is an information contact that involves the knowledge, use, recommendations, interpretation, or instruction in the use of one or more information sources by a member of the library staff.
NOTE: Data include imputations for nonresponse. Detail may not sum to totals because of rounding.
SOURCE: Institute of Museum and Library Services, Public Libraries Survey, fiscal years 2012 and 2013, retrieved March 16, 2016, from http://www.imls.gov/research/public_libraries_in_the_united_states_survey.aspx. (This table was prepared March 2016.)

Table 702.10. Number and percentage of persons age 3 and over using the Internet and percentage distribution by means of internet access from home and main reason for not having high-speed access, by selected age groups and other characteristics of all users and of students: 2013

[Standard errors appear in parentheses]

Selected age group or other characteristic	Total population (in thousands)		Persons using the Internet anywhere — Number (in thousands)		Persons using the Internet anywhere — Percent of population		Among internet users, percent using the Internet from home		Percentage distribution of home internet users, by means of access from home — A regular "dial-up" telephone		High speed (i.e., faster than dial-up)[1]		Don't need it, not interested		Too expensive		Can use it somewhere else		Not available in area		No computer or computer inadequate		Other reasons[2]	
1	2		3		4		5		6		7		8		9		10		11		12		13	
Total, all persons age 3 and over	299,216	(52.0)	213,708	(725.5)	71.4	(0.24)	91.5	(0.18)	1.0	(0.07)	99.0	(0.07)	41.1	(0.64)	33.6	(0.69)	3.2	(0.27)	2.2	(0.21)	11.9	(0.50)	7.9	(0.36)
Sex																								
Male	145,897	(37.9)	103,462	(412.0)	70.9	(0.29)	91.8	(0.22)	1.0	(0.08)	99.0	(0.08)	40.8	(0.75)	33.9	(0.76)	3.3	(0.33)	2.4	(0.23)	11.9	(0.54)	7.8	(0.40)
Female	153,319	(36.9)	110,246	(441.5)	71.9	(0.29)	91.2	(0.20)	1.1	(0.08)	98.9	(0.08)	41.5	(0.67)	33.4	(0.72)	3.0	(0.26)	2.1	(0.22)	11.9	(0.54)	8.0	(0.41)
Race/ethnicity																								
White	188,805	(111.9)	142,313	(487.0)	75.4	(0.25)	93.7	(0.17)	1.1	(0.08)	98.9	(0.08)	47.9	(0.84)	25.6	(0.77)	2.8	(0.26)	3.2	(0.34)	11.3	(0.60)	9.2	(0.49)
Black	35,918	(175.0)	22,996	(273.2)	64.0	(0.74)	83.8	(0.82)	1.2	(0.23)	98.8	(0.23)	35.9	(1.54)	40.5	(1.57)	3.1	(0.51)	0.8 !	(0.27)	12.8	(1.08)	6.9	(0.82)
Hispanic	50,425	(34.5)	30,771	(340.8)	61.0	(0.67)	85.8	(0.58)	0.8	(0.19)	99.2	(0.19)	33.1	(1.20)	43.6	(1.48)	3.3	(0.68)	1.3 !	(0.42)	12.7	(1.09)	6.0	(0.70)
Other[3]	24,068	(176.2)	17,627	(219.7)	73.2	(0.76)	93.7	(0.46)	0.7	(0.19)	99.3	(0.19)	34.2	(2.24)	39.1	(2.67)	5.4	(1.33)	2.1 !	(0.86)	10.7	(1.76)	8.6	(1.31)
Age																								
3 and 4	8,147	(52.0)	2,773	(92.4)	34.0	(1.14)	91.5	(1.19)	1.3 !	(0.56)	98.7	(0.56)	24.8	(2.44)	49.4	(2.74)	6.4	(1.41)	3.0 !	(0.90)	10.8	(1.81)	5.5	(1.04)
5 to 9	20,570	(0.0)	10,795	(168.3)	52.5	(0.82)	91.7	(0.62)	0.7	(0.19)	99.3	(0.19)	24.1	(1.63)	50.1	(1.77)	4.1	(0.72)	2.1	(0.49)	12.3	(1.34)	7.4	(1.14)
10 to 15	24,743	(0.0)	17,657	(163.7)	71.4	(0.66)	92.2	(0.48)	0.8	(0.17)	99.2	(0.17)	26.0	(1.53)	47.4	(1.76)	3.3	(0.71)	3.7	(0.68)	10.6	(1.11)	9.0	(1.14)
16 to 19	16,795	(0.0)	14,205	(108.2)	84.6	(0.64)	91.8	(0.52)	0.9	(0.19)	99.1	(0.19)	28.4	(2.18)	46.2	(2.38)	2.4 !	(0.72)	3.7	(0.80)	12.3	(1.71)	7.0	(1.25)
20 to 24	22,066	(0.0)	18,563	(135.5)	84.1	(0.61)	89.4	(0.54)	0.8	(0.18)	99.2	(0.18)	27.6	(1.82)	44.8	(1.99)	4.8	(0.83)	2.8 !	(0.85)	12.5	(1.30)	7.4	(1.05)
25 to 29	20,877	(0.0)	17,266	(125.9)	82.7	(0.60)	90.3	(0.50)	0.6	(0.15)	99.4	(0.15)	30.0	(1.73)	45.2	(1.94)	5.6	(0.94)	2.0	(0.48)	10.4	(1.29)	6.8	(0.94)
30 to 39	39,842	(0.0)	32,998	(178.5)	82.8	(0.45)	91.9	(0.35)	0.7	(0.13)	99.3	(0.13)	27.6	(1.36)	46.3	(1.51)	4.2	(0.74)	2.3	(0.38)	11.9	(0.98)	7.7	(0.73)
40 to 49	41,357	(0.0)	33,604	(165.7)	81.3	(0.40)	93.5	(0.30)	0.7	(0.10)	99.3	(0.10)	33.9	(1.41)	39.0	(1.41)	3.7	(0.57)	2.9	(0.54)	12.4	(1.00)	8.1	(0.83)
50 to 59	43,244	(78.2)	31,295	(199.9)	72.4	(0.44)	91.7	(0.35)	1.3	(0.15)	98.7	(0.15)	44.1	(1.12)	31.2	(1.25)	2.8	(0.36)	2.9	(0.44)	11.9	(0.79)	7.1	(0.63)
60 to 69	32,588	(124.6)	21,651	(177.5)	66.4	(0.52)	91.6	(0.44)	2.0	(0.21)	98.0	(0.21)	50.9	(1.23)	22.5	(1.03)	2.7	(0.39)	1.8	(0.35)	13.3	(0.93)	8.8	(0.75)
70 or older	28,987	(84.0)	12,899	(179.9)	44.5	(0.62)	87.6	(0.58)	2.3	(0.30)	97.7	(0.30)	66.8	(1.08)	11.4	(0.78)	1.0	(0.17)	0.7	(0.15)	11.4	(0.68)	8.7	(0.57)
Educational attainment of persons age 25 and over																								
Less than high school	39,330	(419.3)	21,063	(286.4)	53.6	(0.62)	85.1	(0.56)	1.2	(0.18)	98.8	(0.18)	43.0	(0.98)	33.3	(1.14)	1.5	(0.27)	1.8	(0.25)	13.3	(0.84)	7.1	(0.55)
High school diploma or equivalent	72,679	(611.1)	46,166	(493.1)	63.5	(0.43)	87.9	(0.32)	1.5	(0.14)	98.5	(0.14)	45.3	(0.78)	30.5	(0.74)	2.3	(0.27)	2.0	(0.22)	12.3	(0.57)	7.6	(0.45)
Some college	46,159	(450.2)	38,219	(443.2)	82.8	(0.41)	91.9	(0.31)	1.2	(0.12)	98.8	(0.12)	41.1	(1.29)	33.1	(1.20)	4.5	(0.51)	2.1	(0.40)	10.7	(0.82)	8.6	(0.73)
Associate's degree	22,427	(304.9)	18,752	(279.0)	83.6	(0.52)	91.9	(0.40)	1.2	(0.15)	98.8	(0.15)	44.0	(1.86)	28.7	(1.78)	4.8	(0.92)	3.5	(0.70)	11.6	(1.21)	7.4	(0.88)
Bachelor's degree	69,248	(549.2)	61,627	(496.6)	89.0	(0.25)	95.4	(0.21)	0.7	(0.09)	99.3	(0.09)	44.8	(1.47)	25.6	(1.28)	6.4	(0.80)	2.8	(0.57)	9.2	(0.92)	11.1	(0.95)
Master's or higher degree	45,322	(410.7)	39,977	(364.8)	88.2	(0.32)	95.1	(0.25)	0.8	(0.11)	99.2	(0.11)	44.1	(1.67)	26.9	(1.63)	6.7	(0.86)	2.8	(0.63)	8.6	(1.01)	10.9	(1.05)
	23,927	(391.2)	21,650	(368.0)	90.5	(0.40)	96.0	(0.31)	0.6	(0.11)	99.4	(0.11)	46.6	(2.32)	22.4	(1.92)	5.7	(1.29)	3.0	(0.85)	10.7	(1.71)	11.7	(1.87)
Family income																								
Less than $10,000	20,430	(594.5)	10,937	(377.5)	53.5	(1.04)	75.1	(1.20)	1.8	(0.43)	98.2	(0.43)	32.3	(1.51)	45.1	(1.71)	2.2	(0.47)	1.5	(0.37)	12.1	(1.02)	6.8	(0.88)
$10,000 to $19,999	31,314	(608.2)	16,419	(468.8)	52.4	(0.81)	81.1	(0.84)	2.1	(0.34)	97.9	(0.34)	42.0	(1.39)	34.9	(1.44)	1.5	(0.35)	1.4	(0.39)	12.3	(0.99)	8.0	(0.75)
$20,000 to $29,999	33,039	(617.8)	19,913	(466.5)	60.3	(0.80)	85.2	(0.64)	2.1	(0.35)	97.9	(0.35)	43.1	(1.43)	33.8	(1.43)	2.5	(0.45)	1.4	(0.38)	12.5	(1.06)	6.6	(0.76)
$30,000 to $39,999	32,893	(634.2)	21,155	(445.8)	64.3	(0.68)	86.1	(0.61)	1.2	(0.23)	98.8	(0.23)	42.8	(1.60)	31.7	(1.55)	3.0	(0.64)	1.9	(0.46)	12.3	(1.09)	8.3	(0.93)
$40,000 to $49,999	24,764	(509.1)	17,786	(422.9)	71.7	(0.75)	92.4	(0.64)	0.8	(0.23)	99.2	(0.23)	44.5	(2.55)	29.4	(2.41)	2.8	(0.75)	2.0 !	(0.71)	12.6	(1.85)	8.7	(1.53)
$50,000 to $74,999	56,781	(699.3)	43,490	(577.0)	76.6	(0.47)	94.1	(0.32)	1.2	(0.18)	98.8	(0.18)	40.7	(2.06)	28.4	(1.91)	6.4	(1.01)	4.3	(0.81)	11.5	(1.56)	8.8	(0.99)
$75,000 to $99,999	36,007	(582.6)	29,429	(479.6)	81.7	(0.52)	96.3	(0.31)	0.6	(0.13)	99.4	(0.13)	44.3	(3.17)	25.9	(2.63)	7.3	(1.90)	7.0	(1.67)	6.7	(1.69)	8.8	(1.93)
$100,000 or more	63,988	(816.4)	54,598	(740.2)	85.3	(0.39)	97.3	(0.20)	0.5	(0.10)	99.5	(0.10)	46.7	(3.37)	20.0	(3.12)	6.5	(1.66)	5.1 !	(1.69)	10.0	(2.01)	11.8	(2.06)
Total school-age population (all 5- to 15-year-olds)	45,313	(0.0)	28,452	(271.1)	62.8	(0.60)	92.0	(0.42)	0.8	(0.15)	99.2	(0.15)	25.1	(1.24)	48.7	(1.40)	3.7	(0.61)	2.9	(0.52)	11.4	(1.01)	8.2	(0.94)
Age																								
5 to 9 years old	20,570	(0.0)	10,795	(168.3)	52.5	(0.82)	91.7	(0.62)	0.7	(0.19)	99.3	(0.19)	24.1	(1.63)	50.1	(1.77)	4.1	(0.72)	2.1	(0.49)	12.3	(1.34)	7.4	(1.14)
10 to 15 years old	24,743	(0.0)	17,657	(163.7)	71.4	(0.66)	92.2	(0.48)	0.8	(0.17)	99.2	(0.17)	26.0	(1.53)	47.4	(1.76)	3.3	(0.71)	3.7	(0.68)	10.6	(1.11)	9.0	(1.14)
Sex																								
Male school-age population	23,146	(0.0)	14,519	(169.9)	62.7	(0.73)	92.2	(0.56)	0.8	(0.19)	99.2	(0.19)	24.9	(1.52)	48.3	(1.85)	4.2	(0.93)	2.9	(0.52)	11.6	(1.24)	8.1	(1.12)
5 to 9 years old	10,508	(0.0)	5,416	(115.8)	51.5	(1.10)	91.6	(0.88)	0.7 !	(0.25)	99.3	(0.25)	23.4	(2.23)	49.7	(2.17)	4.6	(1.05)	1.9	(0.54)	13.1	(1.70)	7.3	(1.40)
10 to 15 years old	12,638	(0.0)	9,103	(102.3)	72.0	(0.81)	92.5	(0.62)	0.9	(0.24)	99.1	(0.24)	26.3	(1.97)	47.0	(2.52)	3.8	(1.04)	3.9	(0.78)	10.1	(1.45)	7.8	(1.42)
Female school-age population	22,167	(0.0)	13,933	(166.1)	62.9	(0.75)	91.8	(0.52)	0.7 !	(0.18)	99.3	(0.18)	25.2	(1.65)	49.2	(1.67)	3.1	(0.60)	3.0	(0.68)	11.2	(1.15)	8.3	(1.07)
5 to 9 years old	10,062	(0.0)	5,379	(102.1)	53.5	(1.01)	91.7	(0.82)	0.7 !	(0.27)	99.3	(0.27)	24.8	(2.19)	50.5	(2.58)	3.6	(0.93)	2.3	(0.65)	11.4	(1.72)	7.4	(1.53)
10 to 15 years old	12,105	(0.0)	8,554	(118.3)	70.7	(0.98)	91.8	(0.65)	0.7 !	(0.22)	99.3	(0.22)	25.6	(2.28)	47.9	(2.31)	2.7	(0.74)	3.6	(0.95)	11.0	(1.43)	9.2	(1.50)

See notes at end of table.

Table 702.10. Number and percentage of persons age 3 and over using the Internet and percentage distribution by means of internet access from home and main reason for not having high-speed access, by selected age groups and other characteristics of all users and of students: 2013—Continued

[Standard errors appear in parentheses]

Selected age group or other characteristic	Total population (in thousands)	Persons using the Internet anywhere — Number (in thousands)	Persons using the Internet anywhere — Percent of population	Among internet users, percent using the Internet from home	Percentage distribution of home internet users, by means of access from home — A regular "dial-up" telephone	High speed (i.e., faster than dial-up)[1]	Don't need it, not interested	Too expensive	Can use it somewhere else	Not available in area	No computer or computer inadequate	Other reasons[2]
1	2	3	4	5	6	7	8	9	10	11	12	13
Race/ethnicity												
White school-age population	24,016 (51.2)	16,262 (189.4)	67.7 (0.77)	95.8 (0.41)	0.8 (0.18)	99.2 (0.18)	27.4 (2.38)	41.2 (2.83)	2.6 (0.73)	5.6 (1.23)	11.0 (1.71)	12.4 (2.06)
5 to 9 years old	10,626 (40.3)	6,119 (117.6)	57.6 (1.10)	95.5 (0.63)	0.9 ! (0.29)	99.1 (0.29)	27.1 (3.01)	42.9 (3.36)	3.0 ! (1.02)	3.0 ! (0.96)	12.2 (2.11)	11.9 (2.45)
10 to 15 years old	13,390 (49.4)	10,143 (129.7)	75.8 (0.90)	95.9 (0.45)	0.7 (0.18)	99.3 (0.18)	27.7 (2.78)	39.5 (3.36)	2.3 (0.69)	8.1 (1.77)	9.8 (2.03)	12.8 (2.39)
Black school-age population	6,221 (55.5)	3,499 (102.5)	56.2 (1.64)	82.6 (1.96)	0.8 ! (0.41)	99.2 (0.41)	22.1 (2.74)	57.0 (3.31)	3.7 (1.10)	‡ (†)	10.6 (2.29)	5.8 (1.54)
5 to 9 years old	2,842 (29.9)	1,320 (63.3)	46.4 (2.19)	83.3 (2.72)	‡ (†)	99.7 (0.26)	18.5 (3.35)	58.5 (4.10)	5.6 ! (1.75)	‡ (†)	11.2 (2.91)	5.5 (1.64)
10 to 15 years old	3,379 (41.8)	2,179 (67.9)	64.5 (1.97)	82.2 (2.11)	‡ (†)	99.8 (0.64)	24.8 (3.27)	55.9 (3.88)	2.3 ! (1.11)	‡ (†)	10.1 (2.37)	6.1 (1.88)
Hispanic school-age population	10,810 (0.0)	5,944 (141.9)	55.0 (1.31)	86.3 (1.16)	0.9 ! (0.36)	99.1 (0.36)	25.0 (1.90)	49.0 (2.23)	4.3 (1.12)	2.0 ! (0.79)	13.0 (1.68)	6.8 (1.33)
5 to 9 years old	5,131 (0.0)	2,307 (90.4)	45.0 (1.76)	85.6 (1.92)	‡ (†)	99.4 (0.36)	23.8 (2.46)	50.9 (2.91)	4.2 (1.24)	1.9 ! (0.78)	13.8 (2.33)	5.3 (1.35)
10 to 15 years old	5,679 (0.0)	3,636 (85.0)	64.0 (1.50)	86.7 (1.19)	1.0 ! (0.45)	99.0 (0.45)	26.1 (2.58)	47.0 (2.73)	4.3 ! (1.38)	2.2 ! (0.95)	12.2 (1.87)	8.2 (1.95)
Family income												
Less than $10,000	3,465 (168.6)	1,559 (110.8)	45.0 (2.28)	69.6 (3.29)	‡ (†)	98.5 (1.00)	17.1 (2.29)	63.9 (3.13)	2.4 ! (0.82)	2.0 ! (0.78)	9.0 (1.72)	5.6 ! (1.69)
$10,000 to $19,999	4,983 (202.3)	2,491 (114.0)	50.0 (2.09)	83.9 (1.99)	1.3 ! (0.65)	98.7 (0.65)	22.6 (2.35)	51.7 (3.28)	1.9 ! (0.78)	2.2 ! (0.98)	9.7 (1.94)	11.9 (2.32)
$20,000 to $29,999	4,837 (196.3)	2,603 (149.1)	53.8 (1.74)	88.5 (1.40)	1.6 ! (0.74)	98.4 (0.74)	25.6 (3.06)	47.8 (3.61)	3.9 (1.13)	‡ (†)	14.6 (2.82)	6.5 (1.80)
$30,000 to $39,999	4,728 (188.0)	2,667 (125.1)	56.4 (1.78)	88.5 (1.64)	‡ (†)	99.5 (0.35)	25.8 (3.39)	45.0 (3.57)	5.7 ! (1.96)	3.3 ! (1.29)	11.4 (2.40)	8.7 (2.45)
$40,000 to $49,999	3,627 (147.7)	2,264 (120.1)	62.4 (1.80)	92.9 (1.62)	‡ (†)	99.1 (0.54)	35.3 (5.90)	37.6 (5.78)	‡ (†)	‡ (†)	16.0 (5.19)	‡ (†)
$50,000 to $74,999	8,279 (221.3)	5,469 (187.8)	66.1 (1.37)	93.9 (1.07)	1.6 ! (0.53)	98.4 (0.53)	29.8 (4.23)	39.8 (4.58)	5.0 ! (2.00)	7.9 ! (2.70)	12.0 (3.53)	5.5 (1.64)
$75,000 to $99,999	5,291 (190.7)	3,791 (190.7)	71.7 (1.42)	98.4 (0.48)	‡ (†)	99.9 (0.07)	32.9 (7.66)	32.8 (7.66)	8.4 ! (3.77)	‡ (†)	‡ (†)	13.5 ! (6.39)
$100,000 or more	10,103 (242.0)	7,609 (215.8)	75.3 (1.10)	97.7 (0.38)	‡ (†)	100.0 (0.01)	37.5 (7.71)	26.8 (7.71)	‡ (†)	‡ (†)	13.3 ! (6.43)	13.8 ! (4.94)
Total, all 16- to 24-year-old students[4]	11,784 (223.2)	10,230 (212.0)	86.8 (0.76)	92.9 (0.61)	0.8 (0.25)	99.2 (0.25)	31.0 (3.19)	44.9 (3.07)	3.1 (0.91)	2.4 (0.72)	10.1 (1.82)	8.5 (1.73)
School level												
High school	4,352 (120.6)	3,553 (116.6)	81.6 (1.32)	91.8 (0.99)	0.7 ! (0.35)	99.3 (0.35)	29.5 (4.07)	50.8 (4.20)	‡ (†)	‡ (†)	11.8 (2.71)	5.5 ! (1.89)
College	7,432 (192.3)	6,677 (182.6)	89.8 (0.78)	93.4 (0.77)	0.9 ! (0.32)	99.1 (0.32)	32.4 (4.29)	39.7 (4.04)	5.2 ! (1.62)	‡ (†)	8.6 (2.27)	11.2 (2.73)
Sex												
Male	5,584 (132.7)	4,793 (132.1)	85.8 (1.11)	91.7 (0.97)	0.7 ! (0.27)	99.3 (0.27)	35.4 (4.35)	45.6 (3.93)	2.5 ! (1.01)	2.2 ! (1.08)	8.7 (2.39)	5.5 ! (1.91)
High school	2,256 (82.5)	1,838 (80.6)	81.5 (1.75)	91.4 (1.43)	‡ (†)	99.9 (0.05)	34.3 (5.74)	52.7 (5.40)	# (†)	‡ (†)	8.3 (3.11)	‡ (†)
College	3,329 (118.0)	2,955 (115.4)	88.8 (1.22)	92.0 (1.18)	1.1 ! (0.43)	98.9 (0.43)	36.5 (5.46)	39.0 (4.93)	4.8 ! (1.92)	‡ (†)	9.2 ! (3.35)	7.3 ! (2.89)
Female	6,200 (150.3)	5,437 (139.9)	87.7 (0.99)	93.9 (0.70)	1.0 ! (0.35)	99.0 (0.35)	26.5 (4.08)	44.2 (4.04)	3.6 ! (1.57)	‡ (†)	11.4 (2.66)	11.5 (2.78)
High school	2,096 (92.4)	1,715 (82.5)	81.8 (1.86)	92.3 (1.34)	1.5 ! (0.72)	98.5 (0.72)	24.4 (5.35)	48.8 (5.78)	‡ (†)	‡ (†)	15.5 (4.35)	7.5 ! (3.14)
College	4,104 (128.8)	3,722 (121.5)	90.7 (1.00)	94.6 (0.90)	0.7 ! (0.36)	99.3 (0.36)	28.4 (5.57)	40.3 (5.47)	5.6 ! (2.71)	‡ (†)	8.0 ! (3.09)	15.0 (4.22)
Race/ethnicity												
White	6,531 (154.0)	5,809 (149.8)	89.0 (0.86)	95.2 (0.59)	‡ (†)	99.5 (0.25)	33.3 (4.48)	38.5 (4.82)	‡ (†)	5.5 ! (1.72)	9.9 (2.82)	10.5 (3.09)
High school	2,245 (85.0)	1,913 (76.6)	85.2 (1.58)	94.0 (1.09)	‡ (†)	99.3 (0.37)	37.1 (6.66)	44.9 (6.56)	‡ (†)	‡ (†)	7.2 ! (3.37)	‡ (†)
College	4,286 (135.8)	3,896 (134.7)	90.9 (0.92)	95.8 (0.71)	‡ (†)	99.6 (0.30)	29.9 (6.47)	32.8 (6.46)	‡ (†)	‡ (†)	12.3 (4.04)	15.3 ! (4.89)
Black	1,602 (87.5)	1,313 (80.5)	81.9 (2.16)	90.6 (1.83)	2.4 ! (1.14)	97.6 (1.14)	21.5 (5.16)	47.4 (6.61)	‡ (†)	# (†)	12.8 ! (4.94)	14.4 ! (5.35)
High school	675 (51.4)	519 (48.9)	76.9 (3.54)	91.0 (2.90)	‡ (†)	97.8 (2.01)	15.2 ! (5.82)	57.4 (9.55)	# (†)	# (†)	16.6 ! (7.68)	‡ (†)
College	928 (69.4)	794 (65.0)	85.6 (2.93)	90.4 (2.38)	‡ (†)	97.8 (1.31)	28.0 (8.13)	37.0 (8.79)	‡ (†)	‡ (†)	10.7 ! (3.22)	18.2 ! (8.28)
Hispanic	2,452 (92.4)	2,047 (89.7)	83.5 (2.04)	86.9 (1.71)	‡ (†)	99.0 (0.54)	32.3 (5.49)	50.3 (5.87)	‡ (†)	‡ (†)	14.1 ! (4.95)	3.7 ! (1.70)
High school	1,014 (63.6)	758 (56.9)	74.7 (3.64)	85.6 (2.88)	‡ (†)	100.0 (0.00)	30.8 (6.76)	52.2 (7.30)	‡ (†)	‡ (†)	‡ (†)	‡ (†)
College	1,437 (71.9)	1,289 (67.4)	89.7 (1.96)	87.7 (2.12)	‡ (†)	98.5 (0.84)	33.8 (6.91)	48.4 (7.86)	‡ (†)	‡ (†)	‡ (†)	‡ (†)
Family income												
Less than $10,000	958 (85.2)	767 (84.7)	80.1 (3.18)	81.0 (3.93)	‡ (†)	98.0 (1.28)	22.5 (6.64)	50.7 (7.10)	‡ (†)	‡ (†)	16.4 (4.92)	7.9 ! (3.58)
$10,000 to $19,999	1,151 (84.9)	906 (71.9)	78.7 (2.59)	84.9 (2.78)	‡ (†)	99.9 (0.11)	24.6 (6.52)	53.6 (7.11)	‡ (†)	‡ (†)	8.3 ! (3.44)	9.6 ! (3.66)
$20,000 to $29,999	1,117 (88.8)	968 (82.5)	86.6 (2.37)	89.1 (1.99)	‡ (†)	96.9 (1.91)	27.0 (7.44)	55.6 (8.30)	‡ (†)	‡ (†)	9.8 ! (4.57)	‡ (†)
$30,000 to $39,999	1,088 (74.9)	916 (67.4)	84.2 (2.58)	89.1 (2.32)	‡ (†)	98.8 (1.09)	38.9 (8.72)	32.2 (7.19)	‡ (†)	‡ (†)	11.2 ! (5.13)	11.5 ! (5.01)
$40,000 to $49,999	922 (69.9)	792 (68.7)	86.0 (2.69)	93.3 (1.81)	# (†)	100.0 (0.00)	41.8 (9.60)	39.6 (9.84)	‡ (†)	‡ (†)	‡ (†)	‡ (†)
$50,000 to $74,999	2,349 (117.4)	2,090 (110.5)	89.0 (1.58)	94.2 (1.34)	‡ (†)	99.3 (0.35)	26.7 ! (9.25)	32.5 (8.41)	11.3 ! (5.23)	‡ (†)	12.5 ! (5.79)	‡ (†)
$75,000 to $99,999	1,378 (86.3)	1,240 (82.4)	90.0 (2.06)	97.1 (1.12)	‡ (†)	99.4 (0.46)	‡ (†)	‡ (†)	‡ (†)	‡ (†)	‡ (†)	‡ (†)
$100,000 or more	2,822 (129.4)	2,551 (118.0)	90.4 (1.29)	98.4 (0.55)	‡ (†)	99.7 (0.32)	‡ (†)	‡ (†)	‡ (†)	‡ (†)	‡ (†)	‡ (†)

†Not applicable.
#Rounds to zero.
!Interpret data with caution. The coefficient of variation (CV) for this estimate is between 30 and 50 percent.
‡Reporting standards not met. Either there are too few cases for a reliable estimate or the coefficient of variation (CV) is 50 percent or greater.
[1]Includes DSL, cable, modem, satellite, wireless, mobile phone or PDA, fiber optics or other broadband, and other.

[2]Includes "Privacy or security concerns" and "Other reason."
[3]Includes persons of all other races and Two or more races.
[4]Includes only those 16- to 24-year-olds who are enrolled in school.
NOTE: Race categories exclude persons of Hispanic ethnicity. Detail may not sum to totals because of rounding.
SOURCE: U.S. Department of Commerce, Census Bureau, Current Population Survey (CPS), July 2013. (This table was prepared May 2015.)

APPENDIX A
Guide to Sources

The information presented in the *Digest of Education Statistics* was obtained from many sources, including federal and state agencies, private research organizations, and professional associations. The data were collected using many research methods, including surveys of a universe (such as all colleges) or of a sample, compilations of administrative records, and statistical projections. Brief descriptions of the information sources, data collections, and data collection methods that were used to produce this report are presented below, grouped by sponsoring organization. Additional details about many of these and other data sets can be found on the Department of Education's Data Inventory website (http://datainventory.ed.gov/).

National Center for Education Statistics (NCES)

Baccalaureate and Beyond Longitudinal Study

The Baccalaureate and Beyond Longitudinal Study (B&B) is based on the National Postsecondary Student Aid Study (NPSAS) and provides information concerning education and work experience after completing a bachelor's degree. A special emphasis of B&B is on those entering teaching. B&B provides cross-sectional information 1 year after bachelor's degree completion (comparable to the information that was provided in the Recent College Graduates study), while at the same time providing longitudinal data concerning entry into and progress through graduate-level education and the workforce, income, and debt repayment. This information has not been available through follow-ups involving high school cohorts or even college-entry cohorts, because these cohorts have limited numbers who actually complete a bachelor's degree and continue their graduate education. Also, these cohorts are not representative of all bachelor's degree recipients.

B&B followed NPSAS baccalaureate degree completers for a 10-year period after completion, beginning with NPSAS:93. About 11,000 students who completed their degrees in the 1992–93 academic year were included in the first B&B cohort (B&B:93). The first follow-up of this cohort (B&B:93/94) occurred 1 year later. In addition to collecting student data, B&B:93/94 collected postsecondary transcripts covering the undergraduate period, which pro-

vided complete information on progress and persistence at the undergraduate level. The second follow-up of this cohort (B&B:93/97) took place in spring 1997 and gathered information on employment history, family formation, and enrollment in graduate programs. The third follow-up (B&B:93/03) occurred in 2003 and provided information concerning graduate study and long-term employment experiences after degree completion.

The second B&B cohort (B&B:2000), which was associated with NPSAS:2000, included 11,700 students who completed their degrees in the 1999–2000 academic year. The first and only follow-up survey of this cohort was conducted in 2001 (B&B:2000/01) and focused on time to degree completion, participation in postbaccalaureate education and employment, and the activities of newly qualified teachers.

The third B&B cohort (B&B:08), which is associated with NPSAS:08, included 18,000 students who completed their degrees in the 2007–08 academic year. The first follow-up took place in 2009 (B&B:08/09), and the second follow-up took place in 2012 (B&B:08/12). The report *Baccalaureate and Beyond: A First Look at the Employment Experiences and Lives of College Graduates, 4 Years On (B&B:08/12)* (NCES 2014-141) presents findings based on data from the second follow-up. It examines bachelor's degree recipients' labor market experiences and enrollment in additional postsecondary degree programs through the 4th year after graduation. In addition, *2008/12 Baccalaureate and Beyond Longitudinal Study (B&B:08/12) Data File Documentation* (NCES 2015-141) describes the universe, methods, and data collection procedures used in the second follow-up. A third and final follow-up (B&B:08/18) to the third B&B cohort is planned for 2018.

Further information on B&B may be obtained from

Aurora D'Amico
Ted Socha
Sample Surveys Division
Longitudinal Surveys Branch
National Center for Education Statistics
550 12th Street SW
Washington, DC 20202
aurora.damico@ed.gov
ted.socha@ed.gov
http://nces.ed.gov/surveys/b&b

Beginning Postsecondary Students Longitudinal Study

The Beginning Postsecondary Students Longitudinal Study (BPS) provides information on persistence, progress, and attainment for 6 years after initial time of entry into postsecondary education. BPS includes traditional and non-traditional (e.g., older) students and is representative of all beginning students in postsecondary education in a given year. Initially, these individuals are surveyed in the National Postsecondary Student Aid Study (NPSAS) during the year in which they first begin their postsecondary education. These same students are surveyed again 2 and 5 years later through the BPS. By starting with a cohort that has already entered postsecondary education and following it for 6 years, the BPS can determine the extent to which students who start postsecondary education at various ages differ in their progress, persistence, and attainment, as well as their entry into the workforce. The first BPS was conducted in 1989–90, with follow-ups in 1992 (BPS:90/92) and 1994 (BPS:90/94). The second BPS was conducted in 1995–96, with follow-ups in 1998 (BPS:96/98) and 2001 (BPS:96/01). The third BPS was conducted in 2003–04, with follow-ups in 2006 (BPS:04/06) and 2009 (BPS:04/09). A fourth BPS was conducted in 2012, with a follow-up in 2014 and one planned for 2017.

Further information on BPS may be obtained from

Aurora D'Amico
Sean Simone
Sample Surveys Division
Longitudinal Surveys Branch
National Center for Education Statistics
550 12th Street SW
Washington, DC 20202
aurora.damico@ed.gov
sean.simone@ed.gov
http://nces.ed.gov/surveys/bps

Common Core of Data

The Common Core of Data (CCD) is NCES's primary database on public elementary and secondary education in the United States. It is a comprehensive, annual, national statistical database of all public elementary and secondary schools and school districts containing data designed to be comparable across all states. This database can be used to select samples for other NCES surveys and provide basic information and descriptive statistics on public elementary and secondary schools and schooling in general.

The CCD collects statistical information annually from approximately 100,000 public elementary and secondary schools and approximately 18,000 public school districts (including supervisory unions and regional education service agencies) in the 50 states, the District of Columbia, Department of Defense (DoD) dependents schools, the Bureau of Indian Education (BIE), Puerto Rico, American Samoa, Guam, the Northern Mariana Islands, and the U.S. Virgin Islands. Three categories of information are collected in the CCD survey: general descriptive information on schools and school districts; data on students and staff; and fiscal data. The general school and district descriptive information includes name, address, phone number, and type of locale; the data on students and staff include selected demographic characteristics; and the fiscal data pertain to revenues and current expenditures.

The ED*Facts* data collection system is the primary collection tool for the CCD. NCES works collaboratively with the Department of Education's Performance Information Management Service to develop the CCD collection procedures and data definitions. Coordinators from state education agencies (SEAs) submit the CCD data at different levels (school, agency, and state) to the ED*Facts* collection system. Prior to submitting CCD files to ED*Facts*, SEAs must collect and compile information from their respective local education agencies (LEAs) through established administrative records systems within their state or jurisdiction.

Once SEAs have completed their submissions, the CCD survey staff analyzes and verifies the data for quality assurance. Even though the CCD is a universe collection and thus not subject to sampling errors, nonsampling errors can occur. The two potential sources of nonsampling errors are nonresponse and inaccurate reporting. NCES attempts to minimize nonsampling errors through the use of annual training of SEA coordinators, extensive quality reviews, and survey editing procedures. In addition, each year, SEAs are given the opportunity to revise their state-level aggregates from the previous survey cycle.

The CCD survey consists of five components: The Public Elementary/Secondary School Universe Survey, the Local Education Agency (School District) Universe Survey, the State Nonfiscal Survey of Public Elementary/Secondary Education, the National Public Education Financial Survey (NPEFS), and the School District Finance Survey (F-33).

Public Elementary/Secondary School Universe Survey

The Public Elementary/Secondary School Universe Survey includes all public schools providing education services to prekindergarten, kindergarten, grade 1–12, and ungraded students. For school year (SY) 2013–14, the survey included records for each public elementary and secondary school in the 50 states, the District of Columbia, the DoD dependents schools (overseas and domestic), the Bureau of Indian Education (BIE), Puerto Rico, American Samoa, the Northern Mariana Islands, Guam, and the U.S. Virgin Islands.

The Public Elementary/Secondary School Universe Survey includes data for the following variables: NCES school ID number, state school ID number, name of the school, name of the agency that operates the school, mailing address, physical location address, phone number, school type, operational status, locale code, latitude, longitude, county number, county name, full-time-equivalent (FTE) classroom teacher count, low/high grade span offered, congressional district code, school level, students eligible for free lunch, students eligible for reduced-price lunch, total students eligible for free and reduced-price lunch, and student totals and detail (by grade, by race/ethnicity, and by sex). The survey also contains flags indicating whether a school is Title I eligible, schoolwide Title I eligible, a magnet school, a charter school, a shared-time school, or a BIE school, as well as which grades are offered at the school.

Local Education Agency (School District) Universe Survey

The coverage of the Local Education Agency Universe Survey includes all school districts and administrative units providing education services to prekindergarten, kindergarten, grade 1–12, and ungraded students. The Local Education Agency Universe Survey includes records for the 50 states, the District of Columbia, Puerto Rico, the Bureau of Indian Education (BIE), American Samoa, Guam, the Northern Mariana Islands, the U.S. Virgin Islands, and the DoD dependents schools (overseas and domestic).

The Local Education Agency Universe Survey includes the following variables: NCES agency ID number, state agency ID number, agency name, phone number, mailing address, physical location address, agency type code, supervisory union number, American National Standards Institute (ANSI) state and county code, county name, core based statistical area (CBSA) code, metropolitan/micropolitan code, metropolitan status code, district locale code, congressional district code, operational status code, BIE agency status, low/high grade span offered, agency charter status, number of schools, number of full-time-equivalent teachers, number of ungraded students, number of PK–12 students, number of special education/Individualized Education Program students, number of English language learner students, instructional staff fields, support staff fields, and LEA charter status.

State Nonfiscal Survey of Public Elementary/ Secondary Education

The State Nonfiscal Survey of Public Elementary/Secondary Education for the 2013–14 school year provides state-level, aggregate information about students and staff in public elementary and secondary education. It includes data from the 50 states, the District of Columbia, Puerto Rico, the U.S. Virgin Islands, the Northern Mariana Islands, Guam, and American Samoa. The DoD dependents schools (overseas and domestic) and the BIE are also included in the survey universe. This survey covers public school student membership by grade, race/ethnicity, and state or jurisdiction and covers number of staff in public schools by category and state or jurisdiction. Beginning with the 2006–07 school year, the number of diploma recipients and other high school completers are no longer included in the State Nonfiscal Survey of Public Elementary/Secondary Education File. These data are now published in the public-use CCD State Dropout and Completion Data File.

National Public Education Financial Survey

The purpose of the National Public Education Financial Survey (NPEFS) is to provide district, state, and federal policymakers, researchers, and other interested users with descriptive information about revenues and expenditures for public elementary and secondary education. The data collected are useful to (1) chief officers of state education agencies; (2) policymakers in the executive and legislative branches of federal and state governments; (3) education policy and public policy researchers; and (4) the public, journalists, and others.

Data for NPEFS are collected from state education agencies (SEAs) in the 50 states, the District of Columbia, Puerto Rico, American Samoa, Guam, the Northern Mariana Islands, and the U.S. Virgin Islands. The data file is organized by state or jurisdiction and contains revenue data by funding source; expenditure data by function (the activity being supported by the expenditure) and object (the category of expenditure); average daily attendance data; and total student membership data from the CCD State Nonfiscal Survey of Public Elementary/Secondary Education.

School District Finance Survey

The purpose of the School District Finance Survey (F-33) is to provide finance data for all local education agencies (LEAs) that provide free public elementary and secondary education in the United States. National and state totals are not included (national- and state-level figures are presented, however, in the National Public Education Financial Survey.

NCES partners with the U.S. Census Bureau in the collection of school district finance data. The Census Bureau distributes Census Form F-33, Annual Survey of School System Finances, to all SEAs, and representatives from the SEAs collect and edit data from their LEAs and submit data to the Census Bureau. The Census Bureau then produces two data files: one for distribution and reporting by NCES and the other for distribution and reporting by the Census Bureau. The files include variables for revenues by source, expenditures by function and object, indebtedness, assets, and student membership counts, as well as identification variables.

Teacher Compensation Survey

The Teacher Compensation Survey (TCS) was a research and development effort designed to assess the feasibility of collecting and publishing teacher-level data from the administrative records residing in state education agencies. Twenty-three states participated in the TCS for school year 2008–09. Participating states provided data on salaries, years of teaching experience, highest degree earned, race/ethnicity, and gender for each public school teacher.

The following text table lists the CCD file versions used in the current edition of the *Digest of Education Statistics*:

Table G. Common Core of Data (CCD) file versions used in the current edition of the *Digest of Education Statistics*: 1986–87 through 2013–14

Year	State Nonfiscal Survey of Public Elementary and Secondary Education	NCES CCD State Dropout and Completion Data	National Public Education Financial Survey	Local Education Agency Universe Survey	School District Finance Survey	Public Elementary/ Secondary School Universe File
1986–87 (FY 1987)..........................	v.1c	†	v.1b–Revised	v.1	†	v.1
1987–88 (FY 1988)..........................	v.1c	†	v.1b–Revised	v.1	†	v.1
1988–89 (FY 1989)..........................	v.1c	†	v.1b–Revised	v.1	†	v.1
1989–90 (FY 1990)..........................	v.1c	†	v.1b–Revised	v.1	v.1a–Final[1]	v.1
1990–91 (FY 1991)..........................	v.1c	†	v.1b–Revised	v.1	†	v.1
1991–92 (FY 1992)..........................	v.1c	†	v.1b–Revised	v.1	v.1a–Final[1]	Revised
1992–93 (FY 1993)..........................	v.1c	†	v.1b–Revised	v.1	†	v.1
1993–94 (FY 1994)..........................	v.1b	†	v.1b–Revised	v.1	†	Revised
1994–95 (FY 1995)..........................	v.1b	†	v.1b–Revised	Revised	v.1d–Revised[1]	Revised
1995–96 (FY 1996)..........................	v.1b	†	v.1b–Revised	v.1	v.1b–Revised[1]	v.1
1996–97 (FY 1997)..........................	v.1c	†	v.1b–Revised	v.1	v.1a–Final[1]	v.1
1997–98 (FY 1998)..........................	v.1c	†	v.1b–Revised	v.1	v.1e–Revised[1]	v.1
1998–99 (FY 1999)..........................	v.1b	†	v.1b–Revised	v.1c	v.1c–Revised[1]	v.1c
1999–2000 (FY 2000)......................	v.1b	†	v.1b–Revised	v.1b	v.1d–Revised[1]	v.1b
2000–01 (FY 2001)..........................	v.1c	†	v.1b–Revised	v.1a	v.1d–Revised[1]	v.1a
2001–02 (FY 2002)..........................	v.1c	†	v.1c–Revised	v.1a	v.1c–Revised[1]	v.1a
2002–03 (FY 2003)..........................	v.1b	†	v.1b–Revised	v.1a	v.1b–Revised[1]	v.1a
2003–04 (FY 2004)..........................	v.1b	†	v.1b–Revised	v.1b	v.1b–Revised[1]	v.1a
2004–05 (FY 2005)..........................	v.1f	†	v.1b–Revised	v.1c	v.1c–Revised[1]	v.1b
2005–06 (FY 2006)..........................	v.1b	v.1b	v.1b–Revised	v.1a	v.1a–Final[1]	v.1a
2006–07 (FY 2007)..........................	v.1c	v.1a	v.1b–Revised	v.1c	v.1a–Final[1]	v.1c
2007–08 (FY 2008)..........................	v.1b	v.1a	v.1a–Final	v.1b	v.1a–Final[1]	v.1b
2008–09 (FY 2009)..........................	v.1c	v.1a	v.1b–Revised	v.1a	v.1a–Final[1]	v.1b
2009–10 (FY 2010)..........................	v.1b	v.1a	v.1a– Provisional	v.2a	v.1a–Provisional[1]	v.2a
2010–11 (FY 2011)..........................	v.1a	v.1a–Provisional[1]	v.1a–Preliminary	v.2a	v.1a–Provisional[1]	v.2a
2011–12 (FY 2012)..........................	v.1a	v.1a–Preliminary	v.1a–Provisional	v.1a	v.1a–Provisional	v.1a
2012–13 (FY 2013)..........................	v.1a	—	v.1a–Provisional	v.1a	v.1a–Provisional	v.1a
2013–14 (FY 2014)..........................	v.1a	—	—	v.1a	—	v.1a

—Not available.

†Not applicable. Survey not conducted.

[1]Data not used in current edition of *Digest of Education Statistics*.

NOTE: Preliminary data have been edited but are subject to further NCES quality control procedures. Provisional data have undergone all NCES data quality control procedures. NCES releases a final data file after a publication using provisional data has been released. If NCES receives revised data from states or discovers errors in the final data file, a revised data file is released.

SOURCE: U.S. Department of Education, National Center for Education Statistics, Common Core of Data (CCD), retrieved May 10, 2016, from http://nces.ed.gov/ccd/ccddata.asp. (This table was prepared May 2016.)

Further information on the nonfiscal CCD data may be obtained from

Patrick Keaton
Administrative Data Division
Elementary and Secondary Branch
National Center for Education Statistics
550 12th Street SW
Washington, DC 20202
patrick.keaton@ed.gov
http://nces.ed.gov/ccd

Further information on the fiscal CCD data may be obtained from

Stephen Cornman
Administrative Data Division
Elementary and Secondary Branch
National Center for Education Statistics
550 12th Street, SW
Washington DC 20202
stephen.cornman@ed.gov
http://nces.ed.gov/ccd

Early Childhood Longitudinal Study, Birth Cohort

The Early Childhood Longitudinal Study, Birth Cohort (ECLS-B) was designed to provide policymakers, researchers, child care providers, teachers, and parents with nationally representative information about children's early learning experiences and their transition to child care and school. From the time the ECLS-B children were infants until they entered kindergarten, their cognitive and physical development was measured using standardized assessments, and information about their care and learning experiences at home, in early care and education settings, and at school was collected through interviews with adults in the children's lives.

Data were collected from a sample of about 14,000 children born in the United States in 2001, representing a population of approximately 4 million. The children participating in the study came from diverse socioeconomic and racial/ethnic backgrounds, with oversamples of Chinese, other Asian and Pacific Islander, and American Indian/Alaska Native children. There were also oversamples of twins and of children born with moderately low and very low birthweight. Children, their parents (including nonresident and resident fathers), their child care and early education providers, and their kindergarten teachers provided information on children's cognitive, social, emotional, and physical development. Information was also collected about the children's experiences across multiple settings (e.g., home, child care, and school).

Information about the ECLS-B children was collected when they were approximately 9 months old (2001–02), 2 years old (2003–04), and 4 years old/preschool age (2005–06). Additionally, in the fall of 2006, data were collected from all participating sample children, approximately 75 percent of whom were in kindergarten or higher. In the fall of 2007, data were collected from the approximately 25 percent of participating sample children who had not yet entered kindergarten or higher in the previous collection, as well as children who were repeating kindergarten in the 2007–08 school year.

In every round of data collection, children participated in assessment activities and parent respondents (usually the mothers of the children) were asked about themselves, their families, and their children. Resident fathers were asked about themselves and their role in the ECLS-B children's lives in the 9-month, 2-year, and preschool collections. Similar information was collected from nonresident biological fathers in the 9-month and 2-year collections. In addition, beginning when the children were 2 years old, their child care and early education providers were asked to provide information about their own experience and training and their setting's learning environment. At 2 years and at preschool, observations were conducted in the regular nonparental care and education arrangements of a subsample of children in order to obtain information about the quality of the arrangements. When the ECLS-B children were in kindergarten, their teachers were asked to provide information about the children's early learning experiences and their school and classroom environments. Also, the before- and after-school care and education providers of children in kindergarten were asked to provide information about their own experience, their training, and their setting's learning environment. School-level data, taken from other NCES datasets (the Common Core of Data and the Private School Universe Survey) and residential ZIP codes collected at each wave are also available.

Further information on the ECLS-B may be obtained from

Gail Mulligan
Sample Surveys Division
Longitudinal Surveys Branch
National Center for Education Statistics
550 12th Street SW
Washington, DC 20202
ecls@ed.gov
http://nces.ed.gov/ecls/birth.asp

Early Childhood Longitudinal Study, Kindergarten Class of 1998–99

The Early Childhood Longitudinal Study, Kindergarten Class of 1998–99 (ECLS-K) was designed to provide detailed information on children's school experiences throughout elementary school and into middle school. The study began in the fall of 1998. A nationally representative sample of about 21,300 children enrolled in 940 kindergarten programs during the 1998–99 school year was selected to participate in the ECLS-K. The children attended both public and private kindergartens and full- and part-day programs. The sample included children from different racial/ethnic and socioeconomic backgrounds and oversamples of Asian and Pacific Islander children and private school kindergartners.

In the kindergarten year (1998–99), base-year data were collected in the fall and spring. In the first-grade year (1999–2000), data were collected again in the fall and spring. In the 3rd-grade (2002), 5th-grade (2004), and 8th-grade (2007) years, data were collected in the spring. The fall 1999 collection drew from a 30 percent subsample of schools; all other collections drew from the full sample of schools.

From kindergarten to 5th grade, the ECLS-K included a direct child cognitive assessment that was administered one on one with each child in the study. The assessment used a computer-assisted personal interview (CAPI) approach and a two-stage adaptive testing methodology. In the 8th grade, a two-stage adaptive paper-and-pencil assessment was administered in small groups. In kindergarten and first grade, the assessment included three cognitive domains: reading, mathematics, and general knowledge. General knowledge was replaced by science in the 3rd, 5th, and 8th grades. Children's height and weight were measured at each data collection point, and a direct measure of children's psychomotor development was administered in the fall of the kindergarten year only. In addition to these measures, the ECLS-K collected information about children's social skills and academic achievement through teacher reports in every grade and through student reports in the 3rd, 5th, and 8th grades.

A computer-assisted telephone interview with the children's parents/guardians was conducted at each data collection point. Parents/guardians were asked to provide key information about the children in the ECLS-K sample on subjects such as family structure (e.g., household members and composition), family demographics (e.g., family members' age, relation to the child being studied, and race/ethnicity), parent involvement, home educational activities (e.g., reading to the child), child health, parental education and employment status, and the social skills and behaviors of their children.

Data on the schools that children attended and their classrooms were collected through self-administered questionnaires completed by school administrators and classroom teachers. Administrators provided information about their schools' populations, programs, and policies. At the classroom level, data were collected from teachers on the composition of the classroom, teaching practices, curriculum, and teacher qualifications and experience. In addition, special education teachers and related services staff provided reports on the services received by children with an Individualized Education Program (IEP).

Further information on the ECLS-K may be obtained from

Gail Mulligan
Sample Surveys Division
Longitudinal Surveys Branch
National Center for Education Statistics
550 12th Street SW
Washington, DC 20202
ecls@ed.gov
http://nces.ed.gov/ecls/kindergarten.asp

Early Childhood Longitudinal Study, Kindergarten Class of 2010–11

The Early Childhood Longitudinal Study, Kindergarten Class of 2010–11 (ECLS-K:2011) provides detailed information on the school achievement and experiences of students throughout their elementary school years. The students who participated in the ECLS-K:2011 were followed longitudinally from the kindergarten year (the 2010–11 school year) through the spring of 2016, when most of them were expected to be in 5th grade. This sample of students is designed to be nationally representative of all students who were enrolled in kindergarten or who were of kindergarten age and being educated in an ungraded classroom or school in the United States in the 2010–11 school year, including those in public and private schools, those who attended full-day and part-day programs, those who were in kindergarten for the first time, and those who were kindergarten repeaters. Students who attended early learning centers or institutions that offered education only through kindergarten are included in the study sample and represented in the cohort.

The ECLS-K:2011 places emphasis on measuring students' experiences within multiple contexts and development in multiple domains. The design of the study includes the collection of information from the students, their parents/guardians, their teachers, and their schools. Information was collected from their before- and after-school care providers in the kindergarten year.

A nationally representative sample of approximately 18,170 children from about 1,310 schools participated in the base-year administration of the ECLS-K:2011 in the 2010–11 school year. The sample included children from different racial/ethnic and socioeconomic backgrounds. Asian/Pacific Islander students were oversampled to ensure that the sample included enough students of this race/ethnicity to make accurate estimates for the group as a whole. Eight data collections have been conducted to date: fall and spring of the children's kindergarten year (the base year), fall 2011 and spring 2012 (the 1st-grade year), fall 2012 and spring 2013 (the 2nd-grade year), spring 2014 (the 3rd-grade year), and spring 2015 (the 4th-grade year). The final data collection was conducted in the spring of 2016. Although the study refers to later rounds of data collection by the grade the majority of children are expected to be in (that is, the modal grade for children who were in kindergarten in the 2010–11 school year), children are included in subsequent data collections regardless of their grade level.

A total of approximately 780 of the 1,310 originally sampled schools participated during the base year of the study. This translates to a weighted unit response rate (weighted by the base weight) of 63 percent for the base year. In the base year, the weighted child assessment unit response rate was 87 percent for the fall data collection and 85 percent for the spring collection, and the weighted parent unit response rate was 74 percent for the fall collection and 67 percent for the spring collection.

Fall and spring data collections were conducted in the 2011–12 school year, when the majority of the children were in the 1st grade. The fall collection was conducted within a 33 percent subsample of the full base-year sample, and the spring collection was conducted within the full base-year sample. The weighted child assessment unit response rate was 89 percent for the fall data collection and 88 percent for the spring collection, and the weighted parent unit response rate was 87 percent for the fall data collection and 76 percent for the spring data collection.

In the 2012–13 data collection (when the majority of the children were in the 2nd grade) the weighted child assessment unit response rate was 84.0 percent in the fall and 83.4 percent in the spring.

Further information on ECLS-K:2011 may be obtained from

Gail Mulligan
Sample Surveys Division
Longitudinal Surveys Branch
National Center for Education Statistics
550 12th Street SW
Washington, DC 20202
ecls@ed.gov
http://nces.ed.gov/ecls/kindergarten2011.asp

EDFacts

EDFacts is a centralized data collection through which state education agencies submit PK–12 education data to the U.S. Department of Education (ED). All data in EDFacts are organized into "data groups" and reported to ED using defined file specifications. Depending on the data group, state education agencies may submit aggregate counts for the state as a whole or detailed counts for individual schools or school districts. EDFacts does not collect student-level records. The entities that are required to report EDFacts data vary by data group but may include the 50 states, the District of Columbia, the Department of Defense (DoD) dependents schools, the Bureau of Indian Education, Puerto Rico, American Samoa, Guam, the Northern Mariana Islands, and the U.S. Virgin Islands. More information about EDFacts file specifications and data groups can be found at http://www.ed.gov/EDFacts.

EDFacts is a universe collection and is not subject to sampling error, but nonsampling errors such as nonresponse and inaccurate reporting may occur. The U.S. Department of Education attempts to minimize nonsampling errors by training data submission coordinators and reviewing the quality of state data submissions. However, anomalies may still be present in the data.

Differences in state data collection systems may limit the comparability of ED*Facts* data across states and across time. To build ED*Facts* files, state education agencies rely on data that were reported by their schools and school districts. The systems used to collect these data are evolving rapidly and differ from state to state.

In some cases, ED*Facts* data may not align with data reported on state education agency websites. States may update their websites on schedules different from those they use to report data to ED. Furthermore, ED may use methods for protecting the privacy of individuals represented within the data that could be different from the methods used by an individual state.

ED*Facts* firearm incidents data are collected in data group 601 within file 094. ED*Facts* collects this data group on behalf of the Office of Safe and Healthy Students in the Office of Elementary and Secondary Education. The definition for this data group is "The number of incidents involving students who brought or possessed firearms at school." The reporting period is the entire school year. Data group 601 collects separate counts for incidents involving handguns, rifles/shotguns, other firearms, and multiple weapon types. The counts reported here exclude the "other firearms" category. For more information about this data group, please see file specification 094 for the relevant school year, available at http://www2.ed.gov/about/inits/ed/edfacts/file-specifications.html.

For more information about ED*Facts*, contact

ED*Facts*
Administrative Data Division
Elementary/Secondary Branch
National Center for Education Statistics
550 12th Street SW
Washington, DC 20202
EDFacts@ed.gov
http://www2.ed.gov/about/inits/ed/edfacts/index.html

Education Longitudinal Study of 2002

The Education Longitudinal Study of 2002 (ELS:2002) is a longitudinal survey that is monitoring the transitions of a national probability sample of 10th-graders in public, Catholic, and other private schools. Survey waves follow both students and high school dropouts and monitor the transition of the cohort to postsecondary education, the labor force, and family formation.

In the base year of the study, of 1,200 eligible contacted schools, 750 participated, for an overall weighted school participation rate of approximately 68 percent (62 percent unweighted). Of 17,600 selected eligible students, 15,400 participated, for an overall weighted student response rate of approximately 87 percent. (School and student weighted response rates reflect use of the base weight [design weight] and do not include nonresponse adjustments.) Information for the study is obtained not just from students and their school records, but also from the students' parents, their teachers, their librarians, and the administrators of their schools.

The first follow-up was conducted in 2004, when most sample members were high school seniors. Base-year students who remained in their base schools were resurveyed and tested in mathematics. Sample freshening was conducted to make the study representative of spring 2004 high school seniors nationwide. Students who were not still at their base schools were all administered a questionnaire. The first follow-up weighted student response rate was 89 percent.

The second follow-up, conducted in 2006, continued to follow the sample of students into postsecondary education, the workforce, or both. The weighted student response rate for this follow-up was 82 percent. The third follow-up, which had a weighted student response rate of 78 percent, was conducted in 2012; the data were released in January 2014.

The postsecondary transcript data collection was conducted in 2013–14. Postsecondary transcripts were requested for each of the ELS:2002 sample members who reported attending an IPEDS postsecondary institution. Transcripts were obtained for 11,623 of 12,549 eligible sample members for a weighted response rate of 77 percent. For more information on the postsecondary transcript data collection, see *Education Longitudinal Study of 2002 (ELS:2002): A First Look at the Postsecondary Transcripts of 2002 High School Sophomores* (NCES 2015-034).

Further information on ELS:2002 may be obtained from

Elise Christopher
Sample Surveys Division
Longitudinal Surveys Branch
National Center for Education Statistics
550 12th Street SW
Washington, DC 20202
elise.christopher@ed.gov
http://nces.ed.gov/surveys/els2002

Fast Response Survey System

The Fast Response Survey System (FRSS) was established in 1975 to collect issue-oriented data quickly, with a minimal burden on respondents. The FRSS, whose surveys collect and report data on key education issues at the elementary and secondary levels, was designed to meet the data needs of Department of Education analysts, planners, and decisionmakers when information could not be collected quickly through NCES's large recurring surveys. Findings from FRSS surveys have been included in congressional reports, testimony to congressional subcommittees, NCES reports, and other Department of Education reports. The findings are also often used by state and local education officials.

Data collected through FRSS surveys are representative at the national level, drawing from a sample that is appropriate for each study. The FRSS collects data from state education agencies and national samples of other educational organizations and participants, including local education agencies, public and private elementary and secondary schools, elementary and secondary school teachers and principals, and public libraries and school libraries. To ensure a minimal burden on respondents, the surveys are generally limited to three pages of questions, with a response burden of about 30 minutes per respondent. Sample sizes are relatively small (usually about 1,000 to 1,500 respondents per survey) so that data collection can be completed quickly.

Further information on the FRSS may be obtained from

John Ralph
Annual Reports and Information Staff
National Center for Education Statistics
550 12th Street SW
Washington, DC 20202
john.ralph@ed.gov
http://nces.ed.gov/surveys/frss

Condition of America's Public School Facilities

Condition of America's Public School Facilities: 1999 (NCES 2000-032) is a report that presents national data about the condition of public schools in 1999. It provides results from the survey "Condition of Public School Facilities, 1999" (FRSS 73), which was conducted by NCES using its Fast Response Survey System (FRSS). The survey collected information about the condition of school facilities and the costs of bringing them into good condition; school plans for repairs, renovations, and replacements; the age of public schools; and overcrowding and practices used to address overcrowding. The results presented in this report are based on questionnaire data for 900 public elementary and secondary schools in the United States. The responses were weighted to produce national estimates that represent all regular public schools in the United States.

In 2013, NCES conducted "Condition of Public School Facilities: 2012–13" (FRSS 105), an FRSS survey covering most of the same topics. The First Look report *Condition of America's Public School Facilities: 2012–13* (NCES 2014-022) is based on results from this FRSS survey.

Further information on these FRSS reports and surveys may be obtained from

John Ralph
Annual Reports and Information Staff
National Center for Education Statistics
550 12th Street SW
Washington, DC 20202
john.ralph@ed.gov
http://nces.ed.gov/surveys/frss

Public School Principals Report on Their School Facilities: Fall 2005

This report (NCES 2007-007) presents information on the extent of the match between the enrollment and the capacity of school buildings, environmental factors that can affect the use of classrooms and school buildings, the extent and ways in which schools use portable buildings and the reasons for using them, the availability of dedicated rooms for particular subject areas (such as science labs or music rooms), and the cleanliness and maintenance of student restrooms.

Results from the FRSS survey "Public School Principals' Perceptions of Their School Facilities: Fall 2005" (FRSS 88) form the basis of the report. The survey was mailed to school principals, who were asked to complete it themselves. The sample included 1,205 public schools in the 50 states and the District of Columbia. The sample was selected from the 2002–03 Common Core of Data (CCD) Public Elementary/Secondary School Universe File, the most current available at the time of selection. Of the 1,205 schools surveyed, 47 were determined to be ineligible. Of the remaining 1,158 schools, responses were received from 1,045. Data have been weighted to yield national estimates of public elementary/secondary schools. The unweighted response rate was 90 percent, and the weighted response rate was 91 percent.

Further information on this report may be obtained from

John Ralph
Annual Reports and Information Staff
National Center for Education Statistics
550 12th Street SW
Washington, DC 20202
john.ralph@ed.gov
http://nces.ed.gov/surveys/frss

Internet Access in U.S. Public Schools and Classrooms: 1994–2005

This report (NCES 2007-020) is based on data collected in the FRSS survey "Internet Access in U.S. Public Schools, Fall 2005" (FRSS 90). The survey was designed to assess the federal government's commitment to assist every school and classroom in connecting to the Internet by the year 2000.

In 1994, NCES began surveying approximately 1,000 public schools each year regarding their access to the Internet, access in classrooms, and, since 1996, their type of internet connections. Later administrations of this survey were expanded to cover emerging issues. The 2003 survey (FRSS 86) was designed to update the questions in the 2002 survey (FRSS 83) and covered the following topics: school connectivity, student access to computers and the Internet, school websites, technologies and procedures to prevent student access to inappropriate websites, and teacher professional development on how to incorporate the Internet into the curriculum.

In 2005, respondents were asked about the number of instructional computers with access to the Internet, the types of internet connections, the technologies and procedures used to prevent student access to inappropriate material on the Internet, and the availability of handheld and laptop computers for students and teachers. Respondents also provided information on teacher professional development in integrating the use of the Internet into the curriculum and using the Internet to provide opportunities and information for teaching and learning.

Use of Educational Technology in Public Schools

In 2008, the NCES survey on educational technology use in public schools was redesigned and expanded to a set of three surveys (i.e., a school-, district-, and teacher-level survey). The three surveys provide complementary information and together cover a broader range of topics than would be possible with one survey alone. The set of surveys collected data on availability and use of a range of educational technology resources, such as district and school networks, computers, devices that enhance the capabilities of computers for instruction, and computer software. They also collected information on leadership and staff support for educational technology within districts and schools.

Educational Technology in U.S. Public Schools: Fall 2008 (NCES 2010-034) is based on the school-level survey, "Education Technology in U.S. Public Schools: Fall 2008" (FRSS 92); *Educational Technology in Public School Districts: Fall 2008* (NCES 2010-003) is based on the district-level school technology survey, "Educational Technology in Public School Districts, Fall 2008" (FRSS 93); and *Teachers' Use of Educational Technology in U.S. Public Schools: 2009* (NCES 2010-040) is based on the teacher-level school technology survey, "Teachers' Use of Educational Technology in U.S. Public Schools, 2009" (FRSS 95).

Further information on internet access and technology use in public schools and classrooms may be obtained from

John Ralph
Annual Reports and Information Staff
National Center for Education Statistics
550 12th Street SW
Washington, DC 20202
john.ralph@ed.gov
http://nces.ed.gov/surveys/frss

Distance Education for Public Elementary and Secondary School Students

The report *Technology-Based Distance Education Courses for Public Elementary and Secondary School Students: 2002–03 and 2004–05* (NCES 2008-008) presented data collected in the FRSS survey "Distance Education Courses for Public Elementary and Secondary School Students, 2004–05" (FRSS 89, 2005). The report included national estimates of the prevalence and characteristics of technology-based distance education courses in public schools nationwide in school year 2004–05. The report also compared those data with the baseline data that were collected in the FRSS survey "Distance Education Courses for Public Elementary and Secondary School Students: 2002–03" (FRSS 84, 2003) and provided longitudinal analysis of change in the districts that responded to both the 2002–03 and 2004–05 surveys.

Distance education courses were defined as credit-granting courses offered to elementary and secondary school students enrolled in the district in which the teacher and student were in different locations. These courses could be delivered via audio, video (live or prerecorded), or Internet or other computer technologies.

Distance Education Courses for Public Elementary and Secondary School Students: 2009–10 (NCES 2012–008) presents national estimates about student enrollment in distance education courses in public school districts. The estimates are based on a district survey, "Distance Education Courses for Public Elementary and Secondary School Students: 2009–10 (FRSS 98, 2010), about distance education courses offered by the district or by any of the schools in the district during the 12-month 2009–10 school year. Distance education courses were defined as courses offered to elementary and secondary school students regularly enrolled in the district that were (1) credit granting; (2) technology delivered; and (3) had the instructor in a different location than the students and/or had course content developed in, or delivered from, a different location than that of the students.

Further information on FRSS reports on distance education may be obtained from

John Ralph
Annual Reports and Information Staff
National Center for Education Statistics
550 12th Street SW
Washington, DC 20202
john.ralph@ed.gov
http://nces.ed.gov/surveys/frss

School Safety and Discipline

The FRSS survey "School Safety and Discipline: 2013–14" (FRSS 106, 2014) collected nationally representative data on public school safety and discipline for the 2013–14 school year. The topics covered included specific safety and discipline plans and practices, training for classroom teachers and aides related to school safety and discipline issues, security personnel, frequency of specific discipline problems, and number of incidents of various offenses.

The survey was mailed to approximately 1,600 regular public schools in the 50 states and the District of Columbia. Recipients were informed that the survey was designed to be completed by the person most knowledgeable about safety and discipline at the school. The unweighted survey response rate was 86 percent, and the weighted response rate using the initial base weights was 85 percent. The survey weights were adjusted for questionnaire nonresponse, and the data were then weighted to yield national estimates that represent all eligible regular public schools in the United States. The report Public School Safety and Discipline: 2013–14 (NCES 2015-051) presents selected findings from the survey.

Further information on this FRSS survey may be obtained from

John Ralph
Annual Reports and Information Staff
National Center for Education Statistics
550 12th Street SW
Washington, DC 20202
john.ralph@ed.gov
http://nces.ed.gov/surveys/frss

Federal Support for Education

NCES prepares an annual compilation of federal funds for education for the *Digest of Education Statistics.* Data for U.S. Department of Education programs come from the *Budget of the United States Government.* Budget offices of other federal agencies provide information for all other federal program support except for research funds, which are obligations reported by the National Science Foundation in *Federal Funds for Research and Development.* Some data are estimated, based on reports from the federal agencies contacted and the *Budget of the United States Government.*

Except for money spent on research, outlays are used to report program funds to the extent possible. Some *Digest of Education Statistics* tables report program funds as obligations, as noted in the title of the table. Some federal program funds not commonly recognized as education assistance are also included in the totals reported. For example, portions of federal funds paid to some states and counties as shared revenues resulting from the sale of timber and minerals from public lands have been estimated as funds used for education purposes. Parts of the funds received by states (in 1980) and localities (in all years) under the General Revenue Sharing Program are also included, as are portions of federal funds received by the District of Columbia. The share of these funds allocated to education is assumed to be equal to the share of general funds expended for elementary and secondary education by states and localities in the same year, as reported by the U.S. Census Bureau in its annual publication, *Government Finances.*

The share of federal funds assigned to education for the District of Columbia is assumed to be equal to the share of the city's general fund expenditures for each level of education.

For the job training programs conducted by the Department of Labor, only estimated sums spent on classroom training have been reported as educational program support.

During the 1970s, the Office of Management and Budget (OMB) prepared an annual analysis of federal education program support. These were published in the *Budget of the United States Government, Special Analyses.* The information presented in this report is not, however, a continuation of the OMB series. A number of differences in the two series should be noted. OMB required all federal agencies to report outlays for education-related programs using a standardized form, thereby assuring agency compliance in reporting. The scope of education programs reported in the *Digest of Education Statistics* differs from the scope of programs reported in the OMB reports. Off-budget items such as the annual volume of guaranteed student loans were not included in OMB's reports. Finally, while some mention is made of an annual estimate of federal tax expenditures, OMB did not include them in its annual analysis of federal education support. Estimated federal tax expenditures for education are the difference between current federal tax receipts and what these receipts would be without existing education deductions to income allowed by federal tax provisions.

Recipients' data are estimated based on *Estimating Federal Funds for Education: A New Approach Applied to Fiscal Year 1980* (Miller, V., and Noell, J., 1982, Journal of Education Finance); *Federal Support for Education,* various years; and the *Catalog of Federal Domestic Assistance* (cfda.gov). The recipients' data are estimated and tend to undercount higher education institutions, students, and local education agencies. This is because some of the federal programs have more than one recipient receiving funds. In these cases, the recipients were put into a "mixed recipients" category, because there was no way to disaggregate the amount each recipient received.

Further information on federal support for education may be obtained from

Tom Snyder
Annual Reports and Information Staff
National Center for Education Statistics
550 12th Street SW
Washington, DC 20202
tom.snyder@ed.gov
http://nces.ed.gov/surveys/AnnualReports/federal.asp

High School and Beyond Longitudinal Study

The High School and Beyond Longitudinal Study (HS&B) is a nationally representative sample survey of individuals who were high school sophomores and seniors in 1980. As a large-scale, longitudinal survey, its primary purpose is to observe the educational and occupational plans and activities of young people as they pass through the American educational system and take on their adult roles. The study contributes to the understanding of the development of young adults and the factors that determine individual education and career outcomes. The availability of this longitudinal data encourages research in such areas as the strength of secondary school curricula, the quality and effectiveness of secondary and postsecondary schooling, the demand for postsecondary education, problems of financing postsecondary education, and the adequacy of postsecondary alternatives open to high school students.

The HS&B survey gathered data on the education, work, and family experiences of young adults for the pivotal years during and immediately following high school. The student questionnaire covered school experiences, activities, attitudes, plans, selected background characteristics, and language proficiency. Parents were asked about their educational aspirations for their children and plans for how their postsecondary education would be financed. Teachers were surveyed regarding their assessments of their students' futures. The survey also collected detailed information, from complete high school transcripts, on courses taken and grades achieved.

The base-year survey (conducted in 1980) was a probability sample of 1,015 high schools with a target number of 36 sophomores and 36 seniors in each school. A total of 58,270 students participated in the base-year survey. Substitutions were made for nonparticipating schools—but not for students—in those strata where it was possible. Overall, 1,120 schools were selected in the original sample and 810 of these schools participated in the survey. An additional 200 schools were drawn in a replacement sample. Student refusals and absences resulted in an 82 percent completion rate for the survey.

Several small groups in the population were oversampled to allow for special study of certain types of schools and students. Students completed questionnaires and took a battery of cognitive tests. In addition, a sample of parents of sophomores and seniors (about 3,600 for each cohort) was surveyed.

HS&B first follow-up activities took place in the spring of 1982. The sample for the first follow-up survey included approximately 30,000 individuals who were sophomores in 1980. The completion rate for sample members eligible for on-campus survey administration was about 96 percent. About 89 percent of the students who left school between the base-year and first follow-up surveys (e.g., dropouts, transfer students, and early graduates) completed the first follow-up sophomore questionnaire.

As part of the first follow-up survey of HS&B, transcripts were requested in fall 1982 for an 18,150-member subsample of the sophomore cohort. Of the 15,940 transcripts actually obtained, 12,120 transcripts represented students who had graduated in 1982 and thus were eligible for use in the overall curriculum analysis presented in this publication. All courses in each transcript were assigned a 6-digit code based on the Classification of Secondary School Courses (a coding system developed to standardize course descriptions; see http://nces.ed.gov/surveys/hst/courses.asp). Credits earned in each course are expressed in Carnegie units. (The Carnegie unit is a standard of measurement that represents one credit for the completion of a 1-year course. To receive credit for a course, the student must have received a passing grade—"pass," "D," or higher.) Students who transferred from public to private schools or from private to public schools between their sophomore and senior years were eliminated from public/private analyses.

In designing the senior cohort first follow-up survey, one of the goals was to reduce the size of the retained sample while still keeping sufficient numbers of various racial/ethnic groups to allow important policy analyses. A total of about 11,230 (93.6 percent) of the 12,000 individuals subsampled completed the questionnaire. Information was obtained about the respondents' school and employment experiences, family status, and attitudes and plans.

The samples for the second follow-up, which took place in spring 1984, consisted of about 12,000 members of the senior cohort and about 15,000 members of the sophomore cohort. The completion rate for the senior cohort was 91 percent, and the completion rate for the sophomore cohort was 92 percent.

HS&B third follow-up data collection activities were performed in spring 1986. Both the sophomore and senior cohort samples for this round of data collection were the same as those used for the second follow-up survey. The completion rates for the sophomore and senior cohort samples were 91 percent and 88 percent, respectively.

HS&B fourth follow-up data collection activities were performed in 1992 but only covered the 1980 sophomore class. These activities included examining aspects of these students' early adult years, such as enrollment in postsecondary education, experience in the labor market, marriage and child rearing, and voting behavior.

An NCES series of technical reports and data file user's manuals, available electronically, provides additional information on the survey methodology.

Further information on HS&B may be obtained from

Aurora D'Amico
Sample Surveys Division
Longitudinal Surveys Branch
National Center for Education Statistics
550 12th Street SW
Washington, DC 20202
aurora.damico@ed.gov
http://nces.ed.gov/surveys/hsb

High School Longitudinal Study of 2009

The High School Longitudinal Study of 2009 (HSLS:09) is a nationally representative, longitudinal study of approximately 21,000 9th-grade students in 944 schools who will be followed through their secondary and postsecondary years. The study focuses on understanding students' trajectories from the beginning of high school into postsecondary education, the workforce, and beyond. The HSLS:09 questionnaire is focused on, but not limited to, information on science, technology, engineering, and mathematics (STEM) education and careers. It is designed to provide data on mathematics and science education, the changing high school environment, and postsecondary education. This study features a new student assessment in algebra skills, reasoning, and problem solving and includes surveys of students, their parents, math and science teachers, and school administrators, as well as a new survey of school counselors.

The HSLS:09 base year took place in the 2009–10 school year, with a randomly selected sample of fall-term 9th-graders in more than 900 public and private high schools that had both a 9th and an 11th grade. Students took a mathematics assessment and survey online. Students' parents, principals, and mathematics and science teachers and the school's lead counselor completed surveys on the phone or online.

The HSLS:09 student questionnaire includes interest and motivation items for measuring key factors predicting choice of postsecondary paths, including majors and eventual careers. This study explores the roles of different factors in the development of a student's commitment to attend college and then take the steps necessary to succeed in college (the right courses, courses in specific sequences, etc.). Questionnaires in this study have asked more questions of students and parents regarding reasons for selecting specific colleges (e.g., academic programs, financial aid and access prices, and campus environment).

The first follow-up of HSLS:09 occurred in the spring of 2012, when most sample members were in the 11th grade. Data files and documentation for the first follow-up were released in fall 2013 and are available on the NCES website.

A between-round postsecondary status update survey took place in the spring of students' expected graduation year (2013). It asked respondents about college applications, acceptances, and rejections, as well as their actual college choices. In the fall of 2013 and the spring of 2014, high school transcripts were collected and coded.

A full second follow-up took place in 2016, when most sample members are 3 years beyond high school graduation. Additional follow-ups are planned, to at least age 30.

Further information on HSLS:09 may be obtained from

Elise Christopher
Sample Surveys Division
Longitudinal Surveys Branch
National Center for Education Statistics
550 12th Street SW
Washington, DC 20202
hsls09@ed.gov
http://nces.ed.gov/surveys/hsls09

High School Transcript Studies

High school transcript studies have been conducted since 1982 in conjunction with major NCES data collections. The studies collect information that is contained in a student's high school record—courses taken while attending secondary school, information on credits earned, when specific courses were taken, and final grades.

A high school transcript study was conducted in 2004 as part of the Education Longitudinal Study of 2002 (ELS:2002/2004). A total of 1,550 schools participated in the request for transcripts, for an unweighted participation rate of approximately 79 percent. Transcript information was received on 14,920 members of the student sample (not just graduates), for an unweighted response rate of 91 percent.

Similar studies were conducted of the coursetaking patterns of 1982, 1987, 1990, 1992, 1994, 1998, 2000, 2005, and 2009 high school graduates. The 1982 data are based on approximately 12,000 transcripts collected by the High School and Beyond Longitudinal Study (HS&B). The 1987 data are based on approximately 25,000 transcripts from 430 schools obtained as part of the 1987 NAEP High School Transcript Study, a scope comparable to that of the NAEP transcript studies conducted in 1990, 1994, 1998, and 2000. The 1992 data are based on approximately 15,000 transcripts collected by the National Education Longitudinal Study of 1988 (NELS:88/92). The 2005 data, from the 2005 NAEP High School Transcript Study, come from a sample of over 26,000 transcripts from 640 public schools and 80 private schools. The 2009 data are from the 2009 NAEP High School Transcript Study, which collected transcripts from a nationally representative sample of 37,700 high school graduates from about 610 public schools and 130 private schools.

Because the 1982 HS&B transcript study used a different method for identifying students with disabilities than was used in NAEP transcript studies after 1982, and in order to make the statistical summaries as comparable as possible, all the counts and percentages in this report are restricted to students whose records indicate that they had not participated in a special education program. This restriction lowers the number of 1990 graduates represented in the tables to 20,870.

Further information on NAEP high school transcript studies may be obtained from

Elise Christopher
Sample Surveys Division
Longitudinal Surveys Branch
National Center for Education Statistics
550 12th Street SW
Washington, DC 20202
elise.christopher@ed.gov
http://nces.ed.gov/surveys/hst

Further information on all other high school transcript studies may be obtained from

Carl Schmitt
Administrative Data Division
Elementary and Secondary Branch
National Center for Education Statistics
550 12th Street SW
Washington, DC 20202
carl.schmitt@ed.gov
http://nces.ed.gov/surveys/hst

Integrated Postsecondary Education Data System

The Integrated Postsecondary Education Data System (IPEDS) surveys approximately 7,500 postsecondary institutions, including universities and colleges, as well as institutions offering technical and vocational education beyond the high school level. IPEDS, an annual universe collection that began in 1986, replaced the Higher Education General Information Survey (HEGIS). In order to present data in a timely manner, *Digest of Education Statistics* tables use "provisional" IPEDS data for the most recent years. These data have been fully reviewed, edited, and imputed, but do not incorporate data revisions submitted by institutions after the close of data collection. Tables are revised with these institutional revisions on a periodic basis.

IPEDS consists of interrelated survey components that provide information on postsecondary institutions, student enrollment, programs offered, degrees and certificates conferred, and both the human and financial resources involved in the provision of institutionally based postsecondary education. Prior to 2000, the IPEDS survey had the following subject-matter components: Graduation Rates; Fall Enrollment; Institutional Characteristics; Completions; Salaries, Tenure, and Fringe Benefits of Full-Time Faculty; Fall Staff; Finance;

and Academic Libraries (in 2000, the Academic Libraries component became a survey separate from IPEDS). Since 2000, IPEDS survey components occurring in a particular collection year have been organized into three seasonal collection periods: fall, winter, and spring. The Institutional Characteristics and Completions components first took place during the fall 2000 collection; the Employees by Assigned Position (EAP), Salaries, and Fall Staff components first took place during the winter 2001–02 collection; and the Enrollment, Student Financial Aid, Finance, and Graduation Rates components first took place during the spring 2001 collection. In the winter 2005–06 data collection, the EAP, Fall Staff, and Salaries components were merged into the Human Resources component. During the 2007–08 collection year, the Enrollment component was broken into two separate components: 12-Month Enrollment (taking place in the fall collection) and Fall Enrollment (taking place in the spring collection). In the 2011–12 IPEDS data collection year, the Student Financial Aid component was moved to the winter data collection to aid in the timing of the net price of attendance calculations displayed on the College Navigator (http://nces.ed.gov/college navigator). In the 2012–13 IPEDS data collection year, the Human Resources component was moved from the winter data collection to the spring data collection, and in the 2013–14 data collection year, the Graduation Rates and Graduation Rates 200% components were moved from the spring data collection to the winter data collection.

Beginning in 2008–09, the first-professional degree category was combined with the doctor's degree category. However, some degrees formerly identified as first-professional that take more than two full-time-equivalent academic years to complete, such as those in Theology (M.Div, M.H.L./Rav), are included in the Master's degree category. Doctor's degrees were broken out into three distinct categories: research/scholarship, professional practice, and other doctor's degrees.

IPEDS race/ethnicity data collection also changed in 2008–09. The "Asian" race category is now separate from a "Native Hawaiian or Other Pacific Islander" category, and a new category of "Two or more races" is added.

The degree-granting institutions portion of IPEDS is a census of colleges that award associate's or higher degrees and are eligible to participate in Title IV financial aid programs. Prior to 1993, data from technical and vocational institutions were collected through a sample survey. Beginning in 1993, all data are gathered in a census of all postsecondary institutions. Beginning in 1997, the survey was restricted to institutions participating in Title IV programs. The tabulations developed for editions of the *Digest of Education Statistics* from 1993 forward are based on lists of all institutions and are not subject to sampling errors.

The classification of institutions offering college and university education changed as of 1996. Prior to 1996, institutions that had courses leading to an associate's or higher degree or that had courses accepted for credit toward those degrees were considered higher education institutions. Higher education institutions were accredited by an agency or association that was recognized by the U.S. Department of Education or were recognized directly by the Secretary of Education. The newer standard includes institutions that award associate's or higher degrees and that are eligible to participate in Title IV federal financial aid programs. Tables that contain any data according to this standard are titled "degree-granting" institutions. Time-series tables may contain data from both series, and they are noted accordingly. The impact of this change on data collected in 1996 was not large. For example, tables on faculty salaries and benefits were only affected to a very small extent. Also, degrees awarded at the bachelor's level or higher were not heavily affected. The largest impact was on private 2-year college enrollment. In contrast, most of the data on public 4-year colleges were affected to a minimal extent. The impact on enrollment in public 2-year colleges was noticeable in certain states, such as Arizona, Arkansas, Georgia, Louisiana, and Washington, but was relatively small at the national level. Overall, total enrollment for all institutions was about one-half of 1 percent higher in 1996 for degree-granting institutions than for higher education institutions.

Prior to the establishment of IPEDS in 1986, HEGIS acquired and maintained statistical data on the characteristics and operations of higher education institutions. Implemented in 1966, HEGIS was an annual universe survey of institutions accredited at the college level by an agency recognized by the Secretary of the U.S. Department of Education. These institutions were listed in NCES's *Education Directory, Colleges and Universities.*

HEGIS surveys collected information on institutional characteristics, faculty salaries, finances, enrollment, and degrees. Since these surveys, like IPEDS, were distributed to all higher education institutions, the data presented are not subject to sampling error. However, they are subject to nonsampling error, the sources of which varied with the survey instrument.

The NCES Taskforce for IPEDS Redesign recognized that there were issues related to the consistency of data definitions as well as the accuracy, reliability, and validity of other quality measures within and across surveys. The IPEDS redesign in 2000 provided institution-specific web-based data forms. While the new system shortened data processing time and provided better data consistency, it did not address the accuracy of the data provided by institutions.

Beginning in 2003–04 with the Prior Year Data Revision System, prior-year data have been available to institutions entering current data. This allows institutions to make changes to their prior-year entries either by adjusting the data or by providing missing data. These revisions allow the evaluation of the data's accuracy by looking at the changes made.

NCES conducted a study (NCES 2005-175) of the 2002–03 data that were revised in 2003–04 to determine the accuracy of the imputations, track the institutions that submitted revised data, and analyze the revised data they submitted. When institutions made changes to their data, it was assumed that the revised data were the "true" data. The data were analyzed for the number and type of institutions making changes, the type of changes, the magnitude of the changes, and the impact on published data.

Because NCES imputes for missing data, imputation procedures were also addressed by the Redesign Taskforce. For the 2003–04 assessment, differences between revised values and values that were imputed in the original files were compared (i.e., revised value minus imputed value). These differences were then used to provide an assessment of the effectiveness of imputation procedures. The size of the differences also provides an indication of the accuracy of imputation procedures. To assess the overall impact of changes on aggregate IPEDS estimates, published tables for each component were reconstructed using the revised 2002–03 data. These reconstructed tables were then compared to the published tables to determine the magnitude of aggregate bias and the direction of this bias.

Since fall 2000 and spring 2001, IPEDS data collections have been web-based. Data have been provided by "key-holders," institutional representatives appointed by campus chief executives, who are responsible for ensuring that survey data submitted by the institution are correct and complete. Because Title IV institutions are the primary focus of IPEDS and because these institutions are required to respond to IPEDS, response rates for Title IV institutions have been high (data on specific components are cited below). More details on the accuracy and reliability of IPEDS data can be found in the *Integrated Postsecondary Education Data System Data Quality Study* (NCES 2005-175).

Further information on IPEDS may be obtained from

Richard Reeves
Administrative Data Division
Postsecondary Branch
National Center for Education Statistics
550 12th Street SW
Washington, DC 20202
richard.reeves@ed.gov
http://nces.ed.gov/ipeds

Fall (12-Month Enrollment)

The 12-month period during which data are collected is July 1 through June 30. Data are collected by race/ethnicity, gender, and level of study (undergraduate or postbaccalaureate) and include unduplicated headcounts and instructional activity (contact or credit hours). These data are also used to calculate a full-time-equivalent (FTE) enrollment based on instructional activity. FTE enrollment is useful for gauging the size of the educational enterprise at the institution. Prior to the 2007–08 IPEDS data collection, the data collected in the 12-Month Enrollment component were part of the Fall Enrollment component, which is conducted during the spring data collection period. However, to improve the timeliness of the data, a separate 12-Month Enrollment survey component was developed in 2007. These data are now collected in the fall for the previous academic year. Of the 7,304 Title IV institutions that were expected to respond to the 12-Month Enrollment component of the fall 2014 data

collection, 7,302 responded, for an approximate response rate of 100.0 percent.

Further information on the IPEDS 12-Month Enrollment component may be obtained from

Chris Cody
Administrative Data Division
Postsecondary Branch
National Center for Education Statistics
550 12th Street SW
Washington, DC 20202
christopher.cody@ed.gov
http://nces.ed.gov/ipeds

Fall (Completions)

This survey was part of the HEGIS series throughout its existence. However, the degree classification taxonomy was revised in 1970–71, 1982–83, 1991–92, 2002–03, and 2009–10. Collection of degree data has been maintained through IPEDS.

Degrees-conferred trend tables arranged by the 2009–10 classification are included in the *Digest of Education Statistics* to provide consistent data from 1970–71 through the most recent year. Data in this edition on associate's and other formal awards below the baccalaureate degree, by field of study, cannot be made comparable with figures from years prior to 1982–83. The nonresponse rate does not appear to be a significant source of nonsampling error for this survey. The response rate over the years has been high; for the fall 2014 Completions component, it rounded to 100.0 percent. Because of the high response rate, there was no need to conduct a nonresponse bias analysis. Imputation methods for the fall 2014 Completions component are discussed in the *2014–15 Integrated Postsecondary Education Data System (IPEDS) Methodology Report* (NCES 2015-098).

The *Integrated Postsecondary Education Data System Data Quality Study* (NCES 2005-175) indicated that most Title IV institutions supplying revised data on completions in 2003–04 were able to supply missing data for the prior year. The small differences between imputed data for the prior year and the revised actual data supplied by the institution indicated that the imputed values produced by NCES were acceptable.

Further information on the IPEDS Completions component may be obtained from

Imani Stutely
Administrative Data Division
Postsecondary Branch
National Center for Education Statistics
550 12th Street SW
Washington, DC 20202
imani.stutely@ed.gov
http://nces.ed.gov/ipeds

Fall (Institutional Characteristics)

This survey collects the basic information necessary to classify institutions, including control, level, and types of programs offered, as well as information on tuition, fees, and room and board charges. Beginning in 2000, the survey collected institutional pricing data from institutions with first-time, full-time, degree/certificate-seeking undergraduate students. Unduplicated full-year enrollment counts and instructional activity are now collected in the 12-Month Enrollment survey. Beginning in 2008–09, the student financial aid data collected include greater detail. The overall unweighted response rate was 100.0 percent for Title IV degree-granting institutions for 2009 data.

In the fall 2014 data collection, the response rate for the Institutional Characteristics component among all Title IV entities was 100.0 percent: Of the 7,389 Title IV entities expected to respond to this component, all responded.

The *Integrated Postsecondary Education Data System Data Quality Study* (NCES 2005-175) looked at tuition and price in Title IV institutions. Only 8 percent of institutions in 2002–03 and 2003–04 reported the same data to IPEDS and Thomson Peterson—a company providing information about institutions based on the institutions' voluntary data submissions—consistently across all selected data items. Differences in wordings or survey items may account for some of these inconsistencies.

Further information on the IPEDS Institutional Characteristics component may be obtained from

Bao Le
Administrative Data Division
Postsecondary Branch
National Center for Education Statistics
550 12th Street SW
Washington, DC 20202
bao.le@ed.gov
http://nces.ed.gov/ipeds

Winter (Student Financial Aid)

This component was part of the spring data collection from IPEDS data collection years 2000–01 to 2010–11, but it moved to the winter data collection starting with the 2011–12 IPEDS data collection year. This move will aid in the timing of the net price of attendance calculations displayed on College Navigator (http://nces.ed.gov/collegenavigator).

Financial aid data are collected for undergraduate students. Data are collected regarding federal grants, state and local government grants, institutional grants, and loans. The collected data include the number of students receiving each type of financial assistance and the average amount of aid received by type of aid. Beginning in 2008–09, student financial aid data collected includes greater detail on types of aid offered.

In the winter 2014–15 data collection, the Student Financial Aid component collected data about financial aid awarded to undergraduate students, with particular emphasis on full-time, first-time degree/certificate-seeking undergraduate students awarded financial aid for the 2014–15 academic year. In addition, the component collected data on undergraduate and graduate students receiving military service members and veterans benefits. Finally, student counts and awarded aid amounts were collected to calculate the net price of attendance for two subsets of full-time, first-time degree/certificate-seeking undergraduate students: those awarded any grant aid, and those awarded Title IV aid. Of the 7,218 Title IV institutions that were expected to respond to the Student Financial Aid component, 7,212 Title IV institutions responded, resulting in a response rate that rounded to 100 percent.

Further information on the IPEDS Student Financial Aid component may be obtained from

Bao Le
Administrative Data Division
Postsecondary Branch
National Center for Education Statistics
550 12th Street SW
Washington, DC 20202
bao.le@ed.gov
http://nces.ed.gov/ipeds

Winter (Graduation Rates and Graduation Rates 200 Percent)

In IPEDS data collection years 2012–13 and earlier, the Graduation Rates and 200 Percent Graduation Rates components were collected during the spring collection. In the IPEDS 2013–14 data collection year, however, the Graduation Rates and 200 Percent Graduation Rates collections were moved to the winter data collection.

The 2014–15 Graduation Rates component collected counts of full-time, first-time degree/certificate-seeking undergraduate students beginning their postsecondary education in the specified cohort year and their completion status as of 150 percent of normal program completion time at the same institution where the students started. If 150 percent of normal program completions time extended beyond August 31, 2014, the counts as of that date were collected. Four-year institutions used 2008 as the cohort year, while less-than-4-year institutions used 2011 as the cohort year. Of the 6,433 institutions that were expected to respond to the Graduation Rates component, 6,430 institutions responded, resulting in a response rate that rounded to 100 percent.

The 2014–15 Graduation Rates 200 Percent component was designed to combine information reported in a prior collection via the Graduation Rates component with current information about the same cohort of students. From previously collected data, the following elements were obtained: the number of students entering the institution as full-time, first-time degree/certificate-seeking students in a cohort year; the number of students in this cohort completing within 100 and 150 percent of normal program completion time; and the number of cohort exclusions (such as students who left for military service). Then the count of additional cohort exclusions and additional program completers between 151 and 200 percent of normal program completion time was collected. Four-year institutions reported on bachelor's or equivalent degree-seeking students and used cohort year 2006 as the reference period, while less-than-4-year institutions reported on all students in the cohort and used cohort year 2010 as the reference period. Of the 5,928 institutions that were expected to respond to the Graduation Rates 200 Percent component, 5,926 institutions responded, resulting in a response rate that rounded to 100 percent.

Further information on the IPEDS Graduation Rates and 200 Percent Graduation Rates components may be obtained from

Andrew Mary
Administrative Data Division
Postsecondary Branch
National Center for Education Statistics
550 12th Street SW
Washington, DC 20202
andrew.mary@ed.gov
http://nces.ed.gov/ipeds/

Winter (Admissions)

For the 2014–15 survey year, an Admissions component was added to the winter data collection. This new component was created out of the admissions data that had previously been a part of the fall Institutional Characteristics component. The moving of these data into a new component in the winter collection will enable all institutions to report data for the most recent fall period.

The Admissions component collects information about the selection process for entering first-time degree/certificate-seeking undergraduate students. Data obtained from institutions include admissions considerations (e.g., secondary school records, admission test scores), the number of first-time degree/certificate-seeking undergraduate students who applied, the number admitted, and the number enrolled. Admissions data were collected only from institutions that do not have an open admissions policy for entering first-time students. Data collected correspond to individuals applying to be admitted during the fall of the 2014–15 academic year (the fall 2014 reporting period). Of the 2,217 Title IV institutions that were expected to respond to the Admissions component, all responded.

Further information on the IPEDS Admissions component may be obtained from

Moussa Ezzeddine
Administrative Data Division
Postsecondary Branch
National Center for Education Statistics
550 12th Street SW
Washington, DC 20202
moussa.ezzeddine@ed.gov
http://nces.ed.gov/ipeds

Spring (Fall Enrollment)

This survey has been part of the HEGIS and IPEDS series since 1966. Response rates for this survey have been relatively high, generally exceeding 85 percent. Beginning in 2000, with web-based data collection, higher response rates were attained. In the spring 2015 data collection, the Fall Enrollment component covered fall 2014. Of the 7,292 institutions that were expected to respond, 7,284 responded, for a response rate that rounded to 100 percent. Data collection procedures for the Fall Enrollment component of the spring 2015 data collection are presented in *Enrollment and Employees in Postsecondary Institutions, Fall 2014; and Financial Statistics and Academic Libraries, Fiscal Year 2014: First Look (Provisional Data)* (NCES 2016-005).

Beginning with the fall 1986 survey and the introduction of IPEDS (see above), the survey was redesigned. The survey allows (in alternating years) for the collection of age and residence data. Beginning in 2000, the survey collected instructional activity and unduplicated headcount data, which are needed to compute a standardized, full-time-equivalent (FTE) enrollment statistic for the entire academic year. As of 2007–08, the timeliness of the instructional activity data has been improved by collecting these data in the fall as part of the 12-Month Enrollment component instead of in the spring as part of the Fall Enrollment component.

The *Integrated Postsecondary Education Data System Data Quality Study* (NCES 2005-175) showed that public institutions made the majority of changes to enrollment data during the 2004 revision period. The majority of changes were made to unduplicated headcount data, with the net differences between the original data and the revised data at about 1 percent. Part-time students in general and enrollment in private not-for-profit institutions were often underestimated. The fewest changes by institutions were to Classification of Instructional Programs (CIP) code data. (The CIP is a taxonomic coding scheme that contains titles and descriptions of primarily postsecondary instructional programs.)

Further information on the IPEDS Fall Enrollment component may be obtained from

Chris Cody
Administrative Data Division
Postsecondary Branch
National Center for Education Statistics
550 12th Street SW
Washington, DC 20202
christopher.cody@ed.gov
http://nces.ed.gov/ipeds

Spring (Finance)

This survey was part of the HEGIS series and has been continued under IPEDS. Substantial changes were made in the financial survey instruments in fiscal year (FY) 1976, FY 1982, FY 1987, FY 1997, and FY 2002. While these changes were significant, considerable effort has been made to present only comparable information on trends in this report and to note inconsistencies. The FY 1976 survey instrument contained numerous revisions to earlier survey forms, which made direct comparisons of line items very difficult. Beginning in FY 1982, Pell Grant data were collected in the categories of federal restricted grant and contract revenues and restricted scholarship and fellowship expenditures. The introduction of IPEDS in the FY 1987 survey included several important changes to the survey instrument and data processing procedures. Beginning in FY 1997, data for private institutions were collected using new financial concepts consistent with Financial Accounting Standards Board (FASB) reporting standards, which provide a more comprehensive view of college finance activities. The data for public institutions continued to be collected using the older survey form. The data for public and private institutions were no longer comparable and, as a result, no longer presented together in analysis tables. In FY 2001, public institutions had the option of either continuing to report using Government Accounting Standards Board (GASB) standards or using the new FASB reporting standards. Beginning in FY 2002, public institutions had three options: the original GASB standards, the FASB standards, or the new GASB Statement 35 standards (GASB35).

Possible sources of nonsampling error in the financial statistics include nonresponse, imputation, and misclassification. The unweighted response rate has been about 85 to 90 percent for most of the historic years presented in the *Digest of Education Statistics*; however, in more recent years, response rates have been much higher because Title IV institutions are required to respond. Beginning with 2002, the IPEDS data collection has been a full-scale web-based collection, which offers features that improve the quality and timeliness of the data. The ability of IPEDS to tailor online data entry forms for each institution based on characteristics such as institutional control, level of institution, and calendar system, and the institutions' ability to submit their data online, are two such features that have improved response.

In the FY 2014 Finance component, of the 7,292 institutions that were expected to respond, 7,284 provided data, resulting in a response rate that rounded to 100 percent. Data collection procedures for the FY 2014 component are discussed in *Enrollment and Employees in Postsecondary Institutions, Fall 2014; and Financial Statistics and Academic Libraries, Fiscal Year 2014: First Look (Provisional Data)* (NCES 2016-005).

The *Integrated Postsecondary Education Data System Data Quality Study* (NCES 2005-175) found that only a small percentage (2.9 percent, or 168) of postsecondary institutions either revised 2002–03 data or submitted data for items they previously left unreported. Though relatively few institutions made changes, the changes made were relatively large—greater than 10 percent of the original data. With a few exceptions, these changes, large as they were, did not greatly affect the aggregate totals.

Further information on the IPEDS Finance component may be obtained from

Bao Le
Administrative Data Division
Postsecondary Branch
National Center for Education Statistics
550 12th Street SW
Washington, DC 20202
bao.le@ed.gov
http://nces.ed.gov/ipeds

Spring (Human Resources)

The Human Resources component was part of the IPEDS winter data collection from data collection years 2000–01 to 2011–12. For the 2012–13 data collection year, the Human Resources component was moved to the spring 2013 data collection, in order to give institutions more time to prepare their survey responses (the spring and winter collections begin on the same date, but the reporting deadline for the spring collection is several weeks later than the reporting deadline for the winter collection).

IPEDS Collection Years 2012–13 and Later

In 2012–13, new occupational categories replaced the primary function/occupational activity categories previously used in the IPEDS Human Resources component. This change was required in order to align the IPEDS Human Resources categories with the 2010 Standard Occupational Classification (SOC) system. In tandem with the change in 2012–13 from using primary function/occupational activity categories to using the new occupational categories, the sections making up the IPEDS Human Resources component (which previously had been Employees by Assigned Position, Fall Staff, and Salaries) were changed to Full-Time Instructional Staff, Full-time Noninstructional Staff, Salaries, Part-Time Staff, and New Hires.

The webpage "Archived Changes—Changes to IPEDS Data Collections, 2012–13" (https://nces.ed.gov/ipeds/Inside Pages/ArchivedChanges?year=2012-13) provides information on the redesigned IPEDS Human Resources component. "Resources for Implementing Changes to the IPEDS Human Resources (HR) Survey Component Due to Updated 2010 Standard Occupational Classification (SOC) System" (https://nces.ed.gov/ipeds/Section/resources_soc) is a webpage containing additional information, including notes comparing the new classifications with the old ("Comparison of New IPEDS Occupational Categories with Previous Categories"), a crosswalk from the new IPEDS occupational categories to the 2010 SOC occupational categories ("New IPEDS Occupational Categories and 2010 SOC"), answers to frequently asked questions, and a link to current IPEDS Human Resources survey screens.

In the 2013–14 collection year, the response rate for the (spring 2014) Human Resources component was 99.9 percent. Data collection procedures for this component are presented in *Enrollment in Postsecondary Institutions, Fall 2013; Financial Statistics, Fiscal Year 2013; and Employees in Postsecondary Institutions, Fall 2013: First Look (Provisional Data)* (NCES 2015-012). Of the 7,292 institutions that were expected to respond to the spring 2015 Human Resources component, 7,284 responded, for a response rate that rounded to 100 percent. Data collection procedures for this component are presented in *Enrollment and Employees in Postsecondary Institutions, Fall 2014; and Financial Statistics and Academic Libraries, Fiscal Year 2014: First Look (Provisional Data)* (NCES 2016-005).

IPEDS Collection Years Prior to 2012–13

In collection years before 2001–02, IPEDS conducted a Fall Staff survey and a Salaries survey; in the 2001–02 collection year, the Employees by Assigned Position survey was added to IPEDS. In the 2005–06 collection year, these three surveys became sections of the IPEDS "Human Resources" component.

Data gathered by the Employees by Assigned Position section categorized all employees by full- or part-time status, faculty status, and primary function/occupational activity. Institutions with M.D. or D.O. programs were required to report their medical school employees separately. A response to the EAP was required of all 6,858 Title IV institutions and administrative offices in the United States and other jurisdictions for winter 2008–09, and 6,845, or 99.8 percent unweighted, responded. Of the 6,970 Title IV institutions and administrative offices required to respond to the winter 2009–10 EAP, 6,964, or 99.9 percent, responded. And of the 7,256 Title IV institutions and administrative offices required to respond to the EAP for winter 2010–11, 7,252, or 99.9 percent, responded.

The main functions/occupational activities of the EAP section were primarily instruction, instruction combined with research and/or public service, primarily research, primarily public service, executive/administrative/managerial, other professionals (support/service), graduate assistants, technical and paraprofessionals, clerical and secretarial, skilled crafts, and service/maintenance.

All full-time instructional faculty classified in the EAP full-time non-medical school part as either (1) primarily instruction or (2) instruction combined with research and/or public service were included in the Salaries section, unless they were exempt.

The Fall Staff section categorized all staff on the institution's payroll as of November 1 of the collection year by employment status (full time or part time), primary function/occupational activity, gender, and race/ethnicity. These data elements were collected from degree-granting and non-degree-granting institutions; however, additional data elements were collected from degree-granting institutions and related administrative offices with 15 or more full-time staff. These elements include faculty status, contract length/teaching period, academic rank, salary class intervals, and newly hired full-time permanent staff.

The Fall Staff section, which was required only in odd-numbered reporting years, was not required during the 2008–09 Human Resources data collection. However, of the 6,858 Title IV institutions and administrative offices in the United States and other jurisdictions, 3,295, or 48.0 percent unweighted, did provide data in the Fall Staff section that year. During the 2009–10 Human Resources data collection, when all 6,970 Title IV institutions and administrative offices were required to respond to the Fall Staff section, 6,964, or 99.9 percent, did so. A response to the Fall Staff section of the 2010–11 Human Resources collection was optional, and 3,364 Title IV institutions and administrative offices responded that year (a response rate of 46.3 percent).

The *Integrated Postsecondary Education Data System Data Quality Study* (NCES 2005-175) found that for 2003–04 employee data items, changes were made by 1.2 percent (77) of the institutions that responded. For all institutions making changes, the changes resulted in different employee counts. For both institutional and aggregate differences, however, the changes had little impact on the original employee count submissions. A large number of institutions reported different staff data to IPEDS and Thomson Peterson; however, the magnitude of the differences was small—usually no more than 17 faculty members for any faculty variable.

The Salaries section collected data for full-time instructional faculty (except those in medical schools in the EAP section, described above) on the institution's payroll as of November 1 of the collection year by contract length/teaching period, gender, and academic rank. The reporting of data by faculty status in the Salaries section was required from 4-year degree-granting institutions and above only. Salary outlays and fringe benefits were also collected for full-time instructional staff on 9/10- and 11/12-month contracts/teaching periods. This section was applicable to degree-granting institutions unless exempt.

Between 1966–67 and 1985–86, this survey differed from other HEGIS surveys in that imputations were not made for nonrespondents. Thus, there is some possibility that the salary averages presented in this report may differ from the results of a complete enumeration of all colleges and universities. Beginning with the surveys for 1987–88, the IPEDS data tabulation procedures included imputations for survey nonrespondents. The unweighted response rate for the 2008–09 Salaries survey section was 99.9 percent. The response rate for the 2009–10 Salaries section was 100.0 percent (4,453 of the 4,455 required institutions responded), and the response rate for 2010–11 was 99.9 percent (4,561 of the 4,565 required institutions responded). Imputation methods for the 2010–11 Salaries survey section are discussed in *Employees in Postsecondary Institutions, Fall 2010, and Salaries of Full-Time Instructional Staff, 2010–11* (NCES 2012-276).

Although data from this survey are not subject to sampling error, sources of nonsampling error may include computational errors and misclassification in reporting and processing. The electronic reporting system does allow corrections to prior-year reported or missing data, and this should help with these problems. Also, NCES reviews individual institutions' data for internal and longitudinal consistency and contacts institutions to check inconsistent data.

The *Integrated Postsecondary Education Data System Data Quality Study* (NCES 2005-175) found that only 1.3 percent of the responding Title IV institutions in 2003–04 made changes to their salaries data. The differences between the imputed data and the revised data were small and found to have little impact on the published data.

Further information on the Human Resources component may be obtained from

Imani Stutely
Administrative Data Division
Postsecondary Branch
National Center for Education Statistics
550 12th Street SW
Washington, DC 20202
imani.stutely@ed.gov
http://nces.ed.gov/ipeds

Library Statistics

In the past, NCES collected library data through the Public Libraries Survey (PLS), the State Library Agencies (StLA) Survey, the Academic Libraries Survey (ALS), and the Library Media Centers (LMC) Survey. On October 1, 2007, the administration of the Public Libraries Survey (PLS) and the State Library Agencies (StLA) Survey was transferred to the Institute of Museum and Library Services (IMLS) (see below).

NCES administered the Academic Libraries Survey (ALS) on a 3-year cycle between 1966 and 1988. From 1988 through 1999, ALS was a component of the Integrated Postsecondary Education Data System (IPEDS) and was on a 2-year cycle. Beginning in the year 2000, ALS began collecting data independent from the IPEDS data collection, but it remained on a 2-year cycle. ALS provided data on approximately 3,700 academic libraries. In aggregate, these data provided an overview of the status of academic libraries nationally and statewide. The survey collected data on the libraries in the entire universe of degree-granting institutions. Beginning with the collection of FY 2000 data, ALS changed to web-based data collection. ALS produced descriptive statistics on academic libraries in postsecondary institutions in the 50 states, the District of Columbia, and the outlying areas. *Academic Libraries: 2012* (NCES 2014-038) presented tabulations for the 2012 survey, the most recent administration of ALS for which data are available. Since 2014, ALS has been reintegrated back into the IPEDS collection as the Academic Libraries component and is collected annually.

School library data were collected on the School and Principal Surveys of the 1990–91 Schools and Staffing Survey (SASS). The School Library Media Centers (LMC) Survey became a component of SASS with the 1993–94 administration of the survey. Thus, readers should refer to the section on the Schools and Staffing Survey, below, regarding data on school libraries. Data for the 2011–12

LMC Survey are available on the NCES website at http://nces.ed.gov/surveys/sass/index.asp.

Further information on library statistics may be obtained from

Bao Le
Administrative Data Division
Postsecondary Branch
National Center for Education Statistics
550 12th Street SW
Washington, DC 20202
bao.le@ed.gov
http://nces.ed.gov/surveys/libraries

National Adult Literacy Survey

The National Adult Literacy Survey (NALS), funded by the U.S. Department of Education and 12 states, was created in 1992 as a new measure of literacy. The aim of the survey was to profile the English literacy of adults in the United States based on their performance across a wide array of tasks that reflect the types of materials and demands they encounter in their daily lives.

To gather information on adults' literacy skills, trained staff interviewed a nationally representative sample of nearly 13,600 individuals ages 16 and older during the first 8 months of 1992. These participants had been randomly selected to represent the adult population in the country as a whole. Black and Hispanic households were oversampled to ensure reliable estimates of literacy proficiencies and to permit analyses of the performance of these subpopulations. In addition, some 1,100 inmates from 80 federal and state prisons were interviewed to gather information on the proficiencies of the prison population. In total, nearly 26,000 adults were surveyed.

Each survey participant was asked to spend approximately an hour responding to a series of diverse literacy tasks, as well as to questions about his or her demographic characteristics, educational background, reading practices, and other areas related to literacy. Based on their responses to the survey tasks, adults received proficiency scores along three scales that reflect varying degrees of skill in prose, document, and quantitative literacy. The results of the 1992 survey were first published in *Adult Literacy in America: A First Look at the Findings of the National Adult Literacy Survey* (NCES 93-275), in September 1993. See the section on the National Assessment of Adult Literacy (below) for information on later adult literacy surveys.

Further information on NALS may be obtained from

Sheida White
Assessments Division
National Assessment Branch
National Center for Education Statistics
550 12th Street SW
Washington, DC 20202
sheida.white@ed.gov
http://nces.ed.gov/naal/nals_products.asp

National Assessment of Adult Literacy

The 2003 National Assessment of Adult Literacy (NAAL) was conducted to measure both English literacy and health literacy. The assessment was administered to 19,000 adults (including 1,200 prison inmates) age 16 and over in all 50 states and the District of Columbia. Components of the assessment included a background questionnaire; a prison component that assesses the literacy skills of adults in federal and state prisons; the State Assessment of Adult Literacy (SAAL), a voluntary survey given in conjunction with NAAL; a health literacy component; the Fluency Addition to NAAL (FAN), an oral reading assessment; and the Adult Literacy Supplemental Assessment (ALSA). ALSA is an alternative to the main NAAL for those with very low scores on seven core screening questions. NAAL assesses literacy directly through the completion of tasks that covered quantitative literacy, document literacy, and prose literacy. Results were reported using the following achievement levels: *Below Basic, Basic, Intermediate,* and *Proficient.*

Results from NAAL and NALS can be compared. NALS offers a snapshot of the condition of literacy of the U.S. population as a whole and among key population subgroups in 1992. NAAL provides an updated picture of adult literacy skills in 2003, revealing changes in literacy over the intervening decade.

Further information on NAAL may be obtained from

Sheida White
Assessments Division
National Assessment Branch
National Center for Education Statistics
550 12th Street SW
Washington, DC 20202
sheida.white@ed.gov
http://nces.ed.gov/naal

National Assessment of Educational Progress

The National Assessment of Educational Progress (NAEP) is a series of cross-sectional studies initially implemented in 1969 to assess the educational achievement of U.S. students and monitor changes in those achievements. In the main national NAEP, a nationally representative sample of students is assessed at grades 4, 8, and 12 in various academic subjects. The assessments are based on frameworks developed by the National Assessment Governing Board (NAGB). Assessment items include both multiple-choice and constructed-response (requiring written answers) items. Results are reported in two ways: by average score and by achievement level. Average scores are reported for the nation, for participating states and jurisdictions, and for subgroups of the population. Percentages of students performing at or above three achievement levels (*Basic, Proficient,* and *Advanced*) are also reported for these groups.

Main NAEP Assessments

From 1990 until 2001, main NAEP was conducted for states and other jurisdictions that chose to participate. In 2002, under the provisions of the No Child Left Behind Act of 2001, all states began to participate in main NAEP, and an aggregate of all state samples replaced the separate national sample. (School district-level assessments—under the Trial Urban District Assessment [TUDA] program—also began in 2002).

Results are available for the mathematics assessments administered in 2000, 2003, 2005, 2007, 2009, 2011, 2013, and 2015. In 2005, NAGB called for the development of a new mathematics framework. The revisions made to the mathematics framework for the 2005 assessment were intended to reflect recent curricular emphases and better assess the specific objectives for students at each grade level.

The revised mathematics framework focuses on two dimensions: mathematical content and cognitive demand. By considering these two dimensions for each item in the assessment, the framework ensures that NAEP assesses an appropriate balance of content, as well as a variety of ways of knowing and doing mathematics.

Since the 2005 changes to the mathematics framework were minimal for grades 4 and 8, comparisons over time can be made between assessments conducted before and after the framework's implementation for these grades. The changes that the 2005 framework made to the grade 12 assessment, however, were too drastic to allow grade 12 results from before and after implementation to be directly compared. These changes included adding more questions on algebra, data analysis, and probability to reflect changes in high school mathematics standards and coursework; merging the measurement and geometry content areas; and changing the reporting scale from 0–500 to 0–300. For more information regarding the 2005 mathematics framework revisions, see http://nces.ed.gov/nationsreportcard/mathematics/frameworkcomparison.asp.

Results are available for the reading assessments administered in 2000, 2002, 2003, 2005, 2007, 2009, 2011, 2013, and 2015. In 2009, a new framework was developed for the 4th-, 8th-, and 12th-grade NAEP reading assessments.

Both a content alignment study and a reading trend or bridge study were conducted to determine if the new assessment was comparable to the prior assessment. Overall, the results of the special analyses suggested that the assessments were similar in terms of their item and scale characteristics and the results they produced for important demographic groups of students. Thus, it was determined that the results of the 2009 reading assessment could still be compared to those from earlier assessment years, thereby maintaining the trend lines first established in 1992. For more information regarding the 2009 reading framework revisions, see http://nces.ed.gov/nationsreportcard/reading/whatmeasure.asp.

In spring 2013, NAEP released results from the NAEP 2012 economics assessment in *The Nation's Report Card: Economics 2012* (NCES 2013-453). First administered in 2006, the NAEP economics assessment measures 12th-graders' understanding of a wide range of topics in three main content areas:

market economy, national economy, and international economy. The 2012 assessment is based on a nationally representative sample of nearly 11,000 12th-graders.

In *The Nation's Report Card: A First Look—2013 Mathematics and Reading* (NCES 2014-451), NAEP released the results of the 2013 mathematics and reading assessments. Results can also be accessed using the interactive graphics and downloadable data available at the online Nation's Report Card website (http://nationsreportcard.gov/reading_math_2013/#/).

The Nation's Report Card: A First Look—2013 Mathematics and Reading Trial Urban District Assessment (NCES 2014-466) provides the results of the 2013 mathematics and reading TUDA, which measured the reading and mathematics progress of 4th- and 8th-graders from 21 urban school districts. Results from the 2013 mathematics and reading TUDA can also be accessed using the interactive graphics and downloadable data available at the online TUDA website (http://nationsreportcard.gov/reading_math_tuda_2013/#/).

The online interactive report *The Nation's Report Card: 2014 U.S. History, Geography, and Civics at Grade* 8 (NCES 2015-112) provides grade 8 results for the 2014 NAEP U.S. history, geography, and civics assessments. Trend results for previous assessment years in these three subjects, as well as information on school and student participation rates and sample tasks and student responses, are also presented. *The Nation's Report Card: 2015 Mathematics and Reading Assessments* (NCES 2015-136) is an online interactive report that presents national and state results for 4th- and 8th-graders on the NAEP 2015 mathematics and reading assessments. The report also presents TUDA results in mathematics and reading for 4th- and 8th-graders. The online interactive report *The Nation's Report Card: 2015 Mathematics and Reading at Grade 12* (NCES 2016-018) presents grade 12 results from the NAEP 2015 mathematics and reading assessments.

NAEP Long-Term Trend Assessments

In addition to conducting the main assessments, NAEP also conducts the long-term trend assessments. Long-term trend assessments provide an opportunity to observe educational progress in reading and mathematics of 9-, 13-, and 17-year-olds since the early 1970s. The long-term trend reading assessment measures students' reading comprehension skills using an array of passages that vary by text types and length. The assessment was designed to measure students' ability to locate specific information in the text provided; make inferences across a passage to provide an explanation; and identify the main idea in the text.

The NAEP long-term trend assessment in mathematics measures knowledge of mathematical facts; ability to carry out computations using paper and pencil; knowledge of basic formulas, such as those applied in geometric settings; and ability to apply mathematics to skills of daily life, such as those involving time and money.

The Nation's Report Card: Trends in Academic Progress 2012 (NCES 2013-456) provides the results of 12 long-term trend reading assessments dating back to 1971 and 11 long-term trend mathematics assessments dating back to 1973.

Further information on NAEP may be obtained from

Daniel McGrath
Assessments Division
Reporting and Dissemination Branch
National Center for Education Statistics
550 12th Street SW
Washington, DC 20202
daniel.mcgrath@ed.gov
http://nces.ed.gov/nationsreportcard

National Education Longitudinal Study of 1988

The National Education Longitudinal Study of 1988 (NELS:88) was the third major secondary school student longitudinal study conducted by NCES. The two studies that preceded NELS:88—the National Longitudinal Study of the High School Class of 1972 (NLS:72) and the High School and Beyond Longitudinal Study (HS&B) in 1980—surveyed high school seniors (and sophomores in HS&B) through high school, postsecondary education, and work and family formation experiences. Unlike its predecessors, NELS:88 began with a cohort of 8th-grade students. In 1988, some 25,000 8th-graders, their parents, their teachers, and their school principals were surveyed. Follow-ups were conducted in 1990 and 1992, when a majority of these students were in the 10th and 12th grades, respectively, and then 2 years after their scheduled high school graduation, in 1994. A fourth follow-up was conducted in 2000.

NELS:88 was designed to provide trend data about critical transitions experienced by young people as they develop, attend school, and embark on their careers. It complements and strengthens state and local efforts by furnishing new information on how school policies, teacher practices, and family involvement affect student educational outcomes (i.e., academic achievement, persistence in school, and participation in postsecondary education). For the base year, NELS:88 included a multifaceted student questionnaire, four cognitive tests, a parent questionnaire, a teacher questionnaire, and a school questionnaire.

In 1990, when most of the students were in 10th grade, students, school dropouts, their teachers, and their school principals were surveyed. (Parents were not surveyed in the 1990 follow-up.) In 1992, when most of the students were in 12th grade, the second follow-up conducted surveys of students, dropouts, parents, teachers, and school principals. Also, information from the students' transcripts was collected. The 1994 survey data were collected when most sample members had completed high school. The primary goals of the 1994 survey were (1) to provide data for trend comparisons with NLS:72 and HS&B; (2) to address issues of employment and postsecondary access and choice; and (3) to ascertain how many dropouts had returned to school and by what route. The 2000 follow-up examined the educational and labor market outcomes of the 1988 cohort at a time of transition. Most had been out of high school for 8 years; many had completed their post-secondary educations, were embarking on first or even second careers, and were starting families.

Further information on NELS:88 may be obtained from

Elise Christopher
Sample Surveys Division
Longitudinal Surveys Branch
National Center for Education Statistics
550 12th Street SW
Washington, DC 20202
elise.christopher@ed.gov
http://nces.ed.gov/surveys/nels88

National Household Education Surveys Program

The National Household Education Surveys Program (NHES) is a data collection system that is designed to address a wide range of education-related issues. Surveys have been conducted in 1991, 1993, 1995, 1996, 1999, 2001, 2003, 2005, 2007, and 2012. NHES targets specific populations for detailed data collection. It is intended to provide more detailed data on the topics and populations of interest than are collected through supplements to other household surveys.

The topics addressed by NHES:1991 were early childhood education and adult education. About 60,000 households were screened for NHES:1991. In the Early Childhood Education Survey, about 14,000 parents/guardians of 3- to 8-year-olds completed interviews about their children's early educational experiences. Included in this component were participation in nonparental care/education; care arrangements and school; and family, household, and child characteristics. In the NHES:1991 Adult Education Survey, about 9,800 people 16 years of age and older, identified as having participated in an adult education activity in the previous 12 months, were questioned about their activities. Data were collected on programs and up to four courses, including the subject matter, duration, sponsorship, purpose, and cost. Information on the household and the adult's background and current employment was also collected.

In NHES:1993, nearly 64,000 households were screened. Approximately 11,000 parents of 3- to 7-year-olds completed interviews for the School Readiness Survey. Topics included the developmental characteristics of preschoolers; school adjustment and teacher feedback to parents for kindergartners and primary students; center-based program participation; early school experiences; home activities with family members; and health status. In the School Safety and Discipline Survey, about 12,700 parents of children in grades 3 to 12 and about 6,500 youth in grades 6 to 12 were interviewed about their school experiences. Topics included the school learning environment, discipline policy, safety at school, victimization, the availability and use of alcohol/drugs, and alcohol/drug edu-

cation. Peer norms for behavior in school and substance use were also included in this topical component. Extensive family and household background information was collected, as well as characteristics of the school attended by the child.

In NHES:1995, the Early Childhood Program Participation Survey and the Adult Education Survey were similar to those fielded in 1991. In the Early Childhood component, about 14,000 parents of children from birth to 3rd grade were interviewed out of 16,000 sampled, for a completion rate of 90.4 percent. In the Adult Education Survey, about 24,000 adults were sampled and 82.3 percent (20,000) completed the interview.

NHES:1996 covered parent and family involvement in education and civic involvement. Data on homeschooling and school choice also were collected. The 1996 survey screened about 56,000 households. For the Parent and Family Involvement in Education Survey, nearly 21,000 parents of children in grades 3 to 12 were interviewed. For the Civic Involvement Survey, about 8,000 youth in grades 6 to 12, about 9,000 parents, and about 2,000 adults were interviewed. The 1996 survey also addressed public library use. Adults in almost 55,000 households were interviewed to support state-level estimates of household public library use.

NHES:1999 collected end-of-decade estimates of key indicators from the surveys conducted throughout the 1990s. Approximately 60,000 households were screened for a total of about 31,000 interviews with parents of children from birth through grade 12 (including about 6,900 infants, toddlers, and preschoolers) and adults age 16 or older not enrolled in grade 12 or below. Key indicators included participation of children in nonparental care and early childhood programs, school experiences, parent/family involvement in education at home and at school, youth community service activities, plans for future education, and adult participation in educational activities and community service.

NHES:2001 included two surveys that were largely repeats of similar surveys included in earlier NHES collections. The Early Childhood Program Participation Survey was similar in content to the Early Childhood Program Participation Survey fielded as part of NHES:1995, and the Adult Education and Lifelong Learning Survey was similar in content to the Adult Education Survey of NHES:1995. The Before- and After-School Programs and Activities Survey, while containing items fielded in earlier NHES collections, had a number of new items that collected information about what school-age children were doing during the time they spent in child care or in other activities, what parents were looking for in care arrangements and activities, and parent evaluations of care arrangements and activities. Parents of approximately 6,700 children from birth through age 6 who were not yet in kindergarten completed Early Childhood Program Participation Survey interviews. Nearly 10,900 adults completed Adult Education and Lifelong Learning Survey interviews, and parents of nearly 9,600 children in kindergarten through grade 8 completed Before- and After-School Programs and Activities Survey interviews.

NHES:2003 included two surveys: the Parent and Family Involvement in Education Survey and the Adult Education for Work-Related Reasons Survey (the first administration). Whereas previous adult education surveys were more general in scope, this survey had a narrower focus on occupation-related adult education programs. It collected in-depth information about training and education in which adults participated specifically for work-related reasons, either to prepare for work or a career or to maintain or improve work-related skills and knowledge they already had. The Parent and Family Involvement Survey expanded on the first survey fielded on this topic in 1996. In 2003, screeners were completed with 32,050 households. About 12,700 of the 16,000 sampled adults completed the Adult Education for Work-Related Reasons Survey, for a weighted response rate of 76 percent. For the Parent and Family Involvement in Education Survey, interviews were completed by the parents of about 12,400 of the 14,900 sampled children in kindergarten through grade 12, yielding a weighted unit response rate of 83 percent.

NHES:2005 included surveys that covered adult education, early childhood program participation, and after-school programs and activities. Data were collected from about 8,900 adults for the Adult Education Survey, from parents of about 7,200 children for the Early Childhood Program Participation Survey, and from parents of nearly 11,700 children for the After-School Programs and Activities Survey. These surveys were substantially similar to the surveys conducted in 2001, with the exceptions that the Adult Education Survey addressed a new topic—informal learning activities for personal interest—and the Early Childhood Program Participation Survey and After-School Programs and Activities Survey did not collect information about before-school care for school-age children.

NHES:2007 fielded the Parent and Family Involvement in Education Survey and the School Readiness Survey. These surveys were similar in design and content to surveys included in the 2003 and 1993 collections, respectively. New features added to the Parent and Family Involvement Survey were questions about supplemental education services provided by schools and school districts (including use of and satisfaction with such services), as well as questions that would efficiently identify the school attended by the sampled students. New features added to the School Readiness Survey were questions that collected details about TV programs watched by the sampled children. For the Parent and Family Involvement Survey, interviews were completed with parents of 10,680 sampled children in kindergarten through grade 12, including 10,370 students enrolled in public or private schools and 310 homeschooled children. For the School Readiness Survey, interviews were completed with parents of 2,630 sampled children ages 3 to 6 and not yet in kindergarten. Parents who were interviewed about children in kindergarten through 2nd grade for the Parent and Family Involvement Survey were also asked some questions about these children's school readiness.

The 2007 and earlier administrations of NHES used a random-digit-dial sample of landline phones and computer-assisted telephone interviewing to conduct interviews. However, due to declining response rates for all telephone surveys and the increase in households that only or mostly use a cell phone instead of a landline, the data collection method was changed to an address-based sample survey for NHES:2012. Because of this change in survey mode, readers should use caution when comparing NHES:2012 estimates to those of prior NHES administrations.

NHES:2012 included the Parent and Family Involvement in Education Survey and the Early Childhood Program Participation Survey. The Parent and Family Involvement in Education Survey gathered data on students who were enrolled in kindergarten through grade 12 or who were homeschooled at equivalent grade levels. Survey questions that pertained to students enrolled in kindergarten through grade 12 requested information on various aspects of parent involvement in education (such as help with homework, family activities, and parent involvement at school) and survey questions pertaining to homeschooled students requested information on the student's homeschooling experiences, the sources of the curriculum, and the reasons for homeschooling.

The 2012 Parent and Family Involvement in Education Survey questionnaires were completed for 17,563 (397 homeschooled and 17,166 enrolled) children, for a weighted unit response rate of 78.4 percent. The overall estimated unit response rate (the product of the screener unit response rate of 73.8 percent and the Parent and Family Involvement in Education Survey unit response rate) was 57.8 percent.

The 2012 Early Childhood Program Participation Survey collected data on the early care and education arrangements and early learning of children from birth through the age of 5 who were not yet enrolled in kindergarten. Questionnaires were completed for 7,893 children, for a weighted unit response rate of 78.7 percent. The overall estimated weighted unit response rate (the product of the screener weighted unit response rate of 73.8 percent and the Early Childhood Program Participation Survey unit weighted response rate) was 58.1 percent.

Data for the 2012 NHES Parent and Family Involvement in Education Survey are available in the First Look report, *Parent and Family Involvement in Education, From the National Household Education Surveys Program of 2012* (NCES 2013-028). Data for the 2012 NHES Early Childhood Program Participation Survey are available in the First Look report *Early Childhood Program Participation, From the National Household Education Surveys Program of 2012* (NCES 2013-029).

Further information on NHES may be obtained from

Andrew Zukerberg
Gail Mulligan
Sample Surveys Division
National Center for Education Statistics
550 12th Street SW
Washington, DC 20202
andrew.zukerberg@ed.gov
gail.mulligan@ed.gov
http://nces.ed.gov/nhes

National Longitudinal Study of the High School Class of 1972

The National Longitudinal Study of the High School Class of 1972 (NLS:72) began with the collection of base-year survey data from a sample of about 19,000 high school seniors in the spring of 1972. Five follow-up surveys of these students were conducted in 1973, 1974, 1976, 1979, and 1986. NLS:72 was designed to provide the education community with information on the transitions of young adults from high school through postsecondary education and the workplace.

In addition to the follow-ups, a number of supplemental data collection efforts were made. For example, a Postsecondary Education Transcript Study (PETS) was conducted in 1984; in 1986, the fifth follow-up included a supplement for those who became teachers.

The sample design for NLS:72 was a stratified, two-stage probability sample of 12th-grade students from all schools, public and private, in the 50 states and the District of Columbia during the 1971–72 school year. During the first stage of sampling, about 1,070 schools were selected for participation in the base-year survey. As many as 18 students were selected at random from each of the sample schools. The sizes of both the school and student samples were increased during the first follow-up survey. Beginning with the first follow-up and continuing through the fourth follow-up, about 1,300 schools participated in the survey and slightly fewer than 23,500 students were sampled. The unweighted response rates for each of the different rounds of data collection were 80 percent or higher.

Sample retention rates across the survey years were quite high. For example, of the individuals responding to the base-year questionnaire, the percentages who responded to the first, second, third, and fourth follow-up questionnaires were about 94, 93, 89, and 83 percent, respectively. The fifth follow-up took its sample from students who had participated in at least one of the prior surveys. In all, 91.7 percent of participants had responded to at least five of the six surveys, and 62.1 percent had responded to all six.

Further information on NLS:72 may be obtained from

Aurora D'Amico
Sample Surveys Division
Longitudinal Surveys Branch
National Center for Education Statistics
550 12th Street SW
Washington, DC 20202
aurora.damico@ed.gov
http://nces.ed.gov/surveys/nls72

National Postsecondary Student Aid Study

The National Postsecondary Student Aid Study (NPSAS) is a comprehensive nationwide study of how students and their families pay for postsecondary education. Data gathered from the study are used to help guide future federal student financial aid policy. The study covers nationally representative samples of undergraduates, graduates, and first-professional students in the 50 states, the District of Columbia, and Puerto Rico, including students attending less-than-2-year institutions, community colleges, and 4-year colleges and universities. Participants include students who do not receive aid and those who do receive financial aid. Since NPSAS identifies nationally representative samples of student subpopulations of interest to policymakers and obtains baseline data for longitudinal study of these subpopulations, data from the study provide the base-year sample for the Beginning Postsecondary Students (BPS) longitudinal study and the Baccalaureate and Beyond (B&B) longitudinal study.

Originally, NPSAS was conducted every 3 years. Beginning with the 1999–2000 study (NPSAS:2000), NPSAS has been conducted every 4 years. NPSAS:08 included a new set of instrument items to obtain baseline measures of the awareness of two new federal grants introduced in 2006: the Academic Competitiveness Grant (ACG) and the National Science and Mathematics Access to Retain Talent (SMART) grant.

The first NPSAS (NPSAS:87) was conducted during the 1986–87 school year. Data were gathered from about 1,100 colleges, universities, and other postsecondary institutions; 60,000 students; and 14,000 parents. These data provided information on the cost of postsecondary education, the distribution of financial aid, and the characteristics of both aided and nonaided students and their families.

For NPSAS:93, information on 77,000 undergraduates and graduate students enrolled during the school year was collected at 1,000 postsecondary institutions. The sample included students who were enrolled at any time between July 1, 1992, and June 30, 1993. About 66,000 students and a subsample of their parents were interviewed by telephone. NPSAS:96 contained information on more than 48,000 undergraduate and graduate students from about 1,000 postsecondary institutions who were enrolled at any time during the 1995–96 school year. NPSAS:2000 included nearly 62,000 students (50,000 undergraduates and almost 12,000 graduate students) from 1,000 postsecondary institutions. NPSAS:04 collected data on about 80,000 undergraduates and 11,000 graduate students from 1,400 postsecondary institutions. For NPSAS:08, about 114,000 undergraduate students and 14,000 graduate students who were enrolled in postsecondary education during the 2007–08 school year were selected from more than 1,730 postsecondary institutions.

NPSAS:12 sampled about 95,000 undergraduates and 16,000 graduate students from approximately 1,500 postsecondary institutions. Public access to the data is available online through PowerStats (http://nces.ed.gov/datalab/).

Further information on NPSAS may be obtained from

Aurora D'Amico
Tracy Hunt-White
Sample Surveys Division
Longitudinal Surveys Branch
National Center for Education Statistics
550 12th Street SW
Washington, DC 20202
aurora.damico@ed.gov
tracy.hunt-white@ed.gov
http://nces.ed.gov/npsas

National Study of Postsecondary Faculty

The National Study of Postsecondary Faculty (NSOPF) was designed to provide data about faculty to postsecondary researchers, planners, and policymakers. NSOPF is the most comprehensive study of faculty in postsecondary education institutions ever undertaken.

The first cycle of NSOPF (NSOPF:88) was conducted by NCES with support from the National Endowment for the Humanities (NEH) in 1987–88 with a sample of 480 colleges and universities, over 3,000 department chairpersons, and over 11,000 instructional faculty. The second cycle of NSOPF (NSOPF:93) was conducted by NCES with support from NEH and the National Science Foundation in 1992–93. NSOPF:93 was limited to surveys of institutions and faculty, but with a substantially expanded sample of 970 colleges and universities and 31,350 faculty and instructional staff. The third cycle, NSPOF:99, included 960 degree-granting postsecondary institutions and approximately 18,000 faculty and instructional staff. The fourth cycle of NSOPF was conducted in 2003–04 and included 1,080 degree-granting postsecondary institutions and approximately 26,000 faculty and instructional staff.

There are no plans to repeat the study. Rather, NCES plans to provide technical assistance to state postsecondary data systems and to encourage the development of robust connections between faculty and student data systems so that key questions concerning faculty, instruction, and student outcomes—such as persistence and completion—can be addressed.

Further information on NSOPF may be obtained from

Aurora D'Amico
Sample Surveys Division
Longitudinal Surveys Branch
National Center for Education Statistics
550 12th Street SW
Washington, DC 20202
aurora.damico@ed.gov
http://nces.ed.gov/surveys/nsopf

Principal Follow-up Survey

The Principal Follow-up Survey (PFS) is a component of the 2011–12 Schools and Staffing Survey (SASS). The 2012–13 PFS was administered in order to provide attrition rates for principals in K–12 public and private schools. The goal was to assess how many of those who worked as a principal in the 2011–12 school year still worked as a principal in the same school in the 2012–13 school year, how many had moved to become a principal in another school, and how many no longer worked as a principal. The PFS sample included all schools whose principals had completed SASS principal questionnaires. Schools that had returned a completed 2011–12 SASS principal questionnaire were mailed the PFS form in March 2013.

Further information on the PFS may be obtained from

Isaiah O'Rear
Sample Surveys Division
Cross-Sectional Surveys Branch
National Center for Education Statistics
550 12th Street SW
Washington, DC 20202
isaiah.orear@ed.gov
http://nces.ed.gov/surveys/sass/

Private School Universe Survey

The purposes of the Private School Universe Survey (PSS) data collection activities are (1) to build an accurate and complete list of private schools to serve as a sampling frame for NCES sample surveys of private schools and (2) to report data on the total number of private schools, teachers, and students in the survey universe. Begun in 1989, the PSS has been conducted every 2 years, and data for the 1989–90, 1991–92, 1993–94, 1995–96, 1997–98, 1999–2000, 2001–02, 2003–04, 2005–06, 2007–08, 2009–10, 2011–12, and 2013–14 school years have been released. A *First Look* report on the 2011–12 PSS data, *Characteristics of Private Schools in the United States: Results From the 2011–12 Private School Universe Survey* (NCES 2013-316) was published in July 2013.

The PSS produces data similar to that of the Common Core of Data for public schools, and can be used for public-private comparisons. The data are useful for a variety of policy- and research-relevant issues, such as the growth of religiously affiliated schools, the number of private high school graduates, the length of the school year for various private schools, and the number of private school students and teachers.

The target population for this universe survey is all private schools in the United States that meet the PSS criteria of a private school (i.e., the private school is an institution that provides instruction for any of grades K through 12, has one or more teachers to give instruction, is not administered by a public agency, and is not operated in a private home).

The survey universe is composed of schools identified from a variety of sources. The main source is a list frame initially developed for the 1989–90 PSS. The list is updated regularly by matching it with lists provided by nationwide private school associations, state departments of education, and other national guides and sources that list private schools. The other source is an area frame search in approximately 124 geographic areas, conducted by the U.S. Census Bureau.

Of the 40,302 schools included in the 2009–10 sample, 10,229 were found ineligible for the survey. Those not responding numbered 1,856, and those responding numbered 28,217. The unweighted response rate for the 2009–10 PSS survey was 93.8 percent.

Of the 39,325 schools included in the 2011–12 sample, 10,030 cases were considered as out-of-scope (not eligible for the PSS). A total of 26,983 private schools completed a PSS interview (15.8 percent completed online), while 2,312 schools refused to participate, resulting in an unweighted response rate of 92.1 percent.

Further information on the PSS may be obtained from

Steve Broughman
Sample Surveys Division
Cross-Sectional Surveys Branch
National Center for Education Statistics
550 12th Street SW
Washington, DC 20202
stephen.broughman@ed.gov
http://nces.ed.gov/surveys/pss

Projections of Education Statistics

Since 1964, NCES has published projections of key statistics for elementary and secondary schools and higher education institutions. The latest report is titled *Projections of Education Statistics to 2024* (NCES 2016-013). The *Projections of Education Statistics* series uses projection models for elementary and secondary enrollment, high school graduates, elementary and secondary teachers, expenditures for public elementary and secondary education, enrollment in postsecondary degree-granting institutions, and postsecondary degrees conferred to develop national and state projections. These models are described more fully in the report's appendix on projection methodology.

Differences between the reported and projected values are, of course, almost inevitable. An evaluation of past projections revealed that, at the elementary and secondary level, projections of enrollments have been quite accurate: mean absolute percentage differences for enrollment ranged from 0.3 to 1.3 percent for projections from 1 to 5 years in the future, while those for teachers were less than 3 percent. At the higher education level, projections of enrollment have been fairly accurate: mean absolute percentage differences were 5 percent or less for projections from 1 to 5 years into the future.

Further information on *Projections of Education Statistics* may be obtained from

William Hussar
Annual Reports and Information Staff
National Center for Education Statistics
550 12th Street SW
Washington, DC 20202
william.hussar@ed.gov
http://nces.ed.gov/pubsearch/pubsinfo.asp?pubid=2016013

Recent College Graduates Study

Between 1976 and 1991, NCES conducted periodic surveys of baccalaureate and master's degree recipients 1 year after graduation with the Recent College Graduates (RCG) Study. The RCG Study—which has been replaced by the Baccalaure-ate and Beyond Longitudinal Study (B&B) (see listing above)—concentrated on those graduates entering the teaching profession. The study linked respondents' major field of study with outcomes such as whether the respondent entered the labor force or was seeking additional education. Labor force data collected included employment status (unemployed, employed part time, or employed full time), occupation, salary, career potential, relation to major field of study, and need for a college degree. To obtain accurate results on teachers, NCES oversampled graduates with a major in education. The last two studies oversampled education majors and increased the sampling of graduates with majors in other fields.

For each of the selected institutions, a list of graduates by major field of study was obtained, and a sample of graduates was drawn by major field of study. Graduates in certain major fields of study (e.g., education, mathematics, and physical sciences) were sampled at higher rates than were graduates in other fields. Roughly 1 year after graduation, the sample of graduates was located, contacted by mail or telephone, and asked to respond to the questionnaire.

The locating process was more detailed than that in most surveys. Nonresponse rates were directly related to the time, effort, and resources used in locating graduates, rather than to graduates' refusals to participate. Despite the difficulties in locating graduates, RCG response rates are comparable to studies that do not face problems locating their sample membership.

The 1976 study of 1974–75 college graduates was the first, and smallest, of the series. The sample consisted of about 210 institutions, of which 200 (96 percent) responded. Of the approximately 5,850 graduates in the sample, 4,350 responded, for a response rate of 79 percent.

The 1981 study was somewhat larger than the 1976 study, covering about 300 institutions and 15,850 graduates. Responses were obtained from 280 institutions, for an institutional response rate of 95 percent, and from 9,310 graduates (about 720 others were found not to meet eligibility requirements), for a response rate of 74 percent.

The 1985 study sampled about 400 colleges and 18,740 graduates, of whom 17,850 were found to be eligible. Responses were obtained from 13,200 graduates, for a response rate of 78 percent. The response rate for colleges was 98 percent. The 1987 study sampled 21,960 graduates. Responses were received from 16,880, for a response rate of nearly 80 percent.

The 1991 study sampled about 18,140 graduates of 400 bachelor's and master's degree-granting institutions, including 16,170 bachelor's degree recipients and 1,960 master's degree recipients receiving diplomas between July 1, 1989, and June 30, 1990. Random samples of graduates were selected from lists stratified by field of study. Graduates in education, mathematics, and the physical sciences were sampled at a higher rate, as were graduates of various racial/ethnic groups, to provide a sufficient number of these graduates for analysis purposes. The graduates included in the sample were selected in proportion to the institution's number of graduates. The unweighted institutional response rate was 95 percent, and the unweighted graduate response rate was 83 percent.

Further information on the RCG Study may be obtained from

Aurora D'Amico
Sample Surveys Division
Longitudinal Surveys Branch
National Center for Education Statistics
550 12th Street SW
Washington, DC 20202
aurora.damico@ed.gov
http://nces.ed.gov/surveys/b&b

School Survey on Crime and Safety

The most recent School Survey on Crime and Safety (SSOCS) was conducted by NCES in spring/summer of the 2009–10 school year. SSOCS focuses on incidents of specific crimes/offenses and a variety of specific discipline issues in public schools. It also covers characteristics of school policies, school violence prevention programs and policies, and school characteristics that have been associated with school crime. The survey was conducted with a nationally representative sample of regular public elementary, middle, and high schools in the 50 states and the District of Columbia. Special education, alternative, and vocational schools; schools in the other jurisdictions; and schools that taught only prekindergarten, kindergarten, or adult education were not included in the sample.

The sampling frame for the 2010 SSOCS was constructed from the 2007–08 Public Elementary/Secondary School Universe File of the Common Core of Data, an annual collection of data on all public K–12 schools and school districts. The sample was stratified by instructional level, type of locale (urbanicity), and enrollment size. The sample of schools in each instructional level was allocated to each of the 16 cells formed by the cross-classification of the four categories of enrollment size and four types of locale. The sample was allocated to each subgroup in proportion to the sum of the square roots of the total student enrollment in each school in that stratum. The effective sample size within each stratum was then inflated to account for nonresponse. Once the final sample sizes were determined for each of the 64 strata, the subgroups were sorted by region and racial/ethnic composition of enrollment, and an initial sample of 3,476 schools was selected. Of those schools, 2,648 completed the survey. In February 2010, questionnaires were mailed to school principals, who were asked to complete the survey or to have it completed by the person at the school most knowledgeable about discipline issues.

Further information about SSOCS may be obtained from

Rachel Hansen
Sample Surveys Division
Cross-Sectional Surveys Branch
National Center for Education Statistics
550 12th Street SW
Washington, DC 20202
rachel.hansen@ed.gov
http://nces.ed.gov/surveys/ssocs

Schools and Staffing Survey

The Schools and Staffing Survey (SASS) is a set of related questionnaires that collect descriptive data on the context of public and private elementary and secondary education. Data reported by districts, schools, principals, and teachers provide a variety of statistics on the condition of education in the United States that may be used by policymakers and the general public. The SASS system covers a wide range of topics, including teacher demand, teacher and principal characteristics, teachers' and principals' perceptions of school climate and problems in their schools, teacher and principal compensation, district hiring and retention practices, general conditions in schools, and basic characteristics of the student population.

SASS data are collected through a mail questionnaire with telephone and in-person field follow-up. SASS has been conducted by the Census Bureau for NCES since the first administration of the survey, which was conducted during the 1987–88 school year. Subsequent SASS administrations were conducted in 1990–91, 1993–94, 1999–2000, 2003–04, 2007–08, and 2011–12.

SASS is designed to produce national, regional, and state estimates for public elementary and secondary schools, school districts, principals, teachers, and school library media centers and national and regional estimates for public charter schools, as well as principals, teachers, and school library media centers within these schools. For private schools, the sample supports national, regional, and affiliation estimates for schools, principals, and teachers.

From its inception, SASS has had four core components: school questionnaires, teacher questionnaires, principal questionnaires, and school district (prior to 1999–2000, "teacher demand and shortage") questionnaires. A fifth component, school library media center questionnaires, was introduced in the 1993–94 administration and has been included in every subsequent administration of SASS. School library data were also collected in the 1990–91 administration of the survey through the school and principal questionnaires.

School questionnaires used in SASS include the Public and Private School Questionnaires; teacher questionnaires include the Public and Private School Teacher Questionnaires; principal questionnaires include the Public and Private School Principal (or School Administrator) Questionnaires; and school district questionnaires include the School District (or Teacher Demand and Shortage) Questionnaires.

Although the four core questionnaires and the school library media questionnaires have remained relatively stable over the various administrations of SASS, the survey has changed to accommodate emerging issues in elementary and secondary education. Some questionnaire items have been added, some have been deleted, and some have been reworded.

During the 1990–91 SASS cycle, NCES worked with the Office of Indian Education to add an Indian School Questionnaire to SASS, and it remained a part of SASS through 2007–08. The Indian School Questionnaire explores the same school-level issues that the Public and Private School Questionnaires explore, allowing comparisons among the three types of schools. The 1990–91, 1993–94, 1999–2000, 2003–04, and 2007–08 administrations of SASS obtained data on Bureau of Indian Education (BIE) schools (schools funded or operated by the BIE), but the 2011–12 administration did not obtain BIE data. SASS estimates for all survey years presented in this report exclude BIE schools, and as a result, estimates in this report may differ from those in previously published reports.

School library media center questionnaires were administered in public, private, and BIE schools as part of the 1993–94 and 1999–2000 SASS. During the 2003–04 administration of SASS, only library media centers in public schools were surveyed, and in 2007–08 only library media centers in public schools and BIE and BIE-funded schools were surveyed. The 2011–12 survey collected data only on school library media centers in traditional public schools and in public charter schools. School library questions focused on facilities, services and policies, staffing, technology, information literacy, collections and expenditures, and media equipment. New or revised topics included access to online licensed databases, resource availability, and additional elements on information literacy. The Student Records and Library Media Specialist/Librarian Questionnaires were administered only in 1993–94.

As part of the 1999–2000 SASS, the Charter School Questionnaire was sent to the universe of charter schools in operation in 1998–99. In 2003–04 and in subsequent administrations of SASS, there was no separate questionnaire for charter schools—charter schools were included in the public school sample instead. Another change in the 2003–04 administration of SASS was a revised data collection procedure using a primary in-person contact within the school intended to reduce the field follow-up phase.

The SASS teacher surveys collect information on the characteristics of teachers, such as their age, race/ethnicity, years of teaching experience, average number of hours per week spent on teaching activities, base salary, average class size, and highest degree earned. These teacher-reported data may be combined with related information on their school's characteristics, such as school type (e.g., public traditional, public charter, Catholic, private other religious, and private nonsectarian), community type, and school enrollment size. The teacher questionnaires also ask for information on teacher opinions regarding the school and teaching environment. In 1993–94, about 53,000 public school teachers and 10,400 private school teachers were sampled. In 1999–2000, about 56,300 public school teachers, 4,400 public charter school teachers, and 10,800 private school teachers were sampled. In 2003–04, about 52,500 public school teachers and 10,000 private school teachers were sampled. In 2007–08, about 48,400 public school teachers and 8,200 private school teachers were sampled. In 2011–12, about 51,100 public school teachers and 7,100 private school teachers were sampled. Weighted overall response rates in 2011–12 were 61.8 percent for public school teachers and 50.1 percent for private school teachers.

The SASS principal surveys focus on such topics as age, race/ethnicity, sex, average annual salary, years of experience, highest degree attained, perceived influence on decisions made at the school, and hours spent per week on all school activities. These data on principals can be placed in the context of other SASS data, such as the type of the principal's school (e.g., public traditional, public charter, Catholic, other religious, or nonsectarian), enrollment, and percentage of students eligible for free or reduced price lunch. In 2003–04, about 10,200 public school principals were sampled, and in 2007–08, about 9,800 public school principals were sampled. In 2011–12, about 11,000 school principals and 3,000 private school principals were sampled. Weighted response rates in 2011–12 for public school principals and private school principals were 72.7 percent and 64.7 percent, respectively.

The SASS 2011–12 sample of schools was confined to the 50 states and the District of Columbia and excludes the other jurisdictions, the Department of Defense overseas schools, the BIE schools, and schools that do not offer teacher-provided classroom instruction in grades 1–12 or the ungraded equivalent. The SASS 2011–12 sample included 10,250 traditional public schools, 750 public charter schools, and 3,000 private schools.

The public school sample for the 2011–12 SASS was based on an adjusted public school universe file from the 2009–10 Common Core of Data, a database of all the nation's public school districts and public schools. The private school sample for the 2011–12 SASS was selected from the 2009–10 Private School Universe Survey (PSS), as updated for the 2011–12 PSS. This update collected membership lists from private school associations and religious denominations, as well as private school lists from state education departments. The 2011–12 SASS private school frame was further augmented by the inclusion of additional schools that were identified through the 2009–10 PSS area frame data collection.

The NCES data product *2011–12 Schools and Staffing Survey (SASS) Restricted-Use Data Files* (NCES 2014-356) is available. (Information on how to obtain a restricted-use data license is located at http://nces.ed.gov/pubsearch/licenses.asp.) This DVD contains eight files (Public School District, Public School Principal, Public School, Public School Teacher, Public School Library Media Center, Private School Principal, Private School, and Private School Teacher) in multiple formats. It also contains a six-volume User's Manual, which includes a codebook for each file.

Further information on SASS may be obtained from

Amy Ho
Sample Surveys Division
Cross-Sectional Surveys Branch
National Center for Education Statistics
550 12th Street SW
Washington, DC 20202
amy.ho@ed.gov
http://nces.ed.gov/surveys/sass

Teacher Follow-up Survey

The Teacher Follow-up Survey (TFS) is a follow-up survey of selected elementary and secondary school teachers who participate in the NCES Schools and Staffing Survey (SASS). Its purpose is to determine how many teachers remain at the same school, move to another school, or leave the profession in the year following a SASS administration. It is administered to elementary and secondary teachers in the 50 states and the District of Columbia. The TFS uses two questionnaires, one for teachers who left teaching since the previous SASS administration and another for those who are still teaching either in the same school as last year or in a different school. The objective of the TFS is to focus on the characteristics of each group in order to answer questions about teacher mobility and attrition.

The 2008–09 TFS is different from any previous TFS administration in that it also serves as the second wave of a longitudinal study of first-year teachers. Because of this, the 2008–09 TFS consists of four questionnaires. Two are for respondents who were first-year public school teachers in the 2007–08 SASS and two are for the remainder of the sample.

The 2012–13 TFS sample was made up of teachers who had taken the 2011–12 SASS survey. The 2012–13 TFS sample contained about 5,800 public school teachers and 1,200 private school teachers. The weighted overall response rate using the initial basic weight for private school teachers was notably low (39.7 percent), resulting in a decision to exclude private school teachers from the 2012–13 TFS data files. The weighted overall response rate for public school teachers was 49.9 percent (50.3 percent for current and 45.6 percent for former teachers). Further information about the 2012–13 TFS, including the analysis of unit nonresponse bias, is available in the First Look report *Teacher Attrition and Mobility: Results From the 2012–13 Teacher Follow-up Survey* (NCES 2014-077).

Further information on the TFS may be obtained from

Isaiah O'Rear
Sample Surveys Division
Cross-Sectional Surveys Branch
National Center for Education Statistics
550 12th Street SW
Washington, DC 20202
isaiah.orear@ed.gov
http://nces.ed.gov/surveys/sass/

Other Department of Education Agencies

National Center for Special Education Research

The National Center for Special Education Research (NCSER) was created as part of the reauthorization of the Individuals with Disabilities Education Act (IDEA). NCSER sponsors a program of special education research designed to expand the knowledge and understanding of infants, toddlers, and children with disabilities. NCSER funds programs of research that address its mission. In order to determine which programs work, as well as how, why, and in what settings they work, NCSER sponsors research on the needs of infants, toddlers, and children with disabilities and evaluates the effectiveness of services provided through IDEA.

Further information on NCSER may be obtained from

Joan McLaughlin
Commissioner
National Center for Special Education Research
550 12th Street SW
Washington, DC 20202
joan.mclaughlin@ed.gov
http://ies.ed.gov/ncser/help/webmail/

The National Longitudinal Transition Study-2

Funded by NCSER, the National Longitudinal Transition Study-2 (NLTS-2) was a follow-up of the original National Longitudinal Transition Study conducted from 1985 through 1993. NLTS-2 began in 2001 with a sample of students who received special education services, were ages 13 through 16, and were in at least 7th grade on December 1, 2000. The study was designed to provide a national picture of these youths' experiences and achievements as they transition into adulthood. Data were collected from parents, youth, and schools by survey, telephone interviews, student assessments, and transcripts.

NLTS-2 was designed to align with the original NLTS by including many of the same questions and data items, thus allowing comparisons between the NLTS and NLTS-2 youths' experiences. NLTS-2 also included items that have been collected in other national databases to permit comparisons between NLTS-2 youth and the general youth population. Information was collected over five waves, beginning in 2001 and ending in 2009.

Further information on NLTS-2 may be obtained from

Jacquelyn Buckley
Office of the Commissioner
National Center for Special Education Research
555 New Jersey Avenue NW
Washington, DC 20208
jacquelyn.buckley@ed.gov
http://www.nlts2.org/

Office for Civil Rights

Civil Rights Data Collection

The U.S. Department of Education's Office for Civil Rights (OCR) has surveyed the nation's public elementary and secondary schools since 1968. The survey was first known as the OCR Elementary and Secondary School (E&S) Survey; in 2004, it was renamed the Civil Rights Data Collection (CRDC). The survey provides information about the enrollment of students in public schools in every state and about some education services provided to those students. These data are reported by race/ethnicity, sex, and disability.

Data in the survey are collected pursuant to 34 C.F.R. Section 100.6(b) of the Department of Education regulation implementing Title VI of the Civil Rights Act of 1964. The requirements are also incorporated by reference in Department regulations implementing Title IX of the Education Amendments of 1972, Section 504 of the Rehabilitation Act of 1973, and the Age Discrimination Act of 1975. School, district, state, and national data are currently available. Data from individual public schools and districts are used to generate national and state data.

The CRDC has generally been conducted biennially in each of the 50 states plus the District of Columbia. The 2009–10 CRDC was collected from a sample of approximately 7,000 school districts and over 72,000 schools in those districts. It was made up of two parts: part 1 contained beginning-of-year "snapshot" data and part 2 contained cumulative, or end-of-year, data.

The 2011–12 CRDC survey, which collected data from approximately 16,500 school districts and 97,000 schools, was the first CRDC survey since 2000 that included data from every public school district and school in the nation. The 2013–14 CRDC survey also collected information from a universe of every public school district and school in the nation.

Further information on the Civil Rights Data Collection may be obtained from

Office for Civil Rights
U.S. Department of Education
400 Maryland Avenue SW
Washington, DC 20202
OCR@ed.gov
http://www.ed.gov/about/offices/list/ocr/data.html

Office of Federal Student Aid

Cohort Default Rate Database

A school's cohort default rate is the percentage of the school's borrowers who enter repayment on certain Federal Family Education Loan (FFEL) program or William D. Ford Federal Direct Loan (Direct Loan) program loans during a particular federal fiscal year and default within the cohort default period. The 2-year cohort default period is the period that begins on October 1 of the fiscal year when the borrower enters repayment and ends on September 30 of the following fiscal year. The 3-year cohort default period is the period that begins on October 1 of the fiscal year when the borrower enters repayment and ends on September 30 of second fiscal year following the fiscal year in which the borrower entered repayment.

The Office of Federal Student Aid's cohort default rate database can be accessed at https://www.nslds.ed.gov/nslds/nslds_SA/defaultmanagement/search_cohort_3yrCY_2012.cfm.

Further information about cohort default rates produced by the Office of Federal Student Aid may be obtained from

http://www2.ed.gov/offices/OSFAP/defaultmanagement/schooltyperates.pdf

http://www2.ed.gov/offices/OSFAP/defaultmanagement/cdr.html

http://ifap.ed.gov/DefaultManagement/CDRGuideMaster.html

Office of Special Education Programs

Annual Report to Congress on the Implementation of the Individuals with Disabilities Education Act

The Individuals with Disabilities Education Act (IDEA) is a law ensuring services to children with disabilities throughout the nation. IDEA governs how states and public agencies provide early intervention, special education, and related services to more than 6.5 million eligible infants, toddlers, children, and youth with disabilities.

IDEA, formerly the Education of the Handicapped Act (EHA), requires the Secretary of Education to transmit to Congress annually a report describing the progress made in serving the nation's children with disabilities. This annual report contains information on children served by public schools under the provisions of Part B of IDEA and on children served in state-operated programs for persons with disabilities under Chapter I of the Elementary and Secondary Education Act.

Statistics on children receiving special education and related services in various settings and school personnel providing such services are reported in an annual submission of data to the Office of Special Education Programs (OSEP) by the 50 states, the District of Columbia, the Bureau of Indian Education schools, Puerto Rico, American Samoa, Guam, the Northern Mariana Islands, the U.S. Virgin Islands, the Federated States of Micronesia, Palau, and the Marshall Islands. The child count information is based on the number of children with disabilities receiving special education and related services on December 1 of each year. Count information is available from http://www.ideadata.org.

Since all participants in programs for persons with disabilities are reported to OSEP, the data are not subject to sampling error. However, nonsampling error can arise from a variety of sources. Some states only produce counts of students receiving special education services by disability category because Part B of IDEA requires it. In those states that typically produce counts of students receiving special education services by disability category without regard to IDEA requirements, definitions and labeling practices vary.

Further information on this annual report to Congress may be obtained from

Office of Special Education Programs
Office of Special Education and Rehabilitative Services
U.S. Department of Education
400 Maryland Avenue SW
Washington, DC 20202-7100
http://www.ed.gov/about/reports/annual/osep/index.html
http://idea.ed.gov/
http://www.ideadata.org

Office of Career, Technical, and Adult Education, Division of Adult Education and Literacy

Enrollment Data for State-Administered Adult Education Programs

The Division of Adult Education and Literacy (DAEL) promotes programs that help American adults get the basic skills they need to be productive workers, family members, and citizens. The major areas of support are Adult Basic Education, Adult Secondary Education, and English Language Acquisition. These programs emphasize basic skills such as reading, writing, math, English language competency, and problem solving. Each year, DAEL reports enrollment numbers in state-administered adult education programs for these major areas of support for all 50 states, the District of Columbia, American Samoa, the Federated States of Micronesia, Guam, the Marshall Islands, the Northern Mariana Islands, Palau, Puerto Rico, and the U.S. Virgin Islands.

Further information on DAEL may be obtained from

Office of Career, Technical, and Adult Education
Division of Adult Education and Literacy
U.S. Department of Education
400 Maryland Avenue SW
Washington, DC 20202
http://www.ed.gov/about/offices/list/ovae/pi/AdultEd/

Other Governmental Agencies and Programs

Bureau of Economic Analysis

National Income and Product Accounts

The National Income and Product Accounts (NIPAs), produced by the Bureau of Economic Analysis, are a set of economic accounts that provide information on the value and composition of output produced in the United States during a given period. NIPAs present measures of economic activity in the United States, including production, income distribution, and personal savings. NIPAs also include data on employee compensation and wages. These estimations were first calculated in the early 1930s to help the government design economic policies

to combat the Great Depression. Most of the NIPA series are published quarterly, with annual reviews of estimates from the three most recent years conducted in the summer.

Revisions to the NIPAs have been made over the years to create a more comprehensive economic picture of the United States. For example, in 1976, consumption of fixed capital (CFC) estimates shifted to a current-cost basis. In 1991, NIPAs began to use gross domestic product (GDP) instead of gross national product (GNP) as the primary measure of U.S. production. (At that time, virtually all other countries were already using GDP as their primary measure of production.) In the 2003 comprehensive revision, a more complete and accurate measure of insurance services was adopted. The incorporation of a new classification system for personal consumption expenditures (PCE) was among the changes contained in the 2009 comprehensive revision. The comprehensive revision of 2013 included the treatment of research and development expenditures by business, government, and nonprofit institutions serving households as fixed investment. As was the case in previous years, the most recent revisions, made in 2015, were the result of the incorporation of newly available and revised source data and the adoption of improved estimating methods.

NIPAs are slowly being integrated with other federal account systems, such as the federal account system of the Bureau of Labor Statistics.

Further information on NIPAs may be obtained from

U.S. Department of Commerce
Bureau of Economic Analysis
www.bea.gov

Bureau of Labor Statistics

Consumer Price Indexes

The Consumer Price Index (CPI) represents changes in prices of all goods and services purchased for consumption by urban households. Indexes are available for two population groups: a CPI for All Urban Consumers (CPI-U) and a CPI for Urban Wage Earners and Clerical Workers (CPI-W). Unless otherwise specified, data in this report are adjusted for inflation using the CPI-U. These values are generally adjusted to a school-year basis by averaging the July through June figures. Price indexes are available for the United States, the four Census regions, size of city, cross-classifications of regions and size classes, and 26 local areas. The major uses of the CPI include as an economic indicator, as a deflator of other economic series, and as a means of adjusting income.

Also available is the Consumer Price Index research series using current methods (CPI-U-RS), which presents an estimate of the CPI-U from 1978 to the present that incorporates most of the improvements that the Bureau of Labor Statistics has made over that time span into the entire series. The historical price index series of the CPI-U does not reflect these changes, though these changes do make the present and future CPI more accurate. The limitations of the

CPI-U-RS include considerable uncertainty surrounding the magnitude of the adjustments and the several improvements in the CPI that have not been incorporated into the CPI-U-RS for various reasons. Nonetheless, the CPI-U-RS can serve as a valuable proxy for researchers needing a historical estimate of inflation using current methods. This series has not been used in NCES tables.

Further information on consumer price indexes may be obtained from

Bureau of Labor Statistics
U.S. Department of Labor
2 Massachusetts Avenue NE
Washington, DC 20212
http://www.bls.gov/cpi

Employment and Unemployment Surveys

Statistics on the employment and unemployment status of the population and related data are compiled by the Bureau of Labor Statistics (BLS) using data from the Current Population Survey (CPS) (see below) and other surveys. The CPS, a monthly household survey conducted by the U.S. Census Bureau for the Bureau of Labor Statistics, provides a comprehensive body of information on the employment and unemployment experience of the nation's population, classified by age, sex, race, and various other characteristics.

Further information on unemployment surveys may be obtained from

Bureau of Labor Statistics
U.S. Department of Labor
2 Massachusetts Avenue NE
Washington, DC 20212
cpsinfo@bls.gov
http://www.bls.gov/bls/employment.htm

Census Bureau

American Community Survey

The Census Bureau introduced the American Community Survey (ACS) in 1996. Fully implemented in 2005, it provides a large monthly sample of demographic, socioeconomic, and housing data comparable in content to the Long Forms of the Decennial Census up to and including the 2000 long form. Aggregated over time, these data serve as a replacement for the Long Form of the Decennial Census. The survey includes questions mandated by federal law, federal regulations, and court decisions.

Since 2011, the survey has been mailed to approximately 295,000 addresses in the United States and Puerto Rico each month, or about 3.5 million addresses annually. A larger proportion of addresses in small governmental units (e.g., American Indian reservations, small counties, and towns) also receive the survey. The monthly sample size is designed to approximate the ratio used in the 2000 Census, which requires more intensive distribution in these areas. The ACS

covers the U.S. resident population, which includes the entire civilian, noninstitutionalized population; incarcerated persons; institutionalized persons; and the active duty military who are in the United States. In 2006, the ACS began interviewing residents in group quarter facilities. Institutionalized group quarters include adult and juvenile correctional facilities, nursing facilities, and other health care facilities. Noninstitutionalized group quarters include college and university housing, military barracks, and other noninstitutional facilities such as workers and religious group quarters and temporary shelters for the homeless.

National-level data from the ACS are available from 2000 onward. The ACS produces 1-year estimates for jurisdictions with populations of 65,000 and over and 5-year estimates for jurisdictions with smaller populations. The 2014 1-year estimates used data collected between January 1, 2014, and December 31, 2014, and the 2010–2014 5-year estimates used data collected between January 1, 2010, and December 31, 2014. The ACS produced 3-year estimates (for jurisdictions with populations of 20,000 or over) for the periods 2005–2007, 2006–2008, 2007–2009, 2008–2010, 2009–2011, 2010–2012, and 2011–2013. Three-year estimates for these periods will continue to be available to data users, but no further 3-year estimates will be produced.

Further information about the ACS is available at http://www.census.gov/acs/www/.

Annual Survey of State and Local Government Finances

The Census Bureau conducts an Annual Survey of State and Local Government Finances as authorized by law under Title 13, United States Code, Section 182. Periodic surveys of government finances have been conducted since 1902 and annually since 1952. This survey covers the entire range of government finance activities: revenue, expenditure, debt, and assets. Revenues and expenditures comprise actual receipts and payments of a government and its agencies, including government-operated enterprises, utilities, and public trust funds. The expenditure-reporting categories comprise all amounts of money paid out by a government and its agencies, with the exception of amounts for debt retirement and for loan, investment, agency, and private trust transactions.

State government finances are based primarily on the Census Bureau Annual Survey of State and Local Government Finances. Census analysts compile figures from official records and reports of the state governments for most of the state financial data. States differ in the ways they administer activities; they may fund such activities directly, or they may disburse the money to a lower level government or government agency. Therefore, caution is advised when attempting to make a direct comparison between states on their state fiscal aid data.

The sample of local governments is drawn from the periodic (years ending in "2" and "7") Census of Governments and consists of certain local governments sampled with certainty plus a sample below the certainty level. Finance data for all school districts are collected on an annual basis and released through the NCES Common Core of Data system. A new sample is usually selected every 5 years (years ending in "4" and "9").

The statistics in Government Finances that are based wholly or partly on data from the sample are subject to sampling error. State government finance data are not subject to sampling error. Estimates of major U.S. totals for local governments are subject to a computed sampling variability of less than one-half of 1 percent. The estimates are also subject to the inaccuracies in classification, response, and processing that would occur if a complete census had been conducted under the same conditions as the sample.

Further information on government finances may be obtained from

Governments Division
Census Bureau
U.S. Department of Commerce
4600 Silver Hill Road
Washington, DC 20233

Local government
ewd.local.finance@census.gov

State government
govs.statefinance@census.gov
http://www.census.gov/govs

Census of Population—Education in the United States

Some NCES tables are based on a part of the decennial census that consisted of questions asked of a 1 in 6 sample of people and housing units in the United States. This sample was asked more detailed questions about income, occupation, and housing costs, as well as questions about general demographic information. This decennial Long Form is no longer conducted and has been replaced by the American Community Survey (ACS).

School enrollment. People classified as enrolled in school reported attending a "regular" public or private school or college. They were asked whether the institution they attended was public or private and what level of school they were enrolled in.

Educational attainment. Data for educational attainment were tabulated for people ages 15 and older and classified according to the highest grade completed or the highest degree received. Instructions were also given to include the level of the previous grade attended or the highest degree received for people currently enrolled in school.

Poverty status. To determine poverty status, answers to income questions were used to make comparisons to the appropriate poverty threshold. All people except those who were institutionalized, people in military group quarters and college dormitories, and unrelated people under age 15 were considered. If the total income of each family or unrelated individual in the sample was below the corresponding cutoff, that family or individual was classified as "below the poverty level."

Further information on the 1990 and 2000 Census of Population may be obtained from

Population Division
Census Bureau
U.S. Department of Commerce
4600 Silver Hill Road
Washington, DC 20233
http://www.census.gov/main/www/cen1990.html
http://www.census.gov/main/www/cen2000.html

Current Population Survey

The Current Population Survey (CPS) is a monthly survey of about 60,000 households conducted by the U.S. Census Bureau for the Bureau of Labor Statistics. The CPS is the primary source of information of labor force statistics for the U.S. noninstitutionalized population (e.g., it excludes military personnel and their families living on bases and inmates of correctional institutions). In addition, supplemental questionnaires are used to provide further information about the U.S. population. Specifically, in October, detailed questions regarding school enrollment and school characteristics are asked. In March, detailed questions regarding income are asked.

The current sample design, introduced in July 2001, includes about 72,000 households. Each month about 58,900 of the 72,000 households are eligible for interview, and of those, 7 to 10 percent are not interviewed because of temporary absence or unavailability. Information is obtained each month from those in the household who are 15 years of age and older, and demographic data are collected for children 0–14 years of age. In addition, supplemental questions regarding school enrollment are asked about eligible household members ages 3 and older in the October survey. Prior to July 2001, data were collected in the CPS from about 50,000 dwelling units. The samples are initially selected based on the decennial census files and are periodically updated to reflect new housing construction.

A major redesign of the CPS was implemented in January 1994 to improve the quality of the data collected. Survey questions were revised, new questions were added, and computer-assisted interviewing methods were used for the survey data collection. Further information about the redesign is available in *Current Population Survey, October 1995: (School Enrollment Supplement) Technical Documentation* at http://www.census.gov/prod/techdoc/cps/cpsoct95.pdf.

Caution should be used when comparing data from 1994 through 2001 with data from 1993 and earlier. Data from 1994 through 2001 reflect 1990 census-based population controls, while data from 1993 and earlier reflect 1980 or earlier census-based population controls. Changes in population controls generally have relatively little impact on summary measures such as means, medians, and percentage distributions. They can have a significant impact on population counts. For example, use of the 1990 census-based population controls resulted in about a 1 percent increase in the civilian noninstitutional population and in the number of families and households.

Thus, estimates of levels for data collected in 1994 and later years will differ from those for earlier years by more than what could be attributed to actual changes in the population. These differences could be disproportionately greater for certain subpopulation groups than for the total population.

Beginning in 2003, race/ethnicity questions expanded to include information on people of Two or more races. Native Hawaiian/Pacific Islander data are collected separately from Asian data. The questions have also been worded to make it clear that self-reported data on race/ethnicity should reflect the race/ethnicity with which the responder identifies, rather than what may be written in official documentation.

The estimation procedure employed for monthly CPS data involves inflating weighted sample results to independent estimates of characteristics of the civilian noninstitutional population in the United States by age, sex, and race. These independent estimates are based on statistics from decennial censuses; statistics on births, deaths, immigration, and emigration; and statistics on the population in the armed services. Generalized standard error tables are provided in the Current Population Reports; methods for deriving standard errors can be found within the CPS technical documentation at http://www.census.gov/programs-surveys/cps/technical-documentation/complete.html. The CPS data are subject to both nonsampling and sampling errors.

Prior to 2009, standard errors were estimated using the generalized variance function. The generalized variance function is a simple model that expresses the variance as a function of the expected value of a survey estimate. Beginning with March 2009 CPS data, standard errors were estimated using replicate weight methodology. Those interested in using CPS household-level supplement replicate weights to calculate variances may refer to *Estimating Current Population Survey (CPS) Household-Level Supplement Variances Using Replicate Weights* at http://thedataweb.rm.census.gov/pub/cps/supps/HH-level Use of the Public Use Replicate Weight File.doc.

Further information on the CPS may be obtained from

Education and Social Stratification Branch
Population Division
Census Bureau
U.S. Department of Commerce
4600 Silver Hill Road
Washington, DC 20233
http://www.census.gov/cps

Dropouts

Each October, the Current Population Survey (CPS) includes supplemental questions on the enrollment status of the population ages 3 years and over as part of the monthly basic survey on labor force participation. In addition to gathering the information on school enrollment, with the limitations on accuracy as noted below under "School Enrollment," the survey data permit calculations of dropout rates. Both status and event dropout rates are tabulated from the October CPS. Event rates describe the proportion of students who leave school each year without completing a high school program. Status rates provide cumulative data on dropouts among all young adults within a specified age range. Status rates are higher than event rates because they include all dropouts ages 16 through 24, regardless of when they last attended school.

In addition to other survey limitations, dropout rates may be affected by survey coverage and exclusion of the institutionalized population. The incarcerated population has grown more rapidly and has a higher dropout rate than the general population. Dropout rates for the total population might be higher than those for the noninstitutionalized population if the prison and jail populations were included in the dropout rate calculations. On the other hand, if military personnel, who tend to be high school graduates, were included, it might offset some or all of the impact from the theoretical inclusion of the jail and prison populations.

Another area of concern with tabulations involving young people in household surveys is the relatively low coverage ratio compared to older age groups. CPS undercoverage results from missed housing units and missed people within sample households. Overall CPS undercoverage for October 2014 is estimated to be about 12 percent. CPS coverage varies with age, sex, and race. Generally, coverage is larger for females than for males and larger for non-Blacks than for Blacks. This differential coverage is a general problem for most household-based surveys. Further information on CPS methodology may be found in the technical documentation at http://www.census.gov/cps.

Further information on the calculation of dropouts and dropout rates may be obtained from *Trends in High School Dropout and Completion Rates in the United States: 1972–2012* (NCES 2015-015) at http://nces.ed.gov/pubs2015/2015015.pdf or by contacting

Joel McFarland
Annual Reports and Information Staff
National Center for Education Statistics
550 12th Street SW
Washington, DC 20202
joel.mcfarland@ed.gov

Educational Attainment

Reports documenting educational attainment are produced by the Census Bureau using March Current Population Survey (CPS) supplement (Annual Social and Economic Supplement [ASEC]) results. The sample size for the 2014 ASEC supplement (including basic CPS) was about 98,000 addresses; the tables may be downloaded at http://www.census.gov/hhes/socdemo/education/data/cps/2014/tables.html. The sample size for the 2015 ASEC supplement (including basic CPS) was about 100,000 addresses. The results were released in *Educational Attainment in the United States: 2015*; the tables may be downloaded at http://www.census.gov/hhes/socdemo/education/data/cps/2015/tables.html. In addition to the general constraints of CPS, some data indicate that the respondents have a tendency to overestimate the educational level of members of their household. Some inaccuracy is due to a lack of the respondent's knowledge of the exact educational attainment of each household member and the hesitancy to acknowledge anything less than a high school education. Another cause of nonsampling variability is the change in the numbers in the armed services over the years.

Further information on educational attainment data from CPS may be obtained from

Education and Social Stratification Branch
Census Bureau
U.S. Department of Commerce
4600 Silver Hill Road
Washington, DC 20233
http://www.census.gov/hhes/socdemo/education

School Enrollment

Each October, the Current Population Survey (CPS) includes supplemental questions on the enrollment status of the population ages 3 years and over. Prior to 2001, the October supplement consisted of approximately 47,000 interviewed households. Beginning with the October 2001 supplement, the sample was expanded by 9,000 to a total of approximately 56,000 interviewed households. The main sources of nonsampling variability in the responses to the supplement are those inherent in the survey instrument. The question of current enrollment may not be answered accurately for various reasons. Some respondents may not know current grade information for every student in the household, a problem especially prevalent for households with members in college or in nursery school. Confusion over college credits or hours taken by a student may make it difficult to determine the year in which the student is enrolled. Problems may occur with the definition of nursery school (a group or class organized to provide educational experiences for children) where respondents' interpretations of "educational experiences" vary.

For the October 2014 basic CPS, the household-level nonresponse rate was 10.56 percent. The person-level nonresponse rate for the school enrollment supplement was an additional 7.8 percent. Since the basic CPS nonresponse rate is a household-level rate and the school enrollment supplement nonresponse rate is a person-level rate, these rates cannot be combined to derive an overall nonresponse rate. Nonresponding households may have fewer persons than interviewed ones, so combining these rates may lead to an overestimate of the true overall nonresponse rate for persons for the school enrollment supplement.

Further information on CPS methodology may be obtained from http://www.census.gov/cps.

Further information on the CPS School Enrollment Supplement may be obtained from

Education and Social Stratification Branch
Census Bureau
U.S. Department of Commerce
4600 Silver Hill Road
Washington, DC 20233
http://www.census.gov/hhes/school/index.html

Decennial Census, Population Estimates, and Population Projections

The decennial census is a universe survey mandated by the U.S. Constitution. It is a questionnaire sent to every household in the country, and it is composed of seven questions about the household and its members (name, sex, age, relationship, Hispanic origin, race, and whether the housing unit is owned or rented). The Census Bureau also produces annual estimates of the resident population by demographic characteristics (age, sex, race, and Hispanic origin) for the nation, states, and counties, as well as national and state projections for the resident population. The reference date for population estimates is July 1 of the given year. With each new issue of July 1 estimates, the Census Bureau revises estimates for each year back to the last census. Previously published estimates are superseded and archived.

Census respondents self-report race and ethnicity. The race questions on the 1990 and 2000 censuses differed in some significant ways. In 1990, the respondent was instructed to select the one race "that the respondent considers himself/herself to be," whereas in 2000, the respondent could select one or more races that the person considered himself or herself to be. American Indian, Eskimo, and Aleut were three separate race categories in 1990; in 2000, the American Indian and Alaska Native categories were combined, with an option to write in a tribal affiliation. This write-in option was provided only for the American Indian category in 1990. There was a combined Asian and Pacific Islander race category in 1990, but the groups were separated into two categories in 2000.

The census question on ethnicity asks whether the respondent is of Hispanic origin, regardless of the race option(s) selected; thus, persons of Hispanic origin may be of any race. In the 2000 census, respondents were first asked, "Is this person Spanish/Hispanic/Latino?" and then given the following options: No, not Spanish/Hispanic/Latino; Yes, Puerto Rican; Yes, Mexican, Mexican American, Chicano; Yes, Cuban; and Yes, other Spanish/Hispanic/Latino (with space to print the specific group). In the 2010 census, respondents were asked "Is this person of Hispanic, Latino, or Spanish origin?" The options given were No, not of Hispanic, Latino, or Spanish origin; Yes, Mexican, Mexican Am., Chicano; Yes, Puerto Rican; Yes, Cuban; and Yes, another Hispanic, Latino, or Spanish origin—along with instructions to print "Argentinean, Colombian, Dominican, Nicaraguan, Salvadoran, Spaniard, and so on" in a specific box.

The 2000 and 2010 censuses each asked the respondent "What is this person's race?" and allowed the respondent to select one or more options. The options provided were largely the same in both the 2000 and 2010 censuses: White; Black, African American, or Negro; American Indian or Alaska Native (with space to print the name of enrolled or principal tribe); Asian Indian; Japanese; Native Hawaiian; Chinese; Korean; Guamanian or Chamorro; Filipino; Vietnamese; Samoan; Other Asian; Other Pacific Islander; and Some other race. The last three options included space to print the specific race. Two significant differences between the 2000 and 2010 census questions on race were that no race examples were provided for the "Other Asian" and "Other Pacific Islander" responses in 2000, whereas the race examples of "Hmong, Laotian, Thai, Pakistani, Cambodian, and so on" and "Fijian, Tongan, and so on," were provided for the "Other Asian" and "Other Pacific Islander" responses, respectively, in 2010.

The census population estimates program modified the enumerated population from the 2010 census to produce the population estimates base for 2010 and onward. As part of the modification, the Census Bureau recoded the "Some other race" responses from the 2010 census to one or more of the five OMB race categories used in the estimates program (for more information, see http://www.census.gov/popest/methodology/2012-nat-st-co-meth.pdf).

Further information on the decennial census may be obtained from http://www.census.gov.

Small Area Income and Poverty Estimates

Small Area Income and Poverty Estimates (SAIPE) are produced for school districts, counties, and states. The main objective of this program is to provide updated estimates of income and poverty statistics for the administration of federal programs and the allocation of federal funds to local jurisdictions. Estimates for 2014 were released in December 2015. These estimates combine data from administrative records, postcensal population estimates, and the decennial census with direct estimates from the American Community Survey to provide consistent and reliable single-year estimates. These model-based single-year estimates are more reflective of current conditions than multiyear survey estimates.

Further information on the SAIPE program may be obtained from

Small Area Estimates Branch
Census Bureau
U.S. Department of Commerce
sehsd.saipe@census.gov
http://www.census.gov/did/www/saipe/data/index.html

Centers for Disease Control and Prevention

National Health Interview Survey

The National Health Interview Survey (NHIS) is the principal source of information on the health of the civilian noninstitutionalized population of the United States and is one of the major data collection programs of the National Center for Health Statistics (NCHS), which is part of the Centers for Disease Control and Prevention (CDC). The main objective of the NHIS is to monitor the health of the U.S. population through the collection and analysis of data on a broad range of health topics. A major strength of this survey lies in its ability to display these health characteristics by many demographic and socioeconomic characteristics.

The NHIS covers the civilian noninstitutionalized population residing in the United States at the time of the interview. The NHIS is a cross-sectional household interview survey. Sampling and interviewing are continuous throughout each year. The sampling plan follows a multistage area probability design that permits the representative sampling of households and noninstitutional group quarters (e.g., college dormitories). The sampling plan is redesigned after every decennial census. The current sampling plan was implemented in 2006. It is similar in many ways to the previous sampling plan, which was in place from 1995 to 2005. The first stage of the current sampling plan consists of a sample of 428 primary sampling units (PSUs) drawn from approximately 1,900 geographically defined PSUs that cover the 50 states and the District of Columbia. A PSU consists of a county, a small group of contiguous counties, or a metropolitan statistical area.

The revised NHIS questionnaire, implemented since 1997, contains Core questions and Supplements. The Core questions remain largely unchanged from year to year and allow for trends analysis and for data from more than one year to be pooled to increase sample size for analytic purposes. The Core contains four major components: Household, Family, Sample Adult, and Sample Child.

The Household component collects limited demographic information on all of the individuals living in a particular house. The Family component verifies and collects additional demographic information on each member from each family in the house and collects data on topics including health status and limitations, injuries, healthcare access and utilization, health insurance, and income and assets. The Family Core component allows the NHIS to serve as a sampling frame for additional integrated surveys as needed.

Data are collected through a personal household interview conducted by interviewers employed and trained by the U.S. Bureau of the Census according to procedures specified by the NCHS.

Further information on the NHIS may be obtained from

Information Dissemination Staff
National Center for Health Statistics
Centers for Disease Control and Prevention
3311 Toledo Road, Room 5407
Hyattsville, MD 20782-2003
(800) 232-4636
nhis@cdc.gov
http://www.cdc.gov/nchs/nhis.htm

Morbidity and Mortality Weekly Report: Summary of Notifiable Diseases

The Summary of Notifiable Diseases, a publication of the Morbidity and Mortality Weekly Report (MMWR), contains the official statistics, in tabular and graphic form, for the reported occurrence of nationally notifiable infectious diseases in the United States. These statistics are collected and compiled from reports sent by state health departments and territories to the National Notifiable Diseases Surveillance System (NNDSS), which is operated by the Centers for Disease Control and Prevention (CDC) in collaboration with the Council of State and Territorial Epidemiologists.

For more information on the MMWR: Summary of Notifiable Diseases, see http://www.cdc.gov/mmwr/mmwr_nd/.

National Vital Statistics System

The National Vital Statistics System (NVSS) is the method by which data on vital events—births, deaths, marriages, divorces, and fetal deaths—are provided to the National Center for Health Statistics (NCHS), part of the Centers for Disease Control and Prevention (CDC). The data are provided to NCHS through the Vital Statistics Cooperative Program (VSCP). In 1984 and earlier years, the VSCP included varying numbers of states that provided data based on a 100 percent sample of their birth certificates. Data for states not in the VSCP were based on a 50 percent sample of birth certificates filed in those states. Population data used to compile birth rates are based on special estimation procedures and are not actual counts.

Race and Hispanic ethnicity are reported separately in the NVSS. Data are available for non-Hispanic Whites and non-Hispanic Blacks for 1990 and later; however, for 1980 and 1985, data for Whites and Blacks may include persons of Hispanic ethnicity. For all years, Asian/Pacific Islander and American Indian/Alaska Native categories include persons of Hispanic ethnicity.

For more information on the NCHS and the NVSS, see http://www.cdc.gov/nchs/nvss.htm.

School-Associated Violent Deaths Study

The School-Associated Violent Deaths Study (SAVD) is an epidemiological study developed by the Centers for Disease Control and Prevention in conjunction with the U.S. Department of Education and the U.S. Department of Justice. SAVD seeks to describe the epidemiology of school-associated violent deaths, identify common features of these deaths, estimate the rate of school-associated violent death in the United States, and identify potential risk factors for these deaths. The study includes descriptive data on all school-associated violent deaths in the United States, including all homicides, suicides, or legal intervention in which the fatal injury occurred on the campus of a functioning elementary or secondary school; while the victim was on the way to or from regular sessions at such a school; or while attending or on the way to or from an official school-sponsored event. Victims of such incidents include nonstudents, as well as students and staff members. SAVD includes descriptive information about the school, event, victim(s), and offender(s). The SAVD study has collected data since July 1, 1992.

SAVD uses a four-step process to identify and collect data on school-associated violent deaths. Cases are initially identified through a search of the LexisNexis newspaper and media

database. Then law enforcement officials are contacted to confirm the details of the case and to determine if the event meets the case definition. Once a case is confirmed, a law enforcement official and a school official are interviewed regarding details about the school, event, victim(s), and offender(s). A copy of the full law enforcement report is also sought for each case. The information obtained on schools includes school demographics, attendance/absentee rates, suspensions/expulsions and mobility, school history of weapon-carrying incidents, security measures, violence prevention activities, school response to the event, and school policies about weapon carrying. Event information includes the location of injury, the context of injury (while classes were being held, during break, etc.), motives for injury, method of injury, and school and community events happening around the time period. Information obtained on victim(s) and offender(s) includes demographics, circumstances of the event (date/time, alcohol or drug use, number of persons involved), types and origins of weapons, criminal history, psychological risk factors, school-related problems, extracurricular activities, and family history, including structure and stressors.

Some 105 school-associated violent deaths were identified from July 1, 1992, to June 30, 1994 (Kachur et al., 1996, School-Associated Violent Deaths in the United States, 1992 to 1994, *Journal of the American Medical Association, 275:* 1729–1733). A more recent report from this data collection identified 253 school-associated violent deaths between July 1, 1994, and June 30, 1999 (Anderson et al., 2001, School-Associated Violent Deaths in the United States, 1994–1999, *Journal of the American Medical Association, 286:* 2695–2702). Other publications from this study have described how the number of events change during the school year (Centers for Disease Control and Prevention, 2001, Temporal Variations in School-Associated Student Homicide and Suicide Events—United States, 1992–1999, *Morbidity and Mortality Weekly Report, 50:* 657–660), the source of the firearms used in these events (Reza et al., 2003, Source of Firearms Used by Students in School-Associated Violent Deaths—United States, 1992–1999, *Morbidity and Mortality Weekly Report, 52:* 169–172), and suicides that were associated with schools (Kauffman et al., 2004, School-Associated Suicides—United States, 1994–1999, *Morbidity and Mortality Weekly Report, 53:* 476–478). The most recent publication describes trends in school-associated homicide from July 1, 1992, to June 30, 2006 (Centers for Disease Control and Prevention, 2008, School-Associated Student Homicides—United States, 1992–2006, *Morbidity and Mortality Weekly Report 2008, 57:* 33–36). The interviews conducted on cases between July 1, 1994, and June 30, 1999, achieved a response rate of 97 percent for police officials and 78 percent for school officials. For several reasons, all data for years from 1999 to the present are flagged as preliminary. For some recent data, the interviews with school and law enforcement officials to verify case details have not been completed. The details learned during the interviews can occasionally change the classification of a case. Also, new cases may be identified because of the expansion of the scope of the media files used for case identification. Sometimes other cases not identified during earlier data years using the independent case finding efforts (which focus on nonmedia sources of information) will be discovered. Also, other cases may occasionally be identified while the law enforcement and school interviews are being conducted to verify known cases.

Further information on SAVD may be obtained from

Jeff Hall
Division of Violence Prevention
National Center for Injury Prevention and Control
Centers for Disease Control and Prevention
4770 Buford Highway NE
Mailstop F63
Atlanta, GA 30341-3742
(770) 488-4648
JHall2@CDC.gov
http://www.cdc.gov/violenceprevention/index.html

Web-based Injury Statistics Query and Reporting System Fatal

WISQARS Fatal provides mortality data related to injury. The mortality data reported in WISQARS Fatal come from death certificate data reported to the National Center for Health Statistics (NCHS), Centers for Disease Control and Prevention. Data include causes of death reported by attending physicians, medical examiners, and coroners and demographic information about decedents reported by funeral directors, who obtain that information from family members and other informants. NCHS collects, compiles, verifies, and prepares these data for release to the public. The data provide information about unintentional injury, homicide, and suicide as leading causes of death, how common these causes of death are, and whom they affect. These data are intended for a broad audience—the public, the media, public health practitioners and researchers, and public health officials—to increase their knowledge of injury.

WISQARS Fatal mortality reports provide tables of the total numbers of injury-related deaths and the death rates per 100,000 U.S. population. The reports list deaths according to cause (mechanism) and intent (manner) of injury by state, race, Hispanic origin, sex, and age groupings.

Further information on WISQARS Fatal may be obtained from

National Center for Injury Prevention and Control
Mailstop K65
4770 Buford Highway NE
Atlanta, GA 30341-3724
(770) 488-1506
ohcinfo@cdc.gov
www.cdc.gov/info
http://www.cdc.gov/injury/wisqars/fatal_help/data_sources.html

Youth Risk Behavior Surveillance System

The Youth Risk Behavior Surveillance System (YRBSS) is an epidemiological surveillance system developed by the Centers for Disease Control and Prevention (CDC) to monitor the prevalence of youth behaviors that most influence health. The YRBSS focuses on priority health-risk behaviors established during youth that result in the most significant mortality, morbidity, disability, and social problems during both youth and adulthood. The YRBSS includes a national school-based Youth Risk Behavior Survey (YRBS), as well as surveys conducted in states and large urban school districts.

The national YRBS uses a three-stage cluster sampling design to produce a nationally representative sample of students in grades 9–12 in the United States. The target population consisted of all public and private school students in grades 9–12 in the 50 states and the District of Columbia. The first-stage sampling frame included selecting primary sampling units (PSUs) from strata formed on the basis of urbanization and the relative percentage of Black and Hispanic students in the PSU. These PSUs are either counties; subareas of large counties; or groups of smaller, adjacent counties. At the second stage, schools were selected with probability proportional to school enrollment size.

The final stage of sampling consisted of randomly selecting, in each chosen school and in each of grades 9–12, one or two classrooms from either a required subject, such as English or social studies, or a required period, such as homeroom or second period. All students in selected classes were eligible to participate. In surveys conducted before 2013, three strategies were used to oversample Black and Hispanic students: (1) larger sampling rates were used to select PSUs that are in high-Black and high-Hispanic strata; (2) a modified measure of size was used that increased the probability of selecting schools with a disproportionately high minority enrollment; and (3) two classes per grade, rather than one, were selected in schools with a high percentage of combined Black, Hispanic, Asian/Pacific Islander, or American Indian/Alaska Native enrollment. In 2013, only selection of two classes per grade was needed to achieve an adequate precision with minimum variance. Approximately 16,300 students participated in the 1993 survey, 10,900 students participated in the 1995 survey, 16,300 students participated in the 1997 survey, 15,300 students participated in the 1999 survey, 13,600 students participated in the 2001 survey, 15,200 students participated in the 2003 survey, 13,900 students participated in the 2005 survey, 14,000 students participated in the 2007 survey, 16,400 students participated in the 2009 survey, 15,400 participated in the 2011 survey, and 13,600 participated in the 2013 survey.

The overall response rate was 70 percent for the 1993 survey, 60 percent for the 1995 survey, 69 percent for the 1997 survey, 66 percent for the 1999 survey, 63 percent for the 2001 survey, 67 percent for the 2003 survey, 67 percent for the 2005 survey, 68 percent for the 2007 survey, 71 percent for the 2009 survey, 71 percent for the 2011 survey, and 68 percent for the 2013 survey. NCES standards call for response rates of 85 percent or better for cross-sectional surveys, and bias analyses are required by NCES when that percentage is not achieved. For YRBS data, a full nonresponse bias analysis has not been done because the data necessary to do the analysis are not available. The weights were developed to adjust for nonresponse and the oversampling of Black and Hispanic students in the sample. The final weights were constructed so that only weighted proportions of students (not weighted counts of students) in each grade matched national population projections.

State-level data were downloaded from the Youth Online: Comprehensive Results web page (http://nccd.cdc.gov/YouthOnline/). Each state and district school-based YRBS employs a two-stage, cluster sample design to produce representative samples of students in grades 9–12 in their jurisdiction. All except a few state samples, and all district samples, include only public schools, and each district sample includes only schools in the funded school district (e.g., San Diego Unified School District) rather than in the entire city (e.g., greater San Diego area).

In the first sampling stage in all except a few states and districts, schools are selected with probability proportional to school enrollment size. In the second sampling stage, intact classes of a required subject or intact classes during a required period (e.g., second period) are selected randomly. All students in sampled classes are eligible to participate. Certain states and districts modify these procedures to meet their individual needs. For example, in a given state or district, all schools, rather than a sample of schools, might be selected to participate. State and local surveys that have a scientifically selected sample, appropriate documentation, and an overall response rate greater than or equal to 60 percent are weighted. The overall response rate reflects the school response rate multiplied by the student response rate. These three criteria are used to ensure that the data from those surveys can be considered representative of students in grades 9–12 in that jurisdiction. A weight is applied to each record to adjust for student nonresponse and the distribution of students by grade, sex, and race/ethnicity in each jurisdiction. Therefore, weighted estimates are representative of all students in grades 9–12 attending schools in each jurisdiction. Surveys that do not have an overall response rate of greater than or equal to 60 percent and that do not have appropriate documentation are not weighted and are not included in this report.

In 2013, a total of 42 states and 21 districts had weighted data. Not all of the districts were contained in the 42 states. For example, California was not one of the 42 states that obtained weighted data, but it contained several districts that did. For more information on the location of the districts, please see http://www.cdc.gov/healthyyouth/yrbs/participation.htm. In sites with weighted data, the student sample sizes for the state and district YRBS ranged from 1,107 to 53,785. School response rates ranged from 70 to 100 percent, student response rates ranged from 60 to 94 percent, and overall response rates ranged from 60 to 87 percent.

Readers should note that reports of these data published by the CDC and in this report do not include percentages for which the denominator includes fewer than 100 unweighted cases.

In 1999, in accordance with changes to the Office of Management and Budget's standards for the classification of federal data on race and ethnicity, the YRBS item on race/ethnicity was modified. The version of the race and ethnicity question used in 1993, 1995, and 1997 was

How do you describe yourself?
  a. White—not Hispanic
  b. Black—not Hispanic
  c. Hispanic or Latino
  d. Asian or Pacific Islander
  e. American Indian or Alaskan Native
  f. Other

The version used in 1999, 2001, 2003, and in the 2005, 2007, and 2009 state and local district surveys was

How do you describe yourself? (Select one or more responses.)
  a. American Indian or Alaska Native
  b. Asian
  c. Black or African American
  d. Hispanic or Latino
  e. Native Hawaiian or Other Pacific Islander
  f. White

In the 2005 national survey and in all 2007, 2009, 2011, and 2013 surveys, race/ethnicity was computed from two questions: (1) "Are you Hispanic or Latino?" (response options were "Yes" and "No"), and (2) "What is your race?" (response options were "American Indian or Alaska Native," "Asian," "Black or African American," "Native Hawaiian or Other Pacific Islander," or "White"). For the second question, students could select more than one response option. For this report, students were classified as "Hispanic" if they answered "Yes" to the first question, regardless of how they answered the second question. Students who answered "No" to the first question and selected more than one race/ethnicity in the second category were classified as "More than one race." Students who answered "No" to the first question and selected only one race/ethnicity were classified as that race/ethnicity. Race/ethnicity was classified as missing for students who did not answer the first question and for students who answered "No" to the first question but did not answer the second question.

CDC has conducted two studies to understand the effect of changing the race/ethnicity item on the YRBS. Brener, Kann, and McManus (*Public Opinion Quarterly, 67*:227–226, 2003) found that allowing students to select more than one response to a single race/ethnicity question on the YRBS had only a minimal effect on reported race/ethnicity among high school students. Eaton, Brener, Kann, and Pittman (*Journal of Adolescent Health, 41*:488–494, 2007) found that self-reported race/ethnicity was similar regardless of whether the single-question or a two-question format was used.

Further information on the YRBSS may be obtained from

Laura Kann
Division of Adolescent and School Health
National Center for HIV/AIDS, Viral Hepatitis, STD,
   and TB Prevention
Centers for Disease Control and Prevention
Mailstop E-75
1600 Clifton Road NE
Atlanta, GA 30329
(404) 718-8132
lkk1@cdc.gov
http://www.cdc.gov/yrbs

Department of Justice

Bureau of Justice Statistics

A division of the U.S. Department of Justice Office of Justice Programs, the Bureau of Justice Statistics (BJS) collects, analyzes, publishes, and disseminates statistical information on crime, criminal offenders, victims of crime, and the operations of the justice system at all levels of government and internationally. It also provides technical and financial support to state governments for development of criminal justice statistics and information systems on crime and justice.

For information on the BJS, see www.ojp.usdoj.gov/bjs/.

National Crime Victimization Survey

The National Crime Victimization Survey (NCVS), administered for the U.S. Bureau of Justice Statistics (BJS) by the U.S. Census Bureau, is the nation's primary source of information on crime and the victims of crime. Initiated in 1972 and redesigned in 1992, the NCVS collects detailed information on the frequency and nature of the crimes of rape, sexual assault, robbery, aggravated and simple assault, theft, household burglary, and motor vehicle theft experienced by Americans and American households each year. The survey measures both crimes reported to the police and crimes not reported to the police.

NCVS estimates presented may differ from those in previous published reports. This is because a small number of victimizations, referred to as series victimizations, are included using a new counting strategy. High-frequency repeat victimizations, or series victimizations, are six or more similar but separate victimizations that occur with such frequency that the victim is unable to recall each individual event or describe each event in detail. As part of ongoing research efforts associated with the redesign of the NCVS, BJS investigated ways to include high-frequency repeat victimizations, or series victimizations, in estimates of criminal victimization. Including series victimizations results in more accurate estimates of victimization. BJS has decided to include series victimizations using the victim's estimates of the number of times the victimizations occurred over the past 6 months, capping the number of victimizations within each series at a maximum of 10. This strategy for counting series victimizations balances the desire to estimate national rates and account for the experiences of persons who have been subjected to repeat victimizations against the desire to minimize the estimation errors that can occur when repeat victimizations are reported. Including series victimizations in national rates results in rather large increases in the level of violent victimization; however, trends in violence are generally similar regardless of whether series victimizations are included. For more information on the new counting strategy and supporting research, see *Methods for Counting High-Frequency Repeat Victimizations in the National Crime Victimization Survey* at http://bjs.ojp.usdoj.gov/content/pub/pdf/mchfrv.pdf.

Readers should note that in 2003, in accordance with changes to the Office of Management and Budget's standards for the classification of federal data on race and ethnicity, the NCVS item on race/ethnicity was modified. A question on Hispanic origin is now followed by a new question on race. The new question about race allows the respondent to choose more than one race and delineates Asian as a separate category from Native Hawaiian or Other Pacific Islander. An analysis conducted by the Demographic Surveys Division at the U.S. Census Bureau showed that the new race question had very little impact on the aggregate racial distribution of the NCVS respondents, with one exception: There was a 1.6 percentage point decrease in the percentage of respondents who reported themselves as White. Due to changes in race/ethnicity categories, comparisons of race/ethnicity across years should be made with caution.

There were changes in the sample design and survey methodology in the 2006 NCVS that may have affected survey estimates. Caution should be used when comparing the 2006 estimates to estimates of other years. Data from 2007 onward are comparable to earlier years. Analyses of the 2007 estimates indicate that the program changes made in 2006 had relatively small effects on NCVS estimates. For more information on the 2006 NCVS data, see *Criminal Victimization, 2006,* at http://bjs.ojp.usdoj.gov/content/pub/pdf/cv06.pdf, the technical notes at http://bjs.ojp.usdoj.gov/content/pub/pdf/cv06tn.pdf, and *Criminal Victimization, 2007,* at http://bjs.ojp.usdoj.gov/content/pub/pdf/cv07.pdf.

The number of NCVS-eligible households in the sample in 2013 was about 107,400. Households were selected using a stratified, multistage cluster design. In the first stage, the primary sampling units (PSUs), consisting of counties or groups of counties, were selected. In the second stage, smaller areas, called Enumeration Districts (EDs), were selected from each sampled PSU. Finally, from selected EDs, clusters of four households, called segments, were selected for interview. At each stage, the selection was done proportionate to population size in order to create a self-weighting sample. The final sample was augmented to account for households constructed after the decennial Census. Within each sampled household, the U.S. Census Bureau interviewer attempts to interview all household members age 12 and older to determine whether they had been victimized by the measured crimes during the 6 months preceding the interview.

The first NCVS interview with a housing unit is conducted in person. Subsequent interviews are conducted by telephone, if possible. About 80,000 persons age 12 and older are interviewed each 6 months. Households remain in the sample for 3 years and are interviewed seven times at 6-month intervals. Since the survey's inception, the initial interview at each sample unit has been used only to bound future interviews to establish a time frame to avoid duplication of crimes uncovered in these subsequent interviews. Beginning in 2006, data from the initial interview have been adjusted to account for the effects of bounding and have been included in the survey estimates. After a household has been interviewed its seventh time, it is replaced by a new sample household. In 2013, the household response rate was about 84 percent and the completion rate for persons within households was about 88 percent. Weights were developed to permit estimates for the total U.S. population 12 years and older.

Further information on the NCVS may be obtained from

Rachel E. Morgan
Victimization Statistics Branch
Bureau of Justice Statistics
rachel.morgan@usdoj.gov
http://www.bjs.gov/

School Crime Supplement

Created as a supplement to the NCVS and co-designed by the National Center for Education Statistics and Bureau of Justice Statistics, the School Crime Supplement (SCS) survey has been conducted in 1989, 1995, and biennially since 1999 to collect additional information about school-related victimizations on a national level. This report includes data from the 1995, 1999, 2001, 2003, 2005, 2007, 2009, 2011, and 2013 collections. The 1989 data are not included in this report as a result of methodological changes to the NCVS and SCS. The SCS was designed to assist policymakers, as well as academic researchers and practitioners at federal, state, and local levels, to make informed decisions concerning crime in schools. The survey asks students a number of key questions about their experiences with and perceptions of crime and violence that occurred inside their school, on school grounds, on the school bus, or on the way to or from school. Students are asked additional questions about security measures used by their school, students' participation in after-school activities, students' perceptions of school rules, the presence of weapons and gangs in school, the presence of hate-related words and graffiti in school, student reports of bullying and reports of rejection at school, and the availability of drugs and alcohol in school. Students are also asked attitudinal questions relating to fear of victimization and avoidance behavior at school.

The SCS survey was conducted for a 6-month period from January through June in all households selected for the NCVS (see discussion above for information about the NCVS sampling design and changes to the race/ethnicity variable beginning in 2003). Within these households, the eligible respondents for the SCS were those household members who had attended school at any time during the 6 months preceding the interview, were enrolled in grades 6–12, and were not home schooled. In 2007, the questionnaire was changed and household members who attended school sometime during the school year of the interview were included. The age range of students covered in this report is 12–18 years of age. Eligible respondents were asked the supplemental questions in the SCS only after completing their entire NCVS interview. It should be noted that the first or unbounded NCVS interview has always been included in analysis of the SCS data and may result in the reporting of events outside of the requested reference period.

The prevalence of victimization for 1995, 1999, 2001, 2003, 2005, 2007, 2009, 2011, and 2013 was calculated by using NCVS incident variables appended to the SCS data files of the same year. The NCVS type of crime variable was used to classify victimizations of students in the SCS as serious violent, violent, or theft. The NCVS variables asking where the incident happened (at school) and what the victim was doing when it happened (attending school or on the way to or from school) were used to ascertain whether the incident happened at school. Only incidents that occurred inside the United States are included.

In 2001, the SCS survey instrument was modified from previous collections. First, in 1995 and 1999, "at school" was defined for respondents as in the school building, on the school grounds, or on a school bus. In 2001, the definition for "at school" was changed to mean in the school building, on school property, on a school bus, or going to and from school. This change was made to the 2001 questionnaire in order to be consistent with the definition of "at school" as it is constructed in the NCVS and was also used as the definition in subsequent SCS collections. Cognitive interviews conducted by the U.S. Census Bureau on the 1999 SCS suggested that modifications to the definition of "at school" would not have a substantial impact on the estimates.

A total of about 9,700 students participated in the 1995 SCS, 8,400 in 1999, 8,400 in 2001, 7,200 in 2003, 6,300 in 2005, 5,600 in 2007, 5,000 in 2009, 6,500 in 2011, and 5,700 in 2013. In the 2013 SCS, the household completion rate was 86 percent.

In the 1995, 1999, 2001, 2003, 2005, 2007, 2009, and 2011 SCS, the household completion rates were 95 percent, 94 percent, 93 percent, 92 percent, 91 percent, 90 percent, 92 percent, and 91 percent, respectively, and the student completion rates were 78 percent, 78 percent, 77 percent, 70 percent, 62 percent, 58 percent, 56 percent, and 63 percent, respectively. For the 2013 SCS, the student completion rate was 60 percent. The overall unweighted SCS unit response rate (calculated by multiplying the household completion rate by the student completion rate) was about 74 percent in 1995, 73 percent in 1999, 72 percent in 2001, 64 percent in 2003, 56 percent in 2005, 53 percent in 2007, 51 percent in 2009, 57 percent in 2011, and 51 percent in 2013.

There are two types of nonresponse: unit and item nonresponse. NCES requires that any stage of data collection within a survey that has a unit base-weighted response rate of less than 85 percent be evaluated for the potential magnitude of unit nonresponse bias before the data or any analysis using the data may be released (U.S. Department of Education 2003). Due to the low unit response rate in 2005, 2007, 2009, 2011, and 2013, a unit nonresponse bias analysis was done. Unit response rates indicate how many sampled units have completed interviews. Because interviews with students could only be completed after households had responded to the NCVS, the unit completion rate for the SCS reflects both the household interview completion rate and the student interview completion rate. Nonresponse can greatly affect the strength and application of survey data by leading to an increase in variance as a result of a reduction in the actual size of the sample and can produce bias if the nonrespondents have characteristics of interest that are different from the respondents.

In order for response bias to occur, respondents must have different response rates and responses to particular survey variables. The magnitude of unit nonresponse bias is determined by the response rate and the differences between respondents and nonrespondents on key survey variables. Although the bias analysis cannot measure response bias since the SCS is a sample survey and it is not known how the population would have responded, the SCS sampling frame has four key student or school characteristic variables for which data are known for respondents and nonrespondents: sex, race/ethnicity, household income, and urbanicity, all of which are associated with student victimization. To the extent that there are differential responses by respondents in these groups, nonresponse bias is a concern.

In 2005, the analysis of unit nonresponse bias found evidence of bias for the race, household income, and urbanicity variables. White (non-Hispanic) and Other (non-Hispanic) respondents had higher response rates than Black (non-Hispanic) and Hispanic respondents. Respondents from households with an income of $35,000–$49,999 and $50,000 or more had higher response rates than those from households with incomes of less than $7,500, $7,500–$14,999, $15,000–$24,999 and $25,000–$34,999. Respondents who live in urban areas had lower response rates than those who live in rural or suburban areas. Although the extent of nonresponse bias cannot be determined, weighting adjustments, which corrected for differential response rates, should have reduced the problem.

In 2007, the analysis of unit nonresponse bias found evidence of bias by the race/ethnicity and household income variables. Hispanic respondents had lower response rates than other races/ethnicities.

Respondents from households with an income of $25,000 or more had higher response rates than those from households with incomes of less than $25,000. However, when responding students are compared to the eligible NCVS sample, there were no measurable differences between the responding students and the eligible students, suggesting that the nonresponse bias has little impact on the overall estimates.

In 2009, the analysis of unit nonresponse bias found evidence of potential bias for the race/ethnicity and urbanicity variables. White students and students of other races/ethnicities had higher response rates than did Black and Hispanic respondents. Respondents from households located in rural areas had higher response rates than those from households located in urban areas. However, when responding students are compared to the eligible NCVS sample, there were no measurable differences between the responding students and the eligible students, suggesting that the nonresponse bias has little impact on the overall estimates.

In 2011, the analysis of unit nonresponse bias found evidence of potential bias for the age variable. Respondents 12 to 17 years old had higher response rates than did 18-year-old respondents in the NCVS and SCS interviews. Weighting the data adjusts for unequal selection probabilities and for the effects of nonresponse. The weighting adjustments that correct for differential response rates are created by region, age, race, and sex, and should have reduced the effect of nonresponse.

In 2013, the analysis of unit nonresponse bias found evidence of potential bias for the age variable in the SCS respondent sample. Students age 14 and those from the western region showed percentage bias exceeding 5 percent; however, both subgroups had the highest response rate out of their respective categories. All other subgroups evaluated showed less than 1 percent nonresponse bias and had between 0.3 and 2.6 percent difference between the response population and the eligible population.

Response rates for most SCS survey items in all survey years were high—typically over 97 percent of all eligible respondents, meaning there is little potential for item nonresponse bias for most items in the survey. Weights were developed to compensate for differential probabilities of selection and nonresponse. The weighted data permit inferences about the eligible student population who were enrolled in schools in all SCS data years.

Further information about the SCS may be obtained from

Rachel Hansen
Sample Surveys Division
Cross-Sectional Surveys Branch
National Center for Education Statistics
550 12th Street SW
Washington, DC 20202
(202) 245-7082
rachel.hansen@ed.gov
http://nces.ed.gov/programs/crime

Federal Bureau of Investigation

The Federal Bureau of Investigation (FBI) collects statistics on crimes from law enforcement agencies throughout the country through the Uniform Crime Reporting (UCR) Program. The UCR Program was conceived in 1929 by the International Association of Chiefs of Police to meet a need for reliable, uniform crime statistics for the nation. In 1930, the FBI was tasked with collecting, publishing, and archiving those statistics. Today, several annual statistical publications, such as the comprehensive *Crime in the United States* (CIUS), are produced from data provided by over 18,000 law enforcement agencies across the United States. CIUS is an annual publication in which the FBI compiles the volume and rate of crime offenses for the nation, the states, and individual agencies. This report also includes arrest, clearance, and law enforcement employee data.

For more information on the UCR Program, see http://www.fbi.gov/about-us/cjis/ucr/ucr.

Supplementary Homicide Reports

Supplementary Homicide Reports (SHR) are a part of the Uniform Crime Reporting (UCR) program of the Federal Bureau of Investigation (FBI). These reports provide incident-level information on criminal homicides, including situation type (e.g., number of victims, number of offenders, and whether offenders are known); the age, sex, and race of victims and offenders; the weapon used; circumstances of the incident; and the relationship of the victim to the offender. The data are provided monthly to the FBI by local law enforcement agencies participating in the UCR program. The data include murders and nonnegligent manslaughters in the United States from January 1980 to December 2012; that is, negligent manslaughters and justifiable homicides have been eliminated from the data. Based on law enforcement agency reports, the FBI estimates that 625,919 murders (including nonnegligent manslaughters) were committed from 1980 to 2011. Agencies provided detailed information on 590,954 of these homicide victims. SHR estimates in this report have been revised from those in previously published reports.

About 90 percent of homicides are included in the SHR program. However, adjustments can be made to the weights to correct for missing victim reports. Estimates from the SHR program used in this report were generated by the Bureau of Justice Statistics (BJS). The SHR data were weighted to compensate for the average annual 10 percent of homicides that were not reported to the SHR. The development of the set of annual weights is a three-step process.

Further information on the SHR program may be obtained from

Communications Unit
Criminal Justice Information Services Division
Federal Bureau of Investigation
Module D3
1000 Custer Hollow Road
Clarksburg, WV 26306
(304) 625-4995
cjis_comm@leo.gov

Department of Defense

Defense Manpower Data Center

The Statistical Information Analysis Division of the Defense Manpower Data Center (DMDC) maintains the largest archive of personnel, manpower, and training data in the Department of Defense (DoD). The DMDC's statistical activities include the personnel survey program, an enlistment testing program to support screening of military applicants, and a client support program to provide statistical support to the Office of the Secretary of Defense. The DMDC collects DoD contract information in support of national economic tables and the Small Business Competitiveness Demonstration Program; it also produces statistics on DoD purchases from educational and nonprofit institutions and from state and local governments.

For more information on the DMDC, see http://www.dhra.mil/website/locations/map_page_dmdc.shtml.

Institute of Museum and Library Statistics

On October 1, 2007, the administration of the Public Libraries Survey (PLS) and the State Library Agencies (StLA) Survey was transferred from the National Center for Education Statistics to the Institute of Museum and Library Statistics (IMLS).

IMLS Library Statistics

Public library statistics are collected annually using the PLS and disseminated annually through the Federal-State Cooperative System (FSCS) for Public Library Data. Descriptive statistics are produced for over 9,000 public libraries. The PLS includes information about staffing; operating income and expenditures; type of governance; type of administrative structure; size of collection; and service measures such as reference transactions, public service hours, interlibrary loans, circulation, and library visits. In the FSCS, respondents supply the information electronically, and data are edited and tabulated in machine-readable form.

The respondents are public libraries identified in the 50 states and the District of Columbia by state library agencies. At the state level, FSCS is administered by State Data Coordinators, who are appointed by the Chief Officer of each State Library Agency. The State Data Coordinator collects the requested data from local public libraries. All 50 states and the District of Columbia submit data for individual public libraries, which are aggregated to state and national levels.

From 1994 through 2006, NCES conducted the StLA Survey for the 50 states and the District of Columbia. A state library agency is the official agency of a state that is charged by state law with the extension and development of public library services throughout the state and that has adequate authority under state law to administer state plans in accordance with the provisions of the Library Services and Technology Act (LSTA) of 2003. The StLA Survey collected data on services, collections, staffing, revenue, and expenditures.

Further information on the Public Library Survey and State Library Agency Survey can be obtained from

Institute of Museum and Library Services
Office of Policy, Planning, Research, and Communication
Research and Statistics Division
955 L'Enfant Plaza North SW
Washington, DC 20024-2135
imlsinfo@imls.gov
http://www.imls.gov/

My Brother's Keeper Initiative

Established by President Obama in 2014, the My Brother's Keeper Initiative is an interagency effort to improve measurably the expected educational and life outcomes for and address the persistent opportunity gaps faced by boys and young men of color. The Initiative established a task force to develop a coordinated federal effort to identify the public and private efforts that are working and how to expand upon them.

The My Brother's Keeper Task Force and the Federal Interagency Forum on Child and Family Statistics have collected federal statistics on a number of national level indicators to provide an initial snapshot of young people's well-being across multiple domains, including health, nutrition, poverty, education, economic opportunity, criminal justice and more. A selection of these data may be accessed at http://www2.ed.gov/rschstat/statistics/surveys/mbk/index.html.

Further information about the My Brother's Keeper Initiative may be obtained from
https://www.whitehouse.gov/my-brothers-keeper.

National Institute on Drug Abuse

Monitoring the Future Survey

The National Institute on Drug Abuse of the U.S. Department of Health and Human Services is the primary supporter of the long-term study titled "Monitoring the Future: A Continuing Study of American Youth," conducted by the University of Michigan Institute for Social Research. One component of the study deals with student drug abuse. Results of the national sample survey have been published annually since 1975. With the exception of 1975, when about 9,400 students participated in the survey, the annual samples comprise roughly 16,000 students in 150 public and private schools. Students complete self-administered questionnaires given to them in their classrooms by University of Michigan personnel. Each year, 8th-, 10th-, and 12th-graders are surveyed (12th-graders since 1975, and 8th- and 10th-graders since 1991). The 8th- and 10th-grade surveys are anonymous, while the 12th-grade survey is confidential. The 10th-grade samples involve about 17,000 students in 140 schools each year, while the 8th-grade samples have approximately 18,000 students in about 150 schools. In all, approximately 50,000 students from about 420 public and private secondary schools are surveyed annually. Approximately 88.4 percent of 8th-grade students, 87.2 percent of 10th-grade students, and 84.7 percent of 12th-grade students surveyed participated in the study in 2010. Beginning with the class of 1976, a randomly selected sample from each senior class has been followed in the years after high school on a continuing basis.

Understandably, there is some reluctance to admit illegal activities. Also, students who are out of school on the day of the survey are nonrespondents, and the survey does not include high school dropouts. The inclusion of absentees and dropouts would tend to increase the proportion of individuals who had used drugs. A 1983 study found that the inclusion of absentees could increase some of the drug usage estimates by as much as 2.7 percentage points. (Details on that study and its methodology were published in *Drug Use Among American High School Students, College Students, and Other Young Adults*, by L.D. Johnston, P.M. O'Malley, and J.G. Bachman, available from the National Clearinghouse on Drug Abuse Information, 5600 Fishers Lane, Rockville, MD 20857.)

The 2014 Monitoring the Future survey encompassed about 41,600 8th-, 10th-, and 12th-grade students in 377 secondary schools nationwide. The first published results were presented in *Monitoring the Future, National Results on Drug Use, 1975–2014: Overview, Key Findings on Adolescent Drug Use*, at http://www.monitoringthefuture.org/pubs/monographs/mtf-overview2014.pdf.

Further information on the Monitoring the Future drug abuse survey may be obtained from

National Institute on Drug Abuse
Division of Epidemiology, Services and
    Prevention Research (DESPR)
6001 Executive Boulevard
Bethesda, MD 20892
mtfinformation@umich.edu
http://www.monitoringthefuture.org

National Science Foundation

Survey of Federal Funds for Research and Development

The annual Survey of Federal Funds for Research and Development is the primary source of information about federal funding for research and development in the United States. It is used by policymakers in the executive and legislative branches of the federal government in determining policies, laws, and regulations affecting science; it is also used by those who follow science trends in every sector of the economy, including university administrators and professors, economic and political analysts, research and development managers inside and outside the government, the science press, and leading members of the science community in the United States and around the world.

The survey's target population consists of the federal agencies that conduct research and development programs, which are identified from information in the President's budget submitted to Congress. In the survey cycle for data collection on fiscal years 2014–16, a total of 28 federal agencies (15 federal departments and 13 independent agencies) reported data. Because multiple subdivisions of a federal department were in some cases requested to complete the survey, there were 72 individual respondents. Federal funds data, as collected, span 3 government fiscal years: the fiscal year just completed, the current fiscal year, and the next fiscal year. Actual data are collected for the year just completed; estimates are obtained for the current fiscal year and the next fiscal year.

The data are collected and managed online; this system was designed to help improve survey reporting by offering respondents direct online reporting and editing.

The federal funds survey has an unweighted response rate of 100 percent with no known item nonresponse. The information included in this survey has been stable since fiscal year 1973, when federal obligations for research to universities and colleges by agency and detailed science and engineering fields were added to the survey.

Further information on federal funds for research and development may be obtained from

Michael Yamaner
Research and Development Statistics Program
National Center for Science and Engineering Statistics
National Science Foundation
4201 Wilson Boulevard, Suite 965
Arlington, VA 22230
myamaner@nsf.gov
http://www.nsf.gov/statistics

Survey of Earned Doctorates

The Survey of Earned Doctorates (SED) has collected basic statistics from the universe of doctoral recipients in the United States each year since 1957. It is supported by six federal agencies: the National Science Foundation, National Institutes of Health, U.S. Department of Education, U.S. Department of Agriculture, National Endowment for the Humanities, and National Aeronautics and Space Administration. With the assistance of institutional coordinators at each doctorate-awarding institution, a survey form is distributed to each person completing the requirements for a research doctorate. Of the 54,070 persons receiving research doctorates granted in 2014, 91 percent responded to the survey. The survey questionnaire obtains information on sex, race/ethnicity, marital status, citizenship, disabilities, dependents, specialty field of doctorate, educational institutions attended, time spent in completion of doctorate, financial support, education debt, postgraduation plans, and educational attainment of parents.

Further information on the Survey of Earned Doctorates may be obtained from

Lynn Milan
Human Resources Statistics Program
National Center for Science and Engineering Statistics
National Science Foundation
4201 Wilson Boulevard
Arlington, VA 22230
lmilan@nsf.gov
http://www.nsf.gov/statistics/srvydoctorates

Survey of Graduate Students and Postdoctorates in Science and Engineering

The Survey of Graduate Students and Postdoctorates in Science and Engineering, also known as the graduate student survey (GSS), is an annual survey of all U.S. academic institutions granting research-based master's degrees or doctorates in science, engineering, or selected health fields. Sponsored by the National Science Foundation and the National Institutes of Health, the survey provides data on the number and characteristics of graduate students, postdoctoral researchers, and doctorate-holding nonfaculty researchers in selected health fields. Results are used to assess shifts in graduate enrollment and postdoctorate appointments and trends in financial support.

Data collection for the 2014 GSS began in fall 2014. The survey universe consisted of 406 doctorate-granting and 300 master's-granting institutions, for a total of 706 institutions. There were 821 schools affiliated with these institutions: 521 at doctorate-granting institutions and 300 at master's-granting institutions.

New procedures to improve coverage of GSS-eligible units were introduced in the 2007 survey cycle and were continued in subsequent cycles. Increased emphasis was given to updating the unit list by providing an exhaustive list of GSS-eligible programs within existing GSS fields. In previous years, only a representative list was provided for each GSS field, which may have resulted in not reporting all eligible units. The set of GSS-eligible fields was also modified. Due to these changes, data for 2007 and later years are not directly comparable with data from previous years. Most recently, in 2014, the survey universe was modified to include 151 new institutions and exclude two for-profit institutions; these changes were the result of a comprehensive frame evaluation study conducted from 2010 to 2013 and the annual frame evaluation conducted in the 2013–14 cycle.

Further information on the Survey of Graduate Students and Postdoctorates in Science and Engineering may be obtained from

Kelly Kang
Human Resources Statistics Program
National Center for Science and Engineering Statistics
National Science Foundation
4201 Wilson Boulevard, Suite 965
Arlington, VA 22230
kkang@nsf.gov
http://www.nsf.gov/statistics/srvygradpostdoc/

Substance Abuse and Mental Health Services Administration

National Survey on Drug Use and Health

Conducted by the federal government since 1971 (annually since 1991), the National Survey on Drug Use and Health (NSDUH) is a survey of the civilian, noninstitutionalized population of the United States age 12 or older. It is the primary source of information on the prevalence, patterns, and consequences of alcohol, tobacco, and illegal drug use and abuse. The survey collects data by administering questionnaires to a representative sample of the population (since 1999, the NSDUH interview has been carried out using computer-assisted interviewing). NSDUH collects information from residents of households, noninstitutional group quarters, and civilians living on military bases. The main results of the NSDUH present national estimates of rates of use, numbers of users, and other measures related to illicit drugs, alcohol, and tobacco products.

Prior to 2002, the survey was called the National Household Survey on Drug Abuse (NHSDA). The 2002 update of the survey's name coincided with improvements to the survey. In light of these improvements, NSDUH data from 2002 and later should not be compared with NHSDA data from 2001 and earlier as a method of assessing changes in substance use over time.

The 2005 NSDUH was the first in a coordinated 5-year sample design providing estimates for all 50 states and the District of Columbia for the years 2005 through 2009. Because the 2005 design enables estimates to be developed by state, states may be viewed as the first level of stratification, as well as a reporting variable.

In the 2014 NSDUH, screening was completed at 127,605 addresses, and 67,901 completed interviews were obtained. The survey was conducted from January through December 2014. Weighted response rates for household screening and for interviewing were 81.9 and 71.2 percent, respectively.

Further information on the NSDUH may be obtained from

SAMHSA, Center for Behavioral Health Statistics
    and Quality
5600 Fishers Lane
Rockville, MD 20857
http://www.samhsa.gov/data/

Other Organization Sources

ACT

ACT assessment

The ACT assessment is designed to measure educational development in the areas of English, mathematics, social studies, and natural sciences. The ACT assessment is taken by college-bound high school students and by all graduating seniors in Colorado and Illinois. The test results are used to predict how well students might perform in college.

Prior to the 1984–85 school year, national norms were based on a 10 percent sample of the students taking the test. Since then, national norms have been based on the test scores of all students taking the test. Beginning with 1984–85, these norms have been based on the most recent ACT scores available from students scheduled to graduate in the spring of the year. Duplicate test records are no longer used to produce national figures.

Separate ACT standard scores are computed for English, mathematics, science reasoning, and, as of October 1989, reading. ACT standard scores are reported for each subject area on a scale from 1 to 36. In 2015, the national composite score (the simple average of the four ACT standard scores) was 21.0, with a standard deviation of 5.4. The tests emphasize reasoning, analysis, problem solving, and the integration of learning from various sources, as well as the application of these proficiencies to the kinds of tasks college students are expected to perform.

It should be noted that graduating students who take the ACT assessment are not necessarily representative of graduating students nationally. Students who live in the Midwest, Rocky Mountains, Plains, and South are overrepresented among ACT-tested students as compared to graduating students nationally. Students in these areas often aspire to public colleges and universities, which in these jurisdictions require the ACT assessment more often than the SAT test.

Further information on the ACT may be obtained from

ACT
500 ACT Drive
P.O. Box 168
Iowa City, IA 52243-0168
http://www.act.org

The College Board

Advanced Placement Exam

The Advanced Placement (AP) program is a curriculum sponsored by the College Board that offers high school students the opportunity to take college-level courses in a high school setting. A student taking an AP course in high school can earn college credit for participation by attaining a certain minimum score on the AP exam in that subject area.

The AP program offers 38 courses in 7 subject areas. Although nearly 60 percent of U.S. high schools in the United States offer AP courses, the College Board does not require students to take an AP course before taking an AP exam. AP exams are offered once a year in May. Most of the exams take 2 to 3 hours to complete. The scores for all AP exams range from 1 to 5, with 5 being the highest score. Over 90 percent of the nation's colleges and universities have an AP policy granting incoming students credit, placement, or both, for qualifying AP exam scores.

SAT

The Admissions Testing Program of the College Board is made up of a number of college admissions tests, including the Preliminary Scholastic Assessment Test (PSAT) and the Scholastic Assessment Test, now known as the SAT. High school students participate in the testing program as sophomores, juniors, or seniors—some more than once during these three years. If they have taken the tests more than once, only the most recent scores are tabulated. The PSAT and SAT report subscores in the areas of mathematics and verbal ability.

Each year, over 2 million students take the SAT examination. SAT results are not representative of high school students or college-bound students nationally, however, since the sample is self-selected (i.e., taken by students who need the results to apply to a particular college or university). In addition, public colleges in many states—particularly those in the Midwest, parts of the South, and the West—require ACT scores rather than SAT scores; thus, the proportion of students taking the SAT in these states is very low and is inappropriate for comparison. The current version of the SAT, which includes an optional writing component among other content, format, and scoring changes, was first administered in March 2016.

Further information on AP and the SAT may be obtained from

The College Board National Office
250 Vesey Street
New York, NY 10281
http://www.collegeboard.org/

Commonfund Institute

Higher Education Price Index

Commonfund Institute took over management of the Higher Education Price Index (HEPI) in 2005 from Research Associates of Washington, which originated the index in 1961. HEPI is an inflation index designed specifically to track the main cost drivers in higher education. It measures the average relative level of prices in a fixed basket of goods and services purchased each year by colleges and universities through current fund educational and general expenditures, excluding research.

The main components of HEPI are professional salaries and fringe benefits of faculty, administrators, and other professional service personnel; nonprofessional wages, salaries, and fringe benefits for clerical, technical, service, and other nonprofessional personnel; contracted services such as data processing, communication, transportation, supplies and materials, and equipment; library acquisitions; and utilities. These represent the major items purchased for current operations by colleges and universities. Prices for these items are obtained from salary surveys conducted by the American Association of University Professors, the College

and University Professional Association for Human Resources, and the Bureau of Labor Statistics (BLS), as well as from price series of components of BLS's Consumer Price Index (CPI) and Producer Price Index (PPI). Since 2009, data have been consistently drawn from the July–June academic fiscal year. Prior to 2009, data were collected from years with varying endpoints.

HEPI measures price levels from a designated reference year in which budget weights are assigned. This base year is FY 1983 and is assigned a price value of 100.0 for index compilation. An index value of 115.0, for example, represents a 15 percent price increase over 1983 values.

Further information on HEPI may be obtained from

Commonfund Institute
15 Old Danbury Road
Wilton, CT 06897
https://www.commonfund.org/commonfund-institute/
higher-education-price-index-hepi/

Council for Aid to Education

Survey of Voluntary Support of Education

The Council for Aid to Education, Inc. (CAE) is a nonprofit corporation funded by contributions from businesses. CAE largely provides consulting and research services to corporations and information on voluntary support services to education institutions. Each year, CAE conducts a survey of colleges and universities and private elementary and secondary schools to obtain information on the amounts, sources, and purposes of private gifts, grants, and bequests received during the academic year.

The annual Voluntary Support of Education (VSE) survey consistently captures about 85 percent of the total voluntary support to colleges and universities in the United States. Institutional reports of voluntary support data from the VSE survey are more comprehensive and detailed than the related data in the Integrated Postsecondary Education Data System (IPEDS) Finance survey conducted by NCES.

The VSE survey is conducted online. All accredited higher education institutions are eligible to participate, and about a quarter of these institutions fill out a survey each year. CAE reviews the survey forms for internal consistency, queries institutions whose data appear out of line with national trends or their own historical data, and makes an effort to clean the data before preparing a computerized database of the results.

Individual institutions and several state systems of higher education use the VSE data to monitor and analyze their fundraising results. CAE uses the data to develop national estimates of giving to education and to report in detail on private support of education. The results from the VSE survey are available to subscribers online and are also published in the annual report *Voluntary Support of Education*, which may be purchased from CAE.

Further information on the VSE survey may be obtained from

Ann Kaplan
Council for Aid to Education
215 Lexington Avenue
16th Floor
New York, NY 10016-6023
vse@cae.org
http://cae.org

Council of Chief State School Officers

State Education Indicators

The Council of Chief State School Officers (CCSSO) is a nonpartisan, nationwide, nonprofit organization of the public officials who head departments of public education in the 50 states, the District of Columbia, the Department of Defense dependents schools, the Bureau of Indian Education, Puerto Rico, American Samoa, Guam, the Northern Mariana Islands, and the U.S. Virgin Islands. The CCSSO State Education Indicators project provides leadership in developing a system of state-by-state indicators of the condition of K–12 education. Indicator activities include collecting and reporting statistical indicators by state, tracking state policy changes, assisting with accountability systems, and conducting analysis of trends in education. *Key State Education Policies on PK–12 Education* is one of the publications issued by the State Education Indicators project. It is intended to inform policymakers and educators about the current status of key education policies that define and shape elementary and secondary education in the nation's public schools. State education staff reported on current policies through a survey, and CCSSO staff collected additional assessment information through state websites.

Further information on CCSSO publications may be obtained from

State Education Indicators Program
Standards, Assessment, and Accountability
Council of Chief State School Officers
1 Massachusetts Avenue NW
Suite 700
Washington, DC 20001-1431
http://www.ccsso.org

Editorial Projects in Education

Education Week

Editorial Projects in Education is an independent, non-profit publisher of *Education Week* and other print and online products on K–12 education.

Further information on Editorial Projects in Education publications may be obtained from

Editorial Projects in Education, Inc.
Suite 100
6935 Arlington Road
Bethesda, MD 20814-5233
http://www.edweek.org/info/about

Education Commission of the States

StateNotes

Education Commission of the States (ECS) regularly issues compilations, comparisons, and summaries of state policies—enacted or pending—on a number of education issues, including high school graduation requirements and school term information. ECS monitors state education activities for changes in education policies and updates ECS state information accordingly.

Further information on ECS StateNotes may be obtained from

Education Commission of the States
700 Broadway, #810
Denver, CO 80203-3442
ecs@ecs.org
http://www.ecs.org

GED Testing Service

GED Testing Service is a joint venture, begun in 2011, between the American Council on Education (ACE) and Pearson. A GED credential documents high school-level academic skills. The test was first administered to World War II veterans in 1942 and was subsequently administered to civilians beginning in 1947. The first four generations of the GED test were the original GED test released in 1942, the 1978 series, the 1988 series, and the 2002 series. In 2014, a new test was implemented. Differences and similarities between the 2014 GED test and the 2002 series test are available at http://www.gedtestingservice.com/uploads/files/2487f6e1ca5659684cbe1f8b16f564d0.pdf.

The annual *GED Testing Program Statistical Report* looks at those who take the GED, test performance statistics, and historical information on the GED testing program.

Attempting to make comparisons in GED testing across jurisdictions is problematic, since each jurisdiction manages its own GED testing program. As such, each jurisdiction develops its own policies, which would be reflected in its testing program outcomes, such as pass rates.

Further information on the GED may be obtained from

GED Testing Service
1919 M Street NW
Suite 600
Washington, DC 20036
http://www.gedtestingservice.com/ged-testing-service

Graduate Record Examinations Board

GRE tests

Graduate Record Examinations (GRE) tests are taken by individuals applying to graduate or professional school. GRE offers two types of tests, the revised General Test and Subject Tests. The revised General Test, which is mainly taken via computer, measures verbal, quantitative, and analytical writing skills. The analytical writing section (which replaced the analytical reasoning section on the general GRE in October 2002) consists of two analytical writing tasks. The Subject Tests measure achievement in biochemistry, cell and molecular biology, biology, chemistry, literature in English, mathematics, physics, and psychology. Each graduate institution or division of the institution determines which GRE tests are required for admission.

Individuals may take GRE tests more than once. Score reports only reflect scores earned within the past 5-year period.

Further information on the GRE may be obtained from

GRE-ETS
Educational Testing Service
P.O. Box 6000
Princeton, NJ 08541
http://www.ets.org/gre

Institute of International Education

Open Doors

Each year, the Institute of International Education (IIE) conducts a survey of the number of foreign students studying in American colleges and universities and U.S. students studying abroad. The results of these surveys are reported in the publication *Open Doors*. All of the regionally accredited institutions in NCES's Integrated Postsecondary Education Data System (IPEDS) are surveyed by IIE. The foreign student enrollment data presented in the *Digest of Education Statistics* are drawn from IIE surveys that ask U.S. institutions for information on enrollment of foreign students, as well as student characteristics such as country of origin. For the 2013–14 survey, 62.0 percent of the 2,814 institutions surveyed reported data. For 2014–15, 58.9 percent of the 2,808 institutions surveyed reported data.

Surveys on the flows of U.S. college students studying abroad have been conducted since 1985–86. Surveys are sent to U.S. institutions asking them to provide information on the number and characteristics of the students to whom they awarded credit for study abroad during the previous academic year. For the 2012–13 academic year, data were obtained from 1,119, or 64.1 percent, of the 1,746 institutions surveyed; for the 2013–14 academic year, data were obtained from 1,116, or 61.3 percent, of the 1,821 institutions surveyed.

Additional information may be obtained from the publication Open Doors or by contacting

Sharon Witherell
Institute of International Education–Public Affairs
809 United Nations Plaza
New York, NY 10017
switherell@iie.org
http://www.iie.org/en/Research-and-Publications/Open-Doors

International Association for the Evaluation of Educational Achievement

The International Association for the Evaluation of Educational Achievement (IEA) is composed of governmental research centers and national research institutions around the world whose aim is to investigate education problems common among countries. Since its inception in 1958, the IEA has conducted more than 30 research studies of cross-national achievement. The regular cycle of studies encompasses learning in basic school subjects. Examples are the Trends in International Mathematics and Science Study (TIMSS) and the Progress in International Reading Literacy Study (PIRLS). IEA projects also include studies of particular interest to IEA members, such as the TIMSS 1999 Video Study of Mathematics and Science Teaching, the Civic Education Study, and studies on information technology in education.

The international bodies that coordinate international assessments vary in the labels they apply to participating education systems, most of which are countries. IEA differentiates between IEA members, which IEA refers to as "countries" in all cases, and "benchmarking participants." IEA members include countries such as the United States and Ireland, as well as subnational entities such as England and Scotland (which are both part of the United Kingdom), the Flemish community of Belgium, and Hong Kong (a Special Administrative Region of China). IEA benchmarking participants are all subnational entities and include Canadian provinces, U.S. states, and Dubai in the United Arab Emirates (among others). Benchmarking participants, like the participating countries, are given the opportunity to assess the comparative international standing of their students' achievement and to view their curriculum and instruction in an international context.

Some IEA studies, such as TIMSS and PIRLS, include an assessment portion as well as contextual questionnaires to collect information about students' home and school experiences. The TIMSS and PIRLS scales, including the scale averages and standard deviations, are designed to remain constant from assessment to assessment so that education systems (including countries and subnational education systems) can compare their scores over time, as well as compare their scores directly with the scores of other education systems. Although each scale was created to have a mean of 500 and a standard deviation of 100, the subject matter and the level of difficulty of items necessarily differ by grade, subject, and domain/dimension. Therefore, direct comparisons between scores across grades, subjects, and different domain/dimension types should not be made.

Further information on the International Association for the Evaluation of Educational Achievement may be obtained from http://www.iea.nl.

Trends in International Mathematics and Science Study

The Trends in International Mathematics and Science Study (TIMSS, formerly known as the Third International Mathematics and Science Study) provides data on the mathematics and science achievement of U.S. 4th- and 8th-graders compared with that of their peers in other countries. TIMSS collects information through mathematics and science assessments and questionnaires. The questionnaires request information to help provide a context for student performance. They focus on such topics as students' attitudes and beliefs about learning mathematics and science, what students do as part of their mathematics and science lessons, students' completion of homework, and their lives both in and outside of school; teachers' perceptions of their preparedness for teaching mathematics and science, teaching assignments, class size and organization, instructional content and practices, collaboration with other teachers, and participation in professional development activities; and principals' viewpoints on policy and budget responsibilities, curriculum and instruction issues, and student behavior. The questionnaires also elicit information on the organization of schools and courses. The assessments and questionnaires are designed to specifications in a guiding framework. The TIMSS framework describes the mathematics and science content to be assessed and provides grade-specific objectives, an overview of the assessment design, and guidelines for item development.

TIMSS is on a 4-year cycle. Data collections occurred in 1995, 1999 (8th grade only), 2003, 2007, and 2011. TIMSS 2015 is the sixth administration of TIMSS since 1995. It consists of five assessments: 4th-grade mathematics; numeracy (a less difficult version of 4th-grade mathematics, newly developed for 2015); 8th-grade mathematics; 4th-grade science; and 8th-grade science. In addition to the 4th- and 8th-grade assessments, TIMSS 2015 includes the third administration of TIMSS Advanced since 1995. TIMSS Advanced assesses final-year (12th-grade) secondary students' achievement in advanced mathematics and physics. The study also collects policy-relevant information about students, curriculum emphasis, technology use, and teacher preparation and training.

Progress in International Reading Literacy Study

The Progress in International Reading Literacy Study (PIRLS) provides data on the reading literacy of U.S. 4th-graders compared with that of their peers in other countries. PIRLS is on a 5-year cycle: PIRLS data collections have been conducted in 2001, 2006, and 2011. In 2011, a total of 57 education systems, including 48 IEA members and 9 benchmarking participants, participated in the survey. The next PIRLS data collection is scheduled for 2016.

PIRLS collects information through a reading literacy assessment and questionnaires that help to provide a context for student performance. Questionnaires are administered to collect information about students' home and school experiences in learning to read. A student questionnaire addresses students' attitudes toward reading and their reading habits. In addition, questionnaires are given to students' teachers and school principals to gather information about students' school experiences in developing reading literacy. In countries other than the United States, a parent questionnaire is also administered. The assessments and questionnaires are designed to specifications in a guiding framework. The PIRLS framework describes the reading content to be assessed and provides objectives specific to 4th grade, an overview of the assessment design, and guidelines for item development.

TIMSS and PIRLS Sampling and Response Rates

As is done in all participating countries and other education systems, representative samples of students in the United States are selected. The sample design that was employed by TIMSS and PIRLS in 2011 is generally referred to as a two-stage stratified cluster sample. In the first stage of sampling, individual schools were selected with a probability proportionate to size (PPS) approach, which means that the probability is proportional to the estimated number of students enrolled in the target grade. In the second stage of sampling, intact classrooms were selected within sampled schools.

TIMSS and PIRLS guidelines call for a minimum of 150 schools to be sampled, with a minimum of 4,000 students assessed. The basic sample design of one classroom per school was designed to yield a total sample of approximately 4,500 students per population.

About 23,000 students in almost 900 schools across the United States participated in the 2011 TIMSS, joining 600,000 other student participants around the world. Because PIRLS was also administered at grade 4 in spring 2011, TIMSS and PIRLS in the United States were administered in the same schools to the extent feasible. Students took either TIMSS or PIRLS on the day of the assessments. About 13,000 U.S. students participated in PIRLS in 2011, joining 300,000 other student participants around the world. Accommodations were not provided for students with disabilities or students who were unable to read or speak the language of the test. These students were excluded from the sample. The IEA requirement is that the overall exclusion rate, which includes exclusions of schools and students, should not exceed more than 5 percent of the national desired target population.

In order to minimize the potential for response biases, the IEA developed participation or response rate standards that apply to all participating education systems and govern whether or not an education system's data are included in the TIMSS or PIRLS international datasets and the way in which its statistics are presented in the international reports. These standards were set using composites of response rates at the school, classroom, and student and teacher levels. Response rates were calculated with and without the inclusion of substitute schools that were selected to replace schools refusing to participate. In TIMSS 2011 at grade 4 in the United States, the weighted school participation rate was

79 percent before the use of substitute schools and 84 percent after the use of replacement schools; the weighted student response rate was 95 percent. In TIMSS 2011 at grade 8 in the United States, the weighted school participation rate was 87 percent before the use of substitute schools and 87 percent after the use of replacement schools; the weighted student response rate was 94 percent. In the 2011 PIRLS administered in the United States, the weighted school participation rate was 80 percent before the use of substitute schools and 85 percent after the use of replacement schools; the weighted student response rate was 96 percent.

Further information on the TIMSS study may be obtained from

Stephen Provasnik
Assessments Division
International Assessment Branch
National Center for Education Statistics
550 12th Street SW
Washington, DC 20202
(202) 245-6442
stephen.provasnik@ed.gov
http://nces.ed.gov/timss
http://www.iea.nl/timss_2011.html

Further information on the PIRLS study may be obtained from

Sheila Thompson
Assessments Division
International Assessment Branch
National Center for Education Statistics
550 12th Street SW
Washington, DC 20202
(202) 245-8330
sheila.thompson@ed.gov
http://nces.ed.gov/surveys/pirls/
http://www.iea.nl/pirls_2011.html

National Association of State Directors of Teacher Education and Certification

NASDTEC Manual/KnowledgeBase

The National Association of State Directors of Teacher Education and Certification (NASDTEC) was organized in 1928 to represent professional standards boards and commissions and state departments of education that are responsible for the preparation, licensure, and discipline of educational personnel. Currently, NASDTEC's membership includes all 50 states, the District of Columbia, the U.S. Department of Defense Education Activity, U.S. territories, and Canadian provinces and territories.

The NASDTEC Manual on the Preparation and Certification of Educational Personnel was printed between 1984 and 2004, when it was replaced by an online publication, KnowledgeBase. KnowledgeBase is an expanded version of the Manual and is the most comprehensive source of state-by-state information pertaining to the certification requirements and preparation of teachers and other school personnel in the United States and Canada.

Further information on KnowledgeBase may be obtained from

Phillip S. Rogers
Executive Director
NASDTEC
1629 K Street NW
Suite 300
Washington, DC 20006
philrogers@nasdtec.com
http://www.nasdtec.net/

National Catholic Educational Association

The United States Catholic Elementary and Secondary Schools

The National Catholic Educational Association (NCEA) has been providing leadership and service to Catholic education since 1904. NCEA began to publish *The United States Catholic Elementary and Secondary Schools: Annual Statistical Report on Schools, Enrollment and Staffing* in 1970 because of the lack of educational data on the private sector. The report is based on data gathered by all of the archdiocesan and diocesan offices of education in the United States. These data enable NCEA to present information on school enrollment and staffing patterns for prekindergarten through grade 12. The first part of the report presents data concerning the context of American education, while the following segment focuses on statistical data of Catholic schools. Statistics include enrollment by grade level, race/ethnicity, and affiliation.

Further information on *The United States Catholic Elementary and Secondary Schools: Annual Statistical Report on Schools, Enrollment, and Staffing* may be obtained from

Sister Dale McDonald
National Catholic Educational Association
1005 North Glebe Road
Suite 525
Arlington, VA 22201
mcdonald@ncea.org
http://www.ncea.org

National Education Association

Estimates of School Statistics

The National Education Association (NEA) publishes *Estimates of School Statistics* annually as part of the report *Rankings of the States & Estimates of School Statistics*. *Estimates of School Statistics* presents projections of public school enrollment, employment and personnel compensation, and finances, as reported by individual state departments of education. The state-level data in these estimates allow broad assessments of trends in the above areas. These data should be looked at with the understanding that the state-level data do not necessarily reflect the varying conditions within a state on education issues.

Data in *Estimates of School Statistics* are provided by state and District of Columbia departments of education and by other, mostly governmental, sources. Surveys are sent to the departments of education requesting estimated data for the current year and revisions to 4 years of historical data, as necessary. Twice a year, NEA submits current-year estimates on more than 35 education statistics to state departments of education for verification or revision. The estimates are generated using regression analyses and are used only if the states do not provide current data.

Further information on *Estimates of School Statistics* may be obtained from

NEA Rankings & Estimates Team—NEA Research
1201 16th Street NW
Washington, DC 20036
http://www.nea.org

Organization for Economic Cooperation and Development

The Organization for Economic Cooperation and Development (OECD) publishes analyses of national policies and survey data in education, training, and economics in OECD and partner countries. Newer studies include student survey data on financial literacy and on digital literacy.

Education at a Glance

To highlight current education issues and create a set of comparative education indicators that represent key features of education systems, OECD initiated the Indicators of Education Systems (INES) project and charged the Centre for Educational Research and Innovation (CERI) with developing the cross-national indicators for it. The development of these indicators involved representatives of the OECD countries and the OECD Secretariat. Improvements in data quality and comparability among OECD countries have resulted from the country-to-country interaction sponsored through the INES project. The most recent publication in this series is *Education at a Glance 2015: OECD Indicators*.

Education at a Glance 2015 features data on the 34 OECD countries (Australia, Austria, Belgium, Canada, Chile, the Czech Republic, Denmark, Estonia, Finland, France, Germany, Greece, Hungary, Iceland, Ireland, Israel, Italy, Japan, the Republic of Korea, Luxembourg, Mexico, the Netherlands, New Zealand, Norway, Poland, Portugal, the Slovak Republic, Slovenia, Spain, Sweden, Switzerland, Turkey, the United Kingdom, and the United States) and a number of partner countries, namely, Argentina, Brazil, China, Colombia, Costa Rica, India, Indonesia, Latvia, Lithuania, the Russian Federation, Saudi Arabia, and South Africa.

The *OECD Handbook for Internationally Comparative Education Statistics: Concepts, Standards, Definitions, and Classifications* provides countries with specific guidance on how to prepare information for OECD education surveys; facilitates countries' understanding of OECD indicators and their use in policy analysis; and provides a reference for collecting and assimilating educational data. Chapter 7 of the *OECD Handbook for Internationally Comparative Education Statistics* contains a discussion of data quality issues. Users should examine footnotes carefully to recognize some of the data limitations.

Further information on international education statistics may be obtained from

Andreas Schleicher
Director for the Directorate of Education and Skills and
    Special Advisor on Education Policy to the OECD's
    Secretary General
OECD Directorate for Education and Skills
2, rue André Pascal
75775 Paris CEDEX 16
France
andreas.schleicher@oecd.org
http://www.oecd.org

Program for International Student Assessment

The Program for International Student Assessment (PISA) is a system of international assessments organized by the Organization for Economic Cooperation and Development (OECD), an intergovernmental organization of industrialized countries, that focuses on 15-year-olds' capabilities in reading literacy, mathematics literacy, and science literacy. PISA also includes measures of general, or cross-curricular, competencies such as learning strategies. PISA emphasizes functional skills that students have acquired as they near the end of compulsory schooling.

PISA is a 2-hour paper-and-pencil exam. Assessment items include a combination of multiple-choice questions and open-ended questions that require students to develop their own response. PISA scores are reported on a scale that ranges from 0 to 1,000, with the OECD mean set at 500 and a standard deviation set at 100. In 2012, mathematics, science, and reading literacy were assessed primarily through a paper-and-pencil exam, and problem-solving was administered using a computer-based exam. Education systems could also participate in optional pencil-and-paper financial literacy assessments and computer-based mathematics and reading assessments. In each education system, the assessment is translated into the primary language of instruction; in the United States, all materials are written in English.

To implement PISA, each of the participating education systems scientifically draws a nationally representative sample of 15-year-olds, regardless of grade level. In the United States, about 6,100 students from 161 public and private schools took the PISA 2012 assessment. In the U.S. state education systems, about 1,700 students at 50 schools in Connecticut, about 1,900 students at 54 schools in Florida, and about 1,700 students at 49 schools in Massachusetts took the 2012 assessment. PISA 2012 was only administered at public schools in the U.S. state education systems.

The intent of PISA reporting is to provide an overall description of performance in reading literacy, mathematics literacy, and science literacy every 3 years, and to provide a more detailed look at each domain in the years when it is the major focus. These cycles will allow education systems to compare changes in trends for each of the three subject areas over time. In the first cycle, PISA 2000, reading literacy was the major focus, occupying roughly two-thirds of assessment time. For 2003, PISA focused on mathematics literacy as well as the ability of students to solve problems in real-life settings. In 2006, PISA focused on science literacy; in 2009, it focused on reading literacy again; and in 2012, it focused on mathematics literacy. PISA 2015 focuses on science, as it did in 2006.

In 2000, 43 education systems participated in PISA. In 2003, 41 education systems participated; in 2006, 57 education systems (30 OECD member countries and 27 nonmember countries or education systems) participated; and in 2009, 65 education systems (34 OECD member countries and 31 nonmember countries or education systems) participated. (An additional nine education systems administered PISA 2009 in 2010.) In PISA 2012, the most recent administration for which results are available, 65 education systems (34 OECD member countries and 31 nonmember countries or education systems), as well as the U.S. states of Connecticut, Florida, and Massachusetts, participated. PISA 2015 assessed students' mathematics, reading, and science literacy in more than 70 countries and educational jurisdictions. The survey also included a collaborative problem-solving assessment and an optional financial literacy assessment. U.S. 15-year-old students participated in this optional assessment.

Further information on PISA may be obtained from

Patrick Gonzales
Assessments Division
International Assessment Branch
National Center for Education Statistics
550 12th Street SW
Washington, DC 20202
patrick.gonzales@ed.gov
http://nces.ed.gov/surveys/pisa

Program for the International Assessment of Adult Competencies

The Program for the International Assessment of Adult Competencies (PIAAC) is a cyclical, large-scale study that aims to assess and compare the broad range of basic skills and competencies of adults around the world. Developed under the auspices of the Organization for Economic Cooperation and Development (OECD), it is the most comprehensive international survey of adult skills ever undertaken. Adults were surveyed in 24 participating countries in 2012 and in an additional 9 countries in 2014.

PIAAC focuses on what are deemed basic cognitive and workplace skills necessary to adults' successful participation in 21st-century society and in the global economy. Skills assessed include literacy, numeracy, problem solving in technology-rich environments, and basic reading skills. PIAAC measures the relationships between these skills and other characteristics such as individuals' educational background, workplace experiences, and occupational attainment. PIAAC was administered on laptop computers or in paper-and-pencil mode. In the United States, the background questionnaire was administered in both English and Spanish, and the cognitive assessment was administered only in English.

The 2012 PIAAC assessment for the United States included a nationally representative probability sample of households. This household sample was selected on the basis of a four-stage, stratified area sample: (1) primary sampling units (PSUs) consisting of counties or groups of contiguous counties; (2) secondary sampling units (referred to as segments) consisting of area blocks; (3) housing units containing households; and (4) eligible persons within households. Person-level data were collected through a screener, a background questionnaire, and the assessment.

Based on the screener data, 6,100 U.S. respondents ages 16 to 65 were selected to complete the 2012 background questionnaire and the assessment; 4,898 actually completed the background questionnaire. Of the 1,202 respondents who did not complete the background questionnaire, 112 were unable to do so because of a literacy-related barrier: either the inability to communicate in English or Spanish or a mental disability. Twenty others were unable to complete the questionnaire due to technical problems. The final response rate for the background questionnaire—which included respondents who completed it and respondents who were unable to complete it because of a language problem or mental disability—was 82.2 percent weighted. The overall weighted response rate for the household sample—the product of the component response rates—was 70.3 percent.

Key to PIAAC's value is its collaborative and international nature. In the United States, NCES has consulted extensively with the Department of Labor in the development of the survey, and staff from both agencies are co-representatives of the United States in PIAAC's international governing body. Internationally, PIAAC has been developed through the collaboration of OECD staff and participating countries' representatives from their ministries or departments of education and labor. Through this cooperative effort, all participating countries follow the quality assurance guidelines set by the OECD consortium and closely follow all agreed-upon standards set for survey design, assessment implementation, and reporting of results.

Further information on PIAAC may be obtained from

Holly Xie
Assessments Division
International Assessment Branch
National Center for Education Statistics
550 12th Street SW
Washington, DC 20202
holly.xie@ed.gov
https://nces.ed.gov/surveys/piaac/
http://www.oecd.org/skills/piaac/

School Bus Fleet

School Bus Fleet magazine is a trade publication serving more than 28,000 school transportation professionals in the United States and Canada that provides information on the management and maintenance of school bus fleets operated by public school districts, private schools, Head Start agencies, and child care centers. The readership includes public operators and contract service providers.

Further information on School Bus Fleet magazine may be obtained from

School Bus Fleet
3520 Challenger Street
Torrance, CA 90503
info@schoolbusfleet.com
http://www.schoolbusfleet.com/

School Transportation News

School Transportation News is a monthly news and feature magazine covering the field of pupil transportation. The publication focuses on school bus and school vehicle safety and reports on transportation-related legislation and environmental issues touching on school transportation. The *School Transportation News* website offers a detailed history of school transportation services in the United States.

Further information about *School Transportation News* may be obtained from

School Transportation News
P.O. Box 789
Redondo Beach, CA 90277
http://stnonline.com/

United Nations Educational, Scientific, and Cultural Organization

Statistical Yearbook and Global Education Digest

The United Nations Educational, Scientific, and Cultural Organization (UNESCO) conducts annual surveys of education statistics of its member countries. Data from official surveys are supplemented by information obtained by UNESCO through other publications and sources. Each year, more than 200 countries reply to the UNESCO surveys. In some cases, estimates are made by UNESCO for particular items, such as world and continent totals. While great efforts are made to make them as comparable as possible, the data still reflect the vast differences among the countries of the world in the structure of education. While there is some agreement about the reporting of primary and secondary data, tertiary-level data (i.e., postsecondary education data) present numerous substantive problems. Some countries report only university enrollment, while other countries report all postsecondary enrollment, including enrollment in vocational and technical schools and correspondence programs. A very high proportion of some countries' tertiary-level students attend institutions in other countries. The member countries that provide data to UNESCO are responsible for their validity. Thus, data for particular countries are subject to nonsampling error and perhaps sampling error as well. Users should examine footnotes carefully to recognize some of the data limitations. UNESCO publishes the data in reports such as the *Statistical Yearbook* and the *Global Education Digest*.

Further information on the *Statistical Yearbook* and the *Global Education Digest* may be obtained from

UNESCO Institute for Statistics
C.P. 6128 Succursale Centre-ville
Montreal, Quebec, H3C 3J7
Canada
http://www.uis.unesco.org

APPENDIX B
Definitions

Academic support This category of college expenditures includes expenditures for support services that are an integral part of the institution's primary missions of instruction, research, or public service. It also includes expenditures for libraries, galleries, audio/visual services, academic computing support, ancillary support, academic administration, personnel development, and course and curriculum development.

Achievement gap Occurs when one group of students outperforms another group, and the difference in average scores for the two groups is statistically significant (that is, larger than the margin of error).

Achievement levels, NAEP Specific achievement levels for each subject area and grade to provide a context for interpreting student performance. At this time they are being used on a trial basis.

   Basic—denotes partial mastery of the knowledge and skills that are fundamental for *proficient* work at a given grade.

   Proficient—represents solid academic performance. Students reaching this level have demonstrated competency over challenging subject matter.

   Advanced—signifies superior performance.

Achievement test An examination that measures the extent to which a person has acquired certain information or mastered certain skills, usually as a result of specific instruction.

ACT The ACT (formerly the American College Testing Program) assessment program measures educational development and readiness to pursue college-level coursework in English, mathematics, natural science, and social studies. Student performance on the tests does not reflect innate ability and is influenced by a student's educational preparedness.

Administrative support staff Staff whose activities are concerned with support of teaching and administrative duties of the office of the principal or department chairpersons, including clerical staff and secretaries.

Advanced Placement (AP) A program of tertiary-level courses and examinations, taught by specially qualified teachers, that provides opportunities for secondary school students to earn undergraduate credits for first-year university courses. The schools and teachers offering AP programs must meet College Board requirements and are monitored.

Agriculture Courses designed to improve competencies in agricultural occupations. Included is the study of agricultural production, supplies, mechanization and products, agricultural science, forestry, and related services.

Alternative school A public elementary/secondary school that serves students whose needs cannot be met in a regular, special education, or vocational school; may provide nontraditional education; and may serve as an adjunct to a regular school. Although alternative schools fall outside the categories of regular, special education, and vocational education, they may provide similar services or curriculum. Some examples of alternative schools are schools for potential dropouts; residential treatment centers for substance abuse (if they provide elementary or secondary education); schools for chronic truants; and schools for students with behavioral problems.

Appropriation (federal funds) Budget authority provided through the congressional appropriation process that permits federal agencies to incur obligations and to make payments.

Appropriation (institutional revenues) An amount (other than a grant or contract) received from or made available to an institution through an act of a legislative body.

Associate's degree A degree granted for the successful completion of a sub-baccalaureate program of studies, usually requiring at least 2 years (or equivalent) of full-time college-level study. This includes degrees granted in a cooperative or work-study program.

Autism See Disabilities, children with.

Autocorrelation Correlation of the error terms from different observations of the same variable. Also called Serial correlation.

Auxiliary enterprises This category includes those essentially self-supporting operations which exist to furnish a service to students, faculty, or staff, and which charge a fee that is directly related to, although not necessarily equal to, the cost of the service. Examples are residence halls, food services, college stores, and intercollegiate athletics.

Average daily attendance (ADA) The aggregate attendance of a school during a reporting period (normally a school year) divided by the number of days school is in session during this period. Only days on which the pupils are under the guidance and direction of teachers should be considered days in session.

Average daily membership (ADM) The aggregate membership of a school during a reporting period (normally a school year) divided by the number of days school is in session during this period. Only days on which the pupils are under the guidance and direction of teachers should be considered as days in session. The ADM for groups of schools having varying lengths of terms is the average of the ADMs obtained for the individual schools. Membership includes all pupils who are enrolled, even if they do not actually attend.

Averaged freshman graduation rate (AFGR) A measure of the percentage of the incoming high school freshman class that graduates 4 years later. It is calculated by taking the number of graduates with a regular diploma and dividing that number by the estimated count of incoming freshman 4 years earlier, as reported through the NCES Common Core of Data (CCD). The estimated count of incoming freshman is the sum of the number of 8th-graders 5 years earlier, the number of 9th-graders 4 years earlier (when current seniors were freshman), and the number of 10th-graders 3 years earlier, divided by 3. The purpose of this averaging is to account for the high rate of grade retention in the freshman year, which adds 9th-grade repeaters from the previous year to the number of students in the incoming freshman class each year. Ungraded students are allocated to individual grades proportional to each state's enrollment in those grades. The AFGR treats students who transfer out of a school or district in the same way as it treats students from that school or district who drop out.

Bachelor's degree A degree granted for the successful completion of a baccalaureate program of studies, usually requiring at least 4 years (or equivalent) of full-time college-level study. This includes degrees granted in a cooperative or work-study program.

Books Nonperiodical printed publications bound in hard or soft covers, or in loose-leaf format, of at least 49 pages, exclusive of the cover pages; juvenile nonperiodical publications of any length found in hard or soft covers.

Breusch-Godfrey serial correlation LM test A statistic testing the independence of errors in least-squares regression against alternatives of first-order and higher degrees of serial correlation. The test belongs to a class of asymptotic tests known as the Lagrange multiplier (LM) tests.

Budget authority (BA) Authority provided by law to enter into obligations that will result in immediate or future outlays. It may be classified by the period of availability (1-year, multiple-year, no-year), by the timing of congressional action (current or permanent), or by the manner of determining the amount available (definite or indefinite).

Business Program of instruction that prepares individuals for a variety of activities in planning, organizing, directing, and controlling business office systems and procedures.

Capital outlay Funds for the acquisition of land and buildings; building construction, remodeling, and additions; the initial installation or extension of service systems and other built-in equipment; and site improvement. The category also encompasses architectural and engineering services, including the development of blueprints.

Career/technical education (CTE) In high school, encompasses occupational education, which teaches skills required in specific occupations or occupational clusters, as well as nonoccupational CTE, which includes family and consumer sciences education (i.e., courses that prepare students for roles outside the paid labor market) and general labor market preparation (i.e., courses that teach general employment skills such as word processing and introductory technology skills).

Carnegie unit The number of credits a secondary student received for a course taken every day, one period per day, for a full year; a factor used to standardize all credits indicated on secondary school transcripts across studies.

Catholic school A private school over which a Roman Catholic church group exercises some control or provides some form of subsidy. Catholic schools for the most part include those operated or supported by a parish, a group of parishes, a diocese, or a Catholic religious order.

Central cities The largest cities, with 50,000 or more inhabitants, in a Metropolitan Statistical Area (MSA). Additional cities within the metropolitan area can also be classified as "central cities" if they meet certain employment, population, and employment/residence ratio requirements.

Certificate A formal award certifying the satisfactory completion of a postsecondary education program. Certificates can be awarded at any level of postsecondary education and include awards below the associate's degree level.

Charter school A school providing free public elementary and/or secondary education to eligible students under a specific charter granted by the state legislature or other appropriate authority, and designated by such authority to be a charter school.

City school See Locale codes.

Class size The membership of a class at a given date.

Classification of Instructional Programs (CIP) The CIP is a taxonomic coding scheme that contains titles and descriptions of primarily postsecondary instructional programs. It was developed to facilitate NCES' collection and reporting of postsecondary degree completions by major field of study using standard classifications that capture the majority of reportable program activity. It was originally published in 1980 and was revised in 1985, 1990, 2000, and 2010.

Classification of Secondary School Courses (CSSC) A modification of the Classification of Instructional Programs used for classifying high school courses. The CSSC contains over 2,200 course codes that help compare the thousands of high school transcripts collected from different schools.

Classroom teacher A staff member assigned the professional activities of instructing pupils in self-contained classes or courses, or in classroom situations; usually expressed in full-time equivalents.

Coefficient of variation (CV) Represents the ratio of the standard error to the estimate. For example, a CV of 30 percent indicates that the standard error of the estimate is equal to 30 percent of the estimate's value. The CV is used to compare the amount of variation relative to the magnitude of the estimate. A CV of 30 percent or greater indicates that an estimate should be interpreted with caution. For a discussion of standard errors, see Appendix A: Guide to Sources.

Cohort A group of individuals who have a statistical factor in common, for example, year of birth.

Cohort-component method A method for estimating and projecting a population that is distinguished by its ability to preserve knowledge of an age distribution of a population (which may be of a single sex, race, and Hispanic origin) over time.

College A postsecondary school that offers general or liberal arts education, usually leading to an associate's, bachelor's, master's, or doctor's degree. Junior colleges and community colleges are included under this terminology.

Combined school A school that encompasses instruction at both the elementary and the secondary levels; includes schools starting with grade 6 or below and ending with grade 9 or above.

Combined school (2007–08 Schools and Staffing Survey) A school with at least one grade lower than 7 and at least one grade higher than 8; schools with only ungraded classes are included with combined schools.

Combined Statistical Area (CSA) A combination of Core Based Statistical Areas (see below), each of which contains a core with a substantial population nucleus as well as adjacent communities having a high degree of economic and social integration with that core. A CSA is a region with social and economic ties as measured by commuting, but at lower levels than are found within each component area. CSAs represent larger regions that reflect broader social and economic interactions, such as wholesaling, commodity distribution, and weekend recreation activities.

Computer science A group of instructional programs that describes computer and information sciences, including computer programming, data processing, and information systems.

Constant dollars Dollar amounts that have been adjusted by means of price and cost indexes to eliminate inflationary factors and allow direct comparison across years.

Consumer Price Index (CPI) This price index measures the average change in the cost of a fixed market basket of goods and services purchased by consumers. Indexes vary for specific areas or regions, periods of time, major groups of consumer expenditures, and population groups. The CPI reflects spending patterns for two population groups: (1) all urban consumers and urban wage earners and (2) clerical workers. CPIs are calculated for both the calendar year and the school year using the U.S. All Items CPI for All Urban Consumers (CPI-U). The calendar year CPI is the same as the annual CPI-U. The school year CPI is calculated by adding the monthly CPI-U figures, beginning with July of the first year and ending with June of the following year, and then dividing that figure by 12.

Consumption That portion of income that is spent on the purchase of goods and services rather than being saved.

Control of institutions A classification of institutions of elementary/secondary or postsecondary education by whether the institution is operated by publicly elected or appointed officials and derives its primary support from public funds (public control) or is operated by privately elected or appointed officials and derives its major source of funds from private sources (private control).

Core Based Statistical Area (CBSA) A population nucleus and the nearby communities having a high degree of economic and social integration with that nucleus. Each CBSA includes at least one urban area of 10,000 or more people and one or more counties. In addition to a "central county" (or counties), additional "outlying counties" are included in the CBSA if they meet specified requirements of commuting to or from the central counties.

Credit The unit of value, awarded for the successful completion of certain courses, intended to indicate the quantity of course instruction in relation to the total requirements for a diploma, certificate, or degree. Credits are frequently expressed in terms such as "Carnegie units," "semester credit hours," and "quarter credit hours."

Current dollars Dollar amounts that have not been adjusted to compensate for inflation.

Current expenditures (elementary/secondary) The expenditures for operating local public schools, excluding capital outlay and interest on school debt. These expenditures include such items as salaries for school personnel, benefits, student transportation, school books and materials, and energy costs. Beginning in 1980–81, expenditures for state administration are excluded.

Instruction expenditures Includes expenditures for activities related to the interaction between teacher and students. Includes salaries and benefits for teachers and instructional aides, textbooks, supplies, and purchased services such as instruction via television, webinars, and other online instruction. Also included are tuition expenditures to other local education agencies.

Administration expenditures Includes expenditures for school administration (i.e., the office of the principal, full-time department chairpersons, and graduation expenses), general administration (the superintendent and board of education and their immediate staff), and other support services expenditures.

Transportation Includes expenditures for vehicle operation, monitoring, and vehicle servicing and maintenance.

Food services Includes all expenditures associated with providing food to students and staff in a school or school district. The services include preparing and serving regular and incidental meals or snacks in connection with school activities, as well as the delivery of food to schools.

Enterprise operations Includes expenditures for activities that are financed, at least in part, by user charges, similar to a private business. These include operations funded by sales of products or services, together with amounts for direct program support made by state education agencies for local school districts.

Current expenditures per pupil in average daily attendance Current expenditures for the regular school term divided by the average daily attendance of full-time pupils (or full-time equivalency of pupils) during the term. See also Current expenditures and Average daily attendance.

Current-fund expenditures (postsecondary education) Money spent to meet current operating costs, including salaries, wages, utilities, student services, public services, research libraries, scholarships and fellowships, auxiliary enterprises, hospitals, and independent operations; excludes loans, capital expenditures, and investments.

Current-fund revenues (postsecondary education) Money received during the current fiscal year from revenue which can be used to pay obligations currently due, and surpluses reappropriated for the current fiscal year.

Deaf-blindness See Disabilities, children with.

Default rate The percentage of loans that are in delinquency and have not been repaid according to the terms of the loan. According to the federal government, a federal student loan is in default if there has been no payment on the loan in 270 days. The Department of Education calculates a *3-year cohort* default rate, which is the percentage of students who entered repayment in a given fiscal year (from October 1 to September 30) and then defaulted within the following 2 fiscal years. For example, the 3-year cohort default rate for fiscal year (FY) 2009 is the percentage of borrowers who entered repayment during FY 2009 (any time from October 1, 2008, through September 30, 2009) and who defaulted by the end of FY 2011 (September 30, 2011).

Degree An award conferred by a college, university, or other postsecondary education institution as official recognition for the successful completion of a program of studies. Refers specifically to associate's or higher degrees conferred by degree-granting institutions. See also Associate's degree, Bachelor's degree, Master's degree, and Doctor's degree.

Degree/certificate-seeking student A student enrolled in courses for credit and recognized by the institution as seeking a degree, certificate, or other formal award. High school students also enrolled in postsecondary courses for credit are not considered degree/certificate-seeking. See also Degree and Certificate.

Degree-granting institutions Postsecondary institutions that are eligible for Title IV federal financial aid programs and grant an associate's or higher degree. For an institution to be eligible to participate in Title IV financial aid programs, it must offer a program of at least 300 clock hours in length, have accreditation recognized by the U.S. Department of Education, have been in business for at least 2 years, and have signed a participation agreement with the Department.

Degrees of freedom The number of free or linearly independent sample observations used in the calculation of a statistic. In a time series regression with t time periods and k independent variables including a constant term, there would be t minus k degrees of freedom.

Department of Defense (DoD) dependents schools Schools that are operated by the Department of Defense Education Activity (a civilian agency of the U.S. Department of Defense) and provide comprehensive prekindergarten through 12th-grade educational programs on military installations both within the United States and overseas.

Dependency status A designation of whether postsecondary students are financially dependent on their parents or financially independent of their parents. Undergraduates are assumed to be dependent unless they meet one of the following criteria: are age 24 or older, are married or have legal dependents other than a spouse, are veterans, are orphans or wards of the court, or provide documentation that they self-supporting.

Dependent variable A mathematical variable whose value is determined by that of one or more other variables in a function. In regression analysis, when a random variable, *y*, is expressed as a function of variables *x1, x2, ... xk*, plus a stochastic term, then *y* is known as the "dependent variable."

Developmental delay See Disabilities, children with.

Disabilities, children with Those children evaluated as having any of the following impairments and who, by reason thereof, receive special education and related services under the Individuals with Disabilities Education Act (IDEA) according to an Individualized Education Program (IEP), Individualized Family Service Plan (IFSP), or a services plan. There are local variations in the determination of disability conditions, and not all states use all reporting categories.

   Autism Having a developmental disability significantly affecting verbal and nonverbal communication and social interaction, generally evident before age 3, that adversely affects educational performance. Other characteristics often associated with autism are engagement in repetitive activities and stereotyped movements, resistance to environmental change or change in daily routines, and unusual responses to sensory experiences. A child is not considered autistic if the child's educational performance is adversely affected primarily because of an emotional disturbance.

   Deaf-blindness Having concomitant hearing and visual impairments which cause such severe communication and other developmental and educational problems that the student cannot be accommodated in special education programs solely for deaf or blind students.

   Developmental delay Having developmental delays, as defined at the state level, and as measured by appropriate diagnostic instruments and procedures in one or more of the following cognitive areas: physical development, cognitive development, communication development, social or emotional development, or adaptive development. Applies only to 3- through 9-year-old children.

   Emotional disturbance Exhibiting one or more of the following characteristics over a long period of time, to a marked degree, and adversely affecting educational performance: an inability to learn that cannot be explained by intellectual, sensory, or health factors; an inability to build or maintain satisfactory interpersonal relationships with peers and teachers; inappropriate types of behavior or feelings under normal circumstances; a general pervasive mood of unhappiness or depression; or a tendency to develop physical symptoms or fears associated with personal or school problems. This term does not include children who are socially maladjusted, unless they also display one or more of the listed characteristics.

   Hearing impairment Having a hearing impairment, whether permanent or fluctuating, that adversely affects the student's educational performance. Also reported in this category is deafness, a hearing impairment so severe that the student is impaired in processing linguistic information through hearing (with or without amplification).

   Intellectual disability Having significantly subaverage general intellectual functioning, existing concurrently with defects in adaptive behavior and manifested during the developmental period, which adversely affects the child's educational performance.

   Multiple disabilities Having concomitant impairments (such as intellectually disabled-blind, intellectually disabled-orthopedically impaired, etc.), the combination of which causes such severe educational problems that the student cannot be accommodated in special education programs solely for one of the impairments. This term does not include deaf-blind students.

   Orthopedic impairment Having a severe orthopedic impairment that adversely affects a student's educational performance. The term includes impairment resulting from congenital anomaly, disease, or other causes.

   Other health impairment Having limited strength, vitality, or alertness due to chronic or acute health problems—such as a heart condition, tuberculosis, rheumatic fever, nephritis, asthma, sickle cell anemia, hemophilia, epilepsy, lead poisoning, leukemia, or diabetes—that adversely affect the student's educational performance.

   Specific learning disability Having a disorder in one or more of the basic psychological processes involved in understanding or in using spoken or written language, which may manifest itself in an imperfect ability to listen, think, speak, read, write, spell, or do mathematical calculations. The term includes such conditions as perceptual disabilities, brain injury, minimal brain dysfunction, dyslexia, and developmental aphasia. The term does not include children who have learning problems that are primarily the result of visual, hearing, motor, or intellectual disabilities, or of environmental, cultural, or economic disadvantage.

   Speech or language impairment Having a communication disorder, such as stuttering, impaired articulation, language impairment, or voice impairment, that adversely affects the student's educational performance.

   Traumatic brain injury Having an acquired injury to the brain caused by an external physical force, resulting in total or partial functional disability or psychosocial impairment or both, that adversely affects the student's educational performance. The term applies to open or closed head injuries resulting in impairments in one or more areas, such as cognition; language; memory; attention; reasoning; abstract thinking; judgment; problem-solving; sensory, perceptual, and motor abilities;

psychosocial behavior; physical functions; information processing; and speech. The term does not apply to brain injuries that are congenital or degenerative or to brain injuries induced by birth trauma.

Visual impairment Having a visual impairment that, even with correction, adversely affects the student's educational performance. The term includes partially seeing and blind children.

Discipline divisions Degree programs that include breakouts to the 6-digit level of the Classification of Instructional Programs (CIP). See also Fields of study.

Disposable personal income Current income received by people less their contributions for social insurance, personal tax, and nontax payments. It is the income available to people for spending and saving. Nontax payments include passport fees, fines and penalties, donations, and tuitions and fees paid to schools and hospitals operated mainly by the government. See also Personal income.

Distance education Education that uses one or more technologies to deliver instruction to students who are separated from the instructor and to support regular and substantive interaction between the students and the instructor synchronously or asynchronously. Technologies used for instruction may include the following: Internet; one-way and two-way transmissions through open broadcasts, closed circuit, cable, microwave, broadband lines, fiber optics, and satellite or wireless communication devices; audio conferencing; and DVDs and CD-ROMs, if used in a course in conjunction with the technologies listed above.

Doctor's degree The highest award a student can earn for graduate study. Includes such degrees as the Doctor of Education (Ed.D.); Doctor of Juridical Science (S.J.D.); Doctor of Public Health (Dr.P.H.); and Doctor of Philosophy (Ph.D.) in any field, such as agronomy, food technology, education, engineering, public administration, ophthalmology, or radiology. The doctor's degree classification encompasses three main subcategories—research/scholarship degrees, professional practice degrees, and other degrees—which are described below.

Doctor's degree—research/scholarship A Ph.D. or other doctor's degree that requires advanced work beyond the master's level, including the preparation and defense of a dissertation based on original research, or the planning and execution of an original project demonstrating substantial artistic or scholarly achievement. Examples of this type of degree may include the following and others, as designated by the awarding institution: the Ed.D. (in education), D.M.A. (in musical arts), D.B.A. (in business administration), D.Sc. (in science), D.A. (in arts), or D.M (in medicine).

Doctor's degree—professional practice A doctor's degree that is conferred upon completion of a program providing the knowledge and skills for the recognition, credential, or license required for professional practice. The degree is awarded after a period of study such that the total time to the degree, including both preprofessional and professional preparation, equals at least 6 full-time-equivalent academic years. Some doctor's degrees of this type were formerly classified as first-professional degrees. Examples of this type of degree may include the following and others, as designated by the awarding institution: the D.C. or D.C.M. (in chiropractic); D.D.S. or D.M.D. (in dentistry); L.L.B. or J.D. (in law); M.D. (in medicine); O.D. (in optometry); D.O. (in osteopathic medicine); Pharm.D. (in pharmacy); D.P.M., Pod.D., or D.P. (in podiatry); or D.V.M. (in veterinary medicine).

Doctor's degree—other A doctor's degree that does not meet the definition of either a doctor's degree—research/scholarship or a doctor's degree—professional practice.

Double exponential smoothing A method that takes a single smoothed average component of demand and smoothes it a second time to allow for estimation of a trend effect.

Dropout The term is used to describe both the event of leaving school before completing high school and the status of an individual who is not in school and who is not a high school completer. High school completers include both graduates of school programs as well as those completing high school through equivalency programs such as the GED program. Transferring from a public school to a private school, for example, is not regarded as a dropout event. A person who drops out of school may later return and graduate but is called a "dropout" at the time he or she leaves school. Measures to describe these behaviors include the event dropout rate (or the closely related school persistence rate), the status dropout rate, and the high school completion rate.

Durbin-Watson statistic A statistic testing the independence of errors in least squares regression against the alternative of first-order serial correlation. The statistic is a simple linear transformation of the first-order serial correlation of residuals and, although its distribution is unknown, it is tested by bounding statistics that follow R. L. Anderson's distribution.

Early childhood school Early childhood program schools serve students in prekindergarten, kindergarten, transitional (or readiness) kindergarten, and/or transitional first (or pre-first) grade.

Econometrics The quantitative examination of economic trends and relationships using statistical techniques, and the development, examination, and refinement of those techniques.

Education specialist/professional diploma A certificate of advanced graduate studies that advance educators in their instructional and leadership skills beyond a master's degree level of competence.

Educational and general expenditures The sum of current funds expenditures on instruction, research, public service, academic support, student services, institutional support, operation and maintenance of plant, and awards from restricted and unrestricted funds.

Educational attainment The highest grade of regular school attended and completed.

Educational attainment (Current Population Survey) This measure uses March CPS data to estimate the percentage of civilian, noninstitutionalized people who have achieved certain levels of educational attainment. Estimates of educational attainment do not differentiate between those who graduated from public schools, those who graduated from private schools, and those who earned a GED; these estimates also include individuals who earned their credential or completed their highest level of education outside of the United States.

1972–1991 During this period, an individual's educational attainment was considered to be his or her last fully completed year of school. Individuals who completed 12 years of schooling were deemed to be high school graduates, as were those who began but did not complete the first year of college. Respondents who completed 16 or more years of schooling were counted as college graduates.

1992–present Beginning in 1992, CPS asked respondents to report their highest level of school completed or their highest degree received. This change means that some data collected before 1992 are not strictly comparable with data collected from 1992 onward and that care must be taken when making comparisons across years. The revised survey question emphasizes credentials received rather than the last grade level attended or completed. The new categories include the following:

- High school graduate, high school diploma, or the equivalent (e.g., GED)
- Some college but no degree
- Associate's degree in college, occupational/vocational program
- Associate's degree in college, academic program (e.g., A.A., A.S., A.A.S.)
- Bachelor's degree (e.g., B.A., A.B., B.S.)
- Master's degree (e.g., M.A., M.S., M.Eng., M.Ed., M.S.W., M.B.A.)
- Professional school degree (e.g., M.D., D.D.S., D.V.M., LL.B., J.D.)
- Doctor's degree (e.g., Ph.D., Ed.D.)

Elementary education/programs Learning experiences concerned with the knowledge, skills, appreciations, attitudes, and behavioral characteristics that are considered to be needed by all pupils in terms of their awareness of life within our culture and the world of work, and that normally may be achieved during the elementary school years (usually kindergarten through grade 8 or kindergarten through grade 6), as defined by applicable state laws and regulations.

Elementary school A school classified as elementary by state and local practice and composed of any span of grades not above grade 8.

Elementary/secondary school Includes only schools that are part of state and local school systems, and also most nonprofit private elementary/secondary schools, both religiously affiliated and nonsectarian. Includes regular, alternative, vocational, and special education schools. U.S. totals exclude federal schools for American Indians, and federal schools on military posts and other federal installations.

Emotional disturbance See Disabilities, children with.

Employees in degree-granting institutions Persons employed by degree-granting institutions, who are classified into the following occupational categories in this publication:

Executive/administrative/managerial staff Employees whose assignments require management of the institution or of a customarily recognized department or subdivision thereof. These employees perform work that is directly related to management policies or general business operations and that requires them to exercise discretion and independent judgment.

Faculty (instruction/research/public service) Employees whose principal activities are for the purpose of providing instruction or teaching, research, or public service. These employees may hold such titles as professor, associate professor, assistant professor, instructor, or lecturer. Graduate assistants are not included in this category.

Graduate assistants Graduate-level students who are employed on a part-time basis for the primary purpose of assisting in classroom or laboratory instruction or in the conduct of research.

Nonprofessional staff Employees whose primary activities can be classified as one of the following: technical and paraprofessional work (which generally requires less formal training and experience than required for professional status); clerical and secretarial work; skilled crafts work; or service/maintenance work.

Other professional staff Employees who perform academic support, student service, and institutional support and who need either a degree at the bachelor's or higher level or experience of such kind and amount as to provide a comparable background.

Professional staff Employees who are classified as executive/administrative/managerial staff, faculty, graduate assistants, or other professional staff.

Employment Includes civilian, noninstitutional people who (1) worked during any part of the survey week as paid employees; worked in their own business, profession, or farm; or worked 15 hours or more as unpaid workers in a family-owned enterprise; or (2) were not working but had jobs or businesses from which they were temporarily absent due to illness, bad weather, vacation, labor-management dispute, or personal reasons whether or not they were seeking another job.

Employment (Current Population Survey) According to the October Current Population Survey (CPS), employed persons are persons age 16 or older who, during the reference week, (1) did any work at all (at least 1 hour) as paid employees or (2) were not working but had jobs or businesses from which they were temporarily absent because of vacation, illness, bad weather, child care problems, maternity or paternity leave, labor-management dispute, job training, or other family or personal reasons, whether or not they were paid for the time off or were seeking other jobs.

Employment status A classification of individuals as employed (either full or part time), unemployed (looking for work or on layoff), or not in the labor force (due to being retired, having unpaid employment, or some other reason).

Endowment A trust fund set aside to provide a perpetual source of revenue from the proceeds of the endowment investments. Endowment funds are often created by donations from benefactors of an institution, who may designate the use of the endowment revenue. Normally, institutions or their representatives manage the investments, but they are not permitted to spend the endowment fund itself, only the proceeds from the investments. Typical uses of endowments would be an endowed chair for a particular department or for a scholarship fund. Endowment totals tabulated in this book also include funds functioning as endowments, such as funds left over from the previous year and placed with the endowment investments by the institution. These funds may be withdrawn by the institution and spent as current funds at any time. Endowments are evaluated by two different measures, book value and market value. Book value is the purchase price of the endowment investment. Market value is the current worth of the endowment investment. Thus, the book value of a stock held in an endowment fund would be the purchase price of the stock. The market value of the stock would be its selling price as of a given day.

Engineering Instructional programs that describe the mathematical and natural science knowledge gained by study, experience, and practice and applied with judgment to develop ways to utilize the materials and forces of nature economically. Includes programs that prepare individuals to support and assist engineers and similar professionals.

English A group of instructional programs that describes the English language arts, including composition, creative writing, and the study of literature.

English language learner (ELL) An individual who, due to any of the reasons listed below, has sufficient difficulty speaking, reading, writing, or understanding the English language to be denied the opportunity to learn successfully in classrooms where the language of instruction is English or to participate fully in the larger U.S. society. Such an individual (1) was not born in the United States or has a native language other than English; (2) comes from environments where a language other than English is dominant; or (3) is an American Indian or Alaska Native and comes from environments where a language other than English has had a significant impact on the individual's level of English language proficiency.

Enrollment The total number of students registered in a given school unit at a given time, generally in the fall of a year. At the postsecondary level, separate counts are also available for full-time and part-time students, as well as full-time-equivalent enrollment. See also Full-time enrollment, Full-time-equivalent (FTE) enrollment, and Part-time enrollment.

Estimate A numerical value obtained from a statistical sample and assigned to a population parameter. The particular value yielded by an estimator in a given set of circumstances or the rule by which such particular values are calculated.

Estimating equation An equation involving observed quantities and an unknown that serves to estimate the latter.

Estimation Estimation is concerned with inference about the numerical value of unknown population values from incomplete data, such as a sample. If a single figure is calculated for each unknown parameter, the process is called point estimation. If an interval is calculated within which the parameter is likely, in some sense, to lie, the process is called interval estimation.

Executive/administrative/managerial staff See Employees in degree-granting institutions.

Expenditures, Total For elementary/secondary schools, these include all charges for current outlays plus capital outlays and interest on school debt. For degree-granting institutions, these include current outlays plus capital outlays. For government, these include charges net of recoveries and other correcting transactions other than for retirement of debt, investment in securities, extension of credit, or as agency transactions. Government expenditures include only external transactions, such as the provision of perquisites or other payments in kind. Aggregates for groups of governments exclude intergovernmental transactions among the governments.

Expenditures per pupil Charges incurred for a particular period of time divided by a student unit of measure, such as average daily attendance or fall enrollment.

Exponential smoothing A method used in time series analysis to smooth or to predict a series. There are various forms, but all are based on the supposition that more remote history has less importance than more recent history.

Expulsion Removing a student from his or her regular school for an extended length of time or permanently for disciplinary purposes.

Extracurricular activities Activities that are not part of the required curriculum and that take place outside of the regular course of study. They include both school-sponsored (e.g., varsity athletics, drama, and debate clubs) and community-sponsored (e.g., hobby clubs and youth organizations like the Junior Chamber of Commerce or Boy Scouts) activities.

Faculty (instruction/research/public service) See Employees in degree-granting institutions.

Family A group of two or more people (one of whom is the householder) related by birth, marriage, or adoption and residing together. All such people (including related subfamily members) are considered as members of one family.

Family income Includes all monetary income from all sources (including jobs, businesses, interest, rent, and Social Security payments) over a 12-month period. The income of nonrelatives living in the household is excluded, but the income of all family members age 15 or older (age 14 or older in years prior to 1989), including those temporarily living outside of the household, is included. In the October Current Population Survey, family income is determined from a single question asked of the household respondent.

Federal funds Amounts collected and used by the federal government for the general purposes of the government. The major federal fund is the general fund, which is derived from general taxes and borrowing. Other types of federal fund accounts include special funds (earmarked for a specific purpose other than a business-like activity), public enterprise funds (earmarked for a business-like activity conducted primarily with the public), and intragovernmental funds (earmarked for a business-like activity conducted primarily within the government).

Federal sources (postsecondary degree-granting institutions) Includes federal appropriations, grants, and contracts, and federally funded research and development centers (FFRDCs). Federally subsidized student loans are not included.

Fields of study The primary field of concentration in postsecondary certificates and degrees. In the Integrated Postsecondary Education Data System (IPEDS), refers to degree programs that are broken out only to the 2-digit level of the Classification of Instructional Programs (CIP). See also Discipline divisions.

Financial aid Grants, loans, assistantships, scholarships, fellowships, tuition waivers, tuition discounts, veteran's benefits, employer aid (tuition reimbursement), and other monies (other than from relatives or friends) provided to students to help them meet expenses. Except where designated, includes Title IV subsidized and unsubsidized loans made directly to students.

First-order serial correlation When errors in one time period are correlated directly with errors in the ensuing time period.

First-professional degree NCES no longer uses this classification. Most degrees formerly classified as first-professional (such as M.D., D.D.S., Pharm.D., D.V.M., and J.D.) are now classified as doctor's degrees—professional practice. However, master's of divinity degrees are now classified as master's degrees.

First-time student (undergraduate) A student who has no prior postsecondary experience (except as noted below) attending any institution for the first time at the undergraduate level. Includes students enrolled in the fall term who attended college for the first time in the prior summer term, and students who entered with advanced standing (college credits earned before graduation from high school).

Fiscal year A period of 12 months for which accounting records are compiled. Institutions and states may designate their own accounting period, though most states use a July 1 through June 30 accounting year. The yearly accounting period for the federal government begins on October 1 and ends on the following September 30. The fiscal year is designated by the calendar year in which it ends; e.g., fiscal year 2006 begins on October 1, 2005, and ends on September 30, 2006. (From fiscal year 1844 to fiscal year 1976, the federal fiscal year began on July 1 and ended on the following June 30.)

Forecast An estimate of the future based on rational study and analysis of available pertinent data, as opposed to subjective prediction.

Forecasting Assessing the magnitude that a quantity will assume at some future point in time, as distinct from "estimation," which attempts to assess the magnitude of an already existent quantity.

Foreign languages A group of instructional programs that describes the structure and use of language that is common or indigenous to people of a given community or nation, geographical area, or cultural traditions. Programs cover such features as sound, literature, syntax, phonology, semantics, sentences, prose, and verse, as well as the development of skills and attitudes used in communicating and evaluating thoughts and feelings through oral and written language.

For-profit institution A private institution in which the individual(s) or agency in control receives compensation other than wages, rent, or other expenses for the assumption of risk.

Free or reduced-price lunch See National School Lunch Program.

Full-time enrollment The number of students enrolled in postsecondary education courses with total credit load equal to at least 75 percent of the normal full-time course load. At the undergraduate level, full-time enrollment typically includes students who have a credit load of 12 or more semester or quarter credits. At the postbaccalaureate level, full-time enrollment includes students who typically have a credit load of 9 or more semester or quarter credits, as well as other students who are considered full time by their institutions.

Full-time-equivalent (FTE) enrollment For postsecondary institutions, enrollment of full-time students, plus the full-time equivalent of part-time students. The full-time equivalent of the part-time students is estimated using different factors depending on the type and control of institution and level of student.

Full-time-equivalent (FTE) staff Full-time staff, plus the full-time equivalent of the part-time staff.

Full-time-equivalent teacher See Instructional staff.

Full-time instructional faculty Those members of the instruction/research staff who are employed full time as defined by the institution, including faculty with released time for research and faculty on sabbatical leave. Full-time counts exclude faculty who are employed to teach less than two semesters, three quarters, two trimesters, or two 4-month sessions; replacements for faculty on sabbatical leave or those on leave without pay; faculty for preclinical and clinical medicine; faculty who are donating their services; faculty who are members of military organizations and paid on a different pay scale than civilian employees; those academic officers whose primary duties are administrative; and graduate students who assist in the instruction of courses.

Full-time worker In educational institutions, an employee whose position requires being on the job on school days throughout the school year for at least the number of hours the schools are in session. For higher education, a member of an educational institution's staff who is employed full time, as defined by the institution.

Function A mathematical correspondence that assigns exactly one element of one set to each element of the same or another set. A variable that depends on and varies with another.

Functional form A mathematical statement of the relationship among the variables in a model.

General administration support services Includes salary, benefits, supplies, and contractual fees for boards of education staff and executive administration. Excludes state administration.

GED certificate This award is received following successful completion of the GED test. The GED program—sponsored by the GED Testing Service (a joint venture of the American Council on Education and Pearson)—enables individuals to demonstrate that they have acquired a level of learning comparable to that of high school graduates. See also High school equivalency certificate.

GED program Academic instruction to prepare people to take the high school equivalency examination. Formerly known as the General Educational Development program. See also GED recipient.

GED recipient A person who has obtained certification of high school equivalency by meeting state requirements and passing an approved exam, which is intended to provide an appraisal of the person's achievement or performance in the broad subject matter areas usually required for high school graduation.

General program A program of studies designed to prepare students for the common activities of a citizen, family member, and worker. A general program of studies may include instruction in both academic and vocational areas.

Geographic region One of the four regions of the United States used by the U.S. Census Bureau, as follows:

Northeast	*Midwest*
Connecticut (CT)	Illinois (IL)
Maine (ME)	Indiana (IN)
Massachusetts (MA)	Iowa (IA)
New Hampshire (NH)	Kansas (KS)
New Jersey (NJ)	Michigan (MI)
New York (NY)	Minnesota (MN)
Pennsylvania (PA)	Missouri (MO)
Rhode Island (RI)	Nebraska (NE)
Vermont (VT)	North Dakota (ND)
	Ohio (OH)
	South Dakota (SD)
	Wisconsin (WI)

South	*West*
Alabama (AL)	Alaska (AK)
Arkansas (AR)	Arizona (AZ)
Delaware (DE)	California (CA)
District of Columbia (DC)	Colorado (CO)
Florida (FL)	Hawaii (HI)
Georgia (GA)	Idaho (ID)
Kentucky (KY)	Montana (MT)
Louisiana (LA)	Nevada (NV)
Maryland (MD)	New Mexico (NM)
Mississippi (MS)	Oregon (OR)
North Carolina (NC)	Utah (UT)
Oklahoma (OK)	Washington (WA)
South Carolina (SC)	Wyoming (WY)
Tennessee (TN)	
Texas (TX)	
Virginia (VA)	
West Virginia (WV)	

Government appropriation An amount (other than a grant or contract) received from or made available to an institution through an act of a legislative body.

Government grant or contract Revenues received by a postsecondary institution from a government agency for a specific research project or other program. Examples are research projects, training programs, and student financial assistance.

Graduate An individual who has received formal recognition for the successful completion of a prescribed program of studies.

Graduate assistants See Employees in degree-granting institutions.

Graduate enrollment The number of students who are working toward a master's or doctor's degree and students who are in postbaccalaureate classes but not in degree programs.

Graduate Record Examination (GRE) Multiple-choice examinations administered by the Educational Testing Service and taken by college students who intend to attend certain graduate schools. There are two types of testing available: (1) the general exam which measures critical thinking, analytical writing, verbal reasoning, and quantitative reasoning skills, and (2) the subject test which is offered in eight specific subjects and gauges undergraduate achievement in a specific field. The subject tests are intended for those who have majored in or have extensive background in that specific area.

Graduation Formal recognition given to an individual for the successful completion of a prescribed program of studies.

Gross domestic product (GDP) The total national output of goods and services valued at market prices. GDP can be viewed in terms of expenditure categories that include purchases of goods and services by consumers and government, gross private domestic investment, and net exports of goods and services. The goods and services included are largely those bought for final use (excluding illegal transactions) in the market economy. A number of inclusions, however, represent imputed values, the most important of which is rental value of owner-occupied housing.

Group quarters Living arrangements where people live or stay in a group situation that is owned or managed by an entity or organization providing housing and/or services for the residents. Group quarters include such places as college residence halls, residential treatment centers, skilled nursing facilities, group homes, military barracks, correctional facilities, and workers' dormitories.

    Noninstitutionalized group quarters Include college and university housing, military quarters, facilities for workers and religious groups, and temporary shelters for the homeless.

Institutionalized group quarters Include adult and juvenile correctional facilities, nursing facilities, and other health care facilities.

Handicapped See Disabilities, children with.

Head Start A local public or private nonprofit or for-profit entity authorized by the Department of Health and Human Services' Administration for Children and Families to operate a Head Start program to serve children age 3 to compulsory school age, pursuant to section 641(b) and (d) of the Head Start Act.

Hearing impairment See Disabilities, children with.

High school A secondary school offering the final years of high school work necessary for graduation. A high school is usually either a 3-year school that includes grades 10, 11, and 12 or a 4-year school that includes grades 9, 10, 11, and 12.

High school (2007–08 Schools and Staffing Survey) A school with no grade lower than 7 and at least one grade higher than 8.

High school completer An individual who has been awarded a high school diploma or an equivalent credential, including a GED certificate.

High school diploma A formal document regulated by the state certifying the successful completion of a prescribed secondary school program of studies. In some states or communities, high school diplomas are differentiated by type, such as an academic diploma, a general diploma, or a vocational diploma.

High school equivalency certificate A formal document certifying that an individual has met the state requirements for high school graduation equivalency by obtaining satisfactory scores on an approved examination and meeting other performance requirements (if any) set by a state education agency or other appropriate body. One particular version of this certificate is the GED test. The GED test is a comprehensive test used primarily to appraise the educational development of students who have not completed their formal high school education and who may earn a high school equivalency certificate by achieving satisfactory scores. GEDs are awarded by the states or other agencies, and the test is developed and distributed by the GED Testing Service (a joint venture of the American Council on Education and Pearson).

High school program A program of studies designed to prepare students for employment and postsecondary education. Three types of programs are often distinguished—academic, vocational, and general. An academic program is designed to prepare students for continued study at a college or university. A vocational program is designed to prepare students for employment in one or more semiskilled, skilled, or technical occupations. A general program is designed to provide students with the understanding and competence to function effectively in a free society and usually represents a mixture of academic and vocational components.

Higher education Study beyond secondary school at an institution that offers programs terminating in an associate's, bachelor's, or higher degree.

Higher education institutions (basic classification and Carnegie classification) See Postsecondary institutions (basic classification by level) and Postsecondary institutions (Carnegie classification of degree-granting institutions).

Higher Education Price Index A price index that measures average changes in the prices of goods and services purchased by colleges and universities through current-fund education and general expenditures (excluding expenditures for sponsored research and auxiliary enterprises).

Historically black colleges and universities Accredited higher education institutions established prior to 1964 with the principal mission of educating black Americans. Federal regulations (20 USC 1061 (2)) allow for certain exceptions of the founding date.

Hours worked per week According to the October Current Population Survey, the number of hours a respondent worked in all jobs in the week prior to the survey interview.

Household All the people who occupy a housing unit. A house, an apartment, a mobile home, a group of rooms, or a single room is regarded as a housing unit when it is occupied or intended for occupancy as separate living quarters, that is, when the occupants do not live and eat with any other people in the structure, and there is direct access from the outside or through a common hall.

Housing unit A house, an apartment, a mobile home, a group of rooms, or a single room that is occupied as separate living quarters.

Income tax Taxes levied on net income, that is, on gross income less certain deductions permitted by law. These taxes can be levied on individuals or on corporations or unincorporated businesses where the income is taxed distinctly from individual income.

Independent operations A group of self-supporting activities under control of a college or university. For purposes of financial surveys conducted by the National Center for Education Statistics, this category is composed principally of federally funded research and development centers (FFRDC).

Independent variable In regression analysis, a random variable, *y,* is expressed as a function of variables *x1, x2, ... xk,* plus a stochastic term; the *x*'s are known as "independent variables."

Individuals with Disabilities Education Act (IDEA) IDEA is a federal law enacted in 1990 and reauthorized in 1997 and 2004. IDEA requires services to children with disabilities throughout the nation. IDEA governs how states and public agencies provide early intervention, special education, and related services to eligible infants, toddlers, children, and youth with disabilities. Infants and toddlers with disabilities (birth–age 2) and their families receive early intervention services under IDEA, Part C. Children and youth (ages 3–21) receive special education and related services under IDEA, Part B.

Inflation A rise in the general level of prices of goods and services in an economy over a period of time, which generally corresponds to a decline in the real value of money or a loss of purchasing power. See also Constant dollars and Purchasing Power Parity indexes.

Institutional support The category of higher education expenditures that includes day-to-day operational support for colleges, excluding expenditures for physical plant operations. Examples of institutional support include general administrative services, executive direction and planning, legal and fiscal operations, and community relations.

Instruction (colleges and universities) That functional category including expenditures of the colleges, schools, departments, and other instructional divisions of higher education institutions and expenditures for departmental research and public service that are not separately budgeted; includes expenditures for both credit and noncredit activities. Excludes expenditures for academic administration where the primary function is administration (e.g., academic deans).

Instruction (elementary and secondary) Instruction encompasses all activities dealing directly with the interaction between teachers and students. Teaching may be provided for students in a school classroom, in another location such as a home or hospital, and in other learning situations such as those involving co-curricular activities. Instruction may be provided through some other approved medium, such as the Internet, television, radio, telephone, and correspondence.

Instructional staff Full-time-equivalent number of positions, not the number of different individuals occupying the positions during the school year. In local schools, includes all public elementary and secondary (junior and senior high) day-school positions that are in the nature of teaching or in the improvement of the teaching-learning situation; includes consultants or supervisors of instruction, principals, teachers, guidance personnel, librarians, psychological personnel, and other instructional staff; and excludes administrative staff, attendance personnel, clerical personnel, and junior college staff.

Instructional support services Includes salary, benefits, supplies, and contractual fees for staff providing instructional improvement, educational media (library and audiovisual), and other instructional support services.

Intellectual disability See Disabilities, children with.

Interest on debt Includes expenditures for long-term debt service interest payments (i.e., those longer than 1 year).

International baccalaureate (IB) A recognized international program of primary, middle, and secondary studies leading to the International Baccalaureate (IB) Diploma. This diploma (or certificate) is recognized in Europe and elsewhere as qualifying holders for direct access to university studies. Schools offering the IB program are approved by the International Baccalaureate Organization (IBO) and their regional office and may use IBO instructional materials, local school materials, or a combination.

International finance data Include data on public and private expenditures for educational institutions. Educational institutions directly provide instructional programs (i.e., teaching) to individuals in an organized group setting or through distance education. Business enterprises or other institutions that provide short-term courses of training or instruction to individuals on a "one-to-one" basis are not included. Where noted, international finance data may also include publicly subsidized spending on education-related purchases, such as school books, living costs, and transportation.

Public expenditures Corresponds to the nonrepayable current and capital expenditures of all levels of the government directly related to education. Expenditures that are not directly related to education (e.g., cultures, sports, youth activities) are, in principle, not included. Expenditures on education by other ministries or equivalent institutions (e.g., Health and Agriculture) are included. Public subsidies for students' living expenses are excluded to ensure international comparability of the data.

Private expenditures Refers to expenditures funded by private sources (i.e., households and other private entities). "Households" means students and their families. "Other private entities" includes private business firms and nonprofit organizations, including religious organizations, charitable organizations, and business and labor associations. Private expenditures are composed of school fees, the cost of materials (such as textbooks and teaching equipment), transportation costs (if organized by the school), the cost of meals (if provided by the school), boarding fees, and expenditures by employers on initial vocational training.

Current expenditures Includes final consumption expenditures (e.g., compensation of employees, consumption of intermediate goods and services, consumption of fixed capital, and military expenditures); property income paid; subsidies; and other current transfers paid.

Capital expenditures Includes spending to acquire and improve fixed capital assets, land, intangible assets, government stocks, and nonmilitary, nonfinancial assets, as well as spending to finance net capital transfers.

International Standard Classification of Education (ISCED) Used to compare educational systems in different countries. ISCED is the standard used by many countries to report education statistics to the United Nations Educational, Scientific, and Cultural Organization (UNESCO) and the Organization for Economic Cooperation and Development (OECD). ISCED was revised in 2011.

ISCED 2011 ISCED 2011 divides educational systems into the following nine categories, based on eight levels of education.

ISCED Level 0 Education preceding the first level (early childhood education) includes early childhood programs that target children below the age of entry into primary education.

ISCED Level 01 Early childhood educational development programs are generally designed for children younger than 3 years.

ISCED Level 02 Pre-primary education preceding the first level usually begins at age 3, 4, or 5 (sometimes earlier) and lasts from 1 to 3 years, when it is provided. In the United States, this level includes nursery school and kindergarten.

ISCED Level 1 Education at the first level (primary or elementary education) usually begins at age 5, 6, or 7 and continues for about 4 to 6 years. For the United States, the first level starts with 1st grade and ends with 6th grade.

ISCED Level 2 Education at the second level (lower secondary education) typically begins at about age 11 or 12 and continues for about 2 to 6 years. For the United States, the second level starts with 7th grade and typically ends with 9th grade. Education at the lower secondary level continues the basic programs of the first level, although teaching is typically more subject focused, often using more specialized teachers who conduct classes in their field of specialization. The main criterion for distinguishing lower secondary education from primary education is whether programs begin to be organized in a more subject-oriented pattern, using more specialized teachers conducting classes in their field of specialization. If there is no clear breakpoint for this organizational change, lower secondary education is considered to begin at the end of 6 years of primary education. In countries with no clear division between lower secondary and upper secondary education, and where lower secondary education lasts for more than 3 years, only the first 3 years following primary education are counted as lower secondary education.

ISCED Level 3 Education at the third level (upper secondary education) typically begins at age 15 or 16 and lasts for approximately 3 years. In the United States, the third level starts with 10th grade and ends with 12th grade. Upper secondary education is the final stage of secondary education in most OECD countries. Instruction is often organized along subject-matter lines, in contrast to the lower secondary level, and teachers typically must have a higher level, or more subject-specific, qualification. There are substantial differences in the typical duration of programs both across and between countries, ranging from 2 to 5 years of schooling. The main criteria for classifications are (1) national boundaries between lower and upper secondary education and (2) admission into educational programs, which usually requires the completion of lower secondary education or a combination of basic education and life experience that demonstrates the ability to handle the subject matter in upper secondary schools. Includes programs designed to review the content of third level programs, such as preparatory courses for tertiary education entrance examinations, and programs leading to a qualification equivalent to upper secondary general education.

ISCED Level 4 Education at the fourth level (postsecondary non-tertiary education) straddles the boundary between secondary and postsecondary education. This program of study, which is primarily vocational in nature, is generally taken after the completion of secondary school and typically lasts from 6 months to 2 years. Although the content of these programs may not be significantly more advanced than upper secondary programs, these programs serve to broaden the knowledge of participants who have already gained an upper secondary qualification.

ISCED Level 5 Education at the fifth level (short-cycle tertiary education) is noticeably more complex than in upper secondary programs giving access to this level. Programs at the fifth level typically provide practically based, occupationally specific content and prepare students to enter the labor market. However, the fifth level may also provide a pathway to other tertiary education programs (the sixth or seventh level). Short cycle-tertiary programs last for at least 2 years, and usually for no more than 3. In the United States, this level includes associate's degrees.

ISCED Level 6 Education at the sixth level (bachelor's or equivalent level) is longer and usually more theoretically oriented than programs at the fifth level, but may include practical components. Entry into these programs normally requires the completion of a third or fourth level program. They typically have a duration of 3 to 4 years of full-time study. Programs at the sixth level do not necessarily require the preparation of a substantive thesis or dissertation.

ISCED Level 7 Education at the seventh level (master's or equivalent level) has significantly more complex and specialized content than programs at the sixth level. The content at the seventh level is often designed to provide participants with advanced academic and/or professional knowledge, skills, and competencies, leading to a second degree or equivalent qualification. Programs at this level may have a substantial research component but do not yet lead to the award of a doctoral qualification. In the United States, this level includes professional degrees such as J.D., M.D., and D.D.S., as well as master degrees.

ISCED Level 8 Education at the eighth level (doctoral or equivalent level) is provided in graduate and professional schools that generally require a university degree or diploma as a minimum condition for admission. Programs at this level lead to the award of an advanced, postgraduate degree, such as a Ph.D. The theoretical duration of these programs is 3 years of full-time enrollment in most countries (for a cumulative total of at least 7 years at the tertiary level), although the length of the actual enrollment is often longer. Programs at this level are devoted to advanced study and original research.

ISCED 1997 ISCED 1997 divides educational systems into the following seven categories, based on six levels of education.

ISCED Level 0 Education preceding the first level (early childhood education) usually begins at age 3, 4, or 5 (sometimes earlier) and lasts from 1 to 3 years, when it is provided. In the United States, this level includes nursery school and kindergarten.

ISCED Level 1 Education at the first level (primary or elementary education) usually begins at age 5, 6, or 7 and continues for about 4 to 6 years. For the United States, the first level starts with 1st grade and ends with 6th grade.

ISCED Level 2 Education at the second level (lower secondary education) typically begins at about age 11 or 12 and continues for about 2 to 6 years. For the United States, the second level starts with 7th grade and typically ends with 9th grade. Education at the lower secondary level continues the basic programs of the first level, although teaching is typically more subject focused, often using more specialized teachers who conduct classes in their field of specialization. The main criterion for distinguishing lower secondary education from primary education is whether programs begin to be organized in a more subject-oriented pattern, using more specialized teachers conducting classes in their field of specialization. If there is no clear breakpoint for this organizational change, lower secondary education is considered to begin at the end of 6 years of primary education. In countries with no clear division between lower secondary and upper secondary education, and where lower secondary education lasts for more than 3 years, only the first 3 years following primary education are counted as lower secondary education.

ISCED Level 3 Education at the third level (upper secondary education) typically begins at age 15 or 16 and lasts for approximately 3 years. In the United States, the third level starts with 10th grade and ends with 12th grade. Upper secondary education is the final stage of secondary education in most OECD countries. Instruction is often organized along subject-matter lines, in contrast to the lower secondary level, and teachers typically must have a higher level, or more subject-specific, qualification. There are substantial differences in the typical duration of programs both across and between countries, ranging from 2 to 5 years of schooling. The main criteria for classifications are (1) national boundaries between lower and upper secondary education and (2) admission into educational programs, which usually requires the completion of lower secondary education or a combination of basic education and life experience that demonstrates the ability to handle the subject matter in upper secondary schools.

ISCED Level 4 Education at the fourth level (postsecondary non-tertiary education) straddles the boundary between secondary and postsecondary education. This program of study, which is primarily vocational in nature, is generally taken after the completion of secondary school and typically lasts from 6 months to 2 years. Although the content of these programs may not be significantly more advanced than upper secondary programs, these programs serve to broaden the knowledge of participants who have already gained an upper secondary qualification.

ISCED Level 5 Education at the fifth level (first stage of tertiary education) includes programs with more advanced content than those offered at the two previous levels. Entry into programs at the fifth level normally requires successful completion of either of the two previous levels.

ISCED Level 5A Tertiary-type A programs provide an education that is largely theoretical and is intended to provide sufficient qualifications for gaining entry into advanced research programs and professions with high skill requirements. Entry into these programs normally requires the successful completion of an upper secondary education; admission is competitive in most cases. The minimum cumulative theoretical duration at this level is 3 years of full-time enrollment. In the United States, tertiary-type A programs include first university programs that last approximately 4 years and lead to the award of a bachelor's degree and second university programs that lead to a master's degree or a first-professional degree such as an M.D., a J.D., or a D.V.M.

ISCED Level 5B Tertiary-type B programs are typically shorter than tertiary-type A programs and focus on practical, technical, or occupational skills for direct entry into the labor market, although they may cover some theoretical foundations in the respective programs. They have a minimum duration of 2 years of full-time enrollment at the tertiary level. In the United States, such programs are often provided at community colleges and lead to an associate's degree.

ISCED Level 6 Education at the sixth level (advanced research qualification) is provided in graduate and professional schools that generally require a university degree or diploma as a minimum condition for admission. Programs at this level lead to the award of an advanced, postgraduate degree, such as a Ph.D. The theoretical duration of these programs is 3 years of full-time enrollment in most countries (for a cumulative total of at least 7 years at levels five and six), although the length of the actual enrollment is often longer. Programs at this level are devoted to advanced study and original research.

Interpolation See Linear interpolation.

Junior high school A separately organized and administered secondary school intermediate between the elementary and senior high schools. A junior high school is usually either a 3-year school that includes grades 7, 8, and 9 or a 2-year school that includes grades 7 and 8.

Labor force People employed (either full time or part time) as civilians, unemployed but looking for work, or in the armed services during the survey week. The "civilian labor force" comprises all civilians classified as employed or unemployed. See also Unemployed.

Lag An event occurring at time $t + k$ ($k > 0$) is said to lag behind an event occurring at time t, the extent of the lag being k. An event occurring k time periods before another may be regarded as having a negative lag.

Land-grant colleges The First Morrill Act of 1862 facilitated the establishment of colleges through grants of land or funds in lieu of land. The Second Morrill Act in 1890 provided for money grants and for the establishment of land-grant colleges and universities for Blacks in those states with dual systems of higher education.

Lead time When forecasting a statistic, the number of time periods since the last time period of actual data for that statistic used in producing the forecast.

Level of school A classification of elementary/secondary schools by instructional level. Includes elementary schools, secondary schools, and combined elementary and secondary schools. See also Elementary school, Secondary school, and Combined school.

Limited-English proficient Refers to an individual who was not born in the United States and whose native language is a language other than English, or who comes from an environment where a language other than English has had a significant impact on the individual's level of English language proficiency. It may also refer to an individual who is migratory, whose native language is a language other than English, and who comes from an environment where a language other than English is dominant; and whose difficulties in speaking, reading, writing, or understanding the English language may be sufficient to deny the individual the ability to meet the state's proficient level of achievement on state assessments as specified under the No Child Left Behind Act, the ability to successfully achieve in classrooms where the language of instruction is English, or the opportunity to participate fully in society. See also English language learner.

Linear interpolation A method that allows the prediction of an unknown value if any two particular values on the same scale are known and the rate of change is assumed constant.

Local education agency (LEA) See School district.

Locale codes A classification system to describe a type of location. The "Metro-Centric" locale codes, developed in the 1980s, classified all schools and school districts based on their county's proximity to a Metropolitan Statistical Area (MSA) and their specific location's population size and density. In 2006, the "Urban-Centric" locale codes were introduced. These locale codes are based on an address's proximity to an urbanized area. For more information see http://nces.ed.gov/ccd/rural_locales.asp.

Pre-2006 Metro-Centric Locale Codes

Large City: A central city of a consolidated metropolitan statistical area (CMSA) or MSA, with the city having a population greater than or equal to 250,000.

Mid-size City: A central city of a CMSA or MSA, with the city having a population less than 250,000.

Urban Fringe of a Large City: Any territory within a CMSA or MSA of a Large City and defined as urban by the Census Bureau.

Urban Fringe of a Mid-size City: Any territory within a CMSA or MSA of a Mid-size City and defined as urban by the Census Bureau.

Large Town: An incorporated place or Census-designated place with a population greater than or equal to 25,000 and located outside a CMSA or MSA.

Small Town: An incorporated place or Census-designated place with a population less than 25,000 and greater than or equal to 2,500 and located outside a CMSA or MSA.

Rural, Outside MSA: Any territory designated as rural by the Census Bureau that is outside a CMSA or MSA of a Large or Mid-size City.

Rural, Inside MSA: Any territory designated as rural by the Census Bureau that is within a CMSA or MSA of a Large or Mid-size City.

2006 Urban-Centric Locale Codes

City, Large: Territory inside an urbanized area and inside a principal city with population of 250,000 or more.

City, Midsize: Territory inside an urbanized area and inside a principal city with population less than 250,000 and greater than or equal to 100,000.

City, Small: Territory inside an urbanized area and inside a principal city with population less than 100,000.

Suburb, Large: Territory outside a principal city and inside an urbanized area with population of 250,000 or more.

Suburb, Midsize: Territory outside a principal city and inside an urbanized area with population less than 250,000 and greater than or equal to 100,000.

Suburb, Small: Territory outside a principal city and inside an urbanized area with population less than 100,000.

Town, Fringe: Territory inside an urban cluster that is less than or equal to 10 miles from an urbanized area.

Town, Distant: Territory inside an urban cluster that is more than 10 miles and less than or equal to 35 miles from an urbanized area.

Town, Remote: Territory inside an urban cluster that is more than 35 miles from an urbanized area.

Rural, Fringe: Census-defined rural territory that is less than or equal to 5 miles from an urbanized area, as well as rural territory that is less than or equal to 2.5 miles from an urban cluster.

Rural, Distant: Census-defined rural territory that is more than 5 miles but less than or equal to 25 miles from an urbanized area, as well as rural territory that is more than 2.5 miles but less than or equal to 10 miles from an urban cluster.

Rural, Remote: Census-defined rural territory that is more than 25 miles from an urbanized area and is also more than 10 miles from an urban cluster.

Magnet school or program A special school or program designed to reduce, prevent, or eliminate racial isolation and/or to provide an academic or social focus on a particular theme.

Mandatory transfer A transfer of current funds that must be made in order to fulfill a binding legal obligation of a post-secondary institution. Included under mandatory transfers are debt service provisions relating to academic and administrative buildings, including (1) amounts set aside for debt retirement and interest and (2) required provisions for renewal and replacement of buildings to the extent these are not financed from other funds.

Margin of error The range of potential true or actual values for a sample survey estimate. The margin of error depends on several factors such as the amount of variation in the responses, the size and representativeness of the sample, and the size of the subgroup for which the estimate is computed. The magnitude of the margin of error is represented by the standard error of the estimate.

Master's degree A degree awarded for successful completion of a program generally requiring 1 or 2 years of full-time college-level study beyond the bachelor's degree. One type of master's degree, including the Master of Arts degree, or M.A., and the Master of Science degree, or M.S., is awarded in the liberal arts and sciences for advanced scholarship in a subject field or discipline and demonstrated ability to perform scholarly research. A second type of master's degree is awarded for the completion of a professionally oriented program, for example, an M.Ed. in education, an M.B.A. in business administration, an M.F.A. in fine arts, an M.M. in music, an M.S.W. in social work, and an M.P.A. in public administration. Some master's degrees—such as divinity degrees (M.Div. or M.H.L./Rav), which were formerly classified as "first-professional"—may require more than 2 years of full-time study beyond the bachelor's degree.

Mathematics A group of instructional programs that describes the science of numbers and their operations, interrelations, combinations, generalizations, and abstractions and of space configurations and their structure, measurement, transformations, and generalizations.

Mean absolute percentage error (MAPE) The average value of the absolute value of errors expressed in percentage terms.

Mean test score The score obtained by dividing the sum of the scores of all individuals in a group by the number of individuals in that group for which scores are available.

Median earnings The amount that divides the income distribution into two equal groups, half having income above that amount and half having income below that amount. Earnings include all wage and salary income. Unlike mean earnings, median earnings either do not change or change very little in response to extreme observations.

Middle school A school with no grade lower than 5 and no grade higher than 8.

Migration Geographic mobility involving a change of usual residence between clearly defined geographic units, that is, between counties, states, or regions.

Minimum-competency testing Measuring the acquisition of competence or skills to or beyond a certain specified standard.

Model A system of postulates, data, and inferences presented as a mathematical description of a phenomenon, such as an actual system or process. The actual phenomenon is represented by the model in order to explain, predict, and control it.

Montessori school A school that provides instruction using Montessori teaching methods.

Multiple disabilities See Disabilities, children with.

National Assessment of Educational Progress (NAEP) See Appendix A: Guide to Sources.

National School Lunch Program Established by President Truman in 1946, the program is a federally assisted meal program operated in public and private nonprofit schools and residential child care centers. To be eligible for free lunch, a student must be from a household with an income at or below 130 percent of the federal poverty guideline; to be eligible for reduced-price lunch, a student must be from a household with an income between 130 percent and 185 percent of the federal poverty guideline.

Newly qualified teachers People who: (1) first became eligible for a teaching license during the period of the study referenced or who were teaching at the time of survey, but were not certified or eligible for a teaching license; and (2) had never held full-time, regular teaching positions (as opposed to substitute) prior to completing the requirements for the degree that brought them into the survey.

Non-degree-granting institutions Postsecondary institutions that participate in Title IV federal financial aid programs but do not offer accredited 4-year or 2-year degree programs. Includes some institutions transitioning to higher level program offerings, though still classified at a lower level.

Nonprofessional staff See Employees in degree-granting institutions.

Nonprofit institution A private institution in which the individual(s) or agency in control receives no compensation other than wages, rent, or other expenses for the assumption of risk. Nonprofit institutions may be either independent nonprofit (i.e., having no religious affiliation) or religiously affiliated.

Nonresident alien A person who is not a citizen of the United States and who is in this country on a temporary basis and does not have the right to remain indefinitely.

Nonsectarian school Nonsectarian schools do not have a religious orientation or purpose and are categorized as regular, special program emphasis, or special education schools. See also Regular school, Special program emphasis school, and Special education school.

Nonsupervisory instructional staff People such as curriculum specialists, counselors, librarians, remedial specialists, and others possessing education certification, but not responsible for day-to-day teaching of the same group of pupils.

Nursery school An instructional program for groups of children during the year or years preceding kindergarten, which provides educational experiences under the direction of teachers. See also Prekindergarten and Preschool.

Obligations Amounts of orders placed, contracts awarded, services received, or similar legally binding commitments made by federal agencies during a given period that will require outlays during the same or some future period.

Occupied housing unit Separate living quarters with occupants currently inhabiting the unit. See also Housing unit.

Off-budget federal entities Organizational entities, federally owned in whole or in part, whose transactions belong in the budget under current budget accounting concepts, but that have been excluded from the budget totals under provisions of law. An example of an off-budget federal entity is the Federal Financing Bank, which provides student loans under the Direct Loan Program.

On-budget funding Federal funding for education programs that is tied to appropriations. On-budget funding does not include the Direct Loan Program, under which student loans are provided by the Federal Financing Bank, an off-budget federal entity. See also Off-budget federal entities.

Operation and maintenance services Includes salary, benefits, supplies, and contractual fees for supervision of operations and maintenance, operating buildings (heating, lighting, ventilating, repair, and replacement), care and upkeep of grounds and equipment, vehicle operations and maintenance (other than student transportation), security, and other operations and maintenance services.

Ordinary least squares (OLS) The estimator that minimizes the sum of squared residuals.

Organization for Economic Cooperation and Development (OECD) An intergovernmental organization of industrialized countries that serves as a forum for member countries to cooperate in research and policy development on social and economic topics of common interest. In addition to member countries, partner countries contribute to the OECD's work in a sustained and comprehensive manner.

Orthopedic impairment See Disabilities, children with.

Other health impairment See Disabilities, children with.

Other professional staff See Employees in degree-granting institutions.

Other religious school Other religious schools have a religious orientation or purpose, but are not Roman Catholic. Other religious schools are categorized according to religious association membership as Conservative Christian, other affiliated, or unaffiliated.

Other support services Includes salary, benefits, supplies, and contractual fees for business support services, central support services, and other support services not otherwise classified.

Other support services staff All staff not reported in other categories. This group includes media personnel, social workers, bus drivers, security, cafeteria workers, and other staff.

Outlays The value of checks issued, interest accrued on the public debt, or other payments made, net of refunds and reimbursements.

Parameter A quantity that describes a statistical population.

Part-time enrollment The number of students enrolled in postsecondary education courses with a total credit load less than 75 percent of the normal full-time credit load. At the undergraduate level, part-time enrollment typically includes students who have a credit load of less than 12 semester or quarter credits. At the postbaccalaureate level, part-time enrollment typically includes students who have a credit load of less than 9 semester or quarter credits.

Pass-through transaction A payment that a postsecondary institution applies directly to a student's account. The payment "passes through" the institution for the student's benefit. Most private institutions treat Pell grants as pass-through transactions. At these institutions, any Pell grant funds that are applied to a student's tuition are reported as tuition revenues. In contrast, the vast majority of public institutions report Pell grants both as federal revenues and as allowances that reduce tuition revenues.

Personal income Current income received by people from all sources, minus their personal contributions for social insurance. Classified as "people" are individuals (including owners of unincorporated firms), nonprofit institutions serving individuals, private trust funds, and private noninsured welfare funds. Personal income includes transfers (payments not resulting from current production) from government and business such as social security benefits and military pensions, but excludes transfers among people.

Physical plant assets Includes the values of land, buildings, and equipment owned, rented, or utilized by colleges. Does not include those plant values that are a part of endowment or other capital fund investments in real estate; excludes construction in progress.

Postbaccalaureate enrollment The number of students working toward advanced degrees and of students enrolled in graduate-level classes but not enrolled in degree programs. See also Graduate enrollment.

Postsecondary education The provision of formal instructional programs with a curriculum designed primarily for students who have completed the requirements for a high school diploma or equivalent. This includes programs of an academic, vocational, and continuing professional education purpose, and excludes avocational and adult basic education programs.

Postsecondary institutions (basic classification by level)

4-year institution An institution offering at least a 4-year program of college-level studies wholly or principally creditable toward a baccalaureate degree.

2-year institution An institution offering at least a 2-year program of college-level studies that terminates in an associate degree or is principally creditable toward a baccalaureate degree. Data prior to 1996 include some institutions that have a less-than-2-year program, but were designated as higher education institutions in the Higher Education General Information Survey.

Less-than-2-year institution An institution that offers programs of less than 2 years' duration below the baccalaureate level. Includes occupational and vocational schools with programs that do not exceed 1,800 contact hours.

Postsecondary institutions (2005 Carnegie classification of degree-granting institutions)

Doctorate-granting Characterized by a significant level and breadth of activity in commitment to doctoral-level education as measured by the number of doctorate recipients and the diversity in doctoral-level program offerings. These institutions are assigned to one of the three subcategories listed below based on level of research activity (for more information on the research activity index used to assign institutions to the subcategories, see http://carnegieclassifications.iu.edu/):

Research university, very high Characterized by a very high level of research activity.

Research university, high Characterized by a high level of research activity.

Doctoral/research university Awarding at least 20 doctor's degrees per year, but not having a high level of research activity.

Master's Characterized by diverse postbaccalaureate programs but not engaged in significant doctoral-level education.

Baccalaureate Characterized by primary emphasis on general undergraduate, baccalaureate-level education. Not significantly engaged in postbaccalaureate education.

Special focus Baccalaureate or postbaccalaureate institution emphasizing one area (plus closely related specialties), such as business or engineering. The programmatic emphasis is measured by the percentage of degrees granted in the program area.

Associate's Institutions conferring at least 90 percent of their degrees and awards for work below the bachelor's level. In NCES tables, excludes all institutions offering any 4-year programs leading to a bachelor's degree.

Tribal Colleges and universities that are members of the American Indian Higher Education Consortium, as identified in IPEDS Institutional Characteristics.

Poverty (official measure) The U.S. Census Bureau uses a set of money income thresholds that vary by family size and composition. A family, along with each individual in it, is considered poor if the family's total income is less than that family's threshold. The poverty thresholds do not vary geographically and are adjusted annually for inflation using the Consumer Price Index. The official poverty definition counts money income before taxes and does not include capital gains and noncash benefits (such as public housing, Medicaid, and food stamps). See also Supplemental Poverty Measure (SPM).

Prekindergarten Preprimary education for children typically ages 3–4 who have not yet entered kindergarten. It may offer a program of general education or special education and may be part of a collaborative effort with Head Start.

Preschool An instructional program enrolling children generally younger than 5 years of age and organized to provide children with educational experiences under professionally qualified teachers during the year or years immediately preceding kindergarten (or prior to entry into elementary school when there is no kindergarten). See also Nursery school and Prekindergarten.

Primary school A school with at least one grade lower than 5 and no grade higher than 8.

Private institution An institution that is controlled by an individual or agency other than a state, a subdivision of a state, or the federal government; that is usually supported primarily by other than public funds; and the operation of whose program rests with other than publicly elected or appointed officials.

Private nonprofit institution An institution in which the individual(s) or agency in control receives no compensation other than wages, rent, or other expenses for the assumption of risk. These include both independent nonprofit institutions and those affiliated with a religious organization.

Private for-profit institution An institution in which the individual(s) or agency in control receives compensation other than wages, rent, or other expenses for the assumption of risk (e.g., proprietary schools).

Private school Private elementary/secondary schools surveyed by the Private School Universe Survey (PSS) are assigned to one of three major categories (Catholic, other religious, or nonsectarian) and, within each major category, one of three subcategories based on the school's religious affiliation provided by respondents.

> ***Catholic*** Schools categorized according to governance, provided by Catholic school respondents, into parochial, diocesan, and private schools.

> ***Other religious*** Schools that have a religious orientation or purpose but are not Roman Catholic. Other religious schools are categorized according to religious association membership, provided by respondents, into Conservative Christian, other affiliated, and unaffiliated schools. Conservative Christian schools are those "Other religious" schools with membership in at least one of four associations: Accelerated Christian Education, American Association of Christian Schools, Association of Christian Schools International, and Oral Roberts University Education Fellowship. Affiliated schools are those "Other religious" schools not classified as Conservative Christian with membership in at least 1 of 11 associations—Association of Christian Teachers and Schools, Christian Schools International, Evangelical Lutheran Education Association, Friends Council on Education, General Conference of the Seventh-Day Adventist Church, Islamic School League of America, National Association of Episcopal Schools, National Christian School Association, National Society for Hebrew Day Schools, Solomon Schechter Day Schools, and Southern Baptist Association of Christian Schools—or indicating membership in "other religious school associations." Unaffiliated schools are those "Other religious" schools that have a religious orientation or purpose but are not classified as Conservative Christian or affiliated.

> ***Nonsectarian*** Schools that do not have a religious orientation or purpose and are categorized according to program emphasis, provided by respondents, into regular, special emphasis, and special education schools. Regular schools are those that have a regular elementary/secondary or early childhood program emphasis. Special emphasis schools are those that have a Montessori, vocational/technical, alternative, or special program emphasis. Special education schools are those that have a special education program emphasis.

Professional staff See Employees in degree-granting institutions.

Program for International Student Assessment (PISA) See Appendix A: Guide to Sources.

Projection In relation to a time series, an estimate of future values based on a current trend.

Property tax The sum of money collected from a tax levied against the value of property.

Proprietary (for profit) institution A private institution in which the individual(s) or agency in control receives compensation other than wages, rent, or other expenses for the assumption of risk.

Public school or institution A school or institution controlled and operated by publicly elected or appointed officials and deriving its primary support from public funds.

Pupil/teacher ratio The enrollment of pupils at a given period of time, divided by the full-time-equivalent number of classroom teachers serving these pupils during the same period.

Purchasing Power Parity (PPP) indexes PPP exchange rates, or indexes, are the currency exchange rates that equalize the purchasing power of different currencies, meaning that when a given sum of money is converted into different currencies at the PPP exchange rates, it will buy the same basket of goods and services in all countries. PPP indexes are the rates of currency conversion that eliminate the difference in price levels among countries. Thus, when expenditures on gross domestic product (GDP) for different countries are converted into a common currency by means of PPP indexes, they are expressed at the same set of international prices, so that comparisons among countries reflect only differences in the volume of goods and services purchased.

R^2 The coefficient of determination; the square of the correlation coefficient between the dependent variable and its ordinary least squares (OLS) estimate.

Racial/ethnic group Classification indicating general racial or ethnic heritage. Race/ethnicity data are based on the *Hispanic* ethnic category and the race categories listed below (five single-race categories, plus the *Two or more races* category). Race categories exclude persons of Hispanic ethnicity unless otherwise noted.

> ***White*** A person having origins in any of the original peoples of Europe, the Middle East, or North Africa.

> ***Black or African American*** A person having origins in any of the black racial groups of Africa. Used interchangeably with the shortened term *Black*.

> ***Hispanic or Latino*** A person of Cuban, Mexican, Puerto Rican, South or Central American, or other Spanish culture or origin, regardless of race. Used interchangeably with the shortened term *Hispanic*.

> ***Asian*** A person having origins in any of the original peoples of the Far East, Southeast Asia, or the Indian subcontinent, including, for example, Cambodia, China, India, Japan, Korea, Malaysia, Pakistan, the Philippine Islands, Thailand, and Vietnam. Prior to 2010–11, the Common Core of Data (CCD) combined Asian and Pacific Islander categories.

Native Hawaiian or Other Pacific Islander A person having origins in any of the original peoples of Hawaii, Guam, Samoa, or other Pacific Islands. Prior to 2010–11, the Common Core of Data (CCD) combined Asian and Pacific Islander categories. Used interchangeably with the shortened term *Pacific Islander.*

American Indian or Alaska Native A person having origins in any of the original peoples of North and South America (including Central America), and who maintains tribal affiliation or community attachment.

Two or more races A person identifying himself or herself as of two or more of the following race groups: White, Black, Asian, Native Hawaiian or Other Pacific Islander, or American Indian or Alaska Native. Some, but not all, reporting districts use this category. "Two or more races" was introduced in the 2000 Census and became a regular category for data collection in the Current Population Survey in 2003. The category is sometimes excluded from a historical series of data with constant categories. It is sometimes included within the category "Other."

Region See Geographic region.

Regression analysis A statistical technique for investigating and modeling the relationship between variables.

Regular school A public elementary/secondary or charter school providing instruction and education services that does not focus primarily on special education, vocational/technical education, or alternative education.

Related children Related children in a family include own children and all other children in the household who are related to the householder by birth, marriage, or adoption.

Remedial education Instruction for a student lacking those reading, writing, or math skills necessary to perform college-level work at the level required by the attended institution.

Resident population Includes civilian population and armed forces personnel residing within the United States; excludes armed forces personnel residing overseas.

Retention in grade Retaining a student in the same grade from one school year to the next.

Revenue All funds received from external sources, net of refunds, and correcting transactions. Noncash transactions, such as receipt of services, commodities, or other receipts in kind are excluded, as are funds received from the issuance of debt, liquidation of investments, and nonroutine sale of property.

Revenue receipts Additions to assets that do not incur an obligation that must be met at some future date and do not represent exchanges of property for money. Assets must be available for expenditures.

Rho A measure of the correlation coefficient between errors in time period t and time period t minus 1.

Rural school See Locale codes.

Salary The total amount regularly paid or stipulated to be paid to an individual, before deductions, for personal services rendered while on the payroll of a business or organization.

Sales and services Revenues derived from the sales of goods or services that are incidental to the conduct of instruction, research, or public service. Examples include film rentals, scientific and literary publications, testing services, university presses, and dairy products.

Sales tax Tax imposed upon the sale and consumption of goods and services. It can be imposed either as a general tax on the retail price of all goods and services sold or as a tax on the sale of selected goods and services.

SAT An examination administered by the Educational Testing Service and used to predict the facility with which an individual will progress in learning college-level academic subjects. It was formerly called the Scholastic Assessment Test.

Scholarships and fellowships This category of college expenditures applies only to money given in the form of outright grants and trainee stipends to individuals enrolled in formal coursework, either for credit or not. Aid to students in the form of tuition or fee remissions is included. College work-study funds are excluded and are reported under the program in which the student is working.

School A division of the school system consisting of students in one or more grades or other identifiable groups and organized to give instruction of a defined type. One school may share a building with another school or one school may be housed in several buildings. Excludes schools that have closed or are planned for the future.

School administration support services Includes salary, benefits, supplies, and contractual fees for the office of the principal, full-time department chairpersons, and graduation expenses.

School climate The social system and culture of the school, including the organizational structure of the school and values and expectations within it.

School district An education agency at the local level that exists primarily to operate public schools or to contract for public school services. Synonyms are "local basic administrative unit" and "local education agency."

Science The body of related courses concerned with knowledge of the physical and biological world and with the processes of discovering and validating this knowledge.

Secondary enrollment The total number of students registered in a school beginning with the next grade following an elementary or middle school (usually 7, 8, or 9) and ending with or below grade 12 at a given time.

Secondary instructional level The general level of instruction provided for pupils in secondary schools (generally covering grades 7 through 12 or 9 through 12) and any instruction of a comparable nature and difficulty provided for adults and youth beyond the age of compulsory school attendance.

Secondary school A school comprising any span of grades beginning with the next grade following an elementary or middle school (usually 7, 8, or 9) and ending with or below grade 12. Both junior high schools and senior high schools are included.

Senior high school A secondary school offering the final years of high school work necessary for graduation.

Serial correlation Correlation of the error terms from different observations of the same variable. Also called Autocorrelation.

Serial volumes Publications issued in successive parts, usually at regular intervals, and as a rule, intended to be continued indefinitely. Serials include periodicals, newspapers, annuals, memoirs, proceedings, and transactions of societies.

Social studies A group of instructional programs that describes the substantive portions of behavior, past and present activities, interactions, and organizations of people associated together for religious, benevolent, cultural, scientific, political, patriotic, or other purposes.

Socioeconomic status (SES) The SES index is a composite of often equally weighted, standardized components, such as father's education, mother's education, family income, father's occupation, and household items. The terms high, middle, and low SES refer to ranges of the weighted SES composite index distribution.

Special education Direct instructional activities or special learning experiences designed primarily for students identified as having exceptionalities in one or more aspects of the cognitive process or as being underachievers in relation to general level or model of their overall abilities. Such services usually are directed at students with the following conditions: (1) physically disabled; (2) emotionally disabled; (3) culturally different, including compensatory education; (4) intellectually disabled; and (5) students with learning disabilities. Programs for the mentally gifted and talented are also included in some special education programs. See also Disabilities, children with.

Special education school A public elementary/secondary school that focuses primarily on special education for children with disabilities and that adapts curriculum, materials, or instruction for students served. See also Disabilities, children with.

Special program emphasis school A science/mathematics school, a performing arts high school, a foreign language immersion school, and a talented/gifted school are examples of schools that offer a special program emphasis.

Specific learning disability See Disabilities, children with.

Speech or language impairment See Disabilities, children with.

Standard error of estimate An expression for the standard deviation of the observed values about a regression line. An estimate of the variation likely to be encountered in making predictions from the regression equation.

Standardized test A test composed of a systematic sampling of behavior, administered and scored according to specific instructions, capable of being interpreted in terms of adequate norms, and for which there are data on reliability and validity.

Standardized test performance The weighted distributions of composite scores from standardized tests used to group students according to performance.

Status dropout rate The percentage of individuals within a given age range who are not enrolled in school and lack a high school credential, regardless of when they dropped out.

Status dropout rate (Current Population Survey) The percentage of civilian, noninstitutionalized young people ages 16–24 who are not in school and have not earned a high school credential (either a diploma or equivalency credential such as a GED certificate). The numerator of the status dropout rate for a given year is the number of individuals ages 16–24 who, as of October of that year, have not completed a high school credential and are not currently enrolled in school. The denominator is the total number of individuals ages 16–24 in the United States in October of that year. Status dropout rates count the following individuals as dropouts: those who never attended school and immigrants who did not complete the equivalent of a high school education in their home country.

Status dropout rate (American Community Survey) Similar to the status dropout rate (Current Population Survey), except that institutionalized persons, incarcerated persons, and active duty military personnel living in barracks in the United States may be included in this calculation.

STEM fields Science, Technology, Engineering, and Mathematics (STEM) fields of study that are considered to be of particular relevance to advanced societies. For the purposes of *The Condition of Education 2015*, STEM fields include agriculture and natural resources, architecture, biology and biomedical sciences, computer and information sciences, engineering and engineering technologies, health studies, mathematics and statistics, and physical and social sciences. STEM occupations include computer scientists and mathematicians; engineers and architects; life, physical, and social scientists; medical professionals; and managers of STEM activities.

Student An individual for whom instruction is provided in an educational program under the jurisdiction of a school, school system, or other education institution. No distinction is made between the terms "student" and "pupil," though "student" may refer to one receiving instruction at any level while "pupil" refers only to one attending school at the elementary or secondary level. A student may receive instruction in a school facility or in another location, such as at home or in a hospital. Instruction may be provided by direct student-teacher interaction or by some other approved medium such as television, radio, telephone, and correspondence.

Student membership Student membership is an annual headcount of students enrolled in school on October 1 or the school day closest to that date. The Common Core of Data (CCD) allows a student to be reported for only a single school or agency. For example, a vocational school (identified as a "shared time" school) may provide classes for students from a number of districts and show no membership.

Student support services Includes salary, benefits, supplies, and contractual fees for staff providing attendance and social work, guidance, health, psychological services, speech pathology, audiology, and other support to students.

Study abroad population U.S. citizens and permanent residents, enrolled for a degree at an accredited higher education institution in the United States, who received academic credit for study abroad from their home institutions upon their return. Students studying abroad without receiving academic credit are not included, nor are U.S. students enrolled for a degree overseas.

Supervisory staff Principals, assistant principals, and supervisors of instruction; does not include superintendents or assistant superintendents.

Supplemental Poverty Measure (SPM) An alternative measure of poverty that supplements the U.S. Census Bureau's official poverty measure by adding to family income the value of benefits—including nutritional assistance, housing subsidies, and home energy assistance—from many government programs designed to assist those with low incomes, subtracting taxes and necessary expenses such as child care costs (for working families) and out-of-pocket medical expenses, and adjusting poverty thresholds for geographic differences in housing costs. See also Poverty (official measure).

Suspension Temporarily removing a student from his or her regular classroom (an in-school suspension) or from his or her regular school (an out-of-school suspension) generally for disciplinary purposes.

Tax base The collective value of objects, assets, and income components against which a tax is levied.

Tax expenditures Losses of tax revenue attributable to provisions of the federal income tax laws that allow a special exclusion, exemption, or deduction from gross income or provide a special credit, preferential rate of tax, or a deferral of tax liability affecting individual or corporate income tax liabilities.

Teacher see Instructional staff.

Technical education A program of vocational instruction that ordinarily includes the study of the sciences and mathematics underlying a technology, as well as the methods, skills, and materials commonly used and the services performed in the technology. Technical education prepares individuals for positions—such as draftsman or lab technician—in the occupational area between the skilled craftsman and the professional person.

Three-year moving average An arithmetic average of the year indicated, the year immediately preceding, and the year immediately following. Use of a 3-year moving average increases the sample size, thereby reducing the size of sampling errors and producing more stable estimates.

Time series A set of ordered observations on a quantitative characteristic of an individual or collective phenomenon taken at different points in time. Usually the observations are successive and equally spaced in time.

Time series analysis The branch of quantitative forecasting in which data for one variable are examined for patterns of trend, seasonality, and cycle.

Title I school A school designated under appropriate state and federal regulations as a high-poverty school that is eligible for participation in programs authorized by Title I of the Reauthorization of the Elementary and Secondary Education Act, P.L. 107-110.

Title IV Refers to a section of the Higher Education Act of 1965 that covers the administration of the federal student financial aid program.

Title IV eligible institution A postsecondary institution that meets the criteria for participating in federal student financial aid programs. An eligible institution must be any of the following: (1) an institution of higher education (with public or private, nonprofit control), (2) a proprietary institution (with private for-profit control), and (3) a postsecondary vocational institution (with public or private, nonprofit control). In addition, it must have acceptable legal authorization, acceptable accreditation and admission standards, eligible academic program(s), administrative capability, and financial responsibility.

Total expenditure per pupil in average daily attendance Includes all expenditures allocable to per pupil costs divided by average daily attendance. These allocable expenditures include current expenditures for regular school programs, interest on school debt, and capital outlay. Beginning in 1980–81, expenditures for state administration are excluded and expenditures for other programs (summer schools and designated subsidies for community colleges and private schools) are included.

Town school See Locale codes.

Traditional public school Publicly funded schools other than public charter schools. See also Public school or institution and Charter school.

Transcript An official list of all courses taken by a student at a school or college showing the final grade received for each course, with definitions of the various grades given at the institution.

Traumatic brain injury See Disabilities, children with.

Trust funds Amounts collected and used by the federal government for carrying out specific purposes and programs according to terms of a trust agreement or statute, such as the Social Security and unemployment trust funds. Trust fund receipts that are not anticipated to be used in the immediate future are generally invested in interest-bearing government securities and earn interest for the trust fund.

Tuition and fees A payment or charge for instruction or compensation for services, privileges, or the use of equipment, books, or other goods. Tuition may be charged per term, per course, or per credit.

Type of school A classification of public elementary and secondary schools that includes the following categories: regular schools, special education schools, vocational schools, and alternative schools. See also Regular school, Special education school, Vocational school, and Alternative school.

Unadjusted dollars See Current dollars.

Unclassified students Students who are not candidates for a degree or other formal award, although they are taking higher education courses for credit in regular classes with other students.

Undergraduate students Students registered at an institution of postsecondary education who are working in a baccalaureate degree program or other formal program below the baccalaureate, such as an associate's degree, vocational, or technical program.

Unemployed Civilians who had no employment but were available for work and: (1) had engaged in any specific job-seeking activity within the past 4 weeks; (2) were waiting to be called back to a job from which they had been laid off; or (3) were waiting to report to a new wage or salary job within 30 days.

Ungraded student (elementary/secondary) A student who has been assigned to a school or program that does not have standard grade designations.

Urban fringe school See Locale codes.

U.S. Service Academies These higher education institutions are controlled by the U.S. Department of Defense and the U.S. Department of Transportation. The 5 institutions counted in the NCES surveys of degree-granting institutions include: the U.S. Air Force Academy, U.S. Coast Guard Academy, U.S. Merchant Marine Academy, U.S. Military Academy, and the U.S. Naval Academy.

Variable A quantity that may assume any one of a set of values.

Visual and performing arts A group of instructional programs that generally describes the historic development, aesthetic qualities, and creative processes of the visual and performing arts.

Visual impairment See Disabilities, children with.

Vocational education Organized educational programs, services, and activities that are directly related to the preparation of individuals for paid or unpaid employment, or for additional preparation for a career, requiring other than a baccalaureate or advanced degree.

Vocational school A public school that focuses primarily on providing formal preparation for semiskilled, skilled, technical, or professional occupations for high school–age students who have opted to develop or expand their employment opportunities, often in lieu of preparing for college entry.

Years out In forecasting by year, the number of years since the last year of actual data for that statistic used in producing the forecast.

APPENDIX C
Index of Table Numbers